AF527381

AN

INDEX TO THE NAMES

IN THE

MAHĀBHĀRATA

AN

INDEX TO THE NAMES
IN THE

MAHĀBHĀRATA

With Short Explanations
and
A Concordance
to the
Bombay and Calcutta Editions and P.C. Roy's Translation

by

S. SÖRENSEN
PH.D.

MOTILAL BANARSIDASS PUBLISHERS
PRIVATE LIMITED • DELHI

*Reprint: Delhi, 1963, 1978, **2006***
First Edition : Delhi, 1904

ISBN: 81-208-2011-8

MOTILAL BANARSIDASS
41 U.A. Bungalow Road, Jawahar Nagar, Delhi 110 007
8 Mahalaxmi Chamber, 22 Bhulabhai Desai Road, Mumbai 400 026
236, 9th Main III Block, Jayanagar, Bangalore 560 011
203 Royapettah High Road, Mylapore, Chennai 600 004
Sanas Plaza, 1302 Baji Rao Road, Pune 411 002
8 Camac Street, Kolkata 700 017
Ashok Rajpath, Patna 800 004
Chowk, Varanasi 221 001

Printed in India
BY JAINENDRA PRAKASH JAIN AT SHRI JAINENDRA PRESS,
A-45 NARAINA, PHASE-I, NEW DELHI 110 028
AND PUBLISHED BY NARENDRA PRAKASH JAIN FOR
MOTILAL BANARSIDASS PUBLISHERS PRIVATE LIMITED,
BUNGALOW ROAD, DELHI 110 007

PREFACE.

THE present work consists of two portions — the Index proper and the Concordance. The Index deals mainly with the proper names occurring in the Mahābhārata. The student should therefore first look for information under such headings as are *names*, and not under narrative headings such as **Indravijaya** and the like.

The paragraph references found under the names in the Index are given sometimes alone [e.g. § 547], and sometimes with the addition of small italic letters [e.g. § 201*b*]. If there is no such addition, the paragraphs (viz. abstracts or paraphrases of the text) are themselves sections of the narrative, and given under the name in question, because the bearer of the name is the principal actor. Such paragraph references, without small italic letters, are often followed by a parenthesis. Thus, under the heading **Agni**, we find the quotation "§§ 254–260 (Khāṇḍavadah.)." Here the references are *suggestive* of a narrative which will be found in full under the heading given within parenthesis, viz. Khāṇḍavadahanaparvan, and the name in question, in this case Agni, is the name of one among several principal actors, so that it would seem arbitrary to refer the narrative to him alone.

A small italic letter after a paragraph reference and followed by a word within parenthesis is used when the name to which it is added does not connote the principal actor or the chief item of the narrative, but is only incidentally mentioned, though the reference is of interest for, and solely, or at least chiefly, concerned with it. If further information is wanted it will have to be looked for under the heading given within parenthesis, where the name in question is mentioned, the small italic letter being added within parenthesis as a kind of cross-reference.

Under **Māhishmatī** we thus find the quotation "§ 282*b* (Sahadeva)" followed by a remark concerning Māhishmatī. Further particulars must then be looked for under **Sahadeva**, where we read, "§ 282: From Kishkindhā Shd. marched towards Māhishmatī (*b*) . . . ."

A small Greek letter indicates that the reference is chiefly of interest on account of the connection in which it occurs, and that further information will be found under the heading referred to within parenthesis, where the same Greek letter has likewise been added, within parenthesis, as a cross-reference.

Take, for instance, the reference given under **Duḥçāsana**, "§ 83 (Ādivaṃçāv.) *α*: I, **63**, 2447" (or, I, **63***α*, 2447). Similarly, we find under **Duḥsaha**, "§ 83 (Ādivaṃçāv.) *α*: I, **63**, 2448." These references show that Duḥçāsana and Duḥsaha are mentioned under the heading **Ādivaṃçāvatāraṇa**, and that no immediate interest attaches to their being referred to in that place. The statement made under **Ādivaṃçāvatāraṇa** runs, "§ 83: the 101 sons of Dhṛtarāshṭra . . . of whom 11 (*α*) . . . are enumerated as mahārathas." Here the *α* indicates that I have not thought it worth while to enumerate those 11 names (they must accordingly be looked for in the Sanskrit texts), but the passage in question has been referred to under the headings of each of them.

To return to the quotation under **Duḥçāsana,** "83 (Ādivamçāv.) *α*: I, **63**, 2447."

The figures **63**, 2447 refer to a passage where Duḥçāsana is actually mentioned.

The small *α* shows that the mention of his name presumably is of little or no general importance, and may be practically neglected from a mythological or legendary point of view.

If the reader nevertheless wishes to know the purport of the reference, the word given within parenthesis shows that information will be found under **Ādivaṃçāvatāraṇa,** and *one* inspection under that heading will show that Duḥçāsana is there only mentioned, among eleven of Dhṛtarāshṭra's sons, as a mahāratha.

The heading **Ādivaṃçāvatāraṇa,** with or without *one* additional inspection of the Concordance under § 83, will at once show the reader who in his memory has a general idea of the contents of the Mahābhārata that the quotation has been taken from a kind of preface or introduction to the principal narrative of the Epos, which is placed after the sections where, not Vaiçampāyana, but Sauti is the speaker. According to his critical disposition he will, or will not, draw conclusions from this fact.

Mere comparisons have been marked by the addition of (*iva*) or the like.

The signs *, **, †, (†), ††, and (††) have a critical value. I have not, of course, allowed the book to be influenced by critical theories. I have only intended to draw attention to such facts as seem to be of critical importance. According to his disposition, the reader may or may not draw conclusions from those signs. The danger is that they may sometimes have been omitted through inadvertence.

The numbers of verses, in ordinary type, refer to the Calcutta edition; the numbers of chapters, in **clarendon type,** to the Bombay text. By using the Concordance it will be possible, with very little uncertainty, to calculate what verse in the Bombay edition corresponds to a given one in the Calcutta Mahābhārata.

The books are quoted in Roman numbers.

The enumeration of verses is, except where the heading is marked by an asterisk, intended to be complete, and I hope that it is so, at least with regard to all instances where there cannot be any doubt that the heading occurs as a *name.* In such cases, on the other hand, where it may have been a matter of subjective feeling during the reading whether a word should be considered as a proper name or as a mere laudatory epithet, I fear that there may be some incompleteness and inconsistency. Thus some synonyms of Agni and Arjuna, which will be found in Mr. Holtzmann's lists, have not been registered

There are also some other inconsistencies, sometimes voluntary, for the sake of convenience, sometimes involuntary, due to the fact that my work has extended over a very great span of time. These latter ones are faults for which I must ask indulgence, but I hope that they will not cause any serious misunderstanding or inconvenience. I do not now venture to correct them, lest the numerous cross-references should be imperilled.

The numerous synonyms, such as *Kirīṭin* for *Arjuna,* have, as a rule, been put together under the principal name; e g. *Kirīṭin,* etc., under *Arjuna.* Such denominations as *Kaurava, Kuruçreshṭha,* etc., have, however, been given separately in their proper places, the principal aim to be held in view with regard to them clearly being to be able to know easily what person is meant in each instance.

In the case of such synonyms, and of articles the contents of which are unimportant, I have only quoted book and verse. In other cases I have usually also added reference to paragraph and chapter. Take, for instance, under the heading **Arjuna**, the quotation § 613 (Gadāyuddh.), IX, **32–33**: **33**, 1890, 1921. Here the explanatory addition (Gadāyuddh.) refers the reader to the heading **Gadāyuddhaparvan**, where a summary of the narrative in question will be found under Book ix, chapters 32–33. The quotation **33**, 1890, 1921 indicates the places where the name Arjuna actually occurs.

In some cases the summary of the narrative has also, for the sake of convenience, been repeated, in a more or less abridged form, under the special heading; thus, in our present case, under Arjuna.

In these, probably not very numerous, cases the reference to the paragraph is only necessary in order to get an idea of the wider connection in which the quotation occurs. In other instances the exposition must almost entirely be looked for in the paragraph quoted. Thus in the case of the quotation §§ 254–260 (Khāṇḍavadah.), I, **222–234**, under the heading **Arjuna**. Here the narrative will be found in §§ 254–260 under the heading Khāṇḍavadahanaparvan. By referring to the Concordance, under the same paragraphs, the place which the narrative occupies in the epic as a whole will immediately be seen.

By arranging in numerical order, i.e. in the order of the Concordance, the paragraphs as given in the Index, we should obtain a synopsis of the contents of the whole epic, in the order of the original. Essentially the same result may be obtained from the article **Arjuna**, where I have introduced more repetitions (i.e. statements which are also found under other headings) than in any other article.

With regard to repetitions, I have thought it more important to enable the reader to use the Index conveniently and without unnecessary waste of time, than to save space. I have not, therefore, strictly avoided them in the principal articles, though I have done so in most cases by referring to paragraph articles and to the headings under which the quotations concerned are first given.

The text on which the Index is based is, on the whole, the Calcutta edition. Readings from other sources (i.e. almost exclusively the Bombay edition) have only been noticed for special reasons.

In transliterating the Sanskrit words, it will be noticed that I have followed the order of the Latin alphabet, without paying any attention to diacritical marks. I have adopted the usual system of transliteration, with some modifications. Thus the palatal mute is given as *c*, *ch* being reserved for the corresponding aspirate; *j* is the palatal media, and *y* the corresponding semi-vowel. The palatal and cerebral *s*-sounds have been transliterated *ç* and *sh* respectively.

The only exception from the strict adherence to the arrangement in accordance with the Latin alphabet is that the letters *ç* and *ṛ* have been treated as separate letters and placed after *c* and *r* respectively. This has been done because these sounds are often transliterated as *ś* and *ṛi* respectively.

In the CONCORDANCE it will be noticed that the mutual relationship between the two divisions in paragraphs and chapters has been indicated in various ways. My principal aim has here been to save space and trouble.

Where the paragraphs are separated from the synopsis of chapters and verses, the headings to which they belong in the Index have simply been printed after the other indications relating to them. E.g., § 19 (*giving the contents of Mhbhr.* I, **5**, 1–11) *will be found under the heading* 'BHṚGU.' *Where the paragraphs are not so separated, it should be generally understood that the title of the minor parvan to which a paragraph belongs is also the heading under which it will be found in the Index. E.g.,* § 249 (*Mhbhr.* I, **215**) *under the heading* 'ARJUNAVANAVĀSAPARVAN.' *If this is not the case, the paragraphs are to be found in the Index under the titles of those chapters of the parvan in question which have been printed with spaced type. E.g.,* § 177 (*Mhbhr.* I, **113**) *under the heading* 'PĀṆḌUDIGVIJAYA,' § 161 (*Mhbhr.* I, **96**) *under the heading* 'MAHĀBHISHOPĀKHYĀNA,' *and not under* 'SAMBHAVAPARVAN.'

My sincere thanks are due to those who have helped me with their advice or have in other ways shown their interest in my work. In this connection I beg to mention Professor V. Fausböll, Professor K. F. Geldner, Professor Ch. R. Lanman, Dr. Sten Konow, and Dr. G. A. Grierson. The valuable suggestions made by Professor Lanman have, in many respects, left material traces in the arrangement of the Index, and certainly rendered it much more convenient and useful to the student than would otherwise have been the case. My young friend Mr. Elof Olesen deserves my warmest thanks for the care and sagacity with which he has assisted me in the revision of the manuscript.

Finally, I tender my respectful thanks for the pecuniary assistance which has rendered the compilation of this work possible, viz., the very liberal support which I have received from the Carlsberg Fond at Copenhagen, and from the Danish Government and the Danish Parliament.

S. SÖRENSEN.

COPENHAGEN.
February, 1902.

LIST OF ABBREVIATIONS.

A. = Açvin.
Ā. = Āditya.
adj. = adjective
all. = allusion.
Aps. = Apsaras.
Arj. = Arjuna.
As. = Asura.
B. = Bombay edition.
Bh. = Bhūta.
Bhīmas. = Bhīmasena.
B.-ṛ = Brahmarshi.
Bṛh. = Bṛhaspati.
C. = Calcutta edition.
Cā. = Cāraṇa.
Çak. = Çakuni.
cf. = compare.
D. = Deva.
Dā. = Dānava.
Dai. = Daitya.
Dhanurv. = Dhanurveda.
Dhārt. = Dhārtarāshṭra.
Dhṛshṭady. = Dhṛshṭadyumna.
Dhṛt. = Dhṛtarāshṭra.
do. = ditto.
D.-ṛ. = Devarshi.
G. = Gandharva.
Gh. = Guhyaka.
Hanūm. = Hanūmat.
I. = Indra.
Janam. = Janamejaya.
Jayadr. = Jayadratha.
K. = Kinnara.
Kp. = Kimpurusha.
Kṛ = Kṛshṇa.
Kub. = Kubera.
LIA. = Lassen's Indische Altertumskunde.
Lp. = Lokapāla.
M. = Marut.
Mhbhr. = Mahābhārata.
M°Pu°st. = Mahāpurushastave.
M.-ṛ. = Maharshi.
MSNSt. = Mahādevasahasranāmastotra.
Mu. = Muni.
M.-U. = Mahoraga.
N. = Nāga.
Nak. = Nakula.
Nīl. = Nīlakaṇṭha.
P. = Pitṛ.
Pāṇd. = Pāṇḍava.
Pa°vra°mā° = Paṭivratāmāhātmyaparvan.
Pç. = Piçāca.
PCR. = Protap Chandra Roy's translation.
pl., plur. = plural.
Pn. = Pannaga.
q.v. = quod vide.
R. = Rudra.
Ṛ. = Ṛshi.
Rā. = Rākshasa.
S. = Sādhya.
Sapt. = Saptarshayaḥ.
sg. = singular.
Shd. = Sahadeva.
Si. = Siddha.
Sp. = Serpent.
Sū. = Sūrya.
Sū. Si. = the Sūrya Siddhānta (Journal of the American Oriental Society, vol. vi, 1860).
U. = Uraga.
V. = Burdwan edition.
V. = Vasu.
Vaiç. = Vaiçampāyana.
Vaiv. = Vaivasvata.
Var. = Varuṇa.
V.-D. = Viçve devāḥ.
VDSNK. = Vishṇor divyasahasranāmakathana.
Ved. = Veda.
Vi. = Viçva.
VP. = the Vishńu Puráńa, translated by H. H. Wilson, edited by FitzEdward Hall, London, 1864–77.
v.s. = vide supra.
Y. = Yaksha.
Yudh. = Yudhishṭhira.

° abbreviation of a word.
[ ] (1) headings not occurring as names in the text; (2) passages of the text in which a synonym is substituted for the name in question; (3) explanatory additions.
( ) headings occurring in the prose remark before the verse quoted.
* (1) a blessing on the reader; (2) headings which are not, or possibly are not, proper names.
** repeated.
† in trishṭubh (or jagatī)
(†) in trishṭubh (or jagatī) mixed with çlokas.
†† prose passage.
(††) mixed prose and çlokas.
> succession.
⁀ married to.
& fights against.
\+ assisted by.
Capitals in italics denote the heading of the article in which they occur.
Numbers of verses (in ordinary type) refer to the Calcutta edition.
Numbers of chapters (**in clarendon type**) refer to the Bombay edition, Çaka 1799.

CONCORDANCE

TO THE BOMBAY AND CALCUTTA EDITIONS AND P. C. ROY'S TRANSLATION.

(a) *Where the paragraphs are separated from the synopsis of chapters and verses, the headings to which they belong in the Index have simply been printed after the other indications relating to them. E.g.,* § 19 *(giving the contents of Mhbhr.* I, **5**, 1–11) *will be found under the heading* 'Bhṛgu.'

(b) *Where the paragraphs are not so separated, it should be generally understood that the title of the minor parvan to which a paragraph belongs is also the heading under which it will be found in the Index. E.g.,* § 249 (*Mhbhr.* I, **215**) *under the heading* 'Arjunavanavāsaparvan.' *If this is not the case, the paragraphs are to be found in the Index under the titles of those chapters of the parvan in question which have been printed with spaced type. E.g.,* § 177 (*Mhbhr.* I, **113**) *under the heading* 'Pāṇḍudigvijaya,' § 161 (*Mhbhr.* I, **96**) *under the heading* 'Mahābhishopākhyāna,' *and not under* 'Sambhavaparvan.'

I. ĀDIPARVAN.

I. Anukramaṇikā-parvan: I, 1.

1, 1-275 (1-268). PCR., pp. 1-21.
§ 1, I, **1,** 1-21 (1-21). pp. 1-2: Anukram. (Ugraçravas).
§ 2, I, **1,** 22-28 (22-28). pp. 2-3: id. (Vishṇu).
§ 3, I, **1,** 29-53 (29-53). pp. 3-4: id. (Bráhman).
§ 4, I, **1,** 54-220 (54-218). pp. 4-17: id. (Mahābhārata).
§ 5, I, **1,** 221-230 (219-224*a*). pp. 17-18: id. (Nārada).
§ 6, I, **1,** 230-251 (224*b*-244). pp. 18-19: id. (Sañjaya).
§ 7, I, **1,** 252-275 (245-268). pp. 19-21: id. (Mahābhārata).

II. Parvasaṅgraha-parvan: I, 2.

2, 1-396 (270-659). PCR., pp. 22-44.
§ 8, I, **2,** 1-16 (270-286*a*). pp. 21-22: Parvasaṅgr. (Paraçu-Rāma).
§ 9, I, **2,** 17-32 (286*b*-302). pp. 22-23: id. (akshauhiṇī).
§ 10, I, **2,** 33-83 (303-358). pp. 23-26: id. (Mahābhārata).
§ 11, I, **2,** 84-396 (359-659). pp. 26-44: id. (Mahābhārata).

III. Paushya-parvan: I, 3.

3, 1-188 (661-850). PCR., pp. 44-60.
§ 12, I, **3,** 1-10 (661-671). pp. 44-45: Paushyaparvan (Janamejaya).
§ 13, I, **3,** 11-20 (672-683). p. 45: id. (id.).
§ 14, I, **3,** 21-33*a* (684-697*a*). pp. 45-46: id. (id.).
§ 15, I, **3,** 33*b*-77 (697*b*-739). pp. 46-51: Upamanyu.
§ 16, I, **3,** 78-82 (740-746). p. 51: Veda.
§ 17, I, **3,** 83-188 (747-850). pp. 51-60: Ut(t)aṅka.

IV. Pauloma-parvan: I, 4-12.

4, 1-12 (851-862). pp. 60-61: Kathāpravoça.
5, 1-34 (863-896). pp. 61-63: [Pulomāgnisaṃvāda].
6, 1-14 (897-910). pp. 63-64: [Agniçāpa].
7, 1-29 (911-938). pp. 65-67: [Agniçāpamocana].
8, 1-27 (939-963). pp. 67-68: [Pramadvarāsarpadaṃça].
9, 1-23 (964-986). pp. 69-70: [Pramadvarājīvana].
10, 1-8 (987-994). pp. 70-71: [Ruru-duṇḍubha-saṃvāda].
11, 1-19 (995-1013). pp. 71-72: [Duṇḍubha-çāpamoksha].
12, 1-6 (1014-1019). pp. 72-73: Sarpasatra-prastāvanā.
§ 18, I, **4,** 1-12 (851-862). pp. 60-61: Paulomaparvan (Ugraçravas).
§ 19, I, **5,** 1-11 (863-873). pp. 61-62: Bhṛgu.
§ 20, I, **5,** 12—**7,** 29 (874-938). pp. 62-67: (*a*) Pulomā, (*b*) Agni.
§ 21, I, **8,** 1-22 (939-959). pp. 67-68: Pramadvarā.
§ 22, I, **8,** 23-27 (960-963). p. 68: id.
§ 23, I, **9,** 1-18 (964-981*a*). pp. 69-70: id.
§ 24, I, **9,** 19—**10,** 8 (981*b*-994). pp. 70-71: Sahasrapād.
§ 25, I, **11,** 1—**12,** 6 (995-1019). pp. 71-73: id.

V. Āstīkaparvan: I, 13-58.

(*a*) I, **13,** 1—**16,** 25 (1020-1093). pp. 73-77.
13, 1-32 (1020-1050). pp. 73-75: [Jaratkāru-tatpitṛ-saṃvāda].
14, 1-7 (1051-1057). p. 75: [Vāsuki-svasṛ-varaṇa].
15, 1-11 (1058-1068). pp. 75-76: [Sarpāṇāṃ mātṛ-çāpa-prastāva].
16, 1-25 (1069-1093). pp. 76-77: [Sarpādīnām utpatti].
§ 26, I, **13,** 1—**15,** 11 (1020-1068). pp. 73-76: Jaratkāru.
§ 27, I, **16,** 1-25 (1069-1093). pp. 76-77: Kaçyapa.

(*b*) *Amṛtamanthana*: I, **17,** 1—**19,** 31 (1094-1188). pp. 78-83.
17, 1-13 (1094-1111). p. 78: Amṛtamanthana.
18, 1-46 (1112-1157). pp. 79-81: id.
19, 1-31 (1158-1188). pp. 81-83: id. [-samāpti].
§ 28, I, **17,** 1—**19,** 31 (1094-1188). pp. 78-83: Amṛtamanthana.

(*c*) *Sauparṇa*: I, **20,** 1—**34,** 26 (1189-1545). pp. 83-112.
20, 1-16 (1189-1204). pp. 83-84.
21, 1-18 (1205-1222). pp. 85-86.
22, 1-12 (1223-1234). pp. 86-87: Samudradarçana.
23, 1-27 (1235-1260). pp. 87-89.
24, 1-20 (1261-1278). pp. 90-91.
25, 1-17 (1279-1295). pp. 91-93.
26, 1-8 (1296-1303). p. 93.
27, 1-16 (1304-1319). pp. 94-95.
28, 1-21 (1320-1339). pp. 95-97.
29, 1-44 (1340-1383). pp. 97-100.
30, 1-52 (1384-1435). pp. 100-104.

31, 1-35 (1436-1470). pp. 104-106
32, 1-25 (1471-1495). pp. 107-108.
33, 1-25 (1496-1519). pp. 109-110.
34, 1-26 (1520-1545). pp. 111-112.
§ 29, I, **20**, 1-16 (1189-1204). pp. 83-84: Kadrū.
§ 30, I, **21**, 1-18 (1205-1222). pp. 85-86: (*a*) Kadrū, (*b*) Samudra.
§ 31, I, **22**, 1-12 (1223-1234). pp. 86-87: (*a*) Kadrū, (*b*) Samudradarçana.
§ 32, I, **23**, 1-15*a* (1235-1249*a*). pp. 87-88: (*a*) Kadrū, (*b*) Garuḍa.
§ 33, I, **23**, 15*b*-27 (1249*b*-1260). pp. 88-89: Garuḍa.
§ 34, I, **24**, 1-5*a* (1261-1264). p. 90: id.
§ 35, I, **24**, 5*b*-20 (1265-1278). pp. 90-91: Aruṇa.
§ 36, I, **25**, 1-6 (1279-1284). p. 91: (*a*) Kadrū, (*b*) Garuḍa.
§ 37, I, **25**, 7-17 (1285-1295). p. 92: Indra.
§ 38, I, **26**, 1-8 (1296-1303). p. 93: Kadrū.
§ 39, I, **27**, 1-10*a* (1304-1313*a*). p. 94: Rāmaṇīyaka.
§ 40, I, **27**, 10*b*—**29**, 5 (1313*b*-1344). pp. 94-97: (*a*) Garuḍa, (*b*) Nishādāḥ.
§ 41, I, **29**, 6-32 (1345-1371*a*). pp. 97-99: (*a*) Garuḍa, (*b*) Supratīka.
§ 42, I, **29**, 33-36*a* (1371*b*-1374). p. 99: Garuḍa.
§ 43, I, **29**, 36*b*—**30**, 31 (1375-1414). pp. 99-102: (*a*) Garuḍa, (*b*) Alamba (?).
§ 44, I, **30**, 32-52 (1415-1435). pp. 102-104: Garuḍa.
§ 45, I, **31**, 1-35 (1436-1470). pp. 104-106: Vālikhilya.
§ 46, I, **32**, 1—**34**, 26 (1471-1545). pp. 107-112: Garuḍa.

(*d*) I, **35**, 1—**51**, 17 (1546-2031). pp. 113-147.
35, 1-19 (1546-1564). p. 113: [Sarpanāmakathana].
36, 1-25 (1565-1588). pp. 114-116: [Çesha-vṛtta-kathana].
37, 1-34 (1589-1621). pp. 116-118: [Vāsuky-ādi-mantraṇa].
38, 1-19 (1622-1640). pp. 118-119: [Elāpatra-vākya].
39, 1-14 (1641-1654). pp. 120-121: [Jaratkārv-anveshaṇa].
40, 1-32 (1655-1686). pp. 121-123: [Parikshid-upākhyāna].
41, 1-33 (1690-1724). pp. 123-125: [Parikshic-chāpa].
42, 1-41 (1725-1765). pp. 125-128: [Kāçyapāgamana].
43, 1-36 (1766-1801). pp. 128-130: [Takshaka-daṃça].
44, 1-11 (1802-1812). pp. 131-132: [Janamejaya-rājyābhisheka].
45, 1-34 (1813-1845). pp. 132-134: [Jaratkāru-pitṛdarçana].
46, 1-23 (1846-1868). pp. 134-136: [Vāsuki-Jaratkāru-samāgama].
47, 1-43 (1869-1911). pp. 136-139: [Jaratkāru-nirgama].
48, 1-22 (1912-1932). pp. 139-140: [Āstīkotpatti].
49, 1-31 (1933-1963). pp. 140-143: [Pārikshitīya].
50, 1-54 (1964-2014). pp. 143-146: [Parikshin-mantri-saṃvāda].
51, 1-17 (2015-2031). pp. 146-147: [Sarpasattropakrama].
§ 47, I, **35**, 1-19 (1546-1564). p. 113: Sarpanāmakathana.
§ 48, I, **36**, 1-25 (1565-1588). pp. 114-116: Çesha.
§ 49, I, **37**, 1—**39**, 14 (1589-1654). pp. 116-121: Vāsuki.
§ 50, I, **40**, 1-4 (1655-1658). p. 121: Jaratkāru (etymology).
§ 51, I, **40**, 5—**43**, 36 (1659-1801). pp. 121-130: Parikshit.
§ 52, I, **44**, 1-11 (1802-1812). pp. 131-132: Janamejaya.
§ 53, I, **45**, 1—**47**, 14*a* (1813-1882*a*). pp. 132-137: Jaratkāru (repetition).
§ 54, I, **47**, 14*b*-43 (1882*b*-1911). pp. 137-139: Jaratkāru.
§ 55, I, **48**, 1-22 (1912-1932). pp. 139-140: Āstīka.
§ 56, I, **49**, 1—**50**, 31 (1933-1991). pp. 140-145: Parikshit.
§ 57, I, **50**, 32-54 (1992-2014). pp. 145-146: Janamejaya.
§ 58, I, **51**, 1-17 (2015-2031). pp. 146-147: id.

(*e*) *Sarpasattra*: I, **52**, 1—**58**, 32 (2032-2197). pp. 148-160.
52, 1-10 (2032-2040). p. 148: Sarpasattr[opakrama].
53, 1-26 (2041-2066). pp. 149-150: id. [Vāsukivākya].
54, 1-30 (2067-2096). pp. 150-152: id. [Āstīkāgamana].
55, 1-17 (2097-2113). pp. 153-154: id. [Āstīka-kṛta-rājastava].
56, 1-27 (2114-2141). pp. 154-156: Āstīkavarapradāna.
57, 1-24 (2142-2165). pp. 157-158: [Sarpanāmakathana].
58, 1-32 (2166-2197). pp. 158-160: Sarpasattra.
§ 58*b*, I, **52**, 1-10 (2032-2040). p. 148: Sarpasattra.
§ 59, I, **53**, 1-10 (2041-2050). p. 149: id.
§ 60, I, **53**, 11—**54**, 30 (2051-2096). pp. 149-152: id.
§ 61, I, **55**, 1-17 (2097-2113). pp. 153-154: id.
§ 62, I, **56**, 1-27 (2114-2141). pp. 154-156: id.
§ 63, I, **57**, 1-7 (2142-2148). pp. 157-158: Sarpasattra (Vāsuki's race).
§ 64, I, **57**, 8-10 (2149-2151). pp. 157-158: id. (Takshaka's race).
§ 65, I, **57**, 11-12*a* (2152-2153*a*). pp. 157-158: id. (Airāvata's race).
§ 66, I, **57**, 12*b*-14*a* (2153*b*-2155*a*). pp. 157-158: id. (Kauravya's race).
§ 67, I, **57**, 14*b*-24 (2155*b*-2165). pp. 157-158: id. (Dhṛtarāshṭra's race).
§ 68, I, **58**, 1-28 (2166-2193). pp. 158-160: Āstīka.
§ 69, I, **58**, 29-32 (2194-2197). p. 160: Sarpasattra.

VI. ĀDIVAṂÇĀVATĀRAṆAPARVAN (C.) = AṂÇĀVATARAṆAPARVAN (B.): **I, 59-64.**

59, 1—**60**, 24 (2197-2230). pp. 161-163: Kathā[nu]-bandha.
61, 1-53 (2231-2282). pp. 163-167: Bhārata-sūtra.
62, 1-53 (2283-2333). pp. 168-171: [Mahā-]Bhārata-praçaṃsā.
63, 1-127 (2334-2455). pp. 171-180: Vyāsādy-utpatti = Ādivaṃçāvatāraṇa.
64, 1-54 (2456-2508). pp. 181-184: [Aṃçāvataraṇa].
§ 70 (*a*), I, **59**, 1-10 (2197-2207). p. 161: Ādivaṃçāvatāraṇa-parvan (Kathābandha (Vyāsa)).
(*b*), I, **60**, 1-24 (2208-2230). pp. 162-163: id. (Kathānu-bandha (Vyāsa)).
§ 71 (*c*), I, **61**, 1-53 (2231-2282). pp. 163-167: id. (Bhārata-sūtra).
§ 72 (*d*), I, **62**, 1-53 (2283-2333). pp. 168-171: id. (Bhārata-praçaṃsā).
(*e*) §§ 73-83. *Ādivaṃçāvatāraṇa.*
§ 73, I, **63**, 1-27 (2334-2360*a*). pp. 171-173: Vasu (Uparicara).
§ 74, I, **63**, 28-33*a* (2360*b*-2365). p. 173: Vasu['s sons].
§ 75, I, **63**, 33*b*-39*a* (2366-2371*a*). pp. 173-174: Vasu (*cf.* Girikā).
§ 76, I, **63**, 39*b*-69*a* (2371*b*-2398). pp. 174-176: Matsya (*cf.* Satyavatī).
§ 77, I, **63**, 69*b*-88 (2399-2417). pp. 176-177: Vyāsa.
§ 78, I, **63**, 89-90 (2418-2419). p. 177: Vyāsa['s pupils].
§ 79, I, **63**, 91 (2420). p. 178: Bhīshma.
§ 80, I, **63**, 92-97*a* (2421-2426*a*). p. 178: Aṇīmāṇḍavya.
§ 81, I, **63**, 97*b*-98 (2426*b*-2427). p. 178: Sañjaya; Karṇa.
§ 82, I, **63**, 99-104*a* (2428-2432). pp. 178-179: Kṛshṇa Vāsudeva.
§ 83, I, **63**, 104*b*-127 (2433-2455). pp. 179-180: Ādivaṃçāvatāraṇa.
§ 84, I, **64**, 1-54 (2456-2508). pp. 181-184: Ādivaṃçāvatāraṇaparvan (Paraçu-Rāma; Kṛta-yuga; Asurā).

VII. Sambhavaparvan: I, **65–140.**

(*a*) [*Aṃçāvataraṇa*]: I, **65,** 1—**67,** 164 (2509–2798). pp. 185–204.

65, 1–56 (2509–2564). pp. 185–188: Ādityādi-vaṃçakathana [Aṃçāvataraṇa].

66, 1–72 (2565–2636). pp. 188–193: [Aṃçāvataraṇa].

67, 1–164 (2637–2798). pp. 193–204: Aṃçāvataraṇa [-samāpti].

§ 85, I, **65,** 1–8 (2509–2516). p. 185: Aṃçāvataraṇa.

§ 86, I, **65,** 9–11*a* (2517–2519*a*). p. 185: id. (Brahmán. Kaçyapa).

§ 87, I, **65,** 11*b*–13 (2519*b*–2521). p. 185: id. (Daksha).

§ 88, I, **65,** 14–16 (2522–2524). p. 185: id. (Ādityāḥ).

§ 89, I, **65,** 17–18 (2525–2526). p. 186: id. (Hiraṇyakaçipu).

§ 90, I, **65,** 19 (2527). p. 186: id. (Prahlāda).

§ 91, I, **65,** 20–21*a* (2528–2529*a*). p. 186: id. (Bali, Bāṇa, Virocana).

§ 92, I, **65,** 21*b*–27 (2529*b*–2535). p. 186: id. (Danu).

§ 93, I, **65,** 28–30 (2536–2538). p. 186: id. (Danu).

§ 94, I, **65,** 31 (2539). p. 186: id. (Siṃhikā).

§ 95, I, **65,** 32 (2540). p. 186: id. (Krūrā).

§ 96, I, **65,** 33 (2541). p. 186: id. (Danāyus).

§ 97, I, **65,** 34–35 (2542–2543). pp. 186–187; id. (Kālā).

§ 98, I, **65,** 36–39 (2544–2547). p. 187: id. (Çukra).

§ 99, I, **65,** 40 (2548). p. 187: id. (Vainateyāḥ).

§ 100, I, **65,** 41 (2549). p. 187: id. (Kādraveyāḥ).

§ 101, I, **65,** 42–44 (2550–2552). p. 187: id. (Muni).

§ 102, I, **65,** 45–48*a* (2553–2556*a*). p. 187: id. (Prādhā).

§ 103, I, **65,** 48*b*–51 (2556*b*–2559). p. 187: id. (Prādhā).

§ 104, I, **65,** 51 (2559). pp. 187–188: id. (Prādhā).

§ 105, I, **65,** 52 (2560). p. 188: id. (Kapilā).

§ 106, I, **65,** 53–56 (2561–2564). p. 188: id.

§ 107, I, **66,** 1*a* (2565*a*). p. 188: id. (Brahmán).

§ 108, I, **66,** 1*b*–3 (2565*b*–2567). p. 188: id. (Sthāṇu).

§ 109, I, **66,** 4 (2568). p. 188: id. (Maharshis, *cf.* § 86).

§ 110, I, **66,** 5 (2569). p. 188: id. (Aṅgiras).

§ 111, I, **66,** 6 (2570). p. 188: id. (Atri).

§ 112, I, **66,** 7 (2571). pp. 188–189: id. (Pulastya).

§ 113, I, **66,** 8 (2572). p. 189: id. (Pulaha).

§ 114, I, **66,** 9 (2573). p. 189: id. (Kratu).

§ 115, I, **66,** 10–17*a* (2574–2581*a*). p. 189: id. (Daksha).

§ 116, I, **66,** 17*b*–30 (2581*b*–2594). pp. 189–190: id. (Vasavaḥ).

§ 117, I, **66,** 31–33 (2595–2597). p. 190: id. (Dharma).

§ 118, I, **66,** 34 (2598). p. 190: id. (Kaçyapa).

§ 119, I, **66,** 35 (2599). p. 190: id. (Açvin).

§ 120, I, **66,** 36 (2600). p. 190: id. (Ādityāḥ).

§ 120 *bis*, I, **66,** 37–41*a* (2601–2605*a*). p. 191: id. (Devagaṇāḥ).

§ 121, I, **66,** 41*b*–43 (2605*b*–2607). p. 191: id. (Bhṛgu, Çukra).

§ 122, I, **66,** 44–49 (2608–2613). pp. 191–192: id. (Cyavana).

§ 123, I, **66,** 50–51 (2614–2615). p. 192: id. (Brahmán, Dhātṛ, Lakshmī).

§ 124, I, **66,** 52 (2616). p. 192: id. (Çukra, Devī, Surā).

§ 125, I, **66,** 53–55 (2617–2619). p. 192: id. (Adharma, Mṛtyu).

§ 126, I, **66,** 56–59 (2620–2623). p. 192: id. (Tāmrā).

§ 127, I, **66,** 60–69*a* (2624–2633*a*). pp. 192–193: id. (Krodhavaçā).

§ 128, I, **66,** 69*b*–70*a* (2633*b*–2634*a*). p. 193: id. (Çyenī).

§ 129, I, **66,** 70*b*–72 (2634*b*–2636). p. 193: id. (Kadrū, Surasā, etc.).

§ 130, I, **67,** 1–128 (2637–2763). pp. 193–201: id. (Bhīshma, Dhṛtarāshṭra, etc.).

§ 131, I, **67,** 129–150 (2764–2784). pp. 201–203: id. (Kuntī, Karṇa).

§ 132, I, **67,** 151–164 (2785–2798). pp. 203–204: id. (Nārāyaṇa, etc.).

(*b*) *Çakuntalopākhyāna*: I, **68,** 1—**74,** 133 (2799–3125). pp. 204–228.

68, 1–15 (2799–2813). pp. 204–205: Çākuntalopākhyāna.

69, 1–31 (2814–2844). pp. 205–207: id.

70, 1–51 (2845–2894). pp. 207–211: id.

71, 1–42 (2895–2936). pp. 211–214: id.

72, 1–19 (2937–2954). pp. 215–216: id.

73, 1–34 (2955–2987). pp. 216–218: id.

74, 1–133 (2988–3125). pp. 219–228: id.

§ 133, I, **68,** 1—**71,** 15 (2799–2909). pp. 204–212: Dushyanta.

§ 134, I, **71,** 16—**72,** 19 (2910–2954). pp. 212–216: Viçvāmitra.

§ 135, I, **73,** 1—**74,** 133 (2955–3125). pp. 216–228: Çakuntalopākhyāna.

(*c*) *Yayāty-upākhyāna*: I, **75,** 1—**85,** 35 (3126–3534). pp. 228–260.

75, 1–58 (3126–3182). pp. 228–232: Yayāty-upākhyāna.

76, 1–72 (3183–3255). pp. 232–238: id.

77, 1–23 (3256–3278). pp. 238–240: id.

78, 1–41 (3279–3318). pp. 240–243: id.

79, 1–13 (3319–3331). pp. 243–244: id.

80, 1–27 (3332–3358). pp. 245–247: id.

81, 1–38 (3359–3396). pp. 247–250: id.

82, 1–27 (3397–3423). pp. 250–252: id.

83, 1–42 (3424–3465). pp. 252–255: id.

84, 1–34 (3466–3499). pp. 255–258: id.

85, 1–35 (3500–3534). pp. 258–260: id.

§ 136, I, **75,** 1–3 (3126–3128). p. 228: Yayāty-upākhyāna.

§ 137, I, **75,** 4–5 (3129–3130). p. 228: Daksha Prācetasa.

§ 138, I, **75,** 6–9 (3131–3134). pp. 228–229: id.

§ 139, I, **75,** 10–18*a* (3135–3143*a*). pp. 229–230: Manu Vaivasvata.

§ 140, I, **75,** 18*b*–24*a* (3143*b*–3148). p. 230: Purūravas.

§ 141, I, **75,** 24*b*–26*a* (3149–3150). p. 230: id.

§ 142, I, **75,** 26*b*–30*a* (3151–3154). p. 230: Nahusha.

§ 143, I, **75,** 30*b*–35 (3155–3160*a*). p. 230: id.

§ 144, I, **75,** 36–58 (3160*b*–3182). pp. 230–232: Yayāti.

§ 145, I, **76,** 1—**77,** 23 (3183–3278). pp. 232–240: Kaca.

§ 146, I, **78,** 1—**81,** 38 (3279–3396). pp. 240–250: Devayānī.

§ 147, I, **82,** 1—**83,** 42 (3397–3465). pp. 250–255: id.

§ 148, I, **84,** 1—**85,** 35 (3466–3534). pp. 255–260: Yayāti.

(*d*) *Uttara-Yayāty-upākhyāna*: I, **86,** 1—**93,** 28 (3535–3690): pp. 261–277.

86, 1–17 (3535–3550). pp. 261–262: Uttara-Ya°-upākhyā° (U°-Yāyātam).

87, 1–13 (3551–3563). pp. 262–263: id. (id.).

88, 1–13 (3564–3576). pp. 263–265: id. (id.).

89, 1–23 (3577–3599). pp. 265–267: id. (id.).

90, 1–27 (3600–3626). pp. 267–270: id. (id.).

91, 1–18 (3627–3644). pp. 270–272: id. (id.).

92, 1–19 (3645–3663). pp. 272–275: id. (id.).

93, 1–28 (3664–3690). pp. 275–277: id. (id.).

§ 149, I, **86,** 1—**93,** 28 (3535–3690). pp. 261–277: Yayāti.

(*e*) *Pūruvaṃçānukīrtana*: I, **94,** 1—**95,** 90 (3691–3842). pp. 278–288.

94, 1–64 (3691–3753). pp. 278–282: Pūruvaṃçānukīrtana.

95, 1–90 (3754–3842). pp. 282–288: id.

§ 150, I, **94,** 1–19 (3691–3709). pp. 278–279: Pūruvaṃç° (from Pūru to Bharata).

§ 151, I, **94**, 20-23 (3710-3713). p. 279 : id. (Bharata).
§ 152, I, **94**, 24-34 (3714-3724). pp. 279-280 : id. (from Bharata to Saṃvaraṇa).
§ 153, I, **94**, 35-48*a* (3725-3737). pp. 280-281 : id. (Saṃvaraṇa).
§ 154, I, **94**, 48*b*-59*a* (3738-3748*a*). p. 281 : id. (from Saṃvaraṇa to Pratīpa, excl.).
§ 155, I, **94**, 59*b*-64 (3748*b*-3753). pp. 281-282 : id. (from Pratīpa to Çāntanu).
§ 156, I, **95**, 1-51 (3754-3804). pp. 282-285 : id. (from Daksha to Vicitravīrya).
§ 157, I, **95**, 52-68 (3805-3820). pp. 285-286 : id. (from Vicitravīrya's death to Pāṇḍu's death).
§ 158, I, **95**, 69-74 (3821-3826). p. 287 : id. (Pāṇḍavāḥ).
§ 159, I, **95**, 75-82 (3827-3834). p. 287 : id. (the Pāṇḍavas' eleven children).
§ 160, I, **95**, 83-90 (3835-3842). pp. 287-288 : id. (from Abhimanyu to Açvamedhadatta).

(*f*) *Mahābhishopākhyāna*: I, **96**.
§ 161, I, **96**, 1-23 (3843-3864). pp. 288-290 : Mahābhishopākhyāna.

(*g*) *Çāntanūpakhyāna*: I, **97**.
§ 162, I, **97**, 1-32 (3865-3895). pp. 290-292 : Çāntanūpākhyāna.

(*h*) *Bhīshmotpatti*: I, **98**.
§ 163, I, **98**, 1-24 (3896-3919). pp. 293-294 : Bhīshmotpatti.

(*i*) *Apavopākhyāna* : I, **99**.
§ 164, I, **99**, 1-49 (3920-3967). pp. 295-297 : Āpavopākhyāna.

(*j*) *Satyavatīlābhopākhyāna* : I, **100**.
§ 165, I, **100**, 1-103 (3968-4066). pp. 298-305 : Satyavatīlābhopākhyāna.

(*k*) *Citrāṅgadopākhyāna* : I, **101**.
§ 166, I, **101**, 1-14 (4067-4080). pp. 305-306 : Citrāṅgadopākhyāna.

(*l*) *Vicitravīryoparama*: I, **102**.
§ 167, I, **102**, 1-73 (4081-4145). pp. 306-311 : Vicitravīryoparama.

(*m*)
I, **103**, 1-26 (4146-4171). pp. 311-313 : Bhīshma-Satyavatī-saṃvāda.
104, 1-56 (4172-4222). pp. 313-317 : id.
105, 1-54 (4223-4273). pp. 317-321 : Satyavaty-upadeça.
106, 1-32 (4274-4304). pp. 321-323 : Vicitravīrya-sutotpatti.
§ 168, I, **103**, 1-26 (4146-4171). pp. 311-313 : Bhīshma-Satyavatī-saṃvāda.
§ 169, I, **104**, 1-8 (4172-4178). p. 313 : Paraçu-Rāma.
§ 170, I, **104**, 9-56 (4179-4222). pp. 313-317 : Dīrghatamas.
§ 171, I, **105**, 1—**106**, 32 (4223-4304). pp. 317-323 : Vicitravīrya-sutotpatti.

(*n*) *Aṇīmāṇḍavyopākhyāna* : I, **107-108**.
§ 172, I, **107**, 1-17 (4305-4321). pp. 323-324 : Aṇīmāṇḍavyopākhyāna.
108, 1-19 (4322-4336). pp. 324-326 : id.

(*o*)
§ 173, I, **109**, 1-26 (4337-4362). pp. 326-328 : Pāṇḍurājyābhisheka.
§ 174, I, **110**, 1-19 (4363-4381). pp. 328-329 : Dhṛtarāshṭravivāha.
§ 175, I, **111**, 1-31 (4382-4411). pp. 329-331 : Aindri-çaktilābha (Karṇa-sambhava).
§ 176, I, **112**, 1-13 (4412-4424). p. 332 : Kuntī-vivāha.
§ 177, I, **113**, 1-45 (4425-4468). pp. 333-336 : Pāṇḍu-digvijaya.
114, 1-14 (4469-4482). pp. 336-337 : Vidura-pariṇaya.
§ 178, I, **114**, 1-11 (4469-4479). pp. 336-337 : Pāṇḍu.
§ 179, I, **114**, 12-14 (4480-4482). pp. 337 : Viduraparinaya.
§ 180, I, **115**, 1-44 (4483-4522). pp. 337-340 : Gāndharīputrotpatti.
§ 181, I, **116**, 1-18 (4523-4539). pp. 340-348 : Duḥçalotpatti.
§ 182, I, **117**, 1-18 (4540-4557). p. 342 : Dhṛtarāshṭraputranāmakathana.

(*p*)
I, **118**, 1—**127**, 32 (4558-4963). pp. 343-373.
118, 1-34 (4558-4591). pp. 343-349 : Pāṇḍu-mṛgaçāpa.
119, 1-50 (4592-4639). pp. 346-349 : Pāṇḍu-carita.
120, 1-41 (4640-4679). pp. 349-353 : Pāṇḍu-Pṛthā-saṃvāda.
121, 1-37 (4680-4715). pp. 353-355 : Vyushitāçvopākhyāna.
122, 1-44 (4716-4758). pp. 355-359 : Kuntī-putrotpattyanujñāna.
123, 1-78 (4759-4835). pp. 359-364 : Pāṇḍavotpatti.
124, 1-32 (4836-4865). pp. 364-366 : id.
125, 1-31 (4866-4896). pp. 367-369 : Pāṇḍūparama.
126, 1-35 (4897-4931). pp. 369-371 : Ṛshisaṃvāda.
127, 1-32 (4932-4963). pp. 371-373 : Pāṇḍu-dāha.
§ 183, I, **118**, 1-34 (4558-4591). pp. 343-345 : (*a*) Pāṇḍu, (*b*) Agastya.
§ 184, I, **119**, 1-50 (4592-4639). pp. 346-349 : Pāṇḍu.
§ 185, I, **120**, 1-41 (4640-4679). pp. 349-353 : (*a*) Pāṇḍu, (*b*) Manu Svāyambhava, (*c*) Çāradaṇḍāyanī.
§ 186, I, **121**, 1-37 (4680-4715). pp. 353-355 : Vyushitāçvopākhyāna.
§ 187, I, **122**, 1-21*a* (4716-4735). pp. 355-357 : (*a*) Pāṇḍu, (*b*) Çvetaketu.
§ 188, I, **122**, 21*b*-31 (4736-4745). p. 357 : Madayantī.
§ 189, I, **122**, 32-44 (4746-4758). pp. 357-359 : Pāṇḍu.
§ 190, I, **123**, 1-46 (4759-4802). pp. 359-362 : (*a*) Pāṇḍavotpatti, (*b*) Yudhishṭhira, (*c*) Bhīmasena, (*d*) Arjuna.
§ 191, I, **123**, 47-78 (4803-4835). pp. 362-364 : (*a*) Pāṇḍavotpatti, (*b*) Arjuna.
§ 192, I, **124**, 1-32 (4836-4865). pp. 364-366 : Pāṇḍavotpatti.
§ 193, I, **125**, 1-31 (4866-4896). pp. 367-369 : Pāṇḍu.
§ 194, I, **126**, 1-35 (4897-4931). pp. 369-371 : id.
§ 195, I, **127**, 1-32 (4932-4963). pp. 371-373 : id.

(*q*)
I, **128**, 1-72 (4964-5033). pp. 373-377 : Bhīmasenarasapāna.
129, 1-43 (5034-5070). pp. 377-380 : Bhīma-pratyāgamana.
§ 196, I, **128**, 1-13 (4964-4976). pp. 373-374 : Vyāsa.
§ 197, I, **128**, 14—**129**, 43 (4977-5070). pp. 374-380 : Bhīmasena-rasapāna.

(*r*)
I, **130**, 1-67 (5071-5133). pp. 380-385 : Droṇa-Bhārgava-saṃvāda (Droṇasya Bhārgavād astraprāpti).

131, 1–79 (5134–5210). pp. 385–391 : Bhīshma-Droṇa-Samvāda (°samāgama).

132, 1–79 (5211–5288). pp. 391–396 : Droṇa-çishya-parīkshā.

133, 1–22 (5289–5311). pp. 397–398 : Droṇa-grāha-mokshaṇa.

§ 198, I, **130**, 1–24*a* (5071–5093). pp. 380–382 : Çaradvat.

§ 199, I, **130**, 24*b*–30 (5094–5099). p. 382 : Droṇa.

§ 200, I, **130**, 31–40 (5100–5108). pp. 382–383 : id.

§ 201, I, **130**, 41–67 (5109–5133). pp. 383–385 : (*a*) Droṇa, (*b*) Drupada.

§ 202, I, **131**, 1–79 (5134–5210). pp. 385–391 : (*a*) Droṇa, (*b*) Açvatthāman.

§ 203, I, **132**, 1–29 (5211–5239). pp. 391–393 : (*a*) Droṇa, (*b*) Arjuna, (*c*) Açvatthāman.

§ 204, I, **132**, 30–60 (5240–5269). pp. 393–395 : Ekalavya.

§ 205, I, **132**, 61–66 (5270–5275). pp. 395–396 : Droṇa.

§ 206, I, **132**, 67 — **133**, 10 (5276–5298). pp. 396–397 : id.

§ 207, I, **133**, 11–22 (5299–5311). pp. 397–398 : Droṇa-grāha-mokshaṇa.

(*s*) *Astradarçana* : I, **134–137**.

§ 208, I, **134**, 1–35 (5312–5346). pp. 398–400 : Astra-darçana.

135, 1–32 (5347–5378). pp. 401–403 : id.

136, 1–41 (5379–5418). pp. 403–406 : id. (Karṇābhisheka).

137, 1–25 (5419–5443). pp. 406–408 : id.

(*t*)

§ 209, I, **138**, 1–77 (5444–5516). pp. 408–413 : Drupada-çāsana.

I, **139**, 1–27 (5517–5542). pp. 413–415 : Dhṛtarāshṭracintā.

§ 210, I, **139**, 1–19 (5517–5533). pp. 413–415 : Sambhava-parvan.

§ 211, I, **139**, 20–27 (5534–5542). pp. 415 : id.

§ 212, I, **140**, 1–93 (5543–5634). pp. 416–424 : Kaṇika-vākya.

VIII. JATUGṚHAPARVAN.

§ 213, I, **141**, 1–38 (5635–5672). pp. 424–427 : Duryodhanershyā.

142, 1–24 (5673–5695). pp. 427–428 : Duryodhanaparā-marça.

143, 1–19 (5696–5714). pp. 429–430 : Vāraṇāvatayātrā.

144, 1–19 (5715–5733). pp. 430–431 : Purocanopadeça.

145, 1–34 (5734–5767). pp. 431–434 : Vāraṇāvata-gamana.

146, 1–31 (5768–5797). pp. 434–436 : Bhīmasena-Yudhi-shṭhira-saṃvāda.

147, 1–20 (5798–5818). pp. 436–438 : Jatugṛhavāsa.

148, 1–22 (5819–5840). pp. 438–439 : Jatugṛhadāha.

149, 1–15 (5841–5855). pp. 439–440 : Gaṅgottaraṇa.

150, 1–26 (5856–5881). pp. 441–442 : Pāṇḍava-vana-praveça.

151, 1–45 (5882–5926). pp. 443–446 : Bhīma-jalāharaṇa.

IX. HIḌIMBAVADHAPARVAN.

§ 214, I, **152**, 1–36 (5927–5961). pp. 446–448 : Hiḍimbā-Bhīma-saṃvāda (Bhīma-Hiḍimbā°).

153, 1–45 (5962–6006). pp. 448–452 : Hiḍimba-[Bhīma-] yuddha.

154, 1–36 (6007–6041). pp. 452–454 : Hiḍimba-vadha.

155, 1–46 (6042–6083). pp. 454–457 : Ghaṭotkacotpatti.

156, 1–19 (6084–6102). pp. 458–459 : Vyāsa-darçana [Ekacakrāpraveçe Vyā°].

X. BAKAVADHAPARVAN.

§ 215, I, **157**, 1–41 (6103–6142). pp. 459–462 : Brāhmaṇa-cintā.

158, 1–38 (6143–6180). pp. 462–465 : Brāhmaṇī-vākya.

159, 1–24 (6181–6204). pp. 465–467 : Brāhmaṇa-kanyā-putra-vākya.

160, 1–17 (6205–6221). pp. 467–468 : Kuntī-praçna.

161, 1–20 (6222–6240). pp. 468–470 : Bhīma-Baka-vadhāṅgīkāra.

162, 1–26 (6241–6266). pp. 470–472 : Kuntī-Yudhishṭhira-vākya (°samvāda).

163, 1–28 (6267–6294). pp. 472–474 : Baka-Bhīma-yuddha.

164, 1–21 (6295–6315). pp. 474–475 : Baka-vadha.

XI. CAITRARATHAPARVAN : I, **165–183** : (*a*) **165–170**.

§ 216, I, **165**, 1–12 (6316–6327). pp. 475–476 : Draupadī-sambhava.

§ 217, I, **166**, 1–28 (6328–6355). pp. 476–479 : id.

§ 218, I, **167**, 1–56 (6356–6409). pp. 479–483 : id. [id.].

§ 219, I, **168**, 1–11 (6410–6420). pp. 483–484 : Pāñcāla-deçayātrā.

§ 220, I, **169**, 1–16 (6421–6436). pp. 484–485 : [Draupadī-janmāntara-kathana].

§ 221, I, **170**, 1–80 (6437–6515). pp. 486–492 : Gandharva-vākya (°parābhava).

(*b*) *Tapaty-upākhyāna* : I, **171–173**.

§ 222, I, **171**, 1–44 (6516–6559). pp. 492–495 : Tapaty-upākhyāna.

172, 1–26 (6560–6583). pp. 495–496 : id.

173, 1–50 (6584–6633). pp. 497–500 : Tāpatya (Tapaty-upākhyānasamāpti).

(*c*) I, **174–183**.

I, **174**, 1–15 (6634–6648). pp. 500–501 : Purohitakaraṇa-kathana.

175, 1–48 (6649–6695). pp. 501–504 : Vāçishṭhe Viçvā-mitraparābhava.

176, 1–49 (6696–6744). pp. 505–508 : Vāçishṭhe Vaçishṭa-çoka.

177, 1–47 (6745–6791). pp. 508–511 : Vāçishṭhe Saudā-sasutotpatti.

178, 1–29 (6792–6819). pp. 512–514 : Aurvopākhyāna.

179, 1–22 (6820–6841). pp. 514–515 : Aurva-vāraṇa.

180, 1–23 (6842–6864). pp. 516–517 : Aurvopākhyāna.

§ 223, I, **174**, 1 — **175**, 48 (6634–6695). pp. 500–504 : Vāsishṭha.

§ 224, I, **176**, 1–42 (6696–6737), pp. 505–507 : Kalmāshapāda.

§ 225, I, **176**, 43 — **177**, 47 (6738–6791), pp. 508–511 : Vāsishṭha.

§ 226, I, **178**, 1–11*a* (6792–6802*a*), p. 512 : Parāçara.

§ 227, I, **178**, 11*b* — **180**, 23 (6802*b*–6864), pp. 513–517 : Aurvopākhyāna.

§ 228, I, **181**, 1–23 (6865–6887). pp. 517–519 : Aurvo-pākhyāna.

§ 229, I, **182**, 1–26 (6888–6912). pp. 519–521 : Vasishṭho-pākhyāna.

§ 230, I, **183**, 1–12 (6913–6924). pp. 521–522 : Dhaumya-purohitakaraṇa.

XII. SVAYAṂVARAPARVAN.

I, **184**, 1–20 (6925–6944). pp. 522–524 : Pāṇḍavagamana.

185, 1–37 (6945–6980). pp. 524–526 : Dhṛshṭadyumna-vākya.

186, 1-24 (6981-7004). pp. 527-528 : Rājanāmakīrtana.
187, 1-29 (7005-7033). pp. 528-530 : [Sarva-]Rāja-parāṇmukha (°parāṅmukhībhavana).
188, 1-28 (7034-7060). pp. 531-533 : Lakshyacchedana.
189, 1-24 (7061-7084). pp. 533-535 : Kṛshṇa-vākya.
190, 1-47 (7085-7130). pp. 535-538 : Pāṇḍavapratyāgamana.
191, 1-25 (7131-7155). pp. 538-541 : Rāma-Kṛshṇāgamana.
192, 1-18 (7156-7173). pp. 541-542 : Dhṛshṭadyumnapratyāgamana.
§ 231, I, **184**, 1 — **185**, 37 (6925-6980). Svayaṃvaraparvan.
§ 232, I, **186**, 1-24 (6981-7004) : id.
§ 233, I, **187**, 1 — **188**, 28 (7005-7060) : id.
§ 234, I, **189**, 1 — **190**, 43 (7061-7126*a*) : id.
§ 235, I, **190**, 43*b* — **191**, 25 (7126*b*-7155) : id.
§ 236, I, **192**, 1-18 (7156-7173) : id.

XIII. VAIVĀHIKAPARVA.

I, **193**, 1-29 (7174-7202). pp. 543-545 : Purohitāgamana (°Yudhishṭhira-saṃvāda).
194, 1-15 (7203-7217). pp. 546-547 : Sāṅgrāmikadravyagrahana (Yudhishṭhirādiparīkshaṇa).
195, 1-33 (7218-7251). pp. 547-550 : Dvaipāyanāgamana.
196, 1-23 (7252-7274). pp. 550-551 : Vyāsa-vākya.
197, 1-53 (7275-7328). pp. 552-557 : Pañcendropākhyāna.
198, 1-18 (7329-7346). pp. 557-559 : Draupadī-vivāha.
199, 1-19 (7347-7365). pp. 559-560 : id.
§ 237, I, **193**, 1 — **196**, 23 (7174-7274) : Vaivāhikaparvan.
§ 238, I, **197**, 1-43 (7275-7318) : Pañcendropākhyāna.
§ 239, I, **197**, 44-53 (7319-7328) : id.
§ 240, I, **198**, 1 — **199**, 19 (7329-7365) : Vaivāhikaparvan.

XIV. VIDURĀGAMANAPARVA.

I, **200**, 1-31 (7366-7395). pp. 561-563 : Duryodhana-vākya.
201, 1-20 (7396-7414). pp. 563-565 : id.
202, 1-25 (7415-7440). pp. 565-566 : Dhṛtarāshṭramantraṇa.
203, 1-19 (7441-7459). pp. 567-568 : Bhīshmavākya.
204, 1-28 (7460-7487). pp. 568-570 : Droṇa-vākya.
205, 1-30 (7488-7517). pp. 570-572 : Viduravākya.
206, 1-26 (7518-7544). pp. 573-574 : Vidura-[Drupada-] saṃvāda.
§ 241, I, **200**, 1 — **204**, 12 (7366-7471) : Vidurāgamanaparvan.
§ 242, I, **204**, 13-25 (7472-7484) : Ambuvīca.
§ 243, I, **204**, 26 — **206**, 26 (7485-7544) : Vidurāgamanaparvan.

XV. RĀJYALĀBHAPARVAN (°LAMBHA°).

(*a*) § 244, I, **207**, 1-52 (7545-7596). pp. 575-579 : Kṛshṇagamana (Puranirmāṇa).
(*b*) § 245, I, **208**, 1-24 (7596-7618). pp. 579-580 : Yudhishṭhira-Nārada-saṃvāda.
(*c*) *Sundopasundopākhyāna* (ch. 209-212).
§ 246, I, **209**, 1-33 (7619-7651). pp. 581-583 : Sundopasundopākhyāna.
210, 1-27 (7652-7678). pp. 583-585 : id.
211, 1-32 (7679-7710). pp. 586-588 : Tilottamā-prasthāpana (Su° Ti°).
212, 1-31 (7711-7742). pp. 588-590 : Sundopasundopākhyāna.

XVI. ARJUNAVANAVĀSAPARVAN.

§ 247, I, **213**, 1-35 (7743-7775). pp. 590-593 : Arjunatīrthayātrā.
§ 248, I, **214**, 1-36 (7776-7811). pp. 593-596 : Ulūpī-saṅga.
§ 249, I, **215**, 1-27 (7812-7838). pp. 596-598 : Citrāṅgadāsaṅgama.
§ 250, I, **216**, 1-23 (7839-7860). pp. 598-600 : Tīrthagrāhavimocana.
217, 1-35 (7861-7884). pp. 600-602 : Arjunatīrthayātrā.
§ 251, I, **218**, 1-21 (7885-7905). pp. 602-603 : Arjuna-Dvārakāgamana.

XVII. SUBHADRĀHARAṆAPARVAN.

§ 252, I, **219**, 1-25 (7906-7930). pp. 603-605 : Yudhishṭhirānujñā.
220, 1-32 (7931-7962). pp. 605-607 : Baladeva-krodha.

XVIII. HARAṆĀHARAṆAPARVAN : I, **221**, 1-89 (7963-8049). PCR., pp. 607-613.

§ 253. (*a*) Haraṇāharaṇaparvan, (*b*) Dhanurveda, (*c*) Kṛshṇā.

XIX. KHĀṆḌAVADAHANAPARVAN : (*a*) I, **222**, 1 — **227**, 52 (8050-8284). PCR., pp. 614-631.

I, **222**, 1-33 (8050-8082). pp. 614-616 : Brāhmaṇarūpy-Analāgamana.
223, 1-83 (8083-8156). pp. 616-622 : Agniparābhava.
224, 1-21 (8157-8173). pp. 622-623 : Arjunāgni-saṃvāda.
225, 1-37 (8174-8210). pp. 623-626 : (Khāṇḍava-dāha) Gāṇḍīvādi-dāna.
226, 1-22 (8211-8232). pp. 626-627 : Indra-krodha.
227, 1-52 (8233-8284). pp. 628-631 : Deva-Kṛshṇārjuna-yuddha.

(*b*) (*Khāṇḍavadahanaparvan*) *Mayadarçanaparvan* : I, **228**, 1 — **234**, 19 (8285-8479). pp. 631-647.

I, **228**, 1-47 (8285-8330). pp. 631-634 : Maya-Dānavatrāṇa.
229, 1-34 (8331-8363). pp. 634-637 : Çāṅgakopākhyāna.
230, 1-22 (8364-8385). pp. 637-639 : Jaritā-vilāpa.
231, 1-18 (8386-8403). pp. 639-640 : Çārṅg[ak]opākhyāna.
232, 1-25 (8404-8428). pp. 641-643 : id.
233, 1-32 (8429-8460). pp. 643-645 : id.
234, 1-19 (8461-8479). pp. 646-647 : [Vara-pradāna].
§ 254, I, **222**, 1 — **223**, 11 (8050-8093). pp. 614-617 : Khāṇḍavadahanaparvan.
§ 255, I, **223**, 12-83 (8094-8156). pp. 617-622 : (*a*) Agniparābhava, (*b*) Durvāsas.
§ 256, I, **224**, 1-21 (8157-8173). pp. 622-623 : (*a*) Agniparābhava, (*b*) Khāṇḍavadah.
§ 257, I, **225**, 1-37 (8174-8210). pp. 623-626 : (*a*) Khāṇḍavadahanap., (*b*) Varuṇa, (*c*) Gāṇḍīva, (*d*) Arjuna's horses, (*e*) Sudarçana, (*f*) Kaumodakī.
§ 258, I, **226**, 1 — **228**, 47 (8211-8330). pp. 626-634 : Khāṇḍavadahanap.

§ 259, I, **229**, 1 — **234**, 4 (8331–8464). pp. 634–646 : (*a*) Çārṅgakopākhyāna, (*b*) Arundhatī.

§ 260, I, **234**, 5–19 (8465–8479). pp. 646–647 : Khāṇḍavadahanap.

II. SABHĀPARVAN.

XX. Sabhākriyāparvan.

§ 261, II, **1**, 1–21 (1–20). pp. 1–2 : Sabhākhyānanirṇaya (°sthāna°).

§ 262, II, **2**, 1–36 (21–57). pp. 3–5 : Bhagavad-yāna.

§ 263, II, **3**, 1–37 (58–95). pp. 5–8 : Sabhānirmāṇa.

§ 264, II, **4**, 1–41 (96–134). pp. 8–10 : Sabhāpraveça.

XXI. Lokapālasabhākhyānaparvan : II, **5**, 1 — **12**, 34 (135–513). PCR., pp. 11–40.

II, **5**, 1–128 (135–263). pp. 11–21 : Nārada-praçnamukhena-rājadharmānuçāsana (Kaccid-adhyāya).

6, 1–19 (264–282). pp. 21–23 : [Yudhishṭhira-]sabhājijñāsā.

7, 1–30 (283–310). pp. 23–25 : Indra-sabhā-varṇana (Çakra°).

8, 1–41 (311–352). pp. 25–28 : Yama-sabhā-varṇana.

9, 1–30 (353–382). pp. 29–30 : Varuṇa-sabhā-varṇana.

10, 1–40 (383–419). pp. 30–33 : Dhanada-sabhā-varṇana (Vaiçravaṇa°).

11, 1–62 (420–478). pp. 33–37 : Brahma-sabhā-varṇana.

12, 1–34 (479–513). pp. 37–40 : Pāṇḍu-sandeça-kathana (Brahma-sabhā-varṇana).

§ 265, II, **5**, 1 — **6**, 19 (135–282). pp. 11–23 : Lokapālasabhākhyānaparvan.

§ 266, II, **7**, 1–30 (283–310). pp. 23–25 : Çakrasabhāvarṇana.

§ 267, II, **8**, 1–41 (311–352). pp. 25–28 : Yama-sabhāvarṇana.

§ 268, II, **9**, 1–30 (353–382). pp. 29–30 : Varuṇa-sabhāvarṇana.

§ 269, II, **10**, 1–40 (383–419). pp. 30–33 : Vaiçravaṇasabhāvarṇana.

§ 270, II, **11**, 1–62 (420–478). pp. 33–37 : Brahma-sabhāvarṇana.

§ 271, II, **12**, 1–34 (479–513). pp. 37–40 : (*a*) Lokapālas°, (*b*) Hariçcandra.

XXII. Rājasūyārambhaparvan.

§ 272, II, **13**, 1–51 (514–564). pp. 40–44 : [Vāsudevāgamana].

§ 273, II, **14**, 1–70 (565–634). pp. 44–49 : Kṛshna-vākya.

§ 274, II, **15**, 1–26 (635–659). pp. 49–51 : id.

16, 1–17 (660–675). pp. 52–53 : Jarāsandha-vadhamantraṇa.

§ 275, II, **17**, 1–52 (676–728). pp. 53–57 : Jarāsandhotpatti.

18, 1–12 (729–740). pp. 57–58 : id.

19, 1–28 (741–767). pp. 58–60 : Jarāsandhapraçaṃsā.

XXIII. Jarāsandhavadhaparvan.

§ 276, II, **20**, 1–30 (768–797). pp. 60–63 : Kṛshṇa-Pāṇḍava-Māgadhayātrā.

§ 277, II, **21**, 1–54 (798–853). pp. 63–67 : Kṛshṇa-Jarāsandha-saṃvāda.

22, 1–36 (854–889). pp. 67–70 : Jarāsandha-yuddhodyoga.

23, 1–35 (890–924). pp. 70–73 : Jarāsandha-klānti.

24, 1–60 (925–982). pp. 73–77 : Jarāsandhavadha.

XXIV. Digvijayaparvan.

II, **25**, 1–11 (983–993). p. 78 : Digvijayasaṅkshepakathana.

26, 1–16 (994–1009). pp. 79–80 : Arjuna-digvijaye Bhagadatta-jaya.

27, 1–29 (1010–1037). pp. 80–82 : Phālguna-digvijaye Nānādeça-jaya.

28, 1–21 (1038–1058). pp. 82–83 : Arjunottaradigvijaya.

29, 1–16 (1059–1074). pp. 84–85 : Bhīma-digvijaya (Prācī-jaya).

30, 1–30 (1075–1104). pp. 85–87 : Bhīma-prācī-digvijaya.

31, 1–78 (1105–1182). pp. 87–93 : Sahadeva(-dakshiṇa)-digvijaya.

32, 1–20 (1183–1203). pp. 93–94 : Nakula-pratīcī-vijaya.

§ 278, II, **25**, 1–11 (983–993). p. 78 : Digvijayaparvan (Pāṇḍavāḥ).

§ 279, II, **26**, 1 — **28**, 21 (994–1058). pp. 79–83 : Arjuna.

§ 280, II, **29**, 1 — **30**, 30 (1059–1104). pp. 84–87 : Bhīmasena.

§ 281, II, **31**, 1–20 (1105–1123). pp. 87–88 : Sahadeva.

§ 282, II, **31**, 21–39 (1124–1143*a*). pp. 89–90 : (*a*) Sahadeva, (*b*) Māhishmatī.

§ 283, II, **31**, 40–50 (1143*b*–1154). pp. 90–91 : (*a*) Sahadeva, (*b*) Agni (enumeration of names).

§ 284, II, **31**, 51–78 (1155–1182). pp. 91–93 : Sahadeva.

§ 285, II, **32**, 1–20 (1183–1203). pp. 93–94 : Nakula.

XXV. Rājasūyikaparvan (°sūya°).

§ 286, II, **33**, 1–55 (1204–1259). pp. 95–99 : Rājasūyadīkshā.

§ 287, II, **34**, 1–25 (1260–1285). pp. 99–101 : Nimantritarājāgamana.

§ 288, II, **35**, 1–19 (1286–1306). pp. 101–102 : Yajña-karaṇa.

XXVI. Arghāharaṇaparvan.

§ 289, II, **36**, 1–32 (1307–1337). pp. 103–105 : Kṛshṇārghadāna.

37, 1–31 (1338–1368). pp. 105–107 : Çiçupāla-krodha.

38, 1–33 (1369–1400). pp. 108–110 : Bhīshma-vākya.

39, 1–18 (1401–1417). pp. 110–111 : Rājamantraṇa.

XXVII. Çiçupālavadhaparvan.

§ 290, II, **40**, 1–15 (1418–1432). pp. 112–113 : Yudhishṭhirāçvāsana.

41, 1–40 (1433–1473). pp. 113–116 : Çiçupala-vākya.

42, 1–20 (1474–1493). pp. 116–117 : Bhīma-krodha.

43, 1–25 (1494–1518). pp. 117–119 : Çiçupālavṛttāntakathana.

44, 1–42 (1519–1560). pp. 119–122 : Bhīshma-vākya.

45, 1–68 (1561–1627). pp. 122–126 : Çiçupāla-vadha.

§ 291, II, **45**, 1–36 (1561–1596*a*) : Çiçupālavadhaparvan.

§ 292, II, **45**, 37–68 (1596*b*–1627) : Rājasūyikaparvan (continued).

XXVIII. Dyūtaparvan.

§ 293, II, **46**, 1–33 (1628–1661). pp. 127–129 : Yudhishṭhira-samaya.

§ 294, II, **47**, 1–40 (1662–1701). pp. 129–132 : Duryodhanasantāpa.

48, 1–23 (1702–1724). pp. 132–133 : id.

49, 1–60 (1725–1785). pp. 134–138 : id.

50, 1–36 (1786–1820). pp. 138–141 : id.

§ 295, II, **51**, 1–35 (1821–1856). pp. 141–143 : id.

52, 1–41 (1857–1907). pp. 144–147 : id.

§ 296, II, **53**, 1-26 (1908-1933). pp. 147-149 : id.
§ 297, II, **54**, 1-11 (1934-1944). pp. 149-150 : id.
55, 1-21 (1945-1965). pp. 150-152 : id.
§ 298, II, **56**, 1-22 (1966-1986). pp. 152-154 : Yudhishṭhirā-nayana.
57, 1-5 (1987-1991). pp. 154-155 : id.
58, 1-38 (1992-2029). pp. 155-158 : Yudhishṭhira-sabhāgamana.
59, 1-21 (2030-2050). pp. 158-160 : [Yudhishṭhira-Çakuni-saṃvāda].
60, 1-9 (2051-2059). pp. 160-161 : Dyūtārambha.
61, 1-31 (2060-2093). pp. 161-164 : Devana.
62, 1-17 (2094-2110). pp. 164-165 : Vidura-hitavākya.
63, 1-10 (2111-2120). pp. 165-166 : Vidura-vākya.
64, 1-20 (2121-2140). pp. 167-169 : Vidura-hitavākya.
65, 1-45 (2141-2185). pp. 169-173 : Draupadī-parājaya.
§ 299, II, **66**, 1-12 (2186-2197). pp. 173-174 : Vidura-vākya.
67, 1-54 (2198-2250). pp. 174-179 : Draupadī-praçna.
68, 1-90 (2251-2339). pp. 179-186 : Draupady-ākarshaṇa.
69, 1-21 (2340-2360). pp. 186-188 : Bhīshmavākya.
70, 1-18 (2361-2378). pp. 188-190 : Bhīma-vākya.
71, 1-36 (2379-2415). pp. 190-193 : Draupadī-varalābha.
72, 1-17 (2416-2432). pp. 193-195 : Bhīma-krodha.
73, 1-18 (2433-2451). pp. 195-196 : Khāṇḍavaprastha-prasthāna (Dhṛtarāshṭra-varapradānapūrvakam Indraprastham prati Yudhishṭhira-gamana).
§ 299, II, **66**, 1 — **68**, 65 (2186-2314) : Dyūtaparvan.
§ 300, II, **68**, 66-87 (2315-2336) : Prahlāda.
§ 301, II, **68**, 88 — **73**, 18 (2337-2451) : Dyūtaparvan.

XXIX. ANUDYŪTAPARVAN.

§ 302, II, **74**, 1-27 (2452-2478). pp. 196-198 : Punar-Yudhishṭhirā-hvāna (Yudhishṭhira-pratyānayana).
§ 303, II, **75**, 1-12 (2479-2490). pp. 198-199 : Gāndhārī-vākya.
76, 1-24 (2491-2513). pp. 200-201 : Punar-Yudhishṭhira-parājaya (°bhava).
§ 304, II, **77**, 1-46 (2514-2559). pp. 202-205 : Dhṛtarāshṭra-samīpagamana (Pāṇḍava-pratijñākaraṇa).
§ 305, II, **78**, 1-24 (2560-2583). pp. 205-207 : Yudhishṭhira-vanaprasthāna.
79, 1-36 (2584-2619). pp. 207-210 : Dhṛtarāshṭra-praçna (Draupadī-Kuntī-saṃvāda).
§ 306, II, **80**, 1-52 (2620-2671). pp. 210-214 : [Vidura-] Dhṛtarāshṭra-[Droṇa-]vākya.
§ 307, II, **81**, 1-39 (2672-2709). pp. 214-216 : Dhṛtarāshṭra-cintā (°Sañjaya-saṃvāda).

III. VANAPARVAN.

XXX. ĀRAṆYAKAPARVAN.

III, **1**, 1-46 (1-46). pp. 1-4 : Paurapratyāgamana.
2, 1-84 (47-130). pp. 4-11 : Pāṇḍavānām-pravrajana.
3, 1-85 (131-218). pp. 11-17 : Kāmyaka-vana-praveça.
4, 1-22 (219-239). pp. 18-20 : Vidura-vākya[-pratyākhyāna].
5, 1-22 (240-261). pp. 20-22 : Vidura-nirvāsa.
6, 1-25 (262-286). pp. 22-24 : Vidura-pratyāgamana.
7, 1-24 (287-310). pp. 24-26 : Vyāsāgamana.
8, 1-12 (311-322). p. 26 : Vyāsavākya.
9, 1-23 (323-345). pp. 27-28 : Surabhy-upākhyāna.
10, 1-39 (346-384). pp. 29-31 : [Maitreyaçāpa].
§ 308, III, **1**, 1—**2**, 14a (1-60). pp. 1-5 : Āraṇyakaparvan.
§ 309, III, **2**, 14b-84 (61-130). pp. 5-11 : Āraṇyakaparvan.
§ 310, III, **3**, 1-85 (131-218). pp. 11-17 : (a) Āraṇyakap., (b) Sūrya.
§ 311, III, **4**, 1-22 (219-239). pp. 18-20 : Āraṇyakap.
§ 312, III, **5**, 1-22 (240-261). pp. 20-22 : Āraṇyakap.
§ 313, III, **6**, 1 — **8**, 12 (262-322). pp. 22-26 : Āraṇyakap.
§ 314, III, **9**, 1-23 (323-345). pp. 27-28 : Āraṇyakap.
§ 315, III, **10**, 1-39 (346-384). pp. 29-31 : Maitreya-çāpa.

XXXI. KIRMĪRA-VADHA-PARVAN.

§ 316, III, **11**, 1-75 (385-460). pp. 31-36 : Vidura-vākya.

XXXII. ARJUNĀBHIGAMANAPARVAN.

(a) *Arjunābhigamanaparvan* : III, **12-13**.
§ 317, III, **12**, 1-136 (461-596). pp. 36-46 : Draupady-āçvāsana.
§ 318, III, **13**, 1-17 (597-613). pp. 46-47 : Vāsudevavākya.
(b) *Saubhavadhopākhyāna* : III, **14-22**.
§ 319, III, **14**, 1-22 (614-635). pp. 47-49 : Saubhavadhopākhyāna.
15, 1-23 (636-658). pp. 49-50 : Saubhavadhopākhyāna.
16, 1-33 (659-691). pp. 50-52 : id.
17, 1-25 (692-716). pp. 53-54 : id.
18, 1-33 (717-749). pp. 54-57 : id.
19, 1-27 (750-776). pp. 57-59 : id.
20, 1-41 (777-817). pp. 59-61 : id.
21, 1-30 (818-848). pp. 62-64 : id.
22, 1-54 (849-902). pp. 64-67 : id.
§ 320, III, **15**, 1—**22**, 43 (636-891) : Saubhavadhopākhyāna.
§ 321, III, **22**, 44-54 (892-902) : id.
(c) *Dvaitavanapraveça* : III, **23-26**.
§ 322, III, **23**, 1-16 (903-918). pp. 68-69 : Dvaitavanapraveça.
24, 1-26 (919-944). pp. 69-71 : id.
§ 323, III, **25**, 1-19 (945-963). pp. 72-73 : id.
§ 324, III, **26**, 1-25 (964-988). pp. 74-75 : id.
(d) *Draupadī-paritāpavākya* : III, **27-35**.
§ 325, III, **27**, 1-40 (989-1028). p. 78 : Draupadī-paritāpavākya.
§ 326, III, **28**, 1-36 (1029-1064). pp. 78-81 : id. Draupadī-vākya.
§ 327, III, **29**, 1-52 (1065-1116). pp. 81-85 : id. Draupadī-Yudhishṭhira-saṃvāda.
30, 1-43 (1117-1159). pp. 85-89 : id. (Draupadī-vākya).
31, 1-42 (1160-1201). pp. 89-92 : Yudhishṭhira-Draupadī-saṃvāda (°vākya).
32, 1-62 (1202-1263). pp. 92-97 : Draupadī-vākya.
33, 1-90 (1264-1353). pp. 97-104 : Bhīma-vākya.
34, 1-22 (1354-1375). pp. 104-106 : Yudhishṭhira-vākya.
35, 1-35 (1376-1410). pp. 107-109 : Bhīma-vākya.
(e) *Kāmyakavanapraveça* : III, **36**.
III, **36**, 1-45 (1411-1455). pp. 109-113 : Kāmyakavanapraveça (°gamana).
§ 328, III, **36**, 1-21 (1411-1431) : Kāmyakavanapraveça.
§ 329, III, **36**, 22-45 (1432-1455) : id.

(*f*) *Indradarçana*: III, **37**.

§ 330, III, **37**, 1-59 (1456-1515). pp. 113-117: Indradarçana.

XXXIII. KAIRĀTAPARVAN.

III, **38**, 1-35 (1516-1550). pp. 118-120: Muni-Çaṅkara-saṃvāda.

39, 1-84 (1551-1635). pp. 120-126: Mahādevastava.

§ 331, III, **38**, 1—**39**, 71 (1516-1622*a*): Kairātaparvan.

§ 332, III, **39**, 72-84 (1622*b*-1635): Mahādevastava.

§ 333, III, **40**, 1-28 (1636-1663). pp. 126-128: Çivaprasthāna.

§ 334, III, **41**, 1-49 (1664-1713). pp. 128-132: Devaprasthāna.

XXXIV. INDRALOKĀBHIGAMANAPARVAN.

§ 335, III, **42**, 1-42 (1714-1755). pp. 132-135: [Çakrapurī-darçana].

§ 336, III, **43**, 1-32 (1756-1787). pp. 135-138: Indrasabhādarçana.

§ 337, III, **44**, 1-11 (1788-1799). pp. 138-139: [Arjunāstrādiçikshā].

§ 338, III, **45**, 1-16 (1800-1816). pp. 140-141: Citrasenorvaçī-saṃvāda.

46, 1-63 (1817-1878). pp. 141-146: Urvaçī-çāpa.

§ 339, III, **47**, 1-35 (1879-1913). pp. 146-148: Lomaçagamana.

§ 340, III, **48**, 1-18 (1914-1931). pp. 149-150: Dhṛtarāshṭravilāpa.

49, 1-23 (1932-1954). pp. 150-152: Dhṛtarāshṭra-kheda.

§ 341, III, **50**, 1-12 (1955-1966). pp. 152-153: Pārthāhārakathana.

§ 342, III, **51**, 1-46 (1967-2012). pp. 154-157: Dhṛtarāshṭravilāpa.

XXXV. NALOPĀKHYĀNAPARVAN.

§ 343, III, **52**, 1-59 (2013-2071). 157-161: [Bṛhadaçva-Yudhishṭhira-saṃvāda].

§ 344, III, **53**, 1-32 (2072-2103). pp. 161-164: Haṃsavākya (°Damayantī-saṃvāda).

§ 345, III, **54**, 1-31 (2104-2134). pp. 164-166: Nala-dautya (Indra-Nārada-saṃvāda).

55, 1-25 (2135-2159). pp. 166-168: Nalasya deva-dautya.

56, 1-31 (2160-2190). pp. 168-170: id. (Nalakartṛka°).

57, 1-47 (2191-2238). pp. 170-173: Damayantī-svayaṃvara.

§ 346, III, **58**, 1-14 (2239-2253). pp. 173-174: Kali-deva-saṃvāda.

59, 1-18 (2254-2271). pp. 174-175: Nala-dyūta.

60, 1-25 (2272-2296). pp. 175-177: id. (Kuṇḍinaṃ prati kumāra-kumarī-prasthāpana).

§ 347, III, **61**, 1-36 (2297-2332). pp. 177-179: Nala-vanayātrā.

62, 1-29 (2333-2361). pp. 180-181: [Nalasya]Damayantī[-pari-]tyāga.

63, 1-39 (2362-2400). pp. 182-184: Damayantī-sarpagrāsamocana (Ajagaragrasta-Damayantī-mocana).

64, 1-132 (2401-2531). pp. 185-194: Damayantī-vilāpa (°sārthavāhasaṅgama).

65, 1-76 (2532-2607). pp. 195-200: Damayantī-Cedirājagṛha-vāsa.

§ 348, III, **66**, 1-26 (2608-2633). pp. 200-202: Nala-Karkoṭaka-saṃvāda.

§ 349, III, **67**, 1-19 (2634-2653). pp. 202-203: Nala-vilāpa.

§ 350, III, **68**, 1-39 (2654-2693). pp. 204-206: Damayantī-Sudevasaṃvāda.

69, 1-50 (2694-2743). pp. 207-210: Nalānveshaṇa.

§ 351, III, **70**, 1-27 (2744-2770). pp. 210-211: Damayantī-punaḥ svayaṃvara-kathana.

71, 1-36 (2771-2807). pp. 212-214: Ṛtuparṇa-Vidarbhagamana.

§ 352, III, **72**, 1-43 (2808-2851). pp. 214-217: [Nala-]Kali-tyāga (°nirgama).

§ 353, III, **73**, 1-36 (2852-2889). pp. 217-220: Bhīmapurapraveça.

74, 1-31 (2890-2920). pp. 220-222: [Nala-]Keçinīvākya (°saṃvāda).

75, 1-28 (2921-2950). pp. 222-224: [Nala-]kanyā-putradarçana.

76, 1-53 (2951-3008). pp. 225-228: Nala-Damayantīmelana (°samāgama).

77, 1-20 (3009-3029). pp. 228-229: Ṛtuparṇa-svadeçagamana.

78, 1-33 (3030-3062). pp. 229-231: Pushkarāçvasana (°parābhava-purvakaṃ rājya pratyānayanaṃ).

79, 1-27 (3063-3089). pp. 232-234: Bṛhadaçva-gamana.

§ 354, III, **78**, 1—**79**, 5*a* (3030-3067*a*): Nalopākhyānaparvan.

§ 355, III, **79**, 5*b*-27 (3067*b*-3089): id.

XXXVI. TĪRTHAYĀTRĀPARVAN.

(*a*): III, **80-95**.

III, **80**, 1-30 (3090-4020). pp. 234-236: Arjunānuçocana.

81, 1-22 (4021-4042). pp. 237-238: Pārtha-Nārada-saṃvāda.

82, 1-128 (4043-5070). pp. 239-249: Nānātīrthakathana (Pulastya-tīrthayātrā).

83, 1-208 (5071-7078). pp. 249-264: id. (id.).

84, 1-163 (7079-8142). pp. 265-276: Tīrthakathana (id.).

85, 1-132 (8143-8275). pp. 276-285: Nāradavākya [id. Nā°].

86, 1-21 (8276-8296). pp. 286-288: Dhaumya-Yudhishṭhira-kathā (°tīrthayātrā).

87, 1-28 (8297-8325). pp. 288-290: Dhaumya-tīrthakathana (id.).

88, 1-27 (8326-8353). pp. 291-293: id. (id.).

89, 1-18 (8354-8371). pp. 293-294: id. (id.).

90, 1-34 (8372-8406). pp. 294-297: id. (id.).

91, 1-25 (8407-8431). pp. 297-298: Lomaça-saṃvāda.

92, 1-27 (8432-8457). pp. 299-300: Yudhishṭhira-tīrthayātrā (Lomaça°).

93, 1-29 (8458-8486). pp. 301-302: id. (id.).

94, 1-22 (8487-8509). pp. 303-304: Yudhishṭhira-tīrthagamana (id.).

95, 1-29 (8510-8539). pp. 304-306: Gayayajñakathana.

§ 356, III, **80**, 1—**82**, 19 (3090-4061): Tīrthayātrāparvan.

§ 357, III, **82**, 20-39 (4062-4081*a*): Pushkara.

§ 358, III, **82**, 40-91 (4081*b*-5033): Tīrthayātrāparvan.

§ 359, III, **82**, 92-99 (5034-5041): Vaḍavā.

§ 360, III, **82**, 100-128 (5042-5070): Tīrthayātrāparvan.

§ 361, III, **83**, 1-8 (5041-5078): Kurukshetra.

§ 362, III, **83**, 9-26*a* (5079-5096*a*): Tīrthayātrāparvan.

§ 363, III, **83**, 26*b*-41*a* (5096*b*-6011*a*): Rāmahradāḥ.

§ 364, III, **83**, 41*b*-115*a* (6011*b*-6085*a*): Tīrthayātrāparvan.
§ 365, III, **83**, 115*b*-134 (6085*b*-7005*a*): Maṅkaṇaka.
§ 366, III, **83**, 135-144 (7005*b*-7015*a*): Tīrthayātrāparvan.
§ 367, III, **83**, 145-149 (7015*b*-7020*a*): Pṛthūdaka.
§ 368, III, **83**, 150-202*a* (7020*b*-7072): Tīrthayātrāparvan.
§ 369, III, **83**, 202*b*-208 (7073-7078): Kurukshetra.
§ 370, III, **84**, 1 — **85**, 45 (7079-8188*a*): Tīrthayātrāparvan.
§ 371, III, **85**, 46-54 (8188*b*-8197*a*): Tuṅgaka.
§ 372, III, **85**, 55-69*a* (8197*b*-8211): Tīrthayātrāparvan.
§ 373, III, **85**, 69*b*-85 (8212-8228*a*): Prayāga.
§ 374, III, **85**, 86-87 (8228*b*-8230*a*): Tīrthayātrāparvan.
§ 375, III, **85**, 88-111 (8230*b*-8254): id.
§ 376, III, **85**, 112-132 (8255-8275): id.
§ 377, III, **86**, 1 — **90**, 34 (8275-8406): Dhaumya-tīrthakathana.
§ 378, III, **91**, 1 — **94**, 22 (8407-8509): Tīrthayātrāparvan.
§ 379, III, **95**, 1-10*a* (8510-8519): id.
§ 380, III, **95**, 10*b*-17 (8520-8527): Brahmasaras.
§ 381, III, **95**, 18-29 (8528-8539): Gaya.

(*b*) *Agastyopākhyāna*: III, **96**, 1 — **99**, 30 (8540-8645).
§ 382 (Agastya).
III, **96**, 1-30 (8540-8569). pp. 307-309: Agastyopākhyāna.
97, 1-25 (8570-8594). pp. 309-311: id. [Lo°tī°yā° Aga°].
98, 1-20 (8595-8614). pp. 311-312: id. [id.].
99, 1-71 (8615-8688). pp. 312-317: Jāmadagnya-tejohānikathana (Lo°tī°yā° Jā°).

(*c*) *Jāmadagnya-tejohānikathana*: III, **99**, 31-71 (8646-8688).
§ 383 (*a*) Tīrthayātrāp., (*b*) Paraçurāma.

(*d*) *Āgastya*: III, **100-109**.
III, **100**, 1-25 (8689-8713). pp. 318-319: Vajranirmāṇakathana (Lo°tī°yā° Va°).
101, 1-23 (8714-8736). pp. 320-321: Vṛtravadhopākhyāna (id. Vṛ°).
102, 1-26 (8737-8762). pp. 322-323: Vishṇu-stava (id. Vi°).
103, 1-18 (8763-8780). pp. 324-325: Agastyamāhātmyakathana (id. Aga°).
104, 1-24 (8781-8804). pp. 325-327: id. (id.).
105, 1-20 (8805-8824). pp. 327-328: Samudrapūraṇamantraṇa (id. Agastyopākhyāna).
106, 1-23 (8825-8848). pp. 329-331: Sagarasantalikathana (id. Sa°).
107, 1-70 (8849-9919). pp. 331-336: Gaṅgāvataraṇa (id. Agastyamāhātmyakathana).
108, 1-27 (9920-9946). pp. 336-338: id. (id. Aga°opākhyāna).
109, 1-21 (9947-9967). pp. 338-340: id. (id. Aga°mā°).
§ 384, III, **100**, 1 — **103**, 18 (8689-8780): Agastyopākhyāna.
§ 385, III, **104**, 1-15 (8781-8795): Vindhya.
§ 386, III, **104**, 16 — **106**, 2 (8796-8827): Agastyopākhyāna.
§ 387, III, **106**, 3 — **107**, 37 (8828-8886): Sagara.
§ 388, III, **107**, 38-45*a* (8887-8894*a*): Asamañjas.
§ 389, III, **107**, 45*b* — **109**, 21 (8894*b*-9967): Gaṅgāvataraṇa.

(*e*) *Ṛshyaçṛṅgopākhyāna*: III, **110-113**.
III, **110**, 1-58 (9968-10026). pp. 340-344: Ṛshyaçṛṅgopākhyāna (Lo°tī°çya°).
111, 1-23 (10027-10050). pp. 345-347: id. (id.).
112, 1-19 (10051-10069). pp. 347-349: id. (id.).
113, 1-25 (10070-10094). pp. 349-351: id. (id.).
§ 390, III, **110**, 1-26 (9968-9994*a*): Tīrthayātrāparvan.
§ 391, III, **110**, 27 — **113**, 25 (9994*b*-10094): Ṛshyaçṛṅga.

(*f*) *Mahendrācalagamana*: III, **114**.
§ 392, III, **114**, 1-30 (10095-10124). pp. 352-354: [Lo°tī°] Mahendrācalagamana.

(*g*): III, **115-117**.
III, **115**, 1-45 (10125-10170). pp. 354-358: [Lo°tī° Kārttavīryopākhyāna] Jamadagnyutpatti.
116, 1-29 (10171-10200). pp. 358-361: [id.] Jamadagnivadha.
117, 1-18 (10201-10213). pp. 361-362: [id.] Jāmadagnyopākhyāna.
§ 393, III, **115**, 1-6 (10125-10130): Paraçurāma.
§ 394, III, **115**, 7-19*a* (10131-10143): Arjuna Kārtavīrya.
§ 395, III, **115**, 19*b*-45 (10144-10170): Jamadagni.
§ 396, III, **116**, 1-18 (10171-10188): id.
§ 397, III, **116**, 19-29 (10189-10195+5): id.
§ 398, III, **117**, 1-15 (10195+6-10210): Paraçu-Rāma.
§ 399, III, **117**, 16-18 (10211-10213): Mahendrācala-gamana.

(*h*) *Vārshṇeya-Yudhishṭhira-saṃvāda*: III, **118-120**.
III, **118**, 1-23 (10214-10236). pp. 363-365: Vārshṇeya-Yudhishṭhira-saṃvāda (Prabhāse Yādava-Pāṇḍava-samāgama).
119, 1-22 (10237-10258). pp. 365-367: Balarāma-vākya.
120, 1-32 (10259-10290). pp. 368-371: Vṛshṇigamana (Lo° Yādavagamana).
§ 400, III, **118**, 1-23 (10214-10236): (*a*) Tīrthayātrāparvan, (*b*) Sūrpāraka.
§ 401, III, **119**, 1-22 (10237-10258): Balarāma.
§ 402, III, **120**, 1-32 (10259-10290): Tīrthayātrāparvan.

(*i*) *Sukanyopākhyāna*: III, **121-125**.
III, **121**, 1-24 (10291-10315). pp. 371-373: Sukanyopākhyāna (Lo° Saukanya).
122, 1-29 (10316-10344). pp. 373-375: id. (id.).
123, 1-24 (10345-10370). pp. 375-377: id. (id.).
124, 1-25 (10371-10395). pp. 377-379: id. (id.).
125, 1-26 (10396-10422). pp. 380-382: id. (id.).
§ 403, III, **121**, 1-15 (10291-10305): (*a*) Tīrth., (*b*) Payoshṇı, (*c*) Gaya.
§ 404, III, **121**, 16-24 (10306-10315): Tīrthayātrāparvan.
§ 405, III, **122**, 1 — **125**, 11 (10316-10406): Sukanyopākhyāna.
§ 406, III, **125**, 12-26 (10407-10422): Tīrthayātrāparvan.

(*k*) *Māndhātrupākhyāna*: III, **126**.
III, **126**, 1-47 (10423-10469). pp. 382-385: [Lo°] Māndhatrupākhyāna.

(*l*) *Jantūpākhyāna*: III, **127-128**.
§ 408, III, **127**, 1-21 (10470-10490). pp. 386-387: [Lo°] Jantūpākhyāna.
128, 1-21 (10491-10512). pp. 388-389: id. (id.).

(*m*): III, **129-131**.
III, **129**, 1-22 (10513-10535). pp. 389-391: Plakshāvataraṇagamana (Lo°).
130, 1-24 (10536-10560). pp. 391-393: [Lo°] Çyenakapotīya.
131, 1-34 (10561-10596). pp. 393-396: [id.] id.
§ 409, III, **129**, 1-22 (10513-10535): Plakshāvataraṇagamana.
§ 410, III, **130**, 1-21*a* (10536-10556): id.
§ 411, III, **130**, 21*b* — **131**, 34 (10557-10596): Çyenakapotīya.

(*n*) *Ashṭāvakrīya*: III, **132-134.**

§ 412, III, **132,** 1-23 (10597-10620). pp. 396-398: [Lo°] Ashṭāvakrīya.

133, 1-30 (10621-10650). pp. 398-401: [id.] id.

134, 1-41 (10651-10691). pp. 401-407: [id.] id.

(*o*) *Yavakrītopākhyāna*: III, **135-138.**

III, **135,** 1-60 (10692-10751). pp. 408-412: [Lo°] Yavakrītopākhyāna.

136, 1-20 (10752-10771). pp. 412-413: [id.] id.

137, 1-19 (10772-10790). pp. 413-415: [id.] id.

138, 1-28 (10791-10819). pp. 415-417: [id.] id.

§ 413, III, **135,** 1-9 (10692-10700): Tīrthayātrāparvan.

§ 414, III, **135,** 10-44 (10701-10735): Yavakrītopākhyāna.

§ 415, III, **135,** 45-55 (10736-10746): Medhāvin.

§ 416, III, **135,** 56—**137,** 19 (10747-10790): Yavakrītopākhyāna.

§ 417, III, **138,** 1-28 (10791-10819): id.

(*p*): III, **139-145.**

III, **139,** 1-20 (10820-10839). pp. 417-419: Yudhishṭhiravākya [Lo° Kailāsādigiripraveça].

140, 1-29 (10840-10870). pp. 419-421: [Lo°] Gandhamādanapraveça.

141, 1-28 (10871-10898). pp. 421-423: [id.] id.

142, 1-63 (10899-10962). pp. 423-427: [id.] id.

143, 1-23 (10963-10985). pp. 427-428: [id.] id.

144, 1-28 (10986-11013). pp. 429-431: [id.] id.

145, 1-54 (11014-11068). pp. 431-434: [id.] id.

§ 418, III, **139,** 1-20 (10820-10839): (*a*) Tīrth., (*b*) Gaṅgā, (*c*) Mandara, (*d*) Kailāsa, (*e*) Kṛshṇā.

§ 419, III, **140,** 1-29 (10840-10870): Gandhamādana-praveça.

§ 420, III, **141,** 1-28 (10871-10898): id.

§ 421, III, **142,** 1-12 (10899-10910): id.

§ 422, III, **142,** 13-28*a* (10911-10926*a*): (*a*) Gandhamādana-praveça, (*b*) Naraka.

§ 422 *bis*, III, **142,** 28*b*-63 (10926*b*-10962): Varāhāvatāra.

§ 423, III, **143,** 1—**145,** 54 (10963-11068): Gandhamādana-praveça.

(*q*): III, **146-150.**

III, **146,** 1-96 (11069-11166). pp. 435-441: [Lo°] Bhīmakhadalī-khaṇḍa-praveça.

147, 1-34 (11167-11200). pp. 441-443: [id.] Hanūmad-Bhīma-saṃvada.

148, 1-22 (11201-11223). pp. 444-445: [id.] id.

149, 1-40 (11224-11264). pp. 445-448: [id. Kadalīshaṇḍa] id.

150, 1-52 (11265-11317). pp. 448-452: [id.] Hanūmad-Bhīma[sena-] saṃvāda.

§ 424, III, **146,** 1—**147,** 25 (11069-11191): Bhīma-khadalī-khaṇḍa-praveça.

§ 425, III, **147,** 26—**148,** 22 (11192-11223): Hanūmad-Bhīma-saṃvāda.

§ 426, III, **149,** 1-23*a* (11224-11246): (*a*) Hanūmad-Bhīma-saṃvāda, (*b*) Kṛta-yuga.

§ 427, III, **149,** 23*b*-26 (11247-11250*a*): Tretā-yuga.

§ 428, III, **149,** 27-33*a* (11250*b*-11256): Dvāpara-yuga.

§ 429, III, **149,** 33*b*-40 (11257-11264): Kaliyuga.

§ 430, III, **150,** 1-52 (11265-11317): Hanūmad-Bhīma-saṃvāda.

(*r*): III, **151-156.**

§ 431, III, **151,** 1-19 (11318-11336). pp. 452-454: Saugandhikāharaṇa (Lo° Gandhamā° Hanūmad-Bhīma-saṃvāda).

§ 432, III, **152,** 1-14 (11337-11350). pp. 454-455: [Lo°] Saugandhikāharaṇa.

153, 1-16 (11351-11366). pp. 455-456: [id.] id.

154, 1-27 (11367-11394). pp. 456-458: [id.] id.

§ 433, III, **155,** 1-34 (11395-11429). pp. 459-461: [id.] id.

§ 434, III, **156,** 1-21 (11430-11450). pp. 461-462: [Lo° punar] [Nara] Nārāyaṇāçramāgamana.

XXXVII. JAṬĀSURAVADHAPARVAN.

§ 435, III, **157,** 1-72 (11451-11523). pp. 462-467: Jaṭāsuravadha.

XXXVIII. YAKSHAYUDDHAPARVAN.

§ 436, III, **158,** 1-103 (11524-11627). pp. 467-473: Gandhamādanaçobhādarçana (°praveça).

159, 1-32 (11628-11660). pp. 473-475: Ārshṭisheṇa-Yudhishṭhira-saṃvāda.

§ 437, III, **160,** 1-77 (11661-11738). pp. 475-480: Maṇimadvadha.

§ 438, III, **161,** 1-63 (11739-11802). pp. 480-484: Kuberadarçana.

162, 1-38 (11803-11840). pp. 484-487: Kuberavākya.

§ 439, III, **163,** 1-42 (11841-11882). pp. 487-489: Merudarçana.

§ 440, III, **164,** 1-20 (11883-11902). pp. 489-491: Maharshigaṇadarçana (Arjunābhigamana).

XXXIX. NIVĀTAKAVACAYUDDHAPARVAN.

§ 441, III, **165,** 1-14 (11903-11916). pp. 491-492: Arjun[asam]āgama[na].

166, 1-17 (11917-11934). pp. 492-493: Indrāgama[na].

§ 442, III, **167,** 1-57 (11935-11991). pp. 493-497: Arjuna-Yudhishṭhirasaṃvāda (Gandhamādanavāse Yudhishṭhirārjunasaṃvāda).

§ 443, III, **168,** 1-86 (11992-12078). pp. 497-503: Arjunavākya.

§ 444, III, **169,** 1-24 (12079-12102). pp. 503-504: Nivātakavaca-vadha (Yuddhārambha).

170, 1-29 (12103-12131). pp. 505-506: Nivātakavacavadha.

171, 1-30 (12132-12161). pp. 506-508: Māyāyuddha.

172, 1-35 (12162-12196). pp. 509-511: Nivātakavacavadha (°yuddha).

§ 445, III, **173,** 1-75 (12107-12273). pp. 511-516: Hiraṇyapura-Daitya-vadha.

§ 446, III, **174,** 1-17 (12274-12290). pp. 516-517: Astradarçana [saṅketa].

§ 447, III, **175,** 1-25 (12291-12315). pp. 517-519: Astradarçana.

XL. ĀJAGARAPARVAN.

§ 448, III, **176,** 1-23 (12316-12338). pp. 519-521: Lomaçagamana (Gandhamādanaprasthāna).

§ 449, III, **177,** 1-24 (12339-12362). pp. 521-523: Punar-Dvaitavana-praveça.

§ 450, III, **178,** 1-33 (12363-12395). pp. 523-525: [Bhīmasy]ājagaragrahaṇa.

179, 1-54 (12396-12449). pp. 526-529: Yudhishṭhira-Bhīma-darçana.

180, 1-38 (12450-12488). pp. 529-532: Ajagara-Yudhishṭhira-saṃvāda.

181, 1-49 (12489-12538). pp. 532-536: Bhīma-mocana.

XLI. MĀRKAṆḌEYASAMĀSYĀPARVAN.

(*a*): III, **182–200.**

§ 451, III, **182,** 1–18 (12539–12556). pp. 536–538: Kāmyaka-pratyāgamana (°vanapraveça).

183, 1–95 (12557–12651). pp. 538–546: [Mārkaṇḍeya-kathā].

§ 452, III, **183,** 1–40 (12557–12596): Mārkaṇḍeyasamāsyā-parvan.

§ 453, III, **183,** 41–95 (12597–12651): id.

§ 454, III, **184,** 1–23 (12652–12676). pp. 546–547: Brāhmaṇamāhātmyakathana.

§ 455, III, **185,** 1–37 (12677–12714). pp. 548–550: id.

§ 456, III, **186,** 1–30 (12715–12745). pp. 551–552: Sarasvatī-Tārkshya-saṃvāda.

§ 457, III, **187,** 1–58 (12745–12804). pp. 552–556: Vaivasvatopākhyāna (Matsyopākhyāna).

188, 1–143 (12805–12949). pp. 556–566: [Mārkaṇḍeya-praçna].

189, 1–59 (12950–13008). pp. 556–571: Mārkaṇḍeya-Nārāyaṇa-saṃvāda (Bhavishyakathana).

§ 458, III, **188,** 1–85 (12805–12890): (*a*) Mārkaṇḍeyasamāsyā-parvan, (*b*) Kali-yuga.

§ 459, III, **188,** 86 — **189,** 59 (12891–13008): Mārkaṇḍeya-samāsyāparvan.

§ 460, III, **190,** 1–97 (13009–13106). pp. 571–579: Kaliyugakṛtyakathana (Bhavishya°).

191, 1–35 (13107–13141). pp. 579–582: Yudhishṭhira-darçāsana. (*a*) Mārkaṇḍeyasamāsyāparvan, (*b*) Kali-yuga, (*c*) Kalkin

§ 461, III, **192,** 1–72 (13142–13211). pp. 582–589: Vāmadevacarita (Maṇḍūkopākhyāna).

§ 462, III, **193,** 1–36 (13212–13247). pp. 589–593: Baka-Çakra-saṃvāda (Brāhmaṇamahābhāgye Ba°).

§ 463, III, **194,** 1–8 (13248–13255). pp. 593–594: Çibi-mahābhāgyakathana (°carita).

III, **195,** 1–6 (13256–13260). pp. 594–595: Nāhushacarit[r]a.

§ 464, III, **195**: Yayāti.

§ 465, III, **196,** 1–13 (13261–13273). pp. 595–596: [Seduka-Vṛshadarbha-carita].

§ 466, III, **197,** 1–28 (13274–13300). pp. 596–599: Çibicarita.

§ 467, III, **198,** 1–27 (13301–13330). pp. 599–602: Rājanyamahābhāgya [kathana] [Çibicarita].

§ 468, III, **199,** 1–18 (13331–13348). pp. 602–605: Indradyumnopākhyāna.

200, 1–129 (13349–13481). pp. 605–617: Dānakathana (°māhātmya).

§ 469, III, **200,** 1–42 (13349–13391): Mārkaṇḍeyasamāsyāp.

§ 470, III, **200,** 43–63 (13392–13412): Yama-loka.

§ 471, III, **200,** 64–80 (13413–13429): Mārkaṇḍeyasamāsyāp.

§ 472, III, **200,** 81–118 (13430–13468): id.

§ 473, III, **200,** 119–129 (13469–13481): id.

(*b*) *Dhundhumāropākhyāna*: III, **201–204.**

III, **201,** 1–34 (13482–13514). pp. 617–619: Dhundhumāropākhyāna.

202, 1–31 (13515–13545). pp. 620–622: id.

203, 1–35 (13546–13581). pp. 622–624: id.

204, 1–45 (13582–13627). pp. 625–628: id.

§ 474, III, **201,** 1–34 (13482–13514): (*a*) Mārkaṇḍeyasamāsyāp., (*b*) Dhundhumāropākhyāna.

§ 475, III, **202,** 1–5 (13515–13519): Dhundhumāropākhyāna.

§ 476, III, **202,** 6 — **203,** 6*a* (13520–13551*a*): id.

§ 477, III, **203,** 6*b*–35 (13551*b*–13581): id.

§ 478, III, **204,** 1–45 (13582–13627): id.

(*c*) *Pativratopākhyāna*: III, **205–206,** and **216**; *Brāhmaṇa-vyādhasaṃvāda*: III, **207–215.**

§ 479, III, **205,** 1–24 (13628–13651). pp. 628–630: Pativratopākhyāna.

206, 1–48 (13652–13700). pp. 630–634: id.

§ 480, III, **207,** 1–99 (13701–13801). pp. 634–643: id. (Brāhmaṇavyādha-saṃvāda).

208, 1–39 (13802–13841). pp. 643–646: id. [Pativratopākhyāna, id.].

209, 1–56 (13842–13897). pp. 646–650: Dvijavyādha-saṃvāda (Brāhmaṇa°).

210, 1–21 (13898–13919). pp. 650–652: id. (Brāhmaṇa-māhātmya).

§ 481, III, **210,** 1–12 (13898–13909): Pativratopākhyāna.

§ 482, III, **210,** 13–21 (13910–13919): id.

§ 483, III, **211,** 1–27 (13920–13946). pp. 652–654: id. Dvijavyādhasaṃvāda (Brāhmaṇa°).

§ 484, III, **212,** 1–12 (13947–13958). pp. 654–655: id. (id.).

§ 485, III, **213,** 1–40 (13959–13999). pp. 655–659: Brāhmaṇa-vyādhasaṃvāda.

214, 1–29 (14000–14029). pp. 659–661: Dvijavyādha-saṃvāda.

215, 1–31 (14030–14062). pp. 662–664: id. (Brāhmaṇa°).

216, 1–37 (14063–14099). pp. 664–667: Pativratopākhyāna (id.).

§ 486, III, **214,** 1 — **215,** 20 (14000–14051*a*): Pativratopākhyāna.

§ 487, III, **215,** 21 — **216,** 37 (14051*b*–14099): id.

(*d*) *Āṅgirasopākhyāna*: III, **217,** or *Āṅgirasa*: III, **218–222.**

§ 488, III, **217,** 1–21 (14100–14121). pp. 667–668: Āṅgirasopākhyāna (Āṅgirasa).

§ 489, III, **218,** 1–8 (14122–14129). p. 669: Āṅgirasa (Āṅgirasopākhyāna).

§ 490, III, **219,** 1–25 (14130–14155). pp. 669–672: id. (id.).

220, 1–20 (14156–14175). pp. 672–673: id. (id.).

221, 1–31 (14176–14207). pp. 674–676: id. (id.).

222, 1–32 (14208–14240). pp. 676–678: id. (id.).

§ 491, III, **220,** 1–10*a* (14156–14165*a*): Āṅgirasa.

§ 492, III, **220,** 10*b*–17 (14165*b*–14172): id.

§ 493, III, **220,** 18 — **222,** 21 (14173–14229*a*): id.

§ 494, III, **222,** 22–32 (14229*b*–14240): id.

(*e*) *Skandotpatti*, etc.: III, **223–232.** (*a*) *Skandotpatti*: III, **223–226.**

223, 1–15 (14241–14256). pp. 679–680: [Āṅgi°] Skandotpatti [Keçiparābhava].

224, 1–42 (14257–14298). pp. 680–683: [id.] id.

225, 1–39 (14299–14338). pp. 683–686: [id.] id. [Kumārotpatti].

§ 495, III, **223,** 1 — **224,** 10 (14241–14266): Skandotpatti.

§ 496, III, **224,** 11 — **225,** 39 (14267–14338): id.

226, 1–29 (14339–14367). pp. 686–688: [Āṅgi°] Skandotpatti [Keçiparābhava].

§ 497, III, **226,** 1–17*a* (14339–14355*a*): Skandotpatti.

§ 498, III, **226,** 17*b*–29 (14355*b*–14367): id.

(β)

§ 499, III, **227,** 1–18 (14368–14386). pp. 688–690: Skanda-Çakra-samāgama (Āṅgi° Indra-Skando°).

(γ) *Skandopākhyāna*: III, **228**–**229**.

§ 500, III, **228**, 1–15 (14387–14401). pp. 690–691: Skandopākhyāna (Āṅgi° Kumārotpatti).

§ 501, III, **229**, 1–52 (14402–14453). pp. 691–695: id. (Āṅgi° Skandop°).

(δ) *Manushyagrahakathana*: III, **230**.

§ 502, **230**, 1–59 (14454–14513). pp. 695–699: [Āṅgi°] Manushyagrahakathana.

(ε) *Skandhayuddha*: III, **231**.

231, 1–113 (14514–14627). pp. 699–707: [Ā°] Skandayuddha (°otpatti) [Mahishāsuravadha].

§ 503, III, **231**, 1–7 (14514–14520): Skandayuddha.

§ 504, III, **231**, 8–17*a* (14521–14530): id.

§ 505, III, **231**, 17*b*–27 (14531–14541*a*): id.

§ 506, III, **231**, 28–57 (14541*b*–14571): id.

§ 507, III, **231**, 58–113 (14572–14627): id.

(ζ) *Kārttikeyastava*: III, **232**.

232, 1–21 (14628–14648). pp. 707–710: [Ā°] Kārttikeyastava.

§ 508, III, **232**, 1–9 (14628–14636): Kārttikeyastava.

§ 509, III, **232**, 10–21 (14637–14648): id.

XLII. Draupadī-Satyabhāmā-saṃvāda-parvan.

§ 510, III, **233**, 1–61 (14649–14709). pp. 710–714: [Draupadī-nijakāryakathana].

234, 1–12 (14710–14721). pp. 714–716: Draupadī-kartavyakathana.

§ 511, III, **235**, 1–18 (14722–14740). pp. 716–717: [Satyabhāmā-]Kṛshṇagamana.

XLIII. Ghoshayātrāparvan.

III, **236**, 1–31 (14741–14771). pp. 717–720: Dhṛtarāshṭrakhedavākya.

237, 1–23 (14772–14795). pp. 721–722: Karṇa-Çakunivākya.

238, 1–24 (14796–14819). pp. 722–724: Ghoshayātrāmantraṇa.

239, 1–29 (14820–14848). pp. 724–726: Duryodhana-Dvaitavana-gamana (°-prasthāna).

240, 1–31 (14849–14879). pp. 726–729: Gandharva-Duryodhanasenā-saṃvāda.

241, 1–32 (14880–14912). pp. 729–731: Karṇa-raṇabhaṅga (°parābhava).

242, 1–22 (14913–14934). pp. 731–733: Duryodhanādiharaṇa.

243, 1–22 (14935–14956). pp. 733–735: Duryodhana-mokshānujñā.

244, 1–22 (14957–14978). pp. 735–736: Pāṇḍava-gandharvayuddha.

245, 1–30 (14970–15009). pp. 736–738: Gandharva-parābhava.

246, 1–27 (15010–15036). pp. 739–741: Duryodhana-mokshaṇa.

247, 1–16 (15037–15052). pp. 741–742: Karṇa-Duryodhana-saṃvāda.

248, 1–16 (15053–15069). pp. 742–743: id. (Duryodhana-vākya).

249, 1–41 (15070–15110). pp. 743–746: id. (Duryodhana-prāyopaveça).

250, 1–13 (15111–15123). pp. 746–747: id. (id.) [Karṇa-vākya].

251, 1–30 (15124–15154). pp. 748–750: Duryodhana-prāyopaveça.

252, 1–52 (15155–15207). pp. 750–754: Duryodhana-purapraveça.

253, 1–29 (15208–15236). pp. 754–756: Karṇa-digvijaya.

254, 1–36 (15237–15272). pp. 756–758: id.

255, 1–25 (15273–15297). pp. 758–760: Duryodhana-yajñ[a-sam]ārambha.

256, 1–27 (15298–15324). pp. 760–762: Duryodhana-yajña[-samāpti].

257, 1–28 (15325–15352). pp. 762–764: Yudhishṭhira-cintā.

§ 512, III, **236**, 1 — **251**, 21*a* (14741–15144*a*): Ghoshayātrāparvan.

§ 513, III, **251**, 21*b* — **252**, 37 (15144*b*–15192*a*): id.

§ 514, III, **252**, 38–52 (15192*b*–15207): id.

§ 515, III, **253**, 1 — **254**, 36 (15208–15272): Karṇa-digvijaya.

§ 516, III, **255**, 1 — **257**, 20 (15273–15344): Duryodhana-yajña.

§ 517, III, **257**, 21–28 (15345–15352): Ghoshayātrāparvan.

XLIV. Mṛgasvapnodbhavaparvan.

§ 518, III, **258**, 1–17 (15353–15369). pp. 764–765: Yudhishṭhira-mṛgasvapnadarçana (Kāmyakapraveça).

XLV. Vrīhidrauṇikaparvan.

§ 519, III, **259**, 1–35 (15370–15404). pp. 765–768: Dānakathana (Dānadushkaratva°).

§ 520, III, **260**, 1–36 (15405–15440). pp. 768–771: Svarga-guṇapraçna (Mudgalopākhyāna).

261, 1–51 (15441–15491). pp. 771–775: Mudgala-jñānaprāpti (°devadūta-saṃvāda).

XLVI. Draupadīharaṇaparvan.

§ 521, III, **262**, 1–28 (15492–15520). pp. 775–777: Durvāsa-ātithya (°upākhyāna).

263, 1–49 (15521–15570). pp. 777–780: Kṛshṇagamana (°upākhyāna).

§ 522, III, **264**, 1–17 (15571–15587). pp. 781–782: Koṭi-kāsyapraçna (Jayadrathāgamana).

265, 1–14 (15588–15601). pp. 782–783: id.

266, 1–9 (15602–15610). pp. 783–784: Draupadī-vākya.

267, 1–28 (15611–15638). pp. 784–786: id. (Jayadratha-Draupadī-saṃvāda).

268, 1–28 (15639–15666). pp. 786–788: Draupadī-haraṇa.

269, 1–28 (15667–15694). pp. 789–791: Pārthāgamana.

270, 1–21 (15695–15715). pp. 792–794: Pārtha-yuddha (Draupadī-vākya).

271, 1–60 (15716–15776). pp. 794–798: Jayadrathagrahaṇa (°palāyana).

XLVII. Jayadrathavimokshaṇaparvan.

III, **272**, 1–81 (15777–15858). pp. 798–804: [Jayadratha-varaprāpti].

§ 523, III, **272**, 1–24*a* (15777–15800*a*): Jayadrathavimokshaṇaparvan.

§ 524, III, **272**, 24*b*–81 (15800*b*–15858): id.

XLVIII. Rāmopākhyānaparvan.

III, **273**, 1–13 (15859–15871). pp. 804–805: Yudhishṭhira-praçna.

274, 1–17 (15872–15888). pp. 805–806: Vaiçravaṇotpatti (Rāma-Rāvaṇayor janmakathana).
275, 1–40 (15889–15928). pp. 806–809: Rāvaṇādi-varaprāpti.
276, 1–16 (15929–15944). pp. 809–810: Vānarādy-utpatti.
277, 1–56 (15945–16000). pp. 811–815: Rāma-vanābhigamana.
278, 1–43 (16001–16044). pp. 815–818: [Mārīca-vadha] Sītāharaṇa.
279, 1–48 (16045–16092). pp. 818–822: Kabandhahanana (Viçvāvasumokshaṇa).
280, 1–74 (16093–16165). pp. 822–827: [Trijaṭā-kṛta-] Sītā-sāntvana.
281, 1–30 (16166–16196). pp. 827–830: Sītā-Rāvaṇa-saṃvāda.
282, 1–71 (16197–16268). pp. 830–835: Hanumat-pratyāgamana.
283, 1–54 (16269–16322). pp. 835–839: Setu-bandhana.
284, 1–41 (16323–16363). pp. 839–842: Laṅkā-praveça.
285, 1–15 (16364–16378). pp. 843–844: Rāma-Rāvaṇ[ādi-] dvandva]-yuddha.
286, 1–29 (16379–16408). pp. 844–846: Kumbhakarṇa-nirgamana.
287, 1–29 (16409–16437). pp. 846–848: Kumbhakarṇādi-vadha.
288, 1–26 (16438–16464). pp. 848–850: Indrajid-yuddha.
289, 1–33 (16465–16497). pp. 851–854: Indrajid-vadha.
290, 1–33 (16498–16530). pp. 854–857: Rāvaṇa-vadha.
291, 1–70 (16531–16601). pp. 857–862: Rāma-[rājya-] abhisheka.
292, 1–14 (16602–16615). pp. 862–863: Yudhishṭhirāçvāsa[na].

§ 525, III, **273**, 1 — **274**, 17 (15859–15888). pp. 804–806: Rāmopākhyānaparvan.
§ 526, III, **275**, 1—**276**, 16 (15889–15944). pp. 806–810: id.
§ 527, III, **277**, 1–39 (15945–15983). pp. 811–813: id.
§ 528, III, **277**, 40–56 (15984–16000). pp. 813–815: (*a*) Rāvaṇagamana, (*b*) Mārīca.
§ 529, III, **278**, 1–43 (16001–16044). pp. 815–818: Sītāharaṇa.
§ 530, III, **279**, 1–48 (16045–16092). pp. 818–822: Viçvāvasumokshaṇa.
§ 531, III, **280**, 1–40 (16093–16132). pp. 822–825: Rāmopākhyānap.
§ 532, III, **280**, 41–74 (16133–16165). pp. 825–827: Sītāsāntvana.
§ 533, III, **281**, 1–30 (16166–16196). pp. 827–830: Sītā-Rāvaṇa-saṃvāda.
§ 534, III, **282**, 1–71 (16197–16268). pp. 830–835: (*a*) Hanumat-pratyāgamana, (*b*) Madhuvana, (*c*) Jaṭāyu, (*d*) Laṅkā.
§ 535, III, **283**, 1–54 (16269–16322). pp. 835–839: Setubandhana.
§ 536, III, **284**, 1–41 (16323–16363). pp. 839–842; Laṅkāpraveça.
§ 537, III, **285**, 1–15 (16364–16378). pp. 843–844: Rāma-Rāvaṇayuddha.
§ 538, III, **286**, 1–29 (16379–16408). pp. 844–846: Kumbhakarṇa-raṇagamana.
§ 539, III, **287**, 1–29 (16409–16437). pp. 846–848: Kumbhakarṇādi-vadha.
§ 540, III, **288**, 1–26 (16438–16464). pp. 848–850: Indrajid-yuddha.
§ 541, III, **289**, 1–33 (16465–16497). pp. 851–854: Indrajid-vadha.
§ 542, III, **290**, 1–33 (16498–16530). pp. 854–857: Rāvaṇa-vadha.
§ 543, III, **291**, 1–70 (16531–16601). pp. 857–862: Rāmābhisheka.
§ 544, III, **292**, 1–14 (16602–16615). pp. 862–863: Yudhishṭhirāçvāsa.

XLIX. Pativratāmāhātmyaparvan.

§ 545, III, **293**, 1–41 (16616–16657). pp. 864–866: Sāvitrī-svayaṃvara (°upākhyāna).
294, 1–33 (16658–16690). pp. 867–869: Sāvitry-udvāha Nāradānumati (id.).
295, 1–23 (16691–16713). pp. 869–871: id. (id.).
296, 1–33 (16714–16746). pp. 871–874: Sāvitryā vanagamana (id.).
297, 1–111 (16747–16857). pp. 875–883: Satyavadāçramāgamana (id.).
298, 1–44 (16858–16901). pp. 884–887: Sāvitrī-kathā (id.).
299, 1–17 (16902–16918). pp. 887–888: Dyumatsena-rājyalābha (id.).

L. Kuṇḍalāharaṇaparvan.

§ 546, III, **300**, 1–9 (16919–16957). pp. 888–891: Sūrya-Karṇa-saṃvāda.
301, 1–18 (16958–16976). pp. 891–893: id.
302, 1–21 (16977–16997). pp. 893–894: id.
§ 547, III, **303**, 1–29 (16998–17026). pp. 895–897: Pṛthopadeça.
304, 1–20 (17027–17046). pp. 897–898: Pṛthā-dvija-paricaryā.
305, 1–23 (17047–17069). pp. 899–900: Pṛthā[yā]mantra-prāpti.
306, 1–28 (17070–17097). pp. 900–903: [Pṛthā-] Sūryāhvāna.
307, 1–28 (17098–17125). pp. 903–905: Pṛthā-Sūrya-samgama (Sūrya-Kuntī-samāgama).
308, 1–27 (17126–17152). pp. 905–907: Pṛthā-mañjūshā-kshepaṇa (Karṇa-parityāga).
309, 1–25 (17153–17177). pp. 907–909: Rādhā-Karṇa-prāpti.
310, 1–42 (17178–17220). pp. 909–912: [Karṇasya]varma-kuṇḍaladāna (kavaca°).
§ 546: Kuṇḍalāharaṇaparvan.
§ 547: Karna.

LI. Āraṇeyaparvan.

III, **311**, 1–21 (17221–17241). pp. 913–914: [Pāṇḍava-] mṛgānveshaṇa.
312, 1–45 (17242–17287). pp. 914–918: Nakulādi-patana (Yudhishṭhira-sarodarçana).
313, 1–133 (17288–17418). pp. 918–930: Yaksha[-Yudhishṭhira]-praçn[ottar]a.
314, 1–29 (17419–17447). pp. 931–933: Nakulādi-jīvan [ādivaraprāpti].
315, 1–31 (17448–17478). pp. 933–935: Ajñātavāsodyoga (°saṃmantraṇa).
§ 548, III, **311**, 1 — **315**, 31 (17221–17478). pp. 913–935: (*a*) Āraṇeyaparvan, (*b*) Pāripātra (°yā°), (*c*) Dharma, (*d*) Indra, (*e*) Vishṇu, (*f*) Agni, (*g*) Aurva, (*h*) Vivasvat.

IV. VIRAṬAPARVAN.

LII. Pāṇḍavapraveçaparvan.

IV, **1**, 1–28 (1–27). pp. 1–3 : Yudhishṭhirādi-mantraṇa.
2, 1–32 (28–59). pp. 3–5 : id.
3, 1–23 (60–82). pp. 5–7 : id.
4, 1–58 (83–140). pp. 7–11 : Dhaumyopadeça.
5, 1–36 (141–177). pp. 11–13 : [Purapraveçe] Astra-saṃsthāpana.
6, 1–35 (178–213). pp. 14–16 : [Çrī] Durgāstava.
7, 1–18 (214–230). pp. 17–18 : Yudhishṭhira-praveça.
8, 1–13 (231–243). pp. 19–20 : Bhīma-praveça.
9, 1–37 (244–279). pp. 20–23 : Draupadī-praveça.
10, 1–16 (280–295). pp. 23–24 : Sahadeva-praveça.
11, 1–14 (296–311). pp. 24–25 : Arjuna-praveça.
12, 1–13 (312–324). pp. 26–27 : Nakula-praveça.
§ 549, IV, **1**, 1 — **12**, 13 (1–324). pp. 1–27 : (*a*) Pāṇḍava-praveçaparvan, (*b*) Agni, (*c*) Arjuna, (*d*) Dhṛtarāshṭra, (*e*) Airāvata (elephant), (*f*) Durgā.

LIII. Samayapālanaparvan.

§ 550, IV, **13**, 1–46 (325–372). pp. 27–30 : Jīmūtavadha.

LIV. Kīcakavadhaparvan.

§ 551, IV, **14**, 1–52 (373–430). pp. 31–35 : Kīcaka-Kṛshṇā-saṃvāda.
15, 1–21 (431–451). pp. 35–36 : Draupadī-surāharaṇa.
16, 1–51 (452–502). pp. 37–40 : Draupadī-paribhava.
17, 1–21 (503–522). pp. 41–42 : Draupadī-Bhīma-saṃvāda.
18, 1–33 (523–556). pp. 42–44 : id.
19, 1–47 (557–603). pp. 44–47 : id.
20, 1–31 (604–640). pp. 48–50 : id.
21, 1–51 (641–693). pp. 50–53 : Draupadī-sāntvana.
22, 1–94 (694–792). pp. 53–60 : Kīcaka-vadha.
23, 1–34 (793–828). pp. 60–62 : [Upa-Kīcaka-vadha].
24, 1–30 (829–860). pp. 62–64 : Kīcaka-dāha.

LV. Goharaṇa-parvan.

§ 552, IV, **25**, 1–22 (861–882). pp. 65–66 : Cārapratyāgamana.
26, 1–18 (883–901). pp. 67–68 : Karṇa-Duḥçāsana-vākya.
27, 1–10 (902–911). pp. 68–69 : [Droṇavākye] Cāra-pratyācāra.
28, 1–33 (912–946). pp. 69–72 : Cārapratyācāre Bhīma-vākya.
29, 1–14 (947–970). pp. 72–73 : id. Kṛpa-vākya.
30, 1–27 (971–999). pp. 74–75 : Suçarmādi-Matsyadeça-yāna (Dakshiṇagograhe Suçarmādi-yāna).
31, 1–35 (1000–1035). pp. 76–78 : [Dakshiṇagograhe] Matsyarājaraṇodyoga.
32, 1–30 (1036–1066). pp. 78–80 : [id.] Suçarma-Virāṭa-(Vi°-Su°-)yuddha.
33, 1–61 (1067–1128). pp. 81–85 : [id.] Suçarma-nigraha.
34, 1–19 (1129–1148). pp. 85–86 : [id.] Virāṭa-jayaghosha.
35, 1–22 (1149–1170). pp. 87–88 : Uttara-praçaṃsā (°gograhe gopavākya).
36, 1–24 (1171–1194). pp. 88–90 : [Uttaragograhe-] Bṛhannalā-sārathyakathana.
37, 1–34 (1195–1229). pp. 90–93 : [id.] Uttara-niryāṇa.
38, 1–51 (1230–1284). pp. 93–97 : [id.] Uttarāçvāsana.
39, 1–17 (1285–1302). pp. 97–99 : [id.] Arjuna-praçaṃsā.
40, 1–8 (1303–1311). p. 99 : [id.] Arjunāstrakathana.
41, 1–12 (1311–1324). p. 100 : [id.] Astrāropaṇa.
42, 1–18 (1325–1342). pp. 101–102 : Uttarāstradarçana (Uttaravākya).
43, 1–23 (1343–1366). pp. 102–104 : [Uttaragograhe] Uttarasyāstradarçana (Āyudhavarṇana).
44, 1–25 (1367–1393). pp. 104–106 : [id.] Arjuna-paricaya.
45, 1–41 (1394–1435). pp. 106–109 : [id.] Arjuna-yuddhā-rambha (Uttarārjunayor vākya).
46, 1–33 (1436–1470). pp. 109–111 : [id.] Utpātadarçana (Autpātika).
47, 1–34 (1471–1506). pp. 112–115 : [id.] Duryodhana-vākya.
48, 1–23 (1507–1529). pp. 115–117 : [id.] Karṇa-vikatthana.
49, 1–23 (1530–1553). pp. 117–119 : [id.] Kṛpa-vākya.
50, 1–28 (1554–1582). pp. 120–123 : [id.] Açvatthāma-bhartsana-vākya (Drauṇivākya).
51, 1–22 (1583–1605). pp. 123–125 : Droṇavākya.
52, 1–23 (1606–1629). pp. 125–127 : Bhīshma-sainyavyūha.
53, 1–25 (1630–1659). pp. 127–129 : [U°] Gonivartana.
54, 1–36 (1660–1695). pp. 130–133 : [U°] Karṇāpayāna.
55, 1–60 (1696–1758). pp. 134–138 : Arjuna-Kṛpa-saṅgrāma.
56, 1–19 (1759–1778). pp. 138–140 : Devāgamana.
57, 1–43 (1779–1822). pp. 140–143 : [U°] Kṛpāpayāna.
58, 1–76 (1823–1900). pp. 143–148 : Droṇāpayāna.
59, 1–21 (1901–1922). pp. 148–150 : [U°] Arjunāçvatthāma-yuddha.
60, 1–27 (1923–1949). pp. 150–152 : Karṇāpayāna.
61, 1–46 (1950–1997). pp. 152–156 : Arjuna-Duḥçāsanādi-yuddha.
62, 1–22 (1998–2020). pp. 156–158 : Arjuna-saṅkulayuddha.
63, 1–14 (2021–2034). [omitted] : id.
64, 1–49 (2035–2085). pp. 158–161 : Bhīshmāpayāna.
65, 1–18 (2086–2104). pp. 162–163 : Duryodhana-palāyana (°āpayāna).
66, 1–30 (2105–2135). pp. 164–167 : Arjuna-yuddha-nivartana (Samasta-Kaurava-palāyana).
67, 1–23 (2136–2159). pp. 167–169 : Uttarāgamana.
68, 1–76 (2160–2240). pp. 169–175 : Virāṭottara-saṃvāda.
69, 1–19 (2241–2259). pp. 175–177 : id.

LVI. Vaivāhikaparvan.

§ 553, IV, **70**, 1–28 (2260–2288). pp. 177–179 : Pāndava-prakāça.
71, 1–36 (2289–2325). pp. 179–182 : Uttarā-vivāha-prastāva.
72, 1–40 (2326–2376). pp. 182–185 : Uttarā-vivāha.

V. UDYOGAPARVAN.

LVII. Sainyodyogaparvan.

§ 554, V, **1**, 1–26 (1–26). pp. 1–3 : Purohitayāna.
2, 1–15 (27–40). pp. 3–5 : [Baladevavākya].
3, 1–23 (41–63). pp. 5–7 : Sātyaki-krodhavākya.
4, 1–26 (64–89). pp. 7–8 : Purohitayāna (Drupada-vākya).
5, 1–18 (90–108). pp. 8–9 : [Pāñcālya-]purohita-yāna.
6, 1–19 (109–128). pp. 10–11 : Purohitayāna.
7, 1–39 (129–171). pp. 11–14 : Kṛshṇasārathyasvīkāra.
§ 555, V, **8**, 1–54 (172–226). pp. 14–18 : Çalya-vākya.
9, 1–59 (227–289). pp. 18–22 : Indravijaya.

10, 1–50 (290–341). pp. 22–26: Vṛtra-vadhe Indravijaya.
11, 1–26 (342–367). pp. 26–27: Indrāṇī-bhaya.
12, 1–32 (368–400). pp. 28–30: Indrāṇī-kāla-[avadhi-]yācana.
13, 1–27 (401–427). pp. 30–32: Upaçruti-yācana.
14, 1–18 (428–445). pp. 32–33: Indrāṇīndra-stava.
15, 1–34 (446–482). pp. 33–36: Bṛhaspaty-Agni-saṃvāda.
16, 1–34 (483–519). pp. 36–38: Indra-Varuṇādi-saṃvāda.
17, 1–22 (520–543). pp. 38–40: Indrāgastya-saṃvāde Nahusha-bhraṃça.
18, 1–25 (544–569). pp. 40–42: Çalya-gamana.
19, 1–33 (570–602). pp. 42–44: Purohitasainyadarçana.

LVIII. SAÑJAYAYĀNAPARVAN.

§ 556, V, **20**, 1–21 (603–623). pp. 44–45: Purohita-vākya (°yāna).
21, 1–21 (624–644). pp. 46–47: Sañjayāhvāna (id.).
22, 1–40 (645–684). pp. 47–51: Dhṛtarāshṭra-kathā (°sandeça).
23, 1–28 (685–712). pp. 51–54: Yudhishṭhira-praçna.
24, 1–10 (713–722). pp. 54–55: Sañjaya-vākya.
25, 1–15 (723–737). pp. 55–56: id.
26, 1–29 (738–766). pp. 57–59: Yudhishṭhira-vākya.
27, 1–27 (767–793). pp. 60–63: Sañjaya-vākya.
28, 1–14 (794–808). pp. 63–65: Yudhishṭhira-vākya.
29, 1–58 (809–866). pp. 65–70: Kṛshṇa-vākya.
30, 1–49 (867–915). pp. 70–75: Yudhishṭhira-vākya (°sandeça).
31, 1–23 (916–938). pp. 76–77: id. (id.).
32, 1–32 (939–970). pp. 77–81: Dhṛtarāshṭra-Sañjaya-saṃvāda.

LIX. PRAJĀGARAPARVAN.

§ 557,[1] V, **33**, 1–123 (971–1093). pp. 81–91: Vidura-hita-vākya (°nīti°).
34, 1–86 (1094–1180). pp. 91–97: Vidura-vākya (id.).
§ 558,[2] V, **35**, 1–77 (1181–1259). pp. 97–103: Vidura-hita-vākya.
§ 559,[1] V, **36**, 1–74 (1260–1333). pp. 103–110: id.
37, 1–64 (1334–1397). pp. 110–116: Vidura-vākya.
38, 1–47 (1398–1445). pp. 116–120: id.
39, 1–86 (1446–1531). pp. 120–127: id.
40, 1–32 (1532–1564). pp. 127–130: id.

LX. SANATSUJĀTAPARVAN.

§ 560, V, **41**, 1–12 (1565–1576). pp. 130–131: Vidura-[kṛta-Sanatsujāta-]prārthana.
42, 1–46 (1577–1620). pp. 131–139: [Sanatsujāta-vākya].
43, 1–63 (1621–1683). pp. 139–149: Sanatsujāta-vākya.
44, 1–31 (1684–1714). pp. 149–154: id.
45, 1–21 (1715–1736). pp. 154–156: id.
46, 1–31 (1737–1790). pp. 157–165: [id.].

LXI. YĀNASANDHIPARVAN.

§ 561, V, **47**, 1–17 (1791–1808). pp. 165–167: Sañjaya-pratyāgamana.
48, 1–109 (1809–1916). pp. 167–177: Sañjaya-vākya (Arjuna-vākya-nivedana).
49, 1–48 (1917–1966). pp. 178–181: Bhīshma(-Droṇa)-vākya.
50, 1–50 (1967–2017). pp. 181–185: Sañjaya-vākya.

[1] Prajāg. [2] Virocana.

51, 1–61 (2018–2084). pp. 185–189: Dhṛtarāshṭra-vākya.
52, 1–20 (2085–2105). pp. 190–191: id.
53, 1–16 (2106–2120). pp. 191–192: id.
54, 1–22 (2121–2142). pp. 193–194: Sañjayavākya.
55, 1–69 (2143–2213). pp. 194–199: Duryodhana-vākya.
56, 1–17 (2214–2231). pp. 199–201: Sañjaya-vākya.
57, 1–62 (2232–2294). pp. 201–205: id.
58, 1–29 (2295–2323). pp. 205–207: Dhṛtarāshṭra-vākya.
59, 1–31 (2323–2358). pp. 207–209: Sañjaya-vākya (Sañjayena-Çrī-Kṛshṇa-vākya-kathana).
60, 1–23 (2359–2381). pp. 210–211: Dhṛtarāshṭra-vivecana.
61, 1–29 (2382–2410). pp. 211–213: Duryodhana-vākya.
62, 1–18 (2411–2428). pp. 213–215: Karṇa[-Bhīshma]-vākya.
63, 1–24 (2429–2454). pp. 215–217: Vidura-vākya.
64, 1–27 (2455–2481). pp. 218–219: id.
65, 1–16 (2482–2497). pp. 220–221: Dhṛtarāshṭra-vākya.
66, 1–15 (2498–2512). pp. 221–222: Sañjaya-vākya.
67, 1–10 (2513–2522). pp. 222–223: id. (Vyāsa-Gāndhāryā-gamana).
68, 1–15 (2523–2537). pp. 223–225: Sañjaya-vākya.
69, 1–21 (2538–2559). pp. 225–227: id.
70, 1–15 (2560–2573). pp. 227–228: id.
71, 1–7 (2574–2580). p. 229: Dhṛtarāshṭra-vākya.

LXII. BHAGAVADYĀNAPARVAN.

§ 562, V, **72**, 1–93 (2581–2674). pp. 229–236: Yudhishṭhira-vākya (Y°-kṛta-Kṛshṇa-preraṇa).
73, 1–42 (2675–2716). pp. 237–239: Kṛshṇa-vākya.
74, 1–23 (2717–2739). pp. 240–241: Bhīma-vākya.
75, 1–23 (2740–2762). pp. 241–243: [Bhīmottejaka-]Çrī-Kṛshṇa-vākya.
76, 1–18 (2763–2781). pp. 243–244: Bhīma[sena]vākya.
77, 1–20 (2782–2801). pp. 244–246: [Çrī-]Kṛshṇa-vākya.
78, 1–19 (2802–2821). pp. 246–247: Arjuna-vākya.
79, 1–21 (2822–2843). pp. 248–249: [Çrī-]Kṛshṇa-vākya.
80, 1–18 (2844–2861). pp. 249–251: Nakula-vākya.
81, 1–9 (2862–2870). p. 251: Sahadeva-[Sātyaki-]vākya.
82, 1–49 (2871–2919). pp. 252–255: Çrī-Kṛshṇa-vākya (Draupadī-Kṛshṇa-saṃvāda).
83, 1–72 (2920–2992). pp. 255–261: Bhagavad-yāna (Çrī-Kṛshṇa-prasthāna).
84, 1–29 (2993–3021). pp. 261–263: id. (Çrī-Kṛshṇa-prayāna).
85, 1–18 (3022–3039). pp. 263–264: id. (Mārge sabhānir-māṇa).
86, 1–21 (3040–3060). pp. 264–266: Dhṛtarāshṭra-vākya.
87, 1–17 (3061–3077). pp. 266–267: Vidura-vākya.
88, 1–23 (3078–3100). pp. 267–269: Duryodhana-vākya.
89, 1–27 (3101–3127). pp. 269–270: Vidura-Bhagavat-saṃvāda (Dhṛtarāshṭra-gṛhapraveça-pūrvakaṃ Çrī-Kṛshṇasya Vidura-gṛha-praveçaḥ).
90, 1–105 (3128–3235). pp. 271–279: Kuntī-Kṛshṇa-(Kṛ°-Ku°)-saṃvāda.
91, 1–41 (3236–3277). pp. 280–283: Çrī-Kṛshṇa-Duryodhana-saṃvāda.
92, 1–30 (3278–3307). pp. 283–285: Çrī-Kṛshṇa-Vidura-saṃvāda.
93, 1–22 (3308–3329). pp. 285–287: id. (°vākya).
94, 1–54 (3330–3383). pp. 287–291: Bhagavad-upaveça (Çrī-Kṛshṇa-sabhāpraveça).

95, 1–63 (3384–3447). pp. 291–296: Bhagavad-(Çrī-Kṛshṇa-)vākya.
§ 563, V, **96**, 1–52 (3448–3500). pp. 296–300: Jāmadagnya-vākya (Dambhodbhavopākhyāna).
§ 564, V, **97**, 1–21 (3501–3521). pp. 300–302: Mātalīyopākhyāna (°li-varānveshaṇa).
98, 1–25 (3522–3546). pp. 302–304: id. (id.).
99, 1–20 (3547–3566). pp. 304–306: id. (id.).
100, 1–19 (3567–3585). pp. 306–308: id. (id.).
101, 1–16 (3586–3601). pp. 308–309: id. (id.).
102, 1–15 (3602–3616). pp. 309–310: id. (id.).
103, 1–26 (3617–3642). pp. 311–312: id. (id.).
104, 1–30 (3643–3673). pp. 312–315: id. (id.).
105, 1–40 (3674–3713). pp. 315–318: id. (id.).
§ 565, V, **106**, 1–27 (3714–3740). pp. 318–321: Gālavacarita.
107, 1–19 (3741–3760). pp. 321–322: id.
108, 1–18 (3761–3778). pp. 323–324: id.
109, 1–21 (3779–3800). pp. 324–327: id.
110, 1–20 (3801–3820). pp. 327–329: id.
111, 1–28 (3821–3849). pp. 329–332: id.
112, 1–22 (3850–3872). pp. 332–334: id.
113, 1–23 (3873–3895). pp. 334–336: id.
114, 1–20 (3896–3916). pp. 336–338: id.
115, 1–21 (3917–3937). pp. 339–340: id.
116, 1–22 (3938–3959). pp. 340–342: id.
117, 1–21 (3960–3980). pp. 342–344: id.
118, 1–21 (3981–4001). pp. 344–345: id.
119, 1–24 (4002–4025). pp. 345–347: id.
120, 1–22 (4026–4047). pp. 347–349: id.
§ 566, V, **121**, 1–28 (4048–4077). pp. 350–352: [Gālavacarite] Yayāti-[svarga-]bhraṃça.
122, 1–18 (4078–4096). pp. 352–353: [Gā°-]Yayātisvargārohaṇa.
123, 1–23 (4097–4120). pp. 353–356: [Gā°-] [id.].
§ 567, V, **124**, 1–62 (4121–4185). pp. 356–361: Bhagavad-vākya.
125, 1–27 (4186–4213). pp. 361–363: Dhṛtarāshṭra-vākya (Bhīshmādi°-).
126, 1–18 (4214–4232). pp. 363–364: Bhīshma-Droṇa-vākya.
127, 1–25 (4232–4258). pp. 364–366: Duryodhana-vākya.
128, 1–50 (4259–4308). pp. 367–370: [Çrī-]Kṛshṇa-vākya.
129, 1–54 (4309–4363). pp. 371–375: Gāndhārī-vākya.
130, 1–53 (4364–4417). pp. 375–379: Vidura-vākya.
131, 1–41 (4418–4458). pp. 379–382: Viçvarūpa-darçana.
132, 1–34 (4459–4493). pp. 382–385: Kuntī-vākya.
§ 568,[1] V, **133**, 1–45 (4494–4538). pp. 385–389: Vidulāputrānuçāsana.
134, 1–41 (4539–4579). pp. 389–392: id.
135, 1–40 (4580–4621). pp. 393–396: id.
136, 1–22 (4622–4643). pp. 397–399: Kuntī-vākya (Vidulāputrānuçasanasamāpti).
§ 569, V, **137**, 1–32 (4644–4675). pp. 399–401: Kuntī-vākya.
138, 1–27 (4676–4703). pp. 401–403: Bhīshma-Droṇa-vākya.
139, 1–22 (4704–4725). pp. 404–406: id.
140, 1–29 (4726–4754). pp. 406–409: Bhagavad-vākya (Çrī-Kṛshṇa°).

[1] Vidulāputraçāsana.

141, 1–57 (4755–4812). pp. 409–415: Karṇa-vākya (°opanivāda).
142, 1–20 (4813–4832). pp. 415–417: [id.] Bhagavad-vākya.
143, 1–52 (4833–4884). pp. 417–421: [id.] Kṛshṇa-Karṇa-saṃvāda.
144, 1–31 (4885–4916). pp. 421–424: Kuntī-Karṇa-samāgama.
145, 1–12 (4917–4928). pp. 424–425: id.
146, 1–27 (4929–4955). pp. 425–427: id.
147, 1–43 (4956–5001). pp. 427–431: Bhagavad-vākya.
148, 1–36 (5002–5034). pp. 431–434: Kṛshṇa-vākya.
149, 1–36 (5040–5076). pp. 434–436: id. (Dhṛtarāshṭra-vākyakathana).
150, 1–20 (5077–5096). pp. 437–438: Bhagavad-vākya (Kṛshṇa°).

LXIII. Sainyaniryāṇaparvan.

§ 570, V, **151**, 1–71 (5097–5169). pp. 438–444: Kurukshetra-praveça.
152, 1–18 (5170–5187). pp. 444–445: Çibirādinirmāṇa.
153, 1–27 (5188–5215). pp. 445–448: Duryodhana-[sainya-]sajjā[-karaṇa].
154, 1–27 (5216–5242). pp. 448–450: Yudhishṭhirārjuna-saṃvāda.
155, 1–35 (5243–5277). pp. 450–453: Duryodhana-sainya-vibhāga.
156, 1–36 (5278–5313). pp. 453–455: Bhīshma-saināpatya.
157, 1–35 (5314–5349). pp. 456–458: [Bala-]Rāma-[tīrthyātrā-]gamana.
158, 1–40 (5350–5390). pp. 458–461: Rukmi-pratyākhyāna.
159, 1–15 (5391–5406). pp. 461–462: Sañjaya-vākya.

LXIV. Ulūkadūtāgamanaparvan.

§ 571, V, **160**, 1–125 (5407–5534). pp. 462–472: Duryodhana-vākya.
161, 1–43 (5535–5577). pp. 472–475: Ulūka-vākya.
162, 1–63 (5578–5642). pp. 475–480: Bhagavad-vākya (Kṛshṇādi°).
163, 1–57 (5643–5701). pp. 480–484: Ulūkāpayāna.
164, 1–12 (5702–5713). pp. 484–485: Senāpatiniyoga.

LXV. Rathātirathasaṅkhyānaparvan.

§ 572, V, **165**, 1–33 (5714–5747). pp. 485–488: [Kauravarathātirathasaṅkhyā].
166, 1–22 (5748–5769). pp. 488–489: [id.].
167, 1–38 (5770–5807). pp. 489–492: [id.].
168, 1–42 (5808–5849). pp. 492–495: Bhīshma-Karṇa-kalaha (°saṃvāda).
169, 1–28 (5850–5878). pp. 495–497: Pāṇḍava-rathātirathasaṅkhyā.
170, 1–14 (5879–5892). pp. 498–499: [id.].
171, 1–27 (5893–5920). pp. 499–500: [id.].
172, 1–21 (5921–5941). pp. 501–502: [id.].

LXVI. Ambopākhyānaparvan.

§ 573, V, **173**, 1–23 (5942–5965). pp. 502–504: [Bhīshma-] Kanyāharaṇa.
174, 1–10 (5966–5975). pp. 504–505: Ambā-vākya.
175, 1–45 (5976–6021). pp. 505–508: Çaikhāvatyāmbā-saṃvāda.

176, 1–59 (6022–6082). pp. 508–512: Akṛtavraṇāmbā-saṃvāda (Hotravahanā°).
177, 1–42 (6083–7024). pp. 513–516: Rāmāmbā-saṃvāda.
178, 1–95 (7025–7123). pp. 516–523: Gaṅgā-vākya (Paraçu-Rāma-Bhīshmayoḥ Kurukshetrāvataraṇa).
179, 1–39 (7124–7162). pp. 523–526: Bhīshma-Rāma-yuddhe (Rā° Bhī°) [Bhīshma-paçcāttāpa].
180, 1–38 (7163–7200). pp. 526–529: Rāma-Bhīshma-yuddha.
181, 1–16 (7201–7216). pp. 529–530: [id. çakti-prakshepa].
182, 1–30 (7217–7247). pp. 530–532: Rāma-Bhīshma-yuddhe [Gaṅgā-hayasaṅgraha].
183, 1–19 (7248–7266). pp. 533–534: Rāma-Bhīshma-yuddhe svapnopadeça (Bhīshma-prasvāpanāstralābha).
184, 1–23 (7267–7289). pp. 534–535: [Rāma-Bhīshma-yuddhe] [Paraspara-]Brahmāstra-prayoga.
185, 1–37 (7290–7327). pp. 535–538: [Rāma-Bhīshma-] yuddhanivṛtti.
186, 1–41 (7328–7369). pp. 538–541: Ambā-tapasyā.
187, 1–19 (7370–7388). pp. 541–542: Ambā-hutāçana-praveça.
188, 1–20 (7389–7408). pp. 542–544: Çikhaṇḍy-utpatti.
189, 1–23 (7409–7433). pp. 544–545: Hiraṇyavarma-dūtāgamana (°ta-preshaṇa).
190, 1–22 (7434–7455). pp. 545–547: Drupada-praçna.
191, 1–30 (7456–7486). pp. 547–549: Sthūṇākarṇa-pratyaksha (°samāgama).
192, 1–70 (7487–7557). pp. 549–554: Çikhaṇḍi-puṃstva-prāpti.
193, 1–22 (7558–7580). pp. 554–556: Bhīshmādi-çaktika-thana.
194, 1–22 (7581–7602). pp. 556–558: Arjuna-vākya.
195, 1–19 (7603–7621). pp. 558–559: Kaurava-sainya-niryāṇa.
196, 1–35 (7622–7657). pp. 560–562: Pāṇḍava-sainya (senā)-niryāṇa.

VI. BHĪSHMAPARVAN.

LXVII. Jambūkhaṇḍa-vinirmāṇa-parvan.

§ 574, VI, **1**, 1–34 (1–35). pp. 1–4: Sainya-çikshaṇa.
2, 1–33 (36–67). pp. 4–6: Çrī-[Veda-]Vyāsa-darçana.
3, 1–85 (68–154). pp. 6–15: Nimittākhyāna.
4, 1–21 (155–175). pp. 15–17: Bhaumaguṇakathana.
5, 1–18 (176–193). pp. 17–19: Sudarçana-dvīpa-varṇana.
6, 1–56 (194–252). pp. 19–24: Bhūmyādi-parimāṇavivaraṇa.
7, 1–32 (253–286). pp. 24–27: Mālyavad-varṇana.
8, 1–22 (287–308). pp. 27–29: Dhṛtarāshṭra-vākya.
9, 1–76 (309–384). pp. 29–34: Bhāratīya-nady-[deç']ādi-nāmakathana.
10, 1–15 (385–400). pp. 34–35: Bhārata[-varshe kṛtā-dyanurodhenā] [dy]āyurnirūpaṇa.

LXVIII. Bhūmiparva.

§ 575, VI, **11**, 1–40 (401–441). pp. 36–39: Çākadvīpa-varṇana.
12, 1–52 (442–494). pp. 39–43: Uttarakurv-ādi-nirūpaṇa (Uttaradvīpādisaṃsthānavarṇana).

LXIX. Bhagavadgītāparvan.

§ 576, VI, **13**, 1–13 (495–507). pp. 44–45: Bhīshma-mṛtyuçravaṇa.
14, 1–80 (508–587). pp. 45–51: Dhṛtarāshṭra-praçna.
15, 1–20 (588–607). pp. 52–53: Duryodhana-Duḥçāsana-saṃvāda.
16, 1–27 (608–635). pp. 53–55: Sainyavarṇana.
17, 1–39 (636–675). pp. 55–59: id.
18, 1–18 (676–694). pp. 59–60: id.
19, 1–45 (695–740). pp. 60–64: Pāṇḍavasainyavyūha.
20, 1–20 (741–759). pp. 64–66: Sainyavarṇana.
21, 1–17 (760–776). pp. 67–68: Yudhishṭhirārjuna-saṃvāda.
22, 1–16 (777–792). pp. 68–70: Çrī-Kṛshṇārjuna-saṃvāda.
23, 1–28 (793–821). pp. 70–73: Durgā-stotra.
24, 1–7 (822–829). pp. 73–74: Dhṛtarāshṭra-Sañjaya-saṃvāda.
25, 1–47 (830–878). pp. 74–78: Çrī-Kṛshṇārjuna-saṃvāde Arjuna-vishāda[-yoga].
26, 1–72 (878–950). pp. 78–86: Çrī° Sāṅkhya-Yoga.
27, 1–43 (951–993). pp. 86–91: Çrī° Karmayoga.
28, 1–42 (994–1035). pp. 91–95: Çrī° Jñānayoga (Yajña-vibhāga°).
29, 1–29 (1036–1064). pp. 95–98: [Çrī° Karma-]Sannyāsa-yoga.
30, 1–47 (1065–1111). pp. 98–102: [Çrī°]ātmasaṃyama-(adhyātma-)yoga.
31, 1–30 (1112–1141). pp. 102–105: Çrī° Jñānayoga.
32, 1–28 (1142–1169). pp. 105–108: Çrī° [Mahāpurusha-yoga].
33, 1–34 (1170–1204). pp. 108–111: [Çrī°] Rājavidyā-rājaguhya-yoga.
34, 1–42 (1205–1246). pp. 111–115: [Çrī°] Vibhūtiyoga.
35, 1–55 (1247–1301). pp. 115–121: [Çrī°] Viçvarūpa-darçana.
36, 1–20 (1302–1321). pp. 121–123: [Çrī° Bhaktiyoga].
37, 1–34 (1322–1355). pp. 123–126: [Çrī°] Kshetra-kshetrajña-[vibhāga-]yoga.
38, 1–27 (1356–1382). pp. 126–129: [Çrī°] Guṇatraya-vibhāga[-yoga].
39, 1–20 (1383–1402). pp. 129–132: [Çrī°] Purushottama-yoga.
40, 1–14 (1403–1426). pp. 132–134: [Çrī°] Daivā (Devā°) sura-Sampatti-(Sampadvibhāga-)yoga.
41, 1–28 (1427–1454). pp. 134–136: [Çrī°] Çraddhā-trayavibhāga[-yoga].
42, 1–78 (1455–1532). pp. 136–143: Çrī° Sannyāsayoga.

LXX. Bhīshmavadhaparvan.

§ 577, VI, **43**, 6–109 (1533–1637). pp. 143–152: Bhīshma-Droṇa-Kṛpa-Çalyābhigamana (Bhīshmādi-saṃmānana).
§ 578, VI, **44**, 1–30 (1638–1669). pp. 152–154: Yuddhā-rambha.
45, 1–87 (1670–1756). pp. 154–161: Dvandvayuddha.
46, 1–50 (1757–1807). pp. 161–165: Saṅkulayuddha.
47, 1–67 (1808–1867). pp. 165–170: Çvetayuddha.
48, 1–121 (1868–1984). pp. 170–178: Çvetavadha.
49, 1–53 (1985–2032). pp. 179–182: Çaṅkhayuddhe prathamadivasāvahāra.
50, 1–58 (2033–2090). pp. 182–187: Krauñcavyūha-nirmāṇa.
51, 1–30 (2091–2120). pp. 187–189: Kaurava-[sainya-] vyūha-[racanā].
§ 579, VI, **52**, 1–72 (2121–2193). pp. 189–194: Bhīsh-mārjuna-yuddha.
53, 1–41 (2194–2234). pp. 194–197: Dhṛshṭadyumna-Droṇa-yuddha.

54, 1–124 (2235–2358). pp. 197–205: [Dvitīyayuddhadivase] Kaliṅgarājavadha.
55, 1–43 (2359–2401). pp. 205–208: Dvitīya[yuddha-]divasāvahāra.
§ 580, VI, **56,** 1–22 (2402–2424). pp. 208–210: Gāruḍārdhacandrayuddha-nirmāṇa (Tṛtīye yuddha-divase parasparavyūharacanā).
57, 1–40 (2425–2461). pp. 210–212: Tṛtīyadivasayuddhā-(Tṛtiye yuddhadivase) [rambhe] [saṅkulayuddha].
58, 1–46 (2462–2507). pp. 212–215: [Tṛtīyayuddhadivase] Bhīshma-Duryodhana-saṃvāda.
59, 1–139 (2508–2650). pp. 216–227: Tṛtīyadivasāvahāra.
§ 581, VI, **60,** 1–29 (2651–2679). pp. 227–231: Bhīshmārjuna-dvairatha.
61, 1–36 (2680–2715). pp. 231–233: [Caturthayuddhadivase] Sāṃyamani-putra-vadha.
62, 1–65 (2716–2779). pp. 233–237: Bhīmasena parākrama (Caturthadivase Bhīmayuddha).
63, 1–33 (2780–2812). pp. 238–240: Sātyaki-Bhūriçravas[oḥ] samāgama.
64, 1–87 (2813–2897). pp. 240–245: Caturtha[yuddha] divasāvahāra.
65, 1–75 (2898–2972). pp. 246–252: Viçvopākhyāna.
66, 1–41 (2973–3013). pp. 252–255: id.
67, 1–25 (3014–3036). pp. 255–257: id.
68, 1–20 (3037–3055). pp. 257–258: id.
§ 582, VI, **69,** 1–34 (3056–3089). pp. 258–261: Pañcamadivasayuddhārambha.
70, 1–29 (3090–3118). pp. 261–263: Saṅkulayuddha.
71, 1–43 (3119–3161). pp. 263–266: id.
72, 1–35 (3162–3196). pp. 266–268: Bhīshmaparākrama (Pañcamadivasa-yuddha).
73, 1–43 (3197–3239). pp. 269–271: Dvandvayuddha.
74, 1–39 (3240–3276). pp. 272–274: Pañcama[yuddha] divasāvahāra.
§ 583, VI, **75,** 1–37 (3277–3313). pp. 274–277: Shashṭadivasayuddhārambha.
76, 1–26 (3314–3336). pp. 277–278: Dhṛtarāshṭracintā.
77, 1–75 (3337–3412). pp. 279–284: [Saṅkulayuddhe] Droṇa-parākrama.
78, 1–17*a* (3413–3429). pp. 284–285:
17*b*–36 (3430–3449). pp. 285–287: Saṅkulayuddha.
79, 1–64 (3450–3511). pp. 287–291: Shashṭhadivasāvahāra.
80, 1–19 (3512–3530). pp. 291–293: Bhīshma-Duryodhana-saṃvāda.
§ 584, VI, **81,** 1–46 (3531–3576). pp. 293–296: Saptamadivasa-yuddhā-(Sa°yu°di°)[rambha].
82, 1–62 (3577–3638). pp. 297–301: Dvairatha.
83, 1–57 (3639–3695). pp. 301–305: Dvandvayuddha.
84, 1–55 (3696–3750). pp. 305–309: [Saptamayuddhadivase] Suçarmārjuna-samāgama.
85, 1–40 (3751–3790). pp. 309–313: [id.] [Citrasenarathabhaṅga].
86, 1–57 (3791–3846). pp. 314–317: Saptamadivasayuddhāvahāra.
§ 585, VI, **87,** 1–40 (3847–3886). pp. 317–320: Ashṭama divasayuddhārambha.
88, 1–44 (3887–3930). pp. 320–323: Ādityaketu-prabhṛti-vadha (Sunābhādi-Dhṛtarāshṭraputravadha).
89, 1–40 (3931–3970). pp. 323–326: Ashṭamadivasayuddha.
90, 1–93 (3971–4063). pp. 326–333: Irāvad-vadha.
91, 1–31 (4064–4095). pp. 333–335: Haiḍimbayuddha.
92, 1–46 (4096–4138). pp. 335–338: id.
93, 1–43 (4139–4181). pp. 338–342: id. (Saṅkulayuddha).
94, 1–50 (4182–4231). pp. 342–345: Haiḍimbamāyā (Ashṭamayuddhadivase Ghaṭotkaca-yuddha).
95, 1–86 (4232–4322). pp. 345–351: Bhagadatta-parākrama (°yuddha).
96, 1–80 (4323–4403). pp. 351–357: Ashṭadivasayuddhāvahāra.
97, 1–43 (4404–4447). pp. 357–360: Bhīshma[m prati] Duryodhana-saṃvāda (°vākya).
98, 1–51 (4448–4499). pp. 360–363: [Bhīshma-]Duryodhana-[Duḥçāsana]-saṃvāda.
§ 586, VI, **99,** 1–30 (4500–4529). pp. 363–366: [Parasparavyūharacanāyām] Utpātadarçana.
100, 1–54 (4529–4583). pp. 366–369: [Navamadivasayuddhārambhe] Alambushābhimanyu-samāgama.
101, 1–59 (4584–4642). pp. 369–373: Saṅkulayuddhe Droṇārjuna-samāgama (Alambushābhimanyu-yuddha).
102, 1–39 (4643–4681). pp. 373–376: Bhīmaparākrama.
103, 1–47 (4682–4728). pp. 376–379: Saṅkulayuddha.
104, 1–38 (4729–4766). pp. 379–382: [Bhīshma-] Vārshṇeya-yuddha.
105, 1–35 (4767–4801). pp. 382–384: [Çalya-Dharmarāja-samāgama].
106, 1–85 (4802–4885). pp. 384–390: Navamadivasayuddhasamāpti.
107, 1–107 (4886–4993). pp. 390–398: Navamadivasā[va]hārottaramantra.
§ 587, VI, **108,** 1–60 (4994–5054). pp. 398–402: [Daçamadivasayuddhārambhe] Bhīshma-Çikhaṇḍi-pralāpa (°samāgama).
109, 1–39 (5055–5093). pp. 402–405: Duryodhana-Bhīshma (Bhī° Du°)-saṃvāda.
110, 1–48 (5094–5139). pp. 405–408: Arjuna-Duḥçāsana-samāgama.
111, 1–58 (5140–5197). pp. 408–412: Dvandvasamāgama (°yuddha).
112, 1–41 (5198–5238). pp. 412–415: Droṇāçvatthāma-saṃvāda.
113, 1–53 (5239–5290). pp. 415–418: Bhīma[sena]parākrama.
114, 1–47 (5291–5334). pp. 418–421: Bhīmārjuna-parākrama.
115, 1–43 (5335–5377). pp. 421–424: Bhīshmopadeça.
116, 1–80 (5378–5451). pp. 424–430: Saṅkulayuddha.
117, 1–65 (5452–5514). pp. 430–434: id.
118, 1–54 (5515–5568). pp. 434–438: Bhīshma-parākrama.
119, 1–122 (5569–5688). pp. 438–446: Bhīshma-nipātana.
120, 1–38 (5689–5727). pp. 447–449.
39–71 (5728–5761). pp. 449–452: Bhīshmopadhānadāna.
§ 588, VI, **121,** 1–57 (5762–5817). pp. 452–456: [Duryodhanaṃ prati] Bhīshma-[çikshā]-kathana (°vākya).
122, 1–39 (5818–5856). pp. 456–459: Bhīshma-Karṇa-samāgama (°saṃvāda).

VII. DROṆAPARVAN.

LXXI. DROṆĀBHISHEKAPARVAN.

§ 589, VII, **1,** 1–53 (1–51). pp. 1–5: Dhṛtarāshṭrapraçna.
2, 1–37 (52–88). pp. 5–9: Karṇa-niryāṇa.
3, 1–25 (89–114). pp. 9–11: Karṇa-vākya.
4, 1–18 (115–133). pp. 11–12: Karṇāçvāsa.

5, 1–21 (134–154). pp. 12–14: Karṇa-vākya.
6, 1–13 (155–168). pp. 14–15: Duryodhana-protsāha (Droṇa-protsāhana).
7, 1–54 (169–223). pp. 15–19: Droṇa-parākrama.
8, 1–36 (224–260). pp. 19–22: Droṇa-vadha çravaṇa.
9, 1–45 (261–305). pp. 22–25: Dhṛtarāshṭra-çoka.
10, 1–77 (306–381). pp. 25–31: Dhṛtarāshṭra-vākya.
11, 1–51 (382–433). pp. 31–35: Dhṛtarāshṭra-vilāpa.
§ 590, VII, **12,** 1–31 (434–464). pp. 35–37: Droṇa-varadāna (°pratijñā).
13, 1–29 (465–494). pp. 37–39: Yudhishṭhira-grahaṇa-pratijñā (Arjuna-kṛta-Yudhishṭhirāçvāsana).
14, 1–87 (495–581). pp. 39–46: Abhimanyu-parākrama.
15, 1–37 (582–618). pp. 46–48: Çalyāpayāna.
16, 1–54 (619–672). pp. 48–52: Arjuna-jaya (Prathama-divasāvahāra).

LXXII. Saṃçaptakavadhaparvan.

§ 591, VII, **17,** 1–49 (673–721). pp. 52–56: Dhanañjayayāna.
§ 592, VII, **18,** 1–31 (722–752). pp. 56–58: Sudhanva-vadha.
19, 1–39 (753–791). pp. 58–61: Arjuna-[Saṃçaptaka-]yuddha.
20, 1–63 (792–855). pp. 61–66: Saṅkulayuddha.
21, 1–65 (856–919). pp. 66–70: Droṇa-yuddha.
22, 1–30 (920–949). pp. 70–73: id.
23, 1–98 (950–1045). pp. 73–79: [Haya-]dhvajādi-kathana.
24, 1–20 (1046–1065). pp. 79–80: Dhṛtarāshṭra-vākya.
25, 1–65 (1066–1128). pp. 81–85: Dvandvayuddha.
26, 1–68 (1129–1194). pp. 85–90: Bhagadatta-yuddha.
27, 1–31 (1195–1225). pp. 90–93: Saṃçaptaka-vadha.
28, 1–30 (1226–1255). pp. 93–95: Bhagadatta-yuddha.
29, 1–51 (1256–1301). pp. 95–98: Bhagadatta-vadha.
30, 1–42 (1302–1343). pp. 98–101: Çakuni-palāyana.
31, 1–29 (1343–1372). pp. 101–103: Nīlavadha.
32, 1–80 (1373–1452). pp. 103–109: Saṅkulayuddha (Dvitīyadivasāvahāra).

LXXIII. Abhimanyuvadhaparvan.

§ 593, VII, **33,** 1–28 (1453–1481). pp. 109–111: Cakravyūhanirmāṇaparāmarça (Abhimanyu-vadha-saṅkshepa-kathana).
34, 1–25 (1482–1506). pp. 111–113: Cakravyūhanirmāṇa.
35, 1–32 (1507–1537). pp. 113–115: Abhimanyu-pratijñā.
36, 1–46 (1538–1584). pp. 115–119: Abhimanyu-parākrama.
37, 1–37 (1585–1622). pp. 120–122: id.
38, 1–24 (1623–1645). pp. 122–124: id.
39, 1–31 (1646–1676). pp. 124–127: Duḥçāsana-yuddha.
40, 1–37 (1677–1713). pp. 127–129: Duḥçāsana-Karṇa-parājaya (Ka°-Du°-parākrama).
41, 1–26 (1714–1740). pp. 129–131: Abhimanyu-parākrama.
42, 1–22 (1741–1762). pp. 131–133: Jayadratha-yuddha.
43, 1–19 (1763–1781). pp. 133–135: id.
44, 1–21 (1782–1802). pp. 135–137: Abhimanyu-parākrama.
45, 1–30 (1803–1832). pp. 137–139: Duryodhana-parājaya.
46, 1–27 (1833–1860). pp. 139–141: Krāthaputra-vadha (Lakshmaṇa-vadha).
47, 1–24 (1861–1884). pp. 141–143: Bṛhadbala-jaya (°vadha).
48, 1–41 (1885–1926). pp. 143–146: Abhimanyu-yuddha (virathakaraṇa).
49, 1–39 (1927–1966). pp. 146–149: Abhimanyu-vadha.
50, 1–15 (1967–1981). pp. 149–151: [Tṛtīyadivasāvahāre] Samara-bhūmivarṇana.
51, 1–21 (1982–2002). pp. 151–152: Yudhishṭhiravi (°pra) lāpa.
§ 594, VII, **52,** 1–45 (2003–2048). pp. 152–156: [Çokāpanodana].
53, 1–23 (2049–2072). pp. 156–157: Mṛtyukathana.
54, 1–58 (2073–2133). pp. 158–162: Mṛtyu-Prajāpati-saṃvāda.
§ 595, VII, **55,** 1–50 (2134–2183). pp. 163–167: Shoḍaça-rājika (°īya).
56, 1–12 (2184–2195). pp. 167–168: id.
57, 1–12 (2196–2208). pp. 168–169: id.
58, 1–15 (2209–2223). pp. 169–170: id.
59, 1–25 (2224–2248). pp. 171–173: id.
60, 1–14 (2249–2262). pp. 173–174: id.
61, 1–12 (2263–2271). pp. 174–175: id.
62, 1–20 (2272–2291). pp. 175–177: id.
63, 1–11 (2292–2302). p. 177: id.
64, 1–17 (2303–2320). pp. 178–179: id.
65, 1–12 (2321–2333). pp. 179–180: id.
66, 1–21 (2334–2355). pp. 180–182: id.
67, 1–21 (2356–2376). pp. 182–184: id.
68, 1–17 (2377–2392). pp. 184–185: id.
69, 1–33 (2393–2426). pp. 185–188: id.
70, 1–25 (2427–2450). pp. 188–190: id.
71, 1–26 (2451–2476). pp. 190–192: id.

LXXIV. Pratijñāparvan.

§ 596, VII, **72,** 1–88 (2477–2565). pp. 192–198: Arjuna-kopa.
73, 1–53 (2566–2612). pp. 198–202: Arjuna-pratijñā.
74, 1–35 (2613–2647). pp. 202–204: Jayadrathāçvāsa.
75, 1–31 (2648–2678). pp. 204–207: Kṛshṇa-vākya.
76, 1–27 (2679–2705). pp. 207–209: Arjuna-vākya.
77, 1–26 (2706–2731). pp. 209–210: Subhadrāçvāsana.
78, 1–44 (2732–2774). pp. 211–214: Subhadrā-[pra]vilāpa.
79, 1–44 (2775–2819). pp. 214–217: Kṛshṇa-Dāruka-sambhāshaṇa.
80, 1–65 (2820–2885). pp. 217–222: Arjuna-svapna [-darçana].
81, 1–25 (2886–2910). pp. 222–224: [Arjunasya punaḥ] Pāçupatāstraprāpti.
§ 597, VII, **82,** 1–35 (2911–2945). pp. 224–226: Yudhishṭhira-sajj[at]ā.
83, 1–28 (2946–2973). pp. 226–228: Çrī-Kṛshṇa-vākya.
84, 1–35 (2974–3009). pp. 228–231: Arjunavākya.

LXXV. Jayadrathavadhaparvan.

§ 598, VII, **85,** 1–54 (3010–3063). pp. 231–234: Dhṛtarāshṭrānutāpa (°vākya).
86, 1–23 (3064–3086). pp. 235–236: Sañjaya-vākya.
87, 1–34 (3087–3120). pp. 236–239: Kaurava-vyūha-nirmāṇa.
88, 1–29 (3121–3149). pp. 239–241: Arjuna-raṇa-praveça.
§ 599, VII, **89,** 1–33 (3150–3182). pp. 241–243: Arjuna-yuddha.
90, 1–34 (3183–3216). pp. 243–245: Duḥçāsana-sainya-parābhava.
91, 1–44 (3217–3260). pp. 246–249: Droṇātikrama.
92, 1–76 (3261–3337). pp. 249–254: Çrutāyudha-Sudakshiṇavadha.
93, 1–70 (3338–3408). pp. 254–259: Ambashṭha-vadha.
94, 1–76 (3409–3485). pp. 259–264: Duryodhana-kavaca-bandh[an]a.
95, 1–51 (3486–3541). pp. 264–268: Saṅkulayuddha.

96, 1–31 (3542–3572). pp. 268–270 : Saṅkula (Dvandva)-yuddha.
97, 1–36 (3573–3608). pp. 270–272 : Saṅkula-yuddha (Droṇa-Dhṛshṭadyumna°).
98, 1–57 (3609–3665). pp. 273–277 : Droṇa-Sātyaki-yuddha.
99, 1–63 (3666–3725). pp. 277–281 : [Vindānuvinda-vadhe] Arjuna-saro [vara-]nirmāṇa[ca].
100, 1–37 (3726–3762). pp. 281–284 : Sainyavismaya.
101, 1–42 (3763–3804). pp. 284–287 : Duryodhanāgam[an]a.
102, 1–38 (3805–3842). pp. 287–289 : Duryodhana-dambha-vākya (°vacana).
103, 1–49 (3843–3890). pp. 290–293 : Duryodhana-parājaya.
104, 1–35 (3891–3925). pp. 293–295 : Saṅkulayuddha.
105, 1–38 (3926–3964). pp. 295–298 : Dhvajavarṇana.
106, 1–47 (3965–4012). pp. 298–301 : Yudhishṭhirāpayāna.
107, 1–39 (4013–4052). pp. 301–304 : Sātyaki-yuddha (Saṅkulayuddha).
108, 1–44 (4053–4096). pp. 304–307 : Alambusha-parājaya.
109, 1–37 (4097–4133). pp. 307–309 : Alambusha-vadha.
110, 1–103 (4134–4238). pp. 309–316 : Yudhishṭhira-vākya.
111, 1–51 (4239–4290). pp. 316–319 : id. [Sātyaki].
112, 1–80 (4291–4371). pp. 319–324 : Sātyaki-praveça.
113, 1–67 (4372–4439). pp. 325–329 : id.
114, 1–103 (4440–4542). pp. 329–336 : [Sātyaki-praveçe] Kṛtavarma-parākrama.
115, 1–61 (4543–4601). pp. 336–340 : [id.] Jalasandhavadha.
116, 1–46 (4602–4647). pp. 340–343 : [id. Duryodhana-] Kṛtavarmaparājaya.
117, 1–36 (4648–4683). pp. 343–346 : [id.] Sātyaki-parākrama.
118, 1–18 (4684–4701). pp. 346–347 : Sudarçana-vadha.
119, 1–55 (4702–4757). pp. 348–351 : [Sātyaki-praveçe] Yavanaparājaya.
120, 1–47 (4758–4805). pp. 351–355 : Sātyaki-praveçe [Duryodhanapalāyana].
121, 1–58 (4806–4863). pp. 355–359 : Sātyaki-praveça.
122, 1–73 (4864–4934). pp. 359–363 : [Sā°-pra°] Droṇa-parākrama.
123, 1–37 (4935–4971). pp. 363–366 : Sā°-pra° Duḥçāsana-parājaya.
124, 1–47 (4972–5016). pp. 366–369 : [Sā°-pra°] Saṅkula-yuddha.
125, 1–78 (5017–5095). pp. 369–374 : Droṇa-parākrama.
126, 1–49 (5096–5143). pp. 375–378 : Yudhishṭhira-cintā.
127, 1–74 (5144–5218). pp. 378–383 : Bhīma[sena-]-praveçe Bhīma-parākrama.
128, 1–56 (5219–5271). pp. 383–386 : [Bhīmasena-pra°] Yudhishṭhira-harsha.
129, 1–39 (5272–5310). pp. 386–389 : [Bhīma-pra°] Karṇaparājaya.
130, 1–44 (5311–5354). pp. 389–392 : Duryodhana-yuddha.
131, 1–58 (5355–5412). pp. 392–396 : Karṇa-parājaya.
132, 3–43 (5413–5454). pp. 396–399 : Bhīma-Karṇa-yuddha.
133, 1–45 (5455–5499). pp. 399–402 : Karṇa-Bhīma-yuddha.
134, 1–35 (5500–5534). pp. 402–404 : [Bhīma-]Karṇā-payāna.
135, 1–40 (5535–5574). pp. 404–407 : Bhīma[sena-]-parākrama.
136, 1–40 (5575–5614). pp. 407–409 : Bhīma-yuddha.
137, 1–53 (5615–5666). pp. 409–413 : id.
138, 1–29 (5667–5695). pp. 413–415 : Bhīma-Karṇa-yuddha.
139, 1–125 (5696–5816). pp. 415–423 : id.
140, 1–25 (5817–5841). pp. 423–425 : Alambushavadha.
141, 1–37 (5842–5878). pp. 425–428 : Sātyaky-Arjuna-darçana.
142, 1–72 (5879–5950). pp. 428–433 : Bhūriçravo-bāhuccheda.
143, 1–72 (5951–6024). pp. 433–439 : Bhūriçravo-vadha.
144, 1–29 (6025–6054). pp. 439–441 : Sātyaki-praçaṃsā.
145, 1–98 (6055–6152). pp. 441–448 : Saṅkulayuddha.
146, 1–144 (6153–6296). pp. 448–458 : Jayadratha-vadha.
147, 1–92 (6297–6387). pp. 458–464 : Karṇa-Sātyaki-yuddha.
148, 1–59 (6388–6450). pp. 464–469 : [Yuddhabhūmi-darçana].
149, 1–62 (6451–6493). pp. 469–472 : Yudhishṭhira-harsha.
150, 1–36 (6494–6528). pp. 472–475 : Duryodhanānutāpa.
151, 1–41 (6529–6569). pp. 475–478 : Droṇa-vākya.
152, 1–36 (6570–6604). pp. 478–480 : Punar-yuddhā-rambha.

LXXVI. GHAṬOTKACAVADHAPARVAN.

§ 600, VII, **153,** 1–44 (6605–6640). pp. 480–483 : Duryodhana-parābhava.
154, 1–41 (6641–6681). pp. 483–486 : Droṇa-yuddha (Rātri°).
155, 1–46 (6682–6728). pp. 486–489 : [Rātriyuddhe] Bhīmaparākrama.
156, 1–190 (6729–6921). pp. 489–503 : [id.] [Açvatthāma-yuddha].
157, 1–49 (6922–6969). pp. 503–506 : [Rā°] Droṇa-Yudhishṭhira-yuddha.
158, 1–70 (6970–7041). pp. 506–511 : [id.] Kṛpa-Karṇa-vākya.
159, 1–100 (7042–7142). pp. 511–518 : [id.] Duryodhana-vākya.
160, 1–60 (7143–7203). pp. 518–522 : [id.] Açvatthāma-parākrama.
161, 1–19 (7204–7223). pp. 522–523 : [id.] Saṅkulayuddha.
162, 1–55 (7224–7278). pp. 523–527 : Rātriyuddhe [Soma-dattavadha].
163, 1–37 (7279–7316). pp. 527–530 : [Rā°] Dīpoddyotana.
164, 1–37 (7317–7354). pp. 531–533 : [id.] Saṅkulayuddha.
165, 1–41 (7355–7396). pp. 533–536 : [id.] Yudhishṭhirā-payāna.
166, 1–64 (7397–7461). pp. 536–540 : [id.] Duryodhanā-payāna.
167, 1–22 (7462–7483). pp. 541–542.
23–50 (7484–7511). pp. 542–544 : [Rā°] Alam-bushaparābhava.
168, 1–47 (7512–7558). pp. 544–547 : [id.] Çatānīkādi-yuddha.
169, 1–50 (7559–7608). pp. 547–550 : Rātri-[yuddhe] Saṅkulayuddha.
170, 1–70 (7609–7679). pp. 550–555 : [Rā°] Saṅkulayuddha.
171, 1–54 (7680–7734). pp. 555–558 : [id.] id.
172, 1–41 (7735–7773). pp. 558–561 : [id.] id.
173, 1–68 (7774–7843). pp. 561–566 : [id.] Ghaṭotkaca-yāna (°protsāhana).
174, 1–45 (7844–7889). pp. 566–569 : [id.] Alambusha-vadha.
175, 1–114 (7890–8003). pp. 569–577 : [id.] Karṇa-Ghaṭotkaca-yuddha.
176, 1–22 (8004–8025). pp. 577–578 : [id.] Alāyudha-yuddha.

177, 1–48 (8026–8073). pp. 578–581 : [id.] id.
178, 1–40 (8074–8114). pp. 582–584 : [id.] Alāyudha-vadha.
179, 1–64 (8115–8177). pp. 584–590 : [id.] Ghaṭotkaca-vadha.
180, 1–33 (8178–8212). pp. 590–592 : [Rā° Gha° Çrī-] Kṛshṇaharsha.
181, 1–33 (8213–8246). pp. 593–595 : [Rā°] Kṛshṇa-vākya.
182, 1–47 (8247–8293). pp. 595–599 : [id.] id.
183, 1–67 (8294–8361). pp. 599–603 : [id.] Vyāsa-vākya.

LXXVII. Droṇavadhaparvan.

§ 601, VII, **184,** 1–56 (8362–8418). pp. 603–607 : [Rā°] Sainyanidrā.
185, 1–37 (8419–8456). pp. 607–610 : [Droṇa-Duryodhana-bhāshaṇa].
§ 602, VII, **186,** 1–60 (8457–8517). pp. 610–614 : Saṅkula-yuddha.
187, 1–55 (8518–8573). pp. 614–618 : Nakula-yuddha.
188, 1–54 (8574–8628). pp. 618–622 : Saṅkula-yuddha.
189, 1–66 (8629–8693). pp. 622–626 : id.
190, 1–59 (8694–8754). pp. 626–631 : Yudhishṭhirā-satyakathana.
191, 1–53 (8755–8808). pp. 631–635 : Saṅkulayuddha (Droṇa-Dhṛshṭadyumna-yuddha).
192, 1–84 (8809–8892). pp. 635–640 : Droṇa-vadha.

LXXVIII. Nārāyaṇāstramokshaparva.

§ 603, VII, **193,** 1–70 (8893–8963). pp. 641–645 : Açvatthāma-krodha.
194, 1–15 (8964–8978). pp. 645–646 : Açvatthāma-vākya (Dhṛtarāshṭra-praçna).
195, 1–50 (8979–9028). pp. 647–650 : Açvatthāma-krodha.
196, 1–53 (9029–9081). pp. 650–654 : Arjuna-vākya.
197, 1–44 (9081–9125). pp. 654–658 : Dhṛshṭadyumna-vākya.
198, 1–68 (9126–9194). pp. 658–663 : Dhṛshṭadyumna-Sātyaki-krodha.
199, 1–63 (9195–9257). pp. 663–667 : Pāṇḍavasainyā-stratyāga.
200, 1–131 (9258–9389). pp. 667–676 : Açvatthāmaparā-krama.
201, 1–100 (9390–9493). pp. 676–685 : Vyāsa-vākya.
202, 1–158 (9494–9649). pp. 685–696 : [Çatarudrīya].

VIII. KARṆAPARVAN.

LXXIX. Karṇaparvan.

§ 604, VIII, **1,** 1–24 (1–24). pp. 1–3 : Janamejaya-vākya.
2, 1–25 (25–50). pp. 3–5 : Sañjaya-Dhṛtarāshṭra (Dh° S°)-saṃvāda.
3, 1–21 (51–72). pp. 5–6 : Sañjaya-vākya.
4, 1–16 (73–89). pp. 7–8 : Dhṛtarāshṭra-çoka.
5, 1–60 (90–150). pp. 8–12 : Sañjaya-vākya.
6, 1–39 (151–189). pp. 12–15 : id.
7, 1–28 (190–217). pp. 15–17 : id.
8, 1–31 (218–249). pp. 17–20 : Dhṛtarāshṭra-vākya.
9, 1–97 (250–343). pp. 20–27 : Dhṛtarāshṭra-praçna.
§ 605, VIII, **10,** 1–56 (344–399). pp. 27–31 : Karṇābhisheka.
11, 1–43 (400–440). pp. 31–34 : Vyūha-nirmāṇa.
12, 1–45 (441–486). pp. 34–38 : Kshemadhūrti-vadha.
13, 1–38 (487–525). pp. 38–40 : Vindānuvinda-vadha.
14, 1–39 (526–565). pp. 40–43 : Citravadha.
15, 1–44 (566–609). pp. 43–46 : Açvatthāma-Bhīmasena-[yor]yuddha.
16, 1–51 (610–660). pp. 46–50 : Açvatthāmārjuna-yuddha (°saṃvāda).
17, 1–26 (661–686). pp. 51–53 : Açvatthāma-parājaya.
18, 1–25 (687–710). pp. 53–56 : Daṇḍavadha.
19, 1–58 (711–769). pp. 56–60 : Saṅkulayuddha.
20, 1–51 (770–820). pp. 61–65 : Pāṇḍya-vadha.
21, 1–40 (821–861). pp. 65–68 : Saṅkula-yuddha.
22, 1–30 (862–892). pp. 68–70 : id.
23, 1–22 (893–914). pp. 71–72 : Sahadeva-Duḥçāsana-yuddha.
24, 1–78 (915–992). pp. 72–77 : Karṇa-yuddha.
25, 1–43 (993–1036). pp. 77–80 : Sutasoma-Saubala-yuddha.
26, 1–38 (1037–1075). pp. 80–82 : Saṅkulayuddha.
27, 1–42 (1076–1118). pp. 83–85 : Saṃçaptaka-jaya.
28, 1–49 (1119–1168). pp. 85–88 : Saṅkulayuddha.
29, 1–36 (1169–1204). pp. 89–91 : id.
30, 1–44 (1205–1248). pp. 91–95 : Prathama(°me)-yuddha-divasa.
31, 1–73 (1249–1323). pp. 95–100 : Karṇa-Duryodhana-saṃvāda.
32, 1–66 (1324–1390). pp. 100–105 : Çalya-sārathya.
§ 606, VIII, **33,** 1–63 (1391–1453). pp. 105–109 : Tripurākhyāna.
34, 1–162 (1454–1619). pp. 109–121 : Tripura-vadhopākhyāna.
35, 1–48 (1620–1669). pp. 121–124 : Çalya-sārathya-svīkāra.
§ 607, VIII, **36,** 1–33 (1670–1703). pp. 124–127 : [Karṇa-] Çalya-saṃvāda.
37, 1–45 (1704–1751). pp. 127–131 : Karṇa-Çalya-saṃvāda.
38, 1–26 (1752–1779). pp. 131–133 : Karṇāvalepa.
39, 1–35 (1781–1815). pp. 133–136 : Karṇa[-Çalya] adhikshepa.
40, 1–56 (1816–1872). pp. 136–140 : Karṇa-Madrādhipa-saṃvāda.
41, 1–87 (1873–1961). pp. 140–146 : [Karṇa-Çalya-saṃvāde] Haṃsa-kākīyopākhyāna.
42, 1–50 (1962–2013). pp. 146–151 : Karṇa-Çalya-saṃvāda.
43, 1–9 (2014–2023). pp. 151–152 : id.
44, 1–47 (2024–2070). pp. 152–156 : id.
45, 1–48 (2071–2121). pp. 156–160 : id.
§ 608, VIII, **46,** 1–87 (2122–2209). pp. 160–166 : id.
47, 1–23 (2210–2233). pp. 167–168 : Saṅkulayuddha.
48, 1–67 (2234–2300). pp. 168–173 : id.
49, 1–92 (2301–2390). pp. 173–180 : id.
50, 1–49 (2391–2439). pp. 180–183 : Karṇāpayāna.
51, 1–81 (2440–2519). pp. 183–188 : Saṅkulayuddha.
52, 1–42 (2520–2562). pp. 188–191 : id.
53, 1–46 (2563–2609). pp. 191–194 : id.
54, 1–42 (2610–2651). pp. 194–197 : id.
55, 1–39 (2652–2691). pp. 197–199 : Pārthāpayāna.
56, 1–147 (2692–2839). pp. 200–210 : Saṅkulayuddha.
57, 1–17 (2840–2856). pp. 210–211 : Açvatthāma-pratijñā.
58, 1–52 (2857–2908). pp. 211–215 : Vāsudeva-vākya.
59, 1–67 (2909–2975). pp. 215–219 : Drauṇy-apayāna.
60, 1–92 (2976–3066). pp. 219–225 : Saṅkulayuddha (Kṛshṇārjuna-saṃvāda).
61, 1–74 (3067–3141). pp. 225–230 : Saṅkulayuddha.
62, 1–34 (3142–3175). pp. 230–233 : id.
63, 1–37 (3176–3214). pp. 233–235 : id. (Dharmāpayāna).
64, 1–70 (3215–3284). pp. 235–240 : id. (Dharmarāja-çodhana).

65, 1–23 (3285–3308). pp. 240–242: id. (Yudhishṭhiraṃ prati Kṛshṇārjunāgama).
66, 1–48 (3309–3356). pp. 242–246: Yudhishṭhira-vākya.
67, 1–23 (3357–3379). pp. 246–248: Arjuna-pratijñā (°vākya).
68, 1–30 (3380–3402). pp. 248–250: Yudhishṭhira[krodha] vākya.
69, 1–88 (3403–3491). pp. 251–258: Kṛshṇārjuna-saṃvāda.
70, 1–60 (3492–3551). pp. 259–264: Yudhishṭhira-prabodhana (°samāçvāsana).
71, 1–40 (3552–3592). pp. 264–267: Yudhishṭhirārjuna-saṃvāda (Arjuna-pratijñā).
72, 1–40 (3593–3633). pp. 267–270: Kṛshṇārjuna-saṃvāda.
73, 1–125 (3634–3750). pp. 270–278: Arjunopadeça (Kṛshṇavākya).
74, 1–58 (3751–3803). pp. 278–282: Arjuna-çlāghā (°vākya).
75, 1–17 (3804–3820). pp. 282–284: Saṅkula-[dvandva-] yuddha.
76, 1–40 (3821–3860). pp. 284–287: Bhīmasena-Viçoka-saṃvāda.
77, 1–79 (3861–3939). pp. 287–293: Saubaleya (Çakuni)-parājaya.
78, 1–64 (3940–4003). pp. 293–297: Saṅkulayuddha.
79, 1–95 (4004–4090). pp. 297–305: id.
80, 1–32 (4091–4122). pp. 305–307: id.
81, 1–57 (4123–4179). pp. 307–311: id.
82, 1–36 (4180–4215). pp. 311–315: Duḥçāsana-Bhīmasena-yuddha.
83, 1–52 (4216–4260). pp. 315–318: Duḥçāsana-vadha.
84, 1–42 (4261–4304). pp. 318–322: Vṛshasenayuddhe Nakulaparājaya.
85, 1–39 (4305–4347). pp. 322–326: Vṛshasena-vadha.
86, 1–23 (4348–4371). pp. 327–328: Karṇārjuna-dvairatha.
87, 1–117 (4372–4489). pp. 328–336: Karṇārjuna[-samāgame] dvairatha.
88, 1–34 (4490–4523). pp. 336–340: Açvatthāma-vākya.
89, 1–97 (4524–7621). pp. 340–350: Karṇārjuna-yuddha (°dvairatha).
90, 1–116 (4622–4747). pp. 350–362: Karṇa-rathacakra-grasana.
91, 1–67 (4748–4817). pp. 362–368: Karṇa-vadha.
92, 1–15 (4818–4833). pp. 368–369: id. (Çalya-pratyāgamana).
93, 1–60 (4834–4894). pp. 369–374: Kauravasainya-palāyana.
94, 1–68 (4895–4963). pp. 374–381: Çibiragamana (Bhūmi-varṇana).
95, 1–18 (4964–4981). pp. 381–382: Kaurava-palāyana (Çibiraprayāṇa).
96, 1–65 (4982–5040). pp. 382–387: Yudhishṭhira-harsha.

IX. ÇALYAPARVAN.

LXXX. ÇALYAPARVAN.

§ 609, IX, **1,** 1–55 (1–56). pp. 1–5: Dhṛtarāshṭra-pramoha.
2, 1–70 (57–125). pp. 5–9: Dhṛtarāshṭra-vilāpa.
§ 610, IX, **3,** 1–61 (126–186). pp. 9–13: Kauravasainyāpayāna.
4, 1–51 (187–238). pp. 14–17: Duryodhana-prabodhana (Kṛpavākya).
5, 1–52 (239–291). pp. 17–21: Duryodhana-vākya.
6, 1–30 (292–320). pp. 21–23: [Çalya] id. (°saṃvāda).
7, 1–46 (321–366). pp. 24–27: Çalya-saināpaty[ābhishek]a.
§ 611, IX, **8,** 1–45 (367–412). pp. 27–30: Vyūhanirmāṇa.
9, 1–47 (413–459). pp. 30–33: Saṅkulayuddha.
10, 1–68 (460–528). pp. 33–38: id.
11, 1–63 (529–592). pp. 38–42: id. (Bhīmasena-Çalya-yuddha).
12, 1–63 (593–655). pp. 42–46: Saṅkulayuddha.
13, 1–48 (656–704), pp. 47–50: Çalya-yuddha.
14, 1–48 (705–752). pp. 50–53: Saṅkula-yuddha.
15, 1–43 (753–795). pp. 53–56: id.
16, 1–68 (796–863). pp. 56–60: Çalya-Yudhishṭhira-yuddha.
17, 1–91 (864–954). pp. 61–68: Çalya-vadha.
18, 1–40 (955–995). pp. 68–71: Saṅkulayuddha.
19, 1–69 (996–1065). pp. 71–75: id.
20, 1–27 (1066–1092). pp. 75–78: Çālva-vadha.
21, 1–37 (1093–1129). pp. 78–80: Kauravasainyāpayāna (Sātyaki-Kṛtavarma-yuddha).
22, 1–49 (1130–1178). pp. 80–84: Saṅkulayuddha.
23, 1–92 (1179–1271). pp. 84–90: id.
24, 1–66 (1272–1337). pp. 90–94: id.
25, 1–63 (1338–1400). pp. 94–98: Duryodhanāpayāna.
26, 1–42 (1401–1442). pp. 98–101: Saṅkulayuddha (Ekādaça-Dhārtarāshṭra-vadha).
27, 1–57 (1443–1500). pp. 101–104: Suçarmavadha.
28, 1–68 (1501–1565). pp. 104–109: Çakuny-Ulūka-vadha.

LXXXI. HRADAPRAVEÇAPARVAN.

(Ch. **29–31.** B. ch. **29.**)

§ 612, IX, **29,** 1–105 (1566–1672). pp. 109–116: [Yuyutsu-gamana].
30, 1–68 (1673–1741). pp. 116–121: [Duryodhanān-veshaṇa].
31, 1–73 (1742–1816). pp. 121–126: Duryodhanabhartsana (Suyodhana-Yudhishṭhira-saṃvāda).

LXXXII. GADĀ[YUDDHA]PARVAN.

(Ch. **32–65.** B. ch. **30–65.**)

§ 613, IX, **32,** 1–71 (1817–1888). pp. 126–131: Yudhishṭhira-Duryodhana-saṃvāda.
33, 1–58 (1889–1946). pp. 131–135: Bhīmasena-Duryodhana-saṃvāda.
§ 614, IX, **34,** 1–22 (1947–1968). pp. 135–136: Baladevāgamana.
§ 615, IX, **35,** 1–90 (1969–2063). pp. 137–143: Baladeva-tīrthayātrāyāṃ Candra-çāpopakhyāna (°Prabhāsotpatti-kathana).
36, 1–54 (2064–2118). pp. 143–146: Ba°tī° Tīrthaka-thana (Tritākhyāna).
37, 1–66 (2119–2185). pp. 147–151: Ba°tī° Sārasvatopākhyāna.
38, 1–59 (2186–2245). pp. 152–156: id.
39, 1–38 (2246–2284). pp. 156–158: id.
40, 1–33 (2285–2317). pp. 159–161: id.
41, 1–40 (2318–2357). pp. 161–164: id.
42, 1–41 (2358–2399). pp. 164–167: id.
43, 1–49 (2400–2449). pp. 167–170: id.
44, 1–53 (2450–2502). pp. 170–174: id. [Kurmārābhishe-kopakrama].
45, 1–115 (2503–2618). pp. 174–181: id. [Skandābhisheka].
46, 1–108 (2619–2727). pp. 181–188: id. [Tāraka-vadha].
47, 1–33 (2728–2761). pp. 188–190: id.

48, 1–68 (2762–2830). pp. 190–195: id. [Badarapācana-tīrthakathana].
49, 1–24 (2831–2853). pp. 195–197: [Ba°] Sārasvatopakhyāna.
50, 1–69 (2854–2924). pp. 197–202: Ba° Sā°.
51, 1–53 (2925–2978). pp. 202–205: id.
52, 1–29 (2979–3007). pp. 205–207: id.
53, 1–26 (3008–3034). pp. 208–209: Ba° [Sā° Kurukshetrakathana].
54, 1–41 (3035–3076). pp. 210–212: Ba° Sā°.
55, 1–51 (3077–3128). pp. 213–216: [Gadā]yuddh[ārambha].
56, 1–46 (3129–3174). pp. 216–219: id.
57, 1–70 (3175–3245). pp. 219–224: Gadāyuddha.
58, 1–63 (3246–3308). pp. 224–228: [Gadāyuddhe] Duryodhana-vadha.
59, 1–31 (3309–3341). pp. 228–231: Yudhishṭhira-vilāpa.
60, 1–48 (3342–3387). pp. 231–234: Baladeva-sāntvana.
61, 1–71 (3388–3459). pp. 234–239: Kṛshṇa-Pāṇḍava-[Duryodhana-]saṃvāda.
62, 1–46 (3460–3502). pp. 239–242: Vāsudeva-vākya.
63, 1–78 (3503–3581). pp. 242–247: Dhṛtarāshṭra-Gāndhārī-prabodhana (°samāçvāsana).
64, 1–43 (3582–3624). pp. 248–251: Duryodhana-vilāpa.
65, 1–46 (3625–3671). pp. 251–254: Açvatthāma-sainā-patyābhisheka.

X. SAUPTIKAPARVAN.

LXXXIII. Sauptikaparvan.

§ 616, X, **1**, 1–69 (1–69). pp. 1–5: Drauṇi-mantraṇā.
2, 1–35 (70–104). pp. 6–8: Drauṇi-Kṛpa-saṃvāda.
3, 1–36 (105–140). pp. 8–11: Drauṇi-mantraṇā.
4, 1–34 (141–175). pp. 11–13: id.
5, 1–40 (176–215). pp. 14–16: Drauṇi-gamana.
6, 1–34 (216–250). pp. 16–19: Drauṇi-cintā.
7, 1–68 (251–318). pp. 19–24: Drauṇi[kṛta-]Çivārcana.
8, 1–159 (319–478). pp. 24–34: Rātriyuddhe Pāñcālādi-vadha.
9, 1–63 (479–542). pp. 35–39: Duryodhana-prāṇatyāga.

LXXXIV. Aishīkaparvan.

§ 617, X, **10**, 1–31 (543–573). pp. 39–42: Yudhishṭhira[sya] çibiradarçana (°praveça).
11, 1–31 (574–605). pp. 42–44: Drauṇi-vadhārtha[ṃ]-Bhīma[sena]gamana.
12, 1–41 (606–645). pp. 44–47: Yudhishṭhira-Kṛshṇa-saṃvāda.
13, 1–22 (646–669). pp. 47–48: Brahmaçiro-'stratyāga.
14, 1–16 (670–686). pp. 49–50: Arjunāstratyāga.
15, 1–35 (687–721). pp. 50–52: Brahmaçiro'strasya Pāṇḍaveya-garbhapraveçana.
16, 1–37 (722–759). pp. 52–55: Draupadī-sāntvanā.
17, 1–26 (760–785). pp. 55–57: Yudhishṭhira-Kṛshṇa-saṃvāda.
18, 1–26 (786–812). pp. 57–59: [Yudhishṭhirārjuna-saṃvāda].

XI. STRĪPARVAN.

LXXXV. Jalapradānikaparvan.

§ 618, XI, **1**, 1–44 (1–45). pp. 1–4: [Dhṛtarāshṭra-]viçoka-[karaṇa].
2, 1–37 (46–83). pp. 4–7: Dhṛtarāshṭra-viçoka-[karaṇa].
3, 1–20 (84–103). pp. 7–8: [id.] id. [id.].
4, 1–20 (104–124). pp. 8–10: [id.] id. [id.].
5, 1–24 (125–148). pp. 10–11: [id.] id. [id.].
6, 1–14 (149–162). p. 12: [id.] id. [id.].
7, 1–29 (163–192). pp. 13–15: [id.] id. [id.].
8, 1–53 (193–245). pp. 15–18: id. id. [id.].
9, 1–23 (246–268). pp. 18–20: [Vidura-vākya].
10, 1–20 (269–288). pp. 20–21: Dhṛtarāshṭra-[nir]gamana.
11, 1–24 (289–312). pp. 22–23: Kṛpa-Drauṇi-Bhoja-darçana.
12, 1–30 (313–342). pp. 23–25: Āyasa-Bhīma-bhaṅga.
13, 1–17 (343–359). pp. 25–27: Dhṛtarāshṭra-kopavimocana.
14, 1–21 (360–380). pp. 27–28: Gāndhārī-sāntvanā.
15, 1–44 (381–426). pp. 29–32: Pṛthā-putradarçana.

LXXXVI. Strīvilāpaparvan.

§ 619, XI, **16**, 1–61 (427–486). pp. 32–36: Strīṇāṃ yuddha-bhūmidarçana (Āyodhanadarçana).
17, 1–32 (487–518). pp. 36–38: Duryodhana-darçana.
18, 1–28 (519–546). pp. 39–41: Gāndhārī-vākya.
19, 1–21 (547–567). pp. 41–42: id.
20, 1–35 (568–602). pp. 42–45: id.
21, 1–14 (603–616). pp. 45–46: id. (Karṇa-darçana).
22, 1–18 (617–634). pp. 46–47: Gāndhārī-vākya.
23, 1–42 (635–676). pp. 47–50: id. (°vacana).
24, 1–30 (677–705). pp. 50–52: Gāndhārī-vākya.
25, 1–50 (706–755). pp. 52–56: Gāndhārī-çāpadāna.

LXXXVII. Çrāddhaparvan.

§ 620, XI, **26**, 1–44 (756–799). pp. 56–59: Kurūṇām aurdhvadehika.
27, 1–30 (800–828). pp. 59–61: Karṇa[sya]gūḍhajatva-kathana.

XII. ÇĀNTIPARVAN.

LXXXVIII. Rājadharmānuçāsanaparvan.

§ 621, XII, **1**, 1–44 (1–45). pp. 1–4: Karṇābhijñāna.
2, 1–29 (46–74). pp. 4–6: Karṇa-çāpa(-kathana).
3, 1–33 (75–107). pp. 6–9: Karṇ[asy]āstra-prāpti.
4, 1–21 (108–128). pp. 9–10: Duryodhanasya svayamvara-(°re) kanyāharaṇa.
5, 1–15 (129–143). pp. 10–11: Karṇa-vīrya-kathana.
6, 1–13 (144–156). pp. 11–12: Strīçāpa.
7, 1–44 (157–200). pp. 12–16: Yudhishṭhira-paridevana.
8, 1–37 (201–242). pp. 16–19: Arjuna-vākya.
9, 1–37 (243–276). pp. 19–22: Yudhishṭhira-vākya.
10, 1–27 (277–304). pp. 22–25: [Bhīmasenavākya].
§ 622, XII, **11**, 1–28 (305–332). pp. 25–28: [Arjunavākye] Ṛshi-çakuni-saṃvāda-kathana.
§ 623, XII, **12**, 1–38 (333–370). pp. 28–31: Nakula-vākya.
13, 1–13 (371–383). pp. 31–33: Sahadeva-vākya.
14, 1–39 (384–423). pp. 33–36: Draupadī-vākya.
15, 1–58 (424–481). pp. 36–41: Arjuna-vākya.
16, 1–29 (482–510). pp. 41–44: Bhīma[sena]-vākya.
17, 1–24 (511–534). pp. 44–46: Yudhishṭhira-vākya.
§ 624, XII, **18**, 1–40 (535–574). pp. 46–50: Arjuna-vākya.
§ 625, XII, **19**, 1–26 (575–600). pp. 50–53: Yudhishṭhira-vākya.
§ 626, XII, **20**, 1–14 (601–614). pp. 53–55: Devasthāna-vākya.

21, 1–20 (615–635). pp. 55–56: id.
§ 627, XII, **22**, 1–15 (636–650). pp. 57–58: Arjuna-vākya.
§ 628, XII, **23**, 1–47 (651–697). pp. 58–61: Vyāsa-vākya.
24, 1–34 (698–730). pp. 61–65: id.
§ 629, XII, **25**, 1–36 (731–767). pp. 65–68: Senajid-upākhyāna.
§ 630, XII, **26**, 1–31 (768–798). pp. 68–71: Yudhishṭhira-vākya.
27, 1–34 (799–832). pp. 71–73: Vyāsa-vākya.
§ 631, XII, **28**, 1–59 (833–892). pp. 74–78: id.
§ 632, XII, **29**, 1–149 (893–1042). pp. 78–91: Shoḍaçarāj[ik]opākhyāna.
§ 633, XII, **30**, 1–44 (1043–1087). pp. 91–94: Nārada-Parvatopākhyāna.
§ 634, XII, **31**, 1–47 (1088–1134). pp. 94–97: S[u]varṇashṭhīvi-sambhavopākhyāna.
§ 635, XII, **32**, 1–25 (1135–1159). pp. 98–100: Prāyaçcittopākhyāna (°vidhi).
33, 1–48 (1160–1207). pp. 100–103: Prāyaçcittīyopākhyāna.
34, 1–32 (1208–1240). pp. 104–106: id. (Prāyaçcittīya).
35, 1–51 (1241–1290). pp. 106–111: id. (id.).
36, 1–50 (1291–1343). pp. 111–116: Vyāsa-vākya.
37, 1–49 (1344–1392). pp. 116–120: Yudhishṭhira[sya-pura-]praveça.
38, 1–37 (1393–1429). pp. 120–122: Cārvākavadha.
§ 636, XII, **39**, 1–12 (1430–1442). p. 123: Cārvākavadhopāya-(°varadānādi-)kathana.
§ 637, XII, **40**, 1–24 (1443–1466). pp. 124–125: Yudhishṭhirābhisheka.
41, 1–19 (1467–1485). pp. 125–127: Bhīmādi-karmaniyoga.
42, 1–12 (1486–1498). pp. 127–128: Çrāddhakriyā (-upākhyāna).
43, 1–17 (1499–1515). pp. 128–130: Vāsudeva-stuti.
44, 1–16 (1516–1531). pp. 130–131: Gṛhavibhāga.
45, 1–20 (1532–1552). pp. 131–133: [Kṛshṇaṃ prati] Yudhishṭhira-praçna (°vākya).
46, 1–35 (1553–1587). pp. 133–136: Mahā-Purushastava [upākhyāna].
47, 1–108 (1588–1697). pp. 136–146: [Bhīshma-]Stavarāja [upākhyāna].
§ 638, XII, **48**, 1–16 (1698–1714). pp. 147–148: Rāmopākhyāna.
49, 1–90 (1715–1805). pp. 148–154: id.
§ 639, XII, **50**, 1–38 (1806–1843). pp. 154–157: Kṛshṇa-vākya.
51, 1–18 (1844–1861). pp. 157–158: id.
52, 1–34 (1862–1895). pp. 158–161: Yudhishṭhirādyāgamana.
53, 1–28 (1896–1924). pp. 161–163: [Kṛshṇādi-]Bhīshma-samīpayāna (°abhigamana).
§ 640, XII, **54**, 1–39 (1925–1963). pp. 163–166: Kṛshṇa-vākya.
55, 1–22 (1964–1986). pp. 166–168: Yudhishṭhirāçvāsana.
56, 1–61 (1987–2046). pp. 168–172: * * *
57, 1–45 (2047–2091). pp. 173–176: * * *
58, 1–30 (2092–2121). pp. 177–179: Yudhishṭhirādisāyaṃ (svasthāna)-gamana.
§ 641, XII, **59**, 1–145 (2122–2267). pp. 179–191: Sūtrādhyāya.
60, 1–54 (2268–2323). pp. 191–197: Varṇāçramadharma-kathana.
61, 1–21 (2324–2344). pp. 197–199: id. (Caturāçramadharmakathana).
62, 1–11 (2345–2355). pp. 199–200: Varṇāçramadharma-kathana.
63, 1–30 (2356–2385). pp. 200–204: id.
64, 1–30 (2386–2416). pp. 204–207: id.
65, 1–35 (2417–2451). pp. 207–210: [Indra-Māndhātṛ-saṃvāda].
66, 1–43 (2452–2494). pp. 211–214: Cāturāçramya-vidhi.
67, 1–39 (2495–2534). pp. 215–218: Rāshṭre rājakaraṇāvaçyakatva-kathana).
68, 1–61 (2535–2595). pp. 218–223: Aṅgiro (Āṅgirasa) vākya.
69, 1–105 (2596–2700). pp. 223–231: * * *
70, 1–14 (2701–2714). pp. 231–232: * * *
71, 1–33 (2715–2748). pp. 232–235: * * *
72, 1–26 (2749–2774). pp. 235–237: * * *
73, 1–32 (2775–2807). pp. 237–241: [Ailakaçyapasaṃvāda].
74, 1–22 (2808–2833). pp. 241–242: Mucukundopākhyāna.
75, 1–37 (2834–2868). pp. 242–245: * * *
76, 1–14 (2869–2882). pp. 245–247: * * *
77, 1–34 (2883–2916). pp. 247–250: Kaikeyopākhyāna.
78, 1–44 (2917–2961). pp. 250–254: * * *
79, 1–21 (2962–2982). pp. 254–256: * * *
80, 1–41 (2983–3023). pp. 256–259: * * *
81, 1–31 (3024–3054). pp. 259–262: Vāsudeva-Nārada-saṃvāda.
82, 1–68 (3055–3124). pp. 262–267: [Amātyaparikshāyāṃ] Kālakavṛkshīyopākhyāna.
83, 1–57 (3125–3182). pp. 268–273: Mantraṇopadeça (Sabhyādilakshaṇakathana).
84, 1–11 (3183–3193). pp. 273–274: [Indra-Bṛhaspati-saṃvāda].
85, 1–34 (3194–3227). pp. 274–277: [Amātyavibhāga].
86, 1–33 (3228–3260). pp. 277–280: Durgaparīkshā.
87, 1–40 (3261–3301). pp. 280–284: [Rāshṭraguptyādi-kathana].
88, 1–33 (3302–3334). pp. 284–287: [Koçasañcayaprakāra-kathana].
89, 1–26 (3335–3361). pp. 287–290: Rāshṭragupti.
90, 1–40 (3362–3402). pp. 290–293: Utathya-gītaḥ.
91, 1–60 (3403–3462). pp. 293–298: id.
92, 1–19 (3463–3481). pp. 299–300: Vāmadeva-gītaḥ.
93, 1–39 (3482–3521). pp. 300–304: id.
94, 1–13 (3522–3534). pp. 304–305: id.
95, 1–22 (3535–3556). pp. 305–307: Vijigīshamāṇavṛtta.
96, 1–24 (3557–3580). pp. 307–310: [id.].
97, 1–32 (3581–3612). pp. 310–312: * * *
98, 1–51 (3613–3663). pp. 312–317: [Indrāmbarīsha-saṃvāda].
99, 1–10 (3664–3681). pp. 317–318: [Vijigīshamāṇavṛtta].
100, 1–50 (3682–3732). pp. 318–324: [Senānītikathana].
101, 1–20 (3733–3751). pp. 324–325: Vijigīshamāṇavṛtta.
102, 1–41 (3752–3793). pp. 326–330: Senānītikathana.
103, 1–53 (3794–3846). pp. 330–335: Indra-Bṛhaspati-saṃvāda.
104, 1–54 (3847–3902). pp. 335–340: Kālakavṛkshīya.
105, 1–25 (3903–3928). pp. 341–343: id.
106, 1–28 (3929–3956). pp. 343–345: id.
107, 1–32 (3957–3988). pp. 345–348: [Gaṇa-vṛtta].
108, 1–33 (3989–4022). pp. 349–351: [Mātṛ-pitṛ-guru-māhātmya].

109, 1–30 (4023–4052). pp. 352–355 : Satyānṛtaka [vibhāga].
110, 1–30 (4053–4082). pp. 355–357 : Durgātitaraṇa.
111, 1–90 (4083–4172). pp. 357–365 : Vyāghra-gomāyu-saṃvāda.
112, 1–21 (4173–4195). pp. 365–367 : Ushṭragrīvopākhyāna.
113, 1–14 (4196–4209). pp. 367–368 : Sarit-sāgara-saṃvāda.
114, 1–21 (4210–4230). pp. 368–370 : Ṭiṭṭibhaka (°upākhyāna).
115, 1–23 (4231–4253). pp. 370–372 : * * *
116, 1–23 (4254–4278). pp. 373–374 : Çva-rshi-saṃvāda.
117, 1–23 (4279–4302). pp. 374–376 : id.
118, 1–28 (4303–4330). pp. 376–379 : id.
119, 1–20 (4331–4350). pp. 379–381 : id.
120, 1–56 (4351–4407). pp. 381–387 : [Rājadharmakathana].
121, 1–60 (4408–4468). pp. 387–393 : Daṇḍa[rūpādi] kathana.
122, 1–56 (4469–4524). pp. 393–398 : Daṇḍotpatti-kathana (upākhyāna).
123, 1–25 (4525–4548). pp. 398–400 : Kamandāñgarishṭa-saṃvāda.
124, 1–71 (4549–4621). pp. 400–406 : Çīlavarṇana.
125, 1–19 (4622–4640). pp. 406–408 : Ṛshabhagītāḥ.
126, 1–19 (4641–4659). pp. 408–409 : id.
127, 1–26 (4660–4686). pp. 409–411 : id.
128, 1–27 (4687–4715). pp. 411–414 : id.
129, 1–11 (4716–4726). pp. 414–415 : Yama-Gautama-saṃvāda.
130, 1–50 (4727–4778). pp. 415–420 : * * *

LXXXIX. ĀPADDHARMAPARVAN.

§ 642, XII, **131**, 1–14 (4779–4792). pp. 420–422 : * * *
132, 1–22 (4793–4814). pp. 422–424 : Rājarshivṛtta.
133, 1–20 (4815–4834). pp. 425–427 : * * *
134, 1–17 (4835–4851). pp. 427–428 : * * *
§ 643, XII, **135**, 1–26 (4852–4877). pp. 428–430 : [Kāyavyacarita].
§ 644, XII, **136**, 1–11 (4878–4888). pp. 431–432 : * * *
§ 645, XII, **137**, 1–24 (4889–4912). pp. 432–434 : Çākulopākhyāna.
§ 646, XII, **138**, 1–221 (4913–5132). pp. 434–451 : Mārjāra-mūshika-saṃvāda.
§ 647, XII, **139**, 1–113 (5133–5246). pp. 451–460 : Brahmadatta-Pūjanī-saṃvāda.
§ 648, XII, **140**, 1–71 (5247–5318). pp. 460–467 : Kaṇikopadeça.
§ 649, XII, **141**, 1–102 (5319–5420). pp. 467–477 : Viçvāmitra-çvapaca-saṃvāda.
§ 650, XII, **142**, 1–38 (5421–5458). pp. 477–480 : * * *
§ 651, XII, **143**, 1–34 (5459–5492). pp. 481–483 : Kapota-lubdhaka-saṃvāda [°upakrama].
144, 1–17 (5493–5509). pp. 483–484 : Bhāryāpraçaṃsā.
145, 1–14 (5510–5523). pp. 485–486 : Kapota-lubdhaka-saṃvāda (Kapotaṃ prati kapotī-vākya).
146, 1–26 (5524–5549). pp. 486–487 : Kapota-lubdhaka-saṃvāda.
147, 1–11 (5550–5560). p. 488 : id. (Lubdhakoparati).
148, 1–12 (5561–5573). p. 489 : Kapotalubdhakasaṃvāda (Kapota-svargagamana).
149, 1–19 (5574–5593). pp. 490–491 : id. (Lubdhaka-svargagamana).

§ 652, XII, **150**, 1–19 (5596–5612). pp. 491–493 : Indrota-Pārīkshitīya-saṃvāda.
151, 1–22 (5613–5634). pp. 494–495 : Indrota-Pārīkshitīya.
152, 1–39 (5635–5674). pp. 495–499 : id.
§ 653, XII, **153**, 1–122 (5675–5800). pp. 499–509 : Gṛdhra-gomāyu-saṃvāda.
§ 654, XII, **154**, 1–21 (5801–5821). pp. 509–510 : Pavana-çālmali-saṃvāda.
155, 1–19 (5822–5840). pp. 510–512 : id.
156, 1–19 (5841–5860). pp. 512–513 : id.
157, 1–16 (5861–5876). pp. 513–515 : id.
§ 655, XII, **158**, 1–35 (5877–5911). pp. 515–518 : [Āpanmūla-bhūta-doshakathana].
159, 1–14 (5912–5925). pp. 518–519 : Ātmajñāna (Ajñāna-māhātmya).
160, 1–38 (5926–5963). pp. 519–523 : Damakathana.
161, 1–13 (5964–5976). pp. 523–524 : Tapaḥ-kathana (°praçaṃsā).
162, 1–26 (5977–6002). pp. 524–526 : Satyakathana (°praçaṃsā).
163, 1–22 (6003–6025). pp. 526–528 : Lobhopākhyāna (°nirūpana).
164, 1–13 (6026–6038). pp. 528–529 : Nṛçaṃsa-kathana (°ākhyāna).
165, 1–78 (6039–6119). pp. 530–538 : Prāyaçcittīya.
§ 656, XII, **166**, 1–89 (6120–6209). pp. 538–545 : Khaḍgotpattikathana.
§ 657, XII, **167**, 1–51 (6210–6263). pp. 545–550 : Shaḍja-gītā.
§ 658, XII, **168**, 1–52 (6264–6316). pp. 550–555 : Kṛtaghnopākhyāna.
169, 1–24 (6317–6341). pp. 555–557 : id.
170, 1–26 (6342–6367). pp. 558–560 : id.
171, 1–35 (6368–6402). pp. 560–562 : id.
172, 1–26 (6403–6429). pp. 563–565 : id.
173, 1–26 (6430–6456). pp. 565–567 : id.

XC. MOKSHADHARMAPARVAN.

§ 659, XII, **174**, 1–63 (6457–6521). pp. 1–8 : Piṅgalā-gītā (Brāhmaṇa-Senajit-saṃvāda-kathana).
175, 1–39 (6522–6561). pp. 8–12 : Pitā-putra-saṃvāda [kathana].
176, 1–23 (6562–6585). pp. 12–14 : Çampāka-gītā.
177, 1–54 (6586–6639). pp. 14–20 : Maṅki-gītā.
178, 1–13 (6640–6652). pp. 20–21 : Bodhya-gītā.
179, 1–37 (6653–6689). pp. 21–25 : Prahrādājagara(A° Pra°) saṃvāda.
180, 1–54 (6690–6744). pp. 25–30 : Çṛgāla-Kāçyapa-saṃvāda.
181, 1–20 (6745–6764). pp. 30–32 : * * *
§ 660, XII, **182**, 1–38 (6765–6803). pp. 32–36 : Bhṛgu-Bharadvāja-saṃvāda.
183, 1–17 (6804–6820). pp. 36–37 : id. [Mānasabhūtotpatti-kathana].
184, 1–44 (6821–6865). pp. 37–40 : Bhṛgu-Bharadvāja-saṃvāda.
185, 1–17 (6866–6882). pp. 41–42 : [id.].
186, 1–15 (6883–6897). pp. 43–44 : Bhṛ° [Jīvasvarūpākshepa].
187, 1–31 (6898–6929). pp. 44–47 : id. [Jīvasvarūpanirūpana].
188, 1–20 (6930–6949). pp. 47–49 : id. [Varṇavibhāga-kathana].

189, 1–18 (6950–6967). pp. 50–52: id. [Varṇasvarūpakathana].

190, 1–16 (6968–6983). pp. 52–54: Bhṛgu-Bharadvāja-saṃvāda.

191, 1–18 (6984–7001). pp. 54–58: id.

192, 1–27 (7002–7031). pp. 58–63: id.

§ 661, XII, **193**, 1–33 (7032–7065). pp. 63–67: [Bhīshma-Yudhishṭhirasaṃvāda] Ācāravidhi.

194, 1–63 (7066–7128). pp. 67–75: [Adhyātma-kathana].

195, 1–22 (7129–7150). pp. 75–77: Adhyātma (Dhyānayogakathana).

196, 1–23 (7151–7173). pp. 77–80: Jāpakopākhyāna.

197, 1–13 (7174–7186). pp. 80–82: id.

198, 1–11 (7187–7197). pp. 82–83: id.

§ 662, XII, **199**, 1–128 (7198–7329). pp. 84–96: id.

200, 1–34 (7330–7364). pp. 96–99: id.

§ 663, XII, **201**, 1–27 (7365–7393). pp. 99–104: Manu-Bṛhaspati-saṃvāda.

202, 1–23 (7394–7416). pp. 104–108: id.

203, 1–23 (7417–7439). pp. 108–111: id.

204, 1–20 (7440–7459). pp. 112–115: id.

205, 1–26 (7460–7485). pp. 115–118: id.

206, 1–32 (7486–7516). pp. 118–122: id.

§ 664, XII, **207**, 1–49 (7517–7566). pp. 122–126: Sarvabhūtotpatti[-kathana].

§ 665, XII, **208**, 1–37 (7567–7603). pp. 127–129: Diça[ṃ] svastika.

§ 666, XII, **209**, 1–36 (7604–7640). pp. 129–132: Antarbhūmivikrīḍita (°ḍana).

§ 667, XII, **210**, 1–46 (7641–7688). pp. 133–137: Vārshṇeyādhyātma[kathana].

211, 1–17 (7689–7706). pp. 137–141: id. [id.].

212, 1–33 (7707–7741). pp. 141–145: id. [id.].

213, 1–21 (7742–7763). pp. 145–149: id. [id.].

214, 1–29 (7764–7792). pp. 149–153: id. [id.].

215, 1–27 (7793–7820). pp. 154–158: id. [id.].

216, 1–20 (7821–7841). pp. 158–161: id. [id.].

217, 1–38 (7842–7880). pp. 161–167: id. [id.].

§ 668, XII, **218**, 1–49 (7881–7929). pp. 167–177: Pañcaçikhavākya [Pāshaṇḍa-khaṇḍana].

219, 1–52 (7930–7983). pp. 177–185: Pañcaçikha-vākya.

§ 669, XII, **220**, 1–20 (7984–8003). pp. 185–187: Damapraçaṃsā.

221, 1–17 (8004–8020). pp. 187–189: Amṛtaprāçnika.

§ 670, XII, **222**, 1–37 (8021–8057). pp. 189–193: Çakra-Prahrāda-saṃvāda.

§ 671, XII, **223**, 1–30 (8058–8087). pp. 193–196: Bali-Vāsava-saṃvāda.

224, 1–60 (8088–8147). pp. 196–202: id.

225, 1–38 (8148–8186). pp. 202–205: Çrī-sannidhānà.

§ 672, XII, **226**, 1–23 (8187–8211). pp. 206–209: Çakra-Namuci-saṃvāda.

§ 673, XII, **227**, 1–119 (8212–8332), pp. 209–219: Bali-Vāsava-saṃvāda.

§ 674, XII, **229** (*sic*), 1–96 (8333–8428). pp. 219–228: Çrī-Vāsava-saṃvāda.

§ 675, XII, **230**, 1–25 (8429–8453). pp. 228–231: Jaigīshavyāsita-saṃvāda.

§ 676, XII, **231**, 1–24 (8454–8477). pp. 231–233: Vāsudevograsena-saṃvāda.

§ 677, XII, **232**, 1–32 (8478–8509). pp. 233–237: Çukānupraçna.

233, 1–43 (8510–8554). pp. 237–245: id.

234, 1–19 (8555–8574). pp. 245–247: id.

235, 1–38 (8575–8612). pp. 247–251: id.

236, 1–32 (8613–8644). pp. 251–255: id.

237, 1–41 (8645–8687). pp. 255–261: id.

238, 1–25 (8687–8712). pp. 261–266: id.

239, 1–21 (8713–8733). pp. 266–270: id.

240, 1–34 (8734–8767). pp. 270–275: id.

241, 1–36 (8768–8803). pp. 276–280: id.

242, 1–20 (8804–8823). pp. 281–283: id.

243, 1–30 (8824–8853). pp. 283–288: id.

244, 1–29 (8854–8883). pp. 288–292: id.

245, 1–31 (8884–8914). pp. 292–297: id.

246, 1–36 (8915–8950). pp. 297–304: id.

247, 1–23 (8951–8973). pp. 304–307: id.

248, 1–25 (8974–8998). pp. 307–310: id.

249, 1–24 (8999–9023). pp. 311–315: id.

250, 1–14 (9024–9037). pp. 315–317: id.

251, 1–25 (9038–9063). pp. 317–320: id.

252, 1–24 (9064–9087). pp. 320–324: id.

253, 1–12 (9088–9100). pp. 324–326: id.

254, 1–15 (9101–9115). pp. 326–329: id.

255, 1–14 (9116–9130). pp. 329–332: id.

256, 1–13 (9131–9143). pp. 332–334: id.

§ 678, XII, **257**, 1–21 (9144–9164). pp. 334–336: [Mṛtyu]-Prajāpati-saṃvād[opakrama].

258, 1–22 (9165–9186). pp. 336–338: Mṛtyu-Prajāpati-saṃvāda.

259, 1–42 (9187–9228). pp. 338–342: id.

§ 679, XII, **260**, 1–27 (9229–9256). pp. 342–346: Dharmalakshaṇa [kathana].

261, 1–20 (9257–9276). pp. 346–350: Dharmalakshaṇakathana (°prāmāṇyākshepa).

§ 680, XII, **262**, 1–51 (9277–9328). pp. 350–354: Tulādhāra-Jājali-saṃvāda.

263, 1–55 (9339 (*sic*)–9395). pp. 354–362: id.

264, 1–42 (9396–9441). pp. 362–370: id.

265, 1–23 (9442–9466). pp. 370–373: id.

§ 681, XII, **266**, 1–14 (9467–9480). pp. 373–375: Vicakhyu (°khnu) gītā.

§ 682, XII, **267**, 1–78 (9481–9558). pp. 375–384: Cirakārikopākhyāna.

§ 683, XII, **268**, 1–36 (9559–9595). pp. 384–389: Dyumatsena-Satyavad-vākya (°t-saṃvāda).

§ 684, XII, **269**, 1–40 (9596–9635). pp. 389–394: Gokapilīya.

270, 1–08 (9636–9706). pp. 394–406: id.

271, 1–47 (9707–9754). pp. 406–414: id.

§ 685, XII, **272**, 1–56 (9755–9810). pp. 414–419: Kuṇḍadhāropākhyāna.

§ 686, XII, **273**, 1–20 (9811–9830). pp. 420–423: Yajñanindā.

§ 687, XII, **274**, 1–24 (9831–9854). pp. 423–426: Catuḥprāçnika.

275, 1–19 (9855–9873). pp. 426–429: Yogācārānuvarṇana.

§ 688, XII, **276**, 1–38 (9874–9913). pp. 429–434: Nāradāsita-saṃvāda.

§ 689, XII, **277**, 1–14 (9914–9927). pp. 435–436: Māṇḍavya-Janaka-saṃvāda.

§ 690, XII, **278**, 1–39 (9928–9966). pp. 436–441: Pitāputra-saṃvāda.

§ 691, XII, **279**, 1–22 (9967–9989). pp. 441–444: Hārīta-gītā.

§ 692, XII, **280**, 1–34 (9990–10024). pp. 445–449: Vṛtragītāḥ.

281, 1–70 (10025–10097). pp. 449–464 : Vṛtra-gītāḥ.
§ 693, XII, **282,** 1–44 (10098–10142). pp. 464–467 : Vṛtra-vadha.
283, 1–65 (10143–10207). pp. 468–473 : id. (Brahma-hatyāvibhāga).
§ 694, XII, **284,** 1–63 (10208–10271). pp. 473–478 : Jvarot-patti.
§ 695, XII, **285,** 1–71 (10272–10345). pp. 478–485 : [Dakshayajñavināça].
§ 696, XII, **285,** 72–208 (10346–10484). pp. 485–502 : Dakshaprokta-Çiva-sahasranāma-stotra (°stava).
§ 697, XII, **286,** 1–46 (10485–10531). pp. 502–508 : Pāñca-bhautika.
§ 698, XII, **287,** 1–21 (10532–10552). pp. 508–511 : Samaṅga-Nārada-saṃvāda.
§ 699, XII, **288,** 1–59 (10553–10611). pp. 511–518 : Çreyovācika.
§ 700, XII, **289,** 1–47 (10612–10658). pp. 519–524 : Sagarā-rishṭanemi-saṃvāda.
§ 701, XII, **290,** 1–38 (10659–10696). pp. 524–527 : Bhava-Bhārgava-samāgamā.
§ 702, XII, **291,** 1–26 (10697–10722). pp. 528–531 : Parāçara-gītā[ḥ].
292, 1–23 (10723–10746). pp. 532–535 : Parāçara-gītā.
293, 1–23 (10747–10769). pp. 535–538 : id.
294, 1–21 (10770–10790). pp. 538–540 : id.
295, 1–31 (10791–10821). pp. 540–544 : id.
296, 1–39 (10822–10860). pp. 544–549 : id.
297, 1–39 (10861–10899). pp. 549–553 : id.
298, 1–41 (10900–10941). pp. 553–558 : id.
299, 1–47 (10942–10991). pp. 558–564 : id.
§ 703, XII, **300,** 1–45 (10992–11036). pp. 564–570 : Haṃsa-gītā[-samāpti].
§ 704, XII, **301,** 1–62 (11037–11098). pp. 570–575 : Yoga-vidhi.
302, 1–116 (11098 (*sic*)–11213). pp. 575–588 : Sāṅkhya-kathana.
§ 705, XII, **303,** 1–49 (11214–11262). pp. 588–593 : Vasishṭha-Karālajanaka-saṃvāda.
304, 1–54 (11263–11316). pp. 593–598 : id.
305, 1–11 (11317–11327). pp. 599–600 : id.
306, 1–39 (11328–11367). pp. 600–604 : id.
307, 1–50 (11368–11417). pp. 604–609 : id.
308, 1–48 (11418–11465). pp. 609–614 : id.
309, 1–51 (11466–11517). pp. 614–620 : id.
§ 706, XII, **310,** 1–25 (11518–11542). pp. 621–624 : Janakānuçāsana.
§ 707, XII, **311,** 1–26 (11543–11568). pp. 624–626 : Yājñavalkya-Janaka-saṃvāda.
312, 1–21 (11569–11589). pp. 626–628 : Janaka-Yājña-valkya-saṃvāda.
313, 1–17 (11590–11606). pp. 628–629 : Yājñavalkya-Janaka-saṃvāda.
314, 1–28 (11607–11634). pp. 630–631 : id.
315, 1–18 (11635–11654). pp. 632–633 : id.
316, 1–20 (11655–11674). pp. 633–636 : id.
317, 1–27 (11675–11702) : pp. 636–639 : [id.].
318, 1–21 (11703–11723). pp. 639–641 : id.
319, 1–112 (11724–11836). pp. 641–654 : id. [-samāpti].
§ 708, XII, **320,** 1–15 (11837–11851). pp. 654–655 : [Bhikshu]-Pañcaçikha-Janaka-saṃvāda.
§ 709, XII, **321,** 1–190 (11852–12043). pp. 656–678 : Sulabhā-Janaka-saṃvāda.
§ 710, XII, **322,** 1–94 (12044–12137). pp. 678–689 : Pāvak[ādhyayana].
§ 711, XII, **323,** 1–20 (12138–12157). pp. 690–691 : Dharma-mūlika.

324, 1–29 (12158–12186). pp. 692–694 : Çukotpatti.
325, 1–27 (12187–12214). pp. 694–696 : id.
326, 1–45 (12215–12259). pp. 696–700 : Çukakṛti (Çukot-patti).
327, 1–51 (12260–12311). pp. 700–705 : id. (id.).
328, 1–53 (12312–12364). pp. 705–709 : [Çukakṛtya].
329, 1–57 (12365–12421). pp. 709–714 : id. (Çukotpatti).
330, 1–59 (12422–12481). pp. 715–721 : [Çuka-Nārada-saṃvāda].
331, 1–30 (12482–12511). pp. 722–725 : Çukābhipatana.
332, 1–65 (12512–12576). pp. 725–733 : id. (Çukābhi-gamana).
333, 1–31 (12577–12607). pp. 733–735 : id.
334, 1–42 (12608–12649). pp. 735–739 : id. (Çukotpatana-samāpti).
§ 712, XII, **324,** 1–**325,** 27 (12158–12214). pp. 692–696 : Çukotpatti.
§ 713, XII, **326,** 1–**327,** 51 (12215–12311). pp. 696–705 : Çukakṛti.
§ 714, XII, **328,** 1–**329,** 57 (12312–12421). pp. 705–714 : Çukakṛtya.
§ 715, XII, **330,** 1–**332,** 45 (12422–12556). pp. 715–730 : Çuka-Nārada-saṃvāda.
§ 716, XII, **332,** 44–**334,** 42 (12557–12649). pp. 730–739 : Çukābhipatana.

---

§ 717, XII, **335,** 1–45 (12650–12695). pp. 739–743 : [Nārāyaṇīya].
336, 1–55 (12296–12751). pp. 743–749 : Nārāyaṇīya.
337, 1–65 (12752–12817). pp. 749–756 : id.
338, 1–41 (12818–12860). pp. 756–760 : id.
339, 1–4 (12861–12864). pp. 760–765 : [id. Mahāpurusha-stava].
340, 1–141 (12865–13006). pp. 765–779 : Nārāyaṇīya.
341, 1–119 (13007–13128). pp. 779–791 : id.
342, 1–59 (13129–13187). pp. 791–796 : id.
343, 1–141 (13188–13303). pp. 796–819 : id.
344, 1–67 (13304–13370). pp. 819–825 : id.
345, 1–27 (13371–13398). pp. 825–828 : id.
346, 1–28 (13399–13426). pp. 828–831 : id.
347, 1–22 (13427–13448). pp. 831–834 : id.
348, 1–96 (13449–13546). pp. 834–843 : id.
349, 1–88 (13547–13636). pp. 843–852 : [id.] Ekānti[ka]-bhāva.
350, 1–74 (13637–13712). pp. 852–860 : [id.] Dvaipāyanot-patti.
351, 1–27 (13713–13739). pp. 860–863 : Nār° [Brahma-Rudra-saṃvāda].
352, 1–23 (13740–13763). pp. 863–866 : Nār°[-samāpti].
§ 718, XII, **353,** 1–11 (13764–13774). pp. 866–867 : Uñchavṛtty-upākhyāna.
354, 1–9 (13775–13783). pp. 867–869 : id.
355, 1–16 (13784–13799). pp. 869–871 : id.
356, 1–11 (13800–13810). pp. 871–872 : id.
357, 1–11 (13811–13821). pp. 872–873 : id.
358, 1–13 (13822–13834). pp. 874–875 : id.
359, 1–13 (13835–13847). pp. 875–876 : id.

360, 1–16 (13848–13863). pp. 876–878 : id.
361, 1–20 (13864–13883). pp. 878–880 : id.
362, 1–16 (13884–13899). pp. 880–882 : id.
363, 1–18 (13900–13917). pp. 882–884 : id.
364, 1–6 (13918–13924). p. 884 : id.
365, 1–10 (13925–13934). pp. 885–886 : id.
366, 1–9 (13935–13943). pp. 886–887 : id.

XIII. ANUÇĀSANAPARVAN.

XCI. Ānuçāsanika-parvan.

§ 719, XIII, **1,** 1–83 (1–83). pp. 1–8 : [Dānadharme] Gautamī-lubdhaka-vyāla-Mṛtyu-Kāla-saṃvāda.
§ 720, XIII, **2,** 1–96 (84–180). pp. 8–14 : [id.] Sudarçanopākhyāna.
§ 721, XIII, **3,** 1–19 (181–199). pp. 14–15 : Viçvāmitropākhyāna.
4, 1–62 (200–262). pp. 15–19 : [Dānadharme] id.
§ 722, XIII, **5,** 1–32 (263–294). pp. 19–21 : [id.] Çuka-Vāsava-saṃvāda.
§ 723, XIII, **6,** 1–49 (295–343). pp. 22–25 : [id.] Daiva-purushakāra[-nirdeça].
§ 724, XIII, **7,** 1–29 (344–373). pp. 25–28 : [id. Karma]-phalikopākhyāna.
8, 1–29 (374–402). pp. 28–31 : Dānadharma (Bhīshma-niçcaya).
§ 725, XIII, **9,** 1–28 (403–432). pp. 31–33 : [id.] Çṛgāla-vānara-saṃvāda.
§ 726, XIII, **10,** 1–74 (433–506). pp. 33–41 : [id.] Çūdra-muni-saṃvāda.
§ 727, XIII, **11,** 1–21 (507–527). pp. 41–43 : [id.] Çrī-Rukmiṇī-saṃvāda.
§ 728, XIII, **12,** 1–54 (528–581). pp. 44–48 : [id.] Bhaṅgā-svanopākhyāna.
§ 729, XIII, **13,** 1–6 (582–587). pp. 48–49 : [do.] Lokayātrā-kathana.
§ 730, XIII, **14,** 1–429 (588–1024). pp. 49–91 : Meghavāhanopākhyāna (°parvākhyāna).
15, 1–11 (1025–1036). pp. 92–93 : id. (id.).
16, 1–70 (1037 1113). pp. 93–101 : id. (id.).
17, 1–182 (1114–1295). pp. 101–140 : [Dānadharme] Mahādeva-sahasranāma-stotra.
18, 1–83 (1296–1380). pp. 140–147 : [id.] Meghavāhanopākhyāna (°parvākhyāna).
§ 731, XIII, **19,** 1–103 (1381–1484). pp. 148–157 : Ashṭā-vakra-dik-saṃvāda.
20, 1–26 (1485–1511). pp. 157–160 : id.
21, 1–19 (1512–1530). pp. 160–161 : id.
§ 732, XIII, **22,** 1–41 (1531–1571). pp. 162–167 : Bahu-prāçnika.
23, 1–103 (1572–1675). pp. 167–180 : [Dānadharme] Dānakathana (Svarga-Naraka-gāmi-varṇana).
24, 1–12 (1676–1687). pp. 180–181 : [do.] Brahmaghna-kathana.
§ 733, XIII, **25,** 1–71 (1688–1757). pp. 181–187 : [id.] Aṅgirasastīrthayātrā (Āṅgirasatī-°).
§ 734, XIII, **26,** 1–106 (1758–1864). pp. 187–198 : [id.] Gaṅgā-māhātmyakathana.
§ 735, XIII, **27,** 1–30 (1865–1895). pp. 198–201 : [id.] Indra-Mataṅga-saṃvāda.
28, 1–16 (1896–1912). pp. 201–202 : [id.] id.
29, 1–26 (1913–1939). pp. 202–205 : [id.] id.
§ 736, XIII, **30,** 1–67 (1940–2007). pp. 205–211 : [id.] Vītahavyopākhyāna.
§ 737, XIII, **31,** 1–36 (2008–2043). pp. 211–215 : [id.] Kṛshṇa-Nārada-saṃvāda.
§ 738, XIII, **32,** 1–39 (2044–2082). pp. 215–218 : [id.] Çyena-kapotākhyāna.
§ 739, XIII, **33,** 1–27 (2083–2109). pp. 218–221 : [id.] Brāhmaṇa-praçaṃsā.
34, 1–31 (2110–2141). pp. 221–224 : [id.] id. (Pṛthivī-Vāsudeva-saṃvāda).
35, 1–23 (2142–2164). pp. 224–227 : [id.] Brāhmaṇa-praçaṃsā.
§ 740, XIII, **36,** 1–19 (2165–2183). pp. 227–229 : [id.] [id.] Indra-Çambara-saṃvāda.
§ 741, XIII, **37,** 1–18 (2184–2201). pp. 229–231 : [id.] Pātraparīkshā.
§ 742, XIII, **38,** 1–30 (2202–2231). pp. 231–234 : [id.] Pañcacūḍā-Nārada-saṃvāda.
39, 1–14 (2232–2246). pp. 234–235 : [id.] Strīsvabhāva-kathana.
§ 743, XIII, **40,** 1–60 (2247–2306). pp. 236–240 : [id.] Vipulopākhyāna.
41, 1–36 (2307–2343). pp. 241–244 : [id.] id.
42, 1–33 (2344–2376). pp. 244–246 : [id.] id.
43, 1–27 (2377 2403). pp. 247–249 : [id.] id.
§ 744, XIII, **44,** 1–56 (2404–2460). pp. 249–257 : [id.] Vivāha[-dharma]-kathana.
45, 1–23 (2461–2483). pp. 257–260 : [id.] Vivāha-dharma-[kathana] Yama-gāthā.
46, 1–15 (2484–2498). pp. 260–262 : [id. Vivāhadharme] Strīpraçaṃsa.
47, 1–61 (2499–2561). pp. 262–268 : [id.] Rikthavibhāga [-kathana].
48, 1–50 (2562–2612). pp. 268–275 : [id.] Varṇasaṅkara-kathana.
49, 1–28 (2613–2640). pp. 275–279 : [id.] Putrapratinidhi-kathana.
§ 745, XIII, **50,** 1–27 (2641–2667). pp. 279–281 : [Dānadharme] Cyavanopākhyāna.
51, 1–48 (2668–2715). pp. 281–285 : [id.] id.
52, 1–39 (2716–2754). pp. 285–288 : [id.] id. (Cyavana-Kuçika saṃvāda).
53, 1–68 (2755–2824). pp. 289–294 : [id.] Kuçikopākhyāna (id.).
54, 1–40 (2825–2866). pp. 294–298 : [id.] Kuçika-Cyavana (Cya° Ku°) saṃvāda.
55, 1–37 (2867–2903). pp. 298–301 : [id.] Cyavana-Kuçika-saṃvāda.
56, 1–21 (2904–2925). pp. 302–303 : [id.] id.
§ 746, XIII, **57,** 1–44 (2926–2969). pp. 304–307 : Dāna-dharma[-kathana].
58, 1–33 (2970–3002). pp. 307–310 : id. [id.] [Ārāma-taḍāga-māhātmya-varṇana].
59, 1–41 (3003–3043). pp. 310–315 : Dānadharma [-kathana].
60, 1–20 (3044–3063). pp. 315–317 : id. [id.].
61, 1–38 (3064–3102). pp. 317–321 : id. [id.].
62, 1–96 (3103–3199). pp. 321–329 : [id.] [-kathana] [Indra-Bṛhaspati-saṃvāda].
63, 1–52 (3200–3251). pp. 330–334 : [id.] [-ka°] [anna-dāna-praçaṃsā].

64, 1–36 (3252–3288). pp. 334–337: [id.] [-ka°] [Nakshatra-yoga-dāna].
65, 1 – 19 (3289 – 3308). pp. 337 – 339: Dānadharma [-kathana].
66, 1–65 (3309–3374). pp. 339–344: id. [id.].
67, 1–19 (3375–3394). pp. 345–346: [id.] [id.] [Pānīyadānamāhātmya].
68, 1–34 (3395–3429). pp. 346–349: [id.] [id.] [Yama-brāhmaṇa-saṃvāda].
69, 1–22 (3430–3451). pp. 350–352: [id.] [id.] [Godāna-māhātmya].
70, 1–33 (3452–3484). pp. 352–355: [id.] [id.] [Nṛgopākhyāna].
71, 1–57 (3485–3541). pp. 355–362: [id.] [id.] [Yama-vākya].
72, 1–12 (3542–3553). pp. 362–363: [id.] [id.] [Gopradānika].
73, 1–51 (3554–3605). pp. 364–370: [id.] [id.] [Pitāmahendra-saṃvāda].
74, 1–16 (3606–3621). pp. 370–372: Dānadharma[-kathana].
75, 1–41 (3622–3664). pp. 372–375: id. [id.].
76, 1–31 (3665–3695). pp. 375–380: id. [Godāna]-ka°.
77, 1–35 (3696–3731). pp. 380–384: id. [Goprabhava] -ka°.
78, 1–25 (3732–3756). pp. 384–387: id. [Gopradānike] [-ka°].
79, 1–27 (3757–3784). pp. 387–390: id. [id.] [id.].
80, 1–17 (3785–3801). pp. 390–391: id. [id.] [id.].
81, 1–47 (3802–3850). pp. 391–396: Dāna°[-ka°] Gopra°.
82, 1–27 (3851–3878). pp. 396–398: Dānadharma[-ka°] [Çrī-go-saṃvāda].
83, 1–52 (3879–3930). pp. 398–402: id. [id.] [Goloka-varṇana].
§ 747, XIII, **84,** 1–82 (3931–4014). pp. 402–409: id. [id.] Suvarṇotpatti.
85, 1–168 (4015–4185). pp. 409–424: id. [id.] id. [-upākhyāna].
§ 748, XIII, **86,** 1–35 (4186–4220). pp. 424–427: id. [id.] Tārakavadhopākhyāna.
§ 749, XIII, **87,** 1–19 (4221–4239). pp. 427–429: [Dānadharme] Çrāddhakathana(°kalpa).
88, 1–15 (4240–4254). pp. 429–431: Dānadharma [-ka°] Çrāddhakalpa.
89, 1–15 (4255–4269). pp. 431–432: id. [id.] id.
90, 1–54 (4270–4325). pp. 432–439: id. [id.] id.
91, 1–45 (4326–4371). pp. 439–443: Çrāddhadharmaka° (Dā° Çrā°).
92, 1–23 (4372–4395). pp. 443–445: Dā° [-ka°] Çrāddhakalpa.
§ 750, XIII, **93,** 1–149 (4396–4546). pp. 445–460: id. [id.] Bisastainyopākhyāna.
§ 751, XIII, **94,** 1–54 (4547–4600). pp. 460–467: id. [id.] [Çapathavidhi].
§ 752, XIII, **95,** 1–28 (4601–4628). pp. 467–469: id. [id.] Chattropānahotpatti.
96, 1–22 (4629–4650). pp. 469–471: id. [id.] Chattropānahadāna-praçaṃsā.
§ 753, XIII, **97,** 1–25 (4651–4676). pp. 471–473: Dānadharma [-ka°] [bali-dānavidhi].
§ 754, XIII, **98,** 1–66 (4677–4742). pp. 473–479: Dā° [-ka°] Suvarṇa-Manu-saṃvāda.
§ 755, XIII, **99,** 1–21 (4743–4771). pp. 479–482: id. [id.] Agastya-Bhṛgu-saṃvāda.
100, 1–41 (4772–4812). pp. 482–485: [id. id.] Nahushopākhyāna (id.).
§ 756, XIII, **101,** 1–29 (4813–4842). pp. 485–488: [Dā°] Rājanya-Cāṇḍāla-saṃvāda.
§ 757, XIII, **102,** 1–63 (4843–4905). pp. 488–496: [Dā°] Hastikūṭa.
§ 758, XIII, **103,** 1–45 (4906–4953). pp. 496–501: [id.] [Tapaḥkathana] Brahma-Bhagīratha-saṃvāda.
§ 759, XIII, **104,** 1–157 (4954–5112). pp. 501–517: [id.] Āyushyākhyāna.
105, 1–20 (5113–5132). pp. 517–520: [id.] Jyeshṭha-kanishṭha-dharma-kathana (°vṛtti).
106, 1–72 (5133–5204). pp. 520–526: [id.] [-ka°] upavāsavidhi.
107, 1–144 (5205–5348). pp. 526–538: [id.] upavāsavidhi.
108, 1–21 (5349–5369). pp. 538–540: [id.] çaucakathana (°ānupṛcchā).
109, 1–17 (5370–5386). pp. 541–542: [id.] Vishṇor dvādaça [nāma] [ka] (-kathana).
110, 1–10 (5387–5396). pp. 542–543: [id.] [Aṅgavidhi].
§ 760, XIII, **111,** 1–133 (5397–5531). pp. 543–554: [id.] Saṃsāracakra [kathana].
112, 1–31 (5532–5563). pp. 554–557: [id. Sa°] [Anna-dānakathana].
113, 1–11 (5564–5574). pp. 557–558: id. [ka°] [Saṃsāra-cakrasamāpti].
§ 761, XIII, **114,** 1–19 (5575–5593). pp. 558–560: [id.] Māṃsavarjana-kathana.
115, 1–85 (5594–5679). pp. 560–567: [id.] Māṃsa-bhakshaṇa-nishedha.
116, 1–42 (5680–5722). pp. 567–570: [id.] Ahiṃsāphala-kathana.
§ 762, XIII, **117,** 1–29 (5723–5751). pp. 570–573: [id.] Kīṭopākhyāna.
118, 1–24 (5752–5776). pp. 573–575: [id.] id.
119, 1–15 (5777–5792). pp. 575–577: [id.] id.
§ 763, XIII, **120,** 1–27 (5793–5820). pp. 577–580: [id.] Maitreya-bhikshā.
121, 1–17 (5821–5837). pp. 580–581: id. [ka°] [id.].
122, 1–20 (5838–5857). pp. 581–583: [id.] id.
§ 764, XIII, **123,** 1–22 (5858–5879). pp. 583–585: [id. Çāṇḍilī-]Sumanā-saṃvāda.
§ 765, XIII, **124,** 1–39 (5880–5918). pp. 585–588: [id.] Hariṇa-Kṛçakākhyāna.
§ 766, XIII, **125,** 1–84 (5919–6004). pp. 588–597: [id.] Crāddhadharmakathana (Pitṛ-rahasya).
126, 1–50 (6005–6054). pp. 597–602: [id.] [ka°] [Deva-rahasya].
127, 1–19 (6055–6075). pp. 602–604: [id.] Dai (De°)va-rahasya.
128, 1–11 (6076–6086). pp. 604–605: [id.] [ka°] [Deva-rahasya].
129, 1–15 (6087–6101). pp. 605–607: [id.] Lomaça-rahasya.
130, 1–40 (6102–6140). pp. 607–610: [id. Arundhatī]-Citragupta-rahasya.
131, 1–12 (6141–6154). pp. 610–611: [id.] Pramatha-rahasya.
132, 1–17 (6155–6172). pp. 612–613: [id.] Diggaj[ānām] rahasya.
133, 1–9 (6173–6181). pp. 613–614: [id.] Mahādeva-rahasya.

134, 1–17 (6182–6198). pp. 614–616: [id. Skanda]-Devarahasya.
§ 767, XIII, **135**, 1–21 (6199–6219). pp. 616–617: [id.] Bhojyābhojyānnakathana.
136, 1–25 (6220–6243). pp. 618–619: [id.] Prāyaçcittakathana (°vidhi).
137, 1–32 (6244–6276). pp. 620–622: [id.] [Dānaphalakathana].
138, 1–11 (6277–6287). pp. 622–623: Dānadharma [-kathana].
§ 768, XIII, **139**, 1–50 (6288–6337). pp. 623–627: [Dāna°] [Ṛshi-Vāsudeva-saṃvāda].
140, 1–51 (6338–6389). pp. 627–631: [Dā°] Umā-Maheçvara-saṃvāda.
141, 1–115 (6390–6505). pp. 632–643: [id.] [id.]
142, 1–59 (6506–6564). pp. 643–649: [id.] id.
143, 1–59 (6565–6623). pp. 649–656: [id.] id.
144, 1–60 (6624–6682). pp. 656–661: [id.] id.
145, 1–64 (6683–6746). pp. 661–667: [id.] id.
146, 1–61 (6747–6805). pp. 667–672: [id.] id.
147, 1–62 (6806–6869). pp. 673–678: [id.] Vishṇu (Purusha) māhātmya[-kathana].
148, 1–66 (6870–6935). pp. 679–684: [id.] Umā-Maheçvara-saṃvāda (Mahāpurusha-prastāva).
§ 769, XIII, **149**, 1–142 (6936–7078). pp. 684–715: [id.] Vishṇor (°ṇu-) [divya-] sahasranāmakathana.
§ 770, XIII, **151** (*sic*), 1–82 (7079–7161). pp. 715–722: [id.] Sāvitrī-vratakathana (°opākhyana).
§ 771, XIII, **152**, 1–23 (7162–7184). pp. 723–725: [id.] Brāhmaṇapraçaṃsā.
§ 772, XIII, **153**, 1–28 (7185–7212). pp. 725–727: [id.] Pavanārjuna-saṃvāda [Brāhmaṇa-māhātmya].
154, 1–19 (7213–7231). pp. 727–729: [id.] id.
155, 1–32 (7232–7264). pp. 729–732: [id.] id.
156, 1–26 (7265–7290). pp. 732–734: [id.] id.
157, 1–35 (7291–7325). pp. 734–737: [id.] id.
158, 1–27 (7326–7353). pp. 737–740: [id.] id.
§ 773, XIII, **159**, 1–46 (7354–7400). pp. 740–746: [id.] Bhagavan-māhātmyakathana (Mahāpurushamāhātmya).
160, 1–56 (7401–7457). pp. 746–750: [id.] Durvāsobhikshā [upākhyāna].
161, 1–44 (7458–7501). pp. 751–754: [id.] Īçvarapraçaṃsā.
162, 1–29 (7502–7531). pp. 754–756: [id.] id. (Maheçvaramāhātmya).
§ 774, XIII, **163**, 1–63 (7532–7596). pp. 757–764: [id.] Dharma [pramaṇa] kathana.
164, 1–14 (7597–7611). pp. 764–766: Nītikathana (Dānadharme dharmapraçaṃsā).
165, 1–15 (7612–7626). pp. 766–768: Dharmakathana (Dānadharme Dharmapraçaṃsā).
§ 775, XIII, **166**, 1–62 (7627–7688). pp. 769–772: [Dā°] Vaṃçānukīrtana.
§ 776, XIII, **167**, 1–17 (7689–7705). pp. 772–774: [id.] Bhīshmānujñā.

XCII. [Bhīshma]-svargārohaṇ[ik]a-parvan.

§ 777, XIII, **168**, 1–52 (7706–7758). pp. 774–778: [Dā°] [Bhīshma-prārthanā].
169, 1–37 (7759–7796). pp. 778–780: Bhīshma-svargārohaṇa (Bhīshma-mukti).

XIV. ĀÇVAMEDHIKAPARVAN.

XCIII. Āçvamedhika-parvan.

§ 778, XIV, **1**, 1–20 (1–19). pp. 1–2: * * *
2, 1–20 (20–40). pp. 2–4: * * *
3, 1–23 (41–63). pp. 4–5: Saṃvartta-Maruttīya.
4, 1–28 (64–91). pp. 5–7: id.
5, 1–28 (92–119). pp. 7–9: id.
6, 1–33 (120–152). pp. 9–11: id.
7, 1–27 (153–179). pp. 11–13: id.
8, 1–38 (180–218). pp. 14–15: id.
9, 1–37 (219–255). pp. 15–19: id.
10, 1–37 (256–292). pp. 19–23: id.
§ 779, XIV, **11**, 1–20 (293–313). pp. 24–25: Kṛshṇa-Dharma-saṃvāda.
12, 1–16 (314–330). pp. 25–26: id.
13, 1–22 (331–353). pp. 26–28: id.
§ 780, XIV, **14**, 1–17 (354–371). pp. 29–30: * * *
§ 781, XIV, **15**, 1–35 (372–406). pp. 30–32: * * *

XCIV. Anugītāparvan.

§ 782, XIV, **16**, 1–46 (407–453). pp. 32–37: * * *
17, 1–42 (454–496). pp. 37–41: * * *
18, 1–35 (497–531). pp. 41–44: * * *
19, 1–66 (532–598). pp. 45–52: * * *
20, 1–28 (599–627). pp. 52–55: Brāhmaṇagītā (Brahmagītāḥ).
21, 1–26 (628–654). pp. 55–59: id. [ḥ].
22, 1–29 (655–683). pp. 59–61: id. [id.]
23, 1–24 (684–710). pp. 61–63: id. [id.]
24, 1–17 (711–727). pp. 63–65: id. [id.]
25, 1–17 (728–745). pp. 65–67: id. [id.]
26, 1–18 (746–763). pp. 67–68: id. [id.]
27, 1–24 (764–787). pp. 68–70: id. [id.]
28, 1–28 (788–816). pp. 70–73: id. [id.]
29, 1–22 (817–838). pp. 73–75: id. [id.]
30, 1–33 (839–872). pp. 75–78: id. [id.]
31, 1–13 (873–886). pp. 78–79: id. [id.]
32, 1–26 (887–912). pp. 79–82: id. [id.]
33, 1–8 (913–921). pp. 82–83: id. [id.]
34, 1–12 (922–933). pp. 83–85: id. [id.]
35, 1–50 (934–986). pp. 85–89: Guru-çishya-saṃvāda.
36, 1–36 (987–1022). pp. 89–92: id.
37, 1–18 (1023–1041). p. 92: id.
38, 1–15 (1042–1057). pp. 92–94: id.
39, 1–25 (1058–1083). pp. 94–98: id.
40, 1–13 (1084–1096). pp. 98–99: id.
41, 1–5 (1097–1101). p. 99: id.
42, 1–67 (1102–1169). pp. 99–105: id.
43, 1–42 (1170–1211). pp. 105–109: id.
44, 1–22 (1212–1233). pp. 109–110: id.
45, 1–25 (1234–1258). pp. 111–113: id.
46, 1–58 (1259–1316). pp. 113–119: id.
47, 1–17 (1317–1333). pp. 119–120: id.
48, 1–13 (1334–1347). pp. 121–122: id.
49, 1–17 (1348–1365). pp. 122–123: id.
50, 1–56 (1366–1423). pp. 123–128: id.
51, 1–52 (1424–1477). pp. 128–133: id.
§ 783, XIV, **52**, 1–58 (1478–1535). pp. 133–138: Kṛshṇa-prayāṇa.

§ 784, XIV, **53,** 1–26 (1536–1562). pp. 138–140: Ut[t]aṅkopākhyāna [Kṛshṇottaṅka-samāgama].
54, 1–23 (1563–1585). pp. 140–142: Ut[t]° [Kṛshṇa-vākya].
55, 1–37 (1586–1624). pp. 142–145: Ut[t]aṅkopākhyāna.
56, 1–35 (1625–1660). pp. 145–148: id. [Kuṇḍalāharaṇa].
57, 1–28 (1661–1689). pp. 148–150: Ut[t]aṅkop°.
58, 1–60 (1690–1750). pp. 151–155: id.
§ 785, XIV, **59,** 1–21 (1751–1772). pp. 156–157: Kṛshṇasya Dvārakā-praveça.
60, 1–36 (1773–1808). pp. 157–160: Vāsudeva-vākya.
61, 1–42 (1809–1849). pp. 160–163: [Vāsudeva-sāntvana].
62, 1–21 (1850–1870). pp. 163–164: [id.].
63, 1–24 (1871–1894). pp. 164–166: [Dravyānayanopakrama].
64, 1–16 (1895–1912). pp. 166–168: [id.] [Suvarṇakoshasamprāpti].
65, 1–23 (1913–1935). pp. 168–170: [Dravyānayana] [id.].
66, 1–29 (1936–1964). pp. 170–172: Parikshij-janmakathana.
67, 1–19 (1965–1983). pp. 172–174: [id.] [Subhadrā-vākya].
68, 1–24 (1984–2008). pp. 174–175: [id.] [Uttarā-vākya].
69, 1–24 (2009–2032). pp. 176–177: Parikshit[aḥ Kṛshṇāt] saṃjīvana.
70, 1–21 (2033–2064). pp. 177–179: Pāṇḍavāgamana.
71, 1–26 (2065–2082). pp. 179–181: Vyāsāgamana (Kṛshṇa-Vyāsānujñā).
72, 1–26 (2083–2109). pp. 181–183: Açvarakshārtham Arjunaniyoga (Yajñasāmagrīsampādana).
73, 1–28 (2110–2140). pp. 183–185: Açvānusāra (°saraṇa).
74, 1–34 (2141–2174). pp. 185–188: id. (Trigarta-parābhava).
75, 1–20 (2175–2194). pp. 188–189: [Açvānusāre] Vajradattayuddha.
76, 1–26 (2195–2220). pp. 189–191: [id.] Vajradatta-parājaya.
77, 1–32 (2221–2252). pp. 191–194: [id.] [Saindhava-yuddha].
78, 1–49 (2253–2301). pp. 194–197: [id.] Saindhava-parājaya.
79, 1–39 (2302–2340). pp. 197–200: [id.] Arjuna-parābhava (°Babhruvāhana-yuddha).
80, 1–61 (2341–2401). pp. 200–204: Açvānusāre (°-saraṇe) Arjuna-pratyujjīvana.
81, 1–32 (2402–2434). pp. 205–207: Açvānusāra (°saraṇa).
82, 1–30 (2435–2465). pp. 207–209: Açv° (id.) Māgadha-parājaya.
83, 1–20 (2466–2485). pp. 209–211: id. (id.).
84, 1–24 (2486–2509). pp. 211–213: id. (id.) [Çakuniputra parājaya].
85, 1–42 (2510–2552). pp. 213–216: [Yudhishṭhira-] Açvamedha-[ārambha].
86, 1–21 (2553–2573). pp. 216–218: [id.] id. [id.]
87, 1–28 (2574–2602). pp. 218–220: Babhruvāhanāgamana (Arjuna-pratyāgamana).
88, 1–40 (2603–2643). pp. 220–223: Açvamedha (°-ārambha).
89, 1–44 (2644–2688). pp. 224–227: Açvamedhasamāpti.
§ 786, XIV, **90,** 1–120 (2689–2809). pp. 227–237: Nakulākhyāna.
91, 1–37 (2810–2845). pp. 238–240: [Hiṃsāmiçradharmanindā].
92, 1–53 (2846–2900). pp. 241–245: Nakulopākhyāna.

XV. ĀÇRAMAVĀSIKAPARVAN.

XCV. Āçramavāsaparvan.

§ 787, XV, **1,** 1–27 (1–28). pp. 1–3: * * *
2, 1–30 (29–59). pp. 3–5: * * *
3, 1–87 (60–147). pp. 5–12: [Dhṛtarāshṭranirveda].
4, 1–22 (148–169). pp. 12–13: [Vyāsānujñā].
5, 1–43 (170–213). pp. 13–17: [Dhṛtarāshṭropadeça].
6, 1–20 (214–234). pp. 17–20: [id.].
7, 1–23 (235–257). pp. 20–22: Dhṛtarāshṭropasaṃvāda.
8, 1–24 (258–282). pp. 23–24: Dhṛtarāshṭra-kṛta-vanagamana-prārthana.
9, 1–18 (283–301). pp. 25–26: Dhṛtarāshṭra-prārthana.
10, 1–53 (302–355). pp. 26–30: Prakṛti-sāntvana.
11, 1–25 (356–381). pp. 30–32: * * *
12, 1–13 (382–394). pp. 32–33: [Yudhishṭhirānumodana].
13, 1–15 (395–409). pp. 33–34: [Vidura-vākya].
14, 1–18 (410–427). pp. 34–36: [Dānayajña].
15, 1–13 (428–440). pp. 36–37: [Dhṛtarāshṭra-niryāṇa].
16, 1–32 (441–473). pp. 37–40: [Kuntī-vana-prasthāna].
17, 1–21 (474–494). pp. 40–42: [Kuntī-vākya].
18, 1–25 (495–519). pp. 42–44: * * *
19, 1–18 (520–537). pp. 44–45: [Çatayūpāçrama-nivāsa].
20, 1–38 (538–575). pp. 45–48: [Nārada-vākya].
§ 788, XV, **21,** 1–16 (576–591). pp. 48–49: * * *
22, 1–26 (592–617). pp. 49–51: [Yudhishṭhira-yātrā].
23, 1–18 (618–635). pp. 51–52: [Dhṛtarāshṭrāçrama-gamana].
24, 1–20 (636–655). pp. 52–53: [Yudhishṭhirādi-Dhṛtarāshṭra-samāgama].
25, 1–19 (656–674). pp. 54–56: [Ṛshīn prati Yudhishṭhirādi-kathana].
26, 1–38 (675–714). pp. 56–59: [Vidura-niryāṇa].
27, 1–26 (715–740). pp. 59–61: [Vyāsāgamana].
28, 1–25 (741–765). pp. 61–63: [Vyāsa-vākya].

XCVI. Putradarçanaparvan.

§ 789, XV, **29,** 1–52 (766–818). pp. 63–67: [Dhṛtarāshṭrādi-kṛta-prārthana].
30, 1–24 (819–842). pp. 67–69: [Vyāsa-Kuntī-saṃvāda].
31, 1–25 (843–867). pp. 69–71: Gaṅgā-tīra-gamana].
32, 1–21 (868–888). pp. 71–72: [Bhīshmādi-darçana].
33, 1–31 (889–919). pp. 72–75: Strīṇām [sva-sva-]pati-samāgama (°lokagamana).
§ 790, XV, **34,** 1–18 (920–938). pp. 75–77: [Janamejayaṃ prati Vaiçampāyana-vākya].
35, 1–18 (939–956). pp. 78–79: Janamejayasya [sva-] pitṛ-darçana.
§ 791, XV, **36,** 1–53 (957–1010). pp. 79–83: Yudhishṭhira-pratyāgama[na].

XCVII. Nāradāgamanaparvan.

§ 792, XV, **37,** 1–45 (1011–1056). pp. 83–86: Vanā (davā°) gninā Dhṛtarāshṭrādi-dāhaḥ.

38, 1–20 (1057–1077). pp. 87–88 : Yudhishṭhira-vilāpa.
39, 1–27 (1078–1105). pp. 88–90 : Çrāddhadāna.

XVI. MAUSALAPARVAN.

XCVIII. Mausalaparvan.

§ 793, XVI, **1**, 1–31 (1–32). pp. 1–3 : Musalotpatti.
2, 1–24 (33–56). pp. 3–5 : [Utpātadarçana].
3, 1–47 (57–104). pp. 5–9 : [Kṛtavarmādīnāṃ parasparahanana].
4, 1–28 (105–132). pp. 9–12 : [Çrī-Kṛshṇasya svalokagamana].
5, 1–15 (133–147). pp. 12–13 : [Arjunāgama].
6, 1–28 (148–176). pp. 13–15 : [Arjuna-Vasudeva-saṃvāda].
7, 1–76 (177–253). pp. 15–20 : [Vṛshṇi-kalatrādy-ānayana].
8, 1–38 (254–292). pp. 20–24 : [Vyāsārjuna-saṃvāda].

XVII. MAHĀPRASTHĀNIKAPARVAN.

XCIX. Mahāprasthānikaparvan.

§ 794, XVII, **1**, 1–46 (1–46). pp. 1–4 : * * *
2, 1–26 (47–72). pp. 4–6 : Draupady-ādi-patana.
3, 1–38 (73–109). pp. 6–10 : Yudhishṭhira-svargāroha.

XVIII. SVARGĀROHAṆAPARVAN.

C. Svargārohaṇaparvan.

§ 795, XVIII, **1**, 1–26 (1–26). pp. 1–3 : [Svarge Nārada-Yudhishṭhira-saṃvāda].
2, 1–54 (27–80). pp. 3–7 : Yudhishṭhira[sya] Naraka-darçana.
3, 1–44 (81–124). pp. 7–10 : Yudhishṭhira-tanu-tyāga.
4, 1–23 (125–147). pp. 10–12 : [Draupady-ādi-svasvasthāna-gamana].
5, 1–68 (148–211). pp. 12–18 : * * *
6, 1–105 (212–312). pp. 18–28 : * * *

INDEX TO THE NAMES

IN THE

MAHABHARATA.

A

Abala. § 492 (Āṅgirasa): III, **220**, 14166 (one of the 15 *yajñamusho devāḥ,* gods that rob the offering, created by *Agni Pāñcajanya* (?)).

Abbhakshāḥ (masc. pl.) (who live upon water). § 623 (Rājadh.): XII, **17**, 521 (a kind of ascetics).

Abhagnaparisaṅkhyāna (No. 3) (whose enumeration or right perception is not interrupted), the "great spirit." § 717*b* (Nārāyaṇīya): XII, **339**, 12864 (Mahāpurushastava).

Abhagnayoga (No. 4) (whose contemplation is not interrupted) = No. 3. XII, 12864.

Abhāsura (No. 5) (shining, see BR.) = No. 3. XII, 12864.

Ābhāsurāḥ, a class of gods. § 730 (Ānuçāsanik.): XIII, **18**, 1372.

Abhaya (one of Dhṛtarāshṭra's 100 sons). § 130 (Aṃçāvat.), I, **67**, 2739 (the 85th); § 182 (Dhṛtarāshṭraputranām.), I, **117**, 4551 (the 89th); § 599 (Jayadrathavadhap.), VII, **127**, 5178νν (attacks Bhīmasena); 5205ξξ (is slain by Bhīmasena).

Abhibhū, (*a*) king of Kāçi. § 599 (Jayadrathavadhap.): VII, **95**, 3528 ? (*Kāçyasyābhibhuvaḥ putraṃ*) (cf. VII, 976, where B. has *Kāçyasyābhibhuvaḥ putraṃ*, whilst C. has *Kāçyasyābhimukhaṃ putraṃ*). § 604 (Karṇap.): VIII, **6**, 173 (*Kāçirājaḥ*, killed by the son of Vasudāna); cf. Vibhu.—(*b*) = Kṛshṇa, XII, 1508.

Abhigamya = Çiva (1000 names [2]).

Abhijit, the 22nd of the 28 nakshatras, when beginning with Açvinī (star of junction Vega or *a* Lyræ, see Whitney to Sū° Si°, VIII, 9). § 502 (Manushyagrahak.): III, **230**, 14461 (*Abhijit spardhamānā tu Rohiṇyāḥ kanyasī svasā icchantī jyeshṭhatām devī tapas taptuṃ vanaṅ gatā*); XIII, 4265 (when one makes a çrāddha under Abhijit, he obtains the best knowledge).

Abhijita, (*a*) the eighth hour of the day. § 190 (Yudhishṭhira): I, **123**, 4764 (*muhūrte 'bhijite 'shṭame, divāmadhyagate sūrye*).—(*b*) a nakshatra (= Abhijit). § 746 (Ānuçāsanik.): XIII, **64**, 3278 (°*e yoge*; when one at that time offers milk with honey and ghee, he, observing religion, becomes honoured in Svargaloka).

Abhimanyor bhāryā = Uttarā.

Abhimanyu, son of Arjuna and Subhadrā, sister of Kṛshṇa (I, **2**, 401; **63**, 2449; **95**, 3830; **221**, 8026), is an incarnation of Varcas, son of Soma (I, **67**, 2748), wherefore he enters Soma after death, after his Karman has elapsed (XVIII, **5**, 165); (false) etymology of his name (I, **221**, 8027); he is the vaṃçakara of the Pāṇḍavas (I, **95**, 3834). In the beginning of the exile of the Pāṇḍavas he is carried to Dvārakā with his mother by Kṛshṇa (III, **22**, 895), where he is educated and protected by Raukmiṇeya (III, **183**, 12584 and 12586; cf. **235**, 14733). After the elapse of the exile he joins the Pāṇḍavas in Upaplavya with Kṛshṇa and Subhadrā (IV, **72**, 2358, cf. 2350), and is there married to Uttarā, daughter of king Virāṭa (I, **2**, 489; IV, **72**, 2355; V, 1). He fights bravely in the great battle, until he on the 13th day, when enjoined by Yudhishṭhira to break Droṇa's cakravyūha (VII, **35**, 1519), is surrounded and killed by Jayadratha and his people, leaving his wife Uttarā with a yet unborn son, Parikshit, the only one left to propagate the race of the Pāṇḍavas. At first he is not seen in Heaven by Yudhishṭhira (XVIII, **1**, 26), but later he is shown to him beside Soma in Heaven (XVIII, **4**, 146). § 4 (Anukram.): I, **1**, 189, 190.—§ 10 (Parvas.): I, **2**, 328 (°*or Vairāṭyā Vaivāhikaṃ parva*), 400, 489 (*Saubhadram*), 532–3.—§ 83*l* (Ādivaṃç.): I, **63**, 2449.—§ 130*g* (Aṃçāv.): I, **67**, 2748.—§ 159 (Pūruvaṃç.): I, **95**, 3830, 3834.—§ 253 (Haraṇāhar.): I, **221**, 8026, 8027.—§ 321 (Saubhavadhop.): III, **22**, 895.—§ 327 (Draupadīparit.): III, **33**, 1275.—§ 402 (Tīrthayātrāp.): III, **120**, 10279.—§ 452 (Mārkaṇḍeyasam.): III, **183**, 12570, 12584–6.—§ 511 (Draupadī-Satyabhāmā-saṃv.): III, **235**, 14733.—§ 553 (Vaivāhikap. 2): IV, **72**, 2344, 2350, 2355, 2358.—§ 554 (Sainyody.): V, **1**, 1, 5.—§ 561 (Yānasandhip.): V, **48**β, 1840; **50**η, 2010; **59**, 2326.—§ 562 (Bhagavadyānap.): V, **82**, 2893, 2908.—§ 569 (do.): V, **140**, 4747.—§ 570 (Sainyaniryāṇap.): V, **151**, 5144.—§ 571 (Ulukadūt.): V, **162**, 5592; **163**, 5677.—§ 572 (Rathātir.): V, **170**, 5880.—§ 573 (Ambop.): V, **104**, 7601.—(*a*) 1st day of the battle: V, **196**θ, 7629 (in the 1st detachment of Yudhishṭhira's army), 7635 (ι).—§ 578 (Bhīshmavadhap.): VI, 45^{3}, 1683 (fights Bṛhadbala); $47c^{26}$, 1814 (attacks Bhīshma; steeds of tawny hue were yoked to his car; his standard was adorned with pure gold and resembled a karṇikāra tree); $48\kappa^{36}$, 1963 (assists Çveta against Bhīshma), 1970.—(*b*) 2nd day of the battle: VI, **50**π, 2082 (placed in the wings of Dhṛshṭadyumna's krauñcavyūha).—§ 579 (do.): VI, **52***a*, 2150 (assists Arjuna against Bhīshma); 55^{17}, 2368 (fights Lakshmaṇa).—(*c*) 3rd day: § 580 (do.): VI, **56**θ, 2418 (is placed in the midst of Arjuna's ardhacandravyūha); 58^{4}, 2468 (fights the Gāndhāras), 2470 (receives Sātyaki in his chariot).—(*d*) 4th day: § 581 (do.): VI, **60**, 2673 (assists his father against Bhīshma); 62^{5}, 2728 (attacks Çalya), 2733, 2744; **63**ι, 2789 (assists Bhīmasena); 64^{13}, 2833, 2854 (assists Bhīmasena against Bhagadatta).—(*e*) 5th day:

§ 582 (do.): VI, **69**a^6, 3081 (assists Bhīmasena against Droṇa, Bhīshma, and Çalya); **73**$^{11-12}$, 3233 (fights Lakshmaṇa).—(*f*) 6th day: § 583 (do.): VI, **77**λ, 3394 (leads the Kaikeyāḥ, etc.), 3396, 3399, 3407 (receives Pārshata, i.e. Dhṛshṭadyumna, in his chariot); **78**^{11}, 3425 (is sent with eleven others to follow Bhīmasena), 3430, 3433 (fights Vikarṇa); **79**ν^{13}, 3470 (fights together with the Kaikeyas, etc.), 3471, 3474 (fights Vikarṇa).—(*g*) 7th day: § 584 (do.): VI, **84**, 3736 (fights Citrasena, Vikarṇa, and Durmarshaṇa), 3739.—(*h*) 8th day: § 585 (do.): VI, **87**θ, 3867 (is placed in Dhṛshṭadyumna's Çṛṅgāṭakavyūha); **89**ο, 3950; **94**, 4188 (assists Bhīmasena against Duryodhana at the head of the Pāṇḍavas), 4209; **95** (δδ, εε), 4254 (fights Bhagadatta), 4271, 4308; **96**, 4340 (is attacked by Ambashṭaka), 4360.—(*i*) 9th day: § 586 (do.): VI, **99**ζ, 4512; **100**η, 4530, 4539; **101**, 4591–2 (fights Alambusha), 4598, 4603, 4607.—(*j*) 10th day: § 587 (do.): VI, **109**ε, 5074; **110** (+ζ), 5107 (attacks Bhīshma, fights Sudakshiṇa); **111**, 5157; **112**θ, 5234 (defends Yudhishṭhira); [**115***d*, 5365: *karṇikāradhvajañ caiva siṃhaketum* — B.: °*tur* — *arindama* | *pratyujjagāma Saubhadraṃ rājaputro Bṛhadbalaḥ*]; **116**, 5378 (fights Duryodhana); **118**υ–φ, 5560 (attacks Bhīshma); **119**ω, 5588 (defends Arjuna with six others).—(*k*) 11th day: § 589 (Droṇābhishek.): VII, **10**κ, 354.—§ 590 (do.): VII, **14**, 545 (fights Paurava, i.e. Lakshmaṇa).—(*l*) 12th day: § 592 (Saṃçaptakavadhap.): VII, **23**ο–π, 983 (his horses are reddish, *piçaṅgāḥ*), 1036 (his standard is *Çārṅgapakshī hiraṇmayaḥ*, "a golden çārṅga fowl").—(*m*) 13th day: § 593 (Abhimanyuvadhap.): VII, **33**, 1471 (is said to have broken Droṇa's Cakravyūha); **34***a*, 1489, 1492; **35** (δ), 1519 (is charged with piercing the array of Droṇa), 1522, 1524; **36**, 1539, 1542, 1549; **37**, 1587, 1588–9, 1604, 1607, 1611; **39**, 1649, 1655, 1673–4; **40**, 1677, 1699, 1701, 1703, 1706; **41**[–**43**], 1715, 1717, 1720, 1722, 1739–40; **44**, 1788, 1790, 1800; **45**[–**46**] (uses the *Gāndharva* weapon), 1804, 1806, 1814; **47**, 1863; **48**, 1909, 1925–6; **49**, 1930, 1959 (slain by Duḥçāsana's son); **50**, 1981; **51**, 1984.—§ 594 (do.): VII, **54**, 2130 (he has disappeared in the lunar essence).—§ 595 (do.): VII, **71**, 2462, 2467 (has attained to that eternal goal which is attained by yogins).—§ 596 (Pratijñāp.): VII, **72**, 2496, 2533, 2546, 2553, 2557–8; **74**, 2616; **75**, 2655; **78**, 2745.—§ 598 (Jayadrathavadhap.): VII, **85**, 3010, 3059.—§ 599 (do.): VII, **143**θθθ, 5994.—§ 600 (Ghaṭotkacavadhap.): VII, **183**, 8334.—§ 602 (Droṇavadhap.): VII, **191**, 8798.—§ 604 (Karṇap.): VIII, **5**, 114; **6**, 159.—§ 608 (do.) ***aa***: VIII, **50**, 2406; **73**, 3658 (has killed Jayatsena), 3710; **74**, 3789; **91**, 4758.—§ 610 (Çalyap.): IX, **5**, 251, 260.—§ 613 (Gadāyuddhap.): IX, **32**δ, 1871–2, 1874.—§ 615 (do.): IX, **61**, 3434.—§ 618 (Jalapradān.): XI, **12**, 321.—§ 619 (Strīvilāp.): XI, **16***a*, 447, 454; **20**, 570, 601.—§ 620 (Çrāddhap.): XI, **26**β, 787; **27**, 821.—§ 630 (Rājadh.): XII, **27**β, 799, 818.—§ 637 (do.): XII, **42**γ, 1489.—§ 785 (Anugītāp.): XIV, **61**δ, 1810, 1837; **62**, 1855, 1857 (°*vinākṛtāḥ*); **66**, 1956–7; **67**, 1970–2, 1978; **68**, 1996, 2007; **69**, 2028 ("Abhimanyu's son," i.e. Parikshit); **72**, 2101 ("the father of A.," i.e. Arjuna); **78**, 2288 (A°'s son Parikshit).—§ 788 (Āçramavāsap.): XV, **21***a*, 587; **25**γ, 670 (°*or bhāryā*, i.e. Uttarā).—§ 795 (Svargārohaṇap.): XVIII, **1**δ, 26; **4**κ, 143 (Saubhadraṃ); **5**μ, 165 (being Soma's son Varcas, he entered Soma).—Cf. Ārjuni, Saubhadra, Kārshṇi, Arjunātmaja, Arjunāvara, Phālguni, Çakrātmajātmaja.

***Abhimanyuja** (= Parikshit): I, **40**, 1673, 1696. XIV, **67**, 1976, 1979; **69**, 2030; **70**, 2043.

***Abhimanyujananī** (= Subhadrā): VIII, **87**, 4448.

Abhimanyuvadha(ḥ) ("the slaughter of Abhimanyu"). § 10 (Parvas.): I, **2** (339: °*aḥ parva*) = Abhimanyuvadhaparvan.

[**Abhimanyuvadhaparvan**(va)] ("the section including the slaughter of Abhimanyu," the 73rd of the minor parvans of Mhbhr.; cf. Abhimanyuvadha). § 593: **The 13th day:** Broken by *Arjuna*, and *Droṇa* having failed to seize *Yudhishṭhira*, the *Kurus* were regarded as defeated; they heard all praising *Arjuna* and *Kṛshṇa*. Next morning *Duryodhana* blamed *Droṇa* for not having seized *Yudhishṭhira*; *Droṇa* said that even D., As., G., Y., N., and Rā. cannot defeat the force protected by *Arjuna* and *Kṛshṇa*, save *Mahādeva*; but to-day he would slay a mighty car-warrior. The *Saṃçaptakas* challenged *Arjuna* and took him away to the southern side of the field. *Abhimanyu's* slaughter by *Duḥçāsana's* son is alluded to by *Sañjaya*. *Dhṛtarāshṭra* grieves. *Sañjaya* relates (VII, **33**). *Sañjaya* praises *Yudhishṭhira*, etc. (***a***). *Droṇa* had formed the great circular array (*cakravyūha*): *Lakshmaṇa* (the grandson of *Dhṛtarāshṭra*) at their head; *Duryodhana*, etc. (β) in the middle; at the head the commander *Droṇa*, etc. (γ) (VII, **34**). The *Pāṇḍavas* were headed by *Bhīmasena*: *Sātyaki*, etc. (δ) & *Droṇa*, whom the *Pāñcālas* and the *Sṛñjayas* could not approach. *Yudhishṭhira* says that only *Abhimanyu*, etc. (ε), can break the array of *Droṇa*, and orders *Abhimanyu* to do it; *Bhīma*, etc. (ζ) followed him; praised by *Yudhishṭhira*, who says that the protectors of *Droṇa's* host resemble S., R., M., V. or *Agni*, or *Āditya*, *Abhimanyu* orders his charioteer *Sumitra* to urge the steeds towards *Droṇa's* army (VII, **35**). *Abhimanyu* (with *Sumitra*), etc., & *Droṇa*, etc.; *Abhimanyu* breaks that part of the *Kuru* army; many steeds of the *Vanāyu*, etc. (η), breeds were deprived of their ornaments, and caused delight to Rā., etc. (VII, **36**). *Duryodhana* & *Abhimanyu*; *Droṇa*, etc. (θ) & *Abhimanyu* rescuing *Duryodhana*; *Duḥsaha* etc. (ι), & *Abhimanyu*, who slew the heir of *Açmaka* *Karṇa*, etc. (κ), & *Abhimanyu*, who slew *Susheṇa*, etc. (λ), and defeated *Çalya*; *Droṇa's* troops fled; P., D., Cā., Si., etc., glorify *Abhimanyu* (VII, **37**). *Abhimanyu* slays *Çalya's* younger brother, whose followers fled. *Abhimanyu*, with the weapons he has received from *Kṛshṇa* and *Arjuna*, defeats all the warriors that encounter him. *Droṇa's* army fled (VII, **38**). *Abhimanyu* & *Droṇa*, etc. (μ). *Droṇa* says that *Abhimanyu* delights *Yudhishṭhira*, etc. (ν). *Duryodhana* told *Karṇa*, etc. (ξ), to crush *Abhimanyu*, whom they attacked; *Duḥçāsana* & *Abhimanyu* (VII, **39**); *Abhimanyu* addresses *Duḥçāsana* (mentioning the dice, etc.); *Duḥçāsana* is borne away by his charioteer; the *Pāṇḍavas* etc. (ο), uttered leonine shouts, and attacked *Droṇa's* array. *Karṇa* (urged by *Duryodhana*) & *Abhimanyu* (desirous of proceeding towards *Droṇa*); when *Karṇa* is in great distress his younger brother encounters *Abhimanyu* (VII, **40**). *Abhimanyu* slays *Karṇa's* younger brother; *Karṇa* flies; the *Kaurava* array breaks, except the *Sindhu*-king (VII, **41**). *Yudhishṭhira*, etc. (π), endeavour to follow *Abhimanyu*. *Jayadratha* checks them with celestial weapons. *Dhṛtarāshṭra* enquires of *Sañjaya* about the source of *Jayadratha's* energy; *Sañjaya* narrates the boon obtained by *Jayadratha* from *Çiva* (VII, **42**). *Jayadratha* vanquishes all the *Pāṇḍava* leaders with his steeds of the *Sindhu*-breed: *Sātyaki*, etc. (ρ); *Bhīma* mounts the car of *Sātyaki*; the path made by *Abhimanyu* is closed up, notwithstanding the *Matsyas*, etc. (σ); they are all checked by *Jayadratha* (VII, **43**). *Abhimanyu* vanquished *Vṛshasena*, who was borne away from the battle, and slew *Vasātiya* and many others (VII, **44**). *Abhimanyu* seized *Satyaçravas* and routed the *Kurus*; *Rukmaratha* (the son of *Çalya*) & *Abhimanyu*, who slew him and his friends (100 princes) with the *Gāndharva*-weapon (*b*), though they were assisted by *Duryodhana*, who was filled with fear and fled (VII, **45**). *Droṇa*, etc. (τ), & *Abhimanyu*, who beats them back except *Lakshmaṇa* (who is followed by *Duryodhana*), who is slain. *Duryodhana* urged the troops to slay *Abhimanyu*; *Droṇa*, etc. (υ), encompassed *Abhimanyu*, who seeks *Jayadratha*; *Krātha's* son was slain, the others fled (VII, **46**). *Droṇa*, etc. (φ), & *Abhimanyu* + *Yudhishṭhira* supporting *Jayadratha*; *Karṇa* has one ear cut off; *Abhimanyu* slew *Vṛndāraka* and *Bṛhadbala* (VII, **47**); *Abhimanyu* once more pierced *Karṇa* in the ear, and slew the son of the *Magadha*-king, and *Açvaketu*, and the *Bhoja* prince of *Mārttikāvata* (bearing the device of an elephant); the son of *Duḥçāsana* & *Abhimanyu*; *Açvatthāman* & do.; *Abhimanyu* & *Çalya*, who mounts another car; *Abhimanyu* slew *Çatruñjaya*, etc. (χ); *Abhimanyu* & *Çakuni*, who tells *Duryodhana* to take counsel with *Droṇa* and *Kṛpa*, etc., about the means of slaying *Abhimanyu*; *Karṇa* asks *Droṇa* about the means of slaying *Abhimanyu*; *Droṇa*, saying that he is gratified by *Abhimanyu's* prowess, tells *Karṇa*, who is very afflicted with arrows, to cut off his bow, etc. *Karṇa* then cut off *Abhimanyu's* bow, *Kṛtavarman* slew his steeds, and *Kṛpa* slew his two *Pārshṇi* charioteers; *Abhimanyu*, then attacked by six car-warriors, fights with the sword, which is cut off by *Droṇa*, while *Karṇa* cut off his shield (VII, **48**); then *Abhimanyu* fought with a wheel; then with a mace; *Abhimanyu* & *Açvatthāman*; *Abhimanyu* slew (? *apothayat*) *Subala's* son *Kālikeya*, and slew 77 *Gāndhāra* followers of his, and 10 *Brahma-Vasātīyas* (*punar Brahma-Vasātīyān*, C.; B. has *punaç caiva Vasātīyān*), 7 *Kaikayas* (*Kaikayānām*, C.; B. has *Kekayānām*), and 10 elephants; *Abhimanyu* & *Duḥçāsana's* son, who slays *Abhimanyu*. Invisible creatures censure the cowardly act of the *Kurus* headed by *Droṇa* and *Karṇa*. The *Pāṇḍava* divisions fly, but are rallied by *Yudhishṭhira* (VII, **49**). In the evening the *Kurus* withdrew to their encampment. Rā. and Pç., etc., on the field of battle (VII, **50**). *Yudhishṭhira* laments on the fall of *Abhimanyu* (VII, **51**).—§ 594. *Vyāsa* comes and consoles him ("death takes all: D., Dā., G., without exception"), relating to him the ancient story of what *Nārada* had said in days of old to *Akampana* (q.v.). "This story is purifying, etc.; cast off thy grief; *Abhimanyu* has attained to heaven; sprung from *Soma*, he has disappeared in the lunar essence, cleansed from all his impurities" (VII, **54**).—§ 595: *Vyāsa* recites to *Yudhishṭhira* the story of *Sṛñjaya* (q.v.), to whom *Nārada* told *Shoḍaçarājika* (VII, **55**–**70**). *Vyāsa* says that *Abhimanyu* has attained to that eternal goal which is attained by *Yogins*, and those that are living in heaven never prefer this world to heaven; "it is the living that stand in need of our grief, and not those who have attained to heaven; his sins increase for whom the living grieve." Then *Vyāsa* disappeared, and *Yudhishṭhira* became free from grief; but—"what shall we say to *Arjuna*?" (VII, **71**).

Ābhīra, a people in the west of India upon the Indus (II, **32**, 1192: *Çūdrā°*) (Digvijayap.); are conquered by Nakula at his Digvijaya (ib.); bring tribute to Yudhishṭhira (II, **51**, 1832) (Dyūtap.). Mārkaṇḍeya prophesies that in the Kali-yuga there shall be many Ābhīra and other barbarous kings (III, **188**, 12840) (Mārkaṇḍeyas.). The Ābhīras are mentioned by Sañjaya in the enumeration of the people of Bhāratavarsha, VI, **9**, 354, 375 (*Çūdrā°*) (Jambūkh.) (cf. Wilson, Vishṇu-purāṇa, ed. by Fitzedward Hall, vol. ii, 133 f., 167 f., 184 f.). They are placed in the eyes of Droṇa's Suparṇavyūha on the twelfth day of the battle, VII, **20**, 798 (*çūdrā°*) (Saṃçaptakavadhap.). From hatred towards them the Sarasvatī disappeared at Vinaçana, IX, **37**, 2119 (*çūdrā°*) (Baladevat.). They have become çūdras, having omitted their duties of kshattriyas from fear of Paraçurāma, XIV, **29**γ, 832 (*Draviḍā°*) (v. Arjuna Kārtavīrya). When Arjuna, after the catastrophe at Dvārakā, is conducting the wives, children, and the old men from thence to Indraprastha, the Ābhīras attack him when he has arrived at Pañcanada, and rob most of the women, XVI, **7**, 223; **8**, 270 (*Pañcajanālayaiḥ*; probably an error for *Pañcanadālayaiḥ*, B.) (Mausalap.).

Abhirāma = Çiva (1000 names[2]).

Abhirāmā, v. Pūrvābhirāmā.

Abhīru, a king (*rājarshisattamaḥ*), who was an incarnation of the sixth of the eight Asuras of the family of the Kāleyāḥ: I, **67**, 2689 (Aṃçāvat., § 130).

Abhisāra, a people (cf. VP., II, 174–5; "bordering on Kashmir, to the south and west") (=Abhī°). Together with other barbarous tribes they fight Arjuna on the 14th day of the great battle, VII, **93**δ, 3380 (printed *Dārvātisāra* . . .) (Jayadrathavadhap.). They are mentioned by Kṛshṇa among the auxiliaries of Duryodhana, VIII, **73**, 3652 (Dārvā°) (Karṇap.), on the 17th day of the battle.

Abhīsāra (=the preced.), enumerated by Sañjaya among the people of Bhāratavarsha: VI, 9, 361 (Ja°kha°).

Abhisārī, a town conquered by Arjuna (q.v.) on his Digvijaya: II, **27**, 1027 (cf. VP., II, 174 f.; ZKdM., II, 45).

Abhishāha, a people (=°bhī°); with other barbarous tribes they attack Arjuna at the instigation of Duḥçāsana on the 10th day of the great battle, VI, **117**ρ, 5485 (B. has *Abhī°*) (Bhīshmav.).

Abhīshāha, a people (=the preced.): (*a*) first day of the battle: VI, **18**δ, 688 (follow the sons of Dhṛtarāshṭra when going to battle) (Bhagavadgītāp.).—(*b*) 9th day; VI, **106**τ, 4809 (defend Bhīshma; otherwise PCR.) (Bhīshmav.).—(*c*) 10th day: VI, **119**αα, 5648 (defend in vain Bhīshma, when he is slain by Arjuna) (Bhīshmav.).—(*d*) 14th day: VII, **91**β, 3254 (attempt to prevent Arjuna from killing Jayadratha) (Jayadrathavadhap.); **93**γ, 3339 (they angrily attack Arjuna, after he has slain Çrutāyudha and Sudakshiṇa) (do.); **150**β[1], 6526 (Duryodhana complains that they have been slain in defending Jayadratha, etc.) (do.); **157**ρ, 6949 (are slain by Yudhishṭhira) (Ghaṭotkacavadhap.); **161**εε, 7207 (are slain by Bhīma) (do.).—After the 15th day: VIII, **5**, 127 (Sañjaya relates to Dhṛtarāshṭra that they have been slain) (Karṇap.).

Ābhishecanika(m) parva: **2**, 350 (*Dharmarājasya dhīmataḥ*), i.e. XII, **40** (Yudhishṭhirābhishekaḥ) (Parvas.).

Abhishyanta, the second of the five sons of Kuru and Vāhinī: I, **94**, 3740 (Pūruvaṃç., § 154).

Abhivādya = Çiva (1000 names).

Acala[1], brother-in-law of Dhṛtārashṭra, brother of Çakuni: II, **34**, 1266 (*A °Vṛshakaç caiva Karṇaç ca* . . .; attends at Yudhishṭhira's rājasūya (Rājasūyikap.).—V, **168**, 5808 (*A °Vṛshakaç caiva sahitau bhrātarāv ubhau* . . . *Gāndhāramukhyau*; a "ratha" of Duryodhana's) (Rathātir.).—VII,

30, 1303 (*Vṛshakācalau*), 1309 (id.), 1310 (id.); *çyālau tava*, i.e. Dhṛtarāshṭra's), 1312 (*Vṛshakā°au*) (slain by Arjuna on the 12th day of the battle) (Saṃçaptakavadhap.).—VIII, **5**, 130 (id.) (Karṇap.).—XI, **26**, 790 (burnt with the others who have fallen in the battle) (Çrāddhap.).—XV, **32**, 879 (together with the others who have fallen in the battle he is conjured by Vyāsa from the Gaṅgā and shown to Dhṛtarāshṭra and Gāndhārī, when towards the close of their lives they visit his hermitage) (Putradarçanap.).

Acala[2], a warrior of Skanda's: IX, **45**, 2576 (Gadāyuddhap.).

Acala[3] = "the Great Spirit": XII, **339**, 12864 (Mahāpurushastava).

Acala[4] = Vishṇu (1000 names).

Acalā, a mātṛ: IX, **46***θ*, 2632 (Skanda).

Acalendra (= Skanda): III, **232**, 14643 (Kārttikeyastava).

Acalopama = Çiva (1000 names).

Ācārya[1] ("the Teacher") = Droṇa: I, 199, 529, 5331, 5413. —III, 1111, 1923.—IV, 913, 986, 1491, 1493, 1496, 1588, 1598, 1628, 1744, 1837 (°*çishyau*, i.e. Droṇa and Arjuna), 2117 (°Çāradvatayoḥ), 2234.—V, 2089, 4236, 4898–9, 5784, 5873, 7562.—VI, 831–2, 1578–9, 1591, 1601, 1992, 2092, 2500, 3073, 3411, 3927, 4113, 4128, 4193, 4644.—VII, 154, 257, 288, 438, 448, 472–3, 716, 858, 878, 1494, 1541, 1661, 1911, 1916, 2566, 2636, 2672, 3223, 3231, 3435, 3482, 3618, 3656, 4262, 4273, 4732, 5022, 5085, 5186–7, 5335, 5860, 5877, 6505, 6583, 6588, 6641, 7128, 7340, 7581, 7621, 8309, 8616, 8618, 8762, 8799, 8836, 8838, 8861, 8869, 8874, 8935, 8958, 8966, 8978, 8991, 9038, 9065, 9071, 9124, 9199, 9224, 9320.—VIII, 1044?, 3693.—IX, 3419.— X, 522, 610, 612.—XII, 812.

Ācārya[2] = Kṛpa: VII, 6320.—IX, 571 (*Gautama*), 3664.

Ācārya[3] = Paraçurāma: XI, 613.

Ācāryamukhya = Droṇa: VII, 8780, 8800.

Ācāryanandana = Açvatthāman: VII, 9406.

Ācāryaputra = Açvatthāman: I, 5228–9, 5708.—IV, 1587, 1594, 1896, 2235.—VI, 675.—VII, 1370, 7169, 9069, 9287, 9398.—VIII, 355, 632, 801, 3361.—X, 338, 674.

Ācāryasattama[1] = Kṛpa: I, 5324.

Ācāryasattama[2] = Açvatthāman: VIII, 790 (*Drauṇiḥ*).

Ācāryasuta = Açvatthāman: VII, 7170.—VIII, 658.— IX, 573.

Ācāryatanaya = Açvatthāman: VII, 9403.—VIII, 361.

Ācāryau = Droṇa and Kṛpa: IV, 1472.

Acintya[1] = Çiva (1000 names[2]).

Acintya[2] = Vishṇu: XII, 13488.—XIII, 7038 (1000 names).

Acyuta ("unfallen"): (*a*) a proper name of (*α*) Kṛshṇa: I, 8476 (°*Ārjunau*); II, 949; V, 4649; VII, 2982 (*Yuyudhānā °Arjunāḥ*), 6502, 7754; VIII, 1245 (°*Ārjunau*); XII, 1810 (°*Yudhishṭhirau*), 13240 (etymology); XIII, 6867, etc.— (*β*) Vishṇu identified with Kṛshṇa (cf. Keçava, e.g. III, 11257); III, 11247; XIII, 6960 (VDSNK), 6984 (ib.), 7008 (ib.).—(*γ*) cf. °ānuja.—(*b*) an adjective (where the person designed is otherwise clearly indicated in the context; especially often in the vocative case), applied to a great many persons (Kṛshṇa, Vishṇu, Balarāma, Arjuna, Bhīmasena, Yudhishṭhira, Duryodhana, Droṇa, Açvatthāman, Bhīshma, Janamejaya, king Parikshit of Ayodhyā (III, 13169), Āpava (XII, 1757), Çiva (X, 305: *Rudraṃ*), Skanda (IX, 2480: *kumārabaram acyutaṃ*), the Highest (XII, 11201: *brahmaṇyaṃ paramaṃ devam anantaṃ param a°*; 13612: *devaṃ paramakaṃ brahma çvetaṃ candrābham a°*)).

Acyutānuja = Bhīmasena: IV, 236.

Acyutāyus, a warrior always named together with Çrutāyus: they attack (VII, **93**, 3344) and wound (VII, 3350) Arjuna, but are slain by him (VII, 3362); their sons (Niyatāyus and Dīrghāyus) will avenge them, but are likewise slain by Arjuna (VII, 3364); VII, **94**, 3438 (Jayadrathavadhap.); VIII, **72***υυυ*, 3613 (Karṇap.); IX, **2**, 75, 91 (Çalyap.).

Açanin = Çiva (1000 names[2]).

Āçāvaha[1]: I, **3**, 42 (Anukram.): according to the explanation of Nīlakaṇṭha, either a synonym of Vāyu (the wind), the tenth of the twelve sons (i.e. "representations," Nīl.) of Heaven (Dyaus) (= Māyā, Nīl.) and Vivasvat (i.e. Brahman, Nīl.), viz., the geniuses of the ten senses and Mind (*manas*) together with Mahya (B. *Sahya*, i.e. Manu, Nīl.), who are all manifestations of the one "Son of Heaven" (*divaḥ putro*),—or (more probably) a Vivasvat or form of the Sun ("*Vivasvataḥ*" being then an irregular nom. plur.; but B. has *putrā* instead of *purā*).

Āçāvaha[2], I, **186**, 6999 (Svayamvarap., § 232): a prince (enumerated among the Vṛshṇis), who has presented himself at the "self-choice" (*svayaṃvara*) of Kṛshṇā.

Açiva, III, **221**, 14177 (Mārkaṇḍeyas.): a form of Agni in the enumeration of Mārkaṇḍeya (*agnir yaç cāçivo nāma çaktipūjāparaç ca saḥ duḥkhārttānāñ ca sarveshāṃ çivakṛt satataṃ çivaḥ*; B. reads more probably: *agnir yaç ca Çivo . .*).

Açleshā (No. 43; cf. No. 44), a nakshatra (the ninth when beginning with Açvinī; its star of junction is supposed to be ε Hydræ; v. Sū° Si°, p. 188). XIII, **64**, 3262 (C. has A°, B. Ā°) (Ānuçāsanik.) (°*yān tu yo rūpyam ṛshabhaṃ vā prayacchati sa sarvabhayanirmuktaḥ sambhavān adhitishṭhati*; "nakshatrayogasya dānakalpam," **63**, 3212); **89**, 4259 (who gives a çrāddha "*āçleshāyām*" procreates intelligent sons) (çrāddhakalpe); **132**, 6162 (Ānuçāsanik.) (C.: *kārttike māsi cāçleshā bahulaç cāshṭamī çivā*. B. has *bahulasyāshṭamī*): on the 8th day of the dark half of the month Kārttika, when the moon is in conjunction with Açleshā, a brahman, kshattriya, vaiçya, or çūdra may, after having fasted at a çrāddha, after the setting of the sun, deposit an offering of black clothes and unguents with flowers in an ant-hill, begging the serpents to hand it over to the world-elephants to increase their strength that it may be equal to the strength of Vishṇu, when he lifted up Earth; the formula is contained in vv. 7163–6; this he should do for a whole year.

Açleshāḥ (plur.) = No. 43: XIII, **110**, 5392 (Ānuçāsanik.) (description of a *cāndra vrata* or religious performance with reference to the moon in the month Mārgaçīrsha, when the moon is in conjunction with the asterism Mūla; the explanation of Nīlakaṇṭha runs thus:—Here is described a *cāndra vrata* to obtain a desired object; on the 1st day of the bright half of Mārgaçīrsha, when there is conjunction (of the moon) with the nakshatra Mūla, one should begin this *cāndra vrata*; it consists in locating the nakshatras in the limbs of the moon, Mūla in his feet, etc., i.e., one should think of Mūla together with its deity as being the feet of the moon; in like manner Rohiṇī, etc., with their deities are to be thought of as being his legs, etc.; everywhere the exchanging of the case-endings is a Vedic liberty; Āshāḍhā, Phālgunī, and Bhādrapadā represent each 2 nakshatras. The *vrata* is performed as follows: after one has had pronounced the wish of a lucky day, etc. (*puṇyāhavācanādipūrvakaṃ*), having taken upon one's self a religious exercise to obtain a desired object, one should fancy the moon and one's self to be one and the same, distribute the nakshatras together with their respective deities in the limbs of the moon, and day after day propitiate them by the muttering of Veda verses and oblations, etc. (*japahomādinā*), with the Veda verses required for each of them (*tattanmantraiḥ*); thus one should go on until the day of the full moon, and when the *vrata* is at an end, one should present the butter (*ghṛta*) left from the oblations to the teacher (*ācārya*); by the words "*samāpte tu ghṛtaṃ dadyāt*" it is indicated that ghṛta is the substance of the oblation. Thus doing even a cripple becomes well-shaped (*sakalāngo*) at the day of the full moon; this is expressed and exemplified by the sentence beginning with "*paripūrṇānga*." Açleshāḥ (C. Ă°, B. Ā°) is to be identified with the nails). (The chapter is in C. called Angavidhi, in B. Dānadharma.)

Açma: XII, **58**γ, 2116 (Rājadh.): praises Bhīshma on his arrow-couch.

Açmaka[1], a rājarshi, son of Vaçishṭha and Madayantī, the wife of Kalmāshapāda: I, **122**, 4737 (Madayantī); **177**, 6791 (Vāsishṭha) (founded Paudanya).

Açmaka[2], a brahman present at the deathbed of Bhīshma: XII, **47**, 1592 (Rājadh.) (°*Sumantunā*).

Açmaka[3] (No. 46), a king of the Açmakāḥ: VII, **37**, 1606 (Abhimanyuvadhap.) (°*sya suto* = No. 48 and No. 49, killed by Abhimanyu; this half-çloka is omitted in B.).

Açmakadāyāda (No. 48): VII, **37**, 1605 (Abhimanyu-vadhap.) (= No. 46, °*sya suto*; the reading of B differs somewhat from that of C.).

Açmakāḥ (No. 47), a people: VII, **85**, 3049 (Jayadratha-vadhap.) (in the army of the Pāṇḍavas); VIII, **8**, 237 (Karṇap.) (conquered and made tributary by Karṇa); cf. No. 49 (the passages seem to contradict one another; cf. Açvakāḥ and VP. II, 164; perhaps dwelling near Avanti or Oojein, LIA. I, 708/857).

Açmakeçvara (No. 49): VII, 1608 (= No. 48).

Açmakī, a Yādavī, the wife of king Prācinvat and mother of Saṃyāti: I, **95** (§ 156), 3766 (Pūruvaṃç.).

Açman, a brahman consulted by Janaka Vaideha: XII, **28**, 834 (Rājadh.) (°*gītam itihāsaṃ purātanam*), 835 (*brāhmaṇam*), (837), 891.

Açmapṛshṭha, a holy stone in Gayā (Nīl. "*Pretaçilā*," the stone of the dead), a visit to which expiates the murder of a brahman: XIII, **25**s, 1728 (Angirasas tīrthayātrāyām, v. Anuçāsanik.). "Pret Silā exists at the present day. It is *not* a stone, but a rocky hill some 300 or 400 feet high." (Grierson.)

Açoka[1], a king: I, **67** (§ 130), 2650 (Aṃçāvat.) (an incarnation of the Asura Açva); XII, **4**, 114 (Rājadh.) (present at the self-choice of king Citrāngada's daughter in Çrīmadrājapura, where Duryodhana carries off the bride).

Açoka[2] = Vishṇu (1000 names).

Açokatīrtha, a tīrtha or holy place in the south: III, **88**, 8338 (Dhaumyatīrthak.) (*bahulāçramam*).

Açrama = Vishṇu (1000 names).

Āçramanivāsa ("the dwelling in the hermitage"). § 795 (Svargārohaṇap.): XVIII, **6**, 278 (°*e havishyaṃ bhojayed dvijān*), i.e. Āçramavāsikaparvan.

Āçramapūjita = Çiva (1000 names[2]).

Āçramastha = Çiva (1000 names[2]).

Āçramasthāna ("the dwelling in the hermitage"). § 4 (Anukram.): I, **1**, 91 (°*saṃçrayaḥ . . . Bhāratadrumaḥ*), i.e. Āçramavāsikaparvan.

Āçramavāsa[1] ("the dwelling in the hermitage") = Āçrama-vāsaparvan. § 10 (Parvas.): I, **2**, 355 (°*ākhyaṃ parva*).

Āçramavāsa[2] (do.) = Āçramavāsikaparvan. § 11 (Parvas.): I, **2**, 611 (°*ākhyaṃ parva*), 617 (do.).

[Āçramavāsaparvan] ("the section relating to the dwelling in the hermitage"), the 95th of the minor parvans of Mhbhr. (cf. Āçramavāsa). § 787: Asked by Janamejaya how the Pāṇḍavas, having acquired their kingdom, conducted themselves towards *Dhṛtarāshṭra*, how Dhṛtarāshṭra and *Gāndhārī* behaved, and for how many years his grandfather ruled the kingdom, Vaiçampāyana said: The Pāṇḍavas ruled, placing Dhṛtarāshṭra at their head; *Vidura*, *Sañjaya*, and *Yuyutsu* used to wait upon Dhṛtarāshṭra; for 15 years they did all things under the advice of the old king; *Kuntī* obeyed Gāndhārī; *Draupadī* and *Subhadrā*, etc., showed the utmost respect for the old king and his queen; the Pāṇḍavas surrounded the old king and his queen with every luxury, and Maireya wines, etc. *Kṛpa* waited upon Dhṛtarāshṭra; *Vyāsa* frequently visited him and recited histories of old Ṛ., celestial ascetics, P., and Rā.; Vidura, under the orders of Dhṛtarāshṭra, superintended religion and law; through his policy the Pāṇḍavas obtained numerous services from their feudatories and followers; Dhṛtarāshṭra liberated prisoners and pardoned those condemned to death; the old king, on his pleasure excursions, was supplied with everything by Yudhishṭhira; the kings who came to Hāstinapura waited upon Dhṛtarāshṭra as before; Kuntī, etc. (*a*), served Gāndhārī like maidservants; *Bhīmasena* alone did not forget his grievances (XV, **1**); Dhṛtarāshṭra was honoured by Ṛ., and used to make gifts to the brahmans in rites for P. and *çrāddhas* for his sons, etc.; Dhṛtarāshṭra also felt great affection for the Pāṇḍavas, and so did Gāndhārī; Gāndhārī performed çrāddhas with gifts; grieved at the remembrance of Duryodhana, Dhṛtarāshṭra every morning blessed the Pāṇḍavas, wishing them victory in battle, etc. Yudhishṭhira became very much liked by all the four castes, and forgot the wrongs inflicted upon him by Dhṛtarāshṭra's sons; from fear of Yudhishṭhira nobody dared to speak evil of Duryodhana or Dhṛtarāshṭra. Bhīma, however, reverenced the old king outwardly, with a very unwilling heart (XV, **2**). While there was no variance in the cordiality between Yudhishṭhira and Dhṛtarāshṭra, the latter could not but feel unfriendly towards Bhīma, and Bhīma, recollecting his foes Duryodhana, Karṇa, and Duḥçāsana, indulged in boastful language about Duryodhana and his brothers whom he had slain. Gāndhārī was not moved. After 15 years Dhṛtarāshṭra, afflicted by the wordy darts of Bhīma, became penetrated with despair and grief; Yudhishṭhira, etc. (*β*), did not know it. Dhṛtarāshṭra opened his heart to his friends (*γ*); now he was observing a vow of fast, which he had concealed from Yudhishṭhira, lying on the earth clad in deerskin; Gāndhārī observed similar vows; now he asked Yudhishṭhira's permission for himself and Gāndhārī to retire into the woods clad in rags and bark in order to practise austerities. Yudhishṭhira lamented (*δ*) ("Let Yuyutsu be made king; I shall go into the woods"); but Dhṛtarāshṭra's resolution remains unaltered; he asked Sañjaya and Kṛpa to speak for him to Yudhishṭhira; leaning on Gāndhārī he looked like one deprived of life; Yudhishṭhira lamented (*ε*), and gently rubbed Dhṛtarāshṭra's breast and face with cold water and revived him by the touch of his hand, on which were jewels and medicinal herbs. Dhṛtarāshṭra said that the touch of Yudhishṭhira was highly gratifying, embraced him, and smelt his head; Vidura, Kuntī, etc., wept; Gāndhārī bore her sorrow with fortitude. Dhṛtarāshṭra renewed his request; Vyāsa came (XV, **3**) and asked

Yudhishṭhira to permit Dhṛtarāshṭra to follow the path of all the ancient R.-ṛ.; "Gāndhārī bears her grief with fortitude." Yudhishṭhira yielded to Vyāsa's intercession; Vyāsa summed up the reasons for Dhṛtarāshṭra's retirement (ζ), and then proceeded to the woods. Yudhishṭhira then said that he would conform to the advice of Vyāsa, etc. (η) (XV, **4**); Dhṛtarāshṭra, Gāndhārī, etc. (η), entering the palace of Dhṛtarāshṭra, ate a little. Then Dhṛtarāshṭra gave Yudhishṭhira advice about how the latter should rule his kingdom (θ) (XV, **5**). Continuation (XV, **6**). Continuation; agreeably to the science known to Uçanas, [arrays called] Çakaṭa, Padma, and Vajra should be formed; "thou hast been instructed in all duties by Bhīshma, Kṛshṇa, and Vidura"; 100 horse-sacrifices and righteous rule are productive of equal merit (XV, **7**). Yudhishṭhira gratefully accepted his instructions, as Bhīshma, etc. (ι), no longer were there to instruct him. Dhṛtarāshṭra wishes to depart soon, and Gāndhārī reminded him that he has got the permission of Vyāsa, and asks him when he would go to the forest with the permission of Yudhishṭhira; he wished first to make gifts for the advancement in the other world of his dead sons and other kinsmen (who were now *pretas*), and assembled all the subjects, while Yudhishṭhira brought all the articles necessary; Dhṛtarāshṭra, in a touching address, took leave of that large concourse of men of all the four castes (κ) (XV, **8**), recapitulating the history of the realm from Çāntanu downwards (λ) (XV, **9**). The citizens were exceedingly agitated upon hearing Dhṛtarāshṭra's address; they charged the learned brahman Çāmba (B. Sāmba) with answering him (μ): "King Duryodhana never did us any wrong; we were well protected and ruled by him; we have also enjoyed great happiness for thousands of years under Yudhishṭhira, who follows the conduct of the R.-ṛ. of old (Kuru, Saṃvaraṇa, Bharata, etc.); the carnage on the field of Kurukshetra was not brought about by Duryodhana, Karṇa, and Çakuni, nor by Dhṛtarāshṭra, but by Destiny, which in 18 days caused 18 *akshauhiṇīs* to be destroyed by Bhīshma, etc. (ν); the Pāṇḍavas are capable of ruling without either thee or ourselves to look after them; Kuntī, etc. (ξ), will not do the least wrong to the people." Then Dhṛtarāshṭra slowly dismissed the assembly, and entered his house with Gāndhārī (XV, **10**). After that night had passed away, Dhṛtarāshṭra sent Vidura to Yudhishṭhira in order to announce that he would set out for the woods on the coming day of the full moon in the month of Kārttika, and to solicit some wealth for performing the *çrāddha* of Bhīshma, etc. (ο). Yudhishṭhira and Arjuna applauded his words; Bhīma was unwilling, recollecting Duryodhana; Arjuna sought to pacify him, applauded by Yudhishṭhira; Bhīmasena maintained that gifts for Bhīshma, etc. (π), should be given by them, and by Kuntī for Karṇa; "Let Duryodhana, etc., sink from a miserable to a more miserable position," reminding his brothers of the woes and disgrace inflicted upon them by those for whose benefit Dhṛtarāshṭra asked for wealth (ρ). Yudhishṭhira rebuked him (XV, **11**). Arjuna urged Bhīma to forget the injuries. Yudhishṭhira said to Vidura that he would give Dhṛtarāshṭra so much wealth as he wished for the obsequies of his sons and Bhīshma, etc., and asked him to tell Dhṛtarāshṭra not to be angry with Bhīmasena (XV, **12**). Vidura reported the speeches of Yudhishṭhira, Arjuna, and Bhīma to Dhṛtarāshṭra. Dhṛtarāshṭra expressed his satisfaction, and set his heart on making large presents on the day of full moon in the month of Kārttika (XV, **13**). Dhṛtarāshṭra invited thousands of deserving brahmans [and] superior R. for Bhīshma, etc.; and made large gifts to them, naming Droṇa, etc. (σ); tellers and scribes appointed by Yudhishṭhira ceaselessly ask the old king as to what should be given to each recipient that presented himself; unto him that was to receive 100 a 1000 were given, and he who was to receive 1000 was presented with 10,000 at the command of Yudhishṭhira; this was given by Dhṛtarāshṭra for the benefit in the other world of his sons and grandsons, as also of himself and Gāndhārī; the donation lasted for 10 days (XV, **14**). On the day of full moon in the month of Kārttika Dhṛtarāshṭra (and Gāndhārī) summoned the Pāṇḍavas, caused the rites to be performed, and his sacred fire to be taken up, put on deerskins and bark, and set out with his daughters-in-law. The ladies uttered loud wails; Yudhishṭhira and Arjuna were pierced with grief; Bhīmasena, etc. (τ), all followed Dhṛtarāshṭra; Kuntī held on her shoulders the hand of Gāndhārī, who walked with her bandaged eyes; Dhṛtarāshṭra walked behind Gāndhārī, placing his hand on her shoulder; Kṛshṇā, etc. (υ), all proceeded with Dhṛtarāshṭra; the citizens of all orders were as distressed as they had been at the departure of the Pāṇḍavas after the match of dice († 431–440) (XV, **15**); Dhṛtarāshṭra left the city through the principal gate, and then asked those who followed him to desist. Vidura and Sañjaya retired with him into the woods; Kṛpa and Yuyutsu he caused to remain, and made them over to Yudhishṭhira. Kuntī retired with Dhṛtarāshṭra, though Yudhishṭhira sought to dissuade her; she said: "Never show any disregard for Sahadeva: he is very much attached to me, and to thee also"; then she reminded him of Karṇa, etc. (φ); Yudhishṭhira reminded her that she had herself formerly recited to them the story of Vidulā, when they were about to set out from the town, and that they had won sovereignty guided by her words communicated through Kṛshṇa. Also Bhīma dissuaded her, pointing out the grief of the sons of Mādrī; but in vain. Draupadī and Subhadrā followed her, and so did the Pāṇḍavas with all their wives and attendants; Kuntī addressed them (XV, **16**), assigning her reasons for her conduct (χ) (XV, **17**). The Pāṇḍavas and Draupadī then desisted from following her. The Pāṇḍavas circumambulated Dhṛtarāshṭra, etc., for taking their leave to return. Dhṛtarāshṭra (with Gāndhārī and Vidura) made a final effort of dissuading Kuntī from retiring into the forest with him, but in vain. The ladies set up a loud wail of grief. Hāstinapura became plunged into sorrow: no festivals were observed. The Pāṇḍavas were without any energy. Dhṛtarāshṭra arrived on the banks of the Bhāgīrathī and took rest there for the night among the brahmans, who there, like himself, ignited their sacred fires; arrangement of the beds of Vidura, etc. (ψ); the Yājaka brahmans, etc., of the king laid themselves down on their respective beds; that night seemed as delightful to them as a Brāhmī night. When the night had passed away Dhṛtarāshṭra, etc., going through their morning acts and rites, continue their journey (XV, **18**). Following the advice of Vidura, Dhṛtarāshṭra took up his abode on the banks of the Bhāgīrathī; many of the four orders came to see him; he gladdened them all by his words. At evening Dhṛtarāshṭra, etc. (ω), bathed in the stream, etc.; Kuntī led him and Gāndhārī. Then he proceeded to Kurukshetra to the retreat of R.-ṛ. Çatayūpa (*b*), who received him with due rites; accompanied by him he proceeded to the retreat of Vyāsa, where he received the initiation [into the forest life]; after having returned he took up his abode in the retreat of Çatayūpa, who instructed him in all the rites of the forest mode of life, at the command of Vyāsa. Dhṛtarāshṭra, etc. (*aa*), began to practise austerities (XV, **19**). Ṛ. Nārada, etc. (*ββ*), came there and gladdened Dhṛtarāshṭra with discourses on religion. Ṛ. Nārada mentioned the kings that attained to heaven after practising penances in that very retreat (*γγ*): Sahasracitya, Çailālaya, Pṛshadhra, Purukutsa, Çaçaloman; "Thou also wilt, with Gāndhārī, through the grace of Vyāsa, attain to a very high goal; dwelling in the presence of Indra, Pāṇḍu always thinks of thee, and will assist thee in the attainment of prosperity; Kuntī, by serving thee and Gāndhārī, will obtain residence with her husband in the other world; we behold all this with our spiritual vision; Vidura will enter into Yudhishṭhira; Sañjaya will ascend to Heaven." Dhṛtarāshṭra, etc., praised Nārada. Çatayūpa asked Nārada what regions (*lokāḥ*) will be acquired by Dhṛtarāshṭra. Nārada said: On a visit to Indra I saw Pāṇḍu; Indra said that after three years Dhṛtarāshṭra and Gāndhārī would go to the abode of Kubera, on a car moving at will, and he would rove through the regions of D., G., and Rā.; this is a mystery of the gods. All the persons present (as also Dhṛtarāshṭra) became highly pleased. Then they went away by the path of the Siddhas (XV, **20**).—§ 788: The anxiety of the Pāṇḍavas and citizens about the fate of Dhṛtarāshṭra, etc., and their despair when they reflected on that terrible slaughter of their kinsmen (*a*); only Parikshit somehow consoled them (XV, **21**); afflicted with grief, they failed to derive pleasure from anything, nor did they attend to their kingly offices, thinking of Kuntī and Gāndhārī. They set their heart upon seeing Dhṛtarāshṭra in his forest retreat. Sahadeva, lamenting the fate of Kuntī, and expressing his longing to see her, proposed a visit to the woods, supported by Draupadī, who mentioned Kuntī and Gāndhārī and Dhṛtarāshṭra. Yudhishṭhira caused his army to be equipped, ordered litters, etc., for the ladies, and proclaimed that they would march out to-morrow, permitting the citizens to follow them. The next morning they set out, then waited five days for such citizens as would accompany them, and then proceeded towards the forest (XV, **22**), headed by Arjuna (on a car with white horses) and Kṛpa (description of the expedition); Bhīma on a gigantic elephant, the twins on two fleet steeds, the ladies in closed litters, scattering showers of wealth as they proceeded, headed by Draupadī. They proceeded slowly. Yuyutsu and Dhaumya protected the city. They reached Kurukshetra, crossed the Yamunā, and approached the retreat of Dhṛtarāshṭra (XV, **23**). The Pāṇḍavas and their followers, alighting from their cars, walked on foot; the ascetics told them that Dhṛtarāshṭra had gone to the Yamunā for his ablutions, etc., and pointed out the way to them. Sahadeva ran with speed towards Kuntī; they both wept; she informed Gāndhārī, and then advanced towards Yudhishṭhira, etc. (*β*), dragging the childless old couple; the Pāṇḍavas fell down at their feet, and took from their hands the jars of water they were carrying. Yudhishṭhira presented all his followers one after another to Dhṛtarāshṭra, mentioning their names and races. Dhṛtarāshṭra rejoiced and went to his retreat that was applauded by Si. and Cā. (XV, **24**). To the ascetics, who had come from various regions in order to see the Pāṇḍavas, Sañjaya pointed out each of them († *γ*); then Dhṛtarāshṭra asked († v. 660–674) (XV, **25**) Yudhishṭhira about the welfare of the Pāṇḍavas and their devotion to P. and D.; Yudhishṭhira answered, enquiring after Vidura, who turned out to be engaged in penances, subsisting on air alone, and was now seen at a distance with matted locks, and gravel in his mouth, and exceedingly emaciated, naked, and besmeared with filth and dust; Vidura fled, pursued by Yudhishṭhira; at last he stood motionless in *yoga*, and entered the body of Yudhishṭhira, who felt that he had become stronger than before and had acquired many additional virtues and accomplishments, and recollected his own state before his birth among men; he had heard of *yoga*-practice from Vyāsa. He desired to cremate the lifeless body of Vidura, but was prevented by an invisible voice which said, that in Vidura (who was Dharma) was Yudhishṭhira's body also, and that Vidura would attain to the regions (*lokāḥ*) called Santānikāḥ. Yudhishṭhira came and informed Dhṛtarāshṭra; all became filled with wonder. They passed that night under a tree (XV, **26**), conversing on morality and wealth. The next morning they surveyed the retreat (description) and the other retreats in the forest. Yudhishṭhira made presents to the ascetics (specification); then he returned to Dhṛtarāshṭra, etc. (*δ*); many **M.-ṛ.** (Çatayūpa, etc.) who dwelt in Kurukshetra came there, as also Vyāsa (XV, **27**), who enquired after Dhṛtarāshṭra's, etc. (*ε*), welfare, and told them who Vidura was, mentioning the curse of Dharma by Māṇḍavya (with an expenditure of his penances); he was superior to Bṛhaspati and Çukra; and how Vyāsa had procreated him upon the soil of Vicitravīrya; he was Dharma in consequence of his practices of *dhāraṇā* and *dhyāna*; from Dharma also Yudhishṭhira took his birth. Vyāsa says that he has come to show a wonderful effect of his own penances: "what dost thou wish to see, or ask, or hear?" (XV, **28**).

Āçramavāsika(ṃ) **parva**(n) ("the section relating to the dwelling in the hermitage"). § 792 (Nāradāgam.): XV, **39**, 1105 (°*e* °*ṇi gandhamālyādikañ caiva havishyaṃ bhojayed dvijān*; not in B.), i.e. Āçramavāsikaparvan.

[Āçramavāsikaparvan] ("the section relating to the dwelling in the hermitage"), the 15th of the greater parvans of Mhbhr.; cf. Āçramanivāsaparvan, Āçramasthāna, Āçramavāsa[2], Āçramavāsika(ṃ) parva(n).

Āçrāvya: II, **7**, 299 (Çakra-sabhā-v.) (a muni in the palace of Indra; cf. v. 291, *devarshayaḥ*).

Açva[1], a Dānava: I, **65** (§ 92), 2532 (Aṃçāvat.) (the 14th of the forty sons of Danu and Kaçyapa); **67** (§ 130), 2649 (do.) (incarnated as king Açoka). XII, **227**, 8264 (among the innumerable governors of Earth before Indra, mentioned by Bali; Bali-Vāsava-saṃv.).

Açva[2] = Çiva (1000 names[2]).

Açvacakra: III, **120**, 10272 (Tīrthayātrāp.) (had been killed by Çāmba).

Açvaçaṅku, brother of Açva: I, **65** (§ 92), 2531 (Aṃçāvat.); cf. Ayaḥçaṅku.

Açvaçiras[1] ("horse-headed"), brother of Açva: I, **65** (§ 92), 2531 (Aṃçāvat.); is incarnated as a king among the Kaikeyas (B. and V., Kekayas); I, **67** (§ 130), 2647 (Aṃçāvat.).

Açvaçiras[2] = Vishṇu: XII, **127**, 4662 (Rājadh.) ("reads the eternal Vedas" in Badarī); **341**, 13100 (Nārāyaṇīya), 13114; **348**, 13454 (Nārāyaṇīya), 13458 (*devasya Harimedhasaḥ*), 13509 ("became the dwelling of the Vedas"), 13524 (*Hariḥ*); these quotations are from the chapter Nārāyaṇīya, where it is related how Vishṇu, assuming a horse-headed form, rescued the Vedas from the "Dānavas" Madhu and Kaiṭabha (who had robbed them from Brahmán just as he had created them and was going to create the worlds), placed the horse-head in the north-eastern sea (cf. VP. II, 125–6), killed Madhu and Kaiṭabha, and gave the Vedas back to Brahmán that he might create the worlds.

Açvaçiras[3] (neut.), the horse-headed form of Vishṇu: III, **315**, 17461.

Açvaçiras[4] (neut.), a sacred place: III, **79**, 3083 (Nalop.) (here Bṛhadaçva bathed after having taught Yudhishṭhira the science of dice; according to Nīl. it means the science of horses—*açvavidyā*—which Bṛhadaçva taught Yudhishṭhira). VII, **81**, 2851 (Pratijñāp.) (°*sthānam*; visited in thought by Arjuna, accompanied by Kṛshṇa, in order to obtain the Pāçupata weapon).

Açvagrīva[1], brother of Açva: I, **65** (§ 92), 2533 (Aṃçāvat.); incarnated as king Rocamāna, I, **67** (§ 130), 2653 (do.); XII, **227**, 8262 (among the innumerable governors of Earth before Indra, mentioned by Bali; Bali-Vāsava-saṃv.).

Açvagrīva[2], a rājarshi = Hayagrīva: XII, **24**, 723 (Hayagrīva) ("having fallen in the combat he rejoices in the world of Heaven"). As to Açvaçiras and Açvagrīva, cf. VP. V, 2–3, and BR. s.v. Hayagrīva.

Açvaka, plur. (°*āḥ*), a people: VI, **9**, 351 (Ja°kha°; B. reads Açmakāḥ) (cf. Açmakāḥ); LIA. I, 859/1031; II, 129, 137, 142 (probably the Ἀσσακηνοί of the Greeks, in eastern Kabulistan and the Khonar valley, with the chief town Massaga, i.e. Maçakāvatī).

Açvaketu: VII, **48**, 1891 (Abhimanyuvadhap.); son of the Magadha king, killed by Abhimanyu on the 13th day of the battle.

Açvakranda: I, **32**, 1488 (Garuḍa) (killed by Garuḍa when seizing upon the ambrosia).

Açvalāyana, a son of Viçvāmitra's: XIII, **4**β, 253 (Viçvāmitrop.).

Açvamedha ("the Horse-sacrifice"). § 4 (Anukram.): I, **1**, 91 (°*āmṛtarasaḥ*, sc. *Bhāratadrumaḥ*), i.e. Āçvamedhikaparvan.

Açvamedhadatta: I, **95** (§ 160), 3838 (Pūruvaṃç.) (son of Çatānīka and Vaidehī, and grandson of Janamejaya).

Açvamedheçvara ("king of Açvamedha," PCR.), a king in the East subdued by Bhīma (*Rocamānaṃ*: II, **29**, 1066) (Bhīmasena).

Açvamedhika (sc. *parvan*; "the section treating of the Horse-sacrifice"). § 795 (Svargārohaṇap.): XVIII, **6**, 278 (°*aṃ samāsādya bhojanaṃ sārvakāmikaṃ*), i.e. Āçvamedhikaparvan.

Açvamedhika(ṃ) parva(n) ("the section treating of the Horse-sacrifice," the 93rd of the minor parvans of Mhbhr.; cf. Āçvamedhika(ṃ) parva(n)). § 778: *Vaiçampāyana* said (**XIV**, 1): After *Dhṛtarāshṭra* had offered libations of water [to Bhīshma], *Yudhishṭhira* fell down in grief on the bank of *Gangā*. Incited by *Kṛshṇa*, *Bhīma* took him up, surrounded by the *Pāṇḍavas*; *Dhṛtarāshṭra* comforts him, saying that it is he and *Gāndhārī* who ought to grieve, and referring to *Vidura's* advice about abandoning *Duryodhana* and his warnings against *Karṇa* and *Çakuni* (**XIV**, 1). *Kṛshṇa* also exhorts him, referring to the duties of the *kshattriyas* expounded by *Bhīshma*, *Vyāsa*, *Nārada*, and *Vidura*. *Yudhishṭhira* cannot forget the slaughter of *Karṇa*. *Vyāsa* also comforts him (XIV, **2**), and reminding him that D. and As. perform sacrifices, and that by sacrifices D. vanquished Dā., he urged him to perform the *Rājasūya*, the Horse-sacrifice, the *Sarvamedha*, and the *Naramedha*; [especially] the Horse-sacrifice after the example of *Rāma Dāçarathi* and *Bharata Daushmánti*, and indicated to him a spot in the *Himavat*, where there was gold in abundance, left behind by the brahmans at the sacrifice of *Marutta* of the *Karandhama* race. Asked by *Yudhishṭhira*, *Vyāsa* told the history of *Marutta* (XIV, **3**) * * i.e. Saṃvartta-Māruttīya (*b*). *Vaiçampāyana* said: †*Yudhishṭhira* was delighted at hearing the speech of *Vyāsa*, and desirous of performing his sacrifices with those riches, he consulted with his ministers (XIV, **4–10**). — § 779: *Vaiçampāyana* said: When *Vyāsa* had concluded his speech, *Kṛshṇa* addressed *Yudhishṭhira*, saying that *Yudhishṭhira's karman* has not yet been annihilated, nor had his foes been subjugated—"How canst thou be ignorant of the enemies in thy own flesh?"—and related the history of *Indra's* war with Vṛtra (*b*) (XIV, **11**). *Kṛshṇa* then expounds that, as physical ailments and health depend on the distribution of the cold, warm, and windy [humours] of the body, so do the mental ailments and health depend on *sattva*, *rajas*, and *tamas* in the soul [mind]; happiness is overcome by sorrow, and sorrow by pleasure; *Yudhishṭhira* should not recall his past sorrows: *Kṛshṇā* in the assembly, etc. (*a*); "the time has now come when thou must fight single-handed with thy mind" (XIV, **12**); salvation is not attained by foregoing external things; *Mṛtyu* (death) is [the thought] "mine," and the eternal *Bráhman* is [the thought] "not mine"; as no creature is ever destroyed, *ahiṃsā* (absence of injury) may exist even when one has pierced [a creature's] body, and *vice versa*; († v. 339–341): † the *yogin* knows *yoga* to be the perfect way, on account of the practices of his many former births; quoting the old verses sung by *Kāma*: "no creature is able to destroy me without [resorting to] the [proper] methods [i.e. subjugation of all desires, practice of *yoga*, etc.] . . . " (XIV, **13**).—§ 780: *Vaiçampāyana* said: Thus *Yudhishṭhira* was consoled, exhorted by *Vishṭaraçravas*, etc. (β); and having again performed the obsequial rites for his relatives, etc., he ruled the earth. He said to *Vyāsa*, *Nārada*, etc., that he would now perform the sacrifice, and said that they would go to the *Himālaya* under the protection of *Vyāsa* [to fetch the gold], according to the words of *Vyāsa*, D.-ṛ. *Nārada*, and *Devasthāna*. Then M.-ṛ. took leave of *Yudhishṭhira*, *Kṛshṇa*, and *Arjuna*. A short time passed away while they performed their purifications after *Bhīshma's* death, and gave large gifts to the brahmans as *çrāddha* (*aurddhvadehikaṃ*) to the *Kurus Bhīshma*, *Karṇa*, etc., accompanied by *Dhṛtarāshṭra*, and then they entered the city of *Hāstinapura* (XIV, **14**). — § 781: Asked by *Janamejaya* what *Kṛshṇa* and *Arjuna* did when the *Pāṇḍavas* had reconquered and pacified their kingdom, *Vaiçampāyana* said: When the *Pāṇḍava*-kingdom had been conquered and pacified *K.* and *A.* travelled with great pleasure amidst picturesque sceneries, like *Indra* and his wife (?, so PCR.) (*deveçvarau*) in heaven, or like the *Açvins* in *Nandana*, and [then] entered the palace of *Indraprastha* in great merriment, reciting the genealogies of Ṛ. and gods, etc., and *Kṛshṇa* consoled *Arjuna* for the death of his relatives (*a*). It was long since he had seen *Vasudeva*, *Baladeva*, and the *Vṛshṇi*-heroes; he, therefore, asked leave to go to *Dvāravatī*, and to accompany him to *Yudhishṭhira* and apprise him of his departure. († v. 404–6): *Arjuna* sorrowfully replied, "Be it so". (XIV, **15**).

Āçvamedhika(ṃ) parva(n) ("the section treating of the Horse-sacrifice"). § 10 (Parvas.): I, **2**, 354 (*tato 'çva°ṃ parva sarvapāpapraṇāçanaṃ*).—§ 11 (do.): I, **2**, 605 (*tato 'çva°*); 609 (*ity Āçva°*), i.e. Açvamedhika(ṃ) parva(n).

Ā[çvamedhikaparvan] ("the section treating of the Horse-sacrifice," the 14th of the great parvans of Mhbhr.; cf. Açvamedha, Āçvamedhika).

Açvanadī, a river (tributary to Carmaṇvatī and through it to Yamunā) upon which Pṛthā set the new-born Karṇa in a chest. § 547 (Karṇa): III, **308**, 17132, 17134, 17147, 17150.

Açvapati[1], brother of Açva[1]: I, **65** (§ 92), 2532 (Aṃçāvat.); incarnate as king Hārdikya, I, **67** (§ 130), 2650 (do.).

Açvapati[2], a king of the Madras, father of Sāvitrī (Pa° vra° mā°): III, **294**, 16621, 16628, (16629); **294**, (16662), (16673), (16678); **295**, (16698), (16700), 16706; **299**, 16914 (with Mālavī he got 100 sons; these are called Mālavāḥ; **297**, 16807).

Açvarāja[1] ("the king of horses") = Ucchaiḥçravas: I, **17**, 1097 (Amṛtam.); **20**, 1191 (Kadrū).

Açvarāja[2]: V, **130**, 4411 (Bhagavadyānap.) (killed by Kṛshṇa).

Açvarathā, a river on the mountain Gandhamādana, near the hermitage of Ārshṭisheṇa: III, **160**, 11681 (Yakshayuddhap.).

Açvasena, a Serpent: I, **3**, 803 (Utaṅka) (praised by Utaṅka: "always follows Takshaka and dwells with him in Kurukshetra on the river Ikshumatī").—§ 258 (Khāṇḍ.): I, **227**, 8237, 8241 (son of Takshaka, rescued by Indra from the Khāṇḍava wood); **228**, 8330; **229**, 8332 (Çārṅgakop.).—VIII, **90**, 4633 (Karṇap.) (angry on account of his mother's death, he has gone to Pātāla; thence he comes, when Arjuna has his last combat with Karṇa, and assumes the form of one of Karṇa's arrows in order to kill Arjuna, who, however, is rescued by Kṛshṇa, and at his instigation kills Açvasena).—IX, **61**, 3423 (Gadāyuddhap.) (*pannagendrasutasya*).

Açvātaka, plur. (°*āḥ*), a people in the army of Duryodhana: VI, **51**ν, 2105 (Bhīshmavadhap.).

Açvatara[1], in the Mhbhr. only appearing in the compound *Kambalā°au* (the "Horsecloth" and the "Mule"): a pair of Serpents: I, **35**, 1555 (Sarpanāmak.) (sons of Kadrū and Kaçyapa); II, **9**, 361 (Varuṇa sabhā-v.) (dwelling in the palace of Varuṇa); V, **103**γ, 3625 (Mātalīyop.) (dwelling in Bhogavatī).

Açvatara[2], a tīrtha: III, **85**, 8219 (Prayāga) (the vedi of Prajāpati).

Açvatīrtha, a holy place on the Gaṅgā in the neighbourhood of Kanyākubja, where Varuṇa gave to Ṛcīka 1000 steeds as a dowry to Gādhi: III, **115**, 10152 (Jamadagni); V, **119**, 4007 (Gālavacar.); XIII, **4**, 216 (Viçvāmitrop.). Cf. VP. IV, 16.

Açvattha[1], one of the 108 names of the Sun in the enumeration of Dhaumya. § 310 (Āraṇyakap., cf. Sūrya): III, **3**, 156.

Açvattha[2] = Çiva (1000 names[2]).

Açvattha[3] = Vishṇu (1000 names).

Açvatthāman[1], son of Droṇa and Kṛpī. § 4 (Anukram.): I, **1**, †211–212.—§ 11 (Parvas.): **2**, 537, 544.—§ 83 (Ādivaṃç.): **63**, 2436.—§ 130 (Aṃçāv.): **67**, 2709 (*Mahādevāntakābhyāñ ca kāmāt krodhāc ca . . . ekatvam upapannānām*).—§ 200 (Droṇa): **130**, 5101.—§ 201*b* (Droṇa): 5115–16 (*A.* was given this name by a voice from the sky, from his neighing like Ucchaiḥçravas as soon as he was born, cf. VII, 9058 f.).—§ 202*b* (Droṇa): **131**, 5182–83 (*A.* weeps when a child seeing the sons of the rich drinking milk, and is deluded by drinking water mixed with powdered rice—*pishṭodaka*—which he takes for milk).—§ 203 (Droṇa): **132** (is sent after water with a Kumbha; separates Bhīma and Duryodhana).—§ 205 (Droṇa): **132**, 5271 (*A.* excelled everyone in the mysteries—*rahasyeshu*).—§ 208 (Astradarçana): **135**, 5349, 5377.—§ 232 (Svayaṃvarap.): **186**, 6986 (at the svayaṃvara of Kṛshṇā).—§ 241 (Vidurāgamanap.): **200**, 7373 (with Duryodhana after the svayaṃvara).—§ 287 (Rājasūyikap.): II, **34**, 1267 (comes to the rājasūya).—§ 288 (do.): **35**, 1290 (is charged with the reception of the brahmans).—§ 289 (Arghāharaṇap.): **37**, 1348.—§ 290 (Çiçupālavadhap.): **44**, 1532.—§ 305 (Anudyūtap.): **78**, 2561.—§ 552 (Goharaṇap.): IV, **38**, 1243; **50–51** (scolds Karṇa, who blames Droṇa, etc.); **52**, 1628 (is placed by Bhīshma on the left); **55**, 1744 (Arjuna will not fight him); **58**, 1897 (cf. VI, 4458) (rescues Droṇa, who is fighting with Arjuna, but is himself conquered by Arjuna when his arrows are consumed, and rescued by Karṇa); **59**, 1916; **68**, 2236.—§ 556 (Sañjayayānap.): V, **25**, †733; **30**, †879.—§ 561 (Yānasandhip.): **47**, 1796 (present in the assembly of Dhṛtarāshṭra to receive Sañjaya when returning from his mission to the Pāṇḍavas); **50**, 1999; **56**, 2194; **57**, 2246 (favours Arjuna), 2268; **58**, 2300 (does not wish the war), 2304; **66** (is celebrated by Bhīshma).—§ 562 (Bhagavadyānap.): **95**, 3402.—§ 567 (do.): **124**, 4138, 4171; **130**, 4457.—§ 569 (do.): **139**, 4707; **143**, 4874 (*raktoshṇīshaḥ*); **148**, 5017.—§ 571 (Ulūkadūt.): **164**, 5707 (Yudhishṭhira, or Dhṛshṭadyumna, opposes Nakula to him before the great battle).—§ 573 (Ambop.): **193**–a (*A.* declares himself to be able to annihilate the Pāṇḍava army in ten days); **195**, 7608.—§ 576 (Bhagavadgītāp.): VI, **17**, 656 (*siṃhalāṅgūlaketunā*); **25**, 837.—§ 578 (Bhīshmavadhap.): **45**, 1715 (fights Çikhaṇḍin, 1st day); **51**, 2092, 2109 (*senāpṛshṭhe*, 2nd day); **52**δ, ζ (assists Bhīshma against Arjuna).—§ 579 (do.): **55**κ, λ (is with Çalya and Kṛpa fighting Dhṛshṭadyumna on the 2nd day).—§ 580 (do.): **56**, 2405 (together with Kṛpa in the head of the Garuḍavyūha, 3rd day); **62** (do.) (is with others fighting Abhimanyu); **73**ii (fights Arjuna).—§ 583 (do.): **75**, 3292 (together with Kṛpa in the eye of the Krauñcavyūha, 6th day).—§ 584 (do.): **81**, 3532; **82**, 3604 (fights Çikhaṇḍin, 7th day).—§ 585 (do.): **89**, 3934, 3970; **92**χ, 4119 (with many others he rescues Duryodhana, who is fighting Ghaṭotkaca, on the 8th day); **94**λ, ω, 4225 (*A.* is fighting Nīla, and thereupon Ghaṭotkaca, who deludes him by his māyā).—§ 586 (do.): **99**, 4504 (together with Somadatta and the two Avantyas he holds the left side of the army, 9th day); **101** (fights Sātyaki); **102**, 4666 (fights Arjuna, 9th day).—§ 587 (do.): **110**, 5109; **111**, 5162, 5165 (defends Bhīshma against Virāṭa and Drupada, and wounds them, 10th day); **112** (is told by his father the ill omens that have appeared, and the irresistibility of Arjuna, etc.); fights Sātyaki (10th day, ch. **115–16**, 5380).—§ 592 (Saṃçaptakavadhap.): VII, **31** (kills Nīla); **32**, 1375 (fights Bhīmasena, 12th day).—§ 593 (Abhimanyuvadhap.): **34**, 1500 (°*purogamāḥ*: the Dhārtarāshṭras with Açvatthāman at their head stand at the side of the Sindhu king in the foremost part of the cakravyūha, 13th day); **37**, 1601 (wounds Abhimanyu, 13th day), 1616; **47**, 1869 (is wounded by Abhimanyu, 13th day), 1874, 1877; **49**, 1930 (*A.* fights Abhimanyu, 13th day).—§ 598 (Jayadrathavadhap.): **85**, 3037 (does not wish the play); **87**, 3098.—§ 599 (do.): **91**, 3221; **94**, 3427; **104**–μ (with Duryodhana, Karṇa, etc., he fights Arjuna); ν **105** (his lion-tailed standard was effulgent as the rising sun, set with gold, floating in the breeze, possessed of the splendours of the rainbow) (cf. VII, ch. **145**); **135**, 5541; **139** (assists Karṇa against Arjuna; but is compelled to retire); **143**, 6004 (attempts in vain to keep Sātyaki from killing Bhūriçravas, 14th day); **145** μμμ, ννν, οοο, 6063, 6097, 6139 (assists Duryodhana, Jayadratha, etc., against Arjuna, and receives Karṇa in his chariot, 14th day); **146** (assists Jayadratha against Arjuna); **147**, 6307 (after the death of Jayadratha he assists Kṛpa against Arjuna, 14th day); **150**, 6498; **151**, 6563 (Droṇa gives him through Duryodhana his last exhortations to fight bravely, etc.).—§ 600 (Ghaṭotkacavadhap.): **155** (6720); **156**, 6803, 6806, 6810, 6824, 6848, 6914 (fights Sātyaki and Ghaṭotkaca, kills the son of Ghaṭotkaca, destroys Ghaṭotkaca's chariot, and fights the rakshas sent by him, fights Bhīma, etc., and kills Drupada's sons, Suratha, etc., together with Çrutāhvaya, etc.; is praised by the Siddhas, etc., 14th day); **159**, 7054, 7083, 7118, 7132, 7136 (scolds Karṇa for scolding Kṛpa, but is restrained by Duryodhana; assists Karṇa against Arjuna, etc., restrains Duryodhana from rashly rushing to combat, is exhorted and praised by Duryodhana); **160**, 7157 (°*mayaṃ lokaṃ*), 7185, 7202 (scolds Duryodhana and fights the Kaikayas, Pañcālas, etc., and combats bravely against Dhṛshṭadyumna); **161** (is assisted by Duryodhana, etc., against Yudhishṭhira, etc.); **165**, 7363 (resists Ghaṭotkaca); **166**, 7409, 7430 (is wounded by Ghaṭotkaca, but after having regained consciousness he turns him to flight).—§ 602 (Droṇavadhap.): **190-192**, 8705, 8709, 8745 (a false rumour of his death causes Droṇa to cease to defend himself, so that he is killed).—§ 603 (Nārāyaṇāstramokshap.): **193**, 8944, 8946, 8950 (hears from Kṛpa the death of Droṇa); **194**, 8964, 8966, 8976, 8978 (in *A.* human and Vāruṇa, etc., weapons are always present, etc.; he has been ordained to be the slayer of Dhṛshṭadyumna); **195** (swears before Duryodhana to kill Yudhishṭhira, tells him how he has acquired the Nārāyaṇa weapon, and makes use of it, sinister omens ensuing); **196**, 9057, 9059 (he is praised by Arjuna); **199** (he renews his oath before Duryodhana); **200**, 9282, 9306, 9311 (when the Pāṇḍava army is fleeing before the Nārāyaṇa weapon, and all cast their weapons away at the instigation of Kṛshṇa in order to neutralize the Nārāyaṇa weapon, Bhīma alone fights bravely against him, and Arjuna, in order to rescue Bhīma, throws the Vāruṇa weapon; Bhīma is rescued, and the Nārāyaṇa once neutralized cannot be used a second time; fights Dhṛshṭadyumna, Sātyaki, Arjuna, etc.); **201**, 9393 (*siṃhalāṅgūlaketanaṃ*: throws the Āgneya weapon against Arjuna; but Arjuna neutralizes it with the Brāhma weapon; *A.* flees and meets with Vyāsa, who tells him the story of Nara and Nārāyaṇa and the Çatarudrīya, and that *A.* is born as a portion of Rudra and has worshipped him in his phallic form for many generations; he thereupon makes a stand in the combat).—§ 604 (Karṇap.): VIII, **6**, 167; **9**, 329; **10** (exhorts Duryodhana to anoint Karṇa as commander-in-chief); **11** (in the head of Karṇa's *makara*-array); **13-14** (attacks Bhīma); **15** (they combat bravely; the Siddhas, etc., praise them; they are both wounded and carried away by their charioteers); **16**, 611, 630, 636, 648, 659 (attacks Kṛshṇa and Arjuna, who are fighting the Saṃçaptakas); **17**, 664, 685 (but is compelled to retire to the army of Karṇa); **20**, 791 (kills Pāṇḍya); **21**, 825.—§ 608 (do.): **46**, 2144.—§ 608 (Karṇap.): **54** (hinders Yudhishṭhira from assisting Çikhaṇḍin against Kṛpa); **55** (fights Sātyaki, etc., and puts Yudhishṭhira to flight); **56**, 2815 (again attacks Kṛshṇa and Arjuna, when they are destroying the army of the Kāmbojas, but is wounded and carried away by his charioteer); **57** (he promises before Duryodhana to kill Dhṛshṭadyumna); **59** (fights Dhṛshṭadyumna and Arjuna, is wounded by Arjuna, and carried away by his charioteer); **64** (is again conquered by Arjuna); **67**, 3371; **73**, 3688, 3693; **78**, 3999; **79** (together with others he attacks Arjuna); **88**, αγ', αδ' (in vain exhorts Duryodhana to make peace with the Pāṇḍavas); **94** (together with others he consoles Duryodhana after the death of Karṇa); **95**, 4971.—§ 609 (Çalyap.): IX, **2**, 73; **6**, 293, 308 (exhorts Duryodhana to make Çalya commander-in-chief).—§ 611 (do.): **8**, 393 (*pṛshṭhato 'bhūt*), 564 (with the sons of Dhṛtarāshṭra he defends Çalya); **14** (kills Suratha the Pāñcālya, and fights Arjuna; description of his person, ib.); **16** (together with others he assists Duryodhana against Bhīma, and in his chariot rescues Çalya from Yudhishṭhira); **17**, 950 (rescues, in his chariot, Kṛtavarman from Yudhishṭhira); **22** (fights Bhīma); **23**, 1186 (rescues Kṛtavarman in his chariot); **25**, 1377, 1383, 1398 (seeks Duryodhana, who has disappeared in the battle); **27**, 1459.—§ 612 (Hradapraveçap.): **29**, 1627 (together with Kṛpa and Kṛtavarman he hears from Sañjaya that Duryodhana has entered the lake, etc., and flees); **30** (with Kṛpa and Kṛtavarman he visits Duryodhana, who is sitting in the lake; their talk is overheard by some hunters and referred to the Pāṇḍavas; when these come to the spot seeking Duryodhana, *A.*, Kṛpa, and Kṛtavarman flee).—§ 615 (Gadāyuddhap.): **61**, 3418; **63** (Kṛshṇa is aware of his project of killing the Pāṇḍavas during night); **64**, 3589, 3609 (learns from the fleeing people the fate of Duryodhana); **65**, 3627 (with Kṛpa and Kṛtavarman he again visits Duryodhana and promises to kill all the Pañcālas; Duryodhana lets Kṛpa anoint *A.* as commander-in-chief).—§ 616 (Sauptikap.): **X, 1** (from fear of the Pāṇḍavas he, with Kṛpa and Kṛtavarman, retires to the wood, where they pass the night under a nyagrodha tree; seeing an owl destroy a great many fowls, he conceives the project of killing the whole Pāṇḍava army during night); **2-5**, 105, 208 (and, notwithstanding the objections of Kṛpa, they proceed to the gate of the encampment); **6-7**, 227, 298 (while Kṛpa and Kṛtavarman are watching the gate he alone penetrates into the encampment, where he meets with Mahādeva, whom he satisfies by being willing to bring himself as an offering; Mahādeva then enters his body and gives him a sword); **8**, 324, 334, 379, 429 (he then first kills Dhṛshṭadyumna, and thereupon Uttamaujas, Yudhāmanyu, and the sons of Draupadī, and Çikhaṇḍin, etc., while Kṛpa and Kṛtavarman at the gate kill the fleeing and set fire to three sides of the encampment, and Rākshasas and Piçācas devour the corpses; when he has killed all in the encampment — the five Pāṇḍavas were absent — he retires with Kṛpa and Kṛtavarman); **9**, 485, 497, 526 (and they visit Duryodhana for the third time; *A.* tells him what he has done, and receives his thanks the moment before he dies).—§ 617 (Aishīkap.): **10**, 545; **11**, 630 (at the instigation of Draupadī he is persecuted by Bhīma with Nakula as his charioteer); **12** (Kṛshṇa narrates to Yudhishṭhira how *A.* has obtained the *Brahmaçiras* weapon from Droṇa on condition not to use it against men, and how he has asked for Kṛshṇa's discus, but has not been able to lift it up); **13** (when sitting on the banks of Gaṅgā in the neighbourhood of Vyāsa and other ṛshis, he sees Bhīma rushing towards him followed by Kṛshṇa and Arjuna, who try to restrain Bhīma; *A.* then lodges the Brahmaçiras weapon in an *ishīkā* reed, with the words "for the total destruction of the Pāṇḍavas," and throws it); **14** (at the instigation of Kṛshṇa, Arjuna also throws the heavenly weapon, i.e. Brahmaçiras, cf. X, 705; he has been taught by Droṇa; the earth trembles and the worlds are in great peril, when Vyāsa and Nārada come to make them cease); **15** (Arjuna immediately recalls his weapon, but *A.* not being able to recall his because of his lack of self-restraint, Vyāsa permits him to let it fall upon the embryos of the Pāṇḍavas, and he gets his life by agreeing to cede his jewel, *maṇi*, that protects against all sorts of danger); **16** (Kṛshṇa, with the assent of Vyāsa, decrees that the unborn son of Uttarā-Parikshit shall be born dead, but be called to life by Kṛshṇa, while *A.*, for having killed an embryo, shall wander about for 3000 years in the wilderness, stinking and oppressed by all sorts of diseases; *A.* delivers up the maṇi and wanders away into the wood); **17** (the true cause of *A.'s* success was the aid of Rudra).—§ 618 (Jalapradānik.): XI, **1**, 3; **9**, 248; **11**, 298 (when Dhṛtarāshṭra with the women goes out to see the field of battle and bury the dead, *A.* with Kṛpa and Kṛtavarman meets with them a little out of the town and narrates the nightly slaughter, etc.; then, from fear of the Pāṇḍavas, they retire, and *A.* betakes himself to the hermitage of Vyāsa).—§ 623 (Rājadh.): XII, **14**, 403.—§ 630 (do.): **27**, 816.—§ 723 (Ānuçāsanik.): XIII, **6**, 327 (*°ā ca Rāmaç ca muniputrau dhanurdharau* | *na gacchataḥ svargalokaṃ svakṛteneha karmaṇā*) —§ 770 (do.): **151**, 7121 (*Rāmo Vyāsas tathā Drauṇir Açvatthāmā ca Lomaçaḥ* | *ity ete munayo divyā ekaikaḥ sapta saptadhā* | *srashṭāraḥ sarvabhūtānāṃ kīrttitā lokapāvanāḥ*); (in B. the order of the verses is inverted; it seems to me that v. 7121*a* has been erroneously inserted; Nīl. is silent).—§ 785 (Anugītāp.): XIV, **66**, 1951.—§ 793 (Mausalap.): XVI, **6**, 164.—Cf. Ācāryanandana, Ācāryaputra, Ācāryasuta, Ācāryatanaya, Ācāryasattama, Drauṇi, Drauṇāyani (Droṇāyani), Droṇaputra, Droṇasūnu, Guruputra, Gurohsuta, Aṅgirasāṃ varishṭhaḥ (VIII, 683), Bhāratācāryaputra.

Açvatthāman[2], an elephant belonging to the Mālava king Indravarman and killed by Bhīma to delude Droṇa and make him believe that his son had been killed. § 602 (Droṇavadhap.): VII, **190**, 8708-10, 8744.—§ 603 (Nārāyaṇāstramokshap.): **193**, 8946, 8948.—§ 630 (Rājadh.): XII, **27**, 816.

Açvavatī, a river. § 775 (Ānuçāsanik.): XIII, **166**, 7651.

Āçvayuj (No. 87), a month=Āçvayuja (No. 88) or Açvina (No. 91). § 746 (Ānuçāsanik.): XIII, **65**, 3298 (he who then gives ghee to Brahmans, to him the Açvins give beauty in this world).

Āçvayuja (No. 88), adj. § 759 (Ānuçāsanik.): XIII, **106**, 5160 (*māsam* = No. 87): Āçvayuj and No. 91: Āçvina: he who then practises austerities (*kshapet*, B. *kshipet*), confining himself to one meal a day (*ekabhaktena*), is born pure (*mṛjāvān*) and rich in carriages and sons.

Açvin (the two), the surgeons of the gods; they are, because of their beauty, often mentioned in comparisons. § 3 (Anukramaṇikap.): I, **1**, 34 (sprung from the mundane egg).—§ 4 (do.): **1**, 112.—§ 15 (Paushyap.): **3**, 721 (*devabhishajau*), 724-8 (have delivered the quail, etc.; cf. Ṛgveda *passim*), 731 (*Nāsatyau*), 732-3, 735-8 (restore Upamanyu, who praises them, to his eyesight).—§ 83 (Ādivaṃç.): **63**, 2445.—§ 119 (Aṃçāvat.): **66**, 2599 (sons of Sūrya and the daughter of Tvashṭṛ in the shape of a female horse).—§ 120 (do.): **66**, 2604.—§ 130 (Aṃçāvat.): **67**, 2746.—§ 145 (Kaca): **76**, 3229.—§ 157 (Pūruvaṃç.): **95**, 3816 (Mādrī by *A.* had Nakula and Sahadeva).—§ 167 (Vicitravīryop.): **102**, 4141 (*°rūpasadṛço*).—§ 191 (Sambhavap.): **123**, 4827.—§ 192 (do.): **124**, 4850, 4852 (they in Mādrī procreate Nakula and Sahadeva).—§ 194 (Pāṇḍu): **126**, 4922.—§ 221 (Caitrarathap.): **170**, 6500 (=Nakula and Sahadeva).—§ 233 (Svayaṃvarap.): **187**, 7010 (present at the Svayaṃvara of Kṛshṇā).—§ 238 (Pañcendrop.): **197**, 7277, 7302.—§ 254 (Khāṇḍavad.): **222**, 8079 (*iva*).—§ 258 (do.): **227**, 8265 (with the other gods they fight Arjuna and Kṛshṇa in order to defend the Khāṇḍava wood from being burnt; their weapons are flaming herbs).—§ 259 (do.): **229**, 8360 (Mandapāla, praising Agni, identifies him with the Açvins, etc.).—§ 270 (Lokapālas.): II, **11**, 460 (in the palace of Brahmán).—§ 309 (Āraṇyakap.): III, **3**, 127 (it is by their wealth of yoga that R., S., Ā., V., and A. rule the creatures).—§ 336 (Indralok.): **43**, 1768 (on the Suravīthī Arjuna met with S., Vi., M., A., Ā., V., R., B.-ṛ., etc.); **46**, 1840 (in the town of Indra).—§ 342 (do.): **51**, 1973 (*iva*).—§ 362 (Tīrthayātrāp.): **83**, 2098 (*A°oḥ sadṛço*).—§ 344 (Nalop.): **53**, 2098 (*A°oḥ sadṛço*).—§ 347 (do.): **62**, 2356.—§ 362 (Tīrthayātrāp.): **83**, 5087 (*°nos tīrtham āsādya rūpavān abhijāyate*).—§ 375 (do.): **85**, 8248 (*Marud°*: have bathed in the tīrthas).—§ 377 (do.): **86**, 8404 (id.).—§ 400 (do.): **118**, 10224 (*°noḥ . . . āyatanāni*, seen at Sūrpāraka by the Pāṇḍavas together with those of V., M., S., etc., etc., etc.).—§ 401 (do.): **119**, 10257.—§ 404 (Sukanyop.): **121**, 10312 (Çaryāti's offering).—§ 405 (do.): **123-125**, 10349, 10360, 10362, 10381, 10384, 10386, 10398, 10400, 10405 (try to seduce Sukanyā, daughter of Çaryāti and wife of Cyavana, but at her request they make Cyavana young again by letting him bathe with them in a lake; Sukanyā chooses to stay with her husband; Cyavana causes Çaryāti to offer Soma also to the Açvins, and compels Indra to agree to it; cf. XIII, ch. **156** and *passim*).—§ 412 (Ashṭāvakrīya): **134**, 10659.—§ 418 (Tīrthay.): **139**, 10834.—§ 421 (do.): **142**, 10905 (they, with the Maruts and Sādhyas, surround Indra, when he is muttering his daily prayer at the Upper Gaṅgā).—§ 438 (Yakshayuddhap.): **162**, 11819.—§ 443 (Nivātakav.): **168**, 12044 (Arjuna in Amarāvatī beheld V., R., S., M.-gaṇas, Ā., and A.).—§ 457 (Mārkaṇḍeyas.): **188**, 12924 (Mārkaṇḍeya beheld, in the body of Nārāyaṇa, i.e. Kṛshṇa, all D.-gaṇas, S., R., Ā., Gh., P., etc., etc., etc.).—§ 545 (Pativratāmāh.): **294**, 16675.—§ 552 (Goharaṇap.): IV, **56**, 1762 (*Viçvā° Marutāṃ gaṇaiḥ*).—§ 561 (Yānasandhip.): V, **61**, 2387, 2399.—§ 564 (Bhagavadyānap.): **105**, 3700.—§ 567 (do.): **131**, 4423 (in the presence of Duryodhana, Agni, Ā., S., V., A., M., V.-D., etc., issue from Kṛshṇa's mouth).—§ 572 (Rathātirathas.): **169**, 5855.—§ 576 (Bhagavadgītāp.): VI, **35**, 1252, 1268 (R., Ā., V., S., Vi., A., M., Ushmapas, G., Y., and the hosts of As. and Si. behold Kṛshṇa and are amazed).—§ 580 (Bhīshmavadhap.): **59**, 2595 (i.e. Nakula and Sahadeva).—§ 581 (do.): **65**, 2958 (are the ears of Kṛshṇa).—§ 592 (Saṃçaptakav.): VII, **23**, 1035 (i.e. Nakula and Sahadeva).—§ 593 (Abhimanyuvadh.): **34**, 1488; **40**, 1694.—§ 595 (do.): **62**, 2273, 2275 (draw Māndhātṛ from the womb of his father).—§ 596 (Pratijñāp.): **76**, 2682 (*Vasavaç ca sahā°naḥ*).—§ 597 (do.): **84**, 2991 (follow Indra to the offering of Çaryāti); **87**, 4418 (V., M., S., R., Vi., A., Agni, Indra, Soma, Pavana, and the ten points of the compass become the partisans of Arjuna, while all Ā. side with Karṇa).—§ 608 (Karṇap.): VIII, **46**, 2205 (*iva*); **56**, 2785 (*iva*); **65**, 3303 (*iva*), 3304 (*iva*).—§ 615*u* (Skanda): IX, **45γ**, 2508 (A., S., etc., etc., etc., come to the investiture of Skanda), 2540 (give Skanda, at his inauguration, Vardhana and Nandana as his followers).—§ 617 (Aishīkap.): X, **13**, 653.—§ 641 (Rājadh.): XII, **64**, 2395 (created by the supreme god in days of old with S., V., R., Vi., the gaṇas of M., and Si., they are all observant of kshattriya duties).—§ 656 (Āpaddh.): **166**, 6141 (*Marud° naḥ*: Ā., S., V., R., M., D., with their preceptors and purohitas, etc., etc., etc., accept the religion of the Vedas).—§ 661 (Mokshadh.): **193**, 7191 (their places, like those of the other gods, are hells — *nirayāḥ* — compared with the place of Paramātman (?)).—§ 665 (do.): **208**, 7583 (*Nāsatyaçcaiva Dasraç ca*), 7589.—§ 668 (do.): **219**, 7950 (*çūdrau*).—§ 673 (do.): **227**, 8220.—§ 692 (do.): **281**, 10052.—§ 694 (do.): **284**, 10215 (*bhishajām varau*).—§ 702 (do.): **296**, 10837 (*Agny°-Mārutāḥ*: Ā., V., R., V.-D., S., P., M.-gaṇas, etc., etc., etc., have all been crowned with success by their penances—*saṃsiddhās tapasā*).—§ 707 (do.): **318**, 11708 (to them the soul—of the yogin?—arrives when going out through the eyebrows).—§ 712 (Çukotp.): **324**, 12176 (Lp., S., V., Ā., R., A., etc., etc., etc., are present when Vyāsa, devoted to the practices of yoga, adores Mahādeva in order to obtain a son — Çuka). — § 717 (Mokshadh.): **341**, 13111 (*°bhyāṃ pataye*, i.e. *Vishṇu*); **343**, 13206.—§ 721 (Ānuçāsanik.): XIII, **3**, 95 (*°sadṛça-dyutiḥ*).—§ 730 (do.): **14**, 731 (*Rudrādityā°*), 985 (Vishṇu says that Ā., V., S., V.-D., A. praise Viçvadeva, i.e. Çiva).—§ 746 (do.): **65**, 3295, 3298 (give him beauty who in the month of Āçvayuj presents the brahmans with ghee).—§ 747 (do.): **84**, 4011 (Ā., V., R., M., A., and S. become afflicted by the Daiteya Asura Tāraka); **85**, 4126 (spring forth, at an offering of Çiva, from the tears [of Brahmán?], v. Agni).—§ 748 (do.): **86**, 4201 (S., V., A., etc., etc., etc., come to see Skanda, when he is born).—§ 759 (do.): **107**, 5299 (of the result of eating only every 21st day), 5330 (of the result of eating only every 29th day). — § 766 (do.): **125**, 5937 (*bhishajāṃ varau*: have permitted the *devadūta* to visit the *pitaraḥ*); **134**, 6186 (of the result of offering in a certain way on the full-moon day). — § 770 (do.): **151**, 7095 (*Nāsatyaç ca Dasraç ca*; Mārtaṇḍa's—the Sun's—sons, sprung from the nose of Sañjñā), †7160 (no disease befalls him who praises them).—§ 772 (do.): **157**, 7306, 7308–9 (*Sūrya-putrau*), 7311, 7313, 7321–2. — § 773 (do.): **159**, 7387 (procreated from and identified with Kṛshṇa); **161**, 7496 (identified with Rudra).—§ 775 (do.): **166**, 7642 (*Rudrāḥ sā °naḥ*).—§ 778 (Açvamedhikap.): XIV, **8**, 184 (*Nāsatyau*: worship Mahādeva on Muñjavat, with R., V., Vi., S., etc., etc., etc.); **9**, 249; **10**, 261.—§ 781 (do.): **15**, 375 (*iva Nandane*). — § 783 (Anugītāp.): **52**, 1514. — § 789 (Putradarçanap.): XV, **31**, 854 (*yamajau*: i.e. Nakula and Sahadeva). — § 793 (Mausalap.): XVI, **4**, 129. — § 794 (Mahāprasthānikap.): XVII, **3**, 95.—§ 795 (Svargārohaṇap.): XVIII, **3**, 87 (when Yudhishṭhira's vision of Hell had ceased M. with Çakra, V., A., S., R., Ā., Si., etc., came to see him); **4**, 133 (Yudhishṭhira sees Nakula and Sahadeva in their dwelling-place in Heaven); **6**, 215.—Cf. Nāsatyau; Açvinīsutau; Sūryaputrau; [Deva]bhishajau; Açvibhyāṃ pati (= Vishṇu).

Āçvina (adj.). § 592 (Saṃçaptakavadhap.): VII, **23**, 1740 (*°dhanuḥ*, i.e. Sahadeva's bow).—§ 759 (Ānuçāsanik.): XIII, **109**, 5382 (*māsi*: *dvādaçyām° e māsi Padmanābheti cārcayet | gosahasraphalaṃ puṇyaṃ prāpnuyān, nātra saṃçayaḥ*); cf. Nos. 87 and 88; it is the sixth month of the solar year beginning with Vaiçākha, or the seventh of the luni-solar year beginning with Caitra; see Whitney to Sū° Si°, I, 51 and XIV, 16 (Açvineya, see Āçvineya, No. 92).

Āçvineya[1] (*°au*) (No. 92) = Nakula and Sahadeva: I, 7083 (printed A°, but B. has Ā°).—§ 569 (Bhagavadyānap.): V, **138**, 4692.

Āçvineya[2] = Sahadeva. § 281 (Sahadeva): II, **31**, 1115.

Açvinī[1], a nakshatra, the first of the younger series, the twenty-seventh of the older, beginning with Kṛttikā (see Whitney to Sū° Si°, VIII, 9; VP. II, ch. 8, vol. ii, p. 261 ff.; junction-star β Arietis).—§ 746 (Ānuçāsanik.): XIII, **64**, 3285 (he who under *A.* gives a carriage yoked with horses is reborn in a family that is rich in elephants, horses, and carriages). — § 749 (do.): **89**, 4268 (plur.: *°shv açvān vindeta*, obtains horses; of the result of bringing a çrāddha "*açvinīyoge*").—§ 759 (do.): **110**, 5390 (*°yāṃ sakthinī caiva*, cf. Açleshāḥ).—Cf. Açvinī[2].

Açvinī[2], a tīrtha (?). § 733 (Ānuçās.): XIII, **25**, 1708 (*°yām*: then a man acquires beauty and glory—*rūpavar-caskam*—after death).

Açvinīsutau = Nakula and Sahadeva: XII, 6238 (properly = Açvinau, see BR. s.v. Açvin).

Açvisutau = Nakula and Sahadeva: XVII, 37.

Aḍambara, a companion of Skanda. § 615*u* (Skanda): IX, **45ζ**, 2541 (*Ḍambarā°au*).

Adambha = Çiva (1000 names[2]).

Ādāna, a name of Earth. § 746 (Ānuçāsanik.): XIII, **62**, 3114.

Adāntanāçana = Çiva (1000 names[1]).

Adbhuta[1] ("Wonderful"), a name of Fire. § 494 (Āngirasa): III, **222**, 14234 (*Adbhutasya Priyā bhāryā, tasya putro Vibhūrasiḥ*), 14237.—§ 496 (Skandotpatti): **224**, 14284 (? *samāhūto Hutavahaḥ so 'dbhutaḥ sūryamaṇḍalāt*, cf. Agni).

Adbhuta[2] = Vishṇu (1000 names).

Adhana = Çiva (1000 names[2]).

Adhara = Çiva (1000 names[1]) (to read *Dharaḥ*?).

Ādhāranilaya = Vishṇu (1000 names).

Adharma ("injustice"). § 125 (Aṃçāv.): I, **66**, 2617 (came to existence owing to creatures eating each other from lust of food; husband of Nirṛti, "ruin," and father of the Nairṛta rakshases and Bhaya, "fear," Mahābhaya, "terror," and Mṛtyu, "death").—§ 189 (Pāṇḍu): **122**, 4755.—§ 641 (Rājadh.): XII, **90**, 3388 (husband of Çrī, "luck," and father of Darpa, "arrogance"), 3390.

Adharmahan = Çiva (1000 names[1]).

Adharshaṇa = Çiva (1000 names[2]).

Adhidaiva ("the governing Deity," see BR., vol. v, p. 971, and Weber, Rāmat. Up., 350): XII, 9175 (*°e niyukto 'smi*, sc. Çiva).

Adhideva ("the Supreme God") = Kṛshṇa: XIII, 7383.

Adhirājan, v. Indra.

Adhirājyam and Adhirājakuçādyaḥ, see Adhivājyakulādyaḥ.

Adhiratha, a sūta in the neighbourhood of Campā and friend of Dhṛtarāshṭra; husband of Rādhā and foster-father of Karṇa, whom he called Vasusheṇa and sent to Hāstinapura to be instructed by Droṇa (III, ch. **308**); at the show of arms he enters the arena to congratulate Karṇa as king of Anga (I, ch. **137**). § 218 (Astradarçana): I, **137**, 5419.—§ 547 (Kuṇḍalāharaṇap.): III, **309**, 17153 ("the friend of Dhṛtarāshṭra"), 17157, 17168.—§ 572 (Rathātirath.): V, **166**, 4759, 4762; **171**, 4918.—§ 588 (Bhīshmavadhap.): VI, **122**, 5826 (printed *Ādhirathiḥ* in C., but in B. *A°rathaḥ*).

Ādhirathi = Karṇa: III, 17179.—V, 4917.—(VI, 5826, read *Adhirathaḥ*.)—VII, 96, 1423, 1426, 1430, 3937, 5417, 5434, 5510, 5512, 5514, 5520, 5535, 5572, 5622–3,

5626, 5693, 5719, 5723, 5725–7, 5750, 5757, 5763, 6326, 7472, 8589.—VIII, 227, 264 (printed *Adhirathir* in C., but B. has *Ādhi°*), 317, 837, 949, 1365, 1687, 1873, 1962, 2162, 2235, 2331, 2344, 2507, 2734, 2741, 2745, 2753, 2758, 3307, 3354, 3395, 3729, 3960, 4176, 4188, 4190, 4199, 4233, 4494, 4525, 4590, 4598, 4606, 4612, 4626, 4703, 4706, 4785, 4818, 4907, 4926, 4969, 5041.—XI, 637.

Adhiroha = Çiva (1000 names [2]).

Adhishṭhāna = Vishṇu (1000 names).

Adhivājyakulādyaḥ, a country. § 574 (Jambūkh.): VI, **9**, 352 (B.: *Adhirājya-kuçādyaḥ*; V.: *Adhirājaṃ Kuçaṭṭāç ca*); cf. VP. II, 165.

Adhivaṅga, a tīrtha. § 370 (Tīrthayātrāp.): III, **84**, 8093 (*tapovanam*; B. *tato vanam*: the reward of visiting it is to rejoice among the Guhyakas).

Adhokshaja [1] ("born under the axle-tree," cf. Hariv. v. 9087 ff., and BR.)=Kṛshṇa: I, 522 (*Kṛshṇaḥ*).—II, 890 (*Yadunandanaḥ*), 1428.—V, 2568 (*adho na kshīyate jātu yasmāt, tasmād A°*), 3080, 5196.—IX, 3539.—XII, 1620, 13241–3 (*pṛthivī nabhasī cobhe viçrute viçvatomukhe | tayoḥ sandhāraṇārthaṃ hi mamādhokshajam añjasā . . .*).—XIII, 659.—XVI, 162.

Adhokshaja [2] = Vishṇu (1000 names).

Adhṛta = Vishṇu (1000 names).

Adhyaksha: XII, 1626 (*jagato 'dhyakshaḥ*, "the surveyor of the world," i.e. Kṛshṇa).

Adhyātmānugata = Çiva (1000 names [2]).

Ādi = Çiva (1000 names [2]).

Ādi(r) devānām [1] = Çiva (1000 names [1]).

Ādi(r) devānām [2] = Vishṇu: XII, 13676.

Ādi(r) viçvasya ("the first of all") = Kṛshṇa: XII, 1658.

Ādideva [1] ("the first god") = the Sun: III, 155 (the 95th name of the Sun in the enumeration of Dhaumya).

Ādideva [2] = Vishṇu: XII, 2395, 2402 (*Nārāyaṇaṃ purāṇam*), 2405–7, 2411 (*Devaçreshṭhaḥ*), 12699, 12864 (Ma° pu° sta°).—XIII, 6854, 6985 (1000 names), 7001 (ib.).

Ādideva [3] = Kṛshṇa: XIII, 6893, 7373.

Ādikara [1] = Çiva (1000 names [2]).

Ādikara [2] = Vishṇu: XII, 13512 (*Purushaṃ*).

Adīna = Çiva (1000 names [2]).

Ādiparvan, the first book of Mhbh. § 11 (Parvas.): I, **2**, 361, 405.

Ādirāja, third son of Avikshit and grandson of Kuru. § 154 (Pūruvaṃç.): I, **94**, 3741.—§ 775 (Ānuçāsanik.): XIII, **166**, 7680 (enumerated among the rājarshis that one should venerate in the evening and morning).

Aditeḥ putra ("the son of Aditi") = Varuṇa: IX, 2841 (*Varuṇaḥ*).

Aditeḥ suta ("the son of Aditi") = the Sun: III, 55 (the 96th of the 108 names of the Sun in the enumeration of Dhaumya).

Āditeya (pl.), the gods: XII, 7614.

Aditi [1], one of the thirteen daughters of Daksha, who were married to Kaçyapa; by him she is mother of the twelve Ādityas. § 87 (Aṃçāv.): I, **65**, 2520.—§ 88 (do.): **65**, 2522.—§ 120 (do.): **66**, 2600.—§ 190 (Pāṇḍavotp.): **123**, 4795.—§ 253 (Haraṇāhar.): **221**, 8040.—§ 270 (Lokapālas.): II, **11**, 456 (in the palace of Brahmán).—§ 317 (Arjunābhigamanap.): III, **12**, 484.—§ 413 (Tīrthayātrāp.): III, **135**, 10694 (at the Maināka mountain she in order to have a son "cooked that food," according to Nīl. "brahmaudanam for the Sādhyas," quoting Taitt. S. 6. 5. 6. 1, cf. XII, 13218–9, *infra*).—§ 515 (Ghoshayātrāp.): **254**, 15264.—§ 524 (Vishṇu): **272**, 15839 (she bore Vishṇu after having been pregnant 1000 years).—§ 548 (Āraṇeyap.): **315**, 17461.—§ 561 (Yānasandhip.): V, **48**, 1887 (Naraka Bhauma in Prāgjyotisha having robbed her ear-drops set with jewels, they are reconquered by Kṛshṇa).—§ 564 (Mātalīyop.): **98**, 3534; **104**, 3689.—§ 565 (Gālavac.): **117**, 3971.—§ 608 (Karṇap.): VIII, **68**, 3393.—§ 615*u* (Skanda): IX, **45**, 2515 (*devamātā*: present at the anointing of Skanda).—§ 637 (Rājadh.): XII, **43**, 1504 (*Adityāḥ saptadhā tvan tu purāṇe garbhatāṃ gataḥ*, i.e. Kṛshṇa; explained by Nīl. to mean, (*a*) two births, viz., the Āditya Vishṇu and the Dwarf, from Aditi herself, and (*b*) Pṛçnigarbha, the three Rāmas, and Kṛshṇa, from Pṛçni and other manifestations of Aditi; it, however, seems more probable that here is an allusion to the older conception of seven Ādityas); **47***a*, 1626 (*hiraṇyavarṇaṃ yaṃ garbham Aditir Daityanāçanaṃ ekaṃ dvādaçadhā jajñe, tasmai Sūryātmane namaḥ*, i.e. Kṛshṇa).—§ 664 (Mokshadh.): **207**, 7543; **340**, 12945, 12955.—§ 717 (Nārāyaṇīya): **343**, 13218–19: "Aditi cooked food for the gods, hoping that, having eaten it, they would kill the Asuras; there Budha . . . said to her, 'Give me alms'; she, saying that it was only to be eaten by the gods, gave him nothing, wherefore he cursed her, saying that she would have a pain—*vyathā*—in her womb; in the second birth—as an egg—of Vivasvat, the egg of his mother Aditi was killed" (so B.); therefore Vivasvat Çrāddhadeva became Mārttaṇḍa. Cf. also § 746 (Ānuçāsanik.): XIII, **83**, 3904, v. *infra*.—§ 719 (Ānuçās.): **1**, 55 (*Vasavo 'ditiḥ*, v. Āditya [4]).—§ 746 (do.): XIII, **83**, 3904 (she is said to have, in the devayuga, when pregnant with Vishṇu, exercised self-tortures, standing on one foot in order to have a son).—§ 768 (do.): **146**, 6752 (*Kaçyapasya*).—Cf. Devamātṛ, Çiva.

Aditi [2], the same identified with a sickness demon. § 522 (*Manushyagrah.*): III, **230**, 14482 (*Aditiṃ Revatīṃ prāhur, grahas tasyās tu Raivataḥ so' pi bālān mahāghoro bādhate vai· mahāgrahaḥ*).

Aditi [3], the same conceived as a manifestation of Çiva (q.v., 1000 names [2]).

Aditinandanau ("the two sons of Aditi," i.e. Indra and Vishṇu): XIII, 986 (*Çatakratuç ca Vishṇuç ca*).

Āditya [1] (plur.), a class of gods, the sons of Aditi and Kaçyapa, manifestations of the Sun. § 308 (Āraṇyakap.): III, **3**, 189 (*kṛtvā dvādaçadhātmānaṃ dvādaçā°tāṃ gataḥ*, sc. the Sun). They are twelve, enumerated § 88 (Aṃçāvat.), I, **65**, 2522, etc. (1, Dhātṛ; 2, Mitra; 3, Aryaman; 4, Çakra; 5, Varuṇa; 6, Aṃça; 7, Bhaga; 8, Vivasvat; 9, Pushan; 10, Savitṛ; 11, Tvashṭṛ; 12, Vishṇu).—§ 191 (Sambhavap.): **123**, 4823–4 (in the order 1, 2, 5, 6, 7, 4, Indra, 8, 9, 11, 10; then, *Parjanyaç caiva Vishṇuç ca Āditya dvādaça* (!) *smṛtāḥ*; perhaps to be read *jaghanyas tv eva Vishṇuç ca*, cf. v. 2524; but cf. also BR. s.v., and *infra*; Nīl. says nothing).—§ 665 (Mokshadh.): XII, **208**, 7581, etc. (in the order 7, 6, 3, 2, 5, 10, 1, 8, 11, 9, 4, Indra, 12).—§ 770 (Ānuçāsanik.): XIII, **151**, 7002, etc. (in the order 6, 7, 2, 5, 1, 3, 8, 10, *Jayanto Bhāskaras tathā*, 11, 9, 4, Indra, 12); cf. BR. s.v., and Muir, Or. S.T., especially iv, pp. 11–15, 54, 114–121; the youngest and most important is (the Dwarf incarnation of) Vishṇu (I, 2522); Indra is the principal, § 120 (Aṃçāvat.), I, **66**, 2600; and the oldest and best is Varuṇa, § 564 (Mātalīyop.), V, **98**, 3534. For their superintendence of the chariot of the Sun, each in one of the twelve months of the year, in the Purāṇas, see VP. II, pp. 285 ff.; the order is, 1, 3, 2, 5, 4, Indra, 8, 9, 10, Parjanya instead of Savitṛ, 6, 7, 11, 12. Of the older conception of six, seven (or eight) Ādityas there seems to be no trace in the Mhbh., unless it be XII, 1504 (v. Aditi); they came into existence from the coals at the sacrifice of Çiva in the shape of Varuṇa (!) § 747 (Suvarṇotpatti), XIII, **85**, 4131 (*ye dhishṇyeshu divi sthitāḥ*). In most cases they are named together with the other *devagaṇas*, etc.; thus, for instance:—

§ 3 (Anukram.): I, **3**, 34 (v Açvin).—§ 44 (Garuḍa): **30**, 1416 (the weapons of V., R., Ā., S., M., and of all the other tribes of the gods began to spend their forces against one another; among the omens appearing amidst the gods at the approaching of Garuḍa).—§ 46 (Garuḍa): **32**, 1487 (they fled for Garuḍa towards the eastern region). — § 84 (Ādivaṃç.): **64**, 2482. — § 88: **65**, 2522 v.s., 2524.— § 120 *bis* (Aṃçāvat.): **66**, 2603 (among the 33 gods; *Bṛhaspatiç ca bhagavān Ādityeshv eva gaṇyate*, which may signify that Bṛh. is on a level with the Ādityas, or allude to his being invoked with Indra; BR., s.v. *Ād.*, explains Ād. to mean generally "the gods").—§ 139 (Manu Vaivasvata): **75**, 3135.—§ 191 (Sambhavap.): **123**, 4824 (v.s.).— § 233 (Svayaṃvarap.): I, **187**, 7010 (Rudrā°; present at the svayaṃvara of Kṛshṇā).—§ 238 (Vaivāhikap.): **197**, 7315. — § 253 (Haraṇāharaṇap.): **221**, 8040. — § 267 (Varuṇasabhāv.): II, **9**, 359 (present in the palace of Varuṇa!).—§ 270 (Brahma-sabhā-varn.): II, **11**, 448 (in the palace of Brahmán), 460; cf. II, 359 ("in the palace of Varuṇa!") (*sādhirājāno*, i.e. *sendrāḥ*, Nīl., cf. I, 2600, *supra*), 460; cf. II, 359 ("in the palace of Varuṇa").—§ 309 (Āraṇyakap.): III, **2**, 127 (sustain the creatures by way of lordship acquired by yoga).—§ 330 (Indradarçana): **37**, 1490 (Kṛshṇa wishes success to Arjuna from V., R., Ā., the gaṇas of M., V.-D., S., etc., when he is departing to see Indra).—§ 336 (Indralokābhig.): III, **43**, 1768 (seen by Arjuna in the town of Indra!).—§ 338 (do.): **46**, 1840 (do.).—§ 347 (Nalop.): **62**, 2356.—§ 356 (Tīrthayātrāp.): **80**, 3091 (*Ādityānāṃ yathā Vishṇuḥ*).—§ 357 (Pushkara): III, **82**, 4064 (Ā. with V., R., S., M.-gaṇas, G., and Aps.).—§ 370 (Tīrthayātrāp.): **84**, 8102 (Ā. with D., Ṛ., V., and R. always adore Janārdana at the tīrtha Nārāyaṇasya sthānam).—§ 375 (do.): III, **85**, 8248 (have bathed in the tīrthas enumerated in the Tīrthayātrāparvan).—§ 377 (Dhaumyatīrthak.): **90**, 8404 (do.).—§ 383 (Paraçu-Rāma): III, **99**, 8673 (with Ā., V., R., S., M.-gaṇas, P., etc., etc., etc.).—§ 400 (Tīrthayātrāp.): III, **118**, 10224 (their altars —*āyatanāni*—are seen by Yudhishṭhira on his tīrthayātrā).— § 412 (Tīrthayātrāp.): **134**, 10669.—§ 443 (Nivātakavacayuddhap.): **168**, 12044 (seen by Arjuna in the town of Indra).—§ 457 (Mārkaṇḍeyas.): III, **188**, 12924 (seen by Mārkaṇḍeya in the belly of Vishṇu).—§ 547 (Kuṇḍalāharaṇap.): **308**, 17139 ("may Ā., V., R., S., *Vi. ca devatāḥ, M.*, etc., etc., protect thee," says Kuntī, consigning the basket with Karṇa to the river Açvanadī).—§ 549 (Pāṇḍavapraveçap.): IV, **2**, 48 (*Ādityānāṃ trayodaçam*, Arjuna).— § 561 (Yānasandhip.): V, **49**, 1919 (adore Brahmán).— § 562 (Bhagavadyānap.): **86**, 3043 (like Ā., V., R., depending on the intelligence of Bṛhaspati). — § 564 (Mātalīyop.): **97**, 3503 (*Ādityānāṃ hi sarveshāṃ Vishṇur ekaḥ sanātanaḥ*; here Ād. rather means "the gods" generally).—§ 567 (Bhagavadyānap.): **128**, 4301.—§ 567 (do.): **131**, 4423 (appear in the body of Kṛshṇa).—§ 570 (Sainyaniryānap.): **153**, 5190.—§ 576 (Bhagavadgītāp.): VI, **34**, 1225 (*Ādityānām ahaṃ Vishṇur*, i.e. Kṛshṇa); **35**, 1252 (appear in the body of Kṛshṇa), 1268.—§ 608 (Karṇap.): VIII, **87**, 4419 (favour Karṇa against Arjuna).— § 615*u* (Skanda): IX, **44**, 2479 (surround Çiva at the consecration of Skanda); **45**, 2508 (with S., Vi., M., V., P., R., etc., etc., and Ā.).—§ 615 (Asita Devala): **50**, 2892 (°*ānāṃ salokatām*).—§ 626 (Rājadh.): XII, **21**, 634 (R., V., Ā., S., and R.-r. adopt the *adroha-dharma*, and, following the *rāja-çāstra*, not nirvāṇa, have attained to Svarga).—§ 656 (Khaḍgotp.): **166**, 6141.—§ 661 (Mokshadh.): **198**, 7192 (*Rudrā° Vasūnām*; their places are "Nirayāḥ" compared with the place of Paramātman).—§ 664 (do.): **207**, 7543 (*devaçreshṭhān; teshāṃ Vishṇur vāmano' bhūd Govindaç cābhavat prabhuḥ*).—§ 665 (Mokshadh.): XII, **208**, 7581, etc. (v.s.; *dvādaça Kaçyapasyātmasambhavān*), 7589 ("*kshattriyāḥ*" among the gods). — § 671 (Bali-Vāsava-saṃvāda): **224**, 8128 (*dvādaçānām*).—§ 673 (do.): **227**, 8220, 8288 (Bali says he had formerly vanquished Ā., R., S., V., and M.).—§ 695 (Mokshadh.): XII, **285**, 10279 (present at the sacrifice of Daksha).—§ 702 (Mokshadharma): **296**, 10837 (Ā., V., R., Agni, A., M., Vi., S., P., M.-gaṇāḥ, Y., R., G., Si., etc., have become perfect by *tapas*).—§ 712 (Çukotpatti): XII, **324**, 12175 (adore and surround Çiva while he is exercising tapas on the Himālaya). — § 717 (Nārāyaṇīya): **340**, 12916 (*dvādaçaiva tathādityān vāmaṃ pārçvaṃ samāsthitān*, sc. of Kṛshṇa).—§ 730 (Meghavāhanop.): XIII, **14**, 611 (do not know the abode of Çiva), 914 (°*ānāṃ Vishṇuḥ*, i.e. Çiva), 985. —§ 746 (Ānuçāsanik.): **62**, 3148.—§ 747 (Suvarṇotp.): **84**, 4011; **85**, 4131 (5260, read "*Ādityaṃ dvādaçe*" with B.). —§ 759 (Ānuçāsanik.): XIII, **107**, 5296 (°*ānāṃ lokān*: are obtained by him who eats only every 20th day for twelve months, abstaining from meat, etc.), 5307 (°*ānām adhivāse*: there he, who for twelve months eats only every 24th day, etc., shall dwell for a long time).—§ 766 (do.): XIII, **134**, 6186 (receive the bali of him who offers cooked food with honey from a vessel of udumbara-wood to the rising moon on the full moon day).—§ 768 (do.): **139**, 6372 (*dvādaçā°-sankāço*). —§ 770 (do.): **151**, 7092, etc. (*dvādaça Kāçyapeyāḥ*).— § 773 (do.): **159**, 7387 (*Rudrā°* identified with Kṛshṇa). —§ 775 (do.): **166**, 7642 (should be invoked for protection). —§ 778 (Açvam. parv.): XIV, **8**, 185 (adore Çiva on the mountain Muñjavat).—§ 785 (Anugītāp.): **64**, 1896 (*svena sainyena saṃvītā yathādityāḥ svaraçmibhiḥ*). — § 793 (Mausalap.): XVI, **4**, 129 (receive Kṛshṇa when arriving to Heaven after death).—§ 795 (Svargārohaṇap.): XVIII, **3**, 88 (receive Yudhishṭhira when returning from Hell); **4**, 130 (*dvādaçā°-sadṛçam*); **6**, 215 ("represented in the Mhbh."; BR. s.v. explains *Ād°* in this passage to mean generally "the gods"; read with B., *Ādityāç cāçvinau*; v.s.). Cf. Kāçyapeyāḥ.

Āditya[2] (°āḥ), the gods in general: I, 2603 (? v. *supra*); V, 3503 (? v. *supra*); XIII, 7280 (they held a sattra, where they were rescued from the Dānavas named Khalins by Vaçishṭha); XVIII, 215 (? v. *supra*).

Āditya[3], plur. (°āḥ), the seven Suns that shall scourge the world at its dissolution and prepare the way for the Saṃvartaka fire: III, 12874.

Āditya[4], the Sun: I, 126, 718 (°*vat*), 899 (°*varcasaṃ*), 1092 (°*rathaṃ*), 1148 (°*pathaṃ*), 1173; II, 947; III, 192, 7054 (°*syāçramo*), 7055 (°*lokam*); VII, 346 (*Yama-Vaiçravaṇā°-Mahendra-Varuṇopamaṃ*); IX, 301, 985, 2071, 2664, 3124 (°*maṇḍalaṃ*), 3138 (*Rāhuç cāgrasadādityam aparvaṇi*), 3631 (*cakram°gocaraṃ*); X, 577 (*rathenā°-varcasā*), 648 (°*odayavarṇasya*); XI, 471 (°*varṇāni vaktrāṇi*), 535 (*dhvajāṃç cā°-sannibhān*); XII, 318 (°-*çaçi-tārakaṃ*), 865 (*candrā°au*), 1591,

1923 (°m patitam yathā), 1930 (id.), 2576 ([bhūmipaḥ] bhavaty Agnis tathā°o Mṛtyur Vaiçravaṇo Yamaḥ), 3758, 5672 (yathā°ḥ prātar udyaṃs tamaḥ sarvam apohati | kalyāṇam ācarann evaṃ sarvapāpaṃ vyapohati), 5693 (ā°o 'yaṃ sthito, i.e. the sun has not yet set), 5782, 6789 (ūrdhvaṃ gater adhastāt tu candrā°au na dṛçyataḥ), 7048 (nekshetā°m udyantaṃ), 7055 (praty ā°ṃ na meheta), 8180, 8182 (Ā°o nāvatapitā kadācin madhyataḥ sthitaḥ), 8562 (yadā°ṃ sthitaṃ madhye gūhanti çikhino 'rcishaḥ | sarvam evedam arcirbhiḥ pūrṇaṃ jājvalyate nabhaḥ, at the dissolution of the world), 8786, 9316, 9380 (pancendriyeshu bhūteshu sarvaṃ vasati daivataṃ | Ā°ç Candramā Vāyur Brahmā Prāṇaḥ Kratur Yamaḥ), 9406–7 (agnau prāstāhutir, brahmann, ā°m upagacchati | ā°j jāyate vṛshṭir), 10438 (candrā° au cakshushī te, i.e. Çiva, 1000 names[1]), 10986 (advaidhamanasaṃ yuktaṃ çūraṃ dhīraṃ vipaçcitaṃ | na çrīḥ santyajate nityam Ā°m iva raçmayaḥ), 11057 (antakāla ivā°ḥ kṛtsnaṃ saṃçoshayej jagat), 11294, 11387 (vidhūma iva saptārcir ā° iva raçmimān vaidyuto' gnir ivākāçe dṛçyate 'tmā tathātmani), 11593 (tataḥ çatasahasrāṃçur avyaktenābhicoditaḥ | kṛtvā dvādaçadhātmānam ā°o jvaladagnivat | caturvidhaṃ, mahīpāla, nirdahaty āçu tejasā, at the dissolution of the world), 11725 (from him Yājñavalkya has obtained the Yajus), 11789, 11976, 12242, 12518, 12568 (ato me rocate gantum ā°ṃ dīptatejasaṃ, says Çuka), 12579, 12932 (°sthaṃ Kapilaṃ), 13063 (°varṇaṃ taṃ Purushaṃ tamasaḥ paraṃ, i.e. Vishṇu), 13254 (°sthaṃ Kapilaṃ, i.e. Kṛshṇa), 13384 (°dagdhasarvāngā adṛçyāḥ kenacit kvacit | paramāṇubhūtā bhūtvā [tu] taṃ devaṃ praviçanty uta), 13597 (°e Savitur jyeshṭhe), 13911 (°pratīkāçaṃ), 13912 (°ābhimukho 'bhyeti gaganaṃ pātayann iva, sc. uñchavṛttiḥ), 13915 (°tāṃ gataṃ, sc. the splendour of the uñchavṛtti); XIII, 55 (Ādityaç Candramā Vāyur Āpo Vishṇuḥ Çatakratuḥ Agniḥ . . . Sarve Kālena sṛjyante hriyante ca punaḥ punaḥ), 731 (Rudrā° Āçvinām vapur dhārayate Bhavaḥ), 888–9 (°-vaktrāya, °-nayanāya, °-varṇāya, °-pratimāya, i.e. Çiva), 1081 (ayam sadevayānānām Ā° dvāram ucyate | ayañ ca pitṛyāṇānāṃ candramā dvāram ucyate), 1089 (candrā°au), 1368 (°-candrau), 1758 (°samatejasam), 1772 (upatasthur yathodyantam Ā°ṃ mantrakovidāḥ), 1832 (divi jyotir yathā°ḥ Pitṛṇāñ caiva candramāh), 2013, 2115 (Ā°ç candramā vāyur . . . sarve brāhmāṇam āveçya sadānnam upabhuñjate), 3150, 3236 (ādatte ca rasān bhaumān Ā°ḥ svagabhastibhiḥ | Vāyur Ā° -taptāṃç ca rasān devaḥ pravarshati), 3916 (taruṇā° varṇāni), 3508 (id.), 3592 (kālajñānaṃ vipragavāntaram hi duḥkhaṃ jñātuṃ Pāvakā °bhūtam, Nīl. is silent), 3823 (taruṇa°-sankāçair), 4171 (°-udayasamprabhe), 4177 (°-odayanaṃ), 4204 (pāvaka°-varcasaṃ kumāraṃ), 4208 (gave to Skanda a brilliant splendour), 4472 (bālā°-vapuḥprakhyaiḥ pushkarair), 4874 (°-devasya pade), 4970 (evam evāparāṃ sandhyāṃ samupāsīta vāgyataḥ | nekshetā°m udyantaṃ nāstaṃ yāntaṃ kadācana), 5029 (praty ā°ṃ praty analam prati gāñ ca prati dvijān | ye mehanti ca panthānam, te bhavanti gatāyushaḥ), 5286 (candrā°au), 5963 (°-tejasā), 6019 (Aindrīṃ sandhyāṃ upāsitvā ā° ābhimukhaḥ sthitaḥ | sarvatīrtheshu sa snāto mucyate sarvakilvishaiḥ), 6116 (parvakāle ca yat kiñcid Ā°ñ cādhitishṭhati | pretalokaṃ gate martye, tat tat sarvaṃ vibhāvasuḥ | pratijānāti puṇyātmā, tac ca tatropayujyate), 6128, 6224 (māṃsapratigrahe caiva madhuno lavanasya ca | a°-odayanaṃ sthitvā pūto bhavati vai dvijaḥ), 6367 (°-sannibhaṃ, of the third eye of Çiva), 6382 (nashṭā°e loke), 6831 (Dakshāyaṇyas tathā°o, Manur Ā°tas tathā), 7114 (°sannibhāḥ), 7126 (°vaṃçaprabhavaṃ, Pṛthuṃ Vainyaṃ (?)), 7155 (Somā°-ānvayāḥ sarve Rāghavāḥ Kuravas tathā), 7268 (°-varcasaṃ), 7295 (candrā°au), 7375 (tasyā°o bhām upayujya bhāti, i.e. Vishṇoḥ), 7386 (candrā°au, identified with Kṛshṇa), 7488 (°varṇena), 7636 (candrā°au prabhākarau), 7711 (dṛshṭvā nivṛttam ā°ṃ pravṛttañ cottarāyaṇaṃ); XIV, 83 (°-sadṛçaḥ), 187 (bālā°-samadyutiḥ), 294 (upaplutam ivā°ṃ), 976, 1070–2 (dṛshṭvā tv ā°m udyantaṃ kucarāṇāṃ bhayaṃ bhavet | adhvagāḥ paritapyeyur ushṇato duḥkhabhāginaḥ | Ā°ḥ sattvam udriktaṃ, kucarās tu tathā tamaḥ paritāpo 'dhvagānāñ ca rajaso guṇa ucyate | prākāçyaṃ [so B.] sattvam Ādityaḥ, santāpo rajaso guṇaḥ | upaplavas tu vijñeyas tāmasas tasya parvasu | evaṃ jyotihshu sarveshu nivartante guṇās trayaḥ), 1200 (cakshuḥsthaç ca sadā°o rūpajñāne vidhīyate), 1214 (bhūmir ādis tu gandhānāṃ, rasanām āpa eva ca | rūpāṇāṃ jyotir Ā°-ḥ, sparçānāṃ vāyur ucyate), 1216 (°o jyotishām ādir), 2235 (Rāhur agrasad Ā°m yugapat Somam eva ca); XV, 628 (rathenā°-varcasā), 815 (°-sannibhaṃ), 854 (dvidhā kṛtvātmano deham Ā°m tapatām varaṃ | lokāṃç ca tāpayānaṃ vai viddhi Karṇañ ca çobhane); XVI, 4, 61 (ratham ā°-varṇaṃ); XVIII, 5, 100 (°tanayaṃ, i.e. Karṇa), 141 (°sadṛço), 239 (uditā°-sankāçam). See Sūrya.

Āditya[5], a Viçvadeva (?): XIII, 4361.

Āditya[6] = Varuṇa: I, 8175 (Varuṇaṃ); XIII, 212 (Varuṇaṃ devam Ā°ṃ patim ambhasāṃ), 214 (Varuṇo deva Ā°o).

Āditya[7] = Vishṇu: XIII, 6954 (VDSNK.), 7009 (ib., bis).

Āditya[8] = Çiva: XII, 10354 (1000 names[1]); XIII, 1181 (MSNST.), 1253 (ib.).

Āditya[9] (adj.): XIII, 5260 (vimānaṃ).

Ādityaketu, one of the 100 sons of Dhṛtarāshṭra: I, 2737 (the 72nd), 4550 (the 76th); VI, 3901 (with six of his brothers he attacks Bhīma to avenge the death of his brother Sunābha), 3904, 3914 (is killed by Bhīma).

Ādityanandana = Karṇa: VI, 5838.

Ādityanayana ("who has the Sun for his eye") = Çiva: XIII, 888.

Adityaparvata, the hermitage of Çiva: XII, 12332 (surrounded by flaming fire).

Ādityapatha ("the way of the Sun") = the sky: I, 1148.

Ādityapati ("the lord of the Ādityas") = Vishṇu: XII, 13110.

Adityapratima ("like unto the Sun") = Çiva: XIII, 889.

Ādityatanaya[1] ("son of the Sun") = Manu: XII, 4507 (Manave).

Ādityatanaya[2] = Karṇa: XVIII, 100.

Āditya-tīrtha ("the holy place of the Sun"), upon the Sarasvatī, § 615ee (Baladevat.): IX, **49**, 2846. There Sūrya, having performed a sacrifice, obtained the sovereignty of all luminous bodies and acquired his great energy. There, on the bank of the river, D. with I., V.-D., M., G., Aps., Vyāsa, Çuka, Kṛshṇa, Y., Rā., Pç., etc., always reside. There Vishṇu, having in days of yore slain As. Madhu and Kaiṭabha, had performed his ablutions. Vyāsa, having bathed in that tīrtha, obtained great Yoga-powers and success (siddhiṃ). And R. Asita Devala (ff.), having bathed in that tīrtha with soul rapt in Yoga, obtained great Yoga-powers.

Ādityavaktra ("having the Sun for his mouth") = Çiva: XIII, 888.

Ādityavarṇa ("having the colour of the Sun") = Çiva: XIII, 889.

[Ādivaṃçāvatāraṇa] ("genealogy"), the fifth chapter of the Ādivaṃçāvatāraṇaparvan (VI), I, **63**; it includes:

§§ 73–4: Vasu Uparicara and his sons.

§ 75: Girikā.

§ 76: Matsya.

§§ 77–8: Vyāsa and his pupils.

§ 79: Bhīshma.
§ 80: Aṇīmāṇḍavya.
§ 81: Sañjaya; Karṇa.
§ 82: Kṛshṇa Vāsudeva.

§ 83. Birth of Sātyaki (son of Satyaka) and Kṛtavarman (son of Hṛdika) (*Nārāyaṇam anuvratau*), Droṇa, Kṛpī, Kṛpa, Açvatthāman, Dhṛshṭadyumna, Kṛshṇā, Nagnajit, and Subala, Çakuni, Gāndhārī, and Dhṛtarāshṭra, Pāṇḍu, and Vidura, and Yudhishṭhira and his brothers, and the 101 sons of Dhṛtarāshṭra (only Duryodhana and the Karaṇa Yuyutsu, born of a Vaiçyā woman, is named), of whom 11 (*a*) (including Yuyutsu) are enumerated as mahārathas, and Abhimanyu, and the sons of Pāñcālī (Draupadī or Kṛshṇā) (enumerated) (*β*), and Ghaṭotkaca, and Çikhaṇḍi(n); "these are only the principal ones of the hundreds of thousands of monarchs who came to fight against each other in that great battle of the Kurus."

Ādivaṃçāvatāraṇa[2] = °**parvan** (B. *ādir aṃçāvatāraṇam*). § 10 (Parvas.): I, **2**, 312.—§ 11 (do.): **2**, 360.

Ādivaṃçāvatāraṇaparvan. § 70: I, **59.** (*a*) Kathābandha: in the intervals of the duties of the snake-sacrifice Vyāsa recited Mahābhārata.

(*b*) Kathānubandha. § 70: I, **60.** Hearing that Janamejaya was installed in the snake-sacrifice, Kṛshṇa Dvaipāyana went thither (his birth, growth, studies, dividing the Vedas into four parts, and his begetting of Pāṇḍu, etc., are mentioned) with his disciples, and asked by Janamejaya about the Kurus and Pāṇḍavas, he directed his disciple Vaiçampāyana to tell their story.

(*c*) Bhāratasūtram. § 71: I, **61.** Vaiçampāyana gives a survey of the history of the Pāṇḍavas.

(*d*) Bhāratapraçaṃsā. § 72: I, **62.** Janamejaya wishes to hear the Mahābhārata in full. Vaiçampāyana describes its virtues (v. 2320: *Bhāratānāṃ mahaj janma Mahābhāratam ucyate*); Kṛshṇa Dvaipāyana had attained his object in three years, rising daily and purifying himself and performing his ascetic devotions he had composed this Mahābhārata; he that gives away a copy of the Bhārata to one that asks for it does indeed make a present of the whole earth with her belt of seas. *Vide* Ādivaṃçāvatāraṇa.

§ 84: I, **64.** Jamadagni's son, after having twenty-one times destroyed the kshattriya race, began ascetic penances on the Mahendra mountain. A new kshattriya caste sprang from the kshattriya ladies and the brahmans. Description of the Kṛta yuga. Then the Daityas being repeatedly defeated by the Ādityas and deprived of heaven, the Asuras began to be born on Earth in such numbers that the Earth became incapable of supporting herself, even with the united strength of the Pannagas (*bhūtasattvaughaḥ*). The Earth then applied to Brahmán, who was surrounded by gods, brahmans, great Ṛshis, Gandharvas, and Apsarases. Brahmán appointed the gods, Gandharvas and Apsarases, to be born on Earth in order to ease her of her burthen by destroying the Asuras. They agreed, and going to Vaikuṇṭha they also prevailed upon Nārāyaṇa to become incarnate.

Adri[1], son of Viçvagaçva, descendant of Ikshvāku. § 475 (Dhundhumārop.): III, **202**, 13517.

Ādri[2] = Kṛshṇa: XII, 1508.

Adrijā ("born from the mountain"), a river? § 775 (Ānuçāsanik.): XIII, **166**, 7648 (Kṛshṇavenā?).

Adrikā, an Apsaras, cursed by Brahmán to become a fish; when dwelling in the Yamunā river she drank the semen of Uparicara, was caught by a fisherman, and gave birth to Matsya and Satyavatī. § 76: I, **63**, 2388–9.—§ 191 (Arjuna): **123**, 4817 (with other Apsarases she sings and dances at the birth of Arjuna).

Adṛçya = Vishṇu (1000 names).

Adṛçyantī, wife of Çaktri (BR. *Çakti*) and daughter-in-law of Vasishṭha, and mother of Parāçara. § 225 (Vāsishṭha): I, **177**, 6755, 6757, 6763; **178.**—§ 226 (Parāçara): **178**, 6792, 6796–7.—§ 565 (Gālavacarita): V, **117**, 3970.

Adṛḍha, son of Jarāsandha (?). § 604 (Karṇap.): VIII, **7**, 207.

Ādya[1] = Çiva (1000 names[2]).

Ādya[2] = Vishṇu: XII, 13290.

Ādya[3], a tīrtha upon the Sarasvatī (?). § 615 (Baladevatīrthay.): IX, **35**, 2062 (*Ā°ṃ Svastyayanañ caiva*).

Ādya(h) Purusha(h) ("the first Spirit") = Vishṇu: I, 22.

Ādyastuti = Çiva (1000 names[2]).

Agama = Çiva (1000 names[2]).

Agastya[1], a ṛshi, brother of Vasishṭha and son of Mitra and Varuṇa;* he is called Maitrāvaruṇi ("son of Mitra and Varuṇa") and Kumbhayoni ("born in a jar") (see below); he once saw his ancestors hanging in a cave, and was urged by them to procure progeny; he then from the most beautiful parts of all animals created Lopāmudrā and let her become the daughter of the king of Vidarbha; when he had married her he, in order to procure riches for her, applied successively to three kings, and then to the Dānava Ilvala, who shaped his own younger brother into a he-goat that was digested by Agastya. Agastya had a son by Lopāmudrā named Dṛḍhasyu or Idhmavāha. *A.* prevailed upon the Vindhya mountain to cease to increase in height "till he had returned from the South," and drunk up the Sea (and digested it), in order that the gods might overcome the Kālakeyas. § 382 (Agastyop.): III, **96–9.**—§§ 384–6 (do.): **101–5.**—§ 183 (Pāṇḍu): I, **118**, 4571 (he hunted and sacrificed wild beasts: *A°ḥ sattram āsīnaç cakāra mṛgayām ṛshiḥ | āraṇyān sarvadaivatyān mṛgān prokshya mahāvane*).—§ 210 (Sambhavap.): I, **139**, 5524 (Droṇa's teacher Agniveça was a pupil of *A.* in the Dhanurveda).—§ 233 (Svayaṃvarap.): **188**, 7047 (all. to his drinking up the Sea).—§ 236 (do.): **192**, 7164 (°*çāstāṃ diçam*, the South).—§ 267 (Yamasabhāv.): II, **8**, 340 (in the palace of Yama).—§ 270 (Brahmasabhāv.): **11**, 439 (in the palace of Brahmán).—§ 316 (Kirmīravadhap.): III, **11**, 422 (*sambhakshya jarayishyāmi yathāgastyo mahāsuram*).—§ 377 (Dhaumyatīrthak.): **87**, 8316 (°*sy-āçramavaro*, in the East); **88**, 8344 (°*syāçramaḥ*, in the South).—§ 380 (Brahmasaras): **95**, 8521 (*Brahmasarottamam | A°o bhagavān yatra gato Vaivasvatam prati*; cf. XIII, 3400).—§ 382 (Agastyop.): **96**, 8540 (°*syāçramam*), 8541–2, 8553; **97**, 8570, 8575–7, 8581; **98**, 8595, 8606; **99**, 8618, 8620, 8622, 8625, 8633, 8644 (°*āçramo*), 8645.—§ 384 (do.): **100**, 8689–90; **103**, 8773, 8774 (°*syāçramaṃ*); **104**, 8788, 8795–6, 8804; v.s.—§ 389 (Gaṅgāvatār.): **109**, 9967 (all. to his destroying Vātāpi).—§ 391 (Ṛshyaçṛṅga): **110**, +10092 (+*Lopāmudrā vā yathā hy Agastyam*).—§ 410 (Plakshāvataraṇa): **130**, 10541 ("this is the great tīrtha of Sindhu, where Lopāmudrā joined herself to *A.* and chose him for her husband").—§ 438 (Yakshayuddh.): **161**, 11788, 11790, 11794 (the Rākshasa Maṇimat having spit

* Natus erat cum fratre Vasishtho semine Mitri et Varuni, quum nympham Urvaçim vidissent, amore incensorum in urceum profluente (Bṛhaddevatā, 5. 30 ff., see BR.).

upon him, he cursed Kubera to see Maṇimat and his (Kubera's) warriors slain by a man—fulfilled by Bhīmasena at the Yaksha combat); **162,** 11839.—§ 450 (Ājagarap.): **179,** 12409 (all. to Nahusha's curse by *A.*); **180,** 12464–5 (do.); **181,** 12525 (do.).—§ 479 (Pativratop.): **206,** 13679 (all. to the destruction of Vātāpi).—§ 551 (Kīcakavadhap.): IV, **21,** 655 (all. to his wife Lopāmudrā).—§ 555 (Indra): V, **17,** 521 (he cursed Nahusha, who was king of the gods in the absence of Indra, to become a serpent for 10,000 years; cf. XIII, ch. 99 f.), 542; **18,** 556.—§ 565 (Gālavacar.): **117,** 3971.—§ 569 (Bhagavadyānap.): **143,** 4876 (*°çāstām diçam*, i.e. the South).—§ 617 (Brahmaçiras): X, **12,** 618 (*Ag.* had taught Droṇa Brahmaçiras).—§ 649 (Āpaddh.): XII, **141,** 5389 (all. to his eating Vātāpi).—§ 656 (Khaḍgotp.): **166**β, 6142 (*Vaçishṭha-Gautamā°āḥ*).—§ 665 (Mokshadh.): **208**η, 7595 (*Mitra-Varuṇayoḥ putraḥ*, one of the seven ṛshis of the South).—§ 677 (Mokshadh.): **245**β, 8899 (one of the authors of the duties of renunciation).—§ 717 (Nārānaṇīya, v. Indra, V, **17**): **343,** 13216 (*Kumbhayonir Maitrāvaruṇiḥ ṛshivaro*).—§ 734 (Ānuçāsanik.): XIII, **26a,** 1761 (with other ṛshis, *A.* comes to see Bhīshma on his arrow-bed).—§ 746 (do.): XIII, **66**ζ, 3332 (visits the sacrifices of the gods on the Himālaya).—§ 747 (Ānuçāsanik.): XIII, **84**β, 3968 (is consulted with others by Paraçurāma, who is anxious to know how to purify himself totally after he has destroyed the kshattriyas; they advise him to offer gold).—§ 751 (Çapathavidhi): XIII, **94,** 4550, 4554–5 (4592) (at Brahmasaras Indra stole a lotus from *A.* in order to hear the wise words of the ṛshis).—§ 755 (Nahushop.): XIII, **99-100,** 4745 (*Nahushasya ca saṃvādam A°sya Bhṛgos tathā*), 4755–6, 4758, 4771 (*Maitrāvaruṇir*); 4785, 4792, 4794, 4800, 4802, 4805 (he cursed Nahusha, who was king of the gods in the absence of Indra, to become a serpent for 10,000 years; cf. V, **16**).—§ 761 (Ānuçāsanik.): XIII, **115,** 5652 (cf. I, 4571); **116,** 5696.—§ 767 (do.): **137a,** 6255 (*Vaidarbhiḥ kanyām A°āya dattvā*).—§ 770 (do.): **151**η, 7113 (*Mitra-Varuṇayoḥ putraḥ*, the seventh of the seven Dharmarājartvijaḥ in the South), 7157 (read with B., *Çukrā°-Bṛhaspatiprabhṛtibhir brahmarshibhiḥ*).—§ 772*k* (Pavanārjuna-s.): Once the gods were vanquished by As. (Dā.); their sacrifices and the svadhā of P. were robbed, and so also the sacrifices of men. Wandering over the earth they met the brahman Agastya, who at their request burned Dā., who, abandoning both the worlds (i.e. the earth and the sky), fled to the South. The Dā. king Bali was performing a horse-sacrifice in the nether regions (*mahīm gataḥ*); the great As., who were under (the earth) and in (?) the earth (*mahīshṭhāç ca*), were not burned, and *A.* could not destroy them, lest his penances should suffer a diminution. "Name thou a kshattriya that is superior to *A.*": XIII, **156,** 7265 (*brāhmaṇasya*), 7268, 7271, 7273, 7277–8.—§ 775 (Ānuçāsanik.): **166**δ, 7666 (*Mitra-Varuṇayoḥ putraḥ*, one of the ṛshis of the South).—§ 786*e* (Anugītāp.): XIV, **92:** In olden days *A.*, devoted to the good of all creatures, entered into a dīkshā for twelve years; many hotṛs were engaged (description). *A.* obtained the food required by lawful means. Numerous ascetics at that time performed large sacrifices; as *A.*, however, was engaged in his (with seeds), Indra did not pour rain. During the intervals of the sacrifice the Mu. spoke about this; *A.* said that if Indra did not pour rain during those twelve years he would perform the mental sacrifice, or the touch-sacrifice, or other sacrifices; then *A.* by his words caused all wealth in the three worlds, all Aps., G., Ku., Viçvāvasu, etc., the wealth of the Northern Kurus, Heaven, the gods, and Dharma, to come to the place of his sacrifice; Ṛ. praised him, but did not wish that his penances should suffer any diminution. Indra poured rain and came with Bṛhaspati and pacified *A.* After the completion of the sacrifice, *A.* duly worshipped those great Mu. and dismissed them: XIV, **92***e*, 2849–50, 2856–8, 2861, 2873, 2882, 2884.—Compare Kumbhayoni, Maitrāvaruṇi, Mitra-Varuṇayoḥ putra.

Agastya[2]: XIII, 3400 (*A°m gotrataç cāpi nāmataç cāpi çarmiṇam*), might allude to a brahman of Agastya's race, named Çarmin (called before Yama to receive instructions and then dismissed); yet III, 8521, the epithet "bhagavān" naturally leads the thought upon Agastya himself; BR. takes *çarmiṇam* to be an adjective—"happy."

Āgastya[1], patron. (*°āḥ*, see BR.) § 324 (Dvaitavanap.): III, **26,** 971.

Āgastya[2], adj. (*°m*) **ākhyāna(m)** = Agastyopākhyāna (Mbh. III, ch. **96** ff.). § 11 (Parvas.): I, **11,** 442.

Āgastya[3], adj. (*°m*) **saras** ("lake of Agastya"), a tīrtha. § 358 (Tīrthayātrāp.): III, **82,** 4085.

Agastyaçishya (disciple of Agastya, whom ?). § 377 (Dhaumyatīrthak.): III, **88,** 8343 (*āçramo°sya*).

Agastyāçrama ("the hermitage of Agastya"). § 382 (Agastyop.): III, **99,** 8632.

Agastyaparvata ("mountain of Agastya"). § 377 (Dhaumyatīrthak.): III, **87,** 8317.

Agastyatīrtha ("holy place of Agastya"). § 250 (Arjunavanavāsap.): I, **216,** 7841 (in the South, one of the five Nārītīrthāni).—§ 377 (Dhaumyatīrthak.): III, **88,** 8339 (*Pāṇḍyeshu*, in the South).—§ 400 (Tīrthayātrāp.): III, **118,** 10217 (*Draviḍeshu, samudram āsadya, Nārītīrthāny atha*).

Agastyavaṭa ("the *Ficus Indica* of Agastya"), a place in or near the Himālaya. § 249 (Arjunavanavāsap.): I, **215** 7813.

[Agastyopākhyāna.] § 382 (Tīrthay.): In the city of *Maṇimatī* there lived formerly a *Daiteya Ilvala*, whose younger brother was *Vātāpi* (*Prāhrādi*, v. 8645). *Ilvala*, inflamed with wrath against all brahmans, because a brahman had refused to grant him a son equal to *Indra*, used to transform *Vātāpi* into a ram and offer his flesh to brahmans as food, and then to recall him to life (whomsoever *Ilvala* summoned with his voice would come back even from the abode of *Yama*), and *Vātāpi*, ripping the flanks of the brahmans, would come out laughing. Thus they killed many brahmans. Meanwhile *Agastya* saw his ancestors hanging in a hole with the heads downwards, and was asked by them to procure offspring to them. As he did not see any wife worthy of himself, he selected the most beautiful parts from various creatures and created an excellent woman, whom he caused to be born as the daughter of the *Vidarbha* king, who was then undergoing ascetic penances for obtaining offspring. She was named *Lopāmudrā*, and was very beautiful. When she attained to puberty no one dared to ask for her hand (III, **96**). When *Agastya* asked the *Vidarbha* king to bestow her upon him, the king and his queen became much afflicted, but at her own request *Lopāmudrā* was bestowed upon *Agastya*, who immediately asked her to discard her ornaments and dress herself in rags and barks and deer-skins and partake of his vows, and proceeding to *Gaṅgādvāra* they practised the severest penances. When at last he summoned her for marital intercourse she made it a condition that he should approach her on a bed like to that which she had in the palace of her father, and that both should be adorned with costly ornaments, and she told him to procure these things without impairing his ascetic merit (III, **97**). *Agastya* then went to King *Çrutarvan* and asked him for wealth, but seeing that his expenditure was equal to his income, he took nothing, but, together with *Çrutarvan*, went to King *Bradhnaçva*, with the same result; then all three went to King *Trasadasyu Paurukutsa* of the line of *Ikshvāku*, with the same result. At the suggestion of the three kings they all four went to *Ilvala* (III, **98**). *Ilvala* went out with his ministers to receive them on the confines of his domain. He prepared the flesh of *Vātāpi* in order to entertain them, at which the kings became sad, but *Agastya* ate it all, and when *Ilvala* summoned *Vātāpi* there came only air out of *Agastya's* stomach, *Vātāpi* having already been digested. Then *Ilvala*, becoming sad, promised to give them wealth if *Agastya* could tell him what he intended to give, and *Agastya* rightly said that he intended to give each of the kings 10,000 cows and as many gold coins, and to *Agastya* twice as much, and a car that would be found to be a golden one, with two steeds (*Virāva* and *Surāva*). The car brought *Agastya* and the kings to *Agastya's* hermitage within the twinkling of an eye. Then the *rājarshis* went away to their cities. When *Agastya* proposed to *Lopāmudrā* to choose between 1000 sons, or 100 each equal to 10, or 10 each equal to 100, or 1 equal to 1000, she chose the last alternative. After she had conceived he retired into the forest. After seven years she gave birth to *Dṛḍhasyu*, who came out as if repeating the *Vedas* with the *Upanishads* and *Angas*; and from carrying, while yet a child, loads of sacrificial fuel to the hermitage of his father, he was called *Idhmavāha*. *Agastya* was highly pleased, and his ancestors obtained the *lokas* they desired.—§ 384: In the kṛta age the *Dānava* tribes named *Kālakeyas* under *Vṛtra* pursued the gods under *Indra*. The gods, on the suggestion of Brahmán, with *Nārāyaṇa* at their head, proceeded to the hermitage of the ṛshi *Dadhīca* on the other bank of *Sarasvatī*, and having prevailed upon him to leave his body, they caused *Tvashṭṛ* to construct of his bones the six-sided (*shaḍaçri*) *vajra* which *Tvashṭṛ* handed to *Indra* that he might slay *Vṛtra* with it (III, **100**). In the encounter that ensued between the gods and the *Kālakeyas* the gods were defeated, until *Nārāyaṇa*, the gods, and the *brahmarshis* had transferred their own vigour to *Indra*. He then hurled the *vajra* against *Vṛtra* and slew him so that he fell headlong like the *Mandara* mountain hurled of yore from *Vishṇu's* hand; but *Indra* fled in fear, desiring to take shelter in a lake, thinking that the *vajra* had not been hurled from his hand and that *Vṛtra* was still alive, while the gods defeated the *Dānavas*, who fled to the depths of the sea. Here they conspired for the destruction of the three worlds, and resolved upon destroying all who were possessed of ascetic virtues (*tapas*), for so the universe would itself be destroyed, as it is supported by asceticism (III, **101**). Remaining in the depths of the sea by day, the *Kāleyas* during the night slew the *munis* in the hermitages and sacred spots (*puṇyeshvāyataneshu*); in the hermitage of *Vasishṭha*, 197 ascetics; in that of *Cyavana*, 100; in that of *Bharadvāja*, 20, without being seen; every morning people saw the dead bodies and mutilated limbs of the *munis* and the disturbed *agnihotras* scattered on the ground. Men fled for their lives into all directions or killed themselves from fear. Some brave bowmen searched in vain for the evildoers. The gods with *Indra* repaired to *Nārāyaṇa* (c) (III, **102**). They did not know by whom the *brahmans* were being killed during the night. *Vishṇu* explained the whole affair to them, and told them to apply to *Agastya* (*Maitrāvaruṇi*) that he might dry up the sea, as no one else was capable of so doing. They then went to the hermitage of *Agastya*, and mentioned to him that he had delivered the gods from *Nahusha* and caused *Vindhya* to cease to increase in height (in competition with the Sun), the world having been covered with darkness (III, **103**).—§ 385: *Vindhya* (q.v.).—§ 386: At the request of the gods *Agastya*, accompanied by *ṛshis*, gods, men, *Uragas* (snakes), *Gandharvas*, *Yakshas*, and *Kimpurushas*, approached the ocean (III, **104**) and drank it up, to the amazement of the gods, who called him *Vidhātṛ* and the creator of the worlds, while the musical instruments of *Gandharvas* were playing, and celestial blossoms were showered upon him. The *Kāleyas*, who had previously been burnt by the *tapas* of the *munis*, were now destroyed by the gods, except some few who, rending asunder the goddess Earth, sought refuge in *Pātāla*. The gods now asked *Agastya* to fill up the ocean again, but he had already digested the water. The gods with *Vishṇu* came to *Brahmán* and spoke to him about replenishing the sea (III, **105**). *Brahmán* dismissed them, saying that only after a long course of time the ocean would be brought to resume its wonted state by the agnates of king *Bhagīratha*.

Agāvaha, a Vṛshṇi hero (cf. BR.). § 589 (Droṇābhishekap.): VII, **11**ξ, 408.

Aghamarshaṇa, a ṛshi (cf. BR.). § 677 (Mokshadh.): XII, **245**β, 8899 (among the authors of the duties of the fourth mode of life).

Aghanta = Çiva (1000 names[1]).

Aghaṇṭin = Çiva (1000 names[1]).

Aghoraghorarūpa = Çiva (1000 names[1]).

***Āgneya**[1] ("belonging to, of the nature of *Agni or Fire"). § 11 (Parvas.): I, **2**, 538 (°*m astram Nārāyaṇam*? Rudramāhātmyam?).—§ 283 (Digvijayap.): II, **31**, 1154 (*ity evaṃ mantram Āgneyam paṭhan yo juhuyād vibhum | ṛddhimān satataṃ dāntaḥ sarvapāpaiḥ pramucyate*).—§ 592 (Saṃçaptakavadhap.): VII, **23**, 1041 (*Raudram Āgneya-Kauveryaṃ Yāmyaṃ Giriçam eva ca | pañcānāṃ Draupadeyānāṃ dhanūratnāni, Bhārata!*).

***Āgneya**[2], astram. § 208b (Arjuna): I, **135**, 5365 (°*enāsṛjad vahniṃ*).—§ 221 (Caitrarathap.): **170**, 6492 (given by Arjuna to Citraratha).—§ 257 (Khāṇḍavadah.): **225**, 8196 (given to Kṛshṇa by Pāvaka, i.e. Agni).—§ 440 (Yakshayuddhap.): III, **164**, 11900 (obtained by Arjuna from Indra, together with all other celestial weapons).—§ 552 (Goharaṇap.): IV, **66**, 1982, 2058.—§ 573 (Ambop.): V, **180**, 7174 (employed by Bhīshma against Rāma).—§ 588 (Bhīshmavadhap.): VI, **121**β, 5801 (enumeration of weapons only known by Dhanañjaya, i.e. Arjuna and Kṛshṇa).—§ 589 (Droṇābhishekap.): VII, **11**, 402 (*Khāṇḍave Pārtha-sahitas toshayitvā Hutāçanam | °m astraṃ durdharshaṃ cakraṃ lebhe mahābalaḥ*, i.e. *Kṛshṇa*).—§ 600 (Ghaṭotkacav.): **157**, 6954.—§ 603 (Nārāyaṇāstramokshap.): **194**, 8965 (*Vāruṇā*°); **201**, 9406 (*devair api sudurdharsham astram Āgneyam ādade*, v. Açvatthāman).—§ 608 (Karṇap.): VIII, **89**, 4540.—§ 730 (Meghavāhanop.): XIII, **14**, 854 (the Pāçupata weapon is superior to the Āgneya, etc.).

Āgneya[3], nakshatra. § 759 (Ānuçāsanik.): XIII, **103**, 5082 (under it one should not make sacrifices).

***Āgneya**[4], ukshan. § 778 (Saṃvartta-Maruttīya): XIV, **10**, 285 (°*m lohitam ukshāṇam ālabhantām*, v. Agni).

***Āgneya**[5], Mātaraḥ. § 615u (Skanda): IX, **46**, 2655 (°*yyaḥ*, sc. Mātaraḥ, in an enumeration).

Āgneya [6], patron = Skanda: I, 5431 (*Āgneyaḥ Kṛttikāputro Raudro Gāṅgeya ity api | çrūyate bhagavān devaḥ sarvaguhyamayo Guhaḥ*).—III, 14630.

Āgneya [7], patron: XIII, 120 (*Sudarçanaḥ*, son of Agni and Sudarçanā).

Āgneya [8], patron: XIII, 4143 (*Aṅgirāḥ*).

Āgneya [9] (plur.). § 515 (Karṇa-Digvijaya): III, **254**, 15256 (a people conquered by Karṇa).

Agni** (Fire). § 4 (Anukram.): I, **1**, 94 (*trīn A°īṃ iva Kauravyān*), 150 (°*ṃ darpitaṃ Khāṇḍave*).—§ 11 (Parvas.): I, **2**, 448 (*Indrāgnī yatra Dharmaç capy ajijñāsan Chibim*), 630–1 (all. to § 794).—§ 17 (Utaṅka): I, **3**, 829 (*yo'çvaḥ, so'gniḥ*).—§ 18 (Ugraçravas): I, **4**, 854 (°*caraṇam*).—§ 20 (Puloma): I, **5**, 884, 889, (893), **6**, 897, 908, 910, **7**, 923, 924, 926, 928, 933, 937, 938 (Bhṛgu's wife Pulomā had first been betrothed to the Rākshasa Puloman, who one day, when Bhṛgu was absent, came to carry her away, and asked the sacrificial fire if she was rightly his or Bhṛgu's wife. The fire answered that she was indeed first chosen by the Rākshasa, but that she was rightly Bhṛgu's, by whom she had been taken with holy rites and invocations. When Puloman began to carry her away Cyavana dropped from her womb, and Puloman was instantly converted into ashes. Of her tears Brahmán formed the river Vadhūsara. Bhṛgu cursed Agni, saying, "thou shalt eat of all things." Agni, enraged at the curse, withdrew himself from the sacrifice, wherefore all creatures became much distressed. Brahmán appeased Agni by promising that only his less noble form (the digestive fire in the stomach of carnivora) should be compelled to eat of all things, and that everything should become pure when burnt by his flames).—§ 29 (Kadrū): I, **20** (will consume the sons of Kadrū). — § 30*b* (Samudra): I, **21**, 1220 (*Vaḍavāmukhadīptā*°).—§ 32*b* (Garuḍa): I, **23**, 1241 (°*rāçir, yugāntā*°), 1244 (1245).—§ 33 (do.): **23**, 1250 (i.e. Garuḍa). —§ 40 (do.): **29**, 1323, 1325.—§ 46 (do.): I, **32**.—§ 49 (Vāsuki): **37**, 1596 ("As the gods in days of yore sought the occult Agni, who held himself concealed").—§ 71 (Bhāratasūtra, v. Ādivaṃçāvatāraṇap.): I, **61**, 2277 (*A.* gives Arjuna the bow Gāṇḍīva, etc.).—§ 83 (Ādivaṃçāvatāraṇa): I, **63**, 2437 (°*samadyutiḥ*).—§ 116 (Vasus): I, **66**, 2587 (one of the Vasus and father of Kumāra, i.e. Skanda, °*eḥ putraḥ, Kumāraḥ*; cf. Anala).—§ 130 (Aṃçāvat.): **67**, 2761 (a part of Agni is Dhṛshṭadyumna).—§ 149 (Yayāti): **88**, 3576 (*prabhur* °*iḥ pratapane*). — § 240 (Tilottamā): **211**, 7682 (by Brahmán).—§ 248 (Arjunavanavāsap.): **214**, 7790 f. (°*kāryam*).—[§ 253*c* (Kṛshṇa): *nakshatre Vahnidaivate*, i.e. Kṛttikāsu (PCR.) (I, **221**, 8045).]—§§ 254–60 (Khāṇḍavadah. and Çārṅgakop.): I, **222–34** (burns the Khāṇḍava forest), 8094, 8220 (*dehavanta ivāgnayaḥ*), 8324, 8350, 8353, 8357, 8400, 8412–13, 8415–17, 8428, 8437, 8461–2.—§ 266 (Çakra-sabhā-v.): II, **7**, 291 (*dīpyamana ivāgnayaḥ*), 307 (do.). — § 274 (Rājasūyārambhap.): **15**, 647 (*traya ivāgnayaḥ*).—§ 276 (Jarāsandhavadhap.): **20**, 770 (do.), 790 (*ravi-somāgni-vapusham*), 990 (°*dattena rathena*).—§§ 282–4 (Sahadeva and Māhishmatī): II, **31–32**, 1133, 1141, 1143–4, 1149–50, 1153 (assists Nīla against Sahadeva; married to Nīla's daughter; praised by Sahadeva; enumeration of names of Agni; spares Sahadeva).—§ 310*b* (Sūrya), identified with the Sun (also the Saṃvartaka Fire): III, **3**, 190.—§ 310*c*, among the 108 names of the Sun (III, **3**).—[§ 317*b* (Kṛshṇa): III, **12**, having been Nārāyaṇa, Kṛshṇa became Anala, etc.]—§ 345 (Nalop.): **54** ff. (A., Indra, Yama, and Varuṇa come to the svayaṃvara of Damayantī—and Nala as their messenger to her—but are rejected), 2127 (*lokapālāçca sāgnikāḥ*), 2138, 2140, 2157, 2224 (°*purogamān devān*), 2227. — § 366 (Tīrthayātrāp.): **83**, 7009 (*Agnitīrthaṃ tato gacchet, tatra snātvā nararshabha | Agnilokam avāpnoti kulañ caiva samuddharet*).—§ 371 (Tuṅgaka): **85**, 8191 (*ṛshayas tatra* (i.e. in Tuṅgaka) *devāç ca Varuṇo 'gniḥ Prajāpatiḥ | Harir Nārāyaṇas tatra Mahādevas tathaiva ca | Pitāmahaç ca bhagavān devaiḥ saha mahādyutiḥ | Bhṛguṃ niyojayām āsa yajanārthaṃ mahādyutim*), 8194 (when the Vedas had been lost).—[§ 383*c* (Jāmadagnyatejohāni-kathana): III, **99**, Hutāçana (i.e. Fire) seen in the body of Rāma Dāçarathi.]—§ 392*aa* (Tīrthayātrāp.): III, **114**, 11021 (i.e. 10121), 11022 (i.e. 10122).—§ 410*g* (Plakshāvataraṇag.): **130f*, 10546 (*Agneç caivātra* (i.e. in Kāçmīramaṇḍala) *saṃvādaḥ Kāçyapasya ca, Bhārata*).—§ 411 (Çyenakapot.): III, **130***f*, 10559 (*kapoto bhūtvā*; Indra in the shape of a hawk and Agni in that of a pigeon come to test king Uçīnara's merit) (cf. § 466).—§ 412 (Ashṭāvakrīya): III, **134**, 10659 (*dvāv Indrāgnī carato vai sakhāyau*).—§ 417 (Yavakrītop.): **138**, 10810 (°*purogamāḥ*), 10814 (°*purogamān devān*). — § 418*b* (Gaṅgā): III, **139**, 10821 ("where," i.e. at Kālaçaila (?), with the sevenfold Gaṅgā, "Agni blazes forth without intermission").—§ 443 (Nivātakavacayuddhap.): **168**, 12020 (°*er*, sc. *astram*). — § 456 (Sarasvatī-Tārkshya-s.): **186**, 12745 (°*mukhāḥ devāḥ*).—§ 459 (Mārkaṇḍeyas.): **189**, 12956 (Agni is the mouth of Nārāyaṇa; the Vaḍavāvaktra Fire and the Saṃvartaka Fire are identified with Nārāyaṇa), 12961. —§ 466 (Çibi-carita): III, **197** (cf. § 411), 13274–5 (*kapotarūpena*).—§ 473 (Mārkaṇḍeyas.): **200**, 13480 (°*er apatyaṃ prathamaṃ suvarṇam*).—§ 474 (Dhundhumārop.): **201***a*, 13498 (*Indra-Somāgni-Varuṇāḥ*, worship Madhusūdana). —§ 480 (Brāhmaṇa-vyādhasaṃvāda): **208**, 13812 (*agnayo māṃsakāmāç ca ity api çrūyate çrutiḥ*).—§ 485 (do.): **213**, 13959, etc. (*çārīro 'gniḥ*, i.e. digestion).—§§ 488–94 (Āṅgirasa): III, **217–22** (Aṅgiras in days of yore practised austerities in his hermitage, so that he excelled Agni, who, thinking that Brahmán had created a new Fire, retired in anger to the forest (*vanam*; Nīl. and PCR., "the waters") to practise austerities; but Aṅgiras asked him to remain and make him (Aṅgiras) his first son. From Aṅgiras (through Bṛhaspati) and others, who are perhaps not connected with him, are descended a great many of Agnis or Fires), 14101–3 (°*eḥ sutaḥ . . . Kumāraḥ*), 14112, 14113, (14114), 14115 (°*ḥ prathamo*; °*tvaṃ*), 14116–17, 14131 (*Bṛhaspateḥ putraḥ Çaṃyur nāma*), 14132 (*cāturmāsyeshu yasyeshṭyām açvamedhe 'grajaḥ paçuḥ*), 14133 (*Agnis tasya*, i.e. *Çaṃyoḥ* (?), *suto dīptas tisraḥ kanyāç ca suvratāḥ*), 14134 (*prathamenājyabhāgena pūjyate yo 'gnir adhvare | Agnis tasya Bharadvājaḥ prathamaḥ putra ucyate*), 14135 (. . . *Bharato*), 14141 (°*r Niçcyavano nāma*), 14142 (*Vipāpo 'gniḥ sutas tasya*), 14143 (°*ḥ . . . Nishkṛtir nāma*), 14146 (*antar Agniḥ smṛto yas tu bhuktaṃ pacati dehinām | sa jajñe Viçvabhuṅ nāma sarvalokeshu, Bhārata!*), 14156 (*Āṅgirasaḥ*, etc.), 14162 (*Vāyur-agnī prāṇato 'srjat*, sc. Pāñcajanyaḥ), 14171 (*tad ete*, i.e. Yajñamushas, *nopasarpanti yatra . . . Agniḥ sthito bhavet*), 14174 (*Rathantaraç ca Tapasaḥ putro 'gnih paripaṭhyate | Mitravindāya vai tasmai havir adhvaryavo viduḥ*), 14189 (*Āgrayaṇo nāma*), 14190 (*Niçā tv ajanayat kanyām Agnī-Shomāv ubhau tathā*), 14227 (*evam Agnir bhagavatā nashṭaḥ pūrvam Atharvaṇā | āhūtaḥ*), 14236 (*agnayaḥ*).—§§ 495–8 (Skandotpatti): III, **223–6**.—§ 499 (Skanda-Çakra-samāgama): III, **227**.—§§ 500–1 (Skandopākhyāna): III, **228–9**. § 502 (Manushyagrahakathana): III, **230**.—§§ 503–7

(Skandayuddha): III, **231**.—§§ 508-9 (Kārttikeyastava): III, **232** (Agni (Adbhuta (?), III, v. 14284) having become enamoured of the wives of the seven Ṛshis, at first entered their gārhapatya fire, then after a long time retired to the forest (*vanam*; Nīl. says nothing) in order to destroy himself; Svāhā, who had loved him in vain, cohabited with him, successively assuming the guise of the wives of the Ṛshis (six of the Kṛttikās or Pleiads) except Arundhatī, and going out of the forest in the guise of a bird (Garuḍī, Suparṇī, Vinatā) she threw the semen in a golden basin on the Çveta mountain; this took place on the Amāvasyā day; on the Pratipad day the semen became an embryo (Skanda); on the fourth day Skanda was fully developed. The six wives of the Ṛshis were divorced by their husbands. Skanda is called the son of Rudra, because Agni is called Rudra by brahmans, and because he was produced by Rudra entering Fire (and Umā coalescing with Svāhā), etc., and the Çveta mountain was formed of Rudra's semen virile. Agni gave to Skanda a red cock, that formed his ensign perched on the top of his chariot. The six divorced wives of the Ṛshis, together with Vinatā, obtained from Skanda that they became his mothers. At the request of Indra they (incl. of Vinatā, see v. 14464 and Nīl., i.e. the Kṛttikās) were placed among the Nakshatras (and presided by Agni) instead of Abhijit (q.v.). Brahmán ordered that time should be reckoned from Dhanishṭhā, while it had formerly been reckoned from Rohiṇī (so Nīl.). Svāhā prevailed upon Skanda that she should live for ever with Agni, in so far as offerings with mantras to the gods and Pitṛs (*havyaṃ kavyaṃ ca*) should always be coupled with the name of Svāhā), 14241 (*Agnīnāṃ vividhā vaṃçāḥ*), 14276, 14294, 14300, (14302), 14305, 14314, 14323 (°*dāyādaḥ*, i.e. Skandaḥ), 14363, 14367 (°*r bhūtrā Naigameyaç*), 14391 (*tataḥ Kumāraṃ pitaraṃ* (B. °*rapitaraṃ*) *Skandam āhur janā bhuvi* | *Rudram Agnim Umāṃ* (B. *Agnimukhāṃ*) *Svāhāṃ*), 14428 (*Rudram Agniṃ dvijāḥ prāhū, Rudrasūnus tatas tu saḥ*), 14434 (*kukkuṭaç cāgninā dattas tasya*, i.e. Skandasya, *ketur alaṅkṛtaḥ*), 14517, 14560 (*cāmare cāpi Vāyuç ca gṛhītvāgniç ca dhishṭhitau*, sc. for Skanda).—§ 526*a* (Rāvaṇādivaraprāpti): III, **276**, 15930 (used by the Brahmarshis, etc., as their spokesman before Brahmán).—§ 543 (Rāmābhisheka): **291** (when Rāma Dāçarathi would repudiate Sītā because she had dwelt with Rāvaṇa, Brahmán, Çakra, Agni, Vāyu, Yama, Varuṇa, and Kubera, and his deceased father Daçaratha bore witness to her innocence), 16548, (16558); Agni says that he dwells within the bodies of all creatures.—[§ 548*f* (Āraṇeyap.): III, **315**, 17463 (Hutāçana, entering into water and remaining in concealment, achieved the purpose of the gods).]—§ 549*b* (Pāṇḍavapraveçap.): IV, **2**, 38 (Agni, desirous of consuming the forest of Khāṇḍava, had formerly appeared in the guise of a brahman before Arjuna while he was staying with Kṛshṇa), 42 (*tejasvināṃ varaḥ*); **4**, 104 (°*rad*).—§ 552 (Gograhaṇap.): shows interest for Arjuna (IV, **46** and **56**), allusion to §§ 254-60 (γ) (IV, **45**); one of Arjuna's preceptors in arms (δ and ε) (IV, **45** and **49**): 1535 (*ekaç cāgnim atarpayat*, sc. Arjunaḥ), 1580 (°*r Vaḍavāmukhaḥ*), 1770 (°*er*, sc. *vimānam*; present at the combat between Arjuna and the Kurus), 1982 (*astram Āgneyam Agneç ca*, sc. *aham*, i.e. Arjuna, *avāptavān*). —§ 555 (Indravijaya): V, **9-18** (when Nahusha had supplanted Indra and had come to Çacī in a chariot drawn by Ṛshis, Bṛhaspati sent Agni to find out Indra. Agni at first, having in an instant searched the whole world, did not dare to enter the waters from fear of being extinguished, but at last he was prevailed upon to do so, and found Indra in a lotus-sucker in the midst of a lake. Bṛhaspati explained how Nahusha had become the king of the gods. Indra bestowed upon Agni a share in great sacrifices, where there should be one share for Indra and Agni (*Aindrāgnyo*)); V, **12**, 395 (*devā Agnipurogamāḥ*, with Çacī); **13**, 409 (do. with Vishṇu); **15**, 479 (did not at first dare to enter the waters), (481), 482 (*adbhyo 'gnir*, sc. *utthitaḥ*).—§ 555*f* (Indravijaya): **16** (Agni is the mouth of all the gods; the carrier of offerings (*Havyavah*), and himself the best of offerings (*havis*); hidden, he sojourns in the interior of all beings like a witness, single and threefold; abandoned by him, the universe would forthwith cease to be; by bowing to him the brahmans with their wives and sons attain to the eternal happiness (*gatim*) acquired by their deeds; having created the three worlds, he, when the hour comes, again consumes them (*pacasi*); the wise call him identical with the clouds and with the lightning; flames issuing from him support all creatures; all the waters are deposited in him, so is this entire world; to him nothing is unknown in the three worlds), 486-8, 517 (cf. Çārṅgakop., I, **229**, 8353-60).—§ 557 (Prajāgarap.): **33**, 1044 (*pañcāgnayo manushyeṇa paricaryāḥ prayatnataḥ* | *pitā mātāgnir ātmā ca guruç ca, Bharatarshabha!*).—§ 560 (Sanatsujātop.): **46**, 1757 (*tasmād*, i.e. from the Eternal Bhagavat, *Agniç ca Somaç ca*).—§ 561 (Yānasandhip.): **49**, 1918 (*Vasavaç cāgninā saha*), they with Bṛhaspati, Uçanas, M., Y., Ā., S., Sapt., Viçvāmitra, Aps., etc., worship Brahmán; **52**, 2094 (*trayastriṃçat samāḥ, sūta! Khāṇḍave 'gnim atarpayat*, sc. Arjunaḥ); **60**, 2366 (°*ḥ saciryakartā syāt Khāṇḍave tat kṛtaṃ smaran*); **61**, 2387 (*yadā hy Agniç ca Vāyuç ca Dharma Indro 'çvināv api* | *kāmayogāt pravarteran*); **61**, 2399 ("A., Vāyvagnī, M., Y., Dharma are not able to rescue those whom I hate," says Duryodhana).—§ 562 (Bhagavadyānap.): **94**, 3335 (*hutā*°).—§ 564 (Mātalīyop.): **99**, 3549 (*Āsuro 'gniḥ*, in Pātāla).—§ 567 (Bhagavadyānap.): **140**, 4741 (*Agniṃ juhotu vai Dhaumyaḥ*); **142**, 4818 (*ubhe cāpy Agni-Mārute*, sc. *astre*).—§ 571 (Ulūkadūt.): **160**, 5512 (°*dattañ ca te*, i.e. Arjuna's, *ratham*).—§ 576 (Bhagavadgītāp.): VI, **35**, 1285 (i.e. Kṛshṇa).—§ 581 (Bhīshmavadhap.): **60**, 2674 (*bhagavān ivāgniḥ*). — § 592 (Saṃçaptakavadhap.): **25**, 1084 (*yathendrāgnī purā Baliṃ*).—[§ 594 (Mṛtyu): VII, **52-54**]: Urged by the Earth, who was afflicted with the heavy weight of creatures, Brahmán became angry and created Fire that was about to consume the whole universe; Çiva then solicited him, so that he extinguished the Fire and created a woman named Mṛtyu (Death) to destroy the creatures. Cf. XII, 257 ff.—§ 597 (Pratijñāp.): **82**, 2924. —§ 600 (Ghaṭotkacavadhap.): **166**, 7451 (°*samaprabham*); **182**, 8284 (*surā iva nir-agnayaḥ*). — § 603 (Nārāyaṇāstramokshap.): **200**, 9260 (*agnāv agnir iva nyasto*), 9263 (*yathā jagdhvā jagat kṛtsnaṃ samaye sacarācaraṃ* | *gacched agnir* (B. °*ed vahnir*) *Vibhor āsyaṃ*), 9264 (*sūryam agniḥ* (so B.) *pravishṭaḥ syād yathā cāgniṃ divākaraḥ*); **201**, †9457 (*Vāgagnī*).— § 606 (Tripurākhyāna): VIII, **34**, 1471 (*çṛṅgam Agnir babhūvāsya*, i.e. on the arrow of Mahādeva), 1503 (*Agnīshomau* (C. *Somaṃ*) *jagat kṛtsnam*).—§ 608 (Karṇap.): **60**, 2983 (*Çakrāgnibhyām iva*); **87**, 4418 (V., M., S., R., Vi., A., *Agnir Indraç ca Somaç ca Pavano 'tha diço daça* | *Dhanañjayasya te pakshe*).—§ 611 (Çalyap.): IX, **14**, 724 (*bhagavān*); **17**, 912 (°*r iva*), 920 (do.); **21**, 1128 (*yathā*). — § 613 (Gadāyuddhap.): **33**, 1921 (*Khāṇḍave 'gnim ivārjunaḥ*).— § 615 (do. brought): **35**, 1985 (°*īn*, from Dvārakā by Balarāma).—§ 615*a* (Skanda): **45**, 2503 (*Bṛhaspatiḥ samiddhāgnau juhāvāgniṃ yathāvidhi*); **46**, 2702 (*çaktyā* . .

°*dattayā*, i.e. the lance of Skanda).—§ 615 (Baladevat.): **47**, 2742 (°*ḥ pranashṭo bhagavān*), 2744 (do.); **54**, 3049 (*Indro 'gnir Aryamā caiva yatra prāk prītim āpnuvan*, i.e. on the Yamunā).—§ 623 (Rājadh.): XII, **15**β, 439 (*hantā*).—§ 637 (do.): **43**, 1506 (i.e. Kṛshṇa); **47**, 1661 (*antarbhūtaḥ*, i.e. Kṛshṇa).—§ 638*b* (Rāmop.): **49**, 1753 (having got alms from Arjuna Kārtavīrya, *A.* burnt villages, etc., and the hermitage of Āpava).—§ 641 (Rājadh.): **68**, 2576 (v. Āditya[4]); **78**, 2922 (*ajo 'gnir Varuṇo meshaḥ . . . na vikreyaḥ kathañcana* = XIII, 3978); **122**, 4511 (*Vibhāvasuḥ*).—§ 656 (Khaḍgotp.): **166**, 6201 (*Aser daivatam*).—§ 658 (Kṛtaghnop.): **171**, 6382 (*Viçve devāḥ sāgnayaḥ*, etc., represented by brahmans fed in the house of Virūpāksha on a certain day of the Kārttika month).—§ 660 (Bhṛgu-Bharadvāja-s.): **182**, 6778 (*Agni-Mārutau*, spring from water), 6779 (*Agni-Māruta-saṃyogāt tataḥ samabhavan mahī*), 6782 (is Brahmán's tejas), 6783 (*Agnī-Shomau tu candrārkau nayane tasya*, i.e. Brahmán's, *viçrute*).—§ 671*b* (Bali-Vāsava-s.): **224**, 8139 (*āhuç cainam*, i.e. Brahmán, *kecid Agniṃ kecid āhuḥ Prajāpatim*).—§ 693 (Vṛtravadha): **283** (in order to deliver Indra from the brahmahatyā that issued from the body of Vṛtra, when he had been killed by Indra, Brahmán divided it in four portions; one-fourth was taken by Agni on the condition that it should immediately enter the man who should abstain from offering, etc.), 10174.—§ 696 (MSNSt.): **283**, 10354 (= Çiva, 1000 names).—§ 700 (Mokshadh.): **289**, 10644 (*Agnī-Shomāv idaṃ sarvam*).—§ 702 (do.): **296**β, 10837 (v. Ādityaḥ).—§ 707 (do.): **318**, 11708 (if at death the soul escapes through the eyes, the man reaches the region of Agni).—§ 717 (Nārāyaṇīya, Mahāpurushastava): **339**, 12864 (*tavāgnir āsyam*, No. 90); **341**λ, 13017 (*kiñ ca Brahmā ca Rudraç ca Çakraç ca Balabhit prabhuḥ | Sūryas Tārādhipo Vāyur Agnir Varuṇa eva ca | Ākāçam Jagatī caiva ye ca çeshā divaukasaḥ | pralayaṃ na vijānanti ātmanaḥ parinirmitam*).—§ 717 (do.): **342**††I): (Agni (digestive Fire, Nīl.) and Soma (food, Nīl.), blending together, become transformed into one and the same substance; it is for this reason that the entire universe is said to be pervaded with them; the deities also are said to have Agni for their mouth. After the dissolution of the universe Brahmán caused Agni (*kshattram*, i.e. the kshattriyas) and Soma (*bráhman*, i.e. the brahmans) to spring from his own eyes; the brahmans became endowed with greater energy than the kshattriyas. He who offers food in the mouth of a brahman pours libations into a blazing fire. Agni is the hotṛ and brahmán of the sacrifice; the brahmans, becoming Agni, uphold the sacrifices and, possessed of learning, further (*bhāvayanti*) Agni; [being] Agni [and] Vishṇu they, entering all creatures, uphold their lifebreaths), 13186 (*Agniḥ Somena saṃyukta ekayonitvam āgataḥ | Agnī-Shomamayaṃ tasmāj jagat kṛtsnaṃ carācaram*), ††13187 (*api hi Purāṇe bhavati, ekayonyātmakāv Agnī-Shomau, devatāç cāgnimukhā iti*); **343**, 13188 (*Agnī-Shomau*), ††13194 (*sa Purushaḥ . . . netrābhyām Agnī-Shomau sasarja*); VII, ††13217 (*brahmavadhyāñ caturshu sthāneshu vanitāgni-vanaspatigoshu vyabhajat*, cf. § 555, V, **15** f.); IX, ††13218 (*Bhṛguṇā çapto 'gniḥ sarvabhakshatvam upanītaḥ*), ††13223 (*tad etad brahmāgnī-Shomīyaṃ, tena jagad dhāryate*), 13225 (*Agnī-Shoma-*, etymology of *Hṛshīkeça*).—§ 719 (Ānuçāsanik.): XIII, **1**, 55 (v. Āditya[4]).—§ 720*b* (Sudarçana): **2** (married Sudarçanā (daughter of king Duryodhana in Māhishmatī and the river Narmadā), and begat with her Sudarçana; he is always present in Māhishmatī; cf. § 282*b*); 104 ff. 132 (°*putre Sudarçane*).—§ 730 (Meghavāhanop.): **14**, 609 (= Çiva), 1003 (do.), 1005 (*sapta . . . agnayaḥ*, lower than Çiva); **16**, 1045 (*Indrāgni-Marutām gatim*, i.e. Çiva); **18**, 1304 (*sāgni-munibhir*).—§ 731*b* (Ashṭāvakra-Dik-s.): **19**, 1472 (*nānilo 'gnir na Varuṇo na cānye tridaçā dvija | priyāḥ strīṇāṃ yathā Kāmo*).—§ 732 (Ānuçāsanik.): **22** (the opinions of Pṛthivī, Kāçyapa, Mārkaṇḍeya, and Agni ("a brahman who, being engaged in study and regarding himself learned with the aid of his learning destroys the reputation of others, falls away from righteousness, and his regions of felicity hereafter —*lokāḥ*—are of short duration—*antavanto*") as to the essential qualities of brahmans), 1540, (1543), 1515.—§ 733 (do.): **25**s, 1729 (°*aḥ pure*—a tīrtha—*naraḥ snātvā Agnikanyāpure vaset*; Nīl. is silent).—§ 737 (do.): **31**, 2031 (*ayonīn Agniyonīṃç ca brahma-yonīṃs tathaiva ca | sarvabhūtātmayonīṃç ca tān namasyāmy ahaṃ sadā*; cf. Nīl. and PCR.).—§ 746 (do.): **63**, 3239 (*sambhavanti tataḥ çukrāt prāṇinaḥ, pṛthivīpate! | Agnī-Shomau hi tac chukraṃ sṛjataḥ pushyataç ca ha*); **79***k*, 3769 (*samānavatsāṃ kṛshṇān tu dhenuṃ dattvā . . . Agniloke mahīyate*); **82**, 3857 (*mayā*, i.e. by Çrī, *'bhipannā devāç ca modante çāçvatīḥ samāḥ | Indro Vivasvān Somaç ca Vishṇur Āpo 'gnir eva ca*).—§ 747*b* (Suvarṇotpatti): **84**, 3977 (*Agnī-Shomātmakaṃ suvarṇam*), 3978 (*ajo 'gnir, Varuṇo meshaḥ*, etc.; cf. XII, **78**, 2922): Brahmán had granted the Asura Tāraka the boon that he could not be slain by gods, Asuras, Rākshasas, etc., and the deities had, in consequence of their endeavour in former times to stop propagation, been cursed by Pārvatī, that they were not to have any offspring; but Agni had not been there; he therefore, said Brahmán, would beget an offspring for the destruction of Tāraka, etc.: "Kāma is Rudra's seed, a portion of which fell into Agni, who will cast it into Gaṅgā. Therefore, make a search for Agni. Agni is the most eternal of all creatures; he is older than Rudra himself," etc. After searching in vain every part of the universe, the gods successively learnt from a frog that had been scorched by the energy of Agni that he was residing in the nethermost regions of the water; from an elephant, that he was within an açvattha tree; and from a parrot, that he had entered the heart of a çamī tree. All frogs, elephants, and parrots were cursed by Agni and blessed by the gods in various ways: the çamī tree the gods made a sacred fuel fit for producing fire in all religious rites; the heated waters that are found in the nethermost regions are vomited forth by the mountain springs. Agni then united himself in spiritual congress with Gaṅgā, who, being unable to bear the seed, cast it off resplendent like gold on the breast of Meru, on a forest of reeds. Hence Agni was called Hiraṇyaretas; Earth, Vasumatī; the child, Skanda and Guha, and, because it was nursed by the Kṛttikās, Kārttikeya; gold, Jātarūpa. It was in this way that gold came into existence as the offspring of Agni; gold is truly the illustrious Agni, the lord of all things, and the foremost of all Prajāpatis; the most sacred of all sacred things is gold; it has for its essence Agni and Soma. In days of yore (*lokādau*, v. 4163) Rudra (who is Brahmán, Çiva, Rudra, Varuṇa, Agni, Prajāpati, etc.), having assumed the form of Varuṇa (cf. v. 4133, *Varuṇaḥ, Pavanātmakaḥ*), performed a sacrifice to which came the munis and all the deities with Agni, etc.; the Lord of all himself poured libations into his own self. Seeing "*devapatnyaç ca kanyāç ca devānāñ caiva mātaraḥ*," the seed (endowed with Sattva, Rajas, and Tamas) of Brahmán fell upon the Earth; Pūshan took it up, and it was taken with the sacrificial ladle and poured as an oblation into the fire; thence Brahmán caused the different beings to spring into existence. From the flames (*bhṛg*) arose Bhṛgu, etc. . . . from the ashes, the Vaikhānasas, honoured by the gaṇas of brahmarshis; from his (Agni's, PCR.) tears, the Açvins; from his organs of sense (*srotobhyas* B., i.e. ears, etc.), the rest of the Prajāpatis (*prajānāṃ patayaḥ*), the Ṛshis from his pores, etc. For this reason Agni is said to be all the deities; the pieces of wood are the months, etc.; his bile (*pittam*) is day and night (B. somewhat differently); "*Raudraṃ lohityam ity āhur, lohitāt kanakaṃ smṛtaṃ | tan Maitram iti vijñeyaṃ, dhūmāc ca Vasavaḥ smṛtāḥ*" (v. 4130); the flames are the Rudras and Ādityas; the planets, stars, etc. (Nīl.), are the charcoal; "*ādikartā ca lokasya tat paraṃ brahma tad dhruvaṃ | sarvakāmadam ity āhus, tad rahasyam uvāca ha*" (v. 4132). Bhṛgu was considered as the offspring of Varuṇa, Aṅgiras as that of Agni, Kavi as that of Brahmán; Bhṛgu, Aṅgiras, and Kavi were all of them *prajānam patayaḥ*; their offspring (v. 4144–52) are called Vāruṇāḥ, and Kavi and Bhṛgu, Vāruṇau. Agni is Brahmán, Paçupati, Sarva, Rudra, Prajāpati; gold is the offspring of Agni (v. 4164); when fire is not obtainable gold is used as a substitute by a *Jāmadagnyaḥ* ("one that knows the identity of gold with fire," PCR.) *Pramāṇajño vedaçrutividarçanāt* (v. 4165), etc. (v. 4166–7); Agni sprang from Brahmán, and from Agni sprang gold (v. 4168); those persons observant of righteousness who make gifts of gold are regarded as giving away all the deities (v. 4169), etc.; he who makes a gift of gold at the second twilight succeeds in attaining to a residence with (*sālokyaṃ*) Brahmán, Vāyu, Agni, and Soma (v. 4173), and in the regions of Indra (*sendreshu caiva lokeshu*, v. 4174), etc.; he has never to fall down from the regions to which he attains (*na ca ksharati tebhyaç ca*, v. 4176). XIII, **85**, 4062, etc., (4065), etc., 4095 (*Hiraṇyaretaḥ*), etc., 4102 (*Īçaḥ Prajāpatiḥ*), 4103 (*Agnī-Shomātmakaṃ jātarūpam*), 4106 (°*purogamāḥ devāḥ*), 4112 (i.e. Çiva), 4128 (*etasmāt kāraṇād āhur Agniṃ sarvās tu devatāḥ*), (4135), etc., 4141 (*Īçvaro*, i.e. Brahmán, *'ṅgirasañ cāgner apatyārtham akalpayat*), etc., 4164, 4173, etc. — § 748*b* (Tārakavadhop.): **86**, 4209 (gave the newborn Skanda a goat), etc. — § 749 (Ānuçāsanik.): **91**, 4348 (*kṛtvāgnau karaṇaṃ pūrvaṃ mantrapūrvaṃ tapodhanāḥ | tato 'gnaye ca Somāya Varuṇāya ca nityaçaḥ | Viçve devāç ca ye nityaṃ Pitṛbhiḥ sahagocarāḥ*, etc., at a çrāddha), 4351 (*udakānayane caiva stotavyo Varuṇo vibhuḥ | tato 'gniç caiva Somaç ca āpyāyyāviha te 'nagha*, at a çrāddha), 4354 (*viçve cāgni-mukhā devāḥ*); **92** (at a çrāddha ordered by Nimi and performed by the maharshis, the Pitṛs and gods became afflicted with indigestion in consequence of the offerings (*nivāpa*) made by persons of the four castes. They repaired to Soma and thence to Svayambhū (Pitāmaha, on the summit of Meru), and thence to Agni. Agni told them to eat these offerings with him. It is for this reason that in making offerings at çrāddhas a share is first offered to Agni; thence also the Brahma-Rākshasas cannot do any injury to the çrāddha; but the Rakshases fly away from it); (v. 4383–4) (Çrāddhakalpa); XIII, **92**, (4381), 4382 (*etasmāt kāraṇāc cāgneḥ prāk tāvad dīyate, nṛpa!*).—§ 758 (do.): **103**, 5142 (°*saṃbhavaḥ*, i.e. Aṅgiras).—§ 766 (do.): XIII, **126** (at Indra's court Agni declared that the Pitṛs of one who raises his feet to kick a cow, or a brahman, or a fire, become filled with fear, and that he himself has to roast in Hell (*Narake pacyate*) for 100 lives), (6033).—§ 772*b* (Pavan-Arjuna-s.): **154**, 7225 (even Agni and Brahmán are brahmans).—§ 773*b* (Kṛshṇa): **159** [†7378, *sa*, i.e. Kṛshṇa, *ekadā kakshagato mahātmā tushṭo vibhuḥ Khāṇḍave dhūmaketuḥ*], †7388 (Kṛshṇa becoming Agni burns the world).—§ 773*d* (Çiva): **161**, 7486 (Çiva slew the Daityas—in Tripura—"*kṛtvā Vishṇum çarottamaṃ | çalyam Agniṃ tathā kṛtvā, puṅkhaṃ Vaivasvataṃ Yamaṃ | Vedān kṛtvā dhanuḥ sarvān jyāñ ca Sāvitrīm uttamām* . . . "), 7496 (i.e. Rudra); **162**, 7503 (do.).—§ 778*b* (Saṃvartta-Maruttīya): XIV, **3–10**: In the Tretā-yuga (v. 80) king Marutta, who rivalled Indra, intended to celebrate a sacrifice on Meru on the northern side of Himavat. Bṛhaspati had expelled his younger brother Saṃvartta, and in allegiance to Indra refused to perform sacrifice for his rival Marutta. Nārada then told Marutta to appeal to Saṃvartta, who was wandering about in the garb of a mad man; he was to prevail upon him to perform his sacrifice, and tell him that Nārada had entered into the fire; Saṃvartta consented to perform his sacrifice, not from any desire of wealth, but only that he might do what was disagreeable to Indra and Bṛhaspati. Marutta succeeded in obtaining from Çiva the gold on Muñjavat, and made arrangements for the sacrifice. Bṛhaspati became sick with jealousy, and Indra therefore despatched Agni to Marutta to say that Bṛhaspati would officiate at his sacrifice and make him immortal, etc. But Marutta answered that he did not desire these things, and Saṃvartta threatened to burn Agni with his fierce evil (*dāruṇena*) eyes if he should ever come again. At last Indra himself directed the sacrifice. Indra told Marutta to offer a red bull consecrated to Agni, and a blue with a variegated skin to V.-D. (v. 285); **9**, (227), (230), (232), (235), (240), (243), (246), (249).—§ 782*b* (Brāhmaṇagītā): **20**, 608 (i.e. the vessel of the body called Piṅgalā, Nīl.; cf. PCR.), 617 (*Vaiçvānaro*, the senses with manas and buddhi are his seven tongues).—§ 782 (Guru-çishya-s.): **42**, 1167 (*mahān ātmā*, i.e. the Emancipate, *sa vai Vishṇuç ca Mitraç ca Varuṇo 'gniḥ Prajāpatiḥ | sa hi Dhātā Vidhātā ca* . . .); **43**, 1177 (Agni is *bhūtapatir nityaṃ*).—§ 784 (Utaṅkop.): **58**, 1746 (the horse which Utaṅka saw in the Nāgaloka turned out to be Agni).—§ 789 (Putradarçanap.): XV, **31**η, 857 (°*er bhāgaṃ Dhṛshṭadyumnaṃ*). — § 793 (Mausalap.): XVI, **3**, 60 (°*dattaṃ Kṛshṇasya cakraṃ*, ascended to heaven).—§ 794 (Mahāprasthānikap.): XVII, **1**: Having heard about the slaughter of the Vṛshṇis and the death of Kṛshṇa, the five Pāṇḍavas with Draupadī and a dog set out to retire from the world. When they had reached the sea of red waters (*lauhityaṃ salilārṇavam*, v. 33, i.e. *udayācalaprāntasthaṃ samudraṃ*, Nīl.; cf. v. 44 ff.), they beheld Agni in the shape of a man, who requested Arjuna to throw the Gāṇḍīva bow and his couple of inexhaustible quivers into the sea, that they might be made over to Varuṇa, from whom Agni had procured them for the use of Arjuna (v. Khāṇḍavadah.): 35, 38, 43.

Cf. the following:—

Adbhuta ("wonderful"): III, 14212, 14234, 14237. *See also* Vishṇu.

Anala (Analā fem., *see* separately): I, 2582 (a Vasu); II, 332 (in the palace of Yama), 1147; III, 480 (=Kṛshṇa), 12967 (*saṃvarttako*); IX, 2506 (*Anilā°au*), 2687, 2743; XII, 11117; XIII, 7094 (the sixth of the eight vasus), 7110 (*Rudrā° - Vasuprabhāḥ ṛshayaḥ*). Also = Çiva and Vishṇu.

***Anilasambhava** ("sprung from the wind"): II, 1151.

***Anilasārathi** ("having the wind for his charioteer"): I, 1058; III, 5001.

*Apāṃ garbha ("the embryo of the waters"): II, 1150.

*Bhagavat ("the holy one"): II, 1143, 1153.

*Bhūritejasa ("of great might"): II, 1148.

*Bhuvanabhartṛ ("the upholder of the world"): III, 14209.

*Citrabhānu ("with brilliant splendour"): I, †2106; II, 1147; XII, 1753–4; XIII, 113 ff.

*Çikhin ("with flames"): I, 932; II, 1147, 1150, 1152; V, 2118 (metaphorically = the Pāṇḍavas).

*Dahana ("burning"): XIII, 111.

*Dhūmaketu ("having the smoke for his standard"): I, 2113; II, 1152; XIV, 228, 231, 238.

*Gṛhapati ("the lord of the house"): III, 14211 (= Adbhuta).

*Havyakavyabhuj ("the eater of offerings"): XII, 10177, 13382 (*bhagavān*), 13452 (*Vishṇor*).

*Havyavah ("the carrier of offerings"): I, 8353; III, 10590; IV, 50; V, 483, 491, 5290 (the best of the Vasus); [XIII, 916 (*Pitṝṇāṃ*, i.e. Çiva)].

*Havyavāha ("the carrier of offerings"): I, 2113, 8416; III, 14107, 14170 (pl.), 14218, 15929; V, 486, †487; VII, 8725; XII, 10176; XIV, 238, 245.

*Havyavāhana ("the carrier of offerings"): I, 845, 8095, 8147, 8157, 8164, 8363; II, 342, 1126, 1130, 1135, 1146 (*vahanād Havyavāhanaḥ*); III, 9972, 10920, 14100; XIII, 106 ff., 4039, 4068 ff.

*Hiraṇyakṛt ("the maker of gold"): II, 1148.

*Hiraṇyaretas ("the golden seed"): I, †2106; XIII, 4095; [XIV, 118 = the Sun].

*Hutabhuj ("the eater of offerings"): I, 927, *2106; III, 14108.

*Hutāça ("the eater of offerings"): I, 8463; II, 1147; III, 2168 (*īçaṃ devānāṃ*).

*Hutāçana ("the eater of offerings"): I, 930, 2584 (*Çāṇḍilyāç ca Hutāçanaḥ*, sc. *putraḥ*), 7790, 8142, 8174 (*bhagavān Dhūmaketur Hutāçanaḥ*), 8193, 8322, 8422, 8474; II, 1707; III, 5000, 14114, 14196 (*çukla-kṛshṇa-gatir devo yo bibharti Hutāçanam*), 14236 (pl.), 14238, 14286, 14288; V, 476, 484; VII, 402; IX, 2535, 2741; XII, 1006, 4497; XIII, 3150, 4022, 4032, 4036, 4042, 4048, 4080, 4116, 4154, [6351 (pl.)].

*Hutahavyavaha ("the carrier of offerings"): I, 2585 (*Dharasya putro Draviṇo*).

*Hutavaha ("the carrier of offerings"): III, 14105, 14284; XII, 10758.

*Jātavedas: I, 883, 888, 891, 8419, 8423; II, 1146 (*Vedās tvadarthaṃ jātā vai Jātavedās tato hy asi*), 1150; V, 657, 1933; XII, 4499 (*īçaṃ Vasūnāṃ*); XIII, 2013, 2871, 3973 (*apulyaṃ J°aḥ . . . suvarṇam*), 4099 (do.), 4191 (*°aḥ garbham*, i.e. Skanda), 4193 (do.), 5167, 5210, etc., 5944, etc.; XIV, 226, 239, 245, 1706; XV, 1035; XVI, 249.

Jvalana ("flaming"): I, 8403, 8437, 8461; II, 1147; III, 5001; V, 516; VIII, 1502, †4542 (°āstram acyutam*); IX, 2746–8.

*Kṛshṇavartman ("whose road is black"): I, †2106, 8422; II, 1145.

*Kumārasū ("the father of Kumāra"): II, 1148

*Lohitagrīva ("with a red neck"): I, 8422.

*Mahāsattva ("the great Being"): II, 1150.

*Pāñcajanya (an Agni): III, 14160 (called so because he had been thought of with the *mahāvyāhṛtibhir*, had five colours, was made by five persons, and was the progenitor of five races) (Āṅgirasa).

*Pāpahan ("slayer of sin"): II, 1151.

*Pāvaka: I, 884–5, 8087, 8175, 8179, 8196–7, 8201, 8205, 8243, 8325, 8328, 8353, 8361, 8466, 8475, 8478; II, 2, 1144–6 (*pāvanāt Pāvakaç cāsi*), 1162; III, 14137 (*Bharato Bharatasyāgneh Pāvakas tu Prajāpateḥ | mahān atyartham ahitas tathā, Bharatasattama!*), 14145 (*yas tu viçvasya jagato buddhim ākramya tishṭhati | taṃ prāhur adhyātmavido Viçvajin nāma pāvakam*), 14153 (*atulyatvāt kṛte devair nāmnā Kāmas tu pāvakaḥ | saṃharshād dhārayan krodhaṃ dhanvī sragvī rathe sthitaḥ*), 14154 (*samaye nāçayec chatrūn Amogho nāma pavakaḥ*), 14297, 14300 (*°ābhyāsam*), 14307, 14342, 14349, 14378 (*°ārcishaḥ*), 14517; IV, 40, 1434, 1439; V, 489, 545, 2945, 4412, 5356, 5382; VII, 159 (*Rudrāṇām iva Kāpālī, Vasūnām iva Pāvakaḥ | Kubera iva Yakshāṇāṃ Marutām iva Vāsavaḥ*, etc.); IX, 2329, 2484, 2489, 2492; X, 226 (*vaḍavāmukhaḥ*), 463 (*yugānte*), 806 (*sa jalaṃ pāvako bhūtvā çoshayati*, sc. the wrath of Rudra); XII, 1006, 2577, 12105, 12334 (*bhagavān*); XIII, 117, 125 (*°suto*, i.e. *Sudar-çanaḥ*), 142 (id.), 914 (*Vasūnām*, i.e. *Çiva*), 4007, 4061 ff.; XIV, 237; XV, 857; XVII, 36; XVIII, 167.

*Piṅgāksha ("with yellow eyes"): I, 8422.

*Piṅgeça (from *piṅga*, "yellow," and *īça*, "lord"): II, 1148.

*Plavaṅga ("who moves skippingly"): II, 1148 (so also B.).

*Pradakshiṇāvartaçikha ("winding his flames from left to right"): I, †2106.

*Pradīpta ("flaming"): I, †2106.

*Rudragarbha ("the embryo of Rudra"): II, 1148.

*Saptārcis ("who has seven flames"): I, 892, 8208 (*Jvalana*).

*Sarvaprāṇishu nityastha ("ever present in all living beings"): II, 1151.

*Sureça ("the Lord of the gods"): II, 1147.

*Sureçvara ("the Lord of the gods"): II, 1150.

*Svargadvārasprça ("touching the doors of Heaven"): II, 1147.

*Tigmāṃçu ("with hot flames"): I, 8421, 8429, 8465 (*bhagavān*).

*Vahni: I, 911, 922, 935, 8141 (*bhagavato °er*), 8147, 8364; II, 1129 (*bhagavān*), 1137, 1140, 1157; III, 14101 (*sa Vahniḥ sa Prajāpatiḥ | prāṇān āçritya yo dehaṃ pravartayati dehinām*), 14285, 14289, 14293, 14296, 14432; IV, 997 (*diçaṃ °er*); V, 493, 3967 (*Svāhāyāñ ca yathā Vahnir . . . reme*); VII, 7978 (*bhagavān*); VIII, †4542; IX, 2657, 2746, 2789 (*bhagavān*), 3658 (*yathā vahnir jagatkshaye*); XII, 1005, 10171, 10175, 10179 (*°vat*), 11611; XIII, 3295, 3304, 4034, 4040, 4051, 4058, 4081, etc., 4148 (*°jāḥ*, the eight sons of Aṅgiras), etc., 4380, etc.; XIV, 229, 247, 270 (*devaḥ*), 1130 (= *vac*).

*Vaiçvānara: I, 811; II, 299 (*muniḥ*), 1148; III, 11046, 13297, 14192, 14670 (*Sūrya - Vaiçvānara - samau*); VII, 3836; VIII, 4788 (*°ārkapratimaṃ*); XII, †8941 (Brahman?), 12180; XIII, 4085 (*°prabhaṃ*), 4093 (*sūrya° samaḥ*), 5329 (*°samaprabhaḥ*); XIV, 617 (*A°*), 618 (*ghrāṇaṃ jihvā ca . . . saptaitā jihvā V°ārcishaḥ*).

*Vātasārathi ("who has the Wind for his charioteer"): I, 8324 (*Agniḥ, çarīravān jaṭī bhūtvā nadann iva balāhakaḥ*).

*Vibhāvasu ("being a treasure of splendour"): I, †2106; II, 1138 (*bhagavān*), 1147; III, 15932.

Cf. Adolf Holtzmann, "Agni nach den Vorstellungen des Mahābhārata," Strassburg, 1878. *See also* Āṅgirasa.

Agniçiras, a tīrtha. § 377 (Dhaumya-tīrthakathana): III, **85**, 8376.

Agnidhārā, a tīrtha. § 370 (Tīrthayātrāp.): III, **84**, 8124.

Agnijvāla = Çiva (1000 names).

Agnikanyāpura, a tīrtha (?). § 733 (Ānucāsanik.): XIII, **25**, 1729 (cf. Agni).

Agnimat, an Agni. § 490 (Āṅgirasa): III, **221**, 14207 (*Agnaye*).

[**Agniparābhava(ḥ)**] ("the defeat of Agni"), a part of Khāṇḍavadahanaparvan. § 255: I, **223**, 8094–8156. Questioned by Janamejaya why Agni desired to consume the forest of Khāṇḍava, Vaiçampāyana related: It has been heard in the Purāṇa that King Çvetaki performed sacrifices so incessantly that his ṛtvijes left him, their eyes being afflicted with the continued smoke; he then had his sacrifice completed by other ṛtvijes. He then desired to perform another sacrifice, which should extend over 100 years. But he could not obtain any priests to assist him; they told him to apply to Rudra. He then went to Kailāsa, and by observing the most rigid austerities he prevailed upon Rudra that his sacrifice should be completed, on the condition that he could for twelve years without intermission pour libations of clarified butter into the fire, himself leading all the while the life of a brahmacārin. When this had been done Rudra said that he would not himself assist at the sacrifice, which properly belonged to the brahmans; but he caused Durvāsas (*b*) to complete it. [When the time came Çvetaki ascended to heaven (Svarga) with the ṛtvijes and sadasyas who had helped him in life, B.] But Agni became sick, because he had drunk clarified butter for twelve years, and applied to Brahmán. Brahmán told him to consume the forest of Khāṇḍava, that abode of the enemies of the gods, which he had of old once burnt to ashes at the request of the gods, together with its living population; then he would regain his own nature. Seven times Agni, assisted by Vāyu, set the forest on fire; but the inhabitants extinguished the fire (the elephants bringing water in their trunks, and the Nāgas in their hoods, etc.) (I, **223**).—§ 256*a*: I, **224**, 8157–8165*a*. Agni again applied to Brahmán, who told him to solicit the old deities Nara and Nārāyaṇa (now Arjuna and Kṛshṇa) to aid him.

Agniputra = Skanda: IX, 2550–4.

Agnī-Shomau (Agni and Soma): II, 302.

Agnīshoma ("belonging to Agni and Soma"). § 753 (Ānuçāsanik., Dānadharma): XIII, **97**, 4660 (*Agnī-Shomaṃ Vaiçvadevaṃ Dhānvantaryam anantaraṃ | Prajānāṃ pataye caiva pṛthak homo vidhīyate*).

Agnīshomīya (do.). § 717 (Nārāyaṇīya): XII, **343**; XIV, ††13223 (*brāhma*).

Agnisuta = Skanda: VII, 6821 (*Krauñcam Agnisuto yathā*).

Agnisvattāḥ. § 267 (Yama-sabhā-v.): II, **8**, 341 (*pitaraḥ*, a kind of Pitṛs in the palace of Yama).—§ 270 (Brahma-sabhā-v.): II, **11**, 462 (Brahmán).

Agnitīrtha, a tīrtha on the Sarasvatī. § 615*b*+*w* (Baladevatīrthay.): IX, **47**, 2740, 2747 (*A.*, frightened with the curse of Bhṛgu, disappeared, concealing himself in the Çamī-wood; *D.* with *I.* searched and found him, with Bṛh. at their head; *A.*, from Bhṛgu's curse, became an eater of everything).

Agniveça, the teacher of Droṇa in arms. § 200 (Droṇa): I, **130**, 5107.—§ 202 (do.): **131**, 5172 (*maharshir*).—§ 210 (Sambhavap.): I, **139**, 5525.—Cf. Agniveçya.

Agniveçya = Agniveça. § 221 (Caitrarathap.): I, **170**, 6465.—§ 599 (Jayadrathavadhap.): VII, **94**, 3476–7.

Āgniveçya. § 785 (Anugītāp.): XIV, **64**, 1903 (i.e. Dhaumya, Nīl.).

Agniyonayaḥ. § 656 (Khaḍgotp.): XII, **166**, 6144 (*ṛshayo*).

Agrāhya[1], the Great Spirit. § 717 (Mokshadh.): XII, **339**, 12864 (Mahāpurushastave).

Agrāhya[2] = Vishṇu (1000 names).

Agraja = Vishṇu (1000 names).

Agraṇī = Vishṇu (1000 names).

Agratīrtha(ḥ), a king incarnated from the Krodhavaça Gaṇa. § 130 (Aṃçāvat.): I, **67**, 2701

Agravara = Çiva (1000 names[2]).

Āgrayaṇa, an Agni. § 490 (Āṅgirasa): III, **221**, 14189 (*Agnir*).

Aha(ḥ) = Vishṇu (1000 names).

Ahaçcara = Çiva (1000 names[2]).

Ahalyā, the wife of the Ṛshi Gautama. § 370 (Tīrthayātrāp.): III, **84**, 8087 (*Ahalyāyā hrade*).—§ 555*d* (Sainyodyogap.): V, **12**, 373 (*ṛshipatnī*): "*A.*, of spotless form, the wife of a ṛshi, was outraged by Indra while her husband was alive."—§ 717 (Nārāyaṇīya): XII, **343**, II), ††13205 (violated by Indra).—§ 784*d* (Utaṅka): XIV, **56** ff. (has brought to her Madayantī's earrings by Utaṅka), (1652), (1654), (1659), 1706.

Ahaṃkāra: XII, 11575, 11578 (*Parameshṭhī*), 11601 (*bhūtātmā Prajāpatiḥ*), 13037, etc.; XIII, 7230 (= Brahmán?).

Ahaṃyāti, a king, son of Saṃyāti and father of Sārvabhauma. § 156 (Pūruvaṃç.): I, **95**, 3767–8.

***Ahar** ("Day"). § 116 (Aṃçāvat.): I, **66** (one of the eight Vasus), 2582, 2584 (son of Ratā), 2587 (his sons).—§ 615*u* (Skanda): IX, **45**, 2517 (*Rātryahanī*, present at the investiture of Skanda).

Ahas[1] = Çiva (1000 names[2]).

Ahas[2] = Vishṇu (1000 names).

Ahi(r) bradhna, v. Ahirbradhna.

Ahicchatrā. § 209 (Drupadaçāsana): I, **138**, 5516 (the town which Droṇa took from Drupada).

Ahicchatra. § 555 (Sainyodyogap.): V, **19**, 599 (among the localities covered by the troops of the Kaurava army).

Ahikshattra. § 515 (Karṇadigvijaya): III, **254**, 15244 (conquered by Karṇa).

Āhiṇḍaka. § 744 (Ānuçāsanik.): XIII, **48**, 2589 (the offspring of a Nishāda with a woman of the Vaidehī caste).

Ahirbradhna, one of the eleven Rudras. § 191 (Arjuna): I, **123***a*, 4826 (came to the birth of Arjuna).—§ 565 (Gālavacar.): V, **114**, 3899 (v. Ajaikapād).—§ 665 (Mokshadh.): XII, **208**, 7585 (cf. Ajaikapād).—§ 770 (Ānuçāsanik.): XIII, **151***β*, 7090 (v. Ajaikapād).

Ahirbudhnya. § 108 (Aṃçāvat.): I, **66**, 2566 (one of the eleven Rudras, sons of Sthāṇu); XIII, 1216 = Çiva (1000 names[2]).

Ahorātra = Çiva: XII, 10439 (1000 names[1]); XIII, 1226 (1000 names[2]).

Ahovīrya. § 677 (Mokshadh.): XII, **245***β*, 8900 (among the brahmans who have adopted the duties of the fourth mode of life, i.e. renunciation).

Āhuka[1], a Yādava prince. § 262 (Bhagavadyānap.): II, **2**, 55 (called the father of Kṛshṇa?).—§ 264 (Sabhākriyāp.): II, **4***β*, 125 (among the kings present when Yudhishṭhira entered his palace).—§ 273 (Rājasūyārambhap.): II, **14**, 597 (°*sutām*, bestowed upon Akrūra by Kṛshṇa), 621 (has

100 sons, each of whom is almost equal to a god).—§ 320 (Saubhavadhap.): III, **15**, 658 (defends Dvārakā against Çālva); **20**, 783 (is charged with the defence of Dvārakā by Kṛshṇa, when Kṛshṇa pursues Çālva); **21**, 828, 829 (*Dvārakāpatir*).—§ 342 (Indralokābhig.): III, **51**, 1994 (named by Kṛshṇa among the allies who will assist him in revenging Yudhishṭhira).—§ 554 (Sainyodyogap.): V, **4**γ, 75 (is to be enlisted in the cause of the Pāṇḍavas).—§ 567 (Bhagavadyānap.): V, **128**, 4297 (father of Ugrasena).—§ 570 (Sainyaniryāṇap.): V, **157**κ, 5331 (*Raukma(!)ṇeyāhuka-sutaiḥ*) came to Yudhishṭhira).—§ 641 (Rājadh.): XII, **81**, 3033 (*Āhukākrūrau*).—§ 730 (Ānuçāsanik.): XIII, **14**γ, 629 (*rājñaḥ*).—§ 793 (Mausalap.): XVI, **1**β, 28 (at the command of *A.*, etc., the manufacture of wines and spirit was forbidden).

Āhuka[2], a tribe. § 562 (Bhagavadyānap.): V, **86**, 3041 (*Āhukānām adhipatiḥ*).—§ 570 (Sainyaniryāṇap.): V, **158**, 5351 (*Āhukānām adhipatir . . . Rukmī*).

Āhuti. § 717 (Nārāyaṇīya): XII, **339**, 12864 (Mahāpurushastave).

Āhutimaya = Çiva. § 696 (Mokshadh.): XII, **72**, 10400 (1000 names[1]).

Āhvāyaka, pl. (°*āḥ*), one of the five brāhmaṇa-cāṇḍālas. § 641 (Rājadh.): XII, **76**, 2874 (dharmādhikāriṇaḥ, Nīl.).

Āhvṛti. § 317 (Arjunābhigam.): III, **12**, 489 (in Arjuna's praise of Kṛshṇa: a prince defeated by Kṛshṇa).

***Aiçvara**, adj. ("sovereign"). § 635 (Rājadh.): XII, **33**, 1177 (*rūpam*, i.e. Kālasya).—§ 717 (Mokshadh.): XII, **348**, 13525 (*rūpam*), 13543 (*vidhim*).

Aikshvākī, a princess, wife of Suhotra, and mother of Ajamīḍha (cf. Suvarṇā Ikshvākukanyā). § 152 (Pūruvaṃç.): I, **94**, 3719.

Aikshvāku[1]. § 632 (Shoḍaçarājop.): XII, **29**, 962 (= Bhagīratha).

Aikshvāku[2] = Sagara. § 632 (Shoḍaçarāj.): XII, **29**, 1023.

Aikshvāku[3] = Triçaṅku. § 721 (Ānuç.): XIII, **3**, 189.

Aila[1] = Purūravas. § 141 (Purūravas): I, **75**, 3149.—§ 155 (Pūruvaṃç.): I, **94**, 3753 (*Ailavaṃçavivardhanāḥ*).—§ 267 (Yamasabhāv.): II, **8**, 327 (in the palace of Yama).—§ 273 (Rājasūy.): II, **14**, 568-9 (*Ailavaṃçyāḥ*).—§ 305 (Anudyūtap.): II, **78**, 2576 (*Purūravasam Ailam*).—§ 574 (Jambūkh.): VI, **9**αα, 315.—§ 641 (Rājadh.): XII, **72**, 2750 (*Purūravasa Ailasya saṃvādaṃ Mātariçvanaḥ*), (2757); **73**, 2780 (*Aila-Kaçyapa-saṃvadam*), (†2781), †2791, (†2792), (†2794), (†2796), (†2798).—§ 673*b* (Bali-Vāsava-s.): XII, **227**α, 8261.—§ 723 (Ānuçāsanik.): XIII, **6**, 325 (attained to Heaven through the intercession of the brahmans).—§ 764 (Ānuçāsanik.): XIII, **115**δ, 5667 (among the kings that did not eat flesh during the month of Kārttika, and as a consequence thereof attained to Brahmaloka).—§ 770 (Ānuçāsanik.): XIII, **151**γ, 7127 (among the kings whose names one should name for success; *Budhasya putram*).—§ 775 (do.): XIII, **166**η, 7678 (among the kings whose names should be recited at sunset and sunrise), 7683.

Aila[2]: XIII, **34**γ, 2126; v. Aina.

Ailavaṃça ("the race descending from Ilā"). § 155 (Pūruvaṃç.): I, **94**, 3753 (°*vivardhanāḥ*).

Ailavila[1] = Kubera. § 564 (Mātalīyop.): V, **102**, 3611.—§ 565 (Gālavac.): V, **111**, 3840 (dwells on Kailāsa).—§ 569 (Bhagavadyānap.): V, **139**, 4717.—§ 615 (Baladevat.): IX, **47**x, 2753 (practising austerities in Kaubera-tīrtha, he obtained the lordship of all treasures—*dhanādhipatyam*—and all kinds of wealth, etc., came to him of their own accord).

Ailavila[2] = Dilīpa. § 595 (Shoḍaçarāj.): VII, **61**, 2263 (*Dilīpa*).

Ailavila[3] = an ancient king. § 656 (Khaḍgotp.): XII, **166**δ, 6195 (received the Sword from Bharata and gave it to Dhundhumāra).

Aina, a people. § 739 (Ānuçās.): XIII, **34**γ, 2126 (vanquished by Bharadvāja.—B. has Ailān).

Aindhana = the Sun. § 210 (Āraṇyakap.): III, **3**, 149 (in Dhaumya's enumeration of the 108 names of the Sun).

***Aindra**, adj. ("belonging to or named after Indra"): I, 4764 (*muhūrte*, v. Yudhishṭhira); IV, 2028 (*Aindram astram* employed by Bhīma); V, 507 (*Aindram padam*, i.e. the sovereignty over the gods); XI, 210 (*Aindrīm sabhām*); XII, 2287 (*Aindro rājanya ucyate*), 5382 (*Aindro dharmaḥ kshattriyāṇām brāhmaṇānām athāgnikaḥ*), 8283 (*sthānāt*), 10129 (*vajram*), 12336 (*diçam*), 13214 (*padam*); XIII, 854, 4766 (*sthānāt*), 5283 (do.), 6019 (*Aindrīm sandhyām*—the morning twilight: by worshipping it with the face directed towards the East one has bathed in all the tīrthas and becomes purified from all sins—*sarvatīrtheshu sa snāto mucyate sarva-kilvishaiḥ*); XIV, †259 (*vākyam*).

Aindradyumna ākhyāna ("the history of Indradyumna"). § 10 (Parvas.): I, **2**, 325.—§ 11 (do.): **2**, 468 (*v.* Indradyumnopākhyāna).

Aindradyumni = Janaka: III, 10624.

Aindrāgna ("belonging to Indra and Agni"). § 555 (Indravijaya): V, **16**, 517 (*bhāgaḥ*).

Aindrāgneya (= preced.): XII, 5413.

Aindrāgnya (= preced.): XII, 2307 (*Aindrāgnyena vidhānena*).

Aindri = Arjuna: I, 2751 (*Aindrir Naras tu bhavitā . . . | so 'rjunety abhivikhyāto*), 5353, †7052; III, 1528; IV, †2112 (K. has *Aindram* referring to *astram*); VI, 2000 (so B.; C. has *Indram*).

Airāvaṇa[1], the elephant of Indra. § 28 (Amṛtam.): I, **18**, 1151.—§ 549 (Pāṇḍavapraveçap.): IV, **2**, 44 (*hastishu varaḥ*).—§ 564 (Mātalīyop.): V, **99**, 3561 (*nāgarāja*).—§ 599 (Jayadrathavadhap.): VII, **112**, 4325 (°*samā yudhi*).—§ 611 (Çalyap.): IX, **20**, 1071, 1077 (*nāgendram Indra-vāhyam*).—§ 673 (Bali-Vāsava-s.). XII, **227**, 8222 (*caturdantam*).—Cf. Airāvata.

Airāvaṇa[2], a snake. § 268 (Varuṇa-sabhā-v.): II, **9**, 360 (in the palace of Varuṇa). Cf. Airāvata.

Airāvata[1], the elephant of Indra. § 17 (Utaṅka): I, **3**, 820.—§ 127 (Aṃçāvat.): I, **66**, 2627 (*devanāgo mahāgajaḥ*).—§ 334 (Kairātap.): III, **41**, 1676 (°*çirogato . . . Çakraḥ*).—§ 335 (Indralokābh.): III, **42**, 1753 (*caturdantam*).—§ 462 (Baka-Çakra-s.): III, **193**, 13219.—§ 496 (Skandotp.): III, **225**, 14321 (?).—§ 499 (Skanda-Çakra-samāg.): III, **227**, 14370.—§ 505 (Skandayuddha): III, **231**, 14531 (his two bells named Vaijayantī).—§ 506 (do.): III, **231**, 14547.—§ 555 (Sainyodyogap.): V, **18**, 544.—§ 564 (Mātalīyop.): V, **99**, 3553 (he takes up water in Pātāla in order to impart it to the clouds, and it is that water which Indra pours down as rain).—§ 572 (Rathātirath.): V, **167**, 5807 (*iva*).—§ 576 (Bhagavadgītāp.): VI, **21**, 475 (*diggajā Vāmanairāvatā-dayaḥ*); **31**, 1231 (*Airāvataṃ gajendrāṇām*, says Kṛshṇa, about himself).—§ 581 (Bhīshmavadhap.): VI, **62**, 2761 (*gajam Airāvatopaman*); **64**, 2865 (one of the world-elephants).—§ 585 (Bhīshmavadhap.): VI, **95**, 4265 (*iva*).—§ 599 (Jayadrathavadhap.): VIII, **121**, 4830 (°*kule*); **148**, 6436 (*Airāvatopamām*).—§ 611 (Çalyap.): IX, **20**, 1067 (°*prakhya*).—§ 615 (Skanda): IX, **45**γ, 2517 (?).—§ 671*b*

(Bali-Vāsav.-saṃv.): XII, **223,** 8069 (°*skandham*).—§ 673*b* (do.): XII, **227,** 8223.—§ 730 (Meghavāhanop.): XIII, **14,** 831.—§ 773 (Kṛshṇa): XIII, **159,** 7391 (identified with Kṛshṇa).—Cf. Airāvaṇa.

Airāvata[2], a serpent. § 17 (Utaṅka): I, **3,** 797 (°*rājānaḥ sarpāḥ*), 798 (°*odbhavaḥ*), 800, 801 (°*jyeshṭhabhrātṛbhyo*).—§ 47 (Sarpanāmakath.): I, **35,** 1551.—§ 49 (Vāsuki): I, **37,** 1590 (°*prabhṛtibhiḥ*).—§§ 65-6 (Sarpasattra): I, **57,** 2153 (°*kulād*).—§ 248 (Arjunavanavāsap.): I, **214,** 7793 (°*kule*).—§ 564 (Mātalīyop.): V, **103**γ, 3627; **103,** 3639 ("Sumukha of the race of Airāvata"); **104,** 3652.—§ 565 (Gālavacar.): V, **109,** 3798.—§ 585 (Bhīshmavadhap.): VI, **90,** 3978.—§ 608 (Karṇap.): VIII, **90,** 4645 (°*vaṃçasambhavam*).—§ 784*b* (Utaṅka): XIV, **58** ("a serpent of Airāvata's race"), 1714, 1732 (°*sutena*), 1740 (°*niveçanam*).

Airāvata[3], plur. (āḥ), the serpents of Airāvata's kind. § 666 (Karṇap.): VIII, **87**γ, 4416 (sided with Arjuna).

Airāvata[4], a varsha. § 574 (Jambūkh.): VI, **6,** 232; **8,** 296. On the north of *Çṛṅgavat* and up to the border of the sea is the *Varsha Airāvata*, superior to all because of the peak (see the note of PCR., p. 28). The sun gives no heat there, and the men are not subject to decay; the moon with the stars is the only source of light. The men have the complexion and the fragrance of the lotus, their eyes do not wink, without food, with agreeable scent, fallen from *Devaloka*, without passions (*virajaso*), living for 13,000 years.

Airāvatapatha, the northern part of the path of the Moon. § 738 (Yakshayuddhap.): III, **162,** 11836 (°*e yathā*).

Aishīka, adj. ("made of a straw"). § 4 (Anukram.): I, **1,** 211 (°*aṃ paramāstram*).

Aishīka ("the section relating to the Aishīka weapon"). § 4 (Anukram.): I, **1,** 90 (*Strīparvaishīka-viçrāmaḥ . . . . Bhāratadrumaḥ*).—§ 10 (Parvas.): I, **2,** 348 (°*aṃ parva*).—§ 11 (do.): I, **2,** 581 (v. Sauptika).—§ 785 (Anugītāp.): **66,** 1952.—§ 795 (Svargārohaṇap.): XVIII, **6,** 276, i.e. Aishīkaparvan.

[Aishīkaparvan] ("the section relating to the Aishīka weapon"), the 84th of the minor parvans of Mhbhr., cf. Aishīka. § 617: The driver of Dhṛshṭadyumna's chariot, who had managed to escape from Kṛtavarman at a time when he was heedless, informs Yudhishṭhira, in the morning, of the extermination of his army. Yudhishṭhira falls down on the earth; Sātyaki holds him in his embrace; Bhīma, etc. (*a*), stretch forth their arms. Having recovered his senses Yudhishṭhira laments (β), and despatches Nakula to bring thither Draupadī and the ladies with her; then he proceeds to view the slaughter in his camp, and falls down on the earth with all his followers (X, **10**). Draupadī arrives from Upaplavya, falls down in the presence of Yudhishṭhira, is comforted by Bhīma, addresses Yudhishṭhira (γ), and resolves to sit in Prāya, if the Pāṇḍavas do not slay Açvatthāman. Yudhishṭhira urged her to forget her sorrows, as Açvatthāman is not to be found. Draupadī insists on Açvatthāman's slaughter and the depredation of the gem on his head, appealing in particular to Bhīmasena (δ). Bhīmasena, making Nakula his charioteer, sets out in pursuit of Açvatthāman, guided by the track of the latter's car-wheels (X, **11**). Kṛshṇa urges Yudhishṭhira to make arrangements for the safety of Bhīma, as Açvatthāman has the Brahmaçiras (*b*) weapon capable of exterminating all foes (X, **12**). The Pāṇḍavas, with Kṛshṇa, proceed on the track of Bhīmasena: Kṛshṇa, Arjuna, and Yudhishṭhira on Kṛshṇa's car with steeds of the Kāmboja breed: Çaibya on the right, Sugrīva on the left, Meghapushpa and Balāhaka being pārshṇivāhas, the standard having been made by Viçvakarman and standing high like Māyā, with Garuḍa. They in vain ask Bhīma to stop. They find Açvatthāman sitting with Vyāsa on the bank of *Gaṅgā* in the midst of many Ṛ.; he is attired in a piece of cloth made of Kuça-grass, etc. . . . . He consecrates a blade of grass with Mantras, and converts it into that powerful celestial weapon, and throws it off with the words "for the destruction of the Pāṇḍavas" (X, **13**). Urged by Kṛshṇa, Arjuna shoots the [Brāhma, PCR.] weapon imparted to him by Droṇa, which was capable of neutralizing all weapons. Extraordinary portents appear in nature. Nārada and Vyāsa, trying to save the three worlds, stand between the two fires (X, **14**). Arjuna withdraws his weapon; but Açvatthāman is incapable of withdrawing his, as no person of uncleansed soul can bring it back, after it has once been let off, but only a brahmacārin (and such a one is Arjuna); otherwise it strikes off his own head. Vyāsa praises Arjuna for not having before used the Brahmaçiras weapon; "that region where Brahmaçiras is baffled by another high weapon, suffers a drought for twelve years"; he proposes to him to give the Pāṇḍavas the gem on his head; then the Pāṇḍavas would in return grant him his life. Açvatthāman surrenders his gem, whose wearer ceases to have any fear from weapons, etc., and from D., Dā., and N., and Rā.; the weapon he throws into the wombs of the Pāṇḍava women (X, **15**). Kṛshṇa says that a brahman at Upaplavya has said to Uttarā, "while the Kuru line will become extinct, a son will be born to thee, and he will for that reason be called Parikshit." Açvatthāman says that his words could not but be fulfilled. Kṛshṇa says that the fœtus will die, but be recalled to a long life; but Açvatthāman shall wander for 3000 years alone, and without being able to talk to anyone; the stench of pus and blood shall emanate from him, and inaccessible forests and dreary moors shall be his abode; he shall wander over the earth with the weight of all diseases on him. Parikshit shall learn the use of all weapons from Kṛpa and rule the earth for sixty years; Kṛshṇa will revive him. Vyāsa approves of Kṛshṇa's curse. Açvatthāman proceeds to the forest. The Pāṇḍavas with Kṛshṇa, Vyāsa, and Nārada, taking with them the gem, come to Draupadī, who is sitting in Prāya. Bhīma comforts Draupadī (η). Draupadī asks Yudhishṭhira to place upon his head the gem taken from Açvatthāman. Yudhishṭhira asks Kṛshṇa (X, **16**) about the true cause of Açvatthāman's success in destroying the Pāṇḍava army (θ). Kṛshṇa ascribes it to the aid of Mahādeva, and relates that when Brahmán, desirous of creating, saw Rudra, he asked him to create living creatures; Rudra promised to do so, and plunged into the waters and practised austerities. Then Brahmán called into existence another being in order to make him the creator of living creatures, and he created Daksha, etc.; but they ran towards their creator from hunger, desirous of devouring him, and he repaired to Brahmán, who assigned herbs, etc., as their food, and the weak beings to the strong ones. The creatures multiplied. Then Rudra rose from the water, became angry, and caused his productive limb to disappear in the earth. He had created food (herbs and plants) for all these creatures. Then he went away, in cheerlessness and rage, to the Muñjavat mountains in order to practise severer austerities (X, **17**). After the Kṛta-age the gods prepared a sacrifice, but not knowing Rudra truly they assigned no share to him. Rudra constructed a bow of two of the four kinds of sacrifices (v. the note of PCR., p. 58), and came as a brahmacārin to the sacrifice; the earth shrank with fear, etc.; Rudra pierced the sacrifice in the heart; it assumed the shape of a deer and fled away with Agni, pursued by Rudra through the skies; the gods were stupefied; Rudra with his bow broke the arms of Savitṛ and plucked out the eyes of Bhaga and the teeth of Pūshan; the gods uttered a cry; the string of his bow burst; the gods and the sacrifice gratified Rudra; he threw his wrath into the water; that wrath, assuming the form of fire, is always employed in consuming the water. He then gave unto Savitṛ his arms, to Bhaga his eyes, and to Pūshan his teeth, and restored the sacrifice. The gods assigned to him all the libations of clarified butter as his share (X, **18**).

Aja[1] ("unborn") = Kṛshṇa: II, 550 (*Harim*); III, 481; V, 2566 (*na jāyate janitrā 'yam, Ajas tasmād . . .*), 5904 (?); XII, 1646 (*ajasya nābhau sambhūtaṃ yasmin viçvaṃ pratishṭhitam*), 13233, 13447.

***Aja**[2] = the Sun. § 310 (Āraṇyakap.: Sūrya): III, **3**, 146.

***Aja**[3] = Çiva: X, 253.—§ 778 (Saṃvartta-Marutt.): XIV, **8a**, 200, 210; XIII, 1159 (1000 names), 7501.

***Aja**[4] = Brahmán: XII, 8537, 8756, 8802.

***Aja**[5] = Vishṇu: XII, 13109; XIII, 6960 (1000 names), 6971 (ib.), 7005 (ib.).

Aja[6], son of Jahnu. § 638 (Rāmopākhy.): XII, **49**, 1717.

Aja[7], a king: XIII, 5668, 7684.

***Aja**[8], adj. § 677 (Mokshadh.): XII, **238**, 8664 (? *pītaçastraḥ = yogin* ?); XII, 11231 (= Hiraṇyagarbha), 12045 (? *devasya*), 12674, 12864 (Mahāpurushastave).

Aja[9], plur. (°*āḥ*), a kind of Ṛshis. § 246 (Sundopasundop.): I, **211a**, 7683.—§ 630 (Rājadh.): XII, **26**, 774.

Ājagara[1](m) *parva*(n). § 10 (Parvas.): I, **2**, 323 = Ājagaraparvan.

Ājagara[2] (named after ajagara, i.e. a boa). § 659 (Mokshadh.): XII, **179**, 6654 (*munir*), 6677 (*vratam*), 6678 (id.), 6679 (id.), 6680 (id.), 6681 (id.), 6682 (id.), 6683 (id.), 6684 (id.), 6685 (id.), 6686 (id.), (cf. 6689: *ajagaracaritaṃ vratam*).

Ajagaraparvan ("the section relating to the Boa"; the 40th of the minor parvans of Mhbhr.). § 448: The Pāṇḍavas spent four years with Arjuna in the gardens of Kubera, which added to the preceding six make ten years of exile. In the eleventh year Yudhishṭhira, advised by Bhīma, took leave of those regions, determining again to practise austerities on the mountain, when he had regained his kingdom; and after Lomaça had returned to the abode of the gods, they with the brahmans proceeded along that very road, carried by Ghaṭotkaca and his followers, and advised also by Ārshṭisheṇa (III, **176**).—§ 449: Having crossed Kailāsa, they passed one night in the hermitage of king Vṛshaparvan (*b*), then one month at Badarī, seeing Kubera's (*c*) favourite lake (*nalinīm*), then crossing the land of Cīna, Tushāra, Darada, and all the regions of Kulinda, and the difficult Himālaya regions, they reached the city of the Kirāta king Subāhu, where they met with their charioteers Viçoka, etc., and their servants Mahendrasena, etc., the cooks and servants of the kitchen. After having stayed there one night, they, dismissing Ghaṭotkaca and his followers, with the charioteers and chariots reached "the king of mountains" near Yamunā (*Yāmunam adrirājam*, i.e. *Yamunodgamam*, Nīl.; "name of a mountain," BR.), where they dwelt for one year, occupied with hunting, in the forest Viçākhayūpa. There in a cavern Bhīma was seized by a snake and rescued by Yudhishṭhira. In the twelfth year of their exile they repaired thence to the borders of the desert, and desirous of dwelling by the Sarasvatī (*d*), they went there, and thence reached the lake of Dvaitavana (III, **177**).—§ 450: At the request of Janamejaya, Vaiçampāyana detailed how Bhīma, when they had come from the rājarshi Vṛshaparvan's hermitage, was hunting with unpoisoned (*çuddhair*) arrows on some spots of Himavat (*b*), was seized by a huge snake, and on account of a boon that had been granted to the serpent was quite unable to extricate himself (III, **178**). The serpent said that he was the rājarshi Nahusha, the son of Āyu, whom Agastya had cursed to become a serpent, out of compassion, however, adding to his curse that the person who would be able to answer his questions would deliver him, and that even stronger beings would, when seized by him, lose their strength. He had retained his recollection of his former existence, and nobody who came within his reach at the sixth division of the day (? *shashṭhe kāle: ashṭadhā vibhaktasyāhno bhāge*, Nīl.) could escape him. Bhīma lamented. Now appeared dreadful omens to Yudhishṭhira there, and having learnt from Draupadī that Bhīma had long been out, he set out with Dhaumya, having directed Arjuna to protect Draupadī, and Nakula and Sahadeva to protect the brahmans; and in the east, following the tracks of Bhīma, he came to the spot (III, **179**). The serpent told Yudhishṭhira who he was, refused other food instead of Bhīma, but promised to deliver him if Yudhishṭhira could answer his questions. The first question was about the characteristics of the brahman, etc. (III, **180**). Yudhishṭhira asked the serpent some questions about the means of salvation, and some other moral and philosophical questions, about the difference between the mind (*manas*) and the intellect (*buddhi*), and what had caused Nahusha's fall. Nahusha told that in heaven he used to exact tribute from brahmarshis, gods, Rākshasas, Gandharvas, Yakshas, Pannagas, etc.; and that such was the spell of his eyes, that on whatever creature he fixed them he instantly destroyed its power; Agastya had foretold that Yudhishṭhira would save him from his curse. He delivered Bhīma unhurt, and, assuming his celestial shape, went back to heaven. Yudhishṭhira returned with Dhaumya and Bhīma, and narrated all that to the brahmans, who censured Bhīma, and warned him against attempting such things again (III, **181**).

Ājagava[1], the bow of Pṛthu Vainya. § 595 (Pṛthu Vainya): VII, **60**, 2406 (*dhanuḥ*).

Ājagava[2], Arjuna's bow. § 599 (Jayadrathavadhap.): VII, **145**, †6148.

Ājagava[3], Māndhātṛ's bow. § 407 (Māndhātrup.): III, **126**, 10456 (*nāma dhanuḥ*).

Ajaikapād, one of the Rudras, sons of Sthāṇu. § 108 (Aṃçāvat.): I, **66**, 2566.—§ 191 (Pāṇḍavotp.): I, **123**, 4826.—§ 565 (Gālavacar.): V, **114**, 3899 (gold is guarded by the Ajaikapād-Ahirbradhnaiḥ and by Dhanada, i.e. Kubera).—§ 665 (Mokshadh.): XII, **208δ**, 7585 (among the deities that are the lords of the three worlds); XIII, 1217 (= Çiva, 1000 names[2]).—§ 770 (Ānuçāsanik.): XIII, **151β**, 7090 (one of the eleven Rudras, the lords of the three worlds).

Ajaka, an Asura incarnated as Çālva. § 130 (Aṃçāvat.): I, **67**, 2652 (*Ajakas tv avaro rājan ya āsīd Vṛshaparvaṇaḥ | sa Çālva iti vikhyātaḥ pṛthivyām abhavan nṛpaḥ*).

Ajamīḍha, an ancient king. § 61 (Sarpasattra): I, **55**, †2101 (°*sya yajñaḥ*).—§ 152 (Pūruvaṃç.): I, **94**, 3720 (son of Suhotra and Aikshvākī), 3721.—§ 156 (do.): I, **95**, 3789 (son of Vikuṇṭhana and Sudevā Dāçārhī), 3790. — § 721 (Ānuçāsanik.): XIII, **4**, 201. — § 730 (Meghavāhanop.): XIII, **18**, 1315.

Ājamīḍha[1] = A°: I, 3126.

Ājamīḍha[2] = Yudhishṭhira: †I, 2102; I, 7150; II, 1601; III, 10093, 10119, 10691, 10697; V, 35, 650; VI, 3781; VIII, 3287; X, 570; XIII, †1373, 3730.

Ājamīḍha[3] = Nakula: V, 2229.

Ajamīḍha[4] = Dhṛtarāshṭra: II, 2484 (?); V, 1332, 2518; VII, 5838, 5840; VIII, 4227.

Ājamīḍha[5] = Vidura: III, 249.

Ājamīḍha[6] (°au) = Duryodhana + Arjuna: IV, 2091.

Ājamīḍha[7] = Saṃvaraṇa: I, 3737.

Ājamīḍha[8], plur. (°*āḥ*): II, 1601 (°*ānām*); V, 2892 (°*kulaṃ praptā*, sc. Kṛshṇā), 3221 (= do.).

Ajātaçatru = Yudhishṭhira: I, 7149, 7152, 7760; II, 522 (*na tasya vidyate dveshṭā, tato 'syājātaçatrutā*), 972, 1863, 1873, 2118 (*Pāṇḍavo*), 2203 (do.), 2434, 2448; III, 232, 251, 988, 1354, 1362, 11739 (*Kaunteyo*), 11906, 12313, 14749 (*Dharmarājaḥ*), 14954, 15022, 17231; IV, 587, 905; V, 27, 645, 662, 677 (*Kuntīputraḥ*), 716, 720, 721, 722, 724, 768, 899, 948, 953, 960, 969, 970, 979, 1095, 1096, 1907, 1984, 3148, 3438, 5198; VI, 2596, 3138, 3769; VII, 312, 445 (°*tā*), 1358, 1379, 1960, 3529 (*Kaunteyam*), 4174 (*Kaunteyaḥ*), 6445 (*Pāṇḍavam*); VIII, 199, 3206, 3298; IX, 557 (*Kaunteyaṃ Yudhishṭhiram*), 999, 1718 (*Kaunteyo*); XII, 603, 698 (*Kaunteyam*); XIII, 7555; XV, 57, 970.

Ajeya, an ancient king. § 6 (Anukram.): I, **1**, 228.

Ajita[1], an ancient king. § 5 (Anukram.): I, **1**, 224*b*.

Ajita[2] = Çiva (1000 names[2]).

Ajitaçatru. § 270 (Brahma-sabhā-v.): II, **11***a*, 442 (in the palace of Brahmán).

Ājyapāḥ ("drinkers of butter"). § 695*b* (Dakshayajñav.): XII, **285***a*, 10280.—§ 730 (Ānuçāsanik., Meghavāhanop.): XIII, **18**λλ, †1372.

***Ākāça** ("space"). § 543 (Rāmarājyābhisheka): III, **291**β, 16554, etc.

Ākāça-Gaṅgā ("the heavenly Gaṅgā"). § 11 (Parvas.). I, **1**, 638.—§ 421 (Gandhamādanaprav.): III, **142**, 10909: In the neighbourhood of the Mandara mountain, the abode of the gods and ṛshis; coming from Badarī, honoured by Vaihāyasas and Vālakhilyas and Gandharvas and singers of Sāmans; there Marīci, Pulaha, Bhṛgu, and Aṅgiras, with the host of M., mutter their daily prayers; S., A., the Moon, the Sun, the stars, and planets circumambulate it; Çiva (*Vṛshāṅkaḥ*) carries its water on his head at Gaṅgādvāra. According to the counsel of Lomaça the Pāṇḍavas adored it, and then continued their journey with the hosts of ṛshis.—§ 714 (Çukakṛtya): XII, **389**, 12410.—§ 717*b* (Nārāyaṇīya): XII, **343**, ††13218 VIII). — § 795 (Svargārohanap.): XVIII, **3**, 108.

Akāçani = Çiva (1000 names[2]).

Akala = Çiva (1000 names[1]).

Akāla = Çiva (1000 names[2]).

Akampana(ḥ), a king. § 594 (Abhimanyuv.): VII, **52**, 2023, 2029; **54**, 2125: In days of old there was a king named Akampana. Once, on the field of battle, he was surrounded by his foes. His son Hari was at last slain in the midst of the army. *A.* grieved day and night. Then the D.-ṛ. Nārada came and told him the origin of death (Mṛtyu, q.v.). "Therefore," said Nārada, "don't indulge in fruitless grief for creatures after they are dead . . . ." Akampana felt consoled, and Nārada went to the woods of Nandana.

Akara = Çiva (1000 names[2]).

Akāra ("the letter *a*"): VI, 1237 (*aksharāṇām akāro 'smi*, says Kṛshṇa about himself).

Akarkara, a serpent. § 47 (Sarpanāmakathana): I **35**, 1561 (*Karkarākarkarau nāgau*).

Ākarsha. § 287 (Rājasūyikap.): II, **34**, 1270 (among the kings who came to Yudhishṭhira's rājasūya).

Akartṛ = Kṛshṇa? XII, 13285.

Ākhaṇḍala = Indra. § 606 (Karṇap.): VIII, **86**τ, 4353 (°*dhanuḥprakhyam* . . . *Karṇam*).—§ 608 (do.): VIII, **90**, 4661 (*harāmbupākhaṇḍalavittagoptṛbhiḥ*). — § 717 (Nārāyaṇīya): XII, **337**, 12755 (*divam Ākhaṇḍalo yathā*); **339**, 12864 (Mahāpurushastave).

Akroça. § 285 (Digvijayap.): II, **32**, 1188 (*rājarshim*, conquered by Nakula).

Akrodhadrohamoha = Kṛshṇa: XII, 1671.

Akrodhana. § 156 (Pūruvaṃç.): I, **95**, ††3774 (son of Ayutanāyin and Kāmā).

Akrūra[1]. § 232 (Svayaṃvarap.): I, **186**, 6998 (comes to the svayaṃvara of Kṛshṇā).—§ 252 (Subhadrāharaṇap.): I, **219**, 7915.—§ 253 (Haraṇāharaṇap.): I, **221**, 7990 (*Vṛshṇivīrāṇāṃ senāpatir*; visited Arjuna at Khāṇḍavaprastha together with Kṛshṇa).—§ 264 (Sabhākriyāp.): II, **4**β, 125 (among the kings present when Yudhishṭhira entered his palace).—§ 320 (Saubhavadhop.): III, **18**, 736 (a Vṛshṇi hero).—§ 342 (Indralokābhigam.): III, **51**, 1994 (°*Gada-Sāmbaiç ca*, a Vṛshṇi hero).—§ 641 (Rājadh.): XII, **81**, 3033 (*Āhukākrūrau*, v. the note by PCR., p. 260), 3037 ("Baladeva and others of the Bhoja race are partisans of Akrūra").—§ 793 (Mausalap.): XVI, **6**κ, 157; **7**, 248 (his widow(s) desire to retire into the woods). — § 795 (Svargārohaṇap.): XVIII, **5**μ, 162 (among the kings that entered the deities, *Viçveshāṃ devatānān te viviçur*).

Akrūra[2] = Vishṇu (1000 names).

Akrūrakarman = Çiva: XIV, 204.

Ākṛshṭa, plur. (°*āḥ*), a sort of Ṛshis. § 656 (Khaḍgotp.): XII, **166**β, 6144 (accepted the religion of the Vedas).

Akṛtavraṇa, a follower of Paraçu-Rāma. § 393 (Paraçu-Rāma): III, **115**, 10127 (*Rāmasyānucaraṃ vīram*), (10129).—§ 394 (Arjuna Kārtavīrya): III, **115** (10133). — § 394*b* (Tīrthayātrāp.): III, **115**: *A.* had followed Rāma Jāmadagnya and been an eye-witness of all his deeds in former days.—§ 395 (Jamadagni): III, **115** (10150).—§ 396 (do.): III, **116** (10171).—§ 573 (Ambop.): V, **176**, 6058 (*Rāmasyānucaraḥ priyaḥ*), 6062, 6063, (6064); **177** (6083), (6091); **179**, 7132 (he acted as Yuyutsu's charioteer, *sakhā Veda-vid atyantaṃ dayito Bhārgavasya ha*); **180**, 7179 (°*prabhṛtayaḥ* . . . . *Rāmasyānucarāḥ*); **184**, 7280 (*sakhā vipro*, sc. *Rāmasya*).—§ 734 (Ānuçāsanik.): XIII, **26***a*, 1765 (among the ṛshis who surround Bhīshma when he lies on his arrow bed).

Akṛti. § 273 (Rājasūyārambhap.): II, **14**, 586 (brother of the Bhoja king Bhīshmaka; like to Rāma Jāmadagnya; has placed himself under Jarāsandha).—§ 284 (Sahadeva): II, **31***a*, 1165 (a king in the south, subjected by Sahadeva; *Ākṛtiṃ Kauçikācāryam* . . . *vaçe cakre* . . . *Surāshṭrādhipatiṃ*).

Aksha. § 615 (Skanda): IX, **45**η, 2560 (among the warriors of Skanda).

Aksha = Çiva (1000 names[2]).

Akshahṛdayaprāpti. § 11 (Parvas.): I, **2**, 437 (all. to the history of Nala).

Akshamālā. § 565 (Gālavacar.): V, **117**, 3970 (*Vasishṭhaç cākshamālayā . . . reme*; PCR. identifies her with Arundhatī).

Akshamālin = Çiva (1000 names[1]).

***Akshara** ("imperishable"): (= Kṛshṇa) XII, 1626, 1635; XII, 2328 (°*sātmatām*), 2323 (id.), 2351 (°*saṃmitāḥ lokāḥ*); (= Hiraṇyagarbha) XII, 11232 (*eko*); (= Vishṇu?) XII, 13115; (= Kṛshṇa?) XII, 13285 (?); (= Çiva) XIII, 1193 (*paramaṃ Brahma?*); (= Vishṇu) XIII, 6951 (1000 names), 7000 (1000 names).

***akshauhiṇī**, an army of a certain kind and magnitude. § 9 (Parvas.): I, **1**, 287, 292, etc.—§ 153 (Saṃvaraṇa): I, **94**, 3723.—§ 570 (Sainyaniryāṇap.): V, **155**, 5267, etc.

Akshīṇa, son of Viçvāmitra. § 721*b* (Viçvāmitrop.): XIII, **4**β, 249.

Akshobhya = Vishṇu (1000 names).

Akūpāra (v. BR.). § 28 (Amṛtamanth.): I, **18**, 1122.—§ 468 (Indradyumnop.): III, **199**, 13337 (a very old tortoise), 13338.

Alakā, the city and tank of Kubera. § 148 (Yayāti): I, **85**, 3508.—§ 269 (Vaiçravaṇasabhā-v.): II, **10**, 390 (*nalinyāç cālakākhyāyāḥ*).

Alakādhipa = Kubera: IX, 583 (*Maheçvarasakham*); XII, 2811 (= *Vaiçravaṇa*), 2822 (id.).

Alakanandā. § 221 (Caitrarathap.): I, **170**, 6456 (*deveshu Gaṅgā, Gandharva! prāpnoty Alakanandatāṃ*).

Alamba (? v. Garuḍa). § 43*b*: I, **29**, 1377: with divine trees (*devavṛkshāḥ*), with golden boughs, and others with fruits of gold and silver and branches of precious gems.

Ālamba. § 264 (Sabhākriyāp.): II, **4***a*, 109 (among the ṛshis who were present when Yudhishṭhira entered his palace).

Alambāyana (= Cāruçīrsha). § 730 (Ānuçāsanik., Meghavāhanop.): XIII, **18**, 1301 (C°).

Alambusha, a rākshasa, variously genealogized and presumably ultimately identical with other similar figures. § 11 (Parvas.): I, **2**, 535 (is killed).—§ 552 (Goharaṇap.): IV, **5**, 1771 (the same?, rather °*ā*: *Alambushograsenānām*, sc. *vimānāni*; Nīl. *tatprabhṛtīnāṃ Gandharvānām*).—§ 572 (Rathātirathas.): V, **167**, 5802 (*Rākshasendraḥ, pūrvavairam anusmaran, Rākshasasainyānāṃ sarveshāṃ rathasattamaḥ*).—§ 578 (Bhīshmavadhap.): VI, **45**, 1711 (*rākshasam*), 1713 (= do.).—§ 581 (do.): VI, **63**, †2808 (*rākshaso*).—§ 584 (do.): VI, **81**, 3560 (= do.); **82**, 3615 (*rākshasaṃ*), 3620 (= do.). — [§ 585 (do.): VI, **90**, c.]: the rākshasa, Ārçyaçṛṅga (v. 4019), who kills Irāvat, is Alambusha. — § 586 (do.): VI, **99**, 4506 (= do.); **100**, 4572 (= do.), 4575 (= do.); **101**, 4584 (= do.: *Ārçyaçṛṅgim*), 4591 (= do.), 4596 (= do.: *Ārçyaçṛṅjim*), 4604 (= do.).—§ 590 (Droṇābhishekap.): **VII**, **14**, 540 (*Haiḍimbālambushau rākshasau*). — § 592 (Saṃçaptakavadhap.): VII, **25**, 1124 (*rākshasas*). — § 599 (Jayadrathavadhap.): VII, **95**, 3537 (*rākshasendraṃ*); **96**, 3559 (= do.); **108**, 4065 (= do.: *Ārçyaçṛṅgim*, v. 4067), 4072 (= do.: recollecting the slaughter of his brother Vaka, v. 4075); **109**, 4097 (= do.), 4099 (= do.), 4101 (= do.), 4105 (= do.), 4106 (*rākshasendraṃ*), †4132 (slain by Ghaṭotkaca: *Ghaṭotkacaḥ . . . abhinananda . . . Alambushaṃ pakvam alambushaṃ yathā*); **140**, 5828 (*rājavaro*, = do.?), 5830 (do. = do.?), 5833 (= do.?); **150**, 6515 (= do.?).—§ 600 (Ghaṭotkacavadhap.): VII, **165**, 7371 (*rākshasendro*); **167**, 7498 (having eight terrible-looking Piçācas yoked to his car; description); **174**, 7856 (= do.? *Jāṭāsurir*), 7857 (*rakshas*), 7858 (= do.), 7861 (= do.), 7864 (= do.), 7870 (= do.), 7872 (*Ghaṭotkacālambushayoḥ*), 7875 (*Alambusha - Ghaṭotkacau*), 7879 (*rākshasendraṃ*). — § 604 (Karṇap.): VIII, **5**, 135 (*rākshasendraḥ, kharabandhurayānavān*, has been killed by Ghaṭotkaca).—§ 609 (Çalyap.): IX, **2**, 76 (*Jalasandho 'thārshyaçṛṅgī rākshasaç cāpy Alāyudhaḥ | Alambusho . . .* sc. have died), 94 (*Alambushas tathā rājā rākshasaç cāpy Alāyudhaḥ | Ārçyaçṛṅgiç ca nihataḥ*).—§ 620 (Çrāddhap.): XI, **26**, 792 (*Ghaṭotkacaṃ rākshasendraṃ Baka-bhrātaram eva ca | Alambushaṃ rākshasendraṃ Jalasandhañ ca pārthivaṃ*, sc. are burnt after death).

Alambushā, an Apsaras. § 103 (Aṃçāvatar.): I, **65**, 2557.—§ 191 (Arjuna): I, **123**, 4817.—§ 549 (Pāṇḍavapraveçap.): IV, **9**, 259.—§ 615 (Baladevatīrthay.): IX, **51**, 2931 (*divyām Apsarasaṃ puṇyāṃ darçanīyām A°ām*), 2937.—§ 731 (Ashṭāvakra-Dik-saṃv.): XIII, **19**, 1424.—§ 775 (Ānuçāsanik.): XIII, **166**, 7641.

Alarka[1], a rājarshi. § 267 (Yama-sabhā-v.): II, **8**, 329 (among the rājarshis in the palace of Yama). — § 323*b* (Dvaitav.): III, **25** (Alarka had renounced his kingdoms and riches, see BR., LIA. I. Anh., xxx f., 2nd ed. xxxiv f.).—§ 760 (Ānuçāsanik.): XIII, **115**, 5666 (*Rāmā°-Nalaiḥ*).—§ 775 (do.): XIII, **166**η, 7678 (among the principal kings whose names are to be recited at sunset and sunrise). — § 782 (Brāhmaṇagītā): XIV, **30**e, 840 (*rājarshim*), (843), 845, (847), 848, (850), 851, (853), 854, (856), 857, (859), 860, (862), 863, 865, 866. The Pitṛs (of Paraçu-Rāma) said: R.-ṛ. Alarka, having with his bow conquered the whole earth, set his mind on what is subtle; he said: "My mind has become strong; having conquered the mind, one's conquest becomes permanent; I shall shoot sharp-pointed arrows at the mind." The mind said: "These arrows will never pierce me, but only slay thyself; do thou look out for other arrows with which to destroy me"; and so also with the nose, the tongue, etc. Then he set himself to penances, but failed to obtain fit arrows. He engaged in *yoga*, and now slew all the senses with one arrow. He complained that he [had lost his time] in courting sovereignty till now; "there is no happiness higher than *yoga*."

Alarka[2], a worm. § 621 (Rājadh.): XII, **3**, 87 (bites Karṇa; originally a Rākshasa, who in the Kṛta-age had ravished the spouse of Bhṛgu and been cursed by him).

Alātākshī, a mātṛ. § 615*u* (Skanda): IX, **46**υ, 2020.

Alāyudha, a Rākshasa. § 599 (Jayadrathavadhap.): VII, **95**υ, 3536 (fights Ghaṭotkaca on the fourteenth day of the battle); **96**, 3568 (do.).—§ 600 (Ghaṭotkacavadhap.): VII, **176**, 8004 (promises Duryodhana to slay Bhīmasena and his brothers in order to avenge his kinsmen Baka and Kirmīra and his friend Hiḍimba, in the night after the fourteenth day of the combat); **177**, 8028 (fights Ghaṭotkaca, etc.), 8033, 8042, 8043 (°*ratham*), 8044, 8046, 8051; **178**ψψ, 8076 (do.), 8078, 8079, 8085, 8101 (*yuddhaṃ Bhaimy-Alāyudhayor*), 8110 (is killed by Ghaṭotkaca), 8114; **179**, 8117; **180**, 8212; **181**, 8236.—§ 609 (Çalyap.): IX, **2**, 76, 94.—§ 611 (do.): IX, **24**, 1299.—§ 789 (Putradarçanap.): XV, **32**, 879.

Alinda, pl. (°*āḥ*), a people in Bharata-varsha. — § 574 (Jambūkh.): VI, **9**, 371 (B. has *Athida*).

Alola = Çiva (1000 names[2]).

Alolupa, (*a*) son of Dhṛtarāshṭra. § 131 (Aṃçāv.): I, **67**, 2738.—§ 182 (Dhṛtarāshṭraputranāmak.): I, **117**, 4551.—§ 606 (Karṇap.): VIII, **84**ξ, 4263 (among ten sons of Dhṛtarāshṭra's killed by Bhīma; C. has *Alulupa*).—(*b*) = the Sun: III, **3**, 153.

Alulupa, v. Alolupa.

Amadhya ("without middle"): XII, 12864 (Mahāpurushastave), 13249 (= Kṛshṇa).

Amāhaṭha, a serpent. § 67 (Sarpasattra): I, **57**, 2157 (of Dhṛtarāshṭra's race).

Amānin = Vishṇu (1000 names).

*__Amara__[1], pl., the gods: IX, 1909, 2450, 2969 (°*prakhyam*), 3243; X, 766 (°*tām*), 789, 804; XI, 295, 494 (°*vat*), etc.; sing., IX, 1899, etc.

Amara[2] = Çiva (1000 names[2]).

*__Amaraçreshṭha__ = Indra.

*__Amarādhipa__ = Indra.

*__Amaradvishaḥ__, the Asuras: IX, 3519.

*__Amaradyuti__ = Çiva: XIII, 7499.

*__Amaraṇa__ = Çiva (1000 names[2]).

*__Amaraprabhu__ = Vishṇu (1000 names).

*__Amararāja__ = Indra.

Amarāvatī, the city of Indra.—§ 225 (Vāsishṭha): I, **177**, 6786 (*Çakreṇevāmarāvatī*).—§ 262 (Sabhākriyā): II, **2**, 46 (*yathā Çakro 'marāvatīṃ*).—§ 335 (Indralokābhig.): III, **42**, 1755 (*Çakrasya purīṃ*). — § 336 (Indralokābh): III, **43**: Amarāvatī was the resort of Siddhas and Cāraṇas, and the Nandana garden of the troops of the Apsarases. The region cannot be seen by those who have not gone through ascetic austerities, etc.—§ 443 (Nivātakavacay.): III, **168**, 12036 (*Çakrasya bhavanam*). — § 445 (do.): III, **173**, 12224 (°*ī-saṅkāçaṃ Hiraṇyapuram*).—§ 564 (Mātalīyop.): V, **103**, 3617 (*devarājasya purī*). — § 589 (Droṇābhishekap.): VII, **11**, 408.—§ 596 (Pratijñāp.): VII, **77**, 2724.—§ 736 (Vītahavyop.): XIII, **30**, 1957.—§ 745 (Cyavana-Kuçika-s.): XIII, **54**, 2841.—§ 768 (Umā-Maheçvara-s.): XIII, **142**, 6545 (by living with deer, etc., one attains to Amarāvatī).

*__Amareçvara__ = Indra.

Amatsyāçin, son of Viçvāmitra. § 721 (Ānuçāsanik.): XIII, **4**β, 258.

*__Amāvasī__, the day of the new moon. § 615 (Prabhāsotpattik.): IX, **35**, 2052, 2058.—§ 717 (Nārāyaṇīya): XII, **343** XI), 13221.

Amāvasu, son of Purūravas and Urvaçī. § 141 (Purūravas): I, **75**, 3149.

Ambā, the eldest daughter of the king of Kāçi, chosen by the Saubha king, carried off by Bhīshma to be married to Vicitravīrya, but released; refused by the Saubha king, etc., reborn as Çikhaṇḍin (v. Ambopākhyānaparvan). § 167 (Vicitravīryoparama): I, **102**, 4136 (*jyeshṭhāṃ Kāçipateḥ sutāṃ*).—§ 290 (Çiçupālavadhap.): II, **41**, 1454.—§ 573 (Ambop.): V, **173**, 5951–2; **175**, 5977, 5985; **176**, 6040, 6068, (6080); **177**, (6087), (7009), (7017); **178**, (7029), (7031), 7033 (*Rāmāmbayoḥ*); **186**, 7367 (only in B., a river in Vatsabhūmi, to which Ambā was changed after death with half her body); **188**, 7408; **192**, 7551.—§ 576 (Bhagavadgītāp.): VI, **14**, 554.—§ 596 (Pratijñāp.): VII, **72**, 2501.

Ambājanman, a tīrtha. § 364 (Tīrthayātrāp.): III, **83**, 6051.

Ambālikā. § 156 (Pūruvaṃç.): I, **95**, 3804.

```
      Çantanu                 Kauçalya Kāçirāja
         |                           |
         |        ___________________|____________________________
(§ 157) Vicitravīrya~(2) Ambikā.  (3) Ambālikā~Vyāsa (§ 171).  (1) Ambā.
                                             |
                                  ___________|___________
                                  Dhṛtarāshṭra (2).  Pāṇḍu (3).
```

§ 167 (Vicitravīryoparama): I, **102**, 4137.—§ 171 (Vicitravīryasutotp.): I, **106**, 4288.—§ 573 (Ambop.): V, **173**, 5951–2 (*rājakanyā yavīyasī*); **175**, 5990; **176**, 6068. Cf. Kausalyā.

Ambarāvṛta = Çiva (1000 names[2]).

Ambarīsha[1], an ancient king. § 4 (Anukram.): I, **1**, 220 *bis* (mentioned by Sañjaya as belonging to the past).—§ 267 (Yama-sabhā-v.): II, **8**, 322 (in the palace of Yama).—§ 409 (Plakshāvataraṇagam.): III, **129**b, 10514 (*Nābhāgaḥ*; had in olden time sacrificed on the Yamunā and given prodigious riches to the sadasyas, and by his sacrifices and austerities he had attained to the highest perfection—*siddhim*). — § 521 (Draupadīharaṇap.): III, **263**, 15553 (*smṛtā 'nubhāraṃ rājarshir Ambarīshasya dhīmataḥ*).—§ 562 (Bhagavadyānap.): V, **90**ν, 3146.—§ 574 (Jambūkh.): VI, **9**aa, 314 (had been king of Bharatavarsha).—§ 595 (Shoḍaçarājika): VII, **64**, 2303, 2314, 2318. *A. N.* fought alone against 1,000,000 kings, who were reduced to subjection, and he, conquering the whole earth, performed 100 sacrifices, etc. (description); in those sacrifices he as sacrificial presents gave the kingdoms of hundreds and thousands of kings to his 10,000,000 of priests, and numbers of princes and kings with their treasuries, etc.—§ 621 (Rājadh.): XII, **8**θ, 238 (the earth had formerly belonged to him).—§ 623 (do.): XII, **14**, 421 (do.).—§ 632 (Shoḍaçarājop.): XII, **29**, 993 (*Nābhāgim*; his magnificent sacrifices, etc.), 995.—§ 641 (Rājadh.): XII, **98**, 3614 (discourse between him and Indra about Sudeva and the sacrifice of battle), 3615 (*Nābhāgiḥ*), (3618), (3625), 3663.—§ 677 (Mokshadh.): XII, **235**, 8597 (having given to the brahmans eleven arbudas of cows, he proceeded to heaven with all the people of his kingdom).—§ 751b (Çapathavidhi): XIII, **94**a, †4551, (4575).—§ 761 (Ānuçāsanik.): XIII, **115**γ, 5661 (*Nābhāgena*; among the ancient kings that had abstained from honey and meat in the month of Kārttika).—§ 767 (do.): XIII, **137**a, 6253 (among the princes that had attained to heaven by charities and penances; *A.* had given away all his kingdom to a brahman).—§ 775 (do.): XIII, **166**η, 7679 (among the principal kings whose names should be recited at sunrise and sunset).—§ 782b (Brāhmaṇagītā): XIV, **31**, 876 (in an ancient kalpa, sung verses), 877, 886.

Ambarīsha[2], a Nāga (Serpent). § 793 (Mausalap.): XVI, **4**η, †120 (among the celestial snakes who received in the Ocean the Nāga that issued from the mouth of Bala-Rāma).

Ambashṭha[1], pl. (°*āḥ*), a people. § 285 (Digvijayap., Nakula): II, **32**, 1189 (in the west, conquered by Nakula).—§ 295 (Dyūtap.): II, **52**, 1871 (among the people who paid tribute to Yudhishṭhira).—§ 576 (Bhagavadgītāp.): VI, **18**, 688 (among the people who protected Bhīshma); **20**, 750 (in the army of Bhīshma).—§ 587 (Bhīshmavadhap.): VI, **117**, 5485 (vanquished by Arjuna on the tenth day of the battle; *Kaikeyaiḥ saha*); **119**aa, 5649 (among the people who abandoned Bhīshma on the tenth day of the battle; do.).—§ 589 (Droṇābhishekap.): VII, **4**β, 120 (had fought Karṇa); **7**, 183 (in the rear of Droṇa's troops).—§ 592 (Saṃçaptakavadhap.): VII, **20**θ, 802 (at the back of Droṇa's array on the twelfth day of the battle).—§ 599 (Jayadrathavadhap.): VII, **121**εε, 4819 (headed by Duryodhana, they, with Çakas, etc., and the Saṃçaptakas, attacked Sātyaki).—§ 600 (Ghaṭotkacavadhap.): VII, **157**ρ, 6948 (Yudhishṭhira began to slay the *A.*; the nightly combat after the fourteenth day); **161**δδ, 7206 (Yudhishṭhira slew the *A.*).—§ 702 (Mokshadh.): XII, **297**γ, 10868 (among the kshatriyas who had sprung from the original orders by intermixture).

Ambashṭha[2], the Ambashṭha king (Çrutāyu). § 585 (Bhīshmavadhap.): VI, **96**, 4360 (*rājānaṃ loke viçrutam* vanquished by Abhimanyu).—§ 592 (Saṃçaptakavadhap.): VII, **25**, 1112 (*rājānaṃ*, vanquished by the Cedi-king), 1113.—§ 599 (Jayadrathavadhap.): VII, **93**, 3397 (*Çrutāyus tathāmbashṭhas*, fights Arjuna), 3399, 3402.—§ 604 (Karṇap.): VIII, **5**, 107 (*Çrutāyur api cāmbashṭhaḥ*, has been killed by Arjuna); **6**, 161 (*°sya sutaḥ*, killed by Duryodhana's son Lakshmaṇa).

Ambashṭhaka, a king. § 585 (Bhīshmav.): VI, **96**, 4340 (fights Abhimanyu on the eighth day of the battle).

Ambashṭhapati ("the lord of the Ambashṭhas"). § 580 (Bhīshmav.): VI, **59**μ, †2584 (*Çrutāyus*, attacks Arjuna on the third day of the battle), †2547 (ρ) (*Çrutāyur*, has been vanquished by Arjuna).

Ambhonidhi[1] = Kṛshṇa.

Ambhonidhi[2] = Vishṇu (1000 names).

Ambhoruha, son of Viçvāmitra. § 721*b* (Viçvāmitrop.): XIII, **4**β, 258.

Ambikā[1], sister of Ambālikā (q.v.). § 156 (Pūruvaṃç.): I, **95**, 3804 (*Ambikāmbālike Kauçalyātmaje Kāçirāja-duhitarau*).—§ 167 (Vicitravīryoparama): I, **102**, 4137.—§ 171 (Vicitravīryasutotp.): I, **106**, 4277.—§ 196 (Vyāsa): I, **128**, 4973, 4975.—§ 573 (Ambop.): V, **173**, 5951, 5952 (*madhyamā*); **175**, 5990; **176**, 6068. *Cf.* Kausalyā.

Ambikā[2], an Apsaras. § 191 (Pāṇḍavotp.): I, **123**, 4818 (among the Apsarases who danced and sang at the birth of Arjuna).

Ambikā[3], a mātṛ. § 615*u* (Skanda): IX, **46**θ, 2630 (enumeration).—§ 770 (Ānuçāsanik.): XIII, **151**ε, 7106 (*Skandaç cāmbikayā saha*; among those the recital of whose names cleanses from all sins).

Ambikābhartṛ = Çiva.

Ambikāsuta = Dhṛtarāshṭra.

Āmbikeya = Dhṛtarāshṭra.

Ambopākhyāna ("episode relating to Ambā"). § 10 (Parvas.): I, **2**, 336 (*°aṃ parva*).—§ 11 (do.): I, **2**, 516, i.e. Ambopākhyānaparvan.

[Ambopākhyānaparvan] ("the section containing the episode of Ambā," the 66th of the minor parvans of Mhbhr. Cf. Ambopākhyāna). § 573. Questioned by Duryodhana why he would not slay Çikhaṇḍin, Bhīshma said: After Çāntanu's death and Citrāṅgada's demise, obedient to the counsels of Satyavatī I installed, according to the ordinance, Vicitravīrya as king. I repaired on a single car to the *svayaṃvara* of the daughters of the king of Kāçi: Ambā (the eldest), Ambikā (the second), and Ambālikā (the youngest), who were *vīryaçalkāḥ*. Challenging all the kings, I took the three maidens upon my car, and repeatedly told my name to the kings, and vanquished them all. Then I came back to Hāstinapura and made over those maidens, intending them for Vicitravīrya, to Satyavatī (V, **173**). Satyavatī became very glad. When the nuptials approached, Ambā said that she had before mentally chosen the Çālva king (the lord of Saubha, v. 6076, etc.) as her lord, and that he, without her father's knowledge, had privately proposed to her (V, **174**). I then laid the matter before Satyavatī and our counsellors (*mantrin*), *ṛtvijes*, and *purohitas*, and permitted Ambā to depart. She came to the city of the Çālva king, escorted by a number of old brahmans, accompanied by her nurse. But he would no longer have her as his wife, because she was to be wedded to another. It was of no avail that she declared she had been carried away by force, weeping and against her will; for Çālva was in terror of Bhīshma. She cursed Bhīshma, her father, herself (because she had not leapt down from Bhīshma's car), Çālva, and Dhātṛ (the creator). She resolved that her vengeance should fall upon Bhīshma. She repaired to a hermitage of ascetics (*tāpasāḥ*), and stayed there that night. There was the great brahman Çaikhāvatya, a preceptor in the scriptures and the Āraṇyakas (*çāstre cāraṇyake guruḥ*) (V, **175**). The ascetics counselled her to repair to her father's abode; but she would not, lest she should be slighted by her relatives; she wished to practise ascetic austerities. Then came her maternal grandfather, the Sṛñjaya king, the R.-ṛ. Hotravāhana, and advised her to go to Rāma Jāmadagnya, who would slay Bhīshma in battle if Bhīshma did not obey his behest; he always dwelt on the Mahendra mountain with R., G., and Aps. While they were speaking there appeared Akṛtavraṇa, a dear companion of Rāma; he said that Rāma would come the next morning to see Hotravāhana; Hotravāhana related the history of Ambā to Akṛtavraṇa (V, **176**). The next day Rāma appeared with his disciples, his bow in hand, etc. (description). Ambā asked him to slay Bhīshma (V, **177**). Rāma said he would not take up arms except at the command of brahmans. Akṛtavraṇa supported the demand of Ambā. The next morning they all set out for Kurukshetra with the maiden, and quartered themselves on the banks of Sarasvatī. On the third day Rāma sent a message to Bhīshma, who came and worshipped him. Rāma demanded that he should bestow Ambā upon Vicitravīrya, which Bhīshma refused. Rāma threatened to slay him in battle; Bhīshma said that Rāma had himself taught him the four kinds of arms (*ishvastraṃ caturvidhaṃ*; see the note of PCR.); and quoted a *çloka* in the Purāṇa, sung by Marutta (v. 7074). Having first gone to Hāstinapura and represented everything to Satyavatī, Bhīshma set out for Kurukshetra on his car (description). Gaṅgā ("worshipped by Si. and Cā," v. 7095) in vain endeavoured to make them desist (V, **178**). Bhīshma asked Rāma to mount on a chariot; but Rāma said that the earth was his chariot, the Vedas his steeds, the wind (Mātariçvan) his charioteer, and the mothers of the Vedas (Vedamātaraḥ; see the note of PCR.) his harness. Bhīshma saw him stationed on an excellent car (description), with Akṛtavraṇa as his charioteer. Bhīshma propitiated Rāma by worshipping him, on foot. The combat lasted for many days; at last Bhīshma, from pity and reverence, would not strike Rāma any longer, and the combat ceased at sunset (V, **179**). Next morning the battle was taken up again. Bhīshma's Vāyavya weapon was neutralized by Rāma's Guhyaka; Bhīshma's Āgneya by Rāma's Vāruṇa. At a momentary swoon of Bhīshma, Akṛtavraṇa, Ambā, etc., were filled with joy; then Rāma fell into a swoon and dropped down; the ascetics and Ambā comforted him. A conflagration was caused in the welkin. At evening Rāma withdrew (V, **180**). The next day they fought again, and at evening they desisted (V, **181**). The next day Bhīshma's charioteer was slain; Bhīshma, pierced by an arrow, fell down to the earth; eight brahmans supported him on their arms in mid-air; Gaṅgā was seen on his car; she had controlled his steeds in the combat. Bhīshma dismissed her and fought till evening. When Rāma for a moment lost his consciousness, Rāhu enveloped the sun, etc. At evening the battle ceased; next day it was taken up again, and lasted for twenty-three days (V, **182**). During the night the above-mentioned eight brahmans appeared to Bhīshma in a dream, comforted him, and said that the weapon Prasvāpa (*Prājāpatyaṃ Viçvakṛtam*, v. 7259; PCR., "appertaining to the lord of all creatures and forged by the divine artificer") would come to his knowledge, for it had been known to him in his former life; neither Rāma nor any person on earth was acquainted with it; Rāma would not be slain by it, but he would fall asleep; "then thou wilt awaken him with the weapon Sambodhana" (V, **183**). Next day Akṛtavraṇa must comfort Rāma. Bhīshma and Rāma both used the Brāhma weapon; the welkin seemed to be ablaze, and D., As., Ṛ., G., and Rā. were greatly afflicted, etc. Then the *mantras* for using the Prasvāpa weapon suddenly came to Bhīshma's mind (V, **184**). Voices in the sky (the gods) and Nārada forbade him to let off the Prasvāpa weapon against Rāma, and the above-mentioned brahmans supported the words of Nārada. Beholding the Prasvāpa weapon withdrawn, Rāma declared himself to be vanquished. Rāma then beheld before him his father and father's father, who forbade him any more to fight with kshattriyas, especially with Bhīshma, whom the gods forbade to fight with Rāma. "Arjuna has been ordained by Svayambhū to be the slayer of Bhīshma." The ascetics with Ṛcīka, Nārada, Gaṅgā, and the Pitṛs succeeded in bringing about peace; the above-mentioned eight brahmans ordered Bhīshma to go to Rāma, who, summoning Ambā, said (V, **185**) that he could do no more for her. Ambā went away, resolved to devote herself to austerities, that she might herself slay Bhīshma. Rāma with the ascetics departed for the Mahendra mountain; Bhīshma entered Hāstinapura, and was blessed by Satyavatī, and he appointed spies to ascertain the doings of Ambā. Bhīshma became afflicted when he heard that she was resolved on ascetic austerities (description), but was consoled by Nārada and Vyāsa. After having lived for six months on air she stood a year in the waters of Yamunā, etc., and thus went on for twelve years. She then went into Vatsabhūmi (resorted to by Si. and Cā.), etc. (*a*). Gaṅgā, angry because she observed these vows for the destruction of Bhīshma, cursed her, saying that after death she would become a river crooked in her course, etc. When Ambā once more came back to Vatsabhūmi she there became the above-mentioned river, but in consequence of her ascetic merit, only with half her body, while as to the other half she remained a maiden as before (V, **186**). To the ascetics in Vatsabhūmi she said that she was resolved to obtain manhood in order to be revenged on Bhīshma. Çiva appeared in his own form in the midst of those great ṛshis, and promised her that she would slay Bhīshma and even obtain manhood, and in a new body remember all the incidents; born in the race of Drupada, she would become a *mahāratha*. Then Çiva disappeared. Ambā burnt herself on the bank of the Yamunā in the very sight of those great Ṛshis (V, **187**). Questioned by Duryodhana how Çikhaṇḍin, having before been born a girl, afterwards became a man, Bhīshma related: The eldest queen of king Drupada was childless. During those years Drupada worshipped Çaṅkara for the sake of offspring, resolving to bring about Bhīshma's destruction, and practising the austerest of penances. He begged Çiva for a son; Çiva said he should have a child who would be both female and male. In due time the queen conceived (as told by Nārada), and gave birth to a daughter, whom Drupada gave out for a son, and called her Çikhaṇḍin. Bhīshma alone, from his spies and from Nārada, knew the truth (V, **188**). In arrows and weapons she became a disciple of Droṇa. They afterwards wedded her to the daughter of the Daçārṇa king Hiraṇyavarman, quite assured that the words of Çiva would become true. Çikhaṇḍin, after marriage, came back to Kāmpilya. At the discovery of Çikhaṇḍin's sex a war was about to break out with Hiraṇyavarman (V, **189**). Drupada was not naturally courageous, and became filled with fear, and, in the presence of others, asked his queen about the truth (though he knew everything) (V, **190**). The queen said that, childless as she was, when her daughter Çikhaṇḍinī was born she had, from fear of her co-wives, told Drupada that it was a son, remembering the words of Çiva. Drupada prepared for war, and, with the queen, prayed to the gods. Çikhaṇḍinī went to a forest, the haunt of the powerful Yaksha (Guhyaka, v. 7480) Sthūṇākarṇa, who was a follower of Kubera, resolved on putting an end to her own life. Repeatedly requested by Sthūṇākarṇa to ask a boon, she told him the matter, and wished to become a man, as long as Hiraṇyavarman had not left the city (V, **191**). He gave her his manhood and took her womanhood for a certain period, i.e. till Hiraṇyavarman should have departed. Çikhaṇḍin went home and informed Drupada, who with his wife recollected the words of Çiva. Hiraṇyavarman sent a brahman as an envoy to Kāmpilya, threatening to exterminate Drupada with his counsellors, sons, etc. Drupada sent a brahman as his envoy to Hiraṇyavarman, maintaining that Çikhaṇḍin was a male; "let it be made clear by means of witnesses; somebody has spoken falsely to thee." Hiraṇyavarman despatched a number of young ladies for ascertaining it, and they attested that he was a male. Hiraṇyavarman then passed some days with Drupada in gladness, gave much wealth to Çikhaṇḍin, and then departed, having rebuked his daughter. Kubera, hearing the matter from the Yakshas, cursed Sthūṇākarṇa, saying that his femininity should remain as it was; as the Yakshas began to soften him, he set a limit to the curse, i.e. Çikhaṇḍin's death. When Çikhaṇḍin came to redeem his pledge, Sthūṇākarṇa related his curse and let him go. Drupada gave Çikhaṇḍin as a pupil to Droṇa, who taught him the fourfold (*catushpādam*) Dhanurveda, along with the Dhārtarāshṭras and Dhṛshṭadyumna. It was Ambā who had been born as Çikhaṇḍin. Bhīshma had made a vow not to shoot weapons against a woman, or one that had before been a woman, or one bearing a feminine name, or one whose form resembled that of a woman (V, **192**). Duryodhana asked in what time Bhīma, etc. (*a*), could annihilate the hostile army. Bhīshma said he could do it in a month; Droṇa said the same; Kṛpa mentioned two months; Açvatthāman, ten nights; Karṇa, five nights. Bhīshma ridiculed Karṇa, saying that he will think otherwise when he had encountered Arjuna and Kṛshṇa (V, **193**). Having learnt this from his spies, Yudhishṭhira asked Arjuna the same question. Arjuna said that with Kṛshṇa as his ally he could exterminate the three worlds with the gods, etc., in the twinkling of an eye; the weapon given him by Paçupati (i.e. Çiva) as a hunter (*Kairāte dvandvayuddhe*), which Paçupati used at the end of the *yuga* for destroying created things, was not known to Bhīshma, etc. (β); he enumerated Yudhishṭhira's allies (γ); Yudhishṭhira was himself competent to exterminate the three worlds (V, **194**). Next morning, under a cloudless sky, the Kaurava army marched (description) to the field, first Vinda, etc. (δ); Açvatthāman, etc. (ϵ), in the second division; in the rear, Kṛtavarman, etc. (ζ), with the Dhārtarāshṭras at their head. Duryodhana's encampment (description) looked like a second Hāstinapura (V, **195**). In the same way Yudhishṭhira also ordered out his troops, headed by Dhṛshṭadyumna, under Dhṛshṭaketu, etc. (η), (description); first Abhimanyu, etc. (θ); then Bhīma and Arjuna in the second division; last of all himself with Virāṭa and Drupada, etc. Then he disposed his divisions in a different order, confounding the Dhārtarāshṭras: the Draupadeyas, etc. (ι), under Bhīmasena; in the middle division, Virāṭa, etc. (κ); in that part where Yudhishṭhira himself was, Cekitāna, etc. (λ). Yudhishṭhira was followed by Saucitti, etc. (μ), (V, **196**).

Ambuçāyin = Çiva (1000 names[1]).

Ambujāla = Çiva (1000 names[2]).

Ambumatī, a river. § 364 (Tīrthayātrāp.): III, **83**, 6026.

Ambupa = Varuṇa.

Ambuvāhinī. § 775 (Ānuçāsanik.): XIII, **166**, 7646 (among the rivers whose names ought to be recited at sunset and sunrise).

Ambuvīca. § 242: I, **204**, 7476: Karṇa spoke contemptuously of Bhīshma and Droṇa, saying that everyone's happiness depended on destiny and not on his friends, etc., mentioning the Magadha king Ambuvīca at Rājagṛha, whose affairs were in the hands of his minister Mahākarṇi, himself never attending to them; his minister appropriated everything belonging to the king (his queen, treasures, and sovereignty), but he did not succeed in acquiring the kingdom.

Aṃça, one of the Ādityas. § 88 (Aṃçāvat.): I, **65**, 2523.—§ 191 (Arjuna): I, **123**α, 4822 (came to the birth of Arjuna).—§ 258 (Khāṇḍavad.): I, **227**, 8267 (seized a lance).—§ 615u (Skanda): IX, **45**γ, 2507δ, 2537 (gave five companions to Skanda).—§ 665 (Mokshadh.): XII, **208**β, 7581 (enumeration).—§ 748 (Tārakavadhop.): XIII, **86**α, 4201 (among those who came to see the newborn Skanda).—§ 770 (Ānuçāsanik.): XIII, **151**γ, 7092 (enumeration of the Ādityas). Cf. Sūrya.

Aṃçāvatāraṇa (the three first chapters of Sambhavaparvan, I, **65–7**). § 11 (Parvas.): I, **2**, 368 (B. has °*tă*°).—§ 289 (Arghāharaṇap.): II, **36**, 1317 (*Aṃçāvatarane yā 'sau Brahmaṇo bhavane*, i.e. *'bhavat*).

[Aṃçāvataraṇa(ṃ)] ("incarnations"), comprehends the three first chapters of Sambhavaparvan (vii), i.e. I, **65–67**. § 85: Conformably to the consultation held between Indra and Nārāyaṇa, the celestials were born in the lines of brahmarshis and rājarshis, and they slew the Dānavas, Rā., G., and Snakes, etc. Janamejaya desired to hear, from the beginning, of the births of D., Dā., G., Apo., men, Y., and Rā.—§ 86: The six spiritual sons of Brahmán; Kaçyapa.—§ 87: The thirteen daughters of Daksha (v. 2520, read Prādhā with B. and V., and v. 2554).—§ 88: The Ādityāḥ (Vishṇu, the youngest and superior to them all).—§ 89: Diti's son Hiraṇyakaçipu and his five sons.—§ 90: Prahlāda's three sons.—§ 91: Virocana—Bali—Bāṇa (a follower of Rudra and called also Mahākāla).—§ 92: Forty sons of Danu (only thirty-two are enumerated, amongst them Sūryā-Candramasau, "not to be confounded with the gods of the same name").—§ 93: Ten more races (*vaṃçāḥ*) of Danu-putrāḥ.—§ 94: Siṃhikā's four sons (Rāhu, etc.).—§ 95: Offspring of Krūrā (i.e. Krodhā, *gaṇaḥ Krodhavaço nāma*, not otherwise enumerated).—§ 96: The four sons of Danāyus.—§ 97: The offspring of Kālā (the Kālakeyāḥ; only four enumerated; instead of "*Krodhaḥ çatruḥ*" read with B. "*Krodhaçatruḥ*").—§ 98: The upādhyāya of the Asuras was Çukra or Uçanas, son of a ṛshi; he had four sons who sacrificed for the Asuras (*Tvashṭā*—so BR.—*Dharas tathātriç ca dvāv* [!] *anyau raudrakarmiṇau*; ought we not to read *Jaṭādharas* or something of the sort? PCR. has: *Tvashṭādhara* . . . *Raudra* and *Karmin*); they were *Brahmaloka-parāyaṇāḥ*. This progeny of the Asuras and gods is related in the Purāṇa.—§ 99: The six Vainateyāḥ.—§ 100: The six Kādraveyāḥ.—§ 101: The sixteen Devagandharvā Mauneyāḥ.—§ 102: The eight daughters of Prādhā and the ten Devagandharvāḥ Prādheyāḥ.—§ 103: Enumeration of thirteen Apsarases, daughters of Prādhā and the Devarshi (i.e. Kaçyapa).—§ 104: The four Gandharvasattamāḥ, apparently sons of Prādhā.—§ 105: *Amṛtaṃ, brāhmaṇā gāvo Gandharvāpsarasas tathā* | *apatyaṃ Kapilāyās tu Purāṇe parikīrtitam*.—§ 106: "Thus I have told you about the birth of all creatures: of Gandharvas, Apsarases, Snakes, Suparṇas, R., and M., etc."* (I, **65**).—§ 107: *Brahmaṇo mānasāḥ putrā viditāḥ shaṇ maharshayaḥ*.—§ 108: The Rudras, sons of Sthāṇu.—§ 109: Enumeration of the six maharshis (cf. § 86).—§ 110: The three sons of Aṅgiras.—§ 111: Atri's many sons (not enumerated) were perfect (*siddhāḥ*) maharshis.—§ 112: Pulastya's offspring were Rā., the monkeys, K., and Y.—§ 113: Pulaha's offspring were the Çalabhas, the lions, Kp., the tigers, Y. (PCR. reads apparently "*ṛkshā*," i.e. bears), and wolves.—§ 114: Kratu's sons were the companions of the Sun (*Pataṅgasahacāriṇaḥ*, i.e. the Vālikhilyas; so Nīl. and PCR.).—§ 115: The ṛshi Prajāpati Daksha sprang from the right toe of Brahmán, and Daksha's wife from the left toe of Brahmán; he had lost his sons (*nashṭaputraḥ*, v. § 138), but had fifty daughters, whom he made his *putrikāḥ*; he bestowed ten of them on Dharma, twenty-seven on Indu (i.e. the Moon), thirteen on Kaçyapa. Enumeration of the ten wives of Dharma (*dvārāṇy etāni Dharmasya vihitāni Svayambhuvā*). The twenty-seven wives of Soma are all junction-stars of the nakshatras (*nakshatra-yoginyaḥ*, VP. ii, p. 28; cf. BR. s.v., and Sūrya-Si°, ch. viii; not enumerated).—§ 116: The Vasus (q.v.) with their mothers and sons and grandsons, etc.; especially Kumāra (*b*), Prabhāsa (*c*), Viçvakarman (*d*).—§ 117: Dharma, assuming a human body, came out through the right breast of Brahmán. His three sons and their wives.—§ 118: From Marīci's son Kaçyapa sprang the gods and Asuras, "*lokānāṃ prabhavas tu saḥ*."—§ 119: Tvāshṭrī, the wife of Savitṛ, in the form of a mare, gave birth to the Açvins in the skies.—§ 120: The sons of Aditi are twelve (not enumerated); the youngest of them is Vishṇu, upon whom the worlds are dependent.—§ 120 *bis*: "*trayaçtriṃçata ity ete devās*—i.e. eight Vasus, eleven Rudras, twelve Ādityas, Prajāpati, and Vashaṭkāra" (Nīl.)—"*teshām ahaṃ tava* | *anvayaṃ saṃpravakshyāmi pakshaiç ca kulato gaṇān* || *Rudrāṇām aparaḥ pakshaḥ Sādhyānāṃ Marutāṃ tathā* | *Vasūnāṃ Bhārgavaṃ vidyād Viçvedevāṃs tathaiva ca* || *Vainateyas tu Garuḍo balavān Aruṇas tathā* | *Bṛhaspatiç ca bhagavān Ādityeshv eva gaṇyate* || *Açvinau Guhyakān viddhi sarvaushadhyas tathā paçūn* | *ete devagaṇā, rājan, kīrtitās te 'nupūrvaçaḥ* || *yān kīrtayitvā manujaḥ sarvapāpaiḥ pramucyate*."—§ 121: Bhṛgu came out ripping open the heart of Brahmán. Bhṛgu's son was Kavi, and Kavi's son was the planet Çukra (or do Kavi, Kaviputra, and Çukra signify one and the same person, which seems to be the opinion of PCR.?), who was appointed by Svayambhū to give and withhold rain, and to inflict and remit calamities, and who by the power of asceticism (*yogācāryo*) became the guru both of the Daityas and of the gods.—§ 122: As he (Çukra) was thus employed by Vidhi (i.e. Brahmán) in seeking welfare (*yogakshemāya*), Bhṛgu begat Cyavana, who, falling out of his mother's womb through anger, released her (cf. § 20). Cyavana's wife was Ārushī, daughter of Manu; their son Aurva came out ripping open the thigh of Ārushī.

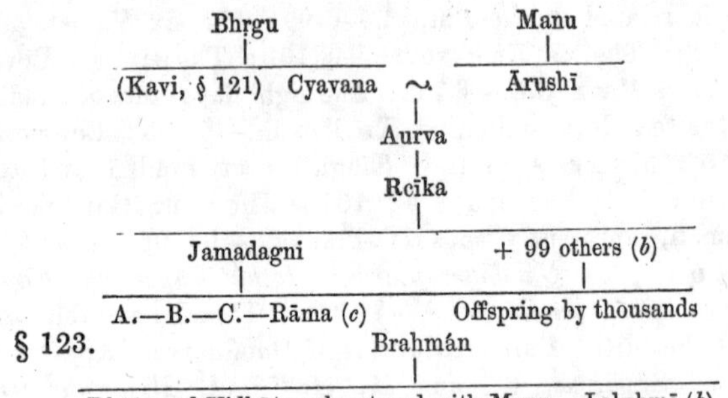

§ 123. Brahmán

Dhātṛ and Vidhātṛ, who stayed with Manu.—Lakshmī (b)

§ 124: Çukra's daughter Devī was the eldest wife of Varuṇa; her children are Bala and Surā ("giving joy unto the gods"). —§ 125: Adharma was born when creatures began to devour each other from want of food. His wife is Nirṛti, whence the Rākshasas, who are called Nairṛtāḥ, and (?) Bhaya, Mahābhaya, and Mṛtyu. Mṛtyu has neither wife nor children.—

§ 126: Tāmrā

Kākī	Çyenī	Bhāsī	Dhṛtarāshṭrī	Çukī
The owls (ulūkāḥ)!	The hawks.	The bhāsas and vultures.	Ducks and swans, and cakravākas.	The parrots.

§ 127: Krodha had nine daughters of wrathful disposition (*Krodhavaçāḥ*): I, Mṛgī (whose offspring are the deer); II, Mṛgamandā (° the bears and sṛmaras); III, Harī (° the monkeys, horses, and golāṅgūlas); IV, Bhadramanas (mother of the elephant Airāvata); V, Mātaṅgī (whose offspring are the elephants); VI, Çārdūlī (° lions, tigers, leopards, and all strong animals); VII, Çvetā (v. 2630: *diçām gajan tu Çvetākhyam . . . ajanayad*); VIII, Surabhi, who has four daughters: (A) Rohiṇī, from whom the cows sprang; (B) Gandharvī, the horses; (C) Vimalā; (D) Analā, whose offspring are the seven sorts of trees that have pulpy fruits—the date, palm, hintala, tali, the little date, the nut, and the cocoanut, according to PCR.—and a daughter, Çukī; IX, Surasā (mother of Kaṅka, i.e. a species of long-feathered birds).—§ 128: Aruṇa's wife, Çyenī, gave birth to Sampāti and Jaṭāyus.—§ 129: Surasā gave birth to the Nāgas, Kadrū to the Pannagas (these names are, however, in reality used indiscriminately), Vinatā to Garuḍa and Aruṇa* (I, **66**).—§ 130: Complying with the wish of Janamejaya, Vaiçampāyana mentions the gods, Dānavas, etc. (see ch. **65–66** = §§ 85–129), who were born among men, and in whom they became incarnated. (*b*) Bhīshma. (*c*) Dhṛtarāshṭra. (*d*) Vidura. Enumeration, among others (*a*) of the 101 sons (*β*) of Dhṛtarāshṭra (v. Dhārtarāshṭra) (they were versed in the Rājaçāstra), including (*e*) Yuyutsu, incarnations of Pulastya's sons (i.e. the Rākshasas), except Duryodhana, who was a portion of Kali, and (*f*) a daughter, Duḥçalā. Nakula and Sahadeva (portions of the Açvins) were the handsomest of all creatures. Soma set a condition for letting his son Varcas be incarnate in Abhimanyu. (*g*) Draupadī's five sons (*h*) (enumerated) were the Viçvas (? *viçvān devagaṇān*).—§ 131 (Kuntī; (*b*) Karṇa). — § 132: Incarnations of Nārāyaṇa (Vāsudeva, i.e. Kṛshṇa), Çesha (Baladeva), Sanatkumāra (Pradyumna), 16,000 portions of the Apsarases (the wives of Vāsudeva; born at the command of Vāsava, i.e. Indra), Çrī (Rukmiṇī, in the line of Bhīshmaka), Çacī (Draupadī), Siddhi and Dhṛti (Kuntī and Mādrī), Mati (Subalātmajā, i.e. Gāndhārī), (I, **67**).

Cf. *ādir amçāvatāraṇa(m)* (so B.; C. ādivamçāvatāraṇam) = [Ādiv]amçāvatāraṇaparvan: I, 312, 360.

Amçu = Çiva (1000 names[2]).

Amçumat[1], a king. § 232 (Svayamvarap.): I, **186**, 6991 (among those who came to the Svayamvara of Kṛshṇā).

Amçumat[2], the son's son of king Sagara. § 387 (Sagara): III, **107**, 8884 (*Asamañjas-sutam*).—§ 389 (Gaṅgāvatar.): III, **107** (brings back the sacrificial horse of Sagara), 8895, 8898, 9901, 9908, 9911, 9914, 9915.

Amçumat[3], a Bhoja king (cf. Amçumat[1]). § 604 (Karṇap.): VIII, **6**, 164 (Bhojarājaḥ, killed by Droṇa).

Amçumat[4], one of the Viçvedevas. § 749 (Ānuçāsanik.): XIII, **91**γ, 4357 (enumerated among 64 Viçvedevas).

Amçumat[5] = Sūrya.

Amçumat[6] = Soma.

Ameyātman[1] = Çiva.

Ameyātman[2] = Vishṇu (1000 names).

Amita = Çiva (1000 names[2]).

Amitāçana = Vishṇu (1000 names).

Amitāçanā, a Mātṛ. § 615*u* (Skanda): IX, **46**θ, 2625 (enumeration).

Amitadhvaja, an ancient king. § 673 (Bali-Vāsava-s.): XII, **227***a*, 8262.

Amitaujas, a king. § 130 (Amçāvat.): I, **67***a*, 2648 (incarnation of the Asura Ketumat).—§ 564 (Sainyodyogap.): V, **4**γ, 75 (among the kings to whom Drupada proposes to send messengers).—§ 572 (Rathātir.): V, **171**, 5903 (among the mahārathāḥ of the Pāṇḍavas, *Pāñcāla-sattamāḥ*).

Amitavikrama = Vishṇu (1000 names).

Amitrajit = Çiva (1000 names[2]).

Amogha[1], a Fire. § 490 (Āṅgirasa): III, **219**, 14154.

Amogha[2], a Yaksha. § 506 (Skandayuddha): III, **231**, 14548 (*mahā-Yaksho*, in the right wing of Skanda's army).

Amogha[3] = Skanda. § 508 (Kārttikeyastava): III, **232**, 14632 (among the names of Skanda).

Amogha[4] = Çiva: X, 256; XIII, 1227 (1000 names[2]).

Amogha[5] = Vishṇu (1000 names).

Amoghā, a Mātṛ. § 615*u* (Skanda): IX, **46**δ, 2639.

Amoghārtha = Çiva (1000 names[2]).

***amṛta**[1], ambrosia (cf. the articles Utaṅka, Amṛtam., Garuḍa, Vālakhilya, Kapilā, etc.). § 615*u* (Skanda): IX, **46**, 2668 (*kamaṇḍalum amritodbhavam*, which Gaṅgā gave to Skanda).—§ 618 (Jalapradānikap.): XI, **2**, 46 (*amṛta-samair vākyair*); **7**, 163 (*vāg*°).

Amṛta[2] = Çiva (1000 names[2]).

Amṛta[3] = Vishṇu (1000 names).

Amṛta[4]: XII, 12864 (Mahāpurushastava).

Amṛtā, a Māgadha princess, wife of Anaçvan. § 156 (Pūruvamç.): I, **95**, ††3794 (*Māgadhīm*).

Amṛtāça = Vishṇu (1000 names).

Amṛtāksha: XII, 12864 (Mahāpurushastava).

[Amṛtamanthana] ("churning of the Amṛta or Ambrosia"). Cf. Āstīkaparvan. § 28: Once the gods having assembled on the summit of Mount Meru, Nārāyaṇa told Brahmán to churn the Ocean with the gods and the Asuras, in order to obtain Amṛta (I, **17**). Vishṇu and Brahmán prevailed upon Ananta (i.e. Çesha), the prince of Snakes, to bring up the mountain Mandara. The gods having obtained from the Ocean the permission to churn it, Indra placed Mandara on the back of the Tortoise-king; Mandara was made the churning staff and Vāsuki the cord, the Asuras holding him by the hood and the gods by the tail, while Ananta, who sided with Nārāyaṇa, at intervals raised the snake's hood and suddenly lowered it. Black vapours with flames issued from Vāsuki's mouth, etc. After some churning the gums of various trees and herbs mingled with the waters of the Ocean, and the milky water produced clarified butter, but even then the Amṛta did not appear. The gods were tired and repaired to Brahmán, who prevailed upon Nārāyaṇa to grant the gods new strength to churn afresh. After a while the Moon, Çrī, Surādevī (wine), Ucchaiḥçravas, and Kaustubha came forth on the side of the gods; then Dhanvantari with a white vessel of Amṛta in his hand; then Airāvaṇa, and at last the poison Kālakūṭa, that Çiva, solicited by Brahmán, swallowed for the safety of the creation; from that time Çiva is called Nīlakaṇṭha ('Blue-neck'). The Asuras preparing to rob the gods of Çrī and the Amṛta, Nārāyaṇa, assisted by his *māyā* ('illusion'), assumed a ravishing female form; the Dānavas and Daityas were infatuated, and placed the Amṛta in her hands (I, **18**). While the Daityas and Dānavas pursued the gods, Vishṇu with Nara let the gods drink of the Amṛta; the Dānava Rāhu also drank of it in the disguise of a god, but was discovered by Sūrya (i.e. the Sun) and Soma (i.e. the Moon); then Nārāyaṇa instantly seized his discus and cut off his head, which to this day swallows Sūrya and Soma. In a dreadful battle on the shores of the salt-water sea the gods, headed by Nārāyaṇa with his discus Sudarçana and Nara with his celestial bow, discomfited the Asuras, who entered the bowels of the earth or plunged into the sea of salt waters. The gods replaced Mandara on its own base, and, headed by Indra, they entrusted the keeping of the vessel of Amṛta to Kirīṭin (i.e. Nara), (I, **19**).

Amṛtāṃçūdbhava = Vishṇu (1000 names).

Amṛtapa[1], a Dānava. § 93 (Aṃçāvat.): I, **65**, 2537 (*Danuputra*).

Amṛtapa[2] = Vishṇu (1000 names).

Amṛtapā = Çiva (1000 names[1]).

Amṛtavapus = Vishṇu (1000 names).

Amṛteçaya: XII, 12864 (Mahāpurushastava).

Amṛtyu = Vishṇu (1000 names).

Amukha = Çiva (1000 names[1]).

Amukhya = Çiva (1000 names[2]).

Amūrtarayas, an ancient king. § 381 (Gaya): III, **95**, 8528 (°*aḥ putro Gayo*).

Amūrtarayasa, an ancient king. § 656 (Khaḍgotp.): XII, **166**δ, 6194 (among those to whom the sword successively passed).

Amūrtarayasa = Gaya.

Amūrti = Vishṇu (1000 names).

Amūrtimat = Vishṇu (1000 names).

Anabhijñeya = Kṛshṇa.

Anaçvan. § 156 (Pūruvaṃç.): I, **95**, 3793, 3794 (cf. Amṛtā).

Anādhṛshṭi[1]. § 150 (Pūruvaṃç.): I, **94**, 3702 (seems to be the same as Ṛceyu).

Anādhṛshṭi[2]. § 253 (Haraṇāharaṇap.): I, **221**, 7990 (a companion of Kṛshṇa).—§ 273 (Rājasūyārambhap.): II, **14**, 623 (a mahāratha among the Vṛshṇis). — § 553 (Vaivāhikap.[2]): IV, **71**, 2357 (a follower of Kṛshṇa).— § 572 (Sainyaniryāṇap.): V, **151**ζ, 5164 (surrounds Kṛshṇa and Arjuna).

Anādhṛshṭi[3], son of Dhṛtarāshṭra (apparently = Anādhṛshya). § 585 (Bhīshmavadhap.): VI, **96**, 4349 (among the sons of Dhṛtarāshṭra who were killed by Bhīmasena).

Anādhṛshṭisuta. § 150 (Pūruvaṃç.): I, **94**, 3703 (*A° tv āsīd rājasūyāçvamedhakṛt Matināra iti khyāto rājā paramadhārmikaḥ*).

Anādhṛshya, a son of Dhṛtarāshṭra (cf. Anādhṛshṭi). § 130 (Aṃçāvat.): I, **67**, 2739.—§ 182 (Dhṛtarāshṭraputranāmak.): I, **117**, 4552.

Anādi[1] = Kṛshṇa.

Anādi[2] = Vishṇu (1000 names).

Anādi[3]: XII, 12864 (Mahāpurushastave).

Anādi-madhya-nidhana = Vishṇu.

Anādi-madhya-paryanta = Kṛshṇa.

Anādi-nidhana = Brahmán, Kṛshṇa, Purushottama, Vishṇu.

Anādya = Kṛshṇa.

Anagha[1]. § 6 (Anukram.): I, **1**, 228 (belongs to the past).

Anagha[2], a Deva-Gandharva. § 191 (Arjuna): I, **123**, 4811 (among the Deva-Gandharvas who sang at the birth of Arjuna).

Anagha[3] = Çiva (1000 names[2], etc.).

Anagha[4] = Vishṇu (1000 names).

Anagha[5] = Skanda.

Anagha[6], a Suparṇa, son of Garuḍa. § 564 (Mātalīyop.): V, **101**, 3597.

Ānakadundubhi = Vasudeva.

Anala[1] ("Fire"), one of the eight Vasus (§ 116), son of Prajāpati (?) or Dharma (?) and Çāṇḍilī, and father of Skanda. See Agni, Vishṇu, Kṛshṇa, Çiva.

Anala[2], a Suparṇa, son of Garuḍa. § 564 (Mātalīyop.): V, **101**, 3594.

Analā. § 127 (Aṃçāvat.): I, **66**, 2632, 2633 (one of the Krodhavaçāḥ).

Analaputra = Skanda.

Analasūnu = Skanda.

Analātmaja = Skanda.

Anāmaya = Vishṇu (1000 names), Skanda.

Ānanda[1], one of the warriors of Skanda. § 615*u* (Skanda): IX, **45**η, 2567.

Ānanda[2] = Vishṇu (1000 names).

Anaṅga[1], son of Kardama. § 641 (Rājadh.): XII, **59**, 2212, 2213 (a protector of creatures; fully conversant with the science of chastisement).

Anaṅga[2] = Kāma, Çiva.

Anaṅgāṅgahara = Çiva.

Ananta[1] ("infinite"), the prince of Snakes. § 28 (Amṛtamanthana): I, **17**, 1107 (? °*kalpam*); **18**, 1118, 1119. —§ 48 (Çesha). I, **36**, 1587 (the same as Çesha), 1588 (Pitāmaha gave him Suparṇa as a friend).—§ 100 (Aṃçāvat.): I, **65**, 2549 (a Kādraveya).—§ 576 (Bhagavadgītāp.): VI, **34**, 1233 (°*asmi Nāgānām*, says Kṛshṇa about himself).—§ 581 (Bhīshmavadhap.): VI, **67**, 3023 (*Çeshaṃ devam*).—§ 585 (do.): VI, **90**, 4044 (*iva vegavān*).—§ 730 (Ānuçāsanik., Meghavāhanop.): XIII, **14**, 915 (*bhujageshu*, i.e. Çiva).— § 770 (Ānuçāsanik.): XIII, **151***a*, 7088 (*mahoragāya*), 7119 ("Dharma, Kāma, Kāla, Vasu, Vāsuki, Ananta, and Kapila are the seven upholders of Earth, *dharaṇīdharāḥ*").—§ 795 (Svargārohaṇap.): XVIII, **5**μ, 169 (incarnate as Balarāma, gone to Rasātala). Cf. Çesha.

Ananta[2], a warrior of Skanda's. § 615*u* (Skanda): IX, **45**η, 2559.

Ananta[3 ff.] = Kṛshṇa, Vishṇu, Çiva, Mahāpurusha, Nārāyaṇa, the Sun (Sūrya).

Anantā, a Mādhava princess, wife of Pūru's son Janamejaya. § 156 (Pūruvaṃç.): I, **95**, †† 3765 (*Mādhavīm*).

Anantabhoga ("with infinite serpent body"). § 552 (Goharaṇap.): IV, **55**, 1719 (*anantabhogo bhujagaḥ krīḍann iva mahārṇave*; presumably allusion to Ananta). See also Mahāpurusha.

Anantaçrī = Vishṇu (1000 names).
Anantagati = Mahāpurusha.
Anantākhya = Mahāpurusha.
Anantaparimeya = Kṛshṇa.
Anantarūpa = Çiva (1000 names [2]), Vishṇu (1000 names), Skanda.
Anantātman = Vishṇu (1000 names).
Anantavijaya, the conch of Yudhishṭhira. § 576 (Bhagavadgītāp.): VI, **25**κ, 845.—§ 578 (Bhīshmavadhap.): VI, **51**aa, 2166.
Anaraṇya. § 6 (Anukram.): I, **1**, 230 (belongs to the past).—§ 760 (Ānuçāsanik.): XIII, **115**γ, 5661 (among the ancient kings who have abstained from meat in the month of Kārttika).—§ 775 (do.): XIII, **166**η, 7684 (among the kings whose names should be recited at sunset and sunrise).
Anartha = Vishṇu (1000 names).
Ānartta [1], pl. (°*āḥ*), a people. § 279 (Arjuna): II, **26**, 997 (conquered by Arjuna).—§ 318 (Arjunābhigam.): III, **13**, 610 (Kṛshṇa said that if he had not been absent from the *A.* country he should have prevented the gambling).—§ 319 (Saubhavadhop.): III, **14**, 622, 631.—§ 320 (Saubhavadhop.): III, **15**, 649 (chase all dancers); **20**, 777 (°*nagaram* = Dvārakā). — § 553 (Vaivāhikap.): IV, **72**, 2350 (many Dāçārhas from the *A.* country came with Kṛshṇa to Upaplavya). — § 562 (Bhagavadyānap.): V, **83**, 2964 (entertained Kuntī). — § 574 (Jambūkh.): VI, **9**, 359 (°*Nairṛtāḥ*).—§ 604 (Karṇap.): VIII, **5**, 96; **7**, †197 (*Ā°vāsī Hṛdikātmajo 'sau . . . Sāttvatānāṃ varishṭhaḥ*).—§ 783 (Anugītāp.): XIV, **52**, 1525, 1535 (°*purīm* = Dvārakā).
Ānartta [2], sg., chief (or country) of the Ānarttas. § 452 (Mārkaṇḍeya-samāsyā-p.): III, **183**, †12582 (*Ānarttaṃ ovābhimukhāḥ çivena gatvā dhanurveda-ratipradhānāḥ | tavātmajā Vṛshṇi-puraṃ praviçya tadaiva tebhyaḥ spṛhayanti, Kṛshṇe*, says Kṛshṇa to Draupadī).—§ 611 (Çalyap.): IX, **17**, 947 (= Sātyaki).
Anaupama = Çiva (1000 names [1]).
Anaushadha = Çiva (1000 names [2]).
Anavadyā, an Apsaras. § 102 (Aṃçāvat.): I, **65**, 2553 (daughter of Prādhā).—§ 191 (Arjuna): I, **123**a, 4817 (among the Apsarases who danced and sang at the birth of Arjuna).
Anāyush (B. *Da*°), erratum for Danāyus.
Aṇḍa = Çiva (1000 names [1]), the Sun.
Aṇḍadhara = Çiva (1000 names [1]).
Aṇḍaja(ṃ janma). § 717b (Nārāyaṇīya): XII, **348**ηη, 13492 (Brahmán's sixth birth); **349** VI), ††13590 (*aṇḍaje janmani*).
Aṇḍajāḥ = Çiva (1000 names [1]).
Aṇḍanāçana = Çiva (1000 names [1]).
Andha, pl. (°*āḥ*), a people, presumably for Andhaka. § 555 (Sainyodyogap.): V, **19**, 586 (*Kṛtavarmā ca Hārddikyo Bhojāndha-Kukuraiḥ saha*).
Andhaka [1], pl. (°*āḥ*), a people. § 82 (Kṛshṇa): I, **63**, 2432 (°*Vṛshṇishu*).—§ 203 (Droṇa): I, **132**, 5220 (became the pupils of Droṇa).—§ 233 (Svayaṃvarap.): I, **187**, †7012 (*Vṛshṇy-Andhakāçca . . . yathāpradhānaṃ*, came to the svayaṃvara of Kṛshṇā).—§ 251 (Arjunavanavāsap.): I, **218**, 7902, 7903 (*Bhoja-Vṛshṇy-Andhakātmajaiḥ*; welcome Arjuna).—§ 252 (Subhadrāharaṇap.): I, **219**, 7906, 7907 (*Bhoja-Vṛshṇy-A*°); **220**, 7942, 7943 (*Vṛshṇy-A*°), 7962.—§ 253 (Haraṇāharaṇap.): I, **221**, 7988, 7993 (*Vṛshṇi-Bhojā*°), 7998 (*Vṛshṇy-A*°), 8002 (id.), 8018 (id.), 8019 (*Kuru-Vṛshṇy-Andhakottamāḥ*), 8022 (*Vṛshṇy-A*°).—§ 275 (Rājasūyārambhap.): II, **19**, 767 (the Kukuras, Andhakas, and Vṛshṇis chose not to fight with Jarāsandha).—§ 289 (Arghāharaṇap.): II, **36**, 1322 (*A°-Vṛshṇīnaṃ vaṃçe*).—§ 295 (Dyūtap.): II, **52**, 1907 (*A°-Vṛshṇayaḥ*).—§ 298 (id.): **62**, 2101 (*Andhakā Yādavā Bhojāḥ sametāḥ Kaṃsam atyajan*).—§ 317 (Arjunābhigam.): III, **12**, 461 (visit the Pāṇḍavas in the great forest).—§ 320 (Saubhavadhop.): III, **15**, 654 (*Vṛshṇy-A°-pure*, i.e. Dvārakā); **48**, 744 (*A°-Vṛshṇayaḥ*). — § 402 (Tīrthayātrāp.): III, **120**, 10278 (*sa-Vṛshṇi-Bhojā*°).—§ 452 (Mārkaṇḍeya-samāsyā-p.): III, **183**, 12588 (*Kukurā*°). — § 511 (Draupadī-Satyabhāmā-saṃvādap.): III, **235**, 14736 (*A°-Vṛshṇayaḥ*). — § 522 (Draupadīharaṇap.): III, **268**, 15654 (*sāndhaka-Vṛshṇi-vīro Janārdanaḥ*).—§ 552 (Vaivāhikap.): IV, **72**, 2360 (*Vṛshṇy-A*°).—§ 554 (Sainyodyogap.): V, **7**, 131 (*Vṛshṇy-A*°). — § 556 (Sañjayayānap.): V, **27**, 768 (*Vṛshṇya°-rājye*); **28**ι, †804, †805 (*Vṛshṇy-A°āḥ . . . Kṛshṇa-praṇītāḥ*).—§ 561 (Yānasandhip.): V, **48**, 1885 (*Vṛshṇy-A*°); **51**, 2056 (*A°-Vṛshṇayaḥ*); **57**, 2233 (*Vṛshṇīnāṃ mukhyaṃ Kṛshṇaṃ*); **65**, 2488 (*A°-Vṛshṇishu*). — § 562 (Bhagavadyānap.): V, **86**, 3043 (*Vṛshṇy-A*°); **128**, 4298 (*A°-Vṛshṇayaḥ*); **131**, 4420 (id.), 4426.—§ 569 (id.): V, **140**, 4738 (*A°-Vṛshṇayaḥ*), 4749 (do.).—[§ 571 (Ulūkadūt.): V, **160**, 5510 (read with B. *Draviḍāndhra Kāñcyaiḥ*; so also v. 5555).] — § 580 (Bhīshmavadhap.): VI, **59**, 2606 (*A°-Vṛshṇi-nātha*, i.e. Kṛshṇa).—§ 599 (Jayadrathavadhap.): VII, **104**, 3891 (*Vṛshṇy-A°-Kurūttamau*, i.e. Kṛshṇa and Arjuna); **142**, 5931 (*Vṛshṇy-A°-vyāghraṃ*, i.e. Sātyaki), 5942 (do.); **143**, 5965 (*Vṛshṇy-A*°). — § 603 (Nārāyaṇāstram.): VII, **198**, 9138 (*A°-Vṛshṇibhiḥ*), 9179 (do.), 9180 (do.); **199**, 9220 (*Vṛshṇy-A°-vṛtaḥ*, i.e. Sātyaki).—§ 611 (Çalyap.): IX, **17**, 911; **21**, 1104 (*Vṛshṇy-A°-mahārathau*, i.e. Sātyaki and Hārdikya).—§ 617 (Aishīkap.): X, **11**, 639 (*Vṛshṇy-A*°).—§ 621 (Rājadh.): XII, **7**, 159 (do., °*pure*).—§ 641 (Rājadh.): XII, **81**, 3031 (*A°-Vṛshṇayaḥ*), 3052 (do.).—§ 785 (Anugītāp.): XIV, **59**, 1768 (*Bhoja-Vṛshṇya*°); **66**, 1959 (*Vṛshṇy-A°-kulaṃ*); **71**, 2066 (°*A°vyāghrair*); **83**, 2480 (*Vṛshṇy-A°-patiḥ*, i.e. Ugrasena?); **86**, 2565 (id. = Kṛshṇa). — § 793 (Mausalap.): XVI, **1**, 12, 14 (*Vṛshṇy-A*°), 19 (*Vṛshṇy-A°-vināçāya*), 26 (id.), 29 (*Vṛshṇy-A°kuleshu*); **2**, 33, 36 (*Vṛshṇy-A*°), 40 (id.), 49 (id.); **3**, 58 (id.), 63 (id.), 64 (*A°-Vṛshṇayaḥ*), 69 (*Vṛshṇy-A*°), 86 (*Bhojā*°), 90, 93, 98 (*Kukurā*°); **4**, 123 (*A°-Vṛshṇi-*); **5**, 134 (*sa-Bhojā°-Kaukurān Vārshṇeyān*), 140 (*Vṛshṇy-A*°); **7**, 186 (id.), 203 (id.), 210 (*A°-Vṛshṇīnām*), 213 (id.), 215 (*Bhoja-Vṛshṇy-A*°), 239 (*Vṛshṇy-A*°); **8**, 263 (*Bhoja-Vṛshṇy-A*°), 279 (*Vṛshṇy-A*°), 292 (id.).—§ 794 (Mahāprasthānikap.): XVII, **1**, 1 (id.).—§ 795 (Svargārohaṇap.): XVIII, **4**, 142 (*Sādhyānām atha devānāṃ Viçveshāṃ Marutām api | gaṇeshu paçya rājendra Vṛshṇy-A°-mahārathān*).
Andhaka [2], an Asura killed by Rudra. § 593 (Abhimanyuvadhap.): VII, **49**, 1937 (*pureva Tryambakāndhakau*).—§ 595 (Rāma Dāçarathi): VII, **59**, 2229 (*pureva Tryambako 'ndhakaṃ*).—§ 600 (Ghaṭotkacavadhap.): VII, **155**, †6726 (*yathā 'ndhake pratinihate Haraṃ surāḥ*); **156**, 6818 (*Maheçvara ivāndhakaṃ*). — § 603 (Nārāyaṇāstram.): VII, **201**, 9463 (*Andhaka-nipātine*, i.e. Rudra).—§ 604 (Karṇap.): VIII, **5**, 146 (*yathā Rudreṇa cāndhakaḥ*).—§ 605 (do.): VIII, **20**, 788 (*Tryambakenāndhako yathā*).
Andhaka-Bhoja. § 273 (Rājasūyārambhap.): II, **14**, 624 (*putrau cāndhakabhojasya vṛddhau*, among the defenders of the fortifications upon the Gomanta mountains, when Jarāsandha made his attack).
Andhaka-ghātin = **Çiva** (1000 names [1]).

Andhakāraka, a mountain in Krauñcadvīpa. § 575 (Bhūmip.): VI, **12**, 459, 463 (°*deçāt*).

Ăndhra, pl. (°*āḥ*), a people. § 284 (Sahadeva): II, **31a**, 1175 (in the South). — § 458 (Kali-yuga): III, **188**, 12839.—§ 569 (Bhagavadyānap.): V, **140β**, 4751.—§ 571 (Ulūkadūt.): V, **160**, 5510 (*Draviḍā° kāñcyaiḥ*; C. °*Ăndhak°*); **161**, 5555 (do.).—§ 574 (Jambūkh.): VI, **9μ**, 357 (a country in Bhārata-varsha). — § 589 (Droṇap.): VII, **4β**, 122 (*Kaliṅgā°*, have been vanquished by Karṇa). — § 641 (Rājadh.): XII, **65θ**, 2439 (°*Madrakāḥ*; among the people mentioned by Indra in setting forth the kshattriya duties).—§ 744 (Ānuçāsanik.): XIII, **48γ**, 2587 (*A° vahirgrāmapratiçrayāḥ*, a mixed caste sprung from the Vaidehika).—§ 785 (Anugītāp.): XIV, **83**, 2476 (towards the southern ocean). Cf. Andhrakāḥ.

Andhraka. § 264 (Sabhākriyāp.): II, **4**, 119 (among the kings present when Yudhishṭhira entered his palace).

Andhrakāḥ, a people. § 287 (Rājasūyikap.): II, **34**, 1270 (in the enumeration of kings who came to Yudhishṭhira's rājasūya). — § 342 (Indralokābh.): III, **51**, 1988 (*Cola-Draviḍā°*).—§ 605 (Karṇap.): VIII, **20δδ**, 779 (*Pulinda-Khasa-Vāhlīka-Nishādā° Kuntalān*, among those slaughtered by Pāṇḍya, in the army of Karṇa).—§ 608 (do.): VIII, **73**, 3653 (mentioned as fighting for the sake of Duryodhana).—§ 664 (Mokshadh.): XII, **207η**, 7559 (mentioned among the sinful creatures of the earth, born in the southern region). Cf. Andhra.

Anekamūrti = Vishṇu (1000 names).

Anenas, son of Āyus and Svarbhānavī. § 141 (Purūravas): I, **75**, 3150.

Aṅga[1], pl. (°*āḥ*), a people (country) descended from Aṅga. § 208 (Astradarçana): I, **136**, 5414 (°*vishaya*; Duryodhana installed Karṇa king of Aṅga), 5415 (°*rājyasya*); **137**, 5422 (°*rājyābhishekārdram*, i.e. Karṇa), 5425 (°*rājyañ ca*), 5435 (°*rājyam*), 5441 (°*eçvaram*, i.e. Karṇa). — § 249 (Arjunavanavāsap.): I, **215**, 7820 (°*Vaṅga-Kaliṅgeshu*). — § 290 (Çiçupālavadhap.): II, **44**, 1527 (*Vaṅgā°-vishayādhyaksham*, i.e. Karṇa).—§ 295 (Dyūtap.): II, **52**, 1872 (among those who brought tribute to Yudhishṭhira).—§ 391 (Ṛshyaçṛṅga): III, **110**, 10008 (°*ānām īçvaro Lomapādaḥ*), 10018 (°*patir* = Lomapāda); **113**, 10077 (°*ādhipateḥ*, i.e. Lomapāda), 10084 (°*rajam* = do.), 10087 (°*patim* = do.). — § 512 (Ghoshayātrāp.): III, **247**, 15052 (°*rājānam* = Karṇa). — § 515 (Karṇadigvijaya): III, **254**, 15243. — § 547 (Kuṇḍalāharaṇap.): III, **309**, 17167.—§ 571 (Jambūkh.): VI, **9μ**, 353 (country in Bharatavarsha).—§ 576 (Bhagavadgītāp.): VI, **17**, 664 (°*patinā* = Karṇa's son Vṛshaketu, PCR.).—§ 589 (Droṇābhishek.): VII, **11γ**, 396 (had been vanquished by Kṛshṇa). — § 595 (Paraçu-Rāma): VII, **70β**, 2436 (*Aṅga-Vaṅga-Kaliṅgāṃç ca*, slain by Paraçu-Rāma). § 599 (Jayadrathavadhap.): VII, **93**, 3368 (they and the Kaliṅga king, on elephants, fought against Arjuna, who caused a great carnage among them, on the fourteenth day of the battle). — § 604 (Karṇap.): VIII, **8**, 236 (caused by Karṇa to pay tribute to Duryodhana, cf. § 515). — § 605 (Karṇap.): VIII, **17**, 671 (*Kaliṅga-Vaṅgāṅga-Nishādavīrāḥ*, attacked Arjuna with a division of elephants, which is broken, on the sixteenth day of the battle); **22ρρ**, 863 (fought against Dhṛshṭadyumna, etc., on the sixteenth day of the battle), 881.—§ 608 (Karṇap.): VIII, **70**, 3500 (*Kaliṅga-Vaṅgā°-Nishāda-Māgadhāḥ*, were being slain by Bhīma on the seventeenth day of the battle).—§ 621 (Rājadh.): XII, **5**, 134 (Karṇa became king not only of the *A.*, but forthwith also over Campā, having vanquished Jarāsandha).—§ 641 (Rājadh.): XII, **122**, 4469 (*Aṅgeshu rājā Vasuhomo*, discourse between him and king Māndhātṛ at Muñjapṛshṭha). — § 743 (Vipulop.): XIII, **42**, 2350, 2351 (°*eçvarasya Citrarathasya*, married to the sister of Ruci), 2352 (°*pater* = do.), 2353 (Aṅgendra-varāṅganā = Prabhāvatī). — § 772c (Kaçyapa): XIII, **154**, 7214 (*tyaktvā mahītvaṃ bhūmis tu spardhayā 'nganṛpasya ha* | *nāçaṃ jagāma, tāṃ vipro vyashṭambhayata Kaçyapaḥ*).—§ 785 (Anugītāp.): XIV, **83**, 2469.

Aṅga[2]. § 6 (Anukram.): I, **1**, 226 (belongs to the past).

Aṅga[3] (= Aṅga[2]?). § 170 (Dīrghatamas): I, **104**, 4219:

Dīrghatamas ~ Sudeshṇā

Aṅga, Vaṅga, Kaliṅga, Puṇḍra, Suhma.

I, 4220 (*Aṅgasyāṅgo'bhavaddeço*, etc.).—§ 267 (Yamasabhā-v.): II, **8**, 326 (in the palace of Yama).

Aṅga[4] (= Aṅga[2]?). § 595 (Paurava): VII, **57**, 2206 (= Paurava); cf. XII, 924, etc. (= Bṛhadratha). — § 632b (Shoḍaçarājika): XII, **29**, 924, 928, 981.

Aṅga[5]. § 768b (Kṛshṇa Vāsudeva): XIII, **147**, 6828 (*Manoḥ putraḥ*, incarnation of Kṛshṇa).

Aṅga[6]. § 772c (Kaçyapa): XIII, **155**, 7232 (wished to give away the whole earth to the brahmans; cf. Aṅgāḥ, XIII, 7214).

Aṅga[7], the Aṅga king at the time of Yudhishṭhira. § 264 (Sabhākriyāp.): II, **4β**, 119, 120 (among the kings present when Yudhishṭhira entered his palace). — § 342 (Indralokābhig.): III, **51**, 1988 (*sa-Baṅgāṅgān mahīpālān*). — § 592 (Saṃçaptakavadhap.): VII, **26**, 1142 (called Mleccha king; was slain by Bhīmasena on the twelfth day of the battle).—§ 605 (Karṇap.): VIII, **22**, 873 (called Mleccha king, and was slain by Nakula on the sixteenth day of the battle), 877, 878. Cf. Aṅgaputra.

Aṅga[8], the Aṅga country or adj. § 170 (Dīrghatamas): I, **104**, 4220 (*Aṅgasyāṅgo 'bhavad deço*).

Aṅga[9], one or the other of the Aṅga kings of the past. § 277 (Jarāsandhavadhap.): II, **21**, 804 (°*Vaṅgādayaḥ rājānaḥ*).

***Aṅga**[10], neut. pl. (°*āni*) = Vedāṅgāni: I, 62 (*sāṅgopanishadāṃ Vedānāṃ*), 645 (do.), 3140 (*sāṅgaṃ Vedaṃ*), 4001 (do.), 4003 (*sāṅgopāṅgaṃ çāstraṃ*), 4150 (*Vedāṅgāni*), 4182 (*shaḍaṅgaṃ Vedaṃ*), 6756 (*shaḍbhir*), 6823 (*shaḍaṅgaḥ vedaḥ*); II, 137 (*shaḍaṅgavid Nāradaḥ*); III, 2417 (*sāṅgopāṅgāḥ Vedāḥ*); VII, 9126 (*sāṅgā vedāḥ*), 9601 (*Vedāṅgāḥ sopanishadaḥ*); XII, 1351 (*Vedān aṅgopavṛṃhitān*), 1569 (*caturo Vedān sā°*), 7201 (*shaḍ°-vid*), 7202 (*shaḍ°*), 7266, 8484 (*Vedān sā° Opanishadāḥ*), 8613 (°*taḥ*), 8730 (*srjata surulo 'ṅgāni tathā Vedā yuge yuge*), 10407 (*Vedāḥ shaḍ°*), 10940 (*shaḍ*), 11772 (*sāṅgopāṅgān Vedān*), 12346 (*sā° vedeshu*), 12674 (*sā° Opāṅgeshu Vedeshu*), 12750 (*sāṅgopanishadaṃ*), 13099 (*sā° Vedān*), 13183 (*Vedān sāṅgopāṅgān*), 13364 (*Vedān sā°*), 13649 (do.); XIII, 1542 (*shaḍbhir*), 1566 (*sā° caturo Vedāḥ*), 4296 (*shaḍ° vid*); XIV, 2628 (*ashaḍ° vid*).

Aṅgada[1], a monkey chief, son of Vālin. § 534 (Hanūmatpratyāgam.): III, **282**, 16224 (*Vāli-putro*). — § 535 (Setubandhana): III, **283β**, 16287 (protected the army of Rāma), 16322 (was sent by Rāma as his envoy to Rāvaṇa). — § 536 (Laṅkāpraveça): III, **284**, 16329, 16341 (his deportment in Laṅkā).—§ 540 (Indrajidyuddha): III, **288**, 16451, 16453 (fought Indrajit).—§ 541 (Indrajidvadha): III, **289a**, 16468, 16477 (was among those who surrounded Rāma and Lakshmaṇa against Indrajit).—§ 542 (Rāvaṇavadha): III, **290a**, 16500 (attacked Rāvaṇa). — § 543 (Rāmābhisheka): III, **291**, 16589 (was installed as yuvarāja in Kishkindhyā).

Aṅgada[2], son of Dhṛtarāshṭra(?). § 592 (Saṃçaptakavadhap.): VII, **25**, 1101 (fought Uttamaujas on the twelfth day of the battle). Cf. Cārucitrāṅgada.

Aṅgaka, pl. (*°āḥ*), a people presumably = Aṅga. § 607 (Karṇap.): VIII, **45**ν, 2101 (praised by Karṇa before Çalya, sixteenth day).

Aṅgalubdha = Çiva (1000 names[2]).

Aṅgaputra = Aṅga[7]. § 605 (Karṇap.): VIII, **22**, 880 (slain by Nakula).

Aṅgāra. § 632 (Shoḍaçarājop.): XII, **29**, 981 (*nṛpatiṃ*), 982 (was vanquished by Māndhātṛ).

Aṅgāraka[1], the planet Mars. § 208 (Astradarçana): I, **134**, 5331 (*sāṅgāraka ivāṃçumān*).—§ 270 (Brahmasabhā-v.): II, **11***a*, 446 (in the palace of Brahmán).—§ 569 (Bhagavadyānap.): V, **143**θ, 4841 (omens).—§ 574 (Jambūkh.): VI, **3***a*, 81 (omens).—§ 578 (Bhīshmavadhap.): VI, **45**[10], 1710 (*A°-Budhāv iva*); **45**[15], 1726 (*Çukrāṅgārakayor iva*).—§ 599 (Jayadrathavadhap.): VII, **109**, 4130 (*bhūmau Aṅgārako yathā*; PCR. translates "charcoal").—§ 605 (Karṇap.): VIII, **15**, 581 (*A°-Budhāv iva*); **19**, 711 (*Aṅgāraka iva grahaḥ*). Cf. Bhauma.

Aṅgāraka[2] = the Sun. § 310 (Āraṇyakap.): III, **3***a*, 147 (in Dhaumya's enumeration).

Aṅgāraka[3], a Sauvīra prince. § 522 (Draupadīharaṇap.): III, **265***a*, 15597 (among Jayadratha's standard-bearers).

Aṅgāraparṇa, a Gandharva king (also name of his forest) = Citraratha. § 11 (Parvas.): I, **2**, 386 (all. to § 221).—§ 221 (Caitrarathap.): I, **170**, 6448 (*Gandharvaṃ*), 6449, 6460 (vanquished by Arjuna), 6473 (*°tāṃ*).

Āṅgarishṭha, an ancient king. § 641 (Rājadh.): XII, **123**, 4534 (discourse between him and the ṛshi Kamanda), 4535.

Aṅgāvaha. § 287 (Rājasūyikap.): II, **34**, 1275 (among the kings, especially Vṛshṇis, who came to Yudhishṭhira's rājasūya).

[Aṅgavidhi] ("the arrangement of the moon's limbs"), i.e. XIII, **110**.

Āṅgeyī = Sudevā, I, 3777.

Aṅghrika, son of Viçvāmitra. § 621 (Rājadh.): XII, **9**, 253 (*Aṅghriko Naikadṛk caiva*).

Āṅgī, an ancient queen, wife of Ariha and mother of Mahābhauma. § 156 (Pūruvaṃç.): I, **95**, 3772.

Aṅgirahsuta = Bṛhaspati. § 693*b* (Vṛtravadha): XII, **280**, 10126.

Āṅgiraja (B. has *°so*): XIII, 2126.

Aṅgiras[1], one of the maharshis, Brahmán's spiritual sons (*mānasāḥ putrāḥ*). § 86 (Sambhavap.): I, **65**, 2518 (six maharshis).—§ 109 (Aṃçāvat.): I, **66**, 2568 (do.).—§ 110 (do.): **66**, 2569 (father of Bṛhaspati, Utathya, and Saṃvartta).—§ 145 (Kaca): I, **76**, 3201 (*ṛsher A°aḥ pautraṃ Kacam*), 3231; **77**, 3257 (*A°aḥ pautra*, i.e. Kaca), 3258 (*ṛshiṛ*).—§ 165 (Satyavatīlābhop.): I, **100**, 4003 (*A°aḥ putraḥ*, i.e. Bṛhaspati).—§ 191 (Arjuna): I, **123***a*, 4808 (among those who came to the birth of Arjuna).—§ 201 (Droṇa): I, **130**, 5122 (*A°aḥ kule*, sc. Droṇa).—§ 270 (Brahmasabhāv.): II, **11***a*, 436 (in the palace of Brahmán).—§ 299 (Dyūtap.): II, **68**, 2335.—§ 371 (Tuṅgaka): III, **85**, 8189 (*muner A°aḥ sutaḥ*, i.e. Sārasvataḥ).—§ 373 (Prayāga): III, **85**, 8214 (*°pramukhāḥ brahmarshayaḥ*; dwelt at Prayāga).—§ 378 (Tīrthayātrāp.): III, **92**, 8437 (had protected the Sun).—§ 421 (Ākāça-Gaṅgā): III, **142**, 10904 (muttered his daily prayers at Ākāça-Gaṅgā).—§ 488 (Āṅgirasa): III, **217**, 14101, 14106, 14107, 14112, (14116), 14117, 14120 (excelled Agni and became his first son).—§ 489 (Āṅgirasa): III, **218**, 14124 (*devī Bhānumatī nāma prathamā 'ṅgirasaḥ sutā*), 14125 (*rāgād Rāgeti yām āhur dvitīyā 'ṅgirasaḥ sutā*), 14126 (Sinīvālī was his third daughter), 14127 (his fourth to sixth daughters were Arcishmatī, Havishmatī, and Mahishmatī; the seventh was Mahāmati), 14129 (his eighth daughter was Kuhū).—§ 491 (do.): **220**, 14164 (*Bhānur Aṅgiraso dhīraḥ putro . . .*).—§ 493 (do.): **221**, 14183 (*Asurāḥ janayan ghorān martyāṃç caiva pṛthagvidhān | tapasaç ca Manuṃ putraṃ Bhānuñ cāpy Aṅgirāḥ sṛjat*).—§ 493 (do.): **222**, 14224 (*Bhṛgv-Aṅgirādibhir bhūyas tapasotthāpitas . . . Çikhī*).—§ 494 (do.): **222**, 14238 (*eka evaisha bhagavān vijñeyaḥ prathamo 'ṅgirāḥ*).—§ 496 (Skandotp.): **225**, 14299 (*Çivā bhāryā tv A°aḥ*), 14301.—§ 570 (Sainyaniryāṇap.): V, **151**, 5114 (*sakhā cā°o nṛpaḥ Drupado*).—§ 581 (Bhīshmavadhap.): VI, **68**γ, 3041 (referred to in a hymn to Nārāyaṇa).—§ 595 (Shoḍaçarāj.): VII, **66**, 2343 (*A° yathā*).—§ 599 (Jayadrathavadhap.): VII, **94**ε, 3453 (invoked by Droṇa when clothing Duryodhana in invulnerable armour), 3475 (Indra gave to *A*. *mantramayaṃ bandhaṃ*), 3476 (*A*. said it to his son Bṛhaspati); **103**, 3861 (*idam A°e prādād Deveço varma bhāsvaraṃ*).—§ 606 (Tripurākhyāna): VIII, **34**, 1497 (*Atharvā°au*), 1505 (*Bhṛgv-Aṅgiro-manyu-bhavaṃ krodhāgniṃ*, sc. *çaraṃ*?).—§ 615*u* (Skanda): IX, **45**γ, 2512 (came to the investiture of Skanda).—§ 637 (Rājadh.): XII, **47**η, 1597 (among those who surrounded Bhīshma on his bed of arrows).—§ 641 (do.): XII, **69**, 2666 (two verses sung by his son Bṛhaspati); **122**, 4505 (Vishṇu made chastisement over to *A*., and *A*. to Indra and Marīci).—§ 656 (Khaḍgotp.): XII, **166***a*, 6135 (among the sons begotten by Brahmán, seven besides Pracetas and Rudra), 6142 (β) (among those who accepted the religion of the Vedas).—§ 664 (Mokshadh.): XII, **207**δ, 7534 (among the seven will-born sons of Brahmán).—§ 665 (do.): XII, **208***a*, 7570 (*Atry-A°au* among Brahmán's seven sons enumerated by Bhīshma, mentioned in the Purāṇas as seven Brahmáns).—§ 677 (do.): XII, **235**, 8602 (Karandhama's son Maruta ascended to heaven, by giving away his daughter to *A*.; cf. XIII, 6260).—§ 694*b* (Jvarotp.): XII, **284***a*, 10218 (*°pramukhāḥ devarshayaḥ*; among those who waited upon Çiva and Pārvatī on Meru).—§ 702 (Mokshadh.): XII, **297**δ, 10877 ("originally only four gotras arose: Aṅgiras, Kaçyapa, Vasishṭha, and Bhṛgu").—§ 717*b* (Nārāyaṇīya): XII, **335***a*, 12685 (among the twenty-one Prajāpatis who were first born).—§ 717*c* (Uparicara): XII, **336**β, 12724 (among the seven ṛshis, etc., who promulgated an excellent treatise on duties on Mount Meru; printed in C. *Ā°*, in B. *A°*); **337**, 12752 (*A°aḥ putre*, i.e. Bṛhaspati).—§ 717*b* (Nārāyaṇīya): XII, **341**, 13040 (among the eight Prakṛtis, i.e. Marīci, etc., and Manu, upon whom all the worlds depend), ξ, 13075 (among the seven Mānasāḥ who will become the preceptors of the Vedas, following the religion of Pravṛtti and created for procreating offspring—*Prājāpatye*).—§ 730 (Ānuçāsanik.): XIII, **14**ββ, 990 (among those who were seen by Kṛshṇa in the presence of Çiva).—§ 733 (do.): **25***a*, 1690 (his enumeration of the sacred waters), 1691, (1694), 1755 (had obtained the discourse from Kaçyapa), 1757 (*°matam*).—§ 734 (do.): **26***a*, 1761 (among the maharshis who had come to see Bhīshma on his arrow bed).—§ 747*b* (Suvarṇotp.): XIII, **85**ζ, 4122 (created by Brahmán from a sacrifice; etymology from *aṅgāra*, 'charcoal'), 4124, 4141 (considered as the offspring of Agni), 4143 (he and Bhṛgu and Kavi were all of them *prajānāṃ patayaḥ*), 4147(θ) (his eight sons called *Vāruṇās*), 4152, 4154 (*jagrāhāṅgirasaṃ* *devaḥ Çikhī* . . . | *tasmād Aṅgirasā jñeyāḥ sarva eva tad-anvayāḥ*).—§ 749 (Ānuçāsanik.): **92**δ, 4392 (among the masters of yoga).—§ 751*b* (Çapathavidhi): **94***a*, †4550 (among the ṛshis assembled at Prabhāsa), 4566(β) (took his oath that he is innocent of the theft of lotus-stalks).—§ 759 (Ānuçāsanik.): **105**, 5141 (his utterance to Bhīshma about the merits of fasting which he had declared formerly to the maharshis), (5143), 5179, 5201, †5203; **107**, 5209 (continuation), 5263.—§ 766 (do.): **127** (6062): recommended standing every night for a full year under a karañjaka tree with a lamp and the roots of a Suvarcala plant.—§ 767 (do.): **137***a*, 6260 (*Maruttaḥ* . . . *kanyām Aṅgirase dattvā divam āçu jagāma saḥ*; cf. XII, 8602).—§ 770 (do.): **151**ζ, 7108 (his son Bala is mentioned among the Mānavāḥ), 7112 (Tṛṇasomā°, the sixth of the seven ṛtvijes of Yama in the South, η), 7157 (ν, among the old brahmarshis who have worshipped certain mantras).—§ 772*d* (Pavanārjunasaṃvāda): The brahmans are always inconquerable in heaven as on earth; in days of yore Aṅgiras drank off the water as milk, but did not feel his thirst slaked, and once more caused the earth to be filled by a great flood. When *A.* became angry with me (i.e. Vāyu), I fled away leaving the world, and dwelled for a long time in the agnihotra from fear of *A.* Kavi (i.e. Agni, Nīl.), who is of the complexion of gold and blazes with effulgence when destitute of smoke, and whose flames, uniting together, burn upwards, when cursed by the angry Aṅgiras, became divested of all these attributes (read *guṇair* with B.): XIII, **154**, 7215 (*apibat tejasā hy apaḥ*), 7217, 7220 (*Kavir Aṅgirasā çapto*).—§ 775 (Ānuçāsanik.): **166**γ, 7664 (among the learned brahmans in the eastern region).—§ 778*e* (Avikshit): XIV, **4**, 85 (the priest of Avikshit Kārandhama); **5**, 95 (*A.*'s sons were Bṛhaspati and Saṃvartta) (v. Saṃvartta-Maruttīya), 99 (was formerly the family priest of king Karandhama, so also of his son Avikshit); **6**, 134 (*Aṅgirasaḥ putraṃ Bṛhaspatim*, had in vain been solicited by Marutta for his sacrifice), 137 (*Aṅgirasaḥ putraḥ Saṃvartto*).—Cf. Agnisambhava.

Aṅgiras[2], pl. (°*aḥ*), the descendants of Aṅgiras. § 206 (Droṇa): I, **132**, 5280 (*Aṅgirasāṃ varaḥ*, i.e. Droṇa).—§ 207 (Droṇa): I, **133**, 5299 (*Aṅgirasāṃ varaḥ*, i.e. Droṇa).—§ 324 (Dvaitavanaprav.): III, **26**, 970 (the Dvaitavana wood became filled with *A.*, etc.).—§ 393 (Paraçu-Rāma): **115**, 10126 (among the ascetics presented to Yudhishṭhira by Lomaça).—§ 406 (Skandotp.): III, **224**, 14270 (*Bhṛgubhiç cāṅgirobhiç ca hutam*).—§ 506 (Skandayuddha): III, **231**, 14555 (*Bhṛgvā° obhiḥ*).—§ 555 (Indra): V, **10**, 511 (*Aṅgirasāṃ varishṭhe Bṛhaspatau*).—§ 578 (Ambop.): **193***a*, 7572 (*Droṇam Āṅgirasāṃ varaṃ*, read with B. *Aṅgi°*).—§ 602 (Droṇavadhap.): VII, **190**, 8728 (*Bhṛgavo 'ngirasaç caiva*, etc., among those who reproach Droṇa for using the Brāhma weapon).—§ 605 (Karṇap.): VIII, **17**, †683 (*Aṅgirasāṃ varishṭhaḥ* – Açvatthāman).—§ 615*a* (Skanda): IX, **45**γ, 2510 (among those who came to the investiture of Skanda).—§ 621 (Rājadh.): XII, **2**δ, 50 (*cakārāṅgirasāṃ çreshṭhād Dhanurvedaṃ guros tadā*, i.e. Karṇa from Droṇa), 59 (do. = do.).—§ 665 (Mokshadh.): XII, **208**δ, 7590 (*Açvinau tu smṛtau çūdrau tapasy ugre samāsthitau* | *smṛtās tv aṅgiraso devā brāhmaṇā iti niçcayaḥ*).—§ 717 (Uparicara): XII, **337**, 12800 (*Aṅgirasāṃ varaṃ* = Bṛhaspati).—§ 795 (Svargārohaṇap.): XVIII, **5**, 159 (*Bṛhaspatim °āṃ varaṃ*).

Aṅgiras[3] = Bṛhaspati. § 145 (Kaca): I, **76**, 3188 (*devā vavrire 'ṅgirasaṃ muniṃ*, perhaps *Āṅgirasaṃ*, i.e. Bṛhaspati).—§ 555 (Indra): V, **11**, 367 (*Bṛhaspater Aṅgirasaḥ*); **18**, 548 (?).—§ 641 (Rājadh.): XII, **68**, 2595 (discourse between him and Vasumanas).—§ 717*b* (Nārāyaṇīya): XII, **343** VI), ††13206 (Aṅgiras Bṛhaspati curses the Ocean that it should be tainted with fishes, etc.).—§ 746 (Ānuçāsanik.): XIII, **62**, 3196 (Indra gave him the whole earth).

Aṅgiras[4] = Sārasvata. § 368 (Tīrthayātrāp.): III, **83**, 7058 (*yatra Sārasvato yātaḥ so 'ṅgirās tapaso nidhiḥ*, i.e. Dadhīcasya tīrthaṃ).

Aṅgiras[5] = Utathya. § 641 (Rājadh.): XII, **90**, 3362 (the duties of kings proclaimed by Aṅgiras Utathya to Māndhātṛ Yauvanāçva).—§ 772 (Utathya): XIII, **155**, 7254 (married to Bhadrā, the daughter of Soma, etc.).

Aṅgiras[6] = Vishṇu. § 493 (Āṇgirasa): III, **221**, 14188 (*Vishṇur nāmeha yo 'gnis tu Dhṛtimān nāma so 'ṅgirāḥ*).

Āṅgirasa[1] = Bṛhaspati. § 145 (Kaca): I, **76**, 3188 (v. Aṅgiras = Bṛhaspati).—§ 168 (Satyavatī): I, **103**, 4151 (*Çukrāṅgirasayor iva*, sc. Bhīshma's knowledge).—§ 488 (Āṅgirasa): III, **217**, 14118 (the firstborn son of Fire).—§ 554 (Sainyodyogap.): V, **6**, 112 (*prajñāyā sadṛçaç cāsi Çukreṇā ṅgirasena ca*, sc. the purohita of Drupada).—§ 589 (Droṇābhishekap.): VII, **5**, 151 (*Çukrāṅgirasadarçanāt*, i.e. Droṇa).—§ 746 (Ānuçāsanik.): XIII, **62**, 3195 (discourse between Indra and Bṛhaspati).—§ 778*b* (Saṃvartta-Maruttīya): XIV, **6**, 121.—§ 782 (Guruçishyas.): XIV, **35** (δ), 962.

Āṅgirasa[2] = Utathya. § 772*j* (Utathya): XIII, **155**, 7260.

Āṅgirasa[3] = Saṃvartta. § 778*b* (Saṃvartta-Maruttīya): XIV, **10**, 281.

Āṅgirasa[4] = Kaca. § 146 (Devayānī): I, **80**, 3335 (*Kacaṃ*).

Āṅgirasa[5] = Sudhanvan. § 300 (Prahlāda): II, **68**, 2315 (*Prahlādasya ca saṃvādaṃ muner Āṅgirasasya ca*).

Āṅgirasa[6] = Cyavana. § 491 (Āṅgirasa): III, **220**, 14156 (*Agnir Āṅgirasaç caiva Cyavanas Trisuvarcakaḥ*).

Āṅgirasa[7] = Bala. § 665 (Mokshadh.): XII, **208**, 7593 (*Balaç cāṅgirasaḥ smṛtaḥ*).

Āṅgirasa[8] = the planet Jupiter. § 605 (Karṇap.): VIII, **17**, 661 (*Çukrāṅgirasavarcasor, Çukrāṅgirasayor iva*, i.e. Arjuna and Açvatthāman).

Āṅgirasa[9], pl. (°*āḥ*), the descendants of Aṅgiras. § 747 (Suvarṇotp.): XIII, **85**, 4154 (the descendants of Fire—or Aṅgiras—are all called Ā°). Cf. Atharvan.

Āṅgirasa[10] (adj.). § 602 (Droṇavadhap.): VII, **191**, 8766 (°*aṃ dhanuḥ*, used by Droṇa).—§ 616 (Sauptikap.): X, **7**, 306 (°*kule*, i.e. Açvatthāman). § 665 (Mokshadh.): XII, **208**, 7590 (cf. Āṅgirasa[7] = Bala).—§ 682 (do.): XII, **267**, 9482 (°*e kule*, said of Cirakārin).—§ 717*c* (Uparicara): XII, **336**, 12749 (*utpanne 'ṅgirase caiva yuge prathamakalpito*; cf. °*Aṅgirasake kāle*, XIII, 4320).—§ 747*b* (Suvarṇotp.): XIII, **85**, 4143 (*Bhārgavāṅgirasau loke lokasantānalakshaṇau*).—§ 772*j* (Utathya): XIII, **155**, 7240 (*Utathyasya jātasy-āṅgirase kule*).

Āṅgirasa[11] (adj.). § 11 (Parvas.): I, **2**, 469 (°*am ākhyānam*, Aṅgirasa or Āṅgirasopākhyāna)

Āṅgirasa(ṃ) ("on the descendants of Aṅgiras"). § 488 (Mārk.): Asked by *Yudhishṭhira*, *Mārkaṇḍeya* related the following "old story" (*itihāsaṃ purātanaṃ*): *Aṅgiras* (the third son of Brahmán, v. 14122) in days of yore practised austerities in his hermitage, so that he excelled *Agni*, who, thinking that *Brahmán* had created a new Fire, was greatly depressed, but *Aṅgiras*, saying that *Agni* had been created by *Brahmán* to officiate as fire, asked him to occupy his proper place, and when *Agni* only wished to be the second or *Prājāpatyaka* fire, at last prevailed upon him to remain and make him (i.e. Aṅgiras) his first son. *Aṅgiras* also had a son, *Bṛhaspati*; knowing him the *Āṅgirasa* to be the firstborn son of Fire, the gods came and learned the matter from *Aṅgiras* (III, **217**).—§ 489: The children of *Aṅgiras* and *Çubhā* (B. *Subhā*): the son *Bṛhaspati*, and the eight daughters, *Bhānumatī*, *Rāgā*, *Sinībālī*, also called *Kapardisutā*, because she was both visible and invisible, *Arcishmatī*, *Havishmatī*, *Mahishmatī*, *Mahāmatī*, and *Kuhū* (III, **218**).—§ 490:

Bṛhaspati ~ Cāndramasī (= Tārā, Nīl., and PCR.).
|
Çaṃyu ~ Satyā Dharmajā.
|
(1) Bharadvāja ~ Vīrā. (2) Bharata ~ (3–5) 3 daughters.
|
Vīra (= Rathaprabhu, Rathādhvāna, Kumbharetas) ~ Çarayū. — Bharata. Bharatī.
|
Siddhi.
Niçcyavana *
|
Vipāpa (Satya, Nīl., and PCR.).
Nishkṛti.†
|
Svana.
Viçvajit.‡
Viçvabhuj ‡ ~ Gomatī.
Vaḍavāgni.‡
Ūrdhvabhāj.‡
Svishṭakṛt.‡
Manyu.‡
Manyantī.‡
Svāhā.‖‡
Kāma.‡
Amogha.‡
Uktha.‡
|
Mahavāc = Samāçvāsa.‡

§ 491: With *Kāçyapa*, *Vāsishṭha*, *Prāṇa*, son of *Prāṇa*, *Agni Āṅgirasa*,‖ and *Cyavana Trisuvarcaka*,‖ he,§ after a penance lasting for many years, obtained the son *Pāñcajanya* ("appertaining to five men and the progenitor of five tribes," v. 14160). *Pāñcajanya* (= *Tapas*, v. 14166–8, 14173, 14174), after 10,000 years of penances, produced the fire of the *Pitṛs*; from his head he created *Bṛhat* and *Rathantara*, from his mouth *Vāta* and *Rasāhara*,¶ in his navel Çiva, from his might (*balād*) *Indra*, from his soul (*prāṇato*) *Vāyu* and *Agni*, from his arms *Anudāttau*,** and *Viçve*†† (!) and the elements (*bhūtāni*), and then the five sons of the *Pitṛs*. *Bṛhadratha's* son was *Praṇidhi*, *Kāçyapa's Mahattara*, *Āṅgiras' Bhānu*, *Varca's Saubhara*, and *Prāṇa's Anudātta*, in all twenty-five. —§ 492: He also produced three times five *devāḥ*: *Yajñamushaḥ* ("who steal the sacrifices"), *Subhīma*, *Atibhīma*, *Bhīma*, *Bhīmabala*, *Abala*, *Sumitra*, *Mitravat*, *Mitrajña*, *Mitravardhana*, *Mitradharman*,* *Surapravīra*, *Vīra*, *Suveça*, *Suravarcas*, and "*Surāṇām api hantṛ*."—§ 493: *Bṛhaduktha* and *Rathantara* (cf. § 491) or *Mitravinda*, sons of *Tapas* (III, **220**). Many "fires" enumerated, among others the five *Ūrjaskarāḥ* (*Purandara*, *Ushman*, *Manu*, *Çambhu*, and *Āvasathya*), sons of *Tapas*; the six sons of *Bhānu* with his wives *Suprajā* and *Bṛhadbhāsā Sūryajā* (*Balada*, *Manyumat*, *Vishṇu* = *Dhṛtimat* = *Aṅgiras*, *Āgrayaṇa*, *Agraha*, *Stubha*). *Niçā* was likewise the wife of *Bhānu*, and gave birth to one daughter, to *Agni* and *Soma*, and to five Fires (*Pāvakān*). The Fire (*Pāvaka*) who in company with *Parjanya* is honoured with the first *havis* at the *Cāturmāsyas* is *Agni Vaiçvānara*. He who is called the lord of all the world is *Viçvapati*, the second son of *Manu*, etc. (III, **221**). Genealogy of the Fires continued. The Fire *Saha*, from fear of his grandson the Fire *Bharata* (*Bhara*, *Niyata*), who burns the dead bodies, hid himself in the sea,† asking *Atharvan* to carry the oblations to the gods. When his place of concealment had been divulged by the fishes, *Saha* cursed them, saying that they should become the food of all creatures in various ways. Then *Saha* gave up his body and entered the earth, where he created various metals: from his pus (*pūyāt*) force (*tejaḥ*) and scent, from his bones the *devadāru*, from his phlegm glass (*sphāṭikaṃ*), from his bile *mārakata*, from his liver the black iron, the clouds from his nails, the corals from his veins, etc., and remained absorbed in meditation, whence he was roused by the *tapas* of *Bhṛgu*, *Āṅgiras*, etc. Seeing the *ṛshi* (i.e. Atharvāṅgirasa, Nīl. = Atharvan, PCR.), he again took refuge in the water. The whole world with the gods sought the protection of *Atharvan*, who searched the sea, and finding the Fire, created the worlds (so Nīl. and PCR.). So *Agni* was formerly destroyed by *Atharvan*, and called back (*āhūtaḥ* (?), PCR.) he carries the oblations, and travelling about various countries and living there (i.e. in the sea, PCR.), he produced the various fires mentioned in the *Vedas*.—§ 494: Enumeration of rivers that are said to be the mothers of the fires. The wife of *Adbhuta* was *Priyā*, and his son *Vibhūrasi* (14234). There are as many *somas* (i.e. kinds of *soma* sacrifices, Nīl. and PCR.) as the number of fires mentioned. Also in the race of *Atri* [these] mind-born sons of *Brahmán* (?)‡ sprang forth. *Atri*, wishing to procreate sons, conceived these [fires] in his mind, and the fires came out of his, the brahman's, body.‖ The powers of these fires are the same as those of the *Adbhuta* fire as related in the *Vedas*, for they are all one and the same, the first *Aṅgiras*, sprung from [his] body in various forms like the *jyotishṭoma* sacrifice (III, **222**).

Āṅgirasa[12]. XIII, 2126 (vanquished the Nīpas, v. Aṅgiraja).

Aṅgirasaka, adj. § 749 (Ānuçāsanik.): XIII, **91**, 4326 (*Bhṛgv-Aṅgirasake kāle*, i.e. in the time when the world was peopled by only the descendants of Bhṛgu and Aṅgiras; cf. *Āṅgirase yuge*, XII, 12749).

Āṅgirasī[1] (a female descendant of Aṅgiras). § 229 (Vaçishṭhop.): I, **182**, 6908 (a brāhmaṇī who cursed Kalmāshapāda).

Āṅgirasī[2] ("daughter of Aṅgiras"). § 489 (Āṅgirasa): III, **218**, 14128 (*mahāmakheshv Āṅgirasī . . . Mahāmatīti vikhyātā saptamī kathyate sutā*, sc. Aṅgiras's).

* We are not told in the text whose son Niçcyavana is. He might be the second son of Bṛhaspati, and that is apparently the opinion of Nīl. and PCR.

† It is not said in the text whose son he is. PCR. takes Nishkṛti to be another name of Satya.

‡ PCR. supposes *Viçvajit* to be *Bṛhaspati's* third son, *Viçvabhuj* the fourth, *Vaḍavāgni* the fifth, *Ūrdhvabhāj* the same as *Vaḍavāgni*, *Svishṭakṛt* the sixth son of *Bṛhaspati*, *Manyu* (fury) as predicate to *Manyantī*, "daughter of *Prajāpati*," *Svāhā* the same as *Manyantī*; *Kāma*, *Amogha*, and *Uktha* the sons of *Svāhā*, by *sattva*, *rajas*, and *tamas* respectively; *Mahāvāc* to mean "the great word, i.e. the word of God," and *Samāçvāsa* ("the means of rest") as epithet of *Uktha*.

‖ Nīl. and PCR. takes "*agnir Āṅgirasaçcaiva*" to be an epithet of *Cyavana*, and *Suvarcaka* (sic!) to stand alone as the fifth name.

§ I.e. Uktha, according to Nīl. and PCR.

¶ Otherwise PCR. and Nīl.

** I.e. Udātta and Anudātta, Nīl. and PCR.

†† I.e. the five senses, Nīl. and PCR.

* Compare the notes of PCR.

† Nīl.: *Bhṛguçāpāddhi sarvabhakshatvaṃ prāpto 'gnir ātmānam bahudhā kṛtā 'gnihotrādishu çmaçānādishu ca sthita ity upākhyāyate.*

‡ *Brahmaṇo* might be an opposition to *Atreḥ*, as in the following verse.

‖ Nīl.: *evam ca ṛshyantarāṇām apy upalakshaṇam, tathā ca sarvaṃ karmāgnidaivatyaṃ sarve brāhmaṇā agnisantatir ity uktaṃ bhavati.*

Āṅgirasopākhyāna, v. Āṅgirasa[11].
Aniça = Vishṇu (1000 names).
Anīkajit = Kṛshṇa: V, 2566.
Anīkasāha = Kṛshṇa: XII, 1506.
Anīkavidāraṇa, brother of Jayadratha. § 522 (Draupadīhar.): III, **265**, 15599 (PCR. translates "Anīka and Vidāraṇa").
***Anila**[1] ("Wind"). § 116 (Aṃçāvat.): I, **66**, 2582 (one of the eight Vasus, son of Prajāpati (?) or Dharma (?) and Çvāsā, husband of Çivā, and father of Manojava and Avijñātagatiḥ), 2589.—§ 485 (Pativratop.): III, **213**, 13959.—§ 615*u* (Skanda): IX, **45**, 2506 (Anilānalau, came to the investiture of Skanda).—§ 770 (Ānuçāsanik.): XIII, **151**δ, 7094 (one of the eight Vasus). Cf. Vāyu.
Anila[2] = Çiva, Vishṇu (1000 names).
Anila[3], a Suparṇa, son of Garuḍa. § 564 (Mātalīyop.): V, **101**, 3594.
Anīla, a Serpent. § 47 (Sarpanāmak.): I, **35**, 1553 (*Nīlānīlau nāgau*).
Anilābha = Çiva (1000 names[2]).
Anilaprabhava = Bhīma, q.v.
Anilasambhava, v. Agni.
Anilasārathi, v. Agni.
Anilātmaja[1] = Bhīma, q.v.
Anilātmaja[2] = Hanūmat, q.v.
***Aṇiman** ("minuteness"). § 705 (Mokshadh.): XII, **303**, 11229 (among the attributes of Çambhu).—§ 707 (do.): XII, **313**, 11602 (among the attributes of Çambhu Prajāpati).
Aṇīmāṇḍavya (a ṛshi, cf. Māṇḍavya). § 11 (Parvas.): I, **2**, 375 (*Dharmasya nṛshu sambhūtir Aṇīmāṇḍavya-çāpajā*).—§ 80: I, **63**, the ṛshi Aṇīmāṇḍavya having been accused of theft, though innocent, and impaled, as a punishment for having in his childhood pierced a little fowl in a reed, cursed Dharma (for having killed a brahman, the most heinous of sins), saying that he should be born on earth in the Çūdra caste. Therefore Dharma was born as Vidura: I, **63**, 2422.—§ 172 (Aṇīmāṇḍavyopākhyāna): I, **108**, 4329 (4333).—§ 264 (Sabhākriyāp.): II, **4***a*, 107 (among the ṛshis who were present when Yudhishṭhira entered the palace).
Aṇīmāṇḍavyopākhyāna(m). § 172 (Sambhavap.): The history of *Māṇḍavya* (§ 80) is more fully described. Suspicion had fallen upon him, because thieves had hid their plunder in his hermitage, while he was sitting for years with his arms upraised observing the vow of silence. When impaled, he by his ascetic power not only preserved his life, but summoned other *ṛshis* to the scene, who came in the night in the shape of birds (I, **107**). Hearing that he was alive, the king asked his pardon and endeavoured to extract the stake from his body, but was obliged to cut it off outside the body. *Māṇḍavya* henceforth walked about with the stake in his life, and thereby conquered *lokas* unattainable by others and was called *Aṇīmāṇḍavya* (v. 4329). He ruled that an act should not be sinful when committed by one below the age of 14 years (I, **108**).
Aṇimat. § 268 (Varuṇa-sabhāv.): II, **9**, 362 (among the Nāgas in the palace of Varuṇa; B. has *Maṇimān*, PCR. has *Matimat*).
Animisha[1], a Suparṇa. § 564 (Mātalīyop.): V, **101**, 3595.
Animisha[2] = Çiva (1000 names[2]), Vishṇu (1000 names).
Anindita = Çiva (1000 names[2]).
Anirdeçyavapus = Vishṇu (1000 names).
Aniruddha[1] (son of Pradyumna). § 262 (Bhagavadyāna): II, **2**, 56.—§ 264 (Sabhākriyāp.): II, **4**β, 123 (among the kings present when Yudhishṭhira entered the palace), 130 (learnt the science of arms from Arjuna).—§ 452 (Mārkaṇḍeyas.): III, **183**, 12584.—§ 581 (Bhīshmavadhap.): VI, **65**ξ, 2968 ("son of Pradyumna and known as the eternal Vishṇu; created Brahmán").—§ 589 (Droṇābhishekap.): VII, **11**ξ, 408 (among those who would take up their position in the Pāṇḍava host).—§ 599 (Jayadrathavadhap.): VII, **110**σ, 4193.—§ 717 (Nārāyaṇīya): XII, **340**η, 12903, 12905 ("Pradyumna or Mind gives origin to Aniruddha or the Creator = Īçvara = Consciousness"), 12937, 12938 ("Brahmán springs from Aniruddha's navel"); **341**, 13036 (= Mahān ātmā or Ahaṅkāra sprang from Avyakta or Pradhāna, and from him sprang Pitāmaha, i.e. Brahmán and the five elements), 13077 (*lokasargakaraḥ prabhuḥ*), 13098 (the Supreme God in the form of Aniruddha showed himself to Brahmán, with a vast horse's head, etc.); **342**, 13144 (from Nārāyaṇa—Aniruddha's grace arose Brahmán, and from his wrath Rudra); **344**, 13309 (Çaunaka asked why Nārada, having seen the Supreme Lord in the form of Aniruddha—*A° tanau sthitam*—again proceeded so quickly to Nara and Nārāyaṇa); **345**, 13385 (the Emancipate entering the Sun; thence reduced to invisible atoms they enter into Nārāyaṇa, and thence into Aniruddha, and thence, transformed into mind alone, into Pradyumna, etc.); **348**, 13466, 13470 (Janamejaya inquires why Hari had appeared to Brahmán in the form of Aniruddha with the horse's head; Brahmán develops into Purusha = Aniruddha = Pradhāna, who, yielding to *yoga*-sleep, lays himself down on the waters reflecting on creation; *A.* develops into Ahaṅkāra = Brahmán, etc. = Hiraṇyagarbha, who takes birth within the lotus that springs from Aniruddha), 13512 (Madhu and Kaiṭabha saw Purusha in the form of Aniruddha in *yoga*-sleep on the water, white, imbued with stainless *sattva*, on the hood of a snake, surrounded with garlands of flames; they awakened him and were slain by him; thence he came to be called Madhusūdana); **352**, 13759 (§ 717*d*: Brahmarudra-saṃvāda: learned brahmans called Mahāpurusha by the name of Aniruddha).—† § 773*b* (Kṛshṇa): XIII, †**159**, †7392 (when Kṛshṇa becomes Jīva, he comes to be called Saṅkarshaṇa; next he transforms himself into Pradyumna, and then into Aniruddha).—§ 793 (Mausalap.): XVI, **3**φ, 101 (slain).
Aniruddha[2] = Vishṇu (1000 names).
Aniruddha[3]. Cf. *Anu°*.
Anirviṇṇa = Vishṇu (1000 names).
Anīti = Çiva (1000 names[2]).
Anivartin = Vishṇu (1000 names).
Aṇīyasām aṇīyān = Kṛshṇa.
Añjana[1], a locality? § 305 (Anudyūtap.): II, **78**, 2574 ("formerly thou wert instructed . . . near *A.* by the great ṛshi Asita . . . ").
Añjana[2], an elephant. § 564 (Mātalīyop.): V, **99**, 3561 (among the elephants in Pātāla, born in the race of the elephant Supratīka).—§ 581 (Bhīshmavadhap.): VI, **64**ν, 2866 (among the Dig-nāgas ridden by Rākshasas).—§ 599 (Jayadrathavadhap.): VII, **112**, 4323 (the Kirātas, q.v., have elephants sprung from the race of *A.*, of impenetrable hides, well trained . . . with armour made wholly of gold, resembling Airāvata, having come from the northern hills, ridden by fierce robbers); **121**ζζ, 4829 (many elephants of the race of *A.*, etc., were slain). Cf. Añjanaka.

Añjanābha, a mountain. § 575 (Ānuçāsanik.): XIII, **166**, 7658 (among the mountains whose names, if recited at morning, etc., remove sin).

Añjanaka (B. *A*°; cf. Añjana). § 599 (Jayadrathavadhap.): VII, **112**, 4307 (*kulam A°aṃ nāma*: Sātyaki, i.e. Yuyudhāna, would crush the elephants of the *A*.-breed mounted by Mlecchas).

Añjanaparvan (son of Ghaṭotkaca). § 573 (Ambop.): V, **194**γ, 7600 (among Yudhishṭhira's allies).—§ 600 (Ghaṭotkacavadhap.): VII, **156**, 6809 (*pautreṇa Bhīmasenasya*), 6811, 6815 (*Ghaṭotkacasutaṃ*), 6817, 6818 (slain by Açvatthāman).

Aṅkṛti. § 264 (Sabhākriyāp.): II, **4**β, 126 (among the kings who were present when Yudhishṭhira entered his palace).

Anna = Çiva (1000 names[1]), Vishṇu (1000 names).

Annabhoktṛ = Çiva (1000 names).

Annabhuj = Çiva (1000 names[1]).

Annada = Çiva (1000 names[1]).

Annāda = Vishṇu (1000 names).

Annapati = Çiva (1000 names[1]).

Annasrashṭṛ = Çiva (1000 names[1]).

Anṛçaṃsa (?) = Çiva.

Antacāra. § 574 (Jambūkh.): VI, **9**o, 375 (a people in Bharatavarsha, in the East and North).

Anta(h)devānāṃ = Çiva (1000 names[1]).

***Antaka**[1] (Death). I, 2708 (*Mahādevāntakābhyān ca Kāmāt Krodhāc ca . . . jajne . . . Açvatthāmā*), 7028 (°*opamah*); III, 1376, 1655 (*murttimantam ivā°m*), † 1931 (*srshto 'ntakaḥ sarvaharo Vidhātrā bhaved yathā*); IV, 763 (*daṇḍapanir ivā°h*), 815 (do.), 817 (*iva*), 1580 (*Pavano Mṛtyuḥ*); V, 3210 (*yathāntakau, Bhīmarjunau*); VI, 2236 (*daṇḍapāṇim ivā°m*), 2790 (*daṇḍapāṇir ivā°ḥ*), 3638 (do.), 4678 (*daṇḍahasta ivā°ḥ*), 4959 (*daṇḍahastam ivā°m*), 4985 (*iva*), 5254 (*Kālā°samadyutiḥ*), 5326 (*iva*); VII, 3135 (*iva*), 4727 (*Kālā°-Yamopamaṃ*), 6099 (*iva*), 7570 (*iva*), † 8168, 8308 (*iva*), 8980 (*iva*); VIII, 596 (*Kālā°-Yamopamau*), 800 (*iva*), 814 (°*daṇḍasannibhān ishūn*), 909 (*Mṛtyu-Kālā°opamaṃ*), 2459 (*Kālā°-Yamopamaṃ*), 2708 (do.), 3995 (*Kālā°vapuḥ*), 4390 (*Yama-Kālā°opamau*); IX, 151 (*daṇḍapāṇir ivāntakaḥ*), 153, 298 (°*pratimaṃ yudhi*), 485 (*atishṭhata raṇe vīraḥ kruddharūpa ivā°ḥ*), 555 (*Kāla-sṛshṭha ivā°ḥ*), 594 (*pāçahastam ivā°m*), 737 (*A°m iva kruddhaṃ*), 870 (*Mṛtyum ivā°m*), 894 (*yathā*), 1044 (*daṇḍapāṇir ivā°ḥ*), 1057 (*mārayaty Antakaḥ sadā*), 1368 (*daṇḍapāṇir ivā°ḥ*), 1402 (*daṇḍahastaṃ yathā kruddham A°m prāṇahāriṇaṃ*), 3270 (*kruddhāv ivā°au*, i.e. Bhīmasena and Duryodhana); X, 40 (*vāyasāntakaḥ*, i.e. the owl), 360 (*Kālasṛshṭa ivā°ḥ*), 395 (do.), 397 (*evaṃ teshāṃ tathā Drauṇir Antakaḥ samapadyata*), 669 (*Kālāntaka-Yamopamaḥ*), 703 (*Pāṇḍaveyānām Antakāyābhisaṃhitaṃ*); XI, 156 (comparison of the human body to a well: *yas tatra vasate 'dhastān mahāhiḥ Kāla eva saḥ | Antakaḥ sarvabhūtānāṃ dehināṃ sarvahāry asau*), 338 (*yathāntakam anuprāpya jīvan kaççin na mucyate*), 404 (*putrāṇām Antake*); XII, 2578, 4264 (*krūraḥ Kāla ivāntakaḥ*), 6164 (*Kālo 'ntaka ivodyataḥ*), 6546 (follows everyone who is born), 6551 (*satyenaivāntakaṃ jayet*), 11061 (*na Yamo nāntakaḥ kruddho na Mṛtyur bhīmavikramaḥ | īçate nṛpate sarve yogasyāmitatejasaḥ*), 11838 (*kair nāpnoti jarāntakau*), 11841 (= do.), 12078 (*purā mṛtaḥ praṇīyase Yamasya rājaçāsanāt | tvam Antakāya dāruṇaiḥ prayatnaṃ ārjave kuru*), 12081 (*Māruto 'ntakaḥ*), 12085 (*purā çarīram Antako bhinatti rogasārathiḥ*), 12107 (*purā karoti so 'ntakaḥ pramādago 'sukhāṃ camūṃ*); XIII, 184 (*Kālāntakopamāḥ*), 803 (*sarpahastam anirdeçyaṃ pāçahastam ivāntakaṃ*), 2226 (*nāgnis tṛpyati kāshṭhānāṃ nāpagānāṃ mahodadhiḥ | nāntakaḥ sarvabhūtānāṃ na puṃsāṃ vāmalocanāḥ*), 2230 (*Antakaḥ Pavano Mṛtyuḥ . . .*), 7497 (*sa Kālaḥ so 'ntako Mṛtyuḥ . . . .*, i.e. Çiva); XIV, 2167 (*Kālāntaka-Yamopamaṃ*).

Antaka[2] = Vishṇu (1000 names).

Antakajvalana (the fire of the universal destruction): I, †1180 (°*samānavarcasaṃ*).

***Antakāla** (the time of universal destruction). § 615*u* (Skanda): IX, **46**κ, 2689.

Antakṛt. § 615*u* (Skanda): IX, **45**, 2560 (a warrior of Skandas; PCR. has *'bhrakṛt*).

Antaradvīpa, pl. (°*āḥ*). § 623 (Rājadh.): XII, **14**, 408 (*dvīpāç ca sāntaradvīpāḥ*).

Antarātman = Çiva (1000 names[2]).

Antardhāman. § 768*b* (Kṛshṇa): XIII, **147**, 6828, 6829 (incarnation of Hari, son of Aṅga and father of Havirdhāman).

Antardhāna ("disappearance"), a celestial weapon. § 334*c* (Kairātap.): III, **41**, 1702 (given by Kubera to Arjuna; *A*. sends the foe to sleep, etc., used to burn the Asuras when Çaṅkara slew Tripura).

Antarhitātman = Çiva (1000 names[2]).

Antarikshacara, pl. (°*āḥ*), ("moving in the air"). § 615*ff* (Asita Devala): IX, **50**, 2879.

Ante'vasāyin, son of a Nishādī and a Cāṇḍāla: XIII, 2590 (*çmaçānagocaraṃ vāhyair api vahishkṛtaṃ*).

Anu, son of Yayāti. § 144 (Yayāti): I, **75**, 3160, 3162 (did not take upon himself his father's decrepitude), (v. Nahusha). — § 147 (Devayānī): I, **83**, 3433 (son of Çarmishṭhā). — § 148*e*: I, **84**, Yayāti cursed his older sons; Anu should be overcome by decrepitude and not be able to perform sacrifices before Agni, and his progeny should die as soon as they attained to youth: I, **84**, 3488 (3489); his sons were the Mlecchāḥ: I, **85**, 3520, 3533.—§ 156 (Pūruv.): I, **95**, 3762.

Aṇu = Çiva (1000 names[1]), Vishṇu (1000 names).

Anucakra, a companion of Skanda. § 615*u* (Skanda): IX, **45**, 2542 (given to him by Tvashṭṛ).

Anūcānā, an Apsaras. § 191 (Arjuna): I, **123**, 4817 (among the Apsarases who danced at the birth of Arjuna).

***Anucara**, pl. ("companions"). § 615*u* (Skanda): IX, **45**γ, 2517 (*Airāvataḥ sānucaraḥ*), 2519 (*Yamasya*), 2537 (δ: Aṃça gave five *anucarān* to Skanda: Paragha, Vaṭa, Bhīma, Dahati, and Dahana), 2539 (ε: Vishṇu gave three *anucarān* to Skanda: Cakra, Vikramaka, and Saṃkrama), 2617 (the companions of Skanda); **46**, 2619 (*Mātṛ-gaṇān Kumārānucarān*). — IX, **45**, 2527 (*caturtham asyānucaraṃ khyātaṃ Kumudamālinaṃ | tataḥ Sthāṇur mahātejā mahāpārishadaṃ prabhuḥ*). — § IX, **45**, 2532 (*tataḥ prādād anucarau Yamaḥ Kālopamāv ubhau*), 2534 (*Somo 'py anucarau çūrau parasainyapratāpinau*), 2535, 2542, 2550.

Anuçāsana ("instruction"). § 11 (Parvas.): I, **2**, 599, 603 (i.e. Ānuçāsanikaparvan).

Anuçāsanika ("relating to instruction"). § 10 (Parvas.): I, **2**, 353 (°*aṃ parva*, i.e. Ānuçāsanikaparvan).

[Ānuçāsanikaparvan] ("the section relating to instruction," the 91st of the minor parvans of Mahābhārata; cf. Anuçāsanika). § 719: *Yudhishṭhira's* despondency at the slaughter of his kinsmen on the field of *Kurukshetra*; he enquired how he might be cleansed of his sins; *Bhīshma* comforted him by telling him that the soul is not the cause of our acts, citing the ancient story Gautamī-lubdhaka-vyāla-Mṛtyu-kāla-saṃvāda (*b*), "This evil has neither been of thy own creation, nor of *Duryodhana's*, but of *Kāla's*." *Yudhishṭhira* became consoled (XIII, 1).—§ 720:

Asked by *Yudhishṭhira* if any householder had ever succeeded in conquering *Mṛtyu* by virtue, *Bhīshma* recited the ancient story Sudarçanopākhyāna (*b*), "To a householder there is no higher divinity than the guest; the blessings of an honoured guest are more efficacious than the merit of 100 sacrifices. Whenever a deserving guest seeks the hospitality of an householder and is not honoured by him, he takes away [with him] all the virtues of the latter, giving him his sins [in return]." Blessing upon the reader (XIII, **2**).—§ 721: *Yudhishṭhira* asked how the *Kshattriya Viçvāmitra* became a brahman, mentioning his destroying of the 100 sons of *Vasishṭha*, etc. (*a*), and comparing the instance of *Matañga*, who was born as a *Caṇḍāla* and could not attain to brahmanhood (XII, **3**). *Bhīshma* related how in olden times *Viçvāmitra* attained to the position of a *brahman* and B.-ṛ, i.e. Viçvāmitropākhyāna (*b*), (XIII, **4**).—§ 722: *Yudhishṭhira* wished to know the merits of compassion and the characteristics of devout men. *Bhīshma* recited the ancient story of the discourse between *Indra* and the parrot (in the territories of the *Kāçi* king) who did not desert the blasted tree wherein it had been born, though the tree had withered, being pierced by a fowler with a poisoned arrow. The parrot, by his penances, knew *Indra* (who came in the shape of a brahman), and, being granted a boon, made *Indra* revive the tree; and after death he came to the region of *Indra* (XIII, **5**).—§ 723: *Yudhishṭhira* enquired which of the two, Exertion and Destiny, is more powerful. *Bhīshma* related the ancient story of the conversation of *Vasishṭha* and *Brahmán*, in which *Brahmán* showed the necessity of exertion, notwithstanding the force of destiny, under reference to the example of the gods, etc. (*a*); *Janamejaya*, who followed in the footsteps of *Indra*, was checked and put down by the gods on account of his having killed a brahman woman; the *viprarshi Vaiçampāyana* was put down by the gods for killing a brahman by ignorance and a child (XIII, **6**).—§ 724: Asked by *Yudhishṭhira*, *Bhīshma* related the various fruits of various good acts. The *Kuru* princes became filled with wonder at his doctrine, as narrated by Ṛ. of old (XIII, **7**). *Yudhishṭhira* enquired who should be honoured and who liked, etc.; *Bhīshma's* answer about the duty of honouring good brahmans (XIII, **8**).—§ 725: *Yudhishṭhira's* enquiry about the misery that awaits those who refuse to make gifts to brahmans after having promised to give them. *Bhīshma* set forth the various kinds of misery that await such men, citing the old narrative of the discourse between a jackal and an ape: While both were human beings they were intimate friends; after death one of them became a jackal and the other an ape, the former because he had not given to a brahman what he had promised to give, the latter because he used to appropriate the fruits belonging to brahmans. *Bhīshma* had heard this from his preceptor and from *Kṛshṇa* (XIII, **9**).—§ 726: *Yudhishṭhira* wished to know whether any fault is incurred by one who gives instruction to a person belonging to a low caste. *Bhīshma* recited what he had heard certain Ṛ. say in days of yore: instruction should not be imparted to one that belongs to a low or mean caste. He related the following instance that occurred in days of old: There was a sacred hermitage on the *Himavat*, inhabited by Si., Cā., *Vālakhilyas*, etc. (description). A *Çūdra* asked the head of the college (*kulapati*) to initiate him into a life of renunciation, but he was refused. He then, at some distance, made a hut, etc., for himself, and began to live according to rigid vows, made sacrifices to the gods, etc. (description). A Ṛ. used to come to him, and, at his request, promised to assist him in *Pitṛ-yajña*. As the *Çūdra* placed the [stool called] *bṛsī* towards the south with its head turned towards the west, Ṛ. told him to place the *bṛsī* with its head turned towards the east, and to sit with his face turned towards the north, and gave him all directions about the *çrāddha* as laid down in the ordinances, and after the rites had been accomplished Ṛ. returned to his own abode. After a long time the *Çūdra* ascetic met with his death in those woods, and in his next life took birth in the family of a great king; the Ṛ. in his next life took birth in the family of a priest, and became well versed in the *Atharvaveda*, etc. (*a*); the reborn *Çūdra* was installed king after his father's death. He appointed the reborn Ṛ. as his priest, and ruled his kingdom righteously; but every day, when he saw his priest, he smiled or laughed. The priest made him swear to tell him the truth, and he was then informed by him about their former births, where the penances of Ṛ. had all been frustrated by the instruction he had given to the *Çūdra*. In order that he might not obtain a still lower birth in his next life, he caused him to relinquish his present office as priest, make gifts, and observe vows, repairing to many sacred places, and at last, his soul having become purified, living in that very asylum where he had lived in his former birth, practising very severe penances; thus he succeeded in attaining to the highest success (XIII, **10**).—§ 727: *Yudhishṭhira* enquired after the nature of the man or the woman in whom the goddess of Prosperity always dwells. *Bhīshma* related the conversation between *Rukmiṇī* (the mother of *Pradyumna* with the *Makara* banner) and the goddess *Çrī*, whom she once asked this question in the presence of *Devakī's* son (XIII, **11**).—§ 728: *Yudhishṭhira* enquired which of the two, man or woman, derives the greater pleasure from sexual union. *Bhīshma* told the old story of the discourse between *Bhañgāsvana* and *Çakra*, i.e. Bhañgāsvanopākhyāna (*b*), (XIII, **12**).—§ 729: *Yudhishṭhira* asked how one should act in order to live happily both here and hereafter; *Bhīshma's* answer indicating the chief duties of commission and omission (XIII, **13**).—§ 730: Asked by *Yudhishṭhira*, *Bhīshma* discoursed about the different names of *Mahādeva* and his puissance, but soon caused *Kṛshṇa* to take up the topic before the conclave of Ṛ. with *Vyāsa*, just as Ṛ. *Taṇḍin*, the offspring of *Brahmán*, had in days of yore told the 1,000 names of *Mahādeva* before *Brahmán* in *Brahmaloka*. "After twelve years had expired from the time when *Pradyumna* (the son of *Rukmiṇī*) slew the *Asura Çambara* in days of yore, my spouse *Jāmbavatī* (seeing the sons of *Rukmiṇī*—*Pradyumna*, *Cārudeshṇa*, etc.) asked me to grant her a heroic son, saying: 'By worshipping *Mahādeva* for twelve years and emaciating thyself in observing vows, thou hast begotten the sons *Cārudeshṇa*, etc., with *Rukmiṇī* (*a*).' She prayed that *Brahmán*, etc. (*β*), would protect me; I took leave of *Āhuka*, etc. (*γ*), and *Garuḍa* bore me to *Himavat*, where I dismissed him; I there saw the asylum (description) of *Upamanyu Vaiyāghrapadya*, reverenced by D., G., and K., adorned with *Gañgā*, etc. *Upamanyu* directed me to devote myself to penances and gratify *Çiva*, here where D. and Ṛ. had in days of yore gratified him, who took his birth as Dā. *Hiraṇyakaçipu* (*b*), who was the father of *Mandāra* (*c*), irresistible even to *Vishṇu's* discus *Sudarçana* (*d*); *Çiva* had further granted boons to the *Dānavas* (or *Asuras*) *Vidyutprabha* (*e*), *Çatamukha* (*f*), and to *Brahmán*, etc. (*δ*); the sacrifice *Saptakapāla*, etc. (*ζ*).

Having narrated his former relations to *Mahādeva*, *Upamanyu* (*g*) there pointed out to me Si., Ṛ., V.-D., Y., G., Aps., etc., and said that in the sixth month from that time I should behold *Mahādeva* and obtain twenty-four boons from him and *Umā*. He gave me certain *mantras*, by reciting which I was sure to behold *Çaṅkara*. On the eighth day I underwent the *dīkshā*, etc. (description); for one month I lived on fruits, etc.; then I beheld *Mahādeva* (description) and *Umā* in a cloud (description), surrounded by 1,100 *Rudras*, etc., praised by Ā., V., V.-D., A., *Indra*, etc. (*ω*), uttered the *Rathantara Sāman* in the presence of *Bhava* (Çiva). Innumerable masters of *Yoga*, etc. (**aa**), were bowing down to him; *Sanatkumāra*, etc. (*ββ*), were beheld by me standing there in their bodily forms; Lp., etc. (*γγ*), were seen to bow down to *Çiva*; G. and Aps. sang and hymned him; V.-D., etc. (*δδ*), were adoring him in thought, word, and deed; *Brahmán*, *Çakra*, etc., looked at me; I, however, had not the power to look at *Mahādeva*. I saluted *Mahādeva*: 'Thou art,' etc. (*εε*). *Çiva* roared like a lion; the innumerable brahmans there present, etc. (*ζζ*), bowed down to *Çiva*. *Çiva*, looking at *Umā*, *Indra*, and myself, told me to ask for eight boons" (XIII, **14**). *Kṛshṇa* went on to enumerate the eight boons, including hundreds upon hundreds of children and (granted by *Umā* in the name of *Çiva*) a son *Çāmba*. "*Umā* also granted me eight boons" (including 100 sons), "and said that I should have 16,000 wives, etc.; and that 7,000 guests would daily feed at my palace. Then *Çiva* and *Umā* disappeared with their *gaṇas*. All this I related to *Upamanyu*" (XIII, **15**). *Upamanyu* said: There was in the *Kṛta* age a Ṛ. *Taṇḍi* who devoutly adored the god [Çiva] for 10,000 years. He succeeded in beholding *Mahādeva* and praised him (*ηη*), and further said: Neither *Brahmán*, etc. (*θθ*), know thee. *Çiva* said that *Taṇḍi* should be imperishable and eternal, etc., and his son become the author of *Sūtras*, etc., and granted him a boon. *Taṇḍi* said: Let my devotion to thee be steady. Then the god disappeared. Then *Taṇḍi* came to my (i.e. Upamanyu's) asylum and told me all that had happened to him. Dost thou hear all those celebrated names [of Mahādeva] that *Taṇḍi* said unto me. *Brahmán* had at one time enumerated 10,000 names of *Mahādeva*; in the scriptures 1,000 names of him occur. They are not known to all, but were uttered in days of yore by *Brahmán* for the purpose of adoring *Çiva*. Having acquired them by the favour of *Brahmán*, *Taṇḍi* communicated them to me (XIII, **16**). *Kṛshṇa* said: "B.-ṛ. *Upamanyu* said: I shall adore [Çiva] with names uttered by *Brahmán*, Ṛ., in the *Vedas* and *Vedāṅgas*, applied by *Taṇḍi*, etc. [i.e. Mahādeva-sahasranāma-stotra]." Blessing upon the reader; "Dā., Y., Rā., Pç., *Yātudhānas*, and Gh. can do no injury to him" (XIII, **17**). *Vyāsa* told *Yudhishṭhira* to gratify *Çiva* with this hymn consisting of 1,008 names; *Vyāsa* had himself recited it in former days, when engaged in penances on *Meru* in order to obtain a son, and he had obtained the fulfilment of all his wishes. After this *Kapila*, etc. (*ιι*), obtained boons from *Çiva*. Then [*Rāma*] *Jāmadagnya*, etc. (*κκ*), narrated to *Yudhishṭhira* the boons they had been granted by *Çiva*. *Vaiçampāyana* continued: Hearing these marvellous feats of *Mahādeva* related by the ascetics, *Yudhishṭhira* became amazed. Then *Kṛshṇa* said to *Yudhishṭhira*: *Upamanyu* said to me: Unrighteous men, stained by *Rajas* and *Tamas*, do not succeed in attaining to *Īçāna* (Çiva); even if a person lives in the enjoyment of every pleasure and luxury, yet he comes to be regarded as the equal of pure-minded forest recluses if he is devoted to the Supreme Deity; if *Rudra* is pleased with a person, he can confer upon him the position of either *Brahmán* or *Keçava* or *Çakra* with all the deities under him, or the sovereignty of the three worlds; a person who devastates the whole universe does not become stained with sin if he adores and worships *Çiva* . . . . Then *Kṛshṇa* said to *Yudhishṭhira*: *Āditya*, etc. (*λλ*), have sprung from that creator of all creatures (Çiva); indeed, that subtle *Brahmán* is the cause of life. Blessing upon the reader (XIII, **18**). [§ 730, i.e. XIII, **14–18**, is called *Meghavāhanopākhyāna*.]—§ 731: *Yudhishṭhira* enquired after the purport of the scriptural injunction to husband and wife about the joint performance of all duties. *Bhīshma* related the old narrative of the discourse between *Ashṭāvakra* and *Diçā*, i.e. Ashṭāvakra-Dik-saṃvāda (*b*), (XIII, **19–21**).—§ 732: Asked by *Yudhishṭhira*, *Bhīshma* discoursed on the question who is worthy of receiving gifts, etc., quoting Ṛ. *Mārkaṇḍeya*, etc. (**a**), (XIII, **22**). Asked by *Yudhishṭhira*, *Bhīshma* discussed the ordinances regulating the actions to be perpetrated towards the deities and the *Pitṛs* on the occasions of *çrāddhas*: "One should carefully perform all acts relating to the deities in the forenoon, and all acts relating to the *Pitṛs* in the afternoon; that gift that is made untimely, etc., is appropriated by Rā."; the brahmans that must not be invited to *çrāddhas*, and those that should be invited, etc.; *Jātakarman*, etc. (XIII, **23**). Asked by *Yudhishṭhira*, *Bhīshma* discussed the circumstances under which a person may become guilty of brahmanicide without actually slaying a brahman (XIII, **24**).—§ 733: Asked by *Yudhishṭhira* about the holy places on earth, *Bhīshma* repeated the enumeration of them (*a*) made by *Aṅgiras* to *Gautama*, who put this same question, especially mentioning the result of bathing in *Candrabhāgā*, etc. (*b*), in *Pushkara*, etc. (*c*), in *Hiraṇyabindu*, etc. (*d*), in *Indratoyā*, etc. (*e*), in *Gaṅgādvāra*, etc. (*f*), at *Saptagaṅga*, etc. (*g*), at *Kanyākūpa*, etc. (*h*), in *Devikā*, etc. (*i*), *Mahāgaṅgā*, etc. (*j*), *Vaimānika*, etc. (*k*), in *Çarastamba*, etc. (*l*), *Citrakūṭa*, etc. (*m*), *Mataṅgavāpī*, etc. (*n*), *Gaṅgāhrada*, etc. (*o*), *Gaṅgā-Yamunayos tīrtham*, etc. (*p*), *Marudgaṇa*, etc. (*q*), *Utpātaka*, etc. (*r*), *Açmapṛshṭha*, etc. (*s*), *Viçālā*, etc. (*t*), *Punarāvartanandā*, etc. (*u*), *Rāmahrada*, etc. (*v*), *Narmadā*, etc. (*w*), *Cāṇḍālikāçrama* (B. *Āñjali°*), etc. (*x*), *Ujjānaka*, etc. (*y*), *Kālodaka*, etc. (*z*). For the purpose of repairing to all the *tīrthas* in the world, one should mentally think of those amongst them that are wholly or almost inaccessible. *Aṅgiras* had obtained this discourse from *Kaçyapa*. Blessing upon the reader (XIII, **25**).—§ 734: *Vaiçampāyana* said: Though equal unto *Bṛhaspati* in intelligence, *Brahmán* in forgiveness, *Indra* in prowess, and *Sūrya* in energy, *Bhīshma* (the son of *Gaṅgā*) had been overthrown in battle by *Arjuna*. Accompanied by his brothers, etc., *Yudhishṭhira* asked him these questions. He was lying on a bed of arrows in expectation of the time of death. Many M.-ṛ. had come there to see him: *Atri*, etc. (**a**). *Yudhishṭhira* with his brothers duly worshipped those Ṛ., who then sat down and conversed about *Bhīshma* (who became delighted), and then, taking leave of *Bhīshma* and the *Pāṇḍavas*, made themselves invisible. The *Pāṇḍavas* then waited upon *Bhīshma*, and seeing the quarters of the sky blazing forth with splendour on account of the penances of the *Ṛshis*, they became filled with wonder, and talked it over with *Bhīshma*. *Vaiçampāyana* continued: After that conversation was over, *Yudhishṭhira* touched *Bhīshma's* feet with his head, and then resumed his questions relating to morality and righteousness. *Yudhishṭhira* asked which countries, retreats, mountains, and rivers are foremost in point of sanctity. *Bhīshma* related the old narrative of a conversation between a brahman who was a *çiloñcha-vṛtti* (subsisting upon gleanings) (or *çilavṛtti*) householder and a *siddha* (crowned with ascetic success) Ṛ., who roamed over the earth and once had passed the night in the house of the *çilavṛtti*, who, when they had conversed on subjects connected with the *Vedas* and *Upanishads*, asked him this very question, and was instructed by him about the superior sanctity of *Gaṅgā*. Then the *siddha* ascended the firmament, and the *çilavṛtti* sought the protection of *Gaṅgā* and attained to great success. *Yudhishṭhira*, etc., were filled with delight. Blessing upon the reader (XIII, **26**).—§ 735: *Yudhishṭhira* asked how a *Kshattriya*, *Vaiçya*, or *Çūdra* may acquire the position of a brahman. *Bhīshma* said that the brahmanhood cannot be acquired except by birth, relating an old story of a conversation between *Mataṅga* and a she-ass, etc., i.e. *Indra-Mataṅga-saṃvāda* (*b*), (XIII, **27–29**).—§ 736: *Yudhishṭhira* mentioned that in former times the position of a brahman was acquired by *Viçvāmitra*, and asked how king *Vītahavya* in ancient times succeeded in obtaining brahmanhood. *Bhīshma* told the Vītahavyopākhyāna (*b*), (XIII, **30**).—§ 737: Asked by *Yudhishṭhira* as to who are worthy of reverent homage, *Bhīshma* repeated the old narrative of the discourse between *Nārada* and *Vāsudeva*, who asked him the above question. *Nārada* answered: "I worship them who constantly worship *Varuṇa*, etc." (*a*), (XIII, **31**).—§ 738: Asked by *Yudhishṭhira* about the merits of those persons who grant protection to living creatures, *Bhīshma* told the Çyenakapotākhyāna (*b*), (XIII, **32**).—§ 739: Asked by *Yudhishṭhira* which act is the most important of all those that have been laid down for a king, *Bhīshma* said it was the worship of *brahmans*; they are older than P., D., men, U., and Rā., and incapable of being vanquished by D., P., G., Rā., As., or Pç.; it is owing to the absence of *brahmans* that the *Kshattriya* tribes, the *Çakas*, etc. (*a*), have become degraded into the state of *Çūdras*; the great Ṛ. have said that brahmanicide is a heinous sin (XIII, **33**); they have *Soma* for their king; "this was said to me by *Nārada*"; *Āditya*, etc. (*β*), enter the body of the brahman and take what the brahman eats; in the house where *brahmans* do not eat, P. refuse to eat; examples of *brahmans* (*γ*) who have conquered *Kshattriyas*; "in this connection the old story of the conversation between *Vāsudeva* and the *Earth*," who instructed the former, is told; examples of discomfiture arising from acts hurtful to the *brahmans* (*δ*), (XIII, **34**). *Bhīshma's* characterisation of *brahmans*; the *Mekalas*, etc. (*ε*), and numerous other *kshattriya* tribes have become degraded to the state of *Çūdras* through the wrath of the *brahmans*; having disregarded the *brahmans*, As. have been obliged to take refuge in the depths of the ocean; through the favour of the *brahmans* D. have become denizens of heaven; comparisons with *brahmans* (*ζ*): the *brahmans* are incapable of being subjugated (XIII, **35**).—§ 740: *Bhīshma* told the old history of the discourse between *Çakra* (in the guise of an ascetic—description—on an ugly car) and As. *Çambara*, who ascribed his success to his never cherishing any ill-feeling towards the *brahmans*, referring to the encounter between D. and As. in days of old; *Çambara's* father had obtained instruction from *Candramas* (*Soma*, the Moon) as to how the *brahmans* attain to success. *Çakra* began to worship the *brahmans*, and therefore succeeded in obtaining the supremacy of the gods (XIII, **36**).—§ 741: Asked by *Yudhishṭhira*, *Bhīshma* discussed the comparative eligibility of *brahmans* for receiving presents; "one pays off the debt one owes to the gods by performing sacrifices, to P. by procreating children, to the *brahmans* by making presents unto them, and to the guests by feeding them" (XIII, **37**).—§ 742: Asked by *Yudhishṭhira* about the disposition of women (who are said to be the root of all evil and exceedingly frail), *Bhīshma* told the old story of the discourse between D.-ṛ. *Nārada* and the courtezan Aps. *Pañcacūḍā*, in ancient times, in the region of *Brahmán* (*Brāhmīṃ*, so PCR.), (XIII, **38**). *Yudhishṭhira* observed that women are in possession of the illusive power of As. *Çambara*, etc. (*a*), and the political knowledge of *Çukra* and *Bṛhaspati*; "it seems to me that *Bṛhaspati* and other great thinkers evolved the science of politics from observation of the understanding of women" (XIII, **39**).—§ 743: *Bhīshma* approved of what *Yudhishṭhira* had said: "There is no creature more sinful than woman; she is the illusion that Dai. *Maya* created, etc.; I am told that all persons of the human race in course of natural progress attain to the state of gods; this circumstance alarmed the gods; they repaired to *Brahmán*, who created women by an *Atharvan* rite; in a previous creation women were all virtuous; but those that sprang from this creation by *Brahmán* with the aid of an illusion became sinful; *Brahmán* bestowed the desire of enjoying all kinds of carnal pleasures upon them." *Bhīshma* repeated the old story of how, in days of yore, *Vipula* had succeeded in restraining his preceptor's spouse, i.e. Vipulopākhyāna (*b*), (XIII, **40–43**).—§ 744: Asked by *Yudhishṭhira*, *Bhīshma* explained upon what person one should bestow one's daughter in marriage; the different forms of marriage (*a*); various ordinances about marriage, quoting *Prajāpati* and *Manu* and the *Maruts* and the *Ṛshis*; what constitutes or completes the union of marriage; the passing and acceptance of a dower do not constitute marriage. *Bhīshma* referred to the opinion of *Bāhlīka* and his own conduct in liberating *Ambā*, whom he had abducted for his brother *Vicitravīrya*, having defeated the *Māgadhas*, etc. (*β*), quoting prince *Satyavat* (XIII, **44**). Asked by *Yudhishṭhira*, *Bhīshma* expounded how a girl's kinsmen should act after having received a dower if the giver goes away without marrying and does not return for some time, comparing the instance of *Sāvitrī* and quoting *Sukratu* (the grandson of the *Videha* king *Janaka*); the unrighteous dereliction of eternal usage is regarded as the practice of the *Asuras*. Asked by *Yudhishṭhira* upon what authority the wealth of men is inherited by others when they happen to have daughters, *Bhīshma* explained the different rules of succession, and recited some verses sung in days of yore by *Yama* about the man who sells his son or bestows his daughter for a dower (he has to sink into seven terrible hells named *Kāla*); the *Ārsha* marriage is also a sale; "even a human being with whom one has no relationship of blood should not form the subject of sale" (XIII, **45**); a verse of [Daksha] *Prācetasa*; how women should be treated; "those houses that are cursed by women meet with destruction and ruin as if scorched by some *Atharvan* rite"; *Manu*, on the eve of his departure for heaven, entrusted women to the care and protection of men; a verse sung by a princess of the house of the *Videha* king *Janaka* on the duties of women (XIII, **46**). Asked by *Yudhishṭhira*, *Bhīshma* discussed the comparative eligibility of different kinds of sons to the father's inheritance, quoting *Manu* and Ṛ., and M.-ṛ. *Kaçyapa* (B. *Kā°*) *Mārīca*; "if a brahman, led by lust, acts in a different way, he shall come to be regarded as a *Caṇḍāla* among brahmans" (XIII, **47**). Asked by *Yudhishṭhira*, *Bhīshma* discussed the duties of persons born in the mixed castes; in the beginning *Prajāpati* created the four castes for the sake of sacrifice; the son begotten by a *brahman* upon a *Çūdra* wife is called *Pāraçava* (etymology); a *Kshattriya's* son with a *Çūdra* wife is called an *Ugra*, etc. (γ); only the duties of the four principal castes have been laid down in the scriptures; as regards the others, the scriptures are entirely silent. Asked by *Yudhishṭhira*, *Bhīshma* discussed the signs by which the origin of men of impure birth may be known (XIII, **48**). Asked by *Yudhishṭhira*, *Bhīshma* discussed the different kinds of sons: *Niruktaja*, etc. (δ), (XIII, **49**).—§ 745: Asked by *Yudhishṭhira* about compassion, etc., *Bhīshma* told the ancient story of a conversation between *Nahusha* and M.-ṛ. *Cyavana*, i.e. Cyavanopākhyāna (*b*), including Cyavana-Kuçika-saṃvāda (XIII, **50-56**). — § 746: *Yudhishṭhira* became stupefied with grief at the thought of the millions of men he had slaughtered; he feared that the *Pāṇḍavas* would have to sink in hell, their heads hanging downwards, and desired to practise severe penances. *Bhīshma* expounded the different rewards of different kinds of acts. *Yudhishṭhira* desired to attain the end that is reserved to heroes, and no longer expressed any disgust at leading a householder's mode of life, and all the *Pāṇḍavas* with *Draupadī* approved of his words (XIII, **57**). Asked by *Yudhishṭhira*, *Bhīshma* spoke of the rewards attached to the planting of trees and the digging of wells and tanks; D., men, G., P., U., and Rā., etc., all resort to a tank full of water as their refuge; the same and Ṛ. all have recourse to trees (XIII, **58**). Asked by *Yudhishṭhira*, *Bhīshma* discussed what gift is distinguished before all other gifts (XIII, **59**). Asked by *Yudhishṭhira*, *Bhīshma* discussed which gift is more meritorious, that bestowed on one who asks for it or that given to an unsoliciting person (XIII, **60**). Asked by *Yudhishṭhira*, *Bhīshma* explained where one meets with the rewards attached to gifts and sacrifices, adducing the instances of king *Çibi* and *Manu* (XIII, **61**). Asked by *Yudhishṭhira* what is the best of all gifts, *Bhīshma* declared it to be earth (called, therefore, *Priyadattā*); *Mṛtyu*, etc. (*a*), are incapable of touching the person that makes a gift of earth; the verse hearing which [*Rāma*] *Jāmadagnya* gave away the whole earth to *Kaçyapa* is quoted; a gift of earth is a high expiation for the sin of those who betake themselves to *Atharvan* rites in order to do injuries to others; Ā., etc. (β), applaud the man who makes a gift of earth; he further told the old narrative of a discourse between *Bṛhaspati* and *Indra*: having adored *Vishṇu* in 100 sacrifices, *Indra* put this same question to *Bṛhaspati*, and was instructed by him; "that man who does not keep a promise of a gift of earth, or who recalls it, is tied with the noose of *Varuṇa* at the command of Death; those men have never to go to *Yama* who honour and worship brahmans, etc."; that king who makes gifts of earth sports in bliss in heaven, adored by D. and G., and is approached by 100 Aps., etc. *Indra* gave the whole earth to *Bṛhaspati*; if these verses are recited at a *çrāddha* neither Rā. nor As. can succeed in appropriating any share of the offerings made (XIII, **62**). Asked by *Yudhishṭhira* as to what gifts kings should make, what gifts immediately gratify the brahmans, what fruits attach to them, what gifts are productive of rewards both here and hereafter, *Bhīshma* related the answer he had received from *Nārada* when he put the same question to him: a gift of food made to even a *Caṇḍāla* or a dog is never lost; in a former *Kalpa* (*purā kalpe*) *Prajāpati* said that food is *amṛta*, etc.; *Agni* and *Soma* in the body create and maintain the vital seed; thus the sun and wind (*Pavanaḥ*) and the vital seed spring and act from food; description of the regions of heaven reserved to those that make gifts of food (XIII, **63**). *Yudhishṭhira* enquired after the conjunctions of the planets and stars in relation to gifts. *Bhīshma* repeated the ancient narrative of the discourse between *Devakī* and Ṛ. *Nārada* at *Dvārakā*, where *Nārada* answered this very question. *Devakī* in her turn told it to her daughters-in-law (XIII, **64**). Various merits of various kinds of gifts, *Bhīshma* referring to *Atri*, etc. (γ); ghee is said to gratify *Bṛhaspati*, etc. (δ), (XIII, **65**). Asked by *Yudhishṭhira*, *Bhīshma* commented on the gift of sandals and shoes, and of sesame, and land, and kine, and food; sesame seeds were created by *Brahmán* as the best food of the *Pitṛs*, etc.; *Āpastamba*, etc. (ε), have all ascended to heaven by means of making gifts of sesame seeds. Once the gods, desirous of performing a sacrifice on the earth, repaired to *Brahmán* on the *Himavat* and obtained from him a clod of earth (which the *munis* should always adore); there came *Agastya*, etc. (ζ); the gods attached one-sixth of the merit arising from their sacrifice to the gift of earth; in days of yore king *Rantideva* performed a grand sacrifice, in which an immense number of kine were slaughtered; from the juice of their skins the river *Carmaṇvatī* was formed; king *Rantideva*, in days of yore, ascended to heaven on account of his having given gifts of food; the cow should never be given away for slaughter; what kine should not be given to brahmans; he referred to *Parāçara*; the seasons when gifts of food produce particular merits (XIII, **66**). Asked by *Yudhishṭhira*, *Bhīshma* dealt with the merits that attach to gifts of drink, quoting *Sāvitrī* and *Lomaça* and *Manu*, and mentioning *Çibi*; *Soma*, etc. (η), has sprung from water; D. have *amṛta* for their food, N. have *Sudhā*, P. have *Svadhā* (XIII, **67**). *Yudhishṭhira* asked about the merits that attach to gifts of sesame and lamps for lighting darkness, as also of food and robes; *Bhīshma* told the narrative of the conversation between a brahman and *Yama*, in ancient times, in the large town of *Parṇaçālā* (inhabited by brahmans) between *Yamunā* and *Gaṅgā*, at the foot of the *Yamunā* hills; one day *Yama* commanded a messenger of his (description) to bring the person named *Çarmin* of *Agastya's* race from this town (*Agastyaṃ gotrataḥ*), not confounding him with another of the same *gotra*; he should be worshipped with respect. The messenger did the very reverse; *Yama* ordered this man to be taken back and *Çarmin* to be brought; the former was, however, first instructed by *Yama* regarding gifts. Then the messenger conveyed him back and fetched *Çarmin*; *Yama*, having given him the same instructions, dismissed him to be taken back to his abode. The giver of a lamp is regarded as benefiting the *Pitṛs* and *Yama*; it enhances the power of vision of D., P., and one's self; citing *Manu* about a gift of gems (XIII, **68**). *Bhīshma*, at *Yudhishṭhira's* solicitation, reverted to the topic of the merits of gifts, with especial reference to the gift of earth; a cow should never be given to a person that is not righteous (XIII, **69**). The tale of the calamity that befell king *Nṛga*, who had unwittingly taken a cow belonging to a brahman and given it away to another brahman. Formerly, when *Dvāravatī* was founded (read with B. *niviçantyām*), a huge lizard was seen (or met with?) in a well; *Kṛshṇa* took it out and learnt that it was king *Nṛga*, who in days of old had performed many sacrifices and repeatedly made gifts of hundreds upon hundreds of thousands of kine to the brahmans; a brahman's cow had accidentally come among *Nṛga's* and been given to another brahman, whose weak child it nourished; neither of them would take the most exorbitant gifts in exchange; after death, when he came to the region of the *Pitṛs*, *Yama* let him choose as his punishment for this little sin to become a lizard for 1,000 years, till he was rescued by *Vāsudeva*. Then *Nṛga* mounted a celestial car and proceeded to heaven; a verse of *Kṛshṇa's* is quoted (XIII, **70**). *Yudhishṭhira* asked *Bhīshma* to further detail the merits attainable by gifts of kine. *Bhīshma* told the old story of Ṛ. *Uddālaki* and his son *Nāciketa*, whom he had cursed to go and see *Yama*, because *Nāciketa* had not found the articles (enumeration) he was sent for, as they had been washed away by the current. *Nāciketa* fell down, deprived of life; *Uddālaki* indulged in lamentations; when the night came, *Nāciketa*, drenched with his father's tears, revived, and in the midst of the *Ṛshis* told that he had been honoured in *Yama's* delightful palace, which extended over 1,000 *yojanas*; "*Yama* said that I was not dead, but had only come to see *Yama* in compliance with the words of my father"; *Yama*, at his request, had caused him to be mounted on a vehicle and showed him all those delightful regions that are reserved for the righteous (description), who make gifts in the world of men, especially gifts of kine, etc. (considerations of propriety or otherwise); in the absence of kine, a person by making gifts of a substitute of kine (e.g. a cow made of ghee) wins the merit of making gifts of kine; gifts of kine on *kāmyāshṭamī*, etc.; "I then took leave of *Yama* and have now come back" (XIII, **71**). *Yudhishṭhira* asked about the regions of kine, which are the residence of givers of kine. *Bhīshma* related the old tale of the conversation between *Brahmán* and *Indra*, who, seeing that the residents of the regions of kine surpassed the denizens of heaven, asked *Brahmán* about them (XIII, **72**). The comments of *Brahmán* to *Indra* on the subject of kine, reference being made to *Ṛshis*, etc. (XIII, **73**). Asked by *Indra*, *Brahmán* spoke about the end of him who consciously steals a cow or sells one from motives of cupidity. *Bhīshma* explained how *Brahmán's* discourse had been handed down from *Indra* to *Bhīshma*: *Brahmán* > *Indra* > *Daçaratha* > *Rāma* [Dāçarathi] > *Lakshmaṇa* > the *Ṛshis* (while dwelling in the woods) > from generation to generation > *Bhīshma's* preceptor > *Bhīshma*. Blessing upon the reader (XIII, **74**). Asked by *Yudhishṭhira*, *Bhīshma* explained the rewards that attach to the observance of different kinds of vows; many millions of Ṛ. are residing in *Brahmaloka* (XIII, **75**). Asked by *Yudhishṭhira*, *Bhīshma* commented upon the ordinances that regulate gifts of kine, quoting the instruction given by *Bṛhaspati* to king *Māndhātṛ*; "kine have that in them that partakes of the nature of both *Sūrya* and *Soma*"; application of the words *bhavitavyā*, etc. (θ); all the three [cow-givers], etc., and he who is well conversant with the *Mahābhārata* attain to the regions of *Vishṇu* and *Soma*; names of kings who have attained to regions of great felicity as the reward of such gifts of kine as they made according to the instructions of *Bṛhaspati*: *Uçīnara*, etc. (ι).—*Vaiçampāyana* said: King *Yudhishṭhira* did all that *Bhīshma* wished; he from that time began always to make gifts of kine and to support himself on grains of barley and on cow-dung as his food and drink, and he began to sleep from that day on the bare earth, and gave up the practice of harnessing kine to his vehicles, and used cars drawn by horses (XIII, **76**). *Vaiçampāyana* continued: Asked by *Yudhishṭhira*, *Bhīshma* once more went into detail on the merits attaching to the gift of kine: a *Kapilā* cow is the best of all kine; *Yudhishṭhira* asked why; *Bhīshma* said he had heard old men tell the following story: In days of yore *Brahmán* commanded *Daksha* to create living creatures; *Daksha*, in the first instance, created food; he drank *amṛta*, a fragrant eructation came out, and gave birth to the cow *Surabhi*, whose daughters came to be regarded as the mothers of the world; they were all *Kapilās*; some froth from the calves fell upon the head of *Mahādeva*, who, filled with wrath, turned his third eye towards them, which produced various complexions in them; some escaped to the region of *Soma* and retained their colour. *Daksha* informed *Çiva* that this froth was *amṛta* and not impure; *Candramas* (the Moon), after drinking the *amṛta*, pours it out again; but it is not, on that account, regarded as impure. *Daksha* then presented *Mahādeva* with a bull and certain kine; *Mahādeva* was gratified and made that bull his vehicle, and after the form of that bull adopted the device on his standard; it was on that occasion also that the gods, uniting together, made *Mahādeva* the lord of animals. Cows yield *Soma* in the form of milk. Blessing upon the reader.—*Vaiçampāyana* continued: *Yudhishṭhira* and his brother began to make gifts of both bulls and cows of different colours to brahmans, *Yudhishṭhira* performing many sacrifices (XIII, **78**). *Bhīshma* said: In days of yore, king *Saudāsa* of *Ikshvāku's* race asked his *purohita* Ṛ. *Vasishṭha* what is most sacred and most productive of merit; *Vasishṭha* enlarged upon the mystery relating to kine; *svāhā* and *vashaṭ* are for ever established in kine; what is meant by *Gomatī* (XIII, **78**). Continuation of *Vasishṭha's* discourse on the pre-eminent sanctity of kine; the diverse merits attaching to gifts of different kinds of kine: *Brahmaloka*, etc. (κ), (XIII, **79**). *Vasishṭha* commented on the purificatory *mantras* having reference to kine; "those who make gifts of 1,000 kine, departing from this world, proceed to the region of G. and Aps., where there are many palatial mansions made of gold, and *Vasor dhārā* (i.e. Mandākinī, Nil.); . . . . by giving away a *Kapilā* cow, etc., one succeeds in entering the palace of *Yama* that is so difficult to enter."—*Bhīshma* said: *Saudāsa*, honouring these words of Ṛ. *Vasishṭha*, made gifts of a very large number of kine unto the brahmans, and attained to many worlds of felicity in the next life (XIII, **80**). *Yudhishṭhira* asked what is the most sacred of all sacred things in the world, and which is the highest of all sanctifying objects. *Bhīshma* said: Kine are the most excellent of all objects, etc.; *Māndhātṛ*, etc. (λ), always used to give away kine in thousands, and have attained to such regions as are unattainable even by the gods; he quoted a discourse delivered of old. *Çuka* (having finished his morning observances) asked Ṛ. *Vyāsa* what is the foremost of all sacrifices, and was instructed by him, who praised kine and described the region of kine which the blessed only attain; Aps. always entertain them there; those regions that have for their lords *Pūshan* and the *Maruts* are attained to by givers of kine; they attain to wealth like that of *Varuṇa* himself; one should daily recite these *mantras* (μ) declared by *Prajāpati* himself. [In this section *Yudhishṭhira* has repeatedly been addressed instead of *Çuka.*] The man who, for a month, subsists upon the gruel of barley picked up every day from cow-dung, becomes free of sins as grave as the slaughter of a brahman: after their defeat at the hands of Dai., the gods practised this penance, owing to which they regained their position; the efficaciousness of the *Gomatī mantras.*—*Bhīshma* said: From that time *Çuka* began to worship kine every day (XIII, **81**). *Yudhishṭhira* asked how it is that the dung of the cow is possessed of *Çrī*. *Bhīshma* told the old story of the conversation between the kine and *Çrī*, who once in a beautiful form entered a herd of cows, saying: "The *Daityas*, forsaken by me, have been lost for ever; the gods *Indra*, etc. (ν), having obtained me, are sporting in joy and will do so for ever; Ṛ. and D. only when they are favoured by me become crowned with success"; she wished to reside in the kine; they refused her, saying she was fickle and restless. *Çrī* said: "D., Dā., G., Pç., U., Rā., and men succeed in obtaining me only after the severest austerities"; they agreed that she should live in their urine and dung (XIII, **82**). *Bhīshma* continued his discourse on kine, repeating the old tale of the discourse between *Brahmán* and *Indra*, after Dai. had been defeated and all creatures grew in prosperity; then once Ṛ., G., K., U., Rā., D., As., the birds, and the *Prajāpatis* all adored *Brahmán*; *Nārada*, etc. (ξ), sang, etc. (ο); *Indra* asked him about the region of kine; *Brahmán* said that *Indra* had always disregarded kine, and commented to him on the superiority of kine. He explained to him why kine have descended to earth: In days of yore, when in the *Deva-yuga* the *Dānavas* became lords of the three worlds, *Aditi* underwent the severest austerities (standing upon one leg for many years) and begot *Vishṇu*; seeing *Aditi* perform penances, *Surabhī*, the daughter of *Daksha*, also underwent austerities on *Kailāsa* (resorted to by D. and G.), in *yoga*, standing upon one leg for 11,000 years; "D., Ṛ., and M.-U. became scorched and repaired thither with me (Brahmán); as she did not herself ask a favour, I granted her the boon of immortality, and that she should dwell in *Goloka*, while her offspring, engaged in doing good acts, would reside in the world of men (description of *Goloka*)." *Bhīshma* continued: From that time *Çakra* began to worship kine every day. Blessing upon the reader, etc. (XIII, **83**).—§ 747: *Yudhishṭhira* asked why gold, in the *Çrutis*, is declared to be even superior to kine as a *dakshiṇā*, and what gold is, etc. *Bhīshma* related the circumstances connected with the origin of gold: "When my father *Çāntanu* was dead, I went to *Gaṅgādvāra* to perform his *çrāddha*; *Gaṅgā* came and rendered me great help (description); a handsome arm, adorned with *aṅgadas*, etc., rose up piercing the ground; the P. did not come in their visible forms to take the cake; I, therefore, disregarding the hand, offered the whole cake on blades of *kuça*-grass, according to rule; then the arm of my father vanished. In that night the *Pitṛs* appeared to me in a dream, pleased by my adherence to the rules, whereby I had honoured the authority of the scriptures, etc. (**a**); I had made gifts of earth and kine; now I should make gifts of gold. Listen now to this old story, that extends the period of life for him who listens to it; it was first recited to *Rāma Jāmadagnya*, who in former days exterminated the *Kshattriyas* twenty-one times; by performing a horse-sacrifice he became free from sin, but he still failed to attain to perfect lightness of heart; he repaired to Ṛ. and D., then to *Vasishṭha*, etc. (β); they told him that in days of yore *Agni* burnt all the world; from his seed sprang gold; he should make gifts of gold; *Vasishṭha* in especial commented on gold: it is the essence of *Agni* and *Soma*, etc. (γ); such is the teaching of the *Smṛtis*; in churning the entire universe a mass of energy (i.e. gold) was found; hence gold is superior; D., G., U., Rā., men, and Pç. keep it with care; *Agni* is all the deities in one, and *Agni* is the essence of gold. I formerly heard this in the *Purāṇa*; it represents the speech of *Prajāpati* himself." Then he related Suvarṇotpatti (*b*), (XIII, **84–85**).—§ 748: Asked by *Yudhishṭhira* (who refers to § 747*b*), *Bhīshma* related Tārakavadhopākhyāna (*b*), (XIII, **86**).—§ 749: Asked by *Yudhishṭhira* (who perhaps refers to § 641 = XII, **60** ff.), *Bhīshma* explained the ordinances respecting the *çrāddha*. D., As., men, G., Pç., K., every one should always worship P. P. are worshipped before the gods. The merits and demerits of the different lunar days for performing the *çrāddha*: 1st–13th days of the bright fortnight are auspicious; all the young men in the family of him who performs it on the 14th day meet with death, and he himself becomes entangled in war; the day of the new moon and 10th–13th days of the dark fortnight are auspicious; the dark fortnight is better than the bright one, the afternoon better than the forenoon (XIII, **87**). Asked by *Yudhishṭhira*, *Bhīshma* explained what, if presented to P., becomes inexhaustible and eternal, and the periods for which different offerings presented at *çrāddhas* gratify the P., quoting some verses [originally] sung by P. and communicated to him by *Sanatkumāra*, recommending *pāyasa* with ghee on the 13th day [of the dark fortnight, PCR.] under *Maghāḥ* during the Sun's southward course, and, under the same constellation, meat of goat, etc., and *çrāddhas* at *Gayā* (*b*), (XIII, **88**); the different merits acquired by persons by performing optional (*kāmyāni*) *çrāddhas* under various *nakshatras*, and which were [first] explained by *Yama* to *Çaçabindu*: by performing such a *çrāddha* under the *Kṛttikās*, "a man acquires the merit of a sacrifice after establishing the sacred fire, and ascends to heaven with his children" (PCR.), etc. (**a**). Having listened to these ordinances about the *çrāddha*, *Çaçabindu* acted accordingly, and easily subjugated and ruled the earth (XIII, **89**). Asked by *Yudhishṭhira*, *Bhīshma* explained to what kinds of brahmans the offerings made at *çrāddhas* should be given away, quoting the *Vaikhānasa Ṛshis* (XIII, **90**). Asked by *Yudhishṭhira* by whom the *çrāddha* was first conceived, etc., in the time when the world was only peopled by the descendants of *Bhṛgu* and *Aṅgiras* (*Bhṛgv-Aṅgirasake kāle*), etc., *Bhīshma* said: *Brahmán* > *Atri* > *Dattātreya* > *Nimi* > *Çrīmat*. After 1,000 years *Çrīmat* died, having undergone the severest austerities; *Nimi*, filled with grief, collected various agreeable objects on the 14th day of the moon, and the next morning he conceived the idea of a *çrāddha*; on the day of the new moon he invited a number of respected brahmans, gave food to seven such brahmans, and made an offering of cakes of rice to his dead son, uttering his name and family (*nāma-gotraṃ*). He then became filled with regret, having done an act that was not laid down in the scriptures [that a father had done with reference to his son what sons ought to do with reference to their fathers, PCR.]; he thought of *Atri*, who came and comforted him, saying that this sacrifice in honour of the *Pitṛs* had been laid down and its rites regulated by *Brahmán* himself in days of yore: one should pour out libations to *Agni*, etc. (β); the gods named *Pitṛs* [and] *Ushṇapas* [so

B. and C.; cf. BR., v. *Ūshmapa*] were created by *Svayambhū* (i.e. Brahmán) and consist of seven classes (*saptakaḥ pitṛvaṃças tu*): when they are honoured by a *çrāddha*, they become freed from sin; the *Viçvedevas* [sixty-four (γ) are enumerated], having *Agni* for their mouth, they are eternal (? *Kālasya gatigocarāḥ*; C. °*syāga*°; "eternal and conversant with all that occurs in time," PCR.). Articles that should not be offered at *çrāddhas*. From the place of a *çrāddha* a *Cāṇḍāla* and a *Çvapaca* should be excluded, as also one who wears yellow clothes (*Kāshāyavāsāḥ*), a leper, an outcast (*patitaḥ*), etc. Having said this to Ṛ. *Nimi*, *Atri* went back to the celestial palace of *Pitāmaha* (Brahmán) (XIII, **91**). After *Nimi* had acted in this way, M.-ṛ. performed a *çrāddha*. The *Pitṛs* and gods became afflicted with indigestion in consequence of the offerings (*nivāpa*) made by persons of the four castes. They repaired to *Soma*, and thence to *Svayambhū* (on the summit of *Meru*), and thence to *Agni*. *Agni* told them to eat those offerings together with him. It is for this reason that in making offerings at *çrāddhas* a share is first offered to *Agni*; then also the *Brahma-Rākshasas* cannot do any injury to the *çrāddha*; but the *Rakshases* fly away from it (v. 4383–4). The cake should first be offered to the [deceased] father, then to the grandfather, then to the great-grandfather; at each cake the *Sāvitrī* should be uttered (*Somāyeti ca vaktavyaṃ tathā pitṛmateti ca*); a woman of another *gotra* (*anyavaṃçajā*), etc., should not assist at a *çrāddha*; while crossing a river, one should offer oblations of water to one's P., and also on the day of the new moon (*māsardhhe kṛshṇapakshasya*); this gives prosperity, etc.; *Brahmán*, etc. (*c*), are great masters of *yoga* and [numbered among] P. (XIII, **92**).—§ 750: Asked by *Yudhishṭhira*, *Bhīshma* said that brahmans who are observant of vows not mentioned in the *Vedas* may eat at *çrāddhas* without incurring sin; but not so those who are observant of vows mentioned in the *Vedas*. Penance is not really identifiable with fast; one should not torment one's own body; renunciation is the best of penances; the brahman should eat *Vighasa* or *Amṛta* (i.e. food that remains after the guests, etc., have eaten); one should only eat morning and evening at the prescribed hours, etc.; such men obtain felicity in the abode of *Brahmán* in the company of Aps. and G. If the giver happens to be unrighteous, the receiver sinks into hell. In this connection an old tale of a conversation between *Vṛshādarbhi* and the seven *Ṛshis* is told: Bisastainyopākhyāna (*b*) (XIII, **93**).—§ 751: *Bhīshma* said: In this connection the old story of the oaths on the occasion of a *tīrthayātrā* [i.e. Çapathavidhi] is told (*b*) (XIII, **94**).—§ 752: Asked by *Yudhishṭhira* by whom the custom of giving umbrellas and sandals at *çrāddhas* was introduced, *Bhīshma* related the story of the discourse between *Jamadagni* and *Sūrya* [i.e. Chattropānahotpatti] (*b*). "Do thou, therefore, give away umbrellas and shoes to brahmans. He who gives away a white umbrella with 100 ribs to a brahman attains to eternal felicity after death in *Çakra-loka*, being respected by brahmans, Aps., and D." (XIII, **95–96**).—§ 753: Asked by *Yudhishṭhira* about the duties of a householder, *Bhīshma* recited the old story of *Vāsudeva* (Kṛshṇa) and the goddess *Pṛthivī* (Earth), who instructed *Vāsudeva* on this very topic: Ṛ., D., P., and men should be worshipped . . . ; he should perform an *Agnī-Shoma*, *Vaiçvadeva*, and *Dhānvantarya* offering, and separately an offering to *Prajānāṃ pati*; and *bali* to *Yama*, etc. (*a*); he should daily perform a *çrāddha* (description); he should take his food last of all (*çishṭāçī*); he should with *madhuparka* honour a king, *ṛtvij*, *guru*, father-in-law, and *snātaka*; in the evening and morning he should place food on the ground for dogs, *çvapacas*, and birds: this is called the *Vaiçvadeva* offering. *Vāsudeva* acted accordingly (XIII, **97**).—§ 754: Asked by *Yudhishṭhira*, *Bhīshma*, in order to explain the gift of lamps, flowers, and incense, told the old story of the discourse between the Prajāpati *Manu Svāyambhuva* and the learned and noble brahman *Suvarṇa* (so called from his golden complexion) on the golden mountain *Meru*. Asked by *Suvarṇa* about the above-named topic, *Manu* related the old history of the discourse between *Çukra Bhārgava* and the *Asura* king *Bali Vairocana*, who ruled the three worlds. Asked by *Bali* about this very topic, *Çukra* discoursed on the plants (having *Soma* for their lord), of which some are *amṛta* (and agreeable to the gods, etc.) and some poison; some are acceptable to As., some to the gods, Rā., U., Y., men, P.; garlands of water flowers should be offered to G., N., and Y.; plants with red flowers and keen scent and having thorns have been laid down in the *Atharvans* as fit for incantation in order to injure foes, etc.; D. become gratified with the scent of flowers, Y. and Rā. with their sight, N. with their touch, men with all three. Among incenses, all exudations (except that of the *Boswellia serrata*) are agreeable to the gods; that of *Aquilaria Agallocha* to Y., Rā., and N.; that of *Boswellia serrata*, etc., to Dai., etc. [For avoiding] *Andhatamas* (B. °*aṃ ta*°; a certain hell, Nīl.), darkness, and the sun's southward course, one should give lights during the sun's northward course (Nīl. and the note of PCR., p. 477); D. are resplendent, Rā. dark; hence one should always give lights, etc.; thereby a man attains to the same world as the celestial lights (*jyotishāṃ sālokyaṃ*). The merits of *bali*-offerings made to D., Y., U., men, *Bhūtas*, and *Rā*. Y., Rā., Pn., D., P., etc., are supported by the food offered by the householder; the *bali* offered to Y. and Rā. should be rich in blood and meat, wines and spirits, etc.; *balis* with lotuses and *utpalas* are agreeable to N.; sesame seeds with sugar to the *Bhūtas*. He who eats without first serving brahmans and gods and guests and children, should be known as a Rā. Thus said *Kāvya Bhārgava* to *Bali*; then *Manu* > *Suvarṇa* > *Nārada* > *Bhīshma* (XIII, **98**).—§ 755: *Yudhishṭhira* (referring to § 754) once more questioned *Bhīshma* on this subject; *Bhīshma* told the old story of the discourse between *Nahusha* and *Agastya* and *Bhṛgu* [i.e. Nahushopākhyāna] (*b*) (XIII, **99–100**).—§ 756: Asked by *Yudhishṭhira* where those men go who steal articles belonging to brahmans, *Bhīshma* related the old conversation between a *Cāṇḍāla* and a *Kshattriya* (*Kshattrabandhoḥ*), who wondered that the old *Cāṇḍāla*, whose body was besmeared with the dust raised by dogs and asses, without minding that dust, was anxious to wash off the small drops of milk that had fallen upon his body; the *Cāṇḍāla* related that formerly some kine belonging to a brahman were stolen, and some milk from them fell upon some *Soma* plants that grew by the roadside; the king who performed the sacrifice with this *Soma*, the brahmans who drank its juice, those who had assisted at the sacrifice, and those who drank milk, etc., in the palace of this king, had to fall into hell, as also the sons and grandsons of those who had stolen them, and the queen, although she treated the animals with great care. The *Cāṇḍāla* himself, who had lived in the observance of *brahmacarya* in that place, and whose alms had been sprinkled with the milk of the kine, had in this life become a *Cāṇḍāla*. It is for this reason that the *Soma* plants become unsaleable, and the persons who sell and who purchase them both sink into the *Raurava* hell, when they repair to the region of *Yama*, etc. "Behold also this miserable dog!" In a former life the *Cāṇḍāla* was born in a noble family, but out of pride he ate the meat attached to the vertebral column of animals, and thence he had attained to his present state; in consequence of some meritorious act in a former life, he had retained the memory of his previous existences. Asked by the *Cāṇḍāla*, the *kshattriya* told him (in order to obtain emancipation (*moksha*) from his state of a *Cāṇḍāla*) to give up his life for the sake of a brahman. This the *Cāṇḍāla* did in a battle for protecting a brahman's wealth, and attained to a desirable end (XIII, **101**).—§ 757: Asked by *Yudhishṭhira* whether there is a difference of position among righteous men after death, *Bhīshma* related the old narrative of the conversation between the muni *Gautama* and *Indra* [i.e. Hastikūṭa] (*b*) (XIII, **102**).—(†) § 758: Asked by *Yudhishṭhira* what constitutes the highest penance, *Bhīshma* said that there is no penance superior to abstention from food, and told the old story of the conversation between king *Bhagīratha* and *Brahmán*. *Bhagīratha* had transcended the world of the gods, that of kine, and that of the *Ṛshis*; beholding this, *Brahmán* asked him how he had attained to that region, where neither gods, nor G., nor men succeed in coming without having practised the severest austerities; *Bhagīratha* enumerated his sacrifices, his penances on the *Jāhnavī* (Gaṅgā), etc. (*a*); those on the banks of *Sarayū*, etc. (*β*), he gave away millions of kine to the brahmans. "It is not through the merits of those acts that I have attained to this region, but through the vow of fast, which had been known to *Indra*, who had kept it secret, but which *Bhārgava Uçanas* had learnt through penance († v. 5945); all brahmans and Ṛ. gratified me, saying that I should repair to *Brahmaloka*." *Bhagīratha* was honoured by *Brahmán* (XIII, **103**).—§ 759: Asked by *Yudhishṭhira*, *Bhīshma* discussed the reason why, a man's period of life being said to extend over 100 years, one becomes short-lived or long lived; one should awake at the *Brāhma muhūrta* [i.e. at the hour when the sun is just below the horizon, PCR.]; Ṛ. by adoring the two twilights became long-lived; one should avoid atheism (*nāstikyam*), calumniating the *Vedas*, censuring the gods, etc.; one should also wash one's feet before sitting down to recite the *Vedas* or to eat any food; one should perform the *homas* for propitiating the gods (*çāntihomān*) and recite the *Sāvitra* mantras (*Sāvitrāṇi ca dhārayet*; i.e. *mantraviçeshāṅ*, Nīl.); persons conversant with ancient history cite a *gāthā* sung by *Yama* in days of old (about running—*prādravati*, B.—or studying with uncleansed mouth); "he who studies at forbidden times, loses his *Veda* and shortens his life" (v. 5026–8); nor should one eat at the *çrāddha* of an enemy; the spots of the hand named *Brāhma tīrtha*, etc. (*a*); having drunk water thrice, etc., one should worship the P. and gods according to the ordinances of the *Vedas* (v. 5065); a brahman should perform [the *ācamana*] (*samupaspṛçet*) in all the purificatory acts with the *Brāhma tīrtha* (v. 5066); one should never perform any act in honour of P. in the night-time (v. 5075); one should wash his head before performing any act in honour of P. or gods (v. 5081); one should never perform [a *çrāddha*] under the constellation of one's nativity, nor under the two *Proshṭhapadas*, nor under *Āgneya* (i.e. *Kṛttikāḥ*, Nīl.), nor under fierce [*nakshatras*, such as *Açleshā*, etc., PCR.], nor under those that are hostile (*pratyarim*), or those mentioned [i.e. forbidden] in the *Jyotisha* (v. 5082–3); a woman of the same *pravara* (*samārshām*), etc., should be avoided [in wedding] (v. 5086); one should accomplish all acts ordained in the *Veda* or by the *Brāhmaṇas* (v. 5092); one should study the *Dhanurveda* and the *Veda* (v. 5100); "you should know the science of reasoning (*Yuktiçāstram*), the science of words (*Çabdaçāstram*), the *Gāndharvaçāstra*, and the [64] *Kalās*, [and] one should always hear the *Purāṇa* and *itihāsas* and the narratives that exist (*ākhyānāni yāni ca*), and the biographies (*caritam*) of high-minded persons" (v. 5102–3); good conduct (*ācāraḥ*) is superior to all lore (*āgamānām*); this fame-producing, etc., [discourse] has been uttered by *Brahmán* out of compassion on all creatures (v. 5112) (XIII, **104**). Asked by *Yudhishṭhira*, *Bhīshma* expounded how the eldest brother should behave towards his younger brothers and the younger ones towards the eldest; "the *upādhyāya* is superior to 10 *ācāryas*; the father to 10 *upādhyāyas*; the mother to 10 fathers or [even] to the whole earth; there is no *guru* equal to the mother" (v. 5126–7) (XIII, **105**). Asked by *Yudhishṭhira* if only brahmans and *kshattriyas* should observe fasts (the very *Mlecchas* observe them), *Bhīshma* related what Ṛ. *Aṅgiras* had said to him in answer [essentially in the negative] to this same question, indicating the merits of fast on different days and different months (*β*), by which fasts the merit of different sacrifices (*γ*) are acquired, or the abode of the Aps., or *Brahmaloka* attained; there is no penance superior to fast: by fasts the gods became denizens of heaven, and Ṛ. attained to the highest success (*siddhim*); witness *Viçvāmitra*, and *Cyavana*, etc. (*δ*), who attained to heaven through fasts. In former days *Aṅgiras* declared so to M.-ṛ.†* (XIII, **106**). *Yudhishṭhira*, saying that sacrifices are incapable of being performed by people that are poor, as they require a large store of diverse kinds of articles, wherefore the merit attaching to them can only be acquired by kings and princes, asked *Bhīshma* about acts fraught with merit equal to that of sacrifices and capable of being performed by persons destitute of means. *Bhīshma* related the ordinances about fasts that were promulgated by *Aṅgiras*; the regions attainable by them (*ε*) and the sacrifices they are equal to (*ζ*) (XIII, **107**). Asked by *Yudhishṭhira* about that which is the foremost of all *tīrthas*, *Bhīshma* mentioned and described *Mānasa tīrtha* [in the figurative sense of the soul]; but also the *tīrthas* of the earth are possessed of merit; by reciting the name of a *tīrtha*, by bathing there, and by gladdening P. there, one casts off one's sins and goes to heaven (v. 5365) (XIII, **108**). Asked by *Yudhishṭhira* as to what is the highest, etc., kind of fast, *Bhīshma* said: [A = "that man who fasts on the 12th day of the moon in the month so called"; B = "and, for the whole day and night, worships *Kṛshṇa* as Keçava, etc."; C = "obtains the merits of the horse sacrifice, etc."; D = "and freedom from sin, etc."]

A.	B.	C.	D.
(1) *Mārgaçīrsha*	*Keçava* ...	Horse sacrifice	becomes free from all his sins.
(2) *Pausha* ...	*Nārāyaṇa* ...	*Vājapeya* ...	the highest success.
(3) *Māgha* ...	*Mādhava* ...	*Rājasūya* ...	rescues his race.
(4) *Phālguna* ...	*Govinda* ...	*Atirātra* ...	*Somaloka.*
(5) *Caitra* ...	*Vishṇu* ..	*Pauṇḍarika* ...	*Devaloka.*
(6) *Vaiçākha* ...	*Madhusūdana*	*Agnishṭoma* ...	*Somaloka.*
(7) *Jyaishṭha* ...	*Trivikrama*	*Gavām medhaḥ*	rejoices with Aps.
(8) *Ashāḍha* ...	*Vāmana* ...	*Naramedha* ...	rejoices with Aps.
(9) *Çrāvaṇa* ...	*Çrīdhara* ...	*Pañcayajñāḥ*	a *vimāna.*
(10) *Bhādrapada*	*Hṛshīkeça* ...	*Santrāmaṇi* ...	becomes purified.
(11) *Āçvika* ...	*Padmanābha*	1,000 cars ...	—
(12) *Kārttika* ...	*Dāmodara* ...	all sacrifices...	—

The result of adoring *Kṛshṇa* as *Puṇḍarīkāksha*, etc. (η). At the conclusion of one's vow, one should feed a number of brahmans or make gifts of ghee to them. *Vishṇu* has said that there is no fast superior to that (XIII, **109**). *Vaiçampāyana* said: Approaching *Bhīshma*, who was lying on his bed of arrows, *Yudhishṭhira* asked how one does acquire beauty, etc. *Bhīshma* said that a *Candravrata* should be commenced in *Mārgaçīrsha*, when the moon comes in conjunction with *Mūla*:

(1) *Mūla* [19]	being in his	feet,
(2) *Rohiṇī* [4]	,,	calf,
(3) *Açvinī* [1]	,,	knee-joints,
(4) *Āshāḍhau* [20–21]	,,	thighs,
(5) *Phālgunī* [11–12]	,,	anus,
(6) *Kṛttikāḥ* [3]	,,	waist,
(7) *Bhādrapada* [26–27]	,,	navel,
(8) *Revatī* [28]	,,	eyes,
(9) *Dhanishṭhāḥ* [24]	,,	back,
(10) *Anurādhā* [17]	,,	belly,
(11) *Viçākhāḥ* [16]	,,	arms,
(12) *Hasta* [13]	,,	hands,
(13) *Punarvasū* [7]	,,	fingers,
(14) *Āçleshāḥ* [9]	,,	nails,
(15) *Jyeshṭhā* [18]	,,	neck,
(16) *Çravaṇa* [23]	,,	ears,
(17) *Pushya* [8]	,,	mouth,
(18) *Svāti* [15]	,,	teeth and lips,
(19) *Çatabhishā* [25]	,,	smile,
(20) *Maghā* [10]	,,	nose,
(21) *Mṛgaçiras* [5]	,,	eye,
(22) *Citra* [14]	,,	forehead,
(23) *Bharaṇī* [2]	,,	head,
(24) *Ārdrā* [6]	,,	hair.

[The figures in brackets indicate the number in the ecliptic; *Abhijit* [22] is wanting.] Then gifts of ghee to learned brahmans; one becomes as accomplished (*paripūrṇāṅgaḥ*) as the full moon (XIII, **110**).—§ 760: *Yudhishṭhira* asked, what regulates rebirth, etc. *Bhīshma* directed him to ask *Bṛhaspati*, as none else was capable of explaining the matter. *Vaiçampāyana* said: While they were thus speaking *Bṛhaspati* came from heaven; *Yudhishṭhira* with *Dhṛtarāshṭra*, etc., honoured him; then *Yudhishṭhira* asked him, what is truly the friend of mortal creatures, and what follows man to the next world. *Bṛhaspati* said: Righteousness. *Yudhishṭhira* asked, how righteousness can accompany the dead body. *Bṛhaspati* said that the soul (*jīva*) obtains a new body according to its merit, *Yama*, etc. (α), being the witnesses, etc. Deities dwelling in the body, viz. earth, etc. (β). After birth *Jīva* receives woe and death from the messengers of *Yama*; if imbued with unrighteousness, *Jīva* has to go to the dominions of *Yama*, and after suffering great misery there, he has to undergo rebirth as an animal, or as some other kind of being, as declared in the *Vedas* and the scriptures (*çāstre*) with the histories (*setihāse*). In the regions of *Yama* there are places worthy of being the abodes even of the deities, and which are equal to *Brahmaloka*, but also such as are worse than [those of animals]. Different forms in which *Jīva* has to take birth in consequence of different acts (e.g. as a *Brahma-Rākshasa*; as *Mlecchas*). [The periods that elapse before one recovers human existence are here generally very short, some few months or years.] "I heard all this in days of old from *Brahmán* himself in the midst of the *surarshis*" (XIII, **111**). Asked by *Yudhishṭhira*, *Bṛhaspati* explained by what acts people, having committed sin, attain to an auspicious end in this world and in heaven, especially recommending gifts of food (praised by D., R., P., and men), citing *Rantideva* (*b*) (XIII, **112**). Asked by *Yudhishṭhira*, *Bṛhaspati* discoursed on the six doors of righteousness (abstention from injury, the observance of the Vedic ritual, meditation, restraining the senses, penances, and obedience to preceptors), saying that the man who practises the religion of universal compassion achieves the highest good, etc. *Vaiçampāyana* said: Then *Bṛhaspati* ascended to heaven. [XIII, **111–113** are called *Saṃsāra-cakra*] (XIII, **113**).—§ 761: *Vaiçampāyana* said: After this *Yudhishṭhira*, addressing *Bhīshma* (lying on his bed of arrows), said: R., D., and brahmans, led by the authority of the *Vedas*, praise the religion of compassion; but how does a man who has injured others in word, thought, and deed, succeed in freeing himself from misery? *Bhīshma* recommended abstention from meat; meat, moreover, enslaves the mind by taste (XIII, **114**). *Yudhishṭhira* (referring to § 749) wondered how, when abstention from injury is the highest religion, persons should make offerings of meat in *çrāddhas* in honour of P. *Bhīshma* referred to the innumerable discourses on this topic that had taken place between R., and strongly recommended abstention from honey and meat, referring to the seven R. (*Saptarshayaḥ*), etc. (α), and quoting *Manu*, etc. (β); he who eats flesh of animals slain by others incurs the sin that attaches to the slaughter; he who purchases flesh slays living creatures through his wealth (the eater's demerit is, however, not so great as the slayer's); by eating flesh left from sacrifices [to D. and P.; v. especially *Agastya*] and of animals that have been slain for feeding brahmans, one incurs a small fault. In old time persons who wanted to attain to regions of merit hereafter, performed sacrifices with seeds. Especially in the month of *Kārttika* or in its bright fortnight one should abstain from [honey and] meat, which many ancient kings have done: *Nābhāga*, etc. (γ); those who abstain from flesh for months or fortnights continuously, have *Brahmaloka* reserved to them. (It is by truthfulness that *Hariçcandra* roves through heaven like a second *Candramas*.) Also the kings *Çyenacitra*, etc. (δ), did not eat flesh during the month of *Kārttika*, and, therefore, attained to *Brahmaloka*, adored by G. and surrounded by 1,000 beautiful damsels. The eaters of meat go to Hell: he who practises the religion of abstention from meat or teaches it to others will never have to go to Hell, even if he be exceedingly wicked in other respects* (XIII, **115**). Asked by *Yudhishṭhira* what can be eaten, etc., *Bhīshma* discoursed on what is flesh, and continued the preceding discourse, again mentioning *Agastya*; snakes, etc. (ϵ), never hurt him who is devoted to compassion; those who are covetous of meat are cooked in the hell called *Kumbhipāka*; etymology of the word *māṃsa* (flesh) (XIII, **116**).—§ 762: Asked by *Yudhishṭhira* what end those attain to who give up their lives in battle, though to give up life is difficult for men, whether they are in prosperity or adversity, *Bhīshma* explained the old narrative of the conversation, in former times, between *Vyāsa* and a worm: Kīṭopākhyāna (*b*) (XIII, **117–119**).—§ 763: Asked by *Yudhishṭhira* about the relative superiority of knowledge, penances, and gifts, *Bhīshma* told the old narrative of the conversation between *Maitreya* and *Vyāsa*: Maitreya-bhikshā (*b*) (XIII, **120–122**).—

§ 764: Asked by *Yudhishṭhira* about the behaviour of good and chaste women, *Bhīshma* said: Once *Sumanā Kaikeyī* in *Devaloka* asked the omniscient *Çāṇḍilī* by what course of acts she had attained to heaven (description). *Çāṇḍilī* said that it was not by wearing yellow robes or barks of trees, or by shaving her head, or by means of matted hair, that she had attained to this state, but by never saying any disagreeable word to her husband; by always worshipping D., P., and brahmans; by always obeying her mother-in-law and father-in-law, etc. (enumeration). By adhering to this path of duty a woman is honoured in heaven like a second *Arundhatī*. Then *Çāṇḍilī* disappeared* (XIII, **123**).—§ 765: Asked by *Yudhishṭhira* which is of superior efficacy, gentleness or gifts, *Bhīshma* said that some become gratified by gentleness, others by gifts, and related the ancient narrative of how a brahman, who had been seized in a forest by a Rā., was released [on account of his gentleness], after answering the question put to him by the Rā., "Why am I pale of hue and so lean?" [a long and very curious enumeration of causes that may render a man pale and lean]. Rā. worshipped that brahman, and making him his friend and bestowing wealth upon him, let him off (XIII, **124**).—§ 766: *Yudhishṭhira* asked about the following "mysteries": how a poor man, desirous of achieving his own good, should act; what is the best of all gifts, and what should be given under various circumstances; and who are truly deserving of honour and worship. *Vaiçampāyana* said: Thus questioned by *Yudhishṭhira*, *Bhīshma* explained those high mysteries. *Bhīshma* said: *Vyāsa* explained them to me in days of yore; it is a mystery to the very gods; *Yama*, by vows and *yoga*, had acquired the knowledge thereof as the fruit of his penances; what pleases each god, etc. (*a*). The scale of sinfulness in the giver is this: 1 [territorial] chief = 10 courtezans; 1 courtezan = 10 drinkers of alcohol; 1 drinker = 10 oilmen; 1 oilman = 10 butchers; a king is reckoned to be half more [sinful as a giver] than these all; hence, one should not accept gifts from such. In the *çrāddha* ritual the mysteries of D., P., and R. have been declared. Once a celestial messenger, sent by the *Açvins*, came to the court of *Indra* (where men, P., and D. assembled together), and, remaining invisible, asked *Indra* why sexual intercourse is interdicted to the man who performs a *çrāddha* and to him who eats a *çrāddha*, and to whom each of the three rice-balls offered separately at a *çrāddha* should be sacrificed. D. (seated towards the east) and P. applauded him. P. said: Lest the P. of that man should have to lie for a whole month on his vital seed; the first rice-ball > the water > the moon > the other gods and P.; the second should be eaten by the spouse; P. confer a son on him who is desirous of a son; the third is thrown into the fire; P. grant all wishes. The *ṛtvij* at a *çrāddha* becomes the P. of the *yajamāna*, and, therefore, should abstain for that day from sexual intercourse. Ṛ. *Vidyutprabha* asked what the atonement is for slaying worms, ants, snakes, sheep, deer, birds, etc. *Indra* answered: "Thinking of *Kurukshetra*, etc." (*β*) (specification); *Vidyutprabha* recommended another rite (specification), and a "mystery" discovered by Ṛ., which he had heard from *Bṛhaspati* in the presence of *Çiva* (standing on one foot on a mountain, etc.). Asked by *Indra*, *Bṛhaspati* discoursed on the wicked persons who make water facing the sun [Sūrya], etc. (*γ*). The D., M., and Ṛ., as to what gifts at a *çrāddha* become inexhaustible. P. said: By setting free dark-coloured bulls, by gifts of sesame seeds and water on the day of new moon, and of lamps in the season of rains, men free themselves from the debt to P. Asked by *Vṛddhagārgya*, P. said: If a blue bull [upon being set free] raises water with its tail, P. become gratified by that [water] for 60,000 years; if the mud from a river bank is attached to its horns, P. go to *Somaloka*; by giving lamps in the season of rain, one shines like the moon; those who on the day of new moon make gifts of sesame seeds and water, mixed with honey, using a vessel of *uḍumbara* (*Ficus glomerata*, PCR. copper), have duly performed a *çrāddha* with its mysteries, and get cheerful and healthy children (XIII, **125**). Asked by *Indra* how he becomes gratified, *Vishṇu* said that he hates the destruction of brahmans; that he is gratified by the worship of brahmans, with those who worship and make offerings in the circle besmeared with cow-dung (because it was with his circular disc that the Dai. were slain), those who reverence their own feet (because it was with his two feet that the world was covered); those who behold a boar that has just emerged from water and on his head carries a quantity of mud from the bank (reminding of the form of a boar in which *Vishṇu* slew *Hiraṇyāksha*), or a brahman that is a dwarf in stature (*Vishṇu* having conquered king *Bali* as a dwarf), have never to meet with any evil (the explanations were given as answer to *Indra*). The man who every day worships the *açvattha* (*Ficus religiosa*) and *gorocana* and the cow is considered to worship the whole universe with D., As., and men; "staying within such, I, in my own form, accept the worship that is offered to them; the worship of other kind I never accept." *Baladeva* points out the importance of touching a cow, ghee, etc., at early dawn. The gods point to the importance of using an *uḍumbara* vessel in presenting offerings to D. and P. *Dharma* said that the offerings in honour of D. and P. should never be given to a brahman who has accepted service under the king, or who rings the bell, etc.; from the house of a person from whom a guest returns unsatisfied, P., D., and the sacred fires all return disappointed. *Agni* declared that P. of one who raises his foot to kick a cow or a brahman or a fire become filled with fear; that D. become highly dissatisfied, and that he himself has to be roasted in hell (*narake pacyate*) for 100 ages; fire refuses to accept his libations. *Viçvāmitra* said: He who offers rice boiled in sugared milk to P., facing the south, at noon, in the first "elephant shade" (*gajacchāyāyāṃ pūrvasyāṃ*, v. BR.), when in the month of *Bhādrapada* [the conjunction of the moon with] *Maghā* takes place in the dark fortnight, has [thereby] performed a great *çrāddha* [every year] for thirteen years [in succession]. The cows said: († v. 6042–5) that man becomes free from his sins who adores a cow, saying: ". . . in *Brahmapura* (the city of Brahmán), in days of yore, thou wast present with thy calf at the sacrifice of *Indra*; thou who stoodst in *Vishṇupada* and in the path of *Agni* (? *Vibhāvasoḥ*), all the gods with *Nārada* call thee *Sarvasahā*"; he attains to the regions (*lokān*) of *Indra*, etc. Then the seven Ṛ. circumambulated *Brahmán*, and *Vasishṭha* asked how poor righteous men may acquire the merits attaching to sacrifices. *Brahmán* answered: If one, in the bright fortnight of the month of *Pausha*, when *Rohiṇī* is in conjunction, purifying himself by a bath, lies under the cope of heaven, clad in a single garment, with faith and concentrated attention, and drinks the rays of the moon, one acquires the merits of great sacrifices. This is a high mystery (XIII, **126**). *Vibhāvasu* recommended to offer a handful of water and *akshatāḥ* (rice-grain) with ghee to the moon on the day of the full moon, and warns against cutting a tree or chewing a tooth-brush on the day of the new moon, lest the *Moon*, P., and D. should be offended. *Çrī* said that D. and P. fly away from that house in which vessels, etc., lie scattered, and in which women are beaten. *Aṅgiras* said that the offspring of that man increases who every night for a full year stands under a *karañjaka* tree with a lamp and the roots of the *Suvarcala* plant. *Gārgya* recommended, for example, that one should always repeat the names of the *Pushkara* lakes; while the merit of even 100 sacrifices is exhausted, the merit resulting from the performance of the duties that he has mentioned becomes inexhaustible; a woman during her season or one whose mother is a leper must not assist at sacred rites, or D. will not eat the libations and P. not become gratified for thirteen years; at a *çrāddha* one should also recite the *Bhārata*. *Dhaumya* warned against broken utensils (which mean *Kali* himself), broken bedsteads (which mean loss of wealth), and trees in the house (under whose roots snakes and scorpions find shelter); when a cock or a dog is in sight, the gods do not eat the offerings made to them. *Jamadagni* said that a man whose heart is not pure is sure to go to hell, even if he performs a horse-sacrifice or 100 *Vājapeyas*; by giving only a *prastha* of powdered barley with a pure heart to a brahman, a very poor brahman attained to *Brahmaloka* (XIII, **127**). *Vāyu* said that he who, during the four months of the rainy season, offers sesames and water, etc., acquires all the merit resulting from 100 sacrifices in which animals are offered up to the gods. When a *Çūdra* ignites the sacred fires, or women are allowed to assist at rites, one is reborn as a *Çūdra*, and P. and D. are never gratified with him; as an expiation, one should for three days pour into the sacred fire libations of the urine of the cow mixed with cow-dung, milk, and ghee; after a year the gods once more accept the offerings of such a man, and P. become gratified (XIII, **128**). *Lomaça* warned against cohabiting with the wives of other people or a barren woman, and against appropriating what belongs to a brahman, or D. and P. will refuse one's offerings, etc. On the 12th lunar day and the day of full moon, one should every month make gifts of ghee and *akshata* to brahmans; thereby *Soma* and the Ocean increases, and *Indra* confers one-fourth of the merit of a horse-sacrifice, and *Soma* grants the fruition of one's wishes. He who, during this *Kaliyuga*, at dawn, in white robes, makes gifts of a vessel of sesame seeds to brahmans, and of water with sesame seeds and honey to P., and who gives lamps and *kṛçara*, acquires, according to the ordinance of *Indra*, the merit of giving cows and land (which merit is eternal) and of an *Agnishṭoma*. This is the ancient ordinance of Ṛ., applauded by P. and D. in heaven and *Pitṛloka* (XIII, **129**). *Bhīshma* said: Ṛ., P., and D. then asked *Arundhatī* (equal to [her husband] *Vasishṭha*; not in C.) about the mysteries of *dharma* [not in C.]. *Arundhatī* said that *dharma* should never be communicated to him who is bereft of faith, full of pride, guilty of having slain a brahman, or who violates the bed of his preceptor. She recommended hospitality as better than giving hundreds of thousands of cows in *Pushkara*, etc.; he who at dawn sprinkles a cow's horns with *kuça*-grass, and causes the water to drip down upon his own head, acquires the merit of bathing in all the *tīrthas* of the three worlds (resorted to by Si. and Cā.). D. and P. applauded her. *Brahmán* granted her that her penances would continually increase. *Yama* related the sayings of *Citragupta*: On days of the full moon and the new moon one's acts are conveyed to the Sun; when a mortal goes into *Pretaloka* (the regions of the dead), *Vibhāvasu* (the Sun) bears witness to all his acts; especially in *Jyeshṭha-Pushkara* one should give a *kapilā* cow to a learned brahman, on *Kaumudī* [the day of full moon in the month of *Kārttika*]; such a man is considered to have given 100 cows with a bull, a gift which is productive of eternal merit. They that are of little understanding become afflicted with hunger and thirst in the regions of the dead, burning in pain, and there is no escape for them (they who make gifts of water, on the other hand, drink of a large river full of excellent water), and have to enter into a thick darkness (but *Soma*, *Sūrya*, and *Agni* always give light to him who has given lamps in this world, and he blazes forth like a second *Sūrya*). One should also give a pair of sandals to a deserving brahman, and an umbrella (thereby comfortable shade is obtained in the next world). *Sūrya's* hair stood on end; applauding the sayings of *Citragupta*, he said to D. and P. that these five should always be avoided: the slayer of a brahman, the slayer of a cow, he who is addicted to sexual intercourse with other people's wives, he who is bereft of faith, and he who derives his living from the misbehaviour of his wife; such persons suffer (*pacyante*) in hell like worms eating pus and blood, and are avoided by P., D., *Snātakas*, etc. (XIII, **130**). Asked by D., P., and Ṛ., the *Pramathas* said that men who are rendered impure by sexual intercourse without having previously purified themselves (*ucchishṭāḥ*), men who insult their superiors, who eat different kinds of meat, and sleep at the foot of a tree, he who keeps flesh under his pillow while lying down to sleep, who places the head where his feet should be placed (in lying down or sleeping), and who throws phlegm, etc., into the water: "these men deserve to be slain and eaten up by us." Means of protection against them are:- *Gorocanā*, [the root of] *vacā* [so B.], ghee with *akshata*, abstaining from meat, ever-burning fire, the skin or teeth of a wolf, a hill-tortoise, [the sacrificial] smoke, a cat, a tawny or black goat; those articles are destructive of Rā. (XIII, **131**). *Brahmán* caused D. together with *Indra* and P. to let the elephant *Reṇuka* in *Rasātala* go and question the *Diggajas* (the elephants who sustain the earth) about the mysteries of *dharma*. Asked by *Reṇuka*, the *Diggajas* recommended a *çrāddha*, with gifts of treacle and rice, on the 8th day of the dark fortnight of *Kārttika*, under the conjunction of the moon with *Āçleshā*, uttering certain *mantras* (mentioning "*Baladeva* and other *Nāgas*," and "*Nārāyaṇa* when he raised the submerged earth"), and making *bali* offerings of blue cloth and fragrant unguents upon an anthill strewn with *gajendra* flowers at sunset. Thereby those beings in the nether regions that bear the weight of the upper regions become pleased, and the *Diggajas* do not feel the weight of upholding the earth. By observing this rule for a whole year, and fasting, the four castes acquire great merit; it is equal to hospitality for 100 years to all the elephants in the three worlds. D., P., and Ṛ. applauded *Reṇuka* (XIII, **132**). *Çiva* recommended to give food to cows every day for a month, contenting oneself with one meal a day; he who gives food to cows even for a single day, receives one-fourth of the merit of all his meritorious acts; cows uphold the three worlds with D., As., and men; *Çiva* had praised them in the *Kṛta* age; at the solicitation of *Brahmán* a bull stands in his banner, and he always sports with cows; only believers should be instructed in these mysteries (XIII, **133**). *Skanda* recommended to smear one's body for three days with earth from the horns of a dark-coloured bull and then to perform one's ablutions; to offer cooked food with honey, in an *udumbara* vessel, as *bali* to the moon on the evening of the day of full-moon, which offer is accepted by Sā., etc. (γ), and whereby *Soma* and the Ocean increase* (spoken by *Vishṇu*). *Bhīshma* said that these mysteries (respected by D. and promulgated by *Vyāsa*) are even superior to the whole earth († v. 6198), and should not be imparted to any unbeliever, etc. (XIII, **134**).—§ 767: Asked by *Yudhishṭhira*, *Bhīshma* enumerated those persons from which a brahman, a *kshattriya*, a *vaiçya*, and a *çūdra* may take his food, etc. (XIII, **135**). Asked by *Yudhishṭhira*, *Bhīshma* expounded the expiations which purify a brahman of the sin he incurs by accepting forbidden food (especially offered to D. and P.); without having performed his ablutions, a brahman should not say his evening prayers, etc.; for this reason the *çrāddha* has been ordained to be performed in the afternoon (XIII, **136**). Asked by *Yudhishṭhira* which is better, charity (*dāna*) or devotion (*tapas*), *Bhīshma* enumerated the pious princes who have attained to heaven (*lokāḥ*) (*a*). "These and many other men (householders) have attained to heaven by charity and penances, and return again and again. As night approaches, I shall explain to thee in the morning whatever doubts may arise in thy mind" (XIII, **137**). Asked by *Yudhishṭhira* (who refers to XIII, **137**), *Bhīshma* discoursed on the five kinds of gifts: from desire of merit, from desire of profit, from fear, from free choice, and from pity; *Brahmán* has said that one should always make gifts according to one's power (XIII, **138**).—§ 768: *Yudhishṭhira*, complaining of the distress of the time, asked *Bhīshma* to discourse on religion and profit in the presence of *Kṛshṇa* and all the kings. *Vaiçampāyana* said that *Bhīshma* recited the discourses on the puissance of *Vishṇu* in days of yore (and the doubt of *Rudra* and his spouse). Once *Kṛshṇa* observed a vow for twelve years in order to obtain a son; *Nārada*, etc. (*a*), came there with Si., etc. (description of their seats); fire issued from the mouth of *Kṛshṇa* and consumed the summit of the mountain with all its living creatures, then it came back and touched his feet; he cast a benignant look upon the mountain, which once more became adorned and peopled as before. Asked by Ṛ., *Kṛshṇa* explained that, in consequence of his penances, his soul became transformed into fire and repaired to *Brahmán* (who told it that half of the energy of *Çiva* would take birth as *Kṛshṇa's* son), and then went back; "I now ask you to tell me something that is highly wonderful, which you have heard of or seen on earth or in heaven." Ṛ. glorified *Kṛshṇa*, and asked by them, *Nārada* described the wonderful incident on *Himavat*, "which was witnessed by Ṛ. on their *tīrthayātrā*" (XIII, **139**). *Bhīshma* said: Then Ṛ. *Nārada*, the friend of *Kṛshṇa*, told the following story of the discourse between *Çiva* and *Umā*: Umā-Maheçvara-saṃvāda (*b*) (XIII, **140–148**). *Bhīshma* said: *Kṛshṇa* paid honour to Ṛ., who praised *Kṛshṇa*, approving of what *Çiva* had said of him, and saying that they had told him [about the discourse of *Çiva* with *Umā*], only to please him, since he had asked them; but "there is nothing in the three worlds that is unknown to thee." Ṛ. took leave of *Kṛshṇa*, promising him that he would soon get an excellent son. *Kṛshṇa* returned to *Dvārakā*. *Rukmiṇī*, after the tenth month, bore a son who is identified with *Kāma*, which exists in every creature and moves within the hearts of both gods and *Asuras*. Praise of *Kṛshṇa* = *Vishṇu Trivikrama* = the thirty-three gods with *Indra* = *Adideva* (the first god), etc. *Bhīshma* congratulated the *Pāṇḍavas*, especially *Arjuna*, and pitied *Duryodhana*; many Dai. and Dā. have been slain by *Kṛshṇa*, witness *Çiva's* utterances (*purāṇam*) on *Himavat* to Ṛ.; the greatness, etc., of *Arjuna* can only come up to one-third of that of *Kṛshṇa*. *Bhīshma* consoled *Yudhishṭhira* (it is Time = *Kṛshṇa* who has slain the warriors), citing *Vyāsa* and *Nārada*. *Nārada* and *Vyāsa* have told me that "*Kṛshṇa* and *Arjuna* (*triyugau*) practised penances in *Badarī* for 10,000 years"; he mentioned his slaying of *Kaṃsa*; the destruction of the *Kurus* is due to *Duryodhana*, etc. (ε). *Yudhishṭhira* remained silent; the kings with *Dhṛtarāshṭra*, and Ṛ. with *Nārada*, applauded *Bhīshma* and worshipped *Kṛshṇa*. When *Bhīshma* had rested and become refreshed, *Yudhishṭhira* once more asked him (XIII, **148**).—§ 769: *Vaiçampāyana* said: *Yudhishṭhira* asked *Bhīshma*: who is the one god, which the foremost of all religions, and by what prayer does one become freed from the bonds of birth and transmigration (*janmasaṃsārabandhanāt*). *Bhīshma* answered: "Always uttering the 1,000 names of the eternal *Vishṇu Purushottama*, the great *Brahmán*, etc., which were sung by the Ṛ." (v. 6949 wants in B.: *Vishṇor nāmasahasrasya Vedavyāso mahān ṛshiḥ | Chando 'nushṭup tathā Devo Bhagavān Devakīsutaḥ*). Then he enumerated Vishṇu's (= *Keçava's* v. 7057 = *Vāsudeva's* v. 7061, 7066, etc. = *Kṛshṇa's* v. 7071) 1,000 names.* "The moveable and immoveable world with D., As., G., Y., U., and Rā., is under the sway of *Kṛshṇa*; R., P., D., etc., have sprung from *Nārāyaṇa*; the *Yoga*, the *Sāṅkhya*, the crafts (*çilpāḥ*), the *Vedas*, the *Çāstras*, etc., have sprung from *Janārdana*; one should recite this hymn in praise of *Vishṇu*, composed (*kīrttitaṃ*) by *Vyāsa*" (XIII, **149**).—§ 770: Asked by *Yudhishṭhira* about the [mantra] which gives righteousness and success on setting out on a journey, or on entering [a new building], or at the commencement of any undertaking, or in sacrifices to D. and P., etc., *Bhīshma* recited a *mantra* promulgated by *Vyāsa* and ordained by *Sāvitrī*, and which purifies from all sins, and which was recited in days of yore by the foremost Ṛ. († v. 7088–9): Salutations (*namaḥ*) to *Vasishṭha*, etc. (*a*); the eleven *Rudras* (the lords of the three worlds) are: *Ajaikapād*, etc. (β); in *Çatarudra* they are 100; *Aṃça*, etc. (γ), are the twelve *Ādityas*, the sons of *Kaçyapa* according to the *Çruti*; *Dhara*, etc. (δ), are the eight *Vasus*; *Nāsatya* and *Dasra* are the two *Açvins*, the sons of *Mārttaṇḍa*, who came out of the nose of *Sañjñā*; *Mṛtyu*, *Kāla*, V.-D., P. (endowed with forms), Mu., and Si. (devoted to penances and emancipation) are the invisible witnesses of all the good and bad acts of all beings, giving the regions of felicity (*lokān etān*) created by *Prajāpati* to those that praise them, and residing in all the worlds; by praising these 33 [i.e. 11 + 12 + 8 + 2] gods (the lords of all hosts of beings) [and] *Nandīçvara*, etc. (ε), one is cleansed of all sins; the Ṛ. [called] *Mānavas* are *Yavakrīta*, etc. (ζ); blazing like *Rudra*, *Anala*, and the *Vasus*, they rejoice in heaven with the gods after having performed good deeds on earth; the seven *gurus* of *Indra* [i.e. presumably Yavakrīta — Bala Āṅgirasa] live in the East, and by praising them one enjoys felicity in *Indraloka*; *Unmucu*, etc. (η), are the seven *ṛtvijs* of *Dharmarāja* [i.e. Yama], and live in the South; *Dṛḍheyu*, etc. (δ), are the *ṛtvijs* of *Varuṇa*, and dwell in the West; *Atri*, etc. (ι), are the seven *gurus* of *Kubera*, and dwell in the North; there are seven other Mu. in all the quarters, bestowers of fame, etc.; *Dharma*, etc. (κ), are upholders of the earth; *Rāma*, *Vyāsa*, *Droṇa's* son *Açvatthāman*, and *Lomaça*; these are the celestial *munis*, distributed into seven groups [of] seven; they are the creators of peace [*çānti-*) and good (*-svasti-*) and the regents of the quarters (*diçām pālāḥ*); one should turn his face in that direction in which one of these Ṛ. live, and take refuge with him; they are the creators of all creatures and the purifiers of the worlds [this is the order in B., where v. 7121: *Rāmo Vyāsas . . . .* is placed before v. 7120: *Çānti-svastikarā loke . . . .*]; *Saṃvartta*, etc. (including *Sāṃkhya* and *Yoga*) (λ), have practised severe penances and are celebrated over the three worlds; there are others resembling *Rudra*, in *Brahmaloka*, through whom the sonless obtains a son, and the poor obtains wealth; one should also praise *Pṛthu*, etc. (μ), [and] *Sāṅkhya* and *Yoga*, *Havya* and *Kavya*, and Supreme *Bráhman*; one should praise them morning and evening; then there is no fear from fire or thieves, nor from Pç. and Rā., etc.; P. eat that man's *kavya*, and the gods his *havya* (so B.), who recites [these names: *Sāvitrī*, v. 7146, 7149, 7158; *mahad bráhma Sāvitrīguṇakīrtanam*, v. 7150; *Sāvitrīṃ paramāṃ gatiṃ*, v. 7155; *Sāvitrī bráhma çāçvatī*, v. 7161] at his rites for D. and P.; they contribute to the peace (*çāntim*) of all the four castes; when setting out on a journey, etc., on every occasion one should recite them; it is a great mystery of Ṛ., etc. This ancient tale contains the opinion of the accomplished (*siddhasya*) *Parāçara*, and in former days was recited to *Indra*; [it is] the veritable eternal *Bráhman*, the heart of all creatures and the eternal *çruti*; all [the princes] of the race of *Sūrya* and of *Soma*, i.e. the *Rāghavas* and the *Kurus*, always recite it after having purified themselves (*çucayaḥ*); there is rescue from every calamity in always reciting [the names of] D., seven Ṛ. (*Saptarshīṇāṃ*), and *Dhruva*; [† v. 7157–8 are each of 38 syllables; † v. 7159–60 are each of 2 × 28 syllables]: the old B.-ṛ. *Kāçyapa*, etc. (ν), have worshipped them; [being] the opinion of *Bhāradvāja* they were obtained by the sons of *Ṛcīka*; having acquired them again from *Vasishṭha*, *Çakra* and the *Vasus* vanquished all Dā.; the man who makes a present of 100 cows with their horns covered with gold to a learned brahman, and he who causes the excellent *Bhārata* story to be always recited, these two acquire [equal] merit; the benefits obtained by praising *Bhṛgu*, etc. (ξ) (XIII, **151**).—§ 771: Asked by *Yudhishṭhira* what course of conduct towards the various classes of persons is regarded faultless, *Bhīshma* eulogised the brahmans, who are attentive to P., D., and guests; who eat the first portions of *havya* and *kavya*; who by their very eating rescue the three worlds from great fear; whose wealth consists in all the *çikshās* and the *çruti*; whose wrath yet burns in the *Daṇḍaka* wood, etc. (XIII, **152**).—§ 772: Asked by *Yudhishṭhira* what is the reward attached to the worship of brahmans, *Bhīshma* told the old narrative of a conversation between *Pavana* (the Wind) and *Arjuna* [Kārtavīrya]: Pavanārjunasaṃvāda (*b*) (XIII, **153–158**). — § 773: Asked by *Yudhishṭhira* about the prosperity resulting from the worship of the brahmans, *Bhīshma*, saying that the time of his death is not distant, and that he has recited all the duties mentioned in the *Purāṇas*, referred him to *Kṛshṇa* (*b*) (XIII, **159**). Asked by *Yudhishṭhira* what prosperity results from the worship of the brahmans, *Kṛshṇa* related what he in former times in *Dvāravatī* had answered his son *Pradyumna*, who was greatly excited by [some] brahmans and put this same question to him; they have *Soma* for their king. He related the visit of *Durvāsas* (*c*) (XIII, **160**). Asked by *Yudhishṭhira* about the knowledge he had acquired from *Durvāsas*, *Kṛshṇa* said that he would recite that *Çatarudrīya* which he repeats every morning, and which was composed by *Prajāpati* at the end of his penances. Then he praised *Çiva* (*d*) (XIII, **161–162**). — § 774: *Vaiçampāyana* said: After *Kṛshṇa* had said these words, *Yudhishṭhira* once more asked *Bhīshma* which of the two, perception (*pratyaksham*) or the scriptures (*āgamaḥ*), should be [regarded as] authoritative for arriving at a conclusion (*kāraṇaṃ bhavet*). *Bhīshma* answered that to affirm that perception is the only authority (as some persons do) is foolish; that knowledge which is derived from reasoning can scarcely be said to be knowledge.—Asked by *Yudhishṭhira* as to [which of these four is most authoritative, viz.] perception (*pratyaksham*), inference (*lokataḥ siddhir*, i.e. *anumānam*, Nīl.), the teaching of the scriptures (*lokaç cāgamapūrvakaḥ*), and the various kinds of good men's practice (*çishṭācāro bahuvidhaḥ*), he declared that as the might of unrighteous persons causes doubts to attach to perception, inference, and good conduct, good people who let themselves be led by the scriptures, and who are ever contented, should be resorted to for the solution of doubts.—As *Yudhishṭhira* remarked that, the *veda*, *pratyaksha*, and *ācāra* being all three *pramāṇa* (authority) [as to what is *dharma*, i.e. righteousness], the one *dharma* would become threefold, *Bhīshma* answered that *dharma* is really one, though capable of being viewed from three different points; he should not engage in such [unfruitful] speculations, but simply follow his instructions like a blind man, knowing that righteousness consists in abstention from injury, truth, absence of wrath, and liberality, and that conduct towards the brahmans that has been observed by his sires and grandsires. The fool who would deny that to be authority that [has always been accepted as] authority, does not deserve to become an authority, for he creates [only] fright.—Asked by *Yudhishṭhira*, *Bhīshma* said that those who hate righteousness have their hearts overwhelmed with passion and darkness and go to hell; those who observe righteousness go to heaven. The brahmans, who are the eldest sons of *Brahmán*, represent righteousness, and, therefore, they are worshipped by the righteous as a ripe fruit by a hungry man.—Asked by *Yudhishṭhira*, *Bhīshma* indicated the acts that are characteristic of wicked and good men (curious enumeration): the good never talk while eating, and never go to sleep with wet hands; two times have been appointed by the deities for taking food, viz. morning and evening, in the meantime, one should not eat anything; when following this rule, one is said to observe a fast; one who never approaches his spouse at any other time save after her courses, is said to observe the vow of *brahmacarya*; *amṛta*, brahmans, and kine are regarded as equal; one does not incur any fault by eating the meat of animals slain in sacrifices with *mantras* from the *Yajurveda*; the flesh of the backbone, or that of animals not slain in sacrifices, is as the flesh of one's own son; one should eat in privacy; well-cooked frumenty, *yāvaka* (B. *yavāgām*), *kṛsara* (C. °*ça*°), and *havis* [should be used in] the *Ashṭakas* of gods and P. and [in] worshipping the planets; one should not shave without calling down a blessing upon oneself; if one sneezes, he should be blessed ("*çataṃ jīva*," Nīl.) by those present; having committed a sin, one should confess it in the presence of those that are good; they would then destroy it; one should achieve righteousness in private, not make a show of righteousness; those are traders in righteousness who draw profit from it; one should lay up for oneself a treasure in the world to come, consisting in gifts made [here] to deserving persons (XIII, **163**). *Yudhishṭhira* observed that the acquisition of wealth very often seems to be independent of exertion and learning, etc.; *Bhīshma* said that when one, notwithstanding great exertion, fails to earn wealth, he should practise severe austerities, make gifts, abstain from cruelty, etc.; then happiness will be obtained [in the next life]; unless seeds be sown, no crops appear; even in the case of insects and ants, their acts [of this and past lives] and Nature are the cause of happiness and woe [i.e., the explanation of what seems unintelligible to *Yudhishṭhira* is to be sought for in the actions in past lives] (XIII, **164**); to put faith in righteousness is the mark of wisdom; Time [which is the supreme disposer of all things] can never make righteousness the cause of misery, and unrighteousness is incapable of touching righteousness, which is protected by time; righteousness is fraught with victory (XIII, **165**).—§ 775: *Vaiçampāyana* said: Desirous of obtaining such goods as are destructive of sins, *Yudhishṭhira* questioned *Bhīshma*, who was lying on a bed of arrows. *Yudhishṭhira* said: What is beneficial for a person in this world? how can one be freed of all one's sins? *Vaiçampāyana* said: In this connection *Bhīshma* recited the names of the gods to *Yudhishṭhira*. *Bhīshma* said: These names of the gods and Ṛ., if recited morning, noon, and evening, become purifiers of sins; then one has never to become blind or deaf, etc., and never takes birth as an animal or in the mixed castes, nor goes to Hell; the names of the gods and Ṛ., etc., rivers, mountains, etc.; *Brahmán*, etc. (*a*); the Aps. (β); learned brahmans in the eastern region (γ), in the southern region (δ), in the western region (ϵ), in the north (ζ); the principal kings (η) (to be recited at sunset and sunrise) (XIII, **166**).—§ 776: *Janamejaya* said: When *Bhīshma* was lying on a bed of arrows, and the *Pāṇḍavas* were sitting around him, my great-grandfather *Yudhishṭhira* heard these expositions of mysteries, etc.; what else did *Yudhishṭhira* do? *Vaiçampāyana* said: When *Bhīshma* became silent, all the kings became silent; then *Vyāsa*, saying that *Yudhishṭhira*, etc., had now been restored to their own nature, asked *Bhīshma* to give *Yudhishṭhira* leave to return to the city, which he did, giving *Yudhishṭhira* some final exhortations, and friendly asking him to return when the hour came for his death. Then *Yudhishṭhira* with his relatives and followers set out for *Hāstinapura*, and entered the city with *Dhṛtarāshṭra*, *Gāndhārī*, Ṛ., the citizens, the inhabitants of the country, and his counsellors (XIII, **167**).

Anūdara, son of Dhṛtarāshṭra. § 131 (Aṃçāvat.): I, **67**, 2734.—§ 182 (Dhṛtarāshṭra-putra-nāma-kathana): I, **117**, 4547.

Anudātta ("the lower accent"), a Fire. § 491 (Āṅgirasa): III, **220**, 14163 (*Anudāttau*, i.e. Udātta and Anudātta PCR., produced by Pāñcajanya from his arms), 14165 (son of Prāṇa).

Anudyūta ("renewal of the gambling"). § 10 (Parvas.): I, **2**, 319 (sc. *parva*, i.e. Anudyūtaparvan).

Anudyūtaparvan. § 302: When the *Pāṇḍavas* had left Hāstinapura with all their wealth and jewels, *Duḥçāsana* complained of it to *Duryodhana*, who, with *Karṇa* and *Çakuni*, quoting the words of *Bṛhaspati* when counselling *Indra* about politics, and declaring that the *Pāṇḍavas* would certainly revenge themselves, prevailed upon *Dhṛtarāshṭra* to invite them a second time to a match of gambling between *Yudhishṭhira* and *Çakuni*, on the condition that the defeated party should repair to the woods for twelve years, dressed in deer-skins, and spend the thirteenth year in some inhabited country unrecognized, and if recognized, be exiled for another twelve years. If the *Pāṇḍavas* should succeed in observing this vow for thirteen years, the *Dhārtarāshṭras* would in the meantime have made alliances and have assembled an invincible army, so that they could defeat them if they reappeared. *Droṇa*, *Somadatta*, *Bāhlīka*, *Gautama*, *Vidura*, *Açvatthāman*, *Vaiçyāputra* (i.e. *Yuyutsu*), *Bhūriçravas*, *Bhīshma*, and *Vikarṇa* dissuaded in vain (II, **74**).—§ 303: *Gāndhārī* reminded *Dhṛtarāshṭra* of the counsel *Vidura* had given, when *Duryodhana* was born, to kill him, and recommended him to do it now, and not to let the gambling match take place, saying that it would cause the destruction of the whole race of the *Kurus*. But *Dhṛtarāshṭra* could not act contrary to the will of his sons (II, **75**).—§ 304: The royal messengers overtook *Yudhishṭhira* when he had already gone a long way. *Yudhishṭhira* having said, "Although a golden animal was an impossibility, *Rāma* suffered himself to be tempted by a golden deer," they returned. The gambling began on the above-mentioned conditions (cf. III, 1362 ff., where the conditions are stated somewhat differently), and *Yudhishṭhira* lost (II, **76**). The *Pāṇḍavas*, casting off their royal robes, attired themselves in deer-skins. *Duḥçāsana* exulted, and exhorted *Kṛshṇā* to abandon the fallen *Pāṇḍavas* and choose a husband among the *Kurus*. As *Bhīma* rebuked him and threatened to slay him with his followers, *Duḥçāsana*, dancing around, said, "O cow! O cow!" *Bhīshma* again swore to drink his blood and to kill all the *Dhārtarāshṭras*. As the *Pāṇḍavas* were going away, *Duryodhana* mimicked the tread of *Bhīma*, who then said: "I will slay *Duryodhana* with my mace, and place my foot on his head. *Dhanañjaya* will slay *Karṇa*, and *Sahadeva* will slay *Çakuni*, and I will drink the blood of *Duḥçāsana*." *Arjuna* and *Sahadeva* approved of it. *Nakula*, "the handsomest of men," vowed to kill all the *Dhārtarāshṭras* that had insulted *Draupadī* (II, **77**).—§ 305: *Yudhishṭhira* bids farewell to *Bhīshma*, *Somadatta*, *Bāhlīka*, *Droṇa*, *Kṛpa*, *Açvatthāman*, *Vidura*, *Dhṛtarāshṭra*, the *Dhārtarāshṭras* *Yuyutsu*, *Sañjaya*, etc. *Vidura* kept *Pṛthā* in his abode, and consoled *Yudhishṭhira*: "Formerly thou wast instructed on the *Himavat* by *Meru-Sāvarṇi*, in *Vāraṇāvata* by *Dvaipāyana*, on *Bhṛgutuṅga* by *Rāma*, on the *Dṛshadvatī* by *Çambhu*, near *Añjana* by the great *ṛshi* *Asita*, by *Bhṛgu* on the banks of *Kalmāshī*; *Nārada* always beholds thee, and this *Dhaumya* is thy *purohita*,—resolve to win victory like *Indra*, to control thy wrath like *Yama*, to give in charity like *Kuvera*, to control all passions like *Varuṇa*." So *Yudhishṭhira* went away, bowing to *Bhīshma* and *Droṇa*, (II, **78**). When *Kṛshṇā* took leave of *Kuntī*, *Kuntī* broke out in complaints, and especially recommended her ever to keep her eye on *Sahadeva*. When *Kuntī* beheld her sons clad in deer-skins, surrounded by rejoicing foes, she embraced them and broke out in complaints, asking why *Kṛshṇa*, who dwells in *Dvārakā*, and is without beginning and without end, does not deliver them from such woe. "O *Sahadeva*! cease to go! thou art my dearest child, O son of *Mādrī*!" The *Pāṇḍavas*, having consoled her, set out for the woods, and *Vidura* led her to his house. The ladies of *Dhṛtarāshṭra's* house wept, blaming the *Kauravas*; and *Dhṛtarāshṭra*, anxious, sent for *Vidura* (II, **79**).—§ 306: Questioned by *Dhṛtarāshṭra*, *Vidura* described the attitude of the *Pāṇḍavas*, etc., when going away (*a*). The citizens cried out in grief, blaming the *Kurus*. Flashings of lightning and other terrible omens appeared. *Nārada* appeared, surrounded by great *ṛshis*, and foreboded that on the fourteenth year thence the *Kauravas* would all be destroyed by *Bhīma* and *Arjuna*. Then he disappeared through the skies. *Duryodhana, Karṇa,* and *Çakuni* offered the kingdom to *Droṇa,* who said that the *Pāṇḍavas* were incapable of being slain; that they would practise the *brahmacarya* for twelve years, and then return in anger; that he (*Droṇa*) would protect the *Dhārtarāshṭras,* who had sought his protection, to the best of his ability; but that he would himself be slain by *Dhṛshṭadyumna,* whom *Drupada* had obtained (together with *Kṛshṇā*) from the fire by the ascetic power of *Yāja* and *Upayāja*; "it is widely known in the world that *Dhṛshṭadyumna* will slay *Droṇa.*" *Dhṛtarāshṭra* sent *Vidura* to bring the *Pāṇḍavas* back, or, if they did not come back, to send them off with respect, with their weapons, cars, and infantry, etc. (II, **80**). — § 307: *Sañjaya* spoke to *Dhṛtarāshṭra* about the perversity of his policy. *Dhṛtarāshṭra* related that when *Kṛshṇā* was dragged into the court the grief was so great that the enraged brahmans did not that evening perform their *agnihotra*; he also related the omens which had appeared on the occasion, etc. (II, **81**).

Anugītā ("repetition of the Bhagavadgītā"). § 10 (Parvas.): I, **2**, 354 (*parva . . adhyātmavācakaṃ,* i.e. Anugītāparvan).

[Anugītāparvan] ("the section containing the repetition of the Bhagavadgītā," the 94th of the minor parvans of Mhbhr.; cf. Anugītā). § 782: *Janamejaya* said: When *Kṛshṇa* and *Arjuna,* after having slain their enemies, dwelt there in the palace, what conversation took place between them? *Vaiçampāyana* said: *Arjuna,* having recovered his kingdom, spent his time joyously in the company of *Kṛshṇa* in that beautiful palace. There they repaired to a particular part of the palace with their friends and relatives. *Arjuna* asked *Kṛshṇa* to repeat to him what he had taught him before the battle [i.e. Bhagavadgītā], especially as he would soon repair to *Dvārakā.* *Kṛshṇa* is discontented because *Arjuna* cannot remember it; he would now, however, recite an old story upon the same topic. "There came a brahman from *Svargaloka* and was honoured by us; hear what he said, asked by us." The brahman said: There came a brahman *Kāçyapa,* possessed of penance, etc., to some other brahman, who had become conversant with all the authorities on religion, etc., crowned with ascetic success (*siddhaṃ*), able to move everywhere at will (*kramamāṇaṃ*), knowing the science of disappearing at will, roving with invisible *Siddhas* and celestial musicians (? *cakradharaiḥ,* PCR.); *Kāçyapa* honoured him as his *guru,* and the brahman spoke to him about transmigration, comparing his own example; at last he had renounced the world and attained to his present success, and should not have to return to this world, but would come to "*Bráhman's* eternal abode"; he promised to answer *Kāçyapa's* questions (XIV, **16**). *Kṛshṇa* said: Asked by *Kāçyapa,* the brahman discoursed on how *Jīva* casts off and then attains to a body, how Emancipation is achieved, and where acts do exist when *Jīva* becomes divested of body, etc.; how death is brought about; the happiness and misery of *Jīva* determined by acts (XIV, **17**); how *Jīva* enters the womb; *Brahmán* first formed a body of his own, then he created *Pradhāna,* the material cause (*prakṛtiṃ*) of all embodied creatures; indifference to pleasure and pain leads to the Supreme Seat (XIV, **18**); who is said to be emancipated; on the science of *yoga*; how *Jīva* attains to emancipation.—*Kṛshṇa* said: Then the brahman disappeared; this discourse was, in fact, what thou (Arjuna) heardst on thy car; this is a great mystery even to the gods; at no time or place has this been heard by man in this world; by adhering to this religion, even those who are of sinful birth, women, *vaiçyas,* and *çūdras,* attain to the highest goal; *yoga* takes place in his case who devotes himself to its constant practice (*nityayuktasya*) for a period of six months (XIV, **19**). In this connection the ancient narrative of a discourse between a married couple is cited: [Brāhmaṇagītā] (*b*) (XIV, **20–34**). Asked by *Arjuna* about *Bráhman, Kṛshṇa* recited the old story of the discourse between a preceptor and his disciple on this subject: Guruçishyasaṃvāda (*g*). Asked by *Arjuna, Kṛshṇa* said that he is the preceptor, and the mind his pupil; "formerly, when the hour of battle came, this very religion was declared by me; and now, it is long since I saw my father; I wish to see him again with thy leave."—*Vaiçampāyana* said: *Arjuna* replied: "We shall go to-day from this town to *Hāstinapura* and inform *Yudhishṭhira*" (XIV, **35–51**).—§ 783: *Vaiçampāyana* said: *Kṛshṇa* caused *Dāruka* to yoke his car, and then set out for *Hāstinapura* with *Arjuna.* *Arjuna* praised *Kṛshṇa,* "the soul of the universe, etc.," as he had learned from *Nārada,* etc. (*a*), saying that *Çrī* is always established in him, and mentioning *Duryodhana,* etc. (*β*). Arrived at *Hāstinapura,* they entered the palace of *Dhṛtarāshṭra,* where they saw *Dhṛtarāshṭra,* etc. (*γ*). *Kṛshṇa* passed the night in the apartments of *Arjuna.* At morning they proceeded to *Yudhishṭhira,* who sat with his ministers; *Yudhishṭhira* mentioned *Vasudeva* (his maternal uncle), etc. (*δ*), and asked *Kṛshṇa* to think of *Yudhishṭhira,* etc. (*ε*), and to come back to his horse-sacrifice. *Kṛshṇa* took no gifts from him, took leave of *Kuntī* (his maternal aunt), *Vidura,* etc., and then set out from *Hāstinapura* with *Subhadrā* on the car, accompanied by *Arjuna, Sātyaki,* etc. (*ζ*); then, having caused them to return, he with *Dāruka* and *Sātyaki* proceeded to the city of the *Ānarttas* (XIV, **52**).—§ 784: *Arjuna* repeatedly embraced *Kṛshṇa,* etc. (omens). As he came to the desert, he beheld *Utaṅka* (*b*) (XIV, **53–58**).—§ 785: *Janamejaya* said: What did *Kṛshṇa* next do, after having granted that boon to *Utaṅka*? *Vaiçampāyana* said: Having granted that boon to *Utaṅka, Kṛshṇa,* accompanied by *Sātyaki,* proceeded to *Dvārakā* on his car, passing many lakes and rivers and forests and hills. He came there when the festival of *Raivataka* had begun; the *Raivataka* hill shone with great splendour (description; the trees looked like the *kalpa*-trees of *Indra's* garden; the mountain looked like *Meru*); gifts were ceaselessly being made to the distressed, or blind, or helpless. *Kṛshṇa* recounted the incidents of the great battle to his father (XIV, **59**). *Vasudeva* said: Tell me about the battle between the *Pāṇḍavas* and *Bhīshma,* etc. (*a*). *Vaiçampāyana* said: *Kṛshṇa* narrated, also in the presence of his mother, how the *Kaurava* heroes had been slain in battle. *Kṛshṇa's* narrative of the battle (*β*). *Vaiçampāyana* said: The *Vṛshṇis* became filled with grief (XIV, **60**). *Kṛshṇa* had passed by the slaughter of *Abhimanyu*; *Subhadrā* noticed it and fell down; *Vasudeva* then also fell down, and then asked *Kṛshṇa* to tell the whole truth (*γ*). *Kṛshṇa* consoled him (*δ*) (XIV, **61**). *Vasudeva* and *Kṛshṇa,* etc. (*ε*), made excellent obsequial offerings to *Abhimanyu,* and *Kṛshṇa* fed six millions of brahmans and gave away heaps of gold, etc. Also the *Pāṇḍavas* at *Hāstinapura* were filled with grief for *Abhimanyu*; *Uttarā* totally abstained from all food, and her relatives feared for her embryo; *Vyāsa* came and predicted to *Pṛthā, Uttarā, Arjuna,* and *Yudhishṭhira,* that the son of *Uttarā* would become a great prince, through the influence of *Kṛshṇa* and *Vyāsa*; *Abhimanyu* had gone to the regions of the gods. *Arjuna* became cheerful; the child in *Uttarā's* womb grew like the moon in the bright fortnight; *Vyāsa* urged *Yudhishṭhira* to perform the horse-sacrifice, and disappeared; *Yudhishṭhira* set his mind on the journey for bringing wealth (XIV, **62**). *Janamejaya* said: Having heard these words of *Vyāsa*, what steps were taken by *Yudhishṭhira*?—how did he succeed in obtaining the wealth of *Marutta*? *Vaiçampāyana* said: Having heard the words of *Vyāsa*, *Yudhishṭhira* summoned all his brothers, reminding them of the words of *Vyāsa*, *Bhīshma*, and *Kṛshṇa* about *Marutta's* gold; *Bhīmasena* was of his opinion, saying that they must worship *Çiva* and his followers; then the K.s, who protected the treasures, would certainly yield; *Yudhishṭhira* was pleased; the others, headed by *Arjuna*, approved. The *Pāṇḍavas* ordered their army to march under the *nakshatra Dhruva* (i.e. *Rohiṇī*, Nīl.), and on the day *Dhruva* (i.e. Sunday, Nīl.), and set out, having worshipped *Çiva* with *modakas*, frumenty, and cakes of meat, taking leave of *Dhṛtarāshṭra*, etc. (ζ), and keeping *Yuyutsu* in the capital (XIV, **63**). Then they set out (description); arrived at the spot, they pitched their camp, placing the brahmans and *Āgniveçya* (i.e. *Dhaumya*, Nīl.) in the van; then the *Pāṇḍavas* and the other kings, and the brahmans and priests, having performed propitiatory rites, and placing the king and his ministers in the middle, caused the camp to be pitched by laying out six roads and nine divisions; king *Yudhishṭhira* caused a separate encampment to be made for the infuriated elephants; the brahmans declared this very day to be an auspicious one; on this day they would live upon water alone, and they should all fast; they passed the night on beds of *kuça*-grass, listening to the discourses of the learned brahmans. When the cloudless morning came, the brahmans told *Yudhishṭhira* (XIV, **64**) to make offerings to *Çiva*. *Dhaumya* performed the rites (description), and gave *bali* to the servants of *Çiva*; offerings were next made to *Kubera*, *Maṇibhadra*, and to the other Y. and lords of Bh. (with *kṛçaras*, and meat, and *nivāpas* mixed with sesame seeds); the king gave thousands of cows to the brahmans; then he ordered *bali* for the night-wandering Bh. Then the king, placing *Vyāsa* ahead, proceeded to the spot where the treasure was, once more worshipping *Kubera*, etc. (η). Numerous costly vessels were dug out and placed in wooden chests, etc.; there were 60,000 camels, 120,000 horses, and 100,000 elephants, etc. (description). Once more worshipping *Çiva*, they set out for *Hāstinapura* with the permission of *Vyāsa*, and placing *Dhaumya* in the van, marched a *goyuta* (four miles, PCR.) every day (XIV, **65**). Meanwhile, *Kṛshṇa* with *Pradyumna*, etc. (δ), came to see *Draupadī*, etc. (ι), and was received by *Dhṛtarāshṭra*, etc. (κ). *Uttarā* gave birth to *Parikshit*, who was born without life, afflicted with the *Brāhma* weapon; *Kuntī*, etc. (λ), lamented, and *Kuntī* asked *Kṛshṇa*, who came with *Yuyudhāna*, to revive him and rescue *Uttarā*, etc. (μ), reminding him that *Abhimanyu* had said to *Uttarā* that her son would learn the art of weapons, etc., by the *Vṛshṇis* and *Andhakas*; *Kṛshṇa* comforted her (XIV, **66**). Then *Subhadrā* lamented (ν) (XIV, **67**). *Kṛshṇa* entered the lying-in room (description; with articles destructive of Rā.); *Uttarā* lamented (ξ) (XIV, **68**), and so did *Kuntī*, etc. *Kṛshṇa* touched water and withdrew the *Brāhma* weapon, and "as *Kaṃsa* and *Keçin* have rightly been slain by me, etc." (*tena satyena*), he revived the child (XIV, **69**). *Parikshit* illumined the lying-in room with his energy; Rā. fled or were destroyed; a voice in the sky applauded *Kṛshṇa*; the *Brāhma* weapon returned to *Brahmán*; at the command of *Kṛshṇa* the brahmans were made to utter benedictions; *Kuntī*, etc. (ο), were glad and praised *Kṛshṇa*, and so did wrestlers, actors, astrologers, etc.; *Kṛshṇa* and the other *Vṛshṇi* chiefs made precious gifts to the child, whom *Kṛshṇa* called *Parikshit* (etymology). When he was a month old, the *Pāṇḍavas* came back with the wealth, and were received by those *Vṛshṇis* and the citizens; *Vidura* ordered various kinds of worship to be offered to the gods in their temples, etc.; with dancers and singers, the city resembled the mansion of *Kubera*, etc. (description) (XIV, **70**). *Kṛshṇa* and his ministers went out to see the *Pāṇḍavas*, who entered the city together with the *Vṛshṇis*, and worshipped *Dhṛtarāshṭra*, etc. (π), and also *Kṛshṇa*, having heard how he had revived *Parikshit*; after a few days *Vyāsa* came and was worshipped by the *Vṛshṇis* and *Andhakas*, and he permitted *Yudhishṭhira* to perform the horse-sacrifice, "a purifier of all sinners." *Yudhishṭhira* asked *Kṛshṇa* to perform the sacrifice; but *Kṛshṇa* told *Yudhishṭhira* to appoint them to whatever tasks he likes; "when thou sacrificest, *Bhīmasena*, etc. (ρ), will be sacrificing" (XIV, **71**). *Yudhishṭhira* asked *Vyāsa* to cause him to be initiated; *Vyāsa* said that he and *Paila* and *Yājñavalkya* would perform the rites; the initiation would be performed on the day of full moon in the month of *Caitra*; "let *sūtas* and brahmans well versed in the science of horses select a worthy horse"; all the articles were duly procured; *Vyāsa* ordained that the *sphya* and the *kūrca* should be made of gold; "let the horse be loosened to-day." Asked by *Yudhishṭhira*, *Vyāsa* ordained that *Arjuna* should protect the horse; *Bhīmasena* the kingdom aided by *Nakula*; *Sahadeva* should attend to all the relatives invited (with the permission of *Dhṛtarāshṭra*); *Yudhishṭhira* asked *Arjuna* to spare all hostile kings as much as possible and to invite them to the horse-sacrifice (XIV, **72**). *Yudhishṭhira* was initiated by the *Ṛtvijs* (description); the horse was let loose. *Arjuna* with *Gāṇḍīva* followed the horse; all *Hāstinapura* came out wanting to behold him; a disciple of *Yājñavalkya* followed him in order to perform auspicious rites for him; and also many brahmans and *kshattriyas*. During the horse's wanderings many great and wonderful battles were fought; the horse wandered over the whole earth; from the north it turned to the east: kings in myriads fought against *Arjuna* because they had lost their kinsmen on the field of *Kurukshetra*, and innumerable *Kirātas*, *Yavanas*, *Mlecchas*, and *Āryas*; "I shall narrate only the principal battles" (XIV, **73**). The *Trigartas* (the sons and grandsons of the slain) attacked *Arjuna*, who in vain asked them to forbear; the *Trigarta* king *Sūryavarman* & *Arjuna*, who slew *Sūryavarman's* younger brother *Ketuvarman*; *Dhṛtavarman* & *Arjuna*, who was wounded in his hand and let fall *Gāṇḍīva*, but took it up again and slew eighteen warriors; the *Trigartas* fled and accepted *Arjuna's* dominion (XIV, **74**). In *Prāgjyotisha*, *Bhagadatta's* son king *Vajradatta* (description) attacked *Arjuna* on his elephant, but, after a fierce battle (XIV, **75**) lasting three days, he on the fourth day had his elephant slain, and he promised to come to the horse-sacrifice (XIV, **76**). Recollecting *Jayadratha*, the *Saindhavas*, mounted on cars, attacked *Arjuna*, who was on foot; a terrible wind began to blow, and *Rāhu* swallowed up both the sun and the moon at the same time, etc.; *Kailāsa* began to tremble; the seven Ṛ. and the other Ṛ. of heaven breathed hot sighs; Indra's bow appeared in the sky, and clouds poured flesh and blood on the earth; *Gāṇḍīva* fell down; the gods, D.-ṛ., *Saptarshis*, and B.-ṛ. recited (*jepuḥ*) "victory" to *Arjuna*, who once more used his bow; the *Saindhavas* fled (XIV, **77**), but once more rallied; *Arjuna* urged them to surrender, but in vain, because they only thought of *Jayadratha*; many were slain; then *Duḥçalā*, taking her grandson, the son of *Suratha* [the son of *Jayadratha*], in her arms, repaired to *Arjuna*; *Arjuna* dropped his bow and asked about *Suratha*; she said that he had died from sorrow when he heard of *Arjuna's* arrival; she drew a parallel between *Suratha's* [orphan] son and *Abhimanyu's* [orphan] son *Parikshit*. Recollecting *Dhṛtarāshṭra* and *Gāndhārī*, and censuring *kshattriya* practices and *Duryodhana*, *Arjuna* consoled and embraced her; *Duḥçalā* asked her warriors to desist, and returned home. At last the horse arrived at *Maṇipūra* (XIV, **78**), where *Babhruvāhana*, *Arjuna's* son by *Citrāṅgadā*, humbly approached *Arjuna*, together with a number of brahmans, bringing treasure in his van; *Arjuna* angrily blamed him for having neglected his duty as a *kshattriya*. *Ulūpī* came from within the earth and beheld her [step-]son standing cheerless, and incited him to fight *Arjuna*, which he did (description of his car); he even caused the sacrificial horse to be seized; gravely wounded, *Arjuna* praised his son highly; he cut off his standard, which was set with gold and resembled a golden palmyra, and then he slew his steeds; at last *Arjuna* fell down in a swoon, and so did *Babhruvāhana*; *Citrāṅgadā* repaired to the battlefield weeping piteously (XIV, **79**); she indulged in copious lamentations, lost her senses, and fell down on the earth; regaining consciousness and seeing *Ulūpī*, she blamed her for having brought about *Arjuna's* slaughter by *Babhruvāhana*, and asked her to revive him; "I do not grieve for my slain son, I only grieve for my husband"; otherwise she would sit in *prāya* and die; the horse she had set free. Regaining consciousness *Babhruvāhana* lamented piteously, saying that now he had slain his father, he would wander over the earth, covering himself with his father's skin, or with the two halves of his head, as an expiation, or else he would die; he took an oath (touching water) that, if *Arjuna* was not revived, he would emaciate his own body, sitting on the field of battle; "I shall without doubt have to sink into hell; he who has slain a heroic *kshattriya* becomes purified by making a gift of 100 cows; I, who have slain my father, cannot be rescued." *Ulūpī* thought of the gem that has the virtue of reviving a dead man; the gem, thus thought of, came there; she said that *Arjuna* had not been vanquished by *Babhruvāhana*, but *Ulūpī* had exhibited this illusion for the benefit of *Arjuna*. As soon as the prince had placed the gem on the breast of *Arjuna* the latter revived. *Indra* poured down celestial flowers, etc. *Arjuna* wondered why the two ladies were present, and why everything seemed to indicate grief, and asked *Babhruvāhana* who told him to question *Ulūpī* (XIV, **80**). Asked by *Arjuna*, *Ulūpī* recited the curse of the *Vasus* (approved by *Gaṅgā*) because *Arjuna* had slain *Bhīshma* in unfair fight (while he was engaged with *Çikhaṇḍin* and had ceased to fight); if *Arjuna* had died without having expiated his sin he would have fallen into Hell; hearing the curse of the *Vasus*, *Ulūpī* had consulted her father, who prevailed upon the *Vasus* that *Arjuna* should be freed from their curses when he had been slain by *Babhruvāhana*. *Arjuna* highly approved of *Ulūpī's* action, and told *Babhruvāhana* to come with his mother and counsellors and officers to the horse-sacrifice; *Babhruvāhana* promised to come and to take upon himself the task of distributing food among the brahmans (*dvijātipariveçakaḥ*). He asked *Arjuna* to pass the night in the city with his two wives; but *Arjuna* was prevented by his vow of following the horse; he took leave and proceeded on his way (XIV, **81**). The horse, having wandered over the whole earth, turned its face towards *Hāstinapura*. At *Rājagṛha*, the *Magadha* king *Meghasandhi*, son of *Sahadeva*, attacked *Arjuna*, who was on foot, from his chariot; *Meghasandhi* was worsted, but spared and told to come to the horse-sacrifice. The horse then proceeded along the sea-coast through the country of the *Vaṅgas*, *Puṇḍras*, and *Koçalas*; in these countries *Arjuna* vanquished innumerable *Mleccha* armies (XIV, **82**). *Arjuna* proceeded towards the south. The horse came to *Cuktimatī*, the beautiful city of the *Cedis*. *Çarabha*, the son of *Çiçupāla*, fought *Arjuna*, and then worshipped him. Then the horse came to the *Kāçis*, *Aṅgas*, *Koçalas*, *Kirātas*, and *Taṅgaṇas*; then to the *Daçārṇas*, whose ruler *Citrāṅgada* was vanquished by *Arjuna*; then to the dominions of the *Nishāda* king, the son of *Ekalavya*, who was vanquished after a furious battle; then towards the southern ocean, where the *Draviḍas*, *Andhras*, *Māhishakas*, and *Kolvagireyas* (B. *Kolla°*) were subjugated; then to the *Surāshṭras*, *Gokarṇa*, *Prabhāsa*, and *Dvāravatī*, where the *Yādava* youths were going to beat the horse, but were forbidden by King *Ugrasena*, who came to *Arjuna* with *Vasudeva*. Then the horse proceeded along the coast of the western ocean to the prosperous country of the five rivers; then to the *Gāndhāras*, where a fierce battle ensued with the *Gāndhāra* king, the son of *Çakuni* (XIV, **83**), who wanted to avenge the slaughter of *Çakuni*; many *Gāndhāras* were slain; at last the king, disregarding *Arjuna's* peaceful advice, fought alone; *Arjuna* shot off his headgear; then he and all the *Gāndhāras* fled; the mother of the king and all the aged ministers came out and forbade her son to fight; *Arjuna* said he had spared him for the sake of *Gāndhārī* and *Dhṛtarāshṭra*, and told him to come to the horse-sacrifice (XIV, **84**). The horse then turned towards the road that led to *Hāstinapura*. As these tidings reached the *Kuru* court through the intelligence-bearers, *Yudhishṭhira* rejoiced, and on the twelfth day of the bright fortnight of *Māgha*, under a favourable constellation, he summoned his brothers (σ), and caused *Bhīma* to let learned brahmans select a beautiful spot for the sacrificial compound (description). Then *Bhīma* sent messengers to invite the kings of the earth; they brought gems, female slaves, horses, and weapons. All the foremost brahmans also came there with their disciples; likewise many dialecticians disputing with each other. All was made of gold. One hundred thousand brahmans were fed; many mountains of food, many large tanks of curds, and many lakes of ghee were seen there. The entire population of *Jambudvīpa* was collected together (XIV, **85**). *Yudhishṭhira* appointed *Bhīmasena* to pay proper honours to the royal guests and to their attendants. *Kṛshṇa* came with the *Vṛshṇis*, *Baladeva*, etc. (τ); *Kṛshṇa* told *Yudhishṭhira* about *Arjuna* (having heard it from a confidential agent of his in *Dvārakā*), that he had become very much emaciated, and that he was near at hand; he had warned against a carnage similar to that at the presenting of the *Arghya*, and he had especially recommended *Babhruvāhana* (XIV, **86**). *Yudhishṭhira* enquired of *Kṛshṇa* why *Arjuna* had to suffer such hardships in life; *Kṛshṇa* attributes it to the elevation of *Arjuna's* cheek-bones; *Draupadī* looked angrily at *Kṛshṇa*, who approved of her love. *Bhīmasena*, etc., became gratified with *Arjuna's* triumphs. A messenger announced the arrival of *Arjuna*, and was presented with large gifts. On the second day *Arjuna* entered the city (description); people said that he had surpassed even *Sagara*, etc. *Arjuna* saluted *Yudhishṭhira*, etc. (υ). *Babhruvāhana* came with his mother and entered the abode of *Kuntī* (XIV, **87**); *Citrāṅgadā* [and *Ulūpī*] saluted *Pṛthā*, etc. (φ); *Babhruvāhana* saluted *Dhṛtarāshṭra*, etc. (χ); *Kṛshṇa* gave him an excellent chariot and steeds, and the others likewise gave him presents. On the third day *Vyāsa* told *Yudhishṭhira* to commence the sacrifice, and to make the *dakshiṇā* threefold. *Yudhishṭhira* underwent the *dīkshā*. The sacrifice was duly performed (description); 300 animals were tied to the stakes in addition to the horse; this sacrifice was honoured by the presence of D.-ṛ., G., Aps., Kp., and Ku.; there were the disciples of *Vyāsa*, etc. (ψ) (XIV, **88**); having cooked the other animals, the priests sacrificed the horse; after having cut it into pieces (B. cooking), they caused *Draupadī* to sit near it; then the brahmans cooked its marrow; *Yudhishṭhira* and his brothers smelled the sin-destroying smoke of that marrow; the limbs (heart, tongue, breast, etc., Nīl.) the sixteen *ṛtvijs* offered into the fire. *Vyāsa* and his disciples eulogised *Yudhishṭhira*, who gave 1,000 crores of golden *nishkas* to the brahmans, and the whole earth as *dakshiṇā* to *Vyāsa*; *Vyāsa* returned it to him, telling him to give the purchasing value instead; *Yudhishṭhira* said that the *dakshiṇā* for the horse-sacrifice is the earth, and that he would enter the woods and tell them to divide it into four parts, one for each of the four principal priests (? *cāturhotrapramāṇataḥ*; PCR. "according to what is done in the *cāturhotra* sacrifice"); his brothers and *Draupadī* approved of his words, as did also a voice in the sky; *Vyāsa* and *Kṛshṇa* prevailed upon him to retain the earth and give away millions of golden coins, trebling the *dakshiṇā* for the horse-sacrifice; no other king would be able to accomplish what *Yudhishṭhira* thus did after the manner of *Marutta*; *Vyāsa* gave the wealth (the price of the earth) to the officiating priests, in four parts, and they distributed it among the brahmans, who were also permitted to take the ornaments of gold, etc.; the remaining wealth was allotted to *kshattriyas*, *Vaiçyas*, *Çūdras*, and *Mlecchas*. *Vyāsa* gave away his own share to *Kuntī*, who devoted it to various meritorious acts. *Yudhishṭhira* performed the final sacrificial bath, and dismissed the kings, etc. (ω), with proper honours and gifts. There were oceans of wine of different kinds, etc. (description); people of different realms speak of this sacrifice to this day. Then *Yudhishṭhira* entered his capital (XIV, **89**).—§ 786: *Janamejaya* said: Tell me of any wonderful incident that occurred in the sacrifice of my grandfather. *Vaiçampāyana* related how a mongoose disparaged the sacrifice: Nakulākhyāna (*b*); then the mongoose disappeared, and the brahmans returned home. "Thou shouldst not think highly of sacrifice; millions of Ṛ. have ascended to Heaven with the sole aid of their penances; abstention from injury, contentment, proper conduct, sincerity, penances, self-restraint, truthfulness, and gifts are each equal in point of merit to sacrifice" (XIV, **90**). Seeing that kings are given to sacrifice, M.-ṛ. to penance, and learned brahmans to tranquillity, etc., *Janamejaya* cannot but think that nothing can be compared with the result of sacrifices, since *Indra* obtained the sovereignty over the gods by his many sacrifices; and when *Yudhishṭhira*, *Bhīma*, and *Arjuna* resembled *Indra*, "why did then that mongoose depreciate *Yudhishṭhira's* horse-sacrifice?" *Vaiçampāyana* said: Formerly, when *Indra* was performing a sacrifice the Ṛ. felt compassion on the animals, and said to *Indra* that the slaughter of animals in sacrifices had not been ordained; according to the [true] scriptural ordinances the sacrifice should be performed with seeds of grain which had been kept for three years. As *Indra* did not accept their words, a great dispute arose; they referred to the *Cedi* king *Vasu*, who declared that a sacrifice may be performed with whichever of the two kinds of objects is ready; he therefore had to enter *Rasātala*; therefore no one should singly be relied upon, when a doubt arises, except *Brahmán*; gifts made by a sinful person and with wealth acquired by unrighteous means became lost; while men possessing the wealth of penances acquired great merit and proceeded to Heaven, by giving away, to the best of their ability, grains of corn, or roots, etc., or water or leaves. The same results are also won by compassion, *brahmacarya*, truthfulness, kindness, fortitude, and forgiveness, which are the eternal foundations of eternal righteousness; having made gifts of articles lawfully acquired, *Viçvāmitra*, etc. (*a*), have attained to high success; those amongst brahmans, *kshattriyas*, *vaiçyas*, and *Çūdras*, who betake themselves to penances, and who purify themselves by gifts and other acts of righteousness, proceed to Heaven (XIV, **91**). *Janamejaya* said: If Heaven is the result of wealth acquired by lawful means, please tell me all about it; thou hast told me the great result that accrued to the brahman living by gleaning grains from his gift of powdered barley. *Vaiçampāyana* cited the old narrative of what occurred in former days at the great sacrifice of *Agastya* (*e*).—Asked by *Janamejaya*, *Vaiçampāyana* explained that the mongoose (v. Nakulākhyāna) with a golden head was *Dharma*, who had been cursed by P., but freed from his curse by disparaging himself in the form of *Yudhishṭhira*; "the mongoose disappeared there in our very sight" (XIV, **92**).

Anugoptṛ, a Viçvadeva. § 749 (Ānuçāsanik.): XIII, **91**γ, 4362.

Aṇuha. § 6 (Anukram.): I, **1**, 226 (belongs to the past).

Anuhlāda (B. °*hrā*°), son of Hiraṇyakaçipu. § 89 (Hiraṇyakaçipu): I, **65**, 2526.—§ 130 (Aṃçāvat.): **67**, 2643 (incarnated as Dhṛshṭaketu).—Cf. Daitya.

Anukampaka. § 678*b* (Mokshadh.): XII, **257**, 9150. *Bhīshma* said: In the *Kṛta*-age king *Anukampaka* (B. *Akampana*) had been brought under the sway of his foes in battle, and his son *Hari*, who was like *Nārāyaṇa* himself, had been slain in that battle with all his followers and troops. The king devoted himself to a life of tranquillity. *Nārada* told him Mṛtyuprajāpatisaṃvāda (*c*).—Cf. § 594 (Akampana).

Anukārin = Çiva (1000 names[2]).

Anukarman, a Viçvadeva. § 749 (Ānuçāsanik.): XIII, **91**γ, 4357.

Anukramaṇī ("table of contents"), the first chapter (Anukramaṇikā-parvan) of Mahābhārata, perhaps also the second (Parvasaṅgrahaparvan): I, **1**, 256.—Compare Anukramaṇikādhyāya; Parvānukramaṇī.

Anukramaṇikādhyāya(ḥ) ("table of contents chapter"), cf. Anukramaṇī: I, **1**, 102 (= Parvasaṅgraha?), 255 (i.e. Anukramaṇikā-parvan?).

[Anukramaṇikā-parvan], the first of the minor parvans (cf. Anukramaṇī). § 1: The Sūta Ugraçravas (Sauti), son of Lomaharshaṇa, had heard the Mahābhārata, which had been composed by Vyāsa, recited—under the direction of Dvaipāyana (i.e. Vyāsa) himself—by Vaiçampāyana, disciple of Vyāsa, at the serpent-sacrifice of king Janamejaya, son of Parikshit; he had thereupon undertaken a pilgrimage to the tīrthas (holy places) and visited Samantapañcaka (*b*); thence he came to the twelve years' sattra (long sacrifice) of

Çaunaka in the Naimisha forest, where he related the Mahābhārata, (§ 2) beginning with the adoration of Vishṇu identified with the Absolute (Brahmán), and (§ 3) a brief exposition of the creation and succession of beings from the Absolute through Brahmán, the 21 Prajāpatis (*a*), gods, etc. (*β*), down to the families of the Kurus, etc. (*γ*), mentioned in the poem.—§ 4: The Mahābhārata contains an enlarged and an abridged form; some make it begin with Manu (i.e. I, **75**, 18 = 3143; otherwise Nīl.), some with Āstīka (i.e. I, **13**, 1 = 1020), and some with Uparicara (i.e. I, **63**, 1 = 2334) (v. 52). Vyasa had composed the Mahābhārata in a moment, and, at the counsel of Brahmán, had Gaṇeça to write it down as fast as he dictated to him. (An enumeration of the first sixteen books is contained in v. 88–91.) The portion destined for men (100,000 çlokas out of six millions) he taught Vaiçampāyana, who narrated it in the intervals between the parts of the serpent-sacrifice of Janamejaya, first giving a survey of the principal contents (*a*), partly in the form of a conversation between Dhṛtarāshṭra and Sañjaya.—§ 5: Sañjaya, in order to console Dhṛtarāshṭra, first enumerated 24 great kings (*a*), who were formerly mentioned by Nārada to Çaivya (B. Çvaitya) when lamenting the loss of a son, and thereupon (§ 6) 66 others (*a*), who had all died.—§ 7: He, who hears or reads the Mahābhārata, is purified from the most atrocious sins (261 ff. = 254 ff.).

Anukūla = Vishṇu (1000 names).

Anumati. § 615*u* (Skanda): IX, **45**γ, 2515 (came to the investiture of Skanda).

Anūpā. § 102 (Aṃçāvat.): I, **65**, 2554 (one of the daughters of Prādhā).

Anūpadeça ("the land lying on the sea-coast"). § 641*f* (Pṛthu Vainya): XII, **59**, 2234 (given by Pṛthu Vainya to Sūta).

Anūpapati ("the lord of the sea-coast") = Arjuna Kārtavīrya: III, 10189.

Anūparāja ("the king of the sea-coast"). § 264 (Sabhākriyāp.): II, **4**β, 123 (*Durdharshaḥ*? among the kings who were present when Yudhishṭhira entered his palace).

Anupāvṛtta. § 574 (Jambūkh.): VI, **9**μ, 356 (*Upāvṛttā°ḥ*, a people in Bharatavarsha).

Anurādhā, a nakshatra. § 569 (Bhagavadyānap.): V, **143**θ, 4841 (omens).—§ 746 (Ānuçasanik.): XIII, **64**, 3273. § 710 (do.): **89**, 4202.—§ 760 (do.): XIII, **110**, 5391 (a candravrata should be instituted, when the moon is in conjunction with Mūla, *A.* being in his belly, etc.).

Anuruddha. § 761 (Ānuçāsanik.): XIII, **115**γ, 5662 (among the kings who had abstained from meat in the Kārttika month; B. has Ani°).

Anurūpa = Kṛshṇa.

Anushṇā. § 574 (Jambūkh.): VI, **9**λ, 331 (among the rivers in Bharatavarsha).

Anushṭubh = Vishṇu (1000 names).

Anuttama = Vishṇu (1000 names).

Anuvākāḥ = Kṛshṇa.

Anuvinda[1]. § 281 (Sahadeva): II, **31**, 1114 (*Vindānuvindāv Āvantyau*, conquered by Sahadeva on his Digvijaya). —§ 290 (Çiçupālav.): II, **44**, 1539 (do.).—§ 561 (Yānasandhip.): V, **66**εε, 2503 (*Vindā°āv Āvantyau*).—§ 572 (Rathāt.): V, **166**, 5753 (do.).—§ 593 (Ambop.): V, **195**δ, 7607 (do.).—§ 576 (Bhagavadg.): VI, **16**, 622 (*Vindānuvindau*); **17**, 673 (*Vindā°āv Āvantyau*).—§ 578 (Bhīshmavadhap.): VI, **45**, (21), 1742 (do.); **51**φ, 2107 (do.).—§ 580 (do.): **56**γ, 2408 (do.); **59**μ, 2584 (*Vindā°au*; ordered to attack Arjuna).—§ 584 (do.): **81***a*, 3533 (*Vindā°āv Āvantyau*), 3557 (1) (do.; fights Irāvat); **83**, 3654 (3) (= do.), 3656; **86**, 3823 (9) (*Vindā°āv Āvantyau*; attacked Dhṛshṭadyumna), 3827 (*Vindā°au*; attacked by Yudhishṭhira, ib. 10).—§ 586 (do.): **102**ι, 4666 (*Vindā°āv Āvantyau*; surrounded Arjuna).—§ 587 (do.): **108**δ, 5051 (do.); **113**ι, 5240 (fought Bhīmasena; do.), 5245 (do.), 5249 (*Vindā°au*), 5261 (*Vindā°āv Āvantyau*); **114**κ, 5309 (do.; fought Arjuna). —§ 590 (Droṇābhish.): VII, **14**, 542 (fought Cekitāna).—§ 592 (Saṃçaptakav.): VII, **25**, 1083 (*Vindā°āv Āvantyau*; fought Virāṭa); **32**ω, *aa*, 1410 (do.).—§ 596 (Pratijñāp.): **74**β, 2629 (do.). — § 598 (Jayadrathav.): **85***a*, 3025 (*Vindā°yoḥ*).—§ 599 (do.): **95**ζ, 3526 (*Vindā°āv Āvantyau*; fought Bhīmasena), 3533 (do.); **99**, 3691 (slain by Arjuna), 3693.—§ 604 (Karṇap.): VIII, **5**, 99 (*Vindā°āv Āvantyau*; "gone to the abode of Yama").—§ 608 (Karṇap.): VIII, **72**υυυ, 3612 (*Vindā°āv Āvantyau*; mentioned as having been vanquished by Arjuna).—§ 619 (Strīvil.): XI, **25**κ, 733 (*Vindā°āv Āvantyau*; lamented as slain).—Cf. Anuvinda[3].

Anuvinda[2], a Kaikeya prince (brother of Vinda). § 605 (Karṇap.): VIII, **13**, 492 (*Vindā°au Kaikeyau*), 507 (*°çiro 'harat*; slain by Sātyaki).

Anuvinda[3], son of Dhṛtarāshṭra (brother of Vinda; among the above quotations those not marked by *Āvantyau* might be referred to these two brothers). § 130 (Aṃçāvat.): I, **67**, 2729 (*Vindānuvindau*). — § 182 (Dhṛtarashṭraputranāmak.): I, **117**, 4542 (do.).—§ 512 (Ghoshayātrāp.): III, **242**, 14920 (*Vindā°āv* . . . ; seized by the Gandharvas).—§ 599 (Jayadrathav.): VII, **127**νν, 5177 (*Vindā°au*; Bhīma passed them and Duḥçala, etc., when he rushed against Droṇa's division), ξξ, 5209 (do.; slain by Bhīma).

Anuyāyin, a son of Dhṛtarāshṭra. § 130 (Aṃçāvat.): I, **67**, 2737 (V. has *Agrayāyin*).—§ 600 (Ghaṭotkacav.): VII, **157**ο, 6938 (slain by Bhīma; C. and PCR. *Ugrayāyy api*).

Anvagbhānu. § 150 (Pūruv.): I, **94**, 3698 (one of the ten sons of Raudrāçva and the Apsaras Miçrakeçī).

Anyagocarā, a Mātṛ. § 615*u* (Skanda): IX, **46**θ, 2645.

Āpa, a Fire. § 493 (Āṅgirasa): III, **222**, 14208 (*Āpasya duhitā*—B. *Muditā—bhāryā Sahasya paramā priyā* . . .).

Āpaddharma ("the duties in cases of need"). § 10 (Parvas.): I, **1**, 351 (*°aḥ parva*).—§ 11 (do.): I, **2**, 595 (*°āḥ*), i.e. Āpaddharmaparvan.

[Āpaddharmaparvan] ("the section relating to the duties in cases of need," the 69th of the minor parvans of Mhbh., cf. Āpaddharma). § 642: *Yudhishṭhira* enquired of *Bhīshma* what should be done by a weak and timid king, as also by one that is in great distress. *Bhīshma's* answer recommending peace and even the surrender of territory. The king should never surrender his person as long as he can avoid doing so. If the invading enemy be righteous, the assailed king should make peace; if otherwise, the assailed should fight bravely and fall (XII, **131**). How a *brahman* should subsist in times of calamity. *Bhīshma* began his exposition of the moral standard of unlucky times; in times of calamity the king may take from the wicked and give it to the good; at such times censurable acts do not become censurable; the king should never oppress *brahmans*, even at such times. Slander should be avoided. The tests of righteousness; difficulty in finding the course of duty. "Some regard ancient usage as the highest test of righteousness; they that are in favour of the conduct of *Caṅkha* towards *Likhita* do not hold this opinion" (XII, **132**). How a king should fill his treasury. The king should establish laws which he should never transgress (XII, **133**). The two duties of a *kshattriya* are the acquisition of religious merit and of wealth. The advantages of Power (XII, **134**).—§ 643: The old story of a robber who having in this world been observant of restraint did not meet with destruction in the next: Kāyavya-carita (*b*) (XII, **135**).—§ 644: What wealth should not be taken by the king (XII, **136**).—§ 645: Who enjoy happiness: Çākulopākhyāna (*b*) (XII, **137**).—§ 646. How a king should behave who is weak and threatened on all sides by powerful foes: the old story of the mouse, the cat, the owl, the mongoose, and the hunter, i.e. Mārjāra-mūshika-saṃvāda (*b*). The moral of the story (XII, **138**).—§ 647: *Bhīshma* related the conversation between the bird *Pūjanī* and king *Brahmadatta*, i.e. Brahmadatta-Pūjanī-saṃvāda (*b*) (XII, **139**).—§ 648: How a king should behave when there is a general decadence of righteousness: the old story of the discourse between *Bhāradvāja* and king *Çatruñjaya*, i.e. Kaṇikopadeça (*b*) (XII, **140**). — § 649: How a *brahman* should live when there is terrible distress around. *Bhīshma* said that the *Kṛta*, etc. (*a*), are all dependent on the king's conduct, citing the old story of the discourse between *Viçvāmitra* and the *Cāṇḍāla* in a hamlet inhabited by *Cāṇḍālas*. Towards the end of *Tretā* and the beginning of *Dvāpara* a frightful drought occurred extending over twelve years; the planet *Bṛhaspati* began to move in a retrograde course, and *Soma* receded towards the south, etc. (description); the *brahmans* abstained from sacrifices and recitations of the *Vedas*, and no longer uttered *vashaṭs*, etc.; the very *Ṛshis*, giving up their vows, began to wander hither and thither. M.-ṛ. *Viçvāmitra*, leaving his wife and son, wandered fireless and homeless, and regardless of food, clean and unclean. One day he came upon a hamlet, in the midst of a forest, inhabited by cruel hunters, etc. (description of a *Cāṇḍāla* hamlet). *Viçvāmitra*, in rage of hunger, wanted to steal a dog's haunch ("theft is allowable in a season of distress even for an eminent person; . . . in the first place one should steal from a low person . . ."). He was discovered and harshly addressed by the owner; but when the *Cāṇḍāla* learned who he was he addressed him respectfully, and dissuaded him from eating dog's meat, as the dog is less clean than a jackal, and the haunch of a dog is much worse than other parts of his body; "only the five kinds of five-clawed animals are clean food for *brahmans* and *kshattriyas* and *vaiçyas*, as laid down in the scriptures" (*yathāçāstraṃ*). *Viçvāmitra* said that it is the duty of the *brahmans* to behave like *Agni* (as it is the duty of the *kshattriyas* to behave like *Indra*), that the *Vedas* are fire, and that fire at times becomes a consumer of everything; "life is better than death; if living one may acquire virtue"; he mentioned that *Agastya*, when hungry, ate up the *Asura Vātāpi* ("a man who is a Ṛshi cannot do what is sinful"). Notwithstanding the warnings of the *Cāṇḍāla*, *Viçvamitra* took away that haunch of dog's meat into the woods and wished to eat it with his wife, having gratified the gods and the *Pitṛs*; igniting a fire according to the *Brāhma* rites and cooking a *caru* according to the *Aindrāgneya* rites, dividing the *caru* into due portions, he invoked the gods, including *Indra*. Meanwhile *Indra* began to pour rain copiously. *Viçvāmitra*, having completed the rites, himself ate that meat. Afterwards he destroyed all his sins by his penances and acquired the most wonderful success (XII, **141**).—§ 650: *Yudhishṭhira* was distressed at the possibility of such acts of impiety being mentioned as a duty. *Bhīshma* said that kings should gather wisdom from various sources, and not from the *Vedas* alone. Those who blame the injunctions of the scriptures, etc., are hucksters in learning and *Rākshasas* among men; it has been heard by us that the texts of morality cannot be understood solely by discussion or by one's own intellect; *Indra* has said that this is the opinion of *Bṛhaspati*; . . . in days of old *Uçanas* told the *Daiteyas* this truth, that scriptures are no scriptures if they cannot stand the test of reason; . . . the sin of killing a person is equal to the sin of not killing one that deserves to be killed. *Indra* has said that in times of distress the great duty of a king is chastising the wicked and protecting the good (XII, **142**).—§ 651: *Yudhishṭhira* enquired after the merits of protecting suppliants. *Bhīshma*, reminded of *Çibi*, etc., told the story (that purifies the heart from every sin) that *Bhārgava* (i.e. *Rāma*, PCR.) had recited to king *Mucukunda*, how a pigeon won success (*siddhi*), i.e. Kapota-lubdhaka-saṃvāda (*b*) (XII, **143–149**). — § 652: Requested by *Yudhishṭhira* about how a person can be purified after having committed sin from want of judgment, *Bhīshma* related the old tale, applauded by R., of what the brahman *Indrota Çaunaka* said to *Janamejaya*, i.e. Indrota-Pārīkshitīya (*b*) (XII, **150–152**).– § 653: Asked by *Yudhishṭhira* if he had ever seen or heard of any mortal restored to life after having succumbed to death, *Bhīshma* related the story of the discourse between a vulture and a jackal as it had happened of old in the forest of *Naimisha*, i.e. Gṛdhra-gomāyu-saṃvāda (*b*) (XII, **153**).—§ 654: *Yudhishṭhira* asked *Bhīshma* as to how a weak king who incurs the wrath of a powerful one should behave in the hour of danger. *Bhīshma* told the story of the discourse between *Pavana* and the *çālmali*, who, having dared the Wind-god, saved himself by causing his branches to be lopped off: Pavana-çālmali-saṃvāda (*b*). "One should overlook the wrongs inflicted by a person of superior strength, and even consider them like the acts of a child, an idiot, or one that is blind or deaf. The eighteen *akshauhiṇīs* were not equal in might to *Arjuna*" (XII, **154–157**).—§ 655: Covetousness is the cause of sin; it is not known in its real nature by D., G., As., M.-U., etc. (XII, **158**). Discourse on ignorance; it has its origin in covetousness; *Janaka*, etc. (*a*), acquired heaven in consequence of their having repressed covetousness (XII, **159**). The moral laws laid down by M.-ṛ. are many; the highest among them all is self-restraint; it surpasses charity and sacrifice and study of the *Vedas* (XII, **160**). Penance (*tapas*) is the root of everything; by penance *Prajāpati* created the universe, etc., and Ṛ. acquired the *Vedas* and acquired their sixfold divine attributes (*aiçvaryaṃ*); renunciation (*saṃnyāsaḥ*) constitutes the highest penance (XII, **161**). Discourse on Truth and its indications; it is applauded by brahmans, Ṛ., and P.; it is *yoga*, it is *Brahmán*, sacrifice, etc.; it has been found to weigh heavier than 1,000 horse-sacrifices (XII, **162**). Discourse on the thirteen vices that are powerful foes of all; all these thirteen faults stained the sons of *Dhṛtarāshṭra* (XII, **163**). The characteristics of malevolent persons (XII, **164**). How *brahmans* should be provided for. At the end of every year one should perform the *Vaiçvānara* sacrifice (*ishṭiṃ Vaiçvānarīṃ*). The practice of an act laid down in an alternative is not destructive of virtue; fearing death, V.-D., Sā., the *brahmans*, and M.-ṛ. make use of the alternative instead of the principal rule in seasons of distress. The five kinds of falsehood that are not sinful. The three sins that cannot be expiated. Acts that are never sinful ("*amṛta,* if extracted from poison, can be quaffed"). Different kinds of expiation for different kinds of sin (XII, **165**).—§ 656: Questioned by *Nakula, Bhīshma* related Khaḍgotpattikathana (q.v.) (XII, **166**).—§ 657: When *Bhīshma* became silent *Yudhishṭhira* returned home. *Yudhishṭhira's* question to *Vidura* and his own brothers about the three things (*trivarga,* i.e. virtue, wealth, and desire). *Vidura* assigned precedence to virtue. *Arjuna* assigned precedence to wealth (or profit). *Nakula* and *Sahadeva* assigned the precedence to both wealth and virtue. *Bhīmasena* assigns precedence to desire ("it is from desire that R. devote themselves to penances"). *Yudhishṭhira* applauded withdrawal from the three things, recommending emancipation (*moksha*) ("we do not know, however, what emancipation is") or extinction (*nirvāṇa*), and quoted *Brahmán.*—All of them were filled with delight and applauded *Yudhishṭhira,* who once more addressed *Bhīshma* (XII, **167**).—§ 658: Asked by *Yudhishṭhira* with whom friendship is delightful, *Bhīshma,* having also stated with whom friendship should be avoided, related an old story that had occurred in the country of the *Mlecchas,* that lies to the north, about an ungrateful person, i.e. Kṛtaghnopākhyāna (*b*). *Bhīshma's* observations on ingratitude (XII, **168-173**).

Apagā[1], a river. § 364 (Tīrthay.): III, **83,** 6038 (*Siddhanishevitā*).

Apagā[2], a river in the country of the Madras. § 607 (Karṇap.): VIII, **44,** 2033.

Apagāsuta ("son of the river") = Bhīshma, q.v.

Apageya ("son of the river") = Bhīshma, q.v.

***Āpaḥ** ("the Waters"). I, †3017 (witness one's actions); III, 147 (= the Sun); III, 16554 (witness one's actions); XII, 11614 (person).

Apakshakshayaṃkara = Çiva (1000 names[1]).

Apāṃ garbha, v. Agni.

Apāṃ hrada, a tīrtha. § 733 (Ānuçāsanik.): XIII, **25,** 1701 (the result of bathing there is equal to that of a horse-sacrifice).

Apāṃ nidhi = Vishṇu (1000 names).

Apāṃ pati ("the lord of the Waters") = Varuṇa. I, 1121; IX, 2723 (*Varuṇaṃ*), 2731, 2737.

Apāṃ prapatana, a tīrtha. § 733 (Ānuçāsanik.): XIII, **251,** 1715 (*Apāṃ prapatanāsevī sevyate so 'psarogaṇaiḥ*).

***Apāna**[1] ("inhalation"). § 660*e* (Bhṛgu-Bharadv.-s.): XII, **185,** 6871: Apāna, having recourse to the heat (*pavakaṃ*) that is in the urethra and the abdominal intestines (*bastimūlaṃ gudaṃ caiva*), moves, engaged in carrying out urine and fæces (cf. Prāṇa).—§ 714 (Çukakṛtya): XII, **329,** 12397 ("the senses are dominated over by the Sādhyas, etc.; these gave birth to an invincible son named Samāna; from Samāna sprang a son called Udāna; from him Vyāna; from Vyāna arose Apāna; and lastly, from Apāna sprang the wind called Prāṇa").

Apāna[2] = Çiva (1000 names[1]).

Apāntaratama(s), son of Sarasvatī. § 717 (Nārāyaṇīya): XII, **350,** 13675 (*Sārasvataḥ,* created by Nārāyaṇa, distributed the Vedas in the Manvantara of Manu Svāyambhuva, and shall do so in each Manvantara, and when Kali-yuga has set in he shall be reborn as Vyāsa, etc.), 13695 (*Sārasvatam ṛshim Apāntarataman tathā*), 13696, 13704 (*Apāntaratamāç caiva Vedācāryaḥ sa ucyate | Prācīnagarbhaṃ tam ṛshiṃ pravadantīha kecana*).

Apara = Çiva (1000 names).

Aparājita[1], a serpent. § 47 (Sarpanāmak.): I, **35,** 1558. —§ 564 (Mātalīyop.): V, **103**γ, 3631.

Aparājita[2], a king, incarnation of the second of the Kāleyas. § 130 (Aṃçāv.): I, **67,** 2685.

Aparājita[3], a son of Dhṛtarāshṭra's. § 130 (Aṃçāv.): I, **67,** 2736.—§ 182 (Dhṛtarāshṭraputranāmak.): I, **117,** 4549. —§ 585 (Bhīshmav.): VI, **88**ι, 3901, 3905, 3908 (slain by Bhīmasena).

Aparājita[4] = Mahāpurusha(°stave), Vishṇu (1000 names).

Aparājitā ("invincible")? III, 14451 (*shashṭhīṃ yāṃ brāhmaṇāḥ prahur Lakshmīm āsāṃ sukhapradāṃ | Sinīvālīṃ Kuhūñ caiva sadṛṭtim aparājitāṃ*).

Aparanandā, a river. § 249 (Arjunavanavās.): I, **215,** 7818 (visited by Arjuna).—§ 390 (Tīrthayātrāp.): III, **110,** 9968 (visited by Yudhishṭhira).—§ 775 (Ānuçāsanik.): XIII, **166***a*, 7654 (among the rivers whose names are to be recited as purifiers of sins).

Aparānta, a people in Bhāratavarsha. § 574 (Jambūkh.): VI, **9**μ, 355.

Aparaseka, pl. (°*āḥ*), a people conquered by Sahadeva on his Digvijaya. § 281 (Sahadeva): II, **31,** 1113.

Aparimita, Aparinirmita, Aparinindita: Mahāpurushastave.

Āpastamba, a brahman. § 545 (Pativratāmāhātmyap.): III, **298,** (16875), (among the brahmans who consoled Dyumatsena).—§ 746 (Ānuçāsanik.): XIII, **66**ε, 3320 (among those who have ascended to heaven by having made gifts of sesame seeds).

Āpava = Vasishṭha. § 163 (Bhīshmotp.): I, **98,** 3918 (had cursed the Vasus).—§ 164 (Āpavopākhy.): I, **99,** 3920, 3924 (*Vasishṭho nāma muniḥ*), 3951, 3955 (cf. § 163).— § 638*b* (Rāmop.): XII, **49,** 1756, 1757 (cursed Arjuna Kārtavīrya, while Agni had burnt his retreat).

Apavarga: XII, 1673 (°*bhūtānāṃparataḥ sthitaḥ,* i.e. Kṛshṇa).

Āpavopākhyāna ("episode relating to Āpava, i.e. Vasishṭha"). § 164 (cf. Bhīshmotp.): *Gaṅgā* fully related to *Çāntanu* the reason why the *Brahmarshi Vasishṭha* (or *Āpava*), the son of *Varuṇa,* had cursed the *Vasus.* When the *Vasus, Pṛthu* (or *Dhara*), etc., were wandering with their wives in the wood near *Vasishṭha's* hermitage, frequented by the *devarshis, Dyaus* was prevailed upon by his wife (assisted by his brothers), in the interest of her friend *Jitavatī,* daughter of *Uçīnara,* to steal *Vasishṭha's homadhenu* [*Nandinī*] (daughter of *Kaçyapa* and *Surabhi,* the daughter of *Daksha*), by drinking whose milk one could remain in unchanged youth for 1,000 years. *Vasishṭha,* however, was prevailed upon to let among them *Dyaus* alone (who was to be conversant with all *çāstras,* etc.) dwell on earth for a long time without marrying. Then *Gaṅgā,* taking with her the child (*Gāṅgeya* or *Devavrata,* i.e. *Bhīshma*), went away, and *Çāntanu* returned to his capital—"I shall now recount the virtues of the *Bhārata Çāntanu,* whose splendid story is called the *Mahābhārata*" (I, **99**). (For continuation v. Satyavatīlabhop.)

Āpoda, v. Āyoda.

Apramada = Çiva (1000 names[1]).

Apramatta = Vishṇu (1000 names).

Aprameya = Vishṇu (1000 names), Skanda.

Aprameyātman = Vishṇu (1000 names).

Apratarkya: Mahāpurushastave.

Apratiratha = Vishṇu (1000 names).

Apratirūpa = Çiva (1000 names[1]).

Aprekshya = Kṛshṇa: XII, 1625.

Apsaras[1], mostly pl. (°*aḥ*). § 11 (Parvas.): I, **2**, 398 (all. to the five *Aps.* in Nārītīrthāni).—§ 21*f* (Pramadvarā): I, **8**, 943, 944, 945, 970 (*Gandharvāpsarasoḥ sutā*, i.e. Pramadvarā). —§ 28 (Amṛtam.): I, **18**, 1113 (on the Mandara mountain). —§ 39 (Rāmaṇīyaka): I, **27**, 1311 (*Gandharvā°āṃ priyaṃ*, sc. Rāmaṇīyakaṃ).—§ 62 (Sarpasattra): I, **56**, 2122 (°*āṃ gaṇaiḥ*).—§ 75 (Vasu): I, **63**, 2366 (*Gandharvā°o*).—§ 76 (Matsya): I, **63**, 2388.—§ 84 (Paraçu-Rāma): I, **64**, 2495, 2503 (*Gandharvā°āṃ gaṇān*).—§ 85 (Aṃçāv.): I, **65**, 2515 (*Gandharvā°āṃ sambhavaṃ*).—§ 102 (do.): I, **65**, 2556 (°*āṃ vaṃçaṃ*).—§ 105 (do.): I, **65**, 2560 (*Gandharvā°aḥ*).— § 106 (do.): **65**, 2561 (*Gandharvā°āṃ sambhavaḥ*).—§ 132 (do.): I, **67**, 2788 (*gaṇas tv A°āṃ*), 2795 (*Gandharvā°ām aṃçāvataraṇaṃ*).—§ 133 (Dushyanta): I, **68**, 2799 (do.); **70**, 2858 (*Gandharvā°āṃ gaṇaiḥ*).—§ 134 (Viçvām.): I, **71**, 2916 (*guṇair A°āṃ divyair*).—§ 135 (Çakuntalop.): I, **74**, 3055 (*shaḍ evāpsarasām varāḥ*), 3063 (*Menakā°āṃ çreshṭhā*).— § 149 (Yayāti): I, **89**, 3595.—§ 165 (Satyavatīl.): I, **100**, 4062.—§ 167 (Vicitravīryop.): I, **102**, 4083 (*Kāçipateḥ kanyās tisro 'psaropamāḥ*).—§ 185 (Sambhavap.): I, **120**, 4649 (*Gandharvā°ām ākrīḍabhūmiṃ*).—§ 191 (Arjuna): I, **123**, 4806 (*Gandharvā°aḥ*), 4808 (do.), 4809 (°*āṃ gaṇāḥ*), 4816 (*Anūcānā*, etc.).—§ 200 (Droṇa): I, **130**, 5103.— § 233 (Svayaṃvarap.): I, **187**, 7011 (*sahasā°obhiḥ*).—§ 250 (Arjunavanavāsap.): I, **217**, 7882.—§ 264 (Sabhākriyāp.): II, **4**, 131 (*Gandharvā°as*).—§ 266 (Çakrasabhāv.): II, **7**, 305.—§ 267 (Yamasabhāv.): II, **8**, 349 (*A°o-gaṇāḥ*).— § 268 (Varuṇasabhāv.): II, **9**, 378 (*Gandharvā°āṃ gaṇāḥ*).— § 269 (Vaiçravaṇas.): II, **10**, 391 (*gaṇair A°ām*), 395 (*Gandharvā°āṃ gaṇāḥ*), 396 (do.).—§ 270 (Brahmasabhāv.): II, **11**, 445 (do.), 472 (*Gandharvā°as*).—§ 271 (Lokapālas.): II, **12**, 481 (do.).—§ 322 (Dvaitavanapr.): III, **24**, 925 (*yaḥ sarvaloka-dvārāṇi nityaṃ sañcarate vaçī | devalokād Brahmalokaṃ Gandharvā°āṃ api*).—§ 335 (Indralokābh.): III, **42**, 1726, 1741 (°*gaṇasaṅkīrṇe*, i.e. Himālaya?), 1750 (°*āṃ gaṇān*).—§ 336 (do.): III, **43**, 1758 (*Nandanaṃ vanam A°gaṇa-sevitaṃ*), 1764, 1786.—§ 338 (do.): III, **45**, 1801 (°*āṃ varām Urvaçīṃ*); **46**, 1836 (°*āṃ vare*, i.e. Urvaçi), 1844 (*sarvā°su*), 1846.—§ 354 (Nalop.): III, **78**, 3043 (*divi Çakram ivāpsarāḥ*).—§ 357 (Tīrthay.): III, **82**, 4064 (*Gandharvā°aḥ*).—§ 359 (Vaḍavā): III, **82**, 5036 (*Gandharvā°āṃ gaṇāḥ*).—§ 361 (Kurukshetra): III, **83**, 5076 (*Gandharvā°*).—§ 370 (Tīrthay.): III, **84**, 8164 (*Kāverīṃ vṛtām A°āṃ gaṇaiḥ*).—§ 373 (Prayāga): III, **85**, 8215 (*Gandharvā°*).—§ 377 (Dhaumyatīrthak.): III, **90**, 8391.—§ 382 (Agastyop.): III, **96**, 8568 (*Satyavatī rūpeṇāpsaraso 'py ati*).—§ 389 (Agastyop.): III, **108**, 9929. —§ 395 (Jamadagni): III, **115**, 10145 (°*samā*, ~ Ṛcīka, i.e. Satyavatī).—§ 423 (Gandhamādanapr.): III, **143**, 10968 (*Gandharvā°āṃ priyaṃ Gandhamādanaṃ*).—§ 424 (Bhīma-kadalīkhaṇḍapr.): III, **146**, 11092 (°*o-nūpuraravaiḥ*).— § 425 (Hanūmad-Bhīma-s.): III, **148**, 11220.—§ 432 (Saugandhikāh.): III, **153**, 11358; **154**, 11372 (*Gandharvā°aḥ*). —§ 436 (Yakshayuddhap.): III, **158**, 11623; **159**, 11645 (*Gandharvā°āṃ gaṇāḥ*), 11653.—§ 438 (Yakshayuddhap.): III, **161**, 11777 (°*āṃ gaṇāḥ*).—§ 441 (Nivātakavacay.): III, **166**, 11920 (*Gandharvā°āṃ gaṇāḥ*).—§ 443 (do.): III, **168**, 12001 (*gaṇāç cā°āṃ*), 12035 (*Gandharvā°āṃ prabhāvam*), 12051.—§ 447 (do.): III, **175**, 12307 (*A°āṃ gaṇāḥ*).— § 450 (Ājagarap.): III, **178**, 12368 (°*gaṇa-sevitān deçān Himavataḥ*).—§ 456 (Sarasvatī-Tārkshya-s.): III, **186**, 12721. —§ 459 (Mārkaṇḍeyas.): III, **188**, 12925 (*Gandharvā°*).— § 474 (Dhundhumārop.): III, **201**, 13485 (*kathāṃ Kinnarā°āṃ*).—§ 501 (Skandop.): III, **229**, 14440 (*A°āṃ gaṇaiḥ*).—§ 502 (Manushyagrahak.): **230**, 14493 (*yā janitrī tv A°āṃ garbham āste pragṛhya*).—§ 505 (Skanday.): III, **231**, 14539.—§ 506 (do.): III, **231**, 14557 (°*āṃ gaṇāḥ*).— § 512 (Ghoshay.): III, **240**, 14870 (*gaṇair A°āñ caiva*); **246**, 15026.—§ 520 (Vrīhidrauṇ.): III, **261**, 15446 (*Gandharvā°as*).—§ 523 (Draupadīhar.): III, **265**, 15589. —§ 533 (Rāmop.): III, **281**, 16178 (do.).—§ 548 (Pāṇḍavapr.): IV, **9**, 257.—§ 552 (Goharaṇap.): IV, **58**, 1895 (*Gandharvā°as*).—§ 555 (Sainyodyogap.): V, **9**, 235, 247; **11**, 354, 356 (*Gandharvā°āṃ gaṇāḥ*); **17**, 541 (°*āṃ gaṇāḥ*); **18**, 544 (*Gandharvā°āṃ gaṇaiḥ*), 546; **29**, 824 (*Gandharva-yakshā°*).—§ 560 (Sanatsujātap.): V, **44**, 1704 (*rūpam A°āṃ abhūt*).—§ 565 (Gālavacar.): V, **111**, 3841 (*atra Vidyutprabhā nāma jajñire 'psaraso daça*).—§ 566 (Yayāti): V, **121**, 4052; **123**, 4100 (*Gandharvā°āṃ gaṇaiḥ*). —§ 573 (Ambop.): V, **176**, 6054 (*Gandharvā°as*).—§ 574 (Jambūkh.): VI, **6**, 212 (°*o-gaṇa-saṃyuktāḥ*), 227 (*striyaç cāpsarasopamāḥ*), 229 (°*āṃ saṅghaiḥ*); **7**, 261 (*striyaç cāpsarasopamāḥ*).—§ 581 (Bhīshmav.): VI, **66**, 2997.— § 595 (Dilīpa): VII, **61**, 2266 (only in B.); VII, **69**, 2403 (*Gandharvā°*; v. Pṛthu Vainya), 2418 (do.).—§ 596 (Pratijñāp.): VII, **80**, 2852.—§ 600 (Ghaṭotkacav.): VII, **156**, 6921; **160**, 7292 (°*āṃ gaṇāḥ*), 7312, 7313 (*Siddhā°āṃ gaṇaiḥ*).—§ 602 (Droṇavadhap.): VII, **188**, 8611.—§ 603 (Nārāyaṇāstram.): VII, **202**, 9617 (*Gandharvā°*).—§ 606 (Tripurākh.): VIII, **34**, 1513 (°*āṃ gaṇāḥ*), 1514 (*āṃ vṛndair*), 1536 (°*āṃ gaṇāḥ*).—§ 608 (Karṇap.): VIII, **49**, 2373 (°*saṅghaiḥ*), 2374 (*gaṇaḥ*); **57**, 2852; **61**, 3098; **69**, 3445 (°*o-gīta-vāditraiḥ*); **87**, 4424 (*Gandharvā°āṃ gaṇāḥ*); **88**, 4490 (*Gandharva-Rakshopsarasāñ ca saṅghaiḥ*); **90**, 4640 (*sabālavyajanair divyair divisthair A°o-gaṇaiḥ*).—§ 610 (Çalyap.): IX, **5**, 275 (°*āṃ gaṇāḥ*), 276.—§ 615*c* (Subhūmika): IX, **37**, 2121, 2123 (°*āñ gaṇāḥ*), 2125; **38***i* (Saptasārasvata), 2194 (°*o-gaṇāḥ*); **42** (Vasishṭhāpavāha), 2397; **45***u* (Skanda), 2509; **46**, 2656 (do.), 2677 (°*o-gaṇāḥ*); **49***ee* (Ādityatīrtha), 2848; **51***gg* (Sārasvata), 2941 (°*āñ gaṇāḥ*); **57** (Gadāyuddhap.), 3243; **58** (do.), 3306; **61** (do.), 3443.—§ 619 (Strīvil.): XI, **20**, 593, 594.—§ 635 (Rājadh.): XII, **33**, 1200.—§ 639 (do.): XII, **52**, 1885 (°*āñ gaṇāḥ*).—§ 641 (do.): XII, **98**, 3657 (*varā°sahasrāṇi*). —§ 656*c* (Daksha): XII, **166**, 6137.—§ 662 (Jāpakop.): **200***δ*, 7343 (°*saṅghāḥ*).—§ 669 (Mokshadh.): **221**, 8019.— § 674*b* (Çrī-Vāsava-s.): XII, **229**, 8346.—§ 677 (Mokshadh.): XII, **244**, 8871 (°*āṃ loke jāmayo*, sc. *prabhuḥ*).—§ 686 (do.): XII, **273**, 9825.—§ 693*b* (do.): XII, **282**, 10114; **283** (Vṛtravadha), 10185, 10187, 10189 (°*āñ gaṇāḥ*).— § 694*b* (Jvarotp.): XII, **284**, 10219 (°*gaṇasaṅghāḥ*).—§ 695*b* (Daksha-yajña-vināça): **285**, 10276 (*Gandharvā°ākīrṇe*), 10279 (*Gandharvā°*).—§ 709*b* (Sulabhā-Janakas.): XII, **321**, 12102 (°*gaṇāḥ*).—§ 712 (Çukotp.): XII, **324**, 12176; **325**, 12200 (°*gaṇāḥ*).—§ 713 (Çukakṛti): XII, **326**, 12249.—§ 714 (Çukakṛtya): XII, **328**, 12315.—§ 716 (Çukābhipat.): XII, **333**, 12591 (*Gandharvā°āñ gaṇāḥ*), 12594 (*sarvā°gaṇāḥ*); **334**, 12624 (°*āñ gaṇāḥ*), 12635 (do.). —§ 717*b* (Nārāyaṇīya): XII, **343** (VII), ††13211 (*deva-striyaḥ*); **351** (§ 717*d*: Brahma-Rudra-s.), 13733.—§ 730 (Ānuçāsanik.): XIII, **14**, 766, 958 (*Gandharvā°*), 995 (do.).—§ 731*b* (Ashṭāvakra-Diks.): XIII, **19**, 1422 (*gaṇāḥ*), 1426.—§ 733*c* (Pushkara): XIII, **25**, 1697, 1710 (°*āṃ nivāse*, a tīrtha?), 1715 (°*āñ gaṇaiḥ*), 1731.—§ 738*b* (Çyenakapotākh.): XIII, **32**, 2075.—§ 742 (Ānuçāsanik.): XIII, **38**, 2208 (°*ottamā*, i.e. Pañcacūḍā).—§ 745*c* (Cyavana-

Kuçika-s.): XIII, 54, 2837 (°*āṃ sanghān*), 2846 (°*āṅ gaṇāḥ*).—§ 746 (Ānuçāsanik.): XIII, 62, 3190; 64, 3268 (°*āṃ loke*), 3282 (°*āṃ gandhān*); 79*b*, 3779 (*Gandharvā°āṃ lokaṃ*); 80, 3789 (*Gandharvā°*); 81, 3832 (°*āṃ gaṇāḥ*).—§ 750 (do.): 93, 4411.—§ 752 (do.): XIII, 96, 4647.—§ 757*d* (Mandākinī): XIII, 102, 4860, 4865 (§ 757*f*: Nandana).—§ 759 (Ānuçāsanik.): XIII, 106, 5168 (°*ām adhivāse nṛtyagīta-*), 5186; 107, 5216, 5222, 5233, 5292 (°*gaṇasevitaṃ*), 5296, 5305 (°*gaṇaiḥ*), 5315 (do.), 5316, 5328; 109, 5378, 5379.—§ 768*b* (Umā-Maheçvara-s.): XIII, 140*a*, 6340 (°*gaṇa-*), 6347 (*pranṛttāpsarasaṃ sadas*); 142, 6547; 145, 6688; 146ε, 6805 (*Gandharvā°*).—§ 772*j* (Utathya): XIII, 155, 7368.—§ 773 (Ānuçāsanik.): XIII, 162, 7518 (*Gandharvā°*).—§ 775 (do.): XIII, 166β, 7640 (°*āṃ gaṇāḥ*; among the names that are to be recited morning, noon, and evening in order to be freed from sins).—§ 778*b* (Saṃv.-Mar.): XIV, 8, 184 (*Gandharvā°*); 10, 262.—§ 782*g* (Guruçishyas.): XIV, 43θ, 1185 (*strīṇām uttamāḥ*).—§ 784*b* (Utaṅka): XIV, 54, 1566.—§ 785 (Anugītāp.): XIV, 88, 2639 (°*āṃ gaṇaiḥ*).—§ 786*e* (Agastya): XIV, 92, 2870 (°*āṃ saṅghāḥ*).—§ 789 (Putradarç.): XV, 31, 848 (*Gandharvā°*); 32, 883 (°*sāṃ gaṇaiḥ*).—§ 793 (Mausalap.): XVI, 3, 62 (Kṛshṇa's and Baladeva's standards were taken away by Aps., who day and night called upon the Vṛshṇis and Andhakas to set out on a pilgrimage to some sacred water); 4θ, 129, 131.—§ 795 (Svargārohaṇap.): XVIII, 3, 104; 5μ, 173 (the 16,000 wives of Kṛshṇa are transformed into Aps.); 6, 217 (§ 795*c*, Mahābhārata ξ: mentioned in the Mhbhr.), 235 (°*gaṇa-saṅkīrṇaṃ*), 242 (*sā°gaṇaṃ*), 248 (°*saṅghaiḥ*), 252.

Apsaras[2] (mostly sing.), special Apsarases, etc. § 21*f* (Pramadv.): I, 8, 943, 944, 945, 970 (i.e. Menakā).—§ 76 (Matsya): I, 63, 2396 (*varā°*=Adrikā), 2388 (do.).—§ 135 (Çakuntalop.): I, 74, 3056 (*Menakā Brahmayonivarāpsarāḥ*), 3057 (*Menakā°*), 3063 (*Menakā°āṃ çreshṭhā*).—§ 150 (Pūruvaṃç.): I, 94, 3698 (*Miçrakeçyāṃ daçāpsarasi sūnavaḥ Raudrāçvasya*).—§ 162 (Çāntanūp.): I, 97, 3894 (Çāntanu asks Gaṅgā if she is an Aps.).—§ 171 (Vicitravīryasutotp.): I, 106, 4297 (*dāsīm Apsaropamāṃ*, i.e. the mother of Vidura).—§ 198 (Çaradvat): I, 130, 5078 (*dṛshṭvā Gautamo 'psarasaṃ vane*, i.e. *Jānapadīṃ*).—§ 200 (Droṇa): I, 130, 5103 (*Bharadvāja iti khyātaḥ . . . dadarçāpsarasaṃ*—C. °*āṃ- . . . Ghṛtācīm*).—§ 217 (Caltrarathap.): I, 100, 6820 (do.).—§ 250 (Arjunavanavāsap.): I, 216, 7853 (Vargā in Nārītīrthāni).—§ 338 (Indralokābhig.): III, 45, 1801 (°*āṃ varām Urvaçīṃ*); 46, 1836 (°*āṃ vare*, i.e. Urvaçi), 1857 (i.e. Urvaçī).—§ 354 (Nalop.): 78, 3043 (*divi Çakram ivāpsarāḥ*).—§ 391 (Ṛçyaçṛṅga): III, 110, 10002 (*dṛshṭvāpsarasam Urvaçīṃ*).—§ 523 (Draupadīhar.): III, 265, 15580 (Koṭikāsya asks Draupadī if she is a D., Y., Dā., or varāpsaras, or a Dai.).—§ 615*aa* (Çrutāvatī): IX, 48, 2826 (*Ghṛtācī*); 51 (§ 615γγ: Sārasvata), 2901 (*Alambushā*), 2937 (id.).—§ 712 (Çukotp.): XII, 325, 12188 (*Ghṛtācīṃ*), 12189, 12191.—§ 721 (Ānuçāsanik.): XIII, 3, 191 (Rambhā).—§ 742 (do.): XIII, 38, 2204 (*Brāhmīṃ Pañcacūḍāṃ*, discourse between her and Nārada), 2205 (do.), 2208 (°*ottamā* = do.).—§ 745*c* (Cyavana-Kuçika-s.): XIII, 53, 2816 (°*sopamāṃ*).

Apsarogaṇasevita = Çiva (1000 names[2]).

Apsuhomya, a. ṛshi. § 264 (Sabhākriyāp.): II, 4*a*, 107 (among the ṛshis who were present when Yudhishṭhira entered his palace).

Apsujātā, a mātṛ. § 615*u* (Skanda): IX, 46, 2622.

Apta, a serpent. § 47 (Sarpanāmak.): I, 35, 1553.—§ 564 (Mātalīy.): V, 103γ, 3628.

Apūraṇa. § 47 (Sarpanāmak.): I, 35, 1551.—§ 564 (Mātalīy.): V, 103γ, 3626.

Āraṇeya = Çuka. § 712 (Çukotp.): XII, 325, 12207.—§ 713 (Çukakṛti): XII, 326, 12253.—§ 714 (Çukakṛtya): XII, 328, 12339.

Āraṇeya ("belonging to or named after the firesticks—*araṇī*"), in the enumerations of the parvans of Mhbhr. § 10 (Parvas.): I, 2, 327 (*parva*).—§ 11 (do.): I, 2, 477 (*upākhyānaṃ*) = Āraṇeyaparvan.

[**Āraṇeyaparvan**] ("the section relating to the wood for producing fire by friction," the 51st of the minor parvans of Mhbhr. = ch. III, 311–315). § 548: Asked by Janamejaya, Vaiçampāyana related what the Pāṇḍavas did after having rescued Kṛshṇā (from Jayadratha). The Pāṇḍavas left Kāmyaka and returned to Dvaitavana with Kṛshṇā. Once a deer carried off a brahman's araṇī and mantha, was pursued by the Pāṇḍavas, and suddenly became invisible. Bhīma repented that he had not slain the prātikāmin, Arjuna that he had not slain Karṇa, and Sahadeva that he had not slain Çakuni. Nakula, Sahadeva, Arjuna, and Bhīma were successively sent to fetch water, but caused to drop down dead by a Yaksha. At last Yudhishṭhira himself went, answered thirty-four questions put by the Yaksha, chose that Nakula should be revived, rescued all his brothers, learnt that the Yaksha was his father Dharma (*c*), was granted the boon that the brahman would recover his araṇī and mantha, that the Pāṇḍavas would manage to live the thirteenth year unrecognized in Virāṭa's kingdom, and that Yudhishṭhira (who was born of Dharma, as Vidura of a portion of Dharma) should overcome covetousness, etc. The Pāṇḍavas asked permission of the brahmans to live the thirteenth year in concealment from the Dhārtarāshṭras, Duryodhana, etc., and Karṇa and Saubala. Dhaumya, etc., consoled Yudhishṭhira: "Even the gods (Indra, *d*; Vishṇu, *e*; Agni, *f*; Aurva, *g*; Vivasvat, *h*) have wandered in disguise for the purpose of overcoming foes." The brahmans (yatis, munis) went back to their homes, and the Pāṇḍavas and Dhaumya set out with Kṛshṇā, and the next day proceeded for a kroça, and then sat down in order to take counsel of each other.

Arāṇi, a son of Viçvāmitra. § 721 (Viçvāmitrop.): XIII, 4β, 257

Araṇīparvan = Āraṇeyaparvan. § 4 (Anukram.): I, 1, 89.—§ 795 (Mahābhārata): XVIII, 6ρ, 268 (at its conclusion waterpots full of water should bo givon away).

Araṇīsuta = Çuka. § 714 (Çukakṛtya): XII, 328, 12342.

Arantuka, a dvārapāla. § 369 (Kurukshetra): III, 83, 7078 (*Tarantukārantukayor yad antaraṃ Rāmahradānāñ ca Macakrukasya ca | etat Kurukshetrasamantapañcakaṃ Pitāmahasyottaravedir ucyate*).—§ 615*kk* (Kurukshetrakathana): IX, 53, 3032 (= do.). Cf. the reading of B. III, 83, 6022.

***Āraṇyaçāstra**, plur. (°*āṇi*) (the rules for the forest mode of life). § 184 (Pāṇḍu): I, 119, 4627.

Araṇyaka[1], the Āraṇyaka or Āraṇyakas, considered as appendices to the Vedas and as containing the rules for the forest mode of life; often called çāstra. § 7 (Anukram.): I, 1, 258 ("better than the Vedas").—§ 18 (Paulomap.): I, 4, 856 (*çāstre cāraṇyake guruḥ*, i.e. Çaunaka).—§ 573 (Ambopākh.): V, 175, 6014 (do., i.e. Çaikhāvatya).—§ 625 (Rājadh.): XII, 19, 591 (*vedavādān . . . çāstrāṇy Ā°ca*).—§ 641 (do.): XII, 61, 2328 (°*çāstrāṇi*).—§ 717*c* (Uparicara): XII, 337, 12762 (no animals were slain in his sacrifice but °*padodbhūtāḥ bhāgās tatropakalpitāḥ*, i.e. presumably that the portions of offerings were made according to the prescripts of the Āraṇyakas; differently PCR.).—§ 717*b* (Nārāyaṇīya): XII, **340**, 12872 (Nārāyaṇa with his mouth uttered the syllable Om, Gāyatrī, the Āraṇyaka, and the four Vedas); **343**χ, 13257 (*sahasraçākhaṃ yat sāma ye vai vedavido janāḥ | gāyanty Āraṇyake viprāḥ*, i.e. Nārāyaṇa); **344**ββ, 13316 ("as the Āraṇyaka from the Vedas . . ."); **349** (IV), 13577 (in that kalpa, when Brahmán took his birth in the ear of Nārāyaṇa; the Āraṇyakas, etc., sprang from Nārāyaṇa's mouth), 13629 ("the Sāṅkhya-yoga, the Veda and Āraṇyakas—*Vedāraṇyakaṃ*—and the Pañcarātra are parts of one whole—*parasparāṅgāni*"); **350**, 13637 (=do.).—§ 787 (Āçramavāsik.): XV, **19**, 532 (Çatayūpa instructed Dhṛtarāshṭra in the *Āraṇyakaṃ vidhiṃ* with the permission of Vyāsa).—§ 788 (do.): XV, **28**, 744 (Vyāsa asked Dhṛtarāshṭra if he followed the rules of the Āraṇyaka—*carasy Āraṇyakaṃ vidhiṃ*?).

Araṇyaka[2] = Āraṇyakaparvan. § 10 (Parvas.): I, **2**, 319 (*parva*).—§ 11 (do.): I, **2**, 417 (*ataḥ paraṃ tṛtīyan tu jñeyam Āraṇyakaṃ mahat* = Vanaparvan), 478 (*etadāraṇyakaṃ parva tṛtīyaṃ parikīrtitam* = Vanaparvan). — § 596 (Pratijñāp.): VII, **81**, 2905 (*varam Āraṇyake dattaṃ*, all. to Kairāṭaparvan, *Ā.* therefore is = Vanaparvan). — § 795*c* (Mahābhārata): XVIII, **6**ρ, 268 (when one has arrived at the *Ā.* one should feed the foremost brahmans with roots and fruits).

Araṇyakaparvan ("section relating to the forest life of the Pāṇḍavas," the 30th of the minor parvans of Mhbhr.). § 308: The *Pāṇḍavas* set out from *Hāstinapura* through the *Vardhamāna* gate with their weapons, accompanied by *Kṛshṇā*, in a northerly direction. *Indrasena* and other servants, 14 in number (see BR. s.v. *pari*; Nīl. and PCR. take it to be = 15), with their wives, followed them on swift cars. The citizens wished to leave the town and follow them, but were prevailed upon by *Yudhishṭhira* to return and cherish *Bhīshma*, *Dhṛtarāshṭra*, *Vidura*, *Kuntī*, etc. About the close of the day the *Pāṇḍavas* reached the banian *Pramāṇa* on the banks of the *Gaṅgā*, purified themselves by touching the water, and passed the night there, taking water alone as their sole sustenance, in the company of brahmans with and without fire, who had followed them (III, **1**). When the day broke in, *Yudhishṭhira* tried to prevail upon the brahmans to leave him, in order that they might not undergo sufferings, living on fruits, roots, and deer. But they declared that they would follow him, themselves providing their own food. — § 309: Then a learned brahman, *Çaunaka*, versed in *Sāṅkhya* and *Yoga*, quoting the çlokas of *Janaka*, told *Yudhishṭhira* not only to retire from the world, but also in his heart not to mind the loss of his wealth. *Yudhishṭhira* declared that it was not from avarice, but only because he could no more support the brahmans, that he regretted his wealth; "nobody should cook his food for himself alone, and nobody should slay an animal without devoting it to the gods, the pitṛs, and guests, nor should one eat of that food which had not been duly dedicated to the gods and the pitṛs." *Çaunaka* said that sacrifices, study, gifts, and penance pave the way to the world of the *Pitṛs*—truth, forgiveness, subduing the senses, and renunciation of desire to the heaven of the gods, and they should be practised without reference to self (*abhimāna*). It was by their wealth of *yoga* that the *Rudras*, *Sādhyas*, *Ādityas*, *Vasus*, and *Açvins* rule over the creatures. So *Yudhishṭhira*, who had already achieved success as to his indebtedness towards his ancestors and as to sacrifices, now ought to seek success in *yoga* and in ascetic austerities; then he would be able to realize all his wishes (III, **2**). — § 310: *Yudhishṭhira* then, having consulted *Dhaumya*, was taught by him (as *Bhīma*, *Kārtavīrya*, *Vainya*, and *Nahusha* had by ascetic meditation delivered the people from affliction) 108 names of *Sūrya* (*a*), [originally] proclaimed by *Svayambhū* (i.e. Brahmán)* (the Sun). *Yudhishṭhira*, touching the water of Gaṅgā, with his senses under control, and feeding upon air alone, stood engaged in *prāṇāyāma*, and began a hymn in praise of *Sūrya* (*b*) (the Sun). The Sun then showed himself to *Yudhishṭhira* and gave him a copper vessel, saying that if *Pāñcālī* (i.e. *Kṛshṇā*) kept this vessel fruits, roots, meat, and vegetables, cooked in their kitchen, would be inexhaustible for twelve years. Then the god vanished. Rising from the water, *Yudhishṭhira* took hold of *Dhaumya's* feet and embraced his brothers. The clean food that was dressed, however little, became inexhaustible, and only after the brahmans, the brothers, *Yudhishṭhira*, and at last *Kṛshṇā* had eaten the day's food became exhausted. Having then performed sacrifices, they set out for the *Kāmyaka* wood, accompanied by *Dhaumya* and the brahmans (III, **3**).—§ 311: *Dhṛtarāshṭra* asked *Vidura* what they should do to secure the good-will of the citizens. *Vidura* said that he must give back to the *Pāṇḍavas* all that had been theirs, let *Duryodhana*, *Çakuni*, and *Karṇa* wait upon them, and *Duḥçāsana* ask their forgiveness in open court, and if *Duryodhana* would not consent to reign in peace jointly with *Yudhishṭhira*, he ought to abandon him and let *Yudhishṭhira* reign alone. *Dhṛtarāshṭra* did not approve, and saying "stay or go, as thou listest," he suddenly rose and went away, and *Vidura* went away to the *Pāṇḍavas* (III, **4**).—§ 312: Starting from the *Gaṅgā*, the *Pāṇḍavas* went to *Kurukshetra*, performed ablutions in the *Sarasvatī*, *Dṛçadvatī*, and *Yamunā*, and, travelling in a westerly direction, they arrived at the *Kāmyaka* wood on the *Sarasvatī*. There *Vidura* came to them in a single car. When seeing him, *Yudhishṭhira* was afraid that he brought an invitation to a new match at dice with *Çakuni* about their weapons. *Vidura* told them that he had been forsaken by *Dhṛtarāshṭra*, and gave them advice how to secure adherents (III, **5**).—§ 313: After *Vidura* had gone *Dhṛtarāshṭra* repented and fell down senseless, and having regained consciousness caused *Sañjaya* to bring *Vidura* back (III, **6**). *Duryodhana*, being afraid because *Vidura* had returned, held counsel with *Çakuni*, *Karṇa*, and *Duḥçāsana*, who were of opinion that the *Pāṇḍavas* would remain the promised space of time in the wood. As *Duryodhana*, however, was not contented, *Karṇa* proposed to set out and slay them. When they had gone out *Kṛshṇa Dvaipāyana* came upon them and commanded them to desist, and then appeared before *Dhṛtarāshṭra* (III, **7**). *Vyāsa* warned *Dhṛtarāshṭra* against permitting *Duryodhana* to try to slay the *Pāṇḍavas* (III, **8**).—§ 314: As *Dhṛtarāshṭra* said he was unable to cast off his senseless son, *Vyāsa* told him: One day, when *Indra* saw *Surabhi* weeping in heaven, and asked her why she wept, she told him that one of her offspring (a cow) was exceedingly harassed by a husbandman; and although she had 1,000 offspring, and her affections flowed equally towards all, yet she felt greater compassion for the weak. *Indra* poured down a shower of rain and caused obstruction to the husbandman's work. "So I feel anxious regarding the *Pāṇḍavas* in distress; let thy affections be greater towards the weak, and let *Duryodhana* make peace with them" (III, **9**).—§ 315: Maitreya-çāpa (q.v.) (III, **10**).

Āraṭṭa, a people. § 584 (Bhīshmavadh.): VI, **85**, 3784 (°*jān vāhān Sindhu-rājasya*).—§ 585 (do.): VI, **90**ρ, 3973 (horses).—§ 592*b* (Bṛhanta): VII, **23**, 1024 (B. °*jāḥ haya-çreshṭhāḥ*; C. *aridhvajāḥ*).—§ 603 (Nārāyaṇāstram.): VII, **193**, 8905 (*Kalingā°-Vāḥlikaiḥ*; among the troops of Kṛtavarman).—§ 607 (Karṇap.): VIII, **44**δ, 2056 (*Āraṭṭā nāma te deçā nashṭadharmā, na tān vrajet*), 2061 (*Āraṭṭā nāma Vāhīkā varjanīyā vipaçcitā*), 2064 (*Āraṭṭā nāma Vāhīkā, na teshv āryo dvy-ahaṃ vaset*), 2068 (*Āraṭṭā nāma te deçā Vāhīkaṃ nāma taj jalaṃ | brahmaṇāpasadā yatra tulyakālāḥ Prajāpateḥ*; v. also 2069), 2070 (*Prasthalā Madra-Gāndhārā Āraṭṭā nāmataḥ Khaçāḥ | Vasāti-Sindhu-Sauvīrā iti prāyo 'tikutsitāḥ*); **45**, 2081 (*satī purā hṛtā kācid Āraṭṭāt kila dasyubhiḥ*, etc.; the Āraṭṭas had been cursed by a chaste woman), 2100 (*Āraṭṭānāṃ* — var. °*kān* — *Pañcanadān dhig astu*), 2110 (*Āraṭṭajān Pañcanadān dhig astu*).

Araudra = Vishṇu (1000 names).

Aravindāksha = Sūrya, Vishṇu (XII, 13586; 1000 names).

Arbuda[1], a Serpent. § 277 (Jarāsandhav.): II, **21**, 806 (among the Nāgas who formerly dwelt at Girivraja).

Arbuda[2], a tīrtha. § 358 (Tīrthay.): III, **82**, 4097 (*Himavat-sutam Arbudaṃ*, "where there was formerly a hole in the earth").

Arcayanty arkam arkiṇaḥ = Çiva (1000 names[1]).

Ārcīkaparvata, a holy place. § 406*b* (Tīrthay.): III, **125**, 10411, 10416: The place of the Maruts, with the caityas of the gods, the tīrtha of the Moon, inhabited by Vaikhānasas, Vālikhilyas, Pāvakas, living upon air; where Çāntanu and Çunaka, Nara and Nārāyaṇa have attained eternity; where gods, Pitṛs, and great Ṛshis have practised austerities.

Arcismantaḥ, one of the three classes of Pitṛs. § 684 (Mokshadh.): XII, **270***a*, 9650.

Arcismat = Vishṇu (1000 names).

Arcismatī, a daughter of Aṅgiras. § 489 (Āṅgirasa): III, **218**, 14127 (*paçyaty A°ībhābhiḥ*).

Arcita = Vishṇu (1000 names).

Ārçyaçṛṅgi, v. Ārshyaçṛṅgi.

Ardana = Çiva (1000 names[2]).

***Ardhacandravyūha**, a certain array. § 580 (Bhīshmav.): VI, **56**, 2418 (employed by Arjuna and Dhṛshṭadyumna); see vyūha.

Ardhakīla, a tīrtha. § 360 (Tīrthayātrāp.): III, **83**, 7024.

Ardhamāsa[1] = Skanda.

***Ardhamāsa**[2], pl. (°*āḥ*), the half-months, person. § 615*u* (Skanda): IX, **45**γ, 2517.

Ārdrā, a nakshatra. § 746 (Ānuçāsanik.): XIII, **64**, 3259 (*Ārdrāyāṃ kṛsharaṃ dattvā tilamiçram uposhitaḥ | naras tarati durgāṇi kshuradhārāṃç ca parvatān*).—§ 749 (do.): XIII, **89**, 4257 (by performing a çrāddha under *Ā.* a man becomes a performer of fierce deeds—*krūrakarmā*).—§ 759 (do.): XIII, **110**, 5395 (description of the candravrata).

Ardracarman = Çiva (1000 names[2]).

Arghābhiharaṇa (the handing over of the gift of honour = Arghāharaṇaparvan). § 10 (Parvas.): I, **2**, 318.

[**Arghāharaṇaparvan**] ("on the handing over of the gift of honour," the 26th of the minor parvans of Mhbhr.). § 289: On the *abhishecanīya* day *maharshis* and *Nārāda* entered the *antarvedi* and sat down together with the *rājarshis* engaged in various topics of conversation and dispute. No *çūdra* was then near the *antarvedi*, nor anybody without vows (*avratin*). *Nārada* sat there with feelings of awe, remembering the words he had heard of old in the mansion of Brahmán regarding the incarnation of the deities, and knowing that *Kṛshṇa* was the incarnation of *Nārāyaṇa* and would himself destroy all these assembled *kshattriyas*. *Bhīshma* then proposed to *Yudhishṭhira* that *arghas* should be offered to the kings, and first to him who was the foremost. As *Bhīshma* declared *Kṛshṇa* to be foremost, he caused *Sahadeva* to present the first *argha* to *Kṛshṇa*, which filled the *Cedi* king *Çiçupāla* with envy (II, **36**). *Çiçupāla* gravely censures *Bhīshma*, *Yudhishṭhira*, and *Kṛshṇa* (saying that he was a servant and cowherd and no king, and speaking depreciatingly of his exploits), and accompanied by the kings left the assembly (II, **37**). *Yudhishṭhira* ran after *Çiçupāla* and spoke sweetly to him in order to conciliate him; *Bhīshma* maintained the fitness of giving *Kṛshṇa* the first *argha* (II, **38**). *Sahadeva* and *Nārada* declared it to be highly improper not to worship *Kṛshṇa*. *Sunītha* (i.e. *Çiçupāla*) stirred the kings up in order to obstruct the completion of the sacrifice (II, **39**).

Arghasaṃvāda = Arghāharaṇaparvan. § 11 (Parvas.): I, **2**, 410 (*rājasūye 'rgha-saṃvāde Çiçupālavadhas tathā*).

Arha[1] = Vishṇu (1000 names).

Arha[2], a people. § 295 (Dyūtap.): II, **52**, 1859 (among the people who brought tribute to Yudhishṭhira).

Ariha[1], son of Avācīna. § 156 (Pūruv.): I, **95**, 3771, 3772.

Ariha[2], son of Devātithi. § 156 (Pūruv.): I, **95**, 3776, 3777.

Ariha[3] ("slayer of foes"), seems to be a son of Dhṛtarāshṭra's. § 611 (Çalyap.): IX, **26**, 1405.

Arimejaya, a Vṛshṇi. § 589 (Droṇābhishek.): VII, **11**ξ, 409.

Arishṭā. § 130 (Aṃçāvat.): I, **67**, 2718 (mother of the Gandharva king Haṃsa, who was reborn as Dhṛtarāshṭra, the son of Vyāsa).

Arishṭanemi[1] ("whose felly is unhurt"), a ṛshi, sometimes identified with Tārkshya and sometimes named together with him. § 99 (Aṃçāvat.): I, **65**, 2548 (*Tārkshyaç cārishṭanemiç ca*, among the Vainateyas, the sons of Vinatā).—§ 191 (Arjuna): I, **123**, 4830 (do.).—§ 267 (Yamasabhāv.): II, **8**, 320 (among the ṛshis in the palace of Yama), 333 (do.).—§ 454 (Brāhmaṇamāhātmyak.): III, **184**, 12660 (as a prince of the Haihayas had killed a brahman by error, the Haihayas repaired to the viprarshi *A.* (*jagmuç cārishṭanemno 'tha Tārkshyasyāçramam añjasā*)).—§ 665 (Mokshadh.): XII, **208**, 7574 (Marīci had a son Kaçyapa or Arishṭanemi).—§ 700 (do.): XII, **289**, 10613 (Bhīshma told Yudhishṭhira the old narrative that was uttered by Tārkshya Arishṭanemi to Sagara).

Arishṭanemi[2]. § 549 (Pāṇḍavapr.): IV, **10**, 284 (Sahadeva introduced himself to Virāṭa as a vaiçya named *A.*).

Arishṭasena. § 610 (Çalyap.): IX, **6**ξ, 294 ("there they passed the night: Çalya, etc.").

Arivindavaktra = Skanda.

Ārjava. § 585 (Bhīshmav.): VI, **90**σ, 3997 (together with his brothers Çakuni, etc., he fought Irāvat, on the eighth day of the battle).

Arjuna[1] Kārtavīrya, Haihaya king. § 169 (Paraçu-Rāma): I, **104**, 4173 (*Haihayādhipatiḥ*; killed by Paraçu-Rāma).—§ 376 (Tīrthay.): III, **85**, 8273 (*Kārtavīryārjuno yathā*).—§ 394 (Tīrthay.): III, **115**: The Haihaya king Arjuna had 1,000 arms, and, by the favour of Dattātreya, he had obtained a golden vimāna that could proceed everywhere without obstruction, and ruled over all beings (*Bhūtān!*). The gods and ṛshis asked Vishṇu to kill him. On his celestial vimāna,

Arjuna affronted Indra, when he was sporting with Çaçī. After having held a consultation with Indra, Vishṇu went to his hermitage Badarī (for continuation v. Jamadagni), 10135 (*Haihayādhipatiḥ*), 10140.—§ 397 (Jamadagni): III, **116**: Once, when the sons of Jamadagni had gone out, Arjuna Kārtavīrya, the lord of the country near the sea-shore (*Anūpapatiḥ*), came to the hermitage, and, being received hospitably by Reṇukā (the wife of Jamadagni), carried off the calf of the *homadhenu* and pulled down the trees. As Jamadagni told Rāma this, Rāma rushed towards Arjuna, and cut down his 1,000 arms with his arrows, and killed him. The heirs of Arjuna came while Rāma was away, and shot Jamadagni to death with their arrows. When they had gone away Rāma returned to the hermitage (III, **116**), 10195.—§ 398 (Paruça-Rāma): III, **117**: After having lamented for and cremated his father, Rāma vowed the slaughter of the entire kshattriya caste, killed Kārtavīrya's sons, etc.—§ 638*b* (Rāmop.): XII, **49**: Meanwhile the virtuous kshattriya, the Haihaya king Arjuna Kārtavīrya, with 1,000 arms through the grace of Dattātreya, having subjugated the whole earth with its mountains and seven islands, became a powerful emperor, and gave away the earth to the brahmans in a horse-sacrifice. Solicited by Agni, he once gave alms to that deity, who sprung from the point of his shaft, i.e. Agni burnt villages, etc., and he burnt also the retreat of Āpava (=Vasishṭha), who cursed Arjuna, saying that Rāma should lop off his arms. Always devoted to peace, always regardful of brahmans, etc., Arjuna did not mind that curse. His sons, always haughty and cruel, seized and brought away the calf of Jamadagni's *homa*-cow, without the knowledge of Arjuna. Rāma lopped off the arms of Arjuna and brought back the calf; the sons of Arjuna came and slew Jamadagni in the absence of Rāma, who vowed to free the earth of kshattriyas, and slaughtered all the sons and grandsons of Arjuna, and 1,000 Haihayas, and freed the earth of all kshattriyas, etc., 1750 (*Kṛtavīryātmajo, Haihayādhipaḥ*), 1757, 1758, 1759, 1763, 1764 (°*sya sutāḥ*).—§ 772*b* (Pavanārjunas.): XIII, **153***ff*: The Haihaya king Arjuna Kārtavīrya with 1,000 arms became the lord of this whole world (i.e. the earth), residing in Māhishmatī; he gave large gifts to Dattātreya, who granted him four boons: that he should have 1,000 arms in battle, but only two at home; that he should subjugate the whole earth righteously; and reign with vigilance; and that whenever he might happen to go wrong, the righteous should set him right. *A.* now regarded himself as having no equal. An invisible voice said that the brahman is superior to the kshattriya; *A.* maintained that the brahmans take refuge with the kshattriyas; "I shall bring the skin-clad brahmans under my sway." Vāyu (Wind) warned *A.*, addressing him from the air, etc. At last Arjuna praised the brahmans, mentioning Dattātreya. Vāyu told him always to protect them; "a terrible danger threatens thee from the Bhṛgus; that will take place after a time," 7186 (*Arjunasya saṃvādaṃ Pavanasya ca*), (7199), 7207, (7211); **154,** 7225; **157,** 7291, 7305; **158,** 7326, 7349, (7350).—§ 782*c* (Brāhmaṇagītā): XIV, **29,** 818, (822): The 1,000 armed king Kārtavīryārjuna conquered the whole earth with his bow; once he showered hundreds of arrows at the ocean. The ocean asked him to desist, as he injured the creatures in the waters; Arjuna asked if there existed any bowman who was his equal in shooting. The Ocean named Rāma Jāmadagnya. Arjuna came and began to trouble him; Rāma burnt his troops and prostrated him with his battle-axe and drove away his kinsmen to the mountain fastnesses; their progeny became Vṛshalas owing to their inability to find brahmans: so the Draviḍas, etc. Cf. Paraçu-Rāma (*d*).—Cf. also Anūpapati, Haihaya, Haihayendra, Haihayādhipati, Haihayarshabha, Haihayaçreshṭha, Kārtavīrya.

Arjuna[2] Pāṇḍava. § 4 (Anukram.): I, **1,** 109, 123, 125, 127, 129, 149, 150, 152, 160, 162, 165, 169, 172, 178, 179, 184, 187, 190, 191, 193, 212.—§ 10 (Parvas.): I, **2,** 315, 320 (°*syābhigamanaṃ parva*).—§ 11 (do.): I, **2,** 386, 389, 438, 439, 459, 493, 505, 546, 622.—§ 71 (Bhāratasūtra): I, **61,** 2267 (*udīcīm*, sc. *ajayat*), 2271, 2274.—§ 83 (Kṛshṇā): I, **63,** 2449 (his son with Subhadrā was Abhimanyu), 2451 (his son with Kṛshṇā was Çrutakīrti).—§ 130 (Aṃçāvat.): I, **67,** 2746 (son of Indra), 2748 (*Abhimanyur Arjunasya suto 'bhavat*), 2751.—[§ 131 (do.): I, **67,** 2779 (for his sake Indra asked Karṇa for his mail and earrings).]—§ 157 (Pūruv.): I, **95,** 3814 (son of Indra and Kuntī).—§ 159 (do.): I, **95,** 3827 (his son with Kṛshṇā was Çrutakīrti), 3830 (his son with Subhadrā was Abhimanyu). After Pāṇḍu had been cursed, that he should have no progeny, he caused Dharma to procreate Yudhishṭhira in Kuntī, then Vayu to procreate Bhīmasena, and then Indra to procreate Arjuna.—§ 190*d* (Pāṇḍavotp.): I, **123**: In order to propitiate *Indra* (before summoning him), *Pāṇḍu*, took counsel with the *maharshis*, and caused *Kuntī* to observe an auspicious vow for a full year, while he himself began to stand upon one leg, etc. After the birth of *A.* a bodyless voice said that he should subjugate the *Madras*, the *Kurus*, the *Somakas*, the *Cedis*, *Kāçis*, and *Karūshas*, and satiate *Havyavāhana* (Fire) in the *Khāṇḍava* wood with the fat of all beings, and, with his brothers, perform three sacrifices; in battle he would gratify *Çaṅkara*, and receive from him the *Pāçupata* weapon, and, at the command of *Indra*, slay the *Nivātakavacas*, and acquire all sorts of celestial weapons: 4791, 4795.—§ 191: On hearing this voice, the ascetics dwelling on *Çataçṛṅga* became exceedingly glad. There was heard the sound of *dundubhis*, and flowers were showered down. The various tribes of celestials (*devagaṇāḥ*), etc. (*a*), came there (enumeration, among others, of *Devagandharvas*, *Apsarases*, the twelve *Ādityas*, the *Rudras*, the *Vainateyas*). Then the Açvins procreated the twins Nakula and Sahadeva in Mādrī.—§ 192 (Pāṇḍavotp.): I, **124,** 4854 (the third son of Kuntī). Having been procreated on Çataçṛṅga in behalf of Pāṇḍu by the gods Dharma (Yudhishṭhira), Vāyu (Bhīmasena), Indra (Arjuna; the mother of these three was Kuntī), and the Açvins (Nakula and Sahadeva, who were twins and sons of Mādrī) in Pāṇḍu's wives Kuntī and Mādrī, the five Pāṇḍavas after the death of Pāṇḍu were brought to Hāstinapura and educated by Droṇa, under the supervision of Bhīshma. Their cousins (the sons of Dhṛtarāshṭra) hated them, especially Duryodhana, who tried to murder Bhīmasena and later on all the Pāṇḍavas and Kuntī (Mādrī had burnt herself with the corpse of Pāṇḍu), and Karṇa hated Arjuna from jealousy.—§ 203*b* (cf. Droṇa): I, **132**: One day *Droṇa* asked his pupils to promise to accomplish what he had on his heart; only *Arjuna* promised it. *Arjuna* became the foremost of all his fellow-pupils. *Droṇa* gave every one of his pupils a narrow-mouthed vessel (*kamaṇḍalu*) for fetching water, in order that much time might be spent in filling it, but to *Açvatthāman* he gave a broad-mouthed vessel (*kumbha*), and in the intervals so gained he used to instruct his son in several superior methods; but *Arjuna* filled the vessel by means of the *Vāruṇa* weapon, and used to come at the same time as *Açvatthāman*. *Droṇa* told the cook never to give *Arjuna* his food in the dark, but not to tell him that it was he (*Droṇa*) that had ordered this. One day a wind put the lamp out when *Arjuna* was taking his food; but his hand went up to his mouth from habit. His attention being thus called to the force of habit, *Arjuna* practised with his bow in the night, and *Droṇa* promised him that there should not be a bowman equal to him in the world. He taught him also to fight on horseback, etc., with the mace, etc.: 5217, 5218, 5224, 5225, 5230, 5232, 5233, 5238.—§ 204 (Ekalavya): I, **132,** 5252 (Droṇa took from Ekalavya as his fee the thumb of his right hand in order that he might not surpass Arjuna).—§ 205*e* (cf. Droṇa): I, **132,** 5273, 5274: Arjuna excelled everyone in every respect, and alone became an *atiratha* ("a charioteer capable of fighting at one time with 60,000 foes," PCR.).—§ 206 (Droṇa): I, **132*f*,** 5293, 5296. One day Droṇa caused an artificial bird to be placed on the top of a tree, and first repeatedly asked Yudhishṭhira to tell what he did see, while aiming at the bird. He answered that he saw the tree, Droṇa, his brothers, and the bird. Droṇa reproachfully told him to stand apart. Then Droṇa repeated the experiment with his other pupils, with the same result (ch. **132**). At last Arjuna's turn came; he said first that he saw only the vulture, and then that he saw only its head, and, when Droṇa gave the order, he struck off its head with his shaft (I, **133**).—§ 207 (do.): I, **133**: Arjuna rescued the life of Droṇa by shooting with five arrows an alligator in the Gaṅgā that had seized his thigh. Droṇa gave him the weapon Brahmaçiras on the condition that he should not use it against a human foe, as it might burn the whole universe. —§ 208*b* (cf. Astradarçana): I, **135**: Then *Arjuna* appeared, while *Kuntī* wept with joy, and *Dhṛtarāshṭra* learned from *Vidura* who it was. By the *Āgneya* weapon *Arjuna* created fire, by the *Vāruṇa* water, by the *Vāyavya* air, by the *Pārjanya* clouds; by means of the *Pārvata* a mountain came into being (v. 5366, read with V. "*abhavadgiriḥ*" or with B. "*asṛjadgirīn*"), and by the *Antardhāna* weapon it again disappeared, etc.; he at one time shot five shafts together into the mouth of a moving iron boar, and discharged twenty-one arrows into the hollow of a cow's horn hung up in a rope and swaying to and fro (v. 5370, instead of "*bale*" read with B. and V. "*cale*").—§ 208 (Astradarçana): I, **137,** 5440, 5442: At the show of arms Karṇa in vain challenged Arjuna.—§ 209 (Drupadaçāsana): I, **138,** 5484, 5492, 5499, 5500, 5501. Arjuna helped Droṇa to subjugate Drupada, which favour Droṇa had asked as his fee.—§ 210*c* (cf. Sambhavaparvan): I, **139**: *Droṇa* taught *Arjuna* Brahmaçiras (that he had learnt from *Agniveça*, the disciple of *Agastya*), on the condition that he should not hurl it at any human being (cf. § 207), and obtained from him as his fee the promise that he would fight with him [in the great battle]. Then *Arjuna* went away to the northern region.—§ 211 (Sambhavap.): I, **139,** 5537, 5538. Headed by Arjuna, the Pāṇḍavas in war slew Sauvīra, who had performed a three years' sacrifice at the inroad of the Gandharvas. The Yavana king, whom even Pāṇḍu had failed to subject, was subdued by Arjuna; as was also the Sauvīra Vitula (B. *Vipula*), who had always shown a disregard for the Kurus; and the Sauvīra Sumitra, called Dattāmitra (LIA. i, pp. 656/804, n. 2); assisted by Bhīma, Arjuna with only a single chariot subjugated all the kings of the east (*prācyāḥ*) backed by 10,000 chariots; and in the same way the south. Dhṛtarāshṭra's sentiments towards the Pāṇḍavas suddenly became poisoned, and from anxiety he could not sleep (I, **139**).—§ 213 (Jatugṛhap.): I, **151,** 5911 (has escaped from the lac house).—§ 214 (Hiḍimbav.): I, **154,** 6019, (6027), (6034), 6039 (*A.* offered to assist Bhīmasena against Hiḍimba, and exhorted him to kill him without delay; then he caused the Pāṇḍavas to proceed to a town not far off); **156,** 6096.—§ 217 (Caitrarathap.): I, **166,** 6346 (a brahman related how Bhīshma prevailed upon Droṇa to teach the princes, etc.; both Arjuna and the others promised to do whatever he might ask as his fee, etc.).—§ 219 (do.): I, **168,** 6419 (the brothers set out for the town of Drupada).—§ 221 (do.): I, **170,** (6451), (6462), (6472), 6474, (6493), 6499 (while the Pāṇḍavas were wandering from Ekacakrā to the town of the Pāñcālas, Arjuna walking before them torch in hand, the Gandharva king Citraratha opposed them at the Gaṅgā, but was vanquished by Arjuna, whom he then gave the Gandharvic māyā called Cākshushī, and on whom and each of his brothers he bestowed 100 Gandharva horses; he gave them the counsel to select a fit purohita; Arjuna in return gave him the Āgneya weapon).—§ 222 (Tapatyup.): I, **171,** (6516) (as Citraratha had called *A.* Tāpatya, Arjuna caused him to relate Tapaty-upākhyāna). **173,** 6633 ("their son was Kuru, the ancestor of Arjuna"). —§ 223 (Vāsishṭha): I, **174,** 6634 (Citraratha told Arjuna about Vasishṭha). **175,** (6649), 6659 (Citraratha related the hostilities between Viçvāmitra and Vasishṭha to Arjuna).—§ 229 (Vasishṭhop.): I, **182,** (6888) (asked by Arjuna, Citraratha related why Kalmāshapāda commanded his queen to go to Vasishṭha, etc.).—§ 230 (Dhaumyapuroh.): I, **183,** (6913), 6915 (according to the counsel of Citraratha, the Pāṇḍavas installed Dhaumya as their purohita, and resolved to go to the svayaṃvara of Kṛshṇā).—§ 231 (Svayaṃvarap.): I, **184**: The Pāṇḍavas went to the Pāñcāla land in the company of brahmans who told them of the svayaṃvara, etc.). **185**: On their way they beheld Vyāsa; they took up their quarters in the house of a potter; and adopting the brahmanical profession, they began to lead an eleemosynary life. Drupada always wished to bestow his daughter on Kirīṭin (i.e. Arjuna), and therefore caused a very stiff bow to be made which was incapable of being bent by anybody except Arjuna.—§ 233 (do.): I, **187**: When Duryodhana, etc., had in vain tried to string the bow, and Karṇa, though having succeeded in stringing it, had, as a sūta, been rejected by Kṛshṇā, Jishṇu (i.e. Arjuna) came forward. **188,** 7049, 7051, 7052: Some of the brahmans spoke reproachingly of Arjuna's daring undertaking, some approved of it. Bending his head unto Īçāna and remembering Kṛshṇa, Arjuna accomplished the task; Kṛshṇā approached Arjuna, who soon after left the lists, followed by her. § 234 (do.): I, **189,** 7075, 7080: When Drupada expressed his desire of bestowing his daughter on that brahman the kings resolved to slay Drupada and burn Kṛshṇā, but spare Arjuna, whom they took for a brahman; Arjuna and Bhīmasena rescued them; Kṛshṇa knew the Pāṇḍavas. **190,** 7086, 7094, 7098, 7099: Karṇa is defeated by Arjuna ("accomplished in the Brāhma and the Paurandara weapons," v. 7105), etc. Bhīmasena and Arjuna with difficulty escaped from the throng, followed by Kṛshṇā.—§ 235 (do.): I, **191,** (7138), 7141: When they came with Kṛshṇā, Kuntī said "enjoy ye all"; Yudhishṭhira declared that Arjuna should wed her, but agreed that she should be the common wife of them all.—§ 236 (do.): I, **192**: Dhṛshṭadyumna secretly followed Bhīmasena and

Arjuna, and from their conversation learned who they were.—§ 237 (Vaivāhikap.): I, **193,** 7192: Dhṛshṭadyumna related what had happened; Arjuna is said to have large red eyes (v. 7175); from their conversation he concluded that they were the Pāṇḍavas of whom it had been heard that they had all escaped from the house of lac. **195,** 7226, 7235, 7237: Drupada vowed to restore Yudhishṭhira on his paternal throne; he became very perplexed at the project of marrying Kṛshṇā to all the five brothers; meanwhile Vyāsa arrived.—§ 241 (Vidurāgam.): I, **200,** 7367: Vidura and Dhṛtarāshṭra became glad at the Pāṇḍavas having won Kṛshṇā; but Duryodhana and Karṇa tried to stir Dhṛtarāshṭra up against them. **201,** 7408: Duryodhana proposed several means of getting the better of the Pāṇḍavas, etc.—§ 244 (Rājyalābhap.): I, **207,** 7547: Dhṛtarāshṭra caused the Pāṇḍavas together with Kuntī and Kṛshṇā to repair to Khāṇḍavaprastha (Indraprastha), giving them half the kingdom. — § 247 (Arjunavanavāsap.): I, **213,** (7774): The Pāṇḍavas reigned in prosperity at Indraprastha; once Arjuna, having violated an established rule regarding Kṛshṇā, set out to live twelve years in the forest.—§ 248 (do.): I, **214,** (7796), 7804: Arjuna was drawn away to the bottom of the water by Ulūpī (upon whom he begat a son); she said that he would be invincible in water.—§ 249 (do.): I, **215**: *A.* visited many tīrthas, married Citrāṅgadā at Maṇipūra, where he dwelled for three years; she gave birth to a son. — § 250 (do.): I, **216***f*, 7850: *A.* visited the tīrthas of the southern ocean, where he liberated the apsaras Vargā, etc., in Nārītīrthāni.—§ 251 (do.): I, **218,** 7890, 7894: *A.* visits Kṛshṇa.—§ 252 (Subhadrāhar.): I, **219,** 7920, (7923), 7928, 7929. **220,** 7961: *A.* carried away Subhadrā, the sister of Kṛshṇa.—§ 253 (Haraṇāharaṇap.): I, **221,** 7969, 7987, 8032, 8039, 8048: Kṛshṇa reconciled *A.* with the Bhojas, etc.; *A.* married Subhadrā and passed a whole year at Dvārakā; then Kṛshṇa remained for some time with *A.* at Indraprastha; Subhadrā brought forth Abhimanyu, who became the favourite of Kṛshṇa and from his father acquired the Dhanurveda. Kṛshṇā also obtained five sons (Çrutakarman by Arjuna), who, after having studied the Vedas, from Arjuna acquired knowledge of all weapons celestial and human.—§§ 254–260 (Khāṇḍavadah.): I, **222–234**: **224,** 8161, 8167; **225,** 8201, (8203); **227,** 8238, 8245, 8247, 8275, 8278, 8282; **228,** 8298, 8301, 8308, 8309, 8310, 8312, 8317, 8322, 8326; **234,** 8466, 8476, 8478: Kṛshṇa and Arjuna assisted Agni in burning the Khāṇḍava forest; Agni caused Varuṇa to give Arjuna the Gāṇḍiva bow, two inexhaustible quivers, and a car yoked with horses; then Agni gave Kṛshṇa the discus Sudarçana; Varuṇa gave Kṛshṇa the mace Kaumodakī; Indra in vain poured down showers of rain in order to prevent the burning. An incorporeal voice said that Kṛshṇa and Arjuna, being really the old ṛshis and gods Nara and Nārāyaṇa, were invincible. Indra appeared and promised to give Arjuna all his weapons (both the Āgneya and the Vāyavya), when Mahādeva had been pleased by him; he granted Kṛshṇa that his friendship with Arjuna should be eternal. The car (I, 8183 ff.) which Varuṇa gave to Arjuna was furnished with celestial weapons, etc., and incapable of being vanquished by gods or Asuras; its banner bore a large monkey; the car was drawn by horses white as silver, born in the region of the Gandharvas (*Gāndharvaiḥ*), and harnessed with gold, and in speed resembling the wind or the mind; its splendour was great, and the sound of its wheels was tremendous; it had been created by the Prajāpati Bhaumana (Viçvakarman) after severe ascetic meditation; no one could gaze at its splendour; it was the very car riding upon which Soma had vanquished the Dānavas; it was furnished with an excellent flagstaff of golden colour, upon which was seen a celestial ape apparently bent upon burning everything it beheld; and upon the flags were seen various creatures of large size whose roars and yells caused the enemy's soldiers to faint.—§ 261 (Sabhākriyāp.): II, **1,** (3), (6): Maya asked Arjuna to tell him what he was to do for him because he had been rescued by him in the Khāṇḍava forest; Arjuna told him to do something for Kṛshṇa, who causes him to build a palace for Yudhishṭhira.—§ 262 (do.): II, **2,** 37 (Kṛshṇa departed for Dvārakā).—§ 263 (do.): II, **3,** 58, 78: Maya told Arjuna about the huge riches on Hiraṇyaçṛṅga, and gave Arjuna the conch-shell Devadatta, etc.; the palace was constructed in fourteen months.—§ 264 (do.): II, **4,** 128: Among those who waited on Yudhishṭhira in the palace were the princes who, dressed in deer-skins, learned the science of arms under Arjuna.—§ 272 (Rājasūyār.): II, **13,** 557: Yudhishṭhira consulted his brothers, etc., as to the rājasūya; all people lived happily; Arjuna protected the people from enemies, etc.—§ 274 (do.): II, **15,** 643: Deliberation about slaying Jarāsandha. **16,** 661: Some objections made by Yudhishṭhira are refuted by *A.*—§ 275 (do.): II, **17,** 676: Approving the words of Arjuna, Kṛshṇa related the origin of Jarāsandha.—§ 276 (Jarāsandhavadhap.): II, **20,** 774, 775, 787: *A.* set out with Bhīmasena and Kṛshṇa to slay Jarāsandha.—§ 277 (do.): II, **21,** 804: They entered the city of Girivraja in the guise of snātakas, etc. **24,** 938, 954, 971: The combat between Bhīma and Jarāsandha having lasted for thirteen days, Bhīma killed him on the fourteenth night; they installed Jarāsandha's son Sahadeva as king of Magadha, then they returned to Indraprastha on Jarāsandha's celestial car; Kṛshṇa set out for Dvārakā.—§ 278 (Digvijap.): II, **25,** (984): Having obtained the bow, *A.*, etc., prevailed upon Yudhishṭhira to let him subdue the north; *A.* set out on that celestial car which he had obtained from Agni and subdued the north, while his brothers subdued the other regions, and Yudhishṭhira stayed at Indraprastha.—§ 279 (cf. Digvijayaparvan): *Arjuna* subdued the *Kulindas, Ānarttas, Kālakūṭas, Sumaṇḍala,* and with him *Çākala-dvīpa* and king *Prativindhya* and the kings in *Çākala-dvīpa* and the Seven Islands (*Saptadvīpeshu,* i.e. the Earth), and together with them he vanquished *Bhagadatta,* king of *Prāgjyotisha* and friend of *Indra,* who was surrounded by *Kirātas, Cīnas,* and other warriors dwelling on the sea-coast; after eight days of combat, *Arjuna* prevailed upon him to give tribute to *Yudhishṭhira* at his will (II, **26**), 999, (1007). Having vanquished all the mountain kings of the north, he subdued *Bṛhanta,* the mountain king dwelling in *Ulūka,* and with him *Senāvindu*; at the command of *Yudhishṭhira,* he stayed at *Devaprastha,* the city of *Senāvindu,* while his troops subjugated *Modāpura, Vāmadeva, Sudāman, Susaṅkula,* and the *Northern Ulūkas.* Then, having vanquished the mountaineers, he conquered the town of the *Paurava* king *Viçvagaçva*; then the seven tribes of the *Utsavasaṅketas,* etc. Having conquered the *Himavat* and *Nishkuṭa* (? see BR.), he came to *Çvetaparvata* (II, **27**). Having crossed *Çvetaparvata,* he subdued the country of the *Kimpurushas* ruled by *Drumaputra,* then by conciliatory proceedings the country named *Hāṭaka* defended by *Guhyakas.* Then he came to the *Mānasa* lake and all the sacred waters (*ṛshikulyāḥ*).

Then he conquered the region of the *Gandharvas*, and took as tribute from the *Gandharva* city horses spotted as partridges and named *maṇḍūkas* ('frogs'). At the entrance to *Northern Harivarsha* he was encountered by huge guardians (*dvārapālāḥ*), who told him that this city could not be conquered, that he who entered it was sure to perish, that nothing might be seen there by one with a human body, for this was the abode of the *Northern Kurus*, but that they would do anything else he would ask of them. At his request they gave him heavenly clothes, etc., as a tribute for *Yudhishṭhira*. Then he returned to *Indraprastha*, and gave all he had won to *Yudhishṭhira* (II, **28**), 1048, 1051.—§ 286 (Rājasūyikap.): II, **33**, 1221, 1234: Under Yudhishṭhira's rule the people were very happy, and great riches filled the treasury; then he resolved to celebrate the rājasūya; he engaged Indrasena and Viçoka and Puru, with Arjuna for his charioteer, to collect food, etc. Kṛshṇa himself had arrived there.—§ 290 (Çiçupālav.): II, **42**, 1475: In the quarrel between Kṛshṇa, etc., and Çiçupāla on the occasion of the handing over of the gift of honour (Arghāharaṇap.), in which Çiçupāla was ultimately killed by Kṛshṇa, Çiçupāla also spoke with depreciation about Arjuna's, etc., slaying Jarāsandha.—[§ 292*a* (Rājasūyikap.): II, **45*a***, 1607 (Dhanañjaya, i.e. Arjuna, followed Yajñasena, i.e. Drupada).]—§ 293 (Dyūtap.): II, **46**, 1610: Terrible omens had appeared at the rājasūya, which Vyāsa explained as foreboding the destruction of the kshattriyas after thirteen years by Bhīma, *A.*, etc.; *A.* prevailed upon Yudhishṭhira to give up his intention to die.—§ 294 (do.): II, **47** ff., 1670, 1755: Bhīma, Arjuna, etc., laughed at Duryodhana's mistakes in the palace; Çakuni caused him to invite the Pāṇḍavas to a match of dice.—§ 295 (do.): II, **52**, 1890 (Kṛshṇa is the soul of Arjuna, and *vice versâ*).—§ 299 (do.): II, **68**, (2257): At the match of dice Yudhishṭhira lost his kingdom, his brothers, himself, and Draupadī, etc.; Bhīma wanted to burn his hands, but was appeased by Arjuna.—§ 301 (do.): II, **70**, 2363, 2376: The admonitions of Arjuna, etc., retained Bhīma from killing the Dhārtarāshṭras. **71**, 2383, 2388, 2399, (2400): Duryodhana said that if Bhīma, Arjuna, and the twins would declare that Yudhishṭhira was not their master, then Draupadī would be free; *A.* said that he was certainly their master before the play; terrible omens appeared; Draupadī was granted a boon, and chose the liberty of Yudhishṭhira and his brothers. **72**, (2423): Bhīma threatened to slay all his foes instantly, but was restrained by Arjuna and Yudhishṭhira. **73**, 2447: Dhṛtarāshṭra sent Yudhishṭhira with his brothers and Kṛshṇā upon their cars to Indraprastha; he said that Arjuna is patient, etc.—§ 304 (Anudyūtap.): II, **77**, (2543), (2545), 2546: Having been vanquished in the second match of dice, the Pāṇḍavas had to live thirteen years in the forest and a fourteenth among men without being recognized; when they were going away they threatened that Arjuna would slay Karṇa, etc.—§ 306 (do.): II, **80*a***, 2634, 2653, 2665: When going away, Arjuna had scattered sand-grains, thus alluding to the arrows he would shower in the battle; terrible omens appeared; Nārada declared that in the fourteenth year hence the Kauravas would all be destroyed by Bhīma and Arjuna.—§ 311 (Āraṇyakap.): III, **4**, 228: Saying that neither Bhīma nor Arjuna would spare their foes, Vidura in vain exhorted Dhṛtarāshṭra to give back to the Pāṇḍavas all they had lost at play.—§ 313 (do.): III, **6**, 275: Dhṛtarāshṭra, who has banished Vidura, sent Sañjaya to the Pāṇḍavas to bring Vidura back; Sañjaya was honoured by Bhīma and Arjuna.—§ 316 (Kirmīrav.): III, **11**, 411, 425: *A.* stringed the Gāṇḍīva against Kirmīra; but Bhīma made him desist and slew him himself.—§ 317 (Arjunābhigam.): III, **12**, 468, (471), 537, 593: Kṛshṇa said: "The earth shall drink the blood of Duryodhana"; Arjuna tried to pacify him by reciting the feats achieved in his former life; then Arjuna, "the soul of Kṛshṇa," became silent, and Janārdana (i.e. Kṛshṇa) replied that he was identical with Arjuna; Kṛshṇā mentioned that *A.* won her at the svayaṃvara; Kṛshṇa promised that she should be avenged; "Arjuna will slay Karṇa, etc."—§ 321 (Saubhavadhop.): III, **22**, 894: Kṛshṇa took leave of *A.*, etc., and set out for Dvārakā.—§ 322 (Dvaitavanapr.): III, **23**, 903, 917: Description of the Pāṇḍavas' going to the forest; *A.* told the citizens, etc., that they would carry off the good name of their enemies into their exile, and asked them to beseech the ascetics to bless them.—§ 325 (Draupadīparitāp.): III, **27**, 1012, 1015: Kṛshṇā lamented their present state (she compared *A.* to Arjuna Kārtavīrya, etc.).—§ 327 (do.): III, **30**, 1123 (discourse between Kṛshṇā and Yudhishṭhira); **33**, 1325 (Arjuna is incomparable in battle).—§ 329 (Kāmyakav.): III, **36**, 1441 (*A.* is a mighty ṛshi, the friend of Nārāyaṇa, ancient, eternal, a god himself).—§ 330 (Indradarçana): III, **37**, 1457, 1504: Yudhishṭhira taught *A.* in private the [Pratismṛti] science, etc., and sent him away to Indra to obtain his weapons.—§ 331 (Kairātap.): III, **38**, 1520, 1527, 1533, 1536, 1537: Arjuna on his way to Indra practised austerities for four months. **39**, 1558, (1576), 1582, 1584, 1601: Combat between *A.* and Çiva in the guise of a Kirāta, etc.; Çiva gave him "*cakshus*."—§ 332 (do.): III, **39**: *A.* worshipped Çiva, (1624).—§ 333 (do.): III, **40**, 1643, 1656, 1661: Çiva said to *A.*: "Thou wast in thy former life Nara, the friend of Nārāyaṇa; in Badarī thou wast engaged in ascetic austerities for thousands of years; the Gāṇḍīva (which I got from thee by my power of illusion) is the bow with which thou assistedst Kṛshṇa in chastising the Dānavas during the coronation of Indra." When granted a boon, Arjuna asked Çiva to give him the Pāçupata weapon named Brahmaçiras (*c*). Having purified himself, he was instructed in its use on the condition that he should not hurl it against any human being, for then it would destroy the universe. The earth trembled, etc.; the gods and Dānavas beheld the weapon in its embodied form by the side of Arjuna. Then Arjuna was touched by Çiva, and all that was bad in his body was dispelled. Having said to Arjuna, "Go thou into heaven," Çiva went up into the skies accompanied by Umā.—§ 334 (do.): III, **41**, 1665, 1672, 1676, 1680, 1705, 1711, 1713: Then the Lokapālas, etc., came to *A.* on the Himavat; they granted him "vision" (*dṛshṭi*) that he might see them; Yama gave him his staff as a weapon, Varuṇa his nooses, Kubera (saying that in ancient kalpas *A.* had ever gone through ascetic austerities along with them) gave him his favourite weapon Antardhāna (*c*), etc.—§ 335 (Indralok.): III, **42**, 1723, (1728), 1733, 1742: *A.* ascended with Mātali to heaven on Indra's car.—§ 336 (do.): III, **43**, 1778: *A.* dwelt with Indra at Amarāvatī.—§ 337 (do.): III, **44**: *A.* dwelt there for five years.—§ 338 (do.): III, **45**, 1812: Urvaçī becomes enamoured of *A.*, who had studied the four Vedas with the Aṅgas and Upanishads and the Ākhyāna (i.e. the Purāṇa) as the fifth. **46**, 1833, (1836), 1852, (1853), (1861), 1867: As Arjuna said that he regarded Urvaçī as his mother, she cursed him, saying that he would have to pass his time among females as a dancer and destitute of manhood; Indra told him that this would come to pass in the thirteenth year of their exile, then he should regain his manhood; (the desire of the man that listens to this history of *A.* never runs after lustful ends, etc.).—§ 339 (do.): III, **47**: One day Lomaça came to the abode of Indra; as Lomaça wondered how *A.*, who was a kshattriya, had attained the seat of Indra, Indra explained to him who Arjuna really was; *A.* had dwelt with Vishṇu in Badarī, which the gods and ṛshis were unable to behold, and whence the Gaṅgā, worshipped by Siddhas and Cāraṇas, springs forth; he and Kṛshṇa had, at Indra's desire, been born on earth and would lighten its burden, etc. Lomaça was sent to Yudhishṭhira in order to bring him news about *A.* and accompany him on a tīrthayātrā.—§ 340 (do.): III, **48**, 1919, 1926: Dhṛtarāshṭra expressed his anxiety at Arjuna's exploits to Sañjaya; **49**, 1952, especially his encounter with Çiva in the guise of a Kirāta, etc.—§ 341 (do.): III, **50**, 1966: Arjuna's absence lasted for five years. —§ 342 (do.): III, **51**, 1973, 1993: Dhṛtarāshṭra expressed his anxiety before Sañjaya.—§ 343 (Nalop.): III, **52**, 2018: One day, when the Pāṇḍavas were grieving for Arjuna, the ṛshi Bṛhadaçva came and told the history of Nala, who was yet more unfortunate than Yudhishṭhira.—§ 356 ff. (Tīrthay.): III, **80**, 4001: The Pāṇḍavas, etc., lamented Arjuna. **81** ff.: Pulastya's enumerations of tīrthas.—§ 377 (do.): III, **86**, 8289, 8295: Yudhishṭhira told Dhaumya that he did not like to live longer in the Kāmyaka wood without Arjuna. **87** ff.: Dhaumya described the tīrthas of the various regions to Yudhishṭhira.—§ 378 (do.): III, **91**, 8424, 8428: Lomaça arrived and told that Arjuna had obtained Brahmaçiras (*b*), learned the Gāndharva Veda, etc. **92**, 8439: Lomaça said that Arjuna had asked him to accompany Yudhishṭhira to all the tīrthas. **93** ff.: Accompanied by Lomaça, the Pāṇḍavas (except Arjuna), etc., visited all the tīrthas.—§ 400 (do.): III, **118**, 10218, 10219, 10220: At the Nārītīrthas they heard of, and praised the deed of Arjuna.—§ 402 (do.): III, **120**, 10282: Kṛshṇa said that Arjuna, etc., would never renounce the rules of his caste.—§ 418 (do.): III, **139**, 10838: Kṛshṇā always sought the protection of Bhīma, whether Arjuna were near or not.—§ 420 (Gandhamādanapr.): III, **141**, 10896: Yudhishṭhira complained to Bhīma that he had not seen Arjuna for five years; they now ought to enter Gandhamādana (*b*) in company with brahmans of strict vows.—§ 424 (Bhīmakadalīkhaṇḍaprav.): III, **146**, 11101: Bhīma thought "as Arjuna has gone to heaven and I have come here for the sake of the flowers, what will Yudhishṭhira do?"—§ 436 (Yakshayuddhap.): III, **159**, 11658: When they had come to the hermitage of Ārshṭisheṇa, Ārshṭisheṇa told the Pāṇḍavas that they must not attempt to proceed further, but wait for Arjuna there.—§ 438 (do.): III, **162**: Arjuna had never uttered an untruth; in heaven he was honoured by gods, Pitṛs, and Gandharvas, and by Çāntanu, who, after having performed seven great sacrifices on the Yamunā, resided in the world of Çakra, and had enquired about his welfare.—§ 440 (do.): III, **164**, 11883, 11902: Since the departure of Arjuna the Pāṇḍavas had not felt joy. After having dwelt in the abode of Indra for five years and obtained all celestial weapons from him, viz., Āgneya, Vāruṇa, Saumya, Vāyavya, Vaishṇava, Aindra, Pāçupata, Brāhmya, Pārameshṭhya, likewise those of Prajāpati, Yama, Dhātṛ, Savitṛ, Tvashṭṛ, and Vaiçravaṇa, Arjuna took leave of Indra and came to Gandhamādana.—§ 441 (Nivātakavacayuddhap.): III, **165** f., 11903: One day the Pāṇḍavas saw Arjuna descending to them with Mātali on Indra's car; *A.* gave Draupadī precious gems, presented to him by Indra; the next morning Indra visited them.—§ 442 (do.): III, **167**, 11937, (11943): When Indra had gone, *A.* related his journey; against the Kirāta he had in vain employed the Vāyavya, Sthūṇākarṇa, Jāla, and the Çalabhāstra, and showers of shafts and stones, as the Kirāta had swallowed them all, and he had in vain discharged the Brahmāstra.—§ 443 (do.): III, **168**: Arjuna continued his tale; he enumerated a great many weapons, the use of which Indra promised to teach him; Mātali wondered that Arjuna was not jerked on the car of Indra, though Indra himself got jerked at the first pull of the steeds; when he had learned the use of the weapons, Indra had said that not even the gods could now conquer him; he had received fifteen weapons and learnt five ways of using them; Indra had asked him as his fee to slay the Nivātakavacas, and had given him the car (conducted by Mātali) upon which he (Indra) had vanquished Bali, etc., and "this" diadem and ornaments of his own and the impenetrable mail, and he had fastened "this" durable (*ajarāṃ*) string to the Gāṇḍīva, and the gods gave him the shell Devadatta by which Indra had conquered the worlds (cf. § 446).—§ 444 (do.): III, **169** f., 12173, 12181: Arjuna related his victory over the Nivātakavacas; Indra had formerly been told by Svayambhū that he himself would destroy them in another body; as the gods were unable to slay them, Indra had presented those weapons to Arjuna in order to have them killed. Then Arjuna and Mātali again went to the abode of the gods.—§ 445 (do.): III, **173**: While returning, *A.* destroyed Hiraṇyapura, inhabited by Paulomas and Kālakhañjas, who could not be slain even by the gods, etc.; therefore Brahmán had determined that Arjuna, a mortal, should kill them; he employed the Raudra weapon. Mātali took Arjuna to the abode of Indra, and in detail related Arjuna's achievement to Indra, and Indra praised him, and said that gods, etc., would not be able to stand him in fight, etc.—§ 446 (do.): III, **174**, 12281, (12289): Indra said that in the battlefield Bhīshma, Droṇa, etc., would not be equal to one-sixteenth part of Arjuna. Then Indra gave him "this" golden garland, the shell Devadatta, etc. (see § 443). Then Indra told him to depart. *A.* promised that he would show Yudhishṭhira all the celestial weapons the next morning.—§ 447 (do.): III, **175**, 12292, 12309: The next morning, when Arjuna was about to show the celestial weapons to Yudhishṭhira, the earth trembled, etc. Vāyu laid celestial garlands on Arjuna; sent by the gods, Nārada came and prevailed upon Arjuna not to charge the celestial weapons without necessity, which would destroy the three worlds; then the gods departed.—§ 448 (Ājagarap.): III, **176**, 12317: The Pāṇḍavas spent four years with Arjuna in the gardens of Kubera.—§ 450 (do.): III, **179**, 12427: Bhīma having been seized by a serpent (Nahusha), Yudhishṭhira directed Arjuna to protect Draupadī, while he himself with Dhaumya set out on the tracks of Bhīma.—§ 452 (Mārkaṇḍeyas.): III, **183**, 12559: In the Kāmyaka wood Kṛshṇa, "the friend of Arjuna," came accompanied by Satyabhāmā, etc.—§ 512 (Ghoshayātrāp.): III, **236**, 14752, 14770: While the Pāṇḍavas were dwelling at the lake [of Dvaitavana], Dhṛtarāshṭra was much afflicted, thinking that Arjuna would not have left heaven, where he received the celestial weapons, if it were not for the purpose of avenging himself and his brothers. **243**, 14941, 14956: Duryodhana, etc.

having set out to insult the Pāṇḍavas under the pretext of supervising their cattle stations, was vanquished by the Gandharva king Citrasena; Duryodhana was made captive, and the soldiers took refuge with Yudhishṭhira, who prevailed upon Arjuna to rescue Duryodhana, he being himself prohibited by a sacrifice. **244:** As the Gandharvas would not set free Duryodhana, etc., as requested by Arjuna, a fierce battle ensued. **245,** 14984, 15001, 15002, 15003, 15004, 15005: The Gandharvas in vain attempted to break the cars of the Pāṇḍavas; especially Arjuna sent millions of them to the abode of Yama by means of his Āgneya weapon. The Gandharvas then rose up to the skies, taking the Dhārtarāshṭras with them, showering maces, darts, etc., upon Arjuna, who killed them with his weapons Sthūṇākarṇa (C. Sthūlā°), Indrajāla, Saura, Āgneya, and Saumya. At last Citrasena rushed at Arjuna, armed with a mace of iron; when Arjuna had cut that mace into seven pieces with his arrows, Citrasena, by means of his science, concealed himself from the view of Arjuna, and thus continued to fight with him; but Arjuna destroyed his power of concealing himself by shooting at him with his celestial arms, guided by the sound (*çabdavedham samāçritya*). Then Citrasena showed himself to Arjuna, reminding him that he was his friend, and the battle was interrupted. **246,** 15010: Citrasena relates that he had been acquainted with the purpose of Duryodhana, etc., and had been requested by Indra to bring Duryodhana thither in chains; Arjuna entreated him to set Duryodhana free, but, at the request of Citrasena, they left the matter to be decided by Yudhishṭhira; Yudhishṭhira then liberated all the Kauravas. **249,** 15070: Duryodhana renounced all food from shame, as he had been liberated by Arjuna.—§ 513 (do.): III, **252,** 15173, 15189: The Dānavas (Daityas) in Pātāla comforted Duryodhana, saying that Naraka, who had been reborn as Karṇa, would slay Arjuna, etc., and that the Saṃçaptakas, possessed by the Rākshasas, were desirous of slaying Arjuna, etc. — § 514 (do.): III, **252,** 15196: Karṇa promised to slay Arjuna; Duryodhana was comforted. — § 518 (Mṛgasvapn.): III, **258:** The Pāṇḍavas left Dvaitavana and repaired to the Kāmyaka forest.—§ 522 (Draupadīharaṇap.): III, **264:** The Sindhu king Jayadratha saw Kṛshṇā and became enamoured of her. **265:** Koṭikāsya introduced him to Kṛshṇā. **266:** She said that her husbands were hunting, Arjuna to the west, etc. **267:** Jayadratha was treated hospitably by Kṛshṇā, and asked her to leave the miserable Pāṇḍavas and become his wife. **268,** 15656: She threatened him with Kṛshṇa and Arjuna, etc., but at last she was obliged to ascend his chariot. **269:** The Pāṇḍavas overtook Jayadratha. **270,** 15695: Kṛshṇā showed Jayadratha each of the five Pāndavas. **271,** 15717, 15759, 15767: Arjuna killed the twelve Sauvīra heroes, etc.; Jayadratha, etc., fled; Arjuna exhorted Bhīma to refrain from slaughtering the remnant of the Saindhava host; Bhīma and Arjuna went in search of Jayadratha; Arjuna killed the horses of Jayadratha, but entreated Bhīma not to kill himself.—§ 524 (Jayadrathavim.): III, **272,** 15805: Jayadratha obtained from Çiva that he should be able to defeat all the five Pāṇḍavas; but Arjuna was invincible, being in reality Nara, who had formerly practised austerities in Badarī, and had acquired the thunderbolt, etc., from the Lokapālas, and was protected by Kṛshṇa. The Pāṇḍavas continued to dwell in Kāmyaka.—§ 546 (Kuṇḍalāharaṇap.): III, **300** ff.: Lomaça had conveyed a message from Indra to Yudhishṭhira: "That intense fear of thine which thou dost never express to anyone I will remove when Dhanañjaya (i.e. Arjuna) has left." After twelve years of the exile of the Pāṇḍavas had passed away, Indra obtained for Arjuna the earrings and mail of Karṇa, giving him a lance instead; **301,** 16974, 16976; **302,** 16984, 16989.—[§ 547 (do.): III, **309:** Karṇa was always desirous of fighting with Phālguna (i.e. Arjuna), and he and Karṇa used to challenge each other.]—§ 548 (Āraṇeyap.): III, **313,** 17409, 17412: When the Pāṇḍavas had left Kāmyaka and returned to Dvaitavana, and a deer carried off a brahman's *araṇī* and *mantha,* Arjuna repented that he had not slain Karṇa; Arjuna and his brothers were sent after water and dropped down dead, until Yudhishṭhira resuscitated them all by answering the questions of the Yaksha (i.e. Dharma).—§ 549 (Pāṇḍavapr.): IV, **1,** 8, (9), (19); **2,** 41, 51, (52), 60; **5,** 149, 150, (154); **11,** 305: Yudhishṭhira asked Arjuna to select some spot where they might dwell during the fourteenth year without being recognized; Arjuna mentioned some countries surrounding the kingdom of the Kurus; Yudhishṭhira chose the city of Virāṭa, where Arjuna presented himself as one of the neuter sex, Bṛhannalā by name, saying that he had been a waiting-maid of Kṛshṇā's; Arjuna carried Kṛshṇā; Arjuna caused them to stow away their weapons on a çamī tree near a cemetery; they assumed secret names, Vijaya (i.e. Arjuna), etc.; Arjuna (§ 549*c*), "who proceeded to the Khāṇḍava forest and gratified Agni on a single car, vanquishing and slaying Nāgas and Rākshasas, and who married the sister of the Nāga king Vāsuki . . . . the tenth Rudra, the thirteenth Āditya, the ninth Vasu, the tenth Graha," said: "I sing, dance, and play on instruments; I will be dancing-master to Uttarā."—§ 550 (Samayapāl.): IV, **13,** 332: Arjuna distributed among his brothers the proceeds of the sale of worn-out clothes which he received in the inner apartments of the palace, etc.; he pleased the king and all the ladies of the inner apartments by singing and dancing.—§ 551 (Kīcakavadhap.): IV, **14–24: 19,** 576; **24,** 846: The senāpati Kīcaka tempted Kṛshṇā, and was slain by Bhīmasena.—§ 552 (Goharaṇap.): IV, **35–69: 35,** 1168; **36,** 1179, 1180, 1188; **37,** 1198, 1206, 1213, 1229; **38,** 1264, 1272; **39,** 1299; **41,** 1324; **43,** 1344, 1355, 1362; **44,** 1368, (1371), (1374), 1375, 1378, (1380), 1387; **45,** (1395), 1398, 1399, 1407, 1425; **46,** 1445, (1446); **47,** 1492; **48,** 1514, 1516; **50,** 1574; **51,** 1602; **53,** 1630, 1640; **54,** 1684; **55,** 1703, 1715, 1726, 1728, (1738); **56,** 1764, 1772; **57,** 1785, 1787, 1790, 1811, 1819; **58,** 1824, [illegible], 1853, 1871, 1873, 1874, 1878, 1882, 1886; **59,** 1901, 1905, 1916; **60,** 1949; **61,** (1963), 1966, 1989, 1992; **62,** 1998, 2014; **64,** 2054, 2065; **65,** 2086, (2101); **66,** 2120, 2122, (2140), 2142: Duryodhana, etc., invaded Virāṭa's country and plundered his cattle and wealth. The Pāṇḍavas helped Virāṭa; Uttara with Bṛhannalā (i.e. Arjuna) for his charioteer encountered the Kurus; Arjuna seized his own weapons, defeated the foes, and was recognized; but the appointed time had passed; the conquered cattle and wealth was recovered and the Kurus fled; when Uttara became afraid he was comforted by Arjuna: (§ 552*d*) "At Indra's command I formerly slew . . . the Paulomas and Kālakhañjas; *aham Indrād dṛḍhāṃ mushṭim, Brahmaṇaḥ kṛtahastatām | prāgaḍhe tumulaṃ citram anividdham* (B. *iti viddhi*) *Prajāpateḥ*; on the other side of the Ocean I vanquished 60,000 of car-warriors residing in Hiraṇyapura . . . I have obtained the Raudra from Rudra, the Vāruṇa from Varuṇa, the Āgneya from Agni, the Vāyavya astra from Mātariçvan, the thunderbolt (*vajra*) and other weapons from

Çakra."—§ 552 (β) (**44**, v. 1375 f.): Enumeration of *A.'s* ten names.—§ 552 (γ) (**45**, v. 1429 ff.): Combat with the Gandharvas on the occasion of the Ghosha-yātrā; conflict at Khāṇḍava against D. and Dā.; combat on behalf of Indra against the Nivātakavacas and Paulomas; svayaṃvara of Kṛshṇā. — § 552 (δ) (**45**, v. 1433 f.): Droṇa, Çakra, Vaiçravaṇa, Yama, Varuṇa, Agni, Kṛpa, Kṛshṇa (Mādhava), Pinākapāṇin (Çiva) [have been my preceptors].—§ 552 (ε) (**49**, v. 1535 ff.): Alone he saved the Kurus (from the Gandharvas), satiated Agni, led the life of a brahmacārin for five years; taking up Subhadrā on his car, he alone challenged Kṛshṇa to single combat; he fought with Rudra as a forester; rescued Kṛshṇā (from Jayadratha); for five years studied the use of arms under Indra; vanquished all foes; vanquished the Gandharva king Citrasena; vanquished the Nivātakavacas and Kālakhañjas.—Arjuna caused Uttara to bring away the white garments of Droṇa and Kṛpa and the yellow ones of Karṇa and the blue ones of Duryodhana and Açvatthaman, but not those of Bhīshma, because he was not stupefied; these garments he presented to Uttarā.—§ 553 (Vaivāhikap.[2]): IV, **70**, 2267, 2289; **71**, (2291), 2297, 2299, 2303, 2306, 2324; **72**, (2327), 2346: After the victory over the Kurus, Arjuna praised Yudhishṭhira before Virāṭa, and showed him all the Pāṇḍavas; Uttara spoke about Arjuna's prowess, and described each of the Pāṇḍavas, especially Arjuna ("it was by him that Bhīshma, Droṇa, and Duryodhana were vanquished"). Virāṭa offered to bestow his daughter Uttarā upon Arjuna, who accepted her for Abhimanyu. The nuptial festival was held at Upaplavya, where a great many kings came with akshauhiṇīs of troops.—§ 554 (Sainyodyogap.): V, **1**, 5; **7**, 140, (167): After the nuptials the assembled kings took counsel of each other about the preparations of war; after Kṛshṇa had set out for Dvārakā, Arjuna and Duryodhana came thither while Kṛshṇa was asleep; Arjuna chose Kṛshṇa himself, who was not to fight, and Kṛshṇa promised to become Arjuna's charioteer; Arjuna came back to Yudhishṭhira with Kṛshṇa and the foremost Daçārhas. —§ 555 (do.): V, **8**, 199, 214, 215; **18**, 561, 567: Çalya came with an army to the Pāṇḍavas, but was enlisted in the cause of Duryodhana; he, however, promised Yudhishṭhira to dispirit Karṇa as his charioteer, and related the misery endured by Indra and his queen.—§ 556 (Sañjayayānap.): V, **20–32**: **22**, 658, 668, 706, 711; **26**, 758, 759; **27**, 785; **29**, 861; **30**, 868: Drupada's purohita was sent as a messenger to Dhṛtarāshṭra; he said, "Nobody can fight Arjuna and Kṛshṇa"; Dhṛtarāshṭra sent Drupada's purohita back to the Pāṇḍavas. Praising Arjuna, etc. (**22**a, etc.), Dhṛtarāshṭra sent Sañjaya to Upaplavya, where he saluted Dhanañjaya (**23**γ); Yudhishṭhira said that by a single effort of his hand (**23**σ) *A.* could shoot sixty-one whetted and keen-edged shafts, furnished with excellent feathers, etc.; Yudhishṭhira demanded Indraprastha, compared Arjuna, etc., with Duryodhana, etc.; the Pāṇḍavas might be compared with a tree of righteousness, whose trunk was Arjuna, etc.; Sañjaya then bade farewell to *A.*, etc. (**30**ν); Yudhishṭhira declared Sañjaya to be as dear to him as Dhanañjaya (i.e. Arjuna); Sañjaya, having returned to Hāstinapura, spoke to Dhṛtarāshṭra about Arjuna's ascending to the very heavens, etc.—§ 561 (Yānasandhip.): V, **47–71**: **48**, 1810, 1815, 1816, 1831; **49**, 1933, 1940, 1963; **51**, 2031, 2037, 2084; **52**, 2092; **53**, 2109, 2111; **54**, 2131, 2135; **55**, 2182, 2184, 2195, 2202; **56**, 2215, 2219; **57**, 2246, 2247, 2292; **59**, 2329, 2352, 2358; **60**, 2366, 2378; **65**, 2497; **66**, 2499; **67**, 2522; **68**, 2523; **69**, 2545: The next morning Sañjaya in the council hall related that Arjuna (! cf. § 556, V, **23–28**) had said with Yudhishṭhira's sanction that Sañjaya should threaten Duryodhana, etc., saying that the Pāṇḍavas only wished for war; Arjuna said (§ 561*b*, V, **48**) that one morning when he had finished his water rites and prayers, a brahman said to him that he would have to fight with his foes, and that either Indra riding on his steed would walk before him, or Kṛshṇa would protect him from behind riding on his car drawn by Sugrīva; and Arjuna had preferred Vāsudeva (Kṛshṇa) as his ally to Indra. Arjuna also said that Duryodhana thought of imprisoning Kṛshṇa and seeks to create a sudden disunion between Kṛshṇa and Arjuna, and relates terrific omens; "I will hurl the Sthūṇākarṇa, Pāçupata, and Brāhma weapons, and all those that Çakra gave me." Bhīshma said that Nara and Nārāyaṇa are Arjuna and Kṛshṇa; Arjuna with an arrow severed in battle the head of the Asura Jambha, etc., and Bhīshma rebuked Karṇa, who had seen his brother in the city of Virāṭa slain by Arjuna; Sañjaya mentioned Arjuna's burning of the Khāṇḍava forest. Dhṛtarāshṭra was most afraid of Bhīma (who in height is higher than Arjuna by the span of the thumb); yet he was also afraid of Arjuna; "33 years have passed away since the burning of the Khāṇḍava forest; we have never heard of his being defeated anywhere"; Duryodhana alluded to the resolution of the Saṃçaptakas to slay Arjuna.—§ 561*h* (Yānas.): V, **56**: *Bhaumana* (i.e. Viçvakarman, Nīl.) and *Çakra* had always created wonderful forms, [he who is] *Tvashṭṛ*, [and] *Dhāṭṛ* (i.e. Prajāpati, Nīl.); for on this (i.e. Arjuna's) flagstaff they (i.e. Tvashṭṛ, Çakra, and Dhāṭṛ, Nīl.) have made forms by divine illusion (*devamāyayā*); and at *Bhīmasena's* request *Hanumat* will also place his own image on it. The banner in all directions both perpendicularly and laterally covered one *yojana*, and even if trees stood in its way its course could not be impeded; it was ever varying like *Çakra's* bow (i.e. the rainbow). And to that chariot were yoked 100 white celestial steeds with the speed of the winds, given by *Citraratha*; neither on earth, nor in the sky, nor in heaven, their course could be impeded; a boon had been granted that their number would always remain full, however often they might be slain. —Arjuna had got Karṇa, Jayadratha, etc., assigned as his share in the combat. Arjuna was protected by the celestials; Sañjaya had seen two straight lines on his foot soles; Agni would help him as in Khāṇḍava; he took up 500 arrows at a time, and Kṛshṇa protected him; on a single chariot Arjuna conquered the whole earth, etc.; he had said that Bhīshma, etc., were all on the eve of death, if they did not give up to Yudhishṭhira his own share of the kingdom. —§ 562 (Bhagavadyānap.): V, **72–95**: **74**, 2739; **77**, 2799; **78**, (2802); **79**, 2838; **81**, 2865; **82**, 2907, 2916; **83**, 2949; **90**, 3156, 3209, 3210: *A.* and Yudhishṭhira were averse from war, and *A.* told Kṛshṇa to exert himself sincerely to bring about peace; if, however, Duryodhana would not give them what they demanded, he would annihilate the Kshattriya race. During Kṛshṇa's embassy Kuntī compared *A.* to Arjuna Kārtavīrya, and mentioned the invisible voices in the night of Arjuna's birth.—§ 563 (Dambhodbhavop.): V, **96**, 3494, 3496 (identified with Nara).—§ 567 (Bhagavadyānap.): V, **124–132**: **124**, 4172, 4173, 4178, 4180; **125**, 4199, 4201; **126**, 4229; **131**, 4425: Kṛshṇa mentioned Arjuna's exploits before Duryodhana, and said that Bhīshma, etc., could not contend with Bhīma and *A.*—§ 569 (do.): V, **137**, 4644, 4663; **138**, 4680; **140**, 4747; **144**, 4887; **145**, 4924,

4925, 4926; **146,** 4949, 4950, 4951: Kuntī asked Kṛshṇa to remind *A.* of the voice heard at his birth, and tell him always to tread in the path pointed out by Draupadī; that Bhīma and Arjuna, like two Yamas, were capable of slaying the very gods, etc. Bhīshma and Droṇa reminded Duryodhana of the exploits of *A.*; Droṇa said that his affection for *A.* was greater than for Açvatthāman. Duryodhana had chosen Karṇa as the antagonist of Arjuna. Kṛshṇa described Arjuna's banner, made by Bhaumana by means of celestial illusion; his Aindra, Āgneya, and Māruta weapons, etc. Karṇa promised Kuntī, that except Arjuna, her other sons should not be slain by him.—§ 570 (Sainyaniryānap.): V, **151–159: 153,** 5197; **154,** 5232; **157,** 5318, 5328: At the commencement of the battle Anādhṛshṭi, etc. (ζ), marched surrounding Kṛshṇa and Arjuna, all of them blowing their conchs on entering Kurukshetra. As Yudhishṭhira complained that he had to slay his preceptors, etc., *A.* reminded him of what Kuntī and Vidura had said through Kṛshṇa. Bhīshma said that he did not know of any warrior upon earth who was equal to him, except Arjuna; but Arjuna would never openly fight with him. Karṇa wanted to fight with Arjuna, but not before Bhīshma was slain. Arjuna "of curly hair" was made the leader of all the leaders of the Pāṇḍava army, and Kṛshṇa the leader of Arjuna and the driver of his steeds. Bhīshmaka's son Rukmin offered Arjuna his assistance if he was afraid; *A.*, mentioning his exploits, and that he had paid his homage to Rudra, etc. (ν), for battle's sake, would not say he was afraid.—§ 571 (Ulūkadūt.): V, **160–164: 160,** 5460, 5513; **161,** 5558; **162,** 5578, 5586, 5640; **163,** 5651, 5695, 5697; **164,** 5704, 5706: Ulūka had to state before *A.* that among the Kuru troops were the Kāmbojas, etc. (γ); "I know that thy Gāṇḍīva is full 6 cubits long"; Ulūka repeated the statement to the Pāṇḍavas, etc., and once more repeated his words to *A.*; *A.* said that Duryodhana's contrivance of seeking cover behind Bhīshma would be of no avail, as he would himself slay Bhīshma.—§ 572 (Rathātirathas.): V, **165–172: 172,** 5935.—§ 573 (Ambop.): V, **173–196: 185,** 7308; **193,** 7560; **194,** 7587: "*A.* had been ordained by Svayambhū to slay Bhīshma." Karṇa having said that he could annihilate Bhīma and Arjuna in the course of five nights, Bhīshma ridiculed him, saying that he would think otherwise when he had encountered Arjuna and Kṛshṇa; to Yudhishṭhira Arjuna said that with Kṛshṇa as his ally he might exterminate the three worlds with the gods, etc., in the twinkling of an eye, etc. In the array of Yudhishṭhira, Bhīma and Arjuna were in the second division, then, with Kṛshṇa, in the middle division together with Virāṭa, etc.—§ 576 (Bhagavadg.): VI, **13–42: 19,** 713, (714), 723; **20,** 754, 759; **21,** 761, 765; **22,** 785; **23,** 793, 795, (796), 813; **25,** 833, 878; **26,** 880, 923, (932); **27,** (951), 957, (986); **28,** (997), 998, 1002, 1030; **29,** 1036; **30,** 1080, 1096, (1097), (1101), 1110; **31,** 1127, 1137; **32,** (1142), 1157, 1168; **34,** (1216), 1236, 1243, 1246; **35,** (1247), 1293, 1296, (1297), 1300; **36,** (1302); **37,** (1322); **38,** (1375); **41,** (1427); **42,** (1455), 1463, 1515, (1527), 1530: Yudhishṭhira told Arjuna to array the troops in a needle-mouthed (*çucīmukha*) array in conformity with the words of M.-ṛ. Bṛhaspati. Arjuna said that he would make a *vajra*-array, which was designed by Indra. Çikhaṇḍin was protected by *A.* Yudhishṭhira sorrowfully addressed Arjuna, who consoled him, mentioning his truthfulness, righteousness, etc. At Kṛshṇa's instance Arjuna recited a hymn to Dūrgā, who appeared and gave him assurance of victory. Arjuna asked Kṛshṇa to place his chariot between the two armies, so that he might see who had assembled to fight. Beholding his relatives, etc., Arjuna was filled with compassion and overcome with despondency, and refused to fight. Kṛshṇa appeals to Arjuna to shake off his despondency, but in vain. Kṛshṇa then explained to Arjuna the nature and the attributes of the soul, and the folly of grieving for the dead, and exhorted him to fulfil the duties of his caste by fighting like a man, and to concern himself with work for work's sake and not for the sake of its results, etc. (Bhagavadgītā). Arjuna praised Kṛshṇa; his delusion was destroyed, and he once more seized the Gāṇḍīva.—§ 577 (Bhīshmav.): VI, **43,** (1543), 1560: Beholding *A.* again seizing the Gāṇḍīva, the Pāṇḍavas and Somakas were filled with joy.—§ 578 (do.), VI, **44–51:** The first day's encounter: **45,** 1678; **49,** 1994, 1998, 2017; **50,** 2072: Bhīshma attacked Arjuna; Abhimanyu was regarded equal to Arjuna; placing himself in front of Çaṅkha, *A.* attacked Bhīshma; Çaṅkha mounted Arjuna's chariot; Bhīshma abandoned Arjuna, and attacked Drupada. The Pāṇḍavas were routed, the sun set, and the Pāṇḍavas withdrew their forces. Arjuna was indifferent; Kṛshṇa consoled Yudhishṭhira, who recommended the array called Krauñcāruṇa. When morning dawned, Dhṛshṭadyumna placed Arjuna in the van of the army; (§ 578*e*, VI, **50**) *A.'s* standard was created at Indra's command by the celestial artificer. *A.* blows the Devadatta.—§ 579 (do.), VI, **52–55:** Second day: **52,** 2128, 2132, 2142, 2144, 2163, 2167, 2168, 2172, 2189; **55,** 2383, 2391, 2393: Bhīshma shot on *A.*, etc. (α); *A.* told Kṛshṇa to drive his chariot before Bhīshma; only Bhīshma, Droṇa, and Karṇa were able to encounter Arjuna; encounter between Bhīshma and *A.*, who was surrounded by Sātyaki, etc.; the Kurus were routed; *A.* and Kṛshṇa blew their conchs.—§ 580 (do.), VI, **56–59:** Third day: **58,** 2487; **59,** 2563, 2586, 2588, 2621, 2639, 2646: Arjuna and Dhṛshṭadyumna formed an array in the shape of the half-moon, with Arjuna on the left wing; Arjuna fought with the Kauravas, who could not be defeated, as they were protected by Droṇa; and the Pāṇḍavas could not be defeated as they were protected by Arjuna and Bhīma; at last Bhīshma, etc. (ι), broke the ranks of the Pāṇḍavas. D., Dā., G., Pç., U., and Rā. eulogized Arjuna. Arjuna routed the Kaurava army, and their flight could not be checked by Bhīshma and Droṇa, but was checked by Duryodhana. Kṛshṇa told Arjuna to fight Bhīshma; he and Arjuna were both wounded by Bhīshma, and the Pāṇḍava army was routed; Bhīshma ordered Droṇa, etc. (μ), to attack Arjuna; the grandson of Çini (i.e. Sātyaki=Yuyudhāna) came to Arjuna's assistance. Kṛshṇa jumped down from the chariot with his discus Sudarçana in his hand, and rushed towards Bhīshma, but was held back by Arjuna; then Duryodhana etc. (ν), attacked Arjuna, who invoked the Māhendra weapon and checked the Kaurava host; *A.* then produced a river of blood, with Rākshasas on its banks. At sunset the Kurus (Bhīshma, etc.) withdrew their forces; Arjuna did the same. There was a great uproar among the Kurus: "the Sauvīras (π) have all been slain by Arjuna, and he has vanquished Çrutāyus, etc. (ρ)."—§ 581 (do.), VI, **60–68** Fourth day: **60,** 2656, 2673; **61,** 2697: Bhīshma, Droṇa etc., attacked Arjuna. Arjuna and Kṛshṇa as incarnations of the old ṛshis Nara and Nārāyaṇa.—§ 582 (do.), VI, **69–74** Fifth day: Bhīshma proceeded in a Makara-array, the Pāṇḍavas in a Çyena-array; Arjuna attacked Bhīshma; Duryodhana protected Bhīshma, who was attacked by the Pāṇḍavas headed by Arjuna. (§ 582*b*, VI, **71**): *A.'s* standard bore the device of a lion's tail and looked like a blazing mountain in the welkin . . . of celestial workmanship . . . with various hues; looking like a rising comet it could not be obstructed by trees. The Kurus were afraid and seemed to melt away. Arjuna encountered Droṇa (ζ). Duryodhana urged 25,000 to slay Arjuna, who, however, slew them all. The Matsyas and Kekayas surrounded Arjuna and Abhimanyu. At sunset both parties withdrew their troops.—§ 583 (do.), VI, **75–80**: SIXTH DAY: **75**, 3303, 3310: The next day the Pāṇḍavas were arranged in the Makara-array, headed by Drupada and Arjuna. The Pāṇḍava army was protected by *A.*; the Kauravas fled, mangled by Bhīma and Arjuna.—§ 584 (do.), VI, **81–86**: SEVENTH DAY: **81**, 3572; **82**, 3584; **84**, 3743, 3748; **85**, 3760; **86**, 3828, 3834: The next day Yudhishṭhira disposed his troops in a *vajra*-array; many kings attacked Arjuna, among others the Trigarta king with his brothers; Arjuna invoked the Aindra weapon; the foes fled and were rescued by Bhīshma. When the Kuru army had been routed by Arjuna, and Bhīshma had proceeded against the chariot of Arjuna, Duryodhana exhorted the kings to protect Bhīshma. Fighting with Alambusha, Sātyaki employed the Aindra weapon which he had obtained from Arjuna, and destroyed the productions of Alambusha's illusive force. Arjuna caused Kṛshṇa to drive the chariot towards Bhīshma; *A.* fought with Suçarman, and slew many. The Trigarta king and thirty-two others attacked Arjuna, who slew sixty of them and then hastened to slay Bhīshma. The Trigarta king attacking Arjuna, Çikhaṇḍin, etc., came to his aid. Arjuna shot at them with the Gāṇḍīva. Duryodhana and Jayadratha, etc., came in order to protect Bhīshma against Arjuna; *A.* fought against many foes. At sunset Arjuna (having vanquished Suçarman, etc.), etc., proceeded to their tents.—§ 585 (do.), VI, **87–98**: EIGHTH DAY: **89**, 3949, 3965; **90**, 3977, 3979, 3981, 3983, 3986, 4022, 4040, 4048, 4052; **95**, 4243, 4322; **96**, 4358; **98**, 4476, 4495: Dhṛshṭadyumna formed a Çṛṅgāṭaka-array: Bhīmasena and Sātyaki, etc., in the wings, next to them Arjuna and Kṛshṇa, etc. *A.*, etc. (ξ), rushed against all the kings under the command of Duryodhana with horses of the Kāmboja, etc. (ρ), breed. Arjuna's son Irāvat (*b*) attacked the Kauravas, but was slain by the Rākshasa, Ṛshyaçṛṅga's son [Alambusha]. Arjuna, etc., slew many; he complained of Irāvat's death before Kṛshṇa; he fought Bhīshma, etc. (ηη). When dark night set in, both parties withdrew their armies. "Yudhāmanyu protects Arjuna's left wheel, Uttamaujas his right wheel, and Arjuna protects Çikhaṇḍin"; *A.* told Dhṛshṭadyumna to place Çikhaṇḍin before Bhīshma; he would himself be his protector.—§ 586 (do.), VI, **99–107**: NINTH DAY: **101**, 4589, 4597, 4622, 4642; **102**, 4650, 4655; **104**, 4729; **106**, 4848, 4871; **107**, 4912, 4924, 4968, 4976, (4989): *A.* fought Bhīshma, Kṛpa, and Droṇa; then the Trigarta king and his son; *A.* employed the Vāyavya weapon; the Trigarta division turned their backs; Duryodhana, etc. (ι), surrounded *A.* *A.* slew all the followers of Suçarman; fought Duryodhana. Kṛshṇa urged Arjuna to slay Bhīshma; Kṛshṇa left the chariot and rushed at Bhīshma, whip in hand, but was brought back by Arjuna. When the sun set, both parties withdrew their forces. Kṛshṇa said that Arjuna, etc. (χ), were invincible; they went to Bhīshma himself in order to ask him about the means of killing him; Bhīshma advised *A.* to fight with him, placing Çikhaṇḍin before him; *A.* grieved at the prospect of killing Bhīshma, but was reminded by Kṛshṇa of his vow to slay Bhīshma. The Pāṇḍavas and Kṛshṇa went away with rejoicing hearts.—§ 587 (do.), VI, **108–120**: TENTH DAY: **108**, 5011; **110**, 5094, 5114, 5115, 5125, 5139; **111**, 5195; **112**, 5213, 5218; **113**, 5284, 5287, 5289, 5290; **114**, 5298, 5308, 5324; **115**, 5340, 5341; **116**, 5428, 5429, 5430, 5433, 5434, 5435; **117**, 5455, 5459, 5465, 5470, 5472; **119**, 5627, 5632, 5642: The Pāṇḍavas went out for battle, placing Çikhaṇḍin in their van; Bhīmasena and Arjuna became the protectors of his wheels, etc.; headed by Arjuna, they proceeded against Bhīshma; Arjuna urged Çikhaṇḍin to slay Bhīshma, while he himself would check Droṇa, etc. (δ); *A.* defeated the Kuru army; Duryodhana complained of *A.* before Bhīshma, etc. Urged by *A.*, Çikhaṇḍin, etc., attacked Bhīshma; Duḥçāsana attacked Arjuna and Çikhaṇḍin; *A.* could not advance further than to the chariot of Duḥçāsana; *A.* compelled Duḥçāsana to turn back, and then crushed the Kuru troops; Duḥçāsana again resisted him; Arjuna and Çikhaṇḍin approached Bhīma (for aid); Duryodhana urged the Trigarta king Suçarman to slay Arjuna and Bhīmasena; *A.* fought Çalya, etc. (κ); Droṇa, etc., fought Arjuna and Bhīmasena; so did Bhīshma; Droṇa, etc. (ξ), fought the Pārthas, especially Arjuna, etc. (ο); the sons of Dhṛtarāshṭra fought with Çikhaṇḍin and *A.*; *A.* fought with Bhīshma and Bhagadatta, and urged Çikhaṇḍin to slay Bhīshma; the Kurus attacked Arjuna; no chariot-warrior ventured to approach Bhīshma except Arjuna and Çikhaṇḍin; Bhīshma did not defend himself against Çikhaṇḍin, whom Arjuna urged quickly to slay Bhīshma; Duḥçāsana fought with Arjuna and all the Pārthas, but was vanquished by *A.*; the Videhas, etc. (ρ), attacked Arjuna, who defeated them all by means of celestial weapons; then *A.* fought with Duḥçāsana, etc., Bhīshma, etc.; Kṛshṇa urged *A.* to slay Bhīshma; the Pāñcāla king Dhṛshṭaketu, etc. (υ), were afflicted by Bhīshma and rescued by Arjuna; protected by Arjuna, Çikhaṇḍin rushed against Bhīshma; *A.* slew all Bhīshma's followers, and then rushed at him himself; Droṇa, etc. (employing celestial weapons), fought with *A.*; Bhīshma said to Duḥçāsana that *A.* was invincible, and that he himself was not able to be vanquished by D., Dā., and Rā.; Dhṛtarāshṭra's sons surrounded Bhīshma, but fled before Arjuna. Bhīshma fell down from his chariot a little before sunset, but put off his death, as the sun was in the southern solstice; both parties desisted from battle; as Bhīshma's head hung down he asked for a pillow; Arjuna supported his head with three arrows shot from the Gāṇḍīva and consecrated by means of mantras, at which Bhīma was highly gratified.—§ 588 (do.), VI, **121–122**: ELEVENTH DAY: **121**, 5776, 5780, 5781: The next morning, as Bhīshma asked for water, Arjuna mounted his chariot and from the Gāṇḍīva shot an arrow consecrated with mantras and identified with the Pārjanya weapon, therewith piercing the earth, and there arose a jet of pure and cold water; Bhīshma praised Arjuna: "even Nārada spoke of thee as an ancient ṛshi . . . "; he said to Duryodhana that the weapons appertaining to Agni, etc., were known only to Arjuna and Kṛshṇa. Bhīshma tried to win over Karṇa to the side of his uterine brothers, but he said that he would fight Arjuna, etc., though protected by Kṛshṇa.—§ 589 (Droṇābhish.), VII, **1–11**: **2**, 67, 82; **3**, 110; **6**, 164; **7**, 197; **8**, 226; **10**, 327; **11**, 419, 422: Karṇa waited upon Bhīshma, mentioning the danger menacing the Kurus from Arjuna with the Gāṇḍīva, etc., Arjuna's battle with Çiva, etc. Yudhishṭhira disposed his troops in the form of a krauñca (crane), with Kṛshṇa and Arjuna at the head. The Pāṇḍavas and Sṛñjayas were defeated by Droṇa; Yudhishṭhira asked *A.* to check Droṇa. Dhṛtarāshṭra regretted that Duryodhana did not know Kṛshṇa and Arjuna.—§ 590 (do.), VII, **12–16**: ELEVENTH DAY (Sañjaya begins his narrative in detail): **12,** 453; **13,** (472): Droṇa promised to seize Yudhishṭhira, if he was not protected by Arjuna (with his weapons received from Indra and Rudra, etc.); Arjuna must therefore be withdrawn from Yudhishṭhira. Yudhishṭhira learnt through his spies that Droṇa had promised to seize him; *A.* consoled him. A fierce battle commenced; protected by Droṇa and Arjuna, both hosts seemed to stand inactive. In order to rescue Yudhishṭhira, *A.* attacked Droṇa's division. When the sun set, both parties withdrew their troops. The Pāṇḍavas, etc., praised Arjuna.—§ 591 (Saṃçaptakavadhap.), VII, **17,** 680, 688, 709: Droṇa confessed his inability of seizing Yudhishṭhira if Arjuna were by; the Trigarta king, saying that Arjuna had always injured them, said that they would take an oath that either Arjuna or the Trigartas should be slain. Then they summoned Arjuna to the southern part of the field. Arjuna told Satyajit to guard Yudhishṭhira, and went out against the Trigartas.—§ 592 (do.), VII, **18–32**: TWELFTH DAY: **18,** 728, 733, 734, 736, 737; **19,** 753, 756, 763, 764, 765, 770, 773; **23,** 1017; **26,** 1130; **27,** 1208, 1212, 1219; **28,** 1232, 1234, 1235, 1241; **29,** 1265, 1266, 1274; **30,** 1303, 1306, 1312, 1319, 1321, 1324, 1325, 1326, 1328, 1329, 1336, 1339; **32,** 1418, 1423, 1426, 1428, 1443: The Saṃçaptakas rejoiced at the prospect of fighting with *A.*, who terrified them with the sound of Devadatta, and attacked them; Subāhu and Suçarman, etc. (*a*), fought with *A.*; they fled to Duryodhana, but, urged by the Trigarta king, they once more returned to the field with the Nārāyaṇa cowherds. Kṛshṇa conveyed Arjuna to the Saṃçaptakas. The Nārāyaṇas fought with Arjuna. *A.* blew the Devadatta and employed the Tvāshṭra weapon, that confounded the foes, who began to strike each other; Arjuna crossed the Lalitthas, etc. (β), and used the Vāyavya weapon to frustrate the downpour of arrows shot by his foes, and Vāyu bore away crowds of Saṃçaptakas with their steeds, etc. Yudhishṭhira disposed his troops in the form of a semicircle. Yudhishṭhira fled. Arjuna's son Çrutakīrti fought with the son of Duḥçāsana. *A.*, etc. (υ), fought with Bhagadatta (upon his elephant). Urged by Arjuna, Kṛshṇa began to proceed against Bhagadatta; the Saṃçaptakas (14,000, including 10,000 Gopālāḥ or Nārāyaṇāḥ) challenged Arjuna, and he encountered them, discharged the Brāhma weapon, defeated and slew them, and then turned against Bhagadatta; but as Suçarman with his brothers followed him from behind, he again attacked Suçarman, and then again Bhagadatta; Bhagadatta, at last, consecrated his hook with mantras so as to become the Vaishṇava weapon; Kṛshṇa received it on his breast, and it became a garland. As *A.* taxed Kṛshṇa for fighting himself, Kṛshṇa related the history of the Vaishṇavāstra (*c*); "the great Asura has now been divested of that supreme weapon; now slay Bhagadatta, that enemy of the gods, just as I formerly slew the Asura Naraka for the good of the worlds"; *A.* then slew both Bhagadatta and the elephant. Then *A.* slew the two brothers Vṛsha and Acala. Dhṛtarāshṭra's sons attacked Arjuna, and Çakuni employed magics in order to confound him and Kṛshṇa: producing clubs, etc., and asses, etc., which *A.* slew with celestial weapons; then darkness, whence harsh voices were heard; this *A.* dispelled with the weapon Jyotishka; then waves of water, which were dried up with the Āditya weapon; Çakuni fled. *A.* slaughtered the Kuru army: some followed Droṇa, others Duryodhana; a fierce battle took place on the southern side between Arjuna and the Kurus. The Pāṇḍavas regretted that Arjuna was engaged on the southern part of the field in slaughtering the Saṃçaptakas and the Nārāyaṇa force. Having slain the Saṃçaptakas, Arjuna fought with Droṇa, etc., employing the Āgneya weapon; *A.* slew three of Karṇa's brothers ($\gamma\gamma$). At sunset the armies retired.—§ 593 (Abhimanyuvadhap.), VII, **33–51**: THIRTEENTH DAY: **33,** 1456, 1466, 1468; **35,** 1520, 1521; **36,** 1545; **40,** 1661; **45,** 1824; **51,** 1989, 1991: Being overcome by *A.*, and Droṇa having failed to seize Yudhishṭhira, the Kurus were regarded as defeated; they heard everybody praise *A.* and Kṛshṇa. Next morning Duryodhana blamed Droṇa for not having seized Yudhishṭhira; Droṇa said that nobody could defeat the force protected by Arjuna and Kṛshṇa, save Mahādeva. The Saṃçaptakas challenged Arjuna and took him away to the southern side of the field. The Pāṇḍavas were headed by Bhīmasena. Abhimanyu defeated all the warriors that encountered him with the weapons he had received from Arjuna and Kṛshṇa. At last Abhimanyu was slain by Duḥçāsana's son, after Jayadratha had checked those who tried to follow Abhimanyu.—§ 595 (do.), VII, **71,** 2465: Vyāsa consoled Yudhishṭhira, who became free from grief; but "what shall we say to Arjuna?" —§ 596 (Pratijñāp.), VII, **72–81**: **72,** 2485, 2537, 2562, 2563; **73,** 2581, 2610; **74,** 2636, 2637; **75,** 2666, 2667, 2672; **76,** (2679), 2704; **77,** 2716; **78,** 2774; **79,** 2775, 2787, 2790, 2791, 2795, 2799, 2801, 2803, 2808; **80,** 2842, 2868, 2872, (2874), 2885; **81,** 2889, 2895, 2905, 2909: In the evening Arjuna, after having slain large numbers of Saṃçaptakas, proceeded towards his tent and told Kṛshṇa that his heart was afflicted; he saw indications of disaster; Abhimanyu did not come out with smiles to receive him, etc. He remembered that Droṇa had this day formed the circular array, which none save Abhimanyu could break; but he had not taught him how to come out of it after having pierced it; he had heard the leonine shouts of the Dhārtarāshṭras, and Kṛshṇa had heard Yuyutsu censuring them for having slain a child instead of Arjuna, and then Yuyutsu had cast up his weapons afflicted with rage and grief. Kṛshṇa consoled Arjuna, talking about the kshattriya duties and heaven. None save Kṛshṇa and Yudhishṭhira (who were always acceptable to him) could address Arjuna. Yudhishṭhira addressed him and told (VII, **72**) him the particulars of Abhimanyu's heroism and fall. Arjuna vowed to slay Jayadratha before the sun set the following day (his oath); even as to As., D., men, birds, snakes, P., wanderers of the night, B.-ṛ., and D.-ṛ., etc., he said that they would not succeed in protecting him, even if he entered Rasātala, or ascended the firmament, or repaired to the city of the gods (*Devapuraṃ*) or the city of Diti (*Diteḥ puraṃ*); if the sun set before he had slain him, he would himself enter the fire. Arjuna bent the Gāṇḍīva, Kṛshṇa blew the Pāñcajanya, Arjuna the Devadatta (VII, **73**). Having been informed by spies, Jayadratha was overwhelmed with sorrow and fear, thinking that not even Droṇa (*a*), not even D., G., As., U., Rā., could protect him against Arjuna. He wished to return home. Duryodhana comforted him saying that he, Karṇa, etc. (β), would protect him. Accompanied by Duryodhana, Jayadratha that very night repaired to Droṇa and questioned him about the difference between himself and Arjuna. Droṇa said they had got the same instruction, but Arjuna was superior to Jayadratha in consequence of yoga and the hard life he had led; Droṇa would, however, protect him, forming an impenetrable array; and, moreover, death ought not to be an object of terror to him (VII, **74**). Kṛshṇa remonstrated with *A.* for his rash vow; the Kurus had expected an attack by *A.*; now they would protect Jayadratha (who had mentioned *A.'s* encounter with Çiva, Hiraṇyapura, etc.); Karṇa, etc. (γ), would be in Jayadratha's van; Droṇa's array would be half a çakaṭa and half a lotus with a needle-mouthed array in the middle (VII, **75**). *A.* assured Kṛshṇa of his competence to accomplish his vow, notwithstanding Droṇa, Sā., R., V., A., M., with Indra, V.-D., D., P., G., Garuḍa, etc., by means of the Gāṇḍīva and the weapons he had obtained from Yama, etc. (δ) (VII, **76**). The gods, including Indra, became very anxious. Sinister omens appeared in nature. Kṛshṇa went to *A.'s* abode and consoled Subhadrā (mentioning the kshattriya duties, etc., and revenge) (VII, **77**). Subhadrā bewailed Abhimanyu, and said "Shame on Bhīmasena, etc. (ε)," because they had not protected him. Draupadī and Uttarā came to her, lamenting. Kṛshṇa said that Abhimanyu had attained the most laudable and enviable goal. Then he returned to *A.* (VII, **78**). *A.* performed his usual nightly sacrifice to Çiva. Kṛshṇa with Dāruka repaired to his own tent. None in the Pāṇḍava camp slept that night, thinking of *A.* In the middle of the night Kṛshṇa said to Dāruka that he had resolved to fight the next day [if necessary]; he must equip his chariot, placing Kaumodakī, etc., on it, making room for Garuḍa, and yoking Balāhaka, etc. (ζ), to it; when hearing Pāñcajanya emitting the shrill Ṛshabha note, he should come to Kṛshṇa (VII, **79**). *A.* saw Kṛshṇa in a dream, who told him not to grieve, and mentioned the Pāçupata weapon (with which Çiva slew all the Daityas in battle); if he remembered it now, he would be able to slay Jayadratha next day; otherwise he must pray to Çiva. At the Brāhma hour *A.* saw himself sojourning through the sky (Himavat, Maṇimat, frequented by Si. and Cā., etc. (η)), with Kṛshṇa, to where Çiva was seated with Pārvatī (description) (θ); Kṛshṇa and *A.* praised Mahādeva (VII, **80**). *A.* beheld the offerings that Çiva made every night to Kṛshṇa, and he mentally adored both Kṛshṇa and Çiva. Çiva told them to bring Çiva's bow and arrow from a lake of amṛta. In the lake they saw two terrible snakes; when they had uttered the Brahma Çatarudriya, the snakes assumed the forms of a bow and arrow; from Çiva's body there came out a brahmacārin with blue throat and red locks, and having showed *A.* the use of the bow and arrow and the mantras, he sped these weapons to that same lake. Having thus once more obtained the Pāçupata weapon, *A.* and Kṛshṇa came back to their own camp (VII, **81**).—§ 597 (do.), VII, **82–84**: FOURTEENTH DAY: **83**, 2958, 2969, 2970; **84**, 2975, 2977, 2982, 2983, 2995, 2998: Yudhishṭhira underwent his morning rites (very copious description); Kṛshṇa visited Yudhishṭhira (VII, **82**). Then also Virāṭa, etc. (**a**), arrived. Yudhishṭhira asked Kṛshṇa to rescue the Pāṇḍavas, quoting Nārada. Kṛshṇa assured Yudhishṭhira of Arjuna's success (VII, **83**). *A.* came and acquainted Yudhishṭhira with his dream, then he and Kṛshṇa and Yuyudhāna (these two on one chariot) set out for *A.'s* pavilion. Kṛshṇa equipped *A.'s* chariot (which had previously been sanctified with mantras), which *A.* circumambulated with his bow and arrow in hand. *A.*, Yuyudhāna, and Kṛshṇa mounted the chariot. Many and auspicious omens appeared. *A.* charged Yuyudhāna to protect Yudhishṭhira in his absence (only he or Pradyumna was able to do it). Yuyudhāna proceeded to Yudhishṭhira (VII, **84**).—§ 598 (Jayadrathavadhap.), VII, **85–88**: **85**, 3047, 3053, 3056; **86**, 3082; **87**, 3095: The warriors of Droṇa shouted in anger "where is *A.*?" etc. (η). After the Rudra-hour had set in, *A.* made his appearance, while omens appeared in nature. Durmarshaṇa (Dhārtarāshṭra) took up his position in the van in order to oppose *A.* *A.* was at the very van of his army. Kṛshṇa and *A.* blew their conchs. The Kuru army was afraid (VII, **88**).—§ 599 (do.), VII, **89–152**: FOURTEENTH DAY: **89**, 3174, 3180; **90**, 3185, 3186; **91**, 3230, 3236, 3241, 3242, (3250), 3256, 3259; **92**, 3265, 3270, 3272, 3286, 3288, 3294, 3297, 3299, 3301; **93**, 3346, 3347, 3366, 3392, 3402, 3405; **94**, 3413, 3436, 3446, 3484; **99**, 3668, 3674, 3677, 3683, 3684, 3694, 3696, 3697, 3700, (3705), 3720, 3721; **100**, 3738, 3743; **101**, 3804; **103**, 3843, 3847, (3853), 3864, 3873, 3876, 3877, 3879, 3880; **104**, 3908, 3913, 3914, 3924; **105**, 3954, 3955, 3956, 3963; **106**, 3965; **110**, 4181, 4198, 4222, 4224, 4233, 4235; **111**, 4264, 4265, 4268, 4272, 4274, 4280; **112**, 4371; **114**, 4467, 4470, 4471, 4473, 4475, 4485; **118**, 4700; **119**, 4713, 4757; **120**, 4758, 4787; **121**, 4806; **124**, 4991, 5014, 5016; **126**, 5110, 5136, 5141; **127**, 5191, 5193; **128**, 5245; **129**, 5279; **130**, 5311, 5317, 5338; **131**, 5357, 5363; **137**, 5629; **139**, 5774, 5780, 5810, 5815; **140**, 5835, 5841; **142**, 5883, 5926, 5928, 5930, 5932, 5933, 5941, 5947; **143**, (5967), (5997), 6007; **145**, 6056, 6066, 6069, 6085, 6088, 6099, 6103, 6127, 6134, 6139, 6145; **146**, 6196, 6204, 6210, 6211, 6252, 6255, 6274, 6288, 6294; **147**, 6324, 6386; **148**, 6394, 6408, 6418; **149**, 6497; **150**, 6522; **151**, 6535, 6549, 6552, 6576; **152**, 6587: *A.* fought with Durmarshaṇa and caused a terrible carnage (VII, **89**); then with Duḥçāsana, whose division was routed (VII, **90**). *A.* met Droṇa and asked leave to slay Jayadratha; Droṇa refused leave and attacked *A.*; *A.* avoided him and penetrated into the Kuru army, the Pāñcāla princes Yudhāmanyu and Uttamaujas being the protectors of his wheels; he was opposed by Jaya, etc. (**a**), and the Abhīshāhas, etc. (β) (VII, **91**). *A.* employed the Brāhma weapon against Droṇa, avoided him again, fought with Kṛtavarman and the Kāmboja king Sudakshiṇa; Kṛtavarman prevented Yudhāmanyu and Uttamaujas from following *A.*, who did not slay Kṛtavarman. Çrutāyudha (*b*) attacked *A.* and was slain by Kṛshṇa. Then *A.* slew Sudakshiṇa; all the troops fled away (VII, **92**). *A.* slew the Abhīshāhas, etc. (γ), and slew Çrutāyus and Acyutāyus with the Aindra weapon, and then their sons Niyatāyus and Dīrghāyus. *A.* caused a great carnage among the Aṅgas (on elephants), the Kaliṅga king, etc. (on elephants), the Mlecchas, Yavanas, etc. (δ); *A.* slew the Ambastha king Çrutāyus (VII, **93**). Droṇa acknowledged his inability to oppose Arjuna, clad Duryodhana in invulnerable armour and urged him to oppose *A.* Duryodhana and the Trigartas, etc., proceeded towards the chariot of *A.* (VII, **94**). *A.* and Kṛshṇa steadily proceeded towards Jayadratha (description). *A.* slew Vinda and Anuvinda. While Kṛshṇa led Arjuna's steeds, *A.* on foot kept the whole Kuru army in check, and piercing the earth with a weapon made a lake for his steeds to drink from and a hall of arrows for them to rest within; Nārada came to see the lake (VII, **99**). Si. and Cā., etc., applauded (VII, **100**). The progress of Arjuna (with Kṛshṇa) became irresistible. Duryodhana (VII, **101**) fought with Arjuna (VII, **102**), who had also got the same invulnerable armour from Indra; *A.* shot terrible shafts consecrated with mantras at Duryodhana; this weapon could not be used again lest it should slay *A.* himself; *A.* deprived Duryodhana of his chariot, steeds, and weapons; when Kṛshṇa blew the Pāñcajanya and *A.* bent the Gāṇḍīva, the Kurus fell down on the ground. The protectors of Jayadratha attacked Kṛshṇa and *A.* (VII, **103**). *A.* fought Bhūriçravas, etc. (μ), (and blew the Devadatta), Duryodhana, Açvatthāman (VII, **104**), and slew many chariot-warriors. *A.'s* standard bore the sign of an ape with fierce face and tail like that of the lion (ν) (VII, **105**). Yudhishṭhira heard the blare of Pāñcajanya and thought *A.* to be in distress; he requested Sātyaki to go to *A.* and bring him intelligence of his safety; *A.* had said in the Dvaita wood to Yudhishṭhira, "even if Kṛshṇa, etc. (σ), assists us, I shall yet appoint Sātyaki for our aid, since there is none equal to him," and Yudhishṭhira had witnessed his reverence for *A.* at Dvārakā, after his return from the tīrthas, etc.; "the day is about to end"; Pradyumna and Sātyaki are equal to *A.* in bravery (VII, **110**). Sātyaki hesitated to comply with Yudhishṭhira's request on the ground of a counter-command by *A.*; "the Sauvīrakas, etc. (τ), D., As., men, Rā., K., M.-U., etc., cannot cope with *A.* in battle" (VII, **111**). Sātyaki agreed to obey Yudhishṭhira's order; "the distance from here is 3 yojanas"; he would crush the elephants of the Añjana breed mounted by Mlecchas (named Rukmarathas), who at Karṇa's command had returned from the pursuit of *A.* and were waiting for Sātyaki, and likewise crush those 700 elephants mounted by Kirātas (*c*) and formerly given by the Kirāta king to *A.* (VII, **112**). Yuyudhāna proceeded towards the chariot of *A.* (VII, **120**). Yudhishṭhira was anxious because he had not obtained any news of *A.* and Sātyaki, and thought of sending Bhīma after Sātyaki; Bhīma penetrated to Arjuna, making his presence known by a roar; *A.* and Kṛshṇa uttered loud roars in return; Yudhishṭhira understood that all was safe, and recalled *A.'s* feats (ππ) (VII, **128**). *A.* bent the Gāṇḍīva, and Kṛshṇa blew the Pāñcajanya (VII, **129**). Yudhāmanyu and Uttamaujas proceeded towards *A.* (VII, **130**). Bhīma was attacked by Karṇa; Kṛshṇa and *A.* became anxious for Bhīma (VII, **132**). Bhīma gladdened *A.*, etc. (ψψ) (VII, **136**). Bhīma's weapons being exhausted, he fled away from Karṇa and defended himself with the bodies of the elephants slain by *A.*; but, recollecting *A.'s* vow, he did not take the life of Karṇa; and Karṇa, recollecting his promise to Kuntī, did not take the life of Bhīma; *A.* then turned Karṇa and then Açvatthāman to flight (VII, **139**). Sātyaki slew the steeds of Duḥçāsana, gladdening *A.* and Kṛshṇa (VII, **140**). Sātyaki approached *A.*, who was anxious for Yudhishṭhira (ccc) (VII, **141**). As Sātyaki succumbed to Bhūriçravas, *A.*, urged by Kṛshṇa, cut off one of the arms of Bhūriçravas (VII, **142**). Bhūriçravas rebuked *A.* (ηηη); *A.* justified his conduct (θθθ). Bhūriçravas (*d*) desired to die in prāya (description); he acknowledged the justice of *A.'s* plea, and was blessed by Kṛshṇa and *A.* (ιι). Though forbidden by Kṛshṇa, etc. (κκκ), Sātyaki slew Bhūriçravas sitting in prāya (VII, **143**). *A.* proceeded to Jayadratha's chariot; Duryodhana, etc. (μμμ), encountered *A.* Duryodhana prevailed upon Karṇa to protect Jayadratha (ννν); *A.* deprived Karṇa of his steeds, chariot, and charioteer. *A.* invoked the Vāruṇa weapon and caused a great carnage (VII, **145**). *A.* employed the Aindra weapon, etc. (description). *A.* cut off Jayadratha's standard and slew his charioteer; Jayadratha was put into their centre by six chariot-warriors. Kṛshṇa covered the sun by means of his yoga power, so that all, except *A.*, thought the sun to have set, and he urged *A.* to cut off Jayadratha's head without delay; *A.* caused such a carnage that the warriors abandoned Jayadratha in fear and fled away; Kṛshṇa again urged *A.* to cut off Jayadratha's head without delay, telling him about the curse of Jayadratha's father Vṛddhakshattra (*g*), who was still engaged in penances outside Samantapañcaka; therefore *A.* should make the head fall upon the lap of Vṛddhakshattra himself, lest *A.'s* head should crack into 100 pieces; this *A.* did, and as the head fell down from Vṛddhakshattra's lap the latter's head split into 100 pieces. Kṛshṇa then withdrew the darkness he had created; Kṛshṇa and *A.* blew their conchs, etc.; *A.* fought with many mighty chariot-warriors (VII, **146**); Kṛpa (at whose death-like swoon *A.* grieved), Açvatthāman (who fled), Karṇa; Kṛshṇa told *A.* to avoid Karṇa, because the latter was still in possession of the lance that Indra had given him. "In this world there are only three mighty archers, Kṛshṇa, *A.*, and Sātyaki," said Sañjaya (VII, **147**). Bhīma tried to induce *A.* to permit him to slay Karṇa; *A.* vowed to slay Karṇa's son Vṛshasena in his presence. Kṛshṇa congratulated *A.* (φφφ), who attributed the victory to Kṛshṇa; Kṛshṇa pointed out to *A.* the results of that day's battle (VII, **148**). Kṛshṇa and *A.* congratulated Yudhishṭhira (ψψψ) (VII, **149**). A fierce battle ensued (VII, **152**).—§ 600 (Ghaṭotkacavadhap.), VII, **153–183**: THE NIGHT COMBAT AFTER THE FOURTEENTH DAY: **159**, 7024, 7044, 7049, 7107; **164**, 7325, 7346, 7350; **165**, 7371; **167**, 7479, 7502, 7503, 7505, 7508; **170**, 7660, 7661; **171**, 7704, 7705, 7706, 7707, 7709; **172**, 7760; **181**, (8213); **182**, 8275; **183**, 8298: A dreadful battle took place between the Pāñcālas and the Kauravas (VII, **153**); *A.*, etc. (β), fought with Droṇa (VII, **154**); do.; Duryodhana urged Çakuni to proceed against *A.* together with Karṇa, etc. (κ) (VII, **156**). Drupada's division, which fled before Droṇa, was rallied by *A.* and Bhīma, followed by the Kaikayas, etc. (σ) (VII, **157**). Karṇa vowed to slay *A.*, etc. (υ) (VII, **158**). Açvatthāman, etc. (ββ), fought with *A.* in order to rescue Karṇa; *A.* slew the steeds and driver of Karṇa, etc.; Duryodhana fought with *A.*; Kṛpa urged Açvatthāman to proceed against *A.*; he made Duryodhana desist from an encounter with *A.* (VII, **159**). *A.* slew the Yaudheyas, etc. (ζζ); the Pāñcālas fled, but were rallied by Bhīma and *A.*; the Kauravas fled (VII, **161**). Kṛshṇa told Yudhishṭhira not to fight with Droṇa, he should go to Duryodhana, *A.*, and Bhīma (VII, **162**). Duryodhana commanded his troops to take up lighted lamps and torches (VII, **163**). "Karṇa will vanquish *A.*, etc.," said Droṇa; *A.* fought against the Kauravas (VII, **164**). Alambusha fought with *A.* (VII, **165**). *A.* vanquished Alambusha and attacked Droṇa (VII, **167**). A new battle ensued (description) (VII, **169**); the Gāṇḍīva and the rattle of *A.'s* chariot were heard; Duryodhana despatched Çakuni against *A.* (VII, **170**). *A.* deprived Çakuni of his chariot, etc.; Kṛshṇa and *A.* blew their conchs (VII, **171**). The Pāṇḍava host fled; *A.* and Kṛshṇa rallied the retreating troops (σσ) (VII, **172**). Dhṛshṭadyumna was deprived of his chariot by Karṇa, and ascended the chariot of *A.* *A.* and Kṛshṇa and Yudhishṭhira conversed about Karṇa; *A.* asked Kṛshṇa to proceed towards Karṇa. Kṛshṇa said that none except *A.* and Ghaṭotkaca could encounter him; but *A.* must not do it as long as he retained the lance presented by Indra; "but Ghaṭotkaca will vanquish Karṇa." They prevailed upon Ghaṭotkaca to encounter Karṇa (ττ) (VII, **173**). Ghaṭotkaca slew Alambusha and fought with Karṇa (VII, **174**). Kṛshṇa urged *A.* to proceed in Bhīma's wake and resist Droṇa's division (VII, **177**). *A.* shot many Kshattriyas (VII, **178**).

Karṇa slew Ghaṭotkaca with his celestial dart (VII, **179**). Kṛshṇa with transports of delight embraced *A.*, because Karṇa's dart could no more kill *A.* (VII, **180**). Kṛshṇa's policy was the reason why Karṇa had never hurled the fatal dart at *A.* (VII, **182**). — § 601 (Droṇavadhap.), VII, **184–185**: CONTINUATION OF THE NIGHT AFTER THE FOURTEENTH DAY: **184**, 8395; **185**, 8431, 8440, 8441, 8445, 8448, 8449: *A.* granted permission to the warriors to sleep. D., Ṛ., and soldiers applauded *A.*; all the combatants lay down on the field to sleep (description); the Kaurava troops blessed *A.* for his act of kindness. When the moon rose, both hosts rose from sleep and again prepared for battle (VII, **184**). Droṇa described the extent of *A.'s* might and prowess (γ); Duryodhana vowed that he would slay *A.* that day. Droṇa was of opinion that it was only right that Duryodhana and Çakuni should proceed against *A.* (VII, **185**).—§ 602 (do.), VII, **186–192**: FIFTEENTH DAY: **186**, 8462, 8465; **187**, 8540, 8543; **188**, 8597, 8605, 8607, 8608, 8610; **189**, 8691; **190**, 8701, 8702; **192**, 8875: When three-fourths of that night had worn away the battle once more commenced. Urged by Kṛshṇa *A.* moved to the left of Droṇa and Karṇa. Bhīma urged *A.* to put forth all his vigour. *A.* fought with Droṇa, Karṇa, etc. (ζ) (description); he was assisted by Drupada, etc. Soon the morning sun arose (VII, **186**). The battle was revived (VII, **187**). D., G., Ṛ., Si., Aps., Y., and Rā. applauded Droṇa and *A.*, saying that "this is no human, etc. (μ), but an exalted Brāhma encounter"; both employed the Brāhma weapon; the engagement became general (VII, **188**). *A.* attacked the Kurus, and Droṇa attacked the Pañcālas (VII, **189**). The Pāṇḍavas feared, thinking that *A.* would not fight with Droṇa. Kṛshṇa told *A.* to abandon virtue and let some one tell Droṇa that Açvatthāman had been slain in battle. *A.* did not approve; others approved, Yudhishṭhira, however, with great difficulty (VII, **190**). A fierce encounter took place between Droṇa and Dhṛshṭadyumna; Sātyaki rescued Dhṛshṭadyumna and was applauded by Kṛshṇa, *A.*, and Si., etc. (VII, **191**). Dhṛshṭadyumna cut off Droṇa's head, though forbidden by *A.* and blamed by everybody (VII, **192**).—§ 603 (Nārāyaṇāstram.), VII, **193–202**: THE LAST PART OF THE FIFTEENTH DAY: **193**, 8957, 8958; **195**, 9002; **196**, 9037, (9054); **197**, 9082, 9119, 9123, 9125; **198**, 9132; **199**, 9246, (9247); **200**, 9259, 9267, †9337; **201**, 9426, 9429, 9431, 9444, 9479; **202**, 9645: Açvatthāman was filled with rage; he said there was none equal to him and *A.* in knowledge of arms; he had a weapon (the Nārāyaṇa weapon) that neither *A.*, etc. (δ), knew, presented by Nārāyaṇa to his father, with the promise that no man should ever be his equal in battle; only this weapon must never be used in haste, etc., and never be hurled upon persons that abandoned their chariots and weapons in battle, etc.; with this he would rout and slay the Pāṇḍavas, etc. (ι) (VII, **195**). Terrible signs appeared in nature. Yudhishṭhira spoke about the matter to *A.* (κ); *A.* in reply described the prowess of Açvatthāman and the unrighteousness of the Pāṇḍavas in slaying Droṇa (λ); "all of us have passed the greater parts of our lives; the days that remain to us are few; this exceedingly unrighteous act has stained what is left; . . . I did not interfere, as he was about to be slain; for this fault I have already sunk into hell, overcome with shame" (VII, **196**). Bhīmasena, reproaching *A.*, vindicated the deed (μ) (VII, **197**). *A.* cast oblique glances upon Dhṛshṭadyumna; Dhṛshṭadyumna taunted Sātyaki for the slaughter of Bhūriçravas (ρ); Sātyaki would slay Dhṛshṭadyumna; Dhṛshṭadyumna asked Bhīma to let him slay Sātyaki (τ); then he and *A.* would slay the enemies. Kṛshṇa and Yudhishṭhira restored peace (VII, **198**). Açvatthāman invoked the Nārāyaṇa weapon (description). Kṛshṇa prevailed upon the troops to lay down their weapons and alight from their chariots; Bhīmasena alone refused to do so. *A.* said that his vow was that the Gāṇḍīva should not be used against the Nārāyaṇa weapon, kine, and brahmans. Bhīma attacked Açvatthāman, but was overwhelmed by the energy of the Nārāyaṇa weapon (VII, **199**). *A.* covered Bhīmasena with the Vāruṇa weapon; he and Kṛshṇa forcibly brought Bhīma down from his chariot, making him abandon his weapons. Then the Nārāyaṇa weapon became pacified. It could not be used twice. *A.*, etc. (γγ), fought with Açvatthāman (VII, **200**). *A.* addressed Açvatthāman in harsh words (δδ), though *A.* and Açvatthāman loved each other. Açvatthāman became angry with *A.* and especially with Kṛshṇa, touched water, and invoked the Āgneya weapon, the result being sinister omens and a great slaughter in the Pāṇḍava army; *A.* invoked the Brāhma weapon; the darkness was dispelled, etc., a full akshauhiṇī of the Pāṇḍava troops had been felled; Kṛshṇa and *A.* were unwounded; Açvatthāman lost heart and ran away; he met Vyāsa, who told him the history of Nārāyaṇa (*b*); "Nara and Nārāyaṇa are *A.* and Kṛshṇa" (VII, **201**). *A.* met with Vyāsa and inquired of him about the invisible person who aided him in the battle. Vyāsa said that it was Mahādeva himself, and related the tale of the sacrifice of Daksha, the destruction of Tripura (*d*), etc. —§ 604 (Karṇap.), VIII, **1–9**: THE NIGHT AFTER DROṆA'S DEATH, AND THE SIXTEENTH MORNING, AND BRIEF ACCOUNT OF THE SIXTEENTH AND SEVENTEENTH DAY: **3**, 72; **5**, 101, 143, 146; **9**, 267, 313: The Kurus made Karṇa their leader; he fought for two days and was then slain by *A.* (VIII, **1**). Sañjaya related to Dhṛtarāshṭra that Karṇa was made generalissimo and slain by *A.* on the second day (VIII, **3**). —§ 605 (do.), VIII, **10–32**: SIXTEENTH DAY: **11**, 428; **16**, 610, 611, 616, 618, 621, 627, 628, 633, 639, 640, 641, 642; **17**, 663, †665, †666, †667, †674, †675, †677, †679, 686; **18**, 688, 694, 695, 697, 708; **19**, 715, 718, 719, 721, 729, 731, 762; **20**, 772, 774; **21**, 821, 824; **26**, 1053; **27**, 1080, 1081; **30**, 1217, 1219, 1223, 1227, 1237, 1245; **31**, 1249, 1257, 1286, 1289, 1295, 1298, 1311, 1315; **32**, 1340, 1344: After Droṇa's fall the Kauravas fought for a long time with the Pāṇḍavas (Arjuna). On the approach of the evening twilight the Kauravas retired to their encampment; they held a consultation in the night; Karṇa was installed as generalissimo (ι) (VIII, **10**). Yudhishṭhira asked *A.* to array the Pāṇḍava army and slay Karṇa. The Pāṇḍava army was arranged after the form of a half-moon, *A.* in the middle (ω); Yudhāmanyu and Uttamaujas became the protectors of *A.'s* chariot-wheels (VIII, **11**). *A.* fought with the Saṃçaptakas (VIII, **13**, **16**) and Açvatthāman (VIII, **16**). The Kaliṅga, Vaṅga, and Nishāda heroes attacked *A.* with a division of elephants, which was broken; Kṛshṇa urged *A.* not to spare Açvatthāman, who was at last borne away by his steeds; Kṛshṇa and *A.* proceeded towards the Saṃçaptakas (VIII, **17**). Urged by Kṛshṇa, *A.* slew the Magadha chief Daṇḍadhāra (lord of Girivraja), (on an elephant), and then his brother Daṇḍa; *A.* once more proceeded against the Saṃçaptakas (VIII, **18**), whom he slaughtered; *A.* slew Ugrāyudha's son; urged by Kṛshṇa, *A.* defeated the remnant of the Saṃçaptakas in order not to lose any time in slaying Karṇa (VIII, **19**). Kṛshṇa said to *A.* that he did not see Yudhishṭhira (VIII, **21**). *A.* fought the Trigartas, etc. (λλ), slew king Çatruñjaya, and Suçruta's son and Candradeva; king Satyasena wounded Kṛshṇa and was slain by *A.*, who then slew Citravarman and Mitrasena, etc., and wounded Suçarman; all the Saṃçaptakas attacked *A.*, who invoked the Aindra weapon (description); the hostile army fled away almost entirely (VIII, **27**). Karṇa slaughtered the Pāñcālas, *A.* the Trigartas, etc., when the sun had passed the meridian (VIII, **28**). In the afternoon *A.* and Kṛshṇa (having said their daily prayers and worshipped Bhava) destroyed the Kurus; *A.* fought Duryodhana, Açvatthāman, Karṇa. At the close of the day both armies withdrew; Rā. and Pç., etc., came (VIII, **30**). Dhṛtarāshṭra exalted the prowess of *A.* (*oo*). Karṇa assured Duryodhana that he would slay *A.* next day; at dawn he repeated his pledge: "*A.* is superior to me only by having Kṛshṇa, the creator of the universe, for his charioteer, the chariot given him by Agni, his steed, and his standard with the ape." He wanted Çalya ("who is superior to Kṛshṇa") as his charioteer (VIII, **31**).—§ 606 (do.), VIII, **35**, 1657: Duryodhana prevailed upon Çalya to be Karṇa's charioteer by relating how Brahmán had acted as such to Rudra, and by pointing to the fact that Kṛshṇa had become the charioteer of *A.*, and would fight if *A.* were slain (VIII, **35**).—§ 607 (do.), VIII, **36–45**: **36**, 1688; **37**, †1722, †1728, †1735, †1740, †1741, †1745; **38**, 1756, 1757, 1758, 1760, 1763, 1766, 1768, 1771, 1774; **39**, 1791, †1794, †1796, †1797, †1798, 1806; **40**, 1818, 1829; **41**, 1958, 1960, 1961; **42**, 1962; **45**, 2111: When the morning came, Duryodhana prevailed upon Çalya to become Karṇa's charioteer. Karṇa told Çalya to urge the steeds that he might slay *A.*, etc. (β) (VIII, **36**). Karṇa boasted (γ); Çalya ridiculed him and praised *A.* (δ). Karṇa proceeded on his chariot and inquired after *A.* (VIII, **37**), promising every Pāṇḍava soldier that he who pointed out to him *A.* would receive whatever wealth he desired (VIII, **38**). Çalya said that Karṇa would have a sight of *A.* without troubling to make a search, and asked him to abandon his desire for a single combat with *A.* (VIII, **39**). Karṇa said that Kṛshṇa and *A.* were well known to him but did not inspire him with fright; notwithstanding the curse of Paraçu-Rāma he would slay *A.*; he would employ the Brāhma weapon, which *A.* would never be able to escape, if only the wheels of Karṇa's chariot did not sink into the earth that day according to the brahman's curse whose homa-cow's calf he had inadvertently struck (VIII, **42**).—§ 608 (do.), VIII, **46–96**: The seventeenth day's battle: **46**, 2130, 2132, 2152, 2154, 2161, 2177, 2193, 2197, 2199, 2201, 2206; **47**, 2212, 2217, 2219; **50**, 2415, 2421; **53**, 2574, 2598, 2604; **56**, 2774, 2784, 2801, 2810, 2828; **57**, 2849; **58**, 2857, 2858, 2894, 2898, 2903; **59**, 2955, 2966, 2970; **60**, 3039, 3055, 3063; **61**, 3079; **62**, 3142; **63**, 3198; **64**, 3217, 3219, 3223, 3230, 3231, 3240, 3241, 3272; **65**, †3292, †3293, †3294, 3307; **66**, 3309, 3317, 3335; **68**, 3386; **69**, (3440), (3470), 3483; **70**, 3492, 3515; **71**, 3562; **72**, 3605, 3615; **73**, 3634; **74**, 3791, 3803; **76**, 3842, 3859, 3860; **77**, 3861, 3862, 3874, 3875, 3876, 3878, 3879, 3881; **79**, 4004, 4025, 4032, 4037, 4066, 4067, 4068, 4072, 4075, 4085; **80**, 4118; **81**, 4124, 4145, 4146, 4157, 4159, 4161; **83**, 4257; **84**, 4301; **85**, 4329, 4340, 4347; **86**, 4349, (4364); **87**, 4383, 4408, 4409, 4415, 4416, 4421, 4423, 4425, 4429, 4430, 4437, 4461, 4462, 4476, 4479; **88**, 4505; **89**, 4524, 4532, 4533, 4534, 4535, 4536, 4539, 4559, 4591; **90**, 4623, 4625, 4626, 4632, 4633, 4635, 4658, 4662, 4664, 4667, 4670, 4671, 4672, 4675, 4685, 4688, 4690, 4696, 4698, 4701, 4715, 4718, 4720, 4725, 4731, 4736, 4741; **91**, 4766, 4780, 4807, 4811, 4816; **92**, 4819, 4826, 4829; **93**, 4834, 4851, 4867; **94**, 4905, 4919, 4947, 4956, 4960; **95**, 4977; **96**, 4990, 4992, 4997, 5008, 5016, 5027: Yudhishṭhira spoke to *A.* of the hostile array; *A.* should proceed against Karṇa, etc.; Çalya pointed out to Karṇa the chariot of *A.* (*b*). *A.'s* chariot of which Agni Vaiçvānara, the first (*pūrvaḥ*), the brahmán, Indu (i.e. Soma), had become the steeds, [and] that was originally (*prathamaṃ*) born from him, [that chariot] the gods and the brahmans knew; which had in days of old borne Brahmán, Īçāna (i.e. Çiva), Indra, and Varuṇa; riding on that primeval (*ādyaṃ*) chariot, Keçava (i.e. Kṛshṇa) and *A.* now proceeded to battle . . . . with white steeds. How the Saṃçaptakas threatened to slay *A.*, etc.; Çalya dissuaded Karṇa from trying to slay *A.* (VIII, **46**). *A.* arrayed his troops, headed by Dhṛshṭadyumna (with steeds white like pigeons); by the side of Dhṛshṭadyumna were the Draupadeyas. *A.* fought the Saṃçaptakas (VIII, **47**). *A.* fought the Saṃçaptakas, etc. (ηη); *A.* fought Suçarman; *A.* repeatedly invoked the Nāga weapon, paralyzing the legs (encircled with snakes) of the Saṃçaptakas; Suçarman invoked the Sauparṇa weapon; birds came down and devoured the snakes; *A.* sat down, recovered, and invoked the Aindra weapon; the battle became awful (VIII, **53**). *A.* fought the Saṃçaptakas; he addressed Kṛshṇa upon beholding Karṇa's (*e*) prowess, and as the Saṃçaptakas were defeated (when the sun had ascended the meridian), *A.* pierced through the Kuru host. Duryodhana once more urged the Saṃçaptakas against him. Having slain 10,000 kshattriyas, *A.* came to the further wing of the Saṃçaptakas, which was protected by the Kāmbojas; the younger brother of the Kāmboja chief Sudakshiṇa was slain by *A.*; the Kāmbojas, etc. (ττ), were slain. *A.* fought Açvatthāman; Si. and Cā. arrived; Kṛshṇa urged *A.* not to spare Açvatthāman, who swooned away and was borne away by his charioteer; *A.* slaughtered the Kuru troops, etc. (VIII, **56**). *A.* pointed out to Kṛshṇa that the Pāṇḍava army was fleeing before Karṇa, and that Yudhishṭhira was nowhere to be seen; "the third part of the day still remains." *A.* proceeded to Yudhishṭhira; Kṛshṇa described the field of battle to *A.* (γγ). A terrible battle ensued (VIII, **58**). A remnant only of the Saṃçaptakas were left unslaughtered. Dhṛshṭadyumna was worsted by Açvatthāman and rescued by *A.*; *A.* proceeded towards the Saṃçaptakas (VIII, **59**). Kṛshṇa pointed out to *A.* that Yudhishṭhira was being pursued by many Dhārtarāshṭras and was in great danger; Karṇa would soon come against *A.* and was protected by Duryodhana; he should be slain. *A.* then destroyed the remnant of his foes; the Saṃçaptakas fled (VIII, **60**). *A.* fought against Açvatthāman (VIII, **61**). *A.* appeared (VIII, **62**). Çalya exhorted Karṇa to fight with *A.*, but in vain; he once more reminded Karṇa of *A.*, etc. (ηη) (VIII, **63**). *A.* fought with Açvatthāman; Açvatthāman employed the Aindra weapon, which *A.* neutralized with a mighty weapon created by Indra; at last Açvatthāman was borne away by his steeds. The Sṛñjayas called upon *A.* and Kṛshṇa. *A.* spoke to Kṛshṇa about Karṇa; Kṛshṇa asked him first to find Yudhishṭhira (VIII, **64**). *A.* met with Bhīma and asked him to bring intelligence of Yudhishṭhira; but they agreed that *A.* should go to Yudhishṭhira while Bhīma should resist the Saṃçaptakas. *A.* and Kṛshṇa found Yudhishṭhira lying on his bed (VIII, **65**). *A.* swore to slay Karṇa and all the foes that day (VIII, **67**). Yudhishṭhira censured *A.*, thinking that he had run away from the battle leaving Bhīma unsupported (λλλ), several times invoking him to give up the Gāṇḍīva to somebody else (VIII, **68**). *A.* drew his sword in order to strike off Yudhishṭhira's head in fulfilment of his vow regarding the person who would tell him to give up the Gāṇḍīva (μμμ); Kṛshṇa addressed *A.* on the nature of truth (ννν); *A.* said he must keep his vow (ξξξ); Kṛshṇa suggested that *A.*, by insulting Yudhishṭhira, by addressing him with "thou," would be regarded as having slain him (οοο) (VIII, **69**). Urged by Kṛshṇa, *A.* insulted Yudhishṭhira in a long speech (πππ); then he became despondent and desired to cut off his own head; Kṛshṇa urged him to utter his own praises, as self-praise was equal to self-destruction. *A.* praised himself (ρρρ) and asked for Yudhishṭhira's forgiveness, promising to slay Karṇa and rescue Bhīma. Kṛshṇa induced him to forgive both himself and *A.* (σσσ) (VIII, **70**). Speeches of Kṛshṇa, *A.*, and Yudhishṭhira on the same topic (τττ) (VIII, **71**). *A.* proceeded to slay Karṇa, having obtained Yudhishṭhira's leave; Kṛshṇa addressed *A.* in order to raise his spirits (υυυ) (VIII, **72**); continuation (υυυ) (VIII, **73**). *A.'s* cheerful reply to Kṛshṇa (ψψψ) (VIII, **74**). Sañjaya related: *A.* slew many (VIII, **75**). Bhīma said to his charioteer Viçoka that he was anxious about *A.* and Yudhishṭhira; Viçoka pointed out to Bhīma that *A.* was returning to battle (ωωω) (VIII, **76**). *A.* and Bhīma attacked the Kaurava army (description) (VIII, **77**). *A.* produced a river of blood (description). Requested by *A.* (ζ'), Kṛshṇa brought him to Karṇa; Duryodhana attacked *A.*; *A.* vanquished Açvatthāman, Kṛpa, and Kṛtavarman; Çikhaṇḍin, etc. (ι'), proceeding towards *A.*, checked the foes (VIII, **79**). *A.*, avoiding Karṇa, proceeded to the rescue of Bhīma; he informed Bhīma that Yudhishṭhira was well; he slew ten sons of Dhṛtarāshṭra (VIII, **80**). *A.* was assailed by ninety Saṃçaptakas as he was proceeding towards Karṇa's chariot; he slew them; so also many Kauravas and a force of Mlecchas, mounted on 1,300 elephants under the command of Duryodhana. Bhīma rushed towards *A.*, and destroyed a small unslaughtered remnant of the Kauravas; then he followed *A.* in his rear (VIII, **81**). Kṛshṇa urged *A.* to slay Karṇa; *A.* proceeded with Bhīmasena (VIII, **82**). Bhīmasena took up a little of Duḥçāsana's blood and drank it (μ'), addressing Kṛshṇa and *A.*, and vowing soon to slay Duryodhana (VIII, **83**). Urged by Bhīma and Nakula, *A.* proceeded towards Vṛshasena (VIII, **84**). *A.* slew Karṇa's son Vṛshasena, and threatened to slay Karṇa, as Bhīma would slay Duryodhana; *A.* attacked Karṇa (VIII, **85**); Kṛshṇa addressed *A.* (τ'); *A.'s* reply (υ') (VIII, **86**); description of *A.* and Karṇa (φ'); As., Yātudhānas, Gh., etc., sided with Karṇa; the Vedas, etc. (χ'), took the side of *A.*; the smaller snakes all sided with Karṇa; V., M., Sā., R., V.-D., A., and Agni, etc. (χ'), sided with *A.*, while all Ā. sided with Karṇa; the Vaiçyas, etc. (ψ'), sided with Karṇa; P., etc. (χ'), with *A.*; the Pretas, Pç., Rā., etc., with Karṇa; D.-ṛ., B.-ṛ., R.-ṛ., with *A.*, as also G. headed by Tumburu. With the Prādheyas and Mauneyas, G., and Aps., and many wise sages, having wolves for their vehicles, came to witness the encounter that was also witnessed by D., Dā., G., N., Y., etc., M.-ṛ., P. (subsisting upon Svadhā), etc., and Brahmán with B.-ṛ., and Prajāpatis, and Bhava. Indra wished that *A.* should vanquish Karṇa; Sūrya, that Karṇa should vanquish *A.*; the gods urged Brahmán that the success of both should be equal, Indra that *A.* and Kṛshṇa should win; Brahmán and Īçāna (i.e. Çiva) said that the victory of *A.* was certain (ω'): "let Karṇa obtain identity with V. or M., let him be worshipped in heaven with Droṇa and Bhīshma." Indra acquiesced by their words. Description of Karṇa's and *A.'s* chariots; the ape on *A.'s* banner attacked the elephant's rope on Karṇa's banner. Kṛshṇa and Çalya darted keen glances at each other, and so did *A.* and Karṇa. Çalya said that he would slay both Kṛshṇa and *A.* if Karṇa was slain; Kṛshṇa said that Karṇa could not slay *A.*; otherwise, the destruction of the universe would be at hand, and he would himself slay Karṇa and Çalya. *A.* said that that day the wives of Karṇa would become widows (*αα'*) (VIII, **87**). In the welkin D., N., As., Si., Y., G., Rā., Aps., and B.-ṛ., etc., looked on. The battle commenced. *A.* defeated Duryodhana, etc. (VIII, **88**); description of the battle between *A.* and Karṇa; *A.* employed an Āgneya weapon, which was neutralized by Karṇa with a Vāruṇa weapon by means of clouds, which was in its turn dispelled by *A.* by means of a Vāyavya weapon; *A.* employed the Aindra weapon (? *dayitaṃ devarājñaḥ; Mahendrasyāstram*), Karṇa the Bhārgava weapon. Seeing *A.'s* weapons neutralized by Karṇa, Bhīma (αε') and Kṛshṇa (αζ') urged *A.* to put forth his strength. *A.* bowed to Brahmán and invoked the Brāhma weapon, which could be applied by the mind alone; Karṇa neutralized it; urged by Bhīma, *A.* applied a second Brāhma weapon, which caused a great carnage among the Kaurava troops (description). *A.* shot at Karṇa and Çalya and slew Sabhāpati, etc. The Kauravas urged Karṇa to slay *A.* Yudhishṭhira appeared in order to witness the encounter. *A.'s* bowstring burst; Karṇa pierced *A.* (αδ'). Karṇa employed five snakes as arrows; they were cut off by *A.*, who slew 2,000 Kurus. The Kurus fled, leaving Karṇa to fight alone with *A.* (VIII, **89**). The snake Açvasena entered into Karṇa's quiver in the form of an arrow. Karṇa and *A.* were fanned and sprinkled with fragrant sandal-water by many Aps., staying in the welkin, and Çakra and Sūrya gently brushed their faces with their hands. Karṇa aimed that arrow which he had long kept for *A.'s* destruction. Omens appeared; Karṇa did not know that Açvasena had entered his arrow. Kṛshṇa with his feet pressed *A.'s* car about a cubit into the earth and the snake-arrow only broke his diadem (made by Svayambhū for Indra > *A.*); incapable of being crushed by Rudra, etc. (αι'). Karṇa would not shoot the same weapon again. Açvasena then of his own accord came towards *A.* in the shape of an arrow; Kṛshṇa informed *A.*; *A.* cut off the snake, and Kṛshṇa raised the chariot from the earth. Once, when Karṇa was stupefied, *A.* did not wish to slay him, but he was taught by Kṛshṇa never to spare an enemy. Karṇa invoked the Brāhma weapon and *A.* the Aindra weapon, which was neutralized by Karṇa; urged by Kṛshṇa to shoot "high weapons," *A.* shot the Brāhma weapon. Karṇa cut off eleven bowstrings of *A.'s* one after another, not knowing that *A.* had 100 strings to his bow; urged by Kṛshṇa to strike Karṇa with "superior weapons," *A.* then consecrated another celestial weapon with mantras, uniting the Raudra weapon with it. At that time the earth swallowed up Karṇa's wheels. Karṇa asked *A.* to wait for a moment till he had raised his sunken wheel (VIII, **90**). Kṛshṇa urged *A.* to pierce Karṇa with a celestial weapon; *A.* kindled with fury; blazing flames of fire seemed to emanate from all the pores of his body. Both Karṇa and *A.* invoked the Brāhma weapon; *A.* shot an Agni weapon, which was neutralized by Karṇa with the Vāruṇa weapon, spreading darkness in all directions, which *A.* dispelled with the Vāyavya weapon. Pierced by a shaft of Karṇa's, *A.* began to reel, etc.; Karṇa in vain endeavoured to extricate his chariot. Recovering his senses, *A.* took up an Añjalika weapon. Urged by Kṛshṇa, *A.* cut off Karṇa's standard, and then struck off Karṇa's head with an Añjalika weapon (the Ṛ. loudly crying out "Peace be to the universe!") (VIII, **91**). *A.* fought the chariots of the Kauravas. *A.* and Kṛshṇa blew their conchs; D., G., men, Cā., M.-ṛ., Y., and M.-U. congratulated *A.* (VIII, **94**). Urged by Kṛshṇa (*αφ'*), *A.* presented himself to Yudhishṭhira, who greeted *A.* and Kṛshṇa. Yudhishṭhira, with Kṛshṇa and *A.*, came back to the field to have a look at Karṇa's body (VIII, **96**).—§ 609 (Çalyap.), IX, **1-2**: **2**, 119: Çalya was made the commander of the army (IX, **1**). Dhṛtarāshṭra's lament (IX, **2**).—§ 610 (do.), IX, **3-7**: **3**, 143, 150; **4**, 207, 208, 234; **5**, 251; **7**, 351: *A.* proceeded towards the chariots; he fought with 25,000 foot-soldiers; Cekitāna, etc. (*κ*), having slain a large number, *A.* attacked the rest (IX, **3**). The troops passed the night at the foot of Himavat (IX, **6**). Kṛshṇa said that Çalya was equal to Bhīshma and superior to *A.* (*χ*) (IX, **7**).—§ 611 (do.), IX, **8-28**: The battle of the forenoon of the eighteenth day: **8**, 398; **9**, 448; **11**, 567; **14**, 705, 708, 710, 714, 730, 737, 749, 750, 751; **18**, 961; **19**, 1015; **24**, 1325; **25**, 1364, 1395; **27**, 1471, 1480, 1485: *A.* went against Kṛtavarman and the Saṃçaptakas (IX, **8**). *A.* and Bhīmasena stupefied their foes (IX, **9**). *A.*, having slaughtered the Saṃçaptakas, encountered Çalya (IX, **10**). Duryodhana fought with *A.* (IX, **11**). *A.* fought with Açvatthāman (IX, **12**). *A.* fought against Açvatthāman and the Trigartas; he destroyed 2,000 cars (IX, **14**). The Pāṇḍavas (in the very sight of Kṛshṇa and *A.*) were afflicted by the Kurus; *A.* fought with Kṛpa and Kṛtavarman. Yudhishṭhira said that *A.* should protect his rear; *A.* began to slay the Kaurava troops (IX, **16**). Yudhishṭhira slew Çalya with a celestial dart (IX, **17**). *A.*, etc. (*ββ*), began to slaughter the Madrakas (IX, **18**). Also the sons of Dhṛtarāshṭra almost all turned away from the fight at midday; *A.* fought against the chariots; Duryodhana rallied a small force by a spirited address (*ζζ*); the Pāṇḍavas, and especially *A.*, rushed against them (IX, **19**). The whole army of Duryodhana fled except Duryodhana (IX, **21**). *A.* (desiring to exterminate the Kurus) addressed Kṛshṇa, recounting the loss sustained by the Kurus (*νν*), and attacked the remnant of the Kuru army, and caused a great slaughter (IX, **24**). *A.* and Bhīma, etc. (*οο*), slew 3,000 elephants, encompassing the Pāṇḍava brothers; *A.* had afflicted Sañjaya's men; Bhīma and *A.* destroyed the elephants (IX, **25**). Kṛshṇa urged *A.* to destroy the remnant of Duryodhana's troops (*σσ*); *A.* ascended his chariot (*ττ*); *A.* fought against Suçarman and Çakuni, the Trigartas, slew Satyakarman, Satyeshu, and the Prasthala ruler Suçarman, and the latter's thirty-five sons, etc., and then proceeded against the remnant of the Bharata host (IX, **27**).—§ 612 (Hradapr.), IX, **29-31**: **29**, 1568, 1600; **30**, 1725: the followers of Çakuni attacked the Pāṇḍavas; *A.* and Bhīmasena came to the rescue of Sahadeva; *A.* slew them. Duryodhana abandoned his slain steed, and fled away without a companion, on foot towards a lake, taking up his mace. The Pāṇḍavas with *A.* baffled the purpose of the Kurus. In Duryodhana's army no great chariot-warrior was alive save Açvatthāman, Kṛpa, and Kṛtavarman (IX, **29**). When the sun had set, *A.*, etc. (*ε*), started towards the lake (IX, **30**). Yudhishṭhira in vain exhorted Duryodhana to come out from the lake and fight with them (IX, **31**).—§ 613 (Gadāyuddh.), IX, **32-33**: **33**, 1890, 1921: Yudhishṭhira (though reproved by Kṛshṇa) granted Duryodhana that if he could slay even one of the five Pāṇḍavas he would continue king (IX, **32**); Bhīmasena undertook to encounter him with the mace (IX, **33**).—§ 614 (do.), IX, **34**: Bala-Rāma (*b*) came to see the encounter.—§ 615 (do.), IX, **35-65**: **58**, 3246; **61**, 3416; **62**, 3474, 3477: According to the proposal of Bala-Rāma, Yudhishṭhira, with his brothers and Duryodhana, proceeded to Samanta-pañcaka (IX, **55**). *A.* inquires of Kṛshṇa about the relative merits of the two combatants. Kṛshṇa said that by fighting fairly Bhīma would never succeed in vanquishing Duryodhana. *A.* struck his own left thigh before the eyes of Bhīmasena, who understood the sign and fractured Duryodhana's thigh with his mace (IX, **58**). Kṛshṇa caused *A.* to take down the Gāṇḍīva and his inexhaustible quivers, and then to dismount; then Kṛshṇa also dismounted; the celestial Ape on his standard disappeared, and the chariot (burnt by Droṇa and Karṇa with the Brāhma weapon) with its steeds, etc., was reduced to ashes. At Kṛshṇa's suggestion the Pāṇḍavas and Sātyaki resolved to pass the night at a spot outside the camp, on the banks of the Oghavatī. They then despatched Kṛshṇa to Hāstinapura in order to pacify the wrath of Gāndhārī and console her and Dhṛtarāshṭra (IX, **62**). Duryodhana induced Kṛpa to instal Açvatthāman as the Kuru generalissimo; then they took leave of Duryodhana and left him alone (IX, **65**).—§ 616 (Sauptikap.), X, **1-9**: **4**, 171; **9**, 509: Açvatthāman, Kṛpa, and Kṛtavarman murdered all who were present in the Pāṇḍava camp during the night. "*A.* is incapable of being vanquished by D., As., G., Y., and Rā." They went to Duryodhana and informed him; Duryodhana died (X, **9**).—§ 617 (Aishīkap.), X, **10-18**: **10**, 550; **13**, 652 (*satya-karmā*); **14**, 670, 671; **15**, 695, 696, 706: The Pāṇḍavas with Kṛshṇa proceeded in the track of Bhīmasena and Nakula in pursuit of Açvatthāman: Kṛshṇa, *A.*, and Yudhishṭhira on Kṛshṇa's chariot. Açvatthāman shot a celestial weapon "for the destruction of the Pāṇḍavas" (X, **13**). Urged by Kṛshṇa, *A.* shot the [Brāhma] weapon. Extraordinary omens appeared in nature; Nārada and Vyāsa, seeking to save the three worlds, stood between the two fires (X, **14**). *A.* withdrew his weapon, but Açvatthāman could not. Vyāsa praised *A.* for not having used the Brahmaçiras weapon before (X, **15**). Kṛshṇa said that Uttarā's son Parikshit would be stillborn, but be brought to life by Kṛshṇa, etc. Açvatthāman's gem was placed upon Yudhishṭhira (X, **16**).—§ 618 (Jala-pradānikap.), XI, **1-15**: **15**, 412: Dhṛtarāshṭra resolved to visit the field of battle accompanied by the Kuru ladies (XI, **10**). Yudhishṭhira and his brothers set out to meet Dhṛtarāshṭra, accompanied by Kṛshṇa, etc. (*κ*); they met the weeping ladies on the way (*λ*), and saluted Dhṛtarāshṭra, who reluctantly embraced Yudhishṭhira and broke an iron statue of Bhīma (XI, **12**). Commanded by Dhṛtarāshṭra, the Pāṇḍava brothers proceeded with Kṛshṇa to see Gāndhārī (XI, **14**). *A.* moved away to the rear of Kṛshṇa (XI, **15**).—§ 619 (Strīvil.), XI, **16-25**: **18**, 540; **23**, 660; **24**, 684, 696: With the Pāṇḍavas and Kṛshṇa and all the Kuru ladies Dhṛtarāshṭra proceeded to the field of battle. The Pañcāla and the Kuru ladies were plunged into unutterable distress (description). Gāndhārī cursed Kṛshṇa.—§ 620 (Çrāddhap.), XI, **26-27**: **27**, 807: Urged by Dhṛtarāshṭra, Yudhishṭhira ordered Sudharman, etc. (*a*), to cause the funeral rites of the slain (*β*) to be duly performed; they burnt them upon funeral pyres. Then Yudhishṭhira and

Dhṛtarāshṭra proceeded towards the Gaṅgā (XI, **26**). The Kuru ladies, etc., performed the water rites for their fallen kinsmen on the Gaṅgā. Kuntī, in a paroxysm of grief, disclosed to her sons the truth about the birth of Karṇa (γ), whom *A.* had slain, being in reality his brother (XI, **27**). — § 621 (Rājadh.): XII, **1**, 13, 34, 36, 39; **2**, 47, 55; **7**, 158 (Yudhishṭhira's lament before *A.*); **8**, 201, (203) (*A.* addressed Yudhishṭhira, justifying the battle and applauding the acquisition of wealth, quoting Nahusha, etc.); **9** (unmoved by *A.'s* words, Yudhishṭhira desired to lead the life of a religious recluse).—§ 622 (do.), XII, **11**, (305), (331): *A.* recited the story of the discourse between Çakra (in the form of a golden bird) and certain youths (Ṛ.) desirous of leading a forest life.—§ 623 (do.), XII, **12**, 333; **15**, 424, (425): *A.* applauded [him who wields] the rod of chastisement; **16**, 482.—§ 624 (do.), XII, **18**, 535, (536), (571): *A.* recited the story of the discourse between the Videha king Janaka and his queen, in which the latter explained the claims of a life of poverty and renunciation.—§ 625 (do.): XII, **19**, 579, 595: Yudhishṭhira's reply to *A.* on the vanity of wealth.—§ 627 (do.): XII, **22**, 636 (*A.* justified before Yudhishṭhira the slaughter of foes in battle, citing Indra).—§ 629 (do.), XII, **25**: Seeing *A.* angry, Yudhishṭhira declared to Vyāsa that earthly rule could not give him any delight. —§ 630 (do.), XII, **27**, 809 (Yudhishṭhira's reply to *A.* approving a life of yoga and austerities).—§ 632 (do.), XII, **29**, (894), 897: *A.* asked Kṛshṇa (who from his earliest years was dearer to Yudhishṭhira than even *A.* himself) to dispel Yudhishṭhira's grief.—§ 635 (do.), XII, **33**, 1175; **37**, 1377: Directed by Nārada to apply to Bhīshma for instruction and exhorted by Jishṇu (Arjuna), etc. (γ), Yudhishṭhira with his brothers, etc., headed by Dhṛtarāshṭra, set out for Hāstinapura. The procession described (δ): *A.* held a white umbrella of great effulgence, etc., over his head. **38**, 1396: The citizens welcomed Yudhishṭhira and Draupadī and *A.*, etc. (ε). Yudhishṭhira entered the palace; the brahmans slew Cārvāka with their yells.—§ 637 (do.), XII, **40*a***, 1445: Bhīma and *A.* sat one on each side of Yudhishṭhira at his installation on the throne. **41**β, [1479: *A.* was appointed to resist hostile forces and chastise the wicked]; **44**δ, 1517, 1524 (obtained the palace of Duḥçāsana), 1530 (Çaurin and Sātyaki entered the palace of *A.*); **47**, [1694 (Yudhishṭhira and *A.* went in one chariot to see Bhīshma, together with Kṛshṇa)]. — [§ 638 (do.), XII, **48**: Kṛshṇa and the Pāṇḍavas, etc., proceeded to Kurukshetra (description).]—§ 639 (do.), XII, [**50**: The Pāṇḍavas and Kṛshṇa, etc., descended from their chariots and approached and saluted the Ṛ., who surrounded Bhīshma on his arrow-bed]. **52**ε: [The Pāṇḍavas, etc., returned to Hāstinapura after having saluted Bhīshma]; **53**, [1910 (Yudhishṭhira asked *A.* to see that his chariot was made ready)], 1914 (the Pāṇḍavas proceeded towards Kṛshṇa's abode; the princes set out to see Bhīshma), [having come to Bhīshma, they alighted from their chariots]. — § 640 (do.), XII, **54*a***, 1929 (the Pāṇḍavas asked Bhīshma to discourse on morality).—§ 654 (Āpaddh.), XII, **157**, 5874 ("the 18 akshauhiṇīs were not equal in might to the single-handed *A.*").—§ 657 (do.), XII, **167**, (6220) (*A.* assigned precedence to Wealth, not to Virtue and Desire). — § 717 (Nārāyaṇīya), XII, **342**, (13133), 13136, 13186: Vaiçampāyana related what Kṛshṇa had said to *A.*, when the latter asked him about the signification of his names mentioned by M.-ṛ. in the Vedas and Purāṇas. **343**, (13188), 13238, (13277): Asked by *A.* about the identical origin of Agni and Soma, Kṛshṇa (in prose) related some ancient stories about the gods, etc.; asked by *A.* about the battle between Rudra and Nārāyaṇa, Kṛshṇa related some particulars thereof: "that being, whom, at the time of all the battles, thou beheldst stalking in thy van, is no other than Rudra . . . . those foes whom thou hast slain, were all, in the first instance, slain by him." **349**, 13554: When the Pāṇḍava and Kuru armies were drawn up for the battle and *A.* became distressed, Kṛshṇa himself explained the religion of Devotion . . . . Pārtha put that question to Nārada in the midst of Ṛ. and in the presence of Kṛshṇa and Bhīshma.—§ 734 (Ānuçāsanik.), XIII, **26**, 1759: Bhīshma had been overthrown in battle by *A.*; he was lying on a bed of arrows in expectation of the time of death; the Pāṇḍavas, etc., waited upon him, while he answered their questions relating to morality and righteousness.—§ 777 (Svargāroh. p.), XIII, **169*a***, 7771: When they burnt the corpse of Bhīshma, Bhīmasena and *A.* held a couple of Yak-tails of pure white in their hands; then the Pāṇḍavas, etc., proceeded to Gaṅgā, where they offered oblations of water to Bhīshma; Gaṅgā wept; Kṛshṇa comforted her; he declared that Bhīshma had not been slain by Çikhaṇḍin, but by *A.*—§ 781 (Açvamedh.), XIV, **15**, 396, 399, 406: Asked by Janamejaya what Kṛshṇa and *A.* did when the Pāṇḍavas had reconquered and pacified their kingdom, Vaiçampāyana said that Kṛshṇa comforted *A.* for the death of his relatives (*a*) and then wished to go to Dvāravatī; *A.* sorrowfully assented.—§ 782 (Anugītāp.), XIV, **16**, 407, 410: When Kṛshṇa and *A.*, after slaying the enemies, dwelt in the palace, *A.* asked Kṛshṇa to repeat the contents [of the Bhagavadgītā], because he would soon repair to Dvārakā. Kṛshṇa was discontented that *A.* could not remember it; he now, however, recited what the brahman Kāçyapa had heard from a brahman crowned with ascetic success about Jīva (the individual Soul), etc. (i.e. Anugītā). — § 782*b* (Brāhmaṇagītā), XIV, **34**, (932): When Kṛshṇa had finished the Brāhmaṇagītā, *A.* asked where that brāhmaṇī and that brahman were now; Kṛshṇa said: "My mind (*manas*) is the brahman, my understanding (*buddhi*) is the brāhmaṇī; he who has been called *kshetrajña*, I am myself." —§ 782 (Anugītāp.), XIV, **35**, (934): Asked by *A.* about Bráhman, Kṛshṇa recited the old history about the discourse between the preceptor and his disciple on this subject (Guruçishyasaṃvāda). **51**, (1470): Asked by *A.*, Kṛshṇa said that he was the preceptor and the mind his pupil; "I wish to see my father again with thy leave"; *A.* replied: "We shall go to-day from this town to Hāstinapura and inform Yudhishṭhira."—§ 783 (do.), XIV, **52**: Kṛshṇa and *A.* set out for Hāstinapura; *A.* praised Kṛshṇa, "the soul of the universe, etc."; they saw Dhṛtarāshṭra, etc. (γ); Kṛshṇa passed the night in the apartment of *A.*; at morning they proceeded to Yudhishṭhira; then they set out from Hāstinapura with Subhadrā, etc.; *A.* returned.—§ 784 (do.), XIV, **53**: *A.* repeatedly embraced Kṛshṇa; as he came upon the desert he beheld Utaṅka.—§ 785 (do.), XIV, **62**: Vyāsa came and predicted to Pṛthā, Uttarā, *A.*, and Yudhishṭhira that the son of Uttarā would become a great prince through the puissance of Kṛshṇa and Vyāsa; *A.* became comforted. **63**, 1874, 1887: Yudhishṭhira summoned all his brothers, and spoke to them about performing the horse-sacrifice, and about obtaining the wealth of Marutta; Bhīmasena proposed to worship Çiva; *A.*, etc., approved. **64**: The Pāṇḍavas, etc., set out for the gold of Marutta. **65**: They made offerings to Çiva, etc.; then they again set out for Hāstinapura. **66**: Meanwhile Kṛshṇa, etc., arrived; Uttarā gave birth to Parikshit, who was still-born. **67**, 1969: Subhadrā lamented (ν). **68**: Kṛshṇa entered the lying-in-room (description). **69**: Kṛshṇa touched water and withdrew the Brāhma-weapon and revived the child. **70**: When Parikshit was a month old, the Pāṇḍavas came back with the wealth. **71**, 2081: *A.*, etc. (ρ), would officiate at Yudhishṭhira's sacrifice. **72**, 2105: According to the counsel of Vyāsa, *A.* was charged with the protection of the horse. **73**, 2115, 2130: Yudhishṭhira asked *A.* to spare all hostile kings as much as possible and to invite them to the horse-sacrifice; *A.* with the Gāṇḍīva followed the horse; all Hāstinapura came out to see him; a disciple of Yājñavalkya followed him in order to perform auspicious rites for him, and also many brahmans and kshattriyas. In course of the horse's wandering many great and wonderful battles were fought. The horse wandered over the whole earth; from the North it turned to the East; myriads of kings fought with *A.*, because they had lost their kinsmen on the field of Kurukshetra, the same did innumerable Kirātas, Yavanas, Mlecchas, and Āryas. **74**: The Trigartas attacked *A.*, who in vain asked them to forbear; the Trigarta king Sūryavarman fought with *A.*, who slew his younger brother Ketuvarman; then he fought Dhṛtavarman, was wounded in his hand and dropped the Gāṇḍīva, but took it up again and slew eighteen warriors; the Trigartas fled and accepted *A.'s* dominion. **75**, 2188, 2190: In Prāgjyotisha, Bhagadatta's son king Vajradatta (description) attacked *A.* on his elephant, but, after a fierce battle—**76**, 2195, 2197, 2207, 2208, 2209—during three days, he on the fourth day had his elephant slain, and promised to come to the horse-sacrifice. **77**: The Saindhavas seated on chariots attacked *A.*, who was on foot, recollecting Jayadratha; omens appeared; the Gāṇḍīva fell down; the gods, etc., shouted "victory" to *A.*, who once more used his bow; the Saindhavas fled. **78**, 2265, 2273, 2280: The Saindhavas once more rallied; *A.* urged them to surrender, but in vain; then Duḥçalā, taking her grandson, the son of Suratha, in her arms, repaired to *A.*; *A.* cast off his bow, and asked after Suratha (the son of Jayadratha); she said that he had died from sorrow when he heard of *A.'s* arrival; *A.* comforted her; Duḥçalā asked her warriors to desist, and returned home; at last the horse arrived at Maṇipūra **79**, 2338—where Babhruvāhana, *A.'s* son by Citrāngadā, approached *A.* with humility; *A.* angrily blamed him for having fallen away from kshattriya duties. Ulūpī pierced through the earth and beheld her [step-]son standing distressed, and incited him to fight *A.*, which he did; he even caused the sacrificial horse to be seized; gravely wounded, *A.* praised his son highly; at last *A.* fell down in a swoon, and so did Babhruvāhana. **80**, 2371: Citrāngadā lamented. At last Ulūpī thought of the gem that has the virtue of reviving a dead man; the gem came; she placed it on the breast of *A.*; he revived. **81**, (2402): Asked by *A.*, Ulūpī recited the curse of the Vasus for *A.'s* having slain Bhīshma in unfair fight; if *A.* had died without having expiated his sin, he would have fallen into Hell; *A.* highly approved of her deed and told Babhruvāhana to come with his mother, etc., to the horse-sacrifice; Babhruvāhana promised to come and to take upon himself the task of distributing food among the brahmans. He asked *A.* to pass the night in the city with his two wives; but *A.* was prevented by his vow of following the horse. **82**, 2456, 2462: The horse at last turned its face towards Hāstinapura; at Rājagṛha, the Magadha king Meghasandhi, the son of Sahadeva, mounted on his chariot, attacked *A.*, who was on foot; he was told to come to the horse-sacrifice. In Vanga, Puṇḍra, and Koçala *A.* vanquished innumerable Mleccha armies. **83**: *A.* proceeded towards the south. At the beautiful city of the Cedis, Çarabha, the son of Çicupāla, fought *A.* and then worshipped him, etc. Citrāngada was vanquished by *A.*; the Nishāda king, the son of Ekalavya, was vanquished after a furious battle, etc. King Ugrasena came to *A.* with Vasudeva. Then along the coast of the western ocean; then to the Gāndhāras, where a fierce battle ensued with the Gāndhāra king, the son of Çakuni. **84**, 2491: At last the king, disregarding *A.'s* peaceful advice, fought alone; *A.* shot off his headgear; the mother of the king came out and forbade her son to fight; *A.* told him to come to the horse-sacrifice. **85**, 2511: At the news of his arrival to Hāstinapura, Yudhishṭhira rejoiced, etc., and made magnificent preparations for the sacrifice. **86**, 2559: Kṛshṇa, etc., came and told about *A.* that he had been very much emaciated, and that he was near at hand. **87**, 2587, 2592, 2593: Yudhishṭhira enquired of Kṛshṇa why *A.* was fated to bear such hardships in life; Kṛshṇa attributed it to the elevation of *A.'s* cheekbones. Bhīmasena, etc., became gratified with *A.'s* triumphs. A messenger announced the arrival of *A.*, and received large gifts. On the second day *A.* entered the city (description). *A.* saluted Yudhishṭhira, etc. **88**: The sacrifice was duly performed; **89**, 2655.—§ 786 (do.), XIV, **91**, 2814: "Yudhishṭhira, Bhīma, and *A.* resembled Indra."—§ 787 (Āçramavāsap.), XV, **1**: For fifteen years the Pāṇḍavas did everything under the advice of Dhṛtarāshṭra; Bhīmasena alone did not forget his grievances. **2**: From fear of Yudhishṭhira nobody dared to speak evil of Duryodhana or Dhṛtarāshṭra. Bhīma, however, reverenced the old king outwardly, but with a very unwilling heart. **3**: After fifteen years Dhṛtarāshṭra, afflicted by the cutting words of Bhīma, asked Yudhishṭhira's permission for himself and Gāndhārī to retire to the woods clad in rags and barks in order to practise austerities; **10**, 333, 346. **11**: Yudhishṭhira and *A.* applauded Dhṛtarāshṭra's intention to perform the çrāddha of Bhīshma, etc., before setting out for the woods; Bhīma was unwilling; *A.* sought to pacify him, seconded by Yudhishṭhira. **12**, (382), 387, 392: *A.* urged Bhīma to forget the injuries of Duryodhana. **13**, 403: Vidura reported the speeches of Yudhishṭhira, *A.*, and Bhīma to Dhṛtarāshṭra. **15**, 434: When Dhṛtarāshṭra and Gandharī set out with his daughters-in-law on the day of full-moon in the month of Kārttika, Yudhishṭhira and *A.* were filled with grief. **16**, 455: Vidura and Sañjaya and Kuntī retired with Dhṛtarāshṭra and Gāndhārī into the woods; Dhṛtarāshṭra caused Kṛpa and Yuyutsu to remain and made them over to Yudhishthira.—§ 788 (do.), XV, **22**: Afflicted with grief, the Pāṇḍavas did not attend to their kingly offices; they set their heart upon seeing Dhṛtarāshṭra, etc., and proceeded towards the forest. **23**, 618, 628: Headed by *A.* (on a chariot with white horses) and Kṛpa, they proceeded slowly (description of the expedition). **24**, 646: Sahadeva and Kuntī informed Gāndhārī of the arrival of the Pāṇḍavas, and then advanced towards *A.*, etc. (β), dragging the childless old couple. **25**, 658, 662: To the ascetics who had come from diverse regions to see the Pāṇḍavas, Sañjaya pointed out each of them (†γ). **26**: Vidura entered the body of Yudhishṭhira, but was not cremated; **28**, 747 (ϵ).—§ 789 (Putradarçanap.), XV, **29**: The Pāṇḍavas passed about a month in that forest; Vyāsa came; Dhṛtarāshṭra wished to see his dead children and kinsmen; the grief of Gāndhārī, etc. (δ), was revived; she said that for sixteen years Dhṛtarāshṭra never slept for grief; and also Kṛshṇā, etc. (ε), grieved exceedingly; asked by Vyāsa to tell what she wished—**30**—Kuntī told the story of Karṇa's birth; Vyāsa promised to show her Karṇa. **31**: They all proceeded towards the Bhāgīrathī, and waited for the advent of night; at sunset they bathed and finished their evening rites. **32**: When night came, Vyāsa plunged into the Bhāgīrathī for a bath and summoned all the deceased warriors, who all rose up from the water with a loud uproar. **33**: When they had sported with one another for that night, Vyāsa dismissed them within the twinkling of an eye.—§ 791 (do.), XV, **36**, 1004 (β): Dhṛtarāshṭra became released from his grief; all returned home; the Pāṇḍavas had passed more than a month in the wood.—§ 792 (Nāradāgamanap.), XV, **37–39**: Two years later the Pāṇḍavas were visited by Nārada, who told them that Dhṛtarāshṭra, etc., had been burnt by a forest conflagration; only Sañjaya had escaped. The Pāṇḍavas and the citizens all proceeded to Gaṅgā in order to offer oblations of water to them, etc.—§ 793 (Mausalap.), XVI, **4**, †107: After the mutual slaughter at Dvārakā, Kṛshṇa sent Dāruka to inform *A.* and tell him to come quickly; Kṛshṇa, entering Dvāravatī, told his father to protect the ladies till *A.* came. Bala-Rāma and Kṛshṇa died. **5**, 135, 138: *A.* with Dāruka proceeded to Dvārakā; when Kṛshṇa's 16,000 wives saw *A.*, they uttered a loud cry. The city seemed to *A.* to be like the terrible river Vaitaraṇī. *A.*, Satyā, and Rukmiṇī fell down and wailed; then praising Kṛshṇa and comforting the ladies, *A.* went to Vasudeva. **6**κ, 151, 153, 154, 157, 169: Vasudeva lamented and said he would die by abstaining from food. **7**, 183, 224, 227, 230, 253: *A.* said that the hour had come also for the Pāṇḍavas to depart [from the world] (λ); he would, however, first move the women, the children, and the aged of the Vṛshṇis to Indraprastha. Then he entered the hall of the Yādavas called Sudharmā (*sudharmāṃ yādavīṃ sabhāṃ*), where he told the citizens and ministers that he would take away with him the remnants of the Vṛshṇis and Andhakas, as the sea would soon engulf the city, etc. *A.* passed that night in the mansion of Kṛshṇa. At dawn Vasudeva by yoga attained to the highest goal; his four wives ascended the funeral pyre. When *A.* had caused Vasudeva and his four wives to be burnt, he visited the place where the Vṛshṇis had been slaughtered, and caused the last rites to be performed and Rāma and Kṛshṇa to be burnt. On the seventh day he set out with the ladies and children, the Yādava troops and other inhabitants, with Kṛshṇa's 16,000 wives, and Vajra; they numbered many millions in all; then the ocean flooded Dvārakā; they proceeded in slow marches; at Pañcanada the Ābhīras (Mlecchas) conspired to rob the cavalcade. *A.* only with great difficulty succeeded in stringing his bow. His celestial weapons would not come to his mind; the women were snatched away by the robbers; *A.'s* shafts soon became exhausted; formerly they had been inexhaustible. *A.* became very distressed; he escorted the remnant of the cavalcade to Kurukshetra; he established the son of Kṛtavarman in the city of Mārttikāvata with the remnant of the women of the Bhoja king; the remainder, with children and old men and women, at Indraprastha with Vajra for their ruler; the son of Yuyudhāna (with old men, etc.) on the banks of the Sarasvatī, etc.; then *A.* entered the retreat of Vyāsa. **8**, 254, 255, (261): *A.* informed Vyāsa of what had passed (ν) ("500,000 warriors have thus been laid down"). Vyāsa said that Kṛshṇa, as also the Pāṇḍavas, had finished their work; "the time has come for your departure from this world," etc. (ξ). *A.* entered Hāstinapura and informed Yudhishṭhira of what had taken place.—§ 794 (Mahāprasthān.), XVII, **1**, 2, 5, 20, 31, 37, 38: The Pāṇḍavas set their heart on leaving the world; the kingdom was made over to Yuyutsu, and Parikshit installed as king in Hāstinapura, while Vajra ruled in Indraprastha. Kṛpa was installed as the preceptor of Parikshit. The subjects tried in vain to dissuade them; they and Draupadī divested themselves of their ornaments and dressed in the barks of trees; then they threw their sacred fires into the water. Then they set out on their journey: the five Pāṇḍavas, Draupadī, and a dog; wandering towards the east they reached the sea of red water. Agni came (*a*) and caused *A.* to throw the Gāṇḍīva and his inexhaustible quiver into the water and thus restore them to Varuṇa. They now proceeded towards the south, etc., wishing to make a round of the whole earth. **2**, 67: Having crossed Himavat, etc., Kṛshṇā dropped down, in consequence of her partiality for *A.*; then Sahadeva, then Nakula, then *A.* fell down; *A.*, because he had said that he would consume all the foes in a single day, but had not accomplished it. **3**, 92: Yudhishṭhira's second test.—§ 795 (Svargārohaṇap.), XVIII, **1–3**: Yudhishṭhira's third test: **2**, 36, 66. **4**, [128: When arrived in heaven Yudhishṭhira saw there Govinda (Kṛshṇa) in his Brāhma-form (description), adored by Phālguna (Arjuna)].—Cf. the following synonyms:—

Aindri ("son of Indra"), q.v.
Bhārata ("descendant of Bharata"), q.v.
Bhīmānuja ("younger brother of Bhīma"): IV, 1668.
Bhīmasenānuja (do.): V, 5759.
Bībhatsu ("loathing"): I, 2273, 2275, 2278, 4809, 5302, 5310, 5364, 5389, 5523, 6492, 7887, 8037, 8063, 8165, 8233, 8243, 8258; II, 523, 1928, 2370; III, 551, 589, †915, 1246, 1275, 1387, 1910, 2020, 2061, 8290, 8292, 8421, 10885, 11429, 11526, 11935, 14833, 17261, 17274; IV, 46, 367, 1184, 1227, 1283, 1307, 1311, 1376 (enumeration of Arjuna's ten names), 1378, 1385 (etymology), 1441, 1474, 1475, 1479, 1486, 1493, 1508, 1512, 1527, 1610, 1625, 1649, 1653, 1698, 1702, 1712, 1718, 1939, 1946, 1988, 1997, 2028, 2038, 2125, 2350; V, †852, 2216, 2672, 2800, 2823, 2855, 2969, 3177, 4649, 4709, 4785; VI, 717, 2020, 2552, 3211, 3746, 4834, 4839, 4973, 5212, 5286, 5488, 5558, 5609, 5612, 5621, 5739, 5788, 5790; VII, 320, 420, 669, 768, 787, 1309, 1995, 2486, 2536, 2561, 2815, 2816, 2823, 2829, 3223, 3240, 3251, 3268, 3293, 3356, 3374, 3685, 4218, 4294, 5354, 6063, 6075, 6091, 6094, 6219, 6283, 6411, 6768, 6780, 6966, 7085, 7088, 7091, 7216, 7714, 7834, 8081, 8289, 8386, 8465, 9007, 9103, 9105, 9115, 9246, 9399, 9402; VIII, 159, 1636, 2129, 2179, 2584, 2863, 3237, 3245, 3578, 3581, 3582, 3751, †3833, 4009, 4112, †4778, 4843; IX, 135, 201, 731, 1570; XI, 376, 662, 689; XII, 652, 819; XIV, 1792, 2155, 2182, 2224, 2230, 2283, 2488, 2506, 2579; XV, 370, 397, 400; XVI, 167, 170, 177.
Bṛhannalā (the name which *A.* gave himself with king Virāṭa): IV, 54, †306, †307, †308, (849), 850, (852), 852, 1186, †1190, 1193, 1205, 1206, 1212, 1214, 1217, 1220, 1222, 1223, 1228, 1229, 1248, 1256, (1259), 1274, 1276, 1314, (1315), 1342, (1343), †2151, †2159, 2167, †2169, †2175, 2181, 2199, 2204, 2214, 2216, 2229.

Çākhāmṛgadhvaja (= Kapidhvaja): VII, 5802.
Çakraja ("son of Indra"): XIV, 2560.
Çakranandana ("son of Indra"): III, 1843.
Çakrasūnu ("son of Indra"): VI, 4731; VII, 1804; VIII, †3345, †3521.
Çakrasuta ("son of Indra"): VI, †3753.
Çakrātmaja ("son of Indra"): III, 1724, 11912; VII, 6575; XIV, 2325.
Çvetāçva ("with white horses"): II, 1683; III, 10881; VI, 5451, 5470; VII, 4712; VIII, 1076, 1578; X, 631; XIV, 2135, 2183; XV, 73.
Çvetahaya ("with white horses"): V, 2133; VII, 1228; VIII, 4346.
Çvetavāha ("with white horses"): III, 10847; V, 5759; XII, 30.
Çvetavāhana ("with white horses"): I, 7374; III, 10532, 10863; IV, 1349, 1375 (enumeration of Arjuna's ten names), 1377, 1382 (etymology), 1648; VII, 3287, 3294, 6584, 7329; VIII, 4475; XII, 25; XIV, 2222, 2466; XVII, 64.
Devendratanaya ("son of Indra"): VII, 7716.
Dhanañjaya ("conqueror of booty"): I, †161, †168, †192, 388, 496, 608, 2292, 2444, 4921, 5272, 5275, 5289, 5483, 5496, 5498, 5531, 5539, 5654, 5741, 6439, 6461, 6468, 6518, 6891, 7124, 7136, 7375, 7503, 7753, 7762, 7766, 7770, 7790, 7822, 7829, 7848, 7851, 7878, 7931, 7972, 7979, 8028, 8034, 8079, 8326, 8472; II, 130 (°*sakhā Tumburuḥ*), 647, 823, 970, 987, 995, 996, 1003, 1010, 1011, 1017, 1478, 1607, 1707, 1716, 1889, 1890, 1920, 2157, 2260, 2411, 2422, 2539, 2569; III, 595, 918, 922, 943, 1361, 1439, 1458, 1469, 1489, 1497, 1506, 1508, 1509, 1517, 1588, 1685, 1710, 1712, 1813, 1818, 1864, 1877, 1888, 1918, †2009, 2016, 2017, 3087, 4021, 8280, 8432, 8446, 10283, 10870, 10872, 10873, 10880, 10898, 11069, 11821, 11833, †11894, †11905, 11917, 11925, 11926, 11931, 11942, 11987, 12011, 12059, 12270, 12284, 12290, 12293, 12295, 12302, 12311, †12316, 12443, 12569, 12579, 14758, 14768, 14791, 14832, 14954, 14972, 14976, 14989, 14991, 15004, 15007, 15012, 15015, 15019, 15065, 15066, (°*sakhātmānaṃ darçayām āsa . . . . Citrasenaḥ*), 15069, †15655, †15673, †15694, †15706, 15742, 15770, 15771, 16606, 16920, 17273, 17294, 17297, 17299; IV, 39, 148, †309, †311, 572, 573, 575, 583, 587, 620, 649, 845, 1211, 1233, 1260, 1265, 1266, 1269, 1271, 1286, 1318, 1376 (enumeration of the ten names of *A.*), 1378, 1380 (etymology), 1391, 1459, 1564, 1569, 1571, 1580, 1582, 1618, 1620, 1638, 1758, 1781, 1822, 1857, 1921, 1995, 2006, 2022, 2024, 2025, 2035, 2044, 2055, 2065, 2083, 2087, 2093, †2110, †2129, 2130, 2318, 2323, 2324, 2346, 2368; V, 130, 134, 144, 146, 150, 620, 629, †677, †688, †724, †736, †763, †872, †1809, †1810, 1956, 1957, 2085, 2099, 2187, 2196, 2199, 2324, †2413, 2480, 2490, 2500, 2508, †2512, 2800, 2974, 3071, 3072, 3162, 3195, 3199, 3200, 3204, 3490, 3496, 3707, 3976, 4171, 4358, 4425, 4652, 4691, 4707, 4708, 4722, 4777, 4817, 4869, 4937, 5136, 5142, 5165, 5167, 5295, 5344, 5370, 5487, 5514, 5559, 5623, 5784, 5868, 5873, 7588, 7630, 7639; VI, 18, 697, 707, 762, 844, 927, 1034, 1118, 1178, 1241, 1260, 1310, 1483, 1526, 1533, 1541, 1554, 1677, 1822, 1982, 1999, 2075, 2115, 2136, 2150, 2153, 2161, 2375, 2425, 2554, 2558, 2565, 2568, †2595, †2633, †2644, †2647, †2679, 3004, 3070, 3088, 3119, 3126, 3163, 3269, 3282, 3557, 3563, 3581, 3586, †3751, †3756, †3757, 3759, †3775, 4323, 4339, 4587, 4618, 4621, 4643, 4645, 4738, 4844, 4944, 4970, 4971, 4988, 5066, 5073, 5118, 5227, 5282, 5288, 5300, 5311, 5325, 5356, 5366, 5487, 5527, 5542, 5548, 5577, 5610, 5647, 5726, 5778, 5803, 5848, 5853; VII, †63, 95, 194, 199, 225, †248, 328, 331, 333, 341, 346, 352, 353, 417, 460, 468, 670, 675, 700, 707, 725, 759, 760, 774, 777, 779, 1063, 1221, 1237, 1246, 1247, 1248, 1249, 1254, 1255, 1307, 1322, 1425, 1491, 1523, 1527, 1637, 1758, 1990, 2476, 2582, 2648, 2655, 2660, 2701, 2706, 2789, 2791, 2804, 2820, 2822, 2827, 2841, 2966, 2974, 2979, 3057, 3089, 3132, 3140, 3154, 3176, 3183, 3193, 3239, 3244, 3253, 3339, 3342, 3344, 3348, 3352, 3353, 3354, 3382, 3395, 3397, 3415, 3417, 3428, 3432, 3434, 3435, 3441, 3648, 3688, 3697, 3706, 3707, 3759, 3763, 3764, 3777, 3798, 3801, 3805, 3811, 3832, 3834, 3874, 3875, 3886, 3889, 3899, 3901, 3902, 3934, 4196, 4197, 4228, 4236, 4243, 4246, 4270, 4281, 4392, 4404, 4480, 4484, 4637, 4708, 4724, 4954, 4971, 5013, 5106, 5131, 5140, 5167, 5168, 5244, 5252, 5255, 5256, 5264, 5324, 5326, 5373, 5451, 5547, 5776, 5805, 5807, 5810, 5812, 5813, 5818, 5824, 5842, 5852, 5885, 5934, 5987, 5989, 6074, 6083, 6113, 6122, 6123, 6140, 6142, 6144, †6153, 6155, 6170, 6172, 6197, 6223, 6244, 6246, 6257, 6275, 6302, 6347, 6391, 6393, 6455, 6473, 6474, 6781, 6849, 7093, 7100, 7108, 7274, 7497, 7670, 7710, 7724, 7781, 7802, 7810, 7817, 8058, 8182, 8189, 8218, 8227, 8264, 8267, 8283, 8288, 8290, 8291, 8293, 8310, 8323, 8347, 8369, 8463, 8471, 8605, 8690, 8706, 8802, 8803, 8804, 8865, 8873, 8945, 9039, 9052, 9082, 9098, 9112, 9258, 9390, 9398, 9495; VIII, 42, 61, 105, 114, 232, 299, 368, 421, 427, 494, 614, 655, 656, 683, †697, †701 (*jighāṃsur Indrāvarajaṃ Dhanañjayaṃ*; so also B. and Nīl., who explains *Indrāvarajaṃ* to be Kṛshṇa; ought we not to read °*suḥ sendrāvarajaṃ Dha*°?), 823, 1093, 1096, 1102, 1166, 1384, 1674, 1689, 1693, 1694, †1739, †1751, 1755, 1763, 1771, 1781, 1782, 1789, 1800, 1803, 1805, 1807, 1809, 1813, 1825, 1956, 1972, 1974, †1980, †1987, 2151, 2159, 2165, 2421, 2607, 2815, 2833, 2960, 2964, 2974, 3041, 3273, 3279, 3281, †3285, 3294, 3309, 3322, 3323, 3324, 3327, 3380, 3388, 3405, 3420, 3433, 3449, †3516, †3520, 3564, 3565, 3568, 3583, 3584, 3586, 3631, 3680, 3797, †3804, †3845, †3850, †3851, †3869, 4026, 4034, 4036, 4043, †4068, †4069, †4077, 4085, †4086, 4091, 4092, 4094, 4097, 4102, 4106, 4114, 4116, 4126, 4130, 4144, 4273, 4274, †4298, †4330, 4350, 4373, 4382, 4395, 4410, 4419, 4429, 4431, 4433, 4473, 4477, †4494, †4504, †4507, †4511, †4525, †4546, †4558, †4590, †4598, †4604, †4612, †4614, †4617, †4622, †4684, †4691, 4768, †4777, †4795, †4805, †4823, 4863, 4866, 4870, †4907, †4920, 4959, 4983, 5011, †5041; IX, 142, 155, 158, 209, 210, 450, 706, 725, 799, 820, 1020, 1026, 1029, 1063, 1286, 1338, 1444, 1477, 1569, 1599, 3252, 3261, 3266, 3318, 3469, 3483; X, 443, 610, 681, 687, 691, 692, 705, 707; XI, 359, 613, 617, 815; XII, 54, 192, 195, 581, 732, 768, 771, 772, 775, 1694, 1911, 1913, 13236, 13250, 13303, 13322; XIII, 6925 (*triyugau puṇḍarīkākshau Vāsudeva-Dhanañjayau*), 7019 (= Vishṇu, 1000 names), 7791; XIV, 372, 373, 417, 933, 1171, 1476, 1482, 1511 (°*gṛhaḥ*), 1512, 1589, 1802, 1807, 2116, 2121, 2123, 2149, 2150, 2152, 2168, 2170, 2171, 2186, 2187, 2213, 2215, 2216, 2267, 2269, 2277, 2283, 2291, 2294, 2298, 2303, 2319, 2336, 2345, 2379, 2396, 2397, 2409, 2416, 2438, 2439, 2465, 2470, 2503, 2516, 2570, 2585, 2586 (°*kathām*, i.e. *A.*'s adventures when following the sacrificial horse); XV, 387, 408, 853 (in reality = Nara); XVI, 112, 145, 156, 171, 182, 210, 220, 236, 240, 244, 287; XVII, 34, 42, 52.
Gāṇḍīvabhṛt ("armed with the Gāṇḍīva"): V, 711; XIV, 2253, 2258, 2445.
Gāṇḍīvadhanvan ("having the Gāṇḍīva for his bow"): I, 524; II, 2083; III, 1269, 1921, 2049, 2060, 11532,

11826, †14760, †15657, 17471; IV, 46, 1401, 1632 (°*inam*; so also B.), †1675, 1692, 1723, 1894, 2112; V, 56, 99, †654, †656, †657, †1815, 2086, 2087, 2294, 2486, 3199, 4796, 5302, 5334, 5773, 5805; VI, 729, 2078, 2142, 2642, 3122, 3199, 3204, 3206, 4741, 5626, 5633; VII, 329, 666, 684, 1486, 1908, 2622, 2746, 2785, 3059, 3131, 3326, 3935, 4877, 6207, 7046, 7111, 8285, 8338, 8443, 9430; VIII, 233 (*Çārṅga-Gāṇḍīvadhanvānau*), 3233, 3307, 3540, 3608, 3610, 4160, 4467, †4678, †4792, 4999, 5025; IX, 225, 841, 3467, 3470, 3471, 3473, 3480, 3482; X, 195, 196, 631, 676, 723 (°*aḥ snushā Virāṭasya sutā*, i.e. Uttarā); XI, 571 (°*aḥ snushā Virāṭa-duhitā*, i.e. Uttarā), 584 (°*aḥ sutaṃ svasrīyaṃ Vāsudevasya*, i.e. Abhimanyu), 605, 653, 818; XII, 52, 142, 1464, 1921; XIII, 6924; XIV, 1783, 2266, 2373, 2429.

Gāṇḍīvadhārin ("holding the Gāṇḍīva"): VIII, 1820.

Gāṇḍīvin ("possessing the Gāṇḍīva"): VIII, 6898 (*Hari° vigrahaṃ*).

Guḍākeça: I, 5524, 7964; III, 1715, 1781, 1905, 10848, 10878, 11833, 12565, 15754, 17263; IV, 45; V, 5328, 5644, 5865; VI, 790, 854, 887, 1253; VII, 3083, 4215, 5134; XII, 651, 893; XIV, 382, 2157, 2168, 2201, 2353, 2486, 2519; XV, 362.

Indrarūpa ("having the form of Indra"), q.v.

Indrasuta ("the son of Indra"), q.v.

Indrātmaja ("the son of Indra"), q.v.

Indrāvaraja (VIII, 701), v. Dhanañjaya.

Jaya ("Victory"): II, 770; III, 10270 (°*ātmajasya*, presumably = Abhimanyu), 11525, 15608; V, 162 (?), †710; VII, 1228 (*Çvetahayaḥ*), 3137, 6304, 6539, 8263; VIII, 625, †4070; XIV, 2296, 2376, 2424; XVI, 252.

Jishṇu ("victorious"): I, 5228, †7014 (*Bhīmaḥ sa°*), †7033, †7078, †7079, 7091, 7130, 7141, †7158, 8244; II, †2229; III, 425, 1401, 1443, 1567, 1593, 1596, 1609, 1790, 1891, 8277, 11818, 11823, †11896, †11897, †12321, †15645, 17297; IV, 1375 (enumeration of Arjuna's ten names), 1378, 1388 (etymology), 1570, †1692, 1702, 1786, 1986, 1990, 2063, †2092, †2147; V, †654, †717, 3161, 3495, 3824, 3840, 4177, 5557; VI, 2074, †2611, †3758, 4982, 5296, 5313, 5315, 5352, 5633; VII, 1240, 1414, 2973, 2978, 6175, 6411, 6413, 6496, 6736, 6775, 6778, 8353; VIII, 711, 1103, 1118, 1435, 2739, †3357, †4560, †4682; XII, 1370 (? *Devasthānena Jishṇunā*), 4079; XIV, 2098, 2124, 2145, 2156, 2165, 2167, 2193, 2384, 2392, 2505, 2560 (*Çakrajaṃ*), 2563, 2577; XV, 410.

Kapidhvaja ("with the ape-banner"): V, 3495; VI, †2659, 5663; IX, 521.

Kapiketana (do.): XIV, 2457.

Kapipravara ("with the excellent ape"): X, 631.

Kapivaradhvaja ("with the excellent ape in his banner"): VII, 326.

Kaunteya ("son of Kuntī"), q.v.

Kaurava, Kauravaçreshṭha, etc.

Kauraveya, Kauravya, q.v.

Kirīṭabhṛt ("wearing the diadem"): XIV, 2436.

Kirīṭamālin ("adorned with a diadem as a garland"): III, †11906, †12570; IV, †1678, 1997, 2068; VI, †2625; VII, 5262, †6296.

Kirīṭavat ("having a diadem"): XI, 696.

Kirīṭin ("having a diadem"): I, †163, 400, 426, 434, 460, 471, 488, 489, 546, 5478, 6952, 7103, 7115, 8024, 8043; II, 1021, 1029, 1888; III, 1928, †1931, †11895, †11905, †11916, †12318, †12578, †15653; IV, †1294, 1375 (enumeration of the ten names of *A.*), 1377, 1384 ("formerly, when I fought the Dānavas, Çakra put a diadem resplendent as the sun on my head, therefore men called me Kirīṭin"), †1661, †1677, †1680, †1684, †1687, †1688, 1720, 1724, 1846, †2100, †2134, †2149; V, 137, 138, 165, 621, 622, 629, †761, †1811, †1814, †1910, 2099, †2104, †2421, 5910, 5930; VI, †1281, 2149, 2380, †2585, †2632, 2635, †2641, †2649, †2650, †2660, †2671, 2692, 3137, 5224, 5231, 5338, 5491, 5557, 5568, 5581, 5584, 5590, 5597, 5650; VII, †81, †83, 105, 287, 419, 486, 663, 723, 741, 1218, 1298, 1332, 1434, 1463, 2987, 3183, 3194, 3200, 3202, 3215, 3429, 3748, 4709, 5821, 5856, 5952, 6072, 6097, 6101, †6149, 6174, 6283, †6445, 6450, 6520, 6527, 6571, 6579, 6965, 6968, 7123, 7135, 7209, 7215, 7219, 8910, 9330; VIII, 154, 285, 428, †673, †704, 763, 826, 1948, 2189, 2219, 2609, 2794, 2906, 3234, †3517, †3530, †3533, †3591, †3832, †3854, †3858, 4041, †4082, 4101, 4109, 4118, 4128, 4143, †4192, †4303, †4304, †4331, †4336, †4343, †4346, 4378, †4561, †4564, †4566, †4575, †4584, †4585, †4608, †4630, †4660, †4683, †4702, †4708, †4780, †4785, †4796, †4809, †4818, 4838; IX, 113, 114, 131, 1340, 1390, 1473; XIV, 2141, 2144, 2145, 2221, 2270, 2322, 2472, 2476, 2481, 2485; XV, 364.

Kṛshṇa, q.v.

Kṛshṇasārathi ("having Kṛshṇa for his charioteer"), q.v.

Kuntīputra ("son of Kuntī"), q.v.

Mahendrasūnu ("son of Indra"), q.v.

Mahendrātmaja ("son of Indra"), q.v.

Nara, q.v.

Pākaçāsani ("son of Indra"), q.v.

Pāṇḍava, Pāṇḍaveya, etc., **Pāṇḍunandana**, etc., q.v.

Pārtha ("son of *Pṛthā*"), q.v.

Paurava ("descendant of Puru"), etc., q.v.

Phālguna: I, 396, 576, 4407, 5228, 5231, 5355, 5362, 5397, 5403, 5414, 5467, 5474, 5528, 5872, 7104, †7137, 7408; II, 977, 1016, 1031, 1651, †2161; III, 469, †1369, 1515, 1547, 1558, 1561, 1562, 1595, 1603, 1612, 1618, 1623, 1634, 1660, 1687, 1750, 1801, 1816, 1832, 1837, 1875, †1878, 1925, 1938, 1953, 1985, 4011, 10882, 10889, 11820 (*Bhīmasenād avarajaḥ*), 11927, 12010, 12070, 12566, 14803, 15190, 15342, 15773, 15782, 16983, 17171; IV, 90, 641, 1299, 1375 (enumeration of *A.'s* names), 1378, 1383 (*Uttarābhyāṃ Phalgunībhyāṃ nakshatrābhyām ahaṃ divā | jāto Himavataḥ pṛshṭhe; tena māṃ Phālgunaṃ viduḥ*), 1816, 1849, 1852, 1875, 2052, †2135, 2153, †2157; V, †657, †660, †760, †852, †858, 2092, 2094, 2132, †2228, 2846, 5518, 5519, 5524, 5526 (°*ānāṃ çatāni vā*), 5563, 5569, 5571 (°*ānāṃ çatāni vā*), 5615, 5639, 5714, 5814, 7587; VI, 606, 707, 2158, 2462, 2465, 2467, †2639, 3200, 3203, 4020, 4148, 4547 (*vi° imaṃ lokaṃ*), 4552, 4740, 4875, 4914, 4918, 4922, 5235 (*dvitīya iva Phālgunaḥ*), 5310, 5477, 5481, 5556, 5585, 5586, 5592, 5594, 5625, 5654, 5730, 5732, 5812, 5833; VII, 461, 718, 761, 1039, 1220, 1269, 1415, 1456, 1519, 2610, 2620, 2635, 2779, 3172, 3228, 3321, 3361, 3432, 3918, 4208, 4247, 4275, 4292, †4685, 4786, 4815, 4878, 4880, 5104, 5118, 5119, 5155, 5187, 5250, 5257, 5258, 5263, 5266, 5267, 5857, 5858, 5990, 6073, 6096, 6101, 6119, 6121, 6128, 6130, 6209, 6290, 6299, 6389, 6553, 6575, 6577, 6767, 6776, 6977, 6987, 6992, 7015, 7053, 7059, 7090, 7099, 7115, 7117, 7119, 7120, 7199, 7757, 7798, 8167 (C. has *Pāṇḍavasya*), 8248, 8249, 8250, 8280, 8287, 8296, 8352, 8392,

9189; VIII, 16, 256, 304, 370, 423, 963, 1301, 1315, 1576, 1645, 1658, †1794, 1824, 1834 (°*ānāṃ çatāni vā*), †1965, †1989, 2311, 2419, 2595, 2825, 3191, 3244, †3344, †3355, †3380, †3533, 3570, 3596, 3767, †4062, 4113, 4129, 4135, †4302, 4365, 4444, †4522, †4600, †4650, 4765, †4804, 5017; IX, 1455, 1830, 1883, 1900, 3521; XII, 32, 51, 57, 602, 1479, 1910, 13131, 13132; XIV, 366, 414, 1475, 1524, 1537, 1954, 2104, 2202, 2240, 2260, 2262, 2274, 2304, 2463, 2588, 2596, 2612; XV, 363, 371, 384, †435; XVI, 204; XVII, 39, 68; XVIII, 128, 165 (°*sya suto*, i.e. Abhimanyuḥ).

Prabhañjanasutānuja: VII, 6268.

Savyasācin ("ambidexter"): I, †198, 459; II, 2621, 2624, 2635, 8235, 8277, 8311; III, †228, 575, 4005, 8412, 12006, 15176, 16974; IV, 1246, 1295, 1376 (enumeration of *A.'s* ten names), 1386 (etymology, v. Gāṇḍīva); V, †657, 2293, 2350, 2477, 3194, 3403, 4649, 4770, 4772, 4786, 4801, 4825, 4950, 5115, 5238, 5241, 5466, †5651; VI, †1279, 2048, 5044; VII, 2661, 2793, 2807, 3011, 3124, 3410, 4465, 4707, 4807, 5255, 5337, 5781, 6328, 7023; VIII, 125, 128, 130, †676, 706, 1949, †3843, †4563, †4577; IX, 1, 133, 167, 215, 732, 1322, 1326, 1327, 1366, 1571 (*lokavīreṇa*), 3485; XI, 607; XIV, 383, 1781, 2108, 2163 (°*karād*), 2231, 2415, 2448, 2451; XV, 35, 816 (*mātaraṃ* °*aḥ*), 1067, 1068; XVI, †116; XVII, 5; XVIII, 35, 118.

Surasūnu ("son of a god"): III, 8282.

Tāpatya ("descendant of Tapatī," cf. Tapatyupākhyāna): I, 6514, 6516, 6517 (*Tapatī nāma kā caishā Tāpatyā yatkṛte vayaṃ*), 6520, 6633.

Tridaçavarātmaja ("son of Indra"): VII, †167.

Vānaradhvaja (= Kapidhvaja): VI, 5490.

Vānaraketana (= Kapidhvaja): XIV, 2430, 2446.

Vānaraketu (= Kapidhvaja): V, 4683.

Vānaravaryaketana (= Kapidhvaja): XIV, 1533.

Vāsavaja ("son of Indra"): IV, †1674.

Vāsavanandana ("son of Indra"), v. Vāsava.

Vāsavasyātmaja ("son of Indra"): VII, 1739 (*Vāsavasyātmajātmajaḥ*, i.e. Abhimanyu).

Vāsavi ("son of Indra"): V, 5115; VII, 1250, 1371, 2583, 2704; XII, 12963; XVI, 143.

Vijaya ("Victory"): I, 5232; III, 15346, 17261; IV, [176 (one of the five secret names which Yudhishṭhira gave to the Pāṇḍavas when with Virāṭa)], [804 (do.)], 1376 (enumeration of *A.'s* ten names), 1377, 1381 (etymology); V, 1995, 5231; VI, 3572, 3578, 4510, 5470; VII, 325, 2819, 4171, 4188, 4203, 6899, 7094, 7754; VIII, 2834, 3143, 3572; IX, 628; XII, 30, 896; XIV, 356, 1907, 2020, 2161, 2162, 2192, 2353, 2423, 2471, 2477, 2512, 2575, 2576, 2587; XV, 480, 1066 (°*sya jananī*).

Arjuna[3], a ṛshi in the palace of Yama. § 267 (Yamasabhāv.): II, **8**, 328.

Arjunābhigamanaparvan. § 317: Hearing that the *Pāṇḍavas* had been banished, the *Bhojas*, *Vṛshṇis*, *Andhakas*, the heirs of *Pañcāla*, the *Cedi* king *Dhṛshṭaketu*, the brothers *Kaikeya* went to see them. As *Kṛshṇa* (*b*) said: "the earth shall drink the blood of *Duryodhana*, etc.," *Arjuna* tried to pacify him by reciting the feats achieved in his former lives (*b*); then *Arjuna*, the soul of *Kṛshṇa*, became silent, and *Janārdana* (i.e. Kṛshṇa) (*b*) replied that he was identical with *Arjuna*. Then *Pāñcālī* (i.e. Kṛshṇā), surrounded by *Dhṛshṭadyumna* and her other brothers, praised *Kṛshṇa* (*b*). She then blamed him and the *Pāṇḍavas* for having let her endure the shame of being dragged in the assembly, etc. ("fie on that *Gāṇḍīva* (*c*)"), and relates the persecutions of *Duryodhana* (cf. § 197) and the valour of *Bhīma* until the *svayaṃvara*. *Kṛshṇa* promised that she should be avenged, and *Dhṛshṭadyumna* said: "I will slay *Droṇa*; *Çikhaṇḍin Pitāmaha* (i.e. Bhīshma); *Bhīmasena Duryodhana*; and *Dhanañjaya* (i.e. Arjuna) *Karṇa*; assisted by *Rāma* and *Kṛshṇa* we are invincible in battle even to *Indra*" (III, **12**). —§ 318: *Kṛshṇa* said that if he had not been absent from *Dvārakā* (v. 610: the *Anartta* country) at that time, he should have come and prevented the gambling by either persuading *Dhṛtarāshṭra* (relating how the son of *Vīrasena* was formerly deprived of his kingdom, etc.), or compelling him by force; on arriving at *Dvārakā* he had learnt from *Yuyudhāna* what had happened and had instantly come to see them (III, **13**). —§§ 319–321: Saubhavadhop. (q.v.).—§§ 322–324: Dvaitavanapraveça (q.v.).—§§ 325–327: Draupadī-paritāpa-vākya (q.v.).—§§ 328–329: Kāmyakavana-praveça (q.v.).—§ 330: Indradarçana (q.v.). For continuation v. Kairātaparvan.

Arjunadāyāda = Abhimanyu. § 581 (Bhīshmav.): VI, **61**, 2689 (γ).—§ 590 (Droṇābhishek.): VII, **14**, 570.

Arjunāgraja = Bhīmasena: I, 5472.

Arjunaka, a hunter. § 719 (Gautamī-lubdhaka-vyāla-Mṛtyu-s.): XIII, **1**, 18, 21, 35, 61, 69, 71, 77, 79, 80.

Arjunanandana = Abhimanyu: VII, 1634.

Arjunapūrvaja = Bhīmasena: VI, 4356.

Arjunasuta: VI, **90**, 4022 (= Irāvat); **100**, 4579 (= Abhimanyu).

Arjunasyābhigamana ("the visit of Arjuna to the heaven of Indra"). § 10 (Parvas.): I, **2**, 320 (*parva* = Arjunābhigamanaparvan).

Arjunasya vanavāsaḥ ("the dwelling of Arjuna in the wood"). § 11 (Parvas.): I, **2**, 363 (= Arjunavanavāsaparvan).

Arjunasya vane vāsaḥ (do.). § 10 (Parvas.): I, **2**, 315 (= do.).

Arjunātmaja[1] = Abhimanyu: VII, 1534, 1591, 1631, 1807, 1893.

Arjunātmaja[2] = Irāvat: VI, 3979, 4048.

Arjunavanavāsaparvan ("the section relating to Arjuna's dwelling in the wood," the 16th of the minor parvans of Mhbhr.). § 247: The *Pāṇḍavas* continued to reside there, and by their prowess they brought many kings under their sway, and on account of their virtue the whole race of the *Kurus* grew in prosperity. After some time robbers lifted the cattle of a *brahman*, who then repaired to *Khāṇḍavaprastha* and reproved the *Pāṇḍavas*. *Arjuna* heard it; but the chamber where the *Pāṇḍavas* had their weapons being then occupied by *Yudhishṭhira* with *Kṛshṇā*, *Arjuna* was obliged to violate the established rule by entering the chamber. Then, armed with the bow and attired in mail and riding on his war-chariot decked with flagstaffs, he pursued the thieves and compelled them to give up the booty. Then, notwithstanding *Yudhishṭhira's* objections, he went to the forest to live there for twelve years (I, **213**).—§ 248: *Arjuna* set out followed by *brahmans* conversant with the *vedas* and *vedāṅgas* and devoted to the contemplation of the Supreme Spirit (*adhyātmacintakāḥ*), by mendicants (*bhaikshāḥ*) devoted to *Bhagavat* (*Bhagavadbhaktāḥ*), by reciters of the *Purāṇas* (*sūtāḥ Paurāṇikāḥ*), and by reciters of sacred stories (*divyākhyānāni*), etc., and settled at *Gaṅgādvāra*, where the *brahmans* performed innumerable *agnihotras*. One day when *Arjuna* had performed his ablutions in the *Gaṅgā*, and offered the oblations of water to his deceased ancestors, and when he was about to rise up from the stream desirous of performing his sacrificial rites before the fire, he was drawn away to the bottom of the water by *Ulūpī*, the daughter of the *Nāga* king *Kauravya* of the lineage of *Airāvata*, urged by the god of desire. There he saw a sacrificial fire, where he performed his sacrificial rites, by which *Agni* was much gratified. *Ulūpī* persuaded him that it was a greater merit to give himself up to her than to keep the vow of a *brahmacārin*, and having spent the night there, he in the morning, accompanied by *Ulūpī*, came back to *Gaṅgādvāra*. *Ulūpī*, taking leave of him there, said that he would be invincible in water (I, **214**).—§ 249: Then he set out towards the *Himavat* and came to *Agastyavaṭa* and the mountain of *Vasishṭha*; in *Bhṛgutuṅga* he bestowed many thousands of kine, etc., on *brahmans* and visited many *tīrthas* (especially all those in *Aṅga*, *Vaṅga*, and *Kaliṅga*). At the gate of the kingdom of *Kaliṅga* the *brahmans* desisted from following him further; he crossed *Kaliṅga*, beheld the *Mahendra* mountain adorned with the ascetics, and went to *Maṇipūra*, proceeding slowly along the seashore. There he married *Citrāṅgadā*, the daughter of king *Citravāhana* (*b*), and dwelt there for three years. When *Citrāṅgadā* had given birth to a son, *Arjuna* set out on his wanderings again (I, **215**).—§ 250: Then *Arjuna* went to the *tīrthas* at the southern ocean. There five *tīrthas* were shunned on account of five crocodiles that seized the devotees: *Agastyatīrtha*, *Saubhadra*, *Pauloma*, *Kārandhama* (giving the results of a horse-sacrifice), and *Bhāradvāja's tīrtha*. *Arjuna* plunged into the *Saubhadra* (so called after a *maharshi*), and was seized by a crocodile, which he dragged to the shore. It then became the *apsaras Vargā*, the friend of *Dhanapati* (Kubera). When she with her four companions (*Saurabheyī*, *Samīcī*, *Vudvudā*, and *Latā*), going to the abode of *Kubera*, had in vain tempted an ascetic *brahman*, that *brahman* had cursed them, saying that they should become crocodiles for 100 years (I, **216**). *Vargā* said: "As we asked the *ṛshi* to grant us pardon, he said: '100 and 100,000 are all indicative of eternity; but the words 100 as employed by me is to be understood as a limited period; you will be delivered by an exalted individual, and those waters shall become sacred and purifying under the name of *Nārītīrthāni*.' The *devarshi Nārada* directed us to these lakes, and said that *Dhanañjaya* (i.e. Arjuna) would soon deliver us." *Arjuna* then also delivered the other four *apsarases*. Then he proceeded to *Maṇipūra* to see *Citrāṅgadā*; with her he had begotten king *Babhruvāhana*. Then he proceeded towards *Gokarṇa* (I, **217**).—§ 251: Then *Arjuna* visited the *tīrthas* on the shores of the western ocean, and arrived at *Prabhāsa*. There *Madhusūdana* (= Kṛshṇa) visited him, and he and *Arjuna*, who were the *ṛshis Nara* and *Nārāyaṇa*, sported there for some time. Then they went to the *Raivataka* mountain, after *Kṛshṇa* had caused this mountain to be well adorned by many artifices; there he saw the performances of the actors and the dancers. The next morning they set out for *Dvārakā*, welcomed by the *Bhojas*, *Vṛshṇis*, and *Andhakas*. There he dwelt in the mansion of *Kṛshṇa* for many days (I, **218**).

Arjunāvara (VII, 1550, "inferior to Arjuna," sc. *Ārjunir*, i.e. Abhimanyu); but B. has *Arjunād varaḥ* ("better than Arjuna").

Ārjuni[1] = Abhimanyu: I, 8027; VI, 1824, 2365, 2373, 2460, 2730, 3223, 3436, 3559, 4560, 4584, 4613, 4747, 5158, 5406; VII, 546, 548, 556, 1509, †1550 (cf. Arjunāvaraḥ), 1553, 1557, 1564, 1579, 1597, 1623, 1626, 1630, 1636, 1659, 1725, 1736, 1768, 1783, 1786, 1803, 1818, 1821, 1840, 1852, 1855, 1856, 1874, 1897, 1898, 1909, 1920, 1963; XIV, 1958.

Ārjuni[2] = Çrutakīrti: III, 14731 (*Çrutakarmā*); VII, 1095 (*Çrutakīrtin tu Draupadeyam*), 4059.

Arjuni[3] = Irāvat: VII, 1738.

***Arka**[1] = Sūrya (the Sun): I, 42, 2771, 4388; III, 146 (Dhaumya's enumeration of the 108 names of the Sun), 192 (Yudhishṭhira's hymn to the Sun); XII, 11744 (has given the Yajurveda to Yājñavalkya).

Arka[2] = Vishṇu (1000 names).

Arka[3], an ancient king. § 6 (Anukram.): I, **1**, 230 (belonging to the past).

Arka[4]. § 130 (Aṃçāvat.): I, **67**, 2668 (a Dānava incarnated as the rājarshi Ṛshika).

Arkaja. § 562 (Bhagavadyān.): V, **74**γ, 2730 (born among the Balīhas).

Arkaparṇa. § 101 (Aṃçāvat.): I, **65**, 2551 (one of the sixteen Devagandharvāḥ Mauneyāḥ).

Arkaputra = Karṇa: I, †7026.

Arṇavālaya = Çiva (1000 names[1]).

Ārohaṇa = Çiva (1000 names[2]).

***Ārsha**, adj. ("belonging to or named after the ṛshis"): XII, 349 (*vidhiḥ*).

Ārshabha. § 596 (Pratijñāp.): VII, **79**, 2813 (practically like the note Ṛshabha).

Arshṭishena[1], a ṛshi. § 11 (Parvas.): I, **2**, 456 (°*āçrame*).—§ 22 (Pramadvarā): I, **8***a*, 962.—§ 434 (Saugandhikāh.): III, **156**, 11445 (°*āçrame*).—§ 436 (Yakshay.): III, **158**, 11626 (°*sya rājarsher āçramam*), 11627; **159**, (11643).—§ 437 (Yakshay.): III, **160**, 11661 (°*āçrame*; here the Pāṇḍavas dwelt for some time), 11666, 11672 (°*āçrame*).—§ 438 (do.): III, **161**, 11741 (the Pāṇḍavas entrusted Draupadī to him); **162**, 11812 (°*sya rājarsheḥ* . . . *āçramam*).—§ 439 (do.): III, **163**, 11841, 11842.—§ 448 (Ājagarap.): III, **176**, †12338.—§ 615 (Baladevatīrth.): IX, **39**, 2270 (had formerly undergone austere penances and acquired Brahmanhood at a certain tīrtha), 2281; **40**, 2285, 2287, 2293 (§ 615*m*). In the *Kṛta* age *Ā.* (*dvijottamaḥ*), though residing for a long time in his preceptor's house, and attending to his lessons every day, could not master any branch of knowledge or the *Vedas*. By austere penances he then acquired the mastery of the *Vedas* and great learning and became perfect (*siddhaḥ*) in that *tīrtha*, and bestowed three boons on it: (1) from this day a person who bathes in this *tīrtha*, shall obtain the benefit of a horse-sacrifice; (2) from this day no fear from snakes and wild beasts will be in this *tīrtha*; (3) small exertions in this place will lead to great results. Then the *muni* proceeded to heaven.—§ 707 (Mokshadh.): XII, **319**β, 11783.—§ 733 (Ānuçāsanik.): XIII, **25**, 1741 (by touching water in his hermitage one is cleansed from all sins).

Ārshṭishena[2], a ṛshi in the palace of Yama. § 267 (Yamasabhāv.): II, **8**, 325.

Ārshyaçṛṅga (B. °*im*): VI, 4019 (= Alambusha).

Ārshyaçṛṅgi: VI, 4039 (kills Irāvat), 4552 (= Alambusha), 4570, 4585 (*Alambushaḥ*), 4593, 4595 (do.), 4601, 5052 (*rākshasam*), 5140; VII, 3980, 4067 (*Alambusham*); IX, 76 (v. Alambusha), 95 (do.).—Cf. °**ga.**

Ārtāyani = Çalya.

Artha (profit). § 641 (Rājadh.): XII, **59**, 2253 (son of Dharma and Çrī), 2254; XII, 10407 (= Çiva, 1000 names[1]); XIII, 1166 (do., 1000 names[2]); XIII, 6995 (= Vishṇu, 1000 names).

***Arthaçāstra** (pl. *-āṇi*) ("the practical sciences"). § 11 (Parvas.): I, **2,** 646 (Mahābhārata).—§ 641 (Rājadh.): XII, **71,** 2728 (*°paraḥ*). — § 645 (Āpaddh.): XII, **137,** 4911.—§ 647 (Brahmadatta-Pūjanī-s.): XII, **139,** 5203.— § 657 (Āpaddh.): XII, **167,** 6219.—§ 663 (Mokshadh.): XII, **201,** 7369.—§ 704 (do.): XII, **302,** 11206.—§ 742 (Ānuçāsanik.): XIII, **39,** 2241.

Arthakara = Çiva (1000 names[2]).

Ārtimat (a mantra?). § 68 (Āstīka): I, **58,** 2188 (who recalled *Ā.* to his mind, would have no fear from serpents).—Cf. Asita[1].

Aruja. § 537 (Rāma-Rāvaṇa-y.): III, **285a,** 16365 (a rākshasa, a warrior of Rāvaṇa's).

Aruṇa[1] (the charioteer of Sūrya). § 27 (Kaçyapa): I, **16,** 1091: Son of Kaçyapa and Vinatā; came out of the egg, though not yet full-grown, and cursed his mother. — § 34 (Garuḍa): I, **24,** 1263, 1264: Carried by Garuḍa and placed in the east.—§ 35: I, **24,** 1275, 1277, 1278: At this time Sūrya, who was in danger of being devoured by Rāhu, and did not obtain any help, became wroth, and from the mountains of the west began to destroy the world with heat. The gods and ṛshis repaired to Brahmán, who ordered Aruṇa to become the charioteer of the Sun and take away the Sun's glow. — § 45 (Vālikhily.): I, **31,** 1469: Begotten in consequence of the Vālikhilyas having cursed Indra, and destined by Kaçyapa to become the brother and helpmate of Indra.—§ 99 (Aṃçāvat.): I, **65,** 2548 (one of the six Vainateyāḥ).—§ 120*b* (Devagaṇāḥ): I, **66,** 2603. — § 128 (Çyenī): I, **66,** 2633 (*Aruṇasya bhāryā Çyenī*; her sons are Sampāti and Jaṭāyus).—§ 129 (Aṃçāvat.): I, **66,** 2634.—§ 191 (Arjuna): I, **123,** 4830 (among the Vainateyas present at the birth of Arjuna).—[§ 370 (Tīrthay.): III, **84,** 8134: v. Aruṇā; B. has *Kauçiky-Aruṇayor.*]—§ 600 (Ghaṭotk.): VII, **175,** 7906 (*Aruṇena yathā Raviḥ*).—§ 602 (Droṇav.): VII, **186,** 8458 (*Ādityasya puraḥsaraḥ*).—§ 605 (Karṇap.): VIII, **32,** 1347 (*Aruṇena yathā . . . Sūryo*), 1349 (*Sūryāruṇau yathā*). —§ 615*u* (Skanda): IX, **45**γ, 2518; **46,** 2652 (the Mātṛs are *aruṇābhās* "of the colour of Dawn"), 2664 (the banner which was given to Skanda had the colour of the Dawn and the Sun), 2669 (*A.* gave Skanda a cock—*tāmracūḍaṃ . . . caraṇāyudham*).—§ 748 (Tārakavadh.): XIII, **86**β, 4207 (gave Skanda a cock of the splendour of Fire).

Aruṇa[2] = Çiva (1000 names[1]), etc.

Aruṇa[3] = Sūrya (the Sun): III, 148 (Dhaumya's enumeration of Sūrya's 108 names).

Aruṇa[4], pl. (*°āḥ*). § 630 (Rājadh.): XII, **26a,** 774 (*Ajāç ca Pṛçnayaç caiva Sikatāç caiva, Bhārata!* | *Aruṇāḥ Ketavaç caiva svādhyāyena divaṃ gatāḥ*; Nīl. *Ajādayo Vālakhilyavad ṛshīṇāṃ gaṇa-viçeshāḥ*).

Aruṇā[1]. § 103 (Aṃçāvat.): I, **65,** 2558 (among thirteen Apsarases, daughters of Prādhā and Kaçyapa).

Aruṇā[2], a river. § 370 (Tīrthay.): III, **84,** 8134 (v. Aruṇa; C. has *Kauçikāruṇayor*: *Kālikā-saṅgame . . . K°yor*).— § 610 (Çalyap.): IX, **5,** 289 (*Aruṇāṃ*—C. has *Ā°*—*Sarasvatīṃ*; PCR. "Sarasvatī of red water").—§ 615*p* (Vasishṭhāp.): IX, **43,** 2429 (in order to cleanse the Rā., Sarasvatī united *A.* with herself), 2430.—§ 615*t* (Indra): IX, **43,** 2439, 2441, 2443: Formerly the presence of that river at its site was concealed. Sarasvatī repaired to the Aruṇā and flooded it with her waters. This confluence of Sarasvatī and Aruṇā is highly sacred. Brahmán caused Indra to bathe in the Aruṇā.—§ 775 (Ānuçāsan.): XIII, **166a,** 7647 (*Tāmrā°*; among the rivers whose names, if recited morning, noon, and evening, become purifiers of sin).

Aruṇānuja = Garuḍa.

Aruṇātmaja = Jaṭāyu (cf. Sampāti).

Arundhatī, the wife of Vasishṭha. § 240 (Vaivāhikap.): I, **199,** 7352 (*Vasishṭhe cāpy A°*).—§ 259 (Çārṅgop.): I, **233b,** 8456: *A.* became jealous of Vasishṭha, one of the seven ṛshis, etc.; in consequence of this her presumption she has become a little star, like fire mixed with smoke, sometimes visible and sometimes invisible: *apadhyānena sā tena dhūmāruṇasamaprabhā* | *lakshyā 'lakshyā nābhirupā nimittam iva paçyati.* — § 270 (Brahma-sabhā-v.): II, **11,** 459 (in the palace of Brahmán).—§ 391 (Ṛshyaçṛṅga): III, **113,** 10092 (*Vasishṭhaṃ yathā*).—§ 410 (Plakshāvataraṇagam.): III, **130,** 10553 (*°sahāyaḥ Vasishṭho*, obtained tranquillity at Ujjānaka).—§ 496 (Skandotp.): III, **225,** 14313 (*A.* was the only one of the wives of the seven ṛshis whose form Svāhā was unable to assume, as a consequence of her ascetic merit and devotion to her husband).—§ 497 (do.): III, **226,** 14346 (the only one of the wives of the seven ṛshis who was not divorced).—§ 565 (Gālavacar.): V, **111,** 3834.—§ 574 (Jambūkh.): VI, **2a,** 65 (*yā caishā viçrutā, rājaṃs! trailokye sādhu-sammatā* | *Arundhatī tayā 'py esha Vaçishṭhaḥ pṛshṭhataḥ kṛtaḥ*, an omen).—§ 599 (Jayadrathav.): VII, **94**ε, 3452 (was invoked by Droṇa to bless Duryodhana).—§ 615*z* (Badarapācana): IX, **48**: *Indra* related to *Çrutāvatī*: In this very *tīrtha* the seven Ṛ. had, on one occasion, left *Arundhatī* while they went to *Himavat* in order to gather fruits and roots. A drought occurred extending for twelve years; the Ṛ., having made an asylum for themselves, continued to live there in a forest of *Himavat*. Seeing *Arundhatī* devoted to penances, *Çiva* in the form of a brahman came to her and asked for alms, and, as her store of food was exhausted, he told her to cook jujubes. While she listened to his discourses and cooked, without food, that twelve years' drought passed away to her as if it were a single day. Then the seven Ṛ. returned; *Mahādeva*, in his own form, said that the ascetic merit of *Arundhatī* was much greater than theirs, and granted her the boon that this spot should become an excellent *tīrtha* named Badarapācana, resorted to by Si. and D.-ṛ., and that he who observes a fast there and resides there for three nights after having cleansed himself should obtain the benefit of a twelve years' fast. Then he repaired to heaven. Ṛ. wondered at the sight of the god and because *Arundhatī* was unfatigued and still possessed the hue of health: 2795, 2798, 2805, 2810, 2814, 2815, 2818. — § 707 (Mokshadh.): XII, **318,** 11711 (one who, having previously seen [the star] *A.*, fails to see it . . . has but one year left to live).—§ 750 (Bisastainyop.): XIII, **93,** 4416, (4445), 4455, 4460, (4497), (4528).—§ 751 (Çapathavidhi): XIII, **94a,** β, 4551, (4584). — § 704 (Ānuçāsan.): XIII, **123,** 5877 (*Arundhatīva . . . Svargaloke mahīyate*).—§ 766 (do.): XIII, **130,** 6102, (6103), 6112: *A.* once explained to Ṛ., P., and D. the mysteries of Dharma; Brahmán granted her that her penances would continually increase.

Arundhatīpati = Vasishṭha: I, 6638.

Arundhatīvaṭa, a tīrtha. § 370 (Tīrthay.): III, **84,** 8019.

Āruṇi[1] Pāñcālya, disciple of the ṛshi Āyoda Dhaumya. § 14: I, **3,** 684, 685, 686, 689, 691, 692: *A.* stopped a break in the dike of a field by laying himself down there, thence he was called Uddālaka.

Aruṇi[2]. § 99 (Aṃçāvat.): I, **65,** 2548 (a Vainateya).—§ 191 (Arjuna): I, **123,** 4830 (= do.); present at the birth of Arjuna.

Āruṇi[3], a serpent. § 67 (Sarpasattra): I, **57**, 2160 (of Dhṛtarāshṭra's race).
Āruṇi[4]. § 600 (Ghaṭotk.): VII, **156**κ, 6851 (attacks Arjuna).
Ārushī. § 122 (Bhṛgu, Cyavana): I, **66**, 2610 (daughter of Manu, wife of Çyavana and mother of [Pramati and] Aurva).
Arvāvasu. § 264 (Sabhākriyāp.): II, **4**, 105 (a ṛshi in the palace of Yudhishṭhira).—§ 414 (Yavakrītop.): III, **135**, 10704 (*Raibhyasya tu sutāv āstām Arvāvasu-Parāvasū*) (hardly the same).—§ 417 (do.): III, **138**, 10792, (10800), 10801, 10804, 10809: Deceived by his brother Parāvasu, he composed the Rahasyaveda of the Sun, etc.—§ 665 (Mokshadh.): XII, **208**ε, 7592 (°*Parāvasū*).—§ 717 (Uparicara.): XII, **337**ε, 12758 (°*Parāvasū*).—§ 770 (Ānuçāsan.): XIII, **151**ζ, 7108 (°*Parāvasū*; among the R. [called] Mānavas).
Arvuka (pl. °*āḥ*), a people. § 281 (Sahadeva): II, **31**γ, 1119 (conquered by Sahadeva).
Āryā[1]. § 500 (Skandop.): III, **228**a, 14396 (a Mātṛ, one of the mothers of Çiçu).—§ 502 (Manushyagrahak.): III, **230**, 14495 (a graha).
Āryā[2] = Umā, q.v.
***Āryāḥ** ("Aryans"): II, 2040 (*nāryā mlecchanti bhāshābhiḥ*).—§ 574 (Jambūkh.): VI, **9**, 321 (*Āryā Mlecchāç ca*); VI, 1636 (*Mlecchāç cāryāç ca*); XIV, 2137 (*mlecchāḥ . . . āryāç ca pṛthivīpālāḥ*).
Āryaka, a serpent. § 47 (Sarpanāmak.): I, **35**, 1552.—§ 197 (Bhīmasenarasap.): I, **128**, 5026 (the great-grandfather of Pṛthā; he caused eight jars of the Serpents' *rasa* to be given to Bhīmasena).—§ 564 (Mātalīyop.): V, **103**γ, 3627, 3635 (Sumukha is the grandson of Ā° Kauravya), 3639; **104**, (3656).
Aryaman[1] ("comrade who negociates wedding"), one of the Ādityas. § 88 (Aṃçāvat.): I, **65**, 2523.—§ 191 (Arjuna): I, **123**a, 4822 (came to the birth of Arjuna).—§ 258 (Khāṇḍavadah.): I, **227**, 8267 (attacked Kṛshṇa and Arjuna with a bludgeon furnished with sharp spikes).—§ 266 (Çakrasabhāv.): II, **7**, 302 (in the palace of Indra).—§ 576 (Bhagavadgītāp.): VI, **34**, 1233 (Kṛshṇa said: *Pitṝṇām Aryamā cāsmi*, i.e. the Sun?).—§ 615u (Skanda): IX, **45**γ, 2507.—§ 615 (Baladevat.): IX, **54**, 3049 (on the Yamunā Indra, Agni, and *A.* in days of yore had obtained great happiness).—§ 665 (Mokshadh.): XII, **208**β, 7581 (an Āditya).—§ 730 (Ānuçāsan.): XIII, **18**λλ, 1368 (has sprung from Çiva).—§ 770 (do.): XIII, **151**γ, 7093 (an Āditya).
Aryaman[2] = the Sun: III, 146 (Dhaumya's enumeration).—§ 630 (Rājadh.): XII, **26**, 776 (*dakshiṇena ca panthānam Aryamṇo ye divaṃ gatāḥ | etān kriyāvatāṃ lokān uktavān pūrvam apy aham*).—§ 665 (Mokshadh.): XII, **208**, 7576 (enumerated by Bhīshma among the Prajāpatis; *A.* and his sons were leaders and creators of all creatures).
Aryaman[3] = Çiva (1000 names [2]).
Aryāvartta, a country in Bharatavarsha, Hindustan (v. BR.). § 713 (Çukakṛti): XII, **326**, 12229 (*imaṃ deçam*).
Asahāya = Çiva: XIII, 1233 (*Nitya Ātmāsahāyaç ca*) (1000 names [2]).
Asahya = Çiva: X, 256.
Asamāmnāya = Çiva (1000 names [2]).
Asamañjaḥsuta = Aṃçumat: III, 8884.
Asamañjas[1]. § 388 (Tīrthay.): III, **107**, 8888, 8891, 8892: At the request of *Yudhishṭhira*, *Lomaça* related: *Asamañjas*, the son of *Sagara* and *Çaibyā*, used to seize the children of the citizens by the throat and throw them into the river. At the request of the citizens, *Sagara* caused his ministers (*sacivān*) to drive *Asamañjas* immediately from the city.—§ 640 (Rājadh.): XII, **57**, 2054, 2055 (the eldest son of Sagara, who exiled him, because he used to drown the children of the citizens in the Sarayū).
Asamañjas[2]. § 298 (Dyūtap.): II, **62**, 2100 (*viditaṃ me, mahāprājña! Bhojeshv evāsamañjasaṃ | putraṃ santyaktavān pūrvaṃ paurāṇāṃ hitakāmyayā*; the last half-çloka is omitted in V.; ought we not to translate "I for my part know that something like the story of Asamañjas has really happened among the Bhojas"?).
Asaṅga ("without affections"), a name of Chastisement. § 641 (Rājadh.): XII, **121**σ, 4430.
Asañjña, v. Mahāpurushastava.
Asaṅkhyeya = Vishṇu (1000 names).
Asat = Çiva (1000 names [2]); = Mahāpurusha, XII, 12864; = Vishṇu (1000 names).—**Asataḥ prabhava-**, etc. = Çiva (1000 names [1]).
Asatyā (?). § 490 (Āṅgirasa): III, **219**, 14133 (*Çamyor apratimā bhāryā Satyā Satyā 'tha Dharmajā*).
Āshāḍha[1]. § 130 (Aṃçāvat.): I, **67**, 2699 (a king, incarnation of the gaṇa Krodhavaçāḥ).—§ 554 (Sainyody.): V, **4**γ, 80.
Āshāḍha[2] = Çiva (1000 names [2]).
Āshāḍha[3], adj. ("named after the nakshatra Āshāḍhāḥ"). § 759 (Ānuçāsanik.): XIII, **106**β, 5157 (*māsaṃ*; the man or woman who during this month subsists upon one meal, obtains incomparable lordship); **109**, 5379 (do.; the man who fasts on the twelfth day of the moon in the month *Ā.*, and for the whole day and night worships Kṛshṇa as Vāmana, attains to the merit of Naramedha and sports with Apsarases).
Āshāḍha[4], pl. (°*āḥ*), a nakshatra (v. Sū. Si.). § 746 (Ānuçāsanik.): XIII, **64**, 3276 (*pūrvāsu*), 3278 (*uttarāsu*).—§ 749 (do.): XIII, **89**a, 4264 ([*pūrvāsu*]-*uttarāsu*).—§ 759 (do.): XIII, **110**, 5390 (do.; at the candravrata the two *Ā.* should be in the moon's thighs).
Āshāḍhī (the day of full-moon of the month of *Ā.*). § 658 (Kṛtaghnop.): XII, **171**, 6384.
Ashṭādaçāvarāḥ. § 273 (Rājasūyār.): II, **14**, 599 (*kulair °aiḥ*, some tribes who thought they would be unable to check Jarāsandha in 300 years), 604 (*saṃgrāme 'shṭādaçāvare*; there Haṃsa is slain by Rāma), 620 (*kshattriyair °aiḥ*, fortify Gomanta).
Ashṭaka. § 149 (Yayāti): I, **86-93**: **86**, 3539 (*rājñā*; Yayāti ascended to Svarga accompanied by *A.*, etc.). **88**, †3569 (*rājarshivaraḥ*; when falling from heaven Yayāti was beheld by *A.*). **89**, (†3579), †3586, †3588, †3589, (†3590): Yayāti, who was the maternal grandfather of *A.*, discoursed with him on haughtiness, etc., and told him his own history. **90**, (†3600), (†3602), (†3605), (†3608), (†3611), (†3615), (†3616), (†3620): Yayāti spoke to *A.* of those who talk about their own merit, etc. **91**, (†3627), (3634), (3636): Continuation. **92**, (3645), (†3650), (†3653), (†3655): Yayāti said that he should now fall into the Bhauma hell. **93**, (3673), (3675), (†3680), †3683, (†3688): The kings, *A.*, etc., offered him their 'lokas,' and would themselves go to hell; Yayāti did not accept the offer; then appeared five golden cars, in which they all five ascended to heaven; Yayāti told them that he was their maternal grandfather, etc.—§ 378 (Tīrthay.): III, **93**, 8465.—§ 467 (Rājanyamāh.): III, **198**, 13301 (to the horse-sacrifice of king *A.* Vaiçvāmitri all kings came), 13304, 13305 (*A.* should first come down from heaven, because he had praised himself for having given away thousands of kine).—§ 552 (Goharaṇap.): IV,

56ζ, 1768.—§ 565 (Gālavacar.): V, **119**, 4019, 4021 (begotten by Viçvāmitra upon Mādhavī; *A.* then went to a certain city).—§ 566 (Yayāti): V, **121**, 4057 (as Yayāti was falling from heaven, he fell among his daughter's sons Pratardana, Vasumanas, Çibi, and *A.*, in the Naimisha wood, where they performed a Vājapeya; they gave him their virtues and the merits of all their sacrifices).—§ 656 (Khaḍgotpattik.): XII, **166**δ, 6200.—§ 751 (Çapathavidhi): XIII, **94**a, 4551, (4582) β.—§ 775 (Ānuçāsan.): XIII, **166**η, 7681 (among the principal kings to be recited at sunset and sunrise as purifiers of sins).

Ashṭāvakra[1], a ṛshi. § 11 (Parvas.): I, **2**, 449 (*viprarshiḥ*).—§ 412 (Ashṭāvakrīya): III, **132**, 10599 (*Kahodasūnuḥ*), †10601, †10603, †10608, †10613, †10614, †10620: Cursed by Kahoda; Çvetaketu informed him who his father was; they both go to the sacrifice of Janaka). **133**, (†10623), (†10626), (†10629), (10631), (†10637), (†10643), (10645), (10647), (10648): *A.* defeats Bandin. **134**, (†10651), †10657, (†10659), (†10661), (†10663), (10665), (†10667), (†10669), (†10670), †10671, †10672, (†10673), (†10676), (10680), †10681, (†10688): Defeated by *A.*, Bandin was merged into the sea; Kahoda let *A.* bathe in the river Samanga, at which all his limbs were immediately made straight.—§ 731 (Ashṭāvakra-Dik-s.): XIII, **19**, 1390 (*Ashṭāvakrasya saṃvādaṃ Diçayā saha*), 1391, 1395, (1406), 1417, (1454), (1469): *A.* asked for Suprabhā and made a journey to the north. **20**, (1496), (1498), (1500), (1505), (1508): Here the goddess of the north put him upon a trial. **21**, 1513, 1521 (*viprarshe*), 1529: *A.* came back to his own hermitage, was wedded to Suprabhā, and continued to dwell in his own hermitage.

Ashṭāvakra[2], a tīrtha. § 733 (Ānuçāsan.): XIII, **25**r, 1727: Bhīshma mentioned the profit of bathing in *A.*, etc.

[Ashṭāvakra-Dik-saṃvāda(ḥ)] ("discourse between Ashṭāvakra and the goddess of the North"). § 731b (Ānuçāsanik.): XIII, **19** ff.: *Bhīshma* said: In days of yore *Ashṭāvakra* (of severe penances) asked Ṛ. *Vadānya* for his beautiful daughter *Suprabhā*. *Vadānya* first caused him to make a journey to the North, indicating the road: (1) *Himavat* (peopled by Si. and Cā.); (2) the sacred river *Bāhudā*, where he bathed in one of the *tīrthas*, etc. (description), and worshipped *Rudra* and *Umā*; (3) *Kailāsa*, where he saw a golden gate, etc. (α), and was honoured by *Kubera* among Y. (with *Maṇibhadra*), G., and K., and where Aps. (β) danced; there he remained a celestial year; (4) having crossed *Kailāsa* and *Mandara* as also the golden mountains, he came to the region where *Mahādeva* resides attired as an ascetic, *Pārshadas* of which are frolicsome and fond of dance and possessed of faces of diverse forms, which was peopled by Si., Cā., and Pç., where *Umā* had practised austerities for the sake of [obtaining] *Çiva*; where, in days of yore, on the *Mahāpārçva* [mountain] (to the north of the god) the Seasons, etc. (α′), in their material forms had adored *Mahādeva*; (5) a beautiful forest (description), where the river *Mandākinī* was seen, with an old and decrepit female ascetic (with many beautiful maidens), who in vain tempted him with love (XIII, **19**), at last appearing in a beautiful form (XIII, **20**). She turned out to be the goddess of the North (*Uttarāṃ diçaṃ*), who, having been gratified by Ṛ. *Vadānya*, had devised this trial and now instructed him, showing him the levity of women, even when aged; "thou hast subjugated all the worlds by thy strength of mind; thy journey back will not be irksome; thou wilt obtain the wife thou hast chosen; she will bear thee a son." *Ashṭāvakra* came back to his own abode, and then to *Vadānya*, who wedded him to the girl. There he continued to dwell joyously in his own hermitage (XIII, **21**).

Ashṭāvakrīya(ṃ) ("episode relating to Ashṭāvakra").—§ 51 (Parvasaṅgr.): I, **2**, 449: *A. atraiva vivādo yatra Bandinā*, etc.—§ 412 (Tīrthay.): III, **132** ff.: *Uddālaka* gave his own daughter *Sujātā* in marriage, together with sacred learning (*çrutaṃ*), to his disciple the brahman *Kahoda*, who had served him long. The embryo in her womb had become versed in the *Çāstras* and the *Vedas* with the *aṅgas*, and blamed *Kahoda*, who had been reading the whole night. The great *ṛshi Kahoda* cursed him to become crooked on eight parts of his body, wherefore he, when born, was called *Ashṭāvakra*. In order to procure wealth for *Sujātā*, *Kahoda* went to king *Janaka* (son of *Indradyumna*, v. **133**, 10624), where he was defeated in a controversy with the *sūta* (v. 10613, etc., *sūtaputram* v. 10671) *Bandin* and was immersed into water. *Uddālaka* prevailed upon *Sujātā* to keep it a secret from *Ashṭāvakra*, who regarded *Uddālaka* as his father and *Çvetaketu*, the son of *Uddālaka*, who was of the same age with himself, as his brother, until in his 12th year *Çvetaketu* in anger happened to disclose the matter to him. He and *Çvetaketu* then went to the sacrifice of *Janaka*, and on being driven from the entrance *Ashṭāvakra* met the king (III, **132**), and in the course of a conversation with him and the doorkeeper he compared *Janaka* to *Yayāti*, and said that he had heard that *Bandin* caused those whom he had vanquished in disputation to be drowned in the sea by men sent by *Janaka*, and he declared that he had come to maintain the unity with *Bráhman* (*Bṛahmādvaitam*) and to defeat *Bandin*; then he answered several enigmatical questions (about the wheel of Time, the thunder and lightning, the fish, egg, stone, and river) and was admitted (III, **133**). Here they disputed in such a way that *Bandin* enumerated things of which there is only 1 (fire, Sun, *Indra*, and *Yama*), *Ashṭāvakra* groups of 2 (*Indra* and *Agni*, 2 devarshis: *Nārada* and *Parvata*, 2 *Açvins*, 2 wheels of a chariot; husband and wife), *Ba*° of 3 (3 times the creatures are born, etc.; see Nīl.), *A*° of 4 (4 are the *āçramas* of the *brahmans*; 4 orders perform this sacrifice (!), etc.), *Ba*° of 5 (5 fires, etc.), *A*° of 6 (6 cows, it is asserted by some, are the *dakshiṇā* for establishing the sacred fire, "*ādhāne*," etc.), *Ba*° of 7 (7 domesticated animals, 7 wild animals, etc.), *A*° of 8 (8 *çāṇas* make a *çalamāna*, see BR., 8 are the legs of the *çarabha*, etc.), *Ba*° of 9 (9 are the *sāmidhenī* verses for the *Pitṛs*, etc.), *A*° of 10 (10 are the cardinal points, etc.), *Ba*° of 11 (11 are the *ekādaçinas* of the creatures, see Nīl., 11 are there the *yūpas*, etc.), *A*° of 12 (12 months, etc.). As *Bandin* had said the first half-*çloka* with 13 (the 13th *tithi* is deemed most auspicious, 13 are the islands of the earth), he stopped, and *Ashṭāvakra* fulfilled the *çloka*. *Bandin* was then deemed to be vanquished, and at the request of *Ashṭāvakra* he merged into the sea, after he had declared himself to be the son of *Varuṇa* and that he had caused the *brahmans* to be drowned in order that they might see the twelve years *sattra* of *Varuṇa* that was performed simultaneously with that of *Janaka*. They at once reappeared, and *Kahoda* let *Ashṭāvakra* bathe in the river *Samaṅgā*, and all his limbs were immediately made straight, and the *Samaṅgā* became a remover of sin. "Therefore you also should bathe there" (III, **134**).

***Asi(ḥ)** ("the sword," person). § 656d (Khaḍgotpattik.): XII, **166**, 6162, 6165, 6166, 6188, *dharmagarbhena*; 6191, its forms are the different sorts of punishment; ib. ε, its eight mysterious names, Asi, etc.; 6203 foll., etc.

Asiknī (a river in Bhāratav.). § 574 (Jambūkh.): VI, **9**λ, 330.

Asiloman (a Dānava). § 92 (Aṃçāvat.): I, **65,** 2531.

Asipatravana ("the forest where the leaves of the trees are like swords," a locality in hell). § 710 (Mokshadh.): XII, **322,** 12075.—§ 795 (Svargāroh.): XVIII, **2,** 49.

Asita[1] or **Asita Devala** (very often *A°o D°aç caiva*) or **Devala,** a ṛshi. § 4 (Anukram.): I, **1,** 106 (*A.D.*).—§ 59 (Sarpasattra): I, **53***a*, 2048 (*A.D.*).—§ 68 (Āstīka): I, **58,** 2188 (*Asitaṃ cārtimantañ ca Sunīthaṃ cāpi yaḥ smaret,* a mantra?).—§ 116 (Aṃçāvat.): I, **66,** 2590 (*Pratyūshasya viduḥ putram ṛshiṃ nāmnā 'tha Devalaṃ*; the same?).—§ 165 (Satyavatīl.): I, **100,** 4045 (*devarshiḥ*; Parāçara had rejected *A.* when he asked for the hand of Satyavatī).—§ 230 (Dhaumya-puroh.): I, **183,** 6914 (*D.*, the elder brother of Dhaumya).—§ 264 (Sabhākriyāp.): II, **4***a*, 105 (*A.D.*).—§ 270 (Brahmasabhāv.): II, **11***a*, 441.—§ 296 (Dyūtap.): II, **53,** 1917 (*A.D.*; sprinkled Yudhishṭhira with sacred water).—§ 298*b* (Dyūtap.): II, **59,** 2038: *A.D.* ("who always perambulates these doors of the worlds") has said that gambling is sinful, as is all deceitfulness.—§ 301 (Dyūtap.): II, **72,** 2420 (*D.*).—§ 317 (Arjunābhigam.): III, **12,** 510 (*A.D.*).—§ 376 (Tīrthay.): III, **85,** 8263 (*A.D.*; among the ṛshis who expected Yudhishṭhira at the tīrthas).—§ 576 (Bhagavadgītāp.): VI, **34,** 1217 (*A.D.*)—§ 581 (Bhīshmav.): VI, **68**ρ, 3042 (*D.*).—§ 599 (Jayadrathav.): VII, **94**ε, 3453 (Droṇa invoked *A.D.*, etc., when casing Duryodhana in invulnerable armour).—§ 615 (Baladevatīrth.): IX, **49,** 2852 (*A.D.* obtained great yoga powers in Ādityatīrtha); **50,** 2854 (*A.D.*), 2859 (*D°asyāçrame*), 2861 (*D.*), 2862 (*D.*), 2863 (*D.*), 2864 (*D.*), 2865 (*D.*), 2868 (*D.*), 2870 (*A.*), 2875 (*A.D.*), 2878 (*D.*), 2880 (*A.D.*), 2887 (*D.*), 2889 (*D.*), 2891 (*D.*), 2892 (*D.*), 2893 (*A.*), 2894 (*A.*), 2895 (*A.*), 2896 (*A.*), 2897 (*D.*), 2898 (*A.*), 2900 (*D.*), 2902 (*A.D.*), 2903 (*D.*), 2905 (*D.*), 2906 (*D.*), 2907 (*D.*), 2908 (*D.*), 2912 (*D.*), 2914 (*D.*), 2916 (*D.*), 2917 (*D.*), 2920 (*A.*) (B.; C. has *yoshitaṃ*), 2922 (*A.*): In *Ādityatīrtha* Ṛ. *A.D.* lived in days of yore, observant of the duties of a householder (description); he always practised the vow of *brahmacarya.* Once the ascetic mendicant (*bhikshukaḥ*) *Jaigīshavya,* devoted to *yoga,* came to *Devala's* hermitage and attained to success (*siddhiṃ*). *Devala* always kept his eyes on him. After a long time, *Devala* on one occasion lost sight of *Jaigīshavya*; at the hour of dinner, however, he approached *Devala* in order to solicit alms, and *D.* worshipped him, after the rites laid down by Ṛ., for many years; but *Jaigīshavya* never spoke a single word to him. *D.* proceeded to the shore of the ocean, journeying through the welkin and bearing his earthen jug with him; there he saw *Jaigīshavya,* who had arrived there before him, at which M.-ṛ. *A.* wondered much. Having finished his ablutions and silent prayers, *D.* returned to his hermitage, bearing with him his earthen vessel filled with water. Entering his own hermitage, he saw *Jaigīshavya* seated there. *D.* then soared aloft into the sky in order to ascertain who *Jaigīshavya* really was. He saw crowds of sky-ranging Si. rapt in meditation, and he saw *Jaigīshavya,* reverentially worshipped by them, and he became filled with wonder at the sight. He saw *Jaigīshavya* set out for the *Pitṛloka > Yāmyaloka,* etc. (μ). At last he was seen to pass into the regions of the *brahmasattvins,* then through three other regions to those of chaste women and such as are devoted to their husbands. At this point *A.* lost sight of him, and enquiring of the foremost of Si. in the regions of the *brahmasattvins,* he was told that *Jaigīshavya* had gone to the eternal region (*loka*) of *Brahman.* *A.* endeavoured to soar aloft; but he soon fell down, and the Si. declared that he was not worthy to proceed thither. *D.* came down, descending from one region to another in due order, to his hermitage, where he again beheld *Jaigīshavya,* who taught him the religion of Emancipation (*moksha*) and the ordinances of *yoga,* etc., and performed all the acts according to the rites for that end. Then all creatures with P. began to weep, saying, "Who will henceforth give us food?" *D.* then thought of renouncing the religion of *moksha*; then all kinds of fruits and roots, etc., began to weep, saying, "The wicked-hearted *D.* will once more pluck and eat us, having once assured all creatures of his perfect harmlessness." Then *D.* abandoned the religion of a householder and adopted that of *moksha,* and obtained the highest success (*siddhi*) and the highest *yoga.* *D.* with Bṛh. applauded *Jaigīshavya*; only *Nārada* contradicted.—§ 621 (Rājadh.): XII, **1,** 34 (*D.*).—§ 637 (do.): XII, **47,** 1594 (*A.*).—§ 664 (Mokshadh.): XII, **207**β, 7521 (*A.D.*).—§ 675 (do.): XII, **230,** 8431 (*A.*), 8432 (*A.D.*), (8433) (*D.*), 8436 (*D.*), 8439 (*D.*).—§ 688 (do.): XII, **276,** 9874 (*A.D.*), 9875 (*D.*), (9877) (*A.*).—§ 702 (do.): XII, **293***a*, 10761 (*A.D.*).—§ 707 (do.): XII, **319,** 11742 (*D.*); β, 11782 (*A.D.*).—§ 730 (Ānuçāsan.): XIII, **18**κκ, 1313 (*A.D.*).—§ 746 (do.): XIII, **66**ζ, 3332 (*A.D.*).—§ 768 (do.): XIII, **139***a*, 6298 (*D.*).—§ 775 (do.): XIII, **166**ζ, 7671 (*D.*).—§ 777 (Svargārohaṇika p.): XIII, **168,** 7718 (*A.D.*); **169**β, 7778 (*A.*).—§ 783 (Anugītāp.): XIV, **52***a*, 1492 (*D.*).—§ 786 (do.): XIV, **91***a*, 2843 (*A.*).—§ 787 (Āçramavāsap.): XV, **20**ββ, 538 (*D.*).—§ 789 (Putradarçanap.): XV, **29***a*, 774 (*D.*).—§ 795 (Mahābhārata): XVIII, **5***c*, 199 (*A°o D°aḥ Pitṝn açrāvayat*).

Asita[2], a king conquered by Māndhātṛ. § 595 (Māndhātṛ): VII, **62***a*, 2282.—§ 632*b* (Shoḍaçarājop., Māndhātṛ): XII, **29,** 981.

Asita[3] = Kṛshṇa: IX, 3351.

Asita[4], a mountain. § 377 (Dhaumyatīrthak.): III, **89,** 8364.

Asitadhvaja. § 191 (Arjuna): I, **123,** 4830 (a Vainateya present at the birth of Arjuna).

Asnehana = Çiva (1000 names[2]).

***Asta,** the place (mountain) in the west where the sun sets: I, 717 (*°ācala*), 1270 (*giriṃ*), 1894 (= do.), 4143 (= do.), 4697 (= do.), 6058 (*prāg A°gamanād raveḥ*); III, 11834 (*girivaraçreshṭhaṃ*), 11850 (*parvatarājānaṃ*), 11870, 16730, 17330, 17331; IV, 1731; V, 7162, 7216, 7246; VI, 2398 (*giriṃ çreshṭhaṃ*), 2401, 3831*a*, *b* (only in B.), 4231 (*Sūryāstamanavelāyāṃ*); VII, 1452 (*giriṃ*), 1969 (*parvataṃ*), 2800, 3666 (*°çikharaṃ*), 5530, 6058, 6059, 6221, 6257 (*mahīdharaṃ çreshṭhaṃ*), 6291, 6410 (*giriṃ*), 6614, 9261 (*giriṃ*); VIII, 704, 1241 (*giriṃ*), 4664, 4705, 4809; IX, 1651, 1654; X, 24 (*parvataçreshṭhaṃ*), 650; XII, 743 (*giriṃ*), [1575 (*astam ite Bhīshme*)], 2119 (*upaiti Savitā hy astaṃ*), [11735 (*astam evābhyavartata*)], [12518], 12519; XV, 867 (*girivaraṃ*).

Āstīka(ḥ). § 3 (Anukr.): I, **1,** 52: "Some read the Mahābhārata beginning with Ā."—§ 25 (Paulomap.): I, **11,** 1013: "The deliverance of the Serpents by the brahman *Ā.*; mighty in spiritual energy (*tapovīrya-balopetād*) and having mastered the Vedas and the Vedāṅgas (*Veda-Vedāṅga-pāragāt*)." I, **12,** 1015 (v. Sahasrapād), 1016 (*°caritaṃ*).—§§ 26–69, cf. Āstīkaparvan.—§ 26: I, **13,** 1021, 1024 (*Āstīkasya purāṇarsher brāhmaṇasya*), 1028 (his father was

Jaratkāru, q.v.); I, **15**, 1060 (his mother was Jaratkāru, q.v.), 1063 (rescued the Serpents at the Snake-sacrifice of Janamejaya, etc.), 1067.—§ 27: I, **16**, 1069: *Ā°sya kaveḥ sādhoḥ*.—§ 49 (Vāsuki): I, **38**, 1634: Destined by Brahmán to rescue the harmless (*dharmacāriṇaḥ*) among the Serpents. —§ 51 (Parikshit): I, **40**, 1660.—§ 55, I, **48**, 1929, 1930: *Ā.* was born and reared in Vāsuki's house; etymology of his name (*astītyuktvā gato yasmāt pitā garbhastham eva taṃ | vanaṃ, tasmād idaṃ tasya nāmāstīketi viçrutaṃ*).—§§ 60–62 (Sarpasattra): How he appeared at the Snake-sacrifice and rescued the remaining Serpents: I, **53**, 2065; **54**, 2069 2083, 2089, 2090, 2093, 2094; **55**, 2097; **56**, 2135, 2138, 2139.—§ 68: The reason why Takshaka had not fallen into the fire was that *Ā.* had said thrice, "Stay." Janamejaya let the sacrifice come to an end; he bestowed wealth upon Lohitāksha, etc. *Ā.* returned home after having promised that he would become a *sadasya* at Janamejaya's horse-sacrifice; he obtained the boon from the Snakes that those, who in the morning or the evening cheerfully read the sacred account of his act, should have no fear from them; nor should those who recall *Asita*, *Ārtimat*, and *Sunītha* to their minds; nor those who would say, "I recall the famous *Āstīka*, etc., to my mind." *Ā.* at last died, leaving sons and grandsons behind him. I, **58**, 2166, 2170, 2172, 2173, 2174, 2180, 2182, 2184, 2186, 2189, 2190, 2191, 2196: *Āstīkasya kaver caritaṃ*.—§ 790 (Putradarçanap.): XV, **35** (on the occasion of the account how Dhṛtarāshṭra, obtaining eyesight, beheld his children, Vyāsa brought Parikshit from Heaven and showed him to Janamejaya; Janamejaya addressed *Ā.*, who praised Vyāsa and mentioned the Snake-sacrifice, etc.); XV, **35**, 948 (*Ā°ṃ Yāyāvarakulotpannaṃ Jaratkārusutaṃ*), 949, 950.—§ 795*b* (Janamejaya): XVIII, **5**, 179 (Sauti said: Hearing this (i.e. the Mahābhārata) at the intervals of sacrificial rites, king Janamejaya became filled with wonder. *Ā.*, having rescued the Snakes, became filled with joy).

Āstīka(m) = Āstīkaparvan: I, **1**, 88 (*Paulomāstīka-mūlavān*, i.e. *Bharatadrumaḥ*); **2**, 304, 312, 360, 365 (*Āstīke sarva-nāgānāṃ Garuḍasya ca saṃbhavaḥ | kshīroda-manthanaṅ caiva janmocchaiḥçravasas tathā | yajataḥ sarpa-satreṇa rājñaḥ Pārīkshitasya ca*). XVIII, **6**, 266: "When the *Ā.* is being recited, [brahmans] should be entertained with fruits and roots, and frumenty, and honey and clarified butter, and rice boiled with raw sugar (*guḍandanaṃ*)."

Āstīka(m) ākhyāna(m) ("the story of Āstīka, cf. Āstīka-parvan): I, **13**, 1023, 1027; **15**, 1068; **16**, 1072; **58**, 2194, 2197.

[Āstīka-parvan(°va)], the 5th of the minor parvans. § 26: I, **13–15**: Sauti related how the ascetic Jaratkāru (q.v.), upon a woman, likewise-named Jaratkāru, being the sister of the Serpent-king Vāsuki, begot a son (Āstīka) destined to neutralise the curse inflicted on the Serpents by their mother (Kadrū).—§ 27 (Kaçyapa): I, **16**: Origin of the Serpents and of Garuḍa and Aruṇa.—§ 28 (Amṛtamanthana): I, **17–19**: In order to explain the origin of Uccaiḥçravas, Sauti related the churning of the Ocean and the consequent production of the Amṛta, etc.—§§ 29–46 (Kadrū, Samudra, Samudradarçana, Garuḍa, Aruṇa, Indra, Rāmaṇīyaka, Supratīka, and Vālikhilya): I, **20–34**: Kadrū and Vinatā made a bet as to the colour of the tail of Uccaiḥçravas, and Vinatā (having been cursed by Aruṇa, § 27) became the slave of Kadrū; Kadrū cursed the Serpents, her sons, to be burnt at the Snake-sacrifice of Janamejaya; exploits of Garuḍa; Aruṇa became the charioteer of the Sun; Garuḍa set out to bring the Amṛta to the Snakes, who had promised that he and his mother should on this condition be freed from bondage; Vibhāvasu and Supratīka, and Garuḍa's meeting with the Vālikhilyas; omens foreboding fear (of losing the Amṛta) appeared among the gods, owing to Indra's having formerly been cursed by the Vālikhilyas; Garuḍa snatched the Amṛta, made friendship with Vishṇu and Indra, and placed the Amṛta before the Snakes, who declared Vinatā to be free; but Indra took it from them. —§ 47: I, **35**: Enumeration of the principal Snakes.—§ 48: Çesha (q.v.).—§ 49: Consultation of the Serpents under Vāsuki (q.v.); it became known that Āstīka would be born and save the harmless serpents.—§ 50: Etymology of Jaratkāru.—§ 51: King Parikshit (q.v.), the son of Abhimanyu, was cursed and consequently struck to death by Takshaka; Kāçyapa was bribed to return without curing him. —§ 52: Janamejaya (q.v.) succeeded his father Parikshit. —§ 53: The story of Jaratkāru repeated (see § 26) and somewhat enlarged.—§ 54: Jaratkāru (q.v.) left his wife.—§ 55: Āstīka (q.v.) was born, and reared by Vāsuki.—§ 56: The ministers of Janamejaya told him about Parikshit (q.v.).—§ 57: The ministers of Janamejaya (q.v.) learned what had happened between Takshaka and Kāçyapa. Janamejaya resolved to avenge his father and Utaṅka.—§ 58: Janamejaya (q.v.) made preparations for a Snake-sacrifice.—§§ 58*b*–69 (Sarpasattra): Janamejaya's Snake-sacrifice (cf. also Āstīka); enumeration of the principal Snakes that fell into the fire, of Vāsuki's (§ 63), Takshaka's (§ 64), Airāvata's (§ 65), Kauravya's (§ 66) and Dhṛtarāshṭra's race (§ 67). § 69: Sauti said. "This story I have told, as Pramati narrated it to Ruru, after having heard what was said by the *ḍuṇḍubha*."

Astradarçana ("the show of arms"). § 208 (Sambhav.): I, **134**: When the princes had become accomplished in arms *Droṇa* addressed *Dhṛtarāshṭra* in the presence of *Kṛpa*, *Somadatta*, *Bāhlīka*, *Bhīshma*, *Vyāsa*, and *Vidura*, asking him to let them show their proficiency. *Vidura* then let *Droṇa* measure out a place, and *Kuntī*, *Gāndhārī*, etc. ("like celestial ladies ascending *Meru*"), and the citizens came out to behold the princes' skill. *Droṇa* and *Açvatthāman* appeared like the Moon (*Aṃçumat*) accompanied by the planet Mars (*Aṅgāraka*). The spectators, seeing the prowess of the princes, fancied they were beholding the city of the *Gandharvas*. *Vidura* described all the feats of the princes to *Dhṛtarāshṭra*, and *Kuntī* to *Gāndhārī* (I, **134**). A combat with maces between *Duryodhana* and *Bhīma* divided the spectators into two parties, until *Droṇa* caused *Açvatthāman* to separate them. The exploits of *Arjuna* (*b*) were quite wonderful. *Droṇa* stood surrounded by the five *Pārthas* like the Moon in conjunction with the five-starred *Sāvitra* (i.e. *Hasta*), and *Duryodhana*, mace in hand, surrounded by his 100 brothers and *Açvatthāman*, was like *Purandara* (i.e. *Indra*) encircled by the hosts of gods on the occasion of the victory over the *Dānavas* (I, **135**). *Karṇa* (*c*) enters and challenges *Arjuna*. The *Dhārtarāshṭras* stood by *Karṇa*, while *Droṇa*, *Kṛpa*, and *Bhīshma* remained with *Arjuna*. *Kuntī* swooned away, and was restored to consciousness by *Vidura*, who caused sandal paste and water to be sprinkled on her person. *Kṛpa* rejects *Karṇa*; but *Duryodhana* then installed *Karṇa* as king of *Aṅga* (I, **136**). The sun went down; *Duryodhana* led *Karṇa* out of the arena, and the *Pāṇḍavas*, accompanied by *Droṇa*, *Kṛpa*, and *Bhīshma*, returned to their abodes (I, **137**).

Asura[1], pl. (°*āḥ*), the enemies of the gods: I, 163, 855.—§ 28 (Amṛtam.): I, **17–19**, 1110, 1125 (°*Dānavāḥ*), 1129 (*surā°gaṇān*), 1130 (*surā°*), 1168, 1170, 1172 (*mahā°*), 1181 (°*gaṇān*), 1182, 1185 (°*gaṇa°*), 1186 (*mahā°*): participated with the gods in the churning of the Ocean, would possess themselves of the ambrosia, but were vanquished.—§ 30 (Samudra): I, **21**, 1211, 1219 (the Ocean is called the "abode of the Asuras": *Asurāṇām ca bāndhavam*, i.e. *çaraṇam*, Nīl., I, **21**, 7).—§ 31 (Samudradarç.): I, **22**, 1231 (*Pātālajvalanāvāsam A°āṇām tathālayam*).—§ 32 (Kadrū, Garuḍa): I, **23**, 1245 (°*ārdanāḥ*, i.e. the gods).—§ 44 (Garuḍa): I, **30**, 1418 (*saṅgrāme devāsure*), 1434 (°*puravidāraṇāḥ surāḥ*).—§ 49 (Vāsuki): I, **39**, 1643 (*devāsurāḥ*).—§ 84 (Ādivaṃç.): I, **64**, 2481 (*jajñire kshetre rājñān tu*), 2483 (*jajñire bhuvi bhūteshu teshu teshv Asurā, vibho!*), 2491 (*mahā°*), 2498 (*surā°-lokānām*).—§ 96 (Aṃçāvat.): I, **65**, 2541 (*Danāyushaḥ punaḥ putrāç catvāro 'surapuṅgavāḥ*).—§ 98 (do.): I, **65**, 2544 (*Asurāṇām upādhyāyaḥ Çukras tv ṛshisuto 'bhavat|khyātāç çoçanasaḥ putrāç catvāro 'sura-yājakāḥ*), 2546.—§ 118 (Aṃçāvat.): I, **66**, 2598 (*Kaçyapasya Surāsurāḥ*).—§ 130 (Aṃçāv.): I, **67**, 2647 (*pañcamahā°*), 2655 (*Tuhuṇḍa ita vikhyāto . . . Asurottamaḥ*, incarnated as king Bṛhadratha), 2656 (*teshām*), 2666 (*teshām*), 2694 (v. Sūrya[2]).—§ 131 (do.): I, **67**, 2781 (*devā°manushyāṇām*).—§ 145 (Kaca): I, **76**, 3187, 3191, 3200 (°*endrapure Çukram dṛshṭvā*), 3219, 3225, 3233, 3238; **77**, 3265.—§ 146 (Devayānī): I, **78**, 3304 (°*mandiram*); **80**, 3340, 3342 (*endrāṇām*); **81**, 3367 (°*guruḥ Çukro*), 3369 (°*endrasutā*, i.e. Çarmishṭhā).—§ 147 (do.): I, **83**, 3442 (°*dharmam*).—§ 165 (Satyavatīl.): I, **100**, 4002, 4047 (*yasya hi tvam sapatnaḥ syā Gandharvasyāsurasya vā*).—§ 166 (Citrāṅgadop.): I, **101**, 4073.—§ 167 (Vicitravīryop.): I, **102**, 4104 (adject.: *devāsura*).—§ 175 (Karṇasambhav.): I, **111**, 4410.—§ 215 (Bakavadhap.): I, **160**, 6208 (*Asurarāṭ* = Baka).—§ 233 (Svayaṃvarap.): I, **187**, †7017.—§ 257 (Khāṇḍavadahanap.): I, **225**, 8202 (*surā°*).—§ 258 (do.): I, **227**, 8256, 8262 (*Asurasūdanaḥ* = Indra).—§ 264 (Sabhākriyāp.): II, **4**, 118 (*yathā°ān Kālakeyān*).—§ 265 (Lokapālasabhākhy°): II, **5**, 141 (*Surā°ān*).—§ 277 (Jarāsandhavadhap.): II, **22**, 872.—§ 298 (Dyūtap.): II, **62**, 2105 (*mahā°*).—§ 310 (Āraṇyakap.): III, **3**, †159.—§ 317 (Arjunābhigamanap.): III, **12**, 487.—§ 320 (Saubhavadhop.): III, **20**, 799.—§ 327 (Draupadīparitāpav.): III, **31**, 1188; **33**, 1323, 1349 (*Asurān iva Vṛtrahā*).—§ 331 (Kairātap.): III, **39**, 1590 (sg.), 1626 (*sadevā°mānushaiḥ*).—§ 334 (do.): III, **41**, 1703 (*Mahā°*).—§ 339 (Indralokābhigamanap.): III, **47**, 1893 (*kecin Nivātakavācāḥ*), 1899.—§ 378 (Tīrthay.): III, **94**, 8492 (*dharman tatyajire*), 8493 (*tīrthāni nāviçan*), 8496 (*Alakshmīr agamad A°ān*).—§ 387 (Sagara): III, **107**, 8873 (*A°oragarakshāṃsi*).—§ 405 (Sukanyop.): III, **124**, 10390 (*surā°aiḥ*).—§ 418 (Tīrthay.): III, **139**, 10834 (*devā°ebhyaḥ*).—§ 436 (Yakshay.): III, **158**, 11530 (*surā°nishevitam*).—§ 444 (Nivātakav.): III, **170**, 12112, 12116, 12121 (*mahā°*); **171**, 12157 (°*ottamāḥ*); **172**, 12182 (°*saṅgheshu*).—§ 445 (do.): III, **173**, 12201, 12206 (*maharshi-Yaksha-Gandharva-Pannagā°-Rākshasaiḥ*), 12209 (*Kālakeyaiç ca Paulomaiç ca mahā°*), 12228, 12257 (*surā°air*), 12264 (*mahā°*), 12269 (*atidevā°karmā*), 12272 (*sa-Yakshā°-Gandharvaiḥ*).—§ 452 (Mārkaṇḍeyas.): III, **183**, †12569 (°*tarjanena Dhanañjayena*).—§ 457 (Vaivasvatop.): III, **187**, 12798 (*sa-devā°-mānushāḥ prajāḥ*).—§ 458 (Mārkaṇḍeyas.): III, **188**, 12817 (*devā°gaṇe*), 12877 (*sa-devā°-D°*).—§ 459 (do.): III, **188**, 12891 (*devā°gaṇe*); **189**, 12995 (*surā°aiḥ*).—§ 462 (do.): III, **193**, 13216 (*devā°saṅgrāmam*).—§ 471 (do.): III, **200**, 13427 (*Vajrapāṇir iv Āsurān*).—§ 474 (Dhundhumārop.): III, **201**, 13494 (*sasurā°-mānavāḥ prajāḥ*), 13498 (*devā°-mahoragāḥ*), 13502.—§ 495 (Skandotp.): III, **223**, 14243 (*devā°āḥ*); **224**, 14262 (*surā°-namaskṛtaḥ*).—§ 496 (do.): III, **224**, 14268 (*devā°ṃ saṅgrāmam*).—§ 507 (Skandayuddha): III, **231**, 14580, 14585 (*mahā°*).—§ 509 (Kārttikeyastava): III, **232**, 14640 (*tvam bhāvanaḥ sarva-surā°āṇām*, i.e. Skanda).—§ 513 (Ghoshayātr.): III, **252**, 15165 (*Bhīshma-Droṇa-Kṛpādīmç ca pravekshyanty apare 'surāḥ*).—§ 516 (Duryodhanayajña): III, **257**, 15341 (°*vratam*, i.e. *surarahitam vratam*, Nīl.).—§ 526 (Rāmopākhyānap.): III, **275**, 15913 (*Gandharva-devā°to*); **276**, 15932 (*devā°aiḥ*).—§ 537 (do.): III, **285**, 16374 (*devā°* = the war between the gods and the Asuras).—§ 543 (do.): III, **291**, 16578 (*mānushā°-bhoginaṃ*), 16579 (*sadevā°-G°*).—§ 544 (do.): III, **292**, 16604 (*surā°*)-§ 548 (Āraṇeyap.): III, **313**, 17319.—§ 549 (Pāṇḍavapr.). IV, **6**, 180.—§ 550 (Samayapāl.): IV, **13**, 340 (*Kālakhañjā ivā°āḥ*).—§ 552 (Goharaṇap.): IV, **32**, 1040 (*devā°samo*); **35**, 1167 (*Vajrapāṇir ivāsurān*); **39**, 1295 (*sarvair api surā°aiḥ*); **50**, 1571; **59**, 1902 (*devā°samaḥ sannipāto*); **61**, 1981 (*Vajrapāṇir ivā°ān*).—§ 555 (Indra): V, **10**, 292 (*sa-devā°-mānusham tribhuvanam*), 309 (= do.); **12**, 369 (*jagad sāsura-G°*); **15**, 459.—§ 558 (Virocana): V, **35**, 1199.—§ 560 (Sanatsujātap.): V, **42**, †1580 (*pramādād vai parābhavan*).—§ 561 (Yānasandhip.): V, **48**, †1887; **49**, 1925, 1927 (*devā°e yuddhe*), 1936 (*surā°*); **61**, 2395 (*devā°-bhāvānām*), 2401.—§ 562 (Bhagavadyānap.): V, **74**, 2728; **78**, 2808.—§ 564 (do.): V, **100**, 3571 (*A° Kālakhañjāç ca tathā Vishṇupadodbhavāḥ*, etc.); **102**, 3612 (*devair A°-saṃhitaiḥ*); **104**, 3645 (*devā°eshu yuddheshu*).—§ 565 (Gālavacarita): V, **107**, 3756 (*sarvān surā°ān*); **108**, 3776; **115**, 3928; **116**, 3940 (*bahu-devā°-ālokā*).—§ 567 (Bhagavadyānap.): V, **124**, 4172 (*sarvair api surā°aiḥ*), 4175 (*sa-Yakshā°-pannagān*); **128**, 4301, 4302 (*devā°-manushyāç ca*); **130**, 4401, 4407 (*mahā°*).—§ 570 (Sainyaniryānap.): V, **156**, 5297 (*sa-surā°-Rākshasam jagat*).—§ 572 (Rathātirath.): V, **165**, 5725 (*devāsureshv api*).—§ 573 (Ambop.): V, **178**, 7031 (*jahi Bhīshmam raṇe Rāma garjantam A°m yathā*); **184**, 7288 (*sa-devā°-Rākshase loke*).—§ 574 (Jambūkh.): VI, **6**, 212 (*G°Ā°Rā°*), 247 (*devāsurāṇām sarveshām Çvetaparvata ucyate*).—§ 576 (Bhagavadgītāp.): VI, **21**, 774 (*surā°*); **35**, †1268 (*G°-Y°-Ās°-Si°-saṅghāḥ*).—§ 578 (Bhīshmavadh.): VI, **45**, 1754 (*praikshanta tad raṇam ghoram devāsura-samam yudhi*); **48**, 1900 (*Cakrapāṇir iv Āsurān*); **50**, 2073 (*yam Bṛhaspatir Indrāya tadā devāsure 'bravīt*).—§ 579 (do.): VI, **52**, 2185 (*devāsura-Gandharvair lokair*).—§ 580 (do.): VI, **58**, 2474 (*yathā devāsuram yuddham*).—§ 581 (do.): VI, **65**, 2970 (*tatrāsuravadham kṛtvā*); **66**, 2980.—§ 583 (do.): VI, **77**, 2348 (*devā°e yuddhe*); **79**, 3474 (do.); **80**, †3529 (*mahā°*).—§ 584 (do.): VI, **82**, 3631 (*Vajrapāṇir ivā°m*); **83**, 3649 (*devā°opamam*); **86**, 3828 (*Vajrapāṇir ivā°ān*).—§ 585 (do.): VI, **94**, 4250; **98**, 4450 (*sa-devā°-G°-lokam*), 4493 (*yathā devā°yuddhe*).—§ 586 (do.): VI, **100**, 4583 (*yathā devā°e yuddhe*); **107**, 4960 (*sendrair api surā°aiḥ*), 4961 (do.).—§ 587 (do.): VI, **108**, 5027 (*Vajrahastam ivā°āḥ*); **116**, 5411 (*yathā devā°e yuddhe*); **118**, 5567 (*yuddhe devā°opame*).—§ 588 (do.): VI, **121**, 5804 (*surā°*).—§ 589 (Droṇābhishek.): VII, **3**, 103 (*Vajrapāṇer ivā°ḥ*); **5**, 154 (*jigīshanto 'surān saṅkhye Kārttikeyam ivāmarāḥ*); **10**, 333 (*devā°air*).—§ 590 (do.): VII,

12, 461 (*sendrair api surā°aiḥ*); **14**, 542 (*yathā devā°e yuddhe*); **15**, 583 (*yuddhaṃ devā°opamaṃ*).—§ 592 (Saṃçaptakavadh.): VII, **19**, 758 (*yathā . . . yuddhe devā°e purā*); **21**, 891 (*surā°*); **25**, 1084 (*yuddham . . . devā°opamam*), 1120 (*Indram A°ān prati jaghnushaṃ*); **29**, 1284. — § 593 (Abhimanyuvadhap.): VII, **33**, 1463 (*sa-surā° G°*); **36**, 1579 (*yathā°balaṃ*); **39**, 1647 (*Skandasyevā°aiḥ saha*); **48**, 1915 (*surā°*).—§ 595 (Rāma Dāçar.): VII, **59**, 2229 (*surā°*).—§ 595 (Māndhātṛ): VII, **62**, 2272 (*devā°-*), 2287 (*devā°-*). — § 595 (Yayāti): VII, **63**, 2295 (*devā°yuddha*). — § 595 (Pṛthu Vainya): VII, **69**, 2403 (*devā°-*), 2413 (*Asurā duduhur madyam āmapātre tu te tadā | dogdhā Dvimūrddhā tatrāsīd vatsaç cāsīd Virocanaḥ*).—§ 596 (Pratijñāp.): VII, **73**, †2607 (*A°sura°-*); **74**, 2623 (*Asuroraga-*); **75**, 2661 (do.); **77**, †2731 (*surā°*); **81**, 2910 (*mahā°nighātinā Bhavena*, i.e. Çiva). — § 599 (Jayadrathavadhap.): VII, **93**, 3378 (*°māyāṃ*); **94**, 3444 (*sā°-surāḥ*); **102**, 3821 (*devā°mṛdhe*); **105**, 3947 (*devā°e yuddhe purā*); **106**, 3968 (*devā°opamaḥ saṅgrāmo*); **111**, 4214 (*sa-devā°-mānushaṃ*), 4268 (*sasurā°mānushā*); **114**, 4495 (*yuddhaṃ devā°opamaṃ*); **115**, 4601 (do.); **120**, 4779 (*devā°raṇaprakhyaṃ*); **122**, 4910 (*devā°e purā yuddhe yathā*); **125**, 5065 (*Çakreṇeva mahā°aḥ*); **128**, 5231 (*yuddhaṃ devā°-opamaṃ*); **133**, 5456 (*sa-Yakshāsura-mānavān*); **134**, 5511 (*vajreṇendra ivā°ān*); **135**, 5545 (*Purandara ivāsuraṃ*, i.e. Vṛtraṃ?); **142**, 5886 (*purā devā°e yuddhe . . . yathā*); **144**, 6048 (*devā° G°*).—§ 600 (Ghaṭotkacavadhap.): VII, **156**, 6853 (*A°ān iva Devendro*), 6854 (*A°ān iva Pāvakiḥ*); **158**, 7014 (*sa devā°mānushaṃ*); **159**, 7048 (*surā°āḥ*), 7075 (*yathā devā°e yuddhe*); **163**, †7317 (*surā°*); **169**, 7582 (*yathā devā°e yuddhe*); **170**, 7673 (*Ā°ān iva Pāvakiḥ*); **181**, 8234 (*surā°*). — § 601 (Droṇavadhap.): VII, **185**, 8425 (*sa-surā° G°*), 8444 (*A°oraga-*). — § 602 (Droṇavadhap.): VII, **192**, 8819 (*yuddhe devā°opame*). — § 603 (Nārāyaṇāstram.): VII, **195**, 9001 (*A°oraga-*), 9019 (*Çacīpatir ivā°*); **197**, 9101 (*D°Ā°oraga-*); **201**, 9442, 9465 (*surā°*), 9473 (*devāsura°*); **202**, 9543, 9547 (*surā°*), 9555 (*°āṇāṃ purāṇi trīṇi*), 9561, 9571 (*°āṇām antakaraḥ*, i.e. Çiva). — § 604 (Karṇap.): VIII, **9**, 254 (*Vajrahasta ivā°ān*).—§ 605 (do.): VIII, **12**, 441 (*devā°samaprabhe*); **14**, 563 (*yathā devā°e yuddhe*); **19**, 769 (*Çakra ivā°ān*); **30**, 1205 (*saṅgrāmaṃ devā°*); **31**, 1319 (*surā°*). — § 606 (Tripurākhy.): VIII, **33**, 1301 (*yuddhe devā°e*), 1393, 1399, 1432; **34**, 1539, 1547, 1566, 1569 (*°gaṇān*), 1574 (*devā°gaṇādhyakshaḥ*, i.e. Maheçvaraḥ), 1578. — § 606*b* (Paraçu-Rāma): VIII, **34**, 1605 (*mahā°*).—§ 606 (Karṇap.): VIII, **35**, 1626.—§ 607 (do.): VIII, **37**, †1742 (*A°-sura-mahoragāḥ*); **41**, 1959 (*devā°-manushyeshu*); **42**, 1978 (*surā°*).—§ 608 (do.): VIII, **46**, 2148 (*devā°camūpamaḥ*), 2199 (*surā°*); **47**, 2233 (*devā°samaḥ*); **48**, 2273 (*devā°opamaṃ*); **51**, 2493 (*vishṇur ivā°ān*); **60**, 3024 (*devā°e mṛdhe*); **61**, 3130 (*vajreṇendra ivā°ān*); **66**, 3310 (*jitā°am ivāmarau* = Vṛtra?); **72**, †3629 (*surā°*); **73**, 3641 (*sa-surā°mānushān*); **74**, †3800; **77**, †3864 (*iva*); **79**, †4056 (*sa-Kālakeyān A°ān sametān*); **82**, †4207 (*yathā*); **86**, 4359 (*sa-D°Ā° Ga°*); **87**, 4412, 4432, 4434 (sided with Karṇa); **88**, †4490 (*D°N°Ās°Si°Y°air*), †4494 (*yathā*), †4498 (*surā°*); **89**, †4568; **91**, †4789 (*nārāçva N°Ā°*), 4791 (*devā°ān*).—§ 609 (Çalyap.): IX, **1**, 9 (*devā°raṇopamaṃ*). —§ 610 (do.): IX, **3**, 185 (do.); **7**, 323 (*sa-surā°mānavaṃ*), 331 (do.).—§ 611 (do.): IX, **9**, 413 (*devā°opamaṃ*), 446 (*devāsuropame*); **10**, 520 (*yathā devā°aṃ yuddhaṃ*); **15**, 795 (*yathā . . . çakrasyā°saṅkshaye*); **23**, 1182 (*devā°-raṇopamam*): **26**, 1436 (*Sahasrāksha ivā°ān*). — § 615*j* (Maṅkaṇaka): IX, **38**, 2236 (*surā°sya jagato gatis tvam asi, Çūladhṛk!*).—§ 615 (Baladevatīrthay.): IX, **41**, 2346, 2347. —§ 615*u* (Skanda): IX, **45**, 2523, 2529 (*devā°e yuddhe*).— § 615*gg* (Sārasvata): IX, **51**, 2951 (*mahā°*).—§ 615 (Gadāyuddhap.): IX, **58**, 3250; **61**, 3455 (*devair A°ghātibhiḥ*); **63**, 3519 (*devā°e yuddhe*).—§ 616 (Sauptikap.): X, **4**, 155 (*mahā°*); **8**, 441.—§ 621 (Rājadh.): XII, **8**, 229 (*devā°ṃ yathā*, i.e. the conduct of D. and A.).—§ 632 (Shoḍacarājop., cf. Bhagīratha): XII, **29**, 957 (*°āṇāṃ sahasrāṇi . . . ajayat Pākaçāsanaḥ*).—§ 632 (do., cf. Yayāti): XII, **29**, 990 (*vyūḍhā°yuddhe*).—§ 635 (Rājadh.): XII, **33**, 1184 (*yuddhe devā°e purā; A°ā bhrātaro jyeshṭhā devā çcāpi yavīyasaḥ*).— § 637 (do.): XII, **47**, 1623 (*surā° G°*).—§ 639 (do.): XII, **50**, 1830.—§ 640 (do.): XII, **58**, 2105 (*utthānenā°āhatāḥ*). —§ 641 (do.): XII, **64**, †2410 (*urvīṃ sā°āṃ*); **90**, 3388 (*devā°*); **121**, 4411 (*sa-surā°mānushaṃ*), 4466 (*sa-surā°-rakshasāṃ lokānāṃ*); **122**, 4497 (*apāṃ rājye 'surāṇāñ ca vidadhe Varuṇaṃ prabhuṃ*).—§ 647 (Āpaddh.): XII, **139**, 5188 (*devā°*).—§ 652*b* (Indrota-Pārikshitīya): XII, **152**, †5667 (*surā°*).—§ 655 (Āpaddh.): XII, **158**, 5890.—§ 656 (Khaḍgotpattik.): XII, **166**, 6150 (*°sattamāḥ*), 6176.— § 660 (Mokshadh.): XII, **188**, 6932 (*Dai° Ā°m-o°*).—§ 664 (do.): XII, **207**, 7545 (*mahāsattvān*).—§ 666 (do.): XII, **209**, 7610 (*Narakādyā mahā°, tathaiva cānye bahavo Dānavā yuddhadurmadāḥ*).—§ 667 (do.): XII, **210**, 7657 (*N° Ā°-manushyāṃç ca*), 7665 (*surā°*); **211**, 7693 (do.); **216**, 7837 (*tapo hy adhishṭhitaṃ devais, tapoghnam A°ais tamas*), 7838 (*devā°guṇān*). — § 671*b* (Bali-Vāsavas.): XII, **223**, 8060 (*devā°*); **225**, 8179 (*devā°ṃ yuddhaṃ*), 8180 (*devā°e yuddhe*) —§ 672*b* (Mokshadh.): XII, **226**, †8201 (*mahā°*).—§ 673*b* (Bali-Vāsavas.): XII, **227**, 8218 (*devā°e yuddhe*), 8289 (*devā°samāgame*), †8330.—§ 674 (Çrī-Vāsavas.): XII, **229** 8359 (*Asureshv avasaṃ pūrvaṃ*, says Çrī), 8416. — § 692 (Mokshadh.): XII, **281**, 10069 (*A°pravīra*, i.e. Vṛtra).— § 693 (Vṛtravadha): XII, **282**, 10108 (*devā°*), 10119 (*Dai° Ā°nibarhaṇa*, i.e. Indra), 10140.—§ 700 (Mokshadh.): XII, **289**, 10652.—§ 701 (do.): XII, **290**, 10660.—§ 702 (do.): XII, **296**, 10800.—§ 714 (Çukakṛtya): XII, **328**, 12323 (*sā°Rā°devagaṇaṃ*).—§ 717*b* (Nārāyaṇīya): XII, **335**, 12665 (*sa-D° Ā° G°*).—§ 717*c* (Uparicara): XII, **338**, 12889 (*surā°gurur Hariḥ*). — § 717*b* (Nārāyaṇīya): XII, **340** 12927 (*surā°gaṇānāṃ varadaḥ*, i.e. Brahmán), 12944 (*sarvalokānāṃ sa-D°Ā°Ra°*), 12992 (*Surā°air yathā*); **341**, 13012 (*sa-sura°-mānavāḥ*).—§ 717*b* (Nārāyaṇīya): XII, **343**, II) ††13205, VII) ††13208, VIII) ††13212 (*A°pakshaḥ*, X) ††13219, ϕ†13249; **347**, ††13445 (*Harir A°vadhakaraḥ*).— § 718*b* (Uñchavṛttyup.): XII, **352**, 13732 (*surā°*); **361**, 13866 (*surā°gaṇānāṃ*); **364**, 13922. — § 728 (Bhaṅgāsvanop.): XIII, **12**, 556 (*Kaçyapasya surā°āḥ*), 557.— § 730 (Ānuçāsanik.): XIII, **14**, 612 (*A°ghnaḥ . . . Bhagavato*, i.e. Çiva), 671 (*°endrān*), 803 (*devā°*), 804, 814 (*surā°*), †1020 (*surā°*); **16**, 1041 (*devā°munīnāṃ*), 1065 (do.), 1074 (*devā°manushyāṇāṃ*), 1075 (*devā°narāḥ*); **17**, 1176 (*A°endrāṇāṃ*), 1233 (*Devāsurapatiḥ* = Çiva 1000 names[2]), 1257 (*devā°parāyaṇaḥ, devā°vinirmātā*, both do. do.), 1258 (*Devā°guru* = do. do.; *Devā°namaskṛta* = do. do.; *Devā°mahāmātra* = do. do.; *Devā°gaṇāçrayaḥ*), 1259 (*Devā°gaṇādhyaksha* = do. do.; *Devā°gaṇāgraṇī* = do. do.; *Devā°varapradaḥ* = do. do.), 1260 (*Devā°eçvara* = do. do.). —§ 735 (Indra-Mataṅgas.): XIII, **27**, 1895 (*devatā°-martyeshu*). — § 736*b* (Vītahavyop.): XIII, **30**, 1959 (*yuddhaṃ . . . devā°samaṃ*). — § 739 (Ānuçāsan.): XIII, **33**, 2098; **35**, 2160 (*brāhmaṇānāṃ paribhavād*

Asurāḥ salileçayāḥ). — § 740 (do.): XIII, **36**, 2175 (*devāsuraṃ purā*).—§ 744 (do.): XIII, **44**, 2410.—§ 746 (do.): XIII, **62**, 3197; **83**, 3886 (*devā° Suparṇāç ca*), 3923 (*A°sūdana*, i.e. Indra). — § 747 (do.): XIII, **84**, 4013; **85**, 4020, 4181 (*jaghāna Tārakaṃ cāpi Daityam anyāṃs tathā Asurān*). — § 748*b* (Tārakavadhop.): XIII, **86**, 4211.— § 749 (Ānuçāsan.): XIII, **87**, 4224 (*devā°manushyāṇām*).— § 766 (do.): XIII, **126**, 6010 (*jagat sa-devā°-mānúshaṃ*); **133**, 6176 (*trīn lokān sa-devā°mānushān*).—§ 768*b* (Kṛshṇa-Vāsudeva): XIII, **147**, 6809 (*romabhyaç ca surāsurāḥ*).— § 768 (Ānuçāsan.): XIII, **148**, 6890.—§ 769 (Ānuçāsan.): XIII, **149**, 7071 (*sa-surā° G°aṃ . . . jagat*).—§ 772*k* (Agastya): XIII, **156**, 7266, 7274, 7275.—§ 772*m* (Atri): XIII, **157**, 7294, 7295, 7301 (*mahā°*), 7302 (*hatā°*).— § 773*b* (Kṛshṇa): XIII, **159**, †7366, †7371 (*Daityān Asurāṃç ca sarvān*), †7373, †7395.—§ 773*d* (Çiva): XIII, **161**, 7467, 7471 (*surā°*), 7482 (*A°āṇāṃ purāṇi trīṇi*), 7488. —§ 775 (Ānuçāsan.): XIII, **166**, 7634 (*devā°-gurur*= Brahmán).—§ 777 (Svargārohaṇ.): XIII, **168**, 7742 (*surā°-namaskṛta*). — § 778 (Açvamedhik.): XIV, **3**, 46.—§ 778*b* (Saṃvartta-Mar.): XIV, **5**, 94; **9**, †224.—§ 782 (Brāhmaṇagītā): XIV, **26**, 752, 755.—§ 782*g* (Guruçishyas.): XIV, **42**, †1169 (*surā°āç ca*); **51**, 1434 (*Pç°ā° Ra°*).—§ 785 (Anugītāp.): XIV, **79**, 2321 (*devā°raṇaprakhyaṃ*).—§ 788 (Āçramavāsikap.): XV, **28**, 753.—§ 789 (Putradarçanap.): XV, **29**, 779 (*devā°vimiçritāḥ*). — § 795*c* (Mahābhārata): XVIII, **6**, 218 (*jagat surā°*, is to be found in the Mahābhārata). — Seems to have been totally synonymous with *Dānava* and *Daitya*.

Asura[2], sg. (cf. Asura[1]): XII, 8164 (v. Çrī), 13918 (v. Uñchavṛtti). — § 747*b* (Suvarṇotp.): XIII, **85**, 4073 (*A°aḥ kaçcit*).—Names of single Asuras:

Açva: I, 2649 (*mahā°*).
Bali: III, †976, 8759 (*mahā°*); XII, 8182 (do.), 8324, 12943 (do.).
Balina: I, 2679 (*°ottamaḥ*).
Bāṇa: I, 2528 (*mahā°*).
Bhagadatta: VII, 1290 (*mahā°*).
Candrahantṛ: I, 2673 (*pravaro 'suraḥ*).
Çarabha: I, 2663 (*mahā°*).
Çatamukha: XIII, 674 (*mahā°*).
Çaṭha: I, 2537 (*mahā°*).
Damça: XII, 93 (*prāg D°; mahā°*).
Dhundhu: III, 13511 (*mahā°*), 13541, 13543 (*mahā°*), 13598, 13613.
Ekacakra: I, 2657 (*mahā°*).
Gavishṭha: I, 2670 (*mahā°*).
Hiraṇyakaçipu: I, 7620.
Hiraṇyāksha: IX, 1751 (*mahā°*).
Ilvala: III, 8545, 8616 (*°çreshṭhaḥ*), 8620, 8625, 8628 (*mahā°*), 8629 (do.).
Jambha: III, 8760; VIII, 3304 (*mahā°*).
Jarāsandha: XII, 12961.
Kaiṭabha: IX, 2850; XII, 13477, 13506.
Kāleyāḥ: I, 2684 (*pravaraḥ . . . mahā°*), 2686 (*mahāmāyo mahā°*), 2688 (*pravaro mahā°*), 2689 (*matimān mahā°*).
Keçin: III, 14255, 14259 (*mahā°*).
Krathana: I, 2693 (*mahā°*).
Krodhahantṛ: I, 2681.
Kupatha: I, 2664 (*mahā°*).
Mada: III, 10389 (*mahā°*); XIV, †251 (*A°ṃ viçvarūpaṃ*).
Madhu: VI, 3025 (*mahā°*); IX, 2850 (*°au M°-Kaiṭabhau*); XII, 7531 (*mahā°*), 13477 (*As°ottamau*, i.e. Madhu and Kaiṭabha), 13506 (*°au*).
Maya: I, 2278 (*mahā°*), 8323; II, 3 (*mahā°*), 66, 76 (*mahā°*); VIII, 1406 (*mahā°*).
Mayūra: I, 2671 (*mahā°*).
Mṛtapā: I, 2669 (*°ottamaḥ*).
Namuci: V, 497 (*mahā°*).
Naraka: XII, 7610 (*N°ādyā mahā°āḥ*).
Nicandra: I, 2661 (*°ottamaḥ*).
Pīṭha: VII, 386 (*mahā°*).
Prahlāda: III, 1030 (*Asurendraṃ*).
Sunda: I, 7616 (*°au*, i.e. S° + Upas°), 7635, 7670 (*maha°au*, i.e. do.), 7698 (*°ābhyāṃ*, i.e. do.), 7720 (do. = do.); IX, 1755 (*°au*, i.e. do.).
Sūrya: I, 2694 (*°āṇāṃ*).
Svarbhānu: I, 2648 (*mahā°*).
Tāraka: XIII, 4011, 4015, 4066, 4068, 4205, 4215.
Upasunda: I, 7616, 7670, 7698, 7720; IX, 1755.— Cf. Sunda.
Vātāpi: III, 422 (*mahā°*), 8549, 8551 (*mahā°*), 8617 (*mahā°*), 8618 (do.), 8623 (*mahā°*), 13679 (do.); XII, 5389.
Viçvarūpa: V, 504 (*Trāshṭro mahā°*).
Vikshara: I, 2677 (*pravaro 'suraḥ*), 2678 (*dvitīyo Viksharāt, mahā°*).
Vināçanaḥ Candrasya: I, 2674 (*mahā°*).
Virūpāksha: I, 2658 (*mahā°*).
Vṛshaparvan: I, 3344 (*mahā°*).
Vṛtra: I, 2680 (*mahā°*; III, †8728 (do.); V, 311, 324 (*mahā°*), 327 (do.), 522; VII, 9038 (*mahā°*); XII, 10069 (*A°pravīro*), 10133 (*A°çreshṭhaṃ*), 10138 (*mahā°*), 10149 (do.), 10204 (do.), 10268 (do.).

Asurā, one of the daughters of Prādhā. § 102 (Aṃçāvat.): I, **65**, 2553.

Āsura, adj.: I, 2962 (sc. *vivāha*), 2964 (do.), 2965 (do.); III, 765 (*°īṃ māyāṃ*), 12227 (*puraṃ*); V, 2242 (*vyūhaṃ*), 3549 (*Agniḥ . . . vāribhojanaḥ*); VI, 696 (*vyūhaṃ*, known by Bhīshma), 757 (= do.), 1181 (*°īṃ prakṛtiṃ . . . çritāḥ*), 1406 (*sampadam °īṃ*), 1407 (*°ī*, sc. *sampad*), 1408 (*dvau bhūtasargau loke 'smin daiva Āsura eva ca*), 1421 (*°īshv eva yonishu*), 1432 (*tān viddhy Āsura-niçcayān*), 3193 (*°īm iva Vṛtrahā*), 5009 (*yuddhān*, performed by Bhīshma); VII, 26 (*Ā°īva yathā senā*), 1581 (*°īṃ camūṃ*), 7084 (do.), 7728 (*senām Ā°īṃ Maghavān iva*), 7815 (*astrāṇi*), 8614 (*yuddhaṃ*); VIII, 562 (*°īṃ camūṃ*), 2125 (*senām Ā°īṃ*), 2242 (do.), 2358 (do.), 3687 (= do.); IX, 1016 (*bale*); XII, 2160, 6735 (*nakshatreshu*), 6736 (*°īṃ yoniṃ*), 7544 (*°ī prajā*), 7839 (*guṇau*), 8151 (*°īṃ*), 10112 (*devā°*), 10811 (*bhāvaḥ*), 10812 (*karmāṇi*), 11105 (*vishayān*); XIII, 1382 (*dharmaḥ*), 2412 (id.), 2468 (id.), 2476 (id.), 4289, 4700 (*mālyāni*).

Asuraçreshṭha: (*a*) = Namuci, IX, 2435; (*b*) = Vṛtra, XII, 10133.

Asurādhipa[1] = Bali: XII, 8082; XIII, 4688.

Asurādhipa[2] = Prahlāda: XII, 6667.

Asuradvish, pl.: I, 7662 (v. Sundopasundop.) = the brahmarshis and brahmans.

Asurahan = Çiva: XIII, 612.

Asurarāj ("king of the As.") = Baka: I, 6208.

Asurārdana ("the tormentor of As.") = Indra: I, 8225 (Çatakratum, etc.).

Asurasūdana ("the slayer of As.") = Indra (I, 8262; XII, 3923); = Vishṇu (V, 299).

Asurāyaṇi, a son of Viçvāmitra. § 721b (Viçvāmitrop.): XIII, 4β, 255 (*ṛshiḥ*).

Asurendra ("king of As."): (*a*) = Bali, XIII, 4290, 4741; (*b*) = Prahlāda, XII, 4602, 8057; (*c*) = Vṛtra, XII, 10028, 10060, 10110; (*d*) °*au* = Madhu and Kaiṭabha, XII, 13518.

Asurendrasutā = Çarmishṭhā: I, 3369.

Asurī ("a female Asura"): I, 3286 (= Çarmishṭhā); III, 12203 (= *Kālakā mahāsurī*); IV, 260.

Āsuri. § 668b (Pañcaçikhavākya): XII, **218**, 7890 (*Ā°eḥ prathamaṃ çishyam*, i.e. Pañcaçikha), 7893, 7894 (his wife was Kapilā).—§ 707 (Mokshadh.): XII, **319**β, 11784.

Asūrya ("sunless"). § 746 (Ānuçāsan.): XIII, **77**, 3700 (*asūryā nāma te lokā gāṃ dattvā tān na gacchati*).

Ataka (*Ā*°?), a Nāga. § 66 (Sarpasattra): I, **57**, 2154 (among the serpents of Kauravya's race that fell into the fire).

Atandrita = Çiva (1000 names[1]).

Atapana = Çiva (1000 names[1]).

Aṭavī. § 284 (Sahadeva): II, **31**a, 1175 (*purīṃ ramyāṃ*, a city conquered by Sahadeva).

Aṭavīçikhara, pl. § 574 (Jambūkh.): VI, **9**μ, 355 (a people—country—in Bharatavarsha).

Atavika, pl. (°*āḥ*) ("people dwelling in the forest"). § 613 (Gadāyuddh.): IX, **32**a, 1820 (*pṛthivī sarvā sa-Mlecchāṭavikā*).

Atharva = Çiva: XIII, 901; do. (C.) or *Ā*° (B.), pl. = Artharvaveda: XIII. 4706.

Atharvaçiras[1], an Upanishad (v. BR.): I, 2882; III, 17066; XIII, 4298. Do.[2] = Mahāpurusha (Ma° Pu°st°).

Atharvaçīrsha = Çiva (1000 names[2]).

Atharvan[1] (a ṛshi). § 493 (Āṅgirasa): III, **222**, 14215 (finds out Agni in the sea), 14218, 14225, 14226, 14227.—§ 560 (Sanatsujātap.): V, **43**, †1670.—§ 606 (Tripurākhy.): VIII, **34**, 1497 (*Atharvāṅgirasau*).—§ 730 (Ānuçāsan.): XIII, **14**ββ, 991 (*sa-Bṛhaspatiḥ*).

Atharvan[2] = Atharvaveda: XII, 13136 (*Ṛgvede sa-Yajurvede 'thaivātharva-Sāmasu*), 13258 (*pañcakalpam Atharvāṇam kṛtyābhiḥ parivṛṃhitam*); XIII, 4590 (*vedam*).

Atharvan[3], pl. = Atharvaveda: III, 12963 (*Atharvaṇaḥ*); V, 1711 (*Atharvasu*); XII, 8613.

Ātharvaṇa ("belonging to or named after Atharvan"): V, 1391; VII, 2051 (*sthānam Ātharvaṇasya*); VIII, 1848, †4625 ("which in efficacy equalled an Atharvan rite," PCR.); XIII, 1086 (*Ātharvaṇā dvijāḥ*).

Atharvāṇa = Atharvaveda: XII, 13259 (°*vidaḥ*).

Atharvāṅgiras = Aṅgiras. § 555 (Indravijaya): V, **18**, 549 (°*e*), 551 (°*am*).

Atharvāṅgirasa[1] = Aṅgiras: II, 437 (?; in the palace of Brahmán); V, 550 (°*o nāma vede 'smin vai bhavishyati*). Do.[2], adj.: VIII, 3488 (*Atharvāṅgirasī çrutiḥ*), 4795 (*kṛtyām °īm iv ogrām*); IX, 907 (= do.).

Atharvāṅgirasaḥ (pl.), a kind of ṛshis? (II, 437; = Atharvaveda?).

Atharvāṅgirasāḥ (pl.): XII, 12736 (*Yajur-Ṛk-Sāmabhir jushṭam Atharvāṅgirasais tathā*, i.e. Atharvaveda).

Atharvaveda: I, 2883 (°*pravarāḥ*); II, 450; III, 15147 (°*proktaiḥ*); V, 548 (°*mantraiḥ*); XIII, 469 (°*vede vede ca*).

Athida, v. Alinda.

Atibāhu. § 103 (Aṃçāvat.): I, **65**, 2559 (among four Gandharvasattamāḥ, whose mother was Prādhā).

Atibala[1]. § 615u (Skanda): IX, **45**, 2546 (given to Skanda by Vāyu).

Atibala[2]. § 641b (Rājadh.): XII, **59**, 2213 (*Anangaputra*): Obtaining an extensive empire after the demise of his father, he became a slave of his passions.

Atibhīma. § 492 (Āṅgirasa): III, **220**, 14166 (among the five yajñamushaḥ devāḥ "of the gods").

Atiçṛṅga. § 615u (Skanda): IX, **45**, 2551 (given to Skanda by Vindhya; PCR. has Agniçṛṅga).

Atidhūmra = Çiva (1000 names[2]).

Atidīpta = Çiva (1000 names[2]).

Atikāla = Çiva (1000 names[1]).

Atikṛcchra = Mahāpurusha (Ma° Pu°st°).

Atīndra = Vishṇu (1000 names).

Atīndriya = Vishṇu (1000 names).

Atiratha. § 150 (Pūruv.): I, **94**. 3704 (among the sons of Matināra).

Atisāra, v. Abhisāra.

Atishaṇḍa. § 793 (Mausalap.): XVI, **4**η, 120 (among the nāgas who received the white Nāga who issued from the mouth of Bala-Rāma).

Atishṭhira. § 615u (Skanda): IX, **45**, 2550 (given to Skanda by Manu).

Ātithi(n). § 632b (Shoḍarājop.): XII, **29**, 917 (*Suhotrañ caivātithinaṃ mṛtaṃ çuçruma Sṛñjaya*); 921 (*atho 'tithiḥ*; = Suhotra).

Ativarcas. § 615u (Skanda): IX, **45**, 2548 (given to Skanda by Himavat).

Ativṛddha = Çiva (1000 names[2]).

Atiyaças = Kṛshṇa: XII, 13139.

Atiyama. § 615u (Skanda): IX, **45**, 2547 (given to Skanda by Varuṇa).

***Ātman**[1] (the Supreme Soul): IX, 2352; do.[2] = Çiva (1000 names[2]), Kṛshṇa (XIV, 1491).

Ātmanirāloka = Çiva (1000 names[2]).

Ātmasambhava = Çiva (1000 names[2]).

Ātmastha = Kṛshṇa: XII, 1641.

Ātmavat = Vishṇu (1000 names).

Ātmayoni[1] = Kṛshṇa: XII, 1623; XIII, 7392, 7395; do.[2] = Vishṇu (1000 names).

Ātreya[1] (descendant or descendants of Atri). § 59 (Sarpasattra): I, **53**a, 2048.—§ 324 (Dvaitavanapr.): III, **26**, 971 (pl.) (in the speech of Baka Dālbhya: perform their religious practice in the forest protected by Yudhishṭhira).—§ 376 (Tīrthay.): III, **85**, 8236 (among the ṛshis who expect Yudhishṭhira at the Tīrthayātrā).—§ 461 (Vāmadevacar.): III, **192**, ††13184 (disciple of Vāmadeva).—§ 559 (Prajāgarap.): V, **36**, 1260 (*Ā°sya ca saṃvādaṃ Sādhyānāṃ ceti*).—§ 637 (Rājadh.): XII, **47**η, 1594 (among the ṛshis who surround Bhīshma on his arrow-bed).—§ 665 (Mokshadh.): XII, **208**ι, 7598 (one of the seven ṛshis in the North).—§ 677 (do.): XII, **285**, 8502 (*Indradamanaḥ*), 8596 (*Sāṅkṛtiḥ*).—§ 767 (Ānuçāsan.): XIII, **137**a, 6247 (among the pious princes, etc., who have attained to heaven by charity and penances).—§ 793 (Mausalap.): XVI, **4**, †124 (i.e. Durvāsas).

Ātreya[2], pl. (°*āḥ*). § 574 (Jambūkh.): VI, **9**o, 376 (among the peoples in Bharatavarsha in the North and East)

Ātreyī[1]. § 268 (Varuṇasabhāv.): II, **9**, 374 (among the rivers in the palace of Varuṇa in their personified forms).

Ātreyī[2] (a kind of menstruating woman, v. BR.). § 655 (Āpaddh.): XII, **165**, 6094 (*dviguṇā brahmahatyā vai Ā° nidhane bhavet*).

Atri[1], a ṛshi. § 30b (Samudra): I, **21**, 1217 (*brahmarshiṇā*).—§ 86 (Aṃçāvat.): I, **65**, 2518 (one of the six maharshis,

Brahmán's spiritual sons).—§ 109 (Aṃçāvat.): I, **66**, 2568 (among the sons of Brahmán, *maharshayaḥ*).—§ 111 (do.): I, **66**, 2570 (has many sons, all of them *siddhāḥ, maharshayaḥ*).—§ 130 (do.): I, **67**, 2721 (his—i.e. Vivasvat's, Nīl.—son is born in the world as Vidura; cf. I, 4807).—§ 191 (Arjuna): I, **123a**, 4807 (*yaç codito bhāskare 'bhūt pranashṭe*).—§ 228 (Aurvop.): I, **181**, 6872 (rescues the Rā. from the sacrifice of Parāçara).—§ 270 (Brahmasabhāv.): II, **11**, 436 (among the *Prajānāṃ patayaḥ*, etc., who surround Brahmán in his palace).—§ 347 (Nalop.): III, **64**, 2462 (*Vaçishṭha-Bhṛgv-Atri-samaiḥ . . . tāpasaiḥ*).—§ 455 (Brāhmaṇamāh.): III, **185**: His discourse with Gautama as to who is to be styled the foremost of sovereigns; he gets large gifts from king Vainya: (12684), 12691, 12709, 12713.—§ 494 (Āngirasa): III, **222**, 14235.—§ 599*e* (Çini): VII, **144**, 6028 (*Atreḥ putro 'bhavat Somaḥ*, etc.).—§ 602 (Droṇavadhap.): VII, **190ν**, 8727.—§ 615 (Baladevatīrthay.): IX, **43**, †2447 (had been the hotṛ at Soma's Rājasūya sacrifice).—§ 615*u* (Skanda): IX, **45γ**, 2512.—§ 656 (Khaḍgotp.): XII, **166a**, 6135 (among the sons of Brahmán); *β*, 6142 (among those who accepted the eternal religion laid down in the Vedas).—§ 664 (Mokshadh.): XII, **207δ**, 7534 (among the spiritual sons of Brahmán).—§ 665 (do.): XII, **208a**, 7570 (among the seven sons of Brahmán), 7572 (°-*vaṃçe*), 7597 (*Atreḥ putraḥ . . . Sārasvataḥ*, among the ṛshis in the West).—§ 667 (do.): XII, **214**, 7786 (*maharshir bhagavān Atrir veda tac-chukra-sambhavaṃ*).—§ 702 (Mokshadh.): XII, **293a**, 10762.—§ 717*b* (Nārāyaṇīya): XII, **335a**, 12685 (among the twenty-one Prajāpatis).—§ 717*c* (Uparicara): XII, **336β**, 12724 (among the seven Ṛshis, the Citraçikhaṇḍins).—§ 717*b* (Nārāyaṇīya): XII, **341ν**, 13040 (among the eight Prakṛtis upon whom all the worlds depend); *ξ*, 13075 (among the seven Mānasāḥ).—§ 730 (Ānuçāsan.): XIII, **14**, 684: The wife of Atri abandoned her husband and sought the protection of Mahādeva, who granted her that she should obtain a son without Atri, 686; *ββ*, 990.—§ 734 (do.): XIII, **26a**, 1761.—§ 746 (do.): XIII, **65γ**, 3289 (*Pitāmahasutaḥ*); **66ζ**, 3332.—§ 747 (Suvarṇotp.): XIII, **85ζ**, 4125.—§ 749 (Ānuçāsan.): XIII, **91**, 4329 (*Svāyambhuvaḥ*), 4343–4, 4371.—§ 750*b* (Bisast.): XIII, **93a**, *γ*, *δ*, *ε*, 4416, 4436, 4458 (°*pramukhāḥ maharshayaḥ*), (4462), 4481, (4482), (4514).—§ 770 (Ānuçāsan.): XIII, **151θ**, *ι*, *ν*, 7115 (°*eḥ putraḥ Sārasvataḥ*, one of the seven *Varuṇasya ṛtvijaḥ*, in the West), 7116 (the first of the seven *Dhaneçvarasya guravaḥ*, in the North), 7157 (*Bhṛgv-Angiro-ādibhiḥ*).—§ 772*j* (Utathya): XIII, **155**, 7243 (gave Bhadrā to Utathya).—§ 772*m* (Pavanārjunas.): Vāyu said: Once the gods and Dā. were fighting each other in the dark. Rāhu pierced both Sūrya (the Sun) and Soma (the Moon) with his arrows. The gods repaired to the brahman Ṛ. Atri, who becoming the Moon and Sun dispelled the darkness and burnt the As., who were now slain by the gods. "Namo thou a kshattriya superior to Atri": XIII, **157**, 7291, 7294, 7298, 7299, 7301–4.—§ 775 (Ānuçāsan.); XIII, **166ε**, *ζ*, 7669 (°*eḥ putraḥ Sārasvataḥ*, among the Ṛshis in the West), 7670 (among the Ṛshis in the North).—§ 782 (Guruçishyas.): XIV, **35δ**, 961.

Atri[2]. § 98 (Aṃçāvat.): I, **65**, 2545 (among the four sons of Çukra who were *Asurayājakāḥ*).

Atri[3] = Çiva (1000 names[2])

Atrisuta = the Moon: VIII, 4594.

Atryānamaskartṛ = Çiva (1000 names[2]).

Atulya = Çiva (1000 names[2]), = Vishṇu (1000 names).

Atyugra: X, 259 = Çiva.

Auçanasa ("belonging to or named after Uçanas"). § 370 (Tīrthay.): III, **84**, 8034 (°*īṃ*).—§ 615 (Baladevatīrthay.): IX, **39**, 2249 (*tīrthaṃ Kapālamocanaṃ nāma*), 2261 (*Sarasvatyās tīrthavaraṃ*), 2263 (*tīrthaṃ*; purifies from every sin).—§ 641 (Rājadh.): XII, **122**, 4479 (*çāstraṃ*).—§ 717 (Uparicara): XII, **336**, 12741 (*çāstraṃ*).—§ 759 (Ānuçāsanik.): XIII, **107ζ**, 5298 (*lokaṃ*).

Auçanasī = Devayānī: I, 3376; VII, 2297.

Auçija. § 264 (Sabhākriyāp.): II, **4a**, 112.—Cf. Aushija.

Auçīnara[1] (= Çibi). § 149 (Yayāti): I, **53**, †3669 (*Çibiḥ*), †3680 (do.).—§ 232 (Svayaṃvarap.): I, **186**, 6996 (*Çibiḥ*).—§ 378 (Tīrthay.): III, **94**, 8503 (do.).—§ 463 (Çibi): III, **194**, 13249 (only B.), 13252 (*mahīpatiḥ*).—§ 466 (do.): III, **197**, ††13274 (*Çibiṃ mahīpatiṃ*)—§ 467 (Rājanyamāh.): III, **198**, ††13302 (*Çibiḥ*).—§ 480 (Pativratop.): III, **208**, 13808 (*Çibiḥ*).—§ 545 (Pativratāmāh.): III, **294**, 16674 (*Çibir Au°o yathā*).—§ 562 (Bhagavadyānap.): V, **90ν**, 3146 (*Çibiḥ*).—§ 566 (Yayāti): V, **121**, 4057 (*Çibiḥ*); **122**, 4085 (do.).—§ 574 (Jambūkh.): VI, **9aa**, 314 (*Çibiḥ*).—§ 589 (Droṇābhishek.): VII, **10**, 373 (*Çaibyāt*).—§ 595 (Shoḍaçarājika; v. Çibi): VII, **58**, 2209, 2216 (*tāvatīr adadad gā vai Çibir Au°o 'dhvare*).—§ 599 (Jayadrathap.): VII, **143**, 5998 (*gaccha puṇyakṛtāl lokān Çibir Au°o yathā*).—§ 632*b* (Shoḍaçarājop.; cf. Çibi): XII, **29**, 932 (*Çibiṃ*), 934 (*Çibiḥ*), 936 (*Çaibyād-rājarsher*).—§ 677 (Mokshadh.): XII, **235**, 8593 (*Çibi*; ascended to heaven, having sacrificed his limbs and his son for the sake of a brahman).—§ 761 (Ānuçāsan.): XIII, **115γ**, 5663 (*Çibinā*).—§ 767 (do.): XIII, **137a**, 6248 (*Çibiḥ*; cf. XII, 8593).—§ 786 (Nakulākhy.): XIV, **90**, 2790 (*Çibiḥ*).

Auçīnara[2], adj. ("belonging to the Uçīnaras"). § 565 (Gālavacarita): V, **118**, 3982 (*nṛpaṃ*, i.e. Uçīnara, king of Bhojanagara).

Auçīnari. § 267 (Yamasabhāv.): II, **8**, 325 (in the palace of Yama).—§ 463 (Çibi): III, **194**, 13249 (B. Auçīnara).

Auçīnarī. § 277 (Jarāsandhavadhap.): II, **21**, 802 (*çūdrāyāṃ*; bore by Gautama the sons Kākshīvat, etc.).

Audbhida. § 575 (Bhūmip.): VI, **12ζ**, 453 (the first varsha in Kuçadvīpa).

Auddālaka. § 370 (Tīrthay.): III, **84**, 8139 (a tīrtha).

Auddālaki. § 412 (Ashṭāvakrīya): III, **132**, 10597 (*Çvetaketuḥ*), 10599 (do.).—§ 615 (Saptasārasvata): IX, **38**, IV) 2207 (a ṛshi).—§ 775 (Ānuçāsan.): XIII, **166ζ**, 7671 (*Çvetaketuḥ*; among the ṛshis of the North).

Audra (pl. °*āḥ*). § 574 (Jambūkh.): VI, **9μ**, 365 (a people in Bharatavarsha; B. has *Auṃdrāḥ*).

Audra (pl. °*āḥ*). § 785 (Anugītāp.): XIV, **83**, 2470 (a people vanquished by Arjuna).

Audumbara (pl. °*āḥ*). § 295 (Dyūtap.): II, **52**, 1869 (among the peoples who bring tribute to Yudhishṭhira).

Aupanishada ("belonging to or named after the Upanishads"): XII, 8898 (*dharmaḥ*; printed *Upa°* in C.).

Auraga ("belonging to or named after the Serpents") XII, 11103 (*vishayān*).

Aurasikāḥ (pl.). § 589 (Droṇābhishekap.): VII, **11ν**, 397 (have been vanquished in battle by Kṛshṇa).

Aurva (a ṛshi). § 61 (Sarpasattra): I, **55**, 2112.—§ 122 (Cyavana): I, **66**, son of Cyavana and Ārushī and father of Ṛcīka: 2610 (*Au°s tasyāṃ*—i.e. Ārushī—*samabhavad ūruṃ bhittvā mahāyaçāḥ*), 2613 (had 100 sons *Jamadagni-purogamaṃ*, i.e. Ṛcīka?).—§ 227 (Aurvop.): I, **179**, 6833; **180**, (6842), 6862 (he throws his wrath into the

Ocean).—§ 548*g* (Āraṇeyap.): III, **315**, 17465 (the office that *A*. at one time performed for the gods, concealed in his mother's thigh).—§ 747 (Suvarṇotp.): XIII, **85**η, 4145 (the fourth of Bhṛgu's seven sons).—§ 772*g* (Pavanārjunas.): XIII, **154**, 7223 (Vāyu said: "The mighty kshattriya Ṭālajangha was destroyed by the single [brahman] *A*.").—Cf. Bhārgava, Bhṛgunandana.

Aurva Ākhyāna ("the story relating to Aurva"). § 11 (Parvas.): I, **1**, 387, i.e. Aurvopākhyāna.

Aurvopākhyāna(m) ("the episode relating to Aurva"). § 227 (Parāçara): King Kṛtavīrya, the *yājya* of the *Bhṛgus*, at the end of the *Soma* sacrifice gratified the *brahmans* with large offerings. After he had ascended to heaven, it came to happen that his descendants were in want of wealth. Knowing that the *Bhṛgus* were rich, they went to them and begged. Some amongst the *Bhṛgus* buried their wealth under the earth, some gave it away to *brahmans*, and some duly gave it to the *kshattriyas*. Some *kshattriyas*, while digging at the house of a *Bhārgava*, came upon a large treasure. The *kshattriyas* then began to kill the *Bhṛgus* with their arrows all over the earth, even the embryos. A *Bhṛgu* woman fled to *Himavat*, holding an embryo in one of her thighs ("for 100 years," v. 6822). From fear a *brahman* woman reported this to the *kshattriyas*. The *kshattriyas* then went to destroy that embryo, which, however, came out, tearing open the thigh and dazzling the eyes of the *kshattriyas* so that they lost their sight. They asked the woman that they might be restored to sight, promising to abstain from their sinful practice (I, **178**). She told them to ask the child, which they did, and regaining their eyesights they went away. The child (*viprarshi*) was named *Aurva*, because he had been born after tearing open his mother's thigh (*ūru*). *Aurva* devoted himself to the austerest of penances with the object of destroying the whole world to gratify his ancestors. The *Pitṛs* then all came from *Pitṛloka*, and said: "Be propitious towards the three worlds. Having grown weary with the long periods of life allotted to us, we desired our own destruction through the *kshattriyas*. Such as commit suicide never attain to regions that are blessed, therefore we abstained from self-destruction" (I, **179**). When *Aurva* replied that his vow must not be in vain, the *Pitṛs* prevailed upon him to throw his wrath into the waters of the ocean, the whole universe being made of water. It became a large horse-head, which, emitting fire from its mouth, consumes the waters of the ocean (I, **180**).—§ 228: Hearing this the *viprarshi* Parāçara controlled his wrath from destroying the worlds. But he performed a great *rākshasa* sacrifice and began to burn the *rākshasas* in it, and *Vasishṭha* did not restrain him. Desirous of ending that sacrifice the *ṛshi Atri* came to that place, and also *Pulastya* and *Pulaha* and *Kratu*, desiring to save the *rākshasas*. Seeing that many *rākshasas* had already been slain, *Pulastya* said: "That which befell thy father was brought about by his own curse! No *rākshasa* was capable of devouring *Çakti*; he himself provided for his own death! *Viçvāmitra* was only a blind instrument in that matter. Both *Çakti* and *Kalmāshapāda* have ascended to heaven, and are enjoying great happiness, as also the other sons of *Vasishṭha*. Abandon this sacrifice of thine." *Parāçara* then brought his sacrifice to an end, and threw the fire into the woods on the north of the *Himavat*, where it may be seen to this day consuming *rākshasas* and trees and stones in all seasons (*parvaṇi parvaṇi*) (I, **181**).

Aushadaçvi. § 149 (Yayāti): I, **93**, †3664 (*Vasumān*), †3688.

Aushadha = Vishṇu (1000 names).

***Aushadhi** (pl. °*ayaḥ*, the herbs, personif.): IX, 2518 (cf. *aushadhībhiḥ*, XIII, 454; *oshadhi*?).

Aushija (B. *Auç*°) (= Kākshīvat): XII, 7593 (*K*°); XII, 7108 (*K*°; printed *Aushīja* in C.); XIII, 7663.

Autanka (adj.): XIV, 1627 (*guruvṛttim*).

Auttānapāda: XIII, 195 (*Dhruvasya*).

Avācīna. § 156 (Pūruv.): I, **95**, ††3770, ††377.

Avaça = Çiva (1000 names²).

Avaçavartin: Mahāpurushastave.

Āvaçīrāḥ (pl.). § 515 (Karṇadigvij.): III, **254**, 15244 (a people of the East conquered by Karṇa).

Āvaha. § 754 (Çukakṛtya): XII, **328***q*, 12401: The second wind called *Ā*. blows with a great noise; it is this wind that causes Soma and the other luminaries to rise and appear. Within the body that wind is called Udāna by the wise.

Avākīrṇa (a tīrtha, only in B.). § 615 (Baladevatīrthay.): IX, **41**, 2318

Avantī (a town, i.e. Ujjayinī, v. VP.). § 347 (Nalop.): III, **61**, 2317.

Avanti, pl. (°*ayaḥ*, the people of Avantī). § 377 (Dhaumyatīrthak.): III, **89**, 8354 (B. *Ānarteshu*) (*A°shu pratīçyām vai*).—§ 549 (Pāṇḍavapraveçap.): IV, **1***a*, 12 (*Surāshṭrāvantayas tathā*).—§ 594 (Jambūkh.): VI, **9**μ, 350 (*Kuntayo 'vantayaç ca*, in Bharatavarsha).

Āvantya (inhabitant or king of Avantī).—*a*) sg.: § 296 (Dyūtap.): II, **53**, 1915 (*A°āḥ tv abhishekārtham āpo*— V. *apo—bahuvidhās tathā*).—§ 561 (Yānasandhip.): V, **55**ν, 2206 (*Āvantyo, 'tha Jayadrathaḥ*); **62**ββ, †2426 (*Āvantya-Kāliṅga-Jayadratheshu*).—§ 576 (Bhagavadgītāp.): VI, **16***a*, 622 (*Āvantyo, 'tha Jayadrathaḥ, Vindānuvindau . . .*).—§ 582 (Bhīshmavadhap.): VI, **71**δ, 3138.—§ 585 (do.): VI, **92**χ, 4118, 4135.—§ 599 (Jayadrathav.): VII, **95**, 3535.—§ 609 (Çalyap.): IX, **2**ζ, 72 (*A°o, 'tha Jayadrathaḥ*).—§ 619 (Strīvil.): XI, **22**, 617 (slain by Bhīma), 620.—β) Dual in the phrase *Vindānuvindāv Āvantyau* (brothers): § 281 (Sahadeva): II, **31**β, 1114.—§ 290 (Çiçupālavadhap.): II, **44***a*, 1539.—§ 561 (Yānasandhip.): V, **66**εε, 2503.—§ 572 (Rathātirath.): V, **166**, 5753.—§ 573 (Ambop.): V, **195**δ, 7607.—§ 576 (Bhagavadgītāp.): VI, **17**γ, 673.—§ 578 (Bhīshmavadhap.): VI, **45**ᵅ, 1740; **51**φ, 2107. § 580 (do.): VI, **56**γ, 2408.—§ 584 (do.): VI, **81***a*, 3533, *a*', 3557; **86**ᵉ, 3823.—§ 586 (do.): VI, **102**ι, 4666.—§ 587 (Bhīshmav.): VI, **108**δ, 5051; **113**ι, 5240, 5245, 5261.—§ 592 (Saṃçaptakav.): VII, **20**ε, 801; **25**, 1083; **32**, 1410.—§ 596 (Pratijñāp.): VII, **74**, 2629.—§ 599 (Jayadrathav.): VII, **95**, 3520, 3503.—§ 601 (Karṇap.): VIII, **5**ζ, 99 (*Vindānuvindāv Āvantyau rājaputrau mahārathau*, have been slain).—§ 608 (do.): VIII, **72**, 3612.—§ 619 (Strīvil.): XI, **25**, 733 (slain).—γ) Dual *Āvantyau* (no doubt = β): § 555 (Sainyodyogap.): V, **19**δ, 593 (*Āvantyau ca mahīpālau mahābalau susamvṛtau | pṛthag akshauhiṇībhyām tāv abhiyātau Suyodhanam*).—§ 584 (Bhīshmavadhap.): VI, **83**, 3650 (*Āvantyau tu maheshvāsau*), 3657 (*Āvantyau rathinām varau*)—§ 584 (Bhīshmav.): VI, **86**ᵍ, 3826.—§ 585 (Bhīshmav.): VI, **94**ω, 4195 (*Āvantyau ca maheshvāsau Kauravam paryavārayan*).—§ 586 (do.): VI, **99**γ, 4504 (*Āvantyau tu mahārathau*).—§ 587 (Jayadrathavadhap.): VI, **114**, 5293 (*Āvantyau mahārathau*), 5309 (do.).—§ 599 (Jayadrathav.): VII, **99**, 3682 (*Āvantyau bhrātarau*).—§ 609 (Çalyap.): IX, **2**ζ, 93.—δ) pl. (°*āḥ*): § 515 (Karṇadigvijap.): III, **254**,

15253 (*Ā°āmç ca vaçe kṛtvā*).—§ 585 (Jayadrathav.): VI, **87**, 3852.—§ 589 (Droṇābhishek.): VII, **11**ν, 397.—§ 599 (Jayadrathav.): VII, **113**, 4408 (*sainyam Āvantyānām*).—§ 604 (Karṇap.): VIII, **8**, 235.—§ 611 (Çalyap.): IX, **24**νν, 1298 (have been slain).

Āvara = Çiva (1000 names[2]).

Avarṇa = Çiva (1000 names[1]).

Āvartana = Vishṇu (1000 names).

Āvasathya. § 490 (Āṅgirasa): III, **221**, 14181 (a Fire, son of Tapas).

Avatata = Çiva (1000 names[1]).

Āveça = Çiva (1000 names[2]).

Āvedanīya = Çiva (1000 names[2]).

Avijñātagati. § 116 (Vasu, pl.): I, **66**, 2589 ("whose ways cannot be explored," son of Anila and Çivā).

Avijñātṛ = Vishṇu (1000 names).

Avijñeya: Mahāpurushastave.

Avikalpana (B. and PCR. °*mp*°). § 717*b* (Nārāyaṇīya): XII, **349**, VI) 13593 (a king).

Avikshit[1]. § 6 (Anukram.): I, **1**, 231 (belongs to the past).—§ 154 (Pūruvaṃç.): I, **94**, 3740, 3741 (son of Kuru and father of Parikshit).

Avikshit[2]. § 778*e* (Saṃvartta-Mar.): XIV, **4**, 82: King *A.* Kārandhama, son of Suvarcas, lived at the beginning of the Tretā age, and was equal to Indra, Bṛhaspati, and Himavat; all kings were under his control; he was given to sacrifices, he performed hundreds of horse-sacrifices, and Aṅgiras himself served as his priest; **5**, 104 (father of Marutta).

Avikshita: VII, 2170 (*Āvikshitām Maruttam*), 2177 (*rājarsheḥ*); XII, 613 (*Marutta*), 910 (id.), 914; XIV, 136, 149, 163, 176, 256, 275

Avimūḍhāḥ (pl.), a kind of ṛshis. § 246 (Sundopasundop.): I, **211**, 7683.

Avimukta. § 370 (Tīrthay.): III, **84**, 8057 (a tīrtha, where by the sight of Devadeva one is purified even after having slain a brahman, and by renouncing one's life there one obtains emancipation—*moksha*).

Avindhya. § 532 (Sītāsāntvana): III, **280**, 16148 (a Rākshasa who had spoken of Rāma, etc.).—§ 534 (Hanūmatpratyāgam.): III, **282**, 16263.—§ 541 (Indrajidvadha): III, **289**, 16492, 16496.—§ 543 (Rāmābhisheka): III, **291**, 16536 (after the slaughter of Rāvaṇa, *A.* came to Rāma with Sītā).

Avisthala (a village). § 562 (Bhagavadyānap.): V, **72**β, 2595; **82**ζ, 2877 (among the five villages, for which Yudh. asks Dury.).

Avṛhaka (PCR. *Vṛhaka*). § 191 (Arjuna): I, **123***a*, 4813 (a Deva-Gandharva?).

Avṛtta (*Vṛtta*?). § 564 (Mātalīyop.): V, **103**γ, 3630 (in an enumeration of the principal Snakes).

Avyakta[1] = Kṛshṇa: XII, 1640, 13285; do.[2], Mahāpurushastave (read *Avyaktamadhya*); do.[3] = Vishṇu (1000 names); do.[4] = Çiva (1000 names[2]).

Avyaktanidhana: Mahāpurushastave.

Avyaktarūpa[1] = Çiva: XIV, 193; do.[2] = Vishṇu (1000 names).

Avyaktayoni = Çiva: XIII, 589.

Avyaṅga = Vishṇu (1000 names).

***Avyaya**[1] ("imperishable"): XII, 1437 (*devo* = Brahman), 1607 (= Kṛshṇa), 7604 (id.), 9218 (*deveçam* = Brahman), 10682 (= Brahman), 11229 (*jyotir avyayam*), 11602 (*Çambhuḥ Prajāpatiḥ . . . jyotir Avyayaḥ*), 12875 (*devānām ādiḥ*, i.e. Vishṇu), 12879 (*Viçvamūrttiḥ* = id.), 13192; XIII, 716 (= Çiva), 1185 (= do., 1000 names[2]), 1262 (*prāṇānām prabhavo 'vyayaḥ* = Çiva, 1000 names[2]), 6951 (= Vishṇu, 1000 names), 6953 (do.), 6995 (*vācam* ? = do.), 7045 (do.); XIV, 206 (= Çiva).—Do.[2], a serpent: I, **57**, 2157.

Ayaḥçaṅku. § 130 (Aṃçāvat.): I, **67**, 2646 (among the great Asuras who were born among the Kekayas).

Ayaḥçiras. § 92 (Aṃçāvat.): I, **65**, 2531 ("*Danor vaṃçe*," a Dānava).—§ 130 (do.): I, **67**, 2646 (cf. Ayaḥçaṅku).

Ayana(m) = Skanda: III, †14639 ("the half year").

Ayati. § 136 (Yayātyup.): I, **75**, 3155 (brother of Yayāti).

Āyāti. § 136 (Yayātyup.): I, **75**, 3155 (brother of Yayāti).

Ayobāhu. § 130 (Aṃçāvat.): I, **67**, 2733 (among the sons of Dhṛtarāshṭra).—§ 182 (Dhṛtarāshtraputranāmak.): I, **117**, 4545 (do.).

Āyoda-Dhaumya(ḥ) (B. Apoda[ḥ] Dhaumya[ḥ]) = Āyoda(ḥ) Dhaumya(ḥ) (q.v.). § 15: I, **3**, 697: *athāparaḥ çishyas tasyaiv Āyodadhaumyasyopamanyur* (B. °*podasya Dhaumyasyo*°) *nāma*.—§ 16: I, **3**, 740: *athāparaḥ çishyas tasyaiv Āyodadhaumyasya* (B. *Āpodasya Dhaumyasya*) *Vedo nāma*.—Ā°'s teeth were of iron (§ 15: I, **3**, 737).

Āyoda(ḥ) Dhaumya(ḥ) (B. Āpoda Dh°), a Ṛshi. § 14: About the time of king Janamejaya, son of Parikshit, there was a Ṛshi named Ā. Dh. (I, **3**, 21 = 684: *ṛshir Dhaumyo nāma Āyodaḥ*) with three disciples: Upamanyu, Āruṇi Pāñcalya, and Veda. I, **3**, 689: *Āyodo Dhaumyaḥ*.—Cf. Āyoda-Dhaumya(ḥ).

Ayodhyā (a city, i.e. Oude, v. VP.). § 225 (Vāsishṭha): I, **177**, 6780 (*khyātām purīm imāṃ lokeshv A°ām*), 6783 (*A°vāsino janāḥ*), 6784.—§ 280 (Bhīmasena): II, **29**, 1076 (here Bhīm. vanquished Dīrghayajña).—§ 346 (Nalop.): III, **60**, 2295.—§ 348 (do.): III, **66**, 2628 (*nagarīm ramyām*; the city of Ṛtuparṇa).—§ 351 (do.): III, **70**, 2745, 2761, 2766 (°*vāsinaṃ nṛpam Ṛtuparṇam*); **71**, 2795 (*A°ādhipatiḥ*).—§ 353 (do.): III, **74**, 2906.—§ 383 (Paraçu-Rāma): III, **99**, 8657 (*A°yām jātam Dāçarathim*), 8659.—§ 425 (Hanūmad-Bhīmas.): III, **148**, 11215 (the capital of Rāma Dāçarathi).—§ 461 (Vāmadevacarita): III, **192**, ††13145 (king Parikshit of the Ikshvāku race).—§ 475 (Dhundhumārop.): III, **202**, 13515 (kings Ikshvāku, Çaçāda, etc.).—§ 534 (Hanūmatpratyāgam.): III, **282**, 16231 (at the return of Hanūmat, Rāma again hopes to rule at *A.*).—§ 543 (Rāmābhisheka): III, **291**, 16567 (*purīm ramyām*), 16568, 16590.—§ 565 (Gālavacarita): V, **115**, 3934 (king Haryaçva Ikshvāku).

Ayodhyādhipati ("the king of Ayodhyā") = Rāma Dāçarathi: XII, 954.

Ayoga (pl. °*āḥ*), a caste: XII, **297**γ, 10869 (among the castes who spring from the original four castes by intermixture).

Āyogava (f. °*ī*) (son [daughter] of a çūdra with a vaiçya woman): XIII, 2574 (*çūdrād Āyogavaç cāpi vaiçyāyām grāmyadharmiṇaḥ*), 2582 (*vāhyānām anujāyante Sairindhryām Māgadheshu ca | prasādhanopacārajñam adāsam dāsajīvanam | ataç cāyogavaṃ sūte vāgurābandhajīvanam*), 2587 (*Āyogavīshu jāyante hīnavarṇās tu te trayaḥ*—sc. one by a Vaidehaka, the Madranābha by a Nishāda, and the Pukkasa by a Cāṇḍāla?).

Ayonija = Vishṇu: XII, 13488; XIII, 7010 (1000 names).

Āyu(s) (gen. °*oḥ* and °*ushaḥ*)[1] (son of Purūravas and Urvaçī, and father of Nahusha, etc.). § 141 (Purūravas): I, **75**, 3149, 3150.—§ 156 (Pūruvaṃç.): I, **95**, ††3760 (*Āyusho Nahusho*, etc.).—§ 450 (Ājagarap.): III, **179**, 12408 (*Nahusho . . . . Āyor vaṃçadharaḥ sutaḥ*).—§ 599*e*

(Çini): VII, **144**, 6029 (*Āyusho Nahushaḥ sutaḥ*).—§ 656 (Khaḍgotp.): XII, **166**δ, 6193 (among those who succeeded each other in the possession of the sword.—§ 702 (Mokshadh.): XII, **297**δ, 10875 (cited by Parāçara in a question of caste).—§ 717 (Nārāyaṇīya): XII, **343**, VII), 13214 (°*shaḥ putro Nahushaḥ*).—§ 761 (Ānuçāsan.): XIII, **115**γ, 5661 (*Āyunāthānaraṇyena*)—§ 768 (Kṛshṇa): XIII, **147**, 6832 (son of Purūravas and father of Nahusha).—§ 775 (Ānuçāsan.): XIII, **166**η, 7682.

Āyu[2] (king of the frogs). § 461 (Vāmadevacar.): III, **192**, ††13173.

Āyu(s)[3] = Çiva (1000 names[2]).

Āyudhin = Çiva (1000 names[2]).

Āyurveda (the science of medicine). § 270 (Brahmasabhāv.): II, **11**, 442 (*Ā°tathāshṭāngo*); XII, 877, 8133 (°*vido janāḥ*), 13137, 13246 (°*vidaḥ*).

Āyutāksha = Çiva: XIII, 7514.

Ayutanāyin. § 156 (Pūruvaṃç.): I, **95**, ††3773 (he brought a myriad of purushamedhas, thence his name). 3774.

B

(What is not found under **B** should be sought for under **V.**)

Bābhravāyaṇi. § 721*b* (Viçvāmitrop.): XIII, **4**β, 256 (a son of Viçvāmitra).

Bābhravya. § 717 (Nārāyaṇīya): XII, **343**ψ, 13262 (. . . . *so 'ham evottare bhāge kramākshharavibhāgavit | Vāmādeçitamārgeṇa mat-prasādān mahātmanā | Pāñcālena kramaḥ prāptas tasmād bhūtāt sanātanāt | Bābhravya-gotraḥ sa babhau prathamaṃ krama-pāragaḥ | Nārāyaṇād varaṃ labdhvā prāpya yogam anuttamaṃ | kramaṃ praṇīya çikshāñ ca praṇayitvā sa Gālavaḥ*).

Babhru[1] (one or more Vṛshṇi or Yādava princes). § 252 (Subhadrāharaṇap.): I, **219**, 7915 (a Vṛshṇi).—§ 291 (Çiçupālavadhap.): II, **45**, 1569 (his wife is ravished by Çiçupāla).—§ 608 (Karṇap.): VIII, **85**, †4322 (°*suta*, slays the elephant of the Kulinda chief; *Devāvṛdha sūnu*, i.e. Babhru, is wounded by the son of Sahadeva).—§ 641 (Rājadh.): XII, **81**, 3040 (°*Ūgrasenayoḥ*; belongs to the opposition against Kṛshṇa).—§ 793 (Mausalap.): XVI, **1**, 17, 29; **3**γ, 72, 102; **4**, 105, 108–9, 110.

Babhru[2], pl. (°*avaḥ*) (the race of Babhru). § 793 (Mausalap.): XVI, **7**λ, 178.

Babhru[3] (son of Viçvāmitra). § 721*b* (Viçvāmitrop.): XIII, **4**β, 249.

Babhru[4] = Çiva (XIII, 589, 1000 names[2]), Vishṇu (1000 names), Kṛshṇa: XII, 1511.

Babhru[5]. § 455 (Brāhmaṇamāh.): III, **186**, 12705 (among honourable appellations of the king).

Babhrumālin. § 264 (Sabhākriyāp.): II, **4***a*, 111.

Babhruvāha. § 11 (Parvas.): I, **2**, 608 (= Babhruvāhana).

Babhruvāhana (the son of Arjuna and Citrāṅgadā, princess of Maṇipūra). § 11 (Parvas.): I, **2**, 398 (°*janma*).—§ 250 (Arjunavanavāsap.): I, **217**, 7884.—§ 785 (Anugītāp.): XIV, **79**, 2302 (king of Maṇipūra and son of Arjuna), 2314, 2317, 2322, 2333–4; **80**, 2360, 2393, 2396; **81**, 2404, 2406, 2426; **86**, 2571 (*Maṇipūrapatiḥ*); **87**, 2600; **88**, 2607; **89**ω, 2677.—Cf. Babhruvāha, Citrāṅgadāsuta, Citrāṅgadātmaja, Dhanañjayasuta, Maṇipūrapati, Maṇipūreçvara.

Badarapācana (a tīrtha on the Sarasvatī). § 615 (Baladevat.): IX, **47**, 2760.—§ 615*y*: IX, **48**, 2762, 2793, 2812: There the beautiful *Çrutāvatī*, *Bharadvāja's* daughter, a *brahmacāriṇī*, practised austerities for many years, desirous of obtaining *Indra* for her husband. *Indra* then came in the guise of B.-ṛ. *Vasishṭha*, and told her that everything is attainable by penances, and asked her to boil five jujubes, when he went away to mentally recite certain *mantras* at *Indratīrtha*, that was not far away. She sat down to boil the jujubes, but in vain; the day was about to wane; her fuel was all consumed; then she first thrust her feet into the fire, without changing a muscle of her face. *Indra* then showed himself in his own proper form, and said that her wish would be accomplished; throwing off her body, she would live with him in heaven as his spouse; and this *tīrtha* would be the foremost in the world and be called *B.*; he granted her a boon superior to that granted to *Arundhatī* (z) by *Mahādeva*: the person who will reside in this *tīrtha* for only one night and bathe there with his soul fixed on meditation, will, after having thrown off his body, obtain many regions of blessedness difficult of acquisition. Then *Indra* went back to heaven; a shower of celestial flowers poured down, etc., and *Çrutāvatī*, throwing off her body, became the spouse of *Indra*.—Cf. Badarīpācana.

Badarī ("Zizyphus Jujuba," a tīrtha and the hermitage of Nara and Nārāyaṇa at the sources of the Gaṅgā; LIA. I, 547/661; VP.). § 48 (Çesha): I, **36**, 1567.—§ 333*b* (Arjunap.): III, **40**, 1636.—§ 339*b* (Arjuna): III, **47**, 1890 (*tad āçramapadaṃ puṇyaṃ V°nāma*).—§ 377 (Dhaumyatīrthak.): III, **90**, 8396, 8397 (*tasyātiyaçasaḥ*—i.e. Vishṇu's —*puṇyāṃ viçālāṃ B°īm anu | āçramaḥ khyāyate puṇyas trishu lokeshu viçrutaḥ*; Gaṅgā, which formerly streamed with cold water, streams here with hot water and carries golden sand, etc.).—§ 394 (Arjuna Kārtt.): III, **115**, 10143 (*ramyām*).—§ 420 (Gandhamādanapraveça): III, **141**, 10893.—§ 421*c* (Ākāça-Gaṅgā): III, **142**, 10902 (the "great river" springs from *B.*, etc.).—§ 423 (Gandhamādanapraveça): III, **145**, 11024 (*te jagmur viçālāṃ B°īṃ prati*; description of the jujube-tree and the hermitage), 11002, 11004 (*Bhāgīrathīṃ . . . vīkshamāṇā . . . viçālāṃ B°īṃ anu*).—§ 432 (Saugandh.): III, **154**, 11367 (*viçālām*).—§ 434 (do.): III, **156**, 11439 ("having passed Gaṅgādvāra they saw many beautiful mountains, among others Himavat; *viçālā Badarī dṛshṭā Nara-Nārāyaṇāçramaḥ*, etc.), 11443 (*Nara-Nārāyaṇasthānaṃ Badarīty abhiviçrutam*).—§ 449 (Ājagarap.): III, **177**, †12346 (*viçālām*), †12349.—§ 457 (Vaivasvatop.): III, **187**, 12749 (*viçālāyāṃ Badaryām*).—§ 524*b* (Arjuna): III, **272**, 15806. § 565 (Gālavacarita): V, **111**, 3824 (*āçramapade*).—§ 636 (Rājadh.): XII, **39**, 1432.—§ 640 (do.): XII, **127**, 4662.—§ 717*b* (Nārāyaṇīya): XII, **335**, 12659 (°*āçramam*), 12663 (id.); **340**, 12975 (°*āçramam*); **343**, 13270 (do.); **344**, 13314 (id.), 13329 (*āçramam*), 13330 (id.), 13337 (*viçālām*).—§ 730 (Ānuçāsanik.): XIII, **14**, 598.—§ 768 (do.): XIII, **148**, 6924.—§ 777 (Svargārohaṇ. p.): XIII, **168**, 7749.

Badarikā = Badarī. § 370 (Tīrthay.): III, **84**, 8155 (°*tīrthe*; by bathing there one obtains a long life and goes to heaven).

Badarīpācana (= °*ra*°). § 360 (Tīrthay.): III, **82**, 7050 (there one should eat jujube).

Badhirāndha ("deaf and blind," a serpent). § 564 (Mātalīyop.): V, **103**γ, 3632 (in Bhogavatī).

Bāheyika ("used among the Bāhīkas"?, v. BR.; Nīl. "used by the slaughter of an ox"): VIII, 2049.

Bahi (a Piçāca, progenitor of the Bāhīkas): VIII, 2064.

Bāhīka, pl. (°*āḥ*). § 578 (Bhīshmavadhap.): VI, **50**π, 2084 (in the wings of Yudhishṭhira's Krauñcāruṇa vyūha, on the first day of the battle; B. *Bālhīkāḥ*).—§ 607 (Karṇap.): VIII, **44**-**45** (should be avoided as being devoid of virtue, etc.; Karṇa had had to live among them; "there is a town Çākala, a river Āpagā, and a V°-clan Jarttikas"; description; do never perform sacrifices and are exceedingly irreligious; they are the offspring of the two Piçācas Bahi and Hīka; they are not created by the Creator; the regions are called Āraṭṭāḥ, the water Bāhīkam; the lowest of brahmans are residing there from very remote times, *tulyakālāḥ Prajāpateḥ*, not possessing the Vedas, etc.); **44**, 2030, 2032, 2033, 2039 (°*dushṭānām*), 2045, 2046, 2048, 2056, 2057, 2058, 2060, 2061 (*Āraṭṭā nāma Bāhīkāḥ*), 2064 (do.), 2065; **45**, 2075, 2076 (sg.), 2078, 2079, 2080, 2098 (*stēnāḥ*), 2108.—§ 714 (Çukakṛtya): XII, **329**, 12384 (*malam pṛthivyā Vāhīkāḥ*).

Bāhīka, a water among the Bāhīkas: VIII, 2068.

Bahīnara. § 267 (Yamasabhāv.): II, **8**, 326 (in the palace of Yama).

Bǎhl° (Vǎhl°), v. **Bǎlh°**.

Bāhu[1]. § 554 (Sainyodyog.): V, **4**γ, 85.—Do.[2] § 562 (Bhagavadyānap.): V, **74**γ, 2731 (among eighteen kings who annihilated their kinsmen, friends, and relatives; was born among the Sundaravaṃçāḥ).—Do.[3] § 640 (Rājadh.): XII, **57**, 2054 (Bāhu's son king Sagara, who exiled his eldest son Asamañjas).—§ 673*b* (Bali-Vāsavas.): XII, **227***a*, 8263.

Bāhubādhāḥ (pl.; B. *Bahuvādyāḥ*; a people in Bhāratavarsha). § 574 (Jambūkh.): VI, **9**, 362.

Bahubhūta = Çiva (1000 names[2]).

Bāhuçālin[1]. § 282 (Svayaṃvarap.): I, **186**, 6983 (among the princes who came to the svayaṃvara of Kṛshṇā). Do.[2] = Çiva: XIV, 203

Bahuçiras = Vishṇu (1000 names).

Bāhudā[1]. § 156 (Pūruv.): I, **95**, ††3795 (*Parīkshit khalu Bāhudām upayeme Suyaçām nāma*; mother of Bhīmasena).

Bāhudā[2] (a sacred river; VP. "two rivers so called"). § 370 (Tīrthay.): III, **84**, 8045 (having dwelled there for one night, one becomes honoured in Heaven).—§ 377 (Dhaumyatīrth.): III, **88**, 8323.—§ 399 (Tīrthay.): III, **95**, 8513.—§ 574 (Jambūkh.): VI, **9**λ, 322 (*mahānadīṃ*?) (in Bhāratavarsha), 337.—§ 628 (Rājadh.): XII, **23**, 669, 689.—§ 731*b* (Ashṭāvakra-Dik-s.): XIII, **19**, 1408.—§ 757*m* (Goloka): XIII, **102***a*, 4887.—§ 758 (Ānuçāsan.): XIII, **103**β, 4944.—§ 775 (do.): XIII, **166***a*, 7653 (*mahānadī*?).

Bahudāmā (a Mātṛ). § 615*u* (Skanda): IX, **46**θ, 2628.

Bāhudantaka. § 641 (Rājadh.): XII, **59**, 2204 (Brahmán's treatise of ethics as abridged by Indra).

Bahudhānindita = Çiva (1000 names[2]).

Bahudhānyaka (a region of the West). § 285 (Nakula): II, **32**, 1187 (conquered by Nakula).

Bahudhara = Çiva (1000 names[2]).

Bahudhātmaka = Hiraṇyagarbha: XII, 11232.

Bahuguṇa (a Devagandharva?, v. BR.). § 191 (Arjuna): I, **123**, 4814 (came to the birth of Arjuna).

Bāhuka[1] (a Nāga). § 66 (Sarpasattra): I, **57**, 2154 (of Kauravya's race).

Bāhuka[2] (Nala = the sūta *B.*). § 348 (Nalop.): III, **66**, 2627.—§ 349 (do.): III, **67**, 2635, 2638, 2640, 2644.—§ 351 (do.): III, **70**, 2748; **71**, 2771, 2772, 2779, 2781, 2782, (2787), 2789, 2794, 2796, 2797, 2800, 2801, 2804, 2806.—§ 352 (do.): III, **72**, 2814, 2816, 2817, 2819, 2823, 2825, 2827, 2828, 2834, 2835, 2836.—§ 353 (do.): III, **73**, 2869, 2883, 2885; **74**, 2894, (2897), (2900), 2902, (2903); **75**, 2922, 2925, 2928, 2933, 2940, 2941, 2942, 2945, 2946; **76**, 2953, 2959, 2960; **77**, 3016.

Bāhuka[3], a prince. § 402 (Tīrthay.): III, **120**, 10277.

Bāhukaṇṭaka (a mode of fighting). § 621 (Rājadh.): XII, **5**, 132 (v. Nīl.).

Bahukarkaça = Çiva (1000 names[2]).

Bahula[1]. § 562 (Bhagavadyānap.): V, **74**γ, 2729 (*Tālajaṅghānāṃ*; among eighteen kings who annihilated their kinsmen, friends, and relatives); do.[2] = Çiva (1000 names[2]).

Bahulā[1] (a Mātṛ). § 615*u* (Skanda): IX, **46**θ, 2621.

Bahulā[2] (a river in Bhāratavarsha). § 574 (Jambūkh.): VI, **9**λ, 334.

Bahumāla = Çiva (1000 names[2]).

Bahumukha = Çiva (1000 names[1]).

Bahumūlaka (a Nāga). § 47 (Āstīkap., Sarpanāmak.): I, **35**, 1561.

Bahunetra = Çiva (1000 names[1]).

Bahuprada = Çiva (1000 names[2]).

Bahuprasāda = Çiva (1000 names[2]).

Bahuputrikā (a Mātṛ). § 615*u* (Skanda): IX, **46**θ, 2621.

Bahuraçmi = Çiva (1000 names[2]).

Bahurūpa = Çiva (1000 names[2], etc.).

Bahuvadyāḥ, v. Bāhubadhyāḥ.

Bahuvedya = Çiva (1000 names[2]).

Bahuyojanā (a Mātṛ). § 615*u* (Skanda): IX, **46**θ, 2627.

Bahvāçin (a son of Dhṛtarashṭra). § 130 (Aṃçāvat.): I, **67**, 2736 (v. Dhārtarāshṭrāḥ).—§ 182 (Dhṛtarāshṭraputranāmak.): I, **117**, 4550.—§ 585 (Bhīshmavadhap.): VI, **88**ι, 3901 (slain by Bhīma on the eighth day), 3904, 3915.

***Bahvṛca** ("one who has studied the Ṛg-Veda"): XV, 312.

Bāhyakarṇa (a Nāga). § 47 (Āstīkap., Sarpanāmakath.): I, **35**, 1554.

Bāhyakuṇḍa (a Nāga). § 564 (Mātalīyop.): V, **103**γ, 3626 (in Bhogavatī).

Baka[1] (a Rākshasa). § 11 (Parvas.): I, **2**, 361 (*Hiḍimba-Bakayor vadhaḥ*), 383 (*Bakasya nidhane*).—§ 71 (Ādivaṃçāvat., Bhāratasūtra): I, **61**, 2258.—§ 158 (Pūruvaṃç.): I, **95**, ††3825 (*tasyām apy Ekacakrāyāṃ Bakaṃ nāma rākshasaṃ hatvā Pāñcālanagaram adhigatāḥ*).—§ 215 (Bakavadhap.): I, **160***ff* (slain by Bhīshma); **160**, 6207; **163**, 6287; **164**, 6295, 6302, 6313 (°*vanam*).—§ 216 (Caitrarathap.): I, **165**, 6316 (°*rākshasam*), 6317 (do.).—§ 315 (Maitreyaçāpa): III, **10**, 368 (the Pāṇḍavas have slain the rākshases, the enemies of the gods, *Hiḍimba-Baka-mukhyānāṃ Kirmīrasya ca rakshasaḥ*).—§ 316 (Kirmīravadhap.): III, **11**, 407, 415 ("*mama bhrātā Bako*," says Kirmīra, alluding to the fact that Bhīma had slain Kirmīra's brother Baka in the Vetrakīya forest), 419, 420.—§ 317 (Arjunābhigam.): III, **12**, 573 (all. to § 215).—§ 435 (Jaṭāsuravadh.): III, **157**, 11496 (*mārgaṃ Baka-Hiḍimbayoḥ*).—§ 562 (Bhagavadyānap.): V, **90**ο, 3151.—§ 585 (Bhīshmavadhap.): VI, **90**, 4019 (*Ārshyaçṛṅgaṃ vairiṇaṃ Bhīmasenasya khyātaṃ Baka-vadhena vai*).—§ 599 (Jayadrathavadhap.): VII, **108**, 4076 (*rākshasapravaro*, brother of Alambusha Ārshyarçṛṅgi; slain by Bhīmasena).—§ 600 (Ghaṭotkacavadhap.): VII, **176**, 8006 (a kinsman of Alāyudha and a friend of Hiḍimba; an eater of brahmans, slain by Bhīma), 8010 (*Hiḍimba-Baka-Kirmīrāḥ*, kinsmen of Alāyudha, and slain by Bhīshma); **178,** 8077 (*°bhrātrā*, i.e. Alāyudha), 8107 (*°jñātiṃ*, i.e. Alāyudha); **180,** †8211 (*rākshasendrā Hiḍimba-Kirmīra-Baka-pradhānāḥ*); **181**δδδ, 8235 (*Hiḍimba-Baka-Kirmīrāḥ*, have been slain by Bhīmasena).

Baka[2] ("crane," Dharma as Yaksha). § 548 (Āraṇeyap.): III, **313,** †17315.

Baka[3] (a Ṛshi, ordinarily called Baka Dālbhya). § 264 (Sabhākriyāp.): II, **4a**, 106 (*D.*).—§ 324 (Dvaitavanaprav.): III, **26,** 968 (*D.*), 984 (*D.*). — § 615 (Baladevatīrthay.): IX, **40,** 2316 (*Bakasyāçramam*), 2317 (*D.*). — § 615*o*: IX, **41,** 2318 (*D.*), 2322 (*D.*), 2330 (*D.*), 2337 (*muniḥ*), 2339: In former times the Ṛ. residing in the *Naimisha* forest had performed a sacrifice which extended over twelve years. After the *Viçvajit* had been completed, the Ṛ. went to the country of the *Pāñcālas* and solicited the king to give them twenty-one calves to be given away as *dakshiṇā*. *Dālbhya Baka* gave them his, and then applied to *Dhṛtarāshṭra*, who, as some of his kine had died, angrily told him to take these. *B.* set his heart upon the destruction of king *Dhṛtarāshṭra*. Cutting the flesh off from the dead animals, having ignited a fire on the *tīrtha* of the *Sarasvatī*, he poured those pieces as libations for the destruction of king *Dhṛtarāshṭra's* kingdom, which began to waste away, until he, reminded by his counsellors, repairing to the bank of the *Sarasvatī*, had gratified Ṛ. *B.*, who, in order to free his kingdom, again poured libations into the fire. Receiving many animals as a gift, he once more proceeded to the *Naimisha* wood, and *Dhṛtarāshṭra* returned to his capital.

Baka[4] (a ṛshi named together with Dālbhya). § 462 (Baka-Çakras.): III, **193,** ††13212 (*Baka-Dālbhyau*), 13215 (*Baka-Çakra-samāgamam*), 13224, 13226, (13228), (13237), 13247.

Baka[5], pl. (*°āḥ*), a people. § 574 (Jambūkh.): VI, **9**λ, 369 (in Bharatavarsha, in the South).

Baka-bhrātṛ ("the brother of *B.*," i.e. probably Alāyudha): XI, 792 (is burnt after death).—Cf. VII, 8077.

Baka-Çakra-saṃvāda(ḥ) ("Conversation between Baka and Indra"). § 462 (Mārk.): III, **193:** *Yudhishṭhira*, having heard that the *ṛshis Baka* and *Dālbhya* were long-lived and friends of *Indra*, asked *Mārkaṇḍeya* about the meeting of *Baka* and *Indra*. *Mārkaṇḍeya* related: After the conflict between the gods and *asuras* was over, and *Indra* had become the ruler of the three worlds, all people were happy and virtuous. Once *Indra*, riding on *Airāvata*, surveyed his happy subjects, and, descending to earth, he made a visit to the *ṛshi Baka*, who had lived for 100,000 years and was adored by gods and *ṛshis* (? *devarshiganasevita*, v. 13236; PCR. has the accus.), in his hermitage in the east by the seaside. *Indra* asked him about the sorrows of those who have a long life. *Baka* mentioned several common disagreeable things, and finally, the having to witness the injustices that take place. *Indra* then asked him about their joys; he mentioned the frugal life of a pious *brahman*, who only eats after having waited on his guest.

Bakanakha (son of Vicvāmitra). § 721*b* (Viçvāmitrop.): XIII, **4**β, 257.

Bakavadha ("the slaughter of Baka"). § 10 (Parvas.): I, **2,** 313 (*Bakavadhaḥ parva*, i.e. Bakavadhaparvan).

Bakavadhaparvan ("the slaughter of Baka," the 10th of the minor parvans of Mhbhr.). § 215: I, **157** ff.: The *Pāṇḍavas* for some time dwelt in the abode of the *brahman*, living on alms; *Bhīma* alone used to eat one-half of the alms. One day *Bhīma* and *Kuntī* overheard the *brahman* complaining (I, **157**), and his wife (I, **158**) and daughter asked to be sacrificed for him to a *rākshasa*, and their little son said that he would slay the *rākshasa* with a blade of grass. *Kuntī* approached (I, **159**), and learned that the *rākshasa Baka* ("king of the *Asuras*," v. 6808), a cannibal, protected the town and the country, receiving as his fee a cartload of rice, two buffaloes, and the human being who brought them to him, from one after another of the householders, while the king, residing in *Vetrakīyagṛha* (see BR.), did nothing to protect the country against him. Now the turn had come for the *brahman*, and as he had no wealth to buy a man, and could not part with any of his family, he would go with all his family to the *rākshasa*, in order that he might devour them all (I, **160**). *Kuntī* said that one of her sons would bring the food to the *rākshasa*. This the *brahman* energetically refused, until she had told him that on account of his strength and *mantras* her son would be safe; but he ought not to disclose this fact to anybody, for then people might trouble them out of curiosity, and if her son imparted his knowledge to anybody he would himself no longer be able to profit by it. *Bhīma* also consented (I, **161**). When the others returned home with their alms, *Yudhishṭhira* blamed his mother for her rash act; but she relied on *Bhīma* (I, **162**). The next morning *Bhīma* set out for the abode of the *rākshasa*, and approaching he began himself to eat the food he carried, loudly calling the *rākshasa* by his name. The *rākshasa* came out in a fury; but *Bhīma*, disregarding his yells and blows, leisurely ate up the whole of that food and washed his hands. Then they began to hurl trees at each other, and thereupon they clasped each other with their arms. At last *Bhīma* pressed *Baka* down to the earth, and placing one knee on the middle of his back, bent him double, while he (*Baka*) roared frightfully and began to vomit blood (I, **163**). *Baka* died uttering frightful yells. The *rākshasas*, his relatives, came and promised never again to kill human beings, and from that day the *rākshasas* of that region were very peaceful towards mankind. *Bhīma* placed the corpse at one of the gates of the town, and went away unobserved. The *brahman* told the citizens that it was a *brahman* skilled in *mantras* (*mantra-siddha*) who had slain the *rākshasa*, and they established a *Brahma* festival (*brahmamahaṃ*) (I, **164**).

Bakula = Çiva (1000 names[2]).

Bala[1] (an Asura, son of Danāyus, and brother of Vṛtra). § 96 (Aṃçāv.): I, **65,** 2541 (*Bala-Vṛtrau*).—§ 277 (Jarāsandhav.): II, **23,** 897 (*Çakram Bala ivāsuraḥ*).—§ 443 (Nivātaka-vacay.): III, **168,** 12073 (*Namuciṃ Bala-Vṛtrau ca Prahlāda-Narakāv api*, and many millions of Daityas had Indra vanquished with this car).—§ 555 (Indra): V, **16,** 497.—§ 578 (Bhīshmav.): VI, **45**", 1711 (*Balaṃ Çakra ivāhave*).—§ 586 (Bhīshmav.): VI, **100,** 4561 (*devasenāṃ yathā Balaḥ*).—§ 590 (Droṇābhishek.): VII, **14,** 542 (*yathā . . . Bala-Çakrau*). — § 592 (Saṃçaptakav.): VII, **30,** 1310 (*Indraṃ Vṛtra-Balā iva*).—§ 599 (Jayadrathavadh.): VII, **109,** 4131 (*Balaṃ hatveva Vāsavaḥ*); **118,** †4698 (*vaktraṃ vicakarta dehāt | yathā purā Vajradharaḥ prasahya Balasya saṃkhye 'tibalasya rājan*).—§ 608 (Karṇap.): VIII, **90,** †4689 (*yathendro Balam ojasā raṇe*). — § 641 (Rājadh.): XII, **98**ξ, 3660.—§ 730 (Ānuçāsan.): XIII, **14**λ, 806 (v. Yaksha). — § 778*b* (Saṃvartta-Mar.): XIV, **5,** 114 (*nihantā tvaṃ Balasya ca*).

Bala[2] (son of Varuṇa and Devī). § 124 (Çukra): I, **66,** 2616.

Bala[3] (an Āṅgirasa). § 665 (Mokshadh.): XII, **208**e, 7593 (*Āṅgirasaḥ*, among the ṛshis in the East).—§ 770 (Ānuçāsan.): XIII, **151**ζ, 7108 (v. Aṅgiras).

Bala[4] (a companion of Skanda). § 615*u* (Skanda): IX, **45**, 2546 (given to Skanda by Vāyu).

Bala[5](**m**) (a Viçvadeva). § 749 (Ānuçāsan.): XIII, **91**γ, 4355.

Bala[6] (a monkey). § 539 (Kumbhakarṇādivadha): III, **287**, 16414

Bala[7] (son of Parikshit, king of Ayodhyā). § 461 (Vāmadevacar.): III, **192**, 13178.

Bala[8] = Baladeva (Bala-Rāma): IX, 2120, 2136, 2145, 2147, 2156, 2178, 2252, 2446, 2759, 2831, 2926, 3045; XIII, 6860 (*halī*).

Bala[9] = Çiva (1000 names[1]); °*m* (1000 names[1]).

Bāla = Çiva (1000 names[1]).

Balabandhu. § 6 (Anukram.): **I, 1,** 230 (belongs to the past).

Balabhadra = Baladeva (Bala-Rāma): IX, 2284.

Bālabhadrāḥ (pl.). § 604 (Karṇap.): VIII, **6**, 153 (the warriors of Balabhadra ?).

Balabhedana = Indra: VIII, 3869.

Balabhid = Indra: I, †1188; III, 10384; V, 2772, 3646; VIII, †4514; IX, 2443; XII, 13016 (*Çakraḥ*); XIV, †288.

Balacārin = Çiva (1000 names[2]).

Balada (an Agni). § 493 (Āṅgirasa): III, **221**, 14186.

Baladeva[1] = Bala-Rāma: I, 2786 (an incarnation—*aṃça*—of the Nāga Çesha), 7117, †7155, †7308 (incarnation of a white hair of Vishṇu, son of Rohiṇī), 7954; III, 502 (°*sahāyavān* has Kṛshṇa performed his exploits as a child), 744, 833, 838; V, 66, 131 (*Mādhave*), †1885 (°*dvitīyo*); VII, 389; VIII, 157; IX, 1988, 3342 (*Mādhavottamaḥ*); XIII, (6021); XIV, 391, 1501, 1523, 1855 (*sa-Sātyakiḥ*), 1932, 2556, 2680.

Baladeva[2] (a Nāga). § 766 (Ānuçāsan.): XIII, **132**, 6163 (°*prabhṛtayo ye Nāgā balavattarāḥ* . . .).

[Baladevatīrthayātrā] ("Baladeva's visit to the sacred places on the Sarasvatī"; cf. *Sārasvataṃ parva*). § 615 (Gadā-y.-p.): *Vaiçampāyana* said: *Baladeva* first proceeded to *Prabhāsa*, where *Uḍurāj* (i.e. Soma), who had been affected with phthisis (*yakshman*), became freed from his curse, whence its name. Asked by *Janamejaya*, *Vaiçampāyana* related *Prabhāsotpattikathana* (q.v.). Thence *Bala-Rāma* proceeded to *Camasodbheda*, where he passed one night and gave away costly gifts. Thence he proceeded to *Udapāna* (*b*) (IX, **35–36**), and thence to *Vinaçana* (IX, **36**), called so by the Ṛ. because the *Sarasvatī* has there become invisible from contempt of *Çūdras* and *Ābhīras*. Thence to *Subhūmika* (*c*), *Gandharvāṇāṃ tīrtha* (*d*), *Gargasrotas* (*e*); thence ("smeared in white sandal-paste and attired in blue robes") to *Çaṅkhatīrtha* (*f*); thence to the *Dvaita* lake; then, along the southern bank of the *Sarasvatī*, to *Nāgadhanvan* (*g*). *Baladeva* then set out with his face towards the East, and one after another reached hundreds and thousands of *tīrthas* that occurred at every step. Bathing in all those *tīrthas*, and observing fasts, etc., as directed by Ṛ., and giving away wealth in profusion, etc., he (always smeared with white sandal-paste) set out for that spot where the *Sarasvatī* turns in an eastward direction in order to behold the Ṛ. in the forest of *Naimisha* (*h*), and he became filled with wonder. "There, at *Kurukshetra*, O foremost one of *Kuru's* race, do thou perform great sacrifices and rites." Thence *Bala-Rāma* went to the *tīrtha Saptasārasvata* (description), resorted to by *Vāneyas* and other ascetics, where the great ascetic crowned with success (*siddhaḥ*) performed his penances (IX, **37**). Requested by *Janamejaya*, *Vaiçampāyana* related the history of *Saptasārasvata* (*i*) and *Maṅkaṇaka* (*j*) (IX, **38**). Having passed one night there, *Bala-Rāma* went to *Auçanasa tīrtha* ("the *tīrtha* of *Uçanas*") *Kapālamocana*; the great *muni Mahodara*, whose thigh had been seized by the head of a Rā. slain by *Rāma* [Dāçarathi], was liberated. There *Kāvya* (i.e. Çukra, Uçanas) had performed *tapas*, and the whole science of politics and morals (*nīti*) was revealed to him, while meditating on the war of Dai. and Dā. Requested by *Janamejaya*, *Vaiçampāyana* related the story of *Mahodara* (*k*). Thence *Bala-Rāma* went to the abode of *Rushaṅgu* (*l*), where *Ārshṭisheṇa* had formerly undergone austere penances, and where the great *muni Viçvāmitra* had become a *brahman*. Then to that *tīrtha* where *Brahmán* (*Lokapitāmahaḥ*) had created the worlds; where the great Ṛ. *Ārshṭisheṇa* had acquired brahmanhood; where the Ṛ.-ṛ. *Sindhudvīpa*, the great ascetic *Devāpi* (both in the *Kṛta* age, IX, **40**, 2294), and the *muni Viçvāmitra* had obtained brahmanhood (**IX, 39**). Requested by *Janamejaya*, *Vaiçampāyana* related the history of *Ārshṭisheṇa* (*m*) and of *Viçvāmitra* (*n*). Thence to the abode of *Baka*, where *Dālbhya Baka* had practised austerities (IX, **40**); which resounded with the chanting of the *Vedas* (*brahmaghoshair avākīrṇaṃ*; B. has *Brahmayoner Avākīrṇaṃ* "from Br. to Av.," Nīl.), where the Ṛ. *Baka Dālbhya* (*o*) poured the kingdom of *Dhṛtarāshṭra Vaicitravīryi* (? *Vaicitravīryiṇaḥ*, genitive) as a libation into the sacrificial fire. In that *tīrtha Bṛhaspati* also poured libations into the sacrificial fire, by means of flesh, in order to destroy the *Asuras*, and the As. began to waste away and were destroyed by the gods. Thence to *Yāyāta tīrtha*, where, at a sacrifice of king *Yayāti Nāhusha*, the *Sarasvatī* produced milk and clarified butter, whereafter *Yayāti* went to heaven. Once again *Yayāti* performed a sacrifice there, and *Sarasvatī* gave to each of the brahmans everything for which he cherished a wish; they regarded the gifts as made to them by the king, and praised and blessed him; D. and G. were pleased. Thence *Baladeva* proceeded to the *tīrtha Vasishṭhāpavāha* (IX, **41**). Requested by *Janamejaya*, *Vaiçampāyana* told the history of *Vasishṭhāpavāha* (*p*), and why it is so rapid, and the brahmanicide of *Indra* (*s*), who was purified by bathing in that *tīrtha*. Thence *Baladeva* went to the *tīrtha* of *Soma*, where in days of yore *Soma* had performed the *Rājasūya* sacrifice, with *Atri* for his *hotṛ*, after which the great battle took place between D. and Dā., Dai., and a Rā., named *Tāraka*, in which *Skanda* (*Mahāsena*) slew *Tāraka* and obtained the command of the celestial forces; in that *tīrtha* is a gigantic *Açvattha* tree, under whose shade *Kārttikeya* (*Skanda*) always resides in person (IX, **43**). Requested by *Janamejaya*, *Vaiçampāyana* related the investiture of *Skanda* (*u*). The *tīrtha*, where in days of yore *Varuṇa*, the lord of the waters, had been installed by the celestials, is named *Taijasa*. Having bathed in that *tīrtha* and adored *Skanda*, *Bala-Rāma* gave gold, etc., to the *brahmans*; passing one night there, he became cheerful and happy (IX, **44–46**). Requested by *Janamejaya*, *Vaiçampāyana* related the installation of *Varuṇa* (*v*) in a former *kalpa*. Thence *Baladeva* ("the slayer of *Pralamba*") proceeded to *Agnitīrtha*, where *Agni*, disappearing, became concealed in the *Çamī* wood, wherefore the gods repaired to *Brahmán*, and asked him to create fire. Requested by *Janamejaya*, *Vaiçampāyana* related the story of *Agnitīrtha* (*w*). Thence he went to *Brahmayoni*, where *Brahmán* had exercised his functions of creation; in days of yore *Brahmán*, having bathed in that *tīrtha* with all the gods, created all the *tīrthas* for the gods, according to due rites. Thence to *Kaubera tīrtha*, where *Ailavila* (i.e. *Kubera*) (*x*), having practised austerities, obtained the mastery of all treasures (*Dhanādhipatyam*), and all kinds of wealth, etc., came to him of their own accord. *Rāma* there beheld the excellent woods of *Kubera*. Thence *Bala-Rāma* went to *Badarapācana*, where the fruits of every season are always to be found (IX, **47**), and where many ascetics and Si. are dwelling. (The story of *Badarapācana* (*y*) and of *Arundhatī* (*z*).) Requested by *Janamejaya*, *Vaiçampāyana* related the birth of *Çrutāvatī* (*aa*). Then *Baladeva* proceeded to *Indratīrtha* (IX, **48**). (The history of *Indratīrtha* (*bb*).) Thence to *Rāmatīrtha* (*cc*), the resort of D. and B.-ṛ. Thence to *Yamunātīrtha* (*dd*). Thence *Baladeva*, adorned with garlands of wild flowers (*vanamālī*), proceeded to *Ādityatīrtha* (*ee*), where also Ṛ. *Asita Devala* obtained great *yoga* powers (IX, **49**). (The history of *Asita Devala* (*ff*).) Thence *Bala-Rāma* went to the *tīrtha* of *Soma* (IX, **50**), where *Soma* had in former days performed the *Rājasūya* sacrifice, and where the great battle was fought about *Tārā* (*Tārakāmayaḥ*). Thence *Bala-Rāma* proceeded to the *tīrtha* of the *muni Sārasvata*, where, during a drought of twelve years, *Sārasvata* in former days taught the *Vedas* to many *brahmans*. Requested by *Janamejaya*, *Vaiçampāyana* related the history of *Sārasvata* (*gg*) and of *Dadhīca* (*hh*). Thence *Bala-Rāma* proceeded to the *tīrtha* of the old maiden (*vṛddhakanyā*) (IX, **51**). Requested by *Janamejaya*, *Vaiçampāyana* related the story of the *vṛddhakanyā* (*ii*). While there, *Baladeva* heard of the slaughter of *Çalya*. Having come out of the environs of *Samantapancaka* (*Samantapañcakadvārāt*), he enquired of the Ṛ. what was the result of a visit to *Kurukshetra*, which they told him (IX, **52**). (*Kurukshetra-kathana* (*kk*) (IX, **53**).) Having visited *Kurukshetra*, *Bala-Rāma* proceeded to a large and exceedingly beautiful hermitage, overgrown with *madhūkas*, etc., and was told by Ṛ.: Here *Vishṇu* in days of yore undertook austere penances and performed duly all the eternal sacrifices. Here a *brāhmaṇī* girl, having from youth observed the vow of *brahmacarya*, was crowned with success (*siddhā*), and, in possession of *yoga* powers, she proceeded to heaven. The beautiful daughter of *Çāṇḍilya*, a *brahmacāriṇī*, who had performed penances difficult to women, went to heaven [here], and was worshipped by the gods and *brahmans*. *Baladeva* then began his ascent of *Himavat*, and soon came to the *tīrtha Plakshaprasravaṇa*, and thence to the *tīrtha Kārapavana* (PCR. °*vapa*°), where he passed one night. > the asylum of *Mitra* and *Varuṇa*. From *Kārapavana* > that spot on the *Yamunā* where in days of yore *Indra*, *Agni*, and *Aryaman* had obtained great happiness. Then he sat down with Ṛ. and Si. in order to listen to their talk. There came Ṛ. *Nārada* (*ll*), and, asked by *Bala-Rāma*, he told him all that had happened to the *Kurus*, including the names of those chiefs that had fallen (*ν*), and of those that were still alive (*ζ*), and asked him to go to the field to witness the mace-encounter between *Bhīma* and *Duryodhana*, which was to take place that very day. *Bala-Rāma* then bade farewell, and dismissed all those that had accompanied him to *Dvārakā*, and descended from *Himavat* and *Plakshaprasravaṇa*, and sang a verse in praise of the *Sarasvatī*. Then he ascended a chariot with goodly steeds, and arrived on the field (IX, **54**).

Bāladhi (a muni). § 415 (Medhāvin): III, **135**, 10736, (10739).

Bālagraha ("demon who seizes children"). § 653*b* (Gṛdhragomāyu-s.): XII, **153**, 5677 (°-*nipīḍitaḥ*; BR. "infantile convulsions").

Balāhaka[1] (a Nāga). § 268 (Varuṇa-sabhāv.): II, **9**, 361 (*nāgau Dhṛtarāshṭra-°au*, in the palace of Varuṇa).

Balāhaka[2] (one of Kṛshṇa's pārshṇivāhas). § 552 (Goharaṇap.): IV, **45**, 1416 (Uttara says his right pārshṇivāha is better than *B.*).—§ 596 (Pratijñāp.): VII, **79**ζ, 2812.—§ 599 (Jayadrathavadh.): VII, **147**ρρρ, 6344 (*kāmagaiḥ Çaibya-Sugrīva-Meghapushpa-Balāhakaiḥ*).—§ 617 (Aishīkap.): X, **13**, 649.—§ 639 (Rājadh.): XII, **53**η, 1917.

Balāhaka[3] (brother of Jayadratha). § 522 (Draupadīharaṇap.): III, **265**, 15599.

Balahan = Çiva (1000 names[2]); do. = Indra: I, 3574 (*Balahā 'pi Çakraḥ*).

Balahantṛ = Indra: VII, 1202; XIII, 7493; XV, 554.

Balāka (a hunter). § 608*f* (Karṇap.) VIII, **69**, 3438, 3440, 3441, 3447: The hunter *Balāka* used to slay animals for the livelihood of his sons and wives, and thus he also supported his parents and others that depended upon him always speaking the truth and never harbouring malice devoted to the duties of his own order. One day, having found no other animal, he slew a blind (*ghrāṇacakshusham*) beast of prey while it was drinking water. A shower of flowers fell from the skies; a celestial chariot took him to heaven, while Aps., etc., were singing. That beast of prey had by austerities obtained a boon, and had become the cause of the destruction of all creatures. For this reason he was made blind by *Brahmán*.

Balākā (a tīrtha). § 733 (Ānuçāsan.): XIII, **25***a*, 1706.

Balākāçva (a king). § 638 (Rāmop.): XII, **49**, 1717 (son of Aja, father of Kuçika, and grandfather of Gādhi).—§ 721 (Viçvāmitrop.): XIII, **4**, 203 (*rājarshiḥ*, son of Sindhudvīpa, grandfather of Kuçika, and great-grandfather of Gādhi).

Balākin (a Dhārtarāshṭra). § 130 (Aṃçāvat.): I, **67**, 2733.—§ 182 (Dhṛtarāshṭra-putranāmak.): I, **117**, 4546.—§ 232 (Svayaṃvarap.): I, **186***a*, 6982.

Bālakrīḍanaka = Çiva (1000 names[1]).

Bālakrīḍanakapriya = Skanda: III, 14634.

Balāksha (a king of the past). § 552 (Goharaṇap.): IV, **56**ζ, 1768.

Balanāçana = Indra: V, 283.

Balandharā (a Kāçi princess, queen of Bhīmasena Pāṇḍava). § 159 (Pūruvaṃç.): I, **95**, 3829 (mother of Sarvaga).

Balānīka. § 600 (Ghaṭotkacav.): VII, **156**λ, 6911 (slain by Açvatthāman); **158**χ, 7011 (named among those who are fighting for the Pāṇḍavas).

Balanisūdana = Indra: III, 13218; V, 240. 421. 4042 (*Çakraḥ*); IX, 3022; XIII, 3893 (*Çakram*)

Balānucaragupta = Çiva (1000 names[1])

Balapramathana = Çiva (1000 names[1])

Bala-Rāma (the elder brother of Kṛshṇa; incarnation of Çesha, or of a white hair of Vishṇu; B. = Bala, R. = Rāma, B.D. = Baladeva, Hal. = Halāyudha, Rauh. = Rauhiṇeya Saṅk. = Saṅkarshaṇa). [§ 11 (Parvas.): I, **2**, 390 (R.). 596 (R.), 621 (R.), 624 (R.).]—[§ 132 (Aṃçāvat.) I, **67**, 2786 (B.D.).]—[§ 210*b* (Bhīmasena): I, **139**, 5520 (Saṅk.).]—[§ 232 (Svayaṃvarap.): I, **186***a*, 6997 (Saṅk.).]—[§ 233 (do.): I, **187**, 7012 (Hal.), 7014 (R.); **189**, 7079 (Hal.), 7080 (Saṅk.), 7084 (Hal.).]—[§ 234 (do.): I, **189**, 7117 (B.D.).]—[§ 235 (do.): I, **191**, †7155 (B.D.).]—[§ 238 (Pañcendrop.): I, **197**, †7308 (B.D.).]—[§ 243 (Vidurāgam.): I, **205**, 7507 (R.).]—

[§ 244 (Rājyalābhap.): I, **207**, 7548 (R.).] —[§ 252 (Subhadrāharaṇap.): I, **219**, 7912 (*Haladharaḥ*); **220**, 7953 (Hal.), 7954 (B.D.), 7955 (R.).]—[§ 253 (Haraṇāharaṇap.): I, **221**, 7987 (R.), 7998 (R.), 8000 (R.), 8015 (R., *Lāṅgalī*, *Haladharaḥ*), 8022 (R.).]—[§ 273 (Rājasūyārambhap.): II, **14**, 598 ("Kaṃsa and Sunāman have been slain by me and R.," says Kṛshṇa; Saṅk.); **15**, 643 (R.).]—[§ 287 (Rājasūyikap.): II, **34**, 1274 (R.).]—[§ 290 (Çiçupālavadhap.): II, **43**, 1508 (Saṅk.), 1509 (R.).]—[§ 317 (Arjunābhigam.): III, **12**, 502 (B.D.; °*sahāyavān*), 595 (R.).]—[§ 320 (Saubhavadh.): III, **18**, 744 (B.D.); **21**, 833 (B.D.), 838 (B.D.).]—[§ 242 (Indralokābhigam.): III, **51**, 1977 (R.), 1993 (R.), †2009 (R.).]—[§ 400 (Tīrthay.): III, **118**, 10231 (R.), 10233 (R.).]—§ 401 (Tīrthay.): III, **119**: *B.* wonders that the righteous Pāṇḍavas are so unhappy while the wicked Duryodhana is ruling the earth, which might make a person of limited sense believe a vicious life to be preferable to a virtuous one: [10240 (*vanamālī halī Rāmo*)].—[§ 402 (Tīrthay.): III, **120**, †10259 (R.), †10260 (R.), †10261 (R.), †10262 (R.), †10267 (R.).]—[§ 420 (Gandhamādanaprav.): III, **141**, 10890 (Saṅk.).]—[§ 511 (Draupadī-Satyabh.): III, **235**, 14736 (R.).] — [§ 549 (Pāṇḍavaprav.): IV, **6**, 187 (*Saṅkarshaṇa*—C. *Ç°*—*samānanā*, i.e. Durgā).]—[§ 553 (Vaivāhikap.): IV, **72**, 2356 (*Vāsudevo Vanamālī Halāyudhaḥ*).]—[§ 554 (Sainyodyog.): V, **1a**, †3 (R.), †4 (Rauh.); **2**, (27) (B.D.); **3**, 44 (*Lāṅgaladhvajaḥ*); **4**, 66 (B.D.); **7**γγ, 131 (B.D.), 155 (Rauh.), 156 (*Çauriḥ*), (157) (B.D.), 162 (Hal.).]—[§ 561*b* (Kṛshṇa): V, **48**, †1885 (B.D.).]—[§ 561 (Yānasandhip.): V, **55**, 2177 (Saṅk.), 2197 (? R.).]—[§ 562 (Bhagavadyānap.): V, **80**ε, 2855 (R.); **90**, 3218 (R.).]—[§ 567 (Bhagavadyānap.): V, **131**o, 4425 (Saṅk.).]—[§ 569 (do.): V, **145**, 4926 (R.).]—[§ 570 (Sainyaniryānap.): V, **157**, 5330 (Hal.), 5335 (do.), 5336 (do.), 5349 (R.); **158**, 5388 (Rauh.).]—[§ 581 (Bhīshmav.): VI, **65**ξ, 2967 (*Saṅkarshaṇaṃ devaṃ*; B. *sṛshṭvā*); **66**, 3012 (Saṅk.); **67**π, 3023 (*agrajaṃ sarvabhūtānāṃ Saṅkarshaṇam*).]—[§ 588 (do.): VI, **121a**, †5797 (R.).]—[§ 589 (Droṇābhishekap.): VII, **11**ξ, 412 (*Vanamālī Halī R.*).]—[§ 592 (Saṃçaptakav.): VII, **23**ρ, 1042 (*Rohiṇīsutaḥ R.*, *Raudraṃ dhanurvaraṃ çreshṭhaṃ lebhe yaṃ Rohiṇī-sutaḥ | taṃ tushṭaḥ pradadau Rāmaḥ Saubhadrāya mahātmane*).]—[§ 599 (Jayadrathavadhap.): VII, **110**σ, 4193 (R.), 4227 (*Saṅkarshaṇasamo bale*).]—[§ 600 (Ghaṭotkacavadhap.): VII, **181**δδδ, 8220 (Rauh.).]—[§ 604 (Karṇap.): VIII, **2**γ, 31 (R.).]—[§ 607 (do.): VIII, **41**ε, 1952 (R.).]—[§ 614*b*: IX, **34**, 1948 (Hal., R.; "his banner bore the device of the palmyra palm, and he owned the plough for his weapon," PCR.).]—[§ 614 (Gadāyuddhap.): IX, **34**, 1950 (R.), 1951 (R.), 1954 (Hal.), 1955 (Hal.), 1957 (Rauh.), 1959 (R., Rauh.), 1960 (R.), 1961 (*Halī*), 1964 (Rauh.), 1965 (R.).]—[§ 615 (Baladevatīrthay.): IX, **35**, 1060 (R.), 1971 (R.), 1972 (R.), 1979 (Rauh.), 1981 (*Haladhara*), 1983 (Rauh.), 1984 (R.), 1994 (Rauh.), †2002 (*Halabhṛt*), †2004 (R.), 2061 (Hal.); **36**, 2064 (Hal.), 2117 (Hal.); **37**, 2119 (Hal.), 2120 (B.), 2128 (*Rohiṇī-sutaḥ*), 2129 (*Haladhara*), 2136 (B.), 2145 (Hal., B.), 2147 (B.), 2156 (*Lāṅgalī*, B.), 2176 (R.), 2178 (B.), 2184 (Hal.); **39**, 2246 (Hal., R.), 2247 (*Lāṅgalī*), 2248 (R.), 2249 (Hal.), 2252 (B.), 2272 (*Haladharaḥ*), 2280 (Hal.), 2284 (*Balabhadraḥ*); **40**, 2314 (R.), 2316 (R.); **43**, †2446 (B.); **46**, 2724 (*Lāṅgalī*), 2725 (do.); **47**, 2754 (do.), 2759 (B.), 2760 (R.); **48**, 2762 (R.); **49**, 2831 (B.), 2844 (*Lāṅgalī*); **50**, †2924 (*Halabhṛt*); **51**, 2926 (B.), †2978 (Rauh.); **52**, 3006 (R., *Mādhavaḥ*).] — [§ 615*kk* (Kurukshetrakath.): IX, **53**, 3008 (R.), (3010 (R.)), 3011 (R.), 3029 (Hal.).]—[§ 615 (Baladevatīrthay.): IX, **54**, 3038 (R., Hal.), 3045 (B.), 3046 (Hal.), 3052 (R.), 3055 (R.), 3057 (Rauh.), 3061 (Rauh.), 3064 (R.), 3067 (R.), 3068 (R.), 3072 (R.).]—[§ 615 (Gadāyuddhap.): IX, **55**, 3078 (R.), 3079 (R.), 3080 (*Lāṅgalī*), 3081 (R.), 3104 (Rauh.), 3121 (R.); **60**, 3342 (B.D.), 3343 (Rauh.), 3344 (R.), 3365 (R.), 3369 (Rauh.), 3370 (R.).] — [§ 616 (Sauptikap.): X, **9**, 505 (R.).]—[§ 617*b* (Brahmaçiras): X, **12**, 638 (R.).]—[§ 641 (Rājadh.): XII, **122**, 4471 (? R.).]—[§ 730 (Ānuçāsan.): XIII, **14**γ, 630 (R.).]—[§ 768*c* (Kṛshṇa): XIII, **147**, 6860 (*Halī*), 6867 (R.), 6868 (*Lāṅgaladhārin*)]: Having a plough for his weapon (*halī*) he will look like a white hill; he will be endowed with might capable of uplifting the whole earth; upon the chariot of that god a tall palmyra, a three-headed golden [palmyra-] tree, will form his standard; the head of that lord of all the worlds will be shaded with great snakes; [all] weapons of attack and defence will come to him as soon as he thinks of them; he is called *Ananta*; once *Garuḍa*, son of *Kaçyapa*, was addressed by the gods in these words: "Do thou see if this one has any end"; *Garuḍa*, however, failed to find out the end of this highest god (*devasya paramātmanaḥ*); supporting the earth on his head (*bhogena*), he resides in the nether regions (*antar vasati*) = *Çesha* = *Vishṇu* = [*Bala-*] *Rāma* = *Kṛshṇa* (XIII, **147**).—[§ 793 (Mausalap.): XVI, **1**, 8 (R.), 20 (R.), 29 (R.), 32 (R.); **2**, 43 (R.); **3**, 62 (R.), 72 (R.), 104 (R.); **4**, 105 (R.), 111 (R.), 112 (R.), 114 (R.), 116 (R.); **5**, 142 (R.); **6**, 172 (R.); **7**, 207 (R.); **8**, 261 (R.).]—[§ 794 (Mahāprasthānikap.): XVII, **1**, 10 (R.).]

Bālārkavarṇa = Çiva (1000 names[1]).

Bālarūpadhara = Çiva (1000 names[1]).

Bālarūpadhṛk = Çiva (1000 names[2]).

Bālasūdana = Indra: I, 1285, 7706; III, 13226, 14411; V, 496, 523; IX, 2777 (*bhagavān*), 3251; XII, 8354, 8357; XIII, 278, 828, 3903, 4592, 7312; XIV, 115.

Balavardhana (a son of Dhṛtarāshṭra's). § 182 (Dhṛtarāshṭraputranāmak.): I, **117**, 4546.

Balavat[1] = Çiva (1000 names[2]).—Do.[2] (?) § 677 (Mokshadh.): XII, **245**β (?), 8901.

Balavīra = Çiva (1000 names[2]).

Balavishṭambha = Çiva (1000 names[1]).

***Bala-Vṛtra-ghna** = Indra: III, 16947; XIII, 2343; XIV, †277.

***Bala-Vṛtra-han** = Indra: III, 2240, 12062: XII, 1113; XIII, 1914, 1934; XIV, 167.

***Bala-Vṛtra-nisūdana** = Indra: II, 306; III, 2126.

***Bala-Vṛtra-sūdana** = Indra: XII, 3835.

Balh-, cf. also **Bahl-**.

Bālhi-jāta (probably [horses] born in Balkh). § 562 (Bhagavadyānap.): V, **86**, 3045.—§ 592 (Saṃçaptakav.): VII, **23**, 973.—§ 758 (Ānuçāsan.): XIII, **103**β, 4921 (*vājināṃ Bāhlijātānām ayutāny adadaṃ daça*, says Bhagīratha).

Bālhika[1] (king(s) who belong(s) to the past). § 5 (Anukram.): I, **1**, 224.—§ 267 (Yamasabhāv.): II, **8**, 327 (in the palace of Yama).

Bālhika[2] (son of the elder Janamejaya and brother of the elder Dhṛtarāshṭra and Pāṇḍu). § 154 (Pūruv.): I, **94**, 3745.

Bālhika[3] ([great-]grandson of the elder Dhṛtarāshṭra and son of Pratīpa, and brother of Devāpi and Çantanu). § 155 (Pūruv.): I, **94**, 3750, 3751 (is made king together with Çantanu).—§ 156 (do.): I, **95**, 3797 (son of Pratipa and Çaibyā Sunandā).—§ 194 (Pāṇḍu): I, **126**, 4911 (*Somadatto* 'tha B°ḥ).—§ 208 (Astradarçana): I, **134**, 5313 (*Kṛpasya, Somadattasya, Bāhlīkasya ca dhīmataḥ . . . sānnidhye*).—§ 213 (Jatugṛhap.): I, **143**, 5707 (*Droṇaṃ ca Bālhīkañ caiva Somadattañ ca Kauravam*). — § 287 (Rājasūyikap.): II, **34**, 1266 (*tathā Çalyaç ca bhagavān Bāhlīkaç ca mahābalaḥ | Somadatto 'tha Kauravyo Bhūrir Bhūriçravāḥ Çalaḥ*).—§ 288 (do.): II, **35**, 1293 (*Bāhlīko Dhṛtarāshṭraç ca, Somadatto Jayadrathaḥ | Nakulena samānītāḥ svāmivat tatra remire*).—§ 296 (Dyūtap.): II, **53**, 1912 (*Vāhlīko ratham āhārshīd jāmbūnada-vibhūshitam*).—§ 298 (do.): II, **58**, 2011 (*Bālhīkena ratham yattam* [i.e. *dattam*, cf. 1912]); **63**, 2112 (*Prātipeyāḥ Çāntanavā Bhīmasenāḥ sa-Vāhlīkāḥ | Duryodhanāparādhena kṛcchram prāpsyanti sarvaçaḥ*).—§ 302 (Anudyūtap.): II, **74**, 2477 (*tato Droṇaḥ, Somadatto, Vāhlīkaç caiva, Gautamaḥ . . .* in vain dissuaded the game). — § 305 (Anudyūtap.): II, **78**, 2560 (Yudhishṭhira said: *āmantrayāmi Bharatāṃs tathā vṛddhaṃ pitāmahaṃ | rājānaṃ Somadattañ ca mahārājañ ca Vāhlīkaṃ*). — § 307 (do.): II, **81**, 2697 (Dhṛtarāshṭra related: *prātishṭhata tato Bhīshmo Droṇena saha Sañjaya | Kṛpaç ca Somadattaç ca Vāhlīkaç ca mahāmanāḥ*).—§ 318 (Arjunābhigamanap.): III, **13**, 599 (among the means of dissuading Dhṛtarāshṭra from permitting the game, Kṛshṇa mentioned *Bhīshma-Droṇau samānāyya Kṛpaṃ Vāhlīkam eva ca*). — § 512 (Ghoshayātrāp.): III, **249**, 15084 (Duryodhana asked Karṇa: "What will Bhīshma, Droṇa, Kṛpa, Drauṇi, Vidura, Sañjaya, Vāhlīka, Saumadatti, etc., say to me when I come to Hāstinapura?").—§ 514 (Ghoshayātrāp.): III, **252**, 15205 (*Bhūriçravāḥ, Somadatto, mahārājaç ca Vāhlikaḥ . . . Kurūdvahāḥ* followed Duryodhana; *kālenālpena rājendra sva-puraṃ viviçus tadā*).—§ 515 (Karṇadigvijaya): III, **254**, 15261 (Duryodhana said to Karṇa when the latter had fulfilled his Digvijaya: "What I have not been able to accomplish through Bhīshma, Droṇa, Kṛpa, and Vāhlika, I have obtained through thee").—§ 552 (Goharaṇap.): IV, **38**, 1243 (Uttara said about the Kuru army: *yatra Droṇaç ca Bhīshmaç ca Kṛpaḥ Karṇo Viviṃçatiḥ | Açvatthāmā Vikarṇaç ca Somadattaç ca Vāhlikaḥ*, etc.).—§ 556 (Sañjayayānap.): V, **23**δ, †693 (Yudhishṭhira asked Sañjaya about the health of Bhīshma, Dhṛtarāshṭra, *mahārājo Vāhlikaḥ Prātipeyaḥ . . . vidvān*, Somadatta, Bhūriçravas, etc.); **30**ξ, †885 (Yudhishṭhira asked Sañjaya to salute Droṇa, Açvatthāman, Kṛpa, etc., *sa Vāhlikānām ṛshabho manīshī*, who never cherishes any other wish than that there should be peace among the Bharatas, and Somadatta, Saumadatti, etc.). — § 561 (Yānasandhip.): V, **47**a, 1796 (Bhīshma, Droṇa, Kṛpa, Çalya, Kṛtavarman, Jayadratha, Açvatthāman, Vikarṇa, Somadatta, Vāhlika, Vidura, Dhṛtarāshṭra, etc., entered the hall for hearing the message of Sañjaya); **55**ν, 2206 (the chief warriors of the Kurus are Bhīshma, Droṇa, Kṛpa, etc., Drauṇi, Vaikartana Karṇa, Somadatta, Vāhlika, *Prāgjyotishādhipaḥ, Çalya, Āvantyo, 'tha Jayadrathaḥ*, etc.); **57**σ, 2289 (Sañjaya should inform *sa-Vāhlikān Kurūn . . . Prātipeyān Çaradvataḥ*, etc.); **58**τ, 2300 (Dhṛtarāshṭra, Vāhlika, Bhīshma, Droṇa, Açvatthāman, Sañjaya, Somadatta, Çala, and Kṛpa, etc., do not wish the combat), ν, 2304 (Duryodhana will challenge the Pāṇḍavas without depending upon Dhṛtarāshṭra, Droṇa, Açvatthāman, Sañjaya, Bhīshma, Kāmboja, Kṛpa, Vāhlika, etc.); **62**ββ, †2426 (Karṇa boasts that he will slay myriads of warriors in the sight of *Āvantya-Kāliṅga-Jayadratheshu . . . Vāhlike ca*); **63**, 2432 (Duryodhana says that he is not dependent on Bhīshma, Droṇa, Kṛpa, Vāhlika, etc.); **65**δδ, 2493 (Dhṛtarāshṭra exhorts Duryodhana to follow himself, Droṇa, Kṛpa, Vikarṇa, Bhīshma, *mahārājañ ca Vāhlikaṃ*); **66**εε, 2501 (Arjuna had said that Bhīshma, Dhṛtarāshṭra, Sañjaya, Droṇa, Kṛpa, Karṇa, *mahārājañ ca Vāhlikaṃ*, etc., were in the greatest danger).—§ 562 (Bhagavadyānap.): V, **80**ζ, 2859 (Vidura, Bhīshma, *Droṇaç ca saha-Vāhlikaḥ* will understand Kṛshṇa); **83**ι, 2966 (Yudhishṭhira tells Kṛshṇa to salute Bhīshma, Droṇa, Kṛpa, *mahārājañ ca Vāhlikaṃ*, Drauṇi, Somadatta, etc.); **89**λ, 3114 (Kṛpa, Somadatta, *mahārājaç ca Vāhlikaḥ* rose from their seats and honoured Kṛshṇa), 3117(μ) (Kṛshṇa accosted *Droṇaṃ sa-Vāhlīkaṃ sa-putrañ ca*, Kṛpa, and Somadatta); **90**ρ, 3180 (Dhṛtarāshṭra, *mahārājaç ca Vāhlīkaḥ*, Kṛpa, Somadatta, and the Kurus had grieved at the dragging of Kṛshṇā at the game); **91**σ, 3271 (Droṇa, Kṛpa, *Bhīshmo, 'tha Vāhlikaḥ*, and [the] Kurus came to Kṛshṇa); **95**ν, 3402 (Duryodhana will be irresistible, when he has Bhīshma, Droṇa, Kṛpa, Karṇa, Viviṃçati, Açvatthāman, Vikarṇa, *Somadatto, 'tha Vāhlikaḥ*, etc.).—§ 567 (do.): V, **124**β, 4138 (Duryodhana does not follow Dhṛtarāshṭra, Bhīshma, Droṇa, Vidura, Kṛpa, *Somadattasya, Vāhlīkasya ca dhīmataḥ*, etc.); **128**θ, 4284 (Duryodhana disregards Vidura, Dhṛtarāshṭra, *mahārājañ ca Vāhlikaṃ*, etc.); **129**, 4350 (Bhīshma, Dhṛtarāshṭra, and Vāhlika have given their share to the sons of Pāṇḍu from fear of disunion); **131**π, 4453 (Kṛshṇa addressed Dhṛtarāshṭra, Droṇa, Bhīshma, Vidura, Vāhlika, and Kṛpa), 4457 (ρ) (Kṛshṇa was followed by Bhīshma, Droṇa, Kṛpa, Vidura, Dhṛtarāshṭra, Vāhlika, etc.).—§ 569 (do.): V, **149**, 5055, 5059, 5066, 5067 (*V.* abandoned his father and brother and obtained the wealthy kingdom of his maternal uncle, permitting Çāntanu to rule the paternal kingdom).—§ 570 (Sainyaniryānap.): V, **155**, 5275 (among the eleven men, Kṛpa, Droṇa, etc., under each of whom Duryodhana placed an akshauhiṇī).—§ 572 (Rathātirathas.): V, **167**, 5797 (is an *atiratha*).—§ 576 (Bhagavadgītāp.): VI, **17**γ, 675 (the Kuru army was arrested by Droṇa, Bhīshma, Açvatthāman, Vāhlīka, and Kṛpa).—§ 578 (Bhīshmavadhap.): VI, **45**[10], 1707 (fights Dhṛshṭaketu = Cedirājaḥ, 1709), 1709; **48**, 1925[349] (he attacked Çveta with Kṛtavarman, Kṛpa, Çalya, Jārāsandhi, Vikarṇa, and Viviṃçati in order to protect Bhīshma).—§ 580 (do.): VI, **59**o, †2643 (at sunset the Kurus *sa-Bhīshmāḥ, sa-Droṇa-Duryodhana-Vāhlikāç ca*, withdrew their troops), †2648 (Droṇa, Kṛpa, *Saindhava-Vāhlikau*, Bhūriçravas, *Çalya-Çalau*, etc., were vanquished by Arjuna).—§ 581 (do.): VI, **60**a, 2652 (Droṇa, Duryodhana, Vāhlika, etc., accompanied Bhīshma).—§ 583 (do.): VI, **76**ι, 3330 (the Kuru army was protected by Droṇa, Bhīshma, Kṛtavarman, Kṛpa, Duḥçāsana, Jayadratha, etc., Bhagadatta, Vikarṇa, Drauṇi, Saubala, and Vāhlika).—§ 584 (do.): VI, **81**a, 3533 (Bhīshma said to Duryodhana that he, Droṇa, Çalya, etc., *Vāhlikaḥ saha Vāhlikaiḥ*, etc., would fight for him).—§ 585 (do.): VI, **92**χ, 4118 (Bhīshma sent Droṇa, Somadatta, *Vāhlīko, 'tha Jayadrathaḥ*, etc., to the rescue of Duryodhana), 4120 (was wounded by Ghaṭotkaca); **96**, 1310 (with Kṛtavarman he fought Sātyaki).—§ 586 (do.): VI, **102**ι, 4666 (Açvatthāman, Çalya, *Kāmbojaç ca Sudakshiṇaḥ | Vindānuvindāv Āvantyau, Vāhlikaḥ saha Vāhlikaiḥ*, surrounded Arjuna); **104**, 4746 (fought Bhīmasena: *Bhīmasenas tu rājānaṃ Vāhlikaṃ prapitāmahaṃ | viddhvānadan mahā-nādaṃ . . .*), 4753, 4754 (mounted upon the chariot of Lakshmaṇa).—§ 592 (Saṃçaptakav.): VII, **20**δ, 800 (Bhūriçravas, Çalya, Somadatta, and Vāhlika were in the right wing of Droṇa's Garuḍa-array on the twelfth day of the battle); **25**, 1081 (fought Drupada); **32**, 1373 (fought Bhīmasena); **39**ξ, 1660 (Duryodhana told Karṇa, Vāhlika, etc., to crush Abhimanyu).

—§ 596 (Pratijñāp.): VII, **74a**, 2619 (Jayadratha said that not even Droṇa, Duryodhana, Kṛpa, *Karṇa-Madreça-Vāhlikāḥ*, etc., could protect him).—§ 598 (Jayadrathavadhap.): VII, **85γ**, 3043 (Dhṛtarāshṭra said that the Pāṇḍavas would hear Çalya, Somadatta, Bhīshma, Droṇa, Vikarṇa, Vāhlīka, Kṛpa, etc.).—§ 599 (Jayadrathav.): VII, **95**, 3527 (*Vāhlīka-rājas tejasvī kulaputro mahārathaḥ . . . Draupadeyān avārayat*), 3534 (fought Çikhaṇḍin); **96**, 3548, 3549 (fought Çikhaṇḍin), 3553 (*Vāhlīka-rājaḥ*, fought the Draupadeyas).—§ 600 (Ghaṭotkacavadhap.): VII, **155δ**, 6720 (in the sight of Karṇa, Drauṇi, Duryodhana, Kṛpa, Somadatta, and Vāhlīka, Bhīmasena slew Dushkarṇa and Durmada); **157**, 6932 (Bhīma made Somadatta, the son of Vāhlīka, insensible), 6933 (wounded by Bhīmasena; wounds—C. *Prātīpīyas* for B. *Prātīpeyas*—Bhīma), 6936 (slain by Bhīmasena), 6937; **158ω**, 7035 (Karṇa said that Bhīshma, Vikarṇa, Citrasena, *Bāhlīkaç ca*, Jayadratha, etc., had been slain by Destiny).—§ 604 (Karṇap.): VIII, **1**, 22 (has been slain); **5ζ**, 119 (Sañjaya said to Dhṛtarāshṭra: *pitāmahas tava tathā Vāhlikaḥ saha Vāhlikaiḥ* has been slain by Bhīmasena); **7**, 180 (the son of Senāvindu has been slain by *Vāhlīkena . . . Kauravendreṇa*).—§ 609 (Çalyap.): IX, **2ζ**, 72 (. . . *Somadatto, 'tha Vāhlikaḥ*, . . . , enumerated by Dhṛtarāshṭra among the kings who had been slain for his sake), 89 (*mahārājaḥ*).—§ 611 (do.): IX, **24νν**, 1299 (*Vāhlike, Somadatte ca*, have been slain).—§ 613 (Gadāyuddhap.): IX, **32β**, 1836 (enumerated by Duryodhana among the kings who had been slain for his sake).—§ 615 (do.): IX, **63**, 3548 (*Bhīshmeṇa, Somadattena, Bāhlīkena Kṛpeṇa ca . . .* have in vain exhorted Dhṛtarāshṭra to make peace, says Kṛshṇa).—§ 616 (Sauptikap.): X, **9κ**, 523 (Açvatthāman said to the dying Duryodhana: *parishvajethā rājānaṃ Bāhlīkaṃ sumahārathaṃ* in heaven).—§ 619 (Strīvilāp.): XI, **22η**, 621 (Gāndhārī said: *Prātipeyaṃ maheshvāsaṃ hataṃ bhallena Vāhlikaṃ*).—§ 744 (Ānuçāsan.): XIII, **44**, 2446 (Bhīshma said: *pitā mama, mahārāja! Bāhlīko vākyam abravīt*).—§ 787 (Āçramavāsap.): XV, **11**, 360 (Dhṛtarāshṭra wished to perform the çraddhā of Bhīshma, Droṇa, Somadatta, Vāhlīka, etc.), 372 (*rājarsheḥ*; enumerated by Bhīmasena among those whose pretakārya the Pāṇḍavas will themselves perform); **15**, 414(σ).—§ 789 (Putradarçanap.): XV, **29ε**, 809 (*yasyās tu çvaçuro dhīmān Vāhlikaḥ sa Kurūdvahaḥ | nihataḥ Somadattaç ca pitrā saha mahāraṇe*); **32θ**, 879.

Bālhīka[4] = Somadatta. § 600 (Ghaṭotkacavadhap.): VII, **162**, 7225 (*Bāhlīkam Kauravādhamam*, i.e. Somadatta, fights Sātyaki), 7241 (*Bāhlīkasya* = Somadattasya).—Cf. XV, 809.

Bālhīka[5]. § 130 (Aṃçāvat.): I, **67**, 2661 (a king, incarnation of Suhara—B. Ahara).—Cf. Bālhīka[3] (?).

Bālhīka[6]. § 130 (Aṃçāvat.): I, **67**, 2696 (incarnation of the gaṇa Krodhavaça).—Cf. Bālhīka[3] (?).

Bālhīka[7] (pl. °*āḥ*), a people (probably Balkh, VP.). § 279 (Arjuna): II, **27**, 1030 (conquered by Arjuna). § 305 (Dyūtap.): II, **52**, 1869 (*Kairātā Daradā Darvāḥ . . . Pāradā Vāhlikaiḥ saha*, etc.; bring tribute to Yudhishṭhira).—§ 559 (Prajāgarap.): V, **39**, 1525 (*malaṃ pṛthivyā Vāhlīkāḥ*, etc.).—§ 573 (Ambop.): V, **195**, 7607 (*Vindānuvindāv Āvantyau Kaikeyā Vāhlikaiḥ saha | prayayuḥ sarva evaite Bhāradvājapurogamāḥ*).—§ 574 (Jambūkh.): VI, **9μ**, 361 (in Bhāratavarsha).—§ 576 (Bhagavadgītāp.): VI, **20ζ**, †750 (in Bhīshma's division were all the Dhārtarāshṭras with *Vāhlīkānām ekadeçaḥ Çalaç ca*, etc.); VI, 2084, v. Bāhīka.—§ 583 (Bhīshmavadhap.): VI, **75γ**, 3293 (Kṛtavarman, accompanied by *Kāmbojavara-Vāhlikaiḥ*, was in the head of Bhīshma's crane-array on the sixth day of the battle); VI, 3533, v. Bālhīka[3]; VI, 4666, v. Bālhīka[3].—§ 587 (Bhīshmavadhap.): VI, **117ρ**, 5484 (many combatants belonging to the Nishādas, Sauvīras, Vāhlīkas, Daradas, etc., fell upon Arjuna).—§ 589 (Droṇābhishekap.): VII, **4β**, 122 (a people vanquished by Karṇa).—§ 599 (Jayadrathavadhap.): VII, **93δ**, 3379 (among the peoples, among whom Arjuna caused a great carnage); **113χ**, 4409 (*Vāhlīkānāṃ mahad balaṃ*; among the peoples that Sātyaki pointed out to his charioteer), 4412 (*nānāpraharaṇodyatāḥ*); **121εε**, 4818 (among the peoples who, headed by Duryodhana, attacked Sātyaki together with the Saṃçaptakas).—§ 600 (Ghaṭotkacavadhap.): VII, **157ρ**, 6949 (among the peoples whom Yudhishṭhira began to slay); **179**, †8159.—§ 602 (Droṇavadhap.): VII, **192π**, 8841 (among the peoples whom Dhṛshṭadyumna began to slay).—§ 603 (Nārāyaṇāstramokshap.): VII, **193β**, 8905 (among the peoples with whom Kṛtavarman fled); VIII, 119, v. Bālhīka[3].—§ 605 (Karṇap.): VIII, **20**, 779 (δδ) (among the peoples that Pāṇḍya was slaughtering).—§ 608 (do.): VIII, **56ρρ**, 2762 (among the peoples that were slaughtered by Bhīma); **74**, †3801 (Arjuna boasts that he will destroy the Kurus and Vāhlikas).

Bālhīka[8] (king or prince of *B.*). § 130 (Aṃçāvat.): I, **67**, 2694 (*Asurāṇān tu yaḥ Sūryaḥ çrīmāṃç caiva mahāsuraḥ | Darado nāma Vāhlīko baraḥ sarvamahīkshitām*).—§ 282 (Svayaṃvarap.): I, **186**, 7001.—§ 287 (Rājasūyikap.): II, **34**, 1272 (*Bāhlīkāç cāpare çūrāḥ rājānaḥ*).—§ 290 (Çiçupālavadhap.): II, **44a**, 1526 (*Daradaṃ stuhi Bāhlīkaṃ imaṃ pārthivasattamaṃ | jāyamānena yeneyam abhavad dāritā mahī*).—§ 458 (Kaliyuga): III, **188**, 12840 (pl.: among barbarous and sinful kings who will rule on earth when kali-yuga sets in).—§ 554 (Sainyodyogap.): V, **4γ**, 77 (among the kings to whom the Pāṇḍavas ought to send messengers for support).

Bālhīka[9] (coming from Bālhīka[7]). § 253 (Haraṇāharaṇap.): I, **221**, 8011 (Kṛshṇa gave 100,000 *pṛshṭhyānām api çāçvānāṃ Vāhlikānāṃ* as kanyādhana).—§ 593 (Abhimanyuvadh.): VII, **36η**, 1574 (*Vāhlikān sādhu-vājinaḥ*, among the steeds of different breeds who were slain).—§ 599 (Jayadrathav.): VII, **121**, 4831 (ηη) (*pārvatīyān atha Vāhlikān*, among the steeds of different races who were slain).

Bālhīka-puṅgava ("the foremost of the *B.*") = Çalya. § 130 (Aṃçāvat.): I, **67**, 2642.—§ 177 (Pāṇḍu-digvijaya): I, **113**, 4427 (= the Madra king Çalya, brother of Pāṇḍu's queen Mādrī).

Bālhikātmaja = Somadatta: VII, 7247.

Bālhikī (= Mādrī). § 193 (Pāṇḍu): I, **125**, 4886.

Bali[1] (an Asura). § 91 (Aṃçāvat.): I, **65**, 2528 (son of Virocana and father of Bāṇa).—§ 209 (Drupadaçāsana): I, **138**, 5484 (*Indra-Vairocanāv iva*).—§ 268 (Varuṇasabhāv.): II, **9**, 364 (*B°r Vairocano rājā*; in the palace of Varuṇa).—[§ 324 (Dvaitavanapr.): III, **26**, †976 (*Asurasya Vairocaneḥ*).] —§ 326 (Draupadīparitāpav.): III, **28**, 1029 (*Prahlādasya ca saṃvādaṃ Baler Vairocanasya ca*), [1044 (*Vairocane*)].—§ 384 (Agastyop.): III, **102**, 8759 (*abadhyaḥ sarvabhūtānāṃ Baliç cāpi mahāsuraḥ*).—§ 435 (Jaṭāsuravadhap.): III, **157**, 11502 (*Balir Vajradharaṃ yathā*).—§ 443 (Nivātakavacayuddhap.): III, **168**, 12068 (*Baliṃ Vairocaniṃ*).—[§ 444 (do.): III, **171**, 12150 (*Vairocaner mahāyuddhaṃ*).]—§ 524*d* (Vishṇu): III, **272**, 15842, 15843, 15844, 15845 (is deluded by Vishṇu in the shape of a dwarf).—§ 548 (Āraṇeyap.): III, **315**, 17462 (do.).—§ 552 (Goharaṇap.): IV, **58**, 1884 (*Bali-Vāsavayor iva*); **64**, 2046 (do.).—§ 555*b* (Vishṇu):

V, **10**, 297 (*Balim baddhvā mahā-Daityam Çakro devādhipaḥ kṛtaḥ*).—§ 556 (Sañjayayānap.): V, **32**, †962 (*rājā*).—§ 559 (Prajāgarap.): V, **38**, 1445 (*aiçvarya-mada-sammūḍham Balim lokatrayād iva*).—[§ 567 (Bhagavadyānap.): V, **130**, 4368 (*Indro Vairocanim yathā*).]—§ 571 (Ulūkadūt.): VI, **160**, 5411 (*yathā devāsure yuddhe Bali-Vāsavayor abhūt*).—§ 589 (Droṇābhishekap.): VII, **1**, 26 (*Āsurīva yathā senā nigṛhīte purā Balau*).—[§ 592 (Saṃçaptakav.): VII, **21**, 859 (*Indra-Vairocanāv iva*)]; **25**, 1084 (*yatherdrāgnī purā Balim*). — [§ 599 (Jayadrathavadhap.): VII, **94**, 3484 (*yathā Vairocanis tathā*)]; **117**, 4649 (*Bali-Vāsavayor iva*); [**136**, 5608 (*Çakra-Vairocanī yathā*)]; **142**, 5886 (*purā devāsure yuddhe Çakrasya Balinā yathā*).—§ 600 (Ghaṭotkacavadhap.): VII, **156**, 6761 (*Baler iva suraiḥ pūrvam trailokya-jaya-kāṅkshayā*); **167**, 7485 (*yādṛçam hy abhavad rājan Bali-Vāsavayoḥ purā*); **172**, 7641 (*Bali-Vāsavayor iva*); [**174**, 7873 (*Indra-Vairocanāv iva*)].—§ 605 (Karṇap.): VIII, **20**, †820 (*jite Balau Vishṇum ivāmareçvaraḥ*). — § 608 (do.): VIII, **79**, †4081 (*tathā yathā Vajradharaḥ purā Baleḥ*); [**87**, 4376 (*trailokya-vijaye yattāv Indra-Vairocanāv iva*); **89**, †4528 (*Sureça-Vairocanayor yathā purā*)]; **90**, †4701 (*tathā yathā Çambarahā purā Balim*); **93**, 4880 (*devān iva purā Baliḥ*); **94**, †4963 (*Balim niyamyeva Sureça-Keçavau*).—§ 610 (Çalyap.): IX, **3**, 171 (*devān iva purā Baliḥ*).—§ 611 (do.): IX, **22**, 1161 (*Balim Çakra ivāhave*).—§ 612 (Hradapraveçap.): IX, **31ζ**, 1750 (*kriyābhyupāyair bahubhir Balir baddho mahātmanā*).—§ 615u (Skanda): IX, **46**, 2700 (*Bāṇo nāmātha Daiteyo Baleḥ putro mahābalaḥ*). — § 639 (Strīvilāp.): XI, **23**, 646 (*Çakrasya Balinā yathā*).—§ 641 (Rājadh.): XII, **90**, 3385 (*Vairocano Baliḥ*; on account of his hatred of the brahmans, Çrī deserted him). — § 656 (Khaḍgotp.): XII, **166γ**, 6146. — § 659 (Mokshadh.): XII, **180a**, 6692. — § 671 (do.): XII, **223**, 8059 (*Vāsavasya ca saṃvādam Baler Vairocanasya ca*).—§ 671b (Bali-Vāsava-s.): XII, **223**, 8060, 8061, 8063, 8064, 8065, 8067, 8068, 8070, [8082 (*Asurādhipa*)], (8083); **224**, 8090, (8092), 8117 (*Vairocano Baliḥ*), 8138; **225**, 8149, 8150, (8151), 8152, 8154 (*Vairocano Baliḥ*), 8156 (*Balinaḥ kṛte*), 8158, 8159, 8177, (8178), 8181, [8182 (*mahāsura*)], 8185 (*Daityendro Baliḥ*), 8186.—§ 673b (do.): XII, **227**, 8218 (*Bali-Vāsava-saṃvādam*), 8223 (*Balim Vairocanim*), 8224, [8227 (*Vairocane*)], 8232 (*Balir Vairocano*), (8233), [8819 (*Vairocane*), 8824 (*Asura*)].—§ 717b (Nārāyaṇīya): XII, **340κ**, 12943 (*Virocanasya balavān Baliḥ putro mahāsuraḥ*), 12947 (*Baliñ caiva karishyāmi Pātāla-talavāsinam | Dānavañ ca Balim çreshṭham abadhyaṃ sarvadaivataiḥ*, says Nārāyaṇa), 12958 (*tataḥ sutam Baler jitvā Vāṇam bāhu-sahasriṇam*). — § 723 (Ānuçāsan.): XIII, **6a**, 329 (*Balir Vairocanir baddho dharmapāçena daivataiḥ*; by Vishṇu's prowess he was made to dwell in Pātāla).—§ 742 (do.): XIII, **39a**, 2238.—[§ 749 (do.): XIII, **90**, 4290 (*Asurendrāya*; what is given in wrath and what is destitute of faith, all this Brahmán made the share of the Asura chief).]—§ 754 (do.): XIII, **98**, 4686 (*Çukrasya ca Baleç caiva saṃvādaṃ vai mahātmanoḥ*), 4687 (*Baler Vairocanasyeha trailokyam anuçāsataḥ*), [4688 (*Asurādhipaḥ*)], (4691), [4741 (*Asurendrāya*)].—§ 766 (do.): XIII, **126**, 6016 (*vāmanam rūpam āsthāya jito rājā mayā Baliḥ*).—§ 772k (Agastya): XIII, **156**, 7274.

Bali[2] (the king who rescued Dīrghatamas). § 170 (Dīrghatamas): I, **104**, 4208, 4209, 4217, 4221.

Bali ∼ Sudeshṇā ∼ Dīrghatamas ∼ çūdrā

Aṅga. Vaṅga. Kaliṅga. Puṇḍra. Suhma ‖ Kākshīvat + 10 sons

Bali[3]. § 264 (Sabhākriyāp.): II, **4a**, 105 (among the ṛshis and kings present when Yudhishṭhira entered his palace).

[Bali-Vāsava-saṃvāda(ḥ)] ("the discourse between Bali and Indra"). (*a*) § 671b (Mokshadh.): One day, after having subjugated all As., *Indra* asked *Brahmán* where *Bali* now was, he who was *Vāyu*, etc. (*a*). *Brahmán* said that *Bali* might now have taken his birth among camels or bulls, etc., and be staying in a deserted house; he told *Indra* not to slay him, but to ask him for instruction in morality. *Indra* roamed over the earth on *Airāvata*, and found *Bali* in a deserted house in the form of an ass. *Indra* scoffed at him, and asked if he did not grieve, and where his 42,000 *Gandharvas* had gone who in former days used to dance before him, and also about the garland given to him by *Brahmán*. *Bali* said: "When thou becomest like me, thou wilt not indulge in speech like this" (XII, **223**). *Bali* said that D., men, P., G., snakes, and Rā. were under his sway in days gone by, and that all creatures used to flatter him; but he did not grieve at all; in reality it is Time that creates and destroys all things, though living creatures brag of doing this or that; "this royal glory (*rājya-çrī*) . . . does not dwell long in one place; she had dwelt in thousands of *Indras* before thee, who were very much superior to thee; . . . knowing thee to be full of vanity, she will very soon desert thee" (XII, **224**). *Indra* saw *Çrī*, adorned with head-plumes, etc., issue out of *Bali*, who did not know whether she was an As. damsel or a celestial one or a human one; *Indra* asked her who she was, as she stood there like *Māyā* herself; she said: "*Virocana* did not know me; *Bali* does not know me; the learned called me *Duḥsahā* ('difficult to be borne'), etc. (*β*); thou knowest me not, O *Indra*, nor does any one of the deities know me; nor the Creator (*Dhātā*), nor the Ordainer (*Vidhātā*) rules over me; it is *Time* that moves me from one place to another; do not disregard *Bali*. *Bali* has fallen off from truth, etc.; formerly he was devoted to the *brahmans*, etc.; but latterly he began to cherish feelings of animosity towards the *brahmans* and touched clarified butter with soiled hands; therefore I desert him and shall henceforth dwell in thee; there is none among D., G., As., or Rā. that can keep me for ever." Requested by *Indra*, she told him how she might be able to reside in him permanently, dividing herself into four parts, according to the ordinance laid down in the *Vedas*: one to be established on earth, one in the waters, one in Fire, one among the good, while *Indra* should continue to protect her. *Bali* said that when the Sun would shine only upon the region of *Brahmán* in the middle of *Sumeru*, then a great battle between the gods and the *Asuras* would again occur, and in that fight *Bali* would certainly vanquish them all. *Indra* said that *Brahmán* had commanded him never to kill him; "never will come the day when the Sun will shine only from the meridian (*madhyataḥ sthitaḥ*); *Brahmán* has before this laid down the laws that regulate the Sun's motions . . . ." *Bali* proceeded towards the South; *Indra* proceeded towards the North and ascended the skies (XII, **225**).—(*b*) § 673b (Mokshadh.): *Bhīshma* said: After the battle between the gods and the *Asuras*, in which a large number of Dai. and Dā. fell, *Bali* became king. He was deceived by *Vishṇu*, who once more established his sway over all the worlds. *Indra* was once more invested with the sovereignty of the gods, etc.; the three worlds once more swelled with prosperity, and *Brahmán* became glad of heart. At that time *Indra*, accompanied by R., V., Ā., A., D.-ṛ., G.,

Si., etc., seated on the four-tusked *Airāvata*, made a progress through all the worlds. Once he saw *Bali Vairocani* within a certain mountain cave on the sea-shore. *Bali* showed no signs of sorrow or agitation. *Indra* asked him how it was that he was so unmoved; "thou art bound with *Varuṇa's* noose and hast been struck with my thunderbolt." *Bali* said: "What I am now, thou wilt be in the future," explaining that only time (not merit) rules the destiny of men; "that thou regardest thyself as the actor is the root of all sorrow"; "in the course of time many thousands of *Indras* and of deities have been swept away *yuga* after *yuga*, and will be swept away in future . . . . , just as *Pṛthu*, etc. (*a*)," though they were devoted to the *Vedas* and *Vedic* rites, etc., and though all of them were the offspring of *Daksha's* daughters; "those 1,000 [celestial years], that are the measure of thy sway, will surely come to an end"; "Ā., R., Sā., V., and M. were all vanquished by me," etc. *Indra's* panegyric on *Bali*. *Indra* left the spot and was praised by the M.-ṛ.; *Fire* once more began to bear the libations [to the gods], etc. (XII, **227**)

Balīha (pl. °*āḥ*) (a people). § 562 (Bhagavadyānap.): V, **74**γ, 2730 (*Arkajaç ca Balīhānām [kulapāṃsanaḥ]*).

Balin = Çiva (1000 names[2])

Balīna (an Asura). § 130 (Aṃçāvat.): I, **67**, 2679 (°*ottamaḥ*, incarnated as Pauṇḍramātsyaka).

Balīvāka (B. °*lī*°). § 264 (Sabhākriyāp.): II, **4***a*, 108.

Bali-Vāsava-saṃvāda, v. before Balīhāḥ.

Ballava, the name which Bhīmasena Pāṇḍava gave himself when dwelling with king Virāṭa: IV, 28, †237, †238, 363, 560, 565, 1020, 1370, 2291; V, 5472.

Ballavāḥ (B.), v. *Mallavāḥ* (C.), a people.

Balotkaṭā (a Mātṛ). § 615*u* (Skanda): IX, **46**θ, 2641.

Bāṇa[1] (an Asura, son of Bali). § 91 (Aṃçāv.): I, **67**, 2528 (*Mahāsura*; a follower of Rudra, and also called Mahākāla; cf. Daitya, pl.).—§ 561 (Yānasandhip.): V, **62**, †2421 (*Vāṇasya Bhaumasya ca Karṇa hantā . . . Vāsudevaḥ*).—§ 567 (Bhagavadyānap.): V, **130**ξ, 4412 (*Vāṇaç ca nihataḥ saṅkhye* by Kṛshṇa).—§ 615*u* (Skanda): IX, **46**, 2700 (v. Bali; he sought refuge in the Krauñca mountain).—§ 673*b* (Bali-Vāsavas.): XII, **227***a*, 8264.—§ 717 (Nārāyaṇīya): XII, **340**, 12957, 12958 (*tataḥ sutaṃ Valer jitvā Vāṇaṃ bāhusahasriṇam*)

Bāṇa[2] (a warrior of Skanda's). § 615*u* (Skanda): IX, **45**η, 2569.

Bāṇahasta = Çiva (1000 names[2]).

Bandhakartṛ = Çiva (1000 names[2]).

Bandhana = Çiva (1000 names[2]).

Bandhana(ḥ) Asurendrāṇām = Çiva (1000 names[2]).

Bāndhava, Ma°pu°st°.

Barbara, pl. ([a] barbarous people[s]). § 223 (Vāsishṭha): I, **175**, 6684.—§ 280 (Bhīmasena): II, **29**, 1088 (vanquished by Bhīmasena).—§ 285 (Nakula): II, **32**, 1199 (vanquished by Nakula).—§ 295 (Dyūtap.): II, **51**, 1843 (among the peoples who brought tribute to Yudhishṭhira).—§ 342 (Indralokābhigam.): III, **51**, 1989 (among the peoples who were present at Yudhishṭhira's rājasūya).—§ 515 (Karṇadigvijaya): III, **254**, 15254.—§ 574 (Jambūkh.): VI, **9**μ, 364 (in Bhārata-varsha).—§ 599 (Jayadrathavadhap.): VII, **119**, 4716, 4722 (ββ), 4747 (γγ); **121**εε, 4819.—§ 641 (Rājadh.): XII, **65**θ, 2429 (*Çavara*°).—§ 664 (Mokshadh.): XII, **207**θ, 7560.—§ 739 (Ānuçāsan.): XIII, **35**ε, 2158 (*Çavara*°).

Bārhadratha[1] (a certain Vedic section). § 560 (Sanatsujātap.): V, **44**, 1711 (Bráhman is not to be found in *B.*, Rathantara, etc.).

Bārhadratha[2] (patron. of Jarāsandha). § 273 (Rājasūyārambhap.): II, **14**, 594 (°*sute*, i.e. Asti and Prāpti, married by Kaṃsa).—§ 274 (do.): II, **15**, 651 (*B*°*o Jarāsandhaḥ*).—§ 277 (Jarāsandhavadhap.): II, **21**, 811 (pl.) (the race of Jarāsandha), 851; **22**, 863; **24**, 966 (°*puram*, i.e. Rājagṛha).

Bārhaspata ("belonging to or named after Bṛhaspati"). § 650 (Āpaddh.): XII, **142**, 5437 (*iti Vārhaspatam jñānam provāca Maghavā svayam*).—§ 746 (Ānuçāsan.): XIII, **76**, †3692 (*Vārhaspatīm bhāratīṃ*).

Bārhaspatya (= Bārhaspata). § 537 (Rāma-Rāvaṇa-y.): III, **285**, 16370 (*Vārhaspatyaṃ vidhiṃ kṛtvā*).—§ 608 (Karṇap.): VIII, **46**, 2149 (*Vārhaspatyaḥ . . . mahā-vyūhaḥ*).—§ 641 (Rājadh.): XII, **59**, 2205 (*Vārhaspatyaṃ yad ucyate*, i.e. the abridgement of Bāhudantaka, which was undertaken by Bṛhaspati).—§ 746 (Ānuçāsan.): XIII, **76**, †3688 (*Vārhaspatyaṃ vākyam*).

Barhin[1]. § 102 (Aṃçāvat.): I, **65**, 2554 (among the ten Devagandharvāḥ Prādheyāḥ).

Barhin[2]. § 775 (Ānuçāsan.): XIII, **166**γ, 7664 (a ṛshi in the East).

Barhishad[1] (pl.) (a kind of Pitṛs or munis). § 267 (Yamasabhāv.): II, **8**, 341.—§ 684 (Mokshadh.): XII, **270***a*, 9650.—§ 717*b* (Nārāyaṇīya): XII, **349**, 13592 (*munayaḥ*).

Barhishad[2]? (a ṛshi). § 665 (Mokshadh.): XII, **208**, 7593 (*ṛshir Medhātitheḥ putraḥ Kaṇvo Barhishadas tathā*; is *Barhishadas* genitive? Westergaard proposes *Nārshadas*, a patron. of Kaṇva; BR. identifies him with Barhin[2]).—§ 770 (Ānuçāsan.): XIII, **151**ζ, 7109 (do.; a Mānava; in the East).

Barhishada?, v. Barhishad[2].

Bāshkala (C. Vā°) (a son of Hiraṇyakaçipu). § 89 (Aṃçāvat.): I, **65**, 2526.—§ 130 (do.): I, **67**, 2645 (C. *Bāsk*°) (incarnated as Bhagadatta).

Bhadra[1] (pl. °*āḥ*) (a people). § 295 (Dyūtap.): II, **52**, 1870 (only B., C. has Madra°).—§ 515 (Karṇadigvijaya): III, **254**, 15256 (conquered by Karṇa).

Bhadra[2]. § 608 (Karṇap.): VIII, **56**νν, 2739 (slain by Karṇa).

Bhadrā[1]. § 186 (Vyushitāçva): I, **121**, 4695 (*Bh*°*ā Kākshīvatī*, the queen of Vyushitāçva), 4698, (4699), 4711, 4713.

Bhadrā[2]. § 240 (Vaivāhikap.): I, **199**, 7352 (*yathā Vaiçravaṇe Bhadrā . . . tvaṃ bhava bhartṛshu*).

Bhadrā[3]. § 291 (Çiçupālavadhap.): II, **45**, 1570 (*esha . . . jahāra Bhadrāṃ Vaiçālīṃ mātulasya*).

Bhadrā[4] (daughter of Soma and wife of Utathya). § 772*j* (Utathya): XIII, **155**, 7241, 7259 (ravished by Varuṇa).

Bhadrā[5] (daughter of Vasudeva) = Subhadrā (q.v.).

Bhadrā[6] (a wife of Vasudeva's). § 793 (Mausalap.): XVI, **7**, 194.

Bhadraçākha (a form of Skanda). § 500 (Skandopākhyāna): III, **228**, 14390, 14400.

Bhadraçālavana, v. °sāla°.

Bhadrāçva (a "dvīpa"). § 574 (Jambūkh.): VI, **6**δ, 207 (a dvīpa near Meru); **7**, 267 (*Meroḥ pārçvam ahaṃ pūrvaṃ vakshyāmy api yathātatham | tasya pūrvābhishekas tu Bh*°*sya . . .* ; B. *mūrdhābhi*°). In *Bh.* is a large forest of *bhadraçālas* and a huge tree *kālāmra*, which always has fruits and flowers, a *yojana* in height, adored by Si. and Cā.

The men there are all white, with great energy and strength; the women of the complexion of lilies (*kumudavarṇāḥ*), very beautiful, etc.; they live 10,000 years. Drinking the juice of the *kālāmra*, they continue youthful for ever.—§ 623 (Rājadh.): XII, **14a**, 407 (to the north of Meru; had been ruled by Yudhishṭhira).

Bhadrakālī[1] (a form of Durgā). § 576 (Bhagavadgītāp.): VI, **23**, 797 (in Arjuna's hymn to Durgā).—§ 695*b* (Dakshayajña-vināça): XII, **285**, 10327.

Bhadrakālī[2] (a Mātṛ). § 615*u* (Skanda): IX, **46θ**, 2629.

Bhadrakāra (pl. °*āḥ*) (a people). § 273 (Rājasūyārambhap.): II, **14**, 590.

Bhadrakarṇeçvara (a tīrtha). § 370 (Tīrthay.): III, **84**, 8017.

Bhadrakṛt = Skanda: III, 14632.

Bhadramanas. § 127 (Aṃçāvat.): I, **66**, 2624, 2627 (one of the nine daughters of Krodha and mother of Airāvata).

Bhādrapadā (two nakshatras, Pūrva- and Uttara-Bh°, with the junction stars α Pegasi and γ Pegasi or α Andromedæ, v. Sū° Si°). § 746 (Ānuçāsan.): XIII, **64**, 3282 (*Pūrva-Bhādrapadā-yoge*).—§ 759 (Ānuçāsan.): XIII, **110**, 5391 (*nābhiṃ Bhādrapade vindyāt*).

Bhādrapada (a month, the 5th of the solar year, the 6th of the luni-solar, Aug.-Sept., v. Sū° Si°). § 759 (Ānuçāsan.): XIII, **109**, 5381 (*māsi*).—§ 766 (do.): XIII, **126**, 6040 (*māsi*).

Bhadrasālavana (C. °*çāla*) ("a forest with beautiful *Shorea robusta*"). § 574*h* (Bhadrāçva): VI, **7**, 268.

Bhadratuṅga (a tīrtha). § 358 (Tīrthay.): III, **82**, 5022.

Bhadravaṭa ("the beautiful fig-tree," a locality). § 506 (Skandayuddha): III, **231**, 14542.—§ 507 (do.): III, **231**, 14625.

Bhaga[1] (an Āditya). § 88 (Aṃçāv.): I, **65**, 2523.—§ 191 (Arjuna): I, **123**, 4822.—§ 258 (Khāṇḍavadah.): I, **227**, 8268.—§ 266 (Çakrasabhāv.): II, **7**, 303 (in the palace of Indra). — § 615*u* (Skanda): IX, **45γ**, 2507. — § 617 (Aishīkap.): X, **18**, 801 (had his eyes plucked out by Rudra), 807 (id.). — § 665 (Mokshadh.): XII, **208β**, 7581.—§ 746 (Ānuçāsan.): XIII, **65δ**, 3295.—§ 770 (do.): XIII, **151γ**, 7092 (C. *Bhāgas*; enumeration of the 12 Ādityas).—§ 773*d* (Çiva): XIII, **161**, 7475 (had his eyes torn out by Rudra).—Cf. Bhaganetra°, etc.—Is often used to signify 'love,' etc. (e.g. XIV, 1184).

Bhaga[2] (the nakshatras Pūrvā and Uttarā Phālgunī). § 574 (Jambūkh.): VI, **3a**, 81 (*Bhagaṃ nakshatram ākramya Sūryaputreṇa pīḍyate*).

Bhaga[3] = the Sun. § 310*b* (Sūrya): III, **3**, 146 (in the enumeration of Dhaumya).

Bhaga[4] (a Rudra). § 108 (Aṃçāvat.): I, **66**, 2567 (son of Sthāṇu).—§ 191 (Arjuna): I, **123**, 4826 (enumeration of 13 Rudras).

Bhagadā (a mātṛ). § 615*u* (Skanda): IX, **46θ**, 2644.

Bhagadaivata ("whose divinity is Bhaga"). § 21 (Pramadvarā): I, **8**, 953 (*nakshatre*, i.e. Uttarā Phālgunī).—§ 759 (Ānuçāsan.): XIII, **106β**, 5153 (°*māsa* = the month Phālguna).

Bhagadatta (king of Prāgjyotisha). § 11 (Parvas.): I, **2**, 531 (*Bh°o mahārājo yatra Çakrasamo yudhi | Supratīkena nāgena sa hi çāntaḥ Kirīṭinā*).—§ 130 (Aṃçāvat.): I, **67**, 2645 (incarnation of the Asura Bāskala).—§ 232 (Svayaṃvarap.): I, **186a**, 6992.—§ 269 (Vaiçravaṇasabhāv.): II, **10**, 409 (*Kinnarāḥ çataças tatra dhanānām īçvaraṃ prabhuṃ | āsate cāpi rājāno Bhagadatta-purogamāḥ*).—§ 273 (Rājasūyārambhap.): II, **14**, 579 (the old friend of Yudhishṭhira's father; he has bowed to Jarāsandha, but loves Yudhishṭhira as a father).—§ 279 (Arjuna): II, **26**, 1001 (is vanquished by Arjuna; king of Prāgjyotisha; surrounded by Kirātas, Cīnas, and other warriors dwelling along the sea-coast; he was a friend of Indra and equal to Indra in battle; friend of the father of Arjuna and beloved by him), (1009); **27**, 1010.—§ 287 (Rājasūyikap.): II, **34**, 1268 (*Prāgjyotishaç ca nṛpatir Bhagadatto mahārathaḥ | sa tu sarvaiḥ saha mlecchaiḥ sāgarānūpavāsibhiḥ*).—§ 290 (Çiçupālavadhap.): II, **44a**, 1538.—§ 295 (Dyūtap.): II, **51**, 1834 (*Prāgjyotishādhipaḥ çūro mlecchānām adhipo balī | Yavanaiḥ sahito rājā Bhagadatto mahārathaḥ*; among those who pay tribute to Yudhishṭhira), 1836 (do.; he brought *açmasāramayaṃ bhāṇḍaṃ çuddhadanta-tsarūn asīn*). — § 513 (Ghoshayātrāp.): III, **252**, 15163 (°*purogamāḥ*).—§ 515 (Karṇadigvijaya): III, **254**, 15241 (*Bhagadattañ ca nirjitya Rādheyo girim āruhat | Himavantaṃ . . .*).—§ 554 (Sainyodyogap.): V, **4γ**, 74 (*Bhagadattāya rājñe ca pūrvasāgaravāsine*).—§ 555 (do.): V, **19**, 584 (gave Duryodhana an akshauhiṇī, crowded with Cīnas and Kirātas).—§ 561 (Yānasandhip.): V, **66εε**, 2502 (on the side of Duryodhana).—§ 571 (Ulūkadūt.): V, **160**, †5531 (°*mārutaṃ . . . purushodadhiṃ*).—§ 572 (Rathātirath.): V, **167**, 5804 (*Prāgjyotishādhipo vīro Bhagadattaḥ pratāpavān | gajāṅkuçadharaçreshṭho rathe caiva viçāradaḥ*; had formerly fought with Arjuna during many days; a friend of Indra; he will fight riding an elephant).—§ 576 (Bhagavadgītāp.): VI, **17γ**, 672 (riding on his elephant), 673.—§ 578 (Bhīshmavadhap.): VI, **45**[13], 1717, 1718, 1719; **51φ**, 2107.—§ 580 (do.): VI, **56β**, 2406.—§ 581 (do.): VI, **64**[15], 2852, 2858, 2863, 2869 ([16]), 2870, 2873 ([17]), 2879; **65ν**, 2929.—§ 583 (do.): VI, **76ι**, 3330.—§ 584 (do.): VI, **83**[3], 3663, 3665, 3670.—§ 585 (do.): VI, **87**, 3854; **89λ**, 3934; **95**, 4247, 4255 (on his elephant Supratīka), 4256, 4263, 4268, 4275, 4282, 4293, 4305, 4312, 4320, 4321 (ζζ); **96ηη**, 4339, 4358.—§ 586 (do.): VI, **99β**, 4503; **102κ**, 4667.—§ 587 (do.): VI, **108**, 5006δ, 5051; **111**, 5146, 5149 (*Prāgjyotisho rājā Mādhavasya mahad dhanuḥ | ciccheda*, etc.); **113ι**, 5239, 5243, 5260, 5273, 5276; **116**, 5429; **119ψ**, 5583.—§ 590 (Droṇābhishekap.): VII, **14**, 534, 535, 536.—§ 592 (Saṃçaptakav.): VII, **26**, 1158, 1161 (*Prāgjyotishaṃ*), 1165, 1166, 1174, 1175, 1189; **27**, 1196, 1203, 1206, 1225; **28**, 1246, 1248, 1249, 1250; **29**, 1256, 1260, 1261, 1267, 1273, 1291 (*mahāsuraṃ*), 1292, 1295, 1297 (is slain by Arjuna), 1298 (do.); [**30**, 1302: *priyam Indrasya satataṃ sakhāyam amitaujasaṃ | hatvā Prāgjyotishaṃ Pārthaḥ pradakshiṇam avartata*].—§ 599 (Jayadrathavadhap.): VII, **147**, 6387 (has been slain).—§ 600 (Ghaṭotkacavadhap.): VII, **158ω**, 7036.—§ 603 (Nārāyaṇāstramokshap.): VII, **197**, 9120 (has been slain by Arjuna, though he was the friend of Arjuna's father). — § 604 (Karṇap.): VIII, **5**, 105, 118 (°*suto*, has been slain by Nakula). — § 605 (do.): VIII, **18**, 688. — § 608 (do.): VIII, **72**, 3612 (νυν).—§ 609 (Çalyap.): IX, **2ζ**, 72, 89.—§ 611 (do.): IX, **24**, 1300 (νν).—§ 613 (Gadāyuddhap.): IX, **32**, 1836.—§ 615 (do.): IX, **64**, 3613 (εε).—§ 619 (Strīvilāp.): XI, **23**, 644 (*Çailālayo . . . gajāṅkuçadharaḥ çreshṭhaḥ*).—§ 620 (Çrāddhap.): XI, **26**, 790 (β).—§ 785 (Anugītāp.): XIV, **76**, 2198 (in Prāgjyotisha, Bhagadatta's son Vajradatta was vanquished by Arjuna).—§ 787 (Āçramavāsap.): XV, **20**, 547 (*Çailālayo rājā Bhagadattapitāmahaḥ*, had gone to the seat of Indra).—§ 789 (Putradarçanap.): XV, **32θ**, 877 (*Jarāsandhir, Bha°o, Jalasandhaç ca . . .*).

Bhagadattaja = Vajradatta: XIV, 2189.
Bhagadattasuta = Vajradatta: XIV, 2177, 2208.
Bhagadattātmaja = Vajradatta: XIV, 2175, 2190, 2220.
Bhagaghna = Çiva: VII, 9538.
Bhagahan = Vishṇu: XIII, 7009 (1000 names).
Bhagahārin = Çiva: XIII, 1190 (1000 names[1]).
Bhāgakara = Çiva: XIII, 1197 (1000 names[2]).
Bhagākshihan = Çiva: XII, 6169.
Bhaganandā (a mātṛ). § 615u (Skanda): IX, **46**θ, 2629.
Bhaganetraghna = Çiva: XIII, 6565, 6806.
Bhaganetrahan = Çiva: II, 420; III, 1649.
Bhaganetrahara = Çiva: I, 4371, 7970; X, 249 (*Haraṃ*); XII, 10344, 13149.
Bhaganetranipātana = Çiva: III, 1624, 15857; VII, 3465.
Bhaganetrāṅkuça = Çiva: XII, 10423 (1000 names[1]).
* **Bhagavadbhakta** (pl. °*āḥ*) ("adoring the Exalted one"). § 248 (Arjunavanavāsap.): I, **214**, 7777.
Bhagavadgītā ("the song of the Exalted one"). § 10 (Parvas.): I, **2**, 338 (*parva*, i.e. Bhagavadgītāparvan).
[Bhagavadgītāparvan(°va)] ("the section including the song of the Exalted one," the 69th of the minor parvans of Mhbhr.; cf. Bhagavadgītā). § 576: *Sañjaya* informs *Dhṛtarāshṭra* of *Bhīshma's* fall in battle (VI, **13**). *Dhṛtarāshṭra's* lament and inquiries (VI, **14**). *Sañjaya*, praising *Vyāsa* for his *yoga*-power, i.e. the celestial vision (description) he had given him, began his discourse on the battle. *Duryodhana* gave *Duḥçāsana* instructions about the protection of *Bhīshma* from *Çikhaṇḍin* (VI, **15**). The two hosts arrayed at sunrise (description). *Çakuni*, etc. (*a*), stood each at the head of an *akshauhiṇī*; the 11th under *Bhīshma* (description) stood in advance of the whole army. The *Sṛñjayas*, headed by *Dhṛshṭadyumna*, looked [beholding *Bhīshma*] like small animals beholding a lion (VI, **16**). On that day *Soma* approached the region of the *Pitṛs*. Omens. Every morning *Bhīshma* and *Droṇa* prayed for victory for the *Pāṇḍavas*, though they must fight for *Dhṛtarāshṭra* according to their pledge: *Bhīshma* briefly addressed the *Kuru* army, mentioning *Nābhaga*, etc. (β), as examples. *Karṇa*, with his friends and relatives, laid aside his weapons owing to *Bhīshma*. Description of the proceedings of the army, especially of *Bhīshma*, etc. (γ) (VI, **17**). *Duḥçāsana*, etc. (δ), protected *Bhīshma* from behind, etc. (VI, **18**). *Yudhishṭhira* told *Arjuna*, according to the words of the M.-ṛ. *Bṛhaspati*, to array the troops in needle-mouthed (*çucīmukha*) array. *Arjuna* said that he would make a *Vajra* array, which was designed by *Indra*; they would all seek shelter with *Bhīma*. The leaders were *Bhīmasena*, etc. (ε). Omens (VI, **19**). When the sun rose the *Kauravas* stood facing the west, the *Pāṇḍavas* facing the east. Disposition of the two armies: *Duryodhana*, etc. (ζ) (VI, **20**). *Yudhishṭhira* sorrowfully addressed *Arjuna*, who consoled him with his truth, righteousness, etc., which *Nārada*, *Bhīshma*, and *Droṇa* knew, and which were a powerful aid towards victory according to *Bráhman's* words to *Indra*, etc., on the occasion of the battle between the gods and the *Asuras*; "victory clings to Kṛshṇa"; it was by choosing him that the gods under *Indra* had vanquished the *Asuras* (VI, **21**). Disposition of the troops in the *Pāṇḍava* army: *Çikhaṇḍin*, etc. (η) (VI, **22**). At *Kṛshṇa's* instance *Arjuna* recited a hymn to *Durgā*. *Durgā* appeared and gave him assurances of victory. Merits of this hymn (VI, **23**). The combatants of both armies were cheerful, etc. (VI, **24**). Before *Droṇa*, *Duryodhana* compared the combatants of the *Pāṇḍava* army: *Bhīma*, etc. (θ), with his own; *Droṇa*, etc. (ι). *Kṛshṇa*, etc., blew *Pāñcajanya*, etc. (κ). *Arjuna* asked *Kṛshṇa* to place his chariot between the two armies, so that he might see who were assembled to fight. Beholding his relatives, etc., *Arjuna* was filled with compassion and overcome with despondency, and refused to fight (VI, **25**). *Kṛshṇa* appealed to *Arjuna* to shake off his despondency, but in vain. *Kṛshṇa* then declared to *Arjuna* the nature and the attributes of the soul, and the folly of grieving for the dead, and exhorted him to comply with the duties of his order by fighting fairly, and to apply himself to work for work's sake, and not for the sake of its results. *Kṛshṇa* spoke of contemplation (VI, **26**); on the *Sāṅkhyas* and *Yogins*; on devotion to work (VI, **27**); on his reiterated births; on the best way (VI, **28**); on abandonment of actions and application to actions; he has the right view who considers *Sāṅkhya* and *Yoga* as one (VI, **29**); on the means of rising to devotion (VI, **30**); on *Kṛshṇa* identified with *Bráhman* (VI, **31**); on the nature of Bráhman (VI, **32**); on *Kṛshṇa* as the pervader of the whole universe, and as the enjoyer of all sacrifice (VI, **33**); on *Kṛshṇa* as the source of the gods, etc. *Arjuna* believed what *Kṛshṇa* said, and what also had been said by all the Ṛ., and the D.-ṛ. *Nārada*, and *Asita Devala* and *Vyāsa*. *Kṛshṇa* declared his divine perfections to *Arjuna* (VI, **34**), and disclosed his supreme sovereign form; he was praised by *Arjuna* (VI, **35**); he discoursed on the two kinds of worshippers (VI, **36**); on the body and the soul, etc., the supreme object of knowledge (VI, **37**); on the three *guṇas* (Goodness, Passion, and Darkness) (VI, **38**); on the symbolical *Açvattha* (VI, **39**); on godlike and demoniac natures and births (VI, **40**); on the threefold nature of faith (VI, **41**); on renunciation and abandonment. —*Arjuna's* delusion is destroyed, and he once more takes up the *Gāṇḍīva* (VI, **42**).
Bhagavadyāna(m) ("the journey of Kṛshṇa"). § 10: I, **2**, 331, i.e. Bhagavadyānaparvan.
Bhagavad-yāna(m) ("the departure of Kṛshṇa"). § 262 (Sabhākr.): *Kṛshṇa*, after some time, desirous of beholding his father, left *Khāṇḍavaprastha*, having taken leave of *Pṛthā*, *Subhadrā*, *Kṛshṇā*, and *Dhaumya*. The *Pāṇḍavas*, etc., followed him half a *yojana*, *Yudhishṭhira* causing *Dāruka* to stand aside and, himself taking the reins, riding on *Kṛshṇa's* golden chariot with *Garuḍa* on the banner, and yoked with *Çaivya* and *Sugrīva*. Then he caused them to retire, and with *Sāttvata* (PCR. has *Sātyaki*) and *Dāruka* reached *Dvārakā*, worshipped by *Ugrasena*, etc.; and having embraced *Pradyumna*, *Çāmba*, *Niçatha*, *Çārudeshṇa*, *Gada*, *Aniruddha*, and *Bhānu*, and having worshipped *Āhuka* and (? BR. here takes *Āhuka* to be the name of his father) his old father and mother and *Bala*, he entered the dwelling of *Rukmiṇī*. *Yudhishṭhira* at *Indraprastha* sported with *Draupadī*, dismissing all his friends, brothers, and sons (II, **2**).
[Bhagavadyānaparvan] ("the section relating to the journey of Kṛshṇa," the 62nd of the minor parvans of Mhbhr.; cf. Bhagavadyāna). § 562: *Yudhishṭhira* spoke to *Kṛshṇa* about the mission of *Sañjaya* and the wickedness of *Duryodhana* and *Dhṛtarāshṭra*; though he was supported by the *Kāçis*, etc. (*a*), he asked for only five villages (*Avisthala*, etc., β) or towns, and complained of the cruel duties of the *kshattriya* order. *Kṛshṇa* said he was willing to go to the *Kuru* court in order to negotiate a peace, and *Yudhishṭhira*, after some hesitation, agreed to the proposal (V, **72**). *Kṛshṇa* mentioned the offences of the *Kauravas*, and said that he thought war to be certain; all the omens pointed in that

direction; therefore *Yudhishṭhira* should collect everything needed for battle (V, **73**). *Bhīma* told *Kṛshṇa* to speak mildly and not threaten the *Kurus* with war. "Just as, when *Dharma* became extinct, *Kali* was born in the race of the *Asuras*, who flourished with prosperity and blazed with energy, so was *Udāvarta* born among the *Haihayas*, etc. (γ). These vile individuals sprang up, at the end of each *yuga*, in their respective races for the destruction of their kinsmen; so has *Duryodhana* been born at the end of the *yuga* among us the *Kurus*. *Yudhishṭhira* and *Arjuna* too are averse from war" (V, **74**). *Kṛshṇa* scoffed at *Bhīma* for his unusual mildness, though he had sworn, as the sun journeyed around *Meru*, to slay *Duryodhana* with his mace (V, **75**). *Bhīma* mentioned his well-known valour, and said that he was for bearing their injuries, only for fear lest the *Bharata* race might be extirpated (V, **76**). *Kṛshṇa* explained that he had only spoken through affection (V, **77**). *Arjuna* told *Kṛshṇa* to strive sincerely to bring about peace; for he was able to do whatever he would; but if *Kṛshṇa* deemed the destruction of the *Kurus* to be preferable, "let it be effected soon"; he mentioned the offences of *Duryodhana* towards themselves and *Draupadī*. At all events, *Kṛshṇa* best knew what was for their good (V, **78**). *Kṛshṇa* said he would try to bring about what was beneficial to both the *Pāṇḍavas* and the *Kurus*; to make peace was within his power; he would do all that could be done by human exertion, but he could not control destiny; *Duryodhana*, etc. (δ), would never make peace by giving up the kingdom; many a time he had tried to withdraw *Kṛshṇa* from *Arjuna*; about a year ago, on the occasion of attacking *Virāṭa's* kine, *Bhīshma* had solicited *Duryodhana* about this very peace (V, **79**). *Nakula* told *Kṛshṇa* to act according to his own opinion, disregarding all he had heard. Their attachment for the kingdom was now greater than ever, as nobody could encounter *Yudhishṭhira*, etc. (ε). He should first speak mildly and then threaten *Duryodhana*. He did not doubt that he would accomplish his object, for *Vidura*, etc. (ζ), would understand him (V, **80**). *Sahadeva* said that *Kṛshṇa* ought to provoke a war, because of the insults to *Draupadī*. *Sātyaki* approved of this, and thus did all the heroes present (V, **81**). *Kṛshṇā* approved of the words of *Sahadeva* and *Sātyaki*, mentioned weeping the injustice of the *Dhārtarāshṭras*, and that they had refused to give even five villages, *Avisthala*, etc. (ζ), and was of opinion that there was no necessity for going thither in order to make peace. *Kṛshṇa* consoled her: "Thou wilt soon see thy husbands slay their enemies, and crowned by prosperity" (V, **82**). *Arjuna* once more besought *Kṛshṇa* to try to make peace. On the next morning, at the *Maitra* hour, in the month of *Kaumuda* (Kārttika), under the constellation *Revatī*, at the season of dews, Autumn having departed (description), *Kṛshṇa* caused *Çini's* grandson *Sātyaki* to prepare his chariot (description); they yoked to it *Çaibya*, *Sugrīva*, *Meghapushpa*, and *Balāhaka*. *Garuḍa* came and perched on the flagstaff. And taking *Sātyaki* also upon it, he set out under auspicious omens; *Vasishṭha*, etc. (η), and D.-ṛ. and B.-ṛ. (*devabrahmarshayaç caiva*) walked around him (*pradakshiṇam avartanta*). *Yudhishṭhira*, etc. (θ), followed him on the way, and told him to salute *Kuntī*, etc. (ι). *Arjuna* said he was for peace, but if *Duryodhana* would not give them what they demanded, he would annihilate the *Kshattriya* race. *Bhīma* uttered a terrible shout, so that the bowmen trembled in fear, and steeds and elephants were seen to void urine and fæces. When all the kings had desisted following him, *Kṛshṇa* set out with *Dāruka*. On his way he met with some *Ṛshis*, and *Jamadagni's* son, the friend of *Brahmán* (*Surāsurapateḥ*), told him that the D.-ṛ., *brahmans*, and R.-ṛ., who had witnessed the former feats of gods and *Asuras* (*devāsurasya drashṭāraḥ purāṇasya*), had come to see and hear the assemblage at *Hāstinapura* (V, **83**). Ten chariot-warriors followed in *Kṛshṇa's* train, and 100 foot-soldiers and attendants by hundreds, carrying provisions in abundance. Sinister omens occurred over *Hāstinapura*; but where *Kṛshṇa* passed everything became auspicious. At *Vṛkasthala* he passed the night (V, **84**). Meanwhile *Dhṛtarāshṭra*, having heard from his spies that *Kṛshṇa* was coming, respectfully addressed *Bhīshma*, etc. (κ), and said to *Duryodhana* and his counsellors that *Kṛshṇa* ("the lord of all creatures," etc.) should be received with the greatest honour; "let pavilions be set up on the road," etc. *Bhīshma*, etc., approved of it, and *Duryodhana* made the arrangements. But *Kṛshṇa* did not even glance at it (V, **85**). When *Kṛshṇa* was staying at *Vṛkasthala* and intended to come to *Hāstinapura* the next morning, *Dhṛtarāshṭra* spoke to *Vidura* about how he intended to treat *Kṛshṇa* in order to honour him (V, **86**). *Vidura* blamed *Dhṛtarāshṭra* for his insincerity; "the right hospitality to be offered to *Kṛshṇa* is to make peace with the *Pāṇḍavas*, and thou wilt not give them even five villages, and seekest only to separate *Kṛshṇa* from the *Pāṇḍavas*" (V, **87**). *Duryodhana* said that it was of no use to bestow wealth and honour upon *Kṛshṇa*, as he could never be separated from the *Pāṇḍavas*, "and he will only think that we are worshipping him out of fear." *Bhīshma* advised them to do as *Kṛshṇa* would say. *Duryodhana* declared that he would imprison *Kṛshṇa*. *Dhṛtarāshṭra* and all his counsellors became deeply afflicted, especially as *Kṛshṇa* came as an ambassador. Inflamed with rage, *Bhīshma* rose and left the place (V, **88**). The next morning *Kṛshṇa* rose at daybreak and arrived in *Hāstinapura*, and was solemnly received by all the *Dhārtarāshṭras* (except *Duryodhana*), etc. (λ), and the citizens (description). Having saluted *Dhṛtarāshṭra*, etc. (μ), he went to the abode of *Vidura* (V, **89**). In the afternoon he visited *Kuntī*, who wept for her sons, comparing *Yudhishṭhira* to *Ambarīsha*, etc. (ν), mentioning the feats of *Bhīmasena* (ο), comparing *Arjuna* to *Kārtavīrya*, etc. (π), and also inquiring about *Sahadeva* and *Nakula*, and likewise about *Draupadī* (whom she had not seen for fourteen long years), mentioning how she was dragged by *Duḥçāsana*, while *Bāhlika*, etc. (ρ), grieved; but especially she praised *Vidura*. "Full 14 years have gone since *Duryodhana* first exiled my son." She mentioned the invisible voice on the night of *Arjuna's* birth, and trusted to *Dharma* and the Creator and *Kṛshṇa*. She asked *Kṛshṇa* to tell her sons that she besought them to avenge themselves and *Draupadī*, as even death was better than a life gained by meanness. *Kṛshṇa* consoled her, and then departed for *Duryodhana's* mansion (V, **90**). *Kṛshṇa* entered *Duryodhana's* palace (description), where he also beheld *Duḥçāsana*, *Karṇa*, and *Çakuni*. *Duryodhana* asked him to dine at his house; but *Kṛshṇa* did not accept the invitation, because he hated the *Pāṇḍavas*, and went to *Vidura's* abode, where *Droṇa*, etc. (σ), came to him (V, **91**). *Vidura* warned *Kṛshṇa* against *Duryodhana*, who would never make peace, because he trusted *Bhīshma*, etc. (τ), and distrusted *Kṛshṇa* (V, **92**). *Kṛshṇa* said that he knew *Duryodhana*; but great would be the merit earned by him who liberates the whole earth from the noose of death; and even if he should meet failure, the merit of that intended act would become his;

"moreover, I have come here in order that unrighteous, foolish, and inimical persons shall not afterwards be free to say that *Kṛshṇa* made no attempt to restrain them from slaughtering one another, though he was competent to do so." Then he laid himself down for sleep (V, **93**). In the morning *Duryodhana* and *Çakuni* came and invited him to go to the council where *Dhṛtarāshṭra* and *Bhīshma*, etc., were present; he rode thither in his chariot with *Dāruka*, putting on his gem *Kaustubha*, and being protected by the *Vṛshṇis*, and he was followed by *Vidura* in his own chariot, and by *Duryodhana* and *Çakuni* in one chariot, and by *Sātyaki* and *Kṛtavarman* and the other chariot-warriors of the *Vṛshṇi* race in chariots and on steeds and elephants (description). Then he entered the court with *Vidura* and *Sātyaki*; before him sat *Karṇa* and *Duryodhana*, behind him the *Vṛshṇis* with *Kṛtavarman*. *Bhīshma*, *Droṇa*, etc., with *Dhṛtarāshṭra* rose up in his honour, etc. He beheld the *Ṛshis* staying in the skies with *Nārada* at their head, and caused *Bhīshma* to offer them seats. *Duḥçāsana* gave a seat to *Sātyaki*, and *Viviṃçati* one to *Kṛtavarman* (V, **94**). *Kṛshṇa* spoke of the just complaints and claims of the *Pāṇḍavas*, and said that with them as his allies *Dhṛtarāshṭra* would become invincible, having *Bhīshma*, etc. (ν). "Let not the peoples of the earth be exterminated! If thou regainest thy natural disposition, the earth may continue to be peopled as now." All the kings there present highly applauded the words of *Kṛshṇa* in their hearts, but none of them ventured to say anything in the presence of *Duryodhana* (V, **95**).—§ 563: *Jāmadagnya* then told Dambhodbhavopākhyāna (q.v.). "Great, indeed, was that feat of old achieved by *Nara*. *Nārāyaṇa* again became superior to *Nara* in consequence of many additional qualities. Therefore, O king, before such weapons as *Kākudika*, etc. (φ), are placed on the string of the *Gāṇḍīva*, go thou to *Dhanañjaya*, laying aside thy pride!" These weapons have other names corresponding to the eight passions (lust, wrath, etc.; description) (V, **96**).—§ 564: Mātalīyopākhyāna (q.v.).—§ 565: After *Kaṇva* had spoken, *Kṛshṇa*, *Bhīshma*, and *Nārada* in vain admonished *Duryodhana*. *Nārada* related the old story Gālavacarita (q.v.), and—§ 566: The fall of *Yayāti* (q.v.).—§ 567: *Dhṛtarāshṭra* complained that *Duryodhana* never listened to his, etc. (α), words, and asked *Kṛshṇa* to admonish him. *Kṛshṇa* reminded *Duryodhana* of what was agreeable to *Dhṛtarāshṭra*, etc. (β), and warned him against *Duḥçāsana*, etc. (γ). *Bhīshma*, etc. (δ), could not fight against *Bhīma* and *Arjuna*, who had vanquished D., G., Y., As., and Pn. at *Khāṇḍavaprastha*; who encountered many at *Virāṭa*'s city, etc. (ε) (V, **124**). *Bhīshma*, *Droṇa*, *Vidura*, and *Dhṛtarāshṭra* recommended *Duryodhana* to follow the counsels of *Kṛshṇa* (V, **125**). *Bhīshma* and *Droṇa* warned *Duryodhana* against *Kṛshṇa*, etc. (ζ) (V, **126**). *Duryodhana* complained that *Kṛshṇa* always censured him; in the match of dice blame could not be attached to him. He quoted this saying of *Mātaṅga*, "one should always keep himself erect . . ." (V, **127**). *Kṛshṇa* indignantly answered *Duryodhana*, mentioning his offences against the *Pāṇḍavas*, *Vāraṇāvata*, etc. (η). *Duḥçāsana* said to *Duryodhana* that the *Kauravas* would bind him, and *Bhīshma*, *Droṇa*, and *Dhṛtarāshṭra* would make *Duryodhana*, *Karṇa*, and *Duḥçāsana* over to the *Pāṇḍavas*. Disregarding *Vidura*, etc. (θ), *Duryodhana* went out of the court in anger. *Kṛshṇa* blamed them for not having forcibly seized and bound *Duryodhana*; "I think the time has come for doing this"; he reminded them of how he had himself slain *Kaṃsa*, and then installed *Ugrasena* on the throne, for the benefit of all the *Yādavas*, *Andhakas*, and *Vṛshṇis*; and that when the gods and *Asuras*, etc. (ι), were arrayed for battle *Parameshṭhin* had commanded *Dharma* to bind the *Daiteyas* and the *Dānavas* and make them over to *Varuṇa*, who having bound them with *Dharma*'s noose and also with his own, kept them within the depths of the ocean. In the same way they ought to bind *Duryodhana*, etc. (κ) (V, **128**). *Dhṛtarāshṭra* caused *Vidura* to fetch *Gāndhārī*, who blamed *Dhṛtarāshṭra*, because he had by his indulgence caused *Duryodhana* now to be the slave of delusion and incapable of being turned back; she then caused *Vidura* to fetch *Duryodhana*, whom she rebuked severely and asked to obey the words of his well-wishers *Dhṛtarāshṭra*, etc. (λ); *Bhīshma* and *Dhṛtarāshṭra* and *Bāhlīka* [formerly] gave the *Pāṇḍavas* their share from fear of a disunion. If *Bhīshma*, etc. (μ), became enraged the population of the earth would be exterminated. The affection of *Bhīshma*, *Droṇa*, and *Kṛpa* towards the *Pāṇḍavas* and the *Dhārtarāshṭras* was equal; "it is never seen in this world that men acquire wealth by avarice" (V, **129**). Disregarding the words of his mother, *Duryodhana* again went away in anger, and began to consult with *Çakuni*, and *Duryodhana*, etc. (ν), resolved upon seizing *Kṛshṇa*; then the *Pāṇḍavas* with the *Somakas* would become depressed. *Sātyaki* knew it, caused *Kṛtavarman* to array the troops at the entrance of the court, and informed *Kṛshṇa*, *Dhṛtarāshṭra*, and *Vidura*, but laughed at the project. *Vidura* told *Dhṛtarāshṭra* that the last hour of all his sons was at hand. *Kṛshṇa* said to *Dhṛtarāshṭra* that if his sons perpetrated such a deed *Yudhishṭhira*'s object would be accomplished, "for this very day, seizing them with all who follow them, I can make them over to the *Pāṇḍavas*; I will not, however, commit any such censurable deed that can proceed only from wrath and a sinful understanding." *Dhṛtarāshṭra* once more caused *Vidura* to fetch *Duryodhana* with his brothers, etc., and rebuked them; "dost thou not know *Kṛshṇa*, who is incapable of being defeated in battle by D., men, G., As., and U.?" *Vidura* reminded *Duryodhana* that at the gates of *Saubha* the monkey *Dvivida* covered *Kṛshṇa* with a shower of stones, but could not seize him; nor could *Naraka* with all the *Dānavas* at *Prāgjyotisha*; slaying *Naraka*, *Kṛshṇa* brought away 1,000 damsels and married them all. In the city of *Nirmocana* 6,000 mighty *Asuras* failed to seize him with their nooses. He also mentioned *Pūtanā Çakunī*, etc. (ξ) (V, **130**). *Kṛshṇa* reminded *Duryodhana* that he was not alone, and from his body issued myriads of gods, etc. (ο); all the kings were terrified and closed their eyes, except *Bhīshma*, *Droṇa*, *Vidura*, *Sañjaya*, and the *Ṛshis*; for *Kṛshṇa* gave them celestial sight, etc. Then he went out with *Sātyaki* and *Kṛtavarman*. The *Ṛshis Nārada*, etc., vanished. He found *Dāruka* waiting with his chariot (description) drawn by *Çaibya*, and *Kṛtavarman*, who had mounted his chariot. *Dhṛtarāshṭra* excused himself, saying that he was powerless. *Kṛshṇa* bade farewell to *Dhṛtarāshṭra*, etc. (π), and set out, followed by *Bhīshma*, etc. (ρ), to the abode of *Kuntī* (V, **131**). *Kuntī* asked him to admonish *Yudhishṭhira* to attend to the duties of his own order, and not contemplate virtue alone ("thy virtue is decreasing greatly"), citing *Mucukunda* (b). It is the king that creates the *Kṛta*, *Tretā*, or *Dvāpara* age; if he creates the *Kṛta* age, he enjoys heaven exceedingly; if he creates the *Tretā*, he enjoys heaven, but not exceedingly; if he causes the *Dvāpara* age to set in, he enjoys heaven according to his due; if he promotes the *Kali* age, he will reside in hell for countless years. "That understanding according to which thou art now acting, is not in accordance with the intentions of *Pāṇḍu*, or myself, or thy grandsire, when we uttered blessings on thee before," etc. (V, **132**). "In this connection is cited an old story: § 568. Vidulāputraçāsana" (q.v.).—§ 569: *Kuntī* asked *Kṛshṇa* to remind *Arjuna* of the voice heard at his birth (that he should rival *Indra*, vanquish the *Kurus*, conquer the earth aided by *Bhīma*; slay the *Kurus* in battle with *Kṛshṇa* as his ally, and recover his share in the kingdom, and, with his brothers, perform three great sacrifices); to *Bhīma* he should say that "the time has come for that in view of which a *kshattriya* lady brings forth a son"; *Kṛshṇā* he should praise for her behaviour towards the *Pāṇḍavas*; he should remind *Nakula* and *Sahadeva*, that they must not forgive the insults towards *Draupadī*, that was worse than the defeat at dice and the exile; *Arjuna* should always tread in the path pointed out by *Draupadī*; *Bhīma* and *Arjuna* are a pair of *Yamas* capable of slaying the very gods; they should revenge the harsh words said by *Duḥçāsana* to *Bhīma*. *Kṛshṇa* bade farewell to *Bhīshma*, etc., took *Karṇa* upon his chariot and set out with *Sātyaki*, deliberating with *Karṇa* for a long time. Then he dismissed *Karṇa*, and driven by *Dāruka* the steeds soon reached *Upaplavya*. The *Kurus* assembled and talked about *Kṛshṇa* (V, **137**). *Bhīshma* and *Droṇa* reminded *Duryodhana* of what *Kuntī* had said to *Kṛshṇa*, and the exploits of *Arjuna*; they recommended peace; fearful omens appeared (V, **138**). *Duryodhana* was cheerless and silent. *Bhīshma* complained. *Droṇa* said that his affection for *Arjuna* was greater than for *Açvatthāman*; *Duryodhana* ought to have followed the counsels of the elders; *Yudhishṭhira* was invincible; the *Pāṇḍavas* had procured wealth from *Kubera's* abode; "the periods of our lives have run out"; etc. (V, **139**). Requested by *Dhṛtarāshṭra*, *Sañjaya* related the conversation between *Kṛshṇa* and *Karṇa* (see the note of PCR.). *Kṛshṇa* disclosed to *Karṇa* that he was virtually the son of *Pāṇḍu*, and on the side of his father was related to the *Pāṇḍavas*, on the side of his mother to the *Vṛshṇis*. He ought to come with him to the *Pāṇḍavas*, being the elder brother of *Yudhishṭhira*, and be installed as king by *Dhaumya*, etc. (*a*), *Yudhishṭhira* being his heir-presumptive and ruling the kingdom under him; "during the sixth period *Draupadī* also will come to thee"; "let the *Draviḍas*, etc. (β), walk before thee" (V, **140**). *Karṇa* admitted that he was virtually the son of *Pāṇḍu*, *Kuntī* having, while a maiden, born him to *Sūrya* and then abandoned him. But the *Sūta Adhiratha* had taken him to his home; from her affection for him *Rādhā's* breasts were filled with milk that very day, and she held his urine and fæces; "how can one like us . . . . deprive her of her *piṇḍa*?" *Adhiratha* regarded *Karṇa* as a son, and *Karṇa* regarded *Adhiratha* as a father; he had caused all the rites of infancy to be performed on *Karṇa* according to the scriptures; he had caused the name *Vasushena* to be bestowed upon him by the *brahmans*; when *Karṇa* attained to youth he married wives according to *Adhiratha's* selection; with them he had begotten sons and grandsons. Through *Duryodhana* he had enjoyed sovereignty for thirteen years. His many sacrifices had always been with *Sūtas*, as had also his family rites and marriage rites. It was only after having got hold of *Karṇa* that *Duryodhana* had decided upon war with the *Pāṇḍavas*, *Karṇa* having been chosen as the antagonist of *Arjuna*. Their discourse ought to be kept secret, lest *Yudhishṭhira* should refuse to accept the kingdom; and "if the empire becomes mine I shall certainly make it over to *Duryodhana* only." He praised *Yudhishṭhira*, etc. (γ), and the weapons of *Arjuna* (δ), comparing the combat to a sacrifice; and *Bhīma's* drinking the blood of *Duḥçāsana* to the *Soma*-drinking, etc. (V, **141**). *Kṛshṇa* said the victory of the *Pāṇḍavas* was very certain; he described *Arjuna's* banner, made by *Bhaumana* by celestial illusion; his *Aindra*, *Āgneya*, and *Māruta* weapons, etc.; "then all signs of the *Kṛta*, *Tretā*, and *Dvāpara* ages will disappear." He forebade *Bhīmasena's* dancing, having quaffed the blood of *Duḥçāsana*, etc. (ε). "Returning hence, say to *Bhīshma*, etc. (ζ), that the present month is a delightful one; 7 days hence it will be the day of the new moon, presided over by *Indra*; let the battle commence then" (V, **142**). *Karṇa* ascribed the approaching destruction to *Çakuni*, etc. (η), and mentioned diverse sinister visions of planets (θ), etc., and he had seen in a vision, foreboding victory, *Yudhishṭhira*, etc. (ι), and the inverse respecting *Bhīshma*, etc. (κ). "*Karṇa* embraced *Kṛshṇa*, descended from his chariot, and riding in his own chariot, which was decked with gold, came back with us" (V, **143**). *Vidura* approached *Kuntī* and spoke of the state and disposition of *Yudhishṭhira*, etc. (λ), and the allies of *Yudhishṭhira* (μ). *Kuntī* thought with grief on those who were going to fight (ν). Especially she was afraid of *Karṇa*; she recollected the boon of *Durvāsas* and its consequences (ξ). She went to *Karṇa*, who was standing performing his prayers on the bank of *Gaṅgā* with his face turned towards the east and his arms upraised; and she stayed behind him, waiting for the completion of his prayers. Then, turning round, he beheld *Kuntī* (V, **144**). *Kuntī* disclosed to *Karṇa* his birth, mentioned the justice of the *Pāṇḍava* cause and the injustice of *Duryodhana's*, and besought him to join the *Pāṇḍavas* (V, **145**). *Sūrya* corroborated the words of *Kuntī*. But *Karṇa* represented to her the great injury she had done him; he could not now frustrate the hope of the *Kauravas*; but "except *Arjuna* thy other sons shall not be slain by me." They then left the spot, turning into different directions (V, **146**). At *Upaplavya Kṛshṇa* represented to the *Pāṇḍavas* all that had happened at *Hāstinapura*. In the night, *Yudhishṭhira* again brought *Kṛshṇa* into their midst, and caused him to repeat what had been said by *Bhīshma*, etc. (ο); *Bhīshma* had related his own life (π); he mentioned a duel with *Rāma* [*Jāmadagnya*], where *Vicitravīrya* fled, having been deserted by his subjects; upon *Vicitravīrya's* death anarchy prevailed in the kingdom, and *Indra* did not give a drop of rain; afflicted by hunger and maladies (very few of them were still alive), the subjects then asked *Bhīshma* —in vain—to ascend the throne; "when *Pāṇḍu* became king, his sons must obtain their paternal inheritance" (V, **147**). *Droṇa* had related the life of *Pāṇḍu*. *Vidura* had asked *Bhīshma* to go to the woods with him and *Dhṛtarāshṭra*, or to bind *Duryodhana* and rule the kingdom with the *Pāṇḍavas*. *Gāndhārī* proved that the kingdom by right belonged to the *Pāṇḍavas* and their sons and grandsons, and to no others (V, **148**). *Dhṛtarāshṭra* had repeated to *Duryodhana* the genealogy of the *Kuru* race from *Soma*, mentioning especially that *Yayāti* (*b*) had placed his youngest son *Pūru* on the throne; and that *Devāpi's* installation was forbidden by the *brahmans* and all aged persons because of a skin disease (leprosy, Nīl.), and as *Bāhlika* abandoned his father and brother and obtained the wealthy kingdom of his maternal uncle, *Çāntanu*, the youngest of the three brothers, became king. "Being defective of a limb, I was likewise excluded by *Pāṇḍu*; at his death the kingdom must pass to his sons . . . . thou art not the son of a king, and therefore hast no right to the kingdom" (V, **149**). *Kṛshṇa* continued his relation; *Duryodhana* had repeatedly instructed the kings, saying: "To-day is *Pushya* [in conjunction with the moon]; march ye." "Eleven *akshauhiṇīs* have been assembled headed by *Bhīshma* (with the device of the palmyra in his banner)" (V, **150**).

***Bhagavat** ("illustrious, holy") is often applied to the names of persons (gods and men) of high merit, especially religious merit, or used to design them alone.—(*a*) The Most High: I, 7777 (°*bhaktāḥ*); III, 13936; V, 1596, 1740, 1742, 1744, 1746, 1748, 1750, 1752, 1754, 1756, 1759, 1761, 1763, 1765, 1767, 1769, 1771, 1773, 1775, 1777, 1779, 1781, 1783; XII, (13095, *Çrī°*), 13097, 13098, (13102, *Çrī°*), 13122, (13136, *Çrī°*), (13189, *Çrī°*), (13278, *Çrī°*), (13295, *Çrī°*), 13307 (Nārāyaṇa), 13313 (Hari), 13318 (= Nārāyaṇa), 13325 (= Kṛshṇa), 13350 (*Paramātmā*), 13358 (do.), 13370 (*Hariḥ*), 13372 (*Purushottamaḥ*), 13393, 13405 (Nārāyaṇa), 13425 (Vishṇu), 13428 (°*ākhyānaṃ*, *Hariṃ*), 13449 (*Paramātmanaḥ*), 13473 (*Anādinidhano*, *Parameshṭhī*), 13496 (*Purushaḥ sarvatomukhaḥ*), 13547 (*Hariḥ*), 13554 (i.e. Kṛshṇa as reciting Bhagavadgītā), 13658, 13663, 13672 (*Madhusūdanaḥ*), 13678 (*Hariḥ*), 13706, 13762 (Purusha).—Cf. Kṛshṇa, Vishṇu, Nārāyaṇa.—(*b*) Kṛshṇa: I, 331 (°*yānaṃ*); II, 25; III, 15542; V, 2534, 2535, (2666, *Çrī°*), (2822, *Çrī°*), (2924, *Çrī°*), 3042 (*trayāṇām api lokānāṃ bhagavān prapitāmahaḥ*), (3308, *Çrī°*), 4435 (voc.), 4966; VI, (933, *Çrī°*), (987, do.), (994), (998), (1037, *Çrī°*), (1065), (1104), (1112), (1144), (1170), (1205), 1218 (voc.), 1221 (voc.), (1223), (1251), (†1278), (†1293), (1298), (1303), (1323), (1356), (1377), (1403), (1428), (1456), 2973; VII, 2699 (voc.); VIII, 3440 (voc.); XIII, 613; XIV, 355 (*Vishṭarasravasā*), 412, (931, *Çrī°*), (933, do.), (1550, do.).—Cf. the Most High, Vishṇu, Nārāyaṇa.—(*c*) Vishṇu: III, 10140 (voc.), 13493, (13571), (13578, *Çrī°*); V, 3695, 3700 (voc.); XIII, 6949 (1000 names), 7009 (1000 names).—Cf. the Most High, Kṛshṇa, Nārāyaṇa.—(*d*) Nārāyaṇa: VII, 9010, 9017.—Cf. the Most High, Kṛshṇā, Vishṇu.—(*e*) Brahmán: I, 2503, 7701 (?); III, 12191; V, 4107 (voc., *Pitāmaha*), 4109 (do.); VIII, 4439; XII, 13726 (*Pitāmahaḥ*, *Prajāpatiḥ*), 13729, 13730.—(*f*) Çiva: I, 7832, 8123, 8124; V, 7393 (voc.); VII, 6041 (voc.); VIII, 4445 (*Vṛshabhadhvajaḥ*), †4569 (*Kirātarūpī*); XIII, 603, 612, 615, 661, 665, 667, 675, 676, 681, 690, 693, 733, 743, 780, 795, 836, 841, 878, 919, 920, 930, 931, (932, *Çrī°*), 939, etc., (1106, *Çrī°*), 1147, 1242 (1000 names [2]), 1267 (ib.), (6390, *Çrī°*), (6419), (6485, *Çrī°*), 7499, 7501; XIV, 186, 191.—(*g*) Indra: V, 325, 446; XIII, 765, 803.—(*h*) Agni, q.v.—(*i*) Kubera: VIII, †4514 (*Yaksharāṭ*).—(*j*) Dharma: XVII, †89.—(*k*) Nārada: III, ††13314, ††13316, ††13317; V, 4121 (voc.).—(*l*) Kaṇva: V, 3676 (voc.).—(*m*) Dhṛtarāshṭra: V, 2897 (*çvaçuro*).

Bhāgavata ("belonging to or named after Vishṇu or Kṛshṇa, etc., an adorer of Bhagavat"). § 717*c* (Uparicara): XII, **336**, 12718 (*tad Bhāgavataṃ sarvam iti tat prokshitaṃ sadā*); **338**, 12818 ("devoted to Nārāyaṇa").—§ 717*b* (Nārāyaṇīya): XII, **341**, 13008 (Parameçvara is devoted to Bhagavat—*Bhāgavata*); **344**, 13358 (Paramātman is *Bhāgavata-priyaḥ-*, i.e. loves the adorers of Bhagavat); **345**, 13387 (*Sāṅkhyā Bhāgavataiḥ saha*).

Bhāgin = Çiva (1000 names [2]).

Bhagīratha (descendant of Sagara). § 5 (Anukram.): I, **1**, 221.—§ 61 (Sarpasattra): I, **55***β*, †2112.—§ 232 (Svayamvarap.): I, **186**, 7001 (*a*).—§ 263 (Sabhākriyāp.): II, **3**, 67.—§ 267 (Yamasabhāv.): II, **8**, 322 (in the palace of Yama).—§ 274 (Rājasūyārambhap.): II, **15**, 649.—§ 296 (Dyūtap.): II, **53**, 1929.—§ 323 (Dvaitavanapr.): III, **25**, 956.—§ 376 (Tīrthay.): III, **85**, 8269 (Nārada exhorts Yudhishṭhira to seek renown by visiting the tīrthas, as *Bh.*, etc.).—§ 377 (Dhaumyatīrth.): III, **87**, 8310 (on the bank of Gaṅgā *Bh.* brought many sacrifices).—§ 378 (Tīrthay.): III, **92**, 8444 (Lomaça exhorts Yudhishṭhira to visit the tīrthas in order to be "liberated," as *Bh.*, Gaya, Yayāti, etc.); **94**, 8504.—§ 386 (Agastyop.): III, **106**, 8826.—§ 387 (Sagara): III, **106**, 8828 (°*pratiçrayāt*).—§ 389 (Gaṅgāvataraṇa): III, **107**, 9918 (son of Dilīpa); **108**, 9940 (Gaṅgā promises him to descend in order to purify his forefathers), 9944 (practises austerities on Kailāsa); **109**, 9947 (°*vacas*; Çiva promises him to sustain the Gaṅgā), 9950, 9959 (Gaṅgā descends), 9961 (fills up the Ocean with the Gaṅgā, whom he made his daughter).—§ 573 (Ambop.): V, **178**, 7096 (°*sutā nadī*, i.e. Gaṅgā).—§ 574 (Jambūkh.): VI, **6**, 238 (*Bh.* dwelled for many years at Bindusaras after having seen Gaṅgā).—§ 595 (Shoḍaç.): VII, **60**, 2249, 2256, 2258; *Bh.* (*Aikshvākaṃ*, v. 2256) caused the shore of Gaṅgā Bhāgīrathī to be covered by flights of steps (*cayanaiḥ*) made of gold; he presented the brahmans with 1,000,000 of damsels decked with ornaments of gold, etc. (description). It is related how Gaṅgā became his daughter and then his "son" (see the note of PCR., p. 173); G. sang all this before Ṛ., D., and men. At last he ascended to Brahmaloka through the grace of the brahmans (v. 2260, v. Nīl.).—§ 599 (Jayadrathav.): VII, **94**, 3450 (*ε*) (a rājarshi).—§ 604 (Karṇap.): VIII, **5***ζ*, 117 (*rājā Bh°o vṛddho*, has been slain).—§ 632 (Shodaçarāj.): XII, **29**, 956, 962 (*Aikshvākuṃ*).—§ 658*b* (Kṛtaghnop.): XII, **170**, 6345 (°*rathākrāntadeçān*).—§ 734 (Ānuçāsan.): XIII, **26**, †1854 (brought down Gaṅgā having gratified all D. by terrible austerities).—§ 746 (do.): XIII, **76***ι*, 3689.—§ 758 (do.): XIII, **103**, 4909 (°*sya saṃvādaṃ Brahmaṇaç ca*), 4910 (transcended the world of the gods, that of kine, and that of the ṛshis), 4911, 4912, (†4913), 4950 (*rājānaṃ*).—§ 767 (do.): XIII, **137***σ*, 6270 (*rājarshiḥ*; attained to the imperishable worlds by giving his daughter Haṃsī to Kautsa), 6271 (attained to the highest worlds by giving 100,000 cows with calves to Kohala).—§ 775 (do.): XIII, **166***η*, 7677.—§ 795 (Svargāroh.): XVIII, **3***θ*, 107.

Bhagīratha-sutā = Gaṅgā: V, 7096.

Bhāgīrathī ("the daughter of Bhagīratha," i.e. Gaṅgā): I, 372, 599 (°*putrāt* . . . *Bhīshmāt*), ††3800 (Çāntanu married *Gaṅgāṃ Bhāgīrathīm* and begat upon her Devavrata or Bhīshma), 3989, 5509, 5845, 6351, 6447, 6459 (°*jalaṃ*), 6917 (°*tīrāt*), †7283; II, 68 (*Gaṅgām*), 370 (*nadī*); III, 4033 (°*tīre*), 8141, 8156, 8319 (*Mahendro* . . . *yatra Bhā°ī puṇyā sarasy—Maṇikarṇik'-ākhye* Nīl.—*āsīd Yudhishṭhira*), 8646 (*puṇyā deva-Gandharva-sevitā*), 10722, 10724, 11054 (*Nara-Nārāyaṇa-sthānaṃ Bhāgīrathyopaçobhitaṃ*), 11063 (*sutīrthāñ ca çītāṃ vimalapaṅkajāṃ*, etc.), 11065 (°*puṇyajale*); V, 4911, 7317 (the mother of Bhīshma); VI, 223 (*Gaṅgā*), 239 (*Gaṅgāṃ*), 5567 (*Bhīshmaṃ Bhāgīrathīputraṃ*); VII, 2249 (*Gaṅgā*), 2254 (*tathā Bhāgīrathī Gaṅgā Urvaçī cābhavat purā*; became the daughter and "son" of king Bhagīratha); X, 659 (°*tīraṃ*); XII, 8 (do.), 961 (*Gaṅgā* sat on the lap of king Bhagīratha, therefore she was formerly [called] Urvaçī), 1118 (°*tīre*), 1350 (°*putraḥ*); XIII, 1702 (*Gaṅgā*), 1726, 1784 (*Gaṅgā*), 4070 (*Gaṅgā*), 6294 (°*putraḥ Bhīshmo*), 7777, 7780; XIV, 2415; XV, 510

(°*tīre*), 520 (do.), 527 (do.), 861, 871 (°*jalaṃ*), 901, 1083 (°*tīre*).

Bhāgīrathī-putra = Bhīshma: I, 599; VI, 5567; XII, 1350; XIII, 6294.

Bhāgīrathī-suta = Bhīshma: XIV, 24.

Bhaima (pl., patron.): III, †10268: *bhīmākramakartāro Bhīmavaṃçajā vā*: Schol.; VII, 4069 (*Bhaimān parijaghānāçu rathāṃs triçatam āhave*).

Bhaimaseni[1] = Divodāsa: V, 3960 (*Divodāsaḥ*).

Bhaimaseni[2] = Ghaṭotkaca: V, 5926 (*Haiḍimbaḥ*); VI, 1713, 2418 (C., *Bhaimi*°), 3668, 3671, 4065 (*Ghaṭotkacaḥ*), 4086, 4222 (*Ghaṭotkacaḥ*), 5106 (*rākshasaṃ*); VII, 4060, 4110, 4121, 4126, 6785, 6806, 6824, 6890, 7367, 7418, 7856, 7861, 7868, 7948, 7968, 7994, 8035, 8039, 8086, 8110, 8117, †8174, 8238 (*Ghaṭotkacaḥ*), 8333.

Bhaimi = Ghaṭotkaca: VII, 8101.

Bhaimī = Damayantī: III, 2083, 2200, 2217, 2225, 2239, 2253, 2267, 2283, 2320, 2355, 2376, 2382, 2411, 2493, 2507, 2585, 2595, 2603, 2663, 2681, 2729, 2744, 2857, 2973, 2994, 2999, 3008, 3042.

Bhairava. § 67 (Sarpasattra): I, 2158 (a Nāga of Dhṛtarāshṭra's race).

Bhaktānāṃ paramā gatiḥ = Çiva (1000 names[2]).

Bhaktavatsala[1] = Mahāpurusha. — Do.[2] = Vishṇu (1000 names).

Bhallāṭa (a mountain). § 280 (Bhīmasena): II, **30**, 1079 (conquered by Bhīmasena).

Bhāluki (a muni). § 264 (Sabhākriyāp.): II, **4***a*, 110.—§ 266 (Çakrasabhāv.): II, **7**, 293 (in the palace of Indra).—§ 324 (Dvaitavan.): III, **26***a*, 985.

Bhāṇḍāyani. § 266 (Çakrasabhāv.): II, **7**, 294 (in the palace of Indra).

Bhaṅga. § 64 (Sarpasattra): I, **57**, 2150 (a serpent of Takshaka's race).

Bhaṅgakāra[1]. § 154 (Pūruv.): I, **94**, 3741 (son of Avikshit).

Bhaṅgakāra[2]. § 252 (Subhadrāharaṇap): I, **219**, 7916 (present at the festival on the Raivataka mountain).

Bhāṅgāsuri = Ṛtuparṇa: II, 326 (in the palace of Yama); III, 2745, 2781, 2809, 2813, 2885, 2900, 2974, 3027.

Bhaṅgāsvana (a rājarshi). § 728*b* (Bhaṅgāsvanop.): XIII, **12**, 529, 530, 557.

[**Bhaṅgāsvanopākhyāna(m)**] ("the episode relating to Bhaṅgāsvana"). § 728*b* (Ānuçāsanik.). *Bhīshma* said: In days of yore lived R.-ṛ. *Bhaṅgāsvana*, who, being childless, from desire of obtaining issue performed the *Agnishṭuta*, that is disliked by *Indra*, but is approved of by men desirous of offspring, in order to purge themselves of their sins (*prāyaçcitteshu*, v. the note of PCR., p. 44). He had 100 sons. *Indra* began to look for an occasion against him. Once, on a hunting expedition, he was bewildered by *Indra*, and, afflicted with thirst, he plunged into a lake after having caused his horse to drink, and found himself changed into a woman. He took leave of his wives and children and retired to the woods, joined an ascetic and bore him 100 sons, whom he took to his former children, and made them all enjoy the kingdom as their joint property. Filled with rage, *Indra*, in the form of a brahman, repaired to *Bhaṅgāsvana's* capital, and, referring them to the example of the gods and the *Asuras* (the children of *Kaçyapa*), caused the half-brothers to slay each other. Then, in the form of a brahman, he came to the spot where *Bhaṅgāsvana* lived as an ascetic lady, afflicted with grief, and told him that he was *Indra*, and why he was angry, but was gratified and granted him a boon. He asked that those sons of his should revive that were born by him as a woman, because the affection entertained by a woman is much greater than that which is entertained by a man. *Indra* revived all his children, and told him to choose whichever sex he liked, that of woman or that of man. He chose to remain a woman, because in sexual intercourse the pleasure that women enjoy is always much greater than what is enjoyed by men. *Indra* proceeded to heaven (XIII, **12**).

Bhānu[1]. § 102 (Aṃçāvat.): I, **65**, 2555 (a Devagandharva Prādheya).

Bhānu[2] (= the Sun): I, 42, 1103 (or 1098), 1273; III, 154 (in the enumeration of Dhaumya), 191; *XII, 150; XVIII, 162.

Bhānu[3] = Çiva (1000 names[1]).—Do.[4] = Vishṇu (1000 names).

Bhānu[5] (a man). § 262 (Bhagavadyāṇa): II, **2**, 56 (*Bhānuñ ca Janārdanaḥ*).—§ 402 (Tīrthay.): III, **120**, 10277.—§ 452 (Mārkaṇḍeyas.): III, **183**, †12584.

Bhānu[6]. § 552 (Goharaṇap.): IV, **56**ζ, 1769 (regarded the battle from a vimāna).

Bhānu[7] (a son of Aṅgiras). § 491 (Āṅgirasa): III, **220**, 14164 (*Bhānur Aṅgiraso dhīraḥ putro*).—§ 493 (do.): III, **221**, 14183 (*Bhānuñ cāpy Aṅgirāḥ srjat*, called by the brahmans Bṛhadbhānu), 14184 (*Bhānor bhāryā suprajā tu Bṛhadbhāsā tu sūrya-jā*), 14186 (*tam Agniṃ Baladaṃ prāhuḥ prathamaṃ Bhānutaḥ sutaṃ*), 14187 (*Agniḥ sa Manumān nāma dvitīyo Bhānutaḥ sutaḥ | darçe ca paurṇamāse ca yasyeha havir ucyate*), 14189 (*Agnir Agrāyaṇo nāma Bhānor evānvayas tu saḥ*), 14190 (*cāturmāsyeshu nityānāṃ havishāṃ yonir Agrahaḥ | caturbhiḥ sahitaḥ putrair Bhānor evānvaya Stubhaḥ*), 14191 (*Niçā tv ajanayat kanyām Agnī-shomāv ubhau tathā | Bhānor evābhavad bhāryā sushuve pañca pāvakān*).

Bhānudeva. § 608 (Karṇap.): VIII, **48**ν, 2248 (slain by Karṇa)

***Bhānumat**[1] (= the Sun): I, †3665; III, 16949; XIV, 892 (*Bhānumantam iva grahaḥ*); XV, 832.

Bhānumat[2]. § 579 (Bhīshmavadhap.): VI, **54**[11], 2268 (king of the Kaliṅgas, fights Bhīma), 2273 (slain by Bhīma).

Bhānumatī[1] (daughter of Kṛtavīrya). § 156 (Pūruv.): I, **95**, 3768 (wife of Ahaṃyāti and mother of Sarvabhauma).

Bhānumatī[2] (daughter of Aṅgiras). § 489 (Āṅgirasa): III, **218**, 14124.

Bhānusena. § 608 (Karṇap.): VIII, **48**, 2260 (a son of Karṇa slain by Bhīma).

Bhara (an Agni). § 493 (Āṅgirasa): III, **222**, 14210 (= Bharata, Nīl.; *agnishṭome ca niyataḥ kratuçreshṭho Bharasya tu*).

Bhārabhṛt = Vishṇu (1000 names).

Bharadvāja[1] (a ṛshi). § 22 (Pramadvarā): I, **8***a*, 962.—§ 83 (Ādivaṃçāvat.): I, **63**, 2434 (*Bharadvājasya ca skannaṃ droṇyāṃ çukram avardhata | maharsher ugratapasas, tasmād Droṇo vyajāyata*).—§ 151 (Pūruv.): I, **94**, 3712 (helped Bharata to get a son Bhumanyu).—§ 191 (Arjuna): I, **123**, 4807 (one of the seven maharshis).—§ 200 (Droṇa): I, **130**, 5102 (*bhagavān ṛshiḥ*), 5103, 5105 (the birth of Droṇa), 5107 (gave the Āgneya weapon to Agniveça).—§ 201 (Drupada): I, **130**, 5109 (°*sakhā . . . Pṛshato*), 5112 (*bhagavān*, "went to Heaven"), 5124 (°*āt samutpannaṃ Droṇaṃ*).—§ 202 (Droṇa): I, **131**, 5183.—§ 217 (Caitrarathap.): I, **166**, 6328, 6333 (C., *Bhā*°), 6336 (°*suto* = Droṇa).—§ 221 (do.): I, **170**, 6464 (Bṛhaspati gave him the Āgneya weapon), 6465 (Agniveça received the Āgneya weapon from *Bh.*).—§ 270 (Brahmasabhāv.): II, **11**, 440 (in the palace of Brahmán).—§ 376 (Tīrthay.): III, **85**, 8264 (among the ṛshis who expected Yudhishṭhira at the tīrthas). — § 384 (Agastyop.): III, **102**, 8741 (*°āçrame*).—§ 414 (Yavakrītop.): III, **135**, 10703 (*Bh°ç ca Raibhyaç ca sakhāyau sambabhūvatuḥ*), (10735).—§ 416 (do.): III, **137**, 10772 (cursed Raibhya), 10780, 10790 (burned the corpse of his son and thereupon himself). — § 417 (do.): III, **138**, 10812 (was revived by Arvāvasu).—§ 545 (Pativratāmah.): III, **298**, 16873 (consoled Dyumatsena).—§ 561 (Yānasandhip.): V, **55**μ, 2191 (*brahmarsheç ca Bharadvājāt Droṇo droṇyām ajāyata*).—§ 570 (Sainyaniryāṇap.): V, **15**β, 5110 (Drupada has learned the art of arms from *Bh.*).—V, 5783 (*°ātmajaḥ* = Droṇa).—VI, 526 (*°ātmaje* = Droṇa), 640 (do.).—§ 580 (Bhīshmavadhap.): VI, **56**, 2404 (*Bh.* and Kṛtavarman were in the eyes of Bhīshma's Garuḍa-vyūha; so both C. and B., but we ought certainly to read *Bhāradvājaḥ*).—§ 602 (Droṇavadhap.): VII, **190**ν, 8727 (only B., C. has *Bhā°*).—§ 615*y* (Badarapācana): IX, **48**, 2763 (father of Çrutāvatī).—§ 615*aa* (Çrutāvatī): IX, **48**, 2826 (*viprarsheḥ*), 2828 (*mahāmuniḥ*). — § 656 (Khaḍgotp.): XII, **166**δ, 6200.—§ 660 (Mokshadh.): XII, **182**, 6769, 6770, 6774.—§ 660*b* (Bhṛgu-Bharadvājas.): XII, **182**, 6787, (6801); **183**, (6808); **184**, (6821), (6826); **185**, (6866); **186**, (6883); **187**, (6900), (6909); **188**, (6935); **189**, (6950); **190**, (6977); **191**, (6984), (6988), (6990); **192**, (7009), 7030.—§ 665 (Mokshadh.): XII, **208**ι, 7593 (among the ṛshis of the North).—§ 667 (do.): XII, **210**, 7662 (knows the science of arms).—§ 677 (do.): XII, **232**, 8481 (*viprarsheḥ*).—§ 702 (do.): XII, **293***a*, 10762.—§ 717*b* (Nārāyaṇīya): XII, **343**, VIII), 13218.— § 734 (Ānuçāsan.): XIII, **26***a*, 1763.—§ 736*b* (Vītahavyop.): XIII, **30**, 1962 (*āçramapadam °sya*; priest of Divodāsa), 1963 (*jyeshṭhaḥ putro Bṛhaspateḥ*), 1967, 1971.—§ 739 (Ānuçāsan.): XIII, **34**γ, 2126 (vanquished the Vītahavyas and the Ainas).—§ 750*b* (Bisastainyop.): XIII, **93***a*, 4416, (4441), (4466), (4488), (4519). — § 751*b* (Çapathavidhi): XIII, **94***a*, †4551 (C. *Bhā°*), (4581).—§ 770 (Ānuçasan.): XIII, **151**, 7116 (*sa° Gautamaḥ*; the fifth of the seven *Dhaneçvarasya guravaḥ*, dwells in the North).—§ 775 (do.): XIII, **166**, 7670 (among the learned brahmans in the North).—§ 782*g* (Guruçishyasaṃvāda): XIV, **35**δ, 960 (*Prajāpati°au*).

Bharadvāja[2] (a Fire). § 490 (Āṅgirasa): III, **219**, 14134 (son of Çaṃyu), 14138 (married to Vīrā and father of Vīra).

Bharadvāja[3] (pl. *°āḥ*) (a people). § 374 (Jambūkh.): VI, **9**, 376 (*Ātreyāḥ sa-Bharadvājāḥ*; in Bhāratavarsha).

Bhāradvāja[1]. § 648*b* (Kaṇikop.): XII, **140**, 5249 (*Bhāradvājasya saṃvādaṃ rājñaḥ Çatruñjayasya ca*), 5250.—§ 250*b* (Nārītīrtha): I, **216**, 7842 (*°sya tīrtha, pāpapraçamanaṃ mahat*).—VII, 8727 (a ṛshi) (*Bha°*, B.).

Bhāradvāja[2] = Yavakrīta: III, 10700, 10701.

Bhāradvāja[3] (descendant of Bharadvāja): XIII, †4551 (*Bha°*, B.), †7158; XVII, 12.

Bhāradvāja[4] = Droṇa: I, †176, †188, 2705, 5096, 5108, 5117, 5121, 5123, 5126, 5134, 5135, 5145, 5147, 5208, 5213, 5305, 5315, 5319, 5349, 5404, 5474, 5526, 6341, 6352, 6353, 6379, 6381, 6389, 6408, 6499, 7536; II, 2264; III, 1683; IV, 1287, 1651, 1828, 1833, 1846, 1852, 1856, 1874, 2056; V, 1961, 4963, 5786, 7607; VI, 1595, 2104, 2201, 2203, 2205, 2208, 2212, 2225, 2230, 2394, 2432, 2879, 2883, 3072, 3078, 3079, 3211, 3292, 3305, 3307, 3308, 3387, 3402, 3555, 3590, 3596, 3599, 3601, 3849, 3853, 3953, 4190, 4206, 4638, 4644, 4645, 5110, 5189, 5715; VII, 178, 201, 230, 259, 279, 281, 435, 467, 493, 644, 648, 792, 795, 796, 820, 881, 883, 920, 924, 946, 1028, 1455, 1462, 1507, 1512, 1513, 1515, 1620, 1624, 1645, 1654, 1665, 2646, 3097, 3115, 3243, 3256, 3495, 3543, 3644, 3787, 3965, 3990, 4010, 4134, 4137, 4141, 4143, 4144, 4155, 4157, 4158, 4252, 4255, 4259, 4261, 4293, 4484 (*°sutaḥ* = *Açvatthāman*), 4557, 4608, 4652, 4660, 4665, 4856, 4860, 4864, 4893, 4904, 4910, 4918, 4933, 5020, 5048, 5049, 5050, 5053, 5068, 5069, 5072, 5087, 5230, 6291, 6292, 6687, 6698, 6762, 6769, 6954, 6966, 7205, 7217, 7259, 7344, 7351, 7438, 8310, 8369, 8442, 8491, 8553, 8719, 8721, 8724, 8761, 8782, 8790, 8821, 8824, 8827, 8828, 8840, 8862, 8865 (*Bhā° sya cātmajaḥ*, i.e. *Açvatthāman*), 8866, 8871, 8878, 8879, 8885, 8900, 9313 (*°sutaṃ*, i.e. *Açvatthāman*); VIII, 165, 188, 1043, 3677; IX, 75 (*Bhīsmaḥ pitāmahaç caiva, Bhāradvājo, 'tha Gautamaḥ* . . .), 124 (*Bhāradvājasya cātmajaḥ*), 627 (*Bhāradvājasya hantāraṃ Dhṛshṭadyumnaṃ*), 740; XII, 2094 (*bhagavān*), 5249, 5250.

Bhāradvāja[5] = Açvatthāman: I, 574 (*°guru* = Droṇa); X, 349, 367, 368, 681.

Bhāradvājaguru = Droṇa: I, 574.

Bhăradvājasuta = Droṇa: I, 6336.

Bhāradvājasuta = Açvatthāman: VII, 4484.

Bharadvājātmaja = Droṇa: V, 5783; VI, 526, 640.

Bhāradvājī (a river). § 574 (Jambūkh.): VI, **9**λ, 336 (in Bhāratavarsha).

Bharaṇī (pl.) (a nakshatra, junction-star 35 or 41 Arietis, Sū° Si°). § 746 (Ānuçāsan.): XIII, **64**, 3286 (when giving kine and sesame to the brahmans, under *Bh.*, one obtains great fame and abundant kine in the next life).—§ 749 (do.): XIII, **89***a*, 4268 (by performing a çrāddha under *Bh.* one attains to longevity).—§ 759 (do.): XIII, **110**, 5394 (*Bh.* should be the head during the candravrata under Mūla).

Bharata[1] (Daushmanti). § 3 (Anukram.): I, **1**, 46 (his race is descended from Sahasrajyotis).—§ 5 (do.): I, **1***a*, 220 bis (has died).—§ 11 (Parvas.): I, **2**, 371 (son of Dushmanta and Çakuntalā; the Bhārata race is named after him).—§ 133 (Dushyanta): I, **69** (called Sarvadamana; became a cakravartin sārvabhauma), 2814.—§ 135 (Çakunt.): I, **74**, 3106 (etymology), 3118, 3122, 3123 (*Bharatād Bhāratī kīrttir*), 3124 (*°syānvavāye hi*), 3126 (*°sya vaṃçam*).—§ 150 (Pūruv.): I, **94**, 3709 (*Dushyantād Bh°o jajñe*).—§ 151 (do.): I, **94**, 3710. With his three wives Bharata begat altogether nine sons, with whom he was not pleased, as they were not like him; their mothers therefore became angry and slew them (*ninyur Yamakshayaṃ*). Bharata then, performing great sacrifices, obtained from Bharadvāja a son named Bhumanyu, who became his heir-apparent; 3712.—§ 153 (Saṃvaraṇa): I, **94**, 3736 (pl. ? *°ādhyushitaṃ pūrvaṃ* . . . *purottamaṃ*).—§ 155 (do.): I, **94**, 3752 (*°syānvaye*).—§ 156 (do.): I, **95**, ††3782 (son of Dushyanta and Çakuntalā), ††3785 (*°tvaṃ*; married Kāçeyī Sārvasenī Sunandā, who bore him Bhumanyu).—§ 171 (Vicitravīryasutotp.): I, **105**, 4226 (*°vaṃçasya*).—§ 177 (Pāṇḍudigvijaya): I, **113**, 4461.—§ 202 (Droṇa): I, **131**, 5156 (*°ānvaye*).—§ 241 (Vidurāgamanap.): I, **202**, 7432.—§ 253 (Haraṇāharaṇap.): I, **221**, 7969 (*°ānvaye*).—§ 267 (Yama-sabhā-v.): II, **8**, 322 (in the palace of Yama).—§ 274 (Rājasūyārambhap.): II, **15**, 649.—§ 377 (Dhaumya-tīrthak.): III, **90**, 8379 (*rājā cakravartī*; performed 35 horse-sacrifices on the Yamunā).—§ 413 (Tīrthay.): III, **135**, 10692 (*Kardamilaṃ* . . . *Bharatasyābhishecanaṃ*). — § 516 (Duryodhanayajña): III, **257**, 15329.—§ 562 (Bhagavadyānap.): V, **90**ν, 3146.—§ 595 (Shoḍaç.): VII, **68**: When a child in the forest *Bh. D.* (*Çākuntalaḥ*, v. 2387) bound the lions and checked the tigers, etc., whence he was called Sarvadamana, and his mother forbade him to torture animals. He performed 100 horse-sacrifices on the banks of the Sarasvatī, and 400 on the banks of the Gaṅgā; then once more 1,000 horse-sacrifices and 100 Rājasūyas, etc., etc.; he gave 10,000 billions of kine of the purest gold to Kaṇva. The gods with Indra and brahmans set up his sacrificial stake (of gold, 100 vyāmas in width). To brahmans he gave horses, elephants, etc.; 2377 (*Daushmantaṃ* — B. *Daushyantiṃ* — *Bharataṃ*), 2387 (*Çākuntalaḥ*).—§ 632*b* (Shoḍaçarājika; cf. § 595, Bharata): XII, **29,** 938 (*Daushmantiṃ Çākuntalam*), 940 (*Daushmantiḥ*), 941, 942.—§ 656 (Khaḍgotpattik.): XII, **166***δ*, 6195 (*Daushmantiḥ*). — § 721 (Viçvāmitrop.): XIII, **4,** 201 (*Bh°syānvaye*). — § 746 (Ānuçāsanik.): XIII, **76** *ι*, 3690 (*cakravartī*).—§ 761 (do.): XIII, **115***δ*, 5666, 5669.—§ 770 (do.): XIII, **151***μ*, 7128 (*triloke viçrutaṃ vīraṃ Bharatañ ca prakīrttayet* | *gavāmayena yajñena yeneshṭaṃ vai Kṛte yuge* | *Rantidevaṃ mahādevaṃ kīrttayet paramadyutim*).—§ 775 (do.): XIII, **166***η*, 7676 (*cakravartī*).—§ 778 (Açvamedhik.): XIV, **3,** 50 (*Daushmantiḥ Çākuntalaḥ*).—§ 795 (Svargārohaṇap.): XVIII, **3***θ*, 107.

Bharata[2] (Dāçarathi). § 525 (Rāmop.): III, **274,** 15878, 15879 (son of Daçaratha and Kaikeyī, and uterine brother of Rāma Dāçarathi).—§ 527 (do.): III, **277** (invested as yuvarāja, when Rāma was exiled), 15970, 15975.—§ 543 (Rāmarājyābhisheka): III, **295** (Rāma saw *Bh.* at Nandigrāma, and has the kingdom made over to him by *Bh.*), 16591, 16592, 16593, 16594, 16595.

Bharata[3] (two or more Fires). § 490 (Āṅgirasa): III, **219,** 14135, 14136, 14137 (*paurṇamāsyeshu sarveshu havishājyaṃ srucodyataṃ* | *Bharato nāmatah so 'gnir dvitīyaḥ Çaṃyutaḥ sutaḥ* | *tisraḥ kanyā bhavanty anyā yāsāṃ sa Bharataḥ patiḥ* | *Bharatas tu sutas tasya Bharaty ekā ca putrikā* | *Bharato Bharatasyāgneḥ pāvakas tu Prajāpateḥ* | *mahān atyartham ahitas tathā Bharatasattama*); **221,** 14176, 14177 (*gurubhir niyamair jāto Bharato nāma pāvakaḥ* | *agniḥ Pushṭimatir nāma tushṭaḥ pushṭiṃ prayacchati* | *bharaty esha prajāḥ sarvās tato Bharata ucyate*).—§ 493 (do.): III, **222,** 14213 (*dahan mṛtāni bhūtāni tasyāgnir Bharato 'bhavat*; v. Bhara).

Bharata[4] (pl. °āḥ) ("descendants of Bharata, or the people and race named *Bh.*"): I, 367 (*katheyaṃ* . . . *Bha°ānāṃ mahātmanāṃ*), 2308 (*°ānāṃ mahaj janma*), 2320 (do.), 2321 (= do.), 3126 (*°ānāṃ svastyayanaṃ*), 4270 (the royal house of Hāstinapura), 5160; II, 2396 (principally the Duryodhanists), 2560, 2650 (principally the Duryodhanists), 2090 (*°ānāṃ striyaḥ*, i.e. those of the Duryodhanists), 2695 (*°ānām abhūtaye*, i.e. do.), 2700 (= do.); III, 1114 (*°ānām abhūtaye*, principally the Duryodhanists), †1361 (those who were assembled in the hall of Dhṛtarāshṭra), †10245 (*°pradhānān*, principally the Duryodhanists), 15155 (*°ānāṃ kulodvaha* = Duryodhana), 17474 (*Pāṇḍavān*); IV, 912 (*Çāntanavo Bhīshmo Bharatānāṃ pitāmahaḥ*), 913, 1838 (principally the Duryodhanists), 2035 (*°ānāṃ pitāmahaḥ Bhīshmo*); V, 2105 (principally the Duryodhanists), 2914 (*°striyaḥ*), 2966 (principally the Duryodhanists), 3399 (i.e. Pāṇḍavāḥ), 4211, 5651 (i.e. the Duryodhanists); VI, 37 (*°ānāṃ pitāmahaḥ*, i.e. Vyāsa), 497 (*Bhīshmo* . . . *Bharatānāṃ pitāmahaḥ*), 1972 (*°ānāṃ pitāmahaḥ* = Bhīshma), 5687, 5736; VII, †59 (i.e. the Duryodh.), 76 (*°striyaḥ*, i.e. of the Duryodh.), 308 (*°striyaḥ*), 1023 (i.e. the Duryodh.), 1240 (do.), 3123; VIII, 738 (*°kshayaḥ*), 1252 (i.e. Pāṇḍavāḥ), †1971 (i.e. Pāṇḍavāḥ), 2866 (*°kshayaḥ*); IX, 122 (the Duryodh.), 1664 (= do., *°kshaye*); X, 681 (*°ānāṃ pitāmahaḥ*, i.e. Vyāsa); XI, 270 (*°striyaḥ*), 440 (id.), 479 (*°yoshitaḥ*), 680 (*°kshayaṃ*), 751 (*°striyaḥ*); XII, 1 (id.), 1588 (*°ānāṃ pitāmahaḥ*, i.e. Bhīshma), 1930 (*°ānāṃ pitāmahaṃ*, i.e. Bhīshma); XIII, 7729, 7768 (*°ānāṃ kulodvahaḥ*, i.e. Bhīshma), 7778 (*°strībhir*); XIV, 1505 (*Subhadrādyāḥ °ānāṃ striyaḥ*), 1549, 2010 (*°striyaḥ*), 2036 (id.), 2038 (*°siṃhānāṃ*); XVII, 46 (*°sattamāḥ*, i.e. Pāṇḍavāḥ).

Bhārata[1] (pl. °āḥ) (= Bharatāḥ): I, 3122 (*pūrve*), 3727 (the people of Bharata), 3731 (v. Saṃvaraṇa: "the *Bh.* dwelt in the forests on the banks of the Sindhu for 1,000 years"), 3732 (the people of *Bh.*), 3733, 3735 (the people of *Bh.*), 4107 (the people of Hāstinapura), 4156 (the people of *Bh.*), 4973 (principally the Duryodh.), 6431 (i.e. Pāṇḍavāḥ), 6439 (do.); II, 2096 (*°ānāṃ kulaghnaḥ* = Duryodhana), 2236, 2656 (i.e. the Duryodh.); III, †1363 (*°ānāṃ carāḥ*, i.e. of the Duryodh.), 11898; V, †684, †698, †885, 923 (*°ānāṃ pitāmahaṃ* = Bhīshma), 966 (*Bhāratānāṃ virodhāt*, i.e. the Pāṇḍavāḥ and the Duryodh.), †2575, 2671 (the Pāṇḍ. and the Duryodh.), 2726, 3009, 4294 (= the Duryodh.), 4298 (*Bhāratāndhaka-Vṛshṇayaḥ*), 4896 (i.e. the Duryodh.), 5314 (*pitāmahaṃ Bhā°ānāṃ* = Bhīshma); VI, 496 (*Bhā°ānāṃ pitāmahaḥ* = Bhīshma), 597 (*°ānām abhūd yuddhaṃ*, i.e. the Pāṇḍ. and the Duryodh.), 3084 (*°ānāṃ pitāmahaḥ* = Bhīshma), 3815 (do.), 4688 (do.), 5203 (*°ānāṃ camūṃ prati* = the Duryodh.), 5327 (*°ānāṃ pitāmahaṃ* = Bhīshma), 5436 (do.), 5677 (do.), 5703 (*°ānāṃ mahattamaṃ* = Bhīshma), 5704 (*°ānāṃ pitāmahe* = Bhīshma), 5733 (*°ānāṃ mahārathaṃ*, i.e. Bhīshma); VII, 96 (*Bhā°ānāṃ pitāmahaṃ*, i.e. Bhīshma), 1424 (*sarva°harshaṇaḥ* = Arjuna), 1736 (*°sainyānāṃ*, i.e. the Duryodh.), 1943 (*°vāhinīṃ*, i.e. the Duryodh.), 3043 (*°ānāṃ mahātmanāṃ*), 5015 (*°sainyasya*, i.e. the Duryodh.), 5640 (i.e. the Duryodh.), 5927 (do.), 6158 (do.), 7519 (*°ānāṃ mahārathaḥ*, i.e. Citrasena), †8155 (i.e. the Duryodh.); VIII, 3645 (*°ānāṃ mahārathau Bhīshma-Droṇau*), †3829 (*°ānāṃ balaṃ*, i.e. the Duryodh.), 4265 (*°ān daça*, i.e. ten Duryodh.), 4958 (*°ānāṃ patiṃ Duryodhanaṃ*), 4976 (i.e. the Duryodh.); IX, 1672; XII, 13680 (*Kuravo nāma*); XIII, 3690, 7756; XIV, 1809? (*Mahābhārata-yuddhaṃ tat*), 2409? (do.).

Bhārata[2] ("a descendant of Bharata"): I, 7446.

Bhārata[3], **°tī** (adj.): I, 371 (*°ṃ kulaṃ*), 534 (*°tī senā* = the army of the Kurus), 2233 (*°tīṃ kathāṃ* = Mahābhārata), 2324 (do.), 2759 (*°ṃ vaṃçaṃ*), 3122 (*°ī kīrttir, °aṃ kulaṃ*), 3870 (*°ṃ kulaṃ*), 4271 (*°ṃ vaṃçaṃ*); II, 676 (*°te vaṃçe*), 1219 (*°ṃ puraṃ*); III, 1930 (*°tī camūḥ*, i.e. the Duryodh.); IV, 1241 (*°īṃ senām*); V, 161 (*°te vaṃçe*), 2102 (*senā°tī*, i.e. the Duryodh.), 2315 (*°tī*, sc. *senā*, i.e. the Duryodh.), 4190 (*°īṃ*, sc. *lakshmīṃ*), 4811 (*Mahābhāratam āhavaṃ*); VI, 130 (*kīrtiçca°ī*), 4548 (*°tī mahācamūḥ* = the Duryodh.), 5229 (*°tīṃ*, sc. *senāṃ*, i.e. the Duryodh.), 5769 (*samitir* . . . *Bhāratī*); VII, 28 (*°tī*, sc. *senā*), 1724 (*senāṃ Bh°īṃ*, i.e. the Duryodh.), 3363 (*°īṃ senāṃ*, i.e. the Duryodh.), 3397 (do. = do.), 4205 (sc. *senāṃ*, i.e. the Duryodh.), 4216 (do. = do.), 4218 (do. = do.), 4873 (*senā*, i.e. the Duryodh.), 5133 (*°īṃ camūṃ*, i.e. the Duryodh.), 5325 (do. = do.), 5846 (*°tī-madhyaṃ*, i.e. the Duryodh.), 5927 (*°īṃ*, sc. *senāṃ*), 6536 (*°tī*, sc. *senā*, i.e. the Duryodh.), 6668 (*°ī senā*), 6671 (*°ī senā*) (principally the Duryodh.?), 6968 (*°tī senā* = the Duryodh.), 7219 (*°tī senā*, i.e. the Duryodh.), 8441 (*°īṃ*, sc. *senāṃ*); VIII, 2850 (*°tī camūḥ* = the Duryodh.), 3037 (*°tī senā*, i.e. Pāṇḍav.), 3525 (*°tī camū*, i.e. the Duryodh.), 3686 (*°tī senā* = the Duryodh.), †3815 (*°tī pṛtanā*), 3843 (*°tīṃ*, sc. *senāṃ*, i.e. the Duryodh.); IX, 1491 (*°tīṃ senāṃ*, i.e. the

Duryodh.); XII, 12228 (*varsham*), 13646 (*ākhyānam*); XVI, 51 (*yuddhe*); XVIII, 192 (°*tvāt*).

Bhārata[4–17] = (1) Abhimanyu Ārjuni, (2) Arjuna Pāṇḍava, (3) Bhīmasena Pāṇḍava, (4) Bhīshma Çāntanava, (5) Çāntanu, (6) Dhṛtarāshṭra Vaicitravīrya, (7) Duḥçāsana Dhārtarāshṭra, (8) Duryodhana Dhārtarāshṭra, (9) Janamejaya Pārikshita, (10) Nakula Pāṇḍava, (11) Pāṇḍu Vaicitravīrya, (12) Sagara, (13) Vidura Vaicitravīrya, (14) Yudhishṭhira Pāṇḍava:—

(1) Abhimanyu: IV, 2325 (Matsya-Bhāratayoḥ).

(2) Arjuna: I, 5398, 5525, 6524, 6621, 6713, 6733, 6762, 6769, 7812; II, 4, 61, 1050, 2425, 2426; III, 507, 1459, 1486, 11948, 11992, 12026, 12192, 12288, 12309, 17268; IV, 17, †1666, †2158 (Bhārata-Matsya-vīrau, i.e. Arjuna and Uttara); V, 2832, 2833, 5512; VI, 892, 896, 975, 1035, 1138, 1252, 1324, 1354, 1358, 1363, 1401, 1405, 1429, 1516, 3582, 3584, 4980, 5736; VII, 5927, 6391, 6428, 7838; VIII, 2827, 2867, 2869, 2878, 2999, 3017, 3021, 3034, 3441, 3486, 3635, 3650, 3651, 3683, 3703, 3719, 3740, 3744, 3746; X, 672; XII, 596, 774, 13159, 13166, 13170, 13171, 13246, 13268, 13297, 13560, 13584; XIV, 390, 2116, 2440; XVI, 169 (ought to have been Vasudeva), 286, 290.

(3) Bhīmasena: I, 4880; II, 2423, 2431; III, 1365, 1415, 1416, 10895, 11222, 11283, 11289, 11326, 17275; IV, 524, 528, 555, 557, 588, 615, 687, 688, 722, 1085; V, 2761, 2790, 5474, 5475; VI, 2275, 3424; VII, 5511; IX, 3402, 3403; X, 756 (?); XI, 393.

(4) Bhīshma: I, 4028, 4034, 4107, 4154, 4231; II, 1352(?), 1355 (?) (Yudhishṭhira ?), 1472, 1481, 1545; V, 6071 (C. Bhārata, voc. instead of nom.), 7023, 7056, 7259; VI, 507, 523, 5462; VII, 98, 108; XII, 1822, 1836, 1837, 1854, 1957, 2126, 2597, 2917, 4210, 4551, (4552), 4716, 4727, 4779, 5247, 5321, 5928, 6026, 6028, 7153, 7641, 7984, 8021, 9259, 9270, 9755, 9855, 11078, 11079; XIII, 374, 1676, 1681, 2631, 2927, 2930, 3065, 3222, 3229, 3235, 3237, 3268, 3375, 3697, 5146, 6199, 6244.

(5) Çāntanu: I, 3963, 3967.

(6) Dhṛtarāshṭra: I, 238, 4516, 4764, 5597, 5686, 7462, 7471, 7493, 7498, 7499, 7509; II, 1756, 1807, 1809, 1812, 1821, 1822, 1875, 1907, 1911, 1928, 1932, 1962, 2095, 2108, †2120, 2433, 2481, 2482, 2630, 2635, 2636, 2641; III, 285, 313, 318, 343, 459, 14837; V, †691 (?), †950, 955 (°āgrya!), 1038, 1066, 1099, 1167, 1256, 1286, 1345, 1388, 1392, 1415, 1431, 1438, 1441, 1444, 1447, 1543, †1553, 1566, 1656, 1691, 1788, 2121, 2142, 2147, 2159, 2163, 2174, 2185, 2189, 2197, 2200, 2203, 2210, 2211, 2272, 2278, 2324, 2384, 2387, 2388, 2391, 2563, 3061, 3386, 3389, 3395, 3409, 3428, 3443, 3494 (?), 4300, 4390, 4391, 4730, 5409, 5410, 5885; VI, 40, 64, 91, 114, 138, 146, 152, 200, 207, 227, 313, 317, 331, 344, 399, 408, 430, 487, 613, 693, 755, 756, 854, 1621, 1660, 1690, 1692, 1700, 1712, 1721, 1775, 1793, 1851, 1862, 1895, 2149, 2203, 2205, 2275, 2284, 2286, 2324, 2359, 2363, 2424, 2449, †2649, †2651, 2727, 2773, 2801, †2807, 2817, 2914, 3077, 3184, 3186, 3244, 3275, 3278, 3311, 3406, 3412, 3447, 3475, 3489, 3550, 3618, 3625, 3627, 3667, 3675, 3717, 3750, †3787, 3831 (only in B.), 3873, 3876, 3969, 3995, 4164, 4314, 4336, 4365, 4370, 4383, 4399, 4400, 4502, 4537, 4546, 4551, 4597, 4628, 4634, 4660, 4686, 4762, 4882, †4884, 4893, 5008, 5010, 5109, 5122, 5163, 5195, 5218, 5337, 5501, 5635; VII, 42, 466, 483, 492, 592, 600, 819, 890, 919, 957, 1041, 1098, 1336, †1452, 1471, 1571, 1630, 1640, 1652, 1655, 1737, 1738, 1757, 1823, 1886, 2915, 3124, 3282, 3302, 3322, 3356, 3364, 3400, 3485, 3520, 3521, 3562, 3639, 3653, 3678, 3752, 3935, 3982, 3994, 4011, 4021, 4026, 4033, 4153, 4494, 4577, †4688, 4816, 4823, 4957, 4968, 4969, 4994, 5074, 5077, 5097, 5222, 5306, 5400, 5426, 5513, 5628, 5640, 5687, 5761, 5827, 5925, 5940 (B.; C. has °aḥ-Yuyudhāna), 6238, 6453, 6615, 6618, 6625, 6636, 6724, 6774, 6861, 6878, 6881, 6897, 6924, 6943, 7100, 7197, 7252, 7253, 7285, 7319, 7369, 7409, 7437, 7439, 7496, 7504, 7520, 7542, 7550, 7594, 7598, 7606, 7608, 7615, 7768, 7794, 7911, 8111, 8392, 8394, 8482, 8520, 8539, 8593, 8608, 8693, 8722, 8816, 8898, 9027, 9279, 9358, 9369, 9415, 9421; VIII, 53, 362, 399, 547, 553, 589, 629, 712, 736, 739, 741, 749, 804, 952, 959, 979, 980, 982, 1007, 1011, 1029, 1038, 1078, 1079, 1117, 1157, 1175, 1190, 1243, 1390, 1675, 2247, 2315, 2365, 2386, 2502, 2527, 2530, 2555, 2559, 2606, 2625, 2676, 2677, 2706, 2742, 2751, 2788, 2835, 2911, 3088, 3093, 3219, 3246, 3283, 3634, 3751, †3815, †3829, 3888, 3898, 3934, 3967, 3992, 3993, 4117, 4379, 4432, †4621, †4702, †4763, 4775, †4787; IX, 32, 39, 136, 190, 328, 371, 384, 407, 417, 422, 427, 431, 456, 681, 718, 721, 738, 839, 855, 952, 971, 981, 1001, 1088 (?), 1133, 1137, 1151, 1167, 1176, 1260, 1356, 1363, 1401, 1402, 1446, 1496, 1506, 1507, 1518, 1533, 1564, 1580, 1581, 1726, 1729, 1759, 1965, 3080, 3189, 3201, 3204, 3296, 3307, 3413, 3444, 3492, 3542, 3543, 3549, 3624; X, 33, 39, 268, 271, 272, 278, 303, 330, 335, 348, 417, 434, 547; XI, 31, 49, 51, 94, 97, 166, 170, 182, 185, 190, 195, 207, 228, 236, 239, 251, 256, 306, 346, 350, 768, 776; XII, 4561, 4566; XV, 404, 749, 750.

(7) Duḥçāsana: III, 15091; VII, 4887.

(8) Duryodhana: II, 1763, 1968, 2092 (?); III, 294, 14773, 14836, 14837, 15031, 15049, 15051, 15225, 15226, 15290, 15293, 15337; IV, 881, 890, 920, 966; V, 2379, 2494, 2922, 3254, 3472, 3494, 3498, 3674, 4129, 4134, 4149, 4163, 4164, 4167, 4200, 4266, 4353, 5069, 5828, 5892, 5896, 5901, 5911, 5935, 5940, 5965, 6012, 6040, 7002, 7048, 7092, 7142, 7159, 7161, 7173, 7179, 7187, 7203, 7204, †7207, 7235, 7267, 7288, 7338, 7367, 7438, 7463, 7482, 7495, †7570, 7571; VI, 3035, 3930, 4443 (PCR.), 4469, 5816; VII, 152, 437, 3449, 5339, 6555, 6561, 6975, 7149, 7151, 7159, 7666, 8445, 8921, 9020; VIII, 359, 1286, 1287, 1291, 1318, 1626, †4829, †4832; IX, 193, 213, 974, 1686, 1768, 1773, 1776, 1777, 1805, 1858, 1876, 3333; X, 506, 529; XII, 4567.

(9) Janamejaya: I, 2175, 2496, 2498, 2521, 2522, 2527, 2529, 2538, 2553, 2609, 2632, 2708, 3110, 3117, 3124, 3125, 3162, 3205, 3207, 3212, 3424, 3712, 3720, 3721, 3749, 3908, 4020, 4040, 4049 (B. *Bhārata*, C. °*taḥ*), 4099, 4146, 4289, 4320, 4373, 4375, 4380, 4383, 4395, 4513, 4539, 4641, 4784, 4936, 4975, 4994, 4996, 5236, 5293, 5312, 5339, 5370, 5391, 5440, 5462, 5511, 5715, 5814, 5899, 5901, 6180, 6185, 6241, 6277, 6284, 6300, 6360(?), 6953, 7206, 7250, 7524, 7528, 7742, 7780, 7783, 7811, 7814, 7816, 7818, 7821, 7858, 7874, 7912, 8023, 8029, 8066, 8069, 8120, 8293, 8327, 8337, 8348, 8435, 8448; II, 15, 75, 101, 135, 514, 541, 762, 821, 834, 943, 970, 976, 981, 1094, 1112, 1156, 1195, 1247, 1263, 1432, 1487, 2052, 2289, 2481, 2492, 2513 (?); III, 262, 410, 426, 1612, 1665, 4038, 10097, 10469, 10972, 10985, 11133, 11341, 11427, 11513, 11709, 11772, 11898, 12441, 13213, 13488, 14860, 14880, 14903, 14958, 14978, 14998, 15104, 15182, 15186, 15272, 15344, 15611, 15801, 16926, 17056; IV, 6, 462, 826, 828, 1005, 1067, 1271, 1599, 1705, 1998, 2014, 2032, 2082, 2348; V, 152, 178, 210, 598, 1572, 1802, 1917, 2212, 3002, 3376, 5243, 5276, 5390, 5696, 5698, 7614, 7622, 7652; VI, 495, 496; VIII, 10, 5041; IX, 1996, 2205, 2207, 2218, 2248, 2270, 2273, 2366, 2368, 2401,

2445, 2498, 2546, 2550, 2568, 2572, 2582, 2586, 2603, 2605, 2607, 2608, 2612, 2620, 2623, 2625, 2626, 2629, 2632, 2641, 2642, 2646, 2649, 2713, 2768, 2772, 2787, 2788, 2851, 2864, 2869, 2913, 2918, 2925, 2959, 2964 (! ?), 3511; XI, 325, 412, 503 (ought to have been Kṛshṇa), 742, 787; XII, 1383, 1395, 1399, 1411, 1466, 5632, 6127, 12999, 13029, 13615, 13632, 13718; XIII, 1304; XIV, 1624, 1627, 1635, 1717, 1738, 1739, 1741, 1759, 1862, 1886, 1887, 1964, 2041, 2045, 2063, 2125 (?), 2145, 2163, 2186, 2205, 2233, 2254, 2258, 2537, 2658 (?), 2692, 2816, 2827, 2845; XV, 134, 174, 513, 524, 589, 619, 727, 774, 917, 1055; XVI, 39, 46, 97, 149, 195, 222; XVIII, 56, 87, 177, 221, 233, 246.

(10) Nakula: V, 5476 (= Ulūka ?), 5477; XII, 6149, 6172.

(11) Pāṇḍu: I, 4478, 4568, 4579, 4682, 4750.

(12) Sagara: III, 8847.

(13) Vidura: I, 7382 (Janamejaya ?), 7521; II, 1782, 2130; III, 256.

(14) Yudhishṭhira: I, 6360 (? one expects Pāṇḍavāḥ); II, 42 (?) (Janamejaya ?), 156, 161, 208, 240, 274, 286, 304, 346, 377, 420, 431, 438, 442, 448, 455, 462, 475, 478, 504, 565, 605, 743, 1327, 1428, 1639, 2445, 2492 (?), 2504 (?), 2513 (?), 2581; III, 128, 142, 618, 715, 797, 802, 812, 813, 828, 844, 995, 1001, 1016, 1120, 1121, 1145, 1251, 1271, 1345, 1351, 2077, 2104, 2135, 2200, 2216, 2219, 2264, 2350, 2391, 2516, 2687, 2705, 2807, 2874, 2919, 2945, 4075, 5010, 5031, 5040, 5052, 5056, 5062, 5076, 5082, 6028, 6030, 6049, 6052, 6058, 6060, 6065, 7006, 7046, 7088, 7089, 7098, 8026, 8029, 8040, 8050, 8060, 8067, 8068, 8101, 8115, 8181, 8184, 8221, 8225, 8260, 8326, 8355, 8357, 8376, 8465, 8493, 8528, 8532, 8562, 8632, 8640, 8643, 8667, 8813, 8832, 9902, 9984, 9985, 10133, 10134, 10201, †10214, 10304, 10316, 10409, 10457, 10497, 10523, 10546, 10704, 10714, 10753, 10764, 10805, 10820, 10830, 10847, 10849, 10861, 10991, 11448, 11485, 11804, 11824, 11882, 11962, 11994, 12009, 12051, 12093, 12100, 12122, 12140, 12142, 12169, 12230, 12252, 12275, †12327, †12328, 12872, 12873, 12888, 12904, 12908, 12976, 13113, 13376, 13422, 13491, 13621, 13647, 14119, 14232, 14432, 15357, 15386, 15952, 16074, 16228, 16505, 16526, 16658, 16712, 17245, 17435; IV, 28, 31, 77, 79, 89, 157, 226, 228, 555; V, 205, 377, 436, †689, 2585, 2688, 2689, 2711, 4470, 5083 (*Bhārata*, B.; C. has °*aṃ*), 5087, 5140, 5427; VI, 1545, 4940; VII, 2010, [illegible], VIII, 2155, †3375, †3503, †3505, 5001; IX, 350 (?), 351 (?), 1748, 1780, 1792, 3482; X, 616, 629, 768, 792; XI, 321, 2742 (ought to have been Kuçika); XII, 47, 82, 110, 115, 117, 118, 133, 290, 338, 344, 371, 376, 381, 397, 409, 410, 440, 477, 536, 606, 620, 702, 703, 1072, 1146, 1147, 1155, 1157, 1159, 1188, 1192, 1205, 1207, 1219, 1240, 1241, 1255, 1433, 1437, 1465, 1515, 1759, 1932 (?), 2044, 2086, 2136, 2248 (?), 2280, 2294, 2304, 2307, 2312, 2468, 2469, 2470, 2476, 2483, 2492, 2536, 2626, 2670, 2720, 2730, 2802, [illegible], 2920, 3055, 3057, 3124, 3128, 3229, 3268, 3281, 3298, 3331, 3354, 3361, 3460, 3461, 3578, 3686, 3692, 3705, 3757, 3769, 3786, 3792, 3961, 3963, 3980, 3989, 3997, 4007, 4023, 4026, 4191, 4197, 4243, (4330), 4351, 4437, 4520, 4524, 4553 (?), 4647, 4735, 4741, 4748, 4772, 4823, 4825, 4877, 4880, 4924, 4927, 4928, 5129, 5132, 5248, 5360, 5414, 5428, 5436, 5440, 5463, 5876, 5902, 5920, 5961, 5979, 5983, 5998, 6040, 6078, 6317, 6351, 6387, 6389, 6448, 6587, 7077, 7093, 7095, 7148, 7537, 7540, 8009, 8088, 8185, 8344, 8431, 9296, 9450 (?), 9548, 9795, 9838, 9847, 9853, 10003, 10146, 10155, 10165, 10185, 10211, 10213, 10221, 10264, 10267, 10347, 10497, 10502, 10533, 11109, 11139, 11160, 11168, 11170, 11171, 11186, 11189, 11194, 11195, 11516, 11545, 11854, 12183, 12204, 12218, 12252, 12259, 12260, 12425, 12577, 12616, 12621, 12645, 12819, 12846, 12988, 13942; XIII, 89, 102, 159, 180, 220, 345, 406, 410, 426, 444, 445, 598, 602, 650, 972, 975, 998, 1033, 1380, 1576, 1578, 1588, 1591, 1607, 1610, 1617, 1635, 1637, 1656, 1658, 1662, 1666, 1672, 1675, 1939, 1947, 1958, 1970, 2084, 2192, 2274, 2349, 2355, 2358, 2427, 2498, 2508, 2513, 2517, 2519, 2554, 2613, 2619, 2630, 2722, 2730, 2762, 2806, 2828, 2833, 2859, 2951, 2995, 3016, 3047, 3076, 3077, 3080, 3081, 3098, 3100, 3282, 3347, 3348, 3364, 3366, 3723, 3831, 3877, 3930, 4320, 4321, 4325, 4374, 4378, 4415, 4422, 4644, 4649, 4652, 4678, 4679, 4755, 4793, 4814, 4910, 5059, 5076, 5080, 5081, 5082, 5083, 5095, 5098, 5103, 5114, 5115, 5128, 5130, 5141, 5146 (?), 5348, 5363, 5433, 5444, 5447, 5464, 5466, 5479, 5492, 5493, 5504, 5523, 5529, 5563, 5611, 5686, 5697, 5706, 5714, 5921, 6280, 6281, 6913, 7134, 7161, 7186, 7370, 7473, 7488, 7538; XIV, 40, 43, 48, 68, 97, 332, 335, 2080; XV, 157, 181, 187, 197, 214, 222, 223, 240, 249, 681, 708, 1024, 1046, 1078; XVII, 90, 94; XVIII, 61, 114.

Bhārata[18] **(m)** (= Mahābhārata): I, 19 (*Bhāratasyetihāsasya*), 52 (*Manv-ādi Bhāratam kecit* . . .), 77 (*Lekhako Bhāratasyāsya*), 85 (°*sūryeṇa*), 92 (°*drumaḥ*), 96 (*abravīd Bhāratam loke mānushye 'smin mahān ṛshiḥ*), 98 (*çrāvayām āsa Bhāratam*), 101 (*caturviṃçatisāhasrīṃ cakre Bhārata-saṃhitām*), 247 (°*ādhyayanam*), 255 (*anukramaṇikādhyāyam Bhāratasyemam āditaḥ*), 257 (°*sya vapuḥ*), 259, 262 (*adhītam Bhāratam tena*), 264 (*ekataç caturo vedān Bhāratam caitad ekataḥ*), 303 (°*ākhyānam*), 308 (*tad etad Bhāratam nāma kavibhis tūpajīvyati*), 311 (*Bhāratasyetihāsasya* . . . *parvasangrahaḥ*), 360 (*samāso Bhāratasyāyam atroktaḥ parvasangrahaḥ*), 516 (*pañcamaṃ parva Bhārate*), 526 (*shashṭham etat samākhyātaṃ Bhārate parva*), 539 (*saptamaṃ Bhārate parva*), 548 (*ashṭamaṃ parva Bhāratacintakaiḥ*), 592 (*çlokasaptaçatī cāpi pañcasaptatisaṃyutā | saṃkhyayā Bhāratākhyānam uktaṃ Vyāsena dhīmatā*), 644 (*etat sarvaṃ samākhyātaṃ Bhārataparvasangrahaḥ*), †655 (*yo Bhārataṃ samadhigacchati* . . .), †658 (°*kathām* . . .), 2202 (*mahat*), 2313 (*yo 'dhīte Bhā°m puṇyaṃ*), 2314 (*Bhā°ṃ paṭhan*), 2329, 2330 (*idaṃ*), 2419, ††3841 (*idaṃ*); XII, 13315 (*çatasahasrād °ākhyānavistarāt*), 13649 (°*ārthān*), 13650 (id.), 13651 (id.); XIII, 3682, 6069 (?), 7159 (°*kathaṃ*); XVIII, 196, 202 (°*ādhyayanāt*), 208 (°*Sāvitrīṃ*), 209, 210 (*ākhyānaṃ*), 211–12, 214, 218, 220, 221 (*çrutvā Bhārata Bh°ṃ*), 233 (id.), 262, 290 (*bhavishyāṃ* ?), 295 (°*çravaṇe*), 296–8, 300.

Bhārata[19] = °*saṃgrāma* ("the war of the Bhāratas"): XII, 1716 (Nīl.).

Bhārata[20] **(m)** (= *Bha°varsha*). § 574 (Jambūkh.). VI, 9, 317; XII, 12228.

Bhāratācārya[1] = Droṇa: II, 1535; IV, 1591, 1592 (*Droṇāt*); X, 618.

Bhāratācārya[2] = Kṛpa: II, 1349 (*Kṛpe*).

Bhāratācāryaputra = Açvatthāman: X, 640.

Bharataçārdūla[1–5] = (1) Bhīmasena Pāṇḍava, (2) Dhṛtarāshṭra, (3) Duryodhana Dhārtarāshṭra, (4) Janamejaya Pārikshita, (5) Yudhishṭhira Pāṇḍava:—

(1) Bhīmasena: II, 1061.

(2) Dhṛtarāshṭra: VI, 4237; VII, 5432; IX, 3557.

(3) Duryodhana: V, 7272.

(4) Janamejaya: I, 2016; XVII, 44.

(5) Yudhishṭhira: III, 8884, 15892; XII, 2189; XIII, 3199, 7087.

Bharataçārdūlau = Bhīmasena and Duryodhana: IX, 3111.

Bharataçreshṭha[1–10] = (1) Arjuna Pāṇḍava, (2) Bhīmasena Pāṇḍava, (3) Bhīshma Çāntanava, (4) Dhṛtarāshṭra Vaicitravīrya, (5) Duḥçāsana Dhārtarāshṭra, (6) Duryodhana Dhārtarāshṭra, (7) Janamejaya Pārikshita, (8) Nakula Pāṇḍava, (9) Parikshit (father of Janamejaya), (10) Yudhishṭhira Pāṇḍava:—

(1) Arjuna: I, 6793, 6892; III, 12207; VIII, 648, 2881, 3037, 3576, 3730, 4129; XIV, 1475, 2279.

(2) Bhīmasena: III, 11208; IV, 591; VIII, 3894; IX, 1924.

(3) Bhīshma: V, 1962, 3100, 5942, 7295; VI, 4486 (Gāṅgeyo), 5568, 5735; VII, 25, 102; IX, 1934 (Gāṅgeya); XII, 1994, 7519, 7522; XIII, 344, 1531, 1760, 2045, 4743, 5880, 7723.

(4) Dhṛtarāshṭra: V, 3437, 3499 (?), 5626, 5736; VI, 102, 173, 381, 410, 475, 491, 1855, 1968, 1971, 2019, 2032, 2033, 2447, 2924, 3447, 3531, 3594, 3642, 3880, 4083, 4085, 4139, 4145, 4312, 5084, 5589, 5783; VII, 28, 789, 794, 1735, 3066, 3888, 3983, 4117, 4240, 5444, 5472, 5661, 5740, 5815, 5901, 6095, 6883, 7348, 7441, 7584, 7601, 7721; VIII, 2482, 2656, 2681, 2698, 2770, 2771; IX, 378, 722, 1006, 1340, 1577, 1591, 1641, 3233.

(5) Duḥçāsana: VII, 4937.

(6) Duryodhana: III, 14842, 15334; V, 3499 (?), 4192, 4205, 4685, 5045, 5966, 5994, 6060, 6097, 7177, 7236, 7509; VI, 4411; VII, 444; VIII, 1663, 2717 (so both C. and B.); IX, 171, 3234, 3637 (*sarvalokeçvareçvaraṃ*).

(7) Janamejaya: I, 3713; III, 13628, 15799, 16922, 17184, 17271; IX, 9, 23, 2094, 2822, 2851, 3003; X, 688; XIII, 7779; XIV, 2176, 2240; XV, 888; XVII, 43; XVIII, 208, 270, 290–1.

(8) Nakula: IX, 504.

(9) Parikshit: I, 1678.

(10) Yudhishṭhira: II, 427, 726; III, 608, 617, 637, 644, 670, 782, 849, 2716, 3097, 8336, 8833, 11650, 13000, 13063, 13377, 13415, 13643, 14286, 15971; VI, 2059; VII, 2974, 3982, 8318, 8357; VIII, 3563; IX, 1749, 1837, 3152; XII, 640, 700, 2267, 3267, 5541, 5798, 5804, 6038, 7536, 7568, 10696, 13938; XIII, 201, 408, 432, 441, 452, 1537, 1724 (ought to have been Gautama), 2122, 4293, 4646, 4650, 4653, 5374, 7554; XIV, 2530, 2652, 2688; XVII, 94; XVIII, 119.

Bhārataçreshṭha = Arjuna Pāṇḍava: XIV, 2482.

Bharataçreshṭhāḥ[1] (pl., "the best of the Bh.") = the Pāṇḍavāḥ: III, 2015, 12555, 15389, 15571.

Bharataçreshṭhāḥ[2] = the Duryodhanists: VII, 22.

Bharataçreshṭhau = Nakula and Sahadeva: VIII, 2701.

Bhāratagoptṛ = Çāntanu: I, 3975.

Bhāratāgrya = (1) Arjuna Pāṇḍava, (2) Duryodhana Dhārtarāshṭra, (3) Janamejaya Pārikshita:—

(1) Arjuna: XV, 434.

(2) Duryodhana: V, 766.

(3) Janamejaya: I, †2097, †2098, †2099, †2100, †2101, †2102, †2103.

Bharatamukhya = (1) Duryodhana Dhārtarāshṭra: V, †915.—(2) Janamejaya Pārikshita: I, 7151.

Bhāratāpasada = Duḥçāsana Dhārtarāshṭra: II, 2307.

Bharatapravarha = Yudhishṭhira: III, †909.

Bharatapravarhāḥ (pl.) = Pāṇḍavāḥ: III, †944.

Bharatapravīra = Bhīmasena Pāṇḍava: III, 1372.

Bhāratarājaputra = Hrīnisheva (?) Ugrāyudha (?): VIII, †207.

Bhāratarathaçreshṭha = Arjuna Pāṇḍava: VII, 1424.

Bharatarshabha[1–15] = (1) Arjuna Pāṇḍava, (2) Bhīmasena Pāṇḍava, (3) Bhīshma Çāntanava, (4) Çāntanu, (5) Dhṛshṭadyumna, (6) Dhṛtarāshṭra Vaicitravīrya, (7) Droṇa, (8) Duryodhana Dhārtarāshṭra, (9) Janamejaya Pārikshita, (10) Nakula Pāṇḍava, (11) Pāṇḍu Vaicitravīrya, (12) Sahadeva Pāṇḍava, (13) Vidura Vaicitravīrya, (14) Vikarṇa Dhārtarāshṭra, (15) Yudhishṭhira Pāṇḍava:—

(1) Arjuna: I, 6492, 6651, 6689, 6874, 7781, 7816, 7839, 7932; II, 988; III, 1467, 1490, 1620, 2018; VI, 991, 1122, 1164, 1347, 1367, 1438, 1490, 5586; VII, 2546, 3849; VIII, 2829, 2997, 3024, 3025, 3030, 3032, 3061, †4578; XIV, 402, 422, 589, 596, 599; XVI, 166, 259.

(2) Bhīmasena: I, 5897; II, 922, 1069, 1079; III, 11126, 11288, 11307, 11697, 11705, 17279; IV, 558, 618; XII, 514; XV, 370.

(3) Bhīshma: I, 4052, 4481; V, 7097, 7257, 7295; VI, 533, 559, †792, 4943, 4952, 5719; VII, †86; XII, 1963, 2132, 2270, 2535, 4913, 4914, 4919, 5877, 6003, 7567, 8213, 10102, 10114, 11837; XIII, 197, 199, 344, 1381, 1688, 1689, 2008, 2970, 3006, 3241, 3955, 4551, 4601, 4677, 5166, 5688.

(4) Çāntanu: I, 3930, 3951.

(5) Dhṛshṭadyumna: VI, 2066.

(6) Dhṛtarāshṭra: I, 7467; II, 1754, 1952, 2407, 2472, 2484, 2506, 2632, 2707; III, 254; V, 995, 1004, 1032, 1044, 1143, 1194, 1319, 1465, 1960, 2001, 2013, 2123, 2134, 2185, 2195, 2386, 2467, 2468, 3395, 3404, 3412, 3419, 3420, 3421, 3426, 3430, 3434, 5626, 5698, 5776, 5859; VI, 46, 163, 271, 274, 281, 365, 387, 391, 497, 647, 654, 713, 733, 734, 735, 790, 826, 1760, 1806, 1810, 1812, 2080, 2178, 2351, 2364, 2889, 3055, 3095, 3127, 3148, 3337, 4097, 4350, 4681, 4769, 4817, 5000, 5014, 5016, 5068, 5085, 5096, 5458, 5462, 5677, 5771; VII, 760, 1597, 1724, 2713, 3065, 3696, 3698, 3932, 3950, 4007, 4129, 4486, 4669, 5066, 5210, 5299, 5356, 5454, 5511, 5601, 5619, 5936, 6362, 6503, 6655, 6669, 6894, 7019, 7072, 7108, 7282, 7476, 7507, 7512, 7571, 7616, 7678, 7723, 8362, 8394, 8522, 8774, 8915, 9214, 9311, 9496; VIII, 402, 486, 997, 1282, 2124, 2228, 2383, 2392, 2397, 2671, 2727, 3114, 3167, 3308, 3403 (so C.; B. °*aṃ*, i.e. Yudhishṭhira), 3564, 3572, 3961, 3964, 4143, 4400, 4407; IX, 25, 38, 341, 343, 397, 405, 406, 408, 454, 459, 511, 622, 707, 728, 731, 757, 932, 1099, 1138, 1163, 1209, 1223, 1274, 1485, 1495, 1712, 1713, 1721, 3288, 3298, 3306, 3467, 3494, 3556; X, 432; XI, 54, 141, 168, 255, 260, 268, 292, 336; XV, 763.

(7) Droṇa: VII, 684.

(8) Duryodhana: II, 1935, 1937, 1944, †2134; III, 372, 15282; V, 161, 937, 1944 (v. 1926, read *Bhīshma uvāca* against B. and C.), 2386, 4132, 4136, 4140, 4150, 4153, 4154, 4155, 4160, 4174, 4202, 4205, 4227, 4229, 4355, 4363, 5941, 5945, 5955, 5962, 5973, 5995, 7105, 7106, 7201, 7225, 7427, 7487; VI, 3015, 5081; VIII, 1310; IX, 227, 3640.

(9) Janamejaya: I, 2235, 2333, 2466, 2472, 2479, 2481, 2762, 3279, 3750, 3927, 4009, 4038, 4041, 4123, 4309, 4396, 4474, 4557, 4643, 5282, 5299, 5502, 5642, 5657, 5716, 5775, 5824, 5889, 5900, 5941, 6109, 6111, 6634, 6974, 8052, 8155, 8209, 8479; II, 8, 885, 979, 1000, 1099, 1142, 1161, 1262, 1660, 2215, 2454; III, 435, 9968, 11395, 11416, 11545, 11670, 11681, 13482, 15188, 15231, 15237, 15330, 15370,

16594; IV, 158, 1034, 1889, 1894, 2010, 2034, 2370; V, 565, 596, 1797, 3007, 3107, 4186, 4439, 5386, 5392; VIII, 77; IX, 53, 54, 110, 1990, 1998, 2340, 2648, 2651, 2655, 2664, 2690, 2723, 2949, 3509; X, 657; XII, 1543; XIV, 1536 (read °*bha*; B. °*āḥ*), 1680, 1750, 1765, 2013, 2032, 2040, 2128, 2195, 2314, 2445, 2550, 2629, 2631, 2647, 2683; XV, 261, 281, 354, 427, 521, 609, 630, 635, 656, 733, 894, 898; XVI, 204; XVII, 21, 156, 158; XVIII, 193 (ought to have been Çaunaka), 221, 263, 283, 293, 298, 300, 308, 311.

(10) Nakula: II, 1203; XII, 6208.

(11) Pāṇḍu: I, 4617, 4653, 4715, 4967.

(12) Sahadeva: II, 1182.

(13) Vidura: IX, 46; XV, 390.

(14) Vikarṇa: II, 2282.

(15) Yudhishṭhira: II, 157, 179, 188, 191, 255, 256, 277, 382, 423, 497, 499, 500, 567, 569, 608, 651, 656, 692, 708, 1639, 2159, 2499, 2568; III, 613, 615, 662, 760, 1206, 1261, 1272, 1281, 2956, 2996, 3068, 4087, 5003, 5005, 5011, 5013, 5020, 5046, 5058, 5094, 7023, 8003, 8052, 8071, 8073, 8098, 8121, 8298, 8309, 8329, 8426, 8534, 8833, 8859, 9919, 9989, 10102, 10169, 10828, 11535, 11784, 11964, 12011, 12031, 12095, 12146, 12241, 12286, 12507, 12790, 12792, 12794, 12833, 12855, 12873, 13016, 13017, 13136, 13555, 13588, 13592, 13603, 13658, 15872, 16568, 16594, 16609, 16614, 16637, 16722, 16859, 17325, 17388, 17424; V, 208, 235, 270, 285, 322, 494, 5322, 5419; VI, 4970; VII, 2011, 8353; VIII, †3292; IX, 347, 1788, 1883, 1893, 1900, 3150; X, 608, 621, 767; XII, 108, 278, 305, 345, 506, 643, 650, 1138, 1177, 1343, 1440, 1571, 1761, 1784, 2154, 2167, 2181, 2606, 2753, 2883, 3261, 3408, 3459, 3558, 3582, 3682, 3753, 4023, 4185, 4196, 4244, 4352, 4412, 4732, 4733, 5035, 5328, 5379, 5454, 5809, 6448, 7549, 7555, 7562, 7565, 7742, 8455, 9771, 9833, 10152, 10155, 10162, 10189, 10251, 10488, 11062, 11066, 11086, 11132, 11181, 11203, 12646; XIII, 109, 260, 386, 407, 437, 442, 445, 458, 459, 460, 461, 468, 472, 477, 507, 1582, 1593, 1594, 1598, 1600, 1604, 1630, 1649, 1650, 1655, 1669, 1723 (ought to have been Gautama), 2085, 2095, 2126, 2129, 2249, 2400, 2418, 2420, 2524, 2552, 2553, 2629, 2643, 2649, 2701 (ought to have been Nahusha), 2708, 2767, 2913 (ought to have been Kuçika), 2934, 3040, 3357, 3360, 3372, 3377, 3616, 3655, 3813, 3829, 3884, 3946, 3950, 3952, 3959, 4647, 4797, 4842, 5085, 5113, 5131, 5140, 5142, 5189 (?), 5492, 5565, 5646, 5882, 7402, 7454, 7457; XIV, 311, 327, 2678; XV, 97, 139, 204, 225, 345, 604, 680, 978, 993, 1082; XVII, 77, 78; XVIII, 98.

Bharatarshabhāḥ (pl.): I, 4966 (Pāṇḍavān), 5334 (the disciples of Droṇa); II, 2497 (= Pāṇḍavāḥ), III, 240 (=Pāṇḍavāḥ), 355 (= do.), 934 (= do.), 1453 (= do.), 2007 (= do.), 6089 (= do.), 6921 (= do.), 10695 (= do.), 11550 (= do.), 11648 (= do.), 11668 (= do.), 11832 (= do.), †12339 (= do.), †12340 (= do.), 13007 (°*au* = Yamau), 14702 (= Pāṇḍavāḥ); IV, 1683 (= the Duryodhanists), 2259 (= Pāṇḍavāḥ), 2295 (°*au* = Nakula and Sahadeva); V, 4456 (= Bhīshma, etc., in the palace of Dhṛtarāshṭra); XI, 445 (= the Duryodhanists); XII, 1519 (= Pāṇḍavāḥ); XIV, 1536 (= Pāṇḍavāḥ; C. °*aḥ*, read probably °*bha*).

Bharatarshabhau = Bhīma and Duryodhana: IX, 3109.

Bharatasattama[1-10] = (1) Arjuna Pāṇḍava, (2) Bhīshma Çāntanava, (3) Çāntanu, (4) Dhṛtarāshṭra Vaicitravīrya, (5) Duryodhana Dhārtarāshṭra, (6) Janamejaya Pārikshita, (7) Pāṇḍu Vaicitravīrya, (8) Sahadeva Pāṇḍava, (9) Vikarṇa Dhārtarāshṭra, (10) Yudhishṭhira Pāṇḍava:—

(1) Arjuna: III, 1540; VI, 1458; VII, 2549, 6224; IX, 3468; XVI, 290.

(2) Bhīshma: I, 5096; XII, 5594, 12709; XIII, 2044, 2202, 3200, 7601.

(3) Çāntanu: I, 3924, 3926.

(4) Dhṛtarāshṭra: V, 4329, 4331; VI, 300, 4240, 4279; VII, 6778, 7349, 7606; VIII, 1001, 1390, 2839; IX, 327, 1175, 1225, 1270, 1349; X, 412, 497.

(5) Duryodhana: V, 1928 (v. 1926, read *Bhīshma uvāca* against B. and C.), 2296, 4203, 4712, 4996, 7104, 7200; VI, 2933; VII, 8998.

(6) Janamejaya: I, 1962, 2217, 2390, 2801, 3900, 4776, 4976, 5108, 8047, 8061; II, 69, 836, 1789; VIII, 75; IX, 2547, 2940; XI, 317; XIV, 1482, 1902, 2061, 2434, 2691, 2857; XV, 618; XVII, 15, 32.

(7) Pāṇḍu: I, 4415, 4891.

(8) Sahadeva: II, 1159.

(9) Vikarṇa: XI, 552.

(10) Yudhishṭhira: II, 625, 691; III, 1024, 4059, 5026, 6012, 6027, 6032, 6047, 6058, 6078, 6080, 7009, 7071, 8041, 8155, 8315, 8385, 10523, 11655, 13019, 13507, 13609, 13661, 13668, 14137, 16728; V, 5451; VII, 8355; VIII, 2993; XII, 383, 418, 2138, 2346, 2387, 3382, 3966, 3978, 5460, 5586, 6041, 6380, 6459, 7624, 10157, 10164, 13766; XIII, 429, 2081, 2287, 2654, 2710, 2807, 2920, 3043, 3339, 3423, 3481, 3804, 3852, 4548, 4650, 5137, 5346; XV, 1080; XVII, 53.

Bhāratasattama = Duryodhana: V, 7283 (so both B. and C.).

Bharatasattamāḥ: I, 7737 (= Pāṇḍavāḥ); III, 11649, 11675; V, 4181 (= the Duryodhanists); VI, 3135 (= Pāṇḍavāḥ); XVII, 46 (= do.).

Bharatasiṃha[1] = Bhīshma Çāntanava: VI, 3810.—Do.[2] = Pāṇḍu: I, 4631.

Bhāratasiṃha = Yudhishṭhira: III, 740.

Bharatavaṃça: I, 3970.

Bhārata(ṃ)varsha(ṃ). § 574 (Jambūkh.): VI, **6**, 201; **9**, 309, 312, 313; **10**, 385, 387.—§ 575 (Bhūmiparvan): VI, **12**, 493.—Cf. Bhārata[20].

Bharatī (?) (an Agni). § 490 (Āṅgirasa): III, **219**, 14136 (v. Bharata).

Bhāratī (a river). § 494 (Āṅgirasa): III, **222**, 14232.

***bhāratī** (voice): XII, 1412; XIII, 3692 (*Bārhaspatīṃ*); XIV, 650 (*gauḥ*), 1192.

Bharga, pl. (°*āḥ*). § 280 (Bhīmasena): II, **29**, 1085 (*Bhargqāṇāṃ adhipañ caiva Nishādādhipatiṃ tathā*) (conquered by Bhīmasena).

Bhārga, pl. (°*āḥ*, B. *Bhargāḥ*). § 574 (Jambūkh.): VI, **9**, 358 (a people in Bhāratavarsha).

Bhārgava[1], pl. (°*āḥ*) (the descendants of Bhṛgu): VIII, 1583 (*Bhārgavāṇāṃ kule jāto . . . Jamadagniḥ*); XIII, 2753 (°*āṇāṃ kulodvahaḥ*, i.e. Cyavana), 4146, 4160.

Bhārgava[2], pl. (°*āḥ*), a people in Bhāratavarsha: VI, 358.

Bhārgava[1], adj. (?): I, 2602 (*Vasūnāṃ Bhārgavaṃ vidyāt*); I, 865 (°*aṃ vaṃçaṃ*), 868 (do.).

Bhārgava[2] (a descendant of Bhṛgu): XI, 661; XII, 60; XIII, 4143 (°*Āṅgirasau*); XIV, 960.

Bhārgava[3] = Aurva: I, 6820, 6828.

Bhārgava[4] = Cyavana: I, 445, 870, 874, 939, 1928; III, 10312, 10314, 10322, 10325, 10327, 10331, 10337, 10338,

10358, 10371, 10377, 10383, 10386, 10387, 10398, 10400, 10402; IV, 550; XII, 1354, 13935, 13937; XIII, 2643, 2692 (*viprarsheḥ*), 2723, 2734, 2746, 2751, 2764, 2765, 2806, 2808, 2858, 2868, 7673 (C.; enumerated among the ṛshis of the North).

Bhārgava[5] = Çaunaka: I, 882, 1117.

Bhārgava[6] = Çiva: VII, 9527; XIV, 200.

Bhārgava[7] = Dadhīca: XII, 13212.

Bhārgava[8] = Devaçarman: XIII, 2268.

Bhārgava[9] = Jamadagni: XII, 1744; XIII, 4607, 4626.

Bhārgava[10] = Mārkaṇḍeya: III, 12617, 12902, 13010; XIII, 1545 (*prakṛshṭāyus*).

Bhārgava[11] = Paraçu-Rāma: I, 275, 2460, 2712, 3175, 4175, 5131, 5132; III, 220 (*prajñā ca te Bhārgavasyeva çuddhā*), 5099, 6009, 8318, 8656, 8658 (*Ṛcīka-nandano Rāmo Reṇukā-sutaḥ*), 8671, 8673, 10128, 10193; V, 1475 (?), 6051, 6085, 7001, 7012, 7022, 7038, 7040, 7065, 7086, 7112, 7119, 7132 (*Akṛtavraṇah . . . sakhā Bhārgavasya*), 7133, 7217, 7223, 7245, 7269, 7303, 7308, 7319, 7326; VI, 557; VII, 2439; VIII, 37, 144, 221? (*cittamoham ivāyuktaṃ Bhārgavasya*), 1294, 1297, 1588, 1592, 1598, 1599, 1605, 1606, 1608, 1613, 3741 (*Rāmāt . . . ṛshisattamāt*), †4710; IX, 2836; XII, 83, 96, 100, 101 (*brahman*), 102, 806, 1566, 1596, 1711, 1769, 1775, 2086? (PCR. Uçanas), 4572? (Uçanas?), 5464 (Rāma, PCR.), 5465 (do.); XIII, 3965, 3972, 4061, 4170; XIV, 828.

Bhārgava[12] = Pramati: I, 952.

Bhārgava[13] = Ṛcīka: III, 10146; XII, 1722, 1723; XIII, 207 (*Ṛ° Cyavanasyātmasambhavaḥ*), 211.

Bhārgava[14] = Uçanas or Çukra: I, 2608, 3221, 3254, 3262, 3338, 3339, 3342, 3344, 3345, 3387, 3390, 3450; III, 7007? (PCR. *°priyakāmyayā*); XII, 2086? (PCR. *çlokaç cāyaṃ purā gīto Bhārgaveṇa mahātmanā | ākhyāne Rāmacarite nṛpatiṃ prati Bhārata*), 4572, 4574 (is consulted by Indra), 4575 (directs Indra to consult Prahlāda), 7662 (PCR. *nītiçāstraṃ jagāda*), 10677 (is swallowed by Mahādeva), 10696; XIII, 1289 (*Taṇḍiḥ provāca Çukrāya, Gautamāya ca Bhārgavaḥ*), 4688, 4741 (*Kāvyaḥ*), †4945 (Çukra knows the highest penance, viz. abstention from food).

Bhārgava[15] = Utaṅka: XIV, 1559, 1576, 1617, 1618, 1644, 1742.

Bhārgava[16] = Vipula: XIII, 2300.

Bhārgava[17], "the potter" (Nīl.): I, 391, 7130, †7131, †7148, 7156, 7157, †7179.

Bhārgava[18] = the planet Venus (cf. Bh° = Uçanas or Çukra): VII, 7546 (*Budha-Bhārgavayor iva*).

Bhārgavaçreshṭha = Paraçu-Rāma: V, 6048.

Bhārgavadāyāda = Uçanas: XII, 10665 (*muniḥ*).

Bhārgavanandana[1] = Jamadagni: III, 10168, 10173.—Do.[2] = Paraçu-Rāma: XII, 108; XIII, 4094.

Bhārgavarshabha = Ṛcīka: XIII, 242.

Bhārgavasattama = Mārkaṇḍeya: III, 13487, 14104.

Bhārgavasattamāḥ (pl.): I, 6805.

Bhārgavāstra (a certain celestial weapon): VIII, 3261 (employed by Karṇa), 3264, 3274, 3756, †4550, †4551.

Bhārgavī = Devayānī: I, 3217, 3419, 3431.

Bhārgavottama = Çaunaka: I, 2195.

Bhartṛ = Vishṇu (1000 names).

Bhartṛshṭhāna (a tīrtha). § 370 (Tīrthay.): III, **84**, 8054.—§ 372 (do.): **85**, 8202.

Bharukaccha (= Bharoch; C., Ma°). § 295 (Dyūtap.): II, **51**, 1830 (*°nivāsinaḥ*, bring tribute to Yudh.).

Bhāruṇḍa (a kind of bird). § 574*g* (Uttarāḥ Kuravaḥ): VI, **7**, 265 (*Bhāruṇḍā nāma çakunās tīkshṇatuṇḍā bhayānakāḥ*).—§ 641 (Rājadh.): XII, **89**, 3357; **93**, 3519.—§ 658 (Kṛtaghnop.): XII, **169**, 6326 (*°āḥ, manushyavadanāḥ*).

Bhāruṇḍasāman (a certain sāman). § 133 (Dushyanta): I, **70**, 2881 (*°gītābhiḥ*, in the hermitage of Kaṇva).

Bhāsa (a mountain). § 782*g* (Guruçishyasaṃv.): XIV, **43**η, 1174.

Bhāshya (commentary). § 270 (Brahmasabhāv.): II, **11**, 453 (*Bhāshyāṇi tarkayuktāṇi dehavanti*, in the palace of Brahman).—§ 289 (Arghāharaṇap.): II, **36**, 1312 (*sarvabhāshyavidāṃ varāḥ*).—§ 709*b* (Sulabhā-Janaka-s.): XII, **321**, 11866 (*sarvabhāshyavidāṃ madhye*).—§ 749 (Ānuçāsan.): XIII, **90**, 4303 (*ye ca bhāshyavidaḥ kecid ye ca vyākaraṇe ratāḥ*, are paṅktipāvanāḥ and should be invited to çrāddhas).

Bhāsī[1]. § 102 (Aṃçāvat.): I, **65**, 2554 (among the eight daughters of Prādhā).—Do.[2] (daughter of Tāmrā, and mother of different birds of prey). § 126 (Tāmrā): I, **66**, 2620, 2621.

***Bhāskara**[1] (= the Sun): I, 5381 (*tīkshṇāṃço Bhāskarasyāṃçaḥ Karṇo 'rigaṇasūdanaḥ*), 5383 (*°syātmasambhavaḥ*, i.e. Karṇa); VI, 2380; VII, 7874 (*Svarbhānu-Bhāskarau*, i.e. Alambusha and Ghaṭotkaca), 7938 (*Svarbhānur iva Bhāskaram*); IX, 261, 535, 1174, 1333, 1640, 1654, 1858, 1919, 2311, 2457, 2846 (*bhagavān*); XI, 811; XII, 148 (*devena*), 4499 (*tejasām īçaṃ*), 11731, 11733; XIII, 4629, 7093 (the eighth of the twelve Ādityas), 7292 (*Soma-°au*).

Bhāskara[2] = Çiva: XIV, 195.

Bhāskaradyuti = Vishṇu (1000 names).

Bhāskari (a muni). § 637 (Rājadh.): XII, **47**η, 1599.

Bhasmabhūta = Çiva: XIII, 1209 (1000 names[2]).

Bhasmāçaya = Çiva: XIII, 1209 (do.).

Bhasmadigdhordhvaliṅga = Kṛshṇa: XII, 1669.

Bhasmagoptṛ = Çiva: XIII, 1209 (1000 names[2]).

Bhasmaguṇṭhita = Çiva: XIII, 695.

Bhāsvara. § 615*u* (Skanda): IX, **45**, 2533 (a companion of Skanda's given to him by Sūrya).

Bhauma[1] = Naraka: III, 477 (*Narakaṃ*), 12590 (= do.); V, †1887 (*Narakaḥ*), †1892 (*Narakaṃ*), 5357 (do.); XII, 12956 (*Narakaṃ*).

Bhauma[2] = the planet Mars. § 775 (Ānuçāsan.): XIII, **166***a*, 7643 (among the deities whose names remove sin).

Bhauma[3] (sc. *astra*, a celestial weapon). § 208*b* (Arjuna): I, **135**, 5366 (employed by Arjuna: *Bhaumena prāviçad bhūmiṃ*).

Bhaumana (= Viçvakarman, Nīl., BR., etc.). § 46 (Garuḍa): I, **32**, 1473 (the keeper of the amṛta).—§ 257 (Arjuna): I, **225**, 8185 (*bhuvanaprabhuḥ*, had fabricated the car which was given to Arjuna by Varuṇa).—§ 561*h* (Arjuna): V, **56**, 2220 (*Tvashṭā, Dhātā*, etc., had decorated the flagstaff of Arjuna), †2223, †2224.

Bhava[1] (an ancient king). § 6 (Anukram.): I, **1**, 226 (belongs to the past).

Bhava[2] = Çiva.

Bhāva[1] = Çiva (1000 names[2]); [2]= Vishṇu (1000 names).

[Bhava-Bhārgava-samāgama(ḥ)] ("the meeting of Çiva and Uçanas"). § 701*b* (Mokshadh.): *Bhīshma* said: *Uçanas* became engaged in doing what was disagreeable to the gods for an adequate cause (v. the note of PCR., p. 524). *Kubera*, the chief of Y. and Rā., is the lord of the treasury of *Indra*. *Uçanas*, by *yoga*, entered *Kubera*, and deprived him of his liberty and robbed him of all his wealth. *Kubera* repaired to *Çiva*, who prepared to slay *Uçanas* with his lance. *Uçanas* placed himself on the point of *Çiva's* lance. *Çiva* bent the lance with his hand (*pāṇinā samanāmayat*), whence it was called *Pināka*, and threw *Uçanas* into his mouth and swallowed him, and *Uçanas* began to wander there. *Mahādeva* entered the waters and remained there like an immovable stake of wood for millions of years. Then he rose from the mighty lake and *Brahmán* approached him. *Çiva* saw that *Uçanas* within his stomach (Nīl.) had become greater in consequence of those penances of his. He once more betook himself to *yoga*-meditation. *Uçanas*, filled with anxiety, began to wander within his stomach, and to sing his praises; but *Rudra* had stopped all his outlets; at last he let him go out through his urethra. Thence he came to be called *Çukra*, and became unable to attain the central point of the firmament. *Umā* prevented *Çiva* from slaying him, and *Uçanas* became her son (XII, **290**).

Bhavabhāvana = Çiva: X, 252.

Bhavadā (a mātṛ). § 615*u* (Skanda): IX, **46**θ, 2631.

Bhavaghna = Çiva: XIII, 908.

Bhāvana[1] = Skanda: III, †14640 (*Bh° sarvasurāsurāṇām*).

Bhāvana[2] = Çiva (1000 names[1-2]); [3] = Vishṇu (1000 names).

Bhāvinī (a mātṛ). § 615*u* (Skanda): IX, **46**θ, 2629.

Bhavishya (a parvan of Harivaṃça). § 10 (Parvas.): I, **2**, 358 (°*ṃ parva*).—§ 11 (do.): I, **2**, 642 (named besides Harivaṃça).—§ 23 (Pramadvarā): I, **9**, 979 (*etad dṛshṭaṃ bhavishye hi Ruror uttamatejasaḥ*).—§ 795*c* (Mahābhārata): XVIII, **6**, 290.

Bhavodbhava = Kṛshṇa: XII, 1509.

Bhaya ("Fear"). § 125 (Adharma): I, **66**, 2619 (son of Adharma and Nirṛti).

Bhayakṛt = Vishṇu: XIII, 7038 (1000 names).

Bhayanāçana = Vishṇu: XIII, 7038 (1000 names).

Bhayaṅkara[1] (a Sauvīra-prince, one of the twelve standard-bearers of Jayadratha). § 522 (Draupadīharaṇap.): III, **265***a*, 15598 (PCR. has *Prabhaṅkara*).—Do.[2], a Viçvadeva. § 749 (Ānuçās.): XIII, **91**γ, 4356.

Bhayaṅkarī (a mātṛ). § 615*u* (Skanda): IX, **46**θ, 2622.

Bhayāpaha = Vishṇu: XIII, 7049 (1000 names).

Bheḍī (a mātṛ). § 615*u* (Skanda): IX, **46**θ, 2631.

Bherīsvanamahāsvanā (a mātṛ). § 615*u* (Skanda): IX, **46**θ, 2644.

Bheshaja(ṃ) = Vishṇu: XIII, 7011 (1000 names).

Bhettṛ = Çiva (1000 names[1]).

Bhikshu = Çiva (1000 names[2]).

Bhikshurūpa = Çiva (1000 names[2]).

Bhīma[1] (an asura). § 702 (Mokshadh.): XII, **295**, 10807 (slain by Çiva).

Bhīma[2] (a companion of Skanda's). § 615*u* (Skanda): IX, **45**δ, 2536 (given to him by Aṃça).

Bhīma[3] (an ancient king). § 673*b* (Bali-Vāsava-s.): XII, **227***a*, 8261.

Bhīma[4] = Vishṇu (1000 names).

Bhīma[5] = Çiva (1000 names[2]).

Bhīma[6] = Bhīmasena (Bhs.) or Bhīma (Bh.) Pāṇḍava. § 4 (Anukram.): I, **1**, 109 (Bhs.), 123 (Bhs.), 129 (Bh.), 134 (Bh.), 153 (Bhs.), 164 (Bh.), 195 (Bh.), 202 (Bh., Bhs.), 211 (Bhs.).—§ 9 (Parvas.): I, **2**, 301 (Bh.; fought mace in hand with Duryodhana for half a day).—§ 11 (do.): **2**, 389 (Bhs.), 411 (Bh.), 425 (Bhs.), 430 (Bh.), 452 (Bhs.), 456 (Bh.), 463 (Bh.), 474 (Bh.), 486 (Bhs.), 534 (Bh.), 554 (Bh.), 556 (Bh.), 558 (Bh.), 574 (Bh.), 575 (Bhs.), 582 (Bhs.).—§ 71 (Ādivaṃç. p.): I, **61**, 2240 (Bh. *Vṛkodaraḥ*) (is poisoned), 2241 (Bh.; is thrown into the Gaṅgā), 2242 (Bhs.), 2255 (Bh.), 2258 (Bhs.), 2267 (Bhs.).—§ 83 (Ādivaṃç.): I, **63**, [2451] (Vṛkodara, i.e. *Bh.*, begat Sutasoma), 2452 (Bh.).—§ 130 (Aṃçāvat.): I, **67**, 2742 (Bhs.), 2746 (*Bhs°n tu Vātasya*, sc. *putram*).—§ 157 (Pūruvaṃç.): I, **95**, ††3814 (*Mārutād Bhīmasenaḥ*).—§ 159 (do.): I, **95** [3827, father of Sutasoma], ††3829 (Bhs. *Kāçyāṃ Balandharāṃ nāmopayeme vīryaçulkāṃ, tasyāṃ putraṃ Sarvagaṃ nāmotpādayām āsa*), ††3833 (*pūrvam eva Hiḍimbāyāṃ rākshasaṃ Ghaṭotkacaṃ putram utpādayām āsa*, Bhs.).—§ 190*c* (Pāṇḍavotpatti): I, **123**, 4772 (Bh.): Vāyu came to Kuntī riding upon a deer; a celestial voice was also heard after the birth of *Bh.*; he fell from the lap of his mother, who had been frightened by a tiger, and broke into 100 fragments the rock on which he fell; he was born on the same day as Duryodhana.—§ 192 (Pāṇḍavotp.): I, **124**, 4854 (Bhs. *tu madhyamaḥ*).—§ 194 (Ṛshisaṃv.): I, **126**, 4920 (*Mātariçvā dadau putram Bhīmaṃ nāma mahābalam*).—§ 197 (Bhīmasenarasapāna): I, **128**, 4979 (Bhs.), 4984 (Bh.), 4988 (Bhs.), 4993 (Bh.), 5008 (Bhs.), 5010 (Bh.), 5014 (Bh.), 5017 (Bh.), 5018 (Bh.), 5022 (Bh.), 5025 (Bh.), 5031 (Bh.), 5033 (Bhs.); **129**, 5034 (Bh.), 5035 (Bhs.), 5038 (Bh.), 5042 (Bhs.), 5043 (Bh.), 5044 (Bh.), 5046 (Bhs.), 5047 (Bh.), 5061 (Bhs.), 5064 (Bhs.), 5066 (Bh.).—§ 205*a* (cf. Droṇa): I, **132**, 5275 (Bhs.), 5288 (*Bhīmādīn*): Duryodhana and Bhīma became very skilled in the use of the mace, and were jealous of each other.—§ 206 (Droṇa): I, **132***f* (Droṇa tests his pupils).—§ 208 (Astradarçana): I, **135**, 5348 (Bh.), 5350 (Bh.) (a combat with maces between Duryodhana and *Bh.*); **137**, 5423 (Bhs.), 5428 (Bhs.).—§ 209 (Drupadaçāsana): I, **138**, 5468 (Bhs.), 5469 (Bhs.), 5470 (Bh.), 5471 (Bhs.), 5500 (Bh.), 5501 (Bhs.).—§ 210*b* (cf. Sambhavaparvan): I, **139**, 5521 (Bh.): Vṛkodara (i.e. *Bh.*) received lessons in arms from Saṅkarshaṇa (i.e. Balarāma), and became like to Dyumatsena himself in strength.—§ 211 (Sambhavap.): I, **139**, 5538 (Bhs.).—§ 213 (Jatugṛhap.): I, **141**, 5654 (Bhs.); **145**, 5741 (Bh.); **146**, 5780 (Bhs.), (5786) (Bhs.); **148**, 5820 (Bhs.), 5828 (Bh.), 5838 (Bhs.); **150**, 5871 (Bh.), 5878 (Bhs.), 5881 (Bhs.); **151**, 5886 (Bh.), 5895 (Bhs.), 5896 (Bh.), 5926 (Bh.).—§ 214 (Hiḍimbavadhap.): I, **152**, 5941 (Bhs.), 5942 (Bhs.), 5946 (Bhs.), 5947 (Bhs.), (5956) (Bhs.), (5959) (Bh.); **153**, 5964 (Bhs.), (5968) (Bh.), 5973 (Bhs.), 5982 (Bh.), 5983 (Bhs.), 5999 (Bhs.), 6000 (Bh.), 6001 (Bh.), 6002 (Bhs.), 6004 (Bhs.); **154**, 6023 (Bh.), 6024 (Bh.), (6026) (Bh.), 6029 (Bh.), 6030 (Bh.), (6032) (Bh.), 6036 (Bhs.), 6037 (Bh.), 6038 (Bhs.), 6039 (Bhs.); **155**, (6042) (Bhs.), 6043 (Bh.), 6046 (Bhs.), 6053 (Bhs.), 6058 (Bhs.), 6059 (Bhs.), 6060 (Bhs.), 6062 (Bhs.), 6071 (Bh.), 6072 (Bhs.); **156**, 6096 (Bhs.).—§ 215 (Bakavadhap.): I, **157**, 6108 (Bh.), 6110 (Bhs.), 6113 (Bh.), (6118) (Bhs.); **162**, 6241 (Bh.), 6243 (Bh.), 6255 (Bh.), 6256 (Bh.), 6259 (Bh.); **163**, 6268 (Bh.), 6270 (Bhs.), 6272 (Bh.), 6275 (Bhs.), 6277 (Bhs.), 6278 (Bhs.), 6281 (Bh.), 6282 (Bh.), 6283 (Bh.), 6284 (Bh.), 6285 (Bh.), 6287 (Bhs.), 6288 (Bhs.), 6289 (Bh.), 6294 (Bh.); **164**, 6297 (Bh.), 6301 (Bh.), 6303 (Bh.).—§ 219 (Caitrarathap.): I, **168**, 6419 (Bhs.).—§ 233 (Svayaṃvarap.): I, **187**, †7014 (Bh.).—§ 234 (do.): I, **189**, †7075 (Bhs.), †7076 (Bh.); **190**, 7088 (Bh.), 7092 (Bhs.), 7111 (Bh.), 7112 (Bhs.), 7113 (Bhs.), 7121 (Bh.), 7124 (Bhs.).—§ 235 (do.): I, **191**, 7138 (Bh.).—§ 236 (do.): I, **192**, 7158 (Bh.), †7161 (Bh.).—§ 237 (Vaivāhikap.): I, **193**, 7194 (Bh.), 7195 (Bh.); **195**, 7226 (Bhs.), 7235 (Bhs.), 7241 (Bhs.).—§ 241 (Vidurāgam.): I, **200**, 7368 (Bh.); **201**, 7405 (Bhs.), 7409 (Bhs.).—§ 243 (do.): I, **205**, 7504 (Bhs.).—§ 244 (Rājyalābhap.): I, **207**, 7547 (Bhs.).—§ 253 (Haraṇāharaṇap.): I, **221**, 8001 (Bh.), 8042 (Bhs.).—§ 262 (Bhagavadyāna):

II, **2**, 38 (Bhs.), 41 (Bhs.).—§ 263 (Sabhākriyāp.): II, **3**, 64 (Bh.), 78 (*gadāñ ca*, Bh.).—§ 272 (Rājasūyārambhap.): II, **13**, 523 (*Bhīmasya paripālanāt*), 556 (Bh.).—§ 274 (do.): II, **15**, 643 (Bhs.), 644 (Bh.), (645) (Bh.); **16**, 661 (*Bhīmārjunāv ubhau netre*).—§ 276 (Jarāsandhavadhap.): II, **20**, 770 (*balaṃ Bhīme*), 772 (Bhs.), 774 (Bhs.), 775 (Bh.), 787 (Bh.), 791 (Bh.).—§ 277 (do.): **21**, 823 (Bh.), 830 (*Pārtha-Bhīmayoḥ*); **23**, 892 (Bhs.), 896 (Bh.), 897 (Bhs.), 898 (Bhs.), 920 (Bh.); **24**, 925 (Bhs.), 928 (Bh.), 929 (Bh.), 932 (Bhs.), 933 (Bhs.), 938 (Bh.), 954 (Bh.), 969 (Bh.), 970 (Bhs.), 971 (Bhs.), 977 (Bhs.).—§ 278 (Digvijayap.): II, **25**, 990 (Bhs.), 992 (Bhs.).—§ 280 (do.): II, **29**, 1059 (Bhs.), 1064 (Bhs.), 1065 (Bh.), 1072 (Bh.), 1073 (Bh.), 1074 (Bh.); **30**, 1081 (Bh.), 1104 (Bh.): *Bh.* vanquished the Pañcālas, etc.; the Daçārṇa king Sudhanvan fought with *Bh.* without weapons, and was therefore appointed commander-in-chief (*adhisenāpati*) by him; the Cedi king Çiçupāla offered his kingdom to *Bh.*, who dwelt with him for thirty nights (II, **29**). *Bh.* vanquished king Çreṇimat of the Kumāra country, etc., and returned to Indraprastha (II, **30**).—§ 286 (Rājasūyikap.): II, **33**, 1221 (Bh.).—§ 290 (Çiçupālavadh.): II, **42**, 1475 (Bhs.), 1478 (Bh.), 1482 (Bhs.), 1487 (Bh.), 1489 (Bhs.), 1491 (Bhs.), 1493 (Bhs.); **44**, 1520 (Bhs.).—§ 292*a* (Rājasūyikaparvan): II, **45**, 1607 (Bhs.): Bhīmasena followed Bhīshma and Dhṛtarāshṭra.—§ 293 (Dyūtap.): II, **46**, 1640 (Bh.).—§ 294 (do.): II, **47**, 1668 (Bhs.), 1669 (Bhs.), 1716 (Bhs.); **50**, 1811 (Bh. *Vṛkodaraṃ*), 1819 (Bhs.).—§ 296 (do.): II, **53**, 1920 (Bhs.).—§ 298 (do.): II, **58**, 2021 (Bhs.); **63**, 2112 (Bhs. pl.); **65**, 2157 (Bhs.), †2163 (Bh.), 2165 (Bhs.).—§ 299 (do.): II, **68**, 2257 (Bhs.), (2260) (Bhs.), 2299 (Bh.), (2300) (Bhs.).—§ 300 (do.): II, **70**, †2363 (Bh.), 2370 (Bhs.), 2371 (Bhs.); **71**, †2383 (Bhs.), †2385 (Bhs.), 2387 (Bhs.), 2388 (Bh.), 2391 (Bh.), 2392 (Bhs.), †2395 (Bhs.), †2399 (Bh.), 2411 (Bhs.); **72**, 2419 (Bhs.), (2425) (Bh.), 2427 (Bhs.); **73**, 2447 (*Bhīmasene parākramaḥ*).—§ 304 (Anudyūtap.): II, **77**, †2528 (Bhs.), (†2533) (Bhs.), †2536 (Bhs.), †2538 (Bh.), 2543 (Bh.), (2544) (Bhs.), 2545 (Bhs.), 2546 (Bh.).—§ 305 (do.): II, **77**, 2553 (Bh.); **78**, 2569 (Bhs.).—§ 306 (do.): II, **80**, 2621 (Bhs.), 2623 (Bh.), 2632 (Bh.), 2633 (Bh.), 2653 (Bh.): Bhīma had gone away looking at his arms, desiring to destroy his enemies.—§ 307 (do.): II, **81**, 2703 (Bhs.), 2705 (Bh.), 2707 (Bh.).—§ 311 (Āraṇyakap.): III, **4**, †228 (Bhs.), †229 (Bh.), †234 (Bhs.).—§ 312 (do.): III, **5**, †246 (Bhs.), †248 (Bhs.).—§ 313 (do.): III, **6**, 275 (Bh.).—§ 315 (Maitreyaçāpa): III, **10**, 369 (Bh.), 370 (Bh.), 379 (Bh.), 382 (Bh.).—§ 316 (Kirmīravadh.): III, **11**, 385 (Bhs.), 386 (Bh.), 411 (Bhs.), 413 (Bhs.), 420 (Bhs.), 423 (Bh.), 425 (Bh.), 427 (Bh.), 430 (Bh.), 436 (Bh.), 442 (Bhs.), 445 (Bh.), †453 (Bh.), †454 (Bh.), 457 (Bh.), 458 (Bh.), 459 (Bh.).—§ 317 (Arjunābhigam.): III, **12**, 527 (Bhs.), 537 (Bh.), 538 (Bhs.), 540 (Bhs.), 541 (Bh.), 543 (Bhs.), 544 (Bhs.), 549 (Bh.), 555 (Bhs.), 556 (Bh.), 557 (Bh.), 560 (Bh.), 564 (Bhs.), 565 (Bhs.), 566 (Bhs.), 567 (Bhs.), 568 (Bhs.), 569 (Bh.), 574 (Bh.), 595 (*Duryodhanaṃ Bhīmasenaḥ . . . hantā*).—§ 321 (Saubhavadhop.): III, **22**, 893 (Bh.).—§ 322 (Dvaitavanapr.): III, **23**, †903 (Bhs.); **24**, †943 (Bh.).—§ 323 (do.): III, **25**, †950 (Bhs.).—§ 325 (Draupadīparitāpavākya): III, **27**, 1008 (Bhs.), 1009 (Bhs.).—§ 327 (do.): III, **30**, 1123 (Bhs.); **34**, †1354 (Bhs.), †1357 (Bhs.), †1359 (Bhs.), †1360 (Bhs.), †1369 (Bh.), †1371 (Bhs.); **35**, (1376) (Bh.).—§ 328 (Kāmyakavanaprav.): III, **36**, 1411 (Bhs.), 1414 (Bhs.), 1431 (Bhs.).—§ 340 (Indralokābhigam.): III, **49**, 1941 (Bh.), 1954 (Bh.).—§ 341 (do.): III, **50**, †1965 (*dakshiṇāṃ Bhīmasenaḥ*).—§ 342 (do.): III, **51**, 1973 (Bh.), 1978 (Bh.), 1979 (Bh.), 1993 (Bh.), 2009 (Bh.).—§ 343 (Nalop.): III, **52**, 2017 (Bh.), 2048 (Bh.), 2052 (Bh.).—§ 356 (Tīrthay.): III, **80**, 4006 (Bhs.), 4016 (*Bhīmād avarajaṃ*, i.e. Arjuna).—§ 378 (do.): III, **93**, 8473 (Bhs.), 8477 (Bh.).—§ 402 (do.): III, **120**, †10282 (Bh.).—§ 406 (do.): III, **125**, 10417 (Bhs.).—§ 418 (do.): III, **139**, 10832 (*Bhīmasenabalena*), †10838 (Bh.).—§ 419 (Gandhamādanapr.): III, **140**, (10847) (Bh.), 10857 (Bh.), 10862 (Bhs.).—§ 420 (do.): III, **141**, 10871 (Bhs.), 10890 (Bh.), 10896 (Bh.).—§ 423 (do.): III, **143**, 10976 (Bhs.); **144**, 10993 (Bh.), 11006 (Bhs.), (11008) (Bhs.), 11012 (Bhs., father of Ghaṭotkaca), 11013 (Bhs.); **145**, 11014 (Bh.), 11016 (Bhs.).—§ 424 (Bhīmakadalīkhaṇḍapr.): III, **146**, 11072 (Bhs.), 11073 (Bh.), 11076 (Bhs.), 11077 (Bh.), 11104 (Bh.), 11108 (Bh.), 11114 (Bhs.), 11117 (Bhs.), 11118 (Bhs.), 11122 (Bh.), 11124 (Bhs.), 11130 (Bh., blows his conch), 11131 (*Bhīmasenaraveṇa*), 11134 (Bhs.), 11135 (Bh.), 11136 (Bh.), 11143 (Bhs.), 11153 (Bh.), 11154 (Bh.); **147**, (11167) (Bhs.), 11169 (*Pāṇḍavo Vāyutanayaḥ*, Bhs.), (11172) (Bhs.), (11174) (Bh.), (11177) (Bhs.), 11183 (Bh.), 11185 (Bh.), 11186 (Bh.), 11187 (Bh.).—§ 425 (Hanūmat-Bhīma-s.): III, **148**, 11218 (Bh.).—§ 426 (do.): III, **149**, 11224 (Bhs.), (11233) (Bhs.).—§ 430 (do.): III, **150**, (11265) (Bhs.), 11266 (Bh.), 11271 (Bh.), 11274 (Bh.), 11275 (Bh.), 11281 (Bh.).—§ 431 (Saugandhikāharaṇap.): III, **151**, 11318 (Bhs.), 11319 (Bh.), 11321 (Bh.), 11325 (Bh.), 11329 (Bhs.), 11332 (Bhs.), 11336 (Bh.).—§ 432 (do.): **152**, 11337 (Bh.), 11343 (Bhs.), 11346 (Bh.); **153**, 11362 (Bh.); **154**, (11367) (Bhs.), 11379 (Bhs.), †11383 (Bhs.), †11385 (Bh.), †11387 (Bh.), †11389 (Bh.), †11392 (Bh.), †11393 (Bh.), †11394 (Bh.).—§ 433 (do.): III, **155**, 11398 (Bh.), 11403 (Bhs.), 11404 (Bh.), 11408 (Bhs.), 11412 (Bh.), 11418 (Bh.), 11420 (Bh.).—§ 434 (do.): III, **156**, 11441 (Bh.), 11450 (Bhs.).—§ 435 (Jaṭāsurav.): III, **157**, 11452 (Bhs.), 11457 (Bhs.), 11461 (Bhs.), 11486 (Bhs.), 11490 (Bh.), 11497 (Bh.), 11500 (Bh.), 11501 (Bh.), 11507 (Bh.), 11517 (Bh.), 11518 (Bhs.), 11519 (Bh.), 11521 (Bhs.).—§ 436 (Yakshayuddhap.): III, **158**, 11600 (Bh.), 11606 (Bh.), 11609 (Bh.), 11621 (Bh.); **159**, 11629 (Bh.).—§ 437 (do.): **160**, 11664 (Bhs.), 11679 (Bhs.), 11685 (Bhs.) 11686 (Bh.), 11706 (Bhs.), 11710 (Bhs.), 11713 (Bhs.), 11717 (Bhs.), 11718 (Bh.), 11724 (Bhs.), 11725 (Bhs.), 11726 (Bhs.), 11729 (Bh.), 11732 (Bh.), 11733 (Bhs.), 11737 (Bhs.).—§ 438 (do.): III, **161**, 11740 (Bhs.), 11742 (Bhs.), 11743 (Bhs.), 11748 (Bh.), 11749 (Bhs.), 11753 (Bhs.), 11754 (Bhs.), 11761 (Bh.), 11778 (Bhs.), 11779 (Bhs.), 11781 (Bh.), 11782 (Bhs.), 11784 (Bhs.), 11785 (Bhs.), 11802 (Bh.); **162**, 11812 (Bhs.).—§ 450 (Ājagarap.): III, **178**, 12363 (Bh.), 12374 (Bh.), 12375 (Bh.), 12379 (Bh.), 12380 (Bhs.), 12381 (Bhs.), 12383 (Bhs.), 12384 (Bh.), 12385 (Bhs.), 12390 (Bh.), 12391 (Bhs.), 12392 (Bhs.), 12393 (Bh.); **179**, 12396 (Bhs.), 12398 (Bhs.), 12403 (Bh.), 12420 (Bhs.), 12441 (Bh.), 12444 (Bhs.); **180**, (12453) (Bhs.); **181**, 12532 (Bhs.), 12537 (Bh.), 12538 (Bh.).—§ 452 (Mārkaṇḍeyas.): III, **183**, 12564 (Bh.), †12578 (Bh.).—§ 512 (Ghoshayātr.): III, **236**, †14753 (Bh.), †14758 (Bh.); **238**, 14803 (Bh.), 14806 (Bhs.); **239**, 14828 (Bhs.); **242**, 14926 (Bhs.), 14934 (Bhs.); **243**, 14950 (Bh.), 14952 (Bh.); **244**, 14957 (Bhs.); **245**, 14986 (Bh.), 15008 (Bh.); **248**, 15063 (Bh.).—§ 516 (Duryodhanayajña): III, **256**, 15312 (Bh.).—

§ 519 (Vrīhidrauṇikap.): III, **259**, 15375 (Bh.).—§ 521 (Draupadīhar.): III, **263**, 15546 (Bhs.; B. *Sahadevam*), 15547 (Bhs.; B. *Sahadevaḥ*), 15557 (Bhs.; B. *Sahadevaḥ*).—§ 522 (do.): III, **266**, †15607 (Bhs.), †15608 (Bhs.); **268**, †15644 (Bhs.), †15658 (Bh.); **269**, †15673 (Bh.), †15691 (Bh.); **270**, 15695 (Bhs.), †15704 (Bh.); **271**, 15717 (Bh.), 15719 (Bh.), 15721 (Bh.), 15722 (Bh.), 15738 (Bhs.), 15739 (Bh.), 15741 (Bh.), 15751 (Bh.), 15754 (Bhs.), 15759 (Bh.), 15767 (Bhs.), 15770 (Bh.), 15775 (Bh.).—§ 523 (Jayadrathavim.): III, **272**, 15778 (Bhs.), 15779 (Bh.), 15781 (Bh.), 15782 (Bhs.), (15783) (Bh.), 15788 (Bh.), 15790 (Bh.), 15791 (Bh.), 15792 (Bh.).—§ 544 (Yudhishṭhirāçvāsa): III, **292**, 16607 (Bh.).—§ 547 (Kuṇḍalāhar.): III, **310**, 17205 (Bhs.).—§ 548 (Āraṇeyap.): III, **312**, (17243) (Bh.), 17274 (Bhs.), 17276 (Bhs.), 17277 (Bh.), 17281 (Bh.); **313**, 17289 (Bhs.), 17299 (Bhs.), 17409 (Bhs.), 17410 (Bh.), 17411 (Bhs.); **315**, 17470 (Bhs.), 17474 (Bhs.).—§ 549 (Pāṇḍavaprav.): IV, **2**, (28) (Bhs.); **5**, 162 (Bhs.), 164 (Bhs.); **8**, (†239) (Bh.), †243 (Bh.).—§ 550 (Samayapālanap.): IV, **13**, 331 (Bhs.), 344 (Bh.), 359 (Bh.).—§ 551 (Kīcakavadhap.): IV, **16**, 464 (Bhs.), 465 (Bh.), 468 (Bh.), 469 (Bhs.); **17**, 506 (Bh.), †508 (Bhs.), 510 (Bh.), 511 (Bh.), 515 (Bhs.), 516 (Bhs.); **18**, 556 (Bh.); **19**, 569 (Bh.), 576 (Bh.), 580 (C. *Bhīmā*), 581 (Bhs.), 589 (Bhs.); **20**, 609 (Bhs.), 619 (Bh.), 636 (Bhs.), 637 (Bhs.); **21**, 659 (Bh.), 660 (Bhs.), 661 (Bh.), 663 (Bh.), 685 (Bhs.), 689 (Bhs.), 690 (Bh.), 693 (Bh.); **22**, 717 (Bh.), (724) (Bhs.), (731) (Bhs.), 734 (Bh.), 737 (Bh.), (744) (Bhs.), 746 (Bh.), 754 (Bh.), 758 (Bh.), 761 (Bh.), 762 (Bh.), 763 (Bh.), 766 (Bh.), 767 (Bh.), 770 (Bh.), 780 (Bhs.), 782 (Bh.); **23**, 795 (Bhs.), 807 (Bh.), 810 (Bhs.), 812 (Bh.), 820 (Bhs.), 821 (Bh.); **24**, 839 (Bhs.), 842 (Bhs.), (844) (Bh.).—§ 552 (Goharaṇap.): IV, **31**, 1024 (Bh.); **33**, 1077 (Bhs.), 1079 (Bhs.), 1080 (Bhs.), 1084 (Bh.), 1085 (Bh.), 1086 (Bh.), 1088 (Bhs.), 1089 (Bh.), 1092 (Bhs.), 1093 (Bhs.), 1099 (Bh.), 1109 (Bh.), 1111 (Bh.), 1112 (Bh.), 1113 (Bhs.), 1115 (Bh.), 1119 (Bh.), 1123 (Bh.), 1124 (Bh.); **40**, 1307 (Bh.), 1311 (Bh.); **43**, 1351 (Bhs.), 1357 (Bh.), 1363 (Bhs.); **44**, 1368 (Bhs.), 1371 (Bhs.); **50**, 1565 (Bh.).—§ 553 (Vaivāhikap.): IV, **71**, 2289 (Bh.), 2291 (Bh.), 2297 (*Bhīmād avarajaḥ . . . Arjunaḥ*), 2313 (Bhs.), 2319 (Bh.).—§ 554 (Sainyodyog.): V, **1**, †5 (Bh.); **3**, 56 (Bh.).—§ 555 (do.): V, **8**, 199 (Bh.); **18**, 561 (Bh.). § 556 (Sañjayayānap.): V, **20**, 619 (Bhs.); **22**, †658 (Bh.), †678 (Bh.); **23**, †688 (Bh.), 707 (Bhs.), 710 (Bhs.), 711 (Bhs.); **24**, †717 (Bhs.); **26**, †762 (Bhs.), †763 (Bhs.); **29**, †827 (Bhs.), †858 (Bh.), †859 (Bhs.), †861 (Bhs., *gadāhastaḥ*); **30**, †868 (Bhs.).—§ 561 (Yānasandhip.): V, **48**, †1816 (Bhs.), †1824 (Bhs.), †1825 (Bhs.), †1826 (Bhs.), †1831 (Bhs.); **49**, †1959 (Bh.); **50**, 1986 (Bhs.); **51**, 2018 (Bh.), 2019 (Bhs.), 2026 (Bh.), 2029 (Bh.), 2030 (Bh.), 2031 (Bh.), 2032 (Bhs.), 2037 (Bhs.), 2040 (Bh.), 2043 (*Bhīmasenamayam*), 2053 (Bhs.); **53**, 2111 (Bhs.); **54**, 2135 (Bh.); **55**, 2176 (Bh.), 2178 (Bh.), 2203 (Bhs.); **56**, 2215 (Bhs.).—§ 561*h* (Arjuna): V, **56**, 2222 (Bhs.).—§ 561*j* (Yanas.): to Bhīmasena's chariot are yoked coursers endued with the speed of the wind and the splendour of the stars (*ṛkshaprakhyāḥ*): V, **56**, †2228 (Bhs.).—§ 561 (do.): V, **57**, 2245 (Bhs.), 2257 (Bh.); **58**, 2317 (Bhs.), 2318 (Bh.), 2319 (Bh.), 2320 (Bhs.), 2321 (Bhs.), 2322 (Bhs.); **62**, †2425 (Bhs.); **65**, 2485 (Bhs.); **69**, 2548 (Bhs.); **74**, (2717) (Bhs.).—§ 562 (Bhagavadyānap.): V, **75**, 2740 (Bh.), 2742 (Bh.), 2743 (Bhs.), 2745 (Bh.), 2747 (Bh.), 2750 (Bh.), 2754 (Bh.), 2760 (Bhs.); **76**, 2766 (Bhs.); **77**, 2785 (Bh.), 2794 (Bhs.), 2799 (Bhs.); **80**, 2845 (Bhs.), 2855 (Bhs.); **81**, 2865 (Bh.); **82**, 2873 (Bhs.), 2901 (Bhs.), 2907 (Bh.), 2911 (Bh.), 2916 (Bh.); **83**, 2949 (Bhs.); **90**, 3150 (Bh.), 3154 (Bh.), 3154 (Bhs.), 3177 (Bhs.), 3210 (Bh.), 3212 (Bhs.), 3213 (Bh.), 3219 (Bh.); **95**, 3403 (Bhs.).—§ 564 (Mātalīyopākhy.): V, **105**, 3707 (Bh.).—§ 567 (Bhagavadyānap.): V, **124**, 4169 (Bhs.); **126**, 4217 (Bhs.), 4218 (Bhs.); **129**μ, 4358 (Bhs.); **131**, 4426 (Bh.).—§ 569 (do.): V, **137**, 4646 (Bhs.), 4654 (Bh.), 4665 (Bh.); **138**, 4680 (Bh.), 4689 (*Bhīmapūrvajaḥ Yudhishṭhiraḥ*), 4690 (Bh.), 4702 (Bh.), 4745 (Bhs.); **141**, 4778 (Bh.), 4781 (Bhs.), 4788 (Bh.), 4804 (Bhs.); **142**, 4822 (Bhs.); **144**, 4887 (Bh.); **146**, 4949 (Bh.).—§ 570 (Sainyaniryānap.): V, **151**, 5101 (Bhs.), (5126) (Bhs.), 5143 (Bhs.); ν, 5152 (Bhs.), 5153 (Bhs.); **153**, 5197 (Bhs.), 5198 (Bhs.); **154**, 5232 (Bh.), 5234 (Bhs.); **157**, 5318 (Bhs.), 5347 (Bhs.).—§ 571 (Ulūkadūt.): V, **160**, 5471 (*Bhīmasenakam*), 5519 (Bhs.), 5522 (Bhs.); **161**, 5544 (Bhs.), 5563 (Bhs.), 5564 (Bhs., *sagadād*), 5568 (Bhs.); **162**, 5581 (Bhs.), 5592 (Bhs.), 5608 (Bhs.), 5614 (Bh.), 5615 (Bhs.), 5617 (Bh.), 5641 (Bhs.), 5642 (Bhs.); **163**, 5657 (Bhs.), 5664 (Bhs.), 5672 (Bhs.), 5696 (Bh.); **164**, 5704 (Bhs.), 5706 (Bh.).—§ 572 (Rathātirathas.): V, **166**, 5759 (Bhīmasenānuja, i.e. Arjuna); **169**, 5853 (Bhs.); **171**, 5913 (Bhs.); **172**, 5922 (Bhs.).—§ 573 (Ambopākhy.): V, **193**, 7560 (Bh.); **194**, 7598 (Bhs.); **196**, 7630 (Bh.), 7637 (Bhs.).—§ 576 (Bhagavadgītāp.): VI, **19**, 702 (Bh.), 705 (Bh.), 709 (Bhs.), 711 (Bh.), 715 (Bhs.), 717 (Bhs.), 724 (Bhs.), 727 (Bhs.), 740 (Bhs.); **20**, 741 (*Bhīmanetrāḥ*); **22**, 779 (Bhs.), 788 (Bhs.); **25**θ, 833 (Bh.), 839 (Bh.).—§ 577 (Bhīshmavadhap.): VI, **43** (1544) (Bhs.), 1560 (Bh.).—§ 578 (do.): VI, **44**, 1640 (Bhs.), 1645 (Bhs.), 1647 (Bhs.), 1660 (Bh.); **45**^{4}, 1688 (Bhs.); **47**, 1833 (Bh.), 1837 (Bh.), 1839 (Bhs.), 1840 (Bhs.), 1865 (Bhs.).—§ 578*d* (do.): VI, **47**: *Bh.'s* standard was made of gold and showed the device of a lion.—§ 578 (do.): VI, **48**$^{36}\chi$, 1962 (Bhs.), 1968 (Bhs.), 1969 (Bhs.); **49**, 1994 (Bh.); **50**, 2049 (Bh.), 2067 (Bh.); π, 2082 (Bhs.; *Bh.* and Dhṛshṭadyumna were the wings of the Krauñcāruṇa vyūha); **51**, 2096 (Bh.); **52**^{1} *a*, 2128 (Bhs.).—§ 579 (do.): VI, **53**$^{5\,f.}$, 2228 (Bhīma attacks Droṇa), 2231 (Bh.), 2234 (Bh.); **54**$^{9\,f.}$, 2237 (Bh.), 2239 (Bhs.), 2240 (Bh.), 2243 (Bhs.), 2250 (Bhs.), 2251 (Bhs.), 2253 (Bh.), 2255 (Bhs.), 2256 (Bh.), 2257 (Bhs.), 2260 (Bh.), 2263 (Bhs.), 2264 (Bhs.), 2265 (Bhs.), 2267 (Bh.); **54**, 2268 (Bh.), 2269 (Bh.), 2271 (Bh.), 2278 (Bh.), 2283 (Bhs.), 2300 (Bhs.), 2301 (Bhs.), 2302 (Bhs.), 2303 (Bhs.), 2304 (Bh.), 2305 (Bh.), 2307 (Bh.), 2311 (Bhs.), 2314 (Bh.), 2316 (Bh.), 2318 (Bh.), 2320 (Bhs.), 2322 (Bhs.), 2323 (Bh.), 2327 (Bhs.), 2328 (Bh.), 2329 (Bhs.), 2331 (Bhs.), 2332 (Bhs.), 2336 (Bh.), 2337 (Bhs.), 2338 (Bhs.), 2339 (Bh.), 2340 (Bhs.), 2343 (Bh.), 2344 (Bhs.), 2346 (Bhs.), 2348 (Bh.), 2350 (Bhs.), 2355 (Bhs.), 2358 (Bh.).—§ 580 (do.): VI, **56**^{2}, 2413 (Bhīmasena on the right horn of Arjuna's and Dhṛshṭadyumna's array after the form of a half-moon); **57**, 2433 (Bh.); χ, 2454 (Bhs.); **58**$^{10\,f.}$, 2475 (Bhs. vanquishes Duryodhana), 2477 (Bhs.), 2480 (Bh.); **59**, †2595 (Bh.).—§ 581 (do.): VI, **62**η, 2733 (Bh.); do.^{6}, 2747 (Bhs. attacks Dury.), 2748 (Bhs.), 2750 (Bhs.), 2753 (Bhs.), 2754 (Bh.), 2756 (Bh.), 2764 (Bhs.), 2765 (Bhs.), 2769 (Bh.), 2770 (Bhs.), 2773 (Bhs.), 2774 (Bhs.), 2777 (Bh.), 2779 (Bh.); **63**^{7}, 2780 (Bhs.), 2781 (Bhs.), 2784 (Bhs.), 2785 (Bhs.), 2786 (Bhs.), 2787 (Bh.), 2789 (Bhs.), 2791 (Bh.), 2795 (Bhs.), 2798 (Bhs.), 2805 (Bhs.); **64**^{12}, 2817 (Bhs.), 2818

(Bhs.), 2819 (Bhs.), 2820 (Bh.), 2825 (Bh.), 2826 (Bh.), 2827 (Bh.), 2831 (Bhs.), 2833 (Bh.), 2835 (Bhs.), 2837 (Bh.), 2839 (Bhs.), 2840 (Bhs.), 2845 (Bhs.), 2846 (Bh.), 2847 (Bhs.), 2848 (Bh.), 2849 (Bh.), 2851 (Bhs.), 2852 (Bh.), 2853 (Bhs.), 2854 (Bhs.), 2860 (Bhs.), 2862 (Bhs.), 2863 (Bh.), 2892 (Bhs.); **65,** 2907 (Bh.).—§ 582 (do.); **69*a*,** 3063 (Bhs. in the beak of the Çyena array), 3068[1] (Bh. attacks Bhīshma), 3079 (Bhs.), 3080 (Bhs.); **70,** 3090 (Bhs.), 3110 (Bh.); **71**δ, 3138 (Bhs. fights with Bhīshma, etc.); **72,** 3165 (Bhs.), 3182 (Bhs.), 3183 (Bh.), 3186 (Bhs.); **73,** 3213 (Bhs.), 3217 (Bhs.), 3218 (Bh.); **74,** 3267 (Bhs.).—§ 583 (do.): VI, **75,** 3283 (Bhs.); η, 3303 (Bhs.), 3305 (Bhs.), 3306 (Bh.), 3307 (Bh.), 3310 (Bh.); **77**[3] κ, 3342 (Bhs.), 3351 (Bhs.), 3353 (Bhs.), 3354 (Bhs.), 3356 (Bh.), 3363 (Bhs.), 3364 (Bh.), 3366 (Bh.), 3368 (Bhs.), 3369 (Bh.), 3371 (Bhs.), 3373 (Bhs.), 3374 (Bhs.), †3375 (Bhs.), †3376 (Bhs.), 3388 (Bh.), 3390 (Bh.), 3391 (Bh.), 3396 (Bhs.), 3408 (Bhs.); **78**[10 f.], 3413 (Bh.), 3414 (Bh.), 3417 (Bhs.), 3422 (Bhs.), 3426 (Bhs.), 3428 (Bh.), 3430 (Bhs.); **79,** 3450 (Bh.), 3451 (Bhs.), 3465 (Bh.), 3468 (Bhs.), 3469 (Bh.); **80,** †3516 (Bh.).—§ 584 (do.): VI, **81,** 3558 (Bhs.), 3563 (Bh.); **82,** 3632 (Bh.), 3634 (Bh.), 3638 (Bhs.); **84,** 3737 (Bh.); **85,** †3764 (Bhs.), †3767 (Bhs.), †3782 (Bhs.), †3785 (Bhs.); **86,** 3836 (Bhs.).—§ 585 (do.): VI, **87,** 3864 (Bhs.); **88,** 3894 (Bhs.), 3895 (Bh.), 3898 (Bh.), 3903 (Bh.), 3905 (Bhs.), 3906 (Bh.), 3908 (Bh. slays Aparājita), 3915 (Bh.), 3917 (Bh.), 3923 (Bhs.), 3928 (Bh.); **89,** 3938 (Bhs.), 3950 (Bhs.), 3956 (Bhs.), 3959 (Bh.); **91,** 4019 (Bhs.), 4057 (Bhs.); **93,** 4145 (Bhs.), 4156 (Bhs.); **94,** 4182 (Bhs.), 4184 (Bhs.), 4186 (Bhs.), 4187 (Bhs.), 4192 (Bhs.), 4197 (Bh.), 4197 (Bhs.), 4201 (Bhs.), 4202 (Bhs.), 4205 (Bhs.), 4207 (Bh.), 4207 (Bhs.), 4210 (Bh.); **95,** 4237 (Bhs.), 4243 (Bhs.); δδ, 4254 (Bhs.), 4263 (Bhs.), 4266 (Bh.), 4267 (Bhs.), 4268 (Bhs.), 4269 (Bhs.), 4270 (Bhs.), 4282 (Bh.), 4304 (Bhs.).—§ 585*b* (Bhīshmav.): VI, **95,** 4307 (Bhīma's standard showed the device of a lion).—§ 585 (do.): VI, **95,** 4310 (Bhs.), 4313 (Bh.), 4316 (Bhs.), 4322 (Bhs.); **96,** 4338 (Bhs.), 4342 (Bhs.), 4345 (Bh.), 4348 (Bhs.), 4351 (Bhs.), 4354 (Bh.).—§ 586 (do.): VI, **99,** 4508 (Bhs.), 4515 (Bhs.); **101,** 4586 (Bh.), 4589 (Bhs.); **102,** 4668 (Bh.), 4671 (Bh.), 4673 (Bhs.), 4675 (Bhs.); **103**γ, 4694 (Bh.); **104,** 4746 (Bhs.), 4753 (Bhs.); **105,** 4799 (Bh.); **106**δ, 4803 (Bh.), 4805 (Bhs.), 4806 (Bhs.); **107**χ, 4912 (Bhs.), 4945 (Bh.).—§ 587 (do.): VI, **108,** 4998 (Bhs.), 5012 (Bh.); **109,** 5073 (Bh.); **110**ζ, 5103 (Bhs.), 5184 (Bh.); **111,** 5183 (Bhs.), 5187 (Bh.); **112**ζ, 5228 (Bhs.); **113,** 5241 (Bhs.), 5242 (Bhs.), 5250 (Bh.), 5251 (Bh.), 5252 (Bhs.), 5255 (Bhs.), 5259 (Bhs.), 5260 (Bh.), 5262 (Bh.), 5264 (Bhs.), 5267 (Bhs.), 5272 (Bh.), 5275 (Bh.), 5279 (Bhs.), 5281 (Bhs.), 5282 (Bh.), 5284 (Bh.), 5286 (Bh.), 5287 (Bhs.), 5289 (Bh.); **114,** 5295 (Bh.), 5298 (Bhs.), 5300 (Bhs.), 5308 (Bh.), 5310 (Bh.), 5316 (Bhs.), 5318 (Bhs.), 5319 (Bh.), 5320 (Bh.), 5322 (Bhs.), 5323 (Bh.), 5325 (Bhs.); **115,** 5353 (Bhs.), 5363 (Bhs.); **116,** 5412 (Bhs.); **118,** 5553 (Bhs.); **119**χ, 5577 (Bh.); ω, 5587 (Bhs.), 5684 (Bhs.); **120,** 5708 (Bhs.).—§ 588 (do.): VI, **121,** †5798 (Bh.), 5809 (Bhs.).—§ 589 (Droṇābhishekap.): VII, **2*a*,** †82 (Bhs.); **8,** 227 (Bhs.), †248 (Bhs.); θ, †251 (Bh.); **10,** 319 (Bhs.).—§ 590 (do.): VII, **14,** 521 (Bhs.), 522 (Bh.), 524 (Bhs.); *a*, 577 (Bh.); **15,** 586 (Bh.), 587 (Bh.), 589 (Bh.), 592 (Bhs.), 594 (*paṭṭair jāmbūnadair baddhā babhūva . . . viddhā Bhīmena mahatī*, sc. *gadā*), 598 (Bhs.), 599 (Bhs.), 601 (Bhs.), 606 (Bh.), 607 (*Bhīma-gadā-*), 614 (Bh.); **16**β, 633 (Bh.).—§ 592 (Saṃçaptakav.): VII, **22,** 935 (Bh.), 943 (Bh.); **23,** 950 (Bh.), 1027 (Bhs.), 1030 (Bhs.); β, 1038 (Bhs.); **25,** 1070 (Bh.), 1071 (Bh.); **26,** 1131 (Bh.), 1134 (Bhs.), 1136 (Bh.), 1137 (Bh.), 1139 (Bh.), 1140 (Bhs.), 1142 (Bh.), 1143 (Bhs.), 1147 (Bh.), 1149 (Bh.), 1152 (Bh.), 1153 (Bh.), 1154 (Bhs.), 1155 (Bh.), 1156 (Bh.), 1174 (Bh.), 1176 (Bh.), 1177 (Bh.); **32**χ, 1376 (Bhs.), 1379 (Bhs.); 1381 (*Bhīmaprabhṛtayaḥ*); ββ, 1427 (Bh.), 1435 (Bh.); ζζ, 1443 (Bh.).—§ 593 (Abhimanyuvadhap.): VII, **34,** 1485 (Bhs.), 1490 (Bhs.); **35,** 1507 (Bhs.); ζ, (1528) (Bh.); **39**ν, 1657 (Bhs.); **40,** 1680 (Bh.), 1685 (Bh.); **42**π, 1743 (Bhs.), 1752 (Bhs.); **43,** 1774 (Bh.), 1775 (Bh.).—§ 596 (Pratijñāp.): VII, **78**ε, 2743 (Bhs.).—§ 597 (do.): VII, **83*a*,** 2949 (Bhs.).—§ 599 (Jayadrathavadhap.): VII, **95**ζ, 3525 (Bhs.); **96**ο, 3572 (Bhs.); **97,** 3574 (Bhs.); **98**κ, 3660 (Bhs.); **106,** 3980 (Bhs.); **108,** 4065 (Bhs.), 4067 (Bh.), 4068 (Bh.), 4069 (Bh.), 4070 (Bh.), 4074 (*Bhīma-cāpa-*), 4075 (Bhs.), 4078 (Bh.), 4079 (Bh.), 4093 (Bhs.), 4094 (Bhs.); **109,** 4107 (*Bhīmasenādayaḥ*), 4113 (Bhs.); **110,** 4151 (Bhs.), 4197 (Bh.), 4204 (Bhs.); **111,** 4281 (Bh.); **112,** 4358 (Bhs.), 4360 (Bh.), 4361 (Bh.), 4362 (Bh.), 4364 (Bh.), 4365 (Bhs.), 4367 (Bh.), 4368 (Bh.); **113,** 4431 (Bh.), 4436 (Bhs.); **114,** 4500 (Bh.), 4505 (Bh.), 4508 (Bhs.), 4511 (Bh.), 4510 (Bhs.), 4514 (Bh.), 4516 (Bh.), 4517 (Bhs.), 4518 (Bhs.); **122**οο, 4877 (Bhs.), 4883 (Bh.); **123,** 4969 (Bhs.); **124**κκ, 4983 (Bhs.), 4987 (Bhs.), 5000 (Bhs.), 5001 (Bhs.); **125,** 5074 (Bhs.); **126,** 5114 (Bh.), 5115 (Bh.), 5118 (Bhs.), 5120 (Bh.), 5122 (Bh.), 5123 (Bh.), 5123 (Bhs.), 5124 (Bh.), 5126 (Bhs.), 5134 (Bh.); **127,** (5144) (Bh.), 5147 (Bhs.), 5159 (Bhs.), 5162 (Bhs.), 5164 (Bh.), 5167 (Bh.), 5170 (Bh.), 5179 (Bhs.), 5182 (Bh.), 5188 (Bhs.), 5190 (Bh.), 5193 (Bh.), 5193 (Bhs.), 5196 (Bh.), 5199 (Bhs.), 5201 (Bh.), 5203 (Bh.), 5206 (Bh.), 5207 (Bh.), 5213 (Bhs.), 5215 (Bh.), 5215 (Bhs.), 5216 (Bhs.), 5217 (Bh.); **128,** 5222 (Bh.), 5227 (Bh.), 5230 (Bh.), 5230 (Bhs.), 5232 (Bh.), 5235 (Bh.), 5236 (Bh.), 5238 (Bhs.), 5241 (Bhs.), 5244 (Bhs.), 5248 (Bhs.), 5250 (*Bhīmasena-ravam*), 5252 (Bhs.), 5254 (Bh.), 5268 (Bhs.); **129,** 5272 (Bhs.), 5273 (Bhs.), 5276 (Bh.), 5277 (Bhs.), 5278 (Bh.), 5279 (Bh.), 5280 (Bh.), 5281 (Bhs.), 5283 (Bh.), 5285 (Bh.), 5286 (Bhs.), 5290 (Bh.), 5291 (Bh.), 5292 (Bhs.), 5293 (Bh.), 5297 (Bh.), 5301 (Bh.), 5305 (Bhs.), 5306 (Bhs.), 5308 (Bh.); **130,** 5311 (Bhs.), 5314 (Bhs.), 5316 (Bh.), 5318 (Bhs.); **131,** 5356 (Bh.); ρρ, 5357 (Bh.), 5358 (Bhs.), 5359 (Bh.), 5361 (Bh.), 5362 (Bh.), 5364 (Bh.), 5365 (Bh.), 5367 (Bhs.), 5368 (Bh.), 5369 (Bh.), 5370 (Bh.), 5371 (Bh.), 5373 (Bhs.), 5375 (Bh.), 5376 (Bh.), 5378 (Bhs.), 5380 (Bhs.), 5384 (Bhs.), 5386 (Bhs.), 5389 (Bhs.), 5393 (Bh.), 5394 (Bhs.), 5395 (Bhs.), 5396 (Bh.), 5397 (Bhs.), 5402 (Bhs.), 5403 (Bh.), 5405 (Bhs.), 5406 (Bh.), 5409 (Bhs.); **132,** 5413 (Bh.), 5414 (Bh.), 5415 (Bhs.), 5417 (Bhs.), 5418 (Bhs.), 5419 (Bh.); σσ, 5423 (Bhs.), 5433 (Bh.), 5434 (Bhs.), 5435 (Bh.), 5439 (Bh.), 5451 (Bh.); **133**ττ, 5455 (Bhs.), 5460 (Bhs.), 5468 (Bh.), 5469 (Bh.), 5470 (Bh.), 5471 (Bh.), 5472 (Bh.), 5473 (Bh.), 5474 (Bhs.), 5476 (Bhs.), 5478 (Bh.), 5479 (Bh.), 5483 (Bh.), 5489 (Bh.), 5494 (Bhs.), 5495 (Bh.), 5496 (Bhs.), 5499 (Bh.); **134,** 5500 (Bh.), 5502 (Bhs.), 5503 (Bh.), 5504 (Bh.), 5507 (Bhs.), 5509 (Bh.), 5511 (Bh.), 5515 (Bh.), 5517 (Bh.), 5524 (Bhs.), 5528 (Bhs.), 5530 (Bh.), 5531 (Bh.), 5532 (Bh.), 5533 (Bhs.); **135,** 5542 (Bh.), 5545 (Bhs.), 5547 (Bh.), 5549 (Bhs.), 5550 (Bhs.), 5552 (Bh.), 5553 (Bh.), 5554 (Bhs.), 5556 (Bh.), 5557 (Bh.), 5563 (Bhs.), 5566 (Bhs.), 5568 (Bh.), 5567 (Bhs.), 5569 (Bhs.), 5570 (Bh.),

5572 (Bhs.), 5573 (Bh.), 5574 (Bhs.); **136,** 5576 (Bh.), 5578 (Bh.), 5581 (Bhs.), 5582 (Bh.), 5584 (Bh.), 5587 (Bhs.), 5589 (Bh.), 5591 (Bhs.), 5595 (Bhs.), 5603 (Bh.), 5609 (Bh.), 5610 (Bh.), 5611 (Bh.), 5612 (Bhs.), 5613 (Bh.); **137,** 5615 (Bhs.), 5616 (Bhs.), 5628 (Bhs.), 5633 (*Bhīma-cāpa-*), 5634 (Bhs.), 5639 (Bhs.), 5640 (Bhs.), 5650 (Bhs.), 5660 (Bhs.), 5665 (Bh.); **138,** 5670 (Bh.), 5671 (Bhs.), 5672 (Bh.), 5674 (*Bhīma-cāpa-*), 5676 (*Bhīma-cāpa-*), 5678 (Bh.), 5679 (Bh.), 5698 (Bh.), 5695 (Bh.); **139,** 5697 (Bhs.), 5701 (Bh.), 5706 (Bh.), 5712 (Bh.), 5717 (Bh.), 5726 (Bhs.), 5729 (Bh.), 5731 (Bh.), 5733 (Bh.), 5734 (Bhs.), 5735 (Bhs.), 5737 (Bh.), 5742 (Bh.), 5747 (Bh.), 5748 (Bhs.), 5749 (Bh.), 5750 (Bh.), 5753 (Bh.), 5755 (Bh.), 5767 (Bhs.), 5768 (Bh.), 5780 (Bh.), 5782 (Bh.), 5785 (Bhs.), 5794 (Bh.), 5797 (Bhs.), 5800 (Bh.), 5805 (Bhs.), 5806 (Bh.); **140,** 5819 (Bh.), †5825 (Bh.); **143,** 5997 (Bh.), 6004 (Bh.); **145,** 6079 (Bhs.), 6094 (Bhs.), 6115 (Bhs.), 6116 (Bhs.); **146,** 6288 (Bhs.); **147,** 6368 (Bh.), 6369 (Bhs.), 6385 (Bhs.); **148,** 6388 (Bh.), 6389 (Bhs.), 6394 (Bh.), 6398 (Bh.), 6402 (Bhs.); **149,** 6482 (Bh.); **150,** 6496 (Bhs.); **152,** 6582 (Bhs.).—§ 600 (Ghaṭotkacavadhap.): VII, **153***α*, 6626 (Bhs.); **154***β*, 6649 (Bhs.); **155,** 6703 (Bhs.), 6704 (Bh.), 6707 (Bhs.), 6708 (Bh.), 6709 (Bhs.), 6714 (Bh.), 6716 (Bh.), 6718 (Bh.), 6719 (Bh.), 6723 (Bh.); **156,** 6763 (Bhs.), 6776 (Bhs.), 6781 (Bhs.), 6809 (*pautreṇa Bhīmasenasya . . . Añjana-parvaṇā*), 6817 (Bh.), 6826 (Bh.), 6853 (Bh.), 6895 (Bh.), 6898 (Bhs.); **157***ξ*, 6923 (Bhs.), 6926 (Bh.), 6929 (Bhs.), 6933 (Bh.), 6934 (Bh.), 6935 (Bh.), 6937 (Bh.), 6939 (Bh.), 6941 (Bh.), 6942 (Bh.), 6943 (Bh.), 6945 (Bhs.), 6964 (Bhs.), 6965 (Bh.); **158,** 7015 (Bh.); **161,** 7204 (Bhs.), 7208 (Bh.), 7215 (Bhs.); **162,** 7247 (Bh.), 7274 (Bh.), 7276 (Bh.); **163***ηη*, 7281 (Bh.); **164,** 7346 (Bhs.); **165,** 7363 (Bhs.); **166,** 7438 (Bhs.), 7439 (Bhs.), 7441 (Bh.), 7442 (Bh.), 7443 (Bhs.), 7444 (Bh.), 7445 (Bhs.), 7446 (Bhs.), 7448 (Bh.), 7452 (Bhs.), 7454 (Bh.), 7455 (Bh.); **170***νν*, 7672 (Bhs.); **172,** 7754 (Bhs.), 7763 (Bh.); **173,** 7814 (Bh.), 7835 (Bhs.); **176,** 8008 (Bh.), 8009 (Bh.), 8016 (Bh.), 8041 (Bhs.), 8043 (Bh.), 8044 (Bhs.), 8047 (Bhs.), 8049 (Bh.), 8051 (Bhs.), 8052 (Bh.), 8054 (Bh.), 8058 (Bh.), 8064 (Bh.), 8065 (Bhs.), 8068 (Bhs.); **177,** 8073 (Bhs.); **178,** 8074 (Bh.), 8075 (Bh.), 8083 (Bh.), 8112 (Bhs.), 8114 (Bhs.); **179,** †8163 (Bh.); **181,** 8227 (Bhs.), 8235 (Bhs.); **183,** 8314 (Bhs.), 8315 (Bh.), 8330 (Bhs.), 8343 (Bhs.).—§ 601 (Droṇa-vadhap.): VII, **184,** 8364 (Bh.).—§ 602 (do.): VII, **186,** 8461 (Bhs.), (8165) (Bhs.), 8168 (Bh.), 8506 (Bhs.), (8508) (Bhs.); **187,** 8544 (Bhs.); **188,** 8581 (Bh.), 8585 (Bh.), 8587 (Bhs.), 8588 (Bh.), 8589 (Bh.), 8590 (Bh.), 8591 (Bh.), 8596 (Bh.); **189,** 8676 (Bhs.), 8678 (Bhs.), 8681 (Bhs.), 8689 (Bhs.), 8690 (Bhs.); **190,** 8707 (Bh.), 8709 (Bhs.), 8710 (Bh.), 8711 (Bhs.), 8735 (Bhs.), 8743 (Bhs.); **191,** 8805 (Bh.); **192,** 8811 (Bhs.), 8834 (Bh.), 8844 (Bh.), 8850 (Bhs.), 8887 (Bhs.), 8888 (Bh.), 8890 (Bh.).—§ 603 (Nārā-yaṇastramokshap.): VII, **193,** 8946 (Bhs.), 8949 (Bh.); **195***θ*, 9007 (Bhs.); **197***μ*, 9083 (Bhs.); **198,** 9133 (Bh.), 9175 (Bhs.), 9177 (Bh.), 9186 (Bh.), 9191 (Bh.); **199,** 9238 (Bhs.), 9247 (Bh.), 9248 (Bh.), 9252 (Bhs.), 9254 (Bh.), 9256 (Bh.), 9257 (Bhs.); **200,** 9261 (Bhs.), 9263 (Bh.), 9265 (Bh.), 9267 (Bh.), 9270 (Bh.), 9279 (Bh.); *γγ*, 9330 (Bhs.), †9337 (Bh.), †9338 (Bhs.), 9344 (Bhs.), 9346 (Bh.), 9348 (Bh.), 9349 (*Bhīmanāmāṅkitā vāṇāḥ*), 9350 (Bh.), 9352 (Bh.), 9357 (Bhs.), 9358 (Bh.), 9360 (Bhs.), 9364 (Bh.), 9369 (Bhs.), 9371 (Bh.), 9372 (Bhs.), 9378 (Bh.), 9381 (Bh.), 9382 (Bhs.), 9385 (Bhs.), 9386 (Bhs.); *εε*, 9401 (Bh.).—§ 604 (Karṇap.): VIII, **3,** 62 (Bhs.); **4,** 89 (Bhs.); **5***ζ*, 98 (Bhs.), 108 (Bhs.), 111 (Bhs.), 119 (Bhs.), 121 (Bhs.), 124 (Bhs.), 131 (Bhs.), 133 (Bhs.); **9,** 297 (Bhs.).—§ 605 (do.): VIII, **11***χ*, 426 (Bhs.); **12,** 472 (Bh.), 473 (Bhs.), 474 (Bh.), 476 (Bh.), 477 (Bhs.), 478 (Bh.), 479 (Bhs.), 481 (Bh.), 482 (Bhs.), 483 (Bh.); **13,** 492 (Bhs.); **14,** 564 (Bhs.); **15,** 566 (Bhs.), 568 (Bhs.), 572 (Bh.), 583 (Bh.), 595 (Bh.), 600 (Bh.); **21,** 829 (Bhs.); **26,** 1053 (Bhs.), 1055 (Bh.); **28,** 1167 (Bhs.); **29,** 1201 (Bh.), 1203 (Bh.).—§ 606 (do.): VIII, **35,** 1637 (Bhs.).—§ 607 (do.): VIII, **36,** 1688 (Bhs.); *α*, 1690 (Bhs.); *β*, 1694 (Bhs.), 1700 (Bh.); **37,** †1728 (Bhs.).—§ 608 (do.): VIII, **46***α*, 2126 (Bhs.), 2156 (Bhs.); **48***ξ*, 2257 (Bhs.), 2262 (Bh.), 2266 (Bhs.), 2280 (Bhs.); *ρ*, 2286 (Bhs.); **49,** 2334 (Bhs.), 2365 (Bhs.), 2386 (Bhs.); **50,** 2393 (Bh.), 2394 (Bh.), 2396 (Bhs.), 2397 (Bh.), 2404 (Bh.), 2409 (Bh.), 2410 (Bhs.), 2415 (Bh.), 2416 (Bhs.), 2418 (Bhs.), 2419 (Bhs.), 2422 (Bh.), 2423 (Bh.), 2424 (Bhs.), 2437 (Bhs.), 2439 (Bhs.); **51,** 2440 (Bh.), 2442 (Bh.), 2444 (Bhs.), 2445 (Bhs.), 2448 (Bhs.), 2451 (Bhs.), 2453 (Bh.), 2454 (Bh.), 2455 (Bh.), 2457 (Bh.), 2459 (Bhs.), 2461 (Bhs.), 2463 (Bh.), 2464 (Bh.), 2465 (Bh.), 2467 (Bh.), 2472 (Bh.), 2474 (Bhs.), 2481 (Bhs.), 2483 (Bh.), 2484 (Bh.), 2490 (Bh.), 2491 (Bh.), 2492 (Bh.), 2494 (Bh.), 2501 (Bh.), 2502 (Bhs.); **54,** 2625 (Bhs.); **56,** 2692 (Bhs.), 2693 (Bhs.), 2694 (Bhs.), 2761 (Bhs.), 2763 (Bh.), 2765 (Bh.), 2766 (Bhs.), 2767 (Bhs.), 2772 (Bhs.); **57***φ*, 2849 (Bhs.); **58,** 2857 (Bhs.), 2901 (Bh.); **60,** 2983 (Bh.), 2995 (Bhs.), 3002 (Bh.), 3008 (Bhs.), 3033 (Bh.), 3035 (Bhs.), 3036 (Bh.), 3037 (Bhs.), 3042 (Bhs.), 3052 (Bh.), 3053 (Bhs.), 3054 (Bh.), 3056 (Bh.), 3062 (Bhs.), 3063 (Bhs.); **61***δδδ*, 3067 (Bhs.), 3069 (Bhs.), 3070 (Bhs.); *εεε*, 3073 (Bhs.), 3081 (Bhs.), 3118 (Bhs.), 3119 (Bhs.), 3120 (Bhs.), 3126 (Bhs.), 3128 (Bh.), 3132 (Bh.), 3133 (Bh.), 3137 (Bhs.), 3139 (Bhs.), 3140 (Bhs.); **62***ζζζ*, 3149 (Bhs.), 3175 (Bh.); **63,** 3178 (Bhs.), 3201 (Bhs.), 3201 (Bh.), 3202 (Bhs.), 3205 (Bh.), 3211 (Bhs.), 3213 (Bh.); **65,** †3287 (Bh.), (3288) (Bhs.), †3291 (Bh.), (†3292) (Bhs.), †3294 (Bhs.), †3295 (Bhs.), 3299 (Bh.), 3301 (Bhs.); **66,** 3322 (Bhs.); **67,** †3378 (Bh.); **68,** †3381 (Bh.), †3382 (Bh.), †3383 (Bhs.); **69,** 3405 (Bhs.), †3476 (Bh.), †3485 (Bh.); **70,** †3493 (Bh.), †3498 (Bhs.), †3499 (Bh.), †3502 (Bh.), †3532 (Bh.), †3537 (Bhs.), †3538 (Bh.); **71,** 3573 (Bh.); **73,** 3651 (Bh.), 3659 (Bh.), 3660 (Bh.), 3745 (Bh.); **74,** 3796 (Bh.), †3803 (Bh.); **75,** †3815 (Bh.), [†3820] (Bh.), †3822 (Bhs.); **76,** †3823 (Bh.), †3824 (Bh.), †3825 (Bh.), †3826 (Bh.), †3827 (Bh.), †3830 (Bhs.), †3839 (Bh.), (†3839) (Bhs.), †3840 (Bhs.), †3841 (Bhs.), †3848 (Bh.), (†3860) (Bhs.); **77,** 3862 (Bh.), 3883 (Bhs.), 3884 (Bhs.), 3885 (Bh.), 3887 (Bh.), 3889 (Bhs.), 3892 (Bh.), 3897 (Bh.), 3899 (Bh.), 3907 (Bhs.), 3908 (Bhs.), 3910 (Bh.), 3911 (Bh.), 3913 (Bh.), 3915 (Bh.), 3918 (Bh.), 3919 (Bhs.), 3920 (Bh.), 3922 (Bhs.), 3928 (Bh.), 3931 (Bhs.), 3932 (Bh.), 3935 (Bh.), 3936 (Bh.); **78,** 3940 (Bhs.), 3946 (Bhs.), 3947 (Bh.), 3948 (Bhs.); *γ*, 3955 (Bh.), 3959 (Bhs.), 3962 (Bhs.), 4003 (Bh.); **79,** 4010 (Bhs.); **80,** 4091 (Bh.), 4111 (Bhs.), 4113 (Bh.), 4114 (Bhs.); **81,** 4143 (Bhs.), 4145 (Bh.), 4146 (Bh.), 4152 (Bh.), 4153 (Bh.), 4155 (Bh.), 4157 (Bhs.), 4168 (Bhs.); **82,** †4193 (Bhs.), †4209 (Bh.), †4213 (Bh.), †4214 (Bh.); **83,** †4216 (Bh.), †4217 (Bh.), †4217 (Bhs.), †4218 (Bhs.), †4220 (Bh.), †4221 (Bh.), †4223 (Bh.), †4224 (Bhs.), †4228 (Bh.), †4236 (Bh.), †4239 (Bh.), †4240 (Bhs.), †4242 (Bh.), †4243 (Bh.), 4248 (Bh.), †4258 (Bhs.); **84,** 4262 (Bh.), 4264 (Bhs.), 4265 (Bh.), 4268 (Bh.), 4270 (Bhs.), 4290 (Bh.),

†4297 (Bhs.), †4298 (Bhs.), †4301 (Bh.); **85**, †4329 (Bh.), †4341 (Bhs.); **89**, †4559 (Bh.), †4572 (Bh.), †4576 (Bh.), †4585 (Bh.); **91**, 4752 (Bhs.); **92**, †4824 (Bh.); **93**, 4848 (Bhs.), 4854 (Bhs.), 4855 (Bhs.), 4856 (Bh.), 4860 (Bhs.), 4861 (Bh.), 4862 (Bh.), 4870 (Bhs.), 4891 (Bhs.).—§ 609 (Çalyap.): IX, **1**, 12 (Bhs.); **2**, 105 (Bhs.).—§ 610 (do.): IX, **3**, 140 (Bhs.), 146 (Bhs.), 147 (Bhs.), 148 (Bh.), 152 (Bh.), 152 (Bhs.), 153 (Bh.), 154 (Bh.), 161 (Bhs.), 181 (Bhs.); **4**, 203 (Bh.), 223 (Bhs.), 234 (Bhs.); **5**, 252 (Bhs.); **7**, 351 (Bh.).—§ 611 (do.): IX, **8**, 381 (Bhs.), 399 (Bhs.); **9**, 448 (Bhs.), 450 (Bhs.); **10**, 516 (Bhs.); **11**λ, 549 (Bhs.), 565 (Bhs.), 569 (Bh.), 573 (Bhs.), 577 (Bh.), 591 (Bhs.); **12**, 595 (Bh.), 598 (Bhs.), 603 (Bh.), 604 (Bh.), 605 (Bh.), 608 (Bhs.), 609 (Bh.), 618 (Bhs.), 646 (Bhs.), 652 (Bhs.); **13**, 656 (Bhs.), 659 (Bhs.), 663 (Bhs.), 667 (Bhs.), 675 (Bhs.), 676 (Bhs.), 679 (Bh.), 687 (Bhs.), 703 (Bhs.); **15**, 768 (Bhs.), 770 (Bhs.), 775 (Bhs.), 779 (Bhs.); **16**, 798 (Bh.), 802 (Bhs.), 806 (Bh.), 820 (Bh.), 831 (Bh.), 834 (Bh.), 835 (Bhs.); **17**χ, 866 (Bhs.), †871 (Bhs.), †873 (Bhs.), †886 (Bh.), †889 (Bhs.), †890 (Bhs.), †891 (Bh.), †892 (Bh.), †892 (Bhs.), †895 (Bh.), †896 (Bh.), †898 (Bh.); **18**ββ, 961 (Bh.); **19**, 1016 (Bh.), 1017 (Bh.), 1017 (Bhs.), 1020 (Bhs.), 1027 (Bhs.), 1037 (Bhs.), 1038 (Bh.), 1039 (Bhs.), 1040 (Bh.), 1042 (Bh.), 1045 (Bh.), 1058 (Bhs.); **20**οο, †1084 (Bh.); **22**λλ, 1138 (Bhs.), 1144 (Bhs.), 1149 (Bhs.); **24**, 1302 (Bhs.); **25**, 1367 (Bhs.), 1370 (Bhs.), 1371 (Bhs.), 1395 (Bhs.), 1397 (Bhs.); **26**, 1401 (Bhs.), 1404 (Bhs.), 1407 (Bh.), 1407 (Bhs.), 1408 (Bh.), 1409 (Bh.), 1409 (Bhs.), 1411 (Bh.), 1413 (Bh.), 1414 (Bh.), 1420 (Bh.), 1421 (Bh.), 1424 (Bhs.), 1427 (Bhs.), 1428 (Bh.), 1429 (Bh.), 1434 (Bhs.), 1435 (Bhs.), 1436 (Bh.), 1439 (Bhs.); **27**, 1455 (Bh.); φφ, 1471 (Bhs.), 1473 (Bhs.), 1491 (Bh.), 1494 (Bh.), 1495 (Bh.), 1496 (Bh.); **28**, 1503 (Bh.), 1506 (Bh.), 1517 (Bhs.), 1527 (Bhs.), 1528 (Bh.), 1529 (Bhs.), 1530 (Bh.).—§ 612 (Hradapraveçap.): IX, **29**, 1568 (Bhs.), 1643 (Bhs.), 1651 (Bhs.); **30**, 1697 (Bhs.), 1706 (Bhs.), 1714 (Bhs.), 1715 (Bhs.), 1718 (Bhs.); ε, 1725 (Bhs.).—§ 613 (Gadāyuddhap.): IX, **32**, 1882 (Bh.); **33**ε, 1893 (Bhs.), 1896 (Bh.), 1900 (Bh.), (1905) (Bhs.), 1918 (Bh.), 1918 (Bhs.), 1930 (Bhs.).—§ 614 (do.): IX, **34**, 1957 (Bhs.).—§ 615 (Baladevatīrthay.): IX, **54**, 3068 (Bh.).—§ 615 (Gadāyuddhap.): **55**, 3078 (Bh.), 3095 (Bh.), 3097 (Bh.), 3101 (Bhs.), 3102 (Bh.), 3122 (Bh.); **56**, 3135 (Bh.), 3157 (Bhs.); **57**, 3175 (Bhs.), 3187 (Bhs.), 3191 (Bhs.), 3200 (Bh.), 3200 (Bhs.), 3201 (Bh.), 3203 (Bhs.), 3206 (Bh.), 3207 (Bhs.), 3212 (Bh.), 3213 (Bh.), 3215 (Bhs.), 3218 (Bh.), 3220 (Bh.), 3221 (Bh.), 3222 (Bh.), 3224 (Bh.), 3224 (Bhs.), 3225 (Bh.), 3228 (Bh.), 3230 (Bhs.), 3234 (Bhs.), 3235 (Bh.), 3235 (Bhs.), †3239 (Bhs.), †3242 (Bh.); **58**, 3248 (Bh.), 3249 (Bhs.), 3251 (Bh.), 3252 (Bh.), 3264 (Bhs.), 3266 (Bhs.), 3267 (Bh.), 3269 (Bhs.), 3272 (Bh.), 3283 (Bhs.), 3285 (Bh.), 3287 (Bhs.), 3290 (Bhs.), 3293 (Bhs.); **59**, 3311 (Bhs.), 3314 (Bh.), †3321 (Bhs.), 3326 (Bh.), 3329 (Bhs.), 3330 (Bhs.); **60**, 3344 (Bhs.), 3345 (Bh.), 3348 (Bh.), 3356 (Bh.), 3357 (Bh.), 3362 (Bhs.), 3373 (Bh.), 3376 (Bhs.), 3379 (Bh.), 3380 (Bhs.); **61**, 3388 (Bhs.), 3389 (Bhs.), 3393 (Bhs.), 3401 (Bh.), 3404 (Bhs.), 3415 (Bh.), 3430 (Bhs.); **62**, 3480 (Bhs.); **63**, 3510 (Bhs.); **64**, 3592 (Bhs.), 3597 (Bhs.), 3612 (Bhs.). — § 616 (Sauptikap.): X, **1**, 7 (Bh.), 15 (Bh.); **1**, 60 (Bhs.); **5**, 198 (Bh.), 199 (Bhs.); **9**, 499 (Bhs.), 500 (Bhs.), 502 (Bhs.).—§ 617 (Aishīkap.): **10**, 550*a* (Bhs.); **11**, 582 (Bhs.), 595 (Bh.), 595 (Bhs.), 601 (Kaunteya, Bhs.); **12**, 608 (Bh.); **13**, 657 (Bhs.), 663 (Bhs.); **15**, 699 (Bhs.), 700 (Bhs.); **16**, 748 (Bhs.).—§ 618 (Jalapradānikap.): XI, **11**, 299 (Bhs.); **12**, 325 (Bh.), 326 (Bhs. °*mayaṃ dāvaṃ*), 327 (Bh.), 329 (Bhs.), 330 (Bh.), 333 (Bh.), 334 (Bhs.), 335 (Bh.), 339 (Bh.), 340 (Bhs.); **13**, 351 (Bh.), 352 (Bhs.), 356 (Bh.), 359ν (Bh.); **14**, 378 (Bh.); **15**, 381ο (Bhs.), 395 (Bhs.).—§ 619 (Strīvilāpap.): **17**, 502 (Bhs.), 503 (Bhs.), 505 (Bhs.); **18**, 519γ (Bhs.), 537 (Bh.), 538 (Bhs.), 543 (Bhs.), 545 (Bhs.), 546 (Bhs.); **20**, 547 (Bh.); **22**, 617η (Bhs.).—§ 621 (Rājadh.): XII, **1**, 13γ (Bh.), 26 (Bh.); **2**, 51 (Bhs.); **10**, 277 (Bhs.).—§ 623 (do.): **16**, 482ν (Bhs.).—§ 635 (do.): **33**, 1175 (Bh.); **37**, 1377 (Bh. Kaunteya); **38**, 1396ε (Bhs.).—§ 637 (do.): **40**, 1445 (Bhs.), 1464 (Bhs., Pāṇḍ.); **41**β, 1475 (Bhs. *Kaunteyaṃ*); **44**, 1517 (Bh.); **47**, 1695 (Bhs.).—§ 639 (do.): **53**ζ, 1914 (Bh.); θ, 1921 (Bh.).—§ 640 (do.): **54**, 1929*a* (Bh.). — § 657 (Āpaddh.): **167**, 6238 (Bhs.), †6252 (Bh.), 6239 (Bhs.).—§ 730 (Ānuçāsan.): XIII, **15**, 1033 (Bh. °*pūrvaja*, i.e. Yudh.). — § 777 (Svargārohaṇikap.): **169**, 7771*a* (Bhs.).—§ 778 (Āçvamedhikap.): XIV, **1**, 3 (Bh.).—§ 780 (do.): **14**, 356β (Bh.); **15**, 384*a* (Bhs.), 389 (Bh.).—§ 783 (Anugītāp.): **52**, 1504ν (Bhs.), 1508 (Bh.), 1524 (Bh.), †1533 (Bh.).—§ 785 (do.): **60**, 1787 (Bh.), 1799 (Bhs.), 1802 (Bhs.); **61**, 1845 (Bh.); **63**, 1874 (Bhs.), 1880 (Bh.), 1881 (Bhs.), 1886 (Bh.); **66**, 1954μ (Bh.); **67**, 1967 (Bhs.), 1969 (Bhs.); **68**, 1997ξ (Bhs.); **71**ρ, 2081 (Bhs.); **72**, 2097 (*Bhīmasenād avarajaḥ*, i.e. Arjuna), 2102 (Bhs.), 2108 (Bh.); **77**, 2223 (*Bhīmasenād anantarād*, i.e. Arjuna); **85**δ, 2514 (Bh.), 2515 (Bh.), 2516 (Bhs.), 2519 (Bh.), 2520 (Bhs.), 2526 (Bhs.), 2537 (Bhs.); **86**, 2553 (Bhs.), 2555 (Bhs.), 2558 (Bh.); **87**, 2586 (Bh.), υ, 2598 (Bh.); **88**χ, 2608 (Bh.), 2612 (Bh.), 2627 (Bhs.), 2632 (Bh.); **91**, 2814 (Bh.).—§ 787 (Āçramavāsik.): XV, **1**, 27 (Bh.); **2**, 35 (Bh.), 57 (Bh.); **3**, 61 (Bh.), 62 (Bhs.), 64 (Bh.), 66 (Bh.), 72 (Bh.), 124 (Bhs.); **10**, 333ν (Bh.), 346 (Bh.); **11**, 362 (Bh.), 363 (Bhs.), 364 (Bh.), 371 (Bhs.); **12**, 382 (Bh.), 386 (Bh.), 387–8 (Bhs.), 389 (Bh.), 391 (Bh.); **13**, 399 (Bh.), 401 (Bh.); **16**, 455φ (Bhs.), 465 (Bh.); **17**, 479 (Bh.), 480 (Bhs.), 483 (Bh.), 494 (Bhs.).—§ 788 (do.): **24**, 646β (Bhs.); **25**, 658 (Bh.); **26**, 710 (Bhs.); **27**, 733 (Bhs.); **28**ε, 737 (Bhs.), 747 (Bh.).—§ 789 (Putradarçanap.): **31**η, 853 (*Marudgaṇād Bhīmasenaṃ*).—§ 791 (do.): **36**, 1003β (Bh.).—§ 792 (Nāradāgamanap.): XV, **37**, 1053 (Bhs.); **38**, 1066 (Bh.), 1073 (Bh.).—§ 793 (Mausalap.): XVI, **7**, 179λ (Bhs.); **8**, 284 (Bh.).—§ 794 (Mahāprasthānikap.): XVII, **1**, 5 (Bhs.), 20 (Bh.), 31 (Bh.), 37*a* (Bhs.); **2**, 50 (Bhs.), 54 (Bh.), 59 (Bh.), 61 (Bhs.), 65 (Bh.), 69 (Bh.); **3**, 92 (Bh.).—§ 795 (Svargārohaṇap.): XVIII, **2**, 36 (Bh.), 66ε (Bhs.); **3**η, 96 (Bh.), 118 (Bh.); **4**κ, 131 (*Bhīmasenaṃ Marudgaṇavṛtaṃ*).

Cf. also the following synonyms:

Acyutānuja ("younger brother of Yudhishṭhira"): IV, 236.
Anilātmaja ("son of the wind"): VI, 5279; VII, 1138.
Arjunāgraja ("elder brother of Arjuna"): I, 5472.
Arjunapūrvaja (do.): VI, 4356.
Ballava (q.v.).
Bhīmadhanvan: X, 663.
Jaya: VII, 5159 (*pradeçitajayo Jayaḥ* (B. *Dayaḥ*) *Bhīmasenaḥ* . . .).
Kaunteya, etc. (q.v.).
Kaurava, etc., **Kuruçārdūla**, etc. (q.v.).

Mārutātmaja ("son of the wind"): IX, 3245 (*Vṛkodaraḥ*).
Māruti (do.): VII, 4509; VIII, 2500, 3051, †4302.
Pāṇḍava, etc. (q.v.).
Pārtha, etc. (q.v.).
Pavanātmaja ("son of the wind"): III, 11275; XV, 626.
Prabhañjanasuta (do.): VII, 6268.
Rākshasakaṇṭaka ("thorn of the Rākshasas"): III, 420.
Samīraṇasya sutaḥ ("son of the wind"): III, †14755.
Vāyuputra (do.): V, 3707.
Vāyusuta (do.): III, 11116.
Vṛkodara ("wolf's belly"): I, 455 (*Jaṭāsurasya ca vadho rākshasasya Vṛkodarāt*), 483 (*dushṭātmano vadho yatra Kīcakasya Vṛkodarāt*), 547, 2240, 2257, 2288, 2444 (*Mārutāc ca Vṛkodaraḥ . . . jajñe*), ††3827 (*Sutasomaṃ Vṛkodaraḥ*, sc. *utpādayām āsa*), 4773, 4777, 4981, 4987, 4990, 4991, 5036, 5040, 5343, 5428, 5473, 5840, 5923, 6035, 6039, 6252, 6256, 6257, 6291, 7107, 7117, 7139, 7408, 8039 (*Sutasomaṃ Vṛkodarāt Pañcālī sushuve*); II, 782, 924, 1810, 1811, †2118, 2221, †2250, 2393, 2534, 2537; III, 421, 440, 444, 446, 449, 533 (*Sutasomo Vṛkodarāt*), 549, 567, 918, 1012, 1246, 1430, 10250, 10253, 10283, 10840, 10875, 10877, 10878, 10879, 10882, 10895, 11105, 11365, 11371, 11411, 11504, 11506, 11607, 11609, 11788, 11815, 11818 (*yathā Jishṇur Mahendrasya, yathā Vāyor Vṛkodaraḥ . . .*), 11830, †11907, †12356, 12367, 12442, 12467, 12488, †14751, †14757, †14760, 14945, 14949, 14953, 15694, †15703, 15720, 15785, 15786, 15789, 17278, 17291; IV, 27, 45, 361, 366, 639, 760, 769, 771, 773, 823, 1104 (*Kuntīputraḥ*), 1121, 2302; V, 653, †724, 1988, 1989 (*Kuntīputraḥ*), 2020, 2024 (*gadāṃ bibhrad*), 2036, 2051, 2173, 2180, 2741, 2786, 2801, 2973, 3155, 3200, 3204, 3213, 4228, 4652, 4867, 5334λ, 5476, 5595; VI, 706, 788, 789, 844, 1554, 2115, 2333, 2751, 2768, 2769, 2803, 3118, 3367, 3372, 3398, 3401, 3511, 3783, 4149, 4355, 4357, 4670, 5234θ, 5236, 5271, 5288; VII, †67, †81, 376 (*sadyo Vṛkodarāj jāto māyāvī rākshasaḥ*, i.e. *Ghaṭotkacaḥ*), 593, 596, 940, 944, 951, 1046δ, 1063, 1145, 1149 (°*rathaṃ*), 1152, 1157, 1158, 1373, 1769ρ, 3047δ, 3082, 3083, 3095η, 5109, 5152, 5169, 5188, 5249, 5326, 5363, 5384, 5392, 5401, 5431, 5436, 5443, 5565, 5578, 5585, 5619, 5624, 5632, 5644, 5653, 5700, 5714 (only in B.), 5789, 5790, 5792, 6403, 6492, 6705, 6712, †6725, †6726, †6727, 6780, 6909, 6966, 7216, 7459, 7732, 7762, 8243, 8310, 8512, 8553, 8583, 9334, 9382; VIII, 168, 453, 461, 484, 582, 2395, 2408, 2411, 2421, 2430, 2696, 2836, 3056, 3129, 3131, 3211, 3896, 4027, †4209, †4212, †4213, †4227, †4233, 4256, †4279, †4303, †4512, †4520, †4584, 4843, 4851, 4857, 4991, 4999, 5030; IX, 135, 143, 149, 560, 588, 599, 600, 761, 838, 1369, 1494, 1716, 1830 (Pārthāt), 1894 (id.), 1902, 1910, 1940, 1953, 3103, 3119, 3148, 3165, 3166, 3173 (*Pāṇḍavaḥ*), 3184, 3189, 3248, 3281, 3289, 3318, 3323, 3346, 3374, 3396, 3596 (*Pāṇḍuputraḥ*); X, 61, 501, 504, 581, 646; XI, 329, 341, 376 (*Pārthaḥ*), 394; XII, 1522; XIV, 3517; XV, 63, 70, 402, 403 (°*kṛte*), 435, 626 (*Pavanātmajaḥ*), 664, 667 (°*sya parigrahaḥ*); XVII, 63.

Bhīma[7], a Deva-gandharva Mauneya. § 101 (Aṃçāvat.): I, **65**, 2551.
Bhīma[8]. § 150 (Pūruvaṃç.): I, **94**, 3708 (brother of Dushyanta).
Bhīma[9], an ancient king (?). § 310 (Āraṇyakap.): III, **3**, 141 (*Bhīmena Kārtavīryeṇa Vainyena Nahusheṇa ca*; had by ascetic meditation delivered the people from affliction; PCR. "the great K.").
Bhīma[10], Vidarbha king. § 344 (Nalop.): III, **53**, 2076 (*Vidarbheshu*, sc. king), 2078 (is granted a boon by Damana).—§ 345 (do.): III, **54**, 2109 (father of Damayantī and her three brothers), 2113 (arranges the svayaṃvara of Damayantī); **54**, 2115; **57**, 2191, 2231 (marries Damayantī to Nala), 2232.—§ 346 (do.): **60**, 2295 (*rājānaṃ*; receives the children of Nala from the charioteer Vārshṇeya).—§ 347 (do.): **64**, 2444 (*Vidarbhādhipatiḥ*), 2476 (*Vidarbheshu mahīpālo Bhīmo nāma mahīpatiḥ*).—§ 350 (do.): **68**, 2654 (sends brahmans to find out Nala), 2682; **69**, 2694 (*Vidarbharājaḥ*), 2708 (*rājñaḥ*, husband of the daughter of the Daçārṇa king Sudāman), 2725.—§ 353 (do.): **73**, 2852 (Ṛtuparṇa comes to him), 2853, 2871, 2878; **76**, 2955 (all but recognizes Nala), 3002; **77**, 3011 (receives the recovered Nala as a son).—§ 354 (do.): **78**, 3030 (after a month Nala departs); **79**, 3064 (Damayantī departs).
Bhīma[11], one of the 15 yajñamushaḥ devāḥ. § 492 (Āṅgirasa): III, **220**, 14166.
Bhīma[12], son of Dhṛtarāshṭra. § 581 (Bhīshmavadhap.): VI, **64**, 2838κ, 2845λ (slain by Bhīmasena).
Bhīmā[1] (= Umā?). § 358 (Tīrthayātrāp.): III, **82**, 5026 (*Bhīmāyāḥ sthānam*, a tīrtha).
Bhīmā[2], a river in Bhāratavarsha. § 574 (Jambūkh.): VI, **9**, 329λ.
Bhīmabala[1], one of the 15 yajñamushaḥ devāḥ. § 492 (Āṅgirasa): III, **220**, 14166.
Bhīmabala[2], a son of Dhṛtarāshṭra. § 130 (Aṃçāv.): I, **67**, 2733.—§ 182 (Dhṛtarāshṭraputranāmak.): I, **117**, 4546.
Bhīmaçara, a son of Dhṛtarāshṭra. § 130 (Aṃçāv.): I, **67**, 2734.
Bhīmadhanvan = Bhīmasena Pāṇḍava: X, 663.
Bhīmadundubhihāsa (°**dundabhi**°, C.) = Çiva (1000 names[1]): XII, 10369.
Bhīmāḥ. § 267 (Yamasabhāvarṇana): II, **8**, 335 (*çataṃ*, in the palace of Yama).
Bhīmajānu. § 267 (Yamasabhāv.): II, **8**, 332 (in the palace of Yama).
Bhīmakadalīkhaṇḍapraveça(ḥ) (Bhīma's entering the plantain thicket). § 424 (cf. Tīrthayātrāp.): There they dwelt for six nights. Suddenly a wind from the north-east brought a celestial lotus of 1,000 petals, which *Kṛshṇā* presented to *Yudhishṭhira*; she sent *Bhīma* to bring others, in order to carry them to their hermitage in *Kāmyaka*. *Bhīma* proceeded along the slopes of the *Gandhamādana* (*b*); the lions, etc., fled; invisible, the wives of *Yakshas* and *Gandharvas* stared at him. After having bathed in a lake, he blew his shell and began to proceed into a plaintain wood, but was arrested by his brother the ape *Hanumat*, who for his good obstructed the way to heaven (*divaṅgamaṃ mārgaṃ*), saying that this was the path to the *devaloka*, impassable by mortals, save the way of *siddhi* (*siddhigatiṃ*) (III, **146**). *Hanumat* said he was suffering from illness and could not rise; but *Bhīma* would not leap over him, and could not remove his tail.—§§ 425–430: *Hanumad-Bhīma-saṃvāda* (q.v.).
Bhīmamukha = Çiva (1000 names[1]).
Bhīmanandinī = Damayantī: III, 2490.
Bhīmaparākrama = Vishṇu (1000 names).
Bhīmapūrvaja = Yudhishṭhira: XIII, 1033.
Bhīmaputrikā = Damayantī: III, 2659.
Bhīmaratha[1], a son of Dhṛtarāshṭra. § 130 (Aṃçāv.): I, **67**, 2738.—§ 182 (Dhṛtarāshṭraputran.): I, **117**, 4551.—

§ 581 (Bhīshmavadhap.): VI, **64,** 2838κ, 2845λ (slain by Bhīmasena).—§ 592 (Saṃçaptakav.): VII, **20**η, 804 (in the bosom of Droṇa's Garuḍavyūha); **25,** 1089 (slays Çālva).

Bhīmaratha[2]. § 264 (Sabhākriyāp.): II, **4**β, 121 (*Cānūro Devarātaç ca Bhojo Bhīmarathaç ca yaḥ*, among the kings who received Yudhishṭhira when he entered his palace).

Bhīmarathī. § 377 (Dhaumyatīrthak.): III, **88,** 8328 (a river in the south). § 574 (Jambūkh.): VI, **9,** 327λ (a river in Bhāratavarsha).—§ 775 (Ānuçās.): XIII, **166,** 7653*a*.

Bhīmasena[1] (Pāṇḍava), v. Bhīma[6].

Bhīmasena[2]. § 12 (Paushyap.): I, **3,** 662 (brother of Janamejaya Pārikshita).

Bhīmasena[3]. § 154 (Pūruv.): I, **94,** 3744γ (son of Parikshit).—§ 156 (do.): I, **95,** 3795–6 (son of Parikshit and grandfather of Pratīpa).

Bhīmasena[4]. § 101 (Aṃçāv.): I, **65,** 2550 (a Devagandharva Mauneya).—§ 191 (Arjuna): I, **123,** 4811*a* (among the Gandharvas who sing at the birth of Arjuna).

Bhīmasenarasapāna(m) ("Bhīma's drinking the magic draught"). § 197 (Sambhavap.): The *Pāṇḍavas* were far superior in strength and skill to the *Dhārtarāshṭras*, and *Bhīma* tormented the *Dhārtarāshṭras*. *Duryodhana* then built a palace (*Udakakrīḍana*) at *Pramāṇakoṭi*, on the banks of the *Gaṅgā*, in order to sport in the water there. There he invited the *Pāṇḍavas* and poured *kālakūṭaka* poison into the food of *Bhīma*, and when *Bhīma* had lost his senses, *Duryodhana* bound him and threw him into the water, where he sunk down to the dwelling of the *Nāgas*, who bit him, but could not penetrate his thick skin. The immovable (i.e. vegetable) *kālakūṭaka* poison was neutralised by the movable (i.e. animal) serpent poison. *Bhīma* awoke and began to crush the serpents, until *Vāsuki* came, and, informed by *Āryaka* that he was the daughter's son of *Āryaka's* daughter's son, let him drink as much of their *rasa* (containing the strength of 1,000 elephants (serpents?) in each *kuṇḍa*) as he could. He drank eight *kuṇḍas*, and then was laid on a bed (I, **128**). When the *Kauravas* and *Pāṇḍavas* had returned to *Hāstinapura*, Yudhishṭhira ("himself unacquainted with wickedness, and regarding others as honest as himself," v. 5037) asked *Kuntī* if *Bhīma* had come home. *Vidura* consoled her. On the eighth day *Bhīma* awoke from his slumber, bathed in the holy waters, ate of the *paramānna* (rice boiled in milk with sugar), etc., and was placed by the *Nāgas* in the same gardens, whence he ran home. *Yudhishṭhira* ordered him to keep silence on this accident, and the *Pāṇḍavas* [with *Vidura's* advice] became very vigilant from this day (the words in brackets are from B., where also v. 5068*a* is placed after v. 5070*a*). [*sārathiṃ cāsya dayitam apahastena jaghnivān* (see BR., s.v. *apahasta*, cf. iii, v. 545). *Duryodhana* again poured *kālakūṭaka* poison into the food of *Bhīma*. *Yuyutsu* informed the *Pāṇḍavas* of this; but *Bhīma* swallowed the poison and digested it, and it produced no change in him.]—*Duryodhana*, *Karṇa*, and *Çakuni* had recourse to numerous other contrivances in order to kill the *Pāṇḍavas*, who, though knowing it, yet, in accordance with the advice of *Vidura*, suppressed their indignation. Seeing the princes passing their time in play, *Dhṛtarāshṭra* appointed *Gautama* (i.e. *Kṛpa*, born in a thicket of reeds and well skilled in the meaning of the *Vedas* and *çāstras*) as their preceptor (I, **129**).

Bhīmasenasuta ("son of Bh.") = Ghaṭotkaca: VI, 5178; VII, 7942.

Bhīmasenātmaja (do.), i.e. Ghaṭotkaca: III, 11451.

Bhīmasūnu (do.) = do.: VII, 8131.

Bhīmasuta (do.) = do.: VIII, 6858.

Bhīmasutā = Damayantī.

Bhīmavega, son of Dhṛtarāshṭra. § 130 (Aṃçāv.): I, **67,** 2733.—§ 182 (Dhṛtarāshṭrap.): I, **117,** 4546.

Bhīmavegarava. § 232 (Svayaṃvarap.): I, **186,** 6981 (present at the Svayaṃvara of Kṛshṇā).

Bhīmavikrama. § 130 (Aṃçāv.): I, **67,** 2733 (a son of Dhṛtarāshṭra).

Bhīmavratadhara = Çiva (1000 names[1]).

Bhīṇī (a Mātṛ). § 615*u* (Skanda): IX, **46**θ, 2645.

Bhishaj ("the physician") = Vishṇu (1000 names).

Bhishajau ("the two physicians") = Açvinau: XII, 12917 (*Nāsatyañ caiva Dasrañ ca*).

Bhishajāvartta (the father of the Açvins, Nīl., i.e. Kṛshṇa): XII, 1510.

Bhīshma. § 4 (Anukram.): I, **1,** 138, †176 (*Çāntanavaṃ*), †177, †180, †182, †183, †184.—§ 9 (Parvas.): I, **2,** 300 (*ahāni yuyudhe Bhīshmo daça vai paramāstravit*).—§ 10 (do.): I, **2,** 336, 353 (*Svargārohaṇikañ caiva tato Bhīshmasya dhīmataḥ*, sc. *parva*).—§ 11 (do.): I, **2,** 373 (°*sya sambhavaḥ*), 523 (Kṛshṇa intends to slay him), 525 (Arjuna felled him, placing Çikhaṇḍin in front of himself), 526 (*çaratalpagataḥ*), 599 (*Bhāgīrathīputrāt*, instructs Yudhishṭhira lying on his arrow-bed), 603 (°*sya samprāptiḥ svargasya*).—§ 61 (Sarpasattra): I, **55,** †2109β.—§ 79 (Ādivaṃç.): I, **63,** 2420, "in like manner Bhīshma, the son of Çāntanu, was born in the womb of Gaṅgā from the seed of the Vasus (*Vasuvīryāt*)."—§ 130*b* (Aṃçāv.): I, **67,** 2711 (the youngest of the Vasus, son of Çāntanu, *Kurūṇām abhayaṅkaraḥ*, fought with Rāma Jāmadagnya).—§ 156 (Pūruv.): I, **95,** 3800 (son of Çāntanu and Gaṅgā; his real name was Devavrata), 3801 (marries his father to Satyavatī).—§ 157 (do.): I, **95,** 3818.—[§ 164 (Āpavop.): I, **99,** 3965, *Dyu-nāmā*, etc.]—§ 165 (Satyavatīlābhop.): I, **100,** 4065 (is called Bhīshma), 4066.—§ 166 (Citrāṅgadop.): I, **101,** 4071 (places Citrāṅgada on the throne), 4077 (*Çāntanavaḥ*; performs the obsequial rites for Citrāṅgada), 4079 (instals Vicitravīrya), 4080 (*Çāntanavaṃ*).—§ 167 (Vicitravīryoparama): I, **102,** 4081, 4082 (marries Vicitravīrya to the princesses of Kāçi), 4087, 4093, 4100, 4103, 4105, 4108 (*Çāntanavaṃ*; is attacked by Çālva), 4110, 4111, 4113, 4115 (*Çāntanavaṃ*), 4116, 4118 (*Çāntanavaḥ*), 4122 (do.; slays the horses of Çālva with the Aindreya weapon), 4125 (returns to Hāstinapura), 4131, 4132 (releases Ambā), 4137, 4145 (performs the obsequies for Vicitravīrya).—§ 168 (Bhīshma-Satyavatīsaṃvāda): I, **103,** 4147, 4164, 4168 (declines to marry the widows of Vicitravīrya).—§ 169 (do.): I, **104,** (4172).—§ 170 (do.): I, **104,** (4199).—§ 171 (Vicitravīryasutotp.): I, **105,** (4223), 4225, 4239, 4240, 4241, 4244, 4253, 4255, 4264, 4271; **106,** 4276.—§ 173 (Pāṇḍu-rājyābhisheka): I, **109,** 4349, 4350, 4353 (is the tutor of Dhṛtarāshṭra, Pāṇḍu, and Vidura), 4360.—§ 174 (Dhṛtarāshṭravivāha): I, **110,** 4372 (*Kurupitāmahaḥ*), 4379.—§ 177 (Pāṇḍudigvijaya): I, **113,** 4425 (*Çāntanavaḥ*), 4427 (marries Pāṇḍu to Mādrī), 4429, 4432, 4436, 4441 (*Sāgaragāsutaḥ*), 4446, 4463 (°*purogamāḥ*).—§ 178 (Pāṇḍu): I, **114,** 4469, 4471.—[§ 179 (Viduraparinaya) [*Āpagāsutaḥ*]: married Vidura to the daughter of king Devaka—*Pārasavīṃ kanyāṃ*: I, **114,** 4480.]—§ 180 (Gandhārīputrotp.): I, **115,** 4507, 4510 (consultation with Dhṛtarāshṭra after the birth of Duryodhana).—§ 184 (Pāṇḍu): I, **119,** 4614.—§ 194 (do.): I, **126,** 4902 (receives the sons of Pāṇḍu, etc.), 4911 (*Çāntanavaḥ*), 4917 (worships the ṛshis).—§ 195 (do.): I, **127,** 4936 (performs the funeral rites for Pāṇḍu), 4947, 4959, 4960.—§ 196 (Vyāsa): I, **128**, 4964 (gives Pāṇḍu a çrāddha), 4975.—§ 199 (Droṇa): I, **130**, 5094 (inquires about teachers for the princes), 5098.—§ 202 (do.): I, **131**, 5168 (engages Droṇa), 5169, 5170, 5177, 5192, 5206, (5208).—§ 203 (do.): I, **132**, 5211, 5212.—§ 208 (Astradarç.): I, **134**, 5323; **136**, 5404 (sides with Arjuna); **137**, 5439.—§ 213 (Jatugṛhap.): I, **141**, 5650 (performs the funeral rites of the Pāṇḍavas, whom he thinks burnt), 5660 (*Çāntanavaḥ*), 5662 (do.), 5666, 5667; **142**, 5688, 5691; **143**, 5707 (*Çāntanavam*); **145**, 5734, 5743, 5762; **146**, 5790 (*pitāmahaḥ*), 5791 (do.); **150**, 5860 (*Çāntanavaḥ*).—§ 217 (Caitrarathap.): I, **166**, 6344.—§ 241 (Vidurāgamanap.): I, **200**, 7371; **202**, 7439; **203**, (7441); **204**, 7461, 7471.—§ 243 (do.): I, **205**, 7489 (*Çāntanavaḥ*); **206**, 7518 (do.), 7535 (do.).—§ 244 (Rājyalābhap.): I, **207**, 7565, 7593.—§ 286 (Rājasūyikap.): II, **33**, 1256.—§ 287 (do.): II, **34**, 1260, 1264.—§ 288 (do.): II, **35**, 1287, 1291.—§ 289 (Arghāharaṇap.): II, **36**, 1327, 1332 (*Çāntanavaḥ*), 1336, 1337; **37**, 1341, 1347 (*Çāntanave*), 1367; **38**, 1371 (*Çāntanavaḥ*), 1373, (1374); **39**, 1401.—§ 290 (Çiçupālavadhap.): II, **40**, 1419, 1422, 1432; **41**, 1437, 1438, 1439, 1440, 1441, 1442, 1444, 1446, 1448, 1453, 1455, 1457, 1460, 1462, 1464, 1465, 1466, 1471, 1472; **42**, 1486, 1487, 1492, 1493; **43**, (1494), (1518); **44**, (1519), 1523, 1524, 1525, 1527, 1530, 1532, 1541, 1542, 1543, 1546, 1548, 1549, 1551, 1553, 1554, 1555, 1556 (*Kurupitāmahaḥ*).—§ 291 (do.): II, **45**, 1561.—§ 292 (Rājasūyikap.): II, **45**, 1607.—§ 294 (Dyūtap.): II, **49**, 1782.—§ 298 (do.): II, **58**, 2014; **60**, 2052; **65**, 2181.—§ 299 (do.): II, **67**, 2237, (2243); **68**, 2263.—§ 301 (do.): II, **69**, (2353); **70**, 2378; **71**, 2379, †2402.—§ 305 (Anudyūtap.): II, **78**, 2583; **79**, 2609.—§ 307 (do.): II, **81**, 2677, 2696.—§ 308 (Āraṇyakap.): III, **1**, 12, 35.—§ 313 (do.): III, **6**, 316, 322.—§ 314 (do.): III, **9**, 324.—§ 315 (Maitreyaçāpa): III, **10**, 347, 360.—§ 317 (Arjunābhigam.): III, **12**, 525.—§ 318 (do.): III, **13**, 599.—§ 328 (Kāmyakavanaprav.): III, **36**, 1419, 1425.—§ 329 (do.): III, **36**, 1435.—§ 330 (Indradarçana): III, **37**, 1459*a*.—§ 333 (Kairātaparv.): III, **40**, 1645, 1648.—§ 334 (do.): III, **41**, 1683.—§ 339 (Indralokābhigam.): III, **47**, 1904.—§ 340 (do.): III, **48**, 1922.—§ 356 (Tīrthay.): III, **81**, 4032, 4038, 4040, 4041, 4042 (*Kurukulaçreshṭham*); **82**, 4045, (4046), 4070.—§ 357 (do.): III, **82**, 4070.—§ 375 (do.): III, **85**, 8254.—§ 376 (do.): III, **85**, 8256, 8259.—§ 377 (Dhaumyatīrthak.): III, **86**, 8283.—§ 401 (Balarāma): III, **119**, 10245.—§ 402 (Tīrthay.): III, **120**, 10274.—§ 446 (Nivātakav.): III, **174**, 12276.—§ 512 (Ghoshayātr.): III, **238**, 14810, 14811; **249**, 15084.—§ 513 (do.): III, **252**, 15165, 15191.—§ 515 (Karṇadigvijaya): III, **253**, 15209, 15211, 15218, 15220, 15221, 15223, 15225; **254**, 15261.—§ 516 (Duryodhanayajña): III, **256**, 15302, 15332.—§ 517 (do.): III, **257**, 15350.—§ 552 (Goharaṇap.): IV, **25**, 867; **28**, 912 (*Çāntanavaḥ, Bhāratānām pitāmahaḥ*), 915; **29**, 958; **35**, 1150*a*; **37**, 1224; **38**, 1240, 1243; **39**, 1286, 1302; **47**, 1471, 1476, 1488; **49**, 1550; **51**, (1583), 1599, 1600 (*Çāntanavaḥ*); **52**, (1606), (1622), 1626, 1627, (1628); **53**, 1643; **54**, †1684; **55**, 1734, 1755; **59**, 1908; **61**, 1951 (*etan mām prāpayānīkaṃ yatra tālo hiraṇmayaḥ | yatra Çāntanavo Bhīshmo rathe 'smākaṃ pitāmahaḥ . . .*) [1751 f., *yas tu nīlānusāreṇa pañcatāreṇa ketunā | . . . | yasya tārārkacitro 'san rathe dhvajavaraḥ sthitaḥ*], 1967, 1984; **64**, 2035 (*Çāntanavaḥ*), 2040, 2042, 2044, 2045, 2046, 2047, 2049, 2051, 2053, 2054, 2056 (*Çāntanavāt*), 2060 (used the Prājāpatya weapon, etc., against Arjuna), 2061, 2063 (his bow was laid with gold), 2064, 2065, 2066, 2068, 2069, 2078 (*Gāṅgeyam*), 2080, 2081 (*Çāntanavaḥ*), 2082; **65**, †2086; **66**, †2108 (*Çāntanavaḥ*), †2118, †2121, †2122, †2129; **68**, 2167 (*Çāntanavam*), 2201, 2203, 2233; **69**, 2244.—§ 554 (Sainyodyogap.): V, **2**, †31β; **3**, 52; **4**, 65; **6**, 118.—§ 556 (Sañjayayānap.): V, **20**, 603; **21**, 624, 631, (639), 641, 642; **22**, †668; **23**, †692δ; **25**, †733*o*, †737; **27**, †790; **29**, †845; **30**, †881ξ (*Kurusattamasya*); **31**, 923 (*Çāntanavam*).—§ 559 (Prajāgarap.): V, **37**, †1376.—§ 561 (Yānasandhip.): V, **47**, 1798*a*; **48**, †1848, †1916; **49**, 1917 (*Çāntanavaḥ*), 1951 (*Çāntanavaḥ*), 1961, 1962 (*Bharataçreshṭhaḥ*), 1965; **50**, 2001ζ, 2033ζ; **51**, 2056, 2062, 2067; **55**, 2149, 2159, 2162, 2164 (*Devavratam*), 2185λ, 2188, 2190μ, 2196, 2200, 2205ν; **57**, 2213 (*Çāntanavaḥ, bhāgaḥ klptaḥ Çikhaṇḍinaḥ*), 2275, 2281ρ, 2291σ; **58**, 2300τ, 2304υ; **59**, 2333, 2345 (*Kurumukhyasya*); **60**, 2368, 2375χ; **62**, 2417, 2424, †2428; **64**, 2478; **65**, 2492δδ (*Çāntanavam*).—§ 562 (Bhāgavadyānap.): V, **73**, 2681, 2693, 2702; **79**, 2841; **80**, 2859ζ; **82**, 2900; **83**, 2966ι, 2989; **85**, 3022κ, 3031, 3052; **88**, 3084 (*Kurupitāmahaḥ*), (3056), 3100; **89**, 3103λ, 3105, 3113, 3115μ; **91**, 3271σ; **92**, 3284τ, 3285; **94**, 3337, 3364, 3365, 3368, 3371 (*Çāntanavam*); **95**, 3402υ.—§ 565 (Bhagavadyānap.): V, **106**, 3717.—§ 567 (do.): V, **124**, 4125*a*, 4170δ; **125**, 4186 (*Çāntanavaḥ*), 4195 (do.), 4197, 4200; **126**, 4214; **127**, 4246; **128**, 4277, 4282, 4284*o*, 4287 (*Çāntanavaḥ*), 4291; **129**, 4329λ, 4330, 4346, 4350, 4358μ, 4360; **131**, 4431, 4453π, 4457ρ.—§ 569 (do.): **137**, 4669; **138**, 4676; **139**, (4706); **141**, 4803; **143**, 4875κ; **147**, 4971; **148**, 5002, 5003 (Devavrata), 5011, 5014, 5015, †5035; **150**, 5077, 5080, 5081, 5082, 5091.—§ 570 (Sainyaniryāṇap.): V, **151**, 5104, 5107, 5110, 5114, 5122, 5129; **154**, 5219, 5223, 5226; **156**, 5278, (5293), 5302 (*Gāṅgeya*), 5303, 5309; **157**, 5314 (*Āpageyaṃ pitāmahaṃ Bhāratānām*, etc.).—§ 571 (Ulūkadūt.): V, **160**, 5501, 5529; **161**, 5546, 5574; **162**, 5606; **163**, 5650; 5655, 5663, 5687; **164**, 5708ε.—§ 572 (Rathātirath.): V, **165**, 5714, 5716, 5718 (*Kuruvṛddhena*), 5719, (5730); **166**, (5748); **167**, (5770); **168**, (5808), 5817, 5826, 5829, 5831, 5834, 5835, 5836, (5837); **169**, (5850), 5877; **170**, (5879); **171**, (5893); **172**, (5921).—§ 573 (Ambop.): V, **173**, (5944), 5956; **174**, (5966), 5970, 5972; **175**, (5976), 5981, 5982, 5986, 5999, (6001), 6000, 6001, 6006, 6008 (*Çāntanavaḥ*), 6009, 6010; **176**, (6022), (6037), 6048, 6070, 6071, 6075, 6076, 6077, 6079; **177**, 6085, 6087, 6089, 6094, 6096, (6097), 7014, 7017, 7020, 7021, 7024; **178**, 7025, 7027, 7029, 7030, 7031, (7033), 7034, 7040, 7044, (7050), 7054, 7066, 7089, 7090, (7092), 7092, 7097, 7114, 7120, 7122; **179**, (7124), 7126; **180**, (7163), 7190; **181**, (7201); **182**, (7217); **183**, (7248), 7262, 7263; **184**, (7267); **185**, (7290), †7297, 7299, 7302, 7304, 7307, 7309, (7310), 7320, 7326; **186**, 7329, 7331, 7333, 7335, 7336, 7345, 7358, 7359, 7362; **187**, (7370), 7371, 7372, 7375, 7379, 7380, 7382, 7388; **188**, (7390), 7393; **189**, (7409); **190**, (7434), (7444); **191**, (7456); **192**, (7487), (7494), (7544), 7556, 7557; **193**, (7565), 7572, 7575 (*Çāntanavaḥ*); **194**, 7599.—§ 576 (Bhagavadgītāp.): VI, **13**, 496 (*Bhāratānām pitāmahaṃ*), 497 (do., *Çāntanavaḥ*), 499 (slain by Çikhaṇḍin); **14**, 508, 509, 524, 526, 529, 531, 532, 540, 541, 542, 547, 554, 555, 560, 564, 565, 568, 569 (*Çāntanunandanāt*), 576, 577, 580 (*Çāntanavāt*), 581, 583, 585; **15**, 599, 601, 603, 607; **16**, 629; **17**, 647, 648, 653γ, 658; **18**, 685; **19**, 696, 713; **20**, †741, †749ζ, 756, 757 (*Çāntanavaḥ*), 758; **21**, 761, 763, 767; **22**, 767,

†791 (*Kuruvaṃçaketuḥ*); **25**, 838ι, 839, 855; **26**, 882; **35**, †1272, †1280.—§ 577 (Bhīshmavadhap.): VI, **43**, 1549β, 1553, 1559, 1562, 1563 (*Çāntanavaṃ*), (1565), (1571), (1574), (1576), 1577, 1618, 1619.—§ 578 (do.): VI, **44**, 1639, 1640; **45**[1], 1680; **46**, 1805, 1807b (*ketunā pañcatāreṇa tālena*); **47**[25], 1809, 1811, 1813, 1814[26], 1815, 1822, 1824, 1828, 1829, 1830, 1831, 1834, 1838[27], 1840, 1841 (*Çāntanavaṃ*), 1863[31]; **48**, 1869 (*Çāntanavaḥ*), 1872, 1891, 1897 (*Çāntanavaṃ*), 1898, 1901, 1904 (*pitā Devavratas tava*), 1905, 1907, 1908, 1912, 1914[33], 1916, 1919, 1920, 1921, 1922, 1923, 1924 (*Çāntanavaḥ*), 1929, 1930, 1931, 1935, 1941, 1943, (*Çāntanavaṃ*), 1944, 1949, 1952, 1953, 1955, 1958[35], 1959, 1965[36], 1978, 1981; **49**, 1992, 1997, 2009[37], 2015[38], 2017[39], 2021[40], 2022[41], 2025, 2026, 2029 (*Çāntanavaḥ*), 2032; **50**, 2033, 2035, 2036, 2040, 2041, 2042, 2047, 2052, 2053, 2054, 2055, 2063 (*Çikhaṇḍī . . . Bhīshmasyāntakaraḥ*), 2070o; **51**, 2096, 2099, 2100, 2101, 2103.—§ 579 (do.): VI, **52**, 2127[1], 2132, 2133, 2135, 2137, 2142, 2143, 2147, 2151[2], 2154, 2161[3], 2164, 2165 (*Çāntanavaḥ*), 2166, 2168, 2169, 2170, 2171, 2179, 2186, 2188; **53**, 2195 (*Çāntanavaḥ*), 2196; **54**, 2300, 2325[13], 2340[14], 2341 (*Gāṅgeyaṃ*), 2349; **55**, 2376[19], 2400.—§ 580 (do.): VI, **56**, 2402[1] (*Çāntanavaḥ*); **57**, 2452ι, 2459; **58**, 2472[5], 2483[7], 2484, 2489[9], 2494 (*Çāntanavaṃ*), 2502, 2506; **59**, 2508[10], 2509, 2527 (*Çāntanavaḥ*), 2531, 2533, 2536, 2539, 2541, 2543, 2551, 2553, 2555, 2556, 2557, 2560, 2561, 2568, 2569, 2570, 2572, 2576, 2578 (*Pitāmahaṃ*), 2580, †2588[11], †2591, †2593, †2594, †2597, †2598, †2608, †2612, †2620ν[12], †2643o, †2649ρ.—§ 581 (do.): VI, **60**, †2651[1], †2670b [†2671 (*pañcatāloochṛtapañcaketuḥ*)], †2675, †2677, †2678, †2679; **63**, 2803[8]; **64**, 2872, 2879, 2883 (*Çāntanavaḥ*); **65**, 2901, 2910, 2922, (2932); **66**, (2973), (2996); **67**, (3015); **68**, (3037), 3049.—§ 582 (do.): VI, **69**, 3059, 3068[1], 3069, 3070[2], 3074[3] (*Pitāmahaṃ*), 3080[5]β, 3082[6], 3085[7], 3087[8], 3088; **70**, 3090 (*Çāntanavaḥ*), 3110, 3117[9], 3118; **71**, 3119, 3128 (*Çāntanavaḥ*), 3137; **72**, 3162, 3182, 3183, 3185, 3187, 3189, 3192 (*Çāntanavaḥ*), 3193, 3194 (*Çāntanavaṃ*), 3195; **73**, 3197, 3238; **74**, 3268.—§ 583 (do.): VI, **75**, 3304θ, 3309[2]; **76**, 3329ι; **77**, 3345[3]; **78**, 3441; **79**, 3509 (*Çāntanavaḥ*).—§ 584 (do.): VI, **81**, 3542, 3546, 3551, 3575 (*Çāntanavaṃ*); **82**, 3581, 3584 (*Çāntanavaḥ*), 3588 (*Çāntanavaṃ*); **84**, 3738, 3744; **85**, †3758, †3761[7], †3764 (*Çāntanavaṃ*), †3770, †3772, †3774, †3775, †3776, †3777, †3780; **86**, 3792 (*Çāntanavaḥ*), 3794 (do.), 3795, 3797, 3798 (*Çāntanavaḥ*), 3800, 3801, 3803, 3804, 3805 (*Çāntanavaṃ*), 3811, 3816, 3817, 3830[13], 3838 (*Çāntanavaṃ*).—§ 585 (do.): VI, **87**, 3849a, 3851 (*pitā tava*, i.e. Dhṛtarāshṭra's), 3852 (*Çāntanavaḥ*), 3884 (*Çāntanavaḥ*); **88**, 3887, 3889, 3890, 3891 (*Çāntanavaḥ*), 3893, 3895, 3897, 3898, 3922; **89**, 3931, 3933λ, 3936μ, 3942, 3945, 3946, 3947, 3948, 3969 (*Çāntanave*)π; **90**, 4052, 4055, 4057; **92**, 4113 (*Çāntanavaḥ*); **95**, 4234 (*Kurupitāmaham*), 4240 (*Çāntanavaḥ*), 4252; **96**, 4337, 4339 (*Çāntanavaḥ*); **97**, 4407κκ, 4411 (*Çāntanavaḥ*), 4413, 4414, 4415, 4416, 4420, 4421, 4426, 4437, 4439, 4447; **98**, 4474, 4478, 4480, 4492, 4496, 4497, 4498.—§ 586 (do.): VI, **99**, 4500 (*Çāntanavaḥ*), 4502a, 4514, 4515; **100**, 4555; **101**, 4590, 4614 (*Çāntanavaḥ*), 4620, 4622; **102**, 4669; **103**, 4682, 4685, 4687, 4690, 4693, 4696, 4724ξ; **104**, 4737, 4740, 4741, 4765; **105**, 4767, 4768, 4770 (*asmākaṃ pitāmahaḥ*), 4771, 4773; **106**, 4809, 4813, 4818, 4821, 4828, 4836, 4837, 4841 (*Kurupitāmahaṃ*), 4842, 4843, 4846, 4847, 4850, 4852, 4853, 4855, 4857, 4859, 4860, 4861, 4863, 4876 (*Çāntanavaḥ*), 4880, 4881, †4884; **107**, 4887, 4888, 4892, 4893, 4898, 4900, 4902, 4903, 4904, 4905, 4912, 4914, 4915, 4923, 4924, 4925 (*Çāntanavaḥ*), 4928, 4930, 4933, 4938 (*Devavrataḥ*), 4942, 4943, 4944 (*Kurupitāmahaḥ*), (4961), 4975 (*Kurupitāmahaṃ*), 4982, 4985, 4986, 4989, 4991.—§ 587 (do.): VI, **108**, 4994, 5004b, 5009 (*Çāntanavaḥ*; every day *Bh.* formed arrays in battle, sometimes after the manner of the Asuras, sometimes after that of the Piçācas, and sometimes after that of the Rākshasas), 5011, 5017, 5021, 5027, 5034, 5037, 5042, 5043, 5045, 5046, 5047; **109**, 5057 (*Çāntanavaḥ*), 5058, 5059, 5062, 5065, 5069, 5086, 5089, 5091; **110**, 5094, 5095, 5097, 5101, 5102, 5104, 5105, 5106, 5107, 5109, 5111, 5112, 5113, 5114, 5115, 5118, 5136, 5137; **111**, 5140, 5157, 5160, 5162, 5166, 5171, 5172, 5174, 5175, 5176, 5179, 5182, 5187, 5188, 5189, 5192, 5193, 5196; **112**, 5201, 5213, 5214, 5215, 5218, 5238; **113**, 5242, 5285; **114**, 5325λ, 5326, 5328, 5330, 5331, 5333, 5334; **115**, 5335, 5336, 5339, 5340, 5341, 5342 (*Çāntanavaḥ*), 5343, 5350, 5351, 5352, 5354, 5356, 5358, 5360 (*Çāntanavaṃ*), 5376; **116**, 5378, 5383, 5405, 5406, 5410, 5416, 5427, 5431, 5433, 5438, 5442, 5447, 5449, 5450; **117**, 5452, 5456, 5457, 5461, 5471, 5476, 5478, 5479, 5480, 5512, 5513; **118**, 5522, 5527, 5536 (*vṛddhaḥ Kurupitāmahaḥ*), 5537, 5541 (slays Çatānīka), 5543, 5547, 5548 (*Çāntanavaḥ*), 5550, 5551, 5555, 5557, 5558, 5560, 5561, 5564, 5567 (*Bhāgīrathīputraṃ*), 5568; **119**, 5572, 5573, 5579, 5580, 5581, 5582, 5590, 5593, 5596, 5598, 5602, 5603, 5606, 5607, 5608, 5609 (*Çāntanavaḥ*), 5611 (*Kurupitāmahaḥ*), 5614, 5615, 5617, 5621 (*Çāntanavaḥ*), 5625, 5634 (*Çāntanavaḥ*), 5641, 5642, 5645, 5650, 5652, 5655, 5656, 5663 (*Kurupitāmahaḥ*), 5665 (do.), 5666, 5669, 5676 (*Kurūṇāṃ çṛṅge*), 5680 (*Çāntanoḥ putre*), 5686; **120**, 5689, 5690, 5692, 5693, 5696 (*Kurupitāmahaḥ*), 5697, 5699 (*Çāntanavaṃ*), 5701 (do.), 5704 (do.), 5710 (*Kauravāṇāṃ pitāmahaḥ*), 5711, 5714, 5718, 5719, 5721 (*Çāntanavaḥ*), 5735, 5750, 5753, 5755, 5756.—§ 588 (do.): VI, **121**, 5769, 5771, 5778, 5785, 5787 (*Kurūṇāṃ ṛshabhaṃ*), †5812; **122**, 5818 (*Çāntanunandane*), 5819, 5840, (5851).—§ 589 (*Droṇābhishekap.*): VII, **1**, 4, 9, 10, 15, 17, 18, 35, 40, 42, 50 (*Kauravāṇāṃ upāçraye*); **2**, †52, †54, †55, †71, †81, †83; **3**, 90 (*Pitāmahaṃ*), 94, 96 (*Bhāratānāṃ pitāmahaṃ*); **5**, 138; **7**, 187, 190; **11**, 425, 427, 428, 430.—§ 592 (Saṃçaptakav.): VII, **23**, 1017 (*Bh°ād avāpya çāstrāṇi*, i.e. Pāṇḍya); **24**, 1056.—§ 598 (Jayadrathavadhap.): VII, **85**, 3036β, 3042γ, 3054; **86**, 3074.—§ 599 (do.): VII, **98**, 3649ι; **110**, 4228; **122**, 4884; **128**, 5270; **131**, 5360; **147**, 6387; **149**, 6479; **150**, 6505 (*mama pitāmahaṃ*, i.e. Duryodhana's); **151**, 6535, (*yac Chikhaṇḍy avadhīd Bh°aṃ*), 6556, 6559.—§ 600 (Ghaṭotkacav.): VII, **158**, 7035ω.—§ 603 (Nārāyaṇāstramokshap.): VII, **196**, 9074; **198**, 9142, 9144 (°*āntakaraḥ . . . Çikhaṇḍī*), 9168 (*Kurupitāmahaḥ*); **199**, 9223χ.—§ 604 (Karṇap.): VIII, **2**, 32γ, 40; **5**, 95; **6**, 153, 186; **7**, 191; **9**, 262, 273, 287 (*Bh° am apratiyudhyantaṃ Çikhaṇḍī sāyakottamaiḥ | pātayām āsa samare*), 294, 310, 341.—§ 605 (do.): VIII, **10**, 362κ, 367, 369, 381; **11**, 411; **20**, 772γγ, 774; **26**, 1057 (*Çikhaṇḍinaṃ Bh°mṛtyuṃ*); **32**, 1332σσ, 1333.—§ 607 (do.): VIII, **36**, 1686a, 1687; **37**, †1715, †1719, †1736, †1745 (*sa-Bhīshmakāḥ*); **41**, 1947ε, 1953; **45**, 2113o.—§ 608 (do.): VIII, **56**, 2745oo; **61**, 3082 (*Çikhaṇḍī . . . Bhīshmahantā*); **66**, 3330ιι; **69**, 3432ννν; **72**, 3612υυυ; **73**, 3644, 3646 (*Çāntanavaṃ*), 3662, 3666, 3673 (slain by Çikhaṇḍin), 3685, 3722, 3734, 3735; **79**, 4035; **87**, 4455; **88**, 4510; **96**, 5013.—§ 609 (Çalyap.): IX, **2**, 75 (*Pitāmaha*), 86 (*lokanātha*), 111, 113.—§ 610 (do.): IX, **4**μ, 197, 224; **6**π, 315; **7**, 340, 349,

360.—§ 611 (do.): IX, **8**, 380, 383, 402θ; **16**, 811σ; **19**, 1001γγ, 1023; **24**νν, 1291, 1292, 1293; **27**ττ, 1456.—§ 612 (Hradapraveçap.): IX, **29**β, 1646.—§ 613 (Gadāyuddhap.): IX, **32**β, 1836.—§ 615*b* (Baladevatīrthay.): IX, **54**ν, 3060.—§ 615 (Gadāyuddhap.): IX, **58**, 3256; **61**φ, 3424, 3428, 3447χ, 3450; **63**ββ, 3548; **64**εε, 3588 (*Çāntanave*), 3593.—§ 616 (Sauptikap.): X, **3**, 137; **5**ε, 196 (*Çāntanavaḥ*).—§ 617 (Aishīkap.): X, **10**β, 563.—§ 618 (Jalapradānikap.): XI, **1**β, 16γ, 29 (*Kuruvṛddhasya*); **12**λ, 320 (*Pitāmahaṃ*); **13**μ, 346.—§ 619 (Strīvilāpap.): XI, **16**, 447**a**, 454; **23**θ, 648 (*bhīshmakṛd āhave*), 656 (*Çāntanavaḥ*); **25**κ, 735.—§ 621 (Rājadh.): XII, **4**, 120; **5**ζ, 140.—§ 623 (do.): XII, **16**γ, 503.—§ 635 (do.): XII, **37**, 1349 (*Kurupitāmahaṃ*) (Vyāsa directs Yudhishṭhira to consult Bhīshma).—§ 637 (do.): XII, **46**ζ, 1563, 1573 (*Gāṅgeyaṃ*), 1575 (*Kauravāṇāṃ dhurandhare*), 1577, 1578, 1580; **47**, 1589 (asked by Janamejaya, Vaiçampāyana related how Bhīshma cast off his body), 1591, 1600, 1603θ, (1604), 1689, 1690, 1691, 1692, 1693.—§ 639 (do.): XII, **50**, 1811, 1817γ, 1823, 1826 (*Çāntanavāt*), 1831, 1836; **51**, 1844δ, (1845), 1856, 1857, 1860; **52**, 1862 (*Çāntanavaḥ*), 1876, 1879, 1882, 1888; **53**, 1905, 1911, 1920.—§ 640 (do.): XII, **54**, 1926 (*Çāntanunandane Gāṅgeye*), 1928 (*Kauravāṇāṃ dhurandhare*), 1932 (*Gāṅgeyaḥ*), 1935, (1941), 1951, 1953, 1955; **55**, (1978), 1984, 1985; **56**, (1996); **57**, (2047); **58**, (2092), 2117, 2118.—§ 641 (do.): XII, **59**, 2123, 2124, 2125, (2134); **60**, (2273); **61**, (2324); **62**, (2346); **63**, (2356); **64**, (2386); **65**, (2448); **66**, (2453); **67**, (2496), (2518); **68**, (2536); **69**, (2598), (2670); **70**, (2702); **71**, (2716); **72**, (2749); **73**, (2775); **74**, (2808), (2827); **75**, (2832), (2849), (2865); **76**, (2870); **77**, (2884), (2914); **78**, (2918), (2920), (2930), (2936), (2955); **79**, (2963), (2971); **80**, (2985); **81**, (3025); **82**, (3055); **83**, (3120), **84**, (3183), (3193); **85**, (3195), (3198); **86**, (3229); **87**, (3262); **88**, (3303); **89**, (3335), (3356); **90**, (3362); **91**, (3461); **92**, (3464); **94**, (3534); **95**, (3536), (3541); **96**, (3557); **97**, (3583); **98**, (3614), (3663); **99**, (3664); **100**, (3683); **101**, (3734); **102**, (3754); **103**, (3795), (3846); **104**, (3848); **107**, (3986); **108**, (3991); **109**, (4026); **110**, (4054); **111**, (4084), (4130); **112**, (4174); **113**, (4197), (4207); **114**, (4211); **115**, (4243); **116**, (4254); **117**, (4279); **118**, (4303); **119**, (4331); **120**, (4353); **121**, (4416); **122**, (4409), (4523); **123**, (4527); **124**, (4552), (4613), (4621); **125**, (4629); **126**, (4641); **127**, (4660); **128**, (4713); **129**, (4718); **130**, (4732).—§ 642 (Āpaddharm.): XII, **131**, (4782), (4788); **132**, (4795); **133**, (4815); **134**, (4835).—§ 643 (do.): XII, **135**, (4852), (4874).—§ 644 (do.): XII, **136**, (4878).—§ 645 (do.): XII, **137**, (4889).—§ 646 (do.): XII, **138**, 4923 (*Çāntanavāt*), (4924), (4994). § 647 (do.): XII, **139**, (5136), (5245).—§ 648 (do.): XII, **140**, (5248).—§ 649 (do.): XII, **141**, (5327), (5410). § 650 (do.): XII, **142**, (5423), (5456).—§ 651 (do.): XII, **143**, (5460), (5464); **144**, (5493); **145**, (5510); **146**, (5524); **147**, (5550); **148**, (5561); **149**, (5574).—§ 652 (do.): XII, **150**, (5595); **151**, (5613); **152**, (5673).—§ 653 (do.): XII, **153**, (5676), (5771), (5784).—§ 654 (do.): XII, **154**, (5804); **156**, (5841), (5845), (5850); **157**, (5861), (5867).—§ 655 (do.): XII, **158**, (5878); **159**, (5913), (5917); **160**, (5930), 5962, 5963; **161**, (5964); **162**, (5979); **163**, (6005); **164**, (6029); **165**, (6039).—§ 656 (do.): XII, **166**, 6128, (6129).—§ 657 (do.): XII, **167**, 6210.—§ 658 (do.): XII, **168**, (6268), (6293); **169**, (6317); **170**, (6342), (6344); **171**, (6368), (6373); **172**, (6403); **173**, (6430), 6456.—§ 659 (Mokshadh.): XII, **174**, (6458), (6463), (6521); **175**, (6523), (6561); **176**, (6563); **177**, (6587); **178**, (6640), (6647); **179**, (6654), (6661), (6689); **180**, (6691); **181**, (6746).—§ 660 (do.): XII, **182**, (6769); **192**, (7030).—§ 661 (do.): XII, **193**, (7033); **194**, (7068); **195**, (7129); **196**, (7156); **197**, (7175), (7186); **198**, (7188).—§ 662 (do.): XII, **199**, (7199), (7215), (7227), (7232), (7285), (7319); **200**, (7332), (7362).—§ 663 (do.): XII, **201**, (7366).—§ 664 (do.): XII, **207**, (7520).—§ 665 (do.): XII, **208**, (7568).—§ 666 (do.): XII, **209**, (7607).—§ 667 (do.): XII, **210**, (7642); **211**, (7689); **212**, (7707), (7734); **213**, (7742); **214**, (7764); **215**, (7793); **216**, (7821); **217**, (7842).—§ 668 (do.): XII, **218**, (7882); **219**, (7930), (7934).—§ 669 (do.): XII, **220**, (7985); **221**, (8005), (8007), (8013).—§ 670 (do.): XII, **222**, (8023).—§ 671 (do.): XII, **223**, (8059), (8069); **224**, (8088); **225**, (8148), (8185).—§ 672 (do.): XII, **226**, (8187).—§ 673 (do.): XII, **227**, (8214).—§ 674 (do.): XII, **229**, (8334).—§ 675 (do.): XII, **230**, (8430), (8434).—§ 676 (do.): XII, **231**, (8455).—§ 677 (do.): XII, **232**, (8483), (8487); **240**, (8734); **242**, (8806); **243**, (8835); **245**, (8884); **256**, (9131), (9142).—§ 678 (do.): XII, **257**, (9150); **260**, (9231).—§ 680 (do.): XII, **262**, (9277), (9289); **263**, (9339), (9342); **264**, (9441); **265**, (9446), (9462).—§ 681 (do.): XII, **266**, (9467), (9480).—§ 682 (do.): XII, **267**, (9482).—§ 683 (do.): XII, **268**, (9560).—§ 684 (do.): XII, **269**, (9598).—§ 685 (do.): XII, **272**, (9756), (9782), (9787), (9801), (9804).—§ 686 (do.): XII, **273**, (9812).—§ 687 (do.): XII, **274**, (9832); **275**, (9856).—§ 688 (do.): XII, **276**, (9874).—§ 689 (do.): XII, **277**, (9916).—§ 690 (do.): XII, **278**, (9929), (9966).—§ 691 (do.): XII, **279**, (9968).—§ 692 (do.): XII, **280**, (9995); **281**, (10085), (10087), (10096).—§ 693 (do.): XII, **282**, (10104), (10124), (10138); **283**, (10143), (10170), (10184), (10189).—§ 694 (do.): XII, **284**, (10211), (10238).—§ 696 (do.): XII, **285**, (10347).—§ 697 (do.): XII, **286**, (10486).—§ 698 (do.): XII, **287**, (10533).—§ 699 (do.): XII, **288**, (10554).—§ 700 (do.): XII, **289**, (10613), (10615).—§ 701 (do.): XII, **290**, (10664), (10680).—§ 702 (do.): XII, **291**, (10699); **298**, (10941); **299**, (10942), (10991).—§ 703 (do.): XII, **300**, (10993), (11036).—§ 704 (do.): XII, **301**, (11038), (11047), (11079); **302**, (11100), (11151), (11181).—§ 705 (do.): XII, **303**, (11220); **309**, (11508).—§ 706 (do.): XII, **310**, (11518), (11542).—§ 707 (do.): XII, **311**, (11545); **319**, (11818).—§ 708 (do.): XII, **320**, (11839). § 709 (do.): XII, **321**, (11854), (11928), (12043).—§ 710 (do.): XII, **322**, (12046), (12137).—§ 711 (do.): XII, **323**, (12139).—§ 712 (do.): XII, **324**, (12163); **325**, (12187).—§ 713 (do.): XII, **326**, (12215); **327**, (12260).—§ 714 (do.): XII, **328**, (12312); **329**, (12365), (12386).—§ 715 (do.): XII, **330**, (12422).—§ 716 (do.): XII, **333**, (12577); **331**, (12608).—§ 717 (do.): XII, **335**, (12654); **336**, †(12696), (12711); **337**, (12752), (12768); **338**, (12819), (12823), (12831), (12859); **339**, (12861); **340**, (12865), (12882), (12974), (12980), (13002); **347**, 13443 (*çṛṇvatoḥ Kṛshṇa-Bhīshmayoḥ*); **349**, 13557 (do.), 13611 (do.).—§ 718 (do.): XII, **353**, (13765); **354**, (13775); **357**, (13818); **358**, (13822); **359**, (13835); **360**, (13848); **362**, (13884); **366**, (13935).—§ 719 (Ānuçāsanik.): XIII, **1**, (15), (33), (49), (61), (69), (80).—§ 720 (do.): XIII, **2**, (87), (173).—§ 721 (do.): XIII, **4**, (200), (212).—§ 722 (do.): XIII, **5**, (264), (282).—§ 723 (do.): XIII, **6**, (296).—§ 724 (do.): XIII, **7**, (345), 371; **8**, (376).—§ 725 (do.): XIII, **9**, (405), (417), (420).—§ 726 (do.): XIII, **10**, (435), (450), (480),

(494).—§ 727 (do.): XIII, **11**, (508).—§ 728 (do.): XIII, **12**, (529), (575).—§ 729 (do.): XIII, **13**, (583).—§ 730 (do.): XIII, **14**, (590), 605 (*Pitāmahaḥ*), (606).—§ 731 (do.): XIII, **19**, (1390), (1407), (1476); **20**, (1485), (1497); **21**, (1513), (1523), (1529).—§ 732 (do.): XIII, **22**, (1532), (1534), (1536), (1539), (1545), (1547), (1549), (1555), (1557), (1563); **23**, (1573), (1621); **24**, (1677).—§ 733 (do.): XIII, **25**, (1690).—§ 734 (do.): XIII, **26**, 1766, 1768 (*Bh° āçritāḥ . . . kathāḥ*), 1769, 1774, 1775, (1777), †(1860), 1863.—§ 735 (do.): XIII, **27**, (1870), (1892); **28**, (1896); **29**, (1913).—§ 736 (do.): XIII, **30**, (1944).—§ 737 (do.): XIII, **31**, (2009).—§ 738 (do.): XIII, **32**, (2046), (2060).—§ 739 (do.): XIII, **33**, (2084); **34**, (2110), (2140); **35**, (2142).—§ 740 (do.): XIII, **36**, (2165), (2183).—§ 741 (do.): XIII, **37**, (2185), (2189).—§ 742 (do.): XIII, **38**, (2203), (2206), (2208).—§ 743 (do.): XIII, **40**, (2247), (2271), (2274); **41**, (2307), (2334); **42**, (2344); **43**, (2377).—§ 744 (do.): XIII, **44**, (2406), (2424), (2434); **45**, (2462), (2471); **46**, (2484); **47**, (2505), (2529), (2547); **48**, (2564), (2602); **49**, (2615), (2619), (2625), (2627), (2632), (2635).—§ 745 (do.): XIII, **50**, (2642); **51**, (2668), (2681), (2688), (2707); **52**, (2722), (2728); **53**, (2756), (2803); **54**, (2825); **56**, (2919).—§ 746 (do.): XIII, **57**, (2931); **58**, (2971); **59**, 3005; **60**, (3045); **61**, (3067); **62**, (3104), (3156); **63**, (3203), (3242); **64**, (3253), (3288); **65**, (3289); **66**, (3310), (3314); **67**, (3377); **68**, (3396), (3418); **69**, (3433), (3444); **70**, (3452); **71**, (3486); **72**, (3546); **74**, (3616); **75**, (3629); **76**, (3666), †3693; **77**, (3699), (3705); **78**, (3732), (3735); **80**, (3801); **81**, (3803); **82**, (3852); **83**, (3879), (3924).—§ 747 (do.): XIII, **84**, (3940); **85**, (4183).—§ 748 (do.): XIII, **86**, (4190).—§ 749 (do.): XIII, **87**, 4222 (*Çāntanavaḥ*), (4223); **88**, (4241); **89**, (4255); **90**, (4271); **91**, (4328); **92**, (4372).—§ 750 (do.): XIII, **93**, (4397), (4399), (4405), (4414), (4449), (4458), (4468), (4481), (4541).—§ 751 (do.): XIII, **94**, (4547), (4588).—§ 752 (do.): XIII, **95**, (4604), (4619); **96**, (4630), (4636), (4641), (4644).—§ 753 (do.): XIII, **97**, (4652), (4675).—§ 754 (do.): XIII, **98**, (4678).—§ 755 (do.): XIII, **99**, (4745); **100**, (4773).—§ 756 (do.): XIII, **101**, (4814), (4841).—§ 757 (do.): XIII, **102**, (4844).—§ 758 (do.): XIII, **103**, (4908), (4950).—§ 759 (do.): XIII, **104**, (4957); **105**, (5114); **106**, 5139 (*Çāntanavaḥ*), (5140); **107**, (5209); **108**, (5350); **109**, (5371); **110**, 5387 (*Kurupitāmahaṃ*), (5389).—§ 760 (do.): XIII, **111**, (5400).—§ 761 (do.): XIII, **114**, (5578); **115**, (5600); **116**, (5686).—§ 762 (do.): XIII, **117**, (5726), (5737); **119**, (5777), (5787), (5789).—§ 763 (do.): XIII, **120**, (5794); **121**, (5821); **122**, (5838).—§ 764 (do.): XIII, **123**, (5859), (5878).—§ 765 (do.): XIII, **124**, (5881).—§ 766 (do.): XIII, **125**, (5922); **126**, (6005), (6015), (6046); **130**, (6102); **131**, (6141); **132**, (6155); **134**, (6196).—§ 767 (do.): XIII, **135**, (6200); **136**, (6222); **137**, (6246); **138**, (6280).—§ 768 (do.): XIII, **139**, 6294 (*Bhāgīrathīputraḥ*), (6295); **140**, (6338), (6388); **146**, (6778), (6804); **148**, (6887), 6934 (*°anuçāsanaṃ*).—§ 769 (do.): XIII, **149**, (6939).—§ 770 (do.): XIII, **151**, (7082).—§ 771 (do.): XIII, **152**, (7163).—§ 772 (do.): XIII, **153**, (7186); **156**, (7265), (7269); **157**, (7291); **158**, (7326).—§ 773 (do.): XIII, **159**, (7356); **160**, 7457.—§ 774 (do.): XIII, **163**, 7532 (*Çāntanavaṃ*), (7534), (7543), (7551), (7560), (7566); **164**, (7608); **165**, (7612).—§ 775 (do.): XIII, **166**, 7627, (7630).—§ 776 (do.): XIII, **167**, 7689 (*Kauravāṇāṃ dhurandhare*).—§ 777 (Svargārohaṇikap.): XIII, **168**, 7713 (*°saṃskaraṇāya*), 7716 (*°syāgnīn*), 7730, (7735), (7742), 7752; **169**, 7759 (*Çāntanavaḥ*), 7766, 7773 (*Kurukulodvahaṃ*), 7792 (*Kuruçārdūlaṃ*).—§ 778 (Açvamedhikap.): XIV, **2**, 24 (*Bhāgīrathīsutāt*).—§ 779 (do.): XIV, **12**, 326 (*Droṇa° bhyāṃ*).—§ 780 (do.): XIV, **14**, 368, 369 (*°Karṇapurogānāṃ Kurūṇāṃ*).—§ 781 (do.): XIV, **15**, 393.—§ 784*b* (Utaṅka): XIV, **53**, 1552.—§ 785 (Anugītāp.): XIV, **60**, 1775α, 1780β (*Kauravyaḥ*); **61**, 1822γ; **63**, 1876; **81**, 2410, 2415 (*Çāntanavaḥ*).—§ 787 (Āçramavāsap.): XV, **3**, 79γ; **7**, 255; **8**, 259ι; **9**, 283λ; **10**, 320, 332ν; **11**, 366 (*°ādīnāṃ*), 371π, 378; **12**, 386 (*°ādīnāṃ*); **14**, 411, 414σ.—§ 789 (Putradarç.): XV, **29**, 797 (*Çāntanavaṃ*); **31**, 858η (*Bhīshmañ ca viddhi Gāṅgeyaṃ Vasuṃ mānushatāṃ gataṃ*); **32**, 874θ.—§ 795 (Svargārohaṇap.): XVIII, **4**, 145 (*Vasubhiḥ sahitaṃ Çāntanavaṃ*); **5**, 148λ, 158μ.

Compare also the following synonyms:—

Āpagāsuta ("son of the river"): I, 4480; VI, 5216.

Āpageya (do.), q.v.

Bhāgīrathīputra ("son of Gaṅgā"): XIII, 6294.

Bhāgīrathīsuta (do.): XIV, 24.

Bhārata, q.v.

Bharataçreshṭha ("the best of the Bh°"), q.v.

Bhāratānāṃ pitāmahaḥ ("the grandfather of the Bh°"), q.v.

Bharatarshabha (do.), q.v.

Bharatasattama (do.), q.v.

Bhīshmaka: V, 5981.

Çāntanava: I, †176, †184, 2261, 2420, 4077, 4080, 4108, 4115, 4118, 4122, 4254, 4425, 4911, 4960, 5660, 5662, 5707, 5860, 7489, 7518, 7535, 7567 (*rājñā?*), 8050 (*rājñaḥ?*); II, 1332, 1347, 1371, 2477; III, 1110 (*Pitāmahaḥ*); IV, 912 (*Bharatānām pitāmahaḥ*), 1176, 1238, 1600, 1734, 1755 (*sarveshāṃ naḥ pitāmahaḥ*, has a golden helm, etc.), 2035 (*Bhāratānāṃ pitāmahaḥ*), 2056, 2068, 2081, †2108, †2124, †2131 (*Pitāmahaṃ vṛddhaṃ*), 2167; V, 89 (*nṛpaḥ*), 642, †790, 923 (*Bhāratānāṃ pitāmahaṃ*), 1897 (*rājñe?*), 1916, 1951, 2213, 2428, 2492 (*vṛddhaṃ . . . Pitāmahaṃ*), 2501εε (*Pitāmahaṃ*), 3371, 3374, 4186, 4195, 4287, 4346, 4367 (*rājñā?*), 4824ε, 4828ζ, 4898 (*Pitāmahaḥ*), †5039, 5278, 5956, 6008, 6070, 7575, 7608ε; VI, 497 (*Bhāratānāṃ pitāmahaḥ*), 516, 524, 552, 568, 570, 572, 575, 580, 628, 654, 675 (*rājñā*), 757, 1563, 1677, 1838, 1841, 1869, 1874, 1897, 1916, 1917, 1924, 1929, 1943, 2029, 2142, 2165, 2195, 2339, 2402, 2403, 2494, 2527, †2585 (*rājñaḥ*), †2604, †2606, †2621, †2623, †2655 (*rājñā*), 2656, †2671, 2849, 2883, 3049, 3090, 3128, 3192, 3194, 3198, 3508, 3575, 3581, 3584, 3588, †3764, †3765, †3769, †3773 (*rājñā*), 3792, 3794, 3798, 3805, 3838, 3852, 3884, 3891, 3969π, 4113, 4240, 4339, 4411, 4476, 4500, 4614, 4876, 4925, 4940, 4954, 5009, 5057, 5092, 5335, 5342, 5360, 5368, 5533 (*pitā Ç°s tava*, i.e. Dhṛtarāshṭra's), 5548, 5609, 5621, 5634, 5670, 5688, 5699, 5701, 5704 (*Bhāratānāṃ pitāmaha*), 5721, 5730, 5764, 5765, 5774, 5776, 5790, †5799; VII, 23, †53, †59, †63, 144; VIII, 22, 93, 3640; IX, 1306, 3588; X, 196; XI, 649, 654, 656; XII, 1826, 1862, 2714, 4923; XIII, 3596, 3598, 4222, 5139, 6936, 7532, 7629, 7697, 7717, 7759, 7767; XIV, 2409, 2414, 2415; XV, 797; XVIII, 145.

Çāntanoḥ putraḥ ("the son of Ç°") = Bhīshma: VI, 5680; IX, 1294; XI, 740.

Çāntanoḥ sutaḥ (do.) = Bhīshma: V, 3707; VI, 2564, 4849, 5079.

Çāntanūja (do.) = Bhīshma: V, †1847.

Çāntanunandana (do.) = Bhīshma: I, 4085; VI, 569, 5818; XII, 1926.
Çāntanusuta (do.) = Bhīshma: XIII, 7761.
Devavrata, the original name of Bhīshma: I, 3800, 3965 (*Gāṅgeyaḥ*), 3987, 4024, 4039; V, 2164, 5003 (*Bh°*), 5020, 5037; VI, 580, 642 (*pitā D°s tava*, i.e. Dhṛtarāshṭra's), 1904 (do.), 1934 (do.), 1948 (do.), 1966 (do.), 1970 (do.), 1973 (do.), 2158 (do.), 2342 (do.), 2345 (do.), 2394 (do.), 2404 (do.), 2511 (do.), 3060 (do.), 3273 (do.), 3291 (do.), 3771, 3807 (*pitā D°s tava*, i.e. Dhṛtarāshṭra's), 3892 (do.), 3925 (do.), 4227, 4619 (*pitā D°s tava*, i.e. Dhṛtarāshṭra's), 4684 (do.), 4877 (do.), 4932, 4938 (*Bh°*), 5078 (*pitā D°s tava*, i.e. Dhṛ°s), 5346 (do.), 5459 (do.), 5694, 5768; VII, 2, 13, 14, 24, 31, 32, 351; XI, 659 (*gate . . . svargaṃ devakalpe*); XII, 1925 (*çaratalpagate 'cyute*).
Gaṅgāsuta = Bhīshma: VI, 3518, 3765, 5770.
Gāṅgeya = Bhīshma: I, 94, 3965 (*sa tu Devavrato nāma Gāṅgeya iti cābhavat Dyu-nāmā Çāntanoḥ putraḥ Çāntanor adhiko guṇaiḥ*), 3987 (*Devavrato Vasuḥ*), 4029, 4049, (4058), 4144, 4147, 4362, 4439, 5096, 5185, 5313; III, 165; IV, 1605, 2038, 2078 (*Bh°*), 2084; V, 2189 (*Pitāmahaḥ*), 4984, 5092, 5302, 5308, 5485, 5649, 5715 (*pitaraṃ*, i.e. Dhṛtarāshṭra's), 5717, 5725, 5820, 5836, 5846, 5943, 5988, 5990, 6073, 7256, 7306, 7307 (*Çāntanoḥ putro Vasuḥ*), 7374, 7559, 7562, 7594β; VI, 607 (*°aṃ*, so B.), 1678, 1679, 1911, 1925, 1936, 1969, 2150, 2156, 2158, 2162, 2168, 2173, 2189, 2341, 2344, 2481, 2532, 3119, 3126, 3531, 3565, 3578, †3763, 3796, 3888, 4252, 4358, 4412, 4430, 4441, 4477, 4487, 4488, 4489, 4490, 4491, 4683, 4692, 4695, 4763, 4921, 4946, 4976, 4983, 4990, 5055, 5071, 5085, 5093, 5096, 5098, 5103, 5116, 5119, 5161, 5308, 5332, 5428, 5453, 5474, 5475, 5532, 5533, 5591, 5612, 5619, 5636, 5638, 5661, 5662, 5685, 5824, 5856; VII, 18, 22, 38; VIII, 152; IX, 1934 (*Bharataçreshṭhaḥ sarveshāṃ naḥ pitāmahaḥ*), 3161, 3407; X, 533; XI, 653; XII, 183, 802, 1573 (*Bh°*), 1810, 1815, 1816, 1817, 1839, 1876, 1877, 1884 (*sa°*), 1891, 1912, 1923, 1926, 1930, 1932, 1986, 2123, 2268 (*Pitāmahaṃ*); XIII, 1759, 1771 (*Kurusattamaṃ*), 1942, 5402 (*Pārtha°yoḥ*), 5920, 6931, 6935, 7693, 7729, 7734, 7754, 7770, 7776, 7777 (*Kuruçreshṭhaṃ*), 7779; XIV, 1783; XV, 359, 858 (*Bh°*).
Jāhnavīputra ("son of Gaṅgā") = Bhīshma: VI, 5746.
Jāhnavīsuta (do.) = Bhīshma: V, 7015; VII, 21, 28.
Kaurava,
Kauravāṇāṃ dhurandharaḥ,
Kauravāṇāṃ pitāmahaḥ,
Kauravāṇām upaçrayaḥ, v. Kaurava.
Kauravādhama.
Kauravanandana.
Kauravya.
Kuruçārdūla.
Kuruçreshṭha.
Kurūdvaha.
Kurukulaçreshṭha.
Kurukulādhama.
Kurukulodvaha.
Kurumukhya.
Kurūṇām abhayaṃkaraḥ
Kurūṇāṃ çṛṅgaṃ } v. Kuru, pl.
Kurūṇām ṛshabhaḥ
Kurunandana.
Kurupati.
Kurupitāmaha.
Kurupravīra.
Kurupuṅgava.
Kururājarshisattama.
Kurusattama.
Kurūttama.
Kuruvaṃçaketu.
Kuruvaraçreshṭha.
Kuruvṛddha.
(Kuruvṛddhatama).
Mahāvrata ("who observes a great religious vow"): V, 5038, 7020 (*Bh°*), 7023, 7583 (*Āpageyaṃ*); VI, †2594, †3770; VII, †57, 95 (*pitaraṃ te*, i.e. Dhṛtarāshṭra's).
Nadīja ("son of the river"): IV, 1294; V, 78 (?), 5030.
Pitāmaha: I, 5790; III, 1110 (*Çāntanavaḥ*); IV, †2131 (do.); V, 2268π, 2492 (*Bh°*), 2501 (*Çāntanavaṃ*); VI, 1909, 1940, 1960, †2806, 4873, 5048, 5061, 5212, 5473, 5563; IX, 75 (*Bh°*), 278, 1789 [1934 (*Gāṅgeyo Bharataçreshṭhaḥ sarveshāṃ naḥ pitāmahaḥ*)], 2190 (*pitāmahasya mahato vartamāne mahāmakhe*), 2196, 2198, 2199, 2200, 3418; XI, 320; XII, 804, 1936, 1987, 1989, 1994, 2119, 2268 (*Gāṅgeyaṃ*), 2272, 2495, 2535, 2669, 2714, 2715, 2831, 2869, 2883, 2962, 2983, 3125, 3228, 3302, 3463, 3540, 3613, 3682, 3794, 4231, 4408 (?), 4622, 4623, 4624, 4717, 4794, 5135, 5247, 5325, etc.
Prapitāmaha: VI, 5538; XII, 6125.
Sāgaragāsuta ("son of the river"): I, 4128, 4111; VI, 4938.
***Satyasandha** ("true"): V, †5652, †5655 (*°aṃ*, so B.); VIII, †3506.
Tāladhvaja ("whose banner is the palmyra palm"): VI, 4742.
Vasu, q.v.

Bhīshma[2] = Çiva (1000 names).
Bhīshma[3] (pl.). § 267 (Yamas.): II, **8**, 335 (200 in the palace of Yama).
Bhīshmābhishecana ("the coronation of Bh°"). § 10 (Parvas.): I, **2**, 336 (*parva*).
Bhīshmahantṛ ("the slayer of Bh°") = Çikhaṇḍin: VIII, 3082.
Bhīshmaka[1] = Bhīshma, q.v.
Bhīshmaka[2]. § 132 (Aṃçāv.): I, **67**, 2790 (*Çriyas tu bhāgaḥ sañjajñe ratyarthaṃ pṛthivītale | Bhīshmakasya kule sādhvī Rukmiṇī nāma nāmataḥ*).—§ 264 (Sabhākriyāp.): II, **4**, 126*a*.—§ 273 (Rājasūyārambhap.): II, **14**[11], 586 (king of the Bhojas, the friend of Indra, etc., obeys Jarāsandha).—§ 281*c* (Sahadeva): II, **31**, 1116 (the combat between Sahadeva—on his Digvijaya—and Bh°, the king of the town of Bhojakaṭa, lasted for two days).—§ 284 (do.): II, **31***a*, 1167 (Sahadeva, *Surāshṭravishayasthaçca preshayām āsa Rukmiṇe | rājñe Bhojakaṭasthāya mahāmātrāya dhīmate | Bhīshmakāya sa dharmātmā sākshād Indra sakhāya vai, sa cāsya pratijagrāha sasutaḥ çāsanaṃ tadā*).—§ 289 (Arghāharaṇap.): II, **37**, 1350 (*durdharshe Pāṇḍuvat kṛtalakshaṇe*).—§ 290 (Çiçupālav.): II, **44**, 1537.—§ 570*c* (Sainyaniryāṇāp.): V, **158**, 5350 (Bhīshmaka or Hiraṇyaroman, the friend of Indra, was the most illustrious of the descendants of Bhoja, and he was the ruler of the whole southern country; his son was Rukmin).—§ 570 (Sainyan.): V, **158**, 5388 (*Bhīshmakasya sute* = Rukmin).—§ 621 (Rājadharm.): XII, **4**, 113ε (present at the svayaṃvara of the daughter of the Kaliṅga king Citrāṅgada at Rājapura).
Bhīshmakātmajā = Rukmiṇī: V, 575.

Bhīshmanihantṛ ("the slayer of Bhīshma") = Çikhaṇḍin: X, 381 (slain by Açvatthāman).

Bhīshmaparvan ("the section treating of Bh°"). § 4 (Anukram.): I, **1,** 89 (°*mahāçākho . . . Bhāratadrumaḥ*).—§ 11 (Parvas.): I, **2,** 519 (*vicitrārtham*), 528 (contains 5884 çlokas—in reality only 5856).—§ 795*c* (Mahābhārata): VIII, **6,** 271 (donations to be given to the brahmans when reciting Bh°).

Bhīshma-Satyavatī-saṃvāda(ḥ) ("conversation of Bh° and S."). § 168 (cf. Vicitravīryoparama): *Satyavatī* in vain asked *Bhīshma* to ascend the throne and marry the widows of *Vicitravīrya*, in order to propagate the race (I, 103). *Bhīshma* adduced the examples of *Paraçu-Rāma* (§ 169) and of *Dīrghatamas* (§ 170).—§ 171: "Thus many kshattriyas have sprung from the seed of brahmans." Vyāsa raised offspring in the widows of *Vicitravīrya* (v. Vicitravīrya-sutotpatti, § 171).

Bhīshmasya Svargārohaṇika(ṃ) parva(n). § 10 (Parvas.): I, **2,** 353.

Bhīshmavadha ("the slaying of Bh°"). § 10 (Parvas.): I, **2,** 338 (°*aḥ parva,* i.e. Bhīshmavadhaparvan).

[Bhīshmavadhaparvan] ("the section relating to the slaying of Bhīshma," the 70th of the minor parvans of Mhbhr.; cf. Bhīshmavadha). § 577: Beholding *Arjuna* again taking up the *Gāṇḍīva,* the *Pāṇḍavas* and *Somakas* were filled with joy and blew their conches, etc. D., G., P., Si., Cā., and Ṛ. came with *Indra* in order to behold the fight. Putting off his coat of mail, etc., *Yudhishṭhira,* followed by his brothers (*a*) (who did not know his intentions) and *Kṛshṇa,* proceeded on foot, with joined hands, to *Bhīshma,* etc. (*β*), one after another, and asked their permission to fight. He also inquired about the means of vanquishing *Bhīshma* and *Droṇa,* and as they said that they were invincible he asked them to indicate the means of killing them. They gave the permission, said they would pray for his victory, though they were bound by the wealth of the *Kurus* to fight for them. *Bhīshma* said that his time of death had not yet come, he must come to see him once more. *Droṇa* said that if he did not give himself up to death and drop his weapons nobody would be able to slay him; he would drop his arms if he heard something very disagreeable from someone whose speech was trustworthy. *Kṛpa* said he was incapable of being slain. *Çalya* renewed his promise to weaken the energy of *Karṇa.* When the *Kauravas* saw *Yudhishṭhira,* they contemned him, believing that he had come in terror. *Kṛshṇa* endeavoured to bring *Karṇa* over to the *Pāṇḍavas,* as long as *Bhīshma* was not slain, but in vain. *Yudhishṭhira* exclaimed, "He who chooses us, him we will choose for our ally"; *Yuyutsu* went over to the *Pāṇḍavas,* and *Yudhishṭhira* said that the propagation of *Dhṛtarāshṭra's* lineage and his çrāddha oblations rested on him. The *Mlecchas* and *Aryans* wept for joy at the behaviour of the *Pāṇḍavas,* and blew their conches, etc. (VI, **43**).—§ 578: The first day's encounter: *Duḥçāsana* advanced with his troops with *Bhīshma* at their head, and the *Pāṇḍavas* headed by *Bhīmasena,* who roared frightfully. *Duryodhana,* etc. (*a*), attacked *Bhīmasena.* The *Draupadeyas,* etc. (*β*), rushed against the *Dhārtarāshṭras.* The disciples of *Droṇa* always hit the mark (VI, **44**). (1) *Bhīshma* attacked *Arjuna*; (2) *Sātyaki* attacked *Kṛtavarman*; (3) *Abhimanyu* fought with *Bṛhadbala*; (4) *Bhīmasena* struggled with *Duryodhana*; (5) *Duḥçāsana* fought with *Nakula*; (6) *Durmukha* fought with *Sahadeva*; (7) *Yudhishṭhira* fought with the *Madra* king (*Çalya*); (8) *Dhṛshṭadyumna* attacked *Droṇa*; (9) *Çaṅkha* encountered *Somadatta's* son; (10) *Dhṛshṭaketu* (the king of the *Cedis*) encountered *Bāhlīka,* they looked like the planets *Aṅgāraka* (Mars) and *Budha* (Mercury); (11) *Ghaṭotkaca* encountered *Alambusha*; (12) *Çikhaṇḍin* encountered *Açvatthāman*; (13) *Virāṭa* attacked *Bhagadatta*; (14) *Kṛpa* attacked the *Kaikeya* king *Bṛhatkshattra*; (15) *Drupada* attacked the *Sindhu* king *Jayadratha,* they resembled the planets *Çukra* (Venus) and *Aṅgāraka* (Mars); (16) *Vikarṇa* (son of *Dhṛtarāshṭra*) attacked *Sutasoma*; (17) *Cekitāna,* who sided with the *Pāṇḍavas,* attacked *Suçarman*; (18) *Çakuni* attacked *Prativindhya*; (19) *Çrutakarman* (the son of *Sahadeva*) attacked the *Kāmboja* king *Sudakshiṇa,* and stood like the *Maināka* mountain; (20) *Irāvat* (son of *Arjuna*) attacked *Çrutāyus*; (21) the two princes of *Avanti, Vinda* and *Anuvinda,* encountered *Kuntibhoja* with his son; (22) the *Kekaya*-brothers encountered the five *Gāndhāra*-princes; (23) *Vīrabāhu* (son of *Dhṛtarāshṭra*) encountered *Uttara* (the son of *Virāṭa*); (24) The *Cedi* king attacked *Ulūka.* Thousands of single combats took place. D.-ṛ., Si., and Cā. beheld the battle, which resembled the combat of D. and As. (VI, **45**). The *Pāṇḍavas* and the *Kurus* fought as if they were possessed by demons. The divisions of the *Pāṇḍavas,* approaching *Bhīshma* (*b*), began to yield (VI, **46**). (25) After the greater part of the forenoon had worn out, *Durmukha,* etc. (*γ*), began to protect *Bhīshma,* who rushed upon the *Cedis,* etc. (*δ*). (26) Then *Abhimanyu* (*c*) attacked *Bhīshma, Kṛtavarman, Çalya, Durmukha* (cutting off the head of his charioteer), and *Kṛpa* (cutting in two his bow); he was regarded as equal to *Arjuna,* and his bow sent forth a twang like that of the *Gāṇḍīva*; he stood firm like the *Maināka* mountain. When *Bhīshma's* standard fell down, *Bhīma* shouted. *Bhīshma* used celestial weapons. (27) In order to protect *Abhimanyu, Virāṭa,* etc. (*ε*), attacked *Bhīshma,* who wounded *Dhṛshṭadyumna* and *Sātyaki,* and they cut off the standard of *Bhīmasena* (*d*), who wounded *Bhīshma* and *Kṛpa* and *Kṛtavarman.* (28) Mounted on an elephant, *Uttara* (the son of *Virāṭa*) attacked the *Madra* king *Çalya,* whose steeds were killed by the elephant; *Çalya,* with a dart, deprived *Uttara* of his senses, and mounted the chariot of *Kṛtavarman.* (29) Seeing his brother *Uttara* slain and *Çalya* staying with *Kṛtavarman, Çveta* (the son of *Virāṭa*) attacked *Çalya.* (30) The *Kosala* king *Bṛhadbala,* etc. (*ζ*), attacked *Çveta* in order to protect *Çalya*; *Çveta* wounded *Rukmaratha,* who was borne away by his charioteer. (31) Then *Duryodhana,* with *Bhīshma,* etc., attacked *Çveta* and rescued *Çalya*; *Bhīshma* shot at *Abhimanyu,* etc. (*η*) (VI, **47**). The *Pāṇḍavas,* with *Çikhaṇḍin,* desired to rescue the generalissimo *Çveta* and attacked *Bhīshma.* The *Kurus* retreated from fear, and abandoned *Bhīshma.* (32) *Duryodhana* averted *Çveta* from *Bhīshma,* and was routed; (33) *Çveta* once more attacked *Bhīshma,* whose standard he cut down; (34) then *Bāhlīka,* etc. (*θ*), attacked *Çveta* in order to protect *Bhīshma,* whose chariot *Çveta* reduced to ashes, with standard, etc.; (35) *Çalya,* etc., rushed to *Bhīshma's* rescue; a voice in the skies admonished *Bhīshma* to hasten the death of *Çveta.* (36) *Sātyaki,* etc. (*κ*), rushed to the rescue of *Çveta. Bhīshma,* etc. (*λ*), checked them. With a shaft endued with the force of the *Brāhma* weapon, seen by D., G., P., U., and Rā., *Bhīshma* shot *Çveta* to death. The *Pāṇḍavas* (with *Çikhaṇḍin*) lamented; the *Kurus* rejoiced; *Duḥçāsana* danced for joy. *Arjuna* and *Kṛshṇa* withdrew the troops, the same did the *Kurus* (VI, **48**). (37) When *Çveta* had been slain,

Virāṭa's son *Çaṅkha*, on beholding *Çalya* standing with *Kṛtavarman*, attacked *Çalya*; (38) *Bhīshma* attacked *Çaṅkha*; (39) *Arjuna* placed himself in front of *Çaṅkha* and attacked *Bhīshma*; (40) *Çalya*, mace in hand, slew the steeds of *Çaṅkha*, who mounted *Arjuna's* chariot. (41) *Bhīshma* with his arrows slaughtered the *Pāñcāla* hosts, etc. (μ), abandoned *Arjuna*, and attacked *Drupada*. The *Pāṇḍavas* were routed, the sun set, and the *Pāṇḍavas* withdrew their forces (VI, **49**). Seeing *Bhīshma's* (and *Droṇa's*) prowess, *Yudhishṭhira* complained before *Kṛshṇa*, and spoke of retiring into the woods. *Bhīma* alone, he said, fought in accordance with *kshattriya* duties; *Arjuna* was indifferent. *Kṛshṇa* consoled him, saying that he had got *Sātyaki*, etc. (ν), and that *Çikhaṇḍin* was certainly the slayer of *Bhīshma*. *Yudhishṭhira* then addressed *Dhṛshṭadyumna*, saying that he himself and *Bhīma*, etc. (ξ), would follow him. *Dhṛshṭadyumna* said that he had been appointed by *Çambhu* to slay *Droṇa* and to fight against *Bhīshma*, etc. (ο). *Yudhishṭhira* recommended the array called *Krauñcāruṇa*, which *Bṛhaspati* had explained to *Indra* in days of old, when the gods and the *Asuras* fought, but which had never been seen before. When morning dawned, *Dhṛshṭadyumna* placed *Arjuna* (e) in the van of the army, and *Drupada* became the head [of the array], etc. (π) (VI, **50**). Seeing the *Krauñca* of the *Pāṇḍavas*, *Duryodhana*, approaching *Bhīshma*, etc. (ρ), gladdened them all, saying that their army, which was protected by *Bhīshma*, was immeasurable, while that of the *Pāṇḍavas*, protected by *Bhīma*, was measurable. The *Saṃsthānas*, etc. (σ), should protect *Bhīshma*. *Bhīshma*, *Droṇa*, and the *Dhārtarāshṭras* formed a mighty array. *Bhīshma* was followed by *Droṇa* with the *Kuntalas*, etc. (τ). *Çakuni* protected *Droṇa*. Followed by his brothers and the *Açvātakas*, etc. (υ), *Duryodhana* advanced against the *Pāṇḍava* host. *Bhūriçravas*, etc. (φ), protected the left flank; *Somadatta*, etc. (χ), the right; *Açvatthāman*, etc. (ψ), were in the rear; behind them *Ketumat*, etc. (ω). *Bhīshma* and the others blew their conches, etc. *Kṛshṇa*, etc. (*aa*), blew their conches (*Kṛshṇa* blew *Pāñcajanya*, etc.). The *Kurus* and *Pāṇḍavas* marched against each other in order to renew the battle (VI, **51**).—§ 579: SECOND DAY: *Duryodhana* began the battle. (1) *Bhīshma* shot at *Abhimanyu*, etc. (*a*); *Arjuna* told *Kṛshṇa* to take his chariot before *Bhīshma*; "protected by *Bhīshma*, *Droṇa*, etc. (β), will slaughter the *Pāñcālas*." Only *Bhīshma*, *Droṇa*, and *Karṇa* could encounter *Arjuna*. *Bhīshma* was protected by *Saindhava* (i.e. Jayadratha), etc. (γ). *Bhīshma*, etc. (δ), struck *Arjuna*, who struck *Bhīshma*, etc. (ε). *Sātyaki*, etc. (ζ), surrounded *Arjuna*. (2) The *Pāñcāla* prince and the *Somakas* attacked *Droṇa*. (3) *Bhīshma* fought with *Arjuna*, at the request of *Duryodhana*, who complained of the absence of *Karṇa*; *Açvatthāman*, etc. (η), stood for battle; *Bhīshma* wounded *Kṛshṇa*; D., G., Cā., and great R. said they would be invincible by all the worlds with D., As., and G. (4) See 2 (VI, **52**): Continuation of the combat between *Droṇa* and *Dhṛshṭadyumna*. (5) *Bhīma* attacked *Droṇa* in order to aid *Dhṛshṭadyumna*, whom he caused to be taken up on another chariot. (6) Urged by *Duryodhana*, the *Kaliṅga* king rushed against *Bhīma* in order to protect *Droṇa*. (7) *Droṇa* abandoned *Dhṛshṭadyumna* and encountered *Virāṭa* and *Drupada*. (8) *Dhṛshṭadyumna* proceeded to support *Yudhishṭhira*. (9) See 6 (VI, **53**): *Bhīmasena* was supported by the *Cedis*; the *Kaliṅga* king by *Ketumat* (son of the *Nishāda* king; *rājaputraḥ*, v. 2354) and *Çrutāyus*. The *Cedis*, etc. (θ), attacked the *Nishādas*. (10) The *Cedis* left *Bhīmasena* and turned back; the *Kaliṅga* king and his son *Çakradeva* fought with *Bhīma*, who slew *Çakradeva* with his mace. (11) *Bhīma* attacked *Bhānumat* (the prince of the *Kaliṅgas*), and slew him with his sword, dividing him in the middle, and made a great slaughter of men and elephants. (12) Beholding *Çrutāyus* (the ruler of the *Kaliṅgas*) at the head of the *Kaliṅga* troops, *Bhīmasena* attacked him, was wounded, and taken into his chariot by the charioteer *Açoka*; once more he fought with *Çrutāyus*, and slew him, and *Satyadeva*, and *Satya*, and *Ketumat*, and routed the *Kaliṅgas*. (13) When, however, the *Kaliṅgas* were rallied again, *Dhṛshṭadyumna*, with *Çikhaṇḍin*, *Yudhishṭhira*, etc., protected one of the wings of *Bhīmasena*; there was nobody on earth, save *Bhīma* and *Sātyaki*, who was dearer to *Dhṛshṭadyumna* than his very life; they beheld *Sātyaki* at a distance; and that [grand]son of *Çini* took up the wing of both *Bhīma* and *Dhṛshṭadyumna*; *Bhīma* caused a bloody river to flow there. (14) *Bhīshma* heard the cries, attacked *Bhīma*, and was attacked by *Sātyaki*, etc. (ι). *Bhīshma* jumped from his chariot, mace in hand, and was taken by *Dhṛshṭadyumna* on his chariot. *Sātyaki* slew the charioteer of *Bhīshma*, who was then carried away from the field of battle by his steeds. The *Kaliṅgas* were totally routed by *Bhīma*, who was praised by the *Pāñcālas* and *Matsyas*, himself embraced *Dhṛshṭadyumna*, and was congratulated by *Sātyaki*, who returned to his own chariot and began to slay the *Kurus* (VI, **54**). (15) When the forenoon of that day had passed away, *Dhṛshṭadyumna* engaged in battle with *Açvatthāman*, etc. (κ); he slew the steeds of *Açvatthāman*, who got up on *Çalya's* car. (16) *Abhimanyu* quickly came up and wounded *Çalya*, etc. (λ), but was, in his turn, wounded by *Açvatthāman*, etc. (μ). (17) *Lakshmaṇa* (the son of *Duryodhana*) attacked *Abhimanyu*. (18) *Duryodhana* attacked *Abhimanyu* in order to aid *Lakshmaṇa*. (19) *Arjuna* engaged in battle with the *Kurus*, headed by *Bhīshma* and *Droṇa*; dust and *Abhimanyu's* arrows produced complete darkness. The *Kurus* were routed. *Arjuna* and *Kṛshṇa* blew their conches. *Bhīshma* suggested to *Droṇa* that they should withdraw the troops, and as the sun set both armies were withdrawn (VI, **55**).—§ 580: THIRD DAY: (1) Next morning *Bhīshma* formed a *Garuḍa* array; at its beak was *Bhīshma* himself; its eyes were formed by *Droṇa* and *Kṛtavarman*; *Açvatthāman*, etc. (*a*), were at its head; *Bhūriçravas*, etc. (β), were placed in its neck; at its back was *Duryodhana* and his followers; *Vinda*, etc. (γ), formed its tail; the *Magadhas*, etc. (δ), formed the right wing; the *Kārūshas*, etc. (ε), were stationed in the left wing. (2) *Arjuna* and *Dhṛshṭadyumna* formed an array in the shape of a half-moon, with *Bhīmasena* in the right horn, etc. (ζ); next to *Nīla Dhṛshṭaketu*, etc. (η); in the middle was *Dhṛshṭadyumna*, etc. (θ); on the left horn was he who had *Kṛshṇa* for his protector. Then the battle commenced (VI, **56**). (3) *Arjuna* fought with the *Kauravas*, who could not be broken, as they were protected by *Droṇa*; and the *Pāṇḍavas* could not be broken, as they were protected by *Arjuna* and *Bhīma*. At last *Bhīshma*, etc. (ι), broke the ranks of the *Pāṇḍavas*. *Bhīmasena*, etc. (κ), attacked the *Kauravas* and fought with *Duryodhana*, *Bhīshma*, and *Droṇa*; *Abhimanyu* and *Sātyaki* attacked *Çakuni* (VI, **57**). D., Dā., G., Pç., U., and Rā. eulogized *Arjuna*. (4) The *Gāndhāras*, with *Çakuni*, fought with *Sātyaki* (the *Vṛshṇi* hero) and *Abhimanyu*, and destroyed the chariot of *Sātyaki*, who mounted *Abhimanyu's* chariot. (5) *Droṇa* and *Bhīshma* attacked *Yudhishṭhira*, and were attacked by him and the sons of *Mādrī*. (6) *Bhīmasena* and *Ghaṭotkaca* fought with *Duryodhana*, who was brought away by his charioteer, and his troops fled, pursued by *Bhīma*. (7) *Dhṛshṭadyumna* and *Yudhishṭhira* slew *Droṇa's* and *Bhīshma's* army, which fled and could not be checked by *Bhīshma* and *Droṇa*. (8) *Abhimanyu* and *Çaineya* began to slaughter the army of *Çakuni*. (9) *Arjuna* routed the *Kaurava* army, and its flight could not be checked by *Bhīshma* and *Droṇa*, but was checked by *Duryodhana*, who blamed *Bhīshma*, saying that he did not sincerely fight with the *Pāṇḍavas*, otherwise his troops could not have been routed while *Bhīshma*, etc. (λ), were alive; had he known this unwillingness of *Bhīshma* to fight, he would have consulted *Karṇa*. *Bhīshma* said that the *Pāṇḍavas* were incapable of being vanquished by the very gods, including *Indra*, but he alone would check them to-day (VI, **58**). (10) After the forenoon of that day had passed away, *Bhīshma* attacked the *Pāṇḍavas*, and a dreadful battle ensued, in which the *Pāṇḍavas* were routed. *Kṛshṇa* told *Arjuna* to strike *Bhīshma*, reminding him of his vow to slay all the warriors of *Dhṛtarāshṭra's* son, headed by *Bhīshma* and *Droṇa*. At the request of *Arjuna*, *Kṛshṇa* drove the steeds to where *Bhīshma* was, and the army of *Yudhishṭhira* rallied for battle. *Arjuna* and *Bhīshma* fought; *Kṛshṇa* displayed great skill in driving the horses; he and *Arjuna* were both wounded by *Bhīshma*, and the *Pāṇḍava* army was routed; *Bhīshma* ordered *Droṇa*, etc. (μ), to attack *Arjuna*. (11) The grandson of *Çini* came to *Arjuna's* rescue; *Kṛshṇa* applauded him, and, saying that he would slay *Bhīshma* and *Droṇa*, etc., he jumped down from the chariot with his discus *Sudarçana* in his hand, and rushed towards *Bhīshma* (who welcomed him), but was held back by *Arjuna*, who said that he would himself slay the *Kurus*; he was then prevailed upon to mount the chariot once more, where he blew the *Pāñcajanya*, while arrows were shot from the *Gāṇḍīva* in all directions. (12) Then *Duryodhana*, etc. (ν), attacked *Arjuna*, who invoked the *Māhendra* weapon and checked the *Kaurava* host. (13) *Virāṭa*, *Drupada*, etc., approached. *Arjuna* caused a river of blood to flow there with *Rākshasas* on its banks. Elated with victory, the *Cedis*, etc. (ξ), set up a loud shout. The *Kurus*, including *Bhīshma*, etc. (ο), got afraid of the *Indra*-weapon, and withdrew their forces at sunset. The same did *Arjuna*. Among the *Kurus* there was a great uproar: "The *Sauvīras*, etc. (π), have all been slain by *Arjuna*, and he has vanquished *Çrutāyus*, etc. (ρ)" (VI, **59**).—§ 581: THE FOURTH DAY: (1) When the night had passed away, *Bhīshma* at the head of the army proceeded against the foe, surrounded by *Droṇa*, etc. (**a**). The array of the *Pāṇḍavas* was like that of the day before. *Bhīshma* (*b*) attacked *Arjuna*, and so did *Droṇa*, etc. (β); *Abhimanyu* rushed out of the ranks and proceeded against all the foes, but *Bhīshma* avoided *Abhimanyu* and fought against *Arjuna* himself (VI, **60**). (2) *Açvatthāman*, etc. (γ), fought with *Abhimanyu*. (3) Urged by *Duryodhana*, the *Trigartas*, etc. (δ), attacked *Arjuna* and *Abhimanyu*. (4) Proceeding towards *Arjuna*, *Dhṛshṭadyumna* attacked the *Madras*, etc. (ε), and slew *Saṃyamani's* son (VI, **61**). *Dhṛshṭadyumna* fought with *Çalya*. (5) *Abhimanyu* attacked *Çalya*. *Duryodhana*, etc. (ζ), protected the chariot of *Çalya*. *Bhīmasena*, etc. (η), fought with them. (6) *Bhīmasena*, with his mace, attacked *Duryodhana*, who advanced with the *Magadha*-division, and placing the ruler of *Magadha* before himself, *Bhīmasena* jumped from his chariot and slew the elephants with his mace; the *Draupadeyas*, etc. (θ), protected *Bhīma's* rear; *Abhimanyu* slew the *Magadha* king after having slain his elephant (VI, **62**). (7) *Duryodhana* commanded his entire army to slay *Bhīmasena*, who crushed them with his mace, without being abandoned by *Dhṛshṭadyumna*, etc. (ι). (8) *Bhīshma* attacked *Bhīmasena*. (9) *Sātyaki* (*Çinipravīraḥ*) attacked *Bhīshma*. (10) Only the Rā. *Alambusha* fought with the grandson of *Çini*. (11) Only *Somadatta's* son *Bhūriçravas* was then of good cheer; he attacked *Sātyaki* (VI, **63**). (12) *Duryodhana* and his brothers surrounded *Somadatta's* son; *Bhīmasena* encountered the *Dhārtarāshṭras*, who were headed by *Duryodhana*; *Nandaka* (Dhārtarāshṭra) also attacked *Bhīmasena*, who addressed his charioteer *Viçoka*, that he should drive the steeds with care; *Duryodhana* also wounded *Viçoka*; *Duryodhana* struck *Bhīmasena* so that he swooned away. (13) The *Pāṇḍava* army, headed by *Abhimanyu*, showered arrows on *Duryodhana*; *Bhīmasena* regained consciousness and fought against *Duryodhana* and *Çalya*, who was borne away from the battle. (14) Fourteen *Dhārtarāshṭras*, viz. *Senāpati*, etc. (κ), encountered *Bhīmasena*, who slew *Senāpati*, etc. (λ); the remaining six fled. (15) Urged by *Bhīshma*, the whole *Dhārtarāshṭra* army attacked *Bhīmasena*; the *Prāgjyotisha* king *Bhagadatta*, on a huge elephant, struck *Bhīmasena*, who fell in a swoon. (16) Then the Rā. *Ghaṭotkaca*, by help of his illusive force, appeared riding on an *Airāvata*, followed by the other *Dignāgas* (μ), each with four tusks and mounted by *Rākshasas*, and attacked *Bhagadatta's* elephant. (17) *Bhīshma* urged *Droṇa* and *Duryodhana* to rescue *Bhagadatta*; all the kings, headed by *Droṇa*, proceeded to aid *Bhagadatta*; *Yudhishṭhira*, with the *Pāñcālas* and *Pāṇḍavas*, pursued them from behind; *Ghaṭotkaca* uttered a fierce roar; *Bhīshma*, addressing *Droṇa*, caused the army to withdraw, and so did the *Pāṇḍavas* with *Bhīmasena* and *Ghaṭotkaca*. *Duryodhana* was afflicted with sorrow (VI, **64**). *Dhṛtarāshṭra* complained to *Sañjaya*, and asked what was the cause of the victory of the *Pāṇḍavas*. *Sañjaya* explained that victory sides with righteousness, and related how *Duryodhana* in the night had enquired of *Bhīshma*, on whom the *Pāṇḍavas* were relying to vanquish *Droṇa*, etc. (ν). *Bhīshma* had related this ancient history: In days of old all the gods and *Ṛshis* were assembled by *Brahmán* upon *Gandhamādana*; and when *Brahmán*, together with the *Ṛshis* and gods, beheld an excellent chariot in the sky, he hymned *Nārāyaṇa* (ξ). ". . . Therefore take birth in the race of *Yadu* and slay the sons of *Diti* . . . Having created the divine *Saṅkarshaṇa* out of thy own self by thyself, thou didst then, O *Kṛshṇa*, create thyself as *Pradyumna*, born of thyself; from *Pradyumna* thou didst then create *Aniruddha*, who is known as the eternal *Vishṇu*; and it was *Aniruddha* who created me as *Brahmán*, the upholder of the Universe. Created out of *Vāsudeva*, I have therefore been created by thee. Dividing thyself into portions, take birth among human beings, and slaughtering the *Asuras* there . . . thou wilt again truly attain to *Yoga* . . ." (VI, **65**). Requested by D., Ṛ., and G., *Brahmán* explained to them who *Nārāyaṇa* is. "Those Dai. and Dā. and Rā. who were slain in battle have been born among men." The old *Ṛshis Nara* and *Nārāyaṇa* are *Arjuna* and *Kṛshṇa*. *Kṛshṇa* should never be disregarded as if he were a man. This was heard by *Bhīshma* from *Ṛshis*, etc. (ο). "Never go to war with *Kṛshṇa* and the *Pāṇḍavas*; on account of thy folly thou couldst not apprehend this; I regard thee, therefore, as a wicked *Rākshasa*." "Where *Kṛshṇa* is, there is righteousness; and victory is where righteousness is . . . It is *Kṛshṇa* who always imparts an understanding endued with righteousness and strength in battle to the *Pāṇḍavas*, and who always protects them from danger . . . He it is who, towards the close of the *Dvāpara yuga* and the beginning of the *Kali yuga*, is hymned by *Saṅkarshaṇa* according to the *Sātvata* ritual" (VI, **66**). *Bhīshma*, on the authority of *Mārkaṇḍeya*, declared the origin and glory of *Kṛshṇa*, his deeds and creations, to *Duryodhana* (π) (VI, **67**). *Bhīshma* cited a hymn to *Nārāyaṇa*, uttered by *Brahmán* himself, and communicated in days of old by B.-ṛ. and G. on earth. *Brahmán*, who quoted *Nārada*, etc. (ρ), hymned *Nārāyaṇa* as the god of D., S., etc. (σ) (VI, **68**).—§ 582: Fifth day: After the night had passed away, *Bhīshma* proceeded in a *Makara* array, the *Pāṇḍavas* in a *Çyena* array, in whose beak, etc., was *Bhīmasena*, etc. (**a**). (1) *Bhīmasena*, penetrating the *Makara* array through its mouth, attacked *Bhīshma*; the *Pāṇḍavas* were confounded. (2) Then *Arjuna* attacked *Bhīshma*. (3) *Duryodhana* addressed *Droṇa*, who attacked *Sātyaki* (the grandson of *Çini*). (4) *Bhīmasena* attacked *Droṇa* in order to protect *Sātyaki*. (5) *Droṇa*, etc. (β), attacked *Bhīmasena*. (6) *Abhimanyu* and the *Draupadeyas* attacked the *Kurus*; *Çikhaṇḍin* attacked *Bhīshma* and *Droṇa*; *Bhīshma* avoided him. (7) Urged by *Duryodhana*, *Droṇa* protected *Bhīshma*; *Çikhaṇḍin* avoided *Droṇa*. (8) *Duryodhana* protected *Bhīshma*, who was attacked by the *Pāṇḍavas* with *Arjuna* at their head (VI, **69**). An awful carnage ensued. (9) *Duryodhana* and the *Kāliṅgas* placed *Bhīshma* at their head and attacked the *Pāṇḍavas*; the *Pāṇḍavas*, supporting *Bhīma*, attacked *Bhīshma* (VI, **70**). *Arjuna* (*b*) attacked *Bhīshma* with the *Gāṇḍīva* (*c*); the *Kurus* were afraid and seemed to melt away. (10) Then, with steeds of the *Kāmboja* breed, the *Kāliṅga* king, etc. (γ), surrounded *Çakuni*. *Bhīshma*, etc., fought with *Arjuna*, etc. (δ); *Drupada*, etc. (ε), fought with *Droṇa*; *Kṛpa* and *Kṛtavarman* attacked *Dhṛshṭadyumna* (VI, **71**). *Arjuna* encountered *Droṇa*, etc. (ζ). *Sātyaki*, etc. (η), attacked *Çalva* and the *Kaikeyas*. *Dhṛshṭaketu* and *Ghaṭotkaca* attacked the chariot-division of the *Dhārtarāshṭras*. *Bhīshma* checked *Bhīmasena*. *Sātyaki* (*Yuyudhāna*) attacked *Bhīshma*, but had his charioteer slain. *Bhīshma* slew the *Pāṇḍava* forces; but the *Pañcālas* and the *Somakas* again attacked *Bhīshma*. (11) *Dhṛshṭadyumna*, etc., attacked *Bhīshma*; *Bhīshma*, *Droṇa*, etc., attacked the *Pāṇḍavas* (VI, **72**).

{ *Virāṭa*. { *Açvatthāman*. { *Duryodhana*.
{ *Bhīshma*. { *Arjuna*. { *Bhīmasena*.

Abhimanyu attacked *Citrasena*, etc. (θ). (12) *Duryodhana* attacked *Abhimanyu*, and so did *Lakshmaṇa* (grandson of *Dhṛtarāshṭra*), who had his steeds and charioteer slain, and was carried away by *Kṛpa* on his chariot. The *Sṛñjayas* fought with the *Kurus* with their fists; *Bhīshma* slew the troops of the *Pāṇḍavas* with his celestial weapons (VI, **73**). (13) *Sātyaki* (*Yuyudhāna*) slew innumerable foes with his arrows; *Duryodhana* despatched 10,000 chariots against him, but he destroyed them all with his celestial weapons. *Sātyaki* & *Bhūriçravas* (*d*); *Sātyaki's* combatants fled and abandoned him; ten sons of *Yuyudhāna* & *Bhūriçravas* (son of *Bāhlīka's* son *Somadatta*) towards the afternoon; *Bhūriçravas* slew them; *Sātyaki* & *Bhūriçravas*, each of them slew the other's chariot-steeds; *Bhīmasena* took *Sātyaki* up on his own chariot, and *Duryodhana Bhūriçravas* on his. (14) The *Pāṇḍavas* & *Bhīshma*; *Duryodhana* urged 25,000 to slay *Arjuna*, who, however, slew them all. The *Matsyas* and *Kekayas* surrounded *Arjuna* and *Abhimanyu*. At sunset *Bhīshma* caused the troops to be withdrawn, and so did the *Pāṇḍavas* and the *Sṛñjayas* (VI, **74**).—§ 583: The sixth day: After the night had passed away, the *Kurus* and the *Pāṇḍavas* once more set out for battle. *Yudhishṭhira* caused *Dhṛshṭadyumna* to dispose the troops in the *Makara* array: *Drupada* and *Arjuna* = head; *Sahadeva* and *Nakula* = two eyes; *Bhīmasena* = beak; *Abhimanyu*, etc. (**a**) = neck; *Virāṭa* and *Dhṛshṭadyumna* = back; five *Kekaya* brothers = left wing; *Dhṛshṭaketu* and *Cekitāna* = right wing; *Kuntibhoja* and *Çatānīka* = two feet; *Çikhaṇḍin*, etc. (β) = tail. *Bhīshma* disposed his army in the form of a huge crane: *Droṇa* = beak; *Açvatthāman* and *Kṛpa* = two eyes; *Kṛtavarman*, etc. (γ) = head; *Çūrasena* and *Duryodhana* = neck; the *Prāgjyotisha* king, etc. (δ) = breast; the *Prasthala* king *Suçarman* = left wing; the *Tushāras*, etc. (ε) = right wing; *Çrutāyus*, etc. (ζ) = rear. The *Pāṇḍava* army was protected by *Bhīmasena*, etc. (η); the *Kaurava* army by *Bhīshma*, etc. (θ). (1) *Bhīmasena* & *Droṇa*, who had his charioteer slain and then himself restrained his steeds. (2) Slaughtered by *Droṇa* and *Bhīshma*, the *Sṛñjayas* and *Kekayas* took to flight; and so did the *Kauravas*, mangled by *Bhīma* and *Arjuna* (VI, **75**). *Dhṛtarāshṭra* recounted the excellency of the *Kaurava* army, protected by *Droṇa*, etc. (ι). Neither men nor *Ṛshis* of old ever beheld such an army. That it should yet be slaughtered, he thought was due only to fate (or to the Creator); *Vidura* had spoken well, but the wicked *Duryodhana* would not accept (VI, **76**). (3) *Bhīmasena* & the younger brothers of *Duryodhana*: *Duḥçāsana*, etc. (κ); *Bhīma* left his chariot and took up his mace. (4) *Dhṛshṭadyumna* (forsaking *Droṇa*) proceeded towards *Çakuni*; seeing *Bhīma's* empty chariot, he became afflicted, but was comforted by the words of *Viçoka*; he took *Bhīma*, who was surrounded by foes on all sides, into his chariot. (5) The *Dhārtarāshṭras* (*Duryodhana*, etc.) & *Dhṛshṭadyumna* (who applied the weapon *Pramohana*). (6) *Droṇa* & *Drupada* (who left the battle); the *Somakas* were struck with fear. (7) *Droṇa*, with the weapon *Prajñā*, neutralized the *Pramohana* weapon in order to rescue *Dhṛtarāshṭra's* sons. (8) *Yudhishṭhira* sent the *Kaikeyas*, etc. (λ), headed by *Abhimanyu*, arrayed in a *Sūcīmukha*, to help *Bhīma* and *Dhṛshṭadyumna*; *Dhṛtarāshṭra's* troops were quite helpless, like a lady in the streets. (9) *Dhṛshṭadyumna*, causing *Bhīma* to be taken into the chariot of the *Kekaya* king, attacked *Droṇa*, who slew his charioteer and steeds; *Dhṛshṭadyumna* ascended the chariot of *Abhimanyu*; *Droṇa* broke the *Pāṇḍava* army (VI, **77**). (10) *Duryodhana* & *Bhīma* (who ascended his own chariot); *Bhīma* & *Citrasena*, etc. (11) *Yudhishṭhira* sent 12 chariot-warriors (*Abhimanyu*, etc.) to follow *Bhīmasena* from behind; seeing them, the *Dhārtarāshṭras* abandoned *Bhīma*. In the afternoon *Duryodhana* attacked *Abhimanyu* and *Bhīmasena*; *Abhimanyu* & *Vikarṇa*, who had his steeds slain and mounted on the chariot of *Citrasena*; *Abhimanyu* & *Durjaya* and *Vikarṇa*; *Duḥçāsana* & the five *Kekaya* brothers; *Draupadeyāḥ* & *Duryodhana* (VI, **78**). *Duryodhana* (*b*) & *Bhīmasena* (who said that he, by slaying *D.*, would dispel the sorrows of *Kuntī*, etc.) (μ). (12) The *Sindhu* king came to the rescue of *Duryodhana*; *Kṛpa* caused *Duryodhana* to mount his own chariot; *Jayadratha* & *Bhīmasena*. (13) *Dhṛshṭaketu*, etc. (ν), & the sons of *Dhṛtarāshṭra*; *Abhimanyu* & *Vikarṇa* (who had his charioteer and steeds slain, and was himself pierced); *Durmukha* & *Çrutakarman* (who had his steeds slain); *Sutasoma* took *Çrutakarman* into his own chariot; *Çrutakīrti* & *Jayatsena* (Dhārtarāshṭra); *Çatānīka* & *Jayatsena*; *Dushkarṇa* & *Çatānīka*, who slew *Dushkarṇa*; *Çatānīka* was surrounded by foes. (14) The five *Kekaya* brothers & the sons of *Dhṛtarāshṭra*: *Durmukha*, etc. (ξ). About sunset *Bhīshma* broke the ranks of the *Pāṇḍavas*; and so did *Yudhishṭhira*, having smelt the heads of *Dhṛshṭadyumna* and *Bhīmasena* (VI, **79**). *Duryodhana* sought *Bhīshma* in the night and gave expression to his grief at the success of the *Pāṇḍavas*; *Bhīshma* promised to do his best, at which *Duryodhana* was delighted (VI, **80**).—§ 584: The seventh day: *Bhīshma* said to *Duryodhana* that he himself, etc. (*a*), were all prepared to battle for his sake; that the *Pāṇḍavas* could not be vanquished by the very gods including *Indra*, having *Kṛshṇa* for their ally, etc.; but that he would either vanquish them or be vanquished by them. He gave *Duryodhana* a herb of great efficacy for healing his wounds. At dawn *Bhīshma* disposed his troops in a *Maṇḍala* array (description), protected by *Bhīshma*, who was again protected by *Citrasena*, etc.; *Duryodhana* looked like *Çakra* himself. Then the *Dhārta-rāshṭras* began to proceed, facing the west. *Yudhishṭhira* disposed his troops in a *Vajra* array. (1) *Droṇa* & the *Matsya* king; *Açvatthāman* & *Çikhaṇḍin*; *Duryodhana* & *Dhṛshṭadyumna*; *Nakula* and *Sahadeva* & the *Madra* king; *Vinda* and *Anuvinda* & *Irāvat*; many kings & *Arjuna*; *Bhīmasena* & *Kṛtavarman Hārdikya*; *Abhimanyu* & *Citrasena*, etc. (*β*) (sons of *Dhṛtarāshṭra*); *Ghaṭotkaca* & the *Prāgjyotisha* king; *Alambusha* & *Sātyaki*; *Bhūriçravas* & *Dhṛshṭaketu*; *Yudhishṭhira* & king *Çrutāyus*; *Cekitāna* & *Kṛpa*. Others proceeded against *Bhīma*, and thousands against *Arjuna*, among others the *Trigarta* king with his brothers. D., D.-ṛ., G., and U. wondered, beholding the two *Kṛshṇas* (i.e. Kṛshṇa and Arjuna). *Arjuna* invoked the *Aindra* weapon; the foes fled, but were rescued by *Bhīshma* (VI, **81**). (2) After *Suçarman* had ceased fighting, and the *Kuru* army had been routed by *Arjuna*, and *Bhīshma* had proceeded against the chariot of *Arjuna*, *Duryodhana* exhorted the kings and *Suçarman* to protect *Bhīshma*, who resembled the planet *Çukra* (Venus) and was surrounded by the *Trigartas*. *Droṇa* & the *Matsya* king (*Virāṭa*), who mounted the chariot of *Çaṅkha* (his son), who was slain by *Droṇa*; *Virāṭa* fled. *Çikhaṇḍin* & *Açvatthāman*; *Çikhaṇḍin* descended, fought first with a sword, then mounted *Sātyaki's* chariot. *Sātyaki* & *Alambusha*; *Sātyaki* employed the *Aindra* weapon which he had obtained from *Arjuna*, and destroyed the creations of *Alambusha's* illusive power; *Alambusha* fled. *Dhṛshṭa-dyumna* & *Duryodhana*, who was forced to descend, mounted *Çakuni's* chariot. *Kṛtavarman* & *Bhīmasena*; *Kṛtavarman* went to the chariot of *Vṛshaka* in the very sight of *Çalya* and *Duryodhana* (VI, **82**). *Dhṛtarāshṭra* spoke to *Sañjaya* about the cheerfulness of the *Pāṇḍavas* and the cheerlessness of the *Kurus*, which he thought was destiny. (3) In the forenoon: The two *Avanti* princes & *Irāvat* (the daughter's son of the king of the *Nāgas*); *Anuvinda* mounted the chariot of *Vinda*; the horses ran away with the chariot. *Ghaṭotkaca* & *Bhaga-datta*; D., G., and Ṛ. came there; except *Ghaṭotkaca*, the other *Pāṇḍava* warriors fled, but rallied. (4) The *Prāgjyotisha* king & *Ghaṭotkaca*, who fled. The ruler of the *Madras* (*Çalya*) & the twins; *Nakula* must mount the chariot of *Sahadeva*; *Çalya* was borne away by his charioteer (VI, **83**). When the sun reached the meridian: *Yudhishṭhira* & *Çrutāyus*; D., G., and Rā. trembled; Ṛ. and D. prayed for the peace of the world; *Çrutāyus* fled, and the troops of *Duryodhana* turned away. *Cekitāna* & *Kṛpa*; *Cekitāna* was forced to descend, and took up a mace, and then a sword; *Karakarsha* took *Cekitāna* into his chariot, and *Çakuni* took *Kṛpa* into his. *Dhṛshṭaketu* & *Bhūriçravas* (the son of *Somadatta*); *Dhṛshṭaketu* mounted the chariot of *Çatānīka*. *Citrasena*, etc. (*γ*), & *Abhimanyu*, who did not slay them, remembering *Bhīma's* words. *Arjuna* caused *Kṛshṇa* to direct the chariot against *Bhīshma*; *Arjuna* & *Suçarman* (VI, **84**); many were slain by *Arjuna*. (5) The *Trigarta* king and thirty-two others attacked *Arjuna*, who slew sixty (so C.) chariot-warriors, and sped to kill *Bhīshma*. (6) The *Trigarta* king attacked *Arjuna*; *Çikhaṇḍin*, etc., came to his rescue; *Arjuna* shot at them with the *Gāṇḍīva*. (7) *Duryodhana*, with *Jaya-dratha*, etc., came to protect *Bhīshma* against *Arjuna*, who, avoiding them, attacked *Bhīshma*, as did also *Yudhi-shṭhira*, etc. (*δ*), avoiding the *Madra* king. *Kṛpa*, etc. (*ε*), shot at the *Pāṇḍavas*. *Çikhaṇḍin* fled, but, rebuked by *Yudhishṭhira*, who reminded him of his oath, he again attacked *Bhīshma*. *Çalya* & *Çikhaṇḍin*, who employed the *Vāruṇa* weapon. *Bhīmasena* (mace in hand) & *Jayadratha*; *Citrasena* & *Bhīmasena* (VI, **85**); *Citrasena* mounted on *Vikarṇa's* chariot. *Bhīshma* & *Yudhishṭhira* (accompanied by the twins), who mounted *Nakula's* chariot. *Yudhishṭhira* urged the kings to slay *Bhīshma*. *Çikhaṇḍin* & *Bhīshma*, who disregarded him, remembering that he had formerly been a wife; the *Sṛñjayas* & *Bhīshma*. (8) *Dhṛshṭadyumna* and *Sātyaki* slaughter the *Kuru* army. (9) *Vinda* and *Anuvinda* attacked *Dhṛshṭa-dyumna*, who mounted *Sātyaki's* chariot. (10) *Yudhishṭhira* attacked *Vinda* and *Anuvinda*, protected by *Duryodhana*. (11) *Arjuna* fought against many foes. (12) *Droṇa* began to consume the *Pāñcālas* like fire a heap of cotton. (13) *Duryodhana* and his brothers surrounded *Bhīshma* and fought against the *Pāṇḍavas*. At sunset Rā., Pç., etc., were seen all around. At sunset *Arjuna* (having vanquished *Suçarman*, etc.), *Yudhishṭhira* with his brothers, *Bhīma-sena* (having vanquished *Duryodhana*, etc.), *Duryodhana* (protecting *Bhīshma*), *Droṇa*, etc., proceeded to their tents (VI, **86**).—§ 585: The eighth day: Having passed the night, the *Kauravas* and *Pāṇḍavas* once more proceeded to battle. *Duryodhana*, etc. (*a*), formed the array, having *Bhīshma* with the *Mālavas*, etc., in the van (*β*); next to him was *Droṇa* with the *Pulindas*, etc. (*γ*); next to *Droṇa* was *Bhagadatta* with the *Magadhas*, etc. (*δ*); behind him was the *Koçala* king *Bṛhadbala* with the *Melakas*, etc. (*ε*); next to him the *Prasthala* king *Traigarta*, etc. (*ζ*); next to the *Trigarta* king was *Açvatthāman*; next to him *Duryodhana* with the whole army and his brothers; behind him *Kṛpa*. Urged by *Yudhishṭhira*, *Dhṛshṭadyumna* formed a *Çṛṅgāṭaka* array: *Bhīmasena* and *Sātyaki*, etc. = the horns; next to them *Arjuna* and *Kṛshṇa*; *Yudhishṭhira*, etc. (*η*) = the centre; *Abhimanyu*, etc. (*θ*) = rear. Description of the battle. *Bhīshma* & *Dhṛshṭadyumna* (VI, **87**). *Yudhishṭhira* & *Bhīshma*. *Bhīmasena* & *Bhīshma*, who was protected by *Duryodhana* and his brothers; the steeds ran away with *Bhīshma*; *Bhīmasena* slew eight sons of *Dhṛtarāshṭra*: *Sunābha*, etc. (*ι*). Then the other sons of *Dhṛtarāshṭra* all fled away. *Duryodhana* urged his brothers to kill *Bhīma*. They remembered the words of *Vidura*. *Duryodhana* blamed *Bhīshma*, who reminded him of the words of *Droṇa*, etc. (*κ*) (VI, **88**). *Dhṛtarāshṭra* complained to *Sañjaya* that his sons, though assisted by *Droṇa*, etc. (*λ*), were still slain; "What can be the reason save fate?" He regretted that the wicked *Duryodhana* had not obeyed *Bhīshma*, etc. (*μ*). *Sañjaya* said that *Dhṛtarāshṭra* ought to have restrained his sons from gambling. At noon the whole *Pāṇḍava* army, at the command of *Yudhishṭhira*—*Dhṛshṭadyumna*, etc. (*ν*)—rushed against *Bhīshma* alone. *Arjuna*, etc. (*ξ*), rushed against all the kings under the command of *Duryodhana*.

A third body was formed of *Abhimanyu*, etc. (*o*). *Droṇa* slew the *Somakas* and *Sṛñjayas*; *Bhīmasena*, principally the elephant division of the *Kurus*; *Nakula* and *Sahadeva*, the cavalry; the *Pāṇḍavas* were destroyed by *Bhīshma*, etc. (π) (VI, **89**). *Çakuni* and *Kṛtavarman Hārdikya* attacked the *Pāṇḍavas*. With horses of the *Kāmboja*, etc. (ρ), breed *Arjuna's* son *Irāvat* (*b*) attacked the *Kauravas*, and with his steeds brought about great confusion in their cavalry. *Çakuni* + his six brothers *Gaja*, etc. (σ), & *Irāvat*, who slew them except *Vṛshabha*. *Duryodhana* urged *Ṛshyaçṛṅga's* son the Rā. (*c*) [*Alambusha*] (who hated *Bhīmasena* because he had killed *Baka*) to slay *Irāvat*; both of them had recourse to magic; *Nāgas* came to the rescue of *Irāvat*, but were consumed by a phantom in the form of *Garuḍa*; then *Irāvat* became confounded and was slain by [*Alambusha*]. *Arjuna*, etc. (τ), slew many. Both armies fought as if they were all possessed by *Rākshasas* and demons (*rakshobhūtair*; B. *rakshobhūtā*) (VI, **90**). *Ghaṭotkaca*, etc., & *Duryodhana* + the *Vaṅga* king with 10,000 elephants; *Duryodhana* slew four Rā.: *Vegavat*, etc. (υ); *Ghaṭotkaca* threatened *Duryodhana* with revenge for the exile of the *Pāṇḍavas*, etc. (φ) (VI, **91**); the *Vaṅga* king, mounted on his elephant, placed himself between *Ghaṭotkaca* and *Duryodhana*; *Ghaṭotkaca* slew the elephant. *Bhīshma* sent *Droṇa*, etc. (χ), to the rescue of *Duryodhana* (VI, **92**). *Bhīma*, urged by *Yudhishṭhira*, came to the rescue of *Ghaṭotkaca*, with *Satyadhṛti*, etc. (ψ). The *Kurus* left *Ghaṭotkaca* and fled (VI, **93**). *Duryodhana* & *Bhīmasena*, who was wounded; *Abhimanyu*, etc., & *Duryodhana*; urged by *Droṇa*, *Somadatta*, etc. (ω), attacked the *Pāṇḍavas*; *Droṇa* & *Bhīma*; *Nīla* & *Açvatthāman*; *Açvatthāman* & *Ghaṭotkaca* + many other Rā.; *Droṇa* & Rā.; *Ghaṭotkaca* confounded *Açvatthāman* by magic; the *Kurus* and *Droṇa*, etc. (*aa*), seemed to fly, etc.; then, towards sunset, the *Kuru* troops fled, notwithstanding the words of *Sañjaya* and *Bhīshma* (VI, **94**). *Duryodhana* complained to *Bhīshma* that he had not himself been able to slay *Ghaṭotkaca*. *Bhīshma* said *Duryodhana* should always battle with *Yudhishṭhira*, etc. (ββ), while *Bhīshma*, etc. (γγ), would battle against *Ghaṭotkaca*; or *Bhagadatta* should fight against *Ghaṭotkaca*. Urged by *Bhīma*, *Bhagadatta*, on his elephant *Supratīka*, set out against the foes. *Bhagadatta* & *Bhīmasena* (*b*), etc. (δδ). *Bhagadatta* & the five *Kekaya* princes, etc. (εε); wounded by the *Prāgjyotisha* king, the elephant of the *Daçārṇa* king fled; *Ghaṭotkaca* & *Bhagadatta*; D., G., and *Munis* wondered; *Bhagadatta* wounded *Viçoka* (*Bhīma's* charioteer); *Bhīma* descended, taking up his mace; *Arjuna* came; *Duryodhana* sent a division; *Bhagadatta* attacked *Yudhishṭhira*; *Bhagadatta* & the *Pañcālas*, etc. (ζζ); *Bhīmasena* told *Kṛshṇa* and *Arjuna* about the slaughter of *Irāvat* (VI, **95**). *Arjuna* complained to *Kṛshṇa* about *Irāvat's* death, the killing of kinsmen, etc., quoting *Vidura*, etc. In the afternoon: *Droṇa* + *Dhṛtarāshṭra's* sons & *Bhīmasena*; *Bhīshma*, etc. (ηη), & *Arjuna*; *Kṛtavarman* + *Bāhlīka* & *Sātyaki*; *Ambastha* & *Abhimanyu*; *Bhīma* felled *Vyūḍhoraska*, etc. (θθ). Then the other sons of *Dhṛtarāshṭra* fled. *Ambastha* got upon the chariot of *Kṛtavarman*. *Dhṛshṭadyumna*, etc., battled with the *Kurus*. When dark set in, both parties withdrew their armies (VI, **96**). *Duryodhana* consulted *Çakuni*, etc. (ιι), as to why *Droṇa*, etc. (κκ), did not resist the *Pārthas*. *Karṇa* asked *Duryodhana* to see *Bhīshma* and solicit him to withdraw from the battle in order to permit *Karṇa* to fight the foe. *Duryodhana* set out for *Bhīshma's* tent (description), and asked *Bhīshma* to retire if he was not competent to slay the *Pāṇḍavas*, etc. (λλ) (VI, **97**). *Bhīshma* spoke to *Duryodhana* about the invincibility of the *Pāṇḍavas*, mentioning the *Khāṇḍava* forest, etc. (μμ), and *Kṛshṇa* (citing *Nārada* and other great Ṛ.); he promised to display all his valour on the next day; only *Çikhaṇḍin*—who was really *Çikhaṇḍinī*—he would not slay. *Duryodhana* told *Duhçāsana* to let all their twenty-two divisions protect *Bhīshma* against *Çikhaṇḍin*, especially *Çakuni*, etc. (νν). Thus they proceeded to battle. "*Yudhāmanyu* protected *Arjuna's* left wheel, *Uttamanjas* his right wheel, and *Arjuna* protected *Çikhaṇḍin*." *Arjuna* told *Dhṛshṭadyumna* to place *Çikhaṇḍin* before *Bhīshma*; he would himself be his protector (VI, **98**).—§ 586: THE NINTH DAY: *Bhīshma* disposed his troops in a *Sarvatobhadra* array: *Kṛpa*, etc. (α), in the van; *Droṇa*, etc. (β), on the right wing; *Açvatthāman*, etc. (γ) = left wing; *Duryodhana*, etc. (δ), in the midst; *Alambusha* and *Çrutāyus* in the rear. *Yudhishṭhira*, etc. (ε), stood in the van; then there were *Dhṛshṭadyumna*, etc. (ζ). The *Kuru* troops were headed by *Bhīshma*, the *Pāṇḍava* troops by *Bhīmasena* (VI, **99**). Description of the heroism of *Abhimanyu*, confounding *Kṛpa*, etc. (η). *Duryodhana* despatched *Alambusha* to slay *Abhimanyu*, while they, headed by *Bhīshma* and *Droṇa*, would slay *Arjuna*. *Alambusha* & *Abhimanyu*; *Alambusha* slaughtered the *Pāṇḍava* host; the *Draupadeyas* (especially *Prativindhya*) & *Alambusha* (VI, **100**). *Dhṛtarāshṭra* asked *Sañjaya* what was done by *Alambusha*, etc. (θ). *Alambusha* & *Abhimanyu*, who defeated him. *Bhīshma* & *Abhimanyu*, who slaughtered the *Kaurava* army. *Arjuna* (surrounded by the *Pāṇḍavas*) & *Bhīshma* (protected by *Dhṛtarāshṭra's* sons); *Kṛpa* & *Arjuna*; *Sātyaki* & *Kṛpa*; *Sātyaki* & *Açvatthāman*; *Droṇa* & *Sātyaki*; *Arjuna* & *Droṇa* (VI, **101**); *Duryodhana* despatched *Suçarman* to take up the wing of *Droṇa*; the *Trigarta* king (and his son) & *Arjuna*; D. and Dā. were highly gratified; *Arjuna* employed the *Vāyavya* weapon, *Droṇa* the *Çaila* weapon; the *Trigarta* division turned away; *Duryodhana*, etc. (ι), surrounded *Arjuna*; *Bhagadatta*, etc. (κ), surrounded *Bhīma*; *Bhūriçravas*, etc. (λ), & the twins; *Bhīshma* (+ the sons of *Dhṛtarāshṭra*) & *Yudhishṭhira*; *Bhīmasena*, with his mace, slaughtered the elephants. *Duryodhana's* troops fled (VI, **102**). *Bhīshma* & the *Somakas*; *Dhṛshṭadyumna*, etc. (μ), & *Bhīshma*; the *Draupadeyas*, etc. (ν), & *Bhīshma*; the *Kuru* army protected *Bhīshma*, who slaughtered the *Pāṇḍava* army; the combatants censured *Duryodhana*, who urged *Bhīshma*, etc. (ξ), to fight (VI, **103**). *Arjuna* slew all the followers of *Suçarman*; *Duryodhana* (+ *Bhīshma*) & *Arjuna*. At noon: *Sātyaki* & *Kṛtavarman*; *Drupada* & *Droṇa*; *Bhīmasena* & *Bāhlīka*; *Abhimanyu* & *Citrasena*, who mounted the chariot of *Durmukha*; *Droṇa* & *Drupada*, who retreated; *Bāhlīka* mounted the chariot of *Lakshmaṇa*; *Sātyaki* & *Bhīshma*; the *Pāṇḍavas* attacked *Bhīshma* in order to rescue *Sātyaki*; battle between them and the *Kurus* (VI, **104**). At the request of *Duryodhana*, *Duhçāsana* protected *Bhīshma*. *Çakuni* checked *Nakula*, etc. (ο). *Duryodhana* despatched 10,000 horsemen, who were checked by *Yudhishṭhira*, etc. (π). *Duryodhana* urged *Çalya* against *Yudhishṭhira*; *Çalya* & *Yudhishṭhira*, etc. (ρ); *Bhīma* came to the rescue of *Yudhishṭhira*. When the sun was sinking, there commenced a fierce and terrible battle (VI, **105**). *Bhīshma* & *Bhīma*, etc. (σ). *Droṇa* & *Sātyaki* (+ *Bhīmasena*). *Bhīshma* & the *Sauvīras*, etc. (τ); *Bhīshma* & 14,000 *Cedis*, etc. (υ), who were slain. *Kṛshṇa* urged *Arjuna* to slay *Bhīshma* (mentioning his words by *Virāṭa*). *Arjuna* & *Bhīshma*. *Kṛshṇa* left his chariot, and rushed at *Bhīshma*, whip in hand, but was brought back by *Arjuna* (VI, **106**). When the sun set, both parties withdrew their forces. The *Pāṇḍavas*, etc. (φ), sat down for a consultation about *Bhīshma*; *Kṛshṇa* said that *Arjuna*, etc. (χ), were invincible, mentioning *Arjuna's* words at *Upaplavya* (ψ). *Yudhishṭhira* proposed to go to *Bhīshma* himself and ask him the means of his death. *Kṛshṇa* approved of the proposal, and they went to the tent of *Bhīshma*, who advised *Arjuna* to fight with him, placing *Çikhaṇḍin* before himself. *Arjuna* grieved at the prospect of striking *Bhīshma*, but was reminded by *Kṛshṇa* of his vow to slay *Bhīshma* (the words of *Bṛhaspati* to *Indra* in days of old also being quoted). The *Pāṇḍavas* and *Kṛshṇa* went away with rejoicing hearts (VI, **107**).—§ 587: THE TENTH DAY: Towards sunrise the *Pāṇḍava* army went out for battle, placing *Çikhaṇḍin* in their van; *Bhīmasena* and *Arjuna* became the protectors of his wheels; in his rear were the *Draupadeyas* and *Abhimanyu*, protected by *Sātyaki* and *Cekitāna*; behind them was *Dhṛshṭadyumna*, protected by the *Pāñcālas*; next to him was *Yudhishṭhira* with the twins; next behind him *Virāṭa*; next to him *Drupada*; the five *Kekaya* brothers and *Dhṛshṭaketu* protected the rear. At their head the *Kurus* had *Bhīshma* (*b*), protected by *Dhṛtarāshṭra's* sons; next behind them *Droṇa* and *Açvatthāman*; next behind was *Bhagadatta* with his elephant division; behind him *Kṛpa* and *Kṛtavarman*; behind them the *Kāmboja* king *Sudakshiṇa*, etc. (*a*). The *Pārthas* with *Arjuna* at their head, placing *Çikhaṇḍin* in the van, proceeded against *Bhīshma*. *Bhīma*, etc. (β), slew many. *Bhīshma* & *Pāṇḍavas*, etc. (γ); *Bhīshma* & *Çikhaṇḍin* (who mentioned *Bhīshma* & *Rāma Jāmadagnya*); *Arjuna* urged *Çikhaṇḍin* to slay *Bhīshma*, while *Arjuna* would check *Droṇa*, etc. (δ) (VI, **108**). *Bhīshma* slew the *Pāñcālas* and the *Pāṇḍava* army. *Arjuna* slew the *Kuru* army. *Duryodhana* complained of *Arjuna* before *Bhīshma*, and of *Sātyaki*, etc. (ε). *Bhīshma* said he would "to-day" either be slain or slay the *Pāṇḍavas*, and he slew hundreds of thousands (VI, **109**). Urged by *Arjuna*, *Çikhaṇḍin*, and so also *Dhṛshṭadyumna*, etc. (ζ), attacked *Bhīshma*; *Citrasena* & *Cekitāna*; *Kṛtavarman* & *Dhṛshṭadyumna*; *Somadatta's* son & *Bhīmasena*; *Vikarṇa* & *Nakula*; *Kṛpa* & *Sahadeva*; *Durmukha* & *Ghaṭotkaca*; *Duryodhana* & *Sātyaki*; the *Kāmboja* king *Sudakshiṇa* & *Abhimanyu*; *Açvatthāman* & *Virāṭa* + *Drupada*; *Droṇa* & *Yudhishṭhira*; *Duḥçāsana* & *Arjuna* + *Çikhaṇḍin*; etc.; *Dhṛshṭadyumna* (exciting the troops for aiding *Arjuna*) & *Bhīshma*; *Arjuna* could not advance further than to the chariot of *Duḥçāsana*, who also shot at *Kṛshṇa*; *Duḥçāsana* for a moment sought refuge by *Bhīshma*; then he again attacked *Arjuna* (VI, **110**); *Alambusha* & *Sātyaki*; *Bhagadatta* & *Sātyaki*; *Duryodhana* & *Sātyaki*; the *Kāmboja* king & *Abhimanyu*; *Çikhaṇḍin* & *Bhīshma*; *Virāṭa* + *Drupada* & *Bhīshma*; *Açvatthāman* & *Virāṭa* + *Drupada*; *Kṛpa* & *Sahadeva*; *Vikarṇa* & *Nakula*; *Durmukha* & *Ghaṭotkaca*; *Kṛtavarman* & *Dhṛshṭadyumna*; *Bhūriçravas* & *Bhīmasena*; *Droṇa* & *Yudhishṭhira*; the *Prabhadrakas* began to tremble; *Citrasena* & *Cekitāna*; *Arjuna* compelled *Duḥçāsana* to retire, and then crushed the *Kuru* troops; *Duḥçāsana* again resisted him (VI, **111**). *Droṇa* became cheerless upon beholding unfavourable omens (η); mentioning *Çikhaṇḍin* and *Yudhishṭhira*, etc. (θ), he urged *Açvatthāman* to attack *Çikhaṇḍin* and *Bhīmasena* (VI, **112**). *Bhagadatta*, etc. (ι) (ten warriors urged by *Droṇa*) & *Bhīmasena*, who was also attacked by *Duryodhana*; *Jayadratha* mounted the chariot of *Citrasena*; *Viçoka* was wounded by *Çalya*; *Arjuna* came, placing *Çikhaṇḍin* before himself, and approached *Bhīma*. Then *Duryodhana* urged the *Trigarta* king (who ruled *Prasthala*) *Suçarman* to slay *Arjuna* and *Bhīmasena*; *Suçarman* & *Arjuna* + *Bhīmasena* (VI, **113**); *Arjuna* & *Çalya*, etc. (κ); *Jayadratha* also attacked *Bhīma*; so did also *Çalya*, who also shot at *Kṛshṇa*; *Droṇa* + the *Māgadha* king *Jayatsena* (commanded by *Duryodhana*) & *Arjuna* + *Bhīmasena*; *Jayatsena* was carried away by his steeds. Then *Bhīshma*, etc. (λ), & *Bhīmasena* + *Arjuna*; *Dhṛshṭadyumna* & *Bhīshma*; *Çikhaṇḍin* & *Bhīshma*; *Yudhishṭhira*, etc. (μ), & *Bhīshma*. A terrible battle ensued, mainly turning upon whether *Bhīshma* should be victorious or vanquished (VI, **114**). At *Bhīshma's* own request: *Yudhishṭhira* + *Arjuna*, etc. (ν), & *Bhīshma*, who gave up all desire of protecting his own life. Urged by *Duryodhana*, *Droṇa*, etc. (ξ) (placing *Bhīshma* in their van), & the *Pārthas* (headed by *Çikhaṇḍin*), especially *Arjuna*, etc. (ο); the grandson of *Çini* (*Sātyaki*) & *Açvatthāman*; *Dhṛshṭaketu* & *Paurava*; *Yudhāmanyu* (B. *Abhimanyu*) & *Duryodhana*; *Virāṭa* & *Jayadratha* (*Vṛddhakshattrasya dāyādam*; I do not understand the doubt of PCR.); *Yudhishṭhira* & *Çalya*; *Bhīmasena* & the elephant division; *Dhṛshṭadyumna* & *Droṇa*; *Bṛhadbala* (*c*) & *Abhimanyu* (*d*); the sons of *Dhṛtarāshṭra*, etc., & *Çikhaṇḍin* + *Arjuna* (VI, **115**); *Abhimanyu* & *Duryodhana*; *Açvatthāman* & *Sātyaki*; *Paurava* & *Dhṛshṭaketu*; *Jayatsena* (*Dhārtarāshṭra*) carried *Paurava* away on his chariot, and *Sahadeva* carried away *Dhṛshṭaketu*; *Citrasena* & *Suçarman*; *Abhimanyu* & *Bṛhadbala* (the *Koçala* king); *Bhīmasena* slaughtered the elephants; *Yudhishṭhira* & *Çalya*; *Jayadratha* & *Virāṭa*; *Droṇa* & *Dhṛshṭadyumna*; *Arjuna* & *Bhīshma*; *Bhagadatta* & *Arjuna*, who urged *Çikhaṇḍin* to slay *Bhīshma*; *Bhagadatta* (leaving *Arjuna*) & *Drupada*; *Arjuna* (placing *Çikhaṇḍin* ahead) & *Bhīshma*; the *Kurus* attacked *Arjuna*; *Çikhaṇḍin* attacked *Bhīshma*; 14,000 *Cedis*, etc. (π), were slain by *Bhīshma*, and so the *Somakas*; no chariot-warrior ventured to approach *Bhīshma* except *Arjuna* (with *Kṛshṇa*) and *Çikhaṇḍin* (VI, **116**). *Bhīshma* did not defend himself against *Çikhaṇḍin*, whom *Arjuna* urged to quickly slay *Bhīshma*, who with his arrows only checked *Arjuna* and slew the *Pāṇḍava* warriors. *Duḥçāsana* & *Arjuna* + all the *Pārthas*; *Duḥçāsana* was vanquished by *Arjuna*; the *Videhas*, etc. (ρ) (urged by *Duryodhana*) & *Arjuna*, who consumed them all by means of celestial weapons; *Arjuna* & *Duḥçāsana*, etc. (σ), who fled (in the forenoon); *Bhīshma* (with a celestial weapon) & *Arjuna*; *Çikhaṇḍin* & *Bhīshma*, who withdrew the celestial weapon (VI, **117**). *Çalya*, etc. (τ), slaughtered the *Pāṇḍava* warriors; *Arjuna* felled a great many *Kurus*. *Dhṛtarāshṭra's* sons & the *Pāṇḍavas*; the *Somakas* and *Sṛñjayas* (urged by *Dhṛshṭadyumna*) & *Bhīshma* (who relied on the instruction he had got from *Rāma*); *Bhīshma* slew 10,000 elephants, etc., and seven *Matsyas* and *Pāñcālas*, and *Çatānīka* (the brother of *Virāṭa*), etc. *Kṛshṇa* urged *Arjuna* to slay *Bhīshma*. The *Pāñcāla* king and *Dhṛshṭaketu*, etc. (υ), were afflicted by *Bhīshma* and rescued by *Arjuna*; *Çikhaṇḍin*, protected by *Arjuna*, rushed against *Bhīshma*; *Arjuna* slew all *Bhīshma's* followers, and then rushed at himself; *Sātyaki*, etc. (φ), attacked *Bhīshma*, who slew seven warriors of *Dhṛshṭadyumna's* division (VI, **118**). Continuation: The extraordinary heroism of *Bhīshma*: he (disregarding the *Pāñcāla* king and *Dhṛshṭaketu*) & *Sātyaki*, etc. (χ); *Arjuna* (with *Çikhaṇḍin* ahead) & *Bhīshma*; *Droṇa*, etc. (ψ) (employing celestial weapons), & *Arjuna*; *Sātyaki*, etc. (ω), & the *Kauravas*, in order to rescue *Arjuna*; *Arjuna* (with *Çikhaṇḍin*) & *Bhīshma*, who (remembering the boon granted by his father) now wished his death, which was approved of by Ṛ. and V. (heard only by *Bhīshma* and *Sañjaya*), etc.; *Bhīshma* said to *Duḥçāsana* that *Arjuna* was invincible, and that he himself could not be vanquished by D., Dā., and Rā. *Yudhishṭhira* urged his troops against *Bhīshma*; *Dhṛtarāshṭra's* sons surrounded *Bhīshma*, but fled for *Arjuna*; the *Sauvīras*, etc. (*αα*), abandoned *Bhīshma*. A little before sunset *Bhīshma* fell down from his chariot with his head to the east; there were heard celestial voices, etc.; as the sun was in the southern solstice, *Bhīshma* postponed his death; *Gaṅgā* sent to him the great Ṛ. in form of swans inhabiting the *Mānasa* lake. The *Kurus*, headed by *Kṛpa* and *Duryodhana*, sighed and wept; the *Pāṇḍavas* and *Sṛñjayas*, etc. (*ββ*), uttered loud shouts. Ṛ. and P. applauded *Bhīshma*, who had recourse to that *Yoga* which is taught in the great *Upanishads* (VI, **119**). *Dhṛtarāshṭra*, mentioning *Bhīshma's brahmacarya* for the sake of his father, and that he had not been slain by *Rāma Jāmadagnya*, grieved that he had been slain by *Çikhaṇḍin*. *Sañjaya* related that *Bhīshma* lay on his bed of arrows, without, however, touching the earth. Both the *Kurus* (*Karṇa*, *Duryodhana*, etc.) and the *Pāṇḍavas* were despondent; the welkin was enveloped with a gloom, etc.; Ṛ., Si., and Cā. mentioned his *brahmacarya* for his father's sake. The *Pāṇḍavas* blew their conches, and *Bhīmasena* sported in great glee. *Duḥçāsana* informed *Droṇa*, who fell down from his chariot, and then ordered the *Kurus* to desist from battle; and so did the *Pāṇḍavas*. Then the kings of both armies all repaired to *Bhīshma*. *Bhīshma's* head hanging down, he asked a pillow; he refused the soft pillows offered him, and asked *Arjuna* to give him a suitable pillow; *Arjuna* supported his head with three arrows shot from the *Gāṇḍīva* and inspired with *mantras*; *Bhīshma* was highly gratified. He caused *Duryodhana* to dismiss the physicians; he asked that a ditch should be dug around him, until the sun should proceed towards the direction occupied by *Vaiçravaṇa* (i.e. the north), and told them to cease fighting. Stationing guards all around for his protection, the heroes repaired for rest in the evening. *Kṛshṇa* congratulated *Yudhishṭhira*, "that canst slay with thy eyes alone"; *Yudhishṭhira* ascribed the victory to *Kṛshṇa* (VI, **120**).—§ 588: THE ELEVENTH DAY: After the night had passed away, maidens came to *Bhīshma* and showered flowers upon him. The *Pāṇḍavas* and *Kauravas* assembled together like brothers around his body. *Bhīshma* asked for water; he refused the excellent viands and water offered him, and asked *Arjuna* to give him water; *Arjuna* mounted his chariot, and from the *Gāṇḍīva* shot an arrow inspired with *mantras* and identified with the *Pārjanya* weapon, piercing therewith the earth, and there arose a jet of pure and cold water; *Bhīshma* praised *Arjuna*: "even *Nārada* spoke of thee as an ancient Ṛshi"; he mentioned his alliance with *Kṛshṇa*, and regretted that *Duryodhana* had not listened to the words of *Bhīshma*, etc. (*α*). He said to *Duryodhana* that the weapons appertaining to *Agni*, etc. (*β*), were known only to *Arjuna* and *Kṛshṇa*, and told him to make peace, as long as *Yudhishṭhira*, etc. (*γ*), did not consume his troops; "let *Yudhishṭhira* go to *Indraprastha*." But *Duryodhana* would not accept his counsels (VI, **121**). All the kings retired. *Karṇa* visited *Bhīshma* in private. *Bhīshma* told *Karṇa* that he was not the son of *Rādhā*, but of *Kuntī*; that he knew from *Nārada* and *Vyāsa*; "sinfully didst thou come into the world; therefore it is that thy heart has been such, and also because thou didst associate with the low"; he mentioned that, proceeding to the city of *Kāçi*, *Karṇa* alone, with his bow, had crushed the kings in battle in order to procure a bride for the *Kuru* king; *Jarāsandha* could not become a match to *Karṇa* in fight. He adjured *Karṇa* to unite with his uterine brothers. *Karṇa* mentioned that *Kuntī* had abandoned him, and his obligations to *Duryodhana*, etc. (*δ*); he would fight *Arjuna* and the *Pāṇḍavas* though they were protected by *Kṛshṇa*. *Bhīshma* gave permission to *Karṇa* to fight, making heaven his goal, and then dismissed him (VI, **122**).

Bhīshmotpatti(ḥ) ("origin of Bhīshma"). § 163 (cf. *Çāntanūp.*): *Gaṅgā* agreed to become the wife of *Çāntanu* on the condition that she would leave him the moment he interfered with her or spoke an unkind word to her. They had eight children; but seven of them were, as soon as they were born, thrown into the water by her. The eighth was rescued by *Çāntanu's* interfering. But then *Gaṅgā*, telling him who she was, and that his sons were the eight *Vasu's* who had been cursed by *Vasishṭha*, left him (I, 98). (For continuation v. Āpavop.)

Bhogavat (a mountain in the east). § 280 (Bhīmasena): II, **30**, 1086 (conquered by Bhīmasena).

Bhogavatī[1] (the city of the Nāgas in Pātāla). § 244 (Rājyalābhap.): I, **207**, 7575 (*Nāgair Bhogavatī yathā*), 7593 (do.).—§ 345 (Nalop.): III, **57**, 2195 (*iva*).—§ 564 (Mātalīyop.): V, **103**, 3617 (*iyam Bhogavatī nāma purī Vāsuki-pālitā, yādṛçī devarājasya purī varyā 'marāvatī*).—§ 565 (Gālavacar.): V, **109**, 3797 (*atra Bhogavatī nāma purī Vāsuki-pālitā | Takshakena ca Nāgena tathaivairāvatena ca | atra niryāṇakāle 'pi tamaḥ samprāpyate mahat | abhedyaṃ bhāskareṇāpi svayaṃ vā kṛshṇavartmanā*).

Bhogavatī[2] (a river = Sarasvatī (Nīl.)). § 322 (Dvaitavanap.): III, **24**, †938 (*manoramāṃ*).

Bhogavatī[3] (a tīrtha = Bh°[2]?). § 373 (Prayāga): III, **85**, 8219 (*tīrthaṃ Bhogavatī caiva, vedir eshā Prajāpateḥ*).—§ 374 (Tīrthay.): III, **85**, 8228 (. . . *Gaṅgā-Yamunā-saṅgame | tatra Bhogavatī Vāsukes tīrtham uttamaṃ*).—§ 573 (Ambop.): V, **186**, 7354.

Bhogavatī[4] (a mātṛ). § 615*u* (Skanda): IX, **46***θ*, 2626.

***Bhogin**, pl. (serpents): III, 14309 (the mountain Çveta is guarded by Bhogins, Rakshases, Piçācas, etc.): IV, 1322 (*Bh°ām iva jṛmbhitāṃ*): VII, 632 (*iva . . . patatrivara-bh°āṃ*), 6100 (*bhujair bhogi-bhogābhaiḥ*): XIII, 4717 (*Yaksha-rākshasabhoginām*), 6164.

Bhogipati ("king of serpents," i.e. the Nāga Padmanābha). § 718*b* (Uñchavṛttyupākhy.): XII, **365**, 13933.

Bhoja, pl. (a people). § 148 (Yayāti): I, **85**, 3500 (*Druhyoḥ sutās tu vai Bhojāḥ*).—§ 251 (Arjunavāsap.): I, **218**, 7902 (*Bhoja-Vṛshṇy-Andhakānāṃ*), 7903 (*Bhoja-Vṛshṇy-Andhaka-tmajaiḥ*).—§ 252 (Subhadrāharaṇap.): I, **219**, 7907 (*Bhoja-Vṛshṇy-Andhakāç caiva*; make a festival on the Mahendra mountain); **220**, 7942 (do.), 7962 (do.).—§ 253 (Haraṇā-haraṇap.): I, **221**, 7993 (*Vṛshṇi-Bhojāndhakās tathā*, bring nuptial presents to Khāṇḍavaprastha), 7998 (do.).—§ 273 (Rājasūyārambhap.): II, **14**, 570 (*Yayāteç caiva Bhojānāṃ vistaro guṇato mahān*), 589 (*udīcyāç ca tathā Bhojāḥ kulāny ashṭādaça prabho | Jarāsandhabhayād eva pratīcīṃ diçam āsthitāḥ*), 596 (*Bhoja-rājanya-vṛddhaiç ca pīḍyamānair durātmanā*, i.e. *Kaṃsena*).—§ 298 (Dyūtap.): II, **62**, 2100 (*viditaṃ me . . . Bhojeshvevāsamañjasaṃ | putraṃ santyaktavān pūrvaṃ paurāṇāṃ hitakāmyayā*), 2101 (*Andhakā Yādavā Bhojāḥ sametāḥ Kaṃsam atyajan*).—§ 402 (Tīrthay.): III, **120**, 10278 (*sa-Vṛshṇi-Bhojāndhaka-yodha-mukhyāḥ*).—§ 553 (Vaivāhikap.): IV, **72**, 2360 (*Vṛshṇyandhakāç ca bahavo Bhojāç ca paramaujasaḥ*, follow Kṛshṇa to Dvārakā).—§ 554 (Sainyody.): V, **7**, 131 (the V°., A°., and Bh°. follow Kṛshṇa to Dvārakā).—§ 555 (do.): V, **19**, 586 (*Kṛtavarmā* *ca Hārdikyo Bhojāndha-Kukuraiḥ saha*). — § 556 (Sañjayayānap.): V, **28**, †804 (*Çaineyo 'yan Cedayaç cāndhakāç ca Vārshṇeya - Bhojāḥ Kukurāḥ Sṛñjayāç ca*). — § 561 (Yānasandhip.): V, **48**, †1881 (*yo*, i.e. Kṛshṇa-*Rukmiṇīm ekarathena Bhojān utsādya rājñaḥ samare prasahya*).—§ 567 (Bhagavadyānap.): V, **128**, 4297 (*Āhukaḥ punar asmābhir jñātibhiç cāpi satkṛtaḥ | Ugrasenaḥ kṛto rājā Bhojarājyasya vardhanaḥ, Kaṃsam ekaṃ parityajya kulārthe sarva-Yādavāḥ . . .*).— § 574 (Jambūkh.): VI, **9**, 348μ.—§ 599 (Jayadrathavadh.): VII, **92**, 3276 (Arjuna *Bhojānīkaṃ vyaçātayat*); **94**, 3409 (°*ānīkaṃ*, i.e. Kṛtavarman's (?), is vanquished by Arjuna); **101**, 3775 (do.); **113**, 4432 (do., Yuyudhāna has fought with Kṛtavarman), 4438 (do., commanded by Kṛtavarman); **114**, 4481; **120**, 4765 (°*ānīkaṃ*) (commanded by Kṛtavarman); **128**, 5240 (°*ānīkaṃ Hārdikyenābhirakshitaṃ*), 5242 (°*ānīkaṃ*). —§ 603 (Nārāyaṇāstramokshap.): VII, **193**, 8905 (°*ānīkena . . . Kṛtavarmā vṛtaḥ*).—§ 605 (Karṇap.): VIII, **20**, 780$\delta\delta$ (are attacked by Pāṇḍya). — § 641 (Rājadh.): XII, **81**, 3052λ.—§ 785 (Anugītāp.): XIV, **59**, 1768 (°*Vṛshṇy-andhakāḥ*, receive Kṛshṇa returning to Dvārakā). —§ 793 (Mausalap.): XVI, **1**, 12*a*, 14; **3**, 86 (°*Andhakāḥ*), 90, 93; **5**, 134 (*sa*° *Andhaka-Kaukurān*); **7**, 215 (° *Vṛshṇyandhaka-*); **8**ν, 263 (° *Vṛshṇyandhakāḥ*).—§ 795 (Svargārohaṇap.): XVIII, **4**, 142 (*gaṇeshu paçya rājendra Vṛshṇyandhaka-mahārathān | Sātyaki-pramukhān vīrān Bhojāṃç caiva mahābalān*).

Bhoja[1] (king of the Bh°). § 232 (Svayaṃvarap.): I, **186**, 6986 (*Açvatthāmā ca Bhojaç ca sarvaçastrabhṛtāṃ varau*; among the kings present at the svayaṃvara of Kṛshṇā).— § 264 (Sabhākriyāp.): II, **4**, 121*a* (among the kings who received Yudhishṭhira when he entered his palace); V, 5904 (cf. Aja).—§ 578 (Bhīshmav.): VI, **44**, 1653*a*.

Bhoja[2] = Bhīshmaka. § 570 (Bhīshmaka): V, **158**, 5351 (. . . *Bhīshmakasya . . . Ahukānām adhipatir Bhojasyātiyaçasvinaḥ | Dākshiṇapateḥ putro dikshu Rukmīti viçrutaḥ*).

Bhoja[3] **Mārtikāvata** (the Bh° from Mṛttikāvatī, a descendant of Mahābhoja). § 593 (Abhimanyuvadhap.): VII, **48**, 1892.

Bhoja[4] = Kṛtavarman: V, 2252 (*Bhojan tu Kṛtavarmānaṃ Yuyudhāno yuyutsati*), 5737; VII, 530, 1650 (?), 1917 (Abhimanyuvadh.), 2628 (?)β, 3278 (Jayadrathav., wounds Arjuna), 3280, 3289, 3292, 3437 (*Hārdikyaḥ*), 3511, 4429 (Jayadrathav.), 4434 (?), 4438, 4517, 4632; VIII, 45 (*Kṛtavarmaṇaḥ*), 197 (do.), 1071, 1332 (?), †4065 (?), †4073 (?), †4080 (?), †4204 (?)μ, †4315, †4503 (?)*a*, β; IX, 73, 569, 1623 (*Kṛtavarmāṇaṃ*), 1982; X, 31, 57, 116, 119, 206, 216, 319, 533; XII, 114 (?), 3037 (?) (*Akrūra*° *prabhavāḥ*), 6199; XIV, 1805 (*Kṛpa*° *ābhyām*).

Bhojā (the queen of Yuyudhāna). § 589 (Droṇabhishekap.): VII, **10**, 338 (Y. had conquered her by defeating the army of the Sauvīra king).

Bhojakaṭa (a city of the Bhojas). § 281*c* (Bhīshmaka): II, **31**, 1115 (*puraṃ*, conquered by Sahadeva). — § 284 (Sahadeva): II, **31***a*, 1166 (v. Bhīshmaka). — § 570*d* (Rukmin): V, **158**, 5364, 5365 (built by Rukmin on the spot, where he was vanquished by Kṛshṇa).

Bhojana[1] = Çiva (1000 names[2]).

Bhojana[2] = Vishṇu (1000 names).

Bhojanagara. § 565 (Gālavac.): V, **118**, 3982 (*Gālavo . . . jagāma Bh°aṃ drashṭum Auçīnaraṃ nṛpam*).

Bhojarāja[1] (the king of Dvārakā): II, 1567 (during the invasion of Çiçupāla).

Bhojarāja[2] = Ugrasena: V, 4295 (*Bhojarājasya vṛddhasya durācāro hy anātmavān | jīvataḥ pitur aiçvaryaṃ hṛtvā mṛtyuvaçaṃ gataḥ | Ugrasena - sutaḥ Kaṃsaḥ parityaktaḥ svabāndhavaiḥ*).

Bhojarāja[3] = Kaṃsa: VII, 388 (Droṇābhishek.) (brother of Sunāman).

Bhojarāja[4] = Aṃçumat: VIII, 164 (v. Aṃçumat).

Bhojarāja[5] = Kṛtavarman (?). § 793 (Mausalap.): XVI, **7**, 245 (*Hārdikyatanayaṃ Pārtho nagaraṃ Mārttikāvatam | Bhojarājakalatrañ ca hṛtaçeshaṃ narottamaḥ*).

Bhojarājanyavardhana = Kṛshṇa: XIV, 2581 (*Vishṇuḥ*).

Bhojasutā = Kuntī: XIV, 1949 (*Kuntī*).

Bhoktṛ = Vishṇu (1000 names).

Bhrājishṇu = Vishṇu (1000 names).

Bhramara. § 522 (Draupadīharaṇap.): III, **265**, 15598 (follows Jayadratha).

Bhṛgos tīrthaṃ. § 383*e* (Tīrthay.): III, **99**, 8650: where Paraçurāma had regained his energy that had been taken away by Rāma Dāçarathi.

Bhṛgu[1] (a maharshi). § 19 (Paulomap.): I, **5**, 869 (*Bhṛgur maharshir bhagavān Brahmaṇā vai Svayambhuvā | Varuṇasya kratau jātaḥ Pāvakād iti naḥ çrutaṃ | Bhṛgoḥ sudayitaḥ putraç Cyavano nāma Bhārgavaḥ*), 870.—§ 20 (Pulomā): I, **5**, 875 (married Pulomā, and became the father of Cyavana), 877, 878, 882, 886, 887, 888, 890, 891, 892, 894, 895, 901, 903, 905, (906), 910, 911, 926, 938 (°*taḥ*). — § 121 (Aṃçāv.): I, **66**, 2605 (*Brahmaṇo hṛdayaṃ bhittvā niḥsṛto bhagavān Bhṛguḥ*), 2606 (*Bhṛgoḥ putraḥ Kavir vidvān*).—§ 122 (do.): I, **66**, 2608 (father of Cyavana).—§ 264 (Sabhākr.): II, **4***a*, 111.—§ 266 (Çakras.): II, **7**, 309.—§ 270 (Brahmas.): II, **11**, 436 (among the maharshis, *Prajānāṃ patayaḥ*).—§ 305 (Anudyūtap.): II, **78**, 2575.—§ 347 (Nalop.): III, **64**, 2462.—§ 371 (Tuṅgaka): III, **85**, 8193.—§ 377 (Dhaumyatīrthak.): III, **90**, 8394. — § 383*c* (Tīrthay.): III, **99**, 8650 (°*os tīrthaṃ*).—§ 383 (Paraçu-Rāma): III, **99**, 8686 (*devayuge*).—§ 395 (Jamadagni): III, **115**, 10155 (*ājagāma Bhṛguḥ çreshṭhaṃ putraṃ*, i.e. Ṛcīka), 10157, (10159), 10163. —§ 405 (Sukanyop.): III, **122**, 10316 (°*or maharsheḥ putro 'bhūc Cyavano*). — § 407 (Mandhātrup.): III, **126**, 10431 (*āçramaṃ Bhṛgoḥ*).—§ 421 (Gandhamādanaprav.): III, **142**, 10904 (among the maharshis).—§ 493 (Āṅgirasa): III, **222**, 14224 (*Bhṛgvaṅgirādibhiḥ*).— § 506 (Skandayuddha): III, **231**, 14555 (*Bhṛgvaṅgirobhiḥ sahitaḥ*). — § 562 (Bhagavadyānap.): V, **83**η, 2946.—§ 585 (Gālavac.): V, **117**, 3971 (*yathā °ḥ Pulomāyām*).—§ 576 (Bhagavadgītāp.): VI, **34**, 1229 (*maharshīṇāṃ Bhṛgur ahaṃ*, says Kṛshṇa).—§ 595 (Shoḍaçarāj., Rāma Jām.): VII, **70**, 2435.—§ 606 (Tripurākhy.): VIII, **34**, 1505 (*Bhṛgv-aṅgiro-manyubhavaṃ krodhāgniṃ*).—§ 615*u* (Skanda): IX, **45**, 2512γ.—§ 615*w* (Agnitīrtha): IX, **47**, 2745 (*Bhṛgoḥ çāpād bhṛçaṃ bhīto Jātavedāḥ . . . | çamīgarbham athāsādya nanāça*), 2749 (*sarvabhakshyaç ca so 'bhavat | Bhṛgoḥ çāpāt*, sc. Agniḥ). — § 615*hh* (Dadhīca): IX, **51**, 2957 (*Prajāpatisutena*). — § 621 (Rājadharm.): XII, **3**, 77 (*āçrame °oḥ*), 93, 94, 96.—§ 641 (do.): XII, **122**, 4505, 4506.—§ 656 (Khaḍgotp.): XII, **166**, 6142β (*Bhṛgv-Atry-Aṅgirasaḥ . . .*).—§ 660 (Mokshadh.): XII, **182**, 6769 (*Bhṛguṇā 'bhihitaṃ çāstraṃ Bharadvājāya pṛcchate*), 6770 (*maharshiṃ*). — § 660*b* (Bhṛgu-Bharadvāja-s.): XII, **182**, (6775), (6788), (6802); **183**, (6809); **184**, (6828), (6830); **185**, (6867); **187**, (6898), (6902), (6917); **188**, (6930), (6939); **189**, (6951); **190**, (6968), (6978); **191**, (6985), (6989), (6991); **192**, (7002), (7010), 7030. — § 677 (Mokshadh.): XII, **232**, 8481.—§ 702 (do.): XII, **297**, 10877.—§ 706 (do.): XII, **310**, 11518 (*ṛshiṃ vaṃçabharaṃ °oḥ*).—§ 707 (do.): XII, **319**, 11783β.—§ 717*b* (Nārāyaṇīya):

XII, **335**, 12685*a*; **343**, ††13218, IX), 13223, XIV).—§ 730*g* (Upamanyu Vaiyāghrapadya): XIII, **14***v*, 873 (*Bhṛgv-ādyā ṛshayaḥ*).—§ 730 (Ānuçāsanik.): XIII, **14**ββ, 991.—§ 734 (do.): XIII, **26**, 1761*a*.—§ 736*b* (Vītahavyop.): XIII, **30**, 1983 (Vītahavya seeks refuge in the hermitage of *Bh.*), 1984, 1986, 1987, 1991, 1992, 1996, 2006.—§ 745*b* (Cyavanop.): XIII, **51**, 2691 (°*oḥ putraṃ Cyavanaṃ*).—§ 746 (Ānuçāsanik.): XIII, **66**, 3332ζ.—§ 747*b* (Suvarṇotp.): XIII, **85**, 4122ζ ("from *bhṛg*"), 4123, 4141 (adopted by Mahādeva in the form of Varuṇa), 4142 (called *Vāruṇaḥ*), 4145η (has seven sons, Cyavana, etc.), 4152, 4153 (cf. 4142).—§ 749 (Ānuçāsanik.): XIII, **91**, 4326 (*Bhṛgv-Aṅgirasake kāle*).—§ 751*b* (Çapathavidhi): XIII, **94**, 4550*a* (4562).—§ 755 (Ānuçāsanik.): XIII, **99**, 4745 (*Nahushasya ca saṃvādam Agastyasya Bhṛgos tathā*).—§ 755*b* (Nahushop.): XIII, **99**, 4756 (4764), 4771; **100**, 4786, 4788, 4791, 4794, 4797, 4799, 4800, (4801), 4804.—§ 759 (Ānuçāsanik.): XIII, **106**, 5200δ.—§ 770 (do.): XIII, **151**, 7157ν (°*Aṅgiro-'try-ādibhiḥ*), 7160ξ.—§ 775 (do.): XIII, **166**, 7664γ (°*Aṅgirās*).—Cf. Bhṛgūdvaha.—Compare the following genealogical table (cf. §§ 19, 20, 21, 121, 122):—

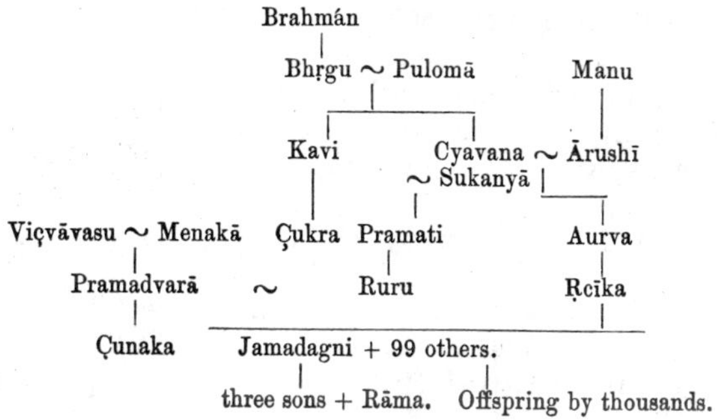

Bhṛgu[2] (a son of Kavi). § 747*b* (Suvarṇotp.): XIII, **85**, 4150ι.

Bhṛgu[3] = Cyavana. § 745*b* (Cyavanopākhyāna): XIII, **51**, 2685.

Bhṛgu, pl. ("descendants of Bhṛgu"). § 227 (Aurvop.): I, **178**, 6802, 6805 (°*ūṇāṃ dhanaṃ*), 6808 (°*veçmani*; sg. ? = a Bhṛgu ?), 6809, 6811, 6822, 6830; **179**, 6834, ? 6836 (°*veçmani*); **180**, 6846, 6847, 6849.—§ 024 (Dvaitavanapr.): III, **26**, 970.—§ 303 (Paraçu-Rāma): III, **115**, 10126.—§ 394 (Arjuna Kārtav.): III, **115**, 10133 (°*ūṇāṃ vaṃçe jātasya Rāmasya Jāmadagnyasya*).—§ 398 (Paraçu-Rāma): III, **117**, 10205 (the forefathers of Paraçu-Rāma).—§ 490 (Skandotp.): III, **224**, 14270 (*Bhṛgubhiç cāṅgirobhiç ca*).—§ 595 (Shoḍaçarāj., Paraçu-Rāma): VII, **70**, 2447 (°*ūṇāṃ kīrttivardhanaḥ*, i.e. Paraçu-Rāma).—§ 602 (Dronavadhap.): VII, **190**, 8728γ.—§ 615*u* (Skanda): IX, **45**γ, 2510 (beings).—§ 739 (Ānuçāsanik.): XIII, **34**, 2196γ (conquered the Tālajaṅghas).—§ 745*e* (Cyavana-Kuçika-s.): XIII, **55**, 2898; **56**, 2905, 2906, 2918, 2924.—§ 772*b* (Pavanārjuna-s.): XIII, **158**, 7353.—§ 786*f* (Jamadagni): XIV, **92**, 2891.

[Bhṛgu-Bharadvāja-saṃvāda(ḥ)] ("the conversation between Bhṛgu and Bharadvāja"). § 660*b* (Mokshadh.): The Primeval Being called *Mānasa* (description) > *Mahat* > Consciousness > Space > Water > Fire and Wind > Earth. The self-born *Mānasa* created a lotus pregnant with Energy > *Brahmán* > all things, *Brahmán* = *Ananta*: *Agni* and *Soma* (= the Sun and the Moon) are his eyes, etc. *Bharadvāja* asked *Bhṛgu* about the extent of the firmament. *Bhṛgu* explained that the firmament or Space is infinite, and is peopled with systems upon systems of self-luminous bodies (*devāḥ*), etc. *Bharadvāja* asked why *Brahmán* is called the first-born and not the Lotus whence he sprang. *Bhṛgu's* answer: The earth is that lotus, created to give rise to that form of *Mānasa* which became *Brahmán*; *Sumeru*, reaching up to heaven, became its pericarp (XII, **182**). *Bharadvāja* asked how *Brahmán*, residing within *Meru*, created all things. *Bhṛgu* said that *Mānasa* [in his form of Brahmán, PCR.] created by fiat of Will, first water, which is the life of all creatures; earth, etc., are transformations of water, and have been produced by the solidification of that element. *Bharadvāja* enquired after the manner and order of the creation of the several elements; *Bhṛgu* explained that in very ancient times (the *Brahmakalpa*) Br.-r., assembled together, felt this very doubt, engaged in contemplation for 1,000 celestial years, and then heard a celestial voice saying: "Formerly there was only infinite Space . . . " (XII, **183**). Asked by *Bharadvāja*, *Bhṛgu* explained why only the five primal elements are called *Bhūtas*. *Bharadvāja* enquired why all the elements are not seen in the immobile objects. *Bhṛgu* explained how all objects consist of all the five primal elements, but in each the proportions are different; as example he adduced the trees, which he showed to be not inanimate, etc.; through the breath called *Prāṇa* living creatures are enabled to move; through *Vyāna* they put forth strength for action; *Apāna* moves downward; *Samāna* resides within the heart; through *Udāna* one eructates and is enabled to utter the seven original notes called *Shaḍja*, etc. (*a*) (XII, **184**). Asked by *Bharadvāja*, *Bhṛgu* explained how fire resides within a living body, and how wind moves the body; *Prāṇa* (*c*), *Samāna* (*d*), *Apāna* (*e*), *Udāna* (*f*), *Vyāna* (*g*) (XII, **185**). *Bharadvāja's* observations on life being worth little if that which is called life be due to the action of fire and wind only (XII, **186**). *Bhṛgu's* observations on the indestructibility of living creatures; *Bharadvāja's* objection; *Bhṛgu's* answer ("it is fire that sustains the breaths *Prāṇa*, etc.; that heat is called life . . . "). *Bharadvāja* enquired on the true nature of life; *Bhṛgu* explained that it is *antarātman* that inspires the body: water—the soul (*ātmā*) = *Brahmán* (in all creatures) = *kshetrajña* and *paramátman* respectively; etc. There is no destruction of the living agent; it is the body that is dissolved in death (XII, **187**). *Bhṛgu* said: *Brahmán* first created only some *brahmans* who were *Prajāpatis*; then Truth, etc. (β); then D., Dā., G., Dai., As., M.-U., Y., Rā., N., Pç., and men with their four divisions: *brahmans* (white), *kshattriyas* (red), *vaiçyas* (yellow), and *çūdras* (black); etc. *Bharadvāja* was unwilling to admit any original distinction between the four castes; *Bhṛgu* admitted that there is no original distinction between them; all the world at first consisted of only *brahmans*; how the different castes gradually rose; those are not *brahmans* that are incapable of understanding that every created thing is the Supreme *Brahmán*; they take birth as Pç., Rā., *Pretas*, and *Mlecchas* (XII, **188**). What acts constitute a *brahman*, a *kshattriya*, a *vaiçya*, a *çūdra*; a *çūdra* may become a *brahman* by adopting the characteristics of a *brahman*, and *vice versa*; the duties that one should observe to become truly righteous; the mind should be united with *Prāṇa*, and *Prāṇa* be held within *Brahmán* (XII, **189**). *Bhṛgu* discoursed on the characteristics of Truth and Untruth; happiness should always be sought; upon what happiness depends; *Bharadvāja* doubted that happiness is the highest aim ("*Brahmán* lives alone, observant of the vow of *brahmacarya*; *Çiva* brought *Kāma* to extinction"); *Bhṛgu's* discourse in explanation of *Bharadvāja's* doubt ("the earth is the progenitrix of all creatures; females partake of her nature; the male animal is like *Prajāpati* himself") (XII, **190**). Asked by *Bharadvāja*, *Bhṛgu* explained the consequences of gifts, of righteousness, of conduct, of penances, of the study of the *Vedas*, and of Sacrifices. Asked by *Bharadvāja*, he then discoursed about the several kinds of duty; then about the four modes of life (laid down in days of old by *Brahmán* for the benefit of the world) and the duties of the several modes (XII, **191**); on the duties of the Forest mode of life; on those of the *Parivrājakas*. *Bharadvāja* enquired about the existence of any region beyond that which we inhabit; *Bhṛgu* indicated the existence in the North (on the other side of *Himavat*) of a region that is the abode of the righteous: "Here *Brahmán* in days of yore, and all the gods with Ṛ., having performed proper penances, became purified and attained to *Brahmán*."—*Bharadvāja* worshipped *Bhṛgu* with veneration (XII, **192**).

Bhṛgu-çārdūla[1] = Cyavana: XIII, 2863.
Bhṛgu-çārdūla[2] = Çaunaka: I, 1068, 1093.
Bhṛgu-çārdūla[3] = Jamadagni: XIII, 2919.
Bhṛgu-çārdūla[4] = Paraçu-Rāma, q.v.
Bhṛgu-çārdūla[5] = Ṛcīka: XII, 1731; XIII, 212.
Bhṛgu-çreshṭha[1] = Çukra: I, 3332 (*Kāvyaḥ*).
Bhṛgu-çreshṭha[2] = Jamadagni: XIV, 2891.
Bhṛgu-çreshṭha[3] = Paraçu-Rāma, q.v.
Bhṛgūdvaha[1] = Bhṛgu. § 736*b* (Vītahavyop.): XIII, **30**, 1995.
Bhṛgūdvaha[2] = Cyavana: XIII, 2709 (*Cy°e*), 2874.
Bhṛgūdvaha[3] = Çaunaka: I, 876.
Bhṛgūdvaha[4] = Çukra: I, 3453, 3458, 3461.
Bhṛgūdvaha[5] = Paraçu-Rāma, q.v.
Bhṛgūdvaha[6] = Utaṅka: XIV, 1570, 1604, 1647, 1729.
Bhṛgūdvaha[7] = Vipula: XIII, 1317.
Bhṛgukulaçreshṭha[1] = Mārkaṇḍeya: III, 13642.
Bhṛgukulaçreshṭha[2] = Paraçu-Rāma: XIII, 4052.
Bhṛgukulakīrtivardhana = Cyavana: XIII, 2824.
Bhṛgukulodvaha[1] = Cyavana: XIII, 2803.
Bhṛgukulodvaha[2] = Çaunaka: I, 898.
Bhṛgukulodvaha[3] = Çukra: XIII, 4687 (*Çukraḥ*).
Bhṛgukulodvaha[4] = Paraçu-Rāma, q.v.
Bhṛgukulodvaha[5] = Utaṅka: XIV, 1705.
Bhṛgumukhya = Cyavana: XIII, 2850.
Bhṛgunandana[1] ("the son of Bhṛgu"): III, 10432 (*maharshiḥ, ishṭiñ cakāra Saudyumner*—i.e. Yuvanāçva's *putrakāraṇāt*).
Bhṛgunandana[2] = Aurva: I, 6830.
Bhṛgunandana[3] = Cyavana, q.v.
Bhṛgunandana[4] = Çaunaka: I, 868, 900, 944, 1470, 1868, 2140.
Bhṛgunandana[5] = Mārkaṇḍeya: III, 13631.
Bhṛgunandana[6] = Paraçu-Rāma, q.v.
Bhṛgunandana[7] = Kuru: I, 973.
Bhṛgunandana[8] = Ṛcīka: XII, 1726; XIII, 2910.
Bhṛgunandana[9] = Uçanas: XII, 10678.
Bhṛgunandana[10] = Utaṅka: XIV, 1559, 1571, 1579, 1580, 1615, 1622, 1736.
Bhṛguputra = Ṛcīka: XII, 1721.
Bhṛgusattama[1] = Paraçu-Rāma: V, 7338.
Bhṛgusattama[2] = Ṛcīka: XIII, 214, 235.
Bhṛgusattama[3] = Vipula: XIII, 2286.
Bhṛgusūnu ("the son of Bhṛgu," a planet, Venus = Çukra): IX, 545.
Bhṛgusuta = Ṛcīka: XIII, 218.
Bhṛgūttama[1] = Jamadagni: XIII, 4641.
Bhṛgūttama[2] = Paraçu-Rāma: XIII, 3982, 4035, 4044.
Bhṛgūttama[3] = Vipula: XIII, 2270.
Bhṛgutuṅga. § 144 (Yayāti): I, **75**, 3181.—§ 249 (Arjunavanavāsap.): I, **215**, 7813.—§ 305 (Anudyūtap.): II, **78**, 2574.—§ 370 (Tīrthay.): III, **84**, 8028 (°*aṃ samāsādya vājimedhaphalaṃ labhet*).—§ 375 (do.): III, **85**, 8234 (on Malaya one should ascend the funeral pyre, in Bh° one should kill himself by hunger; *anāçanaṃ* both C. and B.).—§ 377 (Dhaumyatīrthak.): III, **90**, 8394 (mahāgiriḥ, in the North).—§ 410 (Plakshāvataraṇa): III, **130**, 10555.—§ 413 (Tīrthay.): **135**, 10698 (*parvataṃ*).—§ 442 (Nivātakavacayuddhap.): III, **167**, 11945.—§ 733 (Ānuçāsanik.): XIII, **25**, 1705 (*mahāhrada upaspṛçya Bh°e tv alolupaḥ | trirātroposhito bhūtvā mucyate brahmahatyayā*).
Bhṛguvaṃça ("the family of Bh°"). § 11 (Parvas.): I, **2**, 365.—§ 70 (Ādivaṃç.): I, **59**, 2198.—§ 227 (Aurvop.): I, **179**, 6823.
Bhū[1] ("Earth") = Çiva (1000 names[1]).
Bhū[2] = Kṛshṇa: XII, 1509.
Bhū[3] = Vishṇu (1000 names).
Bhūçaya ("lying on earth") = Vishṇu (1000 names).
Bhūgarbha = Vishṇu (1000 names).
Bhujagapati ("the lord of the serpents") = Padmanābha: XII, 13943.
Bhujagāri ("the enemy of the serpents") = Garuḍa: X, 651.
Bhujagātmajā ("daughter of the serpent") = Ulūpī: XIV, 2403; XVII, 27.
Bhujagendrakanyā ("the daughter of the serpent king") = Ulūpī: XV, 666.
Bhujagottama ("the foremost of serpents") = Vishṇu (1000 names).
Bhujagottamā (do.) = Ulūpī: XIV, 2375.
Bhūliṅga. § 290*d* (Çiçupālavadhap.): II, **44**, 1545 ("on the other side of the Himavat, the bird Bhūliṅga always cries 'Never do anything rashly,' but nevertheless picks from the lion's mouth the pieces of flesh sticking between the teeth, and lives at the lion's pleasure").—§ 658 (Kṛtaghnop.): XII, **169**, 6326 (°*çakunāḥ sāmudrāḥ, parvatodbhavāḥ*).
Bhumanyu[1]. § 151 (Pūruv.): I, **94**, 3712 (son of Bharata through Bharadvāja), 3713 (becomes yuvarāja).—§ 152 (do.): I, **94**, 3714 (has the sons Diviratha, Suhotra (the oldest), Suhotṛ, Suhavis, Suyajus, *Pushkariṇyām Ṛcīkas ca*).—§ 156 (do.): I, **95**, ††3785 (son of Bharata Daushyanti and Sunandā Sārvasenā Kāçeyī), ††3786 (married to Vijayā Dāçārhī, and by her father of Suhotra).
Bhumanyu[2]. § 154 (Pūruv.): I, **94**, 3748 (son of the elder Dhṛtarāshṭra, the brother of Vāhlīka).
Bhūmanyu (B. *Su°*). § 767 (Ānuçāsanik.): XIII, **137*a***, 6266 (went to Heaven for having given Çāṇḍilya mountains of food).
***Bhūmi** ("Earth") personified: I, 3017; V, 3973 (*yathā*, married to Bhūmipati); XIII, 7236, 7237 (*Kāçyapī*), etc.
Bhūmiçaya. § 656 (Khaḍgotp.): XII, **166**, 6194-5 (receives the Sword from Amūrtarayas and transmits it to Bharata).
Bhūmiñjaya[1]. § 552 (Goharaṇap.): IV, **35**, 1157 (a son of Matsya); **40**, 1306 (= Uttara); **44**, 1390 (*ahaṃ Bh°o nāma, nāmnā 'ham api cottaraḥ*).

Bhūmiñjaya[2]. § 592 (Saṃçaptak.): VII, **20**, 804η (in the bosom of Droṇa's Garuḍavyūha).

Bhūmipāla. § 130 (Aṃçāvat.): I, **67**, 2697 (among the kings reborn from the Krodhavaça gaṇa).—§ 554 (Sainyodyogap.): V, **4**γ, 79.

Bhūmiparvan(°**va**) ("the section relating to the earth"; the 68th of the minor parvans of Mhbhr.).—§ 10 (Parvas.): I, **2**, (337).—[§ 575]: *Dhṛtarāshṭra* wishes to hear about the extent of the ocean, of *Çākadvīpa*, etc. (*a*). *Sañjaya* describes the seven [great] islands, the moon and the sun, and *Rāhu*. *Jambu-parvata* (i.e. Jambu-dvīpa, v. Nīl.) extends for 18,600 *yojanas*. The extent of the salt ocean is twice this; it has many kingdoms, mountains, etc., peopled by Si. and Cā., and is circular in form. Then *Çākadvīpa* (*b*) (VI, **11**). In the North is the ocean of clarified butter; then that of curds; then that of wine; then another of water. The extent of the islands is doubled as they proceed further and further towards the North. In the island in the middle is the great mountain *Gaura* of red arsenic; in the western the mountain *Kṛshṇa*, the friend (i.e. favourite abode, PCR.) of *Nārāyaṇa*, where *Keçava* guards celestial gems and bestows happiness on creatures. The clump of *Kuça*-grass in *Kuça-dvīpa* and the *Çālmali* tree in *Çālmalika* are adored. In the *Krauñca* island also the mountain *Mahā-Krauñca* (a mine of all kinds of gems) is always adored by all four castes of men. There is the huge mountain *Gomanta* (consisting of all kinds of metals), whereon, with the emancipated (*mokshibhiḥ*), the puissant *Nārāyaṇa Hari* always resides. In *Kuçadvīpa* are six principal mountains (ε); the intervening spaces increase in the ratio of one to two as they proceed further and further towards the North; and seven *Varshas* (ζ), where D. and G., etc., sport, and the inhabitants never die, and there are no robbers or *Mlecchas*; all the residents are almost white and very delicate. In the *Krauñca* island are six mountains (η); the intervening spaces increase in the ratio of one to two; there are seven countries (*deçāḥ*) (θ), inhabited by D. and G.; the people are almost white. In the island of *Pushkara* is the mountain *Pushkara*, with jewels and gems; there *Prajāpati* always dwells, adored by D. and M.-ṛ.; diverse gems from *Jambu-dvīpa* are used there. In all these islands truth, etc., increase in the ratio of one to two, as the islands become more and more remote. The land in all those islands comprises but one country, for that is said to be one country in which one religion is met with. *Prajāpati* always dwells there, protecting those islands. Cooked food comes there of itself. After these regions is seen *Samā* (*c*). Then he speaks of *Svarbhānu* (*d*; v. Rāhu), *Candramas* (*e*), *Sūrya* (*f*). "I have now told thee the construction of the universe according to the *Çāstras*. Therefore pacify thy son *Duryodhana*." Blessing upon the reader (VI, **12**).

Bhūmipati ("the husband of Earth"): V, 3973 (*yathā Bhūmyāṃ Bhūmipatiḥ*).

Bhūpati. § 749 (Ānuçās.): XIII, **91**γ, 4357 (one of the 64 Viçve devāḥ).

Bhūri (son of Somadatta according to VP. and Hariv.). § 232 (Svayaṃvarap.): I, **186***a*, 6995 (present with Somadatta, Bhūriçravas, and Çala at the svayaṃvara of Kṛshṇā).—§ 287 (Rājasūyikap.): II, **34**, 1267 (comes with the same to the rājasūya of Yudhishṭhira).—§ 593 (Abhimanyuv.): VII, **37**, 15890.—§ 600 (Ghaṭotkacav.): VII, **158**, 7031ψ; **165**, 7361 (*Kauravaḥ*; attacks Çaineya, i.e. Sātyaki); **166**, 7397 (attacks Çaineya).—§ 795 (Svargārohaṇap.): XVIII, **5**, 163μ. Cf. Kaurava.

Bhūribala (son of Dhṛtarāshṭra). § 611 (Çalyap.): IX, **26**, 1404ρρ, 1414 (slain by Bhīma).

Bhūriçravas (v. Bhūri). § 213 (Jatugṛhap.): I, **143**, 5708.—§ 232 (Svayaṃvarap.): I, **186***a*, 6995 (v. Bhūri).—§ 287 (Rājasūyikap.): II, **34**, 1267 (v. Bhūri).—§ 302 (Anudyūtap.): II, **74**, 2477.—§ 314 (Ghoshayātrap.): III, **252**, 15205. § 556 (Sañjayayānap.): V, **23**, †694.—§ 561 (Yānasandhip.): V, **55**, 2185λ, 2208ν; **58**, 2301τ, 2305υ; **66**, 2504εε.—§ 567 (Bhagavadyānap.): V, **124**, 4171δ.—§ 570 (Sainyaniryāṇap.): V, **155**, 5275θ.—§ 572 (Rathātirath.): V, **165***a*, 5742 (*Saumadattiḥ*).—§ 593 (Ambop.): V, **195**ζ, 7612.—§ 576 (Bhagavadgītāp.): VI, **17**, 657γ; **18**δ, 687; **20**ζ, 752.—§ 578 (Bhīshmavadhap.): VI, **51**, 2107φ.—§ 580 (do.): VI, **56**β, 2406 (in the neck of Bhīshma's Garuḍa-vyūha); **59**μ, †2583, †2620ν, †2621, †2622, †2648ρ.—§ 581 (do.): VI, **61**γ, 2680, 2690; **63**, 2811 (*Saumadattiḥ*); **64**, 2813 (attacks Sātyaki); **65**, 2929ν.—§ 582 (do.): VI, **74**, 3246, 3252 (*Yūpaketum*, i.e. having on his standard the sacrificial stake), 3263, 3267.—§ 584 (do.): VI, **81**, 3561; **84**, 3432.—§ 585 (do.): VI, **92**, 4118χ, 4132; **94**, 4194ω.—§ 586 (do.): VI, **99**, 4503β (in the right wing of the Sarvatobhadra of Bhīshma); **102**, 4668λ.—§ 587 (do.): VI, **111**, 5184; **119**, 5583ψ.—§ 590 (Droṇābhishekap.): VII, **14**, 538 (fights Çikhaṇḍin).—§ 592 (Saṃçaptak.): VII, **20**, 800δ (in the right wing of Droṇa's Garuḍa-vyūha).—§ 593 (Abhimanyuv.): VII, **34**, 1504γ; **37**, 1589θ, 1602ι, 1609κ.—§ 596 (Pratijñāp.): VII, **75**, 2673γ.—§ 598 (Jayadrathavadhap.): VII, **85**, 3036β.—§ 599 (do.): VII, **104**, 3894μ, 3916, 3923; **105**, [3948: the standard of *Bh.*—*Saumadatteḥ*, devoted to sacrifices—bore the sign of the sacrificial stake, made of gold]; **137**ωω, 5629; **141**εεε, 5870, 5873, 5876; **142**, 5879, 5899, 5929, 5938, 5940, 5942, 5943, 5944; **143**, (5954), 5955ηηη, 5966θθθ, 6008 (slain by Sātyaki in *prāya*); **144**, 6026, 6027; **145**, 6055 (*Kaurave*), 6056; **147**, 6327, 6334; **151**, 6529, 6531, 6557.—§ 600 (Ghaṭotkacav.): VII, **155**, 6684; **156**, 6743; **158**, 7036ω.—§ 603 (Nārāyaṇāstramokshap.): VII, **198**ρ, 9154, 9168, 9190.—§ 604 (Karṇap.): VIII, **1**, 22; **5**, 106 (*Kauravadāyādaḥ*).—§ 609 (Çalyap.): IX, **2**ζ, 72, 88.—§ 611 (do.): IX, **24**νν, 1298.—§ 613 (Gadāyuddhap.): IX, **32**β, 1837.—§ 615*b* (Baladevatīrthay.): IX, **54**, 3061ν. § 615 (Gadāyuddhap.): IX, **61**φ, 3421, 3447χ; **64**, 3593.—§ 616 (Sauptikap.): X, **5**ε, 197; **9**, 524κ (*svarge*).—§ 619 (Strīvilāpa): X, **24**ι, 679 (son of Somadatta), 685, 687 (°*o bhāryaḥ*).—§ 620 (Çrāddhap.): XI, **26**, 786β.—§ 783 (Anugītāp.): XIV, **52**, 1497β.—§ 787 (Āçramavāsap.): XV, **11**, 372π.—§ 789 (Putradarçanap.): XV, **29**ε, 808 (°*o bhāryā; yasyās tu çvasuro dhīmān Bāhlīkaḥ sa Kurūdvahaḥ*, i.e. grandfather-in-law, PCR.); **32**, 877θ.—§ 793 (Mausalap.): XVI, **3**, 77.—§ 795 (Svargarohaṇap.): XVIII, **5**μ, 163 (entered the deities).

Compare also the following synonyms:—

Bhūridakshiṇa ("rich in sacrificial gifts"): VII, 5927, 5937, 6002, 6044.

Çalāgraja ("the elder brother of Çala"): VII, 5997, 6002.

Kaurava, q.v.

Kauravadāyāda, q.v.

Kauraveya, q.v.

Kauravya, q.v.

Kauravyamukhya, q.v.

Kuruçārdūla, q.v.

Kuruçreshṭha, q.v.
Kurūdvaha, q.v.
Kurupuṅgava, q.v.
Yūpaketana : VII, 5988.
Yūpaketu ("having for his standard the sacrificial stake"): II, 1538; VI, 3252 (*Bhūriçravasaṃ*); VII, 1118 (*Saumadattiḥ*), 5984, 5992, 5996, 6337.

Bhūridakshiṇa[1] = Bhūriçravas, q.v.
Bhūridakshiṇa[2] ("rich in sacrificial gifts") = Vishṇu (1000 names).
Bhūridyumna[1]. § 267 (Yamas.): II, **8,** 330 (in the palace of Yama), 332.—§ 562 (Bhagavadyānap.): V, **83,** 2946η (among the brahmarshis who surround Kṛshṇa).
Bhūridyumna[2] (a prince, son of Vīradyumna). § 641 (Rājadh.): XII, **128,** 4686.
Bhūridyumna[3]. § 746 (Ānuçāsanik.): XIII, **76,** 3689ι.
Bhūridyumnapitṛ ("the father of Bh°") = Vīradyumna (a king): XII, 4673.
Bhūrihan (an ancient ruler) § 673*b* (Bali-Vāsava-s.): XII, **227,** 8263*a*.
Bhūritejas (among the kings reborn from the krodhavaça-gaṇa). § 130 (Aṃçāvat.): I, **67,** 2699.—§ 554 (Sainyodyogap.): V, **4,** 80γ.
Bhūritejasa = Agni, q.v.
Bhūrloka (the lowest of the upper worlds). § 730 (Ānuçāsanik.): XIII, **17,** 1137.
Bhūshaṇa = Vishṇu (1000 names).
Bhūta = Çiva (1000 names[2]).
***Bhūta**, pl. ("beings," "elements"): I, 648 (*pañcabhyaḥ*); II, 71 (surround Bhūtapati); II, 402 (°*saṅghaiḥ*; surround Umāpati, i.e. Çiva); III, 1491 (*divyebhyaḥ*), 1554 (surround Çiva), 1646 (*Dānavān Rākshasāṃs tathā | Bhūtāni ca Piçāçāṃs ca Gandharvān atha Pannagān*), 8168 (*Bhūta-Yaksha-Piçācāç ca*, etc.), 12238 (*svasti bhūtebhyaḥ*), 14310 (. . . *Rakshobhiç ca Piçācaiç ca Raudrair Bhūtagaṇais tathā*, etc.), 14444 (*sarvabhūtagaṇair vṛtaḥ*, i.e. Skanda), 15823 (*sarvabhūtāni*), 15913 (*Sarpa-Kinnara-Bhūtebhyaḥ*); IV, 196 (*Kṛtānuyātrā Bhūtais tvaṃ*), †2148 (*tataḥ sa Vahni-pramito mahākapiḥ sahaiva Bhūtair divam utpapāta*, sc. in the banner of Arjuna); V, 348 (*deva-Dānava-Yakshāṇām Ṛshīṇāṃ Rakshasāṃ tathā | Pitṛ-Gandharva-Bhūtānāṃ cakshurvishaya-vartinām | teja ādāsyase paçyan*, say the gods and ṛshis to Nahusha), 5290 (*Kumāra iva Bhūtānāṃ*), 7249 (. . . *naktañcarāṇāṃ Bhūtānāṃ* . . .); VI, 219 (*Paçupatir divyair Bhūtaiḥ samāvṛtaḥ*), 1195 (*Bhūtāni yānti Bhūtejyā* . . .), 1430 (*pretān Bhūtagaṇāṃç cānye yajante tāmasā janāḥ*), 3833 (*ghoram āyodhanaṃ jajñe Bhūtasaṅghasamākulaṃ*), 4061 (*āvishṭā iva yudhyante raksho-Bhūtair mahābalāḥ*), 5509 (*dṛçyamāneshu Rakshaḥsu Bhūteshu ca nadatsu ca*), 5702 (*ity abhāshanta Bhūtāni*, about Bhīshma when he has fallen); VII, 256 (*tato ninādo Bhūtānām ākāçe samajāyata*), 1221 (*Dhanañjayaṃ Bhūtagaṇāḥ sādhu sādhv ity apūjayan*), 1630 (*sarvabhūtāni*, cry *sādhu* to Abhimanyu), 1947 (*antarikshe ca Bhūtāni prākroçanta*), 2266, 2267 (only in B.), 2736 (*bhūtāni tvāṃ nirīkshante nūnaṃ candram ivoditaṃ*), 2859 (°*saṅghaiḥ*, surround Çiva), 3119 (*iti bhūtāni menire*), 3659 (*ākāçagāny api*), 3791 (*sarva*°), 3988 (*sarva*°-*amanyanta*), 3994 (*sarva*°), 3995 (do.), 4066 (do.), 6188 (*nṛtyat-preta-Piçācādyair Bhūtākīrṇaṃ*, sc. the battlefield), 6282 (*sarvāṇi*), †6921 (°*gaṇāḥ*, etc., applaud Açvatthāman), 7015 (*sa-Bhūta-bhujaga-dvipaṃ* . . . *jagat*), 8170 (*nedur Bhūtāny antarikshe*), 9197 (*Bhūta-pakshi-gaṇākulaṃ*), 9456 (°*saṅghaiḥ*), 9461 (°*saṅghagaṇair vṛtaṃ*, sc. Çiva); VIII, 992 (*Bhūtānīva tamonudaḥ*, sc. scorches), 1039 (*sarva*°), 2555 (*nṛtyanti vai Bhūtagaṇāḥ sutṛptā māṃsaçoṇitaiḥ*), 2852 (*sadaivatāni* . . . *sahāpsarobhiḥ*); IX, 2442 (°*saṅghaçataiḥ*), 2473 (°*saṅghānāṃ*), 2496 [2571, *Bhūtānāṃ Mathanaḥ*], 2675 (*nānābhūtagaṇāḥ*), 2680 (*Bhūtasaṅghānāṃ*), 2911 (*pitṛbhiḥ saha*), 2912 [2915 (*sarva*°)], 3633 (°*gaṇaiḥ*); X (selected quotations), 297 (*mahā*°-*gaṇaiḥ*), 300 (°*saṅghāḥ*), 318 (*adṛçyāni*), 412 (°*saṅghaiḥ*), 460, 571 (°*gaṇānukīrṇam āyodhanaṃ*); XII, 574 (*devatātithi*°), 652, 1703 (?), 4500 (°*ānāṃ rājānaṃ Skandaṃ*), 7551 (? °*mātṛgaṇādhyakshaṃ Virūpākshaṃ*), 9285 (i.e. the Piçācas), 9_87 (i.e. *rakshāṃsi*), 11244 (*sa-Yaksha*° *Gandharve*), 12168 (°*gaṇaiḥ*), 12407 (°*ānāṃ vimānāni*), 13648 (°*air Bhūtapatir yathā*); XIII, 874 (*sarva* °*gaṇāḥ*), 1020 (°*gaṇāḥ*), 4719 (*deva-Dānava*°), 4731, 4738, 6021 (°*pīḍitāḥ*), 6112, 6340(?) (°*saṅghaṃ*), 6341 (do.), 6344 (*raksho*° *gaṇaiḥ*), 6346(?) (°*saṅghaiḥ*), 6407 (do.), 6805 (°*gaṇāḥ*), 6872 (°*saṅghaṃ*); XIV, 182 (?) (*nānā* °*gaṇāvṛtaḥ Çūlī*), 184 (910 ?), 1169 (°*gaṇaḥ*), 1177 (*Agnir* °*patiḥ*), 1226 (*deva-Dānava* °*ānāṃ* . . . *Īçvaraḥ prabhuḥ*), 1919 (°*ānāṃ patayaḥ*), 1921 (*naktañcarāṇāṃ*).
Bhūta, pl. masc. (°*āḥ*): XII, 10477 (*na Rākshasāḥ Piçācā vā na Bhūtā na Vināyakāḥ*), 12396 (*tatra devagaṇāḥ Sādhyā mahābhūtā mahābalāḥ*).
Bhūtabhāvana[1] = Çiva: VI, 220; XIII, 1147, 1219 (1000 names[2]).
Bhūtabhāvana[2] = Vishṇu (1000 names).
Bhūta-bhavya-bhavan-nātha = Vishṇu (1000 names).
Bhūta-bhavya-bhavat-prabhu[1] = Vishṇu (1000 names).
Bhūta-bhavya-bhavat-prabhu[2] = Çiva: X, 297.
Bhūta-bhavya-bhavodbhava = Çiva: XIII, 6759; XII, 10425 (1000 names[1]).
Bhūta-bhavyeça = Indra: XVII, 79.
Bhūta-bhṛt = Vishṇu (1000 names).
Bhūtacārin = Çiva (1000 names[2]).
Bhūtaçarman. § 592 (Saṃçaptakav.): VII, **20,** 797γ (in the neck of Droṇa's Garuḍa-vyūha).
Bhūtadhāman. § 238 (Pañcendrop.): I, **197,** 7304 (one of the five Indras).
Bhūtādhipati ("the Lord of Beings, i.e. of the world"): XV, 924 (*mahābhūtāni nityāni Bh*° *saṃçrayāt*).
Bhūtādi = Vishṇu (1000 names).
Bhūtādinidhana = Kṛshṇa: XII, 1670.
Bhūtagrāma(ç) caturvidha(ḥ) = Çiva (1000 names[2]).
Bhūtakarman. § 592 (Saṃçapkav.): VII, **25,** 1085 (*Sabhāpatiḥ*), 1087 (fights Çatānīka Nākuli and is slain).
Bhūtakṛt[1] = Brahmán: XII, 7073, 8979? (the creator of all things), 10493? (do.).
Bhūtakṛt[2] = Çiva (1000 names[1]).
Bhūtakṛt[3] = Vishṇu (1000 names).
Bhūtakṛt[4] = Vasishṭha: XII, 8601.
Bhūtalaya = Çiva (1000 names[2]).
Bhūtamaheçvara = Vishṇu: XIII, 7001.
Bhūtānām īçvaraḥ = Kṛshṇa: IX, 3471.
Bhūtānāṃ mathanaḥ (a warrior of Skanda): § 615*u* (Skanda): IX, **45,** 2571η.
Bhūtānāṃ patiḥ = Çiva: XIV, 199.
Bhūtanishevita = Çiva (1000 names[2]).
Bhūtāntarātman = Nārāyaṇa: XIII, 13461.
Bhūtapati[1] ("the lord of Beings"): II, 71; XII, 13648.
Bhūtapati[2] = Çiva: III, 1547 (*Umāpati*), 12569; V, 3558; VI, 240; XII, 13648, 13705 (*Umāpatiḥ*); XIII, 1226 (1000 names[2]); XIII, 6358, 6366, 6369, 6641.

Bhūtapati[3] = Kṛshṇa; XII, 7558; XIII, 7396.
Bhūtātman[1] = Çiva (1000 names[1]).
Bhūtātman[2] = Vishṇu (1000 names).
Bhūtātman[3] = Brahmán or Kṛshṇa, etc.: III, 8315 (*Pitāmahaḥ*), 11853 (*Prajāpatiḥ*); XII, 7073, 7365, 7423, 7444, 7525 (= Kṛshṇa), 7635 (= Kṛshṇa, mentioned by Pitāmaha), 8744 (*hṛdayāçritaḥ*), 8745, 8754 (a living creature), 10918 (*paribhramati bhūtātmā dyām irāmbudharo mahān | sa punar jāyate rājan prāpyehāyatanaṃ nṛpa*), 11248 (called *ksharaḥ*), 11601 (*mano grasati bhūtātmā, so 'haṅkāraḥ Prajāpatiḥ*), 11849; XIV, 1486 (*tvattejaḥ-sambhavo nityaṃ bhūtātmā, Madhusūdana!*).
Bhūtavāhanasārathi = Çiva (1000 names[2]).
Bhūtāvāsa = Vishṇu (1000 names).
Bhūteça[1] = Çiva: III, 1513; XIII, 6762.
Bhūteça[2] = Kṛshṇa: XII, 1609.
Bhūteça[3] = Skanda: III, 14630.
Bhūti = Vishṇu (1000 names).
Bhūtilaya (a place among the Bāhikas). § 409 (Plakshāvataraṇag.): III, **129,** 10521.—§ 607 (Karṇap.): VIII, **44,** 2063 (*tadvad Bhūtilaye snātvā kathaṃ Svargaṃ gamishyati?*).
Bhūtitīrthā (a mātṛ). § 615*u* (Skanda): IX, **46***θ*, 2645.
Bhuvabhartṛ: III, 14208, v. Āpa (*Āpasya duhitā*—B. *Muditā—bhāryā Sahasya paramā priyā | Bhūpatir Bhuvabhartā ca janayat Pāvakaṃ paraṃ*); 14212 (*Bhūpatir Bhuvabhartā ca Mahataḥ patir ucyate*).
Bhuvaḥ[1] = Çiva (1000 names[1]).
Bhuvaḥ[2] = Vishṇu (1000 names).
Bhuvana[1] (among those who come to see Bhīshma). § 734 (Ānuçāsanik.): XIII, **26,** 1765*a*.
Bhuvana[2] (one of the 64 Viçvadevas). § 749 (Ānuçāsan.): XIII, **91,** 4360*γ*.
Bhuvanabhartṛ, v. Agni.
Bhuvanaçreshṭha = Vishṇu: XII, 13487.
Bhuvaneçvara[1] = Çiva: XIV, 207.
Bhuvaneçvara[2] = Svayambhū: XIII, 6456.
Bhuvaneçvara[3] = Skanda: III, 14631.
Bībhatsu, v. Arjuna.
Bījādhyaksha, Bījakartṛ = Çiva (1000 names[2]).
Bījam avyayam = Vishṇu (1000 names).
Bījavāhana = Çiva (1000 names[2]).
Bilvadaṇḍa = Çiva: XIV, 196.
Bilvaka[1] (a serpent). § 47 (Sarpanāmak.): I, **35,** 1557.
Bilvaka[2] (a tīrtha). § 733 (Ānuçāsanik.): XIII, **25,** 1700.
Bilvapāṇḍara (a serpent). § 47 (Sarpanāmak.): I, **35,** 1557.
Bilvapattra (a Nāga in Bhogavatī). § 564 (Mātalīyop.): V, **103***γ*, 3630.
Bilvatejas (a serpent of Takshaka's race). § 64 (Sarpasattra): I, **57,** 2150.
Bindu = Çiva (1000 names[2]).
Bindusaras. § 263 (Sabhākriyāp.): II, **3,** 60, 62, 67.—§ 294 (Dyūtap.): II, **50,** 1809 (the palace of Yudhiohṭhira is *kṛtāṃ Bindusaro-ratnaiḥ*).—§ 423 (Gandhamādanap.): III, **145,** 11057 (*çivaṃ*).—§ 574*f* (Jambūkh.): VI, **6,** 238: There king Bhagīratha, beholding Gaṅgā, resided for many years; there innumerable sacrificial stakes made of gems and chaitya trees made of gold may be seen. There Indra (*Sahasrāksha*) reached perfection (*gataḥ siddhiṃ*) by sacrificing; there Çiva (? *Bhūtapatiḥ*), etc. (*ζ*), reside; there Gaṅgā, issuing from Brahmaloka, first showed herself, and then divided herself into seven streams: Vasvaukasārā, etc. (*η*).
[Bisastainyopākhyāna] ("the episode relating to the theft of the lotus-stalks"). § 750*b* (Ānuçāsanik.): *Bhīshma* said: The seven Ṛ. *Kaçyapa*, etc. (*a*), and *Arundhatī* together had one single maidservant, *Gaṇḍā*, who was married to the *çūdra Paçusakha*. While they, in days of old, practised penances, preparing themselves for (*upaçikshanto*) *Brahmaloka* by yoga meditation (*samādhinā*), there occurred a severe drought; *Çibi's* son *Çaibya* had in former times given away a son of his as the sacrificial present to the *ṛtvijes*; that prince now died of starvation; impelled by hunger, the *Ṛshis* cooked his body in a vessel. King *Çaibya Vṛshādarbhi* came and offered to give them kine, etc., but they refused it: that acceptance of gifts from a king was poison; they left the spot abandoning that flesh. The king sent his ministers with figs, some of which were filled with gold; but *Atri*, finding them heavy, refused to take them; and so did all of them (*β*), and left the spot. Filled with wrath, *Vṛshādarbhi*, after having observed penances, poured libations into the fire accompanied by *mantras*; from the fire a hag (*kṛtyā*) sprang forth, whom he called *Yātudhānī*; he ordered her to slay the *Ṛshis*, etc., having ascertained their names. While Ṛ. roved within the forest, subsisting upon fruits and roots, they saw a well-nourished mendicant [called further below *Çunaḥsakha*] with a dog in good condition; *Arundhatī* pointed him out to them, and each of them explained the superior condition of this mendicant with reference to one of the points in which he was better situated than they (*γ*). The wandering mendicant approached them and touched their hand according to custom. One day they beheld a beautiful lake overgrown with lotuses, and desired to gather some lotus-stalks; urged by *Vṛshādarbhi, Yātudhānī*, who guarded the lake, would know their names before they took the stalks; *Atri* knew that she stood there in order to slay them; but they all told their names with their etymological explanations (*δ*); at each explanation *Yātudhānī* declared that she did not understand it, [in some cases] "in consequence of the inflections which the roots had undergone"; *Çunaḥsakha* calls himself *Çunaḥsakha-sakhi*, and as *Yātudhānī* wishes to hear the name once more in order to understand it, he struck her head with his triple stick, at which she was consumed to ashes. Having gathered lotus-stalks, they once more plunged into the lake in order to offer oblations of water to the *Pitṛs*. As they came up, the stalks were nowhere to be seen. They took, each of them, oaths to their innocence (*ε*); but the oath of *Çunaḥsakha* was "no oath at all,' and he confessed that he had stolen the stalks from desire of testing them; he turned out to be *Indra*, who had come to test them, and told them the whole matter about *Yātudhānī*. They then ascended to heaven in the company of *Indra* himself * (XIII, **93**).
Bodha, pl. (°*āḥ*), a people. § 273 (Rājasūyār.): II, **14,** 590 (had emigrated to the West from fear of Jarāsandha).—§ 574 (Jambūkh.): VI, **9,** 347*μ* (a people in Bhārata-varsha).
Bodhya (a ṛshi). § 650 (Mokshadh.): XII, **178,** 6643 (*ṛshiṃ*), (6645).
Bradhnaçva (a king; prob. w.r. instead of Vadhryaçva, BR.). § 382 (Agastyop.): III, **98,** 8601, 8602, 8606.
Brāhma, adj. ("belonging to Brahmán or Bráhman"). § 1 (Anukram.): I, **1,** 19 (*Bhāratasyetihāsasya B°īṃ saṃhitāṃ*).—§ 135 (Çakuntalop.): I, **74,** 2962 (sc. *vivāhaḥ*).—§ 146 (Devayānī): I, **81,** 3371 (*vācaṃ*).—§ 209 (Drupadaçāsana): I, **138,** 5514 (*balaṃ*).—§ 214 (Hiḍimbavadhap.): I, **156,** 6087 (*Vedaṃ*).—§ 218 (Caitrarathap.): I, **167,** 6383 (*tejaḥ*), 6384 (do.).—§ 234 (Svayaṃvarap.): I, **190,** 7105 (*astre*), 7106 (*tejaḥ*).—§ 270 (Brahmasabhāv.): II, **11,** 429

(*Brāhmīṃ*, sc. *sabhāṃ*).—§ 277 (Jarāsandhavadhap.): II, **22,** 889 (*ājñām*).—§ 306 (Anudyūtap.): II, **80,** 2654 (*çriyam*).—§ 330 (Indradarçana): III, **37,** 1460 (sc. *astraṃ*), 1499 (*çriyā*).—§ 356 (Tīrthayātrāp.): III, **81,** 4022 (do.).—§ 423 (Gandhamādanaprav.): III, **145,** 11041 (*lakshmyā*).—§ 468 (Mārkaṇḍeyas.): III, **188,** 12832 (*etat sahasraparyantam aho Brāhmam udāhṛtam*).—§ 482 (Pativratop.): III, **210,** 13912 (*vidyāṃ*).—§ 555*f* (Agni): V, **16,** 490 (*mantraiḥ*).—§ 560 (Sanatsujātap.): V, **44,** †1684 (*vācaṃ*), †1690 (*sthitiṃ*).—§ 561 (Yānasandhip.): V, **48,** 1913 (*astraṃ*). — § 562 (Bhagavadyānap.): V, **84,** 3017 (*vṛttiṃ*).—§ 568 (Vidulāputraçāsana): V, **136,** 4641 (*çriyā*).—§ 569 (Bhagavadyānap.): V, **139,** 4786 (sc. *astraṃ*).—§ 571 (Ulūkadūt.): V, **160,** 5504 (*Brāhme*—sc. *vede*—*dhanushi cācāryaṃ*, i.e. Droṇa); **161,** 5550 (do. = do.).—§ 573 (Ambop.): V, **184,** 7281 (*paramāstraṃ*).—§ 589 (Droṇābhishek.): VII, **9,** 296 (sc. *ghoshaḥ*).—§ 592 (Saṃçaptakav.): VII, **23,** 988 (*Dhanurvede Brāhme Vede ca pāragaṃ*, i.e. Satyadhṛti).—§ 596 (Pratijñāp.): VII, **76,** 2692 (*astreṇa*); **80,** 2842 (*muhūrte*).—§ 599 (Jayadrathavadhap.): VII, **106,** 3998 (*astraṃ*); **125,** 5028 (do.), 5029 (do.), 5030 (*astre*).—§ 600 (Ghaṭotkacavadhap.): VII, **157,** 6959 (*astraṃ*). — § 602 (Droṇavadhap.): VII, **188,** 8615 (sc. *yuddhaṃ*), 8621 (*astraṃ*); **192,** 8833 (do.), 8839 (*astrāṇi*).—§ 603 (Nārāyaṇāstram.): VII, **193,** 8933 (*astraṃ*); **194,** 8965 (do.); **201,** 9426 (do.).—§ 608 (Karṇap.): VIII, **49,** 2338 (do.), 2356 (*bale*).—§ 615*u* (Skanda): IX, **46***ι*, 2655 (°*yaḥ*, sc. *mātaraḥ*).—§ 660*b* (Bhṛgu-Bharadvājas.): XII, **188,** 6939 (*sarvaṃ Brāhmam idaṃ jagat*), 6944 (*sarasvatī*).—§ 661 (Mokshadh.): XII, **196,** 7171 (*tanuṃ*). — § 662*b* (Jāpakop.): XII, **199,** 7203 (*tapaḥ*).—§ 677 (Mokshadh.): XII, **232,** 8495 (*kshape*), 8506 (*divasaṃ*); **234,** 8567 (*sañcaraḥ*). — § 680*b* (Tulādhāra-Jājalisaṃv.): XII, **264,** 9415 (*vedaṃ*).—§ 705 (Mokshadh.): XII, **303,** 11227 (*ahaḥ*).—§ 713 (Çukakṛti): XII, **326,** 12219 (*çriyā*). — § 717*b* (Nārāyaṇīya): XII, **342,** 13144 (*rātrīkshaye*). — § 734 (Ānuçāsanik.): XIII, **26,** †1852 (*sthānakaṃ*).—§ 742 (do.): XIII, **38,** 2204 (°*īm Apsarasaṃ Pañcacūḍāṃ*).—§ 744 (do.): XIII, **44,** 2407 (*dharmaḥ*), 2413 (*brāhmaḥ kshāttro 'tha Gāndharva ete dharmyāḥ*, sc. *vivāhāḥ*).—§ 746 (do.): XIII, **69,** 3434 (*sarasvatiṃ*).—§ 747*b* (Suvarṇotpatti): XIII, **85,** 4143 (*Kaviḥ*, i.e. son of Brahmán).—§ 759 (Ānuçāsanik.): XIII, **104,** 4969 (*muhūrte*), 5058 (*tīrthaṃ*, between the tip and the root of the thumb), 5066 (*tīrthena*).—§ 768*b* (Umā-Maheçvarasaṃv.): XIII, **141,** 6487 (*phenotkaraṃ*).—§ 795 (Svargārohaṇap.): XVIII, **4,** 126 (*vapushā*). Cf. Brāhmya.

Brahmabhavana ("the abode of Brahmán"). § 289 (Arghāharaṇap.): II, **36,** 1309 (*sametā B°e devā Devarshayaḥ*).—§ 520 (Mudgala): III, **261,** 15472. — § 576 (Bhagavadgītāp.): VI, **32,** 1157 (*ā B°ād lokāḥ punar āvartanti*).—§ 755*b* (Nahushop.): XIII, **100,** 4803, 4809. — § 757*n* (Svayambhūbhavana): XIII, **102,** 4895. Cf. Svayambhūbhavana.

Brahmabodhyā, a river. § 574 (Jambūkh.): VI, **9***λ*, 337 (in Bharatavarsha, B. °*vedhyāṃ*).

Brahmacakra = Çiva: VII, 2881 (B. °*vaktrāya*).

Brahmacārin[1], a Gandharva. § 103 (Aṃçāvat.): I, **65,** 2557 (one of the *Devagandharvāḥ Prādheyāḥ*). — § 191 (Arjuna): I, **123***a*, 4814 (among the Gandharvas who sung at the birth of Arjuna).

Brahmacārin[2] = Skanda: III, 14635.

Brahmacārin[3] = Çiva: VII, 2879; VIII, 1448; X, 254, 257, 794; XIII, 1188 (1000 names[2]).

Brahmaçālā, a river. § 377 (Dhaumyatīrthak.): III, **87,** 8319 (*puṇyā*, in the East).

***Brahmaçāpa** ("curse of a brahman"). § 76 (Matsya): I, **63,** 2388 (v. Adrikā).—§ 793 (Mausalap.): XVI, **4,** †107; **7,** 206; **8,** 262 (*vināço B°jaḥ*), 279.

Brahmaçiras, a celestial weapon. § 4 (Anukram.): I, **1,** 212 (repelled by Arjuna).—§ 207 (Droṇa): I, **133,** 5306 (given to Arjuna by Droṇa). — § 210 (Sambhavap.): I, **139,** 5525 (acquired by Droṇa from Agniveça). — § 333*e* (Kairātap.): *B.* (Pāçupata) destroys the entire universe at the end of the yuga. It is not known to Mahendra, nor to Yama, nor to the Yaksha king (i.e. Kubera), nor to Varuṇa, nor to Vāyu. By this Arjuna might obtain victory over Karṇa, Bhīshma, Kṛpa, and Droṇa, and over Dānavas, Rākshasas, Bhūtas, Piçācas, Gandharvas, and Pannagas; when hurled with mantras it produced darts by thousands, maces and arrows. It might be hurled by the eye, by the mind, by words, and by the bow: III, **40,** 1644.—§ 378*b* (Tīrthayātrāp.): III, **91,** 8417: *B.* had sprung from the *amṛta* and came to Rudra in consequence of tapas.—§ 617*b* (Aishīkap.): Droṇa had given *B.* to *Arjuna*; *Açvatthāman* asked him for it, and Droṇa unwillingly gave him it, knowing his restlessness, with the command never to use it against men. Because of the bitter words of his father, *Açvatthāman* began to wander over the earth in grief; coming to *Dvārakā* he said to Kṛshṇa that now he had *B.* (worshipped by D. and G.), which Droṇa had obtained from *Agastya* after austere penances; he asked Kṛshṇa for his discus in exchange for that weapon. He was unable even to move the discus. *Kṛshṇa* praised *Arjuna* (*ε*) and *Pradyumna* (a portion of *Sanatkumāra* and son of *Kṛshṇa* and *Rukmiṇī*), etc. (*ζ*), who had never desired his discus, while *Açvatthāman* confessed that he would have used it against *Kṛshṇa* himself. Then he left *Dvārakā*: X, **12,** 609, 619.—§ 617 (Aishīkap.): X, **13,** 646; **15,** 705, 709.

Brahmaçiropaharta (!) = Çiva: XIII, 905.

***Brahmadaṇḍa**[1] ("curse of a brahman"): I, 619, 1394, 2089, 2165; II, 257 (Nīl. *ābhicārikā vidyā*), 2318 (*iva*); III, 16518 (*çūlam Indrāçaniprakhyaṃ B°m ivodyataṃ*), 16526 (do.); V, 2025 (*B°m ivotthitaṃ*); VI, 5629 (°*samasparçā . . . vāṇāḥ*); VII, 8767 (*çarāṃç ca B°ābhān*); VIII, 1496; IX, 906; XVI, 9, 96. Cf. Brahmaçapa.

Brahmadaṇḍa[2] = Çiva: XIII, 907.

Brahmadaṇḍavinirmātṛ = Çiva (1000 names[2]).

Brahmadarçana. § 747*b* (Suvarṇotpatti): XIII, **85,** 4104 (i.e. the episode XIII, 4104 ff.).

Brahmadatta[1], an ancient king. § 267 (Yamasabhāv.): II, **8,** 331 (in the palace of Yama).—§ 647*b* (Brahmadatta-Pūjanī-saṃv.): XII, **139,** 5136, 5137, 5155, (5156), (5168), (5170), (5175), (5182), 5196, (5208), 5245, 5246.—§ 677 (Mokshadh.): XII, **235,** 8603 (*Pāñcālyaḥ*, went to Heaven after giving the treasure Çaṅkha to the brahmans).—§ 717*b* (Nārāyaṇīya): XII, **343***ψ*, 13264 (*Kaṇḍariko 'tha rājā ca Brahmadattaḥ pratāpavān | jātīmaraṇajaṃ duḥkhaṃ smṛtvā punaḥ punaḥ | saptajātishu mukhyatvād yogānāṃ sampadaṃ gataḥ*).—§ 767 (Ānuçāsanik.): XIII, **137***a*, 6261 (*Pāñcālyaḥ*, attained to Heaven after giving the treasure Çaṅkha).

Brahmadatta[2], pl. (°*āḥ*). § 267 (Yamasabhāv.): II, **8,** 334 (100 Brahmadattas in the palace of Yama).

Brahmadatta-Pūjanī-Saṃvāda(ḥ) ("conversation between Br. and P."). § 647*b*: XII, **139**: As *Bhīshma* had said that from trust great danger arose to kings, *Yudhishṭhira* asked: "But how would the king maintain himself if he were not to trust anybody?" *Bhīshma* related: A bird named *Pūjanī* lived with king *Brahmadatta* in his palace at *Kāmpilya*; like [the bird] *Jīvajīvaka*, it could mimic the cries of all animals (*rutajñā sarvabhūtānām*), etc. At one and the same time P. got an offspring and the king a son. P. used every day to go to the shores of the ocean and bring a couple of fruits, one for her own child and one for the prince. One day the prince, when playing with the offspring of P., killed it, and then came back to his nurse. When P. had returned to the palace, she wept bitterly, and said that nobody should live with a kshattriya or make friends with him; for so long as it suits their purpose, they behave with courtesy; but then they throw off the instrument; they do evil to all, and should never be trusted; even after doing an injury they try to soothe. P. then pierced the eyes of the prince, saying that those who avenge an injury never lose their merit by such conduct. Thinking that the avenger only squares his account, Br. sought to prevail upon P. to remain; "even after a deadly injury, affection and mutual trust arise between two persons residing together (for instance, the *çvapaca* [*cāṇḍāla*, PCR.] and the dog); animosity disappears quickly, like water poured upon the leaf of a lotus; it is Time that does every act; who therefore injures whom? Like fire consuming the fuel, Time consumes all creatures; what thou hast done, has been forgiven by me, do thou also forgive me." P. maintained that the injurer ought to leave his old place and never to place his trust upon the injured; just as the fragments of an earthen vessel cannot be reunited; animosity destroys the very sons and grandsons, and thereby the parties lose the next world as well; animosity can never die; it lies hidden like fire in wood, or like the water-fire (*toyāgniḥ*, i.e. the Aurva-fire) in the ocean; amongst men that have injured one another, therefore, mistrust alone can produce happiness; nor should too much trust be placed upon a person deserving of trust; one should try to inspire others with confidence in one's self, but never repose confidence in others (not even in a wife, son, brother, or friend); the mind of a person who has once injured another becomes naturally filled with mistrust if he sees the injured person worshipping him with gifts and honours. Hostility springs from five causes: woman, land, [harsh] words, natural incompatibility (*sāpatna*, i.e. *jāti-vairam*, [as] that between the cat and the mouse, Nīl.), and injury; if Time be the cause of all acts, why do friends and kinsmen seek to avenge each other? further, why did the gods and the Asuras, in days of yore, smite each other in battle? and what use would there be of medicines? and how could religious merit be acquired by persons performing religious acts (*kasmād dharmo 'sti kartṛshu*)? Men wish for birds either [to kill them] for food or [to keep them in cages] for sport. Misery arises from various sources (decrepitude, loss of wealth, association with something disagreeable, separation from agreeable objects, death [*badha*], immurement [*bandha*], women, natural causes [*sahajam*], [especially the death of] a son; foolish persons say that there is no misery in others' misery; but one that knows the flavour of all [sorts of] misery (*rasajñaḥ sarvaduḥkhasya*), feels the misery of others as his own; [we have this] decision in [our] own practical scriptures, and [according to them] trust is productive of misery (*niçcayaḥ svārthaçāstreshu, viçvāsaç cāsukhodayaḥ*; ought we not to read °*yaç cārtha*°?), and Uçanas did formerly quote two verses (*gāthe*) [to this effect] to Prahlāda(*b*); those who trust [the word], true or false, of a foe, are killed by trusting (*çraddadhānās*) like [a seeker of] honey by dry grass; having conceived (*upagṛhya*) hostilities [people] soothe [their foe], then they dash upon him like a full jar upon stone; if a king does injury to anyone, he should never trust him again. As Br. objected that by mere mistrust one does not obtain his desires, but is like a dead person, P. maintained that it is necessary not to act without an eye to the consequences (for instance, of sore feet, sore eyes, a wicked path, want of rain, injurious food); destiny and exertion are depending upon each other (*daivam purushakāraç ca sthitāv anyonyasamçrayāt*); but those that are high-minded achieve good feats, while eunuchs only pay court to Destiny; knowledge, courage, cleverness, strength, and patience are one's natural (*sahajāni*) friends; house, precious metals (*kupyam*), land (*kshetram*), wife, and friends are secondary (*upahitāni*) and may be obtained everywhere; home-keeping persons (*gṛhasnehāvabaddhānām*) of little understanding are eaten up by a bad wife like the crab by her progeny (*māghamām segavā*—C. *çe*°—*iva*, 89 = 5222, v. Nīl.); one should put a distance between oneself and a bad wife, a bad son, a bad king, a bad friend, a bad alliance (*ku-sambandham*), and a bad country; she only is a wife who speaks what is agreeable; he is a son who makes his sire happy; he is a friend in whom one can trust; that is one's country where one earns one's living; he is a king of strict rule who does not oppress, etc. (95–96 = 5229–5230); the king is the root of the triple aggregate (*trivargasya*, i.e. Virtue, Wealth, and Pleasure); while taking from his subjects a sixth share of their wealth, he should protect them all; otherwise he is a thief, and takes upon himself the sins of all his subjects, and ultimately sinks into Hell (*nirayam prayāti*); the king, on the other hand, who gives protection is said by the Prajāpati ***Manu*** to have seven attributes (*guṇān*): he is a father (by compassion; the man who does not behave rightly towards him takes birth [in the next life] as an animal—*tiryag gacchati*), a mother (by doing good to his subjects—*sambhāvayati*—and by cherishing the poor—*dīnam apy upapadyate*), a preceptor (*guru*) (by giving instruction in morality and virtue—*dharmopadeçena*), a protector, fire (by scorching the wicked — *anishṭān*), *Vaiçravaṇa* (i.e. Kubera) (by making gifts of wealth to those that are dear to him—*ishṭeshu*), and *Yama* (by restraining the sinful—*yamayann asataḥ*) (*c*); that king, whose subjects grow like a large lotus in a lake, obtains every reward [here] and meets with honour in Heaven (*Svargaloke mahīyate*).—Then P. took leave of Br. and proceeded to the region she chose.

Brahmādhipa ("Lord of the Vedas," PCR.) = Çiva: XIII, 1002.

Brahmādistambaparyanta = Çiva: XIII, 1090.

Brahmagarbha = Çiva (1000 names[2]).

Brahmāgrya = Mahāpurusha (Mahāpurushast.).

Brahmaguhā ("the cave of Bráhman"). § 773*b* (Kṛshna Vāsudeva): XIII, **159*a***, 7070 (°*ām purāṇīm pratishṭho mahīsattram Bharatāgre dadarça*, sc. Kṛshṇa).

Brahmahatyā (personif.) = Brahmavadhyā (q.v.): XII, 10160.

Brahmahṛdaya = Vishṇu: XII, 13487.

Brahmaja = Skanda: III, 14638.

Brahmajña[1] = Skanda: III, 14638.

Brahmajña[2] = Vishṇu (1000 names).

Brahmakalpa[1] ("the cosmic period of Brahmán"). § 660*b* (Bhṛgu-Bharadvājas.): XII, **183**, 6809.

Brahmakalpa[2], adj. ("like Brahmán"): I, 2216 (*ṛtvigbhiḥ*), 3124 (*rājasattamāḥ*); III, 2071 (*dvijāgryaiḥ*); V, 535 (*ṛshīn*), 4029 (*ṛshibhiḥ*); XIII, 7720 (*ṛtvigbhiḥ*); XV, 790 (*bhavadbhiḥ*, i.e. Vyāsa, etc.).

Brahmakanyā[1]: XII, 4432 (*tathoktā Brahmakanyeti Lakshmir Vṛttir Sarasvatī*, sc. Nīti, Nīl.).

Brahmakanyā[2]. § 759 (Ānuçāsanik.): XIII, **107**ζ, 5248 (°*nivāse*? "companionship of Brāhmana's daughters," PCR.).

Brahmakāya, pl. ("having mantras for their bodies," PCR.), a class of beings. § 730 (Ānuçāsanik.): XIII, **18**λλ, 1371.

Brahmakāyika = Mahāpurusha (Mahāpurushast.).

Brahmakāyikam agnīnāṃ = Çiva (1000 names[1]).

Brahmakṛt[1] = Çiva (1000 names[2]).

Brahmakṛt[2] = Vishṇu (1000 names).

Brahmakshetra. § 361 (Kurukshetra): III, **83**, 5076 (*tatra*—i.e. in *Kurukshetra—māsaṃ vased vīraḥ Sarasvatyāṃ Yudhishṭhira* | *yatra Brahmādayo devā ṛshayaḥ Siddha-Cāraṇāḥ* | *Gandharvāpsaraso Yakshāḥ Pannagāç ca mahīpate*! | *B°ṃ mahāpuṇyam abhigacchati—abhigacchanti*, B.—*Bhārata*!).—§ 782*g* (Guruçishyasaṃv.): XIV, **44**ι, 1222 (*sthāvarāṇāṃ tu bhūtānāṃ sarveshām aviçeshataḥ* | *B°ṃ sadāpuṇyaṃ plakshaḥ prathamataḥ smṛtaḥ*).

Brahmalaukika (adj.). § 770 (Ānuçāsanik.): XIII, **151**λ, 7124 (sc. *ṛshayaḥ*).

Brahmaloka[1] ("the world of Brahman"). § 4 (Anukram.): I, **1**, †172 (Nārada had seen Kṛshṇa and Arjuna in *B.*).—§ 98 (Aṃçāvat.): I, **65**, 2545 (°*parāyaṇāḥ*). — § 133 (Dushyanta): I, **70**, 2879 (°*pratikāçam āçramaṃ*), 2884 (*iva*), 2892 (°*sthaṃ*). — § 140 (Purūravas): I, **75**, 3146 (Sanatkumāra came from *B.*).—§ 149 (Yayāti): I, **87**, 3552 (visited by Yayāti).—§ 185 (Pāṇḍu): I, **120**, 4646.—§ 246 (Sundopasundop.): I, **209**, 7644; **210**, 7657; **212**, 7735. —[§ 310 (Sūrya): III, **3**, 175 (? *sabrahmakeshu lokeshu saptasu*).]—§ 322 (Dvaitavanaprav.): III, **24**, 925 (Nārada, etc., always wander from Devaloka to *B.*).—§ 327 (Draupadī-paritāpav.): III, **29**, 1103 (*kshamāvatāṃ B°e lokāḥ parama-pūjitāḥ*). — § 357 (Pushkara): III, **82**, 4078. — § 358 (Tīrthayātrāp.): III, **82**, 4085, 5022.—§ 361 (Kurukshetra): III, **83**, 5077.—§ 364 (Tīrthayātrāp.): III, **83**, 6024, 6027, 6043.—§ 366 (do.): III, **83**, 7011.—§ 368 (do.): III, **83**, 7037, 7038, 7053, 7070 (*padmavarṇena yānena B°ṃ pra-padyate*).—§ 370 (do.): III, **84**, 8014, 8036, 8063, 8132.—§ 371 (Tuṅgaka): III, **85**, 8197.—§ 496 (Skandotpatti): III, **224**, 14277 (the residence of Brahmán). — § 556 (Sañjayayānap.): V, **28**, †802 (*Prājāpatyaṃ tridivaṃ B°ṃ nādharmataḥ, Sañjaya, kāmayeyaṃ*); **29**, †833. — § 559 (Prajāgarap.): V, **40**, †1567 (*abrahmaṇyaç cyavate B°āt*).—§ 560 (Sanatsujātap.): V, **42**, 1602; **44**, 1703.—§ 574*f* (Bindusaras): VI, **6**, 242 (*yatra divyā Tripathagā prathamaṃ tu pratishṭhitā B°ād apakrāntā*).—§ 574*j* (Mālyavat): VI, **7**, 283 (°*çyutāḥ*, the inhabitants of Mālyavat).—§ 576 (Bhaga-vadgītāp.): VI, **16**, 627 (*hṛshtā Duryodhanasyārthe B°āya dīkshitāḥ*).—§ 587 (Bhīshmavadhap.): VI, **115**, 5355 (°*parā bhūtvā*); **118**, 5515 (°*parāḥ*), 5530 (°*āya tatparāḥ*).—§ 592 (Saṃçaptakavadhap.): VII, **20**, 805 (°*parishkṛtāḥ*).—§ 595 (Shoḍaçarājika, v. Bhagīratha): VII, **60**, 2259 (°*gataḥ*, sc. Bhagīratha).—§ 599 (Jayadrathavadhap.): VII, **142**, 5907 (°*puraskṛtau*); **143**, 5985 (*yiyāsur B°āya prāṇān prāṇeshv athājuhot*).—§ 602 (Droṇavadhap.): VII, **190**, 8727 (°*aṃ ninīshavaḥ*); **192**, 8864 (Droṇa went to *B.*), 8867, 8869.—§ 603 (Nārāyaṇāstramokshap.): VII, **201**, 9493; **202**, 9646. — § 615*b* (Udapāna): IX, **36**, 2070 (°*jitaḥ*). — § 618 (Jalapradānikap.): XI, **1**, 22 (*vivṛtaṃ B°sya dīrgham adhvānam āsthitaṃ*, sc. Dhṛtarāshṭra); **7**, 187. — § 641 (Rājadh.): XII, **78**, 2947 (those who chastise the enemies of brahmans repair to *B.*); **108**, 3997.—§ 658*b* (Kṛtaghnop.): XII, **169**, 6335.—§ 660*b* (Bhṛgu-Bharadvājas.): XII, **192**, †7008 (°*aṃ çrayate*), 7024 (Prajāpati, etc., attained to *B.*).—§ 667 (Mokshadh.): XII, **214**, 7773 (*samyagvṛtti*, i.e. brahmacarya leads to *B.*). — § 674*b* (Çrī-Vāsavas.): XII, **229**, 8336 (°*nivāsibhiḥ*, sc. *ṛshibhiḥ*).—§ 677 (Mokshadh.): XII, **237**, 8656 (*jīvayukto ratho divyo B°e virājate*); **243**, 8838 (v. Bráhman); **244**, 8870 (*ācāryo B°eçaḥ*, cf. Nīl. and the note of PCR.).—§ 707 (do.): XII, **319**, 11789 (°*gatāç caiva . . . maharshayaḥ*). — § 714 (Çukakṛtya): XII, **328**, 12355.—§ 717*c* (Uparicara): XII, **338**, 12845, 12856 (*saçarīro gataç caiva B°ṃ*, sc. Uparicara), 12858. — § 717*b* (Nārāyaṇīya): XII, **343**, 13298 (*B°ñ ca . . . Golokañ ca*); **348**θθ, 13502 (*B.* is the lower lip of Nārāyaṇa, Goloka the upper). — § 730 (Ānuçāsanik.): XIII, **14**, 607. — § 730*g* (Upamanyu): XIII, **14**, 779, (χ) 917 (*Brahmalokaç ca lokānām ucyase*, sc. Çiva).—§ 730 (Ānuçāsanik.): XIII, **17**, 1118 (°*āvatāritaiḥ*, sc. the 1000 names of Çiva), 1136. — § 733 (do.): XIII, **25**, 1747. — § 746 (do.): XIII, **57**, 2940; **62**, 3127 (°*gatāḥ Siddhāḥ*), 3160 (°*gatāḥ*), 3187, 3190; **66**, 3347 (°*e vasanti*, sc. gāvaḥ); **75**, 3631, 3640, 3658; **79**κ, 3765. — § 750*b* (Bisastainyop.): XIII, **93**, 4418. — § 758 (Ānuçāsanik.): XIII, **103**, 4947. — § 759 (do.): XIII, **106**γ, 5170; **107**ε, 5235, 5262, 5284, 5331, 5332, 5339.—§ 760 (do.): XIII, **111**, 5441 (*Yamasya sadane B°same guṇaiḥ*).—§ 761 (do.): XIII, **115**, 5659 (ordained for those who abstain from flesh), 5670.—§ 763*b* (Maitreyabhikshā): XIII, **122**, 5849.—§ 766 (Ānuçāsanik.): XIII, **127**, 6075. — § 768*b* (Umā-Maheçvaras.): XIII, **142**, 6523, 6557; **143**, 6576.—§ 782 (Anugītāp.): XIV, **16**, 424; **19**, 594 (*parāyaṇāḥ*).—§ 786*b* (Nakulākhyāna): XIV, **90**, 2775 (°*cārāḥ*), 2794. Cf. Brahmaṇo loka(ḥ).

Brahmaloka[2], pl. (°*āḥ*). § 612 (Hradaprav.): IX, **31**, 1810 (only C.; B. has *vrajalokān*).

Brahmaloka[3] = Çiva: XIII, 917, 1257 (1000 names[2]).

Brahmamaya (adj.): V, 2412 (*astram*, i.e. Brahmāstra); XII, 1582 (*nidhiḥ*, i.e. Kṛshṇa), 6811 (*vāṇī*); XIV, 1181 (sc. Brahmán), 1182 (*Vishṇuḥ*), 1227 (do.), 1428 (*rathaḥ*), 1429 (do.).

Brahmamedhyā, a river. § 574 (Jambūkh.): VI, **9**λ, 339 (in Bhāratavarsha).

Brahmán[1], masc., the Creator. § 3 (Anukram.): I, **1**, 32 (*Suraguruḥ* (?), came from the primordial egg).—§ 4 (do.): I, **1**, 57 (*Lokaguruḥ*), 60 (*Parameshṭhinā*), 61 (*Parameshṭhinaṃ*), 62, (71), 74.—§ 19 (Bhṛgu): I, **5**, 869 (*B.* Svayambhu begot Bhṛgu from the fire at the sacrifice of Varuṇa).—§ 20 (Pulomā): I, **6**, 901 (*Sarvalokapitāmahaḥ*), 902 (*Pitāmahaḥ*).—§ 20*b* (Agni): I, **7**, 925.—§ 28 (Amṛtamanthana): I, **17**, 1109; **18**, 1115, 1117, 1118, 1140, 1142, 1153. —[§ 29 (Kadrū): I, **20**, 1197 (Pitāmaha, i.e. *B.*, sanctioned the curse of Kadrū).]—[§ 35 (Aruṇa): I, **24**, 1272, (1274), 1277 (Pitāmaha).]—§ 45 (Vālakhilya): I, **31**, 1453, 1454.—§ 48 (Çesha): I, **36**, (1581), (1584), (1586), 1587.—§ 49 (Vāsuki): I, **38**, (1630), 1635, (1636); **39**, (1648).—§ 51 (Parikshit): I, **42**, 1734.—§ 60 (Sarpasattra): I, **54**, (2079).—§ 77 (Vyāsa): I, **63**, 2417.—§ 84 (Ādivaṃçā-vatāraṇap.): I, **64**, 2491, 2494 (*lokakartāram avyayaṃ*), (2500), 2501, (2504).—§ 86 (Aṃçāvat.): I, **65**, 2518 (*Brahmaṇo mānasāḥ putrā viditāḥ shaṇ maharshayaḥ*, i.e. Marīci, Atri, Aṅgiras, Pulastya, Pulaha, and Kratu).—§ 107 (do.): I, **66**, 2565 (do.).—§ 109 (do.): I, **66**, 2568 (*shaḍ ete Brahmaṇaḥ putrā vīryavanto maharshayaḥ*).—§ 115 (do.):

I, **66**, 2574 (Daksha was born from the right toe of *B.*).—§ 117 (do.): I, **66**, 2595 (Dharma came out through the right breast of *B.*).—§ 121 (do.): I, **66**, 2605 (Bhṛgu came out ripping open the heart of *B.*).—§ 123 (do): I, **66**, 2614 (father of Dhātṛ and Vidhātṛ).—§ 161 (Mahābhishop.): I, **96**, 3845, 3848.—§ 185 (Pāṇḍu): I, **120**, 4644.—§ 223 (Vāsishṭha): I, **174**, 6638 (°*ṇo mānasaḥ putro Vaçishṭho 'rundhatīpatiḥ*).—§ 246 (Sundopasundop.): I, **209**, (7639). —§ 246*b* (Tilottamā): I, **211**, 7697.—§ 256*a* (Agniparābhava): I, **224**, 8143, 8158.—§ 257 (Khāṇḍavadahanap.): I, **225**, 8192 (had made Gāṇḍīva).—§ 263 (Sabhākriyāp.): II, **3**, 72 (with Nara, Nārāyaṇa, Yama, and Sthāṇu he celebrated a sattra at Bindusaras or Hiraṇyaçṛṅga), 84 (°*ṇo*, sc. *sabhā*, cannot compete with the palace of Yudhishṭhira).—§ 264 (do.): II, **4**, 134 (*iva*).—§ 265 (Lokapālasabhākhyānap.): II, **6**, 271 (Nārada travels through the worlds, which are created by *B.*), 275, 276 (°*ṇo*, sc. *sabhām*).—§ 266 (Çakrasabhāv.): II, **7**, 309 (°*ṇaḥ sadṛçā Bhṛguḥ Saptarshayas tathā*).—§ 270 (Brahmasabhāv.): II, **11**, 444, 464, 473 (*Lokapitāmahaḥ*).—§ 310*b* (Sūrya): III, **3**, 148 (= the Sun, in the enumeration of Dhaumya), 185 (*aho B°ṇaḥ proktaṃ sahasrayugasammitaṃ*), 208 (*etad Brahmā dadau pūrvaṃ Çakrāya*, sc. the hymn for praising Sūrya).—§ 317*b* (Kṛshṇa Vāsudeva): III, **12**, 480 (Kṛshṇa was first Nārāyaṇa, then Hari, then Brahmán, etc.), 497 (*yugādau*, *B.* was born from Kṛshṇa's navel; *carācaragurur yasyedaṃ sakalaṃ jagat*), 514 (Kṛshṇa plays with *B.*, Çaṅkara, etc., as with playthings). — § 327 (Draupadīparitāpav.): III, **31**, 1199 (*Brahmā provāca putrāṇām yad ṛshir veda Kaçyapaḥ*).—§ 334 (Kairātap.): III, **41**, 1682 (*niyogād B°as tāta martyatām samupāgataḥ*, sc. Nara).—§ 358 (Tīrthayātrāp.): III, **82**, 5014 (*tatra*—i.e. in Damin—*Brahmādayo devā upāsante Maheçvaraṃ*).—§ 359 (Vaḍavā): III, **82**, 5037.—§ 360 (Tīrthayātrāp.): III, **82**, 5050 (°*ādayo devāḥ*), 5058 (do., adore Keçava).—§ 361 (Kurukshetra): III, **83**, 5075 (do.). —§ 364 (Tīrthayātrāp.): III, **83**, 6043 (°*āṇam adhigatvā*).—§ 365 (Maṅkanaka): III, **83**, 6089 (°*ādibhiḥ suraiḥ*), 6099 (*surā B°ādayaḥ*).—§ 366 (Tīrthayātrāp.): III, **83**, 7006 (°*ādayo devāḥ*).—§ 368 (do.): III, **83**, 7035 (do.), 7040, 7061 (°*ādayo devāḥ*).—§ 370 (do.): III, **84**, 7083 (do.), 8037 (*Brahmā devagaṇaiḥ saha*, always dwells at Naimisha), 8064 (had made a yūpa in Brahmasaras), 8081 (*purusharshabhaṃ*), 8101 (°*ādayo devāḥ*); **85**, 8162, 8167 (°*ādayo devāḥ*).—§ 378 (Prayāga): III, **85**, 8212 (do.).—§ 384 (Agastyop.): III, **100**, 8693.—§ 386 (do.): III, **106**, 8825 (*Lokapitāmahaḥ*).—§ 387 (Sagara): III, **107**, 8855 (°*āṇaṃ çaraṇaṃ jagmuḥ*).—§ 391 (Ṛshyaçṛṅga): III, **110**, 10004 (*lokakartṛṇā*).—§ 422 *bis* (Varāhāvatāra): III, **142**, 10948, 10949, (10953), (10958).—§ 439 (Yakshayuddhap.): III, **163**, 11854 (°*ṇaḥ putrān mānasān Dakshasaptamān*).—§ 445 (Nivātakavacayuddhap.): III, **173**, 12207 (had made Hiraṇyapura for the sake of the Kālakeyas), 12211 (had destined that the Kālakeyas should be slain by a man). —§ 457 (Vaivasvatop.): III, **187**, 12797 (*ahaṃ Prajāpatir Brahmā yat paraṃ nādhigamyate*). — § 458 (Mārkaṇḍeyasamāsyap.): III, **188**, 12807 (*Parameshṭhinaṃ*), 12808 (visited by Mārkaṇḍeya during the cataclysms), 12814 (*kāmarūpiṇaḥ*), 12818 (*padmotpalaniketanaṃ sarvabhūteçaṃ*). —§ 459 (do.): III, **189**, 12954 (*ahaṃ Vishṇur ahaṃ Brahmā*, etc., said Nārāyaṇa to Mārkaṇḍeya), 12991 (*yāvad B°ā na budhyate*), 12996.—§ 477 (Dhundhumārop.): III, **203**, 13560 (born from the lotus in Vishṇu's navel), 13566 (was terrified by Madhu and Kaiṭabha).—§ 478 (do.): III, **204**, 13583 (granted a boon to Dhundhu).—§ 488 (Āṅgirasa): III, **217**, 14110 (*anyo 'gnir lokānāṃ B°ṇā saṃprakalpitaḥ*, i.e. Aṅgiras), 14113 (had created Agni); **218**, 14122 (*Brahmaṇo yas tritīyas tu putraḥ*, i.e. Aṅgiras).—§ 491 (do.): III, **220**, 14157 (*yaçasā B°ṇā samaṃ*, i.e. the desired son of Uktha).—§ 496 (Skandotpatti): III, **224**, (14279).—§ 501 (Skandop.): III, **229**, 14446 (*ayaṃ tasyāḥ patir vihito B°ṇā*, i.e. Skanda). —§ 502 (Manushyagrahak.): III, **230**, 14462, 14463.—§ 504 (Skandayuddha): III, **231**, 14521.—§ 507 (do.): III, **231**, 14619 (°*dattavaraḥ*, sc. Mahisha).—§ 524 (Jayadrathavim.): III, **272**, 15821 (*caturmukho Brahmā nābhipadmād viniḥsṛtaḥ*), 15824 (*sṛjate Brahmamūrttis tu, rakshate Paurushī tanuḥ | Raudrī bhāvena çamayet tisro 'vasthāḥ Prajāpateḥ*). — § 526 (Rāmop.): III, **275**, 15903 (the sons of Pulastya gratified *B.* by a terrible tapas), 15909 (*B.* went and made them desist from this tapas), (15910), (15914), (15919); **276**, 15929 (the brahmarshis, etc., *B°āṇaṃ çaraṇaṃ gatāḥ*), (15932).—§ 543 (Rāmarājyābhisheka): III, **291**, (16560), 16571, 16573.—§ 548 (Āraṇeyap.): III, **313**, 17331 (*Brahmādityam unnayati*).—§ 550 (Samayapālanap.): IV, **13**, 338 (°*ṇaḥ sumahotsavaḥ*), 339 (*samāje Brahmaṇo, rājan, yathā Paçupater iva*).—§ 552*c* (Gāṇḍīva): IV, **43**, 1347 (*B.* had first Gāṇḍīva for 1,000 years).—§ 552*m* (Arjuna): IV, **61**, 1976 (*Brahmaṇaḥ kṛtahastatām*, sc. *vedmi*, said Arjuna).—§ 555 (Indravijaya): V, **12**, 385 (*purā gītaṃ Brahmaṇā*, i.e. v. 386 ff. (*e*)); **13**, 403; **17**, 529 (only *B.*).—§ 561 (Nara-Nārāyaṇau.): V, **49**, 1918 (*Bṛhaspatiç cuçanāç ca B°ṇaṃ paryupasthitau*), 1922, (1923).—§ 561 (Yānasandhip.): V, **55**, 2172 (*Svayambhuvaḥ*).—§ 564 (Mātalīyop.): V, **97**, 3502 (*Lokapitāmahaḥ*); **98**, 3542 (*sṛshṭaḥ prathamataḥ caṇḍo B°ṇā brahmavādinā*, sc. the bow in the lake of Varuṇa); **100**, 3571 (*Brahmapādodbhavāç ca ye*, sc. *Yātudhānāḥ*).—§ 565 (Gālavacarita): V, **111**, 3824 (*çāçvataḥ*, at Badarī).—§ 567 (Bhagavadyānap.): V, **131***o*, 4422 (in the forehead of Kṛshṇa).—§ 569 (do.): V, **145**, 4927 (*devaiḥ parivṛto Brahma vedyām iva mahādhvare*).—§ 574 (Jambūkh.): VI, **6**, 213 (on Meru).—§ 574*f* (Bindusaras): VI, **6ζ**, 241 (at Bindusaras, Nara, Nārāyaṇa, Brahmán, Manu, and Sthāṇu are present).—§ 576 (Bhagavadgītāp.): VI, **17**, 643 (*gacchadhvaṃ tena Çakrasya Brahmaṇaç ca salokatām*, said to the warriors); **28**, 1025 (*evaṃ bahuvidhā yajñā vitatā B°ṇaḥ mukhe*, (?) PCR: in the Vedas); **32**, 1158 (*sahasrayugaparyantam ahar yad Brahmaṇo viduḥ*); **35**, †1261 (*Brahmāṇam Īçaṃ kamalāsanasthaṃ*, seen in the body of Kṛshṇa), †1283 (*Brahmaṇo 'py ādikartre*, i.e. Kṛshṇa).—§ 581 (Bhīshmavadhap.): VI, **65**, 2941 (*dhyānenāredya tad Brahmā*), 2943 (*brahmavidāṃ varaḥ*), 2968 (*Brahmāṇam lokadhāriṇaṃ*, created by Aniruddha); **66**, 2973, 2985 (*yasyāham ātmajo Brahmā sarvasya jagataḥ patiḥ*, i.e. Nārāyaṇa's), 2997 (*kathāṃ tāṃ Brahmaṇā gītāṃ çrutvā prītā divaṃ yayuḥ*), 3001 (*yasya syād ātmajo Brahmā sarvasya jagataḥ pitā*, i.e. Kṛshṇa's); **67**, 3026 (*Madhuṃ . . . Brahmaṇo 'pacitiṃ kurvañ jaghāna Purushottamaḥ*); **68**, 3037 (°*proktaṃ stavaṃ*).—§ 592 (Saṃçaptakavadhap.): VII, **23**, 1039 (had created the bow of Arjuna).—§ 594 (Mṛtyu): VII, **52**, 2041 (*Pitāmahaḥ*, the creatures would not die), 2046 (*Parameshṭhinaṃ*); **53**, (2051); **54**, (2082), (2112), 2123 (°*sṛshṭaṃ*, sc. the death).—§ 599 (Jayadrathavadhap.): VII, **94**, 3449 (*karotu svasti te Brahma Brahmā cāpi dvijātayaḥ | sarīsṛpāç ca ye çreshṭhās tebhyas te svasti, Bhārata!*), 3458 (°*āṇaṃ çaraṇaṃ jagmuḥ*), 3465, 3480 (*yathā ca Brahmaṇā baddhaṃ saṃgrāme Tārakāmaye | Cakrasya kavacaṃ divyaṃ*); **98**, 3641 (*Brahma-Somapurogamāḥ*, sc. *devāḥ*); **103**, 3862 (*Brahmaṇā vā svayaṃ kṛtaṃ*, sc. the armour of Duryodhana);

127, 5144 (*Brahmeçānendravaruṇān avahad yaḥ purā rathaḥ*); **143**, 5999 (*°ādyaiḥ suravṛshabhaiḥ*).—§ 603*b* (Nārāyaṇa): VII, **201**, 9467 (*Kālo Brahmā Brahma ca brāhmaṇāç ca . . .*).—§ 603*d* (Tripura): VII, **202**, 9559 (*°dattavarāḥ, Tripuravāsinaḥ*), 9567 (became Rudra's charioteer in the combat with Tripura), 9578 (*prabhum avyayam*), 9579, 9581 (*brahmavidāṃ varaḥ*), 9582, 9587, (9588).—§ 603 (Nārāyaṇāstram.): VII, **202**, 9628 (*Hara*, i.e. Çiva, vanquished him).—§ 605 (Karṇap.): VIII, **16**, 628 (*Brahmeçānāv iva*); **32**, 1330 (*sa pāhi sarvathā Karṇaṃ yathā Brahmā Maheçvaram*), 1367 (*Brahmaṇā brāhmaṇāḥ sṛshṭā mukhāt kshattrañ ca bāhutaḥ | ūrubhyām asṛjad vaiçyān çūdrān padbhyām iti çrutiḥ*).—§ 606 (Tripurākhyāna): VIII, **33**, 1436 (*°āṇam agrataḥ kṛtvā*, sc. the gods); **34**, 1454, 1555 (*Brahma-Rudrayoḥ*).—§ 606 (Karṇap.): VIII, **34**, 1574 (*yathaiva bhagavān Brahmā lokadhātā Pitāmahaḥ | sārathyam akarot tatra Rudrasya paramo 'vyayaḥ*); **35**, 1620 (became Rudra's charioteer in the combat against *Tripura*), 1665 (do.).—§ 607 (do.): VIII, **45**, 2090.—§ 608*b* (Arjuna): VIII, **46**, 2160–1.—§ 608 (Karṇap.): VIII, **72**, 3617 (had created the creatures and Gāṇḍīva); **87**, 4428 (*Brahmā Brahmarshibhiç sārddhaṃ Prajāpatibhir eva ca*, present at the encounter between Karṇa and Arjuna), 4440 (*Brahmeçānau*), 4456 (do.); **89**, †4573, †4574.—§ 614 (Gadāyuddhap.): IX, **34***a*, 1964 (*°āṇam iva deveçam*).—§ 615*i* (Saptasarasvatī): IX, **38**, VII), 2214.—§ 615*j* (Maṅkanaka): IX, **38**, 2226 (*°ādibhiḥ suraiḥ*), 2238 (*devā Brahmādayaḥ*).—§ 615*n* (Viçvāmitra): IX, **40**, 2303 (*°ṇaḥ sutaḥ*, i.e. Vasishṭha), 2313 (*Sarvalokapitāmahaḥ*).—§ 615*u* (Skanda): IX, **44**, 2457 (*niyogād B°ṇaḥ*), 2479 (*Svayambhur bhagavān saputraḥ*), 2500 (*devā Brahmapurogamāḥ*); **45**, 2524 (*bhagavān Lokapitāmahaḥ*), 2525 (gave four companions to Skanda); **46**, 2670 (gave a black deerskin to Skanda).—§ 615 (Baladevatīrthay.): IX, **47**, 2751 (*sasarja tīrthāni tathā devatānāṃ yathāvidhi*).—§ 615*kk* (Kurukshetrak.): IX, **53**, 3023 (*°ādyaiḥ suraiḥ*), 3034 (*Brahma-Vishṇu-Maheçvaraiḥ*).—§ 617 (Aishīkap.): X, **17**, 782.—§ 618 (Jalapradānikap.): XI, **7**, 186 (*damas tyāgo 'pramādaç ca te trayo Brahmaṇo hayāḥ*, cf. v. 187).—§ 623 (Rājadh.): XII, **15**, 441 (*na Brahmāṇaṃ na Dhātāraṃ na Pūshāṇaṃ*, sc. *janā namasyanti*), †454 (*°ṇā pūrvam uktam*).—§ 627 (do.): XII, **22**, 646 (?, *Indro Brahmaṇaḥ putraḥ*; *Brahmaṇaḥ* = Kaçyapa's, Nīl.).—§ 635 (do.): XII, **35**, 1258 (*B°ṇaḥ çrutiḥ*), 1276 (*°oktena vidhinā*).—§ 636 (do.): XII, **39**, 1433, 1436.—§ 637 (do.): XII, **43**, 1513 (Kṛshṇa identified with *B.*).—§ 639 (do.): XII, **53**, 1920 (*Brahmā devagaṇair yathā*), 1923 (*Brahmāṇam iva Vāsavaḥ*).—§ 641 (do.): XII, **59**, 2143, 2202 (*çāstraṃ mahārthaṃ Brahmaṇā kṛtam*); **63**, †2362 (*Brā°*, C.); **64**, †2403 (cannot obtain a sight of Nārāyaṇa); **72**, 2752 (the brahman sprang from *B.'s* mouth, the kshatriya from his arms, the vaiçya from his thighs, the çudra from his feet), 2756 (*°ānuçāsanam*); **89**, 3342 (created kshatriyas); **121**, 4420 (*°ṇo vacanaṃ mahat*), 4465 (*Pitāmahaḥ pūrvaṃ babhūvātha Prajāpatiḥ*); **122**, 4483 (*bhagavān Sarvalokapitāmahaḥ*), 4486 (Kshupa fell from *B.'s* head and became priest at his sacrifice), 4503 (*°ṇaḥ putram anujātaṃ Kshupam*), 4512 (*°ṇaḥ putro Vyavasāyaḥ sanātanaḥ*), 4515 (*Pitāmahaḥ*).—§ 644 (Āpaddh.): XII, **136**, 4878 (*gāthā B°gītāḥ*).—§ 650 (do.): XII, **142**, 5446 (*ajo 'çvaḥ kshattram ity etat sadṛçaṃ B°ṇā kṛtam*).—§ 653*b* (Gṛdhragomāyusaṃv.): XII, **153***a* 752.—§ 656 (Khaḍgotpattik.): XII, **166**, 6144 (*°ānuçāsane*), 6150 (*bhagavān*), 6152, 6165 (gave the sword to Rudra).—§ 657 (Āpaddh.): XII, **167**, 6224 (*iva*).—§ 658 (Kṛtaghnop.): XII, **169**, 6336 (*Brahmaṇaḥ sakhā*, i.e. Nadījaṅgha); **172**, 6408 (adored by Rājadharman); **173**, 6436 (cursed Rājadharman), 6437, 6445.—§ 660*b* (Bhṛgu-Bharadvāja-saṃv.): XII, **182**, 6780 (sprung from the lotus), 6781, 6800 (*dharmamayaḥ pūrvaḥ Prajāpatiḥ*), 6801; **183**, 6804; **184**, 6821; **187**, 6920 (*tatrātmā mānaso Brahmā sarvabhūteshu lokakṛt*); **188**, 6930 (created the Prajāpatis), 6939 (created only brahmans, from which all four castes arose), 6944; **190**, 6977 (*Trilokakṛt*), 6983; **191**, ††6991 (*°ṇā . . . āçramāç catvāro 'bhinirdishṭāḥ*); **192**, 7028 (*°nirmitaḥ*, sc. *dharmaḥ*).—§ 662*b* (Jāpakop.): XII, **199**, 7320 (*Parameshṭhinam*); **200**, 7350, (7359).—§ 664 (Mokshadh.): XII, **207**γ, 7530 (*sarvabhūtapitāmahaḥ*, sprung from the lotus).—§ 664*b* (Madhu): XII, **207**, 7532 (*Brahmaṇo 'pacitiṃ kurvan jaghāna Purushottamaḥ*, sc. *Madhum*).—§ 664 (Mokshadh.): XII, **207**δ, 7534 (*Brahmā 'nusasṛje putrān mānasān Dakshasaptamān | Marīcim Atryaṅgirasaṃ Pulastyaṃ Pulahaṃ Kratum*), (ε) 7536 (created Daksha from his right toe), 7551 (*Vedavidyāvidhātāram*).—§ 665 (do.): XII, **208***a*, 7569 (*Svayambhuvaḥ*, as his seven sons are enumerated the same as in v. 7534, only with Vasishṭha instead of Daksha).—§ 666 (do.): XII, **209**, 7614, 7615.—§ 669 (do.): XII, **221**, 8019.—§ 671*b* (Bali-Vāsavasaṃv.): XII, **223**, 8061, 8063, 8064, (8065), 8067, (8068), 8082 (*°dattāṃ mālām*), 8083 (do.); **225**, 8181 (*°ṇā samādishṭaḥ*, sc. Indra).—§ 673*b* (Bali-Vāsavasaṃv.): XII, **227**, 8252 (*sarvabhūtabhavaṃ çāçvatam*).—§ 674*b* (Çrī-Vāsavasaṃv.): XII, **229**, 8337 (*iva*).—§ 677 (Mokshadh.): XII, **232**, 8508 (*ahar B°ṇaḥ*), 8509 (*pratibuddhaḥ*); **233**, 8523, 8551 (*°Harādishu*); **237**, 8681, 8687; **243**, 8828 (*yathā vai vihitā vṛttiḥ purastād B°ṇā svayam*); **244**, 8881 (*°ṇā vihitā*).—§ 678*c* (Mṛtyu-Prajāpatisaṃv.): XII, **257**, 9162; **259**, 9199, 9203.—§ 680*b* (Tulādhāra-Jājalisaṃv.): XII, **263***a*, 9380; **265**, 9451 (*gāthā B°gītāḥ*).—§ 692 (Mokshadh.): XII, **281**δ, †10076.—§ 693*b* (Vṛtravadha): XII, **282***a*, 10120, 10134; **283**, 10164, 10171, (10173), 10174, (10175), 10179, (10183), 10184, (10188), 10191, (10193), (10196).—§ 694*b* (Jvarotpatti): XII, **284**, (10253), 10258.—§ 695*b* (Dakshayajñavināça): XII, **285***a*, 10281, 10323 (*°ādayo devāḥ*).—§ 696*b* (Daksha-prokta-Çiva-sahasranāmastotra): XII, **285**, 10440 (*na Brahmā na ca Govindaḥ paurāṇā ṛshayo na te | māhātmyaṃ veditum çaktā yathātathyena te, Çiva!*).—§ 701*b* (Bhava-Bhārgavasaṃv.): XII, **290**, 10681 (*devātidevaḥ*).—§ 702 (Mokshadh.): XII, **296**β, 10839 (created brahmaṇs); **297**, 10870 (*°ṇaikena jātānāṃ nānatvaṃ gotrataḥ katham*).—§ 704 (do.): XII, **301***a*, †11094; **302**β, 11106.—§ 705 (do.): XII, **309**, †11507.—§ 707 (do.): XII, **312**, 11571 (*hiraṇyāṇḍasambhavam*); **313**, 11591; **318**, 11709 (*devāgrajam*, if the jīva-soul escapes through the crown of the head one attains to the region of *B.*; read with B.: *vibhuṃ mūrdhnā*); **319**, †11809 (*°ādīnāṃ khecarāṇāṃ kshitau*), †11813 (*°jāḥ*, sc. *sarve varṇāḥ*), †11814 (*°āsyato brāhmaṇāḥ samprabhūtā bāhubhyāṃ kshatriyāḥ . . . nābhyāṃ vaiçyāḥ pādataç cāpi çūdrāḥ*).—§ 717*b* (Nārāyaṇīya): XII, **335***a*, 12685 (among the Prajāpatis).—§ 717*c* (Uparicara): XII, **336**, 12736 (B. *mayā*—i.e. by Nārāyaṇa—*kṛto Brahmā prasādataḥ*; C. has erroneously *Brahmaprasādataḥ*); **337**, 12742 (*°ṇaḥ putrā mānasāḥ*, i.e. Ekata, Dvita, and Trita).—§ 717*b* (Nārāyaṇīya): XII, **340**θ, 12914 (*Hiraṇyagarbho lokādiç caturvaktro niruktagaḥ*), 12924 (*mayā*—i.e. by Nārāyaṇa—*sṛshṭaḥ purā Brahmā*), 12927, 12929, 12930, 12938 (*Aniruddhāt tathā Brahmā tannābhikamalodbhavaḥ | Brahmaṇaḥ sarvabhūtāni*), 12971, 12978, 12981; **341**, 13013 (*sa-B°kā* *lokāḥ*), (λ), 13016, 13042 (*Lokapitāmahaḥ*), 13044, (13048), 13051, 13052 (°*oktaṃ*), 13055 (*sa-B°kā devāḥ*), 13058 (*Lokagurur Lokapitāmahaḥ*), 13060, 13061, 13079 (*saptaite mānasāḥ proktā ṛshayo Brahmaṇaḥ putrāh*, i.e. Sana, etc. (*o*)), 13083 (*Lokaguruḥ*), 13085 (°*ānuçishṭāḥ*), 13098 (°*aikaḥ*), 13100 (*Lokakartā*), 13105; **342,** 13140 (*yasya*— i.e. Nārāyaṇa's—*prasādajo Brahmā*), 13145 (sprung from the lotus), (*τ*), 13158 (*sa-B°kā devāḥ*), 13164, 13175 (°*ṇaḥ putra ādyaḥ*, i.e. Trita); **343,** I), ††13195 (*bhūtasargaḥ kṛto B°ṇā*), 13201 (*viçvaṃ sṛjat*), VII), ††13211 (*Brāhmaṇaṃ*, C.), ††13212, ††13213 (created the vajra from the bones of Dadhīca), (*aa*), 13281 (fell from his seat during the battle between Rudra and Nārāyaṇa), 13282 (*caturvaktraḥ niruktagaḥ*), 13289, 13292; **344,** 13307 (*sa-B°kaiḥ suraiḥ*, cannot see Nārāyaṇa), 13319 (°*ādayaḥ surāḥ*), (*γγ*), 13365; **346,** 13403 (*Lokapitāmahaḥ*); **348***εε*, 13452 (*Parameshṭhinā*), 13454, 13459, 13469 (*caturmukhaḥ*), 13476 (*sṛjantaṃ Vedān*), 13478, 13479 (was robbed of the Vedas by Madhu and Kaiṭabha), (*ζζ*), (13481), 13485, (*ηη*), (13487), 13508, 13520 (*Brahmaṇo 'pacitiṃ kurvan jaghāna Madhusūdanaḥ*, sc. Madhu and Kaiṭabha), 13521 (created the worlds), 13541 (°*ādīnāṃ salokānāṃ*); **349,** I), 13559 (*mānasaṃ janma Nārāyaṇamukhodgataṃ B°ṇaḥ*, II), 13562 (*cākshushaṃ janma dvitīyaṃ B°ṇaḥ*), III), 13565 (*tritīyaṃ janma B°ṇo . . . vācikaṃ*), IV), 13571 (*çravaṇajā sṛshṭir B°ṇaḥ*), 13573 (*prajāsargakaro . . . jagatpatiḥ*), 13576, 13577, 13579 (*varado Lokapitāmahaḥ*), 13581 (*lokavisargakṛt*), V), 13585 (*nāsatye janmani purā B°ṇaḥ*), 13586, VI), 13590 (*Hariyonaye*), 13591, VII), 13594 (*saptamaṃ janma padmajaṃ B°ṇaḥ*), 13624 (*Lokapitāmahaḥ*); **350,** 13654, 13655, 13661, 13665 (*Parameshṭhinā*), 13705 (*Umāpatir Bhūtapatiḥ Çrīkaṇṭho B°ṇaḥ sutaḥ*); **351,** 13720 (*Brahmaṇā saha saṃvādaṃ Tryambakasya*).—§ 717*d* (Brahma-Rudrasaṃv.): XII, **351,** (13734), 13735, 13736, (13737); **352,** (13740), †13761 (*ādya īçaḥ prajānāṃ*).—§ 723 (Ānuçāsanik.): XIII, **6,** 296 (*Vaçishṭhasya ca saṃvādaṃ Brahmaṇaç ca*), (299).—§ 730 (do.): XIII, **14,** 591 (*Brahma-Vishṇu-Sureçānāṃ srashṭā*, i.e. Çiva; *B°ādayo devāḥ*, adored Çiva), 594 (created by Çiva), 607 (cf. Brahmaloka), (*β*), 624.—§ 730*g* (Upamanyu): XIII, **14***η*, 731 (*Brahma-Vishṇu-Surendrāṇāṃ . . . vapur dhārayate Bhavaḥ*, i.e. Çiva), 791 (*yaḥ*—i.e. Çiva—*pūrvam asṛjad devaṃ Brahmāṇaṃ lokabhāvanaṃ*), (*θ*), 795 (*Bhagavaty uttamaiçvaryaṃ Brahma-Vishṇu puragamaṃ*), 819, (*ι*), 820 (*Brahmendra Mahendra-Vishṇusahitā devāḥ*), (*ξ*), 824, 857 (can be slain by the weapon of Çiva), (*υ*), 869 (*Lokapitāmahaḥ*), (*φ*), 875 (praised Çiva), 877, 910 (*tvaṃ Brahma sarvadevanaṃ*, sc. Çiva), 931 (°*ādibhiḥ suraiḥ*), 940 (*yo*—i.e. Çiva—*'sṛjad dakshiṇād aṅgād Brahmāṇaṃ lokabhāvanaṃ*).—§ 730 (Ānuçāsanik.): XIII, **14***ω*, 986, 1001 (°*ādibhiḥ suraiḥ*), 1003 (Çiva identified with *B.*), 1011; **16,** 1052 (did not know the real nature of Çiva), 1053 (°*ākhyaḥ*, i.e. Çiva), 1058 (Çiva identified with *B.*), 1074 (°*ādibhiḥ Siddhaiḥ*, concealed Çiva), (*θθ*), 1105; **17,** 1115 (°*proktaiḥ*), 1134 (*Sarvalokapitāmahaḥ*), 1267 (°*ādayo devāḥ*), 1283, 1287 (°*ṇo hṛdi*), 1288; **18,** 1361 (°*tvaṃ*), (*λλ*), 1369.—§ 734 (do.): XIII, **26,** 1758 (*kshamayā Brahmaṇaḥ samaṃ*, i.e. Bhīshma), †1853 (°*kāntāṃ Gaṅgāṃ*).—§ 737 (do.): XIII, **31***a*, 2013 (C. has *Brāhmāṇam*). —§ 739 (do.): XIII, **35,** 2153 (°*gītāḥ*, i.e. vv. 2146–2152).—§ 743 (do.): XIII, **40,** 2249 (*pramadāḥ sṛshṭhāḥ °ṇā*).—§ 746 (do.): XIII, **59,** 3042 (? *lokān çucīn Brahmapuraskṛtān*); **62***β*, 3150; **66,** 3325 (*Svayambhuvā*, in C. is printed *Brāhmaṇā*), 3326, (3330); **74,** 3621 (*Parameçvaraḥ*); **79,** 3761; **81,** 3816 (read with B.: *Brahmā tu gāh*, etc.), 3818 (gave horns to the kine); **83,** 3893, (3913).—§ 747 (do.): XIII, **84***a*, 3954 (*Pitāmahaḥ*).—§ 747*b* (Suvarṇotpatti): XIII, **84,** 4014; **85,** (4017), (4022), 4066, 4104 (*Paramātmanaḥ*), (*δ*), 4112, 4117 (created the four castes), 4136 (*Lokagurur Lokapitāmahaḥ*), 4140 (*nisargād B°ṇaḥ*), 4149 (adopted Kavi), 4155 (*Pitāmahaḥ*), 4162 (*Lokapitāmahaḥ*), 4164 (Agni identified with *B.*), 4168 (Agni sprung from *B.*), 4173 (°*vāyvagnisomānāṃ sālokyaṃ*).—§ 749 (Ānuçāsanik.): XIII, **90,** 4290; **91,** 4345.—§ 755*b* (Nahushop.): XIII, **100,** 4809.—§ 758 (Ānuçāsanik.): XIII, **103,** 4909 (*Bhagīrathasya saṃvādaṃ B°ṇaç ca*), 4911, 4920, 4922, 4923, †4938, 4942, 4950.—§ 759 (do.): XIII, **104,** 5112.—§ 760 (do.): XIII, **111,** 5530 (*vadataḥ*).—§ 762*b* (Kīṭop.): XIII, **119,** 5790 (*sālokyaṃ B°ṇaḥ*).—§ 766 (Ānuçāsanik.): XIII, **126,** 6046 (*Padmasambhavaṃ*), 6049, (6050); **130,** (6113); **133,** 6178 (*Padmayoninā*).—§ 768*b* (Umā-Maheçvarasaṃv.): XIII, **141,** 6390 (°*ṇo yoshiduttamā*, i.e. Tilottamā), 6399 (created Surabhi), 6487 (drank *amṛta*); **143,** 6580 (°*ṇā samudāhṛtaṃ*), 6612 (°*ānuçāsanaṃ*), 6617 (*sṛjatā prajāḥ*); **144,** 6682 (°*ṇā samudīritaḥ*, sc. *mārgaḥ*); **145,** 6691 (°*ṇā proktāḥ*); **146***γ*, 6750 (*Sāvitrī Brahmaṇaḥ sādhvī*).—§ 768*b* (Kṛshṇa Vāsudeva): XIII, **147,** 6809 (*Brahmā tasyodarabhavaḥ*, i.e. Kṛshṇa's), 6818 (*Brahmā vasati garbhasthaḥ çarīre*, i.e. in Kṛshṇa), 6843 (*Pitāmahaṃ*), 6846 (°*pūrvo devagaṇaḥ*).—§ 772*i* (Pavanārjunasaṃv.): Vāyu said: A superior brahman is the protector of all creatures and the creator of the living world (cf. Agni), viz. *Prajāpati Brahmán*. Some unwise persons say that *Brahmán* was born from an egg . . . ; this view one should not hold; how can *Brahmán* be born, he who is unborn (*ajaḥ*)? the egg is space (*ākāçaṃ*); from that *Brahmán* was born; if it is objected, that there would be nothing for him to stand upon: there is Ahaṅkāra ("consciousness"), endued with great energy: XIII, **154,** 7227 (*Prajāpatiḥ*), 7228, 7231.—§ 772*b* (Pavanārjunasaṃv.): XIII, **155,** 7233 (°*ṇaḥ sutāṃ*, i.e. Earth).—§ 772*l* (Vasishṭha): XIII, **156,** 7282 (°*dattavaraṃ saras*), 7289 (°*dattavarā Daityāḥ*).—§ 772*p* (Kapa, pl.): XIII, **158,** 7328, (7330).—§ 773*b* (Kṛshṇa Vāsudeva): XIII, **159,** 7388 (*Brahmā bhūtva*, sc. Kṛshṇa).—§ 773*d* (Çiva): XIII, **161,** 7487 (°*āṇaṃ sārathiṃ kṛtvā*, sc. Çiva), 7492 (adored Çiva).—§ 775 (Ānuçāsanik.): XIII, **166***a*, 7635 (°*ṇaḥ satī Sāvitrī*).—§ 782 (Anugītāp.): XIV, **18,** 521 (*Sarvalokapitāmahaḥ*). § 782*b* (Brāhmaṇagītā): XIV, **20,** 609 (°*ādayaḥ*): **23,** (†690), 707 (*Prajāpatiḥ*); **27,** 785.—§ 782*g* (Guruçishyasaṃv.): XIV, **35,** 949 (°*ṇoktam idaṃ*), 962 (*vītakalmashaṃ*); **36,** (967); **37,** (1023); **38,** (1042); **39,** (1058); **40,** (1084); **41,** (1097); **42,** (1102), [33]1133; **43,** (1170); **44,** (1212); **45,** (1234); **46,** (1259); **47,** (1317); **48,** (1334); **50,** (1366); **51,** (1424), 1466, 1467.—§ 784*b* (Uttaṅka): XIV, **54,** 1576 (Kṛshṇa identified with *B.*, Vishṇu, and Indra).—§ 788 (Āçramavāsap.): XV, **28,** 755 (*niyogād B°ṇaḥ*).

Cf. also the following synonyms:

Abjasambhava: I, 2077.
Ādideva: XII, 6949.
Agni: XII, 8139.
Ahaṃkāra, q.v.
Aja, q.v.
Avyaya, q.v.
Bhūmipati: I, 2499.
Bhūtakṛt, q.v.
Bhūtātman, q.v.

Caturmukha, q.v.
Caturvaktra, q.v.
Caturveda, q.v.
Çambhu, q.v.
Devadeva, q.v.
Devādhideva, q.v.
Devāsuraguru, q.v.
Devātideva: XII, 10681.
Devavara, q.v.
Deveça, q.v.
Dhātṛ, q.v.
Hiraṇyagarbha, q.v.
Īça, q.v.
Īçvara, q.v.
Jagannātha, q.v.
Jagatpati, q.v.
Jagatprabhu: XII, 9166.
Lokabhāvana, q.v.
Lokadhātṛ, q.v.
Lokādinidhaneçvara: VII, 2068.
Lokaguru, q.v.
Lokakartṛ, q.v.
Lokakṛt, q.v.
Lokapitāmaha: I, 904, 2074; II, 473; III, 8825; V, 3502, 4107; VII, 2078; IX, 2281, 2524; XII, 2144, 9194, 10180, 10185, 13042, 13058, 13403, 13579, 13624; XIII, 869, 3912, 4136, 4162; XIV, 1347.
Lokasambhava: XIII, 940.
Lokasrashṭṛ: VIII, 1532.
Lokavṛddha: V, 1920.
Lokeça, q.v.
Mahādeva: XII, 9176, 13047.
Mānasa, q.v.
Niruktaga: XII, 12914, 13283.
Padmasambhava: XIII, 6046.
Padmayoni: III, 16547; VII, 9427, 9591; XII, 13371; XIII, 1126, 3546, 6178.
Padmodbhava: XIII, 298.
Parameshṭhin, q.v.
Pitāmaha: I, 32, 902, 935, 1197, 1272, (1274), 1277, 1569, 1570, 1576, 1580, 1588, 1627, 1628, 1629, 1638, 1644, 1645, 1652, 1826, 1915, 2057, 2065, 2075, 2076, 3846, (7279), 7635, 7636, 7637, 7642, (7643), 7644, 7680 (*°sya bhavanaṃ*), 7681, 7683, 7685, 7686, 7687, 7689, 7690, 7696, (7698), 7700, 7708, 7732, 7733, 8157; II, 280, 420 (*°sabhāṃ*), 425 (do.), 465, 467, 482 (*°sabhāyāṃ*), 739 (*°samaḥ*, i.e. Bṛhadratha); III, 7078, 8034 (*Vetasikāṃ P°nishevitāṃ*), 8192 (at Tuṅgaka), 8239, 8253 (*°purogāç ca devāḥ*), 8276 (*°samaṃ Dhaumyaṃ*), 8315 (performed a sacrifice in Prayāga), 8700, 8707 (*yathā*), 8775 (*iva*), 8823, 8827, 8858, 11856 (on Meru), 12152, 12190, 12305, 12809, 13559, 13565, 13585, 14278, 15886, 15934, 15938; V, 1920, 1922, 3604 (*amṛtenā 'bhitṛptasya sāram udgirataḥ purā, P°sya vadanād udatishṭhad aninditā*, i.e. Surabhi), 3835 (*atra*—in the North—*yajñaṃ samāsadya dhruvaṃ sthātā P°ḥ*), 3969 (*yathā Devyāṃ P°ḥ*), 4102, (4111); VI, 2939, 2975, 2977, 5770 (*iva*); VII, 2041, 2071, 2085, 2099, 2101, 6348 (*°purogamā devāḥ*); VIII, 1518, 1526, 1528 (*trilokeçaṃ*), (1530), 1531, 1533, 1574 (*lokadhātā*), 1575, 1622, 1627, 2089, 2091, 4438; X, 769, 771, 776, 784; XII, 1355 (*°sutaṃ jyeshṭhaṃ Kumāraṃ*), 2148, 2514, 4176 (wanting in B.), 4178, 4465, 4490, 4515, 4516, 4519 (*°samaprabhaḥ*), 5847, 6131, 6134, 6145, 6162, 6330 (*°sabhopamaṃ*), 6437, 7355, 7631, (7635), 8060, †8423 (*Svayambhuvaḥ*), 9156, 9159, 9165, 9174, (9195), 9210, 9212, 10052 (identified with Vishṇu), 10113 (*°purogāç ca sarve devāḥ*), 10163, 10164, 10165, 10170, 10177, 10178, 10187, 10191, 10252, 10438 (*hṛdayañ ca P°aḥ*, sc. Çiva's), 12979, 13037, 13045, 13420 (?), 13522, 13562, 13595, 13596, †13686, (13727), 13731, 13764; XIII, 297, 298, 794, 1112, 1517, 2252, 2253, 2255, 2966, 3289 (*Atriḥ P°sutaḥ*), (3554), (3607), 3616, 3884 (*°sya saṃvādam Indrasya ca*), 3887, 3953, 4016, 4020, 4104, 4138, 4142, 4155, 4159, 4160, 4371 (*°sabhāṃ*), 4378, 4392, 4765, 4805, 4807, 4923, 4928, 4933, 6155 (*padmabhūtaḥ*), 6159, 6582, 6807, 6810 (*°gṛhaṃ*, i.e. Kṛshṇa), 6843, 6845, 7229 (born from the *ākāça*), 7635 (*jagannāthaḥ*), 7642; XIV, 525, 689, 784, 2035; XVIII, 170.
Prabhavaḥ sarvabhūtānāṃ: I, 2499.
Prajānām īçvareçvaraḥ: VII, 2085.
Prajāpati, q.v.
Prajeçvara: VII, 2079.
Prapitāmaha: I, 7733; III, 1152, 15916; VI, 1285 (identified with Kṛshṇa); VII, 1626; IX, 2192; XII, 7351, 9161; XIII, 1126; XIV, 966.
Sarvabhūtapitāmaha: I, 2493; IX, 2499; XII, 7530.
Sarvabhūtātman, q.v.
Sarvabhūteça: III, 12818.
Sarvalokakṛt: I, 8145.
Sarvalokapitāmaha: I, 901, 7735; II, 435; III, 8856, 12811, 12997, 13535; VIII, 1620; IX, 2313, 2495, 2742, 2750; XII, 4483, 6140, 13470; XIII, 1134; XIV, 521.
Sarvalokeçvara, q.v.
Sarveça: VII, 2102.
Suraguru: I, 32 (?), 2504.
Suraçreshṭha, q.v.
Surasattama, q.v.
Svayambhū, q.v.
Trailokyakartṛ: XII, 10167.
Tribhuvaneçvara, q.v.
Trilokakṛt: XII, 6977, 10190.
Trilokeça, q.v.
Vedhas, q.v.
Vibudhaçreshṭha, q.v.
Vibudheçvara, q.v.
Viçvakṛt, q.v.
Viçvātman, q.v.
Viçveça, q.v.
Viçveçvara, q.v.
Vidhātṛ, q.v.
Vidhi, q.v.
Viriñci, q.v.

Brahmán[2] = Çiva (1000 names[1–2]). Do.[3] = Vishṇu (1000 names).

Bráhman ("the Absolute, the Vedas, etc."). § 1 (Anukram.): I, **1**, 14 (*°bhūtāḥ*, i.e. the munis present at the sacrifice of Çaunaka).—§ 2 (do.): I, **1**, 22 (*ekāksharaṃ*, etc. = Vishṇu).—§ 3 (do.): I, **1**, 30 (*satyaṃ, jyotir, Brahma sanātanaṃ*, in the primordial egg, whence came Brahmán, etc.).—§ 4 (do.): I, **1**, †109 (*mūlaṃ Kṛshṇo brahma ca brāhmaṇāç ca*).—§ 7 (do.): I, **1**, 250 (*çāçvataṃ, paramaṃ*).—§ 72 (Ādivaṃçāvatāraṇap.): I, **62**, 2317 (*gacchati çāçvataṃ*).—§ 82 (Kṛshṇa Vāsudeva): I, **63**, 2429 (*avyaktyam aksharaṃ*, etc. = Kṛshṇa).—§ 84 (Ādivaṃçāvatāraṇap.): I, **64**, 2474 (*na ca vikrīṇate brahma*, i.e. the Vedas).—§ 135 (Çakuntalop.): I, **74**, 3098 (*satyaṃ paraṃ brahma*).—§ 143 (Nahusha): I, **75**, 3156 (°*bhūtaḥ*, i.e. Yati).—§ 144 (Yayāti): I, **75**, 3176 (*sampadyate tadā*), 3177 (do.).—§ 145 (Kaca): I, **76**, †3229 (? *brahma ca brāhmaṇāç ca*, worship Devayānī), †3245 (°*rāçiṃ*, i.e. Uçanas), †3253 (*brāhmaṇo brahmabhūtaḥ*, i.e. Kaca).—§ 146 (Devayānī): I, **78**, 3315 (*acintyaṃ*, etc.).—§ 148 (Yayāti): I, **85**, 3515 (°*ṇy ādhāya mānasaṃ*).—§ 149 (do.): I, **90**, †3622.—§ 223 (Vāsishṭha): I, **175**, 6691 (?, *mahad āçcaryaṃ B°tejobhavaṃ*), 6692 (°*tejobalaṃ*).—§ 233 (Svayaṃvarap.): I, **188**, 7047 (°*tejasā*).—§ 259 (Çārṅgakop.): I, **232**, 8424 (?, *etad brahma vyāhṛtaṃ tvayā*).—§ 260 (Khāṇḍavadah.): I, **234**, 8463 (?).—§ 277 (Jarāsandhavadhap.): II, **22**, 871 (?, *svargayonir mahad brahma*).—§ 310*b* (Sūrya): III, **3**, 190 (*çāçvataṃ* = Sūrya).—§ 327 (Draupadīparit.): III, **29**, 1101 (*kshamā brahma*, etc.), 1104 (do.), 1105, 1106 (*sampadyate tadā*).—§ 329 (Kāmyakavanaprav.): III, **36**, 1450 (*brahma* = the Pratismṛti knowledge).—§ 330 (Indradarçana): III, **37**, 1466 (do.).—§ 370 (Tīrthayātrāp.): III, **84**, 8043 (°*bhūtaḥ*, cf. Gaṅgodbheda).—§ 377 (Dhaumyatīrthak.): III, **90**, 8400 (*paramaṃ*, i.e. Nārāyaṇa).—§ 383 (Jāmadagnyatejohānik.): III, **99**, 8675 (°*bhūtāḥ*). — § 417 (Yavakrītop.): III, **138**, 10814 (= the Vedas), 10817 (?).—§ 423 (Gandhamādanaprav.): III, **145**, 11047 (°*bhūtāḥ*, at Badarī).—§ 450 (Ājagarap.): III, **180**, 12471 (*paraṃ brahma nirduḥkham asukhañ ca yat*), 12472.—§ 453 (Mārkaṇḍeyas.): III, **183**, 12621 (°*bhūtāḥ*).—§ 456 (Sarasvatī-Tārkshyas.): III, **186**, 12719 (= the Vedas?). — § 459 (Mārkaṇḍeyas.): III, **189**, 12992 (°*rūpiṇā*, i.e. Nārāyaṇa). —§ 474*b* (Dhundhumārop.): III, **201**, 13495 (*Brahma Vedāç ca*, created by Vishṇu).—§ 482 (Pativratop., Brāhmaṇavyādhasaṃv.): III, **210**, 13913 (*mahābhūtātmakaṃ Brahma*). —§ 483 (do., do.): III, **211**, 13934 (°*bhūtasya saṃyogaḥ*).—§ 485 (do., do.): III, **213**, 13962 (°*yoniṃ*, i.e. the soul), 13992 (°*ṇo yogaṃ*), 13997, 13998.—§ 520 (Mudgala): III, **261**, 15482 (*Vishṇoḥ paramaṃ padaṃ, paraṃ brahmeti yaṃ viduḥ*).—§ 552 (Goharaṇap.): IV, **50**, 1559 (?, °*karmāṇi*); **51**, 1592 (*Brahmāstraṃ Brahma Vedāç ca*).—§ 555 (Indravijaya): V, **17**, 534 (*yasmāt pūrvaiḥ kṛtaṃ brahma brahmarshibhir anushṭhitaṃ* | *adushṭam dūshayasi vai*). — § 556 (Sañjayayānap.): V, **29**μ, †861 (*mūlan tvahaṃ brahma ca brāhmaṇāç ca*, said Kṛshṇa, cf. I, 109).—§ 559 (Prajāgarap.): V, **36**, 1282 (°*vittaṃ*); **39**, 1515 (= the Vedas?, *brahma brahmavidām balaṃ*).—§ 560 (Sanatsujātap.): V, **42**, 1580 (*apramādād Brahmabhūtā bhavanti*, sc. the gods), 1610 (*āvasati*); **43**, 1679, 1680, **44**, †1685, †1700, †1707 (*abhyeti*), †1708; **45**, 1722 (°*mukhyānāṃ brāhmaṇānāṃ*), 1736 (*āviçati*); **46**, 1739 (*Brahma çukrāt pravartate, Brahma çukreṇa vardhate*).—§ 561 (Yānasandhip.): V, **53**, 2113 (?, °*varcasī*, i.e. Yudhishṭhira); **63**, 2452 (°*bhūyāya kalpate*). —§ 562 (Bhagavadyānap.): V, **90**, 3234 (*mahat brahma*, identified with Kṛshṇa). — § 569 (do.): V, **140**, 4742 (°*karmaṇy avasthitaḥ*, sc. Dhaumya). — § 573 (Ambopakhyānap.): V, **181**, 7215 (°*rāçiḥ*, i.e. Rāma Jāmadagnya). —§ 576 (Bhagavadgītāp.): VI, **26**, 950 (*nirvāṇaṃ*); **27**, 965 (*karma brahmodbhavaṃ viddhi*); **28**, 1017, 1018 (°*āgnau*), 1024 (*yajñaçishṭāmṛtabhujo yānti brahma sanātanaṃ*); **29**, 1041 (*adhigacchati*), 1045, 1054, 1055, 1056, 1059 (*Brahmanirvāṇaṃ Brahmabhūto 'dhigacchati*), 1060 (*labhante Brahmanirvāṇam ṛshayaḥ kshīṇakalmashāḥ*), 1061 (°*nirvāṇaṃ*), 1091 (°*bhūtaṃ*), 1092; **30**, 1102 (*vimūḍho Brahmaṇaḥ pathi*), 1108 (*çabdabrahma*, i.e. the Vedas); **31**, 1140; **32**, 1142, 1144, 1154 (*om ity ekāksharaṃ brahma*), 1165; **34**, 1216 (*paraṃ*, identified with Kṛshṇa); **37**, 1334 (*paraṃ*), 1351 (*sampadyate tadā*); **38**, 1358 (*mahat*), 1359, 1381 (°*bhūyāya kalpate*), 1382 (*Brahmaṇo hi pratishṭhā 'ham amṛtasyāvyayasya ca*); **41**, 1449 (*oṃ, tat, sad iti nirdeço Brahmaṇas trividhaḥ smṛtaḥ*); **42**, 1504 (*āpnoti*), 1507 (°*bhūyāya kalpate*), 1508 (°*bhūtaḥ*).—§ 581 (Bhīshmavadhap.): VI, **66**, 2987 (*paramakaṃ*, identified with Kṛshṇa); **67**, 3030 (°*bhūtaṃ Keçavaṃ*).—§ 593 (Abhimanyuvadhap.): VII, **42**, 1754 (*gṛṇan Brahma sanātanaṃ*).—§ 595 (Shoḍaçar. v. Pṛthu Vainya): VII, **69**, 2416 (milked from the Earth by the *Saptarshayaḥ*).—§ 596 (Pratijñāp.): VII, **80**, 2862 (*gṛṇan Brahma sanātanaṃ*), 2865 (identified with Çiva); **81**, 2898 (*gṛṇantau vedavidvāṃsau tad Brahma Çatarudriyaṃ*).—§ 599 (Jayadrathavadhap.): VII, **94**, 3449 (v. Brahmán), 3479 (°*sūtreṇa badhnāmi kavacaṃ*).—§ 603 (Nārāyaṇāstram.): VII, **195**, 9009 (°*rūpaḥ*); **201**, 9451 (°*bhūto . . . abhavat*, sc. Nārāyaṇa), †9467 (v. Brahmán), †9470 (*gacchati*).—§ 606 (Tripurākhyāna): VIII, **33**, 1437 (*gṛṇanto Brahma çāçvataṃ*).—§ 607 (Karṇap.): VIII, **42**, †1970 (*abrāhmaṇe Brahma na hi dhruvaṃ syāt*). — § 616 (Sauptikap.): X, **7**η, 257 (identified with Çiva).—§ 618 (Jalapradānikap.): XI, **7**, 192 (*çāçvataṃ*).—§ 621 (Rājadh.): XII, **3**, 105 (i.e. Brahmāstra); **7**, 194 (*sampadyate tadā*).—§ 623 (do.): XII, **12**, 357 (°*bhūtasya dvijāteḥ*); **13**, 374 (*tryaksharaṃ çāçvataṃ*), 375; **15**, 460 (*na Brahma çāpy adhīyīta*, i.e. the Vedas, differently B.); **17**, 532 (°*bhāvaprapannānāṃ*), 533 (*sampadyate tadā*).—§ 626 (do.): XII, **20**, 604 (= the Vedas); **21**, 619 (*sampadyate tadā*).—§ 630 (do.): XII, **26**, 781 (do.), 782 (do.).—§ 635 (do.): XII, **34**, 1213 (°*vikrayī*).—§ 637 (do.): XII, **47**, 1606 (*paraṃ*, identified with Kṛshṇa), 1617 (*bhaumasya*, i.e. the Vedas, the brahmans and the sacrifices, Nīl.), 1619 (*Brahma proktaṃ yugādishu*, sc. Kṛshṇa), 1622 (*ekāksharaṃ*, i.e. Kṛshṇa), 1688 (*Nārāyaṇaparaṃ Brahma*).—§ 640 (do.): XII, **56**, 2012 (*bhaumaṃ*).—§ 641 (do.): XII, **59**, 2142 (i.e. the Vedas), 2143 (do.), 2145 (*sanātanaṃ naralokasthaṃ*), 2146.—§ 641*f* (Pṛthu Vainya): XII, **59**, 2227 (*bhaumaṃ*).—§ 641 (Rājadh.): XII, **63**, 2357 (*shaṭkarma*); **66**, 2489 (*samaçnute*); **77**, 2913 (*yeshāṃ Brahma paraṃ balaṃ*); **108**, 4015 (*yena prīṇāty upadhyāyaṃ tena Brahma pūjitaṃ*); **121**, 4463.—§ 649 (Āpaddharm.): XII, **141**, 5382 (*vahniḥ*).—§ 655 (do.): XII, **160**, 5950 (°*bhūyāya kalpate*), 5957 (*Paitāmahaṃ sthānam Brahmarāçisamudbhavaṃ*); **161**, 5981 (*sanātanaṃ*).—§ 659 (Mokshadh.): XII, **174**, 6510 (*sampadyate tadā*), 6512 (do.); **177**, 6610 (*mano B°ṇi dhārayan*), 6635 (°*pratishṭhaḥ*, sc. Maṅki), 6638 (*mahat sukhaṃ*).—§ 660*b* (Bhṛgu-Bharadvājasaṃv.): XII, **188**β, 6931 (*çāçvataṃ*, i.e. *nityaṃ Vedaṃ*, Nīl., created by Brahmán), 6945 (*brāhmaṇa B°tantrasthās tapas teshāṃ na naçyati* | *Brahma dhārayatāṃ nityaṃ vratāni niyamās tathā*), 6946 (*paraṃ*), 6949 (°*mūlā*, sc. *sṛshṭiḥ*); **189**, 6965 (*prāṇaṃ B°ṇi dhārayet*), 6966 (*nirvedenādhigacchati*); **190**, 6968 (*satyaṃ*).—§ 661 (Mokshadh.): XII, **196**, 7158 (°*ṇy avasthitāḥ*), 7166 (*dhiyā dhyāyati*), 7172 (°*kāyanishevaṇaṃ*); **197**, 7185 (°*ṇi sthitaṃ*).—§ 662 (do.): XII, **199**, 7324 (°*bhūtaḥ*), 7325.—§ 662*b* (Jāpakop.): XII, **199**, 7264 (*ekāksharaṃ*). — § 663 (Mokshadh.): XII, **201**, †7380 (*paraṃ hy upaiti*); **204**, 7456 (*tadā sampadyate*); **205**, 7466 (*abhyeti*), 7469 (*prajñāyate*), 7471 (do.), 7478 (*ninīshet paramaṃ Brahma*), 7480 (*āpnoti*), 7481 (*paramaṃ*); **206**, 7486 (*drakshyate*), 7499 (*paramaṃ*, i.e. Vishṇu), 7502, 7503, †7512 (°*çarīraṃ*), †7516 (*praviçati B° cāvyayaṃ*). — § 667 (do.): XII, **210**, 7649 (*guhyaṃ*), 7650 (°*ṇo mukhaṃ*, i.e. Kṛshṇa), 7651 (*çāçvataṃ*, i.e. Kṛshṇa), 7652, 7655 (*çāçvataṃ*, i.e. Kṛshṇa), 7664 (*anādyaṃ tat paraṃ B° na devā narshayo viduḥ*); **215**, 7813 (°*bhūyāya kalpate*), 7820 (*sanātanaṃ*);

216, 7839 (*paramaṃ*), 7841 (*aksharaṃ*); **217,** 7842 (*paraṃ*), 7844 (*çāçvataṃ*), 7871 (°*bhūtāḥ*).—§ 668*b* (Pānçaçikhavākya): XII, **218,** 7894 (*ekāksharaṃ nānarūpaṃ*). — § 671*b* (Bali-Vāsavasaṃv.): XII, **224,** 8135 (*gambhīraṃ gahanaṃ*). — § 677 (Mokshadh.): XII, **227,** 8488 (*agre sampravartate*), 8499 (*çāçvataṃ*); **233,** 8510 (*tejomayaṃ çukraṃ*), 8540 (*dve brahmaṇī veditavye çabdabrahma*—i.e. the Vedas—*parañ ca yat*), 8541 (*çabdabrahmaṇi nishṇātaḥ paraṃ B°ādhigacchati*); **234,** 8571 (*paraṃ*), 8572, 8573 (°*āvyakte*); **235,** 8596 (*nirguṇaṃ*); **236,** 8629 (°*prāyabhavena*); **238,** 8709 (°*jñānapratishṭhaṃ hi taṃ devā brāhmaṇaṃ viduḥ*); **240,** 8735 (*adhigacchati*), 8751 (°*bhūyase kalpate*), 8754 (*sampadyate tadā*); **241,** 8776 (*tejomayaṃ çukraṃ*); **242,** 8816 (*paramaṃ*); **243,** 8831 (°*bhūyase kalpate*), 8838 (*catushpadī hi niḥçreṇī B°ṇy eshā pratishṭhitā*); **251,** 9054 (°*bhūyān bhavishyasi*), 9060 (*aduḥkham asukhaṃ*); **252,** 9068 (*sampadyate tadā*), 9069 (do.), 9070 (°*bhūyāya kalpate*); **254,** 9115 (*paraṃ*).—§ 680 (do.): XII, **263,** 9355 (*sampadyate tadā*), 9356 (do.); **264,** 9412 (*Brahmaiva vartate loke*), 9415 (*sarvaṃ Brahma Brahmaṇi saṃçritaṃ*).—§ 684 (do.): XII, **270,** 9638 (°*bhūtāḥ*), 9654 (*Brahmaṇi Brahma vindati*); **271,** 9707 (*dve Brahmaṇī*, etc., cf. v. 8540), 9708 (*paraṃ B°ādhigacchati*, cf. v. 8541), 9747, †9753, †9754.—§ 688 (do.): XII, **276,** 9912 (°*tvam upagacchati*), 9913 (°*bhāve*). — § 692 (do.): XII, **280,** 10000 (*prakāçati sanātanaṃ*), 10021 (*aiçvaryaṃ vai mahat B°*); **281,** 10051 (identified with Vishṇu), 10054 (*prakāçate*), †10081 (*dushprāpam abhyeti*).—§ 696*b* (Dakshaprokta-Çivasahasra-nāmastotra): XII, **285,** 10474 (°*sammitaḥ*, sc. *stavaḥ*, i.e. the hymn containing Çiva's 1000 names as recited by Daksha). — § 702 (Mokshadh.): XII, **292,** 10736 (°*çāstrajñāḥ*). — § 703 (Mokshadh.): XII, **300,** †11011 (*guhyaṃ*). — § 704 (do.): XII, **302,** 11198 (*sanātanaṃ*, i.e. the Saṅkhya-system).—§ 705 (do.): XII, **303,** 11224 (*paraṃ sanātanaṃ*); **309,** 11474 (*avyaktaṃ*), †11497 (*sanātanaṃ viçuddham ādyaṃ*), †11502 (*paraṃ*), †11504 (do.), †11506 (*sanātanaṃ*), 11508 (*paraṃ*), 11512 (*sanātanaṃ*).—§ 707 (do.): XII, **311,** 11547 (*avyaktaṃ paraṃ*); **317,** 11692 (*avyayaṃ*), 11699 (*paramam avyayaṃ*); **319,** †11813, 11825. —§ 709*b* (Sulabhā-Janaka-saṃv.): XII, **321,** 11924 (*Brahma Brahmavidāṃ balaṃ*, i.e. the Vedas). — § 713 (Çukakṛti): XII, **326,** 12219 (°-*tulyaparākramaṃ*); **327,** 12279 (°*āçramapade*, i.e. sannyāsa), 12293 (*sampadyate tadā*), 12294 (do.), 12295 (°*tvam açnute*), 12296 (*sampadyate tadā*), 12298 (do.).—§ 714 (Çukakṛtya): XII, **329,** 12370 (i.e. the Vedas).—§ 715 (Çuka-Nāradasaṃv.): XII, **331,** 12498 (*abhyeti*). — § 716 (Çukābhipatana): XII, **334,** 12610 (°*ṇi pratyatishṭhat*), 12627 (°*bhūto 'bhavat*, sc. Çuka), 12642 (°*tejomayaḥ*, i.e. Çuka). — § 717*c* (Uparicara): XII, **336,** 12727; **337,** 12753 (*bṛhad Brahma mahac caiva çabdāḥ paryāyavācakāḥ*, etymology of the name Bṛhaspati), 12802 (°*bhāvam anusthitāḥ*). — § 717*b* (Nārāyaṇīya): XII, **341,** 13116 (*paraṃ*, i.e. Nārāyaṇa); **343,** 13191 (°*bhūtaṃ*), ††13196 (? *Agniḥ*; = brāhmaṇa, Nīl.), 13239 (*paramaṃ*, i.e. nirvāṇa); **348,** 13465 (*tamaso Brahma sambhūtaṃ*), 13481 (*Vēdā me Brahma cottaraṃ*, said Brahmán), 13530 (*agryaṃ*, i.e. Nārāyaṇa); **349,** 13612 (*paramakaṃ*, i.e. Nārāyaṇa).—§ 718*b* (Uñchavṛttyup.): XII, **360,** 13861 (*vartayan*); **362,** 13890 (*āvartayāmi*, i.e. the Vedas).—§ 724 (Ānuçāsanik.): XIII, **7,** 369 (*yena prīṇāti upadhyāyaṃ tena syād Brahma pūjitaṃ*).—§ 730 (do.): XIII, **14,** 593 (*aksharaṃ paramaṃ*, identified with Çiva); **16**ηη, 1044 (*nirguṇaṃ*, i.e. Çiva), 1045 (? °*ṇo gatiṃ* = Çiva), 1061 (*paramaṃ*, i.e. Çiva), 1066 (= Çiva), 1086 (*paraṃ* = Çiva), 1093 (*sanātanaṃ* = Çiva), 1103 (*paramaṃ* = Çiva); **17,** 1118 (do.), 1120 (*sanātanaṃ* = Çiva), 1193 (*paramaṃ* = Çiva (1000 names[2])), 1266 (= do.), 1270 (*paramaṃ, paraṃ*); **18**λλ, †1369 (= the Upanishads, PCR.). — § 733*t* (Viçālā): XIII, **25,** 1730 (°*bhūtāḥ*). — § 746 (Ānuçāsanik.): XIII, **62,** 3138 (°*bhūyaṃ sa gacchati*); **63,** 3232 (i.e. the Vedas).—§ 747*b* (Suvarṇotpatti): XIII, **85,** 4132 (*paraṃ*, i.e. Agni). — § 762*b* (Kītopākhyāna): XIII, **117,** 5728 (°*bhūtasya*, i.e. Vyāsa); **118,** 5775 (°*bhūtaḥ*); **119,** 5790 (*sanātanaṃ*).—§ 768*b* (Umā-Maheçvarasaṃv.): XIII, **141,** 6420 (°*bhūyāya kalpate*); **142,** 6538 (do.); **143,** 6616 (*nirguṇaṃ nirmalaṃ Brahma yatra tishṭhati sa dvijaḥ*), 6621 (°*bhūyāya kalpate*). — § 768*b* (Kṛshṇa Vāsudeva): XIII, **147,** 6817 (°*bhūtasya*, i.e. Kṛshṇa), 6838 (°*bhūtaḥ*, i.e. Kṛshṇa); **148,** 6875 (do.).—§ 769 (Ānuçāsanik.): XIII, **149,** 6944 (*paramaṃ*, i.e. Vishṇu), 7066 (*sanātanaṃ yāti*).—§ 770 (do.): XIII, **151**ζ, 7109 (°*tejomayāh*, i.e. the ṛshis of the East), 7133 (*paramaṃ*), 7150 (*mahad Brahma Sāvitrīguṇakīrtanaṃ*), 7154 (*sanātanaṃ*). — § 773*b* (Kṛshṇa Vāsudeva): XIII, **159,** 7370 (°*guhāṃ pravishṭaḥ*, sc. Kṛshṇa). — § 779 (Açvamedhikap.): XIV, **13,** 333 (*tryaksharaṃ çāçvataṃ*), 334 (°*mṛtyū*).—§ 782 (Anugītāp.): XIV, **16,** 419 (*paraṃ*); **17,** 477 (= jīva); **18,** 502 (*çāçvataṃ* = jīva?); **19,** 545 (*sanātanaṃ paraṃ āpnoti*), 557 (*avyayam āpnoti*), 579 (*āsadayati tad B°*), 582.—§ 782*b* (Brāhmaṇagītā): XIV, **20,** 608 (*nirdvandvaṃ*); **24,** 727 (*sanātanaṃ*); **26,** 753 (*om ity aksharaṃ Brahma*), 761 (°*ṇi sthitaḥ, Brahmabhūtaḥ*), 762 (*Brahmaiva samidhas tasya Brahmāgnir Brahmasambhavaḥ* | *āpo Brahma gurur Brahma sa Brahmaṇi samāhitaḥ*); **27,** 783 (*vāri B°sambhavaḥ*); **32,** 912 (°*lābhyasya*; °*nābhasya*, PCR.); **34,** 925 (°*ṇo liṅgaṃ*).—§ 782 (Anugītāp.): XIV, **35,** 934 (*paraṃ*).—§ 782*g* (Guruçishyasaṃv.): XIV, **35,** 950 (*paraṃ*), 953 (°*bhūyāya kalpate*), 956 (°*bījaḥ*, sc. *vṛkshaḥ*), 969, 973 (°*bhāvāya*); **41,** 1112 (*çubhaṃ yāti*), 1115 (*prakāçate*); **42,** 1153 (°*bhūyāya kalpate*); **47,** 1317 (*param . . . Brahmayonisthāḥ*), 1318, 1324 (°*bhūyāya kalpate*), 1330 (°*vṛkshaḥ*); **48,** 1334 (°*mayaṃ vṛkshaṃ*, °*vanaṃ*); **49,** 1351 (°*jnāḥ*), 1353 (do., C. has *Brā°*); **51,** 1432 (*paraṃ*), 1453 (*tryaksharaṃ . . . çāçvataṃ*), 1460 (*çubhaṃ vetti*). — § 790 (Putradarçanap.): XV, **35,** 940 (°*opanishadaṃ*, i.e. the Vedas and the Upanishads).—§ 795 (Svargārohaṇap.): XVIII, **5,** 187 (°*bhūyāya kalpate*).—§ 795*b* (Mahābhārata): XVIII, **5,** 208 (*paraṃ Brahmādhigacchati*).

Bráhman[2] = Çiva (1000 names[1]). Do.[3] = Vishṇu (1000 names).

Brāhmaṇa[1] = Çiva (1000 names[2]). Do.[2] = Vishṇu (1000 names).

Brāhmaṇa[3] (adj.). § 520 (Mudgala): III, **261,** 15458 (*lokāḥ*).

[Brāhmaṇagītā] ("the instruction given by the brahman"). § 782*b* (Anugītāparvan): *Kṛshṇa* said: A certain brahman's wife asked her husband (who was a complete master of every kind of knowledge and wisdom) to what region she should go, being dependent on him as her husband, who was harsh in his conduct towards her (*kīnāçaṃ*, i.e. *karkaçaṃ niranukroçaṃ*, Nīl.). The brahman discourses on acts; on the seat of the soul, where *Bráhman*, *Soma*, and *Agni*, etc., dwell, and for whose sake *Brahmán*, etc., in *Yoga*, worship the indestructible, etc.; the life-breaths *prāṇa*, etc. (*a*); in the midst of them is *Agni Vaiçvānara*, whose seven flames are the nose, the tongue, the eye, the skin, the ear, the mind, and the understanding (*boddhavyaṃ*), etc. (XIV, **20**). In this connection an ancient story is cited, viz. that of the institution of the ten *hotṛs*, i.e. the ear, the skin, the two eyes, the tongue, the nose, the two feet, the two hands, the genital organ, the lower duct, and speech; sound, etc., are the ten libations; the points of the compass, wind, sun, moon, earth, fire, *Vishṇu*, *Indra*, *Prajāpati*, and *Mitra* are the ten fires, etc. (XIV, **21**); in this connection an ancient story is cited, viz. that of the institution of the seven *hotṛs*, the nose, the eye, the tongue, the skin, the ear, the mind, and the understanding (*buddhiḥ*), not knowing the qualities of one another; the nose, etc., and the understanding never succeed in apprehending doubt, it is the mind [alone] that apprehends it; the nose, etc., and the mind never succeed in apprehending determination; it is the understanding alone that apprehends it; in this connection this ancient narrative of a discourse between the senses and the mind is cited: as the nose does not smell, etc., without the mind, the mind thought itself to be the eternal and foremost one of all the elements; but the senses said that without them the mind would have no enjoyments at all, etc. (XIV, **22**); likewise the ancient story of the institution of the five *hotṛs: Prāṇa, Apāna, Udāna, Samāna*, and *Vyāna*; the wind nursed by *Prāṇa* > *Apāna* > *Vyāna* > *Udāna* > *Samāna*; these asked *Brahmán* in days of yore as to which of them was the foremost; *Brahmán* said that he upon whose extinction all the life-breaths become extinct is the foremost; it turned out (as *Brahmán* said) that they are all foremost and not foremost, as they possess the attributes of one another (XIV, **23**); likewise the ancient story of the discourse between *Nārada* and Ṛ. *Devamata*. *Devamata* said: Which part of a creature that takes birth comes first into existence, is it *Prāṇa* or *Apāna*, etc.? *Nārada* seems to give the following explanation: *kāma* (desire) is (1–2) *samāna* and *vyāna*, which move transversely and alternately [from the man to the woman, and *vice versâ*?] and have sprung from *sattva*; from *kāma* springs the vital seed [in the man] and the *rajas* or blood [in the woman]; from the union of these two springs (3) *prāṇa*, and from the seed being modified by *prāṇa* springs (4) *apāna*; these two move up and down and represent the two libations in the [mystical] fire; from the sexual intercourse of the loving pair springs *harsha* (pleasure), which is (5) *udāna* = the fire between *prāṇa* and *apāna* = the fire between day and night = the fire between *sat* (the existent) and *asat* (the non-existent) = [the union between *Samāna* and (Nīl.)] *Vyāna* = *Çānti* (tranquillity) = eternal *Bráhman* ("as the brahmans know"); in fire the smoke is *tamas* (darkness), and the ashes *rajas* (passion). [Nīl. takes all the expressions figuratively in a philosophical sense; according to him the seed (*çukra*) is = *adṛshṭa*, i.e. the *karman* of past lives, the blood (*çoṇitam*) = attachment to the objects of sense, *prāṇa* = *liṅgātman*, *apāna* = death, etc.] (XIV, **24**); likewise the ancient story of the *Cāturhotra*, i.e. the sacrifice with four *hotṛs*; the instrument, the action, the agent, and emancipation; at the sacrifice of *yoga* the *Prāṇa* is the *Stotra*, etc. (*β*); people knowing *Nārāyaṇa* recite some Ṛcs; to *Nārāyaṇa* animals (i.e. the senses, Nīl.) were offered in days of yore; and some *Sāmans*; *Nārāyaṇa* is the soul of all (XIV, **25**); † there is one ruler, residing in the heart, etc.; instructed by him the seven Ṛ.'s shine in the firmament; having lived with that instructor, *Indra* attained to the sovereignty of all the worlds. There is one enemy, residing in the heart; instructed by him all snakes are always hated († v. 746–750). In this connection the old story of the instruction of the snakes, the gods (and As.), and Ṛ. by *Prajāpati* is cited; asked by them what is highly beneficial, he said *om*, i.e. *Bráhman* in one syllable; then they ran away in various directions from desire of self-instruction; first arose in the snakes the disposition of biting; in the As. the disposition for ostentatious pride; the gods betook themselves to gifts, and M.-ṛ. to self-restraint (XIV, **26**). The brahman compared the world to an impassable fastness (*durgam*), and *Bráhman* to a great forest; asked by his wife, he described this forest copiously (XIV, **27**); "it is not I, but nature that smells scents, etc." In this connection an ancient discourse between an *adhvaryu* and a *yati* is recited: Beholding an animal sprinkled with water at a sacrificial ceremony, a *yati* blamed the *adhvaryu* for that destruction of life. The *Adhvaryu* appealed to the *Vedas*, saying, "This goat will not be destroyed, but will be benefited; that part of it which is of earth will go to earth," etc.; the *yati* said that if the sacrifice was to the benefit of the goat, then the goats ought to give their consent; "abstention from cruelty is alone worthy of approbation; one should be guided by perception"; the *adhvaryu* objected that by smelling what belongs to the earth, etc., one takes life, as all these entities have life; the *yati* distinguished between the indestructible and the destructible of the soul (*ātmanaḥ*); of these only the indestructible is really existent; to him who is freed from all existent objects there is no fear; the *adhvaryu* admires and praises him, and says that he has no fault by performing those rites according to the *mantras*; the *yati* remained silent; the *adhvaryu* proceeded with the sacrifice (XIV, **28**). Follows the ancient story about the 1,000-armed king *Kārtavīryārjuna* and the Ocean; v. *Arjuna Kārtavīrya* (*c*) and *Paraçu-Rāma* (*d*) (XIV, **29**) with *Alarka* (*e*) (XIV, **30**). The brahman said: There are three foes in the world (i.e. ninefold, on account of the three guṇas); exultation, satisfaction, and joy < goodness; desire, wrath, and hatred < passion; lassitude, sloth, and delusion < darkness. Persons conversant with the ancient *kalpas* recite some verses which were sung in days of old by king *Ambarīsha*, who had acquired a tranquil soul: "I have killed all foes, etc., but the greatest vice has not yet been destroyed by me . . . " (XIV, **31**). Then the old narrative of the discourse between a brahman and king *Janaka* (*f*) is cited (XIV, **32–33**). Asked by his wife as to how this knowledge may be acquired, the brahman said: Know that *Brāhmaṇī* (i.e. *buddhi*, Nīl.) is the [lower] *araṇī*, the preceptor the upper *araṇī*; penances and conversance with the scriptures turn the upper *araṇī*; knowledge is the fire produced. Asked by his wife about the symbol (*liṅgam*) of *Bráhman* called *kshetrajña*, the brahman answered that he is without symbols and qualities. *Kṛshṇa* said: Then the mind of that brahman's wife, upon the destruction of the *kshetrajña*, became that which is beyond the *kshetrajñas*, in consequence of the knowledge of *kshetra*. Asked by *Arjuna*, where now that brahman and his wife were, *Kṛshṇa* said: "My mind (*manas*) is the brahman, my understanding (*buddhi*) is the *brahmaṇī*; he who has been called *kshetrajña* is I myself" (XIV, **34**).

Brāhmaṇāḥ = Çiva (1000 names[1]).

Brahmaṇaḥ çāstra(ṃ) ("the Vedas," PCR.). § 702 (Mokshadh.): XII, **292**, 10735 (°*nirdeçāt*).

Brahmaṇaḥ kshaya(ḥ). § 615*kk* (Kurukshetrak.): IX, **53**, 3025. Cf. Brahmakshetra.

Brahmaṇaḥ pada(ṃ). § 480 (Pativratop. Brahmaṇa-vyādhasaṃvāda): III, **209**, 13895 (*āpnoti yat param*).—§ 641 (Rājadh.): XII, **79**, 2982.—§ 677 (Mokshadh.): XII, **236**, 8621 (*ninīshet*); **237**, 8780 (do.).—§ 684 (do.): XII, **271**, 9739 (*anvicchan*).—§ 687 (do.): XII, **275**, 9871 (*ninīshet*).—§ 772*b* (Pavanārjunasaṃv.): XIII, **155**, 7234.—§ 779 (Açvamedhikap.): XIV, **11**, 296.—§ 782 (Anugītāp.): XIV, **16**, 418 (*Brahmaṇaḥ padavedane*; *padiv°*, C.), 449.

Brahmaṇaḥ sadana(ṃ). § 255 (Agniparābhava): I, **223**, 8143.—§ 357 (Pushkara): III, **82**, 4074.—§ 439 (Yakshayuddhap.): III, **163**, 11858 (*Brahmaṇaḥ sadanād tasya* — i.e. Nārāyaṇa's — *paraṃ sthānaṃ prakāçate*).—§ 520 (Mudgala): III, **261**, 15482 (*Brahmaṇaḥ sadanād ūrdhvaṃ tad Vishṇoḥ paramaṃ padaṃ*).—§ 615*ff* (Asita-Devala): IX, **50**, 2904.—§ 618 (Jalapradānikap.): XI, **8ζ**, 216.—§ 734 (Ānuçāsanik.): XIII, **26**, †1851.—§ 750 (do.): XIII, **93**, 4411.—§ 751*b* (Çapathavidhi): XIII, **94**, 4591.

Brahmaṇaḥ saras. § 615*gg* (Sārasvata): IX, **51**, 2943 (thence comes the Sarasvatī).

Brahmaṇaḥ sthāna(ṃ). § 72 (Ādivaṃçāvatāraṇap.): I, **62**, 2297. — § 364 (Tīrthayātrāp.): III, **83**, 6041 (*uttamaṃ*, i.e. Brahmodumbara).—§ 662*b* (Jāpakop.): XII, **199**, 7212.—§ 675 (Mokshadh.): XII, **230**, 8429, 8430, 8452.—§ 680*b* (Tulādhāra-Jājalisaṃv.): XII, **264**, 9420.—§ 691 (Mokshadh.): XII, **279**, 9967.—§ 692 (do.): XII, **281δ**, †10075 (*sthānaṃ . . . devasya Vishṇor atha Brahmaṇaç ca*, etc.).—§ 717*c* (Uparicara): XII, **337**, 12816.—§ 717*b* (Nārāyaṇīya): XII, **340**, 12977.

Brāhmaṇa - māhātmya - kathana. § 454 (Mārk.): Questioned by the *Pāṇḍavas* about the greatness of the *brahmans*, *Mārkaṇḍeya* told: A prince of the *Haihayas* killed a *brahman*, whom he took for a deer, as he was enveloped in the skin of a black antelope. The *Haihayas*, very afflicted, set out inquiring as to whose son the *muni* might be. Arriving at the hermitage of *Tārkshya Arishṭanemi*, they told him the matter, and learnt that it was his son, and that he had been revived, because these *munis* had no fear of death, as they spoke well of *brahmans*, etc. (III, **184**).—§ 455: *Mārkaṇḍeya* continued: When the *rājarshi Vainya* was performing the horse-sacrifice, *Atri* desired to go and ask him for alms, but gave up his desire of wealth and proposed to his wife and sons that they should all retire to the woods. His wife prevailed upon him that (though he had heard from *Gautama* that there were *brahmans* about *Vainya* who were jealous of him) he should first acquire riches and distribute them to his sons and servants, and so he went to *Vainya* and praised him as the foremost of sovereigns and the ruler of their destinies (*vidhātṛ*). The *ṛshi Gautama* blamed him for thus flattering the king, and said that it was *Indra* who was the foremost of sovereigns and ruler of their destinies (*vidhātṛ*). The *munis* (having let the pious *Kāçyapa* inquire about the matter) applied to *Sanatkumāra*, who said that the *brahmans* and *kshattriyas* ought to act together, and that the king (enumeration of honourable appellations) might rightly be styled as *Atri* had done. *Vainya* then gave to *Atri* 1000 maidservants and 100 millions of gold [coins] and ten *bhāras* of gold. Having given this to his sons *Atri* retired to the forest (III, **185**).

Brāhmaṇānāṃ netṛ = Skanda: III, 14638.

Brāhmaṇapriya[1] = Mahāpurusha (Mahāpurushastava).

Brāhmaṇapriya[2] = Vishṇu (1000 names).

Brāhmaṇarūpa = Mahāpurusha (Mahāpurushastava).

Brāhmaṇasavratin = Skanda: III, 14638.

Brahmaṇas tīrtha(ṃ), a tīrtha. § 364 (Tīrthayātrāp.): III, **83**, 6083.

Brāhmaṇa-vyādha-saṃvāda, v. Pativratopākhyāna.

Brāhmaṇī[1], a tīrtha. § 370 (Tīrthayātrāp.): III, **84**, 8036 (by bathing there one attains to Brahmaloka).

Brāhmaṇī[2], a river. § 574 (Jambūkh.): VI, **9λ**, 341 (in Bhāratavarsha, only in B., C. has by error *Brahmāṇīṃ*).

Brahmanirmitaṃ saras ("the lake created by Brahmán"). § 775 (Ānuçāsanik.): XIII, **166*a***, 7655.

Brahmaṇo bhavana(ṃ) = Brahmabhavana. § 289 (Arghāharaṇap.): II, **36**, 1317.

Brahmaṇo 'has ("a day of Brahmán"). § 310*b* (Sūrya): III, **3**, 185 (*yad aho Brahmaṇaḥ proktaṃ sahasrayugasammitaṃ*.).—§ 576 (Bhagavadgītāp.): VI, **32**, 1158 (*sahasrayugaparyantam ahar yat Brahmaṇo viduḥ*).—§ 675 (Mokshadh.): XII, **232**, 8508 (do.).

Brahmaṇo loka(ḥ) = Brahmaloka. § 615*ff* (Asita Devala): IX, **50**, 2901 (*Jaigīshavyaḥ sa vai lokaṃ çāçvataṃ Brahmaṇo gataḥ*).—§ 751*b* (Çapathavidhi): XIII, **94**, 4600.—§ 757*b* (Hastikūṭa): XIII, **102**, 4905 (*sa yāti Brahmaṇo lokaṃ brāhmaṇo Gautamo yathā*).

Brahmaṇya[1] = Skanda: III, 14638; IX, 2670.

Brahmaṇya[2] = Vishṇu (1000 names).

Brahmaṇyā = Durgā (Umā): VI, 802.

Brahmaṇyadeva[1] = Kṛshṇa: XII, 1683.

Brahmaṇyadeva[2] = Mahāpurusha (Mahāpurushastava).

Brahmapraçnānuçāsana. § 10 (Parvasaṅg.): I, **2**, 352 (presumably XII, **257** foll.).

Brahmapriya = Skanda: III, 14638.

Brahmapura. § 659 (Mokshadh.): XII, **177**, 6637 (*prāpyābadhyaṃ B°ṃ*—i.e. Bráhman, Nīl.—*rājeva syāṃ ahaṃ sukhī*).—§ 766 (Ānuçāsanik.): XIII, **126**, 6042 (*yathā B°e . . . Çatakrator Vajradharasya yajñe*).

Brahmapurohita = Mahāpurusha (Mahāpurushastava).

Brahmaputra, pl. (°*āḥ*) ("the son of Brahmán"). § 704 (Mokshadh.): XII, **301*a***, 11094.

Brahmarāçi (a constellation): § 574 (Jambūkh.): VI, **3**, 86 (= Çravaṇa, Nīl.).

Brahmarakshas, pl. (°*āṃsi*). § 760 (Ānuçāsanikap.): XIII, **111**, 5446. Cf. next.

Brahmarākshasa, mostly pl. (°*āḥ*). § 271 (Lokapālasabhākh.): II, **12**, 508 (*yajñaghnāḥ*).—§ 615*p* (Vasishṭhāpavāha): IX, **43**, 2420.—§ 749 (Ānuçāsanik.): XIII, **92**, 4383.—§ 760 (do.): XIII, **111**, 5445 (sg.).—§ 768*b* (Umā-Maheçvarasaṃv.): XIII, **145**, 6744.

Brahmarshi[1], pl. (°*ayaḥ*). § 1 (Anukram.): I, **1**, 17 (heard the Mahābhārata).—§ 3 (do.): I, **1**, 35 (issued from the primordial egg).—§ 7 (do.): I, **1**, 247 (spoken of in the Mahābhārata).—§ 18 (Paulomap.): I, **4**, 861 (i.e. the ṛshis present at the sacrifice of Çaunaka). — § 72 (Ādivaṃçāvatāraṇap.): I, **62**, 2314 (described in the Mahābhārata).—§ 85 (Aṃçāvat.): I, **65**, 2512 (the gods took their births in *B°vaṃçeshu*, etc.).—§ 185 (Pāṇḍu): I, **120**, 4643 (°*sadṛçaḥ*, i.e. Pāṇḍu).—§ 186*b* (Vyushitāçvop.): I, **121**, 4688.—§ 246 (Sundopasundop.): I, **211**, 7681.—§ 266 (Çakrasabhāv.): II, **7**, 307 (*Brahmarājarshayaḥ*, in the palace of Indra).—§ 267 (Yamasabhāv.): II, **8**, 318 (in the palace of Yama).—§ 269 (Vaiçrāvaṇasabhāv.): II, **10**, 401 (in the palace of Kubera). — § 270 (Brahmasabhāv.): II, **11**, 476. — § 336 (Indralokābh.): III, **43**, 1768 (on Suravīthī). — § 357 (Pushkara): III, **82**, 4065 (in Pushkara). — § 369 (Kurukshetra): III, **83**, 7077 (*Kurukshetraṃ B°nishevitaṃ*).—§ 370 (Tīrthayātrāp.): III, **84**, 8140 (*Dharmatīrthaṃ . . . B°sevitaṃ*). — § 373 (Prayāga): III, **85**, 8214 (*Aṅgiraḥpramukhāḥ*, at Prayāga).—§ 377 (Dhaumyatīrthak.): III, **90**, 8392 (*Gaṅgādvāram . . . B°gaṇasevitaṃ*). — § 384 (Agastyop.): III, **101**, 8724. — § 423 (Gandhamādanapr.): III, **145**, 11055 (°*gaṇasevitaṃ*, sc. the hermitage of Nara and Nārāyaṇa). — § 424 (Bhīmakadalīkh.): III, **146,** 11089 (on Gandhamādana).—§ 439 (Yakshayuddhap.): III, **163,** 11861 (on Meru).—§ 444 (Nivātakavacayuddhap.): III, **169,** 12101.—§ 447 (do.): III, **175,** 12302.—§ 450 (Ājagarap.): III, **181,** 12522, 12524.—§ 495 (Skandotpatti): III, **223,** 14242 (*°bhāryābhiḥ*, i.e. the wives of the Saptarshayaḥ).—§ 526 (Rāmopākhyānap.): III, **276,** 15929. —§ 555 (Indravijaya): V, **11,** 350; **17,** 528, 534.—§ 561 (Yānasandhip.): V, **55,** 2190 (*°sadṛçaḥ*, i.e. Droṇa).—§ 562 (Bhagavadyānap.): V, **83**η, 2947 (worshipped Kṛshṇa).— § 574 (Jambūkh.): VI, **6,** 246 (on Nīla).—§ 576 (Bhagavadgītāp.): VI, **r 2,** †783 (praised Yudhishṭhira).—§ 581 (Bhīshmavadhap.: VI, **66,** 2977 (*deva-B°-Gandharvān*).— § 596 (Pratijñāp.): VII, **73,** †2607 (*Brahmadevarshayaḥ*).— § 606 (Tripurākhyāna): VIII, **33,** 1443; **34,** 1513 (praised Çiva).—§ 608 (Karṇap.): VIII, **87**χ, 4428 (present at the encounter between Karṇa and Arjuna); **88,** †4490.—§ 615*u* (Skanda): IX, **45**γ, 2509 (came to the investiture of Skanda). —§ 615*y* (Badarapacana): IX, **48,** 2794 (praised Badarapacana).—§ 615*cc* (Rāmatīrtha): IX, **49,** 2839 (*deva-B°bhiḥ sevite*, sc. Rāmatīrtha).—§ 621 (Rājadh.): XII, **1,** 3 (*siddhā B°sattamāḥ*, i.e. Dvaipāyana, Nārada, Devala, Devasthāna, and Kaṇva). — § 635 (do.): XII, **37,** 1358. — § 656*d* (Daksha): XII, **166,** 6136 (married the daughters of Daksha and begot all creatures: *devāḥ*, etc.). — § 656 (Khaḍgotpattik.): XII, **166,** 6150, 6156.—§ 660*b* (Bhṛgu-Bharadvāja-saṃv.): XII, **183,** 6809; **190,** 6990, ††6993; **192,** ††7003. — § 665 (Mokshadh.): XII, **208**η, 7596 (i.e. Unmuca, etc.). — § 693*b* (Vṛtravadha): XII, **282,** 10123 (*Bṛhaspatipurogamāḥ*). — § 704 (Mokshadh.): XII, **302**β, 11105, (γ) 11126.—§ 712 (Çukotpatti): XII, **324,** 12174; **325,** 12203.—§ 721 (Ānuçāsanik.): XIII, **3,** 185 (*mahān Kuçikavaṃçaç ca B°çatasaṅkulaḥ*), 190 (*°surasevitā*, sc. Kauçikī), 195 (i.e. the *Saptarshayaḥ* (the Great Bear)); **4,** 200 (*°tvam*).—§ 730 (do.): XIII, **14***aa*, 987.—§ 736*b* (Vītahavyop.): XIII, **30,** 1996 (*°tāṃ gataḥ*, sc. Vītahavya). —§ 745 (Ānuçāsanik.): XIII, **52***a*, 2718 (*°vaṃçaḥ*, i.e. Paraçurāma). — § 746 (do.): XIII, **66,** 3347. — § 747*b* (Suvarṇotpatti): XIII, **85,** 4125 (*°gaṇasammatāḥ*, sc. the Vaikhānasas). — § 751*b* (Çapathavidhi): XIII, **94,** 4589 (*°devarshinṛparshimadhye*).—§ 754 (Ānuçāsanik.): XIII, **98,** 4683 (*°deva-Daityānāṃ*).—§ 770 (do.): XIII, **151**ν, 7157 (*Çukrāgastya-Bṛhaspatiprabhṛtibhiḥ*, C. has *Çakr°*). — § 777 (Svargārohaṇikap.); XIII, **169,** 7767. § 705 (Anugītap.): XIV, **77,** 2244.—§ 786*b* (Nakulākhyāna): XIV, **90,** 2775.

Brahmarshi[2] (single Brahmarshis). § 172 (Aṇīmaṇḍavyop.): I, **107,** 4305 (*kasya çāpāç ca B°eḥ çūdrayonāv ajāyata*, sc. Dharma).—Names of single Brahmarshis:

Arvāvasu: III, 10807.
Ashṭāvakra: XIII, 1417, 1478.
Atri: I, 1217.
Aurva: III, 17465 (*Aurveṇa*).
Bharadvāja: V, 2191 (*Bharadvājāt*).
Bhṛgu: XII, 6774.
Cyavana: XIII, 2852.
Çuka: XII, 12302.
Dadhīca: IX, 2937, 2938.
Damana: III, 2077 (*Damano nāma*).
Devaçarman: XIII, 2379.
Gautama: III, 8086 (*Gautamasya*); XII, 4722.
Jājali: XII, 9297.
Kāçyapa: I, 1979.
Kṛpa: I, 2712 (*Kṛpo nāma*).
Likhita: XII, 685.
Lomaça: III, 1885, 1892, 8431.
Maṅkanaka: III, 7002.
Mārkaṇḍeya: III, 12607.
Nārada: II, 264, 281.
Pulastya: III, 4039 (*°sattame*).
Ṛcīka: XIII, 219 (*°sattamaḥ*), 220.
Vaiçampāyana: XII, 13637.
Vasishṭha: I, 3952, 6644 (?).
Viçvāmitra: XIII, 246.
Vyāsa: I, 55, 2212, 4253; VI, 42 (*sattama*); XII, 12195, 12348, 12376 (*Vāçishṭha*), 12383, 12598 (*°putrasya* = Çuka); XV, 890, 961.

[**Brahma-Rudra-saṃvāda(ḥ)**], ("the discourse between Brahmán and Rudra"). § 717*d* (Nārāyaṇīya): *Vaiçampāyana* said: In the midst of the ocean of milk there is a mountain of golden splendour, named *Vaijayanta*, where *Brahmán* (leaving his abode inhabited by D., As., Ṛ., G., and Aps.) often used to sit thinking of *Adhyātma*; once, in days of yore, his son *Çiva* (endued with high *yoga*), who had sprung from his forehead, when proceeding along the sky saw him and dropped down before him, and was instructed by him about the many *Purushas* created by him (Brahmán), and the one *Purusha*, who transcends all *Purushas* and is invisible, etc. (XII, **351**). *Brahmán* discoursed on the indications of *Purusha* (*Mahāpurusha*) (XII, **352**).

Brahmasabhāvarṇana(m) ("description of the palace of Brahmán"). § 270 (Lokapālas.): In the *Kṛta* age, *Āditya* (= the Sun) having seen the *sabhā* of *Pitāmaha* (i.e. *Brahmán*), which is immeasurable and immaterial (*mānasī*), told *Nārada*, who also desired to see it, to perform a *Brahmavrata* for 1,000 years. *Nārada*, then, having repaired to *Himavat*, performed the penance, and then he was taken by *Sūrya* (the Sun) to the *sabhā* of *Brahmán*. Within a moment it assumes a different form, and cannot be described. It is neither cold nor warm, without hunger or thirst, etc.; it is not supported by columns; it is eternal, etc. There *Sarvalokapitāmaha* (i.e. *Brahmán*) is sitting, himself alone incessantly creating by means of his divine illusion (*devamāyayā*), surrounded by the *prajānāṃ patayaḥ* (enumeration), etc. (***a***) (II, **11**).

Brahmasadana. § 620 (Çrāddhap.): XI, **26,** 771 (*gatās te B°ṃ hatā vīrāḥ suvarcasaḥ*). § 717*b* (Nārāyaṇīya): XII, **340,** 12982 (resorted to by *siddhasaṅghāḥ*); **343,** 13205 (*Paushkaro*). — § 700 (Ānuçāsanik.): XIII, **16,** 1099 (*yā gatir B°no sāgatis tvaṃ sanatana*, sc. Çiva).

Brahmasadas. § 430 (Yakshayuddhap.): III, **163,** 11853 (*Mahāmeruḥ . . . . yasmin B°ç caivo Bhūtātmā cāvatishṭhate*). —§ 658*b* (Kṛtaghnop.): XII, **173,** 6444.—§ 789 (Putradarçanap.): XV, **33**κ, 902.

Brahmasadman. § 730 (Ānuçāsanik.): XIII, **17,** 1289 (cf. Tandin).

Brahmasaṅkāça: XII, 6774 (*Brahmarshir B°ḥ*, i.e. Bhṛgu, "who resembled Brahman itself," PCR.).

Brahmasaras, a tīrtha. § 370 (Tīrthayātrāp.): III, **84,** 8063 (there Brahmán had raised a *yūpa*).—§ 377 (Dhaumyatīrthak.): III, **87,** 8304 (in the east).—§ 380 (Tīrthayātrāp.): At *B.*, with holy peaks and resorted to by ṛshis, Agastya had come to Vaivasvata; Dharmarāja (i.e. Yama) himself had dwelt there; there all the rivers take their rise (*samudbhedaḥ*) and *Mahādeva* is always present; there the Pāṇḍavas performed *cāturmāsya* sacrifices together with the great *ṛshiyajña* (v. BR.). There is the Akshayavaṭa ("the imperishable banian"), the imperishable sacrificial platform of the gods, where the merit acquired is imperishable. Here they fasted with concentrated souls, and brahmans by hundred came and performed the *cāturmāsya* sacrifice and talked about various sacred subjects, and the learned and pious Çamatha, who lived in celibacy (*kaumāraṃ vratam āsh̤ṭhitaḥ*), told them of Gaya Āmūrtarayasa: III, **95**, 8520.—§ 595 (Shoḍacarāj., v. Gaya): VII, **66**, 2353.—§ 735 (Ānuçāsanik.): XIII, **25**, 1726 (on Gaṅgā, the results of bathing there), 1744 (*Dharmāraṇyopaçobhitam*).—§ 751*b* (Çapathavidhi): XIII, **74**, 4553.

Brahmasattra, name of a certain religious practice. § 677 (Mokshadh.): XII, **244**, 8857 (°*sattre*, = praṇavopāstau, Nīl.).

Brahmasattrin ("one who performs the Brahmasattra practice"). § 615*ff* (Asita-Devala): IX, **50**, 2894 (°*āṃ lokam*), 2899, 2902.

Brahmasṛj ("creator of Brahmán") = Çiva: X, 257.

Brahmasthāna, a tīrtha. § 370 (Tīrthayātrāp.): III, **84**, 8081; **85**, 8178.

Brahmāstra, a celestial weapon. § 217 (Caitrarathap.): I, **166**, 6340 (acquired by Droṇa from Rāma Jāmadagnya). —§ 218 (Draupadīsambhava): I, **167**, 6378 (known by Droṇa).—§ 320 (Saubhavadhop.): III, **19**, 766 (employed by Pradyumna).—§ 442 (Nivātakavacayuddhap.): III, **167**, 11968 (employed by Arjuna), 11971.—§ 444 (do.): III, **170**, 12120 (°*parimantritaiḥ* . . . . *sāyakaiḥ*).—§ 478 (Dhundhumārop.): III, **204**, 13612 (employed by Kuvalāçva).—§ 526 (Rāmopākhyānap.): III, **275**γ, 15918 (acquired by Vibhīshaṇa).—§ 539 (Kumbhakarṇādivadha): III, **287**, 16426 (employed by Lakshmaṇa).—§ 542 (Rāvaṇavadha): III, **290** 16523 (*vāṇavaryaṃ Rāmeṇa B° nānumantritaṃ*), 16525, 16529, 16530.—§ 552 (Goharaṇap.): IV, **55**, 1590, 1592.—§ 573 (Ambopākhyānap.): V, **184**, 7283 (dual., employed by Bhīshma and Rāma Jāmadagnya); **185**, 7296.—§ 578 (Bhīshmavadhap.): VI, **48**, 1975 (°*ena saṃyuktaṃ çaraṃ*).—§ 592 (Saṃçaptakavadhap.): VII, **27**, 1214 (employed by Arjuna).—§ 599 (Jayadrathavadhap.): VII, **92**, 3269 (°*ṃ samudīrayan*, sc. Arjuna), 3272; **106**, 4000 (employed by Yudhishṭhira); **125**, 5029.—§ 600 (Ghaṭotkacavadhap.): VII, **157**, 6961.—§ 601 (Droṇavadhap.): VII, **185**, 8423 (pl.).—§ 602 (do.): VII, **188**, 8624 (employed by Arjuna); **190**, 8733.—§ 603 (Nārāyaṇāstramokshap.): VII, **193**, 8935; **197**, 9113 (pl.); **199**χ, 9228 (°*vidushā*, i.e. Droṇa).—§ 608 (Karṇap.): VIII, **90**, 4720 (employed by Karṇa), 4724 (°*ṃ* . . . . *sammantrya samayojayat*, sc. Arjuna), **91**, 4768 (employed by Karṇa), 4769 (employed by Arjuna).—§ 615 (Gadāyuddhap.): IX, **62**ω, 3478, 3488.—§ 617 (Aishīkap.): X, **15**, 707 (acquired by Arjuna from Droṇa).—§ 621 (Rājadh.): XII, **2**, 55 (°*ṃ vettum icchāmi*, says Karṇa), 58 (°*ṃ brāhmaṇo vidyāt yathāvaccaritavrataḥ | kshatriyo vā tapasvī yo nānyo vidyāt kathañcana*); **3**, 76 (obtained by Karṇa from Rāma Jāmadagnya), 104 (*yasmān mithyopacarito hy astralobhād iha tvayā | tasmād etan na te mūḍha B°ṃ pratibhāsyati*, says Rāma to Karṇa).—§ 785 (Anugītāp.): XIV, **66**, 1944 (afflicted by *B.*, Parikshit was stillborn); **68**, 1999 (do.), 2005 (do.); **69**, 2024 (Kṛshṇa touched water and withdrew *B.*); **70**, 2033 (do., Parikshit was revived).

Brahmasutā. § 717*b* (Nārāyaṇīya): XII, **343**φ, 13234 (*Ṛtā Brahmasutā sā me Satyā devī Sarasvatī*, says Nārāyaṇa).

Brahmasūtra, a literary work. § 576 (Bhagavadgītāp.): VI, **37**, 1326 (? °*padaiḥ*).

Brahmātman[1] = Çiva (1000 names[1]).

Brahmātman[2] = Kṛshṇa: XII, 1668.

Brahmatuṅga (a mountain). § 596 (Pratijñāp.): VII, **80**, 2850.

Brahma-Vaçātīya, pl., v. Vaçātīya.

Brahmavadhyā ("slaughter of a brahman") (person.). § 693*b* (Vṛtravadha): XII, **283**, 10154, 10159, 10162, 10164, (10167), 10170, 10173, 10176, 10180, 10182, 10186, 10193, 10198, 10199, 10200.

Brahmavaktra = Çiva: VII, 2881 (*Brahmacakrāya*, C.).

Brahmavāluka, a tīrtha. § 360 (Tīrthayātrāp.): III, **82**, 5048.

Brahmavarcasa = Çiva (1000 names).

Brahmāvarta, a tīrtha. § 364 (Tīrthayātrāp.): III, **83**, 6023, 6024 (v. Brahmaloka).—§ 372 (do.): III, **85**, 8021 (v. Somaloka).

Brahmavatāṃ varishṭhaḥ = Skanda: III, 14638.

Brahmavedhyā, a river. § 574 (Jambūkh.): VI, **9**λ, 337 (so B., C. has *Brahmabodhyā*).

Brahmavedī ("the sacrificial altar of Brahmán") = Kurukshetra: III, 7077.

Brahmavedin. § 554 (Sainyodyogap.): V, **6**, 110 (*kartṛshu B°aḥ*, sc. *çreshṭhāḥ*).

Brahmavid[1] = Çiva (1000 names[2]).

Brahmavid[2] = Skanda: III, 14638.

Brahmavid[3] = Vishṇu (1000 names).

Brahmavidāṃ vara(ḥ) = Çiva (1000 names[1]).

Brahmavidyā[1] = Durgā (Umā): VI, 803 (*tvaṃ B°ā vidyānāṃ*).

Brahmavidyā[2] ("knowledge of Bráhman") (personified). § 730 (Ānuçās.): XIII, **14**β, 627.

Brahmavivardhana = Vishṇu (1000 names).

Brahmavrata. § 270 (Brahmasabhāv.): II, **11**, 428 (*varshasahasrikaṃ*).

Brahmayajña. § 659 (Mokshadh.): XII, **175**, 6554 (v. the note of PCR.).

Brahmayoni[1] ("born of Brahman"). (*a*) = Pulastya: III, 16187; (*b*) = Sanatkumāra: IX, 2716; (*c*) = Pracīnabarhi: XII, 7572; (*d*) = Purusha: XII, 13194; (*e*) = Taṇḍin: XIII, 607; (*f*) pl.: XIII, 2031 (*ayonīn Agniyonīṃç ca B°īn*, etc.). Do. fem. = Menakā: I, 3056 (°*varā*).

Brahmayoni[2] (a tīrtha). § 366 (Tīrthayātrāp.): III, **83**, 7010 (after bathing there one goes to Brahmaloka).—§ 615 (Baladevat.): IX, **41**, 2318 (only B., cf. v. 2281); **47**, 2750 (on Sarasvatī, v. Brahmán).

Brahmayoni[3]. § 782*g* (Guruçishyas.): XIV, **42**, 1139 (*dvividhā khalu vijñeyā B°ḥ sanātanī*).

Brahmeçaya[1] = Skanda: III, 14638.

Brahmeçaya[2] = Mahāpurusha (Mahāpurushast.).

Brahmin = Vishṇu (1000 names).

Brahmodumbara (°*oḍ*°, C.) (a tīrtha). § 364 (Tīrthayātrāp.): III, **83**, 6041.

Brahmopanishad? § 790 (Pūtradarçanap.): XV, **35**, 940 (*sa rājā rājadharmāṃç ca B°an tadā avāptavān*, "the Vedas and the Upanishads," PCR.).

Brāhmya, adj. (only C., B. has *Brāhma*). § 440 (Yakshayuddhap.): III, **164**, 11900 (sc. *astraṃ*, in the enumeration of celestial weapons acquired by Arjuna from Indra).—§ 589 (Droṇābhishekap.): VII, **10**, 344 (*astraṃ*?).—§ 602 (Droṇavadhap.): VII, **190**, 8717 (*astram*); **191**, 8773 (do). —§ 604 (Karṇap.): VIII, **9**, 295 (*Jāmadagnyān mahāghoram B°m astram açikshata*, sc. Karṇa).—§ 607 (do.): VIII, **42**, †1995 (*astrāṇi*), †1996 (*astraṃ*).—§ 608 (do.)· VIII, **60**,

2993 (*bale*, opp. to *kshātra*); **89**, 4574 (*astram*), 4576 (*mahāstram*).—§ 730*g* (Upamanyu): XIII, **14***ρ*, 854 (sc. *astram*).—Cf. Brāhma.

Bṛhadaçva[1] (a Ṛshi). § 11 (Parvasaṅg.): I, **2**, 435 (*darçanam B°sya maharsheḥ*). — § 324 (Dvaitavanaprav.): III, **26***a*, 987 (among the Ṛshis, who praised Yudhishṭhira). — § 343 (Nalopākhyānap.): III, **52**, 2052 (*maharshiḥ*), (2063), (2066).—§ 344 (do.): III, **53**, (2072) (related the Nalopākhyāna to Yudhishṭhira). — § 345 (do.): III, **54**, (2104), (2120); **55**, (2135), (2144); **56**, (2160); **57**, (2191). —§ 346 (do.): III, **58**, (2239); **59**, (2254); **60**, (2272). —§ 347 (do.): III, **61**, (2297); **62**, (2335); **63**, (2362); **64**, (2401); **65**, (2532).—§ 348 (do.): III, **66**, (2608).— § 349 (do.): III, **67**, (2634), (2641).—§ 350 (do.): III, **68**, (2654), (2680), (2684).—§ 351 (do.): III, **70**, (2744); **71**, (2771).—§ 352 (do.): III, **72**, (2808).—§ 353 (do.): III, **73**, (2852); **74**, (2912); **75**, (2921), (2939); **76**, (2951); **77**, (3009).—§ 354 (do.): III, **78**, (3030); **79**, (3063).— § 355 (do.): III, **79**, 3082 (taught Yudhishṭhira the science of dice), 3084.

Bṛhadaçva[2], king of Ayodhyā. § 474 (Dhundhumārop.): III, **201**, 13512 (*Ikshvākuḥ*, father of Kuvalāçva).—§ 475 (do): III, **202**, 13518 (son of Çrāvastaka), 13519 (father of Kuvalāçva).—§ 476 (do.): III, **202**, 13521, 13522 (installed Kuvalāçva as king and retired into the wood), 13523.

Bṛhadambālikā, a mātṛ. § 615*u* (Skanda): IX, **46***θ*, 2622.

Bṛhadbala[1], an ancient king. § 6 (Anukram.): I, **1***a*, 230 (among the kings of the past who have died).

Bṛhadbala[2], son of Subala, the Gāndhāra king. § 232 (Svayaṃvarap.): I, **186**, 6985 (*Çakuniḥ Saubalaç caiva Vṛshako 'tha Bṛhadbalaḥ, ete Gāndhārarājasya sutāḥ sarve samāgatāḥ*). Cf. Acala.

Bṛhadbala[3] (presumably the same as next). § 232 (Svayaṃvarap.): I, **186**, 6996.—§ 290 (Çiçupālavadhap.): II, **44***a*, 1538.

Bṛhadbala[4], the Kosala king. § 280 (Bhīmasena): II, **30**, 1075 (*Koçalādhipatim*, vanquished by Bhīmasena on his digvijaya).—§ 287 (Rājasūyikap.): II, **34**, 1269 (came to the rājasūya of Yudhishṭhira). — § 554 (Sainyodyogap.): V, **4***γ*, 85 (the same?).—§ 561 (Yānasandhip.): V, **57**, 2250 (*Saubhadreṇa kṛto bhāgaḥ*).—§ 571 (Ulūkadūt.): V, **161**, 5573 (*°mahocchālam*, sc. *purushodadhim*, i.e. the army of Duryodhana). —§ 572 (Rathātirathas.): V, **166**, 5765 (*Kauçalyo rathasattamaḥ*).—§ 576 (Bhagavadgītāp.): VI, **16***a*, 623 (*Kausalyaḥ*, B.; C. has *Kauravyaḥ*).—§ 578 (Bhīshmavadhap.): VI, **45**[3], 1683 (*Kauçalakaḥ*), 1685 (fights Abhimanyu on the first day of the battle).—§ 580 (do.): VI, **56***c*, 2410.—§ 584 (do.): VI, **81***a*, 3534 (*Kauçalyaḥ*).—§ 585 (do.): VI, **87***δ*, 3855 (*Kauçalyaḥ*, in the array of Bhīshma on the eighth day of the battle), 3856; **92***χ*, 4118, 4136 (*rājaputram*); **94***ω*, 4195. —§ 587 (do.): VI, **108***a*, 5007; **114***λ*, 5325 (*Kauçalyaḥ*); **115**, 5365 (*B.* (*c*) bore a lion on his standard—*siṃhaketuḥ*, so B.—and attacked Abhimanyu); **116**, 5405 (*rājaputram*), 5409 (*rājaputraḥ*).—§ 593 (Abhimanyuvadhap.): VII, **37***θ*, 1589, (*ι*) 1601 (fought Abhimanyu); **39***μ*, 1650; **46***τ*, 1838, (*υ*) 1851; **47***φ*, 1864, 1868, 1878, 1881 (*Koçalānām bhartāram rājaputram*), 1883 (slain by Abhimanyu).—§ 596 (Pratijñāp.): VII, **73**, 2579 (*°m rājānam svargeṇājau prayojya*, sc. Abhimanyu, all. to § 593).—§ 609 (Çalyap.): IX, **2***ζ*, 73, 92 (had been slain).—§ 619 (Strīvilāpap.): XI, **25***κ*, 715 (*Koçalānām adhipatim rājaputram*, bewailed by his widows). Cf. Kausalya, Kausalendra, Kosalaka, Kosalānām adhipati(ḥ), Kosalānam bhartṛ, Kosalarāja.

Bṛhadbhānu[1] = Bhānu[7]: III, 14184.

Bṛhadbhānu[2] = Kṛshṇa: XII, 1506.

Bṛhadbhānu[3] = Vishṇu (1000 names).

Bṛhadbhāsa (son of Aṅgiras). § 489 (Āṅgirasa): III, **218**, 14123 (PCR. takes this as adj. to *Bṛhaspatiḥ*).

Bṛhadbhāsā. § 493 (Āṅgirasa): III, **221**, 14184 (*Sūryajā*, wife of Bhānu[7]).

Bṛhadbrahman (son of Aṅgiras). § 489 (Āṅgirasa): III, **218**, 14123 (PCR. takes this as adj. to *Bṛhaspatiḥ*).

Bṛhaddyumna (*Bṛhadyumnaḥ*, C.), a king. § 417 (Yavakrītop.): III, **138**, 10791, 10792, 10800, 10802.

Bṛhadgarbha, son of Çibi Auçīnara. § 467 (Rājanyamahābh.): III, **198**, ††13321.

Bṛhadguru, an ancient king. § 6 (Anukram.): I, **1***a*, 226 (among the kings of the past who have died).

Bṛhadratha[1], an ancient king. § 6 (Anukram.): I, **1**, 228 (among the kings of the past who have died). — § 267 (Yamasabhāv.): II, **8**, 320 (in the palace of Yama).

Bṛhadratha[2]. § 130 (Aṃçāvat.): I, **67**, 2654 (a king, incarnate of the Asura Sūkshma).—§ 232 (Svayaṃvarap.): I, **186**, 7001 (the same?, among the princes who were present at the svayaṃvara of Draupadī).

Bṛhadratha[3], a Māgadha king. § 74 (Vasu): I, **63**, 2363 (*mahāratho Māgadhānām viçruto yo B°ḥ*, son of king Vasu Uparicara). — § 275 (Rājasūyārambhap.): II, **17**, 688 (*Magadhadhipatiḥ*, father of Jarāsandha), 701, 725; **19**, 742, 755 (*Magadhādhipatiḥ*, installed Jarāsandha as king), 757.— § 277 (Jarāsandhavadhap.): II, **21**, 812 (*B.* had slain a rākshasa named Ṛshabha and made three drums of his hide); **22**, 877 (the same?, had met with destruction); **24**, 950 (his celestial chariot). § 638*b* (Rāmopākhyāna): XII, **49**, 1797 (*B°o mahātejā bhūribhūtiparishkṛtaḥ | golāṅgūlair mahābhāgo Gṛdhrakūṭe 'bhirakshitaḥ*; PCR. is hardly right in connecting this verse with the preceding). Cf. Bṛhadratha[1].

Bṛhadratha[4], a fire? § 491 (Āṅgirasa): III, **220**, 14164 (father of Pranidhi). Cf. Vāsishṭha.

Bṛhadratha[5]. § 573 (Ambopākhyānap.): V, **195**, 7612 (*Kauçalyaḥ*; is not to be read *Bṛhadbalaḥ*?).

Bṛhadratha[6], a king slain by Māndhātṛ. § 595 (Shoḍaçarāj. v. Māndhātṛ): VII, **62***a*, 2281.—§ 632*b* (Shoḍaçarājop., cf. § 595): XII, **29**, 981 (*Aṅgam*?).

Bṛhadratha[7] = Paurava, the Aṅga king. § 632 (Shoḍaçarājop., cf. § 505 under the article Paurava): XII, **30**, 924 (*Aṅgam*).

Bṛhadrūpa = Vishṇu (1000 names).

Bṛhaduktha, a fire. § 493 (Āṅgirasa): III, **220**, 14173 (son of Tapas).

Bṛhadvatī, a river. § 574 (Jambūkh.): VI, **9***λ*, 337 339 (in Bhāratavarsha).

Bṛhajjyotis, Bṛhanmanas, Bṛhanmantra (sons of Aṅgiras). § 489 (Āṅgirasa): III, **218**, 14123 (PCR. takes these words as adjectives to *Bṛhaspatiḥ*).

Bṛhannalā = Arjuna, q.v.

Bṛhanta[1], a king. § 232 (Svayaṃvarap.): I, **186**, 6987 (among the princes who were present at the svayaṃvara of Draupadī).—§ 554 (Sainyodyogap.): V, **4***γ*, 76.

Bṛhanta[2], the Ulūka king. § 279 (Arjuna): II, **27**, 1014 (*Ulūkavāsinam*), 1016, 1017 (fought with Arjuna on his digvijaya). Cf. the prec.

Bṛhanta[3]. § 592*b* (Saṃçapt.): mighty steeds of the *Āraṭṭa* breed bore *B.*, who alone rejecting the opinions of all the *Bharatas*, had from his reverence (*bhaktyā*) for Yudhishṭhira, gone over to him, abandoning all his cherished wishes (*sarvam abhīpsitaṃ*): VII, **23**, 1024.

Bṛhanta[4], a Kuru warrior. § 592 (Saṃçapt.): VII, **25**, 1110 (*Kshemadhūrte-B°au bhrātarau*, attacked Sātyaki).—§ 604 (Karṇap.): VIII, **5**ζ, 132 (among the slain, PCR. has Vṛshanta).—§ 620 (Çrāddhap.): XI, **26**β, 788 (the same?).

Bṛhanta[5], a Pāṇḍava warrior. § 604 (Karṇap.): VIII, **6**, 162 (slain by Duḥçāsana).

Bṛhaspati (the purohita of the gods and the planet Jupiter). § 44 (Garuḍa): I, **30**, 1421, (1423), 1427.—§ 70 (Ādivaṃçāvatāraṇap.): I, **60**, 2218 (*yathā*). —§ 110 (Aṃçāvat.): I, **66**, 2569 (son of Aṅgiras and brother of Utathya and Saṃvartta).—§ 116 (do.): I, **66**, 2590 (*°er bhaginī*, wife of the Vasu Prabhāsa). —§ 120 *bis* (do.): I, **66**, 2603 (*Ādityeshveva gaṇyate*).—§ 130 (do.): I, **67**, 2705 (Droṇa was born from a portion of *B.* (*devarsheḥ*)).—§ 145 (Kaca): I, **76**, 3191 (the purohita of the gods), 3193 (*Kacaṃ . . . jyeshṭhaṃ putraṃ B°eḥ*), 3201, 3203, 3210, 3228 (*°eḥ sutaḥ*, i.e. Kaca), †3231 (son of Aṅgiras and father of Kaca); **77**, 3258, 3277.—§ 146 (Devayānī): I, **80**, 3341 (*iva*).—§ 170 (Dīrghatamas): I, **104**, 4180 (*Utathasya yavīyāṃs tu purodhās tridivaukasāṃ*), 4182, 4184, 4187, 4188, 4189, 4192.—§ 221 (Caitrarathap.): I, **170**, 6464 (*gurur mānyaḥ Çatakratoḥ*, had given the Āgneya weapon to Bharadvāja). —§ 223 (Vāsishṭha): I, **174**, 6644 (*iva*).—§ 253 (Haraṇāharaṇap.): I, **221**, 7991 (*sākshād B°eḥ çishyaḥ*, i.e. Uddhava?).—§ 254 (Khāndavadah.): I, **223**, 8057 (*°samāḥ*, sc. viprāḥ).—§ 259 (Çarṅgakop.): I, **229**, 8360 (Agni identified with *B.*).—§ 265 (Lokapālasabhākh.): II, **5**, 139.—§ 266 (Çakrasabhāv.): II, **7**, 308 (in the palace of Indra). —§ 270 (Brahmasabhāv.): II, **11**, 446 (among the planets in the palace of Brahmán).—§ 290 (Çiçupālavadhap.): II, **40**, 1419 (*B°ṃ bṛhattejāḥ Puruhūta iva*).—§ 294*b* (Vidura): II, **50**, 1793 (*devarshir Vāsavagurur devarājāya dhīmate yat prāha çāstraṃ bhagavān B°ḥ*).—§ 297 (Dyūtap.): II, **55**, 1950 (*āha*).—§ 302 (Anudyūtap.): II, **74**, 2458 (*yaj jagāda B°ḥ Çakrasya nītiṃ pravadan vidvān devapurohitaḥ*, i.e. v. 2459).—§ 310*b* (Sūrya): III, **3**, 147 (Sūrya is identified with *B.*).—§ 377 (Dhaumyatīrthak.): III, **87**, 8297 (*°samo Dhaumyaḥ*).—§ 430 (Hanūmad-Bhīmas.): III, **150**, 11291 (*°samaiḥ*), 11294 (*B°y-Uçanoktaiç ca nayaiḥ*). —§ 455 (Brāhmaṇamahātmyak.): III, **185**, 12703 (among the honourable appellations of the king). —§ 460*c* (Kalkin): III, **190**, 13099 (the planet: *Sūryaçca yadā Candraçca tathā Tishya-B°tī | ekarāçau sameshyanti tadā pravartsyati Kṛtaṃ*).—§ 488 (Āṅgirasa): III, **217**, 14118 (son of Aṅgiras).—§ 489 (do.): III, **218**, 14123 (do.).—§ 490 (do.): III, **219**, 14130 (*B°eç Cāndramasī bharyā 'bhūt*, by her *B.* had six sons and one daughter), 14131 (Çaṃyu was *B.'s* first son).—§ 501 (Skandop.): III, **229**, 14450. —§ 513 (Ghoshayātrāp.): III, **251**, 15146 (*B°y-Uçanoktaiç ca mantraiḥ*).—§ 524 (Jayadrathavim.): III, **272**, 15842.—§ 527 (Ramopākhyānap.): III, **277**, 15954 (*°samaṃ matau*, i.e. Rāma Dāçarathi).—§ 545 (Pativratām.): III, **293**, 16672 (*°samaṃ matau*, i.e. Satyavat).—§ 552 (Goharaṇap.): IV, **58**, 1829 (*°samo naye*, i.e. Droṇa).—§ 555 (Indravijaya): V, **11**, 360, 364, 367; **12**, 377, 381, (383), 391, (392); **13**, 408 (*°niketaṃ*); **15**, 470, 471, 475, 478, 479; **16**, (483), 491, 495, 503, (505), (†507), †511 (*Aṅgirasāṃ varishṭhe*); **18**, 545.—§ 556 (Sañjayayānap.): V, **29**, †822 (*brahmacaryaṃ cacāra*).—§ 557 (Prajāgarap.): V, **33**, 1041 (*āha*).—§ 559 (do.): V, **39**, 1447, 1485 (*°samaiḥ*).—§ 561*d* (Nara-Nārāyaṇau): V, **49**, 1918 (*B°ç c' Oçanā*), 1922, 1926 (*devagaṇaiḥ sarvair B°purogamaiḥ*).—§ 561 (Yānasandhip.): V, **55**, 2209 (*prāha*).—§ 562 (Bhagavadyānap.): V, **86**, 3043 (*yathā būddhiṃ B°ḥ*).—§ 565 (Gālavacarita): V, **108**, 3972 (*yathā . . . B°ç ca Tārāyāṃ*).—§ 570 (Sainyaniryāṇap.): V, **157**, 5315 (*°samaṃ buddhyā*, i.e. Bhīshma).—§ 572 (Rathātirathas.): V, **165**, 5722 (*yathā*).—§ 574 (Jambūkh.): VI, **3**, 81 (the planet, *Çravaṇe ca B°ḥ*, omens), 95 (do., *Viçākhāyāṃ samīpasthau B°-Çanaiçcarau*, omens).—§ 576 (Bhagavadgītāp.): VI, **19**, 698 (*maharsher vacanāt*); **34**, 1228 (*purodhasāñ ca mukhyaṃ māṃ viddhi, Pārtha! B°ṃ*, says Kṛshṇa).—§ 578 (Bhīshmavadhap.): VI, **50**, 2073 (*vyūhaḥ Krauncārūṇo nāma . . . yaṃ B°r Indrāya tadā devāsure 'bravīt*).—§ 586 (do.): VI, **103**, 4703 (*ati nayena ca B°ṃ*); **107**, 4986 (*yathovāca purā Çakraṃ mahābuddhir B°ḥ*).—§ 589 (Droṇābhiskekap.): VII, **9**, 275 (*B°y-Uçanastulyaḥ*, i.e. Droṇa); **11**, 354 (*°samaṃ matau*, i.e. Abhimanyu).—§ 590 (do.): VII, **12**, 447 (*°samaiḥ*).—§ 595 (Shoḍaçarāj., v. Marutta): VII, **55**, 2171, 2172 (*sendrāmaragaṇā B°purogamāḥ*); (do., v. Pṛthu Vainya): VII, **69**, 2416 (milker of the earth).—§ 599 (Jayadrathavadhap.): VII, **94**, 3476 (son of Aṅgiras); **103**, 3861.—§ 603 (Nārāyaṇāstram.): VII, **194**, 8971 (*°samo matau*, i.e. Açvatthāman).—§ 605 (Karṇap.): VIII, **31**οο, 1261 (*vyūhaṃ . . . B°y-Uçanomataṃ*).—§ 607 (do.): VIII, **37**, †1726 (*B°y-Uçanoḥ samaṃ*, i.e. Droṇa).—§ 608 (do.): VIII, **94**, †4945 (the planet, *B°ḥ samparivārya Rohiṇīṃ babhūva Candrārkasamaḥ*, omens).—§ 610 (Çalyap.): IX, **4**, 229 (*nītir eshā B°eḥ*).—§ 615*b* (Udapāna): IX, **36**, 2102 (*devapurohitaḥ*).—§ 615 (Baladevatīrthay.): IX, **41**, 2346.—§ 615*u* (Skanda): IX, **44**, 2470 (performed the *jātakarman*, etc., of Skanda), 2481 (*devarshayaç ca Siddhāç ca B°purogamāḥ*); **45**, 2503; **46**, 2668 (gave to Skanda a *daṇḍa*).—§ 615*w* (Agnitīrtha): IX, **47**, 2748 (*devāḥ . . . B°purogamāḥ*).—§ 615*bb* (Indratīrtha): IX, **49**, 2832 (Indra gave enormous wealth to B.).—§ 615*ff* (Asita Devila): IX, **50**, 2893 (*sthānaṃ B°eḥ*, just under Goloka), 2918 (*devāḥ . . . B°purogamāḥ*). —§ 615 (Gadāyuddhap.): IX, **61**, 3436 (*°y-Uçanaso nopadeçaḥ çrutas tvayā*, says Kṛshṇa to Duryodhana).—§ 626 (Rājadh.): XII, **21**, 615 (*Indreṇa samaye pṛshṭo yad uvāca B°ḥ*).—§ 628 (do.): XII, **23**, 664 (*api gāthām imāñ caiva B°r agāyata*, i.e. v. 665).—§ 632*b* (Shoḍaçarājikop., cf. § 595): XII, **29**, 911 (*°purogamāḥ | devāḥ*), 912 (*Cakrapriyaishī yaṃ*, i.e. Marutta, *vidvān pratyācashṭa B°ḥ*), 913 (*Saṃvarttaḥ . . . yavīyān sa B°eḥ*).—§ 634*b* (Suvarṇashṭhīvisambhavop.): XII, **31**, 1113 (*°mate sthitaḥ*, sc. Indra).—§ 635 (Rājadh.): XII, **35**, 1258 (*°saveneshṭvā surāpo brāhmaṇaḥ punaḥ | samitiṃ brāhmaṇo* [read *Brahmaṇo*, m.] *gacchet*); **37**, 1352 (*°purogāns tu devarshīn*).—§ 637 (do.): XII, **47**η, 1595 (among the ṛshis who surrounded Bhīshma, when lying on his arrow-bed).—§ 640 (do.): XII, **57**, 2052 (*°mate*, cf. Marutta), **58**, 2092, 2104 (*abhāshata*).—§ 641 (do.): XII, **59**, 2205 (abridged the Bāhudantaka and called it Bārhaspatya); **68**, 2536 (his discourse with Vasumanas), 2537 (*maharshiṃ*), 2538, 2539, 2541, (2542); **69**, 2618 (*āha*); **84**, 3183 (*°eç ca saṃvādaṃ Çakrasya ca*), (3185); **98**, 3654 (*°samaḥ*); **103**, 3795 (*°eç ca saṃvādam Indrasya ca*), 3796, (3800), (3839), 3846; **111**, 4145 (*°mater api*); **115**, 4238 (*°samo buddhyā*, i.e. Bhīshma); **120**, 4372; **122**, 4479 (*°er mataṃ . . . adhītaṃ . . . tvayā*); **124**, 4569, 4570, 4571, (4572).—§ 652*b* (Indrota-Pārīkshitīya): XII, **152**, 5667 (*devaguruṃ*), (5669).—§ 658*b* (Kṛtaghnop.): XII, **170**, 6353 (*°mataṃ yathā*).—§ 661 (Mokshadh.): XII, **198***a*, 7191.—§ 663 (do.): XII, **201**, 7366 (*Manoḥ Prajāpater vādaṃ maharsheç ca B°eḥ*), †7367 (*devarshisaṅghapravaro maharshiḥ*), (†7378). — § 667 (do.): XII, **210**, 7661 (*vedavid veda bhagavān Vedāṅgāni B°ḥ*).— § 693*b* (Vṛtravadha): XII, **282**, 10123 (*Brahmarshayaç caiva B°purogamāḥ*), 10129.—§ 710 (Mokshadh.): XII, **322**, 12104 (*salokatāṃ B°eḥ*).—§ 712 (Çukotpatti): XII, **325**, 12209 (preceptor of Çuka).—§ 717*c* (Uparicara): XII, **336**, 12740 (would promulgate a çāstra), 12742 (°*mate*), 12743, 12750 (*Āṅgirase*); **337**, 12753 (etymology, *Aṅgirasaḥ sute . . . devapurohite*), 12756 (*hotṛ* at the sacrifice of king Vasu Uparicara), 12770, 12791, 12812. — § 717*b* (Nārāyaṇīya): XII, **342**, 13178, 13180 (repetition of § 170); **343**, VI), ††13206 (*Aṅgirasaḥ*), VII), ††13214, ††13217. — § 730 (Ānuçāsanik.): XIII, **14**ββ, 991; **18**κκ, 1315 (°*samadyutiḥ*, i.e. Gṛtsamada), (λλ) †1368. — § 734 (do.): XIII, **26**, 1758 (°*samaṃ buddhyā*, i.e. Bhīshma, (*a*), 1762. — § 736*b* (Vītahavyop.): XIII, **30**, 1963 (*Bharadvājo jyeshṭhaḥ putro B°eḥ*). — § 742 (Ānuçāsanik.): XIII, **39**, 2239 (*Uçanā veda yac chāstraṃ yac ca veda B°iḥ*), 2242 (°*prabhṛtibhiḥ*).—§ 745*c* (do.): XIII, **56**, 2915 (°*m ivaujasā*, i.e. Viçvāmitra). — § 746 (Ānuçāsanik.): XIII, **62**, 3153 (°*eç ca saṃvādam Indrasya ca*), 3154, 3156 (*devapurohitaḥ*), (3157); **65**δ, 3295; **76**, 3668 (instructed king Māndhātṛ about kine).—§ 747*b* (Suvarṇotpatti): XIII, **85**θ, 4147 (the first of Aṅgiras' eight sons, called Vāruṇas).—§ 760 (Ānuçāsanik.): XIII, **111**, 5400, 5401, 5402, 5404, (5408), (5418), (5425), (5429), (5433); **112**, (5534); **113**, (5565); **115**β, 5608 (*prāha*).—§ 766 (do.): XIII, **125**, 5972, 5977, (5979). —§ 770 (do.): XIII, **151**ν, 7157 (°*prabhṛtibhir Brahmarshibhiḥ*).—§ 775 (do.): XIII, **166*a***, 7643.—§ 778*e* (Avikshit): XIV, **4**, 83 (°*samo buddhyā*, i.e. Avikshit).—§ 778*b* (Saṃvartta-Maruttīya): XIV, **5**, 95 (son of Aṅgiras and brother of Saṃvartta), 96, 99, 108, 109, 110, 113, 119; **6**, 120 (°*eḥ saṃvādaṃ Maruttasya ca*), 122, (125), (127), 134 (*Aṅgirasaḥ putraṃ devācāryaṃ*), 138; **7**, 164, 165, 170, 172 (°*Purandarau*); **8**, 215, 217; **9**, †219, (†220), (†222), (†224), †226, †227, †233, †234, †235, †236, †237, †238, †239, †240, †244; **10**, †257, †260, †278 (°*er avarajaḥ*, i.e. Saṃvartta), †279 (°*er anujaṃ*, i.e. Saṃvartta).—§ 782*g* (Guruçishyas.): XIV, **43**θ, 1177 (*B.* is the lord of the brahmans).—§ 786*e* (Agastya): XIV, **92**, 2883.—§ 788 (Āçramavāsap.): XV, **27**, 734 (*iva*); **28**ε, 753 (Vidura surpassed *B.* in intelligence).— § 789 (Putradarçanap.): XV, **31**η, 858 (Droṇa was born from a part of *B.*).—§ 795 (Svargārohaṇap.): XVIII, **4**, 145; **5**, 159 (°*ṃ viveçātha Droṇo hy Aṅgirasāṃ varaṃ*). Cf. Aṅgiras[2-3], Āṅgirasa[1], Angirasaḥ putraḥ (I, 4008), Guru.

Bṛhaspati[2] = Çiva (1000 names[1])

Bṛhaspatisuta = Kaca: I, 3199, 3219.

Bṛhat[1]. § 3 (Anukram.): I, **1**, 42 (the first son of Dyau; cf. Āçāvaha).

Bṛhat[2], an Asura. § 130 (Aṃçāvat.): I, **67**, 2691 (the eighth of the Kāleyas).

Bṛhat[3], a Sāman. § 491 (Āṅgirasa): III, **220**, 14162 (°*Rathantaraṃ mūrdhnaḥ*, created by Pāñcajanya). — § 576 (Bhagavadgītāp.): VI, **34**, 1239 (*B°sāma tathā sāmnāṃ*, sc. *asmi*, says Kṛshṇa).—§ 637 (Rājadh.): XII, **47**θ, 1633 (? *Rathantaraṃ B°sāma* = Kṛshṇa).—§ 757*o* (Somapāthin): XIII, **102**, †4896 (*Rathantaraṃ yatra B°c ca gīyate*).

Bṛhat[4] = Bráhman: XII, 12753.

Bṛhat[5] = Mahāpurusha (Mahāpurushastava).

Bṛhat[6] = Vishṇu (1000 names).

Bṛhatketu, an ancient king. § 6 (Anukram.): I, **1*a***, 231 (among the kings of the past who have died).

Bṛhatkīrti, son of Aṅgiras. § 489 (Āṅgirasa): III, **218**, 14123 (PCR. takes this as adj. to *Bṛhaspatiḥ*).

Bṛhatkshattra[1], a Kaikeya prince. § 232 (Svayaṃvarap.): I, **186**, 7001 (the same?).—§ 578 (Bhīsmavadhap.): VI, **45**[11], 1720 (*Kaikeyaṃ*, fought Kṛpa).—§ 592 (Saṃçaptakavadhap.): VII, **23**ο, 972 (*Kaikeyaṃ*, description of his horses). — § 593 (Abhimanyuvadhap.): VII, **35**δ, 1509 (rushed against Droṇa). — § 599 (Jayadrathavadhap.): VII, **106**, 3971 (*Kaikeyānāṃ mahārathaḥ*, fought Droṇa); **107**, 4013 (*Kaikeyaṃ*), 4014, 4017, 4020; **125**, 5021 (*Kaikeyānāṃ mahārathaḥ*), 5027, 5028, 5030, 5035, 5036, 5039 (slain by Droṇa).—§ 604 (Karṇap.): VIII, **5**, 117 (*Kaikeyaḥ*, among the slain of Duryodhana's (!) party). Cf. Kaikeya.

Bṛhatkshattra[2]. § 592 (Saṃçaptakavadhap.): VII, **32**δδ, 1437 (*Naishadaṃ*, slain by Dhṛshṭadyumna).

Bṛhatsena, a king. § 130 (Aṃçāvat.): I, **67**, 2700 (among the kings born from the Krodhavaça gaṇa).—§ 554 (Sainyodyogap.): V, **4**γ, 84.

Bṛhatsenā, the nurse of Damayantī. § 346 (Nalopākhyānap.): III, **60**, 2275, 2276, 2281, 2282.

Bṛṃhitā (C. Bṛṃhilā), a mātṛ. § 500 (Skandop.): III, **228*a***, 14396 (one of the mothers of Çiçu).

Budbudā, an Apsaras (Vudvudā, B.). § 250 (Arjunavanavāsap.): I, **216**, 7858 (among the five Apsarases, delivered by Arjuna from a brahman's curse). — § 269 (Vaiçravaṇasabhāv.): II, **10**, 394 (in the palace of Kubera).

Buddhi. § 115 (Aṃçāvat.): I, **66**, 2579 (daughter of Daksha and wife of Dharma).—§ 637 (Rājadh.): XII, **45**, 1549 (*devī*). — § 705 (Mokshadh.): XII, **303**, 11231 (= Hiraṇyagarbha).—§ 707 (do.): XII, **314**, 11618.

Buddhikāmā, a mātṛ. § 615*u* (Skanda): IX, **46**θ, 2630.

Budha, the planet Mercury. § 270 (Brahmasabhāv.): II, **11**, 446 (among the planets in the palace of Brahmán).—§ 310*b* (Sūrya): III, **3**, 147 (Sūrya is identified with *B.*).—§ 578 (Bhīshmavadhap.): VI, **45**[10], 1710 (*Aṅgāraka-Budhāv iva*). —§ 586 (do.): VI, **101**, 4642 (*yathā Budhaç ca Çukraç ca*); **104**, 4748 (*yathā . . . Budha-Çanaiçcarau*). — § 597 (Pratijñāp.): VII, **84**, 2993 (*sahito Budha-Çukrābhyāṃ tamo nighnan yathā Çaçī*).—§ 599*e* (Çini): VII, **144**, 6028 (son of Soma and father of Purūravas).—§ 600 (Ghaṭotkacavadhap.): VII, **168**, 7546 (*Budha-Bhārgavayor iva*).—§ 605 (Karṇap.): VIII, **15**, 581 (*Aṅgāraka-Budhāv iva*).—§ 677 (Mokshadh.): XII, **245**β, 8900 (? PCR. "learned").—§ 717*b* (Nārāyaṇīya): XII, **343**, X), ††13210. — § 768*b* (Kṛshṇa Vāsudeva); XIII, **147**, 6832 (married to Ilā and father of Purūravas).— § 770 (Ānuçāsanik.): XIII, **151**, 7127 (°*sya putram*, i.e. Purūravas).—§ 775 (do.): XIII, **166*a***, 7643.

C

Caçāti, pl. (°*ayaḥ*), a people: V, †889 (read with *B. Vaçātayaḥ*, q.v.).

Caidya ("king of the Cedis"): I, 129 (= Çiçupāla, slain by Kṛshṇa); II, 1523 (= do.), 1589 (= do.), 1636 (= do.); V, 2526 (= do.), 4780 (= Dhṛshṭaketu); VII, 3049 (= do.), 5047 (= do.); XVI, 158 (= Çiçupāla).

Caidyā ("princess of Cedi"): I, 3831 (= Kareṇumatī, the wife of Nakula).

Caidyādhipati ("king of the Cedis"). § 554 (Saṃyodyogap.): V, **4**γ, 77 (= Dhṛshṭaketu ?).

Caitra ("named after the nakshatra Citrā," name of a certain month). § 360 (Tīrthayātrāp.): III, **82**, 5068 (°*çuklacaturdaçīṃ*).—§ 410 (Plakshāvataraṇag.): III, **130**, 10550 (*māsi*).—§ 759 (Ânuçāsanik.): XIII, **106**β, 5154 (*māsaṃ*, he who during the whole month of Caitra confines himself every day to one meal takes birth in a rich family, etc.); **109**[5], 5376 (he who fasts on the twelfth day of the moon in the month of Caitra and for the whole day and night worships Kṛshṇa as Vishṇu attains the merit of the *Pauṇḍarīka* sacrifice and proceeds to *devaloka*).

Caitraratha[1] ("the wood belonging to Citraratha"). § 76 (Matsya): I, **63**, 2376 (*vanaṃ C°opamaṃ*).—§ 133 (Dushyanta): I, **70**, 2873 (°*prakhyaṃ*, sc. *vanaṃ*).—§ 144 (Yayāti): I, **75**, 3171 (*vane*).—§ 146 (do.): I, **78**, 3282 (*vane C°opame*).—§ 184 (Pāṇḍu): I, **110**, 4637 (in the North, visited by Pāṇḍu).—§ 317*b* (Kṛshṇa Vāsudeva): III, **13**, 482 (*vane*, there Kṛshṇa performed sacrifices), 501 (do.).—§ 356 (Tīrthayātrāp.): III, **80**, 3095 (*vanaṃ C°ṃ yathā*, sc. the Kāmyaka-wood).—§ 449 (Âjagarap.): III, **177**, 12355 (°*prakāçam*), 12358 (*vanāc C°prakāçāt*).—§ 497 (Skandotpatti): III, **226**, 14342 (*vane*).—§ 516 (Duryodhanayajña): III, **257**, 15344 (*praviveça gṛhaṃ yathā C°ṃ prabhuḥ*, i.e. Kubera, PCR.).—§ 565 (Gālavac.): V, **111**, 3831 (in the North).—§ 608 (Karṇap.): VIII, **53**, 2573 (*yathā C°ṃ vanaṃ*).—§ 713 (Çukakṛti): XII, **326**, 12245 (°*opamaṃ*, a garden at the palace of Janaka).

Caitraratha[2]. § 154 (Pūruvaṃç.): I, **94**, 3740 (son of Kuru and Vāhinī).

Caitraratha[3] ("son of Citraratha") = Çaçabindu: XII, 998.

Caitraratha[ṃ] parvan ("the section relating to Citraratha"). § 10 (Parvasaṅgr.): I, **2**, 313 (i.e. Caitrarathaparvan).—§ 11 (do.): I, **2**, 361 (do.).

Caitrarathaparvan ("the section relating to Citraratha," the eleventh of the minor parvans of Mhbhr.). (Cf. Caitraratha[ṃ] parvan.) § 216: Within a few days there came a *brahman* to the abode of their host, whom they asked to narrate the birth of *Dhṛshṭadyumna* from the sacrificial fire, and that of *Kṛshṇā* from the centre of the *vedī*, and that of *Çikhaṇḍin*, and how *Dhṛshṭadyumna* learnt the use of all weapons from *Droṇa*, and how the friendship of *Droṇa* and *Drupada* was broken (I, **165**).—§ 217: The *brahman* related (not mentioning *Açvatthāman*) the birth of *Droṇa* (§ 200), his friendship with *Drupada*, and his visit to *Rāma* (§ 201; he obtained the *Brahmāstra*, v. 6340), the breaking of his friendship with *Drupada* (§ 202), how *Bhīshma* prevailed upon him to teach the princes, etc. (both *Arjuna* and the others promised to give what he might ask for his fee, v. 6346), and the chastisement of *Drupada* (§ 209; *Drupada* resides in *Chattravatī*, v. 6348) (I, **166**).—§ 218: Draupadīsambhava (q.v.).—§ 219: Hearing the words of the *brahman*, the sons of *Kuntī* seemed to be, as it were, pierced with darts. *Kuntī* proposed to *Yudhishṭhira* that they should go to the *Pāñcālas*, a country they had not seen before, and he consented for his part. When the other brothers had likewise consented, they set out for the town of *Drupada* (I, **168**).—§ 220: When they were living disguised, *Vyāsa* came and told them that formerly the daughter of a *ṛshi*, notwithstanding her beauty, obtained no husband, and therefore by austerities propitiated *Çaṅkara* five times, saying "Give me a husband." Accordingly the god said (notwithstanding her objection) that she should in a future life have five husbands. "That damsel is *Kṛshṇā*, appointed to be the wife of ye all; go therefore to the capital of the *Pāñcālas* and dwell ye there." He then left them (I, **169**).—§ 221: After *Vyāsa* had gone away, the *Pāṇḍavas* proceeded [towards the *Pāñcālas*] in a northerly direction, walking day and night till they reached the *tīrtha Somāçrayāyaṇa* ("the shrine of *Rudra* with the crescent mark on his brow," PCR. with Nīl.). Then they arrived at the *Gaṅgā*; *Dhanañjaya* (i.e. *Arjuna*) walked before them, torch in hand. The *Gandharva* king with his wives was then sporting there in the *Gaṅgā*. Bending his bow to a circle, he said, "Excepting the first 80 *lavas*, the *muhūrta* (*prasthānakālaṃ*, Nīl.) that begins with the twilight preceding nightfall has been appointed for the *Yakshas*, *Gandharvas*, and *Rākshasas*, capable of going everywhere at will; the rest has been appointed for man to do his work. If therefore men, wandering during those moments from greed of gain, come near us, both we and the *rākshasas* slay those fools. Therefore persons acquainted with the *Vedas* never applaud those men, who then approach any piece of water. Stay ye at a distance. Know that I am *Aṅgāraparṇa* (= *Citraratha*, v. 6475; cf. LIA. i, 666/814), the friend of *Kubera*, and this my forest is also called *Aṅgāraparṇa*, where neither *kauṇapas* (i.e. *rākshasas*), nor *çṛṅgins* (a horned animal, see BR.; according to Nīl. it is = *kāpālikāḥ*, a Çivaitic sect), nor gods, nor men can come." *Arjuna* replied: "Whether it be day, night, or twilight, who can bar others from the ocean, the *Himālaya*, and *Gaṅgā*?" (*b*). *Arjuna* burnt the *Gandharva's* chariot with the *Âgneya* weapon, given by *Bṛhaspati* (the preceptor of *Indra*) to *Bharadvāja*, by him to *Agniveçya*, by him to *Droṇa*, by *Droṇa* to *Arjuna*, and dragged him, who had become unconscious, by the hair. His wife *Kumbhīnasī* prevailed upon *Yudhishṭhira*, and he commanded *Arjuna* to spare him. He declared that, instead of his former name, *Citraratha* ("who has a variegated chariot"), he should now be called *Dagdharatha* ("whose chariot has been burnt"), and imparted to *Arjuna* the *Gāndharvī vidyā* called *Cākshushī* (*c*). He also gave *Arjuna* and each of his brothers one hundred horses born in the country of the Gandharvas (*Gandharvajānāṃ*), endued with the speed of wind and employed in carrying the gods and Gandharvas, a portion of *Indra's vajra* ("thunderbolt") (*d*). *Arjuna* in return gave him the *Âgneya* weapon, and asked him why they, though skilled in the *Vedas*, had been censured by him. He replied that it was because they were without fires, without sacrifices, and without a *brahman* walking before them. "The *Yakshas*, *Rākshasas*, *Gandharvas*, *Piçācas*, *Uragas*, and *Dānavas* know the history of the *Kuru* race; I have heard from *Nārada* and other *devarshis* the deeds of your ancestors. I have been vanquished by thee in battle on account of the *brahmacarya* being rigidly observed; a *kshattriya*, who is addicted to lust, if he fights in the night, can never escape with life; but even if addicted to lust, he who has a *purohita* may vanquish all wanderers of the night. Therefore, O *Tāpatya*! kings should always select a fit *purohita*" (I, **170**).—§ 222: *Citraratha* related Tapatyupākhyāna (q.v.).—§§ 223–7: Vāsishṭha (q.v.).—§ 228: Aurvopākhyāna (q.v.).—§ 229: Vasishṭopākhyāna (q.v.).—§ 230: Dhaumya-purohitakaraṇa (q.v.).

Caitraseni[1], a prince. § 592 (Saṃçaptakav.): VII, **21**μ, 916 (vanquished by Droṇa).

Caitraseni[2], patron. ("son of Citrasena"). § 592 (Saṃçaptakav.): VII, **25**, 1091 (*Caitrasenir* (C. *Citrasainir*) *mahārāja tava putram* [read *pautram*] *avārayat* (B. *nya°*) | *tau* *pautrau tava*, etc., i.e. the son of Citrasena (the son of Dhṛtarāshṭra) and Çrutakarman, the son of Nakula).

Caitravāhanī ("daughter of Citravāhana") = Citrāṅgadā: I, 7827 (C. °*vāhinīm*); XIV, 2358, 2405 (*Citrāṅgadā*).

Caitrī, the day of full-moon in the month of Caitra. § 641 (Rājadh.): XII, **100**, 3691 (*Caitryāṃ vā Mārgaçīrshyāṃ vā senayogaḥ praçasyate*).—§ 785 (Anugītāp.): XIV, **72**, 2086 (*paurṇamāsyāṃ*, the *dīkshā* of Yudhishṭhira will be performed); **76**, 2219 (*parāṃ C°ṃ*, on this day the açvamedha of Yudhishṭhira will take place, cf. XIV, 2086); **81**, 2425 (do.); **82**, 2462 (do.); **84**, 2509 (do.).

Caitya, a mountain near Girivraja, cf. the following. § 277 (Jarāsandhavadhap.): II, **21**, 814 (°*prākāraṃ*).

Caityaka (= Caitya). § 277 (Jarāsandhavadhap.): II, **21**, 799 (*çubhāç C°pañcamāḥ*, sc. *parvatāḥ*), 811 (*Māgadhānān tu ruciraṃ C°āntaram ādravan*), 815 (*Māgadhānāṃ suruciraṃ C°an taṃ samādravan*), 843 (°*sya gireḥ çṛṅgam*).

Cakra[1], a serpent. § 63 (Sarpasattra): I, **57**, 2147 (of Vāsuki's race).

Cakra[2], companions of Skanda. § 615*u* (Skanda): IX, **45**ε, 2539 (given to Skanda by Vishṇu), 2542 (another, given to Skanda by Tvashṭṛ),

***Cakra**[3], the discus of Kṛshṇa. § 795 (Svargārohaṇap.): XVIII, **4**, 127 (°*prabhṛtibhiḥ purushavigrahaiḥ*).

Cakra[4], pl. (°*āḥ*), a people. § 574 (Jambūkh.): VI, **9**μ, 352 (in Bhāratavarsha).

Cakracara, pl. (°*āḥ*), a sort of ṛshi. § 373 (Prayāga): III, **85**, 8214 (at Prayāga).—§ 768*b* (Umā-Maheçvaras.): XIII, **141**, 6493, 6497.

Cakradeva, a Vṛshṇi warrior. § 273 (Rājasūyārambhap.): II, **14**, 621 (among the seven rathas of the Vṛshṇis).

Cakradhanus, a ṛshi. § 565 (Gālavac.): V, **109**, 3795 (*Sūryajāto mahān ṛshiḥ*, in the south).

Cakradhara, adj. ("armed with the discus"): XIV, 429 (*Siddhaiḥ*).

Cakradhārin = Kṛshṇa, q.v.

Cakradharman, the chief of the Vidyādharas. § 269 (Vaiçravaṇasabhāv.): II, **10**, 408 (*Vidyādharādhipaḥ*, in the palace of Kubera).

Cakradvāra, a mountain and its genius. § 709*b* (Sulabhā-Janaka-saṃv.): XII, **321***a*, 12035.

Cakragadābhṛt = Kṛshṇa, q.v.

Cakragadādhara[1] = Kṛshṇa, q.v.

Cakragadādhara[2] = Vishṇu (1000 names).

Cakraka, son of Viçvāmitra. § 721*b* (Viçvāmitrop.): XIII, **4**β, 253.

Cakramaṇḍa, a serpent. § 793 (Mausalap.): XVI, **4**η, †120 (°*ātishaṇḍau*, issued from the mouth of Balarāma).

Cakranemi, a mātṛ. § 615*u* (Skanda): IX, **46**θ, 2623.

Cakrapāṇi = Kṛshṇa, q.v.

Cakrāti, pl. (°*ayaḥ*), a people. § 574 (Jambūkh.): VI, **9**μ, 352 (only B., C. has *Vakrātapāḥ*).

***Cakravāka**, pl. (°*āḥ*), a sort of goose, *Anas casarca*, Gm. § 126 (Aṃçāvat.): I, **66**, 2622 (born by Dhṛtarāshṭrī).

Cakravyūha, a kind of array. § 130*g* (Abhimanyu): I, **67**, 2754.—§ 593 (Abhimanyuvadhap.): VII, **33**, 1471; **34**, 1494; **35**, 1520, 1521.—§ 599 (Jayadrathavadhap.): VII, **87**, 3108 (*vyūhaḥ sacakraçakaṭaḥ*).

Cakrāyudha = Vishṇu and Kṛshṇa.

Cakrin[1] = Vishṇu (1000 names).

Cakrin[2] = Çiva: XIII, 745.

Cakshurājya = Mahāpurusha (Mahāpurushastava).

Cakshurvardhanikā, a river in Çākadvīpa. § 575*b* (Bhūmip.): VI, **11**γ, 433.

Cakshus[1]. § 3 (Anukram.): I, **1**, 42 (the third son of Heaven; cf. Āçāvaha).

Cakshus[2] = Çiva: XIV, 197.

Cākshusha[1], a Manu. § 730 (Ānuçāsanik.): XIII, **18***a*, 1315 (*Varishṭho nāma bhagavāṃç C°sya Manoḥ sutaḥ*).

Cākshusha[2], adj. ("relating to the eye," viz., one of Brahmán's births). § 717*b* (Nārāyaṇīya): XII, **348**ηη, 13490 (*cākshushaṃ vai me*, i.e. Brahmán's, *dvitīyaṃ janma*); **349**, II), 13562 (*cākshushaṃ janma dvitīyaṃ Brahmaṇaḥ*).

Cākshushā, a Gandharvic science given to Arjuna by Citraratha. § 221 (Caitrarathap.): I, **170**, 6478.—§ 221*b* (Caitrarathap.): *C.* had been communicated by *Manu* to *Soma*, by *Soma* to *Viçvāvasu*, and by *Viçvāvasu* to *Citraratha* after ascetic penances, and when communicated by the preceptor to a man without energy, it becomes fruitless. By means of it one may see whatever one wishes. One can acquire it only by standing on one leg for six months; but *Arjuna* obtained it without any rigid vow. This knowledge makes the *Gandharvas* superior to men and equal to the gods.

Cala = Çiva (1000 names[2]). Do.[2] = Vishṇu (1000 names).

Calācala = Çiva (1000 names[1]).

Camasa (= Camasodbheda), a tīrtha. § 360 (Tīrthayātrāp.): III, **82**, 5053 (where Sarasvatī reappears).

Camasodbheda (= Camasa), a tīrtha. § 360 (Tīrthayātrāp.): III, **82**, 5054 (bathing there one acquires the merit of an agnishṭoma).—§ 410*c* (Plakshāvataraṇag.): III, **130**, 10540 (where Sarasvatī once more becomes visible).—§ 615 (Baladevatīrthay.): IX, **35**, 2060.

Camasodbhedana (= Camasodbheda), a tīrtha. § 377 (Dhaumyatīrthak.): III, **88**, 8345 (in the country of the Surāshṭras).

Campā, the metropolis of the Aṅgas. § 370 (Tīrthayātrāp.): III, **84**, 8141 (*atha Campāṃ samāsādya Bhagīrathyāṃ kṛtodakaḥ* | *Daṇḍārttam abhigatvā tu gosahasraphalam labhet*); **85**, 8156 (*tathā Campāṃ samāsādya Bhagīrathyāṃ kṛtodakaḥ* | *Daṇḍākhyam abhigamyaiva*, etc.).—§ 391 (Ṛshyaçṛṅga): III, **113**, 10084 (the city of king Lomapāda).—§ 547 (Karṇa): III, **308**, 17151 (on Gaṅgā, the city of Adhiratha).—§ 621 (Rājadh.): XII, **5**, 135 (ruled by Karṇa).—§ 743*b* (Vipulop.): XIII, **42**, 2359 (the abode of the ṛshi Devaçarman), 2376. Cf. Mālinī.

Campakāraṇya, a wood. § 370 (Tīrthayātrāp.): III, **84**, 8111 (dwelling there for one night one acquires the merit of giving a thousand kine).

Cāmpeya, son of Viçvāmitra. § 721*b* (Viçvāmitrop.): XIII, **4**β, 257.

Camūhara, a Viçvedeva. § 749 (Ānuçāsanik.): XIII, **91**γ, 4360.

Camūstambhana = Çiva (1000 names[2]).

Caṇḍa[1] = Skanda: III, 14631.

Caṇḍa[2] = Çiva (1000 names[1]).

Caṇḍā = Durgā (Umā): VI, 797.

Caṇḍabala, a monkey. § 539 (Kumbhakarṇādivadha): III, **287**, 16414 (devoured by Kumbhakarṇa).

Caṇḍabhārgava, a brahman. § 59 (Sarpasattra): I, **53**, 2045 (*tatra*—i.e. at the snake sacrifice of Janamejaya—*hotā babhūvātha Caṇḍabhārgavaḥ* | *Cyavanasyānvaye khyāto vipro vedavidāṃ varaḥ*).

Caṇḍadhāra = Çiva (1000 names[1]).

Caṇḍakauçika, a muni, son of Kākshīvat. § 275 (Rājasūyār.): II, **17**, 698 (*Kākshīvataḥ putraṃ Gautamasya*);

19, 741 (*C.* uttered mantras over a mango fruit, which the queens of Bṛhadratha ate up; then Jarāsandha was born).

***Caṇḍāla**[1], name of a caste. § 721 (Ānuçāsanik.): XIII, **3**, 199 (°*yonau jātaḥ*, sc. Mataṅga).—§ 735 (do.): XIII, **27**, 1895 (°*yonau jātena*, sc. Mataṅga); **29**, 1916 (do.).—§ 743*b* (Vipulop.): XIII, **40**, 2276 (°*samadarçanaḥ*, sc. Indra).—§ 744 (Ānuçāsanik.): XIII, **48**, 2589 (the son of a *C.* with a Vaidehī becomes a Saupāka; read *Saupākaḥ* with B.).—§ 749 (do.): XIII, **91**, 4368 (°*çvapacau*, should be excluded from a çrāddha).

Caṇḍāla[2], sg. = Mataṅga: XIII, 1876, 1880, 1881, 1882, 1901.

Cāṇḍāla**[1] (mostly pl., = Caṇḍāla[1]). § 562 (Bhagavadyānap.): V, **92**, 3291.—§ 641 (Rājadh.): XII, **76**, 2874 (*brāhmaṇac°āḥ*).—§ 659 (Mokshadh.): XII, **180**, 6727 (sg.).—§ 702 (do.): XII, **297**γ, 10869; **298**, 10931 (°*tve*).—§ 705 (do.): XII, **303a*, 11245.—§ 744 (Ānuçāsanik.): XIII, **47**, 2535 (*brāhmaṇacāṇḍālaḥ*); **48**γ, 2572 (sg., son of a *çūdra* with a *brāhmaṇī*), 2583 (the son of a *C.* with a Sairandhrī becomes a *çvapāka*), 2588 (the son of a *C.* [with a Nishādī?] becomes a *pāṇḍusaupāka*), 2590; **49**δ, 2613 (son of a *çūdra* with a *brāhmaṇī*).—§ 782*g* (Guruçishyasaṃv.): XIV, **36**, 1016.—§ 784*b* (Uttaṅka): XIV, **55**, 1620 (°*rūpī*, sc. Indra).

Cāṇḍāla[2], sg. (single Cāṇḍālas): (*a*) = Parigha: XII, 4935, 5008, 5028 (*Parighaḥ*), 5034, 5035, 5110. (*b*) (the *C.* who discoursed with Viçvāmitra): XII, 5330, 5353, 5355, 5361, 5362, 5363, 5366, 5373, 5376. (*c*) (the *C.* who conversed with a kshatrabandhu): XIII, 4814 foll.

Cāṇḍālikāçrama, a tīrtha. By repairing to *C.* and bathing in Kokāmukha, after having subsisted upon potherbs and having worn ragged clothes, one is sure to obtain ten maidens (differently Nīl.): XIII, **25**, 1738 (only C.; B. *Āñjalikāçramam*).

Candana = Çiva (1000 names[2]).

Candanin = Çiva (1000 names[2]).

Caṇḍatuṇḍaka, a Suparṇa, son of Garuḍa. § 564 (Mātalīyop.): V, **101**β, 3594.

Caṇḍī = Durgā (Umā): VI, 797.

Caṇḍikaghaṇṭa = Çiva (1000 names[1]).

Candra[1] = Çiva (1000 names[2]).

Candra[2] (the Moon), v. Soma.

Candra[3], an Asura. § 130 (Aṃçāvat.): I, **67**, 2666 (incarnate as Candravarman, king of the Kāmbojas). Cf. Candramas.

Candrabha, a warrior of Skanda. § 615*u* (Skanda): IX, **45**η, 2577.

Candrabhāgā, a river, the present Chenāb. § 268 (Varuṇasabhāv): II, **9**, 371 (among the rivers present in the palace of Varuṇa).—§ 459 (Mārkaṇḍeyas.): III, **188***a*, 12907 (seen by Mārkaṇḍeya in the stomach of Nārāyaṇa).—§ 574 (Jambūkh.): VI, **9**λ, 323, 327 (only C.; B. *Vetravatīm*).—§ 607 (Karṇap.): VIII, **44**θ, 2055 (in the country of the Āraṭṭas).—§ 733*b* (Ānuçāsanik.): Bathing for seven days in the *C.* or the *Vitastā*, one is sure to become purified from all sins and endued with the merits of an ascetic: XIII, **25***a*, 1694.—§ 768*b* (Umā-Maheçvarasaṃv.): XIII, **146**δ, 6764.—§ 775 (Ānuçāsanik.): XIII, **166***a*, 7645.

Candraçilā, a mātṛ. § 615*u* (Skanda): IX, **46**θ, 2629.

Candrāçva, son of Kuvalāçva. § 478 (Dhundhumārop.): III, **204**, 13621.

Candradeva[1], a Kuru warrior. § 605 (Karṇap.): VIII, **47**λλ, 1078 (attacks Arjuna), 1086, 1089 (slain by Arjuna).

Candradeva[2], a Pāñcāla prince. § 608 (Karṇap.): VIII, **49**, 2327 (*Pāñcālyau . . . . Candradevañ ca Daṇḍadhārañ ca*, slain by Karṇa).

Candrahantṛ, an Asura. § 94 (Aṃçāvat.): I, **65**, 2539 (son of Siṃhikā).—§ 130 (do.): I, **67**, 2673 (*Asuraḥ*, incarnate as the rājarshi Çunaka).

Candraka, an owl. § 646*b* (Mārjāramūshikasaṃv.): XII, **138**, 4944.

Candraketu, a Kuru warrior. § 593 (Abhimanyuvadhap.): VII, **48**χ, 1899 (slain by Abhimanyu).

Candramā, a river in Bhāratavarsha. § 574 (Jambūkh.): VI, **9**λ, 337.

Candramas[1] (the Moon), v. Soma.

Candramas[2], an Asura. § 92 (Aṃçāvat.): I, **65**, 2534 (*Sūrya-Candramasau*, sons of Danu), 2535 (do., different from Sūrya-Candramasau among the gods). Cf. Candra.

Candramasas tīrtha(ṃ), a tīrtha. § 406*b* (Ārcīkaparvata): III, **125**, 10412 (on Ārcīkaparvata).

Cāndramasī, the wife of Bṛhaspati. § 490 (Āngirasa): III, **219**, 14130 (*Candramasā ākrāntā Tārā nāma*, Nīl., mother of six fires and one daughter).

Candramaulivibhūshaṇa = Çiva: X, 261.

Candrāṃçu = Vishṇu (1000 names).

Candrānana = Skanda: III, 14632.

Candrapramardana, an Asura. § 94 (Aṃçāvat.): I, **65**, 2539 (son of Siṃhikā).

Candrārdhakṛtaçīrsha = Kṛshṇa: XII, 1669.

Candrasena[1], a prince, son of Samudrasena. § 232 (Svayaṃvarap.): I, **186**, 6991 (*Samudrasenaputraḥ*, came to the svayaṃvara of Draupadī).—§ 280 (Bhīmasena): II, **30**, 1098 (in the East, with Samudrasena he is vanquished by Bhīmasena).—§ 571 (Rathātirathas.): V, **171**, 5911 (among the rathas of the Pāṇḍavas).—§ 592 (Saṃçaptakavadhap.): VII, **23**o, 1007 (*Samudrasenaputram*, proceeded against Droṇa, description of his horses).—§ 600 (Ghaṭotkacavadhap.): VII, **156**ν, 6912 (the same?, slain by Açvatthāman); **158**χ, 7009 (the same?).

Candrasena[2], a Kuru warrior. § 605 (Karṇap.): VIII, **27**, 1084 (attacked Arjuna, PCR. has Candradeva).

Candrasena[3]. § 611 (Çalyap.): IX, **12**, 644 (slain by Yudhishṭhira).

Candrasya vināçana(ḥ), an Asura. § 130 (Aṃçāvat.): I, **67**, 2673 (incarnate as king Jānaki).

Candravaktra = Çiva (1000 names[2]).

Candravarman. § 130 (Aṃçāvat.): I, **67**, 2668 (*Kāmbojānāṃ narādhipaḥ*, incarnation of the Asura Candra).—§ 592 (Saṃçaptakavadhap.): VII, **32**, 1437 (the same?, slain by Dhṛshṭadyumna).

Candrāvarta = Çiva (1000 names[1]).

Candravatsa, pl. (°*āḥ*), a people. § 562 (Bhagavadyānap.): V, **74**γ, 2732 (*Dhāraṇaç C°ānām*).

Candrodaya, a Pāṇḍava warrior. § 600 (Ghaṭotkacavadhap.): VII, **158**χ, 7012 (brother of Virāṭa?).

Caṇūra[1], a prince. § 264 (Sabhākriyāp.): II, **4**β, 121 (among the princes who waited upon Yudhishṭhira, when he entered his palace).

Caṇūra[2]. § 567 (Bhagavadyānap.): V, **130**ζ, 4410 (had been slain by Kṛshṇa).

Caṇūrāndhranishūdana (C. Caṇūrāndhranisū°) = Vishṇu (1000 names).

Capala, an ancient king. § 6 (Anukram.): I, **1***a*, 231 (in the enumeration of Sañjaya).

Capalāksha = Abhimanyu: XIV, 2003, 2004.

Capalekshaṇa = Abhimanyu: XIV, 2021.

Cāpin = Çiva (1000 names [1]).
Carācarasya pratihartṛ = Çiva (1000 names [1]).
Carācarasya srashṭṛ = Çiva (1000 names [1]).
Carācarātman [1] = Çiva (1000 names [2]). — Do.[2] = Sūrya, III, 157.
Cāraṇa, pl. (°*āḥ*), a class of beings. § 76 (Matsya): I, **63**, 2396 (*Siddha-C°patham*).—§ 133 (Dushyanta): I, **70**, 2858 (*Siddha-C°saṅghaiḥ*). — § 162 (Çāntanūp.): I, **97**, 3889 (*Gaṅgām . . . Siddha-C°sevitām*).—§ 173 (Pāṇḍurājyābhisheka): I, **109**, 4346 (*Devarshi-C°aiḥ*).—§ 185 (Pāṇḍu): I, **120**, 4640 (*Siddha-C°saṅghānam*).—§ 194 (do.): I, **126**, 4907 (°*sahasrāṇām*).—§ 233 (Svayaṃvarap.): I, **187**, †7011. —§ 246 (Sundopasundop.): I, **210**, 7655.—§ 310*b* (Sūrya): III, **3**, 170 (*Siddha-C°-Gandharvāḥ*, follow Sūrya).—§ 322 (Dvaitavanapr.): III, **24**, †940 (*C°-Siddhasaṅghāḥ*).—§ 331 (Kairātap.): III, **38**, 1530 (*vanam . . . Siddha-C°sevitam*). —§ 336 (Indralokābhigamanap.): III, **43**, 1756 (*Siddha-C°sevitām*, sc. the city of Indra).—§ 338 (do.): III, **46**, 1830 (*Siddha-C°-Gandharvaiḥ*), 1841.—§ 339 (do.): III, **47**, 1891 (*Gaṅgā . . . Siddha-C°sevitā*).—§ 361 (Kurukshetra): III, **83**, 5075 (*Siddha-C°āḥ*, in Kurukshetra). — § 370 (Tīrthayātrāp.): III, **84**, 7083 (*Siddha-C°-Gandharvāḥ*, in Saugandhikavana); **85**, 8168 (*Siddha-C°-Gandharvamānushāḥ*, in Gokarṇa).—§ 377 (Dhaumyatīrthak.): III, **89**, 8357 (*Siddharshi-C°aiḥ*).—§ 434 (Saugandhikāharaṇa): III, **156**, 11444 (*Siddha-C°sevitam . . . āçramam Vṛshaparvaṇaḥ*).—§ 436 (Yakshayuddhap.): III, **158**, 11561 (*Siddha-C°sevitam . . . Gandhamādanam*).—§ 437 (do.): III, **160**, 11674.—§ 542 (Rāvaṇavadha): III, **290**, 16528 (*Tridaçāḥ saha-Gandharva-C°āḥ*).—§ 566 (Yayāti): V, **123**, 4101 (praised Yayāti in Heaven).—§ 573 (Ambopākhyānap.): V, **186**, 7351 (*Vatsabhūmim Siddha-C°sevitām*). — § 574 (Jambūkh.): VI, **6**, 199 (*parvatāḥ . . . Siddha-C°sevitāḥ*). —§ 574*h* (Bhadrāçva): VI, **7**, 269 (*drumaḥ Siddha-C°sevitaḥ*, i.e. the tree Kālāmra in the region Bhadrāçva).—§ 574*i* (Jambū): VI, **7**, 273 (*Jambūvṛkshaḥ Siddha-C°sevitaḥ*).—§ 575 (Bhūmip.): VI, **11**, 407 (*Siddha-C°saṅkīrṇaḥ*, sc. the salt ocean).—§ 575*b* (Çākadvīpa): VI, **11**, 429 (in Çākadvīpa). —§ 575 (Bhūmip.): VI, **12**, 464 (*Siddha-C°saṅkīrṇaḥ*, sc. Dundubhisvana).—§ 576 (Bhagavadgītāp.): VI, **23**, 808 (*saṅkhye vīkshyase Siddha-C°aiḥ*, sc. Durgā).—§ 577 (Bhīshmavadhap.). VI, **40**, 1500 (*Siddha-C°saṅghāḥ*, came to see the battle).—§ 578 (do.): VI, **45**, 1753 (*Siddha-C°āḥ*).—§ 579 (do.): VI, **52**, 2183 (praise Bhīshma and Arjuna).—§ 587 (do.): VI, **120**, 5704 (*Siddha-C°aiḥ*).—§ 593 (Abhimanyuv.): VII, **37**, †1622 (*Pitṛ-sura-C°-Siddhasaṅghaiḥ*). — § 596 (Pratijñāp.): VII, **80**, 2843 (*Siddha-C°sevitam*, sc. the mountain Maṇimat).—§ 598 (Jayadrathavadhap.): VII, **87**, 3118 (*Siddha-C°saṅghānām*).—§ 599 (do.): VII, **98**, 3642 (*Siddha-C°saṅghāḥ*), 3652 (do.); **100**, 3728 (*Siddha C°saṅghānām*); **107**, 4026 (do.); **110**, 4756 (*C°āḥ saha-Gandharvāḥ*); **124**, 4978; **137**, 5628; **138**, 5692 (*C°-Siddhānām*); **139**, 5769; **143**, 6008 (*Siddha-C°mānavāḥ*); **145**, 6132 (*Siddha-C°vātikaiḥ*, B. °*pannagaiḥ*). —§ 600 (Ghaṭotkacavadhap.): VII, **160**, 7188 (do.).—§ 605 (Karṇap.): VIII, **15**, 599 (*Siddha-C°saṅghānām*); **16**, 626. —§ 608 (do.): VIII, **56**, 2817 (*Siddha-C°saṅghāḥ*); **78**, 3970; **87**, 4400 (*Siddha-C°saṅghānām*), (χ'), 4413 (sided with Arjuna), 4433 (*trayo lokāḥ sahadevarshi-C°āḥ*), 4452 (*trayo lokāḥ saha Devarshi-C°aiḥ*); **94**, 4962 (*deva-Gandharva-manushya-C°aiḥ*).—§ 610 (Çalyap.): IX, **7**τ, 337.—§ 611 (do.): IX, **22**, 1156 (*yuddham . . . Siddha-C°sevitam*). —§ 615 (Gadāyuddhap.): IX, **55**, 3090 (*vātikāḥ*, i.e. *ākāça-cāriṇaḥ*, Nīl.); **58**, 3307 (*vātika-C°āḥ*).—§ 705 (Mokshadh.): XII, **303**, 11244 (*trailokye . . . sa-C°-Paiçāce*).—§ 714 (Çukakṛtya): XII, **328**, 12314 (*Himavantam . . . Siddha-C°sevitam*). — § 717*b* (Nārāyaṇīya): XII, **341**, 13028 (*Merau . . . Siddha-C°sevite*). — § 726 (Ānuçāsanik.): XIII, **10**, 439 (*Siddha-C°saṃyuktam*, sc. *āçramam*).—§ 730*g* (Upamanyu): XIII, **14**η, 741 (*Siddha-C°rūpadhṛk*, i.e. Çiva). —§ 730 (Ānuçāsanik.): XIII, **18**$\lambda\lambda$, †1373 (°*pannagāḥ*).—§ 731*b* (Ashṭāvakra-Dik-saṃv.): XIII, **19**, 1396 (*Rudrasyāyatanam . . . Siddha-C°sevitam*), 1407 (*Himavantam . . . Siddha-C°sevitam*).—§ 733 (Ānuçāsanik.): XIII, **25**, 1748 (*Himavān . . . Siddha-C°sevitaḥ*). — § 766 (do.): XIII, **130**, 6111 (*tīrthāni . . . Siddha-C°jushṭāni*). —§ 768*b* (Umā-Maheçvarasaṃv.): XIII, **140**, 6339 (*Himavati . . . Siddha-C°sevite*). — § 788 (Āçramavāsap.): XV, **24**, 655 (*āçramam . . . Siddha-C°sevitam*).—§ 793 (Mausalap.): XVI, **4**θ, †131 (in Heaven).
Cāritra[m] = Kṛshṇa: XII, 1512.
Carmakāra, a caste: XIII, 2588.
Carmamaṇḍala, pl. (°*āḥ*), a people. § 574 (Jambūkh.): VI, **9**μ, 355 (in Bhāratavarsha).
Carmaṇvatī, a river, now Chambal. § 209 (Drupadaçāsana): I, **138**, 5513 (*dakshiṇāṃç cāpi Pañcālān yāvac C°ī nadī*, ruled by Drupada).—§ 268 (Varuṇasabhāv.): II, **9**, 373 (among the rivers in the palace of Varuṇa).—§ 276 (Jarāsandhavadhap.): II, **20**, 795. — § 281 (Sahadeva): II, **31**, 1111 (on the bank of *C.* Sahadeva vanquished Jambhaka's son).—§ 356 (Tīrthayātrāp.): III, **82**, 4096 (*C°m samāsādya niyato niyatāçanaḥ | Rantidevābhyanujñātam* (C. °*to*) *agnishṭomaphalam labhet*). — § 459 (Mārkaṇḍeyas.): III, **188***a*, 12907.—§ 494 (Āṅgirasa): III, **222**, 14230 (among the rivers who are mothers of fires).—§ 547 (Kuṇḍalāharaṇap.): III, **308**, 17150.—§ 574 (Jambūkh.): VI, **9**λ, 327.—§ 595 (Shoḍaçarāj., v. Rantideva): VII, **67**, 2360 (origin of the name).—§ 632*b* (Shoḍaçarāj., cf. § 595): XII, **29**, 1016 (*mahānadī*, do.).—§ 746 (Ānuçāsanikap.): XIII, **66**, 3351 (*gocarmabhyaḥ pravartitā*).—§ 775 (do.): XIII, **166***a*, 7653.
Carmavāsas = Çiva: VIII, 1449.
Carmavat, brother of Çakuni. § 585 (Bhīshmavadhap.): VI, **90**σ, 3997 (slain by Irāvat).
Carmin = Çiva (1000 names [2]).
Carucelin = Çiva (1000 names [1]).
Cārucitra, son of Dhṛtarāshṭra. § 182 (Dhṛtarāshṭraputranāmak.): I, **117**, 4543.—§ 583 (Bhīshmavadhap.): VI, **77**κ, 3344.—§ 599 (Jayadrathavadhap.): VII, **136**$\chi\chi$, 5594 (among six sons of Dhṛtarāshṭra who are slain by Bhīmasena). Cf. Cārucitrāṅgada.
Cārucitrāṅgada, son of Dhṛtarāshṭra. § 130 (Aṃçāvat.): I, **67**, 2730. Cf. Cārucitra.
Cāruçīrsha, a muni. § 730 (Ānuçāsanik.): XIII, **18**$\iota\iota$, 1300 (*Çakrasya sakhā Ālambāyanaḥ*, had formerly gratified Çiva at Gokarṇa and obtained a hundred sons).
Cāruçravas, son of Kṛshṇa and Rukmiṇī. § 730 (Ānuçāsanik.). XIII, **14***a*, 621.
Cārudeshṇa, son of Kṛshṇa and Rukmiṇī. § 232 (Svayaṃvarap.): I, **186**, 6997 (present at the svayaṃvara of Draupadī).—§ 252 (Subhadrāharaṇap.): I, **219**, 7915.—§ 253 (Haraṇāharaṇap.): I, **221**, 7992.—§ 262 (Bhagavadyāna): II, **2**, 56. — § 273 (Rājasūyārambhap.): II, **14**, 621 (among the seven rathas of the Vṛshṇis).—§ 287 (Rājasūyikap.): II, **34**, 1275 (came to the rājasūya of Yudhishṭhira).—§ 320 (Saubhavadhop.): III, **16**, 667 (sallied

out against Çālva), 680, 681 (fights the Dānava Vivindhya); **18**, 736; **21**, 835.—§ 402 (Tīrthayātrāp.): III, **120**, 10277.—§ 570 (Sainyaniryānap.): V, **157**κ, 5331.—§ 589 (Droṇābhishekap.): VII, **11**ζ, 408.—§ 730 (Ānuçāsanik.): XIII, **14**, 617 (*Pradyumna-C°ādīn Rukmiṇyāḥ putrakān*), (*a*) 621 (enumeration of the sons of Kṛshṇa and Rukmiṇī).—§ 785 (Anugītāp.): XIV, **66**θ, 1938.—§ 793 (Mausalap.): XVI, **3**ζ, 100 (slain).

Cāruliṅga = Çiva (1000 names[2]).

Cārunetrā, an Apsaras. § 269 (Vaiçravaṇasabhāv.): II, **10**, 392 (in the palace of Kubera).

Cāruvaktra, a warrior of Skanda. § 615*u* (Skanda): IX, **45**η, 2575.

Cāruveça, son of Kṛshṇa and Rukmiṇī. § 730 (Ānuçāsanik.): XIII, **14**a, 621.

Cāruyaças, son of Kṛshṇa and Rukmiṇī. § 730 (Ānuçāsanik.): XIII, **14**a, 621.

Cārvāka, a Rākshasa, friend of Duryodhana. § 10 (Parvasaṅg.): I, **2**, 349 (*°sya vadhaḥ parva Rakshaso brahmarūpiṇaḥ*).—§ 615 (Gadāyuddhap.): IX, **64**, 3619 (will avenge the death of Duryodhana).—§ 635 (Rājadh.): XII, **35**, 1414 (*brahmacchadmā Rākshasaḥ*), 1418, 1425 (*Duryodhanasakhā*, slain).—§ 636 (do.): XII, **39**, 1432, 1440.

Cāsavaktra, a warrior of Skanda. § 615*u* (Skanda): IX, **45**η, 2578.

Cāturāçramyanetṛ (C. *°āçrama°*) = Çiva (1000 names[1]).

Caturaçva, an ancient king. § 267 (Yamasabhāv.): II, **8**, 321 (in the palace of Yama).

Caturasra = Vishṇu (1000 names).

Caturātman[1] = Kṛshṇa: XII, 1614.

Caturātman[2] = Vishṇu (1000 names).

Caturbāhu = Vishṇu (1000 names).

Caturbhāva = Vishṇu (1000 names).

Caturbhuja[1] = Vishṇu (1000 names).—Do.[2] = Kṛshṇa: V, †2512.

Caturdaṃshṭra[1], a warrior of Skanda. § 615*u* (Skanda): IX, **45**η, 2564.

Caturdaṃshṭra[2] = Vishṇu (1000 names).

Caturgati = Vishṇu (1000 names).

Cāturhotrapravartaka = Çiva (1000 names[1]).

Cāturmahārājika = Mahāpurusha (Mahāpurushastava).

Caturmukha[1] = Brahmán: III, 13560, 15821, 16547; XII, 13469.

Caturmukha[2] = Çiva (1000 names[1-2]).

Caturmūrti[1] = Brahmán: III, 13560.

Caturmūrti[2] = Vishṇu (1000 names).

Caturmūrtidhṛt = Vishṇu: XII, 13114.

Caturvaktra = Brahmán: XII, 12914, 13283, 13723 (*°sya lalāṭaprabhavaḥ putraḥ Çivaḥ*). Cf. Caturmukha.

Cāturvarṇyakara = Çiva (1000 names[1]).

Caturveda[1], pl. (*°āḥ*), a sort of pitṛs. § 270 (Brahmasabhāv.): II, **11**, 463.

Caturveda[2] = Brahmán: III, 13560.

Caturveda[3] = Çiva (1000 names[1]).

Caturvedavid = Vishṇu (1000 names).

Cāturvidya, n. (the four Vedas): XII, 1574, 1837.

Caturvyūha = Vishṇu: XII, 13604; XIII, 6964 (1000 names), 7031 (do.).

Caturyuga = Çiva (1000 names[1]).

Catushkarṇī, a mātṛ. § 615*u* (Skanda): IX, **46**θ, 2643.

Catushpatha = Çiva (1000 names[2]).

Catushpathaniketā, a mātṛ. § 615*u* (Skanda): IX, **46**θ, 2643.

Catushpatharata = Çiva (1000 names[1]).

Catushpatharatā, a mātṛ. § 615*u* (Skanda): IX, **46**θ, 2645.

Catvaravāsinī, a mātṛ. § 615*u* (Skanda): IX, **46**θ, 2629.

Caura, pl. (*°āḥ*), a people. § 739 (Ānuçāsanik.): XIII, **35**ε, 2158.

Cedi, pl. (*°ayaḥ*), a people. § 73 (Vasu): I, **63**, 2335 (*°vishayaṃ* conquered by Vasu Uparicara), 2342, 2345.—§ 190*d* (Arjuna): I, **123**, 4796 (Arjuna will subjugate *Cedi-Kāçi-Karūshān*).—§ 233 (Svayaṃvarap.): I, **187**, 7028 (*°īnām adhipaḥ*, i.e. Çiçupāla).—§ 273 (Rājasūyārambhap.): II, **14**, 582 (*Purushottamo vijñāto yo asau Cedishu durmatiḥ* (i.e. Pauṇḍraka Vāsudeva?), among the allies of Jarāsandha).—§ 290 (Çiçupālavadhap.): II, **43**, 1494 (*°rājakule jātaḥ*, sc. Çiçupāla), 1508 (*°purīṃ*, i.e. Çuktimatī).—§ 291 (do.): II, **45**, 1595 (after the slaughter of Çiçupāla, his son [Dhṛshṭaketu] was installed as king of the *C.*).—§ 347 (Nalopākhyānap.): III, **65**, 2578 (*°rājapurīṃ*, the capital of king Subāhu).—§ 350 (do.): III, **68**, 2660 (*°purīṃ*, do.).—§ 549 (Pāṇḍavapr.): IV, **1**a, 11 (*Pāñcāla-C°-Matsyāç ca*).—§ 555 (Sainyodyogap.): V, **19**γ, 576 (*°īnām ṛshabhaḥ*), i.e. Dhṛshṭaketu, came with one akshauhiṇī of troops to Yudhishṭhira).—§ 556 (Sañjayayānap.): V, **22**, †669 (*°Karūshakāḥ . . . . bhūmipālāḥ*, took the part of the Pāṇḍavas); **28**ι, 804.—§ 561 (Yānasandhip.): V, **57**, 2264 (among the allies of Yudhishṭhira); **71**a, 2594 (*°Pāñcālaiḥ*, do.).—§ 562 (Bhagavadyānap.): V, **74**γ, 2732 (*Sahajaç C°-Matsyānāṃ*).—§ 569 (do.): V, **140**a, 4743; **144**λ, 4887 (*°Pāñcāla-Kaikayāḥ*), (ν), 4896 (*°Pāñcālāḥ*).—§ 573 (Ambopākhyānap.): V, **196**η, 7623 (*°Kāçi-Karūshāṇāṃ netāraṃ . . . Dhṛshṭaketuṃ*), (λ), 7644 (*Dhṛshṭaketuç ca C°īnāṃ praṇetā*).—§ 574 (Jambūkh.): VI, **9**μ, 348 (*°Matsya-Karūshāç ca*, in Bhāratavarsha).—§ 578 (Bhīshmavadhap.): VI, **47**δ, 1811 (*°Kāçi-Karūsheshu*), (η), 1866.—§ 579 (do.): VI, **52**a, 2129 (*°Matsyeshu*); **54**, 2239, (θ), 2242 (*°Matsya-Karūshāḥ*), 2249, 2250[10].—§ 580 (do.): VI, **56**η, 2415 (*°Kāçi-Karūshaiḥ*), **59**ζ, †2640 (*°Pāñcāla-Karūsha-Matsyāḥ*).—§ 586 (do.): VI, **106**ν, 4819 (*°Kāçi-Karūshāṇāṃ*).—§ 587 (do.): VI, **115**ο, 5360; **116**π, 5446 (*°Kāçi-Karūshāṇāṃ*); **118**φ, 5565 (*Matsya-Pāñcāla-C°īnāṃ*).—§ 589 (Droṇābhish.): VII, **9**, 288 (*°Karūshaiḥ*, attack Droṇa); **10**κ, 348 (*eko 'pasṛtya C°bhyaḥ Pāṇḍavān yaḥ samāçritaḥ | Dhṛshṭaketuṃ* (!)).—§ 592 (Saṃçaptakavadhap.): VII, **21**θ, 877 (*°Kārūsha-Koçalāḥ*, attack Droṇa), (ι), 883; **22**ν, 926 (*°Kekayān*); **23**, 971 (*Dhṛshṭaketuṃ C°īnām ṛshabhaṃ*); **24**σ, 1052 (*°ayaç cāpare*); **32**aa, 1412 (*°Pāñcāla-Pāṇḍūnāṃ*).—§ 596 (Pratijñāp.): VII, **78**ε, 2744.—§ 599 (Jayadrathavadhap.): VII, **106**, 3973 (*Dhṛshṭaketuç ca C°īnām ṛshabhaḥ*); **108**ο, 4087 (*°Pāñcāla-Sṛñjayān*); **114**ω, 4539; **125**, 5042 (*Dhṛshṭaketuç ca C°īnām ṛshabhaḥ*), (μμ), 5069, 5070 (*°Pāñcāla-Sṛñjayāḥ*), 5072, 5073, 5088 (*°Pāñcāla-Sṛñjayān*).—§ 600 (Ghaṭotkacavadhap.): VII, **153**a, 6628; **156**ι, 6779 (*°Kārūsha-Koçalāḥ*); **160**δδ, 7156 (*°Pāñcāla-Somakāḥ*); **166**υ, 7459.—§ 602 (Droṇavadhap.): VII, **186**, 8489, (η), 8490 (*°Kaikeya-Sṛñjayān*), 8500 (*°-Matsyeshu*).—§ 603 (Nārāyaṇāstramokshap.): VII, **193**γ, 8919; **200**γγ, 9330 (*yuvarājaç ca C°īnāṃ*), †9342 (*°prabhuṃ yuvarājaṃ*, = do.; slain by Açvatthāman).—§ 604 (Karṇap.): VIII, **6**, 180 (*Dhṛshṭaketuḥ . . . C°īnāṃ pravaro rathaḥ*).—§ 605 (do.): VIII, **12**ββ, 459 (*°Pāñcāla-Kaikayāḥ*); **30**ζζ, 1231 (*°-Kārūsha-Matsyānāṃ*).—§ 607 (do.): VIII, **45**μ, 2085 (among those who know the eternal religion).—§ 608 (do.): VIII, **47**θ, 2224 (*Pāñcāla-C°īnāṃ*), (μ), 2229; **48**ξ, 2254 (*°Kaikeya-*

Pāñcālāḥ), 2295; **49**ω, 2359 (°*Pāṇḍava-Pāñçālāḥ*); **56**μμ, 2692 (*Pāñcālyaṃ C°-Kaikeyasaṃvṛtam*, i.e. Dhṛshṭadyumna?), 2693, (νν), 2741 (°*īnāñ ca mahārathān*), (οο), 2751 (°*Kaikeya-Pāñcāleshu*), (ππ), 2758 (°*Pāñcāla-Pāṇḍavān*); **60**βββ, 3002; **64**, 3267; **73**, 3639, 3662 (°*-Kāçi-Pāñcālān*), 3668 (°*Pāñcāla-Kaikayān*); **78**β[1], 3949 (°*Pāñcālān*); 3965, 3993.—§ 609 (Çalyap.): IX, **1**γ, 31 (have been slain); **2**ζ, 79 (do.).—§ 610 (do.): IX, **7**τ, 335; **12**ο, 645.—§ 785 (Anugītāp.): XIV, **83**, 2467 (*purīṃ ramyāṃ C°īnāṃ çuktisāhvayāṃ*, i.e. Çuktimatī).—§ 786 (do.): XIV, **91**, 2831 (°*īnām īçvaraḥ*, i.e. Vasu).—§ 791 (Putradarçanap.): XV, **36**a, 990 (do no longer exist). Cf. Cedika.

Cedidhvaja. § 561 (Yānasandhip.): V, **62**ββ, 2426 (cf. the note of PCR.).

Cedija: VI, 4255 (v. Cedipa).

Cedika, pl. (°*āḥ*), a people = Cedi. § 608 (Karṇap.): VIII, **48**, 2245.

Cedipa ("king of the Cedis"): I, 2342 (i.e. Vasu); III, 463 (i.e. Dhṛshṭaketu); V, 2857 (do.), 2950 (do.); VI, 4255 (do.?, C. has *Cedijaḥ*), 4272 (do.); VII, 1509 (do.), 2950 (do.), 9343 (*yuvarājaṃ*, whom?).

Cedipati (do.): I, 2356 (i.e. Vasu), 2361 (do.); II, 1373 (i.e. Çiçupāla), 1430 (do.), 1432 (do.), 1493 (do.), 1519 (do.), 1585 (do.), 1913 (i.e. Dhṛshṭaketu?); III, 2688 (i.e. Subāhu), 10284 (i.e. Dhṛshṭaketu); V, 672 (i.e. Çiçupāla), 2012 (i.e. Dhṛshṭaketu), 5901 (do.); XI, 727 (do.); XIII, 5650 (i.e. Vasu).

Cedipuṅgava[1] = Çiçupāla: **II**, 1412, 1426. Do.[2] = Dhṛshṭaketu: XI, 725.

Cedirāj ("king of the Cedis"): II, 1398 (i.e. Çiçupāla), 1522 (do.), 1561 (do.); III, 898 (i.e. Dhṛshṭaketu); V, 2239 (do.); VI, 1747 (do.).

Cedirāja (do.): II, 1070 (i.e. Çiçupāla), 1072 (do.), 1337 (do.), 1382 (do.), 1429 (do.), 1491 (do.), 1551 (do.), 1575 (do.), 1584 (do.); III, 2531 (i.e. Subāhu), 2576 (do.); V, 5900 (i.e. Dhṛshṭaketu); VI, 1709 (do.), 5398 (do.); VII, 394 (i.e. Çiçupāla, slain by Kṛshṇa), 1113 (i.e. Dhṛshṭaketu?), 4026 (i.e. Dhṛshṭaketu), 5056 (do., slain), †8210 (i.e. Çiçupāla), 8214 (do.), 8217 (do.), 8233 (do.); XI, 728 (i.e. Dhṛshṭaketu), 729 (do.).

Cedivṛsha = Çiçupāla: II, 1071 (*Kuru °aḥ*).

Cekita = Cekitāna[1]. § 556 (Sañjayayānap.): V, **25**η, †932 (*sa-Cekitān*, sc. the Pāṇḍavas).

Cekitāna[1], a Vṛshṇi. § 232 (Svayaṃvarap.): I, **186**, 6991 (present at the svayaṃvara of Draupadī).—§ 264 (Sabhākriyāp.): II, **4**β, 122 (among the princes present when Yudhishṭhira entered his palace).—§ 296 (Dyūtap.): II, **53**, 1916 (at the rājasūya of Yudhishṭhira C. bore Yudhishṭhira's quiver).—§ 556 (Sañjayayānap.): V, **25**ζ, †724 (among the allies of the Pāṇḍavas); **30**ν, †808 (do.).—§ 561 (Yānasandhip.): V, **57**ξ, 2233, 2251.—§ 562 (Bhagavadyānap.): V, **83**θ, 2950.—§ 569 (do.): V, **141**γ, 4780.—§ 570 (Sainyaniryāṇap.): V, **151**a, 5101, (ζ), 5164.—§ 571 (Ulūkadūtāgamanap.): V, **164**ε, 5709.—§ 573 (Ambopākhyānap.): V, **196**λ, 7644.—§ 576 (Bhagavadgītāp.): VI, **19**, 715; **25**θ, 834.—§ 578 (Bhīshmavadhap.): VI, **45**[17], 1728, 1729, 1730 (fights Suçarman).—§ 580 (do.): VI, **57**κ, 2454.—§ 582 (do.): VI, **71**ε, 3140; **72**η, 3172.—§ 583 (do.): VI, **75**a, 3286 (in the right wing of Yudhishṭhira's *makaravyūha*).—§ 584 (do.): VI, **81**[1], 3561 (fights Kṛpa); **84**, 3715 (*Vārshṇeyaḥ*, fights Kṛpa), 3716, 3721, 3723, 3728.—§ 585 (do.): VI, **89**ξ, 3949.—§ 586 (do.): VI, **99**ζ, 4511.—§ 587 (do.): VI, **108**, 4998; **109**ε, 5074; **110**, 5101 (attacked by Citrasena); **111**, 5192, (a), 5193, 5194 (fights Citrasena); **118**υ, 5553, (φ), 5558.—§ 589 (Droṇābhiskekap.): VII, **8**η, 228 (PCR. Citrasena); **10**, 360 (attacks Droṇa).—§ 590 (do.): VII, **14**, 542 (fights Anuvinda).—§ 592 (Saṃçaptakavadhap.): VII, **21**κ, 905 (attacks Droṇa), 916; **23**ο, 994 (proceeded against Droṇa, description of his horses); **26**τ, 1180.—§ 593 (Abhimanyuvadhap.): VII, **35**δ, 1508; **40**ο, 1695.—§ 597 (Pratijñāp.): VII, **83**a, 2950.—§ 598 (Jayadrathavadhap.): VII, **85**δ, 3049.—§ 599 (do.): VII, **95**, 3531 (fights Sañjaya); **125**, 5084 (attacks Droṇa), 5087 (his charioteer is slain by Droṇa).—§ 605 (Karṇap.): VIII, **12**ββ, 454; **22**ηη, 870; **30**ξξ, 1232.—§ 608 (do.): VIII, **49**χ, 2333; **93**aρ, 4873.—§ 610 (Çalyap.): IX, **3**κ, 165.—§ 611 (do.): IX, **12**, 622, 624 (slain by Duryodhana).—§ 789 (Putradarçanap.): XV, **32**θ, 879 (among the slain warriors who arose from the Gaṅgā). Cf. Sāttvata, Vārshṇeya.

Cekitāna[2] = Çiva: VII, 9453; XIII, 1216 (1000 names[1]).

Cetasaka, pl. (°*āni*), v. Vetasaka.

Chada = Çiva (1000 names[2]).

Chāgavaktra = Skanda: III, 14398.

Chandas[1] = Çiva (1000 names[2]). Do.[2] = Vishṇu (1000 names).

Chandodeva. § 735b (Indra-Mataṅga-s.): XIII, **29**, 1937 (*C°a iti khyātaḥ strīṇāṃ pūjyo bhavishyasi*, says Indra to Mataṅga, "deity of a particular measure of verse," PCR.).

Chatravatī, a city (probably instead of Chattravatī, BR.). § 217 (Caitrarathap.): I, **166**, 6348 (the residence of king Drupada). Cf. Ahicchattra.

Chattra[ṃ] = Çiva (1000 names[2]).

[Chattropānahotpatti] ("the origin of giving umbrellas and sandals at *çrāddhas*"). § 752b (Ānuçāsanik.): *Bhīshma* said: In ancient times *Jamadagni Bhārgava* was practising with his bow; [his wife] *Reṇukā* used to pick up the arrows and bring them back to him. One day, at noontide, when the Sun was in *Jyeshṭhāmūla*, *Reṇukā*, her head and feet being scorched by the heat of the Sun, rested for a moment under a tree, whereafter *Jamadagni* threatened to shoot the Sun. The Sun, in the guise of a brahman, approached him and reminded him that the Sun produces food, etc. (XIII, **95**). [Further] questioned by *Yudhishṭhira*, *Bhīshma* said: As *Jamadagni* did not desist from his anger, the brahman reminded him that the Sun is always in motion and cannot therefore be pierced; *Jamadagni*, knowing *Sūrya*, said that the Sun stays at midday for a moment. Then *Sūrya* sought his protection, and *Jamadagni* comforted him, saying "he who would slay one who asks for protection would transcend the simplicity that exists in brahmans, etc. (a)." *Sūrya* presented him with an umbrella and a pair of sandals, saying, "from this day the gift of these articles in all religious rites shall be established as an indispensable usage" (XIII, **96**).

Chāya = Çiva (1000 names[1]).

Chettṛ = Çiva (1000 names[1]).

Chinnasaṃçaya = Mahāpurusha (Mahāpurushastava).—Do.[2] = Vishṇu (1000 names).

Chinnatṛshṇa = Mahāpurusha (Mahāpurushastava).

Cicchila, pl. (°*āḥ*), a people. § 585 (Bhīshmavadhap.): VI, **87**ε, 3855 (in the array of the Kurus, followed Bṛhadbala the Kosala king, only in C.).

Cikura, a serpent, father of the serpent Sumukha. § 564 (Mātalīyop.): V, **103**, 3640 (had been devoured by Garuḍa).

Cīna, pl. (°*āḥ*), a people. § 223 (Vāsishṭha): I, **175**, 6685 (sprung from the froth of the mouth of Vasishṭha's cow).—§ 279 (Arjuna): II, **26**, 1002 (*sa Kirātaiç ca Cīnaiç ca* *vṛtaḥ Prāgjyotishaḥ*, i.e. Bhagadatta).—§ 294 (Dyūtap.): II, **51**, 1843 (bring tribute to Yudhishṭhira), 1846 (only B.: *Bālhī-Cīnasamudbhavam aurṇam*).—§ 342 (Indralokābhigamanap.): III, **51**, 1991 (present at the rājasūya of Yudhishṭhira).—§ 449 (Ājagarap.): III, **177**, †12350 (on their way from Himālaya to king Subāhu the Pāṇḍavas crossed the country of the *C.*).—§ 555 (Sainyodyogap.): V, **19**γ, 584 (*C°aiḥ Kirātaiç ca*, follow Bhagadatta).—§ 562 (Bhagavadyānap.): V, **74**γ, 2730 (*C°ānāṃ Dhautamūlakaḥ*); **86**, 3049 (*vājinām ca sahasrāṇi C°deçodbhavāni ca*).—§ 574 (Jambūkh.): VI, **9**ζ, 373 (*Yavanāç C°-Kāmbojāḥ*, among the peoples of the north), 374.—§ 641 (Rājadh.): XII, **65**θ, 2429.—§ 713 (Çukakṛti): XII, **326**, 12229 (*deçān . . . C°-Hūnanishevitān*).

Cīnaka, pl. (°*āḥ*), a people = the Cīnas. § 604 (Karṇap.): VIII, **8**, 236 (*Puṇḍra-C°ān*, vanquished by Karṇa).

Cintyadyotāḥ, a gaṇa of gods. § 730 (Ānuçāsanik.): XIII, **18**λλ, †1373.

Cirakāri, Cirakārika, Cirakārin, son of Gautama. § 682 (Mokshadh.): XII, **267**, 9482 (°*eḥ*, C. °*aiḥ*, *Āngirase kule*), 9484 (°*ī . . . . Gautamasya sutaḥ*), 9485 (°*ī*), 9489 (°*kaḥ*), 9534–8 (?), 9539 (°*iṃ*), 9540 (°*ī*), 9547 (?).

Cirāntaka, a Suparṇa, son of Garuḍa. § 564 (Mātalīyop.): V, **101**β, 3598.

Cīravāsas[1], a king. § 130 (Aṃçāvat.): I, **67**, 2697 (among the incarnations from the Krodhavaçagaṇa).

Cīravāsas[2], a Yaksha. § 269 (Vaiçravaṇasabhāv.): II, **10**, 399 (among the Yakshas in the palace of Kubera).

Cīravāsas[3] = Çiva: VII, 9504; XIII, 1160 (1000 names[2]); XIV, 196.

Ciriṇī, a river. § 457 (Vaivasvatop.): III, **187**, 12751.

Citibhasmapriya = Çiva (1000 names[1]).

Citra[1], son of Dhṛtarāshṭra. § 130 (Aṃçāvat.): I, **67**, 2730.—§ 182 (Dhṛtarāshṭraputranāmak.): I, **117**, 4543.—§ 599 (Jayadrathavadhap.): VII, **136**χχ, 5594 (among seven sons of Dhṛtarāshṭra slain by Bhīmasena); **137**aaa, 5644 (the same?, among seven sons of Dhṛtarāshṭra slain by Bhīmasena).

Citra[2], a serpent. § 268 (Varuṇasabhāv.): II, **9**, 360 (in the palace of Varuṇa).—§ 496 (Skandotpatti): III, **225**, 14321 (*mahānāgau C°ç cairāvatau*).

Citra[3], a Pāṇḍava warrior. § 592 (Saṃçaptakavadhap.): VII, **23**o, 1013 (proceeded against Droṇa, description of his horses, etc.).

Citra[4], brother of Citrasena, the Abhisāra king. § 604 (Karṇap.): VIII, **11**φ, 420 (*C°ç ca Citrasenaç ca*, in the makaravyūha of the Kurus); **13**, 493; **14**, 545, 546, 551, 553, 554, 557, 559 (slain by Prativindhya).

Citra[5], a Pāñcāla warrior. § 608 (Karṇap.): VIII, **56**νν, 2735, 2740 (slain by Karṇa).

Citrā, a nakshatra (v. Su° Si.). § 569 (Bhagavadyānap.): V, **143**θ, 4842 (°*āṃ pīḍayate grahaḥ*, omens).—§ 574 (Jambūkh.): VI, **3**, 79 (*çveto grahaḥ* (i.e. Ketu, Nīl.) *tathā C°āṃ samatikramya tishṭhati*, omens), 85 (*C°-Svātyantare caiva vishṭhitaḥ* (C. *dhishṭhitaḥ*) *purushagrahaḥ*, do.).—§ 746 (Ānuçāsanik.): XIII, **64**, 3268 (by making a gift of a bull and perfumes under the constellation *C.*, one goes to the world of the Apsarases).—§ 749 (do.): XIII, **89**a, 4261 (by performing çrāddhas under the constellation *C.*, one obtains beautiful children).—759 (do.): XIII, **110**a, 5394 (? C. has *C°ram*, B. *Mitram*, description of the candravrata).

Citrabāhu, son of Dhṛtarāshṭra. § 130 (Aṃçāvat.): I, **67**, 2730.

Citrabarha, a Suparṇa, son of Garuḍa. § 564 (Mātalīyop.): **101**β, 3597 (C. *Citrav°*).

Citrabarhin, son of Garuḍa. § 615u (Skanda): IX, **46**, 2669 (? given by Garuḍa to Skanda; PCR. takes this as an appellative, "a peacock of beautiful feathers").

Citrabhānu[1] = Agni (q.v.)

Citrabhānu[2] = Çiva (1000 names[1]).

Citracāpa, son of Dhṛtarāshṭra. § 130 (Aṃçāvat.): I, **67**, 2733.

Citraçikhaṇḍin[1] = Mahāpurusha (Mahāpurushast.).

Citraçikhaṇḍin[2], pl. (°*aḥ*), = the seven Ṛshis. § 717c (Uparicara): XII, **336**, 12722 (i.e. Marīci, etc.), 12725; **337**, *12754 (*çāstram C°jam*).—Do.[3], pl. (°*aḥ*), = Ekata, Dvita, and Trita.—§ 717c (Uparicara): XII, **337**, 12771 (PCR. translates: well conversant with the science of morality and duties compiled by the seven Ṛshis).

Citraçilā, a river. § 574 (Jambūkh.): VI, **9**λ, 337 (only B.; C. has Antraçilā).

Citrāçva = Satyavat: III, 16670 (etymology); XIII, 7675 (*Satyavān*).

Citradeva, a warrior of Skanda. § 615u (Skanda): IX, **45**η, 2573.

Citradharman, a prince. § 130 (Aṃçāvat.): I, **67**, 2658 (the re-born Asura Virūpāksha).

Citragupta. § 766 (Ānuçāsanik.): XIII, **125**a, 5924 ("the recording assistant of Yama," PCR.); **130**, 6114, 6118, 6120, 6134, 6135.

Citraka[1], son of Dhṛtarāshṭra. § 130 (Aṃçāvat.): I, **67**, 2740.

Citraka[2], pl. (°*āḥ*), a people. § 294 (Dyūtap.): II, **50**, 1804 (are living in the palace of Yudhishṭhira as his bondsmen).

Citraketu[1], a Suparṇa, son of Garuḍa. § 564 (Mātalīyop.): V, **101**β, 3597.

Citraketu[2], a Pāṇḍava warrior. § 585 (Bhīshmavadhap.): VI, **95**εε, 4272.—§ 599 (Jayadrathavadhap.): VII, **122**u, 4903 (brother of the Pāñcala prince Vīraketu and slain by Droṇa).

Citraketusuta = Suketu: VIII, 2630.

Citrāksha, son of Dhṛtarashṭra. § 130 (Aṃçāvat.): I, **67**, 2730.—§ 182 (Dhṛtarāshṭraputranāmak.): I, **117**, 4543.—§ 599 (Jayadrathavadhap.): VII, **136**χχ, 5594 (slain by Bhīmasena).

Citrakuṇḍala, son of Dhṛtarāshṭra. § 182 (Dhṛtarāshṭraputranāmak.): I, **117**, 4545, 4552 (also B.; V. *Dīrghalocana*).

Citrakūṭa, a mountain. § 372 (Tīrthayātrāp.): III, **85**, 8200 (*girivaraçreshṭhe* with the tīrtha Mandākinī).—§ 527 (Rāmopākhyānap.): III, **277**, 15982 (during his exile Rāma dwelt on *C.*).—§ 534 (Hanūmatpratyāgamana): III, **282**, 16266.—§ 733m (Ānuçāsanik.): If one observing a fast bathes at *C.* and Janasthāna, and in the water of Mandākinī, he is sure to obtain royal prosperity: XIII, **25**, 1715.—§ 775 (Ānuçāsanik.): XIII, **166**a, 7658.

Citralekhā, an Apsaras. § 336 (Indralokābh.): III, **43**a, 1785 (in the world of Indra).

Citrāṅga, son of Dhṛtarāshṭra. § 182 (Dhṛtarāshṭraputranāmak.): I, **117**, 4545.

Citrāṅgada[1], son of Çāntanu and Satyavatī. § 11 (Parvasaṅgr.): I, **2**, 374.—§ 156 (Pūruvaṃç.): I, **95**, ††3803 (son of Çāntanu and Satyavatī and brother of Vicitravīrya).—§ 166 (Citrāṅgadop.): I, **101**, 4068 (do.), 4071 (after the death of Çāntanu, *C.* was installed as king), 4072, 4076 (slain by the Gandharva king of the same name).—§ 167

(Vicitravīryop.): I, **102**, 4081 (*hate*).—§ 572 (Rathātirathas.): V, **172**, 5938 (repetition of § 166).—§ 573 (Ambopākhyānap.): V, **173**, 5946 (do.).—§ 787 (Āçramavāsap.): XV, **10**, 320 (*yathā*).

Citrāṅgada[2], a prince. § 232 (Svayaṃvarap.): I, **186**, 7002 (°-*Çubhāṅgadau*, present at the svayaṃvara of Draupadī).

Citrāṅgada[3], a Kuru warrior. § 604 (Karṇap.): VIII, **7**, †209 (in the enumeration of the Kuru warriors who were still alive).

Citrāṅgada[4], a Kaliṅga king. § 621 (Rājadh.): XII, **4**, 109 (*tataḥ kadācid rājānaḥ samājagmuḥ svayaṃvare | Kaliṅgavishaye rājan rājñaç Citrāṅgadasya ca çrīmad Rājapuraṃ nāma nagaraṃ*).

Citrāṅgada[5], a Daçārṇa king. § 785 (Anugītāp.): XIV, **83**, 2471 (when the sacrificial horse, followed by Arjuna, came to the country of the Daçārṇas, their king *C.* was vanquished by Arjuna).

Citrāṅgadā[1], daughter of Citravāhana and mother of Babhruvāhana. § 11 (Parvasaṅg.): I, **2**, 608 (°*āyāḥ putreṇa putrikāyāḥ*, i.e. Babhruvāhana).—§ 249 (Arjunavanavāsap.): I, **215**, 7826 (the only child of king Citravāhana in Maṇipūra, whom he made a putrikā, married to Arjuna).—§ 250 (do.): I, **217**, 7883 (*C.'s* and Arjuna's son Babhruvāhana is installed upon the throne in Maṇipūra).—§ 785 (Anugītāp.): XIV, **79**, 2339; **80**, (2352); **81**, 2405 (*Caitravāhanī*), 2425 (*Kauravyaduhituḥ*); **88**, 2604: In the encounter between Arjuna and Babhruvāhana both fell down in a swoon. Babhruvāhana regained consciousness and *C.* prevailed upon Ulūpī to revive Arjuna.—§ 787 (Āçramavāsap.): XV, **1***a*, 23 (waited upon Gāndhārī); **15**ν, †437 (accompanies Dhṛtarāshṭra and Gāndhārī to the forest).—§ 788 (do.): XV, **25**γ, †666.—§ 794 (Mahāprasthānikap.): XVII, **1**, 28 (sets out for Maṇipūra). Cf. Caitravāhanī.

Citrāṅgadā[2], an Apsaras. § 731*b* (Ashṭāvakra-Diksaṃv.): XIII, **19**β, 1424 (enumeration).

Citrāṅgadāsuta, "son of Citrāṅgadā" = Babhruvāhana: XIV, 2326.

Citrāṅgadātmaja, do. = Babhruvāhana: XIV, 2337, 2431.

Citrāṅgadopākhyāna(ṃ), "episode relating to Citrāṅgada." § 166 (cf. Satyavatīlābhop.): I, **101**. Two sons were born of *Satyavatī*, *Citrāṅgada* and *Vicitravīrya*. Before the last had attained to majority, *Çāntanu* died and ascended to heaven. *Bhīshma* placed *Citrāṅgada* on the throne. *Citrāṅgada* considered nobody his equal, not even the gods and *Asuras*. Therefore the king of the *Gandharvas* bearing the same name fought a three years' battle with him at *Kurukshetra* on the banks of the *Sarasvatī*, where *Citrāṅgada* was slain; then the *Gandharva* ascended to heaven. *Bhīshma* installed *Vicitravīrya*, yet in his minority, on the throne of the *Kurus* and ruled for him. (For continuation v. Vicitravīryop.)

Citraratha[1], king of the Gandharvas. § 101 (Aṃçavat.): I, **65**, 2551 (among the Devagandharvas, sons of Muni).—§ 191 (Arjuna): I, **123**, 4813 (among the Devagandharvas present at the birth of Arjuna).—§ 221 (Caitrarathap.): I, **170**, 6475 (*so 'haṃ C°o bhūtva nāmnā Dagdharatho 'bhavaṃ*, says the Gandharva, who, v. 6448, had named himself Aṅgāraparṇa).—§ 269 (Vaiçravaṇasabhāv.): II, **10**, 407 (among the Gandharvas in the palace of Kubera).—§ 295 (Dyūtap.): II, **52**, 1880 (*rājā C°o Gandharvo Vāsavānugaḥ*, had given 400 horses to Yudhishṭhira).—§ 298 (do.): II, **61**, 2083 (had given horses to Arjuna).—§ 561*h* (Arjuna): V, **56**, †2226 (*sadaçvāḥ . . . . C°ena dattāḥ*, i.e. Arjuna's).—§ 576 (Bhagavadgītāp.): VI, **34**, 1230 (*Gandharvāṇāṃ C°aḥ*, sc. *asmi*, says Kṛshṇa).—§ 595 (Shoḍaçarāj., v. Pṛthu Vainya): VII, **69**, 2418 (when the Gandharvas milked the Earth *C.* was their calf). Cf. Aṅgāraparṇa, Dagdharatha, Gandharva, Gandharvarāja.

Citraratha[2], king of Mṛttikāvatī. § 396 (Jamadagni): III, **116**, 10176 (*Mārttikāvatakaṃ nṛpaṃ*, seeing him bathing, Reṇukā, the wife of Jamadagni, became filled with desire).

Citraratha[3], brother of the Pāñcāla prince Vīraketu. § 599 (Jayadrathavadhap.): VII, **122**ιι, 4903 (slain by Droṇa).

Citraratha[4], an Aṅga king. § 743*b* (Vipulop.): XIII, **42**, 2351 (*Aṅgeçvarasya*, the husband of Prabhāvatī). Cf. Aṅgapati, Aṅgeçvara, Aṅgendra.

Citraratha[5], the great-grandfather of Kṛshṇa. § 768*b* (Kṛshṇa Vāsudeva): XII, **147**, 6839 (son of Rshadgu and father of Çūra).

Citrarathā, a river. § 574 (Jambūkh.): VI, **9**λ, 341 (in Bhāratavarsha).

Citrasaini, v. Caitraseni.

Citrasena[1], son of Dhṛtarāshṭra. § 83 (Ādivaṃçāvatāraṇa): I, **63***a*, 2447 (is a mahāratha).—§ 157 (Pūruv.): I, **95**, ††3810.—§ 232 (Svayaṃvarap.): I, **186**, 6983 (present at the svayaṃvara of Draupadī).—§ 244 (Rājyalābhap.): I, **207**, 7557 (receives the Pāṇḍavas).—§ 298 (Dyūtap.): II, **58**, †2004 (among those who have come to play with Yudhishṭhira).—§ 512 (Ghoshayātrāp.): III, **242**, 14920 (*Viviṃçati-C°au*, were captured by the Gandharvas).—§ 552 (Goharaṇap.): IV, **35***a*, 1151; **54**, 1666 (attacks Arjuna).—§ 556 (Sañjayayānap.): V, **30**, †894 (*durjayo devitavyena*).—§ 561 (Yānasandhip.): V, **47***a*, 1798; **55**ν, 2207; **66**εε, 2503.—§ 576 (Bhagavadgītāp.): VI, **17**γ, 657 (followed Açvatthāman); **18**δ, 686 (protected Bhīshma).—§ 578 (Bhīshmavadhap.): VI, **44***a*, 1653 (attacks Bhīmasena); **48**[34] θ, 1926 (attacks Çveta); **51**σ, 2099.—§ 580 (do.): VI, **59**ρ, †2647 (*Durmarshaṇa-C°au*, have been vanquished by Arjuna).—§ 581 (do.): VI, **60***a*, †2652; **61**[2]γ, 2680 (fights Abhimanyu); **62**[5]ζ, 2731, 2741.—§ 582 (do.): VI, **71**[10]δ, 3139 (fights Çikhaṇḍin); **73**[11]θ, 3220, 3222, 3223 (fights Abhimanyu).—§ 583 (do.): VI, **77**[3]κ, 3343; **78**[10], 3423 (*tava*, i.e. Dhṛtarāshṭra's, *putraṃ*); **79**, 3435 (fights Abhimanyu).—§ 584 (do.): VI, **81***a*, 3534, 3547 (°*ādayaḥ*), β, 3558; **84**γ, 3735; **85**ε, †3768, †3787; **86**, 3791.—§ 585 (do.): VI, **87***a*, 3849; **92**χ, 4119, 4129 (attacked by Ghaṭotkaca); **94**ω, 4195.—§ 586 (do.): VI, **104**, 4747 (fights Abhimanyu).—§ 587 (do.): VI, **108**δ, 5050; **110**, 5101 (fights Cekitāna); **111**, 5192 (*tava sutaḥ*), 5194; **113**ι, 5240, 5243, 5249, 5257, 5261 (fights Bhīmasena); **114**κ, 5293, 5295, 5297 (°*ādayaç caiva putrās tava*); **116**, 5402, 5404 (fights Suçarman); **118**τ, 5519.—§ 589 (Droṇābhishekap.): VII, **7**δ, 181.—§ 596 (Pratijñāp.): VII, **74**β, 2627 (will protect Jayadratha).—§ 598 (Jayadrathavadhap.): VII, **85***a*, 3020.—§ 599 (do.): VII, **95**ζ, 3525; **96**θ, 3572 (fights Bhīmasena); **116***aa*, 4605 (fights Sātyaki), 4608, 4626; **120**δδ, 4767, 4790, 4794 (fights Sātyaki); **127**, 5176; **137***aaa*, 5644 (among seven sons of Dhṛtarāshṭra who are slain by Bhīmasena), 5664 (*hataḥ*); **152**, 6580 (*adya me bhrātaraḥ kshīṇāç C°ādayaḥ*, says Duryodhana).—§ 600 (Ghaṭotkacavadhap.): VII, **158**ω, 7035 (among the dead); **164**θθ, 7337 (? is still living, brother of Duryodhana); **165**, 7370 (fights Çatānīka); **168**, 7512 (do.), 7513, 7514, 7519, 7520, 7521.—§ 604 (Karṇap.): VIII, **5**ζ, 111 (has been slain by Bhīmasena); **7**, †206 (? among other sons of Dhṛtarāshṭra who are staying desirous of battle).—§ 618 (Jalapradānikap.): XI, **1**γ, 28 (had been the counsellor of Duryodhana).—§ 619 (Strīvilāpap.): XI, **19**δ, 557 (*Dhārtarāshṭram*, among the dead).

Citrasena[2], son of the elder Parikshit. § 154 (Pūruvaṃç.): I, **94**, 3743.

Citrasena[3], a Gandharva. § 264 (Sabhākriyāp.): II, **4**, 131 (in Yudhishṭhira's palace).—§ 266 (Çakrasabhāv.): II, **7**, 303 (in the palace of Indra).—§ 269 (Vaiçravaṇasabhāv.): II, **10**, 407 (among the Gandharvas in the palace of Kubera). —§ 337 (Indralokābhig.): III, **44**, 1793, 1795 (Arjuna learnt music and dancing from Citrasena and became his friend).—§ 338 (do.): III, **45**, 1800, 1814; **46**, 1838, 1847, 1868, 1869, 1870, 1876 (*C.* urges Urvaçī to go to Arjuna, who rejects her and is cursed by her).—§ 443 (Nivātakavacayuddhap.): III, **168**, 12048 (*Viçvāvasoç ca vai putraḥ*, became the friend of Arjuna).—§ 512 (Ghoshayātrāp.): III, **241**, 14887, 14888, 14895, 14896, 14901, 14903; **242**, 14918; **245**, 14998, 15006, 15008; **246**, 15010, (15012), 15018, (15019), 15026 (°*mukhāḥ*, sc. *Gandharvāḥ*: When Duryodhana and his brothers had been captured by the Gandharvas, the Pāṇḍavas, in order to deliver them, attacked the Gandharvas. Arjuna vanquished *C.*, who made himself known to him as his friend, and set the captives free).—§ 513 (do.): III, **247**, 15067 (repetition).—§ 552 (Goharaṇap.): IV, **49**, 1538 (had been vanquished by Arjuna, cf. § 512); **64**, 2072 (praises Arjuna).—§ 601 (Droṇavadhap.): VII, **185**, 8435 (*Gandharvān ghoshayātrāyāṃ C°ādayo jitāḥ*, sc. by Arjuna, cf. § 512).—§ 607 (Karṇap.): VIII, **41**, 1952 (*hatvā jitvā ca Gandharvāṃç C°mukhān*, cf. § 512).—§ 623 (Rājadh.): XII, **16**, 501 (°*ena cāhavaṃ*, cf. § 512).—§ 662*b* (Jāpakop.): XII, **200**δ, 7341 (*Gandharvaḥ*).—§ 775 (Ānuçāsanik.): XIII, **166***a*, 7640.—§ 779 (Açvamedhikap.): XIV, **12**, 324 (°*enena çāhavaḥ*, cf. § 512).—§ 785 (Anugītāp.): XIV, **88**ψ, 2642 (among the Gandharvas present at the açvamedha of Yudhishṭhira).—§ 789 (Putradarçanap.): XV, **29***a*, 774. Cf. Gandharva, Gandharvarāj, Gandharvarāja, Gandharvarājan.

Citrasena[4], the general of king Jarāsandha. § 277 (Jarāsandhav.): II, **22**, 885 (formerly named Ḍimbhaka).

Citrasena[5], a prince. § 604 (Karṇap.): VIII, **6**, 165 (*Sāmudraḥ*, he has been slain by Samudrasena, together with his son).

Citrasena[6], king of the Abhisāras, brother of Citra. § 605 (Karṇap.): VIII, **11**φ, 420 (*bhrātarau Citraç Citrasenaç ca*); **13**, 493 (fights Çrutakarman); **14**, 526, [527 (Abhisāraḥ)], 528, 531, 532, 540 (slain by Çrutakarman, while Citra is slain by Prativindhya).

Citrasena[7], a Pāñcāla warrior. § 608 (Karṇap.): VIII, **48**γ, 2248 (among five Pāñcālas slain by Karṇa).

Citrasena[8], brother of Karṇa. § 608 (Karṇap.): VIII, **75**χχχ, †3811 (? fights Yudhāmanyu); **83**, †4243, †4244 (slain by Yudhāmanyu), †4247 (*tasmin hate bhrātari C°e kruddhaḥ Karṇaḥ*).

Citrasena[9], a serpent. § 608 (Karṇap.): VIII, **87**χ[1], 4414 (*Vāsukiç C°ç ca Takshako Maṇikas tathā*, sided with Arjuna).

Citrasena[10], son of Karṇa. § 611 (Çalyap.): IX, **10**, 468 (fights Nakula), 471, 477, 479, 480 (slain by Nakula), [481 (*viçastaṃ bhrātaraṃ dṛshṭvā Karṇaputrau mahārathau*)].

Citrasena[11], various Kuru warriors. § 604 (Karṇap.): VIII, **7**, 209 (PCR. has Citravarman).—§ 605 (do.): VIII, **27**, 1078 (= Çrutasena, v. 1087 ?).—§ 608 (do.): VIII, **61**, 3078 (attacked by Yudhishṭhira = Citrasena[10] ?). —§ 610 (Çalyap.): IX, **6**ξ, 293.

Citrasenā[1], an Apsaras. § 269 (Vaiçvavanasabhāv.): II, **10**, 392 (in the palace of Kubera).—§ 336 (Indralokābh.): III, **43***a*, 1785 (dances in Indra's palace).

Citrasenā[2], a river. § 574 (Jambūkh.): VI, **9**λ, 325 (in Bhāratavarsha).

Citrasenā[3], a mātṛ. § 615*u* (Skanda): IX, **46**θ, 2632.

Citravahā, a river. § 574 (Jambūkh.): VI, **9**λ, 325 (in Bhāratavarsha).—§ 775 (Ānuçāsanik.): XIII, **166***a*, 7652.

Citravāhana, king of Maṇipūra. § 249 (Arjunavanavāsap.): I, **215**, 7826 (*Maṇipūreçvaraṃ*, gave his daughter Citrāṅgadā in marriage to Arjuna).

Citravāṇa (B. °*bāṇa*), son of Dhṛtarāshṭra. § 182 (Dhṛtarāshṭraputranāmak.): I, **117**, 4545. Cf. Citrabāhu.

Citravarman[1], son of Dhṛtarāshṭra. § 130 (Aṃçāvat.): I, **67**, 2732.—§ 182 (Dhṛtarāshṭraputranāmak.): I, **117**, 4545. — § 599 (Jayadrathavadhap.): VII, **136**χχ, 5595 (among seven sons of Dhṛtarāshṭra who are slain by Bhīmasena).

Citravarman[2], a prince. § 554 (Sainyodyogap.): V, **4**γ, 76.

Citravarman[3], brother of Vīraketu. § 599 (Jayadrathavadhap.): VII, **122***u*, 4903 (slain by Droṇa).

Citravarman[4], son of Sucitra. § 604 (Karṇap.): VIII, **6**, 177 (*Sucitraç C°ā ca pitāpitrau mahārathau*, have been slain by Droṇa).

Citravegika, a serpent. § 67 (Sarpasattra): I, **57**, 2159 (of Dhṛtarāshṭra's race).

Citrāyudha[1], son of Dhṛtarāshṭra. § 182 (Dhṛtarāshṭraputranāmak.): I, **117**, 4547. — § 571 (Ulūkadūtāg.): V, **160**, 5531 (in the army of Duryodhana). — § 599 (Jayadrathavadhap.): VII, **136**χχ, 5595 (among seven sons of Dhṛtarāshṭra who are slain by Bhīmasena); **137***aaa*, 5644 (among seven sons of Dhṛtarāshṭra who are slain by Bhīmasena).

Citrāyudha[2], a prince. § 186 (Svayaṃvarap.): I, **186**, 6990 (present at the svayaṃvara of Draupadī).

Citrāyudha[3], one or more princes who sided with the Pāṇḍavas. § 572 (Rathātirathas.): V, **171**, 5909 (*nṛpatiḥ*, is a Ratha and attached to Arjuna). — § 592 (Saṃçaptakavadhap.): VII, **23***o*, 1003 (proceeded against Droṇa, description of his horses), 1011 (do., do., the same ?).—§ 604 (Karṇap.): VIII, **6**, 167 (had been slain by Vikarṇa).— § 608 (do.): VIII, **56**νν, 2740 (slain by Karṇa).

Citrāyudha[4], a Kuru warrior. § 604 (Karṇap.): VIII, **7**γ, †207 (among the Kuru warriors who were still alive).

Citropalā, a river. § 574 (Jambūkh.): VI, **9**λ, 341 (in Bhāratavarsha).

Civuka, pl. (°*āḥ*), a barbarous people. § 223 (Vāsishṭha): I, **175**, 6685 (issued from the froth of the mouth of Vasishṭha's cow).

Cola[1], pl. (°*āḥ*), a people in the present Tanjore (BR.). § 342 (Indralokābh.): III, **34**, 1988 (*mahīpālān . . . . so-Cola-Draviḍāndhrakān*, present at the rājasūya of Yudhishṭhira).—§ 574 (Jambūkh.): VI, **9**ν, 357 (in the south).— § 589 (Droṇābhishekap.): VII, **11**ν, 398 (had been vanquished by Kṛshṇa). — § 605 (Karṇap.): VIII, **12**ββ, 455 (fight on the side of the Pāṇḍavas).

Cola[2], "king of the Colas." § 295 (Dyūtap.): II, **52**, 1893 (°*Pāṇḍyau*, bring tribute to Yudhishṭhira).

Cucuka, pl. (°*āḥ*), a people. § 664 (Mokshadh.): XII, **207**η, 7559 (in the south, only C., B. has *Cūcukāḥ*).

Cūcuka, v. Cucuka.

Cucupa, v. Cūcupa.

Cūcupa, pl. (°*āḥ*), a people. § 569 (Bhagavadyānap.): V,

140β, 4751 (only B., C. has *Cucupāḥ*).—§ 583 (Bhīshmavadhap.): VI, **75**ε, 3297 (only B., C. has *Cūlikaiḥ*).

Culakā, v. Culukā.

Cūlika, v. Cūcupa.

Culukā, a river. § 574 (Jambūkh.): VI, **9**λ, 328 (in Bhāratavarsha, only B., C. has *Culakā*).

Cyavana[1], a ṛshi, son of Bhṛgu. § 11 (Parvasaṅg.): I, **2**, 445 (*Saukanyam api cākhyānaṃ C°o yatra Bhārgavaḥ | Çaryātiyajñe Nāsatyau kṛtavān somapītinau*).—§ 19 (Bhṛgu): I, **5**, 870 (son of Bhṛgu), 871 (father of Pramati).—§ 20 (Pulomā): I, **5**, 874 (°*tvaṃ*); **6**, 898 (dropped—*cyutaḥ*—from the womb of his mother Pulomā and therefore called *C.*), 900 (*Bhārgavaṃ*), 904 (°*syāçramaṃ*, at Vadhūsarā), 905; **7**, 938.—§ 21 (Paulomap.): I, **8**, 939 (*Bhārgavaḥ*, begot on Sukanyā the son Pramati).—§ 55 (Āstīka): I, **48**, 1928 (*Bhārgavāt*, the preceptor of Āstīka).—§ 59 (Sarpasattra): I, **53**, 2045 (*Caṇḍabhārgava*, the hotṛ at the snake-sacrifice of Janamejaya was of *C.*'s race).—§ 122 (Aṃçāvat.): I, **66**, 2609 (son of Bhṛgu and Pulomā, married to Ārushī, the daughter of Manu, and father of Aurva).—§ 270 (Brahmasabhāv.): II, **11**, 440 (in the palace of Brahmán).—§ 377 (Dhaumyatīrthak.): III, **89**, 8365 (°*syāçramaḥ*, in the south).—§ 384 (Agastyop.): III, **102**, 8740 (°*syāçramaṃ*, there 100 ascetics were slain by the Kālakeyas).—§ 404 (Tīrthayātrāp.): III, **121**, 10313.—§ 405 (Sukanyop.): III, **122**, 10316 (*Bhṛgor maharsheḥ putraḥ*, practised austerities), 10338 (*Bhārgavaḥ*), 10341, 10344 (married Sukanyā, the daughter of king Çaryāti); **123**, 10348, 10354, 10356, 10359, 10361, 10366, 10370 (turned into a youth by the grace of the Açvins); **124**, 10371, 10375, 10377 (*Bhārgavaḥ*), 10378, (10380), 10388 (at the sacrifice of Çaryāti *C.* took up soma for the Açvins; Indra forbade it, but *C.* paralysed Indra's arm and created the Asura Mada); **125**, 10397 (then Indra consented to admit the Açvins to the soma sacrifice). — § 491 (Āṅgirasa): III, **220**, 14156 (a fire, *Āṅgirasaḥ*?).—§ 547 (Karṇa): III, **304**, 17035 (*aparādhe 'pi rājendra rājñām açreyase dvijāḥ | bhavanti Cyavano yadvat Sukanyāyāḥ kṛte purā*, cf. § 405).—§ 551 (Kīcakavadhap.): IV, **21**, 650 (*purā Sukanyā bhāryyā ca Bhārgavaṃ C°ṃ vane valmīkabhūtaṃ çāmyantam anvapadyata bhāminī*, cf. § 405).—§ 565 (Gālavac.): V, **117**, 3970 (*Cyavanaḥ Sukanyāyāṃ . . . . yathā*).—§ 573 (Ambop.): V, **186**a, 7353 (°*syāçrame*, visited by Ambā). — § 605 (Rājadh.): XII, **37**, 1354 (*Bhārgavāt*, preceptor of Bhīshma); **47**a, 1595 (among the ṛshis who surrounded Bhīshma on his arrow-bed).—§ 717*b* (Nārāyaṇīya): XII, **343**, III), ††13206 (cf. § 405).—§ 718*b* (Ūnchavṛttyup.): XII, **366**, 13935 (*Bhārgavam*).—§ 721*b* (Viçvāmitrop.): XIII, **4**, 207 (°*syātmasambhavaḥ | Ṛcīka iti vikhyātaḥ*), 212 (°*syātmajuḥ*, i.e. Ṛcīka). —§ 704 (Ānuçāsanik.): XIII, **26**a, 1762.—§ 745 (do.): XIII, **50**, 2642 (*Nahushasya ca saṃvādaṃ maharsheç C°sya ca*).—§ 745*b* (Cyavanop.): XIII, **50**, 2643 (*maharshiç C°o Bhārgavaḥ*), 2659 (*Bhṛgunandanaṃ*), 2665; **51**, 2668, 2669, (2672), (2674), (2676), (2678), (2680), 2691 (*Bhṛgoḥ putraṃ*), 2693, (2705), 2709 (*Bhṛgūdvahaḥ*), 2712 (*C.* having been caught in the net of some fishers, the price of him is settled to be a cow); **52**, 2722 (°*sya saṃvādaṃ Kuçikasya ca*).— § 745*c* (Cyavana-Kuçikasaṃv.): XIII, **52**, 2723, 2725, 2728, 2730, 2734 (*Bhārgavaḥ*), 2750; **53**, 2757, 2774, 2776 (*Bhṛgunandanaḥ*), 2780, 2783, 2809, 2818; **54**, 2844, 2852 (*brahmarsheḥ*), 2854, 2855; **55**, (2867), (2876); **56**, (2904), 2919, 2920, 2922 (*C.* will destroy the race of Kuçika, but is gratified by him, and promises that Viçvāmitra, a descendant of Kuçika, will become a brahman).—§ 747*b* (Suvarṇotpatti): XIII, **85**η, 4145 (the first of the seven sons of Bhṛgu). —§ 759 (Ānuçāsanik.): XIII, **106**δ, 5200 (attained to heaven by fast).—§ 772*n* (Pavanārjunasaṃv.): *Vāyu* said: "According to his promise to the *Açvins*, *C.* ordered *Indra* to let the A. drink soma with the gods; *Indra* refused because A. were not regarded as equal to D.; *C.* maintained that they were gods, being the sons of *Sūrya*. Then *C.* began a religious rite for the benefit of A.; D. became stupefied by him with his *mantras*; *Indra* attacked him with a mountain and his thunderbolt; *C.* paralysed him, sprinkling him with water; from his libations he created a terrible foe to *Indra* named *Mada* (*o*); while standing in the mouth of *Mada*, the gods prevailed upon *Indra* to obey *C.*, who distributed *Mada* into dice, hunting, drinking, and women, which faults lead men to destruction. Name you a *kshatriya* superior to that brahman": XIII, **157**, 7305, 7306, (7309), (7312), 7313, 7314, 7315, 7321, 7322, 7324. — § 772*p* (Kapa, pl.): XIII, **158**, 7327, 7329 (took away the earth from the gods).—§ 775 (Ānuçāsanik.): XIII, **166**ζ, 7673 (*Bhārgavaḥ*, among the ṛshis of the north).—§ 778*b* (Saṃvartta-Maruttīya): XIV, **9**, †249, †250 (cf. § 405). Cf. Āṅgirasa, Bhārgava, Bhṛgu[3], Bhṛguçārdūla[1], Bhṛgūdvaha, Bhṛgukulakīrtivardhana, Bhṛgukulodvaha[1], Bhṛgumukhya, Bhṛgunandana[3], Bhṛgusuta.

Cyavana[2]: XIII, 7676 (error in C. instead of Pavana (B.), PCR. has Yavana).

[Cyavana-Kuçika-saṃvāda(ḥ)], "the discourse between *Cyavana* and *Kuçika*." § 745*c* (Cyavanop.): *Bhīshma* said: *Cyavana Bhārgava* saw the stain that would affect his own race and desired to consume the race of the *Kuçikas*; he came and said to king *Kuçika* that he desired to dwell with him for some time. *Kuçika* and his wife welcomed and honoured him; according to his desire, they promised to serve him, while he observed a vow. Once he slept for twenty-one days, while *Kuçika* and the queen kept themselves awake, foregoing all food; then *Cyavana* went out, followed by the king and the queen, and disappeared (XIII, **52**); the king with the queen sorrowfully returned to the palace, where he found *Cyavana* stretched as before on his bed, and sat by his side, while he slept for twenty-one days, then *Cyavana* ordered them to rub him, and then entered the bathing house, and once more disappeared by means of his *yoga*-power. The next time, *C.* was seen on the throne; then he ordered food (description), but reduced it all to ashes, and disappeared. *Kuçika* with his queen stood there in the same posture the whole night without speaking a word, without giving way to wrath. So it went on every day. *Cyavana* failed to notice any fault in the conduct of the king. Then he ordered them to yoke themselves to a chariot and pull him along; it should be the king's battle-chariot with every weapon, etc., and the goad (description); they must drag him slowly in the sight of the people, who lamented; suddenly he struck them with the goad, so that they were covered with blood; no food had passed their lips for fifty nights; on his way he began to give away very largely of the king's property. Then *Cyavana*, delighted, came down from the chariot, unharnessed the royal couple, and granted them a boon; he softly touched them with his hands, the healing virtues of which were like ambrosia, and all their fatigue, etc., was dispelled, and they once more became endued with youth. He dismissed them till the next day, himself remaining on the banks of the *Gaṅgā*. Meanwhile *Cyavana*, by his *yoga*-power, converted that delightful wood on the bank of the *Gaṅgā* into a retreat full of wealth of every kind and jewels and gems (XIII, **53**). The next morning *Kuçika* came with his wife, and saw that palace made entirely of gold, etc. (description), and Aps. and G., and thought that it was the country of the *Uttara-Kurus* or *Indra's* abode *Amarāvatī*. *Cyavana* lay stretched on a costly and excellent bed, and at the same time on a mat of *kuça*-grass. In a moment everything disappeared, Aps., G., etc. *Cyavana* praised *Kuçika* and his queen; *Kuçika* said that he had a sufficient boon, not having been consumed by the fire of *Cyavana's* penances; he asked him to expound some doubts (XIII, **54**). Asked by *Kuçika*, *Cyavana* explained the reason of his conduct: In days past, when the gods had assembled together, he had heard *Brahmán* say that, owing to a contention between *brahman*- and *kshattriya*-energy, there would occur an intermixture in his race; therefore he had resolved to exterminate the *Kuçikas*, but had failed to find any fault with *Kuçika*; seeing the delightful palace he had created, *Kuçika* had had a foretaste of heaven and had become desirous of the status of a *brahman* and the merit of penances; "the person who will be the third in descent from thee shall attain to the status of a *brahman*; through the energy of the *Bhṛgus*, thy grandson will be an ascetic endued with the splendour of fire; I shall set out on a *tīrthayātrā*." *Kuçika* asked in what way the status of brahmanhood would attach to his race (XIII, **55**). *Cyavana* foretold that the *Kshattriyas* would exterminate the *Bhārgavas*, except *Ūrva*, who would cast the fire of his wrath into the mare's mouth (*Vaḍavā-vaktra*) in the Ocean; he would have a son *Ṛcīka*, to whom *Dhanurveda* in its incarnate form would come in order to exterminate all *Kshattriyas*; he would communicate it to his son *Jamadagni*:

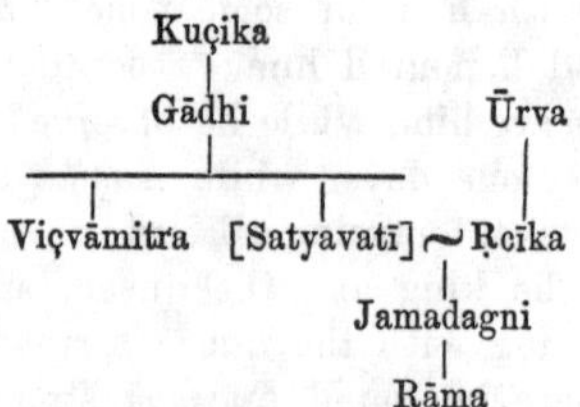

Kuçika became filled with joy; *Cyavana* set out on his *tīrthayātrā*; everything fell out as *Cyavana* had said (XIII, **56**). [Cf. Viçvāmitrop., § 721*b* = XIII, **4**.]

[Cyavanopākhyāna(ṃ)], "the episode relating to Cyavana." § 745*b* (Ānuçāsanik.): *Bhīshma* said: In days past M.-ṛ. *Cyavana Bhārgava* set himself for twelve years to *udavāsa* ("dwelling in water") at the confluence (*madhye*) of the *Gaṅgā* and *Yamunā*, and stood there like a wooden post (description). He was caught in the net (description) of some fishers (*kaivartāḥ*) along with a large number of fish, etc. They were afraid; *Cyavana* said that he would either die with the fishes or be sold with them. With pale faces the fishers repaired to king *Nahusha* (XIII, **50**), who immediately went to *Cyavana* with his ministers and priest; *Cyavana* asked him to pay the price for himself and the fishes; *Nahusha* ordered large sums to be paid to the *Nishādas* for *Cyavana*; but the latter declared that these could not represent his price, even his whole kingdom; *Nahusha* deliberated with his ministers and priests; then there came an ascetic living in the woods, born of a cow, and said that the cow was equal in value to the *brahman*; this *Cyavana* approved of, as *svāhā*- and *vashaṭ-kāra* are always established upon kine, etc. *Cyavana* accepted the cow from the fishermen, and caused them along with the fishes to proceed to heaven. The two Ṛ. gladdened king *Nahusha* by granting him many boons; he accepted the boon that he should himself remain firm in virtue. The two Ṛ. returned each to his own asylum, and *Nahusha* to his city (XIII, **51**). Asked by *Yudhishṭhira* about *Rāma Jāmadagnya*, etc. (*a*), *Bhīshma* recited an old history of the discourse between *Cyavana* and *Kuçika*, i.e. Cyavana-Kuçika-saṃvāda (*c*) (III, **52–56**).

Ç

(What is not found under Ç should be sought for under S.)

Çabala (C. °*va*°), a serpent. § 46 (Sarpanāmak.): I, **35**, 1552.

Çabalāçva (C. °*va*°), a prince. § 154 (Pūruv.): I, **94**, 3741 (son of Avikshit and grandson of Kuru).

Çabalāksha (C. °*va*°), a ṛshi. § 734 (Ānuçāsanik.): XIII, **26***a*, 1764 (among the ṛshis who came to Bhīshma as he lay on his arrow-bed).

Çabara (C. °*va*°), pl. (°*āḥ*), a barbarous people. § 223 (Vāsishṭha): I, **175**, 6683 (their origin), 6684 (do. only in B., C. has *Çarabhān*).—§ 578 (Bhīshmavadhap.): VI, **50**π, 2084 (in the krauñcavyūha of Yudhishṭhira, only in B., C. has *Çaravāḥ*).—§ 599 (Jayadrathavadhap.): VII, **119**$\gamma\gamma$, 4748 (Sātyaki slew thousands of *Ç*., etc.).—§ 615*n* (Viçvāmitra): IX, **40**, 2305 (sprung from the cow of Vasishṭha, cf. § 223).—§ 641 (Rājadh.): XII, **65**θ, 2429 (°*Barbarāḥ*).—§ 652*b* (Indrota-Pārīkshitīya): XII, **151**, 5620 (*Pulinda-Ç°ā iva*).—§ 658*b* (Kṛtaghnop.): XII, **168**, 6299 (°*ālaye*); **171**, 6372 (do.); **173**, 6445 (°*ālayam*).—§ 664 (Mokshadh.): XII, **207**η, 7559 (in the south).—§ 730*g* (Upamanyu): XIII, **14**η, 732 (Çiva assumes the form of the Kirātas and the *Ç*.).—§ 739 (Ānuçāsanik.:) XIII, **35**ϵ, 2158 (°*Barbarāḥ*—kshattriyas who are degraded to çūdras—*vṛshalatvam anuprāptāḥ*).—§ 782*c* (Arjuna Kārtavīrya): XIV, **29**, 832 (*vṛshalatvaṃ parigatāḥ*).

Çabda ("Sound," personif.). § 270 (Brahmasabhāv.): II, **11**, 438 (°*sparçau*, in the palace of Brahmán).

Çabdasaha = Vishṇu (1000 names).

Çabdātiga = Vishṇu (1000 names).

Çacī, the queen of Indra, daughter of Puloman and mother of Jayanta. § 71 (Ādivaṃçāvatāraṇap.): I, **61**, 2274 (*iva Mahendreṇa*).—§ 132 (Aṃçāvat.): I, **67**, 2791 (Draupadī was born from a portion of *Ç*.).—§ 222 (Tapatyup.): I, **173**, 6631 (*yathā Çacyā Marutpatiḥ*).—§ 266 (Çakrasabhāv.): II, **7**, 286 (*Mahendrāṇyā*, in the palace of Indra).—§ 270 (Brahmasabhāv.): II, **10**, 459 (in the palace of Brahmán).—§ 338 (Indralokābhigamanap.): III, **46**, 1854 (*yathendrāṇī*, C. has *Saçī*), 1862 (*yathā*).—§ 344 (Nalop.): III, **53**, 2082 (*iva*).—§ 345 (do.): III, **57**, 2233 (*Çacyeva Balavṛtrahā*).—§ 391 (Ṛshyaçṛṅga): III, **113**, 10092 (*yathā Çacī Vajradharasya*).—§ 394 (Arjuna Kārtavīrya): III, **115**, 10141 (°*sahayaṃ Vāsavaṃ*; *S*°, C.).—§ 443 (Nivātakavacayuddhap.): III, **168**, 12003 (°*sahayaḥ*, sc. Indra).—§ 555*c* (Indravijaya): V, **11**, 360 (*Ç*. says to *Bṛhaspati*: "You always say, O brahman, that I have got on my person all the auspicious marks, being the favourite queen of the divine king;

that I am chaste, devoted to my lord, and destined never to become a widow"); **12**, 389, 390; **13**, 423 (*devī*); **14**, 440; **15**, 446.—§ 561 (Yānasandhip.): V, **55**, 2198 (in order to gratify *Ç.* Indra asked Karṇa for his earrings).—§ 564 (Mātalīyop.): V, **104**, 3651 (*Vāsavasya Çacīm iva*).—§ 565 (Gālavac.): V, **117**, 3967 (*yathā Çacyāñ ca Vāsavaḥ*).—§ 599 (Jayadrathavadhap.): VII, **94**ε, 3452.—§ 615u (Skanda): IX, **45**γ, 2515 (came to the investiture of Skanda).—§ 717b (Nārāyaṇīya): XII, **343**, VII), ††13214–17.—§ 768b (Umā-Maheçvarasaṃv.): XIII, **146**γ, 6750 (*Kauçikasya C°ī satī*).

Cf. also the following synonyms:—

Çakrāṇī: V, 364, 367.

Indrāṇī, "queen of Indra": I, 7351; III, 1854 (*yathā . . . Çacī*); IV, 259; V, 376, 377, 379, 383, 389 (*Çakrasya mahishīṃ priyāṃ*), 392, 395, 399, 406, 429, 432, 438, 440, 454; XII, ††13216.

Mahendrāṇī, "queen of the great Indra": II, 286 (*Çacyā*); III, 1677; V, 547.

Paulomī, "daughter of Puloman": I, 4472 (*Jayantam iva Paulomī*), 8025 (do.); III, 12563 (*Maghavān iva P°yā*), 16570 (*Mahendra iva P°yā*).

Çacīpati = Indra, q.v.

Çaça = Çiva (1000 names[1]).

Çāçabindava[1] (patron.), pl. § 595 (Shoḍaçarājik., v. Çaçabindu): VII, **65**, 2324 (*kumārāḥ*).—Do.,[2] adj. ("relating to Çaçabindu".) § 665 (Mokshadh.): XII, **208**, 7579 (*prajām ācakshate viprāḥ purāṇāḥ Çāçabindavīṃ, sa Vṛshṇivaṃçaprabhavo mahāvaṃçaḥ Prajāpater*, i.e. Çaçabindu's).

Çaçabindu[1] (C. °vi°), an ancient king, son of Citraratha. § 5 (Anukram.): I, **1**a, 221 *bis* (in the enumeration of 24 kings of the past).—§ 61 (Sarpasattra): I, **55**, 2100 (*yajñaḥ Ç°oç ca rājñaḥ*, comparison).—§ 267 (Yamasabhāv.): II, **8**, 328 (in the palace of Yama).—§ 595 (Shoḍaçarāj.): VII, **65**, 2321, 2328, 2331: King *Ç.* was invincible, etc., performed diverse sacrifices, and had 100,000 wives, who bore each 1,000 sons of great prowess, who performed millions of sacrifices (also horse sacrifices). *Ç.* gave away all those sons to the brahmans, each with hundreds upon hundreds of chariots, etc.; upon the completion of his horse sacrifice 13 mountains of food and drink remained. At last he ascended to heaven.—§ 632b (Shoḍaçarājikop., cf. § 595): XII, **29**, 998 (*Caitrarathaṃ*).—§ 665 (Mokshadh.): XII, **208**, 7577 (among the Prajāpatis).—§ 749 (Ānuçāsanik.): XIII, **89**, 4255, 4269 (Yama spoke to him about çrāddhas).—§ 760 (do.): XIII, **115**γ, 5662 (did not eat meat during the month of Kārttika).—§ 775 (do.): XIII, **166**η, 7677.

Çaçabindu[2] = Vishṇu (1000 names).

Çaçabindu[3], pl. (°*avaḥ*), "descendants of Çaçabindu." § 267 (Yamasabhāv.): II, **8**, 338 (1,000 in the palace of Yama).—§ 632b (Shoḍaçarājikop., cf. § 595): XII, **29**, 999 (*sahasran tu sahasrāṇāṃ*).

Çaçāda, an ancient king of Ayodhyā. § 475 (Dhundhumārop.): III, **202**, 13515 (succeeded Ikshvāku), 13516 (father of Kakutstha).

Çaçaka, pl. (°*āḥ*), a people. § 515 (Karṇadigvijaya): III, **254**, 15257 (vanquished by Karṇa).

Çaçalakshaṇa = Soma (the Moon), q.v.

Çaçaloman, an ancient king. § 787 (Āçramavāsap.): XV, **20**γγ, 551 (having undergone severe austerities he ascended to heaven).

Çaçāṅka[1] = Soma: VI, 1285 (identified with Kṛshṇa).

Çaçāṅka[2] = Çiva (1000 names[1]).

Çaçayāna, a tīrtha. § 360 (Tīrthayātrāp.): III, **82**, 5055.

Çaçija, "son of the Moon" = Budha (the planet): IX, 545.

Çaçika, pl. (°*āḥ*), a people. § 574 (Jambūkh.): VI, **9**μ, 354 (in Bhāratavarsha, C. has *Çāçikāḥ*).

Çaçin[1] = Soma (the Moon), q.v.

Çaçin[2] = Çiva (1000 names[2]).

Çaçolūkamukhī, a mātṛ. § 615u (Skanda): IX, **46**θ, 2640.

Çāçvata[1] = Sūrya: III, 151.

Çāçvata[2] = Çiva (1000 names[2]).

Çāçvata[3] = Vishṇu (1000 names).

Çaibāla, pl. (°*āḥ*), v. Çaivala, pl.

Çaibya[1], an ancient king. § 5 (Anukram.): I, **1**a, 223 (in Nārada's enumeration).

Çaibya[2], Govāsana. § 159 (Pūruv.): I, **95**, †3828 (*Govāsanasya*, the father of Devikā, the wife of Yudhishṭhira).—§ 576 (Bhagavadgītāp.): VI, **17**γ, 655 (*Govāsanaḥ*, in the army of Duryodhana).—§ 599 (Jayadrathavadhap.): VII, **95**, 3528 (*Govāsanaḥ*, battled with the son of the Kāçi king); **96**, 3552 (do.).

Çaibya[3], one of Kṛshṇa's horses. § 252 (Subhadrāharaṇap.): I, **220**, 7933 (°*Sugrīvayuktena*, sc. *rathena*).—§ 320 (Saubhavadhop.): III, **20**, 789 (°*Sugrīvayuktena rathena*).—§ 321 (do.): III, **22**, 896 (do.).—§ 452 (Mārkaṇḍeyasamāsyap.): III, **183**, 12562 (do.).—§ 552 (Goharaṇap.): IV, **45**, 1415 (*samaṃ Ç°sya*, one of Uttara's horses).—§ 562 (Bhagavadyānap.): V, **83**, 2938 (°*Sugrīva-Meghapushpa-Balāhakaiḥ*).—§ 567 (do.): V, **131**, 4446 (°*Sugrīvayuktena rathena*).—§ 596 (Pratijñāp.): VII, **79**ζ, 2812.—§ 599 (Jayadrathavadhap.): VII, **147**ρρρ, 6344 (°*Sugrīva-Meghapushpa-Balāhakaiḥ | hayodagraiḥ*).—§ 617 (Aishīkap.): X, **13**, 649 (description of Kṛshṇa's chariot).—§ 635 (Rājadh.): XII, **37**, 1382 (°*Sugrīvayojitaṃ*, sc. *rathaṃ*).—§ 637 (do.): XII, **46**, †1587 (*Sugrīva-C°pramukhair varāçvaiḥ*).—§ 639 (do.): XII, **53**η, 1917.

Çaibya[4], a Vṛshṇi prince. § 264 (Sabhākriyāp.): II, **4**, 130 (among the princes who acquired the science of arms from Arjuna).

Çaibya[5], a prince slain by Kṛshṇa. § 317b (Kṛshṇa Vāsudeva): III, **12**, 489.

Çaibya[6] = Koṭikāsya: III, 15605, 15606, 15610, 15613, 15615.

Çaibya[7], king of the Çibis, various princes at the time of Yudhishṭhira. (*a*) § 264 (Sabhākriyāp.): II, **4**β, 120. Possibly identical with (*b*) or (*c*).—(*b*) (siding with Duryodhana, = Çaibya Govāsana?): § 586 (Bhīshmavadhap.): VI, **99**a, 4501 (stationed in the front of Bhīshma's *sarvatobhadra*-array).—(*c*) (siding with the Pāṇḍavas): § 553 (Vaivāhikap.): IV, **72**, 2351 (came with one akshauhiṇī of troops to Yudhishṭhira).—§ 571 (Ulūkadūtāgamanap.): V, **164**ε, 5707 (is placed against Kṛtavarman).—§ 576 (Bhagavadgītāp.): VI, **25**θ, 834.—§ 578 (Bhīshmavadhap.): VI, **50**π, 2079 (only C., B. has *Caidya*), 2088; **51**aa, 2117.—§ 589 (Droṇābhishekap.): VII, **10**, 374 (grandson of Çibi Auçīnara, attacked Droṇa).—§ 592 (Saṃçaptakavadhap.): VII, **23**o, 1008 (proceeded against Droṇa, description of his horses).

Çaibya[8] = Çibi Auçīnara: III, †10260 (*ye nāthavanto 'dya bhavanti loke te nātmanā karma samārabhante | teshān tu kāryeshu bhavanti nāthāḥ Ç°ādayo, Rāma!, yathā Yayāteḥ*); VII, 373 (*Auçīnarāt*, cf. *Uçīnarasutaḥ*, v. 371); XII, 936 (*Auçīnarāt*), 10754 (?, *tair eva phalapatraiç ca samāṭharam*—

sc. *Sūryaṃ*, Nīl.—*atoshayat | tasmāl lebhe paraṃ sthānaṃ Çaivyo 'pi pṛthivīpatiḥ*).

Çaibya[9] = Vṛshādarbhi: XIII, 4420 (*Çibisūnunā*), 4424 (*V°*).

Çaibya[10]: VII, 2138, v. Çaivya.

Çaibyā[1] ("daughter of the king of the Çibis") = Sunandā: I, 3797 (wife of Pratīpa).

Çaibyā[2] (do.), wife of Sagara. § 387 (Sagara): III, **106**, 8833, 8843.—§ 388 (Asamañjas): III, **107**, 8888 (mother of Asamañjas).

Çaibyā[3] (do.), wife of Dyumatsena. § 545 (Pativratamāhātmyap.): III, **298**, 16859, 16883; **299**, 16911.

Çaibyā[4] (do.), wife of Kṛshṇa. § 793 (Mausalap.): XVI, **7**μ, 249 (when the body of Kṛshṇa was burnt, *Ç.* ascended the funeral pyre).

Çaibyā[5], a river. § 574 (Jambūkh.): VI, **9**λ, 331 (in Bhāratavarsha).

Çaibya-Sugrīvavāhana = Kṛshṇa: II, 35; V, 2977; IX, 3501.

Çaibyātmaja. § 589 (Droṇābhishekap.): VII, **8**θ, †248 (*Kāçirājaḥ* ?, attacked Droṇa).

Çaiçava, pl. (*°āh*), a people. § 295 (Dyūtap.): II, **52**, 1874 (among the peoples who brought tribute to Yudhishṭhira).

Çaiçira, a mountain (= Himavat, PCR.). § 442 (Nivātakavacay.): III, **167**, 11949.—§ 443 (do.): III, **168**, 11999 (*°sya gireḥ pāde*), 12026.—§ 603 (Nārāyaṇāstramokshap.): VII, **199**, 9242 (*samarthau parvatasyāpi Ç°sya nipātane*, says Bhīma about his arms).—§ 714 (Çukakṛtya): XII, **328**, 12313.

Çaiçupāla, v. Çaiçupāli.

Çaiçupāli ("son of Çiçupāla") = Dhṛshṭaketu: III, 15252 (so B.; C. has *Çaiçupālaṃ*, vanquished by Karṇa on his digvijaya); V, 2011, 4221; VII, 1511, 5039, 5045.

Çaikhaṇḍi ("son of Çikhaṇḍin") = Kshattradeva: VII, 955.

Çaikhāvatya, a brahman. § 573 (Ambopākhy.): V, **175**, 6014 (*tapovṛddhaḥ çāstre cāraṇyake guruḥ*, consoled Ambā).

Çaila[1]. § 565 (Gālavacarita): V, **111**, 3830 (*atra*—i.e. in the North—*Kāmaç ca Roṣhaç ca Çailaç*—i.e. Himavat, PCR. —*comā sambabhuḥ*; cf. the note of PCR.).

Çaila[2], a celestial weapon. § 444 (Nivātakavacayuddhap.): III, **171**, 12141 (*mahāstreṇa*, employed by Arjuna).—§ 586 (Bhīshmavadhap.): VI, **102**, 4663 (*ghoram astraṃ*, employed by Arjuna).

Çailābha, a Viçvedeva. § 749 (Ānuçāsanik.): XIII, **91**γ, 4357 (enumeration).

***Çailaguru** = Himavat, q.v.

***Çailāḥ** ("mountains" person.): XII, 12606.

Çailakampin, a warrior of Skanda. § 615*u* (Skanda): IX, **45**η, 2565.

Çailālaya, an ancient king, grandfather of Bhagadatta. § 787 (Āçramavāsap.): XV, **20**γγ, 547 (attained by his penances to the region of Indra).

Çailaputrī = Umā, q.v.

Çailarāj, Çailarāja = Himavat, q.v.

Çailarājasutā[1] ("daughter of Himavat") = Gaṅgā: III, 9950.

Çailarājasutā[2] (do.) = Umā, q.v.

Çailasutā (do.) = Gaṅgā: III, 10836.

Çailendra[1] = Vindhya: III, 8793.

Çailendra[2] = Himavat, q.v.

Çailodā, a river. § 295 (Dyūtap.): II, **52**, 1858 (*Meru-Mandarayor madhye Çailodām abhito nadīṃ | ye te kīcakaveṇūnāṃ chāyāṃ ramyām upāsante*, i.e. the Khasas, etc., who brought pipīlika-gold as tribute to Yudhishṭhira).

Çailūsha, a Gandharva. § 269 (Vaiçravaṇasabhāv.): II, **10**, 406 (in the palace of Kubera).

Çaineya[1] = Sātyaki, q.v.

Çaineya[2], pl. (*°āḥ*), "descendants of Çini." § 793 (Mausalap.): XVI, **3**ε, 93 (slain).

Çaineyanandana = Sātyaki, q.v.

Çairīshaka, name of a place. § 285 (Nakula): II, **32**, 1188 (in the west, conquered by Nakula on his digviyaya).

Çaivala (C. Çaibāla), pl. (*°āḥ*), a people. § 574 (Jambūkh.): VI, **9**μ, 361.

Çaivya[1]. § 5 (Anukram.): I, **1**, 224 (B. *Çvaityāya*, to him Nārada enumerated 24 kings (*a*) who had died).—§ 595 (Shoḍaçarāj.): VII, **55**, 2138 (B. Çaibya, father of Sṛñjaya; PCR. has Çvitya, which seems to be the true reading, as Sṛñjaya is named Çvaitya, q.v.; Nārada related to Sṛñjaya the Shoḍaçarājika).

Çaivya[2], **Çaivyā, Çaivyātmaja** (so C. for Çaib°, q.v.).

Çaka, pl. (*°āḥ*), a people. § 223 (Vāsishṭha): I, **175**, 6683 (their origin).—§ 280 (Bhīmasena): II, **30**, 1088 (in the east, vanquished by Bhīmasena).—§ 285 (Nakula): II, **32**, 1199 (in the west, vanquished by Nakula).—§ 295 (Dyūtap.): II, **51**, 1843, 1850 (among the peoples who brought tribute to Yudhishṭhira); **52**, 1872 (do.).—§ 342 (Indralokābhig.): III, **51**, 1990 (had been present at the rājasūya of Yudhishṭhira).—§ 458*b* (Kaliyuga): III, **188**, 12839 (among the barbarous peoples who in the Kaliyuga will rule the earth).—§ 554 (Sainyodyogap.): V, **4**γ, 78 (their king mentioned among the kings to whom the Pāṇḍavas ought to send messengers).—§ 555 (do.): V, **19**δ, 590 (followed the Kāmboja king Sudakshiṇa).—§ 571 (Ulūkadūtāgamanap.): V, **160**γ, 5510 (in the army of Duryodhana); **161**, 5555 (do.).—§ 573 (Ambopākhyānap.): V, **195**ε, 7609 (do.).—§ 574 (Jambūkh.): VI, **9**μ, 352 (in Bhāratavarsha), 359 (do.).—§ 576 (Bhagavadgītāp.): VI, **20**, †753 (follow Kṛpa).—§ 580 (Bhīshmavadhap.): VI, **56**γ, 2408 (in Bhīshma's garuḍavyūha).—§ 583 (do.): VI, **75**ε, 3297 (in Bhīshma's krauñcavyūha).—§ 587 (do.): VI, **117**ρ, 5485 (attack Arjuna).—§ 589 (Droṇābhishekap.): VII, **7**ε, 182; **11**ν, 399 (have been vanquished by Kṛshṇa).—§ 592 (Saṃçaptakavadhap.): VII, **20**γ, 798 (in Droṇa's garuḍavyūha).—§ 599 (Jayadrathavadhap.): VII, **93**δ, 3379 (attack Arjuna); **112**, 4340 (*Çakratulyaparākramaiḥ*); **119**ββ, 4716, 4722 (many *Ç.*, etc., have been slain by Sātyaki); γγ, 4747 (thousands of *Ç.* have been slain by Sātyaki), 4754; **121**εε, 4818 (attack Sātyaki).—§ 604 (Karṇap.): VIII, **8**, 235 (Karṇa has [formerly] vanquished the *Ç.*).—§ 608 (do.): VIII, **46**ε, 2137 (in Karṇa's array); **56**ττ, 2807 (*ekeshu nihatair açvaiḥ Kāmbojair Yavanaiḥ Çakaiḥ*); **73**, 3652 (have been vanquished by Arjuna); **88**αβ[1], †4506 (attack Arjuna).—§ 609 (Çalyap.): IX, **1**γ, 27 (have been slain); **2**φ, 74 (had taken up arms for the sake of Duryodhana).—§ 611 (do.): IX, **8**γ, 392 (with Kṛpa on the right side of Çalya's array).—§ 641 (Rājadharm.): XII, **65**θ, 2429 (enumeration of barbarous or low peoples).—§ 739 (Ānuçāsanik.): XIII, **33**a, 2103 (among the tribes who have been degraded from kshattriyas to çūdras—*vṛshalatvaṃ parigatāḥ*).

Çāka, a tree in Çākadvīpa. § 575*b* (Çākadvīpa): VI, **11**, 428.

Çākadvīpa, a dvīpa named after the Çāka-tree. § 575 (Bhūmip.): VI, **11**a, 402.—§ 575*b* (do.): *Ç.* is of twice the extent of *Jambudvīpa*, and the ocean also is of twice the extent of that island. *Ç.* is surrounded on all sides by the ocean. The kingdoms there are full of righteousness, and the men never die; there is no famine; the people are all full of forbearance and great energy. There are seven mountains decked with jewels, etc., and many rivers. The mountains are: (1) *Meru*, the abode of D., Ṛ., and G.; (2) *Malaya*, to the east; there the clouds are generated, and thence they disperse on all sides; (3) *Jaladhāra*, whence *Indra* daily takes water, and from that we get showers of rain; (4) *Raivataka*, over which the constellation *Revati* is placed by *Brahmán* himself; (5) on the north of this is *Çyāma*. Because the hue of these mountains is dark, the people residing there are all dark in complexion; (6) *Durgaçaila*; (7) *Keçarin* (B. *Kesara*). The measure of each of these mountains is double that of the one mentioned immediately before. There are seven *Varshas* (β), one for each mountain. In the midst is a large tree called *Çāka*, in height and breadth equal to the *Jambu*-tree in *Jambudvīpa*, and it is always adored by the people. There are many delightful provinces where *Çiva* is worshipped, and thither repair D., Si., and Cā. The people are virtuous, and all the four orders are devoted to their respective occupations. There is no instance of theft. They are free from decrepitude and death, and gifted with long life. The rivers (γ) are full of sacred water whence *Indra* draws water to shower it as rain. *Gaṅgā* herself is among them. They are all sin-cleansing. There are four sacred provinces (δ). There is no king and no punishment, and no person that deserves to be punished: VI, **11**, 408, 411, 413, 441.—§ 623 (Rājadh.): XII, **14a**, 406 (east of Meru, swayed by Yudhishṭhira), 407.

Çākala[1], a city, the capital of the Madras. § 285 (Nakula): II, **32**, 1196 (the city of Çalya, in the west).—§ 607 (Karṇap.): VIII, **44**, 2033 (*nagaram*), 2049 (*nagare*).

Çākala[2], pl. (°*āḥ*), the inhabitants of Çākala. § 607 (Karṇap.): VIII, **44**, 2052.

Çākala(ḥ) dvīpa(ḥ), a country. § 279 (Arjuna): II, **26**, 998 (in the north, conquered by Arjuna on his digvijaya). Cf. next.

Çākaladvīpa (= prec.). § 279 (Arjuna): II, **26**, 999 (*Çākaladvīpavāsāç ca saptadvīpeshu ye nṛpāḥ | Arjunasya ca sainyais tair vigrahas tumulo 'bhavat | sa tān api maheshvāsān vijigye*, sc. *Arjunaḥ*).

Çākalya, a ṛshi. § 730 (Ānuçāsanik.): XIII, **14ζ**, 689 (adored Çiva in a mental sacrifice which lasted for 900 years).

Çākambharī[1], a tīrtha, named after *Ç.* = Durgā. § 370 (Tīrthayātrāp.): III, **84**, 7094.

Çākambharī[2] = Durgā (Umā): III, 7091 (*devyāḥ*), 7094 (origin of the name); VI, 801.

Çākavaktra, a warrior of Skanda. § 615u (Skanda): IX, **45η**, 2578.

Çākha, a son or form of Skanda. § 116b (Kumāra): I, **66**, 2588 (brother of Skanda according to PCR.).—§ 615u (Skanda): IX, **44**, 2487, 2489 (the vāyu form of Skanda).

Çakra[1] = Indra (q.v.).

Çakra[2] = Çiva (1000 names[1-2]).

Çākra (adj.), "belonging to Indra." § 599 (Jayadrathavadhap.): VII, **93**, 3358 (°*m astram*, invoked by Arjuna).

Çakrabhavana, "the abode of Indra." § 339 (Indralokābhig.): III, **47**, 1879 (desiring to see Indra, Lomaça came to *Ç.*).—§ 568 (Vidulāputraçāsana): V, **135**, 4593 (only B.).

Çakradeva, son of the Kaliṅga king. § 579 (Bhīshmavadhap.): VI, **54**[10], 2253 (fought Bhīmasena), 2254, 2256, 2257 (*Kāliṅgasya sutaḥ*, slain by Bhīmasena), 2354.

Çakraja = Arjuna, q.v.

Çakraloka, "the world of Indra." § 4 (Anukram.): I, **1**, †163.—§ 340 (Indralokābhig.): III, **48**, 1915 (°*gatam*, sc. Arjuna).—§ 343 (Nalopākhyānap.): III, **52**, 2013 (*astrahetor gate Pārthe*—i.e. Arjuna—*Ç°m*), 2014 (do.).—§ 368 (Tīrthayātrāp.): III, **83**, 7053 (by bathing in Indramārga—B. Rudramārga—one attains to *Ç.*).—§ 370 (do.): III, **84**, 8118 (*ye tu dānam prayacchanti Nirvīrāsaṅgame narāh | te yanti . . . . Ç°m anāmayam*, differently PCR.), 8131 (by bathing at Stanakuṇḍa one attains to *Ç.*), 8137 (by bathing in Nandā one attains to *Ç.*).—§ 438f (Arjuna): III, **162**, 11828 (*svargajit Ç°sthaḥ*, sc. Çāntanu).—§ 512 (Ghoshayātrāp.): III, **236**, 14768 (*gato hy aranyād api Ç°m Dhanañjayaḥ*, i.e. Arjuna, all. to § 335).—§ 555b (Indravijaya): V, **10**, 310 (pl.).—§ 600 (Ghaṭotkacavadhap.): VII, **156**, 6914 (Açvatthāman despatched Çatruñjaya to *Ç.*).—§ 610 (Çalyap.): IX, **5**, 273 (*gaccheyam C°tām*, says Duryodhana).—§ 613 (Gadāyuddhap.): IX, **32**, 1873 (*nyāyena yudhyatām proktā Ç°gatiḥ purā*).—§ 618 (Jalapradānikap.): XI, **11**, 291 (after death Duryodhana has gone to *Ç.*).—§ 752b (Chattropānahotpatti): XIII, **96**, 4647 (he who gives an umbrella with 100 ribs to a brahman dwells after death in *Ç.*).—§ 757k (Indraloka): XIII, **102**, †4881.—§ 759 (Ānuçāsanik.): XIII, **107ζ**, 5298 (°*ñ ca gacchati*).—§ 768b (Umā-Maheçvarasamv.): XIII, **142**, 6561 (°*gaḥ*), 6564.—§ 770 (Ānuçāsanik.): XIII, **151**, 7111 (*prayataḥ kīrttayān etān*—i.e. the seven gurus of Indra—*Ç°e muhīyate*).

[Çakra-Namuci-saṃvāda(ḥ)], "the discourse between Indra and Namuci." § 672b (Mokshadh.): When the *Asura Namuci*, who was conversant with the birth and death of all creatures, was sitting, divested of prosperity but untroubled at heart, bound with cords, brought under the sway of his foes, etc., *Indra* asked him if he grieved or passed his days cheerfully. *Namuci* answers that he does not grieve, and explains why, citing *Gautama* [the spouse of Ahalyā] (XII, **226**).

Çakranandana = Arjuna, q.v.

Çakrāṇī = Çacī, q.v.

Çakraprastha = Indraprastha, q.v.

Çakrapurī = Indraprastha, q.v.

Çakraputra = Vālin: III, 11194 (*V°*).

Çakra-sabhā-varṇana(m), "description of the palace of Indra." § 266 (Lokapālas.): The sabhā of *Çakra* is built by *Çakra* himself, 100 *yojanas* in breadth, 150 *yojanas* in length, 5 *yojanas* in height, capable of going everywhere at will, named *Pushkaramalinī* (?). There *Indra* sits with *Çacī*, *Çrī*, and *Lakshmī*, the *Maruts*, the *Siddhas*, the *Devarshis*, the *Sādhyas*, the *Devagaṇas*. Enumeration of *Devarshis* and celestial beings (II, **7**).

Çakrasārathi = Mātali, q.v.

Çakrasūnu = Arjuna, q.v.

Çakrasuta = Arjuna, q.v.

Çakrasya tīrtha(m), "the tīrtha of Indra." § 358 (Tīrthayātrāp.): III, **82**, 5023 (?, *Kumārikāṇām Çakrasya tīrtham*, by bathing there one obtains the region of Indra).—§ 615 (Baladevatīrthay.): IX, **49**, 2830 (= *Indratīrtham*, v. 2831).

Çakrātmaja = Arjuna, q.v.

Çakrātmajātmaja, "son of the son of Indra" = Abhimanyu: VII, 1616.

Çakravāpin, a serpent. § 277 (Jarāsandhav.): II, **21**, 806 (*Arbudaḥ Ç°ī ca pannagau*, at Girivraja).

Çakrāvart(t)a, a tīrtha. § 370 (Tīrthayātrāp.): III, **84**, 8007.

Çakta[1], a prince. § 150 (Pūruv.): I, **94**, 3697 (son of Manasyu and Sauvīrī).
Çakta[2] = Çiva (1000 names[2]).
Çākta, Çākteḥ putra(ḥ), Çakteya, v. Çaktr°.
Çakti[1], probably a more correct reading (of B.) instead of Çaktri (q.v.).
Çakti[2]. § 456 (Skandotpatti): III, **226**, 14352 (*devyāḥ* = Durgā?).
Çaktidhara = Skanda: III, 14637.
Çaktija, v. Çaktrija.
Çaktimat: VI, 318; v. Çuktimat.
Çaktimatām çreshṭha(ḥ) = Vishṇu (1000 names).
Çaktiputra, v. Çaktriputra.
Çāktra (B. Çākta), "son of Çakt(r)i" = Parāçara: I, 6885.
Çaktreḥ (B. Cakteḥ) **putra(ḥ)** (do.) = Parāçara: I, 2209 (*P*°).
Çāktreya (B. Cakteya) (do.) = Parāçara: I, 6886 (*P*°).
Çaktri (B., probably more correctly, Çakti), a ṛshi, son of Vasishṭha and father of Parāçara. § 224 (Kalmāshapāda): I, **176**, 6701 (*Vaçishṭha-kulavarddhanaṃ jyeshṭhaṃ putraṃ putraçatād Vaçishṭhasya*), 6709, 6714, 6731 (°*nā*), 6733, 6735, 6736 (C. *Çaktriṃ taṃ*; B. *Çaktinaṃ*), 6737 (°*avarān putrān Vaçishṭhasya*, having cursed Kalmāshapāda to become a rākshasa, *Ç*. himself and all his brothers were devoured by Kalmāshapāda). — § 225 (Vāsishṭha): I, **177**, 6757 (°*eḥ bhāryyā*, i.e. Adṛçyantī), 6758 (*iva*), 6759 (°*eḥ garbhaḥ*, i.e. Parāçara, whom Adṛçyantī bore after the death of *Ç*.).— § 226 (Parāçara): I, **178**, 6792 (Parāçara is born).—§ 228 (Aurvop.): I, **181**, 6867 (°*er vadhaṃ*), 6878, 6879, 6882 (°*avarāḥ putrāḥ Vaçishṭhasya*). — § 229 (Vasishṭhop.): I, **182**, 6892 (°*nā*).—§ 717*b* (Nārāyaṇīya): XII, **350**, 13642 (son of Vasishṭha, father of Parāçara, and grandfather of Vyāsa).—§ 775 (Ānuçāsanik.): XIII, **166**ζ, 7670 (among the ṛshis of the North). Cf. Vāsishṭha.
Çaktrija (B. Çaktija), "son of Çakt(r)i" = Parāçara: I, 6870.
Çaktriputra (B. Çakti°) (do.) = Parāçara: XII, 13642 (*P*°).
[Çākulopākhyāna(m)], "the episode about the Çakula fishes." § 645*b* (Āpaddh.): In a lake that was not very deep and which abounded in fishes, there lived three *Çakula* fishes (*kuçalās* in B. seems only to be a typographical error) that were friends; amongst those three, one had much forethought (*dīrghakālajñaḥ*); another was possessed of great presence of mind (*utpannapratibhaḥ*); the third was procrastinating (*dīrghasūtraḥ*). One day certain fishermen coming to that lake began to bale out its waters to a lower ground through diverse outlets. He of great forethought, having in vain warned the others, immediately set out through a current and reached another deep lake. The procrastinating one was caught with many others and tied to a string. He of presence of mind thrust himself into the company of those so tied, and remained quietly among them biting the string, and escaped when the fishes were removed to a piece of deep water to be washed. The procrastinating one met with his death (XII, **137**).
Çakuna, pl. (°*āḥ*), a people. § 592 (Saṃçaptakav.): VII, **20**ζ, 802 (*Gāndhārāḥ Çakunāḥ*, etc., in the back of Droṇa's garuḍavyūha).
Çakuni[1], son of the Gāndhāra king Subala and brother-in-law of Dhṛtarāshṭra. § 4 (Anukram.): I, **1**, †108, 139.—§ 11 (Parvasaṅgr.): I, **2**, 412 (*Kitavaḥ*, defeats Yudhishṭhira at the play), 426, 553 (°*eç ca vadhah . . . Sahadevena*).— § 83 (Ādivaṃçāvatārana): I, **63**, 2440 (*Gāndhārarājaputraḥ . . . Saubalaḥ*). — § 130 (Aṃçāvat.): I, **67**, 2713 (incarnation of *Dvāpara*).—§ 174 (Sambhavap.): I, **110**, 4377 (*Gāndhārarājasya putraḥ*, gave his sister Gāndhārī in marriage to Dhṛtarāshṭra).—§ 197 (Bhīmasenarasapāna): I, **129**, 5068 (*Saubalaḥ*).—§ 213 (Jatugṛhap.): I, **141**, 5655 (*Saubalaḥ*); **142**, 5674 (do.); **149**, 5849.—§ 215 (Bahavadhap.): I, **162**, 6248.—§ 232 (Svayaṃvarap.): I, **186**, 6985 (*Çakuniḥ Saubalaç caiva Vṛshako 'tha Bṛhadbalaḥ | ete Gāndhārarājasya sutāḥ sarve samāgatāḥ*).—§ 243 (Vidurāgamanap.): I, **205**, 7516 (*Saubalaḥ*).—§ 287 (Rājasūyikap.): II, **34**, 1265 (came to the *rājasūya* of Yudhishṭhira).—§ 290 (Çiçupālavadhap.): II, **44***a*, 1538.—§ 292 (Rājasūyikap.): II, **45**, 1627 (*Saubalaḥ*, remained in the palace of Yudhishṭhira).—§ 293 (Dyūtap.): II, **46**, 1661 (do.).—§ 294 (do.): II, **47**, 1662, 1682; **48**, (1702), (1716), (1720); **49**, 1726 (*Saubalaḥ*), 1727, (1728), 1731, (1762), 1766.— § 298 (do.): II, **56**, (1966), †1977; **58**, †2004 (*Gāndhārarājaḥ*, shall play with Yudhishṭhira), 2007; **59**, 2032 (*Saubalaḥ*), (2033), 2035, (†2036), 2041, (2043), 2049; **60**, 2059; **61**, 2060, 2062, 2066, 2070, 2074, 2078, 2082, 2085, 2090, 2093; **63**, 2120 (*Saubalasya . . . Pārvatīyaḥ*); **65**, (2141), 2142 (*Saubala*), 2145, 2147, 2149, 2151, (2153), 2154, 2156, (2157), (2159), 2161, 2162, 2166, (2167), 2169, 2170, 2172 (gambling with Çakuni, Yudhishṭhira loses all his wealth and also his brethren, himself, and Draupadī).—§ 299 (do.): II, **67**, †2241 (*Gāndhārarājaḥ Subalasya putraḥ*), †2245.—§ 302 (Anudyūtap.): II, **74**, 2456 (*Saubalaḥ*), 2472. — § 303 (do.): II, **76**, 2496 (°*er māyāṃ*), (2499), 2509, (2510), 2513 (the gambling is renewed and *Ç*. again wins).—§ 304 (do.): II, **77**, 2539 (Sahadeva will slay *Ç*.), 2544.—§ 306 (do.): II, **80**, 2655.—§ 311 (Āraṇyakap.): III, **4**, †226, †233.—§ 312 (do.): III, **5**, †247 (*Saubalasya*). —§ 313 (do.): III, **7**, (293).—§ 327 (Draupadīparit.): III, **34**, †1358.—§ 337 (Indralokābh.): III, **44**, 1797 (*Saubalasya*).—§ 446 (Nivātakavacay.): III, **174**, 12276.—§ 512 (Ghoshayātrāp.): III, **236**, †14761; **237**, 14772, 14795; **238**, 14816 (*Gāndhārarājaḥ*); **239**, 14822, (14837), 14841; **240**, 14851; **241**, 14896 (*Saubalaḥ*), 14906 (do.) (*Ç*. follows Duryodhana on the *ghoshayātrā* and is vanquished by the Gandharvas).—§ 513 (do.): III, **251**, 15124 (*Saubalaḥ*), (15125).—§ 515 (Karṇadigvijaya): III, **253**, 15209, 15233; **254**, 15254 (*Saubalaḥ*), 15272.—§ 521 (Draupadīharaṇap.): III, **262**, 15495.—§ 548 (Āraṇeyap.): III, **312**, 17245.— § 551 (Kīcakavadhap.): IV, **21**, 646 (*Saubalasya*).—§ 552 (Goharaṇap.): IV, **50**, 1577 (*Gāndhāraḥ*).—§ 554 (Sainyodyogap.): V, **2**, †37; **3**, 60; **6**, 114.—§ 556 (Sañjayayānap.): V, **21**, 633; **26**, †755; **29**, †854 (*Gāndhārarājaḥ*), (λ) †860; **30**ν, †895 (*Gāndhārarājaḥ*).—§ 558 (Prajāgarap.): V, **35**, 1257.—§ 561 (Yānasandhip.): V, **47***a*, 1798 (*Saubalaḥ*); **49**, 1944 (*Saubalasya*); **58**, 2303 (*Saubalaḥ*); **66**εε, 2502 (*Saubalaḥ*).—§ 562 (Bhagavadyānap.): V, **79**δ, 2829; **91**, 3240 (*Saubalaṃ*); **94**, 3336 (*Saubalaḥ*), 3346 (do.), 3379 (*Gāndhārarājaḥ*).—§ 567 (do.): V, **127**, 4239; **128**, 4306; **130**ν, 4365 (*Saubalena*), 4366 (*Saubalasya*).— § 568 (do.): V, **143**η, 4835.—§ 570 (Sainyaniryānap.): V, **153**, 5195; **154**, 5218, 5227 (*Saubalaḥ*); **155**θ, 5275 (*Saubalaṃ*).—§ 571 (Ulūkadūtāgamanap.): V, **160***a*, 5409, †5532 (*purushodadhim . . . Ç°prapātaṃ*, i.e. the army of Duryodhana); **161**, †5575 (do.); **162**, 5599, 5613, 5614 (Sahadeva promises to slay *Ç*. and his son Ulūka); **163**, 5698; **164**ε, 5709 (Sahadeva is urged against *Ç*.).—§ 572 (Rathātirathas.): V, **167**, 5770 (*mātulas te*—i.e. Duryodhana's—is a *ratha*).—§ 573 (Ambop.): V, **195**ε, 7609 (*Gāndhārarājaḥ*).—§ 574 (Jambūkh.): VI, **9**, 311 (*Saubalaḥ*).—

§ 576 (Bhagavadgītāp.): VI, **14,** 576; **16**a, 622 (do.); **20,** †748 (*taṃ*—i.e. Duryodhana—*sarvataḥ Ç°ḥ Pārvatīyaiḥ sārddhaṃ Gāndhārair yāti Gāndhārarājaḥ*).—§ 578 (Bhīshmavadhap.): VI, **45**[18], 1731, 1733 (fights Prativindhya); **51**σ, 2104.—§ 580 (do.): VI, **57**ι, 2452 (*Saubalaḥ*).—§ 582 (do.): VI, **71**δ, 3140; **72,** 3166 (*Ç°m Ulūkañ ca mahārathaṃ pitāputrau*).—§ 584 (do.): VI, **82,** 3630; **84,** 3729 (*çyālas tava*, i.e. Dhṛtarāshṭra's).—§ 585 (do.): VI, **90,** 3971, 3998 (has six brothers (σ), of whom the five are slain by Irāvat); **96,** 4329 (*Saubalasya*); **97**ιι, 4404 (*Saubalaḥ*); **98**νν, 4489 (*mātulaḥ*).—§ 586 (do.): VI, **99**a, 4501 (in the van of Bhīshma's *sarvatobhadravyūha*).—§ 589 (Droṇābhishekap.): VII, **7**γ, 180 (in the right wing of Droṇa's array).—§ 590 (do.): VII, **14,** 516 (fights Sahadeva).—§ 592 (Saṃçaptakavadhap.): VII, **30,** 1316 (*māyāçataviçāradaḥ*, created illusions), 1329.—§ 593 (Abhimanyuvadhap.): VII, **37**ι, 1602 (fights Abhimanyu); **39**μ, 1650.—§ 598 (Jayadrathavadhap.): VII, **85**ε, 3052 (*Saubalāt*); **86,** 3072.—§ 599 (do.): VII, **95,** 3532 (fights Sahadeva); **96,** 3562 (attacked by Nakula and Sahadeva), 3565; **120**δδ, 4768, 4790 (fights Sātyaki); **130,** 5327 (*°buddhijaṃ*, sc. *dyūtaṃ*), 5328; **151**γ, 6538, 6547.—§ 600 (Ghaṭotkacavadhap.): VII, **155,** 6713; **156,** 6750 (*putrapautraiḥ parivṛto bhrātṛbhiç ca*); **157**π, 6944 (read with B.: *Çakuner bhrātaro vīrā Gavākshaḥ*, etc., five brothers of Ç. are slain by Bhīmasena); **158**ψ, 7030; **165,** 7364 (*Saubalaḥ*, fights Nakula); **169,** 7569 (fights Nakula), 7571; **170**λλ, 7625, (fights Dhṛshṭadyumna); **171,** 7704 (fights Arjuna), 7714, 7716; **182**ζζζ, 8266, (ηηη), 8281; **183**ζζζ, 8294 (*Saubalasya*).—§ 601 (Droṇavadhap.): VII, **185**δ, 8441 (*mātulaç ca me*, i.e. Duryodhana's).—§ 602 (do.): VII, **186**ζ, 8470 (*Saubalaḥ*), (θ), 8504 (do.).—§ 603 (Nārāyaṇāstramokshap.): VII, **193**a, 8901; **200**aa, 9316.—§ 604 (Karṇap.): VIII, **1**a, 5 (*Saubalaḥ*); **4**ε, 83 (*Saubalasya*); **9,** 326 (*Saubalaḥ*).—§ 605 (do.): VIII, **11**ν, 414 (Ç. and Ulūka in the eyes of Karṇa's makaravyūha); **25,** 1010, 1012, 1019 (fights Sutasoma); **32**σσ, 1332.—§ 608 (do.): VIII, **46**γ, 2134 (*°r Ulūkaç ca mahārathaḥ . . . Gāndhāribhir asadbhrāntaiḥ Pārvatīyaiç ca durjayaiḥ*); **47**ι, 2225; **48**ο, 2263; **50,** 2393 (*Saubalaḥ*, rushed against Bhīmasena); **51,** 2494 (*°nirdishṭāḥ sādinaḥ . . . trisāhasrāḥ*); **61,** 3079 (attacked by Sātyaki), 3111, 3114; **64**θθθ, 3249 (*Saubaleyasya*); **77,** 3007, 3011 (fights Bhīmasena), 3914; **78**δ′, 3999; **83**ν′, 4254; **85,** †4323 (*Gāndhārapatiḥ*, fights the Kulinda prince); **91**aκ′, †4749, 4750, 4758; **93**aπ′, 4864 (attacked by Nakula, Sahadeva, and Sātyaki); **95**aυ′, 4969 (*Gandharaṇaṃ sahasreṇa . . . parivāritaḥ*).—§ 609 (Çalyap.): IX, **1**γ, 26 (*Saubalaḥ*, has been slain); **2**ζ, 73 (*Saubalaḥ*), 96 (do.).—§ 610 (do.): IX, **3**ι, 156 (attacked by Nakula and Sahadeva); **6**ξ, 293.—§ 611 (do.): IX, **8,** 400 (attacked by Nakula and Sahadeva); **11**μ; 563 (*Saubalaḥ*), 566; **16,** 800, 832 (*°pramukhān*); **18,** 972 (*Gāndhārarājasya putraḥ*), (977); **19,** 1026, 1064; **22,** 1152 (fights Yudhishṭhira), 1155; **23,** 1204 (*Gāndhārarājasya putraḥ*), 1214 (*Saubalaṃ*), 1215, 1217, 1237, 1241, 1244 (*Saubalaḥ*); **24,** 1274, 1277 (*Saubalaḥ*), 1279; **27**ττ, 1457, (υυ), 1459, 1473; **28,** 1501 (*Saubalaḥ*), 1520 (*°eç ca padānugāḥ*), 1526, 1527, 1529, 1533 (father of Ulūka, who is slain), 1536 (*Saubalaḥ*), 1546, 1555, 1557, †1563, †1564 (Ç. is slain by Sahadeva).—§ 612 (Hradapraveçap.): IX, **29,** 1658 (*nihate*); **31,** 1772 (*Saubalaṃ*), 1797 (*iva*).—§ 613 (Gadāyuddhap.): IX, **32**β, 1837 (*Saubalasya*); **33**ε, 1895, (ι), 1924 (*°buddhijaṃ*, sc. *karma*, all. to the game), 1932 (*dyūte yad vijito rājā Ç°er buddhiniçcayāt*), 1935 (*nihataḥ*).—§ 615 (do.): IX, **56,** 3155 (*°buddhijaṃ*, sc. *karma*), 3162 (*Saubala hataḥ*); **60,** 3384 (has been slain); **61,** 3429 (*°niçcayāt*, Duryodhana had wronged the Pāṇḍavas); **64**εε, 3589, 3613 (*Saubalaṃ*).—§ 618 (Jalapradānikap.): XI, **1**γ, 28; **8**ζ, 223 (*mātulaḥ*, sc. Duryodhana's); **14**ξ, 375 (*Saubalasya*).—§ 619 (Strīvilāpap.): XI, **18**γ, 541; **24**ι, 698 (*Gāndhārarājaḥ . . . nihataḥ Sahadevena bhagineyena mātulaḥ*), 702.—§ 620 (Çrāddhap.): XI, **26**β, 790 (his body is burnt).—§ 768 (Ānuçāsanik.): XIII, **148**ε, 6930.—§ 778 (Açvamedhikap.): XIV, **1,** 13.—§ 785 (Anugītāp.): XIV, **60**β, 1797 (has been slain by Sahadeva), 1798 (*nihate*); **84,** 2486 (*°es tanayo vīro Gāndhārāṇāṃ mahārathaḥ*), 2487 (in order to avenge the slaughter of Ç. the Gāndhāras attack Arjuna), 2494 (*°eḥ putraḥ*, fights Arjuna), 2506 (*°eḥ . . . tanayaṃ*, is vanquished by Arjuna).—§ 789 (Putradarçanap.): XV, **31**η, 852 (is an incarnation of Dvāpara); **32**θ, 876 (among the dead princes who arose from the Gaṅgā).—§ 795 (Svargārohaṇap.): XVIII, **5,** 149 (*Saubalaḥ*, in Heaven), 167 (was absorbed—*prāpa*—into Dvāpara).

Cf. also the following synonyms:—

Gāndhāra, q.v.
Gāndhārapati, q.v.
Gāndhārarāja, q.v.
Gāndhārarājaputra, Gāndhārarājasya putra(ḥ), Gāndhārarājasya suta(ḥ), q.v.
Kitava, q.v.

Pārvatīya ("the Mountaineer"): II, †2120; III, †1357; V, †895.

Saubala ("son of Subala"): I, †157, †206 (*hataṃ saṃgrāme Sahadevena*), 2238, 2279, 2440 (*Ç°iḥ*), 2745, 5068 (*Ç°iḥ*), 5655 (do.), 5674 (do.), 5920, 6985 (*Ç°iḥ*), 7516 (do.); II, 1627 (do.), 1661 (do.), 1698, 1724, 1726 (*Ç°iḥ*), 2032 (do.), 2075, †2120, 2143, 2146, 2179, 2185, 2274, 2275, 2287, 2456 (*Ç°iḥ*), 2513 (do.), 2520, 2551, 2554, 2655 (*Ç°iḥ*); III, †247, 301, †912, 1797 (*Ç°eḥ*), 1954, 2022, 2030, †14771, 14801, 14808, 14810, 14843, 14896 (*Ç°iḥ*), 14906 (do.), 15092, 15124 (*Ç°iḥ*), 15204, 15218, 15272 (*Ç°iḥ*), 15294, 15324, 17453; IV, 646 (*Ç°eḥ*), (**a**), 1150, 1581, 2286; V, †10, †36, 65, 610, 989, 1798 (*Ç°iḥ*), 1944 (*Ç°eḥ*), 2303 (*Ç°iḥ*), 2502 (*Ç°im*), 2932, 3240 (*Ç°iṃ*), 3336 (*Ç°iḥ*), 3346 (do.), 3441, 4167, 4262, 4306 (*Ç°iṃ*), 4365 (*Ç°inā*), 4960 (*Ç°eḥ*), 4800, 5088, 5218 (*Ç°eḥ*), 5227 (*Ç°iḥ*), 5409 (*Ç°iṃ*); VI, 311 (*Ç°iḥ*), 576 (do.), 622 (do.), 1732, 1906, 2452 (*Ç°iḥ*), 2460, 2468, 3134, 3330, 3353, 3455, 3971 (*Ç°iḥ*), 3995 (*°syānujāḥ*, i.e. Gaja, etc.), 4329 (*Ç°eḥ*), 4404 (*Ç°iḥ*), 4668, 5007; VII, 517, 518, 1305, 1306 (*Gāndhārān . . . Saubalapramukhān*), 1327, 1589, 1838, 1900, 2629, 3052 (*Ç°eḥ*), 3061, 3567, 4793, 6746, 6848, 6855, 7055, †7290, 7364 (*Ç°iḥ*), 7559, 7561, 7570, 7669, 7676, 7707, 7715, 7717, 7746, 8294 (*Ç°eḥ*), 8470 (*Ç°iḥ*), 8504 (*Ç°iḥ*), 8544; VIII, 5 (*Ç°iḥ*), 83 (*C°eḥ*), 326 (*Ç°iḥ*), 1017, 1025, 1026, 1032, 1034, 1035, 1274, 1332 (*Ç°iḥ*), 2156, 2225 (*Ç°iḥ*), 2393 (do.), 2507, 2610, 3111, 3112, 3127, †3353, 3763, 3914, 3916, 3921, 3925, 3932, 3940, †4503, †4749 (*Ç°iḥ*); IX, 26 (*Ç°iḥ*, mentioned among the slain), 73 (*Ç°iḥ*), 96 (do.), 373, 396, 563 (*Ç°iḥ*), 626, 1019, 1168 (*°sya sutaṃ*, i.e. Ulūka), 1214 (*Ç°iṃ*), 1218, 1219, 1220, 1236, 1241, 1244 (*Ç°iḥ*), 1264, 1272, 1277 (*Ç°iḥ*), 1361, 1379, 1384, 1399, 1457 (*Ç°eḥ*), 1464, 1472, 1501 (*Ç°iḥ*), 1522, 1524, 1526, 1536 (*Ç°iḥ*), 1538, 1540, 1542, 1543, 1546, 1548, 1556, †1566 (is slain by Sahadeva), 1772 (*Ç°iṃ*), 1837 (*Ç°eḥ*),

3159, 3162 (*Ç°iḥ . . . hataḥ*), 3432, 3613 (*Ç°iṃ*); XI, 375 (*Ç°eḥ*), 790 (*Ç°iṃ*); XII, 182; XV, 329, 336; XVIII, 149 (*Ç°iḥ*).

Saubalaka (do.): III, 1948 (*ye cāsya*—i.e. Duryodhana's—*sacivā mandāḥ Karṇa-S°ādayaḥ*).

Saubaleya (do.): III, 14, †223, 288, 1995, 15135; VI, 2471, 2910; VIII, 1036, 3249 (*Ç°eḥ*), 3909, 3916; IX, 1516.

Subalaja (do.): II, 1681.

Subalaputra (do.): I, 5635; VIII, 2497; IX, 1213.

Subalasya putra(ḥ) (do.): III, †1356.

Subalasya suta(ḥ) (do.): IX, 1153.

Subalātmaja (do.): V, 2253 (chosen by Sahadeva for his antagonist); VI, 4774; VIII, 3919.

Çakuni[2], a serpent. § 67 (Sarpasattra): I, **57**, 2157 (of Dhṛtarāshṭra's race).

Çakuni[3], a demon. § 502 (Manushyagrahak.): III, **230**, 14486 (°*s tām*—i.e. Surabhi—*āruhya saha bhuṅkte çiçūn bhuvi*).

Çakuni[4] = Çiva (1000 names[1]).

Çākuni ("son of Çakuni") = Ulūka: VIII, 997.

Çakunigraha, a demon = Vinatā. § 502 (Manushyagrahak.): III, **230**, 14480 (*Vinatā tu mahāraudrā kathyate Ç°ḥ*).

Çakunikā, a mātṛ. § 615*u* (Skanda): IX, **46**θ, 2633.

Çakuniputra, the son of Çakuni, king of the Gāndhāras. § 785 (Anugītāp.): XIV, **83**, 2485 (*Gāndhārarājena*, vanquished by Arjuna).

Çakunisuta ("son of Çakuni") = Ulūka: VIII, 4307.

Çakunta, son of Viçvāmitra. § 721*b* (Viçvāmitrop.): XIII, **4**β, 249.

Çakuntalā, daughter of Viçvāmitra and Menakā, wife of Dushyanta, and mother of Bharata. § 11 (Parvasaṅgr.): I, **2**, 371. — § 133 (Dushyanta): I, **69**, 2814, 2815 (Dushyanta sees Ç. in the hermitage of Kaṇva); **71**, (2903). —§ 134 (Viçvāmitra): I, **71**, (2912); **72**, 2945 (daughter of Viçvāmitra and Menakā), 2951 (origin of her name: *nirjane tu vane yasmāt çakuntaiḥ parivāritā | Ç°eti nāmāsyāḥ kṛtaṃ cāpi tato mayā*), 2952, (2953).—§ 135 (Çakuntalop.): I, **73**, (2959), (2968), 2977, 2981, (2985), 2987; **74**, 2988, 2997, 2998, 3000, 3003, 3060, (3069), 3101, 3102, 3103 (Dushyanta wedded Ç. according to the Gāndharva form of marriage, and returned to his capital; Ç. brought her son Bharata to Dushyanta, who first did not acknowledge him as his son, until a celestial voice testified the truth of Ç.'s words).—§ 156 (Pūruvaṃç.): I, **95**, ††3782 (*Viçvāmitraduhitaraṃ*), 3783–4 (= vv. 3102–3).—§ 565 (Gālavacarita): V, **117**, 3974 (*reme . . . yathā . . . Çakuntalāyāṃ Dushvantaḥ*).

Çākuntala, "son of Çakuntalā" (metron.) = Bharata: I, 3104, 3105, 3118, 3709; VII, 2387; XII, 938 (*Bh°*); XIV, 50 (*Bh°*).

Çakuntalopākhyāna(ṃ), "episode relating to Çakuntalā." § 133 (Sambhav.): I, **68–70**: *Dushyanta* (q.v.) saw *Çakuntalā* (§ 134), daughter of *Viçvāmitra* (q.v.) and *Menakā*.—§ 135: Enumeration of the eight forms of marriage according to *Manu*. *Dushyanta*, during the absence of *Kaṇva*, wedded *Çakuntalā* according to the *Gāndharva* form, promising her that her son should be the heir apparent, and departing told her that he should send troops to take her to his capital. *Kaṇva*, by his spiritual knowledge, knew what she had done, and approved of it, and bestowed on her the boon that the *Paurava* monarchs might ever be virtuous and never be deprived of their thrones (I, **73**). *Çakuntalā*, after three years, brought forth a beautiful boy, for whom *Kaṇva* caused all the religious rites to be performed, and who, when he was only 6 years of age, used to seize and bind to the trees lions, etc., wherefore he was called *Sarvadamana*. Then *Kaṇva* caused his disciples to bring *Çakuntalā* and the boy to *Hāstinapura* and introduce them to *Dushyanta*. Then they returned to the hermitage. *Dushyanta* feigned not to remember anything. Then *Çakuntalā* became angry ("But knowest thou not the Ancient Wise [*muniṃ purāṇaṃ*, i.e. Nārāyaṇa] who lies in the heart? He who sins is observed by the gods and by him also who occupies every heart. The sun, the moon, the air, fire, earth, sky, water, the heart, *Yama*, the day, the night, both twilights, and *Dharma*, all witness the acts of man. *Yama Vaivasvata* takes no account of the sins of that person with whom [Nārāyaṇa] the witness of all acts is gratified. But that person with whom he [Nārāyaṇa] is not gratified is tortured for his sins by *Yama* . . . The son that is born to persons cognizant of the *Vedic mantras* rescues the spirits of deceased ancestors. Because the son rescues the father from the hell which is called *Put*, therefore he has been called *puttra* by *Svayambhū* himself . . . Even *ṛshis* cannot create creatures without women . . . 'He shall perform a hundred horse sacrifices,' were the words uttered in the skies when I was in the lying-in room . . . *Urvaçī, Pūrvacitti, Sahajanyā, Menakā, Viçvācī*, and *Ghṛtācī*, these are the six foremost *Apsarases*; amongst them, again, *Menakā*, born of *Brahmán*, is the first . . . I can repair to the abodes of *Indra, Kubera, Yama*, and *Varuṇa* . . . The *Pitṛs* have said that the son continues the race, and he is therefore the best of all religious acquirements . . . *Manu* has said that there are five kinds of sons . . ."). Then she left his presence. But a voice from the sky commanded *Dushyanta* to cherish (*bhara*) his son, who should therefore be called *Bharata*. It was this voice of the *Devadūta* that *Dushyanta* had waited for, that the people should not regard his son as of impure birth. *Bharata* reduced to subjection all the kings of the earth and became a *sārvabhauma-cakravartin*, and performed many sacrifices with *Kaṇva* as the chief priest. From him has come the *Bharata* race, of whom the principal ones shall be mentioned (I, **74**).

Çala[1], a serpent. § 63 (Sarpasattra): I, **57**, 2146 (of Vāsuki's race).

Çala[2], son of Dhṛtarāshṭra. § 182 (Dhṛtarāshṭraputranāmak.): I, **117**, 4543.—§ 599 (Jayadrathavadhap.): VII, **127**νν, 5177 (among other sons of Dhṛtarāshṭra who encompass Bhīmasena). —§ 608 (Karṇap.): VIII, **51**δδ, 2447 (among twenty sons of Dhṛtarāshṭra who attack Bhīmasena).

Çala[3], son of Somadatta and brother of Bhūri and Bhūriçravas. § 232 (Svayaṃvarap.): I, **186**, 6995 (present at the svayaṃvara of Draupadī).—§ 287 (Rājasūyikap.): II, **34**, 1267 (came to the rājasūya of Yudhishṭhira).—§ 328 (Kāmyakavanapr.): III, **36**, 1419.—§ 556 (Sañjayayānap.): V, **23**δ, †694.—§ 561 (Yānasandhip.): V, **55**ν, 2208 (among the chief warriors in Duryodhana's army); **58**τ, 2301; **61**ω, 2409; **66**εε, 2502.—§ 571 (Ulūkadūtāgamanap.): V, **160**, 5531 (*Çala-Çalyamatsyaṃ*, sc. *purushodadhiṃ*, i.e. the army of Duryodhana); **164**ε, 5709 (is matched with Cekitāna).— § 573 (Ambopākhyānap.): V, **195**ζ, 7612.—§ 576 (Bhagavadgītāp.): VI, **18**δ, 687 (protected Bhīshma); **20**ζ, †750 (*Vāhlīkānām ekadeçaḥ*).—§ 578 (Bhīshmavadhap.): VI, **51**φ, 2107 (at the left flank of Bhīshma's array).—§ 579 (do.): VI, **52**[1]δ, 2145.—§ 580 (do.): VI, **56**β, 2406 (in the neck of Bhīshma's *garuḍavyūha*); **59**ρ, †2648.—§ 581 (do.): VI, **61**[2]γ, 2690.—§ 584 (do.): VI, **85**[7]ε, †3768.—§ 586 (do.): VI, **102**λ, 4668.—§ 587 (do.): VI, **119**ψ, 5583.—§ 593 (Abhimanyuvadhap.): VII, **37**θ, 1589, (κ), 1609 (attacked Abhimanyu).—§ 596 (Pratijñāp.): VII, **74**β, 2627 (will protect Jayadratha).—§ 599 (Jayadrathavadhap.): VII, **95**η, 3540; **104**μ, 3894; **105**ν, 3949 (*Ç.'s* standard, bearing a huge silvern elephant, was adorned on all sides with peacocks made of gold; C. has by error *Çalyasya*).—§ 600 (Ghaṭotkacavadhap.): VII, **156**η, 6743; **158**ω, 7036.—§ 604 (Karṇap.): VIII, **7**, 208 (? Çala[2]? stays on the field desirous of battle).—§ 609 (Çalyap.): IX, **2**, 72 (among the allies of Duryodhana).—§ 619 (Strīvilāp.): XI, **24**ι, 685 (has been slain).—§ 620 (Çrāddhap.): XI, **26**β, 786 (his body is burnt).—§ 789 (Putradarçanap.): XV, **32**θ, 877 (among the dead warriors who arose from the Gaṅgā).—§ 795 (Svargārohaṇap.): XVIII, **5**μ, 163 (among those who entered the deities).

Çala[4], son of king Parikshit of Ayodhyā and the daughter of the frog-king. § 461 (Vāmadevacarita): III, **192**, ††13177.

Çalabha[1], an Asura. § 92 (Aṃçāvat.): I, **65**, 2534.—§ 130 (do.): I, **67**, 2666 (incarnate as Prahlāda, king of the Bālhīkas).

Çalabha[2], a Pāṇḍava warrior. § 608 (Karṇap.): VIII, **56**νν, 2740 (slain by Karṇa).

Çalabha, pl. (°*āḥ*) ("winged insects," PCR.). § 113 (Aṃçāvat.): I, **66**, 2572 (among the sons of Pulaha).

Çalabhī, a mātṛ. § 615*u* (Skanda): IX, **46**θ, 2624.

Çalāgraja = Bhūriçravas, q.v.

Çālagrāma = Vishṇu: III, 8102.

Çalahara, a serpent. § 64 (Sarpasattra): I, **57**, 2150 (of Takshaka's race).

Çālakaṭaṅkaṭa. § 599 (Jayadrathavadhap.): VII, **109**, 4127 (name of a Rākshasa, BR., but, if a name, it must be a synonym of Alambusha. PCR. translates "resembled a tall çāla uprooten and broken by the wind").

Çāliçiras, a Devagandharva. § 101 (Amçāvat.): I, **65**, 2552 (son of Muni).—§ 191 (Arjuna): I, **123**, 4812 (present at the birth of Arjuna).

Çālihotra, a ṛshi. § 351 (Nalopākhyānap.): III, **71**, 2798 (*hayānām kulatattvavit*).

Çālihotrapitṛ = Kapila: XII, 12759.

Çālihotrasya tīrtha(ṃ), a tīrtha. § 304 (Tīrthayātrāp.): III, **83**, 6077 (read with B. *tīrthe*, named Çālisūrya).

Çālipiṇḍa, a serpent. § 47 (Sarpasattra): I, **35**, 1551.

Çālisūrya, a tīrtha. § 364 (Tīrthayātrāp.): III, **83**, 6077 (= Çālihotrasya tīrtha(ṃ)).

Çālmali[1], son of Avikshit. § 154 (Pūruv.): I, **94**, 3741.

Çālmali[2], one of the seven dvīpas. § 575 (Bhūmip.): VI, **11***a*, 403.

Çālmalika(ḥ) dvīpa(ḥ) (= Çālmali[2]). § 575 (Bhūmip.): VI, **12**, 447 (with a çālmali tree).

Çalu, a river. § 574 (Jambūkh.): VI, **9**λ, 336 (in Bhāratavarsha).

Çālūkinī, a tīrtha. § 362 (Tīrthayātrāp.): III, **83**, 5083.

Çālva[1], pl. (°*āḥ*). § 186 (Vyushitāçvop.): I, **121**, 4714 (the dead Vyushitāçva begat on his wife Bhadrā Kākshivalī three Çālvas and four Madras).

Çālva[2], pl. (°*āḥ*), a people. § 273 (Rājasūyārambhap.): II, **14**, 590 (fled from fear of Jarāsandha).—§ 545 (Pativratāmāhātmyap.): III, **294**, 16664 (had been ruled by Dyumatsena, who was deprived of the kingdom); **299**, 16904 (Dyumatsena was restored into the kingdom). § 549 (Pāṇḍavapraveçap.): IV, **1***a*, 12.—§ 571 (Ulūkadūtāgamanap.): V, **160**γ, †5510 (in the army of Duryodhana); **161**, †5555 (do.).—§ 574 (Jambūkh.): VI, **9**μ, 346 (among the peoples of Bhāratavarsha).—§ 576 (Bhagavadgītāp.): VI, **18***a*, 688 (in the army of Duryodhana); **20**, †752 (do.).—§ 582 (Bhīshmavadhap.): VI, **72**η, 3169 (*Ç°-Kaikayān*, attacked by Sātyaki, etc.).—§ 587 (do.): VI, **117**ρ, 5485 (attack Arjuna); **119***aa*, 5649 (B. has *Çālvāçrayāḥ*, C. *Çālvāḥ Çayāḥ*).—§ 600 (Ghaṭotkacavadhap.): VII, **154**β, 6651 (with the Matsyas they attack Droṇa (!)).—§ 605 (Karṇap.): VIII, **27**λλ, 1077 (attack Arjuna).—§ 607 (do.): VIII, **45**μ, 2084 (among the people who know the eternal religion), (ν), 2106 (*kṛtsnānuçāsanāḥ*).

Çālva[3] ("king of the Çālvas"), name of one or more different princes. § 130 (Aṃçāvat.): I, **67**, 2653 (incarnation of the Asura Ajaka).—§ 233 (Svayaṃvarap.): I, **187**, 7019; **188**, 7051 (present at the svayaṃvara of Draupadī).—§ 287 (Rājasūyikap.): II, **34**, 1268 (came to the rājasūya of Yudhishṭhira).—§ 592 (Saṃçaptakavadhap.): VII, **25**, 1089 (slain by Bhīmaratha, the son of Dhṛtarāshṭra).—§ 611 (Çalyap.): IX, **20**, 1066 (*Mlecchagaṇādhipaḥ*), †1081, †1087, †1091 (is slain by Sātyaki); **21**, 1093 (*nihate*); **24**, 1298 (sc. *hate*). Some of these quotations may perhaps refer to Çālva[4-5].

Çālva[4] (do.), lord of Saubha. § 167 (Vicitravīryop.): I, **102**, 4113, 4116, 4117, 4134 (Ambā would have chosen Çālva for her husband at the svayaṃvara, and he also had chosen her, but with her sisters she was carried off by Bhīshma, who, however, let her free).—§ 573 (Ambopākhyānap.): V, **175**, 5979, 5992, 5994, 5999, 6002, 6003, 6005, 6013, 6019 (having been set free by Bhīshma Ambā repaired to *Ç.*, who, however, did not accept her); **176**, 6076 (Saubhapatiṃ), 6078 (repetition); **177**, 6086, 6092 (do.); **178**, 7027, 7056, 7059. Cf. Çālvapati, Çālvarāja, Saubhapati, Saubharāj, and the next.

Çālva[5] (do.), lord of Saubha, a Daitya slain by Kṛshṇa. § 317*b* (Kṛshṇa): III, **12**, 491 (enumeration of the feats of Kṛshṇa).—§ 319 (Saubhavadhop.): III, **14**, 615 (°*sya nagaraṃ Saubhaṃ*), 618, 633 (hearing the slaughter of Çiçupāla, *Ç.* attacked Dvārakā).—§ 320 (do.): III, **15**, 637, 638, 648 (do.); **16**, 659, 669 (°*sya sacivam* . . . . *Kshemavṛddhiṃ*, fought Çāmba), 675 (°*sya camūpatau*, i.e. Kshemavṛddhi); **17**, 690, 699, 700, 701, 702 (*yuddhaṃ Ç°-Vṛshṇipravīrayoḥ*, i.e. the encounter between *Ç.* and Pradyumna), 705, 708, 711, 714; **18**, 717, 722, 723, 741; **19**, 753, 755, 760, 768 (Kṛshṇa is ordained by Dhātṛ to be the slayer of *Ç.*), 775 (vanquished by Pradyumna, *Ç.* left Dvārakā, having mounted Saubha); **20**, 781, 786 (*sa Ç°ṃ Saubhanagaraṃ*), 792, 793, 798, 808 (*Saubhapatiḥ*, Kṛshṇa set out for Mārttikāvata [the kingdom of *Ç.*] and pursued *Ç.*, who stayed in the midst of the ocean; a long battle ensued); **21**, †819, 822, 827, 830, 839, †847.—§ 321 (do.): III, **22**, 869 (*Saubhapatiṃ*), 870, 884, 885 (slain by Kṛshṇa with the discus), 889.—§ 589 (Droṇābhishekap.): VII, **11**, 395 (*Saubhaṃ Daityapuraṃ Ç°guptaṃ pātayām āsa Mādhavaḥ*, i.e. Kṛshṇa, all. to § 321). Cf. Daiteyāpasada (III, 796), Mārttikāvataka(ḥ) nṛpa(ḥ) (III, 629), Saubha, Saubhādhipati, Saubhapati, Saubharāj.

Çālvaka[1], adj. ("belonging to the Çālvas"). § 556 (Sañjayayānap.): V, **30**, 889 (*rājānaḥ*, in the army of Duryodhana).

Çālvaka[2], pl. (°*āḥ*) (= the Çālvas). § 561 (Yānasandhip.): V, **57**, 2249 (in the army of Duryodhana, assigned to the five Kaikaya princes as their share in the battle).

Çālvapati[1] ("king of the Çālvas") = Çālva[4]: V, 5971,

5977 (°*eḥ puram*), 5980, 5987, 5991, 5995, 5998, 6024, 6074, 7016.

Çālvapati[2] (do.) = Çālva[5]: III, 666.

Çālvaputra ("the son of Çālva"), a prince. § 554 (Sainyodyogap.): V, **4**γ, 86 (among the princes to whom the Pāṇḍavas ought to send messengers).

Çālvarāja[1] ("king of the Çālvas") = Çālva[3]. § 604 (Karṇap.): VIII, **5**ζ, 131 (had been slain by Bhīma in the great battle).

Çālvarāja[2] (do.) = Çālva[4]: I, 4108, 4115, 4120; V, 5974, 6007, 6089, 6093, 6096, 7017.

Çālvarāja[3] (do.) = Çālva[5]: III, 667, 668, 710, 771, 782, 785, 818, 850, 875; V, †1886 (*ayaṃ*—i.e. Kṛshṇa—*Saubhaṃ yodhayām āsa khasthaṃ vibhīshanaṃ māyayā Çālvarājaṃ*, all. to §§ 320–1).

Çālvarāja[4] (do.) = Dyumatsena: XII, 8607 (*D*°); XIII, 6267 (*D*°).

Çālvaseni, pl. (°*ayaḥ*), a people. § 574 (Jambūkh.): VI, **9**μ, 368 (in Bhāratavarsha).

Çālvāyana, adj. ("belonging to the Çālvas"). § 273 (Rājasūyārambhap.): II, **14**, 591 (*rājānaḥ*, fled from fear of Jarāsandha).

Çālveya, pl. (°*āḥ*), a people. § 522 (Draupadīharaṇap.): III, **264**, 15576 (desirous of matrimony, the Sindhu king Jayadratha is going to the Ç.).—§ 561 (Yānasandhip.): V, **54**ι, 2138 (have sided with Yudhishṭhira).—§ 599 (Jayadrathavadhap.): VII, **98**κ, 3662 (°*senāḥ*, attack Droṇa). Cf. Çālva, pl., and the next.

Çālveyaka, pl. (°*āḥ*), a people. § 552 (Goharaṇap.): IV, **30**, 972 (accompanied by the Matsyas and the Ç., Kīcaka had vanquished the Trigartta king Suçarman).—§ 571 (Ulūkadūtāgamanap.): V, **163**, †5652 (Bhīshma promises to slay the Sṛñjayas and the Ç.).

Çalya, king of the Madras, brother of Mādrī, the wife of Pāṇḍu, and father of Rukmaratha. § 9 (Parvasaṅgr.): I, **2**, 301 (*arddhadivasaṃ*, sc. *rarakshа Kuru-vāhinīm*, i.e. on the first half of the eighteenth day of the battle).—§ 11 (do.): I, **2**, 389, 498, 543, 552.—§ 130 (Aṃçāvat.): I, **67**, 2642 (*Bāhlīkapuṅgavaḥ*, incarnation of the Asura Saṃhrāda).—§ 174 (Pāṇḍudigvijaya): I, **113**, 4437, 4438, 4440 (having accepted precious gifts from Bhīshma, Ç. gave his sister Mādrī in marriage to Pāṇḍu).—§ 232 (Svayaṃvarap.): I, **186**, 6993 (*Madrarājaḥ . . . sahaputraḥ | Rukmāṅgadena vīrena tathā Rukmarathena ca*).—§ 233 (do.): I, **187**, †7019, 7032 (*Madrarājaḥ*); **188**, 7037, 7051; **190**, 7092 (*Madrānām īçvaraḥ*), 7107, 7111, 7112, 7113, 7117 (at the svayaṃvara of Draupadī, Ç. with the other kings present fought with the Pāṇḍavas, who disguised as brahmans had won Draupadī).—§ 285 (Nakula): II, **32**, 1197 (coming to Çākala, the city of the Madras, Nakula made his uncle Ç. accept the sway of Yudhishṭhira).—§ 287 (Rājasūyikap.): II, **34**, 1266 (came to the rājasūya of Yudhishṭhira).—§ 289 (Arghāharaṇap.): II, **37**, 1351 (*Madrādhipe*, among the kings, named by Çiçupāla, as passed over by Bhīshma in bestowing the arghā).—§ 290 (Çiçupālavadhap.): II, **44**, 1540 (do.).—§ 296 (Dyūtap.): II, **53**, 1916 (among the kings who waited upon Yudhishṭhira at the rājasūya).—§ 298 (do.): II, **58**, 2015 (present at the game).—§ 554 (Sainyodyogap.): V, **4**γ, 71 (among the kings to whom the Pāṇḍavas ought to send messengers).—§ 555 (do.): V, **8**, 172, 187, 190, (191), (194), 194, 195, 196, 197, 199, (217) (Çalya was coming with one akshauhiṇī of troops to the Pāṇḍavas, but having been honoured by Duryodhana he promised to become the leader of Duryodhana's army; to Yudhishṭhira Ç. promised to dispirit Karṇa, when he became Karṇa's charioteer).—§ 555 (Indravijaya): V, **9**, (228) (Ç. related to Yudhishṭhira the history of Indra's victory (Indravijaya)), (243), (266); **10**, (295), (304), (318); **11**, (342); **12**, (368), (377), (391), (394); **13**, (401); **14**, (428); **15**, (446), (461), (468); **16**, (493), (†511), (518); **17**, (520), (525), (540); **18**, (544).—§ 555 (Sainyodyogap.): V, **18**, 565, 566, (568), 569 (*Madrādhipaḥ*); **19**δ, 585 (joined Duryodhana with one akshauhiṇī of troops).—§ 556 (Sañjayayānap.): V, **25**θ, †733; **27**, †791.—§ 561 (Yānasandhip.): V, **47**α, 1796; **55**λ, 2186, (ν), 2206 (enumeration of the chief warriors of Duryodhana); **57**ρ, 2281; **60**χ, 2375 (*Madrarājaḥ*); **61**ω, 2409.—§ 570 (Sainyaniryānap.): V, **155**θ, 5274 (commanded one akshauhiṇī of troops).—§ 571 (Ulūkadūtāgamanap.): V, **160**, 5502, 5529 (*Karṇa-Ç°jhasāvarttaṃ*, sc. *purushodadhiṃ*, i.e. the army of Duryodhana), 5531 (*Çala-Çalyamatsyaṃ*, do.); **161**, 5547 (= 5529); **164**ε, 5707 (Dhṛshṭaketu is pitted against Ç.).—§ 572 (Rathātirathasaṅkh.): V, **165**, 5739 (*Madrarājaḥ*, is an atiratha), 5740 (*bhāgineyān nijāṃs tyaktvā*).—§ 573 (Ambopākhyānap.): V, **195**ζ, 7612.—§ 576 (Bhagavadgītāp.): VI, **16**α, 622; **17**γ, 657, 662.—§ 577 (Bhīshmavadhap.): VI, **43**β, 1549, 1605, (1607), (1613), 1614, (1615) (Ç. promises to Yudhishṭhira to weaken the energy of Karṇa).—§ 578 (do.): VI, [**45**[7] (Ç. (Madrarājan, Madrapati, v. 1697, Madreçvara, v. 1699) battles with Yudhishṭhira)]; **47**γ[25], 1809, [26]1817, 1826, [28]1843 (battles with Uttara), [30]1862, 1863; **48**, 1868, (θ), [34]1925, (ι), [35]1957, (λ), [36]1963; **49**, [37]2010, 2013 (attacked by Çaṅkha), [40]2019; **50**ο, 2070; **51**ρ, 2092, (φ), 2107.—§ 579 (do.): VI, **52**[1]β, 2134; **55**[15]κ, 2360, 2362, (λ)[16], 2364, (μ), 2365.—§ 580 (do.): VI, **56**[1]β, 2406; **59**ν, †2621, (ρ), †2648.—§ 581 (do.): VI, **60**β, †2672; **61**[2]γ, 2680, 2687, 2689, 2690, (ε), [4]2715; **62**[4], 2723, 2724, 2726, 2745 (*svasrīyau*—i.e. Nakula and Sahadeva— . . . *ānarcchat*); **64**, [13]2836 (pierced by Bhīmasena); **65**ν, 2928.—§ 582 (do.): VI, **69**β, 3080; **71**δ, 3139 (*Madrāṇām ṛshabheṇa*, fought with Yudhishṭhira).—§ 583 (do.): VI, **75**θ, 3304.—§ 584 (do.): VI, **81**α, 3533, [3556 (*Madrarājānam*, attacked by Nakula and Sahadeva)]; [**83** (Madreçvara, v. 3681, 3693, Madrarāja, v. 3687, 3689, 3690, battled with Nakula and Sahadeva)]; **85**ε, †3768, †3777 (fought with Çikhandin); **86**ζ, 3838.—§ 585 (do.): VI, **92**χ, 4118, 4138; **94**ω, 4194; **95**γγ, 4244; **97**κκ, 4407; **98**νν, 4489.—§ 586 (do.): VI, **99**β, 4503 (in the right wing of Bhīshma's sarvatobhadravyūha); **102**ι, 4666; **103**ξ, 4724; **105**, 4794, 4795 (attacked Yudhishṭhira); **113**ι, 5239, 5242, 5247, 5262, 5263, 5272, 5278 (battled with Bhīmasena); **114**κ, 5291, 5296, 5313; [**116** (Madrarājan, v. 5415, Madreçvara, v. 5416, battled with Yudhishṭhira)]; **117**σ, 5496, 5497; **118**τ, 5519; **119**ψ, 5583.—§ 590 (Droṇābhishekap.): VII, **14**, 525 (fought with Nakula—*svasrīyaṃ*), 572, 575, 576 (fought with Abhimanyu); **15**, 585, 587, 588, 595, 596 (°*Vṛkodarau*), 598, 611 (battles with Bhīmasena).—§ 592 (Saṃçaptakavadhap.): VII, **20**δ, 800 (in the right wing of Droṇa's garuḍavyūha); [**25** (Madrarāj, v. 1079, Madreça, v. 1080, battled with Yudhishṭhira)]; **32**ω, 1410.—§ 593 (Abhimanyuvadhap.): VII, **34**γ, 1504; **37**κ, 1609, 1617, 1619 (vanquished by Abhimanyu); **38**, 1625 (*Madreçam; Ç°ād avarajaḥ*, i.e. the younger brother of Ç., attacked Abhimanyu, when Ç. had been vanquished, but was slain); **39**μ, 1650; **45**, 1816 (*Rukmarathaṃ putraṃ Çalyasya*, is slain); **48**, 1897.—§ 596 (Pratijñāp.): VII, **74**, [α, 2619 (Madreçaḥ)], (β), 2627;

[**75**γ, 2673 (Madreçaḥ)].—§ 598 (Jayadrathavadhap.): VII, **85**β, 3036, (γ), 3042; **87**θ, 3098.—§ 599 (Jayadrathavadhap.): VII, **95,** 3529 (*Madrāṇām īçvaraḥ*), (η), 3540; [**96,** 3570 (Madrarājānaṃ)]; **104,** 3915, 3916, 3921 (battles with Arjuna); **105**ν, 3943 (*Madrarājasya*; (*b*): On *Ç*.'s standard-top was a plough-furrow (*sītāṃ*) of gold looking like the presiding goddess of corn (*Sītā*) producing every seed), 3949 (°*sya*, error in C. for *Çalasya* (so B.)); [**119**ββ, 4720 (Madreçvaraḥ)]; **145,** [ννν, 6074 (Madrarājena), 6077 (Madreçena)], 6109, [6139 (Madrarājaḥ), 6142 (Madrarājaṃ)]; **146,** 6206, 6247, 6251 (fought with Arjuna); **147**σσσ, 6363 (*Madrādhipaḥ*); **149**ωωω, 6488; **151**¹γ, 6550. —§ 600 (Ghaṭotkacavadhap.): VII, **156**κ, 6851; [**158**ψ, 7030 (Madrarāja)]; **159**ββ, 7087; **160**γγ, 7146; **163,** †7290; **164,** 7338; [**165,** 7369 (Madrarāja)]; **167,** 7497, 7498 (slaughtered the division of Virāṭa); **170**λλ, 7624.—[§ 602 (Droṇavadhap.): VII, **187**ι, 8545 (Madrarāja).]—§ 603 (Nārāyaṇāstram.): VII, **193***a*, 8903 (*Madrāṇām īçvaraḥ*); [**198**ρ, 9167 (Madrarāja)].—§ 604 (Karṇap.): VIII, **2**γ, 45; **7,** †199 (*tejovadhaṃ Sūtaputrasya pratiçrutyājataçatroḥ purastāt . . . Ç°ḥ*, cf. VI, 1614); **9,** 330 (*Madrarājaḥ*), 334.—§ 605 (do.): VIII, **11**τ, 418 (*senayā sārddhaṃ Madradeça samutthayā*); **13,** 496 (attacked by Çrutakīrti); **31,** 1308, 1309 (Karṇa wants *Ç*. as his charioteer), 1311, 1312, 1314 (has no equal in knowledge of horses—*hayajñāna*); **32**σσ, 1340, 1348 (*Karṇa-Ç°au*), 1354, 1355, (1356), 1376, (νν), 1378, 1381 (etymology of his name: *çalyabhūtas tu çatrūṇām yasmāt tvaṃ yudhi mānada | tasmāc Chalyo hi te nāma kathyate pṛthivītale*), 1384, (φφ), (1387).—§ 606 (Karṇap.): VIII, **34,** 1578, 1583, 1616 (Duryodhana relates to *Ç*. the Tripurākhyāna and the history of Paraçu-Rāma); **35,** (1625), 1643 (*tvam çalyabhūtaḥ çatrūṇām avishahyaḥ parākrame | tatas tvam ucyase rājan Ç°a ity arisūdana*), (1648) (agrees to become Karṇa's charioteer), 1652, 1654, 1656, 1657, 1661 (*Madrādhipaḥ*), (1662), (1666).—§ 607 (do.): VIII, **36,** 1671, 1675, 1680, 1683, 1693, 1694, 1695, (1697); **37,** †1716, †1727, †1730, †1734, (†1739), 1749, 1750 (*çvetāçvaḥ Çalyasārathiḥ*, i.e. Karṇa); [**38,** 1779 (Madrarāja)]; **39,** (1781), 1793 (being the charioteer of Karṇa, *Ç*. praises Arjuna in order to make Karṇa cheerless); **40,** 1816, 1817, 1818, 1819, 1820, 1821, 1825, 1828, 1836 (Karṇa describes the bad practices of the Madrakas, etc.), 1000; **41,** 1873, (1930); **42,** †1962, †1963, †1965, †1968, †1971, †1972, †1987, 1999, 2002, 2006; **43,** 2015, 2020, 2021, 2022 (°*sahasreṇa*); **44,** (2024), 2053; **45,** 2071, 2080, †2087 (Karṇa describes the bad practices of the Madras, etc.), 2092, 2108, (2112), 2119, 2120.—§ 608 (do.): VIII, **46,** 2162, 2197, (2198); **49,** 2330, 2353; **50,** 2395 (*Madrakādhipaḥ*), 2396, (2405), 2409, 2418, 2420, 2422; [**51,** 2460 (Madrarāja)]; [**57,** 2840 (Madrarāja)]; **63,** 3195, 3204, 3205; [**64,** 3257 (Madrarāja)]; **73,** [3647 (Madrarājan)], 3694 (*Madrajanādhipaṃ*), 3728; **78,** 3947, 3949 (*Madrarājaḥ*), 3950; **79**ζ', 4014, 4043, (†4047), †4058, †4062, †4067; **84,** 4268, 4277; **86,** 4349 (*çvetāçvaḥ Çalyasārathiḥ*, i.e. Karṇa); **87,** 4387 (*Kṛshṇa-Ç°rathopetau*, sc. Karṇa and Arjuna), 4462, 4471, 4472, 4473, 4474, (4475), 4478, 4480; **89,** †4586, †4608; **90,** †4649; **92,** †4818 (wanting in B.), †4819; **94,** [†4895 (Madrapati)], †4896, †4917; **95***a*ν, 4967, 4974.—§ 609 (Çalyap.): IX, **1,** 8 (°*ṃ senāpatiṃ kṛtva*, all. to § 610), 10, 26 (*Madrādhipo hataḥ*); **2**ζ, 72, 104.—§ 610 (do.): IX, **6**ξ, 293, 296, (π), 310, 313, 314, (318) (*Ç*. is elected commander (*senāpati*) of Duryodhana's army); **7,** 329, 341 (his investiture), (ν), 345 (*Madrarājaḥ*), 355, 360.—§ 611 (do.): IX, **8,** 372 (*Madrarājaṃ*), (*a*), 373, 380, 381, 384, (ζ), 396, 397; **9,** 452; **10,** 464, 465; **11,** 538, 548, 552, 553, 554, 556, 559, 560, 562, 564, 571 (Sahadeva slew the son of *Ç*.), 576, 586, 587, 590; **12,** 593, 602, 605, 609, 617 (*Madrāṇāṃ vṛshabhaṃ*), 639, 645, 651, 654; **13,** 657, 659 (°*ṃ çalyabhūtaṃ parākrame*), 663, 668, 672, 677, 679, 684, 686, 688, 696, 704; **15,** 761, 763, 767 (*pīḍitas tena svasrīyena*, i.e. by Nakula), 772, 782, 795; **16,** 802, 804, 805, 808, 813, 816, 821, 827, 848, 849, 851, 855, 856, 857; **17,** †883, †885, †886, †892, †900, †901, †912, 924 (is slain by Yudhishṭhira on the eighteenth day of the battle, when *Ç*. had commanded the army of Duryodhana half-a-day), †953; **18,** 955 (*nihate*), 959; **19,** 1000 (*hate*), 1002 (do.), 1005 (do.); **24,** 1298 (do.); **27,** 1457 (*Madrarājo hataḥ*).—§ 613 (Gadāyuddhap.): IX, **32**β, 1837 (*Madrarājasya*); **33**ι, 1934 (*hataḥ*).—§ 615 (Baladevatīrthay.): IX, **52,** 3004 (*hataṃ*), 3005 (*nihataṃ*); **54,** 3065 (*hate*).—§ 615 (Gadāyuddhap.): IX, **56,** 3162 (*hataḥ*); **64**εε, 3589, 3612. —§ 618 (Jalapradānikap.): XI, **1**γ, 29.—§ 619 (Strīvilāpap.): XI, **16***a*, 447; **23,** 635 (*Nakulamātulaḥ*, bewailed as killed), 638, 640 (*Madrarājaṃ*), 642, 643.—§ 620 (Çrāddhap.): XI, **26**β, 786 (his body is burnt).—§ 621 (Rājadharm.): XII, **5**ζ, 140.—§ 785 (Anugītāp.): XIV, **60***a*, 1775, 1797 (*hate*).—§ 789 (Putradarçanap.): XV, **32**θ, 877 (among the dead kings who arose from the Gaṅgā).

Cf. also the following synonyms:—

Ārt(t)āyani: VI, 2146, 2148, 2729; VII, 581, 584; VIII, †198, 1380 (etymology: *ṛtam eva hi pūrvās te vadanti purushottamāḥ | tasmād Ā°iḥ prokto bhavān*); IX, 347, 561.

Bālhīkapuṅgava, q.v.

Madrādhipa ("king of the Madras"): II, 1351 (*Ç*°); V, 569, 2244; VI, 2012, †2623, 2729, 2730, 2732, †3764; VII, 592, 593, 607, 615, 6363 (*Ç*°), 7488, 7494; VIII, 1661 (*Ç*°), †1962 (*Ç*°), 2025, 2395 (*Ç*°), 2438, 3688, †4827; IX, 26 (*Ç*°), 598, 599, 687, 854, 861, †873, †876, †888, †889, †892, †902, †904.

Madrādhipati (do.): I, 7117 (*Ç*°); VI, 1842, 2723; VIII, †4958; IX, 326, 518, †874, †880, †881, †899, †910.

Madraja ("born among the Madras"): VII, 1602.

Madrajanādhipa ("king of the Madras"): VIII, 2026, 3694 (*Ç*°); IX, †875.

Madrajaneçvara (do.): VIII, 2410; IX, 359.

Madraka: VIII, 2019.

Madrakādhama ("lowest among the Madrakas"): VIII, 1868 (Karṇa scolds him).

Madrakādhipa ("king of the Madrakas"): IX, 813.

Madrakeçvara (do.): VI, 1616; VIII, 2006 (*Ç*°).

Madrāṇām adhipa(ḥ) ("the king of the Madras"): VII, 613; VIII, 331 (*Sauvīraḥ*); IX, 332, 674, 782, 784.

Madrāṇām īçvara(ḥ) (do.): I, 7092 (*Ç*°); VII, 3529 (*Ç*°), 8903 (*Ç*°); VIII, 2404, 2408.

Madrāṇām ṛshabha(ḥ) ("the bull of the Madras"): VI, 3138.

Madrāṇāṃ vṛshabha(ḥ) (do.): IX, 617 (*Ç*°).

Madrapa ("king of the Madras"): I, 4432, 4436; VIII, †1747, 1866; IX, 618, †878.

Madrapati (do.): I, 4426 (°*eḥ puraṃ*); VI, 1697; VIII, †1729, †1747, †4833, †4895; IX, 862, 864.

Madrarāj (do.): VI, 1604; VII, 1079, 6062, 6096; VIII, †1738; IX, 570, 678, 916.

Madrarāja (do.): I, †196, †205, 497, 542, 4429, 6993

(Ç°), 7367 (Ç°); V, 188, 198, 566, 2375 (Ç°), 5739 (Ç°); VI, 1849, 1864, 2014, 2728, 3687, 3689, 3690, 4792, 4796, 4798, 4800, 5265, 5363; VII, 589, 600, 606, 1589, 1660, 2673, 3894, 3918, 3943 (Ç°), 5353, 5541, 5629, 6074, 6139, 6142, 7030, 7055, 7369, 7484, 7486, 7491, 7493, 8545, 9167; VIII, 45 (Ç°), 330 (Ç°), 334 (Ç°), 1313, 1323, 1324, 1341, 1390, 1632, 1655, 1656, 1665, 1670, 1672, 1673, 1674, 1679, 1703, 1779, 1869, 2014, 2394, 2460, 2840, 3190, 3193, 3207, 3257, 3949 (Ç°), 4021, †4648, †4815; IX, 120, 121, 321, 342, 345 (Ç°), 349, 352, 354, 358, 372 (Ç°), 377, 385, 388, 391, 409, 451, 460, 463, 466, 512, 515, 539, 540, 541, 589, 590 (Ç°), 600 (°*Vṛkodarau*), 604, 608, 626, 643, 650, 656, 689, 690, 691, 697, 698, 700, 768, 773, 775, 776, 778, 780, 781, 785, 786, 794, 796, 800, 809, 810, 824, 826, 851, 852 (°*Yudhishṭhirau*), †898, †903, 942 (*hate*), 955 (*nihate*), 960, 969 (°*padānugān*, will revenge his death), 978 (do.), 982 (do.), 983 (do.), 990 (°*ānugeshu*), 993, 994 (*nipātitam*), 996 (*pātite*), 998, 1003 (*hate*), 1018 (*hataṃ*), 1023, 1207, 1457 (*hataḥ*), 1837 (Ç°), 3061 (among the fallen); XI, 636 (*nihataḥ çete*), 640, 641.

Madrarājan (do.): VI, 1697, 3556, 5415; VII, 3570; VIII, 1651, 1872, 3647; IX, 685; XIV, 1796.

Madrarājeçvarātmaja (?): VIII, 1386.

Madreça ("king of the Madras"): VII, 1080, 1625, 2619, 6077; VIII, 1345, 1391, 1579, 1749, 2196, †4063; IX, 555, 556, 774, 823, 842, 848, †921 (*praçāntaṃ*); XIV, 1794.

Madreçvara (do.): I, 551; VI, 1699, 3681, 3693, 5269, 5315, 5416; VII, 4720; VIII, 1325, 1327, 1331, 1379, 1793 (Ç°), 4354; IX, 356, 660, 683, 694, 772.

Sauvīra, q.v.

Çalyabhrātṛ ("brother of Çalya"). § 593 (Abhimanyuvadhap.): VII, **38**, 1631 (slain by Abhimanyu; cf. *Çalyād avarajaḥ*, v. 1625).

Çalyānuja ("younger brother of Çalya"). § 611 (Çalyap.): IX, **17**, 931 (slain by Yudhishṭhira). Cf. Madrarājānuja.

Çalyaparvan[1] ("the section relating to Çalya"), the 9th of the greater parvans of Mhbhr. § 4 (Anukram.): I, **1**, 90 (°*sugandhibhiḥ*).—§ 11 (Parvas.): I, **2**, 550, 552.—§ 795*c* (Mahābhārata): XVIII, **6**, 275 (enumeration of what gifts should be given away during the recitation of Ç.).

Çalyaparvan[2], the 80th of the minor parvans of Mhbhr. § 10 (Parvas.): I, **2**, 346.—§ 609: Requested by *Janamejaya* (*a*), *Vaiçampāyana* related *Duryodhana's* grief at *Karṇa's* slaughter, his resolution to continue the battle, his making *Çalya* the commander of the army; that *Çalya*, having made a great carnage, was slain by *Yudhishṭhira* at midnight; that *Duryodhana* fled away from the field, penetrated into a lake, and in the afternoon was summoned and slain by *Bhīmasena*, who had caused the lake to be encompassed by many warriors; that *Açvatthāman*, etc. (β), slaughtered the *Pāñcāla* troops in the night; that *Sañjaya*, next morning, having set out from the camp, entered the city; the grief of the citizens upon hearing *Duryodhana's* fall; that *Sañjaya* informed *Dhṛtarāshṭra* (γ) ("on the side of the *Pāṇḍavas* 7 are alive, amongst the *Dhārtarāshṭras* 3") (δ); *Dhṛtarāshṭra's*, etc. (ε), grief; that *Dhṛtarāshṭra* ordered *Vidura* to let the ladies and *Gāndhārī* retire, and was comforted by *Vidura* (IX, **1**); *Dhṛtarāshṭra's* lament and how he asked *Sañjaya* about the battle (ζ) (IX, **2**). *Sañjaya* begins his narration.—§ 610: The fear of the *Kurus* after the fall of *Karṇa*, and the state of the *Kuru* army (η); *Duryodhana's* resolution to resist the victors (θ); *Bhīma* and *Dhṛshṭadyumna* caused a great carnage; *Arjuna* proceeded towards the car-division; *Nakula*, etc. (ι), & *Çakuni*; 25,000 foot-soldiers & *Arjuna*; they were slain by *Dhṛshṭadyumna* (*b*) and *Bhīma*; the *Kuru* army broke and fled away; *Cekitāna*, etc. (κ), having slain a large number, blew their conchs; *Arjuna* attacked the rest; they fled; *Duryodhana* & the *Pāṇḍavas*; *Duryodhana* rallied his troops (λ); *Duryodhana* (+ all his troops) & the *Pāṇḍavas* (headed by *Yudhishṭhira*) (IX, **3**). *Kṛpa* urged *Duryodhana* to make peace (μ) (IX, **4**); *Duryodhana* refused (ν). The troops were filled with enthusiasm; they took up their quarters about two yojanas distant, and bathed in the *Sarasvatī* of red waters on the sacred and beautiful tableland at the foot of *Himavat* (IX, **5**); there they passed the night: *Çalya*, etc. (ξ), and urged *Yudhishṭhira* to continue the battle. *Duryodhana* addressed *Açvatthāman* (description) (ο), according to whose proposal *Çalya* was made generalissimo (π) (IX, **6**); *Çalya* promised to slay the foes (ρ). *Çalya* was anointed; the troops became cheerful (σ). *Çalya* resolved to slay or be slain (τ). No one any longer felt any grief on account of *Karṇa*; they slept that night happily and became very cheerful. *Yudhishṭhira* asked *Kṛshṇa* his advice (υ); *Kṛshṇa* praised *Çalya* (*Ārtāyani*), saying that he was equal to *Bhīshma*, etc. (φ), and superior to *Çikhaṇḍin*, etc. (χ); he thought only *Yudhishṭhira* was a match for *Çalya*, and urged him to slay him. After *Kṛshṇa* had gone, *Yudhishṭhira* dismissed all his brothers and the *Somakas* and slept happily that night, and so did the *Pāñcālas* and the *Pāṇḍavas*, delighted with *Karṇa's* fall (IX, **7**).—§ 611: The Battle of the Forenoon of the Eighteenth Day. After that night had passed away, the *Kuru* army, urged by *Duryodhana*, prepared for battle; the leaders, *Kṛpa*, etc. (*a*), resolved to fight unitedly ("or be stained with the five great sins and all the minor sins"). Then, with *Çalya* at their head, they quickly proceeded against the foes. Similarly, the *Pāṇḍavas*. Asked by *Dhṛtarāshṭra* about *Çalya's* slaughter by *Yudhishṭhira* and *Duryodhana's* by *Bhīmasena*, *Sañjaya* related: *Çalya* proceeded with horses of the *Sindhu* breed yoked unto his chariot, at the head of the array, accompanied by the *Madrakas* and the sons of *Karṇa*; enumeration of warriors on the left (β), on the right (γ), in the rear (δ), in the centre (ε); *Çakuni* and *Ulūka* surrounded by a large force of cavalry, etc. The mighty bowmen amongst the *Pāṇḍavas* divided themselves into three bodies, and rushed against the *Kurus*; *Dhṛshṭadyumna*, etc. (ζ), against the army of *Çalya*; *Yudhishṭhira* with his troops against *Çalya* alone; *Arjuna* against *Kṛtavarman* and the *Saṃçaptakas*; *Bhīmasena*, etc. (η), against *Kṛpa*; *Nakula* and *Sahadeva* against *Çakuni* and *Ulūka*. Requested by *Dhṛtarāshṭra*, *Sañjaya* enumerated the relative strength of the two armies (θ) (IX, **8**). The commencement of the battle (description); a terrible slaughter on both sides. *Arjuna* and *Bhīmasena* stupefied their foes; *Dhṛshṭadyumna*, etc. (ι), & *Çalya*; *Nakula* and *Sahadeva* proceeded with speed; the *Kurus* fled away (IX, **9**). *Çalya* & *Yudhishṭhira* (+ the *Pāṇḍava* host); *Nakula* & *Karṇa's* son *Citrasena*, whom he slew; *Nakula* & *Citrasena's* brothers *Satyasena* and *Susheṇa*; *Nakula* slew *Satyasena*, mounted the chariot of *Sutasoma*, and slew *Susheṇa*. The *Kurus* were rallied by *Çalya*; a great slaughter took place on both sides. *Sātyaki*, etc. (κ), roared like lions, etc. The *Kurus* surrounded *Çalya*; thither came *Arjuna*, having slaughtered the *Saṃçaptakas*, and the *Pāṇḍavas* headed by *Dhṛshṭadyumna* (IX, **10**). *Çalya* fought with great heroism against the troops of *Yudhishṭhira*; portents appeared on earth and in the skies. *Çalya* & *Yudhishṭhira*, etc. (λ); many were slain; the *Pāṇḍava* army repaired to *Yudhishṭhira*; *Kṛtavarman*, etc. (μ), & *Bhīmasena*, etc.; *Kṛtavarman* & *Bhīmasena*; *Kṛpa* & *Dhṛshṭadyumna*; *Çakuni* & the *Draupadeyas*; *Açvatthāman* & the twins; *Duryodhana* & *Kṛshṇa* and *Arjuna*; the *Bhoja* chief slew the brown steeds of *Bhīmasena*; *Çalya* slew the steeds of *Sahadeva*, who then slew *Çalya's* son; *Kṛpa* & *Dhṛshṭadyumna*; *Açvatthāman* & the *Draupadeyas*; once more the steeds of *Bhīmasena* were slain; he crushed the steeds and chariot of *Kṛtavarman*, who fled away; *Çalya* & *Yudhishṭhira*, etc. (ν); *Bhīma* (with his mace, with which he had challenged *Kubera* and slain Gh. on Gandhamādana) & *Çalya* (IX, **11**); "save *Çalya* or *Rāma* (the delighter of the *Yadus*), none else can venture to encounter *Bhīma*; save *Bhīma*, none can venture to encounter *Çalya*"; *Kṛpa* taking up *Çalya* on his own chariot, bore him away; *Bhīma* had also been made senseless. The *Kurus* (headed by *Duryodhana*) & the *Pāṇḍavas*; *Duryodhana* & *Cekitāna*; *Kṛpa*, etc. (ξ), & *Yudhishṭhira*; *Duryodhana* & *Dhṛshṭadyumna*; *Açvatthāman* (with 3,000 chariots, despatched by *Duryodhana*) & *Arjuna*; *Çalya* + *Candrasena* + *Drumasena* & *Yudhishṭhira* + 25 *Cedis*, etc. (ο); *Yudhishṭhira* was worsted (IX, **12**). *Sātyaki* and *Bhīmasena*, etc. (ο) (+ *Yudhishṭhira*) & *Çalya*; Si., etc., were delighted; *Duryodhana* regarded the *Pāṇḍavas*, *Pāñcālas*, and *Sṛñjayas* as already slain; the *Pāṇḍavas* & *Çalya*, who agitated the whole *Pāṇḍava* army; D. and G. wondered; the *Pāṇḍavas* with *Bhīmasena* at their head and led by *Yudhishṭhira* did not fly (IX, **13**). *Arjuna* & *Açvatthāman* and the *Trigartas*; *Arjuna* destroyed 2,000 chariots; *Açvatthāman* & the *Pāñcāla Suratha*, whom he slew; *Açvatthāman* and the *Saṃçaptakas* & *Arjuna* (IX, **14**). *Duryodhana* & *Dhṛshṭadyumna*; *Çikhaṇḍin* + the *Prabhadrakas* & *Kṛtavarman* and *Kṛpa*; *Çalya* & the *Pāṇḍavas* (with *Bhīma*, etc. (π), and *Sātyaki*); *Nakula* + *Yudhishṭhira* & *Çalya*; *Yudhishṭhira*, etc. (ρ), & *Çalya*; *Çalya* & *Bhīmasena* + *Sātyaki* (whom he deprived of his chariot); *Sātyaki* (on another chariot) & *Çalya* (IX, **15**). The *Pāṇḍavas* (in the very sight of *Kṛshṇa* and *Arjuna*, and though checked by *Bhīmasena*) were afflicted by the *Kurus* (headed by *Çalya*). *Arjuna* & *Kṛpa* and *Kṛtavarman*; *Sahadeva* & *Çakuni*; *Nakula* cast glances on *Çalya* from the side; the *Draupadeyas* checked numerous kings; *Çikhaṇḍin* & *Açvatthāman*; *Bhīmasena* & *Duryodhana*; *Yudhishṭhira* & *Çalya*; *Çalya* alone fought with the whole *Pāṇḍava* army; *Çalya* & *Bhīma*; the *Pāṇḍavas* fled, disregarding the cries of *Yudhishṭhira*, who, summoning all his brothers and *Kṛshṇa*, declared that after *Bhīshma*, etc. (σ), had been slain, *Çalya* only remained as his share; the sons of *Mādrī* should be the protectors of his wheels; *Sātyaki* would protect his right wheel and *Dhṛshṭadyumna* his left, *Arjuna* his rear, *Bhīma* fight in his front. The *Pāṇḍava* troops rejoiced, especially the *Pañcalas*, etc. (τ); *Yudhishṭhira* & *Çalya*; *Bhīma* & *Duryodhana*; *Dhṛshṭadyumna*, etc. (υ), & *Çakuni*, etc.; *Duryodhana* was borne away by his steeds; *Açvatthāman*, etc. (φ), followed him in order to rescue him; the *Kaurava* troops became terrified; *Arjuna* began to slay them; *Çalya* was worsted by *Yudhishṭhira*; the army of *Duryodhana* broke; *Açvatthāman*, taking *Çalya* up on his own chariot, fled away; *Çalya* (on another chariot) & *Yudhishṭhira* (IX, **16**) + *Sātyaki*, etc. (χ); the *Pāṇḍavas*, etc. (ψ), & *Çalya*; the *Kurus* surrounded *Çalya* at the command of *Duryodhana*; *Kṛpa* slew *Yudhishṭhira's* charioteer, and *Çalya* his steeds; *Bhīmasena* slew *Çalya's* charioteer and steeds and cut off his armour; *Dhṛshṭadyumna*, etc. (ω), & *Çalya*; *Yudhishṭhira* slew *Çalya* with a celestial dart (created by *Tvashṭṛ* for the use of *Īçāna*, and always worshipped by the *Pāṇḍavas* with perfumes and garlands and excellent seats and the best kinds of viands and drinks). *Çalya's* younger brother & *Yudhishṭhira*, who slew him; the *Kurus* broke; *Sātyaki* & *Kṛtavarman*, whom *Kṛpa* carried away on his chariot; *Duryodhana* alone withstood the *Pāṇḍava* leaders (*aa*); *Kṛtavarman* (on another chariot) + *Kṛpa* & *Yudhishṭhira*; *Kṛtavarman* was carried away by *Açvatthāman* upon the latter's chariot; *Kṛpa* & *Yudhishṭhira*. The *Pārthas* blew their conchs and applauded *Yudhishṭhira* (IX, **17**). The followers of *Çalya* (1,700 *Madrakas*) resolved to avenge him; *Duryodhana* commanded them not to proceed to battle; they, however, attacked *Yudhishṭhira*; *Arjuna*, etc. (ββ), & the *Madrakas*, whom they began to slaughter; *Duryodhana* in vain tried to prevent them from fighting; then, urged by *Çakuni*, he proceeded to the rescue of the *Madrakas*. The *Pāṇḍavas* arranged themselves in the form called *Madhyama* and slew the *Madrakas*; meteors, etc., were seen; the *Pārthas* encountered a body of horse advancing towards them; the *Kuru* army fled away (IX, **18**). Also the sons of *Dhṛtarāshṭra* almost all turned away from the fight at noon; their fear was like to that after the fall of *Bhīshma*, etc. (γγ); the *Pāñcālas* and the *Pāṇḍavas* pursued them, and congratulated one another (δδ). The *Sṛñjayas* pursued the *Kurus*; *Arjuna* & the chariot-division; *Nakula*, etc. (εε), & *Çakuni*. *Duryodhana* rallied 21,000 foot-soldiers, resisted by *Bhīmasena* and *Dhṛshṭadyumna*; *Bhīma* slew them; *Yudhishṭhira's* troops in vain tried to transgress *Duryodhana*. *Duryodhana* rallied a small force by a spirited address (ζζ); the *Pāṇḍavas*, especially *Arjuna*, rushed against them; *Nakula*, etc. (ηη), against *Çakuni* (IX, **19**). The *Mleccha* king *Çālva* (on an elephant, sprung from a noble breed, and always worshipped by *Duryodhana*) attacked the *Pāṇḍavas* (+ *Somakas* and *Sṛñjayas*), who fled; *Dhṛshṭadyumna* (in order to vanquish the elephant) & *Çālva*; *Dhṛshṭadyumna* had his chariot, steeds, and charioteer destroyed by the elephant; *Bhīma*, etc. (θθ), & *Çālva* (+ the elephant); the *Pāñcālas*, etc. (ιι), lamented; *Dhṛshṭadyumna* slew the elephant with his mace, and *Sātyaki* slew *Çālva* (IX, **20**). *Kṛtavarman*, rallying a portion of the *Kuru* army, resisted the *Pāṇḍavas*; *Sātyaki* & king *Kshemakīrti*, whom he slew; *Kṛtavarman* & *Sātyaki*; the *Pāṇḍavas*, the *Pāñcālas*, etc., became spectators; *Kṛpa* carried *Kṛtavarman* away upon his chariot; the whole army of *Duryodhana* fled except *Duryodhana*, who assailed all the *Pāṇḍavas*, etc. (κκ); then *Kṛtavarman* came (on another chariot) (IX, **21**). *Duryodhana* alone resisted the *Pāṇḍavas*; the *Kuru* army once more rallied and fought; *Duryodhana* & *Yudhishṭhira*, etc. (λλ); *Açvatthāman* & *Bhīmasena*; *Çakuni* & *Yudhishṭhira*, who was carried away by *Sahadeva* on his chariot; *Yudhishṭhira* (on another chariot) & *Çakuni*; Si. and Cā. applauded; *Ulūka* & *Nakula*; *Kṛtavarman* & *Sātyaki*; *Duryodhana* & *Dhṛshṭadyumna*; *Kṛpa* & the *Draupadeyas* (IX, **22**). The *Kurus* were broken by the *Pāṇḍavas*, but rallied by the sons of *Dhṛtarāshṭra*; *Yudhishṭhira* & *Kṛpa* and *Kṛtavarman* (who was carried away by *Açvatthāman*); *Duryodhana* despatched 700 chariots against *Yudhishṭhira*; *Çikhaṇḍin*, etc., came to aid *Yudhishṭhira*; an awful battle ensued; the 700 were slain; the *Pāṇḍavas* and *Pāñcālas* resisted; terrifying omens in nature were seen. *Çakuni* exhorted the others to fight in front; he would himself slay the *Pāṇḍavas* from behind; the *Madrakas* rejoiced, but were slain; *Çakuni* with 10,000 horsemen assailed the *Pāṇḍava* army in the rear; the force of the *Pāṇḍavas* broke down. *Yudhishṭhira* urged *Sahadeva* to slay *Çakuni*, aided by the *Draupadeyas*; *Yudhishṭhira*, with the *Pāñcālas*, would himself destroy the chariot-force. *Sahadeva* (with 700 elephants, 5,000 horses, and 3,000 foot-soldiers) + the *Draupadeyas* & *Çakuni*, who, with 6,000 horses, went away; similarly, the *Pāṇḍava* force, which was reduced to 6,000 horses; the *Draupadeyas* proceeded to *Dhṛshṭadyumna*, *Sahadeva* to *Yudhishṭhira*; *Çakuni* & *Dhṛshṭadyumna's* division; after a terrible battle the *Pāṇḍavas* encompassed *Çakuni* (IX, **23**). *Çakuni* exhorted the remainder of his following, 700 horses, and urged *Duryodhana* to attack the *Pāṇḍavas* (μμ); the remnant of the *Kuru* army attacked the *Pāṇḍavas*; *Arjuna* (desiring to exterminate the *Kurus*) addressed *Kṛshṇa*, recounting the loss sustained by the *Kurus* (νν), and attacked the remnant of the *Kuru* army, and caused a great slaughter (IX, **24**). *Dhṛshṭadyumna*, etc. (ξξ), & the chariot-force; *Duryodhana* escaped on horseback to *Çakuni*; 3,000 elephants encompassed the *Pāṇḍava* brothers, and were slain by *Arjuna* and *Bhīma*, etc. (οο). *Açvatthāman*, etc. (ππ), enquired about *Duryodhana*, pierced through *Dhṛshṭadyumna's* force, and proceeded to *Çakuni*. The *Pāṇḍavas*, headed by *Dhṛshṭadyumna*, assailed the *Kurus*. *Sañjaya* (having joined the five leaders and posted his men, who had been afflicted by *Arjuna*, by *Kṛpa*) & *Dhṛshṭadyumna*; *Sātyaki* & *Sañjaya*, who was made captive; *Bhīma* and *Arjuna* destroyed the elephants; *Açvatthāman*, etc., seeking *Duryodhana*, proceeded to *Çakuni* (IX, **25**). Eleven sons of *Dhṛtarāshṭra*: *Durmarshaṇa*, etc. (ρρ), & *Bhīmasena*, who slew them. *Bhīmasena* then slew 500 chariot-warriors, 10,000 foot, 700 elephants, and 800 horses (IX, **26**). *Duryodhana* and *Sudarça* (the only sons of *Dhṛtarāshṭra* yet unslain) were in the midst of the cavalry. *Kṛshṇa* urged *Arjuna* to destroy the remnant of *Duryodhana's* troops (σσ); *Arjuna* assented (ττ); "only 500 horses form the remnant of the troops of *Çakuni* . . . . . ; there remain also *Açvatthāman*, etc. (υυ)." *Bhīmasena*, etc. (φφ), & *Duryodhana* + *Çakuni*; *Dhṛtarāshṭra's* son *Sudarçana* & *Bhīmasena*; *Suçarman* and *Çakuni* & *Arjuna*; *Duryodhana* (on horseback) & *Sahadeva*. *Arjuna* & the *Trigartas*; *Arjuna* slew *Satyakarman*, *Satyeshu*, and the *Prasthala* ruler *Suçarman*, and the latter's thirty-five sons, etc., and then proceeded against the remnant of the *Bharata* host. *Bhīma* slew *Sudarçana* (Dhārtarāshṭra), and completed the destruction of the *Kaurava* army (IX, **27**). *Çakuni* & *Sahadeva*; *Ulūka* & *Bhīmasena*; *Sahadeva* sat down on his chariot; *Bhīma* and *Sahadeva* & *Çakuni's* men, who fled away, but were rallied by *Duryodhana*; *Sahadeva* + *Nakula* and *Bhīma* & *Çakuni* + *Ulūka*; *Sahadeva* slew *Ulūka*; *Çakuni* (recollecting the words of *Vidura*) & *Sahadeva*; *Çakuni's* division and *Çakuni* himself fled away, pursued by *Sahadeva*, who slew him (IX, **28**).

Çalyaputra[1] = Rukmaratha, q.v.

Çalyaputra[2]: IX, 959 (so C., but read with B. *Dharmaputram*, i.e. Yudhishṭhira).

Çalyasya putra(ḥ) = Rukmaratha, q.v.

Çama[1] ("serenity of mind"). § 116 (Vasu, pl.): I, **66**, 2587 (son of the Vasu Ahas).

Çama[2]. § 117 (Aṃçāvat.): I, **66**, 2596 (son of Dharma), 2597 (husband of Prāpti).

Çama[3] (C. *S°*), a king among the Nandivegas. § 562 (Bhagavadyānap.): V, **74**γ, 2733 (*Samaç ca Nandivegānām*, among the eighteen kings who annihilated their relatives and kinsmen).

Çama[4] = Vishnu (1000 names).

Çamaçam = Çiva (1000 names[1]).

Çamaçama = Çiva (1000 names[1]).

Çamana = Çiva (1000 names[1]).

Çamaṭha, a brahman. § 380 (Brahmasaras): III, **95**, 8527 (*vidyāvratasnātaḥ kaumāraṃ vratam āsthitaḥ*).—§ 381 (Gaya): III, **95**, (8528) (related to Yudhishṭhira the history of Gaya Āmūrtarayasa).

Çāmba[1] (B. Sāmba), son of Kṛshṇa and Jāmbavatī. § 232 (Svayaṃvarap.): I, **186**, 6997 (among the Vṛshṇis who were present at the svayaṃvara of Draupadī).—§ 252 (Subhadrāharaṇap.): I, **219**, 7914.—§ 253 (Haraṇāharaṇap.): I, **221**, 7992 (came to the marriage of Arjuna and Subhadrā).—§ 262 (Bhagavadyāna): II, **2**, 56 (received Kṛshṇa at his return to Dvārakā).—§ 264 (Sabhākriyāp.): II, **4**, 129 (among the princes who received instruction in the use of arms from Arjuna; C. has *S°*).—§ 273 (Rājasūyārambhap.): II, **14**, 622 (one of the seven atirathas among the Vṛshṇis; C. has *S°*).—§ 287 (Rājasūyik.): II, **34**, 1275 (*Gada-Pradyumna-Ç°āç ca*, came to the rājasūya of Yudhishṭhira).—§ 320 (Saubhavadhop.): III, **15**, 644 (*Gada-Çāmboddhavādibhiḥ*, defended Dvārakā); **16**, 667, 669, 672, 673, 674 (fights Kshemavṛddhi), 676, 677 (fights Vegavat); **18**, 735; **21**, 836 (*°prabhṛtayaḥ*).—§ 342 (Indralokābhigamanap.): III, **51**, 1994, 2009 (will assist the Pāṇḍavas in the battle).—§ 400 (Tīrthayātrāp.): III, **118**, †10233 (among the Vṛshṇis whom the Pāṇḍavas met in Prabhāsa).—§ 402*b* (do.): *Ç.*, when still a boy, had routed the army of the Daitya Çambara and killed Açvacakra: III, **120**, 10270, 10272.—§ 510 (Draupadī-Satyabhāmās.): III, **234**, 14719.—§ 553 (Vaivāhikap.): IV, **72**, 2357 (came to the marriage of Abhimanyu and Uttarā).—§ 554 (Sainyodyogap.): V, **1***a*, †5; **2**, 59.—§ 570 (Sainyaniryānap.): V, **157**κ, 5330 (*Gada-Sāmboddhavādibhiḥ*, accompany Balarāma).—§ 589 (Droṇābhishek.): VII, **11**ξ, 408.—§ 599 (Jayadrathavadhap.): VII, **110**σ, 4195.—§ 617*b* (Brahmaçiras): X, **12**ζ, 638 (had never desired the discus of Kṛshṇa).—§ 730 (Ānuçāsanik.): XIII, **14**, 615 (*°hetoḥ*, in order to obtain the son *Ç.* Kṛshṇa performed austerities); **15**, 1028 (Çiva was gratified and granted Kṛshṇa the son *Ç.*).—§ 785 (Anugītāp.): XIV, **66**θ, 1938 (accompanied Kṛshṇa); **86**τ, 2557 (do.).—§ 793 (Mausalap.): XVI, **1**, 16, 19 (*Vāsudevasya dāyādaḥ*), 25; **3**ζ, 100 (is slain).—§ 795 (Svargārohaṇap.): XVIII, **5**, 162 (among those who after death entered the deities). Cf. Jāmbavatīsuta (III, 10271), Jāmbavatyāḥ sutaḥ (III, 670).

Çāmba[2] (B. Sāmba), a brahman. § 787 (Āçramavāsap.): XV, **10**, 312 (the citizens charged *Ç.* to answer Dhṛtarāshṭra, when he took leave with them in order to go to the forest).

Çambara, an Asura. § 92 (Aṃçāvat.): I, **65**, 2530 (the second of the forty sons of Danu).—§ 209 (Drupadaçāsana): I, **138**, 5481 (*Mahendraṃ Çambaro yathā*).—§ 402*b* (Çāmba): III, **120**, †10271 (*Daityasya*, his army has been routed by Çāmba).—§ 443 (Nivātakavacayuddhap.): III, **168**, 12072 (has been vanquished by Indra).—§ 444 (do.): III, **171**, 12149 (*°sya vadhe*, Mātali had acted as the charioteer of Indra).—§ 555 (Indravijaya): V, **16**, 497 (has been slain by Indra).—§ 561 (Yānasandhip.): V, **68**ζζ, 2526 (has been vanquished by Kṛshṇa).—§ 562 (Bhagavadyānap.): V, **72**, 2602 (a sentence of his is quoted).—§ 568 (Vidulāputraçāsana): V, **134**, 4550 (do.).—§ 585 (Bhīshmavadhap.): VI, **100**, 4583 (*yathā devāsure yuddhe Çakra-Ç°yoḥ purā*, sc. *samāgamaḥ*).—§ 592 (Saṃçaptakavadhap.): VII, **25**, 1125 (*yādṛk purā vṛttaṃ Ç°āmararājayoḥ*).—§ 599 (Jayadrathavadhap.): VII, **96**, 3571 (*yathā pūrvam abhūd yuddhaṃ*

Ç°āmararājayoḥ); **106,** 3973 (*Mahendra iva Ç°m*, sc. *abhyadravat*); **109,** 4098 (*kurvator vividhā māyāḥ Çakra-Ç°yor iva*).—§ 600 (Ghaṭotkacavadhap.): VII, **169,** 7582 (*yathā devāsure yuddhe Ç°āmararājayoḥ*, sc. *yuddhaṃ*); **175,** 7914 (*Indra-Ç°yor iva*, sc. *sannipātaḥ*).—§ 605 (Karṇap.): VIII, **13,** 508 (*°sya çiro yadvad nihatasya mahāraṇe*).—§ 608 (do.): VIII, **74,** 3793 (*Ç°m Maghavān iva*, sc. *hatvā*; C. has *S°*); **82,** †4210 (*Çakra-Ç°yor yathā*, sc. *yuddhaṃ*); **87,** 4397 (*sadṛçau yuddhe Ç°āmararājayoḥ*; C. has *S°*), 4463 (*Çakra-Ç°yor iva*, sc. *yuddhaṃ*); **88,** †4498 (*surāsurāḥ Ç°-Vāsavāv iva*, sc. *parivāryya*).—§ 610 (Çalyap.): IX, **7,** 355 (*Maghavān iva Ç°m*, sc. *jahi*).—§ 611 (do.): IX, **15,** 784 (*yādṛço vai purā vṛttaḥ Ç°āmararājayoḥ*).—§ 617 (Aishīkap.): X, **12,** 596 (*Ç°m Maghavān iva*, sc. *jahi*).—§ 641 (Rājadh.): XII, **98ζ,** 3661 (*naikamāyaṃ*, had been slain by Indra); **102,** 3783 (a sentence of his is quoted); **130,** 4761 (*atraitac Chambarasyāhur mahāmāyasya darçanam* (i.e. *çāstram*, Nīl.)). —§ 656 (Khaḍgotpatti): XII, **166γ,** 6146 (a Dānava).—§ 673*b* (Bali-Vāsavasaṃv.): XII, **227*a*,** 8261 (among the ancient rulers of the earth).—§ 730 (Ānuçāsanik.): XIII, **14,** 616 (had been slain by Pradyumna).—§ 740 (do.): XIII, **36,** 2165 (*Çakra-Çambara saṃvādam*), 2166, 2167, (2168).—§ 742 (do.): XIII, **39*a*,** 2237 (*°sya māyā*). Cf. Daitya, Dānavendra (XIII, 2183).

Çambarahan = Indra, q.v.

Çambara-Pākahan = Indra, q.v.

Çambhalagrāma, v. S°.

Çambhu[1], an ancient king. § 6 (Anukram.): I, **1*a*,** 228 (in Sañjaya's enumeration).—§ 761 (Ānuçāsanik.): XIII, **115δ,** 5668.

Çambhu[2] = Brahmán: I, 2499; VI, 2069 (*ahaṃ Droṇāntakaḥ Pārtha, vihitaḥ Ç°nā purā*, says Dhṛshṭadyumna); XII, 11229 (creates Hiraṇyagarbha), 11602.

Çambhu[3] = Vishṇu (Nārāyaṇa, Kṛshṇa): II, 1321 (*Nārāyaṇaḥ* = Kṛshṇa); XII, 1505 (= Kṛshṇa); XIII, 6954 (1000 names); XIV, 1085 (= *mahān ātmā*).

Çambhu[4] = Çiva: III, 499 (*Çūlapāṇis Trilocanaḥ*, born from the forehead of Hari), 1629, 8648 (*°or jaṭābhrashṭā*, sc. Gaṅgā); V, 7395; VII, 9453, 9507, 9582; VIII, 1446; XII, 9164; XIII, 588, 1011.

Çambhu[5], a fire. § 493 (Āṅgirasa): III, **221,** 14181 (the fourth of the five Ūrjaskara fires, sons of Tapas).

Çambhu[6], a Rudra. § 770 (Ānuçāsanik.): XIII, **151β,** 7091 (enumeration).

Çambhu[7], son of Kṛshṇa and Rukmiṇī. § 730 (Ānuçāsanik.): XIII, **14*a*,** 621.

Çambuka. § 653*b* (Gṛdhra-gomāyus.): XII, **153,** 5742 (*çūdre*, slain by Rāma [Dāçarathi, because he performed austerities], then a brahman's child was revived; B. has *J°*).

Çambūka, a warrior of Skanda. § 615*u* (Skanda): IX, **45η,** 2578.

Çamīka[1], a muni, father of Çṛṅgin. § 51 (Parikshit): I, **41,** (1711); **42,** (1727), 1741, 1749 (having disgraced Ç., Parikshit was cursed by Çṛṅgin).—§ 266 (Çakrasabhāv.): II, **7,** 297 (in the palace of Indra, B. has *S°*).—§ 790 (Putradarçanap.): XV, **35,** 946.

Çamīka[2], a Vṛshṇi. § 232 (Svayaṃvarap.): I, **186,** 6999 (came to the svayaṃvara of Draupadī, *S°* both B. and C.).—§ 273 (Rājasūyārambhap.): II, **14,** 623 (is a mahārātha, *S°* both B. and C.).—§ 589 (Droṇābhishek.): VII, **11ζ,** 409 (*Ç°* also B.). The right spelling of this and prec. is *S°*.

Çampāka, a brahman. § 659 (Mokshadh.): XII, **176,** 6568 (*°ena muktena gītam itihāsaṃ purātanam*, i.e. vv. 6565 foll.), 6585 (*Hāstinapure brāhmaṇena upavarṇitam* | *Ç°ena purā mahyaṃ*, i.e. to Bhīshma).

Çamyu, a fire. § 490 (Āṅgirasa): III, **219,** 14131 (the first son of Bṛhaspati), 14133 (Satyā is his wife), 14135 (his children).

Çanaiçcara[1], the planet Saturn, son of Sūrya (the Sun). § 270 (Brahmasabhāv.): II, **11,** 447 (among other planets in the palace of Brahmán).—§ 533 (Sītā-Rāvaṇasamv.): III, **281,** 16171 (*Rohiṇīm etya Ç°a iva grahaḥ*).—§ 569 (Bhagavadyānap.): V, **143θ,** 4840 (*Prājāpatyaṃ hi nakshatraṃ*— i.e. Rohiṇī, Nīl.—*grahas tīkshṇo mahādyutiḥ* | *Ç°ḥ pīḍayati*, omens).—§ 574 (Jambūkh.): VI, **2*a*,** 66 (*Rohiṇīṃ pīḍayann esha sthito . . . C°ḥ*, omens); **3,** 94 (*Viçākhāyām samīpasthau Bṛhaspati-Ç°au*).—§ 586 (Bhīshmavadhap.): VI, **104,** 4748 (*samāgatau . . . yathākāçe . . . sthitau Budha-C°au*).—§ 611 (Çalyap.): IX, **16,** 805 (*candramaso 'bhyāse Ç°a iva grahaḥ*).—§ 717*b* (Nārāyaṇīya): XII, **350,** 13692 (*°ḥ Sūryaputro bhavishyati Manur* (*Manor*, C.) *mahān*).—§ 775 (Ānuçāsanik.): XIII, **166*a*,** 7643 (enumeration). Cf. Sūryaputra.

Çanaiçcara[2] = Sūrya (the Sun): III, 148.

Çānavatya, pl. (*°āḥ*), a people. § 295 (Dyūtap.): II, **52,** 1872 (among the peoples who brought tribute to Yudhishṭhira).

Çāṇḍilī[1], a goddess. § 116 (Vasu): I, **66,** 2584 (wife of Prajāpati and mother of the Vasu Anala).—§ 574 (Jambūkh.): VI, **8ι,** 295 (*tatra*—i.e. on the Çṛṅgavat mountain—*svayamprabhā devī nityaṃ vasati Ç°ī*).

Çāṇḍilī[2], a brāhmaṇī. § 565 (Gālavacarita): V, **113,** 3872 (*brāhmaṇī*, performed austerities on the Ṛshabha mountain), 3890.—§ 764 (Ānuçāsanik.): XIII, **123,** 5859, 5864 (had attained to heaven, discourse between her and Sumanā).

Çāṇḍilya, a ṛshi. § 264 (Sabhākriyāp.): II, **4*a*,** 112 (in Yudhishṭhira's palace).—§ 615 (Baladevatīrthay.): IX, **54,** 3041 (his daughter attained to heaven).—§ 637 (Rājadh.): XII, **47η,** 1593 (among the ṛshis who surrounded Bhīshma on his arrow-bed).—§ 677 (Mokshadh.): XII, **254,** 9114 (*samādhau yogam evaitac Ch°aḥ çamam abravīt*, in the Chāndogya Upanishad, Nīl. and PCR.).—§ 746 (Ānuçāsanik.): XIII, **65,** 3308 (*pradānaṃ sarvadānānāṃ çakaṭasya, viçāmpate* | *evam āha mahābhāgaḥ Ç°o mahān ṛshiḥ*).—§ 767 (do.): XIII, **137*a*,** 6266 (having given food to Ç., Bhumanyu ascended to heaven).

Çani = Çiva (1000 names[2]).

Çaṅkara[1] = Çiva, q.v.

Çaṅkara[2], a Viçvadeva. § 749 (Ānuçāsanik.): XIII, **91γ,** 4360 (enumeration).

Çaṅkaraçvaçura = Himavat: XIII, 1748.

Çaṅkarshaṇa (X, 498), error in C. for Saṅkarshaṇa, q.v.

Çaṅkha[1], a serpent. § 47 (Sarpanāmakath.): I, **35,** 1553. —§ 564 (Mātalīyop.): V, **103,** 3628.—§ 793 (Mausalap.): XVI, **4ε,** 119.

Çaṅkha[2], son of the Matsya king Virāṭa and brother of Uttara. § 232 (Svayaṃvarap.): I, **186,** 0990 (*Virāṭaḥ saha putrābhyāṃ Ç°enaivottareṇa*, present at the svayaṃvara of Draupadī).—§ 556 (Goharaṇap.): IV, **31,** 1015 (*Virāṭasya suto jyeshṭhaḥ*).—§ 561 (Yānasandhip.): V, **57,** 2237 (*Virāṭaḥ saha putrābhyāṃ Ç°enaivottareṇa*, in the army of Yudhishṭhira).—§ 569 (Bhagavadyānap.): V, **141γ,** 4782.—§ 572 (Rathātirathasaṅkh.): V, **171,** 5907 (a ratha among the Pāṇḍavas).—§ 573 (Ambopākhyānap.): V, **194γ,** 7599.—§ 578 (Bhīshmavadhap.): VI, **45**[9], 1704, 1705 (fought with Saumadatti); **49,** 2010 (*Vairāṭiḥ*, not in B.), 2012 (not in B.), 2015, 2017, 2019.—§ 584 (do.): VI, **82**[2], 3595, 3597 (is slain by Droṇa).—§ 604 (Karṇap.): VIII, **6ζ,** 187

(*Virāṭaputraḥ*, mentioned among those who have fallen).—§ 795 (Svargārohaṇap.): XVIII, **5**λ, 148, 164 (among those who entered the deities).

Çaṅkha[3], an ancient ṛshi, brother of Likhita. § 266 (Indrasabhāv.): II, **7**, 292 (*Çaṅkhaç ca Likhitaç ca*, in the palace of Indra).—§ 628 (Rājadharm.): XII, **23**, 668, 670, 671, 672, 673, 675, 687, (688), 690, 692, (694).—§ 746 (Ānuçāsanik.): XIII, **66**ε, 3320 (ascended to heaven by having made gifts of sesame seeds).

Çaṅkha[4], a Daitya. § 268 (Varuṇasabhāv.): II, **9**, 365 (among other Daityas in the palace of Varuṇa).

Çaṅkha[5], a treasure. § 269 (Vaiçravaṇasabhāv.): II, **10**, 418 (*nidhipramukhyau Ç°Padmau dhaneçvarau*, in the palace of Kubera; C. has *S°*).—§ 677 (Mokshadh.): XII, **235**, 8603 (*nidhiṃ*, given by Brahmadatta to the brahmans).—§ 767 (Ānuçāsanik.): XIII, **137***a*, 6261 (do.).—§ 785 (Anugītāp.): XIV, **65**η, 1924 (*°ādīn nidhīn*).

Çaṅkha[6], a prince. § 291 (Çiçupālavadhap.): II, **44***a*, 1539.

Çaṅkhabhṛt = Vishṇu (1000 names).

Çaṅkhacakragadādhara = Kṛshṇa (Vishṇu), q.v.

Çaṅkhacakragadāhasta = Kṛshṇa, q.v.

Çaṅkhaçiras, a serpent. § 47 (Sarpanāmak.): I, **35**, 1557. Cf. next.

Çaṅkhaçīrsha, a serpent. § 564 (Mātalīyop.): V, **103**γ, 3631. Cf. the prec.

Çaṅkhakumbhaçravas, a mātṛ. § 615*u* (Skanda): IX, **46**θ, 2644.

Çaṅkhalikā, a mātṛ. § 615*u* (Skanda): IX, **46**θ, 2644.

Çaṅkhamekhala, a ṛshi. § 22 (Pramadvarā): I, **8***a*, 961.

Çaṅkhamukha, a serpent. § 47 (Sarpanāmak.): I, **35**, 1556.

Çaṅkhapada, son of Manu Svārocisha. § 717*b* (Nārāyaṇīya): XII, **349**, IV), 13583, 13584.

Çaṅkhapiṇḍa, a serpent. § 47 (Sarpanāmak.): I, **35**, 1558.

Çaṅkhatīrtha, a tīrtha on the *Sarasvatī*. § 615*f* (Baladevat.): Here *Baladeva* beheld a gigantic tree, *Mahāçaṅkha*, tall as *Meru*, looking like *Çvetaparvata*, and resorted to by many R.; there dwell Y., Vd., Rā., Pç., and Si., in thousands; all of them, abandoning other kinds of food, observe vows and regulations, and take at due seasons the fruits of that tree for their sustenance, and wander unseen by men: IX, **37**, 2137.

Çaṅkhinī, a tīrtha. § 364 (Tīrthayātrāp.): III, **83**, 6021 (°*ṃ*, but B. has *Çaṅkhinītīrthaṃ*; cf. Devyās tīrtha(ṃ)).

Çaṅku, a Vṛshṇi. § 232 (Svayaṃvarap.): I, **186**, 6999 (present at the svayaṃvara of Draupadī).—§ 253 (Haraṇāharaṇap.): I, **221**, 7992 (came to the nuptials of Arjuna and Subhadrā).—§ 273 (Rājasūyārambhap.): II, **14**, 623.

Çaṅkukarṇa[1], a serpent. § 67 (Sarpasattra): I, **57**, 2156 (of Dhṛtarāshṭra's race).

Çaṅkukarṇa[2], son of Janamejaya. § 160 (Pūruv.): I, **95**, 3838 (son of Janamejaya and Vapushṭamā).

Çaṅkukarṇa[3], a warrior of Skanda. § 615*u* (Skanda): IX, **45**, 2553 (given to Skanda by Parvata), (η), 2558 (enumeration).

Çaṅkukarṇa[4] = Çiva (1000 names[1]).

Çaṅkukarṇeçvara, a tīrtha. § 358 (Tīrthayātrāp.): III, **82**, 5012.

Çānta[1], son of the Vasu Ahas. § 116 (Vasu, pl.): I, **66**, 2587.

Çānta[2] = Çiva (1000 names[1]).

Çānta[3] = Vishṇu: XII, 13112; XIII, 7011 (1000 names), 7048 (do.).

Çāntā, daughter of the Aṅga king Lomapāda and wife of Ṛshyaçṛṅga. § 390 (Tīrthayātrāp.): III, **110**, 9993.—§ 391 (do.): III, **110**, 9996 (*rājaputrī*).—§ 391 (Ṛshyaçṛṅga): III, **113**, †10080, †10088, †10089, †10091, †10093 (Ṛshyaçṛṅga married Ç.).—§ 677 (Mokshadh.): XII, **235**, 8609 (having given his daughter Ç. to Ṛshyaçṛṅga, Lomapāda obtained the fruition of all his wishes).—§ 767 (Ānuçāsanik.): XIII, **137***a*, 6269 (do.).

Çāntabhaya, an ancient king. § 6 (Anukram.): I, **1**, 229 (in Sañjaya's enumeration).

Çāntanava[1] = Bhīshma, q.v.

Çāntanava[2] = Citrāṅgada: I, 4068, 5744.

Çāntanava[3], pl. (°*āḥ*), "the descendants of Çāntanu." § 298 (Dyūtap.): II, **63**, 2112, 2117.

Çāntanoḥ putra(ḥ), Çantanoḥ suta(ḥ) = Bhīshma, q.v.

Çāntanu, son of Pratīpa and father of Bhīshma, Citrāṅgada, and Vicitravīrya. § 11 (Parvas.): I, **2**, 372. — § 70 (Ādivaṃçāvat.): I, **60**, 2213 (°*oḥ santatiṃ*). — § 130 (Aṃçāvat.): I, **67**, 2711 (*jajñire Vasavas tv ashṭau Gaṅgāyāṃ Çāntanoḥ sutāḥ*). — § 155 (Pūruvaṃç.): I, **94**, 3750 (*Pratīpasya trayaḥ putrā jajñire, Bharatarshabha* | *Devāpiḥ Çāntanuç caiva Vāhlīkaç ca mahārathaḥ*), 3751 (became king after Pratīpa had retired to the woods).—§ 156 (do.): I, **95**, ††3797 (son of Pratīpa and Sunandā), ††3798, 3799 (*atrānuvaṃçaçloko bhavati* | "*yaṃ yaṃ karābhyāṃ spṛçati jīrṇaṃ sa sukham açnute* | *punar yuvā ca bhavati tasmāt taṃ Çāntanuṃ viduḥ*" *iti tad asya Çāntanutvaṃ*), ††3800 (married Gaṅgā, by whom he had the son Devavrata or Bhīshma), ††3802 (married Satyavatī, by whom he had the sons Citrāṅgada and Vicitravīrya). — § 161 (Mahābhishop.): I, **96**, 3858 (shall be the father of the Vasus).—§ 162 (Çāntanūp.): I, **97**, 3882 (the reborn Mahābhisha was called Çāntanu, because of the asceticism of his father Pratīpa: *çāntasya jajñe santānas tasmād āsīt sa Çāntanuḥ*), 3883 (*Kurusattamaḥ*), 3884, 3887 (is made king), 3888.—§ 163 (Bhīshmotp.): I, **98**, 3900 (marries Gaṅgā), 3901, 3904, 3909 (seven of the eight children whom Çāntanu begot in Gaṅgā, she threw into the water, but the eighth was saved by Ç.).—§ 164 (Āpavop.): I, **99**, (3920), 3923, 3965, 3966, 3967 (having told Ç. the history of the Vasus, Gaṅgā left him, taking with her the child [Bhīshma]).—§ 165 (Satyavatīlābhop.): I, **100**, 3968, 3969, 3973, 3976, 3981, 3982, 3983, 3989, 3990, 3994, 3996, 3998, 4006, 4009 (°*oḥ putraḥ*, i.e. Bhīshma, was taken by Ç. to the capital and installed as yuvarāja), 4015 (sees Satyavatī), (4020), 4022, 4024, 4027, 4041, 4053 (*nāthaḥ C°oḥ*, i.e. Bhīshma), 4064, 4066 (marries Satyavatī; Bhīshma adopts the vow of brahmacarya, and Ç. grants him that he shall die at his own choice).—§ 166 (Citrāṅgadop.): I, **101**, 4067, 4070, 4071 (having procreated Citrāṅgada and Vicitravīrya, he dies). — § 167 (Vicitravīryop.): I, **102**, 4126 (*Kauravyaḥ*).—§ 168 (Bhīshma-Satyavatīsaṃv.): I, **103**, 4148 (*Kauravyasya*), 4170.—§ 173 (Pāṇḍurājyābhish.): I, **109**, 4359 (°*or vaṃçaṃ*). — § 177 (Pāṇḍudigvijaya): I, **113**, 4461.—§ 198 (Çaradvat): I, **130**, 5084 (brings up Kṛpa and Kṛpī).—§ 253 (Haraṇāharaṇap.): I, **221**, 7969 (°*or anvaye*).—§ 267 (Yamasabhāv.): II, **8**, 336 (in the palace of Yama).—§ 370 (Tīrthayātrāp.): III, **84**, 8012 (*tato Lalitikaṃ gacchet Ç°os tīrtham uttamaṃ*).—§ 406*b* (Ārcīkaparvata): III, **125**, 10414 (had attained the eternal abode at Ārcīkaparvata).—§ 438*f* (Arjuna): III, **162**, 11825 (*pitus tava pitāmahaḥ*, i.e. Arjuna's), 11828 (*adhirājaḥ sa rājaṃs tvāṃ Çāntanuḥ prapitāmahaḥ* | *svargajit Çakralokasthaḥ kuçalaṃ paripṛcchati*, says Kubera to Arjuna).—§ 556 (Sañjayayānap.): V, **31**, 924 (°*or vaṃçaḥ*).—§ 561 (Yānasandhip.): V, **55**, 2189 (*Pitāmaho 'pi Gāṅgeyaḥ Çāntanor adhi*).—§ 569

(Bhagavadyānap.): V, **147**χ, 4973, 4983 (°*oḥ kulavardhana*, i.e. Bhīshma), 4992 (°*unā jātaḥ*, i.e. Bhīshma); **148**, 5003 (*Prātīpaḥ*); **149**, 5055 (*dhṛtimān me pitāmahaḥ*, i.e. Dhṛtarāshṭra's), 5059 (*Vāhlīkaç ca priyo bhrātā Ç°oç ca*), 5067 (*pitṛbhrātṝn parityajya*—sc. Bāhlīka; *Vāhlīkena tv anujñātaḥ Çāntanur . . . | pitary uparate . . . rājyakāmam* (B. *rājā rājyam*) *akārayat*).—§ 573 (Ambop.): V, **173**, 5945 (*mama pitā*, i.e. Bhīshma's).—§ 576 (Bhagavadgītāp.): VI, **14**, 550 (became free from sorrow, etc., when Bhīshma was born).—§ 587 (Bhīshmavadhap.): VI, **120**, 5702 (*ayaṃ*—i.e. Bhīshma—*pitaram ājñāya kāmārttaṃ Çāntanuṃ purā | ūrdhvaretasam ātmānaṃ cakāra*).—§ 615 (Gadāyuddhap.): IX, **56**ρ, 3153 (°*oḥ kulapāṃçanaḥ*, i.e. Duryodhana).—§ 639 (Rājadh.): XII, **50**, 1820 (*varadānāt pituḥ kāmaṃ chandamṛtyur asi prabho | Ç°or dharmanityasya*, says Kṛshṇa to Bhīshma).—§ 717*b* (Nārāyaṇīya): XII, **340**, 12988 (*mama pitā*, i.e. Bhīshma's).—§ 724 (Ānuçāsanik.): XIII, **8**, 387 (*tena satyena gaccheyaṃ lokān yatra sa Ç°uḥ*).—§ 746 (do.): XIII, **59**, 3041 (do.).—§ 747 (do.): XIII, **84**, 3941 (Bhīshma had performed his çrāddha).—§ 775 (do.): XIII, **166**η, 7683 (among the kings whose names, when recited, bestow religious merit).—§ 787 (Āçramavāsap.): XV, **9**λ, 283 (has ruled over the earth); **10**, 320 (do.). Cf. Bhārata, Bhāratagoptṛ, Bharatasattama, Kauravya, Kurusattama, Prātīpa.

Çāntanuja = Bhīshma, q.v.

Çāntanunandana = Bhīshma, q.v.

Çāntanūpākhyāna(ṃ) ("episode relating to Çāntanu"). § 162 (Sambhav.): The *rājarshi Pratīpa* spent many years in ascetic penances at the source of *Gaṅgā*. She sat upon his right thigh and wished him to be her husband. He replied that the left lap was for the wife, but the right for the daughters and daughters-in-law; therefore he accepted her for his son, to which *Gaṅgā* consented on the condition that his son should not be able to judge of the propriety of her acts. Then *Pratīpa*, along with his wife, engaged in ascetic austerities from desire of offspring, and when they had grown old, *Mahābhisha* (v. Mahābhishop.) was born as a son to them and was called *Çāntanu*, because his father had controlled his passion (*çāntasya santānaḥ*, v. 3882, cf. 3799). When *Çāntanu* had grown to become a youth, *Pratīpa* told him about his appointment with the celestial damsel, installed him upon the throne, and retired into the woods. *Çāntanu*, who was addicted to hunting, one day came upon the banks of *Gaṅgā*, frequented by *Siddhas* and *Cāraṇas*, and there he requested *Gaṅgā*, in the form of a lovely maiden, to become his wife (I, **97**). (For continuation v. Bhīshmotpatti.)

Çāntanusuta = Bhīshma, q.v.

Çāntatama = Çiva (1000 names[1]).

Çantātman = Kṛshṇa: XII, 1671.

Çānti[1], an Indra. § 238 (Pañcendrop.): I, **197**, 7304 (the fourth of the five Indras).

Çānti[2], a ṛshi. § 717*c* (Uparicara): XII, **337**ε, 12759 (*ṛshiḥ*, among the sadasyas at king Vasu Uparicara's sacrifice).

Çānti[3], son of Aṅgiras. § 747*b* (Suvarṇotpatti): XIII, **85**θ, 4147 (the fourth son of Aṅgiras).

Çānti[4] = Vishṇu (1000 names).

Çāntida = Vishṇu (1000 names).

Çāntiparvan, the twelfth book of Mhbhr. § 4 (Anukram.): I, **1**, 90 (°*mahāphalaḥ . . . . Bhāratadrumaḥ*).—§ 10 (Parvasaṅgr.): I, **2**, 351 (*yatra Rājadharmānuçāsanaṃ | Āpaddharmaç ca parvoktaṃ Mokshadharmas tataḥ paraṃ*).—§ 11 (do.): I, **2**, 593, 594.—§ 795*c* (Mahābhārata): XVIII, **6**, 277 (during the recitation of *Ç.* brahmans should be fed with *havishya*).

[Çapathavidhi] ("the taking of oaths"). § 751*b* (Anuçāsanik.) (†vv. 4549–4561). *Bhīshma* said: Once B.-ṛ and R.-ṛ. proceeded to the western *Prabhāsa*, and resolved to visit all the sacred waters on earth; there were *Çukra*, etc. (α), and *Indra*; they reached *Kauçikī* on the day of full-moon in the month of *Māgha*, and then *Brahmasaras*, where they gathered and ate the stalks of the lotus; *Agastya's* stalks had been taken away; he complained of the increasing unrighteousness, and thought of going to heaven in order not to live to see yet worse things; the Ṛ. took, each of them, the most frightful oaths to their own innocence (β); but *Indra* uttered "a benediction instead of a curse," and confessed that he had stolen the stalks, not from cupidity, but from desire of hearing what Ṛ. would say. *Agastya* forgave him. Then they proceeded to other *tīrthas* *(XIII, **94**).

Çara = Çiva (1000 names[2]).

Çarabha[1], a serpent. § 64 (Sarpasattra): I, **57**, 2150 (of Takshaka's race).

Çarabha[2], a serpent. § 65 (Sarpasattra): I, **57**, 2152 (of Airāvata's race).

Çarabha[3], an Asura. § 92 (Aṃçāvat.): I, **65**, 2534 (son of Danu).—§ 130 (do.): I, **67**, 2663 (*yas teshāṃ Daiteyānāṃ mahāsuraḥ*, incarnate as the rājarshi Paurava).

Çarabha[4], a ṛshi. § 267 (Çakrasabhāv.): II, **8**, 325 (in the palace of Indra).

Çarabha[5], son of Çiçupāla. § 561 (Yānasandhip.): V, **50**η, 2013 (*Cedipater*—i.e. Dhṛshṭaketu's—*bhrātā . . . . Karakarsheṇa sahitaḥ*, has joined the Pāṇḍavas).—§ 785 (Anugītāp.): XIV, **83**, 2468 (*Çiçupālasutena*, king of the Cedis, vanquished by Arjuna). Cf. Çiçupālasuta.

Çarabha[6], brother of Çakuni. § 600 (Ghaṭotkacavadhap.): VII, **157**π, 6944 (among five brothers of Çakuni who are slain by Bhīmasena).

Çarabha[7] = Vishṇu (1000 names).

Çarabha, pl. (*āḥ*), a people. § 223 (Vāsishṭha): I, **175**, 6684 (only C.; B. has *Çabarāḥ*).

Çarabhaṅga, a ṛshi. § 370 (Tīrthayātrāp.): III, **84**, 8184 (°*āçramaṃ*).—§ 377 (Dhaumyatīrthak.): III, **90**, 8380 (*āçramaḥ Ç°sya*, in the north).—§ 528 (Rāvaṇagamana): III, **277**, 15984 (°*āçramaṃ*), 15985 (worshipped by Rāma Dāçarathi).

Çāradaṇḍāyanī, a kshatriya wife. § 185*e* (Pāṇḍu): When appointed by her husband to raise offspring, *Ç.* went out in the night and waited at a spot where four roads met, and having performed the *puṃsavana* rite had three sons (*Durjaya*, etc. (α)) by a brahman: I, **120**, 4677.

Çaradvat[1], a ṛshi. § 83 (Ādivaṃçāvatāraṇa): I, **63**, 2435 (*Gautamāt*, father of Kṛpa and Kṛpī).—§ 198: *Janamejaya* said: "Tell me the birth of Kṛpa." *Vaiç.* said: The *maharshi* Gotama had a son *Çaradvat*, born with arrows. *Ç.* studied the *Dhanurveda* in preference to the *Vedas*, and by his austerities he came to master all weapons. Indra was afraid of him, and sent the *devakanyā* (cf. v. 5078: *apsarasam*) Jānapadī to disturb him. He fled from her; but from his seed that had fallen upon a clump of reeds (*çarastambe*) sprung two children, whom a soldier found and brought to king *Çāntanu*. *Çāntanu*, from pity (*kṛpā*, v. 5089), brought them up as his own children, whence he called them *Kṛpa* and *Kṛpī*. *Ç.* by his *tapas* learnt what had happened and came to *Çāntanu* and told him his lineage, etc. He then instructed *Kṛpa* in the fourfold *Dhanurveda* and various *çāstras*, and in a short time *Kṛpa* became an eminent teacher, who instructed the *Dhārtarāshṭras, Pāṇḍavas, Yādavas, Vṛshṇis,* and other princes from various countries in the *Dhanurveda*: I, **130,** 5072 (*Gautamaḥ*), 5077, 5083 (*Gautamasya*).—§ 572 (Rathātirathas.): V, **166,** 5768 (*Gautamasya maharsher ya ācāryasya Ç°aḥ çarastambāt suto 'bhavat,* i.e. Kṛpa). Cf. Gautama.

Çaradvat[2] = Kṛpa: I, 7116 (*Kṛpāt*); V, 5734 (*Kṛpasya*); XI, 30 (*Kṛpasya*).

Çaradvat[3], pl. § 561 (Yānasandhip.): V, **57**σ, 2289 (*sa-Bāhlikān Kurūn brūyāḥ Prātipeyān Çaradvataḥ,* (?), = *āyushmataḥ,* Nīl.).

Çāradvata = Kṛpa, q.v.

Çāradvatasūnu: VIII, †4504 (*tatas tu Duryodhana-Bhoja-Saubalāḥ Kṛpeṇa Çāradvatasūnunā saha,* where Ç. must be taken as the name of a son of Kṛpa, but PCR. seems to have read Çāradvatīsūnunā (i.e. Açvatthāman)).

Çāradvatī[1], an Apsaras. § 191 (Arjuna): I, **123,** 4820 (among the Apsarases who sung at the birth of Arjuna).

Çāradvatī[2] = Kṛpī: I, 5114.

Çāradvatīputra ("son of Kṛpī") = Açvatthāman: VII, 6861, 8970.

Çāradvatīsuta, do. = Açvatthāman: VII, 6103, 6802, 6819, 8747; VIII, 2.

Çaradvatsuta = Kṛpa: VIII, †4310.

Çaraṇa[1], a serpent. § 63 (Sarpasattra): I, **57,** 2147 (of Vāsuki's race).

Çaraṇa[2] = Vishṇu (1000 names).

Çaraṇya[1] = Çiva: XIII, 1246 (1000 names[2]); XIV, 212.—Do.[2] = Sūrya: III, 192.

Çarāsana, son of Dhṛtarāshṭra. § 182 (Dhṛtarāshṭraputranāmak.): I, **117,** 4543.—§ 599 (Jayadrathavadhap.): VII, **136**χχ, 5594 (among seven sons of Dhṛtarāshṭra who are slain by Bhīmasena).

Çarastamba, a tīrtha. § 733*b* (Ānuçāsanik.): XIII, **25,** 1714: By bathing in the waterfalls at Ç., Kuçastamba, and Droṇaçarmapada, one becomes worshipped by Apsarases.

Çarava, pl. (°*āḥ*), v. Çabara.

Çaravanālaya = Skanda: I, 2587.

Çaravanodbhava = Skanda: III, 14635.

Çarāvatī, a river in Bhāratavarsha. § 574 (Jambūkh.): VI, **9**λ, 327.

Çārdulī ("tigress"). § 127 (Aṃçāvat.): I, **66,** 2625 (daughter of Krodhavaçā), 2629 (mother of the lions and tigers, etc.).

Çarin = Çiva (1000 names[1]).

Çarīrabhṛt = Vishṇu (1000 names).

Çarīrabhūtabhṛt = Vishṇu (1000 names).

Çarmaka, pl. (°*āḥ*), a people. § 280 (Bhīmasena): II, **30,** 1087 (in the east, conquered by Bhīmasena on his *digvijaya*).

Çarman = Vishṇu (1000 names).

Çarmin, a brahman. § 746 (Ānuçāsanik.): XIII, **68,** 3400 (*Agastyaṃ gotrataḥ,* cf. Agastya[2]), 3419.

Çarmishṭhā, daughter of the Asura king Vṛshaparvan and the second wife of Yayāti. § 143 (Nahusha): I, **75,** 3159, 3160 (mother of Druhyu, Anu, and Pūru).—§ 146 (Devayānī): I, **78,** 3284 (*duhitā Vṛshaparvaṇaḥ*), 3285, (3287), 3290, 3291, 3305 (*duhitrā Vṛshaparvaṇaḥ*), 3306, 3309, 3310 (*Vārshaparvaṇī*), 3312, 3313; **80,** 3347, 3348, 3349, (3351), (3353), (3355); **81,** 3360, 3363, 3365, 3368, 3375, 3393, 3395.—§ 147 (do.): I, **82,** 3399, 3402, 3406, 3407, (3408), (3412), (3415), (3417), 3420, 3421, 3422; **83,** 3424, 3425, (3426), (3429), 3433, 3438, 3440, (3443), 3451, 3458.—§ 148 (Yayāti): I, **84,** 3481 (°*āyāḥ sutaṃ Druhyuṃ*), 3520 (°*āyāḥ suto Druhyuḥ*).—§ 156 (Pūruvaṃç.): I, **95,** ††3761, ††3762 (by Yayāti, mother of Druhyu, Anu, and Pūru).—§ 569*b* (Yayāti): V, **149,** 5044 (*duhitrā Vṛshaparvaṇaḥ,* mother of Pūru).—§ 595 (Shoḍaçarāj., v. Yayāti): VII, **63,** 2297.

Cf. also the following synonyms:—

Asurendrasutā ("daughter of the Asura king"): I, 3369.

Asurī: I, 3286.

Vārshaparvaṇī ("daughter of Vṛshaparvan"): I, 3310, 3393, 3399, 3402, 3411, 3433, ††3762.

Çārṅga, the bow of Kṛshṇa (Vishṇu). § 262 (Bhagavadyāna): II, **2,** 34.—§ 320 (Saubhavadhop.): III, **20,** 795; **21,** 843, 850.—§ 569 (Bhagavadyānap.): V, **131,** 4427.—§ 570*f* (Rukmin): Ç. is said to have been in the possession of Vishṇu; it was held by Kṛshṇa, who obtained it, baffling the nooses of Muru and slaying that Asura, and vanquishing Naraka while recovering the earrings set with gems, with 16,000 girls, etc.: V, **158,** 5353, 5355, 5358.

Çārṅgacakragadādhara = Kṛshṇa, q.v.

Çārṅgacakragadāpāṇi = Kṛshṇa, q.v.

Çārṅgacakrāsipāṇi = Kṛshṇa, q.v.

Çārṅgadhanurdhara = Kṛshṇa, q.v.

Çārṅgadhanvan[1] = Kṛshṇa, q.v.—Do.[2] = Vishṇu (1000 names).

Çārṅgagadāpāṇi = Kṛshṇa, q.v.

Çārṅgagadāsipāṇi = Kṛshṇa, q.v.

Çārṅgakopākhyana(m) ("episode relating to the çārṅgaka birds"). § 259 (Khāṇḍavad.): *Janamejaya* said: "Why did the *çārṅgakas* escape?" *Vaiçampāyana* said: When the *maharshi Mandapāla,* who was an *ūrdhvaretas,* had finished his *tapas,* he left his body and went to *Pitṛloka,* but did not obtain the expected result of his acts, and learned from the gods sitting around *Dharmarāja* that it was because he had no offspring. He then reflected how he could obtain numerous offspring in the shortest time possible; he learnt that the birds were peculiarly prolific, and, becoming a *çārṅgika,* he married the *çārṅgikā Jaritā,* and begat upon her four sons, who were all reciters of the *Vedas.* Then he left her and married *Lapitā.* When *Agni* came to the forest of *Khāṇḍava* to burn it down, *Mandapāla* praised *Agni* (vv. 8353–8360) and prevailed upon him to spare his children (I, **229**). *Jaritā* told her sons (*Jaritāri, Sārisṛkva, Stambamitra,* and *Droṇa*), who would have her to rescue herself by abandoning them, to conceal themselves in the hole of a mouse; but they were afraid of the mouse (I, **230**). Finally *Jaritā* was prevailed upon by her sons to abandon them, and *Agni* approached the spot where the sons were (I, **231**). The four young *ṛshis* praised *Agni,* who promised them safety and granted them a boon. *Droṇa* asked him to consume the cats that troubled them every day (I, **232**). Meanwhile *Mandapāla* addressed *Lapitā,* being anxious about his children. *Lapitā,* from jealousy, told him to go to *Jaritā,* who, she said, was the real cause of his anxiety. When *Agni* had spared the children, *Jaritā* came and embraced them. When *Mandapāla* came they did not speak to him, and *Jaritā,* from jealousy, told him to go to *Lapitā. Mandapāla* declared that nothing was so destructive to the happiness of women as a concubine, except a lover; witness *Arundhatī* (*b*). Then all his children came forward to worship him, and he also spoke kindly to them all (I, **233**). *Mandapāla* told that he had asked *Agni* to protect them, and therefore he had not come earlier. Then he took his wives and sons with him and went away to some other country (I, **234**).

Çārṅgarava, a brahman. § 59 (Sarpasattra): I, **53**, 2046 (among the priests at the snake sacrifice of Janamejaya, only B.; C. has *Sāṅgarevā*, V. *Sāṅgaravo*).

Çārṅgin = Kṛshṇa, q.v.

Çaru, a Devagandharva. § 191 (Arjuna): I, **123a**, 4814 (came to the birth of Arjuna).

Çarva[1] = Çiva, q.v.

Çarva[2] = Vishṇu (1000 names).

Çarvāṇī = Umā: XIII, 1028.

Çarvarīkara = Vishṇu (1000 names).

Çaryāti, an ancient king, son of Manu Vaivasvata. § 5 (Anukram.): I, **1a**, 224 (among the kings of the past in the enumeration of Nārada).—§ 11 (Parvasaṅgr.): I, **2**, 445 (°*yajñe*).—§ 139 (Manu Vaivasvata): I, **75**, 3141 (the seventh son of Manu Vaivasvata).—§ 267 (Yamasabhāv.): II, **8**, 325 (in the palace of Yama) —§ 404*b* (Tīrthayātrāp.): At the sacrifice of *Ç*. Indra drank *soma* with the *Açvins*, and *Cyavana* paralysed Indra and obtained Sukanyā: III, **121**, 10311 (°*yajñasya deçaḥ*).—§ 405 (Sukanyop.): III, **122**, 10320, 10329, 10336, 10341 (gave his daughter in marriage to Cyavana); **123**, 10348 (°*tanayām*, i.e. Sukanyā); **124**, 10371, 10372, 10375, 10376 (description of his sacrifice).—§ 597 (Pratijñāp.): VII, **84**, 2991 (°*er yajñam*; C. has *Sva*°).—§ 736*b* (Vītahavyop.): XIII, **30**, 1945 (Haihaya and Tālajaṅgha were born in the race of *Ç*., the son of Manu).—§ 782*g* (Saṃvartta-Maruttīya): XIV, **9**, 249 (°*yajñam*).

Çaryātitanayā = Sukanyā: III, 10348.

Çaryātivana, a place. § 596 (Pratijñāp.): VII, **80**, 2851 (passed by Kṛshṇa and Arjuna on their way to Çiva's abode).

Çāstṛ = Vishṇu (1000 names).

Çatabalā, a river. § 574 (Jambūkh.): VI, **9λ**, 328 (in Bhāratavarsha).

Çatabhishā, a nakshatra (v. Su. Si.). § 746 (Ānuçāsanik.): XIII, **64**, 3281 (°*yoge*, the result of making gifts under the constellation *Ç*.).—§ 759 (do.): XIII, **110**, 5394 (description of the *candravrata*).

Çatacandra, a Kuru warrior. § 600 (Ghaṭotkacavadhap.): VII, **157**, 6943 (is slain by Bhīmasena), 6944 (cf. Çakuni).

Çataçīrsha, wife of Vāsuki, king of the serpents. § 565 (Gālavac.): V, **117**, 3970 (*reme . . . yatha . . . Vāsukiç Ç°āyām*).

Çataçṛṅga, a mountain. § 184 (Pāṇḍu): I, **119**, 4639 (there Pāṇḍu practised austerities).—§ 185 (do.): I, **120**, 4647 (wishing to visit heaven, Pāṇḍu was setting out from *Ç*. in a northerly direction).—§ 191 (Arjuna): I, **123**, 4804 (°*nivāsinām*, the inhabitants of *Ç*. rejoiced at the birth of Arjuna).—§ 192 (Pāṇḍavotpatti): I, **124**, 4853 (°*nivāsinaḥ*, give names to the sons of Pāṇḍu), 4858 (*ṛshīṇām Ç°nivāsinām*).—§ 194 (do.): I, **126**, 4918.—§ 305 (Anudyūtap.): II, **79**, 2600 (after the death of Pāṇḍu, Kuntī had come back from *Ç*. to Hāstinapura).—§ 596 (Pratijñāp.): VII, **80**, 2851 (Kṛshṇa and Arjuna passed by *Ç*. on their way to Çiva's abode).—§ 604 (Karṇap.): VIII, **68**, 3394 (°*mūrdhni*, the celestial voice at the birth of Arjuna on the top of *Ç*.).—§ 709*b* (Sulabhā-Janaka-saṃv.): XII, **321a**, 12035 (i.e. the genius of the mountain *Ç*., came to the sacrifices of the ancestors of Sulabhā).

Çatadhanvan[1], a prince. § 317*b* (Kṛshṇa): III, **12**, 489 (has been defeated by Kṛshṇa).

Çatadhanvan[2], a prince. § 621 (Rājadh.): XII, **4ε**, 114 (came to the svayaṃvara of the daughter of the Kaliṅga king Citrāṅgada).

Çatadru (or°ū), a river, the modern Sutlej. § 225 (Vāsishṭha): I, **177**, 6753 (*Haimavatīm*, origin of the name *Ç*.).—§ 268 (Varuṇasabhāv.): II, **9**, 371 (among other rivers in the palace of Varuṇa).—§ 459 (Mārkaṇḍeyas.): III, **188a**, 12907 (seen by Mārkaṇḍeya in the stomach of Nārāyaṇa).—§ 574 (Jambūkh.): VI, **9λ**, 322 (°*ūm*, among the rivers of Bhāratavarsha).—§ 607 (Karṇap.): VIII, **44θ**, 2055.—§ 768*b* (Umā-Maheçvaras.): XIII, **146δ**, 6764 (among the rivers who came to Umā).—§ 775 (Ānuçāsanik.): XIII, **166a**, 7645 (enumeration). Cf. next.

Çatadrukā = Çatadru. § 607 (Karṇap.): VIII, **44**, 2040.

Çatadyumna, an ancient king. § 677 (Mokshadh.): XII, **235**, 8606 (having given a mansion made of gold to Mudgala, *Ç*. ascended to heaven).—§ 767 (Ānuçāsanik.): XIII, **137a**, 6265 (do., but with Maudgala instead of Mudgala).

Çataghaṇṭā[1], name of a spear. § 538 (Kumbhakarṇaraṇag.): III, **286**, 16381 ("with hundred bells," PCR.).

Çataghaṇṭā[2], a mātṛ. § 615*u* (Skanda): IX, **46θ**, 2629.

Çataghnin = Çiva (1000 names[2]).

Çataghnīpāçaçaktimat = Çiva (1000 names[2]).

Çatajihva = Çiva (1000 names[1–2]).

Çatajyotis. § 3 (Anukram.): I, **1**, 44 (son of Subhrāj), 45 (father of 100,000 sons).

Çatakratu[1] = Indra, q.v.—Do.[2] = Çiva (1000 names[1]).

Çatakratuprastha = Indraprastha: III, 913.

Çatakumbhā, a river. § 370 (Tīrthayātrāp.): III, **84**, 7088 (a tīrtha).—§ 494 (Āṅgirasa): III, **222**, 14230 (enumeration of rivers who are mothers of fires).—§ 574 (Jambūkh.): VI, **9λ**, 326 (in Bhāratavarsha).

Çatalocana, a warrior of Skanda. § 615*u* (Skanda): IX, **45η**, 2526.

Çatamanyu = Indra: VIII, †3497 (°*vikramaḥ*, sc. Bhīmasena).

Çatamāya, an Asura. § 641 (Rājadh.): XII, **98ξ**, 3660 (slain by Indra, or is perhaps *çatamāyam* an epithet to *Virocanam*?).

Çatamukha, an Asura. § 730*f* (Anuçāsanik.): Dhātṛ created the great Asura *Ç*., who for a hundred years sacrificed the flesh of his own body into the sacrificial fire. Gratified by this, Çiva granted him *yoga* (i.e. *candra-surya-parjanya-pṛthivyādi-shṛshṭi-sāmarthyam*, Nīl.) and eternal power: XIII, **14**, 674 (*mahāsuraḥ*), 675.

Çatamūrt(t)i = Vishṇu (1000 names).

Çatānana = Vishṇu (1000 names).

Çatānanda[1], a ṛshi. § 734 (Ānuçāsanik.): XIII, **26a**, 1705 (among the ṛshis who surrounded Bhīshma as he lay on his arrow-bed).

Çatānanda[2] = Vishṇu (1000 names).

Çatānandā, a mātṛ. § 615*u* (Skanda): IX, **46θ**, 2629.

Çatānīka[1], son of Nakula Pāṇḍava and Draupadī. § 83 (Ādivaṃçāvatāraṇa): I, **63**, 2451 (*Nākuliḥ*).—§ 130 (Aṃçāvat.): I, **67**, 2763 (*Nākuliḥ*, the sons of Draupadī were incarnations of the Viçvadevas).—§ 159 (Pūruvaṃç.): I, **95**, ††3827.—§ 253 (Haraṇāharaṇap.): I, **221**, 8039 (*Nākulim*, his birth, was named *Ç*. after the rājarshi of that name).—§ 511 (Draupadī-Satyabhāmās.): III, **235**, 14731 (*Nākuliḥ*).—§ 583 (Bhīshmavadhap.): VI, **79**[13], 3489, 3492, 3494, 3500.—§ 584 (do.): VI, **84**, 3734.—§ 590 (Droṇābhishekap.): VII, **16**, 625 (*Nākuliḥ*, attacks Vṛshasena).—

§ 592 (Saṃçaptakavadhap.): VII, **23**, 980 (*Nākulim*, description of his horses); **25**, 1085 (proceeded towards Droṇa). — § 598 (Jayadrathavadhap.): VII, **88**, 3128 (*Nākuliḥ*, arranged the divisions of the Pāṇḍavas). — § 599 (do.): VII, **108**ξ, 4055 (*Nākuliḥ*). — § 600 (Ghaṭotkacavadhap.): VII, **165**, 7376 (*Nākulim*); **168**, 7512, 7514, 7520 (fought Citrasena Dhārtarāshṭra).—§ 605 (Karṇap.): VIII, **25**, 1005, 1006, 1009 (fought Çrutakarman, the son of Dhṛtarāshṭra).—§ 608 (do.): VIII, **46**, 2157 (should proceed against Duḥçāsana); **48**π, 2281; **55**λλ, 2665, 2668 (fought Açvatthāman); **60**βββ, 3002; **73**, 3731 (*Nākulim*); **75**, †3813 (*Nākuliḥ*, rushed against Vṛshasena); **82**, †4181; **85**, †4315 (°*matān mahāgajāṃs tathā rathān*), †4327 (°*hatā mahāgajā hayā rathāḥ*), †4329. — § 611 (Çalyap.): IX, **25**ξξ, 1354 (*Nākuliḥ*).—§ 616 (Sauptikap.): X, **8**, 375 (*Nākuliḥ*), 376 (slain by Açvatthāman).

Cf. also the following synonyms :—

Nakuladāyāda ("the son of Nakula"): VII, 1086.
Nakulasya sutaḥ (do.): VII, 7522.
Nakulātmaja (do.): VIII, †4328.
Nākuli (do.): I, 2451 (*Ç*°), 2763 (*Ç*°), 8039 (*Ç*°); III, 533 (*Ç*°), 14731; VI, 3493; VII, 625 (*Ç*°), 980 (*Ç*°), 1985 (*Ç*°), 3128 (*Ç*°), 4055 (*Ç*°), 4061, 7370 (*Ç*°), 7513, 7517, 7519, 7521; VIII, 2756, 3731 (*Ç*°), †3813 (*Ç*°), †4328; IX, 1354 (*Ç*°); X, 375 (*Ç*°).

Çatānīka[2]. § 160 (Pūruvaṃç.): I, **95**, ††3838 (son of Janamejaya Pārikshita and Vapushṭamā, married to Vaidehī, and father of Açvamedhadatta).

Çatānīka[3], a rājarshi of the Kuru race. § 253 (Haraṇāharaṇap.): I, **221**, 8044 (*Ç°sya rājarsheḥ Kauravasya mahātmanaḥ | cakre putraṃ sanāmānaṃ Nakulaḥ kīrttivarddhanaṃ*).

Çatānīka[4], brother of the Matsya king Virāṭa. § 552 (Goharaṇap.): IV, **31**, 1011 (*Virāṭasya priyo bhrātā*), 1012 (*Ç°ād avarajo Madirākshaḥ*), 1019, 1024; **32**, 1054.—§ 583 (Bhīshmavadhap.): VI, **75**β, 3287 (the same?, the sons of Draupadī are mentioned v. 3283, with Kuntibhoja in the feet of Dhṛshṭadyumna's makaravyūha).—§ 587 (do.): VI, **118**, 5541 (*Virāṭasya priyo bhrātā*, was slain by Bhīshma). — § 592 (Saṃçaptakavadhap.): VII, **21**, 879 (*Matsyād avarajaḥ Ç°ḥ*, attacked Droṇa).—§ 600 (Ghaṭotkacavadhap.): VII, **167**, 7490, 7491 (when supporting his brother Virāṭa, *Ç.* was slain by Çalya).

Çatañjayā, v. Çatruñjayā.

Çataparvā, the wife of Çukra. § 565 (Gālavac.): V, **117**, 3972 (*reme . . . yathā . . . Çukraç ca Ç°āyāṃ*).

Çatapatha, i.e. Çatapatha-Brāhmaṇa. § 707 (Mokshadh.): XII, **319**, 11734 (*kṛtsnaṃ Ç°ñ caiva praṇeshyasi*, said Sūrya to Yājñavalkya), 11739 (*Ç°m kṛtsnaṃ sarahasyaṃ sasaṅgrahaṃ . . . . sapariçeshaṃ*), 11746 (composed by Yājñavalkya).—§ 717*b* (Nārāyaṇīya): XII, **343**, I), ††13198 (*brāhmaṇamukhe*, a passage is quoted, cf. Nil. to the next verse).

Çataratha, an ancient king. § 6 (Anukram.): I, **1***a*, 227 (in Sañjaya's enumeration).—§ 267 (Yamasabhāv.): II, **8**, 337 (in the palace of Yama).

Çatarudra, a hymn = Çatarudriya. § 770 (Ānuçāsanik.): XIII, **151**, 7092 (*çatam etat samāmnātaṃ Ç°e mahātmānāṃ*, sc. *Rudrāṇaṃ*).

Çatarudriya, a certain hymn of the Yajurveda [and apparently also name of a certain hymn in Mhbhr., cf. VII, 9639, 9642; XIII, 7461, 7524]. § 596 (Pratijñāp.): VII, **81**, 2898 (*brahma*, recited by Kṛshṇa and Arjuna).—§ 603 (Nārāyaṇāstramokshap.): VII, **202**, 9612 (*Vede cāsya*—i.e. in honour of Rudra—*samākhyātaṃ Ç°m uttamaṃ*), 9639 (*dhanyaṃ yaçasyam āyushyaṃ puṇyaṃ Vedaiç ca sammitaṃ Devadevasya te, Pārtha, vyākhyātaṃ Ç°ṃ*), 9642 (°*drīy*°).—§ 696*b* (Dakshaprokta-Çiva-sahasranāmastotra): XII, **285**, 10413 (identified with Çiva (1000 names[1])). — § 730*g* (Upamanyu): XIII, **14**φ, 876 (*brahma paraṃ*), 915 (*yajushāṃ Ç°ṃ*, sc. *asi*, i.e. Çiva).—§ 773 (Ānuçāsanik.): XIII, **161**, 7461.— § 773*d* (Çiva): XIII, **161**, 7489.—§ 773 (Ānuçāsanik.): XIII, **162**, 7524 (*vede cāsya vidur viprāḥ Ç°m uttamaṃ | Vyāsenoktañ ca yac cāpi avasthāne mahātmanaḥ*).

Çatasahasraka, a tīrtha. § 368 (Tīrthayātrāp.): III, **83**, 7028.

Çatasāhasraka, a tīrtha. § 370 (Tīrthayātrāp.): III, **84**, 8052.

Çatasahasrāṃçu = Soma (the Moon): I, 1145.

Çatāvarta[1] = Çiva (1000 names[1]).—Do.[2] = Vishṇu (1000 names).

Çatayūpa, a Kaikeya prince. § 787*b* (Āçramavāsap.): The R.-ṛ. *Çatayūpa* had been the king of the *Kekayas*; having made over sovereignty to his son he had come into the woods: XV, **19**, 528 (*rājarshiṃ*).—§ 787 (Āçramavāsap.): XV, **19**, 531 (°*āçrame*, *Ç.* received Dhṛtarāshṭra in his hermitage in Kurukshetra and instructed him in the *āraṇyaka vidhi*); **20**, 539, 543 (grandson of Sahasracitya), 560; **23**, 634 (*āçramam . . . . Ç°sya*); **27**, 735, 738.

Çatāyus[1], son of Purūravas. § 141 (Purūravas): I, **75**, 3149 (the sixth son of Purūravas and Urvaçī).

Çatāyus[2], a Kuru warrior, always mentioned together with Çrutāyus. § 578 (Bhīshmavadhap.): VI, **51**χ, 2108 (°*ç ca Çrutāyuç ca*, in the army of Duryodhana). — § 583 (do.): VI, **75**ζ, 3298 (*Çrutāyuç ca Ç°ç ca*).—§ 609 (Çalyap.): IX, **2**ζ, 75 (*Çrutāyuç cācyutāyuç ca Ç°ç ca*, among the slain).

Çaṭha, an Asura. § 93 (Aṃçāvat.): I, **65**, 2537 (*mahāsuraḥ*, son of Danu).

Çatodara = Çiva (1000 names[1]).

Çatodarī, a mātṛ. § 615*u* (Skanda): IX, **46**θ, 2633.

Çatolūkhalamekhalā, a mātṛ. § 615*u* (Skanda): IX, **46**θ, 2628.

Çatru, v. Krodhaçatru.

Çatrughna[1], son of Daçaratha. § 525 (Rāmopākhyānap.): III, **274**, 15878, 15879 (Sumitrā was the mother of Lakshmaṇa and *Ç.*). — § 543 (Rāmābhisheka): III, **291**, 16594 (*Bharata-Ç°au*).

Çatrughna[2] = Vishṇu (1000 names).

Çatruhan = Çiva (1000 names[2]).

Çatrujetṛ = Skanda: III, 14641.

Çatrujit = Vishṇu (1000 names).

Çatrundama = Çiva (1000 names[1]).

Çatruñjaya[1]. § 522 (Draupadīharaṇap.): III, **265**, 15597 (one of Jayadratha's standard-bearers).

Çatruñjaya[2], son of Dhṛtarāshṭra. § 571 (Bhīshmavadhap.): VI, **51**σ, 2098.—§ 583 (do.): VI, **79**ξ, 3503 (*tava putrāḥ*, v. 3501).—§ 599 (Jayadrathavadhap.): VII, **137***aaa*, 5644 (among seven sons of Dhṛtarāshṭra who were slain by Bhīmasena).

Çatruñjaya[3], brother of Karṇa. § 592 (Saṃçaptakavadhap.): VII, **32**, 1433 (*Karṇād avarajaṃ*, v. 1432, slain by Arjuna).

Çatruñjaya[4], a Kuru warrior. § 593 (Abhimanyuvadhap.): VII, **48**χ, 1899 (slain by Abhimanyu).

Çatruñjaya[5], son of Drupada. § 600 (Ghaṭotkacavadhap.): VII, **156**ν, 6910 (*Surathasyānujam*, slain by Açvatthāman), 6914 (the same?, the half-çloka is wanting in B.).

Çatruñjaya[6], a Kuru warrior. § 605 (Karṇap.): VIII, **27**λλ, 1085, 1086, 1088 (was slain by Arjuna).

Çatruñjaya[7], a Sauvīra king. § 648 (Āpaddh.): XII, **140**, 5249 (*Bhāradvājasya saṃvādaṃ rājñaḥ Ç°sya ca*).— § 648*b* (Kaṇikopadeça): XII, **140**, 5250 (*Sauvīreshu*).

Çatruñjayā, a mātṛ. § 615*u* (Skanda): IX, **46**θ, 2624 (so B., C. has *Çatañjayā*).

Çatruntāpa, a Kuru warrior. § 552 (Goharaṇap.): IV, **54**, †1670, †1671 (slain by Arjuna).

Çatrusaha, son of Dhṛtarāshṭra. § 552 (Goharaṇap.): IV, **54**, †1665. — § 583 (Bhīshmavadhap.): VI, **79**ξ, 3503 (*tava putrāḥ*, v. 3501). — § 599 (Jayadrathavadhap.): VII, **137***aaa*, 5644 (among seven sons of Dhṛtarāshṭra who were slain by Bhīmasena).

Çatrutāpana[1], an Asura. § 93 (Aṃçāvat.): I, **65**, 2537 (son of Danu).

Çatrutāpana[2] = Vishṇu (1000 names).

Çatruvināçana = Çiva (1000 names[2]).

Çaunaka[1], a descendant of Bhṛgu, at whose sacrifice Ugraçravas recited the Mhbhr. § 1 (Anukram.): I, **1**, 1 (performed a twelve years' sacrifice in the Naimisha wood; Ugraçravas recited the Mhbhr.).—§ 10 (Parvasaṅgr.): I, **2**, 303.—§ 18 (Paulomap.): I, **4**, ††851, 854, 862.—§ 19 (do., Bhṛgu): I, **5**, (863) (the ancestors of Ç. from Bhṛgu to Çunaka, the *pūrvapitāmaha* of Ç., enumerated).—§ 20 (do., Pulomā): I, **5**, (874).—§ 26 (Āstīkap., Jaratkāru): I, **13**, (1020) (C. has S°), (1024) (do.), 1027 (do.). — § 27 (do., Kaçyapa): I, **16**, (1069).—§ 28 (do., Amṛtamanthana): I, **17**, 1097 (C. has S°).—§ 45 (do., Vālikhilya): I, **31**, (1436).—§ 46 (do., Garuḍa): I, **34**, 1525. — § 47 (do., Sarpanāmak.): I, **35**, (1546).—§ 48 (do., Çesha): I, **36**, (1565).—§ 50 (do., Jaratkāru): I, **40**, 1655. — § 51 (do., Parikshit): I, **40**, 1659, (1660); **43**, 1796. — § 53 (do., Jaratkāru): I, **46**, 1856.—§ 56 (do., Parikshit): I, **49**, (1933).—§ 59 (do., Sarpasattra): I, **53**, 2041 (C. has S°).— § 63 (do., do.): I, **57**, (2142).—§ 68 (do., Āstīka): I, **58**, (2169).—§ 70 (Ādivaṃçāvatāraṇap.): I, **59**, (2198), (2203).— § 717*b* (Nārāyaṇīya): XII, **340**, 13005; **341**, (13007); **344**, (13304), 13311; **347**δδ, 13442; **348**, (13449). — § 795*c* (Mahābhārata): XVIII, **5**, 201. Cf. Bhārgava, Bhārgavottama, Bhṛguçārdūla, Bhṛgūdvaha, Bhṛgukulodvaha, Bhṛgunandana.

Çaunaka[2], a ṛshi. § 309 (Āraṇyakap.): III, **2**, 61 (*Yoge Sāṅkhye ca kuçalaḥ*), (110) (instructs Yudhishṭhira).—§ 310 (do.): III, **3**, 131.—§ 324 (Dvaitavanaprav.): III, **26***a*, 986 (worships Yudhishṭhira). — § 376 (Tīrthayātrāp.): III, **85**, 8264.

Çaunaka[3] = Indrota: XII, 5595 (*I°*), 5601 (*I°*), 5616, 5621, (5622), 5627, (5628), (5665), 5670 (*I°*).

Çaunaka[4]. § 736*b* (Vītahavyop.): XIII, **30**, 2005 (son of Çunaka and grandson of Ruru of Vītahavya's race). Cf. Çaunaka[1].

Çaunakottama = Çaunaka[1]: XII, 13011.

Çauṇḍika, pl. (°*āḥ*), a people. § 739 (Ānuçāsanik.): XIII, **35**ε, 2158 (degraded to çūdras).

Çauri[1], son of Çūra = Vasudeva: I, 623; VII, 6031, 6035 (only C.); XVI, 191 (V°, C. has S°), 195.

Çauri[2], descendant of Çūra = Kṛshṇa Vāsudeva, q.v.

Çauri[3], do. = Balarāma: V, 156.

Çauri[4], do. = Sātyaki (!): VIII, 502.

Çauri[5] = Sūrya: III, 148.

Çauri[6] = Vishṇu (1000 names).

Çavala, Çavalāçva, Çavalāksha, v. Çab°.

Çavara, pl., v. Çabara.

Çaya = Sūrya: III, 154 (so B., C. has *Jayaḥ*).

Çaya, pl. (°*āḥ*), a people. § 587 (Bhīshmavadhap.): VI, **119***aa*, 5649 (so C., differently B., v. Çālva, pl.).

Çayamāna = Çiva (1000 names[1]).

Çayita = Çiva (1000 names[1]).

Çesha, the serpent who carries the earth = Ananta. § 47 (Sarpanāmak.): I, **35**, 1550 (*Çeshaḥ prathamato jāto Vāsukis tadanantaram*). § 48: Ç. left his mother Kadrū and practised hard penances on Gandhamādana, in Badarī, Gokarṇa, the woods of Pushkara, on the foot of Himavat, in order to be emancipated from his body and avoid companionship with his brothers. Brahmán prevailed upon him to pass through a crevice and support the earth, and gave him Suparṇa to help him: I, **36**, 1566, 1570, (1571), 1576, 1578, (1580), 1581, 1582, (†1583), †1584, †1586. — § 100 (Aṃçāvat.): I, **65**, 2549 (*Anantaḥ*, son of Kadrū).—§ 132 (do.): I, **67**, 2786 (a portion of Ç. incarnate as Balarāma). — § 459 (Mārkaṇḍeyasamās.): III, **189**, 12960 (*Çesho bhūtvāham evaitāṃ dhārayāmi vasundharām*, says Nārāyaṇa). — § 477 (Dhundhumārop.): III, **203**, 13557 (*sushvāpa bhagavān Vishṇuḥ . . . . nāgasya bhoge mahati Ç°sya*). — § 524 (Jayadrathavimokshap.): III, **272**, 15815 (Nārāyaṇa slept lying on Ç., description).—§ 564*b* (Mātalīyop.): In consequence of his ascetic austerities Ç. is able to support the earth; he has 1,000 heads; his tongues are blazing like flames of fire, and he is endued with great strength: V, **103**, 3618. — § 581 (Bhīshmavadhap.): VI, **67**π, 3023 (*Ç°ñ cākalpayad devam Anantam iti yaṃ viduḥ, yo dhārayati bhūtāni dharāṃ caiva saparvatām*).—§ 599 (Jayadrathavadhap.): VII, **94**ε, 3456 (*pannagaçreshṭhaḥ*). — § 603*d* (Tripura): VII, **202**, 9563 (was made the aksha of Çiva's chariot in the battle against Tripura). — § 692 (Mokshadh.): XII, **281**δ, 10076 (°*sya sthānam*).—§ 717*b* (Nārāyaṇīya): XII, **340**, 12936 (*asmanmūrttiç caturthī yā sāsṛjac Çesham avyayam*, says Nārāyaṇa). — § 768*c* (Balarāma): XIII, **147**, 6866 (= Balarāma). Cf. Ananta.

Çibi[1] (C. Çivi), a king, son of Uçīnara. § 149 (Yayāti): I, **86**, 3539; **93**, (†3669), †3669 (*Auçīnaraḥ*), (†3671), †3672, †3680 (*Auçīnaraḥ*), †3681 (*Uçīnarasya putraḥ*), †3682 (when Yayāti fell down from heaven, his daughter's sons, Çibi, etc., offered him their worlds, but he would not accept them; then they all ascended to heaven).—§ 232 (Svayaṃvarap.): I, **186**, 6996 (*Auçīnaraḥ*, present at the svayaṃvara of Kṛshṇā) —§ 267 (Yamasabhāv.): II, **8**, 320 (in the palace of Yama).—§ 378 (Tīrthayātrāp.): III, **94**, 8503 (*Ç°r Auçīnaro yathā*).—§ 463: Questioned by the *Pāṇḍavas* about the greatness of the *rājanyas*, *Mārkaṇḍeya* related: Suhotra, one of the Kurus, on his return from a visit to the great *ṛshis*, met *Çibi Auçīnara* seated on his chariot; each of them regarding himself to be the equal of the other, refused to give way. Nārada appeared and prevailed upon Suhotra to give way, quoting three çlokas (v. 13251–3; v. 13253: "one should conquer the mean by charity, the untruthful by truth, the man of wicked deeds by forgiveness, and the dishonest by honesty") and declaring Çibi to be superior: III, **194**, ††13249 (*Auçīnaraḥ*, C. has °*iḥ*), ††13255. —§ 466: Mārkaṇḍeya tells the history of *Çibi Auçīnara* (*Saurastheyam*, v. 13297, i.e. son of Surathā, Nīl.) being tried by Indra and Agni (cf. § 411 (Çyenakapotīya, where the same is told of Uçīnara); v. 13278, the purohita says that the falling (*nipātam*) of a pigeon forebodes a great danger; the pigeon says he is a muni; v. 13283, Çibi wonders that the birds speak a polished language (*vāg ucyamānā çakunena saṃskṛtā*); of the gashes (*peçiṃ*) which the sword had caused on Ç.'s body Agni made an auspicious mark of golden hue and sweet odour; Çibi should have a son Kapotaroman, v. 13299, see Nīl.): III, **197**, ††13274 (*Auçīnaraḥ*), ††13275.—§ 467 (Rājanyamahābh.): III, **198**, ††13302 (*Auçīnaraḥ*), ††13319, ††13320, ††13324, ††13325, ††13326, (††13329), ††13330 (in order to try Ç., Vidhātṛ, in the disguise of a brahman, had ordered Ç. to cook his own son Bṛhadgarbha as food to him. Ç. did so).—§ 480 (Pativratop.): III, **208**, 13808 (*ātmamāṃsapradānena Ç°r Auçīnaro nṛpaḥ svargañ ca dushkaraṃ prāptaḥ kshamāvān*, all. to § 466).—§ 545 (Pativratāmāhātmyap.): III, **294**, 16674 (*Ç°r Auçīnaro yathā*).—§ 552 (Goharaṇap.): IV, **56**ζ, 1768 (came to see the encounter between Bhīshma and Arjuna).—§ 562 (Bhagavadyānap.): V, **90**ν, 3146 (*Auçīnarasya*).—§ 565 (Gālavac.): V, **118**, 4000 (born of Mādhavī, the daughter of Yayāti, to Uçīnara).—§ 566 (Yayāti): V, **121**, 4057 (*Auçīnaraḥ*); **122**, 4085 (*Auçīnaraḥ*, the sons of the daughter of Yayāti, viz. Çibi, etc., caused him to ascend again to heaven by means of their good deeds, cf. § 149).—§ 574 (Jambūkh.): VI, **9**aa, 314 (*Auçīnarasya*).—§ 595 (Shoḍaçarājika): King Ç. *Auçīnara* girded the earth round himself as if it were a leathern girdle (*carmavat paryaveshṭayat*, i.e. *svādhīnām akarot*, Nīl.), performed many sacrifices, etc., and acquired enormous wealth; Çiva granted him the boon that his wealth, etc., should be inexhaustible. Then he left this world for heaven: VII, **58**, 2209 (*Auçīnaram*), 2210, 2214, 2216, 2222.—§ 599 (Jayadrathavadhap.): VII, **143**, 5998 (*Ç°r Auçīnaro yathā*).—§ 632*b* (Shoḍacarājop., cf. § 595): XII, **29**, 932 (*Auçīnaram*), 934 (*Auçīnaraḥ*).—§ 651 (Āpaddh.): XII, **143**, 5461 (*°prabhṛtayo, rājan, rājānaḥ çaraṇāgatān | paripālya mahātmanaḥ saṃsiddhiṃ paramāṅ gatāḥ*).—§ 656 (Khaḍgotpattik.): XII, **166**δ, 6199 (received the sword from the Yadus, from him it came to Pratardana).—§ 677 (Mokshadharm.): XII, **235**, 8593 (*Ç°r Auçīnaro 'ṅgāni sutañ ca priyam aurasaṃ brāhmaṇārtham upāhatya nākapṛshṭham ito gataḥ*, all. to §§ 466 and 467).—§ 746 (Ānuçāsanik.): XIII, **61**, 3093 (a sentence of his is quoted); **67**, 3384 (all. to § 466).—§ 751*b* (Çapathavidhi): XIII, **94**a, †4551, (4572).—§ 760 (Ānuçāsanik.): XIII, **115**γ, 5663 (*Auçīnareṇa*, abstained from meat during the month of Kārttika).—§ 767 (do.): XIII, **137**, 6248 (*Ç°r Auçīnaraḥ prāṇān priyasya tanayasya ca brāhmaṇārtham upākṛtya nākapṛshṭham ito gataḥ*, all. to § 467).—§ 786*b* (Nakulākhyāna): XIV, **90**, 2790 (*Auçīnaraḥ*, all. to § 466). Cf. Auçīnara, Çaibya[8].

Çibi[2] = Uçīnara: I, 448 (read *nṛpaṃ* with B., all. to Çyenakapotīya).

Çibi[3], an Asura. § 89 (Aṃçāvat.): I, **65**, 2526 (*°Bāshkalau*, the fourth and fifth son of Hiraṇyakaçipu).—§ 130 (do.): I, **67**, 2644 (incarnate as king Druma).

Çibi[4], name of an Indra. § 238 (Pañcendrop.): I, **197**, 7304 (the third of the five Indras of old, who are born again as the Pāṇḍavas).

Çibi[5], a prince who sided with Yudhishṭhira. § 589 (Droṇābhishekap.): VII, **8**θ, †248 (fights Droṇa).—§ 590 (do.): VII, **16**δ, 650 (do.).—§ 600 (Ghaṭotkacavadhap.): VII, **155**, 6698, 6700 (slain by Droṇa).

Çibi, pl. (*°ayaḥ*), a people. § 285 (Nakula): II, **32**, 1189 (vanquished by Nakula, in the west).—§ 295 (Dyūtap.): II, **52**, 1870 (among the peoples who brought tribute to Yudhishṭhira).—§ 411 (Çyenakapotīya): III, **131**, 10582 (*rājyaṃ Ç°īnāṃ*, the kingdom of Uçīnara).—§ 466 (Çibi): III, **197**, †13287, †13291, †13296 (ruled by Çibi).—§ 522 (Draupadīharaṇap.): III, **266**, †15602 (*°īnāṃ pravareṇa*, i.e. Koṭikāsya); **267**, 15621 (ruled by Jayadratha); **271**, 15718, 15743 (the Ç° who followed Jayadratha were slain by Arjuna).—§ 556*e* (Nakula): V, **23**, 709 (had been vanquished by Nakula).—§ 573 (Ambopākhyānap.): V, **195**ε, 7609 (in the army of Duryodhana).—§ 576 (Bhagavadgītāp.): VI, **18**δ, 688 (do.).—§ 578 (Bhīshmavadhap.): VI, **51**σ, 2104 (do.).—§ 586 (do.): VI, **106**τ, 4809 (do., protect Bhīshma).—§ 587 (do.): VI, **117**ρ, 5485 (attack Arjuna); **119**aa, 5648 (abandon Bhīshma).—§ 589 (Droṇābhishekap.): VII, **7**ζ, 183.—§ 595 (Shoḍaçarāj., v. Rāma Jāmadagnya): VII, **66**β, 2437 (vanquished by Rāma Jāmadagnya).—§ 599 (Jayadrathavadhap.): VII, **91**β, 3254 (had formerly been vanquished by Karṇa); **93**γ, 3339 (attack Arjuna); **150**, 6526.—§ 600 (Ghaṭotkacavadhap.): VII, **157**ρ, 6948; **161**δδ, 7206.—§ 602 (Droṇavadhap.): VII, **192**π, 8841.—§ 604 (Karṇap.): VIII, **5**ζ, 127 (have been slain).—§ 605 (do.): VIII, **27**λλ, 1077.—§ 607 (do.): VIII, **45**ν, 2106 (described by Karṇa as stupid).

Çibiputra = Gopati: XII, 1794 (*G°*).

Çibisūnu = Vṛshādarbha: XIII, 4420.

Çiçira[1]. § 116 (Vasu, pl.): I, **66**, 2586 (son of Varcas (or of Varcasvin) and Manoharā).

Çiçira[2] = Vishṇu (1000 names).

Çiçu[1]. § 500 (Skandopākhyana): III, **228**, 14396 (*°mātaraḥ*, i.e. Kākī, etc.), 14397 (had the son Çiçu, who was born through the favour of Skanda—*Skandaprasādajaḥ*).

Çiçu[2] = Skanda: III, 14631.

Çiçumāra, name of a star or constellation. § 231 (Svayaṃvarap.): I, **185**, 6960 (*°çiraḥ* — i.e. the north-eastern direction, Nīl.—*prāpya*).

Çiçumāramukhī, a mātṛ. § 615*u* (Skanda): IX, **46**θ, 2640.

Çiçupāla, king of the Cedis, son of Damaghosha. § 130 (Aṃçāvat.): I, **67**, 2641 (incarnation of the Asura Hiraṇyakaçipu).—§ 232 (Svayaṃvarap.): I, **186**, 7003 (present at the svayaṃvara of Draupadī); **187**, 7029 (*Cedīnām adhipaḥ . . . . Damaghoshasutaḥ*).—§ 264 (Sabhākriyāp.): II, **4**β, 124 (among the kings who were present when Yudhishṭhira entered his palace).—§ 273 (Rājasūyārambhap.): II, **14**, 574 (had become the generalissimo of Jarāsandha).—§ 280 (Bhīmasena): II, **29**, 1069, 1074 (vanquished by Bhīmasena on his *digvijaya*).—§ 287 (Rājasūyikap.): II, **34**, 1273 (came to the rājasūya of Yudhishṭhira).—§ 289 (Arghāharaṇap.): II, **36**, 1336; **37**, (1338), 1368; **38**, 1369, 1397, 1400 (did not regard Kṛshṇa as deserving the argha).—§ 290 (Çiçupālavadhap.): II, **40**, 1427, 1428; **41**, (1433); **42**, (1474), 1489 (censured Kṛshṇa); **43**, 1516, 1518 (his former history).—§ 291 (do.): II, **44**, (1524); **45**, 1576 (Ç. is slain by Kṛshṇa, and his son [Dhṛshṭaketu] is installed as king of the Cedis).—§ 294 (Dyūtap.): II, **47**, 1686 (*Sātvatamukhyena*—i.e. by Kṛshṇa—*nipātitaḥ*); **50**, 1812 (*iva*).—§ 317*b* (Kṛshṇa): III, **12**, 489 (all. to § 291).—§ 319 (Saubhavadhap.): III, **14**, 616 (do.), 625, 626 (Çālva will revenge the death of Ç., his relative, *bhrātā*).—§ 556*b* (Sañjayayānap.): In order to enhance the fame and honour of the Pāṇḍavas, Keçava (i.e. Kṛshṇa) formerly smote Ç., who was honoured by the Karūsha king, etc. Then the other kings, deeming Kṛshṇa unassailable when seated on his chariot, left the chief of the Cedis and ran away: V, **22**, †671 (cf. § 291).—§ 567 (Bhagavadyānap.): V, **130**ξ, 4411 (all. to § 291).—§ 592 (Saṃçaptakavadhap.): VII, **23**o, 970 (*putran tu Ç°sya*, different from Dhṛshṭaketu).—§ 604 (Karṇap.): VIII, **6**, 183 (*putras tu Ç°sya Suketuḥ*, slain by Droṇa).—§ 608 (do.): VIII, **49**λ, 2334 (*°sya cātmajaḥ*, i.e. Dhṛshṭaketu).—§ 621 (Rājadh.): XII, **4**ε, 113 (came to the svayaṃvara of king Citrāṅgada's daughter).—§ 717b (Nārāyaṇīya): XII, **340**, 12962 (in a prophecy by Nārāyaṇa, all. to § 291).

Cf. also the following synonyms:—

Caidya, Cedīnām adhipaḥ, Cedipa, Cedipati, Cedipuṅgava, Cedirāj, Cedirāja, Cedivṛsha, q.v.

Çrautaçrava, metron. ("son of Çrutaçravā," cf. Harivaṃça, v. 1930): III, 637.

Damaghoshasuta ("son of Damaghosha"): I, 7029.

Damaghoshātmaja (do.): II, 1594; III, 516.

Çiçupālasuta[1] ("son of Çiçupāla") = Dhṛshṭaketu: V, 5900 (*Dhr°*).

Çiçupālasuta[2] (do.) = Çarabha: XIV, 2468 (*Ç°*).

Çiçupālātmaja (do.) = Dhṛshṭaketu: III, 1994.

Çiçupālavadha = Çiçupālavadhaparvan. § 10 (Parvasaṅgr.): I, **2**, 318.—§ 11 (do.): I, **2**, 410.

Çiçupālavadhaparvan ("of the killing of Çiçupāla," the 27th of the minor parvans of Mhbhr., cf. *Çiçupālavadha*). § 290: As *Yudhishṭhira* was afraid that his sacrifice might be obstructed, *Bhīshma* consoled him, saying that *Kṛshṇa* was invincible (II, **40**). *Çiçupāla* again censured *Bhīshma* and *Kṛshṇa*, and compared *Bhīshma* to the old swan, who always preached of virtue, so that the other birds gave him food and kept their eggs with him; but the old swan used to eat up their eggs, till he was found out and slain (II, **41**). *Çiçupāla* censured *Kṛshṇa's* behaviour towards *Jarāsandha*; *Bhīma* rushed up in anger, but was restrained by *Bhīshma*, while *Çiçupāla* was boasting (II, **42**). *Bhīshma* said: *Çiçupāla* was born with three eyes and four hands, and brayed like an ass; his parents resolved to abandon him, but were prevented by an incorporeal voice who foreboded that that man in whose lap the child would be sitting, when its superfluous arms would fall down and the third eye on its forehead disappear, should be its slayer. Though the child was placed upon the laps of 1,000 kings, this came not to pass until *Rāma* and *Kṛshṇa* went to the capital of the *Cedis* to see their father's sister (the mother of *Çiçupāla*), when the boy was placed on the lap of *Kṛshṇa*; then the arms fell down and the eye disappeared. *Kṛshṇa* granted to *Çiçupāla's* mother the boon that he would pardon 100 offences of *Çiçupāla's* (II, **43**). *Bhīshma* declared that *Kṛshṇa* himself had wanted to provoke the boast of *Çiçupāla*. *Çiçupāla* reproached *Bhīshma* because he did not rather praise the other kings (*a*), such as the *Bālhika* king *Darada* (*b*), or *Karṇa* (*c*), etc.; he compared *Bhīshma* to the bird *Bhūliṅga* (*d*). *Bhīshma* expressed his contempt for such talk. The kings became angry and proposed to kill *Bhīshma*, who relied upon *Kṛshṇa* (II, **44**).—§ 291: *Çiçupāla* challenged *Kṛshṇa*, being desirous to slay him with all the *Pāṇḍavas*. *Kṛshṇa* related (*a*) how *Çiçupāla*, hearing that the *Sātvatas* had gone to *Prāgjyotisha*, came and burnt *Dvārakā*; (*b*) that when king *Bhoja* was sporting on the *Raivataka* hill, he fell upon his attendants and slew many of them and led many away in chains to his own city; (*c*) in order to obstruct the sacrifice of *Kṛshṇa's* father, he stole the sacrificial horse that had been let loose under the guard of armed men; (*d*) that he ravished the reluctant wife of *Babhru* on her way from *Hāstinapura* (so Nīl.) to the *Sauvīras*; (*e*) that disguising himself in the attire of the *Kārūsha* king, he had ravished *Bhadrā Vaiçālī* (i.e. daughter of the king of *Viçālā*, Nīl.); (*f*) that he had desired *Rukmiṇī*, but failed to obtain her; (*g*) that he (*Kṛshṇa*) had promised to pardon him 100 times, and that the number had now become full. *Kṛshṇa* then thought of his discus, which came into his hand; therewith he instantly cut off the head of *Çiçupāla*; the kings beheld a fiery energy issuing out of the body of *Çiçupāla* and entering *Kṛshṇa's* body; the sky, though cloudless, poured showers of rain, etc. *Yudhishṭhira* caused his brothers to perform the funeral rites of *Çiçupāla*, the son of *Damaghosha*; then he, with all the kings, installed the son of *Çiçupāla* in the sovereignty of the *Cedis*.—§ 292, v. Rājasūyikaparvan.

Çiçuroman, a serpent. § 64 (Sarpasattra): I, **57**, 2151 (of Takshaka's race).

Çīghra = Skanda: III, 14631.

Çīghrā, a river. § 574 (Jambūkh.): VI, **9**λ, 336.

Çīghraga = Sūrya: III, 155.

Çikhaṇḍin[1], son (originally daughter) of the Pāñcāla king Drupada, and father of Kshattradeva. § 4 (Anukram.): I, **1**, † 182.—§ 11 (Parvasaṅgr.): I, **2**, 525.—§ 83 (Ādivaṃçāvatāraṇa): I, **63**, 2453 (*Ç°ī Drupadād jajñe kanyā putratvam āgatā*).—§ 130 (Aṃçāvat.): I, **67**, 2761 (incarnation of a Rākshasa).—§ 216 (Caitrarathap.): I, **165**, 6323.—§ 241 (Vidurāgamanap.): I, **200**, 7379.—§ 312 (Arjunābhigamanap.): III, **12**, 594 (will slay Bhīshma).—§ 553 (Vaivāhikap.): IV, **72**, 2352 (came to the marriage of Abhimanyu and Uttarā).—§ 561 (Yānasandhip.): V, **48**β, †1817, †1847 (will slay Bhīshma), †1848; **50**ζ, 2003 (is Ambā re-born (cf. § 573), has vanquished the Kaliṅgas); **57**ξ, 2236, 2243 (*Bhīshmaḥ . . . . bhāgaḥ kṛtaḥ Ç°aḥ*); (*o*), 2263 (in the army of Yudhishṭhira).—§ 562 (Bhagavadyānap.): V, **83**θ, 2950.—§ 567 (do.): V, **126**, 4221.—§ 569 (do.): V, **140***a*, 4748; **141**γ, 4780.—§ 570 (Sainyaniryānap.): V, **151***a*, 5100, 5126 (*Drupadātmajaḥ*, born for the destruction [of Bhīshma]), 5128, 5129, (δ), 5161; **153**, 5193; **157**, 5325.—§ 571 (Ulūkadūtāgamanap.): V, **160**, 5484; **162**, 5591; **163**, 5684, 5697; **164**, 5708 (is placed against Bhīshma).—§ 572 (Rathātirathas.): V, **171**, 5893 (*Pañcālarājasya sutaḥ*); **172**, 5936 (*Pāñcālyam*), 5940 (Bhīshma will not slay Ç. because he has been a woman).—§ 573 (Ambōpākhyānap.): V, **173**, 5942, 5944; **188**, 7389, 7407 (born as a daughter of Drupada); **189**, 7418, 7419 (married to the daughter of king Hiraṇyavarman), 7422, 7426; **190**, 7442, 7446, 7448, 7450; **191**, 7456, 7478, 7482, (7483); **192**, 7487, (7492), 7495, 7496, 7505, †7514, †7515, 7517, †7533, 7539, 7541 (the sex of Ç. having been found out, Hiraṇyavarman prepared for war with Drupada, but Ç. then obtained the manhood of the Yaksha Sthūṇākarṇa), 7544, 7546, 7547, 7548, 7550, 7551 (is Ambā re-born), 7554, 7555; **194**γ, 7598; **196**η, 7624.—§ 576 (Bhagavadgītāp.): VI, **13**, 499 (*çete nihataḥ . . . . Bhīshmaḥ Ç°nā*), 501; **14**, 508, 527 (*Pāñcālyena*), 531, 557, 558 (*Drupadātmajaḥ*); **15**, 602 (*çrūyate strī hy asau pūrvam*), 603, 605, 606; **19**ε, 713; **22**, 779; **25**κ, 846.—§ 578 (Bhīshmavadhap.): VI, **45**[12], 1714, 1715, 1716 (fights Açvatthāman); **48**, 1871 (tried to rescue Çveta), 1981; **50**, 2063 (*Bhīshmasyāntakaraḥ*); **51***aa*, 2117.—§ 579 (do.); VI, **54**[13], 2325.—

§ 580 (do.): VI, **56**θ, 2416.—§ 581 (do.): VI, **63**ι, 2789.—§ 582 (do.): VI, **69**a, 3063, 3082, 3084 (°*naṃ tathāsādya Bhāratānāṃ pitāmahaḥ | avarjayata saṅgrāme strītvaṃ tasyānusaṃsmaran*), 3086; **71**δ, 3139 (fights Citrasena); **72**ε, 3162.—§ 583 (do.): VI, **75**β, 3288.—§ 584 (do.): VI, **81**[1], 3555; **82**, 3602, 3604, 3606, 3611, 3613, 3614; **85**[6], †3759, †3769, †3777; **86**, 3815, 3816 (*strītvaṃ cintya Ç°aḥ*, sc. Bhīshma).—§ 585 (do.); VI, **89**ν, 3946; **98**, 4466, 4468 (*pūrvaṃ hi strī samutpannā*), 4481, 4484 (*strīpūrvakaḥ*), 4488, 4495, 4498 (Bhīshma will not slay Ç.).—§ 586 (do.): VI, **99**ζ, 4510; **103**μ, 4685, 4688, 4690 (attacks Bhīshma); **107**, 4966, 4968 (Bhīshma advises Arjuna to fight with him, placing Ç. before himself), 4989, 4990, 4991.—§ 587 (do.): VI, **108**, 4994, 4996 (in the van of the Pāṇḍavas), 4997, 5011, 5032, 5033, 5034, 5036, 5044 (attacks Bhīshma); **109**, 5055 (*Pāñcālyaḥ*), 5056, 5058; **110**, 5094, 5096, 5110; **111**, 5161; **112**, 5215; **113**, 5285 (*Bhīshmasya nidhanakāṅkshī Ç°naṃ puraskṛtya*, sc. Arjuna); **114**, 5327, 5328, 5329; **115**ν, 5354, 5356, 5359, 5360, 5366; **116**, 5431, 5433, 5436, 5451 (*Pāñcālyena*); **117**, 5452, 5453, 5455, 5458, 5473, 5475, 5513; **118**ν, 5554, 5556, 5564, 5568; **119**, 5569, 5580, 5582, 5590, 5600 (*strībhāvāc ca Ç°aḥ*), 5610, 5616, 5617, 5625, 5627, 5628, 5629, 5630, 5631, 5632 (placing Ç. ahead, Arjuna felled Bhīshma); **120**, 5695 (*sa*—i.e. Bhīshma—*hato Draupadeyena Pāñcālyena Ç°nā*).—§ 589 (Droṇābhishekap.): VII, **1**, 2 (*Pāñcālyena*, had slain Bhīshma); **10**, 350 (*Yājñasenim*), 368.—§ 590 (do.): VII, **14**, 537, 539 (fights Bhūriçravas); (*a*), 577; **16**γ, 645.—§ 592 (Saṃçaptakavadhap.): VII, **21**κ, 903, 909, (μ), 916; **23**ο, 963, 969 (description of his horses), 970, 974 (°*aḥ putraṃ Kshattradevaṃ*); **25**, 1099 (*Yājñasenim*, battles with Vikarṇa).—§ 593 (Abhimanyuvadhap.): VII, **40**ο, 1695; **42**π, 1743; **43**ρ, 1770.—§ 596 (Pratijñāp.): VII, **83**a, 2950.—§ 598 (Jayadrathavadhap.): VII, **85**δ, 3048.—§ 599 (do.): VII, **95**, 3534 (fights Bālhīka); **111**ν, 4283; **114**ψ, 4503 (fights Kṛtavarman), 4520, 4521, 4526, 4527, 4536, 4537; **124**λλ, 5002; **150**, 6506 (has slain Bhīshma); **151**, 6535 (do.), 6554.—§ 600 (Ghaṭotkacavadhap.): VII, **153**a, 6627; **154**β, 6654 (leader of the Prabhadrakas); **156**θ, 6763; **158**χ, 7008; **165**, 7365 (battles with Kṛpa); **169**, 7579, 7580, 7585, 7587, 7589, 7590 (do.); **171**ξξ, 7731; **177**χχ, 8059; **178**ωω, 8082; **179**βββ, 8118; **183**ιι, 8346.—§ 601 (Droṇavadhap.): VII, **184**a, 8366.—§ 603 (Nārāyaṇāstram.): VII, **193**γ, 8918; **195**θ, 9008; **198**, 9144 (*sa cāpi sṛshṭaḥ pitrā te*—i.e. by Drupada—*Bhīshmasyāntakaraḥ kila*).—§ 604 (Karṇap.): VIII, **2**, 36 (*Yajñasenasya putreṇa*, has slain Bhīshma); **9**θ, 287.—§ 605 (do.): VIII, **10**, 370 (*hato Bhīshmo . . . . Ç°naṃ puraskṛtya Phālgunena*), **12**ββ, 454; **13**, 495 (fights Kṛtavarman); **22**ηη, 870, (κκ), 889; **26**, 1057 (*Bhīshmamṛtyuḥ*), 1058 (fights Kṛtavarman), 1067; **30**ξξ, 1230.—§ 608 (do.): VIII, **46**, 2158; **48**ξ, 2253, (ρ), 2281, (σ), 2296; **49**χ, 2333; **54**θθ, 2614, 2615, 2616, 2617, 2620, 2621, 2626, 2632 (fights Kṛpa); **56**ππ, 2756; **60**βββ, 3001; **61**εεε, 3073, 3077, 3082, 3083, 3084, 3088, 3089; **66**ιι, 3319; **70**, †3506 (has slain Bhīshma); **73**, 3644 (do.), 3673 (do.), 3731; **74**, 3796; **75**, †3811 (fights Kṛpa), †3818, †3819; **78**γ′, 3955, 3957, (ε′), 4001; **79**η′, 4028, (ι′), †4087; **82**κ′, †4187, †4188, (λ′), †4195, †4200; **93**aρ′, 4873; **96**βa′, 5031.—§ 609 (Çalyap.): IX, **1**γ, 30 (among the slain); **2**ζ, 87.—§ 610 (do.): IX, **3**κ, 165; **5**, 254; **7**τ, 336, (χ), 351.—§ 611 (do.): IX, **8**ζ, 396; **9**ι, 451; **11**λ, 550; **15**, 759 (fights Kṛtavarman and Kṛpa); **16**, 801 (*Pāñçālyaḥ*, fights Açvatthāman); **17**ω, †894; **18**ββ, 962, 968; **19**δδ, 1021; **20**θθ, †1084; **21**κκ, 1126; **23**, 1190; **25**ξξ, 1353.—§ 612 (Hradapraveçap.): IX, **30**ε, 1725.—§ 615 (Gadāyuddhap.): IX, **61**φ, 3418; **62**ψ, 3462.—§ 616 (Sauptikap.): X, **5**ε, 196 (*Bhīshmaḥ . . . . C°naṃ puraskṛtya hato Gāṇḍīvadhanvanā*); **8**, 368, 383 (is slain by Açvatthāman); **9**ν, 534.—§ 620 (Çrāddhap.): XI, **26**β, 789 (his body is burnt; *Pāñçālyaṃ*).—§ 630 (Rājadh.): XII, **27**β, 803, 809 (*Pāñcālyaṃ*).—§ 777 (Svargārohaṇikaṃ p.): XIII, **169**, 7783 (had slain Bhīshma), 7786, 7787, 7791.—§ 785 (Anugītāp.): XIV, **60**β, 1781, 1786 (all. to the battle); **81**, 2411 (do.).—§ 789 (Putradarçanap.); XV, **31**β, 857 (Vyāsa declares Ç. to have been an incarnate Rākshasa); **32**θ, 878 (°*putrāḥ*).—§ 793 (Mausalap.): XVI, **3**δ, 81.—§ 795 (Svargārohaṇap.): XVIII, **1**δ, 26 (*Pāñcālyaṃ*).

Cf. also the following synonyms:—

Bhīshmahantṛ ("the slayer of Bhīshma"): VIII, 3082.
Bhīshmanihantṛ (do.): X, 381.
Çikhaṇḍinī (*Ç.'s* name as a woman): V, 7421, 7423, 7424, 7440, 7451, 7456, 7457, 7473, 7519, 7527; VI, 4468, 4469, 4484, 5036.
Draupadeya, q.v.
Drupadātmaja, q.v.
Pāñçalya, q.v.
Yājñaseni, q.v.

Çikhaṇḍin[2] = Kṛshṇa: XII, 1511.
Çikhaṇḍin[3] = Çiva (1000 names [1–2]): XIII, 1310.
Çikhaṇḍin[4] = Vishṇu (1000 names).
Çikhaṇḍinī, v. Çikhaṇḍin [1].
Çikhaṇḍitanaya = Kshattradeva: VIII, 176 (*K°*).
Çikhāprokta (adj.), said of Pañcaçikha: XII, 11885 (°-*ena bhikshunā*).
Çikhāvart(t)a, a Yaksha. § 269 (Vaiçravaṇasabhāv.): II, **10**, 398 (in the palace of Kubera).
Çikhāvat, a ṛshi. § 264 (Sabhākriyāp.): II, **4**a, 109.
Çikhin[1] = Agni, q.v.
Çikhin[2], a serpent. § 564 (Mātalīyop.): V, **103**γ, 3628 (enumeration).
Çikhin[3] = Çiva: VII, 9504; XIII, 1171 (1000 names [2]).
Çikshaka, a warrior of Skanda. § 615u (Skanda): IX, **45**η, 2578.
Çīladhārin = Çiva (1000 names [2]).
Çilāyūpa,* a son of Viçvāmitra. § 721b (Viçvāmitrop.): XIII, **4**β, 253.
Çilin, a serpent. § 64 (Sarpasattra): I, **57**, 2150 (of Takshaka's race).
Çilpika = Çiva (1000 names [1]).
Çilpināṃ çreshṭhaḥ = Çiva (1000 names [1]).
Çineḥ pautra(ḥ), Çineḥ putra(ḥ) = Sātyaki, q.v.
Çineḥ suta(ḥ)[1] = Satyaka, q.v.—Do.[2] = Sātyaki, q.v.
Çiner naptṛ = Sātyaki, q.v.
Çini[1], father of Satyaka and grandfather of Sātyaki (Yuyudhāna). § 599e (Jayadrathavadhap.): *Atri* > *Soma* > *Budha* > *Purūravas* > *Āyus* > *Nahusha* > *Yayāti* > *Yadu* (by *Devayānī*) > . . . . *Devamīḍha* > *Çūra* (equal to *Kārtavīrya*) > *Vasudeva*; in *Çūra's* race was born Ç. About this time the svayaṃvara of *Devaka's* daughter *Devakī* took place, whom Ç. took up in his chariot for the sake of Vasudeva. *Somadatta* attacked Ç., who threw him to the earth, seized him by the hair and struck him with his foot, and then let him off. Çiva granted Somadatta that he should

have a son (i.e. Bhūriçravas) who should in like manner strike *Ç*.'*s* son (i.e. grandson = Sātyaki) with his foot: VII, **144**, 6032, 6034, 6035, 6037, 6041 (°*eḥ sutam*, i.e. Sātyaki), 6043 (do.).

Çini[2], pl. (°*ayaḥ*), the race of Çini, a family or tribe. § 561 (Yānasandhip.): V, **48**, †1854 (°*īnām adhipaḥ*, i.e. Sātyaki). —§ 599 (Jayadrathavadhap.): VII, **114**, 4481 (°*īnām pravare rathe*, i.e. Sātyaki); **140**, 5819 (°*inam ṛshabhena*, i.e. Sātyaki). —§ 608 (Karṇap.): VIII, **82**, †4186 (°*īnām ṛshabham*, i.e. Sātyaki), †4203 (°*īnām ṛshabhaḥ*, i.e. Sātyaki).

Çinipravara, Çinipravīra, Çinipuṅgava, Çiniputra, Çinivīra = Sātyaki, q.v.

Çipivishṭa = Kṛshṇa (Vishṇu, Nārāyaṇa): XII, 1506, 13229, 13231 (= Nārāyaṇa, etymology); XIII, 6978 (Vishṇu's 1000 names).

Çirīshaka, a serpent. § 564 (Mātalīyop.): V, **103**γ, 3630.

Çirohārin = Çiva (1000 names[2]).

Çīrshin, a son of Viçvāmitra. § 721*b* (Viçvāmitrop.): XIII, **4**β, 258.

Çishṭakṛt = Vishṇu (1000 names).

Çishṭeshṭa = Vishṇu (1000 names).

Çita, a son of Viçvāmitra. § 721*b* (Viçvāmitrop.): XIII, **4**β, 253.

Çītā, a river (III, 11063), v. Sītā.

Çītāṃçu, Cītaraçmi = Soma (the Moon), q.v.

Çītapūtanā, a female demon. § 502 (Manushyagrahak.): III, **230**, 14481 (*Piçācī*).

Çītavana, v. Sītavana.

Çitikaṇṭha[1] = Çiva, q.v.

Çitikaṇṭha[2], a serpent. § 793 (Mausalap.): XVI, **4**η, †120.

Çitikeça, a warrior of Skanda. § 615*u* (Skanda): IX, **45**η, 2563.

Çitiprabha = Vishṇu: I, 2506.

Çītoshṇakshujjarādhidhṛk = Çiva (1000 names[1]).

Çiva[1], the great god (Mahādeva, or Rudra, etc.), husband of Umā. [§ 2 (Anukram.): I, **1**, 32 (Sthāṇu, i.e. *Ç*., issued from the primordial egg).]—§ 28 (Amṛtamanthana): I, **18**, 1153 (swallowed the poison *Kālakūṭa*, and is therefore called *Nīlakaṇṭha*).—[§ 108 (Aṃçāvat.): I, **66**, 2565 (Sthāṇu, i.e. *Ç*., was father of the 11 Rudras).]—[§ 130 (do.): I, **67**, 2708 (Açvatthāman was born from the union of *Mahādeva* (i.e. *Ç*.), *Antaka*, *Kāma*, and *Krodha*).]—[§ 174 (Dhṛtarāshṭravivāha): I, **110**, 4371 (Hara, i.e. *Ç*., granted Gāndhāri the boon that she should have 100 sons).]—§ 190 (Arjuna): I, **123**, 4794 (°*tulyaparākramaḥ*, i.e. Arjuna; Arjuna will gratify Çaṅkara, i.e. *Ç*., etc., all. to Kairātap.).—[§ 213 (Jatugṛhap.): I, **143**, 5698 (*ayaṃ samājaḥ sumahān ramaṇīyatamo bhuvi | upasthitaḥ Paçupater*—i.e. *Ç*.—*nagare Vāraṇāvate*).]—[§ 220 (Caitrarathap.): I, **169**, 6428 foll. (in a former existence, Draupadī had five times asked Çaṅkara, i.e. *Ç*., for a husband, therefore she became the wife of all the five Pāṇḍavas).]—[§ 238 (Pañcendrop.): I, **197** (*Ç*. confined the five Indras in a cave).]—[§ 239 (do.): I, **197** (repetition of § 220).]—[§ 246 (Sundopasundop.): I, **211** (how *Ç*. got four faces).]—[§ 249 (Arjuna-vanavāsap.): I, **215** (gave a boon to Prabhañjana).]—[§ 255 (Agniparābhava): I, **223** (Çvetaki gratified Rudra, i.e. *Ç*., and obtained Durvāsas (who was a portion of *Ç*.) as his ṛtvij).]—[§ 263 (Sabhākriyāp.): II, **3**, 72 (Sthāṇu, i.e. *Ç*., performs sacrifices at Bir[illegible]ras).]—§ 269 (Vaiçravaṇasabhāv.): II, **10**, 416 (t[illegible]her with Umā and numerous attendants, *Ç*., the friend of Kubera, is sitting in the palace of Kubera).—[§ 273 (Rājasūyārambhap.): II, **14**, 629 (Jarāsandha worshipped Mahādeva, i.e. Çiva).]—[§ 274 (do.): II, **15**, 656 (Jarāsandha kept many kings in the temple of Paçupati, i.e. *Ç*., in order to sacrifice them to *Ç*.).]—§ 293 (Dyūtap.): II, **46**, 1643 (*Vṛshadhvajam*, etc.). —[§ 317*b* (Kṛshṇa Vāsudeva): III, **12** (Kṛshṇa becomes Rudra, i.e. Çiva; Çambhu, i.e. *Ç*., sprung from the forehead of Kṛshṇa; Kṛshṇa plays with Çaṅkara as with a toy).]—§ 330 (Indradarçana): III, **37**, 1513 (*Bhūteçam*, etc.).—[§ 331 (Kairātap.): III, **38–39** (Arjuna fights with *Ç*., disguised as a Kirāta).]—§ 332 (Mahādevastava): III, **39**, 1627 (Arjuna praised *Ç*., *Kapardinam*, etc.).—§ 333 (Kairātap.): III, **40**, †1662 (gave Brahmaçiras (Pāçupata) and Gāṇḍīva to Arjuna).—[§ 360 (Tīrthayātrāp.): III, **82**, 5061 (Rudra, i.e. *Ç*., multiplied himself into ten millions (*koṭi*) of forms, in order that every one of the ten millions of munis who were assembled at Rudrakoṭi might see him first).]—[§ 365 (Maṅkaṇaka): III, **83**, 6089, 6095, 7001, 7005 (Maṅkaṇaka's relations to Mahādeva, i.e. *Ç*.).]—§ 387 (Sagara): III, **106**, 8836 (*Tryaksham Tripuramardanam*, etc., *Ç*. granted Sagara sixty thousand sons by his one wife and one son by the other).—[§ 389 (Gaṅgāvatāraṇa): III, **108–9** (gratified by Bhagīratha, *Ç*. sustained Gaṅgā, when she came down from the sky).]—[§ 392*b* (Vaitaraṇī): III, **114** (how Rudra, i.e. *Ç*., obtained the best part in sacrifices).]—§ 441 (Nivātakavacayuddhap.): III, **165**, 11914 (Arjuna had obtained weapons from *Ç*.); [**167–8** (repetition from Kairātaparvan)].—§ 459 (Mārkaṇḍeyas.): III, **189**, 12955, (identified with Nārāyaṇa).—§ 491 (Āṅgirasa): III, **220**, 14162 (created from the navel of Pāñcajanya). — [§ 501 (Skandop.): III, **229** (Rudra, i.e. *Ç*., is identified with Agni, and Skanda is considered as his son).]—[§ 504 (Skandayuddha): III, **231** (Rudra begat Miñjika and Miñjikā).]—§ 506 (do.): III, **231**, 14567 (accompanied by Umā, etc., *Ç*. proceeded to Bhadravaṭa).—[§ 507 (do.): III, **231** (attacked by Mahisha, *Ç*. was rescued by Skanda, who slew Mahisha).]—[§ 524 (Jayadrathavimokṣh.): III, **272** (Jayadratha sought the protection of *Ç*.).]—[§ 550 (Samayapālanap.): IV, **13**, 339 (*samāje Brahmaṇo rājan yathā Paçupater*—i.e. *Ç*.—*iva*).]—[§ 565 (Gālavac.): V, **111**, 3825, 3828, 3829 (*Maheçvara*, i.e. *Ç*., dwells on Himavat; here *Ç*. (*Mahādevaḥ*) received Gaṅgā on his head; Devī (i.e. Umā) here performed austerities in order to win the affection of Maheçvara (i.e. *Ç*.).]—§ 567 (Bhagavadyānap.): V, **124**, 4177 (*yuddhe yena*—i.e. by Arjuna—*Mahādevaḥ sākshāt santoshitaḥ Çivaḥ*, all. to Kairātaparvan); [**181**, 4422 (*Ç*. (*Rudraḥ*) appeared on the breast of Kṛshṇa)].—§ 573 (Ambopākhyānap.): V, [**187**, 7376 (*Ç*. (*Umāpatiḥ*) promised Ambā that she would become a man in her next birth and slay Bhīshma)]; **188**, 7396 (*Ç*. granted Drupada that he should have a daughter [i.e. Ambā re-born], who would afterwards become a man).—[§ 574 (Jambūkh.): VI, **6**, 213 (*Ç*. (*Rudraḥ*) performs sacrifices on Meru), 219 (accompanied by Umā, *Ç*. (*Paçupatiḥ*) resides on Meru), ζ, 241 (*Ç*. (*Sthāṇuḥ*) performs sacrifices at Bindusaras).]—[§ 575*b* (Çākadvīpa): VI, **11**, 429 (*Ç*. (*Çaṅkaraḥ*) is worshipped on Çākadvīpa).]—§ 594 (Mṛtyu): VII, **52**, 2046 (*Haraḥ*, etc.; *Ç*. asked Brahmán not to destroy the creatures).—[§ 595 (Shoḍaçarājik., v. Pṛthu Vainya): VII, **69**, 2417 (when the puṇyajanas milked the earth, *Ç*. (*Vṛshadhvajaḥ*) acted as their calf).]—§ 596 (Pratijñāp.): VII, **80–81**, 2881 (in the night Arjuna and Kṛshṇa visit and praise *Ç*., who gives the *Pāçupata* weapon to Arjuna).—[§ 599 (Jayadrathavadhap.): VII, **94** (*Ç*. gave an armour to Indra, who then proceeded against Vṛtra).]—

[§ 599e (Çini): VII, **144,** 6039, 6040 (*Ç.* (*Mahādevaḥ*) granted that Somadatta should have a son).] — [§ 603c (Nārāyaṇa): VII, **201** (having become one with Bráhman (*brahmabhūtaḥ*), Nārāyaṇa saw *Ç.*, the master, origin and lord of the universe, the lord of all the gods, the supreme deity (*sarvadevair abhishṭutaṃ*) . . . smaller than the smallest and larger than the largest . . . *Rudra, Hara, Çambhu,* with matted locks on his head, the infuser of life in every form . . . the All-destroyer . . . with the celestial bow and quivers, cased in golden armour . . . who holds Pināka, is armed with thunderbolt, blazing trident, battle-axe, mace and sword . . . who has the moon on his forehead, is clad in tiger-skin . . . who uses snakes as his sacrificial string . . . surrounded by numerous ghosts and spirits, who is the one, the abode of ascetic austerities; . . . who is water, heaven, etc., and who is the measure of the duration of the universe. Persons of wicked behaviour can never obtain a sight of that unborn one, that slayer of all haters of brahmans, that bestower of heaven (*amṛtasya yoniṃ,* so Nīl.), but only brahmans of righteous conduct, when cleansed from their sins and freed from the control of grief, behold him with their mind's eye . . . that being whose body is the universe . . . with a garland of *akshas* round his neck, who sports with the fair Pārvatī . . . the destroyer of the Asura Andhaka . . . the three-eyed, the blue-throated god. *Ç.* granted boons to Nārāyaṇa).]—§ 603 (Nārāyaṇāstramoksh.): VII, **202**ηη, 9504, 9519 (protects Arjuna; Vyāsa praises *Ç.*, and relates how *Ç.* destroyed Daksha's sacrifice).—§ 603d (Tripura): VII, **202,** 9570 (*Ç.* makes war against Tripura).—§ 603 (Nārāyaṇāstramoksh.): VII, **202**ιι, 9594 (Vyāsa praises *Ç.*, and explains some of his names to Arjuna), 9622 (why he is so called). [With ch. **202,** cf. XIII, **161-162,** below.]—[§ 606 (Tripurākhyāna): VIII, **33-34** (*Ç.* makes war against Tripura).]—[§ 606b (Paraçu-Rāma): VIII, **34** (*Ç.* caused Rāma Jāmadagnya to fight with the Dānavas and then gave him celestial weapons).]—§ 608 (Karṇap.): VIII, **86**τ, 4361 (*Mahādevaḥ,* all. to Kairātaparvan); [**87,** 4428 (*Ç.* (*Bhavaḥ*) came to see the encounter between Karṇa and Arjuna)].—[§ 615j (Maṅkaṇaka): IX, **38** (repetition of § 365).]—§ 615u (Skanda): IX, **44**-[**46**], 2483 (Skanda sprung from the seed of *Maheçvara,* i.e. *Ç.* (v. 2455); Skanda honoured *Ç.*, who gave him a powerful companion and the army *Dhanañjayā*). — [§ 615z (Arundhatī): IX, **48** (*Ç.'s* relations to Arundhatī).]—§ 616 (Sauptikap.): X, **7**η, 252 (Açvatthāman praises *Ç.* (*Ugraṃ,* etc.), who appeared and gave Açvatthāman a sword. Then *Ç.* entered Acvatthāman's body).—[§ 617 (Aishīkap.): X, **17-18** (*Ç.* retired to the waters and did not partake in the creation; as no share was assigned to him, *Ç.* came to the sacrifice of the gods, pursued the embodied sacrifice, broke the arms of Savitṛ, and tore out the eyes of Bhaga and the teeth of Pūshan; then the gods assigned a share to him).]—[§ 621b (Rājadh.): XII, **8,** 241 (*Ç.* (*Mahādevaḥ*) at a great sacrifice requiring libations of all kinds, offered all creatures as sacrificial libations and then his own self).]—[§ 626 (do.): XII, **20,** †612 (having sacrificed himself as libation at the sarvayajña, *Ç.* (*Mahādevaḥ*) became the god of the gods).] — [§ 638b (Rāmopākhy.): XII, **49,** 1748 (*Ç.* (*Mahādevaḥ*) gave an axe to Rāma Jāmadagnya).]—§ 641 (Rājadh.): XII, **59,** 2201, 2202 (*Çaṅkaraḥ,* etc., acquired the science of chastisement (*daṇḍanīti*) from Brahmán, abridged it, and handed the abridged work (named *Vaiçālāksha* and consisting of 10,000 adhyāyas) over to Indra); **122,** [4498 (*Ç.* (*Içānaḥ*) was made the chief of the Rudras)], 4516 (*Mahādevaḥ*), 4521 (*Devadevaḥ,* etc.). — [§ 653b (Gṛdhragomāyusaṃv.): XII, **153** (revived a dead child).]—§ 656 (Khaḍgotpattik.): XII, **166,** 6183 (as Brahmán had created the sword, *Ç.* slew the Dānavas with it, and then handed it over to Vishṇu). — § 678c (Mṛtyu-Prajāpatisaṃv.): XII, **257**[**-258**], 9162 (*Harijaṭaḥ Sthāṇur Vedādhvarapatiḥ*), 9163 (asked Brahmán not to destroy the creatures, cf. § 595). — § 693 (Vṛtravadha): XII, **281a,** 10120 (*jagatpatiḥ, Ç.'s* energy assumed the form of fever and penetrated the body of Vṛtra).—[§ 694b (Jvarotpatti): XII, **284** (how fever came into existence from the sweat of *Ç.* when he at Daksha's sacrifice pursued the embodied sacrifice).] — [§ 695b (Dakshayajñavināça): XII, **285** (*Ç.* was not invited to the sacrifice of Daksha; urged by Umā, *Ç.* created *Vīrabhadra* from his wrath; accompanied by *Bhadrakālī* (*Mahākālī*), *Vīrabhadra* destroyed the sacrifice; then *Daksha* praised *Ç.* by reciting his 1,008 names (*Çivasahasranāmastotra*)).] — § 696b (Daksha-prokta-Çivasahasranāmastotra): XII, **285,** 10360, 10370 (1000 names[1]), 10440, 10473 (having recited Çiva's 1,008 names, etc., Daksha obtained boons from *Ç.*). — § 701b (Bhava-Bhārgava-samāg.): XII, **290,** 10669 (*Ç.'s* relations to Uçanas).—§ 702 (Mokshadh.): XII, **295,** 10805 (the gods applied to *Ç.*, who slew three Asuras (so PCR.) together with their leader).—[§ 712 (Çukotpatti): XII, **324-325** (sitting on the top of *Meru, Ç.* was gratified by Vyāsa and granted him that he should get the son Çuka).]—[§ 716 (Çukābhipatana): XII, **334** (when Çuka had entered Bráhman, *Ç.* came and consoled Vyāsa).]—§ 717b (Nārāyaṇīya): XII, **342,** 13152 (*Içānaṃ,* identical with Nārāyaṇa); [**343,** V) (how Rudra's — i.e. *Ç.'s* — throat became blue (*nīla*)), XIV) (Himavat gave his daughter Umā in marriage to Rudra and was therefore cursed by Bhṛgu), (ω) (the battle between Rudra and Nara and Nārāyaṇa)]; **350,** 13705 (*Brahmaṇaḥ sutaḥ,* had promulgated the *Pāçupata* system (*jñānaṃ*)). — § 717d (Brahma-Rudra-saṃv.): XII, **351**[**-352**], 13723 (*Caturvaktrasya*—i.e. Brahmán's—*lalāṭa-prabhavaḥ putraḥ,* discourse between him and Brahman).—§ 730 (Ânuçāsanik.): XIII, **14,** 600 (had been gratified by Kṛshṇa at Badarī), 606, (β), 624, 650 (in order to obtain a son from the grace of *Ç.*, *Kṛshṇa* repaired to the hermitage of *Upamanyu* on *Himavat*), 671 (Upamanyu enumerates the boons granted by *Ç.* to *Hiraṇyakaçipu,* etc.). — § 730g (Upamanyu): XIII, **14,** 716, 793, 821, 878, 911, 938 (Upamanyu relates how *Ç.* showed himself to him and granted him boons).—§ 730 (Ânuçāsanik.): **14,** 963 (Kṛshṇa by his penances succeeded in seeing *Ç.*, whom he praised); [**15** (*Ç.* and *Umā* granted boons to Kṛshṇa)]; **16,** 1105 (Taṇḍin succeeded in seeing *Ç.*, whom he praised); **17,** 1141 (*Çivānāṃ Çivaḥ,* Upamanyu recited to Kṛshṇa the 1,008 names of *Ç.* (i.e. *Mahādevasahasranāmastotra*), which had been uttered by Brahmán and communicated to Upamanyu by Taṇḍin), 1269; **18,** 1362, 1364 (*Vyāsa,* etc., had obtained boons from *Ç.*; conclusion of Upamanyu's discourse).—§ 734 (Ânuçāsanik.): XIII, **26,** †1848 (*divaç cyutā cirasāptā Ç°ena Gaṅgā,* cf. § 389). — [§ 746 (do.): XIII, **77** (Daksha gave to Çiva a bull whom he made his vehicle and banner, therefore he is called *Vṛshabhadhvaja*; the gods made *Ç.* lord of the animals (*Paçupati*)).]—§ 747b (Suvarṇotpatti): XIII, [**84** (having married Umā, *Ç.*, at the request of the gods, drew up his seed (therefore he is named *Ūrdhvaretas*), but a part of it came out, whence Skanda arose)]; **85,** 4109, δ, 4112 (*Ç.* assumed the form of Varuṇa and performed a sacrifice, in which Bhṛgu, Aṅgiras, and Kavi arose from the seed of Brahmán, etc.).—[§ 768*b* (Umā-Maheçvara-saṃv.): XIII, **140–148** (the discourse between Umā and *Ç.*).]—§ 773*d* (Ānuçāsanik.): XIII, **161–162**: Kṛshṇa said (declaring that he would recite the *Çatarudriya*): It is *Çiva* who created all creatures; when he looks angrily on D., As., G., or Pn., they cannot find peace anywhere. He pierced the Prajāpati Daksha's sacrifice; D. and As. became stupefied, etc. (description); the *Ṛshis* performed propitiatory rites; *Çiva* tore out the eyes of *Bhaga* and the teeth of *Pūshan* (with his foot); the gods recited the *Çatarudriya.* At last Çiva became gratified and the gods assigned a large share [of the sacrificial offerings] to him; the sacrifice, which had been severed into two pieces, became once more united. The *Asuras* had in days of yore three cities in the sky (of iron, silver, and gold respectively); *Indra* was unable to pierce them; the gods then repaired to *Rudra* (*Çiva*), who made *Vishṇu* his shaft-head, etc. (γ), and pierced the city and burnt it together with the Asuras. Beholding *Mahādeva* (*Çiva*) transformed into a child with five locks of hair, lying upon the lap of Pārvatī, the latter asked the gods who he was. *Indra* resolved to kill him with his thunderbolt, but the child paralysed his arm; the gods and the *Prajāpatis* could not realise that it was the lord of the universe, but *Brahmán* by his penances found out that it was Mahādeva, and praised him, and so did the gods; Indra's arm became restored. Taking birth as *Durvāsas*, *Çiva* resided for a long time at Dvāravatī in my house. He is *Rudra*, etc. (δ) (XIII, **161**). Kṛshṇa continued: "*Çiva* has two forms: (1) one which is terrible (= *Agni*, lightning, and *Sūrya*) and engaged in all operations of destruction; (2) one which is mild and auspicious (= Righteousness, water, and the moon) and engaged in brahmacarya. These two forms again are subdivided into many forms. Half his body is Agni (fire), half is Soma (the moon)." Then Kṛshṇa enumerated and explained many of *Çiva's* names, (ε) Ṛ., D., G., and Aps. worship that emblem of his which is always erect and upraised. He loves to reside in crematoria, and there he burns and consumes all corpses; those persons who perform sacrifices there attain to the regions set apart for heroes. The brahmans know the *Çatarudriya* in the *Veda* and the adoration (*upasthānaṃ*) [of the same name] which is composed by Vyāsa. *Çiva* created *Agni* from his mouth. The lordship of *Çakra*, etc., is verily his. It is he whose mouth is roaring in the waters of the sea in the form of the huge mare's head (XIII, **162**): XIII, **161**δ, 7496; **162,** 7503, 7511 (why he is so called).—§ 778*b* (Saṃvartta-Maruttīya): XIV, **8***a*, 193, 208, 210 (*Ç.* resides on *Muñjavat*, enumeration of his names (*Çarva*, etc.)).—§ 782*y* (Guruçishyasaṃv.): XIV, **43***o*, 1178 (*paçūnām īçvaraḥ*).—§ 795*c* (Mahābhārata): XVIII, **6,** 258 (°*sya bhavane*).

Cf. also the following synonyms:—

Aja, q.v.

Ambikābhartṛ ("husband of Ambikā, i.e. Umā"): VII, 2879.

Anaṅgāṅgahara ("who deprived Kāma of his body"): XIV, 211.

Ananta: VII, 9612; X, 257; XIV, 206.

Andhakaghātin ("slayer of Andhaka"): VII, 2876; XIII, 805, 908.

Andhakanipātin (do.): VII, 9462.

Atharva: XIII, 901.

Babhru: XIII, 589, 1263 (1000 names[2]).

Bahurūpa: I, †7298; II, 417; III, 8836, 11978; VII, 9523, 9527, 9537, 9619 (etymology); X, 253, 258; XII, 2201, 12173; XIV, 185, 211.

Bhagaghna ("slayer of Bhaga"): VII, 9538. Cf. the next.

Bhagahārin, Bhagākshihan, Bhaganetraghna, Bhaganetrahan, Bhaganetrahara, Bhaganetranipātana ("destroyer of Bhaga's eyes"), q.v.

Bhārgava, q.v.

Bhava: I, †7298; II, 417 (the friend of Kubera), 1641; III, 1520, (1618), (1650), 1662, 8836, †10225 (°*sya*, sc. *āyatanaṃ*, visited by Yudhishṭhira on his tīrthayātrā); VII, 2841, 2867, 2874, 2885, 2898, 2903 (*mantraṃ Bh°proktaṃ*), 2905, 2906, 2909, 2910, 9482 (°*mayaṃ jagat*), 9486, 9588, 9595; **202,** v. 135 (only B., the verse is missing in C. after v. 9628, etymology of the name); VIII, 1217 (worshipped by Kṛshṇa and Arjuna), 1252 (all. to Kairātaparvan), 1437, 1551, 1584, 1611, 1626 (*cakre sārathyaṃ Bh°sya Prapitāmahaḥ*, all. to Tripurākhyāna), †1741 (all. to Kairātaparvan), 4398, 4428 (came to see the encounter between Karṇa and Arjuna), †4573, †5044; X, 296 (°*sayujyam agataḥ*), 785; XII, 10258, 10345, 10356 (1000 names[1]), 10464, 10691, 10694, 11094, 13920; XIII, 605, 668, 686, 690, 696, 731, 738, 793, 803, 805, 848, 875, 908, 986, 995, 1003, 1019, 1058, 1075, 1119, 1145 (1000 names[2]), 1227 (do.), 1275, 1277, 1299, 1308, 3715, 4360 (among the 64 Viçvadevas), 6805, 6880, 7106 (°*ānucarāḥ*); XIV, 197, 208.

Bhavaghna (?): XIII, 908 (PCR. proposes to read Bhagaghna).

Bhīma: VII, 2875; VIII, 4360; XIII, 1144 (1000 names[2]).

Bhūtapati, Bhūteça, q.v.

Brahmacārin, Brahmaçiropaharta, q.v.

Cakrin, Candramaulivibhūshaṇa, Carmavāsas, Cekitāna, Cīravāsas (also VII, 9524, 9534), q.v.

Çambhu, q.v.

Çaṅkara: I, 4800 (*Mahādevaṃ*, all. to Kairātaparvan), 6428, 6429, 7320, 7322, 7323, †7332, 8120; II, 864 (Jarāsandha sacrifices human beings to *Ç.*); III, 514 (cf. Brahmán), 1526 (*Devadevaṃ*), 1561 (*Kirātarūpī*), 1586, 1630, 1633, 1703 (°*eṇa Tripuraṃ nihataṃ*, all. to Tripurakhyāna), 8836, 9945, 11943 (all. to Kairātaparvan), 12007 (do.), 14574; V, 7391; VI, 429 (worshipped in Çākadvīpa), 1227 (*Rudrāṇāṃ Çaṅkaraç cāsmi*, says Kṛshṇa about himself), 2774 (*nṛtyantam iva Ç°ṃ* (at the end of the yuga, PCR.)); VII, 2881, 2905 (*darçanaṃ Ç°sya*, all. to Kairātap.), 3403 (°*sthānaṃ*), 6889 (*ghorām Ç°nirmitāṃ*, sc. *açaniṃ*), 9503, 9521, 9550, 9563, 9618; VIII, 822 (*sarvabhūteshv anujñātaḥ Ç°eṇa*, sc. Arjuna), 1443, 1454, 1457, 1466, 1495, 1586, 1598; X, 632 (all. to Kairātap.); XII, 2201, 4521, 5788, 5789, 5797, 5798, 10293 (°*ād ūrdhvaṃ nānyaṃ paçyāmi daivataṃ*), 10683, 10692, 12639, 13272; XIII, 589 (*Surāsuragurau*), 675, 680, 717, 759, 776, 777, 872, 931, 963, 970, 1022, 1027, 1196 (1000 names[2]), 1215 (do.), 1284 (°*sannidhau*, Brahmán sung the 1000 names of Çiva), 1285, 1400 (Umā had performed austerities on Himavat in order to become the wife of *Ç.*), 1748 (Himavat was the father-in-law of *Ç.*), 4216 (*priyakṛc Ch°sya*, i.e. Skanda), 6338 (°*syomayā sārdhaṃ* *saṃvādaṃ*), 6508, 6768, 6806, 6874, 6920 (°*syomayā sārdhaṃ saṃvādaḥ*), 7477; XIV, 193, 208.

Çarva: III, 1550, 9951, 10549 (may be seen at Vātikakhaṇḍa at the end of every yuga), 11983 (repetition of Kairātap.), 12241; VII, 1754, 1756 (all. to Jayadrathavimokshaṇap.), (3470); VIII, 1251 (all. to Kairātap.), 1562, 1592, 4360; X, 252, 782; XII, 4521, 10356 (1000 names[1]); XIII, 663, 727, 783, 908, 931, 997 (*Tridaçeçvaraḥ*), 1112, 1120, 1215 (1000 names[2]), 6374, 7462 (*asṛjat prajāḥ*); XIV, 191, 208, 210. Cf. Sarva.

Çikhaṇḍin, Çikhin, q.v.

Çitikaṇṭha: VII, 9520; X, 253, 632, 803; XII, 6164, 13164, 13274 (°*tā*, origin of the name: Nārāyaṇa seized Çiva by the throat, which became dark); XIV, 192, 210.

Çmaçānavāsin: X, 254.

Çrīkaṇṭha: XII, 13294 (origin of the name from the mark of Nārāyaṇa's hand on Çiva's throat), 13705 (*Brahmaṇaḥ sutaḥ*); XIII, 6397 (°*tā*, origin of the name: Indra hurled his thunderbolt at Çiva, whose throat was scorched).

Çukra: X, 253; XIV, 210.

Çūlabhṛt ("armed with the trident"): II, 402; VI, 2779 (°*bhūt*, C.).

Çūladhara (do.): III, 1513.

Çūladhṛk (do.): III, 6097; VIII, 1554; IX, 2236.

Çūlahasta (do.): IX, 2483.

Çūlāṅka (do.): X, 296.

Çūlapāṇi (do.): I, 1932 (*iva*), 8128; III, 499 (*Çambhuḥ*), 1594, 1622, 6055 (to be worshipped at Vaitaraṇī), 8836, 11979 (repetition from Kairātaparvan), 15999 (*sthānaṃ . . . . Ç°eḥ*, i.e. Gokarṇa); IV, 1406; V, 1993 (all. to Kairātap.), 7376, 7413; VII, 3136 (*iva*), 9455; IX, 1858 (*iva*); X, 250; XII, 4502 (is appointed chief of the Rudras), 6169, 10809; XIII, 859, 929, †981, 3150, 3991, 6378; XVIII, 137 (*ratyarthaṃ bhavatāṃ hy eshā*—i.e. Draupadī—*nirmitā Ç°nā*).

Çūlin (do.): II, 1642 (°*iṃ*, acc.); III, 8333 (*vishāṇaṃ Ç°ḥ*); VII, 2858, 2878; VIII, 1447, 1589, 1609, 4362; XIII, 32, 858, 867; XIV, 182.

Dakshakratuhara ("destroyer of Daksha's sacrifice"), **Dakshayajñanibarhaṇa** (do.), **Dakshayajñavināça** (do.), **Dakshayajñavināçana** (do.), q.v.

Daṇḍapāṇi, Daṇḍin, q.v.

Devaçreshṭha, Devadeva, Devadeveça, Devādhideva, Devavara, Deveça, q.v.

Dhanadhyaksha: X, 258.

Dhanurdhara, Dhanus, Dhanvācārya, Dhanvantara: VII, 9536.

Dhanvin: VII, 9527, 9536; VIII, 1445; XII, 10361 (1000 names[1]); XIII, 1156 (1000 names[2]); XIV, 197, 200.

Dhruva: XIII, 609.

Dhūrjaṭi: VII, 9621 (etymology); XIII, 7510 (do.).

Digvāsas: XIII, 695, 753, 808, 898, 1155 (1000 names[2]).

Divyagovṛshabhadhvaja: XIV, 209. Cf. Vṛshabhadhvaja.

Durvāsas, q.v.

Ekāksha: XIII, 7503.

Gaṇādhyaksha: X, 258; XII, 10421 (1000 names[1]).

Gaṇanāṃ pati(ḥ): VII, 9589.

Ganeça: III, 1629.

Gaurīça ("husband of Gaurī"): XIV, 210.

Gaurīhṛdayavallabha ("dear to Gaurī's heart"): X, 258.

Giriça: I, 7296; III, 1622, 1662; V, 1993 (*Mahādevaṃ*, all. to Kairātaparvan); VII, 9524; X, 250, 252, 766, 772; XIV, 196.

Girīça: XIII, 6348, 6877; XIV, 1883, 1914.

Govṛshabhāṅka ("having a bull as his mark"): XIII, 6902.

Govṛshadhvaja ("having a bull in his banner"): III, 11978, 11989, 14428; XIII, 4002. Cf. Vṛshadhvaja.

Govṛshottamavāhana ("having the excellent bull as his vehicle"): X, 259.

Haṃsa, q.v.

Hara: I, 4371 (granted Gāndhārī 100 sons), 7970 (*Bhaganetraharaṃ*); II, 754 (*Rudraṃ*, etc.), 1642; III, 1551, 1617, 1624, 1630, 1635, 1666, 8838, 9943, 9955, 9962, 14542, 15855; V, 7116 (°*tulyaparākramaḥ*, i.e. Rāma Jāmadagnya); VII, 1755 (repetition from Jayadrathavimokshaṇaparvan), 2046 (*Çivaḥ*), 3463, †6726 (*yathā*), †8410 (°*vṛshodaragātrasamadyutiḥ*, sc. the moon), 9453, 9505, 9541, 9562, 9583, 9628 (etymology); VIII, 1504, 1506, 1524, †4661; IX, 2512 (?), 2807; X, 249, 253, 291, 293; XII, 8551 (*Brahma-H°ādishu*), 10344, 10457, 13302 (*Viçveçaṃ*); XIII, 772, 774, 775, 779, 813, 826, 968, 980, 1143, 1146 (1000 names[2]), 1156 (do.), 1234 (do.), 1312, †1847 (°*sya bhāryā*, i.e. Gaṅgā), 6361 (°*tulyāmbaradharā*, sc. Umā), 6363, 6364, 6369, 6370, 7106 (°*tulyaparākramāḥ*); XIV, 211.

Harirudra, q.v.

Haryaksha: IX, 595 (*saçūlam iva H°ṃ*).

Īça, Īçāna, Īçvara, q.v.

Jaṭādhara ("wearing matted locks"): III, 1625.

Jaṭila (do.): VII, 9454; X, 254; XII, 10366 (1000 names[1]), 10445.

Jaṭin (do.): VI, 2046; VII, 2858, 2879; XIII, 1145 (1000 names[2]), 1171 (do.).

Kāla, q.v.

Kāmāṅganāça ("who destroyed the body of Kāma"): XIII, 907.

Kapāli[n] ("carrying human skulls"): II, 1641 (°*iṃ*, acc.).

Kāpālin (do.?): VII, 159; XIII, 1217 (1000 names[2]).

Kapardin: III, 1624, 1936, 14126 (°*sutāṃ*); V, 7385; VII, 2875, 9453, 9521, 9530; VIII, 1530, 4360; X, 248, 791; XII, 4521, 13114 (identified with Nārāyaṇa), 13148 (*Rudraḥ*), 13300; XIII, 609, 614, 1159 (1000 names[2]), 6877, 7460; XIV, 192, 1884.

Khaṭvāṅgadhārin: X, 254.

Kirāta, q.v.

Kṛttivāsas ("clad in skins"): II, 1642; VIII, 1449, 1505; X, 256, 789; XIII, 1283, 1348; XIV, 204.

Kumārapitṛ ("father of Kumāra, i.e. Skanda"): VIII, 1450; X, 259.

Lalāṭāksha ("having an eye on his forehead"): III, 1628.

Lelihāna: XIV, 198.

Lokabhāvana, Lokaguru, Lokanātha, Lokeça, Lokeçvara, q.v.

Mahādeva ("the great god"): I, 433 (*Kirātavapushā*), ††678 (°*kṛtyāṃ*), 2708 (°*āntakābhyāṃ*, Açvatthāman was born from a part of *Mahādeva*, etc.), 4800 (*Çaṅkaraṃ*, all. to Kairātap.), 7682, 7706 (*Sthāṇuḥ*, how he got four faces), 8117, 8135, 8470 (all. to Kairātap.); II, 417 (in the palace of Kubera), 467 (*sahomaḥ*, in the palace of Brahmán), 629

(*Umāpatiṃ*, worshipped by Jarāsandha), 754 (*Rudraṃ*), 1642; III, 1544, (1547), 1611, 1622, 1625, 1632, 1642, 1645, 1665, 1688, 1952 (all. to Kairātap.), 4093 (*°prasādāc ca gāṇapatyañ ca vindate*, sc. by bathing in *Rudravaṭa*—B. *Bhadravaṭa*), 5042 (to be worshipped at Rudrapada (? *rudraṃ padaṃ*)), 5064, 6072 (to be worshipped at Mṛgadhūma), 6089, 6095, 7001, 7005, 7042 (to be worshipped at the tīrtha Naraka), 8002, 8105 (to be worshipped at Çālagrāma), 8161 (on Çrīparvata), 8192, 8205 (in Jyeshṭhasthāna), 8210 (to be worshipped at Muñjavaṭa), 8522 (in Brahmasaras), 8847, 11941, 11986, 11994, 11995 (repetition from Kairātap.), 12305 (*sagaṇaḥ*), 14521 (*Tripurārdanaṃ*), 14569; IV, 1298 (*Kirāta-veçmapracchannah*, all. to Kairātap.); V, 1993 (*Giriçaṃ*), 3828 (*atra*—i.e. in the north—*Gaṅgāṃ M°ḥ patantīm gaganāc cyutāṃ pratigṛhya dadau loke mānushe*), 3881, 4177 (all. to Kairātap.), 7381, 7385, 7392; VII, 2052, 2875, 2885, 6039, 6040 (granted a boon to Somadatta), 7047 (all. to Kairātap.), 9504, 9505, 9542, 9560, 9588, 9595, 9602, 9623 (etymology), 9636; VIII, 1466 (Çiva became endued with the half of the united energy of the gods, and from that time he was called *Mahādeva*), 1467, 1511, 1544, 1585, 1592, †4055 (all. to Kairātap.), 4361 (*Çivaḥ*, do.); IX, 2227, 2228, 2233, 2235 (*Rudrāt*), 2240, 2414, 2799, 2801 (gratified by Arundhatī); X, 247, 298, 307, 311, 766, 767, 793, 811; XII, 241 (*Viçvarūpaḥ*), †612 (sacrificed himself at the sarvayajña), 1748 (gave weapons to Rāma Jāmadagnya), 4498 (*Īçānaṃ*, was made lord of the Rudras), 4504, 4516 (Çivaḥ), 4520 (*Prajāpatiḥ*), 6169 (*Çūlapāṇiḥ*, slew the Asuras with the sword), 9168, 10221 (*Paçupatiṃ*), 10226, 10233, 10252, 10254, 10286, 10331, 10461, 10471, 10688, 12168, 12173, 12177 (gratified by Vyāsa, Çiva granted him the son Çuka), 12334, 12335 (performed austerities on the mountain Ādityaparvata), 12639 (consoled Vyāsa after the death of Çuka), 12673 (?); XIII, 590, 664, 679, 683, 685, 695, 696, 719, 724, 737, 757, 758, 762, 769, 795, 797, 837, 855, 865, 875, 880, 927, 934, 943 (*jagatsrashṭā*), 964, 965, 972, 999, 1038, 1039, 1104, 1216 (1000 names[2]), 1271, 1308, 1326, 1328, 1331, 1351, 1365, 1366, 1712 (to be worshipped in the hermitage of the Kṛttikās), 3718, 3723 (made the bull which was given to him by Daksha his vehiele and banner), 3724, 3993, 4133 (assumed the form of Varuṇa and performed a sacrifice), 4902 (*Gaṅgāyāç ca durutsahāṃ mūrdhnā dhārāṃ Mahādevaḥ çirasā yām adhārayat*), 5255, 6484, (6527), 6747, (6748), 6893 (identified with Kṛshṇa), 7129 (? *Rantidevaṃ*), 7463, 7501, 7503, 7509 (etymology); XIV, 203, 206, 212, 1933.

Mahāgaṇapati: X, 254.

Mahāyogin: XIV, 206.

Maheça ("the great Lord"): XIII, 780.

Maheçvara (do.): I, 1154, 7701, 8128; II, 416; III, 883 (*°çaroddhūtaṃ pupāla Tripuraṃ yathā*), 1939 (*ashṭa-mūrtinā*, all. to Kairātap.), 5014 (worshipped in Damin), 5045 (to be worshipped on Devikā), 7048 (do. at Gaṅgāhrada), 9906, 9942 (*Nīlakaṇṭhāt*), 11977 (repetition from Kairātap.), 14500, 14513 (*na spṛçanti grahā bhaktān narān devaṃ M°ṃ*), 14526 (father of Skanda), 14567 (*Çivam ity eva yaṃ prāhur Īçaṃ Rudraṃ Pitāmahaṃ | bhāvais tu vividhākāraiḥ pūjayanti M°ṃ*), 14572, 14617, 14618, 15160 (the Dānavas had formerly obtained Duryodhana from Maheçvara), 16188 (*°sakhaṃ*, i.e. Kubera); V, 2031 (*°samaṃ krodhe*, sc. Bhīma), 3152 (*°samaḥ krodhe*, sc. Bhīma), 3825 (on Himavat), 3829, 7498; VI, 222, 1955 (*yathā*); VII, 2668 (all. to Kairātap.), 2838 (slew the Daityas with the *Pāçupata* weapon), 2908, 3462, 3469, 6818 (*jaghāna . . . . Maheçvara ivāndhakaṃ*), 6864 (all. to Tripurākhyāna), 7131 (*°samo yudhi*), 7979 (all. to Tripurākhyāna), 9513, 9532, 9546, 9553, 9566, 9567, 9583, 9587, 9591, 9601, 9607, 9616 (etymology), 9618, 9629; VIII, 1330 (*yathā Brahmā Maheçvaraṃ*, sc. acted as charioteer to), 1463, 1565, 1570, 1573, (1587), 1598, (1602); IX, 2717 (*kecit M°sutaṃ vadanti*, sc. Skanda), 3034 (*Brahma-Vishṇu-Maheçvaraiḥ*); X, 296; XII, 6205 (*°praṇītaç ca Purāṇe niçcayaṃ gataḥ*, sc. the sword), 10126, (10132), (10232), (10234), 10292, 10303, 10330, 10332, 10426 (1000 names[1]), 10671, 10674, 12183 (granted to Vyāsa the son Çuka), 12957 (protected *Bāṇa*, but was vanquished by *Kṛshṇa*), 13164 (*Devadeve*, identified with Nārāyaṇa), 13686 (*°prasādena*, cf. v. 12183, PCR. has Mādhava); XIII, 599, 600, 700 (*Devadevāt*), 727 (*Viçvarūpaḥ*), 755, 770, 778, 801, 806, 823, 829, 856, 871, 911, 923, 948, 966, 978, 1081, 1163 (1000 names[2]), 1280, 1296, 1322, 1337, 1343, 1348, 1702 (*°sya tristhāne*, a tīrtha on the spot where Gaṅgā flows in a northward direction), 1830 (held Gaṅgā on his head), 3346 (performed austerities surrounded by cows), (6173) (discourses about kine), 6376, (6381), (6399), (6405), (6414), (6424), (6451), 6482, (6509), (6642), (6652), 6664, (6684), (6729), (6737), (6743), 6800, (6807), 6913, 6917, 7470, 7479, 7503, 7507 (etymology), 7519, 7530; XIV, 141 (in Vārāṇasī). 182, 200, 1880 (*suraçreshṭhaṃ*).

Mahishaghna ("slayer of Mahisha"): XIII, 905.

Makhaghna ("destroyer of [Daksha's] sacrifice"): VII, 2876.

Mīḍhvas: III, 1628; VII, 9524; XIV, 195.

Mṛgavyādha: XIV, 197.

Munīndra: XIII, 887.

Nandīçvara: XII, 10481; XIII, 1189 (1000 names[2]), 1747 (*°sya mūrttiṃ*), 7103 (*mahākāyo grāmaṇīr Vṛsha-bhadhvajaḥ*).

Niçācarapati: VII, 2046.

Nīlagrīva ("having a dark neck"): III, 1625; VII, 2876; VIII, 1447; XII, 10359 (1000 names[1]). Cf. the next.

Nīlakaṇṭha (do.): I, 1154 (origin of the name: Çiva swallowed the poison Kālakūṭa, then his throat became dark); II, 1641; VII, 9471, 9541; XII, 13206 (origin of the name: Nārāyaṇa seized Çiva in the throat, which became dark); XIII, 813, 1151 (1000 names[2]). Cf. Çitikaṇṭha.

Nīlalohita: VIII, 1505; XIII, 910 (*Rudrāṇām Nīlalohitaḥ*), 1089.

Paçubhartṛ: IX, 2414; XII, 10291; XIII, 620.

Paçupati: I, 5698 (a festival in honour of him at Vāraṇāvata); II, 402 (in the palace of Kubera), 656 (*°er gṛhe*, Jarāsandha kept the vanquished kings), 1642; III, 14545, 15855; IV, 339 (*P°er iva*, sc. *samāje*); V, 7593 (had given the Pāçupata weapon to Arjuna, all. to Kairātap.); VI, 219 (on Meru); VII, 9615 (etymology); IX, 2661 (gave Skanda an army of bhūtas named *Dhanañjayā*); X, 447 (*nyapātayat . . . . paçūn Pa°ir yathā*); XII, 10221, 10230, 10238, 10692, 13365; XIII, 698, †771, 780, 3724 (origin of the name), 4113, 4115, 4164, 7515 (etymology); XIV, 209.

Parameçvara, q.v.

Pinākadhṛk ("armed with the bow Pināka"): I, 7831; III, 1586, 8522, 11939, 11977; IV, 779 (*iva*); VI, 225, 2770 (*iva*); VII, 9471, 9564, 9636; XII, 10241, 10258; XIII, 1188 (1000 names[2]), 1250 (do.), 4110, 6388, 6651, 7467; XIV, 2299 (*yathā*).

Pinākagoptṛ (do.): III, 1628.

Pinākahasta (do.): XII, 12639.

Pinākapāṇi (do.): III, 1551; IV, 1434; VIII, †1523; X, 134 (*iva*); XIII, 881, 6409.

Pinākin (do.): I, 1491 (*iva*); II, 1642 (°*iṃ*, acc.); III, 1543, 1591, 1615, 1664, 1666, 8836 (°*iṃ*, acc.), 10550, 14559; IV, 1960 (*iva*); V, 5897 (*iva*); VI, 225, 684 (plur.), 2770 (*iva*); VII, 2877, 3465, †9455, 9534; VIII, †3521; IX, 2483; XII, 5793, 10685; XIII, 667, 981, 6806.

Piṅgala: XIII, 882.

Pitāmaha, q.v.

Prajāpati, q.v.

Prajāpatimakhaghna ("destroyer of Prajāpati's [i.e. Daksha's] sacrifice"): VIII, 1446.

Pūshṇo dantabhid: XIV, 193.

Pūshṇo dantavināça(ḥ): VII, 9541.

Rājarāja, q.v.

Rudra: I, 538 (°*māhātmyaṃ*), 569, 1668 (*yathaiva bhagavān Rudro viddhvā yajñamṛgaṃ*), 2529 (°*syānucaraḥ çrīmān Mahākālaḥ*, i.e. Bāṇa), 7971 (?*lokeshu sendra-Rudreshu*), (8116), 8122, (8126), 8127, 8133, 8134, 8136, 8138; II, 754, 862 (Jarāsandha sacrificed the vanquished kings to Rudra), 1642; III, 481 (identified with Kṛshṇa), 1441, 1444, 1592, 5015 (to be worshipped at Damin), 5061 (at Rudrakoṭi), 6097, 7097 (worshipped by Vishṇu at the tīrtha Suvarṇākhya), 8105 (at Çālagrāma), 8416 (had obtained Brahmaçiras and given it to Arjuna), 8417, 8841, 8852, 10101, 10103, 10104, 10105, †10225 (°*sya*, sc. *āyatanaṃ*, visited by Yudhishṭhira on his *tīrthayātrā*), 11938, 12237 (*Devadevāya*), 14103 (*yathā Rudrāc ca sambhūtaḥ*, sc. Skanda), 14391 (= Agni, C., but B. has *Rudram Agnimukhāṃ Svāhāṃ*), 14428 (*Rudram Agniṃ dvijāḥ prāhū, Rudrasūnus tatas tu saḥ*, sc. Skanda, the son of Agni), 14429 (*Rudreṇa çukram utsṛshṭaṃ tac Chvetaḥ parvato 'bhavat*), 14430, 14431 (*anupraviçya Rudreṇa vahniṃ jāto hy ayaṃ çiçuḥ*, i.e. Skanda), 14432, 14495 (*purusheshu yathā Rudras tathāryā pramadāsv api*), 14521, 14522, 14523, 14528 (*Miñjikāmiñjikaṃ mithunaṃ Rudrasambhavaṃ*), 14551 (°*sya çūlaḥ*, named Vijaya), 14553 (°*sya paṭṭiçaḥ*), 14556, 14558, 14564, 14566, 14567, (14571), 14601, 14602, 14605, 14625, 16020 (*anvadhāvad mṛgaṃ Rāmo Rudras tārāmṛgaṃ yathā*); IV, 1536 (all. to Kairātaparvan), 1982 (had given Arjuna the *Raudra* weapon), 2011 (°*parākramaḥ*, i.e. Arjuna); V, 457, 3969 (*reme . . . yathā Rudraç ca Rudrāṇyām*), 4482, 5381, 5604, 5856 (°*vat*), 7378; VI, 213 (on Meru), 2776 (*Pinākam iva Rudrasya*), 2797 (do.), 4679 (°*vat*); VII, 456, 755 (*pātayishyāmi Rudraḥ paçugaṇān iva*), 787 (*ākrīḍa iva Rudrasya ghnataḥ kālātyaye paçūn*), 1289 (*lokeshu sendra-Rudreshu*), 1756 (all. to Jayadrathavimokshaṇaparvan), (2054), 2220 (granted Çibi imperishable wealth), 2574 (*Jayadrathaḥ varadānena Rudrasya*), 2691 (had given a weapon to Arjuna), 2874, 2899, 3676, 5013 (°*syākrīḍasadṛçaḥ*), 5956, 6180 (*ākrīḍanam iva Rudrasya*), 6236 (*nyahan Rudraḥ paçūn iva*), 6416 (°*Çakrāntakopamaṃ*), 6723, 6810 (°*opendravikramaḥ*, sc. Açvatthāman), 6993 (all. to Kairātap.), 7939 (°*opendravikramaḥ*, sc. Karṇa), 7986 (*açanīṃ R°nirmitāṃ*), 8617, 8815 (°*sya* [C. *Ruddhasya*] *nighnataḥ paçūn yathā*), 9453, 9462, 9486 (°*bhaktaḥ Keçavaḥ R°saṃbhavaḥ*), 9490, 9504, 9519, 9520, 9553, 9558, 9561, 9592, 9594, 9609, 9612, 9635 (etymology); VIII, 146 (*kṛtvā mahāyuddhaṃ . . . yathā Rudreṇa cāndhakaḥ*), 1248 (°*syākrīḍasannibhaṃ*), 1447, 1496 (°*daṇḍaḥ*), 1501, 1555, 1559, 1561, 1563, 1575, 1577 (°*kalpaḥ*, sc. Çalya), 1620, 1623, 1629, 2224 (*avadhīt . . . Rudraḥ paçūn iva*), 2742 (*iva*), 3141 (*nighnataḥ sarvabhūtāni Rudrasyeva*), 3667 (*rūpaṃ R°opendrasamaṃ*), †4611 (*iva*); IX, 188 (°*syākrīḍasannibhaṃ*), 722 (°*syākrīḍanaṃ yathā*), 847 (*vyapothayata . . . Rudraḥ paçūn iva*), †911 (*sasarja . . . Rudro 'ndhakāyāntakaraṃ yatheshuṃ*), 1130 (*yathā*), 2235, 2488, 2492, 2507, 2666 (°*tulyabalaiḥ*), 2756 (friend of Kubera); X, 134 (*iva*), 249, 252, 254, 305, 780, 788, 799; XI, 439 (°*ākrīḍanibhaṃ*); XII, 141, 439, †2791, †2792, †2793, 4430 (°*tanayaḥ*, i.e. chastisement), 4472 (*Muñjapṛshṭhaḥ . . . Rudrasevitaḥ*), 4521, 5752, 6135 (the eighth son of Brahmán), 6164 (*Ṛshabhaketave*), 6165, 6172, 6173, 6175, 6183, 6185, 6202, 10284, 10308 (°*tulyā gaṇāḥ*), 10320, 10321, 10322, 10325, 10327, 10669, 11706 (if the soul (*jīva*) escapes through the breast, one goes to Rudra), 11785 (*Viçvarūpasya*), 12177 (on Meru), 12645, 12737 (*krodhajaḥ*), 12915 (*devakrodhād viniḥsṛtaḥ*), 13016, 13043 (created ten other Rudras), 13085 (son of Brahmán, issued from the forehead of Brahmán), 13140, 13146, 13149, 13152, 13155 (identified with Nārāyaṇa), 13156, 13158, †† 13206 (Daksha caused a third eye to appear on the forehead of Rudra), †† 13222 (wooed Umā), †† 13223, 13268, (his encounter with Nara and Nārāyaṇa), 13273, 13274, 13278, 13284, 13289, 13291, 13295, 13300 (*Devadevaṃ*), 13563, (13729), (13735); XIII, 597, 681, 687, 693, † 781, 818 (*Devadevena*), 864, 941, 1003, 1279, 1286, 1361, 1379, 1396 (°*syāyatanaṃ*), 1411, 3723 (made the bull given to him by Daksha his vehicle and banner), † 3727, 3991 (*Çūlapāṇiḥ*), 3993, 3994, 4008, 4025 (°*sya retaḥ praskannam agnau*, whence arose Skanda), 4084, 4105 (*Īçasya*), 4112, 4164 (identified with Agni), 5245 (°*kanyābhiḥ*), 5283 (°*devarshi-kanyābhiḥ*), 5972, 7110 (°*ānala-Vasuprabhāḥ*, sc. *ṛshayaḥ*), 7124 (°*saṅkāçāḥ . . . Brahmalaukikāḥ*), 7475, 7477, 7478, 7480, 7483 (*mahā*°), 7484, 7488, 7493, 7496, 7502, 7508 (etymology); XIV, 192, 1132, 1922.

Ṛshabhaketu ("having a bull for his banner"): XII, 6164.

Sarva (B. has often Çarva): II, 1642 (B. *C*°); VII, 2869 (do.), 2872 (do.), 2874 (do.), 2881, 2888 (B. *Ç*°), 9508, 9523, 9565 (B. *C*°), 9594, 9620 (etymology); IX, 2239; XII, 10363, 10391 (1000 names[1]); XIII, 720, 742, 1036 (B. *Ç*°), 1143 (do.), 1145 (1000 names[2]), 1206 (do.), 1303 (B. *Ç*°), 4164 (do., identified with Agni), 6872 (B. *Ç*°), 7496; XIV, 201.

Sarvabhūtaguru, Sarvabhūtamaheçvara, Sarvabhūtapati, Sarvabhūteça, q.v.

Sarvadeveça, Sarvadeveçvara, q.v.

Sarvalokapitāmaha, Sarvalokeçvara, Sarvalokeçvareçvara, q.v.

Sarvayogeçvareçvara: XII, 10240.

Sthāṇu: I, 32 (came out from the primordial egg), 2565 (father of the eleven Rudras), 7702, 7706; II, 72 (at Bindusaras), 298 (?, in the palace of Indra), 1641; III, 1518, 1935 (*ekādaçatanuḥ*), 4091 (°*os tīrthaṃ*, i.e. Rudravaṭa or Bhadravaṭa), 5092 (*Muñjavaṭaṃ nāma Sthāṇoḥ sthānaṃ*), 7034 (*Yogeçvaraḥ*, at Pañcavaṭi), 8883, 10409 (°*or mantrāṇi*, are to be recited at Pushkara), 12285 (all. to Kairātaparvan); VI, 241 (at Bindusaras); VII, 2046, 2047, (2049), 9488, 9505, 9522, 9538, 9570, 9625 (etymology); VIII, 1434, 1435 (*Īçānaṃ*), (1459), 1508, 1534, 1535, 1554 (*Çūladhṛk*), 1572, 1607, 4362, †4561; IX, 300 (°*or vṛshasya sadṛçaṃ*, sc. Açvatthāman), 2362 (performed austerities at Sthāṇutīrtha), 2363, 2527; X, 252, 773, 788; XII, 2201 (*Çivaḥ*), 4521, (*Çivaḥ*), 9162 (*Çivaḥ*), 9163, (9165), (9170), 9177, 10431 (1000 names[1]), 12685; XIII, 716, 841, 843 (*ashṭādaçabhujaṃ*), 1001, 1144 (1000 names[2]), 2013, 5972 (°*oḥ sthāne*), 6923, 7503, 7512 (etymology); XIV, 194, 210.

Suraçreshṭha, Surasattama, Surāsuraguru, Suravara, Sureça, Sureçvara, q.v.

Svayambhū, Svayambhuva, q.v.

Triçūlahasta ("armed with the trident"): XIV, 207.

Triçūlapāṇi (do.): III, 5045 (°*eḥ sthānaṃ*, on Devikā); VII, 9533.

Tridaçapuṅgava, Tridaçeçvara, q.v.

Trilocana ("having three eyes"): III, 499, 15802; VII, 9563.

Trinayana (do.): IX, 2799; XII, 13724; XIV, 207.

Trinetra (do.): III, 12241; VII, 2878; XII, 10357 (1000 names[1]); XIII, 1241 (1000 names[2]).

Tripuraghātin ("destroyer of Tripura"): X, 255.

Tripuraghna (do.): III, 7098, 12253, 14319, 14427; VII, 3941, 9538; XII, 10357 (1000 names[1]); XIII, 1306; XIV, 207.

Tripuraharta (do.): XIII, 906.

Tripuramardana (do.): III, 8835.

Tripuranāçana (do.): XIII, 6542.

Tripurāntaka (do.): II, 1641.

Tripurāntakara (do.): II, 754.

Tripurārdana (do.): III, 14521, 15855.

Tripuravighna (do.): XIV, 205.

Tryaksha ("having three eyes"): I, 7315 (pl., i.e. the Pāṇḍavas); II, 1504; III, 1513, 1656, 8835; VII, 9504, 9541, 9629 (Çiva created a third eye on his forehead); VIII, 1450, 1571, 4360; XII, 10349 (1000 names[1]).

Tryambaka: I, †160; II, 403 (in the palace of Kubera); III, 1525, 1625, 1660, 1661, 1666, 8836, 11984 (repetition from Kairātap.), 11992, 14624, 15857; VII, 111 (all. to Kairātaparvan), 1464, 1579 (*yathā*), 1937 (*samprajahrāte pureva T°āndhakau*), 2229 (*jaghāna . . . pureva T°o 'ndhakaṃ*), 2875, 2887, 2979 (all. to v. 2820 foll.), 9288, 9564, 9624 (etymology), 9643; VIII, 788 (*yudhyasva T°enāndhako yathā*), 1444, 1452, 1600; IX, 306 (worshipped by Droṇa); X, 801; XII, 1668 (Kṛshṇa identified with *T.*), 10357 (1000 names[1]), 10434, 12184 (granted Vyāsa the son Çuka), 13720 (*Brahmaṇā saha saṃvādaṃ T°sya*); XIII, 684, 7503; XIV, 203, 207, 1913.

Ugra: I, †7298; II, 1642; VII, 9525; VIII, 4360; X, 252; XII, 10369 (1000 names[1]); XIII, 1213 (1000 names[2]); XIV, 198, 204, 210.

Ugreça: III, 8836.

Umāpati ("husband of Umā"): I, 7832; II, 402, 417, 629, 1642; III, 1547, 1656, 4091, 7042 (*Viçveçvaraṃ*, in the tīrtha Naraka), 8169 (worshipped in Gokarṇa), 8836, 14622, 15801, 15855; V, 1994, 7376, 7379; VII, 9519, 9529; VIII, 1440, 1697; IX, 2472; X, 248, 253, 632; XII, 2201, 4521, ††6077 (*Viçveçvara U°ḥ Kāmam abhivartamānam anaṅgatvena çamam anayat*), 10328, 10677, 12173, 13301, 13705; XIII, 1154 (1000 names[2]), 1250 (do.), 7492, 7000; XIV, 180 (on Muñjavat), 185, 209, 211.

Vedhas, Vibhu, q.v.

Viçālāksha: XII, 2093, 2201 (composed the çāstra Vaiçālāksha), 4498; XIII, 753, 1151 (1000 names[2]).

Viçva, Viçvakarman, Viçvamūrti, Viçvarūpa, Viçvasambhava, Viçvasṛj, Viçveça, Viçveçvara, q.v.

Vilohita: VII, 2877; VIII, 1447; X, 256; XII, 10359 (1000 names[1]); XIV, 202.

Virūpāksha: I, 569 (*Rudraṃ*), 7970 (*Haraṃ*); III, 15801 (*Umāpatiṃ*); VII, 9463, 9529; XII, 7551 (*bhūtamātṛgaṇādhyakshaṃ*), 10344 (*Haraḥ*), 10349 (1000 names[1]).

Vṛsha, Vṛshabha, q.v.

Vṛshabhadhvaja ("having a bull in his banner"): III, 1634, 1635, 1664, 5061, 14547; V, 7385; VII, 2839, 2857, 2886, 9489; VIII, 1519, 4445; XII, 10345, 10682; XIII, 3724 (origin of the name), 6357, 6921, 7103; XIV, 1886.

Vṛshabhāṅka ("having a bull as his mark"): XIII, 3725, 6339, 6345, 6360.

Vṛshabhavāhana ("having a bull as his vehicle"): XIII, 4003.

Vṛshadhvaja (= Vṛshabhadhvaja): II, 481, 1640; III, 1642, 6045, 6055, 7034, 7099, 8056, 8069, 8107, 8161, 15802; V, 7380, 7381; VII, 2417 (acted as the calf when the *puṇyajanāḥ* milked the earth), 2879, 2897, 9530, 9593; XII, 12331; XIII, 927, 929, 6322, 6387.

Vṛshaketana (= do.): III, 14561.

Vṛshāṅka (= Vṛshabhāṅka): III, 10907; VII, 2894, 2901, 2980, 9531; VIII, 1436.

Vṛshavāhana (= Vṛshabhavāhana): I, †7298; XIII, 1347.

Yāmya: VII, 9521; XIV, 193.

Yati: XIV, 196.

Yogeçvara, Yogin, q.v.

[*Remarks.*—Besides the above synonyms, numerous epithets of Çiva of minor importance are found in hymns or descriptions of him scattered about in the Mahābhārata; cf. especially the following passages:—III, 1624–1633; VII, 2857–2861, 2863–2868, 2874–2884, 9451–9458, 9460–9463, 9464–9471, 9502–9541, 9588–9589, 9594–9635; VIII, 1445–1452; X, 252–261; XII, 10440–10460; XIII, 731–756, 784–828, 880–923, 936–947, 1002–1018, 1040–1102, 1368–1376, 4111–4112, 7462–7467, 7491–7531; XIV, 191–212.]

Çiva (1000 names [1–2]), v. next, etc.

Çivasahasranāmastotra(m) (= Çiva, 1000 names[1]), the 1,008 names by which Çiva was praised by Daksha. § 696*b* (Dakshaprokta-Çivasahasranāmastotra): XII, **285,** 10346–10439. The names are the following, alphabetically arranged:—*Adāntanāçana*, 10426; *Adhara* or *Dhara* (so B.), 10424; *Adharmahan*, 10429; *Adhayaḥ* (pl.), 10433; *Adīkshita*, 10426; *Ādi(r) devānāṃ*, 10409; *Aditya*, 10354; *Aghuṇṭu*, 10410; *Aghaṇṭaghaṇṭin*, 10377; *Aghoraghora rupa*, 10375; *Agni*, 10354; *Ahorātra(ṃ)*, 10439; *Āhutimaya*, 10100; *Akala*, 10417; *Akāla*, 10418; *Akshamālin*, 10374; *Akshapriya*, v. *Sadākshapriya*; *Amārga* (so B.) or *Mārga*, 10430; *Amṛtapā*, 10435; *Amukha*, 10428; *Anala*, 10395, 10411, 10439; *Ananta*, 10403 (*bhoginām*); *Anaupama*, 10410 (B. has *Ghanuupumaḥ*); *Aṇḍa*, 10358; *Aṇḍadhara*, 10358; *Aṇḍajāḥ* (pl.), 10396; *Aṇḍanāçana*, 10434; *Andhakaghātin*, 10356; *Anilu*, 10430; *Anna(ṃ)*, 10395; *Annabhoktṛ*, 10395; *Annabhuj*, 10382, 10395; *Annada*, 10382, 10395; *Annapati*, 10382; *Annasrashṭṛ*, 10395; *Anto devānāṃ*, 10409; *Aṇu*, 10427; *Apakshakshayaṅkara*, 10418; *Apāna*, 10415; *Apramada*, 10414; *Apratirūpa*, 10360; *Arcayanty arkam arkiṇaḥ*, 10352; *Ārjava(ṃ)*, 10425; *Arṇavālaya*, 10350; *Artha*, 10407; *Aruṇa*, 10409; *Asataç ca sataç caiva . . . prabhavāpyayau*, 10355; *Ātapana*, 10374; *Atikāla*, 10418; *Avarṇa*, 10410; *Avatata*, 10359. *Bahumukha*, 10428; *Bahunetra*, 10376; *Bala(ṃ)*, 10439; *Bāla*, 10437; *Bālakrīḍanaka*, 10384; *Balānucaragupta* (B. °*gopta*), 10384; *Balapramathana*,

10368; *Bālarkavarṇa*, 10383; *Bālarūpadhara*, 10383; *Balavishṭambha*, 10348; *Bhaganetrāñkuça*, 10423; *Bhānu*, 10412; *Bhava*, 10356; *Bhāvana*, 10374; *Bhettṛ*, 10406; *Bhīmadundubhihāsa*, 10369 (C. has °*dundabhi*°); *Bhīmamukha*, 10428; *Bhīmavratadhara*, 10369, 10370; *Bhīshma*, 10370; *Bhū*, 10426; *Bhūta*, 10425; *Bhūtabhavyabhavodbhava*, 10425; *Bhūtagrāma(ç) caturvidha(ḥ)*, 10396; *Bhūtakṛt*, 10425; *Bhūtātman*, 10425; *Bhuvaḥ*, 10426; *Bindu*, 10427 (C. *V*°); *Brahmacarya(ṃ)*, 10425; *Brahmakāyika(ṃ) agnīnāṃ*, 10420; *Brahmán*, 10352, 10354, 10425; *Bráhman*, 10397, 10413; *Brāhmaṇāḥ* (pl.), 10401; *Brahmātman*, 10445; *Brahmavidāṃ vara(ḥ)*, 10397; *Bṛhaspati*, 10354. *Calācala*, 10416; *Caṇḍa*, 10358; *Caṇḍadhāra*, 10429; *Caṇḍikaghaṇṭa*, 10377; *Candrādityau cakshushī te*, 10438; *Candrāvarta*, 10394, 10427; *Cāpin*, 10406; *Carācarasya pratihartṛ*, 10397; *Carācarasya srashṭṛ*, 10397; *Carucelin*, 10419; *Cāturāçramyanetṛ*, 10421 (C. has °*āçrama*°); *Cāturhotrapravartaka*, 10420; *Caturmukha*, 10428; *Cāturvarṇyakara*, 10421; *Caturveda*, 10420; *Caturyuga*, 10420; *Catushpatharatha*, 10389; *Chāya*, 10374; *Chettṛ*, 10406; *Citibhashmapriya*, 10370; *Citrabhānu*, 10412; *Çaça*, 10432; *Çaçāñka*, 10432; *Çakra*, 10437; *Çakuni*, 10429; *Çamaçam*, 10379; *Çamaçama*, 10377; *Çamana*, 10432; *Çañkukarṇa*, 10350; *Çānta*, 10375; *Çāntatama*, 10375; *Çarin*, 10406; *Çarva*, 10356; *Çatajihva*, 10351; *Çatakratu*, 10352; *Çatarudriya(ṃ)*, 10413 (*yajushāṃ*); *Çatāvarta*, 10351, 10384; *Çatodara*, 10351; *Çatrundama*, 10361; *Çayamāna*, 10366; *Çayita*, 10366; *Çikhaṇḍin*, 10434; *Çilpika*, 10422; *Çilpināṃ çreshṭha(ḥ)*, 10422; *Çītoshṇakshujjarādhidhṛk*, 10432; *Çiva*, 10360, 10375; *Çreshṭha*, 10368, 10431; *Çūdrāḥ* (pl.), 10401; *Çukla*, 10359; *Çukladhvajapatākin*, 10364; *Çvetapiñgalanetra*, 10387. *Daçabāhu*, 10369; *Daçalakshaṇasaṃyukta*, 10407; *Daṃshṭrin*, 10371; *Daṇḍa*, 10361, 10372, 10387; *Daṇḍadhāra*, 10434; *Daṇḍin*, 10358, 10420; *Daṇḍimuṇḍa*, 10358; *Dānta*, 10381, 10426; *Deva*, 10435; *Deva-Dānavapūjita*, 10348; *Devadeveça*, 10348, 10396; *Devagaṇeçvara*, 10435; *Devāribalasūdana*, 10348; *Dhanada*, 10411; *Dhanus*, 10404 (*yantrāṇāṃ*); *Dhanvin*, 10361; *Dhara* (so B.) or *Adhara*, 10424; *Dhāraṇa*, 10421; *Dharma*, 10407; *Dharmakāmārthamokshāṇāṃ kathanīyakatha(ḥ)*, 10388; *Dhātṛ*, 10424; *Dhāvamāna*, 10366; *Dhruva*, 10426; *Dhṛti*, 10405; *Dhūmra*, 10359; *Dhūrta*, 10421; *Dīkshita*, 10426; *Dīptasūryajaṭila*, 10392 (°*e*, dat.); *Dravyakarmasamārambha*, 10408; *Duḥsaha*, 10431; *Duratikrama*, 10431; *Durdānta*, 10426; *Durdharsha*, 10432; *Durjaya*, 10432; *Durmukha*, 10428; *Durvāraṇa*, 10431; *Durvisha*, 10432; *Durvis(h)aha*, 10431; *Dushkāla*, 10418; *Dushprakampa*, 10432; *Dvesha*, 10405. *Ekaçīrshan*, 10376; *Ekapād*, 10376. *Gadin*, 10406; *Gajendrakarṇa*, 10351; *Gama*, 10433; *Gaṇādhipa*, 10421, 10429; *Gaṇādhyaksha*, 10421; *Gandha*, 10378; *Gañgā*, 10407; *Gañgātoyārdramūrdhaja*, 10394; *Garbhamāṃsaçṛgāla*, 10380 (B. °*sṛ*°); *Gayanti tvāṃ gāyatriṇaḥ*, 10352; *Gāyatrī*, 10409; *Ghanaupama*, 10410 (so B. instead of *Anaupama* in C.); *Ghaṇṭa*, 10377, 10419; *Ghaṇṭamālapriya*, 10378; *Ghaṭin*, 10419 (C. has by error *Dh*°); *Ghoraghoratara*, 10375; *Ghosha*, 10386; *Ghushya*, 10386; *Girīça*, 10422; *Girika*, 10414; *Girikapriya*, 10422; *Girīṇāṃ çikharāṇi*, 10403; *Girivṛkshālaya*. 10379; *Gītavādanakapriya*, 10417; *Gītavāditraçālin*, 10367; *Gītavāditratattvajña*, 10417; *Gokarṇa*, 10351; *Gomārga*, 10430; *Gonarda*, 10430; *Gopratāra*, 10430; *Govinda*, 10430; *Govṛsha*, 10372; *Govṛsheçvaravāhana*, 10430; *Grahāḥ* (pl.), 10402; *Gūḍhavrata*, 10424; *Guhyatapas*, 10424. *Hariçmaçru*, 10416; *Harikeça*, 10390; *Harita*, 10409; *Hāyi hāyi huvā hoyi huvā hoyi tathāsakṛt gāyanti tvaṃ* . . . *sāmagā brahmavādinaḥ*, 10399; *Hiṇḍuka*, 10414; *Hiraṇyagarbha*, 10362, 10429; *Hiraṇyakavaca*, 10362; *Hiraṇyakṛtacūḍa*, 10362; *Hiraṇyapati*, 10362; *Hiraṇyaretas*, 10437; *Homya*, 10412; *Hotṛ*, 10364, 10412; *Hotra(ṃ)*, 10412; *Huṃhuṃhuṃkārapāra*, 10379; *Huṃhuṃkārapriya*, 10379; *Huta*, 10380, 10412. *Içāna*, 10390; *Icchā*, 10405; *Indra*, 10411. *Jagannātha*, 10435; *Jalacara*, 10417; *Jaleçvara*, 10354; *Jālya*, 10417; *Jarāyujāḥ* (pl.), 10396; *Jaṭila*, 10366; *Jaya*, 10432; *Jayājayau*, 10405; *Jharjharin*, 10406; *Jīrṇadaṃshṭra*, 10437; *Jīva*, 10414; *Jṛmbhita(ṃ)*, 10415; *Jyeshṭha*, 10368; *Jyotishāṃ nidhi(ḥ)*, 10398. *Kadru*, 10410; *Kāla*, 10418; *Kalāḥ* (pl.), 10402; *Kalakala*, 10378, 10386; *Kālanātha*, 10368; *Kālapushpaphalaprada*, 10408 (B. reads *kālaḥ pu*°); *Kali*, 10417; *Kalpa* (so C.) or *Kalya* (so B.), 10368; *Kāma*, 10391, 10407, 10427; *Kāmada*, 10391; *Kāmaghna*, 10391; *Kāmakrodhau*, 10405; *Kampa*, 10431; *Kapālahasta*, 10370; *Kapila*, 10410; *Kapota*, 10410; *Karaṇa(ṃ)*, 10355; *Kāraṇa(ṃ)*, 10355; *Karṇikārasrajapriya*, 10427; *Kārya(ṃ)*, 10355; *Kāshṭhāḥ* (pl.), 10402; *Kaṭakaṭa*, 10364; *Kaṭañkaṭa*, 10372; *Kelikala*, 10417; *Kha(ṃ)*, 10398; *Khaḍgajihva*, 10371; *Khaṭvāñgin*, 10406; *Kilakila*, 10365; *Kriyā*, 10355; *Kṛça*, 10365, 10387; *Kṛçāñga*, 10365; *Kṛçanāça*, 10365 (B. °*nāsa*); *Kṛshṇa*, 10409; *Kṛshṇājinottarīya*, 10389; *Kṛshṇaraktekshaṇa*, 10387; *Kṛtya*, 10418; *Kshamākshame*, 10405; *Kshānta*, 10426; *Kshatriyāḥ* (pl.), 10401; *Kshaya*, 10368; *Kshīrapā*, 10436; *Kshīroda(ḥ) udadhīnāṃ*, 10404; *Kshobhaṇa*, 10384; *Kshubdha*, 10384; *Kshudralubdha*, 10376; *Kshudra*, 10376 (B. has *Rudra*); *Kshura*, 10418; *Kshuta(ṃ)*, 10415; *Kumbhakarṇa*, 10350; *Kuṇḍa*, 10358. *Lambodaraçarīrin*, 10445; *Laṭāḥ* (pl.), 10408; *Lobha*, 10405; *Lohitāntargatā dṛshṭi(ḥ)*, 10416; *Lubdha*, 10384. *Madhuçcyutānām agrapā(ḥ)*, 10436; *Mahādaṃshṭra*, 10419; *Mahākāla*, 10392; *Mahākarṇa*, 10350; *Mahāmeghacayaprakhya*, 10392; *Mahāmūrti*, 10353; *Mahāpārçva*, 10429; *Mahāvaktra*, 10416; *Maheçvara*, 10426; *Mahodadhi*, 10439; *Mahodara*, 10416; *Mahoragapati*, 10429; *Manasaḥ paramā yoni(ḥ)*, 10398; *Mañgala(ṃ)*, 10413 (*mañgalānāṃ*); *Mantra*, 10364; *Mārga* (so C.) or *Amarga* (so B.), 10430; *Marutpati*, 10435; *Māsa*, 10402; *Māsardha(ṃ)*, 10402; *Matsya*, 10417; *Mecaka*, 10410; *Meghāvarta*, 10394; *Meghakāla*, 10419; *Meghasañghāḥ* (pl.), 10401; *Milīmilin*, 10419; *Moha*, 10405; *Mṛgāḥ* (pl.), 10408; *Mṛtyu*, 10418; *Mṛtyupā*, 10436; *Mukhavāditravādin*, 10367; *Muṇḍa*, 10366, 10420; *Muñjakeça*, 10385; *Mūrtau hi te* . . . *sarvā vai devatā*, 10353. *Nābha*, 10364; *Nābhya*, 10364; *Nādyupahāralubdha*, 10367; *Nāgendra*, 10437; *Nakshatrāṇi* (pl.), 10402; *Namas* (?), 10423 (*namo namaḥ*); *Namaskāra*, 10423; *Nandīmukha*, 10428; *Napuṃsaka(ṃ)*, 10437; *Nartanaçīla*, 10367; *Netṛ*, 10406; *Nīla*, 10409; *Nīlagrīva*, 10359; *Nimesha*, 10415; *Nimeshāḥ* (pl.), 10402; *Nimeshonmeshakarman*, 10439; *Nishkampa*, 10431. *Oṃkāra*, 10398, 10409; *Oshadhyaḥ* (pl.), 10408. *Pacapaca*, 10372; *Paçavaḥ* (pl.), 10408; *Paçūnāṃ pati(ḥ)*, 10356; *Paksha*, 10418; *Pakshiṇaḥ* (pl.), 10408; *Paktṛ*, 10395; *Pakvabhuj*, 10395; *Pakvāmamāṃsalubdha*, 10371; *Palvalāni* (pl.), 10407; *Pañcāla*, 10377; *Pāṇikarṇa*, 10351; *Parṇacīrapaṭa*, 10361; *Paṭhyase çrutibhiç* (B. *stuti*°) *caiva Vedopanishadāṃ gaṇaiḥ*, 10400; *Pavana*, 10395; *Pavitra(ṃ)*, 10413 (*pavitrāṇāṃ*); *Pitāmaha*, 10438 (*hṛdayañ ca P°ḥ*, sc. *te*); *Prabhu*, 10412; *Prahartṛ*, 10406; *Prahuta*, 10380; *Pramathanātha*, 10361; *Prāṇa*, 10414, 10415; *Prāṇabhagna*, 10387; *Prāṇaghaṇṭa*, 10378; *Priya*, 10349; *Pudgala*, 10414; *Puṃs*, 10437; *Puṇḍarīkāksha*, 10434; *Puṇḍarīkavanālaya*, 10434; *Purusha*, 10437; *Pushṇo dantavināçana(ḥ)*, 10423. *Rāga*, 10405; *Rajas*, 10414; *Rakta*, 10409; *Raktamālyāmbaradhara*, 10422; *Raktavirakta*, 10374; *Raṇeshv agnimukha(ḥ)*, 10428; *Rathyavirathya*, 10389; *Rohita*, 10409; *Rudra*, 10356, 10376 (only B., C. has *Kshudra*); *Ṛcaḥ* (pl.), 10398; *Ṛṅmaya*, 10400; *Ṛtavaḥ* (pl.), 10402. *Sadākshapriya*, 10421 (*sadā cāksha°*); *Sahasracaraṇa*, 10382; *Sahasraçīrsha*, 10382; *Sahasrādhmātaghaṇṭa*, 10378; *Sahasrāksha*, 10349; *Sahasranayana*, 10383; *Sahasrasūryapratima*, 10393; *Sahasrodyataçūla*, 10383; *Samakarṇa*, 10358; *Samāni* (pl.), 10398; *Samāna*, 10415; *Sambhinna*, 10374; *Saṃhṛshṭa*, 10365; *Sampravartaka*, 10427; *Samudrāḥ* (pl.), 10407; *Samudrāmbarasannibha*, 10352; *Saṃvarta*, 10427; *Saṃvartakabalāhaka* (C. *valā°*), 10419; *Saṃvatsara*, 10402; *Saṃvibhāgapriya*, 10376; *Sandhātṛ*, 10424; *Sandhyārāga*, 10391; *Sāṅkhya*, 10388; *Sāṅkhyamukhya*, 10388; *Sāṅkhyayogapravartin*, 10388; *Santāpitṛ*, 10406; *Sarāṃsi* (pl.), 10407; *Sarasvatī*, 10439; *Saritaḥ*, 10407; *Sarva*, 10363, 10391; *Sarvabhakshya*, 10363; *Sarvabhūtāntarātman*, 10363; *Sarvaçilpapravartaka*, 10422; *Sarvada*, 10391; *Sarvaghna*, 10391; *Sarvam āvṛtya tishṭhasi*, 10350; *Sarvataç çrutimāṃl loke*, 10350; *Sarvataḥ pāṇipādānta(ḥ)*, 10349; *Sarvato 'kshiçiromukha(ḥ)*, 10349; *Sarvavarishṭha*, 10373; *Sattva(ṃ)*, 10414; *Satya(ṃ)*, 10404 (*vratānāṃ*), 10425; *Shaṭkarmatushṭa*, 10385; *Sitāṅga*, 10377; *Soma*, 10354; *Somapā*, 10435, 10436; *Sphoṭana*, 10387; *Sthāṇu*, 10131; *Sthavira*, 10437; *Sthira*, 10431; *Sthita*, 10366; *Sthūla*, 10427; *Sthūlajīrṇajaṭila*, 10392 (°*e*, dat.); *Strī*, 10437; *Stuta*, 10363; *Stutya*, 10363; *Stūyamāna*, 10363; *Sūcīroman*, 10416; *Sumukha*, 10428; *Suraçreshṭha*, 10399, 10435; *Sūrya*, 10360; *Sūryadhvajapatākin*, 10360; *Sūryamāla*, 10360; *Suvarṇa*, 10410; *Suvarṇanāman*, 10411; *Suvarṇapriya*, 10411; *Svadhā*, 10423; *Svāhā*, 10423; *Svar*, 10426; *Svarbhānu*, 10412; *Svedajāḥ* (pl.), 10396. *Tamas*, 10414; *Tapana*, 10381; *Tapas*, 10425; *Taponitya*, 10393; *Tapya*, 10381; *Tara*, 10380; *Tāraka*, 10380, 10424; *Tārakāmaya*, 10424; *Taraṅgāṅkitakeça*, 10355; *Tārkshya*, 10403 (*patatāṃ*); *Taṭa*, 10381; *Taṭānāṃ patiḥ*, 10381; *Taṭya*, 10381; *Tejasvin*, 10438; *Toyātman*, 10446; *Trailokyagoptṛ*, 10430; *Triçīrsha*, 10357; *Triçūlavarapāṇi*, 10357; *Tridaṇḍadhṛk*, 10420; *Trijaṭa*, 10357; *Trikarmanirata*, 10385; *Trinetra*, 10357; *Trisauparṇa(ṃ)* (so B.) or *Trisauvarṇa(ṃ)* (so C.), 10413; *Tryaksha*, 10349; *Tryambaka*, 10357, 10434; *Tryambikāmbikanātha*, 10390; *Tṛpāni* (pl.), 10408; *Tṛptātṛptavicārin*, 10391; *Tumbīvīṇāpriya*, 10371; *Tushitādyapā* (so B.) or *Tushṭajyapā* (so C.), 10436. *Udāna*, 10415; *Udbhidjāḥ* (pl.), 10396 (C. has by error *Udbhijāḥ*), *Ugra*, 10369; *Ugradaṇḍa*, 10434; *Unmādana*, 10394; *Unmesha*, 10415; *Upakshaya*, 10368; *Upaplava*, 10412; *Ūrdhvaṃ kham iva menire*, 10352; *Ūrdhvadaṃshṭrakeça*, 10359; *Ūrdhvakeça*, 10416; *Utthita*, 10366. *Vāc*, 10439; *Vaiçyāḥ* (pl.), 10401; *Vajra*, 10404 (*praharaṇānāṃ*); *Vajrasaṅghāta*, 10390; *Valkalājinadhārin*, 10392; *Valkalājinavāsas*, 10393; *Vallyaḥ* (pl.), 10408; *Vara*, 10373; *Varada*, 10356, 10373, 10411 (only C., B. has *Varuṇa*); *Varamālyagandhavastra*, 10373; *Varātivarada*, 10373 (°*e*, dat.); *Varṇāçramāṇāṃ vidhivat pṛthak karmanivartin*, 10386; *Varṇakāra*, 10410; *Varṇavarāḥ* (pl.), 10401; *Varuṇa*, 10411 (only B., C. has *Varada*); *Vashatkāra*, 10423; *Vāyu*, 10398; *Vibhinna*, 10374; *Vibhīshaṇa*, 10370; *Viçvakartṛ*, 10437; *Viçvakṛt*, 10437, 10438; *Viçvakṛtāṃ vareṇya(ḥ)*, 10438; *Viçvarūpa*, 10438; *Viçvatomukha*, 10438; *Viçvavāha*, 10438; *Vidhātṛ*, 10424; *Vidyutstanitagarjita*, 10401; *Vihṛshṭa*, 10365 (only B.); *Vikṛtavaktra*, 10371; *Vilohita*, 10359; *Virāj*, 10429; *Virūpa*, 10360; *Virūpāksha*, 10349; *Vishāgnipā*, 10436; *Vishāgrapā*, 10435; *Vishṇu*, 10354; *Vṛddha*, 10384; *Vṛksha*, 10414; *Vṛkshāṇāṃ kandado* (B. *kakudo*) *'si tvaṃ*, 10403; *Vṛsha*, 10372; *Vṛshaskhandha*, 10361; *Vṛshya*, 10372; *Vyādhayaḥ* (pl.), 10433; *Vyādhi*, 10433; *Vyādhihan*, 10433; *Vyādhīnām āgama(ḥ)*, 10433; *Vyāghra*, 10403 (*mṛgāṇāṃ*); *Vyaktāvyakta*, 10390; *Vyālayajñopavītin*, 10389; *Vyāna*, 10415; *Vyavasāya*, 10405. *Yajin*, 10380; *Yajña*, 10380; *Yajñādhipa*, 10349; *Yajñamṛgavyādha*, 10433 (*mama*, i.e. Daksha's); *Yajñavāha*, 10381; *Yajurmaya*, 10400; *Yakshādhipapriya*, 10349; *Yama*, 10411; *Yuga(ṃ)*, 10402; *Yugāvarta*, 10394, 10427; *Yuvan*, 10437.

Mahādevasahasranāmastotra (= Çiva, 1000 names[2]), the 1,008 names of Çiva, which were originally uttered by Brahmán and afterwards by Taṇḍin. § 730 (Ānuçāsanikap.): XIII, **17**, 1144*b*–1266. The names are the following, alphabetically arranged: *Abhigamya*, 1206; *Abhirāma*, 1264; *Abhivādya*, 1147; *Acalopama*, 1239; *Acintya*, 1260, 1265; *Açanin*, 1157; *Āçramapūjita*, 1187 (*nityaṃ*); *Āçramastha*, 1210; *Açva*, 1227; *Açvattha*, 1184; *Adambha*, 1192; *Adhana*, 1215; *Adharshaṇa*, 1165; *Adhiroha*, 1238; *Adhyātmānugata*, 1191; *Ādi*, 1150; *Ādikara*, 1150; *Adīna*, 1152; *Aditi*, 1212; *Āditya*, 1181, 1253; *Ādya*, 1207, 1255 (only B., v. the next); *Ādyastuti*, 1255 (so C., B. reads *ādyas tu nirgamaḥ* instead of *ādyastutir gamaḥ*); *Agama*, 1172; *Agnijvāla*, 1196; *Agravara*, 1262; *Ahaçcara*, 1161; *Ahas*, 1255; *Ahirbudhnya*, 1216; *Ahorātra(ṃ)*, 1226; *Aja*, 1159; *Ajaikapād*, 1217; *Ajita*, 1203, 1217; *Akāçani*, 1181 (Nīl. takes *akāçanirvirūpaḥ* as one word); *Akara*, 1182; *Aksha*, 1235; *Akshara(ṃ)*, 1193; *Alola*, 1224; *Amara*, 1177, 1261; *Amareça*, 1216; *Ambujāla*, 1211; *Aṃçu*, 1181; *Amita*, 1163; *Amitrajit*, 1194; *Amogha*, 1227; *Amoghārtha*, 1206; *Amṛta*, 1237, 1253; *Amukha*, 1173; *Amukhya*, 1179; *Anagha*, 1152; *Anala*, 1204, 1214, 1220; *Anantarūpa*, 1248; *Anaushadha*, 1193; *Aṅgalubdha*, 1197; *Anila*, 1214, 1220; *Anilābha* (so C.) or *Nilābha* (so B.), 1216; *Animisha*, 1154; *Anindita*, 1213, 1226; *Anīti*, 1194; *Antarātman*, 1201; *Antarhitātman*, 1149; *Anukārin*, 1212; *Apara*, 1211; *Apsarogaṇasevita*, 1230; *Ardana*, 1147; *Ārdracarmāmbaravṛta*, 1162; *Ārohaṇa*, 1238; *Artha*, 1166; *Arthakara*, 1184; *Aryaman*, 1218; *Asāhaya*, 1233; *Asamāmnāya*, 1236; *Asat*, 1222, 1256; *Āshāḍha*, 1234; *Asnehana*, 1203; *Atandrita*, 1165; *Atharvaçīrsha*, 1205; *Atidhūmra*, 1196; *Atidīpta*, 1183; *Ativṛddha*, 1233; *Ātman*, 1233 (C., B. reads *ātmasahāyaḥ* instead of *ātma, sahāyaḥ*); *Ātmanirāloka*, 1183; *Ātmasahāya*, v. *Ātman*; *Ātmasambhava*, 1260; *Atri*, 1152; *Atryānamaskartṛ*, 1152; *Atulya*, 1177; *Avaça*, 1181; *Avara*, 1166; *Āveça*, 1231; *Āvedanīya*, 1231; *Avyakta(ṃ)*, 1256; *Avyaya*, 1185, 1262; *Āyu(s)*, 1211; *Āyudhin*, 1157. *Babhru*, 1263; *Bahubhūta*, 1163; *Bahudhānindita*, 1215; *Bahudhara*, 1163; *Bahukarkaça*, 1236; *Bahula*, 1243; *Bahumāla*, 1240; *Bahuprada*, 1223; *Bahuprasāda*, 1194; *Bahuraçmi*, 1181; *Bahurūpa*, 1159; *Bahuvidya*, 1223; *Bakula*, 1223; *Bala*, 1155, 1191; *Balacārin*, 1174; *Balahan*, 1166; *Balarūpadhṛk*, 1180; *Balavat*, 1193, 1220; *Balavīra*, 1155; *Balin*, 1171; *Bāṇahasta*, 1156; *Bandhakartṛ*, 1214; *Bandhana*, 1214; *Bandhana(ḥ) asurendrāṇāṃ*, 1176; *Bhagahārin*, 1190; *Bhāgakara*, 1197; *Bhagavat*, 1147, 1242; *Bhāgin*, 1197; *Bhaktānāṃ paramā gatiḥ*, 1266; *Bhasmabhūta*, 1209; *Bhasmāçaya*, 1209; *Bhasmagoptṛ*, 1209; *Bhava*, 1145, 1227; *Bhāva*, 1207; *Bhāvana*, v. *Sabhāvana*; *Bhikshu*, 1185; *Bhikshurūpa*, 1185; *Bhīma*, 1144; *Bhojana*, 1227; *Bhūtabhāvana*, 1147, 1219; *Bhūtacārin*, 1163; *Bhūtālaya*, 1226; *Bhūtanishevita*, 1210;

vardhana, 1189; *Nara*, 1230, 1249, 1254; *Nararshabha*, 1261; *Nartaka*, 1164; *Navacakrāṅga*, 1226; *Niçācara*, 1163, 1182; *Niçācārin*, 1188; *Niçākara*, 1192; *Niçālaya*, 1199; *Nidhi*, 1150, 1157; *Nigraha*, 1179; *Nihantṛ*, 1190; *Nija*, 1263; *Nīla*, 1197; *Nīlābha*, 1216 (so B., C. and Nīl. *Anilābha*); *Nīlakaṇṭha*, 1154; *Nīlamauli*, 1250; *Nilaya*, 1227; *Nimitta(ṃ)*, 1189; *Nimittastha*, 1189; *Nipātin*, 1181; *Nīraja*, 1261; *Nirāmaya*, 1263; *Niravagraha*, 1197; *Nirgama*, 1255 (so B., C. has *Gama*); *Nirjīva*, 1236; *Nirvāṇa(ṃ)*, 1257; *Nīti*, 1194; *Nitya*, 1164, 1233; *Nityanarta*, 1164; *Nivedana*, 1242; *Nivṛtti*, 1146; *Niyama*, 1150; *Niyamāçrita*, 1150; *Niyamendriyavardhana*, 1265; *Niyata*, 1146; *Nṛtyapriya*, 1164; *Nyagrodha*, 1167; *Nyāyanirvapana*, 1239. *Pāça*, 1164; *Paçupati*, 1193, 1249; *Pāda*, 1239; *Padmagarbha*, 1247; *Padmanābha*, 1220; *Padmanālāgra*, 1249; *Paksha*, 1254; *Paksharūpa*, 1183; *Pakshin*, 1183; *Paṇavin*, 1172; *Paṇḍita*, 1239; *Para* (masc.), 1211; *Para(ṃ)*, 1266 (*Bráhma*); *Parā gati(ḥ)*, 1257; *Paraçvadhāyudha*, 1212; *Parama(ṃ) Bráhma*, 1193; *Parama(ṃ) tapas*, 1153; *Paramātman*, 1252; *Paramo mantra(ḥ)*, 1156; *Paridhīpatikhecara*, 1232; *Paryaya*, 1254; *Pati*, 1233; *Paṭṭiçin*, 1157; *Pavitra(ṃ)*, 1150, 1246, 1263; *Payonidhi*, 1201; *Pinākadhṛk*, 1188, 1250; *Pitāmaha*, 1190, 1256; *Pītātman*, 1252; *Pitṛ*, 1256; *Prabhāva*, 1218; *Prabhāvātman*, 1225; *Prabhu*, 1144, 1146; *Praçāntātman*, 1170; *Pradhānadhṛk*, 1252; *Prāgdakshiṇa*, 1184; *Prajābīja*, 1255; *Prajādvāra*, 1256; *Prajāpati*, 1173; *Prakāça*, 1205; *Prakṛshtāri*, 1229; *Pramāṇa(ṃ)*, 1153; *Prāṇadhāraṇa*, 1227; *Prāsānāṃ prabhava(ḥ)*, 1262; *Prasāda*, 1149, 1203, 1206; *Prasanna*, 1203; *Praskandana*, 1177; *Pratyaya*, 1203; *Pravara*, 1144; *Pravṛtti*, 1146; *Prayatātman*, 1252; *Pretacārin*, 1163; *Priya*, 1206; *Puṇyacañcu*, 1220; *Purāṇa*, 1220; *Pushkarasthapati*, 1207. *Rājarāja*, 1263; *Raktāṅga*, 1237; *Rathayogin*, 1235; *Rati*, 1230; *Ratnaprabhūta*, 1237; *Raudrarūpa*, 1181; *Ravi*, 1218; *Rudra*, 1160; *Ṛshasahasrāmitekshaṇa*, 1205; *Ṛtu*, 1254. *Sabhāvana*, 1226; *Sādhyarshi*, 1253; *Sagaṇa*, 1208; *Saha*, 1241; *Sahasrabāhu*, 1246; *Sahasrada*, 1183; *Sahasrahasta*, 1165; *Sahasrāksha*, 1151; *Sahasramūrdhan*, 1245; *Sahasrapād*, 1245; *Sahāya*, 1169, 1233 (B. has *Ātmasa°*); *Sakala*, 1243; *Sakalpa*, 1192; *Samāmnāya*, 1236; *Samaramardana*, 1195; *Samāsya*, 1205; *Sambhagna*, 1183; *Sampanna*, 1210; *Samudra*, 1169; *Saṃvatsara*, 1251; *Saṃvatsarakara*, 1153; *Saṃyata*, 1227; *Saṃyoga*, 1232; *Saṃyugāpīḍavāhana*, 1168; *Saṅgraha*, 1179; *Sānkhyaprasāda*, 1176; *Saṅkhyāsamāpana*, 1254; *Saphalodaya*, 1240; *Sāragrīva*, 1224; *Sāraṅga*, 1226; *Sarga*, 1254, 1263; *Sarpacīranivāsana*, 1179; *Sarva*, 1145, 1206; *Sarvabandhavimocana*, 1175; *Sarvabhāvakara*, 1156; *Sarvabhāvana*, 1145; *Sarvabhūtahara*, 1146; *Sarvabhūtātman*, 1149; *Sarvacārin*, 1177, 1188; *Sarvāçaya*, 1221; *Sarvāçraya*, 1244; *Sarvaçubhaṅkara*, 1159; *Sarvada*, 1180; *Sarvadeva*, 1202; *Sarvadevamaya*, 1245, 1260; *Sarvadhārin*, 1178; *Sarvaga*, 1173, 1218; *Sarvagandhasukhāvaha*, 1231; *Sarvajña*, 1154; *Sarvakālaprasāda*, 1180; *Sarvakāma*, 1162; *Sarvakāmada*, 1179; *Sarvakāmaguṇāvaha*, 1219; *Sarvakāmavara*, 1180; *Sarvakara*, 1145; *Sarvakarman*, 1150; *Sarvalakshaṇalakshita*, 1235; *Sarvalālasa*, 1164; *Sarvalocana*, 1243; *Sarvalokakṛt*, 1246; *Sarvalokaprajāpati*, 1148; *Sarvāṅga*, 1145, 1246; *Sarvāṅgarūpa*, 1214; *Sarvapārçvamukha*, 1252; *Sarvapāvana*, 1263; *Sarvapūjita*, 1209; *Sarvaratnavid*, 1222; *Sarvasādhana*, 1264; *Sarvasādhunishevita*, 1176; *Sarvātman*, 1145; *Sarvātodyaparigraha*, 1174; *Sarvatomukha*, 1180; *Sarvatūryaninādin*, 1171; *Sarvavāsa*, 1177; *Sarvavāsin*, 1182; *Sarvavigraha*, 1171; *Sarvavikhyāta*, 1145; *Sarvayogin*, 1235; *Sarvāyudha*, 1241; *Sarveshāṃ prāṇināṃ pati(ḥ)*, 1221; *Sat*, 1222, 1256; *Satkṛta*, 1228; *Satyavrata*, 1265; *Savitṛ*, 1218; *Senākalpa*, 1238; *Senāpati*, 1160; *Shashṭibhāga*, 1186; *Siddhabhūtārtha*, 1265; *Siddhārtha*, 1159, 1185, 1224, 1265; *Siddhārthakārin*, 1224; *Siddhasādhaka*, 1185; *Siddhayogin*, 1185; *Siddhi*, 1171; *Siṃhaçārdūlarūpa*, 1162; *Siṃhadaṃshṭra*, 1225; *Siṃhaga*, 1225; *Siṃhanāda*, 1225; *Siṃhavāhana*, 1225; *Skanda*, 1217; *Snehana*, 1203; *Soma*, 1151; *Sruvahasta*, 1157; *Sthāṇu*, 1144; *Sthāvarāṇāṃ pati(ḥ)*, 1265; *Sthira*, 1144, 1207; *Stuta*, 1174; *Subala*, 1180; *Subandhanavimocana*, 1214; *Subāndhava*, 1212; *Subīja*, 1154; *Suchattra*, 1244; *Suçārada*, 1212; *Sudarçana*, 1206; *Sugandhāra*, 1242; *Suhṛdaḥ* (pl.), 1214; *Sukhājāta*, 1242; *Sukhāsakta*, 1222; *Sūkshma*, 1262; *Sūkshmātman*, 1253; *Sumahāsvana*, 1251; *Sumukha*, 1241; *Suniçcala*, 1211; *Suparvaṇa*, 1233 (*divi*, Nīl. takes *Suparvaṇaḥ* as genit.); *Surabhi*, 1249; *Surādhyaksha*, 1191; *Suragaṇa*, 1264; *Surārihan*, 1216; *Surūpa*, 1157; *Sūrya*, 1151; *Susaha*, 1166; *Susaṅkshepa*, 1254; *Susaraṇa*, 1173; *Sushāḍha*, 1234; *Susvapna*, 1194; *Sutīkshṇadaçana*, 1168; *Sutīrtha*, 1158; *Suvaktra*, 1158; *Suvarcasa*, 1161; *Suvarcasin*, 1181; *Suvarṇa*, 1198; *Suvarṇaretas*, 1154; *Suvāsa*, 1230; *Suvijñeya*, 1212; *Suyukta*, 1262; *Svarbhānu*, 1163; *Svargadvāra(ṃ)*, 1256; *Svastibhāva*, 1197; *Svastida*, 1197; *Svayambhuva*, 1248; *Svayambhūta*, 1150; *Svayaṃçreshṭha*, 1155. *Tala*, 1243; *Tāla*, 1187, 1243; *Tālin*, 1172; *Tāmroshṭha*, 1211; *Tapaḥsakta*, 1230; *Tapasvin*, 1147; *Tapomaya*, 1262; *Taponidhi*, 1237; *Tāraṇa*, 1232; *Taraṅgavid*, 1175; *Tārkshya*, 1212; *Taru*, 1209, 1225; *Tejas*, 1157; *Tejaskara*, 1157; *Tejopahārin*, 1166; *Tigmamanyu*, 1161; *Tigmatejas*, 1248; *Tīkshṇatāpa*, 1169; *Tīrthadeva*, 1236; *Toraṇa*, 1232 (B. *Tau°*); *Trāsana*, 1207; *Triçaṅku*, 1217; *Triçukla*, 1210; *Tridaça*, 1175; *Trijaṭa*, 1161 (B. *Trijaṭin*); *Trikakud*, 1246; *Trikāladhṛk*, 1175; *Trilocana*, 1241 (only B.); *Trinetra*, 1241 (only C.); *Trivikrama*, 1261; *Trivishṭapa*, 1256; *Triyuga*, 1240; *Tryaksha*, 1252; *Tumbavīṇa*, 1213; *Tvashṭṛ*, 1218. *Udagra*, 1158; *Udbhid*, 1261; *Ugra*, 1213; *Ugratejas*, 1170; *Umādhava*, 1250; *Umākānta*, 1250; *Umāpati*, 1154, 1250; *Unmattaveçapracchanna*, 1148 (B. °*vesha*°); *Unmāda*, 1184; *Upaçānta*, 1220; *Upadeçakara*, 1182; *Upakāra*, 1206; *Ūrdhvaçāyin*, 1160; *Ūrdhvagātman*, 1249; *Ūrdhvaliṅga*, 1160; *Ūrdhvaretas*, 1160, 1213; *Ūrdhvasaṃhanana*, 1243; *Ushaṅga*, 1219; *Ushṇīshin*, 1158; *Utsaṅga*, 1190; *Uttamaḥ sarvakarmāṇāṃ*, 1242; *Uttaraṇa*, 1249. *Vācaspatya*, 1187; *Vaçakara*, 1192; *Vaçīkara*, 1195; *Vaçya*, 1192; *Vaḍavāmukha*, 1169; *Vadha*, 1239; *Vāhitṛ sarvabhūtānāṃ*, 1227; *Vaiçravaṇa*, 1217; *Vaidambha*, 1192; *Vaidya*, 1261; *Vaiṇavin*, 1172 (B. *Ve°*); *Vājasaṇa*, 1187; *Vajrahasta*, 1186; *Vajrin*, 1245, 1262; *Vāma*, 1184; *Vāmadeva*, 1184; *Vāmana*, 1184; *Vaṃça*, 1213; *Vaṃçakara*, 1213; *Vaṃçanāda*, 1213; *Vaṇija*, 1223; *Vapus*, 1234 (*āvartamānebhyaḥ*); *Vara*, 1144, 1151, 1210, 1251, 1252; *Varada*, 1144, 1251; *Varāha*, 1251; *Varcasvin*, 1196; *Vardhakin*, 1223; *Vardhana*, 1232; *Vareṇya*, 1251; *Varṇavibhāvin*, 1219; *Vāsava*, 1177; *Vasu*, 1253; *Vasuçreshṭha*, 1234; *Vasuvega*, 1182; *Vāta*, 1232; *Vātaraṃhas*, 1249; *Vāyu*, 1218, 1243; *Vāyuvāhana*, 1204; *Vedakāra*, 1195; *Vibhāga*, 1173; *Vibhāgajña*, 1177; *Vibhu*, 1160, 1167, 1219, 1227, 1268; *Vibudha*, 1262; *Viçāṃ pati(ḥ)*, 1183; *Viçākha*, 1186; *Viçāla*, 1237; *Viçālaçakha*, 1211; *Viçālāksha*, 1151; *Viçārada*, 1178; *Viçāravid*, 1188; *Viçva*, 1260; *Viçvabāhu*, 1173; *Viçvadeva*, 1216, 1264; *Viçvakarmamati*, 1210; *Viçvakshetra*, 1255; *Viçvarūpa*, 1149,

1155; *Vidhātṛ*, 1219; *Vidvat*, 1195; *Vijaya*, 1165; *Vijayakālavid*, 1170; *Vijayāksha*, 1178; *Vikhyāta*, 1244; *Vikṛta*, 1244; *Vikurvaṇa*, 1244; *Vimarsha*, 1235; *Vimocana*, 1173; *Vimukta*, 1266; *Vinata*, 1158; *Vipaṇa*, 1185; *Viraja*, 1261; *Virāma*, 1264; *Virūpa*, 1181 (Nīl. takes *akāçanirvirūpa* as one word), 1244; *Visarga*, 1241; *Vishaṇṇāṅga*, 1241; *Vishkambhin*, 1186; *Vishṇu*, 1218; *Vishṇuprasādita*, 1169; *Vishvaksena*, 1168; *Vistara*, 1254; *Vistāra*, 1240; *Vivasvat*, 1253; *Vratādhipa*, 1266; *Vṛddha*, 1232; *Vṛksha*, 1223; *Vṛkshākāra*, 1204; *Vṛkshakarṇasthiti*, 1167; *Vṛkshaketu*, 1204; *Vṛsharūpa*, 1148; *Vṛshaṇa*, 1196; *Vṛttāvṛttakara*, 1187; *Vyāghra*, 1261; *Vyākaraṇottara*, 1224; *Vyakta(ṃ)*, 1256; *Vyaktāvyakta*, 1237; *Vyālarūpa*, 1175; *Vyāsa*, 1254; *Vyavasāya*, 1165. *Yaças*, 1184; *Yajña*, 1168, 1169, 1178, 1207; *Yajñabhāgavid*, 1177; *Yajñahan*, 1165; *Yajñapati*, 1268; *Yajñāri*, 1215 (*sa°*); *Yajñasamāhita*, 1207; *Yajuḥpādabhuja*, 1205; *Yoga*, 1238; *Yogādhyaksha*, 1191; *Yogakara*, 1238 (B. *Yuga°*); *Yogin*, 1153; *Yojya*, 1153; *Yugādhipa*, 1228; *Yugarūpa*, 1239; *Yugāvaha*, 1191; *Yukta*, 1233; *Yuktabāhu*, 1233.

Çiva[2], name of a lac-house. § 213 (Jatugṛhap.): I, **146**, 5778 (*nivedayām āsa gṛhaṃ Ç°ākhyam açivaṃ tadā*, sc. Purocana).

Çiva[3], a fire. § 490 (Āṅgirasa): III, **221**, 14177, 14178 (v. Açiva).

Çiva[4] = Kṛshṇa: VI, 3010; XII, 1863.

Çiva[5], pl. (*°āḥ*). § 317*b* (Kṛshṇa Vāsudeva); III, **12**, 513 (*°ānām īçvareçvara*, i.e. Kṛshṇa).—§ 565 (Gālavac.): V, **109**, 3796 (*atra*—i.e. in the south—*siddhāḥ Çivā nāma brāhmaṇā vedapāragāḥ* | *adhītya sakalān Vedān lebhire moksham avyayam*, so B.; for the reading of C. v. Çivā[3]).

Çivā[1], wife of the Vasu Anila. § 116 (Aṃçāvat.): I, **66**, 2589 (wife of Anila and mother of Manojava and Avijñātagati).

Çivā[2], wife of Aṅgiras. § 496 (Skandotpatti): III, **225**, 14299 (*bharyā tv Aṅgirasaḥ*, Svahā assumed her form), 14301 (do.), (14303) (i.e. Svāhā), 14305 (do., cohabited with Agni).

Çivā[3], a brāhmaṇī. § 565 (Gālavac.): V, **109**, 3796 (C. *atra*—i.e. in the south—*siddhā Çivā nāma brāhmaṇī vedapāragā* | *adhītya sakalān Vedān lebhe sandeham akshayam*; for the reading of B. v. Çiva, pl.).

Çivā[4], a river. § 574 (Jambūkh.): VI, **9**λ, 332 (in Bhāratavarsha).

Çivakarṇī, a mātṛ. § 615*u* (Skanda): IX, **46**θ, 2647.

Çivapura ("the city of Çiva"). § 377 (Dhaumyatīrthak.): III, **88**, 8334 (having beheld the image of Çūlin—i.e. Çiva—at Payoshṇī, one attains to Ç.).

Çivi[1–5], **Çiviputra, Çivisūnu**, so C. for Çib°, q.v.

Çivodbheda, name of a place. § 360 (Tīrthayātrāp.): III, **82**, 5053 (there the river Sarasvatī reappears), 5054.

Çmaçānabhāj = Çiva (1000 names[2]).

Çmaçānavāsin = Çiva: X, 254; XIII, 1147 (1000 names[2]).

Çobhana = Çiva (1000 names[2]).

Çobhanā, a mātṛ. § 615*u* (Skanda): IX, **46**θ, 2624.

Çokanāçana = Vishṇu (1000 names).

Çoṇa, a river. § 268 (Varuṇasabhāv.): II, **9**, 373 (among the rivers in Varuṇa's palace).—§ 276 (Jarāsandhavadhap.): II, **20**, 796 (crossed by Kṛshṇa, etc., on their way from Indraprastha to Rājagṛha).—§ 370 (Tīrthayātrāp.): III, **85**, 8150 (*°sya Jyotirathyāyāç ca saṅgame*), 8151 (*°sya Narmadāyāç ca prabhave* (B. *prabhede*) . . . *Vaṃçagulme*). — § 459 (Mārkaṇḍeyas.): III, **188***a*, 12910 (seen by Mārkaṇḍeya in the stomach of Nārāyaṇa).—§ 494 (Āṅgirasa): III, **222**, 14233 (among the rivers who are mothers of fires).—§ 574 (Jambūkh.): VI, **9**λ, 337 (enumeration of the rivers of Bhāratavarsha; both C. and B. have *Çoṇāṃ*).

Çoṇāçva, Çoṇāçvavāha, Çoṇahaya = Droṇa, q.v.

Çoṇitabhṛt = Kṛshṇa: XIII, 7367.

Çoṇitoda, a Yaksha. § 269 (Vaiçravaṇasabhāv.): II, **10**, 399 (in the palace of Kubera).

Çraddhā[1] ('Faith'), daughter of Daksha and wife of Dharma. § 115 (Aṃçāvat.): I, **66**, 2578.

Çraddhā[2] (do.), daughter of Vivasvat. § 680*b* (Tulādhāra-Jājali-saṃv.): XII, **265**, 9449 (*Vaivasvatī Sūryasya duhitā Sāvitrī*, cf. the allegoric explanation of Nīl.), 9450.

Çrāddhadeva[1] = Manu: XII, 4507.

Çrāddhadeva[2] = Vivasvat: XII, ††13219 (*Mārttaṇḍo Vivasvān*).

Çrāddhaparvan (*°va*), "the section relating to the Çrāddha," the 87th of the minor parvans of Mhbhr. § 10 (Parvas.): I, **2**, 349.—§ 620: *Kṛshṇa* censured *Gāndhārī*, saying that this vast carnage had taken place by her fault, through her son *Duryodhana*; and told her not to grieve ("the cow brings forth offspring to bear burthens . . . the *Çūdrā* woman to increase the number of servitors . . . a princess, like thee, brings forth sons to be slaughtered"). *Gāndhārī* remained silent. Requested by *Dhṛtarāshṭra*, *Yudhishṭhira* said that one billion 660,020,000 men had fallen; and 24,165 had escaped; the fallen had all attained to regions like those of *Indra* (specifying those who had attained to G., Gh., *Brahmaloka*, and *Uttarakurus*). *Yudhishṭhira* said that in the forest he had obtained the gift of spiritual vision from D.-ṛ. *Lomaça*. Urged by *Dhṛtarāshṭra*, *Yudhishṭhira* ordered *Sudharman*, etc. (*a*), to cause the funeral rites of the slain (β) to be duly performed; they burned them upon funeral pyres; the *Pitṛmedha*-rites were performed for some of the illustrious dead; by the noise of *sāmans*, *ṛcs*, and lamentations all creatures became stupefied that night. Then *Yudhishṭhira* and *Dhṛtarāshṭra* proceeded towards the *Gaṅgā* (XI, **26**). The *Kuru* ladies, etc., performed the water-rites for their fellow-kinsmen at the *Gaṅgā*. *Kuntī*, in a paroxysm of grief, disclosed the truth about *Karṇa's* birth (γ) to her sons. The *Pāṇḍavas* grieved, and *Yudhishṭhira* lamented, hearing that *Karṇa* was his elder brother (δ). *Yudhishṭhira* caused *Karṇa's* wives, etc., to be brought before him, and with them performed the water-rite in honour of *Karṇa* (XI, **27**).

Çramaṇa = Vishṇu (1000 names).

Çrautaçrava (metron.) = Çiçupāla: III, 637.

Çrāva, king of Ayodhyā. § 475 (Dhundhumārop.): III, **202**, 13517 (son of Yuvanāçva and father of Çrāvastaka).

Çravaṇa, a nakshatra (v. Sū. Si.). § 574 (Jambūkh.): VI, **3**, 81 (*°ṇe ca Bṛhaspatiḥ*, sc. *vakraḥ*, omens), 85 (*vakrānuvakraṃ kṛtvā ca Çravaṇaṃ pāvakaprabhaḥ* | *Brahmarāçiṃ samāvṛtya Lohitāṅgo vyavasthitaḥ*, where according to Nīl. *Brahmarāçi* is another name of Ç., omens). — § 514 (Gadāyuddhap.): IX, **34**, 1952 (*catvāriṃçad ahāny adya dve ca me niḥsṛtasya vai* | *Pushyena samprayāto 'smi Ç°e punar āgataḥ*).—§ 746 (Ānuçāsanik.): XIII, **64**, 3279 (the merit acquired by gifts under the constellation Ç.).—§ 749 (do.): XIII, **89***a*, 4265 (the merit of performing çrāddhas under the constellation Ç.).—§ 759 (do.): XIII, **110**, 5393 (description of the candravrata).—§ 782*g* (Guruçishyasaṃv.): XIV, **44**, 1213 (Ç. is the first of the constellations—*ṛkshāṇi*).

Çrāvaṇa ("named after the nakshatra Çravaṇa," name of

a certain month). § 759 (Ānuçāsanik.): XIII, **106β**, 5158 (*māsaṃ*); **109**, 5379 (*māsi*).

Çravaṇaja, adj. ("springing from the ear," viz. one of Brahmán's births). § 717*b* (Nārāyaṇīya): XII, **349**, IV), 13571 (°*jā sṛshṭir Brahmaṇaḥ*).

Çravas, a ṛshi. § 736*b* (Vītahavyop.): XIII, **30**, 2002 (*ṛshiḥ*, son of Santa and father of Tamas).

Çrāvastaka, king of Ayodhyā. § 475 (Dhundhumārop.): III, **202**, 13518 (son of Çrāva and father of Bṛhadratha, founded Çrāvastī).

Çrāvastī, a city. § 475 (Dhundhumārop.): III, **202**, 13518 (founded by Çrāvastaka).

Çreṇimat, a king. § 130 (Amçāvat.): I, **67**, 2687 (*rājarshisattamaḥ*, incarnation of the fourth of the Kāleyas).—§ 232 (Svayaṃvarap.): I, **186**, 6991 (present at the *svayaṃvara* of Draupadī). — § 280 (Bhīmasena): II, **30**, 1075 (*Kumāravishaye*, vanquished by Bhīmasena on his *digvijaya*). — § 281 (Sahadeva): II, **31**, 1109 (vanquished by Sahadeva on his *digvijaya*).—§ 554 (Sainyodyogap.): V, **4γ**, 84 (among the princes to whom the Pāṇḍavas ought to send messengers).—§ 570 (Sainyaniryānap.): V, **151δ**, 5161 (in Yudhishṭhira's army).—§ 572 (Rathātirathas.): V, **171**, 5919 (*Kauravaçreshṭhaḥ*, so C., but read with B. *Kauravaçreshṭha*, i.e Duryodhana). § 573 (Ambopākhyānap.): V, **196μ**, 7650 (followed Yudhishṭhira). — § 585 (Bhīshmavadhap.): VI, **93ψ**, 4151 (followed Bhīmasena). — § 592 (Saṃçaptakavadhap.): VII, **23ο**, 987 (description of his horses, proceeded against Droṇa); 990 (followed Dhṛshṭadyumna). — § 604 (Karṇap.): VIII, **6**, 185 (has been slain—*gato Vaivasvatakshayam*).

Çreshṭha[1] = Çiva (1000 names[1]). Do.[2] = Vishṇu (1000 names).

Çreshṭha(ḥ) çreyasāṃ = Kṛshṇa; XII, 1613.

Çreyas = Vishṇu (1000 names).

Çrī, the goddess of beauty and prosperity. § 28 (Amṛtamanthana): I, **18**, 1146 (appeared at the churning of the milky ocean—*Çrīr anantaram utpannā ghṛtāt pāṇḍaravāsinī*), 1148.—§ 71 (Ādivaṃçāvatāraṇap.): I, **61**, 2274 (*Çrīr Kṛshṇeneva saṃgatā*, wife of Kṛshṇa).—§ 76 (Matsya): I, **63**, 2373 (*sākshāc Chriyam ivāparāṃ*, sc. Girikā).—§ 132 (Aṃçāvat.): I, **67**, 2790 (a part of Ç. became incarnate as Rukmiṇī).—§ 133 (Dushyanta): I, **71**, 2897 (*Çrīr iva rūpiṇī*, sc. Çakuntalā). — § 162 (Çāntanūp.): I, **97**, 3890 (*sākshāc Chriyam ivāparāṃ*, sc. Gaṅgā).—§ 222 (Tapatyup.): I, **171**, 6540 (*rūpataḥ . . . Çriyaṃ tarkayām āsa*, sc. *Tapatīṃ*). —§ 238 (Pañcendrop.): I, **197**, †7305 (appointed to become the wife of the five Indras [incarnate as the Pāṇḍavas], and therefore re-born as Draupadī).—§ 239 (do.): I, **197**, 7327 (*svarga-Çrīḥ Pāṇḍavārthan tu samutpannā mahāmakhe*, sc. as Draupadī).—§ 246 (Sundopasundop.): I, **211**, 7695 (*vigrahavatīva Çrīḥ*).—§ 266 (Çakrasabhāv.): II, **7**, 286 (in the palace of Indra).—§ 270 (Brahmasabhāv.): II, **11**, 458 (in the palace of Brahmán).—§ 298 (Dyūtap.): II, **65**, 2174 (*rūpeṇa Çrīsamānayā*, sc. Draupadī).—§ 330 (Indradarçanap.): III, **37**, 1488.—§ 344 (Nalop.): III, **53**, 2084 (*atīvarūpasampannā Çrīr iva*).—§ 347 (do.): III, **65**, 2582 (*iva*).—§ 350 (do.): III, **68**, 2664 (*iva*).—§ 436 (Yakshayuddhap.): III, **158**, 11605 (*nalinīṃ . . . sākshāc Chriyam ivāparāṃ*). — § 501 (Skandop.): III, **229**, 14404 (*padmarūpā Çrīḥ svayam eva çarīriṇī*, came to Skanda). — § 545 (Pativratāmāhātmyap.): III, **293**, 16640 (*vigrahavatīva Çrīḥ*), 16645 (*Çrīr iva rūpiṇī*).—§ 549 (Pāṇḍavapraveçap.): IV, **9**, 256 (*rūpeṇa sadṛçā Çriyā*, i.e. Draupadī).—§ 551 (Kīcakavadhap.): IV, **14**, 388 (Kīcaka asks Draupadī if she is Ç.).—§ 559 (Prajāgarap.): V, **39**, 1509, 1511 (*andhā*).—§ 564 (Mātalīyop.): V, **98**, 3534 (*dvitīyāṃ rūpataḥ Çriyaṃ*, sc. Jyotsnākālī).—§ 595 (Sṛñjaya): VII, **55α**, 2143 (Nārada asks if the daughter of Sṛñjaya is Ç.).—§ 615*u* (Skanda): IX, **45γ**, 2515 (came to the investiture of Skanda).—§ 626 (Rājadh.): XII, **20**, †613 (*svayaṃ*, came to the sacrifice of Marutta).—§ 641 (do.): XII, **59**, 2253, 2254 (born from the lotus of Vishṇu, married to Dharma and mother of Artha); **90**, 3385, 3386 (Ç. deserted Bali and went to Indra), 3388 (*Darpo nāma Çriyaḥ putro jajñe 'dharmād iti çrutiḥ*); **124**, 4606, (4610), 4613 (deserted Prahlāda).—§ 671*b* (Bali-Vāsavasaṃv.): XII, **225**, 8148 (deserted Bali), (8154), 8155, (8157), (8159), (8164), (8166), (8169), (8171), (8173), (8175). — § 674*b* (Çrī-Vāsavasaṃv.): XII, **229**, 8335 (*Çriyā Çakrasya saṃvādam*), 8347 (*Padmām*), 8350 (*Devarāja*°), (8352), 8353 (*Padmā*), 8354, (8361), 8422, †8427.—§ 717*b* (Nārāyaṇīya): XII, **340θ**, 12919; **348**, 13536 (*Nārāyaṇaparā*).—§ 727 (Ānuçāsanik.): XIII, **11**, 507 (*Padmā*), †509, †511, (†512) (her discourse with Rukmiṇī).—§ 746 (do.): XIII, **82**, 3852 (*gobhiḥ . . . saṃvādaṃ Çriyā*), 3853, (3856), 3856, 3860, (3863), 3874, (3876), 3877.—§ 766 (do.): XIII, **125α**, 5924; **127**, (6060).—§ 768*b* (Kṛshṇa Vāsudeva): XIII, **147**, 6819 (°*garbhaç Ç*°*sahoshitaḥ*, sc. Kṛshṇa). — § 772*p* (Kapa, pl.): XIII, **158**, 7335. — § 783 (Anugītāp.): XIV, **52**, 1489 (*prasāde cāpi Padmā Çrīr nityaṃ tvayi*, i.e. in Kṛshṇa).—§ 795 (Svargārohaṇap.): XVIII, **4**, 136 (*Draupadīrūpā*, i.e. incarnate as Draupadī). Cf. Lakshmī, Padmā.

Çrīça = Vishṇu (1000 names).

Çrīda = Vishṇu (1000 names).

Çrīdhara = Vishṇu: XIII, 5380, 7014 (1000 names).

Çrīgarbha = Vishṇu (1000 names).

Çrīkaṇṭha = Çiva: XII, 13294, 13705 (*Brahmaṇaḥ sutaḥ*).

Çrīkara = Vishṇu (1000 names).

Çrīkuṇḍa, a tīrtha. § 358 (Tīrthayātrāp.): III, **82**, 5028.

Çrīkuñja, a tīrtha. § 364 (Tīrthayātrāp.): III, **83**, 6078 (on Sarasvatī).

Çrīmadrājapura, a city, the capital of the Kāliṅga king Citrāṅgada. § 621 (Rājadh.): XII, **3**, 100 (*Kaliṅgavishaye Citrāṅgadasya nagaraṃ*).

Çrīmat[1], son of Nimi. § 749 (Ānuçāsanik.): XIII, **91**, 4330, 4340 (the first of all çrāddha oblations was performed to Ç.).

Çrīmat[2] = Çiva (1000 names[2]).

Çrīmat[3] = Vishṇu (1000 names).

Çrīmatāṃ varaḥ = Vishṇu (1000 names).

Çrīmatī, a mātṛ. § 615*u* (Skanda): IX, **46θ**, 2621.

Çrīnidhi = Vishṇu (1000 names).

Çrīnivāsa = Vishṇu (1000 names).

Çrīpadma = Kṛshṇa; XII, 1512.

Çrīpañcamī, a certain lunar day: III, 14453.

Çrīparvata, a mountain. § 370 (Tīrthayātrāp.): III, **85**, 8160, 8161 (the abode of Mahādeva, i.e. Çiva).

Çrīpati = Vishṇu (1000 names).

Çrīvāha, a serpent. § 47 (Sarpanāmak.): I, **35**, 1558 (enumeration).

Çrīvardhana = Çiva (1000 names[2]).

Çrīvāsa[1] = Mahāpurusha (Mahāpurushastava). Do.[2] = Vishṇu (1000 names).

[Çrī-Vāsava-saṃvāda(ḥ)] ("the discourse between Çrī and Indra"). § 674*b* (Mokshadh.): *Bhīshma* said: *Nārada*, who through his penance beholds both this and the other world at once, etc., wandered through the three worlds. Once at dawn he performed his ablutions in the *Gaṅgā*

(*Dhruvadvārabhavām*), and so did *Indra*. They listened to the narratives told by the great D.-ṛ. They hymned the rising Sun, and then in the opposite direction beheld a luminous object riding on *Vishṇu's* vehicle adorned with *Garuḍa* and *Sūrya*; it was *Çrī* with many Aps. (description); her names: *Padmā*, etc. (*a*). She said that they had formerly dwelt with the *Asuras* in consequence of her disposition to be bound by truth and merit; seeing, however, that the *Asuras* had assumed perverse natures, she had left them and wished to reside with *Indra*. Requested by *Indra*, she told that she had dwelt with the *Asuras* on account of their good behaviour, but after they had fallen off from virtue, she had deserted Dai. and Dā. and had come to *Indra*; "there where I reside, the seven other goddesses (*β*) and *Jayā* as the eighth, who love me, etc., desire to live; all of them and myself, having deserted As., have come to thee." D.-ṛ., *Nārada*, and *Indra* gave her a hearty welcome. *Vāyu*, the friend of *Agni*, began to blow gently; all the deities assembled; heaven began to shower nectar upon the region of *Brahmán*, etc.; *Indra* began to pour rain; no one deviated from the path of righteousness, etc.; D., K., Y., Ra. became cheerful, etc. (XII, **229**).

Çrīvatsa, the curl of hair on the breast of Vishṇu (Kṛshṇa): I, 2507 (°*aṅko Hṛshīkeçaḥ*); III, 10960 (on the breast of Vishṇu), 12900 (°*kṛtabhūshaṇaḥ*, i.e. Nārāyaṇa), 12901 (°*dhārī*, do.), 15840 (°*orasi bhūshitaḥ*, Vishṇu as a dwarf), 15851 (°*dhāriṇam*, Vishṇu as Kṛshṇa); V, 2955 (°*kṛtalakshaṇam*, i.e. Kṛshṇa), 3590 (°*lakshaṇāḥ*, sc. the sons of Garuḍa); VI, 2993 (°*āṅkam*, i.e. Kṛshṇa); XII, 13294 (on Nārāyaṇa's breast, its origin from the mark made by Çiva's lance), 13339 (°*lakshaṇau*, sc. Nara-Nārayaṇau); XIII, 6808 (°*āṅko Hṛshīkeçaḥ*).

Çrīvatsavakshas = Vishṇu (1000 names).

Çrīvibhāvana = Vishṇu (1000 names).

Çrīyāvāsin = Çiva (1000 names[2]).

Çrutaçravas[1], a ṛshi. § 13 (Paushyap.): I, **3**, ††674 (father of Somaçravas, the purohita of Janamejaya).—§ 59 (Sarpasattra): I, **53***a*, 2049 (among the sadasyas at the snake-sacrifice of Janamejaya, C. has Çrutaçruvas).—§ 702 (Mokshadh.): XII, **293***a*, 10762.

Çrutaçravas[2], a rājarshi. § 267 (Yamasabhāv.): II, **8**, 319 (in the palace of Yama).

Çrutaçrī, a Daitya. § 564 (Mātalīyop.): V, **105***δ*, 3685 (had been slain by Garuḍa).

Çrutaçruvas, v. Çrutaçravas[1].

Çrutadhvaja, a Pāṇḍava warrior. § 600 (Ghaṭotkacavadhap.): VII, **158***χ*, 7011 (brother of Virāṭa?).

Çrutāhvaya, v. Çrutāyus[4].

Çrutakarman[1], son of Sahadeva and Draupadī. § 159 (Pūruvaṃç.): I, **95**, ††3827.—§ 317 (Arjunābhigamanap.): III, **12**, 534.—§ 578 (Bhīshmavadhap.): VI, **45**[19], 1735 (*Sāhadevam*), 1736 (fights Sudakshiṇa).—§ 583 (do.): VI, **79**[13], 3482, 3484 (fights Durmukha).—§ 592 (Saṃçaptakavadhap.): VII, **23***o*, 981 (description of his horses; PCR. says that Ç. here is the son of Bhīmasena, but this (Sutasoma) is mentioned v. 976); **25**, 1090 (fights Caitraseni).—§ 605 (Karṇap.): VIII, **13**, 493 (fights Citrasena, the Abhishāra king); **14**, 526 (do.), 527, 534, 535, 537 (slays Citrasena), 544.—§ 608 (do.): VIII, **55***λλ*, 2664, 2667 (fights Açvatthāman).—§ 616 (Sauptikap.): X, **8**, 377, 378 (is slain by Açvatthāman). Cf. Çrutasena[3], Draupadeya.

Çrutakarman[2], son of Arjuna and Draupadī. § 253 (Haraṇāharaṇap.): I, **221**, 8039, 8043 (origin of the name: *çrutaṃ karma mahat kṛtvā nivṛttena Kirīṭinā*).—§ 511 (Draupadī - Satyabhāmasaṃv.): III, **235**, 14731. Cf. Çrutakīrti.

Çrutakarman[3], son of Dhṛtarāshṭra. § 605 (Karṇap.): VIII, **25**, 1005 (fights Çatānīka).

Çrutakīrt(t)i, son of Arjuna and Draupadī. § 83 (Ādivaṃçāvatāraṇa): I, **63**, 2451.—§ 130 (Aṃçāvat.): I, **67**, 2763 (the sons of Draupadī are incarnations of the Viçvadevas).—§ 159 (Pūruvaṃç.): I, **95**, ††3827.—§ 317 (Arjunābhigamanap.): III, **12**, 533.—§ 583 (Bhīshmavadhap.): VI, **79**[13], 3487 (fights Jayatsena), 3488.—§ 592 (Saṃçaptakavadhap.): VII, **23***o*, 982 (*Draupadeyaṃ*, description of his horses); **25**, 1095 (*Ārjuniṃ*, fights the son of Duḥçāsana).—§ 605 (Karṇap.): VIII, **13**, 496 (attacks Çalya); **14**, 530 (cf. Nīl., but should not we read *Çrutakarmā* as PCR. has it?); **25**, 1032.—§ 608 (do.): VIII, **49**, 2363; **55***λλ*, 2664, 2667, 2669.—§ 616 (Sauptikap.): X, **8**, 379 (slain by Açvatthāman). Cf. Ārjuni, Çrutakarman[2], Draupadeya.

Çrutānīka, a Pāṇḍava warrior. § 600 (Ghaṭotkacavadhap.): VII, **158***χ*, 7011 (brother of Virāṭa?).

Çrutānta, son of Dhṛtarāshṭra. § 611 (Çalyap.): IX, **26***ρρ*, 1404 (among the eleven sons of Dhṛtarāshṭra who attacked Bhīmasena), 1411 (slain by Bhīmasena).

Çrutarvan[1], a king. § 382 (Agastyop.): III, **98**, 8595, 8601, 8606.

Çrutarvan[2], son of Dhṛtarāshṭra. § 608 (Karṇap.): VIII, **51***δδ*, 2446 (C. has *Çrutavān*).—§ 611 (Çalyap.): IX, **26***ρρ*, 1406 (among the eleven sons of Dhṛtarāshṭra who attacked Bhīmasena), 1413, 1421, 1427, 1431 (slain by Bhīmasena).

Çrutasena[1], brother of Janamejaya Pārikshita. § 12 (Paushyap.): I, **3**, ††662.

Çrutasena[2], a serpent. § 17 (Uttaṅka): I, **3**, 804 (*jaghanyajas Takshakaç ca Çrutaseneti yaḥ sutaḥ | avasad yo Mahadyumni prārthayan nāgamukhyatam*, the true reading seems to be *Takshakasya* ("the younger brother of Takshaka," PCR.).

Çrutasena[3], son of Sahadeva and Draupadī. § 83 (Ādivaṃçāvatāraṇa): I, **63**, 2452.—§ 130 (Aṃçāvat.): I, **67**, 2763 (the sons of Draupadī were incarnations of the Viçvadevas).—§ 253 (Haraṇāharaṇap.): I, **221**, 8040, 8045 (origin of the name: *ajījanat Kṛshṇā nakshatre Vahnidaivate*).—§ 511 (Draupadī-Satyabhāmāsaṃv.): III, **235**, 14732. Cf. Çrutakarman[1].

Çrutasena[4], a Daitya. § 564 (Mātalīyop.): V, **105***δ*, 3685 (had been slain by Garuḍa).

Çrutasena[5], a Kuru warrior. § 605 (Karṇap.): VIII, **27***λλ*, 1087 (= Citrasena, v. 1078?).

Çrutasoma, v. Sutasoma.

Çrutavat, v. Çrutarvan[2].

Çrutāvatī, daughter of Bharadvāja. § 615*y* (Badarapācana): IX, **48**, 2763, 2821 (*Bharadvājasya duhitā*, performed austerities at Badarapācana, gratified Indra by her persevering in boiling five badara-fruits, and became the wife of Indra).—§ 615*aa* (Baladevat.): the viprarshi Bharadvāja saw the Apsaras Ghṛtācī, then his vital seed came out. He caught it in his hand, and then kept it in a funnel of a leaf (*parṇapuṭe*); from that seed was born a girl, whom he in the presence of D. and R. called Ç. Keeping the girl in his hermitage, Bharadvāja repaired to the forest of *Himavat*: IX, **48**, 2829.

Çrutāyudha[1], king of the Kaliṅgas. § 264 (Sabhākriyāp.): II, **4***β*, 121 (*Kāliṅgaḥ*, among the kings who were present when Yudhishṭhira entered his palace).—§ 576 (Bhīshmavadhap.): VI, **16**a, 623 (*Kālingaḥ*, in Duryodhana's army); **17**γ, 657. Cf. Çrutāyus [2], Kalinga, Kālinga, Kalingādhipati, Kalingaka.

Çrutāyudha [2], a king. § 599 (Jayadrathavadhap.): VII, **92**, 3295 (fights Arjuna), 3301, 3303, 3304, 3310 (c) (Ç. was the son of Varuṇa and the river Parṇāçā; at the request of Parṇāçā, Varuṇa had given him a mace and mantras, by means of which he would be invincible in battle, if he did not hurl it at anyone who was not engaged in fighting, for then it would come back and slay himself), 3312, 3314 (Ç. hurled his mace at Kṛshṇa, who did not fight and was himself slain), 3315, 3317, 3320, 3337; **93**, 3338 (*hate*); **94**, 3410 (*nihate Savyasācinā* (!)), 3438 (*nihataḥ*).—§ 611 (Çalyap.): IX, **24**νν, 1297 (*hate*).

Çrutāyu(s) [1], king of the Ambashṭhas. [The quotations not mentioning Ambashṭha or the like might also refer to Çrutāyus [2–5].] § 11 (Parvasangr.): I, **2**, 535. — § 130 (Aṃçāvat.): I, **67**, 2700 (among the kings who were incarnations from the Krodhavaçagaṇa). — § 232 (Svayaṃvarap.): I, **186**, 7001 (present at the svayaṃvara of Draupadī). § 264 (Sabhākriyāp.): II, **4**β, 123 (among the kings who were present when Yudhishṭhira entered his palace).—§ 554 (Sainyodyogap.): V, **4**γ, 86 (among the princes to whom the Pāṇḍavas ought to send messengers).—§ 561 (Yānasandhip.): V, **55**ν, 2207 (in the army of Duryodhana). — § 571 (Ulūkadūtāg.): V, **160**, †5531 (*Çrutāyu - Hārddikya-mahāsamudraṃ*, sc. *puroshodadhiṃ*, i.e. the army of Duryodhana; the half-çloka is wanting in B.).—§ 578 (Bhīshmavadhap.): VI, **45** [20], 1737, 1739 (fights Irāvat); **51**χ, 2108 (on the right flank of Duryodhana's army). — § 580 (do.): VI, **59**μ, †2584 (*Ambashṭhapatiḥ*, attacks Arjuna), (ρ), †2647 (do., vanquished by Arjuna).—§ 583 (do.): VI, **75**ζ, 3298 (in the rear of Bhīshma's *krauñcavyūha*). — § 584 (do.): VI, **81** [1], 3562 (attacked by Yudhishṭhira); **84**, 3696, 3697, 3702, 3709, 3712 (vanquished by Yudhishṭhira).—§ 586 (do.): VI, **99**δ, 4506 (in the rear of Bhīshma's *sarvatobhadra* array); **102**κ, 4667 (attacks Bhīmasena). — § 599 (Jayadrathavadhap.): VII, **91**a, 3253 (resists Arjuna); **93**, 3397 (*Ambashṭhaḥ*, is slain by Arjuna); **94**, 3437 (all. to chap. **93**).—§ 604 (Karṇap.): VIII, **5**ζ, 107 (*Ambashṭhaḥ*, mentioned as slain), 115 (the same?).—§ 611 (Çalyap.): IX, **24**νν, 1207 (*hate*). Cf. Ambashṭha, Ambashṭhapati.

Çrutāyus [2] = Çrutāyudha, the Kalinga king. § 579 (Bhīshmavadhap.): VI, **54**, 2240 (attacks Bhīmasena, his son Çakradeva is slain by Bhīmasena), 2301, 2305 (is slain by Bhīmasena). Cf. Çrutāyus [1].

Çrutāyus [3], brother (?) of Acyutāyus. § 599 (Jayadrathavadhap.): VII, **93**, 3344 (*Ç°ç cācyutāyuç ca*, attack Arjuna), 3348, 3362 (with Acyutāyus he is slain by Bhīmasena), 3364 (Ç. and Acyutāyus' sons are Niyatāyus and Dīrghāyus); **94**, 3438 (all. to chap. **93**).—§ 608 (Karṇap.): VIII, **72**, 3613 (all. to § 599). Cf. Çrutāyus [1].

Çrutāyus [4], a Pāṇḍava warrior. § 600 (Ghaṭotkacavadhap.): VII, **156**ν, 6913 (is slain by Açvatthāman; B. has *Çrutāhvayaṃ*).

Çrutāyus [5], a Kuru warrior. § 604 (Karṇap.): VIII, **7**, †209 (among the remnants of Duryodhana's army).

Çruti, an ancient king. § 6 (Anukram.): I, **1**a, 232 (in Sañjaya's enumeration of kings who have died).

Çrutisāgara = Vishṇu (1000 names).

Çrutivarman, a Kuru warrior. § 604 (Karṇap.): VIII, **7**, †207 (among the remnants of Duryodhana's army).

Çṛgāla, a king. § 621 (Rājadh.): XII, **4**ε, 114 (*Strīrājyādhipatiḥ* (?), came to the *svayaṃvara* of king Citrāngada's daughter).

Çṛgālarūpa = Çiva (1000 names [2]).

Çṛnga, a mountain = Çṛngavat. § 574i (Airāvata): VI, **8**, 295 (*uttareṇa tu Çṛngasya samudrānte janādhipa* | *varsham Airāvataṃ nāma*), 296 (B. *tasmāc Chṛngam ataḥ paraṃ*; C. has *yasmāc Chṛngavataḥ paraṃ*, but cf. the note of PCR.).

Çṛngapriya = Çiva (1000 names [2]).

Çṛngavat, a mountain. § 574 (Jambūkh.): VI, **6**β, 199 (among the six *varshaparvatas*).—§ 574 (Airāvata): VI, **8**, 296 (v. Çṛnga).—§ 775 (Ānuçāsanik.): XIII, **166**a, 7658.

Çṛngavera, a serpent. § 66 (Sarpasattra): I, **57**, 2154 (of Kauravya's race).

Çṛngaverapura, a city. § 372 (Tīrthayātrāp.): III, **85**, 8207 (there Rāma Dāçarathi formerly crossed [the Gangā]).

Çṛngin [1], son of Çamīka. § 51 (Parikshit): I, **40**, 1679, 1683; **41**, 1690, (1695), 1700, (1703), 1706, 1707; **42**, (1725) (Parikshit was cursed by Ç. because he had outraged Çamīka). — § 56 (do.): I, **50**, 1965 (had been born from a cow), 1966 (repetition of § 51). — § 57 (Janamejaya): I, **50**, 2009. — § 790 (Putradarçanap.): XV, **35**, 946 (*Çamīkañ ca mahātmānaṃ putran tañ cāsya Ç°ṇaṃ*, they were beheld by Janamejaya when Vyāsa had caused them to come from heaven).

Çṛngin [2] = Çiva (1000 names [2]).—Do. [3] = Vishṇu (1000 names).

Çubhā, v. Subhā.

Çubhakarman, a companion of Skanda. § 615u (Skanda): IX, **45**, 2544 (given to Skanda by Vidhātṛ).

Çubhāksha = Çiva (1000 names [2]).

Çubhānana = Skanda: III, 14631.

Çubhānga = Vishṇu (1000 names).

Çubhāngada, a king. § 232 (Svayaṃvarap.): I, **186**, 7002 (*Citrāngada-Ç°au*, came to the *svayaṃvara* of Draupadī).

Çubhāngī, a Dāçārha princess, the wife of Kuru. § 156 (Pūruv.): I, **95**, ††3722 (*Dāçārhīṃ*, the mother of Vidura).

Çubhavaktrā, a mātṛ. § 615u (Skanda): IX, **46**θ, 2625.

Çubhekshaṇa = Vishṇu (1000 names).

Çuci [1], a month. § 213 (Jatugṛhap.): I, **151**, 5883 (*Çuci-Çukrāgame yathā; Jyeshṭhāshāḍhayoḥ sangame*, Nīl.). § 294 (Dyūtap.): II, **47**, 1685 (*Çuci-Çukrāgame kāle . . . iva; Jyeshṭhāshāḍau tayoḥ sangame grīshmarttau*, Nīl.). — § 608 (Karṇap.): VIII, **79**, †4072 (*yathograraçmiḥ Çuci-Çukramadhyagaḥ sukhaṃ vivasvān harate jalaughān; Ashāḍajyeshṭhayor madhyagataḥ*, Nīl.), †4075 (*Çuci-Çukramadhyago yathaiva sūryaḥ*).

Çuci [2], a ṛshi. § 267 (Yamasabhāv.): II, **8**, 325 (in the palace of Yama).

Çuci [3], name of a caravan leader. § 347 (Nalopākhyānap.): III, **64**, 2526 (met the wandering Damayantī, who then followed the caravan).

Çuci [4], a fire. § 493 (Āngirasa): III, **221**, 14200, 14202 (among the fires in honour of which *ashṭākapāla* rites are to be performed for the sake of expiation at the time of the *agnihotra*).

Çuci [5] = Sūrya: III, 148.

Çuci [6] = Skanda: III, 14631.

Çuci [7] = Kṛshṇa: XII, 1605.

Çuci [8], a son of Viçvāmitra. § 721b (Viçvāmitrop.): XIII, **4**β, 253.

Çuci [9] = Çiva (1000 names [2]).

Çuci[10], a son of Bhṛgu. § 747*b* (Suvarṇotpatti): XIII, **85**η, 4145 (the third of Bhṛgu's seven sons).

Çuci[11] = Vishṇu (1000 names).

Çuciçravas = Kṛshṇa: XII, 1505, 13250 (etymology).

Çucikā, an Apsaras. § 191 (Arjuna): I, **123**, 4818 (among the Apsarases who danced at the birth of Arjuna).

Çucipada = Kṛshṇa: XII, 1605.

Çucishmitā, an Apsaras. § 269 (Vaiçravaṇasabhāv.): II, **10**, 392 (in the palace of Kubera).

Çucisravas = Vishṇu (1000 names).

Çucivrata, an ancient king. § 6 (Anukram.): I, **1***a*, 230 (in Sañjaya's enumeration of kings who have died).

Çuddha = Çiva (1000 names[2]).

Çuddha, pl. (°*āḥ*), a class of gods. § 730 (Ānuçāsanikap.): XIII, **18**λλ, 1372.

Çuddhātman = Çiva (1000 names[2]).

Çūdra, pl. (°*āḥ*), a people, mostly mentioned together with the Abhīras. § 285 (Nakula): II, **32**, 1192 (°*ābhīragaṇāḥ*, in the west, vanquished by Nakula on his digvijaya).—§ 574 (Jambūkh.): VI, **9**o, 375 (°*ābhīrāḥ*, in the north-east).—§ 589 (Droṇābhishek.): VII, **7**ζ, 183 (in the rear of Droṇa's array). — § 592 (Saṃçaptakavadhap.): VII, **20**γ, 798 (°*ābhīrāḥ*, in the neck of Droṇa's garuḍavyūha). — § 615 (Baladevatīrthay.): IX, **57**, 2119 (°*ābhīrān prati dveshād yatra nashṭā Sarasvatī*, sc. at Vinaçana).

Çūdra[2], pl. (°*āḥ*) = Çiva (1000 names[1]).

Çuka[1], son of Vyāsa. § 4 (Anukram.): I, **1**, 81 (knows 8,800 verses of the Mhbhr.), 103 (Vyāsa taught him an epitome of the Mhbhr.), 106 (revealed 1,400,000 verses of the Mhbhr. to the Gandharvas, etc.).—§ 78 (Vyāsa): I, **63**, 2418 (Vyāsa taught his disciples, and among them his own son Ç., the Vedas, of which the Mhbhr. was the fifth one).—§ 264 (Sabhākriyāp.): II, **4***a*, 106 (among the munis who were present when Yudhishṭhira entered his palace). — § 327 (Draupadīparitāpav.): III, **31**, 1171 (became wise like other ṛshis on account of *dharma*).—§ 615*ee* (Ādityatīrtha): IX, **49**, 2848 (resides in Ādityatīrtha). — § 677 (Mokshadh.): XII, **232**, 8485 (*Vaiyāsakiḥ*, received instruction from Vyāsa), (8486); **238**, (8689); **240**, (8735); **242**, (8804); **243**, (8824), (8833); **246**, (8915); **248**, (8974), (8980); **251**, (9038). — § 707 (do.): XII, **319**β, 11783 (had instructed Viçvāvasu). — § 710 (do.): XII, **322**, 12044 (*Vaiyāsakiḥ*, attained to emancipation—*nirvedam āpannaḥ*).— § 712 (Çukotpatti): XII, **324**, 12158, 12159, 12162, 12167; **325**, 12195, 12197, 12200, 12202 (Vyāsa gratified Çiva, who granted to him that he should have a son. When Vyāsa saw Ghṛtācī transformed to a female parrot, his seed came out, and then Çuka was born from the fire-sticks (*araṇī*)).—§ 713 (Çukakṛti): XII, **326**, 12215, 12218, 12240, 12242, 12243, 12246, 12255; **327**, 12263, 12267, (12270), (12280), (Ç. repaired to king Janaka of Mithilā and received instruction from him).—§ 714 (Çukakṛtya): XII, **328**, 12343; **329**, 12387, 12389, 12391 (Ç. returned to Vyāsa). — § 715 (Çuka-Nāradasaṃv.): XII, **330**, 12422, 12423, 12425 (Nārada instructed Ç.). — § 716 (Çukābhipatana): XII, **332**, 12557, 12573, 12574, 12575; **333**, 12581, (12584), 12585 (*Dvaipāyanātmajaḥ*), 12601, 12604, 12606; **334**, 12608, 12617, 12620, 12623, 12624, 12625, 12626, 12628, 12629, 12630, 12633, 12646 (Ç. obtained emancipation, Vyāsa lamented the death of Ç., but was comforted by Çiva). — § 717*b* (Nārāyaṇīya): XII, **341**μ, 13026 (among the disciples of Vyāsa), 13119; **350**μμ, 13647 (*Vyāsātmajaḥ*, among the disciples of Vyāsa).—§ 746 (Ānuçāsanik.): XIII, **81**, 3808, 3849 (questioned Vyāsa about kine). — § 795*c* (Mahābhārata): XVIII, **5**, 199 (recited the Mhbhr. to the Gandharvas and Yakshas), 203. Cf. Āraṇeya, Araṇīsuta, Dvaipāyanātmaja, Vaiyāsaki, Vyāsātmaja.

Çuka[2], a Rākshasa, a counsellor of Rāvaṇa. § 535 (Setubandhana): III, **283**, 16320.

Çuka[3], name of a weapon. § 563 (Bhagavadyānap.): V, **96**φ, 3490 (will be employed by Arjuna).

Çuka[4], a Gandhāra warrior, the son of Subala. § 585 (Bhīshmavadhap.): VI, **90**σ, 3997 (slain by Irāvat).

* **Çuka**, pl. (°*āḥ*), "parrots." § 126 (Amçāvat.): I, **66**, 2623 (the offspring of Çukī).

Çukābhipatana(m) ("the flying about" of Çuka): XII, **332–334** (12557–12649) (continued from *Çuka-Nārada-saṃvāda*, q.v.). § 716: Hearing the words of *Nārada*, *Çuka* understood that great misery follows the acquisition of children and wives, and that one has to undergo great labour in order to acquire science and Vedic lore. He resolved to attain to the highest end, that is fraught with the greatest felicity, and whence there is no return into the ocean of births; "that cannot be attained without *yoga*; I shall therefore have recourse to *yoga*, and throwing off this body I shall become transformed into wind and enter the Sun; for he does not wane like the Moon (Soma) with the gods; when after death one enters the moon he falls to earth and thence ascends to heaven; with the great Ṛshis I shall enter the energy of the Sun; I declare before all the creatures . . . earth, . . . D., Dā., G., Pç., U., Rā., and Ṛ., that I shall enter all creatures in the world." Obtaining *Nārada's* permission, *Çuka* went to *Vyāsa*, who asked him to stay there for the day that he might behold him for some time. But *Çuka*, only intent on emancipation, immediately left him and proceeded to *Kailāsa*, which was inhabited by crowds of ascetics (XII, **332**). Having reached the summit of *Kailāsa*, *Çuka* set himself to practise *yoga* (description). Having then obtained the permission of *Nārada*, he soared into the skies and identified himself with the element of wind; Aps. (*Pañcacūḍā*, etc.), G., Ṛ., etc., wondered. *Çuka* proceeded in silence, his face turned towards the east, regarding the sun; then to the *Malaya* mountain; *Urvaçī* and *Pūrvacitti*, who always dwell on *Malaya*, wondered. *Çuka* asked the gods, etc., to return his father an answer from him, if he should repeatedly call on him (XII, **333**). *Çuka* freed himself of the four kinds of faults, the eight kinds of *tamas*, the five kinds of *rajas*, the attribute of *sattva*, and then dwelt in *Brahman*. Meteors began to shoot, etc.; *Indra* poured showers of rain; *Himavat* and *Meru* (the one yellow, made of gold; the other white, made of silver), each 100 yojanas in height and breadth, were in close contact with each other. Journeying towards the north, *Çuka* clashed against them, and they were immediately broken in two. He was adored by G., Ṛ., Y., Rā., and *Vidyādharas*. He saw from a high region the celestial stream *Mandākinī* running below, with many Aps. Beholding *Çuka*, who was bodyless, those unclad aërial beings felt no shame. *Vyāsa* followed behind him on the same aërial path, by means of high *Yoga*. *Çuka*, above the region of the wind, identified himself with *Brahman*. Ṛ. represented to *Vyāsa* the achievements of his son. He indulged in lamentations; *Çuka*, who had entered the universe, had become the soul of everything, and had acquired omnipresence, answered by uttering *bho* in the form of an echo, and the entire universe echoed the answer of *Çuka* from that time; mountain caves and mountain sides still echo sounds uttered there. Having cast off all the attributes of sound, etc., and showing his *yoga* prowess in the manner of his disappearance, *Çuka* in this way attained to the highest station. *Vyāsa* sat down and began to think of his son with grief; the Aps. who were sporting on the banks of the celestial stream *Mandākinī* saw him seated there, and all became agitated with shame. *Çiva*, with D., G., and great Ṛ., came and comforted *Vyāsa*, who by the favour of *Çiva* thenceforward always beheld a shadow of his son by his side. "This *Nārada* and *Vyāsa* repeatedly told me in days of yore" (XII, **334**). [PCR. rightly remarks that, according to this story, *Çuka* who recited the Bhāgavata to Parikshit, the grandson of Yudhishṭhira, could not possibly be the *Çuka* who was *Vyāsa's* son.]

Çukakṛti(ḥ) ("the works of Çuka"). § 713 (Mokshadh.): XII, **326–7** (12215–12311) (continuation of *Çukotpatti*). *Bhīshma* said to *Yudhishṭhira*: *Vyāsa* desired *Çuka* to study the *Mokshadharma*; *Çuka* mastered all the treatises on *yoga*, as also the science promulgated by *Kapila*. Then *Vyāsa* caused him to go to *Janaka*, the king of *Mithilā*, and not to the skies (by his *yoga* power); nor should he think himself superior to *Janaka*, though he was only his *yājya*. Crossing the Varshas of *Meru* and *Hari* and *Himavat* (*Meror Hareç ca dve varshe varsham Haimavatan tatah*), *Çuka* came to *Bhāratavarsha*. Having seen many countries inhabited by *Cīnas* and *Hūṇas*, he reached *Āryāvarta*, and at last the country of the *Videhas*, protected by *Janaka*, and then *Mithilā*. He had not been fatigued on the way. He obtained permission to enter the city, but was at first roughly forbidden to enter the palace. At last he was admitted into the first chamber; thence he was led into the second chamber by the minister, and thence into a garden that was like a second *Caitraratha*, with damsels equal to the Aps., who entertained *Çuka* and gave him to eat; he, however, went unaffected through his rites, and in the first part of the night he devoted himself to *yoga* (XII, **326**). The next morning he was received by *Janaka*, and was instructed by him about *moksha* and the duties of a brahman; "ordinarily the purified understanding necessary for attaining *moksha* cannot be obtained without passing through all four stages of religious life; but he who in the course of many births has obtained a pure mind, may attain to *moksha* even in the very first stage (i.e. brahmacarya), and then there is no need for the three other stages," quoting a saying of king *Yayāti*; "through the favour of thy father I have acquired to omniscience; thy knowledge is much greater than what you think it to be" (XII, **327**). (For continuation v. *Çukakṛtya*.)

Çukakṛtya(m) ("the works of Çuka"). § 714 (Mokshadh.): XII, **328–9** (12312–12421) (continuation of *Çukakṛti*). *Bhīshma* said to *Yudhishṭhira*: Having heard the words of *Janaka*, having entered Soul by [his] soul and having seen Self by his self (*ātmānam ātmanāsthāya dṛshṭvā cātmānam ātmanā*), *Çuka* without putting further questions to *Janaka*, proceeded northwards to *Çaiçira* (through the air). At that time *Nārada* proceeded to *Himavat* (*b*). Then *Çuka* came to the asylum of *Vyāsa*. One day the disciples asked *Vyāsa* to let no sixth disciple be skilled in the Veda. *Vyāsa* answered that they ought to multiply, and the Veda to be spread, and taught them the qualifications of persons that can be accepted as disciples, and the rules in respect of the study of the Veda (XII, **328**). The disciples of *Vyāsa* took leave of him and descended from the mountain to the earth for the purpose of subdividing the Vedas; there they performed the agnishṭoma, etc., at the sacrifices of Brahmans, Kshattriyas, and Vaiçyas, and taught the Veda. *Vyāsa* remained with *Çuka*, passing his days in anxious thoughtfulness. *Nārada* came and asked him why Vedic sounds were silent now, so that the mountain now resembled a hamlet of *Nishādas*, and Ṛ., D., and G. did no longer shine as before; and exhorted *Vyāsa* to recite the Veda and thereby dispel the fears arising from Rā. *Vyāsa* and *Çuka* then set themselves to recite the Veda. One day a violent wind arose which *Vyāsa* declared to be an omen that the recitation of the Veda should be suspended; and he explained the *Devayāna* and the *Pitṛyāna*, and the Winds (*Samāna*, etc. [*g*]; cf. *Sādhyāḥ*), especially *Pravaha* (*h*), *Āvaha* (*i*), *Udvaha* (*j*), *Saṃvaha* (*k*), *Vivaha* (*l*), *Parivaha* (*m*), *Parāvaha* (*n*); "this wind is the breath of *Vishṇu's* nostrils." Having said this *Vyāsa* plunged into the celestial Ganges. (For continuation v. *Çuka-Nāradasaṃvāda*.)

Çuka-Nārada-saṃvāda(ḥ) ("conversation between Ç. and N."). § 715 (Mokshadh.): XII, **330–332** (12422–12556) (continued from *Çukakṛtya*). *Bhīshma* said to *Yudhishṭhira*: *Nārada* then came to *Çuka* for the object of asking *Çuka* the meaning of certain portions of the Veda. *Nārada* related what *Sanatkumāra* had said in days of yore to certain Ṛshis about avoiding attachment, etc., in order to attain to final emancipation; "with the aid of such instructions the deities succeeded in leaving the earth and became the denizens of heaven." (For continuation v. *Çukābhipatana*.)

Çukapraçnābhigamana. § 10 (Parvasaṅgr.): I, **2,** 352 (= XII, **232,** foll. ?).

Çūkara, pl. (°*āḥ*), a people. § 295 (Dyūtap.): II, **52,** 1882 (their king gave hundreds of elephants as tribute to Yudhishṭhira).

Çukasya āçrama(m), a tīrtha. § 370 (Tīrthayātrāp.): III, **85,** 8184.

Çukī. § 126 (Aṃçāvat.): I, **66,** 2620 (daughter of Tāmrā), 2623 (mother of the parrots).—§ 127 (Aṃçāvat.): I, **66,** 2633 (the same (?), daughter of Analā).

Çukla [1], one or two Pāṇḍava warriors. § 592 (Saṃçaptakavadhap.): VII, **23***o*, 1006 (description of his horses).—§ 608 (Karṇap.): VIII, **56***vv*, 2736 (among eight Pāñcālas who are attacked by Karṇa).

Çukla [2] = Çiva (1000 names [1–2]).

Çukladhvajapatākin = Çiva (1000 names [1]).

Çukotpatti(ḥ) ("origin of Çuka"). § 712 (Mokshadh.): XII, **324–325** (12158–12214). Questioned by Yudhishṭhira about *Çuka*, whose mind became bent on Bráhman when he was a mere boy, Bhīshma answered: The Ṛ. did not make merit depend upon age, etc., but upon the study of the Vedas and upon tapas; the merit of 1,000 horse-sacrifices or 100 *vajapeyas* cannot come up to even 1/16 of the merit that arises from *yoga*. Once on the summit of *Meru*, *Mahādeva* sported with his followers and *Pārvatī*, while *Vyāsa*, devoted to yoga and dhāraṇā, practised austerities for 100 years for the sake of obtaining a son, subsisting on air alone, adoring *Mahādeva*. Thither went Ṛ., B.-ṛ., Lp., S., V., Ā., R., *Sūrya*, *Candramas*, *Indra*, M., the *Oceans*, the *Rivers*, A., D., G., *Nārada*, *Parvata*, *Viçvāvasu*, Si., and Aps. This has been told to me by *Mārkaṇḍeya*. *Çiva* granted him that he would have a son like to *Fire*, *Wind*, *Earth*, *Water*, and *Space*, and devoted to *Bráhman* (XII, **324**). *Vyāsa* was one day employed in rubbing his sticks to make a fire, when he beheld the Aps. *Ghṛtācī*, and fell in love with her. When she approached, transformed into a she-parrot, he dropped his seed, which became a son, who, from this circumstance, came to be called by the name of *Çuka*. *Gaṅgā* came and bathed him in her waters; G. sung, and Aps. danced, etc. *Viçvāvasu*, *Tumburu*, *Nā.*, *Hāhā*, and *Hūhū* eulogized the birth of *Çuka*; there came Lp. with *Çakra*, D., D.-ṛ., and B.-ṛ.; *Māruta* showered celestial flowers; *Çiva*, together with *Pārvatī*, invested *Çuka* with the sacred thread; *Çakra* gave him a celestial *kamaṇḍalu* and celestial robes, etc. As soon as *Çuka* was born, the Vedas, including the mysteries and abstracts (*sarahasyāḥ sasaṅgrahāḥ*), came to dwell in him, just as they dwelt in his father. *Çuka* selected *Bṛhaspati* for his preceptor, remembering the universal practice. Having studied the Vedas, the tradition (*itihāsam*), and the state policy (*rājaçāstrāṇi*), *Çuka* returned home, after paying his preceptor the tuition fee. Adopting the vow of a brahmacārin he practised the hardest penances, even in his childhood. Taking no pleasure in the three modes of life (the domestic, etc.), he only kept in view the law of emancipation (*mokshadharmānudarçinaḥ*) (XII, **325**). (For continuation v. *Çukakṛti.*)

Çukra[1], the upādhyāya of the Asuras (also named Uçanas) and the planet Venus. § 98 (Aṃçāvat.): I, **65**, 2544 (*Asurānām upādhyāyaḥ Ç°s tv ṛshisuto 'bhavat*, enumeration of his (*Uçanasaḥ*) four sons).—§ 121 (do.): I, **66**, 2606 (*Bhṛgoḥ putraḥ Kavir vidvāñ Chukraḥ Kavisuto grahaḥ*, Çukra became a planet; he divided himself into two persons and became the guru of both the Asuras and the gods).—§ 124 (do.): I, **66**, 2616 (father of Devī, the wife of Varuṇa). — § 145 (Kaca): I, **76**, 3185, 3195, 3200, (3203), 3204 (*Kaviputreṇa Uçanasā*), (3215), (3228), (†3239), (†3241); **77**, 3263 (the Asuras, ruled by Vṛshaparvan, made Ç. (*Kāvyam Uçanasam*) their purohita; by his science Sañjivinī he revived the fallen Asuras; in order to obtain this science Kaca, the son of Bṛhaspati, became the disciple of Ç., and acquired it, after having gratified Devayānī, the daughter of Ç.).—§ 146 (Devayānī): I, **78**, 3297, (3314); **79**, (3319); **80**, (3340), (3343), 3351; **81**, 3367 (*Asuraguruḥ*), 3387 (*Bhārgavaḥ*), (3389), (3391), 3394, 3396 (Çarmishṭhā, the daughter of the Asura king Vṛshaparvan, threw Devayānī into a well. Ç. threatened that he would leave the Asuras; then Çarmishṭhā was given as a maid to Devayānī; Yayāti received Devayānī in marriage).—§ 147 (do.): I, **83**, (3454), (3459), (3462), (3464) (Ç. cursed Yayāti, because he had taken Çarmishṭhā as his second wife).—§ 148 (Yayāti): I, **85**, 3519 (*Çukrasya naptāram . . . Yadum*), 3527 (*Kāvyenoçanasā*), 3530 (all. to § 147).—§ 168 (Bhīshma-Satyavatīsamv.): I, **103**, 4151 (*°āṅgirasayor iva*, sc. Bhīshma).—§ 266 (Çakrasabhāv.): II, **7**, 303 (in the palace of Indra), 308 (do.). — § 270 (Brahmasabhāv.): II, **11**, 446 (among other planets present in the palace of Brahmán).—§ 455 (Brāhmaṇamāhātmyak.): III, **185**, 12703 (among the honourable appellations of a king).—§ 554 (Sainyodyogap.): V, **6**, 112 (*prajñayā sadṛçaç cāsi Çukreṇāṅgirasena ca*, sc. the purohita of Drupada).—[§ 561*d* (Nara-Nārāyaṇau): V, **49**, 1918 (*Bṛhaspatiç coçanā ca*, approached Brahmán).]—§ 562 (Bhagavadyānap.): V, **83**η, 2946 (among the ṛshis who worshipped Kṛshṇa).—§ 564 (Mātalīyop.): V, **98**, 3543 (*etac chāstraṃ narendrāṇām mahac Chukreṇa bhāshitam*).—§ 565 (Gālavacarita): V, **114**, 3898 (?, *nityaṃ Proshṭhapadābhyāñ ca Çukre Dhanapatau tathā | manushyebhyaḥ samādatte Çukraç cintārjitaṃ dhanam*, where, according to Nīl., the first Ç. is = *Çukravāsare* ("on Friday"), the following Ç. = Agni); **117**, 3972 (*reme . . . yathā . . . Çukraç ca Çataparvayā*).—§ 569 (Bhagavadyānap.): V, **149**, 5045 (*Kāvyasya*, father of Devayānī and grandfather of Yadu). — § 574 (Jambūkh.): VI, **3**, 82 (*Çukraḥ Praushṭhapade*—B. *Pro°—pūrve samāruhya virocate | uttare tu parikramya sahitaḥ samudīkshyate*; the planet; omens); [**6**, 216 (on the top of Meru, Uçanas Kāvya [sports] with the Daityas (so B., C. has *divi*); to him (so Nīl.) belong the jewels and the jewel mountains, of which he gives a fourth part to Kubera)].—§ 578 (Bhīshmavadhap.): VI, **45**[15], 1726 (*Çukrāṅgārakayor iva*, sc. *yuddham*, the planet).—§ 586 (do.): VI, **101**, 4642 (*yathā Budhaç ca Ç°ç ca, mahārāja, nabhastale*, the planet).—§ 589 (Droṇābhishek.): VII, **5**, 151 (*°āṅgirasadarçanāt*, sc. Droṇa). — § 597 (Pratijñāp.): VII, **84**, 2993 (*sahito Budha-Çukrābhyāṃ tamo vighnan yathā çaçī*, the planet). — § 605 (Karṇap.): VIII, **17**, 661 (*Çukrāṅgirasavarcasoḥ*, sc. Arjuna and Açvatthāman; *Çukrāṅgirasayor iva*, sc. *yuddham*).—§ 637 (Rājadh.): XII, **47**η, 1595 (among the ṛshis who surrounded Bhīshma as he lay on his arrow-bed), 1677 (C. *vīryaṃ Ç°ḥ Prajāpatiḥ*, B. *vīrye Ç°ḥ pratishṭhitaḥ*, in a hymn to Kṛshṇa).—[§ 641 (Rājadh.): XII, **59**, 2206 (*Kāvya* composed an abridgement of the *Bārhaspatya* çāstra).]—§ 641*f* (Pṛthu Vainya): XII, **59**, 2231 (the purohita of Pṛthu Vainya).—§ 641 (Rājadh.): XII, **100**, 3701 (*yato Vāyur yataḥ Sūryaḥ yataḥ Çukraḥ*—i.e. the planet—*tato jayaḥ*); **124**, 4574 (*Bhārgavāt*, instructed Indra, but said that Prahlāda had better knowledge).—§ 650 (Āpaddh.): XII, **142**, 5454 (a saying of his is quoted). — § 661 (Mokshadh.): XII, **198a**, 7191 (*°sya*, sc. *sthānam*). — § 686 (do.): XII, **273**, 9818 (C. *Çukrasya cāpadhyānāt tu punar ājñāti dharmavit*; B. has more correctly: *Ç°sya punar ājnābhiḥ* (*ājātiḥ*, var. lect., Nīl.) *Parṇādo nāma dharmavit*). — [§ 692 (Mokshadharm.): XII, **280-281** (Uçanas was about to instruct Vṛtra about Vishṇu).] — § 701 (do.): XII, **290**, 10662 (*kathañ cāpy Uçanāḥ prāpya* (B. *prāpa*) *Çukratvam*).—§ 701*b* (Bhava-Bhārgavasamāgama): XII, **290**, 10690 (Uçanas entered the body of Kubera and took his wealth away. Kubera applied to Çiva, who swallowed Uçanas up; Çiva permitted Uçanas to go out through his urethra (therefore Uçanas is named *Çukra*, and is unable to attain to the centre of the firmament); Umā then prevented Çiva from slaying Uçanas, who therefore became her son).—§ 702 (Mokshadh.): XII, **293**, 10760 (*gataḥ Ç°tvam Uçanā Devadevaprasādanāt*, all. to § 701).—§ 707 (do.): XII, **319**β, 11784 (had instructed Viçvāvasu).—[§ 717*b* (Nārāyaṇīya): XII, **343**, V), ††13206 (when Çiva intended to attack Tripura, Uçanas tore a matted lock from his own head and hurled it against Çiva; from it arose serpents who bit Çiva, at which his throat became blue).]—§ 730*g* (Upamanyu): XIII, **14**λ, 805.—§ 730 (Ānuçāsanik.): XIII, **17**, 1289 (*Bhārgavaḥ*, Taṇḍi communicated the 1,000 names of Çiva to Ç., and Ç. to Gautama); **18**λλ, †1368 (*°Bṛhaspatī*). — § 747*b* (Suvarṇotpatti): XIII, **85**η, 4148 (the fifth of the seven sons of Bhṛgu) [(ι), 4150 (Kāvya is the second son of Kavi, Uçanas the fourth)]. — § 751*b* (Çapathavidhi): XIII, **94a**, †4550, (4570). — § 754 (Ānuçāsanik.): XIII, **98**, 4686 (*Ç°sya ca Baleç caiva saṃvādam*), 4687 (*Bhṛgukulodvahaḥ*), (4692).—[§ 758 (do.): XIII, **103**, †4945 (*Indreṇa guhyam*—i.e. the vow of fast, Nīl.—*nihitaṃ vai guhāyāṃ yad Bhārgavas tapasehābhyavindat | jājvalyamānam Uçanastejaseha tat sādhayāmāsam aham* (i.e. Bhagīratha) *vareṇya*).]—§ 775 (do.): XIII, **166a**, 7643 (the planet).—§ 788 (Açramavās.): XV, **28**, 753 (*Asureshu*, Vidura excelled Çukra in intelligence).

Cf. also the following synonyms:—

Bhārgava, Bhārgavadāyāda, q.v.

Bhṛguçreshṭha, Bhṛgūdvaha, Bhṛgukulodvaha, Bhṛgunandana, Bhṛgusūnu, q.v.

Kaviputra ("son of Kavi"): I, 3204 (*Çukrenoçanasā*).

Kavisuta (do.): I, 2606 (*Çukraḥ*).

Kāvya (do.): I, 3188 (*Uçanasam*), 3190, 3192, 3193 (*Uçanasaḥ*), †3233 (*maharshiḥ*), †3238, †3249, 3268, 3304, 3306, 3307, 3332 (*Bhṛguçreshṭhaḥ*), 3388, 3411, 3449 (*Uçanasaḥ*), 3453, 3467 (*Uçanasaḥ*), 3493 (do.), 3499, 3527 (*Uçanasā*); II, 2105 (a çloka recited by him in order to induce the Asuras to abandon Jambha, is quoted); V, 5045 (*Çukrasya*); VI, 216 (*Uçanāḥ Kāvyaḥ*, on Meru); IX, 2551 (had performed austerities at Kapālamocana); XII, 2093 (among the ṛshis who surrounded Bhīshma as he lay on his arrow-bed), 2206, 8900 (went to heaven), 10660 (*Uçanāḥ*); XIII, 4150 (? second son of Kavi), 4741 (*Bhārgavaḥ*); XIV, 1785 (*senāpatir abhūt . . . . Kāvyo Daityapater iva*).

Uçanas: I, 2544 (*Çukraḥ*), 3165 (*muneḥ*), 3188 (*Kāvyam*), 3193 (*Kāvyāt*), 3204 (*Çukreṇa*), †3249, 3411 (*Kāvyaḥ*), 3449 (*Kāvyasya*), 3460, 3467 (*Kāvyasya*), 3493 (do.), 3527 (*Çukreṇa . . . Kāvyena*), ††3761 (°*so duhitā Devayānī*); 4002 (*Uçanā veda yac chāstram*); III, 11294 (*Bṛhaspaty-Uçanoktaiç ca* (°*naḥproktair*, B.) *nayaiḥ*), 15146 (*Bṛhaspaty-Uçanoktaiç ca mantraiḥ*), 16369 (*Uçanā iva cāparaḥ | vyūhya cauçanasaṃ vyūhaṃ*, sc. Rāvaṇa); IV, 1829 (*buddhyā tulyo hy Uçanasā*, sc. Droṇa); V, 1918, 5288 (*bhavān Uçanasā tulyaḥ*, sc. Bhīshma); VI, 216 (*Kāvyaḥ*), 1241 (*kavīnām Uçanā kaviḥ*, sc. *asmi*, says Kṛshṇa); VII, 161 (*Daityānām ivoçanaḥ*), 275 (*Bṛhaspaty-Uçanastulyo buddhyā*, sc. Droṇa); VIII, 1261 (*vyūhaṃ . . . Bṛhaspaty-Uçanomataṃ*), †1726 (*naye Bṛhaspaty-Uçanoḥ sadā samaṃ*, sc. Droṇa); IX, 301 (*buddhyā coçanasā samaṃ*, sc. Açvatthāman), 3259 (a çloka sung by him is quoted), 3436 (*Bṛhaspaty-Uçanasor . . . upadeçaḥ*); XII, 1353 (*Uçanā veda yac chāstram*), 2014 (*maharshiṇā*, two çlokas sung by him are quoted), 2048 (a çloka of his is quoted), 5045 (*buddhyā tvam*—i.e. the mouse Palita—*Uçanāḥ sākshāt*), 5104 (two gāthās of his are quoted), 5203 (two gāthas sung by him to Prahlāda are quoted), 5442 (*Daiteyān Uçanāḥ prāha saṃçayacchedanaṃ purā*), 10004, 10012, (10025) (was about to instruct Vṛtra about Vishṇu), 10028 (*muninā*), 10029, 10217 (*mahāmuniḥ*, worshipped Çiva), 10660 (*devarshiḥ . . . Kāvyaḥ*), 10662, 10670, 10672, 10674, 10678, 10679, 10685, 10687 (*mahāmuniḥ*), 10695, 10760 (*gataḥ Çukratvaṃ*), 12740 (*Uçanā Bṛhaspatiç caiva yadotpattau bhavishyataḥ | tadā pravakshyataḥ çāstraṃ*), 13206; XIII, 1762 (among the ṛshis who surroundod Bhīshma as he lay on his arrow-bed), 2239 (*Uçanā veda yac chāstram*), 4150 (fourth son of Kavi), †4945 (*Bhārgavaḥ*), 5284 (?, C. *Mārutoçanasa*, B. *Mārutauçanase*), 5304 (°*saḥ*, sc. *lokaṃ*); XV, 249 (*Uçanā veda yac chāstraṃ*).

Çukra[2], a month. § 213 (Jatugṛhap.): I, **151**, 5883 (v. Çuci).—§ 294 (Dyūtap.): II, **47**, 1685 (do.).—§ 608 (Karṇap.): VIII, **79**, †4072 (do.), 4075 (do.).

Çukra[3] = Agni: I, 8419, 8427; V, 3899 (according to Nīl.).

Çukra[4] = Sūrya: III, 147; XII, 13906.

Çukra[5] = Çiva: X, 253; XIV, 210.

Çukratanayā ("daughter of Çukra") = Devayānī: I, 3183.

Çuktimat, a mountain. § 280 (Bhīmasena): II, **30**, 1079 (conquered by Bhīmasena on his digvijaya). — § 574 (Jambūkh.): VI, **9**κ, 318 (among the *kulaparvatāḥ* in Bhāratavarsha; C. has *Çaktimat*).

Çuktimatī[1], a river. § 75 (Vasu): I, **63**, 2367 (near the capital of the Cedi king Vasu Uparicara; by the mountain Kolāhala she became the mother of the generalissimo of Vasu and Girikā, the queen of Vasu).—§ 574 (Jambūkh.): VI, **9**λ, 342 (among the rivers of Bhāratavarsha; C. has *Muktimatī*).

Çuktimatī[2], a city. § 321 (Saubhavadhop.): III, **22**, 898 (*purīṃ*, the capital of the Cedi king Dhṛshṭaketu).

Çuktisāhvaya, adj. ("named after the oyster"). § 785 (Anugītāp.): XIV, **83**, 2467 (*Cedīnāṃ purīṃ çuktisāhvayāṃ*, i.e. Çuktimatī).

Çūlabhṛt[1] = Çiva, q.v.

Çūlabhṛt[2] = Kṛshṇa: XIII, 7367.

Çūladhṛk, Çūlahasta, Çūlāṅka, Çūlapāṇi = Çiva, q.v.

Çūlavarāyudha = Vishṇu: XII, 4492, 4495.

Çūlin[1] = Çiva, q.v.—Do.[2] = Kṛshṇa: XII, 1668.

Çūna, an ancient king. § 595 (Shoḍaçarāj., v. Māndhātṛ): VII, **62***a*, 2281 (vanquished by Māndhātṛ, only C., B. has *Pūruṃ*).

Çunaḥçepha (B. °*çepa*), son of Ṛcīka. § 721 (Ānuçāsanik.): XIII, **3***a*, 186 (*Ṛcīkasyātmajaḥ*, had been the sacrificial animal at the sacrifice of Hariçcandra (read *Hariçcandrakratau* with B.), but having pleased the gods, he was delivered and became the son of Viçvāmitra; the translation of PCR. is incorrect).

Çunaḥsakha, the name of Indra, disguised as a mendicant. § 750*b* (Bisastainyop.): XIII, **93**, (4503), (4505), 4507 (°*ā*, nom.), (4533), 4534, (4535).—§ 751*b* (Çapathavidhi): XIII, **94**, (4586) (the name seems to be an error, as *Ç.* does not occur elsewhere in this tale, and Indra speaks, v. 4590).

Çunaka[1], a ṛshi. § 19 (Bhṛgu): I, **5**, 872 (son of Ruru and Pramadvarā, and the great-grandfather (*pūrvapitāmaha*) of Çaunaka[1]).—§ 21 (Pramadvarā): I, **8**, 940 (do.).—§ 264 (Sabhākriyāp.): II, **4***a*, 105, 112 (among the munis present in the palace of Yudhishṭhira). — § 736*b* (Vītahavyop.): XIII, **30**, 2005 (son of Ruru (of Vītahavya's race) and Pramadvarā, and father of Çaunaka[4]).

Çunaka[2], one or more princes. § 130 (Amçāvat.): I, **67**, 2674 (incarnation of the Asura Candrahantṛ). — § 406 (Tīrthayātrāp.): III, **125**, 10414 (*narādhipaḥ*, has obtained eternal regions).—§ 656 (Khadgotpatti): XII, **166**δ, 6198 (received the sword from Hariṇāçva, whereafter it passed to Uçīnara, etc.).

Çuṇḍika, pl. (°*uḥ*), a pooplo. § 515 (Karṇadigvijaya): III, **253**, 15243 (vanquished by Karṇa on his digvijaya; only B., C. has *Maṇḍikān*).

Çūnya = Vishṇu (1000 names).

Çūnyapāla, a ṛshi. § 077 (Mokshadh.): XII, **245**β, 8901 (went to heaven).

Çūra[1], an ancient king. § 6 (Anukram.): I, **1***a*, 225 (in Sañjaya's enumeration of kings who have died).

Çūra[2], a Yādava, father of Vasudeva and Kuntī. § 131 (Kuntī): I, **07**, 2761 (*Yaduçreshṭho Vasudevapitā*, gave his daughter Pṛthā, i.e. Kuntī, as a daughter to Kuntibhoja), 2766.—§ 175 (Karṇasambhava): I, **111**, 4382 (*Yaduçreshṭho Vasudevapitā*), 4383 (repetition from § 131).—§ 547 (Karṇa): III, **303**, 17020 (°*sya sutā*, i.e. Kuntī). — § 562 (Bhagavadyānap.): V, **90**, 3221 (°*sya rājño duhitā*, i.e. Kuntī).—§ 599*e* (Çini): VII, **144**, 6031 (*Yādavaḥ*, son of Devamīḍha and father of Vasudeva), 6032 (*Kārttavīryasamaḥ*, forefather of Çini). — § 768*b* (Kṛshṇa Vāsudeva): XIII, **147**, 6835, 6836 (son of Citraratha and father of Vasudeva).

Çūra[3], son of Ilina. § 150 (Pūruvaṃç.): I, **94**, 3708 (C. *Çu*°).

Çūra[4] = Skanda: III, 14635.

Çūra[5], a Sauvīra, one of the standard-bearers of Jayadratha. § 522 (Draupadīharaṇap.): III, **265,** †15598.

Çūra[6], a prince. § 554 (Sainyodyogap.): V, **4**γ, 75 (PCR. has "the king of the Mallas," among the princes to whom the Pāṇḍavas ought to send messengers).

Çūra[7] = Vishṇu (1000 names).

Çūra[8], pl. (°*āḥ*). § 295 (Dyūtap.): II, **52,** 1868 (among the peoples who brought tribute to Yudhishṭhira).—§ 402 (Tīrthayātrāp.): III, **120,** †10278 (*Sālvata-Çūra-senā*, C. has *Sūra*°; perhaps a certain tribe among the Yādavas?).—§ 607 (Karṇap.): VIII, **45,** 2107 (*sarvajñā Yavanā, rājan, Çūrāç caiva viçeshataḥ*).

Çūrajaneçvara = Vishṇu (1000 names).

Çūraputra ("son of Çūra") = Vasudeva: XVI, 200.

Çūrasena[1], pl. (°*āḥ*), a people. § 273 (Rājasūyārambhap.): II, **14,** 590 (among the peoples who fled from fear of Jarāsandha).—§ 282 (Sahadeva): II, **31,** 1106 (vanquished by Sahadeva; read with B. *Çūrasenān*, C. has *Sūrasenāt*).—§ 549 (Pāṇḍavapraveçap.): IV, **1***a*, 11; **5,** 144 (on their way from Dvaitavana to Upaplavya the Pāṇḍavas pass through the country of the Ç.).—§ 561 (Yānasandhip.): V, **54**ι, 2138 (disregard Duryodhana).—§ 574 (Jambūkh.): VI, **9**μ, 347 (among the peoples of Bhāratavarsha), 360 (do., C. has *S*°).—§ 576 (Bhagavadgītāp.): VI, **18**δ, 688 (in the army of Duryodhana).—§ 578 (Bhīshmavadhap.): VI, **51**σ, 2097 (do.).—§ 579 (do.): VI, **52**[1], 2139 (attacked by Arjuna). —§ 580 (do.): VI, **56**γ, 2408 (in the tail of Bhīshma's *garuḍavyūha*). —§ 586 (do.): VI, **106**τ, 4809 (defended Bhīshma, cf. v. 5649).—§ 587 (do.): VI, 117ρ, 5485 (attacked Arjuna); **119***aa*, 5649 (B. *saṃgrāmena jahur Bhīshmam*, C. *saṁgrāme nājahur*, etc., cf. v. 4809).—§ 589 (Droṇābhishek.): VII, **7**ζ, 183 (followed Duryodhana).—§ 599 (Jayadrathavadhap.): VII, **91**β, 3254 (had formerly been vanquished by Karṇa); **93**γ, 3339 (attacked Arjuna); **141,** 5850 (attacked Sātyaki); **150**β', 6526 (have been slain).—§ 600 (Ghaṭotkacavadhap.): VII, 157ρ, 6949 (were slain by Yudhishṭhira); **161**εε, 7207 (were slain by Bhīmasena).—§ 604 (Karṇap.): VIII, **5**ζ, 126 (mentioned as slain).—§ 607 (do.): VIII, **45**ν, †2098 (perform sacrifices).—§ 608 (do.): VIII, **47**κ, 2227 (in Yudhishṭhira's army, attacked by Çakuni and Kṛpa).—§ 768*b* (Kṛshṇa Vāsudeva): XIII, **147,** 6841 (°*eshu samvṛddhaḥ*, sc. Kṛshṇa). Cf. Çūrasenarāj.

Çūrasena[2], a Kuru warrior. § 583 (Bhīshmavadh.): VI, **75**γ, 3294 (in the neck of Bhīshma's *krauñcavyūha*).

Çūrasena[3], a Pāñcāla warrior. § 608 (Karṇap.): VIII, **48**γ, 2248 (slain by Karṇa).

Çūrasena[4] = Vishṇu (1000 names).

Çūrasenarāj ("king of the Çūrasenas") = Sunāman: VII, 390 (*S*°).

Çūrasenī ("daughter of the Çūrasena king"). § 150 (Pūruv.): I, **94,** 3696 (wife of Pravīra and mother of Manasyu).

Çūrasūnu ("son of Çūra") = Vasudeva: XIV, 391.

Çūrasuta (do.) = Vasudeva: III, 831, 837, 838, 840; XIV, 1521.

Çūrātmaja (do.) = Vasudeva: XIV, 1850.

Çūrpaṇakhā, name of a female Rākshasa. § 526 (Rāmopākhyānap.): III, **275,** 15896 (daughter of Viçravas and Rākā), 15900 (*siddhavighnakarī*), 15907.—§ 528 (Rāvaṇāgamana): III, **277,** 15986, 15989 (when Rāma had slain Khara and Dūshaṇa, Ç. repaired to Rāvaṇa to instigate him to take revenge).

Çūrpāraka, name of a place. § 284 (Sahadeva): II, **31,** 1169 (in the south, conquered by Sahadeva on his digvijaya).—§ 370 (Tīrthayātrāp.): III, **85,** 8185 (*Jāmadagnyasevitam*).—§ 377 (Dhaumyatīrthak.): III, **88,** 8337 (in Ç. are two sacrificial platforms (*vedī*) belonging to Jamadagni and named *Pāshāṇatīrthā* and *Punaçcandrā*). —§ 400 (Tīrthayātrāp.): III, **118,** 10221 (C. *Sū*°; near Ç. Yudhishṭhira saw the sacrificial platform (*vedīṃ*) of Ṛcīka's son, i.e. Jamadagni, etc.), 10227 (C. *Sū*°).—§ 638*b* (Rāmopākhy.): XII, **49,** 1781 (the Ocean created for Rāma Jāmadagnya the region Ç.).—§ 733*w* (Narmadā): XIII, **25,** 1736 (°*odake*, a tīrtha; C. has *Sū*°).

Çvaitya[1] = Sṛñjaya: VII, 2183, 2195, 2208, 2223, 2248, 2262, 2271, 2291, 2302, 2320, 2333, 2355, 2376, 2393, 2426; XII, 1052.

Çvaitya[2]: I, 224 (so B. for Çaivya, q.v.).

Çvāsā. § 116 (Vasu, pl.): I, **66,** 2583 (wife of Prajāpati and mother of Çvasana, i.e. Vāyu).

***Çvasana** = Vāyu (the Wind): I, 1489, 2583 (son of Çvāsā); III, 770; VIII, 1511.

Çvāvillomāpaha, a tīrtha. § 364 (Tīrthayātrāp.): III, **83,** 6031. Cf. next.

Çvāvillomāpanayana = Çvāvillomāpaha: III, 6032.

Çveta[1], one or more ancient kings. § 6 (Anukram.): I, **1***a*, 226 (in Sañjaya's enumeration of departed kings).—§ 653*b* (Gṛdhra-gomāyusaṃv.): XII, **153,** 5743 (*rājarsheḥ*, had revived his dead son).—§ 761 (Ānuçāsanik.): XIII, **115**δ, 5668 (among the kings who abstained from meat during the month of Kārttika).—§ 770 (do.): XIII, **151**μ, 7130 (*rājarshiṃ*; in C. and B. then follows the half-çloka *Sāgarasyātmajā* (C. °*jo*) *yena plāvitās tāritās tathā*, which would refer to Ç., but PCR. inserts two çlokas, the first stating that Ç. gratified Çiva, who for his sake slew Andhaka, the second mentioning Bhagīratha, to whom then the half-çloka quoted above must refer (and so, as a matter of fact, it does, *vide* under the heading Bhagīratha, § 389)).—§ 775 (do.): XIII, **166**η, 7681 (*rājarshisattamaḥ*).

Çveta[2], a muni. § 22 (Pramadvarā): I, **8***a*, 962.

Çveta[3], one of the elephants of the quarters. § 127 (Aṃçāvat.): I, **66,** 2630 (*diçāṃ gajaṃ*, son of Çvetā[1]).

Çveta[4], a prince. § 290 (Çiçupālavadhap.): II, **44,** 1539.

Çveta[5], a mountain. § 418 (Tīrthayātrāp.): III, **139,** 10820 (*giriṃ*, passed by the Pāṇḍavas), 10824 (do.).—§ 436 (Yakshayuddhap.): III, **158,** 11527 (*parvatarājānam*, description), 11540, 11554 (*parvataṃ*).—§ 459 (Mārkaṇḍeyas.): III, **188,** 12917 (seen by Mārkaṇḍeya in the stomach of Nārāyaṇa). —§ 496 (Skandotpatti): III, **225,** 14309 (*parvataṃ*; Svāhā deposited the seed of Agni in a golden lake near Ç.; from that seed Skanda was born), 14331 (*mahāgirau*), 14335 (*gireḥ*; Skanda cleft the peak of Ç. in twain, then the mountain fled).—§ 501 (Skandopākhyāna): III, 14429 (*Rudreṇa çukram utsṛshṭaṃ tac Çhvetaḥ parvato 'bhavat | Pāvakasyendriyaṃ Çvete Kṛttikābhiḥ kṛtaṃ nage*).—§ 541 (Indrajidvadha): III, **289,** 16473 (a Guhyaka came from Ç.). —§ 561 (Yānasandhip.): V, **48,** †1879 (*giriṃ* = Kailāsa, PCR.). —§ 574 (Jambūkh.): VI, **6**β, 198 (*çaçisannibhaḥ*, one of the *varshaparvatāḥ*). —§ 615 (Gadāyuddhap.): IX, **60,** 3349 (°*syeva mahāgireḥ*).—§ 619 (Strīvilāp.): XI, **19,** 567 (*bhāti . . . . agnineva Ç°o giriḥ*).—§ 775 (Ānuçāsanik.): XIII, **166***a*, 7657 (*rajatānvitaḥ*).—§ 782*g* (Guruçishyasaṃv.): XIV, **43**η, 1174 (among the foremost of mountains). Cf. Çvetācala, Çvetaparvata.

Çveta[6] = Çvetagraha. § 559 (Prajāgarap.): V, **37,** †1376

(*Çveto grahas tiryag ivāpatan khe,* "like a comet," PCR.).—§ 574 (Jambūkh.): VI, **3,** 79 (*Çveto grahas tathā Citrāṃ samatikramya tishṭhati,* omens; [= Ketu, Nīl., and PCR.]), 83 (*Çveto grahaḥ prajvalitaḥ sadhūma iva pāvakaḥ | Aindraṃ tejasvi nakshatraṃ Jyeshṭhām ākramya tishṭhati,* omens; [= Ketu, Nīl., and PCR.]). Cf. Çvetagraha.

Çveta[7], a varsha. § 574 (Jambūkh.): VI, **6**γ, 232 (north of the mountain Nīla).

Çveta[8], a Pāṇḍava warrior. § 578 (Bhīshmavadhap.): VI, **47,** 1850 (*Vairāṭiḥ* (!) [Nīl. takes *Vairāṭiḥ* = Çaṅkha, and is right, the whole episode of Çveta being an interpolation, cf. the note of PCR., p. 170, and the note in B. to **47,** 43]), 1852, 1855, 1860; **48,** 1868, 1870, 1892, 1895, 1896, 1905, 1907 (fights Bhīshma), 1908, 1909, 1911, 1914, 1916, 1917, 1918, 1921, 1923, 1927, 1932, 1933, 1935, 1938, 1940, 1947, 1954, 1958, 1961, 1965, 1968, 1969, 1973, 1977 (is slain by Bhīshma), 1980; **49,** 1985 (*nihate*), 1997, 2010.

Çveta[9], a warrior of Skanda. § 615*u* (Skanda): IX, **45**η, 2566.

Çveta[10], an island (= Çvetadvīpa). § 717*b* (Nārāyaṇīya): XII, **336,** †12703 (*Kshīrodadher yottarato hi dvīpaḥ Ç°ḥ sa nāmnā,* it is more than 32,000 yojanas distant from Meru, description of the inhabitants).—§ 717*c* (Uparicara): XII, **337,** 12783 (*mahādvīpam,* had been visited by Ekata, Dvita, and Trita). — § 717*b* (Nārāyaṇīya): XII, **338,** 12859 (*dvīpaṃ*); **339,** 12861 (*mahādvīpaṃ,* Nārada saw there Nārāyaṇa); **340,** 12994 (*mahādvīpaṃ*); **344,** 13334 (do.). Cf. Çvetadvīpa.

Çveta[11] = Vishṇu: XII, 13516, 13612.

Çveta[12], pl. (°*āḥ*) = "the inhabitants of Çvetadvīpa" (?). § 717*b* (Nārāyaṇīya): XII, **349,** 13633 (*Çvetānāṃ Yatīnāñ cāha ekāntagatim avyayām*).

Çvetā[1]. § 127 (Aṃçāvat.): I, **67,** 2625 (daughter of Krodhavaçā), 2630 (mother of Çveta[3]).

Çvetā[2] = Umā: VI, 801.

Çvetā[3], a mātṛ. § 615*u* (Skanda): IX, **46**θ, 2640.

Çvetabhadra, a Yaksha. § 269 (Vaiçravaṇasabhāv.): II, **9,** 397 (among the Yakshas in the palace of Kubera).

Çvetācala, a mountain (= Çveta[5]). § 564*b* (Çesha): V, **103,** 3619 (°*nibhākāraḥ,* sc. Çesha). Cf. Çveta[5], Çvetaparvata.

Çvetāçva = Arjuna, q.v.

Çvetadvīpa, an island (= Çveta[10]). § 717*b* (Nārāyaṇīya): XII, **336,** †12709 (°*vāsinām*). —§ 717*c* (Uparicara): XII, **337,** 12778 (*Kshīrodadher uttarataḥ*), 12781 (°*vāsinaḥ,* description).—§ 717*b* (Nārāyaṇīya): XII, **344**ββ, 13313, 13327, 13330, 13331, 13344, 13350, 13360 (Nārada had seen Nārāyaṇa on Ç.); **345,** 13393. Cf. Cveta[10].

Çvetagraha = Çveta[6]. § 584 (Bhīshmavadhap.): VI, **82,** 3588 (*Çvetagraham evoditaṃ* = Çukra, PCR.).

Çvetahaya = Arjuna, q.v.

Çvetaketu[1], a muni, son of Uddālaka. § 59 (Sarpasattra). I, **53***a*, 2047 (among the sadasyas at the snake sacrifice of Janamejaya).—§ 187*b* (Pāṇḍu): The muni Ç., son of Uddālaka, established the present usage among men that the sin of violating matrimonial chastity is regarded like to that of killing an embryo; this Ç. established from anger, as one day, in the presence of his father, a brahman came and seized his mother by the hand and took her away; Uddālaka, however, excused the fact as it was the practice sanctioned by antiquity: I, **122,** 4724, 4725, 4726, 4728, 4730, 4735 (*Uddālakasya putreṇa*).—§ 266 (Çakrasabhāv.): II, **7,** 294 (in the palace of Indra). — § 412 (Ashṭāvakrīya): III, **132,** †10597 (*Auddālakiḥ*), †10598, †10599 (*Auddālakiḥ*), †10609, †10614, †10615, †10617 (Ç. was of the same age as Ashṭāvakra, the son of Uddālaka's daughter, who regarded Ç. as his brother; Ç. informed Ashṭāvakra that Uddālaka was not his father, then they both repaired to the sacrifice of Janaka).—§ 635 (Rājadharm.): XII, **34,** 1229 (Uddālaka caused his son Ç. to be begotten by a disciple).—§ 640 (do.): XII, **57,** 2056 (Uddālaka cast off Ç. because he deceived brahmans).—§ 775 (Ānuçāsanik.): XIII, **166**ζ, 7671 (*Auddālakiḥ,* among the ṛshis of the north).

Çvetaketu[2] = Çvetaki: I, **223,** v. 69 (the çloka is wanting in C.).

Çvetaki, an ancient king. § 255 (Agniparābhava): I, **223,** 8098 (*Harihayopamaḥ*), 8116, 8119, 8127, 8129, 8137 (Çvetaki could not get any priests to assist him in his sacrifice; he then applied to Çiva, who caused Durvāsas to complete the sacrifice on the condition that Ç. poured libations of clarified butter into the fire for twelve years; from this Agni (fire) became sick; after the completion of the sacrifice Ç. ascended to heaven (only B.)). Cf. Çvetaketu[2].

Çvetaparvata, a mountain (= Çveta[5]). § 279 (Arjuna): II, **27,** 1037; **28,** 1038 (crossed by Arjuna on his digvijaya). —§ 506 (Skandayuddhap.): III, **231,** 14540.—§ 532 (Sītāsāntvana): III, **280,** 16158, 16159 (in a dream Vibhīshaṇa is seen to ascend Ç. together with his counsellors).—§ 555 (Indravijaya): V. **11***a*, 353. — § 574 (Jambūkh.): VI, **6**θ, 247 (the abode of the gods and the Asuras).—§ 596 (Pratijñāp.): VII, **80,** 2845 (passed by Kṛshṇa and Arjuna on their way to the abode of Çiva).—§ 615*f* (Çaṅkhatīrtha) IX, **37,** 2138 (°*saṅkāçam,* sc. Mahāçaṅkha).—§ 618 (Jalapradānikap.): XI, **10,** 278 (°*rūpebhyo gṛhebhyaḥ*). Cf. Çveta[5], Çvetācala.

Çvetapiṅgala = Çiva (1000 names[2]).

Çvetapiṅgalanetra = Çiva (1000 names[1]).

Çvetasiddhi, a warrior of Skanda. § 615*u* (Skanda): IX, **45**η, 2570.

Çvetavāha, Çvetavāhana = Arjuna, q.v.

Çvetavaktra, a warrior of Skanda. § 615*u* (Skanda): IX, **45**η, 2575.

Çvetopākhyāna. § 10 (Parvasaṅgrahap.): I, **2,** 333 (mentioned among the parvans of the fifth book, but it may perhaps refer to ch. **47–49** in the sixth book; B. has *Viçvopākhyānaṃ,* which may refer to ch. **65–68** in the sixth book).

Çyāma, a mountain in Çākadvīpa. § 575*h* (Çākadvīpa): VI, **11,** 419 (*mahāgiriḥ*), 426.

Çyāmā = Draupadī: V, 3215, 4661.

Çyāmāyā āçrama(ḥ), a tīrtha. § 733*m* (Citrakuṭa): XIII, **25,** 1716.

Çyāmāyana, son of Viçvāmitra. § 721*b* (Viçvāmitrop.): XIII, **4**β, 251.

Çyena, a ṛshi. § 266 (Çakrasabhāv.): II, **7,** 293 (in the palace of Indra).

***Çyena,** pl. (°*āḥ*) ("hawks"). § 126 (Aṃçāvat.): I, **66,** 2621 (the offspring of Çyenī).

Çyenacitra, an ancient king. § 761 (Ānuçāsanik.): XIII, **115**δ, 5665 (among the kings who abstained from meat during the month of *Kārttika*).

Çyenajit[1], son of Dala. § 461 (Vāmadevacar.): III, **192,** †13202.

Çyenajit[2], a prince. § 569 (Bhagavadyānap.): V, **141**γ, 4781 (has sided with the Pāṇḍavas).

[Çyena-kapotākhyāna(ṃ)] ("the story of the hawk and the pigeon"). § 738*b* (Ānuçāsanik.): *Bhīshma* said: Once a pigeon, pursued by a hawk, dropped down from the skies and sought the protection of the *Kāçi* king R.-r. *Vrshadarbha* (or *Uçīnara*), etc. [cf. Çyenakapotīya (§ 411 = III, **130** foll.), but here the birds are not *Indra* and *Agni*]. The three worlds together with *Indra* came to behold the king; he was bathed in a shower of nectar, etc.; D., G., and Aps. began to sing and dance around him, just as they do around *Brahmán*; he then ascended a celestial chariot and proceeded to the eternal heaven. Blessing upon the reader.

Çyenakapotīya(m) ("the episode relating to the hawk and the pigeon"). § 11 (Parvasaṅgr.): I, **2**, 448 (°*m upākhyānam*). — § 411 (Plakshāv.): *Indra* in the shape of a hawk and *Agni* in that of a pigeon in fear of the hawk came to test king *Uçīnara's* merit (III, **130**). *Uçīnara* in vain offered the hawk another beast, and thereafter his kingdom, in order that he might spare the pigeon ("he who slays a *brahman*, he who slaughters a cow, the common mother of all the worlds, and he who forsakes one asking for protection, are equally sinful"); at last the hawk agreed upon receiving the pigeon's weight of *Uçīnara's* flesh; *Uçīnara* cut portion after portion of his flesh and placed it in the balance, and as it did not outweigh the pigeon he mounted the scale himself, utterly devoid of flesh. Then *Indra* said: "As long as man shall speak of thee, so long . . . . thou shalt inhabit the holy regions." Saying this *Indra* ascended to heaven, and so did king *Uçīnara* in a radiant shape, after having filled heaven and earth with his merits (III, **131**).

Çyenī. § 126 (Aṃçāvat.): I, **66**, 2620 (daughter of Tāmrā), 2621 (mother of the hawks).—§ 127 (do.): I, **66**, 2632 (wife of Aruṇa and mother of Sampāti and Jaṭāyus).

D

Daçabāhu = Çiva (1000 names[1–2]).

Daçabhuja = Çiva: XIV, 209.

Daçāçva, a king of Māhishmatī. § 720*b* (Sudarçanop.): XIII, **2**, 89 (son of Ikshvāku), 90 (father of Madirāçva).

Daçāçvamedha, a tīrtha. § 362 (Tīrthayātrāp.): III, **83**, 5084.

Daçāçvamedhika, a tīrtha. § 364 (Tīrthayātrāp.): III, **83**, 6034.

Daçaçatāksha, Daçaçatanayana, Daçacatekshaṇa = Indra, q.v.

Daçagrīva[1], a Daitya. § 268 (Varuṇasabhāv.): II, **9**, 367 (in the palace of Varuṇa).

Daçagrīva[2] = Rāvaṇa, q.v.

Daçajyotis, son of Subhrāj. § 3 (Anukram.): I, **1**β, 44, 45 (father of 10,000 sons).

Daçakandhara = Rāvaṇa, q.v.

Daçalakshaṇasaṃyukta = Çiva (1000 names[1]).

Daçamālika, pl. (°*āḥ*), a people. § 574 (Jambūkh.): VI, **9**ξ, 374 (among the peoples of the north).

Daçānana = Rāvaṇa, q.v.

Daçāpārçva, pl. (°*āḥ*), a people. § 574 (Jambūkh.): VI, **9**μ, 363 (only B.; C. has *Daçārṇāḥ*).

Daçaratha, king of Ayodhyā and father of Rāma. § 383*b* (Paraçurāma): III, **99**, 8656 (*Daçarathasya putro Rāmaḥ*), 8660.—§ 391 (Ṛshyaçṛṅga): III, **110**, 10008 (*Lomapādaḥ sakhā D°sya*).—§ 525 (Rāmopākhyānap.): III, **273**, 15877 (son of Aja, husband of Kausalyā, Kaikeyī and Sumitrā, and father of four sons: Rāma on Kausalyā, Bharata on Kaikeyī, Lakshmaṇa and Çatrughna on Sumitrā).—§ 527 (do.): III, **277**, 15947, 15949, 15957, 15974, 15976 (Kaikeyī prevailed upon *D.* to let Bharata be anointed and to banish Rāma; then *D.* died).—§ 530 (Viçvāvasumokshaṇa): III, **279**, 16045 (*sakhā D°sya . . . . Jāṭāyuḥ*), 16064 (*sakhā D°sya*, i.e. Jaṭāyu). — § 543 (Rāmābhisheka): III, **291***a*, 16549, (16556) (*D.* appeared to Rāma and attested the innocence of Sītā, and commanded him to return to Ayodhyā and rule there).—§ 548*e* (Vishṇu): III, **315**, 17467 (*Vishṇunā vasatā cāpi gṛhe D°sya vai*—i.e. incarnate as Rāma Dāçarathi—*Daçagrīvo hataḥ*).—§ 746 (Ānuçāsanik.): XIII, **74**, 3616.—§ 775 (do.): XIII, **166**η, 7677.

Dāçaratha, adj. ("relating to Daçaratha"). § 621 (Rājadh.): XII, **8**, 242 (*panthāḥ*).

Daçarathātmaja = Rāma, q.v.

Dāçarathi[1] = Rāma, q.v.

Dāçarathi[2], dual (°*ī*) = Rāma and Lakshmaṇa: III, 15946 (*Rāma-Lakshmaṇau*).

Daçārdhahavirātmaka = Kṛshṇa: XII, 1630.

Daçārha, pl. (°*āḥ*), a people. § 320 (Saubhavadhop.): III, **19**, 769 (*sarva*°).—§ 402 (Tīrthayātrāp.): III, **120**, †10263 (°*senā*, will assist the Pāṇḍavas in the battle), †10287 (°*vīrāḥ*). — § 451 (Mārkaṇḍeyas.): III, **183**, †12588 (°*yodhāḥ*, will assist Yudhishṭhira), †12591 (°*yodhaiḥ*). Cf. Dāçārha, pl.

Daçārha = Vishṇu (1000 names).

Dāçārha[1] = Kṛshṇa, q.v.

Dāçārha[2] = Sātyaki, q.v.

Dāçārha, pl. (°*āḥ*), a people (= Daçārha, pl.). § 243 (Vidurāgamanap.): I, **205**, 7513 (the followers of Kṛshṇa). — § 271 (Lokapālasabhākh.): II, **12**, 511 (°*nagarīṃ*, i.e. Dvārakā). — § 553 (Vaivāhikap.): IV, **72**, 2350 (many *D.* came from the Ānartta country to Upaplavya along with Kṛshṇa and Abhimanyu). — § 554 (Sainyodyogap.): V, **7**, 171 (°*pravaraiḥ*, follow Kṛshṇa). — § 569 (Bhagavadyānap.): V, **140***a*, 4749.—§ 599 (Jayadrathavadhap.): VII, **110**, 4232 (*na hi D°ā raṇe rakshanti jīvitaṃ*, so B.; C. has *D°o . . . . . rakshati*), 4233 (*bhīrūṇām asatāṃ mārgo naisha D°sevitaḥ*; C. reads *Dāçārha* (i.e. Sātyaki) *sevitaḥ* in two words). — § 608 (Karṇap.): VIII, **65**, 3299 (*sarva-Dā°-mukhyaḥ*, i.e. Kṛshṇa).—§ 773*c* (Durvāsas): XIII, **160**, 7431 (*kecit*). Cf. Daçārha, pl.

Dāçārha, adj. ("belonging to Dāçārha, i.e. Kṛshṇa").—§ 263 (Sabhākriyāp.): II, **3**, 84 (°*ī Sudharmā*, i.e. Kṛshṇa's sabhā).

Daçārhabhartṛ = Kṛshṇa: III, †12579.

Daçārhādhipati = Kṛshṇa: III, †903.

Dāçārhakulavardhana = Kṛshṇa: XII, 1870.

Dāçārhanandana = Kṛshṇa: I, 8076.

Daçārhanātha = Kṛshṇa: VIII, †679.

Dāçārhaputraja = Dhṛshṭaketu: XI, 229 (*Cedirājaṃ*, Nil.: *atra putryāṃ api putraçabdaḥ* the mother of Dhṛshṭaketu must then have been a Daçārha rincess)).

Daçārhasiṃha = Kṛshṇa: III, †12578.

Dāçārhavīra = Kṛshṇa: V, †3303.

Dāçārhī[1] ("daughter of the Daçārha king") = Vijayā, wife of Bhumanyu: I, 3786 (*V°*).

Dāçārhī[2] ("do.") = Sudevā, wife of Vikuṇṭhana: I, 3789 (*S*°).
Dāçārhī[3] ("do.") = Çubhāṅgī, wife of Kuru: I, 3792 (*Ç*°).
Daçārṇa, pl. (°*āḥ*), a people. § 177 (Pāṇḍudigvijaya): I, **113**, 4449 (vanquished by Pāṇḍu on his digvijaya).—§ 280 (Bhīmasena): II, **29**, 1063 (in the east, vanquished by Bhīmasena on his digvijaya).—§ 285 (Nakula): II, **32**, 1189 (in the west, vanquished by Nakula on his digvijaya).—§ 350 (Nalopākhyānap.): III, **69**, 2708 (*tvam tu jātā mayā dṛshṭā* (C. °*tvā*) *D°eshu pitur gṛhe*, says Sunandā's mother, daughter of Sudāman, the king of the Daçārṇas, to Damayantī, the daughter of her sister). — § 549 (Pāṇḍavaprav.): IV, **1*a***, 12; **5**, 144 (*uttareṇa D°āṃs te Pañcālān dakshiṇena ca*).—§ 573 (Ambopākhyānap.): V, **189**, 7420 (ruled by Hiraṇyavarman). — § 574 (Jambūkh.): VI, **9***μ*, 348 (in Bhāratavarsha), 350 (do.), 363 (do., only C.; B. has *Daçāpārçva°*). — § 578 (Bhīshmavadhap.): VI, **51***τ*, 2103 (in the army of Duryodhana, followed Droṇa). — § 592 (Saṃçaptakavadhap.): VII, **26**, 1162 (*rājā D°ānāṃ*, fought Bhagadatta).—§ 605 (Karṇap.): VIII, **22***ζζ*, 864 (attacked the Pāñcālas).—§ 785 (Anugītāp.): XIV, **83**, 2470 (at the time of Yudhishṭhira's horse-sacrifice the *D.* were ruled by Citrāṅgada, who was vanquished by Arjuna).
Daçārṇa ("king of the Daçārṇas") = Hiraṇyavarman: V, 7493 (*pārthive*), 7519.
Dāçārṇa[1] (do.) = Hiraṇyavarman: V, 7445, 7468.
Dāçārṇa[2] (do.) = the king of the Daçārṇas at the time of the great battle. § 585 (Bhīshmavadhap.): VI, **95**, 4276 (fought Bhagadatta).
Daçārṇādhipati[1] (do.) = Sudāman: III, 2707 (*S*°).
Daçārṇādhipati[2] (do.) = Hiraṇyavarman: V, 7417 (°*eḥ sutāṃ*, married to Çikhaṇḍin), 7425, 7459, 7483, 7498, 7500, 7512.
Daçārṇādhipati[3] (do.), the king of the Daçārṇas at the time of the great battle. § 585 (Bhīshmavadhap.): VI, **95***δδ*, 4255 (among the Pāṇḍava warriors) (*εε*), 4271 (attacked Bhagadatta).—§ 592 (Saṃçaptakavadhap.): VII, **26**, 1164 (attacked Bhagadatta).
Dāçārṇaka, adj. ("belonging to the Daçārṇas"). § 280 (Bhīmasena): II, **29**, 1063 (°*o rājā Sudharmā*).—§ 573 (Ambopākh.): V, **189**, 7418 (°*sya nṛpateḥ*, i.e. Hiraṇyavarman, Ç. has *Da*°), 7419 (*Hiraṇyavarmeti nṛpo yo 'sau D°ḥ smṛtaḥ*), 7428 (°*o rājā*, i.e. Hiraṇyavarman); **190**, 7454 (do.); **191**, †7462 (°*e nṛpatau* = do.); **192**, 7499 (°*o rājā* = do.).
Daçārṇanṛpa ("king of the Daçārṇas") = Hiraṇyavarman: V, 7503.
Daçārṇapati (do.) = Hiraṇyavarman: V, 7464, 7509.
Daçārṇarāja (do.) = Hiraṇyavarman: V, 7430.
Dāçārṇarāja (do.) = Hiraṇyavarman: V, 7515.
Dāçārṇeça (do.), the king of the Daçārṇas at the time of the great battle. § 578 (Bhīshmavadhap.): VI, **50***π*, 2080 (in the army of Yudhishṭhira).
Dāçārṇika, adj. ("belonging to the Daçārṇas"). § 573 (Ambopākh.): V, **189**, 7424 (*dhātryaḥ*). Cf. Dāçārṇaka.
Daçāsya = Rāvaṇa, q.v.
Daçāvara, an Asura. § 268 (Varuṇasabhāv.): III, **9**, 367 (among the Daityas and Dānavas in the palace of Varuṇa).
Daçeraka, pl. (°*āḥ*), a people. § 589 (Droṇābhishek.): VII, **11***ν*, 397 (had formerly been vanquished by Kṛshṇa).—§ 592 (Saṃçaptakavadhap.): VII, **20***γ*, 798 (in the army of Duryodhana). Cf. next.
Dāçeraka, pl. (°*āḥ*), a people. § 578 (Bhīshmavadhap.): **50***π*, 2080 (°*gaṇaiḥ*, in the army of Yudhishṭhira).—§ 580 (do.): VI, **56***δ*, 2409 (°*gaṇaiḥ*, in the army of Duryodhana; C. has *Dās*°).—§ 587 (do.): VI, **117***ρ*, 5483 (°*gaṇāh*, attacked Arjuna; C. has *Dās*°). Cf. prec.
Dāçeyī ("daughter of the fisherman") = Satyavatī: I, 4015; V, 5966 (C. *Dās*°).
Daçīvidarbha, pl. (°*āḥ*), a people. § 574 (Jambūkh.): VI, **9***ν*, 372 (in the south; B. has *Ṛshīkā Vidabhāḥ*).
Dadhīca, an ancient ṛshi. § 208 (Astradarçana): I, **137**, 5430 (Indra's *vajra* had been made from the bones of *D.*).—§ 368 (Tīrthayātrāp.): III, **83**, 7057 (°*sya . . . tīrthaṃ*).—§ 378 (do.): III, **92**, 8437 (°*a iva Devendraṃ . . . tathā rakshasva*).—§ 384 (Agastyop.): III, **100**, 8695 (*mahān ṛshiḥ*), 8701 (°*syāçramaṃ*), 8706 (°*āçramaṃ*), 8707, †8709 (requested by the gods, *D.* gave up his life, then *Tvashṭṛ* made the *vajra* from his bones).—§ 615*gg* (Sārasvata): IX, **51**, 2929 (*muniḥ*; when *D.* saw the Apsaras *Alambushā* his vital seed came out; from that seed *Sārasvata* was born by the river *Sarasvatī*), 2952 (the weapons of Indra were made from *D.*'s bones; (§ 615*hh*: *D.* had been begotten by the *paramarshi Bhṛgu* (son of *Prajāpati*) by his penances; of stout limbs and great energy, *D.* was the strongest of the creatures in the world (*lokasāraḥ*) and became tall as the king of the mountains; Indra had always been afraid of his energy).—§ 717*b* (Nārāyaṇīya): XII, **343**, VII), ††13212 (*Bhārgavaḥ*), ††13213 (Dhātṛ made the *vajra* from *D.*'s bones). Cf. Dadhīci.
Dadhīci = Dadhīca. § 695*b* (Dakshayajñavināça): XII, **285**, 10283, 10288, (10293), (when Çiva had not been invited to Daksha's sacrifice, *D.* saw by his power of yoga what would happen, and warned Daksha).—§ 717*b* (Nārāyaṇīya): XII, **343**, 13268 (*D°vacanād Dakshayajñam apāharat*, sc. Rudra, all. to § 695*b*). Cf. Dadhīca.
Dadhimukha[1], a serpent. § 47 (Sarpanāmak.): I, **35**, 1553 (enumeration).—§ 564 (Mātalīyop.): V, **103***γ*, 3628 (enumeration).
Dadhimukha[2], a monkey. § 534 (Setubandhana): III, **283**, 16275 (*harivṛddhaḥ*, came to Rāma with a large army of monkeys).
Dadhivāhanapautra. § 638*b* (Rāmopākhy.): XII, **49**, 1796 (*Dadhivāhanapautras tu putro Divirathasya ca | guptas sa Gautamenāsīd Gaṅgākūle 'bhirakshitaḥ*. PCR. connects this çloka with the next (cf. Bṛhadratha[3]). According to Harivaṃça, v. 1693 foll., the grandson of Dadhivāhana and son of Diviratha is a king [of the Aṅgas?] named Dharmaratha).
Dagdharatha = Citraratha[1] (the king of the Gandharvas): I, 6475.
Dahadahā, a mātṛ. § 615*u* (Skanda): IX, **46***θ*, 2638.
Dahana[1], one of the eleven Rudras. § 108 (Aṃçāvat.): I, **66**, 2567 (son of Sthāṇu).—§ 191 (Arjuna): I, **123***a*, 4826 (present at the birth of Arjuna).
Dahana[2] = Agni, q.v.
Dahana[3], a companion of Skanda. § 615*u* (Skanda): IX, **45***δ*, 2536 (given to Skanda by Aṃça).
Dahati, a companion of Skanda. § 615*u* (Skanda): IX, **45***δ*, 2536 (given to Skanda by Aṃça).
Dāho jatugṛhasya. § 10 (Parvasaṅgr.): I, **2**, 313 (i.e. Jatugṛhaparvan).
Daiteya, pl. (°*āḥ*) ("sons or descendants of Diti"), a class of the enemies of the gods (= Daitya, pl.). § 28 (Amṛtamanthana): I, **18**, 1157 (*Dānava-D°āḥ*, after the churning of the ocean Nārāyaṇa took away the *amṛta* from them).—§ 130 (Aṃçāvat.): I, **67**, 2663 (*Çarabho nāma yas teshāṃ*

D°ānāṃ mahāsurah). — § 320 (Saubhavadhop.): III, **17**, 695 (*Saubhavāsinaḥ*, i.e. the followers of Çālva[5]); **19**, 766 (*°āstraṃ*, employed by Çālva).—§ 334 (Kairātap.): III, **41**, 1694 (*ebhis*—i.e. the nooses of Varuṇa—*tadā mayā vīra saṃgrāme Tārakāmaye | D°ānāṃ sahasrāṇi saṃyatāni mahātmanāṃ*, says Varuṇa). — § 358 (Tīrthayātrāp.): III, **82**, 5017 (*hatvā D°-Dānavān*, sc. Vishṇu).—§ 378 (do.): III, **94**, 8491 (*°ā Dānavāç ca*), 8497 (*°ān Dānavāṃç ca Kalir apy āviçat*).—§ 445 (Nivātakavacayuddhap.): III, **173**, 12215, 12220, 12223, 12226 (i.e. the inhabitants of Hiraṇyapura).— § 512 (Ghoshayātrāp.): III, **245**, 14996 (*dahyamānā . . . D°ā iva Çakreṇa*). — § 513 (do.): III, **251**, 15144 (*°-Dānavāḥ*, summoned Duryodhana into their presence). — § 564 (Mātalīyop.): V, **98**, 3536 (*hṛtarājyānāṃ*); **99**, 3557 (*atra*—i.e. in Pātāla—*te dharmaniratā baddhāḥ kālena pīḍitāḥ | D°ā nivasanti sma Vāsavena hṛtaçrayaḥ*); **105**, 3684 (*°vigrahe*).—§ 567 (Bhagavadyānap.): V, **128**, 4301, 4303, 4304 (Dharma bound the *D.* and the Dānavas and made them over to Varuṇa, who kept them within the depth of the ocean).—§ 581 (Bhīshmavadhap.): VI, **65**, 2965 (*°ānāṃ vadhāya ca*). — § 599 (Jayadrathavadhap.): VII, **122**, 4910 (*petuḥ . . . devāsure purā yuddhe yathā D°-Dānavāḥ*). — § 605 (Karṇap.): VIII, **31**, 1295 (*yathā*).—§ 608 (do.): VIII, **73**, 3690 (*purā Vishṇur iva hatvā D°-Dānavān*).—§ 611 (Çalyap.): IX, **25**, 1352 (*trailokyavijaye yuktā yathā D° - Dānavāḥ*). — § 615 (Baladevatīrthay.): IX, **43**, †2448 (*Dānavānaṃ D°ānāṃ Rākshasānāñ ca devaiḥ . . . yuddhaṃ Tārakākhyaṃ*).— § 615*u* (Skanda): IX, **46**, 2685 (*sarva-D°ā Rākshasā Dānavāḥ*, defeated by the gods commanded by Skanda).— § 632*b* (Shoḍaçarāj., cf. § 595, v. Yayāti): XII, **29**, 990 (*vyūḍhenāsurayuddhena hatvā D°-Dānavān*, sc. Yayāti). — § 650 (Āpaddh.): XII, **142**, 5442 (*°ān Uçanāḥ prāha saṃçayacchedanaṃ purā*). — § 671*b* (Bali-Vāsavas.): XII, **223**, 8074 (*°ā vyatishṭhaṃs tava*—i.e. Bali's—*çāsane*).— § 673*b* (do.): XII, **227*a***, 8266 (*Daiteyā Dānavāç caiva*, enumeration of ancient rulers of the earth).—§ 674*b* (Çrī-Vāsavas.): XII, **229**, 8360 (*hitvā D°-Dānavān*, sc. Çrī).— § 707 (Mokshadh.): XII, **319β**, 11786.—§ 768 (Ānuçāsanik.): XIII, **148**, 6899 (*Daiteyā Dānavendrāç ca . . . cakrāgnau kshayam āpannāḥ*). Cf. Asura, pl.; Daitya, pl.; Dānava, pl.; Ditija, pl.

Daiteya, sg. (cf. Daiteya[1]). Names of single Daiteyas:—

- **Açvapati**: I, 2651 (*A°*).
- **Bāṇa**: IX, 2700 (*B°*).
- **Çibi**: I, 2644 (*Ç°*).
- **Hiraṇyakaçipu**: XII, 12942 (*H°*).
- **Ilvala**: III, 8543 (*I°*), 8552 (*I°*).
- **Maya**: II, 10, 16 (*M°*).
- **Prahlāda**: XII, 8032 (*P°*).
- **Tāraka**: XIII, 4012, 4019.
- **Vegavat**: III, 675 (*V°*).
- **Vipracitti**: XII, 3661 (*V°*).
- **Virocana**: V, 1187 (*V°*).
- **Virūpāksha**: I, 2658 (*V°*).

Cf. Asura, sg.; Daitya, sg.; Dānava, sg.

Daiteya, adj. ("belonging to Diti"). § 664 (Mokshadh.): XII, **207**, 7544 (*°ī prajā*).

Daiteyāpasada = Çālva[5]: III, 796.

Daiteyī = Pulomā: III, 12203 (*P°*).

Daitya, pl. (*°āḥ*) ("sons of Diti"), a class of the enemies of the gods (= Daiteya, pl.). § 11 (Parvasaṅgr.): I, **2**, 369 (*°ānāṃ . . . samudbhavaḥ*). — § 28 (Amṛtamanthana): I, **19**, 1158 (*°-Dānavāḥ*, battled with the gods about the *amṛta*).—§ 32*b* (Garuḍa): I, **23**, 1247 (*ahito D°-Rakshasāṃ*, sc. Garuḍa).— § 84 (Ādivaṃçāvatāraṇap.): I, **64**, 2482 (*Ādityaiḥ . . . nirjitā yudhi*). — § 121 (Aṃçāvat.): I, **66**, 2607 (Uçanas became their guru).—§ 146 (Devayānī): I, **78**, 3297, 3310 (*°ānām asi gāyanaḥ*, sc. Uçanas); **80**, 3343 (*°endrāṇāṃ*); **81**, 3396. — § 147 (do.): I, **82**, 3410 (*°kanyāṃ*, i.e. Çārmishṭhā). — § 190*d* (Arjuna): I, **123**, 4801 (*Nivātakavacā nāma D°āḥ*, will be vanquished by Arjuna, cf. § 443 foll.).—§ 233 (Svayaṃvarap.): I, **187**, †7011 (came to see the svayaṃvara of Draupadī). — § 246 (Sundopasundop.): I, **209**, 7650 (*hṛshtaṃ pramuditaṃ sarvaṃ D°ānām abhavat puraṃ*), 7651; **210**, 7653, 7654 (*°senayā*); **212**, 7730 (*°gaṇaḥ*). — § 257 (Khāṇḍavadah.): I, **225**, 8198 (armed with the discus Kṛshṇa is superior to the *D.*).—§ 258 (do.): I, **227**, 8259 (*°Dānavasaṅghānāṃ cakāra kadanaṃ mahat*, sc. Kṛshṇa); **228**, 8292 (*°āḥ Kṛshṇacakravidāritāḥ*). — § 268 (Varuṇasabhāv.): II, **9**, 368 (*°Dānavasaṅghāḥ*, in the palace of Varuṇa). — § 270 (Brahmasabhāv.): II, **11**, 472 (come as guests to the palace of Brahmán).—§ 271 (Lokapālas.): II, **12**, 480 (*°endrāḥ*, in the palace of Varuṇa). — § 290 (Çiçupālavadhap.): II, **45**, 1580 (*cakraṃ D°garvanisūdanam*, sc. Kṛshṇa's).— § 317*b* (Kṛshṇa Vāsudeva): III, **12**, 478 (*avadhīs tvaṃ*—i.e. Kṛshṇa—*raṇe sarvān sametān D°Dānavān*). — § 334 (Kairātap.): III, **41**, 1669 (accompanied Varuṇa).—§ 345 (Nalopākh.): III, **56**, 2170 (*°Dānavamardanaṃ Mahendraṃ*). — § 357 (Tīrthayātrāp.): III, **82**, 4065 (had performed austerities in Pushkara and attained to godhood). — § 378 (do.): III, **94**, 8499 (*niryaçaskās tathā D°āḥ kṛtsnaço vilayaṃ gatāḥ*), 8509 (*vinaṅkshyanti Daityā iva*). — § 384 (Agastyop.): III, **101**, 8729 (*°vare*, i.e. Vṛtra); **102**, 8744 (i.e. the Kāleyas), [8758 (*Ādidaityaḥ . . . Hiraṇyakaçipuḥ*)]. — § 432 (Saugandhikāh.): III, **154**, †11390 (*sa Çakravad Dānava - D°saṅghān vikramya*). — § 443 (Nivātakavacayuddhap.): III, **168**, 12074 (*sahasrāṇi prayutāny arbudāny api rathenānena D°ānāṃ jitavān Maghavā yudhi*).—§ 444 (do.): III, **169**, 12085 (*°puraṃ*); **171**, 12137 (i.e. the Nivātakavacas); **172**, 12162, 12165, 12186 (*°nāryaḥ*).—§ 445 (do.): III, **173**, 12202 (*°ānāṃ puraṃ*, i.e. Hiraṇyapura), 12222 (i.e. the inhabitants of Hiraṇyapura).—§ 453 (Mārkaṇḍeyas.): III, **183**, 12610.—§ 459 (do.): III, **188**, 12925 (seen by Mārkaṇḍeya in the stomach of Nārāyaṇa); **189**, 12977 (are slain when born among men, by the incarnate Nārāyaṇa [Vishṇu]). — § 474*b* (Dhundhumārop.): III, **201**, 13503 (*°endrāḥ parābhūtāḥ*, sc. by Vishṇu).—§ 476 (do.): III, **202**, 13534 (*avadhyo devatānāṃ hi D°ānāṃ atha*, etc., sc. Dhundhu). — § 495 (Skandotpatti): III, **224**, 14264 (*jetā yo dushṭa-D°ānāṃ*). — § 502 (Manushyagrahak.): III, **230**, 14483 (*°ānāṃ yā Ditir mātā*). — § 507 (Skandayuddha): III, **231**, 14588, 14589, 14595 (*°balāt*), 14603, 14605, 14608 (*°senā*), 14614 (*°gaṇāḥ*, battle with the gods). — § 513 (Ghoshayātrāp.): III, **251**, 15150 (summoned Duryodhana into their presence); **252**, 15172 (*°Rakshogaṇān*, re-born as warriors in the great battle), 15177 (re-born as the Saṃçaptakas), 15181. — § 514 (do.): III, **252**, 15198.—§ 522 (Draupadīharaṇap.): III, **265**, †15589 (Koṭika believes Draupadī to be a *Daityavarāṅganā*); **270**, †15710 (*°senāsu*). — § 524*d* (Vishṇu): III, **272**, 15834 (*°ānām ādipurushaḥ*, i.e. Hiraṇyakaçipu).—

§ 526 (Rāmopākhyānap.): III, **275**, 15927 (°*ānāṃ devānāñ ca balotkaṭaḥ ākramya ratnāny aharat*, sc. Rāvaṇa).—§ 533 (Sītā-Rāvaṇas.): III, **281**, 16175 (°*ānāṃ . . . yoshitaḥ*, wives of Rāvaṇa). — § 542 (Rāvaṇavadha): III, **290**, 16510 (°-*Dānavān*, had been slain by Indra). — § 547 (Karṇa): III, **310**, 17201.—§ 548*e* (Vishṇu): III, **315**, 17461 (*vadhārthaṃ D°ānāṃ*).—§ 552 (Goharaṇap.): IV, **58**, 1887 (*jetāraṃ deva-D°ānāṃ*, i.e. Arjuna).—§ 554*b* (Vishṇu): V, **10**, 297 (had been slain by Vishṇu).—§ 554 (Indravijaya): V, **14**, 445 (°*Dānavasūdana*, i.e. Indra, C. has by error °*aṃ*.).—§ 556 (Sañjayayānap.): V, **22**, †676 (*nirdahetām Indrā-Vishṇū* (*Indro Vishṇur*, C.) *D°senāṃ yathaiva*). — § 561*d* (Nara-Nārāyaṇau): V, **49**, 1929 (*Çakro vijigye D°-Dānavān*).—§ 564 (Mātalīyop.): V, **98**, 3538 (°*jātyaḥ*); **99**, 3547 (*Pātālaṃ . . . D°-Dānavasevitaṃ*); **100**, 3567 (in Hiraṇyapura), 3580.—§ 565 (Gālavac.): V, **110**, 3805 (*atra*—i.e. in the west—*paçcāt kṛtā D°ā Vāyunā saṃyatās tadā | niçvasanto mahāvātair arditāḥ sushupur dvija*). —§ 574 (Jambūkh.): VI, **6**, 216 (only B.: *tasya*—i.e. Meru's—*mūrdhany Uçanāḥ Kāvyo D°aiḥ*—C.: *divi*).—§ 576 (Bhagavadgītāp.): VI, **20**, †745 (°*endraseneva*); **34**, 1234 (*Prahlādaç cāsmi D°ānāṃ*, says Kṛshṇa).—§ 579 (Bhīshmavadhap.): VI, **54**, 2245 (*yathendrasya . . . D°senayā*). —§ 580 (do.): VI, **59**, 2576 (*Bhīshmo nāçayet D°-Dānavān*). § 581 (do.): VI, **66**, 2981 (°-*Danava-Rākshasāḥ*, were re-born among men).—§ 583 (do.): VI, **77**, †3381 (*yadvat*); **80**, †3522 (*sadeva-D°āṃl lokān*). — § 584 (do.): VI, **83**, 3695 (*abhidudrāvatuḥ . . . yathā D°camūṃ rājan Indropendrāv ivāmarau*); **85**, †3768 (*viddhāḥ . . . devā yathā D°gaṇaiḥ*). — § 585 (do.): VI, **87**, 3878 (*yathā D°-devasene*); **90**, 4063 (?, *saṅgrāme D°saṅkāçe*).—§ 586 (do.): VI, **107**, 4924 (°-*Dānavaiḥ*).—§ 587 (do.): VI, **118**, 5546 (*yathā D°camūṃ Çakras tāpayām āsa*).—§ 589 (Droṇābhishek.): VII, **11**, 395 (°*puraṃ Saubhaṃ*). — § 592 (Saṃçaptakavadhap.): VII, **21**, 891 (*yathā D°gaṇe Vishṇuḥ*, sc. *cakāra kadanaṃ*).—§ 596 (Pratijñāp.): VII, **79**, 2798 (°-*Dānavadarpahā*, i.e. Indra); **80**, 2838 (had been slain by Çiva with the Pāçupata weapon).—§ 599 (Jayadrathavadhap.): VII, **126**, 5125; **148**, †6444 (*Çatakratau . . . jaghnushi D°-Dānavān*); **149**, 6464 (*Çakro hatvā D°ān*). — § 600 (Ghaṭotkacavadhap.): VII, **158**, 7021; **159**, 7073 (*Çakraṃ D°ā yathā purā*), 7088 (*Çakraṃ D°camūm iva*); **160**, 7143 (*Indro D°vadhe yathā*), **162**, 7227 (*yathendraṃ . . . D°vadhodyataṃ*).—§ 601 (Droṇavadhap.): VII, **185**, 8131 (had been slain by Arjuna).—§ 603*d* (Tripura): VII, **202**, 9560.—§ 605 (Karṇap.): VIII, **16**, 621 (*trailokyavijaye yadvad D°ānāṃ saha Vajriṇā*); **19**, 716 (do.), 734 (°*ān Indra ivāvadhīt*); **25**, 1035 (*yathā D°camūṃ . . . Devarājo mamarda*). — § 605*c* (Vijaya): **31**, 1293 (°*gaṇān . . . jitavān vai Çatakratuḥ*).—§ 606 (Tripurākhyāna): VIII, **33**, 1394 (*saṅgrāmas Tārakāmayaḥ | nirjitāç ca tato D°āḥ*), 1395, 1400 (*Mayaṃ . . . D°-Dānavapujitam*), 1412 (*trayas te D° rājānaḥ*, i.e. Tārakāksha, Kamalāksha, and Vidyunmālin), 1420; **34**, 1548, 1550 (*Tripuraṃ . . . D°-Dānavarakshitam*). — § 606*b* (Paraçu-Rāma): VIII, **34**, 1595, 1604, 1605, 1606 (were slain by Rāma Jāmadagnya).— § 608 (Karṇap.): VIII, **53**, 2588 (*yathendraḥ samare D°āṃs Tārakasya vadhe purā*); **60**, 2983 (*niruddhā . . . jihīrshavo 'mṛtam D°āḥ Çakrāgnibhyām ivāsakṛt*), 3009 (*Çakreṇa yathā D°ān hanyamānān*); **79**, †4054 (had been slain by Arjuna); **82**, †4204 (*yuyudhe . . . digīçvarair D°patir yathā*).—§ 611 (Çalyap.): IX, **14**, 752 (*Çatakrator yathā pūrvaṃ mahatyā D°senayā*, sc. *vimardaḥ*); **20**, †1071 (*yathā*); **24**, †1337 (*jaghāna D°ān iva Vajrapāṇiḥ*).—§ 612 (Hradapraveçap.): IX, **31**, 1750 (*Indreṇa nihatā D°-Dānavāḥ*), 1757 (*hatāḥ*). — § 615 (Baladevatīrthay.): IX, **39**, 2252 (°-*Dānavavigrahaṃ*); **43**, 2449 (°*āntakartā*, i.e. Skanda); **44**, 2452 (°*ānāṃ . . . kadanaṃ*).—§ 615*u* (Skanda): IX, **45**, 2529; **46**, 2673, 2681, 2692, 2697, 2707, 2712 (battle between the *D.* and the gods), 2722 (°*kulāntakaḥ*, i.e. Skanda). — § 615 (Baladevatīrthay.): IX, **47**, 2730. — § 615*gg* (Sārasvata): IX, **51**, 2960 (°-*Dānavavīrāṇāṃ jaghāna navatīr nava*, sc. Indra).—§ 615 (Gadāyuddhap.): IX, **55**, 3120 (°*āv iva*).—§ 616 (Sauptikap.): X, **4**, 156 (°*senām iva kruddhaḥ sarva-Dānavasūdanaḥ*).— § 623 (Rājadh.): XII, **12**, †369 (*Çakro yathā D°balāni saṅkhye*).—§ 635 (do.): XII, **33**, 1186 (*jaghnur D°āṃs tathā devāḥ*), †189 (*devair D°ā ivolvaṇāḥ*).—§ 637 (do.): XII, **47**θ, 1662.—§ 656 (Khaḍgotpattik.): XII, **166**γ, 6147 (°-*Dānavāḥ*, eight are enumerated).—§ 660*b* (Bhṛgu-Bharadvājasaṃv.): XII, **188**β, 6937.—§ 666 (Mokshadh.): XII, **209**, 7620, 7625 (°-*Dānavān*, destroyed by Vishṇu when incarnate as a boar). — § 671*b* (Bali-Vāsavasaṃv.): XII, **225**, 8177 (*rājā D°ānāṃ Baliḥ*).—§ 673*b* (do.): XII, **227**, 8218 (°-*Dānavasaṃkshaye*), 8267 (°*endrāḥ*, had formerly ruled the earth).—§ 674*b* (Çrī-Vāsavasaṃv.): XII, **229**, 8360 (°-*Dānavān*, deserted by Çrī).—§ 693*b* (Vṛtravadha): XII, **282**, 10119 (°*āsuranibarhaṇa*, i.e. Indra).—§ 717*b* (Nārāyaṇīya): XII, **344**γγ, 13365; **350**, 13666 (°-*Dānava-Gandharva-Rākshasagaṇasamākulā . . . vasumatī*), 13667 (°-*Dānava-Rākshasāḥ*). — § 723 (Ānuçāsanik.): XIII, **6***a*, 312.—§ 730*g* (Upamanyu): XIII, **14**, 734 (Çiva assumes the form of *D.* and Dānavas), 796 (°-*Dānavamukhyānāṃ*), 798 (do.): (ν), 820 (°*eçvarāḥ*). — § 736*b* (Vītahavyop.): XIII, **30**, 1998 (attacked Gṛtsamada, believing him to be Indra).—§ 746 (Ānuçāsanik.): XIII, **81**, 3842 (*parābhavāc ca D°ānāṃ*); **82**, 3856 (deserted by Çrī); **83**, 3885 (*parābhūteshu*).—§ 754 (do.): XIII, **98**, 4683 (*Brahmarshi-deva-D°ānāṃ*, sc. *kathāḥ*), 4717 (°*ānāṃ sallakīyaç ca kāṅkshitaḥ*).— § 766 (do.): XIII, **126**, 6015 (*cakreṇa nihatāḥ*).—§ 772*k* (Agastya): XIII, **156**, 7273 (burnt by Agastya).—§ 772*l* (Vasishṭha): XIII, **156**, 7289 (slain by Vasishṭha). — § 773*b* (Kṛshṇa Vāsudeva): XIII, **159**, †7364 (*sa*—i.e. Kṛshṇa—*eva pūrvaṃ nijaghāna D°ān*), †7371. — § 773*d* (Çiva): XIII, **161**, 7485 (in Tripura).—§ 778*b* (Saṃvartta-Maruttīya): XIV, **5**, 115 (*tvam*—i.e. Indra—*ājahartha D°ānām eko vīraçriyaṃ parām*). — § 784*b* (Uttaṅka): XIV, **54**, 1566.—§ 785 (Anugītāp.): XIV, **60**, 1785 (*Kāvyo D°pater iva*, sc. *senāpatiḥ*).—§ 793 (Mausalap.): XIV, **6**κ, 153. Cf. Asura, pl.; Daitya, pl.; Dānava, pl.; Ditija, pl.

Daitya, sg. (cf. Daitya, pl.). § 450 (Ājagarap.): III, **180**, 12458 (Yudhishṭhira asks the *ajagara* if he is a *D.*).—§ 730*d* (Sudarçana): XIII, **14**, 666 (Çiva slew a *D.* who lived in the water).—Names of single Daityas:—

Bali: XII, 8080, 8225.
Çambara: III, †10271 (*Ç°*).
Dhundhu: III, 13544, 13551, 13612, 13623 (*Dhundhur nāma mahā-D°aḥ*).
Ilvala: III, 8631.
Maya: III, 16237 (*M°*).
Namuci: VI, 3678 (*N°ir D°-sattamaḥ*).
Naraka: III, 10914 (*N°*), 10915.
Prahlāda: II, 2320; XII, 4568 (*P°*).
Rāhu: I, 1165.

Tāraka: VII, 6718 (*T°aṃ D°-sattamaṃ*); IX, 1754 (*Tārakaç ca mahā-D°aḥ*); XIII, 4181 (*T°*).
Vātāpi: III, 8542.
Vṛshaparvan: I, 3337.
Vṛtra: VII, 3457 (*V°*); XII, 10002 (*V°*), 10031, 10046, †10055, †10059, †10061, †10066, 10138, 10148, 10151 (*V°*).
Cf. Asura, Daiteya, Dānava.

Daitya, adj. ("belonging to the Daityas"). § 743*b* (Vipulop.): XIII, **40*a***, 2281 (*vapuḥ*).

Daitya, dual (°*au*) = Sunda and Upasunda: I, 7622, 7656, 7678, 7711.

Daityadvīpa, a Suparṇa, son of Garuḍa. § 564 (Mātalīyop.): V, **101**β, 3596 (enumeration).

Daityahan = Çiva (1000 names[2]).

Daityakanyā = Çarmishṭhā: I, 3410.

Daityanāçana = Kṛshṇa: XII, 1526.

Daityanibarhaṇa = Indra: XVII, 108.

Daityapa ("king of the Daityas") = Bali: XIII, 4698.

Daityapati[1] (do.) = Prahlāda: XII, 8056.

Daityapati[2] (do.) = Vṛtra: XII, 10128.

Daityasattama[1] = Namuci: VI, 3678 (*N°*).

Daityasattama[2] = Tāraka: VII, 6718 (*T°*).

Daityasenā ("the army of the Daityas"), daughter of Prajāpati and sister of Devasenā. § 495 (Skandotpatti): III, **224**, 14257, 14259 (robbed by the Asura Keçin).

Daityeçvara = Bali: XII, 8153.

Daityendra[1] = Bali: IX, 2708 (°*sya sutaṃ*, slain by Skanda); XII, 8182, 8185 (*B°*), 8224; XIII, 4690.

Daityendra[2] = Hiraṇyakaçipu: III, 15834, 15838.

Daityendra[3] = Ilvala: III, 8619 (*I°*).

Daityendra[4] = Naraka: III, 10923 (*N°*).

Daityendra[5] = Nikumbha: I, 7620 (*N°*).

Daityendra[6] = Prahlāda: II, 2315 (*P°*); III, 1030 (*P°*); XII, 4588, 4590, 4592, 4600, 4606, 8057.

Daityendra[7] = Tāraka: IX, 2691.

Daityendra[8] = Virocana: V, 1187.

Daityendra[9] = Vṛtra: XII, 10054.

Daityendra[10], dual (°*au*) = Sunda and Upasunda: I, 7641, 7645.

Daivakīnandana = Vishṇu, v. Devakīnandana.

Daivarāti = Janaka: XII, 11546 (*J°*), 11819.

Daivayāneya ("son of Devayānī") = Yadu: I, 3163.

Daksha[1] **(Prācetasa)**, a Prajāpati. § 3 (Anukram.): I, **1**, 33 (*Prācetasas tathā D°o D°putrāç ca sapta vai*, came out of the primordial egg). — § 87 (Aṃçāvat.): I, **65**, 2519 (thirteen daughters of *D.*, viz. Aditi, etc., married to Kaçyapa). — § 115 (Aṃçāvat.): I, **66**, 2574 (*D.* sprung from the right toe of Brahmán, and his wife from the left toe of Brahmán. *D.* had lost his sons (*nashṭaputraḥ*), (cf. § 138), but had 50 daughters, whom he made his *putrikāḥ*; 10 of them were married to Dharma, 27 to Indu, i.e. the Moon, 13 to Kaçyapa).—§ 136 (Yayātyup.): I, **75**, 3126 (*Prajāpateḥ*). — § 137 (Sambhavap.): Prācetas had 10 sons (*mukhajenāgninā yais te pūrvaṃ dagdhā mahaujasaḥ*, PCR. seems to have followed a different reading), from them sprang the muni *Daksha Prācetasa*, and from him the creatures (*sa hi Lokapitāmahaḥ*): I, **75**, 3130 (*Prācetasaḥ*). — § 138 (do.): *Daksha* had from his wife *Vīriṇī* 1,000 sons, whom *Nārada* taught the *Sāṅkhya* as a means of salvation (*moksham adhyāpayām āsa Sāṅkhya-jñānam anuttamaṃ*). Then *Daksha* made his 50 daughters his *putrikāḥ*, and bestowed 10 of them to Dharma, etc. (cf. § 115); I, **75**, 3131 (*Prācetasaḥ*), 3132 (°*putrān*).—§ 156 (Pūruv.): I, **95**, 3760 (father of Aditi).—§ 164 (Āpavop.): I, **99**, 3927 (°*sya duhitā . . . Surabhī*).—§ 191 (Arjuna): I, **123*a***, 4808 (*Prajāpatiḥ*, came to see the birth of Arjuna). — § 270 (Brahmasabhāv.): II, **11**, 436 (*Pracetāḥ*?, in the palace of Brahmán).—§ 410 (Plakshāvataraṇag.): III, **130**, 10537 (performed a sacrifice at Sarasvatī and pronounced a blessing on the spot).—§ 439 (Yakshayuddhap.): III, **163**, 11854 (the seventh of Brahmán's spiritual sons). — § 496 (Skandotpatti): III, **224**, 14295 (Svāhā was daughter of *D.*).—§ 503 (Skandayuddha): III, **231**, 14516 (°*sya . . . kanyā Svāhā*). —§ 508 (Kārttikeyastava): III, **232**, 14643 (Skanda is identified with *D.*).—§ 564 (Mātalīyop.): V, **105**, 3683 (Garuḍa says: *mamāpi D°sya sutā jananī*, i.e. Vinatā).—§ 581 (Bhīshmavadhap.): VI, **68**ρ, 3040 (*Prajāpatiṃ*, Kṛshṇa is identified with *D.*).—§ 603 (Nārāyaṇāstramoksh.): VII, **202**, 9544 (his sacrifice is destroyed by Çiva, cf. § 695*b*). — § 615 (Prabhāsotpattik.): IX, **35**, 2013 (°*sya tanayāḥ*, twenty-seven in number, married to Soma, i.e. the Moon), 2020, 2021, 2025, 2026, 2042, 2053 (how Soma was cursed by *D.*).—§ 615*i* (Saptasārasvata): IX, **38**, 2213 (performed a sacrifice at Gaṅgādvāra).—§ 615*u* (Skanda): IX, **45**γ, 2512.—§ 617 (Aishīkap.): X, **17**θ, 744 (*sapta D°ādīn Prajāpatīn*, created by the second creator).—§ 628 (Rājadh.): XII, **23**, 666 (°*aḥ Prācetaso yathā*), 695 (do.).—§ 637 (do.): XII, **47**γ, 1597 (among the ṛshis who surrounded Bhīshma, as he lay on his arrow-bed). — § 656*c* (Khaḍgotpattik.): *Daksha* begat sixty daughters, who were all taken as wives by Brahmarshis; from them sprung all creatures (*bhūtāni*): D., P.-gaṇāḥ, G., Aps., diverse kinds of Rā., birds and animals and fishes, etc., and vegetables, and all beings that are oviparous or viviparous or born of filth: XII, **166**, 6136 (*Prācetasaḥ*).—§ 664 (Mokshadh.): XII, **207**δ, 7534 (the seventh of Brahmán's spiritual sons), 7536 (*Prajāpatiḥ*, sprung from the toe of Brahmán), 7539 (his daughters and their offspring). — § 665 (do.): XII, **208**, 7573 (son of the ten Prācetases, and also named Ka). — § 673*b* (Bali-Vāsavasaṃv.): XII, **227*a***, 8262 (among the ancient rulers of earth).—§ 694*b* (Jvarotpatti): XII, **284**, 10226 (*Prajāpatiḥ*, his sacrifice), 10232. — § 695 (Mokshadh.): XII, **285**, 10272 (*Prācetasasya*), 10273.—§ 695*b* (Dakshayajñavināça): XII, **285**, 10275, 10276, (10292), 10294, (†10295), 10303, 10304, 10309, 10323 (*Prajāpatiḥ*), 10329, 10331, 10340 (*Prajāpatiḥ*), 10345 (having not been invited, Çiva destroyed *D.*'s sacrifice, then *D.* praised Çiva).—§ 696 (Mokshadh.): XII, **285**, 10346 (*Prajāpatiḥ*). — § 696*b* (Dakshaprokta-Çiva-sahasranāmastotra): XII, **285**, 10461, 10462, 10465, 10470, 10472 (Daksha hymned Çiva by enumerating Çiva's 1,000 names, etc.).—§ 714*n* (Parāvaha): XII, **329**, 12415 (*yaṃ*—i.e. Parāvaha—*samāsādya vegena diço 'ntaṃ pratipedire | Dakshasya daça putrāṇāṃ sahasrāṇi Prajāpateḥ*). — § 717*b* (Nārāyaṇīya): XII, **335*a***, 12685 (among the twenty-one *Prajāpatis*); **343**, IV), ††13206 (caused a third eye to appear on the forehead of Çiva); XI), ††13219 (repetition from IX, ch. **35**), (ω), 13267 (°*yajñaḥ*), 13268, 13269 (°*yajñaṃ*); **349**, VII), 13596 (*D.* had sixty daughters, the ten last of which were married to Manu).—§ 730 (Ānuçāsanik.): XIII, **14**ββ, 991 (in the abode of Çiva).—§ 746 (do.): XIII, **77**, 3706 (gave a bull to Çiva); **83**, 3906 (°*sya duhitā . . . Surabhī*).—§ 768*b* (Kṛshṇa Vāsudeva): XIII, **147**, 6830 (*Prajāpatiḥ*, son of Pracetas).—

§ 773*d* (Çiva): XIII, **161,** 7468 (*Prajāpateḥ*, his sacrifice is destroyed by Çiva, cf. § 603 and § 695*b*). — § 778*b* (Saṃvartta-Maruttīya): XIV, **5,** 94 (*Asurāç caiva devāç ca D°syāsan Prajāpateḥ | apatyam*).—§ 785 (Anugītāp.): XIV, **88,** 2634 (*çuçubhe cayanaṃ tatra D°asyeva Prajāpateḥ*). Cf. Prajāpati, Prācetasa.

Daksha[2], a Suparṇa, son of Garuḍa. § 564 (Mātalīyop.): V, **101**β, 3597 (enumeration).

Daksha[3] = Skanda: III, 14643.

Daksha[4] = Çiva (1000 names[2]).

Daksha[5], a Viçvadeva. § 749 (Ānuçāsanik.): XIII, **91**γ, 4360 (enumeration).

Daksha[6] = Vishṇu (1000 names).

Daksha[7], a king (perhaps = Daksha[1]). § 775 (Ānuçāsanik.): XIII, **166**η, 7679.

Dakshaduhitṛ ("daughter of Daksha") = Svāhā: III, 14295 (*S*°).

Dakshakanyā (do.): Kadrū: I, 2521 (*K*°).

Dakshakratuhara ("destroyer of Daksha's sacrifice"): X, 253; XII, 13149; XIII, 6565.

Dakshaprokta-Çivasahasranāmastotra ("the 1008 names by which Çiva was praised by Daksha"). § 696*b* (Mokshadh.): Daksha praised Çiva by enumerating his 1008 names (i.e. Çivasahasranāmastotra), and adding some further praises. *Çiva* became gratified and granted *Daksha* some further boons (among those the benefits of the *Paçupata* religion); then Çiva disappeared. Blessing to the reader.

Dakshayāgāpahārin = Çiva (1000 names[2]).

Dakshayajñanibarhaṇa ("destroyer of Daksha's sacrifice") = Çiva: VII, 9529.

Dakshayajñavināça (do.) = Çiva: III, 1627.

[**Daksha-yajña - vināça(ḥ)**] ("the destruction of Daksha's sacrifice"). § 695*b* (Mokshadh.): Vaiçampāyana(!) said: In days of yore *Daksha* made arrangements for performing a sacrifice on the top of *Himavat* in that sacred region inhabited by Ṛ. and Si., G. and Aps., where the *Gaṅgā* issues out of the mountains. The gods, etc. (*a*), came there. Ṛ. *Dadhīca* in wrath and grief said that this was no sacrifice, since *Rudra* (Çiva) was not adored in it, etc.; he, the great *yogin*, saw into the future; he beheld *Çiva* seated with *Nārada* and *Umā*. *Daksha* said he knew the eleven *Rudras* with lances and matted locks, but he did not know who this *Maheçvara* was. *Daksha* said that he would perform the sacrifice unto Vishṇu. Umā felt grief. *Çiva* said that it is to him as the Lord of Sacrifices that the chanters utter their praises in sacrifices, etc. (β). Then he created from his mouth a terrible being (description), and *Umā* herself, assuming the terrible form of *Mahākālī*, proceeded in the company of that being, that was the living embodiment of *Çiva's* wrath and resembled *Çiva* himself, and came to be called *Vīrabhadra*. He then created from the pores of his body a large number of spirit-chiefs named *Raumyas*. These *Rudras* attacked the sacrifice (description; Ṛ., D., and men looked pale) and began to set fire to everything, and tore off the head of the sacrifice. D. and *Brahmán* and *Daksha*, informed by *Vīrabhadra*, hymned *Çiva* (γ), who, asked by *Daksha*, granted to him the boon that his sacrificial articles should be of use to him. Then Daksha knelt down and uttered his 1008 names (v. Daksha-prokta-Çiva-sahasranāmastotra).

Dakshayajñavināçana = Çiva: VII, 3464, 9593.

Dākshāyaṇī[1] ("daughter of Daksha") = Aditi: I, 3135 (mother of the Ādityas); III, 14261 (mother of Indra).

Dākshāyaṇī[2] (do.) = Surabhi: XII, 6432 (*S*°).

Dākshāyaṇī[3] (do.) = Vinatā: I, 1459 (*V*°).

Dākshāyaṇī[4] (do.) = the mother of Rājadharman (Nāḍījaṅgha). § 658*b* (Kṛtaghnop.): XII, **170,** 6343.

Dākshāyaṇī[5], dual (°*yau*) = Kadrū and Vinatā: I, 1227 (*Kadrūçca Vinatā caiva*).

Dākshāyaṇī[6], pl. (°*yaḥ*). § 565 (Gālavac.): V, **108,** 3766 (*atra*—i.e. in the east—*pūrvaṃ prasūtā vai D°yaḥ prajāḥ striyaḥ*). — § 673*b* (Bali-Vāsavasamv.): XII, **227,** 8274 (°*putrāḥ Prājāpatyāḥ*).

Dākshāyaṇya ("son of the daughter of Daksha") = Āditya (the Sun): XIII, 6831.

Dāksheyī ("daughter of the daughter of Daksha") = Çukī: XIII, 227.

Dakshiṇa = Çiva (1000 names[2]). Do.[2] = Vishṇu (1000 names).

Dakshiṇāpatha, the land in south (Dekhan). § 281 (Sahadeva): II, **31,** 1121.—§ 347 (Nalopākhyānap.): III, **61,** 2317, 2319. — § 555 (Sainyodyogap.): V, **19,** 593 (°*vāsibhiḥ*, i.e. the subjects of king Nīla).—§ 664 (Mokshadh.): XII, **207**η, 7559 (°*gāminyaḥ*—so C.; B. has °*janmānaḥ*—i.e. the Āndhrakas, etc.).

Dakshiṇāpatha, pl. (°*āḥ*) ("the inhabitants of Dakshiṇāpatha"). § 576 (Bhagavadgītāp.): VI, **15,** 604 (in Duryodhana's army). Cf. Dākshiṇātya, pl.

Dākshiṇātya, pl. (°*āḥ*) ("the Southerners"). § 515 (Karṇadigvijaya): III, **254,** 15247 (i.e. the subjects of Rukmin).—§ 561 (Yānasandhip.): V, **57,** 2245 (assigned to Bhīmasena as his share of the foes).—§ 571 (Ulūkadūtāgamanap.): V, **160**γ, †5510 (in Duryodhana's army); **161,** †5555 (do.). — § 585 (Bhīshmavadhap.): VI, **87**β, 3852 (followed Bhīshma). — § 589 (Droṇābhishekap.): VII, **7**ζ, 184 (followed Karṇa); **11**ν, 397 (had formerly been vanquished by Kṛshṇa). — § 599 (Jayadrathavadhap.): VII, **113**χ, 4412 (*Sūtaputrapurogamāḥ*).—§ 604 (Karṇap.): VIII, **5**ζ, 138 (have been slain by Arjuna).—§ 605 (do.): VIII, **20**δδ, 780 (slain by the Pāṇḍya king); **22**ζζ, 863 (attacked the Pāñcālas).—§ 607 (do.): VIII, **45,** 2098 (*vṛshalāḥ*).—§ 608 (do.): VIII, **70**πππ, †3511 (have been slain), (ρρρ), †3524 (do.).—§ 609 (Çalyap.): IX, **1**γ, 28 (do.).—§ 641 (Rājadh.): XII, **101**π, 3737 (*asipāṇayaḥ*). Cf. next.

Dākshiṇātya, adj. ("belonging to the Southerners"). § 186 (Vyushitāçvop.): I, **121,** 4690 (*nṛpatīn*, vanquished by Vyushitaçva).—§ 401 (Balarāma): XII, **119,** †10254 (*mahīpān*, had been vanquished by Sahadeva). — § 512 (Ghoshayātrāp.): III, **237,** 14774 (*rājānaḥ*, tributary to Yudhishṭhira).—§ 556 (Sañjayayānap.): V, **30,** †890 (sc. *rājānaḥ*, in Duryodhana's army).—§ 573 (Ambopākhyānap.): V, **195**ζ; 7608 (*nṛpāḥ*, do.).—§ 599 (Jayadrathavadhap.): VII, **93,** 3369 (*nṛpāḥ*, attacked Arjuna); **111,** 4267 (*mahārathāḥ*); **113,** 4408 (*balam*). Cf. prec.

Dākshiṇātya, sg. ("the king of the Southerners"). § 295 (Dyutap.): II, **53,** 1914.

Dākshiṇātyapati (do.) = Bhīshmaka: V, 5351 (°*eḥ putro Rukmī*).

Dakshiṇāyanamṛtyu, pl. (*āvaḥ*) ("who have died during the sun's progress towards the south"). § 267 (Yamasabhāv.): II, **8,** 342.

Dala, son of king Parikshit of Ayodhyā, and Suçobhanā the daughter of the frog-king. § 461 (Vāmadevacarita): III, **192,** ††13178, †13197, †13198, †13199, †13203.

Dālbhya[1] = Baka: II, 106 (*B*°); III, 968 (*B*°), 984 (*B*°), (16874) (the same?); IX, 2317 (*B*°), 2318 (*B*°), 2322 (*B*°), 2325, 2330 (*B*°; C. has by error *Dānbhyaḥ*).

Dālbhya², a tīrtha. § 377 (Dhaumyatīrthak.): III, **90**, 8383 (in the north).
Dālbhya³, a ṛshi named together with Baka. § 462 (Baka-Çakrasaṃv.): III, **193**, 13214 (*Baka-D°au*).
Dālbhyaghosha, a tīrtha. § 377 (Dhaumyatīrthak.): III, **90**, 8383 (in the north).
Dama¹, son of Bhīma, the Vidarbha king. § 344 (Nalopākhyānap.): III, **53**, 2080.
Dama², a ṛshi. § 734 (Ānuçāsanik.): XIII, **26a**, 1762.
Dama³ = Vishṇu (1000 names).
Dāmacandra, a Pāṇḍava warrior. § 600 (Ghaṭotkacavadhap.): VII, **158χ**, 7009.
Damaghoshasuta = Çiçupāla, q.v.
Damaghoshātmaja = Çiçupāla, q.v.
Dāmagranthi, the name which Nakula assumed in the palace of Virāṭa. § 551 (Kīcakavadhap.): IV, **19**, 599.—§ 552 (Goharaṇap.): IV, **31**, 1020. Cf. Granthika.
Damana¹, an ancient king. § 5 (Anukram.): I, **1a**, 224 (in Nārada's enumeration).
Damana², a Brahmarshi. § 344 (Nalopākhyānap.): III, **53**, 2077 (*Brahmarshiḥ*), 2079 (granted the Vidarbha king Bhīma that he should have three sons and a daughter).
Damana³, son of the Vidarbha king Bhīma. § 344 (Nalopākhyānap.): III, **53**, 2080 (second son of Bhīma).
Damana⁴, a Kuru warrior. § 581 (Bhīshmavadhap.): VI, **61⁴ε**, 2699 (*dāyādaṃ Pauravasya*, slain by Dhrshṭadyumna).
Damana⁵ = Çiva (1000 names ²).
Damana⁶ = Vishṇu (1000 names).
Damayantī¹, daughter of the Vidarbha king Bhīma, wife of Nala and mother of Indrasena and Indrasenā. § 11 (Parvasaṅgr.): I, **2**, 436.—§ 240 (Vaivāhikap.): I, **199**, 7351 (°*ī yathā Nale*).—§ 344 (Nalop.): III, **53**, 2080 (her birth according to a boon granted by Damana), 2081, 2087, 2092, 2094, 2097, 2098, 2102.—§ 345 (do.): III, **54**, 2104, 2105, 2108, 2109, 2111, 2113, 2124 (*Vidarbharājño duhitā*), 2130; **55**, 2137, 2139, 2145, 2153; **56**, 2172, 2177, 2183, 2184; **57**, 2192, 2198, 2212, 2220, 2223, 2230, 2231, 2236, 2237 (married to Nala, and mother of Indrasena and Indrasenā).—§ 346 (do.): III, **58**, 2241, 2245; **59**, 2265; **60**, 2272, 2279, 2282, 2292.—§ 347 (do.): III, **61**, 2299, 2303, 2307, 2313, 2320, 2321, 2326, (2328); **62**, 2335, 2338, 2339, 2340, 2345, 2347, 2352; **63**, 2362, 2392, 2396, 2398; **64**, (2413), 2425, 2433 (*Vidarbharājatanayām*), 2443, 2460, 2467, 2484, 2491, 2497 (*Vīrasenanṛpasnushā*), 2499 (*Bhīmasutā*), 2504, 2510, 2521; **65**, 2550, 2560, 2574, 2583, 2598, 2606, 2607.—§ 348 (do.): III, **66**, 2608.—§ 349 (do.): III, **67**, 2652.—§ 350 (do.): III, **68**, 2655, 2657, 2684, 2693; **69**, 2694, 2696, 2697, 2704, 2709, 2710, 2719, (2722), 2725, 2728, 2743.—§ 351 (do.): III, **70**, 2745, 2757, 2765, 2767; **71**, 2772, 2774.—§ 353 (do.): III, **73**, 2855, (2859), 2885, 2889; **74**, 2894, 2895, 2897, 2920; **75**, 2921, 2926, 2927, 2929, 2939, 2943; **76**, 2951, 2952, 2957, 2958, 2959, 2965, 2975, (2976), 2992, 2996, 3002, 3003, 3007; **77**, 3010, 3012, 3017.—§ 354 (do.): III, **78**, 3034, 3041, 3044; **79**, 3063, 3064.—§ 355 (do.): III, **79**, 3072.—§ 391 (Ṛshyaçṛṅga): III, **113**, 10092 (*yathā . . . Nalasya vai D°ī*).—§ 555 (Sainyodyogap.): V, **8**, 223 (*yathā*).—§ 565 (Gālavacarita): V, **117**, 3974 (*reme . . . yathā . . . D°yāṃ Nalaḥ*). Cf. Bhaimī, Bhīmanandinī, Bhīmaputrikā, Bhīmasutā (III, 2273, 2278, 2380, 2499, 2509, 2998), Vaidarbhī, Vidarbhādhipatinandinī, Vidarbharājatanayā, Vidarbhatanayā.

Damayantī²: XII, 8604 (error in C. instead of Madayantī, q.v.).
Damayitṛ = Vishṇu (1000 names).
Dambara, a companion of Skanda. § 615*u* (Skanda): IX, **45ζ**, 2541 (given to Skanda by Dhātṛ).
Dambha = Çiva (1000 names ²).
Dambhodbhava, an ancient king. § 6 (Anukram.): I, **1a**, 227 (in Sañjaya's enumeration).—§ 11 (Parvasaṅgr.): I, **2**, 508 (°*sya cākhyānāṃ*, i.e. Dambhodbhavopākhyāna).—§ 61 (Sarpasattra): I, **51**, 2112 (°*enāsi samo balena*, sc. Janamejaya).—§ 277 (Jarāsandhavadhap.): II, **22**, 877 (*çreyaso hy avamanyeha vineçuḥ*, cf. § 563).—§ 563 (Dambhodbhavop.): V, **96**, 3452, 3473, (3476), 3477.
Dambhodbhavopākhyāna(ṃ) ("the episode relating to Dambhodbhava"). (Cf. Dambhodbhavasya ākhyānaṃ.) § 563 (Bhagavady.): There was a king of yore named *Dambhodbhava*, who was at the head of the earth; his sovereignty extended over the whole world. Every morning he used to ask if there were anyone superior or even equal to himself. Certain brahmans counselled him to curb his pride; and as he continued to ask the brahmans the same question day after day, some high-souled brahmans mentioned to him the ascetics *Nara* and *Nārāyaṇa*, "who have taken their birth in the race of men, and are now practising penances on *Gandhamādana*." The king marched to the spot with a large army, and found them emaciated with hunger and thirst, etc. He desired a battle with them. The *Ṛshis* declined; but as he repeatedly summoned them to fight, *Nara* took up a handful of grass-blades, and therewith baffled all their arrows and cut off the eyes and ears and noses of the warriors. The king fell at the feet of the *Ṛshis* and said, "Let me be blessed." *Nara* then told him to be obedient to the *brahmans* and be virtuous. The king returned to his city, and from that time began to practise righteousness.
Daṃça, an Asura. § 621 (Rājadh.): XII, **3**, 93 (*mahāsuraḥ*, cursed by Bhṛgu to become the worm Alarka, because he had ravished the wife of Bhṛgu).
Damin, a tīrtha. § 358 (Tīrthayātrāp.): III, **82**, 5014.
Dāmodara = Kṛshṇa, q.v.—Do.² = Vishṇu (1000 names).
Dāmoshṇīça (B. °*īsha*), a muni. § 264 (Sabhākriyāp.): II, **4a**, 108 (among the munis who were present when Yudhishṭhira entered his palace).
Daṃshṭrin = Çiva: XII, 10371 (1000 names¹); XIV, 205.
Dānapati = Akrūra: I, 7989 (*A*°).
Dānava, pl. (°*āḥ*) ("sons of Danu"), a class of the enemies of the gods. § 11 (Parvasaṅgr.): I, **2**, 369 (°*ānāṃ . . . samudbhavaḥ*), 460 (*Nivātakavacaiḥ*).—§ 28 (Amṛtamanthana): I, **18**, 1125 (*Asura-D°āḥ*, partake in the churning of the ocean), 1141, 1150, 1155, 1157 (°*Daiteyāḥ*); **19**, 1158 (*Daitya-D°āḥ*, battle with the gods about the *amṛta*), 1159 (°*endrebhyaḥ*), 1167, 1177 (*cakraṃ . . . D°sūdanaṃ*).—§ 43 (Garuḍa): I, **30**, 1396 (*ajeyañ ca deva-D°-Rākshasaiḥ*, i.e. Garuḍa).—§ 84 (Ādivaṃçāvatāraṇap.): I, **64**, 2492 (re-born on earth).—§ 85 (Aṃçāvat.): I, **65**, 2513, 2514, 2515 (*deva-D°saṅghānāṃ . . . sambhavaḥ*).—§ 92 (do.): I, **65**, 2534 (*Danor vaṃçe*, enumeration), 2535 (°*mukhyānāṃ*). § 93 (do.): I, **65**, 2536 (*Danuputrāḥ . . . daça D°vaṃçajāḥ*).—§ 97 (do.): I, **65**, 2542 (i.e. the sons of Kālā).—§ 930 (do.): I, **67**, 2637, 2639, 2698, 2703 (various *D.* incarnate as kings on earth).—§ 133 (Çakuntalop.): I, **68**, 2799 (*deva-D°-Rakshasāṃ*).—§ 145 (Kaca): I, **76**, 3189, 3196, 3209, 3220, 3223, †3252, †3253, 3254.—§ 146 (Devayānī): I, **80**, 3358 (*sarva D°aiḥ*).—§ 208 (Astradarçana): 1, **135**,

5378 (*yathā D°saṃkshaye purā*); **137**, 5430 (*vajraṃ kṛtaṃ D°sūdanaṃ*).—§ 218 (Caitrarathap.): I, **167**, 6401 (*deva-D°-Yakshāṇām īpsitāṃ*, sc. Draupadī).—§ 221 (do.): I, **170**, 6496 (know the history of the Kuru race).—§ 257 (Arjuna): I, **225**, 8182 (*deva D°-Gandharvapūjitaṃ*, sc. the chariot which Varuṇa gave to Arjuna), 8186 (had been vanquished by Soma).—§ 258 (Khaṇḍavadah.): I, **227**, 8259 (*Daitya-D°saṅghānāṃ*, slain by Kṛshṇa in the battle at Khāṇḍava); **228**, 8285, 8291 (*sa-D°-niçācarāḥ*), 8318.—§ 261 (Sabhākriyāp.): II, **1**, 5 (*°ānāṃ Viçvakarmā*, i.e. Maya).—§ 263 (do.): II, **3**, 59 (performed a sacrifice at Bindusaras).—§ 268 (Varuṇasabhāv.): II, **9**, 365 (*Kālakhañjāḥ*, in the palace of Varuṇa), 368 (*Daitya-D°saṅghāḥ*, do.). — § 270 (Brahmasabhāv.): II, **11**, 465 (worship Brahmán).—§ 275 (Rājasūyārambhap.): II, **18**, 731 (*°ānāṃ vināçāya sthāpitā divyarūpiṇī*, sc. Jarā).—§ 277 (Jarāsandhavadhap.): II, **24**, 941 (*Çakro Dānavānāṃ jaghāna navatīr nava*).—§ 317*b* (Kṛshṇa Vāsudeva): III, **12**, 478 (*Daitya-D°ān*, had been slain by Kṛshṇa).—§ 319 (Saubhavadhop.): III, **14**, 634 (i.e. the followers of Çālva).—§ 320 (do.): III, **17**, 710 (*°endrāḥ*, do.); **18**, 726; **20**, 804, 806; **22**, 852 (*°saṅghāḥ*), 854, 877 (*Āgneyam astraṃ . . . D°āntakaraṃ*, i.e. Kṛshṇa's discus Sudarçana), 878, 886. — § 325 (Draupadīparitāpav.): III, **27**, 1014 (*pūjitaṃ deva-D°aiḥ*, sc. Arjuna).—§ 333*b* (Arjuna): III, **40**, 1638 (had been chastised by Nara, i.e. Arjuna).—§ 333*c* (Brahmaçiras): III, **40**, 1646.—§ 333 (Kairātap.): III, **40**, 1659 (*deva D°āḥ*). — § 334 (do.): III, **41**, 1684 (*ye manushyatvam āgatāḥ | Nivātakavacāç caiva*), 1686 (*aṃçāḥ kshitisamprāptā deva - D° - Rakshasāṃ*). — § 335 (Indralokābhigamanap.): III, **42**, 1729.—§ 345 (Nalopākhyānap.): III, **56**, 2170 (*Daitya-D°mardanaṃ | Mahendraṃ*).—§ 378 (Tīrthayātrāp.): III, **94**, 8491, 8497 (*°āṃç caiva Kalir apy āvicat*).—§ 384 (Agastyop.): III, **100**, 8691 (*Kālakeyāḥ*); **101**, 8716; **102**, 8742, 8751. — § 386 (do.): III, **105**, †8811, 8813, 8817 (the Kāleyas were vanquished by the gods). —§ 426*b* (Kṛtayuga): III, **149**, 11236 (did not exist in the Kṛtayuga). — § 432 (Saugandhikah.): III, **154**, †11390 (*sa Çakravad D°-Daityasaṅghān vikramya*).—§ 436 (Yakshayuddhap.): III, **159**, 11655 (on Kailāsa). — § 438 (do.): III, **161**, 11744 (*nihatya . . . D°ān Maghavān iva*).— § 439 (do.): III, **163**, 11859 (*deva-D°aih*).—§ 442 (Nivātakavacayuddhap.): III, **167**, 11990.—§ 443 (do.): III, **168**, 12063 (*Nivātakavacāḥ*), 12075, 12078.—§ 444 (do.): III, **169**, 12085, 12087, 12089, 12097, 12099; **170**, 12105, 12130; **171**, 12140, 12142, 12153, 12161; **172**, 12165, 12169, 12177, 12178, 12195, 12196 (the Nivātakavacas were slain by Arjuna). — § 445 (do.): III, **173**, 12208 (the inhabitants of Hiraṇyapura), 12217 (*°endrāḥ*), 12219, 12242 (*°endrānāṃ*), 12251, 12252, 12258, 12271 (Hiraṇyapura was destroyed by Arjuna). — § 447 (do.): III, **175**, 12292 (*jitāḥ*). — § 456 (Sarasvatī-Tārkshyasaṃv.): III, **186**, †12728 (*°saṃniruddhe . . . Narake*).—§ 458 (Mārkaṇḍeyas.): III, **188**, 12808, 12875.—§ 459 (do.): III, **188**, 12942.—§ 462 (Baka-Çakrasaṃv.): III, **193**, 13233.—§ 474 (Mārkaṇḍeyas.): III, **201**, 13483.—§ 478 (Dhundhumārop.): III, **204**, 13584.—§ 495 (Skandotpatti): III, **223**, 14243, 14245 (defeated the gods).—§ 496 (do.): III, **224**, 14264.—§ 501 (Skandopākh.): III, **229**, 14423 (*°ānāṃ vināçāya*).—§ 507 (Skandayuddha): III, **231**, 14580, 14583, 14584, 14586, 14593, 14594, 14595 (*°endrānāṃ*), 14599, 14613, 14615, 14620, 14621, 14626 (battle with the gods).—§ 513 (Ghoshayātrāp.): III, **251**, 15144 (*Daiteya-D°āḥ*), 15152, 15153 (summoned Duryodhana into their presence); **252**, (15155), 15164 (many D. were re-born on earth), 15167, 15182 (*°arshabhāḥ*), 15191. — § 526 (Rāmopākhyānap.): III, **276**, 15936 (*deva-Gandharva-D°aḥ*, were born on earth in order to slay Rāvaṇa and his followers).— § 533*b* (Rāvaṇa): III, **281**, 16168.—§ 533 (Sītā-Rāvaṇasaṃv.): III, **281**, 16175 (*°kanyāḥ*, wives of Rāvaṇa).— § 542 (Rāvaṇavadha): III, **290**, 16510 (*Çakraḥ . . . Daitya-D°ān . . . jaghnivān*), 16525 (*deva - Dānava-Kinnarāḥ*). — § 543 (Rāmābhisheka): III, **291**, 16561 (*çatruḥ . . . D°ānāṃ*, i.e. Rāvaṇa). — § 547 (Karṇa): III, **310**, †17213.—§ 551 (Kīcakavadhap.): IV, **23**, 821 (*Vajrī D°ān iva*).—§ 552 (Goharaṇap.): IV, **36**, 1177 (*vitrāsayitvā . . . D°ān eva Vajrabhṛt*); **43**, 1346 (*deva-D°-Gandharvaiḥ pūjitaṃ*, sc. Gāṇḍīva); **44**, 1384 (*yudhyato D°arshabhaiḥ*, sc. Arjuna); **45**, 1430 (*deva-D°saṅkule*, all. to Khāṇḍavadahanap.); **49**, 1539 (*Kālakañjāḥ*), 1553 (*D°ā iva Vāsavaṃ*).—§ 554 (Sainyodyogap.): V, **7**, 151 (*purato deva-D°yor api*, sc. Kṛshṇa).—§ 555 (Indravijaya): V, **11**, 348; **14**, 445 (*Daitya-D°sūdana*, i.e. Indra, C. has by error *°aṃ*); **15**, 464; **16**, 499 (*°ān hatva*, sc. Indra). — § 561 (Yānasandhip.): V, **49**, 1929 (*Çakro vijigye Daitya-D°ān*); **51**, 2059 (*Mahendra iva vajreṇa D°ān*).—§ 564 (Mātalīyop.): V, **99**, 3547 (*Pātālaṃ . . . Daitya-D°sevitaṃ*); **100**, 3567 (in Hiraṇyapura), 3569, 3573 (*Nivātakavacāḥ*), 3584 (*deva-D°āḥ*), 3585.—§ 567 (Bhagavadyānap.): V, **128**, 4301, 4303 (*Daiteya-D°ān*), 4304 (do.), 4305 (Dharma bound the Daiteyas and the *D.* and made them over to Varuṇa, who kept them within the depth of the ocean); **130**, 4408 (i.e. the followers of Naraka). — § 569 (do.): V, **138**, 4683 (*Nivātakavacāḥ*). — § 570 (Sainyaniryānap.): V, **158**, 5378 (all. to Khāṇḍavadahanap.), 5379 (*Kālakeyaiḥ*).— § 572 (Rathātirathas.): V, **165**, 5739 (*hanishyati . . . Mahendro D°ān iva*); **169**, 5871 (*°ānāṃ sahasrāṇi Hiraṇyapuravāsināṃ*, all. to § 445); **172**, 5924 (*yotsyati . . . Maghavān iva D°aiḥ*).—§ 573 (Ambopākhyānap.): V, **173**, 5961 (*Devarāḍ iva D°ān*). § 576 (Bhagavadgītāp.): VI, **14**, 535 (*nighnan . . . D°ān iva Vajrabhṛt*), 549 (*vibudhaiḥ . . . D°ān ghnadbhih*); **23**, 806 (*jayasi D°ān*, sc. Umā); **34**, 1218.—§ 580 (Bhīshmavadhap.): VI, **57**, 2455 (*Tridaçā D°ān iva*); **58**, 2467 (applauded Arjuna); **59**, 2576 (*Bhīshmo nāçayed Daitya-D°ān*).—§ 581 (do.): VI, **62**, 2753 (*Vṛtrahā D°eshv iva*); **66**, 2981 (*nihatā ye te Daitya-D°-Rakshasaḥ*); **67**, 3026.—§ 582 (do.): VI, **60**, 3080 (*yuddhaṃ . . . devānāṃ D°air iva*). — § 583 (do.): VI, **77**, 3348 (*yathā Devāsure yuddhe Mahendraḥ prāpya D°ān*), 3367 (*nighnantaṃ . . . D°ān iva Vāsavaṃ*).—§ 584 (do.): VI, **83**, 3666 (*yathā*).—§ 585 (do.): VI, **92**, 4096; **97**, 4442 (*jahi . . . Mahendra iva D°ān*).—§ 586 (do.): VI, **102**, 4660 (witness the battle); **107**, 4924 (*Daitya D°aiḥ*).—§ 587 (do.): VI, **119**, 5589 (*saṅgrāme . . . devānāṃ D°air iva*), 5624.— § 589 (Droṇābhishekap.): VII, **3**, 113 (*deva-D°pujitaḥ*, sc. Rāma Jāmadagnya); **6**, 162 (*jahīndro D°ān iva*); **7**, 215 (*badhyamānā . . . Vāsaveneva D°āḥ*), 219 (*iva*).—§ 590 (do.): VII, **16**, 630 (*yuddhaṃ . . . devānām iva D°aiḥ*), 634 (*yuddhaṃ . . . D°ānāṃ yathā suraiḥ*). — § 592 (Saṃçaptakavadhap.): VII, **21**, 919 (*D°ā ivendreṇa badhyamānāḥ*). — § 594 (Abhimanyuvadhap.): VII, **52**, 2013. — § 596 (Pratijñāp.): VII, **75**, 2669 (*Hiraṇyapuravāsināṃ*, all. to § 445); **79**, 2798 (*Daitya-D°darpahā*, i.e. Indra); **80**, 2864 (*deva-D°-Yakshāṇāṃ . . . sādhanaṃ*, i.e. Çiva). —§ 599 (Jayadrathavadhap.): VII, **119**, 4728 (*hanishyāmi D°ān iva Vāsavaḥ*); **122**, 4910 (*petuḥ . . . devāsure purā yuddhe yathā Daiteya-D°āḥ*); **124**, 4973 (*Mahendro*

D°eshv iva); **144,** 6046; **147,** 6352 (witness the battle); **148,** †6444 (*Çatakratau . . . jaghnushi Daitya-D°ān*); **149,** 6459 (*yathā . . . Dānavān Pākaçāsanaḥ*); **151,** 6536.—§ 600 (Ghaṭotkacavadhap.): VII, **159,** 7075 (*yuddhaṃ . . . yathā devāsure yuddhe Çakrasya saha D°aiḥ*), 7132; **168,** 7540 (*yathendrabhayavitrastā D°ās Tārakāmaye*); **170,** 7620; **181,** 8231. — § 601 (Droṇavadhap.): VII, **185,** 8437 (*Hiraṇyapuravāsinām,* all. to § 445). — § 602 (do.): VII, **186,** 8483 (*D°ā Vāsavaṃ yathā*); **190,** 8694 (*yathā . . . Çakro D°ānāṃ kshayaṃ purā*).—§ 603 (Nārāyaṇāstramokshap.): VII, **196,** 9033.—§ 603*d* (Tripura): VII, **202,** 9574 (in Tripura). — § 603 (Nārāyaṇāstramokshap.): VII, **202,** 9638 (*tvayā*—i.e. by Arjuna—*D°ā hatāḥ*). — § 605 (Karṇap.): VIII, **10,** 377 (*jahi . . . Mahendro D°ān iva*), 378 (*dravishyanti . . . Vishṇuṃ dṛshṭveva D°āḥ*); **18,** †691 (*°nāgasannibhaṃ,* sc. the elephant of king Daṇḍadhāra); **19,** 726 (*jaghnivān . . . Mahendra iva D°ān*).—§ 606 (Tripurākhyāna): VIII, **33,** 1406 (*Mayaṃ . . . Daitya-D°pūjitaṃ*), 1413 (*°mukhyānāṃ,* in Tripura), 1426; **34,** 1455, 1457, 1476, 1523, 1550, 1569 (Çiva destroyed Tripura, cf. § 603*d*).—§ 606*b* (Paraçurāma): VIII, **34,** 1601, 1603, 1607 (had been slain by Rāma Jāmadagnya).—§ 606 (Karṇap.): VIII, **35,** 1653 (*jahi . . . Mahendra iva D°ān*).—§ 608 (do.): VIII, **50,** 2439 (*vyadrāvayat . . . yathendro D°ān purā*); **56,** 2759 (*yādṛk purā vṛttaṃ devānāṃ D°aiḥ saha*), 2799 (*pramamātha . . . D°ān iva Vāsavaḥ*); **73,** 3690 (*purā Vishṇur iva hatvā Daiteya-D°ān*); **87,** 4409, 4426, 4460 (present at the encounter between Karṇa and Arjuna). — § 610 (Çalyap.): IX, **6,** 320 (*jahi . . . Mahendro D°ān iva*). — § 611 (do.): IX, **13,** 701 (*deva-Gandharva-D°āḥ,* witness the battle); **25,** 1352 (*yathā Daiteya-D°āḥ*). — § 612 (Hradapraveçap.): IX, **31,** 1750 (*Indreṇa nihatā Daitya-D°āḥ*), 1757 (*nihatāḥ*).—§ 615 (Baladevatīrthay.): IX, **39,** 2252 (*Daitya-D°vigrahaṃ*); **43,** †2448 (*°ānāṃ Daiteyānāṃ Rākshasānāñ ca devaiḥ . . . yuddhaṃ Tārakākhyaṃ*).—§ 615*u* (Skanda): IX, **44,** 2479, 2491; **46,** 2685 (battle with the gods).—§ 615*dd* (Yamunātīrtha): IX, **49,** 2843 (*saṃgrāmaḥ . . . devānāṃ D°ānāñ ca*).—§ 615*gg* (Sārasvata): IX, **51,** 2949, 2960 (*Daitya-D°vīrāṇāṃ jaghāna navatīr nava,* sc. Indra).—§ 616 (Sauptikap.): X, **3,** 132 (*sūdayishyāmi . . . Maghavān iva D°ān*); **4,** 156 (*sarva-D°sūdanaḥ,* i.e. Indra). — § 617*b* (Brahmaçiras): X, **12,** 622, 642 (*cakraṃ deva-D°pūjitaṃ*).—§ 617 (Aishīkap.): X, **14,** 684 (*deva-D°sammatau,* sc. Nārada and Vyāsa); **15,** 715.—§ 619 (Strīvilāpap.): XI, **25,** 754.—§ 621 (Rājadh.): XII, **2,** 63. — § 632*b* (Shoḍaçarāj.; cf. § 595, v. Yayāti): XII, **29,** 990 (*Daiteya-D°ān,* had been slain by Yayāti). — § 635 (Rājadh.): XII, **33,** 1187 (*Çālavṛkāḥ?*). — § 637 (do.): XII, **47θ,** 1608, 1662.—§ 641 (do.): XII, **64,** 2396.—§ 656 (Khaḍgotpattik.): XII, **166,** 6145 (*°endrāḥ,* sc. Hiraṇyakaçipu, etc. (γ)), 6147 (*Daitya-D°āḥ*), 6173, 6175, 6179, 6182, 6183, 6185 (battled with the gods; Çiva slew the *D.* with the sword).—§ 660 (Mokshadh.): XII, **188β,** 6932.—§ 664*b* (Madhu): XII, **207,** 7533.—§ 664 (Mokshadh.): XII, **207ε,** 7544, 7545 (*Vipracittipradhānān,* are the offspring of Danu).—§ 666 (do.): XII, **209,** 7610 (*°mukhyā . . . Narakādyā mahāsurāḥ*), 7611, 7612, 7613, 7615, 7617, 7622 (*°endrāḥ*), 7623 (do.), 7625 (*Daitya-D°ān*), 7628, 7633, 7635 (*°patīn;* the *D.* were destroyed by Vishṇu when incarnate as a boar).—§ 671*b* (Bali-Vāsavas.): XII, **224,** 8127 (*°eçvarapūjitaṃ,* i.e. Bali). — § 673*b* (do.): XII, **227,** 8218 (*Daitya-D°saṃkshaye*), 8266, 8267 (*°endrāḥ,* have left the earth).—§ 674*b* (Çrī-Vāsavasaṃv.): XII, **229,** 8360 (*Daiteya-D°ān,* deserted by Çrī), 8381, 8394, 8413.—§ 695*b* (Dakshayajñavināça): XII, **285a,** 10278 (came to the sacrifice of Daksha). — § 696*b* (Daksha-prokta-Çiva-sahasranāmastotra): XII, **285,** 10467.—§ 701 (Mokshadh.): XII, **290,** 10661 (*nityaṃ vairanibaddhāç ca D°āḥ surasattamaiḥ*).—§ 702 (do.): XII, **291,** 10709.—§ 705 (do.): XII, **303a,** 11243.—§ 714*b* (Himavat): XII, **328,** 12333. — § 716 (Çukābhipatana): XII, **332,** 12570.—§ 717*c* (Uparicara): XII, **337,** 12811 (worship Nārāyaṇa).—§ 717*b* (Nārāyaṇīya): XII, **340,** 12954 (will be slain by Nārāyaṇa in his incarnation as Kṛshṇa); **344γγ,** 13365; **348,** 13478 (*°çreshṭhau,* i.e. Madhu and Kaiṭabha); **350,** 13666 (*Daitya-D°-Gandharva-Rakshogaṇasamākulā . . . vasumatī*), 13667. — § 730*g* (Upamanyu): XIII, **14η,** 734 (Çiva assumes the forms of Daityas and Dānavas), (θ), 796 (*Daitya-D°mukhyānāṃ*), 798 (do.).—§ 730 (Ānuçāsanik.): XIII, **14δδ,** 996 (worship Çiva); **17,** 1294 (*nāsya vighnaṃ vikurvanti Dānavā Yaksha-Rākshasāḥ,* etc.); **18λλ,** 1373.—§ 743*b* (Vipulop.): XIII, **40,** 2263 (*deva-Gandharva-D°āḥ*).—§ 746 (Ānuçāsanik.): XIII, **82,** 3865 (do.). — § 747*b* (Suvarṇotpatti): XIII, **85,** 4023 (*deva-D°-Rākshasān*). — § 754 (Ānuçāsanik.): XIII, **98,** 4719 (*deva-D°-Bhūtānāṃ*).—§ 759 (do.): XIII, **107,** 5258 (*Rudraṃ . . . deva-D°sammataṃ* (C.*°aḥ*)).—§ 768 (do.): XIII, **148,** 6899 (*°endrāḥ,* had been slain by Kṛshṇa with his discus).—§ 770 (do.): XIII, **151,** 7158 (*jitāḥ,* sc. by Indra and the Vasus). — § 772*k* (Agastya): XIII, **156,** 7267, 7270, 7272, 7277 (burnt by Agastya). — § 772*l* (Vasishṭha): XIII, **156,** 7281 (*Khalino nāma*), 7282.—§ 772*m* (Atri): XIII, **157,** 7292 (battled with the gods), 7293. — § 772*p* (Kapa, pl.): XIII, **158,** 7345. — § 778 (Açvamedhikap.): XIV, **3,** 47 (*devāḥ kriyāvanto D°ān abhyadarshayan*).—§ 778*b* (Samvartta-Maruttīya): XIV, **9,** †248 (*apākarshaṃ D°ān antarikshāt,* says Indra). — § 782*b* (Brāhmaṇagītā): XIV, **26,** 756.—§ 782*g* (Guruçishyasaṃv.): XIV, **43,** 1183 (*deva-D°-Nāgānāṃ . . . īçvaraḥ,* i.e. Vishṇu); **44,** 1226 (*deva-D°-Bhūtānāṃ . . . īçvaraḥ,* i.e. Vishṇu).—§ 785 (Anugītāp.): XIV, **59,** 1768 (*kṛtvā nasukaraṃ karma D°eshv iva Vāsavaḥ*). — § 789 (Putradarçanap.): XV, **31ζ,** 849 (had been incarnate and thus slain in the battle). Cf. Asura, pl.; Daiteya, pl.; Daitya, pl.; Dānaveya, pl.; Danuja, pl.; Danuputra, pl.

Dānava, sg. (cf. Dānava[1]). § 435 (Jaṭāsuravadhap.): III, **157,** 11507 (*saṃkhye deva-D°yor iva*).—§ 551 (Kīcakavadhap.): IV, **23,** 795 (*pothitaṃ . . . Indreṇeva D°m*).—§ 552 (Goharaṇap.): IV, **58,** 1876 (*prahāraḥ . . . deva-D°yor iva*).—§ 578 (Bhīshmavadhap.): VI, **45**[9], 1706 (*yuddhaṃ . . . deva-D°yor iva*), 1733 (*vyadārayata . . . Maghavā iva D°m*).—§ 586 (do.): VI, **101,** 4594 (*samīyatuḥ saṅkhye . . . yathā deva-D°au*). — § 589 (Droṇābhishek.): VII, **11,** 385 (Kṛshṇa slew a Dānava who had assumed the form of a bull).—§ 590 (do.): VII, **13,** 492 (*Mahendram iva D°aḥ*). —§ 599 (Jayadrathavadhap.): VII, **135,** 5548 (*Mahendrasyeva D°ḥ*); **139,** 5773 (*saṅkhye deva-D°yor iva*). — § 608 (Karṇap.): VIII, **60,** 3024 (*devāsure . . . mṛdhe deva-D°yor iva*).—Names of single Dānavas:—

Bali: XII, 8071, 12947 (*B°*).
Çālva: III, 858.
Dīrghajihva: I, 2538 (*D°*).
Durjaya: I, 2531 (*D°*), 2698 (*D°*).
Hara: I, 2659 (*Haraḥ . . . D°ottamaḥ*).
Hiraṇyakaçipu: XIII, 662 (*H°*).

Ilvala: III, 8613 (*I*°).
Kaiṭabha: XII, 8265 (*K*°).
Mada: XIV, †252.
Mahisha: III, 14596 (*M*°).
Maya: I, 8332 (*M*°), 8478 (*M*°); II, **7**, 1709 (*M*°).
Naraka: XII, 12957 (°*ottamaṃ*).
Pīṭha: XII, 12956 (*P*°).
Prahlāda: XII, 6668 (°*ottama*).
Puloman: I, 895, 896 (°*ottama*).
Rāhu: I, 1161 (*R*°), 1162, 1164.
Tāraka: XIII, 4214 (*T*°).
Vipracitti: VI, 4212 (*VI*°).
Vivindhya: III, 680 (*V*°).
Vṛtra: XII, 10004, 10026 (°*sattama*), 10041, 10047 (°*sattama*), 10048, 10136.

Dānava, dual (°*au*): Madhu and Kaiṭabha: III, 498 (*Madhu-Kaiṭabhau*), 13561, 13566; XII, 13482, 13509 (*Madhu-Kaiṭabhau*), 13523.
Dānava, adj. ("belonging to the Dānavas"). § 445 (Nivātakavacayuddhap.): III, **173**, 12221 (*māyāṃ*).—§ 507 (Skandayuddha): III, **231**, 14590 (*sainyaṃ*). — § 608 (Karṇap.): VIII, **87**, 4442 (*pakshaḥ*).
Dānavaçatru = Indra: I, †2164 (*Vajrī*).
Dānavaghna = Indra: XIV, †254.
Dānavanandana = Puloman: I, 893 (*P*°).
Dānavapati = Bali: III, 15844 (*B*°).
Dānavapuṅgava = Arka: I, 2668 (*A*°).
Dānavapura = Hiraṇyapura: III, 12262.
Dānavāri = Indra: XII, 10152 (*Maghavān*).
Dānavarshabha[1] = Dīrghajihva: I, 2675 (*D*°).
Dānavarshabha[2] = Vipracitti: I, 2640 (*V*°).
Dānavarshi, pl. (°*ayaḥ*). § 444 (Nivātakavacayuddhap.): III, **169**, 12101.
Dānavasūdana = Indra: I, 1533; III, 14279, 16989.
Dānaveçvara = Bali: XII, 8078.
Dānavendra[1] = Bali: III, 15841.
Dānavendra[2] = Çambara: XIII, 2183.
Dānavendra[3] = Dhundhu: III, 13531.
Dānavendra[4] = Vṛshaparvan: I, 3368 (*V*°), 3455.
Dānavendra[5] = Vṛtra: XII, 10029, 10030, †10059.
Dānavendra, dual (°*au*) = Madhu and Kaiṭabha: XII, 13515.
Dānavendrāntakaraṇa = Kṛshṇa: XII, 1002.
Dānaveya, pl. (°*āḥ*) = Dānava, pl. § 608 (Karṇap.): VIII, **73**, 3602.
Dānavī (a "female Dānava"). § 162 (Çāntanūp.): I, **97**, 3894 (Çāntanu asks Gaṅgā if she is a *D.*).—§ 522 (Draupadīharaṇap.): III, **265**, †15589 (Koṭika asks Draupadī if she is a *D.*).
Danāyus, daughter of Daksha and wife of Kaçyapa. § 87 (Aṃçāvat.): I, **65**, 2520.—§ 96 (do.): I, **65**, 2541 (mother of four sons, Vikshara, etc.).—§ 130 (do.): I, **67**, 2677 (her sons became incarnate. C. has *Anāyus*).
Daṇḍa[1], brother of the Magadha king Daṇḍadhāra. § 11 (Parvasaṅgr.): I, **2**, 544.—§ 130 (Aṃçāvat.): I, **67**, 2681 (incarnation of the Asura Krodhahantṛ).—§ 232 (Svayaṃvarap.): I, **186**, 6992 (the same (?), son of Vidaṇḍa, present at the svayaṃvara of Draupadī).—§ 280 (Bhīmasena): II, **30**, 1091 (°*ñ ca Daṇḍadhārañ ca*, vanquished by Bhīmasena on his digvijaya).—§ 605 (Karṇap.): VIII, **18**, †701 (his brother Daṇḍadhāra slain by Arjuna), †704 (slain by Arjuna).
Daṇḍa[2], a follower of Sūrya (the Sun). § 310*b* (Sūrya): III, **3**, 198 (*Māṭharāruṇa-D°ādyāḥ*).
Daṇḍa[3], a Pāṇḍava warrior. § 608 (Karṇap.): VIII, **56**νν, 2740 (slain by Karṇa).
Daṇḍa[4] = Çiva (1000 names[1]).
Daṇḍa[5] = Vishṇu (1000 names).
Daṇḍabāhu, a warrior of Skanda. § 615*u* (Skanda): IX, **45**η, 2575.
Daṇḍadhāra[1], king of the Magadhas. § 130 (Aṃçāvat.): I, **67**, 2682 (incarnation of the Asura Krodhavardhana).—§ 232 (Svayaṃvarap.): I, **186**, 6987 (the same (?), present at the svayaṃvara of Draupadī).—§ 280 (Bhīmasena): II, **30**, 1091 (coming to the country of the Magadhas, Bhīmasena vanquished Daṇḍa and Daṇḍadhāra).—§ 554 (Sainyodyogap.): V, **4**γ, 84. — § 572 (Rathātirathasaṅkhyānap.): V, **166**, 5764 (a ratha in the army of Duryodhana).—§ 605 (Karṇap.): VIII, **18**, 687, 689, †695 (king of the Magadhas, brother of Daṇḍa, is slain by Arjuna; cf. Daṇḍasena). Cf. Girivrajeçvara (VIII, †696), Māgadha.
Daṇḍadhāra[2], son of Dhṛtarāshṭra. § 130 (Aṃçāvat.): I, **67**, 2738.—§ 608 (Karṇap.): VIII, **56**, 2727 (rescued Duryodhana); **83**ξ', 4262 (among ten sons of Dhṛtarāshṭra who are slain by Bhīmasena).
Daṇḍadhāra[3], various Pāṇḍava warriors. § 592 (Saṃçaptakavadhap.): VII, **23**o, 1000 (proceeded against Droṇa, description of his horses).—§ 604 (Karṇap.): VIII, **6**, 163 (has been slain by Droṇa).—§ 608 (Karṇap.): VIII, **49**, 2327 (a Pāñcālya, slain by Karṇa).
Daṇḍadhāra[4] = Çiva (1000 names[1]).
Daṇḍagaurī, an Apsaras. § 336 (Indralokābhig.): III, **43**a, 1784 (among the Apsarases who danced in the palace of Indra).
Daṇḍaka[1], pl. (°*āḥ*), a people. § 284 (Sahadeva): II, **31**, 1169 (in the south, vanquished by Sahadeva on his digvijaya).—§ 772*b* (Pavanārjunasaṃv.): XIII, **154**, 7223 (their kingdom had been destroyed by a brahman).
Daṇḍaka[2], a forest. § 479 (Pativratop.): III, **206**, 13678 (*munīnāṃ . . . yeshāṃ krodhāgnir adyāpi D°e nopaçāmyati*). — § 771 (Ānuçāsanik.): XIII, **152**, 7178 (*yeshāṃ kopāgnir adyāpi D°e nopaçāmyati*). Cf. next.
Daṇḍakāraṇya = Daṇḍaka[2]. § 370 (Tīrthayātrāp.): III, **85**, 8183. § 425 (Hanūmad-Bhīmasaṃv.): III, **147**, 11108. — § 527 (Rāmopākhyānap.): III, **277**, 15985. — § 530 (Viçvāvasumokshaṇa): III, **279**, 16070. — § 615*k* (Mahodara): IX, **39**, 2255. Cf. the prec.
Daṇḍaketu, a prince. § 592 (Saṃçaptakavadhap.): VII, **23**o, 1015 (proceeded against Droṇa, description of his horses).
Daṇḍākhya, a tīrtha. § 370 (Tīrthayātrāp.): III, **85**, 8157 (in Campā). Cf. Daṇḍārtta.
Daṇḍapāṇi[1] = Antaka: V, 5779 (*iva*); VI, 1952 (°*r ivāparaḥ*).
Daṇḍapāṇi[2] = Çiva: VII, 9455.
Daṇḍārt(t)a, a tīrtha. § 370 (Tīrthayātrāp.): III, **84**, 8141 (in Campā, PCR. has Daṇḍaparṇa). Cf. Daṇḍākhya.
Daṇḍasena, a prince. § 11 (Parvasaṅgr.): I, **2**, 544 (°*sya vadhaḥ*, seems to allude to VIII, ch. **18**, where is read Daṇḍadhāra; v. Daṇḍadhāra[1]).
Daṇḍimuṇḍa = Çiva (1000 names[1]).
Daṇḍin[1], son of Dhṛtarāshṭra. § 130 (Aṃçāvat.): I, **67**, 2738.
Daṇḍin[2] = Yama: I, 7077 (*Pitṛrājaḥ*).
Daṇḍin[3] = Çiva: XII, 10358 (1000 names[1]), 10420 (do.), 10445; XIII, 1244 (1000 names[2]); XIV, 204.

Dānta[1], a son of the Vidarbha king Bhīma. § 344 (Nalopākhyānap.): III, **53**, 2080.
Dānta[2] = Çiva (1000 names[1]).
Dāntā, an Apsaras. § 731*b* (Ashṭāvakra-Diksaṃv.): XIII, **19**β, 1425 (among the Apsarases who danced in the palace of Kubera).
Dantakrūra. § 595 (Shoḍaçarāj., v. Rāma Jāmadagnya): VII, **70**, 2431 (°*ṃ jaghāna ha.* Nīl. *deçādhipatiṃ*, but cf. BR. s.v. *dantakrūram*).
Dantakūra. § 556*d* (Sahadeva): V, **23**, †708 (*Kaliṅgān samāgatān ajayad D°e. D.* seems to be the name of a place (so also BR.), but Nīl. takes it = *saṃgrāme*).—§ 561*c* (Kṛshṇa Vāsudeva): V, **48**, †1883 (*Kaliṅgān D°e mamarda*, Nīl. as above).
Dantavakra, a king. § 130 (Aṃçāvat.): I, **67**, 2698 (so B.; C. has °*vaktra*, incarnation of the Dānava Durjaya?).—§ 273 (Rājasūyārambhap.): II, **14**, 577 (*Karūshaḥ*?, among the princes who wait upon Jarāsandha).—§ 281 (Sahadeva): II, **31**, 1107 (*Adhirājādhipaṃ*?, vanquished by Sahadeva on his digvijaya).—§ 290 (Çiçupālavadhap.): II, **44**, 1537.—§ 554 (Sainyodyogap.): V, **4**γ, 79.
Dantavaktra, v. Dantavakra.
Dantin. § 269 (Vaiçravaṇasabhāv.): II, **10**, 415 (a being in the palace of Kubera).
Dantolūkhalikāḥ, a kind of ascetics: IX, 2182; XII, 521, 8895; XIII, 647.
Dantolūkhalinaḥ (= the prec.): IX, 2166.
Danu, daughter of Daksha and wife of Kaçyapa, mother of the Dānavas. § 84 (Ādivaṃçāvatāraṇap.): I, **64**, 2486 (°*oḥ putrāḥ*, i.e. the Dānavas, became incarnate on earth).—§ 87 (Aṃçāvat.): I, **65**, 2520 (daughter of Daksha and wife of Kaçyapa).—§ 92 (do.): I, **65**, 2529 (mother of 40 sons, of whom 32 (?) are enumerated), 2534.—[§ 93 (do.): I, **65**, 2536 (v. Danuputra, pl.).]—§ 270 (Brahmasabhāv.): II, **11**, 456 (in the palace of Brahmán).—§ 331 (Kairātap.): III, **39**, 1557 (*Mūkaṃ nāma D°oḥ putraṃ*).—§ 349 (Indralokābhig.): III, **47**, 1895 (*Pātālavāsinaḥ . . . D°oḥ putrāḥ*).—§ 641 (Rājadh.): XII, **98**ξ, 3661 (°*oḥ putrān*).—§ 664 (Mokshadh.): XII, **207**, 7545 (mother of the Dānavas).
Danuja, pl. (°*āḥ*) ("sons of Danu") = Dānava, pl. § 28 (Amṛtamanthana): I, **19**, 1180.
Danuputra, pl. (°*āḥ*) ("sons of Danu") = Dānava, pl. § 93 (Aṃçāvat.): I, **65**, 2536 (°*āḥ, mahārajan, daça Dānavavaṃçajāḥ*, i.e. Ekāksha, etc.).
Darada, pl. (°*āḥ*), a people. § 279 (Arjuna): II, **27**, 1031 (vanquished by Arjuna on his digvijaya).—§ 295 (Dyūtap.): II, **52**, 1869 (among the peoples who brought tribute to Yudhishṭhira).—§ 342 (Indralokābh.): III, **51**, 1990 (had been present at the rājasūya of Yudhishṭhira).—§ 449 (Ājagarap.): III, **177**, 12350 (*Cīnāṃs Tushārān D°ān*, their country crossed by the Pāṇḍavas on their way from Badarī to the capital of Subāhu).—§ 554 (Sainyodyogap.): V, **4**γ, 78 (the king of the *D.* mentioned among the princes to whom the Pāṇḍavas ought to send messengers).—§ 574 (Jambūkh.): VI, **9**ο, 375 (among the peoples in the east and the north).—§ 578 (Bhīshmavadhap.): VI, **51**υ, 2106 (in the army of Duryodhana).—§ 587 (do.): VI, **117**ρ, 5484 (attacked Arjuna).—§ 589 (Droṇābhishekap.): VII, **11**ν, 398 (had formerly been vanquished by Kṛshṇa).—§ 595 (Shoḍaçarāj., v. Rāma Jāmadagnya): VII, **70**β, 2435 (*Kāçmīra-Daradān*, had been slain by Rāma Jāmadagnya).—§ 599 (Jayadrathavadhap.): VII, **93**δ, 3380 (attacked Arjuna); **119**ββ, 4716, 4722 (vanquished by Sātyaki); **121**θθ, 4847 (attacked Sātyaki).—§ 608 (Karṇap.): VIII, **73**, 3652 (among the allies of Duryodhana).—§ 739 (Ānuçāsanik.): XIII, **35**ε, 2158 (have from being kshatriyas been degraded to çūdras).
Darada, a Bālhīka king. § 130 (Aṃçāvat.): I, **67**, 2694 (*Vāhlīkaḥ*, incarnation of the Asura Sūrya).—§ 290*b* (Çiçupālavadhap.): *D.* rent the earth as soon as he was born: II, **44**, 1526 (*Vāhlīkaṃ*).
Dārada, pl. (°*āḥ*), a people = Darada, pl. § 578 (Bhīshmavadhap.): VI, **50**π, 2083 (*Piçācā Dāradāç caiva*, in the army of Yudhishṭhira).
Darbhi(n), an ancient ṛshi. § 368 (Tīrthayātrāp.): III, **83**, 7024, 7027 (made the tīrtha Ardhakīla and brought the four oceans thither).
Darçaka, pl. (°*āḥ*), a people. § 574 (Jambūkh.): VI, **9**μ, 361 (in Bhāratavarsha).
Darçapa, pl. (°*āḥ*), a class of gods. § 730 (Ānuçāsanik.): XIII, **18**λλ, 1372.
Dardura, a mountain. § 269 (Vaiçravaṇasabhāv.): II, **10**, 412 (among the mountains in the palace of Kubera).—§ 295 (Dyūtap.): II, **52**, 1892 (precious gifts from the Malaya and Dardura mountains brought to Yudhishṭhira).—§ 534 (Hanumatpratyāg.): III, **282**, 16239 (in the south).—§ 775 (Ānuçāsanik.): XIII, **166**α, 7658 (only B.; C. has by error *Dururdadaḥ*).
Dari, a serpent. § 67 (Sarpasattra): I, **57**, 2157 (of Dhṛtarāshṭra's race).
Darpa, son of Adharma and Çrī. § 641 (Rājadh.): XII, **90**, 3388 (*D°o nāma Çriyaḥ putro jajñe 'dharmād*), 3390.
Darpada = Vishṇu (1000 names).
Darpahan = Vishṇu (1000 names).
Darpaṇa = Çiva (1000 names[2]).
Dāruka, the charioteer of Kṛshṇa. § 262 (Bhagavadyāna): II, **2**, 36, 50.—§ 292 (Rājasūyikap.): II, **45**, 1620.—§ 320 (Saubhavadhop.): III, **19**, 755 (°*eṇāham utpannaḥ*, says Dāruki), 762 (°*sya sutaḥ*, i.e. Dāruki); **20**, 799, 800; **21**, 821, 822; **22**, 876.—§ 552 (Goharaṇap.): IV, **45**, 1412 (°*o Vāsudevasya yathā*, sc. *sārathiḥ*).—§ 562 (Bhagavadyānap.): V, **83**, 2978; **84**, 3014; **94**, 3341.—§ 567 (do.): V, **131**, 4446.—§ 568 (do.): V, **137**, 4674.—§ 596 (Pratijñāp.): VII, **79**, 2781, 2795, 2796, 2801, 2804, 2805, 2813, 2815, (2818).—§ 597 (do.): VII, **82**, 2911.—§ 599 (Jayadrathavadhap.): VII, **112**, 4350 (°*syānujo bhrātā*, i.e. the charioteer of Sātyaki); **147**, 6338, 6342, 6343 (Sātyaki rode upon the chariot of Kṛshṇa, guided by *D.*), 6351, 6376, 6378 (°*syānujaḥ*, i.e. the charioteer of Sātyaki), 6381.—§ 608 (Karṇap.): VIII, **72**, 3597, 3598, 3599.—§ 615 (Gadāyuddhap.): IX, **62**, 3500; **63**, 3533, 3578.—§ 637 (Rājadh.): XII, **46**, 1584, 1587.—§ 639 (do.): XII, **53**, 1917, 1918.—§ 783 (Anugītāp.): XIV, **52**, 1478, 1534.—§ 793 (Mausalap.): XVI, **3**, 61, 103; **4**, †105, †106, †107, †108; **5**, 133, 136; **7**, 182.
Dārukanandana ("son of Dāruka") = Dāruki: III, 746.
Dārukātmaja (do.) = Dāruki: III, 728, 748.
Dāruki (do.), the charioteer of Pradyumna. § 320 (Saubhavadhop.): III, **18**, 719, 731; **19**, 759. Cf. prec.
Dāruṇa[1], a Suparṇa, son of Garuḍa. § 564 (Mātalīyop.): V, **101**β, 3594.
Dāruṇa[2], pl. (°*āḥ*), a people. § 574 (Jambūkh.): VI, **9**ξ, 373 (in the north).
Dāruṇa[3] = Vishṇu (1000 names).
Darva, pl. (°*āḥ*), a people. § 295 (Dyūtap.): II, **52**, 1869

(among the peoples who brought tribute to Yudhishṭhira).—§ 574 (Jambūkh.): VI, **9**μ, 362.—§ 739 (Ānuçāsanik.): XIII, **35**ε, 2158 (have from being kshatriyas become degraded to çūdras). Cf. next.

Dārva, pl. (°*āḥ*), a people. § 279 (Arjuna): II, **27**, 1026 (in the north, vanquished by Arjuna on his digvijaya). —§ 599 (Jayadrathavadhap.): VII, **93**δ, 3380 (°*ātisārāḥ* (B. °*ābhi*°), attacked Arjuna).—§ 608 (Karṇap.): VIII, **73**, 3652 (°*ābhisārāḥ*, had been vanquished by Arjuna in the battle). Cf. prec.

Darvī (B. *Dā*°), a country (?). § 574 (Jambūkh.): VI, **9**μ, 362.

Darvīsaṃkramaṇa, a tīrtha. § 370 (Tīrthayātrāp.): III, **84**, 8023.

Dāsamīya, pl. (°*āḥ*), a people (?). § 607 (Karṇap.): VIII, **44**, 2056 (*vrātyānāṃ Dāsamīyānāṃ Bāhīkānām ayajvanāṃ | na devāḥ pratigṛhṇanti*, etc. PCR. translates "begotten by Çūdras on the girls of other castes" (agreeable to Nīl., who, however, also gives another explanation: *Dasamadeçodbhāvānāṃ*)), 2069 (*vrātyānāṃ D°ānām annaṃ devā na bhuñjate*, PCR. as above); **45**, 2090 (*vrātyānāṃ D°ānāṃ*, PCR. as above).—§ 608 (do.): VIII, **73**, 3650 (*Govāsa-D°ānāṃ*). Cf. next.

Dāsanīya, a people (?). § 295 (Dyūtap.): II, **51**, 1825 (*Govāsanā brāhmaṇāç ca Dāsanīyāç ca*, Nīl. = *dāsyayogyāḥ çūdrādayaḥ*. BR. compares the preceding).

Dāsarha, v. Dāç°.

Dāseraka, v. Dāç°.

Dāseyī, v. Dāç°.

Dāsī, a river. § 574 (Jambūkh.): VI, **9**λ, 338 (in Bhāratavarsha).

Dasra, one of the Açvins. § 15 (Upamanyu): I, **3**, ††723 (*Nāsatya-D°au*).—§ 608 (Karṇap.): VIII, **89**, †4594 (among the surgeons of Indra, not in B.).—§ 665 (Mokshadh.): XII, **208**γ, 7583 (*Nāsatyaç caiva Dasraç ca smṛtau dvāv Açvināv api*).—§ 717*b* (Nārāyaṇīya): XII, **340**, 12917 (*Nāsatyañ caiva D°ñ ca bhishajau*).—§ 770 (Ānuçāsanik.): XIII, **151**, 7095 (*Nāsatyaç cāpi D°aç ca smṛtau dvāv Açvināv api*).

Dasyu, pl. (°*avaḥ*) ("impious men"): I, 3153 (°*saṅghātān*), 3503, 4308, 4309, 4312, 4315, 4341; II, 1025, 1032; III, 362, 13111 (°*vadhe rataḥ*); IV, 199, 482, 704, 839; V, †1873 (°*saṅghān*), †1889 (°*vadhāya*); VII, 2443 (*nirdasyuṃ pṛthivīṃ kṛtvā*), 4749, 4825, 6790 (°*dharme*); VIII, 0450; XII, 360, 708, †723, 789, 2281 (°*vadhe*), 2284 (°*nibarhaṇāt*), 2431 (°*jīvinaḥ*), 2433 (*sarva*°), 2434, 2437, 2439, 2496, 2554, †2782, †2784, 2835, 2934, 2952 (°*bale*), 2953, 2956, 3255, 3288, 3325, 3342, 3436, 3588, 3684, 3832, 4793, 4825, 4826, 4829, 4831 (sg.), 4833, 4852 (sg.), 4854 (°*tvāt*), 4860 (°*luḥ*), 4861, (4862), 4873, 4875, 4879, 5217, 5324, 5421 (°*maryādā*), 5449 (°*gaṇāḥ*), 6295 (sg.), 6298 (sg.), 6301, 6302, 6305, 6306, 6310, 6411 (sg.), 6422, 6425, 6426, 6573, 6621, 7807, 7808 (sg.), 9563, 9568, 9580 (sg.), 10925, †13204; XIII, 2543, 3047 (°*vat*); XVI, †108, 222, 225, 236, 238.

Dasyumat, a fire. § 493 (Āṅgirasa): III, **221**, 14203 (only C.; B. has Vasumat).

Datta, a ṛshi. § 702 (Mokshadh.): XII, **297**δ, 10875 (among the ṛshis who have obtained their position by way of penances). Cf. Dattātreya.

Dattāmitra = Sumitra: I, 5537.

Dattātman, a Viçvadeva. § 749 (Ānuçāsanik.): XIII, **91**γ, 4359 (enumeration).

Dattātreya, a ṛshi. § 393 (Arjuna Kārtavīrya): III, **115**, 10136 (Arjuna Kārtavīrya, who had 1,000 arms, obtained by the favour of *D.* a celestial chariot (*vimāna*) of gold).—§ 638*b* (Rāmopākhy.): XII, **49**, 1751 (by the favour of *D.* Arjuna Kārtavīrya got 1,000 arms).—§ 749 (Ānuçāsanik.): XIII, **91**, 4329, 4330 (father of Nimi and grandfather of Çrīmat).—§ 772*b* (Pavanārjunasaṃv.): XIII, **153**, 7189 (granted four boons to Arjuna Kārtavīrya: 1,000 arms, etc.; C. has by error °*etāya* instead of °*eyāya*); **154**, 7224 (°*prasādena*); **158**, 7351 (do.).

Dauḥçāsana[1], patron., v. Dauḥçāsani.

Dauḥçāsana[2], adj. ("belonging to Duḥçāsana"). § 608 (Karṇap.): VIII, **83**, †4242 (*rudhiraṃ*, drunk by Bhīmasena).

Dauḥçāsani, patron., the son of Duḥçāsana Dhārtarāshṭra. § 592 (Saṃçaptakavadhap.): VII, **25**, 1096 (fought with Çrutakīrti).—§ 593 (Abhimanyuvadhap.): VII, **33**, 1472; **48**, 1893, 1894; **49**, 1935, 1938 (slew Abhimanyu); **51**, 1988 (had slain Abhimanyu).—§ 596 (Pratijñāp.): VII, **73**, 2577 (do.).—§ 604 (Karṇap.): VIII, **5**ζ, 103 (had been slain by a son of Draupadī); **6**, 160 (all. to § 593).—§ 615 (Gadāyuddhap.): IX, **64**εε, 3615 (among the slain). —§ 620 (Çrāddhap.): XI, **26**β, 787 (his body is burnt; C. has °*naṃ*).—§ 785 (Anugītāp.): XIV, **61**, 1825, 1828 (all. to § 593).

Daurmukhi, a Pāṇḍava warrior. § 600 (Ghaṭotkacavadhap.): VII, **158**χ, 7008 (*Janamejayaḥ* ?).—§ 601 (Droṇavadhap.): VII, **184***a*, 8366.

Dauryodhana, adj. ("belonging to Duryodhana"). § 552 (Goharaṇap.): IV, **55**, 1712 (*bale*).—§ 591 (Saṃçaptakavadhap.): VII, **17**, 720 (*sainyaṃ*).—§ 592 (do.): VII, **18**, 744 (*balaṃ*), 749 (*sainyaṃ*).—§ 608 (Karṇap.): VIII, **93**, 4864 (*balaṃ*).—§ 611 (Çalyap.): IX, **16**, 860 (*sainyaṃ*).—§ 785 (Anugītāp.): XIV, **60**, 1791 (*bale*).

Dauryodhani, patron. ("son of Duryodhana") = Lakshmaṇa: VI, 2367.

Daushmanta, v. Daushyanti.

Daushmanti, v. Daushyanti.

Daushyanta, adj. ("originating from Dushyanta"). § 157 (Pūruvaṃç.): I, **95**, ††3805 (*vaṃçaḥ*).

Daushyanti, patron. ("son of Dushyanta") = Bharata: I, 2989, 3105; VII, 2377 (*Bh*°; C. has *Daushmantaḥ*); XII, 938 (*Bh*°; C. has *Daushmantim*), 940 (*Bh*°; C. has *Daushmantiḥ*), 6105 (*Bh*°; C. has *Daushmantiḥ*); XIV, 50 (*Bh*°; C. has *Daushmantiḥ*); XVIII, 107 (*Bh*°; C. has *Daushmantiḥ*).

Dauvālika, pl. (°*āḥ*), a people. § 295 (Dyūtap.): II, **52**, 1874 (among the people who brought tribute to Yudhishṭhira).

Dayāvāsa = Mahāpurusha (Mahāpurushastava).

Deçarakshin = Çiva: X, 260.

Deha = Çiva (1000 names[2]).

Dehakartṛ = Sūrya (the Sun): III, 157.

Deva[1] = Çiva (1000 names[1-2]).

Deva[2] = Vishṇu (1000 names).

Devabhishagvara, dual (°*au*) = Açvinau: III, 10356.

Devabhishaj, dual (°*au*) = Açvinau: I, 721 (*A*°).

Devabhrāj. § 3 (Anukram.): I, **1**, 43 (son of Mahya (so C., B. Sahya) and father of Subhrāj).

Devabhṛt = Vishṇu (1000 names).

Devācārya ("teacher of the gods") = Bṛhaspati: XIV, 134 (*B*°).

Devaçarman, a ṛshi. § 59 (Sarpasattra): I, **53***a*, 2049 (among the sadasyas at the snake-sacrifice of Janamejaya).—

§ 743b (Vipulop.): XIII, **40,** 2262 (*rshih*), 2264, (2269), (2275), 2287; **41,** 2335, 2341, 2343; **42,** 2355; **43,** 2377, (2378), (2380), 2393 (Vipula, the disciple of *D.*, protected Ruci, the wife of *D.*, against Indra).—§ 775 (Ānuçāsanik.): XIII, **166**ζ, 7672 (one of the ṛshis of the north).

Devaçunī ("the bitch of the gods") = Saramā: I, 671 (*S°*).

Deva-Dānavapūjita = Çiva (1000 names[1]).

Devadāruvana, a tīrtha. § 733k (Vaimānika): XIII, **25,** 1713.

Devadatta, the conch-shell of Arjuna. § 263 (Sabhākriyāp.): II, **3,** 65 (*mahāçaṅkhaḥ*, belonged to Varuṇa (*Vāruṇaḥ*) and was placed in Bindusaras); 78 (Maya fetched *D.* from Bindusaras and gave it to Arjuna).—§ 443 (Nivātakavacayuddhap.): III, **168,** 12076 (*jalodbhavam*, was given to Arjuna by the gods).—§ 444 (do.): III, **169,** 12090.—§ 446 (do.): III, **174,** 12278.—§ 447 (do.): III, **175,** 12296 (*vārijam*).—§ 552 (Goharaṇap.): IV, **57,** 1785 (*çaṅkhavaram*); **66,** †2133.—§ 561 (Yānasandhip.): V, **48,** †1872.—§ 574 (Jambūkh.): VI, **1,** 19.—§ 576 (Bhagavadgītāp.): VI, **25**κ, 844.—§ 578 (Bhīshmavadhap.): VI, **51**aa, 2115.—§ 592 (Saṃçaptakavadhap.): VII, **18,** 729; **19,** 762.—§ 596 (Pratijñāp.): VII, **73,** 2610.—§ 599 (Jayadrathavadhap.): VII, **90,** 3197; **104,** 3902.—§ 608 (Karṇap.): VIII, **53,** 2584; **76,** †3852; **79,** †4054 (all. to § 443); **94,** 4955.

Devadeva[1] ("the god of the gods") = Brahmán (Prajāpati): I, 1628; III, 4062 (*°sya tīrtham . . . Pushkaram*); XII, 7341 (*Prajāpatiḥ*), 9213; XIII, 298 (*Pitāmahaḥ*).

Devadeva[2] = Bṛhaspati: XIII, 3693 (*°opadishṭam dharmam*, so C., but B. has *vedadevo°*).

Devadeva[3] = Çiva: I, 160 (*Tryambakam*), 7324, 7831 (*Pinākadhṛk*), 7832; III, 1525, 1526 (*Çaṅkaram*), 1612, 1625, (1636), 8057 (?), 11992 (*Tryambakasya*), 12237 (*Rudrāya*); V, 1994 (*Umāpatim*), 7393; VII, 9523, 9564 (*Pinākadhṛk*), 9627, 9639; VIII, 1589 (*Çūlinā*), 1605, 1609, 4362 (*Çūlinaḥ*); IX, 2472 (*Umāpatim*); X, 248 (*Umāpatim*); XII, †612 (*hūtvātmānam D°o babhūva*), 4521, 5795, 6184, 10214 (*Pinākadhṛk*), 10328 (*Umāpatim*), 10347, 10679, 10760, 13150 (*Maheçvare*, identified with Nārāyaṇa), 13300 (*Kapardinam*), 13301; XIII, 594 (*Brahmāṇam asṛjat tasmād D°aḥ Prajāpatiḥ*), 603, 698, 700, 726, 800, 818 (*Rudreṇa*), 836, 841, 957, 960, 1035, 1222 (1000 names[2]), 6483, (6627), 6651, (6671), 6766 (*Kapardinaḥ*), 6877; XIV, 195, 1922.

Devadeva[4] = Dharma: III, 17441; XV, 756.

Devadeva[5] = Indra: III, 12001 (?).

Devadeva[6] = Varuṇa: I, 8176.

Devadeva[7] = Vāyu: XII, 9226 (*V°*).

Devadeva[8] = Vishṇu (Kṛshṇa): I, 1533 (*Harim*, not identified with Kṛshṇa), 2785 (*Nārāyaṇaḥ*, a portion of him incarnate as Kṛshṇa), †3594 (?, *°sya niveçane*); III, 8352 (= Kṛshṇa, in Dvāravatī), 10139 (*Vishṇum*), 10934 (*Ādidevam*), 11865, 12948, 13015, 15537 (= Kṛshṇa), 15808 (*Vishṇuḥ*, = do.); V, 410 (*Vishṇunā*), 2954 (= Kṛshṇa); VI, 1219 (= do.), 1259 (= do.), 3040 (= do.), 4462 (= do.), 4864 (= do.); VII, 6467 (= do.); XII, 7653 (*Vishṇoḥ*, = do.), 12716 (*Janārdanam* = do.), 12763 (= do.), 12775 (*Nārāyaṇātmakam*, = do.), 13060 (= do.), ††13205 (= do.?), 13395 (= do.), 13421 (*Vṛshākapiḥ*, = do.); XIII, 6939 (Vishṇu's 1000 names); XIV, 1569 (= Kṛshṇa); XVIII, 170 (*Nārāyaṇaḥ*, Kṛshṇa entered into that god).

Devadeva, dual (*°au*) = Brahmán and Çiva: VIII, 4456.

Devadeveça[1] ("lord of the chiefs of the gods") = Çiva: I, 8123; II, 416 (*Ç°*); VII, 9560; IX, 2812; X, 632 (*Çitikaṇṭham*); XII, 10338, 10348 (1000 names[1]), 10396 (do.); XIII, 930; XIV, 1884 (*Kapardinam*).

Devadeveça[2] = Indra: III, 17191.

Devadeveça[3] = Mahāpurusha (Mahāpurushastava).

Devadeveça[4] = Vishṇu (Kṛshṇa): III, 8762; VII, 2963 (= Kṛshṇa), 8860; XII, 7742 (= Kṛshṇa).

Devadeveçvara (do.) = Vishṇu (Kṛshṇa): VI, 3038 (= Kṛshṇa).

Devādhideva[1] = Brahmán: XIII, 5285 (?, *°sya kumāryaḥ*).

Devādhideva[2] = Çiva: VIII, 1445; XIII, 880, 962.

Devādhideva[3] = Vishṇu: XII, 7624.

Devādhipa[1], a prince. § 130 (Aṃçāvat.): I, **67,** 2663 (incarnation of the Asura Nikumbha).

Devādhipa[2] = Indra, q.v.

Devādhipati = Çiva (1000 names[2]).

***Devadūta**[1] ("messenger of the gods"): I, 636, 969, (969), (973), 975, 977, 3108; III, 2156, 15434, 15437, (15441), 15477, 15478, (15482), 15485; VI, 1966; XIII, 7640; XVIII, 40, 41, 42, 52, 54, 77.—Do.[2] (pl.): XIV, 2774.

***Devadūtaka** (= the prec.): III, 15438.

***Devagaṇa,** pl. (*°āḥ*) ("troops of gods"). § 120 *bis* (Aṃçāvat.): I, **66,** 2604 (the text of this section (vv. 2601–2605) is not clear, and Nīl. is silent, but cf. the translation of PCR.).

Devagandharva, pl. (*°āḥ*) ("celestial Gandharvas"). § 101 (Aṃçāvat.): I, **66,** 2552 (enumeration of 16 *D.*, sons of Muni—*Mauneyāḥ*).—§ 102 (do.): I, **66,** 2556 (enumeration of 10 *D.*, sons of Prādhā—*Prādheyāḥ*).—§ 191 (Arjuna): I, **123,** 4815 (present at the birth of Arjuna; the enumeration is somewhat different from that of §§ 101–102). Cf. Gandharva, pl.

Devagaṇeçvara[1] ("the lord of the divine hosts") = Indra: I, 4788; XIV, 116.

Devagaṇeçvara[2] (do.) = Vishṇu: III, 10921 (*V°*).

Devagaṇeçvara[3] (do.) = Çiva (1000 names[1]).

Devagiri = Himavat (?): XIII, 6872.

Devagraha, a demon of disease. § 502 (Manushyagrahak.): III, **230,** 14501.

Devaguru[1] ("the preceptor of the gods") = Bṛhaspati: V, 480; XII, 1353, 5667 (*B°*).

Devaguru[2] = Çiva: XIII, 696.

Devahavya, a ṛshi. § 266 (Çakrasabhāv.): II, **7,** 300 (in the palace of Indra).

Devahotra, a ṛshi. § 717c (Uparicara): XII, **337**ε, 12760 (among the sadasyas at the sacrifice of king Vasu Uparicara).

Devahrada, name of various tīrthas. § 370 (Tīrthayātrāp.): III, **85,** 8162, 8180 (*Kṛshṇaveṇājalodbhave*).—§ 372 (do.): III, **85,** 8199.—§ 730t (Viçālā): XIII, **25,** 1730.

Devāhvaya, an ancient king. § 6 (Anukram.): I, **1**a, 228 (in Sañjaya's enumeration).

Devaka[1], a Gandharva king. § 130 (Aṃçāvat.): I, **67,** 2704 (*Gandharvapatiḥ*, re-born on earth, presumably as one of the princes mentioned under the heading Devaka[2]).

Devaka[2], one or more princes. § 179 (Viduraparinaya): I, **114,** 4480 (*mahīpateḥ*, Vidura married his daughter, who was a *pāraçavī*).—§ 554 (Sainyodyogap.): V, **4**γ, 80 (among the princes to whom the Pāṇḍavas ought to send messengers).—§ 599e (Çini): VII, **144,** 6033 (father of Devakī, the wife of Vasudeva).

***Devakanyā** ("a celestial maiden"): III, 10004 (sg., transformed into a hind she became the mother of Ṛshyaçṛṅga); IV, 258 (sg.); IX, 2468 (pl.); XI, 564 (pl.); XIII, 626 (pl.), 5238 (pl.). Cf. Apsaras.

Devakī, daughter of Devaka, wife of Vasudeva, and mother of Kṛshṇa. § 82 (Kṛshṇa Vāsudeva): I, **63**, 2428 (*Vishṇuḥ . . . Vasudevāt tu D°yāṃ prādurbhūtaḥ*). — § 238 (Pañcendrop.): I, **197**, †7308 (the black hair of Vishṇu entered *D.* and was born as Kṛshṇa).—§ 599*e* (Çini): VII, **144**, 6034 (*Devakasya . . . duhituḥ*), 6035 (won at a svayaṃvara by Çini for Vasudeva).—§ 637 (Rājadh.): XII, **47**θ, 1616 (*yaṃ devaṃ D°ī ajījanat*, i.e. Kṛshṇa).—§ 746 (Ānuçāsanik.): XIII, **64**, 3253 (°*yāç caiva saṃvādaṃ maharsher Nāradasya ca*), 3254.—§ 783 (Anugītāp.): XIV, **52**δ, 1522.—§ 785 (do.): XIV, **66**, 1950; **71**, 2074.—§ 793 (Mausalap.): XVI, **7**, 194 (among the widows of Vasudeva).

Devakīmātṛ, Devakinandana, Devakīnandana[1] = Kṛshṇa, q.v.

Devakīnandana[2] (Dai°, C.) = Vishṇu (1000 names).

Devakīputra, Devakīsuta, Devakītanaya = Kṛshṇa, q.v.

Devakūṭa, a sacred mountain. § 370 (Tīrthayātrāp.): III, **84**, 8119.

Devala, v. Asita Devala.

***Devaloka** ("the world of the gods"): I, 1352, 2866 (°*pratikāçaṃ*), 3552, †7302; III, 925, 1727, 11163, 11533, †12719, †12723, ††13342, 16957; VI, 260, 299, 3986; VIII, †4921; IX, 2990, 3085; XII, †725, †726, †727, †729, †730, †764, †765, †766, 1047, 1866, †10068, 10096 (pl.), 12958; XIII, 1714, 1739, 2994, 7562; XIV, †235, 436, 1765 (*iva*); XV, 895, 902; XVII, †85; XVIII, 197, 237.

Devamata, a ṛshi. § 782*b* (Brāhmaṇagītā): XIV, **24**, 711 (*Nāradasya ca saṃvādam ṛsher Devamatasya ca*), (712).

Devamātṛ[1] ("the mother of the gods") = Aditi: IX, 2515 (*A*°).

Devamātṛ[2], pl. (°*araḥ*): XIII, 626.

Devamīḍha, a Yādava prince. § 599*e* (Çini): VII, **144**, 6030 (father of Çūra and grandfather of Vasudeva).

Devamitrā, a mātṛ. § 615*u* (Skanda): IX, **46**θ, 2632.

***Devanadī** ("celestial river"): I, 6458 (i.e. Gaṅgā); II, 372; III, 9948 (i.e. Gaṅgā), 9989 (*Kauçikī*), 11622 (i.e. Gaṅgā), 15548, 15557; XIII, 101 (*Narmadā*), 7655.

Devanagara ("the city of the gods"). § 444 (Nivātakavacayuddhap.): III, **172**, 12187. Cf. Devapura.

Devapatha, a tīrtha. § 370 (Tīrthayātrāp.): III, **85**, 8187.

Devapati = Indra, q.v.

Devāpi, son of Pratīpa. § 155 (Pūruvaṃç.): I, **94**, 3750 (eldest son of Pratīpa), 3751 (renounced the world—*pravavrāja*). — § 156 (do.): I, **95**, ††3797, ††3798 (being yet a child *D.* retired to the woods, and Çāntanu therefore became king).—§ 569 (Bhagavadyānap.): V, **149**, 5055, 5056, 5057, 5062, 5066 (on account of a skin disease *D.'s* installation on the throne was forbidden by the brahmans; *D.* then retired to the woods).—§ 615 (Baladevatīrthayātrāp.): IX, **39**, 2282; **40**, 2280, 2294 (had become a brahman).—§ 619 (Strīvilāpap.): XI, **23**, 651 (°*inā samaṃ*, sc. Bhīshma).

Devaprastha, a city. § 279 (Arjuna): II, **27**, 1022 (the capital of Senābindu, conquered by Arjuna on his digvijaya).

Devapura ("the city of the gods"). § 596 (Pratijñāp.): VII, **73**, 2608 (in Arjuna's oath). Cf. Devanagara.

Devapurohita ("the priest of the gods") = Bṛhaspati: II, 2458 (*B*°); IX, 2102 (*B*°); XII, 12752.

Devarāj[1] = Indra, q.v.

Devarāj[2] = Nahusha, q.v.

Devarāja[1] = Indra, q.v.

Devarāja[2] = Nahusha, q.v.

Devarāja[3] = Vasishṭha: XIII, 6256 (*V*°).

Devarāja[4], an ancient king. § 267 (Yamasabhāv.): II, **8**, 337 (in the palace of Yama).

Devarājābhinandana = Arjuna: III, 1858.

Devarājan[1] = Indra, q.v.

Devarājan[2] = Nahusha, q.v.

***Devāraṇya**, pl. (°*āni*) ("the forests of the gods"): I, 6069, 7853 (°*vihāriṇī*, sc. Vargā); V, 433, 7354; VII, 2297.

Devarāta[1], a prince. § 264 (Sabhākriyāp.): II, **4**β, 121 (waited upon Yudhishṭhira).

Devarāta[2], a muni, son of Viçvāmitra. § 637 (Rājadh.): XII, **47**η, 1593 (among the ṛshis who surrounded Bhīshma as he lay on his arrow-bed).—§ 721 (Ānuçāsanik.): XIII, **3***a*, 188 (fifty sons of Viçvāmitra were cursed to become *çvapacas* because they did not honour their eldest brother *D.*).—§ 721*b* (Viçvāmitrop.): XIII, **4**β, 249 (enumeration of the sons of Viçvāmitra).

Devāribalasūdana = Çiva (1000 names[1]).

Devarshi[1], pl. ("celestial ṛshis," or "gods and ṛshis"). § 7 (Anukram.): I, **1**, 248.—§ 20*b* (Agni): I, **7**, 936.—§ 70 (Ādivaṃçāvatāraṇap.): I, **60**, 2219 (°*gaṇapūjitaṃ*, sc. Vyāsa).—§ 155 (Pūruv.): I, **94**, 3752 (°*kalpāḥ . . . rājasattamāḥ*).—§ 164 (Āpavop.): I, **99**, 3930 (°*sevitaṃ*, sc. *vanaṃ*).—§ 165 (Satyavatīlābhop.): I, **100**, 3983.—§ 171 (Vicitravīryasutotpatti): I, **105**, 4273.—§ 173 (Pāṇḍurājyābhisheka): I, **109**, 4346 (°-*Cāraṇaiḥ*).—§ 186*b* (Vyushitāçvop.): I, **121**, 4687.—§ 221 (Caitrarathap.): I, **170**, 6497 (*Nāradaprabhṛtīnāṃ*).—§ 233 (Svayaṃvarap.): I, **187**, †7011, †7017 (°*Gandharvasamākulaṃ*).—§ 246 (Sundopasundop.): I, **211**, 7679.—§ 266 (Çakrasabhāv.): II, **7**, 289 (in the palace of Indra), 291 (do.), 307 (do.).—§ 269 (Vaiçravaṇasabhāv.): II, **10**, 401 (in the palace of Kubera).—§ 270 (Brahmasabhāv.): II, **11**, 468.—§ 289 (Arghāharaṇap.): II, **36**, 1309.—§ 336 (Indralokābhigamanap.): III, **43**, 1775 (*Çakrāsane D°gaṇasevite*).—§ 356 (Tīrthayātrāp.): III, **81**, 4034 (*deçe . . . D°sevite*).—§ 358 (do.): III, **82**, 4082 (*Jambūmārgaṃ . . . D°-Pitṛ-sevitaṃ*).—§ 360 (do.): III, **82**, 5049 (*Devikā . . . D°sevitā*).—§ 370 (do.): III, **84**, 8119 (*Devakūṭaṃ . . . D°gaṇasevitaṃ*).—§ 377 (Dhaumyatīrthak.): III, **87**, 8302 (°*jushṭāyāṃ*, sc. *diçi prācyāṃ*), 8303 (*Gomatī . . . D°sevitā*); **88**, 8347 (°*vīreṇa Nāradena*); **89**, 8361 (°*sevite*, sc. the mountain Vaidūryaçikhara); **90**, 8402 (in Badarī).—§ 378 (Tīrthayātrāp.): III, **94**, 8487 (°*sattamu*, i.e. Lomaça), 8508.—§ 383 (Paraçurāma): III, **99**, 8675.—§ 412 (Ashtāvakrīya): III, **134**, 10659 (*dvau devarshī Nārada-Parvatau*).—§ 421 (Gandhamādanapr.): III, **142**, 10902 (*mahānadī Badarīprabhavā . . . D°gaṇasevitā*).—§ 423 (do.): III, **143**, 10966 (*deçān D°gaṇasevitān*); **145**, 11054 (*deva-D°pūjitaṃ Nara-Nārāyaṇasthānaṃ*), 11065 (°*carite deçe*).—§ 432 (Saugandhikāharaṇap.): III, **154**, 11371.—§ 434 (do.): III, **156**, 11439 (*divyapushkariṇī . . . siddha-D°pūjitā*).—§ 436 (Yakshayuddhap.): III, **159**, 11651 (*paramasiddhānāṃ*).—§ 439 (do.): III, **163**, 11855 (*sapta Devarshayaḥ . . . Vaçishṭhapramukhāḥ*, on Mahāmeru).—§ 444 (Nivātakavacayuddhap.): III, **169**, 12101 (°*ayaç caiva Dānavarshayaḥ*).—§ 447 (do.): III, **175**, 12303.—§ 450 (Ājagarap.): III, **178**, 12368 (*deçān girer Himavataḥ . . . D°-Siddhacaritān*).—§ 462 (Baka-Çakrasaṃv.): III, **193**, 13236 (°*gaṇasevita*, sc. Baka).—§ 496 (Skandotpatti): III, **224**, 14281 (*Vaçishṭapramukhāḥ*).—§ 505 (Skandayuddha): III, **231**, 14538.—§ 525 (Rāmopākhyānap.): III, **273**, 15862 (°*ṇāṃ tvaṃ khyāto bhūtabhavishyavit*, sc. Mārkaṇḍeya).—§ 526 (do.): III, **276**, 15929.—§ 547 (Karṇa): III,

310, †17219 (°*iṇāṃ caritam*, told by Mārkāṇḍeya to the Pāṇḍavas).—§ 555 (Indravijaya): V, **10,** 341; **12,** 378 (°*sattama*, i.e. Bṛhaspati), 382 (do.); **16,** 496 (°-*Gandharvaiḥ*), 498, 505 (°*gaṇatejasā*); **17,** 528.—§ 562 (Bhagavadyānap.): V, **83,** 2985.—§ 564 (Mātalīyop.): V, **98,** 3528 (°*sadṛçīṃ pūjāṃ*).—§ 565 (Gālavacarita): V, **109,** 3783 (in the east). —§ 576 (Bhagavadgītāp.): VI, **34,** 1230 (°*iṇāṃ Nāradaḥ*, sc. *asmi*, says Kṛshṇa).—§ 578 (Bhīshmavadhap.): VI, **45,** 1753 (came to see the battle).—§ 584 (do.): VI, **81,** 3571.—§ 596 (Pratijñāp.): VII, **73,** 2607 (*Brahma-devarshayaḥ*).—§ 599 (Jayadrathavadhap.): VII, **139,** 5746 (applauded the combatants).—§ 600 (Ghaṭotkacavadhap.): VII, **163,** †7292 (°-*Gandharva-surarshisaṅghāḥ*). — § 605 (Karṇap.): VIII, **16,** 626 (°*saṅghāḥ*).—§ 608 (do.): VIII, **87,** 4423 (*Deva-Brahma-nṛparshīṇāṃ gaṇāḥ*), 4433 (*saha-D°-Cāraṇāḥ*), 4452 (*saha-D°-Cāraṇaiḥ*). — § 615*u* (Skanda): IX, **44,** 2481; **45**γ, 2509.—§ 615*z* (Arundhatī): IX, **48,** 2812 (*siddha-D°dayitaṃ . . . Badarapācanaṃ*).—§ 615*aa* (Çrutāvatī): IX, **48,** 2829 (°*gaṇasaṃsadi*).—§ 618 (Jalapradānikap.): XI, **8**ζ, 214 (*Nāradapramukhāç ca sarva-D°ayaḥ*). — § 621 (Rājadh.): XII, **10,** 298.—§ 624 (do.): XII, **18,** 543.—§ 635 (do.): XII, **37,** 1352 (*Bṛhaspatipurogān*).—§ 637 (do.): XII, **47**θ, 1607 (surrounded Bhīshma as he lay on his arrow-bed). — § 641 (do.): XII, **91,** 3460 (°-*Pitṛ-Gandharvāḥ*); **122,** 4473 (°*sadṛçaḥ*, sc. Vasuhoma).—§ 663 (Mokshadh.): XII, **201,** †7367 (°*saṅghapravaro maharshiḥ* | *Bṛhaspatiḥ*). — § 666 (Mokshadh.): XII, **209,** 7612.—§ 667 (do.): XII, **210,** 7663 (°*caritaṃ Gārgyaḥ*, sc. *veda*).—§ 674*b* (Çrī-Vāsavasaṃv.): XII, **229,** 8339 (°*jushṭāyāḥ*, sc. *Gaṅgāyāḥ*), 8341 (°*kathitāḥ kathāḥ*).—§ 677 (Mokshadh.): XII, **233,** 8523 (°*Pitṛmānavān*); **235,** 8587 (°*Pitṛgur-vartham*).—§ 694*b* (Jvarotpatti): XII, **284,** 10218 (*Aṅgiraḥ-pramukhāḥ*). — § 704 (Mokshadh.): XII, **302**β, 11106 (°*vishayān*).—§ 712 (Çukotpatti): XII, **324,** 12178 (*vane . . . deva-D°saṅkule*); **325,** 12203.—§ 714 (Çukakṛtya): XII, **329,** 12378 (°*gaṇajushṭaḥ*, sc. *parvataḥ*; C. has by error °*guṇa*°).—§ 717*b* (Nārāyaṇīya): XII, **341,** 13062, 13093. — § 718*b* (Uñchavṛttyup.): XII, **362,** 13866.—§ 721 (Ānuçāsanik.): XIII, **3,** 190 (°*sevitā*, sc. *Kauçikī*).—§ 730 (do.): XIII, **14***aa*, 987.—§ 751*b* (Çapathavidhi): XIII, **94,** †4589 (*Brahmarshi-D°-nṛparshimadhye*).—§ 759 (Ānuçāsanik.): XIII, **107,** 5319 (°*caritaṃ*), 5322 (do.), 5335 (*Rudra-D°kanyābhiḥ*).—§ 760 (do.): XIII, **112,** 5543 (°*Pitṛ-mānavāḥ*). — § 768*b* (Umā-Maheçvarasaṃv.): XIII, **140***a*, 6347 (°*gaṇasevitaṃ*, sc. *sado Vṛshabhāṅkasya*, on Himavat).—§ 768*b* (Kṛshṇa Vāsudeva): XIII, **148,** 6817 (°*çaraṇasya*, i.e. Kṛshṇa). — § 775 (Ānuçāsanik.): XIII, **166,** 7686.—§ 778*b* (Saṃvartta-Maruttīya): XIV, **7,** 157 (°*sattamaḥ*, i.e. Nārada).—§ 778*f* (Muñjavat): XIV, **8,** 184 (on Muñjavat).—§ 782*b* (Brāhmaṇagītā): XIV, **26,** 751 (*Prajāpatau pannagānāṃ D°iṇāñ ca saṃvidam*), 752, 756 (*sarpa-D°-Dānavāḥ*).—§ 785 (Anugītāp.): XIV, **77,** 2237, 2244; **88,** 2638 (°*saṅkulaḥ*, sc. the açvamedha of Yudhi-shṭhira).—§ 787 (Āçramavāsap.): XV, **1,** 14 (*kathāḥ . . . purāṇarshi-D°-Pitṛ-Rakshasām*).—§ 788 (do.): XV, **27,** 736 (*Vyāsaḥ . . . D°gaṇasevitaḥ*).—§ 789 (Putradarçanap.): XV, **31**ζ, 848, 849 (have been incarnate as warriors in the battle).—§ 794 (Mahāprasthānikap.): XVII, **3,** 95, 106.

Devarshi², sg. Names of single Devarshis:—

Asita: I, 4045 (*A*°).

Bhūrbhuva: XIII, 5285 (read with B. *Bhūrbhuvaṃ cāpi*).

Bṛhaspati: I, 2705 (*B*°); II, 1793 (*B*°); V, 378 (°*sattama*), 382 (do.).

Kaçyapa: I, 2557.

Lomaça: III, 8471 (*L*°), 8487 (°*sattama*); XI, 775 (*L*°).

Nārada: I, 7342 (?), 7604 (*N*°), 7605, 7609, 7740 (*N*°), 7874 (*N*°), 7875; II, 145, 268, 2654; III, 4022, 8261 (°*caritaṃ*), 8347 (°*vīreṇa*), 12603 (*N*°), 12605 (do.), 16662; V, 3583, 3637; VI, 1217 (*N*°); VII, 2034 (*N*°), 2035, 2127, 2144, 2168 (*N*°); IX, 3056; XI, 14 (*N*°); XII, 144 (*N*°), 1074 (*N*°), 3029, 5829, 7038 (*N*°), 7520 (*N*°), 7564 (*N*°), 8348 (*N*°), 8418 (*N*°), 10555 (*N*°), 11510, 12314 (*N*°), 12423 (*N*°), 12583 (*N*°), 12647 (*N*°), 12893, 13772; XIII, 2204 (*N*°), 2208, 2209, 2210, 2222, 2227, 3255 (*N*°), 6337 (*N*°); XIV, 130 (*N*°), 157 (°*sattamaḥ*), 364 (*N*°); XV, 542 (*N*°), 562, 574, 1011 (*N*°).

Parvata: III, 8483 (*P*°).

Tanu: XII, 4679.

Uçanas: XII, 10660 (*Uçanāḥ*).

Vasishṭha: III, 16600; XIII, 3968 (*V*°).

Devarshi³ = Çiva (1000 names²).

Devasārathi = Mātali: III, 12254.

Devasenā ("the army of the gods"), the wife of Skanda. § 495 (Skandotpatti): III, **224,** 14257 (*Prajāpateḥ* (i.e. Kaçyapa's) *kanyā*, sister of Daityasenā; Indra liberated her from Keçin), 14278 (Brahmán selected the son whom Agni would beget (i.e. Skanda) to become her husband).—§ 501 (Skandop.): III, **229,** 14446, 14447 (Skanda married *D.*), 14450, 14452.

Devasenāpati ("general of the army of the gods," or "husband of Devasenā") = Skanda: III, 14454, 14455, 14568.

Devasenāpriya = Skanda: III, 14635.

Devasiṃha = Çiva (1000 names²).

Devasthāna, a Brahmarshi. § 621 (Rājadharm.): XII, **1**β, 4.—§ 626 (do.): XII, **20,** 601, (602); **21,** (615).—§ 637 (do.): XII, **37**γ, 1370; **47**η, 1592.—§ 640 (do.): XII, **58**γ, 2116.—§ 780 (Açvamedhikap.): XIV, **14**β, 355, 364.

Devāsura, adj. ("concerning the gods and the Asuras"): I, 1418 (*abhūtapūrvaṃ saṃgrāme tadā D°e 'pi ca*), 4104 (*yuddhaṃ . . . D°opamaṃ*); III, 12269 (*atidevāsuraṃ karma*), 13216 (*saṃgrāme*), 14268 (*saṃgrāmaṃ*), 16374 (sc. *yuddhe*); IV, 1040 (°*samaḥ*, sc. *samāgamaḥ*), 1902 (°*samaḥ sannipātaḥ*); V, 1927 (*yuddhe*), 2986 (°*sya drashṭāraḥ*, sc. *yuddhasya*), 3645 (*yuddheshu*), 4299 (*yuddhe*); VI, 768 (*yuddhe*), 1754 (*raṇaṃ . . . D°opamaṃ*), 2073 (sc. *yuddhe*), 2474 (*yathā D°ṃ yuddhaṃ*), 3474 (*yathā D°e yuddhe*), 3649 (°*opamaṃ*, sc. *janakshayaṃ*), 4493 (*yathā D°e yuddhe*), 4583 (do.), 5411 (do.), 5567 (*yuddhe D°opame*); VII, 542 (*yathā D°e yuddhe*), 583 (*yuddhaṃ D°opamaṃ*), 758 (*yathā . . . yuddhe D°e*), 1084 (*yuddhaṃ . . . D°opamaṃ*), 2295 (*yuddhe*), 3821 (*mṛdhe*), 3947 (*yathā D°e yuddhe*), 3968 (*saṅgrāmaḥ . . . D°opamaḥ*), 4495 (*yuddhaṃ . . . D°opamaṃ*), 4601 (°*opamaṃ*), 4910 (*yuddhe*), 5231 (*yuddhaṃ D°opamaṃ*), 5886 (*yuddhe . . . yathā*), 7075 (*yathā D°e yuddhe*), 7582 (do.), 8819 (*yuddhe . . . D°opame*); VIII, 516 (*yathā D°e yuddhe*), 565 (do.), 1205 (*saṅgrāmaṃ . . . D°opamaṃ*), 1391 (*yathā . . . yuddhe D°e*), 2233 (*saṃgrāmaḥ . . . D°opamaḥ*), 2273 (*yuddhaṃ . . . Devāsuropamaṃ*), 3024 (°*e . . . mṛdhe . . . iva*); **IX,** 2529 (*yuddhe*), 3519 (*yuddhe*); XIII, 2175 (sc. *yuddhaṃ*).

Devāsuragaṇāçraya = Çiva (1000 names²).

Devāsuragaṇādhyaksha = Çiva: VIII, 1574; XIII, 1259 (1000 names[2]).

Devāsuragaṇāgraṇī = Çiva (1000 names[2]).

Devāsuraguru[1] = Brahmán: XIII, 7634.

Devāsuraguru[2] = Çiva (1000 names[2]).

Devāsuramahāmātra = Çiva (1000 names[2]).

Devāsuramaheçvara = Çiva (1000 names[2]).

Devāsuranamaskṛta = Çiva (1000 names[2]).

Devāsuraparāyaṇa = Çiva (1000 names[2]).

Devāsurapati = Çiva (1000 names[2]).

Devāsuravarapradа = Çiva (1000 names[2]).

Devāsuravinirmātṛ = Çiva (1000 names[2]).

Devāsureçvara = Çiva (1000 names[2]).

Devasya tīrtham = Brahmasaras: XIII, 4553.

Devatātman = Çiva (1000 names[2]).

Devātideva[1] = Brahmán: XII, 10681 (*B*°).

Devātideva[2] = Çiva (1000 names[2]).

Devātithi, a prince. § 156 (Pūruvaṃç.): I, **95**, ††3775 (son of Akrodhana and Karambhā), ††3776 (husband of Maryādā and father of Ariha).

Devavana, name of a sacred place. § 377 (Dhaumyatīrthak.): III, **87**, 8322 (*rāmyaṃ tāpasair upaçobhitaṃ*, in the east).

Devavara[1] = Sūrya: III, 161.

Devavara[2] = Vishṇu: III, 13580.

Devavara[3] = Brahmán: XIII, 4949.

Devavara[4] = Çiva: XII, 10805 (*Ç*°).

Devavrata = Bhīshma, q.v.

Devāvṛdha, a prince. § 6 (Anukram.): I, **1***a*, 228 (in Sañjaya's enumeration of departed kings).—§ 608 (Karṇap.): VIII, **85***ρ*′, †4307 (*Krātha-D*°*au*, among the *Kuru* warriors; but should we not read *Daivāvṛdha*? cf. *Devāvṛdhasūnuḥ*, v. 4322).—§ 677 (Mokshadh.): XII, **235**, 8595 (by having given a costly umbrella to a brahman *D.* attained to heaven).—§ 767 (Ānuçās.): XIII, **137***a*, 6251 (do.).

Devāvṛdhasūnu = Babhru: VIII, †4322.

Devayājin, a warrior of Skanda. § 615*u* (Skanda): IX, **45***η*, 2572.

***Devayāna**, subst. (or adj., sc. *pathin*) ("the way that leads to the gods"): I, 3681; III, 123 (sc. *caturvargaḥ*?), 10100, 10104, 10106, 15442 (°*caraḥ*); V, †793; XII, 525, 9609 (pl.), 12394 (°*caraḥ*); XIII, 1081 (°*ānām āditye dvāram ucyate*), †4312, †4318; XIV, 980 (pl.); XV, 930 (pl.).

Devayānī, daughter of Uçanas (Çukra) and wife of Yayāti. § 143 (Nahusha): I, **75**, 3159 (mother of Yadu and Turvasu).—§ 145 (Kaca): I, **76**, 3186, 3197, 3198, 3205, 3206, 3207, 3208, 3212, (3213), 3222, 3226, †3229, (†3231), †3238, †3239, (†3240), †3241 (prevailed upon *Uçanas* to revive *Kaca*); **77**, (3256), 3263, (3264), (3271), 3273, 3276 (*Kaca* would not accept her as his wife, because he, being a disciple of Uçanas, regarded her as his sister; *D.* then cursed *Kaca*).—§ 146: When *Kaca* had imparted to the gods the *Sañjīvanī* they set out with *Indra* at their head to defeat the *Asuras*. In a wood like *Caitraratha*, *Indra* transformed himself into wind and mixed up the clothes of some bathing maidens. A quarrel about the clothes resulted in *D.'s* being thrown into a well by *Çarmishṭhā*, the daughter of *Vṛshaparvan*. *Yayāti* found her and drew her up by her right hand, and then returned to his capital. *Devayānī* sent *Ghūrṇikā* to inform *Çukra* of what had passed (I, **78–79**). *Çukra* threatened *Vṛshaparvan* that he would leave the Asuras, until *Çarmishṭhā*, together with 1,000 maidens, was given to *D.* (I, **80**). Surrounded by *Çarmishṭhā* and 2,000 maidens, *Devayānī* one day again met *Yayāti*, who at her request received her in marriage from *Çukra*, and promised that he would never invite *Çarmishṭhā* to share his bed (I, **81**): I, **78**, 3284, 3285, (3285), 3290, (3297), 3302, (3303), 3307, (3309), 3314; **79**, 3319, 3321, (3326); **80**, 3341, 3343, 3344, (3345), 3346, (3347), 3348, 3350, 3351, (3354), 3356, (3357); **81**, 3359, 3363, 3364, (3367), (3370), (3373), (3375), 3376, (3377), (3379), (3382), (3385), 3386, (3388), 3392, 3395.—§ 147: *Devayānī* gave birth to a son. After 1,000 years had elapsed, *Çarmishṭhā* attained to puberty and prevailed upon Yayāti to beget a son also with her (I, **82**); to *Devayānī* she said that she had born the child to a *ṛshi* whose name she had not dared to ask. The sons of *Devayānī* were *Yadu* and *Turvasu*, those of *Çarmishṭhā* were *Druhyu*, *Anu*, and *Pūru*. One day, when *Devayānī* was walking in the wood together with *Yayāti*, she met the children of *Çarmishṭhā* and asked them: "Who is your father?" They then pointed to *Yayāti*. *Devayānī* in anger withdrew to *Uçanas*, followed by *Yayāti*. *Uçanas* cursed *Yayāti* to be overcome by decrepitude, yet with the permission of transferring it to someone else, and he added that that son of *Yayāti* who would give him his own youth should succeed *Yayāti* on the throne, etc. (I, **83**): I, **82**, 3397, 3398, 3400, 3401, 3404, 3411, 3419; **83**, 3424, 3425, (3425), (3428), (3430), 3432, 3434, (3436), (3437), 3439, (3442), 3446, (3451), 3461.—§ 148 (Yayāti): I, **85**, 3519 (°*yāḥ sutaṃ* . . . *Yaduṃ*).—§ 156 (Pūruvaṃç.): I, **95**, ††3761 (*Uçanaso duhitā*), 3762 (*Yaduñ ca Turvasuñ caiva D*°*ī vyajāyata*).—§ 569 (Bhagavadyānap.): V, **149**, 5045 (*Yaduḥ* . . . *D*°*yāḥ sutaḥ*).—§ 595 (Shoḍaçarāj., v. Yayāti): VII, **63**, 2297 (wife of Yayāti).—§ 599*e* (Çini): VII, **144**, 6030 (*Yayāter D*°*yān tu Yadur jyeshṭo 'bhavat sutaḥ*). Cf. Auçanasī, Bhārgavī, Çukratanayā.

Devayuga = Kṛtayuga. I, 1073; II, 421; III, 8492, 8686; X, 786; XII, 93; XIII, 3903.

Deveça[1] ("lord of the gods") = Brahmán: I, 1647; III, 10949 (*B*°); VI, 5770 (*Pitāmahaṃ*); VII, 2081; IX, 1964 (*B*°), 2494; XII, 9218, 10187, 10195; XIII, 1113 (*B*°), 2256, 3890, 4925, 4943, 6845 (*Pitāmahaḥ*).

Deveça[2] (do.) = Çiva: I, 1932 (*Çūlapāṇiḥ*), 2315, 7322; III, 1545, 1631, 7034 (*Sthāṇuḥ*); VII, 1758, 1759 (all. to Jayadrathavimokshaṇaparvan); VIII, 1457, 1465, 1512, 1516, 1536, 1541, 1544, 1545, 1590, 1601, 1612; IX, 2050 (?), 2483 (*Çūlahastaṃ*); X, 251; XII, 10675, 12172; XIII, 744, 794, 796, 876, 922, 923, 6665, 6760, 6804 (read *Deveçaḥ* with B.).

Deveça[3] (do.) – Daksha. IX, 2044.

Deveça[4] (do.) – Indra: I, 3844 (?), 4400, 8225 (*Çatakratuṃ Sahasrākshaṃ*); III, 1771 (*Pākaçāsanaṃ*), 8413, 12010 (*Maghavān*), 14374, 14376, 16990 (*Purandaraṃ*); V, 525, 3664, 3682; VII, 37, 3861; VIII, 1670; IX, 2832; XII, 8414; XIII, 2307, 5972 (*Çacīpate*).

Deveça[5] (do.) = Kṛshṇa or Vishṇu: III, 10120 (not = Kṛshṇa?), 12947 (do.?), 15535; V, 411 (not = Kṛshṇa); VI, †1271, †1283, †1291, †2604, 2963; XII, 12714, 12804, 12874, 13001, 13363, 13415, 13581 (*Hariṃ Nārāyaṇaṃ*), 13657, 13658; XIII, 1113 (according to the reading of C.; B. has *Deveçaḥ* = Brahmán), 6887 (*Yādavaṃ*), 7801 (Vishṇu's 1000 names).

Deveça[6] (do.) = Yama: III, 16757.

Deveça[7], dual (°*au*) = Brahmán and Çiva: III, 499.

Deveçaya = Mahāpurusha (Mahāpurushastava).

Deveçī = Umā: XII, 10301.

Deveçvara[1] = Çiva: VIII, 1469.

Deveçvara[2] = Indra: II, 286, 1800 (?, *yathā*); III, †10257, 17192; VII, 9053 (*yathā*); XII, 12205 (*Çakraḥ*).
Devendra[1] = Indra, q.v.
Devendra[2] = Nahusha, q.v.
Devendra[3] = Çiva (1000 names [1–2]).
Devendratanaya = Arjuna: VII, 7716.
Devī[1], an Apsaras. § 191 (Arjuna): I, **123**, 4818 (among the Apsarases who danced at the birth of Arjuna).
Devī[2] = Umā (Durgā), q.v.
Devī[3], the wife of Varuṇa. § 124 (Aṃçāvat.): I, **66**, 2616 (the eldest daughter of Çukra; mother of Bala and Surā).
Devī[4] = Sāvitrī (the wife of Brahmán): V, 3969 (*reme . . . yathā D°yāṃ Pitāmahaḥ*); XII, 7204, 7205 (*Vedamātā*), 7206, 7207, 7209, 7210, 7211, 7335.
Devikā[1], wife of Yudhishṭhira. § 159 (Pūruvaṃç.): I, **95**, ††3828 (daughter of Govāsana Çaibya, wife of Yudhishṭhira, and mother of Yaudheya).
Devikā[2], a river. § 360 (Tīrthayātrāp.): III, **82**, 5044 (a tīrtha), 5045, 5049. — § 494 (Āṅgirasa): III, **222**, 14229 (among the rivers who are mothers of fires).—§ 574 (Jambūkh.): VI, **9**λ, 324 (in Bhāratavarsha). — § 733c (Pushkara): XIII, **25**, 1696 (a tīrtha).—§ 733i (Ānuçāsanik.): By bathing in *D.* and in Sundarikāhrada, as also in the tīrtha Açvinī, one acquires great beauty after death: XIII, **25**, 1707.—§ 768b (Umā-Maheçvarasaṃv.): XIII, **146**δ, 6764 (among the rivers who are present with Umā).— § 775 (Ānuçāsanik.): XIII, **166a**, 7645.
Devyās tīrtha(ṃ), a tīrtha. § 364 (Tīrthayātrāp.): III, **83**, 6064, 6072 (the same ?).
Dhāma, pl. (°*āḥ*), a class of celestial beings, mostly mentioned together with the Yāmas. § 520 (Mudgala): III, **261**, 15446 (*Yāmā Dh°āç ca*).—§ 565 (Gālavacarita): V, **111**, 3837 (*munayaḥ*, only in B.).—§ 615u (Skanda): IX, **44**, 2482 (*Yāmā Dh°āç ca*).
Dhamadhamā, a mātṛ. § 615u (Skanda): IX, **46**θ, 2638.
Dhāmakeçin = Sūrya (the Sun): III, 193.
Dhāman[1] = Kṛshṇa: XII, 1513.
Dhāman[2] = Vishṇu (1000 names).
Dhāmavid = Kṛshṇa: XII, 1513.
Dhanada[1] = Kubera, q.v.
Dhanada[2], a follower of Kubera. § 269 (Vaiçravaṇasabhāv.): II, **10**, 397 (among the Yakshas in the palace of Kubera).
Dhanada[3], a mountain (?). § 731b (Ashṭāvakra-Diksamvāda): XIII, **19**, 1396 ("the dominions of the Lord of Treasures," PCR.).
Dhanada[4] = Çiva (1000 names [1]).
Dhanadā, a mātṛ. § 615u (Skanda): IX, **46**θ, 2631.
Dhanadeçvara, Dhanādhigoptṛ, Dhanādhipa, Dhanādhipati = Kubera, q.v.
Dhanādhyaksha[1] = Kubera, q.v.
Dhanādhyaksha[2] = Çiva: X, 258.
Dhanadodyāna ("the garden of Kubera"). § 430 (Hanūmad-Bhīmasaṃv.): III, **150**, 11287 (*rakshitaṃ Yaksha-Rākshasaiḥ*, in the north).
Dhanānām īçvara(ḥ) = Kubera, q.v.
Dhanañjaya[1] = Arjuna, q.v.
Dhanañjaya[2], a serpent. § 47 (Sarpanāmak.): I, **35**, 1550 (enumeration).—§ 268 (Varuṇasabhāv.): II, **9**, 361 (in the palace of Varuṇa).—§ 564 (Mātalīyop.): V, **103**γ, 3625 (enumeration). — § 606 (Tripurākhyāna): VIII, **34**, 1483 (among the serpents who became the cords with which the manes of the steeds of Çiva were bound).
Dhanañjaya[3] = Vishṇu (1000 names).
Dhanañjaya[4], pl. (°*āḥ*), a family of brahmans. § 286 (Rājasūyikap.): II, **33**, 1238 (°*ānām ṛshabhaḥ Susāmā*).
Dhanañjayā, name of an army. § 615u (Skanda): IX, **46**, 2665 (given to Skanda by Çiva).
Dhanañjayāgraja ("elder brother of Arjuna") = Bhīmasena: IX, 3238.
Dhanañjayasuta ("son of Arjuna") = Babhruvāhana: XIV, 2380.
Dhanapati = Kubera, q.v.
Dhanaprada = Mahāpurusha (Mahāpurushastava).
Dhaneça = Kubera, q.v.
Dhaneçvara[1] = Kubera, q.v.
Dhaneçvara[2] = Vishṇu (1000 names).
Dhaneçvarākrīḍa ("the sporting place of Kubera"). § 448 (Ājagarap.): III, **176**, 12317 (on Gandhamādana ?).
Dhanin, the messenger of the Kapas. § 772p (Kapa, pl.): XIII, **158**, 7333, 7341, 7342.
Dhanishṭhā, sg. or pl., a nakshatra = Çravishṭhā, BR. (v. Su. Si.). § 502 (Manushyagrahak.): III, **230**, 14463 (°*ādis tato kālo Brahmaṇā parikalpitaḥ*, cf. Nīl.). — § 746 (Ānuçāsanik.): XIII, **64**, 3280 (pl., merit of making gifts under the constellation *Dh.*).—§ 749 (do.): XIII, **89a**, 4266 (sg., merit of performing a çrāddha under the constellation *Dh.*).—§ 759 (do.): XIII, **110**, 5391 (pl., description of the candravrata).
Dhanurdhara[1], a son of Dhṛtarāshṭra. § 182 (Dhṛtarāshṭraputran.): I, **117**, 4550. Cf. Dhanurgraha.
Dhanurdhara[2] = Çiva: VII, 9536.
Dhanurdhara[3] = Vishṇu (1000 names).
Dhanurgraha, a son of Dhṛtarāshṭra. § 130 (Aṃçāvat.): I, **67**, 2738.—§ 608 (Karṇap.): VIII, **84**ξ′, 4262 (among ten sons of Dhṛtarāshṭra who are slain by Bhīmasena). Cf. next.
Dhanurgrāha, a son of Dhṛtarāshṭra. § 608 (Karṇap.): VIII, **51**δδ, 2447 (attacked Bhīmasena). Cf. prec.
Dhanurvaktra, a warrior of Skanda. § 615u (Skanda): IX, **45**η, 2564.
Dhanurveda[1] ("the science of arms"). § 56 (Parikshit): I, **49**, 1945 (°*e tu çishyo 'bhūn nṛpaḥ Çāradvatasya*, sc. Parikshit). — [§ 71 (Ādivaṃçāvatāraṇap.): I, **61**, 2236 (*vidvāṃso Vede dhanushi ca*).]—§ 130 (Aṃçāvat.): I, **67**, 2707 (°*e ca Vede ca . . . varishṭhaṃ Droṇam*).—§ 173 (Pāṇḍurājyābhisheka): I, **109**, 4355 (°*e ca Vede ca . . . pāragāḥ*, sc. Dhṛtarāshṭra, Pāṇḍu, and Vidura). — § 198 (Çaradvat): I, **130**, 5073 (mastered by Çaradvat), 5075, 5085, 5088, 5091 (*caturvidhaṃ*, Çaradvat taught it to Kṛpa), 5092 (Kṛpa taught it to his disciples).—§ 199 (Droṇa): I, **130**, 5099 (Droṇa taught it to Dhṛtarāshṭra's and Pāṇḍu's sons).—§ 201 (do.): I, **130**, 5117 (°*paraḥ*, sc. Droṇa), 5119, 5132 (Droṇa learnt the *Dh.* from Rāma Jāmadagnya).—§ 202 (do.): I, **131**, 5172 (°*cikīrshayā*).—§ 203 (do.): I, **132**, 5223 (do.).—§ 204 (Ekalavya): I, 5240, 5255 (°*kṛtaçramaṃ*, sc. Ekalavya).—§ 210 (Sambhavap.): I, **139**, 5524 (Agniveça was the disciple of Agastya in the *Dh.*).—§ 233 (Svayaṃvarap.): I, **188**, 7051 (°*paraiḥ*).—§ 234 (do.): I, **190**, 7101 (*sākshāt*), 7104.—§ 253b (Haraṇāharaṇap.): The *Dh.* is both celestial and human, and consists of four branches (*catushpādaṃ*) and ten divisions (*daçavidhaṃ*): I, **221**, 8032 (acquired by Abhimanyu from Arjuna).—§ 264 (Sabhākriyāp.): II, **4**, 128 (Arjuna instructed the young princes in the *Dh.*).— § 265 (Lokapālasabhākhyānap.): II, **5**, 256 (°*sya sūtram*).— § 329 (Kāmyakavanapr.): III, **36**, 1454 (°*parāḥ*).—§ 330 (Indradarçana): III, **37**, 1459 (*catushpādaḥ*). — § 383

(Paraçurāma): III, **99**, 8676 (visible in the body of Rāma Dāçarathi).—§ 395 (Jamadagni): III, **115**, 10169 (*tan*— i.e. Jamadagni — *tu kṛtsno Dh°aḥ pratyabhāt*). — § 407 (Māndhātrup.): III, **126**, 10455 (*Vedāh sa-Dh°āḥ*, learnt by Māndhātṛ).—§ 449, (Ājagarap.): III, **177**, †12359 (*sadā-Dh°ratipradhānāḥ*). — § 453 (Mārkaṇḍeyas.): III, **183**, †12580 (*°ratipradhānāḥ*), †12582 (do.).—§ 487 (Pativratop.): III, **215**, 14054 (*°parāyaṇaḥ*). — § 515 (Karṇadigvijaya): III, **253**, 15216.—§ 527 (Rāmop.): III, **277**, 15948 (pl.). —§ 552 (Goharaṇap.): IV, **58**, 1830 (*°aç ca kārtsnena yasmin* —i.e. in Droṇa—*nityaṃ pratishṭhitaḥ*).—§ 570*d* (Rukmin): V, **158**, 5352 (*kṛtsnaṃ Dh°ṃ catushpādam avāptavān*, sc. Rukmin). — § 573 (Ambop.): V, **192**, 7548 (*pratipede catushpādaṃ Dh°ṃ*, sc. Çikhaṇḍin). — § 581 (Bhīshmavadhap.): VI, **61**, 2692 (*°vidaḥ*).—§ 582 (do.): VI, **74**, 3271 (*°viçāradāḥ*).—§ 592 (Saṃçaptakavadhap.): VII, **23**ₒ, 988 (*astrāṇāñ ca Dh°e Brāhme Vede ca pāragam . . . Satyadhṛtim*).—§ 599 (Jayadrathavadhap.): VII, **112**, 4311 (*°e gatāḥ pāraṃ*, sc. the Rukmarathas), 4333 (*°e ca nishṭhitaḥ*); **130**, 5318 (*°sya pāragaḥ*, sc. Droṇa).—§ 603 (Nārāyaṇāstramoksh.): VII, **194**, 8967 (*yena*—i.e. by Droṇa—*Rāmād avāpyeha Dh°ṃ mahātmanā proktāny astrāṇi divyāni putrāya guṇakāṅkshiṇā*), 8975 (*°e ca pāragaḥ*, sc. Açvatthāman).— § 604 (Karṇap.): VIII, **2**, 37 (*sākshād Rāmeṇa yo bālye Dh°e upākṛtaḥ*, sc. Bhīshma); **9**, 328 (*yasya çikshām upāsate Dh°ṃ cikīrshantaḥ*, i.e. Açvatthāman's), 329 (*ācāryo yo Dh°e Gautamo rathasattamaḥ | Kṛpaḥ*). — § 606*b* (Paraçu-Rāma): VIII, **34**, 1613 (*Bhārgavo*—i.e. Rāma Jāmadagnya—*'pi dadau divyaṃ Dh°ṃ mahātmane Karṇāya*).—§ 608 (Karṇap.): VIII, **74**, †3799.—§ 615*u* (Skanda): IX, **44**, 2471 (*catushpādaḥ*, came in bodily form to Skanda).—§ 621 (Rājadh.): XII, **2**, 50 (*cakārāṅgirasāṃ çreshṭhād*—i.e. from Droṇa—*Dh°ṃ*, sc. Karṇa), 54; **3**, 77.—§ 638*b* (Rāmop.): XII, **49**, 1747 (*°sya pāragaṃ Rāmaṃ kshatriyahantāraṃ*).—§ 639 (Rājadh.): XII, **50**, 1828 (*°e Vede ca*).—§ 641*f* (Pṛthu Vainya): XII, **59**, 2220 (*°e ca pāragaḥ*, sc. Pṛthu Vainya). — § 656 (Khaḍgotpatti): XII, **166**, 6128 (*°sya pāragaḥ . . . Bhīshmaḥ*).—§ 720*b* (Sudarçanop.): XIII, **2**, 91 (*°e ca Vede ca tirato yo 'bhavat sadā*, sc. Madirāçva).—§ 736*b* (Vītahavyop.): XIII, **30**, 1948 (*°e ca Vede ca sarvatraiva kṛtaçramāḥ*, sc. the sons of Haihaya), 1970 (*Vedāñ cāpi jagau kṛtsnaṃ Dh°ñ ca*, sc. Pratardana).—§ 745*c* (Cyavana-Kuçikasaṃv.): XIII, **56**, 2910 (*sākshāt kṛtsno Dh°aḥ samupasthasyate*, sc. to Ṛcīka). § 759 (Ānuçāsanik.): XIII, **104**, 5100 (*°e ca Vede ca*).—§ 785 (Anugītāp.): XIV, **66**, 1959 (*°ṃ grahīshyati*, sc. Parikshit).

Dhanurveda[2] = Vishṇu (1000 names).

Dhanur yantrāṇāṃ = Çiva (1000 names[1]).

Dhanus = Çiva: VII, 9536.

Dhanushākhya, a ṛshi. § 717*c* (Uparicara): XII, **337**ε, 12758. Cf. next.

Dhanushāksha, a ṛshi. § 415 (Medhāvin): III, **135**, 10741, 10743, 10746. Cf. prec.

Dhanvācārya = Çiva: VII, 9536.

Dhanvantara[1] = Çiva: VII, 9536.

Dhanvantara[2], v. Dhanvantari.

Dhanvantari[1], the celestial physician. § 28 (Amṛtamanthana): I, **18**, 1149 (when the gods churned the ocean, *Dh.* arose having a white vessel of amṛta in his hand).— § 753 (Ānuçāsanik.): XIII, **97**, 4662 (B. *Dh°eḥ*, but C. reads *Dh°re* (from *Dhanvantara*), the bali sacrifice to *Dh.* shall be performed in the north-eastern region).

Dhanvantari[2] = Sūrya: III, 155.

Dhanvantari[3] = Çiva (1000 names[2]).

Dhānvantarya, a sacrifice. § 753 (Ānuçās.): XIII, **97**, 4660.

Dhanvin[1] = Çiva, q.v.

Dhanvin[2] = Vishṇu (1000 names).

Dhara[1], one of the Vasus. § 116 (Vasu, pl.): I, **66**, 2582, 2583 (son of Prajāpati (?) and Dhūmrā), 2585 (father of Draviṇa and Hutahavyavaha).—§ 164 (Āpavop.): I, **99**, 3956 (*°ādayaḥ*, sc. the Vasus).—§ 770 (Ānuçāsanik.): XIII, **151**δ, 7094 (enumeration of the Vasus). Cf. Pṛthu.

Dhara[2], a Pāṇḍava warrior. § 600 (Ghaṭotkacavadhap.): VII, **158**χ, 7009.

Dhara[3] = Çiva (1000 names[1-2]).

Dhara[4] = Vishṇu (1000 names).

Dhara[5], v. Tvashṭādhara.

***Dharā** ("the Earth," personif.): I, 1584, 2485.

Dhārā, a tīrtha. § 370 (Tīrthayātrāp.): III, **84**, 8003.

Dharādhara[1] ("supporter of the earth") = Balarāma (Çesha): XIII, 6860, 6867.

Dharādhara[2] = Vishṇu (1000 names).

Dhāraṇa[1], a prince. § 562 (Bhagavadyānap.): V, **74**γ, 2732 (*Candravatsānāṃ*, among eighteen vile kings who annihilated their kinsmen, etc.).

Dhāraṇa[2], a serpent. § 564 (Mātalīyop.): V, **103**γ, 3632.

Dhāraṇa[3] = Çiva: XII, 10424 (1000 names[1]); XIV, 208.

Dharaṇī = Skanda: III, 14641.

Dharaṇīdhara, pl. (*°aḥ*) ("supporters of the earth"). § 770 (Ānuçāsanik.): XIII, **151**κ, 7119 (*sapta*, i.e. Dharma, etc.).

Dharaṇīdhara[1] = Çiva: XIV, 208.

Dharaṇīdhara[2] = Vishṇu (1000 names).

Dharāputra ("the son of the Earth") = Aṅgāraka (the planet Mars). § 611 (Çalyap.): IX, **11**, 545 (*Bhṛgusūnu-Dharāputrau Çaçijena samanvitau*, omens).

Dharma[1], the god of justice (sometimes co-ordinate to Yama). § 4 (Anukram.): I, **1**, 112, †166.—§ 11 (Parvasaṅgr.): I, **2**, 375, 448, 477, 635, 638. — § 72 (Ādivaṃçāvatāraṇap.): I, **62**, 2291 (*suto Dh°sya . . . Yudhishṭhiraḥ*).— § 80 (Aṇīmāṇḍavya): I, **63**, 2422, 2423, 2425 (cursed by Aṇimāṇḍavya to be born by a çūdra-woman, cf. § 172).— § 83 (Ādivaṃçāvatāraṇa): I, **63**, 2444 (father of Yudhishṭhira, cf. § 190).—§ 115 (Aṃçāvat.): I, **66**, 2577 (married ten daughters of Daksha), 2578 (*°patnyaḥ*, the ten wives of *Dh.* are enumerated), 2579 (?, *dvārāṇy etāni Dharmasya vihitāni Svayambhuvā*).—[§ 116 (Vasu, pl.): I, **66**, 2582 (according to Nīl., *Dh.* here, as in other passages, is stated to be the father of the Vasus).]—§ 117 (Aṃçāvat.): I, **66**, 2595 (sprang in human form out from the right breast of Brahmán; he has three sons, *Çama*, *Kāma*, and *Harsha*).— § 130 (do.): I, **67**, [2721 (*Atreḥ . . . putraṃ*, incarnate as Vidura)], 2745 (a part of *Dh.* incarnate as Yudhishṭhira). —§ 135 (Çakuntalop.): I, **74**, †3017 (*°aç ca jānati narasya vṛttaṃ*).—§ 138 (Daksha Prācetasa): I, **75**, 3133 (married ten daughters of Daksha). — § 157 (Pūruvaṃç.): I, **95**, 3814 (father of Yudhishṭhira, cf. § 190).—§ 171 (Vicitravīryasutotpatti): I, **106**, 4302 (reborn as Vidura).—§ 172 (Aṇīmāṇḍavyop.): I, **107**, 4305; **108**, 4329 (*sadanaṃ . . . Dh°sya*), 4330, (4332), 4333, 4335 (Aṇīmāṇḍavya regarded the punishment which *Dh.* had inflicted on him as too severe, and cursed *Dh.* to be born by a çūdra-woman. Then *Dh.* was born as Vidura).—§ 189 (Pāṇḍu): I, **122**, 4754, 4755, 4756, 4757 (Pāṇḍu prevailed upon Kuntī to summon *Dh.*).—§ 190 (Pāṇḍavotpatti): I, **123**, 4759 (read *Dharmam acyutaṃ* with B.), 4760, 4761, 4762 (*Dh.* then begat

Yudhishṭhira on Kuntī).—§ 213 (Jatugṛhap.): I, **151**, 5908 (°*ād Indrāc ca Vātāc ca sushuve yā sutān imān*, i.e. Kuntī).—§ 286 (Rājasūyikap.): II, **33**, 1250 (°*o vigrahavān iva*, sc. Yudhishṭhira).—§ 299 (Dyūtap.): II, **68**, 2295, 2297 (when the attire of Draupadī was torn away, *Dh.* repeatedly covered her with another). — § 317*b* (Kṛshṇa Vāsudeva): III, **12**, 480 (Kṛshṇa became *Dh.*, etc.).—§ 370 (Tīrthayātrāp.): III, **84**, 7079 (performed austerities in Dharmatīrtha), 8077 (present in Dharmaprastha), 8080 (i.e. an image of *Dh.*).—§ 377 (Dhaumyatīrthak.): III, **88**, 8350, 8351 (Kṛshṇa identified with *Dh.*).—§ 392 (Tīrthayātrāp.): III, **114**, 10098 (performed a sacrifice on the Vaitaraṇī). — § 401 (Balarāma): III, **119**, †10258 (°*sya sute*, i.e. Yudhishṭhira). — § 408 (Jantūpākhyāna): III, **128**, (10504). — § 438 (Yakshayuddhap.): III, **162**, 11818 (°*sya . . . sutaḥ*, i.e. Yudhishṭhira).—§ 448 (Ājagarap.): III, **176**, †12332 (°*sya sutaḥ*, i.e. Yudhishṭhira). — § 455 (Brāhmaṇamāhātmyak.): III, **185**, 12703 (?, among the honorific appellations of a king). — § 548 (Āraṇeyap.): III, **312**, 17242 (°*s tu vibhajaty artham ubhayoḥ puṇyapāpayoḥ*); **313**, 17331 (Dharma causes the sun to set); **314**, 17424 (*c*: Dharma says: Fame, truth, self-restraint, purity, candour, etc., are my body; abstention from injury, etc., are the doors (through which I am accessible)), 17428, (17443), 17444; **315**, 17448 (in the shape of a Yaksha *Dh.* put Yudhishṭhira, etc., to test; then he granted him some boons, among those that the Pāṇḍavas might live unrecognized during the thirteenth year).—§ 549 (Pāṇḍavaprav.): IV, **1**, 4, 9 (all. to § 548).—§ 550 (Samayapālanap.): IV, **13**, 327 (*prasādāc ca Dh°sya*, all. to § 548). — § 551 (Kīcakavadhap.): IV, **16**, 477 (°*pāça*°). — § 561 (Yānasandhip.): V, **60**, 2367 (*Dh.*, etc., will from parental affection assist the Pāṇḍavas); **61**, 2387, 2399. — § 562 (Bhagavadyānap.): V, **90**, 3196 (*dhārayati prajāḥ*), 3197. — § 564 (Mātalīyop.): V, **105**ε, 3708.—§ 565 (Gālavac.): V, **106**, 3721, 3728, 3730, 3731 (in the shape of Vasishṭha *Dh.* put Viçvāmitra to test, who then from a kshatriya became a brahman); **108**, 3764 (*cakshushī . . . Dh°sya*, in the east); **109**, 3782 (*etad dvitīyaṃ Dh°sya dvāraṃ*, sc. the south); **112**, 3850 (°*sya cakshushī*, in the east); **113**, 3881; **117**, 3974 (Dhṛti is his wife).—§ 567 (Bhagavadyānap.): V, **128**, 4303, 4304, 4305 (*Dh.* bound the Asuras with his nooses and made them over to Varuṇa).—§ 592 (Saṃçaptakavadhap.): VII, **23**, 1035 (°-*Māruta-Çakrāṇām Açvinoḥ*, their images on the standards of the five Draupadeyas).—§ 593 (Abhimanyuvadhap.): VII, **40**ο, 1694 (do.). — § 603*b* (Nārāyaṇa): VII, **201**, 9447 (Nārāyaṇa took birth as the son of *Dh.*).—§ 603 (Nārāyaṇāstramoksh.): VII, **202**, 9627 (°*aç ca Vṛsha ucyate*).—§ 608 (Karṇap.): VIII, **69**, 3460 (?, *dhāraṇād Dharmam ity āhur, Dharmo dhārayati prajāḥ*).—§ 615*u* (Skanda): IX, **45**γ, 2519 (different from Yama, came to the investiture of Skanda), (κ) 2682 (?).—§ 617 (Aishīkap.): X, **10**, 569 (*dharmena Dh°pratimasya rājñaḥ*, i.e. Yudhishṭhira).—§ 641 (Rājadharm.): XII, **59**, 2253 (married to Çrī, and father of Artha), 2254; **72**, 2773 (the king is *Dh.*); **90**, 3377 (*Vṛsho hi bhagavān Dh°ḥ*), 3379 (etymology: *dhanāt sravati Dh°o hi dhāraṇād veti niçcayaḥ*); **122**, 4512 (*vinayātmakaḥ*); **128**, 4710 (assumed the shape of a muni named Tanu).—§ 661 (Mokshadh.): XII, **198**, 7188 (Yudhishṭhira had sprung from a portion of Dharma).—§ 662*b* (Jāpakop.): XII, **199***a*, 7213 (different from Yama), 7217, (7218), 7218, 7221, (7222), 7223, (7224), (7226), 7231, 7251, 7265, (7276), 7276, 7316; **200***a*, 7332, 7363.—§ 664 (Mokshadh.): XII, **207**, 7539 (married ten daughters of Daksha, cf. § 115), 7540 (father of the Vasus, cf. § 116). —§ 680*b* (Tulādhāra-Jājalisaṃv.): XII, **265**, 9446 (?, °*sya vacanāt*).—§ 686 (Mokshadh.): XII, **273**, 9827, 9829 (in the shape of a deer *Dh.* put the brahman Satya to the test).—§ 704 (do.): XII, **301***a*, 11094. — § 717*b* (Nārāyaṇīya): XII, **335**, 12666 (Nārāyaṇa took birth as *Dh.*'s son in a quadruple form), (*a*) 12685 (among the twenty-one Prajāpatis; different from Yama); **343**, XI), ††13219 (married ten daughters of Daksha, cf. § 115), 13266 (Nārāyaṇa took birth as Dharma's son in a double form, viz. as Nara and Nārāyaṇa), 13286 (*Naro Nārāyaṇaç caiva jātau Dh°kulodvahau*); **348**εε, 13449 (*janma Dh°gṛhe caiva Nara-Nārāyaṇātmakaṃ*).—§ 720*b* (Sudarçanop.): XIII, **2**, 162 (in the shape of a brahman *Dh.* put Sudarçana to the test).—§ 721*b* (Viçvāmitrop.): XIII, **4**, 204 (*sākshād Dh°a ivāparaḥ*).—§ 736*b* (Vītahavyop.): XIII, **30**, 1952 (do.).—§ 766 (Ānuçāsanik.): XIII, **126**, (6028).—§ 770 (Ānuçāsanik.): XIII, **151**κ, 7119 (among the seven *dharaṇīdharāḥ*). —§ 782*f* (Janaka): XIV, **32**, 911 (in the shape of a brahman *Dh.* examined Janaka).—§ 784 (Uttaṅka): XIV, **54**, 1573 (the eldest son of Kṛshṇa (Vishṇu)).—§ 786*b* (Nakulākhyana): XIV, **90**, 2771, 2788, 2795, 2797 (in the shape of a brahman *Dh.* put a brahman family to the test).—§ 786*e* (Agastya): XIV, **91**, 2872. — § 786*f* (Jamadagni): XIV, **91**, 2888, 2889, 2897, 2899 (in order to put Jamadagni to test *Dh.* assumed the form of Krodha; at last Krodha was cursed to become a mungoose).—§ 787 (Āçramavāsap.): XV, **20**, 556 (Yudhishṭhira is identified with *Dh.*).—§ 788 (do.): XV, **28**, 751, 752, 754, 756, 758, 759, 761 (has been born as Vidura through the curse of Māṇḍavya, cf. § 172).—§ 789 (Putradarçanap.): XV, **30**, 824 (°*sya jananī*, i.e. Kuntī, *Dh.* = Yudhishṭhira); **31**η, 851 (Vidura and Yudhishṭhira had been born from portions of *Dh.*).—§ 794 (Mahāprasthānikap.): XVII, **3**, 89 (followed the Pāṇḍavas on their mahāprasthāna in the shape of a dog), (90), 95.—§ 795 (Svargārohaṇap.): XVIII, **2**, 76; **3**, 82, 110, 120, 123; **5**, 169 (after death Vidura and Yudhishṭhira entered *Dh.*). Cf. Dharmarāja, Vṛsha, Yama.

Dharma[2] = Sūrya: III, 191.

Dharma[3] = Skanda: III, 14643.

Dharma[4] = Kṛshṇa: XII, 1996, 2273.

Dharma[5] = Çiva (1000 names[1]).

Dharma[6] = Vishṇu (1000 names).

Dharmada, a warrior of Skanda. § 615*u* (Skanda): IX, **45**η, 2574.

Dharmadeva = Çesha: I, 1586.

Dharmadhvaja[1] = Sūrya: III, 149.

Dharmadhvaja[2] = Janaka: XII, 11855.

Dharmādhyaksha = Vishṇu (1000 names).

Dharmagupta = Vishṇu (1000 names).

Dharmaja[1] ("son of Dharma") = Yudhishṭhira: VII, 6955 (only B.); VIII, 3555; XII, 1813; XIV, 2114, 2556, 2560; XV, 58, 346, 711; XVIII, 58.

Dharmaja[2] (do.) = Kṛshṇa (Nārāyaṇa): XII, 13266.

Dharmajā ("daughter of Dharma") = Satyā, the wife of Çaṃyu: III, 14133.

Dharmakāmārthamokshāṇāṃ kathanīyakathaḥ = Çiva (1000 names[1]).

Dharmakṛt = Vishṇu (1000 names).

Dharmakshetra = Kurukshetra: VI, 830 (*K*°); XIV, 2712 (*K*°).

Dharmanandana ("son of Dharma") = Yudhishṭhira: VIII, 3578, 4987.

Dharmanetra, grandson of the elder Dhṛtarāshṭra. § 155

(Pūruvaṃç.): I, **94**, 3749 (according to B. a son of Dhṛtarāshṭra; cf. Dhārtarāshṭrasuta, pl.).

Dharmaprabhava ("son of Dharma") = Yudhishṭhira: III, †14745.

Dharmaprastha, a tīrtha. § 370 (Tīrthayātrāp.): III, **84**, 8077 (there Dharma is always present).

Dharmaputra = Yudhishṭhira, q.v.

Dharmarāj[1] = Dharma or Yama: I, 4163 (*dharmaṃ jahyāc ca Dh°*).

Dharmarāj[2] = Yudhishṭhira: I, 634, 639, 6095; II, 53, 1659; III, 2053, 4023, 15728, 15730; IV, 330; V, 2830; X, 759; XII, 12998; XIII, 7720; XIV, 2113, 2530; XV, 401.

Dharmarāj[3] = Rājadharman (Naḍījaṅgha): XII, 6350 (*Kāçyapaḥ*).

Dharmarāja[1] = Dharma or Yama: I, 976, (977), 2107 (*Yamaḥ*); **107**, v. 13 (only B., the verse omitted in C.), 8338; II, 344; III, 1442, 1674 (*Vaivasvataḥ*), 8521 (*sanātanaḥ*), 10506, (10507), 16788 (*°tā*, etymology), 16802, 16808; XII, 4723, 5747; XIII, 3405, 3419, 3420, 3471, 3475, †3501, †3512, 3526, †3529, †3541, 7113 (*°rtvijaḥ sapta*, i.e. Unmucu, etc., in the south).

Dharmarāja[2] = Yudhishṭhira: I, †159, †166, †204, †205, 350, 378, 430, 471, 530 (*Pāṇḍuputrasya*), 545, 552, 555, 593, 616, 627, 2270, 5043, 5067, 5747, 5771, 5881, †7206, †7333, 7365, 7754, 7767, 7769, 7796, 7930, 8018, 8058, 8066; II, 10, 14, 22, 43, 44, 52, 95, 115, 264, 273, 278, 542, 544, 556, 558, 976, 978, 987, 991, 993, 1021, 1051, 1058, 1059, 1069, 1073, 1104, 1105, 1123, 1182, 1204, 1216, 1236, 1248, 1251, 1256, 1262, 1263 (*Pāṇḍavaṃ*), 1279, 1284, 1296, 1297, 1315, 1326, 1327, 1337, 1422, 1603, 1612, 1621, 1630, 1633, 1658, 1680, †2008, 2180, 2217, 2350, †2364, 2372, 2377, †2400 (*Kuntīsutaḥ*), 2450, 2629; III, 39, 163, 356, 406, 410 (*Pāṇḍavaḥ*), 454, 464, 467, 893, †908, †911, †913, †914, 922, †951, 968, 990, 1449, 1456, 1458, 1471, 1913 (*Kaunteyaṃ*), 1963, 2000, 2008, 2048, 2052, 4021, 4027, 8456, 10211, †10280, †10289, 10977, 11000, 11006, 11019, 11051, 11074, 11076, 11367, 11374 (*°sya bhrātāraṃ*, i.e. Bhīmasena), 11422, 11427, 11430, 11462, 11917, 11923, 12291, †12326, †12329, †12333, 12398, 12441, 12452, 12464, 12528, †12574, †12588, †12593, 12597, 12805, 13213, 14100, †14749, 14806, 14828, 14878 (*°niveçanaṃ*), 14974, 15018, 15019, 15020, 15041, 15312, 15360, 15643, 15665 (*°purogamān*, sc. the Pāṇḍavas), †15699, 15749, 15860; IV, 158, 645, 684, 903, 925, 1083, 1364 (*Kauravasya*), 2175, 2275, 2324; V, †14, 45, 115, 577, †665, †1834, 2017, 2292, 2660, 2832, 2837, 2842, 2844, 2858, 2865, 4226, 4717, 5136, 5221, 5234, 5238, 5333, 5374, 5375 (*Paṇḍavaṃ*), 5389, 5601, 5621, 5678, 5696; VI, 697, 700, 1540, 1993 (*Pāṇḍavaḥ*), 2034, 2233, 2326, 2417, 2472, 2540, 3284, 3426, 3511, †3776, 4212, 4776 (*Paṇḍavaṃ*), 4790, 4945, 5099, 5758, †5813; VII, 193, 284, 443, 451, 457, 466, 679, 710, 720, 794, 1038, 1079, 1538, 1679, 1959, 1962, 2134, 2581, 2945, 2965, 3003, 3220, 3815, 3986, 3990, 3995, 4004, 4240, 4252, 4253, 4254, 4291, 4293, 4358, 4371, 4372, 4404, 4501, 4508 (*°purogamāḥ*, sc. the Pāṇḍavas), 4880, 4983 (*Pāṇḍavaḥ*), 5001, 5099, 5102, 5103, 5122, 5126, 5148, 5150, 5154, 5155, 5649, 5651, 5858, 5868, 5876, 5877, 5889, 5997, 6372, 6853, 7003 (*Pāṇḍavaṃ*), 7129, 7275, 7380, 7672, 8362, 8363, 8739, 8820, 8850, 8866 (*Pāṇḍavaḥ*), 8947, 8992, 9192, 9218; VIII, 305, 421, 427, 1120, 1125, 1174, 1191, 1198, 1199, 1232, 1260, 1689, 2159, 2204, 2281, 2287, 2328, 2363, 2659 (*Pāṇḍavaḥ*), 2662, 2671, 2754, 2860, 2976 (*Kaunteyaṃ*), 3163, 3168, 3171, 3191, 3282, †3302, 3305, 3473, 3487, 3489, †3490, †3492, †3533 (*Pāṇḍavaḥ*), 3547, 3552, 3562, 3564, 3565, 3568, 3601, †3628, †3833, 4028, 4489 (*Pāṇḍavaṃ*), †4595, 4986, 5014, 5018, 5027; IX, 10, 363, 381, 451, 463, 541, 626, 639, 643, 656, 668, 677, 692, 702, 703, 764, 809, 827, 856, †899, †900, †902, †906, †911, 916, 926 (slays Çalya), 1143, 1321, 1711, 1716, 1727, 1906, 1911, 1914, 1917, 3143, 3255, 3257, 3323, 3372, 3378, 3381, 3486, 3503, 3516, 3532, 3556; X, 543, 589 (*Pāṇḍavaṃ*); XI, 233, 313, 322, 325, 361, 389, 530, 635, 762, 782, 798, 824; XII, 3, 152, 200, 384, 897, 1089, 1291, 1383, 1460, 1466, †1515, 1551, 1583, 1873, 1908, 1975, 2125, †6253, 13611 (C. *°ājaḥ*, but read with B. *Dharmarājñe*); XIII, †3693, †3698, 5574, 7723, 7739; XIV, 28, 384, 1507, 1513, 1514, 1528, 1806, 1862, 1870, 1873, 1909, 1928, 1969, 2111, 2119, 2131, 2147, 2148, 2219, 2261, 2350, 2513, 2531, 2534 (only C.; B. has *dharmajñāya*), 2535, 2547, 2563, 2565, 2573, 2598, 2612, 2632, 2647, 2652 (*Bharataçreshṭhaṃ*), 2661, 2670, 2682, 2689, 2692; XV, 7, 26, 35, 41, 153, 261, 268, 370, 387, 398, 449, 459, 702, 704 (*Pāṇḍavaḥ*), 706, 709, 767, 1056, 1073; XVII, 10, 69, 74, †82, †89; XVIII, 4, 54, 80, 81 (*Pārthe*), 122.

Dharmarājan[1] = Dharma or Yama: III, 10503; XIII, 3406.

Dharmarājan[2] = Yudhishṭhira: I, 8051; II, 146, 968, 1825; III, 8830, 11010, 11426, 11453; VI, 1623, †2661; VIII, 3593, 3600; IX, 1190; XII, 1450, 13611 (only B.; C. has *Dharmarājaḥ*); XIV, 59, 1997, 2017, 2259; XV, 89, 118, 1002; XVII, 50.

Dharmāraṇya**, one or more sacred woods. § 368 (Tīrthayātrāp.): III, **82**, 4087 (at the hermitage of Kaṇva).—§ 370 (do.): III, **84**, 8063 (*Brahmasaras . . . Dh° opaçobhitaṃ*).—§ 528 (Rāvaṇagamana): III, **277**, 15988.—§ 733*q* (Marudgaṇa): XIII, **25**, 1744 (*°opaçobhitaṃ . . . Brahmasaras*).—§ 775 (Ānuçāsanik.): XIII, **166*a, 7655.—§ 786 (Anugītāp.): XIV, **92**, 2898.

Dharmasādharaṇa = Çiva (1000 names[2]).

Dharmasūnu, Dharmasuta, Dharmatanaya = Yudhishṭhira, q.v.

Dharmatīrtha, name of two tīrthas. § 370 (Tīrthayātrāp.): III, **84**, 7079 (there Dharma performed austerities), 8140 (*Brahmarshisevitaṃ*).

Dharmātmaja[1] ("son of Dharma") = Nārāyaṇa: XII, 12657 (*N°*), 13400.

Dharmātmaja[2] = Yudhishṭhira, q.v.

Dharmātman[1] = Skanda: III, 14630, 14633.—Do.[2] = Kṛshṇa: XII, 1639.

Dharmavid = Vishṇu (1000 names).

Dharmavyādha ("the virtuous fowler"). § 480 (Pativratop.): III, **207**, 13710, 13760; **208**, 13802; **209**, 13842.—§ 483 (do.): III, **211**, 13920.—§ 484 (do.): III, **212**, 13947.—§ 485 (do.): III, **214**, 14000, 14007, 14013, 14017; **216**, 14097.

Dharmayuga = Kṛtayuga: XII, 11858.

Dharmayūpa = Vishṇu (1000 names).

Dharmendra = Yama: VII, 160 (*Pitṛṇām iva Dh°ḥ*).

Dharmeyu. § 150 (Pūruvaṃç.): I, **94**, 3701 (the ninth son of Raudrāçva).

Dharmin = Vishṇu (1000 names).

Dharshaṇātman = Çiva (1000 names[2]).

Dhārshṭhadyumna or **Dhārshṭadyumni** ("son of Dhṛshṭadyumna"). § 608 (Karṇap.): VIII, **82**, †4188 (*°eḥ*, slain by Karṇa), †4189 (*°ne nihate*).

Dhārtarāshṭra, pl. (°*āḥ*) ("sons of Dhṛtarāshṭra[1]," very often, especially in books v–ix, applied to the followers of Duryodhana): I, 100, 114, †190, 2289, 4558 (°*ānām ārshaḥ sambhavaḥ*), 4978, 4979, 4987, 5012, 5214, 5275, 5287, 5312, 5404, 5444, 5645 (*sahānugāḥ*), 6089, 6253, 6984 (came to the svayaṃvara of Draupadī; the names of twenty-three of them are enumerated), 7127, 7380; II, 1699, 1947, †2121, 2377, †2381, †2396, 2417, 2452, 2519, 2535 (Bhīmasena promises to slay the *Dh.*), 2557, 2558 (*nir-Dh°āṃ pṛthivīṃ karttāsmi*, says Nakula), 2561, 2615 (°*striyaḥ*), 2630, 2658; III, 1 (*sahāmatyaiḥ*), 9, 305, 463, 523, 535, 1063, 1273, 1279, 1315 (°*balaṃ*), 1397, 1420 (*Duryodhanapurogamāḥ*), 1475 (*vadhāya Dh°āṇāṃ*), 2022 (*sa-Saubalāḥ*), 2028, 2029, 2030 (*sa-Saubalān*), 8508, †10276, †10280 (*mahīṃ . . . nir-Dh°āṃ*), 11327, 12613, 14728 (°*vadhaṃ*), 14883, 14886 (*sarājakāḥ*), 14889, 14890, 14914, 15208, 15314, 15316 (? °*puraṃ*), 15342, 15494 (*Duryodhanādayaḥ*), 15569, †17217, 17451; IV, 1569 (*kshayāya Dh°āṇāṃ*), 2012, 2038, 2137; V, 610 (*sa-Saubalaiḥ*), †659, †678, †721, †762, †764, †857, †858, 864, †911, †1331, †1354, 1378, †1816, †1827, †1830, †1842 (*sasainyān*), †1843 (do.), †1850, †1867, †1899, †1904 (*sa-Karṇān*), †1908, 1947, 2343, 2662, 2680, 2683, 2743, 2881 (°*balaṃ*), 2902, 2917, 2921, 3103, 3105, 3185, 3189, 3285 (*sa-Karṇānāṃ*), 3288, 3297, †3302, 3320, †3327, 4243, 4826 (*vāhinīṃ Dh°āṇāṃ*), 4924, 4939, 4943 (°*opajīvināṃ*), 5089, 5139, 5142, 5145 (°*balaṃ*), 5464, 5473, 5676 (*sarveshāṃ Dh°āṇām ahaṃ mṛtyuḥ*, says Bhīmasena), 5735, 7613; VI, †745, †746, †750, 762, 793 (°*balaṃ*), 848, 849, 866, 867, 877, †884, †1643 (*samāgame Pāṇḍava-D°yoḥ*), 1656, 1827 (*mahārathaiḥ*, i.e. Bhīshma, etc.), 2134 (*Duryodhanapurogamāḥ*), 2427 (i.e. the party of Duryodhana), 2685 (*dhvajinīṃ Dh°āṇāṃ*), 2734 (*daça rathān*, i.e. Duryodhana, etc.), 2821, 2849 (several of Dhṛtarāshṭra's sons slain by Bhīmasena), 3058, 3345, 3350, 3352, 3358, †3377 (*jyeshṭhājñāya coditāḥ*), 3395, 3551 (°*āṇāṃ vyūḍhaḥ . . . maṇḍalaḥ*), 3693, 3928 (several of Dhṛtarāshṭra's sons slain by Bhīmasena), 4048 (*sarājakāḥ*), 4146 (*mahārathaiḥ*), 4196, †4528 (*anīkāni . . . Pāṇḍava-Dh°yoḥ*), 4669 (*sasainikāḥ*), 4914, 4974, 5246 (*mahārathān*), 5479, 5696, 5762; VII, 105, 617, 984, 1434, 1874, 1948 (*shaḍbhiḥ*, i.e. Droṇa, Karṇa, etc.), 2000 (read *mahābalān* (so B.) instead of *mahābalāt* (so C.)), 2535, 2586, 2653, 2816, 2831, 3513, 3778 (*shaḍbhiḥ*), 4171, 4206 (°*balaṃ*), 4210, 5909, †6145, 6412 (°*balaṃ*), 6476 (do.), 6504, 6723, 7831, †8162 (*Kuravaḥ*), 8334, 8684, 8932, 9037, 9394; VIII, 16, 147, 266, 432, 1946, 2158 (*çishṭān*), 2323 (°*balaṃ*), 2362, 2394, 2861, 2977, 2982, 2996, 2997, 3042, 3045, 3049, 3060, 3172 (*sarājakaḥ*), 3174, 3253 (°*balaṃ*), 3311, 3313, †3378, 3405, †3499, 3778, 3790 (*nir-Dh°āṃ . . . dāsyāmi medinīṃ*), †3822, 3923, 3931, 3935, 3936, 3970, 3988, 4037, †4762, †4824; IX, 35 (the party of Duryodhana, only three alive, sc. Açvatthāman, Kṛpa, and Kṛtavarman), 330, 357 (°*balaṃ*), 386, 1039, 1146, 1184 (*sarājakān*), 1294, 1446, 1544, 1564, 1912 (*tvayā*—i.e. Bhīmasena—*nihatāḥ sarve Dh°āḥ*), 3063 (°*bale çeshās trayaḥ*, i.e. Açvatthāman, Kṛpa, and Kṛtavarman), †3319; X, 66 (the party, *trayaḥ çishṭāḥ*, cf. IX, 35), 440, 527 (the party, three still alive, cf. IX, 35); XI, 744, 817; XII, 20 (*āçrayo Dh°āṇāṃ*, i.e. Karṇa), 39, 278, 6024; XIII, 7, 334; XIV, 386, 1554 (°*āçca nihatāḥ sarve sasutabāndhavāḥ*); XV, 68, 876 (*Duḥçāsanādayaḥ*, among the dead warriors who, summoned by Vyāsa, arose from the Gaṅgā); XVIII, 124 (in heaven). Cf. Dhṛtarāshṭraja, pl., Dhṛtarāshṭraputra, pl., Dhṛtarāshṭrasuta, pl., Dhṛtarāshṭrātmāja, pl.

Note.—A list of the names of the 101 sons of Dhṛtarāshṭra is given: I, 2728–2741 and 4541–4553.

Dhārtarāshṭra, sg. ("son of Dhṛtarāshṭra[1]"): (1) Citrasena, (2) Duryodhana, (3) Vikarṇa, (4) Yuyutsu:

(1) = Citrasena: XI, 557 (*C°*).

(2) = Duryodhana: I, 377, 393 (? is not to be read *Dhṛtarāshṭreṇa*, cf. I, 7524), 422, 555, 2254 (?), 4988, 4998, 5802, 5807, 5859, 5887 (?), 5919, 6114; II, 1664 (*mahīpatiḥ*), 1679 (*D°*), †2214, †2242, †2361, 2516 (*rājñaḥ*); III, 378, †912, 991, 1157, 1349, 1701 (*anīkāni Dh°sya*), 8286, †10263, †10264, †12590 (*Suyodhanaḥ*), 14856, 14868, 14881, 14890, 14903, 14913, 14921 (*sainyaṃ . . . Dh°sya*), 14923, 14981, 15023, 15041 (*Suyodhanaḥ*), 15058 (*Duryodhano rājā*), 15150 (*rājānaṃ*), 15188, 15203 (*janādhipaḥ*), 15211, 15218 (*janeçvaraḥ*), 15219, 15221 (*janeçvaraḥ*), 15234, 15259 (*janādhipaḥ*), 15283, 15294 (*mahīpatiḥ*), 15298, 15300 (*nṛpaçreshṭhaḥ*), 15302, 15308 (*janeçvaraḥ*), 15315, 15335 (*mahārājaḥ*), 15349 (*nṛpatiḥ*), 17171; IV, 337, 865, 1302, 1516, 1562, 1603, 2013, †2102, †2123; V, 67, 156, 203, 583, 608, 615, 617, †699, †714, †734 (*rājñaḥ*), †755 (*mantriṇo Dh°sya*), †761, †765, †785, †844, †851, †859, †889, †895, †906, †913, †914 (*Suyodhanaṃ*), †1811, †1815, †1818, †1819, †1820, †1822, †1824, †1826, †1827, †1829, †1831, †1832, †1833, †1834, †1835, †1837, †1839, †1840, †1841, †1842, †1843, †1844, †1845, †1846, †1848, †1849, †1850, †1854, †1858, †1863, †1864, †1865, †1866, †1867, †1872, †1873, †1874, †1895, †1902, †1915, 1948, 2241 (°*sya vāhinīṃ*), 2279, 2382, †2505, †2507, 2513 (*D°*), 2583, 2597, 2666, 2738, 2972, 3240, 3241, 3242, 3255, 3259, 3269 (°*niveçanāt*), 3280, 3287, 3311, 3319, 4204 (*D°*), 4283 (*Suyodhanaḥ*), 4289, 4404 (*D°*), 4418 (do.), 4771, 4783, 4797, 4800, 4804, 4839, 4849, 4852 (°*sya sainyeshu*), 4853 (do.), 4861, 4875, 4899, 4900, 4922, 4966, 5027, 5141, 5174 (°*sya sainikān*), 5212 (*nagaraṃ Dh°sya*), 5537, 5540, 5618, 5650, †5651 (*Suyodhanaṃ*), 5679 (do.), 5766, 5837, 5846 (*rājā*), 7582 (°*sya sainyeshu*), 7584, 7603, 7612 (?), 7655 (*Suyodhanaṃ*); VI, 6 (°*sya vāhinīṃ*), 14, 760 (°*sya senāṃ*), 853, 1551 (°*camūṃ* ?), 1552 (°*sya sainikāḥ*), 1620, 1627, 2551 (°*sya sainikān*), 2851 (°*sya sainikāḥ*), 3565 (*sainyāni Dh°sya*), 4001 (°*sya yodhāḥ*), 4333 (°*camūṃ* ?), 4424, 4836 (°*sya sainikān*), 5210 (°*sya sainyena*), 5229, †5797; VII, †73, 119, 474, 658 (*rājā*), 659, 2588, 2651 (°*sya çivire*), 2679 (*shaḍ rathān Dh°sya*), 2969 (°*sya sainyāni*), 3617 (*rājñaḥ*), 3753, 3806, 3821, 3853, 4224 (°*sya balaṃ*), 4237 (*balaṃ . . . Dh°sya*), 4316, 4334 (*akshauhiṇyaḥ . . . Dh°sya*), 4771 (°*sya yad balaṃ*), 6415, 6562, 8216, 8314 (°*sya vāhinīṃ*), 8889, 9055, 9227; VIII, 431, 1790, 1860 (*sakhā . . . Dh°sya*, i.e. Karṇa), 2021 (*rājñaḥ*), 2120, 2312, 2987 (*anīkan tu Dh°sya*), 3022, 3035 (*senā hi Dh°sya*), 3061 (*akshauhiṇyas tathā tisro Dh°sya saṃhatāḥ*), 3066 (°*sya . . . camūṃ*), 3106 (*senāṃ Dh°sya*), 3196, 3201 (*rājñā*), 3335, †3343, 3624, 3634, 3679 (*balaṃ . . . Dh°sya*), 3684 (*camūḥ . . . Dh°sya*), 3700 (*narendrasya*), 3701, 3703, 3704, 3705, 3777, 3780, 4254, 4275, 4353; IX, 4 (*Suyodhanaḥ*), 240, 345, 356, †1068, 1290 (*balaṃ Dh°sya*), 1291, 1310, 1311, 1321, 1460 (*balaṃ . . . Dh°sya*), 1468, 1573, 1722, 1739, 1743, 1744, 1857, 1907, 1915, 1921 (*Suyodhane*), 1927, 1970, 1977, 3066, 3151, 3173, 3188, 3199, 3248, 3265 (*Kauravo rājā*), 3367 (*hato rājā*), 3453, 3510 (*D°*), 3628 (*nipātitaṃ*); X, 700; XI, 508, 611; XII, 118, 4626; XIII, 8; XIV, 56, 399 (*hato rājā*), 1798 (*rājā*), 1802 (*nihato rājā*).

(3) = Vikarna: II, 2279.

(4) = Yuyutsu: I, 2726 (*vaiçyāputro Yuyutsuḥ*), 2741 (do.); XII, 1541 (*Y°*).

Dhārtarāshṭra, adj. ("belonging to Dhārtarāshṭra (= Duryodhana), or to the Dhārtarāshṭras"). § 342 (Indralokābhigamanap.): III, **51**, 1996 (*çriyam*).—§ 512 (Ghoshayātrāp.): III, **241**, 14905 (*anīkeshu*).—§ 552 (Goharaṇap.): IV, **61**, 1983 (*vanam*).—§ 569 (Bhagavadyānap.): V, **143**, 4847 (*sainyeshu*), 4873 (do.).—§ 576 (Bhagavadgītāp.): VI, **16**, 628 (*mahācamūḥ*); **19**, 697 (*anīkāni*).—§ 584 (Bhīshmavadhap.): VI, **83**, 3662 (*mahācamūḥ*).—§ 585 (do.): VI, **93**, 4181 (*sainyam*).—§ 587 (do.): VI, **112**, 5230 (*sarvasainyāni*).—§ 589 (Droṇābhishekap.): VII, **2**, †72 (*paurushe*).—§ 599 (Jayadrathavadhap.): VII, **92**, 3294 (*anīkeshu*).—§ 605 (Karṇap.): VIII, **10**, 376 (*senām*); **11**, 422 (*senā*), 423 (*mahācamūḥ*).—§ 607 (do.): VIII, **37**, †1727 (*paurushe*).—§ 608 (do.): VIII, **50**, 2439 (*mahācamūm*); **60**, 3047 (*mahācamūḥ*), 3051 (do.); **64**, 3248 (do.); **73**, 3655 (°*m. udagram hi vyūḍham . . . mahābalam*); **76**, †3821 (read *camūm* with B.; C. has by error *camām*); **78**, 3947 (*sainyam*); **79**, 4025 (*senā*).

Dhārtarāshṭrasuta[1], pl. (°*āḥ*) ("grandsons of Dhṛtarāshṭra[4]"). § 155 (Pūruvamç.): I, **94**, 3748 (C. *Dhārtarāshṭrasutān āhus trīn etān prathitān bhuvi | Pratīpam Dharmanetram Sunetram cāpi*, presumably as the sons of Kuṇḍika; B., however, reads *Dhṛtarāshṭrasutānām tu trīn*, etc.; Pratīpa, etc., must then also be sons of Dhṛtarāshṭra and brothers of Kuṇḍika).

Dhārtarāshṭrasuta[2], pl. (°*āḥ*) ("grandsons of Dhṛtarāshṭra[1]"). § 611 (Çalyap.): IX, **27**, 1455 (had been slain by Bhīma, so C., but read with B. *Dhṛta*°).

Dhātṛ[1] ("the Creator, the Orderer," mostly identical with Brahmán). § 17 (Uttaṅka): I, **3**, 828 (*Dhātā Vidhātā ca*, seen by Uttaṅka in the world of the nāgas in the shape of two women).—§ 33 (Garuḍa): I, **23**, 1251 (*Dhātā Vidhātā ca*, identified with Garuḍa).—§ 82 (Kṛshṇa Vāsudeva): I, **63**, 2431 (identified with Kṛshṇa).—§ 88 (Amçāvat.): I, **65**, 2523 (the first of the Ādityas).—§ 123 (do.): I, **66**, 2614 (*Dhātā Vidhātā ca*, sons of Brahmán).—§ 149 (Yayāti): I, **89**, †3586.—§ 191 (Arjuna): I, **123**, 4822 (the first of the Ādityas, present at the birth of Arjuna).—§ 215 (Bakavadhap.): I, **157**, 6137 (*bhartur arthāya nikshiptām nyāsam Dhātrā*, says the brahman about his daughter).—§ 222 (Tapatyup.): I, **171**, 6547 (*lokam nirmathya Dhātredam rūpam āvishkṛtam kṛtam*).—§ 258 (Khāṇḍavadahanap.): I, **227**, 8266 (attacked Arjuna).—§ 259 (Çārṅgakop.): I, **229**, 8360 (Agni identified with *Dh.*).—§ 277 (Jarāsandhavadhap.): II, **21**, 851 (*svavīryam kshatriyāṇān tu bāhvor Dhātā nyavoçayat*). § 208 (Dyūtap.): II, **57**, †1990 (*Dhātrānuçishṭasya* (°*ā tu dish*°, B.) *vaçe kiledam sarvam jagat* (*gajat*, C. by error) *tishṭhati* (*ceshṭati*, B.)); **58**, †2005 (do., as in B.), 2009 (°*uç ca vaçam*).—§ 303 (Anudyūtap.): II, **76**, 2493 (°*ur niyogāt*).—§ 305 (do.): II, **79**, 2605 (*Dhātrā kim nu pramādataḥ mamānto naiva vihitaḥ*).—§ 317*b* (Kṛshṇa Vāsudeva): III, **12**, 480 (Kṛshṇa became Hari, Dhātṛ, etc.).—§ 320 (Saubhavadhop.): III, **19**, 773 (*mṛtyur asya*—i.e. Çālva's—*Devakinandanaḥ Kṛshṇaḥ samkalpito Dhātrā*).—§ 323 (Dvaitavanapr.): III, **25**, †958 (*Dhātrā vidhir yo vihitaḥ purāṇaiḥ*), †959 (*nideçe . . . Dhātuḥ*).—§ 327 (Draupadīparitāp.): III, **30**, 1117 (*namo Dhātre Vidhātre ca yau mohañ cakratus tava*), 1138, 1143 (°*ur ādeçam*), 1145, 1148, 1154, 1156, 1157; **31**, 1174, 1180, 1200 (*īçvaram sarvabhūtānām*); **32**, 1208 (*Dhātā Vidhātā ca*), 1222, 1224, 1237.—§ 330 (Indradarçana): III, **37**, 1488 (*namo Dhātre Vidhātre ca*).—§ 350 (Nalopākhyānap.): III, **69**, 2700 (°*trā vinirmitaḥ*).—§ 377 (Dhaumyatīrthak.): III, **90**, 8401 (identified with Kṛshṇa).—§ 400 (Tīrthayātrāp.): III, **118**, †10225 (°*uḥ*, sc. *āyatanam*, visited by Yudhishṭhira on his tīrthayātrā).—§ 406 (do.): III, **125**, 10419 (*yatra*—i.e. at *Prasravaṇam Indrasya—Dhātā Vidhātā ca Varuṇaç cordhvam āgatāḥ*).—§ 440 (Yakshayuddhap.): III, **142**, 11901 (°*uḥ*, sc. *astram*, obtained by Arjuna).—§ 455 (Brāhmaṇamāhātmyak.): III, **185**, 12703 (among the honourable appellations of a king).—§ 459 (Mārkaṇḍeyas.): III, **189**, 12955 (*aham Dhātā Vidhātā ca*, says Nārāyaṇa), 13004 (*esha Dhātā Vidhātā ca*, i.e. Kṛshṇa).—§ 480 (Pativratop., Brāhmaṇavyādhas.): III, **208**, 13821 (*Dhātrā vidhir ayam dṛshṭaḥ*).—§ 522 (Draupadīharaṇap.): III, **265**, †15591 (*Dhātur Vidhātuḥ*, sc. *sadanāt*).—§ 546 (Kuṇḍalāharaṇap.): III, **300**, 16951 (a çloka sung by *Dh.* is quoted).—§ 549 (Pāṇḍavapr.): IV, **9**, 259 (Sudeshṇā asks Draupadī if she is [the wife] of *Dh.*, etc.).—§ 551 (Kīcakavadhap.): IV, **20**, 617 (°*ur mayā vipriyam kṛtam*).—§ 552 (Goharaṇap.): IV, **56**ζ, 1770 (*Dhātur Vidhātuç ca*, sc. *vimānāni*, present at the encounter between Arjuna and Bhīshma).—§ 556 (Sañjayayānap.): V, **31**, 916.—§ 559 (Prajāgarap.): V, **39**, †1446 (*Dhātrā tu dishṭasya vaçe kṛto 'yam*).—§ 560 (Sanatsujātap.): V, **45**, 1658 (°*kṛtam vṛttam*).—§ 561 (Yānasandhip.): V, **51**, 2045 (*niyatam coditā Dhātrā*).—§ 561*h* (Arjuna): V, **56**, 2220 (*Tvashṭā, Dhātā*, decorated the flagstaff of Arjuna; or is *Dh*° = Tvashṭṛ (Bhaumana)(?); PCR. seems to have another reading (*Dhātrā*?); cf. Nīl.).—§ 562 (Bhagavadyānap.): V, **73**, 2678 (*jayo vadho vā saṅgrāme Dhātrā dishṭaḥ*).—§ 564 (Mātalīyop.): V, **105**, 3677 (*āhāro vihito Dhātrā*).—§ 570 (Sainyaniryānap.): V, **151**, 5133 (*esha Dhātā Vidhātā ca*, i.e. Kṛshṇa).—§ 571 (Ulūkadūtāg.): V, **160**, 5464 (*manasaiva hi bhutāni Dhātaiva kurute vaçe*); **163**, 5687 (*aham Bhīshmavadhāt srshṭo nūnam Dhātrā*, says Çikhaṇḍin).—§ 573 (Ambopākhyānap.): V, **175**, 6007 (*dhig Dhātāram*).—§ 576 (Bhagavadgītāp.): VI, **33**, 1187 (? = Kṛshṇa); **34**, 1237 (do.).—§ 583 (Bhīshmavadhap.): VI, **76**, 3336 (*purā Dhātrā yathā sṛshṭam*).—§ 587 (do.): VI, **108**, 5036 (*yaiva hi tvam kṛtā Dhātrā saiva hi tvam Çikhaṇḍinī*); **112**, 5215 (*strī hy eshā vihitā Dhātrā*, sc. Çikhaṇḍinī).—§ 588 (do.): VI, **121**β, 5802 (°*uḥ*, sc. *astram*, known by Arjuna).—§ 599 (Jayadrathavadhap.): VII, **94**ε, 3454 (*Dhātā Vidhātā*, blessing to Duryodhana); **143**, 6011 (*vihito hy asya*—i.e. Bhūriçravas'—*Dhātraiva mṛtyuḥ Sātyakiḥ*).—§ 606 (Tripurākhyāna): VIII, **33**, 1428 (*purāṇi varadattāni Dhātrā*, sc. the three cities of the Asuras; = Brahmán?).—§ 608 (Karṇap.): VIII, **88**αγ, †4511 (*yathā na kuryāt . . . Dhātā*).—§ 610 (Çalyap.): IX, **6**o, 303 (°*trā yatnād vinirmitam*, sc. Açvatthāman).—§ 612 (Hradapraveçap.): IX, **31**, 1777 (*eshu te puranu dharmaḥ sṛshṭo Dhātrā*).—§ 615*u* (Skanda): IX, **45**γ, 2506 (*Dhātā Vidhātā ca*, came to the investiture of Skanda), (ζ) 2541 (gave five companions to Skanda).—§ 615 (Gadāyuddhap.): IX, **59**, 3332 (*Dhātropadishṭam . . . phalam*); **65**, 3648 (*īdṛço martyadharmo 'yam Dhātrā nirdishṭā ucyate*).—§ 618 (Jalapradānikap.): XI, **1**β, 20 (*yena mām duḥkhabhāgeshu Dhātā karmasu yuktavān*); **7**, 174 (°*trābhilikhitāny āhuḥ sarvabhūtāni karmaṇā*).—§ 621 (Rājadh.): XII, **10**, 295 (*Dhātā tatra na garhyate*).—§ 623 (do.): XII, **15**, 441 (*na Brahmāṇam na Dhātāram na Pūshāṇam*, sc. *namasyanti janāḥ*).—§ 626 (do.): XII, **20**a, †610 (*yajñāya sṛshṭāni dhanāni Dhātrā*).—§ 630 (do.): XII, **26**, †792 (do.), 793 (*dhanaṃ . . . Dhātā dadāti martyebhyo yajñārthaṃ*); **27,** 832 (*sṛshṭo 'si . . . Dhātrā karmasu*).—§ 637 (do.): XII, **47θ**, 1606 (= *Nārāyaṇo Hariḥ*, i.e. Kṛshṇa).—§ 641 (do.): XII, **66,** 2477 (*dharme Dhātrā sṛshṭe*); **91,** 3414 (*durbalārthaṃ balaṃ sṛshṭaṃ Dhātrā*); **104,** 3877 (°*āraṃ garhate nityaṃ*).—§ 651*b* (Kapotalubdhakas.): XII, **143,** 5486 (°*trā . . . nirmitaḥ*).—§ 664 (Mokshadh.): XII, **207,** 7550 (*adhyakshaṃ sarvabhūtānāṃ . . . Brahmāṇaṃ*, created by Vishṇu, i.e. Kṛshṇa).—§ 665 (do.): XII, **208β**, 7581 (the seventh of the Ādityas).—§ 667 (do.): XII, **210,** 7665 (= *Nārāyaṇaḥ*, i.e. Kṛshṇa).—§ 671*b* (Bali-Vāsavas.): XII, **225,** 8157 (*na Dhātā na Vidhātā māṃ*—i.e. *Çrī*—*vidadhāti kathañcana | Kālas tu*, etc.).—§ 672*b* (Çakra-Namucis.): XII, **226,** 8198 (*yatra yatraiva saṃyukto Dhātrā garbhe punaḥ punaḥ*), 8208 (pl.).—§ 677 (Mokshadh.): XII, **233,** 8528 (= Brahmán?); **236,** 8629 (*Dhātrā sṛshṭāni bhūtāni*).—§ 679 (do.): XII, **261,** 9252 (*etasmāt kāraṇād Dhātrā kuçidaṃ sampravarttitaṃ*).—§ 683 (do.): XII, **268,** 9573 (°*çāsanaṃ*).—§ 700 (do.): XII, **289,** 10629 (*Dhātrā vihitabhakshyāṇi sarvabhūtāni*).—§ 717*b* (Nārāyaṇīya): XII, **335,** 12674 (= Nārāyaṇa); **341,** 13102 (? *Dhātā tvaṃ sarvabhūtānāṃ*, sc. Brahmán), 13108 (= Vishṇu); **343,** VII), 13213 (made the vajra).—§ 717*d* (Brahma-Rudras.): XII, **352,** 13757 (*Dhātur ādyaṃ vidhānaṃ*).—§ 719 (Ānuçāsanik.): XIII, **1,** 13 (*nūnaṃ hi pāpakarmāṇo Dhātrā sṛshṭāḥ smahe*).—§ 730 (do.): XIII, **14εε**, 1003 (identified with Çiva); **16,** 1059 (do.); **18κκ**, 1324 (? *paraṃ Dhātā Vidhātā ca*, sc. Çiva), (λλ), †1368.—§ 739 (do.): XIII, **35,** 2145 (*sṛshṭvā dvijātīn Dhātā*).—§ 768*b* (Umā-Maheçvaras.): XIII, **141,** 6451 (*brāhmaṇā lokasāreṇa sṛshṭā Dhātrā*).—§ 770 (Ānuçāsanik.): XIII, **151γ**, 7093 (the fifth of the Ādityas).—§ 773*d* (Çiva): XIII, **161δ**, 7498 (identified with Çiva).—§ 782*g* (Guruçishyasaṃv.): XIV, **42ε**, 1167 (= *mahān ātmā*).—§ 785 (Anugītāp.): XIV, **80,** 2355 (*sakhyañ caitat kṛtaṃ Dhātrā*).

Dhātṛ[2] = Sūrya: III, 148.

Dhātṛ[3] = Çiva (1000 names [1–2]).

Dhātṛ[4] = Vishṇu (1000 names).

Dhātu = Vishṇu (1000 names).

Dhaumra, a ṛshi. § 637 (Rājadh.): XII, **47η**, 1598 (among the ṛshis who surrounded Bhīshma as he lay on his arrow-bed).

Dhaumya[1], the purohita of the Pāṇḍavas, younger brother of Asita Devala. § 11 (Parvasaṅgr.): I, **2,** 420.—§ 230 (Dhaumyapurohitakaraṇa): I, **183,** 6914 (*yavīyān Devalasyaisha . . . bhrātā*), 6918 (°*āçramaṃ*), 6919 (became the purohita of the Pāṇḍavas).—§ 240 (Vaivāhikap.): I, **198,** †7338 (performed the nuptial rites of the Pāṇḍavas).—§ 253 (Haraṇāharaṇap.): I, **221,** 8047 (performed the *cūḍopanayanāni* of the Pāṇḍavas' children).—§ 254 (Khāṇḍavadahanap.): I, **222,** 8057 (°*ādayo viprāḥ*).—§ 262 (Bhagavadyāna): II, **2,** 27, 28.—§ 264 (Sabhākriyāp.): II, **4a**, 107 (the same?).—§ 272 (Rājasūyārambhap.): II, **13,** 542 (°*Dvaipāyanādyaiḥ*).—§ 277 (Jarāsandhavadhap.): II, **24,** 977.—§ 286 (Rājasūyikap.): II, **33,** 1220, 1233, 1239 (acted as *hotṛ* at the rājasūya of Yudhishṭhira).—§ 296 (Dyūtap.): II, **53,** 1917 (sprinkled water over Yudhishṭhira).—§ 305 (Anudyūtap.): II, **78,** 2570 (*brahmaviduttamaḥ*), 2575.—§ 306 (do.): II, **80,** 2622, (*a*), 2627, 2641, 2642 (*Dh.* went away holding *kuça* grass, which pointed to the south-west (*Nairṛtāṃ*), and singing *sāmans* relating to *Yama*, and indicating the songs which would be sung when the Bharatas had been slain in battle).—§ 310 (Āraṇyakap.): III, **3,** 134, (135), 145, (146) (communicated to Yudhishṭhira a hymn to the Sun (*Sūrya*)), 162, 209 (had obtained the hymn from Nārada), 211, 218.—§ 316 (Kirmīravadhap.): III, **11,** 403 (*Rākshasīṃ māyāṃ . . . mantraiḥ . . . nāçayām āsa*).—§ 317 (Arjunābhigamanap.): III, **12,** 577.—§ 321 (Saubhavadhop.): III, **22,** 894.—§ 323 (Dvaitavanapr.): III, **25,** †947, †963.—§ 330 (Indradarçana): III, **37,** 1492.—§ 377 (Dhaumyatīrthak.): III, **86,** 8276 (*Pitāmahasamaṃ*); **87,** 8297 (*Bṛhaspatisamaṃ*); **88,** (8326); **89,** (8354); **90,** (8372) (Dhaumya describes to Yudhishṭhira various tīrthas).—§ 378 (Tīrthayātrāp.): III, **91,** 8407; **92,** 8447; **93,** 8470, 8474, 8483.—§ 419 (Gandhamādanapr.): III, **140,** 10843.—§ 423 (do.): III, **143,** 10977; **144,** 11000; **145,** 11019.—§ 434 (Saugandhikāh.): III, **156,** 11448 (*dvijaḥ*).—§ 436 (Yakshayuddhap.): III, **158,** 11558; **159,** 11630, 11637.—§ 438 (do.): III, **161,** 11740.—§ 439 (do.): III, **163,** 11841, 11842, 11843 (describes the *Mandara* mountain, etc., to Yudhishṭhira).—§ 440 (do.): III, **164,** †11896.—§ 441 (Nivātakavacayuddhap.): III, **165,** †11906.—§ 450 (Ājagarap.): III, **179,** 12442; **181,** 12534.—§ 451 (Mārkaṇḍeyas.): III, **182,** 12556; **183,** 12565, †12578.—§ 522 (Draupadīharaṇap.): III, **264,** 15575 (*purodhasaḥ*); **268,** †15661, †15663, (15664), 15666; **269,** †15691, †15692; **271,** 15749, 15756 (tries to protect Draupadī against Jayadratha).—§ 548 (Āraṇeyap.): III, **315,** 17457, 17469, 17476.—§ 549 (Pāṇḍavapr.): IV, **4,** 88, (89), 136, 139 (in the thirteenth year *Dh.*, with the sacred fires of the Pāṇḍavas, set out towards the Pāñcālas).—§ 567 (Bhagavadyānap.): V, **126,** 4215 (*yāvad Dh°o na medhāgnau juhotīha dvishadbalaṃ*).—§ 569 (do.): V, **140a**, 4741 (*agniṃ juhotu vai Dh°aḥ*).—§ 620 (Çrāddhap.): XI, **26a**, 779, 782 (performed the çrāddha of the fallen).—§ 635 (Rājadh.): XII, **38,** 1409.—§ 637 (do.): XII, **40a**, 1447, 1454; **41β**, 1480; **44δ**, 1529, 1538; **47η**, 1598 (the same?, among the ṛshis who surrounded Bhīshma as he lay on his arrow-bed).—§ 734 (Ānuçāsanik.): XIII, **26a**, 1765 (the same?, among the ṛshis who had come to see Bhīshma).—§ 768 (do.): XIII, **139a**, 6298 (the same?).—§ 787 (Āçramavāsap.): XV, **15τ**, 435.—§ 788 (do.): XV, **23,** 632.—Some of these quotations may perhaps refer to one of the ṛshis under the heading Dhaumya[2]. Cf. Āgniveçya.

Dhaumya[2], name of one or more ṛshis. § 545 (Pativratāmāhātmyap.): III, **298,** (16876).—§ 665 (Mokshadh.): XII, **208θ**, 7596 (one of the ṛshis of the west).—§ 730*g* (Upamanyu): XIII, **14,** 702 (son of Vyāghrapāda).—§ 766 (Ānuçāsanik.): XIII, **127,** (6070).—§ 775 (do.): XIII, **166ζ**, 7672 (one of the ṛshis of the north).—Some of these quotations may also refer to Dhaumya[1].

Dhaumya Āyoda, v. Āyoda Dhaumya.

[Dhaumya-purohitakaraṇa] ("the Pāṇḍavas' making Dhaumya their purohita"). § 230 (Caitrarathap.): *Arjuna* gave his *Āgneya* weapon to the *Gandharva Citraratha* and said: "Let the horses you give us remain with you for some time; when occasion comes we will take them from you." Then the *Pāṇḍavas* took leave of the *Gandharva*, and left the banks of the Bhāgīrathī. At that time *Dhaumya*, the younger brother of *Devala*, was dwelling at the *tīrtha* named *Utkocaka*, engaged in ascetic penances. According to the counsel of the *Gandharva*, the *Pāṇḍavas* installed *Dhaumya* in the office of their *purohita*, and became his *yājyas*. Then they resolved to go to the *svayaṃvara* of *Pāñcālī* (i.e. *Kṛshṇā*) (I, **183**).

[Dhaumya-tīrthakathana] ("Dhaumya's enumeration of tīrthas"). § 377 (Tīrthay.): *Yudhishṭhira* told *Dhaumya* that, missing *Arjuna*, he does not like to live longer in the *Kāmyaka* wood, and asked him to tell them of some other dwelling-place (III, **86**). *Dhaumya* described to *Yudhishṭhira* the *tīrthas*, etc., of the eastern quarter (III, **87**), then of the south and of *Surāshṭra* (III, **88**), then of the west in the country of the *Avantis* (B. *Ānartteshu*) (III, **89**), and then of the north (III, **90**).

Dhaundhumāra(ṃ) upākhyāna(ṃ) ("the episode relating to Dhundhumāra," i.e. Dhundhumāropākhyāna). § 11 (Parvasaṅgr.): I, **2**, 468.—§ 474 (Mārkaṇḍeyas.): III, **201**, 13488 (related by Mārkaṇḍeya to Yudhishṭhira). —§ 478 (Dhundhumārop.): III, **204**, 13625 (the merit of hearing it).

Dhautamūlaka, a king. § 562 (Bhagavadyānap.): V, **74**γ, 2730 (*Cīnānāṃ*, among the vile kings who annihilated their kinsmen and relatives).

Dhāvamāna = Çiva (1000 names[1]).

Dhenuka[1]. § 567 (Bhagavadyānap.): V, **130**ξ, 4410 (had been slain by Kṛshṇa).

Dhenuka[2], a tīrtha. § 370 (Tīrthayātrāp.): III, **84**, 8065. —§ 594 (Mṛtyu): VII, **54**, 2088 (there Mṛtyu performed austerities).—§ 678*c* (Mṛtyu-Prajāpatisaṃv.): XII, **259**, 9201 (do.).

Dhenukāçrama = Dhenuka[2]. § 594 (Mṛtyu): VII, **54**, 2080.

Dhīmat. § 141 (Purūravas): I, **75**, 3149 (second son of Purūravas and Urvaçī).

Dhīroshṇin, a Viçvadeva. § 749 (Ānuçāsanik.): XIII, **91**γ, 4357 (enumeration).

Dhishaṇā, name of a female deity (PCR. the day of the full moon, person.). § 615*u* (Skanda): IX, **45**γ, 2516 (among the wives of the gods, came to the investiture of Skanda).

Dhruva[1], one of the eight Vasus. § 116 (Vasu, pl.): I, **66**, 2582, 2583 (his mother named Dhūmrā?).—§ 770 (Ānuçāsanik.): XIII, **151**δ, 7094 (enumeration).

Dhruva[2], son of Nahusha. § 143 (Yayāti): I, **75**, 3155 (sixth son of Nahusha).

Dhruva[3], an ancient ṛshi. § 267 (Yamasabhāv.): II, **8**, 321 (in the palace of Yama).

Dhruva[4], the Polar star. § 574 (Jambukh.): VI, **3**, 84 (omens).—§ 641 (Rājadh.): XII, **127**, 4685 (*saptarshaya iva Dhruvaṃ*, sc. *parivārya upāviçan*).—§ 707 (Mokshadh.): XII, **318**, 11711 (one who fails to see *Dh.* has but one year to live).—§ 717*b* (Nārāyaṇīya): XII, **340**, 12920 (*jyotishāṃ çreshṭhaṃ*).—§ 721 (Ānuçāsanik.): XIII, **3***a*, 195 (*Auttānapādasya*).—§ 770 (do.): XIII, **151**, 7156.

Dhruva[5], a Pāṇḍava warrior. § 600 (Ghaṭotkacavadhap.): VII, **158**χ, 7009.

Dhruva[6], a Kuru warrior. § 600 (Ghaṭotkacavadhap.): VII, **155**, 6708 (slain by Bhīmasena).

Dhruva[7], a ṛshi. § 734 (Ānuçāsanik.): XIII, **26***a*, 1762 (among the ṛshis who came to see Bhīshma as he lay on his arrow-bed).

Dhruva[8] = Çiva (1000 names[1-2]).

Dhruva[9] = Kṛshṇa: XII, 1510.

Dhruva[10] = Vishṇu (1000 names).

Dhruvadvāra, name of a place (?). § 674*b* (Çrī-Vāsavasaṃv.): XII, **229**, 8338 (*°bhavāṃ Gaṅgāṃ*).

Dhruvaka, a warrior of Skanda. § 615*u* (Skanda): IX, **45**η, 2567.

Dhruvaratnā, a mātṛ. § 615*u* (Skanda): IX, **46**θ, 2622.

Dhṛshṇu[1], son of Manu Vaivasvata. § 139 (Manu Vaivasvata): I, **75**, 3140 (the second son of Manu).

Dhṛshṇu[2], son of Kavi. § 747*b* (Suvarṇotpatti): XIII, **85**, 4150 (the third son of Kavi).

Dhṛshṭadyumna, son of the Pāñcāla king Drupada and brother of Draupadī (Kṛshṇā). § 4 (Anukram.): I, **1**, 199. —§ 11 (Parvasaṅgr.): I, **2**, 384, 429, 564, 570, 572.—§ 83 (Ādivaṃçāvatāraṇa): I, **63**, 2437 (born from the fire, cf. § 218).—§ 130 (Aṃçāvat.): I, **67**, 2761 (born from a portion of Agni).—§ 216 (Caitrarathap.): I, **165**, 6323 (*°sya cotpattiṃ*, related to the Pāṇḍavas by a brahman), 6325 (*Drupadaputrasya Dh°sya pāvakāt . . . sambhavaḥ*, do.).— § 218 (Draupadīsambhava): I, **167**, 6406 (in order to have a son who could slay Droṇa, Drupada held a sacrifice, where *Dh.* arose from the sacrificial fire; the brahmans gave him the name *Dh.* (etymology)), 6408 (instructed by Droṇa in the use of weapons).—§§ 231–236 (Svayaṃvarap.): I, **184**, 6932 (*°sya bhaginī*, i.e. Draupadī); **185**, 6977; **186**, (6981); **192**, 7156, †7168, †7169 (Draupadī's svayaṃvara).—§ 237 (Vaivāhikap.): I, **193**, †7174 (*Somakānāṃ prabarhaḥ*), (†7175); **195**, 7249; **196**, (7261), 7273 (*Pārshataḥ*) (Draupadī's marriage with the five Pāṇḍavas).—§ 241 (Vidurāgamanap.): I, **200**, 7379; **204**, 7464.—§ 243 (do.): I, **205**, 7508 (*°mukhā vīrā bhrātāro Drupadātmajāḥ*).— § 292 (Rajasuyikap.): II, **45***a*, 1606 (accompanied Virāṭa).— § 296 (Dyūtap.): II, **53**, 1926 (had been present at the rājasūya of Yudhishṭhira).—§ 306 (Anudyūtap.): II, **80**, 2662 (all. to his birth, cf. § 218), 2663 (*Pārthānāṃ çyālaḥ*), 2667 (*°o Droṇamṛtyur iti viprathitaṃ vacaḥ*):—§ 317 (Arjunābhigamanap.): III, **12**, 508 (*°mukhair bhrātṛbhiḥ parivāritā | Pāñcālī*), 521 (*°sya bhaginī*, i.e. Draupadī), (594) (promised to slay Droṇa).—§ 321 (Saubhavadhop.): III, **22**, 897 (took the sons of Draupadī with him to his own city, when the Pāṇḍavas retired to the forest).—§ 325 (Draupadīparitāpav.): III, **27**, 1023 (*°sya bhaginīṃ*, i.e. Draupadī).— § 327 (do.): III, **31**, 1191 (*yathā jāto Dh°aḥ*, all. to § 218). —§ 342 (Indralokābh.): III, **51**, 1983 (*Drupadasya tathā putrā Dh°purogamāḥ*, had visited the Pāṇḍavas in the Kāmyaka forest), 1994, 1997, 2000.—§ 553 (Vaivāhikap.): IV, **72**, 2353 (came to the marriage of Abhimanyu and Uttarā).—§ 554 (Sainyodyogap.): V, **3**, 57 (*Pārshataṃ*).— § 556 (Sañjayayānap.): V, **22**β, †661 (in the army of Yudhishthira); **25**ζ, †725 (*Pārshataṃ*).—§ 561 (Yānasandhip.): V, **48**β, †1817, †1849; **50**, 1975 (*°sya sainyena*), 1982; **53**θ, 2110 (*Pāñcālyaḥ*); **55**κ, 2145 (*Pārshataḥ*), 2202 (among the chief warriors of the Pāṇḍavas); **57**ξ, 2235 (*daçabhis tanayair vṛtaḥ*—sc. Drupada—*Satyajitpramukhair vīrair Dh°purogamaiḥ*), 2242 (acquainted with human, celestial, Gāndharva, and Āsura arrays), 2251 (*Draupadeyāḥ . . . Dh°mukhāḥ*), 2262 (*Pārshataḥ*, instead of the second *Dhṛshṭadyumnaḥ* read with B. *Dhṛshṭaketuḥ*), 2278, 2288; **65**γγ, 2487 (*Pāñcālyaḥ*).—§ 562 (Bhagavadyānap.): V, **80**ε, 2856; **82**, 2891 (*°sya bhaginī*, i.e. Draupadī); **83**θ, 2951. —§ 567 (do.): V, **126**, 4220 (*Pārshataḥ*); **129**μ, 4358.— § 569 (do.): V, **141**γ, 4779 (*Pāñcālyaḥ*), 4799 (*vaitānike karmamukhe jāto yaḥ, Kṛshṇa! pāvakāt*, all. to § 218).— § 570 (Sainyaniryānap.): V, **151***a*, 5100 (leader of one akshauhiṇī), 5122, 5124, 5143, 5146 (Yudhishṭhira will appoint *Dh.* as his generalissimo), (γ), 5152 (*Pārshataḥ*), (ε), 5163 (*°sya cātmajāḥ*); **152**η, 5175 (*Pārshataḥ*); **153**, 5193 (*Pāñcālyaḥ*); **157**, 5324 (*Pāñcālyaṃ*), 5326 (was appointed as generalissimo (*sarvasenāpatiṃ*) of Yudhishṭhira's army); **162,** 5591, 5618; **163,** 5688, 5697; **164,** 5702, 5704, 5705, 5712 (*senāpatipatiḥ*, selected Droṇa as his own match in the battle).—§ 572 (Rathātirathas.): V, **171,** 5896 (*senānīḥ* . . . *Droṇaçishyo*, is an atiratha), 5899 (*Kshattradharmā* . . . *Dh°sya tanayaḥ*), 5917.—§ 573 (Ambopākhyānap.): V, **192,** 7548 (*Pārshataḥ*, instructed by Droṇa in the Dhanurveda); **193,** 7560; **194**γ, 7598 (*Pārshataḥ*); **196,** 7622 (*°mukhān vīrān*), (θ), 7629 (*°mukhān*, sc. the Draupadeyas, etc.), 7633.—§ 576 (Bhagavadgītāp.): VI, **16,** 631 (*Sṛñjayāḥ* . . . *Dh°purogamāḥ*), 632 (*°mukhāḥ*); **19**ε, 709, 712 (*Pāñcālyaḥ* . . . *sahitaḥ* . . . *Prabhadrakaiḥ*), 722; **22**η, 779; **25**κ, 846.—§ 577 (Bhīshmavadhap.): VI, **43,** 1632 (*°ādayaḥ*).—§ 578 (do.): VI, **44**β, 1655 (*Pārshataḥ*); **45**[8], 1700 (attacks Droṇa); **47**ε[27], 1837 (*Pārshataḥ*, attacks Bhīshma), (η[31]), 1866 (do., pierced by Bhīshma); **48**κ, 1962 (do.), 1972; **49,** 2003; **50**ν, 2060 (*Pārshataḥ*), 2062 (do.), 2063, 2064 (*Pārshata*), 2069, 2082 (*Pārshataḥ*, formed the *krauñcāruṇa* array); **51**αα, 2117.—§ 579 (do.): VI, **52**[1]α, 2128 (*Pārshate*, pierced by Bhīshma), (ζ), 2149 (*Pārshataḥ*, attacks Droṇa); **53,** 2198, 2199, 2200, 2201, 2204, 2206, 2209, 2215, 2227 (encounter with Droṇa; *Dh.* is rescued by Bhīmasena), 2233; **54**[13], 2332, 2333 (rescues Bhīmasena), (ι[14]), 2340 (*Pārshataḥ*, attacks Bhīshma), 2347, 2352, 2353; **55**[15], 2363 (fights Açvatthāman).—§ 580 (do.): VI, **56**[2], 2411 (Arjuna and *Dh.* formed the *ardhacandra* array), (θ), 2416.—§ 581 (do.): VI, **61,** 2706 (*Pārshataḥ*, slew Sāṃyamani's son); **62,** 2723, 2726, 2728 (encounter with Çalya), (η), 2733 (*Pārshataḥ*), 2740 (pierced by Duryodhana), (θ), 2755, 2760 (*Pārshatena*); **63**ι, 2788 (*Pārshataḥ*).—§ 582 (do.): VI, **69**α, 3063 (do., in the one eye of the *çyena* array); **71,** 3141 (attacked by Kṛpa and Kṛtavarman); **72**ε, 3171 (*senāpatiḥ*, engaged in battle with Droṇa), 3194 (*°mukhāḥ* . . . *Pārthāḥ*).—§ 583 (do.): VI, **75,** 3280, 3281 (formed the *makara* array), (α), 3285; **77**[4], 3353 (*Pārshataḥ*), 3355, 3357, 3362 (*Pārshataḥ*, rescued Bhīmasena), ([7]), 3388 (had used the *Pramohana* weapon against Droṇa, etc.), ([8]), 3396, 3398; **79,** 3511 (*°-Vṛkodarau*).—§ 584 (do.): VI, **82,** 3624, 3625, 3626 (encounter with Duryodhana); **86**[8], 3819 (*Pāñcālyaḥ*), (ζ[13]), 3839 (*Pārshataḥ*).—§ 585 (do.): VI, **87,** 3885 (*Pāṇḍavānāṃ rathāḥ* . . . *Dh°purogamāḥ*); **89**ν, 3946 (attacks Bhīshma); **96,** 4365 (*°mukhāḥ*); **98,** 4498.—§ 586 (do.): VI, **99**ζ, 4509; **103**μ, 4685 (attacks Bhīshma), 4686, 4689, 4695 (*Pāñcālān Dh°purogamān*); **106**σ, 4804 (pierced by Bhīshma), 4805 (pierced Bhīshma).—§ 587 (do.): VI, **108,** 4999 (*Pāñcālair abhirakshitaḥ*); **109**ε, 5075; **110**ζ, 5097 (attacks Bhīshma), 5102, 5113; **111,** 5179 (fights Kṛtavarman); **112**θ, 5234; **114,** 5326 (*Pārshataḥ*, attacks Bhīshma), 5332; **115**ν, 5351; **118**υ, 5553 (*Pārshataḥ*), (φ), 5558 (do.); **119**χ, 5578 (*Pārshataṃ*), (ω), 5587 (*Pārshataḥ*).—§ 589 (Droṇābhishek.): VII, **7,** 215 (*Pāñcālāḥ* . . . *Dh°purogamāḥ*); **8,** 225; **9,** 287 (had slain Droṇa, cf. § 602); **10,** 365 (*g*: *Dh.* overthrew in a battle at *Vārāṇasī* the son of the *Kāçi* king, who was desirous of seizing a maiden for his wife).—§ 590 (do.): VII, **13,** 493 (*°balaṃ*); **14**α, 577.—§ 591 (Saṃçaptakavadhap.): VII, **17,** 679.—§ 592 (do.): VII, **20,** (814), 817, 818; **21**κ, 905 (pierces Droṇa), (μ), 916 (defeated by Droṇa); **23**ο, 953 (*Pāñcālarājasya sutaḥ*, description of his horses; proceeded against Droṇa), 989 (*Pāñcālasenanīḥ*, do.), 993 (followed by the Prabhadrakas), 1028; **31**φ, 1348, 1351 (*Pāñcālyaḥ*); **32**ββ, 1427 (attacks Karṇa), 1437 (slew Bṛhatkshatra and Candravarman), (ζζ), 1443.—§ 593 (Abhimanyuvadhap.): VII, **35**δ, 1508 (attacks Droṇa), (ζ), 1528; **40**ο, 1695; **42**π, 1743; **43**ρ, 1769 (pierced by Jayadratha).—§ 597 (Pratijñāp.): VII, **83**α, 2949.—§ 598 (Jayadrathavadhap.): VII, **85**δ, 3048; **88,** 3128 (*Pārshataḥ*, arrayed the Pāṇḍava army).—§ 599 (do.): VII, **95,** 3490 (*°mukhāḥ Pārthāḥ*), 3501, 3502, 3510, 3512, 3514 (encounter with Droṇa), 3535 (*Pāñcālyaṃ*, resisted by Āvantya); **97,** 3575, 3593, 3595, 3604, 3608 (fights Droṇa and is rescued by Sātyaki); **98,** 3609, (κ), 3661 (*°mukhaiḥ*); **110,** 4148 (*Pāñcālyaṃ*), 4162; **111,** 4286, 4290; **114**ψ, 4502 (pierced Kṛtavarman); **122**ιι, 4912, 4917, 4920, 4921, 4922, 4924, 4929, 4930 (defeated by Droṇa); **124**κκ, 4983, (λλ), 5002 (pierced by Duryodhana); **125,** 5074; **127,** 5146, 5147, 5152, 5153, 5154 (protects Yudhishṭhira); **151**γ', 6554.—§ 600 (Ghaṭotkacavadhap.): VII, **153**α, 6627 (pierced by Duryodhana); **154**β, 6650 (proceeded against Droṇa); **155,** 6696 (*°sya cātmajān*, killed by Droṇa); **156,** 6754, (ι), 6782, 6890, 6891, 6895 (fights with Açvatthāman), 6917; **157**β, 6923 (*Pārshataḥ*); **158**χ, 7008; **160,** 7164, 7166, 7168, 7170, 7174 (fights with Açvatthāman); **164,** 7342, 7343, 7345; **165,** 7372 (*Pāñcālyaḥ*, resisted Droṇa); **170,** 7609 (proceeded against Droṇa), 7611, 7616, 7617, (λλ), 7622, 7623, 7627, 7628 (slays Drumasena), 7635, 7638, 7664 (*Pārshataṃ*), 7678, 7679 (fights with Droṇa, etc.); **171,** 7724 (fights with Droṇa), 7726, 7730, (ξξ), 7731; **173,** 7775 (fights with Karṇa), 7777 (*Pāñcālamukhyasya*), 7779, 7833 (*Pārthā* . . . *Dh°purogamāḥ*); **177**χχ, 8059; **178,** 8082 (*°-Çikhaṇḍyādīn Pāñcālānāṃ mahārathān*); **179**βββ, 8118 (pierced by Karṇa).—§ 601 (Droṇavadhap.): VII, **184,** 8364.—§ 602 (do.): VII, **186,** 8501 (Droṇa slays Virāṭa and Drupada and three grandsons of Drupada (sons of Dhṛshṭadyumna?); *Dh.* vows to slay Droṇa on the same day), 8506, 8513 (*Pāñcālyaḥ*); **189,** 8628 (defeats Duḥçāsana), 8642, 8644, 8692 (*Pāñcālān* . . . *Dh°purogamān*); **190,** 8735, 8753; **191,** 8755 (*Pāñcālarājasya sutaḥ*, rushes at Droṇa), 8766, 8767, 8769, 8772, 8773, 8776, 8787, 8796, 8800 (fights with Droṇa); **192,** 8842, 8854, 8856, 8864, 8876 (when Droṇa had devoted himself to *yoga* and was proceeding to Brahmaloka, *Dh.* cut off his head), 8878, 8887 (*Pārshataḥ*).—§ 603 (Nārāyaṇāstramoksh.): VII, **194**ε, 8964, 8966, 8976, 8977 (*°sya yo mṛtyur dṛshṭaiḥ* (read *sṛshṭaḥ* with B.)); **195**ν, 8990, 8994; **196,** 9036, (κ), 9038; **197,** (9105) (tries to justify his conduct); **198,** (9151) (quarrels with Sātyaki); **199,** 9220; **200,** 9293, 9302, 9327 (fights with Açvatthāman), 9387 (*°rathaṃ*); **201**εε, 9401 (*parājite*).—§ 604 (Karṇap.): VIII, **2,** 39 (*Droṇaṃ nihataṃ* . . . *Dh°ena*); **9**θ, 289 (*nihataḥ khaḍgam udyamya Dh°ena*, sc. Droṇa).—§ 605 (do.): VIII, **10**κ, 372 (*nihato vṛddho Dh°ena*, i.e. Droṇa); **11**λ, 426; **12**ββ, 454; **13,** 495 (proceeds against Kṛpa); **22**ζζ, 862; **26,** 1037, 1039, 1051, 1055 (defeated by Kṛpa).—§ 606 (do.): VIII, **35,** 1640 (*Sṛñjayāç cetare sarve Dh°purogamāḥ*).—§ 608 (do.): VIII, **46,** 2122 (*vyūhaṃ* . . . *Pārthānāṃ Dh°ābhirakshitaṃ*), (α), 2126 (*Pāṇḍavān Dh°mukhān*), 2207 (*Drupadaputrāç ca Dh°purogamāḥ*); **47,** 2213 (*°mukhaṃ vyūhaṃ*); **48,** 2236 (*°mukhān Pārthān*), (ξ), 2253, (ρ), 2285; **49**χ, 2333; **50,** 2398 (*Pārshataṃ*); **54,** 2621, 2622, 2640, 2642, 2644, 2645, 2650, 2651 (defeated Kṛtavarman); **56,** 2711, 2717, 2720, 2722, 2728 (defeated Duryodhana), (ππ), 2755, 2757; **57,** 2846 (*nyastaçastro mama pitā Dh°ena pātitaḥ*, i.e. Droṇa), 2848 (Açvatthāman vows not to doff his armour before he has slain *Dh.*), 2849; **58**χχ, 2902 (*°purogamāḥ*), 2905; **59,** 2912, 2915, 2919 (fights with Karṇa), 2934, 2936, 2939, 2943, 2947, 2952, 2960, 2961 (fights with Açvatthāman);

60ββ, 3002, 3031 (°*ratham*); **61**, 3073, 3077, 3091, 3093, 3094, 3095, 3097, 3099 (fights with Duḥçāsana); **62**ζζζ, 3148 (*Pārshataḥ*); **63**ηηη, 3200; **66**ιιι, 3319; **67**κκκ, †3373; **73**, 3644 (°-*Çikhaṇḍibhyām Bhīshma-Droṇau nipātitau*), 3678; **74**, 3796 (°-*Çikhaṇḍibhyām*); **78**γ′, 3955, 3957 (pierces Karṇa), (ε), 4001 (°-*Çikhaṇḍinau*); **79**, 4028 (*Pārshatam*); **82**, †4182; **87**, 4401 (*Pāṇḍavā . . . Dh°purogamāḥ*); **93**, 4854 (*Pārshataḥ*), 4863, 4869, 4871; **96**αχ′, 4991, (βα′), 5031.—§ 609 (Çalyap.): IX, **1**γ, 30 (mentioned among the slain); **2**, 123 (do.).—§ 610 (do.): IX, **3**, 146 (*Pārshataḥ*), 155, 162 (*putraḥ Pāñcālarājasya*), 163 (*b*: To *Dh.*'s chariot were yoked steeds who were white as pigeons, and his standard was made of a lofty *kovidāra*); **5**, 254; **7**τ, 336, (χ), 351.—§ 611 (do.): IX, **8**ζ, 396; **9**ι, 451 (°-*Çikhaṇḍinau*); **10**, 522 (*Pāṇḍavāḥ sarve Dh°purogamāḥ*); **11**λ, 550, 566, 571 (fights with Kṛpa); **12**ξ, 627 (*Bhāradvājasya hantāram*); **15**, 753 (*Pārshataḥ*), 756 (fights with Duryodhana); **16**σ, 819; **17**ω, †894, (*aa*), 946 (*Pārshatam*); **18**ββ, 962, 967; **19**δδ, 1020 (*Pārshataḥ*), (εε), 1037 (do.), 1046; **20**, †1082 (fights with Çālva); **21**κκ, 1125 (*Pārshatam*); **22**λλ, 1139, 1161, 1162 (fights with Duryodhana); **23**, 1242 (*Pāñcālyaḥ*), 1244 (°*sya vāhinīm*); **25**ξξ, 1353 (*Pāñcālyaḥ*), 1356, (οο), 1374, 1375, 1385 (C. has by error *Dhu*°), 1390, 1392. —§ 612 (Hradapraveçap.): IX, **29**, 1590, 1597 (*Pāṇḍavās . . . Dh°purogamāḥ*), 1603, 1604; **30**ε, 1725 (*Pāñcālyaḥ*).—§ 615 (Gadāyuddhap.): IX, **61**, 3419 (all. to § 602); **62**ψ, 3462.—§ 616 (Sauptikap.): X, **3**, 132 (°*purogamān*), 138 (Açvatthāman will slay *Dh.*); **4**δ, 167; **5**ε, 194, (ζ), 209; **8**, 329, 330 (slain by Açvatthāman in the nightly encounter), 348, 352, 366; **9**, 523 (*hatam*), (μ), 529 (°*sya cātmajāḥ*, slain by Açvatthāman in the nightly encounter), 531 (*māritaḥ*).—§ 617 (Aishīkap.): X, **10**, 543 (°*sya sārathiḥ*); **17**, 763. —§ 618 (Jalapradānikap.): XI, **11**ι, 300 (*Pāñcālā nihatāḥ sarve Dh°purogamāḥ*).—§ 619 (Strīvilāpap.): XI, **23**θ, 670 (*bāṇair bhinnatanutrāṇam Dh°ena*, sc. Droṇa). — § 620 (Çrāddhap.): XI, **26**β, 789 (*Pārshatam*, his body is burnt). — § 630 (Rājadh.): XII, **27**β, 799 (mentioned among the slain).— § 637 (do.): XII, **43**γ, 1489 (a çrāddha is performed for him).— § 785 (Anugītāp.): XIV, **60**, 1787 (*netā Pāṇḍavānām*), 1790 (*Droṇaḥ pariçrānto Dh°vacam gataḥ*, all. to § 602).—§ 787 (Āçramavāsap.): XV, **10**ν, 332.—§ 789 (Putradarçanap.): XV, **31**η, 857 (had been born from a portion of Fire—*Agner bhāgam*); **32**θ, 878 (°*sya cātmajāḥ*). — § 793 (Mausalap.): XVI, **3**δ, 81. — § 795 (Svargārohaṇap.). XVIII, **1**δ, 24 (°*sya cātmajān*), **2**ε, 67; **5**, 167 (after death *Dh.* entered Fire — *Pāvakam prāpa*).

Cf. the following synonyms:—

Bharatarshabha, q.v. (C. wrongly, instead of *purusharshabha*, B.).

Draupadi ("son of Drupada"): VIII, 288.

Droṇahantṛ ("the slayer of Droṇa"): VII, 9395; VIII, 2729; IX, 755.

Pāñcāla, Pāñcāladāyāda, Pāñcālakulavardhana, Pāñcālamukhya, Pāñcālaputra, Pāñcālarāja, Pāñcālarājan, Pāñcālatanaya, Pāñcālya, Pāñcālyaputra, q.v.

Pārshata, q.v.

Yājñasenasuta, Yājñaseni, q.v.

Dhṛshṭadyumnapitṛ = Drupada: VII, 6652.

Dhṛshṭadyumnasuta = Kshatradharman: VII, 5083.

Dhṛshṭadyumnasuta, pl. (°*āḥ*) ("the sons of Dhṛshṭadyumna"). § 619 (Strīvilāpap.): XI, **25**κ, 718 (have been slain by Droṇa). Cf. next.

Dhṛshṭadyumnatanūja, pl. (°*āḥ*) (do.). § 608 (Karṇap.): VIII, **73**, 3731. Cf. the prec. and next.

Dhṛshṭadyumnātmaja, pl. (°*āḥ*) (do.). § 589 (Droṇābhishekap.): VII, **10**λ, 359 (four enumerated). Cf. the prec.

Dhṛshṭaketu[1], an ancient king. § 6 (Anukram.): I, **1***a*, 231 (in Sañjaya's enumeration).

Dhṛshṭaketu[2], king of the Cedis, son of Çiçupāla. § 130 (Aṃçāvat.): I, **67**, 2642 (incarnation of the Asura Anuhlāda). — [§ 290 (Çiçupālavadhap.): II, **45** (when Çiçupāla had been slain by Kṛshṇa, *Dh.* was installed as king of the Cedis).]—§ 317 (Arjunābhigamanap.): III, **12**, 462 (*Cedipaḥ*, came to the Pāṇḍavas in the forest).—§ 321 (Saubhavadhop.): III, **22**, 898 (*Cedirāṭ*, returned to his city Çuktimatī, taking with him his sister [Kareṇumatī, the wife of Nakula]).—§ 342 (Indralokābhigamanap.): III, **51**, 1983 (had come to the Pāṇḍavas in the forest, cf. § 321).—§ 554 (Sainyodyogap.): V, **4**γ, 71 (among the princes to which the Pāṇḍavas ought to send messengers), 83 (do., the same?).—§ 555 (do.): V, **19**γ, 576 (*Cedīnām ṛshabhaḥ*, came with an akshauhiṇī of troops to Yudhishṭhira). — § 561*g* (Sahadeva): V, **50**, 1999.—§ 561 (Yānasandhip.): V, **50**η, 2010 (*Çaiçupāliḥ*, among the allies of Yudhishṭhira); **55**κ, 2145; **57**ξ, 2239 (*Cedirāṭ*, has joined the Pāṇḍavas with an akshauhiṇī), (ο), 2262 (only B., C. has by error *Dhṛshṭadyumnaḥ*). —§ 562 (Bhagavadyānap.): V, **80**ε, 2857 (*Cedipam*); **83**θ, 2950 (*Cedipaḥ*).—§ 570 (Sainyaniryānap.): V, **151**δ, 5160, (ζ), 5164 (the same?); **157**, 5324 (commanded one division of Yudhishṭhira's army).—§ 571 (Ulūkadūtāgamanap.): V, **162**, 5592; **164**ε, 5707 (is pitted against Çalya).—§ 572 (Rathātirathas.): V, **171**, 5900 (*Çiçupālasuto vīraç Cedirājaḥ . . . sambandhī Pāṇḍavasya*, is a *mahāratha*).—§ 573 (Ambopākhyānap.): V, **196**η, 7623 (*Cedi-Kāçi-Karūshāṇām netāram*), 7644. — § 576 (Bhagavadgītāp.): VI, **19**ε, 709, 715; **25**θ, 834.—§ 578 (Bhīshmavadhap.): VI, **45**[11], 1707, 1708 (battles with Bāhlīka); **48**κ, 1963. — § 580 (do.): VI, **56**ζ, 2415 (on the right horn of the ardhacandravyūha, *Cedi-Kāçi-Karūshakaiç ca Pauravaiç cābhisamvṛtaḥ*).—§ 582 (do.): VI, **72**η, 3170.—§ 583 (do.): VI, **75**, 3286; **77**λ, 3394; **79**ν[13], 3470.—§ 584 (do.): VI, **81**[1], 3561 (battles with Bhūriçravas); **84**, 3730 (do.), 3732, 3734.—§ 585 (do.): VI, **89**ν, 3948.—§ 587 (do.): VI, **108**, 5002 (in the rear of the Pāṇḍava army); **115**, 5361 (fights with Paurava); **116**, 5388, 5389, 5390, 5397, 5401 (do.); **118**υ, 5552; **119**χ, 5576.—§ 589 (Droṇābhishekap.): VII, **8**η, 228; **10**, 348 (*c*: *Dh.* had deserted the Cedis and alone joined the Pāṇḍavas). — § 590 (do.): VII, **14**, 527, 528 (fights with Kṛpa), (*a*), 577.—§ 592 (Saṃçaptakavadhap.): VII, **23**ο, 963 (accompanied Virāṭa), 971 (proceeded against Droṇa, description of his horses); **26**τ, 1180, (υ), 1186.—§ 593 (Abhimanyuvadhap.): VII, **35**δ, 1509 (*Cedipaḥ*); **40**ο, 1695; **42**π, 1744.—§ 597 (Pratijñāp.): VII, **83***a*, 2950 (*Cedipam*).—§ 599 (Jayadrathavadhap.): VII, **106**, 3973 (*Cedīnām ṛshabhaḥ*); **107**, 4021, 4026 (slays Vīradhanvan); **111**υ, 4284; **125**, 5042 (*Cedīnām ṛshabhaḥ*), 5051, 5055 (is slain by Droṇa).—§ 604 (Karṇap.): VIII, **6**, 180 (mentioned among the slain). — § 619 (Strīvilāpap.): XI, **25**κ, 725 (*Cedipuṅgavam*), 727 (*Cedipatiḥ*).—§ 620 (Çrāddhap.): XI, **26**β, 787 (his body is burnt).—§ 630 (Rājadh.): XII, **27**β, 800 (sc. *hate*).—§ 787 (Āçramavāsap.): XV, **1***a*, 24 (°*oç ca bhaginī*, i.e. Kareṇumatī; C. has by error Dhṛtaketu).—§ 789

(Putradarçanap.): XV, **32**θ, 878 (among the dead warriors who, summoned by Vyāsa, arose from the Gaṅgā).—§ 795 (Svargārohaṇap.): XVIII, **1**δ, 25; **5**λ, 142, (μ), 162 (among those who after death entered the deities).

Cf. also the following synonyms:—

Caidya, Cedija, Cedipa, Cedipati, Cedipuṅgava, Cedirāj, Cedirāja, q.v.
Çaiçupāli, Çiçupālasuta ("son of Çiçupāla"), q.v.
Çiçupālasya . . . ātmajaḥ (do.): VIII, 2334.
Çiçupālātmaja (do.), q.v.
Daçārhaputraja (?): XI, 729.

Dhṛshṭaratha, a king. § 775 (Ānuçāsanik.): XIII, **166**η, 7676.

Dhṛtāçis = Vishṇu (1000 names).

Dhṛtaketu (XV, 24), error in C. for Dhṛshṭaketu, q.v.

Dhṛtarāshṭra[1], son of Vyāsa with Ambikā, the widow of Vicitravīrya. § 4 (Anukram.): I, **1**, 95 (all. to § 171), †108, 135, 136, 140, 217, 218.—§ 7 (do.): I, **1**, 245.—§ 10 (Parvasaṅgr.): I, **2**, 330.—§ 11 (do.): I, **2**, 376, 413, 421, 434, 501, 502, 503, 582, 583, 584, 585, 611.—§ 70 (Ādivaṃçāvatāraṇap.): I, **60**, 2213 (son of Vyāsa).—§ 71 (do.): I, **61**, 2247, 2251, 2261.—§ 83 (Ādivaṃçāvatāraṇa): I, **63**, 2441 (son of Vyāsa), 2446 (father of 100 sons, of whom eleven are enumerated).—§ 130 (Aṃçāvat.): I, **67**, 2719 (*c:* The Gandharva king Haṃsa, son of Arishṭā, was reborn as *Dh.*, the son of Vyāsa. *Dh.* became blind in consequence of a fault of his mother and the wrath of Vyāsa, cf. § 171), 2727 (enumeration of the names of *Dh.'s* 101 sons and his daughter).—§ 157 (Pūruvaṃç.): I, **95**, ††3808 (son of Vyāsa), ††3809 (father of 100 sons), ††3810.—§ 158 (do.): I, **95**, ††3822.—§ 171 (Vicitravīryasutotpatti): I, **106**, 4301 (Vyāsa begat sons with the widows of Vicitravīrya, Dhṛtarāshṭra with Ambikā, Pāṇḍu with Ambalikā. *Dh.* was born blind because his mother had closed her eyes when Vyāsa approached her; afterwards Vyāsa begat Vidura with the maid of Ambikā).—§ 173 (Pāṇḍurājyābhisheka): I, **109**, 4353, 4357, 4361 (on account of *Dh.'s* blindness Pāṇḍu became king).—§ 174 (Dhṛtarāshṭravivāha): I, **110**, 4374, 4375, 4378 (married Gāndhārī, the daughter of Subala).—§ 177 (Pāṇḍudigvijaya): I, **113**, 4446.—§ 178 (Pāṇḍu): I, **114**, 4469, 4473, 4479.—§ 180 (Gāndhārīputrotpatti): I, **115**, 4483, 4490, 4493, 4510, 4519, 4520, 4521, 4522 (*Dh.* begat 100 sons with Gāndhārī and the son Yuyutsu with a vaiçya woman).—§ 181 (Duḥçalotpatti): I, **116**, 4523 (had the daughter Duḥçalā).—§ 182 (Dhṛtarāshṭraputranāmak.): I, **117**, 4540 (°*sya putrān*, enumeration of *Dh.'s* 101 sons), 4556 (gave wives to his sons), 4557 (married his daughter Duḥçalā to the Sindhu king Jayadratha).—§ 184 (Pāṇḍu): I, **119**, 4634.—§ 194 (do.): I, **126**, 4902 (after the death of Pāṇḍu the five Pāṇḍavas were brought back to Hāstinapura), 4913 (°*sya dāyādāḥ*).—§ 195 (do.): I, **127**, (4932).—§ 208 (Astradarçana): I, **134**, 5312 (*janeçvaram*), (5315), 5346; **135**, 5360, (5363).—§ 210 (Sambhavap.): I, **139**, 5517 (installed Yudhishṭhira as yuvarāja).—§ 211 (do.): I, **139**, 5541 (became afraid of the prowess of the Pāṇḍavas).—§ 212 (Kaṇikavākya): I, **140**, 5543 (*mahīpālaḥ*), 5544, (5545), (5566), 5634 (*Kauravyaḥ*, his discourse with Kaṇika).—§ 213 (Jatugṛhap.): I, **141**, 5636 (*Kauravyam*), 5640, 5649, 5659, 5662, 5664; **142**, 5673, 5675, 5676, (5677), (5687); **143**, 5697, 5699, (5702), 5706, 5710 (persuades the Pāṇḍavas to set out for Vāraṇāvata); **144**, 5720; **145**, 5735 (*rājñaḥ*), 5740 (*Kauravyaḥ*), 5742, 5745; **148**, 5833; **150**, 5861, 5864, 5865, 5870 (*Ambikāsutaḥ*, offered oblations of water to the Pāṇḍavas, who were thought to have been burnt to death); **151**, 5917.—§ 235 (Svayaṃvarap.): I, **191**, †7154 (°*sya putraḥ*, i.e. Duryodhana).—§ 237 (Vaivāhikap.): I, **195**, 7233 (*nareçvaram*).—§ 241 (Vidurāgamanap.): I, **200**, 7371 (*Kauravam*), 7381, (7387), 7391; **201**, (7396); **202**, 7437, 7440; **203**, 7441, 7442; **204**, 7460.—§ 243 (do.): I, **206**, (7518), 7524, 7529, 7533, 7537, 7543 (consents to give the Pāṇḍavas the half of the kingdom).—§ 244 (Rājyalābhap.): I, **207**, 7556, 7565, 7566, 7567, (7568).—§ 245 (do.): I, **208**, 7600.—§ 254 (Khāṇḍavadahanap.): I, **222**, 8050 (*rājñaḥ*).—§ 286 (Rājasūyikap.): II, **33**, 1259.—§ 287 (do.): II, **34**, 1260, 1264 (came to the rājasūya of Yudhishṭhira).—§ 288 (do.): II, **35**, 1293.—§ 292 (do.): II, **45***a*, 1607 (accompanied by Bhīmasena).—§ 294 (Dyūtap.): II, **47**, 1681 (°*sya putraḥ*, i.e. Duryodhana), 1701; **48**, 1724 (*Kurumukhyāya*); **49**, 1727 (*janādhipam*), (1730), 1766, (1768), 1772, 1775, 1777, (1780); **50**, 1790 (*Ambikāsutaḥ*, sends Vidura to invite Yudhishṭhira to the gambling, but then advises Duryodhana to desist from the gambling).—§ 297 (do.): II, **54**, (1934).—§ 298 (do.): II, **56**, (1970), (1975), (†1979), †1981, †1985; **57**, 1987, (†1990) (sends Vidura to Yudhishṭhira); **58**, †1992, †1995, †2000, †2006, 2012, 2018, 2024 (*snushās tā Dh°sya*); **60**, 2051; **63**, †2111 (°*sya putraḥ*, i.e. Duryodhana); **65**, 2183.—§ 299 (do.): II, **66**, †2190 (°*sya putraḥ*, i.e. Duryodhana), †2195 (do.), †2196 (do.); **67**, †2198 (do.), †2201; **68**, 2263, 2306.—§ 301 (do.): II, **70**, †2362 (°*sya putraḥ*, i.e. Duryodhana); **71**, †2401, (†2404), †2405, (2406), (2410), (2412); **72**, 2432; **73**, 2434 (when Yudhishṭhira had lost his brothers and himself at dice, *Dh.* granted Draupadī their liberty).—§ 302 (Anudyūtap.): II, **74**, 2453, 2457 (*Vaicitravīryam*), (2475), 2478 (summoned again Yudhishṭhira to come to gamble).—§ 303 (do.): II, **75**, 2479; **76**, 2491.—§ 304 (do.): II, **77**, †2527 (°*sya putraḥ*, i.e. Duḥçāsana), 2559.—§ 305 (do.): II, **78**, 2561; **79**, 2617, 2619.—§ 306 (do.): II, **80**, 2620 (*Ambikāsutaḥ*), (2621), (2628), 2651, 2670 (discourse with Vidura, etc.).—§ 307 (do.): II, **81**, 2672, 2673, (2675), (2689) (discourse with Sañjaya).—§ 311 (Āraṇyakap.): III, **4**, (†220), (†235), †239 (dismisses Vidura).—§ 312 (do.): III, **5**, †250, †251, †252, †255, †256, †257.—§ 313 (do.): III, **6**, 262, 277 (*Ambikāsutaḥ*), 280, 286 (calls Vidura back); **7**, 289 (*mantrī Dh°sya*); **8**, 311; **9**, (323).—§ 315 (Maitreyaçāpa): III, **10**, (346), 353 (*Ambikāsutaḥ*), 380.—§ 316 (Kirmīravadhap.): III, **11**, (385).—§ 317 (Arjunābhigamanap.): III, **12**, 525 (°*sya . . . snushā*, i.e. Draupadī).—§ 327 (Draupadīparitāp.): III, **34**, †1356 (°*sya putrāt*, i.e. Duryodhana), †1360 (°*sya putraḥ* = do.), †1361 (do.); **35**, 1405.—§ 330 (Indradarçana): III, **37**, 1461 (°*sya putreṇa*, i.e. Duryodhana).—§ 340 (Indralokābhigamanap.): III, **48**, 1914, (1916); **49**, (1945).—§ 341 (do.): III, **50**, 1955.—§ 342 (do.): III, **51**, 1968 (*Ambikāsutaḥ*), (2011).—§ 377 (Dhaumyatīrthak.): III, **86**, 8283 (°*sya putreṇa*, i.e. Duryodhana).—§ 378 (Tīrthayātrāp.): III, **92**, 8453.—§ 446 (Nivātakavacayuddhap.): III, **174**, 12287 (°*sya putrān*).—§ 450 (Ājagarap.): III, **179**, 12429 (°*sya putram*, i.e. Duryodhana).—§ 512 (Ghoshayātrāp.): III, **237**, 14772; **238**, 14798; **239**, 14820, 14821, 14822, (14825), 14841 (permitted Duryodhana, etc., to undertake the ghoshayātrā); **242**, 14942 (°*sya putrāṇām*).—§ 515 (Karṇadigvijaya): III, **254**, 15264, 15270, 15271.—§ 516 (Duryodhanayajña): III, **255**, 15286; **256**, 15302, 15318.—

§ 547 (Karṇa): III, **309**, 17153 (°*sya sakhā*, i.e. Adhiratha).—§ 554 (Sainyodyogap.): V, **1**, †16 (°*sya putraiḥ*); **3**, 60 (°*sya putram*, i.e. Duryodhana), 62; **4**, 65, 88, 89; **5**, 95; **6**, 113, 116, 122.—§ 556 (Sañjayayānap.): V, **20**, 603, 606, 607 (°*sya ye putrāḥ*); **21**, 641; **22**, (†645), †682 (sends Sañjaya to the Pāṇḍavas); **23**, 685, †688, †693, †700, †702, †704, †712 (°*sya putram*, i.e. Duryodhana); **24**, †715, †722; **25**, †723, †726; **26**, †743, †748, †749, †750, †752, †753, †756, †757; **29**, †809, †811, †840 (°*sya putraḥ*, i.e. Duryodhana), †841 (°*sya putre* = do.), †846, †860, †862, †865; **30**, †875, †883 (*jyeshṭhaḥ putro Dh°sya*), †906; **31**, 919; **32**, 939, 941, (†944), (†948), (†970) (Sañjaya's return). —§ 557 (Prajāgarap.): V, **33**, 971, 972, (975), 977, (979), (985), 986, 1071; **34**, (1094), 1178.—§ 558 (do.): V, **35**, 1181.—§ 559 (Prajāgarap.): V, **36**, (†1281), (†1308), 1319, 1320; **37**, (1342); **39**, (1446), 1453, (1454), 1529; **40**, (1562) (discourse with Vidura).—§ 560 (Sanatsujātap.): V, **41**, (1565), 1566, (1568), (1571), 1574; **42**, 1577, (1578), (†1592), (†1594), (†1597), (†1601); **43**, (†1621), (†1623), (†1626), (†1631), (1634), (1661); **44**, (†1684), (†1686), (†1688), (†1708) (discourse with Sanatsujāta). —§ 561 (Yānasandhip.): V, **47**, 1793 (°*mukhāḥ*), (*a*), 1798, 1808; **48**, (†1809), †1861 (°*sya putraḥ*, i.e. Duryodhana); **49**, 1949, 1951, 1961; **50**, (1967), (1975), (1979), 1980; **51**, (2018); **52**, (2085); **53**, (2106); **55**, 2151, 2158; **57**, (2232), (2257), (2274); **58**, (2295), (2313); **59**, (2324), 2345; **64**, 2468, 2481; **65**, (2482); **66**, 2498, (*εε*), 2501; **67**, (†2516), 2522; **69**, (2538), (2542), (2544), (2546), 2549, 2544; **70**, (2560); **71**, (2574) (*Dh.* wishes to keep peace with the Pāṇḍavas).—§ 562 (Bhagavadyānap.): V, **72**, 2586, 2587, 2589, 2590, 2591, 2655; **73**, 2708; **77**, 2796; **78**, 2803; **80**, 2860; **82**, 2875 (°*sya putreṇa*, i.e. Duryodhana), 2900; **83**, 2924, 2965 (*Kauravyaḥ*); **85**, 3022, 3032, 3038; **86**, (3040); **88**, 3093, 3094, 3096; **89**, 3111, 3115, 3118, 3119 (°*purohitāḥ*), 3121; **90***ρ*, 3180; **91**, 3250 (*sambandhī dayitaç cāsi Dh°sya, Mādhava*, i.e. Kṛshṇa); **92**, †3300 (°*sya putraḥ*, i.e. Duryodhana); **94**, 3337, 3364, 3366, 3367; **95**, 3385. —§ 567 (do.): V, **124**, (4121), (*β*), 4137, 4183; **125**, 4190, 4208; **126**, 4214; **127**, 4255; **128**, 4284; **129**, 4309, 4314, (4315), 4319, 4322, 4325; **130**, 4367, 4372, 4376, 4381, 4387, 4393, 4396, 4403; **131**, (4434), 4436, 4437, 4438, 4448, (*π*), 4453, 4455, (*ρ*), 4457.—§ 569 (do.): V, **140**, (4726); **141**, 4767 (°*kule*), 4805; **146**, 4946 (°*sya putrāṇām*); **147**, 4963; **148**, 5005, 5008, 5009, 5012, 5024, 5027, †5034, †5039; **149**, 5040; **150**, 5077, 5083, 5091.—§ 570 (Sainyaniryāṇap.): V, **159**, 5392 (Sañjaya relates the events of the battle to Dhṛtarāshṭra from here to X, **9**, incl.).—§ 571 (Ulūkadūtāgamanap.): V, **162**, 5610, 5611.—§ 572 (Rathātirathasaṅkhyānap.): V, **165**, 5714.—§ 573 (Ambopākhyānap.): V, **196**, 7634 (°*sya putrāṇām*).—§ 574 (Jambūkh.): VI, **2**, (42), 49; **3**, 115, 118, 127, (128), (132); **4**, 155; **5**, (176); **6**, (194); **7**, (253); **8**, (287), 305; **9**, (309); **10**, (385) (Sañjaya describes to *Dh.* the earth, etc.).—§ 575 (Bhūmip.): VI, **11**, (401), (413), (421); **12**, (480) (continuation).—§ 576 (Bhagavadgītāp.): VI, **13**, 496; **14**, (508); **19**, (695), 717 (°*sya dāyādāḥ*); **20**, (†741); **24**, (822); **25**, (830); **35**, †1272 (°*sya putrāḥ*).—§ 577 (Bhīshmavadhap.): VI, **43**, 1626 (*trayi*—i.e. in Yuyutsu—*tantuç ca piṇḍaç ca Dh°sya dṛçyate*).—§ 578 (do.): VI, **44**, (1638); **48**, (1868); **49**, (1985).—§ 579 (do.): VI, **52**, (2121); **53**, (2194); **54**, (2235); **59**, (2508).—§ 580 (do.): VI, **62**, (2716); **65**, (2898).—§ 583 (do.): VI, **76**, (3314).—§ 584 (do.): VI, **83**, (3639).—§ 585 (do.): VI, **89**, (3931); **91**, (4064); **96**, 4325.—§ 586 (do.): VI, **101**, (4584); **102**, (4643); **103**, 4721.—§ 587 (do.): VI, **108**, (4994), (5017); **109**, (5055); **115**, (5335); **120**, (5689).—§ 589 (Droṇābhishekap.): VII, **1**, 3, 6, 8, (10), 47, (48); **9**, (261); **10**, 306, (312); **11**, (382).—§ 590 (do.): VII, **15**, (582).—§ 592 (Saṃçaptakavadhap.): VII, **22**, (920); **23**, (950); **24**, (1046); **26**, (1129); **29**, (1256); **31**, (1344).—§ 593 (Abhimanyuvadhap.): VII, **33**, (1475); **34**, (1492); **38**, (1623); **39**, (1646); **40**, 1679; **42**, (1741), (1749); **46**, (1833); **47**, 1861.—§ 596 (Pratijñāp.): VII, **79**, 2789 (°*sya putreṇa*, i.e. Duryodhana).—§ 598 (Jayadrathavadhap.): VII, **85**, (3010).—§ 599 (do.): VII, **90**, (3183); **98**, (3609); **100**, 3751; **105**, (3926); **106**, (3965); **110**, (4134); **114**, (4440); **121**, (4806); **124**, (4972), (4995); **129**, (5272); **131**, (5357); **132**, (5413); **133**, (5455); **135**, (5535); **138**, (5667); **140**, (5817); **144**, (6025); **145**, (6055); **147**, (6297), (6334), (6375); **148**, (6388); **151**, (6529), 6547.—§ 600 (Ghaṭotkacavadhap.): VII, **154**, (6641); **155**, (6682); **159**, (7090); **163**, (7287); **164**, (7327); **175**, (7890); **179**, (8134); **182**, (†8247), 8260, (8263); **183**, (8294), (8303).—§ 601 (Droṇavadhap.): VII, **185**, 8451.—§ 603 (Nārāyaṇāstramoksh.): VII, **194**, (8964); **196**, (9035), 9074; **198**, (9126); **200**, (9289); **201**, (9398); **202**, (9494).—§ 604 (Karṇap.): VIII, **1**, 17; **2**, 26, (34), (50); **4**, 73 (*Ambikāsutaḥ*); **5**, 90 (do.); **6**, (151); **7**, 190, (†213), 214, 216; **8**, 224, 226, (227); **9**, (252), 282, (283).—§ 605 (do.): VIII, **11**, (400); **16**, (610); **20**, (770); **21**, (821); **29**, (1169); **31**, (1249), (1265).—§ 607 (do.): VIII, **40**, 1868; **44**, 2026, 2027 (°*niveçane*).—§ 608 (do.): VIII, **46**, (2126); **47**, (2210); **48**, (2234); **51**, (2440); **60**, 2991 (°*sya putraiḥ*); **61**, (3067); **66**, 3334 (*saputreṇa*); **73**, 3718; **74***φφφ*, 3759, 3760, 3770, 3782; **75**, (†3804); **78**, (3940); **83**, 4256; **93**, (4834); **96**, 5035 (*Ambikāsutaḥ*).—§ 609 (Çalyap.): IX, **1***ε*, 40, 44, 51; **2**, 57 (*Ambikāsutaḥ*), (59), 109 (*Ambikāsutaḥ*), (111).—§ 610 (do.): IX, **4**, 235.—§ 611 (do.): IX, **8**, (380), (402); **19***δδ*, 1011.—§ 612 (Hradapraveçap.): IX, **29**, (1586); **30**, (1673).—§ 613 (Gadāyuddhap.): IX, **32**, (1817); **33***ι*, 1923, 1930.—§ 615 (do.): IX, **35**, 1973, 1974; **55**, 3077, (3078); **56**, 3129, 3154; **59***σ*, 3319 (°*sya putrāḥ*), 3339 (*snushāç ca prasnushāç caiva Dh°sya*); **60**, (3342); **61**, (3388); **63**, 3537, 3539, 3541, 3560, 3572, 3576, 3578 (after the slaughter of Duryodhana, *Dh.* was comforted by Kṛshṇa and Vyāsa); **64**, (3582).—§ 616 (Sauptikap.): X, **1**, (7); **2**, 101; **6**, (216); **8**, (319), (470) (end of Sañjaya's narrative).—§ 618 (Jalapradānikap.): XI, **1**, 1, 4, (11) (comforted by Sañjaya); **3**, (84); **4**, (104); **5**, (125); **6**, (149); **7**, (163) (discourse with Vidura); **8**, 196, 203, 205, (*ζ*), 218 (°*sya putrāṇām yas tu jyeshṭhaḥ çatasya vai*), 242, 245 (comforted by Vyāsa); **9**, 246, 249; **11**, 307; **12**, 335 (broke the iron statue of Bhīmasena); **13**, 354; **14**, 360, 374.—§ 619 (Strīvilāpap.): XI, **16**, 435, 483; **17**, 495.—§ 620 (Çrāddhap.): XI, **26**, 762, (766), (773), (776), 799.—§ 621 (Rājadh.): XII, **7**, 178 (°*sya putreshu*), 182, 190.—§ 635 (do.): XII, **37**, 1373.—§ 637 (do.): XII, **40**, 1447 (*Kauravaḥ*), 1448, 1458; **41**, 1470, 1472; **42**, 1487, 1494; **44**, 1522; **45**, 1542.—§ 640 (do.): XII, **54***a*, 1929.—§ 641 (do.): XII, **124**, 4552, 4555, (4556), (4562), (4567), (4615), (4620), 4621 (discourses to Duryodhana about behaviour (*çīla*)).—§ 760 (Ānuçāsanik.): XIII, **111**, 5403 (°*purogamaḥ*).—§ 768 (do.): XIII, **148**, 6932 (°*ādayo nṛpāḥ*).—§ 776 (do.): XIII,

167, 7704.—§ 777 (Svargārohaṇikam p.): XIII, **168,** 7714, 7726, 7734, 7741, 7754; **169,** 7772, 7776 (°*mukhāḥ*).—§ 778 (Açvamedhikap.): XIV, **1,** 1, 6.—§ 780 (do.): XIV, **14,** 369, 370.—§ 783 (Anugītāp.): XIV, **52,** 1502, (γ), 1503, 1504, 1506, 1509.—§ 784*b* (Uttaṅka): XIV, **53,** 1547 (°*syātmajāḥ*).—§ 785 (Anugītāp.): XIV, **63**ζ, 1893; **66,** 1941; **71**π, 2059, 2060; **72,** 2109; **78,** 2294; **84,** 2508; **87**ν, 2597; **88,** 2608.—§ 787 (Āçramavāsap.): XV, **1,** 1, 4, 5, 11, 15, 19, 20, 28; **2,** 32, 39, 44 (*Ambikāsutaḥ*), 47, 56, 58; **3,** 62, 65, 74, (76), (116), 118 (*Ambikāsutaḥ*), (129), 135, 139, 146, 147; **4,** 148; **5,** 170; **6,** (214); **7,** (235); **8,** (265), 272, 282; **9,** (283); **10,** 303, 309, 310, 353; **11,** 356 (*Ambikāsutaḥ*), 358, 366, 376; **12,** 382 (*rājarshiḥ*); **13,** 395, 409; **14,** 410, 423; **15,** 428, 436; **16,** 445, 446; **18,** 498 (*Ambikāsutaḥ*), 506, 510; **19,** 533; **20,** 541, 559, 562, 568, 570, 575 (*Dh.* retires into the forest together with Gāndhārī; Nārada prophesies that after death they will go to the world of Kubera).—§ 788 (do.): XV, **22,** 599, 610; **23,** 622, 634; **24,** 638; **26,** (675), 691; **27,** 718, 720, (δ), 730, 738; **28**ε, 742 (the Pāṇḍavas visit *Dh.* in the forest).—§ 789 (Putradarçanap.): XV, **29,** 766, 775, 804; **31**η, 850 (was an incarnation of the Gandharva king of the same name, cf. § 130*c*), 863; **32,** 869, 884, 888 (sees his dead sons, etc.).—§ 790 (do.): XV, **35,** 941.—§ 791 (do.): XV, **36,** 957, 959, 961, 962 (*Kauravanandana*).—§ 792 (Nāradāgamanap.): XV, **37,** 1016, 1050 (*Dh.* and Gāndhārī and Kuntī died in a forest conflagration); **39,** 1094, 1102 (the funeral rites in honour of *Dh.*, etc.).—§ 795 (Svargārohaṇap.): XVIII, **2,** 71 (°*sya putraḥ Suyodhanaḥ*); **5**λ, 148, 160 (attained to the world of *Dhaneçvara*, i.e. Kubera).

Cf. also the following synonyms:—

Ājamīḍha, q.v.

Ambikāsuta ("son of Ambikā"): I, 420, 2248, 5701, 5870 (*Dh*°); II, 1790 (do.), 2620 (do.); III, 277 (do.), 606, 1915, 8456; VI, 127 (*Dh*°); VIII, 18, 73 (*Dh*°), 90 (do.), 214 (do.), 217 (do.), 226 (do.), 5035 (do.); IX, 57 (do.), 109 (do.), 3500; XV, 18, 29, 44 (*Dh*°), 55, 118 (*Dh*°), 176, 356 (*Dh*°), 427, 428 (*Dh*°), 498.

Āmbikeya (do.): III, †219, †250 (*Dh*°), †253, 598; V, †688 (*Dh*°), †1092, †1397; VII, 8 (*Dh*°).

Bhārata, Bharataçārdūla, Bharataçreshṭha, Bharatarshabha, Bharatasattama, q.v.

Kaurava, Kauravaçreshṭha, Kauravarāja, Kauravendra, Kauravya, q.v.

Kuruçārdūla, Kuruçreshṭha, Kurūdvaha, Kurukulaçreshṭha, Kurukulodvaha, Kurumukhya, Kurunandana, Kurupravīra, Kurupuṅgava, Kururāja, Kurusattama, Kuruvaṃçavivardhana, Kuruvīra, Kuruvṛddha, Kuruvṛddhavarya, q.v.

Vaicitravīrya ("son of Vicitravīrya"): I, 500, 7382; II, †2139, 2457 (*Dh*°); III, 326, 600, †14744, †14747; V, †31, †38, †693 (*Dh*°), †945, 1334, 1353, †2411, †2428 (°*sya sutaḥ*, i.e. Duryodhana), 2551, 3084, 3112; VI, 38, 131; VIII, †1732 (°*sya sutaḥ*, i.e. Duryodhana); IX, 233; XI, 46, 93; XV, 46, †431, 709, 1058, 1078.

Dhṛtarāshṭra[2], a serpent-king. § 17 (Uttaṅka): I, **3,** 800.—§ 47 (Sarpanāmakath.): I, **35,** 1558 (enumeration of serpents).—§ 67 (Sarpasattra): I, **57,** 2155 (enumeration of the serpents of *Dh.'s* race).—§ 268 (Varuṇasabhāv.): II, **9,** 361 (among the nāgas in the palace of Varuṇa).—§ 549*d* (Pāṇḍavapr.): *Dh.* is the first of all nāgas: IV, **2,** 44.—§ 564 (Mātalīyop.): V, **103**γ, 3631 (enumeration).—§ 595 (Shoḍaçarāj., v. Pṛthu Vainya): VII, **69,** 2415 (when the serpents milked the earth, *Dh.* was their milker).—§ 606 (Tripurākhyāna): VIII, **34,** 1481 (*daça nāgapatīn* . . . *Dh°mukhān*, became the pole of Çiva's chariot).—§ 793 (Mausalap.): XVI, **4**η, †119.

Dhṛtarāshṭra[3], a Gandharva. § 100 (Aṃçāvat.): I, **65,** 2550 (among the Devagandharvas, the sons of Muni).—§ 191 (Arjuna): I, **123,** 4811 (among the Devagandharvas who were present at the birth of Arjuna).—§ 778*b* (Samvartta-Maruttīya): XIV, **10,** †257, †258, (†259), †259 (*Gandharvam*), †264 (messenger of Indra).—§ 789 (Putradarçanap.): XV, **31,** 850 (*Gandharvarājaḥ*, incarnate as Dhṛtarāshṭra[1]).—§ 795 (Svargārohaṇap.): XVIII, **4,** 139 (*Gandharvarājānam*, identical with Dhṛtarāshṭra[1]). Cf. Gandharva, Gandharvarāj, Gandharvarāja, Gandharvarājan.

Dhṛtarāshṭra[4], a king, son of the elder Janamejaya. § 154 (Pūruvaṃç.): I, **94,** 3745, 3747 (father of Kuṇḍika, etc.).

Dhṛtarāshṭra[5], Vaicitravīryi, an ancient king (properly identical with Dhṛtarāshṭra[1]). § 615*o* (Baka[3]): IX, **41,** 2319 (*Vaicitravīryinaḥ*), 2324, 2328, 2329, 2331, 2343.

Dhṛtarāshṭra[6], a king. § 757*b* (Hastikūṭa): XIII, **102,** 4848, 4849, (†4853), (†4855), (†4857), †4857, (†4859), †4859, (†4861), (†4863), (†4866), †4866, (†4869), †4870, (†4872), †4873, (†4875), †4875, (†4878), †4879, (†4881), †4881, (†4883), (†4885), 4890, (4894), 4895 (in the shape of *Dh.* Indra put Gautama to test).

Dhṛtarāshṭra, pl. (°*āḥ*). § 267 (Yamasabhāv.): II, **8,** 334 (100 Dhṛtarāshṭras in the palace of Yama).

Dhṛtarāshṭraja[1] ("son of Dhṛtarāshṭra[1]") = Duḥçāsana: II, 2298, 2303.

Dhṛtarāshṭraja[2] (do.) = Duryodhana: I, 2240; II, †2226; IV, 867 (*Kauravyam*); V, 98, 4960, 4961, 4964, 4971, 5278; VII, 6985; IX, 1453, 1916; XIV, 1495 (*Kauravyaḥ*).

Dhṛtarāshṭraja[3] (do.) = Vikarṇa: II, 2261, 2281; IV, 1992 (*V*°).

Dhṛtarāshṭraja[4] (do.) = Yuyutsu: XIV, 1894 (*Y*°).

Dhṛtarāshṭraja, pl. (°*āḥ*) ("the sons of Dhṛtarāshṭra[1]"): I, 6250; II, 2556; III, 60, 596, 14897, 14955, 14975, 15243; VI, 1624 (only B., C. has *Dhār*°). Cf. Dhārtarāshṭra, pl.

Dhṛtarāshṭrajā ("daughter of Dhṛtarāshṭra[1]") = Duḥçalā: XIV, 2275 (*D*°), 2285.

Dhṛtarāshṭraputra ("son of Dhṛtarāshṭra[1]") = Duryodhana: IV, †2086, †2105; V, †28, †38, †2411.

Dhṛtarāshṭraputra, pl. ("the sons of Dhṛtarāshṭra[1]"): III, †10278; V, †15, †21, †32, †2417, †2595. Cf. Dhārtarāshṭra, pl.

[Dhṛtarāshṭra-putranāma-kathana] ("enumeration of the names of Dhṛtarāshṭra's sons"). § 182 (Sambhavap.): Enumeration of the children of *Dhṛtarāshṭra* (*a*) according to the succession of their birth (cf. § 130). Worthy wives were in time selected for all of them, and *Duḥçalā* was given to *Jayadratha* (I, **117**).

Dhṛtarāshṭrasūnu ("son of Dhṛtarāshṭra[1]") = Duryodhana: VIII, †4533.

Dhṛtarāshṭrasūnu, pl. (°*avaḥ*) ("the sons of Dhṛtarāshṭra[1]"): VIII, †1744.

Dhṛtarāshṭrasuta[1] ("son of Dhṛtarāshṭra[1]") = Duryodhana: I, 4508; III, 14874 (*D*°), 14879; IV, 1747 (*Suyodhanaḥ*); V, 163, 4835 (*D*°); VIII, †1743.

Dhṛtarāshṭrasuta[1] (do.) = Yuyutsu: I, 4486.

Dhṛtarāshṭrasuta[1], pl. (°*āḥ*) ("sons of Dhṛtarāshṭra[1]"): III, 14974, 14988; V, 104; VIII, 3775; IX, 1455 (only B., C. has by error *Dhārta°*), 3375; XV, 54. Cf. Dhārtarāshṭra, pl.

Dhṛtarāshṭrasuta[2], pl. (°*āḥ*) ("sons of Dhṛtarāshṭra[4]"): I, 3748 (only B., v. Dhārtarāshṭrasuta[1], pl.).

Dhṛtarāshṭrātmaja ("son of Dhṛtarāshṭra[1]") = Duryodhana: II, 1819; III, 287; V, 132, 5303; IX, 1706.

Dhṛtarāshṭrātmaja, pl. (°*āḥ*) ("sons of Dhṛtarāshṭra[1]"): I, 4836, 5093; IV, 1996 (dual °*au* = Viviṃçati and Duḥsaha); XVIII, 168 (after death they became Yātudhānas). Cf. Dhārtarāshṭra, pl.

[Dhṛtarāshṭra-vivāha(ḥ)] ("marriage of Dhṛtarāshṭra[1]"). § 174 (Sambhavap.): *Bhīshma* proposed to marry the two princes to *Yādavī* (i.e. Kuntī), and to the daughter of the *Gāndhāra* king *Subala* (i.e. Gāndhārī), and to the daughter of the *Madra* king. *Gāndhārī* had obtained from *Çiva* (cf. § 180) the boon that she should have 100 sons. She now was brought to the *Kurus* by her brother *Çakuni* (who then returned home), and given to *Dhṛtarāshṭra*. From love for her future husband she had bandaged her own eyes with cloth (I, **110**).

Dhṛtarāshṭrī. § 126 (Aṃçāvat.): I, **66**, 2620 (daughter of Tāmrā), 2622 (her offspring are the ducks and the swans).

Dhṛtasena, a Kuru warrior. § 610 (Çalyap.): IX, **6**ξ, 294.

Dhṛtātman = Vishṇu (1000 names).

Dhṛtavarman, a Trigarta warrior. § 785 (Anugītāp.): XIV, **74**, 2156, 2157, 2159, 2161, 2164, 2168 (vanquished by Arjuna).

Dhṛtavatī, a river. § 574 (Jambūkh.): VI, **9**λ, 331 (only C., B. has *Ghṛtavatī*), 339 (only B., C. has *Dhṛtimatī*).

Dhṛtāyudha, a Kuru warrior. § 604 (Karṇap.): VIII, **7**, 209 (PCR. has *Çrutāyudha*).

Dhṛti[1] ("resolution," personif.). § 115 (Aṃçāvat.): I, **66**, 2578 (daughter of Daksha and wife of Dharma).—§ 132 (do.): I, **67**, 2794 (Siddhi and Dhṛti became incarnate as Kuntī and Mādrī).—§ 330 (Indradarçana): III, **37**, 1488 (only B., C. has Dyuti).—§ 565 (Gālavac.): V, **117**, 3974 (*reme . . . yathā . . . Dhṛtyāṃ Dharmaç ca*, wife of Dharma).—§ 595 (Sṛñjaya): VII, **55***a*, 2143 (Parvata asks if the daughter of Sṛñjaya is *Dh°*, etc.).—§ 606 (Tripurākhyāna): VIII, **34**, 1484 (was transformed into a skin to cover the chariot of Çiva).—§ 615*u* (Skanda): IX, **46**κ, 2682.

Dhṛti[2] = Çiva (1000 names[1]).

Dhṛti[3], a Viçvadeva. § 749 (Ānuçās.): XIII, **91**γ, 4355 (enumeration).

Dhṛtimat[1], a fire. § 493 (Āṅgirasa): III, **221**, 14188.

Dhṛtimat[2], a varsha in Kuçadvīpa. § 575 (Bhūmip.): VI, **12**ζ, 454 (the fifth varsha in Kuçadvīpa).

Dhṛtimat[3] = Çiva (1000 names[2]).

Dhṛtimatī, a river. § 574 (Jambūkh.): VI, **9**λ, 339 (only C., B. has Dhṛtavatī).

Dhūmaketana = Çiva (1000 names).

Dhūmaketu[1] = Agni, q.v. (add I, 8174).

Dhūmaketu[2] = Sūrya (the Sun): III, 155.

Dhūmaketu[3] = Çiva (1000 names[2]).

Dhūmavatī, a tīrtha. § 370 (Tīrthayātrāp.): III, **84**, 8000.

Dhūminī, wife of Ajamīḍha. § 152 (Pūruvaṃç.): I, **94**, 3722 (mother of Ṛksha).

Dhūmorṇā[1], wife of Mārkaṇḍeya. § 768*b* (Umā-Maheçvaras.): XIII, **146**γ, 6750 (*Mārkaṇḍeyasya Dh°ṇā*, sc. *sādhvī*).

Dhūmorṇā[2], wife of Yama. § 775 (Ānuçāsanik.): XIII, **166***a*, 7637 (*Yamo Dh°ayā saha*).

Dhūmra[1], a warrior of Skanda. § 615*u* (Skanda): IX, **45**η, 2566.

Dhūmra[2] = Çiva: VII, 2876; XII, 10359 (1000 names[1]).

Dhūmrā. § 116 (Vasu, pl.): I, **66**, 2583 (mother of the Vasu Dhara (and the Vasu Dhruva?)).

Dhūmrāksha, a Rākshasa. § 538 (Kumbhakarṇavadha): III, **286**, 16383, 16388, 16392, 16393 (*Rākshasottamaṃ*, slain by Hanumat), 16396 (*nihataṃ*).—§ 540 (Indrajidvadha): III, **288**, 16438 (*hataṃ*).

Dhūmrākshī = Durgā (Umā): VI, 801.

Dhundhu[1], an Asura, son of Madhu and Kaiṭabha. § 474*b* (Dhundhumārop.): III, **201**, 13511 (*mahāsuraḥ*).—§ 475 (do.): III, **202**, 13532 (*Madhu-Kaiṭabhayoḥ putraḥ*), 13545.—§ 478 (do.): III, **204**, 13582, 13586, 13587 (*Madhu-Kaiṭabhayoḥ putraḥ*), 13598 (*mahāsuraḥ*), 13599, 13602, 13603, 13614 (slain by Kuvalāçva), 13623 (*mahā-Daityaḥ*). Cf. Asura.

Dhundhu[2], an ancient king. § 761 (Ānuçāsanik.): XIII, **115**δ, 5668 (among the kings who did not eat meat during the month of Kārttika).

Dhundhumāra ("slayer of Dhundhu") = Kuvalāçva. § 474 (Mārkaṇḍeyas.): III, **201**, 13486 (°*tvaṃ*).—§ 474*b* (Dhundhumārop.): III, **201**, 13489, 13490 (°*tvaṃ*), 13514.—§ 478 (do.): III, **204**, 13595, 13615 (origin of the name), 13625.—§ 599 (Jayadrathavadhap.): VII, **94**ε, 3450.—§ 656 (Khaḍgotpatti): XII, **166**δ, 6196 (*Dh.* received the sword from Ailavila, from *Dh.* it passed into the hands of Kāmboja).—§ 723 (Ānuçāsanik.): XIII, **6***a*, 333 (*Dh°aç ca rājarshiḥ sattreshv eva jarāṅ gataḥ | prītidāyaṃ parityajya sushvāpa sa Girivraje*).—§ 751*b* (Çapathavidhi): XIII, **94***a*, 4551, (4567).—§ 775 (Ānuçāsanik.): XIII, **166**η, 7675 (enumeration).

[Dhundhumāropākhyāna(m)] ("the episode about the slayer of Dhundhu"). Cf. Dhaundumāra(m) upākhyāna(m). § 474 (Mārkaṇḍ.): The great *ṛshi Uttaṅka*, in his hermitage in the wilderness, by severe penances for numberless years obtained that *Vishṇu* appeared to him, and having been praised by him (vv. 13494–13503) (*a*), granted him that he should always remain virtuous and devoted to *Vishṇu*, and that he should obtain a *yoga* power and urge *Kuvalāçva* (son of *Bṛhadaçva* of *Ikshvāku's* race), who had been furnished with *yoga* power from *Vishṇu*, to kill the Asura *Dhundhu* (III, **201**).—§ 475: After the death of *Ikshvāku*, *Çaçāda* was king in *Ayodhyā*. List of Çaçāda's descendants: *Çaçāda* > *Kakutstha* > *Anenas* > *Pṛthu* > *Viçvagaçva* > *Adri* > *Yuvanāçva* > *Çrāva* > *Çrāvastaka* (who built *Çrāvastī*) > *Bṛhadaçva* > *Kuvalāçva* > 21,000 sons.—§ 476: Having installed *Kuvalāçva* on the throne, *Bṛhadaçva* retired into the forest as an ascetic. Then *Uttaṅka* asked him first to slay the *Daitya* chief *Dhundhu* (son of *Madhu* and *Kaiṭabha*), who dwelt underground in the sea *Ujjalaka*, which was full of sand, in the desert, practised austerities with a view to destroy the gods and the three worlds, *Brahmán* having granted him that he could not be slain by gods, *Daityas*, *Rākshasas*, *Yakshas*, and *Gandharvas*. "Every year, when he sleeps covered with sand and begins to breathe, the earth trembles for seven days, and the sand raised by his breath shrouds the sun." He then told him the boon granted by *Vishṇu* (see § 474) (III, **202**). They agreed that *Kuvalāçva* should slay the *Daitya*, and *Bṛhadaçva* retired to the forest.—§ 477: Asked by *Yudhishṭhira*, *Mārkaṇḍeya* related: During the cataclysm, when *Vishṇu*, wearing a crown and the *Kaustubha*, and dressed in yellow (*pīta*) silk, stretched over many *yojanas*, lay sleeping on the hood of *Çesha,* who encircled the earth, and a lotus sprang from his navel, and from that lotus *Brahmán,* who is the four *Vedas* with four faces, the *Dānavas Madhu* and *Kaiṭabha* began to terrify *Brahmán. Vishṇu* awoke, and offered to grant them a boon, and as they wished to grant him a boon, he chose that they should be slain by him, and at their request he promised to slay them on a wholly uncovered spot, and that they should become his sons; as only his thighs were uncovered, he there cut off their heads with his discus (III, **203**).—§ 478: Their son was *Dhundhu.* Description of his penances, and the boon he obtained from *Brahmán,* etc. (see § 476). When *Kuvalāçva,* with his 21,000 sons and his troops, and *Uttaṅka* set out, an aërial voice was heard, the gods showered flowers, etc., and the gods, *Gandharvas,* and great *ṛshis* came to behold the encounter. At the request of *Uttaṅka, Vishṇu* filled *Kuvalāçva* with his own energy. He let his sons excavate the sea of sands in seven days, and then they aroused the *Dānava,* assailing him with arrows, etc. He swallowed the arrows and vomited flames, which consumed all the sons of *Kuvalāçva,* but were extinguished by a stream of water flowing from the body of *Kuvalāçva,* who then burnt him with the *Brahmāstra,* whence he was named *Dhundhumāra* ("slayer of Dhundhu"). The gods and great *ṛshis* granted him the boon that he should always be able to give wealth to brahmans, etc. Then the gods and great *ṛshis* went away to their abodes. *Kuvalāçva* had three sons left—*Dṛḍhāçva, Kapilāçva,* and *Candrāçva,* from whom sprang the *Ikshvāku* kings. Blessing upon the reader (III, **204**).

Dhurandhara, pl. (°*āḥ*), a people. § 574 (Jambūkh.): VI, **9**μ, 349 (in Bhāratavarsha).

Dhūrjaṭi = Çiva: VII, 9621 (etymology); XIII, 7510.

Dhūrta[1], an ancient king. § 6 (Anukram.): I, **1a**, 231 (in Sañjaya's enumeration).

Dhūrta[2] = Çiva (1000 names[1]).

Dhūrtaka, a serpent. § 66 (Sarpasattra): I, **57,** 2154 (of Kauravya's race).

Dhūrya = Vishṇu (1000 names).

Dhūtapāpā, a river. § 574 (Jambūkh.): VI, **9**λ, 325.

Dhvajavatī. § 565 (Gālavac.): V, **110,** 3813 (*atra—in the west—Dh°ī nāma kumārī Harimedhasaḥ | ākāçe tishṭha tishṭheti tasthau Sūryasya çāsanāt*).

Dhvajin, an ancient king. § 267 (Yamasabhāv.): II, **8,** 324 (in the palace of Yama).

Dhvajinyutsavasaṅketa, pl. (°*āḥ*), a people. § 574 (Jambūkh.): VI, **9**ν, 368 (in the south). Cf. Utsavasaṅketa, pl.

Diç, a river. § 574 (Jambūkh.): VI, **9**λ, 327.

Diçā ("quarter," viz. the northern, personif.). § 731*b* (Ashṭāvakra-Diksaṃv.): XIII, **19,** 1390 (*Ashṭāvakrasya saṃvādaṃ D°ayā saha*).

Diçācakshu(s), a Suparṇa, the son of Garuḍa. § 564 (Mātalīyop.): V, **101**β, 3595.

***diçaḥ** ("the quarters," personif.): IX, 2514; XII, 11613, 11707, 12606.

Diçaḥ[1] = Skanda: III, 14639. Do.[2] = Vishṇu (1000 names).

Diçāṃ gaja(ḥ) = Mahāpurusha (Mahāpurushastava).

Diçāṃ pati(ḥ) = Çiva: XIV, 198, 201.

Diganta = Çiva: X, 256.

Digbhānu = Mahāpurusha (Mahāpurushastava).

Diggaja, pl. (°*āḥ*) ("the elephants of the quarters"). § 766 (Ānuçāsanik.): XIII, **132,** (6162).

Digvāsas = Çiva: XIII, 695, 753, 808, 898, 1155 (1000 names[2]).

Digvijaya[1] ("conquest of the four quarters of the world"). § 11 (Anukram.): I, **1,** 409 (*Pāṇḍavānāṃ,* i.e. Digvijayaparvan). Do.[2], adj. (sc. *parvan,* i.e. Digvijayaparvan). § 10 (Anukram.): I, **1,** 317, 318.

[Digvijayaparvan] ("the section treating of the conquest of the four quarters"), the 24th of the minor parvans, II, **25-32.** (Cf. Digvijaya.) § 278: Arjuna, having obtained his bow, etc., prevailed upon Yudhishṭhira to let him subdue the North. Arjuna set out on the celestial chariot which he had obtained from Agni, and subdued the North ("the region presided over by Dhanada"), while Bhīmasena subjugated the East, Sahadeva the South, and Nakula the West, and Yudhishṭhira stayed within Khāṇḍavaprastha (II, **25**).—§ 279: The campaign of Arjuna (q.v.) is narrated in full (II, **26-28**).—§ 280: Full description of Bhīmasena's (q.v.) campaign towards the East (II, **29-30**).—§ 281: Full narration of Sahadeva's (q.v.) campaign towards the South (II, **31,** 1105–1123).—§ 282: *a,* v. Sahadeva; *b,* v. Māhishmatī (II, **31,** 1124–1143, *a*).—§ 283: *a,* v. Sahadeva; *b,* v. Agni (enumeration of names) (II, **31,** 1143, *b*–1154).—§ 284: v. Sahadeva (II, **31,** 1155–1182).—§ 285: Full description of the campaign of Nakula (q.v.) towards the West (II, **32**).

Dikpati = Mahāpurusha (Mahāpurushastava).

Dīkshita = Çiva (1000 names[1]).

Dilīpa[1], an ancient king, the father of Bhagīratha. § 61 (Sarpasattra): I, **55,** †2109 (*Khaṭṭāṅga-Nābhaga-Dilīpakalpa,* i.e. Janamejaya).—§ 267 (Yamasabhāv.): II, **8,** 325 (in the palace of Yama).—§ 336 (Indralokābhig.): III, **43,** 1769 (*rājarshayaḥ . . D°pramukhāḥ*).—§ 389 (Gaṅgāvataraṇa): III, **107,** 9915 (son of Aṃçumat), 9916, 9919 (father of Bhagīratha).—§ 562 (Bhagavadyānap.): V, **90**ν, 3146.—§ 573 (Ambopākhyānap.): V, **186,** 7355 (°*syāçrame*).—§ 574 (Jambūkh.): VI, **9aa,** 316.—§ 595 (Shoḍaçarāj.): *D. Ailavila* (*Khaṭṭāṅgasya* (B. °*ṭvā*°), v. 2269) performed 100 sacrifices (description); at his sacrifices the road was made of gold. The gods, headed by Indra, regarded him as Dharma himself, and used to come to him; when he fought on the water his two wheels never sank in. Those who saw him attained to heaven (VII, **61**): VII, **61,** 2263 (*Ailavilam*), 2265, 2268.—§ 621 (Rājadh.): XII, **8**θ, 238.—§ 632*b* (Shoḍaçarāj., v. § 595): XII, **29,** 964, 970, 971, 972.—§ 746 (Ānuçāsanik.): XIII, **76,** †3691 (attained to heaven on account of gifts of kine).—§ 751*b* (Çapathavidhi): XIII, **94a,** †4551, (4568).—§ 761 (Ānuçāsanik.): XIII, **115**γ, 5661.—§ 775 (do.): XIII, **166**η, 7675. Cf. Ailavila, Khaṭvāṅga.

Dilīpa[2], a serpent. § 564 (Mātalīyop.): V, **103**γ, 3631.

Ḍimbhaka, a follower of Jarāsandha. § 273 (Rājasūyārambhap.): II, **14,** 576 (*Haṃsa-Ḍ°au,* among the allies of Jarāsandha), 601 (do.), 605, 607 (on the false report of the death of Haṃsa, *Ḍ.* commits suicide).—§ 275 (do.): II, **19,** 765 (*Haṃsa-Ḍ°au,* followers of Jarāsandha).—§ 276 (Jarāsandhavadhap.): II, **20,** 768 (do.).—§ 277 (do.): II, **22,** 886 (the same as Citrasena, the senāpati of Jarāsandha).

Dīnakṛt = Sūrya (the Sun): III, 192.

Dīnasādhaka = Çiva (1000 names[2]).

Diṇḍika, a mouse. § 571 (Ulūkadūtāgamanap.): V, **160,** 5440, 5442, 5443, 5446 (the story of the wicked cat).

Dīpaka, a Suparṇa, the son of Garuḍa. § 564 (Mātalīyop.): V, **101**β, 3596.

Dīpta = Çiva: XIV, 202.
Dīptaçakti = Skanda: III, 14632.
Dīptaketu, an ancient king. § 6 (Anukram.): I, **1***a*, 231 (in Sañjaya's enumeration).
Dīptakīrti = Skanda: III, 14630.
Dīptāksha, pl. (°*āḥ*), a people. § 562 (Bhagavadyānap.): V, **74**γ, 2731 (°*āṇāṃ Purūravaḥ*).
Dīptāksha = Çiva: XIV, 202.
***Dīptāṃçu** = Sūrya (the Sun): I, 6532; III, 148.
Dīptamūrti = Vishṇu (1000 names).
Dīptaroman, a Viçvadeva. § 749 (Ānuçāsanik.): XIII, **91**γ, 4356 (enumeration).
Dīptasūryāgnijaṭila = Çiva (1000 names[1]).
Dīptavarṇa = Skanda: III, 14631.
Dīpti, a Viçvadeva. § 749 (Ānuçāsanik.): XIII, **91**γ, 4359 (enumeration).
Dīptoda, a tīrtha. § 383 (Paraçu-Rāma): III, **99**, 8685 (on Vadhusarā, there Bhṛgu performed austerities). Cf. Bhṛgos tīrtha(m).
Dīrgha[1], a Māgadha king. § 177 (Pāṇḍudigvijaya): I, **113**, 4451 (*goptā Magadharāshṭrasya D°o Rājagṛhe*, slain by Pāṇḍu).
Dīrgha[2] = Çiva (1000 names[2]).
Dīrghabāhu, son of Dhṛtarāshṭra. § 130 (Aṃçāvat.): I, **67**, 2740.—§ 182 (Dhṛtarāshṭraputranāmak.): I, **117**, 4553.—§ 585 (Bhīshmavadhap.): VI, **96**θθ, 4349 (among other sons of Dhṛtarāshṭra, who are slain by Bhīmasena).—§ 599 (Jayadrathavadhap.): VII, **127**νν, 5177 (among several sons of Dhṛtarāshṭra who encompass Bhīmasena).—§ 600 (Ghaṭotkacavadhap.): VII, **164**θθ, 7337.
Dīrghajihva, an Asura, son of Danu. § 93 (Aṃçāvat.): I, **65**, 2538 (*Dānavaḥ*).—§ 130 (do.): I, **67**, 2675 (*Dānavarshabhaḥ*, incarnate as Kāçirāja).
Dīrghajihvā[1], a Rākshasī. § 544 (Yudhishṭhirāçvāsa): III, **292**, 16605 (*Rākshasī*, had been slain by Indra).
Dīrghajihvā[2], a mātṛ. § 615*u* (Skanda): IX, **46**θ, 2641.
Dīrghalocana, son of Dhṛtarāshṭra. § 130 (Aṃçāvat.): I, **67**, 2739.—§ 209 (Drupadaçāsana): I, **138**, 5461.—§ 585 (Bhīshmavadhap.): VI, **96**θθ, 4349 (among other sons of Dhṛtarāshṭra who are slain (?) by Bhīmasena).—§ 593 (Abhimanyuvadhap.): VII, **37**κ, 1610, (λ), 1614 (slain by Abhimanyu).—§ 599 (Jayadrathavadhap.): VII, **127**νν, 5178. Cf. next.
Dīrghanetra = Dīrghalocana. § 599 (Jayadrathavadhap.): VII, **127**ξξ, 5204 (slain by Bhīmasena).
Dīrghaprajña, a king. § 130 (Aṃçavat.): I, **67**, 2052 (incarnation of the Asura Vṛshaparvan).—§ 554 (Sainyodyogap.): V, **4**γ, 75 (among the princes to whom the Pāṇḍavas ought to send messengers). Cf. Dīrghayajña.
Dīrgharoma, son of Dhṛtarāshṭra. § 182 (Dhṛtarāshṭraputranāmak.): I, **117**, 4552.
Dīrghasattra, a tīrtha. § 360 (Tīrthayātrāp.): III, **82**, 5050, 5051.
Dīrghatamas, a ṛshi. § 170 (cf. Bhīshma-Satyavatī-saṃvāda): *Bhīshma* continued: The *ṛshi Utathya* had a wife named *Mamatā*; his younger brother *Bṛhaspati*, the *purohita* of the gods, approached *Mamatā*, who by *Utathya* was pregnant with a child, who even while being in his mother's womb had studied the *Vedas* and the six *Aṅgas*. The embryo kicked him out with his foot, and the semen fell upon the earth. *Bṛhaspati* cursed him; so he was born blind, and came to be called *Dīrghatamas* ("*tamo dīrghaṃ pravekshyasi*"). The wife of *Dīrghatamas* was a *brāhmaṇī*, *Pradveshī* by name. With her he begat *Gautama* and other sons; and he (*Dīrghatamas*), who knew the *Vedas* and *Aṅgas*, having learnt the *Godharma* (i.e. *prakāçamaithuna*, Nīl.) from *Saurabheya* (i.e. son of the *Kāmadhenu*, Nīl.) began to practise it. He therefore was excluded by the *ṛshis* from the asylum, and accosted in harsh words by his wife, who said that she would no more support him and his children. *Dīrghatamas* then established the rule that from that day every woman should have to adhere to one husband for life, whether he were dead or alive, etc. She then caused her sons to tie him on a raft and throw him into the *Gaṅgā*. Drifting along, he passed through the territories of many kings, until he was taken up by king *Bali*, who wanted him to raise up offspring. But *Bali's* queen *Sudeshṇā*, who saw that he was blind, sent a *Çūdra* woman in her stead, who was her nurse, with whom the *ṛshi* begat eleven sons, *Kākshīvat*, etc. As these sons were his own and not *Bali's*, *Bali* sent *Sudeshṇā* to him, and *Dīrghatamas*, after merely touching her person, told her: "Thou shalt have five children named *Aṅga*, *Vaṅga*, *Kaliṅga*, *Puṇḍra*, and *Suhma*." Their dominions have come to be called after their names: I, **104**, 4192, 4198, (4202), 4218.—§ 266 (Çakrasabhāv.): II, **7**, 293 (in the palace of Indra).—§ 717*b* (Nārāyaṇīya): XII, **342**, 13182 (originally he, on account of his blindness, was called *D.*, but when he had been cured by invoking Nārāyaṇa as Keçava, he was called Gotama).—§ 775 (Ānuçāsanik.): XIII, **166**ε, 7668 (among the ṛshis of the west). Cf. Autathya (see Additions), Gotama, Utathyaputra.
Dīrghaveṇu, pl. (°*avaḥ*), a people. § 295 (Dyūtap.): II, **52**, 1859 (brought tribute to Yudhishṭhira).
Dīrghayajña, king of Ayodhyā. § 280 (Bhīmasena): II, **30**, 1076 (*Ayodhyāyāṃ*, vanquished by Bhīmasena on his digvijaya). Cf. Dīrghaprajña.
Dīrghāyus, son of Açyutāyus. § 599 (Jayadrathavadhap.): VII, **93**, 3364 (slain by Arjuna).
Diti, the daughter of Daksha, the wife of Kaçyapa and mother of the Daityas. § 84 (Ādivaṃçāvatāraṇap.): I, **64**, 2486 (°*eḥ putrāḥ*, i.e. the Daityas).—§ 87 (Aṃçāvat.): I, **65**, 2520 (daughter of Daksha and wife of Kaçyapa).—§ 89 (do.): I, **65**, 2525 (mother of Hiraṇyakaçipu).—§ 130 (do.): I, **67**, 2641 (°*eḥ putro Hiraṇyakaçipuḥ*).—§ 237 (Vaivāhikap.): I, **193**, †7176 (*cakrāma Vajrīva D°eḥ suteshu*—i.e. the Daityas—*sarvaiç ca devair ṛshibhiç ca jushṭāḥ*).—§ 270 (Brahmasabhāv.): II, **11**, 456 (in the palace of Brahmán).—§ 310 (Āraṇyakap.): III, **3***a*, 155 (°*eh sutaḥ* = Sūrya, but read with B. '*diteḥ sutaḥ*).—§ 422*b* (Naraka): III, **142**, 10917 (°*eḥ sutaḥ*, i.e. Naraka).—§ 441 (Nivātakavacayuddhap.): III, **165**, †11909 (*sapta pūgān Diteḥ sutānāṃ*, i.e. the Daityas, slain by Indra).—§ 444 (do.): III, **169**, 12094 (°*eḥ putrāḥ*, i.e. the Nivātakavacas).—§ 565 (Gālavacarita): V, **110**, 3808 (*atra*—i.e. in the west—*devīṃ Ditim atmaprasavadhāriṇīṃ | vigarbhām akāroc Chakro yatra jāto Marudgaṇaḥ*).—§ 596 (Pratijñāp.): VII, **73**, 2608 (°*eḥ puraṃ*).—§ 608 (Karṇap.): VIII, **68**κ, †3393 (*tava Kunti putro jāto Diter Vishnur ivārihantā*, but read '*diter* with B.).—§ 664 (Mokshadh.): XII, **207**ε, 7537 (eldest daughter of Daksha), 7545 (mother of the Asuras).—§ 714 (Çukakṛtya): XII, **329**, 12417 (*evam ete D°eḥ putrā Mārutāḥ paramādbhutāḥ*, i.e. the winds; B. and Nīl. read '*diteḥ*, but cf. V, 3808).—§ 719*b* (Gautamī-lubdhaka-vyāla-Mṛtyu-Kāla-saṃv.): XIII, **1***a*, 55 (PCR. has Aditi).—§ 730*g* (Upamanyu): XIII, **14**θ, 796 (°*eḥ sutān*, i.e. the Daityas).

Ditija, pl. (°*āḥ*) ("the sons of Diti") = Daitya, pl. § 28 (Amṛtamanthana): I, **19,** †1180 (*Diti-Danujān*, vanquished by Nārāyaṇa).—§ 130 (Aṃçāvat.): I, **67,** 2667 (°*çreshṭhaḥ . . . Candraḥ*). — § 333 (Kairātap.): III, **40,** †1662 (°-*Piçācasūdanaṃ . . . Gāṇḍīvaṃ*).—§ 359 (Vaḍavā): III, **82,** 5037. — § 558 (Virocana): V, **35,** 1188. — § 564 (Mātalīyop.): V, **97,** 3518.—§ 589 (Droṇābhishek.): VII, **6,** 161 (°*ānām ivoçanāḥ çreshṭhaḥ*).—§ 608 (Karṇap.): VIII, **89,** †4594 (*yathā Sureço D°aiḥ kshatāṅgaḥ*).—§ 666 (Mokshadh.): XII, **209,** 7619 (*antarbhūmiṃ sampraviçya jagāma D°ān prati*, sc. Vishṇu incarnate as a boar).—§ 730 (Ānuçāsanik.): XIII, **14,** 971 (°*saṅghānāṃ mardanaṃ*, i.e. Çiva).

Ditija[1] ("son of Diti") = Hiraṇyakaçipu: III, 15836.

Ditija[2] (do.) = Vṛtra: XII, 10137.

Ditijāntaka = Skanda: III, 14644.

Ditinandana[1] ("son of Diti") = Hiraṇyakaçipu: III, 15834; XII, 12943.

Ditinandana[2] (do.) = Vātāpi: III, 8544.

Divākara[1], a Suparṇa, the son of Garuḍa. § 564 (Mātalīyop.): V, **101***β*, 3599.

Divākara[2] = Sūrya (the Sun), q.v.

Divaspati = Mahāpurusha (Mahāpurushastava).

Divaspṛç[1] = Kṛshṇa: XII, 1511.

Divaspṛç[2] = Vishṇu (1000 names).

Divaukasāṃ pushkariṇī, a tīrtha. § 370 (Tīrthayātrāp.): III, **84,** 8096.

Diviratha[1], the son of Bhumanyu. § 152 (Pūruvaṃç.): I, **94,** 3714 (son of Bhumanyu and Pushkariṇī (?)).

Diviratha[2], the son of Dadhivāhana. § 638*b* (Rāmopākhyāna): XII, **49,** 1796 (*Dadhivāhanapautras tu putro D°sya ca*, cf. Dadhivāhana-pautra).

Divodāsa, king of the Kāçis, son of Bhīmasena or Sudeva. § 267 (Yamasabhāv.): II, **8,** 322 (in the palace of Yama).—§ 565 (Gālavacarita): V, **116,** 3959; **117,** 3960 (*Kāçīnām īçvaraḥ . . . Bhaimasenih*), (3963), 3977 (begat Pratardana with Mādhavī), 3978, 3980.—§ 641 (Rājadh.): XII, **96,** 3577 (having subjugated his foes, *D.* took away their sacrificial fires, etc.; therefore he was deprived of the merit of his conquests). — § 730*b* (Vītahavyop.): XIII, **30,** 1949 (°*pitāmahaḥ | Haryaçvaḥ*), 1954 (*Saudevaḥ Kāçīçaḥ*), 1955 (rebuilt the city Vārāṇasī), 1959, 1961, 1936 (*D.* was vanquished by the Haihayas (Vītahavyas); in order that *D.* might have a son Bharadvāja performed a sacrifice; then Pratardana was born who defeated the enemies), 1985 (°*ātmajaḥ*, i.e. Pratardana).—§ 775 (Ānuçāsanik.): XIII, **166***η*, 7682. Cf. Bhaimaseni, Kāçīça, Saudeva, Sudevatanaya.

Divodāsātmaja ("the son of Divodāsa") = Pratardana: XIII, 1985.

Divya = Kṛshṇa: XII, 1635.

Divyacakshus = Çiva: XII, 2878.

Divyagovṛshabhadhvaja = Çiva: XIV, 209.

Divyakarmakṛt, a Viçvadeva. § 749 (Ānuçāsanik.): XIII, **91***γ*, 4360 (enumeration).

Divyakaṭa, a city. § 285 (Nakula): II, **32,** 1193 (*puraṃ*, in the west, conquered by Nakula on his digvijaya).

Divyasūnu, a Viçvadeva. § 749 (Ānuçāsanik.): XIII, **91***γ*, 4355 (enumeration).

Divyātman = Kṛshṇa: XII, 1667.

Drasṭhātman = Kṛshṇa: XII, 1651.

Drauṇaputra, v. Droṇaputra.

Drauṇāyani ("son of Droṇa") = Açvatthāman: I, †7019; VI, 4201; VII, 1095, 1367 (C. by error *Dro°*), 9109, 9331, †9337; VIII, †665, 2655, 2662, 2670; X, 463; XI, 586.

Drauṇi (do.) = Açvatthāman: I, †196, †200, 302, 562, 563, 567, 569, 575, 577; II, 1287, 1530, 2014; III, 8283, 15084; IV, 1150, 1302, 1488, 1550 (C. by error *Dro°*), 1583, 1596, 1624, 1643, 1733, 1899, 1901, 1906, 1909, †2117, †2131, 2203; V, 2159, 2185, 2189, 2192, 2201, 2206 (C. by error *Dro°*), 2281, 2375, 2502, 2966, 4796, 7563, 7576, 7585 (promised to slay the army of Yudhishṭhira in ten days); VI, 1714, 2145, 2160, 2361, 2362, 2363, 2365, 2497, 2680, 2687, 2690, 2910, 2928, 3199, 3205, 3206, 3212, 3330, 3555, 3602, 3607, 3608, 3610, 3613, 3838, 3857, 3858, 4133, 4210 (attacked by Nīla), 4211, 4214, 4218 (attacked by Ghaṭotkaca), 4221, 4223, 4244, 4458 (all. to Goharaṇaparvan), 4545, 4626, 4627, 4629, 4633, 4635, 4636, 5164, 5167, 5364, 5384; VII, 633, 1093, 1366, 1368, 1377, 1410, 1589, 1609, 1650, 1838, 1864, 1873, 1875, 1876 (read *Drauṇiṃ* with B.), 1896, 2575, 2629, 2673, 3023, 3539, 3865, 3894, 3913, 3918, 3922, 3923, 3937, 4310, 5629, 5809, 5810, 5812, 5813, 5818, 6075, 6077, 6107, 6108, 6124, 6205, 6247, 6252, 6299, 6303, 6371, 6784, 6800, 6806, 6808, 6809, 6814, 6815, 6817, 6819, 6825, 6829, 6830, 6832, 6834, 6835, 6837, 6838, 6844, 6854, 6856, 6859, 6860, 6866, 6869, 6872, 6875, 6877, 6878 (C. by error *Dro°*), 6879 (do.), 6880, 6882 (C. by error *Dro°*), 6887 (do.), 6889, 6892 (C. by error *Dro°*), 6894, 6896, 6907, 6908, 6909, 6911, 6913, 6917, 6921, 7031, 7042, 7043, 7057, 7087, 7124, 7133, 7143, 7163, 7164, 7165, 7166, 7168, 7171, 7173, 7175, 7176, 7184, 7187, 7194, 7197, 7199, 7200, †7290, 7345, 7351, 7414, 7415, 7416, 7419, 7421, 7424, 7425, 7426, 7428, 7434, 7435, 7627, 7734, 8031, 8309, 8544, 8797, 8853, 8962, 8979, 9034, 9061, 9110, 9209, 9223, 9240, 9244, 9250, 9265, 9271, 9289, 9295, 9298, 9299, 9300, 9302, 9317, 9319, 9323, 9333, 9334, 9335, 9336, †9338, †9339, 9345, 9346, 9347, 9348, 9350, 9351, 9354, 9355, 9359, 9361, 9364, 9366, 9373, 9375, 9381, 9382, 9387, 9403, 9405, 9435, 9437, 9514; VIII, 45, 492, 564, 566, 568, 570, 572, 574, 575, 582, 587, 600, 631, 633, 636, 640, 642, 645, 657, 660, 663, †667, †674, †677, †680, †681, †682, †684, 772, 781, 790, 794, 796, 797, 799, 802, 803, 805, 808, †810, †812, 1126, 1224, 1225, 1332 (C. by error *Drā°*), 1947, 2507, 2610, 2652, 2663, 2670, 2672, 2673, 2674, 2677, 2680, 2690, 2810, 2814, 2819, 2823, 2825, 2829, 2831, 2845, 2904, 2928, 2929, 2932, 2933, 2934, 2942, 2944, 2947, 2950, 2953, 2956, 2957, 2958, 2959, 2961, 2962, 2966, 2989, 3215, 3221, 3225, 3229, 3231, 3233, †3239, 3242, 3243, †3285, †3358, †3359, 3646, 3706, †3819, 3941, 4012, 4035, †4077, †4079, †4231, †4307, †4316, †4338; IX, 36, (310), 373, 566, 705, 706, 725, 735, 736, 739, 740, 742, 744, 749, 861, 1447, 1622, 1681 (only B., C. has by error *Droṇaḥ*), 1692, 1734, 3575, 3637, 3658, 3668; X, 16, 28, 45, 148, 161, 215, 216, 217, 225, 226, 227, 231, (252), 299, 302, (306), 310, 327, 331, 337, 340, 355, 361 (C. by error *Dro°*), 373, 377, 386, 390, 391, 392, 397 (C. by error *Dro°*), 398, 401, 405, 435, 448, 450, 461, 470, 475, 586, 587, 588, 592, 600, 607 (C. by error *Dro°*), 629, 641, 645, 660, 662, 664, 665, 670, 689, 697, 698, (714), 721, 722, 726, 742, 761, 765, 811; XI, 289, 309, 312; XIII, 7121 (*A°*); XIV, 1805, 1974, 2000; XV, 858 (*Rudrajaṃ*).

Draupada ("son of Drupada") = Çikhaṇḍin: VI, 4966 (*Ç°*, only B., C. has by error *Drupadaḥ*); VIII, †3506 (*Ç°*).

Draupadeya, pl. (°*āḥ*) ("sons of Draupadī"), the five sons of the Pāṇḍavas and Draupadī. § 4 (Anukram.): I, **1,** 210 (all. to § 616).—§ 11 (Parvasaṅgr.): I, **2,** 429 (read with B. *nayanam* instead of *tayanam*, all. to § 321), 570 (all. to § 616).—§ 130 (Aṃçāvat.): I, **67**, 2762 (*pañca*, incarnations of the *Viçvadevagaṇa*; their names are: Prativindhya, Sutasoma (C. *Sutā°*), Çrutakīrti, Çatānīka (*Nākuliḥ*), and Çrutasena, cf. v. 2451).—§ 253 (Haraṇāharaṇap.): I, **221**, 8046 (born with intervals of one year; their names are: Prativindhya (by Yudhishṭhira), Sutasoma (by Bhīmasena), Çrutakarman (by Arjuna), Çatānīka (by Nakula), and Çrutasena (by Sahadeva)).—§ 292 (Rājasūyikap.): II, **45**a, 1609 (accompanied the Parvatīyas, etc.).—§ 321 (Saubhavadhop.): III, **22**, 897 (when the Pāṇḍavas went to the forest, Dhṛshṭadyumna took the *D.* with him to his capital).—§ 554 (Sainyodyogap.): V, **1**, †6 (*kumārāḥ*).—§ 556 (Sañjayayānap.): V, **22**, †684 (*pañca*).—§ 561 (Yānasandhip.): V, **48**, †1839; **50**η, 2008; **56**, †2231 (*kumārān*); **57**, 2251.—§ 569 (Bhagavadyānap.): V, **141**, 4737 (*pañca*), 4743 (do.), 4748 (do.), 4778.—§ 570 (Sainyaniryānap.): V, **151**, 5144; **152**γ, 5152.—§ 571 (Ulūkadūtāg.): V, **162**, 5592; **164**ε, 5709 (are pitted against the Trigartas).—§ 572 (Rathātirathas.): V, **170**, 5879 (*pañca*, regarded as *mahārathas*).—§ 573 (Ambopākhyānap.): V, **184**θ, 7629, (ι), 7635.—§ 576 (Bhagavadgītāp.): VI, **19**, 711 (protected Bhīmasena); **25**θ, 835, 847.—§ 578 (Bhīshmavadhap.): VI, **50**ξ, 2068 (π), 2082 (in the wings of Yudhishṭhira's array); **51**aa, 2118.—§ 579 (do.): VI, **52**ζ, 2150.—§ 580 (do.): VI, **57**κ, 2454.—§ 581 (do.): VI, **62**η, 2733; **63**ι, 2789.—§ 582 (do.): VI, **69**a, 3066 (in the back of Yudhishṭhira's array), 3081.—§ 583 (do.): VI, **75**a, 3283 (in the neck of the Pāṇḍavas' *makaravyūha*); **77**λ, 3394; **78**, 3438 (fought with Duryodhana); **79**ν, 3470.—§ 585 (do.): VI, **87**θ, 3867; **89**ξ, 3949; **95**δδ, 4254, (εε), 4271, 4310 (*pañca*, fought with Bhagadatta).—§ 586 (do.): VI, **100**, 4565, 4566 (fought with Alambusha).—§ 587 (do.): VI, **108**, 4998; **118**υ, 5554.—§ 589 (Droṇābhishekap.): VII, **8**η, 228; **10**, 356 (proceeded against Droṇa).—§ 590 (do.): VII, **14**a, 578; **16**, 626, 628 (fought with Vṛshasena), (γ), 646.—§ 592 (Saṃçaptakavadhap.): VII, **23**, 1035 (description of their standards: *pañcānāṃ D°ānāṃ pratimā dhvajabhūshaṇaṃ | Dharma-Māruta-Çakrāṇām Açvinoç ca mahātmanoḥ*), 1041 (enumeration of their bows: *Raudram Āgneyaṃ Kauberyam Yāmyam Giriçam eva ca | pañcānāṃ D°ānāṃ dhanūratnāni, Bhārata!*); **25**, 1095 (fought with Açvatthāman; PCR. reads *Draupadeyaḥ* = Prativindhya), **20**ι, 1100.—§ 596 (Abhimanyuvadhap.): VII, **35**δ, 1511; **40**o, 1691, 1694 (description of their standards: *Dharma-Māruta-Çakrāṇām Açvinoḥ pratimās tatha | dhārayanto dhvajāgreshu D°āḥ*); **43**ρ, 1770.—§ 597 (Pratijñāp.): VII, **83**a, 2951.—§ 598 (Jayadrathavadhap.): VII, **85**δ, 3050.—§ 599 (do.): VII, **95**ζ, 3527 (fought with Bālhīka); **96**, 3553 (do.); **106**, 3979 (fought with Saumadatti, i.e. Bhūriçravas); **108**, 4053 (do.); **109**π, 4111, 4113; **111**υ, 4282; **114**ψ, 4502; **124**λλ, 5002.—§ 600 (Ghaṭotkacavadhap.): VII, **153**a, 6628; **154**β, 6652; **156**θ, 6764; **158**χ, 7013; **177**χχ, 8060.—§ 601 (Droṇavadhap.): VII, **184**a, 8367.—§ 603 (Nārāyaṇāstram.): VII, **197**, 9123.—§ 605 (Karṇap.): VIII, **12**ββ, 454; **21**εε, 845; **22**ηη, 870, (κκ), 888; **30**ξξ, 1230.—§ 608 (do.): VIII, **46**, 2158, 2206 (*pañca . . . Arjunasamāḥ*); **47**, 2215 (protected Dhṛshṭadyumna); **48**ξ, 2253, (π), 2280 (ρ), 2286; **49**χ, 2333, (ω), †2360; **55**κκ, 2652, 2661; **56**ππ, 2755; **59**ψψ, 2946; **61**, 3079; **66**, 3319; **73**, 3731; **78**γ, 3955, 3958 (so B., C. has *Draupadeyaḥ*), 3964, (ε), 4002; **79**η', 4029; **93**aρ', 4873.—§ 609 (Çalyap.): IX, **1**γ, 32 (lamented for as slain); **2**ζ, 79.—§ 610 (do.): IX, **3**κ, 165; **7**τ, 335.—§ 611 (do.): IX, **11**λ, 550, 561, 566, 572; **16**, 801; **17**ω, †894; **18**ββ, 962, 967, 968; **21**κκ, 1126; **22**λλ, 1139, 1143, 1164; **23**, 1214, 1217, 1242.—§ 612 (Hradapraveçap.): IX, **30**ε, 1726.—§ 615 (Gadāyuddhap.): IX, **62**ψ, 3462.—§ 616 (Sauptikap.): X, **8**, 366, 371 (slain by Açvatthāman in the night encounter), 476 (*nihatāḥ*); **9**, 479 (*hatvā . . . D°ān*), 529 (*hatāḥ*).—§ 617 (Aishīkap.): X, **10**, 544 (*hatāḥ*).—§ 618 (Jalaprādānikap.): XI, **11**ι, 300 (*pātitāḥ*); **12**λ, 321.—§ 620 (Çrāddhap.): XI, **26**β, 790 (their bodies are cremated); **27**δ, 821 (*°vadhena*).—§ 621 (Rājadh.): XII, **1**γ, 15 (*°āṃç ca ghātayitvā*).—§ 637 (do.): XII, **42**γ, 1490 (their çrāddha is performed).—§ 788 (Āçramavāsikap.): XV, **21**a, 588 (*°ānāṃ . . . vadhaṃ saṃsmṛtya*).—§ 789 (Putradarçanap.): XV, **32**θ, 875 (among the dead warriors who, summoned by Vyāsa, arose from the Gaṅgā); **33**ι, 892 (do.).—§ 793 (Mausalap.): XVI, **3**δ, 81 (all. to § 616).—§ 795 (Svargārohaṇap.): XVIII, **1**δ, 26; **3**ε, 67, (ξ), 69.

Draupadeya, dual (*°au*). § 599 (Jayadrathavadhap.): VII, **147**, 6330 (follow Sātyaki; it seems that Yudhāmanyu and Uttamaujas are meant, who possibly were sons or grandsons of Drupada).

Draupadeya[1], sg. § 604 (Karṇap.): VIII, **5**ζ, 103 (who?, had slain Dauḥçāsani).

Draupadeya[2] = Çikhaṇḍin (!): VI, 5695 (*Ç°*).

Draupadeya[3] ("son of Draupadī") = Çrutakarman: VII, 981 (*Ç°*, son of Sahadeva?).

Draupadeya[4] (do.) = Çrutakīrti: VII, 982 (*Ç°*, son of Arjuna?), 1095 (*Ārjuniṃ Çrutakīrtiṃ*).

Draupadeya[5] = Sutasoma: IX, 502 (*S°*).

Draupadi ("son of Drupada") = Dhṛshṭadyumna: VIII, 288.

Draupadī, the wife of the Pāṇḍavas (her proper name was Kṛshṇā (K.); as daughter of the Pāñcāla king Drupada she was named Draupadī, Pāñcālī (P.), Pārshatī (Pār.), and Yājñasenī (Y.)).—§ 4 (Anukram.): I, **1**, [125 (K.), 148 (K.)], 152, 155, [167 (K.)].—§ 10 (Parvasaṅgr.): I, **2**, [314 (P.)].—§ 11 (do.): I, **2**, [361 (P.), 384 (K.)], 385, 388, 392, 394, 395, 402 (*°yās tanayān*), 413, [427 (P.), 430 (K.)], 452, [456 (P.)], 469, 473, [483 (P.)], 573, 574, 578, 630, 632.—§ 71 (Ādivaṃçāvatāraṇap.): I, **61**, [2259 (K.)], 2260 (all. to § 231 foll.).—§ 72 (do.): I, **62**, 2289 (*Kṛshṇā*). § 83 (Ādivaṃçāvataraṇa): I, **63**, [2438 (K., all to § 218)], 2450 (*Pāñcālyām*, mother of five sons: Prativindhya from Yudhishṭhira, Sutasoma from Bhīmasena, Çrutakīrti from Arjuna, Çatānīka from Nakula, and Çrutasena from Sahadeva).—§ 132 (Aṃçāvat.): I, **67**, 2701 (born from a portion of Çacī).—§ 158 (Pūruvaṃç.): I, **95**, ††3826 (wife of the Pāṇḍavas, mother of Prativindhya, Sutasoma, Çrutakīrti, Çatānīka, and Çrutakarman).—§ 216 (Caitrarathap.): I, **165**, [6322 (*Yājñasenyaḥ svayaṃvaraṃ*), 6323 (*ayonijatvaṃ Kṛshṇāyā Drupadasya mahāmakhe*, all. to § 218), 6325 (*vedīmadhyāc ca Kṛshṇāyāḥ sambhavaḥ*, all. to § 218)], 6327 (*°sambhavaṃ*).—[§ 218 (Draupadīsambhava): I, **167**, 6398 (P.), 6402 (K.), 6407 (origin of the name Kṛshṇā: *kṛshṇā bhūtā hi varṇataḥ*; *D.* arose from the centre of the *vedī* at the sacrifice of Drupada).]—[§ 220 (Caitrarathap.): I, **169**, 6434 (K., Pār., in a former existence *D.* five times had asked Çiva for a husband, therefore she was destined to become the wife of the five Pāṇḍavas).]—[§ 230 (Dhaumyapurohitak.): I, **183**, 6920 (P.), 6924 (*Pāñcālyās taṃ svayaṃvaraṃ*).]—§§ 231–236 (Svayaṃvarap.): I, **184**, 6925, 6934, [6942 (K.)]; **185**, [6952 (K.)], 6974, [6977 (K.),

†6979 (K.)]; **187,** [†7007 (K.), †7008 (*Drupadātmajāṃ*), †7009 (K. *Drupadātmajārthaṃ*), †7015 (K.)], †7016, [†7024 (K.)], †7027; [**188,** †7059 (K.)]; **189,** 7062; [**190,** 7123 (P.), 7125 (K.)]; **191,** [†7131 (Y.), †7132 (K.), †7133 (Y.), 7141 (P.), 7142 (K.)], 7143, [7144 (P.)], 7146; [**192,** †7159 (*Drupadātmajāṃ*), †7164 (K.), †7167 (K.), †7169 (K.), †7171 (K.)] (at *D.'s* svayaṃvara she was won by Arjuna; when the Pāṇḍavas brought her home Kuntī said "enjoy ye all").—§ 237 (Vaivāhikap.): I, [**193,** †7174 (K.), †7177 (K.), †7179 (K.), †7181 (K.), †7182 (K.), †7183 (K.), †7198 (K.)]; [**194,** †7203 (K.), †7205 (K.), †7211 (K.)]; **195,** [7221 (K.), 7227 (K.), 7235 (K.), 7239 (K.)], 7240, [7243 (K.)]; **196,** 7255, [7263 (K.)] (Yudhishṭhira asked *D.* from Drupada as wife for himself and his brothers in common).—§ 238 (Pañcendrop.): I, **197,** 7310 (incarnation of Çrī).—[§ 239 (do.): I, **197,** 7326 (K., P., is the incarnate Çrī destined to become the wife of the five Pāṇḍavas; in a former existence *D.* had five times asked Çiva for a husband).]—§ 240 (Vaivāhikap.): I, [**198,** †7331 (K.), †7332 (K.), †7333 (K.), †7334 (K.), †7339 (K.)]; **199,** [7349 (K.)], 7350 (married to the five Pāṇḍavas).—§ 241 (Vidurāgamanap.): I, **200,** 7366, 7374, 7375, 7380, [7383 (*Drupadakanyayā*)], 7384 (*Kṛshṇā*); [**201,** 7404 (K.), 7411 (K.)]; [**202,** 7422 (K.), 7423 (K.)]; **204,** 7466.—§ 243 (do.): I, **206,** [7521 (K.), 7522 (*Drupadakanyām*)], 7525, 7531, [7541 (K., P.), 7544 (K.)].—§ 244 (Rājyalābhap.): I, **207,** 7555 (*Kṛshṇām*).—§ 245 (do.): I, **208,** 7597, [7598 (K.), 7599 (K.), 7600 (K.), 7607 (K.)], 7608, [7611 (K.), 7612 (P.)].—§ 246 (do.): I, **212,** 7737, 7740 (the Pāṇḍavas establish a rule among themselves regarding *D.*).—[§ 247 (Arjunavanavāsap.): I, **213,** 7744 (K.), 7754 (K.) (Arjuna violates that rule).]—§ 248 (do.): I, **214,** 7801.—§ 253 (Haraṇāharaṇap.): I, **221,** 7977, 7978, [7979 (K.)], 7983, [7984 (K.), 8038 (P.), 8045 (K.)] (*D.* bore Prativindhya to Yudhishṭhira, Sutasoma to Bhīmasena, Çrutakarman to Arjuna, Çatānīka to Nakula, and Çrutasena to Sahadeva).—§ 254 (Khāṇḍavadah.): I, **222,** 8072.—§ 262 (Bhagavadyāna): II, **2,** [27 (K.)], 28, 53.—§ 277 (Jarāsandhavadhap.): II, **24,** [976 (K.)], 981.—§ 292 (Rājasūyikap.): II, **45,** 1618.—§ 294 (Dyūtap.): II, **48,** 1705; **49,** 1814.—[§ 295 (do.): II, **52,** 1906 (Y.).]—§ 298 (do.): II, **58,** †2008, 2023, [2024 (Y.)]; **65,** [2172 (K., P.)], 2179 (*Pāñcālyā*) (Yudhishṭhira loses *D.* at dice).—§ 299 (do.): II, **66,** †2186 (*bhāryāṃ sammatāṃ Pāṇḍavānāṃ*), [2189 (K.)]; **67,** †2199, †2201 (*Yājñasenī*), (†2202), (2204), 2206, 2207, [2209 (P.)], 2210, (†2212), [†2214 (Y.)], †2215, [2216 (P.), 2217 (K.), †2220 (*Drupadātmajāyāḥ*, K.), †2221 (Y.)], †2222, [†2223 (K., P.), †2227 (K.), †2229 (K., Y.), †2230 (Y.), †2231 (K.)], (†2232), [†2239 (K.), †2240 (K.), †2242 (K.)], †2246 (*D.* was forcibly dragged by Duḥçāsana); **68,** 2254, [2261 (P.), 2262 (Y.)], 2266, 2272 [2274 (K.), 2278 (K. *Drupadātmajāṃ*), 2280 (K.), 2281 (K.)], 2282, 2283, 2288, 2290, 2291, [2294 (Y.), †2295 (Y.)], 2296, 2298, 2308 (ordered by Karṇa, Duḥçāsana repeatedly tore the robe from *D.*, but at her invoking Kṛshṇa (*Dvārakāvāsin*), Dharma each time covered her with another).—§ 301 (do.): II, [**68,** 2337 (K.), 2338 (K.)]; **69,** (2340), (2344), [2358 (P.); **70,** †2363 (Y.), †2364 (P.), 2374 (P.)]; **71,** [†2383 (Y.), 2388 (K.)], 2391, [†2399 (Y.)], †2404, [†2405 (K., P.), 2406 (P.)], (2407), (2411), (2413); **72,** 2417 (*Draupadī . . . Kṛshṇā*), [2418 (P.); **73,** 2451 (K.)], (Karṇa declared *D.* to be a dāsī and ordered Duḥçāsana to take her away, etc.; *D.* was declared not to have been won, and Dhṛtarāshṭra granted her the liberty of her husbands).—§ 302 (Anudyūtap.): II, **74,** 2467.—§ 303 (do.): II, [**76,** 2502 (K.)].—§ 304 (do.): II, **77,** [†2523 (P., Y.), †2524 (Y.)], 2558.—§ 305 (do.): II, **78,** 2570; **79,** [2584 (K.)], 2586, [2604 (K.), 2615 (K.)].—§ 306 (do.): II, **80,** 2622, [2626 (K.)], 2638, 2662 (all. to § 218).—§ 307 (do.): II, **81,** 2677, [2683 (P.), 2686 (P.), 2688 (K.), 2690 (K.)], 2692, [2698 (K., P.), 2700 (K.), 2701 (P.)].—§ 308 (Āraṇyakap.): III, [**1,** 10 (K.)].—§ 309 (do.): III, **2,** 55.—§ 310 (do.): III, **3,** [202 (P.)], 212, 215 (*Pārshatī*).—§ 312 (do.): III, **5,** 245.—§ 316 (Kirmīravadhap.): III, **11,** [400 (K.), 440 (K.), 453 (K.)], 455, 456.—§ 317 (Arjunābhigamanap.): III, **12,** [509, (P.)], (510), [582 (K.), 583 (P.), 591 (K.)], 592 (*Pāñcālī*), 593.—§ 321 (Saubhavadhop.): III, **22,** 894.—[§ 322 (Dvaitavanapr.): III, **23,** †903 (K.), †918 (Y.); **24,** †943 (K.).]—§ 323 (do.): III, **25,** 950 (*Kṛshṇāṃ*).—§ 325 (Draupadīparitāpav.): III, **27,** [989 (K.), 990 (K.)], (991).—§ 326 (do.): III, **28,** (1029).—§ 327 (do.): III, **29,** 1072, 1075, [1078 (K.), 1093 (K.)], 1094, [1099 (K.), 1105 (K.)], 1109; **30,** (1117); **31,** [1160 (Y.), 1162 (K.), 1164 (K.), 1182 (K.)], 1183, [1189 (K.), 1191 (K.), 1199 (K.), 1201 (K.)]; **32,** (1202); [**33,** 1264 (Y.)]; **34,** †1360, [†1371 (Y.)]; **35,** 1402, [1403 (K.)] (*D.'s* discourse with the Pāṇḍavas).—[§ 330 (Indradarçana): III, **37,** 1479 (K.), (1479) (K.), 1492 (K.).]—§ 340 (Indralokābhig.): III, **49,** [1933 (K.)], 1940, 1941, [1945 (K.)].—§ 341 (do.): III, **50,** 1964.—§ 342 (do.): III, **51,** 1975, [2001 (P.), 2003 (K.), 2005 (P.)].—[§ 343 (Nalop.): III, **52,** 2014 (K.), 2015 (K.).—§ 355 (do.): III, **79,** 3070 (K.).]—§ 356 (Tīrthayātrāp.): III, **80,** [4000 (P.)], 4006; [**81,** 4021 (K.)].—§ 377 (Dhaumyatīrthak.): III, **86,** [8293 (K.)]; **87,** 8299.—§ 378 (Tīrthayātrāp.): III, [**91,** 8415 (K.)]; **93,** 8475, [8481 (K.)].—[§ 383 (do.): III, **99,** 8651 (K.).]—§ 392 (do.): III, **114,** 10107.—§ 400 (do.): III, **118,** [†10219 (K.), †10229 (K.)], †10232.—[§ 402 (do.): III, **120,** †10282 (K. *Drupadātmajā*).]—[§ 406 (do.): III, **125,** 10417 (K.).]—[§ 418 (do.): III, **139,** †10837 (K.), †10838 (K.).]—§ 419 (Gandhamādanapr.): III, **140,** [10842 (K.)], 10846, [10849 (K.), 10855, (P.), (10858, P.), 10859 (K.), 10860 (K.)], 10868, [10869 (K.)].—[§ 420 (do.): III, **141,** 10871 (P.), 10874 (Y.).]—§ 423 (do.): III, [**143,** 10976 (K.)]; **144,** 10986, [10987 (P.), 10997 (K.), 11003 (P.), 11004 (K.), 11007 (K.)]; **145,** [11015 (P.), 11019 (K.), 11021 (K.), 11052 (K.), 11058 (K.)], 11062, [11067 (K.)].—§ 424 (Bhīmakadalīkh.): III, **146,** [11071 (P.)], 11081, 11100, 11104 (despatched Bhīma to find saugandhikas).—§ 432 (Saugandhikāharaṇap.): III, **152,** 11346; [**154,** 11368 (P.)] (Bhīma's encounter with the Krodhavaças on account of the saugandhikas).—§ 433 (do.): III, **155,** [11403 (K.), 11404 (P.), 11406 (K.)], (11407), [11412 (K.)].—[§ 434 (do.): III, **156,** 11430 (K.), 11450 (P.).]—§ 435 (Jaṭāsuravadhap.): III, **157,** [11453 (K.)], 11455, 11459, 11475, 11478, 11487, 11489, [11494 (K.)] (carried away by Jaṭāsura, but delivered by Bhīmasena).—§ 436 (Yakshayuddhap.): III, **158,** 11525, [11558 (K.)], 11565; [**159,** 11629 (K.)].—§ 437 (do.): III, **160,** 11679 (*Kṛshṇā*), 11687, 11693.—§ 438 (do.): III, **161,** [11740 (K.)], 11741, [11786 (K.)].—[§ 441 (Nivātakavacayuddhap.): III, **165,** †11907 (K.).]—[§ 442 (do.): III, **167,** 11935 (K.).]—[§ 447 (do.): III, **175,** 12315 (K.).]—§ 450 (Ājagarap.): III, **179,** 12441, [12442 (P.)], 12443; **181,** 12536.—§ 452 (Mārkaṇḍeyas.): III, **183,** [12557 (K.)], 12565, 12567,

[†12571 (K.), †12576 (K.), †12578 (K.), †12579 (K., Y.), †12580 (K., Y.), †12581 (K.), †12582 (K.), †12584 (K.), †12587 (Y.)], 12602.—§ 459 (do.): III, **189**, 13007.—§ 510 (Draupadī-Satyabhāmāsaṃv.): III, **233**, 14649, 14652 (*Yājñasenī*), [14656 (P.)], 14657, [14708 (K., P.), 14709 (P., Y.)]; **234**, (†14710).—§ 511 (do.): III, **235**, [14724 (*Drupadātmajām*), 14725 (K.), 14728 (*Drupadātmaje*), 14730 (K.), 14738 (K.)], 14739 (discourse between *D.* and Satyabhāmā).—§ 512 (Ghoshayātrāp.): III, [**236**, †14746 (K.), †14751 (K.), †14753 (K.)]; [**237**, 14792 (K.)]; **238**, [14803 (K.)], 14805 (*Drupadātmajām*); **240**, 14865; **246**, 15014, [15019 (K.)].—§ 519 (Vrīhidrauṇikap.): III, **259**, 15375.—§ 521 (Draupadīharaṇap.): III, [**262**, 15493 (K.)]; **263**, [15521 (K.)], 15526, 15537 (*Kṛshṇayā*), 15539, [15540 (K.), 15541 (K.), 15542 (K.), 15543 (K.)], 15563, 15566, 15568 (visit of Durvāsas). — § 522 (do.): III, **264**, 15575, 15578; **266**, †15602, [†15606 (K.), †15610 (*Drupadātmajā*)]; **267**, [15611 (K.)], 15615 (*Kṛshṇā*), 15617, [15619 (K.)], (15620), [15636 (K.), 15637 (K.)]; **268**, [†15639 (*Drupadātmajā*), †15648 (K.)], †15649 (*Kṛshṇe*), (†15651), †15663 (K.); **269**, †15677, [†15681 (K.), †15682 (Y.), †15683 (K.), †15693 (Y.)]; **270**, [†15696 (Y.), †15697 (K.)], (†15698); **271**, [15747 (K.)], 15748, 15749, 15755, 15756, 15759, [15762 (K.)], 15764, 15765, 15766 (K.) (carried away by Jayadratha, but delivered by her husbands). — § 523 (Jayadrathavimoksh.): III, **272**, [15783 (K.)], 15792, 15794.—§ 525 (Rāmopākhyānap.): III, **273**, [15859 (K.), 15860 (K.)], 15866. — § 544 (Yudhishṭhirāçvāsa): III, **292**, 16611 (*Kṛshṇām*).—§ 545 (Pativratāmāhātmyap.): III, [**293**, 16616 (*Drupadātmajām*), 16617 (K.), 16618 (*Drupadātmajā*)]; **299**, 16916. — [§ 547 (Karṇa): III, **310**, †17219 (K.).]—[§ 548 (Āraṇeyap.): III, **311**, 17221 (K.), 17222 (K.), 17224 (K.); **312**, 17243 (*prātikāmy anayat Kṛshṇām*, all. to § 299); **315**, 17476 (K.).]—§ 549 (Pāṇḍavapr.): IV, **1**, 2; **2**, 58; **3**, 74 (*Kṛshṇā*), (77), 78, [81 (K.)]; **4**, 86, [90 (K.), 138 (Y.)]; **5**, [146 (K.), 148 (P.)], 149; **9**, [245 (K.), 250 (*Drupadātmajām*)], 260, [263 (K.)], (273), [279 (K.)] (in the thirteenth year *D.* served Sudeshṇā as a *sairindhrī*).—§ 550 (Samayapālanap.): IV, **13**, [335 (K.), 337 (K.)], 370.—§ 551 (Kīcakavadhap.): IV, **14**, [374 (Y.), 375 (P.), 376 (*Drupadātmajām*), 383 (K.)], (412), 417; [**15**, 434 (K.), 451 (K.)]; **16**, (455), (457), [464 (K.), 472 (*Drupadātmajā*)], (473), [485 (K.), 487 (K.), 490 (K.), 497 (K.)], (500); [**17**, 503 (K.), 504 (*Drupadātmajā . . . Kṛshṇā*), 508 (K.), 512 (P.), 513 (P.), 515 (P.), 521 (K.)]; **18**, (523); **19**, (557), [594 (Y.), 595 (P.)]; **20**, (604), [636 (K.)], (638); **21**, [644 (K.)], (659), [690 (K.), 691 (*Drupadātmajām*)]; **22**, [695 (Y.)], 700, (705), (709), [711 (K.)], 717, (730), [735 (P.), 768 (K.), 773 (K.), 780 (K.)], 781 (*Pāñcālī*), [783 (P.)], 786 (*Kṛshṇām*); **23**, [796 (K.), 801 (K.), 803 (K.)], (804), [807 (K.)], 820, [822 (K.)], 823 (*Pāñcālīm*); **24**, [839 (K.), 842 (P.), 846 (K.)], 855 (Kīcaka became enamoured with *D.*, and was therefore slain by Bhīmasena). — § 552 (Goharaṇap.): IV, [**25**, 876 (K.)]; **36**, [1181 (P.), 1182 (K.), 1184 (P.)], (1191); **44**, 1370 (*Pāñcālī . . . Kṛshṇā*), 1372; [**45**, 1432 (*svayaṃvare tu Pāñcālyāḥ*)]; [**49**, 1537 (K.)]; **50**, [1566 (K.)], 1569, [1576 (K.)]; **68**, 2210.—§ 553 (Vaivāhikap.): IV, **71**, 2290, [2292 (K., all. to Saugandhikāharaṇap.)], 2296, [†2305 (K.)]; **72**, 2352 (°*yāç ca sutāḥ*), [2367 (K.)]. — § 554 (Sainyodyogap.): V, **3**, 58.—§ 555 (do.): V, **8**, [201 (K.), 222 (K.)], 223; **18**, 554, 558.—§ 556 (Sañjayayānap.): V, **23**, †680 (*Kṛshṇā*); [**25**, †725 (Y.)]; **29**, †845, [†847 (K.), †849 (K.), †850 (K.), †851 (Y.), †854 (K., Y.)]; [**31**, †928 (K.), †931 (K.)].—§ 559 (Prajāgarap.): V, **36**, †1329.—[§ 561ε (Bhīmasena): V, **50**, 1988 (Y., all. to § 522), 1990 (*Kṛshṇāyāç caratā prītiṃ yena Krodhavaçā hatāḥ*, all. to § 432).]—[§ 561 (Yānasandhip.): V, **59**, 2326 (K.), 2329 (K.), 2349 (K.).]—§ 562 (Bhagavadyānap.): V, **73**, 2692; **78**, 2819; [**81**, 2864 (P.)]; [**82**, 2871 (K.), 2897 (P.), 2912 (K.), 2914 (K.), 2919 (K.)]; **90**, 3171, 3173, 3174, 3175, 3176, [3177 (K.)], 3178, [3185 (K., all. to Dyūtap.)], 3209, [3211 (K., all. to § 299), 3215 (*Çyāmā*, do.), 3217 (K.), 3228 (K.)]; [**95**, 3442 (K., all. to Dyūtap.)].—§ 567 (do.): V, **128**, 4266 (all. to Dyūtap.).—§ 569 (do.): V, **137**, [4655 (K.), 4659 (P.), 4661 (*Çyāmā*), 4662 (K.)], 4663, [4665 (K.), 4666 (K.)]; **138**, 4679; **139**, 4716, 4721, 4740.—§ 570 (Sainyaniryānap.): V, **151**, 5157 (*Pāñcālī*). —§ 571 (Ulūkadūtāgamanap.): V, **160**, 5478 (K.), 5489 (K.), 5495 (K.), 5497 (K.), 5519 (K.), 5520 (Pār.); **161**, [5541 (K., all. to § 299)], 5543, [5564 (K.), 5565 (Pār.)].—§ 572 (Rathātirathas.): V, **165**, 5744 (°*haraṇe*, all. to § 522); **169**, 5864.—§ 573 (Ambopākhyānap.): V, **194**, 7601 (°*yāḥ pañca cātmajāḥ*).—§ 580 (Bhīshmavadhap.): VI, **56**θ, 2417 (do.).—§ 583 (do.): VI, **78**, 3439 (°*yās tanayān*); **79**μ, 3453.—§ 585 (do.): VI, **91**, 4090 (*Kṛshṇā*, all. to § 299).—§ 586 (do.): VI, **103**ν, 4694 (°*yāḥ pañca cātmajāḥ*); [**107**, 4907 (K., all. to Dyūtap.)].—§ 587 (do.): VI, **118**ρ, 5560 (°*yāḥ pañca cātmajāḥ*).—§ 593 (Abhimanyuvadhap.): VII, [**40**, 1684 (K.)]; **42**, 1752 (°*haraṇe*, all. to § 522). —§ 596 (Pratijñāp.): VII, **72**, 2501, 2534; [**78**, 2766 (P.), 2770 (P.).—§ 599 (Jayadrathavadhap.): VII, **102**, 3818 (K., all. to Dyūtap.), 3825 (K.)]; **122**, 4871 (°*yāç ca parikleçaḥ*); **127**, 5167; [**132**σσ, 5425 (K., all. to Dyūtap.), 5428 (K., do.); **137**βββ, 5656 (K., P., do.), 5658 (K., do.); **151**γ', 6543 (K., do.)].—§ 600 (Ghaṭotkacavadhap.): VII, **159**, 7129; [**183**, 8324 (P.)].—§ 603 (Nārāyaṇāstramoksh.): VII, **197**μ, 9090 (all. to Dyūtap.), 9123; **198**ρ, 9165 (all. to § 299), [9166 (K.)]; [**199**, 9226 (K., all. to Dyūtap.)].—[§ 604 (Karṇap.): VIII, **1**, 7 (K., do.); **9**, 308 (K., P., do.), 310 (K., do.).—§ 608 (do.): VIII, **50**ββ, 2412; **66**ι, †3346 (K., all. to Dyūtap.), †3353 (Y., do.)]; **70**, †3505; [**73**, 3716 (K., do.), 3717 (K., do.)]; [**74**φφφ, 3770 (K., do.), 3773 (P., do.)]; **85**, 4253 (all. to Dyūtap.); [**87**, 4180 (K.)]; [**80**αε', †4562 (*Kṛshṇāparikleçam*)]; **91**, †4749 (all. to Dyūtap.), [(κκ'), 4754 (K., do.), 4755 (K., do.), 4756 (K., do.)]; [**96**, 5002 (K., do.)].—§ 609 (Çalyap.): IX, **2**, 123 (°*yāḥ pañca cātmajāḥ*). — § 610 (do.): IX, **5**ν, [248 (K., all. to Dyūtap.), 255 (K., do.)], 257 (*Kṛshṇā*, do.), [259 (K., do.)].—§ 611 (do.): IX, **11**, 585 (all. to § 432); **10**δδ, 1021 (°*yās tanayāḥ pañca*).—§ 612 (Hradapr.): IX, **31**, 1814 (all. to Dyūtap.).—§ 613 (Gadāyuddhap.): IX, **33**ι, 1931 (do.), 1937 (do.).—§ 614 (do.): IX, **34**α, 1956 (°*yāḥ pañca cātmajāḥ*).—§ 615 (do.): IX, **56**, 3158 (all. to Dyūtap.), 3163 (do.); **59**, 3312 (do.), †3318 (*Yājñasenīm*, do.); **61**, [3431 (Y., do.), 3433 (K., all. to § 522)].—§ 617 (Aishīkap.): X, **11**, [577 (K.), 579 (K.), 582 (K.), 589 (K., Y.)], 590, (593), [594 (K.)] (asked for the gem on the head of Açvatthāman); **16**, 744, 746 (*Kṛshṇām*), (756), 757, [759 (K.)] (Yudhishṭhira placed the gem on his own head).—§ 618 (Jalapradānikap.): XI, **12**κ, 316; [**13**, 352 (P., all. to Dyūtap.)]; **15**, [386 (P., do.)], 388 (do.), 398 (do.), 417 (*Pāñcālīm*), (418), [420 (Y.)]. — § 619 (Strīvilāpap.): XI, **18**γ, 538, [539 (P., all. to Dyūtap.), 540 (P.)]; **22**η, 628 (K., all. to § 522), [629 (C. *Kṛshṇā* by error instead of *Kṛshṇa* (so B.))].—§ 621 (Rājadh.): XII, **1**γ, 17 (*hataputrā*).—§ 623 (do.): XII, **14**, 385, (389), [413 (P.)]; [**15**, 424 (Y.)]; **16**, [499 (K., all. to Dyūtap.)], 502 (all. to § 551), 509.—§ 630 (do.): XII, **27**β, 799 (°*yās tanayeshu*), 820.—§ 635 (do.): XII, **37**β, 1368, (δ), [1384 (K.)]; [**38**, 1397 (P.), 1398 (K.)].—§ 637 (do.): XII, [**40**, 1456 (K. *Drupadātmajām*)]; **42**, 1490.—§ 746 (Ānuçāsanik.): XIII, **57**, 2969.—[§ 779 (Açvamedhikap.): XIV, **12**a, 322 (K., all. to Dyūtap.), 325 (Y., all. to § 551).]—[§ 780 (do.): XIV, **14**β, 356 (K.).]—[§ 783 (Anugītāp.): XIV, **52**γ, 1505 (K.).]—§ 785 (do.): XIV, **61**, 1833; **66**ι, 1940, (λ), 1948, 1953; **67**ν, 1973; **68**, 1992; [**69**, 2020 (P.)]; [**70**, 2038 (*Drupadaputrī*)]; **87**, 2584 (*Kṛshṇā*); **88**, [2604 (K.)], 2606; **89**, [2645 (*Drupadātmajām*)], 2657.—§ 787 (Āçramavāsap.): XV, **1**, 9, (*a*), 23; **3**β, 73, 92; [**10**ξ, 348 (P.)]; **11**, 376, [377 (*Pañcālaputryā*)]; **15**υ, †437 (*Kṛshṇā*); **16**φ, 455, 471; [**18**, 495 (P.)].—§ 788 (do.): XV, **21**a, 590; **22**, 605, 609; **23**, 629; [**24**, 654 (K.)]; **25**, 658, 659, [(γ), †664 (K.)].—§ 789 (Putradarçanap.): XV, **29**β, 778, (γ), 783, [801 (*Drupadaputryāḥ*)], (ε), 806 (*Kṛshṇā*); **31**ζ, 844, 857.—§ 791 (do.): XV, **36**, 1007 (°*pramukhāḥ Kauravayoshitaḥ*).—[§ 793 (Mausalap.): XVI, **7**, 179 (Y.).]—§ 794 (Mahāprasthānikap.): XVII, **1**, 20, 23, [24 (K.)], 29, 32; [**2**, 49 (Y.), 50 (Y.), 51 (K.), 58 (K.)]; **3**, [77 (K.), †86 (K.)], 109 (*D.* fell down during the mahāprasthāna).—§ 795 (Svargārohaṇap.): XVIII, **1**, 9 (*Pāñcālī*), 16; **2**, [37 (P.)], (ε), 67, [69 (P.)]; **3**η, 97 (*Kṛshṇā*), 114, [119 (K.)]; **4**, [134 (P.)], 136 (incarnation of Çrī), 138 (the sons of *D.* after death became Gandharvas). Cf. Madhusūdanī, Sutasomamātṛ.

Draupadīharaṇa(ṃ) parva. § 10 (Parvasaṅgr.): I, **2**, 325 (i.e. Draupadīharaṇaparvan).

[Draupadīharaṇaparvan] ("the carrying away of Draupadī," the 46th of the minor parvans of Mhbhr.). (Cf. Draupadīharaṇa(ṃ) parva.) § 521: While *Duryodhana*, *Duḥçāsana*, *Karṇa*, and *Çakuni* were longing to harm the *Pāṇḍavas*, *Durvāsas* arrived with 10,000 disciples, and harassed *Duryodhana* with his whimsical and insolent behaviour; but as *Duryodhana* was neither angered nor annoyed, he granted him a boon. According to what had been agreed upon between himself and *Karṇa* and *Duḥçāsana*, *Duryodhana* asked *Durvāsas* to visit the *Pāṇḍavas* with his disciples, when *Draupadī*, after having regaled the *brahmans*, etc., with food, would have gone to rest. *Durvāsas* promised to do so (III, **262**). Then *Durvāsas* one day came to the *Pāṇḍavas* with 10,000 disciples, when the meal was over and *Kṛshṇā* was reposing. *Kṛshṇā* then praised *Kṛshṇa*, who, leaving *Rukmiṇī*, who was sleeping by his side, came to her and demanded something to eat. *Draupadī* became embarrassed, because the sun-given vessel only remained full till she had finished her meal, and therefore now was empty. At the request of *Kṛshṇa* she, however, fetched the vessel, and *Kṛshṇa* found a particle of rice and vegetable sticking at its rim, and swallowing it he said to her: "May it please the god who is the soul of the universe (*viçvātmā*), and may the partaker of sacrifices (*yajñabhuk*) be satisfied." Then he ordered *Bhīma* (B. *Sahadeva*) to invite the *munis* to dinner. Meanwhile those ascetics, having bathed in the river, observed that their stomachs were full, and as *Durvāsas* feared that the *Pāṇḍavas* would destroy them, looking down upon them with angry eyes, because the repast had been uselessly prepared for them ("I am afraid," said *Durvāsas*, "of men that are devoted to *Hari*"), they all ran away, so that *Bhīma* (B. *Sahadeva*) sought for them in vain. As the *Pāṇḍavas* were afraid that the *munis* might return at night and curse them, *Kṛshṇa* suddenly appeared and consoled them. Then he repaired to his capital (III, **263**).—§ 522: One day when the *Pāṇḍavas* had gone a-hunting, leaving *Draupadī* in the hermitage with the permission of the great *ṛshi Tṛṇabindu* and of *Dhaumya*, the king of *Sindhu* (of *Sauvīra*, v. 15599; of the *Çibis*, *Sauvīras*, *Sindhus*, etc., 15621), *Jayadratha Vārddhakshattri*, who, with a view of matrimony, was on his way to the king of the *Çālveyas*, halted in the wood of *Kāmyaka*, and seeing *Draupadī* standing at the threshold of the hermitage, he fell in love with her, and sent king *Koṭikāsya* (king *Suratha's* son, v. 15593; the foremost of the Çibis, v. 15602) to inquire who she was (III, **264**). *Koṭikāsya* introduced himself to *Draupadī* and showed her the Trigarta king *Kshemaṅkara*, and the son of the king of the *Kulindas* ("who always lives in the mountains"), and the son of *Subala* (B. *Subhava*) of the race of *Ikshvāku*; he said that *Jayadratha* was there at the head of 6,000 chariots, etc., followed by twelve *Sauvīra* princes as his standard-bearers (*Aṅgāraka*, etc., enumerated) (*a*), and his brothers (*Balāhaka*, *Anīka*, *Vidāraṇa*, etc.) (III, **265**). *Draupadī* told *Koṭikāsya* who she was, and that her husbands were out a-hunting (*Yudhishṭhira* to the east, *Bhīma* towards the south, *Arjuna* to the west, and the *Açvins* towards the north), and invited them to alight and await the return of the *Pāṇḍavas* (III, **266**). *Koṭikāsya* told *Jayadratha* the words of *Draupadī*, and exhorted him to take her with him to the *Sauvīras*. *Jayadratha* introduced himself to *Draupadī*, who offered him water for washing his feet, and promised him fifty animals for breakfast and various kinds of deer, etc., etc. (enumerated), when *Yudhishṭhira* returned. *Jayadratha* asked her to leave the miserable *Pāṇḍavas* and become his wife (III, **267**), but was severely rebuked by *Draupadī*, who threatened him with the *Pāṇḍavas*. As *Jayadratha* said, "We too belong by birth to the seventeen high clans, and look down upon the *Pāṇḍavas*," she threatened him with *Kṛshṇa* and *Arjuna*, and the *Andhakas*, *Vṛshṇis*, and *Kaikeyas*, and called upon *Dhaumya*. *Jayadratha* seized her by her upper garment; *Draupadī* pushed him so that he fell upon the ground; but at last she was obliged to ascend his chariot, while *Dhaumya* followed amidst *Jayadratha's* infantry (III, **268**). When the *Pāṇḍavas* again met, *Yudhishṭhira* knew from the shrill cries of the birds that the forest had been invaded by hostile intruders, and he caused them to give up the chase and drive home on their great chariots drawn by *Saindhava* horses. A yellow jackal on their left indicated the violence done. *Indrasena* learned what had happened from the weeping foster-sister of *Draupadī*, and then they pursued and overtook *Jayadratha*, who was greatly alarmed (III, **269**). *Draupadī*, asked by *Jayadratha*, pointed out to him each of the five *Pāṇḍavas*, and advised him to throw down his arms and seek the protection of *Yudhishṭhira*, at the top of whose flagstaff two tabours called *Nanda* and *Upananda* are constantly played. The *Pāṇḍavas*, leaving the panic-stricken infantry alone, rushed upon the charioteers [so PCR., who seems to have read *rathānīkam*, which is, to be sure, the right reading, instead of *yathānīkam*, which occurs both in C. and B.] (III, **270**). *Bhīma* with his iron mace (*sarvaçaikyāyasīm gadām*), embossed with gold, rushed towards *Jayadratha*, who was defended by *Koṭikāsya*. The *Trigarta* king, who had killed the four steeds of

Yudhishṭhira with his mace, was himself killed by *Yudhishṭhira*, who then, together with *Indrasena*, mounted the chariot of *Sahadeva*. *Nakula* killed *Kshemaṅkara* and *Mahāmukha*, and was compelled by the Trigarta king *Suratha* (whom he killed ?) to mount *Bhīma's* chariot. *Bhīma* put *Koṭikāsya* to flight and slew him. *Arjuna* killed the twelve *Sauvīra* heroes, etc.; *Jayadratha* put *Draupadī* down and fled. *Yudhishṭhira*, seeing *Draupadī* and *Dhaumya* walking in front, caused her to be taken up on the chariot of *Sahadeva*. *Arjuna* advised *Bhīma* to refrain from slaying the remnant of the *Saindhava* host. *Bhīma* prevailed upon *Yudhishṭhira* to return to the hermitage with the twins and *Draupadī* and *Dhaumya*, while he himself would find out and slay *Jayadratha*. *Yudhishṭhira* entreated him not to slay him, remembering *Duḥçalā* and *Gāndhārī*; but *Draupadī* indignantly required that he should be slain, and *Bhīma* and *Arjuna* went in search of him. In the hermitage *Yudhishṭhira* found *Mārkaṇḍeya* and many other *brahmans* and ascetics, who were greatly bewailing the lot of *Draupadī*. Meanwhile *Arjuna* killed the horses of *Jayadratha*, though they were a full *kroça* ahead of him. *Jayadratha* was then overtaken by *Bhīma*, but *Arjuna* entreated *Bhīma* not to kill him (III, **271**).

Draupadīja, pl. (°*āḥ*) ("sons of Draupadī") = Draupadeya, pl.: VIII, †4202.

[Draupadīparitāpavākya(m)] ("the complaints of Draupadī"; cf. Arjunābhigamanaparvan). § 325: While they were conversing in the evening, filled with sorrow, *Kṛshṇā*, who wondered at the hardheartedness of *Duryodhana*, *Karṇa*, *Çakuni*, and *Duḥçāsana*, who were the only four that did not shed tears at their being exiled, and who lamented their present state so different from their former happiness, tried to excite *Yudhishṭhira* to revenge himself (III, **27**).—§ 326: *Draupadī* related the old story of the conversation between *Prahlāda* (the chief of the *Asuras* and the *Dānavas*, well versed in the mysteries of the science of duty) and his grandson *Bali Vairocana*, in which *Prahlāda* told *Bali* that neither might nor forgiveness is invariably meritorious, and then she said: "I therefore consider, O king! that time has come for thee to put forth thy might" (III; **28**).—§ 327: *Yudhishṭhira* maintained that a wise man should ever forgive his persecutor; that wrath has been given to man for the destruction of the world; and cited *gāthās* of the forgiving *Kāçyapa*: "Forgiveness is virtue, sacrifice, the *Vedas*, etc.; men of forgiveness obtain regions in the *Brahmaloka*; when one forgives everything, then he becomes *brāhman* (*brahma sampadyate*); this and the other world belongs to him who forgives; etc." (III, **29**). From the fact that pious persons are often unhappy (v. 1133, *Yudhishṭhira* is said to have performed the *açvamedha* (!), *rājasūya*, *puṇḍarīka*, and *gosava* sacrifices) and vicious persons happy, *Draupadī* concludes that *Dhātṛ* and *Vidhātṛ* have clouded *Yudhishṭhira's* senses, that it is folly to aspire to final emancipation (*moksha*), that the consequences of acts are inevitable, that God (*Īçvara*, *Dhātṛ*, *Svayambhū Prapitāmaha*) makes creatures to work as a wooden doll is made to move its limbs by a wire-puller, etc., and causes them to destroy each other, that God does not behave towards his creatures like a father or mother, but like a vicious person; either God is sinful, or Might (and not God) is the true cause of acts, and then those are to be pitied that have no might (III, **30**). *Yudhishṭhira* censured *Kṛshṇā* for her atheism (*nāstikya*), saying that one should not act virtuously from the desire of reaping fruits, but because it is ordained so by the *Veda*, the ancient religion revealed by the *ṛshis*, and because it is the conduct of the good and wise; neither should one doubt virtue or religion nor censure God, by whose grace mortal man, by piety, acquires immortality. For though we may not see the results, being mysterious even to the gods, and the illusion (*māyā*) of the gods is mysterious to us, yet virtue and vice are not fruitless, as may be seen from the examples of *Vyāsa*, *Vasishṭha*, *Maitreya*, *Nārada*, *Lomaça*, *Çuka*, and other *ṛshis*, who by virtue have become superior even to the gods; as also from her own and *Dhṛshṭadyumna's* birth; nor would men have practised virtue, generation after generation, if asceticism, etc., were useless, and no one would pursue salvation (*nirvāṇa*), but they would live like beasts, and why should *ṛshis*, gods, *Gandharvas*, *Rākshasas*, and *Asuras*, who are above human conditions (*īçvarāḥ*), cherish virtue? He who, trusting the proofs of his own reasoning, rejects other authority or doubts religion and virtue, loses this and yonder world, and is lower than even çūdras and robbers (III, **31**). *Kṛshṇā* said that she did not slander religion nor disregard God (*Īçvara*, *Prajāpati*, *Maheçvara*); it was affliction that had extorted these words from her. She maintained that besides what a man obtains from Necessity (*haṭha*), Fate (*daiva*), Accident (*svabhāva*), and deeds in a former life (*karman*) (all of which might be reduced to the last item, also called *adṛçya*), which God distributes, there are also things of which man himself is the cause, working through his own intelligence and exertion. It is by exertion (*utthāna*; the explanation of Nīl. here seems to be inadmissible) that all creatures live, even *Dhātṛ* and *Vidhātṛ*, as well as the crane on the water. Those who believe only in Destiny (*dishṭa*) or Necessity are both the meanest among men. On the other hand, if God were not the giver of good and bad fruits, there would not be any creature that was miserable, and all exertions would be successful. *Manu* himself declares that a man should act; and if he works, even if he be not successful, his debt is cancelled. "Having exerted thyself, thou wilt know what the fruit of thy exertions will be. The tiller tills the soil with the plough, and sows the seed thereon; he then sits silent, for the clouds are now the cause; and if no rain favours him, the tiller is without blame . . . If, however, no exertion is made, there can be no success . . . All this, uttered by *Bṛhaspati* himself, a learned brahman said to my father and my brothers; from them I heard it" (III, **32**). *Bhīma* tried to prevail upon *Yudhishṭhira* that (especially as they had lost the sovereignty by his carelessness) he should make war with the *Dhārtarāshṭras*, aided by the *Sṛñjayas* and *Kaikeyas* and *Kṛshṇa*, maintaining that a man should practise virtue (*dharma*) for the sake of gaining wealth (*artha*), and acquire wealth for the sake of pleasure (*kāma*), but neither for its own sake; that might and energy (and the protecting of the subjects) constitute the virtue of the *Kshatriya*, and that deviation from the virtues of one's own order is never laudable; that the *Asuras*, though elder brothers in possession of power and abundance, were all vanquished by the gods through stratagem; that as wealth should be spent by one who wishes to increase his wealth, just as seeds are scattered on the ground, thus a person who throws away a little of his virtue like seeds (*dharma*) in order to gain a larger measure of virtue is regarded as wise, and that whatever sin a monarch commits in acquiring dominion, he cancels it all afterwards by sacrifices and by bestowing villages, etc., on brahmans (III, **33**). *Yudhishṭhira* declared that he was unable to violate the pledge, and that it was now too late for *Bhīma* to use harsh words (III, **34**). *Bhīma* said that only he whose life is unlimited, or who knows what the period of his life is, has time to wait; they ought to strive for the possession of the kingdom before they died; "if a man, slaying his injurer, goes the very day into hell, that hell becomes heaven to him; the pain one feels in having to suppress his wrath is more burning than fire itself; . . . thou art kind like a brahman, how hast thou been born in the *Kshatriya* order? those who are born in this order are generally of cruel hearts; thou hast heard the duties of kings, as promulgated by *Manu*, cruel and fraught with crookedness and opposed to tranquillity (*çama*); moreover, we will not be able to live unknown, as we are known all over the world, and many kings, who have been expelled by us from their kingdoms, and robbed and exiled by us, will assist *Duryodhana* and set against us numerous spies in disguise; we have now lived in the woods for thirteen months, which may be regarded as so many years, as *pūtikas* (see BR. and Nīl.) are a substitute for the *soma*; or one may free himself from this sin by offering food to a bull" (see Nīl.) (III, **35**).

Draupadīputra, pl. ("the sons of Draupadī") = Draupadeya, pl.: VI, 1655, 2755; X, 365.

[Draupadī - sambhava(ḥ)] ("origin of Draupadī"). § 218 (Caitrarathap.): Distressed and thinking of revenging himself on *Droṇa*, not contented with his children and relatives, king *Drupada* wandered along the *Yamunā* and the *Gaṅgā* and came to a hermitage of *brahmans*, and prevailed upon *Yāja* (*b*) to perform a sacrifice for him, assisted by his brother *Upayāja*, in order to obtain a son who might slay *Droṇa*. Then *Yāja* summoned the queen (*Pṛshatī*, v. 6390; *Pārshatī*, v. 6405; "daughter-in-law of *Pṛshata*," PCR.), but she said that she was not fit for accepting the offspring (?), her mouth being unclean (*avalipta*) and her person perfumed. *Yāja* replied: "Since the sacrifice has been prepared (*çrapitaṃ*) by *Yāja* and sanctified by *Upayāja's* invocations (*abhimantritaṃ*), it shall produce its effect whether thou comest or waitest." Then arose from the flames a boy with a crown on his head, his body being arrayed in excellent armour, sword in hand and carrying a bow and arrows, sending forth loud roars, and immediately ascending a chariot. A great invisible being in the skies said that he would destroy *Droṇa*, etc. After this *Pāñcālī* arose from the centre of the *vedī*, and a voice, not coming from a visible body, said that she would be the cause of the destruction of many *kshatriyas*. At the birth of both children the *Pāñcālas* shouted with joy. The queen was regarded as their mother. Then the *brahmans* gave to the boy the name of *Dhṛshṭadyumna*, on account of his audacity, etc. (*dhṛshṭatvād atidhṛshṇutvād dyumnādyutsambhavād api*, v. 6406), and to the girl that of *Kṛshṇā*, on account of her dark complexion (v. 6407). *Droṇa* brought *Dhṛshṭadyumna* to his own abode, and taught him the use of all weapons, considering that destiny is inevitable (I, **167**).

[Draupadī - Satyabhāmā - saṃvādaparvan] ("conversation between Draupadī and Satyabhāmā," the 42nd of the minor parvans of Mhbhr.). § 510: After the *brahmans* and *Paṇḍavas* had taken their seats, *Draupadī* and *Satyabhāmā Sātrājitī*, the favourite wife of *Kṛshṇa*, entered the hermitage. *Satyabhāmā* asked *Draupadī* how she made the *Pāṇḍavas* obedient to her, in order that she herself might by the same means secure the affection of *Kṛshṇa*. *Draupadī* warned her against using drugs, incantations, etc., which were used by wicked women, and said that she kept aloof from vanity and served the *Pāṇḍavas* with devotion, etc. Formerly, in the palace of *Yudhishṭhira* at *Indraprastha*, food was daily given to 8,000 *brahmans*, 80,000 *snātakas* with thirty serving-maids assigned to each, 10,000 *yatis*; he had 100,000 well-dressed serving-maids with bracelets, etc., all skilled in singing and dancing; 100,000 maidservants who day and night used to feed guests; 100,000 horses, and 100,000 elephants. And it was *Draupadī* who had the supervision of all this; she knew the names and features of all the girls, and knew everything about them, and even about the cowherds and shepherds. She alone knew the income and expenditure of the king and what their whole wealth was, bearing hunger and thirst, and being the first to wake up and the last to go to bed (III, **233**). *Draupadī* said that for women there is no god equal to the husband, as it is from him the wife obtains offspring, articles of enjoyment, fame, and heaven itself hereafter. In order to attract the heart of *Kṛshṇa*, *Satyabhāmā* ought to let him understand that she adored him with all her heart by promptly, when she saw him enter her chamber, offering him a seat and water to wash his feet; and even if he ordered a maidservant to do anything, she ought to get up and do it herself; not to blab of whatever he should speak before her; feed those that were dear to him, and keep herself aloof from those that were hostile to him; not to stay or converse in private even with her sons *Pradyumna* and *Çāmba*; and shun wicked women (III, **234**).—§ 511: Then *Kṛshṇa* bade farewell to the *Pāṇḍavas* and to *Mārkaṇḍeya*, etc., and called for *Satyabhāmā*. *Satyabhāmā* comforted *Draupadī*, saying that she would soon recover her ancient happiness, and relating of *Prativindhya*, *Çrutasoma*, and *Çrutakarman* (her son by *Arjuna*), and *Çatānīka* (her son by *Nakula*), and *Çrutasena* (her son by *Sahadeva*), that they were well and skilled in weapons and, like *Abhimanyu*, delighted with staying at *Dvāravatī*, and were loved by *Subhadrā*, *Pradyumna*, *Kṛshṇa*, with his son *Bhānu*, etc., and her mother-in-law, and all the *Andhakas* and *Vṛshṇis*, with *Rāma*, etc. Then *Satyabhāmā* mounted the chariot of *Kṛshṇa* and they set out for his city (III, **235**).

Draupadī - Satyabhāmayoḥ saṃvāda(ḥ). § 10 (Parvasaṅgr.): I, **2**, 324 (*parva*, i.e. Draupadī-Satyabhāma-saṃvādaparvan).

Draupadīsuta, pl. ("the sons of Draupadī") = Draupadeya, pl.: VII, 1179.

Draviḍa, pl. (°*āḥ*), a people. § 284 (Sahadeva): II, **31**, 1174 (in the south, vanquished by Sahadeva on his digvijaya).—§ 400 (Tīrthayātrāp.): III, **118**, †10217.—§ 569 (Bhagavadyānap.): V, **140**β, 4751.—§ 571 (Ulūkadūtāgamanap.): V, **160**γ, †5510 (in the army of Duryodhana); **161**, †5555 (do.).—§ 739 (Ānuçāsanik.): XIII, **35**ε, 2158 (had become çūdras—*vṛshalatvam anuprāptāḥ*).—§ 782*c* (Arjuna Kārtavīrya): XIV, **29**γ, 832 (°*ābhīrāḥ*, had become çūdras—*vṛshalatāṃ gatāḥ*).—§ 785 (Anugītāp.): XIV, **83**, 2476. Cf. next.

Drāviḍa, pl. (°*āḥ*), a people = Draviḍa, pl. § 223 (Vāsishṭha): I, **175**, 6683 (created from the udder of Vasishṭha's cow).—§ 287 (Rājasūyikap.): II, **34**, 1271 (came to the rājasūya of Yudhishṭhira).—§ 342 (Indralokābhigamanap.): III, **51**, 1988 (had been present at the rājasūya of Yudhishṭhira).—§ 556 (Sañjayayānap.): V, **22**, †656 (*senānugān D°āṃç cakre*, sc. Arjuna).—§ 574 (Jambūkh.): VI, **9**ν, 366 (among the peoples of the south).—§ 604 (Karṇap.): VIII, **5**ζ, 137 (had been slain by Savyasācin, i.e. Arjuna).—§ 605 (do.): VIII, **11**ββ, 454 (in the army of Yudhishṭhira).—§ 608 (do.): VIII, **49**τ, 2304 (do.).—§ 739 (Ānuçāsanik.): XIII, **33**a, 2104 (have been degraded to çūdras — *vṛshalatvaṃ parigatāḥ*). Cf. the prec.

Draviṇa, son of the Vasu Dhara. § 116 (Vasu, pl.): I, **66,** 2585.

Draviṇādhipati = Kubera, q.v.

Draviṇaprada = Vishṇu (1000 names).

Dravyakarmasamārambha = Çiva (1000 names [1]).

Droṇa,[1] the preceptor of the Dhārtarāshṭras and the Pāṇḍavas, Dhṛshṭadyumna, etc., son of Bharadvāja, husband of Kṛpī, and father of Açvatthāman. § 4 (Anukram.): I, **1,** 138, †186, †194, †196, †199 (*Ācāryaṃ*), †201.—§ 9 (Parvasaṅgr.): I, **2,** 300.—§ 11 (do.): I, **2,** 537.—§ 83 (Ādivaṃçāvatāraṇa): I, **63,** 2436 (father of Açvatthāman), 2438 (Dhṛshṭadyumna was born for the destruction of *D.*).—§ 130 (Aṃçāvat.): I, **67,** 2705 (*Bhāradvājaṃ*, born from a portion of Bṛhaspati), 2707 (*Dhanurvede Vede ca yaṃ taṃ Vedavido viduḥ varishṭhaṃ*). —§ 199 (Sambhavap.): *Bhīshma* prevailed upon *D.* to accept the Pāṇḍavas and the Kauravas as his pupils in the *Dhanurveda*: I, **130,** 5096 (*Bhāradvājāya*).—§ 200 (do.): Janamejaya said: "Tell me about the birth of *Droṇa* and of his son *Açvatthāman*." Vaiçampāyana said: The ṛshi *Bharadvāja* who dwelt at *Gaṅgādvāra* one day saw the Apsaras *Ghṛtācī* coming from her bath; then his seed came out, but was preserved by him in a vessel (*droṇa*); from that seed sprang *D.*, who studied the *Vedas* and the *Vedāṅgas*. *Bharadvāja* had taught *Agniveça* the use of the *Āgneya* weapon, and the muni who had sprung from Fire (i.e. Agniveça) now taught it to *D.*: I, **130,** 5100, 5106.—§ 201 (do.): *D.* was a friend of Drupada (q.v.). Droṇa remained in the hermitage of his father and practised austerities. With *Kṛpī Çāradvatī* he had the son *Açvatthāman* (*b*). *D.* studied the *Dhanurveda*. About this time *Rāma Jāmadagnya* desired to distribute his wealth among the brahmans, and *Droṇa* (of the race of *Aṅgiras*, v. 5122) with his disciples set out for the mountain Mahendra to have his share in the wealth and learn from Rāma the *Dhanurveda*, the use of celestial weapons, and the *nītiçāstra*. When he arrived, *Rāma* had already given his wealth to the brahmans and the earth to *Kaçyapa*; he then asked *D.* to choose either his body or his weapons. *Droṇa* accepted the weapons and the *Dhanurveda*, and then repaired to *Drupada*: I, **130,** 5110, 5114, 5122, 5124, 5130, (5131).—§ 202 (do.): As *Drupada* rebuked him for calling him his friend, *D.*, filled with wrath, went to Hāstinapura, where he for some time lived privately in the house of *Kṛpa* (his brother-in-law), while *Açvatthāman*, being unknown, taught the *Pārthas* (i.e. the Pāṇḍavas) the use of arms. One day, when *D.* had by means of blades of grass, which were consecrated by mantras, recovered a ball which the princes had lost in a well, and, by means of an arrow, his ring which he had thrown into the well, he was called to *Bhīshma*, whom he told that he had applied to *Drupada* in order to obtain milk for *Açvatthāman* (*b*), but had been rebuked by him. *Bhīshma* asked *D.* to make the princes accomplished in arms: I, **131,** 5136, 5155, 5158, (5160), 5162, 5164, 5167, (5168), 5170, 5171, (5172), 5177, 5188.—§ 203 (do.): *Bhīshma* presented *D.* with a pretty house, etc., and gave the *Dhārtarāshṭras* and the *Pāṇḍavas* to him as his pupils. *Arjuna* (*b*) became the foremost of *D.'s* pupils, even superior to *Açvatthāman* (*c*). Also the *Vṛshṇis* and the *Andhakas* and princes from various countries became his pupils. Even *Karṇa* came to learn the *Dhanurveda*; he, supported by *Duryodhana*, frequently defied *Arjuna*: I, **132,** 5211, 5214, (5216), 5219, 5220, 5223, 5225, 5228, 5230, 5231, 5236, (5237), 5238, 5239.—§ 204 (Ekalavya): I, **132,** 5241, 5243, 5246, 5255 (°*çishyaṃ*, i.e. Ekalavya), 5256, 5260, 5262, 5263, 5264, 5266, 5269 (*D.* asked the thumb of the right hand of *Ekalavya* as his tutorial fee, in order that *Ekalavya* might not surpass the Pāṇḍavas). — § 205 (Sambhavap.): The foremost pupils of *Droṇa* were *Duryodhana*, *Bhīmasena*, *Açvatthāman* (*b*), *Nakula* (*c*) and *Sahadeva* (*c*), *Yudhishṭhira* (*d*), and *Arjuna* (*e*). The *Dhārtarāshṭras* became very jealous of *Bhīma* and *Arjuna*: I, **132,** 5270.—§ 206 (do.): One day *D.* caused an artificial bird to be placed on the top of a tree, and first repeatedly asked *Yudhishṭhira*, when he stood aiming at the bird, what he did see. He answered that he saw the tree, *D.*, his brothers, and the bird. *D.* reproachingly told him to stand apart. Then *D.* repeated the experiment with his other pupils with the same result (I, **132**). At last *Arjuna's* turn came; he said first that he saw only the vulture, and then that he saw only its head, and when *D.* gave the order he struck off the head of the bird with his shaft: I, **132,** 5276, (5278), 5282, (5284), 5286; **133,** 5289, 5292, 5293, 5294, 5296.—§ 207 (do.): *Arjuna* rescued the life of *D.* by shooting with five arrows an alligator in the *Gaṅgā*, which had seized the thigh of *D.* *D.* gave *Arjuna* the weapon *Brahmaçiras* on condition that he should not use it against a human foe, as it might consume the whole universe (I, **133**): I, **133,** 5300, 5303.—§ 208 (Astradarçana): I, **134,** 5312; **135,** (5350), 5352, 5376; **136,** 5384, 5390, 5399; **137,** 5433, 5439 (the disciples of *D.* displayed their prowess in the use of arms).—§ 209 (Drupadaçāsana): I, **138,** 5445, 5447, 5454, 5466, 5502, 5503, 5511, 5513, 5515, 5516 (assisted by his pupils, *D.* vanquished *Drupada*, but restored the half of his kingdom to him, and thenceforth he himself ruled the other half, residing in Ahicchatra).—§ 210*c* (Arjuna): I, **139,** 5523, 5524, 5529, 5533 (*D.* had obtained the *Brahmaçiras* from Agniveça and given it to Arjuna (cf. § 207); Arjuna promised to fight with *D.* [in the great battle]).—§ 213 (Jatugṛhap.): I, **142,** 5688, 5691, 5692; **143,** 5707; **145,** 5735; **150,** 5860.—§ 216 (Caitrarathap.): I, **165,** 6326 (preceptor of Dhṛshṭadyumna).—§ 217 (do.): I, **166,** 6332, 6334, 6335, 6336, (6338), 6339, 6340, 6345, 6347, 6349, (6350), 6352, 6354 (repetition of the history of *D.* from his birth to the division of Drupada's kingdom, cf. §§ 200–9). — § 218 (Draupadīsambhava): I, **167,** 6358, 6359, 6366, 6377, 6378, 6380, 6385 (°*āntakaṃ*), 6386, 6397 (°*vadhāya*), 6409 (Drupada performed a sacrifice in order to obtain a son who might slay *D.*; then Dhṛshṭadyumna arose from the fire. *D.* became his preceptor).—§ 221 (Caitrarathap.): I, **170,** 6465 (had learnt the use of the *Āgneya* weapon from *Agniveça*, and again taught it to *Arjuna*).—§ 231 (Svayaṃvarap.): I, **184,** 6932 (*Dhṛshṭadyumnasya* . . . *D°çatroḥ*).—§ 234 (do.): I, **190,** 7116.—§ 241 (Vidurāgamanap.): I, **202,** 7439; **204,** (7460).—§ 243 (do.): I, **204,** (7485); **205,** 7490; **206,** 7518 (*ṛshiḥ*), 7536 (*Bhāradvājaḥ*). — § 244 (Rājyalābhap.): I, **207,** 7557.—§ 286 (Rājasūyikap.): II, **33,** 1259.—§ 287 (do.): II, **34,** 1267 (came to the rājasūya of Yudhishṭhira). —§ 288 (do.): II, **35,** 1287, 1291.—§ 289 (Arghāharaṇap.): II, **37,** 1345.—§ 290 (Çiçupālavadhap.): II, **44***a*, 1530, 1532 (°*sya hi samaṃ yuddhe na paçyāmi narādhipaṃ*).—§ 292 (Rājasūyikap.): II, **45***a*, 1608 (Sahadeva accompanied *D.* and his son).—§ 294 (Dyūtap.): II, **48,** 1712 (*saha putreṇa*, among the allies of Duryodhana); **49,** 1782.—§ 298 (do.): II, **58,** 2014; **60,** 2052 (present at the game); **65,** 2181.—§ 299 (do.): II, **67,** †2237.—§ 301 (do.): II, **69,** 2359; **70,** 2378; **71,** †2402.—§ 302 (Anudyūtap.): II, **74,** 2476.—§ 305 (do.): II, **78,** 2561, 2583; **79,** 2609.—§ 306 (do.): II, **80,** 2655, 2656 (all. to § 218), 2667 (*Dhṛshṭadyumno D°mṛtyur iti viprathitaṃ vacaḥ*), 2670.—§ 307 (do.): II, **81,** 2677, 2696.—§ 308 (Āraṇyakap.): III, **1,** 12.—§ 313 (do.): III, **8,** 316, 322.—§ 314 (do.): III, **9,** 324 (had not wished the game).—§ 315 (do.): III, **10,** 347.—§ 317 (Arjunābhigamanap.): III, **12,** 594 (Dhṛshṭadyumna vows to slay *D.*).—§ 318 (do.): III, **13,** 599.—§ 328 (Kāmyakavanapr.): III, **36,** 1419 (will fight with the Pāṇḍavas), 1425.—§ 329 (do.): III, **36,** 1435.—§ 330 (Indradarçana): III, **37,** 1459 (the fourfold Dhanurveda dwells in Droṇa, etc.).—§ 333*c* (Brahmaçiras): III, **40,** 1645, 1648.—§ 339 (Indralokābhigamanap.): III, **47,** 1904.—§ 340 (do.): III, **48,** 1922.—§ 377 (Dhaumyatīrthak.): III, **86,** 8282 (*Bhīshma-D°āv atirathau*).—§ 401 (Balarāma): III, **119,** †10245 (*vipraḥ*).—§ 402 (Tīrthayātrāp.): III, **120,** †10269, †10274 (*°ṃ ca Bhīshmaṃ ca mahārathau*).—§ 446 (Nivātakavacayuddhap.): III, **174,** 12276.—§ 512 (Ghoshayātrāp.): III, **249,** 15084.—§ 513 (do.): III, **252,** 15165 (Asuras will possess *D.*, etc.: *Bhīshma-D°-Kṛpādīṃç ca pravekshyanty apare 'surāḥ*), 15191 (*Bhīshma-D°-Kṛpādyāç ca Dānavakrāntacetasaḥ*).—§ 515 (Karṇadigvijaya): III, **253,** 15209; **254,** 15261.—§ 516 (Duryodhanayajña): III, **256,** 15302; **257,** 15332.—§ 517 (Ghoshayātrāp.): III, **257,** 15350.—§ 546 (Kuṇḍalāharaṇap.): III, **302,** 16985 (had been the preceptor of Karṇa in the use of arms).—§ 547 (Karṇa): III, **309,** 17169 (do.), 17170 (do.).—§ 552 (Goharaṇap.): IV, **25,** 867; **27,** 902; **28,** 915 (*brāhmaṇaḥ*); **30,** 986 (*Ācāryaḥ*); **35*a*,** 1150 (took part in the robbing of Virāṭa's kine); **36,** 1176 (*saha putreṇa*); **37,** 1224 (*Bhīshma-D°mukhān Kurūn*); **38,** 1238 (*saputreṇa*), 1243; **39,** 1286 (*Bhīshma-D°mukhāḥ . . . Kuravaḥ*), 1302; **45δ,** 1433; **46,** (1460); **47,** 1471, 1488, 1494; **49,** 1550; **50,** 1575; **51,** 1592 (*Brahmāstraṃ Brahma Vedāç ca naitad anyatra dṛçyate | anyatra Bhāratācāryāt D°āt purushasattamāt*), 1593 (*Vedāntāç ca Purāṇāni itihāsaṃ purātanaṃ | Jāmadagnyam ṛte, rājan, ko D°ād adhiko bhavet*), 1599, (1600); **52,** 1624; **53,** 1632, (1633), 1643; **54,** †1688; **55,** 1732, 1740 (on his standard was a waterpot (*kamaṇḍalu*) of gold), 1742, 1748 (*°sya çishyāṇāṃ*); **58,** 1823, 1826, 1834, 1838, 1839, 1843, 1844, 1849, 1859, 1862, 1865, 1868, 1873, 1877, 1882, 1884, 1885, 1886, 1888, 1893, 1894, 1899 (on *D.'s* standard there was seen a golden altar decked with flags; *D.* fought with *Arjuna*); **59,** 1908; **63,** 2021, 2024 (*rathināṃ varaḥ*); **66,** †2109 (protects Duryodhana), †2131; **68,** 2168, 2201, 2203, 2235 (*°ena . . . samāgamaḥ*); **69,** 2244.—§ 554 (Sainyodyogap.): V, **2β,** †31 (*saputraṃ*); **3,** 52; **4,** 65, 89 (*rathināṃ varaḥ*); **5,** 95 (*ācāryayoḥ sakhā cāsi D°sya ca Kṛpasya ca*, sc. Drupada); **6,** 118.—§ 556 (Sañjayayānap.): V, **22,** †668 (Sātyaki had obtained arms from *D.*, etc.); **23δ,** †694 (*saputraḥ*); **25θ,** †733 (among the allies of the Kurus); **26,** †759; **27,** †790 (*sahaputraḥ*); **30ξ,** †878 (*Ācarya ishṭo nayago vidheyo Vedān abhīpsan brahmacaryaṃ cacāra | yo 'stram catushpāt punar eva cakre*).—§ 559 (Prajāgarap.): V, **37,** †1376 (*kopaḥ . . . D°sya*).—§ 561 (Yānasandhip.): V, **47*a*,** 1796; **48,** †1849 (had imparted to Dhṛshṭadyumna the mysteries of the science of arms), †1850, †1897 (*sahaputrāya*), †1916 (*saputraḥ*); **49,** 1965; **51,** 2062 (*vipraḥ*); **52,** 2088; **55,** 2149, 2159, (λ), 2185, 2189, 2191 (*Brahmarshер Bharadvājāt D°o drauṇyāṃ ajāyata*, cf. § 200), 2192 (father of Açvatthāman), 2196, 2201, (ν), 2205; **57,** 2251 (headed by Dhṛshṭadyumna the Draupadeyas will proceed against Droṇa), (π), 2268, (ρ), 2281, (σ), 2290; **58τ,** 2300, (υ), 2304; **59,** 2333, 2345; **60,** 2368, (χ), 2375; **61ω,** 2409 (*astreshu yat prajānanti*, sc. Droṇa, etc.); **62,** †2416; **63,** 2432; **64,** 2478 (all. to § 552); **65δδ,** 2493; **66εε,** 2501.—§ 562 (Bhagavadyānap.): V, **73,** 2681, 2685, 2693 (all. to Dyūtaparvan); **80ζ,** 2859; **83ι,** 2966, 2989; **85κ,** 3023; **89λ,** 3103, 3105, 3113, 3117; **91σ,** 3271; **92τ,** 3284, 3285; **94,** 3364, 3365, 3368; **95υ,** 3402.—§ 567 (do.): V, **124β,** 4137, (δ), 4170; **125,** 4194; **126,** 4214; **127,** 4246; **128,** 4277, 4282, (θ), 4284, 4291; **129λ,** 4329, 4330, 4346, (μ), 4358, 4360; **131,** 4431, (π), 4453, (ρ), 4457.—§ 569 (do.): V, **138,** 4676; **139,** (4707); **141,** 4795 (*°çishyāḥ*), 4796, 4803 (*yadā D°ñ ca Bhīshmañ ca Pāñcālyau patayishyataḥ*); **142,** 4824, (ζ), 4828; **143κ,** 4875; **144,** 4899 (*Acāryaḥ*); **148,** 5002, (5003), 5015, 5018; **150,** 5077, 5082.—§ 570 (Sainyaniryāṇap.): V, **151,** 5110, 5112 (all. to § 218), 5114, 5121 (*jajñe D°vināçāya*, sc. Dhṛshṭadyumna, all. to § 218); **154,** 5226; **155θ,** 5274; **157,** 5327 (*°āntahetor utpanno ya iddhāj jātavedasaḥ*, sc. Dhṛshṭadyumna, all. to § 218); **158μ,** 5372, 5376 (*°ṃ vyapadiçan çishyo*, i.e. Arjuna).—§ 571 (Ulūkadūtāgamanap.): V, **160,** 5458 (*°ād astrāṇi samprāpya*, sc. Yudhishṭhira), 5483, 5503 (*Çacīpatisamaṃ*), 5505, 5529 (*°grāhadurāsadaṃ*, sc. *purushodadhim*, i.e. the army of Duryodhana); **161,** 5548 (= v. 5503), 5550 (cf. v. 5505), 5574 (= v. 5529); **163,** †5653 (*°ṃ ṛte*), 5663, 5689 (Dhṛshṭadyumna once more vows to slay *D.*); **164,** 5705, (ε), 5711 (Dhṛshṭadyumna reserved *D.* as his own share in the battle).—§ 572 (Rathātirathasaṅkhyānap.): V, **165,** 5726, 5734 (*°çishyāḥ*, i.e. the Dhārtarāshṭras); **167,** 5775 (*°enānugṛhītaç ca divyair astraiḥ*, sc. Açvatthāman); **168,** 5815 (*sarvaçastrabhṛtāṃ varaḥ*); **171,** 5896 (*°çishyaḥ*, i.e. Dhṛshṭadyumna), 5914 (Çikhaṇḍin became the disciple of *D.*).—§ 573 (Ambopākhyānap.): V, **189,** 7410 (do.); **192,** 7547 (do.); **193,** 7572 (*Aṅgirasāṃ varaḥ*; C. by error *Āṅgi°*), 7573; **194,** 7584 (promises to annihilate the army of Yudhishṭhira within a month), (β), 7594, 7599.—§ 576 (Bhagavadgītāp.): VI, **14,** 525; **17,** 660 (*Ācāryamukhyasya*, his standard [bore the device of] a golden altar (*vedī*) with a waterpot (*kamaṇḍalu*)), 675; **20,** †751 (rode in a golden chariot (*rukmarathaḥ*) with red horses (*çoṇair hayaiḥ*)); **21,** 767; **25,** 855; **26,** 882; **35,** †1272, †1280.—§ 577 (Bhīshmavadhap.): VI, **43β,** 1549, 1579, (1581), (1587), (1590), (1592) (Yudhishṭhira asked Droṇa to tell by which means he could be put to death; *D.* answered that he could not be slain if he did not give himself up to death (*prāyagataṃ*) and drop his weapon; this he would do if he heard something very disagreeable from a trustworthy person).—§ 578 (do.): VI, **44,** 1658 (*°çishyāḥ*); **45**[8], 1700, 1703 (encounter with Dhṛshṭadyumna); **48λ,** 1963; **50,** 2052, 2053, 2069 (*ahaṃ D°āntakaḥ, Pārtha! vihitaḥ Çambhunā purā*, says Dhṛshṭadyumna), (ο), 2070; **51,** 2100.—§ 579 (do.): VI, **52β,** 2134, 2143, (δ), 2144, (ε), 2148, 2150, 2156 (*rathināṃ vare*), 2193; **53,** 2194, 2198, 2200, 2207, 2209, 2210, 2211, 2212, 2215, 2217, 2224, 2229, 2232 (*rathināṃ varaḥ*, encounter with Dhṛshṭadyumna); **55**[19], 2376, 2400 (*Ācāryasattamaṃ*).—§ 580 (do.): VI, **57ι,** 2452, 2459; **58**[5], 2472, 2473 (*°ānīkaṃ*), ([7]), 2481, 2483, ([9]), 2489, (λ), 2496, 2497; **59,** 2551, (μ), †2583, †2593, †2594, (ο), †2643, (ρ), †2648.—§ 581 (do.): VI, **60*a*,** †2652, (β), †2672; **64π,** 2872; **65,** 2910, 2922, (ν), 2928.—§ 582 (do.): VI,

69, 3076, 3077, 3079, (β), 3080, 3082, 3085, 3086; **71**ε, 3141; **72**ζ, 3163, 3171 (encounter with Dhṛshṭadyumna), 3195; **73**, 3209 (Açvatthāman had obtained all weapons (*astragrāmam*) from *D.*), 3210 (°*syātipriyaḥ sutaḥ*, i.e. Açvatthāman).—§ 583 (do.): VI, **75**θ, 3304, 3305 (*Bhāradvājasya*), 3306, 3309; **76**ι, 3329; **77**, 3353, (⁶), 3383, 3384, 3385 (defeated Drupada), (⁷), 3386, 3387, (⁹), 3401, 3404, 3405, 3409, 3410 (encounter with Dhṛshṭadyumna, etc.).—§ 584 (do.): VI, **81***a*, 3532; **82**, 3592, 3594 (encounter with Virāṭa), 3600 (slew Çaṅkha, the son of Virāṭa); **86**, 3829, (ζ), 3838.—§ 585 (do.): VI, **87**, 3854; **88**κ, 3926; **89**, 3931, (λ), 3933, 3942, 3952, 3954, (π), 3969; **90**, 4058, 4060; **92**χ, 4118; **94***aa*, 4225; **95**γγ, 4244; **96**, 4338, 4352, 4353, 4354, 4355 (encounter with Bhīmasena); **97**κκ, 4407; **98**, 4457 (all. to § 552), (νν), 4489.—§ 586 (do.): VI, **99**β, 4503; **100**η, 4545, 4555; **101**θ, 4590, 4641, 4642; **102**, 4643, 4646, 4648, 4650, 4651, 4662, 4663 (encounter with Arjuna); **103**ξ, 4724; **104**, 4745, 4751 (encounter with Drupada); **106**, 4806, 4808, 4836.—§ 587 (do.): VI, **108**, 5005 (*putraç cāsya*), (δ), 5050; **111**, 5190, 5191; **112**, 5200 (became dejected seeing the bad omens); **113**, 5239; **114**, 5317, 5322 (pierced Bhīmasena); **115**ξ, 5357 (*saha putreṇa*); **116**, 5420, 5421, 5422, 5423, 5424, 5425, 5426, 5427 (encounter with Dhṛshṭadyumna); **119**ψ, 5583; **120**, 5712 (°*ānīkam*), 5714, 5715.—§ 588 (do.): VI, **121***a*, †5707.—§ 589 (Droṇābhishekap.): VII, **1**, 4; **5**, 150 (*çastrabhṛtām varaḥ*), 151 (*Çukrāṅgirasadarçanāt*), 152 (Karṇa proposes to choose *D.* to become the generalissimo of Duryodhana's army); **6**, 155, 166, 168; **7**, 169, 173, 174, 175, 177, 192, 212, 213, 214, 215, 216, 217, 218, 220, 221 (*D.* was installed as the generalissimo of Duryodhana's army, arrayed the troops, and afflicted the Pāñcālas headed by Dhṛshṭadyumna); **8**, 224, 232, 237, 238, 241, 243, 244, 245, †247, †249, †251, †252, 253 (brief description of the slaughter of Droṇa); **9**, 261, 262, 266, 267 (*astraṃ caturvidhaṃ vīre yasminn āsīt pratishṭhitam*), 269, 271, (ι), 273, 282, [283 (*Rukmaratham*)], 285, 286, 297, 298, 301, 302; **10**κ, 312, 318, 330, 335, 341, 347, 348, 349, 351, 355, 356, 357, 359, 360, 362, 364, 366, 367, 368, 375, 377 (enumeration of the warriors who attacked Droṇa); **11**, 425 (*vadhaḥ . . . D°sya*), 427 (*Bhīshma-D°au hatau*), 428 (*Bhīshma-D°vadhena*), 430 (*Bhīshma-D°au nipātitau*).—§ 590 (do.): VII, **12**, 434, 446, 452, (453), 462, 463 (the narrative in detail begins; *D.* promises to seize Yudhishṭhira); **13**, 465, 468, 469, 471, 475, 477, 484, 485, 491 (the battle begins); **14**, 495, 512, 514, 520; **16**β, 633, 636, 638, 639, 641, 642, 652, 653, 654, 658, 659, 663, 668 (*D.* seeks to seize Yudhishṭhira, of whose protectors *D.* slays several).—§ 591 (Saṃçaptakavadhap.): VII, **17**, 674, 683, 714, 715.—§ 592 (do.): VII, **19**, 790 (rushes against Yudhishṭhira); **20**, 794 (formed a garuḍavyūha), 806, 815, 816, 817, 818, 821, 822, 855 (rushes against Yudhishṭhira); **21**, 856, 858, 860, 863, 864, 866, 867, 868, 869, 870, 871, 872, 873, 876, 877, 879, 880, 882, 889, 891, 898, 900, 901, 903, 905, 906, 912, 913, 914, 915, 917 (*D.* slays Vṛka, Satyajit, Çatānīka, Kshema, Vasudāna, etc., who protected Yudhishṭhira); **22**, 922, 926, 927, 930, 931, 933, 934, 936, 944, 947, 948, 949; **23**, 950, (ο), 952, 989 (*yaḥ . . . D°m aṃçam akalpayat*, i.e. Dhṛshṭadyumna), 1017 (Sāraṅgadhvaja had obtained weapons from *D.*), 1020, 1044, 1045 (enumeration of the warriors who rushed against *D.*); **24**σ, 1054, 1055, 1056; **25**, 1066, 1067, 1070, 1074, 1077, 1088, 1096, 1097, 1102, 1104, 1106, 1111, 1113, 1117, 1123, 1127 (enumeration of the warriors who protected Droṇa); **28**, 1226 (°*ānīkāya*), 1227; **30**, 1331, 1335; **31**, 1346, 1349, 1350, 1351, 1354, 1359, 1360, 1361; **32**, 1374, 1377, 1381, 1382, 1408, (ω), 1410, 1411, 1412, 1414, (εε), 1441.—§ 593 (Abhimanyuvadhap.): VII, **33**, 1453, 1457, 1468, 1470 (*D.* had failed to seize Yudhishṭhira); **34**, 1502; **35**, 1514, 1515, 1516, 1517, 1518, 1523, 1524, 1530, 1535, 1537 (Abhimanyu proceeds against the army of *D.*); **36**, 1538, 1541, 1542, 1546, 1547, 1548, †1550, 1553; **37**, 1586, (θ), 1589, 1593, (ι), 1600, (κ), 1609; **39**μ, 1650, 1659, 1664; **40**, 1696, 1703, 1704; **43**, 1781; **46**τ, 1838, (υ), 1851; **47**φ, 1864, 1868, 1877; **48**, 1901, 1902, 1903, 1909, 1922, 1924; **49**, 1948 (°*Karṇamukhaiḥ shaḍbhir Dhārtarāshṭrair mahārathaiḥ*); **51**, 1985 (°*ānīkam*), 1988 (°*ānīka*°).—§ 596 (Pratijñāp.): VII, **72**, 2497 (°*ena cakravyūho nirmitaḥ*), 2525; **73**, 2567, 2569, 2575 (cf. v. 1948), 2589; **74***a*, 2619, (β), 2629, 2633, 2634, (2637) (comforts Jayadratha); **75**, 2671 (*sahaputreṇa*), 2674 (description of his vyūha); **76**, 2681, 2686; **79**, 2798, 2799 (will protect Jayadratha).—§ 598 (Jayadrathavadhap.): VII, **85***a*, 3028, (β), 3037, (γ), 3043, 3054; **86**, 3074; **87**, 3087, 3096, 3109, 3111 (description of his vyūha), 3116, 3117 (*b*: *D.* was clad in white armour and had an excellent turban, and stood stretching his large bow like Antaka himself in wrath. *D.*'*s* chariot had a beautiful standard and red horses yoked to it (*çoṇahayam*), and his banner bore the device of a sacrificial altar (*vedī*) and a black deerskin), 3118.—§ 599 (do.): VII, **90**, 3184, 3216; **91**, 3217 (°*ānīkam*), 3218, 3224, 3225, 3226, 3227, 3229, 3232, 3238, 3239, 3240, 3241, 3242, 3244, 3245, 3247, 3248, 3249 (encounter with Arjuna); **92**, 3261, 3267, 3270, 3271, 3273, 3275, 3276, 3277 (do.); **94**, 3409, 3411, 3412, 3417, (3427), (3441), 3447, (3449), (3473), 3478 (*D.* cases Duryodhana in an invulnerable armour); **95**, 3487, 3490, 3491, 3497, 3498, 3500, 3501, 3504, 3510, 3511, 3512, 3518, 3520, 3521, 3523; **96**, 3543 (*Bhāradvājam*), 3544, 3567; **97**, 3575, 3578, 3579, 3593, 3595, 3597, 3599, 3600, 3601, 3605, 3606, 3608; **98**, 3610, 3615, 3619, 3620, 3624, 3641, 3644, 3646, 3647, 3649, 3652, 3655, 3662, 3663 (encounter with Sātyaki); **101**, 3769, 3772, 3773, 3774, 3775, 3784, 3785, 3786, 3788, 3789, 3791, 3796, 3799; **103**, 3853, 3854, 3858 (all. to ch. **94**); **106**, 3966, 3967, 3969, 3970, 3975, 3982, 3983, 3984, 3985, 3986, 3991, 3995, 3997, 3999, 4000, 4001, 4004, 4008, 4009 (encounter with Yudhishṭhira); **107**, 4014 (°*ānīkam*), 4021, 4051 (rushed against Sātyaki); **108**, 4094 (°*ānīkam*); **110**, 4135, 4136, 4138, 4140, 4149, 4150, 4153, 4154, 4156, 4159, 4161, 4162, 4163, 4164, 4165, 4166, 4168, 4202, 4204, 4213, 4219, 4228 (encounter with Sātyaki, etc.); **111**, 4251, 4252, 4254, 4257, 4265, 4273, 4285, 4286, 4288 (*esha D°vināçāya samutpanno hutāçanāt*, sc. Dhṛshṭadyumna, all. to § 218), 4290; **112**, 4300 (°*ānīkam*), (φ), 4329, 4360; **113**, 4373, 4392, 4394, 4396, 4397, 4399, 4400, 4401, 4407, 4415, 4434 (encounter with Sātyaki); **114**, 4454, 4479, 4482, 4483, 4484; **115**, 4551 (°*ānīka*°), 4554 (°*ānīkasya . . . Rukmarathaḥ*), 4598, 4600, 4601 (followed by the Kurus, *D.* attacked Sātyaki); **116***aa*, 4603; **117**, 4649, 4650, 4653, 4654, 4656, 4657, 4659, 4660, 4664, 4666, 4669, 4670, 4672, 4674, 4676, 4678, 4679 (C. by error *Dra*°), 4681, 4683 (defeated by Sātyaki); **118**, †4684; **119**, 4705 (°*ānīka*°), 4707, (ββ), 4720 (*rathināṃ çreshṭhaḥ*); **120**, 4765 (°*ānīkam*); **121**, 4813, 4852, 4857 (*sarvaçastrabhṛtāṃ varam*), 4862, 4863; **122**, 4890, 4891, 4892, 4894, 4895, 4896, 4897, 4898, 4902, 4906, 4907, 4912, 4913,

4915, 4919, 4922, 4924, 4925, 4927, 4929, 4930, 4932 (slays Vīraketu, etc., fights with Dhṛshṭadyumna); **123,** 4953; **124,** 4979 (*vyūho . . . D°ena vihitaḥ*), 5011, 5015, 5016; **125,** 5017, 5023, 5024, 5026, 5028, 5029, 5031, 5033, 5034, 5035, 5036, 5040, 5041, 5042, 5043, 5044, 5045, 5046, 5055, 5057, 5058, 5059, 5060, 5061, 5062, 5063, 5064, 5065, 5066, 5070, 5071, 5073, 5074, 5077, 5078, 5080, 5084, 5089 (*ākarṇapālitaḥ çyāmo vayasāçītipañcakaḥ*), 5090, 5095 (*D.* slew Bṛhatkshattra, Dhṛshṭaketu with his son, the son of Jarāsandha, and Kshatradharman); **126,** 5098; **127,** 5147 (wishes to seize Yudhishṭhira), 5153, 5182, 5185, 5191, 5193, 5196, 5197, 5198, 5218 (Bhīmasena proceeds against the division of *D.*); **128,** 5220, 5230, 5232, 5234, 5235, 5236 (encounter with Bhīmasena); **130,** 5311, 5313, 5318, (5323); **131**ρρ, 5360; **135**υυ, 5546; **137,** 5652; **141**δδδ, 5857, (εεε), 5870, 5878 (wishes to seize Yudhishṭhira); **143**ηηη, 5956; **144,** 6025; **146,** 6292, 6294; **147,** 6313 (*°sya sakhā*, i.e. Kṛpa); **149**ωωω, 6485; **150**α, 6498, 6503; **151,** 6530, 6533, (6534), 6569; **152,** 6570, (δ), 6572, 6574, 6575, 6576, 6578, 6581, 6587, 6589, 6590.—§ 600 (Ghaṭotkacavadhap.): VII, **153,** 6636, 6638; **154,** 6642, 6648, 6649, 6651, 6652, 6653, 6654, 6655, 6662, 6675, 6679, 6681; **155**γ, 6695, 6696, 6699, 6701 (slew the Kaikeyas, Dhṛshṭadyumna's sons, and Çibi); **156,** 6759, 6760, 6766, 6767, 6768, 6769, 6771, 6772, 6773, 6774, 6775, 6776, 6777, 6778; **157,** 6952, 6953, 6959, 6961, 6963, 6964, 6969 (encounter with Yudhishṭhira, etc.); **158**ψ, 7030; **159,** 7055; **160,** 7177, 7178 (Dhṛshṭadyumna has vowed to slay *D.*); **161,** 7214, 7219, 7220; **162,** 7258, 7260, 7264, 7265, 7268, 7270, 7271, 7278 (encounter with Yudhishṭhira); **163**ηη, 7281, †7290, †7298; **164,** 7329, 7330, 7332, 7336, 7338, 7341, 7342, 7343, 7348; **165,** 7357, 7358, 7360, 7362, 7368, 7369, 7370, 7372, 7396; **166,** 7460; **167,** 7462, 7484, 7508; **168,** 7524; **169,** 7577 (*°ānīkāya*), 7578, 7579, 7580; **170,** 7609, 7610, 7611, 7612 (*Ācāryasattamam*), 7614, 7615, 7616, 7617, 7618, 7620, (λλ), 7624, 7626, 7627, 7663, 7666 (*°ānīkāya*); **171,** 7724, 7725, 7726, 7727, 7734; **172,** 7736, (ππ), 7745, 7747, 7748, 7749, 7756, 7758, 7761, 7763, 7765, 7766; **173,** 7797, 7804, 7833, 7838; **174,** 7853; **177**φφ, 8031, 8061 (*camūṃ D°puraskṛtāṃ*); **178,** 8085; **181**δδδ, 8229, 8246; **183,** 8306, 8307, 8308, 8328, 8331, 8335, 8340, 8341, 8343.—§ 601 (Droṇavadhap.): VII, **184,** 8365 (*tvaṃ hi D°vināçāya samutpanno hutāçanāt*, sc. Dhṛshṭadyumna, all. to § 218), 8370, 8372; **185,** 8419, 8427, 8440, 8456.—§ 602 (do.): VII, **186,** 8461, 8463, 8468, 8480, 8482, 8486, 8487, 8489, 8490, 8492, 8493, 8494, 8496, 8497, 8498, 8501, 8502, 8503, 8504, 8505, 8510, 8511, 8512, 8513 (*D.* arrayed the army, slew three grandsons of Drupada, and then Drupada and Virāṭa; Dhṛshṭadyumna then proceeded against *D.*); **187,** 8540, (ι), 8543, (κ), 8551 (encounter with Arjuna); **188,** 8597, 8601, 8602, 8603, 8605, 8606, 8608, 8613, 8616, 8621, 8626 (do.); **189,** 8632, 8634, 8642, 8644, 8645, 8688, 8689, 8691, 8692; **190,** 8694, 8695, 8696, 8698, 8700, 8702, 8709, 8711, 8713, 8716, 8717, 8718, 8719, 8723, 8726, 8729, 8730, 8734, 8737, 8739, 8740, 8741, 8745, 8747, 8751 (*D.* was falsely told that Açvatthāman had been slain in the battle; Yudhishṭhira certified the report and *D.* became cheerless); **191,** 8756 (*ya ishṭvā manujendreṇa Drupadena mahāmakhe labdho D°vināçāya*, i.e. Dhṛshṭadyumna), 8758, 8768, 8778, 8779, 8784, 8785, 8786, 8789, 8794, 8797, 8801 (encounter with Dhṛshṭadyumna); **192,** 8822, 8831, 8835, 8838, 8840, 8841, 8843, 8844, 8850, 8855, 8856, 8857, 8864, 8876, 8880, 8882, 8884 (believing Açvatthāman to have been slain, *D.* laid his weapon aside and sat down in yoga, and then proceeded to Brahmaloka; Dhṛshṭadyumna cut off *D.'s* head).—§ 603 (Nārāyaṇāstramokshap.): VII, **193,** 8893 (*hate*), 8906 (*nipātitam*), 8908 (do.), 8910 (do.), 8929 (*nipātitaḥ*), (δ), 8930, 8933, 8934, 8935, 8936, 8940, 8941, 8949 (brief description of the slaughter of *D.*); **194,** 8970, 8977 (*yathā D°sya Pāñcālyaḥ*, sc. *mṛtyuḥ*); **195,** 8998 (*keçagrahaṇam āptavān*, all. to § 602); **196,** 9038 (*Ācārye nihate*), 9047 (*hate*), 9051 (do.), 9057 (gave 1,000 kine to the brahmans upon the birth of Açvatthāman), 9063 (*nipātite*), 9074, 9078 (*ghātitaḥ*); **197,** 9106 (*hataḥ*), 9116 (*°çiraḥ*); **198**ξ, 9127 (*maharshitanaye*), 9129, 9155 (*nihataḥ*), 9159; **199,** 9204 (*°sya nidhanena*), 9223; **200,** 9289 (*hate*); **201,** 9395 (*°hantā*, i.e. Dhṛshṭadyumna), 9492 (*nipātite*), 9493 (*Brahmalokaṃ gataḥ*); **202,** 9494 (*nihate*), 9495 (do.). — § 604 (Karṇap.): VIII, **1,** 1 (*hate*), 2, 18 (*hatam*), 22; **2**γ, 30, 32, 34, 39 (*nihatam*), 40, 41 (*nihatam*), 44 (*hate*); **3**δ, 51 (do.), 54 (*hatam*), 58 (*nihate*); **5**ζ, 94 (*Rukmaratho hataḥ*), 95; **6,** 154 (had slain Satyajit), 155 (had slain the Pāñcālas), 156 (had slain Virāṭa and Drupada), 164 (had slain Maṇimat and Daṇḍadhāra), [165 (*Bhāradvājena*, had slain Aṃçumat)], 171 (had slain the two Rocamānas), 173 (had slain Purujit and Kuntibhoja), 176 (had slain Mitravarman and Kshatradharman), 178 (had slain Sucitra and Citravarman), 183 (had slain Suketu), 184 (had slain Satyadhṛti, Madirāçva, and Sūryadatta), 189 (had slain Vasudāna); **7,** 191 (*Bhīshma-D°au hatau*), †195; **9**θ, 262 (*°vadhena*), 288 (all. to § 602), 290 (*Bhīshma-D°au nipātitau*), 294, 295, 310, 341 (*Bhīshma-D°au nipātitau*), 342 (*hate*).—§ 605 (do.): VIII, **10,** 344 (*hate*), (κ), 362 (do.), 367 (*Bhīshma-D°au hatau*), 371, 381 (*hate*); **11,** 411, 436; **20**γγ, 772, 774; **26,** 1040 (*°sya nidhanāt*); **32**σ, 1332, 1333.—§ 607 (do.): VIII, **36**α, 1686; **37**γ, †1715, †1722, †1723, †1729, †1730; **41**ε, 1947, 1953.—§ 608 (do.): VIII, **55,** 2682 (*°çishyaḥ . . . Yudhishṭhiraḥ*); **56,** 2729 (*°hantāram*, i.e. Dhṛshṭadyumna), (οο), 2745; **59,** 2931 (*yathā*), 2937, 2940 (*nihataḥ*); **66**ιι, 3330; **72**υυυ, 3612; **73,** 3644 (*Bhīshma-D°au nipātitau*), 3645, 3646, 3675, 3679, 3680 (*hataḥ*), 3685 (*Bhīshma-D°au hatau*), 3692, 3706, 3713, 3722, 3736; **79**η', 4035; **87,** 4455 (worshipped in Heaven); **96,** 5013.—§ 609 (Çalyap.): IX, **2,** 87 (*nihataḥ*), 111 (*Bhīshma-D°au hatau*), 113 (*hataḥ*).—§ 610 (do.): IX, **4,** 197 (*hate*), 216; **6,** 306 (*ārādhya Tryambakaṃ yatnād vratair mahātapāḥ | ayonijāyām utpanno D°enāyonijena yaḥ*, i.e. Açvatthāman), 315; **7**τ, 340, (φ), 349 (*yathā*), 360.—§ 611 (do.): IX, **8,** 380 (*°sya*, sc. *patanam*), 383 (*hate*), (θ), 402; **16**σ, 811, 829; **19**γγ, 1001, (δδ), 1023; **24**νν, 1295 (*nihate*), 1306; **27**ττ, 1456 (*hataḥ*).—§ 612 (Hradapraveçap.): IX, **29**β, 1646; **30,** 1681 (so C., but read *Drauṇiḥ* with B.); **31**θ, 1789 (*saṃçānte*).—§ 613 (Gadāyuddhap.): IX, **32**β, 1836; **33**ι, 1934 (*hataḥ*).—§ 615 (do.): IX, **54**ν, 3060 (*hataḥ*); **56,** 3162 (do.); **61,** 3407, 3427 (C. by error *Drau°*), 3428 (*Bhīshma-D°au nipātitau*), (χ), 3447; **62**ψ, 3472, 3488; **63**ββ, 3548; **64**εε, 3589, 3593, 3612 (*svargatam*).—§ 616 (Sauptikap.): X, **4**δ, 166 (*hataḥ*).—§ 617 (Aishīkap.): X, **10**β, †560.—§ 617*b* (Brahmaçiras): X, **12,** 609, 614 (*Guruḥ*, *D.* had obtained the Brahmaçiras and given it to Arjuna and, but unwillingly, to Açvatthāman).—§ 617 (Aishīkap.): X, **14,** 671 (*astram . . . D°opadishṭam*, i.e. Brahmaçiras); **17**θ, 763.—§ 618 (Jalapradānikap.): XI, **1**β, 18, (γ), 30; **12**λ, 320; **13**μ, 346.—§ 619 (Strīvilāpap.): XI, **16**α, 447, 454;

20ε, 586, 598 (had slain Virāṭa); **23**θ, 660, 661, 663, 665, 668, 669, 670, 672, 674, 675, 676 (lamented for by his wife Kṛpī, etc.); **25**κ, 718, 719, 720, 722, 725, 726, 730, 735 (had slain the sons of Dhṛshṭadyumna, Drupada, and Dhṛshṭaketu).—§ 621 (Rājadh.): XII, **2**, 54 (preceptor of Karṇa), 57; **4**, 120, (ζ), 141.—§ 623 (do.): XII, **14a**, 403; **16**, 503.—§ 630 (do.): XII, **27**β, 819.—§ 637 (do.): XII, **42**γ, 1488 (his çrāddha is performed). — § 656b (Nakula): XII, **166**, 6127 (°*çishyaḥ*, i.e. Nakula).—§ 656 (Khaḍgotpattik.): XII, **166**, 6200 (received the sword from Bharadvāja, from *D.* it passed to Kṛpa).—§ 702 (Mokshadh.): XII, **297**δ, 10875 (*vadatāṃ varaḥ*, among the ṛshis who had obtained their position by way of penances). — § 779 (Açvamedhikap.): XIV, **12a**, 326. — § 785 (Anugītāp.): XIV, **60a**, 1775, (β), 1785, 1788, 1789, 1790 (brief description of the battle); **61**γ, 1821, 1822, (δ), 1825, 1827, 1830. —§ 787 (Āçramavāsap.): XV, **1**, 13 (*çyālo D°sya*, i.e. Kṛpa); **3**γ, 79; **10**ν, 332; **11**ο, 360, (π), 372, 378; **14**σ, 410 (among those whose çrāddha was performed).—§ 788 (do.): XV, **25**, †670 (°*ādibhiḥ*, had slain Abhimanyu).— § 789 (Putradarçanap.): XV, **29**γ, 797; **31**η, 858 (born from a portion of Bṛhaspati); **32**θ, 874 (among the dead warriors who, summoned by Vyāsa, arose from the Gaṅgā).— § 791 (do.): XV, **36a**, 989.—§ 795 (Svargārohaṇap.): XVIII, **3**, 95 (all. to § 602); **4**, 145 (seen by the side of Bṛhaspati in heaven); **5**λ, 148, 159 (after death *D.* entered Bṛhaspati).

Cf. also the following synonyms:—

Ācārya, Ācāryamukhya, q.v.
Bhāradvāja, Bharadvājasuta, Bharadvājātmaja, q.v.
Bhāratācārya, q.v.
***Çoṇāçva** ("having red horses"): IV, 1823. ***Çoṇāçvavāha** (do.): IV, 1677. ***Çoṇahaya** (do.): VII, 637.
Guru, q.v.
***Rukmaratha** ("having a golden chariot"): VII, 283, 488, 4554, 8911.

Droṇa², a çārṅgaka, a son of Mandapāla and Jaritā. § 259 (Çārṅgakop.): I, **230**, 8373 (*brahmavidāṃ varaḥ*, fourth son of Mandapāla and Jaritā); **232**, (8408), (8418), 8423, 8424 (*ṛshiḥ*), 8426, (8427); **233**, 8434.

Droṇa³, a mountain. § 709b (Sulabha-Janakas.): XII, **321a**, 12035 (accompanied Indra).

Droṇābhishecana(ṃ) ("the inauguration of Droṇa"). § 10 (Parvasaṅgr.): I, **2**, 338 (°*aṃ parva*, i.e. Droṇābhishekaparvan).

[Droṇābhishekaparvan] ("the section relating to the inauguration of Droṇa," the 71st of the minor parvans of Mbhbr.; cf. Droṇābhishecana). § 589: *Janamejaya* enquired of the state of *Dhṛtarāshṭra* on the receipt of intelligence of *Bhīshma's* death. *Vaiçampāyana's* answer: *Dhṛtarāshṭra* asked *Sañjaya* about what the *Kauravas* did after the fall of *Bhīshma*. *Sañjaya* mentioned the arrow-pillow, etc. (cf. § 587 foll.), and that the warriors once more went to battle. The *Kurus* desired to make *Karṇa* their generalissimo (mentioning his enmity with *Bhīshma*) (VII, **1**). *Karṇa* eulogised *Bhīshma*, and promised to be their leader, mentioning the prowess of *Yudhishṭhira*, etc. (**a**); he commanded his charioteer to make his chariot ready (VII, **2**). *Karṇa* waited upon *Bhīshma* (mentioning the danger to the *Kurus* from *Arjuna* with the *Gāṇḍīva*, etc.; *Arjuna's* battle with *Çiva*; *Kṛshṇa*; *Bhīshma's* battle with *Rāma*) (VII, **3**). *Bhīshma*, mentioning *Karṇa's* prowess against the *Kāmbojas*, etc. (β), urged him to fight for the victory of *Duryodhana*. Then *Karṇa* saluted *Bhīshma*, and, at his return, was worshipped by *Duryodhana* and the *Kauravas* (VII, **4**). *Duryodhana* asked *Karṇa's* advice as to who should become the generalissimo of the *Kuru* army. *Karṇa* proposed *Droṇa* (VII, **5**). *Duryodhana* requested *Droṇa* to take the command (VII, **6**). *Droṇa*, mentioning his knowledge of the *Veda* and the *Çaiva* weapon, etc., and his inability to slay *Dhṛshṭadyumna*, accepted the request. *Duryodhana* and the kings performed the inauguration of *Droṇa*, at which the army rejoiced. *Droṇa* arrayed the troops: the *Sindhu* king, etc. (γ), in the right wing, supported by *Çakuni*, etc.; *Kṛpa*, etc. (δ), in the left wing, supported by the *Kāmbojas*, etc. (ε); the *Madras*, etc. (ζ), in the rear; *Karṇa* at the head of all the bowmen. The array was in the form of a *çakaṭa* (cart). *Yudhishṭhira* disposed his troops in the form of a *krauñca* (crane), with *Kṛshṇa* and *Arjuna* at the head. Omens appeared when *Droṇa* proceeded to battle. The *Pāṇḍavas* and *Sṛñjayas* were broken by *Droṇa*. *Dhṛshṭadyumna* & *Droṇa* (VII, **7**). *Yudhishṭhira* urged *Dhṛshṭadyumna* and *Arjuna* to check *Droṇa*. The *Kekaya* princes, etc. (η), "achieved diverse feats." *Droṇa* put the *Pāṇḍava* troops to rout. *Droṇa* & the *Kekaya* princes, etc. (θ). At last *Droṇa*, having slain more than two *akshauhiṇīs*, "proceeded hence to heaven" ("attained to the highest state") slain by *Dhṛshṭadyumna*. D., P., etc., beheld him (VII, **8**). *Dhṛtarāshṭra* asked *Sañjaya* the particulars of *Droṇa's* heroism and slaughter (mentioning his knowledge of the *Vedas*; his ability to remove *Meru*; his equality to *Bṛhaspati* or *Uçanas*; his horses of the *Sindhu* breed, etc. (ι)) (VII, **9**). *Dhṛtarāshṭra* swooned away, and was restored to consciousness by the *Bharata* ladies. Then he enquired of *Sañjaya* about *Yudhishṭhira*, etc. (κ), especially *Yuyudhāna Sātyaki* (*b*), and *Dhṛshṭaketu* (*c*), and *Ketumat* (*d*); and the children of *Dhṛshṭadyumna*, *Kshatrañjaya*, etc. (λ), who, giving up all sports for twelve years, and observing excellent vows, waited upon *Bhīshma* for the sake of weapons; and the five *Kaikeya* brothers (*e*); and *Yuyutsu* (*f*), and *Dhṛshṭadyumna* (*g*) (VII, **10**). *Dhṛtarāshṭra* recited the feats of *Kṛshṇa*: the killing of *Hayarāja*, etc. (μ), that he had vanquished in battle the *Aṅgas*, etc. (ν), and that if *Kṛshṇa* would summon them, *Gada*, etc. (ξ), would take up their position in the *Pāṇḍava* host; and regretted that *Duryodhana* did not know *Kṛshṇa* and *Arjuna*; the destruction of the *Kurus* he attributed to himself or to Destiny (VII, **11**).—§ 590: *Sañjaya* begins his narrative in detail. THE ELEVENTH DAY'S BATTLE: *Duryodhana*, having consulted with *Karṇa* and *Duḥçāsana*, etc., asked *Droṇa* to seize *Yudhishṭhira* alive. *Droṇa* became very glad because *Duryodhana* had not asked him to slay *Yudhishṭhira*. *Duryodhana* explained that if *Yudhishṭhira* were slain, the other *Pāṇḍavas*, who were invincible, would avenge him; but taken alive, he might be once more vanquished at dice, and so all the *Pāṇḍavas* be obliged once more to go to the woods. *Droṇa* said that he would seize *Yudhishṭhira* if not protected by *Arjuna* (with his weapons from *Indra* and *Rudra*, etc.); *Arjuna*, therefore, must be withdrawn from *Yudhishṭhira*. *Duryodhana* proclaimed the promise of *Droṇa* to all his troops, in order to make him stick to his promise (VII, **12**). *Yudhishṭhira* learned through his spies that *Droṇa* had promised to seize him, and addressed his brothers and allies; *Arjuna* consoled him. A fierce battle commenced. Protected by *Droṇa* and *Arjuna,* both hosts seemed to stand inactive. The *Pāṇḍavas* could not withstand *Droṇa,* who began to consume the division of *Dhṛshṭadyumna* (VII, **13**). *Droṇa* caused a river of blood to flow there. *Yudhishṭhira* & *Droṇa*; *Çakuni* & *Sahadeva*; *Droṇa* & *Dhṛshṭadyumna*; *Bhīmasena* & *Viviṃçati*; *Çalya* & *Nakula*; *Dhṛshṭaketu* & *Kṛpa*; *Sātyaki* & *Kṛtavarman*; *Senāpati* & *Suçarman*; *Virāṭa* (with the *Matsyas*) & *Karṇa*; *Drupada* & *Bhagadatta*; *Bhūriçravas* & *Çikhaṇḍin*; *Ghaṭotkaca* & *Alambusha*; *Cekitāna* & *Anuvinda*; *Lakshmaṇa* & *Kshatradeva*; *Paurava* & *Abhimanyu*; *Paurava* was rescued by *Kṛtavarman,* and then by *Jayadratha*; *Abhimanyu* (letting *Paurava* alone) & *Jayadratha,* who was vanquished; *Çalya* & *Abhimanyu*; *Virāṭa,* etc. (**α**), praised *Abhimanyu*; *Dhṛtarāshṭra's* sons + *Çalya* & *Abhimanyu* (VII, **14**); *Bhīmasena* + *Abhimanyu* & *Çalya*; *Bhīmasena* (causing *Abhimanyu* to stand aside) & *Çalya*; both fell down; *Kṛtavarman* took *Çalya* away on his chariot; the *Pāṇḍavas* vanquished the *Dhārtarāshṭras* (VII, **15**). *Karṇa's* son *Vṛshaseṇa* attacked the *Pāṇḍava* army; *Nakula's* son *Çatānīka* & *Vṛshasena*; the *Draupadeyāḥ* + the *Pāṇḍavas* & *Vṛshasena* + *Açvatthāman,* etc.; especially *Bhīma,* etc. (β). The *Kuru* army was broken. *Droṇa* & *Yudhishṭhira*; the *Pāñcāla* prince *Kumāra* (the protector of *Yudhishṭhira's* car-wheels) & *Droṇa*; *Droṇa* & *Çikhaṇḍin,* etc. (γ); *Droṇa* caused *Yugandhara* to fall down from the seat of his chariot; *Virāṭa,* etc. (δ), & *Droṇa*; *Vyāghradatta* (the *Pāñcāla* prince) & *Droṇa*; *Siṃhasena* & *Droṇa,* who slew both *Siṃhasena* and *Vyāghradatta*; *Arjuna,* in order to rescue *Yudhishṭhira,* attacked *Droṇa's* division. Just then the sun set. *Droṇa* and *Duryodhana,* etc., withdrew their troops, and so did *Arjuna.* The *Pāṇḍavas,* etc. (ε), praised *Arjuna* (VII, **16**).

Droṇaçarmapada, a tīrtha. § 733*b* (Çarastamba): XIII, **25,** 1714 (by bathing there, one attains to the region of the Apsarases).

Droṇahantṛ = Dhṛshṭadyumna, q.v.

Droṇaja ("son of Droṇa") = Açvatthāman: VIII, 2822.

Droṇanandana (do.) = Açvatthāman: VII, 9195.

Droṇaparvan, the seventh book of Mhbhr. § 4 (Anukram.): I, **1,** 89 (°*palāçavān* . . . *Bhāratadrumaḥ*).—§ 11 (Parvasaṅgr.): I, **2,** 529, 536, 540, 541 (the number of çlokas in *D.* is said to be 8,909, in reality C. has 9,649 çlokas).—§ 795*c* (Mahābhārata): XVIII, **6,** 272.

Droṇaputra ("son of Droṇa") = Açvatthāman: I, †201, †204, †210, †213, 578, 5691; III, 1112, 1419, 1435, 1459; IV, 1920, 1921, 2244; V, †696, 3284, 5275, 5772; VI, 658 (°*purogamāḥ*), 1716, 2360, 4194, 4204, 4631, 5050, 5361, 5387; VII, 627, 801, 1363, 1851, 3021, 3024, 3935, 6142, 6363, 6804, 6821, 6827, 6865, 6873, 6874, 6877, 6884, 6885, 6886, 6918, 6922, 7201, 7204, 7412, 7436, 8918, 8921, 8925, 8927, 8929, 8961, 9024, 9027, 9035, 9098, 9102, 9204, 9239 (°*āstram*), 9248, 9253, 9260 (°*āstra*°), 9262, 9281, 9293, 9297, 9326, 9343, 9345, 9347, 9353, 9371, 9377 (°*vadhepsayā*), 9378, 9380, 9383, 9388, 9389, 9417, 9426, 9490; VIII, 1, 43, 65, †196, 328, 344, 415, 569, 608, 2623, 2660, 2675, 2679, 2680, 2681, 2683, 2686, 2688, 2690, 2824, 2827, 2858, 2935, 2963, 2966, 2967, 2971, 2972, 3079, 3217, 3220, 3232, 3234, 3237, 3245, 3283, †3364, †3365, †3811, †4918 (°*pramukhāḥ*); IX, 313, 628, 708 (°*purogamāḥ*), 733, 748, 801, 840, 1149, 1602, 1674, 3064, 3623, 3624, 3663, 3666; X, 33, 56, 205, 233, 251, 304, 319, 323, 334, 346, 368, 373, 382 (C. by error *Drau*°), 423, 427, 431, 439, 471, 473, 539, 593, 602, 605, 667, 677, 744, 754, 762; XI, 306; XIV, 1803, 1967, 1970, 1971, 1997, 2002; XV, 989; XVI, 83 (°*sahāyena Kṛtavarmaṇā*).

Droṇasūnu (do.) = Açvatthāman: VIII, †3365.

Droṇasuta (do.) = Açvatthāman: I, 572; V, 7594; VI, 4211, 4628; VII, 7203, 9376; VIII, 793, 798, 2157, 2682, †4073, †4076, †4509; X, 244; XI, 736; XIV, 1974.

Droṇatanaya (do.) = Açvatthāman: VII, 6838; VIII, 789.

Droṇātmaja (do.) = Açvatthāman: VIII, 635.

Droṇavadha ("the slaughter of Droṇa"). § 10 (Parvasaṅgr.): I, **2,** 345 (°*aḥ parva,* i.e. Droṇavadhaparvan).

[Droṇavadhaparvan] ("the section including the slaughter of Droṇa," the 77th of the minor parvans of Mhbhr.; cf. Droṇavadha). § 601: CONTINUATION OF THE NIGHT AFTER THE FOURTEENTH DAY: According to the words of *Vyāsa, Yudhishṭhira* refrained from himself seeking to slay *Karṇa,* but was filled with grief and anger because *Karṇa* had slain *Ghaṭotkaca.* Beholding the *Kurus* held in check by *Bhīma,* he told *Dhṛshṭadyumna,* etc. (**α**), to attack *Droṇa,* who received them; *Duryodhana,* etc., came to *Droṇa's* rescue; a fierce battle ensued between the two hosts; both armies became sorely afflicted with fatigue and blind with sleep. *Arjuna* granted permission to the warriors to sleep. D., Ṛ., and the soldiers applauded *Arjuna*; the *Kurus* asked *Karṇa* and *Duryodhana* to abstain from the fight; all the combatants laid themselves down on the field to sleep (description); the *Kaurava* troops blessed *Arjuna* for his act of kindness. When the moon rose, both hosts, rising from sleep, again prepared for battle (VII, **184**). *Duryodhana* taxed *Droṇa* wrathfully for his kindness to the *Pāṇḍavas* (β); *Droṇa* in wrath promised to slay all the *Pāñcālas,* and described the measure of *Arjuna's* might and prowess (γ). *Duryodhana* vowed that he, etc. (δ), that very day would slay *Arjuna,* dividing the *Bharata* host into two divisions. *Droṇa* ridiculed *Duryodhana* (ε), saying that it was only right that *Duryodhana* or *Çakuni,* who were the root of the hostility, should proceed against *Arjuna,* instead of causing all the unoffending *Kshatriyas* to be slain, and that he should accomplish his boasting vow before *Dhṛtarāshṭra,* and that he and *Karṇa* and *Duḥçāsana* would slay the *Pāṇḍavas*; moreover, he had done all in life that one should do. The army then was divided into two bodies, and the battle commenced (VII, **185**).—§ 602: THE FIFTEENTH DAY: When three-quarters of that night had worn away, the battle once more commenced. At sunrise both hosts, alighting from their chariots, etc., uttered the prayers of the twilight. After the *Kuru* army had been divided into two bodies, *Droṇa,* with *Duryodhana* before him, proceeded against the *Somakas,* the *Pāṇḍavas,* and the *Pāñcālas.* Urged by *Kṛshṇa, Arjuna* moved to the left of *Droṇa* and *Karṇa. Bhīma* urged *Arjuna* to put forth all his vigour. *Arjuna* & *Droṇa* & *Karṇa,* etc. (ζ) (description). *Droṇa* moved away towards the north; the *Pāṇḍava* troops began to tremble; the *Pāñcālas* & *Droṇa*; *Drupada* and *Virāṭa* + the three grandsons of *Drupada* + the *Cedis* & *Droṇa,* who slew the three grandsons of *Drupada,* vanquished the *Cedis,* etc. (η), and slew *Drupada* and *Virāṭa. Dhṛshṭadyumna* swore to slay *Droṇa* that very day; *Drupada* with his division (from one side) + *Arjuna* (from another side) & *Droṇa* + *Duryodhana,* etc. (θ); *Bhīma* urged *Dhṛshṭadyumna,* and they both attacked *Droṇa's* division (description); soon the morning sun arose (VII, **186**). The warriors adored the Sun, as he rose, and the battle once more commenced (description); neither *Karṇa,* etc. (ι), could be seen for dust. *Duryodhana,* etc. (κ), engaged in battle with four of the *Pāṇḍava* warriors: *Duryodhana* + his brothers & *Nakula* and *Sahadeva*; *Karṇa* & *Bhīma*; *Droṇa* & *Arjuna*; *Nakula* was worsted by *Duryodhana* (VII, **187**); *Sahadeva* slew *Duḥçāsana's* driver; *Duḥçāsana* was worsted by *Sahadeva*; *Bhīma* jumped into the chariot of *Nakula*; *Droṇa* invoked the *Aindra*, etc. (λ), weapons; D., G., Ṛ., Si., Aps., Y., and Rā. applauded *Droṇa* and *Arjuna*, saying that "this is no human, etc. (μ), but a high *Brāhma* encounter"; both employed the *Brāhma* weapon; the engagement became general (VII, **188**). *Duḥçāsana* & *Dhṛshṭadyumna*, who vanquished him and proceeded against *Droṇa*. *Kṛtavarman* + three of his brothers & *Dhṛshṭadyumna* + *Nakula* and *Sahadeva*, who checked them (enumeration of unfair weapons that were not used); *Dhṛshṭadyumna* proceeded towards *Droṇa*. *Dhṛshṭadyumna* + *Sātyaki* & *Droṇa* + *Duryodhana* (who grieved on account of his former friendship with *Sātyaki*); *Duryodhana* was worsted by *Sātyaki*; *Karṇa* rushed to the rescue of *Duryodhana*; *Bhīma* rushed towards *Karṇa*. *Yudhishṭhira* urged his warriors to rush to the rescue of *Sātyaki*, *Bhīma*, and the twins; *Arjuna* attacked the *Kurus*, and *Droṇa* attacked the *Pāñcālas* (VII, **189**). *Droṇa* caused a great carnage among the *Pāñcālas*; the *Pāñcālas* and *Sṛñjayas* & *Droṇa*; the *Pāṇḍavas* feared, thinking that *Arjuna* would not fight with *Droṇa*. *Kṛshṇa* told *Arjuna* to abandon virtue and let some man tell *Droṇa* that *Açvatthāman* had been slain in battle. *Arjuna* did not approve of it; others approved of it, but *Yudhishṭhira* with great difficulty. *Bhīma* slew with a mace an elephant named *Açvatthāman* belonging to the *Mālava* chief *Indravarman*, and exclaimed before *Droṇa*: "*Açvatthāman* has been slain." *Droṇa* did not believe *Bhīma*, but attacked *Dhṛshṭadyumna* and slew the *Pāñcālas* (and *Somakas*) with the *Brāhma* weapon, and cut off the head of *Vasudāna*, and slew 500 *Matsyas*, etc. The Ṛ. *Viçvāmitra*, etc., etc. (ν), appeared in the welkin and reproved *Droṇa* for using the *Brāhma* weapon against persons not acquainted with it, and called upon *Droṇa* to lay aside his weapons and leave the earth soon. *Droṇa* asked *Yudhishṭhira* whether the report about *Açvatthāman's* death was true; *Kṛshṇa* urged *Yudhishṭhira* to save his army by an untruth; *Bhīma* urged him to do the same; *Yudhishṭhira* distinctly said that *Açvatthāman* was dead, adding indistinctly the word "elephant"; before this *Yudhishṭhira's* chariot had stayed at a height of four fingers' breadth from the surface of the earth; after this untruth his animals touched the earth. *Droṇa* became quite dejected, also after the words of the Ṛ., and beholding *Dhṛshṭadyumna* before him, could not fight as before (VII, **190**). *Dhṛshṭadyumna* & *Droṇa*; the celestial weapons no longer appeared at *Droṇa's* bidding; his weapons, that had not been exhausted for four days and one night, now became exhausted on the third part of the fifth day. *Droṇa* took up another celestial bow which *Aṅgiras* had given him; a fierce encounter took place between *Droṇa* and *Dhṛshṭadyumna*; none else had arrows of that kind that *Droṇa* used in close fight except *Kṛpa*, etc. (ξ); *Sātyaki* rescued *Dhṛshṭadyumna* and was applauded by *Kṛshṇa* and *Arjuna*, and the Si., etc. (VII, **191**). *Duryodhana*, *Karṇa*, and *Kṛpa* + *Dhṛtarāshṭra's* sons & *Sātyaki* + *Yudhishṭhira*, etc. (o); *Yudhishṭhira* urged his troops against *Droṇa* (in order to aid *Dhṛshṭadyumna*), who again used the *Brāhma* weapon; *Bhīma* took up *Dhṛshṭadyumna* on his own chariot, and urged him to slay *Droṇa* quickly; both *Dhṛshṭadyumna* and *Droṇa* invoked the *Brāhma* weapon, etc.; *Dhṛshṭadyumna* began to slay the *Vaçātis*, etc. (π); *Bhīma* again reminded *Droṇa* of *Açvatthāman's* death, calling upon *Karṇa*, *Kṛpa*, and *Duryodhana* to exert carefully in battle. *Droṇa* laid his weapons aside, devoted himself to *yoga*, and proceeded to heaven (*Brahmaloka*) in the company of the foremost of Ṛ., in a blaze of light, that only *Sañjaya*, etc. (ρ), saw; *Dhṛshṭadyumna* cut off *Droṇa's* head—though forbidden by *Arjuna* and blamed by everybody—and threw it down amongst the *Kurus*, who ran away in all directions, except *Açvatthāman*. *Sañjaya*, through the grace of *Vyāsa*, beheld *Droṇa's* proceeding after he had ascended the sky. The *Kurus*, the *Pāṇḍavas*, and the *Sṛñjayas* all became dejected and ran away; *Bhīmasena* and *Dhṛshṭadyumna* embraced each other, *Bhīmasena* expecting the slaughter of *Karṇa* and *Duryodhana* (VII, **192**).

Droṇāyani, v. Drauṇāyani.

Droṇi, v. Drauṇi.

Druhyu[1], son of Yayāti and Çarmishṭhā. § 143 (Nahusha): I, **75**, 3160 (enumeration of the sons of Yayāti; C. has by error *Du*°).—§ 144 (Yayāti): I, **75**, 3162 (all. to § 148; C. *Du*°).—§ 147 (Devayānī): I, **83**, 3433 (eldest son of Çarmishṭhā by Yayāti).—§ 148 (Yayāti): I, **84**, 3481 (*Çarmishṭhāyāḥ sutam*), 3482, (3484) (will not take over the decrepitude from Yayāti, and is therefore cursed), 3485 (*d*: *D.* would be called a Bhoja without really being king of that region, where there is no roads, etc., but which is only to be crossed by means of rafts and floats; read with B. *arājā Bhojaçabdaṃ tvam*); **85**, 3520 (*Çarmishṭhāyāḥ sutaḥ*), 3525, 3533 (*d*: *D.'s* sons are the Bhojas).—§ 156 (Pūruvaṃç.): I, **95**, ††3762 (enumeration of the sons of Yayāti).—§ 632*b* (Shoḍaçarāj., v. Yayāti): XII, **29**, 991 (all. to § 148).

Druhyu[2], son of Matināra. § 150 (Pūruvaṃç.): I, **94**, 3704.

Druma[1], an ancient king. § 6 (Anukram.): I, **1a**, 227 (in Sañjaya's enumeration of departed kings).

Druma[2], a prince. § 130 (Aṃçāvat.): I, **67**, 2644 (incarnation of the Asura Çibi).

Druma[3], king of the Kimpurushas. § 269 (Vaiçravaṇasabhāv.): II, **10**, 410 (*Kimpurusheçaḥ*, in the palace of Kubera).—§ 289 (Arghāharaṇap.): II, **37**, 1350 (*Kimpurushācāryam*).—§ 290 (Çiçupālavadhap.): II, **44**, 1534 (do.).—§ 570*d* (Rukmin): V, **158**, 5356 (*Kimpurushasiṃhasya*, v. 5352; had given the bow Vijaya to Rukmin).

Drumada, a ṛshi. § 702 (Mokshadh.): XII, **297***b*, 10875 (among the ṛshis who had obtained their position by means of penances; PCR. has Drupada).

Drumaputra, king of the Kimpurushas. § 279 (Arjuna): II, **28**, 1038 (*Kimpurushavāsaṃ D°ena rakshitam*). Cf. Druma.

Drumasena, a prince. § 130 (Aṃçāvat.): I, **67**, 2671 (incarnation of the Asura Gavishṭha).—§ 600 (Ghaṭotkacavadhap.): VII, **170**, 7629, 7631 (slain by Dhṛshṭadyumna).

Drupada, king of the Pāñcālas, son of Pṛshata, father of Dhṛshṭadyumna, Çikhaṇḍin, Draupadī, etc. § 11 (Parvasaṅgr.): I, **2**, 391, 536.—§ 83 (Ādivaṃçāvatāraṇa): I, **63**, 2453 (father of Çikhaṇḍin, cf. § 573).—§ 130 (Aṃçāvat.): I, **67**, 2715 (has been born from the Maruts).—§ 132 (do.): I, **67**, 2791 (Draupadī was born in the race of *D.* from a portion of Çrī).—§ 201: *D.* (*Yajñasena*, v. 5174, *Saumaki*, v. 5192), son of *Pṛshata*, the friend of *Bharadvāja*, used every day to come to the hermitage to play and study together with *Droṇa*. After the death of *Pṛshata*, *D.* became king of the northern *Pāñcālas*. About the same time *Bharadvāja* also ascended to heaven: I, **130**, 5109, 5111.—§ 201 (Droṇa): I, **130**, 5133.—§ 202 (do.): I, **131**, 5134, (5137), 5194,

5195, 5206 (rebuked Droṇa for calling him his friend).—§ 207 (do.): I, **133,** 5298.—§ 209 (Drupadaçāsana): I, **138,** 5446 (*Pāñcālarājam*), 5448 (*nagaram D°sya*), 5457, 5459, 5499 (*nagaram D°sya*), 5500 (*sambandhī Kuruvīrāṇām*), 5502 (*Yajñasenam*), 5503, (5510), 5513 (assisted by his pupils, Droṇa vanquished *D.*, but restored half his kingdom to him. *D.* thenceforth resided in Kāmpilya).—§ 216 (Caitrarathap.): I, **165,** 6323 (*Dhṛshṭadyumnasya cotpattim utpattiñ ca Çikhaṇḍinaḥ | ayonijatvam Kṛshṇāyā D°sya mahāmakhe*, all. to §§ 218 and 573).—§ 217 (do.): I, **166,** 6333 (son of Pṛshata), 6335, 6341, (6342), 6345, 6348, 6349 (brief repetition of §§ 201–8).—§ 218 (Draupadīsambhava): I, **167,** 6356, 6368, 6369, 6389, 6406, 6407 (*°sya mahāmakhe*; in order to get a son who might slay Droṇa, *D.* held a sacrifice, where Dhṛshṭadyumna arose from the sacrificial fire, and Kṛshṇā (Draupadī) from the centre of the vedi).—§ 219 (Caitrarathap.): I, **168,** 6420 (*nagarīm . . . D°sya*, i.e. Kāmpilya).—§ 220 (do.): I, **169,** 6434 (*°sya kule jajñe*, sc. Draupadī).—§§ 231–6 (Svayaṃvarap.): I, **184,** 6929 (*°sya niveçane*), 6931 (*Yajñasenasya duhitā*); **185,** 6945 (*rājñā dakshiṇa - Pāñcālān D°enābhirakshitān*), 6947 (*°kshayam*), (6955), 6956, 6958, 6980 (*°sya putraḥ*, i.e. Dhṛshṭadyumna); **188,** 7057; **189,** 7072, 7073; **191,** †7134 (*kanyā D°sya*, i.e. Draupadī); **192,** †7168 (at the svayaṃvara of Draupadī, *D.* (*Yajñasenaḥ*, v. 6952), who wished to bestow his daughter on Arjuna, caused a bow to be made which only Arjuna could bend. Arjuna then won Draupadī).—§ 237 (Vaivāhikap.): I, **193,** †7187, †7191 (*Pāṇḍur hi rājā D°sya hi rājñaḥ sakhā*), †7192, †7194 (*purodhā D°sya*), †7196, †7199; **194,** †7203, †7211 (*°sya niveçane*), †7217 (*°sya putraḥ*, i.e. Dhṛshṭadyumna); **195,** 7230, 7233, 7234, (7239), (7244), (7249); **196,** (7258) (*D.*, who wished to bestow his daughter on Arjuna, tries to ascertain who has won her. Yudhishṭhira tells who they are, and asks for Draupadī as wife for all the five Pāṇḍavas in common).—§ 238 (Pañcendrop.): I, **197,** †7316 (Vyāsa told *D.* the history of the five Indras).—§ 239 (do.): I, **197,** 7326, †7328 (Svayambhū had destined Draupadī to become the common wife of the five Pāṇḍavas).—§ 240 (Vaivāhikap.): I, **198,** (†7329), †7343; **199,** 7347, 7348 (Draupadī is married to the five Pāṇḍavas).—§ 241 (Vidurāgamanap.): I, **200,** 7378, 7379 (*°syātmajān*), 7385, 7389; **201,** 7400, 7414; **202,** 7434; **204,** 7462, 7464, 7468.—§ 243 (do.): I, **205,** 7508, 7512; **206,** 7526, 7531 (*°sya ca putrāṇām*), 7532.—§ 244 (Rājyalābhap.): I, **207,** (7545), 7550, (7551), 7554.—§ 248 (Arjunavanavāsap.): I, **214,** 7800 (*°syātmajām*, i.e. Draupadī).—§ 289 (Arghāharaṇap.): II, **37,** 1344.—§ 290 (Çiçupālavadhap.): II, **44a,** 1538.—§ 294 (Dyūtap.): II, **48,** 1705 (*°sya sutaiḥ*), 1716 (*°aç ca sahātmajaiḥ*).—§ 299 (do.): II, **71,** 2384 (*°syātmajām*, i.e. Draupadī).—§ 311 (Āraṇyakap.): III, **4,** †234 (do.).—§ 317 (Arjunābhigamanap.): III, **12,** 574 (*°sya puram*, i.e. Kāmpilya).—§ 325 (Draupadīparitāpav.): III, **27,** 1022 (*°sya kule jātām snushām Pāṇḍoḥ*, i.e. Draupadī).—§ 342 (Indralokābhigamanap.): III, **51,** 1983 (*°sya putrā Dhṛshṭadyumnapurogamāḥ*).—§ 423 (Gandhamādanapr.): III, **144,** 10998 (*°rājena pitrā dattā*, sc. Draupadī).—§ 515 (Karṇadigvijaya): III, **254,** 15237 (*°sya puram*, i.e. Kāmpilya, attacked by Karṇa), 15239 (paid tribute to Duryodhana).—§ 522 (Draupadīharaṇap.): III, **266,** †15606 (*apatyam asmi D°sya rājñaḥ*, says Draupadī).—§ 525 (Rāmopākhyānap.): III, **273,** 15863 (*°sya sutā*, i.e. Draupadī).—§ 549 (Pāṇḍavapr.): IV, **4,** 84 (Dhaumya, etc., went to the abode of *D.*).—§ 551 (Kīcakavadhap.): IV, **20,** 614 (*°sya duhitā*, i.e. Draupadī).—§ 552 (Goharaṇap.): IV, **36,** 1181 (*°sya sutām*, i.e. Draupadī).—§ 554 (Sainyodyogap.): V, **1,** †3, †5 (*sutāḥ sarve D°sya*); **4,** (64); **5,** 102; **6,** (109), 127 (sends his purohita to Hāstinapura).—§ 555 (do.): V, **19,** 580 (*°sya . . . senā*, joined the Pāṇḍavas).—§ 556 (Sañjayayānap.): V, **20,** 603 (*°sya purohitaḥ*).—§ 561 (Yānasandhip.): V, **48,** †1843 (*Virāṭa-D°au mahārathau*), †1844; **57**ξ, 2236 (*Pāñcālyo daçabhis tanayair vṛtaḥ | Satyajitpramukhair vīrair Dhṛshṭadyumnapurogamaiḥ | D°o vardhayan mānam Çikhaṇḍiparipālitaḥ*, had joined the Pāṇḍavas with one akshauhiṇī of troops), (ο), 2262; **64,** 2480.—§ 562 (Bhagavadyānap.): V, **80**ε, 2856 (*sahāmatyam*); **82,** 2872 (*sutā D°rājasya*, i.e. Draupadī), 2891 (do.); **83**θ, 2950.—§ 570 (Sainyaniryānap.): V, **151a,** 5100, 5113 (*çvaçuraḥ*), 5144; **153,** 5189 (*Virāṭa-Drupadābhyāñ ca saputrābhyām*), 5192, 5199; **157,** 5324 (among the commanders of the divisions of Yudhishṭhira's army), 5336.—§ 571 (Ulūkadūtāgamanap.): V, **160,** 5479; **161,** 5539 (*saputrasya*); **162,** 5585 (do.); **163,** 5683, 5696.—§ 572 (Rathātirathasaṅkhyānap.): V, **170,** 5886 (*Virāṭa-Drupadau*, are mahārathas); **171,** 5916 (father of Satyajit).—§ 573 (Ambopākhyānap.): V, **187,** 7383 (*°sya kule jātā*, sc. Ambā); **188,** 7390, 7391, 7397 (*patnī D°rājasya*), 7399, 7401, 7402, 7403, 7404; **189,** 7409, (7413), 7418, 7429; **190,** 7434, 7438, 7444, 7445; **191,** †7461 (*Yajñasenaḥ*), 7478 (*Çikhaṇḍī sā D°syātmajā*); **192,** 7497, 7500 (*Pāñcālarājam*), 7504, 7509, 7511, 7512, 7514, 7527 (*°sya sutā . . . Çikhaṇḍinī*), 7546, 7549, 7551 (*°sya kule jātā Çikhaṇḍī*, sc. Ambā; being yet childless, *D.* had worshipped Çiva, who promised that *D.* should have a daughter who afterwards would become a son. Then Çikhaṇḍin (who was the reborn Ambā) was born as a female, but afterwards became a male); **194**γ, 7599; **196**η, 7624, 7632.—§ 576 (Bhagavadgītāp.): VI, **25**θ, 833, (κ), 847.—§ 578 (Bhīshmavadhap.): VI, **45**[15], 1723, 1724 (fights with Jayadratha); **49,** 2003 (*°syātmajaḥ*, i.e. Dhṛshṭadyumna), 2023 (*Pāñcālyam*), 2025 (*sainyāni D°sya*, vanquished by Bhīshma); **50**ν, 2060, (π), 2079.—§ 579 (do.): VI, **53**[7], 2232 (*Virāṭa-D°au*, attacked by Droṇa).—§ 580 (do.): VI, **56**ζ, 2414; **59**[13], 2629 (*Pāñcālarājaḥ*).—§ 582 (do.): VI, **69a,** 3065 (*saha putreṇa*); **71**ε, 3140.—§ 583 (do.): VI, **75,** 3282; **77,** †3376 (*°sya putraḥ*, i.e. Dhṛshṭadyumna), †3379 (*°sya putram*, do.), ([6]), 3383, 3384, 3385 (vanquished by Droṇa).—§ 584 (do.): VI, **82,** 3624 (*°syātmajaḥ*, i.e. Dhṛshṭadyumna); **85,** †3774 (*°sya putra*, i.e. Çikhaṇḍin), †3778 (*°sya putraḥ*, do.).—§ 585 (do.): VI, **89**ν, 3947.—§ 586 (do.): VI, **99**ζ, 4512; **103**μ, 4685, 4686, 4690, 4692 (fights with Bhīshma); **104,** 4745, 4751, 4752; **107,** 4966 (so C., but read with B. *Draupadaḥ*, i.e. Çikhaṇḍin).—§ 587 (do.): VI, **108,** 5001; **110**ζ, 5098, 5108 (Virāṭa and *D.* fight with Açvatthāman); **111,** 5161, 5164, 5166 (do.); **116,** 5432 (*°sya ratham*); **118**φ, 5559, 5564 (*°ānīke*); **119**χ, 5578, ω, 5587.—§ 589 (Droṇābhishekap.): VII, **8,** 227 (*°syātmajaḥ*, i.e. Dhṛshṭadyumna); **10**κ, 367 (*utsaṅga iva saṃvṛddham D°sya*, sc. Çikhaṇḍin).—§ 590 (do.): VII, **14,** 534, 535, 536 (fights with Bhagadatta), (*a*), 577; **16**δ, 650.—§ 592 (Saṃçaptakavadhap.): VII, **20,** 816 (*°sya sutaḥ*, i.e. Dhṛshṭadyumna); **23**ο, 961 (*Pāñcālyaḥ*, description of his horses); **25,** 1081 (fights with Bālhīka).—§ 593 (Abhimanyuvadhap.): VII, **35**δ, 1508; **42**π, 1743; **43**ρ, 1770.—§ 597 (Pratijñāp.): VII, **83a,** 2950.—§ 598 (Jayadrathavadhap.): VII, **85**δ, 3050.—§ 599 (do.): VII, **114**ψ, 4503; **124**λλ, 5002; **125,** 5091, 5094 (attacked Droṇa).—§ 600 (Ghaṭotkacavadhap.): VII, **153a,** 6627; **154**β, 6651; **155**ε, 6726; **156**θ, 6764, 6910 (father of Suratha); **157,**

6922 (°*syātmajān*), 6963 (°*vāhinī*); **158**χ, 7010 (°*sya tathā putrā D°ç ca*); **165**, 7368 (fights with Vṛshasena); **168**, 7524, 7530, 7532, 7534, 7537 (defeated by Vṛshasena).—§ 601 (Droṇavadhap.): VII, **184***a*, 8368.—§ 602 (do.): VII, **186**, 8487, 8488 (°*sya pautrāḥ*), 8489 (°*pautrāṇām*), 8491, 8492, 8493, 8496, 8499 (is slain by Droṇa), 8500 (°*sya naptṛshu*), 8508 (°*sya kule jātaḥ*, sc. Dhṛshṭadyumna); **191**, 8756 (*ya ishṭvā manujendreṇa D°ena mahāmakhe | labdho Droṇavināçāya samiddhād dhavyavāhanāt*, i.e. Dhṛshṭadyumna, all. to § 218); **192**, 8831 (*sainyair D°sya*).—§ 604 (Karṇap.): VIII, **6**, 156 (has been slain).—§ 605 (do.): VIII, **26**, 1060 (°*syātmajaḥ*, i.e. Çikhaṇḍin), 1074 (°*syātmaje*, do.).—§ 608 (do.): VIII, **85**, †4306 (°*sutavarishṭhāḥ pañca Çaineyashashṭā D°duhitṛputrāḥ pañca*).—§ 616 (Sauptikap.): X, **8**, 385 (°*sya ca putrāṇaṃ pautrāṇām suhṛdām api*, are slain by Açvatthāman).—§ 617 (Aishīkap.): X, **10**, 544 (°*syātmajaiḥ*); **17**θ, 762 (°*syātmajāḥ*).—§ 618 (Jalapradānikap.): XI, **11**ι, 300 (do.).—§ 619 (Strīvilāpap.): XI, **16***a*, 447; **25**κ, 722 (*pātitam*), 724.—§ 620 (Çrāddhap.): XI, **26**β, 788 (his body is burnt).—§ 630 (Rājadh.): XII, **27**β, 799 (sc. *hate*).—§ 637 (do.): XII, **42**γ, 1490 (his çrāddha is performed).—§ 789 (Putradarçanap.): XV, **32**θ, 875 (among the dead warriors who, summoned by Vyāsa, arose from the Gaṅgā).—§ 795 (Svargārohaṇap.): XVIII, **1**δ, 25; **4**, 137 (Çrī was born in Drupada's race [as Draupadī]); **5**λ, 148, 162 (among those who after death entered the deities).

Cf. also the following synonyms:—

Dhṛshṭadyumnapitṛ ("the father of Dhṛshṭadyumna"), q.v.

Pāñcāla, Pāñcālanṛpa, Pāñcālapati, Pāñcālarāja, Pāñcālya, q.v.

Pārshata ("son of Pṛshata"), **Pṛshatātmaja** (do.), q.v.

Saumaki, q.v.

Yajñasena: I, 5174 (disciple of Agniveça), 5452, 5453, 5502 (*D°*), 6416, 6931 (°*sya duhitā Drupadasya*, i.e. Draupadī), 6935 (°*sya ca sutām*, do.), 6952, 7236, †7334, 7524, 7525, 7538; II, 126 (*Saumakiḥ*, C. has by error *Jajñasenaḥ*), 1268, 1607, 1886, †2523 (*Saumakiḥ*), 2556 (*sutā . . . Y°sya*, i.e. Draupadī); III, †12581, 14828 (°*sya duhitā*, i.e. Draupadī); IV, 2352; V, 7461 (*D°*); VI, 720 (*Pāñcālyaḥ*); VII, 7525, 7526; VIII, 36 (°*sya putreṇa . . . Çikhaṇḍinā*).

[Drupadaçāsana(m)] ("the chastising of Drupada"). § 209 (Sambhavap.): *Droṇa* now one day asked the *Dhārtarāshṭras* and *Pāṇḍavas* for his fee as their instructor, saying: "Seize ye the *Pāñcāla* king *Drupada* in battle and bring him to me." *Duryodhana, Karṇa, Yuyutsu, Duḥçāsana, Vikarṇa, Jalasandha, Sulocana, Subāhu, Dīrghalocana*, etc., smote the *Pāñcālas* and conquered the capital of *Drupada*, while *Arjuna*, etc., waited outside the town at a distance of half a *kroça*, thinking that the others were not able to seize *Drupada*. Defeated by *Drupada*, they fell back upon the *Pāṇḍavas*. *Arjuna*, bidding *Yudhishṭhira* not to engage in the fight, appointed the sons of *Mādrī* his *cakrarakshas*, while *Bhīmasena*, mace in hand, ran ahead to slay the elephants, while *Arjuna* attacked the *Pāñcālas* and *Sṛñjayas* and felled *Drupada* from his elephant. *Drupada* and *Satyajit* rushed at *Arjuna*. *Satyajit* had his bows repeatedly cut in twain and his horses, etc., slain, and desisted from the fight. *Drupada* also had his bow cut in twain, etc., by *Arjuna*, who then took a scimitar and, leaping from his own chariot upon that of his foe, seized *Drupada*, while the *Pāñcālas* ran away. *Bhīma*, etc., began to lay waste his capital, but were prevented by *Arjuna*. *Droṇa* prevailed upon *Drupada* to accept his friendship, and restored half his kingdom to him, viz., that part of it that lay on the southern side of the *Bhāgīrathī*, with the southern *Pāñcālas*, up to the banks of the *Carmaṇvatī* river, where *Drupada* thenceforth resided sorrowfully in *Kāmpilya* in *Mākandī*, on the banks of *Gaṅgā*, while *Droṇa* (because *Drupada* had said that only a king could be the friend of a king) retained that half that lay to the north of the *Bhāgīrathī*, and thenceforth continued to reside in *Ahicchatra* (I, **138**).

Drupadaduhitṛputra, pl. (°*āḥ*) ("the sons of the daughter of Drupada") = Draupadeya, pl.: VIII, †4306 (*pañca*).

Drupadakanyā ("daughter of Drupada") = Draupadī: I, 7383, 7522.

Drupadaputra ("son of Drupada") = Dhṛshṭadyumna: I, 6325 (*Dh°*); VI, 832 (disciple of Droṇa), 1703, 2210, 2217; VII, 3601, 7199, 9131; XI, 668 (the slayer of Droṇa).

Drupadaputra, pl. (°*āḥ*) ("the sons of Drupada"). § 241 (Vidurāgamanap.): I, **204**, 7467.—§ 608 (Karṇap.): VIII, **46**η, 2207 (*Dhṛshṭadyumnapurogamāḥ*); **85**π′, †4306 (°*varishṭhāḥ pañca*). Cf. Drupadasuta, pl., Drupadātmaja, pl.

Drupadaputrī ("daughter of Drupada") = Draupadī: XIV, 2038; XV, 801.

Drupadasuta, pl. (°*āḥ*). § 605 (Karṇap.): VIII, **30**, †1216 (°*mukhaiḥ*, sc. the army of Yudhishṭhira, or does *D.* only refer to Dhṛshṭadyumna?).

Drupadātmaja[1] ("son of Drupada") = Çikhaṇḍin: V, 5126 (*Ç°*), 7550 (*Ç°*); VI, 558 (*Ç°*), 5690.

Drupadātmaja[2] (do.) = Dhṛshṭadyumna: VI, 2704, †3380; VII, 8874; IX, †1088 (*Pāñcālaputraḥ*).

Drupadātmaja, pl. (°*āḥ*) ("the sons of Drupada"). § 243 (Vidurāgamanap.): I, **205**, 7508 (*Dhṛshṭadyumnamukhāḥ*).—§ 589 (Droṇābhishekap.): VII, **8**θ, †248. Cf. Drupadaputra, pl.

Drupadātmajā ("daughter of Drupada") = Draupadī: I, †7008, †7009, †7159; II, †2220, 2278; III, †10282, 14724, 14728, 14805, †15610, †15639, 16616, 16618; IV, 250, 376, 472, 501, 691, XII, 1456; XIV, 2645.

Dṛḍha[1], son of Dhṛtarāshṭra. § 599 (Jayadrathavadhap.): VII, **137***aaa*, 5644 (among seven sons of Dhṛtarāshṭra, who are slain by Bhīmasena); **157***o*, 6938 (the same?, among ten sons of Dhṛtarāshṭra who attacked Bhīmasena). Cf. Dṛḍhahasta, Dṛḍhakshatra, Dṛḍhasandha, Dṛḍhavarman, Dṛḍhāyudha.

Dṛḍha[2] = Vishṇu (1000 names).

Dṛḍhāçva, son of Kuvalāçva. § 478 (Dhundhumārop.): III, **200**, 10021.

Dṛḍhadhanvan, a prince. § 232 (Svayaṃvarap.): I, **186**, 6995 (*Pauravaḥ*?, present at the svayaṃvara of Draupadī).

Dṛḍhahasta, a son of Dhṛtarāshṭra. § 130 (Aṃçāvat.): I, **67**, 2737.—§ 182 (Dhṛtarāshṭraputranāmak.): I, **117**, 4549. Cf. Dṛḍha[1].

Dṛḍhakshatra, a son of Dhṛtarāshṭra. § 130 (Aṃçāvat.): I, **67**, 2734.—§ 182 (Dhṛtarāshṭraputranāmak.): I, **117**, 4547. Cf. Dṛḍha[1].

Dṛḍharatha[1], a son of Dhṛtarāshṭra. § 130 (Aṃçāvat.): I, **67**, 2739.—§ 600 (Ghaṭotkacavadhap.): VII, **152**κ, 6851 (the same?, follows Çakuni); **157***o*, 6938 (among seven sons of Dhṛtarāshṭra who attacked Bhīmasena). Cf. Dṛḍharathāçraya.

Dṛḍharatha[2], an ancient king. § 775 (Ānuçāsanik.): XIII, **166**η, 7678.

Dṛḍharathāçraya, a son of Dhṛtarāshṭra. § 182 (Dhṛtarāshṭraputranāmak.): I, **117**, 4551. Cf. Dṛḍharatha[1].

Dṛḍhasandha, a son of Dhṛtarāshṭra. § 130 (Aṃçāvat.): I, **67**, 2735. — § 182 (Dhṛtarāshṭraputranāmak.): I, **117**, 4548. Cf. Dṛḍha[1].

Dṛḍhasena, a Pāṇḍava warrior. § 592 (Saṃçaptakavadhap.): VII, **21**κ, 906 (slain by Droṇa).

Dṛḍhasyu, a ṛshi, son of Agastya and Lopāmudrā. § 382 (Agastyop.): III, **99**, 8640 (called Idhmavāha).

Dṛḍhavarman, a son of Dhṛtarāshṭra. § 130 (Aṃçāvat.): I, **67**, 2734.—§ 182 (Dhṛtarāshṭraputranāmak.): I, **117**, 4547. Cf. Dṛḍha[1].

Dṛḍhavrata, a ṛshi. § 665 (Mokshadh.): XII, **208**η, 7595 (one of the ṛshis of the south). Cf. Dṛḍhavya, Dṛḍhāyu[3].

Dṛḍhavya, a ṛshi. § 770 (Ānuçāsanik.): XIII, **151**η, 7112 (one of the seven *Dharmarājartvijah* in the south). Cf. Dṛḍhavrata, Dṛḍhāyu[3].

Dṛḍhāyu(s)[1], son of Purūravas and Urvaçī. § 141 (Purūravas): I, **75**, 3149.

Dṛḍhāyu(s)[2], a king. § 554 (Sainyodyogap.): V, **4**γ, 86 (among the princes to whom the Pāṇḍavas ought to send messengers).

Dṛḍhāyu(s)[3], a ṛshi. § 775 (Ānuçāsanik.): XIII, **166**δ, 7666 (one of the ṛshis of the south). Cf. Dṛḍhavrata, Dṛḍhavya.

Dṛḍhāyudha, a son of Dhṛtarāshṭra. § 130 (Aṃçāvat.): I, **67**, 2734. Cf. Dṛḍha[1].

Dṛḍheshudhi, an ancient king. § 6 (Anukram.): I, **1**a, 231 (in Sañjaya's enumeration of departed kings).

Dṛḍheyu, a ṛshi. § 770 (Ānuçāsanik.): XIII, **151**θ, 7114 (one of the seven *ṛtvijah* of Varuṇa, in the west).

Dṛpta[1] = Çiva: X, 254.

Dṛpta[2] = Vishṇu (1000 names).

Dṛptātman = Kṛshṇa: XII, 1662.

Dṛshadvat, a prince. § 156 (Pūruvaṃç.): I, **95**, ††3767 (father of Varāṅgī, the wife of Saṃyāti).

Dṛshadvatī, a river. § 305 (Anudyūtap.): II, **78**, 2574 (there Yudhishṭhira had been instructed by Çambhu, i.e. Brahmán ?).—§ 312 (Āraṇyakap.): III, **5**, 241 (*Sarasvatī-D°yau*; C. has by error *Dṛçad°*). — § 361 (Kurukshetra): III, **83**, 5074 (*dakshiṇena Sarasvatyā D°yuttareṇa ca . . . Kurukshetre*).—§ 364 (Tīrthayātrāp.): III, **83**, 6057 (merit of bathing there), 6065 (*Kauçikyāḥ saṅgame . . . D°yāç ca*).—§ 369 (Kurukshetra): III, **83**, 7075 (*uttareṇa D°yā dakshiṇena Sarasvatīṃ . . . Kurukshetre*). — § 377 (Dhaumyatīrthak.): III, **90**, 8382 (in the north).—§ 574 (Jambūkh.): VI, **9**λ, 323.—§ 640 (Rājadh.): XII, **58**, †2121.—§ 652b (Indrota-Pārīkshitīya): XII, **152**, 5647 (*Sarasvatī-D°yoḥ saṅgamaḥ*). —§ 757m (Goloka): XIII, **102**a, 4889.—§ 775 (Ānuçāsanik.): XIII, **166**a, 7648.

Dṛshṭipa, pl. (°*āḥ*), a class of gods. § 730 (Ānuçāsanik.): XIII, **14**λλ, †1372 ("that live upon vision," PCR.).

Duḥçala, a son of Dhṛtarāshṭra. § 130 (Aṃçāvat.): I, **67**, 2728. — § 182 (Dhṛtarāshṭraputranāmak.): I, **117**, 4541 (only B., C. has by error *Suhçalaḥ*).—§ 599 (Jayadrathavadhap.): VII, **127**νν, 5176 (among several sons of Dhṛtarāshṭra who attack Bhīmasena).—§ 604 (Karṇap.): VIII, **7**, 208 (among those warriors of Duryodhana who still stay in the field).

Duḥçalā, daughter of Dhṛtarāshṭra and Gāndhārī. § 130 (Aṃçāvat.): I, **67**, 2740, 2744 (married to Jayadratha).—§ 181 (Duḥçalotpatti): I, **116**, 4527, 4539 (birth of *D.*).—§ 182 (Dhṛtarāshṭraputranāmak.): I, **117**, 4553, 4557 (married to Jayadratha).—§ 522 (Draupadīharaṇap.): III, **271**, 15758 (Yudhishṭhira orders to save Jayadratha for the sake of *D.*).—§ 523 (Jayadrathavimokshaṇap.): III, **272**, 15782 (do.). — § 615 (Gadāyuddhap.): IX, **64**εε, 3617.—§ 619 (Strīvilāpap.): XI, **22**η, 629, 632.—§ 785 (Anugītāp.): XIV, **78**, 2275 (*Dhṛtarāshṭrajā*, came with her grandson, the son of her son Suratha), 2280, 2294, 2297; **89**, 2678 (her little grandson installed as king of the Sindhus).

[Duḥçalotpatti(ḥ)] ("birth of Duḥçalā"). § 181 (Sambhavap.): That *Gāndhārī* also had a daughter (*Duḥçalā*) was due to the circumstance that Vyāsa, when he divided the lump of flesh (knowing that *Gāndhārī* wished to have a daughter), assigned one part in excess of the hundred to become a daughter (I, **116**).

Duḥçāsana, a son of Dhṛtarāshṭra. § 4 (Anukram.): I, **1**, †108, †156 (all. to § 299), †202 (Bhīmasena drank his blood, all. to § 608), †204. — § 11 (Parvasaṅgr.): I, **2**, 547 (Bhīmasena drank his blood, all. to § 608).—§ 71 (Ādivaṃçāvatāraṇap.): I, **61**, 2247. — § 83 (Ādivaṃçāvatāraṇa): I, **63**a, 2447.—§ 130 (Aṃçāvat.): I, **67**, 2725 (*D.* and his brothers (except Duryodhana) were incarnations of the Paulastyas), 2728 (enumeration of Dhṛtarāshṭra's 100 sons). —§ 157 (Pūruvaṃç.): I, **95**, 3810 (among the four principal sons of Dhṛtarāshṭra).—§ 182 (Dhṛtarāshṭraputranāmak.): I, **117**, 4541 (enumeration of Dhṛtarāshṭra's 100 sons).—§ 209 (Drupadaçāsana): I, **138**, 5449, 5461. — § 213 (Jatugṛhap.): I, **141**, 5635; **142**, 5674.—§ 232 (Svayaṃvarap.): I, **186**, 6981 (came to the svayaṃvara of Draupadī). —§ 241 (Vidurāgamanap.): I, **200**, 7374; **204**, 7469.—§ 288 (Rājasūyikap.): II, **35**, 1290 (at the rājasūya of Yudhishṭhira *D.* superintended [the distribution of] food, etc.).—§ 298 (Dyūtap.): II, **58**, 2016; **65**, 2184.—§ 299 (do.): II, **66**, †2195; **67**, †2221, †2225, †2227, (†2230), †2231, †2240, †2241, †2249 (ordered by Duryodhana, *D.* dragged Draupadī into the sabhā); **68**, 2288, 2290, 2304 (pulled off the clothes of Draupadī; Bhīmasena vows to drink his blood).—§ 301 (do.): II, **68**, 2338, 2339 (drags Draupadī); **69**, 2340.—§ 302 (Anudyūtap.): II, **74**, 2453, (2455).—§ 304 (do.): II, **77**, 2515, 2532, 2533, 2542, 2544 (when Yudhishṭhira had been defeated in gambling and the Pāṇḍavas were going to the wood, *D.* exulted. Bhīmasena [once more] vows to drink the blood of *D.*).—§ 306 (do.): II, **80**, 2656.—§ 308 (Āraṇyakap.): III, **1**, 14.—§ 311 (do.): III, **4**, 234.—§ 313 (do.): III, **7**, 288, (297), 301. —§ 316 (Kirmīravadhap.): III, **11**, 401 (°*karotsṛshṭavipra-kīrṇaçiroruhā*, sc. Kṛshṇā, all. to § 299).—§ 317 (Arjunābhigamanap.): III, **12**, 465.—§ 325 (Draupadīparitāpav.): III, **27**, 996.—§ 329 (Kāmyakavanapr.): III, **36**, 1435.—§ 337 (Indralokābhigamanap.): III, **44**, 1797 (°*vadha*°).—§ 340 (do.): III, **49**, 1934 (all. to § 299 ?).—§ 342 (do.): III, **51**, 1995.—§ 402 (Tīrthayātrāp.): III, **120**, †10270.—§ 512 (Ghoshayātrāp.): III, **236**, †14757, †14761; **238**, 14808; **239**, 14843; **241**, 14897; **242**, 14919, 14924; **249**, 15081, 15091, 15097, 15104; **251**, 15133, 15134 (on the ghoshayātrā Duryodhana and his brothers are made prisoners by the Gandharvas, but delivered by the Pāṇḍavas. *D.* tries to console the mourning Duryodhana). — § 514 (do.): III, **252**, 15205 (°*ādayaç cāsya* — i.e. Duryodhana's — *bhrātaraḥ*). — § 515 (do.): III, **253**, 15219. — § 516

(Duryodhanayajña): III, **256**, 15304 (gives order to invite the Pāṇḍavas to Duryodhana's sacrifice).—§ 521 (Draupadīharaṇap.): III, **262**, 15495, 15497, 15509 (counsellor of Duryodhana); **263**, 15536 (all. to § 299).—§ 551 (Kīcakavadhap.): IV, **21**, 647 (do.).—§ 552 (Goharaṇap.): IV, **26**, 895 (*bhrātā*, sc. Duryodhana's); **30**, 991 (arrays the forces of Duryodhana when he sets out to rob the kine of Virāṭa); **35***a*, 1150; **55**, 1733 (pierced by Arjuna); **61**, 1988, 1989 (fights with Arjuna); **63**, 2021 (defeated by Arjuna); **66**, †2109 (protects Duryodhana). — § 556 (Sañjayayānap.): V, **26**, †755 (counsellor of Duryodhana); **29**, †847 (all. to § 299), †853 (cf. II, 2526), †860 (cf. I, 108); **30**, †884 (*bhrātā kanīyān api tasya*, i.e. Duryodhana's); **31**, 931 (all. to § 299). —§ 557 (Prajāgarap.): V, **33**, 989.—§ 558 (do.): V, **35**, 1257.—§ 561 (Yānasandhip.): V, **47***a*, 1798; **49**, 1945; **55**ν, 2207; **57**, 2250 (°*sya*, sc. *sutāḥ*, destined to become Abhimanyu's share in the battle), (σ), 2290; **58**, 2303, 2309; **63**, 2433; **66**εε, 2502.—§ 562 (Bhagavadyānap.): V, **73**, 2692 (all. to § 299); **79**δ, 2829; **82**, 2906 (all. to § 299), 2909; **86**, 3058 (°*sya ca gṛhaṃ*); **90**, 3211 (all. to § 299); **91**, 3240; **94**, 3377.—§ 567 (do.): V, **124**γ, 4167; **128**, 4268 (all. to § 304), 4270, 4280, (κ), 4306; **129**μ, 4357; **130**ν, 4366, 4397.—§ 569 (do.): V, **137**, 4665 (all. to § 299); **141**, 4802 (Bhīmasena will drink the blood of *D.*); **142**ε, 4822 (do.): **143**η, 4835; **144**, 4890.—§ 570 (Sainyaniryāṇap.): V, **153**, 5195; **154**, 5227. — § 571 (Ulūkadūtāgamanap.): V, **160***a*, 5409, 5411, 5473 (°*sya rudhiraṃ pīyatām*), 5531 (°*aughaṃ*, sc. *purushodadhiṃ*, i.e. the army of Duryodhana); **161**, 5544 (= v. 5473); **162**, 5605 (Bhīmasena will drink the blood of *D.*), 5641 (do.); **163**, 5657 (do.), 5675 (do.), 5698. — § 572 (Rathātirathasaṅkhyānap.): V, **165***a*, 5732 (is a ratha); **166**, 5761 (°*sya*, sc. *putraḥ*). — § 576 (Bhagavadgītāp.): VI, **14**, 577 (*kitavaḥ*); **15**, 598, 599, 607 (deputed to protect Bhīshma); **18**δ, 686 (protects Bhīshma). — § 578 (Bhīshmavadhap.): VI, **44**, 1639, (*a*), 1652; **45**[5], 1690 (attacks Nakula); **48**, 1980; **49**, 1996; **51**ρ, 2093, (σ), 2098.—§ 581 (do.): VI, **62**ζ, 2731 (protects Çalya), 2742 (pierces Dhṛshṭadyumna).—§ 582 (do.): VI, **71** [10]γ, 3133 (protects Çakuni). —§ 583 (do.): VI, **76**ι, 3329; **77**κ, 3343; **78**, 3437 (fights with the five Kekaya princes).—§ 585 (do.): VI, **95**γγ, 4245 (*tava ca bhrātaraḥ çūrā D°purogamāḥ*); **97**ι, 4404, 4418, 4423; **98**, 4477, 4470, 4490 (protects Bhīshma).— § 586 (do.): VI, **105**, 4768, 4773 (do.).—§ 587 (do.): VI, **110**, 5111, 5118, 5120, 5124, 5125, 5129 (encounter with Arjuna); **111**, 5196; **115**ξ, 5358; **117**, 5464, 5466 (defeated by Arjuna), 5493, 5497 (his steeds and charioteer felled by Arjuna); **118**τ, 5520; **119**, 5622, 5626; **120**, 5711, 5714 (*Kauravaḥ*). — § 589 (Droṇābhishekap.): VII, **7**δ, 181.— § 590 (do.): VII, **12**, 438.—§ 593 (Abhimanyuvadhap.): VII, **34**β, 1501; **37**ι, 1600; **39**ξ, 1660, 1666, 1672 (C. by error *Duç°*), 1674 (encounter with Abhimanyu); **40**, 1677, 1686, 1689, 1690, 1699 (defeated by Abhimanyu); **51**, 1987 (C. by error *Duç°*, do.).—§ 596 (Pratijñāp.): VII, **74***a*, 2619, (β), 2629.—§ 598 (Jayadrathavadhap.): VII, **85**, 3034, (ε), 3052, (ζ), 3061; **87**θ, 3107.—§ 599 (do.): VII, **90**, 3187 (attacked Arjuna), 3189, 3215, 3216 (*D.* and his force defeated by Arjuna); **91**, 3217 (°*balam*); **95**, 3530 (attacks Sātyaki); **96**, 3555 (do.); **98**, 3662; **112**, 4313 (°*m anuvratāḥ*, sc. the Rukmarathas); **116***aa*, 4605 (pierces Sātyaki); **120**δδ, 4767, 4790, 4795, 4796 (encounter with Sātyaki); **121**, 4823, 4833, 4834, 4862 (*D.* and his force defeated by Sātyaki); **122**, 4864, 4865, 4868; **123**, 4935, 4939, 4940, 4943, 4944, 4945, 4955, 4957, 4959, 4963, 4970 (*D.* once more defeated by Sātyaki); **127**, 5201 (attacks Bhīmasena); **132**, 5426 (all. to § 299); **135**νν, 5552, 5553; **140**, †5838, †5840 (encounter with Sātyaki); **141**, 5842 (°*rathaṃ*); **145**ννν, 6075; **147**, 6368 (*putrān tava . . . D°mukhān*); **151**γ[1], 6548, 6559.—§ 600 (Ghaṭotkacavadhap.): VII, **156**κ, 6850; **158**ψ, 7030; **165**, 7366 (fights with Prativindhya); **168**, 7545, 7547, 7549 (do.); **170**λλ, 7624, (μμ), 7671; **174**, 7845; **182**ζζζ, 8266, (ηηη), 8281.—§ 601 (Droṇavadhap.): VII, **185**δ, 8441, (ε), 8452.—§ 602 (do.): VII, **187**ι, 8544, (κ), 8551; **188**, 8574, 8576, 8577 (defeated by Sahadeva); **189**, 8628, 8629, 8631, 8632 (defeated by Dhṛshṭadyumna).—§ 603 (Nārāyaṇāstramokshap.): VII, **193***a*, 8907; **200***aa*, 9309. — § 604 (Karṇap.): VIII, **1***a*, 5; **4**, 88 (had been slain by Bhīmasena); **5**ζ, 108 (do.); **6**, 163 (had slain Bṛhanta); **9**θ, 271, 318, 320 (*nihataṃ*). — § 605 (do.): VIII, **13**, 496 (fights with Sahadeva); **23**, 893, 897, 900, 908 (defeated by Sahadeva); **30**νν, 1226.—§ 608 (do.): VIII, **42**, 2142, 2157 (Çatānīka shall proceed against *D.*); **48**ο, 2263, 2278 (rescues Vṛshasena), 2283 (deprived of his chariot by Sātyaki); **61**, 3077, 3092, 3093, 3099 (fights with Dhṛshṭadyumna), 3127; **75**, †3815 (attacks Bhīmasena); **78**, 3941, (δ'), 3998; **80**, 4116 (°*ād avarajaiḥ*); **83**, †4216, †4224, †4225, †4226, †4228, †4229, †4232, †4233, †4239 (slain by Bhīmasena, who drank his blood), 4248, †4258; **84**, 4271 (°*sya rudhire pīyamāne*), (ο'), †4282 (°*syāpacitiṃ*); **88**, *a*δ', †4520; **91**, *a*κ', †4749, 4754 (all. to § 299). — § 609 (Çalyap.): IX, **2**ζ, 105 (lamented for as slain).—§ 610 (do.): IX, **4**μ, 217; **5**ν, 255, 278.—§ 611 (do.): IX, **19**δδ, 1017 (°*vadhe*, all. to § 608); **24**νν, 1300 (*nihate*).—§ 615 (Gadāyuddhap.): IX, **60**, 3384 (°*prabhṛtayah . . . nihatāḥ*); **61**, 3399 (°*sya rudhiraṃ dishṭyā pītaṃ tvayā*, all. to § 608); **64**εε, 3614 (°*purogamāṃç ca bhrātṝn*); **65**, 3640.—§ 617 (Aishīkap.): X, **16**η, 753 (°*sya rudhiraṃ pītaṃ visphurato mayā*, all. to § 608).—§ 618 (Jalapradānikap.): XI, **1**β, 17 (°*vadhaṃ*), (γ), 28; **14**ξ, 375; **15**ο, 393 (*apibaḥ çoṇitaṃ saṅkhye D°çarīrajaṃ*, all. to § 608).—§ 619 (Strīvilāpap.): XI, **18**γ, 537 (*pītaçoṇitasarvāṅgo yudhi Bhīmena pātitaḥ*), 545 (*nihataḥ*), 546 (°*sya yat kruddho 'pibac choṇitam āhave*, all. to § 608).—§ 637 (Rājadh.): XII, **44**, 1523 (his palace is given to Arjuna), 1525.—§ 768 (Ānuçāsanik.): XIII, **148**ε, 6930. — § 787 (Āçramavāsap.): XV, **3**, 65; **17**χ, 484, 486 (all. to § 299).—§ 789 (Putradarçanap.): XV, **31**η, 852 (*D.*, etc., were incarnations of Rākshasas); **32**θ, 876 (°*ādayaḥ Dhārtarāshṭrāḥ*, among the dead warriors who, summoned by Vyāsa, arose from the Gaṅgā). Cf. Bhārata, Bharataçreshṭha, Bhāratāpasada, Dhṛtarāshṭraja, Kaurava, Kauravya, Kuruçārdūla.

Duḥsaha[1], son of Dhṛtarāshṭra. § 83 (Ādivaṃçāvatāraṇa): I, **63***a*, 2447 (among eleven sons of Dhṛtarāshṭra, who were mahārathas).—§ 130 (Aṃçāvat.): I, **67**, 2725 (*D.* and his brothers, except Duryodhana, were incarnations of the Paulastyas), 2728 (enumeration). — § 182 (Dhṛtarāshṭraputranāmak.): I, **117**, 454 (do.).—§ 552 (Goharaṇap.): IV, **35***a*, 1151; **55**, 1733 (pierced by Arjuna); **61**, 1988, 1994 (defeated by Arjuna).—§ 561 (Yānasandhip.): V, **47***a*, 1799; **55**ν, 2207; **66**ε, 2504. — § 576 (Bhagavadgītāp.): VI, **18**δ, 686.—§ 578 (Bhīshmavadhap.): VI, **44***a*, 1652.— § 581 (do.): VI, **62**ζ, 2731, 2741 (pierces Dhṛshṭadyumna). —§ 582 (do.): VI, **72**ε, 3165.—§ 583 (do.): VI, **77**κ, 3343.—§ 593 (Abhimanyuvadhap.): VII, **37**ι, 1599.—§ 599 (Jayadrathavadhap.): VII, **116***aa*, 4603, 4608 (encounter with Yuyudhāna); **120**δδ, 4768, 4791, 4794, 4796 (do.);

127νν, 5177; **135**φφ, 5564 (among five sons of Dhṛtarāshṭra who are slain by Bhīmasena).—§ 604 (Karṇap.): VIII, **5**ζ, 121 (bewailed as slain).—§ 619 (Strīvilāpap.): XI, **19**δ, 565, 566, 567 (*gatāsuḥ*).

Duḥsaha[2] = Çiva (1000 names[1]).

Duḥsvapnanāçana = Vishṇu (1000 names).

Duliduha, an ancient king. § 6 (Anukram.): I, **1**, 227 (in Sañjaya's enumeration of departed kings).

Dundubhi[1] = Kṛshṇa: XII, 1511.

Dundubhi[2], an Asura (?). § 730*g* (Upamanyu): XIII, **14**λ. 805.

Dundubhī, a female Gandharva. § 526 (Rāmopākhyānap.): III, **276**, 15937 (*Gandharvī*), 15938 (do., reborn as Mantharā).

Dundubhisvāna, a region in Krauñcadvīpa. § 575 (Bhūmip.): VI, **12**θ, 464.

Durādhana, a son of Dhṛtarāshṭra. § 130 (Aṃçāvat.): I, **67**, 2736. Cf. next.

Durādhara, a son of Dhṛtarāshṭra. § 182 (Dhṛtarāshṭraputranāmak.): I, **117**, 4549. Cf. the prec.

Durādharsha = Vishṇu (1000 names).

Durārihan = Vishṇu (1000 names).

Durāsada, a prince. § 589 (Droṇābhishekap.): VII, **10**, 349 (*rājaputram*, had been slain by Ketumat; PCR. has *Durjaya*).

Duratikrama[1] = Çiva (1000 names[1]). Do.[2] = Vishṇu (1000 names).

Durāvāsa = Vishṇu (1000 names).

Durdānta = Çiva (1000 names[1]).

Durdhara[1], a son of Dhṛtarāshṭra. § 599 (Jayadrathavadhap.): VII, **135**φφ, 5564 (among four sons of Dhṛtarāshṭra who are slain by Bhīmasena). —§ 604 (Karṇap.): VIII, **51**δδ, 2446 (among several sons of Dhṛtarāshṭra who attack Bhīmasena).

Durdhara[2] = Vishṇu (1000 names).

Durdharsha[1], a son of Dhṛtarāshṭra. § 130 (Aṃçāvat.): I, **67**, 2729. — § 182 (Dhṛtarāshṭraputranāmak.): I, **117**, 4542.—§ 600 (Ghaṭotkacavadhap.): VII, **164**θθ, 7337.—§ 611 (Çalyap.): IX, **27**, 1443 (only C., B. has *Sudarça*, q.v.). Cf. Durdharshaṇa.

Durdharsha[2] = Çiva (1000 names[1]).

Durdharshaṇa, a son of Dhṛtarāshṭra (?). § 599 (Jayadrathavadhap.): VII, **120**δδ, 4768.

Durga = Vishṇu (1000 names).

Durgā[1], a goddess, the same as Umā (q.v.). § 549*f* (Pāṇḍavapraveçap.): Yudhishṭhira praises *D.* (supreme goddess of the universe, born of Yaçodā and rejoicing in the boons bestowed upon her by Nārāyaṇa; she sprang from the race of the cowherd Nanda, terrified Kaṃsa, destroyed the Asuras, and ascended to the sky when dashed [by Kaṃsa] on a stony platform; she was the sister of Vāsudeva, etc.) with the hymn IV, vv. 184–203: IV, **6**, 178, 198 (etymology), 203.—[§ 549 (Pāṇḍavapraveçap.): IV, **6**, 204 (*Devī*, i.e. Durgā, then showed herself to Yudhishṭhira and promised him victory).]—§ 576 (Bhagavadgītāp.): VI, **23**, 793 (°*stotram*), 803 (Arjuna praised *D.* with the hymn VI, vv. 796–808; the goddess then showed herself to Arjuna and promised him victory).—For the names occurring in the two hymns v. the synonyms enumerated under the heading Umā.

Durgā[2], name of two rivers. § 574 (Jambūkh.): VI, **9**λ, 337, 341.

Durgaçaila, a mountain in Çākadvīpa. § 575*b* (Çākadvīpa): VI, **11**, 423.

Durgala (B. Durgāla), pl. (°*āḥ*), a people. § 574 (Jambūkh.): VI, **9**μ, 359.

Durgama = Vishṇu (1000 names).

Durjaya[1], an Asura. § 92 (Aṃçāvat.): I, **65**, 2531 (son of Danu).—§ 130 (Aṃçāvat.): I, **67**, 2698 (*Dānavaḥ*, incarnate as Dantavakra?, or is *D.* name of a king? Cf. Durjaya[4]).

Durjaya[2], son of Çāradaṇḍāyanī. § 185*c* (Çāradaṇḍāyanī): I, **120**, 4679.

Durjaya[3], son of Dhṛtarāshṭra. § 512 (Ghoshayātrāp.): III, **242**, 14924 (made prisoner by the Gandharvas).—§ 583 (Bhīshmavadhap.): VI, **78**, 3436 (pierced Abhimanyu); **79**ξ, 3502 (proceeded against the five Kekaya princes).—§ 592 (Saṃçaptakavadhap.): VII, **25**, 1108.—§ 599 (Jayadrathavadhap.): VII, **133**, 5492, 5493, 5496 (slain by Bhīmasena). —§ 604 (Karṇap.): VIII, **5**ζ, 122 (mentioned among the slain). Cf. Kuruvardhana.

Durjaya[4], a king. § 554 (Sainyodyogap.): V, **4**γ, 79 (among the princes to whom the Pāṇḍavas ought to send messengers).

Durjaya[5] = Çiva (1000 names[1]).

Durjaya[6] = Sudurjaya: XIII, 95.

Durjaya[7] = Vishṇu (1000 names).

Durjayā, name of a place. § 382 (Tīrthayātrāp.): III, **96**, 8540 (there Yudhishṭhira dwelt in the hermitage of Agastya; according to Nīl. *D.* is = Maṇimatī, the city of Vātāpi).

Durlabha = Vishṇu (1000 names).

Durmada, son of Dhṛtarāshṭra. § 130 (Aṃçāvat.): I, **67**, 2731.—§ 182 (Dhṛtarāshṭraputranāmak.): I, **117**, 4544.—§ 583 (Bhīshmavadhap.): VI, **77**κ, 3343.—§ 599 (Jayadrathavadhap.): VII, **135**φφ, 5564.—§ 600 (Ghaṭotkacavadhap.): VII, **155**, 6716, 6717, 6719, 6721, 6722 (*D.* and Dushkarṇa fight with Bhīmasena).—§ 608 (Karṇap.): VIII, **51**δδ, 2447 (among several sons of Dhṛtarāshṭra who attacked Bhīmasena).

Durmarshaṇa[1], son of Dhṛtarāshṭra. § 83 (Ādivaṃçāvatāraṇa): I, **63***a*, 2447 (among eleven sons of Dhṛtarāshṭra, who were mahārathas).—§ 130 (Aṃçāvat.): I, **67**, 2730.—§ 182 (Dhṛtarāshṭraputranāmak.): I, **117**, 4542. — § 571 (Ulūkadūtāgamanap.): V, **160**, 5532 (°*odam*, sc. *purushodadhim*, i.e. the army of Duryodhana); **161**, 5575 (do.).—§ 578 (Bhīshmavadhap.): VI, **44***a*, 1652.—§ 580 (do.): VI, **59**ρ, †2647.—§ 581 (do.): VI, **60***a*, 2652; **62**ζ, 2731, 2741 (pierces Dhṛshṭadyumna). — § 583 (do.): VI, **79**ξ, 3502.—§ 584 (do.): VI, **81**β, 3558; **84**ν, 3735.—§ 587 (do.): VI, **113**ι, 5240, 5245, 5249, 5261 (encounter with Bhīmasena); **114**κ, 5293. — § 592 (Saṃçaptakavadhap.): VII, **25**, 1070 (fights with Bhīma). — § 598 (Jayadrathavadhap.): VII, **87**θ, 3106 (*putraḥ . . . tava*, i.e. Dhṛtarāshṭra's); **88**, 3130 (in the van of Duryodhana's army, will fight with Arjuna). — § 599 (do.): VII, **89**, 3150, 3151 (encounter with Arjuna); **116***aa*, 4603, 4609 (pierced by Sātyaki); **135**φφ, 5564 (slain by Bhīmasena). — § 604 (Karṇap.): VIII, **5**ζ, 122 (mentioned among the slain); **9**, 321 (*hatam*). — § 611 (Çalyap.): IX, **26**ρρ, 1404, 1409 (among eleven sons of Dhṛtarāshṭra who attack Bhīmasena and are slain by him).—§ 637 (Rājadh.): XII, **44**, 1525 (his palace is given to Nakula).

Durmarshaṇa[2] = Vishṇu (1000 names).

Durmukha[1], son of Dhṛtarāshṭra. § 130 (Aṃçāvat.): I, **67**, 2725 (*D.* and his brothers, except Duryodhana, were incarnations of the Paulastyas), 2728 (enumeration), 2730 (do.). — § 182 (Dhṛtarāshṭraputranāmak.): I, **117**, 4542 (do.).—§ 232 (Svayaṃvarap.): I, **186**, 6981 (came to the svayaṃvara of Draupadī). — § 512 (Ghoshayātrāp.): III, **242**, 14924 (made prisoner by the Gandharvas).—§ 552 (Goharaṇap.): IV, **35***a*, 1151.—§ 561 (Yānasandhip.): V,

47a, 1799; **55**ν, 2207; **66**εε, 2503 (*Kauravam*).—§ 576 (Bhagavadgītāp.): VI, **18**δ, 686.—§ 578 (Bhīshmavadhap.): VI, **44**a, 1652; **45**[6], 1694, 1695 (fights with Nakula); **47**γ[25], 1809, ([26]), 1819 (encounter with Abhimanyu).—§ 581 (do.): VI, **62**ζ, 2731, 2741 (pierced Dhṛshṭadyumna); **64**κ, 2838 (among fourteen sons of Dhṛtarāshṭra, who attacked Bhīmasena).—§ 583 (do.): VI, **79**[13], 3482, 3485 (encounter with Çrutakarman), ([14] ξ), 3502.—§ 586 (do.): VI, **104**, 4750 (Citrasena mounted the chariot of *D.*).—§ 587 (do.): VI, **110**, 5106 (attacks Ghaṭotkaca); **111**, 5177, 5178 (encounter with Ghaṭotkaca).—§ 592 (Saṃçaptakavadhap.): VII, **20**, 818, 819 (fights with Dhṛshṭadyumna); **25**, 1103, 1104 (fights with Purujit).—§ 596 (Pratijñāp.): VII, **74**β, 2628.—§ 598 (Jayadrathavadhap.): VII, **85**a, 3020.—§ 599 (do.): VII, **106**, 3977 (fights with Sahadeva); **107**, 4031, 4032, 4033, 4034, 4037 (defeated by Sahadeva); **116**aa, 4605; **120**, 4797 (pierced Sātyaki); **127**νν, 5177; **134**, 5515, 5516, 5517, 5519, 5520, 5521 (slain by Bhīmasena); **135**νν, 5540; **147**, 6386 (Bhīmasena has slain thirty-one of Dhṛtarāshṭra's sons, among them *D.*).—§ 600 (Ghaṭotkacavadhap.): VII, **158**ψ, 7030 (still living(!)).—§ 604 (Karṇap.): VIII, **5**ζ, 121 (mentioned among the slain); **6**, 170 (had slain Janamejaya Pārvatīya).—§ 619 (Strīvilāpap.): XI, **19**ζ, 553 (*hataḥ*), 556 (do.).—§ 637 (Rājadh.): XII, **44**δ, 1527 (his palace is given to Sahadeva). Cf. Kaurava, Kurumukhya.

Durmukha[2], a king. § 264 (Sabhākriyāp.): II, **4**β, 116 (among the kings who were present when Yudhishṭhira entered his palace).

Durmukha[3], an Asura. § 268 (Varuṇasabhāv.): II, **9**, 365 (among the Daityas and Dānavas in the palace of Varuṇa).

Durmukha[4], a Pāṇḍava warrior. § 608 (Karṇap.): VIII, **73**, 3732.

Durmukha[5] = Çiva (1000 names[1]).

Durmukha[6], a serpent. § 793 (Mausalap.): XVI, **4**η, †120.

Durnivārana = Çiva: X, 256.

Dururduda (XIII, 7658), error in C. for Dardura, q.v.

Durvāraṇa[1] = Çiva: VIII, 1448; XII, 10431 (1000 names[1]).

Durvāraṇa[2] (so B.) or **Durvāri** (so C.), pl., name of a tribe among the Kāmbojas. § 599 (Jayadrathavadhap.): VII, **112**, 4333 (°ṇā (°yo, C.) *nāma Kāmbojāḥ*).

Durvāsaḥsaṃvāda. § 10 (Parvasaṅgr.): I, **2**, 352 (*prādurbhāvaç ca Durvāsaḥsaṃvādaç caiva Māyayā*, i.e. XIII, chap. **160** ?).

Durvāsas[1], a ṛshi. § 11 (Parvasaṅgr.): I, **2**, 473 (°o *'py upākhyānam*, i.e. § 521).—§ 131 (Kuntī): I, **67**, 2768 (taught Kuntī a mantra).—§ 175 (Karṇasambhava): I, **111**, 4385, 4393 (do.).—§ 189 (Pāṇḍu): I, **122**, 4748 (do.).—§ 190 (Paṇḍavotpatti): I, **123**, 4760 (do., *japyaṃ D°ā dattaṃ purā*).—§ 256 (Agniparābhava): I, **223**, 8132 (*b*: *D.* was a portion of Çiva himself), 8136, 8140 (completed the sacrifice of Çvetaki).—§ 266 (Çakrasabhāv.): II, **7**, 293 (among the ṛshis in the palace of Indra).—§ 270 (Brahmasabhāv.): II, **11**, 440 (in the palace of Brahmán).—§ 358 (Tīrthayātrāp.): III, **82**, 5006 (had at Varadāna granted a boon to Vishṇu).—§ 376 (do.): III, **85**, 8265 (among the ṛshis who expected Yudhishṭhira on his tīrthayātrā).—§ 520 (Mudgala): III, **260**, 15415 (*digvāsāḥ*), 15425, 15434 (put Mudgala to the test).—§ 521 (Draupadīharaṇap.): III, **262**, 15499, (15507), 15515, 15518; **263**, 15521, 15548, 15550, (15552), 15563 (in order to favour Duryodhana, *D.* and his 10,000 disciples visit the Pāṇḍavas at the time when their supply of food was exhausted. Kṛshṇa, however, came to the assistance of Draupadī).—§ 569 (Bhagavadyānap.): V, **144**ξ, 4903 (all. to §§ 131 and 175).—§ 589 (Droṇābhishekap.): VII, **11**μ, 390 (had granted boons to Kṛshṇa).—§ 734 (Ânuçāsanik.): XIII, **26**a, 1763 (among the ṛshis who came to see Bhīshma as he lay on his arrow-bed).—§ 770 (do.): XIII, **151**λ, 7123.—§ 773*b* (Kṛshṇa Vāsudeva): XIII, **159**a, †7382.—§ 773*c* (Ânuçāsanik.): *Kṛshṇa* said: [Formerly] I put up in my house the brahman *Durvāsas*, who was green and tawny, clad in rags (*cīravāsāḥ*), who had a stick of *Bilva* (*Ægle marmelos*, Linn.), a long beard, who was emaciated, taller than the tallest men; he wandered over all the celestial and human worlds, singing this verse at congregations and in public squares: "Who would cause the brahman *D.* to dwell in his house? He becomes enraged with everyone even at the slightest transgression; he that would give me shelter should not anger me." As no one took notice of him (read with B. °*n nādriyate*), I invited him. Sometimes he would eat food sufficient for many thousand persons, sometimes very little, and [sometimes] he would not return home; he would laugh and weep without any visible reason; no one at that time was equal to him in years; [one day] he burnt all the beds and coverlets and all the well-adorned damsels, and then went out; then he asked for rice-milk (*pāyasa*); having previously caused every kind of food and drink to be kept ready, I caused hot rice-milk to be brought; having eaten some, he ordered me to smear my limbs with the remnant, which I did; then he smeared *Rukmiṇī*, and causing her to be yoked to a chariot, he, ascending that chariot, set out of my house striking her with the hook, and proceeded along the high road; the *Dāçarhas* became angry; as *Rukmiṇī* tottered, he struck her [with the whip]; then he leapt down from the chariot and fled towards the south on foot, followed by us Then he became gratified because I had subdued my anger, and said: "As long as gods and men will continue to entertain a liking for food, so long will everyone among them cherish the same liking for thee; so long as there will be righteous [men] (*puṇyāḥ*) in the worlds, so long will thy fame last; agreeable thou shalt be to all persons; whatever articles of thine have been broken or burnt or destroyed, thou shalt see restored or even better; thou wilt have no fear of death through such parts of thy body as have been smeared [with the rice-milk]; thou oughtest to have smeared also the soles of thy feet." I saw my body endued with great beauty and splendour. He also blessed *Rukmiṇī*, saying: "Thou shalt be the foremost of women in fame, etc., free from decrepitude or diseases or loss of complexion, possessed of a fragrant odour, the foremost of *Kṛshṇa's* 60,000 wives, and [after death] thou shalt dwell in the same world as *Kṛshṇa*." Having recommended me to be always thus disposed towards the brahmans, he disappeared. I and *Rukmiṇī* took the vow of always satisfying the brahmans. Having entered our house, I saw that everything which *D* had broken or burnt had become renewed. From that day forth I have always worshipped the brahmans: XIII, **160**, 7416, 7449.—§ 773 (Ânuçāsanik.): XIII, **161**, 7458 (°*aḥ prasādāt*).—§ 773*d* (Çiva): XIII, **161**, 7494 (is a form of Çiva).—§ 789 (Putradarçanap.): XV, **30**, 820 (repetition from § 131).—§ 793 (Mausalap.): XVI, **4**, †123 (had made Kṛshṇa invulnerable except on the soles of the feet, cf. § 773*c*). Cf. Atreya (XVI, †124).

Durvāsas[2] = Çiva (1000 names[2]).

Durvibhāga, pl. (°*āḥ*), a people. § 295 (Dyūtap.): II, **52**, 1869 (among the peoples who brought tribute to Yudhishṭhira).

Durvigāha, a son of Dhṛtarāshṭra. § 182 (Dhṛtarāshṭraputranāmak.): I, **117**, 4544.

Durvimocana, a son of Dhṛtarāshṭra. § 182 (Dhṛtarāshṭraputranāmak.): I, **117**, 4545 (PCR. has *Durvilocana*).—§ 599 (Jayadrathavadhap.): VII, **127**$\nu\nu$, 5177, ($\xi\xi$), 5205 (slain by Bhīmasena).—§ 611 (Çalyap.): IX, **26**$\rho\rho$, 1405, 1416 (the same?, slain by Bhīmasena). Cf. next.

Durvirocana, a son of Dhṛtarāshṭra. § 130 (Aṃçāvat.): I, **67**, 2732. Cf. the prec.

Durvisha = Çiva (1000 names[1]).

Durvishaha[1], a son of Dhṛtarāshṭra. § 232 (Svayaṃvarap.): I, **186**, 6981 (came to the svayaṃvara of Draupadī).—§ 512 (Ghoshayātrāp.): III, **242**, 14924 (made prisoner by the Gandharvas).—§ 567 (Bhagavadyānap.): V, **124**γ, 4167.—§ 576 (Bhagavadgītāp.): VI, **18**δ, 686.—§ 583 (Bhīshmavadhap.): VI, **77**κ, 3343. — § 600 (Ghaṭotkacavadhap.): VII, **170**$\mu\mu$; 7671. — § 604 (Karṇap.): VIII, **5**ζ, 122 (mentioned among the slain).—§ 611 (Çalyap.): IX, **26**$\rho\rho$, 1405 (C. has °*isa*°), 1420 (slain by Bhīmasena).

Durvishaha[2] = Çiva (1000 names[1]).

Duryodhana[1], the eldest son of Dhṛtarāshṭra and Gāndhārī, and the enemy of the Pāṇḍavas. § 4 (Anukram.): I, **1**, 108, 130, 139, 143, †174, †207.—§ 9 (Parvasaṅgr.): I, **2**, 301.—§ 10 (do.): I, **2**, 377, 411, 414, 422, 424, 484, 493, 496, 507, 510, 530, 558, 562.—§ 71 (Ādivaṃçāvatāraṇap.): I, **61**, 2238, 2239, 2279, 2281.—§ 83 (Ādivaṃçāvatāraṇa): I, **63**, 2441 (°*sya jananī*, i.e. Gāndhārī, the daughter of Subala), 2446 (the eldest of Dhṛtarāshṭra's 100 sons).—§ 130 (Aṃçāvat.): I, **67**, 2722 (born from a portion of Kali), 2726, 2728 (enumeration of Dhṛtarāshṭra's 100 sons). — § 131*b* (Karṇa); I, **67**, 2784 (°*sya sacivaṃ*, i.e. Karṇa).—§ 157 (Pūruvaṃç.): I, **95**, ††3810, ††3820.—§ 180 (Gāndhārīputrotpatti): I, **115**, 4506, 4507 (*D.* was born on the same day as Bhīmasena; as soon as he was born he cried like an ass; Vidura in vain told Dhṛtarāshṭra to abandon *D.*).—§ 182 (Dhṛtarāshṭraputranāmak.): I, **117**, 4541 (enumeration of Dhṛtarāshṭra's 100 sons).—§ 190 (Pāṇḍavotpatti): I, **123**, 4777 (Bhīmasena was born on the same day as *D.*).—§ 194 (Pāṇḍu): I, **126**, 4913 (*Dhṛtarāshṭrasya dāyādā D°purogamāḥ*).—§ 197 (Bhīmasenarasapāna): I, **128**, 4993, 4998, 5008, 5011, 5017, 5036, 5047, 5064, 5068 (gave Bhīmasena poison in the food).—§ 203 (Droṇa): I, **132**, 5222 (disciple of Droṇa; Karṇa and *D.* disregarded the Pāṇḍavas).—§ 205 (do.): I, **132**, 5270 (Duryodhana and Bhīmasena became very skilled in the use of the mace, and were jealous of each other).—§ 206 (do.): I, **132**, 5287.—§ 208 (Astradarçana): I, **135**, 5350, 5377 (combat between *D.* and Bhīmasena with the mace); **136**, 5389, 5391, (5392), (5394), 5400 (installs Karṇa as king of the Aṅgas); **137**, 5427, 5438, 5442 (sides with Karṇa against the Pāṇḍavas).—§ 209 (Drupadaçāsana): I, **136**, 5449, 5461, 5463 (with the assistance of his pupils Droṇa defeated Drupada). — § 213 (Jatugṛhap.): I, **141**, 5635, 5654, (5666); **142**, 5674, 5675, 5676, (5683), (5691); **143**, 5696; **144**, 5715, (5717), 5733; **148**, 5832; **149**, 5849; **150**, 5858 (*D.* orders Purocana to construct the lac house in Vāraṇāvata and to burn the Pāṇḍavas to death).—§ 215 (Bakavadhap.): I, **162**, 6248.—§ 231 (Svayaṃvarap.): I, **185**, 6957 (°*purogamāç ca sa-Karṇāḥ Kuravaḥ*, came to the svayaṃvara of Draupadī). — § 232 (do.): I, **186**, 6981.— § 233 (do.): I, **187**, †7019; **188**, 7051.—§ 234 (do.): I, **190**, 7093, 7116, 7118.—§ 241 (Vidurāgamanap.): I, **200**, 7373, 7383, 7384, 7391; **201**, (7399); **202**, 7416; **203**, 7443, 7445; **204**, 7464.—§ 243 (do.): I, **205**, 7498, 7516, 7517.—§ 287 (Rājasūyikap.): II, **34**, 1265 (came to the rājasūya of Yudhishṭhira).—§ 288 (do.): II, **35**, 1287, 1295 (received the tributes brought to Yudhishṭhira). — § 289 (Arghāharaṇap.): II, **37**, 1349 (*rājendre*). — § 292 (Rājasūyikap.): II, **45**, 1627 (remained in the palace of Yudhishṭhira).—§ 293 (Dyūtap.): II, **46**, 1640 (°*āparādhena*), 1661. — § 294 (do.): II, **47**, 1662, 1676, 1677 (*nṛpateḥ*), 1679 (*Dhārtarāshṭraḥ*), 1681 (*Dhṛtarāshṭrasya, putraḥ*), 1682, (1683); **48**, 1702, (1714), (1719), 1723, (1724); **49**, 1726, 1727, 1728, 1730, (1736), 1766, (1770), 1772, 1775; **50**, 1790, (1801) (*D.*'s mistakes in the palace of Yudhishṭhira; *D.* becomes jealous of the Pāṇḍavas. Çakuni suggests to invite the Pāṇḍavas to a match of dice, to which Dhṛtarāshṭra consents). — § 295 (do.): II, **51**, (1821); **52**, (1857).—§ 296 (do.): II, **53**, (1908).—§ 297 (do.): II, **55**, (1945).—§ 298 (do.): II, **56**, (1969), (1971), (†1977); **58**, 2015; **59**, (2049), (2058); **62**, 2096, 2097; **63**, †2111 (*Dhṛtarāshṭrasya putraḥ*), 2112 (°*āparādhena*), 2113, †2115; **64**, (†2121) (at the game Yudhishṭhira loses his brothers, himself, and Draupadī).—§ 299 (do.): II, **66**, (2186); **67**, (2199), †2201, (2209), 2210, 2215, †2219, (†2221), †2223 (orders Draupadī to be brought into the sabhā).—§ 301 (do.): II, **70**, (†2363); **71**, 2387, (†2399), †2404; **73**, 2444 (Bhīmasena vows to break the thigh of Duryodhana (v. 2393)).—§ 302 (Anudyūtap.): II, **74**, 2454, 2456, (2458) (persuades Dhṛtarāshṭra to invite Yuhhishṭhira once more to a match of dice).—§ 303 (do.): II, **75**, 2480 (all. to § 180).—§ 304 (do.): II, **77**, †2536, 2539 (Bhīmasena vows to slay *D.*), 2544, 2549, 2556.—§ 306 (do.): II, **80**, 2653, 2655, 2656; **81**, 2678 (all. to § 299), 2688 (do.), 2695 (all. to § 301).—§ 308 (Āraṇyakap.): III, **1**, 14, 16, 17 (*nṛpaḥ*).—§ 311 (do.): III, **4**, †232, †233, †237.—§ 313 (do.): III, **7**, 298, 300 (*D.* and his counsellors set out to slay the Pāṇḍavas, but are warned by Vyāsa); **8**, 312.—§ 314 (do.): III, **9**, 325, 345.—§ 315 (Maitreyaçāpa): III, **10**, 348, 350, 363, 364, 374, 376, 384 (disregards Maitreya, who curses him, saying that Bhīmasena shall break his thigh).—§ 316 (Kirmīravadhap.): III, **11**, 440.—§ 317 (Arjunābhigamanap.): III, **12**, 465, 538, 595 (Bhīmasena will slay *D.*).—§ 318 (do.): III, **13**, 598.—§ 325 (Draupadīparitāpav.): III, **27**, 996.—§ 327 (do.): III, **33**, 1266, 1344.—§ 328 (Kāmyakavanapr.): III, **36**, 1420, 1422, 1424, 1429.—§ 329 (do.): III, **36**, 1435 (*nṛpasutāt*).—§ 330 (Indradarçana): III, **37**, 1463.—§ 340 (Indralokābhigamanap.): III, **49**, 1932, 1941 (all. to § 301).—§ 341 (do.): III, **50**, 1956.—§ 342 (do.): III, **51**, 1980, 1995, 2002.—§ 343 (Nalopākhyānap.): III, **52**, 2030, 2038 (Bhīmasena will slay *D.*).—§ 383 (Tīrthayātrāp.): III, **99**, 8651. — § 401 (Balarāma): III, **119**, †10242, †10243, 10258.—§ 402 (Tīrthayātrāp.): III, **120**, †10268. — § 424 (Bhīmakadalīkh.): III, **146**, 11100. — § 431 (Saugandhikāharaṇa): III, **151**, 11328. — § 512 (Ghoshayātrāp.): III, **236**, †14761, †14771; **237**, 14772; **238**, 14796, 14813; **239**, 14824, 14841, 14848; **240**, 14849, 14866, 14871 (*nṛpaḥ*), 14875; **241**, 14880, 14883, 14896, 14906; **242**, 14914, 14916, 14918, 14925, 14926; **243**, 14939; **246**, 15012, 15015, 15030, 15033; **247**, 15039, 15045, 15052; **248**, (15053), 15058 (*rājā Dhārtarāshṭraḥ*); **249**, (15070); **250**, 15123; **251**, 15124 (*rājānam*), 15136 (*rājā*) (on the ghoshayātrā *D.* and his followers are made prisoner by the Gandharvas, but set free by the Pāṇḍavas; at this *D.* becomes dejected and is resolved to give up his life).—§ 513 (do.): III, **251,** 15145, 15154; **252,** 15185 (the Daityas and Dānavas summon *D.* into their presence, and tell him that they in former days had obtained him from Maheçvara by means of tapas, etc., and that incarnate Asuras will assist him in the battle).—§ 514 (do.): III, **252,** 15192 (returns to Hāstinapura). — § 515 (Karṇadigvijaya): III, **253,** 15223 (Karṇa conquers the whole earth and causes it to pay tribute to *D.*). — § 516 (Duryodhanayajña): III, **255,** 15273, 15274 (*Kaurava*); **256,** 15306 (*nṛpasattamaḥ*); **257,** 15343 (*D.* performs the Vaishṇava sacrifice). — § 518 (Mṛgasvapnodbhavap.): III, **258,** 15353.—§ 521 (Draupadīharaṇap.): III, **262,** 15494 (*Dhārtarāshṭrāḥ* . . . *D°ādayaḥ*), 15497, 15500, 15502, 15506 (*nṛpaḥ*), 15519 (gratifies Durvāsas and sends him to annoy the Pāṇḍavas). — § 547 (Karṇa): III, **308,** 17169 (Karṇa became the friend of *D.*). — § 548 (Āraṇeyap.): III, **313,** 17309. — § 549 (Pāṇḍavapraveçap.): IV, **1,** 1. — § 551 (Kīcakavadhap.): IV, **22,** 728.—§ 552 (Goharaṇap.): IV, **25,** 868; **26,** 883 (*rājā*); **30,** 973, 990 (*rājā*); **35*a*,** 1149; **36,** 1176; **38,** 1238, 1244; **39,** 1299, (1300); **47,** 1471 (*rājā*); **48,** 1527; **49,** 1550; **51,** (1598), 1599, 1601, 1604; **52,** (1621); **53,** 1652; **54,** †1660, †1661, †1664; **55,** 1696 (*°purogamāḥ*), [1746 (on the top of *D.'s* standard was an elephant)], 1756; **63,** 2021; **65,** †2090, †2091, †2097, †2100, †2103 (*°tvā*), †2104; **66,** †2107, †2108, †2109, †2128, †2129, †2132; **68,** 2168, 2203, 2238; **69,** 2245 (on the expedition to rob the kine of Virāṭa, *D.* is defeated by Arjuna).—§ 554 (Sainyodyogap.): V, **1,** †13, †23; **2,** †27, †30, †39; **4,** 64, 68, 72, 89; **5,** 99; **7,** 139, 152, 153, 160, 165 (*D.* chooses to get the Nārāyaṇas for his allies).—§ 555 (do.): V, **8,** 178, 179, 182, 186, 187, (189), 191, (193), 194, 210, 211 (prevails upon Çalya to join him with his troops); **18,** 557, 561 (*°āparādhena*), 569; **19*δ*,** 586, 587, 596 (eleven akshauhiṇīs joined *D.*). — § 556 (Sañjayayānap.): V, **20,** 615; **21,** 631, 633, 635, 637; **22,** †651, †652, †678; **26,** †760; **27,** †791; **29,** †859; **31,** 927.—§ 557 (Prajāgarap.): V, **33,** 989.—§ 558 (do.): V, **35,** 1257. — § 559 (do.): V, **36,** †1329, †1333; **38,** 1444; **39,** 1450, 1476; **40,** 1563.—§ 561 (Yānasandhip.): V, **47,** 1799 (*Kururājam*); **48,** †1810, †1870, †1901; **49,** 1917, 1941, 1950; **51,** 2028; **52,** 2098; **54,** 2136 (*°mukhāḥ* . . . *Kauravāḥ*); **55,** (2143), 2176, 2183; **56,** (2214), (2219); **57,** 2245 (destined to become the adversary of Bhīmasena in the battle), 2250 (*°sutaḥ*), (2267), 2289, 2290 (*nṛpam*); **58,** 2296, (2304), 2313; **60,** 2362, 2363; **62,** †2424, †2428; **63,** (2429); **64,** 2477; **65,** 2482; **67,** 2510 (*Dhārtarāshṭre*); **69,** 2544, (2545).—§ 562 (Bhagavadyānap.): V, **72,** 2664; **73,** 2697, 2703, 2709, †2716; **74,** 2718, 2724, 2726, 2734, 2736; **75,** 2752; **81,** 2866; **82,** 2878, 2901; **83,** 2932; **85*κ*,** 3023, 3033 (*rājā*), 3038 (do.); **86,** 3050, 3058 (*°gṛhāt*), 3060; **87,** 3076; **88,** (3078), (3089), 3094; **89,** 3103; **90,** 3188, 3212, 3235 (*°gṛhān*); **91,** 3236 (*°gṛham*), 3241, 3246 (*rājā*), 3247, 3269; **92,** †3299, †3301, †3303; **93,** 3316, 3321; **94,** 3336, 3346, 3363, 3378; **95,** 3392 (*putrās tava* . . . *D°purogamāḥ*). — § 564 (Mātalīyop.): V, **97,** 3501 (Kaṇva told *D.* the Mātalīyopākhyāna); **105,** 3711.—§ 567 (Bhagavadyānap.): V, **124,** 4123, 4126, 4128, 4129; **125,** 4186, 4194, 4204, 4205, 4208, 4209, 4212; **126,** 4214; **127,** 4233; **128,** 4259, 4280, 4306, 4308; **129,** 4313, 4325, 4328, 4329 (*D.* will not make peace with the Pāṇḍavas); **130*ν*,** 4366, 4395, 4396, 4404, 4405 (plans to seize Kṛshṇa); **131,** 4418.—§ 569 (do.): V, **137,** 4671; **138,** 4676; **140,** 4767, 4769, 4776; **141,** 4804 (Bhīmasena will slay *D.*); **142,** 4832 (*rājāno rājaputrāç ca D°vaçānugāḥ*); **143,** 4835, 4837 (*rājāno rājaputrāç ca D°vaçānugāḥ*), 4870; **147,** 4962, 4972; **148,** 5002, 5021, 5023, †5031, †5034; **149,** 5040, 5041.—§ 570 (Sainyaniryāṇap.): V, **153,** 5190 (*rājā*), 5195; **154,** 5218; **155,** 5243 (*rājā*, arrayed his troops), 5271, 5272 (*rājā*); **157,** 5342, 5347 (has been the disciple of Balarāma); **158,** 5386 (rejected Rukmin); **159,** 5396, 5398. — § 571 (Ulūkadūtāgamanap.): V, **160,** 5408 (*rājā*), 5410 (do.) (*D.* sends Ulūka to the Pāṇḍavas); **161,** 5536; **162,** 5597, 5626; **163,** 5643; **164*ε*,** 5706 (Bhīmasena is pitted against *D.*).—§ 572 (Rathātirathasaṅkhyānap.): V, **165,** 5714 (*me mandāḥ putrā D°ādayaḥ*), 5719, (5725); **168,** 5819, 5826 (Bhīshma enumerates to *D.* the rathas and atirathas of both armies).—§ 573 (Ambopākhyānap.): V, **173,** (5942), 5944 (Bhīshma relates to *D.* the tale of Ambā); **188,** (7389) (Bhīshma relates to *D.* the tale of Çikhaṇḍin); **192,** 7557 (*Kauravyo rājā*); **193,** 7572 (*rājā*); **194,** 7583; **195,** 7603, (ζ), 7611 (*nṛpatiḥ*), 7614, 7619 (*rājā*, the army of *D.* took up its position at one end of Kurukshetra).—§ 574 (Jambūkh.): VI, **1,** 16; **9,** 309, 311.—§ 575 (Bhūmip.): VI, **12,** 490.—§ 576 (Bhagavadgītāp.): VI, **14,** 530, 540, 570, 576, 583; **15,** 588, 598; **16,** 625 (*°vaçānugāḥ* | *rājāno rājaputrāç ca*), 627; **17,** 661 (the device of *D.'s* standard was an elephant set with gems (*maṇimayaḥ*)); **19,** 704 (*Kuravaḥ* . . . *D°purogamāḥ*); **20*ζ*,** †747 (description of his elephant); **25,** 831 (*rājā*).—§ 577 (Bhīshmavadhap.): VI, **43,** 1620 (*°hitaishiṇam*, sc. Karṇa).—§ 578 (do.): VI, **44*a*,** 1652; **45**[4], 1688 (fights with Bhīmasena); **48**[31], 1902, ([32]), 1910, ([33]), 1922; **49,** 1995, 2005, 2007; **50,** 2033; **51*ν*,** 2105 (*rājā*). — § 579 (do.): VI, **52,** 2123 (*putras* . . . *tava*), 2133, (β), 2134 (*Dhārtarāshṭrāḥ* . . . *D°purogamāḥ*), (δ), 2145, ([3]), 2154 (*rājā*), (ζ), 2160; **53**[6], 2230; **55**[18], 2372 (*rājā*, father of Lakshmaṇa).—§ 580 (do.): VI, **56*γ*,** 2407 (*rājā*); **57,** 2458 (*putraḥ* . . . *tava*); **58**[6], 2475, 2477, 2478 (*rājā*, fights with Ghaṭotkaca and Bhīmasena; is pierced by Bhīmasena and swoons away), ([9]), 2489, 2490 (*rājā*); **59,** †2607, (ν [12]), †2621, †2622 (fights with Arjuna), (ο), 2643.—§ 581 (do.): VI, **60*a*,** †2652, (β), †2672; **62,** 2720, (ζ), 2731, 2740 (pierces Dhṛshṭadyumna), ([6]), 2747, 2749 (attacks Bhīmasena); **63**[7], 2780 (*putraḥ* . . . *tava*); **64**[12], 2815 (*rājā*), 2817, 2819, 2825 (fights with Bhīmasena, who swooned away), ([13]), 2835 (pierced by Bhīmasena), ([17]), 2895 (*nṛpatiḥ*); **65,** 2909, 2925, (2928); **67,** (3014) (Bhīshma relates to *D.* the glory of Kṛshṇa).—§ 582 (do.): VI, **69**[3], 3072 (*rājā*); **70**[9], 3117 (do.); **71*c*,** 3140; **72,** 3165 (Bhīmasena proceeds against *D.*); **73,** 3213 (fights with Bhīmasena); **74**[13], 3244 (*rājā*), 3270.—§ 583 (do.): VI, **75*γ*,** 3294, (θ), 3304; **76,** 3334; **77,** 3337, ([3]), 3342 (*°ānujān*), ([9]), 3403; **78**[10], 3413 (*rājā*), 3417 (do.), 3419 (fights with Bhīmasena), 3420 (*°ānujāḥ*), 3431, 3438; **79,** 3450 (*rājā*), ([12]), [3464 (*b*: *D.'s* (*Kurupateḥ*) standard bore the device of an elephant set with gems)], 3466, 3467, 3468 (fights with Bhīmasena); **80,** †3518, †3523.—§ 584 (do.): VI, **81,** 3549, ([1]), 3556 (attacks Dhṛshṭadyumna (?)); **82,** 3579 (*rājā*); **84,** 3713 (*°balam*); **85**[7], †3761, †3767; **86**[13], 3830 (*°purogamās tu putrās tava*), 3831 (*rājā*), 3836 (*°mukhān rathān*), 3837 (*nṛpatiḥ*).—§ 585 (do.): VI, **87*a*,** 3849 (*rājā*), 3858 (do.), 3859; **88.** 3897 (*rājā*, protected Bhīshma), 3917 (*rājā*), 3922 (do., censures Bhīshma); **89,** 3936, 3949; **90,** 4018 (*sutaḥ* . . . *tava*); **91,** 4072 (*rājā*), 4076, 4081, 4083 (*putraḥ* . . . *tava*), 4087, 4088, 4094 (fights with Ghaṭotkaca, etc.); **92,** 4103, 4108, 4114 (*rājñā*), 4120 (*putram* . . . *tava*), 4123 (°*balasya*); **93,** 4139; **94,** 4182 (*rājā*, attacks Bhīmasena), 4192, 4201 (*rājā*), (*aa*), 4225 (defeated); **95,** 4232 (*rājā*), 4240, 4318 (*rājā*); **96,** 4329 (°*āparādhena*); **97**ι, 4404 (*rājā*), 4406 (do.), 4417 (*putraḥ* . . . *tava*), 4446 (do.); **98,** 4451, 4475, 4477, 4490, 4494 (*rājā*). — § 586 (do.): VI, **99**δ, 4505; **100,** 4530 (°*balam*), 4552; **102,** 4651 (*rājā*), (ι), 4665, 4681 (°*balam*); **103,** 4720 (°*āparādhena*), 4723 (*putraḥ* . . . *tava*); **104,** 4737 (do.); **105,** 4768, 4777, 4791; **107,** 4931.—§ 587 (do.): VI, **109,** 5069, 5079; **111,** 5154; **113,** 5287 (*rājā*); **114,** 5317; **115,** 5361 (attacked Yudhāmanyu (B. Abhimanyu)); **116,** 5379, 5380 (fights with Ābhimanyu); **119,** 5678.—§ 588 (do.): VI, **120,** 5710, 5749 (*putraḥ* . . . *tava*); **121,** †5798, †5799 (*Kauravendraḥ*), 5800; **122,** 5841 (°*aiçvaryam*), 5843.—§ 589 (Droṇābhishekap.): VII, **1,** 39; **4,** 121 (Karṇa had made many peoples to acknowledge *D.'s* sway, cf. § 515), 123 (°*hitaishiṇā*, sc. Karṇa), 124 (*yathā*), 125, 126 (*yathā*), 128 (do.), 131 (*Kuravaḥ* . . . *D*°*purogamāḥ*); **5,** 134, (138), 154; **6,** 155 (*rājā*), (156), 167, 168; **7,** 174 (°*mukhā nṛpāḥ*, made Droṇa the leader of his army); **10**κ, 315 (°*balam*), 324 (°*purogamān*), 366; **11,** 421.—§ 590 (do.): VII, **12,** 438 (*rājā*), 442, 464; **13,** 471; **16,** 668.—§ 591 (Saṃçaptakavadhap.): VII, **17,** 674. — § 592 (do.): VII, **20,** 796 (*rājā*); **22,** 924 (°*hitaishiṇam Bhāradvājam*), 929, (930), 948 (*rājā*); **24,** 1053, 1057, 1058; **25,** 1068; **26,** 1138, 1142 (fights with Bhīmasena); **30,** 1332; **32**χ, 1376 (*rājā*), 1377 (fights with Bhīmasena), (εε), 1441. — § 593 (Abhimanyuvadhap.): VII, **33,** 1457; **34**β, 1500; **37,** 1585 (attacks Abhimanyu), 1591, (ι), 1602, (κ), 1611; **39**μ, 1650, 1660, 1666; **40,** 1698; **45,** 1820, 1830, 1831; **46,** 1835, (τ), 1838, 1841, 1850 (his son Lakshmaṇa is slain by Abhimanyu); **48,** 1900; **51,** 2001.—§ 596 (Pratijñāp.): VII, **74***a*, 2619, 2625, 2633; **79,** 2796. — § 598 (Jayadrathavadhap.): VII, **85,** 3014, 3031, 3032, (ε), 3052, 3054, 3060; **86,** 3069, 3072; **87,** 3112.—§ 599 (do.): VII, **93,** 3369; **94,** (3435) (Droṇa cases *D.* in an invulnerable armour); **95,** 3486; **100,** 3751 (°*āparādhena*), 3760; **101,** 3799 (*rājā*), 3802, 3804; **102,** 3832, 3838; **103,** 3851, 3858, 3867, 3873 (fights with Arjuna); **104,** 3906, 3912; **105**ν, [3951 (on the standard of *D.* (*rājñaḥ*), which was set with gold, there was an elephant adorned with gems (*maṇimayaḥ*) and tinkling with the sound of a hundred bells)], 3959 (°*mukhānām*); **112,** 4322, 4340; **114,** 4468, 4494 (*rājā*); **115,** 4555; **116*aa*,** 4606, 4621, 4625 (*putraḥ* . . . *tava*, encounter with Sātyaki); **119,** 4733 (*rājā*), 4737 (do.); **120**δδ, 4767, 4788 (*rājā*), 4794, 4797 (encounter with Sātyaki); **121,** 4816, 4818; **124,** 4993, 4995, 4999; **125,** 5092; **128,** 5261, 5266, 5267 (*rājā*), 5268, 5269, 5276; **130,** 5335, 5339 (*Bhārataḥ*), 5342, 5346, 5348 (fights with Yudhāmanyu and Uttamaujas); **131,** 5366; **132,** 5413; **133**ττ, 5463, 5492 (*nṛpaḥ*); **134,** 5515, 5516; **135**υυ, 5537, 5538, 5540; **136,** 5592 (*rājā*); **137,** 5631 (*rājā*), 5634, 5654; **141,** 5865; **145**μμμ, 6062, 6064 (*rājā*), 6079, (οοο), 6096, 6109, 6133 (encounter with Arjuna); **146,** 6227; **147,** 6366; **148,** 6408; **150,** (6505); **151,** 6530, (γ'), 6534, 6541, 6568; **152,** 6570 (*rājā*), 6571 (*putraḥ* . . . *tava*).—§ 600 (Ghaṭotkacavadhap.): VII, **153,** 6615, 6637 (defeated by Yudhishṭhira); **154,** 6641, 6674; **155**γ, 6683, 6685, 6702, (δ), 6720; **156,** 6750, 6844, (6847); **158,** 6970, 7002, (ψ), 7030, 7038, 7041; **159,** 7051 (*rājā*), (7054), 7067, 7082, 7109 (*rājā*), 7125, (7128); **160,** 7143, 7160 (*putram* . . . *tava*); **161,** 7205 (*rājā*); **162,** †7291; **164,** 7328, 7336, 7348 (*putraḥ* . . . *tava*); **165,** 7363 (attacks Bhīmasena); **166,** 7438 (*rājā*), 7439, 7441 (*rājā*), 7443, 7444, 7445, 7453 (defeated by Bhīmasena); **170**λλ, 7625, 7654; **171,** 7693 (*rājā*), 7694, 7695, 7703 (defeated by Sātyaki); **174,** 7849, 7882, 7884; **176,** 8009, 8014; **177,** 8027 (*tava putrās te D*°*purogamāḥ*), 8033; **178,** 8110, 8111; **181**δδδ, 8215; **182**ζζζ, 8266, (ηηη), 8281 (°*purogamāḥ*); **183**ζζζ, 8294, 8309 (°*purogamāḥ*).—§ 601 (Droṇavadhap.): VII, **184,** 8372 (*rājā*, protects Droṇa), 8391; **185,** 8419, (8420), 8427, (γ), 8428.—§ 602 (do.): VII, **186,** 8461 (°*purogamāḥ*), (ζ), 8470, (θ), 8504; **187**ι, 8544, (κ), 8551, 8552, 8567, 8570 (*rājā*, fights with Nakula); **189,** 8646, 8649 (*rājā*), (8655), 8663, 8671, 8672 (fights with Sātyaki); **192,** 8809 (°*ādayaḥ*), 8812 (do.), 8851. — § 603 (Nārāyaṇāstramokshaṇap.): VII, **193*a*,** 8909, 8921, 8925; **195,** 8981; **199**χ, 9224 (*rājñaḥ*); **200,** 9281, (9287), (ω), 9289, (*aa*), 9308.—§ 604 (Karṇap.): VIII, **1,** 1 (°*mukhā nṛpāḥ*), 6 (°*niveçane*), 19 (*Karṇam D*°*hitaishiṇam*); **2**γ, 45; **3**δ, 56 (*rājā*); **4**ε, 85; **5**ζ, 98 (*parikleçān D*°*kṛtān*); **7,** †204; **8,** 230, 234, 238; **9**θ, 269, 273, 284, 321, 324, 325.—§ 605 (do.): VIII, **10,** 351 (*rājā*), 363, 364, (λ), 385 (*nṛpaḥ*), 387 (°*mukhāḥ* . . . *rājānaḥ*); **11**π, 415 (*rājā*); **13,** 494; **19,** 738, 764 (°*bale*); **23,** 913 (°*balam*); **28,** 1119 (*rājā*), 1122 (fights with Yudhishṭhira); **29,** 1174, 1180 (*rājā*), 1182, 1190 (*rājā*), 1195, 1197 (fights with Yudhishṭhira); **30,** 1222, 1224 (fights with Arjuna); **31**οο, 1253, 1262, (ππ), 1265, 1269, 1270, 1271, 1273, 1284, 1298, (1321); **32,** 1354.—§ 606 (do.): VIII, **33,** (1391) (related the Tripurākhyāna to Çalya); **34,** (1454), (1465), (1591) (related to Çalya how Rāma Jāmadagnya obtained weapons from Çiva), (1611); **35,** (1620), 1652, 1654, 1656, 1661.—§ 607 (do.): VIII, **36,** (1670), 1673, 1686, 1696; **38,** 1776; **42,** †1991, †1994.—§ 608 (do.): VIII, **46,** 2142 (*nṛpaḥ*); **47**λ, 2228; **50,** 2391, 2400: **51**γγ, 2441, 2442; **56,** 2698 (fights with Nakula and Sahadeva), 2723 (defeated by Dhṛshṭadyumna), 2726 (*d*: the standard of *D.* (*Kurupateḥ*) was set with golden *aṅgadas*, and bore the device of an elephant worked in jewels (*maṇimayam*)), 2767 (°*balam*); **57,** 2840, 2844, 2845 (°*bale*); **58**χχ, 2866; **60,** 2980 (*rājā sarvasya lokasya*), 2986, (ωω), 2988, 2989, 3025; **61,** 3128 (pierced by Bhīmasena); **62,** 3144, 3153 (pierced by Sahadeva), 3156, 3175; **63,** 3181, 3205 (defeated by Bhīmasena); **64,** 3253, 3256; **66**ι, 3314, †3344; **74**φφφ, 3759, 3761, 3779 (*rājā*); **75**χχχ, †3811; **77,** 3889 (*rājā*), 3907, 3933 (*putraḥ* . . . *tava*); **78,** 3940, 3989; **79**ζ', 4011 (*rājā*); **83,** †4259; **84**ο', 4270, 4272; **85,** †4307, †4338, †4341, †4342; **88**αβ, †4503, †4510; **89,** †4618; **92,** †4820, †4827, †4833 (when Karṇa had been slain *D.* became dejected); **93,** 4849, 4880, 4882; **94,** †4895, †4916, †4917, †4958 (*patim* . . . *Bhāratānām*); **95**αν', 4967 (*putraḥ* . . . *tava*), 4973 (*nṛpatiḥ*). —§ 609 (Çalyap.): IX, **1*a*,** 11 (*rājā*), 29 (*hato rājā*, all. to § 615), 39; **2,** 104 (*hataḥ*, do.), 106 (°*vadhena*), 115 (°*āparādhena*), 122 (*nihataḥ*).—§ 610 (do.): IX, **3,** 141, 171, 173, 175, 186 (*putraḥ* . . . *tava*); **4,** 192, (μ), 193; **5,** 286; **6,** 298, 314, (319); **7,** 321, (ρ), 322, 326 (appointed Çalya leader of his army).—§ 611 (do.): IX, **8,** 367 (*rājā*), (ε), 381, 392; **11,** 567; **12,** 620 (°*purogamāḥ*), 621 (°*purogamān*, slays Cekitāna), 627 (fights with Dhṛshṭadyumna); **13,** 686 (*rājā*); **15,** 753, 756 (fights with Dhṛshṭadyumna); **16,** 834 (defeated by Bhīmasena), 855; **17,** †874, 943 (°*balam*), 945; **18,** 956, 957, 971, 973, (976), 994 (°*balam*); **19**δδ, 1010, 1016, 1027, 1050 (*putram* . . . *tava*), 1053; **21,** 1123 (°*balam*), 1124 (*nṛpam*), 1128 (*rājā*); **22,** 1135, 1136, 1141, 1161; **23,** 1187 (*rājā*), 1207 (°*balam*); **24,** 1279, 1280, 1316,

1320; **25**, 1360 (deprived of his chariot by Dhṛshṭadyumna), 1376, 1377, 1380, 1398; **26**, 1403 (*Kauravye*); **27**, 1443, 1444, (σσ), 1447, 1448 (°*balaṃ*), 1449, 1461, 1467, 1470 (°*balaṃ*), 1471, 1477 (fights with Sahadeva); **28**, 1520 (*rājā*), 1551.—§ 612 (Hradapraveçap.): IX, **29**, 1572 (*rājā*), 1582, 1585, 1587, 1591, 1593 (*putraḥ . . . tava*, being alone left of the whole army *D.* fled and entered the Dvaipāyana lake), 1601, 1609, 1618 (*tava sutaḥ*), 1625 (*rājā*), 1626, 1637 (°*āmātyāḥ*), 1645, 1649, 1658 (*rājā*); **30**δ, 1674 (*rājā*), 1678 (°*vadhepsayā*), 1684, (1687), 1698, 1704 (*nṛpaḥ*), 1705, 1709, 1711 (*nṛpaṃ*), 1714 (do.), 1717, 1724, 1728, 1731 (*rājā*), 1736 (found by the Pāṇḍavas); **31**, 1742, (1780), (1786), 1796 (*tava sutaṃ*).—§ 613 (Gadāyuddhap.): IX, **32**, (1844), 1860 (*putraḥ . . . tava*), (1863), 1864 (do.), (1868), 1881 (do., will fight with the mace against one of the Pāṇḍavas); **33**, 1889, 1899, 1914, 1929, 1930, (1940), 1945 (*nṛpaṃ*; Bhīmasena will fight with *D.*).—§ 614 (do.): IX, **34**, 1951 (*Kauravyaṃ*), 1953.—§ 615 (do.): IX, **35**, 1982.—§ 615 (Baladevatīrthayātrā): IX, **54**, 3065. —§ 615 (Gadāyuddhap.): IX, **55**, 3079 (*putraḥ . . . tava*), 3088 (*rājā*), 3097, 3101 (*rājā*), 3103, 3119, 3120, 3123; **56**, 3157, 3167, 3172 (the encounter between Bhīmasena and *D.* begins); **57**, 3175, 3184, 3201, 3221, 3222, 3230; **58**, 3280, 3285, 3287, 3292 (Bhīmasena breaks the thighs of *D.* with his mace), 3305; **59**, 3311, †3320, 3330 (Bhīmasena struck *D.'s* head with his foot); **60**, 3367 (*hato rājā Dhārtarāshṭraḥ*), 3373; **61**, 3388 (*hataṃ*), 3389 (do.), 3396, 3398 (°*çiraḥ . . . pādena mṛditaṃ*), 3401, 3403 (°*vadhe*), (φ), 3410 (*nṛpaḥ*), 3414, (3438), 3446, 3459 (*nihataṃ*); **62**ψ, 3463, 3465 (°*puraḥsarāḥ*); **63**, 3505 (*hate*), 3510 (*hataṃ . . . Dhārtarāshṭraṃ*), 3524 (*hate*), 3564; **65**, 3626 (*hataṃ*), 3636, 3670 (orders Kṛpa to install Açvatthāman as generalissimo).—§ 616 (Sauptikap.): X, **1**a, 16, 59 (*hataḥ . . . rājā*); **2**, 94; **3**, 137; **5**, 198; **8**, 321; **9**, 479 (*hataḥ*), 489 (do.), 505, 508, 511, 527, 532, 537 (died and went to heaven).—§ 617 (Aishīkap.): X, **16**η, 753 (*hataḥ*). —§ 618 (Jalapradānikap.): XI, **1**a, 1 (*hate*), (β), 17; **8**ζ, 218 (*Dhṛtarāshṭrasya putrāṇāṃ yas tu jyeshṭhaḥ*); **9**η, 249 (*hate*); **11**, 292 (°*balāt*); **13**μ, 350; **14**ξ, 375 (°*āparādhena*), 378; **15**ο, 387, 391 (*hatvā D°ṃ*).—§ 619 (Strīvilāpap.): XI, **16**, 456; **17**β, 487, 488, 498, 503 (*nihataṃ Bhīmasenena*), 505, 511 (°*çubhāṅkagāṃ . . . Lakshmanamātaraṃ*), 514; **18**γ, 541 (*nṛpaṃ*); **25**κ, 732 (father of Lakshmaṇa), 736.—§ 620 (Çrāddhap.): XI, **26**, 757, (β), 786 (his body is cremated); **27**, 809 (°*balaṃ*).—§ 621 (Rājadh.): XII, **1**γ, 28 (*nṛpaṃ*), 41 (°*hitaishiṇaḥ*, i.e. Karṇa); **2**δ, 53 (friend of Karṇa); **3**, 107; **4**, 108, 111, 119 (*Kauravyaḥ*), 123, 128 (ravished the daughter of Citrāṅgada at her svayaṃvara); **5**, 135; **7**η, 189.—§ 623 (do.): XII, **14**a, 392; **16**, 509 (*nihataḥ*).—§ 635 (do.): XII, **38**, 1415 (°*sakha*, i.e. Cārvāka), 1425 (°*sakhā Cārvāko nāma*).—§ 636 (do.): XII, **39**, 1438 (*rājā*).—§ 637 (do.): XII, **44**, 1521 (°*gṛhaṃ*, given to Bhīmasena), 1523 (do.).—§ 641 (do.): XII, **124**, 4552, 4554, 4555, (4559), (4566), 4613 (discourse between Dhṛtarāshṭra and *D.*).—§ 719 (Ānuçāsanikap.): XIII, **1**, 10 (*nihataḥ*), 82.—§ 768 (do.): XIII, **148**, 6898, 6929, (ε), 6930 (°*āparādhena*). —§ 777 (Svargārohaṇika(ṃ) p.): XIII, **168**, 7746.—§ 778 (Açvamedhikap.): XIV, **1**, 11 (°*āparādhena*), 17; **3**, 55 (°*āparādhena*), 56.—§ 783 (Anugītāp.): XIV, **52**β, 1496 (°*sya . . . vadhopāyaḥ*).—§ 787 (Āçramavāsap.): XV, **2**, 56; **3**, 65, 69 (*nītaḥ kshayaṃ*), (γ), 77 (°*ṃ Kauravāṇām ādhipatye 'bhyashecayaṃ*, says Dhṛtarāshṭra), 111 (°*ādayaḥ*); **8**, 279 (°*aiçvaryāt*); **9**λ, 286; **10**μ, 317, 321 (*rājñā*), 327, 329; **11**, 363, 374 (°*ādayaḥ*); **14**σ, 415 (*rājānaṃ*).—§ 789 (Putradarçanap.): XV, **31**η, 852 (incarnation of Kali); **32**θ, 876 (among the dead warriors who, summoned by Vyāsa, arose from the Gaṅgā).—§ 791 (do.): XV, **36**, 975 (°*prabhṛtayo . . . lokāntaraṃ gatāḥ*).—§ 795 (Svargārohaṇap.): XVIII, **1**, 4, 6, (a), 7, 12 (*nṛpaṃ*), 13 (*rājā*), 18 (*rājñā*), 20; **6**, 174 (the followers of *D.* had been Rākshasas).

Cf. the following synonyms:—

Ājamīḍha[6], q.v.

Bhārata, Bharataçardūla, Bharataçreshṭha, Bhāratāgrya, Bharatarshabha, Bharatasattama, Bhāratasattama, q.v.

Dhārtarāshṭra, Dhṛtarāshṭraja, Dhṛtarāshṭraputra, Dhṛtarāshṭrasūnu, Dhṛtarāshṭrasuta, Dhṛtarāshṭrātmaja, q.v.

Gāndhāri ("son of Gāndhārī"): II, 1791; III, 14842, 15046, 15301; V, 190, †1838, 3031, 3706, 4118, 5049, 5730, 5806, 7108; VI, 3454, 4464, 4470; VII, 3457, 6544, 7125, 8449; VIII, 383, 1356, 1363, 1375, 1387, 1648, 1662; IX, 1850 (*Suyodhana*), 1851, 3427; X, 511.

Gāndhārīputra (do.): II, 1725.

Kaurava, Kauravaçreshṭha, Kauravanandana, Kauravātmaja, Kauravendra, Kauraveya, Kauravya, q.v.

Kuru, Kuruçreshṭha, Kurūdvaha, Kurukulaçreshṭha, Kurukulādhama, Kurumukhya, Kurunandana, Kurupati, Kurupravīra, Kurupuṅgava, Kururāja, Kurusattama, Kurusiṃha, Kurūttama, Kuruvardhana, q.v.

Suyodhana: I, 470, 497, 553, 5343, 5417, 5443, 5783, 5789, 5792, 5794, 5809, 6040, 7398; II, 1668, 2102, 2541 (Bhīmasena will slay *S.* and place his foot on his head); III, 890, 1080 (°*vadhāt*), 1115, 1156, †1356, †1367, 1481, 2040, 2046, 2049, 2051, †10286, 10887, †12323, †12326, †12590 (*Dhārtarāshṭraḥ*), 14876, 14941, 14944, 14948, 14950, 14951, 14968, 14975, 15011, 15018, 15041, 15104, 15151 (*rājā*), 15155, 15187, 15192, 15199, 15204, 15210, 15310 (*rājā*), 15314, 15509, 15515, 15516, 17292, 17453; IV, 646, 1645, 1648 (*rājā*), 1747 (do.), 2285; V, 136, 145, 594, †697, †749, †759, †762, †766, †860, †883, 935, 1954, 2281, 2498, †2506, 2592, 2663, 2673, 2816, 2830, 2842, 2854, 2860, 2864, 2879, 2880, 2922, 2958, 3191, 3509, 3743, 4283 (*Dhārtarāshṭraḥ*), 4094, 4410, 4451, 4461, 4824 (*rājānaṃ*), 4886, 4970 (*rājā*, read *Suyodhanaḥ* with B.), 5086, 5088, 5225, 5583, 5598, 5621, 5629, 5636, †5651 (*Dhārtarāshṭraṃ*), 5656, 5658, 5661, 5664, 5666, 5673, 5676, 5678, 5679 (*Kauravyaṃ Dhārtarāshṭraṃ*), 5681, 5688, 5693 (*rājā*), 5655 (*Dhārtarāshṭraṃ*); VI, 2494 (*rājā*), 2750 (do.), 2872 (*rājānaṃ*), 3459, 3925, 4330 (only B.), 4463, 5050, 5844; VII, 792, 2657 (°*āmātyāḥ*), 2659, 2664, 2687, 2697, 2803, 3805, 3813, 3823, 4202, 4215 (°*balaṃ*), 4714 (°*purogamaḥ*), 4717 (do.), 4729, 4731, 4735, 4736, 4873 (*rājā*), 4884, 4885, 5270, 5459, 5882 (*Kururājaṃ*), 6065 (*rājā*), 6247, 6310 (all. to Gāndhārīputrotpatti), 6477, 6494 (*putras tava*), 6591, 7127, 7272 (*rājā*), 7455, 8005, 8217, 8243 (Bhīmasena will slay *S.*), 8331 (*rājā*), 8341; VIII, 5 (*rājā*), 73 (*hataṃ*), 311, 1178, 2156, 2710 (*rājā*), †3342, †3351, †3395, 3630, 3647, 3654, 3669, 3698, 3699, 3715, 3729, †4231, †4233, †4749; IX, 2, 4 (*Dhārtarāshṭraḥ*), 1292, 1303, 1315, 1451, 1701, 1749, 1759, 1761, 1771, 1772, 1774, 1784, 1798, 1840, 1850, 1871, 1896 (*rājā*), 1900 (do.), 1906, 1909, 1921 (*Dhārtarāshṭre*), 1923, 3144, 3145 (*Kauravendre*), 3206, 3207, 3249, 3252,

3258, 3262, 3263, 3356 (Bhīmasena had vowed to break his thighs, cf. II, 2393), 3366, 3386 (*hato rājā*); XII, 185, 4624; XIII, 6901 (°*balam*); XIV, 12 (*rājā*), 385 (do.), 1806 (*nihate Kauravendre*); XV, 110; XVIII, 6, 10, 71 (*rājā*).

Duryodhana[2], king of Māhishmatī. § 720*b* (Sudarçanop.): XIII, **2**, 96 (son of Sudurjaya), 117 (gave his daughter Sudarçanā in marriage to Agni).

Duryodhanapitr̥ ("father of Duryodhana[1]") = Dhr̥tarāshṭra: III, 382; XV, 60.

Duryodhanasuta ("son of Duryodhana[1]") = Lakshmaṇa: VIII, 102, 161 (*L*°).

Duryodhanasuta, pl. (°*āḥ*) ("the sons of Duryodhana[1]"). § 795 (Svargārohaṇap.): XVIII, **5**, 149.

Duryodhanasutā ("daughter of Duryodhana[2]") = Sudarçanā: XIII, 104, 112.

Duryodhanāvara = Vikarṇa: II, 2280.

[Duryodhana-yajña(ḥ)] ("the sacrifice of Duryodhana"). § 516 (Ghoshay., cf. Karṇadigv.): *Karṇa* proposed to *Duryodhana* that he should celebrate a *rājasūya* sacrifice like *Yudhishṭhira*. But as the *purohita* told him that so long as *Yudhishṭhira* and *Dhr̥tarāshṭra* were living he could not undertake the *rājasūya* sacrifice, and advised him to cause the tributary kings to pay him tribute in gold, and with that gold to make a plough, and to plough the sacrificial compound with it, and then to perform a *Vaishṇava* sacrifice that nobody had performed before save the ancient *Vishṇu* (v. 15292, cf. v. 15329 foll.) which was equal to the *rājasūya*, this plan was agreed upon. *Duryodhana* appointed persons to their respective tasks, and desired all the artisans to construct the plough, etc. (III, **255**). When *Vidura* had announced to *Dhr̥tarāshṭra* that the preparations had been made, messengers were dispatched to invite the princes and the *brahmans*. *Duḥçāsana* ordered one messenger to invite the *Pāṇḍavas*, but *Yudhishṭhira* replied that they could not come before the completion of the thirteenth year. *Bhīma* threatened; the other *Pāṇḍavas* said nothing unpleasant. *Vidura* was charged with the distribution of food to the guests. After the completion of the sacrifice, all the kings having been dismissed, *Duryodhana*, with his brothers and *Karṇa* and *Çakuni*, entered *Hāstinapura* (III, **256**). *Duryodhana* was praised by most of the citizens, and his friends compared him to *Yayāti*, *Nahusha*, *Māndhātr̥*, and *Bharata*, who had gone to heaven after celebrating this sacrifice (v. 15329 foll., cf. v. 15292). *Karṇa* said that when *Duryodhana* had slain the *Pāṇḍavas* in battle and completed the *rājasūya* sacrifice he would once more honour him thus, and promised that until he had slain *Arjuna* he would not allow his feet to be washed, nor taste meat, and he would observe the *Asura* vow (i.e. not to drink intoxicating liquors, Nīl.), and never refuse to give to whoever might solicit him.

Dūshaṇa, a Rākshasa. § 528 (Rāvaṇagamaṇa): III, **277**, 15988 (°*ñ ca Kharañ ca*, slain by Rāma Dāçarathi), 15996.

Dūshaṇānuja, dual (°*au*) ("the younger brothers of Dūshaṇa") = Vajravega and Pramāthin: III, 16407, 16429, 16431.

Dūshaṇāvaraja ("the younger brother of Dūshaṇa") = Pramāthin: III, 16435 (*P*°, C. has by error *Du*°).

Dūshaṇāvaraja, dual (°*au*) ("the younger brothers of Dūshaṇa") = Vajravega and Pramāthin: III, 16405 (*Vajravega-Pramāthinau*).

Dushkāla = Çiva (1000 names[1]).

Dushkarṇa, a son of Dhr̥tarāshṭra. § 130 (Aṃçāvat.): I, **67**, 2730.—§ 182 (Dhr̥tarāshṭraputranāmak.): I, **117**, 4542 (C. has *Duḥk*°).—§ 583 (Bhīshmavadhap.): VI, **77**κ, 3344 (C. has *Duḥk*°); **79**[13], 3493 (fights with Çatānīka), 3495, 3498, 3499 (is slain by Çatānīka).—§ 600 (Ghaṭotkacavadhap.): VII, **155**, 6717, 6719, 6721, 6722 (assisted by Durmada he fights with Bhīmasena).

Dushkr̥tihan = Vishṇu (1000 names).

Dushmanta, v. Dushyanta.

Dushparājaya, a son of Dhr̥tarāshṭra. § 182 (Dhr̥tarāshṭraputranāmak.): I, **117**, 4548.

Dushpradharsha, a son of Dhr̥tarāshṭra. § 581 (Bhīshmavadhap.): VI, **64**κ, 2838 (among fourteen sons of Dhr̥tarāshṭra, who attacked Bhīmasena).—§ 608 (Karṇap.): VIII, **51**δδ, 2447. — § 611 (Çalyap.): IX, **26**ρρ, 1405 (attacked Bhīmasena), 1418 (is slain by Bhīmasena). Cf. next.

Dushpradharshaṇa, a son of Dhr̥tarāshṭra. § 130 (Aṃçāvat.): I, **67**, 2729.—§ 182 (Dhr̥tarāshṭraputranāmak.): I, **117**, 4542.—§ 232 (Svayaṃvarap.): I, **186**, 6981 (came to the svayaṃvara of Draupadī).—§ 600 (Ghaṭotkacavadhap.): VII, **170**μμ, 7671. Cf. next.

Dushpraharsha, a son of Dhr̥tarāshṭra. § 130 (Aṃçāvat.): I, **67**, 2731.

Dushprakampa = Çiva (1000 names[1]).

Dushvanta, v. Dushyanta.

Dushyanta[1], an ancient king, the husband of Çakuntalā and the father of Bharata. § 11 (Parvasaṅgr.): I, **2**, 371 (C. *Dushmantāt*).—§ 133: The founder of the Paurava line was *D.*, who ruled the whole world, even the Mlecchas. Description of his happy rule. *D.* could take up the mountain Mandara and support it in his arms (I, **68**). One day *D.* went a hunting (I, **69**). Having come to a forest, which was situated near the river Mālinī and was the resort of ascetics, Cāraṇas, Gandharvas, Apsarases, monkeys, Vālakhilyas, etc. (I, **70**), *D.*, in the hermitage of the R̥shi *Kaṇva Kāçyapa*, saw *Kaṇva's* adopted daughter *Çakuntalā*: I, **68**, 2801 (*Pauravāṇāṃ vaṃçakaraḥ*); **69**, 2815, 2833, 2834; **71**, 2898, 2909.—§ 134 (Viçvāmitra): I, **71**, (2910).—§ 135 (Çakuntalop.): I, **73**, (2955), (2960), 2970, 2981, 2985, 2987; **74**, 3001, 3023, (3060), 3070, 3100, 3101, 3102, 3104, 3113, 3117 (*rājarshiḥ*; *D.* wedded *Çakuntalā* according to the *Gāndharva* form of marriage and returned to his capital. *Çakuntalā* brought her son *Bharata* to *D.*, who did not at first acknowledge him as his son, until a celestial voice corroborated the truth of *Çakuntalā's* words).—§ 150 (Pūruvaṃç.): I, **94**, 3707 (son of Īlina), 3708, 3709 (father of Bharata).—§ 156 (do.): I, **95**, ††3781 (son of Īlina), ††3782 (married to Çakuntalā), 3783 (father of Bharata).—§ 267 (Yamasabhāv.): II, **8**, 326 (in the palace of Yama).—§ 565 (Gālavacarita): V, **117**, 3974 (*reme . . . yathā . . . Çakuntalāyāṃ D°ḥ*, C. *Dushv*°).—§ 761 (Ānuçāsanik.): XIII, **115**δ, 5666 (among the kings who did not eat meat during the month of Kārttika; C. has *Dushmantaḥ*).—§ 775 (do.): XIII, **166**η, 7676.

Dushyanta[2], son of Ajamīḍha. § 152 (Pūruvaṃç.): I, **94**, 3722 (*D.* and Parameshṭhin were the sons of Ajamīḍha with Nīlī), 3723 (the offspring of *D.* and Parameshṭhin were all the Pāñcālas).

Dvādaça = Çiva (1000 names[2]).

Dvādaçabhuja, a warrior of Skanda. § 615*u* (Skanda): IX, **45**η, 2559.

Dvādaçāksha, a warrior of Skanda. § 615*u* (Skanda): IX, **45**η, 2560.

Dvādaçanetrabāhu = Skanda: III, 14646.

Dvādaçātman = Sūrya: III, 156.

Dvaipāyana[1] = Vyāsa, q.v.

Dvaipāyana[2], a lake. § 612 (Hradapraveçap.): IX, **30**, 1721 (*hradaṃ*, there Duryodhana concealed himself when he had been defeated); **31**, 1743 (do.).—§ 615 (Baladevatīrthayātrāp.): IX, **54**ζ, 3065 (*hradaṃ D°aṃ nāma*, do.).—§ 785 (Anugītāp.): XIV, **60**, 1799 (*hrade*, do.). Cf. next.

Dvaipāyanahrada = Dvaipāyana[2]: IX, 1728.

Dvaipāyanasuta ("son of Dvaipāyana," i.e. Vyāsa) = Çuka: XII, 12603.

Dvaipāyanātmaja (do.) = Çuka: XII, 12585 (*Ç*°).

Dvaitavana[1], name of a forest. § 11 (Parvasaṅgr.): I, **2**, 429, 470 (C. by error *Dve*°).—§ 316 (Kirmīravadhap.): III, **11**, 453 (the Pāṇḍavas entered *D.*).—§ 322 (Dvaitavanapr.): III, **24**, 934.—§ 324 (do.): III, **26**, 964, 969.—§ 329 (Kāmyakavanapr.): III, **36**, 1451 (*vanāt*; the Pāṇḍavas left *D.* and entered the Kāmyaka forest). — § 449 (Ājagarap.): III, **177**, 12360 (the Pāṇḍavas again entered *D.*).—§ 512 (Ghoshayātrāp.): III, **238**, 14800, 14814, 14818; **246**, 15036.—§ 516 (Duryodhanayajña): III, **256**, 15305.—§ 517 (Ghoshayātrāp.): III, **257**, 15349 (*vanaṃ*).—§ 518 (Mṛgasvapnodbh.): III, **258**, 15354, 15357 (the Pāṇḍavas left *D.* and went to the Kāmyaka forest).—§ 547 (Karṇa): III, **310**, †17220 (the Pāṇḍavas again entered *D.*).—§ 548 (Āraṇeyap.): III, **311**, 17223 (do.), 17225.—§ 549 (Pāṇḍavapr.): IV, **4**, 87 (the Pāṇḍavas left *D.* and went to the capital of Virāṭa).—§ 556 (Sañjayayānap.): V, **23**, †710 (all. to § 512).—§ 599 (Jayadrathavadhap.): VII, **110**, 4196.—§ 607 (Karṇap.): VIII, **41**, 1950 (all. to § 512).—§ 608 (do.): VIII, **68**λλ, †3383, †3384.—§ 615 (Baladevatīrthay.): IX, **37**, 2145 (on the Sarasvatī, visited by Balarāma).—§ 623 (Rājadh.): XII, **14**, 391.—§ 794 (Mahāprasthānikap.): XVII, **3**, 91 (all. to Āraṇeyaparvan).—§ 795 (Svargārohaṇap.): XVIII, **3**, 113 (do.).

Dvaitavana[2], name of a lake (in the Dvaitavana forest). § 322 (Dvaitavanapr.): III, **24**, 928 (°*ṃ nāma saraḥ*), 930 (*saraḥ*), 931 (do.).—§ 324 (do.): III, **26**, 965 (do.).—§ 449 (Ājagarap.): III, **177**, 12359 (do., on Sarasvatī).—§ 512 (Ghoshayātrāp.): III, **237**, 14784 (*saraḥ*); **239**, 14844 (do.), 14848 (do.); **240**, 14861 (do.), 14867 (do.), 14868 (do.), 14873 (do.).

Dvaitavanapraveça(ḥ) ("proceeding to the Dvaitavana forest") (cf. Arjunābhigamanap.). § 322: The *Pāṇḍavas*, with *Kṛshṇa* and *Dhaumya*, on costly chariots yoked with excellent steeds, went into the forest, distributing nishkas of gold, etc., to brahmans versed in *Çikshā* (i.e., vedic pronunciation, PCR., or "grammar and the other vedāṅgas," Nīl.), *akshara* (= vedic orthography, PCR.; = veda, Nīl.), and *mantras* (= *praṇava*, i.e. the syllable *oṃ*, Nīl.), and followed by twenty attendants with bows, etc., while *Indrasena*, with the princess's (i.e. *Subhadrā's*, Nīl.) clothes and ornaments and the nurses and maidservants, followed in a chariot. The citizens walked round *Yudhishṭhira*, and the brahmans and principal men of *Kurujāṅgala* of all castes saluted him and blamed the *Dhārtarāshṭras*, etc. *Arjuna* told them that after their exile they would take away the good name of their enemies, and asked them to beseech the ascetics for their good. At last they returned to their respective abodes (III, **23**). After a conference between *Yudhishṭhira* and *Arjuna*, they resolved upon dwelling for these twelve years at the sacred lake *Dvaitavana* (see BR.) in the forest of the same name (copious description), on the banks of *Bhogavatī* (i.e. Sarasvatī, Nīl.), surrounded by many brahmans, and saluted by hosts of *Cāraṇas* and *Siddhas*, who came to see *Yudhishṭhira* (III, **24**).—§ 323: While they were dwelling there, *Dhaumya* performed their *ishṭis* (i.e. *darça-paurṇamāsa*, etc., Nīl.) and offerings to the *Pitṛs*, etc. Once the old *ṛshi Mārkaṇḍeya* came to them and smiled, recollecting *Rāma Dāçarathi*, whom he had seen on the top of the *Ṛshyamūka*, and comforted *Yudhishṭhira* by reminding him of the aforesaid *Rāma*, *Nābhāga*, *Bhagīratha*, etc., and *Alarka*, the king of the *Kāçis* and the *Karūshas* (*b*), the seven *ṛshis*, who had followed the ordinance of the Creator and therefore blazed in the firmament; "so you will regain prosperity." Then he went away in a northerly direction (III, **25**).—§ 324: The *Dvaitavana* forest becoming filled with brahmans (*Bhṛgus*, *Āṅgirasas*, *Vāsishṭhas*, *Kāçyapas*, *Āgastyas*, *Ātreyas*, etc.), and always resounding with Vedic recitations, mingling with the twangs of the bows of the *Pāṇḍavas*, a beautiful union of *brahman* and *kshatriya* customs was produced. Therefore one evening the *ṛshi Baka Dālbhya* represented to *Yudhishṭhira* that the *kshatriya* should always consult with a brahman, as did the *Asura* king *Bali*, the son of *Virocana*, who went to no other *tīrtha* than the brahmans, and then had all his wishes gratified, but who met with destruction when he began to act unjustly towards them. Then all those brahmans, *Dvaipāyana*, *Nārada*, *Jāmadagnya*, etc. (enumeration) (*a*), praised *Yudhishṭhira* (III, **26**).

Dvāpara[1], name of a yuga. § 8 (Parvasaṅgr.): I, **2**, 272 (*Tretā-D°yoḥ sandhau*, Rāma Jāmadagnya slew the kshatriyas), 282 (*antare Kali-D°yoḥ*, the battle between the Kurus and the Pāṇḍavas took place).—§ 310 (Āraṇyakap.): III, **3**, 150 (among the 108 names of Sūrya (the Sun)).—§ 374 (Tīrthayātrāp.): III, **85**, 8233.—§ 404 (do.): III, **121**, 10310 (*sandhir esha, naraçreshṭha, Tretāyā D°sya ca | enam āsādya, Kaunteya, sarvapāpaiḥ pramucyate*).—§ 406 (do.): III, **125**, 10409 (*sandhir dvayor, naraçreshṭha, Tretāyā D°sya ca | ayaṃ hi dṛçyate, Pārtha, sarvapāpapraṇāçanaḥ*).—§ 426 (Hanūmad-Bhīmasenas.): III, **149**, 11230.—§ 428: In the *D.* religion (*dharma*) decreases by a half; Nārāyaṇa is yellow; the Veda becomes divided into four parts, etc.: III, **149**, 11250 (*yuge*), 11256.—§ 458 (Mārkaṇḍeyas.): III, **188**, 12828 (comprises 2,000 years, its sandhyā and sandhyāṃça each 200 years).—§ 459 (do.): III, **189**, 12981 (in the *D.* Kṛshṇa is red (*raktaḥ*)).—§ 460 (do.): III, **190**, 13018; **191**, 13120.—§ 567 (Bhagavadyānap.): V, **132**, 4475 (*rājā . . . srashṭā . . . Dvāparasya*), 4477.—§ 574 (Jambukh.): VI, **10**, 387, 388, 390 (comprises 2,000 years), 397, 400 (*asmin*).—§ 581 (Bhīshmavadhap.): VI, **66**, 3012 (°*sya yugasyānte ādau Kaliyugasya ca | Sātvataṃ vidhim āsthāya gītaḥ Saṅkarshaṇena yaḥ*, i.e. Kṛshṇa).—§ 641 (Rājadh.): XII, **69**, 2684, 2693 (*rājā . . . srashṭā . . . Dvāparasya*), 2695; **91**μ, 3408.—§ 649 (Āpaddh.): XII, **141**a, 5328, 5331 (*Tretā-D°yoḥ sandhau*, there was a drought which extended for twelve years), 5332 (°*pratipādane*).—§ 664 (Mokshadh.): XII, **207**, 7557.—§ 677 (do.): XII, **232**, 8496, 8504, 8505; **233**, 8543, 8546 (*yuge*); **239**, 8719, 8726 (*yuge*), 8727.—§ 679 (do.): XII, **261**, 9264.—§ 683 (do.): XII, **268**a, 9592.—§ 717*b* (Nārāyaṇīya): XII, **340**, 12948 (*sandhyāṃçe samanuprāpte Tretāyā(ṃ) D°sya ca*, Nārāyaṇa will be born as Rāma Dāçarathi), 12953 (°*sya Kaleḥ sandhau*, Nārāyaṇa will be born as Kṛshṇa Vāsudeva); **341**, 13091.—§ 773*b* (Kṛshṇa Vāsudeva): XIII, **159**, †7363.

Dvāpara[2], a term of dice. § 130 (Aṃçāvat.): I, **67**, 2713 (personif.; incarnate as Çakuni).—§ 346 (Nalopakhyānap.): III, **58**, 2239, 2240, 2251, 2252; **59**, 2254.—§ 552 (Goharaṇap.): IV, **50**, 1578 (*nākshān kshipati Gāṇḍīvaṃ na*

Kṛtaṃ Dvāparaṃ na ca).—§ 569 (Bhagavadyānap.): V, **142**, 4819, 4821, 4823, 4825, 4827. — § 789 (Putradarçanap.): XV, **31**η, 852 (personif.; incarnate as Çakuni). — § 795 (Svargārohaṇap.): XVIII, **5**, 167 (personif.; Çakuni entered (*prāpa*) *D.*).

Dvāparayuga, v. Dvāpara[1].

Dvārakā, the capital of the Vṛshṇis (= Dvāravatī). § 41 (Anukram.): I, **1**, †149.—§ 11 (Parvasaṅgr.): I, **2**, 400, 428 (*purīṃ*).—§ 251 (Arjunavanavāsap.): I, **218**, 7899, 7901 (°*vāsinaḥ*).—§ 252 (Subhadrāharaṇap.): I, **220**, 7937, 7939 (*purīṃ*).—§ 262 (Bhagavadyāna): II, **2**, 49, 51 (C. has *Dvārikāṃ*). — § 272 (Rājasūyārambhap.): II, **13**, 553 (°*vāsinaṃ Kṛshṇaṃ*). — § 291 (Çiçupālavadhap.): II, **45**, 1567 (had been burnt by Çiçupāla).—§ 292 (Rājasūyikap.): II, **45**, 1611, 1615 (*purī*), 1617.—§ 299 (Dyūtap.): II, **68**, 2291 (°*vāsin Kṛshṇa*).—§ 305 (Anudyūtap.): II, **79**, 2606 (*Kṛshṇa D°vāsin*).—§ 317*b* (Kṛshṇa Vāsudeva): III, **12**, 493 (Kṛshṇa will submerge *D.* in the ocean).—§ 318 (Arjunābhigamanap.): III, **13**, 597, 611.—§ 319 (Saubhavadhop.): III, **14**, 618.—§ 320 (do.): III, **15**, 658; **16**, 665, 686 (°*vāsi tad balaṃ*); **19**, 776; **20**, 778, 779 (°*opavanāni*); **21**, 830, 832, 834; **22**, 874.—§ 321 (do.): III, **22**, 896.—§ 554 (Sainyodyogap.): V, **5**, 101; **7**, 130, 133 (*purīṃ*), 135.— § 592 (Saṃçaptakavadhap.): VII, **23***o*, 1018 (Sāraṅgadhvaja had wished to destroy *D.*). — § 599 (Jayadrathavadhap.): VII, **110**, 4198 (had been visited by Yudhishṭhira on his tīrthayātrā). — § 615 (Gadāyuddhap.): IX, **35**, 1985. — § 615 (Baladevatīrthayātrā): IX, **54**, 3071.—§ 615 (Gadāyuddhap.): IX, **60**, 3369.—§ 617 (Aishīkap.): X, **12**, 616, 639 (°*vāsibhiḥ*).—§ 621 (Rājadh.): XII, **1**, 16 (°*vāsinī*, i.e. Subhadrā, differently Nīl. and PCR.).—§ 717*b* (Nārāyaṇīya): XII, **340**, 12955 (*Kuçasthalīṃ*, there Kṛshṇa Vāsudeva will take up his residence), 12965 (°*āyāḥ . . . karishye pralayaṃ ghoraṃ ātmajñānābhisaṃvṛtaṃ*, sc. as Kṛshṇa Vāsudeva, says Nārāyaṇa, cf. III, 493).—§ 746 (Ānuçāsanik.): XIII, **64**, 3254.—§ 768*b* (Kṛshṇa Vāsudeva): XIII, **147**, 6841.—§ 768 (Ānuçāsanik.): XIII, **148**, 6888.—§ 781 (Açvamedhikap.): XIV, **15**, 403.—§ 782 (Anugītāp.): XIV, **16**, 413.—§ 783 (do.): XIV, **52**, 1500.—§ 784 (do.): XIV, **53**, 1536.— § 784*b* (Uttaṅka): XIV, **55**, 1600.—§ 785 (Anugītāp.): XIV, **59**, 1752; **86**, 2561 (°*vāsī*). — § 793 (Mausalap.): XVI, **1**, 15; **3**, 57; **5**, 136, 142, 144; **7**, 196 (°*vāsinaḥ*), 217 (the ocean flooded *D.*), 219 (°*vāsinaḥ*), 252 (°*vāsinaḥ*).— § 794 (Mahāprasthānikap.): XVII, **1**, 45 (*sāgareṇa pariplutāṃ*). Cf. Dvāravatī, Kuçasthalī.

Dvārakādhipati ("king of Dvārakā") = Āhuka: III, 829.

dvārapāla ("doorkeeper"), said of various Yakshas: II, 1194; III, 5079 (*Maṅkanakaṃ . . . Yakshaṃ*), 5085 (*Tarantukaṃ*), 6022 (*Tarandakaṃ* — B. *Arantukaṃ* — . . . *Yakshendrasya*), 7070 (*Macakrukaṃ*).—Do., pl.: II, 1045.

Dvāravatī, the capital of the Vṛshṇis (= Dvārakā). § 11 (Parvasaṅgr.): I, **2**, 622, 625.—§ 71 (Ādivaṃçāvatāraṇap.): I, **61**, 2272.—§ 159 (Pūruvaṃç.): I, **95**, ††3830.—§ 244 (Rājyalābhap.): I, **207**, 7595.—§ 253 (Haraṇāharaṇap.): I, **221**, 8021. — § 273 (Rājasūyārambhap.): II, **14**, 632 (*purīṃ*, the Yādavas fled from Mathurā to *D.*). — § 290 (Çiçupālavadhap.): II, **43**, 1507.—§ 292 (Rājasūyikap.): II, **45**, 1621 (*purīṃ*), 1626.—§ 320 (Saubhavadhop.): III, **15**, 637 (*purīṃ*); **20**, 785 (do.).—§ 358 (Tīrthayātrāp.): III, **82**, 5007 (in *D.* is the tīrtha Piṇḍāraka). — § 377 (Dhaumyatīrthak.): III, **88**, 8349 (in the country of the Surāshṭras). — § 511 (Draupadī-Satyabhāmās.): III, **235**, 14733.—§ 549 (Pāṇḍavapr.): IV, **4**, 85.—§ 552 (Goharaṇap.): IV, **25**, 876.—§ 554 (Sainyodyogap.): V, **6**, 131.—§ 615 (Gadāyuddhap.): IX, **60**, 3370. — § 617*b* (Brahmaçiras): X, **12**, 617.—§ 746 (Ānuçāsanik.): XIII, **70**, 3453 (when *D.* was being founded Nṛga was liberated); **72**, 3544.— § 773 (do.): XIII, **160**, 7403.—§ 773*d* (Çiva): XIII, **161**, 7494. — § 781 (Açvamedhikap.): XIV, **15**, 392 (*purīṃ*), 397 (do.). — § 783 (Anugītāp.): XIV, **52**, 1521 (do.). — § 785 (do.): XIV, **59**, 1753 (do.); **84**, 2478 (*Vṛshṇivīrābhipālitāṃ*).—§ 793 (Mausalap.): XVI, **4**, †111 (*purīṃ*); **6**, 167 (do., will be swallowed up by the ocean). Cf. Dvārakā, Kuçasthalī.

Dvārikā, v. Dvārakā.

Dvesha = Çiva (1000 names[1]).

Dvetavana, v. Dvaitavana.

***dvijarshi** (= Brahmarshi): (1) sg., XIII, 3541 (i.e. Uddālaka); (2) pl., XIII, 4548.

Dvimūrdhan, an Asura. § 595 (Shoḍaçarāj., v. Pṛthu Vainya): VII, **69**, 2413 (when the Asuras milked the earth *D.* was their milker).

Dvīpicarmanivāsin = Çiva: VII, 9532.

***dvīpin**, pl. (°*naḥ*) ("leopards"). § 127 (Aṃçāvat.): I, **66**, 2629 (among the offspring of Çārdūlī).

Dvirvyūha = Vishṇu: XII, 13603 (°*sañjñitaḥ*).

Dvita, a ṛshi, brother of Ekata and Trita. § 615*b* (Udapāna): IX, **36**, 2071 (Ekata, *D.*, and Trita were the sons of Gautama), 2078, 2083, 2085, 2091 (Trita cursed Ekata and *D.* to become wolves and having golāṅgūlas, bears, and apes for their offspring, on account of their deserting him when he had fallen into a hole).—§ 665 (Mokshadh.): XII, **208**θ, 7597 (*Ekataç ca D°ç caiva Tritaç caiva maharshayaḥ*, among the ṛshis of the west).—§ 717*c* (Uparicara): XII, **337**, 12757 (*Prajāpatisutāḥ . . . Ekataç ca D°ç caiva Tritaç caiva maharshayaḥ*, among the sadasyas at the sacrifice of Vasu Uparicara), 12771 (*Ekata-D°-Tritāḥ . . . Citraçikhaṇḍinaḥ*), 12812. — § 717*b* (Nārāyaṇīya): XII, **340**, 12876 (*Ekataç ca D°ç caiva Tritaç caiva maharshayaḥ*), 12950 (*Ekato 'tha D°s tathā . . . Prajāpatisutau*, will become apes and their offspring will assist Rāma Dāçarathi, cf. § 615*b*); **342**, 13174 (*Tritaṃ . . . Ekata-D°pātitaṃ*, cf. § 615*b*).—§ 770 (Ānuçāsanik.): XIII, **151**θ, 7114 (*Ekataç ca D°ç caiva Tritaç caiva*, among the seven *Varuṇasyartvijaḥ*). — § 775 (do.): XIII, **166**ε, 7668 (do., among the ṛshis of the west).

Dvivida, a monkey chief. § 282 (Sahadeva): II, **31**, 1122 (at Kishkindh(y)ā Sahadeva fought with the monkey kings *D.* and Mainda). — § 531 (Rāmopakhyānap.): III, **280**, 16115 (Mainda and *D.* were among the counsellors of Sugrīva). —§ 535 (Setubandhana): III, **283**β, 16287 (among the allies of Rāma Dāçarathi). — § 541 (Indrajidvadha): III, **289***a*, 16468, (β), 16477. — § 567 (Bhagavadyānap.): V, **130**, 4405 (at the gate of Saubha *D.* covered Kṛshṇa with a mighty shower of stones).

Dviyodha (Dviyodhin, B.) = Arjuna: II, 937.

Dyaus[1] (Div, Dyu, "Heaven"). § 3 (Anukram.): I, **1**β, 42 (*Divaḥ putro Bṛhadbhānuḥ*, etc., v. Āçāvaha). — § 135 (Çakuntalop.): I, **74**, 3017 (among the witnesses of the acts of men).—§ 615*u* (Skanda): IX, **45**γ, 2514.

Dyaus[2] (do.), a Vasu. § 164 (Āpavop.): I, **99**, 3934 (*Dyave*, dat.), 3936, 3945, 3946, 3957, 3963, 3965 (reborn as Bhīshma).

Dyumatsena, king of the Çālvas, husband of Çaibyā, and father of Satyavat. § 210 (Sambhavap.): I, **139**, 5521 (*Bhīmaḥ . . . D°samo bale*, the same?). — § 264 (Sabhākriyāp.): II, **4**β, 126 (the same?). — § 545 (Pativratāmāhātmyap.): III, **294**, 16664 (*Çālveshu*); **295**, 16693

(°*āçramam*), (†16699), (16703); **296,** (16718), (16720), 16721, (16740); **298,** 16858, 16883, 16890; **299,** 16903, 16911. — § 683 (Mokshadh.): XII, **238,** 9560 (°*sya saṃvādaṃ rājñā Satyavatā saha*), (9563), (9576).

Dyumatsenasuta ("the son of Dyumatsena") = Satyavat: III, 16675; IV, 655 (*S*°).

Dyūtaparvan ("the section relating to the gambling," the 28th of the minor parvans of the Mhbhr.). § 10 (Parvas.): I, **2,** 319. — § 293: When *Vyāsa* with his disciples came to take leave, *Yudhishṭhira* asked him about the celestial, atmospherical, and terrestrial portents which, according to the statement of *Nārada*, had happened at the *rājasuya*. *Vyāsa* said that in thirteen years they would be fulfilled by the destruction of all the *kshatriyas*, and that *Yudhishṭhira* would that very night see *Çiva* gazing incessantly towards the direction presided over by the king of the *Pitṛs* (i.e. the south). Then *Vyāsa* with his disciples proceeded towards *Kailāsa*. *Yudhishṭhira* resolved to die in order that he might not be the cause of the destruction of the *kshatriyas*, but called back from his intention by *Phālguna* (i.e. Arjuna), he took upon him the vow not to speak a harsh word to his brothers or to any of the kings. Then, having gratified the *Pitṛs* and gods, he entered his own palace, accompanied by his ministers (II, **46**).—§ 294: *Duryodhana*, accompanied by *Çakuni*, by and by beheld all the *sabhā*; he mistook a piece of crystal for water and drew off his clothes, mistook a lake for land and fell in, etc., and was laughed at by *Bhīma*, *Arjuna*, the twins, and the menials of the palace. Filled with wrath and jealousy he became pale, and returned to *Hāstinapura*, together with *Çakuni* (II, **47**). *Çakuni* told him to ask *Yudhishṭhira*, who was very fond of gambling and did not know how to play, to play at dice; then he (*Çakuni*), who was skilled in dice, would win his kingdom and prosperity for *Duryodhana* (II, **48**). *Çakuni* told *Dhṛtarāshṭra* that *Duryodhana* was pale and depressed; *Dhṛtarāshṭra* asked *Duryodhana* the cause; *Duryodhana* told him that *Yudhishṭhira* supported 88,000 *snātakas*, giving to each of them thirty slave-girls; that 10,000 other brahmans daily ate at his palace the best food off golden plates; that the king of *Kāmboja* sent to him innumerable skins, etc.; that the Ocean brought the *Vāruṇa* nectar to him in a vessel of copper, as the celestial wives (*amarastriyaḥ*) to *Indra*; that *Vāsudeva*, having brought an excellent conch, bathed him with sea-water brought in 1,000 jars of gold, etc., from the eastern, southern, and western oceans; that the conches, which were blown when 100,000 brahmans were fed, could be heard there almost incessantly, etc. *Duryodhana* proposed to *Dhṛtarāshṭra* to invite *Yudhishṭhira* to a game at dice with *Çakuni*, and prevented him from consulting *Vidura* till he had had a *sabhā* built. Then he ordered *Vidura*, who dissuaded him in vain, to invite *Yudhishṭhira*. *Vidura* in great sorrow went to *Bhīshma* (II, **49**).—At the request of *Janamejaya*, *Vaiçampāyana* related that *Dhṛtarāshṭra*, having ascertained the opinion of *Vidura* (*b*), sought to bring *Duryodhana* back from his purpose to play at dice; but *Duryodhana* would not give way, relating that the *Nīpas*, *Citrakas*, the *Kaukuras*, the *Kāraskaras*, and the *Lohajaṅghas* were like bondsmen in the house of *Yudhishṭhira*, and that *Bhīma*, *Arjuna*, and *Draupadī* had laughed at his mistake regarding the crystal, etc. (II, **50**).—§ 295: *Duryodhana* enumerated to *Dhṛtarāshṭra* the articles brought as tribute from various peoples to *Yudhishṭhira*. *Yājñasenī* (i.e. Kṛshṇā) daily (during the *rājasūya*) took care that everybody, including the deformed and the dwarfs, had eaten before she herself took her meal. Only two peoples did not pay tribute to *Yudhishṭhira*, the *Pāñcālas*, in consequence of their relationship by marriage, and the *Andhaka - Vṛshṇis*, in consequence of their friendship (II, **52**).—§ 296: *Duryodhana* continued to enumerate kings, etc., who waited upon *Yudhishṭhira* at the *rājasūya*. The Ocean brought that *Vāruṇa* conch (*çaikyaṃ*, "in a sling," PCR., i.e. in a strap, cf. BR.), which *Viçvakarman* had constructed with 1,000 *nishkas*, and which *Prajāpati* had in a former *kalpa* presented to *Indra*; with that conch *Kṛshṇa* anointed (*abhishiktaḥ*) *Yudhishṭhira*. When the conches were blown, those among the kings who were weak fell down, and *Dhṛshṭadyumna*, *Sātyaki*, the *Pāṇḍavas*, and *Keçava* laughed; then *Bībhatsu* (= Arjuna) gave to the principal brahmans 500 bullocks with horns plated with gold, and *Yudhishṭhira* obtained, like *Hariçcandra*, such prosperity that he surpassed *Rantideva*, *Nābhāga*, *Yauvanāçva*, *Manu*, *Pṛthu Vainya*, *Bhagīratha*, *Yayāti*, and *Nahusha* (II, **53**).—§ 297: Continuation of the conversation between *Dhṛtarāshṭra* and *Duryodhana* (II, **54, 55**). —§ 298: As *Çakuni* recommended the match of dice and praised his own dexterity in gambling, and *Duryodhana* spoke reprovingly of *Vidura* on account of his fondness for the *Pāṇḍavas*, etc., *Dhṛtarāshṭra* reluctantly caused the *sabhā* (called *Toraṇasphāṭikā*) to be built, with 1,000 columns adorned with gold and lapis lazuli, a *kroça* in length and breadth, and then ordered *Vidura* to bring *Yudhishṭhira* and his brothers (II, **56, 57**). *Vidura* arrived at the palace of *Yudhishṭhira* and invited him. *Yudhishṭhira*, having learned that he should have to play with *Çakuni*, *Viviṃçati*, *Citrasena*, *Satyavrata*, *Purumitra*, and *Jaya*, "the most desperate and terrible gamblers, always depending upon deceit," was unwilling to come; but as he had made the vow never to refuse when challenged, he set out for *Hāstinapura* the next day with his relatives, *Draupadī*, brahmans, etc., riding on the chariot taken charge of (so BR.) by *Bāhlīka*, and when he had arrived he saluted *Bhīshma*, *Droṇa*, *Karṇa*, *Kṛpa*, *Açvatthāman*, *Somadatta*, *Duryodhana*, *Çalya*, *Saubala*, *Duḥçāsana*, *Jayadratha*, etc., and *Gāndhārī* and *Dhṛtarāshṭra* (II, **58**). *Çakuni* exhorted *Yudhishṭhira* to gamble. *Yudhishṭhira* quoted *Asita Devala* (*b*), but he was obliged to assent; *Duryodhana* said that he himself would supply jewels, etc., and that it was for him that *Çakuni* would play (II, **59**). The play began, the stake being a wreath of pearls, which *Çakuni* won (II, **60**). *Çakuni* then won from *Yudhishṭhira* his treasury, slave - girls, serving - men, elephants, chariots, the *Gandharva* horses which *Citrasena* had given to *Arjuna*, his warriors, and *nidhis* (II, **61**). *Vidura*, addressing *Dhṛtarāshṭra*, quoted the words of *Kāvya*, and reminded him that among the *Bhojas* they had abandoned an unworthy (*asamañjusam*) son; the *Andhakas*, *Yādavas*, and *Bhojas* had abandoned *Kaṃsa*, and when he had been slain by *Kṛshṇa* the whole tribe became glad for a hundred years; "[likewise] let *Arjuna* slay this *Suyodhana* at thy command"; he quoted what *Kāvya* said to the *Asuras* in order to induce them to abandon *Jambha*, and related how a king from greediness after gold killed some gold-vomiting fowls that dwelt in his house, and so destroyed both his present and future wealth (II, **62**). *Vidura* warned against the gambling, and suggested to *Dhṛtarāshṭra* rather to win the *Pāṇḍavas* than their wealth, and to let *Çakuni*, the hill-king (*Pārvatīyaḥ*), return whence he came (II, **63**). *Duryodhana* blamed *Vidura* for his partiality towards the *Pāṇḍavas*, and said that he would only follow the advice of his own intellect.

Vidura complained of the ingratitude of kings and their fondness of flattery (II, **64**). *Yudhishṭhira* lost his wealth, kine, horses, goats, and sheep, "from *Parṇāçā* to the eastern bank of the *Sindhu*," his city, country, lands, and the wealth of all dwelling therein, except that of the brahmans, and all those persons themselves except the brahmans, the ear-rings and *nishkas* and other ornaments of the princes who were present, then *Nakula, Sahadeva, Arjuna, Bhīma*, himself, and *Draupadī*; now *Bhīshma, Droṇa, Kṛpa, Vidura*, etc., all gave way to grief, but *Dhṛtarāshṭra, Karṇa, Duḥçāsana*, etc., were glad (II, **65**).—§ 299: *Duryodhana* ordered *Kshattṛ* (i.e. *Vidura*) to bring hither *Draupadī* to sweep the chambers and stay with the servant maids; *Vidura* declared that having lost himself, *Yudhishṭhira* could not lawfully stake *Draupadī*, and said: "A goat had once swallowed a knife, and when it was pierced by it the hunter placed the head of the animal on the ground, and when drawing the knife out he tore its throat frightfully; therefore do not swallow the wealth of the *Pāṇḍavas*" (II, **66**). Then *Duryodhana* ordered the *prātikāmin* (a *sūta*) to bring *Draupadī*; she ordered him to ask *Yudhishṭhira* whether he had lost himself or her first; as *Yudhishṭhira* said nothing, *Duryodhana* ordered that *Draupadī* should come and put her question in the assembly; she sent the *sūta* back to the assembly saying that she would do what aged and virtuous persons would tell her; all sat without uttering a word; but *Yudhishṭhira* sent a trusted messenger to *Draupadī*, directing that, although in consequence of her season having come she was attired in one piece of cloth only, she should come before her father-in-law weeping bitterly. *Duryodhana* again ordered the *prātikāmin* to bring her, and as he seemed irresolute, he asked *Duḥçāsana* to do so. As she would flee to the ladies' household, *Duḥçāsana* dragged her in by her hair, while she was praying to *Kṛshṇa* and *Jishṇu* (i.e. *Arjuna*), who were *Nārāyaṇa* and *Nara*, and blaming *Droṇa, Bhīshma, Vidura*, etc., for looking silently on this crime. As she was casting a glance upon her enraged lords, *Duḥçāsana*, dragging her still more forcibly, addressed her, "Slave! slave!" and laughed aloud, applauded by *Karṇa, Çakuni*, and *Duryodhana*, while all the others were filled with sorrow. *Bhīshma* declared himself to be unable to decide the question she had put. As she then asked the others present to decide it, *Duḥçāsana* spoke many harsh words, and *Bhīma*, looking at *Yudhishṭhira*, gave way to wrath (II, **67**). *Bhīma* blamed *Yudhishṭhira*, and ordered *Sahadeva* to bring fire, as he wanted to burn the hands of *Yudhishṭhira*, but *Arjuna* appeased him. *Vikarṇa* repeatedly appealed to those present to decide the question, and as they did not say one word, he declared that as *Yudhishṭhira* must be regarded as of no authority, because he had shown himself addicted to the vice of gambling, etc., he regarded *Draupadī* as not won. All applauded him, except *Karṇa*, who maintained that she had been justly won, and as, contrary to the ordinance of the gods that a woman should have only one husband, she had five husbands, there was no impropriety in dragging her to the assembly, and even to uncover her. *Karṇa* then asked *Duḥçāsana* to take off the robes of the *Pāṇḍavas* and the attire of *Draupadī*. The *Pāṇḍavas* took off their upper garments, and *Duḥçāsana* began to drag off the attire of *Draupadī*. But as she thought of and cried to *Hari* (i.e. *Kṛshṇa*), *Dharma* continually covered her anew with excellent clothes. *Bhīma* swore that he would drink the blood of *Duḥçāsana*. All blamed *Duḥçāsana* and *Dhṛtarāshṭra*. *Vidura* exhorted the assembly to answer the question put by *Draupadī*, and related the dialogue of *Prahlāda* (q.v.) and *Āṅgirasa* (i.e. *Sudhanvan*) (§ 300).—§ 300: v. *Prahlāda*.—§ 301: The kings answered not a word, and *Karṇa* told *Duḥçāsana* to take away the slave-woman *Kṛshṇā* to the inner apartments (II, **68**). Dragged by *Duḥçāsana, Draupadī* saluted the assembly, complained of being exposed to the gaze of the crowd, and again asked them to answer her question. *Bhīshma* again declared himself unable to decide it, but thought *Yudhishṭhira* ought to decide it (II, **69**). *Duryodhana* said to *Draupadī*: "Let thy husbands decide the question, and, by making *Yudhishṭhira* the just a liar, free thee from slavery." *Bhīma* said that only his obedience to *Yudhishṭhira* and the admonitions of *Arjuna* retained him from killing the wretched sons of *Dhṛtarāshṭra*. *Bhīshma, Droṇa*, and *Vidura* asked him to forbear (II, **70**). *Karṇa* exhorted *Draupadī* to choose a new husband among the sons of *Dhṛtarāshṭra*, and *Duryodhana*, after having exhorted *Yudhishṭhira* to decide the question, uncovered his left thigh and showed it to *Draupadī*. *Bhīshma* swore that he would break this thigh of his. *Vidura* warned them, and was of opinion that *Yudhishṭhira* had no right to stake her. *Duryodhana* said that if *Bhīma, Arjuna*, and the twins declared that *Yudhishṭhira* was not their master, then *Draupadī* should be free. *Arjuna* said that he was certainly their master before the play, "but having lost himself, let all the *Kauravas* judge whose master he could be after that." Just then a jackal began to cry near the *agnihotra* of *Dhṛtarāshṭra*, and other terrible omens were heard. On that account *Gāndhārī* and *Vidura* remonstrated with *Dhṛtarāshṭra*, who blamed *Duryodhana* and granted a boon to *Kṛshṇā*. She chose that *Yudhishṭhira* should become free from slavery. As she was granted a second boon, she asked that *Bhīma* and his brothers with their chariots and bows should regain their liberty. She refused to ask a third boon (II, **71**). *Karṇa* praised *Draupadī* for having saved her husbands. *Bhīma* threatened to slay all his foes instantly, but was retained by *Arjuna* and *Yudhishṭhira* (II, **72**). *Dhṛtarāshṭra* sent *Yudhishṭhira* with his brothers and *Kṛshṇā* upon their chariots to *Indraprastha*, having asked him not to remember the harshness of *Duryodhana* (II, **73**).

Dyutidhara = Vishṇu (1000 names).

Dyutimat[1], king of the Madras. § 159 (Pūruvaṃç.): I, **95**, ††3832 (*Madrarājasya*, father of Vijayā, the wife of Sahadeva).

Dyutimat[2], a mountain in Kuçadvīpa. § 575 (Bhūmip.): VI, **12**ε, 451 (*hemaparvataḥ*, the second mountain in Kuçadvīpa, differently PCR.).

Dyutimat[3], king of the Çālvas. § 677 (Mokshadh.): XII, **235**, 8607 (*Çālvarājaḥ*, gave his kingdom to Ṛcīka and gained an abode of blessing).—§ 767 (Ānuçāsanik.): XIII, **137**a, 6267 (do.).

Dyutimat[4], king of Māhismatī. § 720*b* (Sudarçanop.): XIII, **2**, 92 (son of Madirāçva), 93 (father of Suvīra).

E

Edī, a mātṛ. § 615*u* (Skanda): IX, **46**θ, 2631.

* **Eka** ("the only one"): XII, 11232 (= Hiraṇyagarbha); XIII, 7027 (= Vishṇu, 1000 names).

Ekacakra, an Asura. § 92 (Aṃçāvat.): I, **65**, 2533 (son of Danu).—§ 130 (do.): I, **67**, 2657 (*mahāsuraḥ*, incarnate as king Prativindhya).

Ekacakrā, a city. § 11 (Parvasaṅgr.): I, **2**, 382 (all. to § 215). — § 71 (Ādivaṃçāvatāraṇap.): I, **61**, 2255, 2257 (do.).—§ 158 (Pūruvaṃç.): I, **95**, ††3824, ††3825 (do.).—§ 214 (Hiḍimbavadhap.): I, **156**, 6094.—§ 215 (Bakavadhap.): I, **157**, 6103, 6104; **164**, 6306 (the Pāṇḍavas and Kuntī lived for some time at *E.* in the house of a brahman. Bhīmasena slew the Rākshasa Baka).—§ 231 (Svayaṃvarap.): I, **184**, 6928.—§ 317 (Arjunābhigamanap.): III, **12**, 571, 572 (all. to § 215). — § 567 (Bhagavadyānap.): V, **128**, 4272 (do.).

Ekacūḍā, a mātṛ. § 615*u* (Skanda): IX, **46**θ, 2623.

Ekaçīrshan = Çiva (1000 names[1]).

Ekaçṛṅga, pl. (°*āḥ*), a class of Pitṛs. § 270 (Brahmasabhāv.): II, **11**, 463 (in the palace of Brahmán).

Ekaçṛṅga = Vishṇu (Kṛshṇa): XII, 13114, 13251 (origin of the name: Vishṇu assumed the form of a boar with a single tusk).

Ekahaṃsa, a tīrtha. § 362 (Tīrthayātrāp.): III, **83**, 5090.

Ekajaṭa, a warrior of Skanda. § 615*u* (Skanda): IX, **45**η, 2560.

Ekāksha[1], an Asura. § 93 (Aṃçāvat.): I, **65**, 2537 (son of Danu).

Ekāksha[2], a warrior of Skanda. § 615*u* (Skanda): IX, **45**η, 2560.

Ekāksha[3] = Çiva: XIII, 7503.

Ekalavya, a Nishāda prince. § 130 (Aṃçāvat.): I, **67**, 2699 (among the incarnations from the Krodhavaçagaṇa).—§ 204: Among the kings and princes who flocked to *Droṇa* by thousands to learn the *Dhanurveda* was *E.*, the son of the *Nishāda* king *Hiraṇyadhanus*. Not admitted, because he was a *Naishādi*, he in the forest practised weapons before a clay image of *Droṇa* and became very skilled in shooting. One day when the sporting dog of the princes came upon him he shot seven arrows into its mouth, and thus pierced the dog came back to the *Pāṇḍavas*, who highly admired the precision of the archer. In order that he might not surpass *Arjuna*, *Droṇa* took from *E.* the thumb of his right hand as his tutorial fee: I, **132**, 5241 (*Nishādarājasya Hiraṇḍhanushaḥ sutaḥ*), (5255), 5257, 5261, 5262, 5264, 5265, (5265), 5266.—§ 289 (Arghāharaṇap.): II, **37**, 1351.—§ 290 (Dyūtap.): II, **53**, 1915 (among the kings who waited upon Yudhishṭhira at the rājasūya).—§ 554 (Sainyodyogap.): V, **4**γ, 80 (among the kings to whom the Pāṇḍavas ought to send messengers). — § 561*c* (Kṛshṇa Vāsudeva): V, **48**, 1884 (*ayaṃ sma yuddhe manyate 'nyair ajeyaṃ tam Ekalavyaṃ nāma Nishādarājaṃ | vegeneva* (B. °*naiva*) *çailam abhihatya Jambhaḥ çete sa Kṛshṇena hataḥ parāsuḥ*. The text is not clear, but seems to indicate that *E.* has been slain by Kṛshṇa).—§ 600 (Ghaṭotkacavadhap.): VII, **180**, †8210 (*Nishādaḥ*, had been slain [by Kṛshṇa?]); **181**δδ, 8231 (all. to § 204; *E°ṃ hi sāṅgushṭham açaktā deva-Danavāḥ | sa-Rākshasoragāḥ, Pārtha, vijetuṃ yudhi karhicit*).—§ 785 (Anugītāp.): XIV, **83**, 2472 (*Nishādarājño vishayam*).—§ 793 (Mausalap.): XVI, **6**κ, 159 (*Naishādim*, had been slain by Kṛshṇa). Cf. Naishādi, Nishāda, Nishādarāja.

Ekalavyasuta ("the son of Ekalavya"). § 785 (Anugītāp.): XIV, **83**, 2473 (is vanquished by Arjuna).

Ekānaṃçā = Kuhū: III, 14129.

Ekāntadarçaṇa = Mahāpurusha (Mahāpurushastava).

Ekapad[1], an Asura. § 92 (Aṃçāvat.): I, **65**, 2533 (son of Danu, only in C., B. has *Ishupād*).

Ekapad[2] = Çiva (1000 names[1]).

Ekapad[3] = Vishṇu (1000 names).

Ekapāda, pl. (°*āḥ*), a people. § 295 (Dyūtap.): II, **52**, 1868

Ekaparvataka (?), a mountain. § 276 (Jarāsandhavadhap.): II, **20**, 794 (PCR. "on the same mountain").

Ekāsana, pl. (°*āḥ*), a people. § 295 (Dyūtap.): II, **52**, 1859 (among the peoples who brought tribute to Yudhishṭhira).

Ekata, a ṛshi, brother of Dvita and Trita. § 615*b* (Udapāna): IX, **36**, 2071 (v. Dvita), 2078, 2083, 2085, 2091 (v. Dvita).—§ 665 (Mokshadh.): XII, **208**θ, 7597 (do.). — § 717*c* (Uparicara): XII, **337**, 12757 (do.), 12771 (do.), 12812 (do.).—§ 717*b* (Nārāyaṇīya): XII, **340**, 12876 (do.), 12950 (do.); **342**, 13174 (do.).—§ 734 (Ānuçāsanik.): XIII, **26a**, 1764 (*dvijaḥ* (*Dvitaḥ*, PCR.), among the ṛshis who came to see Bhīshma as he lay on his arrow-bed).—§ 770 (do.): XIII, **151**θ, 7114 (v. Dvita).—§ 775 (do.): XIII, **166**ε, 7668 (do.).

Ekātman = Vishṇu (1000 names).

Ekatvacā, a mātṛ. § 615*u* (Skanda): IX, **46**θ, 2642.

Ekavaktrā, a mātṛ. § 615*u* (Skanda): IX, **46**θ, 2648.

Ekavyūhavibhāga = Vishṇu (Nārāyaṇa): XII, 13603.

Elāpatra, a serpent. § 47 (Sarpanāmak.): I, **35**, 1551.—§ 49 (Vāsuki): I, **38**, 1622, 1638; **39**, 1641, 1648 (*nāgena*), 1651.

Elapatra = Elāpatra. § 564 (Mātalīyop.): V, **103**γ, 3626.—§ 603*d* (Tripura): VII, **202**, 9564 (Çiva made *E.* and Pushpadanta the pins of his yoke; C. has by error °*pu*°).

Elaputra, v. Elapatra.

Elavila, v. Ailavila.

Eraka, a serpent. § 66 (Sarpasattra): I, **57**, 2154 (of Kauravya's race).

Etāvarṇau (dual) = Nara and Nārāyaṇa: III, 8384 (*avarṇau*, cf. Nīl.; PCR. Etāvarṇa and Avavarṇa).

G

Gabdhakālī (I, 3801), v. Gandhakālī.

Gabhasti = Çiva (1000 names[2]).

Gabhastimat = Sūrya (the Sun): III, 146.

Gabhastinemi = Vishṇu (Kṛshṇa): XII, 1512; XIII, 7001 (1000 names).

Gabhīra = Vishṇu (1000 names).

Gabhīrātman = Vishṇu (1000 names).

Gada, a Vṛshṇi, the younger brother of Kṛshṇa. § 232 (Svayaṃvarap.): I, **186**, 6997 (*sa-G°ḥ*, among the Vṛshṇis who were present at the svayaṃvara of Draupadī).—§ 252 (Subhadrāharaṇap.): I, **219**, 7915.—§ 253 (Haraṇāharaṇap.): I, **221**, 7992 (*vidushāṃ varaḥ*, came to the marriage of Arjuna and Subhadrā).—§ 262 (Bhagavadyāna): II, **2**, 56 (received Kṛshṇa on his return to Dvārakā).—§ 264 (Sabhākriyāp.): II, **4**β, 125 (among the princes who waited upon Yudhishṭhira when he entered his palace).—§ 287 (Rājasūyikap.): II, **34**, 1275 (°-*Pradyumna-Çāmbāç ca*, came to the rājasūya of Yudhishṭhira).—§ 320 (Saubhavadhop.): III, **15**, 644 (°-*Çāmboddhavādibhiḥ*, defended Dvārakā); **18**, 733 (°*āgrajaḥ* . . . *Mādhavaḥ*, i.e. Kṛshṇa), 736 (°*Sāraṇau*).—§ 342 (Indralokābhigamanap.): III, **51**, 1994 (*Akrūra-G°-Sāmbaiḥ*, will assist the Pāṇḍavas in battle).—§ 402 (Tīrthayātrāp.): III, **120**, †10277 (°*olmukau*).—§ 452 (Mārkaṇḍeyas.): III, **183**,

†12570 (°*āgrajāya*, i.e. Kṛshṇa).—§ 554 (Sainyodyogap.): V, **1**, †27 (°*pūrvajasya*, i.e. Kṛshṇa); **3**, 59 (°-*Pradyumna-Çāmbāç ca*).—§ 570 (Sainyaniryāṇap.): V, **157**κ, 5330 (°-*Sāmboddhavādibhiḥ*, accompany Balarāma).—§ 577 (Bhīshmavadhap.): VI, **43**, 1617 (°*āgrajaḥ*, i.e. Kṛshṇa).—§ 589 (Droṇābhishekap.): VII, **11**ξ, 408.—§ 599 (Jayadrathavadhap.): VII, **110**σ, 4194.—§ 617*b* (Brahmaçiras): X, **12**, 638 (had never desired the discus of Kṛshṇa).—§ 641 (Rājadh.): XII, **81**, 3030 (*saukumāryaṃ punar G°e*). — § 730 (Ānuçāsanik.): XIII, **14**γ, †630.—§ 785 (Anugītāp.): XIV, **66**θ, 1938 (accompanied Kṛshṇa); **86**τ, 2557 (came to the açvamedha of Yudhishṭhira).—§ 793 (Mausalap.): XVI, **3**γ, 72, 101 (is slain).

Gadādhara[1] = Vishṇu (1000 names).—Do.[2] = Kubera: VI, 2039.

Gadāgraja[1] = Kṛshṇa, q.v.—Do.[2] = Vishṇu (1000 names).

Gadāparvan ("the section treating of the combat with the mace"). § 795*c* (Mahābhārata): XVIII, **6**, 275 (i.e. Gadāyuddhaparvan).

Gadapūrvaja = Kṛshṇa: V, †27.

Gadāvasāna, name of a place near Mathurā. § 275 (Rājasūyārambhap.): II, **19**, 764 (Jarāsandha hurled a mace towards Mathurā; the place where it fell was named *G.*).

Gadāyuddha ("the combat with the mace"). § 10 (Parvasaṅgr.): I, **2**, 346 (i.e. Gadāyuddhaparvan).

[Gadāyuddhaparvan (°*va*)] ("the section relating to the battle with maces"). Cf. Gadāparvan, Gadāyuddha. § 613: Requested by *Dhṛtarāshṭra* (**a**), *Sañjaya* related: *Duryodhana* agreed to fight his foes, one at a time (β); *Yudhishṭhira* granted his request, adding that if he could slay even one of the five *Pāṇḍavas* he would remain king. *Duryodhana* rose from the lake and challenged the *Pāṇḍavas* (γ); *Yudhishṭhira* taunted him with his unfair conduct in slaying *Abhimanyu* (δ) (IX, **32**). *Kṛshṇa* reproved *Yudhishṭhira* for his rashness in staking everything on the result of such a single combat with *Duryodhana* (ε); *Bhīmasena* assured *Kṛshṇa* that *Duryodhana* would be no match for him in an encounter with the mace (ζ); *Kṛshṇa* applauded *Bhīma*, and exhorted him to slay *Duryodhana* (η); *Sātyaki*, etc. (θ), applauded *Bhīma*; *Bhīma's* boastful address (ι) to *Yudhishṭhira* and *Duryodhana*; *Duryodhana's* dignified reply, applauded by the *Pāṇḍavas* and *Sṛñjayas*; the elephants began to grunt and the steeds to neigh; the weapons of the *Pāṇḍavas* blazed forth of their own accord (IX, **33**).—§ 614: When the battle between *Bhīma* and *Duryodhana* was about to commence, *Bala-Rāma* (*b*), having heard that that battle between his two disciples was about to begin, came and was worshipped by the *Pāṇḍavas*, *Kṛshṇa*, etc. (**a**); he said that forty-two days had passed since he departed, having set out under the constellation *Pushya* and come back under the constellation *Çravaṇa*; he was clad in blue robes and of fair complexion. Then that dreadful encounter took place (IX, **34**).—§ 615: Requested by *Janamejaya* (**a**), *Vaiçampāyana* related how *Bala-Rāma* had determined upon and set out (under the constellation *Maitra*) on a pilgrimage to the *tīrthas* on the *Sarasvatī* (β), having let the sacred fire be brought from *Dvārakā* and the priests, and having given away rich donations to everyone who wished for them, accompanied by priests, friends, brahmans, chariots, elephants, steeds, and servants, visiting all the sacred places along her course. In the course of his wanderings he at last came to *Kurukshetra*. Requested by *Janamejaya* (γ), *Vaiçampāyana* related the *Baladevatīrthayātrā* (q.v.) (IX, **35-54**). Requested by *Dhṛtarāshṭra*, *Sañjaya* related: Beholding *Bala-Rāma*, *Duryodhana* rejoiced. According to the proposal of *Bala-Rāma*, *Yudhishṭhira* with his brothers and *Duryodhana* proceeded westwards to *Samantapañcaka* on the southern side of the *Sarasvatī*. D. and Cā. praised *Duryodhana*. Description of *Bhīma* and *Duryodhana* (ο). *Duryodhana* told *Yudhishṭhira* (who was standing among his brothers and *Kṛshṇa* and *Rāma*) to behold the battle, protected by the *Kaikeyas*, etc. (π). That large assembly of kings sat down, as did also *Bala-Rāma*, who was worshipped by all around him. *Bhīma* and *Duryodhana* stood inciting each other with violent speeches (IX, **55**). The dispute between the two heroes (ρ). At last *Duryodhana* said, "What is the use of bragging? fight with me," and was applauded by the *Somakas*, etc. The elephants grunted aloud and the steeds neighed repeatedly; the weapons of the *Pāṇḍavas* blazed forth of their own accord (IX, **56**). Description of the combat; D., G., and men wondered; the *Pāṇḍavas* and the *Somakas* feared; adopting the manœuvre called *Kauçika*, *Duryodhana* baffled *Bhīma's* mace; as *Duryodhana* once fell down to the earth, the *Sṛñjayas* cried aloud, so also did the *Pāṇḍavas*; *Bhīmasena* then had his coat of mail fractured and was prostrated on the ground, but rose, steadying himself with great effort (IX, **57**). *Arjuna* inquired of *Kṛshṇa* about the relative merits of the two combatants; *Kṛshṇa* said that their training had been equal, but *Bhīma* was superior in strength; *Duryodhana* was superior in skill and had had more practice; by fighting fairly *Bhīma* would never succeed in winning, but by fighting unfairly he would surely be able to slay *Duryodhana*, just as the *Asuras* were vanquished by the gods, *Virocana* and *Vṛtra* by *Indra* with the aid of deception; "*Bhīma* has vowed to break the thighs of *Duryodhana* with his mace; let him accomplish that vow of his"; he censured *Yudhishṭhira* for his folly, and quoted a verse uttered by *Uçanas*; "*Duryodhana* has practised with the mace for full thirteen years." *Arjuna* struck his own left thigh before the eyes of *Bhīmasena*, who understood the sign. As *Duryodhana* set his heart on the manœuvre called *dvasthāna* and jumped upwards, *Bhīmasena* hurled his mace at the thighs of *Duryodhana* and fractured them. Portents appeared; showers of blood and showers of dust were poured by *Indra*; a loud noise was made by Y., Rā., and Pç. (description of the portents); the *Pāñcālas* and the *Pāṇḍavas* were filled with anxiety; D., G., Si., and Cā. went away (IX, **58**). The *Pāṇḍavas* and *Somakas* rejoiced; *Bhīmasena* rebuked *Duryodhana*, and touched his head with his left foot, which was censured by *Yudhishṭhira*, who grieved for *Duryodhana* (σ) (IX, **59**); *Baladeva's* wrath was excited upon seeing *Duryodhana* struck below the navel; he rushed on to slay *Bhīma*, but was seized and pacified by *Kṛshṇa* (τ). *Baladeva* praised *Duryodhana* and cursed *Bhīmasena*, and then ascended his chariot and proceeded towards *Dvārakā*. The *Pāñcālas*, etc. (υ), became dejected; *Kṛshṇa* and *Yudhishṭhira*, *Bhīmasena*, etc., and *Duryodhana* spoke about what had passed (IX, **60**) (*Kṛshṇa* asking the *Pāṇḍava* warriors to forbear insulting *Duryodhana*; *Duryodhana's* angry reply to *Kṛshṇa*, charging him with every unfair act in course of the battle; *Kṛshṇa* reminded *Duryodhana* of his own evil acts, and referred to his miserable end as the inevitable consequence of those acts; *Duryodhana's* boast with reference to his end, which he pronounced to be most glorious) (φ). Celestial showers descended on *Duryodhana's* head; G., Aps., and Si. praised him. The *Pāṇḍavas* and *Kṛshṇa* became ashamed; but *Kṛshṇa* justified the use of unfair means for the slaughter of the *Kuru* warriors (χ) (IX, **61**). The *Pāṇḍava* warriors proceeded to the *Kuru* camp, which was entirely deserted (ψ); *Kṛshṇa* caused

Arjuna to take down the *Gāṇḍīva* and his inexhaustible quivers, and then to dismount; then *Kṛshṇa* also dismounted; the celestial ape disappeared, and the chariot (burnt by *Droṇa* and *Karṇa* with the *Brāhma* weapon), with its steeds, etc., was reduced to ashes. *Kṛshṇa* congratulated *Yudhishṭhira* on his victory, and *Yudhishṭhira* attributed that victory to *Kṛshṇa's* power (ω). In the encampment of the *Kurus* they found great wealth; at *Kṛshṇa's* suggestion the *Pāṇḍavas* and *Sātyaki* resolved to pass the night at a spot outside the camp, on the banks of the *Oghavatī*. They then dispatched *Kṛshṇa* to *Hāstinapura* in order to pacify the wrath of *Gāndhārī*, and to comfort her and *Dhṛtarāshṭra*. He set out with *Dāruka* upon his chariot, yoked with *Çaibya* and *Sugrīva* (IX, **62**). Asked by *Janamejaya*, *Vaiçampāyana* said that the reason why *Yudhishṭhira* sent *Kṛshṇa* to *Hāstinapura* was his fear that *Gāndhārī*, by means of her ascetic merit, should reduce the *Pāṇḍavas* to ashes, because *Duryodhana* had been slain unfairly (***aa***); "*Vyāsa* will be there." *Kṛshṇa* caused *Dāruka* to equip his chariot, and quickly set out for *Hāstinapura*. He arrived at *Dhṛtarāshṭra's* palace, where *Vyāsa* had arrived before him; he comforted *Dhṛtarāshṭra* (ββ) and *Gāndhārī* (γγ), who said that her heart had again become steady (δδ). Then *Kṛshṇa* came to know the evil that was meditated by *Açvatthāman*, and suddenly took leave, requested by *Dhṛtarāshṭra* and *Gāndhārī* to protect the *Pāṇḍavas*, and proceeded with *Dāruka*. *Vyāsa* comforted *Dhṛtarāshṭra*. *Kṛshṇa* arrived at the camp and informed the *Pāṇḍavas* (IX, **63**). Requested by *Dhṛtarāshṭra*, *Sañjaya* narrated the lamentations of *Duryodhana* while lying on the field with his thighs broken (εε); he thought himself happy, and asked *Sañjaya* to bring his message to his parents and to *Açvatthāman*, etc. (ζζ) ("you should never place any confidence in the *Pāṇḍavas*"), and took leave of the message-bearers (εε); he was confident that *Cārvāka*, the mendicant devotee, would avenge his death. Thousands of men, with eyes full of tears, fled away; the earth trembled, etc. The messengers went and informed *Açvatthāman* and then went away (IX, **64**). *Açvatthāman*, etc. (ζζ), came to *Duryodhana*, who lay surrounded by carnivorous animals, etc. *Açvatthāman's* lament and *Duryodhana's* reply (ηη); *Açvatthāman* vowed to slay all the *Pāñcālas*; *Duryodhana* let *Kṛpa* install *Açvatthāman* as the *Kuru* generalissimo; then they took leave of *Duryodhana* and left him alone (IX, **65**).

Gādheyī ("the daughter of Gādhi") = Satyavatī: XIII, 242.

Gādhi or **Gādhin**, a king of Kanyakubja, the son of Kuçika and the father of Viçvāmitra and Satyavatī. § 223 (Vāsishṭha): I, **175**, 6651 (*Kānyakubje mahān āsīt pārthivo, Bharatarshabha | Gādhīti viçruto loke Kuçikasyātmasambhavaḥ*, father of Viçvāmitra).—§ 395 (Jamadagni): III, **115**, 10145 (°*īti viçrutaḥ*, went to the woods), 10146 (°*iḥ*, Ṛcīka married his daughter [Satyavatī], having given 1,000 horses as a dowry).—§ 565 (Gālavac.): V, **110**, 1005 (°*eḥ Satyavatīṃ sutāṃ*, repetition from § 395).—§ 574 (Jambūkh.): VI, **9*aa***, 315 (°*eḥ*).—§ 615*n* (Viçvāmitra): IX, **40**, 2296 (°*iḥ*, father of Viçvāmitra), 2299 (do.), 2300 (do., having installed Viçvāmitra on the throne, *G.* went to heaven).—§ 638*b* (Rāmopākhyāna): XII, **49**, 1720 (*Gādhir nāmābhavat putraḥ Kauçikaḥ Pākaçāsanaḥ*, Indra was born as *G.*), 1721 (°*iḥ*, Satyavatī was given in marriage to Ṛcīka, cf. § 395), 1722 (°*eḥ*), 1727 (°*iḥ*), 1745 (do., birth of Viçvāmitra).—§ 721*b* (Viçvāmitrop.): XIII, **4**, 205 (*Kuçikasyātmajaḥ* . . . *G°ir nāma*), 208 (°*iḥ*), (211) (do.), 217 (°*aye*), 218 (°*iḥ*, Satyavatī was given in marriage to Ṛcīka, who had given 1,000 horses as a dowry), 246 (°*bhāryā*, birth of Viçvāmitra).—§ 745*c* (Cyavana-Kuçikasaṃv.): XIII, **56**, 2914 (°*er duhitaraṃ*, i.e. Satyavatī), 2915 (*Viçvāmitraṃ* . . . *G°eḥ putraṃ*). Cf. Kauçika.

Gādhija ("the son of Gādhi") = Viçvāmitra: IX, 2306 (*V°*), 2311, 2394.

Gādhin, v. Gādhi.

Gādhinandana ("the son of Gādhi") = Viçvāmitra: I, 6663.

Gādhisutā ("the daughter of Gādhi") = Satyavatī: III, 10153.

Gadin = Çiva (1000 names[1]).

Gaganamūrdhan, an Asura. § 92 (Aṃçāvat.): I, **65**, 2532 (among the sons of Danu).—§ 130 (do.): I, **67**, 2646 (incarnate as one of the five Kaikaya princes).

Gahana = Vishṇu (1000 names).

Gaja, a Gāndhāra warrior, the younger brother of Çakuni. § 585 (Bhīshmavadhap.): VI, **90**σ, 3997 (among six younger brothers of Çakuni (Saubalasyānujāḥ, v. 3995), is slain by Irāvat).

Gajaçiras, a warrior of Skanda. § 615*u* (Skanda): IX, **45**η, 2562.

Gajahan = Çiva (1000 names[2]).

Gajāhvaya ("named after the elephant") = Hāstinapura: II, 2600, 2640; III, 279; V, 6071; XII, †2121 (*puraṃ*); XIV, 370; XV, †439; XVIII, 181.

Gajakarṇa, a Yaksha. § 269 (Vaiçravaṇasabhāv.): II, **10**, 397 (among the Yakshas in the palace of Kubera).

Gajānīka, a Pāṇḍava warrior. § 600 (Ghaṭotkacavadhap.): VII, **158**χ, 7011 (brother of Virāṭa ?).

Gajapura = Hāstinapura: XIII, 7711.

Gajarāja = Airāvata: XII, 8330 (°*vāhanaḥ*, i.e. Indra).

Gajasāhvaya ("named after the elephant") = Hāstinapura: I, 1700 (*svanagaraṃ*), 3000, 4360, 4441 (*purīṃ*), 4460 (*puraṃ*), 4468, 5034, 5149 (*nagaraṃ*); II, 1676, 2647; III, 9, 1348; V, 6092, 7106; XIV, 1476 (*nagaraṃ*), 1479 (do.); XV, 443, 653, 971; XVII, 25.

Gajendra = Airāvata (?): IX, †1074.

Gajendrakarṇa = Çiva (1000 names[1]).

Gajodara, a warrior of Skanda. § 615*u* (Skanda): IX, **45**η, 2562.

Gālava, a ṛshi. § 10 (Parvasaṅgr.): I, **2**, 331 (*caritaṃ G°sya*, i.e. Gālavacarita).—§ 11 (do.): I, **2**, 509 (*maharsheç cāpi caritaṃ* . . . *G°sya*, do.).—§ 264 (Sabhākriyāp.): II, **4*a***, 110 (among the munis who waited upon Yudhishṭhira).—§ 200 (Çakrasabhāv.): II, **7**, 292 (in the palace of Indra).—§ 376 (Tīrthayātrāp.): III, **85**, 8263 (among the brahmarshis who stayed in expectation of Yudhishṭhira).—§ 565 (Gālavacarita): V, **106**, 3720, 3727 (*muniḥ*), 3732 (disciple of Viçvāmitra), 3733, 3738, 3739, 3740; **107**, 3741, 3743, 3760; **108**, 3761, 3762, 3778; **109**, 3792, 3794, 3799; **110**, 3814, 3820; **111**, 3822, 3830, 3834, 3838, 3839, 3846; **112**, (3850), 3854 (*muniḥ*), (3855), 3869, 3872; **113**, 3874, 3877, 3891, 3894, 3895; **114**, 3896, 3907, 3911; **115**, 3919, 3928, 3931, 3932, 3933, 3936; **116**, 3942, 3944, 3946, 3947, 3951 (*muniḥ*), 3953, 3955, 3958; **117**, (3960), 3965, 3978, 3980; **118**, 3981, 3982, 3989, 3992, 3996, 3997, 4001; **119**, 4002, 4003, 4004, 4006, 4010, 4012, 4016, 4021, 4025 (the history of Gālava).—§ 566 (Yayāti): V, **121**, 4076; **123**, 4116 (all. to § 565).—§ 615 ff. (Asita Devala): IX, **50**, 2919 (only C. by error for *Nāradaḥ*).—§ 637 (Rājadh.): XII, **47**η, 1597 (among the ṛshis who surrounded Bhīshma as he lay on his arrow-bed). — § 699 (Mokshadh.): XII, **288**, 10555 (°*sya ca saṃvādaṃ devarsher Nāradasya ca*), 10556, 10564.—§ 717*b* (Nārāyaṇīya): XII, **343**, 13263 (*Vāmādeçitamārgeṇa* *matprasadān* (i.e. Nārāyaṇa's) *mahātmanā* | *Pāñcālena kramaḥ prāptaḥ tasmād bhūtāt sanātanāt* (i.e. from the horse head of Nārāyaṇa) | *Bābhravyagotraḥ sa babhau prathamaṃ krama-pāragaḥ* | *Nārāyaṇād varaṃ labdhvā prāpya yogam anuttamaṃ* | *kramaṃ praṇīya çikshāñ ca praṇayitvā sa Gālavaḥ*).—§ 721*b* (Viçvāmitrop.): XIII, **4**β, 251 (among the sons of Viçvāmitra). — § 730 (Ānuçāsanik.): XIII, **18,** (1349) (Çiva restored his father to life).—§ 734 (do.): XIII, **26*a***, 1763 (among the ṛshis who came to see Bhīshma). — § 751*b* (Çapathavidhi): XIII, **94*a***, †4551 (*ṛshiḥ*), (4583). Cf. Pañcāla, Pāñcāla.

[Gālavacarita(m)] ("the history of Gālava"; cf. Gālavasya caritaṃ). § 565 (Bhagavady.): In ancient times, in order to try *Viçvāmitra*, who was then engaged in ascetic austerities, *Dharma* in the form of the *Ṛshi Vasishṭha*, and feigning himself hungry, came to his hermitage. *Viçvāmitra* cooked *caru*, but could not approach *Dharma* before his guest had dined with the other hermits. *Dharma* said, "I have already dined; wait here," and went away. *Viçvāmitra*, bearing that food on his head and himself subsisting on air, waited a hundred years, while the ascetic *Gālava* waited on him. Then *Dharma* accepted that food, which was still warm and fresh, and called *Viçvāmitra* a *viprarshi*, whereby he became a *brahman*. *Gālava* repeatedly asked *Viçvāmitra* to take a gift from him as his preceptor, and at last *Viçvāmitra*, seeing his persistency, requested him to give 800 white steeds each with one black ear (V, **106**). *Gālava* got troubled and was gradually reduced to a skeleton. He thought of repairing to *Vishṇu* (or *Kṛshṇa*), when his friend *Garuḍa* came, and said he had spoken to *Vishṇu* in his behalf, and that he would bear him (V, **107**). *Garuḍa* described the East: here *Savitṛ* first rises, and the *tapas* of the *Sādhyas* is performed at eve; . . . the two eyes of *Dharma*; . . . here the daughters of *Daksha* in primeval times gave birth to their children, and here the sons of *Kaçyapa* first multiplied; here *Çakra* was first anointed as king of the gods; here is the *tapas* of *Indra* and the gods, all their religious ceremonies; here the Creator (*bhagavān Lokabhāvanaḥ*) first sang the *Vedas*; here *Sāvitrī* was first said by *Savitṛ* to the reciters of the *Vedas* (*brahmavādishu*), and here the Yajurveda (*yajūṃshi*) was given by *Sūrya*; here the *Soma* juice was first drunk by the gods, etc.; it was here that *Varuṇa*, repairing to *Pātāla*, obtained prosperity (*çriyam*); here the birth, growth, and death of the ancient *Vasishṭha* took place; here first grew the hundred branches (*sṛtayaḥ*) of *oṃ*; here the *Munis* called *dhūmapāḥ* first imbibed the smoke of the *havis*; here the thousand-rayed Sun slays, rising, the wicked and ungrateful men and *Asuras*; here is the gate of the three worlds and the path to heaven and to felicity (V, **108**). *Garuḍa* mentioned the remarkable subjects in the South (*dakshiṇā diç*, so called because *Vivasvat* gave it away as a *dakshiṇā*): *Pitṛpakshas trailokasya*; *Ūshmapāḥ devāḥ*; the *Viçvedevas* with the *Pitṛs*, with whom they equally share the sacrifices in all the worlds; the second door of *Dharma* . . .; the *Devarshis*, *Pitṛlokarshis*, and *Rājarshis*, who dwell here in great happiness . . .; it is the region whither all must repair; . . . there are *Nairṛtāḥ* to be seen by the sinful; the *Gandharvas* chanting on *Mandara* and in the abodes of the *viprarshis*; *Raivata* who, hearing the *Sāmans*, retired to the woods, leaving wife and friends and kingdom; *Sāvarṇi* and *Yāvakrīta* setting a limit to *Sūrya* (the southern tropical circle, PCR.); *Rāvaṇa* soliciting immortality from the gods; *Vṛtra* incurring the enmity of *Çakra*; *Vaitaraṇī* filled with the bodies of persons condemned to hell . . .; reaching this region the sun drops sweet water (i.e. the beginning of the rainy season, Nīl.), and thence, proceeding again to the *Vāsishtha* direction (*Vāsishṭhīṃ kāshṭhāṃ* = the quarter of the seven Ṛshis, i.e. the North, Nīl), once more drops dew (*himaṃ*); there is *Garuḍa* obtaining for food an enormous elephant and tortoise; the great *Ṛshi Cakradhanus*' birth from *Sūrya* took place here (he was afterwards known as *Kapila* who burned *Sagara's* sons); the perfect (*siddhāḥ*) brahmans, named *Çivāḥ*, who fully had mastered the *Vedas*, here obtained liberation (*moksha*); here is *Bhogavatī*, ruled by *Vāsuki*, *Takshaka*, and *Airāvata*. Those that have to journey hither encounter here a thick gloom, so that it cannot be penetrated by either the Sun or by *Agni*; "even thou shalt have to pass this road" (V, **109**). *Garuḍa* mentioned the remarkable subjects and occurrences of the West: *Varuṇa's* origin; his instalment by *Kaçyapa*; the Moon, quaffing all the six juices of *Varuṇa*, becomes young again in the beginning of the bright fortnight; the *Daityas* being routed and bound fast by *Vāyu*; the mountain *Asta*; Night and Sleep; *Çakra* beholding the goddess (*devīṃ*) *Diti* asleep, and cutting off her fœtus, whence sprang the *Maruts*; the roots of *Himavat* stretching towards the eternal *Mandara* (sunk in the Ocean, Nīl.), the end of which is not to be reached by journeying for even 1,000 years; *Surabhi* milking on the shores of the lake with golden lotuses; in the midst of the Ocean the headless trunk of *Svarbhānu*; the chanting of the *Vedas* by *Suvarṇa-çiras* (invisible, and whose hair is eternally yellow); *Dhvajavatī*, the daughter of the *muni Harimedhas*, remaining in the air in consequence of *Sūrya's* injunction, 'stay'; . . . the sources of the rivers; here, in the abode of *Varuṇa*, are the waters of the three worlds; the abode of *Ananta*, and of *Vishṇu*, and of *Pavana* (the friend of *Agni*), and of the *Maharshi Kaçyapa Mārīca* (V, **110**). The North (*uttara*) has its name from saving (*uttāraṇa*) from sin; it is also called *madhyama*, i.e. between the East and the West. None can live there that is unamiable, etc. *Garuḍa* mentioned its remarkable subjects and places: *Badarī*, the asylum of *Nārāyaṇa*, *Kṛshṇa*, *Jishṇu*, and *Brahmán*; *Maheçvara* with the effulgence of the *Yugānta* fire; *Purusha* dwelling with *Prakṛti*, invisible to *munis*, D. with I., G., Y., and Si., except *Nara* and *Nārāyaṇa*; there *Vishṇu* appears alone, having 1,000 heads and 1,000 legs; there *Candramas* (the Moon) was installed in the sovereignty over the *brahmans*; *Mahādeva* receiving *Gaṅgā* on his head; *Devī* practising austerities for obtaining *Maheçvara*; *Kāma*; the wrath (of *Çiva*, PCR.); here took place *Kubera's* instalment, on the breast of *Kailāsa*, in the sovereignty of Rā., Y., and G.; *Caitraratha*; here is the asylum of the *Vaikhānasas*; *Mandākinī*; *Mandara*; *Saugandhikavana*, guarded by *Nairṛtas*; the plantain forest (*kadalī-skandhaṃ*), etc.; the *Siddhas*; the seven *Ṛshis* with *Arundhatī*; *Svāti*; *Brahmán* near *Yajña* . . . the *munis* named *Dhāmā* (? so B.) (whose origin, etc., are not known) guarding *Gāyantikādvāra* (B. *Gaṅgāmahādvāraṃ*); the man who passes beyond them will certainly meet with destruction, except *Nārāyaṇa* and *Nara* or *Jishṇu*; here is *Kailāsa*, the abode of *Ailavila*; the origin of the ten *Apsarases Vidyut-prabhāḥ*; *Vishṇupada*, made by *Vishṇu*, when he, in his covering the worlds with three steps, stepped on the northern region; here took place king *Marutta's* sacrifice at *Uçīrabīja*, by the side of the golden lake; here was *Himavat's* gold-mine, that exhibited itself to the *viprarshi Jīmūta*, who gave away the whole wealth to the brahmans, and had it called after his name (*Jaimūta*); here morning and evening the *Lokapālas* (*diçām pālāḥ*) proclaim "what business of what person shall we do?"; it is called *uttara* (North) because it is superior (*uttara*) to all (V, **111**). At the request of *Gālava*, *Garuḍa* carried him (description) to the East, and laughed at his foolish thoughts of casting away his life. At the mountain *Ṛshabha* they rested for some time (V, **112**). On the peak of the *Ṛshabha* they met with a brahman lady, *Çāṇḍilī*, engaged in penances; she gave them cooked food; they fell asleep. As *Garuḍa* awoke, his wings had fallen off. It was because he had, out of pity, thought of carrying the lady to the place where *Mahādeva*, *Vishṇu*, etc. (*a*), live together. She gave him his wings back, having warned him not to contemn women, and they set out, but failed to find the steeds. *Viçvāmitra* met them, and said the time had already passed, but promised to wait for some time more (V, **113**). *Garuḍa* explained the etymology of *hiraṇya* (gold) and *dhana* (wealth), and why gold is not easily obtainable (see the note of PCR. from Nīl.); it is guarded by the *Ajaikapād-Ahirbradhnāḥ* and by *Dhanada* (i.e. *Kubera*). They went to *Garuḍa's* friend, the *Rājarshi Yayāti Nāhusha* (of the Lunar race), in *Pratishṭhāna*, and told him the matter, and that *Gālava*, when he had paid off his debt, would devote himself to severe ascetic penances and give *Yayāti* a portion of his wealth of asceticism; "as many hairs as there are in a horse's body, so many regions of bliss are attained by him that gives away a horse" (V, **114**). *Yayāti*, the performer of 1000 sacrifices, the liberal ruler of all the *Kāçis*, in view of the fact that they had come to him, passing over all the kings of the Solar race, not having the steeds, gave to *Gālava* his daughter *Mādhavī*, always solicited by gods, men, and *Asuras*. *Garuḍa* went away to his own abode, and *Gālava* offered *Mādhavī* to king *Haryaçva* of *Ikshvāku's* race at *Ayodhyā*, who was desirous of offspring (V, **115**), on the condition that he gave as her dower the 800 steeds of the kind wanted. *Haryaçva* had but 200 steeds of this kind; he therefore got the maiden—who by a brahman had been granted the boon that after each delivery she would be a maiden again—in order to beget only one son upon her, for his 200 steeds. This son was *Vasumanas*. Then *Gālava* offered her to king *Divodāsa* (V, **116**), the *Kāçi* king, son of *Bhīmasena*. The same arrangement was made as with *Haryaçva*. She bore him *Pratardana* (V, **117**). Then *Gālava* came to king *Uçīnara* in the city of the *Bhojas*, with whom the same arrangement was made. To him she bore *Çibi*. Then *Gālava* took the maiden and went to see *Garuḍa* (V, **118**). *Garuḍa* said that the remaining 200 steeds were unobtainable. For in days of yore *Ṛcīka* sought at *Kānyakubja Gādhi's* daughter *Satyavatī* in marriage, and was requested by *Gādhi* to give 1000 steeds of this kind. *Ṛcīka* obtained them at *Açvatīrtha*, and gave them to the king. Performing the sacrifice *Puṇḍarīka*, the king gave them away to the *brahmans*. The three kings had each purchased 200 of them from the *brahmans*, but the remaining 400, while being transported over the *Vitastā*, were taken by the river (so B.). *Viçvāmitra*, instead of obtaining the 200 steeds wanting, begot *Ashṭaka* upon *Mādhavī*, and gave him the steeds; *Ashṭaka* then went to a certain city (*puram prāyāt tadā Somapuraprabham*) and *Kauçika* (i.e. *Viçvāmitra*) to the woods. *Gālava* dismissed *Garuḍa*, and returning the maiden to her father, he went into the woods (V, **119**). *Yayāti* went to a hermitage on the confluence of the *Gangā* and *Yamunā*, taking *Mādhavī*, *Pūru*, and *Yadu* with him, desirous of again disposing of his daughter in a *svayamvara*. There was assembled a vast concourse of N., Y., G., men, etc., and numerous *Ṛshis* resembling *Brahmán* himself. *Mādhavī* selected the forest as her lord, practised *tapas*, and adopted a deer's mode of life (*mṛgacāriṇī*). King *Yayāti* died after having lived for many thousands of years. The progeny of *Pūru* and *Yadu* multiplied greatly. *Yayāti*, resembling a *maharshi*, enjoyed the highest bliss in heaven for many thousands of years. On one occasion, while seated among the *Rājarshis* and *Maharshis*, king *Yayāti* mentally disregarded all the gods and *Ṛshis* and men. *Indra* at once read his heart; the dwellers of heaven did not longer know him, and he was soon divested of his splendour (V, **120**). For continuation v. Yayāti (§ 566).

Gālavasambhava ("born from Gālava") = Prākçṛngavat: IX, 2992.

Gālavi ("the son of Gālava") = Prākçṛngavat: IX, 2995, 2997.

Gama = Çiva (1000 names [1-2]).

Gambhīra = Çiva (1000 names [2]).

Gambhīrabalavāhana = Çiva (1000 names [2]).

Gambhīraghosha = Çiva (1000 names [2]).

Gaṇa = Çiva (1000 names [2]).

Gaṇā, a mātṛ. § 615*u* (Skanda): IX, **46**θ, 2645.

Gaṇādhipa = Çiva (1000 names [1]).

Gaṇādhyaksha = Çiva: X, 258; XII, 10421 (1000 names[1]).

Gaṇakāra = Çiva (1000 names [2]).

Gaṇakartṛ = Çiva (1000 names [2]).

Gaṇanayaka = Gaṇeça: I, 77.

Gaṇapati = Çiva (1000 names [2]).

Gaṇḍā, the wife of the çūdra Paçusakha. § 750*b* (Bisastainyop.): XIII, **93**, 4417, (4446), (4499), (4530).

Gaṇḍaka, pl. (°*āḥ*), a people. § 280 (Bhīmasena): II, **29**, 1062 (in the east, vanquished by Bhīmasena on his digvijaya).

Gaṇḍakaṇḍa, a Yaksha. § 269 (Vaiçravaṇasabhāv.): II, **10**, 397 (among the Yakshas in the palace of Kubera).

Gaṇḍakī, a river. § 221*b* (Gangā): I, **170**, 6455.—§ 276 (Jarāsandhavadhap.): II, **20**, 794 (crossed by Kṛshṇa, etc., on their way from Indraprastha to Girivraja). — § 370 (Tīrthayātrāp.): III, **84**, 8091 (*sarvatīrthajalodbhavam*, a tīrtha).—§ 574 (Jambūkh.): VI, **9**λ, 325 (among the rivers of Bhāratavarsha).—§ 775 (Ānuçāsanik.): XIII, **166a**, 7647.

Gaṇḍalin = Çiva (1000 names [2]).

Gaṇḍasāhvayā, a river. § 494 (Āngirasa): III, **222**, 14230 (among the rivers who are mothers of fires, = Gaṇḍakī?).

Gandha [1] (personif.), II, 438.—[2] = Çiva (1000 names [1]).

Gandhadhārin = Çiva (1000 names [2]).

Gandhakālī = Satyavatī: I, ††3801 (C. has by error *Gabdha*°).

Gandhamādana, a mountain. § 11 (Parvasangr.): I, **2**, 451, 452, 462.—§ 43 (Garuḍa): I, **30**, 1392 (*parvataçreshṭham*, there Kaçyapa was engaged in austerities).—§ 48 (Çesha): I, **36**, 1567 (there Çesha performed austerities).—§ 184 (Pāṇḍu): I, **119**, 4637 (having crossed Himavat, Pāṇḍu went to *G.*).—§ 269 (Vaiçravaṇasabhāv.): II, **10**, 412 (among the mountains in the palace of Kubera).—§ 317*b* (Kṛshṇa Vāsudeva): III, **12**, 471 (Kṛshṇa dwelt 10,000 years on *G.*).—§ 330 (Indradarçana): III, **37**, 1496 (on the way to the world of Indra Arjuna crossed Himavat and *G.*).—§ 419 (Gandhamādanapr.): III, **140**, 10861 (the Pāṇḍavas set out for *G.*).—§ 420 (do.): III, **141**, 10892 (*b*: *G.* cannot be reached by means of vehicles, nor by bad people; the impure alone meet with flies, gadflies, etc.), 10898.—§ 423 (do.): III, **143**, 10964 (*b*: *G.* is inhabited by ṛshis, Siddhas, gods, Gandharvas, Apsarases, and Kinnaras), 10969, 10985.—§ 423 (do.): III, **145**, 11015.—§ 424 (Bhīmakadalīkhaṇḍapr.): III, **146**, 11084, 11088 (*b: G.* is frequented by Kinnaras, Yakshas, Gandharvas, gods, Brahmarshis, and Apsarases), 11099, 11119 (°*sānushu*, on *G.* Bhīmasena met with Hanūmat).—§ 432 (Saugandhikāharaṇap.): III, **152**, 11337 (near *G.* Bhīmasena slew the Krodhavaças).—§ 435 (do.): III, **155**, 11429 (°*sānushu*).—§ 436 (Yakshayuddhap.): III, **158**, 11540, 11542 (the hermitage of Vṛshaparvan was situated on the slope of Himavat and near *G.*).—§ 436*b* (do.): *G.* is frequented by Kimpurushas, Siddhas, Cāraṇas, Vidyādharas, Kinnarīs, etc. (very copious description): III, **158**, 11561, 11563, 11571, 11582 (°*sānushu*), 11600 (°*kānanaṃ*), 11603 (°*sānushu*), 11608.—§ 436 (do.): III, **159**, 11656.—§ 437 (do.): III, **160**, 11662, 11702 (°*sambhavaḥ . . . mārutaḥ*, Bhīma there slew the Rākshasa Maṇimat, etc.).—§ 438 (do.): III, **161**, 11768.—§ 440 (do.): III, **164**, 11902 (Arjuna came from the world of Indra to *G.*).—§ 446 (Nivātakavacayuddhap.): III, **174**, 12283.—§ 459 (Mārkaṇḍeyas.): III, **188**, 12918 (seen by Mārkaṇḍeya in the stomach of Nārāyaṇa).—§ 512 (Ghoshayātrāp.): III, **244**, 14965 (°*vāsinaḥ*, i.e. the Gandharvas).—§ 526 (Rāmopākhyānap.): III, **275**, 15901 (°*parvate*, the abode of Viçravas), 15921 (having lost Laṅkā, Kubera began to live on *G.*).—§ 535 (Setubandhana): III, **283***a*, 16273 (°*vāsī . . . Gandhamādanaḥ*).—§ 561*e* (Bhīma): V, **50**, 1991 (*Kṛshṇāyāç caratā prītiṃ yena*—i.e. Bhīma—*Krodhavaçā hatāḥ* | *praviçya vishamaṃ ghoraṃ parvataṃ G°ṃ*, all. to § 432 or § 437).—§ 561 (Yānasandhip.): V, **64**, 2471 (description).—§ 563 (Dambhodbhavop.): V, **96**, 3462 (on *G.* Nara and Nārāyaṇa practised austerities), 3464.—§ 570*d* (Rukmin): V, **158**, 5352 (*Kimpurushasiṃhasya G°vāsinaḥ*, i.e. Druma).—§ 571 (Ulūkadūtāgamanap.): V, **160**, 5501 (*ārurukshur yathā mandaḥ parvataṃ G°ṃ*); **161**, 5546 (do.).—§ 574 (Jambūkh.): VI, **6**, 203 (*paraṃ Mālyavataḥ*), 204 (the half-verse not in B.).—§ 574*e* (do.): On the summits of *G. Kubera*, the lord of the *Guhyakas*, many *Rākshasas* and *Apsarases* live in joy. Beside *G.* there are many smaller mountains and hills. The measure of human life there is 11,000 years. There the men are cheerful and endued with great energy and strength, and the women are all of the complexion of the lotus and highly beautiful: VI, **6**, 229, 230.—§ 574 (Jambūkh.): VI, **9**κ, 318 (among the seven *kulaparvatāḥ* in Bhāratavarsha; B., however, has *Ṛkshavān*).—§ 581 (Bhīshmavadhap.): VI, **65**, 2939 (on *G.* the gods, ṛshis, etc., worshipped *Pitāmaha*, i.e. Brahmán).—§ 585 (do.): VI, **92**, 4099 (*āçīvishā iva kruddhāḥ parvate G°e*).—§ 599 (Jayadrathavadhap.): VII, **125**, 5022 (*mahāmegho yathā varshaṃ vimuñcan G°e*).—§ 600 (Ghaṭotkacavadhap.): VII, **183**, 8324 (°*yātrāyāṃ durgebhyaç ca sma tāritāḥ* | *Pāñcālīñ ca pariçrāntā(ṃ) pṛshṭhenodvahatātmanā*, sc. Ghaṭotkaca, all. to § 423).—§ 603*d* (Tripura): VII, **202**, 9562 (Çiva made *G.* and Vindhya his *vaṃçadhvajau* when he proceeded against Tripura).—§ 607 (Karṇap.): VIII, **45**, 2104 (protected by Guhyakas).—§ 611 (Çalyap.): IX, **11**, 584 (*yayā māyāmayān dṛptān subahūn G°e* | *jaghāna Guhyakān kruddho mandarārthe mahābalaḥ*, sc. Bhīmasena, all. to § 432 or § 437).—§ 638*b* (Rāmopākhyāna): XII, **49**, 1748 (Rāma gratified Mahādeva on *G.*).—§ 717*b* (Nārāyaṇīya): XII, **335**, 12662; **343**, 13267 (the Ṛshis Nara and Nārāyaṇa practised austerities on *G.* (in Badarī)); **344**, 13336 (do.).—§ 731*b* (Ashṭāvakra-Diksaṃv.): XIII, **21**, 1526 (in the north).—§ 733*e* (Indratoyā): XIII, **25**, 1698 (°*sannidhau Indratoyāṃ*).—§ 768*b* (Kṛshṇa Vāsudeva): XIII, **147**, 6850 (Sanatkumāra, etc., dwell on *G.*).—§ 775 (Ānuçāsanik.): XIII, **166***a*, 7658.

Gandhamādana[2], a monkey chief. § 535 (Setubandhana): III, **283***a*, 16273 (dwelt on the mountain Gandhamādana, came with 100,000 crores of monkeys to Rāma).

Gandhamādana[3] = Rāvaṇa(?): II, 410 (*Rākshasādhipatiḥ?*).

[Gandhamādana-praveça(ḥ)] ("proceeding to the Gandhamādana"). § 419 (cf. Tīrthayātrāp.): *Yudhishṭhira* in vain proposed that *Bhīma* should return with *Kṛshṇā*, *Sahadeva*, *Dhaumya*, the charioteers, cooks, etc., to *Gaṅgādvāra*, while *Yudhishṭhira* should proceed with *Nakula* and *Lomaça*. *Bhīma* promised to carry *Kṛshṇā* and the twins. *Kṛshṇā* said that she would be able to go. They entrusted to the *Pulinda* king (v. 10866, *Kulindānāṃ*) *Subāhu* on the *Himavat* (inhabited by *Kirātas*, *Taṅgaṇas*, and *Pulindas*), the servants *Indrasena*, etc., the cooks and stewards, and *Draupadī's* accoutrements, and began to proceed (III, **140**).—§ 420: *Yudhishṭhira* complained to *Bhīma* that he had not seen *Arjuna* for five years. They now should, in company with brahmans of strict vows, enter *Gandhamādana* (*b*), etc. (III, **141**).—§ 421: Exhorted by *Lomaça*, when they were about to go to the mountain *Mandara* (*b*), they adored *Ākāçagaṅgā* (v. 10902, read with B. °*puṇyā* for *puçyā*) (*c*), and then proceeded with the *ṛshis*.—§ 422: Then they saw the bones of the *Daitya Naraka* (*b*) like to a white mountain.—§ 422 *bis*: Varāhāvatāra (q.v.), III, **142**.—§ 423: As they, with the brahmans, entered *Gandhamādana* (*b*) a terrible wind arose, followed by showers of rain, lightning, and torrents, during which they took shelter under trees, etc., *Sahadeva* carrying the sacred fire (*agnihotrāṇi*). When the tempest was over and the sun reappeared, they continued their journey (III, **143**). When they had proceeded only a *kroça*, *Draupadī* sank down. *Nakula* ran forward and supported her, and the others hastily came, and *Yudhishṭhira* took her on his lap and lamented. *Dhaumya* and the other brahmans comforted and blessed him, and by reciting *mantras* capable of dispelling *Rākshasas*, and by performing ceremonies, while she was touched and fanned by the *Pāṇḍavas*, they made her regain her senses. The twins pressed her feet with their hands. *Bhīma* promised *Yudhishṭhira* to carry them all over the snowy mountains, "or *Ghaṭotkaca* will carry us all." With *Yudhishṭhira's* permission *Bhīma* thought of *Ghaṭotkaca*, who immediately came and was embraced by *Bhīma* (III, **144**). *Ghaṭotkaca* carried *Kṛshṇā* through the air, and hundreds of other *Rākshasas* carried the *Pāṇḍavas* and the brahmans, while *Lomaça* moved along the path of the *Siddhas*. So they proceeded through regions inhabited by *Mlecchas*, *Vidyādharas*, monkeys, *Kinnaras*, *Kimpurushas*, *Gandharvas*, etc., and the northern *Kurus*, towards *Kailāsa* and *Badarī* (*c*), where they were received by the numerous *ṛshis*, and where they dwelt, beholding *Maināka*, *Hiraṇyaçikkara*, *Bindusaras*, and *Bhāgīrathī*, and offering oblations, etc. (III, **145**).

Gandhapāḥ, a class of gods. § 730 (Ānuçāsanik.): XIII, **18**λλ, †1372.

Gandhapālin = Çiva (1000 names[2]).

Gāndhāra, pl. (°*āḥ*), a people. § 304 (Anudyūtap.): II, **77**, 2552 (°*ānāṃ yaçohara*, i.e. Çakuni).—§ 562 (Bhagavadyānap.): V, **94**, 3379 (*Gāndhārarājaḥ Çakunir G°air abhirakshitaḥ*).—§ 574 (Jambūkh.): VI, **9**μ, 361 (among the peoples of Bhāratavarsha).—§ 576 (Bhagavadgītāp.): VI, **20**, †748 (followed Çakuni).—§ 578 (Bhīshmavadhap.): VI, **45**[22], 1744 (five Gāndhāras fought with the five Kaikeya princes); **51**σ, 2104 (followed Bhīshma).—§ 580 (do.): VI, **58**[4],

2468 (*saha-Saubalāḥ*, fought with Sātyaki and Abhimanyu).—§ 582 (do.): VI, **71**[10]γ, 3132.—§ 585 (do.): VI, **90**, 4000 (i.e. Gaja, etc., the brothers of Çakuni).—§ 589 (Droṇābhishekap.): VII, **4**β, 120 (had formerly been vanquished by Karṇa).—§ 592 (Saṃçaptakavadhap.): VII, **20**ζ, 802 (in the back of Droṇa's garuḍavyūha); **30**, 1306 (*Saubalapramukhān*), 1307 (500 Gāndhāras slain by Arjuna). — § 593 (Abhimanyuvadhap.): VII, **49**, 1933 (seventy-seven Gāndhāras, followers of Kālikeya, slain by Abhimanyu).—§ 598 (Jayadrathavadhap.): VII, **87**, 3102 (follow Jayadratha).—§ 604 (Karṇap.): VIII, **8**η, 235 (had formerly been vanquished by Karṇa and caused to pay tribute to Duryodhana); **9**θ, 283 (do.). — § 607 (do.): VIII, **44**λ, 2070; **45**, 2078 (follow bad practices).—§ 608 (do.): VIII, **79**, 4040 (had formerly been vanquished by Karṇa); **95**, 4969 (°*ānāṃ sahasreṇa Çakuniḥ parivāritaḥ*).—§ 611 (Çalyap.): IX, **19**, 1019 (*nihate Saubale vīre G°eshu ca*).—§ 613 (Gadāyuddhap.): IX, **33**η, 1913 (mentioned among the slain).—§ 641 (Rājadh.): XII, **65**θ, 2429; **101**ο, 3735 (°*āḥ Sindhusauvīrā nakharaprāsayodhinaḥ*).—§ 664 (Mokshadh.): XII, **207**θ, 7560 (*uttarāpathajanmānaḥ . . . Yauna-Kāmboja-G°āḥ*).—§ 785 (Anugītāp.): XIV, **83**, 2484 (°*vishayam*); **84**, 2486 (*Çakunes tanayo G°ānāṃ mahārathaḥ*), 2492, 2493, 2498 (caused by Arjuna to pay tribute when he followed the sacrificial horse); **85**, 2512 (°*vishaye*).—§ 793 (Mausalap.): XVI, **6**, 159 (had been vanquished by Kṛshṇa). Cf. Gāndhāraka, pl.; Gāndhari, pl.

* **Gāndhāra**[1], name of a note: IV, 515; XII, 6859; XIV, 1419.

Gāndhāra[2] = Çakuni: II, 2529 (°*vidyayā*); IV, 1577 (*Ç°*); IX, 1464.

Gāndhāra[3] = Çiva (1000 names[2]).

Gāndhāra, dual (°*au*) = Acala and Vṛshaka: VII, 1311.

Gāndhārādhipati, a certain king of the Gāndhāras. § 407 (Māndhātrup.): III, **126**, 10465 (*Somakulotpannaḥ*, slain by Māndhātṛ).

Gāndhāraka[1], pl. (°*āḥ*), a people = Gāndhāra, pl. § 589 (Droṇābhishekap.): VII, **7**γ, 180 (*vimalaprāsayodhibhiḥ*, followed Çakuni). — § 599 (Jayadrathavadhap.): VII, **95**, 3532 (*saptaçataiç cāpaçaktyasipāṇibhiḥ*).—§ 607 (Karṇap.): VIII, **40**, 1845 (*Madrakeshu ca saṃsṛshṭaṃ çaucaṃ G°akeshu ca*).

Gāndhāraka[2], adj. ("originating from the country of the Gāndhāras"). § 611 (Çalyap.): IX, **28**, 1545 (*açvaiḥ*).

Gāndhāramukhya, dual (°*au*) = Acala and Vṛshaka: V, 5809.

Gāndhārapati ("lord of the Gāndhāras") = Çakuni: VIII, †4065, †4323.

Gāndhārarāj ("king of the Gāndhāras") = Çakuni: VII, 1609.

Gāndhārarāja[1] (do.) = Çakuni: I, 146; III, 14816 (*Ç°*), 17309; V, †31, †854 (*Ç°*), †895 (*Çakuniḥ Pārvatīyaḥ*), 3379 (*Ç°*), 7609 (do.); VI, †748 (*Çakuniḥ Pārvatīyaiḥ sārdhaṃ Gāndhāraiḥ*); VII, 1504 (*Kitavaḥ*), 8901 (*Ç°*); VIII, †200, †3812, 4872; IX, 164, 1208, 1209; XI, 698.

Gāndhārarāja[2] (do.) = Subala: I, 4373; VII, 1303 (°*sya sutau . . . Vṛshakācalau*).

Gāndhārarāja[3] (do.) = the father of Gāndhārī[4], the wife of Kṛshṇa: VII, 391 (°*sya sutāṃ*, i.e. Gāndhārī[4]).

Gāndhārarāja[4] (do.) = the son of Çakuni: XIV, 2485 (*Çakuniputreṇa*), 2504 (°*sya jananī*).

Gāndhārarājaduhitṛ ("daughter of the king of the Gāndhāras") = Gāndhārī[1]: I, 4524.

Gandhārarājaputra ("son of the king of the Gāndhāras") = Çakuni: I, 2440 (*Ç°*).

Gāndhārarājaputra (do.) = the son of Çakuni: XIV, 2499.

Gandhārarājasya putra(ḥ) (do.) = Çakuni: I, 4377 (*Ç°*).

Gāndhārarājasya putra(ḥ) (do.) = Çakuni: IX, 972 (*Ç°*), 1204 (*Ç°*).

Gāndhārarājasya suta(ḥ) (do.) = Çakuni: V, †35.

Gāndhāri = Duryodhana, q.v.

Gāndhāri, pl. (°*ayaḥ*), a people (= Gāndhāra, pl.). § 608 (Karṇap.): VIII, **46**γ, 2135 (followed Çakuni and Ulūka).

Gāndhārī[1], the daughter of the Gāndhāra king Subala, the wife of Dhṛtarāshṭra[1], and the mother of Duryodhana, etc. § 4 (Anukram.): I, **1**, 99, †214.—§ 11 (Parvasaṅgr.): I, **2**, 585, 587, 611. —[§ 83 (Ādivaṃçāvatāraṇa): I, **63**, 2441 (*Duryodhanasya jananī*).]—[§ 132 (Aṃçāvat.): I, **67**, 2794 (*Subalātmajā*, incarnation of the goddess Mati).] — § 157 (Pūruvaṃç.): I, **95**, 3809 (*tatra Dhṛtarāshṭrasya rājñaḥ putraçataṃ babhūva G°yāṃ varadānād Dvaipāyanasya*, all. to § 180).—§ 174 (Dhṛtarāshṭravivāha): I, **110**, 4371 (*Subalātmajāṃ*), 4372, 4374, 4375, 4380 (*G.*, who from Çiva had obtained the boon that she should have 100 sons, was married to Dhṛtarāshṭra; because Dhṛtarāshṭra was blind, *G.* bandaged her eyes). — § 180 (Gāndhārīputrotpatti): I, **115**, 4483, 4485, 4486, 4489, 4491, 4493, (4497), 4520 (birth of the 100 sons of *G.* and Dhṛtarāshṭra). — § 181 (Duḥçalotpatti): I, **116**, 4530 (mother of Duḥçalā).—§ 190 (Pāṇḍavotpatti): I, **123**, 4759.—§ 192 (do.): I, **124**, 4838. —§ 194 (Pāṇḍu): I, **126**, 4912.—§ 208 (Astradarçana): I, **134**, 5326, 5346.—§ 213 (Jatugṛhap.): I, **143**, 5709 (C. by error *Ga°*).—§ 298 (Dyūtap.): II, **58**, 2018, 2020.—§ 303 (Anudyūtap.): II, **75**, 2479, 2489 (recommended Dhṛtarāshṭra to abandon Duryodhana). — § 307 (do.): II, **81**, 2690. — §. 314 (Āraṇyakap.): III, **9**, 324. — § 515 (Karṇadigvijaya): III, **254**, 15264, 15270.—§ 516 (Duryodhanayajña): III, **256**, 15302.—§ 522 (Draupadīharaṇap.): III, **271**, 15758 (mother-in-law of Jayadratha, cf. I, **117**).—§ 561 (Yānasandhip.): V, **67**, †2518, 2520; **69**, 2546, (2547) (rebuked Duryodhana). — § 567 (Bhagavadyānap.): V, **124**a, 4125; **125**, 4205; **129**, 4310, 4314, 4315, 4317, (4318), 4327 (rebuked Duryodhana).—§ 569 (do.): V, **141**, 4806; **147**ο, 4963, 5000; [**148**, (rebuked Duryodhana)]; **149**, 5040; **150**, 5077, 5083.—§ 578 (Bhīshmavadhap.): VI, **49**, 1901.—§ 585 (do.): VI, **88**κ, 3926; **89**μ, 3937.—§ 604 (Karṇap.): VIII, **4**ε, 77 (lamented for Karṇa).—§ 608 (do.): VIII, **96**, 5036 (do.), 5038.—§ 609 (Çalyap.): IX, **1**, 23 (do.), 42, 50, 52 (*G.*'s lament when she is informed of the result of the battle).—§ 615 (Gadāyuddhap.): IX, **62**, 3501, 3502; **63**, 3503, 3512, 3513, 3515, 3525, 3529, 3530, 3531, 3539, 3554, (γγ), 3561, 3567, 3571, 3572, 3576 (comforted by Kṛshṇa after the slaughter of Duryodhana); **64**, 3618.—§ 616 (Sauptikap.): X, **2**, 101; **9**, 508, 512 (*hataputrā*).—§ 618 (Jalapradānikap.): XI, **1**γ, 29; **8**ζ, 222 (*Kaler aṃçaḥ samutpanno G°yā jaṭhare*, sc. as Duryodhana); **10**, 270, 272; **11**ι, 293; **14**, 360, 361, 366, 368, 369, 372, (373); **15**, 381, (392), 400, (402), 405, 409, 413, 421 (*G.*, by a wrathful glance of her eyes, burnt the nail of a toe of Yudhishṭhira). — § 619 (Strīvilāpap.): XI, **16**, 427 (saw with her spiritual eye the slaughter of the Kurus); **17**β, 487, 489; **18**γ, (519); **19**δ, (547); **20**ε, (568); **21**, (603); **22**η, (617); **23**θ, (635); **24**ι, (677); **25**κ, (706), 742, (744), 752 (having lamented for the dead warriors, *G.* cursed Kṛshṇa that he and his kinsmen should perish after thirty-six years).—§ 620 (Çrāddhap.): XI, **26**, 756, 761.—§ 635 (Rājadh.): XII, **37**, 1383.—§ 637 (do.): XII, **40***a*, 1448; **42**γ, 1494; **45**ε, 1542.—§ 776 (Ānuçāsanik.): XIII, **167**, 7704.—§ 777 (Svargārohaṇik. p.): XIII, **168**, 7714.—§ 778 (Açvamedhikap.): XIV, **1**, 9.—§ 783 (Anugītāp.): XIV, **52**, 1505, 1506 (°*paricārakāḥ*), 1507.—§ 785 (do.): XIV, **71**π, 2060 (*Subalātmajām*); **78**, 2294; **84**, 2508.—§ 787 (Āçramavāsap.): XV, **1**, 2, 8, 11; **2**, 40, 45 (*Saubaleyī*), 47, 57; **3**, 65, 71, 80, 85, 87, 91, 94, 96, 111, 121, 126, 137; **4**, 150, 163; **5**, 170, 174; **8**, 262, 263, 265, 275, 278; **9**, 291, 300; **10**, 306, 355; **14**, 424; **15**, 429, 436 (retired to the woods with Dhṛtarāshṭra and Kuntī); **16**, 449, 457; **18**, 498, 502, 514; **19**, 523, 525, 534; **20**, 553, 555, 570.—§ 788 (do.): XV, **21**, 578, 584; **22**, 598, 608; **24**, 645, 649, 654; **27**δ, 730; **28**, 744.—§ 789 (Putradarçanap.): XV, **29**, 778, 782, 800, 814; **31**, 843; **32**, 870, 885 (sees her dead sons arise from the Gaṅgā).—§ 791 (do.): XV, **36**, 981, 983, 984, 1005.—§ 792 (Nāradāgamanap.): XV, **37**, 1017, 1021, 1024, 1027, 1039, 1041, 1045, 1049, 1051 (together with Dhṛtarāshṭra and Kuntī, *G.* burnt to death in a wood flagration); **38***a*, 1062; **39**, 1090, 1092 (the funeral rites of *G.*, etc., are performed).—§ 793 (Mausalap.): XVI, **2**, 53 (the curse of *G.* (cf. XI, **25**) is fulfilled); **4**, †122 (do.); **6**κ, 163 (do.).—§ 795 (Svargārohaṇap.): XVIII, **5**μ, 161 (in heaven).

Cf. also the following synonyms:—

Gāndhārarājaduhitṛ, q.v.
Saubaleyī ("the daughter of Subala"): I, 4496, 4499, 4526; IX, 3561; XV, 45 (*G*°), 503.
Saubalī (do.): I, 4504, 4536.
Subalajā (do.): XV, 25.
Subalasya putrī (do.): V, †5031.
Subalasyātmajā (do.): I, 4367.
Subalātmajā (do.): I, 2794 (incarnation of Mati), 4371 (*G*°); II, †2402; XI, 442; XIV, 2060 (*G*°).

Gāndhārī[2], wife of Ajamīḍha. § 156 (Pūruvaṃç.): I, **95**, ††3790.

Gāndhārī[3], a goddess. § 506 (Skandayuddha): III, **231**, 14562 (followed Pārvatī).

Gāndhārī[4], wife of Kṛshṇa. [§ 589 (Droṇābhishek.): VII, **11**μ, 391 (*tathā Gāndhārarājasya sutām vīraḥ svayaṃvare* | *nirjitya pṛthivīpālān avahat Pushkarekshaṇaḥ*—i.e. Kṛshṇa | *amṛshyamāṇā rājāno yasya jātyā hayā iva* | *rathe vaivāhike yuktāḥ pratodena kṛtavraṇāḥ*).]—§ 793 (Mausalap.): XVI, **7**μ, 249 (among the wives of Kṛshṇa who ascended his funeral pyre).

Gāndhārīputra = Duryodhana, q.v.

[Gāndhārīputrotpatti(ḥ)] ("birth of Gāndhārī's sons"). § 180 (Sambhavap.): One day *Dvaipāyana*, gratified with *Gāndhārī's* hospitality, granted her the boon that she should have 100 sons (cf. § 174). She had borne the burden in her womb for two years, when she heard that *Kuntī* had brought forth a son; she then struck her womb violently, and there came out a hard mass of flesh like an iron ball. When she was about to throw it away, *Vyāsa* appeared and caused her to put the ball of flesh, sprinkled with cool water and divided into 101 parts (each of the size of a thumb), into 101 pots filled with clarified butter, which were placed in a concealed spot. After having said that she should open the covers of the pots after two years, *Vyāsa* retired to *Himavat* in order to devote himself to asceticism. *Duryodhana* was younger than *Yudhishṭhira*, being born on the same day as *Bhīma*. As soon as *Duryodhana* was born he began to cry like an ass, and ill-portending omens appeared. *Vidura*, etc., in vain told *Dhṛtarāshṭra* to abandon him. Within a month the 100 sons of *Dhṛtarāshṭra* and one daughter were born. During the pregnancy of *Gāndhārī*, *Dhṛtarāshṭra* begot the *Karaṇa Yuyutsu* upon a maidservant of the *Vaiçya* class (I, **115**).

Gandharva[1], pl. (°*āḥ*), the celestial musicians or singers. § 4 (Anukram.): I, **1**, 105 (1,400,000 verses of the Mhbhr. are known among the *G.*), 106 (Çuka recited the Mhbhr. to the *G.*, the Yakshas, and the Rakshases), †165 (all. to § 512).—§ 11 (Parvasaṅgr.): I, **2**, 369, 470 (all. to § 512).—§ 18 (Paulomap.): I, **4**, 855 (*manushyoraga-G°kathā veda*, sc. Çaunaka).—§ 28 (Amṛtamanthana), I, **17**, 1099 (*Merum . . . deva-G°sevitam*).—§ 39 (Rāmaṇīyaka): I, **27**, 1311 (°*āpsarasām priyam*, sc. the forest on Rāmaṇīyaka).—§ 45 (Vālakhilya, pl.): I, **31**, 1440.—§ 46 (Garuḍa): I, **32**, 1486 (fled before Garuḍa towards the east).—§ 75 (Vasu): I, **63**, 2366 (°*āpsarasaḥ*, worshipped Vasu Uparicara).—§ 84 (Ādivaṃçāvatāraṇap.): I, **64**, 2495 (°*āpsarobhiḥ*, worship Brahmán), 2503 (°*āpsarasām gaṇān*, were re-born among men).—§ 85 (Aṃçāvat.): I, **65**, 2513, 2514, 2515.—§ 104 (do.): I, **65**, 2559 (°*sattamāḥ*, enumeration of four *G.*, sons of Prādhā).—§ 105 (do.): I, **65**, 2560 (*amṛtaṃ brāhmaṇā gāvo G°āpsarasas tathā* | *apatyaṃ Kapilāyās tu Purāṇe parikīrtitam*).—§ 106 (do.): I, **65**, 2561 (*sambhavaḥ . . . G°āpsarasām*).—§ 130 (do.): I, **67**, 2637 (°*oraga-Rakshasām . . . sambhavaḥ*).—§ 131 (Karṇa): I, **67**, 2781 (°*oraga-Rakshasām*).—§ 132 (Aṃçāvat.): I, **67**, 2795 °*āpsarasām . . . aṃçāvatāraṇam*), 2798 (*aṃçāvatāraṇam . . . deva-G°āpsarasām*).—§ 133 (Dushyanta): I, **68**, 2799 (*aṃçāvatāraṇam . . . G°āpsarasām*); **70**, 2858 (°*āpsarasāṅ gaṇaiḥ*).—§ 142 (Nahusha): I, **75**, 3152 (°*oraga-Rākshasān*).—§ 149 (Yayāti): I, **88**, 3565, †3567 (*surarshi G°-nara°*).—§ 175 (Karṇasambhava): I, **111**, 4410 (°*oraga-Rakshasām*).—§ 185 (Pāṇḍu): I, **120**, 4649 (*ākrīḍabhūmiṃ devānāṃ G°āpsarasām tathā*, in the north).—§ 191 (Arjuna): I, **123**, 4806 (°*āpsarasaḥ*, present at the birth of Arjuna), 4808 (do.), 4810 (enumeration).—§ 211 (Sambhavap.): I, **139**, 5534 (*trivarshakṛtayajñas tu G°āṇām upaplave . . . Sauvīraḥ*).—§ 214 (Hiḍimbavadhap.): I, **152**, 5960.—§ 221 (Caitrarathap.): I, **168**, 6444 (*muhūrtaṃ . . . vihitaṃ kāmacārāṇām Yaksha-G°-Rakshasām*), 6483 (°*jānām açvānām*, Citraratha gives 100 horses, born among the *G.*, to each of the Pāṇḍavas), 6484 (°*deva-G°vāhāḥ*, sc. *hayāḥ*), 6489 (°*jāḥ . . . hayāḥ*), 6496 (*Yaksha-Rākshasa-G°āḥ*, know the history of the Kurus).—§ 222 (Tapatyup.): I, **173**, 6616 (*giriçreshṭhe deva-G°sevite*). § 233 (Svayaṃvarap.): I, **187**, †7011 (*Viçvāvasur Nārada-Parvatau ca G°mukhyāḥ*, present at the svayaṃvara of Draupadī), †7017 (*devarshi-G°samākulam . . . antarīksham*).—§ 246 (Sundopasundop.): I, **212**, 7713 (*deva-G°-Yakshāṇām . . . sarvaratnāni*).—§ 252 (Subhadrāharaṇap.): I, **219**, 7912 (? "musicians," PCR.), 7913 (do.), 7917 (do.).—§ 257*c* (Gāṇḍīva), I, **225**, 8182 (*deva-Dānava-G°aiḥ pūjitam*, sc. *Gāṇḍīvam*).—§ 258 (Khāṇḍavadah.): I, **227**, 8256 (attack Kṛshṇa and Arjuna); **228**, 8304 (*Yaksha-Rākshasa-G°-nara-Kinnara-pannagaiḥ*).—§ 264 (Sabhākrīyap.): II, **4**, 131 (°*āpsarasaḥ*, together with Citrasena, present in the palace of Yudhishṭhira), 132.—§ 265 (Lokapālasabhākhy.): II, **5**, 135 (in the palace of Yudhishṭhira).—§ 266 (Çakrasabhāv.): II, **7**, 305 (in the palace of Indra).—§ 267 (Yamasabhāv.): II, **8**, 349 (in the palace of Yama).—§ 268 (Varuṇasabhāv.): II, **9**, 378 (°*āpsarasāṃ gaṇaiḥ*, in the palace of Varuṇa).—§ 269 (Vaiçravaṇasabhāv.): II, **10**, 391 (in the palace of Kubera), 395 (°*āpsarasāṅ gaṇāḥ*, do.), 396 (*Kinnarā nāma G°ā Narā nāma tathāpare*, do.), 401, 406 (°*āṇāṃ patayaḥ*, sc. Viçvāvasu, etc.), 407, 411. — § 270 (Brahmasabhāv.): II, **11**, 445 (°*āpsarasāṃ gaṇāḥ*, in the palace of Brahmán), 472 (°*āpsarasaḥ*, do.).—§ 271 (Lokapālasabhākh.): II, **12**, 481 (°*āpsarasaḥ*, in the palace of Kubera), 483 (in the palace of Indra).—§ 279 (Arjuna): II, **28**, 1042 (°*rakshitaṃ deçaṃ*, in the north, conquered by Arjuna).—§ 310*b* (Sūrya): III, **3**, 170 (*Siddha-Cāraṇa-G°āḥ*, follow the chariot of the Sun).—§ 322 (Dvaitavanaprav.): III, **24**, 925 (°*āpsarasāṃ*, sc. *lokaṃ*).—§ 327 (Draupadīparitāpav.): III, **31**, 1188 (°*āsura-Rākshasāḥ*).—§ 335 (Indralokābh.): III, **42**, 1726 (accompanied Indra).—§ 336 (do.): III, **43**, 1764 (in the world of Indra), 1765, 1783 (*Tumburuçreshṭhāḥ*).—§ 337 (do.): III, **44**, 1788.—§ 338 (do.): III, **46**, 1830 (*Siddha-Cāraṇa-G°aiḥ*), 1843.—§ 357 (Tīrthayātrāp.): III, **82**, 4064 (°*āpsarasaḥ*, in Pushkara).—§ 359 (Vaḍavā): III, **82**, 5036 (°*āpsarasāṃ gaṇaiḥ*, in Vaḍavā).—§ 361 (Kurukshetra): III, **83**, 5076 (°*āpsarasaḥ*, in Kurukshetra).—§ 370 (Tīrthayātrāp.): III, **84**, 7083 (*Siddha-Cāraṇa-G°āḥ*, in Saugandhikavana), 8024 (*Sindhoḥ prabhavaṃ . . . Siddha-G°sevitaṃ*); **85**, 8168 (*Siddha-Cāraṇa-G°-mānushāḥ*, in Gokarṇa).—§ 373 (Prayāga): III, **85**, 8215 (in Prayāga).—§ 377 (Dhaumyatīrthak.): III, **90**, 8391 (°*Yaksha-Rakshobhiḥ . . . sevitaṃ . . . çailaṃ*).—§ 383*b* (Gaṅgā): III, **99**, 8646 (*Bhāgīrathī . . . deva-G°sevitā*).— § 383 (Paraçurāma): III, **99**, 8674 (seen in the body of Rāma Dāçarathi).—§ 386 (Agastyop.): III, **104**, 8800 (*manushyoraga-G°-Yaksha-Kimpurushāḥ*), 8804 (*devāḥ sa-G°mahoragāḥ*); **105**, †8810 (°*tūryeshu*).—§ 387 (Sagara): III, **107**, 8854 (°*Rākshasān*). — § 389 (Gaṅgāvataraṇa): III, **109**, 9954 (°*oraga-Yakshāḥ*).—§ 418*c* (Mandara): III, **139**, 10825 (on Mandara). — § 423 (Gandhamādanapr.): III, **143**, 10968 °*āpsarasāṃ priyaṃ . . . Gandhamādanaṃ*); **145**, 11027, 11036 (*deçe . . . deva-G°sevite*). — § 424 (Bhīmakadalīkhaṇḍapr.): III, **146**, 11089 (*Yaksha-G°-sura-Brahmarshigaṇasevitaṃ*), 11098 (*Yaksha-G°yoshābhiḥ*).—§ 425 (Hanūmad-Bhīmasenasaṃv.): III, **148**, 11220.—§ 426*b* (Kṛtayuga): III, **149**, 11236 (did not exist in the Kṛtayuga).—§ 432 (Saugandhikāharaṇa): III, **153**, 11358 (*ākrīḍaṃ rājarājasya Kuberasya . . . G°aiḥ . . . paramārcitaṃ*); **154**, 11372 (°*āpsarasaḥ*).—§ 436 (Yakshayuddhap.): III, **158**, 11620, 11623 (°*āpsarobhiḥ*); **159**, 11645 (°*āpsarasāṃ gaṇāḥ*).—§ 437 (do.): III, **160**, 11682 (°*oraga-Rakshaṃsi*), 11708 (*Yaksha-Rākshasa-G°āḥ*).—§ 438 (do.): III, **161**, 11765 (*deva-G°āḥ*), 11773 (*Yaksha-G°āḥ*), 11777; **162**, 11813 (°*Yakshāḥ*), 11824. § 440 (do.): III, **164**, †11884 (°*saṅghāḥ*).—§ 441 (Nivātakavacayuddhap.): III, **166**, 11920 (°*āpsarasāṃ gaṇāḥ*).—§ 443 (do.): III, **168**, 12001 (*gaṇāḥ . . . G°āṇām*), 12021 (°*oraga Rakshasāṃ*), 12035 (°*āpsarasāñ caiva prabhāvaṃ*), 12045 (*deva-G°pūjitāṃ*), 12047 (*deva-G°aiḥ*).—§ 445 (do.): III, **173**, 12246, 12272 (*sa-Yakshāsura-G°aiḥ*).—§ 446 (do.): III, **174**, 12280 (°*çiçubhiḥ*).—§ 447 (do.): III, **175**, 12304 (*Yaksha-Rākshasa-G°āḥ*), 12307.—§ 449 (Ājagarap.): III, **177**, †12362 (*Yaksha-G°maharshikāntāṃ . . . Sarasvatīṃ*).—§ 450 (do.): III, **178**, 12367 (*vanaṃ ramyaṃ deva-G°sevitaṃ*); **179**, 12427 (*deva-G°-Rākshasāḥ*); **181**, 12522 (*Brahmarshi-deva-G°-Yaksha-Rākshasa-pannagāḥ*).—§ 458 (Mārkaṇḍeyas.): III, **188**, 12877 (*sadevāsura-G°ṃ . . . jagat*).—§ 459 (do.): III, **188**, 12925 (°*āpsarasaḥ*), 12942 (°*nāgāḥ*); **189**, 12979 (°*oraga-Rākshasān*).—§ 474 (do.): III, **201**, 13485 (*kathāṃ . . . deva-G°-Yakshāṇāṃ*).—§ 476 (Dhundhumārop.): III, **202**, 13535 (*sarpa-G°-Rakshasāṃ*).—§ 478 (do.): III, **204**, 13584 (do), 13619.—§ 501 (Skandopākhyāna): III, **229**, 14440 (*deva-G°gītaiḥ*).—§ 502 (Manushyagrahak.): III, **230**, 14492 (°*āṇāṃ yā mātā sā garbhaṃ gṛhya gacchati*), 14505 (°*āç cāpi yaṃ divyāḥ saṃviçanti naraṃ bhuvi | unmadyati sa tu kshipraṃ graho Gāndharva eva sa*).—§ 505 (Skandayuddha): III, **231**, 14539.—§ 506 (do.): III, **231**, 14557.—§ 512 (Ghoshayātrāp.): III, **240**, 14868, 14873, 14875, 14879; **241**, 14881, 14885, 14886, 14888, 14889, 14891, 14893, 14894, 14895, 14899, 14900, 14901, 14904, 14907, 14911; **242**, 14913, 14915, 14916, 14919, 14921, 14923, 14924, 14927, 14929; **243**, 14944, 14955; **244**, 14963, 14969, 14972, 14975, 14977, 14978; **245**, 14979, 14980, 14981, 14982, 14984, 14985, 14986, 14988, 14991, 14993, 14994, 14996, 14998; **246**, 15010 (°*sainyānāṃ*), 15022, 15026, 15027; **247**, 15046 (*kāmarūpinaḥ*), 15048; **248**, 15053, 15054, 15059, 15062, 15063, 15068; **249**, 15074, 15078 (Duryodhana and his brothers were made captives by the *G.*, headed by Citrasena, but were liberated by the Pāṇḍavas).—§ 515 (Karṇadigvijaya): III, **253**, 15214 (°*āṇāṃ tadā raṇāt*, all. to § 512). — § 520 (Mudgala): III, **261**, 15446 (°*āpsarasaḥ*).—§ 526 (Rāmopākhyānap.): III, **275**, 15913 (°*devāsurataḥ*), 15921 (°*Yakshānugataḥ*, sc. Kubera); **276**, 15936 (*deva-G°-Dānavāḥ*).—§ 533 (Sītā-Rāvaṇasaṃv.): III, 16168, 16175 (°*āṇāṃ yoshitāḥ*, wives of Rāvaṇa), 16178 (°*āpsarasaḥ*). — § 542 (Rāvaṇavadha): III, **290**, 16524 (*deva-G°āḥ*), 16528 (*tridaçāḥ saha G°-Cāraṇaiḥ*). — § 543 (Rāmābhisheka): III, **291**, 16533, (*a*), 16550, 16578 (*deva-G°-Yakshāṇāṃ*), 16579 (*sa-devāsura-G°āḥ*). — § 548 (Āraṇeyap.): III, **313**, 17319.—§ 549 (Pāṇḍavapr.): IV, **8**, 235 (Virāṭa considers Bhīmasena to be either the king of the Gandharvas or Indra); **9**, 273 (Draupadī says that she is the wife of five *G.*), 274 (*putrā G°rājasya mahāsattvasya kasyacit*, do.), 275, 277; **12**, †323 (°*varopamaḥ*, i.e. Nakula).—§ 551 (Kīcakavadhap.): IV, **14**, 426 (*patayo mama*, i.e. Draupadī's); **16**, 493 (*patayas tava*, i.e. Draupadī's), 495; **21**, 664 (°*āṇām ahaṃ bhāryā pañcānāṃ*, says Draupadī), 665, 666, 667; **22**, 706, 710, 721, 787 (*patibhir mama*, i.e. Draupadī's, said to have slain Kīcaka); **23**, 806; **24**, 829, 832, 837, 838, 841, 843 (°*rājāya*), 857, 858, 859 (do.).—§ 552 (Goharaṇap.): IV, **25**, 863, 881 (do.); **30**, 975 (do.); **43**, 1346 (*deva-Dānava-G°aiḥ pūjitaṃ*, sc. *Gāṇḍīvam*); **45**, 1406 (°*rājapratimaṃ*, sc. Arjuna), 1429 (all. to § 512); **50**, 1572; **56**, 1762 (*deva Yaksha-G°-mahoragasamākulaṃ maṇḍalaṃ*), 1767 (came to see the encounter between Bhīshma and Arjuna); **58**, 1895 (°*āpsarasaḥ*, applauded Arjuna).—§ 553*b* (Yudhishṭhira): IV, **70**, 2271 (°-*Yakshapravarāḥ*).—§ 555 (Indravijaya): V, **10**, 301, 303, 311, 332; **11**, 348 (*Pitṛ-G°-Bhūtānāṃ*), 356 (°*āpsarasāṃ gaṇāḥ*); **12**, 369 (*jagat . . . sāsura-G°ṃ*), 379, 391; **15**, 464 (*deva-Dānava-G°āḥ*); **16**, 496 (*Devarshi-G°aiḥ*), †507 (°*mukhyāḥ*); **17**, 541; **18**, 544 (°*āpsarasaṃ gaṇaiḥ*), 546.—§ 556 (Sañjayayānap.): V, **29**, †824 (°*Yakshāpsarasaḥ*); **30**, †879 (°*putrapratimaṃ*, sc. Açvatthāman).—§ 560 (Sanatsujātap.): V, **44**, 1704 (°*āṇāṃ . . . rūpaṃ*).—§ 561 (Yānasandhip.): V, **61**, 2401; **64**, 2471 (*Gandhamādanaṃ . . . Siddha-G°sevitaṃ*)—§ 564 (Mātalīyop.): V, **97**, 3518.—§ 565 (Gālavacarita): V, **109**, 3787 (*gāyanti gāthā G°āç cittabuddhiharāḥ*, in the south); **111**, 3826 (°*Yaksha-Siddhaiḥ*, cannot see Purusha), 3830 (ruled by Kubera); **116**, 3940 (*bahu-G°darçanā*, sc. Mādhavī); **120**, 4028 (°*mṛgapakshiṇāṃ*). — § 565 (Yayāti): V, **123**, 4100 (°*apsarasāṃ gaṇaiḥ*, worship Yayāti).—§ 567 (Bhagavadyānap.): V, **124**, 4172, 4175 (had been vanquished by

Arjuna, all. to § 258?); **128**ι, 4302 (*°oraga-Rākshasāḥ*); **130**, 4401; **131**o, 4424 (appeared in the body of Kṛshṇa).—§ 570 (Sainyaniryāṇap.): V, **158**, 5377 (had been vanquished by Arjuna, all. to § 512).—§ 572 (Rathātirathas.): V, **167**, 5787 (*deva-G°-mānushān*).—§ 573 (Ambopākhyānap.): V, **176**, 6054 (*°āpsarasaḥ*, on the mountain Mahendra); **184**, 7285 (present at the encounter between Bhīshma and Rāma Jāmadagnya). — § 574 (Jambūkh.): VI, **6**, 212 (*°āsura-Rākshasāḥ*, on Meru), (θ), 247 (on the mountain Nishadha).—§ 575*b* (Çākadvīpa): VI, **11**, 415 (on Meru in Çākadvīpa).—§ 575 (Bhūmip.): VI, **12**, 455 (*deva-G°āḥ*, in Kuçadvīpa), 465 (*deçāḥ . . . deva-G°sevitāḥ*, in Krauñcadvīpa.).—§ 576 (Bhagavadgītāp.): VI, **34**, 1230 (*°āṇām Citrarathaḥ*, sc. *asmi*, says Kṛshṇa); **35**, †1268 (*°Yakshāsura-Siddhasaṅghāḥ*).—§ 577 (Bhīshmavadhap.): VI, **43**, 1536 (came to see the battle).—§ 578 (do.): VI, **48**, 1975 (*deva-G°āḥ*).—§ 579 (do.): VI, **52**, 2183 (*devāḥ sa-G°āḥ*), 2185 (*sadevāsura-G°air lokaiḥ*). — § 580 (do.): VI, **58**, 2467 (*deva-Dānava-G°āḥ*, applaud Arjuna).—§ 581 (do.): VI, **65**ξ, 2961 (*deva-G°āḥ*); **66**, 2975 (*Devarshi-G°āḥ*), 2977 (*deva-Brahmarshi-G°ān*), 2997.—§ 584 (do.): VI, **83**, 3665 (*devāḥ sa-G°āḥ*, had come to see the battle); **84**, 3704 (*deva-G°-Rākshasāḥ*).—§ 585 (do.): VI, **95**, 4303 (*devāḥ sa-G°āḥ*); **98**, 4450 (*sadevāsura-G°aṃ lokaṃ*).—§ 593 (Abhimanyuvadhap.): VII, **33**, 1463 (*sasurāsura-G°āḥ . . . lokāḥ*). — § 593*b* (Gandharvāstra): VII, **45**, 1824 (*Tumburupramukhebhyaḥ*, from them Arjuna had obtained the *Gāndharvam astraṃ* by means of *tapas*).—§ 594 (Abhimanyuvadhap.): VII, **52**, 2013 (*deva-Dānava-G°ān Mṛtyur harati*).—§ 595 (Shoḍaçarāj., v. Paurava): VII, **57**, 2199 (?*naṭanartana-G°aiḥ*, present at the sacrifice of Paurava, "singers," PCR.); (do., v. Bhagīratha): VII, **60**, 2255 (sung a gāthā); (do., v. Māndhātṛ): VII, **62**, 2287 (*°oragapakshiṇaḥ*, came to the sacrifices of Māndhātṛ); (do., v. Pṛthu Vainya): VII, **69**, 2403 (*°āpsarasaḥ*), 2418 (the *G.* and Apsarases milked perfumes from the earth into a vessel made of a lotus leaf; Citraratha became their calf and Viçvaruci their milker).—§ 596 (Pratijñāp.): VII, **74**, 2623; **75**, 2661; **76**, 2683; **79**, 2806 (*sa-G°āḥ . . . lokāḥ*).—§ 597 (do.): VII, **82**, 2938 (?"singers," PCR.).—§ 599 (Jayadrathavadhap.): VII, **98**, 3651; **110**, 4167 (*devāḥ sa-G°āḥ*); **119**, 4756 (*Cāraṇāḥ saha-G°āḥ*. applaud Sātyaki); **126**, 5125 (*devān sa-G°ān*, had been vanquished by Arjuna, all. to § 258); **139**, 5746 (applaud Karṇa and Bhīmasena); **144**, 6046 (*deva-Dānava-G°āḥ*), 6048 (*devāsura-G°āḥ*); **147**, 6339, 6352 (*deva-G°-Dānavāḥ*).—§ 600 (Ghaṭotkacavadhap.): VII, **156**, †6921 (*Siddha-G°-Piçācasaṅghāḥ*, applaud Açvatthāman); **158**φ, 6985 (*hriyamāṇe tadā, Karṇa, G°air Dhṛtarāshṭraje*, all. to § 512), 7004 (*deva-G°-Yakshāṇāṃ*), 7021 (*devaiḥ . . . sa-Daitya-Yaksha-G°aiḥ*); **163**, †7292 (*Devarshi-G°-surarshisaṅghāḥ*), †7312 (*°Yakshāḥ*), †7313 (*deva-G°samākulaṃ*); **164**, 7320 (*deva-G°dīpādyaiḥ*); **170**λλ, 7620 (*deva-°G-Dānavaḥ*).—§ 601 (Droṇavadhap.): VII, **185**, 8432, 8435 (*°ā ghoshayātrāyāṃ Citrasenādayo jitāḥ*, all. to § 512).—§ 602 (do.): VII, **188**, 8610 (in the welkin).—§ 603 (Nārāyaṇāstramokshaṇap.): VII, **195**, 9001; **196**, 9033 (*deva-Dānava-G°ās trastāḥ*); **201**, 9442.—§ 603*b* (Nārāyaṇa): VII, **201**ζζ, 9465 (*°Yakshān*), 9472 (*deva-G°yonishu*), 9473.—§ 603 (Nārāyaṇāstramokshap.): VII, **201**, 9543, (κκ), 9617 (*°āpsarasaḥ*, worship the liṅga of Çiva).—§ 606 (Tripurākhyāna): VIII, **34**, 1536 (praised Çiva).—§ 607 (Karṇap.): VIII, **41**ϵ, 1950 (*Dvaitavane . . . G°aiḥ samabhidrutaḥ . . . tvam*—i.e. Karṇa—*prathamaṃ palāyitaḥ*, all. to § 512), †951 (*Citrasenamukhān*, were vanquished by Arjuna, do.).—§ 608 (do.): VIII, **72**υυυ, 3615 (*devān sa-G°ān*); **86**τ′, 4359 (*sadevāsura-G°āṃs trīṃl lokān*); **87**, 4409 (*deva-Dānava-G°āḥ*), (χ′), 4423 (*Tumburumukhāḥ*, sided with Arjuna), 4424 *Prādheyāḥ saha-Mauneyā G°āpsarasāṃ gaṇāḥ*), 4426 (*deva-Dānava-G°āḥ*), 4460 (do.); **88**, †4490 (*°āpsarasāṃ saṅghaiḥ*); **94**, †4948 (*deva-G°-manushyapūjitaṃ . . . Karṇaṃ*); †4962 (*deva-G°-manushya-Cāraṇaiḥ*).—§ 611 (Çalyap.): IX, **13**, 701 (*deva-G°-Dānavāḥ*).—§ 615*c* (Subhūmika): IX, **37**, 2122 (*devāḥ sa-G°āḥ*), 2123, 2127 (*deva-G°-Rakshasāṃ*, in the tīrtha Subhūmika).—§ 615*d* (Gandharvāṇāṃ tīrthaṃ): IX, **37**, 2128 (*Viçvāvasumukhās tatra*—i.e. in Gandharvāṇāṃ tīrthaṃ—*G°āpsarasaḥ*). — § 615ι (Saptasārasvata): IX, **38**, 2194 (present at the sacrifice of Brahmán in Pushkara).—§ 615 (Baladevatīrthayātrā): IX, **41**, 2356 (*devāḥ sa-G°āḥ*, in Yāyātaṃ tīrthaṃ).—§ 615*p* (Vasishṭhāpavaha): IX, **42**, 2397 (*°āpsarasaḥ*). — § 615*u* (Skanda): IX, **44**, 2467 (praise Skanda), 2480 (*Nāradapramukhāç cāpi deva-G°sattamaḥ*), 2496 (*deva-G°-Rakshasāṃ*), 2502 (*deva-G°āḥ*); **45**γ, 2509 (came to the investiture of Skanda), 2531; **46**, 2677 (*deva-G°āḥ*, sang), 2715.—§ 615*ee* (Ādityatīrtha): IX, **49**, 2848 (*°āpsarasaḥ*, in Ādityatīrtha). — § 615*gg* (Sārasvata): IX, **51**, 2941 (*°āpsarasāṅ gaṇāḥ*).—§ 615 (Gadāyuddhap.): IX, **57**, 3183 (*deva-G°-mānavāḥ*); **58**, 3306 (*°āpsarasaḥ*); **61**, 3443 (beat musical instruments).—§ 616 (Sauptikap.): X, **8**, 441.—§ 617*b* (Brahmaçiras): X, **12**, 619 (*Brahmaçiraḥ . . . deva-G°pūjitaṃ*), 622 (*deva-Dānava-G°-manushya-patagoragāḥ*).—§ 620 (Çrāddhap.): XI, **26**, 768 (the fallen warriors have attained to the companionship of the *G.*).—§ 621 (Rājadharm.): XII, **2**, 62 (on the mountain Mahendra).—§ 632*b* (Shoḍaçarāj., cf. § 595, v. Marutta): XII, **29**, 916; (do., v. Bṛhadratha) XII, **29**, 929; (do., v. Dilīpa) XII, **29**, 968 (*deva-G°āḥ*, danced at the sacrifice of Dilīpa).—§ 637 (Rājadh.): XII, **47**θ, 1608 (*deva-Dānava-G°āḥ*), 1623 (*surāsura-G°āḥ*), 1662 (do not know Kṛshṇa truly).—§ 639 (do.): XII, **50**, 1830 (*devān sa-G°ān*).—§ 641 (do.): XII, **72**, 2768 (*°oraga-Rākshasāḥ*, depend upon sacrifices); **91**, 3460 (*Devarshi-Pitṛ-G°āḥ*); **99**, 3667 (*lokāḥ . . . pūrṇā G°kanyābhiḥ*).—§ 651*b* (Kapotalubdhakasaṃv.): XII, **149**, 5587 (*Yaksha-G°-Siddhānāṃ madhye*).—§ 655 (Āpaddh.): XII, **158**, 5890.—§ 656*c* (Daksha.): XII, **166**, 6137 (*°āpsarasaḥ*, among those who were begotten by the Brahmarshis on the daughters of Daksha).—§ 656 (Khaḍgotpatti): XII, **166**, 6162 (*maharshi-sura-G°ān*).—§ 660*b* (Bhṛgu-Bharadvājasaṃv.): XII, **188**, 6932 (*deva-Dānava-G°āḥ*, created by Brahmán).—§ 664 (Mokshadh.): XII, **207**ϵ, 7542 (born by a daughter of Daksha).—§ 671*b* (Bali-Vāsavasaṃv.): XII, **223**, 8079 (sang before Bali); **224**, 8116 (*°oraga-Rākshasāḥ*).—§ 673*b* (do.): XII, **227**, 8221.—§ 675 (Mokshadh.): XII, **230**, 8453.—§ 683 (do.): XII, **268**, 9580 (*°-Pitṛṇāṃ*).—§ 686 (do.): XII, **273**, 9825 (*vimānāni . . . G°āṇāṃ*).—§ 693*b* (Vṛtravadha): XII, **282**, 10114 (*°āç ca vimānāgraiḥ*)—§ 695*b* (Dakshayajñavināça): XII, **285**, 10276 (*°āpsarasākīrṇe*, sc. *deçe*), (*a*), 10278 (*deva-Dānava-G°āḥ*), 10279 (*°āpsarasaḥ*), 10336 (*Yaksha-G°saṅghaiḥ*).—§ 702 (Mokshadh.): XII, **291**, 10709 (*deva-G°-Dānavāḥ*); **296**β, 10838 (*Yaksha-Rākshasa-G°āḥ*).—§ 704 (do.): XII, **301**, †11097 (*°saṅghāḥ*).—§ 705 (do.): XII, **303***a*, 11244 (*trailokye . . . sa-Yaksha-Bhūta-G°e*).—§ 712 (Çukotpatti): XII, **324**, 12176 (*deva-G°āḥ*); **325**, 12200 (sang).—§ 714 (Çukakṛtya): XII, 12379.—§ 716 (Çukābhipātana): XII, **332**, 12570 (*deva-Dānava-G°ān*); **333**, 12591 (*°āpsarasāṅ gaṇāḥ*); **334**, 12620, 12621, 12638 (*deva-G°vṛtaḥ*, sc. Çiva).—§ 717*b* (Nārāyaṇīya): XII, **344**, 13319 (*ṛshayaç ca sa-G°āḥ*), (γγ), 13366.—§ 717*d*

Brahma-Rudrasaṃv.): XII, **351**, 13733.—§ 718*b* (Uñcha-vṛttyup.): XII, **364**, 13922.—§ 730 (Ānuçāsanik.): XIII, **14**, 634 (*pūjitaṃ deva-G°aiḥ*, sc. the hermitage of Upamanyu). —§ 730*g* (Upamanyu): XIII, **14**η, 741 (*ṛshi-G°rūpaḥ*, sc. Çiva), 766 (*divya-G°nāditaiḥ*), 800 (*pūjitaṃ Siddha-G°aiḥ*, sc. Çiva), (μ), 813 (*ṛshi-G°-Siddhaiḥ*).—§ 730 (Ānuçāsanik.): XIII, **14**, 958 (*°āpsarasaḥ*), (γγ), 995 (do.); **18**, 1373 (*Suparṇa - G° - Piçāca - Dānavāḥ*). — § 731*b* (Ashṭāvakra-Diksaṃv.): XIII, **19**, 1421 (*Yaksha-G°-Kinnarāḥ*, in the palace of Kubera), 1426 (*avādayan . . . vādyāni*).—§ 734 (Ānuçāsanik.): XIII, **26**, 1816.—§ 738 (do.): XIII, **32**, 2075 (*deva-G°saṅghātaiḥ*).—§ 739 (do.): XIII, **33**, 2098.— § 743*b* (Vipulop.): XIII, **40**, 2263 (*deva-G°-Dānavāḥ*).— § 745*c* (Cyavana-Kuçikasaṃv.): XIII, **54**, 2837 (*saṅghān G°āṇām*), 2847.—§ 746 (Ānuçāsanik.): XIII, **58**, 2977; **62**, 3189 (*deva- G°pūjitaḥ*); **79**, 3779 (*°āpsarasām lokān*), 3789 (*°āpsarasaḥ*); **83**, 3886 (*ṛshayaḥ sa - G°āḥ*), 3907 (*Kailāsaçikhare ramye deva-G°sevite*).—§ 747 (do.): XIII, **84**, 3981 (*°oraga-Rākshasāḥ*). — § 747*b* (Suvarṇotpatti): XIII, **85**, 4023.—§ 748*b* (Tārakavadhop.): XIII, **86**, 4203 (praised Skanda).—§ 749 (Ānuçāsanik.): XIII, **87**, 4224 (*°oraga-Rākshasām*).—§ 750 (do.): XIII, **93**, 4411.—§ 754 (do.): XIII, **98**, 4705 (*°nāga - Yakshebhyaḥ*), — § 757*d* (Mandākinī): XIII, **102**, †4860 (*°-Yakshaiḥ*, at Mandākinī). —§ 757*f* (Nandana): XIII, **102**, †4865 (in Nandana).— § 758 (Ānuçāsanik.): XIII, **103**, 4912.—§ 759 (do.): XIII, **107**ε, 5268 (*gīta-G°ghoshaiḥ*), 5293 (*°air upagītam*), (ζ), 5296, 5316, 5328 (*°air abhināditam*).—§ 760 (do.): XIII, **115**, 5671.—§ 768*b* (Umā-Maheçvarasaṃv.): XIII, **140*a***, 6344 (*Yaksha-G°aiḥ*); **142**, 6543; **146**, 6805 (*°āpsarasaḥ*).— § 769 (Ānuçāsanik.): XIII, **149**, 7071 (*sasurāsura-G°m . . . jagat*).—§ 773*b* (Kṛshṇa Vāsudeva): XIII, **159**, †7368.— § 773*d* (Çiva): XIII, **161**, 7467: **162**, 7518 (worship the liṅga of Çiva).—§ 778*b* (Saṃvartta-Maruttīya): XIV, **7**, 177 (*devān sa-G°ān*). — § 778*f* (Muñjavat): XIV, **8**, 184 (*°āpsarasaḥ*, worship Çiva on Muñjavat).—§ 778*b* (Saṃvartta-Maruttīya): XIV, **10**, †282.—§ 782*g* (Guruçishyasaṃv.): XIV, **43**, 1183 (*°oraga-Raksasām . . . īçvaraḥ*, sc. Vishṇu); **51**, 1434.—§ 784*b* (Uttaṅka): XIV, **54**, 1566 (*Yaksha-G°-Rākshasān*), 1580 (*yadā G°yonau vā vartāmi . . . tadā G°vat sarvam ācarāmi*, says Kṛshṇa).—§ 785 (Anugītāp.): XIV, **88**, 2639 (*°gaṇasaṅgītaḥ*), 2643 (*gītakuçalā nṛtyeshu ca viçāradāḥ*). — § 786*b* (Nakulākhyāna): XIV, **90**, 2774 (*surarshi-deva-G°āḥ*).—§ 786*e* (Agastya): XIV, **92**, 2870.— § 787 (Āçramavāsap.): XV, **20**, 572 (*lokāṃç ca deva-G°-Rakshasām*). — § 789 (Putradarçanap.): XV, **29**γ, 785 (*deva-G°āḥ*); **31**ζ, 848 (*°āpsarasaḥ*, had been incarnate among the warriors of the great battle); **32**, 883 (*°air upagīyantaḥ*). — § 793 (Mausalap.): XVI, **4**θ, †129 (*°mukhyāḥ*), †131 (*°āgryaiḥ*). — § 795 (Svargārohaṇap.): XVIII, **3**, 104 (*deva G°āḥ*); **4**, 108 (the five sons of Draupadī after death became *G.*), 146.—§ 795*c* (Mahābhārata): XVIII, **6**ζ, 216 (*Guhyakāç ca sa-G°āḥ*), 248, 252 (*gītakuçalaiḥ*), 255. Cf. Devagandharva, pl.

Gandharva [2], dual (*°au*) = Hāhā and Hūhū: III, 1769; XII, 10278, 12202.

Gandharva [3], sg. § 165 (Satyavatīlābhop.): I, **100**, 4047 (*yasya hi sapatnaḥ syā G°syāsurasya vā | na sa jātu ciraṃ jīvet tvayi*—i.e. Bhīshma—*kruddhe, parantapa*).—§ 510 (Draupadī-Satyabhāmasaṃv.): III, **233**, 14671.—§ 551 (Kīcakavadhap.): IV, **22**, 792 (Kīcaka is supposed to have been slain by a *G.*); **23**, 819 (Bhīmasena is taken for a *G.*).—§ 553 (Vaivāhikap.): IV, **71**, 2293 (*°a esha vai hantā Kīcakānām*, sc. Bhīmasena).— § 565 (Yayāti): V, **121**, 4063 (Yayāti is questioned if he is a *G.*).—§ 619 (Strīvilāpap.): XI, **19**, 564 (*krīḍantam iva G°m devakanyāḥ sahasraçaḥ*, sc. *paryupāsante*).—§ 671*b* (Bali-Vāsavasaṃv.): XII, **225**, 8164 (*naiva devo na G°o nāsuro na ca Rākshasaḥ | yo mām eko visahituṃ çakyaḥ kaçcit*, says Çrī).

Names of individual Gandharvas—

Aṅgāraparṇa (Citraratha): I, 6448 (*A°*), 6456, 6462, 6463, 6466, 6467, 6472, (6473), 6490, (6491), 6493, 6494, (6495), 6518, (6519), (6560), (6584), (6632), 6634, 6635, (6638), (6650), (6669), (6673), (6675), (6679), (6696), (6725), (6745), (6760), (6769), (6779), (6792), (6865), (6885), (6891), 6913, (6914), 6915, 6916 (*°sattama*), 6917; II, 1880 (*C°*).

Citrāṅgada: I, 3803, 4074, 4075, 4076.

Citrasena: III, 1837, 1876, 14939, 15022, 15071 (*°sattama*), 15072, 15073; IV, 2073; XII, 7341 (*C°*).

Dhṛtarāshṭra: XIV, †259, (†263).

Tumburu: II, 1881 (*T°*); IV, 1771 (*T°*).

Viçvāvasu: I, 970 (*°āpsarasoḥ sutā*, i.e. Pramadvarā); III, 16086 (*V°*); XII, 10218 (*V°*), 11749, 11754 (*°sattamaḥ*), 11755, 11772 (*°sattama*), 11773 (do.), 11792 (do.), 11793, 12176 (*V°*), 12201 (*V°*).

Gandharva [4] = Çiva (1000 names [2]).

Gāndharva, adj. ("belonging to the Gandharvas"). § 135 (Çakuntalop.): I, **73**, 2958 (*vivāhena*), 2962 (sc. *vivāhaḥ*), 2966 (*°Rākshasau*, sc. *vivāhau*), 2967 (*vivāhena*), 2980 (*vivāhaḥ*). —§ 221 (Caitrarathap.): I, **170**, 6474 (*māyayā*).—§ 222 (Tapatyup.): I, **172**, 6577 (*vivāhena*), 6578 (*vivāhānāṃ hi . . . G°aḥ çreshṭha ucyate*).—§ 257 (Arjuna): I, **225**, 8183 (*açvaiḥ*).—§ 298 (Dyūtap.): II, **61**, 2083 (*açvān*).—§ 337 (Indralokābhigamanap.): III, **44**, 1798 (*°m atulaṃ nṛtyaṃ vāditraṃ copalabdhavān*, sc. Arjuna).—§ 378 (Tīrthayātrāp.): III, **91**, 8421 (*°ṃ vedam āptavān*, sc. Arjuna, cf. 337).— § 502 (Manushyagrahak.): III, **230**, 14505 (*Gandharvāç cāpi yaṃ divyāḥ saṃviçanti naraṃ bhuvi | unmadyati sa tu kshipraṃ graho G°a eva saḥ*).—§ 572 (Rathātirathas.): V, **165**, 5723 (*vyūhānāñ ca samārambhān daiva-G°-mānushān* (C. has *Ga°*).—§ 576 (Bhagavadgītāp.): VI, **19**, 696 (*vyūham*), **20**, 757 (do.).—§ 593*b* (Gandharvāstra): VII, **45**, 1823 (*astram*, acquired by Arjuna from the Gandharvas).—§ 599 (Jayadrathavadhap.): VII, **147**, 6048 (sc. *yuddham*).— § 602 (Droṇavadhap.): VII, **188**μ, 8615 (do.). § 704 (Mokshadh.): XII, **302**β, 11103 (*°vishayān*). — § 731*b* (Ashṭāvakra-Diksaṃv.): XIII, **19**, 1429 (*vishayaḥ . . . G°o nāma*). — § 744 (Ānuçāsanik.): XIII, **44*a***, 2409 (*dharmam*), 2413 (sc. *dharmaḥ*).

Gāndharva ("song, music"). § 443 (Nivātakavacayuddhap.): III, **168**, 12049 (*sa*—i.e. Citrasena—*ca G°m akhilaṃ grāhayām āsa mām*, says Arjuna).—§ 667 (Mokshadh.): XII, **210**, 7662 (*°ṃ Nārada veda*).—§ 731*b* (Ashṭāvakra-Diksaṃv.): XIII, **19**, 1427.—§ 759 (Ānuçāsanik.): XIII, **104**, 5103 (*°çāstram*).

Gandharvaloka ("the world of the Gandharvas"). § 140 (Purūravas): I, **75**, 3148 (*sa hi G°sthān Urvaçyā sahito virāṭ | ānināya kriyārthe 'gnīn yathāvad vihitāṃs tridhā*, sc. Purūravas).

Gandharvanagara ("the city of the Gandharvas," Fata morgana). § 194 (Pāṇḍu): I, **126**, 4931 (*°ākāram . . . antarhitam*).—§ 208 (Astradarçana): I, **134**, 5338 (*kumāra-balaṃ . . . G°ākāram*). — § 279 (Arjuna): II, **28**, 1043 (from *G.* Arjuna received horses as tribute). — § 445 (Nivātakavacayuddhap.): III, **173**, 12262 (*Dānavapuram*

. . . *G°ākāraṃ*).—§ 569 (Bhagavadyānap.): V, **143**θ, 4854 (omens).—§ 578 (Bhīshmavadhap.): VI, **50**, 2077 (*ketuḥ . . . G°opamaḥ*).—§ 586 (do.): VI, **103**, 4701 (*rathāḥ . . . G°opamāḥ*). — § 592 (Saṃçaptakavadhap.): VII, **19**, 780 (*°ākārān . . . rathān*).—§ 593 (Abhimanyuvadhap.): VII, **36**, 1569 (do.); **43**, 1765 (*°ākāraṃ . . . rathaṃ*).—§ 605 (Karṇap.): VIII, **16**, 654 (*°ākārān rathān*); **27**, 1112 (*°ākāraṃ ghoram āyodhanaṃ*).—§ 607 (do.); VIII, **36**, 1676 (*jaitraṃ rathavaraṃ G°opamaṃ*).—§ 608 (do.): VIII, **46**, 2188 (*°ākārā rathāḥ*); **81**, 4140 (*rathāḥ . . . G°ākārāḥ*).—§ 679 (Mokshadh.): XII, **261**, 9269 (*°ākāraḥ*, sc. *dharmaḥ*).—§ 745c (Cyavana-Kuçikasaṃv.): XIII, **54**, 2826 (*prāsādaṃ . . . G°opamaṃ*).

Gandharvāṇāṃ tīrthaṃ, a tīrtha on the Sarasvatī. § 615d (Baladevatīrthay.): There many Gandharvas, headed by Viçvāvasu and possessed of ascetic merits, pass their time singing and dancing: IX, **37**, 2128. Cf. Gandharvatīrtha.

Gandharvapati [1] ("Lord of the Gandharvas") = Devaka: I, 2704 (*D°*).

Gandharvapati [2] (do.) = Haṃsa: I, 2718 (*H°*).

Gandharvapati [3] (do.) = Aṅgāraparṇa (Citraratha): I, 6637.

Gandharvarāj [1] ("king of the Gandharvas") = Citrasena: III, 14951.

Gandharvarāj [2] (do.) = Dhṛtarāshṭra [3]: XIV, 243.

Gandharvarāja [1] (do.) = Viçvāvasu: I, 943 (*V°*), 975.

Gandharvarāja [2] (do.) = Citrāṅgada: I, 4073.

Gandharvarāja [3] (do.) = Angāraparṇa (Citraratha): I, 6440.

Gandharvārāja [4] (do.) = Citrasena: III, 1801, 1803, 14869, 14887, 14955, 14966, 14973, 15002; VII, 5261.

Gandharvarāja [5] (do.) = Dhṛtarāshṭra [3]: XV, 850 (*Dh°*).

Gandharvarājan [1] (do.) = Citrasena: IV, 1538 (*C°*).

Gandharvarājan [2] (do.) = Dhṛtarāshṭra [3]: XVIII, 139 (*Dh°*).

[Gandharvāstra(ṃ)]. § 593b (Abhimanyuvadhap.): By practising ascetic penances *Arjuna* had obtained the *G.* (*Gāndharvam astraṃ*, v. 1823) from the Gandharvas (Tumburu, etc.) (VII, **44**).

Gandharvatīrtha = Gandharvāṇāṃ tīrthaṃ: IX, 2131.

Gandharvendra ("king of the Gandharvas") = Viçvāvasu: XII, 11760.

Gandharvī [1], the mother of the horses. § 127 (Aṃçāvat.): I, **66**, 2631 (daughter of Surabhi), 2632 (her offspring are the horses).

Gandharvī [2] ("female Gandharva"). § 162 (Çāntanūp.): I, **97**, 3894 (Gaṅgā is questioned if she is a *G.*).—§ 221 (Caitrarathap.): I. **170**, (6470), 6470 (*nāmnā Kumbhanasī*).—§ 222 (Tapatyup.): I, **171**, 6523, 6553.—§ 549 (Pāṇḍavapraveçap.): IV, **9**, 257 (Draupadī is questioned if she is a *G.*), 260.

Gandhavatī = Satyavatī [1], q.v.

Gandhavatīsuta = Vyāsa: XII, 13434.

Gāṇḍīva, the bow of Arjuna. § 4 (Anukram.): I, **1**, †178.—§ 11 (Parvasaṅgr.): I, **2**, 625, 631.—§ 71 (Ādivaṃçāvatāraṇap.): I, **61**, 2277 (given to Arjuna by Agni, all. to § 257).—§ 257 (Khāṇḍavadahanap.): I, **225**, 8178 (*c: G.* had been given by Soma to Varuṇa, and cannot be met with other weapons, being alone equal to 100,000 bows; it is variegated with excellent colours, well-adorned and beautiful, and honoured by gods, Dānavas, and Gandharvas), 8192 (had been made by Brahmán), 8205 (at the instigation of Agni Varuṇa gave *G.* to Arjuna).—§ 263 (Sabhākriyāp.): II, **3**, 64.—§ 294 (Dyūtap.): II, **48**, 1707 (Arjuna has got *G.* from Agni).—§ 302 (Anudyūtap.): II, **74**, 2463.—§ 307 (do.); II, **81**, 2704.—§ 311 (Āraṇyakap.): III, **4**, †228 (*lokasāraṃ*).—§ 312 (do.): III, **5**, †248.—§ 316 (Kirmīravadhap.): III, **11**, 424 (*vajranishpeshagauravaṃ*).—§ 317 (Arjunābhigamanap.): III, **12**, 527 (*dhik Pārthasya ca G°ṃ*), 537 (*c:* "none else can string *G.* save Arjuna and thyself, oh Madhusūdana").—§ 327 (Draupadīparitāp.): III, **33**, 1350.—§ 330 (Indradarçana): III, **37**, 1473.—§ 331 (Kairātap.): III, **39**, 1559, 1576, 1589 (snatched by Çiva in the shape of a Kirāta).—§ 333b (Arjuna): III, **40**, 1639.—§ 333 (Kairātap.): III, **40**, †1662 (*dhanur mahad Ditija-Piçācasūdanaṃ*, returned by Çiva to Arjuna).—§ 342 (Indralokābhigamanap.): III, **51**, 1979.—§ 377 (Dhaumyatīrthak.): III, **86**, 8288.—§ 437 (Yakshayuddhap.): III, **160**, 11683.—§ 443 (Nivātakavacayuddhap.): III, **168**, 12067 ("Indra fastened this durable —*ajarām*—string to *G.*," says Arjuna).—§ 444 (do.): III, **170**, 12108, 12125; **171**, 12154; **172**, 12163, 12175.—§ 445 (do.): III, **173**, 12241, 12253 (*°āstra-°*).—§ 447 (do.): III, **175**, 12296.—§ 512 (Ghoshayātrāp.): III, **236**, †14770. — § 522 (Draupadīharaṇap.): III, **268**, †15655, †15656.—§ 549 (Pāṇḍavapr.): IV, **5**, 152, 160.—§ 551 (Kīcakavadhap.): IV, **21**, 641.—§ 552 (Goharaṇap.): IV, **40**, 1308; **41**, 1321; **43**, 1343, 1344 (*c:* Brahmán had first possessed the *G.* during 1000 years, then Prajāpati, Çakra, Soma, and Varuṇa during 503, 85, 500, and 100 years respectively, finally Varuṇa handed it over to Arjuna 65 years ago); **44**, 1386 (*ubhau me dakshiṇau pāṇī G°sya vikarshaṇe | tena devamanushyeshu Savyasācīti māṃ viduḥ*); **45**, 1423; **46**, 1454, 1458; **50**, 1578, 1579; **53**, 1631, 1635, 1657; **54**, †1687, †1695; **55**, 1699; **57**, 1794 (*paramāyudhaṃ*), 1800; **58**, 1855, 1888; **59**, 1910; **60**, 1945; **61**, 1957, 1969 (*suvarṇapṛshṭhaṃ*); **62**, 2007, 2020; **63**, 2028 (*tataḥ prahasya Bībhatsur divyam Aindraṃ mahārathaḥ | astram Ādityasaṅkāçaṃ G°e samayojayat*), 2030, 2032 (when falling *G.* covered all the ten regions); **64**, 2049, 2070, 2077; **65**, †2098; **66**, †2113, †2132.—§ 556 (Sañjayayānap.): V, **23**, †705; **26**, †762.—§ 561 (Yānasandhip.): V, **48**, †1860, †1863, †1869, †1872, †1909; **52**, 2096, 2101; **54**, 2121, 2132; **57**, 2258; **59**, 2350; **60**, 2370.—§ 563 (Bhagavadyānap.): V, **96**φ, 3489.—§ 564 (Mātālīyop.): V, **98**, 3540 (*Gāṇḍivaṃ dhanuḥ*, the knotty bow (*gāṇḍimayaç cāpaḥ*) which lies in the abode of Varuṇa and was kept for the destruction of the world).—§ 567 (Bhagavadyānap.): V, **126**, 4215.—§ 569 (do.): V, **138**, 4680, 4702; **141**δ, 4785; **142**, 4819; **143**, 4877.—§ 570 (Sainyaniryāṇap.): V, **158**, 5353, 5354, 5356 (*c: G.* is one of the three celestial bows (cf. Vijaya and Çārṅga); it belonged to Varuṇa, but was obtained by Arjuna from Agni on the occasion of the burning of the Khāṇḍava forest), 5377, 5382.—§ 571 (Ulūkadūtāgamanap.): V, **160**, †5515 (*tālamātraṃ*), 5518, 5519 (*Phālgunād vā sa-G°āt*); **161**, †5560 (*tālamātraṃ*), 5563, 5564 (*Pārthād vāpi sa-G°āt*); **162**, 5622.—§ 572 (Rathātirathas.): V, **169**, 5869.—§ 576 (Bhagavadgītap.): VI, **22**, †786; **25**, 860.—§ 578 (Bhīshmavadhap.): VI, **45** [1], 1678; **47**, 1823.—§ 580 (do.): VI, **59**, †2619, †2624, †2627, †2628, †2629, †2630.—§ 581 (do.): VI, **60**, †2676.—§ 582 (do.): VI, **69**, 3064; **71**, 3120, 3123 (*b:* the back of *G.*'s staff was decked with pure gold (*rukmapṛshṭhaṃ*)), 3130.—§ 583 (do.): VI, **78**, 3442.—§ 584 (do.): VI, **85**, †3761.—§ 587 (do.): VI, **112**, 5211; **117**, 5489; **119**, 5612; **120**, 5733.—§ 588 (do.): VI, **121**, 5781.—§ 589 (Droṇābhishek.): VII, **3**, 103, 104, 108; **7**, 197; **10**, 325, 327, 332.—§ 592 (Saṃçaptakavadhap.): VII, **19**, 761; **30**, 1333, 1334.—§ 596 (Pratijñāp.): VII, **73**, 2609; **75**, 2667; **76**, 2690, 2698.—§ 598 (Jayadrathavadhap.): VII, **88**, 3139.—§ 599 (do.): VII, **90**, 3197, 3199; **92**, 3323; **93**, 3342, 3370; **99**, 3706; **103**, 3849, 3880; **105**, 3957, 3960; **110**, 4171; **114**, 4457; **119**, 4712; **126**, 5101; **129**, 5308; **139**, 5804, 5809, 5813; **142**, 5949; **145**, 6107, †6147, †6151; **146**, 6194, 6255, 6274; **152**, 6586 —§ 600 (Ghaṭotkacavadhap.): VII, **170**, 7653, 7654, 7655, 7659; **180**, 8195.—§ 603 (Nārāyaṇāstramokshaṇap.): VII, **199**, 9246, 9247.—§ 604 (Karṇap.): VIII, **9**, 312, 313.—§ 605 (do.): VIII, **16**, 651; **17**, †681; **30**, 1219.—§ 605c (Vijaya): VIII, **31**, 1296.—§ 605 (Karṇap.): VIII, **31**, 1303.—§ 607 (do.): VIII, **36**, 1699; **39**, 1811; **40**, 1829.—§ 608 (do.): VIII, **46**, 2183, 2194; **47**, 2217; **53**, 2563; **56**, 2828; **59**, 2962; **64**, †3238; **66**, †3349; **68**, †3396 (*tālamātram*), †3399, †3401; **69**, 3411, †3475; **70**, 3541; **72**, 3617; **73**, 3722; **74**, 3752, 3758, 3763, 3772, 3792, †3801; **76**, †3848; **79**, 4023, †4052, †4070, †4071, †4075; **80**, 4105, 4107; **81**, 4138; **82**, †4191; **89**, †4537, †4546, †4547, †4578; **90**, 4721; **91**, †4778 (*çlathahasta-G°ḥ*, sc. *Arjuno*), †4793; **93**, 4866, 4876; **94**, †4922.—§ 610 (Çalyap.): IX, **3**, 158; **4**, 203, 204, 220.—§ 611 (do.): IX, **14**, 731; **18**, 960; **19**, 1064; **24**, 1328, 1330; **25**, 1338; **28**, †1564.—§ 612 (Hradapraveçap.): IX, **29**, 1569, 1599.—§ 615 (Gadāyuddhap.): IX, **62**, 3468.—§ 785 (Anugītap.): XIV, **73**, 2118, 2119; **74**, 2162; **75**, 2178, 2179, 2188; **76**, 2204; **77**, 2241; **79**, 2328; **82**, 2445, 2465; **84**, 2491, 2501.—§ 793 (Mausalap.): XVI, **7**, 230, 236; **8**, 275.—§ 794 (Mahāprasthānikap.): XVII, **1a**, 34, 39, 41 (Agni caused Arjuna to throw *G.* and his inexhaustible quivers into the ocean that they might be restored to Varuṇa).

Gāṇḍīvabhṛt, Gāṇḍīvadhanvan, Gāṇḍīvadhārin, Gāṇḍivin = Arjuna, q.v.

Gaṇeça[1], a god. § 4 (Anukram.): I, **1**, 74, 79, 83 (wrote the Mhbhr.); IV, 1; V, 1. Cf. Gaṇanāyaka, Gaṇeçāna, Heramba, Vighneça.

Gaṇeça[2] = Çiva: III, 1629.

Gaṇeçāna = Gaṇeça: I, 75.

Gaṇeçvara = Vishṇu (1000 names).

Gaṅgā[1], the river Ganges. § 11 (Parvasaṅgr.): I, **2**, 386.—§ 17 (Uttaṅka): I, **3**, 799 (*bahūni nāgaveçmāni G°āyās tīra uttare*).—§ 71 (Ādivaṃçāvatāraṇap.): I, **61**, 2241.—§ 79 (Bhīshma): I, **63**, 2420 (mother of Bhīshma).—§ 130 (Aṃçāvat.): I, **67**, 2710 (the eight Vasus were born as sons of Gaṅgā and Çāntanu, cf. § 163).—§ 133 (Dushyanta): I, **70**, 2872 (*Nara-Nārāyaṇasthānaṃ G°ayevopaçobhitaṃ*).—§ 149 (Yayāti): I, **87**, 3555 (Yayāti gave to Pūru the whole country *G°-Yamunayor madhye*).—§ 156 (Pūruvaṃç.): I, **95**, 3800 (*Çāntanuḥ khalu Gaṅgāṃ Bhāgīrathīṃ upayeme | tasyām asya jajñe Devavrato nāma yam āhur Bhīshmam iti*, cf. § 163).—§ 161 (Mahābhishop.): I, **96**, 3846, v. 7 (only B., one çloka and a half are wanting in C. after v. 3848), (together with Mahābhisha *G.* is cursed to become born among men) (3857), (3859), (3861), 3864 (the Vasus made the arrangement with *G.* that, having born them to Çāntanu, she should throw them into the water, the eighth child excepted).—§ 162 (Çāntanūp.): I, **97**, 3865, 3866 (settled with Pratīpa that she should marry his son, i.e. Çāntanu), 3889.—§ 163 (Bhīshmotpatti): I, **98**, 3903 (*Tripathagāminī*), 3908, 3913 (*Jahnusutā*), 3919 (*°dattaṃ*, i.e. Bhīshma; Çāntanu married *G.*; seven of the eight children whom Çāntanu begot with *G.* she threw into the water, the eighth (Bhīshma) was saved by Çāntanu).—§ 164 (Āpavop.): I, **99**, 3923 (*Jāhnavī*), (3924), 3961 (*G.* told Çāntanu the history of the Vasus, then she disappeared, taking the child with her).—§ 165 (Satyavatīlābhop.): I, **100**, 3989 (*Bhāgīrathīṃ*), 3993, 3996, 3997, (3999) (*G.* restored Bhīshma to Çāntanu).—§ 170 (Dīrghatamas): I, **104**, 4204, 4205.—§ 195 (Pāṇḍu): I, **127**, 4947.—§ 197 (Bhīmasenarasapāna): I, **128**, 4992, 4999.—§ 200 (Droṇa): I, **130**, 5103.—§ 207 (do.): I, **133**, 5299.—§ 209 (Drupadaçāsana): I, **138**, 5512 (*Mākandīm atha G°āyās tīre*).—§ 213 (Jatugṛhap.): I, **149**, 5851, 5853, 5854, 5855; **150**, 5874.—§ 217 (Caitrarathap.): I, **166**, 6329.—§ 218 (do.): I, **167**, 6360.—§ 221 (do.): I, **170**, 6439, 6440, 6449, 6452, 6454 (*b*: *G.* issues from Hemaçṛṅga (cf. Harivaṃça, v. 12850, PCR.: 'the golden peaks') of the Himavat, and falls into the ocean divided into seven streams. Gaṅgā, Yamunā, Sarasvatī (*plakshajātāṃ*, i.e. who issues from the plaksha, v. BR.), Rathasthā, Sarayū (C. *Ç°*), Gomatī and Gaṇḍakī destroy the sins of those who drink of their water; in the celestial regions *G.* is called *Alakanandā*, and among the Pitṛs it becomes the *Vaitaraṇī*, which is difficult to cross for sinners (such is the statement of Kṛshṇa-Dvaipāyana); this celestial river (*devanadī*) is without hindrance).—§ 238 (Pañcendrop.): I, **197**, 7284 (*devīṃ*), 7285 (do.).—§ 248 (Arjunavanavāsap.): I, **214**, 7786.—§ 249 (do.): I, **215**, 7818.—§ 258 (Khāṇḍavadah.): I, **228**, 8316 (*°odadhicarā jhashāḥ*).—§ 263 (Sabhākriyāp.): II, **3**, 68 (*Bhāgīrathīṃ*).—§ 275 (Rājasūyārambhap.): II, **17**, 695 (*°-Yamunayor madhye*).—§ 276 (Jarāsandhavadhap.): II, **20**, 796.—§ 290 (Çiçupālavadhap.): II, **42**, 1484 (*Trikūṭasthāṃ . . . Tripathagāṃ*).—§ 317 (Arjunābhigamanap.): III, **12**, 542.—§ 335 (Indralokābhigamanap.): III, **42**, 1733.—§ 339 (do.): III, **47**, 1891 (*Siddha-Cāraṇasevitā*, its source near Badarī).—§ 364 (Tīrthayātrāp.): III, **83**, 6071.—§ 370 (do.): III, **84**, 8013 (*°-Yamunayor madhye*), 8016 (*°āyāç ca . . . Sarasvatyāç ca saṅgame*), 8059 (*Gomatī G°ayoç caiva saṅgame*); **85**, 8146 (*°āyāḥ sāgarasya ca saṅgame*).—§ 372 (do.): III, **85**, 8209.—§ 373 (Prayāga): III, **85**, 8217 (*Yamunā G°ayā sārdhaṃ saṅgatā*, at Prayāga), 8218 (*°-Yamunayor madhye* (so C., but read *madhyaṃ* with B.) *pṛthivyā jaghanaṃ smṛtaṃ*), 8228 (*°-Yamunā-saṅgame*).—§ 374 (Tīrthayātrāp.): III, **85**, 8230.—§ 375 (do.): III, **85**, 8230, 8231, 8232, 8233 (*Gaṅgā Kaliyuge smṛtā*, sc. *puṇyā*), 8234 (*Magadheshu*), 8236, 8238, 8239, 8240.—§ 377 (Dhaumyatīrthak.): III, **87**, 8310 (*yasyās tīre Bhagīrathaḥ | ayajat*), 8314 (*°-Yamunayor . . . saṅgamaṃ*); **88**, 8334; **90**, 8392 (*bibheda tarasā Gaṅgā Gaṅgādvāraṃ*), 8397 (*ushṇatoyavahā G°ā çītatoyāvahā purā*).—§ 378 (Tīrthayātrāp.): III, **93**, 8467.—§ 379 (do.): III, **95**, 8515 (*°-Yamunayoç caiva saṅgame*).—[§ 383b (do.): Issuing from the matted locks of Çambhu (i.e. Çiva) *G.* floods the southern country: III, **99**, 8648 (*Samudra mahishī*)].—§ 389 (Gangāvataraṇa): III, **107**, 9917 (*°āvataraṇe*); **108**, 9923, 9933, (9934), 9940, 9946; **109**, 9952, 9954 (*Himavataḥ sutā*), 9955 (*yuganamekhalāṃ*), 9962, 9963, 9964 (*G.* promised to Bhagīratha to descend and besprinkle the bodies of Sagara's sons; Bhagīratha gratified Çiva, who received the weight of *G.* when she fell from the sky on his forehead; *G.* fell down to the earth divided into three streams, and was led by Bhagīratha to the ocean where the bodies of Sagara's sons lay, then Bhagīratha adopted her as his daughter).—§ 392 (Tīrthayātrāp.): III, **114**, 10096 (falls into the ocean).—§ 395 (Jamadagni): III, **115**, 10153 (*°āyāṃ* (so B.) *Kānyakubje*).—§ 412 (Ashṭāvakrīya): III, **134**, †10656 (*nadīshu Gaṅgā pravarā yathaiva*).—§ 413 (Tīrthayātrāp.): III, **135**, 10696.—§ 414 (Yavakrītop.): III, **135**, 10723, 10727.—§ 418 (Tīrthayātrāp.): III, **139**, 10821 (*saptavidhā*, *b*: there Agni blazes forth without intermission, a wonder which no man is able to see), 10833, †10835.—§ 436 (Yakshayuddhap.): III, **158,** 11622 (*mahā°*, *b*: the celestial river, frequented by ṛshis and Kinnaras).—§ 457 (Vaivasvatop.): III, **187,** 12764 (*Samudramahishīṃ*), 12766, 12768, 12769.—§ 459 (Mārkaṇḍeyas.): III, **188*a*,** 12907 (seen by Mārkaṇḍeya in the stomach of Nārāyaṇa). — § 488 (Āṅgirasa): III, **217,** 14103 (*yathā Rudrāc ca sambhūto G°āyāṃ Kṛttikāsu ca*, sc. Skanda).—§ 494 (do.): III, **222,** 14230 (among the rivers who are mothers of fires).—§ 514 (Ghoshayātrāp.): III, **252,** 15201 (*°aughapratimā*).—§ 547 (Karṇa): III, **308,** 17150 (the basket with Karṇa passed from Yamunā into the *G.*).—§ 555 (Sainyodyogap.): V, **19,** 599 (*°kūlañ ca*, is filled up by the army of Duryodhana).—§ 561 (Yānasandhip.): V, **51,** 2052 (*°vega iva*).—§ 565 (Gālavacarita): V, **111,** 3828 (*atra*—i.e. in the north—*G°āṃ Mahādevaḥ patantīṃ gaganāc cyutāṃ | pratigṛhya dadau loke mānushe*, cf. § 389); **120,** 4026 (*°-Yamunā-saṅgame*).—§ 566 (Yayāti): V, **121,** 4060 (*°āṃ gām iva gacchantīm ālambya*, sc. Yayāti). — § 568 (Vidulāputraçāsana): V, **135,** 4598 (*gatvā Gaṅgeva sāgaraṃ*).—§ 569 (Bhagavadyānap.): V, **139,** 4714 (*°vega iva*); **144,** 4912 (*°tīre*).—§ 570 (Sainyaniryāṇap.): V, **151,** 5151 (*°eva pūrṇā*); **158,** 5362 (*°ayeva pravṛddhayā*).—§ 579 (Ulūkadūtāgamanap.): V, **160,** 5422 (*°tīre*).—§ 572 (Rathātirathasaṅkhyānap.): V, **166,** 5757 (*makarā iva . . . G°āṃ vikshobhayishyanti*).—§ 573 (Ambopakhyānap.): V, **178,** 7122 (appeared to Bhīshma in order to make him desist from fighting with Rāma Jāmadagnya); **196,** 7633 (*°eva pūrṇā*).—§ 574 (Jambūkh.): VI, **6,** 223 (*c*: coming from the summit of the mountain, *Gaṅgā Bhāgīrathī* falls into the lake of *Candramas*. *Çiva* kept the *G.* on his head for 100,000 years).—§ 574*f* (Bindusaras): VI, **6,** 239 (*Bhāgīrathīṃ*), (*η*) 243 (coming from Brahmaloka, *G.* divided herself into seven streams: Vasvaukasārā, etc.), 245 (pl., *sapta*).—§ 574 (Jambūkh.): VI, **9***λ*, 321, 344 (only B.).—§ 575*b* (Çākadvīpa): VI, **11,** 432 (in Çākadvīpa).—§ 576 (Bhagavadgītāp.): VI, **18,** 694 (*adṛçyata . . . G°eva Yamunāntare* (B. *°rā*)); **19,** 708 (*°eva pūrṇā*).—§ 584 (Bhīshmavadhop.): VI, **83,** 3643 (*°āyāḥ suranadyā vāi svādubhūtaṃ yathodakam*).—§ 587 (do.): VI, **119,** 5664 (*Himavataḥ sutā*). — § 589 (Droṇābhishekap.): VII, **10,** 370 (*°srotaḥsu*). — § 591 (Saṃçaptakavadhap.): VII, **17,** 721 (*°-Sarayvau vegena pravṛshīva*).—§ 592 (do.): VII, **30,** 1331 (*iva*).—§ 594 (Mṛtyu): VII, **54,** 2096.—§ 595 (Shoḍaçarāj. v. Bhagīratha): VII, **60,** 2249 (*Bhāgīrathī*), 2254 (*tasyāṅke nishasāda ha | tathā Bhāgīrathī G°ā Urvaçī cābhavat purā*), 2256 (became the adopted daughter of Bhagīratha); (do., v. Bharata): VII, **68,** 2384. — § 596 (Pratijñāp.): VII, **80***η*, 2847 (in the north).—§ 600 (Ghaṭotkacavadhap.): VII, **156,** 6795 (*iva*). — § 605 (Karṇap.): VIII, **28,** 1162 (*unmatta-G°pratimaṃ*). — § 606 (Tripurākhyāna): VIII, **34,** 1477.—§ 607 (Karṇap.): VIII, **44***η*, 2029 (*bahishkṛtāḥ . . . G°ayā*),—§ 608 (do.): VIII, **46,** 2209 (*°-Yamunāvat*); **60,** 3048 (*iva*).—§ 611 (Çalyap.): IX, **18,** 965 (*iva*).—§ 615 (Baladevatīrthayātrāp.): IX, **37,** 2168 (*iva*).—§ 615*u* (Skanda): IX, **44,** 2457, 2458, 2463, 2469, 2484, 2489, 2492 (the birth, etc., of Skanda); **46,** 2668 (gave to Skanda a *kamaṇḍalu*), 2717 (some call Skanda the son of *G.*).—§ 618 (Jalapradānikap.): XI, **11,** 307; **12,** 317; **14,** 363.—§ 619 (Strīvilāpap.): XI, **23***θ*, 676.—§ 620 (Çrāddhap.): XI, **26,** 799; **27,** 800, 804, 805 (*°tīraṃ*), 828.—§ 621 (Rājadh.): XII, **1,** 23 (*°srotasi*).—§ 632*b* (Shoḍaçarāj., cf. § 595 v. Bharata): XII, **29,** 939; (do. v. Bhagīratha): XII, **29,** 961 (*yasyāṅke nishasāda ha | Gaṅgā Bhāgīrathī tasmād Urvaçī hyabhavat purā*), 962 (*trilokapathagā*, became the adopted daughter of Bhagīratha); (do., v. Gaya): XII, **29,** 1011 (*yāvatyaḥ sikatāḥ . . . G°ayāḥ*). — § 637 (Rājadh.): XII, **46***ζ*, 1568 (*yaṃ G°ā garbhavidhinā dhārayām āsa*, i.e. Bhīshma).—§ 638*b* (Rāmop.): XII, **49,** 1796 (*°kūle*). —§ 641 (Rājadh.): XII, **109,** 4030; **113,** 4202, (4203) (discourse between the ocean and the rivers). — § 658*b* (Kṛtaghnop.): XII, **170,** 6345 (*deçān G°nishevitān*). — § 674*b* (Çrī-Vāsavasaṃv.): XII, **229,** 8338 (*Dhruvadvārabhavāṃ*).—§ 678*c* (Mṛtyu-Prajāpatisaṃv.): XII, **259,** 9208. —§ 694*b* (Jvarotpatti): XII, **284,** 10224 (*saritāṃ çreshṭhā sarvatīrthajalodbhavā*).—§ 712 (Çukotpatti): XII, **325,** 12198 (*saritāṃ çreshṭhā Meruprshṭhe*).—§ 717*b* (Nārāyaṇīya): XII, **348,** 13500 (Gaṅgā and Sarasvatī are the hips of Nārāyaṇa). § 718*b* (Uñchavṛttyup.): XII, **354,** 13775 (*Mahāpadme purottame G°āyā dakshiṇe tīre*); **356,** †13810 (*°hrada-*).—§ 721*b* (Viçvāmitrop.): XIII, **4,** 202 (became the daughter of Jahnu); 215, 216 (near Kānyakubja is situated the tīrtha Açvatīrtha on the bank of the *G.*, there the 1000 horses which Varuṇa gave to Ṛcīka, arose from the river).—§ 733*f* (Gaṅgādvāra): XIII, **25,** 1702 (*yatra Bhāgīrathī G°ā patate diçam uttaraṃ*).—§ 734 (Ānuçāsanik.): XIII, **26,** 1784 (*Bhāgīrathī*), 1785, 1788, 1790, 1791, 1792, 1793, 1794, 1795, 1797, 1798, 1799, 1800, 1801, 1802, 1803, 1804, 1805, 1806, 1807, 1808, 1809, 1810, 1811, 1814, 1815, 1816, 1817, 1818, 1819, 1820, 1821, 1822, 1823, 1824, 1825, 1826, 1827, 1828, 1829, 1830, 1832, 1833, 1834, 1836, 1837, 1838, †1839, †1840, †1841, 1842, †1844, †1846, †1847, †1848, †1849, †1850, †1852, †1853, †1854, †1856, †1858, †1859, 1861, 1862, 1863, 1864 (very copious description). — § 736*b* (Vītahavyop.): XIII, **30,** 1950 (the country between the *G.* and the Yamunā ruled by the Kāçi king Haryaçva), 1957 (*°āyā uttare kūle*), 1977.—§ 739 (Ānuçāsanik.): XIII, **35,** 2161 (*adhāryā setunā*).—§ 743*b* (Vipulopākhyāna): XIII, **43,** 2394 (*°kūle*).—§ 745*b* (Cyavanop.): XIII, **50,** 2646 (*°-Yamunayor madhye*), 2648, 2655 (*°-Yamunayor vāri*).—§ 745*c* (Cyavana-Kuçikas.): XIII, **53,** 2810 (*°tīraṃ*), **54,** 2847 (*°kūlaṃ*). — § 746 (Ānuçāsanik.): XIII, **68,** 3397 (*grāmaḥ . . . G°-Yamunayor madhye Yāmunasya girer adhaḥ*); **73,** †3596 (*yathā hi G°ā saritāṃ varishṭhā*); **77,** †3703 (do.). —§ 747*b* (Suvarṇotpatti): XIII, **85,** 4026 (*Rudrasya retaḥ . . . Agniḥ . . . G°āyāṃ janayishyati*), 4070 (*Bhāgīrathīṃ*), 4072, 4073, 4074, 4085, 4088 (the birth of Skanda).—§ 757*m* (Goloka): XIII, **102*a*,** 4888.—§ 758 (Ānuçāsanik.): XIII, **103,** 4929 (*srotasaç ca yāvad G°āyāḥ*), (*a*), 4932 (*dīrghakālaṃ Himavati G°āyāç ca durutsahāṃ | mūrdhnā dhārāṃ Mahādevaḥ çirasā yām adhārayat*, cf. § 389), (*β*), 4944.—§ 766 (do.): XIII, **125***β*, 5967.—§ 768*b* (Umā-Maheçvarasaṃv.): XIII, **146***δ*, 6765 (*gaganād gāṃ gatā devī*), 6767 (*°ādyāḥ saritāṃ varāḥ*), 6770 (*devanadī*), 6772, 6778.—§ 772*l* (Vasishṭha): XIII, **156,** 7287.—§ 775 (Ānuçāsanik.): XIII, **166*a*,** 7638, 7646.—§ 777 (Svargārohaṇikaṃ p.): XIII, **169,** 7794 (the mother of Bhīshma).—§ 778 (Açvamedhikap.): XIV, **1,** 2 (*tīre G°āyāḥ*).—§ 782*g* (Guruçishyasaṃv.): XIV, **44,** 1225 (*Tripathagā G°ā nadīnām agrajā smṛtā*).—§ 785 (Anugītap.): XIV, **81,** 2413 (after the fall of Bhīshma *G.* sanctioned the Vasus' curse upon Arjuna), 2414.—§ 787 (Āçramavāsap.): XV, **19,** 523, 525 (*°tīraṃ*).—§ 789 (Putradarçanap.): XV, **31,** 862, 864.—§ 792 (Nāradāgamanap.): XV, **37,** 1015, 1016 (*°tīravāsinaḥ*), 1028, 1043 (*°kūle*); **39,** 1088.—§ 794 (Mahāprasthānikap.): XVII, **1,** 27,—§ 795 (Svargārohaṇap.): XVIII, **3,** 119 (*trilokagāṃ*, in heaven), 121 (*devanadīṃ*). Cf. Ākāçagaṅgā, Bhagīrathasutā, Bhāgīrathī, Çailarājasutā,

Çailasutā, Devanadī, Haimavatī, Jāhnavī, Jahnukanyā, Jahnusutā, Samudramahishī, Tripathagā, Tripathagāminī.

Gaṅgā[2] = Çiva (1000 names[1]).

Gāṅga, adj. ("belonging to Gaṅgā"). § 557 (Prajāgarap.): V, **33**, 996 (°*o hrada iva*).—§ 571 (Ulūkadūtāgamanap.): V, **160**, 5511 (°*m yathā vegam*); **161**, 5556 (do.).—§ 587 (Bhīshmavadhap.): VI, **119**, 5643 (°*a ivāvartaḥ*).—§ 593 (Abhimanyuv.): VII, **36**, 1551 (do.): § 595 (Shoḍaçarāj. v. Çibi Auçīnara): VII, **58**, 2215 (*yāvatyaḥ sikitā Gāṅgyaḥ*). —§ 659 (Mokshadh.): XII, **177**, 6613 (°*m ivodakam*).

Gaṅgādvāra, name of the place where the Gangā enters the plains. § 162 (Çāntanūp.): I, **97**, 3865 (there Pratīpa practised austerities).—§ 200 (Droṇa): I, **130**, 5102 (the abode of Bharadvāja).—§ 217 (Caitrarathap.): I, **166**, 6328 (do.). — § 248 (Arjunavanavāsap.): I, **214**, 7781, 7785 (visited by Arjuna on his tīrthayātrā), 7810.—§ 356 (Tīrthayātrāp.): III, **81**, 4034 (*devā-Gandharvasevite*, a tīrtha).— § 370 (do.): III, **84**, 8005 (a tīrtha).—§ 377 (Dhaumyatīrthak.): III, **89**, 8368 (in the west!); **90**, 8392 (*çailam bibheda tarasā Gaṅgā G°m*, in the north).—§ 382 (Agastyop.): III, **97**, 8580. — § 419 (Gandhamādanapr.): III, **140**, 10846.—§ 421 (do.): III, **142**, 10907 (*etasyāḥ*—i.e. Gangā's—*salilam mūrdhnā Vṛshāṅkaḥ*—i.e. Çiva—*paryadhārayat G°e*).— § 434 (Saugandhikāharaṇa): III, **156**, 11438.—§ 524 (Jayadrathavimokshaṇap.): III, **272**, 15801 (there Jayadratha gratified Çiva). — § 615*i* (Saptasārasvata): IX, **38**, 2213 (there Daksha held a sacrifice).—§ 694*b* (Jvarotpatti): XII, **284**, 10229 (do.). — § 695*b* (Dakshayajñavināça): XII, **285**, 10275 (do., *Himavataḥ pṛshṭhe*).—§ 733*f* (Ānuçāsanik.): By bathing in *G.* and Kuçāvarta and Bilvaka on Nīlaparvata, and also in Kanakhala one is freed from his sins and ascends to heaven; by bathing in Apāṃ hradaḥ one obtains the merit of a horse sacrifice. Gaṅgā flows in a northerly direction; by bathing in Tristhāna, which belongs to Maheçvara, during a month, one becomes able to see the gods): XIII, **25**, 1700. —§ 747 (Ānuçāsanik.: XIII, **84**, 3941 (Bhīshma performed the çrāddha of Çāntanu at *G.*).—§ 775 (do.): XIII, **166***a*, 7652.—§ 792 (Nāradāgamanap.): XV, **37**, 1020; **39**, 1091, 1092 (at *G.* Dhṛtarāshṭra, Kuntī, and Gāndhārī were burnt to death).

Gaṅgāhrada, a tīrtha. § 368 (Tīrthayātrāp.): III, **83**, 7047, 7071.—§ 733*o* (Ānuçāsanik.: By bathing in *G.* and at Utpalāvana one obtains the merit of a horse-sacrifice: XIII, **25**, 1720.

Gaṅgāmahādvāra, v. Gāyantikādvāra.

Gaṅgāsuta = Skanda: III, 14642.

Gaṅgātoyārdramūrdhaja = Çiva (1000 names[1]).

[Gaṅgāvataraṇa(m)] ("descent of the Gaṅgā"). § 389 (Sagara): Asked by *Sagara* to bring back the horse and deliver him from hell (*Narakād*), *Aṃçumat* went to the spot where the earth had been excavated, entered the sea by that very way, and beheld *Kapila* and the horse. As he bowed his head before *Kapila*, etc., *Kapila* granted him the horse, and that his fathers should be purified and go to heaven, when his son's son, by the favour of *Çiva*, brought *Tripathagā* (i.e. Gaṅgā) from heaven. When he had brought the horse back to the sacrificial yard and narrated all the events to *Sagara*, *Sagara* grieved no more, but praised *Aṃçumat* and finished the sacrificial rites. *Sagara* was greeted by all the gods and converted the sea into a son of himself (*putratve kalpayām āsa*), and after a long reign placed his grandson on the throne and ascended to heaven. *Aṃçumat* ruled the whole earth like *Sagara*, and died after he had placed his son *Dilīpa* on the throne. *Dilīpa* in vain tried to effect the descent of *Gaṅgā* in order to raise his forefathers. He then anointed his son *Bhagīratha* as king, and practised austerities in the forest, and then ascended to heaven (III, **107**). *Bhagīratha* made over his kingly duties to his minister (*sacive*), and (*b*) practised austerities on the *Himavat* during 1000 celestial years, living upon fruits, roots, and water. Then *Gaṅgā Haimavatī* appeared in a material form (*mūrtimatī*), and promised to besprinkle the bodies of his forefathers and carry them to heaven, and as there existed none in the three worlds except *Çiva*, who was able to sustain her fall, she caused *Bhagīratha* to go to *Kailāsa*, where he, by his austerities, obtained the favour of *Çiva* (III, **108**), who, surrounded by his awful attendants (*pārishadaiḥ*), came to *Himavat*. There he caused *Bhagīratha* to pray to *Gaṅgā*. *Gaṅgā* immediately came down from the sky, in the presence of the gods, *maharshis*, *Gandharvas*, *snakes*, and *Yakshas*, and *Çiva* received her on his forehead, whence she fell to the earth, divided into three streams. At her request *Bhagīratha* led her to the spot where the bodies of *Sagara's* sons lay, while *Çiva* went to *Kailāsa* with the celestials. *Gaṅgā* filled the sea, and *Bhagīratha* adopted her as his daughter and offered libations of water to his forefathers (III, **109**).

Gaṅgā-Yamunayos tīrtham, a tīrtha. § 733*p* (Ānuçāsanik): By bathing in *G.* and at the mountain Kalañjara and offering to the Pitṛs, one obtains the merit of ten horse-sacrifices; by bathing in Shashṭihrada one obtains great merit on the day of full moon in the month of Māgha; thirty millions and ten thousands of tīrthas come together in Prayāga, and by bathing there during the month of Māgha one attains to heaven: XIII, **25**, 1721.

Gāṅgeya[1] = Bhīshma, q.v.

Gāṅgeya[2] = Skanda: I, 5431; IX, 2465; XIII, 4096.

Gāṅgeya[3], adj. ("belonging to the Gaṅgā"). § 310 (Āraṇyakap.): III, **3**, 165 (read with B.: °*aṃ vāry upaspṛçya*).—§ 734 (Ānuçāsanik.): XIII, **26**, 1786 (*toyaiḥ*), 1787 (do.), 1789 (do.), 1796 (*jalam*).

Gaṅgodbheda, a tīrtha. § 370 (Tīrthayātrāp.): III, **84**, 8043.

Gaṇita, a Viçvadeva. § 749 (Ānuçāsanik.): XIII, **91**γ, 4361.

Garbhacārin = Çiva (1000 names[2]).

Garbhamāṃsaçṛgāla (B. °*sṛgāla*) = Çiva (1000 names[1]).

Gardabhi, a son of Viçvāmitra. § 721*b* (Viçvāmitrop.): XIII, **4**β, 258.

Garga, a ṛshi. § 615*e* (Gargasrotas): IX, **37**, 2132 (*atra*— i.e. in Gargasrotas—*G°ena vṛddhena . . . kālajñānagatiç caiva jyotishāṃ vyatikramaḥ | utpātā dāruṇāç caiva çubhāç ca*), 2135. —§ 615*ii* (Vṛddhakanyā): IX, **52**, 2981 (*Kuṇiḥ*), 2982 (do.).—§ 641*f* (Pṛthu Vainya): XII, **59**, 2232 (the astrologer (*sāṃvatsaraḥ*) of Pṛthu Vainya).—§ 707 (Mokshadh.): XII, **319**ρ, 11783 (had instructed Viçvāvasu).—§ 730 (Ānuçāsanik.): XIII, **18**κκ, (1334) (Çiva bestowed on *G.*, who gratified him on the bank of Sarasvatī, the knowledge of time with its sixty-four branches (*catuḥshashṭyaṅgam . . . kālajñānam*) and 1000 sons; through the grace of Çiva the life-time of *G.* and his sons became extended to ten millions of years).

Garga, pl. ("the descendants of Garga"), a family of ṛshis. § 602 (Droṇavadhap.): VII, **190**ν, 8728.

Gargasrotas ("the stream of Garga"), a tīrtha on the Sarasvatī. § 615*e* (Baladevatīrthayātrāp): At *G. Garga*, of venerable years and purified by way of ascetic penances, obtained the knowledge of time and its course, of the movements of the stars, and of all auspicious and unauspicious portents; thence its name *G.*; there the ṛshis always waited upon Garga in order to obtain a knowledge of time); IX, **37**, 2132, 2134.

Gārgya, one or more ṛshis. § 667 (Mokshadh.): XII, **210**, 7663 (*Devarshicaritaṃ veda*).—§ 717*b* (Nārāyaṇīya); XII, **340**, 12959 (°*tejo'bhisambhṛtaḥ Kālayavanaḥ*). — § 721*b* (Viçvāmitrop.): XIII, **4**β, 254 (a son of Viçvāmitra).—§ 766 (Ânuçāsanik.): XIII, **125**, 5996 (*vṛddha*°); **127** (6063).

Gārgya, pl. (°*āḥ*), a people. § 589 (Droṇābhishekap.): VII, **11**ν, 397 (*Vātsya-G°-Karūshān*, had been vanquished by Kṛshṇa).

Gārhapatya, pl. (°*āḥ*), a class of Pitṛs. § 270 (Brahmasabhāv.): II, **11**, 462.

Garishṭha, an ancient ṛshi. § 266 (Çakrasabhāv.): II, **7**, 294 (in the palace of Indra).

Garīyasāṃ garishṭha(ḥ) = Kṛshṇa: XII, 1613.

Gārtsamada, adj. ("belonging to Gṛtsamada"). § 736*b* (Vītahavyop.): XIII, **30**, 2006 (*vaṃçaḥ*).

Garuḍa, the son of Kaçyapa and Vinatā, the vehicle of Vishṇu (Kṛshṇa), or the emblem of his flagstaff. § 11 (Anukram.): I, **2**, 365.—§ 27 (Kaçyapa): I, **16**, 1092 (son of Kaçyapa and Vinatā).—§ 32*b* (Kadrū): In the meantime *G.* came out bursting the egg and ascended the skies. The gods thought that it was Agni, but were undeceived): I, **23**, 1239, 1245, 1248.—§ 33 (Âstīkap.): Then the gods and the ṛshis praised *G.* and prevailed upon him to diminish his own energy and splendour: I, **23**, †1255.—§ 34 (do.): Bearing his brother Aruṇa on his back *G.* went from his father's home and arrived at his mother's side on the other shore of the ocean and placed Aruṇa in the east: I, **24**, 1262.—§ 36*b* (Kadrū): *G.* carried the snakes on his back, but ascended too near to the Sun so that the snakes became scorched by the rays of the Sun: I, **25**, 1283.—§ 40 (Âstīkap.): The serpents promised that if *G.* brought them the amṛta he and his mother should be freed from bondage (I, **27**). Having been directed by Vinatā to live upon the Nishādas (*b*) but not to injure the brahmans, and being taught by her how to know who is a brahman, he set out, and, having come to the Nishādas, he raised a great quantity of dust, and opened his mouth; there the Nishādas entered by thousands, being blinded by the dust, and were devoured (I, **28**). A brahman who, with his wife of the Nishāda caste, entered the throat of *G.*, and began to burn him, was recognized and relieved with his wife by *G.* (I, **29**): I, **28**, 1320, (1327); **29**, (1343), 1344.—§ 41 (do.): As *G.'s* hunger was not appeased Kaçyapa told him of the elephant Supratīka (*b*) and the tortoise Vibhāvasu: I, **29**, (1348).—§ 42 (do.): Then Kaçyapa blessed *G.*: I, **29**, 1371.—§ 43 (do.): *G.* then seized the elephant and the tortoise and came to the tīrtha Alamba (? Nīl. and BR., "without reposing") (*b*). A banyan-tree invited him to sit on one of its huge branches, but the branch broke (I, **29**). *G.* caught the branch with his beak, and perceiving Vālakhilyas suspended therefrom with their head downwards he continued to fly with the branch, the elephant, and the tortoise, fearing to kill the Vālakhilyas if he should throw away the branch. The Vālakhilyas therefore gave him the name Garuḍa (etymology: *guruṃ bhāraṃ samāsādyoḍḍīnaḥ*, v. 1390). On Gandhamādana he saw Kaçyapa engaged in ascetic devotions. Kaçyapa propitiated the Vālakhilyas (*c*) for him, then they abandoned the bough and went to Himavat to practise ascetic penances. According to the advice of Kaçyapa *G.* flew away for a hundred thousand of yojanas to a mountain without human beings, there he threw down the bough and ate the tortoise and the elephant. Then he again rose on his wings: I, **29**, 1375; **30**, 1384, 1390, 1400, 1407, 1413.—§ 44 (do.): Omens foreboding fear began to appear among the gods. Bṛhaspati declared that it was owing to the fault of Indra and the ascetic penances of the Vālakhilyas (cf. § 45) that *G.* now approached to take away the soma. Indra then caused the gods to surround and watch the amṛta (I, **30**).—§ 45 (Vālakhilya, pl.): I, **31**, 1436, 1469, 1470 (by the penances of the Vālakhilyas *G.* had been born as the lord of winged creatures (*patatrīṇām indraḥ*, v. 1455)).—§ 46 (Âstīkap.): *G.* attacked the gods, whom he blinded with dust, and Bhaumana lay as dead on the field. Indra caused Vāyu to dispel the dust. The Sādhyas and the Gandharvas fled eastwards, the Vasus and the Rudras towards the south, the Âdityas towards the west, and the Açvins towards the north. *G.* then slew nine Yakshas, Açvakranda, etc. (*a*), who guarded the amṛta. The amṛta on all sides was surrounded with fire. *G.* then divided his mouth into 8100 mouths, and taking water from many rivers he extinguished the fire. Then he assumed a diminutive body (I, **32**), and passed through the spokes of the revolving keen-edged wheel of steel placed before the soma. Then there were two great snakes, who would reduce to ashes everyone who might be seen by them. *G.* covered their eyes with dust, and unseen by them mangled them to pieces. He then flew away with the amṛta, not drinking it himself. He met with Vishṇu on his way and they agreed that *G.* should stay above Vishṇu, sitting on the flagstaff of his chariot and be his vehicle, and be immortal and free from disease without drinking amṛta. While *G.* was flying Indra hurled his thunderbolt at him. *G.* did not feel the slightest pain, but in honour of Dadhīca and Indra and the thunderbolt *G.* dropped a feather, and from its beauty he gained the name Suparṇa (I, **33**). Indra and *G.* made friendship with each other, and agreed that *G.* should not give the soma to anyone for drink. Indra should bring it away after it had been put down by *G.*, and *G.* should feed on the snakes. The snakes declared Vinatā to be free; *G.* placed down the soma on some kuça grass, and while the snakes were performing their ablutions, their daily devotions, and other religious rites, Indra took up the amṛta and returned to heaven. When the snakes licked the kuça grass their tongues were divided in twain, and the kuça grass, from the contact with the amṛta, became sacred from this time (I, **34**): I, **32**, 1471 (*pakshirāṭ*), 1477, 1485, 1494; **33**, 1509, 1513; **34** (1520), (1528), 1534, 1543. — § 99 (Aṃçāvat.): I, **65**, 2548 (among the Vainateyas). — § 120 *bis* (do.): I, **66**, 2603 (*Vainateyaḥ*, reckoned among the Âdityas).—§ 129 (do.): I, **66**, 2635 (°*āruṇau*, sons of Vinatā).—§ 191 (Arjuna): I, **123**, 4830 (present at the birth of Arjuna).—§ 244 (Rājyalābhap.): I, **207**, 7575 (*dvipaksha - G°prakhyair dvāraiḥ*). — § 289 (Arghāharaṇap.): II, **38**, 1395 (*patatāṃ mukhaṃ*).—[§ 277 (Jarāsandhavadhap.): II, **24**, 945, 946 (*Garutmān*, took his seat on the flagstaff of Kṛshṇa)].—§ 512 (Ghoshayātrāp.): III, **241**, 14897 (*rathair G°niḥsvanaiḥ*).—§ 549 (Pāṇḍavapr.): IV, **2**, 51 (*patatām iva*, sc. *varaḥ*).—§ 561 (Yānasandhip.): V, **71**, 2578 (Kṛshṇa identified with Arishṭanemi, Garuḍa, Suparṇa).—§ 564 (Mātaliyop.): V, **101**, 3600 (°*ātmajāḥ*, enumeration of his descendants); **105**, 3674, (3676), 3704, 3705 (*G.* who wished to devour the serpent Sumukha was humiliated by Vishṇu, who then threw Sumukha upon the breast of *G.*).—§ 565 (Gālavacarita): V, **107**, 3757; **112**, 3854 (the friend of Gālava, whom he assisted in his search for 1000 horses).—§ 574 (Jambūkh.): VI, **3**, 152 (*Vainateyaḥ . . . Suparṇaḥ*); [**6**, 208 (*Suparṇasya*, father of Sumukha)]. —§ 593 (Abhimanyuvadhap.): VII, **36**, 1565 (*pannagaiç chinnair G°eneva*); **37**, 1605 (*°ānilaraṃhobhiḥ . . . hayaiḥ*).—§ 599 (Jayadrathavadhap.): VII, **109**, 4124 (*udvavarha . . . pannagaṃ G°o yathā*); **143**, 6000 (*bhava G°ottamāṅgayānaḥ*, says Kṛshṇa to Bhūriçravas).—§ 600 (Ghaṭotkacavadhap.): VII, **174**vv, 7873 (°-*Takshakau*).—§ 603 (Nārāyaṇāstramokshaṇap.): VII, **201**, 9416 (*°ānilaraṃhasaḥ*).—§ 605 (Karṇap.): VIII, **12**, 446 (*°prahitair ugrair pañcāsyair uragair iva*); **18**, 688 (*turagān G°ānilaraṃhasaḥ*).—§ 607 (Haṃsakākīyop.): VIII, **41**, 1888 (*°sya gatau tulyāḥ*, sc. *haṃsāḥ*).—§ 608 (Karṇap.): VIII, **59**, 2955 (*°syeva patato çighṛkshoḥ pannagottamam*); **65**, 3300 (*vājibhir G°opamaiḥ*); **77**, 3882 (*°syeva patato pannagārthe yathā purā*); **87**, 4468 (*yathā*); **90**, †4679 (*nāgaḥ svayaṃ ya āyād G°sya vaktraṃ*).—§ 615u (Skanda): IX, **45**γ, 2518 (came to the investiture of Skanda), 2585 (*°ānanāḥ*, sc. the warriors of Skanda); **46**, 2669 (gave his favourite son, a peacock, to Skanda).—§ 717c (Uparicara): XII, **338**, 12852 (carried Uparicara up to the welkin).—[§ 730 (Ānuçāsanik.): XIII, **14**δ, 682 (the Vālakhilyas by their penances created *Suparṇaṃ somahartāraṃ*, cf. § 45)].—§ 785 (Anugītāp.): XIV, **88**, 2635 (*rukmapaksho nicitas trikoṇo G°ākṛtiḥ*). Cf. Aruṇānuja, Bhujagāri, Garutmat, Kāçyapeya, Khagarāj, Pakshirāj, Pakshirāja, Patagapati, Patageçvara, Suparṇa, Tārkshya, Vainateya, Vinatānandavardhana, Vinatāsūnu, Vinatāsuta, Vinatātmaja.

Garuḍa[2], name of a vyūha. § 580 (Bhīshmavadhap.): VI, **56**, 2404 (formed by Bhīshma).

Garuḍa, pl. (*°āḥ*) (birds of Garuḍa's race): III, 12245; VIII, †1742 (°-*Piçācasayaksha-Rākshasān*), 2172 (*iva*).

Gāruda, adj. ("shaped like the bird Garuḍa"). § 580 (Bhīshmavadhap.): VI, **56**, 2403 (*mahāvyūhaṃ*, formed by Bhīshma).

Garuḍadhvaja ("having Garuḍa on his banner") = Kṛshṇa (Vishṇu): II, 30; VII, 2821; XIII, 511, 6987 (1000 names).

garuḍī, said of Svāhā: III, 14307, 14343.

Garutmat = Garuḍa: I, 1510, 1517, 8253; II, 51 (*iva*), 945, 946 (*pannagāçanaḥ*, took his seat on the flagstaff of Kṛshṇa); III, 550 (*Vainateyo yathā pakshī G°ān patatāṃ varaḥ*), 11734 (*abhidudrāva . . . G°ān iva pannagaṃ*); IV, 1519 (*°ān iva pannagaṃ*), 1572 (*vṛkshuṃ G°an vegena*, sc. *iva*), 1681 (*nāgaṃ G°ān iva*); V, 3692, 3703, 3850; VI, 2841 (*°ān iva vegitaḥ*), 3690 (*°ān iva vegavān*); VII, 5052 (*chinnau sarpāv iva G°tā*), 5805 (*°ān ivākāçe prārthayan bhujagottamaṃ*); VIII, 2758 (*°ān iva pannagaṃ*, C. has by error *°tvān*); IX, 3095 (*sadṛçaṃ hi G°taḥ*), 3271 (dual, *yathā*); XII, 12317 (*pakshirājaḥ*, on Himavat), 12850, 12853.

Garutmat, pl. (*°aḥ*) (= Garuḍa, pl.): VI, 4778.

Gatādhvara = Mahapurusha (Mahāpurushastava).

Gatāgata = Çiva (1000 names[2]).

Gati = Çiva (1000 names[2]).

Gatisattama = Vishṇu (1000 names).

Gatitālin, a warrior of Skanda. § 615u (Skanda): IX, **45**η, 2569.

Gaura, a mountain. § 575 (Bhūmip.): VI, **12**, 445 (*°s tu madhyame dvīpe girir mānaḥçilo mahān*).

Gauraçiras, a muni. § 266 (Çakrasabhāv.): II, **7**, 292 (*muniḥ*, in the palace of Indra).—§ 640 (Rājadh.): XII, **58**β, 2094 (*muniḥ*, among the authors—*praṇetāraḥ*—of rājaçāstras).

Gaurāçva, an ancient king. § 267 (Yamasabhāv.): II, **8**, 329 (so B., C. has *Go°*; in the palace of Yama).

Gauramukha, a disciple of Çamīka. § 51 (Parikshit): I, **42**, 1738, 1740, (1741), 1751, 1752. § 56 (do.): I, **50**, 1975.

Gauraprshtha, an ancient king. § 267 (Yamasabhāv.): II, **8**, 332 (in the palace of Yama).

Gauravāhana, a king. § 287 (Rājasūyikap.): II, **34**, 1271 (*pārthivaḥ*, came to the rājasūya of Yudhishṭhira).

Gaurī[1] = Umā: III, 8129 (*çikharaṃ vai Mahādevyā G°yāḥ*); IV, †2305 (*mūrtimatīva G°ī*).

Gaurī[2], a goddess in the retinue of Umā. § 506 (Skandayuddha): III, **231**, 14562 (followed Pārvatī, i.e. Umā).

Gaurī[3], the wife of Varuṇa. § 565 (Gālavacarita): V, **117**, 3968 (*reme . . . Varuṇaç ca yathā G°yāṃ*).—§ 768b (Umā-Maheçvarasaṃv.): XIII, **146**γ, 6751 (*Varuṇasya*, sc. *sādhvī*).—§ 775 (Ānuçāsanik.): XIII, **166**a, 7637 (*Varuṇaḥ saha G°yā*).

Gaurī[4], a river. § 574 (Jambūkh.): VI, **9**λ, 333 (in Bhāratavarsha).

Gaurī[5] = the Earth (so Nīl. and PCR.). § 768b (Umā-Maheçvarasaṃv.): XIII, **146**, 6756.

Gaurīça ("the husband of Gaurī") = Çiva: XIV, 210.

Gaurīhṛdayavallabha ("dear to Gaurī's heart") = Çiva: X, 258.

Gautama[1] ("descendant of Gotama"), name of one or more ṛshis. § 22 (Pramadvarā): I, **8**a, 962 (came to see the dead Pramadvarā).—§ 170 (Dīrghatamas): I, **104**, 4194 (the eldest son of Dīrghatamas and Pradveshī), 4205 (with his brothers he threw Dīrghatamas into the Gaṅgā).—§ 191 (Arjuna): I, **123**, 4807 (among the seven ṛshis, present at the birth of Arjuna).—§ 264 (Sabhākriyāp.): II, **4**a, 112 (among the munis who were present when Yudhishṭhira entered his palace).—§ 266 (Çakrasabhāv.): II, **7**, 298 (*Kākshīvān?*, in the palace of Indra).—§ 270 (Brahmasabhāv.): II, **11**, 436 (in the palace of Brahmán).—§ 275 (Rājasūyārambhap.): II, **17**, 698 (*Kākshīvataḥ*).—§ 277 (Jarāsandhavadhap.): II, **21**, 802 (near Rājagṛha *G.* begat, with the çudrā Auçīnarī, the sons Kākshīva, etc.), 803, 804, 805.—§ 370 (Tīrthayātrāp.): III, **84**, 8086 (*Brahmarsher G°sya vanaṃ*, a tīrtha).—§ 376 (do.): III, **85**, 8263 (among the ṛshis who expected Yudhishṭhira on his tīrthayātrā).—§ 455 (Brahmamāhātmyak.): III, **185**, 12684, 12685, (12691), 12692, (12693), 12698, 12699.—§ 545 (Pativratāmāhātmyap.): III, **298**, (16868), (16890).—§ 602 (Droṇavadhap.): VII, **190**ν, 8727.—§ 615b (Udapāna): IX, **36**, 2073 (father of Ekata, Dvita, and Trita).—§ 637 (Rājadh.): XII, **47**η, 1597 (among the ṛshis who surrounded Bhīshma).—§ 638b (Rāmopākhyāna): XII, **49**, 1796 (*Dadhivāhanapautras tu putro Divirathasya ca | guptas sa G°enāsīd Gaṅgākūle 'bhirakshitaḥ*).—§ 641 (Rājadh.): XII, **129**, 4718 (*°sya ca saṃvādaṃ Yamasya ca*), 4719, 4721, (4724).—§ 656 (Khaḍgotpatti): XII, **166**β, 6142.—§ 658b (Kṛtaghnop.): XII, **168**, 6298, 6300, 6301, 6302, 6305, 6307; **169**, 6317, 6327, 6331, 6332, 6333, 6339; **170**, 6342, 6346, 6348, 6350, 6351, 6358, 6362, 6363, 6366; **171** ((6372), 6394, 6396, 6398; **172**, 6412, 6415, 6417; **173**, 6439, 6441, 6442, 6445 (the story of the ingratitude of *G.*).—§ 665 (Mokshadh.): XII, **208**ι, 7699 (one of the ṛshis of the north).—§ 672b (Çakra-Namucisaṃv.): XII, **226**, †8206 (not in the text of B., but mentioned by Nīl. as *varia lectio*, according to Nīl. the husband of Ahalyā).—§ 682 (Mokshadh.): XII, **267**, 9484 (father of Cirakārin), 9488, 9525 (*Medhātithiḥ*), 9539, 9541, 9546, 9548 (when Indra had violated the wife of *G.* (i.e. Ahalyā, Nīl.), he commanded his son Cirakārin to slay her. Cirakārin hesitated to do so, and *G.* meanwhile repented that he had given the order).—§ 707 (do.): XII, **319**β, 11783 (had instructed Viçvāvasu).—§ 717*b* (Nārāyaṇīya): XII, **343,** II), ††13205 (the husband of Ahalyā whom Indra violated; *G.* then cursed Indra to wear a green beard). — § 730 (Ānuçāsanik.): XIII, **17,** 1289 (Çukra communicated the 1000 names of Çiva to *G.*), 1290 (*G.* again communicated them to Manu Vaivasvata).—§ 733 (do.): XIII, **25,** 1691 (questioned Aṅgiras about the tīrthas), 1755.—§ 734 (do.): XIII, **26***a*, 1761 (among the ṛshis who surrounded Bhīshma).—§ 743*b* (Vipulop.): XIII, **41,** 2328 (°*enāsi yan mukto bhagāṅgaparicihnitaḥ* (*bhagāṅka*°, B.), sc. Indra; "that Gautama had cursed thee, in consequence of which thy body became disfigured with a thousand sex-marks, which, by the Ṛshi's mercy, were afterwards changed into organs of vision," PCR.). — § 746 (Ānuçāsanik.): XIII, **66**ε, 3320 (*maharshiḥ*, ascended to heaven by making gifts of sesame seeds).—§ 750*b* (Bisastainyop.): XIII, **93***a*, 4416, (β), (4442), (γ), (4467), (δ), (4490), 4491 (etymology, B. has *Gotamam*), (ε), (4523).—§ 751*b* (Çapathavidhi): XIII, **94***a*, 4550, (β), 4565.—§ 757*b* (Hastikūṭa): XIII, **102,** 4845 (°*sya munes tāta saṃvādam Vāsavasya ca*), 4846, 4849, (†4854), †4855, (†4856), (†4858), (†4860), (†4862), (†4865), (†4867), (†4871), (†4874), (†4877), (†4880), (†4882), (†4884), 4891, (†4896), (†4899), (†4901), 4904, 4905.—§ 759 (Ānuçāsanik.): XIII, **106**δ, 5200.—§ 770 (do.): XIII, **151**ι, 7116 (one of the ṛshis of the north).—§ 772*e* (Pavanārjunasaṃv.): Indra coveting Ahalyā was cursed by Gautama, but, for the sake of righteousness, he was not hurt (*hiṃsitaḥ*): XIII, **154,** 7218. —§ 775 (Ānuçāsanik.): XIII, **166**ε, 7668 (one of the ṛshis of the west).—§ 782*g* (Guruçishyasaṃv.): XIV, **35**δ, 960.—§ 784*b* (Uttaṅka): XIV, **56,** 1628 (the preceptor of Uttaṅka), 1629, 1638, (1643), (1646), 1657, 1660 (the husband of Ahalyā); **58,** 1707, 1733, 1747.

Gautama[2] ("son of Gotama") = Çaradvat: I, 2435 (°*ān mithunaṃ jajñe çarastambāc Charadvataḥ*), 5072 (*Gotamasya . . . Çaradvān nāma G°aḥ putraḥ*), 5075, 5077, 5078, 5083 (Ç°), 5088, 5090; V, 2192 (*Kṛpaḥ . . . maharsher G°āt*, sc. *jajñe*), 5768.

Gautama[3] ("grandson of Gotama") = Kṛpa: I, 302, 5070 (*çarastambe samudbhūtam*), 5147, 5433 (*Gotamasyānvaye ca çarastambāc ca*), 5688, 7557 (*K*°); II, 1712, †2402, 2476; III, 12; IV, 1802 (*K*°), 1803, 1808; V, 5707 (Uttamaujas is pitted against *G.*), 7585, 7594; VI, †753 (*Çāradvataḥ Çakaiḥ Kirāta-Yavanaiç ca sārdham*), 1549, 1602, 1604, 1721, 3234, 3715, 3719, 3720, 3721, 3722, 3723, 3724, 3729, 4358, 4624, 4625, 4627, 5251, 5253, 5273; VII, 797, 1917, 3922, 3940 (*K*°), 6322, 7000, 7025, 7026, 7029, 7580, 7585, 7588, 7589, 8812; VIII, †201 (*Çāradvataḥ*), 329 (*Ācāryaḥ*), 417, 1038, 1039, 1041, 1043, 1047, 1056, 2614, 2628, 2631, 2633, 2635, 2639, 3080, 5013 (*K*°, C. has by error *Go*°); IX, 75, 239, 393 (*Çakaiç ca Yavanaiḥ saha*), 399, 571 (*Ācāryaḥ*), 759, 949, 1164, 1603 (*K*°), 3589; X, 139, 545 (*K*°); XV, †435, 623 (*K*°).

Gautama[4] = Çiva (1000 names[2]).

Gautamī[1] (female descendant of Gotama), name of one or more women. § 270 (Brahmasabhāv.): II, **11,** 457 (in the palace of Brahmán). — § 635 (Rājadh.): XII, **38,** 1397 (*maharshīn iva G°ī*, cf. Gautamī[2]).—§ 719*b* (Gautamī-lubdhaka-vyāla-Mṛtyu-Kālasaṃv.): XIII, **1,** 16 (*saṃvādaṃ Mṛtyu-G°yoḥ kāla-lubdhakapannagaiḥ*), 17, 18, (21), (†26), (†29), †30, (†31), 33, 77, (78), 80.

Gautamī[2] (do.) = Jaṭilā: I, 7265 (*J*°, married seven ṛshis).

Gautamī[3] (do.) = Kṛpī: I, 5115, 5182.

Gautamī[4], a river. § 775 (Ānuçāsanik.): XIII, **166***a*, 7647.

[Gautamī - lubdhaka - vyāla - Mṛtyu - Kāla-saṃ - vāda(ḥ)] ("the conversation between Gautamī, the fowler, the serpent, Death, and Time"). § 719*b* (Ānuçāsanik.): *Bhīshma* said: An old brahman lady named *Gautamī* found her son dead, bitten by a serpent; an angry fowler, *Arjunaka*, bound the serpent with a string and brought it before *Gautamī*; she told him to release it, as *brahmans* do not harbour resentment, and there is no good in tormenting and killing an enemy; the fowler mentioned how *Indra* killed *Vṛtra* and *Mahādeva* destroyed a sacrifice. The serpent said that *Mṛtyu* had sent him on this errand. *Mṛtyu* (masc.) appeared and said that *Kāla* (Time) was the real promoter; *Sūrya*, etc. (*a*) are created and destroyed by *Kāla*. *Kāla* came and said that it was the child's *karman* (deeds in the past) that was the cause; this was approved of by *Gautamī* and the fowler.

Gautaminandana ("the son of Gautamī, i.e. Kṛpī") = Açvatthāman: VII, 6847.

Gautamīsuta (do.) = Açvatthāman: VII, 6857, 7131, 7161.

Gavāksha[1], a monkey chief. § 535 (Setubandhana): III, **283,** 16272 (*golāṅgulaḥ*, came to Rāma with 60,000 crores (*koṭi*) of monkeys).

Gavāksha[2], a Gandhāra warrior, son of Subala and brother of Çakuni. § 585 (Bhīshmavadhap.): VI, **90**σ, 3997 (slain by Irāvat, cf. Gaja).—§ 600 (Ghaṭotkacavadhap.): VII, **157**π, 6944 (read with B.: *Çakuner bhrātaro vīrā Gavākshaḥ . . . tāḍayan*, among five brothers of Çakuni who were slain by Bhīmasena, C., however, has only three names).

Gavalgana, the father of the sūta Sañjaya. § 81 (Sañjaya): I, **63,** 2426.

Gāvalgani = Sañjaya, q.v.

***Gavām aya(ḥ),** name of a sacrifice: III, 8176; XIII, 7128.

Gavāṃ bhavana(m), a tīrtha. § 364 (Tīrthayātrāp.): III, **83,** 6020.

Gavāṃ loka(ḥ), v. Goloka.

Gavāṃ pati(ḥ)[1] = Çiva: VII, 9526, 9540; VIII, 1451; XIII, 1186 (1000 names[2]).

Gavāṃ pati(ḥ)[2] = Sūrya (the Sun): III, 192.

Gavāṃ tīrtha(m), a tīrtha. § 379 (Tīrthayātrāp.): III, **95,** 8512.

Gavaya, a monkey chief. § 535 (Setubandhana): III, **283,** 16271 (together with Gaya he came to Rāma with 100 crores (*koṭi*) of monkeys).

Gaveshaṇa, a Vṛshṇi prince. § 232 (Svayaṃvarap.): I, **186,** 6999 (came to the svayaṃvara of Draupadī).

Gavija, a muni. § 745 (Cyavanop.): XIII, **51,** 2709, 2712 ("born of a cow," PCR.).

Gavijāta = Gavija: XIII, 2682, 2688 ("born of a cow," PCR.).

Gavishṭha, an Asura. § 93 (Aṃçavat.): I, **65,** 2538 (among the sons of Danu). — § 130 (do.): I, **67,** 2670 (*mahāsuraḥ*, incarnate as king Drumasena).

Gaya[1], an ancient king, son of Amūrtarayas. § 5 (Anukram.): I, **1***a*, 220 (in Nārada's enumeration of deceased kings).—§ 11 (Parvasaṅgr.): I, **2,** 441 (*yajñavibhūtiç ca G°sya*, all. to § 381).—§ 61 (Sarpasattra): I, **55,** †2100 (°*sya yajñaḥ*, comparison). — § 243 (Vidurāgamanap.): I, **205,** 7492 (*anavarau . . . G°āt*).—§ 267 (Yamasabhāv.): II, **8,** 329 (in the palace of Yama).—§ 378 (Tīrthayātrāp.): III, **94,** 8504 (has practised austerities and visited tīrthas).—§ 379 (do.): III, **95**, 8518 (*mahīdharaṃ . . . abhisaṃskṛtaṃ . . . G°ena*), 8527 (*Āmūrtarayasaṃ*).—§ 381 (Tīrthayātrāp.): At Brahmasaras the rājarshi *G.*, the son of Amūrtarayas, many times performed sacrifices distinguished by hundreds of mountains of food and thousands of lakes of clarified butter, many hundred rivers of curds, and streams of curries by the thousand; at the time when the gifts (*dakshiṇāḥ*) were given nothing could be heard but the chaunting of the Vedas (*brahmaçabdena*) and in all lands people sung these songs: "In the sacrifice of Gaya," etc. (v. 8535–8539*a*): III, **95**, 8528, 8535, 8536, 8539 (°*yajñe*).—§ 403*b* (Payoshṇī): III, **121**, 10297 (performed sacrifices on the Payoshṇī), 10300, 10303.—§ 552 (Goharaṇap.): IV, **56**ζ, 1768 (came to see the fight between Bhīshma and Arjuna). — § 562 (Bhagavadyānap.); V, **83**η, 2946 (among the ṛshis who worshipped Kṛshṇa).—§ 595 (Shoḍaçarāj. v. Māndhātṛ): VII, **62**, 2281 (vanquished by Māndhātṛ). — § 595 (Shoḍaçarāj.): *G.* Āmūrtarayasa did not eat anything during a hundred years but remains from libations of clarified butter. Agni offered to grant him a boon. *G.* then desired to have a thorough knowledge of the Vedas through ascetic penances, etc., inexhaustible wealth without injury to others, always to be able to make gifts to brahmans, and to have sons begotten of wives of his own order. (Description of his sacrifices and gifts.) In his horse-sacrifice the sacrificial stakes were of gold decked with gems, and were given to the brahmans, etc. His sacrificial altar was 30 yojanas long by 26 yojanas broad and 24 yojanas high, of solid gold, decked with pearls, etc.; upon the completion of that sacrifice twenty-five hills of food remained and also many lakes and rivulets of savoury drinks, etc. In consequence of his glory [the place named] Gaya became renowned in the three worlds; there is the eternal-making banyan-tree (*vaṭaç cākshayyakaraṇaḥ*) and Brahmasaras: VII, **66**, 2334 (*Āmūrtarayasaṃ*), 2235, 2239, 2345, 2346, 2348, 2350. — § 615*i* (Saptasārasvata): IX, **38**, 2205 (performed a sacrifice in Gayā), 2206.—§ 632*b* (Shoḍaçarāj. v. Māndhātṛ, cf. § 595): XII, **29**, 981 (vanquished by Māndhatṛ).—§ 632 (Shoḍaçarāj., cf. § 595): XII, **29**, 1004 (*Āmūrtarayasaṃ*), 1005, 1011 (*Āmūrtarayasaḥ*). —§ 677 (Mokshadh.): XII, **235**, 8600 (gave the earth to the brahmans). — § 761 (Ānuçāsanik.): XIII, **115**γ, 5661 (among the kings who abstained from meat during the month of Kārttika). Cf. Āmūrtarayasa (III, 8527, 10293; VII, 2334; XII, 1004, 1011).

Gaya[2], a sacred mountain. § 370 (Dhaumyatīrthak.): III, **87**, 8304 (*tasyāṃ*—i.e. in the east—*girivaraḥ puṇyo G°o rājarshisatkṛtaḥ çivaṃ Brahmasaro yatra*).—§ 595 (Shoḍaçarāj. v. Gaya): VII, **66**, 2353 (?, *yasya*—i.e. king Gaya's—*prabhāvāc ca Gayas trishu lokeshu viçrutaḥ | vaṭaç cākshayyakaraṇaḥ puṇyaṃ Brahmasaraç ca tat*). Cf. Gayā, Gayaçiras.

Gaya[3], a monkey chief. § 535 (Setubandhana): III, **283***a*, 16271 (together with Gavaya he came to Rāma with 100 crores (*koṭi*) of monkeys).

Gaya, pl. (°*āḥ*), a people, the inhabitants of Gayā. § 295 (Dyūtap.): II, **52**, 1872 (among the peoples who brought tribute to Yudhishṭhira).—§ 615*i* (Saptasārasvata): IX, **38**, 2205.

Gayā, a sacred place (the present Gayā). § 249 (Arjunavanavāsap.): I, **215**, 7818 (visited by Arjuna). — § 370 (Tīrthayātrāp.): III, **84**, 8061 (*tatrākshayavaṭo nāma trishu lokeshu viçrutaḥ*), 8074, 8075 (*eshṭavyā bahavaḥ putrā yady apy eko Gayāṃ vrajet | yajeta vāçvamedhena nīlaṃ vā vṛsham utsṛjet*). —§ 377 (Dhaumyatīrthak.): III, **87**, 8305 (do.).—§ 733*s* (Açmapṛshṭha): XIII, **25**, 1728. — § 735 (Ānuçāsanik.): XIII, **29**, 1917.—§ 749 (do.): XIII, **88**, 4253 (*b*: *eshṭavyā bahavaḥ putrā yady apy eko Gayāṃ vrajet | yatrāsau prathito lokeshvakshayyakaraṇo vaṭaḥ*). — § 766 (do.): XIII, **125**β, 5967.—§ 775 (do.): XIII, **166***a*, 7655.

Gayaçiras, a hill near Gayā. § 377 (Dhaumyatīrthak.): III, **87**, 8307 (*yatrāsau kīrtyate viprair akshayyakaraṇo vaṭaḥ*). —§ 379 (Tīrthayātrāp.): III, **95**, 8519 (*nagaḥ*, visited by Yudhishṭhira on his tīrthayātra). — § 757*m* (Goloka): III, **102***a*, 4888.

Gāyana, a warrior of Skanda. § 615*u* (Skanda): IX, **45**η 2569.

Gāyantikādvāra, name of a place. § 565 (Gālavacarita): V, **111**, 3836 (in the north, B. has *Gaṅgāmahādvāraṃ*).

Gāyanti tvāṃ gāyatriṇaḥ = Çiva (1000 names[1]).

Gāyatrī, name of a metre, and also of a certain verse (= Sāvitrī ?). § 289 (Arghāharaṇap.): II, **38**, 1395 (*chandasāṃ mukhaṃ*).—§ 370 (Tīrthayātrāp.): III, **85**, 8172. —§ 472 (Mārkaṇḍeyas.): III, **200**, 13432 (*devīṃ G°īṃ Vedamātaraṃ* = Sāvitrī ?, but cf. the note of PCR.).—§ 574 (Jambūkh.): VI, **4**, 172, 173 (the universe consisting of nineteen classes of beings and five elements is spoken of as the *G.* (of twenty-four aksharas).—§ 576 (Bhagavadgītāp.)): VI, **34**, 1239 (*G°ī chandasām ahaṃ*, sc. *asmi*, says Kṛshṇa).— § 603*d* (Tripura): VII, **202**, 9567 (Çiva made the *G.* and the Sāvitrī his reins).—§ 606 (Tripurākhyāna): VIII, **34**, 1489 (Çiva made the *G.* his goad-string).—§ 772*b* (Pavanārjunasaṃv.): XIII, **153**, 7204 (*kanyayā*, spoke from heaven to Arjuna Kārtavīrya).

Gāyatrī[2] = Çiva (1000 names[1]).

Gāyatryāḥ sthāna(m), a tīrtha. § 370 (Tīrthayātrāp.): III, **85**, 8171

Ghanaupama = Çiva (1000 names[1]) (only C.).

Ghaṭajānuka, a muni. § 264 (Sabhākriyāp.): II, **4***a*, 108 (only B., C. has *Varajānukaḥ*)

Ghaṇṭa = Çiva (1000 names[1]).

Ghaṇṭakarṇa, a companion of Skanda. § 615*u* (Skanda): IX, **45**, 2526 (given to Skanda by Brahmán).

Ghaṇṭāmālāpriya = Çiva (1000 names[1]).

Ghaṇṭin = Çiva (1000 names[1]).

Ghaṭasṛñjaya, pl. (°*āḥ*), a people. § 574 (Jambūkh.): VI, **9**ν, 371 (in the south).

Ghaṭin = Çiva (1000 names[1]).

Ghaṭodara, an Asura. § 268 (Varuṇasabhāv.): II, **9**, 366 (among the Daityas and Dānavas in the palace of Varuṇa).

Ghaṭotkaca, a Rākshasa, son of Hiḍimbā and Bhīmasena Pāṇḍava. § 4 (Anukram.): I, **1**, †197 (*Devarājena dattāṃ divyāṃ çaktiṃ vyaṃsitāṃ Mādhavena G°e Rākshase*, all. to § 600), †198.—§ 11 (Parvasaṅgr.): I, **2**, 381, 536.—§ 71 (Ādivaṃçāvatāraṇap.): I, **61**, 2255 (son of Hiḍimbā and Bhīmasena). — § 84 (do.): I, **64**, 2452 (do.). — § 159 (Pūruvaṃç.): I, **95**, ††3833 (do.).—§ 214 (Hiḍimbavadhap.): I, **155**, 6079 (born to Bhīmasena by Hiḍimbā, etymology of his name), 6080, 6082.—§ 317 (Arjunābhigamanap.): III, **12**, 570 (*Hiḍimbām agrataḥ yasyāṃ jāto G°aḥ*, all. to § 214).—§ 423 (Gandhamādanapr.): III, **144**, 11009, 11010; **145**, 11016, (11019), 11021 (carried Draupadī). — § 433 (Saugandhikāh.): III, **155**, 11412 (do.).—§ 435 (Jaṭāsuravadhap.): III, **157**, 11457.—§ 437 (Yakshayuddhap.): III, **160**, 11671.—§ 448 (Ājagarap.): III, **176**, †12336 (*G.* and his followers carried the Pāṇḍavas, Kṛshṇā, and the brahmans). — § 449 (do.): III, **177**, †12353 (*sānucaram*). — § 569 (Bhagavadyānap.): V, **141**, 4798 (*çāmitraṃ karishyati*, sc. in the battle represented as a sacrifice).—§ 571 (Ulūkadūtāgamanap.): V, **162,** 5591 (*Rākshasaḥ*, in the army of Yudhishṭhira).—§ 578 (Bhīshmavadhap.): VI, **45**[11], 1711 (fights with Alambusha).—§ 580 (do.): VI, **57**κ, 2454 (*Rākshasaḥ*), 2458; **58**[6], 2475 (fights with Duryodhana).—§ 581 (do.): VI, **64**[16], 2863, 2868 (creating illusions he fights with Bhagadatta), 2887, 2889, 2892.—§ 582 (do.): VI, **72,** 3170 (*Rākshasaḥ*).—§ 583 (do.): VI, **75**α, 3283 (do.).—§ 584 (do.): VI, **83,** 3670 (fights with Bhagadatta).—§ 585 (do.): VII, **87**θ, 3867 (*Rākshasaḥ*); **91,** 4065 (*Bhaimaseniḥ*), 4072 (fights with Duryodhana, etc.); **92,** 4105, 4111 (fights with the Vaṅga king, etc.); **93,** 4154 (*Rākshasendram*), 4157 (rescued by Bhīmasena, etc.); **94,** 4187, 4218, 4222 (fights with Açvatthāman), 4228 (°*prayuktā*, sc. *māyā*), 4230; **95,** 4233, 4237, (δδ), 4254 (*Rākshasaḥ*), 4294, 4316 (*pitāputrau . . . Bhīmasena-Gh°au*).—§ 586 (do.): VI, **99**ζ, 4510 (*Rākshasaḥ*); **101**θ, 4586.—§ 587 (do.): VI, **109**ε, 5075; **111,** 5176 (fights with Durmukha); **118**υ, 5554; **119**ω, 5587.—§ 589 (Droṇābhishekap.): VII, **8**η, 227; **10,** 377 (*sadyo Vṛkodarāj jātaḥ . . . māyāvī Rākshasaḥ*).—§ 592 (Saṃçaptakavadhap.): VII, **23**ο, 1022 (proceeded against Droṇa, description of his horses), (π), 1037 (on his standard there was a vulture), (ρ), 1040 (possessed the bow Paulastya); **25,** 1123 (fights with Alambusha).—§ 593 (Abhimanyuvadhap.): VII, **35**δ, 1509.—§ 599 (Jayadrathavadhap.): VII, **95,** 3536 (*Rākshasam*, attacked by Alāyudha); **96,** 3568 (fights with Alāyudha); **109,** 4099 (encounter with Alambusha), 4100, 4104, 4120 (*Haiḍimbaḥ*), 4127 (slew Alambusha), 4132; **111**υ, 4283; **114**ψ, 4502 (pierced Kṛtavarman).—§ 600 (Ghaṭotkacavadhap.): VII, **153**α, 6629 (pierced by Duryodhana); **154**β, 6652 (*Rākshasaḥ*); **156,** 6794 (*Rākshasendram*), 6796, 6800 (*māyām Gh° vinirmitām*), 6801, 6804, 6807, (6821), 6829, 6833, 6840, 6857, 6859, 6866, 6867, 6882, 6915 *G.'s* son Añjanaparvan is slain by Açvatthāman, and *G.* himself is defeated by the same); **158**χ, 7013 (*Rākshasaḥ*); **166,** 7411, 7414, 7417 (*Rākshasendram*), 7426, 7432, 7436 (*Rākshasendram*, defeated by Açvatthāman); **173,** †7810 (*Rākshasāt*), 7813, 7814, 7820, 7829, 7834, 7835, (7838) (Kṛshṇa urged *Gh.* to proceed against Karṇa); **174,** 7844, 7853, 7855, 7858, 7860, 7863, 7866, 7869, 7871, 7872, 7875, 7878, 7880, 7882 (encounter with Alambusha, whom *Gh.* slew); **175,** 7890 (*Rākshasaḥ*), 7923, 7924 (*prāduç cakre tato māyām Rākshasīm Rākshaseçvaraḥ*), 7927, 7931 (*māyām Gh° vinirmitām*), 7932, 7934, 7935, 7938, 7939, 7940, 7945, 7959, 7961, 7967, 7969, 7971, 7972, 7974, 7980 (encounter with Karṇa); **176,** 8017 (*yādṛçena*), 8021 (*yathā*), †8022; **177,** 8037, 8038, 8042, 8044 (encounter with Alāyudha); **178,** 8074, 8077, 8085, 8094 (slew Alāyudha); **179,** 8115, †8126, 8132, †8145, †8153 (*Gh.* again proceeded against Karṇa, who slew him, hurling the dart which was given to him by Indra, and with which he had intended to slay Arjuna); **180,** 8184 (*hatam*), 8190 (*çaktim Gh°enemām vyaṃsayitvā*), 8192, 8199, 8212 (mentioned among the slain); **181**δδ, 8238 (*nihataḥ*, has hated the brahmans and the sacrifices); **182**εε, 8252 (*sā çaktir Vāsudevena vyaṃsitā ca Gh°e*), 8253, †8255, †8256, 8258, (ηη), 8288 (°*e vyaṃsitām*, sc. *çaktim*); **183,** 8303 (*hatvā*), 8311 (°*vadhena*), 8312 (*hate*), 8326 (*Rākshasendre*).—§ 601 (Droṇavadhap.): VII, **184,** 8363 (*nihate*).—§ 604 (Karṇap.): VIII, **3,** 63 (has been slain by Karṇa); **5**ζ, 135 (has slain Alambusha); **9,** 299 (°*m Rākshasendram Çakraçaktyā nijaghnivān*, sc. Karṇa).—§ 605 (do.): VIII, **35,** 1635 (*hataḥ*).—§ 608 (do.): VIII, **50,** 2406 (*hate . . . Rākshase*).—§ 609 (Çalyap.): IX, **2,** 79 (*Rākshasam*).—§ 615 (Gadāyuddhap.): IX, **61,** 3421 (*vadhārtham Pāṇḍuputrasya yācitām çaktim eva ca | G°e vyaṃsayataḥ*, sc. Kṛshṇa).—§ 620 (Çrāddhap.): XI, **26**β, 792 (*Rākshasendram*, his body is cremated).—§ 789 (Putradarçanap.): XV, **32**θ, 875 (*Rākshasaḥ*, among the dead warriors who, summoned by Vyāsa, arose from the Gaṅgā).—§ 795 (Svargārohaṇap.): XVIII, **5**λ, 150, 174 (after death *Gh.*, etc., entered the gods and Yakshas),

Cf. also the following synonyms:—

Bhaimaseni, Bhaimi, Bhīmasenasuta, Bhīmasenātmaja, Bhīmasūnu, Bhīmasuta, q.v.

Haiḍimba ("the son of Hiḍimbā"): III, 11009, 11017, 11415; V, 5926 (*Bhaimaseniḥ . . . Rākshaseçvaraḥ*), 7599; VI, 2476, 2873, 2883, 3559 (*Rākshaseçvaraḥ*), 3663 (*Rākshasendraḥ*), 3665, 3678, 3950, 993, 4114, 4149, 4153, 4231, 4248, 5177; VII, 540 (*Rākshasau raudrakarmāṇau H°ālambushau*), 4101, 4113, 4117, 4120 (*Gh°*), 6841, 7435, 8031, 8034, 8078, 8133, 8178, 8184, 8185, 8236, 8237, †8254, 8305, 8315, 8332.

Haiḍimbi (do.): VII, 4097, 4123 (C. has by error Haiḍam°), 6822 (do.), 6823 (do.), 6898, 6908, 7819, 7822, 7828, 7841, 7856, 7868, 8002, 8012, 8073, 8093, 8105.

Rakshas, Rākshasa, Rakshādhipa, Rākshasapuṅgava, Rākshaseçvara, Rākshasendra, q.v.

Ghaṭotkacasuta ("the son of Ghaṭotkaca") = Añjanaparvan: VII, 6808, 6815.

Ghaṭotkacavadha ("the slaughter of Ghaṭotkaca"). § 10 (Parvasaṅgr.): I, **2,** 339 (i.e. Ghaṭotkacavadhaparvan).

[Ghaṭotkacavadhaparvan (°va)] ("the section including the slaughter of Ghaṭotkaca," the 76th of the minor parvans of Mhbhr.; cf. Ghaṭotkacavadha). § 600: THE NIGHTLY COMBAT AFTER THE FOURTEENTH DAY: A dreadful battle took place between the *Pāñcālas* and the *Kauravas*. *Duryodhana* penetrated into the midst of the *Pāṇḍava* host, and caused an immense slaughter. *Bhīmasena*, etc. (α) & *Duryodhana*; *Yudhishṭhira* made *Duryodhana* insensible; *Droṇa* advanced to the rescue of *Duryodhana*; the *Pāṇḍavas* & *Droṇa* (VII, **153**). *Arjuna*, etc. (β) & *Droṇa*. (Description of the awful night) (VII, **154.**) *Dhṛtarāshṭra* asked *Sañjaya* about the battle (γ). *Sañjaya* related: *Droṇa* slew the *Kaikeyas* and the sons of *Dhṛshṭadyumna*, etc., and *Çibi*; *Duryodhana* sent *Droṇa* a driver for his chariot; the *Kaliṅga* prince attacked *Bhīma* (and *Viçoka*) and was slain by *Bhīma* with his bare fists); *Karṇa* and *Dhruva* (the brother of the *Kaliṅga* prince) & *Bhīma*, who slew *Dhruva* with his fist, and then *Jayarāta* with a slap of his palm; *Çakuni* rescued *Karṇa*; *Dhṛtarāshṭra's* sons & *Bhīma*; *Durmada* mounted the chariot of *Dushkarṇa*; then, before the eyes of *Karṇa*, etc. (δ), *Bhīma*, by a kick of his foot, caused that chariot to sink into the earth, and with his fists crushed *Durmada* and *Dushkarṇa*. All the kings fled away; *Bhīma* repaired to *Yudhishṭhira*; *Nakula*, etc. (ε) paid their adorations to *Bhīma*. The *Dhārtarāshṭras* + *Droṇa* & *Bhīma* (VII, **155**). *Somadatta* rebuked *Sātyaki* for having slain *Bhūriçravas* while sitting in *prāya* (ζ); *Sātyaki's* reply (η). *Somadatta* + *Duryodhana* and *Çakuni* & *Sātyaki* + *Dhṛshṭadyumna*; *Somadatta* was carried away by his driver. *Droṇa* & *Sātyaki* + *Yudhishṭhira*, etc. (θ); the *Pāṇḍava* host fled away; *Arjuna* + *Bhīma* (+ *Viçoka*) + the *Pāñcālas*, etc. (i) & *Droṇa* + *Açvatthāman*. *Ghaṭotkaca* (description of his chariot) + Rā. & *Açvatthāman*; description of the battle of Rā.; the sons of *Dhṛtarāshṭra*, etc., and *Karṇa* fled away, but not *Açvatthāman*, who soon dispelled the illusive creations of *Ghaṭotkaca*; *Açvatthāman* & *Ghaṭotkaca* + the latter's son *Añjanaparvan*, who was slain by *Açvatthāman*; *Ghaṭotkaca* created illusions; *Açvatthāman* invoked the *Vajra* weapon and then the *Vāyavya* weapon; the followers of *Ghaṭotkaca* were *Paulastyas* and *Yātudhānas*. *Duryodhana* was afraid of them, but quieted by *Açvatthāman* he urged *Çakuni* to proceed against *Arjuna* with *Karṇa*, etc. (κ), and a great force; and he should also slay *Bhīma*, etc. (λ). *Çakuni* proceeded quickly. *Ghaṭotkaca* & *Açvatthāman*, who burnt a full *akshauhiṇī* of Rā. troops and destroyed the chariot of *Ghaṭotkaca*, who mounted *Dhṛshṭadyumna's* chariot. *Bhīmasena* + *Ghaṭotkaca* + *Dhṛshṭadyumna*, etc. (μ), & *Açvatthāman*, who destroyed the Rā. host and caused a river of blood, and slew *Drupada's* son *Suratha*, and then *Suratha's* younger brother *Çatruñjaya*, etc. (ν); *Ghaṭotkaca* was made insensible by *Açvatthāman* and borne away by *Dhṛshṭadyumna*; *Yudhishṭhira's* chariots turned away. Si., G., Pç., N., birds, P., etc., Aps., and the gods applauded *Açvatthāman* (VII, **156**). Beholding the sons of *Drupada* and *Kuntibhoja* and Rā. in thousands slain by *Açvatthāman*, *Yudhishṭhira*, etc. (ξ), set their hearts firmly on battle. *Somadatta* & *Yuyudhāna* + *Bhīma*, who made *Somadatta* insensible, and slew *Pratīpa's* son *Bāhlīka* (the father of Somadatta), ten sons of *Dhṛtarashṭra*; *Nagadatta*, etc. (ο), & *Bhīma*, who slew them. *Vṛkaratha* (the brother of *Karṇa*) & *Bhīma*, who slew him, and thereupon seven brothers of *Çakuni*, and pressed *Çatacandra* down into the earth. *Çakuni's* five brothers, *Gavāksha*, etc. (π) & *Bhīma*, who slew them. *Yudhishṭhira* & *Droṇa*; *Yudhishṭhira* began to slay the *Ambashṭhas* (ρ); *Droṇa* and *Yudhishṭhira* employed the *Vāyavya* weapon; then *Droṇa* employed the *Vāruṇa*, *Yāmya*, *Āgneya*, *Tvāshṭra*, and *Sāvitra*, which were all baffled by *Yudhishṭhira*; then *Droṇa* invoked the *Aindra* and the *Prājāpatya* weapons, and *Yudhishṭhira* the *Māhendra*; then both employed the *Brāhma* weapon. *Droṇa* (with the *Vāyavya* weapon, abandoning *Yudhishṭhira*) & *Drupada's* division, who fled, but were rallied by *Arjuna* and *Bhīma*, who attacked *Droṇa* from two sides, and were followed by the *Kaikayas*, etc. (σ). The *Kurus* fled; *Droṇa* and *Duryodhana* in vain tried to rally them (VII, **157**). *Duryodhana* urged *Karṇa* to defeat the *Pāṇḍavas* (*Pāñcālas*, etc. (τ)); *Karṇa* vowed to slay *Arjuna*, etc. (υ), and was ridiculed by *Kṛpa* (φ), who said that *Dhṛshṭadyumna*, etc. (χ), were all fighting for the *Pāṇḍavas*; *Karṇa* vowed to cut off *Kṛpa's* tongue if *Kṛpa* addressed him again in the same strain, naming *Duryodhana*, etc. (ψ), as invincible, and saying that *Bhīshma*, etc. (ω), had been slain by the work of destiny (VII, **158**). *Açvatthāman* in rage rebuked *Karṇa* (αα); *Duryodhana* and *Kṛpa* pacified *Karṇa* and *Açvatthāman*. *Karṇa* & the *Pāṇḍavas* + *Pāñcālas*, who were vanquished and slaughtered. Urged by *Duryodhana*, *Açvatthāman*, etc. (ββ), & *Arjuna* in order to rescue *Karṇa*; *Arjuna* slew the steeds and driver of *Karṇa* and made him loose his bow; *Karṇa* took shelter in *Kṛpa's* chariot. *Duryodhana* (rallying the troops) & *Arjuna*; *Kṛpa* urged *Açvatthāman* to proceed against *Arjuna*. *Açvatthāman* made *Duryodhana* desist from an encounter with *Arjuna*; *Duryodhana* urged *Açvatthāman* to slay the *Pāñcālas* and the *Somakas* (VII, **159**). *Açvatthāman* said that he, etc. (γγ), could destroy the foe within the twinkling of an eye, and promised to fight with the *Pāñcālas*, etc. (δδ). *Açvatthāman* routed the *Pāñcālas*, etc. *Dhṛshṭadyumna* & *Açvatthāman*; Si. and Cā., etc., applauded them; *Açvatthāman* cut off the bow, the standard, the drivers, and the steeds of *Dhṛshṭadyumna*; the *Pāñcālas* and *Sṛñjayas* fled away (VII, **160**). *Yudhishṭhira* and *Bhīma* & *Açvatthāman* + *Duryodhana*; *Yudhishṭhira* slew the *Ambashṭhas*, etc. (δδ), *Bhīma* the *Abhīshāhas*, etc. (εε), *Arjuna* the *Yaudheyas*, etc. (ζζ). *Droṇa* employed the *Vāyavya* weapon; the *Pāñcālas* fled, but were rallied by *Bhīma* and *Arjuna*, who attacked *Droṇa* from both sides together with the *Sṛñjayas*, etc.; the *Kauravas* fled; *Duryodhana* and *Droṇa* endeavoured in vain to rally them (VII, **161**). *Sātyaki* (with white steeds of the *Sindhu* breed) + *Bhīmasena* & *Somadatta* (*Bāhlīka's* son), who was slain by *Sātyaki*. *Yudhishṭhira* + *Pāṇḍavas* + *Prabhadrakas* & *Droṇa*; *Droṇa* and *Yudhishṭhira* employed the *Vāyavya* weapon. *Kṛshṇa* dissuaded *Yudhishṭhira* from fighting with *Droṇa*; he should go to *Duryodhana*, *Arjuna*, and *Bhīma* (VII, **162**). *Droṇa*, etc. (ηη), afflicted one another and the troops; both armies were dejected. The remnants of the slaughtered army were once more disposed in array; *Droṇa* in the van, *Çalya* in the rear, *Açvatthāman* and *Çakuni* on the right and left flanks; *Duryodhana* protected all the troops. *Duryodhana* ordered his troops to take up lighted lamps and torches. D., Ṛ., G., D.-ṛ., V.-D., Aps., N., Y., U., and K. also took up lamps, and many lamps came from *Nārada* and *Parvata* for *Duryodhana's* sake. (Description); the glare reached the skies, and awakened by it, D., G., Y., Ṛ., etc., and Aps. came there (VII, **163**). *Duryodhana* appointed his brothers *Vikarṇa*, etc. (θθ), to protect *Droṇa* from the rear; *Kṛtavarman* should protect his right wheel, and *Çala* his left. The remnants of the *Trigartas* he placed in the van; especially *Droṇa* should be protected against *Dhṛshṭadyumna*; "*Karṇa* will vanquish *Arjuna*, *Bhīmasena*, and others." *Arjuna* & the *Kauravas*; *Açvatthāman* & the *Pāñcāla* ruler; *Droṇa* & the *Sṛñjayas* (VII, **164**). *Yudhishṭhira* commanded all his warriors to proceed against *Droṇa* alone. The *Pāñcālas* & the *Somakas* & *Droṇa*; *Kṛtavarman* & *Yudhishṭhira* (advancing against *Droṇa*); *Yuyudhāna* & *Bhūri*; *Karṇa* & *Sahadeva* (advancing in order to get at *Droṇa*); *Duryodhana* & *Bhīmasena*; *Çakuni* & *Nakula*; *Kṛpa* & *Çikhaṇḍin*; *Duḥçāsana* & *Prativindhya*; *Açvatthāman* & *Ghaṭotkaca*; *Vṛshasena* & *Drupada* (advancing against *Droṇa*); *Çalya* & *Virāṭa* (advancing in order to slay *Droṇa*); *Citrasena* & *Nakula's* son *Çatānīka* (advancing in order to slay *Droṇa*); *Alambusha* & *Arjuna*; *Dhṛshṭadyumna* & *Droṇa*, etc.; *Yudhishṭhira* retreated, and *Kṛtavarman* once more began to protect the wheel of *Droṇa's* chariot (VII, **165**). *Bhūri* & *Satyaki* who slew him. *Açvatthaman* & *Sātyaki*; *Ghaṭotkaca* & *Açvatthāman*, who swooned away, but then made *Ghaṭotkaca* insensible, who was borne away by his charioteer. *Bhīma* crushed the steeds, the charioteer, and the chariot of *Duryodhana*, who ascended *Nandaka's* chariot, and was regarded as slain, also by *Yudhishṭhira*, who rushed to *Bhīma*. The *Pāñcālas*, etc. (ιι), & *Droṇa* (VII, **166**). *Karṇa* & *Sahadeva*, who was worsted by *Karṇa*, who touched him with his bow and scoffed at him (κκ), but did not slay him, recollecting the words of *Kuntī*; *Sahadeva* ascended the chariot of the *Pāñcāla* prince *Janamejaya*. *Virāṭa* & *Çalya*, who deprived him of his chariot and then slew *Virāṭa's* brother *Çatānīka*; once more *Virāṭa* (ascending *Çatānīka's* chariot) & *Çalya*, who made him insensible; *Virāṭa* was carried away by his charioteer; the host fled away. *Alambusha* (with terrible-looking *Piçācas* of equine faces yoked to his chariot; description) & *Arjuna* (+ *Kṛshṇa*), who vanquished him; *Alambusha* fled away. *Arjuna* quickly proceeded towards *Droṇa*, slaughtering men, etc.; they all fled (VII, **167**). *Citrasena* (Dhārtarāshṭra) & *Nakula's* son *Çatānīka*, who vanquished him; *Citrasena* ascended

Kṛtavarman's chariot; *Vṛshasena* & *Drupada*, who swooned and was carried off by his charioteer; *Vṛshasena* caused a great slaughter among the *Pāñcālas* and the *Somakas*, and then proceeded to *Yudhishṭhira*. *Duḥçāsana* (Dhārtarāshṭra) & *Prativindhya*, who was vanquished by him and rescued by his brothers, ascended the chariot of *Sutasoma* and continued to fight *Duḥçāsana*, to whose assistance many warriors rushed, and a fierce battle ensued (VII, **168**). *Nakula* & *Çakuni*, who was carried away by his charioteer; *Nakula* proceeded towards *Droṇa*. *Çikhaṇḍin* (proceeding towards *Droṇa*) & *Kṛpa*; (*Çikhaṇḍin* was carried away by his charioteer); the *Pāñcālas* and *Somakas* surrounded him, and *Dhṛtarāshṭra's* sons surrounded *Droṇa*. A battle commenced once more (description) (VII, **169**). *Dhṛshṭadyumna* (+ the *Pāñcālas* and *Pāṇḍavas*) & *Droṇa*; D., G., and Dā. wished prosperity to *Droṇa*; *Karṇa*, etc. (λλ) (in order to rescue *Droṇa*) & *Dhṛshṭadyumna*; *Dhṛshṭadyumna* & *Drumasena*, whom he slew; the six chariot warriors & *Dhṛshṭadyumna*; *Sātyaki* (in order to rescue *Dhṛshṭadyumna*) & *Karṇa*; the sons of *Dhṛtarāshṭra*+*Karṇa*+ *Karṇa's* son *Vṛshasena* & *Dhṛshṭadyumna* + *Sātyaki*; *Gāṇḍīva* was heard, and the sound of *Arjuna's* chariot. *Karṇa* counselled *Duryodhana* to encompass and slay *Dhṛshṭadyumna* and *Sātyaki*; *Duryodhana* dispatched *Çakuni* with a large force (also *Duḥçāsana*, etc. (μμ)) against *Arjuna*, to slay *Arjuna*, etc. (νν); a great fight commenced. *Çakāuni*, etc., & *Sātyaki*; *Droṇa* & *Dhṛshṭadyumna* + the *Pāñcālas* (VII, **170**). *Sātyaki* was surrounded by many leaders of the *Kuru* army; *Duryodhana* & *Yuyudhāna*, who forced him to fly away (having mounted the chariot of *Kṛtavarman*), and routed the foes with whom he was engaged. *Arjuna* & *Çakuni* (+ his son *Ulūka*), whom he deprived of his chariot; *Çakuni* ascended the chariot of *Ulūka*; *Arjuna* slew the *Kuru* army. *Kṛshṇa* and *Arjuna* blew their conches. *Dhṛshṭadyumna* & *Droṇa*, whom *Dhṛshṭadyumna* checked and caused an immense carnage. *Dhṛshṭadyumna*, etc. (ξξ), blew their conches (VII, **171**). *Duryodhana* in anger addressed *Droṇa* and *Karṇa* (οο), who furiously attacked and routed the *Pāṇḍava* army; *Droṇa*, etc. (ππ); the *Pāṇḍava* host fled, throwing down their torches before the eyes of *Bhīmasena*, etc. (ρρ), pursued by *Droṇa* and *Karṇa*; *Arjuna* and *Kṛshṇa* rallied the retreating troops (σσ); a wild battle ensued between the *Kurus* (especially *Droṇa* and *Karṇa*) and the *Pāṇḍavas* (especially *Yudhishṭhira*) (description) (VII, **172**). *Karṇa* & *Dhṛshṭadyumna*, who was deprived of his chariot by him, but then slew his steeds and ascended the chariot of *Arjuna* and desired to proceed, but was stopped by *Yudhishṭhira*. *Karṇa* routed the *Pāñcālas*, who, with the *Somakas*, attacked *Karṇa*. Meanwhile *Karṇa's* charioteer had yoked other white steeds of the *Sindhu* breed to his chariot. The *Pāñcāla* host (and the *Sṛñjayas*) fled (description); others, only observed by *Droṇa*, fled away on all sides. *Yudhishṭhira* and *Arjuna* (and *Kṛshṇa*) conversed about *Karṇa*; *Arjuna* asked *Kṛshṇa* to proceed towards *Karṇa*. *Kṛshṇa* said that none except *Arjuna* and *Ghaṭotkaca* could encounter him; but *Arjuna* must not do it, as long as he had the lance given him by *Indra*; "but *Ghaṭotkaca* (who had celestial weapons, as also those used by Rā. and As.), would vanquish *Karṇa*." They prevailed upon *Ghaṭotkaca* to encounter *Karṇa* (ττ); "thou, O *Ghaṭotkaca*, *Sātyaki*, and *Bhīmasena* are the foremost among all our warriors; *Sātyaki* will protect thy rear." *Ghaṭotkaca* & *Karṇa* (VII, **173**). *Duryodhana* urged *Duḥçāsana* to protect *Karṇa* against *Ghaṭotkaca*. Meanwhile the Rā. *Jaṭāsura's* son *Alambusha* said to *Duryodhana* that he wished to slay the *Pāṇḍavas* in order to avenge his father, whom they had slain, performing some Rā.-slaying incantations. *Duryodhana* urged him to slay *Ghaṭotkaca*. *Alambusha* & *Ghaṭotkaca*; both resorted to their power of illusion (υυ); *Ghaṭotkaca* slew *Alambusha* and threw his head upon *Duryodhana's* chariot, promising that he should also see the slaughter of *Karṇa* and then his own. *Ghaṭotkaca* & *Karṇa* (VII, **174**). Requested by *Dhṛtarāshṭra*, *Sañjaya* described *Ghaṭotkaca's* person, armour, weapons, and chariot; then the encounter between *Karṇa* & *Ghaṭotkaca*, who employed Rā.-illusion, and even destroyed the celestial weapon of *Karṇa*; a *Vāyavya* weapon was employed by *Karṇa* to destroy clouds; *Ghaṭotkaca* was once seen on a chariot, created by illusion, yoked with a number of asses, looking like elephants, and having the faces of *Piçācas*; *Ghaṭotkaca* employed an *açani* of *Rudra's* workmanship, furnished with eight wheels; there appeared many Rā., Pç., and *Yātudhānas*, etc. (VII, **175**). Meanwhile, the Rā. *Alāyudha*, with many thousands of Rā., came to *Duryodhana*, and said that he wished to avenge his kinsmen *Baka* and *Kirmīra*, and his friend *Hiḍimba*, and the marriage of *Hiḍimbā*, by slaying all the sons of *Kuntī*, especially *Bhīma*, with *Kṛshṇa*, *Ghaṭotkaca*, etc. *Duryodhana* urged him to slay *Bhīma*. *Alāyudha's* chariot, steeds, weapons, etc., were pretty much as those of *Ghaṭotkaca's* (description) (VII, **176**). The *Kurus* with *Duryodhana* welcomed *Alāyudha*, having been (with *Droṇa*, etc. (φφ)), very anxious about *Karṇa*, who was engaged with *Ghaṭotkaca*. *Alāyudha* & *Ghaṭotkaca* (abandoning *Karṇa*); *Karṇa* & *Bhīmasena*; *Bhīma* (disregarding the advancing *Karṇa*) & *Alāyudha* (abandoning *Ghaṭotkaca*) + all the other Rā. (who fled away); the Rā. attacked the elephants, the *Pāñcālas*, and the *Sṛñjayas*. *Kṛshṇa* urged *Arjuna* to proceed in *Bhīma's* wake, and to let *Dhṛshṭadyumna*, etc. (χχ), proceed against *Karṇa*, *Nakula*, etc. (ψψ), slay the other Rā.; *Arjuna* himself should resist *Droṇa's* division; then *Kṛshṇa* dispatched *Ghaṭotkaca* to protect *Bhīmasena* (VII, **177**). *Ghaṭotkaca* (abandoning *Karṇa*) & *Alāyudha* (brother of *Baka*). Meanwhile, *Yuyudhāna*, etc. (ωω), & the Rā. of *Alāyudha*; *Arjuna* shot many *kshatriyas*, *Karṇa* many *Pāñcālas* headed by *Dhṛshṭadyumna*, *Çikhaṇḍin*, etc. *Bhīma* + *Nakula*, etc. (**ααα**) (having slain the Rā.) & *Karṇa*; the *Pāñcālas* & *Droṇa*; *Alāyudha* resorted to his power of illusion, and so did *Ghaṭotkaca*, who cut off the head of *Alāyudha* and threw it down before *Duryodhana*, who, with all his troops, became full of anxiety, while the *Pāñcālas* and *Pāṇḍavas* roared like lions (VII, **178**). *Karṇa* & the *Pāñcālas*, etc. (βββ); many of them entered the force of *Yudhishṭhira*. *Ghaṭotkaca* & *Karṇa*, who had his steeds and charioteer slain by *Ghaṭotkaca*, who then disappeared from view, and created a terrible illusion (description), which severely afflicted the *Kuru* host, which at last fled; *Karṇa* alone kept his ground, looked at by all the *Saindhavas* and *Bāhlikas*; *Karṇa's* steeds were again slain by *Ghaṭotkaca*, and his celestial weapon was baffled by *Ghaṭotkaca's* illusion. The *Kauravas* urged him to slay *Ghaṭotkaca* with the dart presented to him by *Indra*, without minding *Bhīma*, etc. (γγγ). When *Karṇa* held the dart in his hands *Ghaṭotkaca* began to fly away in fear, all creatures in the skies uttered loud cries, etc.; *Karṇa* hurled the dart, and *Ghaṭotkaca* was slain, and falling upon the *Kaurava* army with his gigantic body, he slew a full *akshauhiṇī*, desirous of benefiting the *Pāṇḍavas*. The *Kauravas* uttered loud shouts of joy; *Karṇa* ascended the chariot of *Duryodhana* and entered the *Kuru* host (VII, **179**). The *Pāṇḍavas* were filled with grief; only *Kṛshṇa* with transports of delight raised his warcry, embracing *Arjuna*, to whom he explained that he rejoiced because *Karṇa's* dart could not now kill *Arjuna*, having been employed against *Ghaṭotkaca*; he recited to *Arjuna* how he had gradually caused all the foes of the *Pāṇḍavas* to be slain (VII, **180**), which he explained more explicitly (δδδ) (VII, **181**). Requested by *Dhṛtarāshṭra* why *Karṇa* had not hurled the fatal dart at *Arjuna*, *Sañjaya* assigned *Kṛshṇa's* policy as the reason (εεε), though it had formed the subject of deliberation with *Duryodhana*, etc. (ζζζ), every night. *Sātyaki* asked *Kṛshṇa* why *Karṇa* had not hurled his dart at *Arjuna*; *Kṛshṇa* said that *Duḥçāsana*, etc., had frequently discussed this subject, and *Karṇa* had approved of it; but *Kṛshṇa* always used to stupefy him; *Kṛshṇa* had neither sleep nor joy in his heart, as long as he could not frustrate that instrument for killing *Arjuna* (VII, **182**). Concluding from *Karṇa's* not using the dart (εεε, ζζζ), *Dhṛtarāshṭra* attributed the ill success of the *Kurus* to Destiny, their own folly, and the policy of *Kṛshṇa*, and asked *Sañjaya* about the battle (ηηη). *Sañjaya* related: All the *Kauravas* uttered loud shouts and began to slay the *Pāṇḍava* troops. *Yudhishṭhira* told *Bhīmasena* to resist the *Dhārtarāshṭra* host, himself sitting down with tearful face; *Kṛshṇa* comforted him, but *Yudhishṭhira* remembered the many services *Ghaṭotkaca* had rendered them (θθθ); *Droṇa* and *Açvatthāman* were the real cause of *Abhimanyu's* slaughter, but it was *Jayadratha* who was slain; "*Droṇa* and *Karṇa* are the root of our woes"; therefore *Yudhishṭhira* will slay *Karṇa*, *Bhīmasena* being engaged with *Droṇa's* division. *Yudhishṭhira* quickly proceeded against *Karṇa*, followed by the *Pāñcālas*, etc. (ιιι). *Vyāsa* approached *Yudhishṭhira* and congratulated him upon *Karṇa's* having employed his dart against *Ghaṭotkaca*; "on the 5th day from hence the earth will be thine." Then he disappeared (VII, **183**).

Ghora[1], name of a weapon. § 563 (Bhagavadyānap.): V, **96**φ, 3491 (will be employed by Arjuna).

Ghora[2], son of Aṅgiras. § 747*b* (Suvarṇotpatti): XIII, **85**θ, 4148 (the fifth son of Aṅgiras, PCR. has Dhīra).

Ghora[3] = Çiva (1000 names[2]).

Ghoraghoratara = Çiva (1000 names[1]).

Ghoraka, pl. (°*āḥ*), a people. § 295 (Dyūtap.): II, **52**, 1870 (among the peoples who brought tribute to Yudhishṭhira).

Ghoratapas = Çiva (1000 names[2]).

Ghorātman = Kṛshṇa: XII, 1045.

Ghosha = Çiva (1000 names[1]).

Ghoshayātrā = Ghoshayātrāparvan. § 10 (Parvasaṅgr.): I, **2**, 324 (*parva*).

ghoshayātra ("the expedition to the cattle station," as related in Ghoshayātrāparvan): I, †165, 470; III, 14814, 14815, 14818; IV, 1430; V, †710, 1958, 4684, 5378; VII, 8435.

[Ghoshayātrāparvan] ("the expedition to the cattle station"), the 13rd of the minor parvans of Mhbhr. (cf. Ghoshayātrā). § 512: When the *Pāṇḍavas* had arrived at the lake (of *Dvaitavana*, Nīl.), and were dwelling in the woods visited by *veda*-knowing ascetics, there came to them a brahman, who afterwards went away to *Dhṛtarāshṭra* and told him how the *Pāṇḍavas* had become emaciated and reduced by wind and sun. *Dhṛtarāshṭra* was much afflicted, considering that *Yudhishṭhira*, who had formerly used to sleep on beds of *raṅku* skins and to be wakened by *sūtas* and *māgadhas*, now slept on the bare ground; he lamented the treatment he had permitted to be meted out to the *Pāṇḍavas*, and feared lest they would avenge themselves; *Arjuna*, he thought, would not have left heaven, where he received the celestial weapons, if it were not for this purpose. This *Çakuni* told to *Duryodhana*, who was sitting with *Karṇa*, and *Duryodhana* was filled with grief (III, **236**). *Çakuni* and *Karṇa* proposed to *Duryodhana* that they should go to *Dvaitavana* to exult over the *Pāṇḍavas* (III, **237**). *Duryodhana* gladly approved the proposal, but feared that he might not obtain the permission of *Dhṛtarāshṭra*, who thought that the *Pāṇḍavas* had become more powerful than before in consequence of their ascetic austerities. He asked them, with *Duḥçāsana*, to find out some skilful pretext. The next morning *Karṇa* and *Çakuni* agreed with *Duryodhana* that they should go there under the pretext of supervising their cattle stations (III, **238**). They then all saw *Dhṛtarāshṭra*. A cowherd, named *Samaṅga*, who had been instructed beforehand, came to the king and spoke to him of the cattle. *Karṇa* and *Çakuni* asked him to give permission to *Duryodhana* to go thither. *Dhṛtarāshṭra* suggested to send some faithful men, fearing some collision with the *Pāṇḍavas* if they were to go thither themselves; for though *Yudhishṭhira* would not suffer his wrath to be awakened, *Bhīma* and *Draupadī* were naturally passionate. *Çakuni* promised that they would not go to the spot where the *Pāṇḍavas* resided, and obtained the permission. *Duryodhana* then started with *Karṇa*, *Duḥçāsana*, *Çakuni*, etc., and ladies by the thousand, followed by the citizens and their wives, with 8,000 chariots, etc., and took up his quarters at the distance of a *gavyūti* from the lake of *Dvaitavana* (III, **239**). Having caused the calves to be marked, etc., *Duryodhana*, etc., began to sport and go a-hunting, and came to the lake. *Yudhishṭhira* was then, together with *Draupadī*, celebrating the diurnal *rājarshi* sacrifice according to the ceremonial used in the forest. When the attendants of *Duryodhana* came to the banks of the lake to construct pleasure-houses, they were forbidden to enter by a number of *Gandharvas*, who told them that the king of the *Gandharvas* had come from the abode of *Kubera*, with his followers and several hosts of *Apsarases*, etc., and when *Duryodhana* sent a number of his warriors, they also were prevailed upon by the *Gandharvas* to return (III, **240**). A battle ensued between the soldiers of *Duryodhana* and the *Gandharvas*, headed by their king *Citrasena*; the soldiers of *Duryodhana* fled, except *Karṇa*, who killed hundreds of *Gandharvas*. *Duryodhana*, *Çakuni*, *Duḥçāsana*, and *Vikarṇa* returned to assist *Karṇa*, and the battle was renewed. *Citrasena* made use of illusion; it seemed as if every warrior of the *Kuru* army were surrounded by ten *Gandharvas*. The entire army of *Duryodhana* again fled, except *Karṇa*. The *Gandharvas* then destroyed the chariot of *Karṇa*, who, mounting the chariot of *Vikarṇa*, was forced to drive away (III, **241**). *Duryodhana* refused to fly, but the *Gandharvas* destroyed his chariot and slew his charioteer and horses; thereupon *Citrasena* took him prisoner, and *Duḥçāsana*, who was seated on his chariot, and *Citrasena*, *Viviṃçati*, *Vinda*, and *Anuvinda*, and the royal ladies, were taken by other Gandharvas, [and *Durvishaha*, *Durmukha*, and *Durjaya*, v. 14924]. The flying soldiers and ministers of *Duryodhana* took refuge with *Yudhishṭhira* (III, **242**). *Yudhishṭhira*, saying that the honour of the family was being destroyed by the *Gandharvas'* seizing *Duryodhana*, etc., in their presence, prevailed upon his brother to rescue *Duryodhana*, etc. (v. 14947: "the liberation of a foe from distress is equal to the bestowal of a boon, sovereignty, and the birth of a son, all the three put together"), if possible, by conciliation or lightly skirmishing, otherwise by all means, *Yudhishṭhira* being prohibited from partaking in the combat by his sacrifice. *Arjuna* promised to rescue *Duryodhana* or kill the king of the *Gandharvas* (III, **243**). The four *Pāṇḍavas*, cased in mail and riding in chariots drawn by fleet horses, encountered the *Gandharvas*; as these would not set *Duryodhana*, etc., free, as requested by *Arjuna*, a fierce battle ensued (III, **244**). The *Gandharvas*, in vain, attempted to break the chariots of the *Pāṇḍavas*; especially *Arjuna*, by means of his *Āgneya* weapon, sent millions of them to the abode of *Yama*. The *Gandharvas* then rose up to the skies, taking the *Dhārtarāshṭras* with them, and showering maces, darts, etc., upon *Arjuna*, who killed them with his weapons *Sthūlākarṇa* (B. Sthūṇākarṇa), *Indrajāla*, *Saura*, *Āgneya*, and *Saumya*. At last *Citrasena* rushed at *Arjuna*, armed with a mace of iron; as *Arjuna* cut that mace in seven pieces with his arrows, *Citrasena*, by means of his science, concealed himself from the view of *Arjuna*, and thus continued to fight with him; but *Arjuna* destroyed his power of concealing himself by shooting at him with his celestial arms guided by the sound (*çabdavedhaṃ samāçritya*). Then *Citrasena* showed himself to *Arjuna*, reminding him of his being his friend, and there was put an end to the battle (III, **245**). *Citrasena* related to *Arjuna* that, staying in his abode, he had become acquainted with the purpose of *Duryodhana*, etc., and had been requested by *Indra* to bring *Duryodhana* thither in chains together with his counsellors. *Arjuna* entreated him to set *Duryodhana* free, but, at the request of *Citrasena*, they left it to be decided by *Yudhishṭhira*; *Yudhishṭhira* then liberated all the *Kauravas*. The *Gandharvas* went away with the *Apsarases*, and *Indra* revived the slain *Gandharvas* by sprinkling *amṛta* upon them. Friendly admonished by *Yudhishṭhira*, *Duryodhana*, overwhelmed with shame, returned to his capital (III, **246**). When *Duryodhana*, afflicted with grief, was approaching *Hāstinapura* with his army, *Karṇa* congratulated him on the honourable victory over the *Gandharvas* (III, **247**). *Duryodhana* told *Karṇa* that, as the *Gandharvas* had resorted to illusion and ascended the skies, he had been captured with his army, and that it was the *Pāṇḍavas* who had vanquished the *Gandharvas* (III, **248**). *Duryodhana* continued his narrative and declared that he would stay there abstaining from food, and that the others, headed by *Duḥçāsana*, should go to *Hāstinapura*. He then offered the royal power to *Duḥçāsana*. *Duḥçāsana*, his voice choked in tears, refused to accept it. *Karṇa* reproached them for weeping thus, and declared that the *Pāṇḍavas*, who resided in the dominions of *Duryodhana* and enjoyed happiness under his protection, only did their duty in liberating him (III, **249**). *Karṇa* continued explaining his opinion, that those who resided in the king's realm should always exert themselves to the best of their ability for the king; if the *Pāṇḍavas* had not followed *Duryodhana* to the battle it would have been an improper act on their part. *Duryodhana*, firmly resolved to leave the world, desired not to rise from where he sat (III, **250**). *Çakuni* reproached *Duryodhana* for his foolish despair, saying that he ought rather to reward the *Pāṇḍavas* by granting them their paternal kingdom. *Duryodhana* embraced *Duḥçāsana*, but did not waver from his purpose; he spread *kuça* grass on the earth, etc., and began to pray and worship mentally.—§ 513: The *Daiteyas* and *Dānavas* who had formerly been vanquished by the gods and were dwelling in *Pātāla*, having ascertained *Duryodhana's* purpose, commenced a sacrifice with formulas, revealed by *Bṛhaspati* and *Uçanas*, according to the rites indicated in the *Atharvaveda* and the *Upanishad*, assisted by *brahmans* of rigid vows, well versed in the *Vedas* and the *Vedāṅgas*. After these rites were ended a sorceress (*kṛtyā*) arose, whom the *Daityas* caused to bring *Duryodhana* to them in the night (III, **251**). The *Dānavas* said to him: "Do not do such a rash act as the vow of starvation. The suicide ever sinks into hell (*adho yāti*), and is blamed . . . In days of old we had obtained thee by ascetic austerities from *Maheçvara*; the upper part of thy body is wholly made of *vajras*, and is, therefore, invulnerable to weapons of every description; the lower part of thy body was made of flowers by *Devī* herself . . . Brave *kshatriyas*, headed by *Bhagadatta*, will slay thy foes . . . In order to aid thee many *Dānavas* (v. 15172: *Daityas* and *Rakshases*) have been born on earth. Other *Asuras* will also possess *Bhīshma*, *Droṇa*, *Kṛpa*, and others; possessed by those *Asuras* these heroes will abandon their kindness and fight with thy foes . . . We have already settled the means of slaying *Arjuna*; the slain *Naraka* has assumed the form of *Karṇa*; recollecting his former hostility he will encounter both *Keçava* (i.e. Kṛshṇa) and *Arjuna*, and vanquish *Arjuna* in battle. *Indra* in disguise will deprive *Karṇa* of his earrings and coat of mail. We also have appointed innumerable *Daityas* and *Rākshasas*, the so-called *Saṃçaptakas*, who will slay *Arjuna* . . . Thou art ever our refuge, as the *Pāṇḍavas* are the refuge of the gods." Then the *Dānavas* embraced and cheered him, and that very goddess (*kṛtyā*) carried him back to the spot where he had sat down intent upon putting an end to his life, and there she vanished. Now *Duryodhana* considered all as a dream, and thought he should defeat the *Pāṇḍavas* in battle. And also *Karṇa*, being possessed by the soul of *Naraka*, and the *Saṃçaptakas*, possessed by the *Rākshasas*, were desirous of slaying *Arjuna*; and *Bhīshma*, *Droṇa*, *Kṛpa*, etc., influenced by the *Dānavas*, were not so affectionate towards the *Pāṇḍavas* as they had been. *Duryodhana* did not tell anyone of this.—§ 514: When the night had passed away *Karṇa* again exhorted *Duryodhana*, and promised to slay *Arjuna* in battle. *Duryodhana* arose and arranged his army, and went to *Hāstinapura*, accompanied by *Karṇa*, *Çakuni*, his brothers headed by *Duḥçāsana* and *Bhūriçravas*, and *Somadatta*, and *Bāhlīka* (III, **252**).—§ 515: *Karṇadigvijaya* (q.v.).—§ 516: *Duryodhanayajña* (q.v.).—§ 517: Hearing the vow of *Karṇa*, *Yudhishṭhira*, filled with anxiety, made up his mind to abandon *Dvaitavana*. *Duryodhana* with his brothers, and *Bhīshma*, *Droṇa*, *Kṛpa*, and *Karṇa* ruled the earth justly and worshipped the brahmans by sacrifices and profuse gifts (III, **257**).

Ghrāṇaçravas, a warrior of Skanda. § 615*u* (Skanda): IX, **45**η, 2559.

Ghṛtācī, an Apsaras, wife of Pramati. § 19 (Bhṛgu): I, **5**, 871 (wife of Pramati and mother of Ruru). — § 21 (Pramadvarā): I, **8**, 940 (do.). — § 135 (Çakuntalop.): I, **74**, 3055 (among the six principal Apsarases). — § 191 (Arjuna): I, **123**, 4821 (among the Apsarases who sang at the birth of Arjuna).—§ 200 (Droṇa): I, **130**, 5103 (when Bharadvāja saw *Gh.* his seed issued, from that seed Droṇa was born).—§ 217 (Caitrarathap.): I, **166**, 6329 (do.).—§ 269 (Vaiçravaṇasabhāv.): II, **10**, 392 (among the Apsarases in the palace of Kubera).—§ 336 (Indralokābh.): III, **43***a*, 1784 (among the Apsarases who danced in the palace of Indra).—§ 615*aa* (Çrutāvatī): IX, **48**, 2826 (*Apsarasaṃ*, when Bharadvāja saw *Gh.* his seed issued, from that seed Çrutāvatī was born).—§ 712 (Çukotpatti): XII, **325**, 12188 (*Apsarasaṃ*), 12190, 12193 (*Gh.* transformed herself into a she-parrot (*çukī*); when Vyāsa saw her his seed issued, from that seed Çuka was born). — § 731*b* (Ashṭāvakra-Diksaṃv.): XIII, **19**β, 1424 (among the Apsarases who danced in the palace of Kubera).—§ 736*b* (Vītahavyop.): XIII, **30**, 2004 (wife of Pramati and mother of Ruru).—§ 775 (Ānuçāsanik.): XIII, **166**β, 7641 (enumeration).

Ghṛtapāḥ (pl.), a class of ṛshis. § 656 (Khaḍgotpattik.): XII, **166**β, 6143.

Ghṛtārcis = Kṛshṇa (Vishṇu): XII, 1505, 13244.

Ghṛtavatī, a river. § 574 (Jambūkh.): VI, **9**λ, 331 (only B., C. has *Dhṛtavatī*).

Ghūrṇiā, the maidservant of Devayānī. § 146 (Devayānī): I, **78**, 3302, 3303, 3304.

Ghushya = Çiva (1000 names[1]).

girayaḥ (pl.) ("the mountains," personif.). § 615*u* (Skanda): IX, **45**, 2556 (gave companions to Skanda).

Giriça[1] = Çiva, q.v.

Giriça[2], name of a bow. § 592 (Saṃçaptakavadhap.): VII, **23**o, 1041 (among the bows held by the five Draupadeyas).

Girīça = Çiva, q.v.

Girigahvara, pl. (°*āḥ*), a people. § 574 (Jambūkh.): VI, **9**o, 375 (in the north-east).

Girika = Çiva (1000 names[1]).

Girikā, the wife of Vasu Uparicara. § 75 (Vasu): I, **63**, 2371 (daughter of the mountain Kolāhala and the river Çuktimatī).—§ 76 (Matsya): I, **63**, 2373, 2377, 2384.

Girikapriya = Çiva (1000 names[1]).

Girīṇāṃ çikharāṇi = Çiva (1000 names[1]).

Girirāj = Himavat: VI, 3419 (?).

Girirāja = Himavat: VIII, †4321 (°*vāsinaṃ*, i.e. the Kulinda prince).

Giriruha = Çiva (1000 names[2]).

Girisādhana = Çiva (1000 names[2]).

Girisutā = Umā: XIII, 6368.

Girivarātmajā = Umā: IX, 2488.

Girivraja, the capital of the Māgadhas. § 11 (Parvasaṅgr.): I, **2**, 409.—§ 273 (Rājasūyārambhap.): II, **14**, 627 (Jarāsandha confined the defeated kings in his capital *G.*).—§ 275 (do.): II, **19**, 762 (from *G.* Jarāsandha threw a mace against Mathurā).—§ 277 (Jarāsandhavadhap.): II, **21**, 800 (protected by five mountains), 810; **24**, 937, 951 (Kṛshṇa, Arjuna, and Bhīma came to *G.*, Bhīma slew Jarāsandha, and the confined kings were liberated).—§ 280 (Bhīmasena): II, **30**, 1091 (at *G.* Bhīma vanquished the son of Jarāsandha).—§ 589 (Droṇābhishekap.): VII, **4**β, 120 (? °*gatāç cāpi Nagnajitpramukhā nṛpāḥ*, vanquished by Karṇa).—§ 717*b* (Nārāyaṇīya): XII, **340**, 12961 (the capital of Jarāsandha).—§ 723 (Ānuçāsanik.): XIII, **6**a, 333 (there Dhundhumāra fell asleep). Cf. Rājagṛha.

Girivrajeçvara ("the Lord of Girivraja") = Daṇḍadhāra: VIII, †696.

Girivṛkshālaya = Çiva (1000 names[1]).

Gītapriyā, a mātṛ. § 615*u* (Skanda): IX, **46**θ, 2625.

Gītavādanakapriya = Çiva (1000 names[1]).

Gītavāditraçālin = Çiva (1000 names[1]).

Gītavāditratattvajña = Çiva (1000 names[1]).

***go**, pl. (°*āvaḥ*) ("kine"). § 105 (Aṃçāvat.): I, **65**, 2560 (the offspring of Kapilā).—§ 127 (do.): I, **66**, 2632 (the offspring of Rohiṇī). Cf. Surabhi—**go**[2] (sg.), v. Gonāman.

Gocara = Çiva (1000 names[2]).

Gocarmavasana = Çiva (1000 names[2]).

Goçabdātmaja ("the son of Aditi") = Indra: VIII, †4668.

Goçṛṅga, a mountain. § 281 (Sahadeva): II, **31**, 1109 (*parvataṃ*, in the south, conquered by Sahadeva on his digvijaya).

Godāvarī, a river. § 268 (Varuṇasabhāv.): II, **9**, 372 (among the rivers present in the palace of Varuṇa).—§ 370 (Tīrthayātrāp.): III, **85**, 8176 (*Siddhasevitāṃ*, a tīrtha).—§ 377 (Dhaumyatīrthak.): III, **88**, 8327 (in the south).—§ 400 (Tīrthayātrāp.): III, **118**, †10216 (visited by Yudhishṭhira, falls into the ocean).—§ 459 (Mārkaṇḍeyas.): III, **188**a, 12908 (among the rivers seen by Mārkaṇḍeya in the stomach of Nārāyaṇa).—§ 494 (Āṅgirasa): III, **222**, 14231 (enumeration of rivers who are mothers of fires).—§ 528 (Rāvaṇagamana): III, **277**, 15985 (where Rāma Dāçarathi lived for a time).—§ 574 (Jambūkh.): VI, **9**λ, 322 (among the rivers of Bhāratavarsha).—§ 775 (Ānuçāsanik.): XIII, **166**a, 7648 (enumeration).

Godha, pl. (°*āḥ*), a people. § 574 (Jambūkh.): VI, **9**μ, 349 (only B., C. has *Sodhāḥ*).

godharma ("rule of cattle"). § 170 (Dīrghatamas): I, **104**, 4195 (Dīrghatamas learnt from Saurabheya the godharma (i.e. *prakāçamaithunaṃ*, Nīl.) and practised it).

Goghnata, pl. (°*āḥ*), a people. § 574 (Jambūkh.): VI, **9**μ, 351 (only C., B. has *Gomantāḥ*).

Gograhaṇa ("the robbing of the kine"). § 10 (Parvasaṅgr.): I, **2**, 328 (*parva*, i.e. Goharaṇaparvan).

Goharaṇaparvan ("the section relating to the robbing of the kine of Virāṭa," the 55th of the minor parvans of Mhbhr.; cf. Gograhaṇa). § 552: Meanwhile the spies of Duryodhana returned to Hāstinapura and informed Duryodhana, who was sitting with Droṇa, Karṇa, Kṛpa, Bhīshma, his brothers, and the Trigartas, that they had not found out the Pāṇḍavas, but that Kīcaka (*b*) had been slain (IV, **25**). Kārṇa and Duḥçāsana proposed that the other spies should be sent (IV, **26**). Droṇa said: "People like the Pāṇḍavas never perish, let the abode which the Pāṇḍavas are to occupy now be settled" (IV, **27**). Bhīshma applauded Droṇa (IV, **28**). Kṛpa recommended precautions (IV, **29**). The Trigarta king, Suçarman, supported by Karṇa, proposed to invade the city of Virāṭa and to rob his kine and wealth, and thus to take revenge for the invasions of the Matsyas headed by Kīcaka. Duryodhana caused Duḥçāsana to array their forces. Suçarman set out towards the south-east on the seventh day of the dark fortnight, and the Kauravas on the eighth day (IV, **30**). After Kīcaka had been slain, Virāṭa began to rest his hopes on the Pāṇḍavas. His brothers, Çatānīka and Madirāksha, and the king himself, and Sūryadatta and Çaṅkha, the eldest son of Virāṭa, put on their coats of mail. Virāṭa also caused Çatānīka to order chariots for Kaṅka, Vallava, Tantripāla, and Dāmagranthi (i.e. Yudhishṭhira, Bhīmasena, Nakula, and Sahadeva in disguise) (IV, **31**). The Matsyas overtook the Trigartas shortly before sunset. Çatānīka and Viçālāksha penetrated into the heart of the Trigarta host. Virāṭa, with Sūryadatta in his van and Madirāksha in his rear, began a single combat from chariots against Suçarman (IV, **32**). The night interrupted the battle for a while, but it began once more when the moon arose. Suçarman and his younger brother made Virāṭa prisoner, and the Matsyas began to fly; Bhīma would uproot a tree, but was prevented by Yudhishṭhira, lest the people should recognize them; then Bhīma, with Nakula and Sahadeva as protectors of his wheels, rushed against Suçarman, and the Matsya warriors, Virāṭa's son, and Yudhishṭhira, etc., followed him; the charioteer of Suçarman was dragged to the ground. Madirāçva came to the aid of Bhīma. Virāṭa leapt down from the chariot of Suçarman, seizing the mace of the latter, and ran in pursuit of him; Suçarman was seized by Bhīma, but set free by Yudhishṭhira (IV, **33**). The Pāṇḍavas passed the night on the field of battle honoured by Virāṭa. As proposed by Yudhishṭhira, Virāṭa ordered messengers to proclaim the victory in the city. The messengers repaired to the city that very night, and at sunrise they proclaimed the victory at the city gates (IV, **34**). Meanwhile Duryodhana, etc. (*a*), invaded the Matsya country and took away the kine. Hearing this, Bhūmiñjaya (i.e. Uttara), who had been left by the king in the empty city (IV, **35**), and whose charioteer had been slain in a great battle, followed the advice of Kṛshṇa (who had been instigated by Arjuna) and sent Uttarā (IV, **36**), who prevailed upon Bṛhannalā (= Arjuna in disguise) to become the charioteer of Uttara. Uttarā and her maidens asked Arjuna to bring fine clothes for their dolls when he had vanquished the Kurus (IV, **37**). Seeing the host of the Kurus, Uttara became agitated with fear and jumped down from the chariot and began to flee, but was seized by Arjuna and made to hold the reins, while Arjuna had to fight (IV, **38**). Bhīshma, Droṇa, etc., suspected the comer to be Arjuna, and many portents were explained by Droṇa in that sense. Karṇa blamed Droṇa, and Duryodhana said that if it were Arjuna the Pāṇḍavas must go into exile for twelve more years (IV, **39**). Having reached the *çamī* tree, Arjuna ordered Uttara to fetch the weapons of the Pāṇḍavas, including Gāṇḍīva, which were deposited there (IV, **40**). Believing that a corpse had been tied up in the tree, Uttara refused, but as Arjuna said: "There are only bows in that tree and no corpse," he climbed up and unwrapped and untied the bows (IV, **41**). Arjuna explained to him to whom the different bows belonged, first mentioning the Gāṇḍiva (*c*), which is honoured by the gods, the Dānavas, and the Gandharvas (IV, **42–43**). He then revealed to Uttara that they were the Pāṇḍavas and confirmed it by telling his ten names (*β*) (IV, **44**). Arjuna took off the bracelets from his arms, etc., recalled to his mind all his weapons, and twanged the Gāṇḍīva with a dreadful sound, whence the Kurus knew that he was Arjuna, then he comforted Uttara by mentioning his former exploits (*γ*) and his preceptors in arms (*δ*) (IV, **45**). Having taken down the banner with the figure of a lion he set up his own flagstaff bearing the figure of an ape with a lion's tail, which was a celestial illusion (*māyā*) contrived by Viçvakarman himself, for as soon as he thought of the gift of Agni, Agni ordered the superhuman creatures to take their usual place on that banner, which then fell down from the air on his chariot (read *rathe* with B.). Droṇa concluded from various omens that it was Arjuna (IV, **46**). Duryodhana repeated to Bhīshma, Droṇa, and Kṛpa, his and Karṇa's opinion, that Arjuna must have broken his pledge, and asked Bhīshma to calculate the time. Karṇa blamed Droṇa for praising Arjuna (IV, **47**), and declared that he would throw Arjuna down from his chariot that very day (IV, **48**). Kṛpa blamed Karṇa and warned him from fighting alone with Arjuna, mentioning his exploits (*ε*); they ought all to fight with Arjuna and not Karṇa alone (IV, **49**). Açvatthāman blamed Karṇa for his vain boast and declared that he would not fight with Arjuna (IV, **50**). Bhīshma tried to mediate between Açvatthāman and Kṛpa on one side and Karṇa on the other side; he was of opinion that fight they must, and therefore this was not the time for quarrel. "The Brāhmāstra and the Vedas are never to be seen combined anywhere else than in Droṇa (and Açvatthāman)." He was supported by Açvatthāman and Duryodhana. Droṇa said: "Let such arrangements be made that Arjuna may not be able to approach Duryodhana in battle, and that Duryodhana may not be captured by the foe" (IV, **51**). Having calculated the time ("an excess of five months and twelve nights in thirteen years"), Bhīshma declared that the Pāṇḍavas had not broken the pledge. Duryodhana said: "I will not give back the kingdom to the Pāṇḍavas." Bhīshma proposed that Duryodhana should proceed towards the capital with one-fourth of the army, and that one-fourth should escort the kine, while he, Droṇa, Karṇa, Açvatthāman, and Kṛpa should withstand the foes. This proposal was accepted; Bhīshma placed Droṇa in the centre, Açvatthāman on the left wing, Kṛpa on the right wing, and Karṇa in the van, and would himself stand in the rear (IV, **52**). Droṇa recognized the top of Arjuna's banner, etc. Arjuna directed Uttara to the spot where Duryodhana was; the soldiers became so confounded that they could not even fly, and the kine turned back along the southern road (IV, **53**). As Arjuna was advancing towards Duryodhana the Kurus fell upon him, especially Karṇa, who was supported by Citrasena, Saṅgrāmajit (the brother of Karṇa), Çatrusaha, Jaya, and Vikarṇa; Vikarṇa fled; Çatruntapa and many others were slain by Arjuna, so also Saṅgrāmajit; at last Karṇa took to flight (IV, **54**). Duryodhana, etc., attacked Arjuna; Arjuna shot at Droṇa, Duḥsaha, Açvatthāman, Duḥçāsana, and Kṛpa, and wounded Bhīshma, Duryodhana, and Karṇa. Then Arjuna described to Uttara the banners, etc., of Kṛpa, Droṇa, Açvatthāman, Duryodhana, Karṇa, and Bhīshma (IV, **55**). Indra, the gods, the Viçvas, the Açvins, the Maruts, the Yakshas, the Gandharvas, the Mahoragas, the Nāgas, the Rākshasas, the serpents, the Pitṛs, and the maharshis came to see the combat, likewise, sitting on the chariot of Indra, king Vasumanas, etc. (*ζ*); also Agni, Çiva, Soma, Varuṇa, Prajāpati, Dhātṛ, Vidhātṛ, Kubera, Yama, Alambusha, Ugrasena, Tumburu, etc., came there (IV, **56**). Arjuna attacked Kṛpa, announced his name, and blew the Devadatta; at last Kṛpa was led away by his soldiers (IV, **57**). Droṇa attacked Arjuna; Arjuna said: "I will not strike thee unless thou strikest me first"; with his own weapons Arjuna baffled the Aindra, Vāyavya, and Āgneya weapons, which were shot by Droṇa; a voice was heard in the sky applauding Droṇa; then Açvatthāman attacked Arjuna, which gave Droṇa an opportunity to leave the field (IV, **58**). Açvatthāman cut off the string of the Gāṇḍīva and was applauded by the gods, and by Droṇa, Bhīshma, Karṇa, and Kṛpa. Arjuna attached a fresh string to the Gāṇḍīva. As Açvatthāman's arrows became exhausted Karṇa attacked Arjuna (IV, **59**), who challenged him to a single combat and rebuked him, because he had fled after the slaughter of his younger brother. At last Karṇa, wounded, fled in a northern direction (IV, **60**). Then Arjuna ordered Uttara to take him to Bhīshma; Uttara became afraid and was comforted by Arjuna (*d*), who enumerated some of his exploits and weapons. Duḥçāsana, Vikarṇa, Duḥsaha, and Viviṃçati rushed towards Arjuna; Duḥçāsana fled; Vikarṇa fell down; Duḥsaha and Viviṃçati were taken away by their warriors (IV, **61**). At last the Kauravas fled (IV, **62**); Duryodhana, Karṇa, and Duḥçāsana attempted in vain to defeat Arjuna (IV, **63**). Then Bhīshma and Arjuna fought with the Prājāpatya, Aindra, Āgneya, Raudra, Kaubera, Vāruṇa, Yāmya, and Vāyavya weapons; the Gandharva Citrasena showed the two combatants to Indra, who showered celestial flowers down upon them;

at last Bhīshma, wounded, lost consciousness and was led away by his charioteer (IV, **64**). Duryodhana and then Vikarṇa attacked Arjuna; Vikarṇa ran back and ascended the chariot of Viviṃçati; Duryodhana was wounded and fled, and so did all the warriors (IV, **65**). Stung by the censure of Arjuna, Duryodhana returned, and Karṇa, Bhīshma, Droṇa, Kṛpa, Viviṃçati, and Duḥçāsana rushed forwards to protect Duryodhana. Arjuna employed the weapon Sammohana which he had obtained from Indra, and blew his conch so that the Kurus were deprived of their senses. Then he caused Uttara to take away the white garments of Droṇa and Kṛpa, the yellow ones of Karṇa, and the blue ones of Duryodhana and Açvatthāman, but not those of Bhīshma, because he had not been stupefied. Arjuna wounded Bhīshma, who told Duryodhana to go back to his city, which they all did; Arjuna followed them for a while and worshipped Bhīshma, Droṇa, Açvatthāman, and Kṛpa; then he, with an arrow, broke the crown of Duryodhana and blew the Devadatta. Then he ordered Uttara to turn back. The gods returned to their respective abodes (IV, **66**). A large number of Kuru soldiers issuing from the forest stood before Arjuna with joined palms and were spared. Arjuna said to Uttara: "Do not eulogize the Pāṇḍavas, but say that the feat is thy own." Then he replaced the weapons on the *çamī* tree; the monkey ascended to the sky, together with the other creatures on the flagstaff, the illusion (*māyā*) melted away, and Uttara's own banner was replaced upon the chariot. Arjuna entered the city in the guise of Bṛhannalā, having sent the cowherds to announce the victory (IV, **67**). Virāṭa entered his city, followed by the four Pāṇḍavas, and dispatched an army to protect Uttara, though Yudhishṭhira said that, protected by Bṛhannalā, he was able to vanquish even the gods, the Asuras, the Siddhas, and the Yakshas. Meanwhile the messengers of Uttara came and Virāṭa ordered the highways to be decorated, etc., and began to play at dice with Yudhishṭhira, who again repeatedly praised Bṛhannalā. Virāṭa struck Yudhishṭhira with a die, but the blood was prevented from falling on the ground and was washed away by Kṛshṇā, who also, at the injunction of Yudhishṭhira, let Uttara enter alone, that Bṛhannalā should not see him bleeding. Uttara prevailed upon Virāṭa to ask Yudhishṭhira's pardon. When the bleeding had stopped, Bṛhannalā entered (IV, **68**). Uttara said: "All this has been accomplished by a *devaputra* ('son of a deity') who then disappeared." Arjuna gave to Uttarā the garments he had brought (IV, **69**).

Gohita = Vishṇu (1000 names).

Gokarṇa[1], name of a tīrtha belonging to Çiva. § 48 (Çesha): I, **36**, 1567 (there Çesha practised austerities).—§ 250 (Arjunavanavāsap.): I, **217**, 7884 (visited by Arjuna on his tīrthayātrā). § 370 (Tīrthayātrāp.): III, **85**, 8166 (*samudra-madhye*, there Brahmán, etc., worship Umāpati, i.e. Çiva).—§ 377 (Dhaumyatīrthak.): III, **88**, 8341 (in the south).—§ 528 (Rāvaṇagamana): III, **277**, 15999 (the abode of Marīca).—§ 574 (Jambūkh.): VI, **6**θ, 246 (? mentioned among the mountains north of Bhāratavarsha, C. *G°e ca tapodhanāḥ*, B. *G°ṃ ca tapovanaṃ*).—§ 594 (Mṛtyu): VII, **54**, 2098 (visited by Mṛtyu).—§ 730 (Ānuçāsanik.): XIII, **18**u, 1301 (there Cāruçīrsha worshipped Çiva).—§ 785 (Anugītāp.): XIV, **83**, 2478 (the sacrificial horse proceeded from *G.* to Prabhāsa).

Gokarṇa[2] = Çiva (1000 names[1]).

Gokarṇā, a mātṛ. § 615*u* (Skanda): IX, **46**θ, 2643.

Gokarṇāsanamardana = Arjuna: VIII, †4669 (Gokarṇāsana = Çiva?, differently Nīl. and PCR.).

Gokula, name of a place (?). § 604 (Karṇap.): VIII, **5**ζ, 128 (*°e nityasaṃvṛddhāḥ*, i.e. the Nārāyaṇas, PCR.).

***golāṅgūla**, pl. (*°āḥ*), a kind of monkey. § 127 (Aṃçāvat.): I, **66**, 2628 (the offspring of Harī).

Goloka ("the world of kine"). [§ 615*ff* (Asita Devala): IX, **50**, 2894 (*gavāṃ lokaṃ*).]—§ 717*b* (Nārāyaṇīya): XII, **343**, 13298 (*sanātanaṃ*); **348**θθ, 13502 (the upper lip of Nārāyaṇa).—§ 746 (Ānuçāsanik.): XIII, **72** [3545 (*gavāṃ lokaṃ*)], 3547 (*°vāsināṃ*); [**73**, †3566 (*lokaṃ gavāṃ*), †3568 (*gavāṃ lokaṃ*)]; **83**, [3891 (*gavāṃ loke*)], 3915, 3922.—§ 752 (do.): XIII, **96**, 4649.—[§ 757*m* (Hastikūṭa)]: *Gautama* said: Next [to *Prājāpatyā(ḥ) lokāḥ*] blaze eternal redolent regions, free from passion and sorrow, the world of kine, difficult to attain. *Dhṛtarāshṭra* said: He who possessing 1,000 kine gives away 100 every year, etc., the brahmans who grow old practising brahmacarya, who obey the declarations of the Vedas (*brāhmīṃ vācaṃ*), and, endued with intelligence, betake themselves to tīrthayātrās, dwell here in felicity; likewise those who repair to Prabhāsa, etc. (**a**): XIII, **102**, 4884 (*gavāṃ loke*).—[§ 758 (Ānuçāsanik.): XIII, **105**, 4910 (*gavāṃ lokaṃ*).]

Gomahishadā, a mātṛ. § 615*u* (Skanda): IX, **46**θ, 2646.

Gomanda, v. Gomanta[2].

Gomanta[1], a mountain. § 273 (Rājasūyārambhap.): II, **14**, 618 (near Dvārakā?).

Gomanta[2], a mountain on Krauñcadvīpa. § 575 (Bhūmip.): VI, **12**, 449 (so B., C. has *Gomandaḥ*).

Gomanta, pl. (*°āḥ*), a people. § 574 (Jambūkh.): VI, **9**μ, 351 (only B., C. has *Goghnatāḥ*).

Gomārga = Çiva (1000 names[1]).

Gomatī, a river. § 221*b* (Gaṅgā): I, **170**, 6455.—§ 268 (Varuṇasabhāv.): II, **9**, 375 (among the rivers present in the palace of Varuṇa).—§ 370 (Tīrthayātrāp.): III, **84**, 8051 (*Rāmatīrthe . . . G°yāṃ*), 8059 (*Mārkaṇḍeyasya . . . tīrthaṃ . . . G°-Gaṅgayoç caiva saṅgame*).—§ 377 (Dhaumyatīrthak.): III, **87**, 8303 (in the east).—§ 379 (Tīrthayātrāp.): III, **95**, 8511 (visited by Yudhishṭhira, etc., on his tīrthayātrā).—§ 490 (Āṅgirasa): III, **219**, 14148 (*nadī*, the wife of the fire Viçvabhuj).—§ 543 (Rāmābhisheka): III, **291**, 16600 (Rāma Dāçarathi performed ten horse-sacrifices on the banks of the *G.*).—§ 551 (Kīcakavadhap.): IV, **17**, 513 (*sa lateva mahāçalaṃ phullaṃ G°tīrajaṃ purishujati*).—§ 574 (Jambūkh.): VI, **9**λ, 325 (among the rivers of Bhāratavarsha).—§ 718*b* (Uñchavṛttyup.): XII, **356**, 13801 (*Naimishe Gomatītīre tatra Nāgāhvayaṃ puraṃ*); **358**, 13833; **360**, 13861; **362**, 13887.—§ 736*b* (Vītahavyop.): XIII, **30**, 1957 (the kingdom of Divodāsa stretched from the northern bank of the Gaṅgā to the southern bank of the *G.*).—§ 757*m* (Goloka): XIII, **102***a*, 4889 (a tīrtha).—§ 768*b* (Umā-Maheçvarasaṃv.): XIII, **146**δ, 6764.

Gomukha[1], a king. § 130 (Aṃçāvat.): I, **67**, 2099 (among the kings who were incarnations of the Krodhavaçagaṇa).

Gomukha[2], the son of Mātali. § 564 (Mātalīyop.): V, **100**, 3574.

Gonāman. § 268 (Varuṇasabhāv.): II, **9**, 381 (*Gonāmnā Pushkareṇa ca*, ? in the palace of Varuṇa, PCR. translates "a sacred water called Go").

Gonanda, a warrior of Skanda. § 615*u* (Skanda): IX, **45**η, 2567.

Gonarda = Çiva (1000 names[1]).

Gopa, pl. (*°āḥ*) ("cowherds") = Nārāyaṇa, pl.: VI, 3131.

Gopāla, pl. (°*āḥ*) ("cowherds") = Nārāyaṇa, pl.: VII, 752 (*N*°), 3255 (*N*°): VIII, 416 (*Nārāyaṇabalaiḥ*, followed Kṛtavarman).

Gopāla = Kṛshṇa: III, 15530.

Gopālakaksha, a country. § 280 (Bhīmasena): II, **30**, 1077 (in the east, conquered by Bhīmasena on his digvijaya).

Gopālakaksha, pl. (°*āḥ*), a people. § 574 (Jambūkh.): VI, **9**μ, 364.

Gopāli = Çiva (1000 names[2]).

Gopālī[1], an Apsaras. § 336 (Indralokābh.): III, **43***a*, 1785 (among the Apsarases who danced in the palace of Indra).

Gopālī[2], a mātṛ. § 615*u* (Skanda): IX, **46**θ, 2622.

Goparāshṭra, pl. (°*āḥ*), a people. § 574 (Jambūkh.): VI, **9**μ, 351.

Gopati[1], a Gandharva. § 101 (Aṃçāvat.): I, **65**, 2550 (among the Devagandharvas, sons of Muni).—§ 191 (Arjuna): I, **123**, 4811 (among the Gandharvas who were present at the birth of Arjuna).

Gopati[2] = Sūrya (the Sun): I, 6615; II, 425; III, 16941, 16977, 16978, †17091.

Gopati[3], a prince (?). § 317*b* (Kṛshṇa Vāsudeva): III, **12**, 492 (had been slain by Kṛshṇa).

Gopati[4] = Varuṇa: V, 3532 (*V*°), 3801 (*V*°).

Gopati[5], a son of Çibi. § 638*b* (Ramopākhyāna): XII, **49**, 1794 (*Çibiputro mahatejā G°r nāma nāmataḥ | vane saṃvardhito gobhiḥ*).

Gopati[6] = Çiva (1000 names[2]).

Gopati[7] = Vishṇu (1000 names).

Gopendra = Kṛshṇa: VI, 799 (°*syānuje jyeshṭhe*, i.e. Durgā).

Gopījanapriya = Kṛshṇa: II, 2291.

Gopratāra[1], a tīrtha on the Sarayū. § 370 (Tīrthayātrāp.): III, **84**, 8048 (*Sarayvās tīrthaṃ*, there Rāma ascended to heaven), 8050.

Gopratāra[2] = Çiva (1000 names[1]).

Goptṛ[1] = Çiva: XIII, 609.

Goptṛ[2] = Vishṇu (1000 names).

Goptrātman = Kṛshṇa: XII, 1659.

Goputra = Karṇa: VIII, †4668 (v. Nīl.).

Gorāçva, v. Gaurāçva.

Goratha, a mountain near Girivraja. § 276 (Jārasandhavadhap.): II, **20**, 797 (*giriṃ*).

Goshṭha = Çiva: XIV, 198.

Gostanī, a mātṛ. § 615*u* (Skanda): IX, **46**θ, 2621.

Gotama, a ṛshi. § 198 (Çaradvat): I, **103**, 5072 (*maharsheḥ*, father of Çaradvat).—§ 208 (Astradarçana): I, **137**, 5433 (Kṛpa was born in the race of *G.*).—§ 717*b* (Nārāyaṇīya): XII, **342**, 13184 (*sa*—i.e. the blind Dīrghatamas—*cakshumān samabhavad Gotamaç cābhavat punaḥ*).—§ 770 (Ānuçasanik.): XIII, **151**ν, 7157. Cf. Dīrghatamas.

Govardhana[1], a mountain. § 290 (Çicupālavadhap.): II, **41**, 1441 (*valmīkamātraḥ saptāhaṃ yady anena*—i.e. by Kṛshṇa—*dhṛto 'calaḥ | tadā G°aḥ*, says Çiçupāla).—§ 567 (Bhagavadyānap.): V, **130**, 4410 (°*o dhāritaç ca gavārthe*, sc. by Kṛshṇa).

Govardhana[2], name of a banyan-tree in the country of the Bāhīkas. § 607 (Karṇap.): VIII, **44**, 2031 (°*o nāma vaṭaḥ*, PCR. follows the interpretation of Nīl.: *govardhanaḥ gocchedanasthānaṃ*).

Govāsa, pl. (°*āḥ*) = Govāsana, pl.: VIII, 3650.

Govāsana = Çaibya[2]: I, ††3828 (*Ç*°); VI, 655 (*Ç*°); VII, 3528 (*Ç*°), 3552 (*Ç*°).

Govāsana, pl. (°*āḥ*). § 295 (Dyūtap.): II, **51**, 1825 (? *brāhmaṇāḥ*: "clad in cow-skins," BR., "engaged in rearing cattle," PCR., brought tribute to Yudhishṭhira).

Govidām pati(ḥ) = Vishṇu (1000 names).

Govinda[1] = Kṛshṇa (Vishṇu), q.v.

Govinda[2], a mountain in Krauñcadvīpa. § 575 (Bhūmip.): VI, **12**η, 460 (*girir uttamaḥ*).

Govinda[3] = Çiva (1000 names[1]).

Govitata, a kind of horse-sacrifice: I, 3122 (°*ṃ nāma vājimedhaṃ*).

Govraja, a warrior of Skanda. § 615*u* (Skanda): IX, **45**η, 2568.

Govṛsha = Çiva (1000 names[1]).

Govṛshabhāṅka, Govṛshadhvaja = Çiva, q.v.

Govṛsheçvara = Çiva: XIII, 1253.

Govṛsheçvaravāhana = Çiva (1000 names[1]).

Govṛshottamavāhana = Çiva, q.v.

graha[1], mostly pl. (°*āḥ*) ("planets"). I, 66 (°*nakshatratārāṇāṃ*), 7677 (*candrādityau g° ās tārā nakshatrāṇi*); II, 304; III, 842 (sg., *prapatan . . . kshīṇapuṇya iva grahaḥ*), 2555 (°*ā na viparītāḥ*), 8674, 10906, 12550 (°*nakshatraiḥ*), 14340, 14368 (°*āḥ sopagrahāḥ*), 14558, 15813 (°*nakshatra*°), 16198 (°*nakshatratārābhiḥ*), 16285 (*vṛtau . . . candrasūryau g°airiva*); IV, 48 (°*āṇāṃ daçamaṃ*, said of Arjuna, the ordinary number being nine), 1606; V, 1148 (*tāpyate . . . nakshatrāṇi g°air iva*), 3504, 4842 (sg., *Citrāṃ pīḍayate grahaḥ*, i.e. Mahāpātākhya, Nīl.), 7322 (°*ān ashṭāv iva*), 7626 (*iva*); VI, 404 (*candrādityau grahās tathā*), 637 (*sampetur divi sapta mahāgrahāḥ*), 3216 (*sūryo grahair iva samāvṛtaḥ*), 3304 (°*air dyaur iva saṃvṛtā*), 4399 (°*nakshatraçabalā dyaur iva*), 4436 (*candramā yukto dīptair iva mahāgrahaiḥ*), 4566 (*dudruvuḥ . . . grahāḥ pañca raviṃ yathā*), 4567 (*pīḍitaḥ . . . yathā yugakshaye ghore candramāḥ pañcabhir grahaiḥ*); VII, 1031 (*somaṃ grahagaṇānvitaṃ*), 2856 (°*nakshatra-somānāṃ*), 3455, 4828, 5636 (*pīḍayan . . . prajāsaṃharaṇe, rājan, somaṃ sapta grahā iva*), 5691 (*dyaur iva grahaiḥ*), 6902 (*dyaur iva . . . grahakīrṇā yugakshaye*), 7212 (*dyaur iva . . . pahaiḥ kīrṇā yugakshaye*), 7538 (*dyaur iva grahaiḥ*), 9603 (*sarvair grahair gṛhītān*); VIII, 170 (*grahāv iva*), 662 (do.), †690 (*vikaco yathā grahaḥ*) †813 (*arka-candra-graha-pāvaka-tvishaṃ*), 1479 (became the anukarsha of Çiva's chariot), 1485 (°*nakshatra-tārābhiḥ . . . nabhastalaṃ*), 1707 (*sapta mahāgrahāḥ*), †4904 (*dyaur grahair amalapradīptaiḥ*); IX, 1363 (*iva*), 2513 (came to the investiture of Skanda); X, 25 (°*nakshatra-tārābhiḥ*), 290 (*sārkendu-g°-nakshatrāṃ dyāṃ*); XI, 796 (*iva*); XII, 909 (*krūragrahābhiçamanaṃ*), 1600 (*vṛtaç candra iva grahaiḥ*), 3271 (sg., *nakshatrāṇām iva grahaḥ*), 3399, 6133, 10047, 10312; XIII, 625, 665 (sg., said of Mandara), 669 (do.), 670 (do.), 913 (°*āṇāṃ Sūrya ucyate*, sc. Çiva), 988, 1089, 4201, †7386 (°*nakshatra-tārāḥ*, identif. with Kṛshṇa), 7499 (identif. with Çiva), 7584 (°*āṇām abhipūjanaṃ*), 7660; XIV, 1175 (*Sūryo grahāṇām adhipaḥ*), 1430, 2674 (*iva*); XVI, 48; XVIII, 217.

do. (sg.) of special planets:—

Budha: VIII, †4943 (*Somasya putraḥ*).

Çanaiççara: III, 16171 (*Ç*°); V, 4840 (*Ç*°); IX, 805 (*Ç*°).

Çukra: I, 2606 (*Çukraḥ Kavisutaḥ*).

Çveta: V, 1376 (*Ç*°); VI, 79 (*Ç*°), 83 (*Ç*°).

Rāhu: I, 1267, 2676 (*grahan tu sushuve yan tu Siṃhikā arkendumardanaṃ*), 6771 (*grastaḥ . . . graheṇeva parvakāle divākaraḥ*); VI, 86 (*parushagrahaḥ*), 480 (only B.), 482

(*Svarbhānuḥ*); XIII, 1151 (identif. with Çiva, 1000 names [2]), 6230 ("eclipse," PCR.); XIV, 892 (*agacchad bhānumantam iva grahaḥ*).

graha [2], sg. and pl. (°*āḥ*) ("sickness demons"): III, 14479 (sg. = Skandāpasmāra), 14480 (*Çakunigrahaḥ, Pūtanāgraham*), 14482 (sg. *Raivataḥ*), 14483 (sg. = do.), 14485 (*sumahāgrahāḥ*, i.e. the Kumāras and the Kumarīs), 14490 (*ashṭādaça*), 14496 (*mahāgrahāḥ*), 14497 (pl. *Skandagrahāḥ*), 14501 (*Devag°ṃ*), 14502 (*Pitṛg°ḥ*), 14503 (*Siddhag°ḥ*), 14504 (*Rākshasag°ḥ*), 14505 (°*o Gāndharvaḥ*), 14506 (°*aḥ Paiçācaḥ*), 14507 (*Yakshag°ḥ*), 14510 (*trividho grahaḥ*), 14511 (°*tulyo bhavet jvaraḥ*), 14512 (pl.), 14513 (°*oddeçaḥ*), 14564 (*Rākshaso grahaḥ*); XI, 109 (pl.); XII, 5677 (*bālagrahanipīḍitaḥ*); XIII, 752*b* (pl.).

graha [3], pl. (°*āḥ*) = Çiva (1000 names [1]).

Grahagaṇeçvara = Soma (the Moon): XIII, 3386.

Grahapati [1] = Soma (the Moon): XII, 4317, 6288.

Grahapati [2] = Çiva (1000 names [2]).

Grāma = Çiva (1000 names [2]).

Grāmaṇī [1] = Vishṇu (1000 names).

Grāmaṇī [2], a follower of Çiva (?). § 770 (Ānuçāsanik.): XIII, **151**, 7103 (*vṛshabhadhvajaḥ*, or is Çiva himself meant?).

Grāmaṇīya, pl. (°*āḥ*). § 285 (Nakula): II, **32**, 1191 (in the west, *Sindhukūlāçritā ye*, vanquished by Nakula on his digvijaya). § 552 (Goharaṇap.): IV, **32**, 1038 (? "combatants," PCR.).

Granthika = Dāmagranthi (the name which Nakula assumed in the palace of Virāṭa). § 549 (Pāṇḍavapraveçap.): IV, **3**, 63; **12**, †319.

***gṛdhra**, pl. (°*āḥ*) ("vultures"). § 126 (Aṃçāvat.): I, **66**, 2621 (the offspring of Bhāsī).

[Gṛdhra-gomāyu-samvāda(ḥ)] ("the discourse between a vulture and a jackal"). § 653*b* (Āpaddh.): *Bhīshma* related: The young child of a *brahman* died and was taken to the burning-place; a vulture caused the lamenting kinsmen to leave the child, as the sun was soon to set, saying that the child could not be revived by their lingering. A jackal, black as a raven, rebuked them for not waiting till the sun had set, as the child might possibly revive. The vulture and the jackal alternately endeavoured to persuade them. The jackal mentioned that by *Rāma's* [i.e. *Dāçarathi's*] slaying the *Çūdra* named *Çambuka*, a *brahmaṇa* child was restored to life; similarly the son of R.-ṛ. *Çveta*. The vulture said that if only *Rudra*, etc. (*a*), would grant him a boon, the child might come back to life, and mentioned the spirits and Y. and Rā., etc., who haunt the burning place, while the jackal reminded them that it was here on this "quiet and peaceful" spot that the *Pitṛs* by thousands took leave of the world. The jackal and the vulture continued to dispute, exhausted with hunger and thirst, wishing to get opportunity of devouring the child. Then *Çaṅkara* (i.e. *Çiva*) exhorted by his consort came, and, taking up a quantity of water in his hands, restored the child to life for a hundred years, and to the jackal and the vulture he granted a boon, in consequence of which their hunger was appeased. Blessing upon the reader (XII, **153**).

Gṛdhrakūṭa, a mountain. § 638*b* (Rāmopākhyāna): XII, **49**, 1797 (there [the Māgadha king] Bṛhadratha was protected by golāṅgulas).

Gṛdhrapatra, a warrior of Skanda. § 615*u* (Skanda): IX, **45**η, 2576.

Gṛdhravaṭa, a tīrtha. § 370 (Tīrthayātrāp.): III, **84**, 8069 (*sthānaṃ devasya*, i.e. Çiva's (Vṛshabhadhvaja)).

Gṛhadevī. § 275 (Rājasūyārambhap.): II, **18**, 730 (°*iti nāmnā vai purā sṛshṭā Svayambhuvā*, sc. the Rākshasī Jarā).

Gṛhānāṃ pravibhāga(ḥ) ("the division of the houses"). § 10 (Parvasaṅgr.): I, **2**, 350 (*parva*, i.e. XII, **44**).

Gṛhapati = Agni, q.v.

***gṛhayajña**: X, 790.

Gṛtsamada, a ṛshi. § 730 (Ānuçāsanik.); XIII, **18**κκ, 1314 (*ṛshiḥ Çakrasya dayitaḥ sakhā*; cursed by Varishṭha, *G.* became a deer, then he sought the protection of Çiva).—§ 736*b* (Vītahavyop.): XIII, **30**, 1997 (son of Vītahavya, the Daityas once took him for Indra), 1999, 2000 (father of Sucetas).

Guḍākeça = Arjuna, q.v.

Gūḍhavrata = Çiva (1000 names [1]).

Guha [1] = Skanda, q.v.

Guha [2] = Kṛshṇa: XII, 1507.

Guha [3] = Çiva (1000 names [2]).

Guha [4] = Vishṇu (1000 names).

Guha, pl. (°*āḥ*), a people. § 664 (Mokshadh.): XII, **207**η, 7559 (among the barbarous people of the south).

Guhāpāla(ḥ)praveçināṃ = Çiva (1000 names [2]).

Guhāvāsin = Çiva (1000 names [2]).

Guhya [1] = Çiva (1000 names [2]).

Guhya [2] = Vishṇu: XII, 13115; XIII, 7007 (1000 names).

Guhya [3] = Mahāpurusha (Mahāpurushastava).

Guhya, pl. = Guhyaka, pl.: III, 173; XV, 848 (°*Rākshasāḥ*).

Guhyaka, pl. (°*āḥ*), a class of beings, followers of Kubera. § 3 (Anukram.): I, **1***a*, 35.—§ 120 *bis* (Aṃçāvat.): I, **66**, 2604.—§ 194 (Pāṇḍu): I, **126**, 4930.—§ 213 (Jatugṛhap.): I, **146**, 5779 (*viviçuḥ . . . Kailāsam iva G°āḥ*).—§ 214 (Hiḍimbavadhap.): I, **155**, 6070 (Bhīmasena sported with Hiḍimbā in the abodes of the *G.*).—§ 233 (Svayaṃvarap.): I, **187**, †7011 (came to see the svayaṃvara of Draupadī).—§ 269 (Vaiçravaṇasabhāv.): II, **10**, 385 (°*air uhyamānā*, sc. the palace of Kubera).—§ 270 (Brahmasabhāv.): II, **11**, 465 (in the palace of Brahmán).—§ 271 (Lokapālasabhākhyānap.): II, **12**, 481 (in the palace of Kubera).—§ 279 (Arjuna): II, **28**, 1040 (*Hāṭakaṃ nāma deçaṃ G°rakshitaṃ*, in the north).—§ 310*b* (Sūrya): III, **3**, 170 (follow Sūrya).—§ 334 (Kairātap.): III, **41**, 1674.—§ 335 (Indralokābhigamanap.): III, **42**, 1750.—§ 359 (Vaḍavā): III, **82**, 5036 (at Vaḍavā).—§ 370 (Tīrthayātrāp.): III, **84**, 8093 (*Adhivaṅgaṃ, dharmajña, samāviçya tapovanaṃ* | *G°eshu, mahārājan, modate*).—§ 445 (Nivātakavacayuddhap.): III, **173**, 12247 (°*ānāñ ca saṅgrāme*).—§ 459 (Mārkaṇḍeyas.): III, **188**, 12921 (seen by Mārkaṇḍeya in the stomach of Nārāyaṇa). § 573 (Ambopākhyānap.). V, **192**, 7532 (followed Kubera).—§ 574 (Jambūkh.): VI, **6**, 236 (*yatra*—i.e. on Kailāsa—*Vaiçravaṇo, rājan, G°aiḥ saha modate*), (θ), 246 (reside on Hemakūṭa).—§ 607 (Karṇap.): VIII, **45**ξ, 2104 (protect Gandhamādana).—§ 608 (do.): VIII, **87**χ [1], 4412 (sided with Karṇa).—§ 611 (Çalyap.): IX, **11**, 584 (had on Gandhamādana been slain by Bhīmasena, all. to Yakshayuddhaparvan).—§ 620 (Çrāddhap.): XI, **26**, 769 (some of the fallen warriors attained to [the world of] the *G.*).—§ 694*b* (Jvarotpatti): XII, **284**, 10216 (*Vaiçravaṇo rājā G°air abhisaṃvṛtaḥ*).—§ 730 (Ānuçāsanik.): XIII, **14**δδ, 996; **17**, 1294.—§ 768*b* (Umā-Maheçvarasaṃv.): XIII, **142**, 6555 (*ātmānam upajīvan yo dīkshāṃ dvādaçavarshikīṃ* | *açmanā caraṇau bhittvā G°eshu sa modate*).—§ 795 (Svargārohaṇap.): XVIII, **4**, 147 (some of the fallen kings attained to [the status of] the *G.*).—§ 795*c* (Mahābhārata): XVIII, **6**ξ, 216. Cf. Guhya, pl.

Guhyaka, sg. § 424 (Bhīmakadalīkh.): III, **147**, 11190

(Bhīshma asks Hanumat if he is a *G.*, etc.).—§ 541 (Indrajidvadha): III, **289,** 16473 (a *G.* came as messenger from Kubera).—§ 573 (Ambopākhyānap.): V, **191,** 7480 (i.e. Sthūṇākarṇa), 7486 (do.).

Guhyaka, name of a Yaksha. § 269 (Vaiçravaṇasabhāv.): II, **10,** 397 (among the Yakshas in the palace of Kubera).

Guhyakādhipa ("the king of the Guhyakas") = Kubera: III, 11834; VI, 229 (*K*°).

Guhyakādhipati (do.) = Kubera: II, 1760.

Guhyakāstra ("the weapon of the Guhyakas"). § 573 (Ambop.): V, **180,** 7173 (employed by Rāma Jāmadagnya).

Guhyatapas = Çiva (1000 names[1]).

Guṇabhṛt = Vishṇu (1000 names).

Guṇabuddhi, Guṇādhika, Guṇākara = Çiva (1000 names[2]).

Guṇakeçī, the daughter of Mātalī. § 564 (Mātalīyop.): V, **97,** 3513, 3520; **103,** 3637; **104,** 3647, 3650.

Guṇamukhyā, an Apsaras. § 191 (Arjuna): I, **123,** 4817 (among the Āpsarases who danced at the birth of Arjuna).

Guṇātman = Kṛshṇa (Vishṇu): XII, 13140 (*Nārāyaṇāya*).

Guṇaushada = Çiva (1000 names[2]).

Guṇāvarā, an Apsaras. § 191 (Arjuna): I, **123,** 4817 (among the Apsarases who danced at the birth of Arjuna).

Gupta = Vishṇu (1000 names).

Guptaka, one of the standard-bearers of Jayadratha. § 522 (Draupadīharaṇap.): III, **265,** †15597.

Guru[1] = Bṛhaspati: II, 303 (in the palace of Indra): VIII, 3304; XII, 5333 (*pratilomo 'bhavad Guruḥ*, i.e. the planet Jupiter).

Guru[2] = Droṇa: I, 574 (°*oḥ sutaṃ*, i.e. Açvatthāman); VII, †6727, 7272; VIII, 4066 (°*oḥ sutaṃ*, i.e. Açvatthāman); X, 614 (*D*°), 757, 764 (°*oḥ sutaḥ*, i.e. Açvatthāman). Cf. Ācārya.

Guru[3] = Çiva: XIII, 696, 1245 (1000 names[2]).

Guru[4] = Vishṇu (1000 names).

Gurubhāra, a Suparṇa, the son of Garuḍa. § 564 (Mātalīyop.): V, **101**β, 3598.

Guruçaktidhārin = Skanda: III, 14642.

[Guruçishyasaṃvāda] ("discourse between a preceptor and his disciple"). § 782*g*. (Anugītāparvan): *Kṛshṇa* said: Asked by his disciple "Whence am I? whence art thou?" etc., the preceptor said: This was declared by *Brahmán* himself to Ṛ.; it was known to the conclaves of Si. in the ancient *kalpas.* In days of old Ṛ. *Bṛhaspati*, etc. (δ) assembled together for asking one another, tired with their acts; placing Ṛ. *Āṅgirasa* at their head, they beheld, in the abode of *Brahmán, Brahmán* free from sin, and were instructed by him about how a good man should act, about Emancipation, etc. "Truth is the universe of being," light, ether, sun, wind, *Indra* and *Prajāpati* are not seen as long as one has not attained to *Adhyātma*; religion has faith (*çraddhā*) for its indication; the number of elements (*tattva*) are twenty-four and one more (XIV, **35**). *Brahmán* discoursed on the city of nine gates, the three qualities, etc., the qualities belonging to darkness (birth as *Cāṇḍālas*, etc.); Ṛ., Mu., and D. become deluded, desirous of pleasure (XIV, **36**). *Brahmán* discoursed on passion (XIV, **37**) and *sattva* (XIV, **38**); the qualities are not completely separated from one another, etc. (XIV, **39**); from the unmanifest first sprang the great soul, the source of all intelligence, the source of all qualities, called *Mahān ātmā, Vishṇu, Jishṇu, Çambhu, Buddhi*, etc., pervading everything in the universe, stationed in the heart of all, endued with minuteness, lightness, and affluence (*prāpti*); this is said to be the first creation (XIV, **40**); the great (*Mahān*), who was first produced and called *Ahaṅkāra*, is the second creation, the source of all creatures, a god, the creator of gods, etc. (XIV, **41**); from *Ahaṅkārā* was born the five great elements; the *prāṇas*, etc.; the eleven organs sprung from *Ahaṅkāra*:—

	Entity (*bhūtas*).	On the Self (*adhyātmam*).	Among Objects (*adhibhūtam*).	Among Gods (*adhidaivatam*).
1.	ether (*ākāça*)	ear (*çrotra*)	sound (*çabda*)	the Quarters (*Diçaḥ*).
2.	wind (*māruta*)	skin (*tvac*)	objects of touch (*sprashṭavya*)	Lightning (*Vidyut*).
3.	light (*jyotis*)	eye (*cakshus*)	form and colour (*rūpa*)	the Sun (*Sūrya*).
4.	water (*āpaḥ*)	tongue (*jihvā*)	taste (*rasa*)	*Soma.*
5.	earth (*pṛthivī*)	nose (*ghrāṇa*)	scent (*gandha*)	the Wind (*Vāyu*).
6.		feet (*pādau*)	motion (*gantavyam*)	*Vishṇu.*
7.	*Apāna*	anus (*pāyu*)	excreta (*visarga*)	*Mitra.*
8.		organ of generation (*upastha*)	vital seed (*çukra*)	*Prajāpati.*
9.		hands (*hastau*)	actions (*karmāṇi*)	*Çakra* (Indra).
10.		speech (*Vāc: Vaiçvadevī*)	what is spoken (*vaktavyam*)	*Vahni* (Agni).
11.		mind (*manas*)	mental operation (*saṅkalpa*)	the Moon (*Candramas*).
12.		egoism (*ahaṅkāra: sarvasaṃsārakārakam*)	consciousness of self (*abhimāna*)	*Rudra.*
13.		understanding (*buddhi: shaḍindriyavicāriṇī*)	what is to be understood (*mantavyam*)	*Brahmán.*

Three are the seats of all existent objects: land, water, and ether; the mode of birth is fourfold (from eggs, germs, filth, or wombs) (specification); etc.; on the means of attaining to *Brahmán*; on the body; the emancipated one is *Vishṇu*, etc. (ε); † him praise brahmans, D., As., Y., Pç., P., birds, Rā., Bh., and M.-ṛ. († v. 1169) (XIV, **42**); the *kshatriya*, elephant, lion, sheep, snake, bull, and male are of middle quality [i.e. *rajas*]; the *nyagrodha*, etc. (ζ) are the foremost among trees; *Himavat*, etc. (η) are the foremost among mountains; M. are the foremost of the *gaṇas*, etc. (θ); [in v. 1201 it is *Vāyu* who resides in the skin and is employed in the perception of touch, etc.] (XIV, **43**); the day was first, then arose the night, etc.; the months are said to begin with the bright fortnights; the constellations begin with *Çravaṇa*; the seasons with winter (*çiçira*), etc. (ι) (XIV, **44**); on the wheel of life (XIV, **45**); on the duties that men should observe (XIV, **46**); on renunciation, knowledge, and power (XIV, **47**); on the different conceptions of *Bráhman* (a tree, a forest, unmanifest, etc.); it is impossible to attain to *Purusha* by any other means than goodness; some assert the unity of *Kshetrajña* and *sattva*; this is not correct; the relation of *Purusha* to *sattva* is like that of the gnat to the *udumbara*, or that of water-drops on the leaf of a lotus. The Ṛ. once more asked (XIV, **48**) about the diversities of practice observed by men, and about the connection between the *Kshetrajña* and *sattva* (XIV, **49**). *Brahmán*, quoting what was said by a preceptor to a disciple, said that abstention from harming any creature is the foremost of all duties, and the relation between *sattva* and *Kshetrajña* (*Purusha*) is that of the object (*vishaya*) to the subject (*vishayitva*), or like that of the matter to the maker, or like that of a lamp (with oil and wick) to him who lights it; *sattva* is manifest, while *Purusha* is unmanifest; knowledge is indispensable for attaining to felicity; from *pradhāna* develops *mahat*, from *mahat ahaṅkāra*, from *ahaṅkāra* the five elements; the qualities of the elements are the following:—

Elements.	Qualities.				
ether (space)					sound.
wind				touch	sound.
light			*rūpa*	touch	sound.
water		taste	*rūpa*	touch	sound.
earth	smell	taste	*rūpa*	touch	sound.
	1. agreeable 2. disagreeable 3. sweet 4. sour 5. pungent 6. diffusive 7. compact 8. oily 9. dry 10. clear	1. sweet 2. sour 3. pungent 4. bitter 5. astringent 6. saline	1. white 2. dark 3. red 4. blue 5. yellow 6. grey (?) 7. short 8. long 9. minute 10. gross 11. square 12. circular	1. rough 2. cold 3. hot 4. tender 6. hard 8. smooth 9. slippery 7. oily 10. painful 5. clear 11. soft 12. ?	1. *Shaḍja.* 2. *Ṛshabha.* 3. *Gāndhāra.* 4. *Madhyama.* 5. *Pañcama.* 6. *Nishāda.* 7. *Dhaivata.* 8. agreeable. 9. disagreeable. 10. compact.

Space (ether) is the highest of the elements > (i.e. above it is) *ahaṅkāra* > *buddhi* > *ātman* (the soul) > the unmanifest *avyaktaṃ* > *Purusha* (XIV, **50**). *Brahmán* said: The body is called the carriage of *Bráhman*, on which the individual soul drives about; the senses are the steeds; the mind is the charioteer, called also the *bhūtātman* (the individual soul), because it is the ruler of the elements (*bhūtāni*); the reins are the *buddhi*, called also *kshetrajña* (the individual soul), because it "proclaims power." The order of the dissolution is: 1, the creatures; 2, their qualities; 3, the elements; D., men, G., Pç., As., and Rā. have all sprung from Nature (*svabhāvataḥ*), and not from actions, nor from a cause; [the elements are called] the brahmans, who are creators of the universe [and] are born here again and again; all that springs from them is dissolved in those very five great elements like billows in the ocean; [beyond] those elements that compose the universe (*viçvasṛgbhyas tu bhūtebhyaḥ*, i.e. the gross elements) are the five great elements (i.e. the subtle elements; read °*bhūtās* with B.), and higher than these is the way of the emancipated (read *mukto* with B.); *Prajāpati* created all this by the mind alone; in the same manner Ṛ. attained to [the status of] D. by the aid of penance; (the wonderful effects of penance, by which one may be cleansed from the most horrible sins, etc.; men, P., deities, etc., have been crowned with success by penance alone); different degrees of bliss after death (*Prajāpati*; the great highest region—*mahāntaṃ lokam uttamaṃ*; the unmanifest accumulation of happiness—*sukhopacayam avyaktaṃ*; the unmanifest, i.e. the highest region of the great ones—*avyaktaṃ mahatāṃ lokam uttamaṃ*), according as one performs acts with expectation, being full of egoism (*ahaṅkāra-samāyuktāḥ*), or is devoid of selfishness (*nirmamāḥ*), and freed from egoism (*nirahaṅkṛtāḥ*) through *yoga*; freed from darkness and passion and adhering only to goodness, one becomes released from every sin and creates all things: such a one should be known to be [perfect] *kshetrajña*: he who knows him knows the *Veda*; that which begins with the unmanifest and ends with the gross qualities (°*viçeshāntaṃ*), has ignorance for its indication; selfishness (*mama*) is death, the reverse (*na mama*) is the eternal [*Bráhman*]; the high-minded ancients never applaud action: by action a creature is born with body; the indication of tranquillity is like what takes place in a dream; this is the goal of the emancipated ones who are intent on knowledge. The preceptor said: Thus addressed by *Brahmán*, Mu. acted accordingly and attained to felicity (*lokaṃ*). *Kṛshṇa* said: The pupil acted accordingly and then attained to emancipation (XIV, **51**).

Guruputra[1] ("the son of Guru, i.e. Droṇa" = Açvatthāman): I, 5351; VI, 4640; VIII, 646, †4522; IX, 309, 732; X, 756.

Guruputra[2] = Çuka: XII, 12261, 12262 (Ç°).

Guruskandha, a mountain. § 782*g* (Guruçishyasaṃv.): XIV, **43**η, 1174.

Gurutama = Vishṇu (1000 names).

H

Hāhā (or **Hahā**), a Gandharva always mentioned together with Hūhū. § 104 (Aṃçāvat.): I, **65**, 2559 (*Hāhā-Hūhūḥ*, among the sons of Pradhā).—§ 191 (Arjuna): I, **123**, 4815 (*Hāhā-Hūhū*, so C., B. has *Ha*°, among the Devagandharvas present at the birth of Arjuna).—§ 269 (Vaiçravaṇasabhāv.): II, **10,** 406 (*Hāhā-Huhūḥ* (*Ha°* B.) in the palace of Kubera).—§ 336 (Indralokābhigamanap.): III, **43,** 1769 (*Hāhā-Hūhū* (*°ūḥ*, B.)).—§ 574 (Jambūkh.): VI, **6,** 214 (*Hāhā-Huhū* (B. *Hahā-Huhūḥ*) on Meru).—§ 662 (Mokshadh.): XII, **200**δ, 7340 (*Hāhā-Huhūḥ*, B. has *Ha°*).—§ 695*b* (Dakshayajñavināça): XII, **285,** 10278 (*Hāhā-Hūhūç ca Gandharvau*).—§ 712 (Çukotpatti): XII, **325,** 12202 (do.).—§ 746 (Ānuçāsanik.): XIII, **83**ζ, 3887 (*Hahā-Huhūḥ*).—§ 775 (do.): XIII, **166a,** 7639 (do.).

Haiḍambi, v. Haiḍimbi.

Haiḍimba[1], adj. ("relating to Hiḍimba"). § 10 (Parvasaṅgr.): I, **2,** 313 (*parva*, i.e. Hiḍimbavadhaparvan).

Haiḍimba[2] = Ghaṭotkaca, q.v.

Haiḍimbasūnu ("the son of Haiḍimba [i.e. Ghaṭotkaca]") = Añjanaparvan: VII, 6813.

Haiḍimbi = Ghaṭotkaca, q.v.

Haihaya, pl. (*°āḥ*), a people. § 11 (Parvasaṅgr.): I, **2,** 444 (*Kārtavīryavadhaḥ . . . H°ānāñ ca*, all. to § 393 foll.).—§ 387 (Sagara): III, **106,** 8832 (Sagara subdued the *H.* and the Tālajaṅghas).—§ 454 (Brāhmaṇamāhātmyak.): III, **184,** 12654 (*°ānāṃ kulakaro rājā parapurañjayaḥ kumāro rūpasampannaḥ*, slew the son of Tārkshya Arishṭanemi), 12657 (*rājñāṃ*).—§ 562 (Bhagavadyānap.): V, **74**γ, 2729 (*°ānām Udāvartaḥ*, so B., C. has *°ānāṃ Mudā°*).—§ 570*b* (Sainyaniryāṇap.): It is heard that the brahmans, raising a standard of kuça-grass, encountered the kshatriyas of the Haihaya clan in battle; the vaiçyas and the çūdras joined the brahmans. In the battles, however, the three castes repeatedly broke down, while the kshatriyas, though alone, vanquished their large army because they obeyed the commands of only one person, while the other three castes acted each acccording to his individual understanding. The brahmans then appointed one among themselves as their commander, and thus succeeded in vanquishing the kshatriyas: V, **156,** 5281. — § 595 (Shoḍaçarāj. v. Rāma Jāmadagnya): VII, **70,** 2432 (had been slain by Rāma Jāmadagnya on account of the slaughter of his father [Jamadagni]).—§ 638*b* (Rāmopākhyāna): XII, **49,** 1768 (*°sahasrāṇi*, slain by Rāma Jāmadagnya as the sons of the Haihaya king Arjuna [Kārtavīrya] had ravished the cow of Jamadagni and afterwards slain Jamadagni himself), 1790 (some kshatriyas of the *H.* tribe were preserved, having been concealed among women).—§ 641 (Rājadh.): XII, **126,** 4648 (*°ānāṃ kule jātaḥ Sumitro Mitranandanaḥ*).—§ 736*b* (Vītahavyop.): XIII, **30,** 1951 (i.e. the sons of Vītahavya, attacked the Kāçi king Haryaçva), 1958 (do., attacked the Kāçi king Dīvodāsa).

Haihaya[1], a son of Vatsa. § 736*b* (Vītahavyop.): XIII, **30,** 1946 (son of Vatsa and brother of Tālajaṅgha), 1947 (had ten wives and a hundred sons, apparently the same as Vītahavya). Cf. Vītahavya.

Haihaya[2] ("king of the Haihayas") = Arjuna Kārtavīrya: XII, 1756; XIII, 7188, 7261.

Haihaya[3] (do.) = Sumitra: XII, 4630 (*Sumitro nāma rājarshiḥ*).

Haihayaçreshṭha (do.)=Arjuna Kārtavīrya: XIII, 7291.

Haihayādhipati (do.) = Arjuna Kārtavīrya: I, 4172 (had been slain by Rāma Jāmadagnya); III, 10134 (*Kārtavīryasya*), 10135 (*A°*), 10140.

Haihayarshabha (do.) = Arjuna Kārtavīrya: XIII, 7267.

Haihayeçapramāthin ("the destroyer of the lord of the Haihayas [i.e. Arjuna Kārtavīrya]") = Rāma Jāmadagnya: V, †7212.

Haihayendra ("king of the Haihayas") = Arjuna Kārtavīrya: XII, 1762 (*Kārtavīryeṇa*).

Haima[1], a mountain. § 731*b* (Ashṭāvakra-Diksaṃv.): XIII, **19,** 1434 (in the north, crossed by Ashṭāvakra).

Haima[2] = Çiva (1000 names[2]).

Haimavata[1] ("named after Himavat," viz. a varsha). § 574 (Jambūkh.): VI, **6**γ, 201 (north of Himavat); **10,** 385, 400. —§ 713 (Çukakṛti): XII, **326,** 12228 (*varsham*, crossed by Çuka on his way from Meru to Mithilā).

Haimavata[2], adj. ("belonging to Himavat"). § 192 (Pāṇḍavopatti): I, **124,** 4864 (*girau*).—§ 225 (Vāsishṭha): I, **177,** 6752 (*nadīṃ H°īṃ*, i.e. Çatadru).—§ 233 (Svayaṃvarap.): I, **187,** 7006 (*yathā H°ā gajendrāḥ*). — § 271 (Jarāsandhavadhap.): II, **21,** 825 (*siṃhā H°ā yathā*).—§ 304 (Anudyūtap.): II, **77,** †2528 (*siṃho yathā H°ḥ*).—§ 330 (Indradarçana): III, **37,** 1495 (*parvataṃ*).—§ 437 (Yakshayuddhap.): III, **160,** 11664 (*girau*). — § 522 (Draupadīharaṇap.): III, **268,** †15643 (*upatyakāṃ*, C. has *upe°*). — § 552 (Goharaṇap.): IV, **54,** †1675 (*nāgā yathā H°āḥ*).—§ 565 (Gālavacarita): V, **111,** 3844 (*kanakākaraḥ*).—§ 608 (Karṇap.): VIII, **85,** †4309 (*gajāḥ*); **89,** †4525 (*yathā gajau H°au*).—§ 610 (Çalyap.): IX, **6,** 292 (*prasthe*). — § 615*i* (Saptasārasvata): IX, **38,** 2215 (*girau*, there Sarasvatī appeared as Vimalodā).—§ 615*u* (Skanda): IX, **44,** 2501 (*Sarasvatīṃ*).—§ 641 (Rājadh.): XII, **82,** 3094 (*guhāṃ H°īm iva*).

Haimavata, pl. (*°āḥ*) ("the inhabitants of Himavat"). § 295 (Dyūtap.): II, **51,** 1844 (brought tribute to Yudhishṭhira). Cf. Haimavatika, pl.

Haimavatī[1] ("the daughter of Himavat") = Gaṅgā: III, 9935.

Haimavatī[2], the wife of Kauçika. § 565 (Gālavacarita): V, **117,** 3972 (*reme . . . yathā . . . H°yāñ ca Kauçikaḥ*).

Haimavatī[3], one of the wives of Kṛshṇa. § 793 (Mausalap.): XVI, **7**μ, 249 (among the wives of Kṛshṇa who, after his death, ascended his funeral pyre).

Haimavatika, pl. (*°āḥ*) ("the inhabitants of Himavat"). § 515 (Karṇadigvijaya): III, **254,** 15242 (vanquished by Karṇa). Cf. Haimavata, pl.

Hairaṇvatī, a river. § 574 (Jambūkh.): VI, **8,** 290 (in the varsha Hiraṇmaya).

Hairaṇyagarbha ("the son of Hiraṇyagarbha [i.e. Brahmán]") = Vasishṭha: XII, ††13209 (*V°*).

Hairaṇyaka, name of a varsha (= Hiraṇmaya). § 574 (Jambūkh.): VI, **6**γ, 231 (north of the varsha Çveta).

Halabhṛt ("plough-holder") = Balarāma: IX, †2002, †2924.

Haladhara (do.) = Balarāma: I, 7912, 8015; IX, 1981, 2129, 2272.

Haladharānuja ("the younger brother of Haladhara [i.e. Balarāma]") = Kṛshṇa: II, 889.

Halāyudha[1] ("having a plough for his weapon") = Balarāma: I, 7012, 7079, 7084; III, †12589; IV, 2356; V, 162, 5330, 5335, 5336; IX, 1948, 1954, 1955, 2061, 2064, 2117, 2119, 2145, 2184, 2246, 2249, 2280, 3004, 3029, 3038, 3046, 3345; XVI, 21.

Halāyudha[2] = Vishṇu (1000 names).

Halika, a serpent. § 47 (Sarpanāmak.): I, **35,** 1561 (enumeration).

Halimā, a mātṛ. § 500 (Skandopākhyāna): III, **228a,** 14396 (one of the mothers of Çiçu).

Halīmaka, a serpent. § 63 (Sarpasattra): I, **57,** 2146 (of Vāsuki's race).

Halin ("ploughman") = Balarāma: III, 10240; V, 4425; VII, 412; IX, 1961; XIII, 6860.

Haṃsa[1] ("the swan," also a name of the supreme soul, as becoming the individual soul): I, 2431 (*Nārāyaṇam*, identif. with Kṛshṇa); XII, 1505 (= Kṛshṇa), 1605 (do.), 8765, 8766 (°*tvaṃ*, etymology), 8767, 10993 (*Sādhyānām iha saṃvādaṃ h°sya*), 10994 (Prajāpati assumed the shape of a golden swan, (10998), (11031), (11033), (11035), ††12864 (= Mahāpurusha), 12967 (the first avatāra of Vishṇu); XIII, 6970 (= Vishṇu, 1000 names).

Haṃsa[2], a Gandharva king, the son of Arishṭā. § 130 (Aṃçāvat.): I, **67**, 2718 (*Arishṭāyās tu yaḥ putro H°a ity abhiçrutaḥ | sa Gandharvapatir jajñe Kuruvaṃçavivardhanaḥ | Dhṛtarāshṭra ity khyātaḥ Kṛshṇa-Dvaipāyanātmajaḥ*, i.e. as Dhṛtarāshṭra[1]).

Haṃsa[3], follower of Jarāsandha. § 273 (Rājasūyārambhap.): II, **14**, 576 (°*Ḍimbhakau*, among the allies of Jarāsandha), 601 (do.), 604 (vanquished by Balarāma), 605, 606 (on the false report of the death of *H.*, his friend Ḍimbhaka plunged into the Yamunā), 607 (then also *H.* committed suicide by plunging into the Yamunā).—§ 275 (do.): II, **19**, 765 (°*Ḍimbhakau*, followers of Jarāsandha).—§ 276 (Jarāsandhavadhap.): II, **20**, 768 (do.).—§ 277 (do.): II, **22**, 886 (the same as Kauçika, the senāpati of Jarāsandha).

Haṃsa[4] = Sūrya (the Sun): III, 191.

***haṃsa**, pl. (°*āḥ*) ("swans"). § 126 (Aṃçāvat.): I, **66**, 2622 (the offspring of Dhṛtarāshṭrī).

Haṃsacūḍa, a Yaksha. § 269 (Vaiçravaṇasabhāv.): II, **10**, 398 (among the Yakshas in the palace of Kubera).

Haṃsaja, a warrior of Skanda. § 615*u* (Skanda): IX, **45**η, 2570.

Haṃsakākīya(m) ākhyāna(m). § 11 (Parvasaṅgr.): I, **2**, 543 (i.e. Haṃsakākīyopākhyāna).

[Haṃsakākīyopākhyāna(m)] ("the story of the crow and the swans"). § 606 (Karṇap.): There lived on the other side of the ocean a rich *vaiçya* with many children, kind to all creatures. A crow lived upon the refuse of the dishes set before these children. The crow, becoming arrogant, came to disregard all birds. Once, certain swans, having their abodes in the *Mānasa* lake, came to that side of the ocean. The crow challenged their leader, saying that he would display 101 different kinds of motion, doing every 100 *yojanas* in a separate kind of motion: rising up and swooping down, etc. One of the swans said that they knew but that one kind of motion that all birds know, at which the assembled crows laughed aloud. The swans in vain tried to dissuade the crow. They began to fly. Beholding the diverse kinds of flight of the crow, the crows loudly rejoiced, while the swans laughed in mockery. For a moment the swan, with that one kind of slow motion, seemed to yield to the crow. As the swan flew westwards to the ocean, the crow was anxious and became almost senseless at not seeing any islands or trees whereon to perch when tired. At last the swan asked: "What is this kind of flight that thou hast now adopted? thou touchest the waters with thy wings and beak repeatedly." The crow suddenly fell down, and imploring the swan, prevailed upon him to take him on his back and carry him to the shore, and promised never to disregard others.

Haṃsakāyana, pl. (°*āḥ*), a people. § 295 (Dyūtap.): II, **52**, 1870 (brought tribute to Yudhishṭhira).

Haṃsakūṭa, a mountain. § 184 (Pāṇḍu): I, **119**, 4639 (in the north, crossed by Paṇḍu).

Haṃsamārga, pl. (°*āḥ*), a people. § 574 (Jambūkh.): VI, **9**o, 377 (only C., in the north-east). Cf. Haṃsapatha.

Haṃsapada, v. Haṃsapatha.

Haṃsapatha, pl. (°*āḥ*), a people. § 592 (Saṃçaptakavadhap.): VII, **20**γ, 798 (in the army of Duryodhana, only B., C. has Haṃsapadāḥ). Cf. Haṃsamārga.

Haṃsaprapatana, a tīrtha. § 374 (Tīrthayātrāp.): III, **85**, 8229.

Haṃsātman = Kṛshṇa: XII, 1634.

Haṃsavaktra, a warrior of Skanda. § 615*u* (Skanda): IX, **45**η, 2574.

Haṃsī, a daughter of Bhagīratha. § 767 (Ānuçāsanik.): XIII, **137***a*, 6270 (given to Kautsa).

Haṃsikā, a celestial cow, daughter of Surabhi. § 564 (Mātalīyop.): V, **102**, 3609 (in the southern quarter).

Hanūmad-Bhīma-saṃvāda(ḥ) ("conversation between Hanūmat and Bhīma"). § 425 (Bhīmakadalīkhaṇḍapraveça): *Hanūmat* said that he was the son of *Vāyu* with the wife of *Keçarin*, and the friend of the Sun's son *Sugrīva*, who, together with *Çakra's* son *Vālin*, used to be waited upon by all monkeys; further, that *Sugrīva* had been driven out by his brother, and dwelt for a long time with *Hanūmat* at *Ṛshyamūka*, when *Rāma Dāçarathi*, who was *Vishṇu* in human shape, with his wife and younger brother resided in the *Daṇḍaka* forest, and the *Rākshasa Rāvaṇa* carried away *Sītā*, *Rāma's* queen, from *Janasthāna*, assisted by the *Rākshasa Mārīca*, in the form of a deer marked with gems and gold (III, **147**). *Rāma* slew *Vālin* and installed *Sugrīva* in the kingdom; *Sugrīva* sent monkeys to inquire after *Sītā*, and according to the communications of the vulture *Sampāti*, *Hanūmat* crossed the ocean, extending over 100 *yojanas*, saw *Sītā* in the abode of *Rāvaṇa*, burnt *Laṅkā*, and returned to *Rāma*. *Rāma* constructed a bridge across the deep, and, followed by myriads of monkeys, he slew *Rāvaṇa*, his brother, sons, and kindred, together with all the *Rākshasas*, and installed the pious *Rākshasa* chief *Vibhīshaṇa* in the kingdom in *Laṅkā*, and then returned with *Sītā* to his city *Ayodhyā*, and was established in the kingdom. *Rāma* granted to *Hanūmat* that he should live as long as the history of *Rāma's* deeds is remembered on earth. *Rāma* went to his own abode after having reigned 11,000 years. From that time all excellent objects of entertainment were, through the grace of *Sītā*, supplied to *Hanūmat*, who constantly stayed there hearing the deeds of *Rāma* sung by *Apsarases* and *Gandharvas* (cf. v. 11,323). He had obstructed this path of the gods to *Bhīma* with the view that none might defeat or curse him (III, **148**).—§ 426: When *Bhīma* asked *Hanūmat* to show him the form he had when crossing the ocean, *Hanūmat* declared this to be impossible, as all things diminish according to the different *yugas*, even the *Siddhas*, gods, and great *ṛshis*. Then he described the *Kṛtayuga* (*b*) and the *Tretā* (q.v., § 427), *Dvāpara* (q.v., § 428), and *Kaliyuga* (q.v., § 429).—§ 430: *Hanūmat* was prevailed upon to grant the request of *Bhīma* (see § 426), and showed himself as great as the *Vindhya* or the *Maināka* mountain, and said that he might become as long as he wished; he had himself been able to slay *Rāvaṇa*, but would not obscure the glory of *Rāma*. He pointed out to *Bhīma* the way to the *Saugandhikavana* and the garden of *Kubera*, which was guarded by *Yakshas* and *Rākshasas*, and warned him against plucking the flowers himself, delivering a discourse upon the duties of the four castes, etc. (III, **150**).

Hanumat or **Hanūmat**, name of a monkey, the son of Vāyu (the Wind). § 11 (Parvasaṅgr.): I, **2**, 453.—§ 424

(Bhīmakadalīkhaṇḍapraveça): III, **146,** 11134 (*kapiḥ*, obstructed the way to Heaven to Bhīmasena), 11138 (*vānaraḥ*), 11155, (11156); **147,** 11170 (*Vāyutanayaḥ*), (11171), (11173), 11175 (*iva*), (11176), 11176, 11177 (*bhrātā mama* — i.e. Bhīmasena's — *guṇaçlāgho buddhisattvabalānvitaḥ | Rāmāyaṇe 'tivikhyātaḥ çrīmān vānarapuṅgavaḥ*), 11181, (11182), 11183 (Bhīmasena could not even move the tail of *H.*). — § 425 (Hanūmad-Bhīmasaṃv.): III, **147,** 11192 (Hanūmat tells his name and his story to Bhīmasena, cf. § 531 foll.), 11193 (begotten by Vāyu on the wife of Keçarin); **148,** (11201).—§ 426 (do.): III, **149,** 11225, (11229), (11234) (described the different yugas to Bhīmasena). —§ 430 (do.): III, **150,** 11272 (showed his former shape to Bhīmasena), 11275 (*tad adbhutaṃ mahāraudraṃ Vindhyaparvatasannibhaṃ . . . H°o varshma*), 11276, 11281 (*plavagottamaḥ*).—§ 431 (Saugandhikāharaṇa): III, **151,** 11329, 11332 (promised to stand on the flagstaff of Arjuna—*Vijayasya dhvajasthaḥ*; cf. V, 2222), 11335.—§ 531 (Rāmopākhyānap.): III, **280,** 16102 (counsellor of the monkey king Sugrīva), 16115 (*Anilātmajaḥ*), 16125. — § 534 (Hanūmatpratyāgamana): III, **282,** 16227 (*°pramukhāḥ . . . plavaṅgamāḥ*, despatched to seek Sītā), 16229, 16263 (reached Laṅkā and consoled Sītā).—§ 535 (Setubandhana): III, **283,** 16284 (*Mārutātmajaḥ*, commanded the monkey force). — § 538 (Kumbhakarṇaraṇagamana): III, **286,** 16385 (*Mārutātmajaḥ*), 16389 (*Pavanātmajaḥ*), 16392 (*Mārutātmajaḥ*, slew the Rākshasa Dhūmrāksha).—§ 539 (Kumbhakarṇādivadha): III, **287,** 16434 (*Mārutātmajaḥ*, slew the Rākshasa Vajravega).—§ 541 (Indrajidvadha): III, **289*a*,** 16468, (*β*), 16477.—§ 542 (Rāvaṇavadha): III, **290*a*,** 16500.— § 543 (Rāmābhisheka): III, **291,** 16576 (shall live as long as Rāma's fame), 16591 (sent as messenger from Rāma to Bharata).—§ 561*h* (Arjuna): V, **56,** 2222 (*Mārutātmajaḥ*, had promised to Bhīmasena to place an image of himself on the standard of Arjuna, cf. III, 11332).—§ 599 (Jayadrathavadhap.): VII, **139,** 5777 (*°ān iva parvataṃ*, sc. *udyamya*, cf. the note of PCR.).

Cf. also the following synonyms:—

Anilātmaja ("the son of the Wind"): III, 16115 (*H°*), 16233.

Mārutātmaja (do.): III, 11280, 16258 (*H°*), 16284 (*H°*), 16385 (*H°*), 16392 (*H°*), 16434 (*H°*); V, 2222 (*H°*).

Pavanātmaja (do.): I, 452 (*H°*); III, 16223, 16386, 16389 (*H°*).

Vāyuputra (do.): III, 16592.

Vāyutanaya (do.): III, 11170.

Hanūmatpratyāgamana ("the returning of Hanūmat"). § 534: Rāma and Lakshmaṇa were dwelling on the mountain Mālyavat. Rāma sent Lakshmaṇa to Kishkindhyā to threaten Sugrīva. Sugrīva, however, said that he had despatched monkeys in all directions to find out Sītā. After a month those who had been sent to the north, the east, and the west returned. After two months Hanūmat, Aṅgada, etc., returned from the south, after having pillaged Madhuvana (*b*). Hanūmat told that in a cavern of the palace of Maya the ascetic Prabhāvatī had shown them the way; on the shore they had seen the mountains Sahya, Malaya, and Dardura, then they had met Sampāti, the brother of Jaṭāyu(s) (*c*), and had informed him of everything; Sampāti then had directed them to Laṅkā (*d*), whereafter Hanūmat had crossed the ocean and slain the Rākshasī of the water, and had been recognized by Sītā from the words of Avindhya; Sītā had given him a jewel as a credential and told him, as a token, that Rāma on the mountain Citrakūṭa had shot a blade of grass at a crow; Hanūmat then had caused himself to be seized by the soldiers of Rāvaṇa, and set fire to Laṅkā.

Hanyamāna, pl. (*°āḥ*), a people: VI, 377 (only B., C. has Haṃsamārga, q.v.).

Hara[1], an Asura. § 130 (Aṃçāvat.): I, **67,** 2659 (*Dānavottamaḥ*, incarnate as king Subāhu).

Hara[2], Çiva, q.v.

Hara[3], a Rudra. § 665 (Mokshadh.): XII, **208** *δ*, 7585.

Harāhara, an Asura. § 92 (Aṃçāvat.): I, **65,** 2533 (so B.: *Virūpāksha-Harāharau*, C. has *Virūpāksha-Mahodarau*; is there not to be read *Virūpākshā Harāharau*? cf. Hara, v. 2659, and Ahara (C. Suhara), v. 2660).

Hārahūṇa, pl. (*°āḥ*), a people. § 285 (Nakula): II, **32,** 1194 (in the west, vanquished by Nakula on his digvijaya.)— § 295 (Dyūtaparvan): II, **51,** 1844 (brought tribute to Yudhishṭhira). — § 342 (Indralokābhigamanap.): III, **51,** 1991 (had been present at the rājasūya of Yudhishṭhira). Cf. Hūṇa, pl.

Haraṇāharaṇa. § 11 (Parvasaṅgr.): I, **2,** 363 (i.e. Haraṇāharaṇaparvan).

[Haraṇāharaṇaparvan] ("the section relating to the handing over the gift of honour," the 17th of the minor parvans of the Mhbhr.). § 253: *Kṛshṇa* said that *Arjuna* had not insulted their family, but had rather enhanced their respect, and prevailed upon them that they, by conciliation, brought *Arjuna* back to *Dvārakā*, where he was united in marriage with *Subhadrā* and passed a whole year. The last time of his exile he passed in *Pushkara*. After the twelve years were complete he came back to *Khāṇḍavaprastha*. *Draupadī* at first was jealous, but then embraced *Subhadrā*. *Kṛshṇa* visited them at *Indraprastha* with *Rāma*, *Akrūra Dānapati* (the *senāpati* of the *Vṛshṇis*), *Anādhṛshṭi*, *Uddhava* (a disciple of *Bṛhaspati* himself), *Satyaka* and *Sātyaki*, and *Kṛtavarman Sātvata*, and *Pradyumna*, *Çāmba*, *Niçaṭha*, *Çaṅku*, *Cārudeshṇa*, *Jhillin*, *Vipṛthu*, *Sāraṇa*, *Gada*, etc., bringing with them many nuptial presents. *Yudhishṭhira* sent the twins out to receive them. *Kṛshṇa* gave them 10,000 kine from the country of *Mathurā*, and *Bālhika* horses as *kanyādhana*, etc. *Rāma* gave *Arjuna* as a wedding present (*pāṇigrahaṇika*) 1,000 elephants. Having spent many days in sports and merriment there, the *Vṛshṇis* returned to *Dvāravatī* with *Rāma* in the van, carrying with them the gems that had been given them by *Yudhishṭhira*. But *Kṛshṇa* remained with *Arjuna* at *Indraprashtha*, and they went a-hunting over the borders of the *Yamunā*. *Subhadrā* brought forth *Abhimanyu*, so called because he was fearless (*abhī*) and wrathful (*manyumat*, v. 8027). Upon his birth *Yudhishṭhira* gave away 10,000 kine and *nishkas* to the *brahmans*. The child became the favourite of *Vāsudeva*, etc., and acquired from his father the *Dhanurveda* (*b*). — *Pāñcalī* (*Kṛshṇā*, v. 8045) also obtained five sons (see § 159): *Prativindhya*, *Sutasoma*, *Çrutakarman*, *Çatānīka*, *Çrutasena*. They were born each at the interval of one year. Their *jātakarman*, *cūḍa*, and *upanayana* were performed by *Dhaumya*. After having studied the *Vedas* they acquired from *Arjuna* knowledge of all weapons celestial and human (I, **221**).

Haraṇāhārika (*°kā*, B.). § 10 (Parvasaṅgr.): I, **2,** 313 (i.e. Haraṇāharaṇaparvan).

Harasulocana = Çiva (1000 names[2]).

Hārdikya[1] = Kṛtavarman, q.v.

Hārdikya[2], a prince. § 130 (Amçāvat.): I, **67**, 2651 (incarnation of the Asura Açvapati).—§ 554 (Sainyodyogap.): V, **4**γ, 75 (among the princes to whom the Pāṇḍavas ought to send messengers).

Hārdikyatanaya (the son of Kṛtavarman). § 793 (Mausalap.): XVI, **7**, 245 (installed as king of Mārttikāvata).

Hari[1] = Vishṇu (Kṛshṇa), q.v.

Hari[2], a Rākshasa. § 537 (Rāma-Rāvaṇayuddha): III, **285a**, 16365 (followed Rāvaṇa).

Hari[3], a Suparṇa, the son of Garuḍa. § 564 (Mātalīyop.): V, **101**β, 3598.

Hari[4], the son of Akampana (Anukampaka). § 594 (Akampana): VII, **52**, 2030 (*Nārāyaṇasamaḥ*).—§ 678*b* (Anukampaka): XII, **257**, 9151.

Hari[5], an Asura, the son of Tārakāksha. § 606 (Tripurākhyāna): VIII, **33**, 1417, 1419.

Hari[6], a Pāṇḍava warrior. § 608 (Karṇap.): VIII, **56**νν, 2740 (slain by Karṇa).

Hari[7], a warrior of Skanda. § 615*u* (Skanda): IX, **45**η, 2563.

Hari[8] = Indra: VIII, †4700 (*vidhya . . . Namucim yathā H°ḥ*).

Hari[9] = Çiva (1000 names[2]).

***hari**, pl. (°*ayaḥ*), the horses of Indra: III, †11903, 11921, 12003, 12215; XII, †8421 (°*açva*°); XIV, †274, †275, †286 (°*mān Devarājaḥ*, i.e. Indra), 1720.

Harī, a daughter of Krodhavaçā. § 127 (Amçāvat.): I, **66**, 2624, 2627 (mother of the *harayaḥ* (?horses, PCR.), the *vānarāḥ* and the *golāngūlāḥ*).

Haribabhru, a muni. § 264 (Sabhākriyāp.): II, **4a**, 111.

Hariçcandra, an ancient king. § 266 (Çakrasabhāv.): II, **7**, 294 (*rājarshiḥ*, in the palace of Indra).—§ 271*b* (Lokapālasabhākhyānap.): *H.* is the only king who lives in the palace of Indra, and the reason is that *H.* had formerly brought the whole earth with its seven islands under his sway, and had performed the *rājasūya* sacrifice, to which all the kings of the earth brought wealth at his command, and having concluded the *rājasūya*, he was installed in the sovereignty of the earth (*sāmrājyena*). All princes who perform a *rājasūya* or are slain in battle without turning their backs, or yield up their lives after severe ascetic penances, attain to the region of Indra; II, **12**, 484 (*rājarshiḥ*), 488, 496, 497.—§ 271 (do.): II, **12**, 502, 504 (Pāndu wished to obtain the same regions as *H.*, therefore Yudhishṭhira must perform the *rājasūya*).—§ 272 (Rājasūyārambhap.): II, **13**, 516 (*rājarshim*).—§ 296 (Dyūtap.): II, **53**, 1931 (*rājasūyam avāpyaivam H°a iva prabhuḥ*).—§ 626 (Rājadh.): XII, **20**, †614 (°*aḥ pārthivendraḥ çrutas te yajñair ishṭvā puṇyabhāg vītaçokaḥ | ṛddhyā Çakram yojayan mānushaḥ san*). § 721 (Ānuçāsanik.): XIII, **3a**, 187 (read with B. *H°akratau*, and cf. Çunaḥçepha).—§ 746 (do.): XIII, **65**γ, 3200 (a sentence of his is quoted).—§ 761 (do.): XIII, **115**γ, 5663 (among the kings who abstained from meat during the month of Kārttika), 5664 (*carati vai divi satyena candravat*).—§ 775 (Ānuçāsanik.): XIII, **166**η, 7678 (enumeration).—§ 795 (Svargārohaṇap.): XVIII, **3**, 106 (°*samāḥ*, sc. *lokāḥ*, won by Yudhishṭhira).

Hariçmaçru[1], a ṛshi. § 702 (Mokshadh.): XII, **293a**, 10762 (praised Vishṇu and attained to great success).

Hariçmaçru[2] = Indra: XII, ††13205 (°*tām Indraḥ prāptaḥ*, on account of the curse of Gautama).

Hariçmaçru[3] = Çiva (1000 names[1]).

Hariçrāvā, a river. § 574 (Jambūkh.): VI, **9**λ, 336.

Haridraka, a serpent. § 47 (Sarpanāmak.): I, **35**, 1557 (enumeration).

Harigiri, a mountain on Kuçadvīpa. § 575 (Bhūmip.): VI, **12**ε, 452.

Harihaya[1] = Indra, q.v.

Harihaya[2] = Mahāpurusha (Mahāpurushastava).

Harijaṭa = Çiva: XII, 9162.

Harikeça[1] = Kṛshṇa: VI, 2949.

Harikeça[2] = Çiva: X, 770; XII, 10390 (1000 names[1]); XIII, 1158 (1000 names[2]); XIV, 194.

Harimat[1], a rite (according to Nīl.). § 270 (Brahmasabhāv.): II, **11**, 447 (in the palace of Brahmán).

Harimat[2] = Indra: XIV, †286.

Harimedha = Mahāpurusha (Mahāpurushastava).

Harimedhas, an ancient king. § 61 (Sarpasattra): I, **55**, 2099 (*yajño H°asaç ca yathā*).—§ 565 (Gālavacarita): V, **110**, 3813 (the same?, father of Dhvajavatī).

Harimedhas[2] = Vishṇu: XII, 12764, 13458 (*Açvaçirasaḥ*), 13576, 13696.

Hariṇa[1], a serpent. § 63 (Sarpasattra): I, **57**, 2152 (of Vāsuki's race).

Hariṇa[2], name of an ichneumon, v. Harita.

Hariṇa[3] = Çiva (1000 names[2]).

Hariṇāçva, a prince. § 656 (Khaḍgotpattik.): XII, **166**, 6198 (received the sword from Raghu, from him it passed over to Çunaka).

Hariṇāksha = Çiva (1000 names[2]).

***harīndra** ("king of the monkeys," or "lions"): VIII, 2474 (°*yor iva*, sc. *yuddham*, perhaps all. to the combat between Vālin and Sugrīva).

Harinetra = Çiva: VII, 9522; XIV, 194.

Haripiṇḍā, a mātṛ. § 615*u* (Skanda): IX, **46**θ, 2642.

Harirudra (i.e. Vishṇu and Çiva in one person). § 332 (Mahādevastava): III, **39**, 1627 (said of Çiva).

Harita[1], name of an ichneumon. § 646*b* (Mārjāramūshikasamv.): XII, **138**, 4942 (only C., B. has Hariṇa).

Harita[2] = Çiva (1000 names[1]).

Hārita, a muni. § 691 (Mokshadh.): XII, **279**, 9988. Cf. Hārīta.

Hārīta, a muni. § 324 (Arjunābhigamanap.): III, **26a**, 986 (praised Yudhishṭhira).—§ 637 (Rājadh.): XII, **47**η, 1594 (among the ṛshis who surrounded Bhīshma).

Harivāhana = Indra, q.v.

Harivamça, the appendix of Mhbhr. § 10 (Parvasaṅgr.): I, **2**, 357 (°*as tataḥ parva Purāṇam khilasamjñitam*).—§ 11 (do.): I, **2**, 642 (*khileshu H°aç ca*), 643 (*khileshu H°e ca*, said to contain 12,000 çlokas, in reality C. has 16,374 çlokas).—§ 795*c* (Mahābhārata): XVIII, **6**, 280 (°*samāptau tu sahasram bhojayed dvijān*), 283 (*parvaṇi*).

Harivarsha, name of a varsha. § 279 (Arjuna): II, **28**, 1044 (on his digvijaya Arjuna reached *uttaram Harivarsham*, the abode of the *Uttarāḥ Kuravaḥ*, where he could not enter).—§ 574 (Jambūkh.): VI, **6**γ, 202 (north of the mountain Hemakūṭa); **10**, 386, 400.

Harivāsa = Kṛshṇa: VI, 2949.

Harsha ("joy"), a son of Dharma. § 117 (Amçāvat.): I, **66**, 2596 (the third son of Dharma), 2597 (the husband of Nandā).

Haryaçva[1], king of Ayodhyā. § 565 (Gālavacarita): V, **115**, 3934 (*Ikshvākum . . . Ayodhyāyām*), 3936, 3937; **116**, 3938, 3944, 3951, 3952, 3957 (obtained Madhavī by giving 200 horses to Gālava, and begat with her the son Vasumanas).—§ 761 (Ānuçāsanik.): XIII, **115**δ, 5669 (the same(?), among the kings who abstained from meat during the month of Kārttika).

Haryaçva [2], king of the Kāçis, father of Sudeva and grandfather of Divodāsa. § 736*b* (Vītahavyop.): XIII, **30**, 1949 (*Divodāsapitāmahaḥ*), 1952 (°*sya dāyadaḥ . . . Sudevaḥ*).

Haryaçva [3] = Çiva (1000 names [2]).

Haryaksha = Çiva: IX, 595 (*saçūlam*); XIII, 1245 (1000 names [2]).

Haryakshan = Çiva: XIV, 192.

Hasana, a warrior of Skanda. § 615*u* (Skanda): IX, **45**η, 2569.

Hasinī, an Apsaras. § 731*b* (Ashṭāvakra-Diksaṃv.): XIII, **19**β, 1425 (among the Apsarases who danced in the palace of Kubera).

Hasta, a nakshatra (v. Sū. Si.). § 749 (Ānuçāsanik.): XIII, **89***a*, 4260 (performing of çrāddhas under the nakshatra *H.*).—§ 759 (do.): XIII, **110**, 5392 (description of the candravrata). Cf. Sāvitra.

Hastibhadra, a serpent. § 564 (Mātalīyop.): V, **103**γ, 3629.

Hastīçvara = Çiva (1000 names [2]).

Hastikāçyapa, a ṛshi. § 768 (Ānuçāsanik.): XIII, **139***a*, 6298. § 775 (do.): XIII, **166**ζ, 7672 (among the ṛshis of the north).

[Hastikūṭa] ("the artifice concerning the elephant"). § 757*b* (Ānuçāsanik.): *Bhīshma* said: A brahman *Gautama* nursed an infant elephant that had lost its mother, till it was ten years old, huge as a hill, etc.; he looked upon it as a son, and it brought him his fuel and water. *Indra*, in the shape of king *Dhṛtarāshṭra*, seized this young elephant, offering to give to *Gautama* great riches instead; "what use can brahmans have of elephants?" († vv. 4850 and 4852–86). *Gautama* said he would take the elephant from him even in [*Yamaloka*] (*c*), *Mandākinī* (*d*), the woods of *Meru* (*e*), *Nandana* (*f*), *Uttarāḥ Kuravaḥ* (*g*), [*Somaloka*] (*h*), [*Sūryaloka*] (*i*), [*Varuṇaloka*] (*j*), [*Indraloka*] (*k*), *Prājāpatyāḥ lokāḥ* (*l*), [*Goloka*] (*m*), *Svayambhubhavana* (*n*), († vv. 4896–4902), the world of the *Somapīthin* (*yatropayāti haribhiḥ somapīthī*, B.; C. *yatropayānti haribhiḥ somavīthīṃ*) (*o*); *Dhṛtarāshṭra*, as regards *c–k*, said that he would go to higher regions, and as regards *l–n*, that he would not go (or be) there; having mentioned (*o*), *Gautama* recognized *Indra*; they asked each other's benediction; *Indra* returned the elephant, and as *Gautama* alone of all R. had been able to recognize him, he took *Gautama* and the elephant with him and proceeded to heaven * (XIII, **102**).

Hastin [1], a son of the elder Dhṛtarāshṭra. § 154 (Pūruvaṃç.): I, **94**, 3747 (the second son of Dhṛtarāshṭra).

Hastin [2], a son of Suhotra. § 156 (Pūruvaṃç.): I, **95**, ††3787 (son of Suhotra and Suvarṇā, founded Hāstinapura); ††3788 (married Yaçodharā and begat with her Vikuṇṭhana).

Hāstinapura, the capital of the Kurus, on the river Gaṅgā. § 11 (Parvasaṅgr.): I, **2**, 512, 514. — § 13 (Paushyap.): I, **3**, ††672 (the capital of king Janamejaya).—§ 17 (Uttaṅka): I, **3**, ††832, 833.—§ 71 (Ādivaṃçāvatāraṇap.): I, **61**, 2261.—§ 156 (Pūruvaṃç.): I, **95**, ††3787 (founded by Hastin, the son of Suhotra and named after him). — § 157 (do.): I, **95**, ††3819 (C. by error *Ha*°). § 165 (Satyavatīlābhop.): I, **100**, 3978 (*Kurūṇāṃ puṭabhedane*), 4023, 4064.—§ 167 (Vicitravīryoparama): I, **102**, 4125.—§ 213 (Jatugṛhap.): I, **143**, 5705.—§ 241 (Vidurāgamanap.): I, **200**, 7377.—§ 244 (Rājyalābhap.): I, **207**, 7558.—§ 286 (Rājasūyikap.): II, **33**, 1258.—§ 287 (do.): II, **34**, 1260.—§ 298 (Dyūtap.): II, **58**, 2013.—§ 319 (Saubhavadhop.): III, **14**, 635.—§ 342 (Indralokābhigamanap.): III, **51**, 1996. — § 512 (Ghoshayātrāp.): III, **247**, 15039.—§ 515 (Karṇadigvijaya): III, **253**, 15210.—§ 516 (Duryodhanayajña): III, **256**, 15324. — § 552 (Goharaṇap.): IV, **47**, 1490; **50**, 1554; **67**, 2152; **69**, 2246. — § 555 (Sainyodyogap.): V, **19**, 597. — § 556 (Sañjayayānap.): V, **32**, 940.—§ 562 (Bhagavadyānap.): V, **84**, 3002. — § 569 (do.): V, **147**, 4956. — § 570 (Sainyaniryāṇap.): V, **156**, 5313. — § 573 (Ambopākhyānap.): V, **173**, 5964; **195**, 7614.—§ 604 (Karṇap.): VIII, **2**, 26.—§ 612 (Hradapraveçap.): IX, **29**, 1654, 1662.—§ 615 (Gadāyuddhap.): IX, **35**, 1974; **63**, 3535, 3580. — § 618 (Jalapradānikap.): XI, **11**, 309. — § 659 (Mokshadh.): XII, **176**, 6584.—§ 787 (Āçramavāsap.): XV, **18**, 508. — § 791 (Putradarçanap.): XV, **36**, 1010 (C. by error *Ha*°).—§ 794 (Mahāprasthānikap.): XVII, **1**, 9. Cf. Gajāhvaya, Gajapura, Gajasāhvaya, Nāgāhvaya, Nāgapura, Nāgasāhvaya, Vāraṇāhvaya, Vāraṇasāhvaya.

Hastipāda, a serpent. § 47 (Sarpanāmak.): I, **35**, 1554 (enumeration).

Hastipiṇḍa, a serpent. § 47 (Sarpanāmak.): I, **35**, 1559 (enumeration).

Hastisomā, a river. § 574 (Jambūkh.): VI, **9**λ, 327.

Hāṭaka, a country. § 279 (Arjuna): II, **28**, 1040 (°*aṃ nāma deçaṃ*, protected by Guhyakas, conquered by Arjuna).

Hāṭaka, pl. (*āḥ*), the inhabitants of Hāṭaka. § 279 (Arjuna): II, **28**, 1042 (°*ān abhitaḥ . . . Gandharvarakshitaṃ deçaṃ*, conquered by Arjuna).

Havana, a Rudra. § 770 (Ānuçāsanik.): XIII, **151**β, 7091 (enumeration).

Havidhra, an ancient king. § 775 (Ānuçāsanik.): XIII, **166**η, 7683.

Haviḥçravas, a son of the elder Dhṛtarāshṭra. § 154 (Pūruvaṃç.): I, **94**, 3748 (the sixth son of Dhṛtarāshṭra).

Havirdhāman. § 768*b* (Kṛshṇa Vāsudeva): XIII, **147**, 6829 (*Prajāpatiḥ*, son of Antardhāman and father of Pracīnabarhis).

Havis [1] = Çiva (1000 names [2]). Do. [2] = Vishṇu (1000 names).

Havishmat, a ṛshi. § 266 (Çakrasabhāv.): II, **7**, 294 (in the palace of Indra).

Havishmatī, a daughter of Aṅgiras. § 489 (Āṅgirasa): III, **218**, 14127 (*havirbhiç ca*, sc. *paçyati*, the fifth daughter of Aṅgiras).

Havyakavyabhuj [1] = Vishṇu (Hayaçiras): XII, 13382, 13452.

Havyakavyabhuj [2] = Agni, q.v.

Havyavah, Havyavāha, Havyavāhana = Agni, q.v.

Haya, pl. (°*āḥ*), a family (?). § 267 (Yamasabhāv.): II, **8**, 333, 335 (in the palace of Yama).

***hayaçāstra:** V, 7102 (°*vidā*).

Hayaçiras ("having a horse's head"), a form of Vishṇu. § 564 (Mātalīyop.): V, **99**, 3551 (*atra*—i.e. in Pātāla—*Ādityo H°āḥ kāle parvaṇi parvaṇi uttishṭhati suvarṇākhyaṃ vāgbhir āpūrayañ jagat*).—§ 641 (Rājadh.): XII, **122**, 4515 (sc. *jāgarti*).—§ 717*b* (Nārāyaṇīya): XII, **340**, 12923 (*ahaṃ H°ā bhūtva samudre paçcimottare pibāmi suhutaṃ havyaṃ kavyañ ca çraddhayānvitaṃ*, says Nārāyaṇa, cf. v. 13508); **341**, 13104; [**343**, 13260 (Kṛshṇa identified with the horse's head); **348**, 13451 (*hayaçiro mahat | Havyakavyabhujo Vishṇoḥ*), 13498 (when Madhu and Kaiṭabha had robbed the Vedas Vishṇu assumed a horse's head), 13503 (in that shape Vishṇu recovered the Vedas), 13508 (Vishṇu then placed the horse's head in the north-eastern (*udakpūrve*) region of the ocean), 13523 (*hayaçirastanum*), 13527 (*hayaçiraḥ*)]. Cf. Açvaçiras, Hayamukha, Vaḍavāmukha.

Hayaçiras[2] = Mahāpurusha (Mahāpurushastava)

Hayaçirodhara ("having a horse's head") = Vishṇu: XII, 13459, 13507, 13526. Cf. Hayaçiras[1].

Hayagardhabhi = Çiva (1000 names[2]).

Hayagrīva[1], a Videha king. § 562 (Bhagavadyānap.): V, **74**γ, 2731 (*Videhānām*, among the wicked kings who annihilated their kinsmen, etc.).

Hayagrīva[2], an Asura. § 567 (Bhagavadyānap.): V, **130**, 4415 (in a later birth he was slain by Kṛshna. Cf. Hariv., 3109–10).

Hayagrīva[3], an ancient king. § 628*b* (Rājadh.): The ancient king *H.*, after having slain a large number of his foes in battle, was himself defeated and slain, being once without a follower at his side. He acquired great fame from the battles he fought. This was his sacrifice, and having completed it by yielding up his life-breaths, he is now sporting in the regions of the gods. He protected his kingdom, performed sacrifices, was possessed of learning, etc. He drank soma in the sacrifices, gratified the brahmans, etc., therefore he won heaven: XII, **24**, 720 (*rājarsheḥ*).

Hayamukha ("having a horse's face") = Vishṇu: I, 1250 (Garuḍa identified with *H.*).

Hayarāja ("the king of the horses"). § 589 (Droṇābhishekap.): VII, **11**μ, 384 (had been slain by Kṛshṇa).

Hāyi hāyi huvā hoyi huvā hoyi tathā 'sakṛd gāyanti tvām sāmagā brahmavādinaḥ = Çiva (1000 names[1])

Hemā, a river. § 574 (Jambūkh.): VI, **9**λ, 331.

Hemaçṛṅga, a mountain. § 221*b* (Gaṅgā): I, **170**, 6454 (?, *purā Himavataç caishā H°ād viniḥsṛtā Gaṅgā*).

Hemaguha, a serpent. § 47 (Sarpanāmak.): I, **35**, 1554 (enumeration).

Hemakampana, a Kuru warrior. § 600 (Ghaṭotkacavadhap.); VII, **156**κ, 6851 (only B., C. has *Hemapuñjakaḥ*).

Hemakara = Çiva (1000 names[2]).

Hemakūṭa. § 390*b* (Tīrthayātrāp.): On the mountain *H.* the utterance of words (so PCR., who follows the various reading cited by Nīl., "*vācā yatra bhavan,*" instead of "*vātābaddha bhavan*") caused the gathering of clouds and stones by thousands. There the recitation of the sacred scriptures was heard, but nobody was seen; in the evening and the morning there was seen fire, and biting flies would interrupt the austerities. Lomaça explained that formerly on this *Ṛshabhakūṭa* (i.e. Hemakūṭa) dwelt a great and resentful ṛshi, who was many hundred years old, and was named Ṛshabha. When practising austerities he had been spoken to by others, and in wrath he ordered the mountain to throw stones on him who should utter any word there, and forbade the wind to make any noise. Therefore, as soon as a man utters any word here he is forbidden by a roaring cloud. Formerly, when the gods came to the *Nandā*, many men came to see them, but the gods with Indra at their head did not like to be seen, and therefore they rendered the spot inaccessible by raising obstructions in the form of mountains, and from that day onwards men could not see that hill, far less ascend it. Lomaça further said: "Here all the gods performed the best sacrifices, and the marks thereof may be seen to this day, the grass resembling *kuça* grass, and many trees resembling *yūpas*; the gods and ṛshis dwell there to this day, and it is their fire which is seen in the evening and the morning. By bathing here one's sins are destroyed": III, **110**, 9969 (*parvatam*, near the River Nandā and Aparanandā, visited by Yudhishṭhira, etc., on his tīrthayātrā).—§ 459 (Mārkaṇḍeyas.): III, **188**, 12917 (*parvatam*, seen by Mārkaṇḍeya in the stomach of Nārāyaṇa).—§ 574 (Jambūkh.): VI, **6**β, 198 (the second of the six *varshaparvatāḥ* of Jambudvīpa), 202 (beyond *H.* lies Harivarsha), 236 (identified with Kailāsa, q.v.), (θ), 246 (inhabited by Guhyakas).

Hemanetra, a Yaksha. § 269 (Vaiçravaṇasabhāv.): II, **10**, 398 (among the Yakshas in the palace of Kubera).

Hemāṅga = Vishṇu (1000 names).

Hemapuñjaka, a Kuru warrior. § 600 (Ghaṭotkacavadhap.): VII, **156**κ, 6851 (only C., B. has *Hemakampanaḥ*).

Hemavarman = Hiraṇyavarman: V, 7493, 7518.

Hemavarṇa[1], a Suparṇa, the son of Garuḍa. § 564 (Mātalīyop.): V, **101**β, 3599.

Hemavarṇa[2], the son of Rocamāna. § 592 (Saṃçaptakavadhap.): VII, **23**o, 1014 (*Rocamānasya sutam*, proceeded against Droṇa, description of his horses).

Heramba = Gaṇeça: I, 75.

Herambaka, pl. (°*āḥ*), a people. § 281 (Sahadeva): II, **31**, 1118 (in the south, vanquished by Sahadeva on his digvijaya).

Hetu = Vishṇu (1000 names).

Hetvātman = Kṛshṇa: XII, 1650.

Hiḍimba, a Rākshasa, slain by Bhīmasena. § 11 (Parvasaṅgr.): I, **2**, 361 (°*Bakayor vadhaḥ*), 381 (°*sya vadhaḥ*).—§ 71 (Ādivaṃçāvatāraṇap.): I, **61**, 2253 (*Rakshaḥ*, slain).—§ 158 (Pūruvaṃç.): I, **95**, ††3824 (*hatvā*).—§ 214 (Hiḍimbavadhap.): I, **152**, 5927 (°*o nāma Rākshasaḥ*), 5940 (brother of Hiḍimbā), 5950 (°*o nāma Rākshasaḥ*); **153**, 5962 (*Rākshaseçvaraḥ*), 5974, 5981, 5984, (5995), 6004; **154**, 6011, 6038 (is slain by Bhīmasena).—§ 215 (Bakavadhap.): I, **162**, 6256 (°*sya vadhāt*).—§ 315 (Maitreyaçāpa): III, **10**, 368 (*Rakshasām . . . H-Bakamukhyānām*).—§ 316 (Kirmīravadhap.): III, **11**, 416 (had been the friend of Kirmīra), 451 (°*Bakayoḥ . . . açrupramārjanam*).—§ 317 (Draupadīparitāpav.): III, **12**, 553 (°*vanam*, all. to § 214), 568 (*Bhīmasena-H°ayoḥ*, do.), 573.—§ 435 (Jaṭāsuravadhap.): III, **157**, 11496 (*mārgam Baka-H°ayoḥ*).—§ 551 (Kīcakavadhap.): IV, **22**, 726 (*hatvā H°m*).—§ 561 (Yānasandhip.): V, **50**, 1987 (all. to § 214).—§ 562 (Bhagavadyānap.): V, **90**ν, 3151 (°*sya*, sc. *hantā*, i.e. Bhīmasena).—§ 600 (Ghaṭotkacavadhap.): VII, **176**, 8010 (°*-Baka-Kirmīrā nihatā mama bāndhavāḥ*, says Alāyudha); **180**δδδ, †8211 (*nihatā Rākshasendrā H°-Kirmīra-Bakapradhānāḥ*); **181**, 8235 (°*-Baka-Kirmīrā Bhīmasenena pātitāḥ*).—§ 617 (Aishīkap.): X, **11**δ, 598 (all. to § 214).

Hiḍimbā, a Rākshasī, sister of Hiḍimba and by Bhīmasena, mother of Ghaṭotkaca. § 11 (Parvasaṅgr.): I, **2**, 380.—§ 71 (Ādivaṃçāvatāraṇap.): I, **61**, 2255 (*prāptā H°ā Bhīmena yatra jāto Ghaṭotkacaḥ*).—§ 83 (Ādivaṃçāvatāraṇa): I, **63**, 2452 (by Bhīmasena, mother of Ghaṭotkaca).—§ 159 (Pūruvaṃç.): I, **95**, ††3833 (do.).—§ 214 (Hiḍimbavadhap.): I, **152**, 5940 (fell in love with Bhīmasena); **153**, 5964, (5972), 5981, 6006; **154**, 6007, (6011), 6041 (*Rākshasī*); **155**, 6042, 6045, 6057, 6062 (*Rākshasī*), 6081 (bore Ghaṭotkaca to Bhīmasena).—§ 317 (Draupadīparitāpav.): III, **12**, 554 (*Rākshasī*), 562, 570 (cf. § 214).—§ 600 (Ghaṭotkacavadhap.): VII, **176**, 8010 (*parāmarshaḥ kanyāyā H°āyāḥ kṛtaḥ purā*, says Alāyudha).

[Hiḍimbavadhaparvan] ("the section relating to the killing of Hiḍimba," the 9th of the minor parvans of Mhbhr.) (cf. Hiḍimba). § 214 (cf. III, 553 ff.): Not far from that place dwelt on a *çāla* tree the *Rākshasa Hiḍimba*, a cannibal with eight long and sharp-pointed teeth, etc. Scenting the odour of man, he sent his sister *Hiḍimbā* to slaughter them and bring them unto him. She fell in love with *Bhīma*, and, assuming a beautiful form, she asked him to become her husband, and promised to rescue him and his brothers and mother from her brother; but *Bhīma* ("neither men nor *Gandharvas*, nor *Yakshas* are able to bear my might," v. 5960) refused to awaken them (I, **152**). Seeing that his sister did not return soon enough, *Hiḍimba* proceeded quickly to the spot, and, abusing his sister, he rushed at her, but was seized by *Bhīma* and dragged to a distance, lest his yells should awaken the brothers of *Bhīma*; fighting they broke down the trees, etc., and at those sounds the *Pāṇḍavas* woke up with their mother, and saw *Hiḍimbā* sitting before them (I, **153**). She made herself and her love for *Bhīma* known to them. *Arjuna* offered to assist *Bhīma*; but *Bhīma* refused. *Arjuna* then said: "The morning twilight is about to set in; during the twilights *Rākshasas* become stronger; kill him without delay." Then *Bhīma* threw the *Rākshasa* to the ground, and he, dying, sent forth a terrible yell; then he doubled up his body and broke it in the middle. *Arjuna* thought there was a town not far off. Thereto they proceeded, followed by *Hiḍimbā* (I, **154**). *Bhīma* would also have slain *Hiḍimbā*, but was prevented by *Yudhishṭhira*. It was agreed upon, that she should have *Bhīma* for her husband, until she got a son, sporting with him during the day, but bringing him back every evening. She then flew away with him, and sported with him on mountains, etc., until she had brought forth (the *Rākshasa* women bring forth the very day they conceive (v. 6077) a bald-headed son, whom they, on account of his baldness, called *Ghaṭotkaca* (*ghaṭo hāsyotkaca iti*, v. 6079), who developed into a young man the very hour he was born, excelled all *Piçācas*, etc., in strength, and soon acquired high proficiency in all weapons. *Hiḍimbā* then went away; and also *Ghaṭotkaca*, who promised that he would come when wanted for business, went away northwards. It was *Indra* who had created *Ghaṭotkaca* as an antagonist for *Karṇa*, in consideration of the latter's lance (I, **155**). The *Pāṇḍavas* proceeded from forest to forest in the garb of ascetics, studying the *Brāhma Veda*, and the *Vedāṅgas*, and the *nītiçāstra*, through the countries of the *Matsyas*, *Trigartas*, *Pañcālas*, and *Kīcakas*. Then they met *Vyāsa*, who comforted them and led them into the town of *Ekacakrā* to the house of a brahman. He ordered them to wait here, till he came back, and then went away (I, **156**).

Hīka, a Piçāca. § 607 (Karṇap.): VIII, **44**, 2064 (*Bahiç ca nāma Hīkaç ca Vipāçāyāṃ Piçācakau | tayor apatyaṃ Bāhīkā naishā sṛshṭiḥ Prajāpateḥ*).

Himālaya=Himavat: VI, 1229 (*sthāvarāṇāṃ H°ḥ*, sc. *asmi*, says Kṛshṇa).

Himavadgirisaṃçraya = Çiva (1000 names[2]).

Himavat, the Himalaya mountains. § 43 (Garuḍa): I, **30**, 1401 (the Vālakhilyas repaired to *H.* to perform austerities).—§ 48 (Çesha): I, **36**, 1567 (*°as taṭe*, there Çesha performed austerities). — § 134 (Viçvāmitra): I, **72**, 2946 (*prasthe H°o ramye Mālinīm abhito nadīm*, there Menakā gave birth to Çakuntalā). — § 135 (Çakuntalop.): I, **74**, 3057 (*°aḥ prasthe*, do.), 3061 (*°aḥ pṛshṭhe*).—§ 178 (Pāṇḍu): I, **114**, 4476 (*dakshiṇaṃ pārçvaṃ ramyaṃ H°o gireḥ*). — § 180 (Gāndhārīputrotpatti): I, **115**, 4505 (Vyāsa repaired to *H.*).—§ 184 (Pāṇḍu): I, **119**, 4637 (crossed by Pāṇḍu).—§ 214 (Hiḍimbavadhap.): I, **155**, 6067 (*°girikuñjeshu*).—§ 221 (Caitrarathap.): I, **170**, 6451 (*°pārçve*). — § 221*b* (Gaṅgā): I, **170**, 6454 (*purā H°aç caishā Hemaçṛṅgād viniḥsṛtā Gaṅgā*).—§ 227 (Aurvop.): I, **178**, 6811 (the women of the Bhṛgus fled to *H.*).—§ 228 (do.): I, **181**, 6885 (Parāçara threw the fire which he had kindled for the purpose of his snake sacrifice on the northern side of *H.*).—§ 232 (Svayaṃvarap.): I, **185**, 6966 (*°cchikharair iva*).—§ 233 (do.): I, **188**, 7042 (*iva*).—§ 249 (Arjunavanavāsap.): I, **215**, 7812 (*°pārçvaṃ*, visited by Arjuna). — § 269 (Vaiçravaṇasabhāv.): II, **10**, 412 (among the mountains (personified) present in the palace of Kubera). — § 270 (Brahmasabhāv.): II, **11**, 428 (*°pṛshṭhe*, there Nārada performed the brahmavrata).—§ 277 (Jarāsandhavadhap.): II, **24**, 933.—§ 279 (Arjuna): II, **27**, 1037 (*sa-Nishkuṭaṃ*, conquered by Arjuna on his digvijaya).—§ 280 (Bhīmasena): II, **30**, 1078 (*°aḥ pārçvaṃ*, conquered by Bhīmasena on his digvijaya).—§ 287 (Rājasūyikap.): II, **34**, 1283 (*°cchikharān iva*).—§ 290*d* (Bhūliṅga): II, **44**, 1546 (*Bhūliṅgaçakunir nāma pārçve H°aḥ pare*).—§ 294 (Dyūtap.): II, **50**, 1805 (*°sāgarānūpāḥ sarve ratnākarāḥ*).—§ 295 (do.): II, **51**, 1861 (*°pushpajaṃ . . . kshaudraṃ*), 1864 (*parārdhe H°aḥ*).—§ 304 (Anudyūtap.): II, **77**, 2548 (*caled hi H°ān*).— § 305 (do.): II, **78**, 2573 (on *H.* Yudhishṭhira had been instructed by Merusāvarṇi). — § 317 (Arjunābhigamanap.): III, **12**, 591 (*°ān çīryet*).—§ 320 (Saubhavadhop.): III, **16**, 671 (*iva*).—§ 327 (Draupadīparitāpav.): III, **32**, 1211 (*kshīyeta H°ān api*); **35**, 1398.—§ 331 (Kairātap.): III, **38**, 1528 (*°cchikharaṃ prati*), 1533 (*°pṛshṭhe*), 1544 (*°pṛshṭhaṃ*); **39**, 1589 (*°cchikharāçrayaḥ*, i.e. Çiva as the Kirāta; Arjuna's encounter with Çiva on *H.*). — § 389 (Gaṅgāvatāraṇa): III, **108**, 9922 (Bhagīratha went to *H°pārçvaṃ*), 9923 (*b*: description, inhabited by Kinnaras, Apsarases, and Vidyādharas), 9931; **109**, 9949, 9954 (*Gaṅgā H°aḥ sutā*, held by Çiva).—§ 419 (Gandhamādanapr.): III, **140**, 10865 (the kingdom of Subāhu, the Pulinda king, was situated near *H.*), 10867 (the Pāṇḍavas started for *H.*).—§ 424 (Bhīmakadalīkhaṇḍapr.): III, **146**, 11152 (*iva*).— § 434 (Saugandhikāharaṇa): III, **156**, 11438 (the Pāṇḍavas had visited *H.*).—§ 436 (Yakshayuddhap.): III, **158**, 11541 (*pṛshṭhaṃ H°aḥ*), 11542 (the Pāṇḍavas came to the hermitage of Vṛshaparvan, *pṛshṭhe H°aḥ*).—§ 437 (do.): III, **160**, 11669 (*°pṛshṭhe*). — § 449 (Ājagarap.): III, **177**, †12350 (crossing *H.*, the Pāṇḍavas returned to the kingdom of Subāhu).—§ 450 (do.): III, **178**, 12368 (on *H.* Bhīmasena was seized by an ajagara; *b*: *H.* was frequented by Devarshis and Siddhas); **179**, 12425 (*sudurgo 'yaṃ Yaksha-Rākshasa-saṅkulaḥ*). — § 457 (Vaivasvatop.): III, **187**, 12792 (*°aḥ çṛṅgaṃ*), 12794 (*baddhā . . . naur matsyasya vacaḥ çrutvā çṛṅge H°as tadā | tac ca Naubandhanaṃ nāma çṛṅgaṃ H°aḥ paraṃ | khyātam adyāpi*).—§ 459 (Mārkaṇḍeyas.): III, **188**, 12917 (seen by Mārkaṇḍeya in the stomach of Nārāyaṇa).—§ 468 (Indradyumnop.): III, **199**, ††13334 (the abode of the owl Prāvārakarṇa).—§ 496 (Skandotpatti): III, **225**, 14331 (*çailaṃ Krauñcaṃ H°aḥ sutaṃ*).—§ 512 (Ghoshayātrāp.): III, **249**, 15101 (*°āṃç ca parivrajet*).—§ 515 (Karṇadigvijaya): III, **254**, 15241 (conquered by Karṇa on his digvijaya).—§ 531 (Ramopākhyānap.): III, **280**, 16102 (*iva*).—§ 538 (Kumbhakarṇaraṇagamana): III, **286**, 16380 (*iva*).—§ 547 (Karṇa): III, **308**, 17146 (*°vanabhūtaṃ siṃhaṃ keçariṇaṃ yathā*). — § 548 (Āraṇeyap.): **313**, 17318 (four mountains enumerated).—§ 549*c* (Arjuna): IV, **2**, 50 (*°ān iva çailānāṃ*, sc. Arjuna). — § 552 (Goharaṇap.): IV, **39**, 1298 (*girau*, all to § 331); **44**, 1383 (*jāto H°aḥ pṛshṭhe*, sc. Arjuna).—§ 555 (Indravijaya): V, **11*a***, 353 (*°pṛshṭhe*);

14, 433.—§ 561 (Yānasandhip.): V, **55,** 2181 (*°ān api parvataḥ*).—§ 562 (Bhagavadyānap.): V, **76,** 2772; **82,** 2918 (*caled hi H°ān*).—§ 565 (Gālavacarita): V, **110,** 3809 (*atra* — i.e. in the west — *mūlaṃ H°o Mandaraṃ yāti çāçvataṃ*); **111,** 3825 (*°pṛshṭhe*, the abode of Maheçvara).—§ 570 (Sainyaniryāṇap.): V, **157,** 5315 (*iva*). — § 574 (Jambūkh.): VI, **3,** 104 (omens); **6**β, 198 (among the *varshaparvatas* of Jambudvīpa), (θ), 246 (the abode of Rakshases).—§ 576 (Bhagavadgītāp.): VI, **13,** 502 (*iva*).—§ 587 (Bhīshmavadhap.): VI, **119,** 5664 (*Gaṅgā H°aḥ sutā*). — § 588 (do.): VI, **121,** 5795 (*girīṇāṃ H°ān varaḥ*).—§ 592 (Saṃçaptakavadhap.): VII, **21,** 890 (*vedīṃ . . . H°cchikharākārāṃ*).—§ 594 (Mṛtyu): VII, **54,** 2097 (*°o mūrdhni yatra devāḥ purāyajan*).—§ 595 (Shoḍaçarāj., v. Marutta): VII, **55,** 2172 (*haimaṃ H°aḥ pādaṃ*).— § 596 (Pratijñāp.): VII, **75,** 2668 (*girau*, all. to § 331); **80,** 2843 (*°aḥ pādaṃ*, reached by Arjuna and Kṛshṇa on their way to the abode of Çiva).—§ 599 (Jayadrathavadhap.): VII, **91,** 3236 (*haṃsā H°aḥ prasthe vāriviprahatā iva*); **105,** 3955 (*iva*).—§ 605 (Karṇap.): VIII, **19,** 718 (*iva*).—§ 606 (Tripurākhyāna): VIII, **34,** 1475 (*adhisthāne H°ān Vindhyaparvataḥ*, description of the chariot of Çiva).—§ 607 (Karṇap.): VIII, **42,** †1983 (*iva*); **44,** 2029 (*bahishkṛtā H°ā*, sc. the Bāhīkas); **45,** 2073 (*°aḥ çṛṅgaṃ*, there Karṇa had lived for a long time), 2104 (protected by Rakshases and Piçācas).—§ 608 (do.): VIII, **79,** †4061 (*calet svadeçād H°ān*).—§ 610 (Çalyap.): IX, **5,** 289 (*prasthe H°aḥ çubhe aruṇāṃ* (*ā°*, C.) *Sarasvatīṃ prāpya*); **6,** 295.—§ 611 (do.): IX, **9,** 424 (*haṃsā H°aḥ prasthe pibanta iva medinīṃ*). — § 613 (Gadāyuddhap.): IX, **33,** 1941 (*°cchikharākārāṃ . . . gadāṃ*).—§ 615i (Saptasārasvata): IX, **38,** 2207 (*sarit sā H°pārçvāt prasrutā*, sc. Viçālā). — § 615u (Skanda): IX, **44,** 2458 (Gaṅgā threw the embryo from which Skanda was born on *H.*); **45,** 2504 (gave a seat to Skanda), (γ), 2516 (came to the investiture of Skanda), 2549 (gave Skanda two companions, viz. Ativarcas and Suvarcas). — § 615z (Arundhatī): IX, **48,** 2795 (the seven Ṛshis went to *H.*); 2796 (*°vane*), 2808 (*°pṛshṭhe*).—§ 615aa (Çrutāvatī): IX, **48,** 2829 (*°vanaṃ*, Bharadvāja repaired to *H.*).—§ 615b (Baladevatīrthayātrā): IX, **54,** 3043 (*parçve H°aḥ*, Balarāma came to *H.*).—§ 615 (Gadāyuddhap.): IX, **58,** 3279 (*°i pushpitāv iva kiṃçukau*).—§ 617 (Aishīkap.): X, **12,** 635 (*°pārçvam āsthāya*, Kṛshṇa performed austerities for twelve years).—§ 619 (Strīvilāpap.): XI, **21,** 610 (*iva*).—§ 638b (Ramopākhyāna): XII, **49,** 1758 (*°vanam*, the abode of Āpava).—§ 640 (Rājadh.): XII, **57,** 2075 (*iva*).—§ 641f (Pṛthu Vainya): XII, **59,** 2239 (*acalottamaḥ*, bestowed inexhaustible wealth upon Pṛthu Vainya).—§ 641 (Rājadh.): XII, **122,** 4471 (*çṛṅge H°o Merau kanakaparvate yatra Muñjāvaṭo Rāmo jaṭāharaṇam ādiçat*); **126,** 4653 (*mahāçailaḥ*); **128,** 4714 (*iva*).—§ 654 (Pavanaçālmalisaṃv.): XII, **154,** 5805; **156,** 5842 (*°pṛshṭha°*).—§ 650 (Khadgotpattik.): XII, **166,** 6151 (*°aḥ çṛṅge*, there Brahmán performed a sacrifice). — § 660b (Bhṛgu-Bharadvājasaṃv.): XII, **192,** 7010 (*uttare H°pārçve*, description).— § 662b (Jāpakop.): XII, **199,** 7202 (*°pādasaṃçrayaḥ*). — § 663 (Mokshadh.): XII, **203,** 7422 (*yathā H°aḥ pārçvaṃ . . . na dṛshṭapūrvaṃ manujaiḥ*).—§ 672b (Çakra-Namucisaṃv.): XII, **226,** †8202 (*iva*).—§ 678b (Mṛtyu-Prajāpatisaṃv.): XII, **259,** 9209 (*°mūrdhni yatra devāḥ samījire*).—§ 695b (Dakshayajñavināça): XII, **285,** 10275 (*°aḥ pṛshṭhe . . . Gaṅgādvāre*, there Daksha performed his sacrifice).—§ 714 (Çukakṛtya): XII, **328,** 12314 (*b*: *H.* is frequented by Siddhas, Cāraṇas, Apsarases, Kinnaras, and various species of birds. There dwells Garuḍa (*Garutmān*); the four lokapālas, the gods, and Ṛshis used to repair thither. There Vishṇu (*c*) performed austerities; there Kumāra (*d*) threw his dart, which Vishṇu (*e*) shook, and which Prahlāda (*f*) could not raise. North of *H.* lies *Ādityaparvata*, the hermitage of Çiva (*Vṛshadhvajaḥ*), where he remained for a thousand celestial years, standing on one leg. It is surrounded on all sides with fire and cannot be approached by Yakshas, Rākshasas, and Dānavas, because the god of fire (*Pāvakaḥ*) himself removes all impediments from Çiva. At the slope of the mountain Vyāsa taught the Vedas to his disciples: Sumantu, etc. (*a*)), 12344 (*°pṛshṭhe*).—§ 716 (Çukābhipatana): XII, **334,** 12612 (*iva*), 12615 (*saçṛṅge . . . H° Merusambhave*, broken in twain by Çuka).—§ 717b (Nārāyaṇīya): XII, **343,** XIV), ††, 13222 (*gireḥ*, father of Umā, whom he bestowed upon Çiva), ††13223 (Bhṛgu therefore cursed *H.*, that it should have no gems (*ratnāni*), (*aa*), 13281 (burst at the encounter between Rudra and Nārāyaṇa); **347,** 13429 (the āçrama of Nārada is situated on *H.*); **350,** 13645 (*°pāda āsaṭaḥ*, sc. Vyāsa), 13648 (*°pāde*). — § 726 (Ānuçāsanik.): XIII, **10,** 438 (*pārçve H°aḥ*).—§ 730 (do.): XIII, **14,** 632 (the āçrama of Upamanyu was situated on *H.*).—§ 730g (Upamanyu): XIII, **14,** 917 (*çailānāṃ H°ān*, sc. *asi*, i.e. Çiva).— § 731b (Ashṭāvakra-Diksaṃv.): XIII, **19,** 1396 (crossed by Ashṭāvakra), 1407 (*Siddha-Cāraṇasevitaṃ*), 1408.—§ 733z (Kālodaka): XIII, **25,** 1748 (the father-in-law of *Çiva*, *Çaṅkaraçvaçuraḥ*). — § 736b (Vītahavyop.): XIII, **30,** 1980 (*iva*).—§ 739 (Ānuçāsanik.): XIII, **35,** 2161 (*acālyo H°ān giriḥ*). — § 746 (do.): XIII, **66,** 3334 (*acalottame*, there the gods performed a sacrifice).—§ 747b (Suvarṇotpatti): XIII, **84,** 3991 (there Rudra wedded his spouse (Umā)). — § 758 (Ānuçasanik.): XIII, **103,** 4932 (there Bhagīratha had dwelt).—§ 768 (do.): XIII, **139,** 6335.—§ 768b (Umā-Maheçvarasaṃv.): XIII, **140,** 6339 (*Siddha-Cāraṇasevite*), 6363 (*°pārçvaṃ*), 6372 (consumed by Çiva), 6375 (restored to his former condition). — § 768 (Ānuçāsanik.): XIII, **148,** 6902 (*°pṛshṭhe*), 6923.—§ 770 (do.): XIII, **151**ε, 7105.—§ 775 (do.): XIII, **166**a, 7656.—§ 778 (Açvamedhikap.): XIV, **3,** 60 (there Marutta performed a sacrifice, from which gold was left behind by the brahmans). — § 778b (Saṃvartta-Maruttīya): XIV, **4,** 83 (*iva*), 88 (*Meruṃ . . . H°pārçva uttare*).—§ 778f (Muñjavat): XIV, **8,** 180 (*°aḥ pṛshṭhe Muñjavān nāma parvataḥ*).—§ 780 (Açvamedhikap.): XIV, **14,** 362.—§ 782g (Guruçishyasaṃv.): XIV, **53**η, 1173 (among the principal mountains).—§ 785 (Anugītāp.): XIV, **78,** 2253 (*yathā*). — § 792 (Nāradāgamanap.): XV, **37,** 1044 (Sañjaya repaired to *H.*).—§ 793 (Mausalap.): XVI, **7,** 251 (the widows of Kṛshṇa crossed *H.* and took their abode in Kalāpagrāma).—§ 794 (Mahāprasthānikap.): XVII, **2,** 47 (on their way to Heaven the five Pāṇḍavas and Draupadī crossed *H.*).—§ 795c (Mahābhārata): XVIII, **5,** 209 (*yathā*).

Cf. also the following synonyms:—

* **Çailaguru**: IX, 2958 (?)
Çailarāj: IX, 3096 (?).
Çailarāja: I, 4648 (?), 4653 (?); III, 8126 (?); XII, 12331, 12336; XIV, 181.
Çailendra: IX, 2500.
Girirāj: VI, 3419.
Girirāja: VIII, †4321.
Himālaya, q.v.

Himavatparvatātmajā = Umā: XIII, 6746
Himavatsuta = Arbuda: III, 4097 (*A*°).
Hiṇḍuka = Çiva (1000 names [1]).
Hiraṇmaya [1], a ṛshi. § 266 (Çakrasabhāv.): II, **7**, 299 (in the palace of Indra).
Hiraṇmaya [2], a varsha. § 574 *i* (Jambūkh.): To the south of Nīla and the north of Nishadha is the varsha *H.* with the River Hairaṇvatī; it is the abode of Garuḍa (*pakshirāṭ*), the people are all followers of the Yakshas (*Yakshānugāḥ*), wealthy, and handsome, of great strength and cheerful, their life lasting for 12,500 years. The three summits [of Çṛṅgavat, Nīl.] are beautiful: one is made of jewels, another of gold, and the third of all kinds of gems, and adorned with palaces; there the self-luminous (*svayamprabhā*) goddess Çāṇḍilī always lives: VI, **8**, 290.
Hiraṇmaya [3] = Çiva: I, 1932.
Hiraṇmaya [4]: Mahāpurusha (Mahāpurushastava).
Hiraṇvatī, name of a river. § 570 (Sainyaniryāṇap.): V, **152**, 5176 (runs through Kurukshetra, there the Pāṇḍavas encamped). — § 571 (Ulūkadūtāgamanap.): V, **160**, 5407 (do.).—§ 574 (Jambūkh.): VI, **9**λ, 333.—§ 775 (Ānuçāsanik.): XIII, **166***a*, 7651.
Hiraṇyabāhu [1], a serpent. § 63 (Sarpasattra): I, **57**, 2147 (of Vāsuki's race).
Hiraṇyabāhu [2] = Çiva: XIII, 1229 (1000 names [2]); XIV, 198.
Hiraṇyabindu, a tīrtha. § 249 (Arjunavanavāsap.): I, **215**, 7815 (°*os tīrthe*, visited by Arjuna).—§ 377 (Dhaumyatīrthak.): III, **87**, 8317 (°*ḥ kathito girau Kalañjare mahān*, in the east).—§ 733*d* (Ānuçāsanik.): By stirring (*vikshobhya*) the waters of *H.* and reverencing the god, who lies in the kuça grass (?, *kuçeçayaṃ*, PCR. translates quite differently), one is cleansed of his sins: XIII, **25**, 1697.
Hiraṇyaçikhara, a mountain. § 423 (Gandhamādanapr.): III, **145**, 11057 (PCR. takes *hiraṇyaçikharaṃ* ("of golden summits") as an adj. to *Maināked*). Cf. the next.
Hiraṇyaçṛṅga, a mountain. § 263 (Sabhākriyāp.): II, **3**, 67 (near Maināka).—§ 574 (Jambūkh.): VI, **6**, 237 (do., PCR. takes Maṇimaya to be the name and *hiraṇyaçṛṅgaḥ* as as adj. ("of golden summits")). Cf. the preceding.
Hiraṇyadhanus, king of the Nishādas and father of Ekalavya.—§ 204 (Ekalavya): I, **132**, 5241 (*Nishādarājasya H°aḥ sutaḥ | Ekalavyaḥ*), 5255 (*Nishādapateḥ . . . H°aḥ sutaṃ*, i.e. Ekalavya).
Hiraṇyagarbha [1] ("the golden fetus") ≐ Brahmán. § 4 (Anukram.): I, **1**, 59.—§ 599 (Jayadrathavadhap.): VII, **94**, 3479 (*brahmasūtreṇa badhnāmi kavacaṃ tava, pārthiva | H°eṇa yathā baddhaṃ Vishṇor purā raṇe*).—§ 621 (Rājadh.): XII, **43**, 1513 (Kṛshṇa identified with *H.*). — § 705 (Mokshadh.): XII, **303**, 11231 (with various names in the different philosophical systems); **309**, †11506 (instructed Vasishṭha), 11511 (do.). — § 717*b* (Nārāyaṇīya): XII, **340**θ, 12914 (*Brahmā*), (ι), 12933 (°*o bhagavān esha chandasi sushṭutaḥ | so 'ham yogaratir, brahmán, yogaçāstreshu çabditaḥ*, says Nārāyaṇa); **343**χ, 13255 (°*o dyutimān yo esha chandasi stutaḥ | yogaiḥ sampūjyate nityaṃ sa evāhaṃ bhuvi smṛtaḥ*, says Kṛshṇa); **348**, 13470 (born from the primeval lotus, which sprang from [the navel of] Aniruddha); **350**, 13703 (promulgator of the Yoga system, read with B. *yogasya* instead of *lokasya*).—§ 730 (Ānuçāsanik.): XIII, **14**, 610 (°*pramukhā devāḥ*).
Hiraṇyagarbha [2] = Çiva (1000 names [1]). Do. [3] = Vishṇu (1000 names).
Hiraṇyahasta, a brahman. § 677 (Mokshadh.): XII, **235**, 8608 (the rājarshi Madirāçva gave his daughter to *H.*, and therefore went to worlds praised by the very gods).—§ 767 (Ānuçāsanik.): XIII, **137***a*, 6268 (do.).
Hiraṇyakaçipu, an Asura. § 89 (Aṃçāvat.): I, **65**, 2525 (son of Diti and father of five sons, Prahlāda, etc.).—§ 130 (do.): I, **67**, 2641 (*Diteḥ putraḥ*, incarnate as Çiçupāla).—§ 246 (Sundopasundop.): I, **209**, 7620 (*mahāsurasyānvaye H°oḥ purā Nikumbho nāma Daityendraḥ*).—§ 384*c* (Vishṇu): III, **102**, 8758 (*ādi-Daityaḥ*, had been slain by Vishṇu in his nṛsiṃha form).—§ 493 (Āṅgirasa): III, **221**, 14194 (?*kanyā sā Rohiṇī nāma H°oḥ sutā | karmaṇā 'sau babhau bhāryā*, according to Nīl. and PCR. *H.* is another name of the fire Manu, who married his own daughter Svishṭakṛt, i.e. Rohiṇī).—§ 524*d* (Vishṇu): III, **272**, 15835 (slain by Vishṇu in his nṛsiṃha form).—§ 602 (Droṇavadhap.): VII, **191**, 8790 (*yathā rūpaṃ purā Vishṇor H°or vadhe*).—§ 603 (Nārāyaṇāstramokshaṇap.): VII, **197**, 9104 (*saṃkruddham iva garjantaṃ H°r Haviṃ*). — § 612 (Hradapraveçap.): IX, **31**ζ, 1751 (had been slain).—§ 656 (Khaḍgotpattik.): XII, **166**γ, 6146. — § 673*b* (Bali-Vāsavasaṃv.): XII, **227***a*, 8265 (among the ancient rulers of the earth).—§ 714*f* (Prahlāda): XII, **328**, 12330 (°*oḥ sutaḥ*, i.e. Prahlāda). — § 717*b* (Nārāyaṇīya): XII, **340**κ, 12942 (Nārāyaṇa prophesies that he, in the shape of a nṛsiṃha, will slay *H.*); **343**, VII), ††13208, ††13209, ††13210 (cursed by Vasishṭha and slain [by Vishṇu in the shape of a nṛsiṃha]).—§ 730*b* (Ānuçāsanik.): The Dānava *H.*, whose strength was so great that he could shake the very mountain of Meru, obtained from Çiva the lordship of all gods (*sarvāmaraiçvaryaṃ*), which he enjoyed for ten millions of years. His son was Mandāra: XIII, **14**, 662. Cf. Daiteya, Daityendra, Dānava, Ditija, Ditinandana.
Hiraṇyakavaca = Çiva: X, 261; XII, 10362 (1000 names [1]).
Hiraṇyakavacodbhava = Çiva (1000 names [2]).
Hiraṇyākhya, v. Hiraṇyāksha.[1]
Hiraṇyakṛt = Agni, q.v.
Hiraṇyakṛtacūda = Çiva (1000 names [1]).
Hiraṇyāksha [1], an Asura. § 590 (Droṇābhishekap.): VII, **14**, 543 (*yathā Vishṇuḥ purā rājan H°eṇa saṃyuge*).—§ 603 (Nārāyaṇāstramokshaṇap.): VII, **193**, 8896 (*yathā . . . H°e purā hate*).—§ 612 (Hradapraveçap.): IX, **31**ζ, 1751 (*mahāsuraḥ*, had been slain).—§ 656 (Khaḍgotpattik.): XII, **166**γ, 6146.—§ 717*b* (Nārāyaṇīya): XII, **340**κ, 12942 (Nārāyaṇa prophesies that he will slay *H.*—so B., C. has *H°ākhyaṃ—Daiteyaṃ*).—§ 766 (Ānuçāsanik.): XIII, **126**, 6016 (slain by Vishṇu in the shape of a boar (*vārāhaṃ rūpaṃ āsthāya*).
Hiraṇyāksha [2], a son of Viçvāmitra. § 721*b* (Viçvāmitrop.): XIII, **4**β, 256 (enumeration).
Hiraṇyākshī = Durgā (Umā): VI, 801.
Hiraṇyanābha = Vishṇu (1000 names).
Hiraṇyapaksha(ḥ) çakuni(ḥ) = Kṛshṇa: XII, 1634.
Hiraṇyapati = Çiva (1000 names [1]).
Hiraṇyapura, a city of the Asuras. § 11 (Parvasaṅgr.); I, **2**, 459 (°*vāsibhiḥ*, vanquished by Arjuna). — § 445 (Nivātakavacayuddhap.): III, **173**, 12209 (in the air, inhabited by the Kālakeyas and the Paulomas), 12214, 12264, 12266 (is destroyed by Arjuna).—§ 552*d* (Arjuna): IV, **61**, 1977 (on the other side of the ocean Arjuna destroyed 6000 inhabitants of *H.*, all. to § 445). — § 561 (Nara-Nārāyaṇau): V, **49**, 1932 (*esha*—i.e. Nara (= Arjuna)—*pāre samudrasya H°m ārujat*, all. to § 445).—§ 564 (Mātalīyop.):

V, **100**, 3567 (in Pātāla, inhabited by Daityas and Dānavas, built by Viçvakarman and planned by Maya).—§ 572 (Rathātirathasaṅkhyānap.): V, **169**, 5871 (*Dānavānāṃ sahasrāṇi H°vāsinām*, slain by Arjuna, all. to § 445).—§ 593 (Abhimanyuvadhap.): VII, **51**, 1998 (*Mahendraçatravo yena* —i.e. by Arjuna—*H°vāsinaḥ . . . Paulomāḥ saganā hatāḥ*, all. to § 445).—§ 596 (Pratijñāp.): VII, **75**, 2669 (*Dānavānāṃ sahasrāṇi H°vāsinām*, slain by Arjuna, all. to § 445).— § 601 (Droṇābhishekap.): VII, **185**γ, 8437 (do., do.). Cf. Dānavapura.

Hiraṇyaretas[1] = Agni, q.v.

Hiraṇyaretas[2] = Çiva (1000 names[2]).

Hiraṇyaroman = Bhīshmaka: V, 5350 (*Bh°*).

Hiraṇyasaras, a tīrtha. § 717*b* (Nārāyaṇīya): XII, **343**, XI), ††13220 (*tīrthaṃ* = Prabhāsa, there Soma bathed).

Hiraṇyātman = Kṛshṇa: XIII, 7745.

Hiraṇyavarman[1], king of the Daçārṇas. § 573 (Ambopākhyānap.): V, **189**, 7419 (*°eti nṛpaḥ . . . Dāçārṇakaḥ*), 7420, 7423 (the daughter of *H.* was married to Çikhaṇḍin, whom she found not to be a man), 7428, [7429 (*Kāñcanavarmaṇaḥ*); **190**, 7439, 7447 (marched with an army against Drupada); **192**, [7493 (*Hemavarmaṇi*), 7506 (*Kāñcanavarmaṇā*)], 7511, [7518 (*Hemavarmaṇi*)] (when Çikhaṇḍinī had become a man and was proved to be so, *H.* made peace and retired).—Cf. Daçārṇa, Dāçārṇa, Daçārṇādhipati, Dāçārṇaka, Daçārṇanṛpa, Daçārṇapati, Daçārṇarāja, Dāçārṇarāja, Hemavarman, Kāñcanavarman.

Hiraṇyavarman[2] = Çiva: VII, 9454.

Hiraṇyavarṇa = Çiva: VII, 2884.

Hiraṇyavarṇa(ḥ) garbha(ḥ) = Kṛshṇa: XII, 1626.

Hiraṇyeçaya = Mahāpurusha (Mahāpurushastava).

Hlādana(ṃ) = Çiva (1000 names[2]).

Homātman = Kṛshṇa: XII, 1632.

Homya(ṃ) = Çiva (1000 names[1]).

Hotra(ṃ) = Çiva (1000 names[1]).

Hotravāhana[1], a Brahmarshi. § 324 (Dvaitavanapr.): III, **26***a*, 987.

Hotravāhana[2], a Rājarshi (king of the Sṛñjayas?). § 573 (Ambopākhyānap.): V, **176**, 6037 (*rājarshiḥ*), 6041 (do.), 6050 (the maternal grandfather of Ambā), (6053), 6058 (consoled Ambā and directed her to Rāma Jāmadagnya), 6059 (*Sṛñjayaḥ*), 6062 (*rājarshiḥ*), (6067), 6080 (*Sṛñjayaḥ*).

Hotṛ = Çiva: XII, 10364 (1000 names[1]), 10412 (do.); XIII, 609

* **hrada**, pl. (*°āḥ*) ("lakes," personif.). § 615*u* (Skanda): IX, **45**γ, 2514.

Hrāda, a serpent. § 793 (Mausalap.): XVI, **4**η, †120.

Hradapraveçana(m) ("Duryodhana's entering the lake"). § 10 (Parvasaṅgr.): I, **2**, 346 (*parva*, i.e. Hradapraveçaparvan).

[Hradapraveçaparvan] ("the section containing Duryodhana's entering the lake," the 81st of the minor parvans of Mhbhr.; cf. Hradapraveçana). § 612: The followers of *Çakuni* attacked the *Pāṇḍavas*; *Arjuna* and *Bhīmasena* came to the rescue of *Sahadeva*; *Arjuna* slew them; *Duryodhana* rallied the remnants of his chariots (many hundreds), etc., and urged them against the *Pāṇḍavas* and *Dhṛshṭadyumna*; they were exterminated in a moment by the *Pāṇḍavas* and the *Sṛñjayas*. Only *Duryodhana* remained alive. Requested by *Dhṛtarāshṭra*, *Sañjaya* recounted the numbers of the remnants of the *Pāṇḍava* army. *Duryodhana* abandoned his slain steeds and fled away on foot without a companion, towards a lake, taking up his mace, recalling the words of *Vidura*. The *Pāṇḍavas* (headed by *Dhṛshṭadyumna*) with *Arjuna* (with *Gāṇḍīva*) baffled the *Kurus*. In *Duryodhana's* army no great chariot-warrior was alive save *Açvatthāman*, etc. (*a*). Urged by *Dhṛshṭadyumna*, *Sātyaki* was about to slay *Sañjaya*; but *Vyāsa* came and caused him to be let off alive. He met with *Duryodhana*, whom he told the state of things, and who asked him to inform *Dhṛtarāshṭra*. Then *Duryodhana*, having charmed the waters, entered the lake. *Sañjaya* then met with *Açvatthāman*, etc. (*a*), and informed them; they fled away, at sight of the *Pāṇḍavas*, to the *Kuru* camp, taking *Sañjaya* up in the chariot of *Kṛpa*. The sun had set a little before. The outposts of the camp wept aloud. The old men proceeded towards the city with the princesses (description); also the camp-guards fled towards the city, and so did also the cowherds, etc., from fear of *Bhīmasena*. *Yuyutsu* reflected (β). With the permission of *Yudhishṭhira* he supervised the removal of the ladies. The sun was setting. Having entered *Hāstinapura* with the ladies, he informed *Vidura* (γ); urged by *Vidura*, he passed that night in his own abode, while *Vidura* went to the cheerless mansion of *Dhṛtarāshṭra* (IX, **29**). Requested by *Dhṛtarāshṭra* (δ), *Sañjaya* related: The *Pāṇḍavas* wandered over the field in search of *Duryodhana*; tired, they took rest in their camp with all their soldiers. Then *Açvatthāman*, etc. (*a*) proceeded towards the lake and urged *Duryodhana* to fight with them against *Yudhishṭhira*. *Duryodhana* said that he would rest for that night and fight the next morning. *Açvatthāman* swore to slay the *Pāṇḍavas* and all the *Pāñcālas* in this night. Certain hunters who used every day to procure a basketful of meat for *Bhīmasena* overheard the conversation between *Duryodhana* and *Açvatthāman*, etc. (*a*), and informed *Bhīmasena*. The *Pāṇḍavas* all (*Arjuna*, etc. (ε) with *Yudhishṭhira*) started towards the lake (*Dvaipāyana*); hearing the noise caused by them *Açvatthāman*, etc. (*a*), took leave from *Duryodhana* and went away, and stopped under a banyan (IX, **30**). *Kṛshṇa* advised *Yudhishṭhira* to slay *Duryodhana* by putting forth his own powers of illusion (ζ). *Yudhishṭhira* tauntingly addressed *Duryodhana* for having fled from battle (η); *Duryodhana* said that he had entered the lake not from fear, but in order to take rest. *Yudhishṭhira* asked *Duryodhana* to come out immediately and fight his foes. He answered that his kingdom might be taken by his foes, his own desire being to enter the woods and retire from the world (θ); *Yudhishṭhira* taunted him for such an answer, refusing to take the kingdom in gift from one who was unable to retain it by might (IX, **31**).

Hradodara, a Daitya. § 615*u* (Skanda): IX, **46**, 2693 (slain by Skanda).

Hrī ("shame," personif.). § 270 (Brahmasabhāv.): II, **11**, 458 (in the palace of Brahmán). — § 330 (Indradarçana): III, **37**, 1488. § 615*u* (Skanda): IX, **45**γ, 2515 (came to the investiture of Skanda).

Hrīmat, a Viçvadeva. § 749 (Ānuçāsanik.): XIII, **91**γ, 4356 (enumeration).

Hrīnisheva, a Daitya (?). § 673*b* (Bali-Vāsavasaṃv.): XII, **227***a*, 8263 (among the ancient rulers of the earth).

Hṛcchaya = Kāma: I, 878, 880.

Hṛdika, father of Kṛtavarman. § 83 (Ādivaṃçāvatāraṇa): I, **63**, 2434.

Hṛdika, pl. (*°āḥ*), the family of Kṛtavarman. § 605 (Karṇap.): VIII, **26**, 1058 (*°ānāṃ mahārathaḥ*, i.e. Kṛtavarman).

Hṛdikasuta, Hṛdikātmaja = Kṛtavarman, q.v.

Hṛdya, a Ṛshi. § 266 (Çakrasabhāv.): II, **7**, 295 (in the palace of Indra).

Hṛshīkeça = Kṛshṇa (Vishṇu), q.v.

Hṛshīkeça, pl. (°*āḥ*) a class of beings (cf. the prec.).—§ 616 (Sauptikap.): X, **6**, 224 (hundred thousand of *H.* issued from the being who resisted Açvatthāman).

Hūhū, a Gandharva always mentioned together with Hăhā, q.v.

Hūṃhūṃhūṃkārapāra = Çiva (1000 names[1]).

Hūṃhūṃkārapriya = Çiva (1000 names[1]).

Hūṇa, pl. (*āḥ*), a people. § 223 (Vāsishṭha): I, **175**, 6685 (among the barbarous peoples created from the froth of the mouth of Vasishṭha's cow, C. by error has *Hūnān*).—§ 342 (Indralokābhigamanap.): III, **51**, 1991 (only C., B. has *Muṇḍān*, had been present at the rājasūya of Yudhishṭhira).—§ 574 (Jambūkh.): VI, **9**ξ, 373 (in the north, C. has by error *Hūnāḥ*).—§ 713 (Çukakṛti): XII, **326**, 12229 (*deçān* . . . *Cīna-H°nishevitān*, opposed to Āryavarta). Cf. Hārahūṇa, pl.

Huṇḍa, pl. (°*āḥ*), a people. § 578 (Bhīshmavadhap.): VI, **50**π, 2081 (only C., B. has *Pauṇḍrāḥ*, in the army of Yudhishṭhira).

Huta = Çiva (1000 names[1-2]).

Hutabhuj[1] = Agni, q.v. Do[2] = Vishṇu (1000 names).

Hutāça = Agni, q.v.

Hutāçana[1] = Agni, q.v.—Do.[2] = Çiva (1000 names[2]).

Hutāçanasahāya = Çiva (1000 names[2]).

Hutāçanasuta = Skanda: IX, 2549.

Hutahavyavaha = Agni, q.v.

Hutavaha = Agni, q.v.

I

Ī = Çiva (1000 names[2]).

Icchā = Çiva (1000 names[1]).

Īça[1] ("the Lord") = Brahmán: I, 2499; VI, †1261 (*B*°); XII, 11094 (*B*°).

Īça[2] (do.) = Çiva: III, 14567; IV, 1770 (?); VII, 4381; XII, 10288; XIII, 588, 610, 726, 783 (?), 820, 822, 931, 941.

Īça[3] (do.) = Vishṇu (Nārāyaṇa, Kṛshṇa): XII, 11120 (*Nārāyaṇe*), 12700, 13249 (*aham Īçaḥ*, says Kṛshṇa), 13285, 13318, 13556 (*Nārāyaṇena*); XVI, 132.

Īça[4] (do.), the Supreme Being, in general: V, †1764.

Īça[5], a Viçvadeva.—§ 749 (Ānuçāsanik.): XIII, **91**γ, 4360

Īça(ḥ) paçūnāṃ = Kṛshṇa: XIII, †7370.

Īçāna[1] ("the Lord") = Brahmán: XII, 11229 (?), 11602 (*Çambhuḥ Prajāpatiḥ*).

Īçāna[2] (do.) = Çiva: III, 8169 (worshipped in Gokarṇa), 8836 (*Çaṅkaraṃ Bhavaṃ*), 9953, 15887 (friend of Kubera); VII, 2863, 2876, 5144 (*Brahme°endra-Varuṇān*), 9453, 9462, 9503, 9504, 9534, 9595; VIII, 628 (*Brahme°āv iva*), 1435 (*Sthāṇuṃ*), 1489, 1531, 1665, 2161 (*Brahme°endra-Varuṇān*), 4361, 4440 (*Brahme°au*), 4456 (*Brahme°ānuçāsanaṃ*); IX, 908; X, 252; XII, 4498 (*Rudrāṇāṃ . . . goptāraṃ*), 10141, 10330, 10390 (1000 names[1]), 13152, 13292; XIII, 658, 728, 828, 908, 924, 956, 998, 1015, 1042, 1103, 1188 (1000 names[2]), 1273, 1305, 1331, 1359, 7497; XIV, 208.

Īçāna[3] (do.) = Vishṇu (Nārāyaṇa, Kṛshṇa): I, 22; XII, 12903 (in the form of Aniruddha), 12982, 13063, 13226, 13480, 13695; XIII, 6957 (1000 names); XIV, 1088 (= *mahān ātmā*).

Īçāna[4] (do.) = the Supreme Being, in general: III, 1139: V, 917, 1751; XII, 11692.

Īçānādhyushita, a tīrtha. § 370 (Tīrthayātrāp.): III, **84**, 7086.

Īçvara[1] ("the Lord") = Brahmán: VI, 470 (*Prajāpatiḥ*); VII, 2682 (? *viçve devāḥ sahe°āḥ*); XII, 2146.

Īçvara[2] (do.) = Çiva: I, 320, 6430, 6615 (*Gopatiṃ*), 7320, 7321, 7832; II, 1486; III, 1663, 15162; VII, 2907, 9452, 9534, 9606, 9609, 9634; VIII, 1504, 1623; X, 252, 318; XII, 6135 (*Rudraṃ*), 13156 (do.); XIII, 658 (*Īçānaṃ*), 772 (*an°bhaktaḥ*), 827, 838, 940 (created Vishṇu), 960, 1040 (*Purushaṃ*), 1048, 1069, 1123, 1131, 1135, 1188 (1000 names[2]), 1359, 3725, 4140 (as Varuṇa), 4141 (?), 7529, 7530; XIV, 210.

Īçvara[3] (do.) = Indra: I, 2354 (*haṃsarūpena*), 6781; IX, 2436; XII, 8057, †8331, †8332; XVII, 107 (*Devendraṃ*).

Īçvara[4] (do.) = Skanda: IX, 2460 (*Analātmajaṃ*), 2693; XIII, 4211.

Īçvara[5] (do.) = Visṇu (Nārāyaṇa, Kṛshṇa): II, 1325 (*Hariṃ*); III, 11866, 13509, 15538 (*Keçavaḥ*), 15546 (*Hariḥ*); V, 3503 (*Vishṇuḥ*); XII, 7522 (*Keçavaḥ*), 7604 (*Kṛshṇaṃ*), 7640, 12857 (*Hariḥ*), 12905 (in the form of Aniruddha), 13036, 13117 (*Hariḥ*), †13447, 13460, 13461 (*Nārāyaṇo Virāṭ*), 13603 (*Hariḥ*), 13656 (*Hariṃ*), 13661; XIII, 1357, 6005, 6953 (1000 names), 6958 (do.): XIV. 1600.

Īçvara[6] (do.) = the Supreme Being, in general: III, 1138, 1141, 1142, 1144, 1146, 1148, 1158, 1202, 1222; V, 1373, 3713; VI, 1349, 1390, 1399, 1410, 1515; XII, 4449, (among the names of Chastisement), 8507, 8536, 8555, 10497, 11039 (*an°ḥ*), 11360, 11408, 11604; XIV, 42.

Īçvara[7], a son of Pūru. § 150 (Pūruvaṃç.): I, **94**. 3695 (son of Pūru and Paushṭi).

Īçvara[8], a prince. § 130 (Aṃçāvat.): I, **67**, 2701 (among the kings who were incarnations from the Krodhavaçagaṇa).

Īçvara[9], name of a Rudra. § 108 (Aṃçāvat.): I, **66**, 2567 (enumeration of the eleven sons of Sthāṇu).—§ 191 (Arjuna): I, **123**, 4826 (enumeration of the Rudras present at the birth of Arjuna).—§ 770 (Ānuçāsanik.): XIII, **151**β, 7091 (enumeration).

Īçvara[10], a Viçvadeva. § 749 (Ānuçāsanik.): XIII, **91**γ, 4362 (enumeration).

Īçvareçvara = Vishṇu (1000 names).

Iḍā ("libation," or "earth"?): III, 10122.

Idhmavāha = Dṛḍhasya: III, 8642; XII, 7595 (one of the ṛshis of the south).

Īḍya = Çiva (1000 names[2]).

***īhāmṛga**, pl. (°*āḥ*) ("wolves"). § 113 (Aṃçāvat.): I, **66**, 2572 (descendants of Pulaha).

Ījaka, pl. (°*āḥ*), a people. § 574 (Jambūkh.): VI, **9**μ, 360 (only C., B. has *Ījikāḥ*).

Ījika, pl. (°*āḥ*), v. Ījaka, pl.

Ijya = Vishṇu (1000 names).

Ikshulā, a river. § 574 (Jambūkh.): VI, **9**λ, 324 (only B., C. has *Ikshumālavīṃ*).

Ikshumālavī, a river. § 574 (Jambūkh.): VI, **9**λ, 324 (only C., B. has *Ikshulāṃ Kṛmiṃ*).

Ikshumatī, a river in Kurukshetra. § 17 (Uttaṅka): I, **3**, 803 (*Kurukshetre ca vasatām*—sc. Takshaka and Açvasena—*nadīm I°īm anu*).

Ikshvāku[1], an ancient king, the son or great-grandson of Manu Vaivasvata. § 3 (Anukram.): I, **1**γ, 47 (*Yayāti°-vaṃçaḥ*, descended from Daçajyotis, etc.). § 5 (do.): I, **1**α, 220 (in Nārada's enumeration of departed kings).—§ 139 (Manu Vaivasvata): I, **75**, 3140 (the fifth son of Manu Vaivasvata).—§ 161 (Mahābhisha): I, **96**, 3843 (*°vaṃçaprabhavaḥ . . . Mahābhishaḥ*).—§ 224 (Kalmāshapāda): I, **176**, 6696 (*°vaṃçajaḥ*, sc. *Kalmāshapādaḥ*).—§ 225 (Vāsishṭha): I, **177**, 6778 (*°kulavṛddhaye*).—§ 273 (Rājasūyārambhap.): II, **14**, 568 (*°vaṃçasya*—i.e. the Solar race—opp. to *Ailasya*, i.e. the Lunar race).—§ 348 (Nalopākhyānap.): III, **66**, 2629 (*°kulajaḥ*, sc. Ṛtuparṇa).—§ 376 (Tīrthayātrāp.): III, **85**, 8270 (*yathā*).—§ 378 (do.): III, **94**, 8506 (*yathā*).—§ 407 (Māndhātrup.): III, **126**, 10427 (*°vaṃçaprabhavo Yuvanāçvaḥ*).—§ 461 (Vāmadevacarita): III, **192**, ††13145 (*Ayodhyāyām I°kulodvahaḥ pārthivaḥ Parikshin nāma*).—§ 475 (Dhundhumārop.): III, **202**, 13515 (succeeded by Çaçāda in the kingdom of Ayodhyā).—§ 525 (Rāmopākhyānap.): III, **274**, 15877 (*Ajaḥ . . . I°vaṃçajaḥ*).—§ 574 (Jambūkh.): VI, **9**αα, 314.—§ 576 (Bhagavadgītāp.): VI, **28**, 994 (*imaṃ Vivasvate yogaṃ proktavān ahaṃ avyayam | Vivasvān Manave prāha Manur Ikshvākave 'bravīt*, sc. the contents of Bhagavadgītā, cf. XII, 13598).—§ 656 (Khaḍgotpattik.): XII, **166**δ, 6193 (obtained the sword from Kshupa, from *I.* it passed over to Purūravas), 6198 (*°vaṃçajaḥ . . . Hariṇāçvaḥ*).—§ 662 (Mokshadh.): XII, **199**, 7198 (*Kāla-Mṛtyu-Yamānān te I°or brāhmaṇasya ca | vivādaḥ*), 7199.—§ 662*b* (Jāpakop.): XII, **199**, 7233 (the tale of *I.* and the brahman who was a jāpaka).—§ 717*b* (Nārāyaṇīya): XII, **349**, VII), 13598 (learnt the [Sātvata, cf. v. 13575 (only B.) and 13580] religion (*dharma*) from Manu, cf. VI, 994).—§ 720*b* (Sudarçanop.): XIII, **2**, 88 (the son of Manu and the father of 100 sons, among whom Daçāçva was the tenth).—§ 746 (Ānuçāsanik.): XIII, **78**, 3732 (*°vaṃçajo rājā Saudāsaḥ*, i.e. Kalmāshapāda).—§ 761 (do.): XIII, **115**δ, 5668 (among the kings who did not eat meat during the month of Kārttika).—§ 775 (do.): XIII, **166**γ, 7684 (enumeration).—§ 778*b* (Saṃvartta-Maruttīya): XIV, **4**, 66 (son of Kshupa and grandson of Prasandhi, the son of Manu), 67 (father of 100 sons, among whom Viṃça was the eldest).

Ikshvāku[2], pl. (*°āḥ*) ("the descendants of Ikshvāku," also name of a people). § 223 (Vāsishṭha): I, **174**, 6642 (had Vasishṭha for their purohita).—§ 225 (do.): I, **177**, 6777 (the ancestors of Kalmāshapāda).—§ 273 (Rājasūyārambhap.): II, **14**, 569 (*Ailavaṃçyāç ca ye*—i.e. the Lunar race—*rājan, tathaive°avo nṛpāḥ*—i.e. the Solar race—*tāni caikaçataṃ viddhi kulāni*).—§ 382 (Agastyop.): III, **98**, 8608 (*°rājasattamaḥ*, i.e. Trasadasyu).—§ 383 (Paraçurāma): III, **99**, 8664 (the family of Rāma Dāçarathi).—§ 387 (Sagara): III, **106**, 8831 (*°ūṇāṃ kule jato Sagaraḥ*).—§ 461 (Vāmadevacarita): III, **192**, †13198 (ruled by Çala and Dala, the sons of Parikshit [of Ayodhyā]), †13204, †13206, †13209 (*°rājyam*).—§ 478 (Dhundhumārop.): III, **204**, 13621 (said of the descendants of Kuvalāçva's sons).—§ 522 (Draupadīharaṇap.): III, **265**, ††15596 (*°rājñaḥ Subalasya* (B. *Subhavasya*) *putraḥ*, a follower of Jayadratha); **271**, 15743 (*Çibīn I°mukhyāṃç ca*, followed Jayadratha and was vanquished by Arjuna).

Ikshvāku[3], sg. ("descendant of Ikshvāku or king of the Ikshvākus") = Kuvalāçva; III, 13486 (*K*°), 13490 (*K*°).

Ikshvāku[4], sg. (do.) = Bṛhadaçva: III, 13512 (*B*°).

Ikshvāku[5], sg. (do.) = Haryaçva: V, 3934 (*H*°).

Ikshvākukanyā ("daughter of the king of the Ikshvākus") = Suvarṇā: I, ††3787 (*S*°).

Ikshvākunandana[1] ("son of the king of the Ikshvākus") = Lakshmaṇa, the son of Daçaratha: III, 16507 (*Saumitriḥ*).

Ikshvākunandana[2] (do.) = Rāma, the son of Daçaratha: III, 16472 (*R*°), 16538.

Ikshvākuvara = Mitrasaha (Kalmāshapāda): XIV, 1690.

Ilā, the daughter of Manu Vaivasvata and the mother of Purūravas.—§ 139 (Manu Vaivasvata): I, **75**, 3141 (the eighth child of Manu Vaivasvata).—§ 140 (Purūravas): I, **75**, 3143 (at one time the father and the mother of Purūravas).—§ 156 (Pūruvaṃç.): I, **95**, 3760 (daughter of Manu and mother of Purūravas).—§ 748*b* (Tārakavadhop.): XIII, **86**, 4209 (presented Skanda with a great many of flowers and fruits).—§ 768*b* (Kṛshṇa Vāsudeva): XIII, **147**, 6831 (*Manoç ca vaṃçaja Ilā Sudyumnaç ca bhavishyati*, wife of Budha and mother of Purūravas). Cf. Sudyumna.

Ilāspada, a tīrtha. § 364 (Tīrthayātrāp.): III, **83**, 6047 (cf. BR., s.v. *iḍ*).

Ilāvṛta, name of a varsha. § 574 (Jambūkh.): VI, **6**, 233 (in the middle of Jambudvīpa).

Īlina, an ancient king. § 150 (Pūruvaṃç.): I, **94**, 3706 (son of Taṃsu), 3707 (husband of Rathantarī and father of five sons, Dushyanta, etc.).—§ 156 (do.): I, **95**, 3780 (son of Taṃsu and Kāliṅgī), ††3781 (husband of Rathantarī and father of five sons, Dushyanta, etc.)

Ilopahūta = Kṛshṇa (Vishṇu): XII, 13226.

Ilvala, an Asura, the brother of Vātāpi. § 382 (Agastyop.): III, **96**, 8543 (*Daiteyaḥ*, dwelt in the city of Maṇimatī), 8546 (*brahmahā 'suraḥ*), 8550, 8552 (*Daiteyaḥ*, killed brahmans by offering them Vātāpi as food); **98**, 8613 (*Dānavaḥ*), 8614; **99**, 8615, 8619, 8620, 8623, 8625, 8627 (did not succeed in killing Agastya, who had totally digested Vātāpi, and gave much wealth to Agastya, etc.).—§ 612 (Hradapraveçap.): IX, **31**ζ, 1755 (C. has by error *Illalaḥ*, among other Asuras who had been slain by the aid of tricks). Cf. Asura, Daiteya, Daitya, Daityendra, Dānava.

Indra, the chief of the devas, lord of rain, esp. named Çakra. [§ 4 (Anukram.): I, **1**, 112 (*Çakrasya*, father of Arjuna), †161 (*Çakrāt*), †185 (*Çakra-Sūryau*), †191 (*Devarājena*).]—§ 11 (Parvasaṅgr.): I, **2**, [441 (*Purandaraḥ*)], 448 (*°āgnī*), [476 (*Purandaraḥ*)], 499 (*°vijayam*), 500 (do.), [638 (*Devarājñā*)], 639 (*sendraiḥ suragaṇaiḥ*).—§ 17 (Uttaṅka): I, **3**, ††794, ‖830, ‖831 (praised, with the çlokas 810 ff., by Uttaṅka, *I.* helped Uttaṅka to recover the ear-rings which had been stolen by Takshaka).—§ 19 (Bhṛgu): I, **4**, 867 (*devaiḥ sendraiḥ*).—§ 28 (Amṛtamanthana): I, **18**, 1123 (placed the mountain Mandara on the back of the tortoise, when the gods intended to churn the ocean), 1136 (*vāriṇā meghajenendro çamayām āsa*), [1151 (*Vajrabhṛta*, got the elephant Airāvaṇa, who emerged at the churning of the ocean), **19**, 1188 (*Balabhid*)].—§ 33 (Garuḍa): I, **23**, 1250 (Garuḍa is identified with *I.*).—[§ 37 (cf. Kadrū): *I.* (*Çakra*, v. 1285) was praised by Kadrū with the hymn vv. 1285*b*–1295.]—[§ 38 (Kadrū): I, **26**, 1295 (*Harivāhanaḥ*), 1301 (*Vāsave*, caused an immense downpour of rain.]—§ 44 (Garuḍa): I, **30**, 1415 (1422), 1428 (*Vajrī*, fought with Garuḍa).—§ 45 (Vālakhilya, pl.): I, **31**, 1448, 1449, 1453, 1457, 1468 (had formerly disregarded the Vālakhilyas, who cursed him that there should arise another *I.*; Kaçyapa, however, pacified the Vālakhilyas, who consented that the coming Indra—i.e. Garuḍa—should become the Indra only of the winged creatures).—§ 46 (Garuḍa): I, **33**, 1512, 1513 (hurled his vajra at Garuḍa, who had robbed the amṛta); [**34,** 1520 (*Purandara,* made friendship with Garuḍa, and recovered the amṛta)].—§ 60 (Sarpasattra): I, **53,** 2056 (protected Takshaka). — § 61 (do.): I, **55,** [†2098 (*Çakrasya yajñaḥ çatasaṅkhya uktaḥ*)], †2110 (°*tvasamam*).—§ 62 (do.): I, **56,** †2118 (°*sya bhavane*), †2120, 2125 (°*sya bhavane*), 2129 (deserted Takshaka).—§ 68 (Āstīka): I, **58,** 2167 (°*hastāc cyutaḥ,* sc. Takshaka), 2170 (°*hastād visrastaṃ,* sc. Takshaka). —§ 73 (Vasu Uparicara): I, **63,** 2335, 2337 (°*tvaṃ*), (2339) (Vasu obtained from *I.* a chariot (*vimāna*), and the garland Indramāla, and a bamboo pole which he erected in worship of *I.* (from that time kings raise such a pole in order to worship *I.*); *I.* (*īçvaraḥ,* v. 2354) came there in the shape of a swan).—§ 74 (do.): I, **63,** 2361 (°*prītyā,* °*mahaṃ*).— § 75 (do.): I, **63,** 2366 (°*prāsāde*).—§ 83 (Ādivaṃçāvatāraṇa): I, **63,** 2444 (father of Arjuna).—§ 84 (Ādivaṃçāvatāraṇap.): I, **64,** 2508 (headed by *I.*, the gods prevailed upon Nārāyaṇa to become incarnate).—§ 85 (Aṃçāvat.): I, **65,** 2509.— [§ 88 (do.): I, **65,** 2523 (*Çakraḥ,* the fourth of the Ādityas).] — [§ 120 (do.): I, **66,** 2600 (*Āditeḥ putrāḥ Çakramukhyāḥ*).]—[§ 130 (do.): I, **67,** 2746 (*Devarājasya,* father of Arjuna).]—§ 131*b* (Karṇa): I, **67,** 2779 (in the shape of a brahman *I.* asked Karṇa for his ear-rings and natural armour and gave him a dart—cf. § 547).—§ 134 (Viçvāmitra): I, **71, 72** (from fear of the ascetic penances of Viçvāmitra *I.* (*Çakraṃ Suragaṇeçvaraṃ,* v. 2914) despatched the Apsaras Menakā to tempt Viçvāmitra).—§ 139 (Manu Vaivasvata): I, **75,** 3136 (*Ādityān . . . Indrādin,* sons of Kaçyapa and Dākshāyaṇī, i.e. Aditi). — § 142 (Nahusha): I, **75,** 3157 (*kārayām āsa cendratvam,* sc. Nahusha).—§ 145 (Kaca): I, **76,** 3229 (*sendrā devāḥ*), †3234 (*api*), †3241.— § 146 (Devayānī): I [**78** (*I.* (*Çatakratuṃ,* v. 3280) set out to defeat the Asuras; changing himself into a wind he mixed up the clothes of some bathing maidens; from this arose the dispute between Devayānī and Çarmishṭhā)]; **80,** 3341 (*yogakshemakaraḥ . . . I°syeva Bṛhaspatiḥ*).—§ 147 (do.): I, **82,** 3408 (°*sya . . . gṛhe*).—§ 148 (Yayāti): I, **85,** 3504 (*sākshād I°iva āparaḥ,* sc. Yayāti).—§ 149 (do.): I, [**86**–] **88,** (†3564), (†3566), (†3568), †3574 (°*samaprabhāva*) (*I.* (*Çakra,* v. 3537) discoursed with Yayāti, who from pride of his ascetic merits disregarded all others and therefore fell down to earth); [**92,** 3652 (*Çakrāc ca labdho hi varaḥ,* sc. by Yayāti)]; **93,** †3672 (°*pratimaprabhāvaḥ*), †3683 (°*kalpaṃ*). § 150 (Pūruvaṃç.): I, **94,** 3701 (°*vikramaḥ,* sc. Satyeyu).— [§ 157 (do.): I, **95,** ††3814 (*Çakrāt,* father of Arjuna).]— § 175 (Karṇasambhava): I, **111,** 4407 (*brāhmaṇo bhūtvā,* repetition from § 131*b*).—§ 186 (Vyushitāçvop.): I, **121,** 4687 (*devāḥ sendrāḥ*), 4688 (*amādyad I°aḥ somena,* at the sacrifices of Vyushitāçva).—§ 190 (Pāṇḍavotpatti): I, **123,** 4779 (*rājā devānāṃ,* begot Arjuna on Kuntī).—§ 191 (Arjuna): I, **123** *a*, 4804 (*sendrāṇāṃ divaukasāṃ,* present at the birth of Arjuna), 4823 (the seventh of the Ādityas).—[§ 192 (Pāṇḍavotpatti): I, **124,** 4846 (*prāpyādhīpatyam I°eṇa yajñaiḥ*). — § 194 (Pāṇḍu): I, **126,** 4921 (*Puruhūtāt,* father of Arjuna).]—[§ 198 (Çaradvat): I, **130** (from fear of the penances of Çaradvat, *I.* (*Devarājaṃ,* v. 5075) sent the Apsaras Jānapadī to tempt Çaradvat).]—§ 208 (Astradarçana): I, **135,** 5355 (*sendrāyudhataḍit-sasandhya iva toyadaḥ*), 5401 (*sendrāyudhapurogamaiḥ . . . meghaiḥ*), [5402 (*Harihayaṃ*)]. § 209 (Drupadaçāsana): I, **138,** 5484 (*vyakshobhayetāṃ . . . I°-Vairocanāv iva*). — § 213 (Jatugṛhap.): I, **151,** 5908 (*Dharmād I°ācca Vātāc ca sushuve yā sutān imān,* sc. Kuntī, cf. § 190).—§ 214 (Hiḍimbavadhap.): I, **153,** 5971 (*vikramaṃ me yathe°sya*); [**156** (the birth of Ghaṭotkaca had been caused by *I.* (*Maghavatā,* v. 6083), in order that Karṇa might use his dart in slaying Ghaṭotkaca and Arjuna be saved)].— [§ 221 (Caitrarathap.): I, **170,** 6500 (*Çakraṃ,* father of Arjuna).]—§ 233 (Svayaṃvarap.): I, **188,** 7035 (*Pārtham I°ketusamaprabhaṃ,* i.e. Arjuna).—§ 238 (Pañcendrop.): I, **197,** [†7304] (the Indra Çibi), †7316 (°*rūpāṃ,* sc. Arjuna) (*I.* (*Vajrī,* v. 7287) was paralysed by Çiva, and together with four Indras of old confined in a cave, then the five Indras became incarnate as the five Pāṇḍavas).—[§ 241 (Vidurāgamanap.): I, **202,** 7432 (*vikramena ca lokān trīn jitavān Pākaçāsanaḥ*)]. — § 244 (Rājyalābhap.): I, **207,** 7593 (°*kalpaiḥ,* sc. the Pāṇḍavas).—[§ 246*b* (Tilottamā): I, **211** (how *I.* (*Mahendrasya,* v. 7705) got 1,000 eyes).]—§ 246 (Sundopasundop.): I, **212,** 7735 (°*e trailokyam ādhāya,* sc. Brahmán).—§ 253 (Haraṇāharaṇap.): I, **221,** 7971 (*lokeshu sendra-Rudreshu*).—§§ 254–8 (Khāṇḍavadahanap.): I, **222–8,** 8088, 8172 (protecting the Khāṇḍava wood, Indra and the other gods fight with Arjuna and Kṛshṇa, who assist Agni).—[§ 260 (do.): I, **234** (*I.* (*Çakrāt,* v. 8469) promises to give Arjuna celestial weapons when he has gratified Çiva, cf. Kairātaparvan foll.).]—[§ 263 (Sabhākriyāp.): II, **3,** 70 (*Sahasrākshaḥ Çacīpatiḥ,* performed sacrifices at Bindusaras).] — § 265 (Lokapālasabhākhyānap.): II, **6,** 275 (°*sya,* sc. *sabhāṃ*).—§ 266 (Çakrasabhāv.): II, **7,** 302 (°*āgnī,* copious description of the palace of *I.*).—[§ 270 (Brahmasabhāv.): II, **11,** 466 (*Purandaraç ca Devendraḥ,* repairs to the palace of Brahmán).]—§ 271*b* (Hariçcandra): II, **12,** 499.—§ 273 (Rājasūyārambhap.): II, **14,** 585 (°*sakhaḥ,* sc. *Bhīshmaka*). —[§ 277 (Jarāsandhavadhap.): II, **24,** 950 (*Vāsavāt,* Vasu obtained a chariot from *I.*, cf. § 73).]—§ 284 (Sahadeva): II, **31,** 1167 (°*sakhāya,* sc. Bhīshmaka).—§ 289 (Arghāharaṇap.): II, **36,** 1323 (*sendrāḥ surāḥ,* worship Hari).— § 295 (Dyūtap.): II, **52,** 1842 (°*āyudhanibhān*).—[§ 297 (do.): II, **55,** 1957 (*adrohasamayaṃ kṛtvā cicheda Namuceḥ çiraḥ / Çakraḥ,* cf. § 615*s*).]—§ 299 (do.): II, **67,** †2232 (°*kalpāḥ*); **70,** †2365 (°*kalpaḥ*).—§ 314 (Āraṇyakap.): III, **9,** 327, 328 (*Surabhyāç caiva saṃvādam I°sya ca*), 329, (330), 339 (*I.'s* discourse with Surabhi).—§ 317*b* (Kṛshṇa Vāsudeva): III, **12,** [479 (Kṛshṇa bestowed the sovereignty of the universe (*sarveçvaratvaṃ*) on Çacīpati, i.e. Indra)], 484 (*Vishṇuḥ . . . I°ād avarajaḥ*).—§ 317 (Arjunābhigamanap.): III, **12,** 566 (°*āçanisamasparçaṃ*).—§ 320 (Saubhavadhop.): III, **15,** 653 (*yathendrabhavanaṃ*); **19,** 770 (*devagaṇāḥ sarve sendrāḥ*); **22,** 865 (°*dayitam . . . vajraṃ*).—§ 323 (Dvaitavanapraveça): III, **25,** 945 (°*pratimāḥ,* sc. the Pāṇḍavas).— § 327 (Draupadīparitāpav.): III, **34,** †1374 (do.).—§ 329 (Kāmyakavanapraveça): III, **36,** 1444 (Arjuna shall receive celestial weapons from *I.*, etc.).—§ 330 (Indradarçana): III, **37,** 1469 (possessed all celestial weapons, as the gods had invested him with all their might; Arjuna, on his way to heaven, meets Indra (*Çakraḥ,* v. 1505), who tells him first to gratify Çiva).—[§ 334 (Kairātap.): III, **41** (when Arjuna had gratified Çiva, the Lokapālas (among them *I.* (*Çakraḥ,* v. 1677)) appeared; *I.* promised to send his chariot to take Arjuna to heaven).] — §§ 335–9 (Indralokābhigamanap.): III, **42–7,** 1724 (*ratham I°sya*), 1767, 1882 (°*āsane*) (the chariot of *I.* takes Arjuna to heaven, where he enters the palace of *I.* and obtains celestial weapons from *I.*; Lomaça saw Arjuna on the seat of Indra).—§ 345 (Nalopākhyānap.): III, [**54** (Nārada tells *I.* about the svayaṃvara of Damayantī, and the Lokapālas headed by *I.* repaired there)]; **55,** 2138 (Nala is despatched to Damayantī as the messenger of the gods); **56**, 2179 (*devāç cendrapurogamāḥ*); [**57** (*I.* (*Çakraḥ, Çacīpatiḥ*, v. 2226) bestowed a boon upon Nala)].—§ 346 (do.): III, **58**, 2242.—§ 356 (Tīrthayātrāp.): III, **80**, 3092 (°*samavīryeṇa*, i.e. Arjuna). — § 377 (Dhaumyatīrthak.): III, **86**, 8282 (°*ād anavaraḥ*, sc. Arjuna; Arjuna has been sent to acquire weapons from *I.*), 8288 (°*āyudholvaṇaḥ*); **87**, 8313 (at Kānyakubja Viçvāmitra drank soma with *I.*); **90**, 8377 (°*gītā* . . . *gāthā*, i.e. v. 8378), 8386 (*devāḥ sendrāḥ*, practised austerities at Viçākhayūpa).—§ 378 (Tīrthayātrāp.): III, **91**, 8419 (°*ād* . . . *astrāṇy avāptavān Pārthaḥ*, i.e. Arjuna); **92**, 8439 (°*sya vacanāt*).—§ 382 (Agastyop.): III, **96**, 8544 (°*tulyam*).—§ 384 (do.): III, **100–3**, †8730 (from the bones of Dadhīca Tvashtṛ formed the vajra with which Indra slew Vṛtra, after the gods had invested him with their energy).—§ 391 (Ṛshyaçṛṅga): III, **113**, †10088 (*yathā*).—[§ 394 (Arjuna Kārtavīrya): III, **115** (Arjuna Kārtavīrya affronted *I.* (*Vāsavam*, v. 10141), who then applied to Vishṇu).] —§ 400 (Tīrthayātrāp.): III, **118**, †10224 (°*sya*, sc. *āyatanam*, visited by Yudhishṭhira), †10234 (*yathā*), †10235 (°*sya* . . . *niveçanam*).—§ 403 (do.): III, **121**, 10292 (*devaiḥ sahendraiḥ*, performed sacrifices).—[§ 404 (do.): III, **121** (*Kauçikaḥ*, v. 10312, all. to § 405).]—§ 405 (Sukanyop.): III, **124** [**-125**], 10378, (10379), 10382, 10386 (at the sacrifice of Çaryāti Cyavana paralysed *I.*, and created the Asura Mada who rushed forwards to devour *I.*, who then allowed the Açvins to become partakers of the soma).—§ 406 (Tīrthayātrāp.): III, **125**, 10418 (*prasravaṇam* . . . *I°sya*, a tīrtha). —§ 407 (Māndhātrup.): III, **126**, 10453 (*sendrā divaukasaḥ*, Māndhātṛ sucked the forefinger of *I.* and obtained the seat beside *I.* (*Çakrasyārdhāsanam*, v. 10460).—§ 409 (Plakshāvataraṇagamana): III, **129**, 10524 (*Prabhāsam* . . . *I°sya dayitam*).—§ 411 (Çyenakapotīya): III, **130**, 10559; **131**, 10590 (*I.* in the shape of a hawk and Agni in the shape of a pigeon put Uçīnara to the test).—§ 412 (Ashṭāvakrīya): III, **133**, †10622 (*api*); **134**, †10659 (°*āgnī*). — § 414 (Yavakrītop.): III, **135**, 10708, 10709, (10713), 10721, (10727), (10729), 10732 (alarmed at the penances of Yavakrīta, *I.* in the shape of a brahman made him to desist).—§ 417 (do.): III, **138**, 10818 (*devāḥ sendrapurogamāḥ*).—§ 418 (Tīrthayātrāp.): III, **139**, †10835 (°*sya jāmbunadaparvatāt*, i.e. Meru, Nīl.).—[§ 422*b* (Naraka): III, **142** (for the sake of Indra (*Surarāja*°, v. 10915), Vishṇu slew Naraka, who desired the position of Indra (*Aindram* . . . *sthānam*, v. 10916).] — § 424 (Bhīmakadalīkhaṇḍapr.): III, **146**, 11139 (*lāṅgūlam I°āçanisamaniḥsvanam*); **147**, 11186 (°*āyudham ivocchritam*).—§ 437 (Yakshayuddhap.): III, **160**, 11736 (°*āçanir ivendreṇa visṛshṭā*).—[§ 438 (do.): III, **162**, 11807 (*deçakālāntaraprepsuḥ kṛtvā Çakraḥ parākramam / samprāptas tridive rājyaṃ Vṛtrahā Vasubhiḥ saha*).]—§ 439 (do.): III, **163**, 11845 (*I.* and Kubera reside on the mountain Mandara).—[§ 440 (do.): III, **164** (in the abode of Indra (*Vāsavam*, v. 11898) Arjuna had acquired celestial weapons).]—§ 441 (Nivātakavacayuddhap.): III, **165**[**-166**], †11909 (°*vāham*), †11915 (*surāḥ* . . . *sahendrāḥ*) (Arjuna returns on the chariot of *I.*, next day *I.* visited the Pāṇḍavas). —§§ 442–5 (do.): III, **167–73**, 12000 (*stutayaç cendrayuktāḥ*), (12016), (12019), 12102 (*yathendram Tārakāmaye*), 12130 (°*āçanisamasparçaiḥ*, sc. *bāṇaiḥ*), 12139 (at the command of *I.*, Arjuna destroyed the Nivātakavacas and the inhabitants of Hiraṇyapura). — § 446 (do.): III, **174**, 12278 (gave Arjuna a golden garland, the conch-shell Devadatta, an impenetrable armour and a diadem), 12280 (°*sya bhavane*), 12282 (do.).—§ 448 (Ājagarap.): III, **176**, †12317 (°*samena*, sc. *Arjunena*).—§ 455 (Brāhmaṇamāhātmyak.): III, **185**, 12692 (*yathaivendraḥ Prajāpatiḥ*).—§ 456 (Sarasvatī-Tārkshyasaṃv.): III, **186**, 12745 (*devāḥ sendrāḥ*).—§ 462 (Baka-Çakrasaṃv.): III, **193**, 13216 (*vṛtte Devāsure* . . . *saṅgrāme* . . . *trayāṇām api lokānām I°o lokādhipo 'bhavat*), (13236) (discourse with Baka).—§ 466 (Çibi): III, **197**, ††13274 (*Agnīndrau*, *I.* in the shape of a hawk and Agni in the shape of a pigeon put Çibi to the test), ††13275 (*çyenarūpeṇa*), ††13286 (*devāḥ sendrāḥ*).—§ 474*b* (Dhundhumārop.): III, **201**, 13498 (°*Somāgni-Varuṇaḥ*, worship Vishṇu).—§ 479 (Pativratop.): III, **206**, 13673 (*api*).—§ 491 (Āṅgirasa): III, **220**, 14162 (a fire (?) created by Pāñcajanya from his energy—*balāt*).—§ 493 (do.): III, **221**, 14188 (°*eṇa sahitam yasya havir āgrayaṇam smṛtam* | *agnir Āgrayaṇo nāma*, name of a fire (?)).—§ 495 (Skandotpatti): III, [**223**-]**224**, (14261), (14263), 14266 (delivers Devasenā from Keçin and takes her to Brahmán, who appoints Skanda as her husband). —[§ 498 (do.): III, **226** (*I.* (*Vāsavam*, v. 14355) did not venture to encounter Skanda).] — § 499 (Skanda-Çakrasamāgama): III, **227**, 14385 (encounter with Skanda).— § 501 (Skandop.): III, **229**, 14408 (appellatively?), 14409 (do.), 14410 (do., *b*: *I.* may officiate for the sun and the moon in places where there is no sun or moon; when required he even acts for fire, air, earth, and water (v. 14412)), 14413 (appellatively?), 14414 (do.), 14415 (do.), 14417 (do., °*tvam*), 14420 (do.), (14421), 14421 (the gods, headed by Çakra, asked Skanda to become the Indra of the gods; Skanda, however, only accepted the leadership of the army of the gods, and was married to Devasenā).—§ 505 (Skandayuddha): III, **231**, 14540 (*sendram jagat*). — § 506 (do.): III, **231**, 14545 (*sendracāpe ghane yathā*).—§ 507 (do.): III, **231**, 14600 (*sendrā divaukasaḥ*, in the battle between the gods and the Dānavas, Skanda slew the Asura Mahisha and was praised by *I.*).—§ 509 (Kārttikeyastava): III, **232**, 14643 (Skanda is identified with *I.*).—§ 512 Ghoshayātrāp.): III, **236**, †14745 (°*kalpaḥ*, sc. Yudhishṭhira); [**244** (at the command of *I.* (*Sureçvarāt*, v. 14971) the Gandharvas made the Dhārtarāshṭras captives), **246** (do. (*Sureçvaraḥ*, v. 15014))]. — § 520 (Mudgala): III, **260**, 15411 (*sahito devaiḥ*, came to the sacrifice of Mudgala).—§ 522 (Draupadīharaṇap.): III, **264**, 15573 (°*pratimāḥ*, sc. the Pāṇḍavas); **269**, †15684 (°*kalpāḥ*, do.); **270**, †15715 (*Pārthāḥ panca pañcendrakalpāḥ*).—[§ 526 (Rāmopākhyānap.): III, **276** (*I.* (*Çakram*, v. 15934) and other gods became incarnate on earth and begot monkeys and bears).]—§ 538 (Kumbhakarṇaraṇagamana): III, **286**, 16390 (°-*Prahlādayor iva*, sc. *yuddham*).—[§ 540 (Indrajidyuddha): III, **288** (*I.* (*Vajradharam, Sahasrāksham, Çacīpatim*, v. 16440) had been vanquished by Indrajit).]—§ 541 (Indrajidvadha): III, **290**, 16495 (*sendrāḥ* . . . *tridaçāḥ*). — § 542 (Rāvaṇavadha): III, **290**, 16518 (*çūlam I°āçaniprakhyam*). — [§ 543 (Rāmābhisheka): III, **291**, 16548 (*Çakraḥ*).]—§ 544 (Yudhishṭhirāçvāsa): III, **292**, 16604 (*sendrā api surāsurāḥ*).—§ 546 (Kuṇḍalāharaṇap.): III, **301**, 16975 (having ascertained the intention of *I.* to ask Karṇa for his ear-rings and coat of mail, Sūrya advised Karṇa to ask a dart from *I.*).—§ 547 (Karṇa): III, **309**, 17177 (*brāhmaṇo bhūtvā*); **310**, (17204) (*I.* in the shape of a brahman obtained the ear-rings and the coat of mail of Karṇa and gave him a dart).—§ 548 (Āraṇeyap.): III, **315**, 17460 (*d*: *I.* went to the mountain Nishadha (differently B.) and lived there in disguise until he had destroyed his foes).—§ 549*c* (Arjuna): IV, **2**, †46 (°*ād anavaraḥ*, sc. Arjuna).—§ 551 (Kīcakavadhap.): IV, **20**, 622 (°*samāḥ*, sc. the Pāṇḍavas); **23**, 795 (°*ṇeva*

Dānavam, sc. *pothitam*).—§ 552 (Goharaṇap.): IV, **37,** †1198 (*yathendralakshmīḥ*); **45,** 1405 (°*eṇa vā samam,* sc. Arjuna); **48,** 1518 (°*āçanisamasparçam*); **49,** 1541 (*api*); [**56** (*I.* (*Çakraḥ,* v. 1761) and the gods came to see the encounter)].—§ 552*d* (Arjuna): IV, **61,** 1975 (all. to Nivātakavacayuddhaparvan), 1976 (*aham I°ād dṛḍhām mushṭim,* says Arjuna).—§ 552 (Goharaṇap.): IV, **63,** 2030 (°*āyudham ivātatam*).—§ 553*b* (Yudhishṭhira): IV, **70,** 2268 (°*syārdhāsanam*).—§ 553 (Vaivāhikap.): IV, **72,** 2369 (*rūpam I°sya*).—§ 555 (Sainyodyogap.): V, **8,** 226 (*Devarājena*).—§ 555 (Indravijaya): V, **9,** 227, 228, 229, 233, 243, (259), (261), 277 (°*çatro,* sc. Vṛtra; *I.* slew Viçvarūpa Triçiras, the son of Tvashṭṛ, Tvashṭṛ then created Vṛtra, who attacked Indra); **10,** (290), 299, 316 (*I.* slew Vṛtra with a mass of froth, and then concealed himself in the water, the murder of Vṛtra being equal to the murder of a brahman); **11,** 359 (appellative = Nahusha), 365 (Nahusha then was appointed as Indra, and coveted Çacī, the wife of Indra).—§ 555*d* (Ahalyā): V, **12,** 372, 373 (Ahalyā had been outraged by *I.* while her husband was alive).—§ 555 (Indravijaya): V, **12,** 374, 380.—§ 555*e* (Brahmán): V, **12,** 388 (*sendrāḥ devāḥ*).—§ 555 (Indravijaya): V, [**13** (*I.* was liberated from the sin of brahman murder)]; **14,** 440 (*I.* was found out by Çacī); **15,** 456; **16,** (506), †515 (found out by Agni, installed the Lokapālas); **17,** (524) (cursed by the Ṛshis, Nahusha fell down from heaven); **18,** 552, 553, 562 (°*vijayam, I.* then again became the king of the gods).—§ 556 (Sañjayayānap.): V, **22,** †657 (*devān sendrān,* all. to Khāṇḍavadahanaparvan), †667 (*Pāṇḍyaḥ . . . samitīndrakalpaḥ*), †676 (*yathā*); **24,** †720 (°*kalpāḥ,* sc. the Pāṇḍavas); **25,** †732 (*api*); **26,** †763 (do.); **29,** †838.—§ 557 (Prajāgarap.): V, **33,** †1092 (*Pāṇḍoḥ putrāḥ pañca pañcendrakalpāḥ*); **34,** 1130.—§ 559 (do.): V, **37,** †1376 (°*kalpa,* sc. Dhṛtarāshṭra).—§ 561 (Yānasandhip.): V, **48**β, †1817 (°*kalpena,* sc. Yudhishṭhira).—§ 561*b* (Arjuna): V, **48,** †1876 (*Harimān Vajrahastaḥ,* will protect Arjuna).—§ 561 (Yānasandhip.): V, **48,** †1915 (*devān I°pramukhān*).—§ 561*d* (Nara-Nārāyaṇau): V, **49,** 1930 (worshipped Nara and Nārāyaṇa, who then assisted him in slaying the Daityas and Dānavas, Nara (i.e. Arjuna) slew the Paulomas and Kālakañjas (cf. § 445)), 1933 (had been vanquished by Arjuna, cf. Khāṇḍavadahanaparvan), 1936 (*sendrair api surāsuraiḥ*).—§ 561 (Yānasandhip.): V, **52,** 2096 (*yathendrasya jayaḥ*); **53**θ, 2108 (*sendrān imāṃl lokān*).—§ 561*f* (Nakula): V, **56,** 2230 (*Vṛtraçatrum yathendram*).—§ 561 (Yānasandhip.): V, **57,** 2265 (*api*), 2269 (*sahito devaiḥ*); **59,** 2333 (°*Vishṇusamau,* sc. Arjuna and Kṛshṇa), 2342 (°*vīryopamaḥ Kṛshṇaḥ*); **61,** 2387.—§ 562 (Bhagavadyānap.): V, **72,** 2610 (*sendrān . . . devān*); **74,** 2725 (°*jyeshṭhā iva*); **92,** 3297 (*api*); **95,** 3401 (do.).—[§ 564 (Mātalīyop.): V, **100,** 3570 (*Çakreṇa*), 3573 (*Çakraḥ,* could not vanquish the Nivātakavacas, etc.); **104** (Mātalī took Sumukha to *I.* (*Vasāvam,* v. 3662), who bestowed upon him a long life); **105** (therefore Garuḍa was incensed with wrath against *I.* (*Vāsavam,* v. 3675), but was humiliated by Vishṇu).]—[§ 565 (Gālavacarita): V, **110,** 3808 (*Çakraḥ,* cut up the foetus of Diti, whence sprang the Maruts).]—§ 567 (Bhagavadyānap.): V, **130,** 4368 (°*o Vairocanim yathā,* sc. *nigṛhṇīma*), [4413 (*Çacīpatiḥ,* had been vanquished by Kṛshṇa, who then brought the Pārijāta down from heaven)]; **131**o, 4424 (*Marutaḥ sahendreṇa,* seen in the body of Kṛshṇa).—§ 568 (Vidulāputraçāsana): V, **134,** 4562 (*Indro Vṛtravadhenaiva Mahendro samapadyata*); **135,** 4593 (°*salokatām*).—§ 569 (Bhagavadyānap.): V, **141,** 4781 (°*āyudhasavarṇaḥ,* °*āḥ,* C.); **142,** †4816 (°*ketuprakāçāḥ*).—§ 570 (Sainyaniryāṇap.): V, **151,** 5138 (*api*); **153,** 5192 (*devān sendrān api*).—§ 570*c* (Bhīshmaka): V, **158,** 5350 (°*sakhasya,* i.e. Bhīshmaka).—§ 572 (Rathātirathasaṅkhyānap.): V, **166,** 5749 (*parākramam yathendrasya*).—§ 573 (Ambopākhyānap.): V, **178,** 7110 (*devāḥ sendragaṇāḥ*); **184,** 7271 (°*āçanisamasparçām*).—[§ 574 (Jambūkh.): VI, **6,** 213 (*Çakraḥ, Sureçvaraḥ,* performs sacrifices on Meru).]—[§ 574*f* (Bindusaras): VI, **6,** 240 (*Sahasrākshaḥ,* performed sacrifices at Bindusaras).]—§ 574 (Jambūkh.): VI, **9***aa*, 313 (*varsham . . . Bhāratam / priyam I°sya devasya*).—§ 576 (Bhagavadgītāp.): VI, **14,** 555 (°*samakarmāṇam,* sc. Bhīshma).—[§ 577 (Bhīshmavadhap.): VI, **43,** 1537 (*Çatakratum,* came to see the battle).]—§ 578 (do.): VI, **50,** 2073 (*yam Bṛhaspatir I°āya tadā Devāsure 'bravīt,* sc. the krauñcāruṇa-vyūha), 2076 °*āyudhasavarṇābhiḥ patākābhiḥ*).—§ 579 (do.): VI, **54,** 2245 (*yathendrasya . . . mahatyā Daityasenayā,* sc. *yuddham*).—§ 581 (do.): VI, **62,** 2764 (°*o girīn iva,* sc. *mṛdnan*), 2774 (°*āçanisamasvanām . . . gadām*); **63,** 2798 (°*āçanisamaprabhām . . . gadām*); **64,** 2871 (°*āçanisamasvanaḥ*); **66,** 2990 (*surāsuraiḥ sarvaiḥ sendraiḥ*).—§ 582 (do.): VI, **74,** 3248 (°*āyudhasavarṇam . . . dhanuḥ*).—§ 584 (do.): VI, **83,** 3678 (*yathendrasya raṇāt purā Namucir Daityasattamaḥ,* sc. *prādravat*), 3695 (*yathā Daityacamūm . . . I°opendrāv ivāmarau,* sc. *abhidudrāvatuḥ*).—§ 585 (do.): VI, **91,** 4086 (*cāpam I°āçanisamaprabham*); **92,** 4111 (*bāṇam I°āçaniprabham*); **94,** 4183 (*cāpam I°āçanisamaprabham*), 4214 (*dhanuç citram I°āçanisamasvanam*); **95,** 4249 (*vārayasva . . . yathendras Tārakam purā*), 4306 (*cāpam I°āçanisamaprabham*); **97,** 4440 (*sendrān api surāsurān*).—§ 586 (do.): VI, **107,** 4928 (*sendrān api raṇe devān*), 4960 (*sendrair api surāsuraiḥ*), 4961 (do.).—§ 587 (do.): VI, **119,** 5657 (°*dhvaja ivotsṛshṭaḥ*).—§ 589 (Droṇābhishekap.): VII, **2,** †86 (*yathā*); **6,** 162 (*jahīndro Dānavān iva*).—§ 590 (do.): VII, **12,** 454 (*sendrair devāsuraiḥ*), 456 (Arjuna had obtained weapons from *I.,* etc.), 461 (*sendrair api surāsuraiḥ*); **15,** 610 (°*dhvajāv iva*).—§ 592 (Saṃçaptakavadhap.): VII, **21,** 859 (°*Vairocanāv iva,* sc. *yuyudhāte*), 919 (*Dānavā ivendreṇa vadhyamānāḥ*); **23**o, 995 (°*āyudhasavarṇaiḥ . . . hayottamaiḥ*), 1003 (°*āçanisamasparçāḥ,* sc. *açvāḥ*), 1027 (*sendrā iva divaukasaḥ*); **25,** 1084 (*yathendrāgnī purā Balim,* sc. *ārchatām*), 1120 (°*m ivāyantam Asurān prati*); **27,** 1198 (°*ād anavaraḥ,* sc. Bhagadatta); **28,** 1249 (*iva*).—§ 592*c* (Vaishṇavāstra): VII, **29,** 1289 (*lokeshu sendra-Rudreshu*).—§ 592 (Saṃçaptakavadhap.): VII, **29,** †1301 (°*vikramam sakhāyam I°sya,* i.e. Bhagadatta); **30,** 1302 (*priyam I°sya satatam sakhāyam,* i.e. Bhagadatta), 1310 (°*m Vṛtra-Balā(v)iva,* sc. *nijaghnatuḥ*); **32,** 1439 (°*samadyutiḥ,* sc. Sātyaki).—§ 593 (Abhimanyuvadhap.): VII, **49,** 1938 (°*dhvajāv ivotsṛshṭau*).—§ 594 (do.): VII, **52,** 2037 (°-*Vishṇusamadyutiḥ,* sc. Abhimanyu).—§ 595 (Shoḍaçarāj., v. Marutta): VII, **55,** 2172 (*sendrāmaragaṇāḥ,* came to the sacrifice of Marutta), [2180 (*Çakreṇa*)]; (do., v. Bhagīratha): VII, **60,** 2257 (*sendraiḥ suragaṇaiḥ*); (do., v. Dilīpa): VII, **61,** 2266 (*sendrā devāḥ*); (do., v. Māndhātṛ): VII, **62,** 2277 (Māndhātṛ sucked the fingers of *I.*), 2279; (do., v. Bharata): VII, **68,** 2389 (*sendrair devaiḥ*).—§ 596 (Pratijñāp.): VII, **76,** 2682 (*Marutaç ca sahendreṇa*), 2691 (Arjuna had obtained weapons from *I.,* etc.); **81,** 2910 (°*Vishṇū yathā prītau Jambhasya vadhakāṅkshiṇau*).—§ 597 (do.): VII, **83,** 2972 (*devāḥ . . . . sendrāḥ*); **84,** 2991 (*Çaryāter yajñam āyantam yathendram* (so B.) *devam Açvinau,* cf. § 405).—§ 598 (Jayadrathavadhap.): VII, **86,** 3093 (*ucchritendradhvajopamaiḥ*).—§ 599 (do.): VII, **93,** 3406 (°*dhvajākārau,* sc. *bhujau*), 3407 (°*dhvaja ivotsṛshṭaḥ*).—§ 599*c*

(Vṛtra): VII, **94**, 3458 (*sendrā divaukasaḥ*), 3461 (*devāḥ sahendrāḥ*, C. has by error *mahe°*), [3471 (*Çakra*, Çiva gave to *I.* an armour with mantras, protected by this *I.* proceeded against Vṛtra and slew him, then he gave the mantras and the armour to Aṅgiras)].—§ 599 (Jayadrathavadhap.): VII, **99**, 3676 (*°sya*, sc. *ratham*); **105**, 3932 (*°āyudhasavarṇābhāḥ patākāḥ*); **106**, 4005 (*dhanuç cendradhvajopamam*); **109**, 4109 (*dhanur ghoram I°āçanisamasvanam*); **117**, 4652 (*bāṇān . . . I°āçanisamasvanān*); **118**, †4690 (*Vṛtrendrayor yuddham iva*), †4696 (*naptā Çiner I°samānavīryaḥ*); **120**, 4774 (*vikrāntam I°syeva*); **127**, 5144 (*Brahmeçanendra-Varuṇān avahad yaḥ rathaḥ*, i.e. the chariot of Arjuna), 5162 (*sendrāyudha ivāmbudaḥ*); **128**, 5223 (*°āçanir ivendreṇa*); **134**, 5511 (*vajreṇendra ivāsurān*, sc. *jaghāna*); **146**, 6174 (*sendradhanvāmbudaḥ*), 6253 (*°āçanisamaprakhyam*, sc. *çaram*), 6273 (*°āçanisamasparçam*, sc. *çaram*); [**149**, 6461 (*tvatprasādāt, Hṛshīkeça* (i.e. Kṛshṇa), *Çakraḥ Suragaṇeçvaraḥ* | *trailokyavijayam çrīmān prāptavān raṇamūrdhani*), 6464 (*tvatprasādasamutthena vikrameṇārisūdana* | *Sureçatvam gataḥ Çakro hatvā Daityān sahasraçaḥ*)].—§ 600 (Ghaṭotkacavadhap.): VII, **156**, 6751 (*°vikramaiḥ*), 6810 (*Rudropendrendravikramaḥ*, sc. Açvatthāman), 6836 (*toyado bhūtvā nīlaḥ sendrāyudho divi*, sc. Ghaṭotkaca), 6842 (*°vikramaiḥ*), 6845 (do.), 6890 (*dhanur ghoram . . . I°āyudhopamam*); **158**, 7008 (*°vīryāḥ*), 7048 (*sendrā api surāsurāḥ*); **160**, 7143 (*°o Daityavadhe yathā*); **162**, 7227 (*yathendram harayo, rājan, purā Daityavadhodyatam*); **168**, 7540 (*yathendrabhayavitrastā Dānavās Tārakāmaye*); **170**, 7669 (*yathendraḥ samare, rājan, prāha Vishṇum mahāyaçāḥ*); **174**, 7873 (*°Vairocanāv iva*, sc. *yuyudhāte*); **175**, 7914 (*°Çambarayor iva*, sc. *sannipātaḥ*), 7939 (*Rudropendrendravikramaḥ*, sc. Karṇa), 7965 (*toyado bhūtvā nīlaḥ sendrāyudho divi*, sc. Ghaṭotkaca), 7975 (*°āyudham ivocchritam*); **179**, †8155 (*sendrā devāḥ*), [†8167 (*Çakraḥ*, Karṇa employed the dart, which had been given him by *I.*, against Ghaṭotkaca)].—§ 601 (Droṇavadhap.): VII, **185ε**, 8444.—§ 603 (Nārāyaṇāstramokshap.): VII, **196**, 9050 (*sendrān apy eva lokāṃs trīn*); **197**, 9101 (*sendrān devān*); **200**, †9340 (*°ketuprakāçau bhujau*; *°samānavīryaḥ*, sc. Açvatthāman).—[§ 603*d* (Tripura): VII, **202** (*I.* was unable to destroy the three cities of the Asuras, which Çiva then destroyed, *I.* was paralysed by Çiva)].—§ 603 (Nārāyaṇāstramokshap.): VII, **202α**, 9594 (Çiva is identified with *I.*), 9605 (*sendrādishu deveshu*), 9628.—§ 604 (Karṇap.): VIII, **8η**, 221 (*iva*); **9**, 292 (*°opamam vīram*, sc. Karṇa).—§ 605 (do.): VIII, **16**, 635 (*jaitreṇa vidhinā hūtam Vāyur I°m ivādhvare*, sc. *avahat*); **17**, †678 (*Dhanadendrakalpau*, sc. Kṛshṇa and Arjuna).—§ 605*c* (Vijaya): VIII, **31**, 1292 (the bow Vijaya had been made by Viçvakarman for the sake of *I.*; *I.* afterwards gave it to Rāma Jāmadagnya), 1295 (*yotsye . . . yathendraḥ samare sarvān Daityān*).—§ 606 (Tripurākhyāna): VIII, [**33**, 1426 (*Çakraḥ*, could not destroy the three cities of the Asuras)]; **34**, 1488 (*vidyud-I°dhanurnaddham ratham*, i.e. the chariot of Çiva).—§ 607 (Karṇap.): VIII, **36**, 1683 (*°agnī stūyamānāv ivādhvare*); **42**, †1988 (*Pāṇḍavam I°kalpam*, i.e. Arjuna).—§ 608*b* (Arjuna): VIII, **46**, 2161 (*Brahmeçānendra-Varuṇān kramaço yo 'vahat purā*, sc. the chariot of Arjuna).—§ 608 (Karṇap.): VIII, **46**, 2208 (*iva*); **51**, 2487 (*jaghne vajreṇendra ivācalān*); **53**, 2588 (*yathendraḥ samare Daityāṃs Tārakasya vadhe purā*, sc. *avadhīt*); **64**, 3239 (*jālam athendrayuktam*, so B., C. has by error *jālamahe°*; cf. *Indrajāla°*, v. 3238); **66**, †3356 (*Vṛtre hate 'sau bhagavān ivendraḥ*); **87**, 4391 (*°Vṛtrāv iva kruddhau*), 4406 (*prajihīrshantāv I°-Vṛtrāv iva*) (χ^1), 4418 (sided with Arjuna in the fight between Karṇa and Arjuna), 4458 (*I.* asked Brahman and Īçāna for the victory of Arjuna, and it was granted); **90**, †4657 (*kirīṭam asya I°dattam*, with an arrow Karṇa broke the diadem, which *I.* had given to Arjuna), †4689 (*yathendro Balam*, sc. *bibheda*), 4718 (*°āçanisamān*, sc. *çarān*).—§ 610 (Çalyap.): IX, **4**, 202 (*°ketum ivocchritam*); **5ν**, 280 (*°sadmasv adhisthitāḥ*).—§ 611 (do.): IX, **12**, 615 (*°dhvajāv iva*); **17**, 916 (*°dhvaja ivocchritaḥ*), 921 (*cāpam . . . I°dhanuḥprabham*), †954 (*purā kṛte Vṛtravadhe yathendram*); **20**, †1077 (*Jambho yathā Çakrasamāgamād vai nāgendram Airāvaṇam I°vāhyam*, sc. *pratyudyayau*); **24**, 1328 (*°āçanisamasparçāḥ . . . çarāḥ*); **25**, 1339 (*°āçanisamasparçān*, sc. *bāṇān*); **27**, 1495 (*°āçanisamasparçaiḥ*, sc. *bāṇaiḥ*).—§ 612 (Hradapraveçap.): IX, **31ζ**, 1750 (*kriyābhyupāyair I°eṇa nihatā Daitya-Dānavāḥ*), 1756 (*kriyābhyupāyair I°eṇa tridivam bhujyate*).—§ 613 (Gadāyuddhap.): IX, **32**, 1851 (*api*).—§ 614 (do.): IX, **34**, 1964 (*Brahmāṇam iva Deveçam I°opendrau*, sc. *pūjayām āsatuḥ*).—§ 615*s* (Baladevatīrthayātrā): In days of yore *Namuci* had entered a ray of the sun from fear of *I.* *I.* then made friends with *Namuci* and entered into an agreement with him, saying: "I shall not slay thee with anything wet or dry, in the night or in the day." One day *I.* beheld a fog and cut off the head of *Namuci* with foam of water. The severed head of *Namuci* thereupon pursued *I.*, saying: "O slayer of a friend, O wretch!" *I.* repaired to *Brahmán*, who caused him to perform a sacrifice and bathe in *Aruṇā* (*t*). Thus *I.* became free from the sin of brahman murder and returned to heaven. The head of *Namuci* also fell into that stream and obtained eternal regions, granting every wish: IX, **43**, 2434.—§ 615*u* (Skanda): IX, [**44**, 2480 (*Çakraḥ*, came to see the new-born Skanda)]; **45γ**, 2506 (*°Vishṇū*, came to the investiture of Skanda), [2538 (*Vāsavaḥ*, gave two companions to Skanda); **46**, 2662 (*Pākaçāsanaḥ*, gave Skanda a dart and a banner)].—[§ 615*y* (Badarapācana): IX, **48** (in the tīrtha Badarapācana *Çrutāvatī* gratified *I.* by persevering in boiling five badara-fruits, and became the wife of *I.*).]—§ 615*bb* (Indratīrtha): IX, **49**, [2833 (*Çakraḥ*, at Indratīrtha *I.* performed 100 sacrifices, therefore he came to be called Çatakratu)].—[§ 615*gg* (Sārasvata): IX, **51** (from fear of the austerities of *Dadhīca*, *I.* despatched the Apsaras *Alambushā* to tempt *Dadhīca*, thus Sārasvata was born, afterwards *Dadhīca* gave his bones, of which the *vajra* of *I.* was made).]—§ 615*kk* (Kurukshetrakathana): IX, **53**, 3012 (sanctified *Kurukshetra*).—§ 615 (Baladevatīrthayātrā): IX, **54**, 3049 (*°o 'gnir Aryamā caiva yatra prāk prītim āpnuvan*).—§ 615 (Gadāyuddhap.): IX, **57**, 3177 (*°Prahrādayor iva*, sc. *yuddham*), 3186 (*°āçanim ivodyatām*), 3202 (*°āçanisamām*, sc. *gadām*); **61**, 3395 (*iva*).—§ 616 (Sauptikap.): X, **6**, 231 (*°ketunibhām gadām*).—§ 617 (Aishīkap.): X, **10β**, †565 (*°opamān*); **17**, 766 (*api*).—§ 618 (Jalapradānikap.): XI, **2δ**, 60 (*°syātithayaḥ*, sc. the fallen warriors).—§ 622 (Rājadh.): XII, **11**, 307 (in the shape of a golden bird *I.* discoursed with some ṛshis).—§ 623 (do.): XII, **15**, 438 (*°o Vṛtravadhena Mahendraḥ samapadyata*), [439 (*Çakraḥ*, among the gods who are slaughterers)].—§ 626 (do.): XII, **20**, †611 (*yajñair I°o vividhai ratnavadbhir devān sarvān atyayād bhūritejāḥ* | *tenendratvam prāpya bibhrājate 'sau*); **21**, 615 (*°eṇa samaye pṛshṭo yad uvāca Bṛhaspatiḥ*).—§ 627 (do.): XII, **22**, 646 (*°o vai Brahmaṇaḥ sutaḥ kshatriyaḥ karmaṇā 'bhavat*), 647 (*°tvam samāpede devanām*, sc. Indra), 648 (*yathā*).—§ 632*b* (Shoḍaçarāj., cf. § 595, v. Marutta): XII, **29**, 911 (*sendrāḥ . . . devāḥ*); (do., v. Paurava): XII, **29**,

928 (*amādyad I°o somena*); (do., v. Çibi): XII, **29,** 936 (°*vikramāt*, sc. Çaibya); (do., v. Bhagīratha): XII, **29,** 956 (drank soma); (do., v. Māndhātṛ): XII, **29,** 977 (*Çatakratuḥ*, Māndhātṛ sucked the finger of Indra), 978, 979, 980 (°*samaṃ*, sc. Māndhātṛ); (do., v. Rantideva): XII, **29,** [1013 (*Çatakratuḥ*, granted a boon to Rantideva)].—§ 634 (Suvarṇasthīvisambhavop.): XII, **31,** 1106 (*I.* caused Suvarṇasthīvin to be killed by a tiger).—§ 635 (Rājadh.): XII, **33,** 1205 (*yathā*); **37,** 1351 (*devān sarvān I°purogamān*); **38,** 1403 (*yathendras tridivaṃ*, sc. *pālaya*).—§ 637 (do.): XII, **47θ,** 1618 (*ati-Vāyv-I°karmāṇaṃ*, sc. *Govindaṃ*).—[§ 638*b* (Rāmopākhyāna): XII, **49,** 1720 (*Pākaçāsanaḥ*, incarnate as Gādhi).]—[§ 640 (Rājadh.): XII, **58β,** 2093 (*Sahasrāksho Mahendraḥ*, among the authors of rājaçāstras).]—[§ 641 (do.): XII, **59,** 2204 (*Purandaraḥ*, abridged the Vaiçālāksha çāstra and called it Bāhudantaka).]—§ 641*f* (Pṛthu Vainya): XII, **59,** 2219 (*rūpeṇendra ivāparaḥ*, sc. Pṛthu Vainya), [2239 (*Çakraḥ*, bestowed wealth on Pṛthu Vainya)].—§ 641 (Rājadh.): XII, **64,** (†2402), (†2407), **65,** (†2417), (2433), (2440) (discourse between *I.* and Māndhātṛ); **67,** 2498 (°*m eva pravṛṇute yad rājānam iti çrutiḥ* | *yathaivendras tathā rājā sampūjyaḥ*), 2505; **71,** 2748 (°*ṃ tarpaya somena*); **72,** 2773 (°*o rājā*); [**84** (discourse between *I.* and Bṛhaspati)]; [**90,** 3386 (*tasmād*, i.e. from Bali, *apākramya sā 'gacchat Pākaçāsanaṃ*, sc. Çrī, cf. § 671*b*)]; **96,** 3575 (*anena*—sc. *vṛttena*—*I°vishayaṃ vijigīshanti pārthivāḥ*); **97,** 3589 (*prāpnoti I°salokatāṃ*), 3601 (*devā I°purogamāḥ*), 3611 (*prāpnotīndrasya sālokyaṃ*); **98,** 3614 (*Ambarīshasya saṃvādam I°sya ca*), (3623), (3626) (discourse between *I.* and Ambarīsha); **102,** 3758 (°*dhanūṃshi*); **103,** 3795 (*Bṛhaspateç ca saṃvādam I°sya ca*), (3797), (3838) (discourse between *I.* and Bṛhaspati); **121,** 4446 (*prītāç ca devatā nityam I°e parivadanty api* | *annaṃ dadāti Çakraç cāpy anugṛhṇann imāḥ prajāḥ*); **122,** [4495 (*devānāṃ īçvaraṃ cakre devaṃ Daçaçatekshaṇaṃ*, sc. Vishṇu)], 4505 (°*Marīcibhyāṃ*), 4511; **124,** 4571 (Prahlāda deprived *I.* of his sovereignty; disguised as a brahman *I.* then was instructed by Prahlāda about his behaviour, whereafter Prahlāda lost his sovereignty).—§ 649 (Āpaddh.): XII, **141,** 5414 (*devān I°ādīn*).—§ 651 (Kapotalubdhakasaṃv.): XII, **149,** 5587 (°*vat*).—§ 654 (Āpaddh.): XII, **155a,** 5831.—[§ 656 (Khaḍgotpattik.): XII, **166,** 6186, 6187 (the ṛshis gave the sword to *I.* (Vāsava), from him (Mahendra) it passed over to the Lokapālas).]—§ 658*b* (Kṛtaghnop.): XII, **173,** 6436 (told Virūpāksha how Rājadharman had been cursed, and restored Gautama to life). —§ 659 (Mokshadh.): XII, **180,** 6693 (°-*Kāçyapasaṃvādaṃ*), 6696 (*çrgālarūpeṇa*), 6713 (°*tāṃ*), 6714 (°*tvaṃ*), 6743 (*devānāṃ devaṃ . . . Çacīpatiṃ . . . Harivāhanaṃ*) (discourse between *I.* in the shape of a jackal and Kāçyapa).—[§ 662*b* (Japakop.): XII, **200,** 7338 (*Tridaçeçvaraḥ*).]—[§ 664 (Mokshadh.): XII, **207,** 7553 (*Vāsavaṃ sarvadevānām adhyaksham akarot prabhuḥ*, sc. Kṛshṇa).]—§ 665 (do.): XII, **208β,** 7582 (the eleventh of the Ādityas).—§ 667 (do.): XII, **214,** 7786 (*tribījam I°daivatyaṃ tasmād indriyam ucyate*, sc. *çukraṃ*).—§ 670 (do.): XII, **222,** 8023 (*Prahrādasya ca saṃvādam I°sya*, discourse between Indra and Prahlāda).—§ 671*b* (Bali-Vāsavasaṃv.): XII, **[223-]225,** 8185 (discourse between *I.* and Bali).—[§ 672*b* (Çakra-Namucisaṃv.): XII, **226** (discourse between *I.* and Namuci).]—§ 673*b* (Bali-Vāsavasaṃv.): XII, **227,** 8224 (*Surendraṃ*), 8279, 8283, 8284, 8286 (discourse between *I.* and Bali).—[§ 674*b* (Çri-Vāsavasaṃv.): XII, **229,** (discourse between *I.* and Çrī).]—[§ 682 (Mokshadh.): XII, **267,** 9527 (*Trilokeçaḥ Purandaraḥ*), 9530 (*Tridaçeçvaraḥ*, had violated the wife of Gautama, i.e. Ahalyā).]—§ 693*b* (Vṛtravadha): XII, **282,** 10104; **283,** 10186 (*I.'s* encounter with Vṛtra, whom he slew, how *I.* was liberated from the sin of brahman murder).—§ 695*b* (Dakshayajñavināça): XII, **285a,** 10280, †10298 (*sendrā devāḥ*).—§ 701*b* (Bhava-Bhārgavasamāgama): XII, **290,** 10666.—§ 707 (Mokshadh.): XII, **314,** 11610 (the adhidaivata of the hands); **318,** 11706 (°*tvaṃ*, when the soul escapes through the navel it becomes *I.*, likewise when escaping through the arms).—[§ 712 (Çukotpatti): XII, **325,** 12206 (*Deveçvaraḥ Çakraḥ*, gave a kamaṇḍalu to Çuka).]—[§ 717*c* (Uparicara): XII, **336,** 12717 (*Devarāṭ*, shared with Vasu Uparicara his own seat and bed).]—§ 717*b* (Nārāyaṇīya): XII, [**340** (Nārāyaṇa prophesies that Bali will deprive *I.* (*Çakraṃ*, v. 12944) of his kingdom, but that Vishṇu will restore it to him)]; **343,** II), ††13205 (cursed by Gautama on account of his violating Ahalyā, *I.* came to wear a green beard; cursed by Kauçika to lose his testicles, *I.* obtained those of a ram), [III), ††13206 (*Purandarasya*, Cyavana paralysed his arms, cf. § 405)], VII), ††13211, ††13212, ††13213, ††13214, ††13216, ††13217, ††13218 (how Indra slew Viçvarūpa and Vṛtra, Nahusha's becoming king of the gods and falling down again to the earth, *I.'s* regaining the sovereignty, cf. § 555 (somewhat different)).—[§ 718*b* (Uñchavṛttyup.): XII, **353-66** (Nārada told the Uñchavṛttyupākhyāna to *I.*).]—§ 720*b* (Sudarçanop.): XIII, **2,** 95 (°*vapushaḥ*, sc. *Durjayasya*).—[§ 722 (Ānuçāsanik.): XIII, **5** (discourse between *I.* and a parrot).]—§ 728*b* (Bhaṅgāsvanop.): XIII, **12,** 531 (*agnistutam I°dvishṭaṃ*), 532, 534, 558, 559, 566, 567, 568, 569, 572, 575 (discourse between *I.* and Bhaṅgāsvana).—§ 730 (Ānuçāsanik.): XIII, **14,** 610 (*devāḥ sendrāḥ*).—[§ 730*c* (Mandāra): XIII, **14,** 664 (*Çakraṃ*, Mandāra fought with *I.* during 1,000 years).]—§ 730 (Ānuçāsanik.): XIII, **14,** [681 (*Maghavatā*, disregarded the Vālakhilyas, cf. § 45).]—§ 730*g* (Upamanyu): XIII, **14,** [763 (Çiva assumed the form of Çakra, i.e. Indra)], (λ), 806 (*yajñendrabalarakshaḥsu*, so C., but B. reads *Yakshendra*°), 809 (Civa in the shape of *I.*), (ν), 820 (*Brahmendra-Mahendra-Vishnusahitā devāḥ*, so C., but B. has *Hutāça* instead of *Mahendra*), 849 (°*āyudhasavarṇābhaṃ dhanuḥ*).—§ 730 (Ānuçāsanik.): XIII, **14,** 976 (°*āyudhapinaddhāṅkaṃ*); **16ηη,** 1045 (°*āgni-Marutāṃ . . . gatiḥ*, i.e. Çiva), 1058 (*Skandendrau*, identified with Çiva); **17,** 1282 (°*kalpena*, sc. Taṇḍin), [1288 (Brahman communicated the 1000 names of Çiva to Çakra, i.e. Indra, who again communicated them to Mṛtyu)]; [**18,** 1313, (*Çakrasya*, had cursed Asita Devala)].—§ 734 (do.): XIII, **26,** 1826 (*devaiḥ sendraiḥ*), †1841 (do.).—[§ 735*b* (Indra - Mataṅgasaṃv.): XIII, **27-9** (discourse between Indra and Mataṅga).]—§ 736*b* (Vītahavyop.): XIII, **30,** 1997 (*rūpeṇendra ivāparaḥ*, sc. Gṛtsamada).—§ 738 (Ānuçāsanik.): XIII, **32,** 2073 (*sendrās trayo lokāḥ*).—[§ 739 (do.): XIII, **34,** 2137 (*bhagasahasreṇa Mahendraḥ paricihnitaḥ* | *teshām eva prabhāvena Sahasranayano hy asau* ‖ *Çatakratur samabhavat*, cf. v. 2328, s.v. Gautama).]—[§ 740 (do.): XIII, **36** (discourse between *I.* and Çambara).]—[§ 743*b* (Vipulop.): XIII, **40-3** (how Vipula protected Ruci, the wife of Devaçarman, against *I.*).]—§ 746 (Ānuçāsanik.): XIII, **60,** 3060; **62,** 3153 (*Bṛhaspateç ca saṃvādam I°sya*, discourse between *I.* and Bṛhaspati); [**72-**]**74,** (3606), 3616 (discourse between *I.* and Brahmán); **82ν,** 3857; **83,** 3884 (*Pitāmahasya saṃvādam I°sya ca*), 3890 (discourse between *I.* and Brahman about kine).—§ 747*b* (Suvarṇotpatti): XIII,

85, 4174 (*sendreshu lokeshu*), 4180 (*devaiḥ . . . sendraiḥ*).—[§ 748*b* (Tārakavadhop.): XIII, **86*a***, 4201 (*Vāsavaḥ*, came to see Skanda), 4210 (*Surendraḥ*, gave lions, etc., to Skanda), 4215 (*Surendraḥ*, Skanda restored the sovereignty of the gods to *I.*).]—[§ 750*b* (Bisastainyop.): XIII, **93** (in the shape of Çunaḥsakha *I.* put the seven ṛshis, etc., to the test).]—§ 751*b* (Çapathavidhi): XIII, **94,** (4593) (do.).—§ 755*b* (Nahushop.): XIII, **99,** 4752 (*Indro 'ham*, sc. Nahusha), 4765 (*karishye 'nindram*, sc. *Nahusham*), 4766; **100,** 4772 (*anindratvaṃ*; Nahusha became *I.*, but cursed to become a serpent he fell down to the earth, cf. also § 555 (somewhat different)).—[§ 757*b* (Hastikūṭa): XIII, **102** (discourse between Gautama and *I.* in the shape of Dhṛtarāshṭra).]—§ 757*k* (Indraloka): XIII, **102,** 4880 (°*sya lokāḥ*).—§ 758 (Ānuçāsanik.): XIII, **103,** †4945 (°*eṇa guhyaṃ nihitaṃ vai guhāyām*, i.e. the vow of fast, Nīl.).—§ 759 (do.): XIII, **107,** 5224 (°*kanyādhirūḍhañ ca vimānaṃ labhate naraḥ*).—§ 766 (do.): XIII, [**125,** (5967) (*Çakraḥ*)]; **126,** (6013).—§ 768*b* (Umā-Maheçvarasaṃv.): XIII, **141,** 6394 (*pūrveṇa vadanenāham I°tvam anuçāsmi ha*, says Çiva), 6397 (°*eṇa ca purā vajraṃ kshiptaṃ çrīkāṅkshiṇā mama* | *dagdhvā kaṇṭhan tu tad yātaṃ tena Çrīkaṇṭhatā mama*, says Çiva).—§ 768 (Ānuçāsanik.): XIII, **148,** 6893 (*sendrā devās trayastriṃçat*).—§ 770 (do.): XIII, **151**γ, 7093 (the eleventh of the Ādityas), [7111 (*Mahendrasya sapta guravaḥ*, i.e. the seven ṛshis of the east)].—[§ 772*e* (Gautama): XIII, **154,** 7218 (*Purandaraḥ*; coveting Ahalyā *I.* was cursed by Gautama, but not hurt).]—§ 772*l* (Vasishṭha): XIII, **156,** 7289 (*sendrāḥ . . . tridivaukasaḥ*, protected by Vasishṭha).—§ 772*n* (Cyavana): XIII, **157,** (7307), (7311), 7314, 7316 (Cyavana paralysed the arm of *I.* and created Mada. *I.* then allowed the Açvins to become partakers of the soma, cf. § 405).—§ 772*p* (Kapa, pl.): XIII, **158,** 7327 (*sendrā divaukasaḥ*), 7330 (do., when the gods had entered the mouth of Mada, Cyavana took away from them the earth).—§ 773*d* (Çiva): XIII, **161,** [7490 (*Çakrasya*, Çiva paralysed the arm of *I.*, cf. § 603*d*)], 7496 (Çiva identified with *I.*).—§ 778*e* (Avikshit): XIV, **4,** 80 (°*ād anavaraḥ*, sc. Avikshit), 82 (°*samaḥ*, sc. Avikshit).—§ 778*b* (Samvartta-Maruttīya): XIV, **5,** 98 (*Vāsavo 'py Asurān sarvān nirjitya ca nipātya ca* | *I°tvam prāpya lokeshu tato vavre purohitam*, sc. Bṛhaspati), 110 (°*tvaṃ prāptavān eko*, says Indra); **7,** 178; **9,** (†219), (†221), (†223), (†226), 230, (†242), (†247); **10,** (†250), †270, †271, †277, (†279), †283 (*I.'s* relations to Bṛhaspati, Saṃvarta, and Marutta).—§ 779*b* (Vṛtra): XIV, **11,** 298 (°*sya saha Vṛtreṇa yuddhaṃ*, *I.'s* encounter with Vṛtra).—§ 782*b* (Brāhmaṇagītā): XIV, **21,** 631.—§ 782*g* (Guruçishyasaṃv.): XIV, **35,** 976; [**42,** 1129 (*Çakraḥ*, the adhidaivata of the hands)]; **43**η, 1176 (*Marutaṃ rājā*).—[§ 784*b* (Uttaṅka): XIV, **55** (in the shape of a Caṇḍāla *I.* offered Uttaṅka *amṛta* in the form of his urine)]; **56** (in the shape of a brahman *I.* assisted Uttaṅka).—[§ 786 (Anugītāp.): XIV, **91** (the dispute of the ṛshis at the sacrifice of *I.*).]—§ 786*e* (Agastya): XIV, **92,** 2867, 2868 (Agastya caused *I.* to pour down rain).—§ 787 (Āçramavāsap.): XV, **17,** 477 (°*samāḥ*, sc. the Pāṇḍavas).—[§ 793 (Mausalap.): XVI, **4** (received Kṛshṇa in heaven).]—§ 794 (Mahāprasthānikap.): XVII, **3,** (†82), (†85) (put Yudhishṭhira to the test).—§ 795 (Svargārohanap.): XVIII, **2**δ, 36 (°*saṅkāçam*, sc. Arjuna) (*I.* put Yudhishṭhira to the test); **4,** 135 (*Devarāṭ*).

Cf. also the following synonyms:—

Aditinandana: XIII, 986 (°*au*, i.e. Indra and Vishṇu).

Akhaṇḍala, q.v.

Amaraçreshṭha: I, 1136; III, 1725 (*Çatakratuḥ*): XIII, 3905.

Amarādhipa: III, 6076 (to be worshipped in *Amarāṇāṃ hrada(ḥ)*); VIII, †1212 (°*sainyasaprabham*); XII, 3825, 8131, 10134.

Amararāja: I, †3569 (°*jushṭān . . . lokān*), †3575 (°*kalpa*); VII, 1125 (*yādṛk purā vṛttaṃ Çambara-°yoḥ*, sc. *yuddham*), 3571 (*yathā pūrvam abhūd yuddhaṃ Çambara-°yoḥ*); VIII, †1740 (*Tridivam ivā °rakshitam*), †3857 (°*tejasā*), 4397 (*sadṛçau yuddhe Çambara-°yoḥ*); IX, 784 (*yādṛço vai purā vṛttaḥ Çambara-°yoḥ*), 2832.

Amareça: VI, †784 (*iva*).

Amareçvara: I, 8226, 8306; VII, 3005; VIII, †820 (*iva*); XII, 3845.

Amarendra: I, †2121.

Amarottama: I, 1287.

Asurārdana, Asurasūdana, q.v.

Balabhid, Balahan, Balahantṛ, Balajit (cf. Additions), **Balanāçana, Balanisūdana, Balasūdana,** q.v.

Bala-Vṛtraghna, Bala-Vṛtrahan, Bala-Vṛtranisūdana, Bala-Vṛtrasūdana. q.v.

Bhūtabhavyeça, q.v.

Çacīpati ("the husband of Çacī"): I, 1286, 7103, 8159, 8240; II, 70 (*Sahasrākshaḥ*); III, 479, 1884, 2226, 10387, 10693, †13297 (*Vajrahastaḥ*), 14624, 16440 (*Sahasrākshaṃ*, C. has by error *S°*); V, 256, 422, 538, 3574 (*Devarājaḥ*), 4413, 5503 (°*samaṃ*, sc. *Droṇam*), 5548 (do.); VII, 9019 (°*ir ivāsurān*), 9087 (*Çakrasya*); IX, 1914; XII, 1200, 6743, 8066, 8109, 8118, 8132, 8142, 8289, 8413, 12945, ††13214, 13770; XIII, 283, 2318, 3573, 3575, 3913, 5972 (*Deveça*), 5980, 6155 (*Vāsavaṃ*), 7637; XIV, 1615; XV, 567 (*Çakraṃ*).

Çakra: I, 112 (father of Arjuna), †161, †185 (°*Sūryau*), 222 (°*pratimatejasaḥ*), 531 (°*samaḥ*, sc. *Bhagadattaḥ*), 1285 (praised in the hymn vv. 1285*b*–95), 1426, 1441, 1442, 1446, 1466, (1519), 1523, (1530), 1532, 1539, 2058 (*bhavane . . . Ç°sya*), †2098 (°*sya yajñaḥ çatasaṅkhyaḥ*), †2108 (*Vajrapāṇir yathā*), 2218 (*yathā Ç°o Bṛhaspateḥ*, sc. *āsanaṃ kalpayām āsa*), 2245 (*yathā*), 2336 (*devāḥ Ç°purogāḥ*), 2351, 2359, 2300 (°*utsavena*), 2504 (°*ādayaḥ*), 2510, 2523 (one of the Ādityas), 2600 (*Aditeh putrāḥ Ç°mukhyāḥ*), 2780, 2914, 2907, 2916 (°*saṃsadaṃ*), 3121 (*yathā Ç°o Marutpatiḥ*), 3315, 3432 (°*Vishṇū ivāparau*), 3537, 3553, (3554), †3567, †3572, †3574 (*Balahā*), †3652, 3094 (°*pratimatejasaḥ*), ††3814 (father of Arjuna), †3976 (°*pratimatejasā*, i.e. Çāntanu), 4408, (4785), 4791 (begot Arjuna), 4794, 4801, 6500 (among the fathers of the Pāṇḍavas), 6586 (°*dhvajam ivocchritam*, C. has by error *S°*), 6786 (*açobhata . . . C°eṇevāmarāvatī*), 7059 (°*pratimaṃ*, i.e. Arjuna), †7277, †7288, †7291, †7293, †7309 (°*syāṃçaḥ Pāṇḍavaḥ Savyasācī*, i.e. Arjuna), †7314 (°*prakhyān*), 8090, 8187 (°*āyudhasamau*), 8261, 8272, 8274, 8276, 8281, 8469; II, 29 (*iva*), 46 (*prayayau . . . yathā Ç°a Amarāvatīm*), 103 (*yathā*), 263 (°*sya salokatām*), 283 (°*sya sabhā*), 291, 483 (°*sya sabhāyām*), 485, 505 (°*sya saṃsadi*), 897 (*pratyudyayau . . . Ç°m Bala ivāsuraḥ*), 939 (°*Vishṇū . . . Tārakāmaye*), 911, 1005 (°*ād anavaraḥ*, i.e. Bhagadatta), 1257 (°*syeva Tripishṭape*), 1684 (*yathā*), 1751 (do.), 1957 (slew Namuci), 2458 (°*sya nītim*), 2572 (°*eṇāpi samaḥ*); III, 3 (°*pratimatejasaḥ*), 208, 209 (obtained a hymn to Sūrya from Brahmán and communicated it to Nārada, C. has by error *S°*), 338 (discourse with Surabhi), 514

(*Brahma-Çaṅkara-Ç°ādyair devavṛndaiḥ*), †939 (*iva*), †955 (°*sya samaprabhāvaḥ*), 1269, 1469, 1470, 1505, 1515, 1526 (*Sureçvaraṃ*), 1606 (°*āçanisamair mushṭibhiḥ*), 1638 (°*ābhisheke*), 1677, 1726, 1755 (°*sya purīṃ tām Amarāvatīṃ*), 1762 (°*sya dayitāṃ purīṃ*), 1775 (°*āsane*), 1777 (°*āsanaṃ*), 1788, 1791, 1793, 1800, 1813, 1847, 1849 (°*tulyaṃ*, sc. Arjuna), 1870, 1875, 1881, 1882 (°*āsanaṃ*), 1884 (*Vṛtranisūdanaḥ, Çacīpatiḥ*), 2123, 2125, 2140, 2141, 2145, 2157, 2226 (*Çacīpatiḥ*), 2240 (*Bala-Vṛtrahā*), 2241, 3043 (°*m ivāpsarāḥ*, sc. *upatishṭhati*), 8282, 8289, 8408 (*iva*), 8411 (°*sya bhavanaṃ*), 8412, 8712, 8723, 8724, 8725, †8728 (°*vajrābhihataḥ*, sc. Vṛtra), †8729, 8762, 9980 (*devāḥ Ç°purogamāḥ*), 9995, 10141, 10383, 10402, 10404, 10425 (°*samadyuteḥ*, sc. Māndhātṛ), 10434 (°*samaṃ*), 10448, 10451, 10452, 10454 (*pradeçinīṃ Ç°dattāṃ*, given to Māndhātṛ to suck), 10457, 10460 (°*syārdhāsanaṃ*), 10516 (*spardhamānasya Ç°eṇa*, sc. *Yayāteḥ*), 10714, 10723, 10724, 10881 (°*ād anavaraḥ*, sc. Arjuna), 10918, 10923, 11052 (°*sadanaprakhyaṃ*, sc. the hermitage of Nara and Nārāyaṇa), 11139 (°*dhvajam ivocchritaṃ*), †11390 (°*vat*), 11684 (°*tulyabalopamaṃ*), 11807 (*Vṛtrahā*), 11824 (°*sadmani*), †11912 (°*ripupramāthī*, i.e. Arjuna), †11914, 11933, 11935, 11939, 12015, 12022, 12032, 12036 (°*sya bhavanaṃ . . . Amarāvatīṃ*), 12046, 12050 (°*sya bhavane*), 12076, 12193, 12265, 12279, 12281, 12413 (Nahusha fell from the seat of Ç.), 12703 (a king is like to Ç.), 12923 (°*ādīn . . . devagaṇān*, seen by Mārkaṇḍeya in the stomach of Nārāyaṇa), 12954 (°*ç cāhaṃ Surādhipaḥ*, says Nārāyaṇa), 13215 (*Baka-Ç°-samāgamaṃ*), 14019 (*trayastriṃçad yathā devāḥ sarve Ç°-purogamāḥ*), 14251, 14272, 14356, 14357, 14358, 14373, 14381, (14414), 14415, (14416), 14421, 14460, 14464, 14532, 14547 (*Airāvataṃ samāsthāya*), 14561, 14585, 14586, 14996 (*Daiteyā iva Ç°eṇa*, sc. *dahyamānāḥ*), 15035 (*iva*), 15275 (*yathā*), †15591 (°*sya . . . sadanāt*), 15757, 15846 (Vishṇu gave the earth to Ç.), 15934, 15939 (°*prabhṛtayaḥ . . . surasattamāḥ*), 15954 (°*ād anavaraṃ*, sc. Daçaratha), 16150 (°*pratimatejasā*, sc. Sugrīva), 16482 (°*Prahlādayor iva*, sc. *yuddhaṃ*), 16510, 16524 (*deva-Gandharvāḥ Ç°purogamāḥ*), 16548, 16571 (*devaiḥ Ç°purogamaiḥ*), 16577 (*devāḥ . . . Ç°purogamāḥ*), 16923, 16944, 16975, 16992, 17191, 17193, (17195), 17211, †17216, 17288 (°*pratimagauravān*, sc. the brothers of Yudhishṭhira), 17464 (°*sya vajraṃ*); IV, 50 (*Tridaçānāṃ yathā Ç°ḥ*), 187 (*vipulau bāhū* — sc. Durgā's — *Ç°dhvajasamucchrayau*), 1348 (held Gāṇḍīva eighty-five years), 1384 (gave a diadem to Arjuna), 1412 (°*sya*—sc. *sārathiḥ—Mātaliḥ*), 1433, 1537 (Arjuna had learnt the use of [celestial] weapons from Ç.), 1724, 1761 (came to see the fight), 1935, 1982 (Arjuna had learnt the use of [celestial] weapons from Ç.), 2274 (°-*Vaiçravaṇopamaḥ*, sc. Yudhishṭhira), 2280 (*iva*); V, 233, 240, 247, 251, 255, 262, (263), 272, 275, 279, 281, 284, 287, 297, 302, 303, 304, 306, 309, 312, 317, 321, 323, 328, 335, 345, 358 (°*sya mahishī*, i.e. Çacī), 366, 389 (°*sya mahishīṃ*, i.e. Çacī), 398, 405, 409, 411 (*Suragaṇeçvaraḥ*), 414, 417, 423, 431, 444, 471, 474, 475, 492, 497, 498, 501, †507, †508, †512, †513, †515, †516, 517, 519, 527, 538, 544, 546, 555, 559, †677 (°*samo Dhanañjayaḥ*, i.e. Arjuna), †821 (*devaḥ*), †1375 (*devāḥ sa-Ç°āḥ*), 1800 (*viviçuḥ . . . surāḥ Ç°sado yathā*), †1888 (*devāḥ saha Ç°eṇa*), †1913 (had given weapons to Arjuna), 1926, 1928, 1929, 2021 (°*pratimatejasaḥ*, i.e. Bhīmasena), 2195, 2220 (*Bhaumanaḥ saha Ç°eṇa*), 3152 (°*samaḥ*, sc. Bhīmasena), 3338 (*iva*), 3570, 3573, 3643 (°*sya dayitaḥ suhṛt*, sc. *Mātaliḥ*), 3644 (°*syāyaṃ* — i.e. Mātali — *sakhā caiva mantrī sārathir eva ca*), 3656 (°*sya sakhā*, i.e. Mātali), 3665 (*Devarājaṃ*), 3671, 3674, 3708 (will side with the Pāṇḍavas), 3767 (*yatra*—i.e. in the east—*Ç°o 'bhyashicyata*), 3791 (*atra*—i.e. in the south—*vṛttena Vṛtro 'pi Ç°çatrutvam īyivān*), 3808 (*atra*—i.e. in the west—*devīṃ Ditiṃ suptām ātmaprasavadhāriṇīṃ vigarbhām akaroc Ch°o yatra jāto Marudgaṇaḥ*), 4042 (*Balanisūdanaḥ*), 4151 (°*samān*, sc. the Pāṇḍavas), 4537 (*iva*), 4830 (*saptamāc cāpi divasād amāvāsyā bhavishyati | saṅgrāmo yujyatāṃ tasyāṃ, tām āhuḥ Ç°daivatāṃ*), 5291 (*iva*), 5381, 7602 (°*samadyute*, i.e. Yudhishṭhira); VI, 102 (*ulkāḥ . . . Ç°āçanisamaprabhāḥ*), 213 (performed sacrifices on Meru), 244 (only C., B. has *satraṃ*), 506 (*iva*), 522 (do.), 643 (°*sya . . . salokatāṃ*), 775 (°*ādibhiḥ suraiḥ*), 780 (*iva*), †784 (°*a ivāmareçaḥ*), 1648 (°*āçanisamasvanaṃ*), 1711 (*Balaṃ Ç°a ivāhave*), 1967 (°*cāpasamaprabhaṃ*, sc. the bow of Çveta), 2011 (°*cāpopamaṃ*, sc. the bow of Çaṅkha), 2202 (°*āçanisamasparçaṃ*), 2672 (°*pratimānakalpaṃ Indrātmajaṃ*, i.e. Arjuna), 3124 (*iva*), 3221 (°*samaḥ*, sc. Abhimanyu), 3365 (*devāḥ Ç°purogamāḥ*), 3549 (*yathā Ç°as Trivishṭape*), 4212 (*yathā Ç°ḥ . . . purā vivyādha Dānavaṃ | Vipracittiṃ*), 4299 (*mahāçanir yathā bhrashtā Ç°muktā*), 4429 (*iva*), 4583 (*yathā Devāsure yuddhe Ç°-Çambarayoḥ purā*, sc. *samāgamaḥ*), 4605 (*Mayaṃ Çakra ivāhave*), 4626 (°*āçanisamadyutiṃ*), 4703 (°*samāḥ*), 4986 (*yathovāca purā Ç°ṃ mahābuddhir Bṛhaspatiḥ*), 5028 (°*āçanisamasparçān*), 5029 (°*cāpopamaṃ*, sc. the bow of Bhīshma), 5123 (*Maya-Ç°au yathā purā*), 5412 (*yathā Ç°o Vajrapāṇir dārayan parvatān uttamān*), 5546 (*yathā*), 5787 (*iva*); VII, 174 (°*mukhāḥ surāḥ*), 282 (*iva*), 293 (do.), 404, 542 (*yathā Devāsure yuddhe Bala-Ç°au*), 605 (°*āçaniravopamaḥ*), 758 (*yathā Ç°rathaḥ*), 782 (°*āçanihatā drumavanta ivācalāḥ*), 788 (°*syātithitāṃ gatāḥ*, C. has by error *Çakta*°), 811 (*iva*), 1035 (v. Draupadeya, pl.), 1223, 1494 (°*opamāḥ*), 1543 (*Airāvatagataṃ*), 1694 (v. Draupadeya, pl.), 1804 (*iva*), 1964 (°*sadmagataḥ*, sc. Abhimanyu), †1981 (°*samaṃ*, sc. Abhimanyu), 2030 (°*opamaḥ*, sc. Hari, the son of Akampana), 2135 (°*pratimavikramāḥ*), 2180, 2616 (father of Arjuna), 2866 (°*Sūryaguṇodayaṃ*, sc. Çiva), 3460 (°*ādīṃç ca surottamān*), 3471, 3561 (°*Jambhau yathā purā*), 3779 (*devagaṇaiḥ saha*), 3936 (°*dhvajasamaprabhaṃ*, sc. the standard of Açvatthāman), 4096 (*Prahlādaṃ samare jitvā yathā Çakraṃ Marudgaṇāḥ*), 4098 (°*Çambarayor iva*, sc. *yuddhaṃ*), 4340 (°*tulyaparākramaiḥ*, sc. *Çakaiḥ*), †4692 (°*pratimaḥ . . . Sātyakiḥ*), †4697 (*bhallena Ç°āçanisannibhena*), 4925 (*trailokyakāṅkshiṇor āsīc Ch°-Prahlādayor iva*, sc. *yuddhaṃ*), 4973 (°*tulyabalaḥ*, sc. Sātyaki), 5008 (*yathā Vṛtravadhe devāḥ purā Ç°ṃ maharshayaḥ*, sc. *parivavruḥ*), 5065 (*iva*), 5192, 5608 (°-*Vairocanī yathā*, sc. *yuyudhāte*), 5732 (°*cāpam ivāparaṃ*), 5886 (*purā Devāsure yuddhe Ç°sya Balinā yathā*), 6153 (°*āçanisphoṭasamaṃ*, sc. *ninādaṃ*), 6416 (*balaṃ . . . Rudra-Ç°āntakopamaṃ*), 6461 (*tvatprasādāt, Hṛshīkeça, Ç°ḥ Suragaṇeçvaraḥ | trailokyavijayaṃ çrīmān prāptavān*), 6464 (*Sureçatvaṃ gataḥ Ç°o hatvā Daityān sahasraçaḥ*), 6856 (°-*Prahlādayor iva*, sc. *yuddhaṃ*), 6973 (°*opamāḥ*), 6977 (*Amoghāṃ . . . çaktiṃ Ç°vinirmitāṃ*, i.e. the dart of Karṇa), 7022 (*Amoghā datteyaṃ çaktiḥ Ç°eṇa*, = do.), 7032 (°*tulyabalaḥ*), 7061 (*iva*), 7073 (°*ṃ Daityā yathā purā*, sc. *ayodhayanta*), 7075 (*yathā Devāsure yuddhe Ç°sya saha Dānavaiḥ*), 7088 (°*aṃ Daityacamūm iva*, sc. *āyāntaṃ*), 7426 (°-*Prahrādayor iva*, sc. *yuddhaṃ*), 7731 (*iva*), 7843 (°-*Prahrādayor iva*, sc. *yuddhaṃ*), †8167 (*yāṃ vai prādāt Sūryaputrāya*—i.e. Karṇa—*Ç°ḥ kuṇḍalābhyāṃ nimāya* (C. *ninâya*), sc. *çaktiṃ*, i.e. Amoghā), †8172 (°*çaktyā*, = do.), †8177 (*yathā Ç°o Vṛtravadhe Marudbhiḥ*, sc. *pūjyamānaḥ*), 8196, 8197, 8208 (°*dattayā*, sc. *çaktyā*, i.e. Amoghā), 8221 (°*muktā ivāçaniḥ*),

8240 (°dattā, sc. çaktiḥ, i.e. Amoghā), 8250 (°dattayā, sc. çaktyā, = do.), 8302 (Pārthe vā Ç°kalpe, i.e. Arjuna), 8694 (yathā kruddho raṇe Ç°o Dānavānāṃ kshayaṃ purā), 8744 (gajah Ç°gajopamaḥ), 9087 (iva), 9243 (yathā), 9372 (°cāpam ivāparaṃ), 9576 (°sya vajreṇa), 9578, 9582 (°ādīṃç ca surottamān), 9590; VIII, †199 (°samānavīryaḥ Çalyaḥ), 299 (°çaktyā, i.e. Amoghā), 516 (yathā Devāsure yuddhe Jambha-Ç°au), 769 (°a ivāsurān, sc. chittvā), 960 (yathaiva cāsito meghaḥ Ç°cāpena — i.e. by the rainbow — çobhitaḥ), 1103 (Jishṇuḥ Ç°tulyaparākramaḥ), 1268 (°Vishṇusamaṃ, sc. vīryaṃ), 1288 (°çaktivinākṛtaṃ, sc. Karṇa), 1294 (Vijaya, the bow of Karṇa, had been given by Ç. to Rāma Jāmadagnya), 1352 (devatānāṃ . . . sa-Ç°āṇāṃ), 1426 (Marudvṛtaḥ), 1436 (devāḥ Ç°purogamāḥ), 1668 (°sya sārathye . . . Mātalivat), 2703 (dhanushī çreshṭhe Ç°cāpanibhe), 2904 (°tulyaparākramaḥ, sc. Drauṇiḥ), 2983 (niruddhāḥ . . . jihīrshavo 'mṛtaṃ Daityāḥ Ç°āgnibhyāṃ ivāsakṛt), 2987, 3009 (°eṇeva yathā Daityān hanyamānān), 3011 (yathā), 3065 (°syātithitāṃ gatvā, sc. the Saṃçaptakas), 3304 (hate mahāsure Jambhe Ç°-Vishṇū yathā Guruḥ, sc. abhyanandat), 3332 (°tulyabalaḥ, sc. Karṇa), †3392 (çauryeṇa Ç°sya), 3611 (°tulyaparākramāḥ), 3645 (°tulyaparākramau), 3687 (iva), 3691 (prayaccha medinīṃ rājñe Ç°āyaiva Harir yathā), 3756 (°eṇeva yathāçaniṃ), †3842 (iva), †4199 (°cāpapratimena dhanvanā), †4206 (iva), †4210 (Çambara-Ç°yor yathā, sc. yuddhaṃ), †4334 (viddhveva Ç°ṃ Namuciḥ), 4429, 4442, 4463 (°Çambarayor iva, sc. yuddhaṃ), †4569 (°o Namucer ivāreḥ), †4646 (Lokapālāḥ sa-Ç°āḥ), †4697 (dhanuç ca tac Ch°çarāsanopamaṃ), 4777 (°āçaniprakhyaruciḥ, sc. sāyakaḥ); IX, 17 (°tulyabalāḥ), 433 (yathā Ç°dhvajaiḥ), 746 (°āçanir ivotsṛshṭaḥ), 795 (yathā pūrvaṃ Ç°syāsurasaṃkshaye), 1016 (°eṇevāsure bale, sc. hate), †1077 (Jambho yathā Ç°samāgamād vai nāgendram Airāvaṇam Indravāhyaṃ, sc. pratyudyayau), 1161 (Baliṃ Ç°a ivāhave, sc. yodhayan), 1849, 1925 (°o Vṛtram ivāhvayan), 2432, 2437, 2440, 2480, 2657 (°vīryopamāḥ), 2733 (yathā . . . Surarāṭ), 2770, 2771, 2930, 2950, 2951, 2955, 3011, 3014, 3016, 3017, 3019, 3021, 3023, 3028 (Surādhipaḥ), 3034, 3084, 3128 (Vṛtra-Ç°au yathāhave), 3156 (yuddhāya Ç°o Vṛtram ivāhvayan), 3250 (Virocanas tu Ç°eṇa māyayā nirjitaḥ), 3261, 3402, 3645 (°vispardhinaḥ); X, 155 (yathā Ç°ḥ sādayitvā mahāsurān), 2571 (Çiva is identified with Ç.); XI, 646 (°sya Balinā yathā, sc. yuddhaṃ); XII, 305, 330 (tridivaṃ . . . Ç°sya), 360 (°o Devapatir yathā), †369 (°o yathā Daityabalāni, sc. nihatya), 439, †613, †614, 892 (°opama), 912 (Devarājaṃ Purandaraṃ), 967 (devāḥ . . . Ç°çreshṭhāḥ), 1013, 1116, 1199 (Marudgaṇair vṛtaḥ), 1356 (Bhīshma had obtained weapons from Ç.), 1807 (iva), 1850, 2196 (devān . . . Ç°purogamān), 2237, 2239, 3183 (Bṛhaspateç ca saṃvādaṃ Ç°sya ca), (3184), 3185, 3186, 3190, 3193, 3610 (°syaiti salokatāṃ), 3615, 3663, 3817, †4397, 4446, 4474 (sakhā Ç° sya . . . Māndhata), 4509, 4598, 4610, 4790 (°syaiti salokatāṃ), 7626 (devāḥ Ç°purogamāḥ), 8028, 8048, 8050, 8052, (8053), 8054, 8056, (8067), 8068, (8071), 8088, (8089), 8092, 8093, 8112, 8113, 8120, 8121, 8122, 8132, 8143, 8144, 8147, (8150), (8152), 8155, (8156), 8157, (8158), 8162, (8163), (8165), (8167), 8169, (8170), 8171, (8172), 8173, (8174), 8175, (8176), (8181), 8191, 8222, 8233, 8238, 8240, 8245, 8251, 8276, 8289, 8293, 8294, 8299, 8335 (Çriyā Ç°sya saṃvādaṃ), (8351), (8360), †8427 (°pramukhaiç ca daivataiḥ), 8741 (°bale), 10101, 10102, 10107, 10109, 10110, 10119, 10121, 10123, 10132, (10137), 10141, 10142, 10148, 10150, 10158, 10161, 10163, 10170, 10173, 10190, 10204, 10206 (°kathāṃ), 10207, 10227 (devāḥ sarve Ç°purogamāḥ), 10230 (devāḥ Ç°purogamāḥ), 10267, 11117, 12202 (°purogāç ca Lokapālāḥ), 12205 (Deveçvaraḥ), 12944, 12946 (Vishṇu will bestow the sovereignty on Ç.), 12951 (°tulyaparākramāḥ), 13016, ††13216, ††13217, 13767, 13878 (°pratispardhī, sc. Rāvaṇa); XIII, 272, 274, 282, 293 (°salokatāṃ), 330, 529, 534, 571, 574, 577, 579, 664 (attacked by Mandara), 694 (adored Çiva), 763 (Çiva assumed the form of Ç.), 768, 770, 772, 777 (783), 793, 801, 803, 817, 818, 828 (Çiva then assumed his own form), 861 (°tulyaparākramaḥ, sc. Māndhātṛ), 873 (°ādyā devatāḥ), 876, 880 (Çiva is identified with Ç.), 916 (°o 'si Marutāṃ, sc. Çiva), 998 (sa-Prajāpati-Ç°āntaṃ jagat), 1288 (learnt the 1000 names of Çiva), 1300 (Cāruçīrshaḥ . . . Ç°sya dayitaḥ sakhā), 1313 (çāpāc Ch°sya), 1314 (Gṛtsamadaḥ . . . Ç°sya dayitaḥ sakhā), 1361 (°tvaṃ), 1369, 1758 (parākrame Ç°samaṃ, sc. Bhīshma), 1897, 1914, (1916), (1920), 1930, (1937), 1955 (Divodāsa built Vārāṇasī at the injunction of Ç.), 1957 (°syevāmarāvatīṃ), 1998 (Gṛtsamada was meant to be Ç.), 2165 (°Çambarasaṃvādaṃ), (2167), 2183, 2273, 2274 (māyāṃ Ç°sya), 2284, 2291, 2315, 2326, 2328, 2332, 2334, 2338, 3170, 3172, 3186, 3187, 3235 (varshati), 3337 (vasati . . . Ç°eṇa saha), 3362 (°eṇa saha modate), †3520 (°yajña°), (3547), 3555, 3563, 3571, 3576, †3581, †3595, 3614, 3661 (yathā), 3885 (Tribhuvaneçvaraḥ), 3893 (Balanisūdanam), 3900, 3922, 4010 (devāḥ Ç°purogamāḥ), (4590), 4662 (prācyāṃ Ç°āya, sc. balikarma prayojayet), 4805, 4807, 4848, †4868 (varshati), †4901, 4927 (°tulyaprabhāvāṇāṃ), 5964, (5967), 5982, 5984, 7153, 7157 (only C., read Çukra° with B.), 7158 (°-Vasubhiḥ), 7285, 7320, 7321, †7366 (Kṛshṇa identified with Ç.), †7381 (paralysed by Kṛshṇa), 7490, 7528 (°ādishu deveshu), 7637 (Çacīpatiḥ); XIV, 107, 119, 166, 177, 179, †232, †238, †244, (†245), †246, †255, †267, 268, †281, †283, †286 (Harimān), 310, 312, †749 (gataḥ Sarvalokāmaratvaṃ), 1129, 1502 (°gṛhopamaṃ), 1576 (Kṛshṇa identified with Ç.), 1766 (°sadmapratikāçāḥ), 2163 (sadṛçaṃ rūpaṃ Ç°cāpasya), 2388, 2496 (°samakarmāṇaṃ, sc. Arjuna), 2649 (°tejasaḥ, sc. Yudhishṭhira), 2817, 2821, 2825, 2827 (°yajñe), 2828; XV, 567 (°sadaḥ . . . Ç°ṃ Çacīpatiṃ), 569; XVII, 65 (°tejasi, sc. Arjuna), 73, (77), (†80), †88, 95; XVIII, 34, 81 (devāḥ Ç°purogamāḥ), 87, 89 (Surapatiḥ), 240 (°sya bhavane), 256 (°eṇa saha modate).

Çambarahan ("the slayer of Çambara"): III, 14773 (yathā); VIII, †4701 (yathā Ç°ā purā Baliṃ, sc. avidhyat; C. has S°)

Çambara-Pākahan ("the slayer of Çambara and Pāka"): XII, 8339 (Sahasranayanaç cāpi Vajrī).

Çatakratu ("performer of a hundred sacrifices"): I, 1421, 1423, 1450, 1465, 1515, 1521, 2470 (Sahasrākshaḥ . . . varshenāpālayat prajāḥ), 3280, 4042 (sākshād api Ç°ḥ), 6464 (gurur mānyaḥ Ç°oḥ, i.e. Bṛhaspati), 8166, 8225 (Sahasrākshaṃ Deveçaṃ), 8278, 8298, 8299; II, 286, 305 (Devarājaṃ), 310 (°oḥ, sc. sabhā), 689 (°r ivāparaḥ), 872 (Asurān parājitya jagat pāti Ç°ḥ), 2375 (api); III, 1725 (Amaraçreshṭhaḥ), 1770 (Devarājaḥ), 3062 (iva), 4024 (iva), 8699, 10395, 10396, 11778 (yathā), 11901 (Arjuna obtained celestial weapons from Ç.), 11940, 11943, 13219 (Devarājaḥ), 13222, 13243, 13417 (āsanena Ç°ḥ, sc. tṛptaḥ), 14253, 14269, 14280, 14283 (devāḥ Ç°purogamāḥ), 14445, 14882, 15093 (iva), †15710 (karma . . . Ç°or vā Daityasenāsu saṅkhye), 16495 (sākshād api Ç°ḥ), 16988; IV, 1406 (devaṃ vāpi Ç°ṃ), 1625; V, 280, 438, 442, 493, 498, 547, 551, 3523 (çāsanād vā Ç°oḥ), 4089, 4443 (iva), 4535 (do.); VI, 528 (°parākramaṃ, sc. Bhīshma), 1537 (came to see the battle), 1574 (*api sākshāt Ç°ḥ*), 4422 (*iva*); VII, 93 (°*m ivācintyaṃ purā Vṛtreṇa nirjitaṃ*), 2522, 2667 (*sākshād api Ç°ḥ*), 5275 (do.), †6444 (°*au cāpi devasattame*), 9076 (*api*); VIII, 385 (*iva*), 1228 (*iva*), 1293 (*yena*—i.e. with the bow (*Vijaya*) of Karṇa—*Daityagaṇān, rājan, jitavān vai Ç°ḥ*), 1698 (*api . . . sākshāt Ç°oḥ*), 2144 (*iva*), †4085 (°*ṃ Vṛtranijaghnushaṃ yathā*), †4948 (*yathā purā Vṛtravadhe Ç°ḥ*); IX, 752 (°*or yathā pūrvaṃ mahatyā Daityasenayā*, sc. *vimardaḥ*), 2430 (*Devarājaḥ*), 2739 (*yathā*), 2833 (origin of the name), 3013, 3015; X, 692 (*sākshād api Ç°uḥ*); XII, 139 (*māyayā ca Ç°oḥ*), 977, 1198 (*kratum āhṛtya çatakṛtvaḥ*), 1812 (*iva*), 2523 (*iva*), 3625, 4574, 5478, 8123, 8148, 8180, 8187 (°*oç ca saṃvādaṃ Namuceç ca*), 8219 (*Devarāje*), 8225, 8268 (*sarvaiḥ kratuçatair ishṭaṃ, na tvam ekaḥ*—sc. *Çakra*—*Ç°ḥ*), 8301, †8330, 10118, 10129, 10205 (*yathā*), 12104 (*salokatāṃ . . . Ç°oḥ*); XIII, 55, 555 (*Devarājaḥ*), 986 (°*ç ca bhagavān Vishṇuç cāditinandanau*), 1022, 1052, 1105, 1316 (°*or acintyasya sattre varshasahasrike*), 1927, 2138, 2279, †2824 (*puri Ç°or api*), 3101 (*iva*), 3156, 3546, 3554, 3569, 3585, 3604, 3615, 3901, †4552 (*Vṛtrahaṇaṃ*), 4766, 4802, †4897 (*Vṛtrahaṇaṃ*), (†4898), (†4900), (†4902), 5970, 5976 (*Devarājaḥ*), †6042 (*yathā . . . Ç°or Vajradharasya yajñe*), 7792 (*sākshād api Ç°ḥ*); XIV, 100 (*iva*), 300, 303, 305, 307, 309, 312, 563 (*sākshād api Ç°oḥ*), †1535 (*yāthā nihatyārigaṇān Ç°r divaṃ*, sc. *yayau*), 1769 (*iva*), 2195 (*Vṛtreṇeva Ç°oḥ*, sc. *yuddhaṃ*), 2826; XVIII, 79 (*Devarājaḥ*).

Çatamanyu: VIII, †3497 (°*vikramaḥ*).

Daçaçatāksha ("having thousand eyes"): VII, †8409; XIII, 277.

Daçaçatanayana (do.): VIII, †4647.

Daçaçatekshaṇa (do.): XII, 4495.

Daityanibarhaṇa: XVII, 108.

Daityāsuranibarhaṇa: XII, 10119.

Dānavaçatru, Dānavaghna, Dānavāri, Dānavasūdana, q.v.

Devaçreshtha, Devadeva, q.v.

Devādhipa ("the king of the gods"): V, 297; IX, †1092 (*vajreṇa D°coditena*).

Devagaṇeçvara, q.v.

Devapati ("the lord of the gods"): III, 2073 (*yathā*), †10264 (*jahi . . . Vṛtraṃ yathā D°r Mahendraḥ*), 12068 (*ajayad D°r Baliṃ Vairocaniṃ purā*); IV, 727 (*Vṛtraṃ D°r yathā*, sc. *jaghāna*); VII, 3475 (slew Vṛtra); XII, 360 (*Çakro D°r yathā*), 3796; XIII, 7717 (*yathā*).

Devarāj ("the king of the gods"): III, 3065 (°*ād iva Nandane*), 8272 (*iva*), 10383, 13224, 15027; V, 324, 547, 2487 (*muñcan D°ād açanīm iva*); VI 4901 (*Vajrapāṇiḥ*); X, 148 (*api*); XII, 12717, ††13217; XIII, †32 (*Vṛtraṃ hatvā*), 4588 (*Sahasrākshaḥ*); XVIII, 135 (*I°*).

Devarāja (do.): I, †150, †197 (°*ena dattām divyāṃ çaktiṃ*), 1448, 1450 (*Çatakratuḥ*), 1451, 1455, 2704 (°*samadyutiḥ*), 2746 (father of Arjuna), 2826 (°*pratimaṃ*), 2934, 3185 (°*samadyutiḥ*), †3567, 3888 (°*samadyutiḥ*), 3904 (°*samadyuteḥ*), 3979 (°*sadṛçaḥ*), 4001 (°*samo yudhi*), 4272 (°*samaprabhaṃ*), 4560 (°*parākramāḥ*), 4787, 5075, †7290, †7291, †7297, 8163, 8229, 8245, 8308, 8309; II, 280, 290, 305 (*Çatakratuṃ*), 1760, 1793; III, 1518, 1706, 1714 (°*rathaṃ*), 1770 (*Çatakratuṃ*), 1880, 1971 (°*samadyuti*), 2117 (°*sya bhavanaṃ*), 2127, 2480 (*samadyutiḥ*), 2797 (*Mātalir ayaṃ D°sya sārathiḥ*), 8181 (at Jātismarahrada *D.* went to heaven after having performed 100 sacrifices), 8445 (read *yaṃ* instead of *'yaṃ*), 10346 (°*sutām iva*). 10369, 10397, †10658, 10718, 10719, 10827, 11920, 11922 (*Purandaraḥ*), 11923, 11925, 11927, 11928, 11929 (*Purandaraḥ*), 11937, 11941, 12005, 12024, 12030, 12046 (*Sahasrākshaṃ*), 12061, 12069, 12087, 12122 (*astraṃ . . . dayitaṃ D°sya*), 12149, 12174 (*vajraṃ . . . D°sya dayitaṃ bhīmam astraṃ*), 12189, 12264 (°*sya bhavanaṃ*), 12268, 12274, 12428 (*api*), 13214 (*Baka-Dālbhyau . . . sakhāyau D°sya*), 13219 (*Çatakratuḥ*), 15016, 16972, 16993 (*çaktir D°sya*, i.e. Amoghā), 17178; IV, 1432, 1766 (*vimānaṃ D°sya*), 1769 (*vimānan* (B. °*ne*) *D°sya*), 2074, 2080; V, 226, 246, 248, 261 (*I°*), 341, 362 (°*sya dayitām*, sc. Çacī), 450, 475, 479, 500, 520, 547 (*Çatakratuḥ*), 551 (do.), †1814 (*yathā*), 3574 (*sahaputraḥ Çacīpatiḥ*), 3617 (°*sya purī varyā 'marāvatī*), 3665 (*Çakraṃ*), 3673, 3679, 4053; VI, 705 (*iva*), †2653 (*iva*), 3985 (°*niveçane*); VII, 1501 (°*opamaḥ*), 2669, 3951 (*yathā . . . D°camū*), 6171 (°*pratimaṃ*), †6296 (*devaçatrūn iva D°ḥ Kirīṭamālī*), 7809 (*iva*); VIII, 104 (°*sya . . . sakhā*, sc. Bhagadatta), 763, 1035 (*yathā Daityacamūṃ . . . D°o mamarda ha*), †1965; IX, 2430 (*Çatakratuḥ*), 2764; XI, 767; XII, 141, †613 (*Çakraṃ . . . Purandaraṃ*), 1102 (°*samadyutiṃ*), 1103, 1104 (°*samadyutiḥ*), 1117 (°*samadyutiṃ*), 1121 (°*sya māyayā*), 1405 (°*gṛhopamaṃ*), 1564 (*api*), 1866 (°*samīpataḥ*), 3622, 6435, 8124, 8128, 8143, 8219 (*Çatakratau*), 13769 (°*ālayaṃ*), 13939; XIII, 94 (°*a ivāparaḥ*, 276, 555 (*Çatakratuḥ*), 768 (Çiva disguised as Indra), 877 (*Kauçikaḥ*), 2284, 2288, 2322, 2819 (°*vat*), 5976 (*Çatakratuḥ*); XIV, 106, 121, 125, 168, 217, †220, †231, †235, †275, †276, 280, 286, 1514 (*iva*), 2422 (*api*), 2813 (*Sahasrākshaḥ*), 2814 (*sadṛço D°ena*), 2880 (*Purandaraḥ*); XVII, 103 (do.); XVIII, 39, 79 (*Çatakratuḥ*), 116 (°*ena Mahendreṇa*).

Devarājan (do.): I, 638; V, 365 (*I°*); VIII, †4546 (*astraṃ dayitaṃ D° jñaḥ*); XIV, 113, †232.

Deveça, q.v.

Devendra ("chief of the gods"): I, 1423, 1525, 4790, 4791 (father of Arjuna), 8263; II, 466 (*Purandaraḥ*), 484, 1919 (*Mahendraṃ iva*); III, 333, 1452 (*yathā*), 1776, 8437 (*Dadhīca iva D°ṃ*, sc. *rakshasva*), 10206, 10715, 10924, 11996, 12265, 13225, 13247, 14260, 14281, 14356; IV, 1265 (*iva*); V, 253, 276, 280, 336, 337, 494, 521, 548; VI, †745 (°*seneva*), 5793; VII, 4213 (*api*), 6853 (*Asurān iva D°ḥ*, sc. *jahi*), 7673 (*iva*); VIII, 268 (°*eṇa ivācalaḥ*, sc. *nihataḥ*), †3863 (*Jambhaṃ jighānsuṃ . . . D°m iva*); IX, 2439, 2442; XII, 1112, 2529 (*iva*), 3813, 4570, 8166, 8279, 8281, 8413, 10115, 10117, 10119, 10159, 10162, 10198, 13938 (°*sya niveçane*); XIII, 554, 577, 767 (Çiva in the shape of Indra), 818 (do.), 830 (do.), 2286, 2313, 2895 (°*tvaṃ*), 3158, 3188, 3190, 3913 (*Çacīpate*); XIV, 117, †225, †246, 1614, 1616, 2537 (*iva*); XVII, 107; XVIII, 110.

Goçabdātmaja, q.v.

Hari: VIII, †4700 (*Namuciṃ yathā H°ḥ*, sc. *vidhya*).

Hariçmaçru ("having a yellow beard"): XII, ††13205 (°*tāṃ*, origin of the name).

Harihaya ("having bay horses"): I, 2685 (°*opamaḥ*), 5402, 7101, 7351 (*yathendrāṇī H°e*), 8098 (°*opamaḥ*).

Harimat (do.): V, †1876 (*I°*); XIV, †286 (*Devarājaḥ*).

Harivāhana (do.): I, 1296, 8227; III, 1870, 12053; XII, 6743; XIII, 1889; XIV, 108.

Içvara, q.v.

Jagadīçvara, q.v.

Kāçyapa, q.v.

Kauçika, q.v.

Kirīṭin, q.v.

Kuçikottama, q.v.

Lokatrayeça ("the lord of the three worlds"): I, 811 (*Purandarāya*).

Lokeçvareçvara: XII, 1720.

Maghavat (rarely *Maghavan*): I, 2358, 2360, 3281, 6083 (Ghaṭotkaca was created by *M.*, that Karṇa might use his dart Amoghā in slaying him), †7302 (among those who procreated the five Indras as the Pāṇḍavas), 7503 (*api*), 8037 (*iva*); III, 1809 (*rakshitā caiva tridivaṃ M°ān iva*), 2118 (°*vā* (nom. from the stem Maghavan)), 2119, 2123, 2137, 10380, 10457, 10719, 11744 (*Dānavān M°ān iva*, sc. *nihatya*), 11833 (*sākshān M°tā sṛshṭaḥ . . . Dhanañjayaḥ*, i.e. Arjuna), 12010 (*Deveçaḥ*), 12072 (*jitavān Çambaraṃ yudhi*), 12075 (*pureva M°ān*, sc. *vijetā*), 12277, 12563 (°*ān iva Paulomyā sahitaḥ*), 13239, 14424 (anointed Skanda), 16510 (*Maghonaḥ*, from the stem Maghavan), 16957; IV, 1788 (*sṛshṭo M°tā vajraḥ prapatann iva parvate*), 1895; V, 271, 295, †822 (*rājyaṃ M°ān prāpa mukhyaṃ*), 5924 (°*ān iva Dānavaiḥ*, sc. *yotsyati*); VI, 1733 (*vyadarata . . . M°ān* (so B., C. has °*vā*, from the stem Maghavan) *iva Dānavān*), 3622 (*ajeyaṃ . . . M°tāpi ca*); VII, 219 (°*ān samabhikruddhaḥ sahasā Dānaveshv iva*, sc. *bāṇavarshaṃ sumahad asṛjat*), 321 (*varshāṇi M°ān iva*, sc. *visṛjan*), 3855 (*na çaktaṃ bhettuṃ . . . svayaṃ M°tāpi*), 5175 (°*antam ivāmarāḥ*, sc. *pṛshṭhato 'nuyayuḥ*), 7728 (*vyadhamat . . . senām Āsurīṃ M°ān iva*), 9557 (*na çakyas tāni M°ān bhettuṃ* (so B., C. has °*vā netum*—from the stem Maghavan)); VIII, 2125 (*vyadhamat . . . senām Āsurīṃ M°ān iva*), 2242 (*jaghāna . . . senām Āsurīṃ M°ān iva*), 3793 (*hatvā . . . Çambaraṃ* (C. *S°*) *M°ān iva*), †4280 (*purā jighāṃsur M°eva* (from the stem Maghavan) *Jambhaṃ*), 4438 (°*vā*, from the stem Maghavan); IX, 355 (*jahi . . . M°ān iva Çambaraṃ*), 551 (*iva*), 828 (*vavarsha . . . varsheṇa M°ān iva*), 3297 (*vavarsha M°ān*); X, 132 (*sūdayishyāmi . . . M°ān iva Dānavān*), 534, 596 (*jahi . . . Çambaraṃ M°ān iva*), 599 (*Paulomīṃ M°ān iva*, sc. *uddhṛtavān kṛcchāt*); XI, 610 (*iva*); XII, 918 (*vavṛshe M°vā*, from the stem Maghavan), 920 (°*vā*, from the stem Maghavan), 1522 (*iva*), 5437 (*provāca M°vā* (from the stem Maghavan) *svayaṃ*), 8065, 8102, 8115, 8349, 8420 (*Lakshmīsahitaṃ*), 10152 (*Vṛtraṃ hatvā M°ān Dānavāriḥ*), 12035; XIII, 681 (disregarded the Vālakhilyas), 790 (Çiva in the shape of Indra), 803 (do.), 3154 (°*vā*, from the stem Maghavan), (3155) (do.), †4589 (do.), †4898 (do.), 7483 (*naçakat tāni M°ā* (from the stem Maghavan) *bhettuṃ* (B. *jetuṃ*); XIV, †222, †225.

Mahendra ("the great Indra"): I, 434 (°*lokagamanaṃ*), 2274 (*Çacīva M°eṇa*, sc. *yuyuje*), 2355, 2358, 2857 (*pādapaiḥ . . . M°dhvajasannibhaiḥ*), 3072, 3397 (°*purasannibhuṃ*), 4345 (do.), 5481 (*abhidudrāva M°ṃ Çambaro yathā*), 6485 (°*sya vajraṃ*), †7078 (°*karmā*, sc. Arjuna), 7705 (how he got 1,000 eyes), 8094; II, 507 (°*sya . . . salokatāṃ*), 1005 (°*sya sakhā*, sc. Bhagadatta), 1919 (°*m iva Devendraṃ divi saptarshayo yathā*, sc. *abhijagmuḥ*); III, 171 (*devāḥ . . . sa-M°āḥ*), 1441, 1508, 1651 (*api*), 1812 (°-*Varuṇopamaḥ*), †1816, 1839, 1848, 1910, 2139 (*lokapālā M°ādyāḥ*), 2170 (°*ṃ sarvadevānāṃ*), 8692 (°*pramukhān surān*), †8727, 8754 (*tridaçāḥ . . . sa-M°āḥ*), †10264 (*jahi . . . Vṛtraṃ yathā Devapatir M°ḥ*), 10312, 10452, †10656 (*pravaraḥ surāṇāṃ*), 11818 (father of Jishṇu, i.e. Arjuna), 11846, †11903 (°*vāhaṃ*), †11906 (°*vāhāt*), 12002 (°*ānucarāḥ*), 12133 (°*āstrapracoditāḥ*), 12195, 12691 (*prajāpatiḥ*), 14863 (°*a iva Vajrabhṛt*), †15640 (°*kalpān*), †15693 (°*opamavikramāṇāṃ*), 16570 (°*a iva Paulomyā . . . sameyivān*), 16672 (°*a iva vīraḥ*), 16924, 17139; IV, †298 (*sutaṃ M°sya*, i.e. Arjuna), 1518 (°*samatejasaṃ . . . Pārthaṃ*), 2304 (*Vishṇu-M°kalpau*), 2368 (*sutām iva M°sya*); V, 332, 353, 418, 499 (*Dānavān hatvā*), 502, †512, †513, 518 (*Pākaçāsanaḥ*), 687 (°*kalpaṃ*, sc. Yudhishṭhira), 1900 (*devair M°pramukhaiḥ*), 1918, 2059 (°*a iva vajreṇa Dānavān*), 2198 (had asked Karṇa for his ear-rings for the sake of Çacī), 2378 (°*opendravikramaṃ*, sc. *Arjunaṃ*), †2419 (had given the dart Amoghā to Karṇa), 3158 (°*samavikramaḥ*, i.e. Arjuna), 3361 (°*sadanaprakhyāṃ . . . sabhāṃ*), 3528 (°*sadṛçīṃ*, sc. *pūjāṃ*); 3553 (*pravarshati*), 4562 (*Indro Vṛtravadhenaiva M°ḥ samapadyata*), 5190 (°*m iva cādityair abhiguptaṃ*), 5316 (*iva*), 5739 (*hanishyati . . . M°o Dānavān iva*), 5930 (*iva*); VI, 502 (°*sadṛçaḥ çaurye*, sc. Bhīshma), 620 (°*ketavaḥ çubhrā M°sadaneshv iva*), 682 (do.), 768 (°*ādīn divaukasaḥ*), †788 (°*pratimānakalpaṃ*), 2543 (°*samavīryeṇa*), 3348 (*yathā Devāsure yuddhe M°ḥ*), †3381 (*Daityeshu yadvat samare M°ḥ*), 3539 (°*samavikramāḥ*), †3778 (°*pratimaprabhāvaḥ*), 4442 (*jahi . . . M°a iva Dānavān*), 4602 (°*pratimaṃ Kārshṇiṃ*), 4828 (°*samavīryeṇa*), 4916 (*iva*), 5183 (*yathā Vṛtra-M°yoḥ*, sc. *yuddhaṃ*); VII, 92 (°*eṇaiva Maināka asahyaṃ bhuvi pātitaṃ*), 346 (*Yama-Vaiçravaṇāditya-M°-Varuṇopamaṃ*, sc. *Uttamaujas*), 403 (°*bhavanād vīraḥ Pārijātam upānayat*, sc. Kṛshṇa), 492 (*iva*), 1998 (°*çatravaḥ . . . Hiraṇyapuravāsinaḥ*), 2475 (°*pratimaujasāṃ*), 3971 (*bāṇān M°āçanisannibhān*), 3973 (°*a iva Çambaraṃ*, sc. *abhyadravat*), 4973 (°*o Dānaveshv iva*), 5548 (*iva*), 5798 (*jayājayau M°sya loke dṛshṭau*), 6028 (°*ābhaḥ . . . Purūravāḥ*), †6151 (°*cāpapratimaṃ . . . Gāṇḍīvaṃ*), 6671 (°*āçaninisvanaḥ*); VIII, 143 (°*eṇa yathā Vṛtraḥ*, sc. *hataḥ*), 212 (*yathā*), 228 (*çatror api M°sya*), 240 (*vṛsho M°o deveshu*), 242 (*varo M°o devānāṃ*), 377 (*jahi . . . M°o Dānavān iva*), 726 (°*a iva Dānavān*, sc. *nijaghnivān*), †813 (°*vajra-*), 1057 (°*o Namuciṃ yathā*, sc. *trasayām āsa*), 1653 (*jahi . . . M°o Dānavān iva*), †1717 (°*ād api Vajrapāṇeḥ*), †1720 (°-*Vishṇupratimau*), †3238 (*varāstraṃ . . . M°sṛshṭaṃ*), †4214 (*çarāṃ . . . M°vajrāçanipātaduḥsahaṃ*), †4318 (°*vajraprahataḥ . . . yathā . . . gairikaparvataḥ*), †4501 (*samīyatur M°-Jambhāv iva*), †4530 (°-*Vṛtrāv iva samprajaghnatuḥ*), †4550 (°*çastrābhimukhān . . . ishusaṅghān*), †4551 (°*karmā*, i.e. Arjuna (?)), †4665 (°*vajraḥ çikharottamaṃ yathā*), †4787 (°*vajrānaladaṇḍasannibhaṃ*), †4798 (*çiro jahāra Vṛtrasya vajreṇa yathā M°ḥ*), †4950 (°*vāhapratimena*, °*vīryapratimānapaurushau*); IX, 209 (°*sadṛçaprabhaṃ*), 320 (*jahi . . . M°o Dānavam iva*), †878 (°*vajrāçanitulyaniḥsvanaḥ*), †885 (*yathā M°o Namuciṃ*, sc. *vivyādha*), †915 (°*vāhapratimaḥ*), †1070 (°*vajrapratimaiḥ*), †1072 (*yathā M°sya yujum*), 2538; X, 172 (*api*), †564 (*nihatya çatrūn sarvān*); XII, 438 (*Indro Vṛtravadhenaiva M°ḥ samapadyata*), 2093 (*Sahasrākshaḥ*), 2105, 2520 (*anuyāsyanti M°m iva devatāḥ*), 2526 (*iva*), 2931 (do.), †4195 (°*pratimaprabhāva*), 4568 (*Prāhrādena hṛtaṃ rājyaṃ M°sya*), 6187, 8069, 10018, 13769; XIII, 820 (*Brahmendra-M°-Vishṇusahitā devāḥ*, so C., but B. has *Hutāça*, instead of *M°*), 887 (Çiva is identified with *M.*), 1340 (°*sya dayitaḥ*, sc. Vyāsa), 1934, 1939, 2137 (*tathā bhagasahasreṇa M°ḥ parivihnitaḥ | teshām eva prabhāvena Sahasranayano hy asau*), 2183 (°*tvaṃ*), 4596, 5768 (*yathā*), 7111 (°*guravaḥ sapta prācīṃ vai diçam āçritaḥ*, sc. Yavakrīta, etc.), 7126 (°*samavikramaṃ*), 7381 (Kṛshṇa is identified with *M.*); XIV, †234, †249, †262 (*devaçreshṭhaṃ*), †263, 1830 (°*pratimāḥ*), 2169 (°*vajrapratimaiḥ . . . çaraiḥ*), 2251 (°*a iva Vajrabhṛt*), 2633 (°*ānugatā devāḥ*), 2673 (*çuçubhe M°as tridaçair iva*); XV, 546 (°*sadane*), 547 (°*sadanaṃ*), 564 (°*sya salokatāṃ*), †663 (*Vishṇu-M°kalpau*); XVII, †83; XVIII, 72 (*iva*), 116 (*Devarājena*), 161 (*Pāṇḍur M°sadanaṃ yayau*), 175 (*bhavanañ ca M°sya*).

Marutpati ("lord of the Maruts"): I, 3121 (*yathā Çakro M°ḥ*), 6631 (*yathā Çacyā M°ḥ*, sc. *sahitaḥ*), 8474 (*saha devaiḥ*); II, 2110 (*Marudbhiḥ sahito, rājan, api sākshād M°ḥ*); IV, 2204 (*Marudgaṇaiḥ parivṛtaḥ sākshād api M°ḥ*); VIII, †3398 (*ahanishyat . . . M°r Vṛtram ivāttavajraḥ*); X, 473 (*api*); XII, 1798 (*°samāḥ*), ††13217 (*Indram*).

Marutvat ("attended by the Maruts"): III, 12003; VIII, †3869 (*yathā M°ān Balab'hedane purā*).

Mukuṭin ("wearing a diadem"): XIII, 2276.

Namucighna ("the slayer of Namuci"): I, 1286.

Namucihan (do.): I, 8231.

Pākaçāsana ("punisher of Pāka"): I, 7432 (*lokāṃs trīn jitavān*), 8277, 8279, 8329; III, 340 (*pravavarsha*), 1727, 1771 (*Deveçam*), 9998 (*nāvarshat*), 10314, 10711, 10730, 12854 (*yathartuvarshī bhagavān na tathā P°ḥ*), 14251, 14259, 15017, 16932, 17190; V, 257, 414, 518 (*Mahendraḥ*), 2357 (*samayavarshīva gagane P°ḥ*), 5806 (friend of Bhagadatta); VII, 6459 (*jeshyāmahe . . . yathā . . . Dānavān P°ḥ*); IX, 2662, 2766, 2779, 2931; XII, 957 (*Surasattamaḥ*), 1198 (*Çatakratuḥ*), 1720 (*Lokeçvareçvaraḥ*, incarnate as Gādhi), 3386, 4576, 8149, 8300 (*Sahasrākshaḥ*), 8416, 10125; XIII, 271, 289, 2264 (*Vṛtrahā*), 2275, 2285, 2290, 2292, 7306; XIV, 116, 2394 (*vavrshe*).

***Parjanya:** I, ††829, 2808 (*kālavarshī*), 4338 (*yathartuvarshī*), 4824 (one of the Ādityas, but Indra is already mentioned; is not to be read *jaghanyajaḥ*, as in v. 2523); II, 1205 (*nikāmavarshī*), 1624 (*iva*); III, 10012 (*pravarshet P°ḥ*), 10016 (do.), 13079 (*akālavarshī*), 13100 (*kālavarshī*), 13217, 13473 (C. has by error *Pary°*), 14192 (*°sahitaḥ . . . Agnir Vaiçvānaraḥ*), 14559; IV, 43 (*varshatāṃ varaḥ*), 931 (*samyagvarshī*), 1898 (*°a iva vṛshṭimān*), 2031 (*yathā varshati P°e*); V, 1131 (*°nāthāḥ paçavaḥ*), 2398 (*nikāmavarshī*), 2997 (*prāvarshat*); VI, 2804 (*°a iva vṛshṭimān*), 5659 (*abhyavarshat*); VII, 320 (*iva*), 2188 (*yasmai*—i.e. Suhotra—*vavarsha P°o hiraṇyam*), 2190 (*kāmān varshati P°ḥ*), 3153 *°a iva vṛshṭimān*), 9595 (Çiva identified with *P.*, C. has by error *Pary°*); X, 709 (*nābhivarshati*); XII, 946 (*kālavarshī*), 1365 (*°m iva nāthamānā upāsate*), 3403 (*kālavarshī*), 3595 (*iva*); XIII, 55 (different from Indra?), 2013, 6257 (*avarshati P°e*), 6871 (*vavrshe*); XIV, 2859 (*na ca varshati P°ḥ*), 2882 (*nikāmavarshī*).

Purandara ("destroyer of fortresses"): I, 441, 476, 811, 1287, 1445, 1518 (*Sahasrākshaḥ*), 1520, 2054 (*°niveçanam*), 2055, 2127, 2128, 2215 (*iva*), 2915, 3280, 3992 (*yathā devam P°m*), 4007 (*purīm . . . P°puropamām*), 4417 (*°m ivāparam*), 4456 (*iva*), 5378 (*babhau yathā Dānavasaṃkshaye purā P°ḥ*), 7999 (*°gṛhopamam*), 8067 (*°puropamam*), 8307, 8467; II, 466 (*Devendraḥ*); III, 274 (*iva*), 988 (*iva*), 1471 (*devam*), 1473, 1789 (*°niveçanam*), 1792, 1879, 8693, †8713, 8721 (*Sahasrākshaḥ*), 8722 (*devaḥ*), 10291, 10381, 10403, 10891, 11922 (*Devarājaḥ*), 11925, 11929 (*Devarājaḥ*), 12072 (*yathā devam P°m*), 12188 (*°purāt*), 12267 (*Sahasrākshaḥ*), †12729 (*lokam . . . P°sya*), 14179 (? name of a fire), 14244, 14248, 14582 (*devaḥ*), 14618, 16935, 16973, 16990 (*Deveçam*), 17088 (*vibudhāḥ sarve P°mukhāḥ*); IV, 235; V, 184, 440 (*devaḥ*), 1993 (had been vanquished by Arjuna, all. to Khāṇḍavadahanaparvan), 2351 (*api sākshāt P°ḥ*), 3237 (*°gṛhopamam*), 3667, 3669, 4179 (*api sākshāt P°ḥ*), 7024 (*jahi . . . yathā Vṛtram P°ḥ*); VI, 3721 (*vadhakāṅkshī Vṛtrasyeva P°ḥ*), 4247 (*°samaḥ*, sc. Bhagadatta), 4265 (*iva*), 5138 (*avārayat . . . yathā Vṛtram P°ḥ*); VII, 3436 (*api . . . Vajrahastaḥ P°ḥ*), 3814 (*jahy enam . . . yathā Vṛtram P°ḥ*), 3861, 5476 (*visṛjya . . . P°a ivāçanim*), 5545 (*ajayat . . . P°a ivāsuram*), 6500 (*sākshād api P°ḥ*), 6633 (*Vṛtrahatyai yathā devāḥ parivavruḥ P°m*), 6934 (*vicakhāna . . . P°a ivāçanim*), 6974, 7089 (*pratyudyayau . . . yathā Vṛtram P°ḥ*), 8971 (*°samaḥ*), 9288 (*api*), 9581; VIII, 293 (all. to Kuṇḍalāharaṇaparvan), †708 (*iva*), 1262 (*°samam*), 1427, 1641 (*Vajrahastam*), †1726 (*Vishṇu-P°opamam*), 3061 (*°same*), †3592 (*jahi . . . P°o Vṛtram iva*), 4465 (*°dhanuḥprakhyā*), †4659, 4721 (*vyasṛjat . . . varshāṇīva P°ḥ*); IX, 1942 (*api*), 3488 (*sākshād api Vajrī P°ḥ*); XII, 912 (*Çakram Devarājam*), 1719 (*Sahasrākshaḥ*), 2204, 3386, 3799, 3804, 3829, †3846, 6440, 8087, 8113, 8164, 8185, 8188, 8233, 8260, 9527 (*Trilokeçaḥ*), 10052, ††13206 (all. to Sukanyopākhyāna); XIII, 788 (Çiva in the shape of Indra), 799 (do.), 1892, 1931, 1936, 2265, 2270, 2322, 2324, 2327, †2957 (*lokam . . . P°sya*), 3162, 3169, 3179, 3193, 3911, 4541, †6044 (*lokān . . . P°sya*), 7218 (*çaptaç ca bhagavān Gautamena P°ḥ | Ahalyāṃ kāmayānaḥ*); XIV, 172 (*Bṛhaspati-P°au*), †250, †261, 1180 (*devatānām*, sc. *rājā*), 1613 (*Vajrapāṇiḥ*), 2247 (*vavarsha . . . varshān iva P°ḥ*), 2822, 2880 (*Devarājaḥ*); XV, 545 (*°sya saṃsthānam*); XVII, 76, 103 (*Devarājaḥ*); XVIII, 256 (*°pure*).

Puruhūta ("invoked by many"): I, †3592 (*purīm P°sya*), 4921 (father of Arjuna); II, 1419 (*iva*); III, 8414; VI, 2076 (*çāsanāt P°sya nirmito Viçvakarmaṇā*, sc. the standard of Arjuna); XII, 10193; XIII, 1050 (*°namaskṛta*, sc. Çiva), 1357 (*°m iveçvaraḥ*, sc. *abravīt*); XIV, †227, †277; XVI, †132.

Pūshānuja ("the younger brother of Pūshan"): VIII, 798 (only B., C. has by error *Pūshātmajaḥ*).

Pushkarekshaṇa ("lotus-eyed"): XIII, 3922.

Sahasradṛç ("thousand-eyed"): III, 670 (*yathā*), 1781, 13088 (*akālavarshī*); IX, 548 (*iva*); XIV, 2444 (do.).

Sahasrāksha (do): I, 1286, 1291, 1478 (*devaḥ*), 1518 (*Purandaraḥ*), 1529, 2470 (*Çatakratuḥ*), 6621 (*na vavarsha*), 6630 (*pravavarsha*), 8244; II, 70 (*Çacīpatiḥ*), 1527 (*°samam*), 1625 (*iva*); III, 1506, 1509, 1777, 8721 (*Purandaraḥ*), 8770, 10011 (*na vavarsha*), 11899 (*°niveçane*), 11901 (*Çatakratum*), 11922, 11932, 12046 (*Devarājam*), 12052, 12267 (*Purandaraḥ*), 16440 (*Çacīpatim*), 16991, 17295 (*°ād anavaraḥ*, sc. Arjuna); IV, 47 (*°sya veçmani*), 1651 (*devāt*); V, 4645 (*°samaḥ*); VI, 240; VII, 117 (*iva*), 2955 (do.), 5133 (do.), 6008 (*°samam*); IX, 1436 (*pīḍayām āsa . . . S°a ivāsurān*), 2820 (*devaḥ*), 3017; XII, 1718 (*°samaḥ*), 1719 (*Purandaraḥ*), 2093 (*Mahendraḥ*), 3447, 5333 (*na vavarsha*), 8186, 8300 (*Pākaçāsanaḥ*); XIII, 204 (*°samadyutiḥ*), 288, 2323, 3165, 3182, 3558, 3601, 3918, 3924, †4588 (*Devarāṭ*); XIV, 2813 (*Devarājaḥ*), 2825, 2857 (*na vavarsha*); XVII, 74.

Sahasralocana (do.): XII, †8421.

Sahasranayana (do): XII, 8339 (*Vajrī*), 13880 (*°opamaḥ*); XIII, 799 (Çiva in the shape of Indra), 2137 (how Indra got 1,000 eyes).

Sahasranetra (do.): I, 7706 (how Indra got 1,000 eyes); III, 954 (*°pratimaḥ*); IV, †238 (do.); VII, †4688 (*°pratimaprabhāvam*); VIII, †4260 (*Vṛtram nihatyeva S°ḥ*), †4789 (*°āçanitulyavīryam*), †4817 (*°pratima-*); IX, 882 (*°pratimaprabhāvaḥ*); XIII, 6045 (*°sya . . . lokam*); XVII, 81.

Sarvadānavasūdana: X, 156.

Sarvadeveça: I, 1285.

Sarvalokāmara: XIV, 749.

Suraçreshṭha, q.v.

Surādhipa ("the king of the gods"): III, 333, 8282, 11938, 12954 (*Çakraḥ*, Nārāyaṇa is identified with Indra);

IX, 3028 (*Çakraḥ*); XII, 8093, †8330, 10121, 10122; XIII, 3898; XIV, 111.

Suragaṇeçvara ("the lord of the gaṇas of gods"): I, 2914 (*Çakraṃ*); III, 10731; V, 411 (*Çakraḥ*); VII, 6461 (do.).

Surāṇāṃ pati(ḥ) ("the lord of the gods"): VIII, 1485 (*Surāmbupretavittānāṃ patīn*, i.e. Indra, Varuṇa, Yama, and Kubera).

Surapati (do.): I, 4409 (all. to Kuṇḍalāharaṇaparvan), 8473; V, 3535 (*°eḥ sakhe*, i.e. Mātali), 3662 (*Vāsavaṃ*); VI, 3666 (*yathā S°ḥ kruddhas trasuyām āsa Dānavān*); VII, 3862; VIII, 1213 (*°samavikramaḥ*), 1428, 1741 (*°vīrya-sama-*): XVIII, 89 (*Çakraḥ*).

Surapuṅgava: III, 12018.

Surarāj ("the king of the gods"): VI, 2101 (*iva*); IX, 2733 (*Çakraḥ*).

Surarāja (do.): III, 10915, †11910 (*°tulyaṃ*), †12321 (*°kalpau*, sc. *Yamau*); VI, †3785 (*°kalpaḥ*); VII, †4699 (do.).

Surārihan: I, 6629 (*yathā*); V, 272.

Surarshabha, Surasattama, Sureça, Sureçvara, q.v.

Surendra ("chief of the gods"): I, 2934; III, 10012 *pravarshaṇe S°sya*), 10142; IV, †2123 (*°kalpaṃ*); VII, †7203; XII, 136 (all. to Kuṇḍalāharaṇaparvan), 4611, 8224 (*I°*), 13773; XIII, 731 (*Brahma-Vishṇu-S°āṇāṃ*, sc. *vapuḥ*), 2289, 2295, 3156, 3166, 4048 (*°dvirada*, i.e. Airāvata), 4210, 4215, †4899 (*°nāgaṃ*, i.e. Airāvata), †4901, 6005; XIV, †278, †280.

Surottama: I, 1290; XII, 3817, 3825.

Trailokyapati ("king of the three worlds"): XII, 8057.

Trailokyarāja (do.): V, 3682.

Tribhuvaneçvara (do.): IX, 2771 (*Çakraḥ*), 2790; XIII, 3885 (*Çakraḥ*).

Tridaçāḍhipa ("the king of the gods"): III, 331, 1510, 8726; V, †2419 (*Mahendraḥ*); VIII, †4612 (*°opamaṃ*); XII, 3844; XIII, 580, 2315, 3354 (a sentence of his is quoted).

Tridaçāḍhipati (do.): VIII, †4647; IX, 2767.

Tridaçeça, Tridaçeçvara (do.): q.v.

Tridaçendra (do.): V, 1041; IX, 2662; XII, 10165; XIII, 4181, 4541.

Tridiveçvara (do.): I, 1529; III, †11191; VI, 776 (?); IX, 2444.

Trilokarāja (do.): V, 3512.

Trilokeça (do.), q.v.

Vajrabhṛt ("carrying the thunderbolt"): I, 1151, 2133, 7457 (*api V°ā svayaṃ*), 8089; III, 837 (*api V°ā svayaṃ*), 10922, 14863 (*Mahendra iva V°t*), 15261 (*paçya . . . Aditiṃ V°d yathā*); IV, 1177 (*vitrāsayitvā . . . Dānavān iva V°t*), 1615 (*api V°tā guptaṃ*), 1777; V, 5431 (*iva*); VI, 535 (*nighnan . . . Dānavān iva V°t*), 811 (*api V°taḥ svayaṃ*), 2074 (*tathoktaḥ . . . Jishṇur V°teva ha*), 2884 (*api V°ā svayaṃ*), 5623 (*api*); VII, 476 (*svayaṃ*); VIII, 290 (do.), 4983 (*hato V°tā Vṛtraḥ*); IX, 1746 (*svayaṃ*); XIV, 2251 (*Mahendra iva V°t*).

Vajradhara (do.): I, 8167 (pl.); II, 118 (*kampayām āsa . . . yathāsurān Kālakeyān devo V°ḥ*); III, 1780, †10092 (*yathā Çacī V°sya*), 10293, 10884 (*api*), 11502 (*abhidudrāva Balir V°ṃ yathā*), 11905 (*Dhanañjayo V°prabhāvaḥ*, i.e. Arjuna), 14381, 16440; V, 630 (*api V°ḥ sākshāt*); VI, 672 (*yathā*), 3664 (*yathā V°ḥ pūrvaṃ saṅgrāme Tārakāmaye*), 4960, 4985 (*api V°ḥ svayaṃ*); VII, 3603 (*yathā*), †4698 (*yathā purā V°ḥ . . . Balasya saṅkhye*), †5826 (*nadan yathā V°s tapānte*), 9051 (*°sya vinādaḥ*); VIII, †4081 (*yathā V°ḥ purā Baleḥ*), †4674 (*svayaṃ*); IX, 1071 (*yathā purā V°sya Daityāḥ*), 2821; XII, †8422; XIII, 6042 (*yathā purā Brahmapure . . . Çatakrator V°sya yajñe*); XV, 548 (*°opamaḥ*).

Vajradhārin (do.): VI, 4493 (*yathā*).

Vajradhṛk (do.): XII, 8096; XIII, 2276.

Vajrahasta (do.): III, †13297 (*Çacīpatiḥ*); V, †1814 (*yathā . . . Devarājasya*), †1876 (*I°*), †1877 (*Mahendrāt*); VI, 5027 (*samavartanta V°m ivāsurāḥ*); VII, 3436 (*api . . . V°ḥ Purandaraḥ*), 5091, 9038 (*nihato V°ena yathā Vṛtre*); VIII, 254 (*mohayitvā . . . V°a ivāsurān*), 562 (*vyadrāvayat . . . camūṃ V°a ivāsurīṃ*), 1641 (*Purandaraṃ*), 2358 (*nyahaṇat . . . senāṃ V°a ivasurīṃ*); XIII, 881 (Çiva in the shape of Indra).

Vajrapāṇi (do.): I, †2108 (*Çakraḥ sākshād V°r yathā*), 2823 (*°ṃ menire*), 5771 (*iva*), †7296, †7303; III, 10464 (*mishato V°naḥ*), 11942, †12329 (*sākshād api V°ḥ*), 13427 (*nihanyur . . . V°r ivāsurān*), 16605 (*nihato Vṛtraḥ . . . V°nā*), 16969; IV, 1167 (*jitvā . . . V°r ivāsurān*), 1551 (*iva*), 1981 (*saṅkālayishyāmi V°r ivāsurān*); VI, 701 (*vyūhaṃ . . . Vajrākhyaṃ vihitaṃ V°nā*), 2039, 3474 (*yathā Devāsure yuddhe V°r mahāsurān*), 3631 (*nyahanat . . . sainyaṃ V°r ivāsurān*), 3828 (*ayodhayata . . . V°r ivāsurān*), 4901 (*Devarāt*), 5412 (*yathā Çakro V°r*); VII, 103 (*°er ivāsurāḥ*); VIII, 1689 (*°r ivāparaḥ*), †1717 (*Mahendrāt*); IX, †1337 (*jaghāna Daityān iva V°ḥ*); X, 141 (*api svayaṃ*), 157 (do.); XIII, 763 (Çiva in the shape of Indra); XIV, 1613 (*Purandaraḥ*), 1720, 1724.

Vajrāyudha (do.): V, 5384 (*api svayaṃ*); VI, 2772 (*iva*).

Vajrin (do.): I, 1428 (*I°*), †7176 (*iva*), †7287, 7569 (*iva*), 8202, 8241; II, 296 (*īçānaṃ sarvalokasya*), †2164 (*yathā*), 2319; III, 8714 (*Balabhid*), 10453, 14250, 15176 (all. to Kuṇḍalāharaṇaparvan, v. Karṇa), 16608 (*°aḥ senāṃ*), 16986, 16987, 17421 (*Tridaçeçvaraḥ*); IV, 821 (*dravataḥ . . . V°ī Dānavān iva*), 1489 (*api*); V, 414, 2772 (*Balabhit svayaṃ*); VII, 2555 (*api*), 9592; VIII, 621 (*trailokyavijaye yadvad Daityānāṃ saha V°ṇā*, sc. *yuddhaṃ*), 653 (*°vajra-pramathitā yathaivādricayāḥ*), 657 (*nirbibheda . . . V°īva parvataṃ*), 716 (*trailyokyavijaye yādṛg Daityānāṃ saha V°ṇā*, sc. *yuddhaṃ*), 3053 (*°vajranihatānīva çikharāṇi*), 3284, 3375 (*saṅkhye Vṛtreṇa V°īva*); IX, 3488 (*sākshād api V°ī Purandaraḥ*); XII, 8122, 8223, 8238, 8339 (*Çambara-Pākahā*), 10157; XIII, 2276, 4904; XIV, †266, 1826.

Varada, q.v.

Vāsava: I, 1301 (*varshati*), 1482 (*vibudhāḥ . . . sa-V°āḥ*), 2710 (*niyogād V°sya ha*), 2788 (do.), 3565, †3570, (*°tulyarūpaḥ*), 3702 (*iva*), 3932 (*°vikrama*), 4784, 4787, 5022 (*°opamaṃ*), 7779 (*Marudbhir iva V°ḥ*, sc. *vṛtaḥ*), 8228, 8301, 8305; II, 280 (*Devarājaṃ*), 914 (*Vṛtra-V°yor iva*, sc. *saṃyuge*), 950, 1529 (*°pratimaḥ*), 1880 (*Citrarathaḥ . . . V°ānugaḥ*); III, 336, 568 (*Vṛtra-V°yor iva*, sc. *yuddhaṃ*), 681 (*Vṛtra-V°yoḥ . . . yathā*, sc. *yuddhaṃ*), 702 (*Bali-V°yor iva*, sc. *yuddhaṃ*), 1427 (*api devaiḥ sa-Vāsavaiḥ*), 1608 (*Vṛtra-V°yor iva*, sc. *yuddhaṃ*), 1777 (*dvitīya iva V°ḥ*), 1800, 1880, 8254 (*°opama*), 8545 (*°sammitaṃ*), 9991 (*varshayām āsa V°ṃ*, sc. Ṛshyaçṛṅga), 10141, 10313, 10557, 11487 (*iva*), 11523 (*Marudbhir iva V°ḥ*, sc. *stūyamānaḥ*), 11682 (all. to Khāṇḍavadahanaparvan), 11898, 12047, 13411 (*devāḥ sarve sa-V°āḥ*), 14249, 14252, 14255, 14355, 14375, 14460, 14782 (*Marudbhir iva V°aḥ*, sc. *vṛtaḥ*), 16444 (had been vanquished by Indrajit), 16997, 17197, 17198, 17199, †17215; IV, 356 (*Vṛtra-V°yor* *iva*, sc. *saṃyuge*), 1296 (°*pratimaḥ*), 1498 (*varshati*), 1553 (*yudhyāmahe . . . Dānavā iva V°ṃ*), 1674 (°*tulyavīryaḥ*), 1767 (*devāḥ . . . saha-V°āḥ*), 1868 (*Vṛtra-V°yor iva*, sc. *yuddhaṃ*), 1884 (*Bali-V°yor iva*, sc. *yuddhaṃ*), 1903 (*Vṛtra-V°yor iva*, sc. *sannipātaḥ*), 2046 (*Bali-V°yor iva*, sc. *yuddhaṃ*), 2073 (*devāḥ sa-V°āḥ*); V, 284 (*yuddhaṃ Vṛtra-V°yoḥ*), 308, 333, 412, 420, 530, 532, †659 (°*enāpi sākshāt*), 2012 (*iva*), 2171 (*api*), 2927 (*iva*), 3162 (do.), 3277 (*Marudbhir iva V°ḥ*), 3557 (*Daiteyā nivasanti sma V°ena hṛtaçriyaḥ*), 3644, 3646, 3651 (°*sya Çacīm iva*), 3662, 3675, 3680, 3682, 3688, 3826 (*devaiḥ sa-V°aiḥ*), 3967 (*reme . . . yathā Çacyāñ ca V°aḥ*), 4400 (*devair api sa-V°aiḥ*), 4940 (*Vasavo V°ṃ yathā*), 5115 *Vāsavir V°samaḥ*, i.e. Arjuna), 5289 (*iva*), 5332 (*Marudbhir iva V°ḥ*, sc. *abhiguptaḥ*), 5807 (*Airāvatagato rājā devānām iva V°ḥ*), 7072 (*bhayād V°syāpi*); VI, 417, 434 (*varshati*), 508 (°*opamaḥ*), 1226 (*devānām asmi V°ḥ*, says Kṛshṇa), 1913 (*ayudhyetām . . . yathā vā Vṛtra-V°au*), 2197 (*devair api sa-V°aiḥ*), 2503 (*do.*), 3367 (*nighnantaṃ . . . Dānavān iva V°ṃ*), 3538 (*devair api sa-V°aiḥ*), 3930 (*do.*), 4029 (*vyavatishṭhetāṃ yathā vai Vṛtra-V°au*), 4338 (*Vasavo V°ṃ yathā*, sc. *parivārya*), 4427 (*iva*), 4460 (*api*), 4541 (*savajra iva V°ḥ*), 4549 (*Mayaṃ jitveva V°ḥ*), 4580 (*yuddhaṃ Vṛtra-V°yor iva*), 5115 (*api*), 5220 (*devair api sa-V°aiḥ*), 5411 (*yathā Devāsure yuddhe Bali-V°yor abhūt*); VII, 158 (*iva*), 159 (*Marutām iva V°ḥ*), 189 (*devān sa-V°ān*), 215 (°*eneva Dānavāḥ*, sc. *vadhyamānāḥ*), 1222 (*iva*), 1236 (do.), 1337 (do.), 1739, 2276, 2298 (*dvitīya iva V°ḥ*), 2707 (*devāḥ sa-V°āḥ*), 2992 (*Mātalir V°m iva* (B. °*syeva*) *Vṛtraṃ hantuṃ prayāsyataḥ*), 3101 (*devāḥ sa-V°āḥ*), 3135 (*savajra iva V°ḥ*), 3389 (*varshati V°e*), 3650 (*devāḥ sa-V°āḥ*), 4131 (*Balaṃ hatveva V°ḥ*), 4351 (*iva*), 4649 (*Bali-V°yor iva*, sc. *samprahāraḥ*), 4728 (*hanishyāmi Dānavān iva V°ḥ*), 5463 (*devair api sa-V°aiḥ*), 6396 (*api*), 6560 (*devair api sa-V°aiḥ*), 6976 (*iva*), 7021 (*devair api sa-V°aiḥ*), 7022 (*çaktyā V°dattayā*, i.e. *Amoghā*), 7139 (only B., *devāḥ sa-V°āḥ*), 7197 (°*syeva saṃyuge*), 7485 (*yādṛçaṃ . . . Bali-V°yoḥ purā*, sc. *yuddhaṃ*), 7641 (*Bali-V°yor iva*, sc. *samāgamaḥ*), 7656 (*iva*), 7908 (°*āçaninirghoshaṃ . . . kārmukaṃ*), 7971 (*Marudbhir iva V°ṃ*; sc. *vṛtaṃ*), †8164 (*çaktyā . . . dattayā V°ena*), 8194, 8199 (°*ena . . . prāptā*, sc. *çaktiḥ*), 8283 (*iva*), 8295 (*devair api sa-V°aiḥ*), 8483 (*na . . . çaṃsire jetuṃ Dānavā V°ṃ yathā*), 8703 (*devair api sa-V°aiḥ*), 8899 (°*syeva nirjayaṃ*), 9051, 9558 (*devāḥ sa-V°āḥ*); VIII, 65 (*Vishṇu-V°yor iva*), 315 (*devair api sa-V°aiḥ*), 565 (*Vṛtra-V°yor iva*, sc. *samāgamaḥ*), 1316 (*devā api sa-V°āḥ*), †1737 (*Yama-Varuṇa-Kubera-V°ā vā*), 1998 (*savajrād vā'pi V°āt*), 2016 (*devatāḥ . . . sa-V°āḥ*), 2799 (*Dānavān iva V°aḥ*, sc. *pramamātha*), 3303 (*Açvināv iva V°m*, sc. *abhyupagatau*), 3314 (*devair api sa-V°aiḥ*), †3389 (°*vikramaḥ*), 3625 (*devair api sa-V°aiḥ*), 3642 (°*opamaḥ*), 3675 (*Vṛtraḥ prāpyeva V°ṃ*), 4019 (°*āçanitulyasya*), 4431 (*Sūryasya . . . vivādo V°sya ca*), †4498 (*surāsurāḥ Çambara-V°āv iva*, sc. *parivārya*), †4831 (*Kubera-Vaivasvata-V°ānāṃ tulyaprabhāvāḥ*), †4951 (*samānayānāv iva Vishṇu-V°au*), †4961 (*sadasyahūtāv iva Vishṇu-V°au*); IX, 358 (*jahi . . . V°o Namuciṃ yathā*), 594 (*savajram iva V°ṃ*), 815 (*api*), †1071 (*Airāvaṇasthasya camūvimarde* (C. *camūr vi*°) *Daityāḥ purā V°syeva*), 1425 (*yādṛçaṃ samare pūrvaṃ Jambha-V°yoḥ*), 2433, 2434, 2436 (slew Namuci), 2531 (*devāḥ sarve sa-V°āḥ*), 2538, 2677 (*sarve devāḥ sa-V°āḥ*), 2746 (*devāḥ sarve sa-V°āḥ*), 2748 (*devāḥ sarve . . . sa-V°āḥ*), 2847 (*sarve devāḥ sa-V°āḥ*), 3105 (*sadṛçakarmāṇau Yama-V°yoḥ*), 3198 (*Vṛtra-V°yor iva*, sc. *yuddhaṃ*), 3212 (do.); X, 147 (*api*), 653 (*açobhetāṃ . . . abhitaḥ sthitau . . . Açvināv iva V°ṃ*); XI, 564 (°*yoshitaḥ*, only C.); XII, 39 (*api*), 1128 (°*ānumate*), 1831 (°*opamaḥ*), 1923 (*Brahmāṇam iva V°ḥ*, sc. *abhyājagāma*), 3458 (*vṛttaṃ . . . V°sya*), 3617, 3621, 3796 (*Devapatiḥ*), 3805, 5415 (*pravavarsha sa V°ḥ*), 6186, 6441, 7553 (°*ṃ sarvadevānām adhyaksham akarot prabhuḥ*, i.e. Kṛshṇa), 8059 (°*sya ca saṃvādaṃ Baleḥ*), 8060, 8068, 8083, 8116, 8129, 8142, 8149, 8151, 8155, 8162, 8218 (*Bali-V°saṃvādaṃ*), 8258, 8282, 8286, †8332, 8418 (*Vṛtrahantā*), †8424 (*vavarsha*), 10124, 10130, 10136, 10200, 10201, 10209, 10809 (*abhishicya rājye tu devānāṃ V°ṃ | saptarshayaḥ*), 12175, 12614 (*vavarsha*); XIII, 97 (*pravarshati*), 173, 264 (°*sya ca saṃvādaṃ çukasya ca*), 273, 328 (*dvitīya iva V°ḥ*), 571, 577, [1177 (= Çiva, 1000 names [2])], 1517 (*devāḥ sa-V°āḥ*), 1805 (*devaiḥ sa-V°aiḥ*), 1919, 1938, 2089 (*iva*), 2112 (do.), 2330, 3164, 3195, 3559, 3895, 3899, 3901, 3919, 3920, 4201, 4539, 4808 (*abhishiktaḥ . . . devarājye*), 4845 (*Gautamasya munes tāta saṃvādaṃ V°sya ca*), 5214 (*yajñaṃ . . . V°priyaṃ*), 5936, 5969, 5981, 6093 (*açvamedhacaturbhāgaṃ phalaṃ sṛjati*), 6155 (*Çacīpatiṃ*), 6351 (*Viçvedevāḥ sa-V°āḥ*), 7284, 7285, 7319 (*sarve devāḥ sa-V°āḥ*); XIV, 98 (*Indratvaṃ prāpya*), 105 (°*tulyaḥ*), 106 (*api*), 161, 165, 169, †243, †258, †263, †264, †270 (*varshatu*), 1541 (*vavarsha*), 1619, 1768 (*kṛtvā nasukaraṃ karma Dānaveshv iva V°ḥ*), 1780 (*iva*), 2384 (*devaiḥ sa-V°aiḥ*), 2862 (*na varshishyati*), 2863 (do.), 2864 (do.); XV, 478 (°*opamaḥ*), 480 (do.); XVI, †129.

Vibudhaçreshṭha ("best of the gods"): XIII, 3159.

Vibudhādhipa ("the king of the gods"): III, 12018; IX, 2780; XII, 8146.

Vibudhādhipati (do.): I, 5532 (*nītiṃ V°eḥ*); III, 11948.

Vibudheçvara (do.): III, 11899; XII, 1200.

Viçvabhuj ("all-enjoying"): VI, 776 (*Tridaçeçvaraḥ*).

Vṛshākapi ("man-ape"): XII, 8331.

Vṛtraçatru ("the enemy of Vṛtra"): III, 1778; V, †2230 (*I*°).

Vṛtrahan ("the slayer of Vṛtra"): I, †2104 (°*aḥ kratuṃ yathā*), 4163 (*vikramaṃ V°ā jahyāt*), 8227; III, 596 (*api*), 1349 (*Marudbhir iva V°ā*, sc. *parivṛtaḥ*), 1512, 1781, 8271 (*yathā*), 11807 (*samprāptas tridive rājyaṃ V°ā Vasubhiḥ saha*), 15093 (*Maruto V°ā yathā*, sc. *pālaya*); V, 2399 (*Marudbhiḥ saha*); VI, 2753 (°*ā Dānaveshv iva*), 3193 (*avadhīt . . . senām Āsurīm iva V°ā*), 3903 (*vivyādha . . . Namuciṃ V°ā yathā*); VII, 4646 (*hitvā V°evāsurīṃ camūṃ*), 8942 (*api*); VIII, 4363 (*jahi . . . Namuciṃ V°ā yathā*); IX, 655 (*hatavikrānto Jambho V°nā yathā*); XII, 10157; XIII, 2264 (*Pākaçāsanaḥ*), 3157, †4552 (*Çatakratuṃ*), †4897 (do.).

Vṛtrahantṛ (do.): III, †12316 (*bhavanād V°uḥ*); XII, 8418 (*Vāsavaḥ*).

Vṛtranis(h)ūdana (do.): I, 2350; III, 1884 (*Çakraḥ*); V, 431 (*Çakraṃ*), 546 (*Çakraḥ*); VI, †2588 (*cakāra sāhāyyaṃ . . . Vishṇur yathā V°sya*).

Indra, pl. (°*āḥ*). § 11 (Parvasaṅgr.): I, **2**, 392 (*pañcendrāṇām upākhyānaṃ*, i.e. Pañcendropākhyāna). — § 238 (Pañcendrop.): I, **197**, (†7302) (*pūrvendrāḥ*), †7310 (five incarnate as the Pāṇḍavas), †7316 (*pūrvendrān*). — § 671*b* (Bali-Vāsavasaṃv.): XII, **223**, 8142 (*bahūnīndrasahasrāṇi samatītāni*), 8146 (°*sahasreshu*).—§ 673*b* (do.): XII, **227**, 8251 (*çataiḥ*), 8253 (*bahūnīndrasahasrāṇi daivatānāṃ yuge yuge*).— § 773*b* (Kṛshṇa Vāsudeva): XIII, **159**, †7370.

Indra [2] = Skanda: III, 14643.

Indra [3] = Sūrya: III, 148.

Indra [4] = Çiva (1000 names [1]).

Indrābha, son of the elder Dhṛtarāshṭra. § 154 (Pūruvaṃç.): I, **94**, 3748 (seventh son of Dhṛtarāshṭra).

Indradamana, a prince, a descendant of Atri. § 677 (Mokshadh.): XII, **235**, 8592 (*Ātreyaḥ*, attained to infinite worlds by giving wealth). Cf. Ātreya.

[Indradarçana(ṃ)] ("seeing Indra," cf. Arjunābhigamanap.). § 330: After some time *Yudhishṭhira* taught *Arjuna* in private the [Pratismṛti] science (*upanishad*, i.e. *rahasyavidyā*, Nīl.; *bráhman*) that would reveal the whole universe to him, and told him to practise severe austerities; *Bhīshma*, etc. (*a*), know the fourfold (*catushpāda*) *Dhanurveda*, the *Brāhma* weapon, etc.; all celestial weapons are in the possession of *Indra*, imparted to him by the celestials from fear of *Vṛtra*. Then *Arjuna* took up the *Gāṇḍīva*, etc., blessed by brahmans, *Siddhas*, and invisible spirits (*bhūtāni*), and by *Kṛshṇā* (she said: "Let no one amongst us be ever again born in the order of *kshatriyas*, but as brahmans; it is my great grief that in the assembly *Duryodhana* called me a 'cow' (i.e. 'to be enjoyed by many men,' Nīl.); but the grief of parting with thee is far greater"), who wished him success from *Dhātṛ*, *Vidhātṛ*, *Hrī*, *Çrī*, *Kīrti*, *Dhṛti*, *Pushṭi*, *Umā*, *Lakshmī*, *Sarasvatī*, the *Vasus*, *Rudras*, *Ādityas*, the hosts (*gaṇān*) of the *Maruts*, the *Viçvedevas*, and the *Sādhyas*, and wished him safety from the spirits (*bhūtebhyaḥ*) of the sky, earth, and heaven, and all other enemies; and having walked round (*pradakshiṇaṃ kṛtvā*) his brothers and *Dhaumya*, he set out towards the north. All creatures left the path of *Arjuna*, who was urged by the desire of beholding *Indra* (? *yuktasyaindreṇa yogena*). He passed over many mountains, and reached *Himavat* in one day by means of his *yoga*; then he passed over *Gandhamādana*, etc., and reached *Indrakīla*, walking night and day untiringly. Here he was addressed by a voice in the skies, and beheld *Indra* in the guise of a brahman, who told him to throw away his bow as of no use there, as this was the abode only of peaceful brahmans, and advised him to wish for heavenly bliss (*lokāḥ*); but *Arjuna* only asked for the celestial weapons, which *Indra* said he should obtain when he had seen *Çiva* (*Tryaksha*, *Çūladhara*, *Bhūteça*, *Parameshṭhin*). Then *Indra* disappeared, and *Arjuna* remained, devoted to *yoga* (III, **37**).

Indradyumna[1], a rājarshi. § 267 (Yamasabhāv.): II, **8**, 332 (in the palace of Yama).—§ 317*b* (Kṛshṇa Vāsudeva): III, **12**, 491 (the same?, had been slain by Kṛshṇa).—§ 168 (Indradyumnop.): III, **199**, ††13332 (*rājarshiḥ*), ††13336, ††13337, ††13338, ||13339, ††13342, ††13348 (having fallen from heaven, *I.* regained it).—§ 469 (Mārkaṇḍeyas.): III, **200**, 13349 (all. to § 468).—§ 474 (do.): III, **201**, 13482 (do.).

Indradyumna[2], a brahman. § 324 (Dvaitavanapr.): III, **26***a*, 985 (among the brahmans who worshipped Yudhishṭhira).

Indradyumna[3], a lake. § 468 (Indradyumnop.): III, **199**, ††13337 (°*ṃ nāma saraḥ*, there king Indradyumna had performed sacrifices, and the lake had been excavated by the cows, which were given away to the brahmans). Cf. next.

Indradyumnasaras, a lake. § 184 (Pāṇḍu): I, **119**, 4639 (in the north, visited by Pāṇḍu). Cf. the prec.

[Indradyumnopākhyāna(ṃ)] ("history of Indradyumna"). § 468 (Mārk.): The *Pāṇḍavas* asked *Mārkaṇḍeya* "Is there anybody that is older than thou?" He related: "The *rājarshi Indradyumna*, who had fallen from heaven, complained that his fame must have passed away, and asked me if I recognized him; as I did not, he became a horse and carried me to the *Himavat* to the owl *Prāvārakarṇa*, who was older than I; the owl we took to the lake *Indradyumna* to the crane *Nāḍījaṅgha*, who was older than the owl; the crane indicated us the tortoise *Akūpāra* in the same lake. *Akūpāra* knew *Indradyumna*, and said that *Indradyumna* had planted the *yūpa* 1,000 times, and that this lake had been excavated by the feet of the cows given away by him to the brahmans. Then a chariot came from heaven, and a celestial voice called *Indradyumna* back to heaven (vv. 13343–5, three *çlokas* are cited; v. 13343: 'The report of a virtuous deed reaches heaven and earth; as long as that report is heard, so long is the doer said to be in heaven'). He first brought me and the owl to our respective places, and then went away in that chariot." The *Pāṇḍavas* praised *Mārkaṇḍeya* for having caused *Indradyumna* to regain his sphere; he said that *Kṛshṇa* also had raised the *rājarshi Nṛga* from hell and caused him to regain heaven (III, **199**).

Indrajāla, a celestial weapon. § 512 (Ghoshayātrāp.): III, **245**, 14995 (*Sthūlā* (B. °*ṇā*-) *karṇendrajālañ ca*, employed by Arjuna).—§ 571 (Ulūkadūtāgamanap.): V, **160**, 5461 (?, "conjuror's tricks," PCR.), 5525 (?, do.); **161**, 5570 (?, do.).—§ 580 (Bhīshmavadhap.): VI, **59**[13], 2633 (*nihatendrajālāḥ*). — § 608 (Karṇap.): VIII, **60***aaa*, 2998 (*Sthūṇākarṇendrajālena*); **64**, 3238. — § 785 (Anugītāp.): XIV, **77**, 2251 (°*pratimaṃ bāṇajālaṃ*). Cf. Aindra.

[Indrajidvadha(ḥ)] ("the slaughter of Indrajit"). § 541: Indrajit tied Rāma and Lakshmaṇa in a network of those arrows of his which he had obtained as boons. Sugrīva and the monkeys Susheṇa, etc. (*a*), surrounded them. Vibhīshaṇa came and roused them with the Prajñāstra; Sugrīva extracted the arrows and applied the medicine *viçalyā*; from the mountain Çveta a Guhyaka of Kubera's brought water, by rubbing one's eyes with which all invisible creatures became visible. Rāma, Lakshmaṇa, Sugrīva, etc. (*β*), rubbed their eyes. Having informed Rāvaṇa, Indrajit returned without having completed his daily sacrifice; receiving a hint from Vibhīshaṇa, Lakshmaṇa killed Indrajit. Rāvaṇa would kill Sītā, but was dissuaded by Avindhya (III, **289**).

[Indrajidyuddha(ṃ)] ("the encounter with Indrajit"). § 540: Rāvaṇa sent Indrajit (who had vanquished Indra and received celestial weapons as boons) to fight Rāma, Lakshmaṇa, and Sugrīva. He first fought with Lakshmaṇa, then with Aṅgada, then he became invisible, but continued to fight (III, **288**).

Indrajit, a Rākshasa, son of Rāvaṇa. § 537 (Rāma-Rāvaṇayuddha): III, **285***β*, 16371 (fought with Lakshmaṇa), 16376.—§ 540 (Indrajidyuddha): III, **288**, 16439 (son of Rāvaṇa, had formerly vanquished Indra), 16452 (fought with Lakshmaṇa and Aṅgada), 16455, 16456. — § 541 (Indrajidvadha): III, **289**, 16466, 16479, 16483 (is slain by Lakshmaṇa). Cf. Rāvaṇātmaja, Rāvaṇi.

Indrakarman = Vishṇu (1000 names).

Indrakīla, a mountain. § 269 (Vaiçravaṇasabhāv.): II, **10**, 413 (among the mountains present in the palace of Kubera) — § 330 (Indradarçana): III, **37**, 1497 (on his way to Indra's world Arjuna passed Himavat and Gandhamādana and then came to *I.*).—§ 331 (Kairātap.): III, **39**, 1562 (°*samaprabhaḥ*).

Indraloka ("the world of Indra"). § 238 (Pañcendrop.): I, **197**, †7301 (*āgantāraḥ punar eve* °*ṃ*, sc. the five Indras).—§ 246 (Sundopasundop.): I, **210**, 7658 (conquered by Sunda and Upasunda).—§ 345 (Nalopākhyānap.): III, **54**, 2116 (on their wanderings Nārada and Parvata came to *I.*).—§ 512

(Ghoshayātrāp.): III, **239**, 14832 (*ushito hi mahābāhur I°e Dhanañjayaḥ*).—§ 585*b* (Irāvat): VI, **90**, 3981 (Arjuna dwelt for some time in *I.*).—§ 608 (Karṇap.): VIII, **79**, †4054 (in *I.* Arjuna slew the Daityas, etc., all. to Nivātakavacayuddhaparvan).—§ 641 (Rājadh.): XII, **77**, 2916 (*prāpnoti °tām*).—§ 677 (Mokshadh.): XII, **244**, 8871 (*atithis tv I°sya*, sc. *prabhuḥ*).—§ 746 (Ānuçāsanik.): XIII, **79**κ, 3768.—[§ 757*k* (Hastikūṭa): Gautama said: "Next [to Varuṇaloka] are Indra's regions (*lokāḥ*), free from passion and sorrow, difficult of access, and coveted by men." Dhṛtarāshṭra said: "He who lives for 100 years, who is a hero, who studies the Vedas and performs sacrifices with devotion, goes to Çakraloka": XII, **102**, †4880 (*Indrasya lokāḥ*), †4881 (*Çakralokam*).]—§ 759 (Ānuçāsanik.): XIII, **107**, 5219, 5238 (*Marutām lokam*). Cf. Çakraloka.

Indralokābhigamana ("Arjuna's journey to the world of Indra"). § 10 (Parvasaṅgr.): I, **2**, 321 (*parva*, i.e. Indralokābhigamanaparvan).

[Indralokābhigamanaparvan] ("the section relating to Arjuna's journey to the world of Indra," the 34th of the minor parvans of Mhbhr.). § 335: After the *Lokapālas* had gone away, *Arjuna* began to think of the chariot of *Indra*, which, guided by *Mātali*, came down full of swords, missiles, maces, thunderbolts, etc. (description), and great *Nāgas* with fiery mouths, and drawn by 10,000 horses of golden hue, and with the flagstaff *Vaijayanta* (described). *Mātali*, descending, invited him to ascend the chariot, as *Indra* waited to behold him, surrounded by gods, *ṛshis*, *Gandharvas*, and *Apsarases*. As that chariot cannot be obtained even by hundreds of *rājasūyas* and horse-sacrifices, and as even gods and *Dānavas* are not competent to ride in it, and as he that has no ascetic merit is not competent even to see or touch it, *Arjuna* first let *Mātali* ascend it and control the horses. Then he purified himself in the *Gaṅgā*, repeated his prayers (*japyam*), gratified the *Pitṛs*, and bade farewell to the *Mandara* mountain (*b*). Then he ascended, in the chariot, through the sky and beheld thousands of *vimānas* of extraordinary beauty; there was no sun or moon or fire, but they blazed in light of their own, generated by virtue and ascetic merit; and the stars, which from earth look small in consequence of their distance, but are very large, were seen by him in their places; and *rājarshis* who had attained *siddhi* (*siddhāḥ*), and heroes fallen in battle, and those that had obtained heaven by *tapas*; and *Gandharvas*, and *Guhyakas*, and *ṛshis*, and *Apsarases*. *Mātali* explained to him that the stars were virtuous persons (*sukṛtinaḥ*) stationed in their respective places (*dhishnyeshu*). At the gates he beheld *Airāvata* with four tusks equal to *Kailāsa*. Continuing along the path of the *Siddhas*, he passed through the regions (*lokān*) of [virtuous] kings, and thus passing through *Svargaloka* he beheld *Amarāvatī* (*b*), the city of *Indra* (III, **42**).—§ 336: When *Arjuna* had entered the city, praised by *Apsarases*, *Gandharvas*, *Siddhas*, great *ṛshis*, and gods, he, at the request of *Indra*, went to the large starry way (*nakshatramārga*) named *Suravīthī*, where he met with the *Sādhyas*, *Viçvas*, *Maruts*, *Açvins*, *Ādityas*, *Vasus*, *Rudras*, *Brahmarshis*, *Rājarshis* with *Dilīpa* at their head, *Tumburu*, *Nārada*, *Hāhā*, and *Hūhū*. Then he beheld *Indra*, eulogized by *Gandharvas* headed by *Viçvāvasu*, etc., and was seated on *Indra's* own seat; and *Gandharvas*, headed by *Tumburu*, sang to them, and thousands of *Apsarases* (enumeration of seventeen) (*a*) danced there (III, **43**).—§ 337: The gods and *Gandharvas* offered him *arghya*, etc., and caused him to enter the palace of *Indra*. There he received *Indra's* weapons, the thunderbolt (*vajra*) and lightning (*açanīḥ*). At the request of *Indra* he dwelt there for five years, and learned the dance and music of the *Gandharvas* from *Citrasena*, whom *Indra* gave him as a friend, but he was longing for his brothers and *Kuntī* and thirsting for revenge (III, **44**).—§ 338: In the beginning, seeing that the eyes of *Arjuna* were fixed upon *Urvaçī*, *Indra* despatched *Citrasena* to *Urvaçī*, who gladly consented to choose *Arjuna* (*b*) for her lover (III, **45**). *Urvaçī* related to *Arjuna* that as he had looked on her only in a solemn assembly of celestials held on account of his coming, where the *Rudras*, *Ādityas*, *Açvins*, *Vasus*, *Maharshis*, *Rājarshis*, *Siddhas*, *Cāraṇas*, *Yakshas*, and *Mahoragas* (i.e. great serpents) were present, and the *Gandharvas* played the *vīṇās*, and the *Apsarases* danced, *Indra* had caused *Citrasena* to send her to him, and that she was herself in love with him. *Arjuna* declared that he regarded her as the wife of his *guru*, and that he had been gazing at her because she was the mother of the *Paurava* race. She replied that the sons and grandsons of *Pūru's* race, that had come thither in consequence of ascetic merit, did all sport with the *Apsarases* without incurring any sin. But *Arjuna* swore that he regarded her as his mother. She then cursed him, saying that he should have to pass his time among females as a dancer and destitute of manhood, and then went away. *Indra* told him that this would come to pass in the thirteenth year of their exile, when they would live unknown to all, but having passed one year thus he would regain his manhood. The desire of the man that listens to this history of *Arjuna* never runs after lustful ends, etc. (III, **46**).—§ 339: One day the *brahmarshi Lomaça* in the course of his wanderings went to the abode of *Indra*. As *Lomaça* within himself wondered how *Arjuna*, being a *kshatriya*, had attained the seat of *Çakra*, who was worshipped by the gods themselves, *Çakra*, knowing his thoughts, explained to him who *Arjuna* (*b*) really was; that moreover the *Asuras*, the sons of *Danu*, named the *Nivātakavacas*, who dwell in *Pātāla*, proud of a boon they had acquired, were planning the destruction of the gods, and could not be slain by others than either *Kṛshṇa* (*c*) or *Arjuna*; but *Madhusūdana* (i.e. Kṛshṇa) should not be urged when the task was insignificant, lest his energy should consume the whole universe; therefore *Arjuna* should slay them. At the request of *Indra*, seconded by *Arjuna*, *Lomaça* went to the *Kāmyaka* wood to *Yudhishṭhira* in order to bring him news about *Arjuna* and recommend him to visit the *tīrthas*, and follow him and protect him from the *Rākshasas* (*d*) (III, **47**).—§ 340: As *Dhṛtarāshṭra* learnt from *Dvaipāyana* of *Arjuna's* arrival and stay at *Indra's* abode, he expressed his anxiety to *Sañjaya* (III, **48**). Conversation of *Sañjaya* and *Dhṛtarāshṭra* about *Arjuna's* encounter with *Çiva* in the guise of a *Kirāta*, etc. (III, **49**).—§ 341: During the five years of *Arjuna's* absence the *Pāṇḍavas* fed themselves and 10,000 *snātaka* brahmans, some with and some without fire, by killing deer, *Yudhishṭhira* going towards the east, *Bhīma* towards the south, and the twins towards the west and north (III, **50**).—§ 342: Having heard of the way of life of the *Pāṇḍavas*, *Dhṛtarāshṭra* expressed his anxiety before *Sañjaya*, fearing *Bhīma* with his iron (*çaikya*) mace, etc. *Sañjaya* commemorated how *Kṛshṇa*, *Dhṛshṭadyumna*, *Virāṭa*, *Dhṛshṭaketu*, and the *Kaikeyas* had visited the *Pāṇḍavas* in the *Kāmyaka* wood, whose conversations *Sañjaya* had learnt through spies and formerly told *Dhṛtarāshṭra*. *Sañjaya* further related that *Kṛshṇa* had consented to become the charioteer of *Arjuna* (enumeration of kings seen by *Kṛshṇa* at the *rājasūya*) and to assist the *Pāṇḍavas* in the battle, together with *Rāma*, *Akrūra*, *Gada*, *Çāmba*, *Pradyumna*, *Āhuka*, *Dhṛshṭadyumna*, and the son of *Çiçupāla*, and *Yuyudhāna*, and the *Kaikeya* and *Pāñcāla* princes and the *Matsya* king, and *Kṛshṇa* had declared that *Yudhishṭhira* should, along with his brothers living at *Hāstinapura*, rule the earth (III, **51**).

Indramālā ("the garland of Indra"). § 73 (Vasu Uparicara): I, **63**, 2349 (given by Indra to Vasu as his emblem).

Indramārga, a tīrtha. § 368 (Tīrthayātrāp.): III, **83**, 7052 (only C., B. has *Rudramārga*).—§ 733*c* (Pushkara): XIII, **25**, 1696.—§ 733*g* (Saptagaṅga): XIII, **25**, 1703.

[Indra-Mataṅga-saṃvāda(ḥ)] ("the conversation between Indra and Mataṅga"). § 735*b* (Ānuçāsanik.): *Bhīshma* said: Once a brahman obtained a son named *Mataṅga*, who, though procreated by a person of a different order, had, however, the rites of infancy and youth performed according to the ordinances laid down for brahmans. His father, desiring to perform a sacrifice, ordered him to collect the articles, and he set out riding in a car drawn by a young ass, that bore away the car to its mother; *Mataṅga* repeatedly struck the animal with his goad on its nose; but the old she-ass consoled it, saying, "A *Cāṇḍāla* it is that is driving thee; there is no severity in a brahman." Asked by *Mataṅga*, the she-ass revealed to him that his father was a *Çūdra* following the profession of a barber, who begat him upon a brahman woman excited with desire; "thou art, therefore, a *Cāṇḍāla* by birth." *Mataṅga* returned home, told his father what he had heard, retired to the forest, and began to undergo the austerest penances in order to acquire the status of a brahman, so that he scorched the very deities. *Indra* came and offered him boons, but the status of a brahman, he said, could not be won by penances (XIII, **27**). *Mataṅga* then stood for 100 years on one foot. *Indra* came once more and said: "From the order of brute life one attains to the state of humanity; if born as a human being, one is sure to take birth as a *Pukkaça* or a *Cāṇḍāla*; after 1,000 years one attains to the status of a *Çūdra*; then after 30,000 years that of a *Vaiçya*; after a period that is sixty times longer, that of a *kshatriya*; after a period that is sixty times longer than this, to that of a fallen *brahman*; after a period 200 times as long, to that of a brahman living by the profession of arms; after a period 300 times as long, to that of a brahman reciting the *Gāyatrī* and sacred *mantras*; after a period 400 times as long, to that of a brahman conversant with the entire *Vedas* and the scriptures" (XIII, **28**). *Mataṅga* then practised austerer penances, standing on one foot for 1,000 years in *yoga*-meditation. *Indra* once more came and said the same. *Mataṅga* then repaired to *Gayā*, and there passed 300 years on one foot in *yoga*, and was reduced to only skin and bones, and dropped down on the ground from sheer exhaustion. *Indra* came quickly; now *Mataṅga* accepted the boons that he should be celebrated as *chandodeva*, and obtain the worship of all women, and his fame should become unrivalled in the three worlds (XII, **29**).

Indrāṇī = Çacī, q.v.

Indrānuja = Kṛshṇa (Vishṇu), q.v.

Indraparvata, a mountain. § 280 (Bhīmasena): II, **30**, 1089 (near *I.* Bhīmasena vanquished seven Kirāta kings).

Indraprabhava ("son of Indra") = Arjuna: III, 14745.

Indraprastha, the capital of the Pāṇḍavas. § 4 (Anukram.): I, **1**, †149.—§ 244 (Rājyalābhap.): I, **207**, 7580 (*Tripishṭapasaṅkāçam*, description).—§ 245 (do.): I, **208**, 7596.—§ 252 (Subhadrāharaṇap.): I, **219**, 7930.—§ 253 (Haraṇāharaṇap.): I, **221**, 7987.—§ 254 (Khāṇḍavadahanap.): I, **222**, 8050.—§ 272 (Rājasūyārambhap.): II, **13**, 554, 555.—§ 277 (Jarāsandhavadhap.): II, **24**, 968.—§ 285 (Nakula): II, **32**, 1201.—§ 301 (Dyūtap.): II, **73**, 2451 (*purottamam*).—§ 342 (Indralokābhigamanap.): III, **51**, 1987.—§ 510 (Draupadī-Satyabhāmasaṃv.): III, **233**, 14698 (°*nivāsinaḥ*).—§ 512 (Ghoshayātrāp.): III, **237**, 14776.—§ 551 (Kīcakavadhap.): IV, **18**, 538, 548.—§ 552 (Goharaṇap.): IV, **50**, 1565.—§ 556 (Sañjayayānap.): V, **26**, †766.—§ 561 (Yānasandhip.): V, **55**, 2146.—§ 562 (Bhagavadyānap.): V, **95**, 3440.—§ 588 (Bhīshmavadhap.): VI, **121**, †5813.—§ 641 (Rājadh.): XII, **124**, 4553.—§ 781 (Açvamedhikap.): XIV, **15**, 376.—§ 793 (Mausalap.): XVI, **7**, 181, 248 (Vajra [the son of Aniruddha] was installed as king of the Yādavas in *I.*).

Cf. also the following synonyms:—

Çakraprastha: I, 8023; II, 1057; XVI, 186, 187 (there the rest of the Yādavas settled, ruled by Vajra); XVII, 9.

Çakrapurī: V, †915.

Çatakratuprastha: III, †913.

Khāṇḍavaprastha: I, 394, 2262, 2263, 2264 (*nagaram*), 7568, 7569, 7571, 7593 (°*vāsinaḥ*), 7600, 7748, 7976, 7993, 7995; II, 21, 993 (°*madhyasthaḥ*, sc. Yudhishṭhira), 1184, 1783, 2448; III, †15606; IV, 1189 (? = the Khāṇḍava forest?); V, 4175 (do.).

Indrasena[1], a son of the elder Parikshit. § 154 (Pūruvaṃç.): I, **94**, 3744 (fifth son of Parikshit).

Indrasena[2], the charioteer of Yudhishṭhira. § 272 (Rājasūyārambhap.): II, **13**, 554 (sent by Yudhishṭhira to fetch Kṛshṇa).—§ 286 (Rājasūyikap.): II, **33**, 1234.—§ 378 (Tīrthayātrāp.): III, **93**, 8485 (°*ādibhir bhṛtyaiḥ*).—§ 419 (Gandhamādanapr.): III, **140**, 10867 (°*mukhāṃç cāpi bhṛtyān*, left by the Pāṇḍavas in the capital of king Subāhu).—§ 449 (Ājagarap.): III, **177**, †12352 (B. *sahendrasenaiḥ paricārakaiḥ*, C. has by error *ma*°, the Pāṇḍavas came back to the capital of Subāhu).—§ 512 (Ghoshayātrāp.): III, **243**, 14943 (°*ādibhiḥ sūtaiḥ*).—§ 518 (Mṛgasvapnodbhavap.): III, **258**, 15367 (°*ādibhiç caiva preshyaiḥ*).—§ 522 (Draupadīharaṇap.): III, **269**, †15676, †15682 (*sārathim*); **271**, 15730.—§ 549 (Pāṇḍavapraveçap.): IV, **4**, 85 (°*mukhāḥ*, shall take the chariots of the Pāṇḍavas to Dvārakā), 140 (°*ādayaḥ*).—§ 553 (Vaivāhikap.): IV, **72**, 2358 (°*ādayaḥ*, came to Upaplavya).—§ 620 (Çrāddhap.): XI, **26*a***, 780 (°*mukhāṃç caiva bhṛtyān*), 782 (°*ādayaḥ*).

Indrasena[3], the son of Nala and Damayantī. § 345 (Nalopākhyānap.): III, **57**, 2237.—§ 346 (do.): III, **60**, 2294.—§ 352 (do.): III, **72**, 2841 (°*sya jananī*, i.e. Damayantī).

Indrasena[4], a Kuru warrior. § 600 (Ghaṭotkacavadhap.): VII, **156**κ, 6851.

Indrasenā[1], the daughter of Nala and Damayantī. § 345 (Nalopākhyānap.): III, **57**, 2237.—§ 346 (do.): III, **60**, 2294.—§ 353 (do.): III, **75**, 2945 (*saha bhrātrā*).

Indrasenā[2], the daughter of Nārāyaṇa and the wife of Mudgala. § 391 (Ṛshyaçṛṅga): III, **113**, †10093 (*Nārāyaṇī ve°ā babhūva vaçyā nityaṃ Mudgalasya*).—§ 551*c* (Kīcakavadhap.): *I.*, the daughter of Nārāyaṇa, who was renowned for her beauty, followed her husband, who was 1,000 years old: IV, **21**, 651 (*Nārāyaṇī*).

Indrasuta ("the son of Indra") = Arjuna: V, 3707 (*Dhanañjayaḥ*).

Indratāpana, an Asura. § 268 (Varuṇasabhāv.): II, **9**, 367 (among the Daityas and Dānavas in the palace of Varuṇa).

Indratīrtha, a tīrtha. § 615*y* (Badarapācana): IX, **48**, 2779 (near Badarapācana). —§ 615 (Baladevatīrthayātrā): IX, **49**, 2831 (visited by Balarāma).—§ 615*bb* (do.): There *Indra* had performed 100 horse-sacrifices, and given away enormous wealth to Bṛhaspati, etc. On account of this *Indra* came to be called *Çatakratu*, and the tīrtha to be called *Indratīrtha*: IX, **49**, 2834.

Indrātmaja ("the son of Indra") = Arjuna: VI, †2672.

Indratoyā, a tīrtha. § 733*e* (Ānuçāsanik.): By bathing in *I.*, near Gandhamādana, and in Karatoyā in Kuraṅga, after three days' fasting, one acquires the merit of a horse-sacrifice: XIII, **25**, 1698 (*Gandhamādanasannidhau*).

Indrāvaraja = Kṛshṇa (Vishṇu), q.v.

Indravarman, a Mālava king. § 602 (Droṇavadhap.): VII, **190**, 8708 (*Mālavasya*, his elephant named Açvatthāman is slain by Bhīmasena), 8744 (do.).—§ 603 (Nārāyaṇāstramokshap.): VII, **193**, 8949 (do.).

[Indravijaya(ḥ)] ("the victory of Indra"). § 555: Questioned by Yudhishṭhira about the misery endured by Indra and Çacī, Çalya related: Once the Prajāpati Tvashṭṛ, from antipathy to Indra, created a son who had three heads (one for reading the Vedas; the second for drinking wine; with the third he looked as if he were about to absorb the four quarters), called Viçvarūpa. Beholding his austerities, Indra became alarmed, and in vain caused Apsarases to tempt him; then he slew him with his thunderbolt (thinking, "I shall afterwards perform some religious ceremony"), but was yet afraid of his appearance, and prevailed upon a carpenter to cut off the heads (promising, "in sacrifices men will give thee the head of the sacrificial animal as thy share"); out flew birds—(1) partridges, (2) sparrows and hawks, (3) quails. Then Tvashṭṛ created Vṛtra, who swallowed up Indra. The gods created Jṛmbhikā ("yawning"); Vṛtra yawned (therefore yawn attaches itself to the living breath of animated beings), and Indra emerged. Tvashṭṛ strengthened Vṛtra; Indra returned; the gods consulted with the munis, and sitting on Mount Mandara, they thought of Vishṇu (V, **9**). Indra, with D. and Ṛ., repaired to Vishṇu (*b*), who taught them, with Ṛ. and G., to make eternal friendship between Indra and Vṛtra ("I may not be killed either by what is dry or wet, stone, wood, weapons, by day or night, by Indra or D.," said Vṛtra). Indra then slew him in the evening with froth blended with the thunderbolt, in which Vishṇu had entered. D., G., Y., Rā., M.-U., and Ṛ. glorified Indra. But Indra was overpowered by falsehood (*anṛta*) and brahmanicide (*brahmahatyā*), and became bereft of his consciousness, and lay concealed in water; the earth became treeless, the rivers were interrupted, the rains ceased (V, **10**). Then Ṛ. and D. (also P. and G., ch. **16**) crowned Nahusha as king of D., giving him their tapas: "whatever being may stand within thy sight—D., Dā., Y., Rā., P., G., Bh.—thou shalt absorb his power." Nahusha then assumed a sensual turn of mind, amusing himself with Aps. and devakanyāḥ and Viçvāvasu, Nārada, G., and the six seasons, in Nandana, and on Kailāsa, Himavat, Mandara, Çveta, Sahya, Mahendra, Malaya, etc. He ordained that Çacī should wait upon him. Çacī (*c*) repaired to Bṛhaspati, who promised soon to unite her with Indra (V, **11**). Nahusha became enraged; the earth, with As., G., K., M.-U., trembled; Nahusha reminded of Indra's behaviour towards Ahalyā (*d*), etc.; at last the gods promised to bring him Çacī; but Bṛhaspati, as a brahman, would not abandon her, quoting a saying of Brahmán (*e*); he told her to ask for time from Nahusha, and so did the gods, led by Agni (V, **12**). Çacī obtained the boon from Nahusha, and returned to Bṛhaspati. D., with Agni, repaired to Vishṇu, who said: "Let Indra offer sacrifice to me; having performed the horse-sacrifice, he will regain his dignity." D. and Ṛ. and Bṛhaspati proceeded to the spot where Indra was, performed a horse-sacrifice, and divided the *brahmahatyā* among trees and rivers and mountains and earth and women; and Indra was free from fever, but vanished again from fear of Nahusha. Çacī worshipped Niçā (Night), who caused Upaçruti to appear, and Çacī prayed to Upaçruti (V, **13**). Upaçruti, followed by Çacī, crossed the heavenly groves and many mountains and came to the northern side of Himavat, and thence to the sea; in an island there was a large lake with an assemblage of lotuses; there they found Indra in the fibres of a lotus-stalk, and, praising him, Çacī implored his help against Nahusha (V, **14**). Indra said that Nahusha had been strengthened by the Ṛ. with the merits of offerings to D. and P. Çacī should tell Nahusha to visit her on a vehicle borne by Ṛ. Nahusha consented. Çacī prevailed upon Bṛhaspati to find out Indra, which he did by means of a sacrifice, prevailing upon Agni to search for him. Agni came back within the twinkling of an eye, having searched everywhere except in the waters, which he dared not enter ("fire rose from water, the kshatriya caste from the brāhmaṇa caste, and iron from stone; the power of these, which can penetrate all other things, has no operation upon the sources from which they sprang") (V, **15**). Bṛhaspati praised Agni (*f*) and strengthened him with hymns of the Veda; Agni then found out Indra (cf. ch. **14**), and soon returned and informed Bṛhaspati. This came with D.-ṛ. and G., and praised Indra by referring to his former deeds (that he had killed the great Asura Namuci and the Asura Çambara and Vala and Vṛtra, as *supra*). Indra increased little by little, and having assumed his original form he grew strong, and asked what business yet remained, as he had killed Viçvarūpa and Vṛtra. Bṛhaspati told him of Nahusha, who had been strengthened by the power of the D.-ṛ., etc. (v. ch. **11**), and how Nahusha, carried by M.-ṛ., journeyed from world to world. Lp. Kubera and Yama Vaivasvata and Soma and Varuṇa came and rejoiced that Viçvarūpa and Vṛtra had been killed, and they and Agni promised him their assistance against Nahusha on the condition that they and Agni should have their shares in sacrifices, and that Kubera (*g*), Yama (*h*), and Varuṇa (*i*) should this day be crowned along with Indra (V, **16**). While Indra, with Lp. and D., was considering the means of slaying Nahusha, the M.-ṛ. Agastya came and rejoiced that Viçvarūpa and Vṛtra had been killed, and related how Nahusha had been hurled from heaven (Svarga). The D.-ṛ. and B.-ṛ., weary with carrying him, had questioned him if certain mantras (*prokshaṇe gavām*) pronounced by Brahmán (so B.) were authentic (*pramāṇam*), to which Nahusha, bewildered by the dark principle (*tamas*), had answered in the negative; Ṛ. reproached him, as M.-ṛ. had formerly declared them to be authentic. Nahusha touched Agastya's head with his foot, and instantly lost his power and luck (*çrī*), and was agitated with fear. Then Agastya cursed him: "Fall thou from heaven, the effect of all thy good deeds (*puṇya*) has been exhausted; for 10,000 years thou shalt be a snake upon earth; then thou mayst come back to Svarga." D., M.-ṛ., P., Y., Sp. (*bhujagāḥ*), Rā., G., devakanyāḥ, and the bands of Aps., and tanks, rivers, mountains, and the sea came and rejoiced (V, **17**). Indra, glorified by G. and Aps., mounted Airāvata. Agni, the M.-ṛ., Bṛhaspati, Yama, Varuṇa, and Kubera accompanied him. Indra went to the three worlds with D., G., and Aps., and was praised by Aṅgiras (i.e. Bṛhaspati?) with hymns of the Atharvaveda. Then he granted Atharvāṅgiras (= Aṅgiras) the boon that his name would be connected with this Veda and that he would get a share in sacrifices. United with Çacī he protected the world virtuously (V, **18**).

Indriya(ṃ) sarvadehināṃ = Çiva (1000 names[2]).

Indrota, a brahman, descendant of Çunaka. § 652 (Āpaddh.): XII, **150**, 5595 (*Çaunako vipraḥ*). — § 652*b* (Indrota-Pārīkshitīya): XII, **150**, 5601 (*Çaunakaṃ*); **152**, 5672 (instructed king Janamejaya Pārikshit and assisted him in his horse-sacrifice).

[Indrota-Pārīkshitīya(ṃ)] ("the narrative of Indrota and Janamejaya Pārikshit"). § 652*b* (Āpaddh.): *Bhīshma* said: There was, in days of yore, a king *Pārikshit* (! so B.; C. °*rī*°) *Janamejaya*; from want of judgment he became guilty of killing a brahman; then all the brahmans, with his priests, abandoned him; burning day and night with regret, the king retired into the woods; deserted by his subjects also, and consumed by repentance, he underwent the most rigid austerities. In order to purify himself of the sin of brahmanicide he interrogated many brahmans, and wandered from country to country over the whole earth. One day he met *Indrota Çaunaka*, who rebuked him for his brahmanicide and reminded him of the messengers of *Yama* in the abode of *Yama* (XII, **150**). *Janamejaya* meekly listened to the reproof, saying that he was much afraid of *Yama*; he knew that, according to the Vedas, wretches like himself had forfeited all claim to the respect of the world, and had after death to dwell in hell like *Pulindas* and *Çabaras* (so C. and B.; PCR. *Khasas*), and he sought instruction from *Indrota*, who told him to repent and, knowing the Vedas, etc., act in such a way that the brahmans might not be angry with him; *Çaunaka* said that his kinsmen and friends would call him sinful because he instructed *Janamejaya*. *Janamejaya* swore never again to injure the brahmans (XII, **151**). *Indrota* discoursed to the repentant king on the means of cleansing himself, quoting a verse sung by *Yayāti* about the sacredness of *Kurukshetra*, etc. (*α*), and recommending him to go to *Mahāsaras*, etc. (*β*), quoting also a saying of *Manu* and a verse of *Satyavat*. *Mahāsaras*, etc. (*γ*), are so sacred that one guilty of fœticide becomes cleansed at even 100 yojanas from them. *Manu* has said that by diving in water after thrice reciting the *Aghamarshaṇa* [*mantras*] (v. the note of PCR., p. 498), one reaps the fruits of the final bath in a horse-sacrifice. The gods and *Asuras* in days of yore were instructed by M.-ṛ. *Bṛhaspati*, the preceptor of the gods, how one should cleanse himself from sin. *Indrota* then assisted *Janamejaya*, cleansed of his sins, in the horse-sacrifice (XII, **152**).

Indu = Soma (the moon), q.v.

Irā, an Apsaras. § 269 (Vaiçravaṇasabhāv.): II, **10**, 393 (among the Apsarases in the palace of Kubera).

Irā, a goddess. § 270 (Brahmasabhāv.): II, **11**, 456 (in the palace of Brahman). Cf. Ilā.

Irāmā, a river. § 459 (Mārkaṇḍeyas.): III, **188*a***, 12909 (seen by Mārkaṇḍeya in the stomach of Nārāyaṇa).

Irāvat, a son of Arjuna Pāṇḍava. § 578 (Bhīshmavadhap.): VI, **45**[21], 1737 (fought with Çrutāyus).—§ 580 (do.): VI, **56**θ, 2418 (in the array of the Pāṇḍavas).—§ 583 (do.): VI, **75**β, 3288 (do.).—§ 584 (do.): VI, **81**[1], 3557 (attacked by Vinda and Anuvinda (*Āvantyau*)); **83**[3], 3650 (fought with Vinda and Anuvinda), 3651, 3654, 3657, 3659, [3661 (*Nāgarājasutāsutaḥ*, vanquished Vinda and Anuvinda)].—§ 585*b* (do.): *I.* was begotten by *Arjuna* on the daughter (so C. (*sutāyāṃ*) and PCR., B. has *snushāyāṃ*) of the king of the *Nāgas*; when her husband had been slain by *Garuḍa*, childless as she was, she was bestowed upon *Arjuna* by *Airāvata*. *I.* grew up in the Nāgaloka, protected by his mother, and when his wicked uncle (*pitṛvyeṇa*) had abandoned him from hatred of *Arjuna*, *I.* went to Indraloka, having heard that *Arjuna* had gone thither. There he gladdened *Arjuna*, who, dismissing him, told him to render him assistance in the battle: VI, **90**, 3977 (*Arjunasyātmajaḥ*), 3983.—§ 585 (do.): VI, **90**, 4000 (fought with the brothers of Çakuni), 4002, 4004, 4006, 4008, 4011, 4012 (slew the brothers of Çakuni, except Vṛshabha), 4024 (attacked by Alambusha), 4025, 4030, 4032, 4036, 4040, 4042, 4046 (is slain by Alambusha), 4047; **91**, 4064 (*nihataṃ*), 4065 (do.); **96**, 4323 (do.). Cf. Arjunasuta, Arjunātmaja, Ārjuni.

Irāvatī, a river, the present Rāvi. § 268 (Varuṇasabhāv.): II, **9**, 372 (among the rivers present in the palace of Varuṇa). — § 317 (Kṛshṇa Vāsudeva): III, **12**, 492 (at *I.* Kṛshṇa slew Bhoja). — § 571 (Jambūkh.): VI, **9**λ, 324.—§ 607 (Karṇap.): VIII, **44**θ, 2040.—§ 768*b* (Umā-Maheçvara-saṃv.): XIII, **146**δ, 6764 (among the rivers with whom Umā held a consultation). Cf. Airāvatī (VIII, 2055).

Īrin, pl. (°*ṇaḥ*), a family. § 267 (Yamasabhāv.): II, **8**, 334 (100 *I.* in the palace of Yama).

Ishṭa = Vishṇu (1000 names).

***Ishṭākṛta**, a sacrifice: III, 10513 (*sattraṃ*).

***Ishṭīkṛta**, a sacrifice: III, 15408 (*sattraṃ*).

Ishupa, v. Ishupad.

Ishupad, an Asura. § 92 (Aṃçāvat.): I, **65**, 2533 (among the sons of Danu, only B., C. has *Ekapād*).—§ 130 (do.): I, **67**, 2656 (incarnate as king Nagnajit, C. has *Ishupaḥ*).

Ishvastrottamabhartṛ = Çiva: X, 260.

***itihāsa**[1] ("tradition, legend, history"): I, 19 (*Bhāratasya*, i.e. Mhbhr.), 50 (pl.), 63 (°-*purāṇānāṃ*), 259 (pl.), 260 (°-*purāṇābhyāṃ*), 306, 2210 (pl.), 2229 (i.e. Mhbhr.), 2301 (do.), ††3810, 4356 (°-*purāṇeshu*), 7619 (°*aṃ purātanaṃ*); II, 136 (°-*purāna-jñaḥ*, sc. Nārada); III, 1029 (°*aṃ purātanaṃ*), 14105 (do.); IV, 1593 (do.); V, 228, etc. (do.); VII, 2023 (do.); VIII, 1498 (°-*yajurvedau*); XII, 1841 (°-*puraṇa*°), 2202 (pl.), 7660 (*vedān setihāsān*), 11206 (pl.), 12211 (sg.), 13020 (°-*kathanāt*), ††13205; XIII, 264, 296, etc.; XIV, 120, etc. Cf. Jaya[14].

Itihāsa[2] = Çiva (1000 names[2]).

J

Jābāli, a ṛshi, son of Viçvāmitra. § 376 (Tīrthayātrāp.): III, **85**, 8265 (among the ṛshis who expected Yudhishṭhira on his tīrthayātrā; C. has *Jāv*°).—§ 721*b* (Viçvāmitrop.): XIII, **4**β, 254 (enumeration of the sons of Viçvāmitra).

Jagadādija = Vishṇu (1000 names).

Jagadanvaya = Mahāpurusha (Mahāpurushastava).

Jagadīçvara = Indra: I, 811.

Jagannātha[1] = Brahmán: VII, 2062; XII, 9176; XIII, 7635 (*Pitāmahaḥ*).

Jagannātha[2] = Kṛshṇa (Vishṇu): XII, 13133, 13309, 13436 (read °*nāthāt* with B.); XIII, 6947.
Jagannātha[3] = Çiva: VII, 9509; XII, 10435 (1000 names[1]).
Jagat = Çiva (1000 names[2]).
Jagataḥ kosha(ḥ) = Kṛshṇa: XII, 1621.
Jagataḥ prabhavāvyaya(ḥ) = Kṛshṇa (Vishṇu): XII, 4076 (*devaṃ Nārāyaṇaṃ*).
Jagataḥ prabhu(ḥ) = Kṛshṇa: XVI, 25, 158, 163.
Jagataḥ setu(ḥ) = Vishṇu (1000 names).
Jagatī ("the earth," personif.). § 592c (Vaishṇavāstra): VII, **29,** 1285 (mother of Naraka). Cf. Bhūmi.
Jagatkāla = Çiva (1000 names[2]).
Jagatpati[1] = Brahmán: I, 8144; IX, 2492 (*Pitāmahaṃ*); XII, 1434, 7631, 13573 (*B°*); XIII, 4021, 4929.
Jagatpati[2] = Çiva: VII, 9589; IX, 2414 (*Mahādevaṃ*); XII, 10120 (*Ç°*), 10127; XIII, 588, 682, 930, 1268.
Jagatpati[3] = Kāma: XIII, 4031, 4032.
Jagatpati[4] = Kṛshṇa (Vishṇu): XII, 1602 (*Jishṇuṃ Vishṇuṃ*), 13406; XIII, 6858; XIV, 2560.
Jagatpati[5] = Mahāpurusha (Mahāpurushastava).
Jagatpati[6] = Nahusha: V, 449, 454.
Jagatprabhu[1] = Brahmán: III, 15908; XII, 9166.
Jagatprabhu[2] = Vishṇu: XIII, 6939.
Jagatprakṛti = Mahāpurusha (Mahāpurushastava).
Jaguḍa, pl. (°*āḥ*), a people. § 342 (Indralokābhigamanap.): III, **51,** 1991 (had been present at the rājasūya of Yudhishṭhira).
Jāhnavī ("the daughter of Jahnu") = Gaṅgā: I, 3922, 3923; III, 41 (°*tīre*), 240 (°*kūlāt*), 8211, 8216, 17153, 17156; V, 3969 (*reme . . . J°yāṃ yathodadhiḥ*), 7094; VI, 1235; VII, 3495 (°*Yamune*); XIII, 1812 (°*pulina-*), 1813 (°*tīra-*), †1851, 3942 (mother of Bhīshma), 4075, 4915 (°*tīra-*), 5272 (°*vālukākīrṇe*), 7680 (*Jahnur J°isevitaḥ*), 7795; XV, 907 (°*jalaṃ*), 908 (do.), 1082 (°*kakshe*).
Jāhnavīdhṛk = Çiva (1000 names[2]).
Jāhnavīputra, Jāhnavīsuta = Bhīshma, q.v.
Jāhnavīya, adj. ("belonging to Jāhnavī, i.e. Gaṅgā"). § 734 (Ānuçāsanik.): XIII, **26,** †1857 (*guṇān*).
Jahnu[1], an ancient king. § 152 (Pūruvaṃç.): I, **94,** 3722 (son of Ajamīḍha and Keçinī), 3723 (his offspring were the Kuçikas).—§ 638b (Rāmop.): XII, **49,** 1717 (father of Aja, whose son was Balākāçva, whose son was Kuçika).—§ 721b (Viçvāmitrop.): XIII, **4,** 202 (son of Ajamīḍha and father of Sindhudvīpa, whose son was Balākāçva, whose son was Vallabha, whose son was Kuçika; Gaṅgā became the daughter of *J.*).—§ 775 (Ānuçāsanik.): XIII, **166**η, 7680 (*Jāhnavisevitaḥ*).
Jahnu[2] = Vishṇu (1000 names).
Jahnukanyā ("the daughter of Jahnu") = Gaṅgā: XIII, †645.
Jahnusutā (do.) = Gaṅgā: I, 3912.
Jaigīshavya, a muni. § 270 (Brahmasabhāv.): II, **11,** 441 (in the palace of Brahmán).—§ 615*ff* (Asita Devala): IX, **50,** 2859 (*muniḥ*), 2860 (*mahāmuniṃ*), 2862 (*munivaraṃ*), 2869, 2873, 2876, 2878, 2879, 2880, 2882 (*mahāmuniṃ*), 2889, 2891, 2892, 2895, 2896, 2897, 2899, 2901, 2904, 2906, 2907, 2908, 2919, 2920, 2921 (*mahāmuniṃ*), 2922 (*J.'s* relations to Asita Devala).—§ 675 (Mokshadh.): XII, **230,** 8431 (°*sya saṃvādaṃ Asitasya ca*), 8432, (8435) (discourse between *J.* and Asita Devala).—§ 707 (do.): XII, **319**β, 11782 (had instructed Viçvāvasu).—§ 730 (Ānuçāsanikap.): XIII, **18,** (1333) (Çiva bestowed the eightfold superhuman power upon him).
Jaimini, a ṛshi, disciple of Vyāsa. § 59 (Sarpasattra): I, **53,** 2046 (*Kautsaḥ*?, acted as *udgātṛ* at the snake-sacrifice of Janamejaya; differently PCR.).—§ 78 (Vyāsa): I, **63,** 2418 (Vyāsa taught his disciples the Vedas, of which Mhbhr. was the fifth one).—§ 264 (Sabhākriyāp.): II, **4***a*, 106 (*Sumantur J°ḥ Pailo Vyāsaçishyās tathā vayaṃ*, says Vaiçampāyana, enumeration of the munis who waited upon Yudhishṭhira).—§ 637 (Rājadh.): XII, **47**η, 1593 (among the ṛshis who surrounded Bhīshma as he lay on his arrow-bed).—§ 707 (Mokshadh.): XII, **319,** 11743.—§ 714 (Çukakṛtya): XII, **328,** 12338 (enumeration of the disciples of Vyāsa).—§ 717b (Nārāyaṇīya): XII, **341**μ, 13025 (do.); **350,** 13647 (do.).
Jaitra, a son of Dhṛtarāshṭra. § 611 (Çalyap.): IX, **26**ρρ, 1404, 1414 (is slain by Bhīmasena).
***jaitra** ("victorious"), said of various chariots: II, 490 (*rathaṃ*, viz. Hariçcandra's), 940 (*rathena*, viz. Indra's), 2064 (*rathavaraḥ*, viz. Yudhishṭhira's); III, 16510 (*Maghonaḥ*—i.e. Indra's—*syandanottamaḥ*); V, 3645 (*rathottamaṃ*, viz. Indra's); VII, 2479 (*rathaṃ*, viz. Arjuna's); VIII, †3526 (do., do.).
Jājali, a brahman. § 680b (Tulādhāra-Jājalisaṃv.): XII, **262,** 9277 (*Tulādhārasya vākyāni dharme J°nā saha*), 9278 (*dvijaḥ*), 9285, 9287, 9288, 9290, 9301, 9303, 9308, 9309, 9311, 9313, 9314, 9317, 9318; **263,** 9339, (9340), 9343, 9344, 9345, 9348, 9349, 9350, 9351, 9360, 9373, 9375, 9386, 9390, 9392, 9393; **264,** (9396), 9399, 9402, 9416, 9424, 9426, 9431, (†9433), 9439, 9440; **265,** 9445, 9446, 9460, 9461 (Tulādhāra's discourse to *J.*).
Jajñasena (II, 126), v. Yajñasena.
Jala ("water," personif.). § 270 (Brahmasabhāv.): II, **11,** 438 (in the palace of Brahmán).
Jalā, a river. § 410 (Plakshāvataraṇag.): III, **130,** 10556 (*Jalāñ copajalāñ caiva Yamunām abhito nadīṃ*).
Jāla, a celestial weapon. § 442 (Nivātakavacayuddhap.): III, **167,** 11967 (i.e. *Vāruṇa(ṃ)*, Nīl., employed by Arjuna).
Jalacara = Çiva (1000 names[1]).
Jalada, a mountain (?) in Çākadvīpa. § 575b (Çākadvīpa): VI, **11**β, 425 (= Malaya (v. 416)?).
Jaladhāra, a mountain in Çākadvīpa. § 575b (Çākadvīpa): VI, **11,** 417 (*mahāgiriḥ | yatra nityam upādatte Vāsavaḥ paramaṃ jalaṃ*), (β), 426.
Jalādhipa = Varuṇa, q.v.
Jalajakusumayoni = Brahmán: VIII, †4647. Cf. Padmayoni.
Jalandhama, a warrior of Skanda. § 615u (Skanda): IX, **45**η, 2559.
Jalapradānika, adj. ("relating to the gift of water to the deceased"). § 10 (Parvasaṅgr.): I, **2,** 348 (°*ṃ parva*, i.e. Jalapradānikaparvan).
[Jalapradānikaparvan] ("the section relating to the gift of water to the deceased," the 85th of the minor parvans of the Mhbhr.; cf. Jalapradānika). § 618: *Janamejaya* inquired of *Vaiçampāyana* as to what *Dhṛtarāshṭra*, etc. (*a*), did after the death of *Duryodhana*. *Dhṛtarāshṭra's* grief; *Sañjaya* comforted him, and suggested the performance of the obsequious rites of the fallen heroes. *Dhṛtarāshṭra* lamented (β); *Sañjaya* rebuked and consoled him (γ). *Vidura* addressed *Dhṛtarāshṭra* (XI, **1**) and comforted him (δ) (XI, **2**); charmed by *Vidura's* discourse, *Dhṛtarāshṭra* asked him to continue his observations on the vanity of human life; *Vidura* continued his discourse, and described human life as it runs (XI, **3**) from the very beginning (XI, **4**), comparing it to a wilderness

abounding with dangers (XI, **5**), explaining the comparison according to the religion of *Moksha* (XI, **6**); asked by *Dhṛtarāshṭra*, *Vidura* continued his discourse on human life (XI, **7**). *Dhṛtarāshṭra* swooned away, but was comforted by *Vyāsa*, etc. (ε), wept and lamented; *Vyāsa* comforted him by explaining the secret history of the slaughter (he had seen the Earth in *Indra's* hall, complaining before the gods and D.-ṛ. and *Nārada*, and *Vishṇu* consoling her, saying that *Duryodhana* would cause her burden to be lightened by a battle in *Kurukshetra*), etc. (ζ). *Dhṛtarāshṭra* promised to live; *Vyāsa* disappeared (XI, **8**). Requested by *Janamejaya* (η), *Vaiçampāyana* related: After *Duryodhana* had been slain, and all the troops slaughtered, *Sañjaya*, deprived of his spiritual sight, came back to *Dhṛtarāshṭra*, and recommended him to cause the obsequial rites to be performed. *Dhṛtarāshṭra* swooned away; *Vidura* comforted him ("Time drags all kinds of creatures away," etc.) (XI, **9**). *Dhṛtarāshṭra* resolved to visit the field of battle with the *Kuru* ladies in his company. The *Kuru* ladies (*Gāndhārī*, *Kuntī*, etc.) were placed in chariots under *Vidura's* supervision; the royal household, with a large number of the citizens, started from *Hāstinapura* (XI, **10**). Having proceeded a *kroça*, *Dhṛtarāshṭra* met with *Açvatthāman*, etc. (ϑ). *Kṛpa* related to *Gāndhārī* the fall of *Duryodhana* in unfair fight, and their nightly attack on the camp of the *Pāṇḍavas* (ι); then *Açvatthāman*, etc., took leave of *Dhṛtarāshṭra* in order to conceal themselves from the wrath of the *Pāṇḍavas*, and urged their steeds towards the banks of the *Gaṅgā*, where they separated from one another: *Kṛpa* went to *Hāstinapura*; *Kṛtavarman* to his own kingdom; *Açvatthāman* set out for the abode of *Vyāsa*; "before the sun rose; it was after this that the sons of *Pāṇḍu* encountered *Açvatthāman* and vanquished him" (XI, **11**). *Yudhishṭhira* and his brothers set out in order to meet *Dhṛtarāshṭra*, accompanied by *Kṛshṇa*, etc. (κ); they met the weeping ladies of the royal house on the way (λ), and saluted *Dhṛtarāshṭra*, who reluctantly embraced *Yudhishṭhira*, and broke an iron statue of *Bhīma* (that had been kept ready by *Kṛshṇa*), mistaking it for *Bhīma* himself; he then grieved for having slain *Bhīma*, fell down, and was raised by his charioteer *Sañjaya*; *Kṛshṇa* enlightened him, and told him not to cherish wrath (XI, **12**). Certain maid servants came and washed *Dhṛtarāshṭra*; then *Kṛshṇa* again addressed him, assuring him that the *Pāṇḍavas* were perfectly innocent (μ), then *Dhṛtarāshṭra* embraced *Bhīma*, etc. (ν) (XI, **13**). Commanded by *Dhṛtarāshṭra*, the *Pāṇḍava* brothers with *Kṛshṇa* then proceeded to see *Gāndhārī*, who wished to curse *Yudhishṭhira*. The great Ṛ. *Vyāsa*, capable of proceeding everywhere with the fleetness of the wind, and capable of seeing the heart of every creature with his spiritual vision, understood her evil intentions, and having cleansed himself by the water of the *Gaṅgā*, he suddenly appeared, and told her not to be angry with the *Pāṇḍavas*, but remember that she had every day for the eighteen days that battle lasted, when *Duryodhana* asked her to bless him, said: "Thither goes victory where righteousness is." *Gāndhārī* admitted that she and *Dhṛtarāshṭra* should protect the *Pāṇḍavas* with as much care as *Kuntī* herself protected them, the fault being with *Duryodhana*, etc. (ξ); but *Bhīma's* unfair combat with *Duryodhana* in the presence of *Kṛshṇa* moved her wrath (XI, **14**). *Bhīma* addressed *Gāndhārī*, and extenuated his fault in having slain *Duryodhana* unfairly ("*Duryodhana* had formerly himself vanquished *Yudhishṭhira* unfairly," etc.) (ο). *Gāndhārī* then blamed *Bhīma* for drinking *Duḥçāsana's* blood, when *Vṛshasena* had deprived *Nakula* of his steeds; *Bhīma* denied that he had really drunk *Duḥçāsana's* blood; "*Karṇa* knew this well; seeing *Nakula* deprived by *Vṛshasena* of his steeds, I caused the rejoicing brothers to be filled with dread; when the tresses of *Draupadī* were seized, I uttered certain words in rage; I dared not leave that vow unaccomplished lest I should be regarded as having swerved from the duties of a *kshatriya*." *Gāndhārī* then inquired after *Yudhishṭhira*, who appeared before her and invoked her curses on himself for his sinful slaughter of all her sons; *Gāndhārī's* glance (under the cloth that covered her eyes) blasted a nail of *Yudhishṭhira's* toe. *Arjuna* moved away to the seat of *Kṛshṇa*, and also the other *Pāṇḍavas* became restless. *Gāndhārī* then comforted the *Pāṇḍavas* and dismissed them. They then met with their mother *Kuntī*, who wept seeing their many scars. *Draupadī* wept for her children and *Abhimanyu*; *Kuntī* consoled her, and so did *Gāndhārī* (mentioning *Vidura's* predictions) (XI, **15**).

Jalasandha[1], a Magadha king. § 11 (Parvasaṅgr.): I, **2**, 535.—§ 232 (Svayaṃvarap.): I, **186**, 6992 (present at the svayaṃvara of Draupadī).—§ 328 (Kāmyakavanapr.): III, **36**, 1419 (has sided with Duryodhana, or is here the son of Dhṛtarāshṭra meant?).—§ 561 (Yānasandhip.): V, **66**εε, 2504 (*pārthivaṃ*, has sided with Duryodhana).—§ 572 (Rathātirathasaṅkhyānap.): V, **167**, 5793 (in the army of Duryodhana).—§ 598 (Jayadrathavadhap.): VII, **87**ι, 3112 (do.).—§ 599 (do.): VII, **95**, 3511; **97**, 3574 (attacked by Bhīmasena); **114**, 4454 (°*mahāgrāhaṃ . . . sainyārṇavaṃ*); **115**, 4569, 4575, 4576, 4578, 4580, 4582, 4585, 4589, 4590, 4593, 4594, 4597 (*J.* (*Māgadha*, vv. 4573, 4578, 4583) is slain by Sātyaki); **119**, 4705; **120**, 4766; **141**δδ, 5865 (*nihatya-J°ṃ . . . Sātyakiḥ*); **147**, 6355 (*nidhanaṃ Kauravya-J°yoḥ*); **150**, 6514 (*Sātyakinā hataṃ*).—§ 600 (Ghaṭotkacavadhap.): VII, **158**ω, 7036 (mentioned among the slain).—§ 604 (Karṇap.): VIII, **5**ζ, 134 (*hataḥ Sātyakinā*).—§ 609 (Çalyap.): IX, **2**, 76 (had sided with Duryodhana), 90 (*hataḥ, Pauravaḥ*?).—§ 611 (do.): IX, **24**, 1297 (sc. *hate, Paurave*?).—§ 615 (Gadāyuddhap.): IX, **64**εε, 3613 (among the slain).—§ 620 (Çrāddhap.): XI, **26**β, 792 (his corpse is burnt).—§ 789 (Putradarçanap.): XV, **32**θ, 877 (among the dead warriors who, summoned by Vyāsa, arose from the Gaṅgā). Cf. Māgadha.

Jalasandha[2], a son of Dhṛtarāshṭra. § 130 (Aṃçāvat.): I, **67**, 2029 (enumeration). — § 182 (Dhṛtarāshṭraputranāmak.): I, **117**, 4541 (do.). — § 209 (Drupadaçāsana): I, **138**, 5449.—§ 581 (Bhīshmavadhap.): VI, **64**[14], 2837 (among fourteen sons of Dhṛtarāshṭra who attacked Bhīmasena), 2842 (is slain by Bhīmasena).—§ 608 (Karṇap.): VIII, **51**δδ, 2447 (among twenty sons of Dhṛtarāshṭra who attacked Bhīmasena).

Jaleçaya = Çiva (1000 names[2]).

Jaleçvara[1] = Varuṇa, q.v.

Jaleçvara[2] = Çiva (1000 names[1]).

Jalelā, a mātṛ. § 615u (Skanda): IX, **46**θ, 2634.

Jaleyu, a son of Raudrāçva. § 150 (Pūruvaṃç.): I, **94**, 3700 (sixth son of Raudrāçva).

Jalodbhava = Çiva (1000 names[2]).

Jālya = Çiva (1000 names[1]).

Jamadagni, a ṛshi, the son of Ṛcīka and Satyavatī and the father of Rāma[1] (Paraçu-Rāma). § 122 (Aṃçāvat.): I, **66**, 2611 (son of Ṛcīka), 2612 (father of four sons, among whom Rāma was the youngest), 2613 (the eldest of the 100 sons of Aurva, i.e. Ṛcīka).—§ 191 (Arjuna): I, **123**, 4807 (one of the seven ṛshis(?) present at the birth of Arjuna).—§ 270

(Brahmasabhāv.): II, **11**, 440 (in the palace of Brahmán).—§ 377 (Dhaumyatīrthak.): III, **88**, 8337 (*vedī Çūrpārake tāta J°er mahātmanaḥ | vamyā Pāshāṇatīrthā ca Punaçcandrā ca*); **90**, 8387 (performed sacrifices at Palāçaka), 8390.—§ 395: At this time (cf. Arjuna Kārtavīrya, § 394), while *Gādhi*, the king of *Kānyakubja*, was dwelling in the wood, there was born to him a beautiful daughter, *Satyavatī*, whom *Ṛcīka Bhārgava* asked in marriage. *Gādhi* said that, according to a family custom, the bridegroom must give a dowry of 1,000 brown steeds with a single sable ear each (so PCR. translates *ekataḥ çyāmakarṇānām*, cf. V, 3740, and Gālavacarita). *Ṛcīka* obtained them from *Varuṇa* (the spot where the horses appeared was thence named Açvatīrtha) and married *Satyavatī* in *Kānyakubja* on the *Gaṅgā*, the very gods being companions of the bridegroom (*janyāḥ*). Then his father *Bhṛgu* came to see him and his wife, and being pleased with *Satyavatī*, granted her the boon that a son should be born to herself and to her mother, telling her that during their season they should embrace, her mother an *açvattha* tree and herself an *udumbara* tree, and eat two pots of rice and milk (*caru*) which he had prepared, having ransacked the whole universe. Then *Bhṛgu* disappeared. They, however, made an interchange both of the pots and of the trees which they embraced. Knowing this by his divine knowledge, *Bhṛgu* came once more and told *Satyavatī* that she had been deluded by her mother, and that therefore she would give birth to a brahman of kshatriya character (*kshatravṛttiḥ*) and her mother to a kshatriya of brahman character (*brāhmaṇācāraḥ*). At her repeated entreaties, however, he granted her that not her son but her grandson should be of that description. The son of *Satyavatī* was *J.*, who excelled many ṛshis in Vedic lore (*Vedādhyayanena*), and to whom the whole Dhanurveda appeared spontaneously (*pratyabhāt*), and likewise the four kinds of weapon (*astrāṇi*): III, **115**, 10167.—§ 396: *J.* devoted himself to the study of the *Veda* and to penances. He married *Reṇukā*, the daughter of king *Prasenajit*, and lived with her in his hermitage practising austerities. She gave birth to five sons, of whom *Rāma* was the youngest. Once when *Reṇukā* had been filled with desire, seeing the *Mārttikāvata* king *Citraratha* bathing, together with his wife, *J.* ordered his sons *Rumaṇvat* (the eldest), *Sushena*, *Vasu*, and *Viçvāvasu* to kill their mother, but as they refused to do so he cursed them, so that they lost their senses and behaved like beasts and birds. Then he ordered *Rāma* to do it, and he immediately severed her head with an axe, and then prevailed upon *J.* to grant him that *Reṇukā* might be restored to life and not remember that she had been slain, that he himself might not be affected by this sin, that his brothers might recover their former state, and that he himself might be unrivalled on the field of battle and obtain a long life: III, **116**, 10183, 10185, 10188.—§ 397: Once when the sons of *J.* had gone out, *Arjuna Kārtavīrya*, the lord of the country near the seashore (*Anūpapatiḥ*), came to the hermitage, and, though he was praised by *Reṇukā*, he carried away the calf of the *homadhenu* and pulled down the trees. *J.* told this to *Rāma*, who then rushed towards *Arjuna* and cut down his 1,000 arms with his arrows and at last killed him. Then the sons of *Arjuna* came while *Rāma* was away, and with their arrows killed *J.*, who did not fight, but repeatedly shouted the name of *Rāma*. When they had gone away, *Rāma* returned to the hermitage: III, **116**, 10196, 10197.—§ 602 (Droṇavadhap.): VII, **190**ν, 8727.—§ 606*b* (Paraçu-Rāma): VIII, **34**, 1583 (*Bhārgavāṇām kule jātaḥ*, father of Paraçu-Rāma).—§ 638*b* (Rāmop.): XII, **49**, 1744 (*Bhārgavam*, son of Ṛcīka and Satyavatī), 1746 (father of Rāma), 1761 (°*dhenvāḥ . . . vatsam*), 1765 (slain by the sons of Arjuna Kārtavīrya; cf. §§ 395–7).—§ 665 (Mokshadh.): XII, **208**ι, 7600 (*Ṛcīkasya putraḥ*, one of the ṛshis of the north).—§ 702 (do.): XII, **293**a, 10762 (had praised Vishṇu).—§ 721*b* (Viçvāmitrop.): XIII, **4**, 245 (his birth; cf. § 395).—§ 733 (Rāmahrada): XIII, **25**, 1734 (°*gatim labhet*, sc. by bathing in Mahāhrada).—§ 745*c* (Cyavana-Kuçikasamv.): XIII, **55**, 2912 (*Bhṛguçārdūlaḥ*, Ṛcīka will beget *J.*, who will master the Dhanurveda).—§ 750*b* (Bisastainyop.): XIII, **93**a, 4416, (4444), (4464), (4495) (etymology of his name), (4521).—§ 751*b* (Çapathavidhi): XIII, **94**a, †4550, (4571).—§ 752*b* (Chattropānahotpatti): XIII, **95**, 4606 (°*eç ca samvādam Sūryasya ca*), (4618); **96**, 4629, 4630, (4633), 4636 (terrifies the Sun (Sūrya), who in order to pacify him gives him an umbrella and a pair of sandals).—§ 759 (Ānuçāsanik.): XIII, **106**δ, 5200 (among the ṛshis who have attained to heaven through observance of fasts).—§ 766 (do.): XIII, **127**, (6073).—§ 770 (do.): XIII, **151**ι, 7117 (*Ṛcīkatanayaḥ*, one of the gurus of Dhaneçvara in the north).—§ 775 (do.): XIII, **166**ζ, 7670 (*Ṛcīkaputraḥ*, one of the ṛshis of the north).—§ 782*c* (Arjuna Kārtavīrya): XIV, **29**, 823 (father of Rāma).—§ 786*f* (Nakulākhyāna): In former times *J.* purposed to perform a *çrāddha*; his *homa*-cow came to him, and he milked her himself. Assuming the form of *Krodha* (anger), *Dharma* entered the vessel of milk, desirous of putting *J.* to the test, and spoiled the milk. *J.* was not enraged. *Krodha*, in the form of a brahman lady, then said to him that the saying was false that the *Bhṛgus* were wrathful, since he had been subdued by *J.*, and asked his forgiveness. *J.* said that as the milk had been destined to the *Pitṛs*, *Krodha* ought to introduce himself to them. Through the curse of the *Pitṛs*, *Krodha* became a mungoose until he had spoken disrespectfully of *Dharma*. Then he wandered about to sacrifices and other sacred places, employed in censuring great sacrifices, until he came and censured the horse-sacrifice of *Yudhishṭhira*, who was *Dharma's* self; then he became freed from his curse: XIV, **92**, 2887, (2894). Cf. Ārcīka (V, 3972), Bhārgava, Bhārgavanandana, Bhṛguçārdūla, Bhṛguçreshṭha, Bhṛgūttama, Ṛcīkaputra, Ṛcīkatanaya.

Jāmadagni, a ṛshi. § 734 (Anuçāsanik.): XIII, **26**a, 1763 (among the ṛshis who surrounded Bhīshma as he lay on his arrow-bed).

Jamadagnisuta = Rāma[1]: V, 6057.

Jāmadagnya[1] = Rāma[1], q.v.

Jāmadagnya[2] = Rumaṇvat: III, 10180 (*R*°).

Jāmadagnyam upākhyāna(m). § 10 (Parvasaṅgr.): I, **2**, 332 (? in the enumeration of parvans entered between two parvans of the fifth book of Mhbhr., but not found there; perhaps referring to III, **115–17**).

Jāmbavat, the king of the bears. § 531 (Rāmopākhyānap.): III, **280**, 16115 (*ṛksharājaḥ*).—§ 535 (Setubandhana): III, **283**a, 16276 (came to Rāma with 100,000 crores of black bears).—§ 541 (Indrajidvadha): III, **289**β, 16477.—§ 542 (Rāvaṇavadha): III, **290**a, 16500.

Jāmbavatī, wife of Kṛshṇa and mother of Çāmba. § 730 (Ānuçāsanik.): XIII, **14**, 616 (desired to have a son and got Çāmba).—§ 793 (Mausalap.): XVI, **7**μ, 249 (among the wives of Kṛshṇa who after his death ascended his funeral pyre). Cf. Kapīndraputrī.

Jāmbavatīsuta ("the son of Jāmbavatī") = Çāmba: III, 10271.

Jāmbavatyāḥ suta(ḥ) (do.) = Çāmba: III, 670.

Jambha[1], an Asura. § 298 (Dyutap.): II, **62**, 2105 (*iti sma bhāshate Kāvyo J°tyāge mahāsurān*).—§ 384*c* (Vishṇu): III, **102**, 8760 (*Asuraḥ*, has been slain by Vishṇu).—§ 561*c* (Kṛshṇa Vāsudeva): V, **48**, †1884 (*vegeneva—°aiva*, B.—*çailam abhihatya J°ḥ*, cf. Ekalavya).—§ 561*d* (Nara-Nārāyaṇau): V, **49**, 1931 (had been slain by Nara (= Arjuna) while about to swallow him).—§ 589 (Droṇābhishekap.): VII, **11**, 386 (has been slain by Kṛshṇa).—§ 596 (Pratijñāp.): VII, **81**, 2910 (*Indra-Vishṇū yathā prītau J°vadhakāṅkshiṇau*).—§ 599 (Jayadrathavadhap.): VII, **96**, 3561 (*yathā Çakra-J°au*); **102**, 3821 (*yathendreṇa hataḥ pūrvaṃ J°o Devāsure mṛdhe*).—§ 605 (Karṇap.): VIII, **13**, 516 (*yathā Devāsure yuddhe J°-Çakrau mahābalau*).—§ 608 (do.): VIII, **65**, 3304 (*hate mahāsure J°e Çakra-Vishṇū yathā Guruḥ*); **77**, †3863 (*°ṃ jighāṃsuṃ pragṛhītavajraṃ jayāya Devendram iva*); **84**, †4280 (*purā jighāṃsur Maghaveva J°ṃ*); **88**, †4501 (*Mahendra-J°āv iva*).—§ 611 (Çalyap.): IX, **12**, 655 (*hatavikrānto J°o Vṛtrahaṇā yathā*); **20**, †1077 (*°o yathā Çakrasamāgamād vai nāgendram Airāvaṇam Indravāhyaṃ*, sc. *pratyudyayau*); **26**, 1425 (*yādṛçaṃ samare pūrvaṃ J°-Vāsavayoḥ*).—§ 641 (Rājadh.): XII, **98**ξ, 3660 (had been slain by Indra). Cf. Asura.

Jambha[2], a Rākshasa. § 537 (Rāma-Rāvaṇayuddha): III, **285***a*, 16365 (follower of Rāvaṇa).

Jambhaka, a prince. § 281*b* (Sahadeva): The son of *J.* lived on the banks of Carmaṇvatī, and had been spared by Vāsudeva in their former hostilities: II, **31**, 1111 (*°syātmajaṃ nṛpaṃ*, vanquished by Sahadeva).

Jambū. § 574*i* (Jambūkh.): On the south of Nīla and the north of Nishadha there is a huge eternal *jambū* tree (*Eugenia jambolana*, rose-apple), named *Sudarçana*, and adored by Si. and Cā.; it grants every wish, and after it *Jambūdvīpa* has its name; the tree is 1,100 *yojanas* high and touches the very heavens. The circumference of a fruit of that tree measures 2,500 cubits; when ripe the fruit bursts, and pours out a silvery juice which becomes a river, which passes round *Meru* and comes to the northern *Kurus*; the drinking of that juice conduces to peace of mind, no thirst is felt ever after, nor decrepitude. On that spot there is found a species of gold, called *jāmbūnada*, used for celestial ornaments and like the complexion of *indragopaka* (cochineal) insects. The men who live there are of the complexion of the morning sun: VI, **7**, 270 (*°-vṛkshuh*).—§ 757*e* (Meru): XIII, **102**, †4862.

Jambŭdvīpa, name of the dvīpa south of Meru, and also of the whole circular central dvīpa. § 354 (Nalopākhyānap.): III, **79**, 3066.—§ 574 (Jambūkh.): VI, **1**, 9 (*°sya maṇḍalaṃ*); **6**δ, 207 (beside Meru lie four dvīpas—Bhadrāçva, Ketumāla, Jambudvīpa, and Uttarāḥ Kuravaḥ; *J.* therefore in this passage cannot design the whole central dvīpa, the centre of which is Meru).—§ 574*i* (Jambū): VI, **7**, 274 (named after the *jambū* tree Sudarçana).—§ 575*b* (Çākadvīpa): VI, **11**, 409 (i.e. the central dvīpa opp. to Çākadvīpa), 428.—§ 575 (Bhūmip.): VI, **12**, 467 (i.e. the central dvīpa).—§ 623 (Rājadh.): XII, **14**, 404, 405 (beside Meru lie Jambudvīpa, Krauñcadvīpa (to the south!), Çākadvīpa (to the east!), and Bhadrāçva (to the north!), cf. VI, 207).—§ 759 (Ānuçāsanik): XIII, **107**ζ, 5338.—§ 785 (Anugītāp.): XIV, **85**, 2548. Cf. Jambūkhaṇḍa, Jambuparvata.

Jambuka[1], a warrior of Skanda. § 615*u* (Skanda): IX, **45**η, 2576.

Jambuka[2], v. Çambuka.

Jambūka, a warrior of Skanda. § 615*u* (Skanda): IX, **45**η, 2578.

Jambūkhaṇḍa = Jambūdvīpa: VI, 226 (beside Meru), 401 (i.e. the central dvīpa). Cf. next.

Jambūkhaṇḍavinirmāṇa ("the measurement of Jambūkhaṇḍa"). § 10 (Parvasaṅgr.): I, **2**, 337 (*°ṃ parva*).—§ 11 (do.): I, **2**, 520 (i.e. Jambūkhaṇḍavinirmāṇaparvan).

[Jambūkhaṇḍavinirmāṇaparvan (*°va*)**]** ("the section relating to the measurement of Jambūkhaṇḍa," the 67th of the minor parvans of Mhbhr.; cf. °vinirmāṇa). § 574: *Janamejaya* inquired how the *Kurus* and the *Pāṇḍavas* and *Somakas* fought on *Kurukshetra*. *Vaiçampāyana* began the description of the battle. The *Pāṇḍavas* occupied the western part, turned towards the east, beyond *Samantapañcaka*. The force was collected from the whole of *Jambudvīpa*. *Yudhishṭhira* and *Duryodhana* fixed watchwords. Seeing *Duryodhana* (description), the *Pāñcālas* were filled with joy, and blew their conches, etc.; *Arjuna* and *Kṛshṇa* also blew their conches *Devadatta* and *Pāñcajanya*, at which the *Kurus* were alarmed. Various ill omens were beheld. Both parties settled rules and made covenants regarding the different kinds of combat (VI, **1**). *Vyāsa* visited *Dhṛtarāshṭra*, and offered to grant him spiritual vision that he might witness the battle. *Dhṛtarāshṭra* did not like to see the slaughter of his kinsmen. *Vyāsa* then granted it to *Sañjaya*, that he might narrate everything to *Dhṛtarāshṭra*; weapons would not hurt him; he would come out of the battle with life. *Vyāsa* informed *Dhṛtarāshṭra* of the omens (*a*), and appealed to him for peace; but *Dhṛtarāshṭra* urged the disobedience of his sons. *Vyāsa* enumerated to *Dhṛtarāshṭra* the omens that indicate victory, and recommended negotiation, as victory was uncertain (VI, **2**, **3**). Then *Vyāsa* departed. Seeing the many hundreds of millions of men that had come together at *Kurujāṅgala* to lay down their very lives for the sake of the earth, *Dhṛtarāshṭra* inquired of *Sañjaya* after the attributes of Earth, and the details about the countries and cities from which they had come. *Sañjaya* discoursed on the merits of the earth, and the various classes of creatures inhabiting it. Their twenty-four constituents are described as *Gāyatrī* (VI, **4**). *Dhṛtarāshṭra* inquired about the rivers, mountains, and provinces of the earth, and their dimensions. *Sañjaya* spoke of the five elements and their attributes, earth being the foremost. Then he began the description of the dvīpa of *Sudarçana* (VI, **5**). *Sañjaya* discoursed on the six mountains (*varshaparvatāḥ*, B.) that extend from the eastern to the western ocean, and are the resort of Si. and Cā.: *Himavat*, etc. (β), and the *varshas* between them—*Bhārata-varsha*, etc. (γ); *Mālyavat*, *Gandhamādana*; *Meru* (description); the four islands beside *Meru*—*Bhadrāçva*, etc. (δ); the bird *Sumukha* (*b*); on *Meru* sport D., G., As., Rā., and Aps., and *Brahmán*, *Rudra*, and *Çakra* perform sacrifices; *Tumburu*, etc. (ε), adore the gods with hymns; the seven *Ṛshis* and *Kaçyapa* repair thither on every *parvan*-day (i.e. the day of full moon and that of new moon); upon the summit is *Uçanas* with the *Daityas*; the jewels, etc., come from *Meru*, one-fourth part being enjoyed by *Kubera*, who gives only one-sixteenth to men. On the northern side of *Meru* is a forest of *karṇikāras*; there *Paçupati* (the creator of all things), together with his celestial attendants and *Umā*, sports, bearing a chain of *karṇikāra* flowers reaching down to his feet, and his three eyes resembling three suns; the *Siddhas* can behold him, but not persons of wicked conduct; from the summit of that mountain *Gaṅgā* (*c*) falls down. On the western side of

Meru is *Ketumāla* (*d*), and also *Jambūkhaṇḍa, Gandhamādana* (*e*). The last *varsha* in the north and *Bharata's varsha* in the south are both of the form of a bow. Amongst these seven *varshas* that which is further north excels the one to its immediate south in respect of longevity, stature, health, righteousness, pleasure, and profit. The huge mountains of *Hemakūṭa* are also called *Kailāsa*, where *Vaiçravaṇa* (i.e. Kubera) lives in joy with Gh. To the north of *Kailāsa* and near the mountains of *Maināka* there is the huge and beautiful mountain *Hiraṇyaçṛṅga*. Beside this the delightful lake *Bindusaras* (*f*), with golden sands. Rā. reside on *Himavat*, etc. (*θ*). The two dvīpas *Nāgadvīpa* and *Kaçyapadvīpa* are the two ears of this hare-shaped region; the beautiful mountains of *Malaya*, having rocks like copper plates, form another part of *Jambūdvīpa*, making it resemble a hare (VI, **6**). *Dhṛtarāshṭra* asked *Sañjaya* about the regions to the north and the east side of *Meru*, and about the mountains of *Mālyavat*. *Sañjaya* told about the *Uttarakurus* (*Uttarāḥ Kuravaḥ*) (*g*). East of *Meru* the foremost region is *Bhadrāçva* (*h*). The *jambū* tree (*i*). *Mālyavat* (*j*) (VI, **7**). *Dhṛtarāshṭra* inquired about the names of all the *varshas* and mountains. *Sañjaya* related of *Ramaṇaka*, etc. (*ι*). *Dhṛtarāshṭra* became absorbed in meditation about his sons; then he said: "Time destroys and creates everything; *Nara* and *Nārāyaṇa*, omniscient, destroying all creatures (*sarvabhūtahṛt*), the gods call him *Vaikuṇṭha*, men call him *Vishṇu*" (VI, **8**). *Dhṛtarāshṭra* asked about *Bhārata-varsha* (*k*), about which *Duryodhana* and the *Pāṇḍavas* are so covetous. *Sañjaya* said that the *Pāṇḍavas* were not covetous about it, but *Duryodhana, Çakuni*, etc.; then he mentioned in *Bhārata-varsha*, the beloved land of *Indra*, etc. (**aa**), inhabited by *Aryans* and *Mlecchas*, the mountains—*Mahendra*, etc. (*κ*); rivers ("all mothers of the universe and productive of great merit")—*Gaṅgā*, etc. (*λ*); countries—*Kuru-Pāñcālāḥ*, etc. (*μ*); and countries in the south—*Draviḍāḥ*, etc. (*ν*); the tribes of the north—*Mlecchāḥ*, etc. (*ξ*); and in the east and the north—*Çūdrābhīrāḥ*, etc. (*ο*) (VI, **9**). *Dhṛtarāshṭra* inquired about life, strength, etc., in *Bhārata-varsha*, and of *Haimavata-varsha* and *Harivarsha*. *Sañjaya* related of the four *yugas*—*Kṛta*, etc. (*π*). The portion that remains of the *Dvāpara* age is small. *Haimavata-varsha* is superior to *Bhārata-varsha*, and *Harivarsha* superior to *Haimavata-varsha*, in every respect (VI, **10**).

Jambūmārga, a tīrtha. § 358 (Tīrthayātrap.): III, **82**, 4082, 4084.—§ 377 (Dhaumyatīrthak.): III, **89**, 8366 (in the west).—§ 730*w* (Narmadā): XIII, **25**, 1737.—§ 775 (Ānuçāsanik.): XIII, **166*a***, 7650.

Jāmbūnada, son of the elder Janamejaya. § 154 (Pūruvaṃç.): I, **94**, 3745 (fifth son of Janamejaya).

Jāmbūnada(ṃ) saras, a lake. § 565 (Gālavacarita): V, **111**, 3843 (on the mountain Uçīrabīja in the north).

Jāmbūnadaparvata, a mountain. § 418 (Tīrthayātrāp.): III, **139**, †10835 (*Indrasya*, = Meru, Nīl.).

Jambūnadī, a river. § 574*f* (Bindusaras): VI, **6***η*, 243 (one of the seven streams of Gaṅgā).

Jāmbūnadī, a river. § 574 (Jambūkh.): VI, **9***λ*, 338 (among the rivers of Bhāratavarsha).

Jambuparvata. § 575 (Bhūmip.): VI, **11**, 405 (*ashṭādaça sahasrāṇi yojanānāṃ viçāmpate | shaṭçatāni ca pūrṇāni vishkambho Jambuparvataḥ*, Nīl. takes Jambuparvata = Jambūdvīpa, but ought there not to be read *Jambuparvaṇaḥ* (gen. from Jambuparvan = Jambūkhaṇḍa = Jambūdvīpa)).

Janadeva (XII, 7883, 7930), v. Janaka.

Janajanmādi = Vishṇu (1000 names).

Janaka, one or more Videha kings in Mithilā. § 11 (Parvasaṅgr.): I, **2**, 449 (°*syādhvare*, all. to Ashṭāvakrīya (§ 412)).—§ 267 (Yamasabhāv.): II, **8**, 330 (in the palace of Yama).—§ 280 (Bhīmasena): II, **30**, 1087 (*Vaidehakañ ca rājānaṃ*, vanquished by Bhīmasena on his digvijaya).—§ 309 (Āraṇyakap.): III, **2**, 66 (some çlokas sung by him are quoted).—§ 370 (Tīrthayātrāp.): III, **84**, 8089 (°*sya tu rājarsheḥ kūpaḥ*, a tīrtha).—§ 412 (Ashṭāvakrīya): III, **132**, †10601 (°*sya yajñe*), †10612, †10618 (*yajñaṃ J°sya*), †10619 (do.); [**133**, †10624 (*Janakendraṃ*)]; **134**, †10672 (*yajñe J°sya*), †10674, †10678, (†10679), 10682, 10684, †10686, †10687 (the events at *J.*'s sacrifice).—§ 425 (Hanūmad-Bhīmasenasaṃv.): III, **148**, 11207 (*sutāṃ Janakarājasya Sītāṃ*).—§ 480 (Pativratop.): III, **207**, 13706 (*Mithilāṃ J°ena surakshitāṃ*), 13728, 13729, 13738 (description of *J.*'s virtuous rule).—§ 525 (Rāmopākhyānap.): III, **274**, 15880 (*Videharājaḥ*, father of Sītā, the wife of Rāma Dāçarathi).—§ 551 (Kīcakavadhap.): IV, **21**, 652 (*duhitā J°sya*, i.e. Sītā).—§ 576 (Bhagavadgītāp.): VI, **27**, 970 (*karmaṇaiva hi saṃsiddhim āsthitā J°ādayaḥ*).—§ 623 (Rājadh.): XII, **17**, 528 (a gāthā sung by him is quoted (v. 529 = v. 6641)).—§ 624 (do.): XII, **18**, 538 (*mauṇḍyam āsthitaḥ*), 571 (*J.* adopted the life of a mendicant, his discourse with his wife Kausalyā).—§ 631 (do.): XII, **28**, 835 (*Vaidehaḥ*), (836) (instructed by Açman). —§ 641 (do.): XII, **99**, 3665 (*Maithilaḥ*, battle between *J.* and Pratardana), 3666; [**105–6** (*Vaidehaḥ*, Kshemadarçin's relation to *J.*)]. —§ 655 (Āpaddh.): XII, **159*a***, 5924 (having repressed covetousness, *J.* attained to heaven).—§ 659 (Mokshadh.): XII, **177**, 6600 (*pratishṭhatā mahāraṇyaṃ J°sya niveçanāt*, sc. Çuka, cf. §§ 713–14, differently PCR.); **178**, 6640 (*Videharājena*, an itihāsa sung by *J.* is quoted (v. 6641 = v. 529)).—§ 668 (do.): XII, **218**, 7881 (*Mithilādhipaḥ*).—§ 668*b* (Pañcaçikhavākya): XII, **218**, 7883 (*janadevaḥ*, Nīl. and PCR. Janadeva of Janaka's race), 7898, 7899; **219**, 7930 (*janadevaḥ*), (7931) (instructed by Pañcaçikha).—§ 702 (Mokshadh.): XII, **291**, 10699 (questioned Parāçara); **297**, (10861), (10870), (10879), (10891), (10895); **299**, 10942 (*Mithilādhipaḥ*), (10943), 10991 (instructed by Parāçara).—§ 705 (do.): XII, **303**, 11120 (*Vasishṭhasya ca saṃvādaṃ Karāla-Janakasya ca*), 11221, 11223 (*Karāla-J°ḥ*); **306**, (11328); **307**, 11368; [**309**, †11504 (*Karāla*) ([Karāla-] *J.* is instructed by Vasishṭha)].—§ 707 (do.): XII, **311**, 11545 (*Yājñavalkyasya saṃvādaṃ J°sya ca*), 11546 (*Daivarātiḥ*), (11547); **315**, (11648); **319**, †11833, †11836 (°*nṛpasya*) (*J.* Daivarāti is instructed by Yājñavalkya).—§ 708 (do.): XII, **320**, 11839 (*Pañcaçikhasyeha saṃvādaṃ J°sya ca*), 11840 (*Vaidehaḥ*, discourse with Pañcaçikha).—§ 709*b* (Sulabhā-Janakasaṃv.): XII, **321**, 11854 (°*sya saṃvādaṃ Sulabhāyāç ca*), 11855 (*Maithilo J°o nāma Dharmadhvaja iti çrutaḥ*), 11860, (11871), 11999 (*J.*'s discourse with Sulabhā). —§ 713 (Çukakṛti): XII, **326**, 12220 (*Mithileçvaraṃ*), 12233 (*dharmarājena*); **327**, 12260, 12265, 12270 (*Videharājaḥ*), (12274), (12282) (visited by Çuka, whom he instructs).—§ 714 (Çukakṛtya): XII, **328**, 12343 (°*rājena*). —§ 718*b* (Uñchavṛttyup.): XII, **366**, 13937 (°*sya niveçane*, Cyavana told the Uñchavṛttyupākhyāna to Nārada).—§ 744 (Ānuçāsanik.): XIII, **45**, 2466 (*Sukratuḥ . . . naptā Videharājasya J°sya*).—§ 761 (do.): XIII, **115***δ*, 5667 (among the princes who abstained from meat during the month of Kārttika). —§ 775 (do.): XIII, **166***η*, 7676. —§ 782*f* (Brāhmaṇagītā): The brahman said: King *J.*, who was desirous of punishing a brahman for an offence, forbade him to dwell within his dominions. The brahman then asked him about the limits of his territories; *J.'s* understanding at first became clouded, then he said that he failed to find his dominion in the kingdom, in *Mithilā*, and among his own children; "even this body is not mine, or the whole earth is mine, and as much mine as it is of others; do remain as long as you please." Asked by the brahman, he explained how he had come to this result, and got rid of the idea of "mine"; "all my acts are for the sake of the gods, P., Bh., and the guests." The brahman turned out to be *Dharma* (XIV, **32**), who described himself as emancipated, and said that *J.* would enter his soul (XIV, **33**): XIV, **32**, 887 (*brāhmaṇasya saṃvādaṃ J°sya ca*), 888, (894), (901), 911.—§ 786 (Anugītāp.): XIV, **41*a***, 2843 (attained to success by making gifts).

Cf. also the following synonyms:—

Aindradyumni: III, 10624.
Daivarāti: XII, 11546.
Dharmadhvaja: XII, 11855.
Karāla, Karālajanaka, q.v.
Maithila ("king of Mithilā"): III, 10655; XII, 3664, 3665 (*J°*), 3666 (do.), 3951, †7981, 7983, 11458 (= Karālajanaka), 11484 (do.), 11556 (= *J.* Daivarāti), 11684 (*°sattama*), 11688, 11855 (*J°*), 11969, 11980, 12013, 12025, 12042.
Mithilādhipa (do.): XII, 7881 (*J°*), 10942 (do.), 11725 (= *J.* Daivarāti), 11821 (do.).
Mithilādhipati (do.): XII, 11818 (= *J.* Daivarāti).
Mithileçvara (do.): XII, 11381 (= Karālajanaka), 11709 (= *J.* Daivarāti), 11859, 11863.
Vaideha, Videharāja, q.v.

Janaka, pl. (*°āḥ*), the family of Janaka. § 412 (Ashṭāvakrīya): III, **133**, †10637 (*°ānāṃ varishṭha*, i.e. Janaka).

Janakanṛpa, Janakarāja, v. Janaka.

Janakātmaja = Vasumat: XII, 11518.

Janakātmajā = Sītā, q.v.

Janakendra, v. Janaka.

Jānaki, a prince. § 130 (Aṃçāvat.): I, **67**, 2675 (incarnation of the Asura Vināçanaḥ Candrasya).—§ 554 (Sainyodyogap.): V, **4γ**, 83 (among the princes to whom the Pāṇḍavas ought to send messengers).

Jānakī = Sītā, q.v.

Janamejaya[1], son of Parikshit and Mādravatī, and the husband of Vapushṭamā; at his snake-sacrifice Vaiçampāyana recited the Mhbhr. for the first time (cf. Janamejaya[10]). § 1 (Anukram.): I, **1**, 9 (*°sya rājarsheḥ sarpasattre*), 20 (*rājñaḥ*).—§ 4 (do.): I, **1**, 97.—§ 10 (Parvasangr.): I, **2**, 303 (*°sya . . . sattre*).—§ 12 (Paushyap.): I, **3**, ††661 (*Pārikshitaḥ*), ††663, ††665, ††668, ††671 (together with his brothers Çrutasena, Ugrasena, and Bhīmasena, *J.* is cursed by Saramā).—§ 13 (do.): I, **3**, ††673 (*Pārikshitaḥ*), ††675 (do.), ††677, ††680 (gets Somaçravas as his purohita).—§ 16 (Veda): I, **3**, ††746 (makes Veda his upādhyāya, C. has by error *Janameyaḥ*).—§ 17 (Uttanka): I, **3**, 833 (*rājānaṃ*), 837 (*rājā*), (†838) (coming to Hāstinapura, Uttanka urges *J.* to burn Takshaka in a snake-sacrifice, reminding him that Takshaka had stung Parikshit dead).—§ 25 (Paulomap., Sahasrapad): I, **11**, 1012 (*°sya yajñe 'smin sarpāṇāṃ hiṃsanaṃ purā*), 1014 (*rājā*).—§ 26 (Āstīkap.): I, **13**, 1020 (*rājā*); **15**, 1058 (*°sya . . . yajñe*, the serpents will be burnt there).—§ 29 (Kadrū): I, **20**, 1196 (*sarpasattre . . . J°sya rājarsheḥ Pāṇḍaveyasya*, do.).—§ 49 (Vāsuki): I, **37**, 1596 (*yajñaḥ . . . J°sya*), 1598; **38**, 1623 (*Pāṇḍaveyaḥ*).—§ 52 (cf. Āstīkap.): *J.*, the minor son of Parikshit, is made king and married to Vapushṭamā, the daughter of the Kāçi king Suvarṇavarman: I, **44**, 1807 (*Kurupravīraṃ*).—§ 56 (Parikshit): I, **49**, 1933 (*rājā*), (1935), 1937 (*rājānaṃ*), 1945, (†1951); **50**, 1977 (the ministers of *J.* told him how Parikshit had been stung by Takshaka, and how Takshaka had induced the brahman Kāçyapa not to help Parikshit).—§ 57 (cf. Āstīkap.): The menial of a brahman who gathered sacrificial fuel in the banyan-tree, which was burnt by Takshaka and revived by Kāçyapa, was equally burnt to ashes and revived, and had told to the ministers of *J.* what had happened between Takshaka and Kāçyapa. *J.* resolved to avenge his father and Uttanka: I, **50**, 1992, 2004, (2007).—§ 58 (do.): As there was a snake-sacrifice read of in the *Purāṇa*, *J.* caused the preparations for such a sacrifice to be made. When the sacrificial platform was being constructed, the *Sūta Lohitāksha*, versed in the rules of building, announced that both the soil and the time of the sacrifice foreboded that a brahman would come to prevent the completion of the sacrifice. *J.* therefore gave orders not to admit anybody without his knowledge (I, **51**).—§ 59 (Sarpasattra): I, **53**, 2041 (*Pāṇḍaveyasya*, description of his snake-sacrifice).—§ 60 (do.): I, **53**, 2054; **54**, 2073, 2086, 2093 (*°sya taṃ yajñaṃ*, Āstīka came to the sacrifice).—§ 61 (do.): I, **55**, †2113 (*rājā*, Āstīka gratified *J.*).—§ 62 (do.): I, **56**, (†2114), (†2117), (2125), 2126, (†2131), 2135 (*J.* granted Āstīka a boon, and Āstīka asked that the sacrifice should be stopped).—§ 68 (do.): I, **58**, 2167 (*rājā*), 2175 (*Bhārataḥ*, thus the sacrifice ceased), 2190 (*°sya yajñānte*).—§ 70 (Ādivaṃçāvatāraṇap.): I, **59**, 2203; **60**, 2208 (*sarpasattrāya dīkshitaṃ*), 2214 (*rājarsheḥ*), 2215, 2217 (*rājarshiḥ*), 2221, 2223, (2224) (requested by *J.* at the snake-sacrifice, Vyāsa causes Vaiçampāyana to tell the history of the dissension between the Kauravas and the Pāṇḍavas).—§ 72 (do.): I, **62**, (2283) (*J.* wishes to hear the Mhbhr. in full, Vaiçampāyana begins his narrative).—§ 84 (do.): I, **64**, (2456).—§ 85 (Sambhavap., Aṃçāvat.): I, **65**, (2515).—§ 130 (do., do.): I, **67**, (2637), (2727).—§ 133 (do., Dushyanta): I, **68**, (2799); **69**, (2814).—§ 134 (do., Çakuntalop.): I, **74**, 2989.—§ 137 (do., Daksha Prācetasa): I, **75**, 3133.—§ 145 (do., Kaca): I, **76**, (3183), 3186.—§ 149 (do., Yayāti): I, **86**, (3540).—§ 150 (do., Pūruv.): I, **94**, (3691), 3708.—§ 156 (do., do.): I, **95**, (3754).—§ 160 (do., do.): I, **95**, ††3837 (son of Parikshit and Mādravatī, husband of Vapushṭamā, and father of Çatānīka and Çankukarṇa).—§ 167 (do., Vicitravīryop.): I, **102**, 4096.—§ 172 (do., Aṇīmāṇḍavyop.): I, **107**, (4305).—§ 181 (do., Duḥçalotpatti): I, **116**, (4523).—§ 182 (do., Dhṛtarāshṭraputranāmak.): I, **117**, (4540).—§ 183 (do., Pāṇḍu): I, **118**, (4558).—§ 190 (do., Pāṇḍavotpatti): I, **123**, 4759.—§ 198 (do., Çaradvat): I, **130**, (5071).—§ 200 (do., Droṇa): I, **130**, (5100).—§ 213 (Jatugṛhap.): I, **141**, (5651).—§ 215 (Bakavadhap.): I, **157**, (6103).—§ 216 (Caitrarathap.): I, **165**, (6316).—§ 231 (Svayaṃvarap.): I, **185**, 6945, 6953.—§ 245 (Rājyalābhap.): I, **208**, (7596).—§ 248 (Arjunavanavāsap.): I, **214**, 7782.—§ 251 (do.): I, **218**, 7897, 7900.—§ 252 (Subhadrāharaṇap.): I, **220**, 7931.—§ 253 (Haraṇāharaṇap.): I, **221**, 7986.—§ 255 (Khāṇḍavadah., Agniparābhava): I, **223**, (8094).—§ 259 (do., Çārngakop.): I, **229**, (8331); **232**, 8428.—§ 271 (Lokapālasabhākhyānap.): II, **12**, 512.—§ 277 (Jarāsandhavadhap.): II, **21**, 830.—§ 279 (Digvijayap., Arjuna): II,

26, (994).—§ 280 (do., Bhīmasena): II, 29, 1069.—§ 282 (do., Sahadeva): II, 31, 1128, (1129).—§ 284 (do., do.): II, 31, 1182.—§ 294 (Dyūtap.): II, 50, (1786).—§ 302 (Anudyūtap.): II, 74, (2452).—§ 308 (Āraṇyakap.): III, 1, (1).—§ 310 (do.): III, 3, (143).—§ 331 (Kairātap.): III, 38, (1516).—§ 340 (Indralokābhigamanap.): III, 48, (1914).—§ 341 (do.): III, 50, (1955).—§ 343 (Nalopākhyānap.): III, 52, (2013).—§ 356 (Tīrthayātrāp.): III, 80, (3090), 3096.—§ 378 (do.): III, 93, 8486.—§ 392 (do., Mahendrācalagamana): III, 114, 10095.—§ 401 (do., Balarāma): III, 119, (10237). — § 447 (Nivātakavacayuddhap.): III, 175, 12300.—§ 448 (Ājagarap.): III, 176, (†12316).—§ 450 (do.): III, 178, (12363).—§ 451 (Mārkaṇḍeyas.): III, 182, 12554.—§ 461 (do., Vāmadevacarita): III, 192, (13142) (wanting in B.).—§ 512 (Ghoshayātrāp.): III, 236, (†14741); 237, 14795; 239, 14820; 247, (15037).—§ 515 (do., Karṇadigvijaya): III, 253, (15208).—§ 518 (Mṛgasvapnodbhavap.): III, 258, (15353). —§ 521 (Draupadīharaṇap.): III, 262, (15492).—§ 525 (Rāmopākhyānap.): III, 273, (15859).—§ 546 (Kuṇḍalāharaṇap.): III, 300, (16919).—§ 547 (Karṇa): III, 303, (16998); 310, (†17218).—§ 548 (Āraṇeyap.): III, 311, (17221).—§ 549 (Pāṇḍavapraveçap.): IV, 1, (1); 9, †279. —§ 550 (Samayapālanap.): IV, 13, (325).—§ 551 (Kīcakavadhap.): IV, 14, 374.—§ 562 (Bhagavadyānap.): V, 84, (†2995).—§ 565 (Gālavacarita): V, 106, (3714).—§ 570 (Sainyaniryāṇap.): V, 153, (5188); 157, (5314); 159, (5391). —§ 574 (Jambūkh.): VI, 1, (2). —§ 589 (Droṇavadhap.): VII, 1, (2).—§ 604 (Karṇap.): VIII, 1, (18); 4, 87; 8, (218).—§ 609 (Çalyap.): IX, 1, (1), 24.—§ 615 (Gadāyuddhap.): IX, 35, (1969).—§ 615 (Baladevatīrthayātrā): IX, 35, (2006), (2011), 2063; 36, (2068); 37, 2133, (2157), 2172; 38, (2186); 39, (2254); 40, (2285); 41, 2336; 42, (2358); 43, (2432), 2443; 44, (2450), 2453; 45, 2580, 2581; 47, (2728), (2744); 48, (2825); 49, 2843; 50, 2862, 2872; 51, (2928); 52, (2979); 54, 3035.—§ 615 (Gadāyuddhap.): IX, 55, 3077; 56, 3129; 63, (3503).—§ 617 (Aishīkap.): X, 11, 574.—§ 618 (Jalapradānikap.): XI, 9, (246).—§ 637 (Rājadh.): XII, 45, (1532); 47, (1588).—§ 640 (do.): XII, 54, (1925).—§ 658 (Āpaddh.): XII, 173, 6456.—§ 695 (Mokshadh.): XII, 285, (10272).—§ 717*b* (Nārāyaṇīya): XII, 340, 12998, 13003; 341, 13011, 13012, (13013); 342, (13129); 344, (13316); 348, (13459); 349, (13547), (13614), (13627); 350, (13637), (13642); 351, (13713).—§ 776 (Ānuçāsanik.): XIII, 167, (7689).—§ 781 (Açvamedhikap.): XIV, 15, (372). —§ 782 (Anugītāp.): XIV, 16, (407). —§ 784*b* (Uttaṅka): XIV, 55, 1596; 56, (1625), 1626, 1628, 1655; 57, 1681; 58, 1725, 1740, 1748, 1749.—§ 785 (Anugītāp.): XIV, 59, (1751); 63, (1871); 66, 1943 (birth of *J.'s* father Parikshit).—§ 786 (do.): XIV, 90, (2689); 91, (2810); 92, (2846), 2882, (2885).—§ 787 (Āçramavāsap.): XV, 1, (1); 13, 409.—§ 789 (Putradarçanap.): XV, 29, (766), 800; 32, 873.—§ 790 (do.): XV, 34, 920, 922; 35, (942), 945, 947, 955 (at the request of *J.*, Vyāsa showed him his father Parikshit, etc.).—§ 791 (do.): XV, 36, (957).—§ 793 (Mausalap.): XVI, 1, (12), (14); 7, 239.—§ 794 (Mahāprasthānikap.): XVII, 1, (1).—§ 795 (Svargārohaṇap.): XVIII, 1, (1); 5, (148), 172.—§ 795*b* (do.): Sauti said: Hearing this, at the intervals of the sacrificial rites, king *J.* became filled with wonder. The sacrificial priests finished the rites. *Āstīka*, having rescued the snakes, became filled with joy. *J.* gratified all the brahmans with copious presents, then they returned home. *J.* came back from Takshaçilā to Hāstinapura: XVIII, 5, 178, 181.—§ 795 (do.): XVIII, 6, (212).

Cf. also the following synonyms:—

Bhārata, Bharataçārdūla, Bharataçreshtha, Bhāratāgrya, Bharatarshabha, Bharatasattama, q.v.

Kaurava, Kauravaçārdūla, Kauravanandana, Kauravendra, Kauravya, q.v.

Kuruçārdūla, Kuruçreshṭha, Kurūdvaha, Kurukulaçreshṭha, Kurukulodvaha, Kurunandana, Kurupravīra, Kurupuṅgavāgraja, Kurusattama, q.v.

Pāṇḍava, Pāṇḍavanandana, Pāṇḍaveya, q.v.

Pārikshita ("the son of Parikshit"): I, 10, 366 (*sarpasattreṇa rājñaḥ P°sya*), ††661 (*J°*), ††673 (*J°*), ††675 (*J°*), 2016 (*rājā*), 2050 (*sattre P°sya*), 2063 (*°sya yajñaḥ*), †2097, †2098, †2099, †2100, †2101, †2102, †2103, 2136, 2139 (*rājā*), 2166 (*rājñā*), 2175 (*Pāṇḍaveyasya rājñaḥ*), 2331; III, †10215; XII, 13311 (*rājñaḥ*), 13457 (do.).

Paurava, q.v.

Janamejaya[2], one or more ancient kings. § 5 (Anukram.): I, 1*a*, 221*bis* (in Sañjaya's enumeration of deceased kings).—§ 267 (Yamasabhāv.): II, 8, 331 (in the palace of Yama).—§ 595 (Shoḍaçarāj., v. Māndhātṛ): VII, 62*a*, 2281 (vanquished by Māndhātṛ).—§ 641 (Rājadh.): XII, 124, 4564 (won the world in the course of three nights).—§ 677 (Mokshadh.): XII, 235, 8598 (attained to heaven by giving his body for the sake of a brahman).—§ 723 (Ānuçāsanik.): XIII, 6, 330 (*Çakrasyodgamya çaraṇam prasthito J°ḥ | dvijastrīṇāṃ vadhaṃ kṛtvā kiṃ daivena na vāritaḥ*).—§ 767 (do.): XIII, 137, 6253 (attained to heaven by giving a chariot and kine to a brahman; PCR. connects the first pāda *Sāvitraḥ kuṇḍalaṃ divyaṃ* with the rest, but *Sāvitra* is = Karṇa; cf. also XII, 8598). The passages quoted here might as well refer to one of the princes mentioned under the headings Janamejaya[4–7].

Janamejaya[3], a prince, contemporary of the great war. § 130 (Aṃçāvat.): I, 67, 2698 (read with B. *J°aḥ*, among the kings who were incarnations from the Krodhavaça gaṇa).—§ 554 (Sainyodyogap.): V, 4γ, 79 (among the princes to whom the Pāṇḍavas ought to send messengers).

Janamejaya[4], son of Kuru. § 154 (Pūruv.): I, 94*a*, 3740 (the fifth son of Kuru and Vāhinī).

Janamejaya[5], son of the elder Parikshit. § 154 (Pūruv.): I, 94γ, 3742 (*°ādayaḥ sapta . . . Parīkshito 'bhavan putrāḥ*), 3744 (father of the elder Dhṛtarāshṭra, etc.).

Janamejaya[6], son of Pūru. § 156 (Pūruv.): I, 95, ††3764 (son of Pūru and Kausalyā), ††3765 (husband of Anantā and father of Prācinvat).

Janamejaya[7], a king of the Nīpas. § 562 (Bhagavadyānap.): V, 74γ, 2729 (*Nīpānāṃ J°ḥ*, among the vile kings who annihilated their kinsmen and relatives).

Janamejaya[8], one or more Pāñcāla princes in the army of Yudhishṭhira. § 592 (Saṃçaptakavadhap.): VII, 23*o*, 998 (*Pāñcālānāṃ naravyāghraḥ*, proceeded against Droṇa, description of his horses).—§ 600 (Ghaṭotkacavadhap.): VII, 158χ, 7008; 167, 7483 (*Pāñcālyasya*).—§ 601 (Droṇavadhap.): VII, 184*a*, 8366.—§ 608 (Karṇap.): VIII, 48ξ, 2253; 49χ, 2335 (*Pāñcālyaḥ*); 56$\pi\pi$, 2756; 73, 3732; 82, †4181, (λ), †4195. Cf. Pāñcālya.

Janamejaya[9], king of the mountaineers (Pārvatīya). § 604 (Karṇap.): VIII, **6**, 169 (in the army of Yudhishṭhira, had been slain by Durmukha).

Janamejaya[10], Pārikshit. § 652*b* (Indrota-Pārīkshitīya): XII, **150**, 5595, 5596 (*Pārīkshit*, B. has *Pāri°*), 5600; **151**, 5613, (5627), (5634); **152**, 5638, 5642, 5673 (*J.* had slain a brahman, but was instructed by Indrota Çaunaka about the means of cleansing himself; Indrota then assisted *J.* in his horse-sacrifice. *J.* here belongs to the past (cf. also Harivaṃça, vv. 1608 ff.), but seems originally to be identical with Janamejaya[1] (Pārikshita)).

Janamejaya, pl. (°*āḥ*). § 267 (Yamasabhāv.): II, **8**, 334 (eighty *J.'s* in the palace of Yama).

Janana = Vishṇu (1000 names).

Jānapadī, an Apsaras. § 198 (Çaradvat): I, **130**, 5076 (sent by Indra to tempt Çaradvat).

Janārdana = Kṛshṇa (Vishṇu), q.v.

Janārdana, pl. (°*āḥ*). § 616 (Sauptikap.): X, **6**, 233.

Jānārdani ("the son of Janārdana, i.e. Kṛshṇa") = Pradyumna: III, 723.

Janasthāna, name of a place. § 425 (Hanūmad-Bhīmasaṃv.): III, **147**, 11199 (there Sītā was carried off by Rāvaṇa).—§ 528 (Rāvaṇagamana): III, **277**, 15986 (°*vāsinā*, sc. Rāma Dāçarathi, there Sītā was robbed).—§ 595 (Shoḍaçarāj., v. Rāma Dāçarathi): VII, **59**, 2226 (there Rāma slew Rākshasas), 2241 (do.).—§ 615*k* (Mahodara): IX, **39**, 2256 (the head of a Rākshasa, which Rāma had cut off at *J.*, fell upon the thigh of Mahodara).—§ 733*l* (Citrakūṭa): XIII, **25***a*, 1715 (a tīrtha).

Janeçvara = Vishṇu (1000 names).

Jāṅgala, pl. (°*āḥ*), a people. § 561 (Yānasandhip.): V, **54**, 2127 (*Kuravas te sa-J°āḥ*).—§ 574 (Jambūkh.): VI, **9**μ, 346 (*Mādreya-J°āḥ*), 364. Cf. Kurujāṅgala, pl.

Jaṅgama = Çiva (1000 names[2])

Jaṅghābandhu, a muni. § 264 (Sabhākriyāp.): II, **4***a*, 111 (among the brahmans who waited upon Yudhishṭhira when he entered his palace).

Jaṅghāri, a son of Viçvāmitra. § 721*b* (Viçvāmitrop.): XIII, **4**β, 256.

Janmamṛtyujarātiga = Vishṇu (1000 names).

Jantu, son of king Somaka. § 408 (Jantūp.): III, **127**, 10473, 10475, 10476, 10483, 10488, 10490; **128**, 10492, 10498.

Jantūpākhyāna(m) ("episode relating to Jantu"). § 11: I, **2**, 447.—§ 408 (Tīrthay.): Questioned by *Yudhishṭhira*, *Lomaça* said: King *Somaka* had 100 wives, but was a long time sonless. At last, when he and his wives were old, he got a son *Jantu*, whom all the wives surrounded with the utmost care. One day when *Jantu* had been stung by an ant at his hip and cried, *Somaka*, afraid of losing him, inquired of his *ṛtvij* if there were a ceremony by which a man might get 100 sons. He was told to sacrifice *Jantu* and let his wives take a smell of the smoke of his fat; then 100 sons would be born to him, and *Jantu* himself would be born once more of the same mother, with a mark of gold on his back (III, **127**). The sacrifice was performed notwithstanding the screams of the wives, and after ten months 100 sons were born, of whom *Jantu* was the eldest and most beloved and superior in merit, and had that mark of gold. When the *guru* and *Somaka* had died, the *purohita* was grilled in a terrible hell for having performed that sacrifice, and *Somaka* prevailed upon *Dharmarāja* (who said "one cannot enjoy or suffer for another person's acts") that he should be likewise tormented for the same period before he entered the blessed regions. Here they (the Pāṇḍavas, etc.) spent six nights (III, **128**).

Jānujaṅgha, an ancient king. § 6 (Anukram.): I, **1***a*, 230 (in Nārada's enumeration).—§ 775 (Ānuçāsanik.): XIII, **166**η, 7684.

Janya = Çiva (1000 names[2]).

[Jāpakopākhyāna(m)] ("the episode about the reciter of sacred mantras"). § 662*b* (Mokshadh.): A brahman, who was a reciter, conversant with the six *Aṅgas*, of the *Kuçika* race and son of *Pippalāda*, acquired spiritual insight into the *Aṅgas*; at the foot of *Himavat* he was devoted to the *Vedas*; silently reciting *Gāyatrī*, he practised austerities for 1,000 years in order to attain to *Bráhman*. Then *Gāyatrī* (*Sāvitrī*) appeared and granted him the boon that his wish for recitation should go on increasing, and his absorption into meditation (*samādhi*) be more complete. She added that he should not have to go to hell, thither where great brahmans go, but to the region of *Brahmán*, and that *Dharma*, etc. (*a*), would come to him in person. He continued engaged in recitation for 1,000 celestial years. Then *Dharma* came to him and told him to cast off his body in order to win regions of bliss; but he did not wish to reside in heaven except with his body, but only took pleasure in recitation. *Time*, *Mṛtyu*, and *Yama* came and told him the same. The brahman gave them *arghya* and *pādya*. *Ikshvāku*, who had set out on a *tīrthayātrā*, came and was given *arghya* and *pādya*. The brahman wished to give him something; *Ikshvāku*, as a kshatriya, would not take anything except battle, but only himself give; at last, however, he asked to be allowed to enjoy the fruits of the brahman's recitations, but when the brahman consented he would not take them, and asked the brahman what those fruits were. The brahman did not know, as his recitations had never been connected with any special purpose; he told the king that Truth required that he should take them as he had asked for them (the signification of Truth). *Dharma* and Heaven (*Svargaḥ*) seconded the brahman. *Ikshvāku* wished to give his own merits instead, but in vain; then *Ikshvāku* agreed to accept half the brahman's merit on the condition that the brahman should take half of his own, but he was refused. At this time two ungainly individuals came there, *Virūpa* and *Vikṛta* (afterwards disclosed to be *Desire* and *Wrath*). *Virūpa* said that he owed *Vikṛta* the merits of the gift of a cow, but that *Vikṛta* refused to take repayment (in the form of the merit of having given two *kapilā* cows with calves to an *uñchavṛtti*); *Vikṛta* declared that *Virūpa* owed him nothing; they asked *Ikshvāku* to decide the question. *Ikshvāku* hesitated; the brahman threatened to curse him. *Ikshvāku* would give him some drops of water that had fallen upon his hand. *Virūpa* approved of this arrangement, and said that *Vikṛta* really did not owe him anything; "we appealed to thee for thy own sake." *Bhīshma* said that a reciter goes to *Brahmán*, or *Agni*, or *Sūrya*, whose attributes he catches stupefied by attachment (*rāgeṇa*), and so also if he goes to *Soma*, etc. (β); if, however, he goes to those regions after having freed himself from attachment, he enters the Supreme and Imperishable, and becomes *Bráhman* (XII, **199**). The brahman accepted, worshipped *Dharma*, etc. (γ), and set himself to his recitations again. Asked by *Ikshvāku*, he agreed that he should go half and half with the king. *Indra* came there with D., Lp., Sā., Vi., etc. (δ), and said to the brahman and the king that they had attained to success ([*saṃ*]*siddhaḥ*). Those two withdrew their senses from the objects of the world; fixing *Prāṇa*, etc. (ε), in the heart, they concentrated the mind in *Prāṇa* and *Apāna* united together, etc. (description). *Brahmán* welcomed the fiery flame that had issued from the head of the brahman, saying: "Reciters attain to the same end as the *yogins*; but as regards reciters, the honour is ordained for them that *Brahmán* himself shall advance to receive them"; then he once more imparted consciousness into that splendour; the brahman then entered the mouth of *Brahmán*, and so did the king. The deities rejoiced. *Brahmán* said that so also would he that reads "the great *Smṛti*" and "the *Anusmṛti*" (i.e. resp. "the six *Añgas* and *Manu*, etc.," Nīl.) in this way attain to the same region with *Brahmán*; and so also he who is devoted to *Yoga*. Then *Brahmán* disappeared, and the deities, having honoured *Dharma*, returned to their respective abodes (XII, **200**).

Jarā, a female Rākshasa. § 275 (Rājasūyārambhap.): II, **17**, 715 (*rākshasī*, united the two half-parts of Jarāsandha); **18**, 729 (created by Svayambhū and named Gṛhadevī), 739 (°*ayā sandhito yasmāj Jarāsandho bhavatv ayam*). — § 600 (Ghaṭotkacavadhap.): VII, **181**, 8224 (in a battle between Jarāsandha and Balarāma, *J.* (who had united Jarāsandha) was slain together with her sons and relatives).—§ 621 (Rājadh.): XII, **5**, 132 (fighting with Jarāsandha, Karṇa was about to sever the two parts of Jarāsandha's body which had been united by *J.*). Cf. Gṛhadevī, Rākshasī.

Jaras, the hunter who wounded Kṛshṇa. § 793 (Mausalap.): XVI, **4**, 126, 127, 128 (wounded Kṛshṇa, piercing him at the heel; Kṛshṇa comforted him and ascended to heaven).

Jarāsandha[1], king of the Māgadhas, son of Bṛhadratha. § 4 (Anukram.): I, **1**, 129, †153 (*Māgadhānāṃ varishṭhaṃ*).—§ 130 (Aṃçāvat.): I, **67**, 2640 (incarnation of the Asura Vipracitti).—§ 232 (Svayaṃvarap.): I, **186**, 7003 (present at the svayaṃvara of Draupadī).—§ 233 (do.): I, **187**, 7030. — § 273 (Rājasūyārambhap.): II, **14**, 571, 574, 576, 582, 588, 589, 593, 599, 602, 608, 610, 618, 626, 628, 631, 633 (*J.'s* great might, his allies; many peoples fled from fear of him; Kaṃsa married the daughters of *J.*, Asti and Prāpti, who when he had been slain by Kṛshṇa, urged *J.* to attack the Yādavas, who fled from Mathurā to Dvārakā; *J.* worshipped Çiva; the defeated kings he kept enclosed in Girivraja). — § 274 (do.): II, **15**, 641, 651 (*Bārhadrathaḥ*), 653, 655, 658, 659 (kept the kings in the temple of Çiva in order to sacrifice them, and must be defeated that Yudhishṭhira might perform his rājasūya); **16**, 662, 673.—§ 275 (do.): II, **17**, 686, 687 (*J.'s* birth; the two wives of Bṛhadratha bore each one-half of a child; the Rākshasī Jarā united the two halves); **18**, 739 (because he had been united (*sandhitaḥ*) by Jarā he was named *J.*); **19**, 756, 757, 758, 760 (after the slaughter of Kaṃsa, *J.* hurled a mace toward Mathurā).—§ 276 (Jarāsandhavadhap.): II, **20**, 768, 778, 791 (Kṛshṇa, Arjuna, and Bhīma set out for Girivraja to slay *J.*); **21**, 808, 815, 818, 819, 821, 824, 829, 835, 837, 839 (receives Kṛshṇa, Arjuna, and Bhīma disguised as brahmans); **22**, (854), 865, (880), 884, 888 (challenged to fight, *J.* installed his son Sahadeva as king); **23**, 890, 892 (*Māgadhaḥ*), 893, 894, 897, 898, 923, 924 (engaged in a wrestling encounter with Bhīmasena); **24**, 925, 927, 928, 929, 932 (Bhīmasena at last killed *J.*), 935 (description of his chariot), 950, 955, 969, 972 (*kshīṇe*), 975.—§ 289 (Arghāharaṇap.): II, **37**, 1360 (had been slain by Kṛshṇa (!)).—§ 290 (Çiçupālavadhap.): II, **42**, 1474, 1475, 1476, 1478 (all. to § 277); **44**, 1529 (had been vanquished by Karṇa in a wrestling encounter and slain (? *dehabhedañ ca lambhitaḥ*, cf. XII, 132)).—§ 307 (Anudyūtap.): II, **81**, 2706 (had been slain by Bhīmasena).—§ 315 (Maitreyaçāpa): III, **10**, 371 (do.).—§ 317*b* (Kṛshṇa Vāsudeva): III, **12**, 489 (had been slain by Kṛshṇa (!)).—§ 561 (Yānasandhip.): V, **51**, 2055 (*Māgadhendreṇa*, had subdued the whole earth and had been slain by Bhīmasena).—§ 567 (Bhagavadyānap.): V, **130**ζ, 4411 (had been slain by Kṛshṇa (!)).—§ 588 (Bhīshmavadhap.): VI, **122**, 5834 (could not vanquish Karṇa).—§ 589 (Droṇābhishekap.): VII, **11**, 387 (*Kaṃsaḥ . . . J°ena pālitaḥ*), 393 (°*m . . . Janārdanaḥ . . . ghātayām āsa*).—§ 600 (Ghaṭotkacavadhap.): VII, **180**, †8210 (had been slain by Kṛshṇa (!)); **181**δδ, 8213 (do.), 8217, 8220, 8224, 8225, 8227, 8228 (*J.* hurled a mace against Balarāma, who baffled it with his Sthūṇākarṇa weapon; the mace fell down on earth and slew the Rākshasī Jarā (who had united *J.*), together with her sons and relatives. Deprived of his mace, *J.* was afterwards slain by Bhīmasena). — § 621 (Rājadh.): XII, **4**ε, 113 (present at the svayaṃvara of the daughter of the Kaliñga king Citrāñgada); **5**, 129 (*rājā Māgadhaḥ*, challenged Karṇa, who in a wrestling encounter vanquished him (? *bibheda sandhiṃ dehasya Jarayā çleshitasya hi*, v. 132); *J.* then gave the town Mālinī to Karṇa).—§ 717*b* (Nārāyaṇīya): XII, **340**, 12960 (*Asuraḥ sphīto bhūmipālo Girivraje*, incarnate as Kṛshṇa Nārāyaṇa will slay him). — § 768*b* (Kṛshṇa Vāsudeva): XIII, **147**, 6839 (Kṛshṇa will vanquish *J.* and liberate the imprisoned kings). — § 788 (Āçramavāsap.): XV, **25**, †668 (*Magadhādhipasya sutā J°a iti çrutasya*, i.e. the wife of Sahadeva Pāṇḍava). Cf. Bārhadratha, Māgadha, Magadhādhipa, Magadhādhipati, Magadheçvara.

Jarāsandha[2], a son of Dhṛtarāshṭra. § 130 (Aṃçāvat.): I, **67**, 2735.—§ 182 (Dhṛtarāshṭraputranāmak.): I, **117**, 4548.

Jarāsandhasuta ("the son of Jarāsandha"). § 599 (Jayadrathavadhap.): VII, **125**, 5058 (is slain by Droṇa, = Sahadeva ?). Cf. Jārāsandhi.

Jarāsandhasutā ("the daughter of Jarāsandha"). § 787 (Āçramavāsap.): XV, **1**α, 24 (i.e. the wife of Sahadeva Pāṇḍava, cf. v. 668).

Jarasandhātmaja ("the son of Jarāsandha") = Sahadeva: II, 962 (*S*°), 965. Cf. Jārāsandhi.

Jarāsandhavadha ("the killing of Jarāsandha"). § 10 (Parvasaṅgr.): I, **2**, 317 (*parva*, i.e. Jarāsandhavadhaparvan). — § 11 (do.): I, **2**, 408 (= do.).

[Jarāsandhavadhaparvan] ("the section relating to the killing of Jarāsandha," the 23rd of the minor parvans of Mhbhr.; cf. Jarāsandhavadha). § 276: As *Kṛshṇa* thought that *Jarāsandha* was incapable of being vanquished in battle even by all the gods and *Asuras*, but might be vanquished in a personal struggle with bare arms (*prāṇayuddha*, PCR.), and as there was in himself policy, in *Bhīma* strength, and in *Arjuna* ability to protect them, he thought that *Jarāsandha* should be made to challenge *Bhīma*, and *Kṛshṇa* therefore obtained the permission of *Yudhishṭhira* that *Bhīma* and *Arjuna* followed him. They set out in the garb of *snātakas*, with *Bhīma* in the van, from the land of the *Kurus* to the *Padmasaras*, over *Kālakūṭa*, *Gaṇḍakī*, *Mahāçoṇa*, *Sadānīrā* (v. 794 runs thus in V.: *Gaṇḍakīñca Sadānīrāṃ Çarkarāvarttam eva ca*), the rivers on the *Ekaparvataka* (? see BR.) and *Pūrvā* (i.e. Eastern) *Koçalā* (B. has *pūrvāṃç ca Koçalān*), *Mithilā*, *Mālā*, *Carmaṇvatī*, *Gañgā*, *Çoṇa*, towards the east, dressed in garments of *kuça*-grass (instead of *kuçacīracchadā* V. has *Kuçāmboraḥsthalaṃ*), to the *Māgadha* land. When they came to the mountain of *Goratha*, they beheld the *Māgadha* town (II, **20**).—§ 277: *Girivraja* is surrounded by the five large hills of *Vaihāra*, *Varāha*, *Vṛshabha*, *Ṛshigiri*, and *Caityaka*. It was there that *Gautama* begat *Kākshīvat*, etc., upon the *çūdra* woman *Auçīnarī*, and was visited by the kings of *Aṅga*, *Vaṅga*, etc. There dwell the *Nāgas Arbuda*, *Çakravāpin*, *Svastika*, and *Maṇināga*. *Manu* had ordered the *Māgadhas* never to be afflicted with drought; *Kauçika* and *Maṇimat* had favoured the country. The *Pāṇḍavas* and *Kṛshṇa* entered the city by breaking down the peak of *Caityaka*, worshipped by the *Bārhadrathas* and the citizens with perfumes and flower garlands, where *Bṛhadratha* had slain the cannibal *Ṛshabha*, and made of his hide (*māsatālābhiḥ*, see BR.; Gauḍapātha : *māṃsanālābhiḥ*, Nīl.) three drums [which the brothers broke, v. 814, not in V.]. As evil omens had been seen, the *purohitas* made *Jarāsandha* mount an elephant and carried fire about him (*paryagnyakurvan*), and he entered upon (*dīkshitaḥ*) a sacrifice with vows (*niyamasthaḥ*) and fasts (*upavāsaparaḥ*). *Kṛshṇa*, *Bhīma*, and *Dhanañjaya* entered the city without weapons in the guise of *snātakas*, snatched from the flower-vendors the garlands they had exposed for sale, and attired in robes of various colours and decked with garlands and ear-rings they entered the abode of *Jarāsandha*, who welcomed them, and hearing from *Kṛshṇa* that *Bhīma* and *Arjuna* in consequence of a vow would not speak before night, quartered them in the sacrificial apartments (*yajñāgāre*) and retired to the palace (*rājagṛham*). At midnight he came to them, as he always observed the vow, that as soon as he should hear of the arrival of *snātakas*, even at midnight, he would immediately come out and grant them an audience. As he questioned them about their strange attire, which was unsuitable for *snātakas*, and their breaking down the *Caityaka* peak, and why they would not accept the worship he offered, *Kṛshṇa* gave him some explanations (v. 848 ff.: *snātakavratino, rājan! brāhmaṇā, kshatriyā, viçaḥ | viçeshaniyamāç caishām aviçeshāç ca santy uta | viçeshavāṃç ca satataṃ kshattriyaḥ çriyam ṛcchati*), and declared that they had come as his foes (II, **21**). As *Jarāsandha* said that he did not remember to have injured them, *Kṛshṇa* told him that they were sent by *Yudhishṭhira* to set at liberty the princes whom *Jarāsandha* intended to slaughter as a sacrifice to *Çiva*, because sacrificing human beings to the gods was never used (v. 864); he reminded him of the destruction of *Dambhodbhava*, *Kārtavīrya*, *Uttara*, and *Bṛhadratha*, and challenged him to set free the monarchs or to fight. *Jarāsandha* chose to fight, and ordered *Sahadeva* to be installed on the throne. Then he thought of his generals *Kauçika* and *Citrasena*, who had formerly been *Haṃsa* and *Ḍimbhaka*. *Kṛshṇa*, remembering that, according to the command of *Brahmán*, *Jarāsandha* was not to be slain by him or by the *Madhus*, did not himself desire to slay him (II, **22**). *Jarāsandha* having chosen to fight with *Bhīma*, the *purohita* brought pigment, garlands, etc., and propitiatory ceremonies (*kṛtasvastyayanaḥ*) were performed by a brahman; and likewise *Bhīma*, having consulted with *Kṛshṇa*, had propitiatory ceremonies pronounced (*kṛtasvastyayanaḥ*). When *Jarāsandha* had taken off his crown and arranged his hair, they fought with their clenched fists as their only weapons. The combat began at the first day of the month *Kārttika*, and lasted, without intermission or food, till the thirteenth; on the fourteenth night *Jarāsandha* desisted from fatigue, and *Kṛshṇa* obscurely intimated that he should now be killed (II, **23**). At the instigation of *Kṛshṇa*, *Bhīma* threw *Jarāsandha* into the air a hundred times, pressed his knee against his backbone and broke his body in two with a terrible roar, so that the citizens became dumb with terror and many women were prematurely delivered. Leaving the lifeless body at the palace gate, they went out of the town riding on *Jarāsandha's* celestial chariot, which *Kṛshṇa* caused to be made ready, it being adorned with a celestial flagstaff and incapable of being vanquished by any king, upon which *Indra* and *Vishṇu* had fought in the battle about *Tārakā*, riding upon which *Indra* had slain ninety-nine (*navatīr nava*) *Dānavas*, which had been obtained by king *Vasu* from *Vāsava* (i.e. Indra), from *Vasu* by *Bṛhadratha*, and from him by *Jarāsandha*. And *Kṛshṇa* thought of *Garuḍa*, who sat upon the chariot along with the frightfully roaring creatures on its flagstaff. *Kṛshṇa* then released his relatives and ordered them to assist *Yudhishṭhira* at his *rājasūya*. Stopping on a level plain outside the town, he was adored by the citizens, and he installed *Sahadeva*, the son of *Jarāsandha*, in the sovereignty of the *Magadhas*. Then they arrived at *Indraprastha*. Thereupon *Kṛshṇa*, having taken leave of *Yudhishṭhira*, etc., set out for his own city, riding upon that same celestial chariot that had been given to him by *Yudhishṭhira*, the *Pāṇḍavas* having circumambulated him (*pradakshiṇam akurvanta*) (II, **24**).

Jārāsandhi ("the son of Jarāsandha") = Sahadeva or Jayatsena. § 277 (Jarāsandhavadhap.): II, **22**, 966 (i.e. Sahadeva, is anointed as king).—§ 280 (Bhīmasena): II, **30**, 1092 (is vanquished by Bhīmasena on his digvijaya).—§ 555 (Sainyodyogap.): V, **19**γ, 577 (*Jayatsenaḥ*, joined Yudhishṭhira).—§ 561 (Yānasandhip.): V, **50**η, 2014 (*°ḥ Sahadevo Jayatsenaç ca tāv ubhau*, do.); **57**ξ, 2239 (*Māgadhaḥ*, do.).—§ 578 (Bhīshmavadhap.): VI, **48**θ, 1926 (in the army of Duryodhana).—§ 599 (Jayadrathavadhap.): VII, **125**, 5061 (is slain by Droṇa).—§ 604 (Karṇap.): VIII, **5**ζ, 120 (*Jayatsenaḥ*, had been slain by Abhimanyu); **7**, †207 (in the army of Duryodhana).—§ 789 (Putradarçanap.): XV, **32**θ, 877 (among the dead warriors who, summoned by Vyāsa, arose from the Gaṅgā). Cf. Jarāsandhasuta, Jarāsandhātmaja.

Jaratkāru[1], a ṛshi, husband of Jaratkāru and father of Āstīka. § 26 (cf. Āstīkap.): Sauti said: The ascetic *J.*, when going about and practising religious austerities, one day saw his ancestors, the Yāyāvaras, hanging, heads down, in a great hole by a rope of *vīraṇa* fibres, which was eaten into on all sides by a rat; he was told that it was because he had no offspring. He then promised to marry, if he might get a wife of the same name as his own, and who would be given to him in charity (I, **13**). At last he married Jaratkāru, the sister of Vasuki, the king of serpents (I, **14**), who intended by this marriage to neutralize the curse inflicted on the serpents by their mother (Kadrū, q.v.). Having begotten Āstīka, *J.* ascended to heaven together with his ancestors (I, **15**): I, **13**, 1029 (*Yāyāvarāṇām pravaraḥ*), 1034, 1037, (1041), 1041, 1045; **14**, 1054, 1055, 1056; **15**, 1067, 1068.—§ 49 (Vāsuki): I, **38**, 1633, 1634, 1635 (it had been destined by Brahmán that *J.* should marry Vāsuki's sister Jaratkāru and beget Āstīka on her); **39**, 1650, 1653, 1654.—§ 50 (cf. Āstīkap.): Etymology of the name *J.* (*jareti kshayam āhur vai, dāruṇaṃ kārusaṃjñitaṃ | çarīraṃ kāru tasyāsīt tat sa dhīmāñ chanaiḥ çanaiḥ | kshapayām āsa tīvreṇa tapasā . . . Vāsuker bhaginī tathā*): I, **40**, 1655, 1656.—§ 51 (Parikshit): I, **40**, 1661 (*ṛshim*).—§ 53 (cf. Āstīkap.): The story of *J.* repeated (cf. § 26) and somewhat enlarged: I, **45**, 1813, 1831 (*Veda-Vedāṅgapāragaḥ*), 1839, 1843; **46**, 1846, (1847), 1848, (1850), 1864; **47**, 1869 (*ṛshim*), 1872, 1875.—§ 54 (cf. Āstīkap.): One day *J.*, sleeping on the lap of his wife when the sun was setting, was awakened by her, lest the twilight should pass away without his prayers being said. *J.* felt insulted, as he believed that the sun had no power to set in the usual time if he was asleep. He therefore left her and again began to practise austerities: I, **47**, 1882, 1891, 1897, 1901, 1911.—§ 60 (Sarpasattra): I, **53**, 2064; **54**, 2079.—§ 68 (Āstīka): I, **58**, 2189 (*yo J°unā jātaḥ Jaratkārau*, i.e. Āstīka).—§ 565 (Gālavacarita): V, **117**, 3975 (*reme . . . yathā . . . J°ur Jaratkārvām*).

Jaratkāru[2], sister of Vāsuki, the king of serpents, wife of Jaratkāru, and mother of Āstīka. § 26 (Jaratkāru): I, **14**, 1056 (given in marriage to Jaratkāru).—§ 49 (Vāsuki): I, **38**, 1637 (*Vāsukeḥ sarparājasya . . . svasā*), 1639; **39**, 1642.—§ 50 (Jaratkāru): I, **40**, 1658.—§ 54 (do.): I, **47**, 1888, 1895, 1901, 1909 (offends her husband by awaking him).—§ 55 (Āstīka): I, **48**, 1912, 1919, (1920) (relates to Vāsuki the departure of her husband, and that he had said that she should give birth to a son).—§ 60 (Sarpasattra): I, **54**, 2067 (*bhujaṅgamā*), 2070 (*bhaginī nāgarājasya*), (2071), 2079 (related to her son Āstīka the curse of the serpents and their hope that he should deliver them).—§ 68 (Āstīka): I, **58**, 2189 (v. Jaratkāru[1]).—§ 565 (Gālavacarita): V, **117**, 3975 (v. Jaratkāru[1]).

Jaratkārusuta ("the son of Jaratkāru") = Āstīka: XV, 948 (*A°*).

Jarāyu, a mātṛ. § 615*u* (Skanda): IX, **46***θ*, 2637.

Jarāyujāḥ (pl.) = Çiva (1000 names[1]).

Jaritā, a çārṅgikā, wife of Mandapāla. § 259 (Çārṅgakop.): I, **229**, 8346 (*çārṅgikām*), 8349; **230**, 8365 (8366), (8379); **231**, (8386), (8390), (8396); **233**, 8441, 8445, 8449, 8452.

Jaritāri, the eldest son of Mandapāla and Jaritā. § 259 (Çārṅgakop.): I, **230**, 8372; **231**, 8403; **232**, (8404), (8410); **233**, 8434.

Jarjarānanā, a mātṛ. § 615*u* (Skanda): IX, **46***θ*, 2637.

Jartika, pl. (*°āḥ*), a tribe of the Bāhīkas. § 607 (Karṇap.): VIII, **44**, 2033 (*°ā nāma Bāhīkāḥ*).

Jārūthī (name of a city, Nīl.). § 317*b* (Kṛshṇa Vāsudeva): III, **12**, 489 (at *J.* Kṛshṇa slew Āhvṛti, etc.).

Jaṭādhara[1], a warrior of Skanda. § 615*u* (Skanda): IX, **45***η*, 2563.

Jaṭādhara[2] = Çiva: III, 1625; XIII, 1241 (1000 names[2]).

Jaṭālikā, a mātṛ. § 615*u* (Skanda): IX, **46***θ*, 2641.

Jaṭāsura[1], a Rākshasa. § 11 (Parvasaṅgr.): I, **2**, 455 (*°sya ca vadho Rākshasasya*).—§ 435 (Jaṭāsuravadhap.): III, **157**, 11455, 11521 (*J.* carries away Draupadī, the three Pāṇḍavas and their arms, but is checked and slain by Bhīmasena).—§ 551 (Kīcakavadhap.): IV, **21**, 685 (all. to § 435).—§ 555 (Sainyodyogap.): V, **8**, 223 (do.).—§ 600 (Ghaṭotkacavadhap.): VII, **174**, 7850 (*Rākshasāgryaḥ*, the father of Alambusha).—§ 623 (Rājadh.): XII, **16**, 501 (all. to § 435).—§ 779 (Açvamedhikap.): XIV, **12***a*, 324 (do.). Cf. Rakshas, Rākshasa.

Jaṭāsura[2], a prince. § 264 (Sabhākriyāp.): II, **4***β*, 119 (in the palace of Yudhishṭhira).

Jaṭāsurasuta ("the son of Jaṭāsura") = Alambusha: VII, 7848.

Jaṭāsuravadha(ḥ) ("the killing of Jaṭāsura"). § 10 (Parvasaṅgr.): I, **2**, 322 (*°aḥ parva*, i.e. Jaṭāsuravadhaparvan).

[Jaṭāsuravadhaparvan] ("the section treating of the killing of Jaṭāsura," being the 37th of the minor parvans of Mhbhr.). (Cf. Jaṭāsuravadha.) § 435: One day, after the *Rākshasas* with *Ghaṭotkaca* had departed, while *Bhīma* was a-hunting, and *Lomaça* and the other ṛshis had gone away to bathe and collect flowers, the *Rākshasa Jaṭāsura*, who had followed *Yudhishṭhira* in the guise of a brahman versed in all the *çāstras*, with the object of possessing himself of the arms of the *Pāṇḍavas* and of *Draupadī*, began to flee away with the arms and *Draupadī* and the three *Pāṇḍavas*. *Sahadeva* extricated himself, and snatching the sword *Kauçika*, he began to call *Bhīmasena*. *Yudhishṭhira* reproached him, saying that the *Rākshasas* are the root of virtue and know virtue (*dharmam*) best, and that the *Rākshasas*, gods, *Pitṛs*, *Siddhas*, *Ṛshis*, *Gandharvas*, etc., depend for their lives on men, etc. *Yudhishṭhira* then made himself ponderous. *Sahadeva* was about to attack the *Rākshasa*, when *Bhīma* appeared mace in hand. The *Rākshasa* set them down, and he and *Bhīma* began to fight with trees, like *Vālin* and *Sugrīva*, and then with rocks, and at last by wrestling, till *Bhīma*, having dealt a blow on the neck of the *Rākshasa*, lifted him up, and dashed him on the ground and severed his head from his body, and then presented himself before *Yudhishṭhira* (III, **157**).

Jāṭāsuri ("the son of Jaṭāsura") = Alambusha: VII, 7856, 7865, 7868, 7869.

Jātavedas = Agni, q.v.

Jātavedasī = Durgā (Umā): VI, 802.

Jaṭāyu(s), a vulture, brother of Sampāti. § 128 (Aṃçāvat.): I, **66**, 2634 (*°usham*, son of Aruṇa and Çyenī, and brother of Sampāti). § 525 (Rāmopākhyānap.): III, **275**, 15873 (*gṛdhram J°usham*, had been slain by Rāvaṇa, cf. § 530).—§ 529 (Sītāharaṇa): III, **278**, 16043 (*gṛdhro J°uḥ*).—§ 530 (Viçvāvasumokshaṇa): III, **279**, 16045 (*sakhā Daçarathasyāsīj J°r Aruṇātmajaḥ | gṛdhrarājo mahāvīraḥ Sampātir yasya sodaraḥ*, tried to deliver Sītā, but was slain by Rāvaṇa).—§ 534 (Hanūmatpratyāgamana): III, **282**, 16242 (*gṛdhrasya J°oḥ*), 16244 (*°oḥ*), 16246 (*°ushaḥ, c.:* once *J.* and his elder brother Sampāti, competing with each other, flew towards the sun; Sampāti's wings were burnt, but those of *J.* not), 16249.

Jaṭhara, pl. (*°āḥ*, a people). § 574 (Jambūkh.): VI, **9***μ*, 350 (in Bhāratavarsha).

Jāṭhara[1], a warrior of Skanda. § 615*u* (Skanda): IX, **45***η*, 2564.

Jāṭhara[2] = Sūrya (the Sun): III, 149 (*agniḥ*).

Jaṭila = Çiva, q.v. (add. XIII, 981, 6386).

Jaṭilā, a female descendant of Gotama. § 237 (Vaivāhikap.): I, **196**, 7265 (*Gautamī*, in the Purāṇas it is related that she married seven ṛshis). Cf. Gautamī.

Jaṭin[1] = Çiva, q.v.

Jaṭin[2], a warrior of Skanda. § 615*u* (Skanda): IX, **45***η*, 2563.

Jātismara, a tīrtha. § 370 (Tīrthayātrāp.): III, **84**, 8106 (by bathing there one *jātismaratvam apnoti*).

Jātismarahrada, a tīrtha. § 370 (Tīrthayātrāp.): III, **85**, 8180.

[Jatugṛhaparvan] ("the section relating to the lac-house," the 8th of the minor parvans of Mhbhr.). (Cf. Jatuveçmākhya[m parva].) § 213: *Vaiçampāyana* briefly related the plan of *Saubala*, *Duryodhana*, *Duḥçāsana*, *Karṇa*, and *Dhṛtarāshṭra* to burn the *Pāṇḍavas* and *Kuntī* in a lac-house, and their escape. Asked by *Janamejaya*, he then began to relate it more fully. The *Pāṇḍavas* frustrated all the plans of murdering them laid by *Duryodhana*, etc., without speaking of them, in obedience to the counsels of *Vidura*. People began to speak in all public places of installing *Yudhishṭhira* on the throne instead of *Dhṛtarāshṭra*. *Duryodhana* represented to *Dhṛtarāshṭra* that this would for ever exclude himself and his brothers from the throne (I, **141**). *Duryodhana, Karṇa, Çakuni,* and *Duḥçāsana* held a consultation together, and *Duryodhana* prevailed upon *Dhṛtarāshṭra* to exile the *Pāṇḍavas* to *Vāraṇāvata* ("*Açvatthāman* is on my side; with him follow *Droṇa* and *Kṛpa*; *Vidura* is dependent on us for his means of life, though he is covertly with the foe") (I, **142**). *Duryodhana* and his brothers began gradually to win over the people to their side by grants of wealth and honours, while *Dhṛtarāshṭra* suggested to the *Pāṇḍavas* to visit the festival of *Paçupati* at *Vāraṇāvata*. Fully understanding the motives of *Dhṛtarāshṭra, Yudhishṭhira* let *Bhīshma, Vidura, Droṇa, Bāhlīka, Somadatta, Kṛpa, Açvatthāman, Bhūriçravas, Gāndhārī,* etc., give them their benedictions, and the *Pāṇḍavas* having performed propitiatory rites in order to obtain the kingdom, set out for *Vāraṇāvata* (I, **143**). *Duryodhana* prevailed upon *Purocana* to reach *Vāraṇāvata* that very day upon a swift chariot, and to construct a house of inflammable materials and burn the *Pāṇḍavas* and *Kuntī* (I, **144**). The people, who were distressed by the departure of the *Pāṇḍavas,* and angry with *Dhṛtarāshṭra,* were calmed by *Yudhishṭhira*. *Vidura,* in obscure words (cf. *Mlecchavācā,* v. 5803), warned *Yudhishṭhira,* who explained the meaning to *Kuntī*. They set out on the 8th day of the month of *Phālguna* when *Rohiṇī* was ascendant (I, **145**). They were received with great honours by the citizens of *Vāraṇāvata* and installed by *Purocana* first in a palace that had been built for them, and after ten days in the lac-house called *Çiva* (*Çivākhyam*). *Yudhishṭhira* scented the smell of fat, etc., and told it to *Bhīma,* but resolved to seem unsuspicious (I, **146**). A miner, sent by *Vidura,* told *Yudhishṭhira* that *Purocana* would put fire to the house on the fourteenth night of the dark lunation, and made a large subterranean passage (I, **147**). They lived there for a year. Then on a certain night *Kuntī* fed a large number of *brahmans*; and there came also a *Nishāda* woman with her five sons, who became intoxicated and lay down in the house to sleep. The *Pāṇḍavas* then set fire to the house and burnt *Purocana* and the *Nishādas,* while they themselves escaped through the subterranean passage and fled in haste, *Bhīma* carrying his mother and brothers (cf. III, v. 546 foll.). The citizens thought they had been burnt to death (I, **148**). A person sent by *Vidura* took the *Pāṇḍavas* and *Kuntī* to the other side of the *Gaṅgā* in a boat (I, **149**). The miner had covered the hole he had dug with ashes, and the townspeople thought that the *Nishāda* woman with her five sons were *Kuntī* and the *Pāṇḍavas,* and sent to *Dhṛtarāshṭra* to inform him that they had been burnt to death together with *Purocana*. *Dhṛtarāshṭra* wept in deep sorrow, and caused the funeral rites to be performed. Meanwhile the *Pāṇḍavas* having crossed the *Gaṅgā* proceeded in the darkness to the south and reached a dense forest. *Yudhishṭhira* then prevailed upon *Bhīma* to carry *Kuntī* and his brothers (I, **150**). The motion of *Bhīma's* legs raised a wind like that of the months of *Çuci* and *Çukra,* while he trod down the trees and swam across streams. Towards evening they sat down in a terrible forest under a banyan-tree. *Kuntī* was thirsty, and *Bhīma* proceeded to a pool at a distance of a *gavyūti,* and brought water by soaking his upper garments. When he found them sleeping from fatigue, he lamented that *Yudhishṭhira* would not yet allow him to slay *Duryodhana,* etc., and sat there awake keeping watch over them (I, **151**).

Jātūkarṇa, a ṛshi. § 264 (Sabhākriyāp.): II, **4***a*, 109 (in the palace of Yudhishṭhira).

Jatuveçmākhya ("named from the lac-house," sc. parva). § 11 (Parvasaṅgr.): I, **2**, 361 (i.e. Jatugṛhaparvan).

Jāvāli, v. Jābāli.

Javana, a warrior of Skanda. § 615*u* (Skanda): IX, **45**η, 2577.

Jaya[1], a son of Dhṛtarāshṭra, or an adherent of Duryodhana. § 83 (Ādivaṃçāvatāraṇa): I, **63***a*, 2448 (enumeration of eleven sons of Dhṛtarāshṭra who were *mahārathas*).—§ 298 (Dyūtap.): II, **58**, †2004.—§ 552 (Goharaṇap.): IV, **54**, 1666 (attacks Arjuna).—§ 561 (Yānasandhip.): V, **58**τ, 2301.—§ 576 (Bhagavadgītāp.): VI, **18**δ, 687; **20**, †752.—§ 578 (Bhīshmavadhap.): VI, **44***a*, 1653.—§ 583 (do.): VI, **77**κ, 3343.—§ 592 (Saṃçaptakavadhap.): VII, **20**η, 804; **25**, 1108 (son of Dhṛtarāshṭra).—§ 596 (Pratijñāp.): VII, **74**β, 2628.—§ 598 (Jayadrathavadhap.): VII, **85**β, 3036.—§ 599 (do.): VII, **91***a*, 3253; **135**$\phi\phi$, 5564 (son of Dhṛtarāshṭra).—§ 600 (Ghaṭotkacavadhap.): VII, **156**κ, 6851; **158**ψ, 7030, (ω), 7036.—§ 604: VIII, **7**, †207.

Jaya[2] ("victory"), a god. § 258 (Khāṇḍavadahanap.): I, **227**, 8266 (armed with a mace *J.* partook in the encounter between the gods and Arjuna and Kṛshṇa). Cf. Jayanta.

Jaya[3], an ancient king. § 267 (Yamasabhāv.): II, **8**, 326 (in the palace of Yama).

Jaya[4] = Sūrya: III, 154 (only C., B. has *Çayaḥ*).

Jaya[5] = Arjuna, q.v.

Jaya[6] (one of the occult names which Yudhishṭhira gave to the Pāṇḍavas). § 549 (Pāṇḍavapraveçap.): IV, **5**, 176.—§ 551 (Kīcakavadhap.): IV, **23***a*, 804.

Jaya[7], a serpent. § 564 (Mātalīyop.): V, **103**γ, 3632.—§ 615*u* (Skanda): IX, **45**, 2554 (given to Skanda by Vāsuki).

Jaya[8], a Pāṇḍava warrior. § 600 (Ghaṭotkacavadhap.): VII, **156**, 6911 (is slain by Açvatthāman).

Jaya[9], a Pāñcāla prince. § 608 (Karṇap.): VIII, **56**, 2735 (fights with Karṇa).

Jaya[10] ("Victory," personif.). § 615*u* (Skanda): IX, **46**κ, 2682.

Jaya[11] = Çiva (1000 names[1]).

Jaya[12] = Vishṇu (1000 names).

Jaya[13], name of a muhūrta. § 554 (Sainyodyogap.): V, **6**, 125 (*muhūrtena*).

Jaya[14] ("victory"), said of the Mhbhr.: I, 2302 (*jayo nāmetihāso 'yam*); XVIII, 194 (do.). Cf. also the introductory çloka of the single books (*Nārāyaṇaṃ namaskṛtya Narañ caiva narottamam | devīṃ Sarasvatīñ caiva tato jayam udīrayet*), and XVIII, 232 (do.).—Do., said of the episode Vidulāputrānuçāsana: V, 4639 (*jayo nāmetihāso 'yam*).

Jayā = Durgā (Umā): IV, 194; VI, 798.

Jayāçva, a Pāṇḍava warrior. § 600 (Ghaṭotkacavadhap.): VII, **158**χ, 7012 (brother of Virāṭa?).

Jayadbala (one of the occult names which Yudhishṭhira gave to the Pāṇḍavas): § 549 (Pāṇḍavapr.): IV, **5**, 176.—§ 551 (Kīcakavadhap.): IV, **23***a*, 804.

Jayadharman, a Kuru warrior. § 600 (Ghaṭotkacavadhap.): VII, **156**κ, 6852.

Jayadratha[1], king of the Sindhus, son of Vṛddhakshatra. § 11 (Parvasaṅgr.): I, **2**, 473, 532, 533.—§ 130 (Aṃçāvat.): I, **67**, 2745 (married Duḥçalā, the daughter of Dhṛtarāshṭra).—§ 182 (Dhṛtarāshṭraputranāmak.): I, **117**, 4557 (do.).—§ 232 (Svayaṃvarap.): I, **186**, 7001 (present at the svayaṃvara of Draupadī).—§ 287 (Rājasūyikap.): II, **34**, 1267 (*Saindhavaḥ*, came to the rājasūya of Yudhishṭhira, C. has by error *Draya°*).—§ 288 (do.): II, **35**, 1293 (do.).—§ 290 (Çiçupālavadhap.): II, **44a**, 1534.—§ 298 (Dyūtap.): II, **58**, 2017 (present at the gambling).—§ 522 (Draupadīharaṇap.): III, **264**, 15581 (*rājā Sindhūnāṃ Vārddhakshatriḥ*); **265**, †15599 (*Sauvīrarājaḥ*); **267**, 15618, (15631); **268**, (†15648), †15662, 15664; **269**, †15683, †15693; **270**, †15696; **271**, 15747 (*Sindhurājaḥ*), 15750, 15751, 15752 (*J.* sees Draupadī and carries her off, but is overtaken by the Pāṇḍavas; after a battle *J.* took to flight). —§ 523 (Jayadrathavimokshanap.): III, **272**, 15777, 15788, 15791, 15796, 15800 (*J.* is seized by *Bhīmasena*, but set free again).—§ 524 (do.): III, **272**, (15804), 15858 (gratified Çiva, who granted him the boon that he might vanquish the Pāṇḍavas, except Arjuna).—§ 525 (Rāmopākhyānap.): III, **273**, 15860 (*vinirjitya J°ṃ*), 15867 (all. to § 522).—§ 544 (Yudhishṭhirāçvāsa): III, **292**, 16611 (do.).—§ 545 (Pativratāmāhātmyap.): III, **293**, 16617 (*°ena hṛtā*, sc. Draupadī, all. to § 522).—§ 551 (Kīcakavadhap.): IV, **21**, 686 (*°n tathaiva tvam ajaishīḥ*, sc. Bhīmasena, all. to § 523).—§ 555 (Sainyodyogap.): V, **19δ**, 588 (came with one akshauhiṇī of Sindhus and Sauvīras to Duryodhana).—§ 561 (Yānasandhip.): V, **47a**, 1796; **55λ**, 2186 (*Sindhurājaḥ*), (ν), 2206; **57ξ**, 2246 (assigned to Arjuna as his match in the battle), (π), 2268, (σ), 2290; **62ββ**, †2426; [**66εε**, 2504 (*Saindhavaṃ*)].—§ 562 (Bhagavadyānap.): V, **92τ**, 3284; [**95ν**, 3403 (*Saindhavaḥ*)] —§ 567 (do.): V, **124δ**, 4171.—§ 569 (do.): V, **142ε**, 4824; **144**, 4890.—§ 570 (Sainyaniryāṇap.): V, **155θ**, 5274 (*Saindhavaṃ*, commander of one akshauhiṇī of Duryodhana's army).—§ 571 (Ulūkadūtāgamanap.): V, **160**, †5532 (*°ādriṃ*, sc. *purushodadhiṃ*, i.e. the army of Duryodhana); **161**, †5575 (do.); [**164ε**, 5708 (*Saindhavāya*, Sātyaki is pitted against *J.*)].—[§ 572 (Rathātirathasaṅkhyānap.): V, **165**, 5743 (*Sindhurājaḥ*, equal to two *rathas*, all. to §§ 522, 523)].—§ 573 (Ambopākhyānap.): V, **195ε**, 7608 (*Saindhavaḥ*, in the army of Duryodhana).—§ 576 (Bhagavadgītāp.): VI, **16a**, 622 (commander of one akshauhiṇī of Duryodhana's army); **17**, 665 (on his standard there was a boar of silver); **25ι**, 837; **35**, †1280.—§ 578 (Bhīshmavadhap.): VI, **45**^{15}, 1723 (*Saindhavaṃ*, fought with Drupada); **50o**, 2070.—§ 580 (do.): VI, **56β**, 2407 (in the neck of Bhīshma's gāruḍavyūha); **57ι**, 2452 (*Saindhavaḥ*); **59μ**, †2583.—§ 581 (do.): VI, **60a**, †2652; **65**, 2910.—§ 582 (do.): VI, **71**^{10}γ, 3133, [3138 (*Saindhavaḥ*, fought with Bhīmasena). —§ 583 (do.): VI, **76ι**, 3329; **79**^{12}, 3469 (attacked Bhīmasena).—§ 584 (do.): VI, **85**^{7}, †3762, †3782 (fought with Bhīmasena).—§ 585 (do.): VI, **92χ**, 4118, [4134 (*Sindhurājñaḥ . . . varāhaṃ* (B. *vā°*) *svarṇabhūshitaṃ*)]; [**94ω**, 4195 (*Saindhavaḥ*)].—[§ 586 (do.): VI, **99a**, 4501 (*Saindhavaḥ*, in the van of Bhīshma's *sarvatobhadra* array); **100η**, 4545 (*Saindhavaṃ*).]—§ 587 (do.): VI, **108δ**, 5050 (*Saindhavaṃ*); **113ι**, 5240 (*Saindhavaḥ*), 5250 (pierced by Bhīmasena); **114κ**, 5292 (*Saindhavaṃ*, pierced by Arjuna), 5295 (pierces Arjuna and Bhīmasena), 5309 (*Saindhavaḥ*); **115**, 5362 (*Vṛddhakshatrasya dāyādaṃ*, attacked by Virāṭa); [**116**, 5417 (*Saindhavaḥ*, encounter with Virāṭa]; **119φ**, 5583 (*Saindhavaḥ*).—[§ 589 (Droṇābhishekap.): VII, **7γ**, 179 (*Saindhavaḥ*).]—§ 590 (do.): VII, **14**, 556, 560, 570 (is vanquished by Abhimanyu).—§ 592 (Saṃçaptakavadhap.): VII, **20η**, 804 (in Droṇa's gāruḍavyūha); [**25**, 1074 (*Saindhavaḥ*, fought with Kshatravarman)]; **32ω**, 1410, (εε), 1441; [**34**, 1503 (*Sindhurājaḥ*), 1505 (*Sindhurājasya*)]. —§ 593 (Abhimanyuvadhap.): VII, **42**, 1747 (*Saindhavasya putraḥ*), 1755, 1756 (*Sindhurājaḥ*), 1758 (had obtained the boon from Çiva that he should check the four Pāṇḍavas, cf. § 524); [**43** (vanquishes the Pāṇḍavas)].—§ 594 (do.): VII, **52**, 2007 (*Saindhavena*, *J.* had prevented the Pāṇḍavas from rescuing Abhimanyu).—§ 596 (Pratijñāp.): VII, **73**, 2574 (*Saindhavako rājā*, do.), 2586, 2587, 2588, 2595, 2597, 2600, 2603, 2605 (Arjuna promises to slay *J.*); **74**, 2613; **75**, 2657, 2674, 2676 (six of the Kuru chariot-warriors promise to protect *J.*); **76**, 2680, 2702; [**77**, 2723 (*Saindhavo bālaghātakaḥ*), 2725 (*Saindhavasya*)]; **79**, 2796, 2797, 2800; **80**, 2830, 2839.—§ 598 (Jayadrathavadhap.): VII, **87**, 3097, 3102 (*Sindhurājaḥ*), 3104 (description of his horses), (ι) 3114.—§ 599 (do.): VII, **91**, 3223, 3251 (*Bībhatsur J°vadhotsukaḥ*), 3260; **94**, 3414, 3416, 3425; **100**, 3749, 3759; **101**, 3777, 3792, 3793; **103**, 3883; **104μ**, 3894, 3912, 3917 (pierced Arjuna); **105ν**, 3946 (on the top of the standard of *J.* there was a silver boar, decked with golden garlands and of the splendour of white crystal (read *dhvajāgre 'lohitārkābho*, with B.)), 3961; **110**, 4209; **111**, 4246, 4249, 4250, 4254; **112**, 4300, 4302; **124**, 4979, 4985; **128**, 5264; **137ωω**, 5629; **141**, 5872; [**143κκκ**, 6005 (*Saindhavena*)]; **145**, 6057, 6061, 6065, †6066, 6072, 6074, 6076; **146**, 6196, 6200, 6205, 6222, 6229, 6230 (Arjuna vanquishes all the protectors of Jayadratha).—§ 599g (Vṛddhakshatra): VII, **146**, 6259, 6265 (Vṛddhakshatra, the father of *J.*, had pronounced the curse that the head of that person who would cause the head of *J.* to fall to the earth should break into pieces).—§ 599 (Jayadrathavadhap.): VII, **146**, 6267, 6286 (Arjuna cut off the head of *J.*, Kṛshna caused it to fall on the lap of Vṛddhakshatra, from there it fell on the earth; according to the curse the head of Vṛddhakshatra broke to pieces); **148**, †6445 (*hataṃ*); **149ψψψ**, 6475; **150a**^{1}, 6501 (*hataḥ*), (β^{1}), 6507 (do.); 6526 (do.); **152δ**^{1}, 6580.—§ 600 (Ghaṭotkacavadhap.): VII, **158**, 7035 (mentioned among the slain); **159**, 7046 (*Gāṇḍīvadhanvā hatavān . . . J°ṃ*); [**182ηηη**, 8281 (*Saindhavaḥ*)].—§ 603 (Nārāyaṇāstramokshap.): VII, **197**, 9118 (*°çiro yathā*).—§ 604 (Karṇap.): VIII, **5ζ**, 100 (*Sindhurāshṭramukhānīha daça rāshṭrāṇi yāni ha | vaçe tishṭhanti vīrasya yaḥ sthitaḥ tava çāsane | akshauhiṇīr daçaikāñ ca vinirjitya çitaiḥ çaraiḥ | Arjunena hato, rājan, mahāvīryo J°ḥ*).—§ 608 (do.): VIII, **73**, 3676 (had been protected by Droṇa), 3681.—§ 609 (Çalyap.): IX, **2ζ**, 72 (had sided with Duryodhana), 90 (*nihataḥ*).—§ 610 (do.): IX, **4**, 198 (*hate*), 217, 219 (*hataḥ*); **5ν**, 278 (has been slain).—§ 611 (do.): IX, **24νν**, 1299 (*nihate*), **27ττ**, 1457 (*hataḥ*).—§ 613 (Gadāyuddhap.): IX, **32β**, 1836.—§ 615 (do.): IX, **61**, 3433 (*°ena pāpena yat Kṛshṇā kleçitā vane*, all. to § 522); **64εε**, 3614 (*Saindhavaṃ*).—§ 618 (Jalapradānikap.): XI, **12λ**, 320 (*hatvā . . . J°ṃ*).—§ 619 (Strīvilāpap.): XI, **16a**, 454; **20ε**, 585; **22η**, 624, 625 (*Sindhu-Sauvīrabhartāraṃ*), 628, 629 (lamented for as dead).—§ 620 (Çrāddhap.): XI, **26β**, 787 (his body is cremated).—§ 785 (Anugītāp.): XIV, **77**, 2231 (*Sindhurājasya*, the Sindhus attacked Arjuna in order to revenge the death of *J.*); **78**, 2269 (*°ṃ hataṃ smṛtvā*), 2287 (the son of *J.* and Duḥçalā had died, leaving a son who was yet a little child); **84**, 2497 (*apāharat . . . J°çiro yathā*, sc. Arjuna).—§ 787 (Āçramavāsap.): XV, **14σ**, 415 (Yudhishṭhira caused the çrāddha of *J.*, etc., to be performed).—§ 795 (Svargārohaṇap.): XVIII, **5λ**, 150.

Cf. also the following synonyms :—

Saindhava, Saindhavaka, q.v.
Sauvīra, Sauvīraka, Sauvīrarāja, q.v.
Sindhupati, Sindhurāj, Sindhurāja, Sindhurājan, Sindhu-Sauvīrabhartṛ, q.v.
Suvīra, Suvīrarāshṭrapa, q.v.
Vārddhakshatri ("the son of Vṛddhakshatra"): III, 15576 (*rājā Sindhūnām*), 1558 (*J*°); VI, †752; VII, 1748; XI, 623.

Jayadratha[2], an ancient king. § 267 (Yamasabhāv.): II, **8**, 337 (in the palace of Yama).

Jayadrathavadha(ḥ) ("the slaughter of Jayadratha"). § 10 (Parvas.): I, **2**, 339 (°*aḥ parva*, i.e. Jayadrathavadhaparvan).

[**Jayadrathavadhaparvan**] ("the section including the slaughter of Jayadratha," the 75th of the minor parvans of Mhbhr.; cf. Jayadrathavadha). § 598: *Dhṛtarāshṭra* lamented the slaughter of his troops; "formerly in the abode of *Somadatta*, who was devoted to truth, I used to hear delightful sounds" (instead of grief and lamentations, as now in the houses of *Viviṃçati*, etc. (*a*)); then he mentioned *Kṛshṇa's* ambassadorship, the match at dice, that he and *Vidura*, etc. (β) did not approve of; "possessed of sovereignty, the *Pāṇḍavas* will ever listen to the voice of *Çalya*, etc." (γ); "none can fight *Bhīmasena*, etc. (δ); only *Duryodhana*, etc. (ε), would venture to resist them"; he asked what the principal leaders (ζ) did (VII, **85**). *Sañjaya* rebuked *Dhṛtarāshṭra* for his folly in bringing about the battle (VII, **86**). *Droṇa* arrayed his divisions. The warriors shouted in anger "where is Arjuna?" etc. (η). *Droṇa* assured *Jayadratha* of protection by *Somadatta's* son, etc. (θ). *Droṇa's* array was in part a *çakaṭa* and in part a circle, 48 miles long, and the width of its rear was 20 miles; in the rear was another impenetrable array in the form of a lotus; and within that a needle, in the mouth of the needle was *Kṛtavarman*; next came the *Kāmboja* king, etc. (ι); behind them all was *Jayadratha* at one side of the needle. At the head of the *çakaṭa* was *Droṇa* (*b*). Si. and Cā. wondered. *Duryodhana* rejoiced (VII, **87**). After the *Rudra*-hour (*Raudre muhūrte*) had set in *Arjuna* made his appearance, while portents appeared in nature. Then *Nakula's* son *Çatānīka* and *Dhṛshṭadyumna* arrayed the divisions of the *Pāṇḍavas*. *Durmarshaṇa* (Dhārtarāshṭra) took up his position in the van in order to oppose *Arjuna*; *Arjuna* was at the very van of his army. *Kṛshṇa* and *Arjuna* blew their conches. The *Kuru* army was afraid (VII, **88**).—§ 599: THE FOURTEENTH DAY'S BATTLE. *Arjuna* & *Durmarshaṇa*; a terrible carnage was caused by *Arjuna*; *Durmarshaṇa's* division fled away (VII, **89**). *Duḥçāsana* & *Arjuna*; *Duḥçāsana's* division was slaughtered and routed; he sought protection with *Droṇa* (VII, **90**). *Arjuna* met with *Droṇa* and prayed for leave to slay *Jayadratha*; *Droṇa* refused leave and attacked *Arjuna*; unable to vanquish *Droṇa*, *Arjuna* avoided him from fear of losing time, and penetrated into the *Kuru* army, the *Pāñcāla* princes, *Yudhāmanyu* and *Uttamaujas*, being the protectors of his wheels; *Jaya*, etc. (*a*), opposed *Arjuna*, and so did the *Abhīshāhas*, etc. (β), with *Droṇa* at their head (VII, **91**). *Droṇa* & *Arjuna*, who employed the *Brāhma* weapon. *Arjuna* avoided *Droṇa*, began to slaughter the *Bhojas*, and took up his position between *Kṛtavarman* and the *Kāmboja* king *Sudakshiṇa*. *Arjuna* & *Kṛtavarman*, who was stupefied; *Arjuna* proceeded to the division of the *Kāmbojas*. *Kṛtavarman* & *Yudhāmanyu* + *Uttamaujas*, who were prevented by *Kṛtavarman* from following *Arjuna*, who did not slay *Kṛtavarman*. *Çrutāyudha* (*b*) & *Arjuna* (+ *Kṛshṇa*); *Çrutāyudha* attacked *Kṛshṇa* with his mace, which returned and slew *Çrutāyudha* himself; all the troops fled away. The *Kāmboja* king *Sudakshiṇa* & *Arjuna*, who slew him; all the troops fled away (VII, **92**). *Arjuna* slew the *Abhīshāhas*, etc. (γ). *Çrutāyus* + *Acyutāyus* & *Arjuna*, who slew them both with the *Aindra* weapon. *Niyatāyus* + *Dīrghāyus* (the sons of *Çrutāyus* and *Acyutāyus*) & *Arjuna*, who slew them both. The *Aṅgas* (on elephants) + the *Kaliṅga* king, etc. (on elephants; urged by *Duryodhana*), & *Arjuna*, who caused a great carnage among them, as also among the *Mlecchas*, *Yavanas*, etc. (δ). The *Ambastha* king *Çrutāyus* & *Arjuna* (+ *Kṛshṇa*), who slew him (VII, **93**). *Duryodhana* addressed *Droṇa* in wrath and affection. *Droṇa* acknowledged his inability to oppose *Arjuna* on account of his own old age. *Droṇa* cased *Duryodhana* in invulnerable armour (invoking the *Vedas*, *Nahusha*, etc. (ε)) and urged him to oppose *Arjuna*; with this armour he need have no fear from As., D., Y., U., Rā., men, etc. It was the armour that *Çiva* had given to *Indra*, by means of which he slew *Vṛtra* (*c*); *Indra* > *Aṅgiras* > *Bṛhaspati* > *Agniveçya* > *Droṇa*. It was put on, its pieces being joined with *Brāhma* strings. *Brahmán* had himself put it on *Vishṇu* in days of yore, and on *Indra* in the flight about *Tārakā*. *Duryodhana* + *Trigartas*, etc., proceeded towards the chariot of *Arjuna* (VII, **94**). The *Pāṇḍavas* (headed by *Dhṛshṭadyumna*) + *Somakas* & *Droṇa*; a fierce battle ensued in front of the *Kuru* array; *Droṇa* & *Dhṛshṭadyumna*; *Droṇa's* host became divided into three bodies: one which retreated towards *Kṛtavarman*, another towards *Jalasandha*, another towards *Droṇa* himself; *Viviṃçati*, etc. (ζ), & *Bhīmasena*; king *Bāhlīka* & the *Draupadeyas*; the *Govāsana* chief *Çaibya* & the *Kāçi* king; the *Madra* king *Çalya* & *Yudhishṭhira*; *Duḥçāsana* & *Sātyaki*; *Sañjaya* & *Cekitāna*; *Çakuni* (+ 700 *Gāndhāras*) & *Sahadeva*; *Vinda* and *Anuvinda* & *Virāṭa*; king *Bāhlīka* & *Çikhaṇḍin*; the *Avanti* chief + the *Sauvīras* and *Prabhadrakas* & *Dhṛshṭadyumna*; *Alāyudha* & *Ghaṭotkaca*; *Kuntibhoja* and Rā. *Alambusha*. *Jayadratha* remained in the rear, protected by *Kṛpa*, etc., and the protectors of his wheels were *Açvatthāman* on the right and *Karṇa* on the left; his rear was protected by *Kṛpa*, etc. (η), headed by *Somadatta's* son (VII, **95**). *Droṇa*, in front of his array, fought the *Pārthas*. *Vinda* and *Anuvinda* & *Virāṭa*; *Çikhaṇḍin* & *Bāhlīka*; the *Govāsana* king *Çaibya* & the *Kāçi* king; the *Bāhlīka* king & the *Draupadeyas*; *Duḥçasana* & *Sātyaki*; *Kuntibhoja* & *Alambusha*; *Nakula* and *Sahadeva* & *Çakuni*, who fled towards *Droṇa*; Rā. *Ghaṭotkaca* & Rā. *Alāyudha*; *Yudhishṭhira* & *Çalya*; *Viviṃçati*, etc. (θ), & *Bhīmasena* (VII, **96**). *Bhīmasena* & *Jalasandha*; *Yudhishṭhira* & *Kṛtavarman*; *Dhṛshṭadyumna* & *Droṇa*; *Dhṛshṭadyumna* mounted *Droṇa's* chariot, had his *pārshṇi* charioteers slain, etc., but was rescued by *Sātyaki*; *Droṇa* & *Sātyaki* (VII, **97**). *Sātyaki* (*Yuyudhāna*) & *Droṇa*; D. (headed by *Brahmán* and *Soma*), Si., Cā., Vd., M.-U. looked at; *Droṇa* acknowledged in *Sātyaki* the force of *Rāma*, etc. (ι); D. (with *Indra*), G., Si., and Cā. admired him; *Droṇa* invoked the *Āgneya* weapon, *Sātyaki* the *Vāruṇa* weapon. Just at that time the sun went down in his course. *Yudhishṭhira*, etc. (κ) (in order to protect *Sātyaki*), & *Droṇa* (protected by *Duḥçāsana*, etc.) (VII, **98**). *Arjuna* and *Kṛshṇa* steadily proceeded towards *Jayadratha* (description). *Vinda* and *Anuvinda* & *Arjuna*, who slew them both. While *Kṛshṇa* groomed *Arjuna's* steeds, *Arjuna* on foot held the whole *Kuru* army in check, and piercing the earth with a weapon made a lake for his steeds to drink from, and an arrow hall for them to rest within; *Nārada* came to see the lake (VII, **99**). The Si. and Cā., etc., applauded. The *Kurus* fiercely attacked *Arjuna* while he was on foot; *Arjuna* beat back all his assailants; the *Kurus* applauded his prowess, blaming *Duryodhana*. After finishing the grooming *Kṛshṇa* reharnessed the steeds and proceeded with great speed. *Duryodhana* followed (VII, **100**). The progress of *Arjuna* (with *Kṛshṇa*) became irresistible. *Duryodhana* outran *Arjuna* in a single chariot, and then turned back, facing *Kṛshṇa* (VII, **101**). *Kṛshṇa* pointed out *Duryodhana* to *Arjuna* and urged him to slay him ("the three worlds with D., As., and men cannot vanquish thee, what need be said of *Duryodhana*?"), mentioning *Duryodhana's* injuries (λ); *Arjuna* promised to slay him; *Arjuna* & *Duryodhana* (VII, **102**). *Arjuna* failed to pierce *Duryodhana* in consequence of the latter's invulnerable armour; "the chief of the gods gave this invulnerable armour to *Aṅgiras* > *Bṛhaspati* > *Indra* > *Arjuna*." *Arjuna* shot strong arrows, strengthened by *mantras*, at *Duryodhana*, which were cut off by *Açvatthāman*; this weapon could not be used again lest it should slay *Arjuna* himself. *Arjuna* deprived *Duryodhana* of his chariot, and steeds, and weapons; when *Kṛshṇa* blew *Pāñcajanya* and *Arjuna* drew *Gāṇḍīva*, the *Kurus* fell down on the ground. The protectors of *Jayadratha* attacked *Kṛshṇa* and *Arjuna* (VII, **103**). *Bhūriçravas*, etc. (μ) (with *Saindhava* horses, etc.), & *Arjuna*, who blew *Devadatta*, as *Kṛshṇa* blew *Pāñcajanya*; *Duryodhana* + *Bhūriçravas*, etc. (μ), & *Arjuna*; *Açvatthāman* & *Arjuna* (+ *Kṛshṇa*) (VII, **104**). *Sañjaya* described to *Dhṛtarāshṭra* the standards (ν). *Arjuna*, assailed by many chariot-warriors, slew many of them (VII, **105**). In the afternoon: The *Pāñcālas* and the *Pāṇḍavas* (desirous of slaying *Droṇa*) & the *Kurus*; *Bṛhatkshattra* (among the *Kaikayas*) & *Droṇa*; *Kshemadhūrti* & *Bṛhatkshattra*; *Dhṛshṭaketu* (the *Cedi*) & *Kshemadhūrti*; *Vīradhanvan* & *Dhṛshṭaketu*; *Yudhishṭhira* & *Droṇa*; *Vikarṇa* (Dhārtarāshṭra) & *Nakula*; *Durmukha* & *Sahadeva*; *Vyāghradatta* & *Sātyaki*; *Bhūriçravas* & the *Draupadeyas*; Rā. *Alambusha* (*Ṛshyaçṛṅga's* son) & *Bhīmasena*; *Yudhishṭhira* & *Droṇa*; *Yudhishṭhira* displayed great heroism; both he and *Droṇa* invoked the *Brāhma* weapon; *Yudhishṭhira*, in distress, getting upon the chariot of *Sahadeva* is borne away from the field (VII, **106**). *Kshemadhūrti* & the *Kaikaya* prince *Bṛhatkshattra*, who slew *Kshemadhūrti*; *Vīradhanvan* & *Dhṛshṭaketu* (advancing against *Droṇa*); Si. and Cā. wondered; *Vīradhanvan* was slain by *Dhṛshṭaketu*; *Durmukha* (Dhārtarāshṭra) & *Sahadeva*; *Durmukha* mounted the chariot of *Niramitra*, who was slain by *Sahadeva*; *Nakula* & *Vikarṇa* (Dhārtarāshṭra), whom he vanquished; *Vyāghradatta* (*Magadha* prince) & *Sātyaki*, who slew him; the *Magadhas* & *Sātyaki*, who nearly exterminated them; the *Kurus* were routed; *Droṇa* & *Sātyaki* (VII, **107**); *Bhūriçravas* & the *Draupadeyas*; *Çatānīka* (the son of *Nakula*), etc. (ξ), & *Bhūriçravas*, who was slain by the son of *Sahadeva*; Rā. *Alambusha* (son of *Ṛshyaçṛṅga*; recollecting the slaughter of his brother *Baka*) & *Bhīmasena*; *Alambusha* resorted to illusive tricks and caused a river of blood with Rā., etc., wafting away countless *Cedis*, etc. (ο); *Bhīma* employed the *Tvāshṭra* weapon; *Alambusha* fled to *Droṇa* (VII, **108**). *Ghaṭotkaca* & *Alambusha*; both availed themselves of their illusive power; the *Pāṇḍavas* (*Bhīmasena*, etc.) & *Alambusha*; *Bhīmasena's* son, etc. (π), & do., who was slain by *Ghaṭotkaca* (VII, **109**). *Yuyudhāna* & *Droṇa*; *Yudhishṭhira* urged *Dhṛshṭadyumna* and all his troops, headed by *Bhīmasena*, to rescue *Yuyudhāna*; *Yudhishṭhira* (with all his troops) & *Droṇa*, who slew many and vanquished the *Pāṇḍavas*, etc. (ρ); *Yudhishṭhira* heard the sound of *Pāñcajanya* and thought *Arjuna* to be in distress; he requested *Sātyaki* to go to *Arjuna* and bring him news of his safety; *Arjuna* had said in the *Dvaitavana* to *Yudhishṭhira*, "even if *Kṛshṇa*, etc. (σ), assist us, I shall yet appoint *Sātyaki* for our aid, since there is none equal to him," and *Yudhishṭhira* had witnessed his reverence for *Arjuna* at *Dvārakā* when returning from the *tīrthas*, and at *Upaplavya* his affection for the *Pāṇḍavas*: "the day is about to end"; amongst the *Vṛshṇis* two were regarded as *atirathas*: *Pradyumna* and *Sātyaki* (in weapons equal to *Nārāyaṇa*, in strength to *Saṅkarshaṇa*, in bravery to *Arjuna*, surpassing *Bhīshma* and *Droṇa*) (VII, **110**). *Sātyaki* hesitated to comply with *Yudhishṭhira's* request on the ground of the counter-commands of *Arjuna* ("only *Pradyumna* and *Sātyaki* are a match for *Droṇa* in battle"); "the *Sauvīrakas*, etc. (τ), D., As., men, Rā., K., M.-U., etc., are no match for *Arjuna* in battle." *Yudhishṭhira* pressed his request, saying that *Bhīma*, etc. (υ), will protect him during *Sātyaki's* absence (VII, **111**). *Sātyaki* agreed to obey *Yudhishṭhira*; "the distance from here is three *yojanas*"; he would crush the elephants of the *Añjana* breed, mounted by *Mlecchas* (named *Rukmarathas*), commanded by *Karṇa* and devoted to *Duḥçāsana*, at *Karṇa's* command returning from the pursuit of *Arjuna* and waiting for *Sātyaki*, and also ordered by *Duryodhana*; he would also crush those 700 elephants ridden by *Kirātas* (sprung from the race of *Agni*) (c) and formerly given by the *Kirāta* king to *Arjuna*; obtaining these and *Kṛpa*, etc. (φ), *Duryodhana* thought lightly of the *Pāṇḍavas*; "also the *Kāmbojas* (a full *akshauhiṇī*) are on the alert with their eyes on me." Then *Sātyaki* directed his chariot to be properly equipped; "I shall also have to encounter the *Çakas*." *Yudhishṭhira* caused quivers, etc., to be placed on *Sātyaki's* chariot (with steeds of the *Sindhu* breed); then *Sātyaki* set out (description) with his charioteer and friend, the younger brother of *Dāruka*. *Bhīmasena* also set out with *Sātyaki*, but was prevailed upon by *Sātyaki* to return and protect *Yudhishṭhira* (VII, **112**). *Yudhishṭhira* followed *Sātyaki* in order to reach the chariot of *Droṇa*. *Dhṛshṭadyumna* and king *Vasudāna* urged the warriors to protect *Sātyaki*. *Sātyaki* made the *Kurus* flee away. *Droṇa* & *Sātyaki*, who then, like *Arjuna*, avoided *Droṇa*, pointing out to his charioteer the *Avantis*, etc. (χ), and then smiting the great host of *Karṇa*. *Kṛtavarman* & *Sātyaki*, who slew *Kṛtavarman's* charioteer and issued out of the *Bhoja* division, while *Kṛtavarman* (himself urging his steeds) attacked *Bhīmasena*. *Yuyudhāna* & the *Kāmbojas*. *Droṇa* (making the *Bhoja* king protect his troops) pursued *Yuyudhāna*, while the *Pāṇḍava* host began to resist him. The *Pāñcālas* (headed by *Bhīmasena*) & *Kṛtavarman* (VII, **113**). *Dhṛtarāshṭra* wondered before *Sañjaya* that even such an army as his should be slain ("it must be Destiny"), and asked about what passed. *Sañjaya*, quoting *Vidura*, rebuked *Dhṛtarāshṭra*, and then related: the *Pārthas* (ψ) (headed by *Bhīmasena*) & the *Bhoja* king *Kṛtavarman*; *Çikhaṇḍin* was brought away from the battle by his charioteer; *Kṛtavarman* vanquished all the *Pārthas*, etc. (ω) (VII, **114**). *Sātyaki* turned back to check *Kṛtavarman*, whom he deprived of his chariot; then he broke the hostile division and proceeded on his way. *Sātyaki* & *Rukmaratha* (with the *Trigartas* and elephants, to the left of *Droṇa's* host; urged by *Duryodhana* they waited for *Sātyaki*); this elephant division fled away. The *Magadha* king *Jalasandha* (on an elephant) & *Yuyudhāna* (with white steeds), who slew him; the *Kurus* fled away. *Droṇa* & *Yuyudhāna* (VII, **115**). *Droṇa*, etc. (**aa**) & *Yuyudhāna*; *Duryodhana* fled away, mounting the chariot of *Citrasena*. *Kṛtavarman* & *Yuyudhāna*, who made him fall on his knees (VII, **116**). *Droṇa* & *Sātyaki*, whose driver swooned away; *Sātyaki*, acting as his own driver, continued to fight with *Droṇa*, who was carried away by his steeds; the troops broke. *Droṇa* returned to the front of the array in order to check the *Pāṇḍavas* (VII, **117**). King *Sudarçana* & *Sātyaki*, who slew him (VII, **118**). *Sātyaki's* driver pronounced an eulogy (ββ) upon him. *Sātyaki* urged him to take him to the *Kāmbojas*; *Yuyudhāna* & the *Yavanas*, who fled away; thousands of *Kāmbojas*, etc. (γγ), were similarly slain by *Sātyaki*; Cā. and G. applauded him (VII, **119**). *Yuyudhāna* proceeded towards *Arjuna*; *Duryodhana*, etc. (δδ), followed him behind and attacked him as he proceeded slowly; an awful carnage set in; *Duryodhana's* chariot was taken away by the steeds; the others then fled away. *Yuyudhāna* proceeded towards the chariot of *Arjuna* (VII, **120**). *Dhṛtarāshṭra* wondered before *Sañjaya* at the feats of *Yuyudhāna* ("I think Destiny is now unpropitious"). *Sañjaya* blamed *Dhṛtarāshṭra* and *Duryodhana*, and then continued his narrative. At the command of *Duryodhana* the *Saṃçaptakas* rallying, with a number of *Çakas*, etc. (εε) (headed by *Duryodhana*), attacked *Sātyaki*; *Duḥçāsana* (with a large force of robbers) & *Sātyaki*; many elephants of the race of *Añjana*, etc. (ζζ), were slain, and many steeds of the *Vanāyu* race, etc. (ηη), and many thousands of warriors; many *Daradas* & *Sātyaki*; they fled away. *Droṇa*, hearing the noise, told his charioteer to take the chariot to the spot where *Yuyudhāna* was; the charioteer remarked that the *Pāñcālas* and *Pāṇḍavas* were rushing against *Droṇa*; suddenly *Sātyaki* appeared, and the broken troops and *Duḥçāsana*, all struck with panic, rushed towards *Droṇa's* division (VII, **121**). *Droṇa* rebuked *Duḥçāsana* for his cowardice (quoting his words to *Draupadī*), and told him to make peace with the *Pāṇḍavas* (θθ). *Duḥçāsana* (with *Mlecchas*) & *Sātyaki*. *Droṇa* & the *Pāñcālas* + the *Pāṇḍavas*, etc. (ιι); *Droṇa* slew the *Pāñçāla* prince *Vīraketu*, and his brothers *Citraketu*, *Sudhanvan*, *Citravarman*, and *Citraratha*; *Dhṛshṭadyumna* mounted *Droṇa's* chariot, but was then carried away by his own steeds; having caused a great carnage *Droṇa* once more took up his station in the midst of his own array (VII, **122**). *Duḥçāsana* & *Sātyaki*; the warriors of *Duḥçāsana* (but not himself) fled away. *Duryodhana* urged a body of 3,000 *Trigartas* towards *Yuyudhāna*, who slew 500; then they turned towards *Droṇa*. While *Sātyaki* was proceeding towards *Arjuna* he was again attacked by *Duḥçāsana*, who was taken up by the *Trigarta* leader on his chariot; *Sātyaki* did not slay him, recollecting the words of *Bhīmasena*, but quickly proceeded along the track of *Arjuna* (VII, **123**). D. and Cā. wondered. *Bhīmasena*, etc. (κκ), & the *Kauravas*. *Sātyaki* proceeded towards *Arjuna*. *Duryodhana* & the *Pāṇḍavas* (λλ); *Duryodhana* caused a great carnage. *Droṇa* (in order to rescue *Duryodhana*) & the *Pāñcālas*; a dreadful carnage took place. Then there arose a loud uproar from the place where *Arjuna* was (VII, **124**). In the afternoon: *Droṇa* & the *Somakas* (and *Pāṇḍavas*); *Bṛhatkshattra* (of the *Kekayas*) & *Droṇa*; both invoked the *Brāhma* weapon; *Bṛhatkshattra* was slain by *Droṇa*, who then slew the *Cedi Dhṛshṭaketu* (the son of *Çiçupāla*; with steeds of the *Kāmboja* breed), and then *Dhṛshṭaketu's* son, and the son of *Jarāsandha*. The *Cedis*, etc. (μμ), & *Droṇa*, who slew them, especially the foremost among the *Cedis*. The *Pāñcālas* began to tremble and loudly called for *Bhīmasena* and *Dhṛshṭadyumna*. *Droṇa* slew *Kshatradharman* (*Dhṛshṭadyumna's* son), and caused *Cekitāna* to be carried away by his steeds. *Drupada* (censuring *Duryodhana*) (placing the *Pārthas* at his head) & *Droṇa* (then 85 years of age, with white locks, but behaving like a youth of 16) (VII, **125**). *Yudhishṭhira* was anxious at not having obtained any intelligence of *Arjuna* and *Sātyaki*, and thought of sending *Bhīma* after *Sātyaki*, asking him to send him a message by uttering a leonine roar (VII, **126**). *Bhīma* requested *Dhṛshṭadyumna* to protect *Yudhishṭhira*, and prepared to set out (description) after *Sātyaki* and *Arjuna*; the fierce blasts of *Pāñcajanya* were heard, filling *Yudhishṭhira* with fear. *Bhīma* (with his charioteer *Viçoka*) broke through the head of the *Kuru* array; the *Pāñcālas* and *Somakas* followed him behind; the brothers *Duḥçala*, etc. (νν), (with celestial weapons) he passed, and rushed against *Droṇa's* division; *Droṇa* & *Bhīmasena*; *Bhīma's* mace pressed *Droṇa's* chariot down into the earth; *Droṇa*, who had previously alighted, was saved; *Bhīma* slew eleven sons of *Dhṛtarāshṭra*: *Kuṇḍabhedin*, etc. (ξξ); *Dhṛtarāshṭra's* sons and the soldiers fled away. *Bhīmasena* then passed towards the division of *Droṇa* (VII, **127**). *Bhīma* & *Droṇa*; *Bhīma* passing through the *Bhoja*, etc. (οο), division and beholding *Sātyaki*, proceeded with great speed and sighted *Arjuna*, to whom he made his presence known by a roar; *Arjuna* and *Kṛshṇa* uttered loud roars in return; *Yudhishṭhira* understood that all was safe, and thought of *Arjuna's* feats (ππ) (VII, **128**). *Karṇa* & *Bhīmasena*; *Karṇa* mounted the chariot of *Vṛshasena*; *Bhīma* uttered a loud roar that gratified *Yudhishṭhira*. *Arjuna* stretched *Gāṇḍīva* and *Kṛshṇa* blew *Pāñcajanya* (VII, **129**). *Duryodhana* saw *Droṇa*, and affectionately chided him for his having allowed *Sātyaki* and *Bhīma* to penetrate the *Kuru* host and approach to the aid of *Arjuna*. *Droṇa* counselled *Duryodhana* to make effective arrangements for the protection of *Jayadratha*. While going back towards *Jayadratha*, *Duryodhana* encountered the two brothers, the *Pāñcāla* princes, *Yudhāmanyu* and *Uttamaujas*, the protectors of the wheels of *Arjuna's* chariot, who had formerly, while *Arjuna* penetrated the *Kuru* host, been checked in their progress by *Kṛtavarman*, and were now proceeding towards *Arjuna* by the flank of the *Kuru* army. *Uttamaujas* ascended the chariot of *Yudhāmanyu*, which *Duryodhana* pressed down into the earth with his mace, and then *Duryodhana* ascended the chariot of the *Madra* king; *Yudhāmanyu* and *Uttamaujas*, ascending two other chariots, proceeded towards *Arjuna* (VII, **130**). *Karṇa* proceeded against *Bhīma*. *Dhṛtarāshṭra* inquired about the battle (ρρ). *Sañjaya* related: *Bhīma* desired to avoid *Karṇa* and to proceed towards *Arjuna*; *Karṇa* insultingly challenged *Bhīma*, who turned back and encountered *Karṇa*; a fierce battle ensued between *Bhīma* and *Karṇa*, whom *Bhīma* deprived of his steeds and chariot. *Karṇa* mounted another chariot (VII, **131**). Continuation of the battle between *Karṇa* and *Bhīma*, who recollected the woes in *Virāṭa's* city, etc. (σσ). *Bhīma's* horses of the hue of bears and *Karṇa's* of the hue of swans mingled together; *Kṛshṇa* and *Arjuna* became anxious for *Bhīma*; a great carnage took place (VII, **132**). *Dhṛtarāshṭra's* eulogy on *Bhīma* (ττ); *Karṇa* was capable of encountering D., As., and men. *Sañjaya* continued: *Bhīma* again deprived *Karṇa* of his steeds and driver. *Duryodhana* dispatched his brother *Durjaya* to rescue *Karṇa*; *Bhīma* slew *Durjaya*; *Karṇa* wept (VII, **133**). Riding upon another chariot *Karṇa* again encountered *Bhīma*, who again deprived him of his chariot. *Duryodhana* dispatched his brother

Durmukha to rescue *Karṇa*; *Bhīma* slew *Durmukha*, upon whose chariot *Karṇa* mounted, weeping; *Karṇa* fled, carried away by his steeds (VII, **134**). *Dhṛtarāshṭra's* observations on *Bhīma's* victory over *Karṇa* (υυ); "I think Destiny reigns supreme." *Sañjaya* called *Dhṛtarāshṭra* "the root of this destruction of the world"; then he related: five brothers of *Duryodhana* (φφ) + *Karṇa* & *Bhīmasena*, who slew the five brothers, resisting *Karṇa* the while (VII, **135**). *Karṇa* became despondent of his life; *Bhīma* again deprived *Karṇa* of his steeds, driver, and bow; *Karṇa* once more fled on foot; *Duryodhana* dispatched other brothers of his against *Bhīma*, who slew them all (χχ). *Karṇa* wept, recollecting the words of *Vidura*; then, riding upon another chariot he encountered *Bhīma* (description), who gladdened *Arjuna*, etc. (ψψ) (VII, **136**). *Karṇa* sorrowfully surveyed the slain brothers of *Duryodhana*, and was hard pressed by *Bhīma*, who was applauded by Cā., *Bhūriçravas*, etc. (ωω); *Duryodhana* dispatched seven of his brothers to the rescue of *Karṇa*; they were all slain by *Bhīma* (**aaa**); *Bhīma* lamented the death of *Vikarṇa*, who was dear to him. Then he with a shout gladdened *Yudhishṭhira*, who rushed against *Droṇa*. Beholding the slaughter of thirty-one of his brothers by *Bhīma*, *Duryodhana* recollected the words of *Vidura* (βββ) (VII, **137**). *Bhīma* & *Karṇa*; a great carnage was caused by both (*Sindhus, Sauvīras, Kauravas*); Cā. and Si. were amazed (VII, **138**). Continuation: D-ṛ., Si., G., and Vd. applauded the two combatants. Pierced by *Karṇa*, *Bhīma's* driver sought refuge in *Sātyaki's* chariot; *Karṇa* cut off *Bhīma's* weapons; *Bhīma* leaped into the sky in order to snatch *Karṇa* off his chariot; *Karṇa* concealed himself on his vehicle; the *Kurus* and Cā. applauded *Bhīma*; *Bhīma's* weapons being exhausted he fled away from *Karṇa* and defended himself with the bodies of the elephants slain by *Arjuna*; but, recollecting *Arjuna's* vow, he did not take the life of *Karṇa*; and *Karṇa*, recollecting his promise to *Kuntī*, did not take the life of *Bhīma*, whom he touched with the end of his bow and insulted with his speech. *Arjuna* then forced *Karṇa* to fly, and speeded a terrible shaft after him when he was retreating, which was cut off by *Açvatthāman*, whom *Arjuna* then forced to flee away (VII, **139**). *Dhṛtarāshṭra* lamented (γγγ). *Sañjaya* related: *Sātyaki* followed *Bhīma*; *Alambusha* (*rājavaro*, v. †5828) & *Sātyaki*, who slew him (!), and then proceeded, with his steeds of the *Sindhu* breed, towards *Arjuna*; *Duḥçāsana* and the *Dhārtarāshṭras* & *Sātyaki*, who slew the steeds of *Duḥçāsana*, gladdening *Arjuna* and *Kṛshṇa* (VII, **140**). Fifty *Trigarta* princes & *Sātyaki*, who made them flee away, and then, passing through the *Çūrasenas* and *Kaliṅgas*, approached *Arjuna*, and was eulogized (δδδ) by *Kṛshṇa*. *Arjuna* was not pleased with the arrival of *Sātyaki* on account of his anxiety for *Yudhishṭhira* (εεε) (VII, **141**). *Bhūriçravas* & *Sātyaki*; they mutually addressed (ζζζ) and challenged each other, whereafter the fight began; each deprived the other of his chariot, then they fought with swords, then with fists and hands (descriptions); *Kṛshṇa* urged *Arjuna* to protect the tired *Sātyaki* against *Bhūriçravas*, who was fresh; *Sātyaki* succumbed to *Bhūriçravas*; *Arjuna* cut off one of the arms of *Bhūriçravas* (VII, **142**). *Bhūriçravas* rebuked *Arjuna* for his unrighteous feat (ηηη); *Arjuna* justified his conduct (θθθ). *Bhūriçravas* (*b*), abandoning *Yuyudhāna*, desired to die in *prāya* (description); he acknowledged the justice of *Arjuna's* plea, and was blessed by *Arjuna* and *Kṛshṇa* (ιι). Though forbidden by *Kṛshṇa*, etc. (κκκ), *Sātyaki* slew *Bhūriçravas* sitting in *prāya*. The warriors did not applaud *Sātyaki*; Si., Cā., men, and D. applauded *Bhūriçravas*; the soldiers thought that it had been ordained by the Creator that it should be so. *Sātyaki* justified his conduct (λλλ), quoting *Vālmīki* (VII, **143**). *Dhṛtarāshṭra* asked *Sañjaya* how *Sātyaki* could be humiliated by *Bhūriçravas*. *Sañjaya* related the history of *Çini* (*e*) and of *Somadatta*, and praised the *Vṛshṇi* heroes, vanquishers of the very D., Dā., G., As., Y., U., and Rā. (VII, **144**). *Arjuna* proceeded to *Jayadratha's* chariot. *Duryodhana*, etc. (μμμ) & *Arjuna* (μμμ). *Duryodhana* prevailed upon *Karṇa* to protect *Jayadratha* (ννν); *Karṇa* promised to do his best (ξξξ); *Duryodhana*, etc. (οοο) (also *Açvatthāman*) (*f*) & *Arjuna* (+ *Bhīmasena* and *Yuyudhāna*); Si., Cā., and Pn. applauded *Karṇa* and *Arjuna*. *Arjuna* deprived *Karṇa* of his steeds, chariot, and driver. *Açvatthāman* made *Karṇa* ride on his chariot. *Arjuna* invoked the *Vāruṇa* weapon; he caused a great carnage (VII, **145**). *Arjuna* employed the *Aindra* weapon, etc. (description). *Arjuna* & *Jayadratha* (+ οοο); *Arjuna* cut off *Jayadratha's* standard and slew his driver; *Jayadratha* was placed by six chariot warriors in their midst. *Kṛshṇa* covered the sun by means of his *yoga* power, so that all, except *Arjuna*, thought the sun to have set, and he urged *Arjuna* to cut off *Jayadratha's* head without delay; *Arjuna* caused such a carnage that the warriors abandoned *Jayadratha* in fear and fled away; *Kṛshṇa* again urged *Arjuna* to cut off *Jayadratha's* head without delay, telling him of *Jayadratha's* father *Vṛddhakshatra* (*g*), who was still engaged in penances outside *Samantapañcaka*; *Arjuna* should make the head fall upon the lap of *Vṛddhakshatra* himself, lest his own head should crack in 100 pieces; this *Arjuna* did, and as the head fell down from *Vṛddhakshatra's* lap the latter's head split into 100 pieces. *Kṛshṇa* then withdrew the darkness created by him; *Kṛshṇa* and *Arjuna* blew their conches, and *Bhīma*, by a tremendous shout, communicated to *Yudhishṭhira* the message of victory. *Yudhishṭhira* & *Droṇa*, after the sun had set; and *Arjuna* fought with many mighty chariot warriors (VII, **146**). *Kṛpa* + *Açvatthāman* & *Arjuna*; *Kṛpa* was carried away by his driver, and *Açvatthāman* fled. *Arjuna*, grieved at *Kṛpa's* death-like swoon (πππ), *Karṇa* & *Arjuna* + *Sātyaki* + the two *Pāñcāla* princes (*Arjuna's* wheel protectors). *Kṛshṇa* told *Arjuna* to avoid *Karṇa* because the latter had yet the lance that *Indra* had given him. *Karṇa* & *Sātyaki* (upon *Kṛshṇa's* chariot with *Dāruka* and the horses *Çaibya*, etc. (ρρρ), *Kṛshṇa* having known before the encounter that *Sātyaki* would be deprived of his chariot by *Bhūriçravas*, and having therefore ordered *Dāruka* to let his chariot be equipped the next day, and now calling *Dāruka* by blowing his conch in the *Ṛshabha* note; neither D., G., Y., U., Rā., nor men could conquer the two *Kṛshṇas*; D. with *Brahmán* and Si. knew their prowess); *Yudhāmanyu* and *Uttamaujas* (abandoning *Arjuna's* chariot) & *Karṇa*; such a battle had never been heard of even between D., G., As., U., or Rā.; D., G., and Dā. looked at; *Sātyaki* slew *Karṇa's* charioteer and steeds. *Vṛshasena*, etc. (σσσ), & *Sātyaki*. *Karṇa* ascended the chariot of *Duryodhana*. *Sātyaki* did not slay the *Dhārtarāshṭras* (*Duḥçāsana*, etc.) on account of the vow of *Bhīmasena*. *Açvatthāman*, *Kṛtavarman*, etc., were all vanquished by *Sātyaki* with only one bow; "in this world there are only three mighty bowmen: *Kṛshṇa*, *Arjuna*, and *Sātyaki*," said Sañjaya. The younger brother of *Dāruka* soon brought another chariot (description) to *Sātyaki*; *Sātyaki* ascended it, and *Dāruka* went to *Kṛshṇa*. A new chariot was brought for *Karṇa* also. *Sañjaya* told *Dhṛtarāshṭra* that thirty-one of his sons had been slain by *Bhīmasena*, etc. (τττ) (VII, **147**). Insulted by *Karṇa*, *Bhīma* addressed *Arjuna* in order to induce the latter to permit him to slay *Karṇa*; *Arjuna* rebuked *Karṇa* (υυυ), and vowed to slay his son *Vṛshasena* in his presence. *Kṛshṇa* congratulated *Arjuna* (φφφ), who attributed the victory to *Kṛshṇa*; *Kṛshṇa* pointed out to *Arjuna* the results of that day's battle; then he blew *Pāñcajanya* and went and informed *Yudhishṭhira* (VII, **148**). *Kṛshṇa* congratulated *Yudhishṭhira*, who attributed the success to *Kṛshṇa's* grace (χχχ); *Kṛshṇa* and *Arjuna* once more congratulated him (ψψψ); then *Bhīma* and *Sātyaki*, whom *Yudhishṭhira* congratulated (ωωω) and embraced (VII, **149**). *Duryodhana's* despondency (*a*′) and cheerless address to *Droṇa* (β′), whom he censured for treating *Arjuna* leniently; "it seems that *Karṇa* only now wishes us victory" (VII, **150**). *Droṇa's* reply to *Duryodhana* (γ′); he vowed to slay all the *Pāñcālas* before doffing his armour; he asked *Duryodhana* to tell *Açvatthāman* to avenge himself on the *Somakas*, etc., even at the risk of his life. Then he proceeded against the *Pāṇḍavas* (VII, **151**). *Duryodhana* communicated to *Karṇa* his suspicions about *Droṇa's* sincerity (δ′); *Karṇa* removed *Duryodhana's* suspicions of *Droṇa* (ε′), and attributed the ill-success of the *Kurus* to destiny. Meanwhile the *Pāṇḍava* divisions appeared for battle, and a fierce battle ensued (VII, **152**).

Jayadrathavimokshaṇa(m) ("the setting free of Jayadratha"). § 10 (Parvasaṅgr.): I, **2**, 325 (i.e. Jayadrathavimokshaṇaparvan).

[Jayadrathavimokshaṇaparvan] ("the setting free of Jayadratha," the 47th of the minor parvans of Mhbhr.). (Cf. Jayadrathavimokshaṇa.) § 523 (cf. Draupadīhar.): *Bhīma* seized *Jayadratha* by the hair, and holding him high up in the air thrust him on the ground, etc., and regretted that *Yudhishṭhira* had forbidden to kill him. He then with his arrow shaved *Jayadratha's* head, leaving only five tufts of hair, and made him promise to say in public assemblies, "I am the slave of the *Pāṇḍavas*." They then bound him and thrust him into the chariot; then they drove towards the hermitage and presented him to *Yudhishṭhira*. *Yudhishṭhira* and *Draupadī* set him free with his army. § 524: *Jayadratha* went to *Gaṅgādvāra*, and pleased *Çiva* so that he deigned to accept his offerings in person and granted him a boon. *Jayadratha* asked that he might be able to defeat in battle all the five *Pāṇḍavas* on their chariots. This *Çiva* declared to be impossible, as *Arjuna* (*b*) was invincible, and was protected by *Kṛshṇa*, who was *Vishṇu* (*c*). *Çiva* then briefly reminded *Jayadratha* of four incarnations of *Vishṇu* (*d*). "Thou shalt, however, be able to vanquish for a single day only the rest of *Yudhishṭhira's* forces and the four *Pāṇḍavas*, but not *Arjuna*." Then *Çiva* vanished with *Umā*, *Jayadratha* returned home, and the *Pāṇḍavas* continued to dwell in *Kāmyaka* (III, **272**).

Jayājayau = Çiva (1000 names[1]).

Jayānīka[1], a Pāṇḍava warrior. § 600 (Ghaṭotkacavadhap.): VII, **156**ν, 6911 (is slain by Açvatthāman).

Jayānīka[2], a Pāṇḍava warrior. § 600 (Ghaṭotkacavadhap.): VII, **158**χ, 7011 (brother of Virāṭa?).

Jayanta[1], son of Indra and Çacī. § 177 (Pāṇḍudigvijaya): I, **114**, 4472 (°*m iva Paulomī parishvajya*).—§ 253 (Haraṇāharaṇap.): I, **221**, 8025 (°*m iva Paulomī*, sc. *ajījanat*).

Jayanta[2] (one of the occult names which Yudhishṭhira gave to the Pāṇḍavas). § 549 (Pāṇḍavapr.): IV, **5**, 176.—§ 551 (Kīcakavadhap.): IV, **23***a*, 801.

Jayanta[3], a Pāñcāla prince. § 572 (Rathātirathas.): V, **171**, 5903 (a mahāratha in the army of Yudhishṭhira).

Jayanta[4], a Rudra. § 665 (Mokshadh.): XII, **208**δ, 7586.

Jayanta[5] = Vishṇu (1000 names).

Jayanta[6], one of the Ādityas. § 770 (Ānuçāsanik.): XIII, **151**γ, 7093.

Jayantī, a river(?). § 362 (Tīrthayātrāp.): III, **83**, 5089 (°*yām* . . . *Somatīrtham samāviçet*).

Jayapriya, a Pāṇḍava warrior. § 600 (Ghaṭotkacavadhap.): VII, **158**χ, 7011 (brother of Virāṭa?).

Jayapriyā, a mātṛ. § 615*u* (Skanda): IX, **46**θ, 2630.

Jayarāta, a Kuru warrior. § 600 (Ghaṭotkacavadhap.): VII, **155**, 6710 (is slain by Bhīmasena).

Jayasena[1], a Māgadha prince. § 264 (Sabhākriyāp.): II, **4**β, 121 (*Māgadhaḥ*, waited upon Yudhishṭhira). Cf. Jayatsena[1].

Jayasena[2], a son of Dhṛtarāshṭra. § 583 (Bhīshmavadhap.): VI, **77**κ, 3343 (attacked Bhīmasena). Cf. Jayatsena[4].

Jayātmaja ("the son of Jaya, i.e. Arjuna") = Abhimanyu: III, †10270.

Jayatsena[1], a Māgadha king, the son of Jarāsandha. § 130 (Aṃçāvat.): I, **67**, 2684 (incarnation of the eldest of the Kālakeyas).—§ 232 (Svayaṃvarap.): I, **186**, 6988 (*Sahadeva-J°au*, present at the svayaṃvara of Draupadī). — § 290 (Çiçupālavadhap.): II, **44**, 1538 (*Māgadham*). — § 554 (Sainyodyogap.): V, **4**γ, 71, 82.—§ 555 (do.): V, **19**γ, 577 (*Māgadhaḥ* . . . *Jārāsandhiḥ* (C. *Ja°*), came with one akshauhiṇī of troops to Yudhishṭhira).—§ 561 (Yānasandhip.): V, **50**η, 2014 (*Jārāsandhiḥ Sahadevo J°aç ca tāv ubhau*, had sided with Yudhishṭhira); **66**εε, 2503 (*pārthivam*, the same?, among the allies of Duryodhana).—§ 573 (Ambopākhyānap.): V, **196**ν, 7637 (in the army of Yudhishṭhira). —§ 576 (Bhagavadgītāp.): VI, **16***a*, 623 (*pārthivaḥ*, the same?, with one akshauhiṇī of troops in the army of Duryodhana). — § 587 (Bhīshmavadhap.): VI, **108***a*, 5007 (*Māgadhaḥ*, in the army of Duryodhana); **114**, 5319 (fought with Bhīmasena).—§ 592 (Saṃçaptakavadhap.): VII, **25**, 1109 (fought with a son of Dhṛtarāshṭra).—§ 604 (Karṇap.): VIII, **5**ζ, 120 (*Jārāsandhiḥ* . . . *Māgadhaḥ*, had been slain by Abhimanyu).—§ 608 (do.): VIII, **73**, 3657 (*Māgadhānām adhipatiḥ*, had seven days before been slain by Abhimanyu).—§ 610 (Çalyap.): IX, **6**ζ, 291 (the same?). § 619 (Strīvilāpap.): XI, **25**κ, 712 (*Māgadhānām adhipatim*, had been slain).—§ 795 (Svargārohaṇap.): XVIII, **5**λ, 149. Cf. Jārāsandhi, Māgadha.

Jayatsena[2], son of Sarvabhauma and Sunandā Kaikeyī. § 156 (Pūruvaṃç.): I, **95**, ††3769, ††3770 (married to Suçravā Vaidarbhī and father of Avacīna).

Jayatsena[3], one of the occult names which Yudhishṭhira gave to the Pāṇḍavas. § 549 (Pāṇḍavapr.): IV, **5**, 176.—§ 551 (Kīcakavadhap.): IV, **23***a*, 801.

Jayatsena[4], a son of Dhṛtarāshṭra. § 583 (Bhīshmavadhap.): VI, **79**[13], 3487 (*sutam tava*, i.e. Dhṛtarāshṭra's), 3491, 3492 (fought with Çrutakīrti and Çatānīka).—§ 587 (do.): VI, **116**, 5400 (*tanayas tava*, rescued Paurava).—§ 611 (Çalyap.): IX, **26**ρ, 1405 (among eleven sons of Dhṛtarāshṭra who attacked Bhīmasena), 1411 (slain by Bhīmasena). Cf. Kaurava.

Jayatsenā, a mātṛ. § 615*u* (Skanda): IX, **46**θ, 2624.

Jayāvatī, a mātṛ. § 615*u* (Skanda): IX, **46**θ, 2622.

Jayin = Vishṇu (1000 names).

Jetā ripūṇām = Skanda: III, 14644.

Jetṛ = Vishṇu (1000 names).

Jharjharin = Çiva (1000 names[1]).

Jhillin, a Vṛshṇi prince. § 232 (Svayaṃvarap.): I, **186,** 7000 (present at the svayaṃvara of Draupadī). — § 253 (Haraṇāharaṇap.): I, **221,** 7992 (came to the nuptials of Arjuna and Subhadrā).—§ 589 (Droṇābhishekap.): VII, **11**ξ, 409.

Jillika (*Jh°*, B.), pl. (*°āḥ*), a people. § 574 (Jambūkh.): VI, **9**ν, 367 (in the south).

Jīmūta[1] = Sūrya (the Sun): III, 152.

Jīmūta[2], name of an athlete. § 550 (Samayapālanap.): IV, **13,** 347 (*mallam*), 362 (vanquished and slain by Bhīmasena).

Jīmūta[3], a ṛshi. § 565 (Gālavacarita): V, **111,** 3843 (*viprarsheḥ*, a gold-mine of Himavat presented itself to *J.*, after whom gold is named *jaimūta*).

Jīrṇadaṃshṭra = Çiva (1000 names[1]).

Jishṇu[1] = Arjuna, q.v.

Jishṇu[2] = Vishṇu (Kṛshṇa): V, 2571 (= Kṛshṇa, etymology); VI, 2074 (°*r Vajrabhṛteva*, sc. *uktaḥ*, only C.; B. has *Vi°*); VII, 2963 (*Vishṇo*, = Kṛshṇa); VIII, †4060 (*Vishṇoḥ*, = Kṛshṇa); XII, 1503 (*Vishṇo*, = Kṛshṇa), 1602 (*Vishṇum*, = Kṛshṇa); XIII, 7106 (*Vishṇuḥ*); XIV, 1085 (*Vishṇuḥ*, = *mahān ātmā*).

Jishṇu[3], a Pāṇḍava warrior. § 608 (Karṇap.): VIII, **56**νν, 2739 (slain by Karṇa).

Jishṇukarman, a Pāṇḍava warrior. § 608 (Karṇap.): VIII, **56**νν, 2739 (slain by Karṇa).

Jita[1] = Çiva (1000 names[2]).

Jita[2] = Vishṇu (1000 names).

Jitakāma = Çiva (1000 names[2]).

Jitakrodha = Vishṇu (1000 names).

Jitamanyu = Vishṇu (1000 names).

Jitāmitra = Vishṇu (1000 names).

Jitāri, son of Avikshit and grandson of Kuru. § 154 (Pūruvaṃç.): I, **94,** 3741 (the eighth son of Avikshit).

Jitātman, a Viçvadeva. § 749 (Ānuçāsanik.): XIII, **91,** 4356 (enumeration).

Jitavatī. § 164 (Āpavop.): I, **99,** 3940 (daughter of Uçīnara and friend of the wife of the Vasu Dyaus).

Jitendriya = Çiva (1000 names[2]).

Jīva[1] = Çiva (1000 names[1]).

Jīva[2] = Vishṇu (1000 names).

Jīvala, a charioteer of King Ṛtuparṇa. § 349 (Nalopākhyānap.): III, **67,** 2640, 2641, 2644.

Jīvana[1] = Sūrya (the Sun): III, 152.

Jīvana[2] = Çiva (1000 names[2]).

Jīvana[3] = Vishṇu (1000 names).

Jñānagamya = Vishṇu (1000 names).

Jñāna(m) uttama(ṃ) = Vishṇu (1000 names).

Jñānapāvana, a tīrtha. § 370 (Tīrthayātrāp.): III, **84,** 7081.

Jñānātman = Kṛshṇa: XII, 1666.

Jñeyātman = Kṛshṇa: XII, 1629.

Jṛmbhaka, pl. (*°āḥ*), a kind of being. § 506 (Skandayuddha): III, **231,** 14548 (followed Rudra, *grahaviçeshaiḥ*, Nīl.).

Jṛmbhikā ("yawning," personif.). § 555 (Indravijaya): V, **9,** 282 (*Vṛtranāçinīm*, created by Indra), 283 (*tataḥ prabhṛti lokasya J°ā prāṇasaṃçritā*).

Jṛmbhita = Çiva (1000 names[1]).

Jvālā, daughter of Takshaka. § 156 (Pūruvaṃç.): I, **95,** ††3778 (*Takshakaduhitaram*, wife of Ṛksha and mother of Matināra).

Jvālājihva, a companion of Skanda. § 615*u* (Skanda): IX, **45,** 2535 (given to Skanda by Agni; C. has by error *°ām*).

Jvalana = Agni, q.v.

Jvalanāstra ("the weapon of Fire"). § 608 (Karṇap.): VIII, **89,** 4542 (employed by Arjuna). Cf. Āgneya[2].

Jvalanasūnu = Skanda: IX, 2554.

Jvalanātmaja = Skanda: IX, 2459; XIII, 4202.

Jvalin = Çiva (1000 names[2]).

Jvara ("fever"). § 694*b* (Jvarotpatti): XII, **284,** 10255, 10259, 10262, foll.

[Jvarotpatti(ḥ)] ("the origin of fever"). § 694*b* (Mokshadh.): *Bhīshma* said: In days of yore there was a summit of *Meru*, named *Jyotishka*, belonging to *Savitṛ* (*Sāvitram*). There *Çiva* used to sit with *Pārvatī*, waited upon by D., V., etc. (*a*). After some time the *Prajāpati Daksha* commenced to perform a sacrifice, whither all the gods headed by *Indra*, with the permission of *Çiva*, repaired mounted on their chariots, proceeding to that spot whence the *Gaṅgā* is said to issue. *Pārvatī* asked why *Çiva* did not himself proceed thither, and was told that in days of yore the deities made an arrangement in consequence of which no share was assigned to *Çiva* of offerings in sacrifices. He was filled with grief. *Çiva* ordered *Nandin* to wait there, and summoning all his *yoga* force, he, with all his terrible followers, came and destroyed that sacrifice (description); it assumed the form of a deer and tried to fly away through the skies, pursued by *Çiva* with bow and arrow. A drop of sweat fell from his forehead down on the earth; there appeared a terrible fire, whence issued a dreadful being of very short stature, etc. (description), who consumed the embodied form of sacrifice and then attacked D. and R., who fled in all directions. The earth began to tremble, etc. *Brahmán* appeased *Çiva* by promising him a share of the sacrificial offerings; the being that had sprung from his sweat should be distributed among all creatures as fever (description of the distribution). Blessing upon the reader (XII, **284**).

Jyaishṭha, name of a month. § 759 (Ānuçāsanik.): XIII, **109,** 5378.

Jyeshṭha[1], a brahman. § 717*b* (Nārāyaṇīya): XII, **349,** I), 13593 (*sāmavedagataṃ dvijaṃ J°nāmābhivikhyātaṃ*, obtained the cult of Nārāyaṇa from the Barhishads and communicated it to King Avikalpana).

Jyeshṭha[2] = Çiva (1000 names[1]).

Jyeshṭha[3] = Vishṇu (1000 names).

Jyeshṭhā, a nakshatra (v. Su. Si.). § 569 (Bhagavadyānap.): V, **143** θ, 4841 (*kṛtvā cāṅgārakaṃ vakraṃ J°āyāṃ*, omens).—§ 574 (Jambūkh.): VI, **3,** 83 (*çveto grahaḥ prajvalitaḥ sadhūma iva pāvakaḥ | Aindraṃ tejasvi nakshatraṃ J°ām ākramya tishṭhati*, omens). — § 746 (Ānuçāsanik.): XIII, **64,** 3274 (result of making gifts under the constellation of *J.*).—§ 749 (do.): XIII, **88***a*, 4263 (result of performing a çrāddha under the constellation of *J.*).—§ 752*b* (Chattropānahotpatti): XIII, **95,** 4609 (*madhyāhnam ārūḍhe J°mūle divākare*).—§ 759 (Ānuçāsanik.): XIII, **106**β, 5156 (*°mūlam . . . māsam*, i.e. the month of Jyaishṭha); **110,** 5393 (description of the cāndravrata). Cf. Aindra.

Jyeshṭhapushkara, a tīrtha. § 471 (Mārkaṇḍeyas.): III, **200,** 13415 (*kapilāyāṃ dattāyāṃ yat phalaṃ J°e*).—§ 766 (Ānuçāsanik.): XIII, **130,** 6107, 6132 (*tasmāt tu kapilā deyā Kaumudyāṃ J°e*). Cf. Pushkara.

Jyeshṭhasāman, name of a sāman. § 717*b* (Nārāyaṇīya): XII, **349,** VI), 13593 (*°vrato Hariḥ*).—§ 730*y* (Upamanyu): XIII, **14**φ, 876 (sung by Nārāyaṇa).—§ 749 (Ānuçāsanik.): XIII, **90,** 4296 (*°gaḥ*).

Jyeshṭhasthāna, a tīrtha. § 372 (Tīrthayātrāp.): III, **85,** 8204.

Jyeshṭhila, a tīrtha. § 370 (Tīrthayātrāp.): III, **84,** 8112.

Jyeshṭhilā, a river. § 268 (Varuṇasabhāv.): II, **9,** 373 (among the rivers present in the palace of Varuṇa).

Jyotika, a serpent. § 47 (Sarpanāmak.): I, **35,** 1558 (enumeration). Cf. Jyotishka.

Jyotirathā, a river. § 574 (Jambūkh.): VI, **9**λ, 334 (in Bhāratavarsha). Cf. next.

Jyotirathyā, a river. § 370 (Tīrthayātrāp.): III, **85,** 8150 (*Çoṇasya J°yāyāḥ saṅgame*). Cf. the prec.

Jyotis[1] ("Light"), son of the Vasu Ahas. § 116 (Vasu, pl.): I, **66,** 2587.

Jyotis[2], a companion of Skanda. § 615*a* (Skanda): IX, **45,** 2535 (given to Skanda by Agni).

Jyotis[3] = Kṛshṇa: XII, 1643. Do.[4] = Vishṇu (1000 names).

***jyotis,** pl. (°*īṃshi*) (the heavenly bodies), selected passages: III, 13085 (°*īṃshi pratikūlāni*); VI, 1225 (°*shāṃ ravir aṃçumān*, sc. *asmi* says Kṛshṇa); IX, 2133 (°*shāṃ vyatikramaḥ*), 2513 (came to the investiture of Skanda), 2847 (°*shām ādhipatyaṃ*, sc. the Sun's); XII, 4514, 4515, 13536 (°*shām ayanaṃ*); XIII, 4730 (°*shāñ caiva salokyaṃ*); XIV, 1177 (°*shām Induḥ*, sc. *rājā*).

Jyotishām ayana(ṃ) = Çiva (1000 names[2]).

Jyotishāṃ nidhiḥ = Çiva (1000 names[1]).

Jyotishka[1], a serpent. § 564 (Mātalīyop.): V, **103**γ, 3631 (enumeration). Cf. Jyotika.

Jyotishka[2], a weapon. § 592 (Saṃçaptakavadhap.): VII, **30,** 1315 (*uttamāstre*, Arjuna dispelled the darkness by means of *J.*).

Jyotishka[3], a summit of Meru. § 694*b* (Jvarotpatti): XII, **284,** 10212 (*Meroḥ Çṛṅgaṃ Sāvitraṃ*).

Jyotsnākālī, a daughter of Soma. § 564 (Mātalīyop.): V, **98,** 3534 (wife of Pushkara, the son of Varuṇa). Cf. Somaputrī.

K

Ka[1] ("who") = Brahmán. § 3 (Anukram.): I, **1,** 32 (issued from the primordial egg).

Ka[2] = Daksha: XII, 7573.

Ka[3] = Vishṇu (1000 names).

Kabandha[1], a Rākshasa. § 530 (Viçvāvasumokshaṇa): III, **279,** 16072, 16083 (slain by Rāma and Lakshmaṇa; from his body then issued the Gandharva Viçvāvasu, who on account of a curse had become a Rākshasa).

***Kabandha**[2], the trunk of Rāhu: III, 13087 (°*āntarhito Bhānuḥ*), V, 3811 (°*aḥ . . . Svarbhānoḥ*).

Kaca, a brahman, the son of Bṛhaspati. § 145 (Sambhavap.): *Janamejaya* said: How did *Yayāti* get *Devayānī*? *Vaiçampāyana* related: In the many battles between the gods and the *Asuras*, the gods had for their purohita *Bṛhaspati Āṅgirasa*, and the *Asuras Uçanas Kāvya* (i.e. *Çukra*). As *Uçanas*, by his science *Sañjīvinī*, restored the fallen *Dānavas* to life, and *Bṛhaspati* was unable to revive the fallen gods, the gods prevailed upon *Bṛhaspati's* son *Kaca* to repair to *Uçanas* and conciliate him and his daughter *Devayānī* and learn the *Sañjīvinī*. *K.* then repaired to the capital of *Vṛshaparvan*, the king of the *Dānavas*, and promising to practise *brahmacarya* for 1,000 years he was accepted by *Uçanas* as his pupil. Young as he was he, by singing and dancing and playing on instruments, etc., soon gratified *Devayānī*. After 500 years the *Dānavas*, having discovered who he was, slew him, and one time hacked his body to pieces and gave it to wolves and jackals, another time they pounded it into paste and mixed it with the waters of the ocean, but both times *Devayānī* prevailed upon *Uçanas* to restore *K.* to life by the *Sañjīvinī*, summoning him and saying, "Come." Then slaying him for the third time they burned the body and mixed the ashes with the wine (*surā*) which *Uçanas* drank. As *Devayānī* again asked her father to revive *K.*, *Uçanas* said: "It is of no use, as he is always killed again; thou art always worshipped by the Bráhman (i.e. the Veda, Nīl.), the brahmans, the gods including *Indra*, the *Vasus*, the *Açvins*, the enemies of the gods and the whole world, therefore do not grieve for a mortal." As *Devayānī* said she would starve, *Çukra* imparted the *Sañjīvinī* to *K.*, who, though reduced to powder, remembered everything. *K.* then came out, ripping open the stomach of *Çukra* and then revived *Çukra* by the *Sañjīvinī*. *Uçanas* declared that henceforth that brahman who would drink wine should be reckoned to have committed the sin of slaying a brahman. *K.* stayed with *Çukra* for 1,000 years (I, **76**). When *K.* was about to return to the gods *Devayānī* asked him to become her husband, and as he refused (saying that she was a sister to him) she cursed him, saying that his science should bear no fruit. *K.* again cursed *Devayānī*, saying that no ṛshi's son should take her hand, and that his science should bear fruit, if not to himself, at least to him to whom he might impart it. Then he went to the abode of *Indra*, and the gods declared that he should become a sharer with them in sacrificial offerings (I, **77**): I, **76,** 3199 (*jyeshṭhaṃ putraṃ Bṛhaspateḥ*), 3199 (*Bṛhaspatisutaḥ*), 3201 (*ṛsher Aṅgirasaḥ pautraṃ putraṃ sākshād Bṛhaspateḥ*), 3203, 3204, 3209, 3212, 3213, 3214, 3215, 3216, 3219 (*Bṛhaspatisutaḥ*), 3223, 3226, 3227, 3228 (*Bṛhaspateḥ sutaḥ*), †3232, (†3237), †3239, †3240, †3241, †3244, †3245, †3248, †3253, 3255; **77,** (3261), 3265, (3267), 3271, (3272), 3276, 3277.—§ 146 (Devayānī): I, **78,** 3279; **80,** 3335 (*Āṅgirasaṃ*, all. to § 145).—§ 637 (*Rājadh.*): XII, **47**η, 1596 (among the ṛshis who surrounded Bhīshma.)—§ 734 (Ānuçāsanik.): XIII, **26*a*,** 1765 (do.). Cf. Āṅgirasaḥ pautra(ḥ), Āṅgirasa, Bṛhaspatisuta.

Kaccha, pl. (°*aḥ*), a people. § 571 (Jambūkh.): VI, **9**μ, 364 (only B., C. has *Kakshāḥ*)

Kacchapa, a serpent. § 191 (Arjuna): I, **123*a*,** 4828 (present at the birth of Arjuna).

kāçakuçādayaḥ ("kāça-grass, kuça-grass, etc.," personif.): II, 336 (in the palace of Yama), 343 (do.).

Kāçapauṇḍra, pl. (°*āḥ*), a people. § 607 (Karṇap.): VIII, **45**μ, 2081.

Kaçeraka, a Yaksha. § 269 (Vaiçravaṇasabhāv.): II, **10,** 397 (in the palace of Kubera).

Kāçeyī ("the daughter of the Kāçi king") = Sunandā: I, ††3875 (*S*°).

Kāçi, pl. (°*ayaḥ*), a people. § 177 (Pāṇḍu): I, **113,** 4456 (vanquished by Pāṇḍu).—§ 190*d* (Arjuna): I, **123,** 4796 (it is prophesied that Arjuna shall vanquish the *K.*, etc.).—§ 561*e* (Bhīmasena): V, **50,** 1986 (had been vanquished by Bhīmasena).—§ 561*g* (Sahadeva): V, **50,** 1997 (had been vanquished by Sahadeva).—§ 561 (Yānasandhip.): V, **57**o, 2264 (among the allies of Yudhishṭhira).—§ 562 (Bhagavadyānap.): V, **72*a*,** 2594 (do.).—§ 565 (Gālavacarita): V, **117,** 3960 (°*īnām īçvaraḥ*, sc. Divodāsa).—§ 573 (Ambopākhyānap.):

V, **176,** 6033 (°*nagaram*, i.e. Vārāṇasī); **196,** 7623 (*Cedi-Kāçi-Karūshāṇām netāram . . . Dhṛshṭaketum*). — § 574 (Jambūkh.): VI, **9**μ, 347 (°*Koçalāḥ*, only C., B. has *Kānti-Kosalāḥ*), 349 (*Kāçayo 'para-Kāçayaḥ*).—§ 576 (Bhagavadgītāp.): VI, **13,** 500 (°*puryām*, i.e. Vārāṇasī).—§ 578 (Bhīshmavadhap.): VI, **47**δ[25], 1811 (*Cedi-K°-Karūsheshu*, in the army of Yudhishṭhira, attacked by Bhīshma).—§ 580 (do.): VI, **56**η, 2415 (*Cedi-K°-Karūshaiḥ*, followed Dhṛshṭaketu).—§ 586 (do.): VI, **106**υ, 4819 (*Cedi-K°-Karūshāṇāṃ sahasrāṇi caturdaça*, are slain by Bhīshma).—§ 587 (do.): VI, **116**π, 5446 (do.).—§ 588 (do.): VI, **122,** 5832 (°*puram*, i.e. Vārāṇasī).—§ 589 (Droṇābhishekap.): VII, **11**ν, 397 (°-*Kauçalān*, had been vanquished by Kṛshṇa). —§ 599 (Jayadrathavadhap.): VII, **125**μμ, 5069 (°*Koçalāḥ*, attacked Droṇa).—§ 604 (Karṇap.): VIII, **8**η, 236 (°-*Koçalān*, vanquished by Karṇa and caused to pay tribute to Duryodhana).—§ 608 (do.): VIII, **73,** 3662 (*Cedi-K°-Pañcālān*, had been vanquished by Bhīshma in the great battle). — § 722 (Ānuçāsanik.): XIII, **5,** 265 (*vishaye K°rājasya*).—§ 736*b* (Vītahavyop.): XIII, **30,** 1949 (ruled by Haryaçva, then by Sudeva, then by Divodāsa), 1990 (*vishayaḥ K°īnām*).—§ 738 (Ānuçāsanik.): XIII, **32,** 2052 (°*rājyam*, ruled by Vṛshadarbha Uçīnara), 2080 (°*īnām īçvaraḥ*, i.e. Vṛshadarbha Uçīnara).—§ 744 (do.): XIII, **44**β, 2441 (had been defeated by Bhīshma at the svayaṃvara of Ambā, etc.).—§ 777 (do): XIII, **169,** 7785 (°*puryām*, i.e. Vārāṇasī, do.).—§ 785 (Anugītāp.): XIV, **83,** 2469 (the sacrificial horse proceeded to the *K.*, etc.). Cf. Kāçika, pl., Kāçya, pl.

Kāçīça[1] ("the king of the Kāçis"), contemporary with the great battle. § 609 (Çalyap.): IX, **2,** 73 (among the allies of Duryodhana).

Kāçīçā[2] (do.) = Divodāsa: XIII, 1954 (*D°*).

Kāçīçvarasya tīrtha(m) (B. °*āni*). § 364 (Tīrthayātrāp.): III, **83,** 6027.

Kāçika ("the Kāçi prince"?). § 572 (Rathātirathasaṅkhyānap.): V, **171,** 5907 (a ratha in the army of Yudhishṭhira).

Kāçika, pl., a people = Kāçi, pl. § 592 (Saṃçaptakavadhap.): VII, **24**σ, 1052 (only B., C. has *Koçikāḥ*, among the allies of Duryodhana).—§ 604 (Karṇap.): VIII, **6,** 173 (followed Abhibhū).

Kāçikanyā ("the daughter of the Kāçi king") = Ambā: V, 2000 (re-born as Çikhaṇḍin), 7030, 7043, 7179, 7352, 7356, 7364.

Kāçikarūsharāja ("the king of the Kāçis and the Karūshas") = Alarka: III, †957 (*A°*).

Kāçin, a son of Kavi. § 747*b* (Suvarṇotpatti): XIII, **85**ι, 4150 (the seventh son of Kavi).

Kāçinagara ("the city of the Kāçis") = Vārāṇasī: V, 6033.

Kāçinandana ("the son of the Kāçi king") = Sudeva: XIII, 1953.

Kāçipa ("the king of the Kāçis") = Suvarṇanāman: I, †1809 (*S.*, father of Vapushṭamā, the wife of Janamejaya Pārikshita).

Kāçipati[1] (do.), the father of Ambā, Ambikā, and Ambālikā. § 167 (Vicitravīryop.): I, **102,** 4083 (°*eḥ kanyāḥ*, robbed by Bhīshma and given in marriage to Vicitravīrya), 4132 (°*eḥ sutā jyeshṭhā*, i.e. Ambā), 4136 (*jyeshṭhām Ambām K°eḥ sutām*).—§ 171 (Vicitravīryasutotp.): I, **106,** 4298 (°*eḥ sutā*, i.e. Ambikā). — § 573 (Ambopākhyānap.): V, **173,** 5953 (°*eḥ purīm*, i.e. Vārāṇasī); **174,** 5967 (°*eḥ kanyāḥ*, robbed by Bhīshma), 5969 (*jyeshṭhā K°eḥ sutā*, i.e. Ambā); **175,** 5994 (°*eḥ sutām*, = do.), 5996 (*jyeshṭhā K°eḥ sutā*, = do.); **186,** 7367 (°*eḥ sutā*, = do.); **192,** 7551 (*jyeshṭhā K°eḥ kanyā Ambā*). Cf. Kāçirāja.

Kāçipati[2] (do.), contemporary of the great battle. § 561 (Yānasandhip.): V, **50**η, 2007 (*Vārāṇasyām*, has sided with Yudhishṭhira, C. has by error *Kāçī°*).—§ 589 (Droṇābhishekap.): VII, **8**θ, †248 (*Çaibyātmajaḥ*?, attacked Droṇa). Cf. Kāçirāja[5], Kāçya[2].

Kāçipati[3] (do.) = Pratardana: XII, 8594 (*P°*); XIII, 6249 (*P°*).

Kāçipura ("the city of the Kāçis") = Vārāṇasī: VI, 5832.

Kāçipurī (do.) = Vārāṇasī: VI, 500; XIII, 7785.

Kāçirāja[1] ("the king of the Kāçis"), one or more princes. § 130 (Aṃçāvat.): I, **67,** 2676 (incarnation of the Asura Dīrghajihva). — § 589 (Droṇābhishekap.): VII, **10,** 364 (*yaḥ* — i.e. Dhṛshṭadyumna — *putram K°sya Vārāṇasyām mahāratham | samare strīshu gṛdhyantam bhallenāpāharad rathāt*).—§ 793 (Mausalap.): XVI, **6**κ, 159 (had been slain by Kṛshṇa).

Kāçirāja[2] (do.), the father of Ambā, Ambikā, and Ambālikā. § 167 (Vicitravīryop.): I, **102,** 4093 (held a svayaṃvara, at which Bhīshma robbed his three daughters).—§ 572 (Rathātirathasaṅkhyānap.): V, **168,** 5842 (°*svayaṃvare*, all. to § 167). Cf. Kāçipati[1].

Kāçirāja[3] (do.), the father of the two wives of Bṛhadratha. § 275 (Rājasūyārambhap.): II, **17,** 692 (°*sya sute yamaje*, mothers of Jarāsandha).

Kāçirāja[4] (do.) = Subāhu: II, 1080 (*S°*, vanquished by Bhīmasena on his digvijaya).

Kāçirāja[5] (do.), contemporary of the great battle. § 553 (Vaivāhikap.): IV, **72,** 2351 (came to Yudhishṭhira with one akshauhiṇī of troops; C. has by error *Kāçī°*).—§ 562 (Bhagavadyānap.): V, **80**ε, 2857 (among the allies of Yudhishṭhira); **83**θ, 2950.—§ 576 (Bhagavadgītāp.): VI, **25**θ, 834 (in the army of Yudhishṭhira).—§ 578 (Bhīshmavadhap.): VI, **50**π, 2088 (in the krauñcavyūha of Yudhishṭhira); **51***aa*, 2117.—§ 582 (do.): VI, **71,** 3138 (fights with Āvantya).—§ 589 (Droṇabhishekap.): VII, **8**θ, †251.—§ 604 (Karṇap.): VIII, **6,** 173 (*Abhibhūḥ*?, has been slain by the son of Vasudāna). Cf. Abhibhū, Kāçipati[2], Kāçya[2].

Kāçirāja[6] (do.) = Sudeva: XIII, 1952 (*S°*).

Kāçirājaduhitarau ("the two daughters of the Kāçi king") = Ambikā and Ambālikā: I, ††3804 (*Ambikāmbālike*).

Kāçirājan = Kāçirāja[2] (?): V, 6040.

Kāçirājasutā ("the daughter of the Kāçi king") = Ambā: V, 6067, 7004, 7054, 7118.

Kāçirājasutāḥ ("the daughters of the Kāçi king") = Ambā, Ambikā, and Ambālikā: V, 5950.

Kaçirājasute[1] ("the two daughters of the Kāçi king") = Ambikā and Ambālikā: I, 4154.

Kāçirājasute[2] (do.) = the wives of Bṛhadratha: II, 726.

Kāçisuta ("the daughter of the Kāçi king") = Ambā: V, 7345, 7388 (*jyeshṭhā*).

Kāçisute ("the two daughters of the Kāçi king") = Ambikā and Ambālikā: I, 4360.

Kāçmīra, pl. (°*āḥ*), a people (the inhabitants of Kashmir). § 295 (Dyūtap.): II, **52,** 1870 (brought tribute to Yudhishṭhira). — § 358 (Tīrthayātrāp.): III, **82,** 5032 (°*eshv eva nāgasya bhavanam Takshakasya ca | Vitastākhyam iti khyātam sarvapāpapramocanam*). — § 574 (Jambūkh.): VI, **9**μ, 361 (ο), 375.—§ 595 (Shoḍaçarāj., v. Rāma Jāmadagnya): VII, **70**β, 2435 (°-*Daradān*, had been vanquished by Rāma Jāmadagnya). Cf. Kāçmīraka, pl.

Kāçmīra, adj. ("belonging to the Kāçmīras"): § 549 (Pāṇḍavapraveçap.): IV, **9,** 254 (*°īva turaṅgamī*).

Kāçmīraka, adj. (do.). § 279 (Arjuna): II, **27,** 1025 (*°ān vīrān kshatriyān*, vanquished by Arjuna on his digvijaya).—§ 287 (Rājasūyikap.): II, **34,** 1271 (*rājā*, came to the rājasūya of Yudhishṭhira).

Kāçmīraka, pl. (*°āḥ*), a people, = Kāçmīra, pl. § 342 (Indralokābhigámanap.): III, **51,** 1991 (had been present at the rājasūya of Yudhishṭhira).—§ 589 (Droṇābhishekap.): VII, **11**ν, 397 (had been vanquished by Kṛshṇa).

Kāçmīramaṇḍala ("the region of the Kāçmīras"). § 410 (Plakshāvataraṇagamana): III, **130,** 10545 (*g*: Here took place a conference between Agni and Kāçyapa, and between Nahusha's son and the ṛshis of the north).—§ 733*b* (Candrabhāgā): XIII, **25,** 1695 (with many rivers, which fall into the Indus).

Kāçya[1] ("the king of the Kāçis"), the father of Ambā, Ambikā, and Ambālikā. § 167 (Vicitravīryop.): I, **102,** 4128 (*°sya sutāḥ*, i.e. Ambā, etc.).—§ 573 (Ambopākhyānap.): V, **178,** 7067 (*sutāṃ K°sya*, i.e. Ambā). Cf. Kāçipati, Kāçirāja.

Kāçya[2] (do.), the Kāçi king at the time of Yudhishṭhira. § 296 (Dyūtap.): II, **53,** 1916 (waited upon Yudhishṭhira at the rājasūya).—§ 299 (Dyūtap.): II, **68,** 2252.—§ 554 (Sainyodyogap.): V, **4**γ, 82 (among the princes to whom the Pāṇḍavas ought to send messengers).—§ 570 (Sainyaniryāṇap.): V, **151**δ, 5160 (*putraḥ K°sya vā Vibhuḥ* (*cābhibhuḥ*, B.)).—§ 572 (Rathātirathasaṅkhyānap.): V, **171,** 5915 (a ratha in the army of Yudhishṭhira).—§ 573 (Ambopākhyānap.): V, **196**μ, 7650 (*putraḥ K°sya vā vibhuḥ* (so also B.)).—§ 576 (Bhagavadgītāp.): VI, **25**κ, 846 (in the army of Yudhishṭhira).—§ 578 (Bhīshmavadhap.): VI, **51**ω, 2110 (*putraḥ K°sya vā Vibhuḥ* (*cābhibhūḥ*, B.)).—§ 585 (do.): VI, **93**ψ, 4151 (do. (do.)).—§ 592 (Saṃçaptakavadhap.): VII, **23**ο, 976 (*°syābhimukhaṃ*—B. *°bhuvaḥ—putraṃ*, description of his horses), 990 (*°sya putraḥ me Vibhuḥ* (*cābhibhūḥ*, B.), followed Dhṛshṭaketu); **25,** 1109 (three sons of Dhṛtarāshṭra resisted *Nīla-K°-Jayatsenān*). — § 599 (Jayadrathavadhap.): VII, **85**δ, 3049 (*putraḥ K°sya vā Vibhuḥ* (*cābhibhūḥ*, B.)); **95,** 3528 (*°syābhibhuvaḥ putraṃ*, attacked by Çaibya Govāsana); **96,** 3552 (*°putraṃ*, do.). Cf. Abhibhū, Kaçipati[2], Kaçirāja[5].

Kāçya[3] = Babhru[7] (v. Additions): V, †806 (*B°*).

Kāçya[4], a ṛshi. § 637 (Rājadh.): XII, **47**η, 1597 (among the ṛshis who surrounded Bhīshma).—§ 730 (Ānuçāsanik.): XIII, **14**ββ, 991.

Kāçya, pl. (*°āḥ*), a people, = Kāçi, pl. § 608 (Karṇap.): VIII, **47***a*, 2226 (*°-Matsyaiḥ*).

Kāçyā[1] ("daughter of the Kāçi king") = Balandharā, the wife of Bhīmasena: I, ††3829 (*B°*).

Kāçyā[2] (do.) = Ambā: V, 7026, 7188, 7362.

Kaçyapa, a ṛshi and prajāpati, son of Marīci. § 27 (cf. Āstīkap.): Sauti related: Kadrū and Vinatā, the daughters of Prajāpati, obtained from their husband *K.* the boon that Kadrū would have 1,000 snakes as her offspring, and Vinatā two sons, who would surpass the 1,000 sons of Kadrū. Then *K.* went to the forest. After a long time Kadrū brought forth 1,000 eggs and Vinatā two. After 500 years the 1,000 eggs of Kadrū burst, but the twins of Vinatā did not yet appear. Vinatā then broke one of the eggs, and out came Aruṇa (who afterwards became the charioteer of the Sun (*Sūrya*)). His lower extremities were yet undeveloped, and he cursed his mother, saying that she should serve as a slave, but be delivered by her other son, if she would wait 500 years patiently without breaking the egg. After the expiration of the 500 years Garuḍa came out of the egg (I, **16**): I, **16,** 1074 (*Prajāpatisamaḥ*), 1075, 1078, 1081.—§ 29 (Kadrū): I, **20,** 1202, 1204 (*Prajāpatiṃ*, received from Brahmán the knowledge of neutralizing poisons—*vishaharīṃ vidyāṃ*, cf. Kāçyapa[1]).—§ 33 (Garuḍa): I, **23,** 1257 (*ṛsheḥ sutaḥ . . . K°sya*, i.e. Garuḍa).—§ 35 (Aruṇa): I, **24,** 1275 (*°sya suto dhīmān Aruṇety abhiviçrutaḥ*).—§ 41 (Garuḍa): I, **29,** (1347) (*mahān ṛshiḥ*), (1352) (told Garuḍa of Supratīka and Vibhāvasu).—§ 43 (do.): I, **30,** 1393, 1397, (1398), 1399, (1400), 1402, 1404 (propitiated the Vālakhilyas for Garuḍa).—§ 44 (do.): I, **30,** 1425 (*°sya muneḥ putraḥ*, i.e. Garuḍa).—§ 45 (Vālakhilya, pl.): I, **31,** 1437, 1440 (*Prajāpateḥ*), 1441, 1450, 1451 (*Prajāpatiḥ*), 1452 (do.), 1456, 1460, 1463 (at the sacrifice which *K.* performed in order to have a son, Indra disregarded the Vālakhilyas, who cursed him saying that there should arise another Indra; according to this *K.* begat on Vinatā an Indra of the winged creatures (viz. Garuḍa) and Aruṇa).—§ 48 (Çesha): I, **36,** 1574 (*varadānāt . . . K°sya*).—§ 49 (Vāsuki): I, **37,** 1619 (*prasādanaṃ . . . K°sya*).—§ 86 (Aṃçāvat.): I, **65,** 2519 (*Marīceḥ K°ḥ putraḥ*, progenitor of the creatures).—§ 115 (do.): I, **66,** 2577 (married thirteen daughters of Daksha).—§ 118 (do.): I, **66,** 2598 (*Marīceḥ K°ḥ putraḥ*, from him the gods and Asuras were born).—§ 138 (Daksha Prācetasa): I, **75,** 3134 (married thirteen daughters of Daksha). — § 139 (Manu Vaivasvata): I, **75,** 3135 (upon the best of the daughters of Daksha (i.e. on Aditi) *K.* begat the Ādityas). — § 164 (Āpavop.): I, **99,** 3927 (had begotten [Nandinī] the homa cow of Vasishṭha with Surabhi).—§ 191 (Arjuna): I, **123,** 4807 (among the seven maharshis, present at the birth of Arjuna).—§ 201 (Droṇa): I, **130,** 5128 (Rāma Jāmadagnya gave the whole earth to *K.*, cf. § 398).—§ 270 (Brahmasabhāv.): II, **11,** 436 (among the *prajānāṃ patayaḥ* in the palace of Brahmán).—§ 300 (Prahlāda): II, **68,** 2320, (2323), 2334 (answered a question put by Prahlāda).—§ 317*b* (Kṛshṇa): III, **12,** 512 (worshipped Kṛshṇa). — § 327 (Draupadīparitāpav.): III, **31,** 1199 (*ṛshiḥ*).—§ 376 (Tīrthayātrāp.): III, **85,** 8262 (among the ṛshis who expect Yudhishṭhira on his tīrthayātrā).—§ 392*e* (Svayambhuvo vanaṃ): III, **114,** 10112, 10115 (Brahmán gave the earth to *K.* as dakshiṇā; resenting this, the earth sank to Rasātala, but was appeased by *K.*).—§ 090 (Paraçu-Rāma): III, **117,** 10207, 10208, 10209 (Rāma gave to *K.* the earth, etc.).—§ 459 (Mārkaṇḍeyas.): III, **189,** 12955 (*Prajapatiḥ*, identif. with Nārāyaṇa).—§ 491 (Aṅgirasa): III, **220,** 14164 (name of a fire, but read with B. *Kaçyapasya*).—§ 524*d* (Vishṇu): III, **272,** 15839 (begat upon Aditi the dwarf incarnation of Vishṇu).—§ 564 (Mātalīyop.): V, **101,** 3589 (through Vinatā the progenitor of the Suparṇas (through Garuḍa)); **103,** 3633 (progenitor of the serpents); **105,** 3683 (Garuḍa and Indra are both sons of *K.* and a daughter of Daksha).—§ 565 (Gālavac.): V, **108,** 3766 (the children of *K.* first multiplied (*pravṛddhāḥ*) in the east); **110,** 3803 (*bhagavān devaḥ*, anointed Varuṇa as king [of the west]—read with B. *Varuṇaṃ smābhyasecayat*), 3819 (*maharsheḥ K°syātra*—i.e. in the west—*Mārīcasya niveçanaṃ*); **117,** 3971 (*reme . . . Adityāṃ K°o yathā*). — § 574 (Jambūkh.): VI, **6,** 215 (*Prajāpatiḥ*, repairs to Meru on the parvans). — § 595 (Shoḍaçarāj., v. Rāma Jāmadagnya): VII, **70,** 2442, 2443 (C. by error *Kā°*), 2446 (*K.* received from Rāma Jāmadagnya a golden altar, eighteen nalas high, and the earth; moreover, at his horse-sacrifice 100,000 elephants; *K.* then ordered Rāma to go out of the earth).—§ 599 (Jayadrathavadhap.): VII, **94**ε, 3453 (mentioned in a blessing to Duryodhana).—§ 602 (Droṇābhishekap.): VII, **190**ν, 8727.—§ 615u (Skanda): IX, **45**γ, 2512 (came to the investiture of Skanda), 2525 (anointed Skanda).—§ 615bb (Rāmatīrtha): IX, **49**, 2837 (*munisattamaṃ*, assisted Rāma Jāmadagnya at his sacrifices and received as dakshiṇā the earth with her oceans).—§ 638 (Rāmopākhyānap.): XII, **49**, 1779, 1782, 1787, 1789, 1803 (when Rāma Jāmadagnya had given the earth to *K.* as dakshiṇā *K.* ordered Rāma to quit his territory and repair to the bank of the southern ocean, where Rāma took up his abode in Çūrpāraka. *K.* gave the earth to the brahmans; when the earth had sunk to Rasātala, *K.* held her on his lap (*ūruṇā*), therefore she was called Urvī; the earth begged of *K.* a king; *K.* then sought out those kshatriyas who had been preserved, and installed them as kings).—§ 641 (Rājadh.): XII, **73**, 2780 (*Aila-K° saṃvādaṃ*), (†2782), †2792, (†2793), (†2795), (†2797), (†2799) (discourse between Aila and *K.*).—§ 658b (Kṛtaghnop.): XII, **169**, 6336 (*°syātmasambhavaḥ*, sc. Rājadharman (Nāḍījaṅgha), the king of the cranes); **170**, 6343 (*°sya putro 'haṃ mātā Dākshāyaṇī ca me*, says Rājadharman). —§ 659 (Mokshadh.): XII, **180**, 6728 (read *Kāçyapa* with B.).—§ 664 (do.): XII, **207**, 7535 (son of Marīci, C. has *Kā°*); 7538 (*Mārīcaḥ*, married thirteen daughters of Daksha, among whom Diti was the eldest; his progeny, C. has *Kā°*). —§ 665 (do.): XII, **208**a, 7574 (son of Marīci; some call him *K.*, others Arishṭanemi), (β), 7582 (father of the twelve Ādityas (enumerated)).—§ 666 (do.): XII, **209**, 7609 (*maharshiṇā*, narrated the history of the boar incarnation of Vishṇu).—§ 702 (do.): XII, **297**δ, 10874 (among the ṛshis who have obtained their positions by way of penances, but B. has *Kā°* (= Ṛshyaçṛṅga?)), 10877 (originally only four gotras arose: Aṅgiras, *K.*, Vasishṭha, and Bhṛgu; C., however, has *Kā°*). —§ 707 (do.): XII, **319**β, 11785 (*pituḥ*, sc. Viçvāvasu's, had instructed Viçvāvasu). —§ 717b (Nārāyaṇīya): XII, **340**, 12945 (Nārāyaṇa says that he will take birth as the twelfth Āditya, son of Kaçyapa and Aditi); **343**, XI), ††13219 (married thirteen daughters of Daksha), 13248 (*Prajāpatiḥ*, called Kṛshṇa Vṛshākapi). —§ 728b (Bhaṅgāsvanop.): XIII, **12**, 556 (*°sya*—sc. *putrāḥ*—*surāsurāḥ*), 557 (*°sya surāç caiva Asurāç ca sutās tathā*).—§ 730 (Ānuçāsanik.): XIII, **14**ββ, 991 (praised Çiva).—§ 744 (do.): XIII, **47**, 2561 (*maharshir api caitad vai Mārīcaḥ K°o*—B. *Kā°*—*'bravīt*).—§ 746 (do.): XIII, **66**, 3318 (*maharsheḥ*, sesame seeds sprung from the limbs of *K.*).—§ 747b (Suvarṇotpatti): XIII, **85**, 4124 (*Mārīcaḥ*).—§ 749 (Ānuçāsanik.): XIII, **92**δ, 4392 (*mahān ṛshiḥ*, among the masters of yoga).—§ 750b (Bisastainyop.): XIII, **93**a, 4416, (β), (4440), (γ), (4465), (δ), (4486), 4486 (etymology of his name), (ε), (4517).—§ 751b (Çapathavidhi): XIII, **94**a, †4550, (β), (4564).—§ 768b (Umā-Maheçvarasaṃv.): XIII, **146**γ, 6752 (husband of Aditi).—§ 768c (Balarāma): XIII, **148**, 6864 (*Suparṇaḥ . . . K°syātmajaḥ*, i.e. Garuḍa). —§ 770 (Ānuçāsanik.): XIII, **151**ι, 7116 (among the seven gurus of Dhaneçvara in the north).—§ 772c (Pavanārjunasaṃv.): Vāyu said: The earth vying with the *Aṅga* king abandoned her character as earth (*tyaktvā mahītvaṃ*) and disappeared (? *nāçaṃ jagāma*). *K.* then paralysed her (XIII, **154**). Vayu repeated: Once a king named *Aṅga* wished to give away the whole earth as dakshiṇā to the brahmans. The goddess of the earth, 'Brahmán's daughter,' then left this king and his kingdom to meet with destruction, and departed for the region of Brahmán. Leaving his body by way of yoga (*samāhitaḥ*), *K.* then entered the earth, which penetrated by *K.* (*Kāçyapī*) grew in prosperity and righteousness for 30,000 celestial years, then the goddess came to *K.* and became his daughter (*Kāçyapī*): XIII, **154**, 7214; **155**, 7235, 7238, 7239.—§ 775 (Ānuçāsanik.): XIII, **166**a, 7643 (*Mārīcaḥ*).—§ 782g (Guruçishyasaṃv.): XIV, **35**δ, 961. Cf. Devarshi, Kāçyapa, Maharshi, Mārīca, Prajāpati.

Kāçyapa[1], one or more brahmarshis of Kaçyapa's race. § 17 (Uttaṅka): I, **3**, 844 (all. to § 51).—§ 51 (Parikshit): I, **42**, 1757 (*dvijasattamaḥ*), 1760, (1762), (1765); **43**, 1766, (1768), 1769, 1771, 1772, 1774 (*dvijasattamaḥ*), 1781, 1783, 1784, 1785 (*K.* was going to Hāstinapura to cure Parikshit from the bite of Takshaka; on the way he met with Takshaka, to whom he showed his power by reviving a banyan-tree which was bit by Takshaka. Then Takshaka gave *K.* much wealth and prevailed upon him to return home).—§ 56 (do.): I, **50**, 1979 (*Brahmarshiḥ*), (1980), 1983, 1984, 1987 (repetition of § 51).—§ 57 (Janamejaya): I, **50**, 1994, 1998 (*saṃvādaṃ pannagendrasya K°sya ca*), 2010, 2011, 2012 (*dvijasattamaṃ*, repetition from § 51).—§ 324 (Dvaitavanapr.): III, **26**a, 986 (among the brahmans who waited upon Yudhishṭhira).—§ 327 (Draupadīparitāpav.): III, **29**, 1099 (some gāthās (vv. 1100–8) of his are quoted), 1109.—§ 410g (Kāçmīramaṇḍala): III, **130**, 10546 (*Agneḥ saṃvādaṃ K°sya*, in the country of the Kāçmīras).—§ 455 (Brāhmaṇamāhātmyak.): III, **185**, 12697.—§ 459 (Mārkaṇḍeyas.): III, 189, 12955 (read with B. *Ka°*, q.v.).—§ 595 (Shoḍaçarāj., v. Rāma Jāmadagnya): VII, **70**, 2443 (read with B. *Ka°*, q.v.).—§ 637 (Rājadh.): XII, **47**η, 1597 (among the ṛshis who surrounded Bhīshma).—§ 659 (Mokshadh.): XII, **180**, 6693 (*Indra-K°-saṃvādaṃ*), 6694 (*ṛshisutaṃ*), 6698, 6708, 6721, 6728 (C. by error *Ka°*), 6741, 6743 (discourse between *K.* and Indra in the shape of a jackal).—§ 664 (Mokshadh.): XII, **207**, 7535 (read with B. *Ka°*, q.v.), 7538 (do.).—§ 665 (do.): XII, **208**ι, 7598 (among the ṛshis of the north).—§ 702 (do.): XII, **297**, 10874 (only B., C. has *Ka°*, q.v.), 10877 (only C., but read with B. *Ka°*, q.v.).—§ 732 (Ānuçāsanik.): XIII, **22**a, 1540, (1542), 1545 (discourse between the Earth, Agni, *K.*, and Mārkaṇḍeya).—§ 733 (do.): XIII, **25**, 1755 (had discoursed to Aṅgiras about the tīrthas).—§ 734 (do.): XIII, **26**a, 1762 (among the ṛshis who came to see Bhīshma).—§ 744 (do.): XIII, **47**, 2561 (only B., C. has *Ka°*, q.v.).—§ 746 (do.): XIII, **62**, 3136 (Rāma Jāmadagnya had given the earth to *K.* as dakshiṇā, cf. Kaçyapa).—§ 747 (do.): XIII, **84**β, 3968 (questioned by Rāma Jāmadagnya; is not *Ka°* to be read?).—§ 768 (do.): XIII, **139**a, 6298 (came to see the penances of Kṛshṇa).—§ 770 (do.): XIII, 151ν, 7157.—§ 775 (do.): XIII, **166**ε, 7668 (one of the ṛshis of the west).—§ 782 (Anugītāp.): XIV, **16**, 425, 429, 432, 453; **17**, (455) (instructed by an ascetic). Cf. Kaçyapa and the following headings.

Kāçyapa[2] ("son or descendant of Kaçyapa") = Kaṇva: I, 2870, 2874 (*maharshiṃ K°ṃ . . . Kaṇvaṃ*), 2876 (*muniṃ*), 2893, †2894, 2975.

Kāçyapa[3] (do.) = Vibhāṇḍaka: III, 9990 (*āçramaḥ . . . K°sya*), 9992 (*°sya sutaḥ*, i.e. Ṛshyaçṛṅga), 10001, 10030 (*°āçramāt*), 10031, †10047 (*V°*), †10075, †10077 (*°syaikaputraṃ*, i.e. Ṛshyaçṛṅga), †10085.

Kāçyapa[4] (do.) = Rājadharman (Nāḍījaṅgha): XII, 6350, 6352, 6374.

Kāçyapa[5] (do.) = Viçvāvasu: XII, 11777, 11802, 11805.

Kāçyapa[6] (do.) = Indra (?): XIII, 624.

Kāçyapa[7], name of a fire. § 491 (Āṅgirasa): III, **220**, 14156 (= Uktha, Nīl.), 14164 (C. by error *Ka°*).

Kāçyapa, dual (°*au*) ("descendants of Kaçyapa"), = Yaja and Upayaja: I, 6363 (*gotrataḥ K°au*).

Kāçyapa, pl. (°*āḥ*) (do.). § 324 (Dvaitavanapr.): III, **26**, 970 (accompany Yudhishṭhira).—§ 393 (Tīrthayātrāp.): III, **115**, 10126.—§ 656*b* (Khaḍgotpattik.): XII, **166**β, 6142.

Kaçyapadvīpa (B. *Kā°*). § 574 (Jambūkh.): VI, **6**, 251 (*K.* and Nāgadvīpa are the two ears [of the hare-shaped Jambudvīpa]).

Kāçyapanandana, pl. (°*āh*) = the gods: XIII, 3330.

Kāçyapaputra ("the son of Kāçyapa [i.e. Vibhāṇḍaka]") = Ṛshyaçṛṅga: III, †10037.

Kāçyapātmaja (do.) = Ṛshyaçṛṅga: III, 9994 (*Ṛ°*).

Kāçyapeya[1] ("the son of Kaçyapa") = Garuḍa: I, 1247.

Kāçyapeya[2] ("descendant of Kaçyapa") = Dāruka: VII, 6352.

Kāçyapeya, pl. (°*āḥ*) ("the sons of Kaçyapa") = the Ādityas: XIII, 7094 (*A°*).

Kāçyapi ("the son of Kaçyapa") = Rājadharman (Nāḍījaṅgha): XII, 6346.

Kāçyapī ("the daughter of Kaçyapa") = the Earth: XIII, 3164, 4350 (*Vaishṇavī K°ī*), 7237 (*Bhūmiḥ*), 7238.

Kādraveya, pl. (°*āḥ*) ("sons or descendants of Kadrū") = the serpents. § 49 (Vāsuki): I, **37**, 1597 (held a consultation about the means of being delivered from death at the snake-sacrifice).—§ 100 (Aṃçāvat.): I, **65**, 2549 (six *K.s* enumerated).—§ 191 (Arjuna): I, **123**, 4806 (present at the birth of Arjuna).—§ 608 (Karṇap.): VIII, **87**χ, 4415 (sided with Arjuna). Cf. Kadrūja, pl., Kadrūputra, pl., Nāga, pl., Sarpa, pl.

Kadru = Çiva (1000 names[1]).

Kadrū, daughter of Daksha, wife of Kaçyapa, and mother of the serpents. § 27 (Kaçyapa): I, **16**, 1074 (daughter of Prajāpati (i.e. Daksha), married to Kaçyapa), 1076 (chose to have 1,000 nāgas as her sons), 1080.—§ 27*b* (do.): After a long time *K.* brought forth 1,000 eggs, which burst after 500 years: I, **16**, 1082.—§ 29 (cf. Āstīkap.): Once *K.* and Vinatā bet about the colour of Uccaiḥçravas, and she who lost should become the other's slave, Vinatā asserting that he was all white, *K.* that he was black in his tail. *K.* ordered her sons to transform themselves into black hair and cover the horse's tail. When they refused she cursed them, saying that the Fire (*Pāvaka*) should consume them at the snake-sacrifice of Janamejaya. Seeing that the snakes had multiplied exceedingly, Brahmán, with all the gods, sanctioned this curse, which had been "indicated in the Purāṇas" (so PCR., *dṛshṭaṃ purātanaṃ*, v. 1204), and propitiated Kaçyapa by bestowing upon him the knowledge of neutralizing poisons: I, **20**, 1190, (1192), 1194, 1197, 1201.—§ 30 (do.): In the morning *K.* and Vinatā went to inspect Uccaiḥçravas. Description of Samudra (the Ocean) (*b*); I, **21**, 1205.—§ 31 (do.): The Nāgas (serpents), notwithstanding their refusal, went and became hairs in the horse's tail. Second description of the Ocean, v. Samudradarçana (*b*): I, **22**, 1227 (*K°ç ca Vinatā caiva Dākshāyaṇyau*).—§ 32 (do.): Vinatā, having lost the wager, became the slave of *K.* [but was afterwards released by] Garuḍa (*b*): I, **23**, 1235, 1237.—§ 36 (do): Some time afterwards *K.* ordered Vinatā to carry her to a remote place, inhabited by the Nāgas, in the midst of the Ocean; the snakes which were carried by Garuḍa (*b*) became scorched by the rays of the sun: I, **25**, 1281.—§ 37 (Indra): I, **25**, 1285 (*K.* then praised Indra).—§ 38 (cf. Āstīkap.); Indra then caused a downpour of rain, and the snakes with their mother reached Rāmaṇīyaka: I, **26**, 1296.—§ 47 (Sarpanāmak.): I, **35**, 1547 (enumeration of the principal sons of *K.*).—§ 48 (Çesha): I, **36**, 1566 (Çesha left his mother *K.*).—§ 49 (Vāsuki): I, **38**, 1628 (all. to § 29).—§ 60 (Sarpasattra): I, **54**, 2071 (*Pannagānāṃ* . . . *mātā*, repetition from § 29).—§ 87 (Aṃçāvat.): I, **65**, 2521 (*Dakshakanyā*, wife of Kaçyapa).—§ 129 (do.): I, **66**, 2634 (Surasā gave birth to the Nāgas, Kadrū to the Pannagas).—§ 270 (Brahmasabhāv.): II, **11**, 457 (°*uḥ*, in the palace of Brahmán).—§ 502 (Manushyagrahak.): III, **230**, 14471 (*K.* introduces herself in a subtle form into the body of a pregnant woman and causes the destruction of the fœtus, and the mother is caused to give birth to a nāga (serpent)).

Kadrūja, pl. (°*āḥ*) ("the sons of Kadrū") = the serpents. § 775 (Ānuçāsanik.): XIII, **166*a***, 7644 (*pannagāḥ*). Cf. Kādraveya, pl., Kadruputra, pl.

Kadrūputra, pl. (°*āḥ*) (do.) = the serpents. § 27 (Kaçyapa): I, **16**, 1077 (°*ādhikau bale*, sc. Garuḍa and Aruṇa), 1084.—§ 39 (Rāmaṇīyaka): I, **27**, 1312.—§ 46 (Garuḍa): I, **34**, 1531. Cf. Kādraveya, pl., Kadrūja, pl.

Kāhali = Çiva (1000 names[2]).

Kahoḍa, a brahman, father of Ashṭāvakra. § 412 (Ashṭāvakrīya): III, **132**, †10603 (disciple of Uddālaka, whose daughter Sujātā he married; on her he begot Ashṭāvakra), †10612 (went to the sacrifice of Janaka, where he was vanquished by Bandin in a controversy, and drowned); **134**, †10681 (when Bandin had been vanquished by Ashṭāvakra *K.* arose from the water), (10683).

Kahoḍasūnu ("the son of Kahoḍa") = Ashṭāvakra: III, †10599 (*A°*).

Kaiçika, pl. (°*āḥ*), a people. § 273 (Rājasūyārambhap.): II, **14**, 585 (*Pāṇḍya-Kratha-K°ān*, had been vanquished by Bhīshmaka).

Kaikaya (B., probably more correctly Kekaya), pl. (°*āḥ*), name of a people (= Kekaya, pl.), especially five brothers who joined Yudhishṭhira (the rest followed Duryodhana). § 130 (Aṃçāvat.): I, **67**, 2647 (five Asuras were re-born among the *K.*).—§ 295 (Dyūtap.): II, **52**, 1870 (*Madra-K°āḥ*, among the peoples who brought tribute to Yudhishṭhira).—§ 556 (Sañjayayānap.): V, **22**, †664 (v. Kaikeya, pl.).—§ 561 (Yānasandhip.): V, **57**ξ, 2248 (*bhrātaraḥ pañca*, have chosen the *Kaikeyāḥ* (*Kekayāḥ*, B.) in Duryodhana's army as their share); **61**ψ, 2406 (among the allies of Yudhishṭhira; the five brothers ?).—§ 562 (Bhagavadyānap.): V, **83**θ, 2951 (worshipped Kṛshṇa; the five brothers ?).—§ 569 (do.): V, **144**λ, 4887 (among the allies of Yudhishṭhira).—§ 576 (Bhagavadgītāp.): VI, **18**δ, 688 (in the army of Duryodhana); **20**, †752 (*bhrātaraḥ*, do.).—§ 581 (Bhīshmavadhap.): VI, **61**[3]δ, 2691 (attacked Arjuna), (ε), 2695 (attacked by Dhṛshṭadyumna).—§ 582 (do.): VI, **72**η, 3169 (attacked by Sātyaki, etc.); **75**[2], 3309 (vanquished by Droṇa and Bhīshma).—§ 585 (do.): VI, **97**λλ, 4443 (Bhīshma had promised to slay the *K.*, etc.).—§ 587 (do.): VI, **117**ρ, 5485 (attacked Arjuna); **119*aa***, 5649 (abandoned Bhīshma).—§ 589 (Droṇābhishekap.): VII, **8**θ, †247 (°*ānāṃ pravarāṃç ca pañca*, in Yudhishṭhira's army).—§ 590 (do.): VII, **16**, 629 (in Yudhishṭhira's army).—§ 592 (Saṃçaptakavadhap.): VII, **20**γ, 799 (in the army of Duryodhana); **21**ι, 883 (defeated by Droṇa) (λ), 915 (do.), 919 (do.); **23**ο, 963 (followed Virāṭa), 966 (*bhrātaraḥ pañca*, description of their horses); **25**, 1085 (*yuddhaṃ* . . . *Matsyānāṃ K°aiḥ* *sārdham*), 1105 (*bhrātṛn pañca*, fought with Karṇa).—§ 593 (Abhimanyuvadhap.): VII, **35** δ, 1511 (proceeded against Droṇa); **40** o, 1695 (in the army of Yudhishṭhira); **42** π, 1743 (do.); **43** ρ, 1770 (do.), (σ),1780 (do.); **49**, 1934 (°*ānāṃ rathān sapta*, slain by Abhimanyu).—§ 596 (Pratijñāp.): VII, **78** ε, 2744 (in Yudhishṭhira's army).—§ 597 (do.): VII, **83**, 2950 (*sa-K°ṃ*, do.).—§ 598 (Jayadrathavadhap.): VII, **85** δ, 3049 (in Yudhishṭhira's army).—§ 599 (do.): VII, **91** β, 3255 (in Duryodhana's army); **98** κ, 3661 (*sa-K°ḥ*, proceeded against Droṇa); **106**, 3971 (*Bṛhatkshattraḥ K°ānāṃ mahārathaḥ*, proceeded against Droṇa); **110** ρ, 4165 (defeated by Droṇa); **111** ν, 4283 (*bhrātaraḥ pañca*, protect Yudhishṭhira); **114** ω, 4539 (vanquished by Kṛtavarman); **125**, 5021 (*Bṛhatkshattraḥ K°ānāṃ mahārathaḥ*, attacks Droṇa), 5040 (are slain by Droṇa). — § 600 (Ghaṭotkacavadhap.): VII, **154** β, 6650 (*sa-K°ḥ*, proceeded against Droṇa); **155** γ, 6696 (are slain by Droṇa), (ε), †6726 (*Drupada-Virāṭa-K°āḥ*); **156** ι, 6779 (followed Bhīmasena); **157** σ, 6967 (followed Bhīmasena and Arjuna); **159**, 7135 (in Yudhishṭhira's army); **160** δδ, 7155 (do.).—§ 601 (Droṇavadhap.): VII, **184** a, 8368 (do., shall proceed against Droṇa).—§ 603 (Nārāyaṇāstram.): VII, **193** δ, 8934 (defeated by Droṇa); **195** ι, 9018 (in Yudhishṭhira's army).—§ 604 (Karṇap.): VIII, **3** δ, 70 (do., defeated by Karṇa); **8**, 235 (in C. is printed *Kakaiyaḥ*, probably for *Kaikayaiḥ*, had formerly been vanquished by Karṇa); **9**, 283 (°*aiḥ*).—§ 605 (do.): VIII, **12** ββ, 459 (in Yudhishṭhira's army); **30** ξξ, 1231 (attacked Karṇa).—§ 608 (do.): VIII, **46**, 2143 (protected Duryodhana); **47** κ, 2226 (in Yudhishṭhira's army, attacked by Kṛpa, etc.); **49** υ, 2309 (checked Karṇa); **54** ιι, 2625 (resisted by Karṇa); **56**, 2695 (are slain by Karṇa), (ρρ), 2762 (fought with Bhīmasena); **63**, 3176 (attacked by Karṇa); **73**, 3662 (had been slain by Bhīshma), 3668 (do.). Cf. Kaikeya pl., Kekaya pl.

Kaikaya[1] = Bṛhatkshattra: VII, 4013 (*B°*, but B. has *Kaikeyaḥ*), 4015 (B. has *Kaikeyasya*); VIII, 117 (*B°*, but B. has *Kekayaḥ*).

Kaikaya[2] = Vinda: VIII, 521 (B. has *Kekayaḥ*).

Kaikaya[3]. § 590 (Droṇābhishekap.): VII, **14** a, 577 (read for *Kaikayo Kaikeyā(ḥ)*, B. has *Kekayā(ḥ)*).—§ 599 (Jayadrathavadhap.): VII, **106**, 3983 (read *Kaunteyena* with B.).

Kaikaya[4], a king of the Kekayas. § 641 (Rājadh.): XII, **77**, 2912 (seized by a Rākshasa). Cf. Kaikeya, Kaikeyarāja.

Kaikaya, dual (°*au*) = Vinda and Anuvinda: VIII, 497 (only C., B. has *Kaikeyau*).

Kaikayarājaputra (B. *Ke°*) ("the son of the king of the Kekayas"). § 604 (Karṇap.): VIII, **7**, †202 (in Duryodhana's army).

Kaikayarājaputra (B. *Ke°*), pl. (°*āḥ*) ("the sons of the king of the Kekayas"). § 342 (Indralokābh.): III, **51**, 2009 (will join the Pāṇḍavas).

Kaikeya (B. mostly Kekaya), pl. (°*āḥ*), in most passages denoting five brothers, sons of the king of the Kekayas, but sometimes the people (= Kekaya, pl.). § 264 (Sabhākriyāp.): II, **4** β, 126 (among the princes who waited upon Yudhishṭhira). — § 317 (Arjunābhigamanap.): III, **12**, 462 (*bhrātaraḥ*, came to the Pāṇḍavas in the wood).—§ 321 (Saubhavadhop.): III, **22**, 899 (= do., took leave of the Pāṇḍavas). — § 327 (Draupadīparitāpav.): III, **33**, 1352 (also B., will assist the Pāṇḍavas). — § 342 (Indralokābhigamanap.): III, **51**, 1983 (all. to § 317), 1991 (had been present at the rājasūya of Yudhishṭhira). — § 522 (Draupadīharaṇap.): III, **268**, †15654 (will assist the Pāṇḍavas).—§ 554 (Sainyodyogap.): V, **4** γ, 71 (among the princes to whom the Pāṇḍavas ought to send messengers.) — § 555 (do.): V, **19** a, 594 (*sodaryāḥ pañca*, came to Duryodhana with one akshauhiṇī of troops).—§ 556 (Sañjayayānap.): V, **22**, †664 (five brothers had been expelled (*avaruddhāḥ*) from the *K.*; in order to recover the kingdom they joined the Pāṇḍavas). — § 561 (Yānasandhip.): V, **57** ξ, 2240 (*bhrātaraḥ pañca*, joined the Pāṇḍavas with one akshauhiṇī of troops), 2248 (chosen by the five Kaikeya (B. *Kekaya*) brothers as their share in the battle).—§ 570 (Sainyaniryāṇap.): V, **151** δ, 5160 (followed Yudhishṭhira; the five brothers ?); **153**, 5189 (do., do.).—§ 571 (Ulūkadūtāgamanap.): V, **162**, 5591 (*bhrātaraḥ pañca*, in Yudhishṭhira's army).—§ 572 (Rathātirathasaṅkhyānap.): V, **171**, 5906 (*pañca . . . bhrātaraḥ*, among the rathas of the Pāṇḍavas).—§ 573 (Ambopākhyānap.): V, **195** δ, 7606 (in the army of Duryodhana).—§ 576 (Bhagavadgītāp.): VI, **16** a, 622 (also B., in the army of Duryodhana).—§ 578 (Bhīshmavadhap.): VI, **45**[22],1744 (*bhrātaraḥ pañca*, fought with five Gāndhāra princes); **48** κ[36], 1964 (rescued Çveta, the five brothers; B., however, has *Kaikeyo* = Dhṛshṭaketu ?). —§ 580 (do.): VI, **56** a, 2405 (also B., in the army of Duryodhana), (θ), 2418 (followed Bhīmasena, the five brothers ?).—§ 583 (do.): VI, **75** a, 3285 (*bhrātaraḥ pañca*, in the left wing of the Pāṇḍavas' makaravyūha); **77** λ[8], 3394 (the five brothers ?); **78**, 3437 (*pañca*, fought with Duḥçāsana).—§ 585 (do.): VI, **89** ν, 3948 (proceeded against Bhīshma, the five brothers ?); **99** ζ, 4512 (*bhrātaraḥ*, in the army of Yudhishṭhira); **103** ν, 4694 (*bhrātaraḥ pañca*, rushed towards Bhīshma). — § 587 (do.): VI, **108**, 5002 (*bhrātaraḥ pañca*, in the rear of the Pāṇḍava army); **118** υ, 5553 (*pañca*, rescued by Arjuna).—§ 589 (Droṇābhishekap.): VII, **8** η, 227 (in Yudhishṭhira's army); **9**, 288 (do., surround Droṇa); **10**, 360 (*e*: the five *K.* brothers, resembling the insects called indragopakas, with red coats of mail, red weapons, and red banners, the maternal cousins of the Pāṇḍavas); **16** δ, 650 (surrounded Droṇa).—§ 598 (Jayadrathavadhap.): VII, **85** a, 3025 (in Yudhishṭhira's army). —§ 599 (do.): VII, **110**, 4164 (°*ānāṃ çataṃ*, are slain by Droṇa); **125**, 5039 (*Bṛhatkshattre hate . . . K°ānāṃ mahārathe*).—§ 600 (Ghaṭotkacavadhap.): VII, **153** a, 6628 (the five brothers ?, pierced by Duryodhana); **158** τ, 6972 (only B., C. has *Kekayaiḥ*, in the army of Yudhishṭhira); **160**, 7161 (also B., attack Açvatthāman); **169** ιι, 7459 (proceeded against Droṇa). — § 602 (Droṇavadhap.): VII, **186** η, 8490 (also B., vanquished by Droṇa), 8499 (sc. *hateshu*).—§ 604 (Karṇap.): VIII, **5** ζ, 136 (have been slain by Arjuna); **6**, 168 (*Vṛkodarasamo yuddhe vṛtaḥ K° yodhibhiḥ | Kaikeyena ca vikramya bhrātā bhrātrā nipātitaḥ*).—§ 605 (do.): VIII, **13**, 511 (°*ānāṃ mahārathaḥ*, i.e. Vinda), 524 (defeated by Sātyaki).—§ 608 (do.): VIII, **48** ξ, 2254 (attack Karṇa); **49** χ, 2334 (attack Vasusheṇa); **56** μμ, 2692 (attack Karṇa), (ππ), 2751 (also B., are slain by Karṇa); **62**, 3173 (*çatāḥ saptadaça*, checked the Dhārtarāshṭras); **82**, †4183 (°*senāpatiḥ*, named Ugrakarman ?, attacked Prasena). — § 611 (Çalyap.): IX, **21** κκ, 1126 (attacked by Duryodhana). Cf. Kaikaya pl., Kekaya pl.

Kaikeya, dual (°*au*) = Vinda and Anuvinda: VIII, 492 (*Vindānuvindau*), 497 (B. two times, C. in the latter passage has *Kaikayau*).

Kaikeya[1] = Bṛhatkshattra: VI, 1720 (*B°ḥ*); VII, 972 (*B°ṃ*), 4013 (*B°*, only B., C. has *Kaikayaḥ*), 4015 (only B., C.

C. has *Kaikayasya*); VII, 5029, 5032, 5033, 5035. Cf. Kaikaya.

Kaikeya[2] = Vinda: VIII, 513, 518, 519. Cf. Kaikaya.

Kaikeya[3] = Kaikaya[4]: XII, 2911.

Kaikeya,[4] one or more Kekaya princes. § 576 (Bhagavadgītāp.): VI, **19**, 715 (*Dhṛshṭaketuḥ* ?, but is not *Kaikeyāḥ* to be read? cf. V, 5160; VI, 3948).—§ 578 (Bhīshmavadhap.): VI, **47**ε, 1837 (only C., B. has *Kekayāḥ*), 1866 (= Bṛhatkshatra?); **48a**[36], 1964 (only B., but C. seems to be right in reading *Kaikeyāḥ*, cf. VI, 715), 1972 (both C. and B., is not *Kaikeyāḥ* to be read with PCR.?).—§ 579 (do.): VII, **52a**, 2128 (= Bṛhatkshattra?). — § 582 (do.): VI, **69a**, 3066 (*akshauhiṇīpatiḥ* = do.?).—§ 583 (do.): VI, **77**, 3401 (= do.?).—§ 604 (Karṇap.): VIII, **6**, 169 (*K°ena ca vikramya bhrāta bhrātrā nipātitaḥ*).

Kaikeyaputra ("son of the Kekaya king") = Viçoka: VIII, †4182.

Kaikeyarāja = Kaikaya[4]: XII, 2888.

Kaikeyī[1] ("daughter of the Kekaya king") = Sunandā, the wife of Sarvabhauma: I, ††3769 (*S°*, mother of Jayatsena).

Kaikeyī[2] (do.), wife of Ajamīḍha. § 156 (Pūruvaṃç.); I, **95**, ††3790.

Kaikeyī[3] (do.) = Kumārī, the wife of Bhīmasena Pārikshita: I, †3796 (*K°*, mother of Pratiçravas).

Kaikeyī[4] (do.), wife of Daçaratha. § 525 (Rāmopākhyānap.): III, **274**, 15879 (mother of Bharata); **277**, 15960, 15961, 15975, 15980 (prevailed upon Daçaratha to banish Rāma and install Bharata as heir apparent. Bharata, however, would only keep the realm for Rāma).

Kaikeyī[5] = Sudeshṇā, the wife of Virāṭa. IV, 249 (*Virāṭabhāryā*), 432, 562, 563, 661, 669.

Kaikeyī[6] (do.) = Sumanā: XIII, 5859.

Kaikeyīnandivardhana ("the son of Kaikeyī[5]") = Uttara: IV, 2231.

Kailāsa, a mountain, the abode of Kubera and Çiva. § 11 (Parvasaṅgr.): I, **2**, 457 (*°ārohaṇaṃ*).—§ 213 (Jatugṛhap.): I, **146**, 5779 (*°m iva Guhyakāḥ*, sc. *viviçuḥ*; C. has *°āça°*).—§ 231 (Svayaṃvarap.): I, **185**, 6963 (*°çikharaprakhyaiḥ*, sc. *prāsādaiḥ*; C. has *°āça°*). — § 252 (Subhadrāharaṇap.): I, **220**, 7950 (*°çikharopamaḥ*, sc. Balarāma, C. has *°āça°*).—§ 255 (Agniparābhava): I, **223**, 8117 (Çvetaki performed austerities on *K.* in order to gratify Çiva; C. has *°āça°*).—§ 263 (Sabhākriyāp.): II, **3**, 59 (*uttareṇa tu K°ṃ Mainākaṃ parvataṃ prati*, there Maya had gathered a bhāṇḍa of jewels), 66 (*uttareṇa tu K°ṃ Mainākaṃ parvataṃ prati*, Hiraṇyaçṛṅga, etc., is situated there).—§ 265 (Lokapālasabhākhyānap.): II, **6**, 275 (*°nilayasya*, i.e. Kubera).—§ 269 (Vaiçravaṇasabhāv.): II, **10**, 384 (*°çikharopamā*, sc. the palace of Kubera), 412 (among the mountains present in the palace of Kubera).—§ 287 (Rajasuyikap.): II, **34**, 1279 (*°çikharaprakhyān*, sc. *āvasathān*).—§ 293 (Dyūtap.): II, **46**, 1643 (*°kūṭapratimam*, sc. *Çivaṃ*), 1645 (*parvataṃ*), 1646 (do., Vyasa went to *K.*).—§ 295 (do.): II, **52**, 1862 (*uttarād api K°ād oshadhīḥ*).—§ 317*b* (Kṛshṇa Vāsudeva): III, **12**, 503 (*°bhavane*, Kṛshṇa had dwelt on *K.*). — § 334 (Kairātap.): III, **41**, 1697 (*°nilayo Dhanādhyakshaḥ*, i.e. Kubera).—§ 335 (Indralokābhigamanap.): III, **42**, 1753 (*°ṃ iva çṛṅgiṇaṃ*).—§ 387 (Sagara): III, **106**, 8834 (*giriṃ*, Sagara went to *K.* to gratify Çiva).—§ 389 (Gaṅgāvataraṇa): III, **108**, 9944 (*parvataṃ*, Bhagīratha went to *K.* to gratify Çiva); **109**, 9963 (the abode of Çiva).—§ 418*d* (Tīrthayātrāp.): The mountain *K.* is six yojanas high, there the gods assemble, there is Viçālā (i.e. Badarī, Nīl.), there live innumerable Yakshas, Rākshasas, Kinnaras, Nāgas, Suparṇas, and Gandharvas, near the abode of Kubera; III, **139**, 10830.—§ 419 (Gandhamādanapr.): III, **140**, 10842.—§ 422 (do.): III, **142**, 10913 (*°çikharopamaṃ*, sc. the bones of Naraka).—§ 423 (do.): III, **145**, 11031 (*parvatottamaṃ*, with Badarī, etc., reached by the Pāṇḍavas).—§ 432 (Saugandhikāharaṇa): III, **153**, 11351 (*°çikharābhyāse*, there the lotus-lake of Kubera is situated); **154**, 11389 (the abode of Kubera, to whom the Krodhavaças repaired, having been defeated by Bhīmasena).—§ 436 (Yakshayuddhap.): III, **158**, 11540 (seen by the Pāṇḍavas on their journey to the hermitage of Vṛshaparvan).—§ 436*d* (do.): Beyond *K.* is the path of the all-perfect (*paramasiddhānāṃ*) Devarshis, if anyone goes beyond this the Rākshasas slay him with iron darts and other weapons; III, **159**, 11651.—§ 449 (Ājagarap.): III, **177**, †12340 (*Kuberakāntaṃ*, on their way from the hermitage of Ārshṭisheṇa the Pāṇḍavas saw *K.*), †12344.—§ 555 (Indravijaya): V, **11a**, 353.—§ 562 (Bhagavadyānap.): V, **94**, 3360 (*rathāt . . . K° çikharopamāt*).—§ 565 (Gālavacarita): V, **111**, 3830 (on *K.* Kubera was installed into the sovereignty of Rākshasas, Yakshas, and Gandharvas), 3840 (*sthānam Ailavilasya*, i.e. Kubera's). — § 570 (Sainyaniryāṇap.): V, **157**, 5332 (*°çikharopamaḥ*, sc. Balarāma).—§ 574 (Jambūkh.): VI, **3**, 104 (*°Mandarābhyān tū tathā Himavato gireḥ sahasraço mahāçabdaḥ khacarāṇi patanti ca*, omens); **6**, 236 (= Hemakūṭa, inhabited by Kubera with the Guhyakas), 237 (*abhyuttareṇa K°ṃ Mainākaṃ parvataṃ prati*, there Hiraṇyaçṛṅga, etc., is situated).—§ 581 (Bhīshmavadhap.): VI, **62**, 2748 (*°m iva çṛṅgiṇaṃ*, sc. Bhīmasena).—§ 585 (do.): VI, **94**, 4204 (do., do.).—§ 589 (Droṇābhishekap.): VII, **11**, 412 (*°çikharopamaḥ*, sc. Balarāma).—§ 611 (Çalyap.): IX, **11**, 583 (*yayā*—so B., sc. *gadayā*; C. has *yathā* — *K°bhavane Maheçvarasakhaṃ* — i.e. Kubera—*balī* | *āhvayām āsa Kaunteyaḥ*—i.e. Bhīmasena—*saṃkruddham Alakādhipaṃ*, all. to Yakshayuddhaparvan); **12**, 594 (*saçṛṅgaṃ iva K°ṃ*, sc. Çalya). — § 613 (Gadāyuddhap.): IX, **33**, 1927 (*°m iva çṛṅgiṇaṃ*, sc. Duryodhana), 1929 (do., do.).—§ 615*u* (Skanda): IX, **45**, 2534 (*°çṛṅgasaṅkāçau*, sc. *Maṇi* and *Sumaṇi*).—§ 615 (Gadāyuddhap.): IX, **56**, 3156 (*°m iva çṛṅgiṇaṃ*, sc. Duryodhana).—§ 637 (Rājadh.): XII, **44**, 1528 (*mumude tad labdhvā K°ṃ Dhanado*—i.e. Kubera—*yathā*). — § 660*b* (Bhṛgu-Bharadvājasaṃv.): XII, **182**, 6770 (*°çikhare*, there Bhṛgu was sitting).—§ 694*b* (Jvarotpatti): XII, **284**, 10216 (*Vaiçravaṇaḥ . . . K°nilayaḥ*). — § 716 (Çukabhipatana): XII, **332**, 12576 (*°pṛshṭhaṃ*, Çuka proceeded to *K.*); **333**, 12586 (*°pṛshṭhāt*, from *K.* Çuka soared into the sky).—§ 731*b* (Ashṭāvakra-Diksaṃv.): XIII, **19**, 1411 (the abode of Kubera), 1434 (crossed by Ashṭāvakra).—§ 746 (Ānuçasanik.): XIII, **83**, 3907 (*°çikhare deva-Gandharvasevite*, there Surabhi performed austerities). — § 772*b* (Vasishṭha): XIII, **156**, 7287 (*°ṃ prasthitāñ caiva nadīṃ Gaṅgāṃ*).—§ 785 (Anugītāp.): XIV, **77**, 2236 (*mahagireḥ*, trembled).—§ 795*c* (Mahābhārata): XVIII, **6**, 241 (*°çikharākāraṃ*, sc. *vimānaṃ*, so B.).

Kailāsa, pl. (VIII, 110), v. Kosala, pl.

Kailāsagirivāsin = Çiva (1000 names[2]).

Kailāsaka, a serpent. § 564 (Mātalīyop.): V, **103**γ, 3627.

Kailāsanilaya = Kubera: II, 275; III, 1697; XII, 10216.

Kailātaka, adj.: VII, 4353 (*madhu*, B. has *kairātakaṃ*), 5157 (do., do.).

Kairāta, adj. ("belonging to a Kirāta"). § 10 (Parvasaṅgr.): I, **2**, 320 (*parva K°sañjñitaṃ*, i.e. Kairātaparvan). — § 331 (Kairātap.): III, **39**, 1552 (*°ṃ veçam āsthāya*, sc. Çiva). — § 340 (Indralokābhigamanap.): III,

49, 1936 (do., all. to § 331).—§ 442 (Nivātakavacayuddhap.): III, **167,** 11954 (*bhūtaṃ mahat K°saṃsthitaṃ*, i.e. Çiva, repetition of § 331).—§ 573 (Ambopākhyānap.): V, **194,** 7592 (*°e dvandvayuddhe*, all. to Kairātaparvan). — § 731*b* (Ashṭāvakra-Diksaṃv.): XIII, **19,** 1434 (*°ṃ sthānaṃ*, i.e. the abode of Çiva).

Kairāta, pl. (*°āḥ*), a people, = Kirāta, pl. § 295 (Dyūtap.): II, **52,** 1869 (brought tribute to Yudhishṭhira).

Kairātaka, adj. ("belonging to the Kirātas"). § 295 (Dyūtap.): II, **52,** 1867 (*°īnām ayutaṃ dāsīnaṃ*, brought as tribute). Cf. also Kailātaka.

Kairātaparvan ("the section treating of the Kirāta"), the 33rd of the minor parvans of Mhbhr., forming an episode to Arjuna's journey to the abode of Indra (cf. Kairāta). § 331. It is anew related how *Arjuna* set out from the *Kāmyaka* wood towards the north; he entered a terrible forest (description), resorted to by *Siddhas* and *Cāraṇas*, and then proceeded to the *Himavat* (description). For four months he practised austerities (specified), until the *ṛshis* made representations about it to *Çiva*, who dismissed them after having removed their fears (III, **38**). Then *Çiva* with his bow and arrows, in the guise of a *Kirāta*, accompanied by *Umā* in the guise of a *Kirāta* woman, by merry spirits (*bhūtaiḥ*), and thousands of women, approached *Arjuna* as he was about to kill *Mūka*, a son of *Danu*, who in the form of a boar would have killed *Arjuna*. *Arjuna* and *Çiva* at the same time pierced *Mūka* with their arrows, and killed him; when dying he again assumed his *rākshasa* form; then they fought against each other, first with arrows, then with the very bows, then with swords, then with trees and stones, then with the fists, and then by clasping each other; at last *Arjuna* lost his senses, and was almost reduced to a ball of flesh; when he regained consciousness he made a clay image of *Çiva*, which he worshipped with a garland, which then appeared on the head of the *Kirāta*; he thus learned that it was *Çiva*, and prostrated himself at his feet. *Çiva* declared that *Arjuna's* prowess was equal to his own, promised to give him his weapon, and gave him 'eye' (*cakshus*), so that he beheld him in his true form, together with *Umā*.—§ 332: *Arjuna* then fell on his knees and worshipped him, saying: "O *Kapardin*! etc." (v. *Mahādevastava*) (III, **39**).—§ 333: Çiva said that *Arjuna* (*b*) was in a former life *Nara*, etc. When granted a boon, *Arjuna* asked *Çiva* to give him the *Pāçupata* weapon named *Brahmaçiras* (*c*). Having purified himself he was instructed in its use on the condition that he should not hurl it against a human being, for then it would destroy the universe. The earth trembled, etc. The gods and *Dānavas* beheld the weapon in its bodily shape standing by the side of *Arjuna*. When *Arjuna* had been touched by *Çiva*, all that was evil in his body was dispelled. Having said to *Arjuna*, "Go thou into heaven," *Çiva* went up into the skies accompanied by *Umā* (III, **40**).—§ 334: Then *Arjuna* was on the *Himavat* visited by the *Lokapālas*, viz., *Varuṇa* (blue as lapis lazuli), together with rivers, *Nāgas*, *Daityas*, and *Sādhyas*; *Kubera*, who dwells on *Kailāsa*, golden-coloured (*jāmbūnadavapuḥ*), accompanied by *Yakshas*; *Yama*, with staff in hand (*daṇḍapāṇiḥ*), illuminating the three worlds, and the *Guhyakas*, *Gandharvas*, and *Nagās*, accompanied by those lords of the creation (*lokabhāvanaiḥ*) the *Pitṛs*; further *Çakra*, with *Māhendrāṇī*, mounted on the neck of *Airāvata*, and surrounded by the gods, and eulogized by *Gandharvas* and *ṛshis*. Each of them occupied a particular summit of *Himavat* (*Yama* to the south, *Varuṇa* to the west). They granted him 'sight' (*dṛshṭi*), that he might see them. *Yama* said that *Arjuna* would defeat the *Nivātakavacas*, etc., and gave him his irresistible staff (*daṇḍa*) as a weapon. *Varuṇa* (*b*) gave him his irresistible nooses. *Kubera* said that in bygone *kalpas Arjuna* had always gone through ascetic austerities along with them, and gave him his favourite weapon *Antardhāna* (*c*). *Indra* said he would descend to earth in his chariot with *Mātali* as his charioteer, and taking him to heaven grant him all his celestial weapons (III, **41**).

Kaiṭabha, a Dānava. § 317*b* (Kṛshṇa Vāsudeva): III, **12,** 498 (*Dānavau Madhu-K°au*, tried to slay Brahmán, cf. § 477).—§ 476 (Dhundhumārop.): III, **202,** 13532 (*Madhu-K°yoḥ putro Dhundhuḥ*).—§ 477 (do.): III, **203,** 13562 (*Madhuç ca K°aç ca*), 13565 (*Madhu-K°yoḥ*), (13573) (*Madhu-K°au*), 13580 (*Madhu-K°yoḥ*; when Vishṇu during the cataclysm slept on the hood of Çesha, Madhu and *K.* terrified Brahmán, Vishṇu awoke, and obtained from them the boon that he should become their slayer, then Vishṇu on his thighs cut off their heads).—§ 478 (do.): III, **204,** 13590 (*Madhu-K°yoḥ putro Dhundhuḥ*), 13623 (*Dhundhur nāma . . . Madhu-K°yoḥ putraḥ*). — § 567 (Bhagavadyānap.): V, **130,** 4414 (*ekārṇave ca svapatā*—sc. Kṛshṇa (Vishṇu) — *nihatau Madhu-K°au*, cf. § 477). — § 615*ee* (Ādityatīrtha): IX, **49,** 2850 (*Asurau Madhu-K°au*, had been slain by Vishṇu, cf. § 477).—§ 615 (Gadāyuddhap.): IX, **55,** 3106 (*sadṛçau tau*, sc. Bhīmasena and Duryodhana . . . *Madhu-K°yor yudhi*).—§ 673*b* (Bali-Vāsavasaṃv.): XII, **227*a*,** 8265 (*Dānavaḥ*, among the ancient rulers of the earth).—§ 717*b* (Nārayaṇīya): XII, **348,** 13475 (originated from rajas and arose from a drop in the primeval lotus, *K.* and Madhu robbed the Vedas from Brahmán), 13509 (*Madhu-K°au . . . Dānavau*), 13519 (*rajastamovishṭatanū . . . Madhu-K°au*, are slain by Nārāyaṇa (Vishṇu)). Cf. Asura, Dānava (dual).

Kaiṭabhanāçinī ("destroyer of *K.*") = Durgā (Umā): VI, 801.

Kaitava = Ulūka, q.v.

Kaitava, pl. (*°āḥ*) a people. § 576 (Bhagavadgītāp.): VI, **18***δ*, 689 (in the army of Duryodhana). Cf. Kaitavya, pl.

Kaitavya = Ulūka, q.v.

Kaitavya, pl. (*°āḥ*), a people. § 604 (Karṇap.): VIII, **7,** †208 (*°ānām adhipatiḥ*, i.e. Ulūka?, in the army of Duryodhana).

* **kaivarta,** pl. (*°āḥ*) ("fishermen"), name of a caste: XIII, 2655, 2672, 2702.

Kāka, pl. (*°āḥ*), a people. § 574 (Jambūkh.): VI, **9***ν*, 372 (only B., C. has *Kāntikāḥ*).

Kākī [1] ("female crow"). § 126 (Aṃçāvat.): I, **66,** 2620 (daughter of Tāmrā), 2621 (mother of the owls).

Kākī [2], one of the mothers of Çiçu. § 500 (Skandopākh.): III, **228*a*,** 14396 (enumeration).

Kaksha, pl. (*°āḥ*), a people. § 574 (Jambūkh.): VI, **9***μ*, 356, 364 (only C., B. has *Kacchāḥ*).

Kakshaka, a serpent. § 63 (Sarpasattra): I, **57,** 2147 (of Vāsuki's race).

Kakshasena, name of one or more princes. § 154 (Pūruvaṃç.): I, **94,** 3743 (son of the elder Parikshit).—§ 264 (Sabhākriyāp.): II, **4***β*, 117 (waited upon Yudhishṭhira).—§ 267 (Yamasabhāv.): II, **8,** 329 (in the palace of Yama).—§ 377 (Dhaumyatīrthak.): III, **89,** 8365 (*āçramaḥ K°sya*, in the west).—§ 767 (Ānuçāsanik.): XIII, **137*a*,** 6259 *°o rājarshiḥ Vaçishṭhāya mahātmane nyāsaṃ yathāvat saṃnyasya jagāma sumahāyaçāḥ*).—§ 775 (do.): XIII, **166***η*, 7685 (*rājarshiḥ*, enumeration).—§ 786 (Anugītāp.): XIV, **91a**, 2843 (had attained to high success by way of gifts).

Kaksheyu, a prince. § 150 (Pūruvaṃç.): I, **94**, 3700 (son of Raudrāçva and Ghṛtācī).—§ 775 (Ānuçāsanik.): XIII, **166η**, 7682 (the same?).

Kākshīva = Kākshīvat. § 277 (Jarāsandhavadhap.): II, **21**, 802 (*çūdrāyāṃ Gautamo yatra*—i.e. at Rājagṛha—*mahātmā saṃçitavrataḥ | Auçīnaryām ajanayat K°ādyān sutān muniḥ*, cf. I, 4213).

Kakshīvat, a ṛshi. § 770 (Ānuçāsanik.): XIII, **151**, 7108 (*Aushijaḥ* (B. *Auç°*), among the *Mahendraguravaḥ* in the east). —§ 775 (do.): XIII, **166γ**, 7663 (*Aushijaḥ* (B. *Auç°*), among the ṛshis of the east). Cf. next and prec.

Kākshīvat = Kakshīvat. § 5 (Anukram.): I, **1**, 224 (in Nārada's enumeration of ancient kings (!), B. has *Auçijaṃ* for *Mahādyutim*, which follows in C.).—§ 170 (Dīrghatamas): I, **104**, 4213 (*°ādayaḥ*, *K.*, etc., were begotten by Dīrghatamas on a çūdrā), 4215.—§ 264 (Sabhākriyāp): II, **4a**, 112 (*Aushijaḥ* (B. *Auç°*) waited upon Yudhishṭhira). — § 266 (Çakrasabhāv.): II, **7**, 299 (*Gautamaḥ*? in the palace of Indra). — § 275 (Rājasūyārambhap.): II, **17**, 698 (*°taḥ putraṃ Gautamasya . . . Caṇḍakauçikaṃ*). — § 370 (Tīrthayātrāp.): III, **84**, 8083 (*°ān iva modate*, sc. by bathing at Rājagṛha).—§ 665 (Mokshadh.): XII, **208ε**, 7593 (*Aushijaḥ* (B. *Auç°*), among the ṛshis of the east).—§ 702 (do.): XII, **293a**, 10761 (had obtained great success by adoring Vishṇu); **297δ**, 10874 (*°Kamaṭhādayaḥ*, among those ṛshis who had obtained their position by way of penances). Cf. the prec.

Kākshīvatī ("a female descendant of Kakshīvat") = Bhadrā: I, 4695.

Kakubha = Çiva (1000 names[2]).

Kākudika, name of a weapon. § 563 (Bhagavadyānap.): V, **96φ**, 3490 (will be employed by Arjuna).

Kakutstha, an ancient king in Ayodhyā. § 6 (Anukram.): I, **1a**, 226 (in Sañjaya's enumeration of departed kings).—§ 475 (Dhundhumārop.): III, **202**, 13516 (son of Çaçāda and father of Anenas).

Kākutstha[1] ("son of Kakutstha") = Anenas: III, 13516 (*A°*).

Kākutstha[2] ("descendant of Kakutstha") = Rāma, the son of Daçaratha: III, 16013, 16063, 16068, 16079, 16106, 16130, 16221, 16312, 16323, 16510, 16514, 16523, 16537, 16558, 16560.

Kākutstha[3] (do.) = Lakshmaṇa, the son of Daçaratha: III, 16207.

Kāla[1] (Time, Death, personif.): I, 223 (*°vaçaṃ gataḥ*), 240–4 (?) 299, 984 (*°daṇḍopamam*), 1335 (*°a ivāntako 'puraḥ*), 2542 (*°kalpāḥ*), 2585 (son of Dhruva), 5470 (*°rūpadhṛk*), 7669 (*iva*), 8264 (*°daṇḍaṃ Yamaḥ*, sc. *jagrāha*), 8293 (*°vat*), 8313 (*°hatā iva*); II, 295 (in the palace of Indra), 340 (in the palace of Yama), 1485 (*°syeva jighatsataḥ*), 1651 (*°ena nirmitaḥ*), 2682 (*daṇḍam udyamya*); III, 481 (identified with Kṛshṇa), 879 (*cakram K°āntaka-Yamopamaṃ*), 1013 (*°āntaka-Yamopamaḥ*), 1376 (*Antakena*), 1377, 8286 (*nisṛshṭa iva K°ena yugānte jvalanaḥ*), 10783 (*°āntaka-Yamopamaṃ*), 11494 (?), 11500 (*°āntakopamaḥ*), 11783 (*°ena . . . hatāḥ*), 12107 (*°rūpāḥ*), 12389 (*°āntaka - Yamopamaṃ*), 15864, 17314 (*°āntaka - Yamāt*), 17403 (?); IV, 1090 (*°āntaka-Yamopamaṃ*), 1726 (*Arjunarūpeṇa samharantam iva prajāḥ*), 2015 (*nadīṃ . . . yugānte K°nirmitāṃ*); V, 57 (*Yama-K°opamadyutī*), 59 (*°vajrānalopamān*), †1868 (*vyāttānanaḥ K°a iva*), 2082 (*°vaçaṅgatāḥ*), 4037 (*yuyuje K°dharmaṇā*) 7185 (*°sammitam*), †7205 (*°otsṛshṭāṃ prajvalitām ivolkāṃ*), 7276 (*°āntakopamaṃ*): VI, 119 (?), 122, 306 (?), 567, 802 (*°pāçena*), 1234 (*°ḥ kālayatām ahaṃ*, sc. *asmi*, says Kṛshṇa), 1677 (*°daṇḍopamaṃ*), 1701 (*°daṇḍam ivāparaṃ*), 1943 (*°daṇḍopamāṃ*), 2280 (*°āntaka - Yamopamaḥ*), 2338, 2396 (*°āntaka-Yamopamaṃ*), 2426 (*°eneva yugakshaye*), 2705 (*°otsṛshṭam ivāntakaṃ*), 2792 (*yugānte K°vat*), 2799 (*iva*), 2831 (*°Mṛtyusamaprabhaṃ*), 2858 (*°otsṛshṭa ivāntakaḥ*), 2874 (*°Mṛtyusamaprabhau*), †3374 (*gadāhastaṃ K°m ivāntakāle*), 3714 (*vyāttānano yathā K°ḥ*), 3772 (*yathā*), 3801 (*°sammitaṃ*), 3956 (*kruddhaḥ K°a ivāparaḥ*), 4071 (*°āntaka-Yamopamaḥ*), 4087 (*°sṛshṭam ivāntakaṃ*), 4202 (*°āntaka-Yamopamaḥ*), 4203 (*°daṇḍopamāṃ*), 4351 (*iva*), 4656 (*°eneva yugakshaye*), 4732 (do.), 5034 (*°sṛshṭham ivāntakaṃ*), 5067 (*°vat*), 5254 (*°āntakasamadyutiḥ*); VII, 238 (*°vat*), 2644 (*°ena balinā hatāḥ*), 2717 (*°nirmitā*), 2825, 2866 (*°kopaṃ*), 3035, 3135 (*Mṛtyuḥ K°ena coditaḥ*), 3379 (*°kalpāḥ*), 3514, 4341 (*°kalpaiḥ*), 4668 (*°sannibhā*), 4726 (*°āntaka-Yamopamaṃ*), 4853 (*°vat*), 5196 (*°daṇḍam ivāntakaḥ*), 5274 (read *°syeva*), 5278 (*iva*), 5475 (*°çaktim ivāparāṃ*), 5543 (*Yama-K°āntakopamaṃ*), 5556 (*iva*), 7090 (*°āntaka - Yamopamaṃ*), 7112 (*vikramaṃ . . . K°syeva yugakshaye*), 7926 (*°daṇḍogradhāriṇaṃ*), †8154, 8356, 8655, 9195 (*°sṛshṭa ivāntakaḥ*), 9240 (*°vat*), 9441, †9467 (identif. with Çiva), 9596 (do.); VIII, 270, 596 (*āntaka-Yamopamau*), †692 (*°vaktravat*), 848 (*°daṇḍair iva*), 909 (*Mṛtyu - K°āntakopamaṃ*), 1022 (*°daṇḍopamaṃ*), 1135 1496 (*°daṇḍaḥ*), 1501, 2214 (*°o vigrahavān iva*), 2459 (*°āntaka-Yamopamaṃ*), 2708 (do.), 2933 (*iva*), 2967 (*°sammitaṃ; °daṇḍam ivāparaṃ*), †3828 (*°a ivāttadaṇḍaḥ*), †3829, 3888 (*°syeva yugakshaye*), 3995 (*°āntakavapuḥ*), 3996 (*yathā*), 4153 (*°daṇḍodyataṃ Yamaṃ*), 4265 (*iva*), †4279 (*°m ivāttadaṇḍam*), 4390 (*Yama-K°āntakopamau*), 4469 (*°pāçopamau*); IX, 17, 38 (*°ena nihataṃ*), 352 (*°ḥ kruddhaḥ . . . iva*), 555 (*°sṛshṭa ivāntakaḥ*), 570 (*°o daṇḍam ivodyamya*), 574 (do.), 2519 (*°o Yamaç ca Mṛtyuç ca*), 2532 (*°opamau*), 3108 (*°sya samau*), 3454 (*daṇḍinā*), 3547 (*°opasṛshṭena*), 3590, 3591; X, 315, 326 (*°vat*), 360 (*°sṛshṭa ivāntakaḥ*), 365 (*°vat*), 395 (*°sṛshṭa ivāntakaḥ*), 500, 501, 669 (*°āntaka-Yamopamaḥ*); XI, 50, etc., 68, etc., 91, 114, 156, 174, 258, etc., 649 (*yugānta iva K°ena patitaṃ sūryaṃ*); XII, 440 (*hantā*), 445 (*yathāgataḥ*), 1132 (*°dharmam upeyivān*), 1702 (*āpānabhūmiṃ K°sya*), 2674 (?), 2675 (*°sṛshṭaṃ*), 4264 (*°a ivāntakaḥ*), 4501 (*sarveçaṃ*), 4520, 5468 (*°sammitaḥ*), 5469 (do.), 5686 (*°dharmam upāgataḥ*), 5717 (*°vaçaṃ yāti*), 5718, 6164 (*°o 'ntaka ivodyataḥ*), 6755, 7156, 7195, 7198, etc., 7496, 7497, 7499, 8058 (*°daṇḍa°*), 8106, etc., 8241, etc., 8570, 9877, 9878, 9879 (*°shashṭān*, the great elements), 9882, 10060 (?), 10497, 10502, 11227, 11960, 12119, †12135, 12148, 13300 (= Rudra); XIII, 7 (*°manyuvaçāṃ gatāḥ*), 16, 50, 51, etc. (70), 184 (*°āntakopamāḥ*), 907 (*°daṇḍadharāya*, sc. Çiva), 6908, 6909 (*lohitaraktākshaḥ*, identif. with Kṛshṇa), 7098, 7111 (one of the seven *dharaṇīdharāḥ*), 7497 (= Rudra), 7768 (*samayujyata K°ena*); XIV, 1584 (*°dharmaṇā*), 1840 (do.), 2167 (*°āntaka-Yamopamaṃ*); XVI, 88 (*°dharmaṇā*), 142 (*°paçagrahāṃ Vaitaraṇīṃ*), 287, etc.; XVII, 3 (*°pāçaṃ*). Cf. Antaka, Mṛtyu, Yama.

Kāla[2] = Sūrya (the Sun): III, 146. — Do.[3] = Çiva (1000 names[1–2]).—Do.[4] = Vishṇu (1000 names).

Kālā, daughter of Daksha and wife of Kaçyapa. § 87 (Aṃçāvat.): I, **65**, 2520 (enumeration of the daughters of Daksha, who were married to Kaçyapa). — § 97 (do.): I, **65**, 2542 (her offspring were the *Kālakeyāḥ*, only four are enumerated; read with B. *Krodhaçatruḥ* instead of *Krodhaḥ Ç°*).

Kala, pl. (*āḥ*), a class of pitṛs. § 270 (Brahma-sabhā-varṇana): II, **11**, 463.

Kalā = Sūrya (the Sun): III, 150 (read *kalākāshṭhā(ḥ)* in one word ?).

Kalā, pl. (*āḥ*) ("minutes," personif.): IX, 2517.—Do.[2] = Çiva (1000 names [1–2]).

Kālacakra(ḥ) = Sūrya (the Sun): III, 151.

Kalaça, a serpent. § 564 (Mātalīyop.): V, **103**γ, 3627 (enumeration).

Kālaçaila, a mountain. § 418 (Tīrthayātrāp.): III, **139**, 10820, 10823 (passed by Yudhishṭhira, etc., on their way to Gandhamādana). Cf. Kālaparvata.

Kalaçapotaka, a serpent. § 47 (Sarpanāmak.): I, **35**, 1552 (enumeration).

Kalaçī, a tīrtha. § 364 (Tīrthayātrāp.): III, **83**, 6050.

Kalaçodara, a warrior of Skanda. § 615*u* (Skanda): IX, **45**η, 2574 (C. has *Kalaso°*).

Kalada, pl. (*āḥ*), a people. § 574 (Jambūkh.): VI, **9**ν, 370 (only B., C. has *Kalavāḥ*).

Kāladantaka, a serpent. § 63 (Sarpasattra): I, **57**, 2147 (of Vāsuki's race).

Kālādhyaksha = Sūrya (the Sun): III, 152.

Kālaghaṭa, a brahman. § 59 (Sarpasattra): I, **53**, 2048 (*dvijaḥ*, among the sadasyas at the snake sacrifice of Janamejaya).

kālāgni ("the fire that is to destroy the world"): I, 2091 (*°samatejasaṃ*); III, 10393 (*°sannibhaṃ*), 14434 (*iva*), 15809 (*yugāntakāle samprāpte k°r dahate jagat*); IV, 1702 (*iva*); V, 2934 (*iva*), 6048 (*°samatejasaṃ*); VI, 281 (*nāmnā Saṃvartakaḥ*), 520 (*iva*), 4110 (*°samatejasaṃ*); VII, 586 (*iva*), 1686 (*°agnyanilavarcasaṃ*), 3518 (*iva*), 9574 (*çaraṃ k°saṃyuktaṃ*); XII, 6170 (*°samavarcasaṃ*), 10150 (*°sadṛçopamaḥ*), 10320 (*°sadṛçopamaḥ*), 11597; XIII, 7271 (*iva*), 7488 (*°samatejasā*).

kalahaṃsa, pl. (*°āḥ*) (probably "whistling swans"). § 126 (Aṃçāvat.): I, **65**, 2622 (the offspring of Dhṛtarāshṭrī).

kālajñāna ("knowledge of time"): IX, 2133, 2135.

Kālajoshaka, pl. (*°āḥ*), a people. § 574 (Jambūkh.): VI, **9**μ, 354 (only C., B. has *Kālatoyakāḥ*).

kālajvalana = kālāgni: VII, 3672 (*°sannibhāḥ*), 7427 (*°sannibhaiḥ*).

Kālakā, a female Asura. § 445 (Nivātakavacayuddhap.): III, **173**, 12203 (*mahāsurī*, mother of the Kālakeyas). Cf. Kālā.

Kālakāksha[1], a Daitya. § 564 (Mātalīyop.): V, **105**δ, 3685 (had been slain by Garuḍa).

Kālakāksha[2], a warrior of Skanda. § 615*u* (Skanda): IX, **45**η, 2571.

Kalakala = Çiva (1000 names [1]).

Kālakañja or **Kālakhañja**, pl. (*°āḥ*), a tribe of Asuras. § 268 (Varuṇasabhāv.): II, **9**, 365 (*Dānavāḥ*, in the palace of Varuṇa; *°kh°* both B. and C.).—§ 445 (Nivātakavacayuddhap.): III, **173**, 12198 (in Hiraṇyapura; *°k°* both B. and C.), 12208 (the offspring of Kālakā? *°k°* both B. and C.), 12211 (destroyed by Arjuna; *°k°* both B. and C.).—§ 550 (Samayapālanap.): IV, **13**, 340 (*°ā ivāsurāḥ*; *°kh°* both B. and C.).—§ 552 (Goharaṇap.): IV, **49**ε, 1539 (*Dānavaḥ*, had been vanquished by Arjuna; *°kh°* B, *°k°* C.).—§ 552*d* (Arjuna): IV, **61**, 1976 (had been vanquished by Arjuna; *°kh°* B., *°k°* C.).—§ 561*d* (Nara-Nārāyaṇau): V, **49**, 1930 (had been vanquished by Nara (i.e. Arjuna); *°kh°* B., *°k°* C.).—§ 564 (Mātalīyop.): V, **100**, 3571 (*Asurāḥ . . . Vishṇupadodbhavāḥ*, in Hiraṇyapura; *°kh°* B., *k°* C.). Cf. Kālakeya, pl.

Kālakaṇṭha, a warrior of Skanda. § 615*u* (Skanda): IX, **45**η, 2571.

Kālakaṭaṅkaṭa = Çiva (1000 names [2]).

Kālakavṛkshīya, a muni. § 266 (Çakrasabhāv.): II, **7**, 299 (*muniḥ*, in the palace of Indra).—§ 641 (Rājadh.): XII, **82**, 3059 (*muniḥ*, instructed Kshemadarçin), 3060, 3118, 3123 (became the *purohita* of Kshemadarçin); **104**, 3849, 3858 (instructed Kshemadarçin).

Kālakeya, pl. (*°āḥ*), a tribe of Asuras. § 4 (Anukram.): I, **1**, †162.—§ 11 (Parvasaṅgr.): I, **2**, 460).—§ 97 (Aṃçāvat.): I, **63**, 2543 (the offspring of Kālā, four are enumerated).—§ 264 (Sabhākriyāp.): II, **4**, 118 (*yathāsurān K°ān devo Vajradharaḥ*, sc. *kampayām āsa*).—§ 364 (Agastyop.): III, **100**, 8691, (followed Vṛtra); **101**, 8715 (do.).—§ 445 (Nivātakavacayuddhap.): III, **173**, 12207, 12209 (in Hiraṇyapura, cf. Kālakañja, pl.).—§ 570 (Sainyaniryāṇap.): V, **158**, 5379 (*Dānavaiḥ*, had been vanquished by Arjuna, cf. § 445).—§ 593 (Abhimanyuvadhap.): VII, **51**, 1997 (had been slain by Arjuna).—§ 599 (Jayadrathavadhap.): VII, **128**ππ, 5260 (*°sahasrāṇi caturdaça*, do.).—§ 608 (Karṇap.): VIII, **79**, †4054 (had been slain by Arjuna), †4056 (*sa-K°ān Asurān*, do.); **89**αε′, †4561 (*pūrvaṃ devair ajitaṃ K°aiḥ*, sc. Arjuna).—§ 778*b* (Saṃvartta-Maruttīya): XIV, **9**, 248 (*pravrājayeyaṃ K°ān pṛthivyāṃ*, says Indra). Cf. Kālakañja, pl.

Kālākhya = Çiva: XIII, 1053.

Kālakhañja, pl., v. Kālakañja, pl.

Kālakīrti, a prince. § 130 (Aṃçāvat.): I, **67**, 2673 (incarnation of the Asura Suparṇa).

Kālakoṭi, a tīrtha. § 379 (Tīrthayātrāp.): III, **95**, 8513 (visited by Yudhishṭhira on his tīrthayātrā).

Kālakūṭa[1], a poison. § 28 (Amṛtamanthana): I, **18**, 1152 (produced by the churning of the ocean, but swallowed up by Çiva).—§ 317 (Arjunābhigamanap.): III, **12**, 540 (*bhojane Bhīmasenasya pāpaḥ*—i.e. Duryodhana—*prakshepayad vishaṃ K°m*, cf. Kālakūṭaka).—§ 599 (Jayadrathavadhap.): VII, **135**, 5561 (*pītvā K°m*). Cf. Kālakūṭaka.

Kālakūṭa[2], a mountain. § 184 (Pāṇḍu): I, **119**, 4637, (crossed by Pāṇḍu on his way to Çataçṛṅga).—§ 276 (Jarāsandhavadhap.): II, **20**, 793 (passed by Kṛshṇa, etc., on their way from Indraprashtha to Girivraja (Rājagṛha)).—§ 555 (Sainyodyogap.): V, **19**, 599 (among the regions which were occupied by Duryodhana's army).

Kālakūṭa, pl. (*°āḥ*), a people, the inhabitants of Kālakūṭa. § 279 (Arjuna): II, **26**, 997 (in the north, vanquished by Arjuna on his digvijaya).

Kālakūṭaka, a poison = Kālakūṭa. § 197 (Bhīmasenarasapāna): I, **128**, 5008 (*vishaṃ*), 5019 (do., Duryodhana poured *K.* into the food of Bhīmasena).

Kālāmra, a tree in the varsha Bhadrāçva. — § 574*h* (Bhadrāçva): VI, **7**, 268 (*mahādrumaḥ*), 272 (description).

Kālamukha, pl. (*°āḥ*), a people. § 284 (Sahadeva): II, **31**, 1171 (*nara-Rākshasayonayaḥ*, in the south, vanquished by Sahadeva on his digvijaya).

kālānala = kālāgni: I, 2163 (*°vishāḥ*, sc. *sarpāḥ*); III, 10959 (*iva*), 13604 (*°samadyutiḥ*), 14384 (*°samadyutim*); V, 7245 (*°opamaṃ*); VI, †1271 (*°sannibhāni*), 3612 (*°samaprabhaṃ*), 4582 (*°samau*); VII, †4697 (*°sannibhena*, C. has by error *kālānila°*), 5755 (*°dyutiḥ*), †5834 (*°sannibhena*), 9116 (*°samaṃ*), 9396 (*°samaprakhyaṃ*); XII, 10247 (*°opamaḥ*); XIII, 851 (*°samadyutiḥ*).

Kālanātha = Çiva (1000 names [1]).

Kālanemi, an Asura. § 130 (Aṃçāvat.): I, **67**, 2703 (*Dānavānāṃ mahābalaḥ*, incarnate as Kaṃsa).

Kālanemihan = Vishṇu (1000 names).

Kālañjara, a mountain. § 372 (Tīrthayātrāp.): III, **85**, 8198 (*parvataṃ*). 8199 (with the tīrtha Devahrada).—§ 377

(Dhaumyatīrthak.): III, **87**, 8317 (*Hiraṇyabinduḥ kathito girau K°e mahān*, in the east).—§ 677 (Mokshadh.): XII, **247**, 8959 (comparison). — § 733p (Gaṅgā-Yamunayos tīrtham); XIII, **25**, 1721 (*girau*, a tīrtha).

Kalāpa, a muni. § 264 (Sabhākriyāp.): II, **4a**, 113 (in the palace of Yudhishṭhira).

Kalāpagrāma, a city (?). § 793 (Mausalap.): XVI, **7**, 251 (crossing Himavat the widows of Kṛshṇa retired to *K.*).

Kālaparvata, a mountain. § 528 (Rāvaṇāgamanap.): III, **277**, 15998 (starting from Laṅkā, Rāvaṇa crossed Trikūṭa and *K.*, and then came to the ocean).—§ 596 (Pratijñāp.): VII, **80**, 2850 (crossed by Kṛshṇa and Arjuna on their way to the abode of Çiva). Cf. Kālaçaila.

Kālapatha, a son of Viçvāmitra. § 721 (Viçvāmitrop.): XIII, **4β**, 249 (enumeration).

Kālapṛshṭha, a serpent. § 606 (Tripurākhyāna): VIII, **38**, 1483 (among the serpents who became the *vālabandhanāḥ* of Çiva's horses).

Kālapūjita = Çiva (1000 names [2]).

Kālapushpaphalaprada(ḥ) = Çiva (1000 names [1]) (B. *kālaḥ pu° aḥ*).

Kālarātrī ("the night of destruction"): VI, 4762 (°*ir yathā*); VII, 5048 (°*īm ivodyatām*), 7585 (°*nibhā*), 8301 (°*īm ivodyatām*); VIII, 1502, 4147 (°*īm ivātyugrām*), 4151 (°*īva durdṛçā*); IX, 578 (°*īm ivodyatām*), 906 (°*īm iva pāçahastām*), 1539 (°*īm ivodyatām*); X, 388 (description), 402; XII, 13502 (*guṇottarā*); XIII, 1401, 4454 (°*īva*).

Kālārka = Kālasūrya: V, †7206 (°*dīptām*).

Kālasāhvaya, a hell. § 744 (Ānuçāsanikap.): XIII, **44**, 2479.

Kalasodara, v. Kalaçodara.

Kālasūrya ("the sun at the end of the world"): V, 278 (*iva*); VII, †252 (do.), 633 (do.), 3769 (°*āv iva*), 4683 (*iva*); VIII, 938 (°*āv iva*); IX, 3115 (do.); XIII, 863 (*iva*).

Kālatīrtha, a tīrtha. § 370 (Tīrthayātrāp.): III, **85**, 8153.

Kālātman = Kṛshṇa: XII, 1655.

Kālatoyaka, pl. (°*āḥ*), a people. § 574 (Jambūkh.): VI, **9μ**, 354 (so B., C. has *Kālajoshakāḥ*).

Kālava, pl. (°*āḥ*), a people. § 574 (Jambūkh.): VI, **9ν**, 370 (only C., B. has *Kāladāḥ*).

kālavahni = kālāgni: XII, 8293.

Kālavega, a serpent. § 63 (Sarpasattra): I, **57**, 2147 (of Vāsuki's race).

Kālaviṅka, a tīrtha. § 733 (Ānuçāsanik.): XIII, **25**, 1720.

Kālayavana, a prince. § 717b (Nārāyaṇīya): XII, **340**, 12959 (*yaḥ K°ḥ khyāto Gārgyatejobhisambhṛtaḥ*, will be slain by Nārāyaṇa incarnate as Kṛshṇa, cf. Harivaṃça, v. 6425 foll.).

Kālayogin = Çiva (1000 names [2]).

Kālohikā, a mātṛ. § 615u (Skanda): IX, **46θ**, 2641.

Kāleya, pl. (°*āḥ*), a tribe of Asuras. § 130 (Aṃçāvat.): I, **67**, 2683 (°*ānān tu yo putrāḥ*, eight became incarnate), 2684 (*ashṭānām*), 2691.—§ 270 (Brahmasabhāv.): II, **11**, 472 (the same ?, in the palace of Brahmán).—§ 384 (Agastyop.): III, **101**, 8719 (*hemakavacāḥ*, = the Kālakeyas, defeated the gods), 8722 (only B.); **102**, 8737 (in the ocean; slew the munis), 8743 (*Kālopasṛshṭāḥ*), 8748; **103**, 8769 (°*aḥ . . . gaṇaḥ*).—§ 386 (do.): III, **104**, 8796, †8798 (°*samjñān*); **105**, 8816, 8818 (when Agastya drank up the ocean the *K.* were destroyed except a few, who sought refuge in Pātāla).—§ 459 (Mārkaṇḍeyas.): III, **188**, 12925 (seen by Mārkaṇḍeya in the stomach of Nārāyaṇa). Cf. Asura, Kālakeya, pl.

Kali [1], name of the fourth yuga. § 8 (Parvasaṅgr.): I, **2**, 282 (*antare K°-Dvāparayoḥ*, the great battle took place).—§ 458b (Kaliyuga): III, **188**, 12837 (°*au yuge*). — § 567 (Bhagavadyānap.): V, **132**, 4477 (°*eḥ pravartanāt*).—§ 641 (Rājadh.): XII, **69**, 2686 (*daṇḍanītim parityajya yadā kārtsnyena bhūmipaḥ | prajāḥ kliçnāty ayogena, pravarteta tadā K°ḥ*), 2687, 2695 (°*eḥ pravartanāt*); **91**, 3408 (*Kṛtam Tretā Dvāparañ ca K°ç ca . . . rājavṛttāni*), †3430. — § 649 (Āpaddh.): XII, **141**, 5328 (*Kṛtam Tretā Dvāparañ ca K°ç ca rājamūlāni*).—§ 677 (Mokshadh.): XII, **232**, 8496, 8505; **239**, 8719 (°*jāḥ sasamçayāḥ*), 8727 (*dṛçyante nāpi dṛçyante K°er ante punaḥ*, sc. the Vedas).—§ 683 (do.): XII, **268**, 9564 (°*au yuge*).—§ 717b (Nārāyaṇīya): XII, **340**, 12953 (*Dvāparasya K°eç caiva sandhau*, Kṛshṇa will be born).—§ 773b (Kṛshṇa); XII, **159**, 7363 (in the *K. yuga* Kṛshṇa is *adharma*; read with B. *Kalāv adh°*, instead of *Kalavadh°*, C.). Cf. Kaliyuga.

Kali [2], a term of dice (also personif.) and name of 'ill luck' in general. § 130 (Aṃçāvat.): I, **67**, 2722 (Duryodhana was born from a portion of *K.*), 2723 (°*pūrushaḥ*, i.e. Duryodhana).—§ 294 (Dyūtap.): II, **49**, 1777 (°*dvāram*).—§ 346 (Nalopākhyānap.): III, **58**, 2239, 2240, 2241, 2243, 2245, 2249, 2250, 2251, 2252; **59**, 2254, 2255, 2256, 2259, 2262, 2270 (possessed Nala, who was then defeated in gambling).—§ 347 (do.): III, **62**, 2346, 2347, 2357, 2358, 2360, 2361.—§ 352 (do.): III, **72**, 2837, 2838, 2839, 2840, 2846, 2847, 2849, 2851 (when Nala had acquired the science of dice, *K.* left him).—§ 353 (do.): III, **76**, 2967, 2969.—§ 354 (do.): III, **78**, 3051.—§ 355 (do.): III, **79**, 3073 (°*nāçanam*).—§ 378 (Tīrthayātrāp.): III, **94**, 8497 (possessed the Asuras). — § 446 (Nivātakavacayuddhap.): III, **174**, 12282 (*dyūtajam K°m*).—§ 562 (Bhagavadyānap.): V, **72**, 2629 (*yuddhe . . . K°r nityam*); **74**, 2728 (*paryāyakāle dharmasya prāpte Kalir ajāyata*). — § 568 (Vidulāputraçāsana): V, **133**, 4523 (°*m putrapravādena . . . ajījanam*, says Vidulā).—§ 570 (Sainyaniryāṇap.): V, **154**, 5136 (°*r mahān*). — § 618 (Jalapradānikap.): XI, **8ζ**, 222 (Duryodhana was born from a portion of *K.*). — § 623 (Rājadh.): XII, **12**, 361 (*açaraṇyaḥ prajānām yaḥ sa rājā K°r ucyate*), 363 (pl., *rājakalayaḥ*).—§ 732 (Ānuçāsanik.): XIII, **23**, 1575 (°*pūrvam*).—§ 746 (do.): XIII, **77**, †3728 (*vimucyate K°kalushena*).—§ 766 (do.): XIII, **127**, 6071 (*bhinnabhāṇḍe K°m prāhuḥ*). —§ 789 (Putradarçanap.): XV, **31η**, 852 (incarnate as Duryodhana). Cf. Kali [1].

Kali [3], a Devagandharva. § 101 (Aṃçāvat.): I, **65**, 2552 (the 15th in the enumeration of the Devagandharvas, sons of Muni).—§ 191 (Arjuna): I, **123**, 4813 (the 15th in the enumeration of the Devagandharvas who were present at the birth of Arjuna).

Kali [4], = Sūrya (the Sun): III, 150 (*sarvamalāçrayaḥ*, i.e. Kaliyuga).

Kali [5], = Çiva (1000 names [1-2]).

Kālī [1] = Satyavatī, the wife of Çantanu. I, 2209 (*janayām āsa yam K°ī Çaktreḥ putrāt Parāçarāt*, sc. Vyāsa), 4244; V, 4975, 4987, 5976 (*Gandhavatī*); VI, 5601.

Kālī [2] = Durgā (Umā): IV, 195; VI, 796; X, 387.

Kālikā [1], a goddess. § 270 (Brahmasabhāv.): II, **11**, 457 (among the goddesses in the palace of Brahmán).

Kālikā [2], a river (?). § 370 (Tīrthayātrāp.): III, **84**, 8134 (°*saṅgame snātvā Kauçikāruṇayor gataḥ*).

Kālikā [3], a mātṛ. § 615u (Skanda): IX, **46θ**, 2632.

Kālikāçrama, a tīrtha. § 733 (Ānuçāsanik.): XIII, **25a**, 1710 (on the river Vipāçā).

Kālikāsaṅgama, v. Kālikā [2].

Kālikeya, a Kuru warrior, son of Subala. § 593 (Abhimanyuvadhap.): VII, **49,** 1933 (*Subaladāyadam*, defeated by Abhimanyu).

Kalinda, a warrior of Skanda. § 615*u* (Skanda): IX, **45**η, 2566 (only C., B. has *Kaliṅgaḥ*).

Kalinda, pl. (XIII, 2104) v. Kaliṅga, pl.

Kālindī = Yamunā. II, 371; IV, 141.

Kaliṅga[1]. § 170 (Dīrghatamas): I, **104,** 4219 (son of Dīrghatamas on Sudeshṇā the wife of King Bali), 4220 (*Kaliṅgavishayaç caiva K°sya ca sa smṛtaḥ*).

Kaliṅga[2] (B. often *Kā°*), the king of the Kaliṅgas at the time of Yudhishṭhira. § 232 (Svayaṃvarap.): I, **186,** 6993 (also B., present at the svayaṃvara of Draupadī).—§ 562 (Bhagavadyānap.): V, **95**ν, 3403 (also B., in the army of Duryodhana).—§ 579 (Bhīshmavadhap.): VI, **54**[9], 2235 (B., *Kā°*), 2252 (do.), ([12]), 2301 (do.), 2302 (do., named Çrutāyus), 2307 (do.).—§ 589 (Droṇābhishekap.): VII, **7**γ, 179 (also B., on the right wing of Droṇa's array).—§ 596 (Pratijñāp.): VII, **74**β, 2629 (*udāyudhaḥ*, will protect Jayadratha; B. has *Kā°*).—§ 599 (Jayadrathavadhap.): VII, **93,** 3369 (*°pramukhā nṛpāḥ*, attacked Arjuna). — § 600 (Ghaṭotkacavadhap.): VII, **155,** 6703 (*°sya sutaḥ*, fought with Bhīmasena; B. has *Kā°*).—§ 604 (Karṇap.): VIII, **5,** 123 (*°-Vṛshakau bhrātarau* (?)). Cf. Kāliṅga.

Kaliṅga[3], a warrior of Skanda § 615*u* (Skanda): IX, **45**η, 2566 (so B., C. has *Kalindaḥ*).

Kaliṅga, pl. (*°āḥ*), a people. § 130 (Aṃçāvat.): I, **67,** 2701 (*°eshu narādhipaḥ*, named Kuhara (?), among the incarnations from the Krodhavaça gaṇa).—§ 170 (Dīrghatamas): I, **104,** 4220 (*°vishayaç caiva Kaliṅgasya ca sa smṛtaḥ*).—§ 249 (Arjunavanavāsap.): I, **215,** 7820 (*Aṅga-Vaṅga-K°eshu yāni tīrthāni kānicit*, visited by Arjuna), 7821 (*°rāshṭradvāreshu*), 7823.—§ 284 (Sahadeva): II, **31,** 1175 (vanquished by Sahadeva on his digvijaya).—§ 295 (Dyūtap.): II, **52,** 1874 (among the peoples who brought tribute to Yudhishṭhira.)—§ 392 (Tīrthayātrāp.): III, **114,** 10097 (on his tīrthayātrā Yudhishṭhira came to the country of the *K.*), 10098.—§ 515 (Karṇadigvijaya): III, **254,** 15243 (vanquished by Karṇa on his digvijaya).—§ 554 (Sainyodyogap.): V, **4**γ, 87 (*°ānām īçvaraḥ*, among the princes to whom the Pāṇḍavas ought to send messengers).—§ 556*d* (Sahadeva): V, **23,** †708 (Sahadeva had vanquished the *K.* in Dantakūra.).—§ 561*c* (Kṛshṇa Vāsudeva): V, **48,** †1883 (Kṛshṇa had destroyed the *K.* in Dantakūra).—§ 561*e* (Bhīmasena): V, **50,** 1986 (had been vanquished by Bhīmasena).—§ 561*g* (Sahadeva): V, **50,** 1997 (had been vanquished by Sahadeva).—§ 561 (Yānasandhip.): V, **50,** 2002 (had been vanquished by Çikhaṇḍin).—§ 574 (Jambūkh.): VI, **9**μ, 347 (only C., B. has *Pulindāḥ*), 349 (only *B.*, C. has *Bhujiṅgāḥ*), 353, (*o*), 376 (in the north-east (!) of Bhāratavarsha). — § 576 (Bhagavadgītāp.): VI, **17,** 668 (*patiḥ sarva - K°ānāṃ*, in Duryodhana's army). — § 579 (Bhīshmavadhap.): VI, **53**[6], 2231 (*senā K°ānāṃ*, attacked Bhīmasena), ([9]), 2234 (fought with Bhīmasena); **54**[9], 2238 (*°ānāṃ mahācamūṃ*), 2239, 2241 (*°ānāṃ janādhipaḥ*, i.e. Çrutāyus), 2249, ([10]), 2250, 2252, 2259 (*°ānāṃ mahārathaḥ*, i.e. Çrutāyus), ([11]), 2270 (*°ānāṃ varūthinīṃ*), ([12]), 2299 (*senā K°ānāṃ*), 2300 (*°sainyānāṃ*), 2302, 2311, 2312, 2314, 2315 ([13]), 2329, 2336, 2337 (headed by Çrutāyus the *K.* fought with Bhīmasena who slew them).—§ 580 (do.): VI, **56**δ, 2409 (in Bhīshma's gāruḍavyūha).—§ 585 (do.): VI, **87**δ, 3854 (followed Bhagadatta).—§ 587 (do.): VI, **117**ρ, 5483 (attacked Arjuna).—§ 589 (Droṇābhishekap.): VII, **4**β, 122 (*°āndhrāḥ*, had formerly been vanquished by Karṇa); **11**ν, 397 (had formerly been vanquished by Kṛshṇa).—§ 592 (Saṃçaptakavadhap.): VII, **20**γ, 798 (in the neck of Droṇa's gāruḍavyūha), (ζ), 802 (in the back of do.).—§ 595 (Shoḍaçarāj., v. Rāma Jāmadagnya); VII, **70**β, 2436 (*Aṅga-Vaṅga-K°ān*, have been vanquished by Rāma Jāmadagnya).—§ 599 (Jayadrathavadhap.): VII, **141,** 5851 (fought with Sātyaki), 5852. — § 600 (Ghaṭotkacavadhap.): VII, **155,** 6703 (*°ānāñ ca sainyena*), 6705 (Bhīmasena fought with the *K.*, headed by the son of their slain king, and slew also the latter).—§ 603 (Nārāyaṇāstramokshap.): VII, **193**β, 8905 (*°āraṭṭa-Bāhlikaiḥ*, followed Kṛtavarman).—§ 604 (Karṇap.): VIII, **5**ζ, 127 (*Çibayaḥ . . . K°sahitāḥ*, have been vanquished in the battle); **8**η, 237 (had formerly been vanquished by Karṇa).—§ 605 (do.): VIII, **17,** 671 (*°-Vaṅga-Nishādavīrāḥ* attack Arjuna); **22**ζζ, 864 (attack Dhṛshṭadyumna) (θθ), 882 (attack Nakula).—§ 608 (do.): VIII, **68**λλλ, †3390 (it had been prophesied that Arjuna would subjugate the *K.*, etc.); **70**πππ, 3500 (slain by Bhīmasena).—§ 613 (Gadāyuddhap.): IX, **33**η, 1913 (had been slain in the battle).—§ 621 (Rājadh.): XII, **4,** 109 (*°vishaye*, ruled by Citrāṅgada).—§ 739 (Ānuçāsanik.): XIII, **33***a*, 2104 (among the kshatriyas who have been degraded to çūdras). Cf. Kāliṅga, pl.

Kāliṅga[1] ("the king of the Kaliṅgas," named Çrutāyudha or Çrutāyus). § 264 (Sabhākriyāp.): II, **4**β, 121 (*Çrutāyudhaḥ*, in the palace of Yudhishṭhira).—§ 290 (Çiçupālavadhap.): II, **44,** 1540. — § 561 (Yānasandhip.): V, **62**ββ, 2426 (*Āvantya-K-Jayadratheshu*).—§ 576 (Bhagavadgītāp.): VI, **16***a*, 623 (*Çrutāyudhaḥ*, commanded one *akshauhiṇī* of Duryodhana's army); **17,** 662 (*Paurava-K°āḥ*, in the van of Duryodhana's army).—§ 579 (Bhīshmavadhap.): VI, **53**[6], 2230; **54**[9], 2236 (i.e. Çrutāyus, proceeded against Bhīmasena), 2254, 2258 (*°sya sutaḥ*, i.e. Çakradeva), 2262, 2265, ([12]), 2305, 2308 (is slain by Bhīmasena), 2309 (the protectors of his wheels are slain).—§ 619 (Strīvilāpap.): XI, **25**κ, 711 (mentioned among the slain). Cf. Kaliṅga, Kaliṅgādhipa, Kaliṅgādhipati, Kaliṅgaka, Kāliṅgaka, Kaliṅgarāja.

Kāliṅga[2] ("son of the king of the Kaliṅgas") = Çakradeva: VI, 2354 (*Ç°*).

Kāliṅga, pl. (*°āḥ*), a people = Kaliṅga, pl. § 579 (Bhīshmavadhap.): VI, **54**[12], 2319 (*sarvā-K°sainyānāṃ*), 2324 (*sarva-K°yodheshu*) ([13]), 2332, 2333, 2338 ([14]), 2351 (*sarva-K°ān hatvā*, sc. Bhīmasena), 2354.—§ 582 (do.): VI, **70**[9], 3117 (follow Duryodhana); **71**γ[10], 3132 (*sarva-K°mukhyaiḥ*, supported Çakuni).—§ 593 (Abhimanyuvadhap.): VII, **46**ν, 1854 (attacked Abhimanyu).—§ 607 (Karṇap.): VIII, **44**κ, 2066 (among the peoples who have no religion—*durdharmān*), **45**μ, 2084 (know the eternal religion—*dharmaṃ*).—§ 793 (Mausalap.): XVI, **6**κ, 159 (had been destroyed by Kṛshṇa).

Kaliṅgādhipa ("king of the Kaliṅgas"). § 233 (Svayaṃvarap.): I, **187,** †7020 (*°-Vaṅgādhipa-Pāṇḍya-Pauṇḍrāḥ*, present at the svayaṃvara of Draupadī). Cf. Kāliṅga.

Kaliṅgādhipati (do.). § 582 (Bhīshmavadhap.): VI, **71**γ, 3132 (supported Çakuni). Cf. Kāliṅga.

Kaliṅgaka (do.). § 576 (Bhagavadgītāp.): VI, **17,** 670 (= Çrutāyudha?). Cf. Kāliṅga.

Kāliṅgaka (do.). § 287 (Rājasūyikap.): II, **34,** 1270 (came to the rājasūya of Yudhishṭhira). Cf. Kāliṅga.

Kaliṅgarāja (do.). § 579 (Bhīshmavadhap.): VI, **54,** 2354 (i.e. Çrutāyus, slain by Bhīmasena). Cf. Kāliṅga.

Kāliṅgī[1] ("daughter of the king of the Kaliṅgas") = Karambhā: I, ††3775 (*K°*, wife of Akrodhana).

Kāliṅgī[2] (do.). § 156 (Pūruvaṃç.): I, **95,** 3780 (wife of Taṃsu and mother of Īlina).

Kāliya, a serpent. § 47 (Sarpanāmak.): I, **35**, 1551 (enumeration).—§ 564 (Mātalīyop.): V, **103**γ, 3625 (do.).

Kālīyaka, a serpent. § 47 (Sarpanāmak.): I, **35**, 1555 (enumeration).

Kaliyuga, the fourth yuga. § 375 (Tīrthayātrāp.): III, **85**, 8233 (in the *K.* the Gaṅgā is sacred). § 429 (cf. Hanūmad-Bhīmasaṃvāda). In the *K.* only a quarter of virtue (*dharma*) abides, Nārāyaṇa is black, etc.: III, **149**, 11257 (*tāmasaṃ yugaṃ*), 11261.—§ 458 (Mārkaṇḍeyas.): III, **188**, 12829 (comprises 1,000 [celestial] years), 12831 (*b*: description of *K.* (many Mleccha, Āndhra, Çaka, Pulinda, Yavana, Kāmboja, Bāhlika, Çūra, and Ābhīra kings will then rule, etc.)).—§ 459 (do.): III, **189**, 12981 (in the *K.* Nārāyaṇa becomes black (*kṛshṇa*)).—§ 460 (do.): III, **190**, 13011 [13019 (*tāmasaṃ yugaṃ*)] (*b*: description of the *K.*: at the end of the yuga the best robes will be made of flax (*vastrāṇāṃ pravarā çaṇī*, v. 13027) and *koradūshakāḥ* (the fruits of *Paspalum frumentaceum*) will be the best grains, men will live on fish and milk, goats and sheep, for the cows will be extinct (cf. v. 13035: "they will employ cows and calves that are only one year old to draw the plough"); men will resort to those countries where wheat and barley form the staple food (v. 13052); the highest lifetime will become sixteen years; renouncing the gods men will worship bones (i.e. relics; *eḍūkān*, v. 13074); in the hermitages of the great ṛshis and the schools and colleges of brahmans, and in places sacred to the gods, and in the sacrificial compounds (*caityeshu*), and in the dwellings of the nāgas (i.e. the sacred tanks), the earth will be dotted with *eḍūkāḥ*, and not graced with temples of the gods (*devagṛha*); at last seven suns will appear).—§ 581 (Bhīshmavadhap.): VI, **66**, 3012 (*Dvāparasya yugasyānte ādau K°sya ca*, then Kṛshṇa is hymned).—§ 615 (Gadāyuddhap.): IX, **60**, 3364 (*prāptaṃ K°ṃ viddhi*).—§ 664 (Mokshadh.): XII, **207**, 7557 (*°e . . . dvandvam āpedire janāḥ*).—§ 677 (do.): XII, **232**, 8504 (*anye*—sc. *dharmāḥ — K°e*); **233**, 8543 (*Dvāpare viplavaṃ yānti yajñāḥ K°e tathā*), 8546 (*dṛçyante na ca dṛçyante Vedāḥ K°e 'khilāḥ*); **239**, 8727 (*Dvāpare viplavaṃ yānti Vedāḥ K°e tathā*).—§ 679 (do.): XII, **261**, 9264 (*anye K°e dharmāḥ*).—§ 683 (do.): XII, **268***a*, 9593.—§ 766 (Ānuçāsanik.); XIII, **129**, 6095 (*imaṃ K°ṃ prāpya*). Cf. Kali[1].

Kalkala, pl. (*āh*), a people. § 574 (Jambūkh.): VI, **9**", 369 (in the south; only C., B. has *Valkalāḥ*).

Kalkin, a brahman. § 460 (Mārkaṇḍeyas.): When the Sun, the Moon, and *Bṛhaspati* (i.e. the planet Jupiter) simultaneously enter the constellation of Pushya, the Kṛta age will begin again (v. 13099), and commissioned by Time a brahman named Kalkin Vishṇuyaças (cf. the note of PCR.), born in Sambhalagrāma, in the house of a brahman, will, surrounded by brahmans, exterminate all the Mleccha crowds (III, **190**). Having exterminated the thieves and the robbers, *K.* will, at a great horse sacrifice, duly give away this earth to the brahmans and then enter a delightful forest, and the *Kṛtayuga* will be re-established. This is said in the Purāṇa (praised by the ṛshis) which is narrated by Vāyu: III, **190**, 13101 (*°ī Vishṇuyaçā nāma*); **191**, 13111 (°ī B., C. has °*iḥ*).—§ 717*b* (Nārāyaṇīya): XII, **340**, 12968 (the tenth avatāra of Vishṇu).

Kalmāsha, a serpent. § 47 (Sarpanāmak.): I, **35**, 1552 (°*Çabalau*, enumeration).

Kalmāshapāda, Saudāsa (also named Mitrasaha), king of Ayodhyā and husband of Madayantī. § 188 (Madayantī): I, **122**, 4737 (being himself unable to beget children *K.* urged Madayantī to go to Vasishṭha, who begat Açmaka on her, cf. § 225). — § 224 (Vāsishṭha): The rājarshi of the race of *Ikshvāku Kalmāshapāda* (whose sacrifices *Viçvāmitra* had desired to perform) once when hunting met the viprarshi *Çaktri*, the eldest of Vasishṭha's 100 sons, and ordered him to stand out of his way, and as *Çaktri* did not yield *K.* struck him with his whip. *Çaktri* then cursed him, saying: "From this day thou shalt be a *rākshasa*, eating human flesh." The king began humbly to propitiate the ṛshi, but *Viçvāmitra* (between whom and Vasishṭha there was a dispute about *K.*, whom they both wanted as their yājya) passed before them without being seen, and caused a *rākshasa* named *Kiṅkara* to enter the king. *Viçvāmitra* then went away. At this time a hungry brahman beheld in the wood *K.*, who was terribly afflicted by the *rākshasa*, and asked the king for some food with meat. *K.* asked him to stay there for a moment, and having roved for some time at pleasure at last entered his inner apartments. When waking at midnight and remembering his promise, he summoned his cook, and as the cook did not find any meat *K.* said: "Feed him with human flesh." The cook then took human flesh from the place where the executioners were, and offered it to the hungry brahman. Seeing with his spiritual power of vision (*siddha-cakshushā*) what kind of food it was, the brahman in anger said that the king himself should take a fancy to such food and wander over all the earth alarming all creatures. The curse on the king, being thus repeated a second time, became very strong, and possessed by the *rākshasa* the king lost all his senses. A while after *K.*, beholding *Çaktri*, in order to revenge himself for the curse slew him and ate him up. And *Viçvāmitra* caused that *rākshasa* also to devour the other sons of Vasishṭha: I, **176**, 6696 (*Ikshvākuvaṃçajaḥ*), [6720 (*Mitrasahaḥ* B., C. has *mitrasahaṃ* as adj. to *dvijaṃ*)].—§ 225 (Vāsishṭha): I, **177**, 6761, 6768 (Vasishṭha delivered *K.* from the curse of Çaktri, and then at the request of *K.* begat Açmaka on Madayantī, the queen of *K.*).—§ 228 (Aurvop.): I, **181**, 6881 (attained to heaven). — § 229 (Vasishṭhop.): I, **182**, 6888, 6904 (*rājarshiṃ*, it is related why *K.* caused Vasishṭha to beget a son on his wife).—[§ 480 (Pativratop., Brāhmaṇavyādhasaṃv.): III, **208**, 13817 (*Saudāsena*, all. to § 224).]—§ 607 (Karṇap.): VIII, **45**, 2092 (*Rākshasaḥ*, a sentence of his is quoted; read with B. *K°aḥ sarvasi*, instead of *K°usurusi*).—[§ 638*b* (Rāmopākhyāna): XII, **49**, 1792 (*dāyādaḥ Saudāsasya . . . Sarvakarmā*, had been protected by Parāçara).]—[§ 723 (Ānuçāsanik.): XIII, **6***a*, 326 (*Koçalādhipaḥ . . . Saudāsaḥ*, had become a *Rākshasa* through a curse, all. to § 224).] — [§ 677 (Mokshadh.): XII, **235**, 8604 (*rājā Mitrasahaç cāpi Vasishṭhāya mahātmane Madayantīṃ* (*Dama*°, C.) *priyāṃ dattvā tayā saha divam gataḥ*, cf. § 225).]—[§ 746 (do.): XIII, **78**, 3732 (*Ikshvākuvaṃçajo rājā Saudāsaḥ*), (3734) (*Saudāsaḥ*, questioned Vasishṭha about kine).]—§ 767 (Ānuçāsanik.): XIII, **137***a*, 6262 (*rājā Mitrasahaḥ*).]—[§ 784*b* (Uttaṅka): XIV, **56**, 1654 (*Saudāsapatnī*°), 1656 (*Saudāsaṃ purushādaṃ*); **57**, (1672) (*Saudāsaḥ*), (1674) (do.), (1679) (do.), 1681 (*Saudāsa*°); **58**, 1690 (*Mitrasahaṃ*), (1691) (*Saudāsaḥ*), (1694) (do.), (1700) (do.), (1704) (do.) (caused Madayantī to give Uttaṅka her ear-rings).] Cf. Ikshvākuvara, Koçalādhipa, Mitrasaha, Rākshasa, Saudāsa.

Kalmāshapadasaras (VIII, 2092), v. Kalmāshapāda.

Kalmāshī, a river (= Yamunā, Nīl.). § 218 (Draupadīsambhava): I, **167**, 6360 (*abhitaḥ so 'tha K°īṃ Gaṅgākūle paribhraman*, sc. Drupada).—§ 305 (Anudyūtap.): II, **78**,

2575 (°*tīrasaṃsthasya gatas tvaṃ* — sc. Yudhishṭhira—*çishyatām Bhṛgoḥ*).

Kālodaka, a tīrtha. § 652*b* (Indrota-Pārīkshitīya): XII, **152**β, 5647.—§ 733*i* (Ānuçāsanik.): By bathing in *K.* and Nandikuṇḍa and Uttaramānasa, etc., one is cleansed from the sin of fœticide; XIII, **25**, 1746 (°*m* . . . *abhyetya yojanaçatāt*).

***kalpa** (a period of time): II, 136 (*purāk°viçeshavid*, sc. Nārada); III, 1699 (*purāk°eshu*); V, 1352 (*purāk°e*); VI, 2953 (°*saṅkshepatatpara*, sc. Kṛshṇa); VII, 892 (°*ānte*); IX, 2732 (*pūrvak°e*); XII, 11227 (*yugaṃ dvādaçasāhasraṃ kalpaṃ viddhi caturyugaṃ | daçakalpaçatāvṛttam ahas tad Brāhmam ucyate*), 12752 (*atīte mahāk°e*), 12925 (°*ādau*), 12939 (°*ādishu*), 12980 (*mahāk°sahasrāṇi mahāk°çatāni ca samatītāni*), 13034 (°*ādau*), 13074 (*yāvat k°kshayāt*), 13319 (°*ānte*); XIII, 3230 (*purāk°e*), 5281 (*mahākalpaṃ*); XIV, 876 (*purāk°vidaḥ*), 958 (*purāk°m*, adj.).

Kalpa = Çiva (1000 names[1–2]).

kalpavṛksha ("wishing-tree"): III, 16170 (°*sadṛçaḥ*); VII, 7529 (°*āv iva*), 7564 (do.); VIII, 4938; XIV, 1756 (pl.).

Kalyāṇī, a mātṛ. § 615*u* (Skanda): IX, **46**θ, 2625.

***Kāma**[1] ("love," personif.). § 117 (Aṃçāvat.): I, **66**, 2596 (son of Dharma), 2597 (husband of Rati). — § 130 (do.): I, **67**, 2708 (Açvatthāman sprung from Mahādeva, Antaka, Kāma, and Krodha). — § 223 (Vāsishṭha): I, **174**, 6639 (°-*Krodhau*, used to shampoo the feet of Vasishṭha).—§ 436 (Yakshayuddhap.): III, **158**, 11590 (°*syeva çarotkarān*).—§ 531 (Rāmopākhyānap.): III, **280**, 16095 (°*bāṇābhisantaptaḥ*).—§ 533 (Sītā-Rāvaṇasaṃv.): III, **281**, 16167 (°*bāṇārttaḥ*).—§ 565 (Gālavac.): V, **111**, 3830 (*atra*—i.e. in the north—*Kāmaç ca Roshaç ca Çailaç comā sambabhuḥ*).—§ 660*b* (Bhṛgu-Bharadvājasaṃv.): XII, **190**, ††6977 (*Viçveçvara Umāpatiḥ K°m abhivartamānam anaṅgatvena çamam anayat*). — § 662*b* (Jāpakop.): XII, **199**, 7316 (*Kāma-Krodhau* = Virūpa and Vikṛta), 7317 (do.).—§ 743 (Ānuçāsanik.): XIII, **40**, 2256 (*Krodhaṃ K°sya Deveçaḥ sahāyañ cāsṛjat prabhuḥ*), 2257 (°-*Krodhavaçaṅgaṭāḥ*). — § 747*b* (Suvarṇotpatti): XIII, **85**, 4025 (*sanātano hi saṃkalpaḥ K°a ity abhīdhīyate | Rudrasya retaḥ praskannam agnau*).—§ 770 (Ānuçāsanik.): XIII, **151**, 7119 (a muni, one of the seven *dharaṇīdharāḥ*).—§ 779 (Açvamedhikap.): XIV, **13**, 342 (*gāthāḥ K° gītāḥ*, quoted).

Cf. also the following synonyms:—

***Anaṅga** ("bodyless"): III, 11591 (°*çarākarān*): IV, 389 (°*vihāriṇī*); V, 5985 (°*çarapīḍitā*); XII, ††6977 (°*tvena*, origin of the name); XIII, 808 (°*ḥ kena nirjitaḥ*, sc. as by Çiva), 2314.

Jagatpati, q.v.

***Kandarpa**: I, †7009 (°*bāṇa*°), †7016 (do.), 7794 III, 2086 (*iva*), 16168; VI, 1232 (Kṛshṇa identif. with *K.*).

Makaradhvaja, q.v.

***Manmatha**: I, †2935, 6014 (°*ena vaçānugā*), 6555 (*iva*), 6611; III, 1818, 1826, 2131 (*iva*), 2665 (°*sya Ratīm iva*), 11588 (*iva*); IV, 398 (°*sya çarotkarān*), 418.

***Manobhava**: I, 7143.

***Saṃkalpaja**: I, †7007.

***Smara**: VII, †8410.

Kāma[2], name of a fire. § 490 (Āṅgirasa): III, **219**, 14153.

Kāma[3], a companion of Skanda. § 615*u* (Skanda): IX, **45**, 2528 (given to Skanda by Sthāṇu).

Kāma[4] = Çiva (1000 names[1–2]).

Kāma[5] = Vishṇu (1000 names).

Kāmā, daughter of Pṛthuçravas and wife of Ayutanāyin. § 156 (Pūruvaṃç.): I, **95**, ††3774 (mother of Akrodhana).

Kāmacarī, a mātṛ. § 615*u* (Skanda): IX, **46**θ, 2641.

kāmaçāstra ("treatise on love"): I, 646 (i.e. Mhbhr.); XII, 9123.

Kāmada[1] = Sūrya (the Sun): III, 154.

Kāmada[2] = Skanda: III, 14631.

Kāmada[3] = Çiva (1000 names[1]).

Kāmadā, a mātṛ. § 615*u* (Skanda): IX, **46**θ, 2645.

Kāmadeva = Vishṇu (1000 names).

***kāmadugha** ("milking desires"): III, 15460 (*lokāḥ*); VII, 2397 (*gāvaḥ*); IX, 2445 (*lokān*); XI, 60 (do.); XIII, 3165 (*sarvak°ām dhenuṃ*, i.e. the earth).

***kāmaduh** (do.): I, 3928 (*sarvak°hāṃ varā*), 3933 (*sarvak°guttamāṃ*, sc. *Nandinīṃ*), 6657 (*dhenur Vasishṭhasya*); III, 2121; VI, 379 (*dhenuḥ*, i.e. the earth), 1232 (*dhenūnām asmi k°k*, says Kṛshṇa); VII, 2397; XIII, 2700 (*gāvaḥ*); XIV, 642.

***kāmaduha** (do.): III, 12725 (*gauḥ*); XIII, 2953 (do.).

Kāmaghna = Çiva (1000 names[1]).

Kāmahan = Vishṇu (1000 names).

Kāmajit = Skanda: III, 14631.

Kāmākhya, a tīrtha. § 360 (Tīrthayātrāp.): III, **82**, 5047 (*Rudrasya tīrthaṃ*).

Kāmakrodhau = Çiva (1000 names[1]).

Kāmakṛt = Vishṇu (1000 names).

Kamalā, a mātṛ. § 615*u* (Skanda): IX, **46**θ, 2627.

Kamalāksha[1], a Kuru warrior. § 600 (Ghaṭotkacavadhap.): VII, **156**κ, 6852.

Kamalāksha[2], an Asura. § 603*d* (Tripura): VII, **202**, 9556 (lord of the gold city, one of the three cities of the Asuras).—§ 606 (Tripurākhyāna): VIII, **33**, 1395 (second son of Tāraka), 1412 (lord of the silver city).

Kamalākshī, a mātṛ. § 615*u* (Skanda): IX, **46**θ, 2624.

Kāmanāçaka = Çiva (1000 names[2]).

Kāmaṇḍa, a ṛshi. § 641 (Rājadh.): XII, **123**, 4535 (*ṛshiṃ*), (4538) (discourse between *K.* and Āṅgarishṭha).

Kāmaṇḍaka = Kāmaṇḍa: XII, 4534 (°*sya saṃvādam Āṅgarishṭhasya ca*).

Kamaṇḍaludhara = Çiva (1000 names[2]).

Kamaṇḍalunishaṅga[1] = Kṛshṇa: XII, 1668. — Do.[2] = Çiva (1000 names[1]).

Kāmāṅganāça = Çiva (q.v. p. 206): XIII, 907.

Kāmapāla = Vishṇu (1000 names).

Kāmaprada = Vishṇu (1000 names).

Kāmaratha, a Pāṇḍava warrior. § 600 (Ghaṭotkacavadhap.): VII, **158**χ, 7012 (brother of Virāṭa ?).

Kāmāri = Çiva (1000 names[2]).

Kamaṭha[1], a king. § 264 (Sabhākriyāp.): II, **4**β, 117 (*Kambojarājaḥ*? in the palace of Yudhishṭhira).

Kamaṭha[2], a ṛshi. § 702 (Mokshadh.): XII, **297**, 10874 (*Kākshīvat-K°ādayaḥ*, among the ṛshis who had obtained their position by way of tapas).

Kāmaṭhaka, a serpent. § 67 (Sarpasattra): I, **57**, 2157 (of Dhṛtarāshṭra's race).

Kāmātman = Kṛshṇa: XII, 1640.

Kambala[1], a serpent. § 47 (Sarpanāmak.): I, **35**, 1555 (°*āçvatarau*, enumeration).—§ 268 (Varuṇasabhāv.): II, **9**, 361 (do., in the palace of Varuṇa).—§ 564 (Mātalīyop.): V, **103**, 3625 (do., enumeration).

Kambala[2], a tīrtha. § 373 (Prayāga): III, **85**, 8219 (°*āçvatarau*). Cf. the prec.

Kambala[3], a varsha on Kuçadvīpa. § 575 (Bhūmip.): VI, **12**ζ, 454 (the fourth varsha on Kuçadvīpa).

Kāmboja, pl. (°*āḥ*), a people. § 130 (Aṃçāvat.): I, **67,** 2668 (*Candravarmā . . . K°ānāṃ narādhipaḥ*). — § 279 (Arjuna): II, **27,** 1031 (together with the Daradas the *K.* are vanquished by Arjuna), 1033 (*parama-K°ān*, vanquished by Arjuna).—§ 296 (Dyūtap.): II, **53,** 1912 (°*jair hayaiḥ*).—§ 458*b* (Kaliyuga): III, **188,** 12840 (among the barbarous people who will obtain sovereignty in Kaliyuga). —§ 554 (Sainyodyogap.): V, **4**γ, 81.—§ 571 (Ulūkadūtāgamanap.): V, **160**γ, 5510 (in the army of Duryodhana); **161,** 5555 (do.).—§ 572 (Rathātirathas.): V, **166,** 5750 (ruled by Sudakshiṇa).—§ 574 (Jambūkh.): VI, **9**ξ, 373 (in the north). — § 576 (Bhagavadgītāp.): VI, **17,** 662 (°*āḥ sa-Sudakshiṇāḥ*, in Duryodhana's van). — § 578 (Bhīshmavadhap.): VI, **45**[19], 1734 (*Sudakshiṇam . . . K°ānāṃ mahāratham*), 1736 (°*ānāṃ mahāratham*, i.e. Sudakshiṇa).— § 580 (do.): VI, **56**γ, 2408 (in the tail of Bhīshma's gāruḍavyūha). — § 583 (do.): VI, **75**γ, 3293 (°*vara-Bāhlīkāḥ*, in Bhīshma's array).—§ 585 (do.): VI, **87**ζ, 3856 (followed the Trigarta king). — § 589 (Droṇābhishekap.): VII, **4,** 119 (going to Rājapura Karṇa vanquished the *K.*); **7**ε, 182 (*Sudakshiṇapuraḥsarāḥ*, in Droṇa's array); **11**ν, 398 (had formerly been vanquished by Kṛshṇa). — § 592 (Saṃçaptakavadhap.): VII, **20**γ, 798 (*Yavana-K°āḥ*, in the neck of Droṇa's gāruḍavyūha); **23**ο, 992 (*Prabhadrakāḥ*, follow Dhṛshṭadyumna).—§ 599 (Jayadrathavadhap.): VII, **91,** 3255 (°*ānāṃ . . . gaṇāḥ*, attack Arjuna); **92,** 3286 (°*ānām anīkinīṃ*, their king Sudakshiṇa is slain); **112,** 4333 (*Durvārayo* (B. °*ṇā*) *nāma*), 4338; **113,** 4432 (°*ānāṃ mahācamūṃ*, attacked by Sātyaki); **119,** 4715, 4721, 4728 (γγ), 4747 (Sātyaki slew thousands of *K.*, etc.), 4754 (°*sainyaṃ*); **120,** 4758 (*jitvā Yavana-K°ān*, sc. Sātyaki), 4766 (°*ānāñ ca vāhinīṃ*); **121**εε, 4818 (*Çaka-K°-Bāhlīkāḥ*, attack Sātyaki), **128**οο, 5242 (°*ānāñ ca vāhinīṃ*).—§ 604 (Karṇap.): VIII, **7,** †200 (*Nadī-K°-Vanāyujaiḥ*, sc. *açvaiḥ*); **8,** 235 (have formerly been vanquished by Karṇa and caused to pay tribute to Duryodhana); **9**θ, 283 (do.).—§ 608 (Karṇap.): VIII, **46**ε, 2137 (in Karṇa's array); **56,** 2798 (°*rakshitaṃ*, sc. *pratyakshaṃ*), (ι), 2807 (the younger brother of Sudakshiṇa is slain); **69**πππ, †3495 (adj.?, sc. horses?); **79,** 4040 (have formerly been vanquished by Karṇa); **88**αβ, †4506 (°*varaiḥ*, attacked Arjuna).—§ 609 (Çalyap.): IX, **1**γ, 27 (have been slain); **8**δ, 393 (in the rear of Çalya's array, followed Açvatthāman).—§ 619 (Strīvilāpap.): XI, **22,** 627 (*Yavana-K°striyaḥ*, wait upon the dead Jayadratha).—§ 641 (Rājadh.): XII, **65**θ, 2430 (enumeration of barbarous or low peoples); **101**π, 3737 (*Yavana-K°-āḥ*, skilled in fighting with the bare arms).—§ 664 (Mokshadh.): XII, **207**θ, 7560 (*Yauna-K°-Gāndhārāḥ*, among the barbarous peoples of the north).—§ 789 (Ānuçāsanik.): XIII, **33a,** 2103 (*Yauna-K°āḥ*, have been degraded to çūdras).

Kāmboja[1] ("king of the Kāmbojas") = Sudakshiṇa: I, 6995 (*S*°); II, 1747 (gave Yudhishṭhira tribute of skins and blankets), 1823 (do.); V, 590 (*S*°), 2304, 3403 (*S*°), 5274 (do.), 5529 (°*vaḍavāmukhaṃ*, sc. *puroshodadhiṃ*, i.e. the army of Duryodhana), 5574 (do.), 5748 (*S*°); VI, 622 (do.), 2108 (do.), 2928 (do.), 4501 (do.), 4666 (do.), 5051 (do.), 5108 (do.); VII, 801 (do.), 2628 (do.), 3112 (C. by error °*au* instead of °*o*), 3253, 3277 (*S*°), 3330 (do.), 3337 (do., is slain by Arjuna), 6515 (*nihataṃ*); VIII, 3612 (*S*°); IX, 74 (do., had joined Duryodhana), 1300 (*S°e*, sc. *nihate*); XI, 601 (*S*°, mentioned among the slain), 706. Cf. Kāmbojarāja.

Kāmboja[2] (do.) = the father of Sudakshiṇa. § 599 (Jayadrathavadhap.): VII, **94,** 3410 (°*sya dāyāde hate . . . Sudakshiṇe*). Cf. Kāmbojarāja.

Kāmboja[3] ("son of the Kāmboja king") = the younger brother of Sudakshiṇa. § 608 (Karṇap.): VIII, **56,** 2804 (*Sudakshiṇād avarajaṃ*, is slain by Arjuna).

Kāmboja[4], an ancient king. § 656 (Khaḍgotpattik.): XII, **166,** 6196 (received the sword from Dhundhumāra, from *K.* it passed over to Mucukunda).

Kāmboja, adj. ("belonging to or originating from [the country of] the Kāmbojāḥ"). § 582 (Bhīshmavadhap.): VI, **71,** 3131 (*açvaiḥ*).—§ 585 (do.): VI, **90,** 3973 (°*mukhyānāṃ . . . vājināṃ*). — § 592 (Saṃçaptakavadhap.): VII, **23**ο, 956 (sc. *açvāḥ*, bore Nakula), 972 (*çabalair açvaiḥ*, sc. Dhṛshṭaketu's); 991 (*yuktaiḥ parama-K°aiḥ*, sc. *açvaiḥ*).— § 593 (Abhimanyuvadhap.): VII, **36**η, 1574 (sc. *açvān*).— § 599 (Jayadrathavadhap.): VII, **92,** 3333 (°*āstaraṇocitaḥ*, sc. Sudakshiṇa); **121**ηη, 4831 (*hayavarān*); **125,** 5041 (*javanair hayaiḥ*). — § 607 (Karṇap.): VIII, **38,** 1776 (*yuktaṃ parama-K°aiḥ*, sc. *açvaiḥ*).—§ 617 (Aishīkap.): X, **13,** 648 (*yuktaṃ parama-K°ais turagaiḥ*, sc. the chariot of Kṛshṇa).—§ 619 (Strīvilāpap.): XI, **25**κ, 706 (*Kāmbojaṃ . . . K°āstaraṇocitaṃ*, i.e. Sudakshiṇa).—§ 635 (Rājadh.): XII, **35,** 1254 (sc. *açvān*).

Kāmbojarāja[1] ("king of the Kāmbojas" = *Kamaṭha*?). § 264 (Sabhākriyāp.): II, **4**β, 117 (B. has *Ka*°).

Kāmbojarāja[2] (do.) = Sudakshiṇa. VI, 5007 (*S*°), 5158.

Kāmbojarāja[3] (do.) = the father of Sudakshiṇa. § 599 (Jayadrathavadhap.): VII, **92,** 3327 (°*sya putraḥ . . . Sudakshiṇaḥ*), 3335 (*putraḥ K°sya*, i.e. Sudakshiṇa).

Kāmin = Vishṇu (1000 names).

Kampa[1], a Vṛshṇi prince. § 795 (Svargārohaṇap.): XVIII, **5**μ, 162 (among the Vṛshṇi heroes who after death entered the deities; read *Kaṅkaḥ*?).

Kampa[2] = Çiva (1000 names[1]).

Kampana, a king. § 264 (Sabhākriyāp.): II, **4**β, 117 (*satataṃ kampayām āsa Yavanān eka eva yaḥ*, in the palace of Yudhishṭhira).

Kampanā, a river. § 370 (Tīrthayātrāp.): III, **84,** 8094 (*nadīṃ Siddhanishevitāṃ*, a tīrtha).—§ 574 (Jambūkh.): VI, **9**λ, 333 (in Bhāratavarsha).

Kāmpilya, the capital of the Pāñcālas. § 209 (Drupadaçāsana): I, **138,** 5512 (*puruttamam*, the residence of Drupada). —§ 573 (Ambopākhyānap.): V, **189,** 7422 (the residence of Drupada); **192,** 7500 (do.).—§ 647*b* (Brahmadatta-Pūjanīsaṃv.): XII, **139,** 5137 (the residence of Brahmadatta).

Kaṃsa, son of Ugrasena, king of Mathurā, enemy of Kṛshṇa. § 10 (Anukram.): I, **2,** 357 (°*vadhaḥ*, related in Harivaṃça). —§ 130 (Aṃçāvat.): I, **67,** 2703 (*Ugrasenasutaḥ*, incarnation of the Asura Kālanemi). — § 273 (Rājasūyārambhap.): II, **14,** 594 (married Asti and Prāpti, the daughters of Jarāsandha), 598 (Kaṃsa and [his brother] Sunāman were slain by Kṛshṇa and Balarāma), 610 (°*bhāryā*, the widow of *K.* urged Jarāsandha to attack Mathurā).—§ 275 (do.): II, **19,** 761 (*nihate Vāsudevena tadā K°e*).—§ 276 (do.): II, **20,** 768 (*hataḥ*).—§ 290 (Çiçupālavadhap.): II, **41,** 1443 (*yasya cānena*—i.e. by Kṛshṇa—*dharmajña bhuktam annaṃ balīyasaḥ sa cānena hataḥ K°ḥ*).—§ 298 (Dyūtap.): II, **62,** 2100 (the Andhakas, the Yādavas, and the Bhojas abandoned *K.*, who was then slain by Kṛshṇa).—§ 549*f* (Durgā): IV, **6,** 180 (°*vidrāvaṇakarīṃ*, sc. Durgā).—§ 561 (Yānasandhip.): V, **68**ζζ, 2526 (all. to his slaughter).—§ 567 (Bhagavadyānap.): V, **128,** 4296 (*Ugrasenasutaḥ K°ḥ parityaktaḥ svabāndhavaiḥ*

. . . *mayā*—i.e. by Kṛshṇa—*hataḥ*), 4298; **130ξ**, 4411 (*nihataḥ*).—§ 571 (Ulūkadūtāgamanap.): V, **160**, 5470 (°*bhṛtye*, sc. Kṛshṇa).—§ 580 (Bhīshmavadhap.): VI, **59**, †2609 (*tyaktas tu K°o Yadubhiḥ*).—§ 589 (Droṇābhishekap.): VII, **11**, 387 (*Jarāsandhena pālitaḥ . . . Kṛshṇena pātitaḥ*), 388 (*Sunāmā . . . bhrātā K°sya*).—§ 615 (Gadāyuddhap.): IX, **61**, 3414 (°*dāsadāyāda*, sc. Kṛshṇa).—§ 717*b* (Nārāyaṇīya): XII, **340**, 12954 (Nārāyaṇa will be incarnate as Kṛshṇa in order to slay *K.*).—§ 768 (Ānuçāsanik.): XIII, **148**, 6926 (*kadanaṃ cakāra K°sya . . . Puṇḍarīkākshaḥ*, i.e. Kṛshṇa).—§ 785 (Anugītāp.): XIV, **69**, 2031 (*nihato mayā*, i.e. by Kṛshṇa).—§ 793 (Mausalap.): XVI, **6**κ, 158 (°*ñ ca vikramya*, sc. Kṛshṇa).—§ 795 (Svargārohaṇap.): XVIII, **5**μ, 163 (among those who after death entered the deities). Cf. Bhojarāja, Ugrasenasuta.

Kaṃsa-Keçinisūdana = Kṛshṇa: III, 623.

Kaṃsanisūdana = Kṛshṇa: III, 15528 (*K°*).

Kāmya = Çiva: VII, 9522.

Kāmyā, an Apsaras. § 191 (Arjuna): I, **123**, 4820 (among the Apsarases who danced at the birth of Arjuna).

Kāmyaka[1], name of a forest. § 11 (Parvasaṅgr.): I, **2**, 432, 464 (°*āgamanaṃ*), 472 (*kānanaçreshṭhe*).—§ 310 (Āraṇyakap.): III, **3**, 218 (*vanaṃ*).—§ 312 (do.): III, **5**, 242 (°*ṃ nāma vanaṃ*), 244 (*vanaṃ*), †245).—§ 313 (do.): III, **6**, 272.—§ 316 (Kirmīravadhap.): III, **11**, 387 (°*ṃ nāma tad vanaṃ*), 407.—§ 321 (Saubhavadhop.): III, **22**, 901.—§ 329 (Kāmyakavanapraveça): III, **36**, 1451 (°*ṃ nāma tad vanaṃ*), 1453.—§ 399 (Indralokābhigamanap.): III, **47**, 1902, 1912 (*vanaṃ*).—§ 341 (do.): III, **50**, †1966.—§ 342 (do.): III, **51**, †1982.—§ 343 (Nalopākhyānap.): III, **52**, 2014.—§ 356 (Tīrthayātrāp.): III, **80**, 3090, 3093, 4004, 4011, 4016.—§ 377 (Dhaumyatīrthak.): III, **86**, 8293, †8296 (*vane*).—§ 378 (Tīrthayātrāp.): III, **92**, 8457; **93**, 8476.—§ 424 (Bhīmakadalīkhaṇḍapr.): III, **146**, 11074 (*āçrame*), 11075 (*āçramaṃ*).—§ 440 (Yakshayuddhap.): III, **164**, †11897.—§ 441 (Nivātakavacayuddhap.): III, **166**, 11930 (*āçramaṃ*).—§ 442 (do.): III, **167**, 11945.—§ 451 (Mārkāṇḍeyas.): III, **182**, 12556 (*vanaṃ*); **183**, 12557.—§ 518 (Mṛgasvapnodbhavap.): III, **258**, 15365 (*kānanottamaṃ*), 15368.—§ 522 (Draupadīharaṇap.): III, **264**, 15571, 15577; **268**, †15660; **269**, 15671.—§ 524 (Jayadrathavimokshaṇap.): III, **272**, 15858.—§ 545 (Pativratāmāhātmyap.): III, **299**, 16917.—§ 547 (Karṇa): III, **310**, 17219 (*āçramāt*).—§ 548 (Āraṇeyap.): III, **311**, 17222.—§ 600 (Ghaṭotkacavadhap.): VII, **183**, 8323.

Kāmyaka[2], a lake. § 295 (Dyūtap.): II, **52**, 1877 (*saraḥ*).

[Kāmyakavanapraveça(ḥ)] ("proceeding to the Kāmyaka-wood," cf. Arjunābhigamanap.). § 328: As *Yudhishṭhira* declared that *Bhūriçravas*, *Çala*, *Jalasandha*, etc., and *Karṇa* (master of all weapons, etc.), and the *Dhārtarāshṭras*, together with the kings who had been injured by the *Pāṇḍavas*, could not now be vanquished, that all the *Kaurava* soldiers and their families had been honoured with wealth and luxuries by *Duryodhana*, and would sacrifice their lives for him, and that, although *Bhīshma*, *Droṇa*, and *Kṛpa*, all knowing celestial weapons and being invincible, behaved equally towards both parties, they would certainly, to pay off the royal favours they enjoyed, lay down their very lives in battle, *Bhīma* remained silent.—§ 329: While they were conversing thus *Vyāsa* appeared, and, taking *Yudhishṭhira* into a corner, taught him, after he had purified himself (*çuddhaye*), the science of *Pratismṛti*, by means of which *Arjuna* (*b*) should proceed to *Mahendra*, *Rudra*, *Varuṇa*, *Kubera*, and *Yama*, to receive weapons from them. He also advised him to go to some other forest in order not to cause uneasiness to the ascetics and exterminate the deer and destroy the plants. Then *Vyāsa* disappeared. The *Pāṇḍavas* went to the forest of *Kāmyaka* on the banks of the *Sarasvatī*, followed by numerous brahmans versed in *çikshā* and *akshara* (see § 322), and lived there devoted to the *Dhanurveda*, and sacrificing to the *Pitṛs*, the gods, and the brahmans (III, **36**).

Kanaka = Çiva (1000 names[2]).

Kanakadhvaja, a son of Dhṛtarāshṭra. § 182 (Dhṛtarāshṭraputranāmak.): I, **117**, 4553.—§ 232 (Svayaṃvarap.): I, **186**, 6983 (present at the svayaṃvara of Draupadī).—§ 585 (Bhīshmavadhap.): VI, **96**, 4349 (is slain by Bhīmasena).

Kanakāksha, a warrior of Skanda. § 615*u* (Skanda): IX, **45**η, 2576.

Kanakāṅgada, a son of Dhṛtarāshṭra. § 130 (Aṃçāvat.): I, **67**, 2740 (enumeration). Cf. Kanakadhvaja.

Kanakāṅgadin = Vishṇu (1000 names).

kanakaparvata ("the golden mountain"), said of Mahāmeru: XII, 2240.

Kanakāpīḍa, a warrior of Skanda. § 615*u* (Skanda): IX, **45**η, 2568.

Kanakāvatī, a mātṛ. § 615*u* (Skanda): IX, **46**θ, 2626.

Kanakāyu(s), a son of Dhṛtarāshṭra. § 130 (Aṃçāvat.): I, **67**, 2734. Cf. Karakāyu.

Kanakhala, name of a tīrtha. § 370 (Tīrthayātrāp.): III, **84**, 8008.—§ 375 (do.): III, **85**, 8231.—§ 377 (Dhaumyatīrthak.): III, **90**, 8393 (in the north).—§ 733*f* (Gaṅgādvāra): XIII, **25**, 1700. Cf. the next.

Kanakhala, pl. (°*āḥ*), a range of mountains. § 413 (Tīrthayātrāp.): III, **135**, 10696 (*ete K°ā, rājan, ṛshīṇāṃ dayitā nagāḥ*). Cf. the prec.

***kānana**, pl. (°*āni*) ("forests," personif.): XII, 12606.

Kāñcana, a companion of Skanda. § 615*u* (Skanda): IX, **45**, 2549 (given to Skanda by Meru).

Kāñcanacchavis = Çiva (1000 names[2]).

Kāñcanāksha, a warrior of Skanda. § 615*u* (Skanda): IX, **45**η, 2559.

Kāñcanākshī, one of the seven Sarasvatīs. § 615*i* (Saptasārasvata): IX, **38***a*, 2189, 2204 (the River Sarasvatī appeared at Naimisha as *K.*).

Kāñcanashṭhīvin = Suvarṇashṭhīvin: XII, 1043, 1045, 1111.

Kāñcanavarman = Hiraṇyavarman: V, 7429, 7506.

Kāñci, pl. (°*ayaḥ*), a people. § 223 (Vāsishṭha): I, **175**, 6684 (sprung from the urine of Vasishṭha's cow). Cf. the next.

Kāñcya, pl. (°*āḥ*), a people. § 571 (Ulūkadūtāgamanap.): V, **160**γ, 5510 (*Draviḍāndhra-°K°āḥ*, in the army of Duryodhana); **161**, 5555 (do.).—§ 605 (Karṇap.): VIII, **12**ββ, 459 (in the army of Yudhishṭhira).

Kandarā, a mātṛ. § 615*u* (Skanda): IX, **46**θ, 2627.

Kaṇḍarīka, a brahman. § 717*b* (Nārāyaṇīya): XII, **343**, 13264 (°*o 'tha rāja ca Brahmadattaḥ pratāpavān | jātīmaraṇajaṃ duḥkhaṃ smṛtvā smṛtvā punaḥ punaḥ | sapta jātishu mukhyatvād yogānāṃ sampadaṃ gataḥ*, cf. Harivaṃça, v. 1256 foll.).

Kandarpa = Kāma, q.v.

Kaṇḍūti, a mātṛ. § 615*u* (Skanda): IX, **46**θ, 2632.

Kaṇika, the minister of Dhṛtarāshṭra. § 212 (Kaṇikavākya): I, **140**, 5544, 5545, (5547), (5567), (5590), 5634.—§ 213 (Jatugṛhap.): I, **142**, 5673.

Kaṇikavākya(ṃ) ("the speech of Kaṇika"). § 212

(Sambhavap.). *Dhṛtarāshṭra* consulted the minister *Kaṇika*, who, after having expounded some very Machiavellian principles of policy, and told the fable of the jackal, the tiger, the mouse, the wolf, and the mongoose, concluded by advising him to destroy the *Pāṇḍavas* (I, 140).

[Kaṇikopadeça(ḥ)] ("the teachings of Kaṇika"). § 648*b* (Āpaddh.): The *Sauvīra* king *Çatruñjaya* questioned Ṛ. *Bhāradvāja* about the acquisition of profit, etc., and was taught by him; the king should have the rod of chastisement always uplifted in his hands; the different other duties of the king. *Çatruñjaya* obeyed these instructions and obtained prosperity (XII, **140**).

Kanishṭha = Çiva (1000 names[2]).

Kaṅka[1], an ancient king. § 6 (Anukram.): I, **1***a*, 227 (in Sañjaya's enumeration of departed kings).

Kaṅka[2], a Vṛshṇi prince. § 232 (Svayaṃvarap.): I, **186**, 6999 (present at the svayaṃvara of Draupadī). — § 273 (Rājasūyārambhap.): II, **14**, 623 (among the seven mahārathas of the Vṛshṇis).—§ 287 (Rājasūyikap.): II, **34**, 1274 (came to the rājasūya of Yudhishṭhira). Cf. Kampa[1].

Kaṅka[3], the name which Yudhishṭhira assumed when he lived disguised as a brahman in the palace of Virāṭa. § 549 (Pāṇḍavapraveçap.): IV, **1**, 23; **7**, †224 (*Vaiyāghrapadyaḥ*), †227.—§ 551 (Kīcakavadhap.): IV, **18**, 548 (*devitā rājñaḥ*); **21**, 674, 675.—§ 552 (Goharaṇap.): IV, **31**, 1020; **68**, 2191, (2195), 2220, 2229.—§ 553 (Vaivāhikap.): IV, **70**, 2265. Cf. Vaiyāghrapadya.

Kaṅka[4] ("heron"). § 127 (Aṃçāvat.): I, **66**, 2633 (son of Surasā).

Kaṅka, pl. (°*āḥ*), a people. § 295 (Dyūtap.): II, **51**, 1850 (brought tribute to Yudhishṭhira). § 641 (Rājadh.): XII, **65**θ, 2429 (enumeration of barbarous or low peoples).

Kaṅkanā, a mātṛ. § 615*u* (Skanda): IX, **46**θ, 2634.

Kānta[1] = Skanda: III, 14631.

Kānta[2] = Çiva (1000 names[2]).

Kānta[3] = Vishṇu (1000 names).

Kaṇṭakinī, a mātṛ. § 615*u* (Skanda): IX, **46**θ, 2634.

Kāntāraka, pl. (°*āḥ*), a people. § 281 (Sahadeva): II, **31**, 1117.

Kānti, pl. (°*ayaḥ*), a people. § 574 (Jambūkh.): VI, **9**μ, 347 (only B.: °-*Kosalāḥ*, C. has *Kāçi-Koçalāḥ*).

Kāntika, pl. (°*āḥ*), a people. § 574 (Jambūkh.): VI, **9**ν, 372 (only C., B. has *Kākāḥ*).

Kaṇva, a ṛshi. § 11 (Parvasaṅgr.): I, **2**, 370 (*maharsher āçramapade K°sya*). — § 133 (Dushyanta): I, **70**, 2874 (*maharshiṃ Kāçyapaṃ*); **71**, 2902 (*ṛshiṃ*), 2909 (°*syāhaṃ bhagavato . . . duhitā matā*, says Çakuntalā, whom Dushyanta sees in the hermitage of *K.*).—§ 134 (Viçvāmitra): I, **71**, (2914); **72**, (2937) (told a brahman the story of the birth of Çakuntalā, whom he had adopted), 2953 (*sutāṃ K°sya māṃ viddhi*, sc. Çakuntalā), 2954.—§ 135 (Çakuntalop.): I, **73**, 2977, 2978, (2986); **74**, 2992 (°*āçramapadaṃ prati*), 2994 (°*āçramanivāsinaḥ*), 2997, 3005 (°*āçramapadaṃ prati*), 3122 (when Çakuntalā had born Bharata, *K.* sent them to Dushyanta; *K.* afterwards became the priest of Bharata, who gave him 1,000 padmas (coins of gold) as dakshiṇā).—§ 564 (Mātalīyop.): V, **97**, 3501 (*ṛshiḥ*), (3502) (related to Duryodhana the Mātalīyopākhyāna), (3518); **98**, (3522); **103**, (3634), (3638); **104**, (3653), (3661); **105**, (3674), (3691), (3706), 3712 (*ṛshiḥ*).—§ 576 (Bhagavadgītāp.): VI, **23**, 819 (all. to § 564).—§ 595 (Shoḍaçarāj., *v.* Bharata): VII, **68**, 2387 (Bharata gave *K.* 1,000 padmas as dakshiṇā).—§ 604 (Karṇap.): VIII, **2**γ, 31 (all. to § 564).—§ 621 (Rājadh.): XII, **1**β, 4 (among the ṛshis who came to see Yudhishṭhira).—§ 632*b* (Shoḍaçarāj., *v.* Bharata, cf. § 595): XII, **29**, 942 (repetition from § 595).—§ 665 (Mokshadh.): XII, **208**ε, 7593 (*ṛshir Medhātitheḥ putraḥ ?*, among the ṛshis of the east, cf. Barhishad[2]).—§ 717*c* (Uparicara): XII, **337**ε, 12760 (among the sadasyas of Vasu Uparicara).—§ 734 (Ānuçāsanik.): XIII, **26***a*, 1764 (among the ṛshis who came to see Bhīshma).—§ 746 (do.): XIII, **66**ζ, 3332.—§ 770 (do.): XIII, **151**ζ, 7109 (*ṛshir Medhātithiḥ* (°*eḥ*, B.) *putraḥ ?*, among the ṛshis of the east, cf. Barhishad[2]).—§ 775 (do.): XIII, **166***a*, 7664 (among the ṛshis of the east).—§ 793 (Mausalap.): XVI, **1**, 15 (the Vṛshṇis attempted to deceive Viçvāmitra, *K.*, and Nārada, who then pronounced a curse on Çāmba, etc.). Cf. Kāçyapa.

Kaṇvāçrama ("the hermitage of Kaṇva"), a tīrtha. § 358 (Tīrthayātrāp.): III, **82**, 4087.—§ 377 (Dhaumyatīrthak.): III, **88**, 8337 (in the south).

Kanyā, a tīrtha. § 370 (Tīrthayātrāp.): III, **84**, 8115 (= Kanyāsaṃvedya ?).

Kanyābhartṛ = Skanda: III, 14633.

Kanyāçrama, a tīrtha. § 368 (Tīrthayātrāp.): III, **83**, 7059.

Kanyāhrada, a tīrtha. § 733 (Ānuçāsanik.): XIII, **25**, 1739.

Kanyakāguṇa, pl. (°*āḥ*), a people. § 574 (Jambūkh.): VI, **9**μ, 360 (in Bhāratavarsha).

Kānyakubja, a city, the present Kanauj. § 223 (Vāsishṭha): I, **175**, 6651 (the capital of Gādhi). — § 377 (Dhaumyatīrthak.): III, **87**, 8313 (at *K.* Kauçika, i.e. Viçvāmitra, drank soma together with Indra).—§ 395 (Jamadagni): III, **115**, 10144 (the capital of Gādhi), 10153 (on the Gaṅgā).—§ 565 (Gālavacarita): V, **119**, 4005 (the capital of Gādhi).—§ 721*b* (Viçvāmitrop.): XIII, **4**, 216 (*adūre K°sya . . . Açvatīrthaṃ*).

Kanyākūpa, a tīrtha. § 733*h* (Ānuçāsanik.): By bathing in *K.* and Balākā one acquires great fame among the gods: XIII, **25**, 1706.

Kanyāsaṃvedya, a tīrtha. § 370 (Tīrthayātrāp.): III, **84**, 8114. Cf. Kanyā.

Kanyātīrtha, one or more tīrthas. § 364 (Tīrthayātrāp.): III, **83**, 6082.—§ 370 (do.): III, **85**, 8165 (*tīre samudrasya*).—§ 379 (do.): III, **95**, 8512 (visited by Yudhishṭhira on his tīrthayātrā).

Kapa, pl. (°*āḥ*), a class of demons. § 772*p* (Pavanārjunasaṃv.): Vāyu said: When the gods with *Indra* were in the mouth of *Mada*, *Cyavana* took away from them the earth, and they had been deprived of the heaven by the *K.* *Brahmán* told the gods to seek the protection of the brahmans. The brahmans commenced a rite for the destruction of the *K.* The *K.* then sent *Dhanin*, who told the brahmans to desist, as the *K.* were equal to M.-ṛ. and very pious in all respects (enumeration). As the brahmans refused, the *K.* attacked them, but the brahmans destroyed them by creating blazing fires. The gods having slain many Dā. in battle did not know that the *K.* had been slain by the brahmans, but were informed by Nārada; then their energy increased and they obtained immortality: XIII, **158**, 7329, 7331–4, 7339, 7341–6.

Kapālahasta = Çiva (1000 names[1]).

Kapālamālin = Çiva: X, 249; XIV, 202.

Kapālamocana, a tīrtha. § 366 (Tīrthayātrāp.): III, **83**, 7007.—§ 615 (Baladevatīrthayātrā): IX, **39**, 2248, 2254.—§ 615*k* (Mahodara): IX, **39**, 2264 (origin of the name).

Kapālavat = Çiva (1000 names).
Kāpālī = Durgā (Umā): VI, 796.
Kapāli(n) = Çiva, q.v.
Kapālin, name of a Rudra. § 108 (Aṃçāvat.): I, **66**, 2567 (enumeration of the Rudras, the sons of Sthāṇu).—§ 191 (Arjuna): I, **123a**, 4826 (among the Rudras present at the birth of Arjuna).
Kāpālin = Çiva, q.v.
Kapardin[1] = Çiva, q.v.—Do.[2] = Vishṇu: XII, 13114.
Kapardin, pl. (°*naḥ*) = the Rudras: XII, 10292.
Kapardisutā = Sinīvalī: III, 14126.
Kapaṭa, an Asura. § 92 (Aṃçāvat.): I, **65**, 2534 (son of Danu).
Kapi = Vishṇu (1000 names).
Kāpī, a river. § 574 (Jambūkh.): VI, **9λ**, 331 (in Bhāratavarsha).
Kapiça = Çiva (1000 names[2]).
Kapidhvaja, Kapiketana = Arjuna, q.v.
Kapila[1], a ṛshi (Prajāpati), promulgator of the Sāṅkhya system and identified with Vishṇu (Kṛshṇa). § 339 (Indralokābh.): III, **47**, 1896 (°*o nāma . . . Hariḥ | yena pūrvaṃ mahātmanaḥ khanamānā Rasātalam | darçanād eva nihatāḥ Sagarasyātmajāḥ*, all. to § 387).—§ 387 (Sagara): III, **107**, 8877, 8879, 8880 (*munisattamaḥ | Vāsudeveti yam āhuḥ*, *K.* burnt the sons of Sagara to ashes, as they on their search for the sacrificial horse of Sagara did not heed *K.* in Pātāla).—§ 389 (Gaṅgāvataraṇa): III, **107**, 9900, 9901, 9903 (*munipuṅgavaḥ*), 9908 (returned the horse to Aṃçumat and granted him that the slain sons of Sagara should be purified when Gaṅgā was brought down from heaven); **108**, 9921, 9935, 9937 (*devaṃ*, all. to § 387).—§ 478 (Dhundhumārop.): III, **204**, 13608 (all. to § 387).—§ 493 (Āṅgirasa): III, **221**, 14197 (°*ṃ paramarshiñ ca yaṃ prāhur yatayaḥ sadā | agniḥ sa Kapilo nāma Sāṅkhyayogapravartakaḥ*, in the enumeration of fires).—§ 565 (Gālavacarita): V, **109**, 3976 (*atra*—i.e. in the north—*Cakradhanur nāma Sūryāj jāto mahān ṛshiḥ | vidur yaṃ K°ṃ devaṃ yenārttāḥ Sagarātmajāḥ*, all. to § 387).—§ 576 (Bhagavadgītāp.): VI, **34**, 1230 (*siddhānāṃ K°o muniḥ*, sc. *asmi*, says Kṛshṇa).—§ 637 (Rājadh.): XII, **43**, 1510 (Kṛshṇa is identified with *K.*); **47η**, 1595 (among the ṛshis who surround Bhīshma).—§ 668b (Pañcaçikhavākya): XII, **218**, 7889 (*yam āhur K°ṃ Sāṅkhyāḥ paramarshiṃ Prajāpatiṃ*, sc. Pañcaçikha); **219**, †7983 (i.e. Pañcaçikha).—§ 684 (Mokshadh.): XII, **269**, 9600 (°*sya goç ca saṃvādaṃ*), 9602, (9607); **270**, (9636), (9655), (9685); **271**, (9707), (9742), (9745) (discourse between *K.* and a cow about sacrifices). — § 704 (do.): XII, **302**, 11100 (*sūkshmaṃ Sāṅkhyānāṃ . . . vihitaṃ yatibhiḥ sarvaiḥ K°ādibhiḥ*).—§ 707 (do.): XII, **319β**, 11783 (had instructed Viçvāvasu).—§ 717c (Uparicara): XII, **336ε**, 12759 (*ṛshiçreshṭhaç ca K°ḥ Çālihotrapitā smṛtaḥ*, among the sadasyas at the sacrifice of Vasu Uparicara). — § 717b (Nārāyaṇīya): XII, **340**, 12932 (*vidyāsahāyavantañ ca ādityasthaṃ samāhitaṃ K°ṃ prāhur ācāryāḥ Sāṅkhyaniçcitiniçcayāḥ*, sc. Nārāyaṇa); **341** *o*, 13078 (among the seven mind-born sons of Brahmán); **343φ**, 13254 (*vidyāsahāyavantaṃ māṃ ādityasthaṃ sanātanaṃ K°ṃ prāhur āçāryāḥ Sāṅkhyā niçcitiniçcayāḥ*, says Kṛshṇa); **350**, 13703 (*Sāṅkhyasya vaktā K°ḥ paramarshiḥ sa ucyate*), 13718 (*ṛshibhiḥ K°ādibhiḥ*).—§ 721b (Viçvāmitrop.): XIII, **4β**, 255 (*mahān ṛshiḥ*, among the sons of Viçvāmitra).—§ 730g (Upamanyu): XIII, **14**, 916 (*Sāṅkhyānāṃ K°o hy asi*, sc. Çiva).—§ 730 (Ānuçāsanik.): XIII, **18ι**, 1299 (*Sāṅkhyarshiḥ*).—§ 770 (do.): XIII, **151κ**, 7119 (among the seven upholders of the earth—*dharaṇīdharāḥ*).—[§ 772f (Pavanārjunasaṃv.): Vāyu said: Behold the great ones—i.e. the sons of Sagara, Nīl.—who adored (? *ye hāsanta*, so Nīl.) the ocean, pulverized, being cursed by the brahman of golden complexion (? *suvarṇadhāriṇā*, so Nīl.), i.e. Kapila: XIII, **154**, 7221.]
Kapila[2], a serpent king. § 370 (Tīrthayātrāp.): III, **84**, 8010 (*nāgarājasya . . . K°sya tīrtham*).
Kapila[3] = Sūrya: III, 154.
Kapila[4] = Çiva (1000 names[1–2]).
Kapila[5] = Vishṇu (1000 names). Cf. Kapila[1].
Kapilā[1], daughter of Daksha and wife of Kaçyapa. § 87 (Aṃçāvat.): I, **65**, 2520 (enumeration of Daksha's daughters).—§ 105 (do.): I, **65**, 2560 (her offspring were the amṛta, the brahmans, the kine, the Gandharvas, and the Apsarases, as recorded in the Purāṇa).
Kapilā[2], a river. § 494 (Āṅgirasa): III, **222**, 14233 (among the rivers who are mothers of fires).—§ 574 (Jambūkh.): VI, **9λ**, 335 (among the rivers of Bhāratavarsha).
Kapilā[3] = Durgā (Umā): VI, 796.
Kapilā[4], a brahman woman, wife of Āsuri. § 668b (Pañcaçikhavākya): XII, **218**, 7895 (Pañcaçikha sucked *K.*, thence he was named Kāpileya).
Kāpila, a varsha in Kuçadvīpa. § 575 (Bhūmip.): VI, **12ζ**, 455 (the seventh varsha in Kuçadvīpa).
Kāpila, adj. ("belonging to or relating to Kapila"). § 387 (Sagara): III, **107**, 8885 (*tejas*).—§ 668b (Pañcaçikhavākya): XII, **218**, 7891 (*maṇḍalaṃ*, i.e. a concourse of munis who followed the system of Kapila).—§ 713 (Çukakṛti): XII, **326**, 12218 (sc. *çāstraṃ*). — § 717b (Nārāyaṇīya): XII, **343**, 13253 (°*ṃ jñānacintakaiḥ*).
Kāpila, pl. ("followers of the system of Kapila") = the Sāṅkhyas: XII, 11151 (*Sāṅkhyāḥ*), 11182.
Kapilācārya = Vishṇu (1000 names).
Kapilāçva, a king. § 478 (Dhundhumārop.): III, **204**, 13621 (the second son of Kuvalāçva Dhundhumāra).—§ 673 (Bali-Vāsavasaṃv.): XII, **227a**, 8263 (among the ancient rulers of the world, the same ?).
Kapilāhrada, a tīrtha. § 370 (Tīrthayātrāp.): III, **84**, 8056.
Kapilasya kedāra(ḥ), a tīrtha. § 364 (Tīrthayātrāp.): III, **83**, 6042 (*kedāre . . . Kapilasya*), 6044 (*Kapilasya ca kedāraṃ*, so C., but B. has *Kapishṭhalasya kedāraṃ*).
Kapilātīrtha, a tīrtha. § 364 (Tīrthayātrāp.): III, **83**, 6017.
Kapilavaṭa, a tīrtha. § 370 (Tīrthayātrāp.): III, **84**, 8009.
Kāpileya ("the son of Kapilā") = Pañcaçikha: XII, 7886 (*P*°), 7896 (*P.* is named so because he sucked Kapilā), 7897, 7899.
Kapīndra = Vishṇu (1000 names).
Kapīndraputrī ("the daughter of the monkey king") = Jāmbavatī: XIII, †629.
Kapiñjalā, a river. § 574 (Jambūkh.): VI, **9λ**, 334.
Kapipravaraketana = Arjuna, q.v.
Kapirājaketu ("having an ape in his banner") = Arjuna: VI, †2657, †2670, †2677, †2678.
Kapishṭalasya kedāra(ḥ), a tīrtha. § 364 (Tīrthayātrāp.): III, **83**, 6044 (only B., C. has *Kapilasya ca kedāram*).
Kapivaradhvaja = Arjuna, q.v.
Kapota[1], a Suparṇa, son of Garuḍa. § 564 (Mātalīyop.): V, **101β**, 3598 (enumeration).

Kapota[2] = Çiva (1000 names[1]).

[Kapota-lubdhaka-saṃvāda(ḥ)] ("the conversation between the dove and the fowler"). § 651*b* (Āpaddh.): *Bhārgava* related: A cruel fowler (description) was surprised in the forest by a great storm (description); the paths of the forest were all submerged; he caught a she-pigeon and immured her in a cage; when the sky cleared he passed the night under a tree, having bowed down to the deities that had this tree for their resort (XII, **143**). In one of the branches of that tree the male pigeon lamented the loss of his wife (XII, **144**). The she-pigeon answered him from within the hunter's cage, telling him to do the duties of hospitality to the fowler (XII, **145**). The male pigeon welcomed the fowler, who was stiff with cold, by igniting a fire; as the fowler was hungry, the pigeon (quoting R̥., D., and P.) himself entered the fire, at which the fowler became terrified, thinking of his own cruel life (XII, **146**), expressed his repentance, and set at liberty the she-pigeon, etc. (XII, **147**). The she-pigeon lamented for the death of her spouse; then she threw herself into the blazing fire; the couple of pigeons ascended to heaven (XII, **148**). The fowler took to rigid penances, perished in a forest conflagration, and beheld himself in heaven in splendour like *Indra* among Y. and G. and Si. (XII, **149**).

Kapotaroman, one or more princes. § 267 (Yamasabhāv.): II, **8**, 328 (in the palace of Yama).—§ 466 (Çibi): III, **197**, ††13299 (son of Çibi Auçīnara), ††13300 (°*ānaṃ çibinaudbhidaṃ prāpsyati* (°*si*, B.), sc. Çibi).—§ 621 (Rājadh.): XII, **4**ε, 113 (came to the svayaṃvara of the daughter of the Kaliṅga king Citrāṅgada).

Kāpoti, a brahman. § 786*b* (Nakulākhyāna): XIV, **90**, 2712 (? Nīl. takes it as an appellative: *yaḥ kapotavad ekaikaṃ kaṇaṃ ādatte*, observed the uñchavr̥tti vow).

Karabha, a king. § 273 (Rājasūyārambhap.): II, **14**, 577 (among the allies of Jarāsandha).

Karabhañjaka, pl. (°*āḥ*), a people. § 574 (Jambūkh.): VI, **9** o, 377 (in the north-east of Bhāratavarsha).

Karahāṭaka, a country (?). § 284 (Sahadeva): II, **31**, 1173 (*pāshaṇḍaṃ* ?, in the south, conquered by Sahadeva on his digvijaya).

Karaka, pl. (°*āḥ*), a people. § 574 (Jambūkh.): VI, **9**ν, 368 (in the south of Bhāratavarsha).

Karakāksha, a Kuru warrior. § 592 (Saṃçaptakavadhap.): VII, **20**γ, 797 (in the neck of Droṇa's gāruḍavyūha).

Karakarsha, a Pāṇḍava warrior. § 561 (Yānasandhip.): V, **50**η, 2014 (followed Çarabha, the brother of the Cedi king (Dhr̥shṭaketu)).—§ 584 (Bhīshmavadhap.): VI, **84**, 3727 (rescued Cekitāna).

Karakāyu(s), a son of Dhr̥tarāshṭra. § 232 (Svayaṃvarap.): I, **186**, 6982 (among the sons of Dhr̥tarāshṭra who were present at the svayaṃvara of Draupadī). Cf. Kanakāyu(s).

Karāla[1], a Devagandharva. § 191 (Arjuna): I, **123**, 4813 (present at the birth of Arjuna).

Karāla[2] = Çiva: VII, 9521; XIV, 192.

Karāla[3] = Kr̥shṇa (Vishṇu): XIII, 7367.

Karāla[4] = Karālajanaka: XII, †11504.

Karāladanta, a r̥shi. § 266 (Çakrasabhāv.): II, **7**, 296 (in the palace of Indra).

Karālajanaka, a king. § 705 (Mokshadh.): XII, **303**, 11220 (*Vasishṭhasya saṃvādaṃ K°sya ca*), 11223. Cf. Janaka, Karāla[4].

Karālāksha, a warrior of Skanda. § 615*u* (Skanda): IX, **45**, 2563.

Karālī = Durgā (Umā): VI, 798.

Karambhā, daughter of the Kaliṅga king and wife of Akrodhana. § 156 (Pūruvaṃç.): I, **95**, ††3775 (*Kāliṅgīṃ*, mother of Devātithi).

Karaṇa ("a man of a certain mixed caste") = Yuyutsu: I, 2446 (*Y*°), 4521 (*Y*°).

***Karaṇa**, pl. (°*āḥ*), name of a caste. § 702 (Mokshadh.): XII, **297**γ, 10869 (among the castes who sprang from the intermixture of the four original castes).

Karaṇa(m) = Çiva (1000 names[1]).—Do.[2] = Vishṇu (1000 names).

Kāraṇa(m) = Çiva (1000 names[1]).—Do.[2] = Vishṇu (1000 names).

Karandhama, an ancient king (= Suvarcas), grandfather of Marutta. § 267 (Yamasabhāv.): II, **8**, 327 (in the palace of Yama).—§ 677 (Mokshadh.): XII, **235**, 8602 (°*sya putraḥ* (!) . . . *Marutaḥ* (!)).—§ 767 (Ānuçāsanik.): XIII, **137**, 6260 (°*sya pautras tu Marutto Vikshitaḥ* (read '*vikshitaḥ*) *sutaḥ*).—§ 778*b* (Saṃvartta-Maruttīya): XIV, **4**, 79 (= Suvarcas, origin of the name *K.*); **5**, 99 (had Aṅgiras for his purohita; read *pūrvaṃ* with B. instead of *putraṃ*); **6**, 122 (°*sutātmajaḥ*, i.e. Marutta).

Kārandhama[1], a tīrtha. § 250 (Arjunavanavāsap.): I, **216**, 7841 (one of the five Nārītīrthāni, visited by Arjuna).

Kārandhama[2] ("the son of Karandhama") = Avikshit: XIV, **63**, 80 (born at the beginning of the Tretā yuga), 214 (°*ātmajaḥ*, i.e. Marutta).

Kārapavana, a tīrtha. § 615 (Baladevatīrthayātrā): IX, **54**, 3046 (*tīrthaṃ*, visited by Balarāma), 3049 (on Yamunā ?).

Kāraskara, pl. (°*āḥ*), a people. § 294 (Dyūtap.): II, **50**, 1804 (among the peoples who live in the palace of Yudhishṭhira as his bondsmen).—§ 607 (Karṇap.): VIII, **44**κ, 2066 (among the peoples who have no religion—*durdharmān*).

Karasthālin = Çiva (1000 names[2]).

Karaṭa, pl. (°*āḥ*), a people. § 574 (Jambūkh.): VI, **9**ν, 370 (in the south of Bhāratavarsha).

Karatoyā, a river. § 268 (Varuṇasabhāv.): II, **9**, 374 (among the rivers present in the palace of Varuṇa).—§ 370 (Tīrthayātrāp.): III, **85**, 8145 (a tīrtha).—§ 574 (Jambūkh.): VI, **9**λ, 343 (among the rivers of Bhāratavarsha).—§ 733*e* (Indratoyā): XIII, **25**, 1699 (a tīrtha, *Kuraṅge* ?).—§ 775 (Anuçāsanik.): XIII, **166***a*, 7646 (enumeration). Cf. next.

Karatoyinī, a river = Karatoyā. § 757*m* (Goloka): XIII, **102***a*, 4887.

Kārāvara, name of a caste: XIII, 2588.

Karavīra, a serpent. § 47 (Sarpanāmak.): I, **35**, 1557 (enumeration).—§ 564 (Mātalīyop.): V, **103**γ, 3630.

Karavīrapura, a city. § 733*t* (Viçālā): XIII, **25**, 1730 (a tīrtha, on the Viçālā ?).

Kardama[1], a serpent. § 47 (Sarpanāmak.): I, **35**, 1561 (enumeration).

Kardama[2], a Prajāpati. § 270 (Brahmasabhāv.): II, **11**, 437 (in the palace of Brahmán).—§ 641 (Rājadh.): XII, **59**, 2211 (son of Kīrtimat), 2212 (*Prajāpateḥ*, father of Anaṅga).—§ 717*b* (Nārāyaṇīya): XII, **335***a*, 12686 (enumeration of twenty-one Prajāpatis).

Kardamila, a sacred place. § 413 (Tīrthayātrāp.): III, **135**, 10692 (*Bharatasyābhishecanaṃ* ?).

Kareṇumatī, daughter of the Cedi king and wife of Nakula Pāṇḍava. § 159 (Pūruvaṃç.): I, **95**, ††3831 (*Caidyāṃ*, mother of Niramitra).

Karīshaka, pl. (°*āḥ*), a people. § 574 (Jambūkh.): VI, **9**μ, 363 (in Bhāratavarsha).

Kārīshi, a son of Viçvāmitra. § 721*b* (Viçvāmitrop.): XIII, **4**β, 254 (enumeration).

Karīshiṇī, a river. § 574 (Jambūkh.): VI, **9**λ, 325, 330 (in Bhāratavarsha).

Karīti, pl. (°*ayaḥ*), a people. § 574 (Jambūkh.): VI, **9**μ, 351 (in Bhāratavarsha).

Karkakhaṇḍa, pl. (°*āḥ*), a people. § 515 (Karṇadigvijaya): III, **254**, 15244 (in the east, vanquished by Karṇa on his digvijaya).

Karkara, a serpent. § 47 (Sarpanāmak.): I, **35**, 1561 (°*ākarkarau*, enumeration).

Karkoṭaka, a serpent. § 47 (Sarpanāmak.): I, **35**, 1550 (°-*Dhanañjayau*, enumeration).—§ 191 (Arjuna): I, **123**, 4828 (*sarpaḥ*, present at the birth of Arjuna). — § 268 (Varuṇasabhāv.): II, **9**, 361 (°*Dhanañjayau*, in the palace of Varuṇa). — § 348 (Nalopākhyānap.): III, **66**, 2611 (*nāgam*), 2617 (*nāgaḥ*), 2621 (do., Nala is bitten by *K.*).—§ 352 (do.): III, **72**, 2838 (°*visham*; Kali, who had possessed Nala, vomited the poison of *K.*).—§ 355 (do.): III, **79**, 3072 (*nāgasya*).—§ 564 (Mātalīyop.): III, **103**γ, 3625 (°*Dhanañjayau*, enumeration).—§ 606 (Tripurākhyāna): VIII, **34**, 1483 (do., among the serpents who became the *vālabandhanāḥ* of Çiva's horses).—§ 793 (Mausalap.): XVI, **4**η, †119.

Karkoṭaka, pl. (°*āḥ*), a people. § 607 (Karṇap.): VIII, **44**κ, 2066 (among the peoples who have no religion—*durdharmān*).

Karmakālavid = Çiva (1000 names[2]).

Karman = Çiva (1000 names[2]).

Karmin, a son of Çukra (so PCR.). § 98 (Aṃçāvat.): I, **65**, 2545 (? *dvāv anyau Raudrakarmiṇau*, enumeration of the sons of Çukra).

Karṇa[1], son of Sūrya with Kuntī, adopted by the Sūta Adhiratha and his wife Rādhā, and the counsellor of Duryodhana. § 4 (Anukram.): I, **1**, †108, 139, †165, †174, †177, †195, †196, †198, †203.—§ 9 (Parvasaṅgr.): I, **2**, 301 (*ahanī yuyudhe dve tu K°ḥ*, sc. as leader of Duryodhana's army).—§ 10 (do.): I, **2**, 334 (*vivādaparvātra K°sya*, cf. V, **62** or **168**).—§ 11 (do.): I, **2**, 389, 422, 441, 476, 510, 511, 543, 545, 548, 589.—§ 71 (Ādivaṃçāvatāraṇap.): I, **61**, 2238 (counsellor of Duryodhana).—§ 81*b* (do.): *K.* was born of Kuntī and Sūrya, with his armour and ear-rings: I, **63**, 2427.—§ 131*b* (Kuntī): When Kuntī had thrown her child into the water, it was taken up by the husband of Rādhā and called Vasusheṇa. He grew very strong and soon mastered the vedāṅgas; there was nothing he would not give to the brahmans. In order to benefit Arjuna, Indra in the guise of a brahman obtained his ear-rings and armour, and in return gave him a lance with which he could slay any one amongst gods, Asuras, men, Gandharvas, and Rākshasas. Because he took off (*utkṛtya*) his natural armour and ear-rings he was called Vaikartana Karṇa. He was the friend and counsellor of Duryodhana: I, **66**, [2776 (*Vasusheṇeti . . . viçrutam*)], 2780, 2782 (*Vaikartanaḥ*), 2783.—§ 175 (Karṇasambhava): I, **111**, 4399, 4408, 4411 (*Vaikartanaḥ*; repetition of § 131).—§ 197 (Bhīmasena-rasapāna): I, **129**, 5068.—[§ 203 (Droṇa): I, **132**, 5221 (*Sūtaputraç ca Rādheyaḥ*, became the disciple of Droṇa in the Dhanurveda).]—§ 208*c* (Astradarçana): When the exhibition had nearly ended there was heard proceeding from the gate the slapping of arms like to the roar of thunder. Then *K.* (the son of *Pṛthā* and the Sun) proceeded with his natural mail and ear-ring and bowed to *Droṇa* and *Kṛpa*. Having spoken disdainfully to *Arjuna*, at which *Duryodhana* was filled with delight, he then, with the permission of *Droṇa*, did all that *Arjuna* had done before. *Duryodhana* and his brothers in joy embraced *K.* *K.* asked for a single combat with *Arjuna*, who rebuked him. *Droṇa* gave his consent to the encounter. *Indra* covered *Arjuna* with clouds, while the Sun dispersed the clouds from *K.*, who remained visible, surrounded by the rays of the Sun. When *Kṛpa* asked *K.* to tell his lineage ("sons of kings never fight with men of inferior lineage," v. 5411) *K.* was ashamed, but *Duryodhana* (saying, "The origin of kings is, according to the *çāstras*, threefold—persons of noble blood, heroes, and those who lead an army," v. 5413) immediately installed *K.* king of the Aṅgas (I, **136**). Then *Adhiratha* entered the lists and embraced *K.* as his son *Bhīmasena*, seeing this, scoffed at *K.* as the son of a charioteer (*sūta*), but was reprimanded by *Duryodhana* ("the origin of heroes and rivers is always unknown," examples: the fire that rises from the water; the thunderbolt (*vajra*) that was made from the bones of *Dadhīca*; *Guha*, i.e. Skanda, is named the son of *Agni* or of the *Kṛttikāḥ* or of *Rudra* or of *Gaṅgā*; *Viçvāmitra* and other kshatriyas who became brahmans; *Droṇa* and *Kṛpa*). When the sun went down *Duryodhana* led *K.* out of the arena. *Kuntī* had recognized *K.* as her son and was pleased at his success. *Duryodhana* banished his fear of *Arjuna* when he had obtained *Karṇa's* friendship (I, **137**): I, **136**, 5379, 5381, 5390, 5391, (5393), 5395, 5396, (5397), 5400, 5403, 5404, 5412, 5415, 5418; **137**, 5420, 5426, 5438, 5440, 5442, 5443.—§ 209 (Drupadaçāsana): I, **138**, 5449, 5463 (assisted by his pupils, and among those by *K.*, Droṇa vanquished Drupada).—§ 213 (Jatugṛhap.): I, **141**, 5635, 5655 (*Vaikartanaḥ*), 5674; **149**, 5849; **151**, 5920.—§ 214 (Hiḍimbavadhap.): I, **155**, 6083 (Ghaṭotkaca was destined to become the antagonist of *K.* and to be killed with his dart (*çakti*), which could only slay one person, so that Arjuna might be saved).—§ 231 (Svayaṃvarap.): I, **185**, 6957 (*Duryodhana-purogamāç ca sa-K°āḥ Kuravaḥ*, came to the svayaṃvara of Draupadī).—§ 232 (do.): I, **186**, 6984.—§ 233 (do.): I, **187**, †7019, †7025, [†7026 (*Arkaputram*)], †7027 (rejected by Draupadī); [**188**, 7051 (*Rādheya*)]. — § 234 (do.): I, **190**, 7089, 7091, 7094 (*Vaikartanam*), 7098 (*Vaikartanaḥ*), (7100), 7104, 7106 (*Rādheyaḥ*), 7113, †7155 (encounter with the Pāṇḍavas at the svayaṃvara of Draupadī).—§ 241 (Vidurāgamanap.): I, **200**, 7373; **202**, (7416).—§ 242 (do., Ambuvīca): I, **204**, (7472).—§ 243 (Vidurāgamanap.): I, **204**, 7486; **205**, 7490, 7516.—§ 280 (Bhīmasena): II, **30**, 1092, 1093, 1094 (vanquished by Bhīmasena on his digvijaya).—§ 287 (Rājasūyikap.): II, **34**, 1266 (came to the rājasūya of Yudhishṭhira).—§ 289 (Arghāharaṇap.): II, **37**, 1353.—§ 290 (Çiçupālavadhap.): II, **44**, 1527 (*c*: the ruler of the country of the Vaṅgas and the Aṅgas (*Vaṅgāṅgavishayādhyaksham*), with natural ear-rings and armour, by whom Jarāsandha was vanquished and mangled (? *dehabhedam lambhitaḥ*) in a wrestling encounter).—[§ 294 (Dyūtap.): II, **48**, 1712 (*Sūtaputraç ca Rādheyaḥ*, among the allies of Duryodhana).]—§ 298 (do.): II, **58**, 2014 (present at the game); **65**, 2184.—§ 299 (do.): II, **67**, †2241; **68**, (2277) (declared Draupadī to be forfeited).—§ 301 (do.): II, **68**, 2338 (declared Draupadī to be a dāsī and ordered Duḥçāsana to drag her away); **71**, (2379) (told Draupadī to select another husband); **72**, 2416.—§ 302 (Anudyūtap.): II, **74**, 2456.—§ 304 (do.):

II, **77**, 2539 (Arjuna will slay *K.*), 2544, 2545, 2546.—§ 306 (do.): II, **80**, 2655, 2656.—§ 307 (do.): II, **81**, 2688.—§ 308 (Āraṇyakap.): III, **1**, 14.—[§ 311 (do.): III, **4**, †233 (*Sūtaputraḥ*).]—§ 313 (do.): III, **7**, 288, (298), 300, 301 (*K.* suggested the slaying of the Pāṇḍavas; he and Duryodhana, etc., set out, but on their way they were warned by Vyāsa).—§ 317 (Arjunābhigamanap.): III, **12**, 465, 586, 595.—§ 322 (Dvaitavanapr.): III, **23**, †912.—§ 325 (Draupadīparitāpav.): III, **27**, 996.—§ 328 (Kāmyakavanapr.): III, **36**, 1419, 1428.—§ 330 (Indradarçana): III, **37**, 1459.—§ 333*c* (Brahmaçiras): III, **40**, 1645.—§ 334 (Kairātap.): III, **41**, 1685 (Arjuna shall slay *K.*).—§ 340 (Indralokābhigamanap.): III, **48**, 1922, 1923; **49**, 1934, 1945, 1948 (°-*Saubalakādayaḥ*).—§ 342 (do.): III, **51**, 1995.—§ 343 (Nalopākhyānap.): III, **52**, 2024, 2030.—§ 377 (Dhaumyatīrthak.): III, **86**, 8285 (*Sūtaputraḥ*), 8288 (°*pāvakam*, sc. *Arjunodīrito meghaḥ çamayishyati*).—§ 378 (Tirthayātrāp.): III, **91**, 8426, 8429.—§ 402 (do.): III, **120**, †10269.—§ 446 (Nivātakavacayuddhap.): III, **174**, 12276.—§ 512 (Ghoshayātrāp.): III, **236**, †14771; **237**, 14772, 14795; **238**, 14796, 14797, 14805, 14812, 14813; **239**, 14842; **240**, 14851; **241**, 14898, 14906 (*Vaikartanaḥ*); **242**, 14913; **245**, 14981; **246**, 15012; **247**, 15043, 15052; **249**, 15081, 15092, 15105; **250**, (15111), 15123; **251**, 15125, 15135 (at the ghoshayātrā *K.* fled, vanquished by the Gandharvas; when Duryodhana, etc., had been set free with the assistance of the Pāṇḍavas, *K.*, etc., reproached Duryodhana for his intention to leave the world).—§ 513 (do.): III, **252**, 15174 (*hatasya Narakasyātmā K°mūrtim upāçritaḥ*), 15177 (Indra will take away his ear-rings and coat of mail, cf. § 547), 15187, 15189 (*āvishṭacittātmā Narakasyāntarātmanā*), 15192 (*Vaikartanaḥ*, possessed by Naraka, *K.* was desirous of slaying Arjuna).—§ 514 (do.): III, **252**, 15204 (promised to slay Arjuna).—§ 515 (Karṇadigvijaya): III, **253**, 15209, 15215 (*Sūtaputrasya*), 15216, 15219, (15223), 15231, 15234; **254**, 15237, 15247, 15251, 15260, 15262, 15264, 15267, 15272 (*K.* subdued the earth for Duryodhana).—§ 516 (Duryodhanayajña): III, **255**, (15274), 15276, 15279, 15283, 15294; **256**, 15302, 15324; **257**, 15337, 15340, 15342 (advised Duryodhana to perform the rājasūya, swears that he will slay Arjuna).—§ 517 (Ghoshayātrāp.): III, **257**, 15347, 15350 (*Sūtaputreṇa*).—§ 521 (Draupadīharaṇap.): III, **262**, 15495, 15497, 15509, 15510, 15517, (15517).—§ 546 (Kuṇḍalāharaṇap.): III, **300**, 16921, 16923, 16924, 16927, 16936, 16938, (16939), (16941); **301**, 16958, 16973, 16976; **302**, (16977), 16980, 16992, 16994, 16996 (Sūrya appeared to *K.* in a dream and dissuaded him from giving away his ear-rings and coat of mail; when *K.* refused to break his vow, Sūrya advised him to ask Indra for the dart Amoghā).—§ 547 (cf. Kuṇḍalāharaṇap.): Asked by *Janamejaya*, *Vaiçampāyana* related the secret which was not revealed to *K.* by *Sūrya*. *Pṛtha* (i.e. *Kuntī*), the sister of *Vasudeva* and the daughter of the *Vṛshṇi Çūra* and adopted by King *Kuntibhoja*, was ordered by *Kuntibhoja* to wait upon a brahman of fierce energy (III, **303, 304**). After a year the brahman gave her a mantra (*Atharvaçirāsi çrutam*), by which she might invoke the gods (III, **305**). When she at the time of her seasons saw the sun's orbit she became possessed of celestial power of vision, and beheld *Sūrya* with his coat of mail and his ear-rings and invoked him. By way of *yoga* he divided himself into two, one of whom appeared before *Kuntī*. At first *Kuntī* was frightened (III, **306**), but *Sūrya* reassured her, saying: "Thou shalt remain a virgin after having gratified me, and thy son shall have the ear-rings and the coat of mail, made of amṛta, that have been given to me by *Aditi*," etc.; then he entered her by virtue of *yoga* (III, **307**). This happened in the bright fortnight of the tenth month (*çukle daçottare pakshe*). Except her nurse nobody else knew about the matter; when the child was born she consulted with her nurse and placed it in a box on the river *Açvanadī*, imploring protection from *Varuṇa*, *Sūrya*, A., V., R., S., V.-D., M., *diçaḥ*, *digīçvarāḥ*, I., etc.; from *Açvanadī* the basket floated to the river *Carmaṇvatī*, thence to the *Yamunā*, and so on to the *Gaṅgā*, to the town of *Campā*, in the country of the *Aṅgas* (III, **308**), ruled by the sūta *Adhiratha* (the husband of *Rādhā*), who was childless. They adopted the child and called him *Vasusheṇa* and *Vṛsha* (only afterwards he was named *K.*). After having adopted *K.*, *Adhiratha* had other sons begotten by himself. When *K.* had grown up he was sent to *Hāstinapura*, and acquired the four kinds of weapons from *Droṇa*, *Kṛpa*, and *Rāma*, and became the friend of *Duryodhana*, but was intent on injuring the *Pāṇḍavas*, especially *Arjuna*. *Yudhishṭhira* was afraid of him. When *K.* after rising from the water at noon worshipped *Sūrya*, brahmans used to solicit him for wealth, and there was nothing that he would not give away to the brahmans (III, **309**). *Indra* in the guise of a brahman appeared before him, asked him for his coat of mail, and gave him instead a dart (*Vāsavī*), which could not be baffled and which, in the hands of *Indra*, destroyed the *Daityas* and then returned to him. "This dart can only slay one powerful enemy of thine and then it will return to me, but it will not be that one which thou seekest to slay, for he is protected by *Kṛshṇa*." *K.* cut the coat of mail and ear-rings off his person, *Indra* having granted him that his body thus disfigured should not become unsightly. Gods and men and *Dānavas* raised a leonine roar. For this feat he was called *Karṇa*. The *Dhārtarāshṭras* became distressed and the *Pāṇḍavas* were filled with joy. Having rescued *Kṛshṇā* from *Jayadratha* and listened to the ancient stories recited by *Mārkaṇḍeya*, the *Pāṇḍavas* returned from *Kāmyaka* to *Dvaitavana* (III, **310**): III, **303**, 16998; **309**, 17172, 17173 (*Sūryasambhavaḥ*), 17175; **310**, (17183), 17184, 17190, 17196, 17197, (17198), 17199, 17200, (17203), (17206), 17208, 17209, (17211), †17213, †17214, †17215, †17216, †17217.—§ 548 (Āraṇeyap.): III, **315**, 17453.—§ 551 (Kīcakavadhap.): IV, **21**, 646.—§ 552 (Goharaṇap.): IV, **25**, 867; **26**, 890, 897 (recommended to inquire about the Pāṇḍavas); **30**, 973, 977, 984, 990 (*Vaikartanasya*, recommended to undertake the expedition for ravishing the cattle of Virāṭa); **35*a***, 1150; **36**, 1176 (*Vaikartanam*); **38**, 1238, 1243; **39**, (1299); **47**, 1472; **48**, (1507) (promised to slay Arjuna); **49**, 1540, 1547, 1551; **50**, 1554; **51**, 1583, 1587, 1599; **52**, 1624, 1629 (*Sūtaputraḥ*, in the van of Duryodhana's array); **53**, 1643; **54**, †1666, †1682, †1685, †1687, †1689 (*Vaikartanam*), †1690, †1692, †1693 (is defeated by Arjuna); **55**, 1734, 1735, 1750 (*Vaikartanaḥ*, on the top of his standard there was the device of an elephant's rope, *nāgakakshā*); **59**, 1908, 1917, 1919, 1921 (Arjuna rushed towards *K.*); **60**, 1923, 1924, 1930, (1931), 1939, 1940, 1943, 1944, 1946, 1947 (is defeated by Arjuna); **63**, 2021, 2024; **66**, †2107, †2117 (stupefied by Arjuna, who caused Uttara to bring *K.*'s yellow robes away); **68**, 2168, 2232 (*padam padasahasreṇa yaç caran nāparādhnuyāt*).—§ 553*b* (Yudhishṭhira): IV, **70**, 2286.—§ 554 (Sainyodyogap.): V, [**2**, †31 (*sa-Sūtaputram*)]; **3**, 60; [**4**, 65 (*Rādheya-Saubalau*)].—§ 555 (do.): V, **8**, 214 (Çalya promises Yudhishṭhira to weaken the energy of *K.*, when he becomes his charioteer in the encounter between *K.* and Arjuna); **18,** 557, 567 (do.).—§ 556 (Sañjayayānap.): V, **21,** 631; **22,** †651; **23**δ, †697; [**25**θ, †733 (*Rādheyaguptān*)]; **26,** †758, †759; **27,** †791; **29,** †852, †860; [**30,** †896 (*Vaikartanaḥ*).—§ 557 (Prajāgarap.): V, **33,** 989.—§ 558 (do.): V, **35,** 1258.—§ 559 (do.): V, **37,** 1377.—§ 561 (Yānasandhip.): V, **47**α, 1799; **48,** [†1812 (*Sūtaputrasya*)], †1904 (*Dhārtarāshṭrān sa-K°ān*); **49,** 1944 (*Sūtaputrasya*, has been cursed by Rāma, cf. § 621), (1946), 1951; **52,** 2088, 2089; **55**λ, 2185, (μ), 2196 (ν), 2206 (*Vaikartanaḥ*); **57**ζ, 2246 (*Vaikartanaḥ*), (π), 2268, (ρ), 2281, [(σ), 2290 (*Sūtaputram*); **58,** 2303, (υ), 2306, 2309; **59,** 2333; **62,** †2411, †2417, †2420, †2421, (†2422), †2428 (had been cursed by Rāma Jāmadagnya, from whom he acquired the Brahmāstra (cf. § 621), possessed the dart which had been given to him by Indra, and a shaft which he worshipped with flower garlands; disregarded by Bhīshma, he vowed not to fight until Bhīshma had been quieted); **63,** 2433 (*Vaikartanaḥ*); **66**ε, 2501.—§ 562 (Bhagavadyānap.): V, **79**υ, 2829 (*Sūtaputraḥ*)]; **83,** 2932; **90,** 3211 (all. to Dyūtap.); **91,** 3240, 3248; **92**τ, 3284, 3285, 3287, †3302; **93,** 3316; **94,** 3363, 3378; **95**υ, 3402.—§ 567 (do.): V, **124**γ, 4167, (δ), 4170; **127,** 4246; **128,** 4270, (κ), 4306; **130**ν, 4366, 4397.—§ 569 (do.): V, **137,** 4669, 4672; **138,** 4684; **140,** 4728, 4732, 4734, [4752 (*Vasusheṇasya*)]; **141,** (4755), [4764 (*nāma vai Vasusheṇeti*)]; **142,** 4813, †4814, 4828; **143,** 4833, 4878, 4880, 4882 (discourse between Kṛshṇa and *K.*, who knows that he is a son of Kuntī, but nevertheless he wants to fight with the Pāṇḍavas); **144,** 4890, 4899, 4902, 4913; **145,** (4917), 4917 (*Rādheyo 'ham Ādhirathiḥ*, says *K.*), 4918 (*Kaunteyas tvaṃ na Rādheyaḥ*, says Kuntī to *K.*), 4920, 4925 (*°Ārjuna-samāgamam*), 4926, 4927 (Kuntī discloses to *K.* that he is her son); **146,** 4929, 4930, 4931, 4951, 4952, 4953, 4955 (promises to Kuntī to save the Pāṇḍavas except Arjuna); [**150,** 5088 (*Rādheyam*)].—§ 570 (Sainyaniryāṇap.): V, **153,** 5195; **154,** 5218, 5224, 5227; **155**θ, 5275; **156,** 5301 (*Sūtaputraḥ*), (5302), 5311; **158,** 5372. — § 571 (Ulūkadūtāgamanap.): V, **160**α, 5410, 5411, [5502 (*Sūtaputram*)], 5529 (*°Çalyajhashāvartam*, sc. *purushodadhiṃ*, i.e. the army of Duryodhana); **161,** [5547 (*Sūtaputram*)], 5574 (= v. 5529); [**162,** 5599 (*Sūtaputrasya*)]; **163,** [5663 (*Sūtaputre*)], 5698, 5700, 5701; [**164,** 5706 (*Sūtaputrāya*, is pitted against Arjuna)].—§ 572 (Rathātirathasaṅkhyānap.): V, **168,** 5811 (*Vaikartanaḥ*), 5812 (Bhīshma estimates *K.* to be only a half ratha, incensed at this *K.* will not fight as long as Bhīshma lives).—§ 573 (Ambopākhyānap.): V, **193**α, 7563, 7577 (*Sūtaputrasya*, pledged himself to annihilate the Pāṇḍava army in five nights); **194,** 7586 (do.).—§ 576 (Bhagavadgītāp.): VI, **14,** 576; **17,** 648 (*Vaikartanaḥ*, did not fight from hatred of Bhīshma); **25**ι, 837; **35,** [†1272 (*Sūtaputraḥ*)], 1280.—§ 577 (Bhīshmavadhap.): VI, **43,** (1614 (*Sūtaputrasya*, Çalya promises Yudhishṭhira to weaken the energy of *K.*)], 1618, (1620) (Kṛshṇa in vain exhorts *K.* to join the Pāṇḍavas).—§ 578 (do.): VI, **49,** 1996 (*°sya matam*).—§ 579 (do.): VI, **52,** 2157 (did not fight, *nyastaçastraḥ*).—§ 580 (do.): VI, **58,** 2500.—§ 583 (do.): VI, **79,** 3455 (*°sya matam*).—§ 585 (do.): VI, **96,** 4329 (*°durmantritena*); **97,** 4408, (4411), 4417, 4419, 4445 (will not fight until Bhīshma has retired from the battle); **98,** [4455 (*Sūtaputre Rādheye*, all. to § 512)], 4459 (all. to § 552).—§ 587 (do.): VI, **120,** 5710.—§ 588 (do.): VI, **122,** 5825, [5826 (*Kaunteyaḥ*)], 5833 (had in Kāçipura crushed the assembled kings in order to procure a bride for the Kuru king, and had vanquished Jarāsandha), (5840) (*Kaunteyaḥ*), 5851, 5855 (when Bhīshma had become quiet *K.* obtained his forgiveness). — § 589 (Droṇābhishekap.): VII, **1,** 32, 33, 35, 36, 41, 43, 44, 45, 47, 48 (*Vaikartanam*), 49 (only C.), 51 (*K.* had not fought for ten days; after Bhīshma had been slain the Kurus set their hopes on *K.*); **2,** †53, (†55), †59, †87 (started for the battle); **3,** 98 (visits Bhīshma); **4,** 119, 121, 123, 129 (*Vaikartanaḥ*), 132 (Bhīshma enumerates *K.'s* feats, etc.); **5,** 134, (136), 139, 140 (only C.), 141, 146 (suggests to elect Droṇa to be leader of the army); **6,** 155; **7,** 185 (*Vaikartanaḥ*, at the head of the rearguard of Duryodhana's army), 187, 188, 189 (*çakto jetuṃ devān sa-Vāsavān*), 190, 199, 200.—§ 590 (do.): VII, **12,** 438; [**14,** 532 (*Vaikartanam*), 533 (*Sūtaputrasya*, resisted by Virāṭa)]; **16**β, 633.—§ 592 (Saṃçaptakavadhap.): VII, **20,** 803 (*Vaikartanaḥ . . . saputrajñātibāndhavaḥ*, in the tail of Droṇa's gāruḍavyūha); **22,** 929, 935 (937); **23**ο, 1017 (*astraiḥ samatvaṃ samprāpya Rukmi-K°ārjunācyutaiḥ*, sc. the Pāṇḍya king); **25,** 1105, 1107 (fought with the Kaikayas); **27,** 1210: **32,** 1373, (χ), 1375, 1377 (encounter with Bhīmasena), (ω), 1410, 1422, 1427, 1431, 1432 (his younger brother is slain), 1435, 1436, 1438, 1440, 1442 (encounter with Arjuna, etc.; *K.* is rescued by Duryodhana, etc.).—§ 593 (Abhimanyuvadhap.): VII, **34**β, 1501; **37**θ, 1589, (κ), 1609, 1612, 1614, 1615 (encounter with Abhimanyu); **39**μ, 1650, (ξ), 1660 (do.); **40,** 1701, 1705, 1708, 1710, 1711, 1712 (do.); **41,** 1718 (his younger brother is slain by Abhimanyu), 1719, 1721 (do.); **46**τ, 1838 (υ), 1851 (do.); **47**φ, 1864, 1870, 1878 (do.); **48,** 1885, 1887, 1889, 1902 (*Vaikartanaḥ*), 1909, 1911, 1916 (*Vaikartanaḥ*) (do.); **49,** 1948 (*Droṇa-K°mukhaiḥ shaḍbhir Dhārtarāshṭrair mahārathaiḥ*).—§ 596 (Pratijñāp.): VII, **72,** 2525; **73,** 2575; **74**α, 2619, (β), 2627 (*Vaikartanaḥ*); **75**γ, 2673; **79,** 2803.—§ 598 (Jayadrathavadhap.): VII, **85,** 3034 (*°sya matam*), (ε), 3052 (ζ), 3060; **86,** 3072 (*°sya . . . matam*); **87**θ, 3098 (ι), 3112 (in the array of Droṇa).—§ 599 (do.): VII, **91,** 3256 (had formerly vanquished the Abhishāhas, etc.) [**95,** 3539 (*Sūtaputraḥ*, one of the *cakrarakshau* of Jayadratha)]; **96,** 3563; **104**μ, 3894, 3915, 3917, 3920 (encounter with Arjuna); **105**ν, [3937 (*Ādhiratheḥ*)], 3938 (*K.'s* standard bore the mark of an elephant-rope, made of gold; it seemed in battle to fill the whole welkin, it was adorned with gold and floral garlands and moved by the wind); **111**τ, 4267 (*°mukhāḥ*); **112,** 4301, 4313, 4314, (φ), 4329; **113**χ, 4409, [4412 (*Dākshiṇātyāḥ . . . Sūtaputra-purogamāḥ*)], 4414, 4416; **114,** 4454 (*°candrodayoddhatam*, sc. *sainyārṇavam*, i.e the army of Duryodhana); **129,** 5281, 5282, 5284, 5285, 5290, 5291, 5292, 5293, 5294, 5295, 5298, 5300, 5302, 5305, 5306 (fought with Bhīmasena and was deprived of his chariot); **131,** 5357, 5358, 5360, 5362, 5365 (his promise to Kuntī, cf. § 569), 5366, (5376), 5378, 5380, 5383, 5385, 5388, 5389, 5390, 5391, 5392, 5393, 5394, 5395, 5400, 5402 (*Vaikartanaḥ*), 5404, 5406, 5407, 5409, 5410, 5411 (fought with Bhīmasena and was again deprived of his chariot); **132,** 5414, 5416, 5426, 5429 (all. to Dyūtaparvan), 5432, 5433, 5437, 5439, 5440, 5443 (*K.* again fought with Bhīmasena); **133,** 5455, 5456 (*tridaçān api codyuktān sarvaçastradharān yudhi | vārayed yo raṇe K°ḥ sa-Yakshāsuramānavān*), 5459, 5460, 5461, 5462, 5469, 5470, 5478, 5481, 5490 (*Vaikartanaḥ*), 5492, 5493, 5497, 5499 (continuation of the encounter between *K.* and Bhīmasena, *K.* is once more deprived of his chariot); **134,** 5500, 5502,

5504, 5513, 5517, 5518, 5522, 5532 (is vanquished by Bhīmasena); **135**υυ, 5536, 5539, 5541, 5544, 5545, 5551, 5553, 5563, 5569, 5574; **136,** 5575, 5577, 5579, 5581, 5582, 5584, 5587, 5591, 5597, 5603, 5610, 5611, 5612, 5613 (continuation of the encounter between *K.* and Bhīmasena); **137,** 5618, 5619, 5620, 5621, 5625, 5626, 5627, 5632, 5656 (all. to Dyūtaparvan) (do.); **138,** 5670, 5671, 5672, 5677, 5678, 5679, 5685, 5695 (do.); **139,** 5696, 5698, 5699, 5704, 5705, 5706, 5709, 5721, 5727, 5729, 5731, 5735, 5740, 5745, 5748, 5752, 5754, 5757, 5758, 5760, 5762, 5764, 5765, 5766, 5769, 5773, 5777, 5778, 5779, 5781, 5783 (*Kuntyā vacaḥ smaran*, all. to § 569), 5784, 5797, 5800, 5801, 5804, 5806, 5807, 5809, 5810 (end of the encounter between *K.* and Bhīmasena, whom he vanquished but did not slay); **140**γγγ, 5818, 5825 (*Vaikartana°*); **143**κκκ, 6005; **145**μμμ, 6062, 6065, 6066 (*Vaikartana*), 6070, 6072, 6077, 6087 (σσσ), 6096, 6109, 6116, 6117, 6118, 6119 (*Vaikartanaṃ*), 6126, 6128, 6130, 6135 (fought with Arjuna); **146,** 6206, 6227, 6247, 6250 (do.); **147,** 6329, 6330, 6332, 6334, 6353 (*°Çaineyayor raṇam*), 6354, 6355, 6356, 6359, 6362, 6365, 6367, 6370, 6375, 6382, 6384 (assisted by his son Vṛshasena *K.* fought with Sātyaki); **148,** 6389, 6391, 6394, 6395 (*Sūtaputra*), 6417 (Arjuna rebukes *K.* and vows to slay Vṛshasena); **149**ωωω, 6488; **150**α′, 6501 (*nirjitaḥ*), 6502 (do.), (β′), 6523; **151**γ′, 6548, 6550; **152,** 6571, 6583.—§ 600 (Ghaṭotkacavadhap.): VII, **155,** 6707 (attacked Bhīmasena), 6711, 6712, (δ), 6720; **156**η, 6746, 6799 (fled), (κ), 6849; **157,** 6941 (*°sya dayitaṃ putraṃ Vṛshasenaṃ*), 6942 (*Vṛkaratho nāma bhrātā K°sya*); **158,** 6970, 6971, (6974), 6981, 6982, 6983, 6985, 6986, 6988, 6989, 6992, 6994, 7004, 7017, 7019 (*Rādheyaḥ*, promised to slay Arjuna with the dart which had been given to him by Indra); **159,** 7043, 7050, (7052), 7055, 7061, 7062, 7064, 7074, 7078, 7080, 7082, 7083, 7084, 7085, 7089, 7090 (*Vaikartanaḥ*), 7092 (do.), 7093, 7094, 7095, 7102, 7103 (fought with Arjuna, who vanquished him); **160**γγ, 7146, 7151; **163**ηη, 7281; **164,** 7346; **165,** 7362 (*Vaikartanaḥ*, resisted Sahadeva); **167,** 7462 (do.), 7464, 7465, 7466, 7469, 7470, 7471, 7475, 7480, 7482 (fought with Sahadeva); **170**λλ, 7621, 7623, 7627, 7634, 7636, 7641, 7642, 7644, 7645, 7646, 7647, 7649, 7650, 7651, 7669 (*°sya mataṃ*) (*K.* fought with Dhṛshṭadyumna and Sātyaki); **171,** 7733; **172,** 7736, (ππ), 7746, 7756 (*Droṇa-K°au*), (σσ), 7758 (do.), 7763 (do.), 7765 (do.), 7766; **173,** 7774, 7776, 7777, 7780, 7782, 7785, 7787, 7790, 7794, 7795, 7796 (defeated Dhṛshṭadyumna and the Pāñcālas), 7798, 7799, 7802, 7803, 7805, 7807, 7809, 7815, 7822, 7823, 7831, 7833, 7836, 7837, 7838, 7841, 7843 (urged by Arjuna Ghaṭotkaca advanced towards *K.*); **174,** 7844, 7845, 7846, 7847 (*Vaikartanaḥ*), 7848, 7853, 7856, 7863, 7887, 7888 (assisted by Alambusha *K.* fought with Ghaṭotkaca); **175,** 7900, 7909, 7913, 7914 (*sannipātaḥ K°-Rākshasayoḥ*), 7921 (*°-Rākshasayor mṛdhe*), 7923, 7931, 7933, 7937, 7938, 7940, 7942, 7943, 7946, 7947, 7956, 7959, 7960, 7961, 7963, 7964 7966 (*Vaikartano Vṛshaḥ*), 7967, 7972, 7974, 7975, 7986, 7988, 7989, 7991, 7994, 7996, 7998, 8000, 8002 (*Vaikartanaḥ*, encounter with Ghaṭotkaca); **176,** 8004 (*°Rākshasayor mṛdhe*); **177,** 8029 (*yuddhe . . . K°-Rākshasayoḥ*), 8032, 8034 (*Vaikartanaḥ*), 8037 (*Vaikartanaṃ*), 8039, 8041 (is supported by Alāyudha), 8060, 8063 (*Vaikartanaṃ*); **178,** 8076, 8077, 8082, 8083, 8085; **179,** 8117, †8127 (*Vaikartanaṃ*), 8132, †8136, †8143, †8157, †8159, †8162, †8164, †8165, †8170, †8177 (slew Ghaṭotkaca with the dart which Indra had given him); **180**δδδ, 8190, 8191, 8193, 8194, 8197 (*Vaikartanaḥ*, all. to § 547), 8198, 8199, 8202 (*Vṛshaḥ*), 8206; **181**δδδ, 8237, 8242 (*Vaikartanaṃ*); **182**εεε, †8255 (*Vaikartanaḥ*), 8257, 8259, 8264 (ζζζ), 8267, 8272, 8277, 8279, 8280 (*Sūtaputreṇa*), 8281, 8282, 8285, 8292; **183**ζζζ, 8294, (εεε), 8296, 8298, 8299, 8300, 8301, 8304, (ηηη), 8309, 8312, 8316, 8328 (*Droṇa-K°au*), 8331, 8336, 8340 (*Droṇa-K°au*), 8344, 8352.—§ 601 (Droṇavadhap.): VII, **184,** 8362, 8391; **185**δ, 8441, 8451, 8452.—§ 602 (do.): VII, **186,** 8463 (*Droṇa-K°au*), 8468 (*°Droṇau*), (ζ), 8470, (θ), 8504; **187**ι, 8543, (κ), 8551 (engaged in battle with Bhīmasena); **188,** 8582, 8583, 8584, 8587, 8590, 8591, 8592, 8594 (fought with Bhīmasena; **189,** 8676, 8677, 8679, 8681 (do.); **191,** 8800, 8801; **192,** 8810, 8812, 8851.—§ 603 (Nārāyaṇāstramokshap.): VII, **193,** 8924 (*°prabhṛtayaḥ*); **200**αα, 9307, 9308; **202,** 9514 (*Drauṇi-K°-Kṛpaguptāṃ*, sc. *senāṃ*).—§ 604 (Karṇap.): VIII, **1,** 11, 15 (*senāpatau*), 19 (*nihataṃ*), 21; **2,** 25 (*hate*), 45; **3,** 60 (*Vaikartanaṃ*), 68 (had been made generalissimo of Duryodhana's army), 69; **5,** 95 (*Vaikartano hataḥ*), 113 (his son Vṛshasena had been slain), 143 (*°ārjunasamāgame*), 147; [**7,** 199 (*tejovadhaṃ Sūtaputrasya saṅkhye pratiçrutya*, sc. Çalya, cf. § 555)]; **8**η, 218 (*hataṃ*), 220 (*°sya nidhanaṃ*), 224 (*°sya vadhaṃ*), 231, 239 (*Vaikartano Vṛshaḥ*), 240 (*Vṛshaḥ*), 242, 244; **9**θ, 252, 256, 257, 258, 262, 267, 285, 291, 294, 301, 319, 326, 329, 330, 331, 333, 336, 337, 341, 343.—§ 605 (do.): VIII, **10**κ, 359, 361, 362, 365, 381, 382, (383), (λ), 386 (is installed as commander of Duryodhana's army), 398, 399; **11,** 400 (*Vaikartanaḥ*), 402, 410, 412, 413 (μ), 414, 421, 422 (arrayed the army of Duryodhana in a *makaravyūha*), 432, 436, 438 (read with B. *Karṇa-Pāṇḍavau* instead of *Kuru-P°*); **13,** 487, 488, 490 (attacked by Nakula); **17,** †683 (*°sya balaṃ*), †684; **19,** 733; **20**γγ, 772, 775, 806; **21,** 821, 825, 830, 838, 839, 840, 844, 845; **22,** 892; **24,** 915 (*Vaikartanaḥ*), 916, 924, 926, 927, 929, 929 bis (*Vaikartanaḥ*), 931, 933, 939, 942, 947, 951, 957, 961, 967, 986, 987 (fought with Nakula, etc.); **28**μμ, 1126, 1166; **30,** 1205, (νν), 1227, 1228, 1229, 1230, 1233, 1234, 1235, 1236, 1237; **31,** 1256, 1262, 1263, (ππ), 1265 (*Vaikartanaṃ*), 1267 (*Vaikartanaḥ*), 1268, 1269, 1271, 1272, 1275, 1283, (1285), 1320, 1321, 1322 (Karṇa pledges either to slay Arjuna or to be slain himself, and asks for Çalya as his charioteer); **32**σσ, 1326, 1329, 1330, 1332, 1339, 1340, 1342, 1346, 1347, 1348, 1350, 1351, (ττ), 1367, 1370, 1384, 1385, 1386, 1390 (Çalya makes it a condition that he may in *K.'s* presence utter whatever he desires).—§ 606 (do.): VIII, **34,** 1576, 1578, 1580, 1613, 1614, 1615, 1616 (*Sūtakulodbhavaḥ*), 1619 (*Vaikartano Vṛshaḥ*); **35,** 1622, 1633 (*Vaikartanaḥ*), 1645, 1651, 1652, 1653, 1654, 1657, 1658, 1664, 1665 (Çalya becomes the charioteer of *K.*).—§ 607 (do.): VIII, **36,** 1670, 1674, 1675, 1677, 1679, 1680, 1683, 1684 (proceeds against Arjuna); **37,** 1704, 1706, 1710, †1739, (†1748), 1749; **38,** 1752, 1774; **39,** 1791, 1793, †1797, 1800, 1802, 1803, 1805, 1807, 1808, 1811 (in order to weaken the energy of *K.* Çalya praises Arjuna); **40,** (1817) (describes the bad practices of the Madrakas), 1871; **41,** 1873, 1877, 1882, 1922 (Çalya related the Haṃsakākīyopākhyāna to *K.*), 1945, 1946, 1950, 1951, 1952, 1957; [**42,** 1962 (*Ādhirathiḥ*) (*K.* tells how he had been cursed by Rāma Jāmadagnya and by a brahman, cf. § 621 below)]; **43,** 2019; **44,** 2024 (*°sahasreṇa*), 2025, (2026) (describes the bad practices of the Bāhīkas, the Madras, etc.); **45,** (2071) (do.), 2112, 2114, 2118, 2119 (*Rādheyaṃ*), 2120.—§ 608 (do.): VIII, **46,** 2122, 2129, 2139 (with his sons in the centre of Duryodhana's army), 2151, 2152, 2164,

2166, 2167, 2169, 2170, 2173, 2175, 2177, 2178, 2192, 2196 (in order to weaken the energy of *K.* Çalya praises Arjuna); **47,** 2210, 2230 (attacks Yudhishṭhira); **48,** 2234, 2235, 2236, 2242, 2243, 2247 (*Vaikartano Vṛshaḥ*), 2250, 2251 (father of Susheṇa and Satyasena), 2252 (father of Vṛshasena), 2259 (father of Bhānusena), 2264, 2266, 2268, 2283, 2285, 2289, 2297 (accompanied by his sons *K.* attacks the Pāṇḍavas); **49,** 2301, 2304, 2305, 2307 (*Vaikartanaṃ*), 2310, 2311, 2314, 2321, 2323, 2329, 2332, 2335, 2337, 2339, 2341, 2346, 2347, 2350 (*c*: on *K.'s* hand were the auspicious signs of a thunderbolt, an umbrella, a hook, a fish, a flag, a tortoise, and a conch-shell), 2353, 2360, 2363 (vanquishes and disparages Yudhishṭhira); **50,** 2394, 2395, 2397, 2401, 2405, 2406, 2408, 2420, 2423, 2425, 2426 (*Vaikartano Vṛshaḥ*), 2428, 2429, 2432, 2435, 2436, 2438, 2439 (vanquished by Bhīmasena); **51,** 2440, 2441, 2462, 2464, 2466, 2468, 2471, 2472, 2473, 2474, 2475, 2476, 2478, 2481, 2498, 2502, 2503, 2507 (fights with Yudhishṭhira and Bhīmasena, whom he vanquishes); **54** [*θθ*, 2610 (*Sūtaputraḥ*)], 2625 (*Vaikartanaḥ*); **56,** 2693, 2694, 2696, 2728, 2731, 2732, 2734, 2737, 2742, 2743, 2748, 2749, 2750, 2751, 2752, 2754, 2757, 2759, 2776 (*e*: *K.'s* standard bears the device of an elephant's rope), 2777, 2778 (*K.* slew the Pāñcālas, etc.); **57,** 2840, 2841; **58,** 2857, 2859, 2901, 2903; **59,** 2910, 2912, 2913, 2914, 2920, 2922, 2924, 2927, 2969 (fights with Dhṛshṭadyumna, etc.); **60***ωω*, 2989, 2990, 2994, 2997, 3001, 3003, 3005, 3006, 3010, 3012, 3016, 3018, 3021, 3024, 3031, 3049; **61,** 3071, 3077, 3082, 3083, 3085, 3086, 3087, 3088, 3089 (fights with Çikhaṇḍin), 3090; **62,** 3150 (*Vaikartanaḥ*), 3160, 3162, 3163, 3164, 3168, 3170 (fights with Yudhishṭhira); **63,** 3176, 3177, 3178, 3179, 3183, 3193, 3195, 3199, 3207 (fights with Yudhishṭhira and the twins, but leaves them in order to rescue Duryodhana); **64***θθθ*, 3249, 3253, 3254, 3266, 3267, 3273, 3277, 3279, 3280, 3281 (*K.* slays the Pāñcālas, etc., with the Bhārgava weapon); **65,** †3288, †3289, †3291, 3305; **66***ιιι*, 3310, 3316, 3320, 3325, 3326, 3327, 3329, 3331, 3335, 3336, †3338, †3345, †3346 (all. to Dyūtaparvan), †3347, †3350, †3351, †3355; **67***κκκ*, †3368, †3369, †3370, †3372, †3373, †3376, †3377; **68,** †3380, †3381, †3383, †3384, †3397, †3398; **69***οοο*, †3479, †3480, †3481, †3482, †3491; **70,** †3527, †3528 (Arjuna promises to slay *K.*); **71,** 3560, 3568, 3573, 3575, 3576, 3577, 3579, 3583, 3588, 3589, 3590, 3592 (do.); **72,** 3601, 3602 (Arjuna advances towards *K.*), 3607, 3619, 3621, †3627, 3632, 3633 (*Vaikartanaṃ*); **73,** 3634, 3688, 3696, 3698, 3699, 3700, 3701, 3702, 3703, 3704, 3710, 3713, 3715, 3716 (all. to Dyūtaparvan), 3719, 3722, 3724, 3725, 3730, 3732, 3733, 3738, 3740, 3741, 3743, 3744, 3745, 3746, 3749, 3750 (Kṛshṇa exhorts Arjuna to slay *K.*); **74,** 3752 (*φφφ*), 3754, 3755, 3756, 3757, 5758, 3761, 3762, 3764, 3766, 3770, 3772, 3774, 3775, 3777, 3778, 3780, 3782, 3784, 3787, 3793, 3795, 3797, †3803 (Arjuna promises to slay *K.*); **75,** †3804, †3812 (°*sya putraṃ Susheṇaṃ*), †3814 (attacked by Dhṛshṭadyumna), †3817 (his son Susheṇa is slain by Uttamaujas); **77,** †3869, 3936, 3938; **78,** 3941, 3943 (*Rādheyaḥ*), 3945, 3947, 3948, 3953, 3956, 3958, 3966, 3969, 3971, 3972, 3973, 3974, 3975, 3977, 3978, 3981, 3984, 3987, 3996, 3998; **79,** 4011, 4012, 4015, 4017, 4021, 4022, 4024, 4031, 4036, (4043), †4047, (†4048), †4049, †4064, †4068; **81,** 4125, 4126 (is protected by the Saṃçaptakas), 4165, 4167, 4169, 4170, 4172, 4173, 4174, 4175, 4177, 4178; **82,** †4180, †4184 (slew the Kaikayas Viçoka and Ugrakarman), †4186 (his son Prasena is slain), †4187, †4189, †4193, †4195, †4196 (*Vaikartanaṃ*), †4202, †4203, †4204; **83***μ*, 4231, †4247; **84,** 4267, 4269, †4280 (°*sya putraṃ*, i.e. Vṛshasena), †4283 (°*sya putraḥ* = do.); †4284 (°*sya sutaḥ* = do.), †4298; **85,** †4337, †4338, †4346 (*K.'s* son Vṛshasena is slain by Arjuna); **86,** 4350, 4352 (°*sya nāgakaksham*), 4353, 4356, 4359, 4363, 4365, 4366, †4371; **87***φ*[1], 4373, 4378, 4381, 4383, 4395, 4400, 4202, 4408, 4409, 4412, 4416, 4419, 4422, 4425, 4429, 4430, 4431, 4433, 4434, 4437, 4442, 4454, 4461, 4462, 4465, 4467, 4473, 4475, 4477, 4478, 4480, 4484, 4486, 4487 (the encounter between *K.* and Arjuna begins; the gods, etc., side some with *K.*, others with Arjuna; Brahmán declares that *K.* will be vanquished, but obtain the same worlds as the Vasus or the Maruts); **88,** †4501, †4516, †4521, †4522; **89,** †4531, †4533, †4534, †4535, †4538, †4539, †4540, †4542, †4545, †4548, †4549, †4550, †4553, †4555, †4556, †4557, †4558, †4563, †4566, †4567, †4568, †4575, †4579, †4585, †4586, †4588, †4590, †4591, †4597, †4603, †4604, †4605, †4606, †4607, †4608, †4610, †4611, †4613, †4615, †4616, †4617, †4620, †4621; **90,** †4623, †4625, †4627, †4632, †4635, †4636, †4637, †4642, †4643, †4644, †4648, †4649, †4651, †4654, †4670, †4671, †4672, †4673, (†4675), †4676, †4677, †4684, †4686, †4688, †4690, †4694, †4695, †4696, †4700, †4701, †4702, †4704, †4705, †4707, †4709, †4713, 4719, 4722, 4723, 4725, 4727, 4728, 4729, 4731, 4735 (the serpent Açvasena became the arrow of *K.*; *K.* forgot the Brahmāstra in consequence of the curse of Rāma Jāmadagnya, and his chariot wheel sank into the earth in accordance with the curse of a brahman, cf. § 612); **91** *ακ*[1], 4749, 4751, 4754, 4757, 4763, 4768, 4770, 4771, †4777, †4787, †4794, †4795, †4796, †4802, †4803 (the head of *K.* is struck off by Arjuna), †4804 (*nihate*), †4807, †4808, 4810, 4811, 4812, 4814, †4815, †4816; **92,** †4818 (*nihate*), †4819, †4821, †4823, †4824 (*hate*), †4826 (*hataḥ*), †4829; **93,** 4834, 4836 (*hate*), 4837 (do.), 4852; **94,** †4905, †4918, †4921, †4923, 4934, 4936 (*saputraḥ*), 4938 (*hato Vaikartanaḥ K°ḥ saputraḥ*), †4943 (*hate*), †4946 (do.), †4947, †4948, †4960, †4962; **95***αν*[1], 4965 (*nihataṃ*), 4976 (*nipātitaṃ*), 4977, 4979 (*hate*); **96***αφ*[1], 4982 (*nipātite*), 4983 (*hataḥ*), 4984, 4986 (*vadhaṃ K° sya*), 4987, 4997 (°*sya nidhanaṃ*), 5013, 5014 (*hate*), 5017, 5018, 5020, 5023 (*hate*), 5028 (*nihataṃ*), 5036 (°*sya nidhanaṃ*).—§ 609 (Çalyap.): IX, **1***a*, 1 (*nipātite*), 4 (*hate*), 5, 24 (°*sya nidhanaṃ*); **2,** 82, 114 (*hataḥ K°ḥ Sūtaputraḥ*), 119 (*nipātite*).—§ 610 (do.): IX, **3***η*, 128 (*hate*), 130 (do.), (*θ*), 144; **4***μ*, 197 (*hate*), 225; **5***ν*, 278; **6,** 295 (*hate*); **7,** 341, (*φ*), 349, 360, 365.—§ 611 (do.): IX, **8,** 386 (*hate*), (*θ*), 402 (do.); **16***σ*, 811; **19***δδ*, 1023; [**24***νν*, 1295 (*nihate . . . Rādheye*)]; **27***ττ*, 1456 (°*o Vaikartano hataḥ*).—§ 612 (Hradapraveçap.): IX, **31***η*, 1772, (*θ*), 1789 (*nihate*).—§ 613 (Gadāyuddhap.): IX, **32***β*, 1836; **33***ι*, 1934 (*hataḥ*). —§ 615 (Baladevatīrthayātrā): IX, **54***ν*, 3060 (*hato Vaikartanaḥ K°ḥ putrāç cāsya*).—§ 615 (Gadāyuddhap.): IX, **56***ρ*, 3162 (*hataḥ*); [**60,** 3384 (*Rādheyaḥ*, had been slain)]; **61,** 3422, 3424 (*patite cakre*, all. to § 608), 3428 (*nihataḥ*), (*χ*), 3447; **62***ψ*, 3472 (*Droṇa-K°ābhyāṃ*), 3488 (*pramuktaṃ Droṇa-K°ābhyāṃ Brahmāstraṃ*); **64***εε*, 3588, 3593, 3612; **65***ηη*, 3640. —§ 616 (Sauptikap.): X, **3***β*, 137; **5***ε*, 195 (*patite cakre . . . hataḥ Gāṇḍīvadhanvanā*, all. to § 608); **9***ν*, 533.—§ 617 (Aishīkap.): X, **10***β*, 558.—§ 618 (Jalapradānikap.): XI, **1***β*, 17 (°*sya viparyayaṃ*), [(*γ*), 28 (*Rādheyaḥ*, counsellor of Duryodhana)]; **8***ζ*, 223 (*paramaḥ sakhā*, sc. Duryodhana's); **14***ξ*, 375.—§ 619 (Strīvilāp.): XI, **16***a*, 447, 454; **18***γ*, 539; **20***ε*, 585; **21,** 604 (*Vaikartanaṃ*), 612 (°*sya patnīṃ Vṛshasenasya* *mātaram*), 614 (father of Sushena), 616 (lamented for as dead); **25**κ, 735 (*Vaikartanāt*).—§ 620 (Çrāddhap.): XI, **26**β, 791 (*Vaikartanam*, his corpse is burnt); **27**δ, 813, 819 (*Kuntīsutāt*), 821, 823, 826 (Kuntī discloses that *K.* was her son).—§ 621 (Rājadh.): XII, **1**, 34 (*hate*), 38, 39, 40, 42; **2**δ, 47, 54, 57, 62, 66, 74 (when Droṇa refused to teach *K.* the Brahmāstra *K.* repaired to Rāma Jāmadagnya, and told him that he was a brahman; when *K.* from inadvertence slew the *homa* cow of a brahman, the brahman imprecated a curse on him in consequence of which the wheel of his chariot would sink into the earth when he fought with Arjuna); **3**, 75, 77, 78, 79, 80, 83, 86, 98, 100, 101 (*Rādheyaḥ*, *K.* learnt the Brahmāstra from Rāma, but having discovered that *K.* was not a brahman, Rāma imprecated a curse on him in consequence of which he would forget it at the time of his death); **4**, 108, 111, 121, 123, 124, 126, 128 (accompanied and assisted Duryodhana at the svayaṃvara of the Kaliṅga king's daughter); **5**, 129, 132, 133, 134 (*K.* vanquished Jarāsandha (? *bibheda sandhiṃ dehasya Jarayā çleshitasya*), who gave him the town Mālinī (= Campā); *K.*, the king of the Aṅgas, then ruled in Campā agreeably to the wishes of Duryodhana), 142 (*hato Vaikartanaḥ K°ḥ*); **7**, 157.—§ 623 (do.): XII, **14**α, 403.—§ 630 (do.): XII, **27**β, 817 (*aghātayaṃ yat K°m . . . jyeshṭhaṃ bhrātaraṃ*, says Yudhishṭhira).—§ 637 (do.): XII, **42**γ, 1488 (Yudhishṭhira gave much wealth away for the sake of *K.*, etc.).—§ 641 (do.): XII, **124**, 4555 (°*sahitaṃ Duryodhanaṃ*).—§ 768 (Ānuçāsanik.): XIII, **148**ε, 6930.—§ 778 (Açvamedhikap.): XIV, **1**, 13; **2**, 32 (*pātayitvā . . . K°ṃ*).—§ 780 (do.): XIV, **14**, 369 (*aurdhvadehikaṃ . . . Bhīshma-K°purogamānāṃ Kurūṇāṃ*).—§ 783 (Anugītāp.): XIV, **52**, 1497 (°*vadhopāyaḥ*).—§ 785 (do.): XIV, **59**α, 1775, 1791, 1794 (all. to the great battle); **60**, 1821, 1822, 1825, 1830 (do.).—§ 787 (Āçramavāsap.): XV, **3**, 65; **10**, 329, 332, 336; **11**, 373; **16**, 451, [452 (*Sūryajaṃ*), 453 (*Sūryajaḥ*), 454 (*Sūryajasya*)].—§ 788 (do.): XV, **21**, 587.—§ 789 (Putradarçanap.): XV, **30**, 833 (the birth of *K.* related, cf. § 547); **31**ζ, 844, (η), 855 (was a portion of Āditya, i.e. the Sun), **32**θ, 876 (among the dead warriors who, summoned by Vyāsa, arose from the Gaṅgā); **33**ι, 892, 893.—§ 795 (Svargārohaṇap.): XVIII, **1**δ, 23 (*Kaunteyaṃ*): **2**, [27 (*Rādheyaṃ*)], 32, 34 (ε), 60 (ζ), 69; **3**, 99, 118 (in heaven); **4**, 130, [140 (*Kaunteyaḥ . . . Sūryaputraḥ . . . Rādheyaḥ*)]; **5**, 167 (after death he entered the Sun (*Raviṃ*)).

Cf. also the following synonyms:—

Ādhirathi, q.v.

Ādityanandana ("the son of the Sun"): VI, 5838.

Ādityatanaya (do.): III, 8428; XVIII, 100.

Aṅgarājan ("king of the Aṅgas"): III, 15052.

Aṅgeçvara (do.): I, 5441.

Arkaputra ("the son of the Sun"): I, †7026.

Bharatarshabha: VIII, 1690 (error in C. for *purusharshabha*, B.).

Goputra, q.v.

Kaunteya, Kuntīsuta, q.v.

Kurūdvaha (only C.), **Kurupṛtanāpati, Kuruvīra, Kuruyodha**, q.v.

Pārtha, q.v.

Pūshātmaja ("the son of Pūshan [i.e. the Sun]"): VIII, †4600.

Rādhāsuta ("the son of Rādhā"): I, 7115 (*K°*), 7490 (do.); VIII, 4351.

Rādhātmaja (do.): VIII, 5024.

Rādheya (do.): I, 5221 (*Sūtaputraḥ*), 7051, 7095, 7106, 7391, 7398, 7408, 7412, 7415, 7437; II, 1712 (*Sūtaputraḥ*), 2276, 2391; III, 14822, 14827, 14891, 14892, 15053, 15241, 16968, 16997, 17177, 17186; IV, 1300, 1530, 1696, 1750, 1918, 1926, 1928, 1937, 1945; V, 65, 639, 641, †733 (°*guptān*), 4673, 4727, 4730, 4731, 4883, 4917 (*Ādhirathiḥ*), 4918 (*Kaunteyas tvaṃ na Rādheyaḥ*), 5088, 5817, 7579; VI, 1617, 1618, 1619, 4455 (*Sūtaputre*), 5819, 5822, 5826, 5856; VII, 34, 48 (*Sūtaputraṃ*), 60, 191, 930, 948, 1428, 1432, 1441, 1698, 1703, 1707, 1886, 1914, 1923, 5310, 5356, 5358, 5373, 5374, 5384, 5396, 5399, 5418, 5475, 5476, 5493, 5513, 5515, 5527, 5567, 5578, 5579, 5593, 5615, 5633, 5648, 5717, 5751, 5756, 5767, 5775, 5785, 6025, 6064, 6073, 6078, 6134, 6324, 6325, 6346, 6347, 6396, 6398, 6498, 6573, 6982, 6990, 7019 (*K°*), 7056, 7065, 7073, 7078, 7108, 7463, 7476, 7633, 7639, 7786, 7803, 7814, 7912, 8286, 8553, 8585, 8588, 8595; VIII, 65, 136 (*Sūtaputraḥ*), 192, 238, 364, 368, 391, 393, 396, 397, 841, 958, 1226, 1266, 1320, 1329, 1331, 1357, 1383, 1388, 1576, 1624, 1649, 1660, 1674, 1686, 1689, 1690, 1693, 1699, 1779, 1782, 1809, 1816, 1871, 1906, 2014, 2119, 2121, 2126, 2131, 2156, 2174, 2194, 2254, 2292, 2294, 2296, 2297, 2325, 2350, 2400, 2408, 2409, 2417, 2442, 2443, (*Sūtaputraṃ*), 2444, 2497, 2501, 2738, 2755, 2761, 2915, 2945, 2991, 3008, 3013, 3020, 3026, 3072, 3108, 3152, 3153, 3156, 3178, 3182, 3184, 3186, 3190, 3193, 3197, 3202, 3204, 3256, 3334, †3398, 3545, 3587, 3625, 3739, 3747, 3773, 3785, 3943, (*K°*), 3945 (*Ādhirathiḥ K°ḥ*), 3956, 3959, 3961, 3975, 3984, 3986, 3991, 4016, 4024, 4034, 4041, 4254, 4269, 4276, 4355, 4420, 4483 (°*bhāryāṇāṃ*), 4724, 4730, 4733, 4734, 4736, †4748, 4753, 4755, 4757, 4772, 4927, 4995 (*nihataṃ*), 5023; IX, 380, 1295, 3384; XI, 28, 807; XII, 23 (*Sūtaputraṃ*), 101 (*K°*); XVIII, 27, 140 (*Kaunteyaḥ . . . Sūryaputraḥ*).

Ravisūnu ("the son of the Sun"): VII, 8131 (*Ravi-Bhīmasūnvoḥ*, i.e. Karṇa and Ghaṭotkaca); VIII, †4676 (°*sattamaḥ*).

Sauti, q.v.

Sāvitra, Sāvitrin, Sūryaja, Sūryaputra, Sūryasambhava ("the son of the Sun"), q.v.

Sūta, Sūtanandana, Sūtaputra, Sūtasūnu, Sūtasuta, Sūtatanaya, Sūtatmaja, q.v.

Vaikartana: I, 2782 (*K°*, origin of the name), 4411 (do., origin of the name), 5655 (*K°*.), 7094 (do.), 7098 (do.); III, 14899, 14906 (do.), 15192 (do.), 15209 (do.); IV, 990 (do.), 1176 (do.), †1677 (°*bhrātuḥ*, i.e. Saṅgrāmajit), †1678 (*Sūtaputraḥ*), †1679, †1680, †1686, †1687, †1688, †1695, 1750 (*K°*), 1950, 2203; V, †896, 2206 (do.), 2246 (do.), †2427, 2433 (do.), 4282, 4916 (*Vṛshaḥ*), 5811 (*K°*); VI, 648 (do.), 2143; VII, 48 (do.), 129 (do.), 185 (do.), 532, 803 (do.), 1902 (do.), 1916 (do.), 2627 (do.), 5283, 5402 (do.), 5419, 5471, 5472, 5474, 5490 (do.), †5825, 6066, 6119 (do.), 7090 (do.), 7092 (do.), 7094 (only B.), 7362 (*K°*.), 7462 (do.), 7468, 7847 (do.), 7890 (do.), 7966 (*Karṇo V°o Vṛshaḥ*), 8002 (*K°*), 8034 (do.), 8037 (do.), 8063 (do.), 8123, †8124, †8125, †8127 (do.), †8168, 8197 (do., origin of the name), 8242 (*K°*.), †8255, 8797; VIII, 60 (do.), 87 (*hataḥ*), 91 (*hataṃ*), 95 (*Karṇo V°o hataḥ*), 239 (*Karṇo V°o Vṛshaḥ*), 320 (*hataṃ*), 327 (do.), 333 (do.), 335, 400 (*K°*), 915 (do.), 929 *bis* (do.), 1265 (do.), 1267 (do.), 1351 (do.), 1389, 1619 *Karṇo V°o Vṛshaḥ*), 1633 (*K°*), 1650, †1715, 2247 (*Karṇo V°o Vṛshaḥ*), 2307 (*K°*), 2426 (*Karṇo V°o Vṛshaḥ*), 2625 (*K°*), 2692, 3150 (*K°*), 3633 (do.), 3646, 3771 (*hate V°e*

Karṇe), †4196 (*K*°), 4454 (do.), †4524 (*Sūtaputraḥ*), †4583, †4799, 4932 (*hataḥ*), 4938 (*hato V°aḥ Karṇaḥ*), 4964 (*hate*), 5001 (*hate V°ḥ Sūtaputraḥ*); IX, 1456 (*Karṇo V°o hataḥ*), 3060 (*hato V°aḥ Karṇaḥ*); XI, 603, 604 (*K*°), 735 (do.), 791 (do.); XII, 142 (*hato V°aḥ Karṇaḥ*).

Vaivasvata, q.v.

Vasushena, the original name of Karṇa: I, 2776, 2782 (*Vaikartanaḥ Karṇaḥ*); III, 17165, 17166; V, 4752, 4764; VII, 5482, 5538; VIII, †1215, 2335, 2837; XII, 800.

Vṛsha: I, 2247, 5416; III, 16995, 17166 (*Vasushenaḥ*); V, 4916; VI, 5821; VII, 5666, 5794, 6134, 6328, 7966 (*Karṇo Vaikartanaḥ*), 8200, 8202 (*K*°, origin of the name), 8250; VIII, 16, 240 (*?°ḥ Karṇo nareshv api*), 245, 1619 (*Karṇo Vaikartanaḥ*). 1875, 2247 (*Karṇo Vaikartanaḥ*), 2265, 2302, 2426 (*Karṇo Vaikartanaḥ*), 4176 (*Ādhirathiḥ*), †4661, †4687, 4727, †4781, 4939 (*hataḥ*), 5019; XIV, 1786.

Karṇa[2], son of Dhṛtarāshṭra. § 130 (Aṃçāvat.): I, **67**, 2730 (enumeration of the sons of Dhṛtarāshṭra).—§ 182 (Dhṛtarāshṭraputranāmak.): I, **117**, 4542 (do.).—§ 583 (Bhīshmavadhap.): VI, **77**κ, 3344 (among other sons of Dhṛtarāshṭra, who are attacked by Bhīmasena).

Karṇaçravas, a brahman. § 324 (Dvaitavanapraveça): III, **26**α, 986 (among the brahmans who waited upon Yudhishṭhira).

[Karṇa-digvijaya(ḥ)] ("subjection of the earth by Karṇa"). § 515 (Ghoshay.). When *Duryodhana* had come to *Hāstinapura*, *Bhīshma* said to him that, as he had told him before, this journey did not please him, and advised him to make peace with the *Pāṇḍavas*. *Duryodhana* laughed and sallied out with *Çakuni*, followed by *Karṇa* and *Duḥçāsana*. When *Bhīshma*, ashamed, had gone away, they returned and began to consult. *Karṇa* complained of the partiality of *Bhīshma* for the *Pāṇḍavas*, and promised to conquer the world for *Duryodhana*. *Duryodhana* gladly accepted his offer, and on an auspicious lunar day, etc., *Karṇa* set out (III, **253**). *Karṇa*, surrounded by a large army, first made *Drupada* and the princes that were under him pay tribute. He then successively conquered the north (*Bhagadatta*, the kings inhabiting the *Himavat*), the east (the *Aṅgas, Vaṅgas, Kaliṅgas, Maṇḍikas* (B. *Çuṇḍika*), *Mithilas, Māgadhas, Karkakhaṇḍas, Āvaçīras, Yodhyas, Ahikshattra, Vatsabhūmi, Kevalī, Mṛttikāvatī, Mohana, Pattana, Tripurā, Koçalā*), the south (*Rukmin*, the *Pāṇḍya* mountain, *Kerala, Nīla*, the son of *Veṇudāri, Çaiçupāla*, the *Āvantyas*, the *Vṛshṇis*, etc.), and the west (*Yāvanas, Barbaras*, etc.), with the *Mlecchas*, the mountaineers, *Bhadras, Rohitakas, Āgneyas, Mālavas, Çaçakas, Nagnajit*, etc. Having returned to *Hāstinapura*, he was highly praised by *Duryodhana* and *Dhṛtarāshṭra*, who sat with *Gāndhārī* (III, **254**).

Karṇanirvāka, a muni. § 677 (Mokshadh.): XII, **245**β, 8901.

Karṇaparvan ("the section relating to Karṇa," the 8th of the greater and the 79th of the minor parvans of Mhbhr.). § 4 (Anukram.): I, **1**, 90 (*°sitaiḥ pushpaiḥ*).—§ 10 (Parvas.): I, **2**, 346.—§ 11 (do.): I, **2**, 542, 549.—§ 604: THE NIGHT AFTER DROṆA'S DEATH, AND THE SIXTEENTH MORNING, AND BRIEF ACCOUNT OF THE SIXTEENTH AND SEVENTEENTH DAYS. After *Droṇa's* death the *Kuru* warriors in grief, with *Duryodhana* at their head, repaired to *Açvatthāman*. When night came(!) they proceeded to their tents, but could not sleep (*a*); they (*a*) passed that night together in *Duryodhana's* tent, reflecting (β). When morning came they rose and performed their customary rites. Arranging their troops they proceeded to battle, making *Karṇa* their leader. The *Pāṇḍavas* also proceeded to battle. *Karṇa* fought for two days and was then slain by *Arjuna*. *Sañjaya* repaired to *Hāstinapura* and informed *Dhṛtarāshṭra* of *Karṇa's* fall. *Janamejaya* inquired about *Dhṛtarāshṭra* and the details of the battle (VIII, **1**). *Vaiçampāyana* said: After the fall of *Karṇa*, *Sañjaya* set out that night for *Hāstinapura* and spoke with *Dhṛtarāshṭra* (γ) (VIII, **2**). *Sañjaya* related the discouragement of the *Kuru* army after the fall of *Droṇa*; *Duryodhana's* spirited address; *Karṇa* was made generalissimo but slain by *Arjuna* on the second day (δ) (VIII, **3**). Hearing of *Karṇa's* fall in battle, *Dhṛtarāshṭra* swooned away; he and the ladies were restored to their senses; *Dhṛtarāshṭra* inquired whether *Duryodhana* was still alive; *Sañjaya* informed him of *Duḥçāsana's* slaughter (ε) (VIII, **4**). Requested by *Dhṛtarāshṭra*, *Sañjaya* recounted the names of those that had fallen and those that were still alive; *Dhṛtarāshṭra* once more swooned away (ζ) (VIII, **5-7**). *Dhṛtarāshṭra's* lament for *Karṇa* (η) (VIII, **8**); *Sañjaya* endeavoured to comfort him; continuation of *Dhṛtarāshṭra's* lament (θ) (VIII, **9**).—§ 605. THE SIXTEENTH DAY: After *Droṇa's* fall the *Kauravas*, having fled and been rallied by *Duryodhana*, fought for a long time with the *Pāṇḍavas* (*Arjuna*). On the approach of the evening twilight(!) the *Kauravas* retired to their encampment; they held a consultation in the night; *Duryodhana* inquired of his counsellors as to what should next be done. *Açvatthāman* suggested the installation of *Karṇa* as generalissimo (ι). *Duryodhana* offered *Karṇa* the command, which *Karṇa* accepted, promising to slay the *Pāṇḍavas* (κ). *Karṇa* was installed in the command and blessed by the brahmans, and ordered the troops to be arrayed at the rise of the sun (λ) (VIII, **10**). Beholding *Karṇa*, none recked the loss of *Bhīshma* or *Droṇa*, etc. He formed a *makara* array: the tip (μ), the two eyes (ν), the head (ξ), the neck (ο), the middle (π), the left foot (ρ), the right foot (σ), the left hind-foot (τ), the right hind-foot (υ), the tail (φ). *Yudhishṭhira* asked *Arjuna* to array the *Pāṇḍava* army and slay *Karṇa* ("incapable of being vanquished by . . . D., As., G., K., and M.-U."). The *Pāṇḍava* troops were arrayed in the shape of the half-moon; the left side (χ), the right side (ψ), the middle (ω), the rear (*aa*); *Yudhāmanyu* and *Uttamaujas* became the protectors of *Arjuna's* chariot wheels, and did not quit him for a moment. Then commenced the battle (VIII, **11**). A fierce slaughter on both sides (description). *Dhṛshṭadyumna*, etc. (ββ), headed by *Bhīmasena* & *Kshemadhūrti* (*Kulūtādhipatiḥ*), who was slain by *Bhīmasena*. The *Kurus* fled away (VIII, **12**). *Nakula* & *Karṇa*; *Bhīmasena* & *Açvatthāman*; *Sātyaki* & the *Kaikaya* princes (brothers) *Vinda* and *Anuvinda*; King *Citrasena* & *Çrutakarman*; *Prativindhya* & *Citra*; *Duryodhana* & *Yudhishṭhira*; *Arjuna* & the *Saṃçaptakas*; *Dhṛshṭadyumna* & *Kṛpa*; *Çikhaṇḍin* & *Kṛtavarman*; *Çrutakīrti* & *Çalya*; *Sahadeva* & *Duḥçāsana*. *Anuvinda* was slain by *Sātyaki*, and so was *Vinda*; *Sātyaki* got upon the chariot of *Yudhāmanyu*, then upon another chariot; the *Kaikeyas* fled (VIII, **13**). *Çrutakarman* & the *Abhisāra* king *Citrasena*, whom he slew and then he pursued his flying troops. *Prativindhya* & *Citra*, whom he slew. The *Kurus* fled; only *Açvatthāman* & *Bhīmasena* (VIII, **14**); Si., Cā., D., and M.-ṛ. applauded them; both were borne away insensible by their drivers (VIII, **15**). *Arjuna* & the *Saṃçaptakas*; Si., D.-ṛ., and Cā. applauded him, etc. *Açvatthāman* & *Arjuna* (+ *Kṛshṇa*), who fought also the *Saṃçaptakas* (VIII, **16**); the *Kaliṅga, Vaṅga,* and *Nishāda* heroes attacked *Arjuna* with a division of elephants, which was broken; *Kṛshṇa* urged *Arjuna* not to spare *Açvatthāman*, who at last was borne away by his steeds and entered the army of *Karṇa*; *Kṛshṇa* and *Arjuna* proceeded towards the *Saṃçaptakas* (VIII, **17**). The *Magadha* chief (lord of *Girivraja*) *Daṇḍadhāra* massacred the *Pāṇḍava* army. *Arjuna* (urged by *Kṛshṇa*) & *Daṇḍadhāra* (on an elephant), whom he slew; his brother *Daṇḍa* & *Arjuna* (+ *Kṛshṇa*), who slew him; the hostile force broke up; *Arjuna* proceeded once more against the *Saṃçaptakas* (VIII, **18**), whom he slaughtered; *Ugrāyudha's* son & *Arjuna*, who slew him; urged by *Kṛshṇa*, *Arjuna* smote the remnant of the *Saṃçaptakas*, hastening in order to kill *Karṇa*; *Kṛshṇa* described the dismal sights of the field of battle "for the sake of *Duryodhana* alone". The army of *Duryodhana* was defeated by *Pāṇḍya* (VIII, **19**), who regarded himself as superior to *Bhīshma*, etc. ($\gamma\gamma$), and was slaughtering the army of *Karṇa*, the *Pulindas*, etc. ($\delta\delta$); *Açvatthāman* & *Pāṇḍya* (*b*), who employed the *Vāyavya* weapon; meanwhile *Karṇa* began to rout the elephant force of the *Pāṇḍavas*; *Pāṇḍya* ascended a riderless elephant and split *Açvatthāman's* diadem; then *Açvatthāmán* slew him, who had given numerous steeds, men, and elephants as food to the Rā. *Duryodhana* and his brothers worshipped *Karṇa* (VIII, **20**). *Kṛshṇa* said to *Arjuna* that he did not see *Yudhishṭhira*; the *Pāṇḍavas* had retreated, and *Karṇa* was slaying the *Sṛñjayas*. The *Kurus* (headed by *Karṇa*) & the *Pāṇḍavas* (headed by *Bhīmasena*); *Karṇa* caused a great carnage among the *Pāṇḍavas, Sṛñjayas,* and *Pāñcālas*. The *Pāñcāla* chief, etc. ($\epsilon\epsilon$), & *Karṇa* (VIII, **21**); *Dhṛshṭadyumna* & the *Aṅgas*, etc. ($\zeta\zeta$); the *Pāṇḍavas* and the *Pāñcālas* come to the aid of *Dhṛshṭadyumna*; *Nakula*, etc. ($\eta\eta$), overloaded the elephants with their weapons; *Sātyaki* killed the elephant of the *Vaṅga* king and felled the rider; *Sahadeva* & *Puṇḍra*, whose elephant he slew, and then proceeded towards the *Aṅga* chief; *Nakula* & the *Aṅga* king (*Mleccha* king), whom he slew; the elephant-men of the *Aṅgas* + *Mekalas*, etc. ($\theta\theta$), & *Nakula*; then the *Pāṇḍavas*, etc. ($\iota\iota$), rushed to the rescue of *Nakula*; *Sahadeva* slew eight elephants and *Nakula* many; *Dhṛshṭadyumna*, etc. ($\kappa\kappa$), overloaded the elephants with arrows; the hostile army fled away and the *Pāṇḍava* warriors rushed against *Karṇa* (VIII, **22**). *Sahadeva* & *Duḥçāsana*, who was taken away by his charioteer; *Sahadeva* crushed *Duryodhana's* division (VIII, **23**). *Karṇa* & *Nakula*; both the *Somakas* and *Kurus* were greatly afflicted; *Nakula* fled on foot; *Karṇa* pursued him and placed his stringed bow around his neck, but let him escape, recollecting the words of *Kuntī*; *Nakula* in great shame proceeded towards *Yudhishṭhira's* chariot, which he ascended. *Karṇa* at noon made a great slaughter among the *Pāñçālas* and the *Sṛñjayas*, and pursued them (VIII, **24**). *Ulūka* & *Yuyutsu*, who was vanquished and mounted another chariot. *Ulūka* slaughtered the *Pāñcālas* and the *Sṛñjayas*. *Çrutakarman* (*Dhārtarāshṭra*) & *Çatānīka*; both were deprived of their chariots and retired; *Çrutakarman* mounted the chariot of *Viviṃça*, *Çatānīka* that of *Prativindhya*. *Çakuni* & *Sutasoma*, who was deprived of his chariot, but contended on foot with *Çakuni*, who fought from his chariot; the Si., etc., were highly pleased; *Sutasoma* went to the chariot of *Çrutakīrti*; *Çakuni* slew many of the *Pāṇḍava* army (VIII, **25**). *Kṛpa* & *Dhṛshṭadyumna*, who got bewildered and let his charioteer carry him to *Bhīmasena*, pursued by *Kṛpa*. *Kṛtavarman* (the *Bhoja* king) & *Çikhaṇḍin*, who fell into a swoon, and was borne away by his charioteer; the *Pāṇḍava* army fled (VIII, **26**). *Arjuna* & the *Trigartas*, etc. ($\lambda\lambda$); *Arjuna* slew king *Çatruñjaya*, and *Suçruta's* son, and *Candradeva*; King *Satyasena* wounded *Kṛshṇa* and was slain by *Arjuna*, who then slew *Citravarman* and the *Saṃçaptakas* in hundreds and thousands, and *Mitrasena*, and wounded *Suçarman*; all the *Saṃçaptakas* attacked *Arjuna*, who invoked the *Aindra* weapon (description); the hostile army fled away almost entirely (VIII, **27**). *Duryodhana* & *Yudhishṭhira*, who deprived him of his chariot; *Karṇa*, etc. ($\mu\mu$), rushed to his aid; the other sons of *Pāṇḍu* surrounded *Yudhishṭhira*; the *Pāñcālas* & the *Kauravas* (description); *Karṇa* slaughtered the *Pañcālas*, *Arjuna* the *Trigartas*, *Bhīmasena* the *Kurus* and their elephant division, when the sun had passed the meridian (VIII, **28**); *Duryodhana* (on another chariot) & *Yudhishṭhira*; *Duryodhana* swooned away; *Bhīmasena* prevented *Yudhishṭhira* from slaying *Duryodhana*; *Kṛtavarman* & *Bhīmasena* in the afternoon (VIII, **29**). The *Kurus* (placing *Karṇa* at their van) & the *Pāṇḍava* army (and *Sātyaki*); *Karṇa* & *Sātyaki*; many *Kurus* came to rescue *Karṇa*, but fled away before the *Pāṇḍavas*, who were headed by the sons of *Drupada*; *Arjuna* and *Kṛshṇa* (having said their daily prayers and worshipped *Bhava*) destroyed the *Kurus*; *Duryodhana* & *Arjuna*; *Arjuna* & *Açvatthāman* + *Kṛpa*, etc. ($\nu\nu$); *Sātyaki*, etc. ($\xi\xi$), & *Karṇa*, who vanquished them; *Arjuna* & *Karṇa*; many *Kurus* fled away. At the close of the day both armies withdrew; Rā. and Pç., etc., appeared (VIII, **30**). *Dhṛtarāshṭra* exalted the prowess of *Arjuna* ($o o$). The *Kurus*, in grief, took counsel of one another; *Karṇa* assured *Duryodhana* that he would slay *Arjuna* on the morrow. On the morrow they beheld an invincible array formed by *Yudhishṭhira* according to the rules of *Bṛhaspati* and *Uçanas*. *Duryodhana* and his troops put confidence in *Karṇa*. *Dhṛtarāshṭra's* grief ($\pi\pi$); *Sañjaya* rebuked him by reminding him of his evil acts ($\rho\rho$). At dawn *Karṇa* repeated before *Duryodhana* his pledge to slaughter *Arjuna*; "my bow *Vijaya* (*c*) is the foremost of all weapons; . . . *Arjuna* is superior to me only by having *Kṛshṇa* ('the Creator of the Universe') for his charioteer, the chariot given him by *Agni*, his steed, and his standard with the Ape." He desired to have *Çalya* ("who is superior to *Kṛshṇa*") to drive his chariot; *Duryodhana* solicited *Çalya* (VIII, **31**) to comply with *Karṇa's* wishes ($\sigma\sigma$); *Çalya* took offence at the proposal ($\tau\tau$); *Duryodhana* repeated his request in honorific words ($\upsilon\upsilon$), and *Çalya* accepted on the condition that he might, in *Karṇa's* presence, utter whatever he desired ($\phi\phi$) (VIII, **32**). § 600: *Duryodhana* related to *Çalya* Tripurākhyāna (q.v.), which the great Ṛ. *Mārkaṇḍeya* had narrated to his father. "As *Brahmán*, . . . the Supreme Deity acted as the driver of *Rudra*, so do thou restrain the steeds of *Karṇa*" (VIII, **33**). He then related a story of *Paraçu-Rāma* (*b*), which a virtuous brahman had recited in the presence of his father. *Rāma* gave the *Dhanurveda* to *Karṇa*, "whom I do not think to have been born in the *Sūta* order, but to be the son of a god, born in the *Kshatriya* order and abandoned in infancy" (VIII, **34**). *Duryodhana* said: "So did *Brahmán* act as *Rudra's* driver; the driver should be superior to the warrior; thou art selected by us as superior to *Karṇa*." *Çalya* said that many a time he had heard this history recited to him, and *Kṛshṇa*, knowing the same, had become the charioteer of *Arjuna*, and would fight if *Arjuna* were slain. *Duryodhana* eulogized *Karṇa* (*a*) and then *Çalya* (etymology) as superior to *Kṛshṇa*. *Çalya* repeated his promise and condition. *Duryodhana* embraced

Karṇa, and, requested by him, once more obtained the promise of *Çalya*, who embraced *Duryodhana* and asked their forgiveness for the words he might speak to *Karṇa* for his good; "what I shall say, in order to inspire thee confidence, is fraught with self-adulation; I am a driver like *Mātali* himself" (VIII, **35**). —§ 607: *Duryodhana* said to *Karṇa*: "*Çalya*, who is superior to *Kṛshṇa*, will act as a driver, like *Mātali* to *Indra*." When the morning came, *Duryodhana* again successfully asked *Çalya* to become *Karṇa's* charioteer. *Karṇa* having worshipped the chariot (which had in days of old been sanctified by a priest), they both ascended it. *Duryodhana* once more addressed *Karṇa* (*a*). *Karṇa* told *Çalya* to urge the steeds that he might slay *Arjuna*, etc. (*β*); *Çalya* endeavoured to inspire *Karṇa* with fear by eulogizing the *Pāṇḍavas* (VIII, **36**). When *Karṇa* set out there appeared ill omens. The *Kuru* army, however, was filled with joy. *Karṇa* reflected and boasted (*γ*). *Çalya* ridiculed him and praised *Arjuna* (*δ*). *Karṇa* proceeded on his chariot with white steeds and tiger-skins, slaying large numbers in battle along his way, and inquired after *Arjuna* (VIII, **37**), promising every *Pāṇḍava* soldier that he met that unto him who pointed out *Arjuna* to him he would give whatever wealth he desired. *Duryodhana* and the troops rejoiced; *Çalya* scornfully laughed, and said (VIII, **38**) that *Karṇa* would get to see *Arjuna* without the trouble of seeking him, and asked him to abandon his desire for a single combat with *Arjuna*. *Karṇa* repeated his resolution, and *Çalya* insulted him in a long speech (VIII, **39**). *Karṇa* replied angrily, describing the disreputable practices of the *Madrakas* (and the *Gāndhārakas* and *Sindhu-Sauvīras*) (VIII, **40**). *Çalya* answered by praising himself and his accomplishments as a charioteer (description), and by reciting the story of the crow and the swan (*Haṃsakākīyopākhyāna*, q.v.): "Even as that crow, fed upon the remains of the dinners of the *Vaiçya* children, disregarded his equals and superiors, so dost thou, that art fed by the sons of *Dhṛtarāshṭra* upon the remains of their dishes, disregard all," etc. (*ε*) (VIII, **41**). *Karṇa* said that *Kṛshṇa* and *Arjuna* were well known to him, but did not make him afraid. The curse, however, of [*Paraçu-*]*Rāma* pained him greatly. He dwelt, disguised as a brahman, with *Rāma* in former days, desirous of obtaining celestial weapons from him. *Indra*, as a worm, began to pierce his thigh, on which was lying the head of the sleeping *Rāma*; therefore he did not move. But *Rāma*, witnessing his patience, discovered that he was not a brahman, and cursed him, saying that this weapon would never, in the time of need, when the hour of his death came, occur to his memory. He had forgotten the weapon, but would, notwithstanding, slay *Arjuna*; he suspected *Çalya* of secret friendship with the *Pāṇḍavas*; he would employ the *Brāhma* weapon, which *Arjuna* would never be able to escape, if only the wheels of *Karṇa's* chariot did not sink into the earth that day; he would not take fright at *Yama* himself with his rod, or *Varuṇa* with his noose, or *Kubera* with his mace, or *Indra* with the thunderbolt. "Once upon a time, while wandering for the sake of practising with my bow *Vijaya*, I had heedlessly struck the calf of a brahman's *homa* cow; the brahman cursed me, saying that my wheel would sink into the earth in a battle when I was in great danger. The kings of the Lunar race offered to give that brahman 1,000 kine and 600 bulls, but in vain," etc. (VIII, **42**). *Karṇa* said that it was in vain that *Çalya* tried to frighten him (*ζ*) (VIII, **43**). *Karṇa* said that in *Dhṛtarāshṭra's* abode the brahmans used to give accounts of various delightful regions and many kings of ancient times; an old brahman had said, blaming the *Madrakas* and the *Bāhīkas*, that they should be avoided as being out of the pale of virtue and living away from *Himavat*, etc. (*η*), but between Sindhu and its tributary rivers. On some very secret mission *Karṇa* had to live among the *Bāhīkas*, and therefore their conduct was well known to him; "there is a town *Çākala*, a river *Āpagā*, and a *Bāhīka* clan *Jarttikas*; the practices of these people are very censurable" (description; an example is cited of a *Bāhīka* who happened to live for some days in *Kurujāṅgala*, and a Rā. woman in *Çākala*; the rivers *Çatadru*, etc. (*θ*), in the countries of the *Āraṭṭas*, regions without virtue and religion). "D., P., and brahmans never accept gifts from those that are fallen, or those that are begotten by *Çūdras* on the girls of other castes, or the *Bāhīkas*, who never perform sacrifices and are exceedingly irreligious." He mentioned three impure places (*ι*) (v. the note of PCR., p. 155). There were two *Piçācas* in the river *Vipāçā*, named *Bahi* and *Hīka*; the *Bāhīkas* are the offspring of those two Pç.; they are not creatures created by the Creator. The *Kārashkaras*, etc. (*κ*), and other peoples of no religion one should always avoid; even thus did a Rā. woman speak to a brahman who went to that country for bathing in sacred water and passed a single night there. The regions are called *Āraṭṭāḥ*, the water *Bāhīka*; the lowest brahmans have resided there from very remote times (*brāhmaṇāpasadā yatra tulyakālāḥ Prajāpateḥ*), without the *Vedas*, etc. The *Prasthalas*, etc. (*λ*), are almost as blameable in their practices (VIII, **44**). *Karṇa* continued his description of the *Bāhīkas* (and *Gāndhāras* and *Madrakas*). The *Āraṭṭas* had been cursed by a chaste woman. The *Kauravas*, etc. (*μ*), know what the eternal religion is. *Brahmán*, even in the *Kṛta* age, had censured the practices of the country of the five rivers. *K.* quoted a saying of the Rā. *Kalmāshapāda*, declared by the *Rākshasa* to be the formula for curing a person possessed by a Rā. or killed by poison. Remarks on the *Pāñcālas*, etc. (*ν*), on *Agni*, etc. (*ξ*). *Çalya* spoke in disparagement of the *Aṅgas* (*o*). *Duryodhana* restored peace between *Karṇa* and *Çalya* (VIII, **45**).—§ 608: THE SEVENTEENTH DAY'S BATTLE. Beholding the array of the *Pārthas* made by *Dhṛshṭadyumna*, *Karṇa* proceeded to battle and assailed *Yudhishṭhira*. *Dhṛtarāshṭra* inquired about the disposition of the *Kuru* forces (*a*). *Sañjaya* described the *Kaurava* array: right wing (*β*); on the right of these (*γ*); the left side (*δ*); on their left (*ε*); in the centre at the head *Karṇa* with his sons; in the rear *Duḥçāsana*; and behind him *Duryodhana* and his brothers, protected by the united *Madrakas* and *Kekayas*; *Açvatthāman*, etc., with *Mlecchas* on elephants followed behind. The array was formed according to the plan of *Bṛhaspati*. *Yudhishṭhira*, beholding *Karṇa*, spoke to *Arjuna* of the hostile array: *Arjuna* should proceed against *Karṇa*; *Bhīmasena* against *Duryodhana*; *Nakula* against *Vṛshasena*; *Sahadeva* against *Çakuni*; *Çatānīka* against *Duḥçāsana*; *Sātyaki* against *Kṛtavarman*; *Pāṇḍya* against *Açvatthāman*; *Yudhishṭhira* against *Kṛpa*; the *Draupadeyas* with *Çikhaṇḍin* against the rest of the *Dhārtarāshṭras*, etc. *Çalya* pointed out to *Karṇa* the chariot of *Arjuna* (*b*) and various omens, etc. (*ζ*); how the *Saṃçaptakas* threatened to slay *Arjuna* and the other heroes of the *Pāṇḍava* army (*η*), and he dissuaded him from trying to slay *Arjuna*. Meanwhile the two armies mingled fiercely in battle (VIII, **46**). *Dhṛtarāshṭra* asked *Sañjaya* about *Arjuna*, the *Saṃçaptakas*, and *Karṇa*. *Sañjaya* related: *Arjuna* arrayed his troops, headed by *Dhṛshṭadyumna* (with steeds white as pigeons); by the side of *Dhṛshṭadyumna* the *Draupadeyas*. *Arjuna* & the *Saṃçaptakas*. The *Pāñcālas*, etc. (θ), & the *Kurus*; *Kṛpa*, etc. (ι), & the *Koçalas*, etc. (κ); the battle became conducive to fame, heaven, and virtue for the *kshatriya*, *vaiçya*, and *çūdra* heroes that engaged in it. *Duryodhana*, etc. (λ) + *Karṇa* & the *Pāṇḍavas*, etc. (μ); *Karṇa* harassed *Yudhishṭhira*; fierce battle between the *Kurus* and the *Sṛñjayas* (VIII, **47**). *Dhṛtarāshṭra* inquired about the particulars of *Karṇa's* encounter with *Yudhishṭhira*. *Sañjaya* related: *Karṇa* attacked the *Pāñcālas* (and *Prabhadrakas* and *Cedis*) and made a great slaughter; among others he slew the five *Pāñcālas Bhānudeva*, etc. (ν). The protectors of *Karṇa's* chariot-wheels were his sons *Susheṇa* and *Satyasena*, and his eldest son *Vṛshasena* protected his rear. *Dhṛshṭadyumna*, etc. (ξ), & *Karṇa* + *Karṇa's* sons; *Susheṇa* & *Bhīmasena*, who pierced him with seventy arrows and then slew *Karṇa's* son *Bhānusena*; *Bhīmasena* & *Kṛpa*, etc. (ο); *Bhīmasena* & *Susheṇa* + *Karṇa*; *Susheṇa* & *Nakula* + *Sahadeva*; *Sātyaki* & *Vṛshasena*, who was taken up by *Duḥçāsana* on the latter's chariot, borne away, and caused to ride in another chariot; *Vṛshasena* & the *Draupadeyas*, etc. (π); *Yuyudhāna* & *Duḥçāsana*, whom he deprived of his chariot, etc., but who got another chariot and fought from within the division of *Karṇa*; *Karṇa* & *Dhṛshṭadyumna*, etc. (ρ); at last *Karṇa's* assailants gave way; *Karṇa* & *Yudhishṭhira* + the *Cedis*, etc. (σ) (VIII, **48**); the *Drāviḍas*, etc. (τ), & *Karṇa*, who crushed them; *Karṇa* & *Yudhishṭhira*, etc. (υ); *Yudhishṭhira* addressed *Karṇa* in rage (φ); *Karṇa* swooned away, but recovered and slew *Yudhishṭhira's* wheel-protectors, the *Pāñcāla* princes *Candradeva* and *Daṇḍadhāra*; *Yudhishṭhira* struck *Susheṇa* and *Satyasena*, etc.; *Sātyaki*, etc. (χ), & *Karṇa*, who invoked the *Brāhma* weapon; *Karṇa* deprived *Yudhishṭhira* of his chariot; *Yudhishṭhira* fled, riding in another chariot with the white steeds with black hair on their tails that used to bear him, pursued by *Karṇa* (c), who touched him with his hand, but remembered the words of *Kuntī* and was withheld by *Çalya*, but insulted *Yudhishṭhira* (ψ) and let him escape. The *Cedis*, etc. (ω), followed *Yudhishṭhira*; *Karṇa* made a great slaughter of the *Pāṇḍava* forces; *Yudhishṭhira* urged his forces to proceed against *Karṇa*, which they did, headed by *Bhīmasena* (+ *Sātyaki*) (description); the *Kurus* broke and fled away (VIII, **49**). *Duryodhana* in vain tried to stop the flying troops. Then *Çakuni*, etc. + *Karṇa* & *Bhīmasena*, who let *Sātyaki* and *Dhṛshṭadyumna* protect *Yudhishṭhira*; *Çalya* pointed out *Bhīma* to *Karṇa* (**αα**); *Karṇa* replied (ββ); *Karṇa* swooned and was brought away by *Çalya* (VIII, **50**). Requested by *Dhṛtarāshṭra* (γγ), *Sañjaya* related: Urged by *Duryodhana*, several *Kuru* leaders (δδ) assailed *Bhīma*, who slew, among others, six sons of *Dhṛtarāshṭra* (εε). The other sons of *Dhṛtarāshṭra* fled away. *Karṇa* & *Bhīmasena*, whom he deprived of his chariot, but who then with his mace killed elephants and men by hundreds, among others fifty-two elephants belonging to *Çakuni*; next 3,000 horsemen dispatched by *Çakuni*, then he mounted another chariot and proceeded against *Karṇa*. *Karṇa* & *Yudhishṭhira*, whom he pursued as he was flying away; *Bhīmasena* & *Karṇa*; *Sātyaki* & *Karṇa*. Beholding *Çakuni*, etc. (ζζ), the *Kurus* rallied when the sun had reached the meridian. Fierce battle (VIII, **51**); (description) (VIII, **52**). *Arjuna* & the *Saṃçaptakas*, etc. (ηη); *Arjuna* (+ *Kṛshṇa*) & *Suçarman*; *Arjuna* repeatedly invoked the *Nāga* weapon, paralysing the legs (encircled with snakes) of the *Saṃçaptakas*; *Suçarman* invoked the *Sauparṇa* weapon; birds came down and devoured the snakes; *Arjuna* sat down, recovered, and invoked the *Aindra* weapon; the battle became awful (VIII, **53**). *Kṛtavarman*, etc. (θθ), began a fierce battle; *Kṛpa* & *Çikhaṇḍin* (+ the *Sṛñjayas*); *Çikhaṇḍin* was deprived of his chariot and made inactive; *Dhṛshṭadyumna* proceeded against *Kṛpa*; *Kṛtavarman* & *Dhṛshṭadyumna*; *Açvatthāman* & *Yudhishṭhira* (proceeding towards the chariot of *Kṛpa*); *Duryodhana* & *Nakula* and *Sahadeva*; *Karṇa* & *Bhīmasena*, etc. (ιι); *Kṛpa* & *Çikhaṇḍin*; *Suketu* (the son of *Citraketu*) & *Kṛpa*; *Çikhaṇḍin* retreated; *Kṛpa* slew *Suketu*, whose troops fled away; *Kṛtavarman* & *Dhṛshṭadyumna*, who made him driverless and was assailed by the *Kurus* (VIII, **54**). *Açvatthāman* & *Yudhishṭhira*, etc. (κκ) (description); *Prativindhya*, etc. (λλ), & *Açvatthāman*; *Sātyaki* had his driver slain; *Yudhishṭhira* went away, leaving his division, against the *Kurus*; *Açvatthāman* also left the spot (VIII, **55**). *Karṇa* & *Bhīmasena*, etc. (μμ), who, avoiding *Karṇa*, proceeded against the *Kurus*; *Arjuna* & the *Saṃçaptakas*; *Bhīmasena* & the *Kauravas*; *Karṇa* & the *Pāñcālas*; *Duryodhana* & *Nakula* and *Sahadeva*; *Dhṛshṭadyumna* (in order to rescue *Nakula* and *Sahadeva*) & *Duryodhana* (d), who was rescued by his brothers and borne away by *Daṇḍadhāra* upon the latter's chariot. *Karṇa* (having vanquished *Sātyaki* and desirous of rescuing *Duryodhana*) & *Dhṛshṭadyumna* + *Sātyaki* (pursuing *Karṇa* from behind) + the *Pāñcālas*; a fierce battle between the two armies when the sun had ascended the meridian; *Karṇa* & *Vyāghraketu*, etc. (νν) (description) (οο). *Yudhishṭhira*, etc. (ππ), & *Karṇa*. *Bhīmasena* slew the *Kurus*: *Bāhlīkas*, etc. (ρρ) (description) (σσ). *Arjuna* addressed *Kṛshṇa* upon beholding *Karṇa's* (e) prowess, and seeing that the *Saṃçaptakas* were broken. *Arjuna* (and *Kṛshṇa*) broke through the *Kuru* host. *Duryodhana* once more urged the *Saṃçaptakas* against him. Having slain 10,000 *kshatriyas*, *Arjuna* came to the further wing of the *Saṃçaptakas*, which was protected by the *Kāmbojas*; the younger brother of the *Kāmboja* chief *Sudakshiṇa* was killed by *Arjuna*; the *Kāmbojas*, etc. (ττ), were slain. *Açvatthāman* & *Arjuna* (+ *Kṛshṇa*); Si. and Cā. came; *Kṛshṇa* urged *Arjuna* not to spare *Açvatthāman*, who swooned and was carried away by his driver; *Arjuna* slew the *Kuru* troops. *Arjuna* had routed the *Saṃçaptakas*, *Bhīmasena* the *Kurus*, *Karṇa* the *Pāñcālas*. *Yudhishṭhira*, pained by his wounds, had retreated a *kroça* (VIII, **56**). *Duryodhana* addressed the *Kuru* leaders (υυ). *Açvatthāman* swore to slay *Dhṛshṭadyumna* or not to doff his armour (φφ). A fierce battle commenced. D., Aps., etc., came; Aps. rained flowers, etc., on the combatants (VIII, **57**). *Arjuna* pointed out to *Kṛshṇa* that the *Pāṇḍava* army was flying away, *Karṇa* slaying their warriors, and *Yudhishṭhira* nowhere to be seen; "the third part of the day still remains." *Arjuna* proceeded to *Yudhishṭhira* (+ *Sṛñjayas*); *Kṛshṇa* described the field of battle to *Arjuna* (χχ). A terrible battle commenced (VIII, **58**). The *Kurus* (headed by *Karṇa*) & the *Sṛñjayas* (*Pārthas*, headed by *Yudhishṭhira*); a remnant only of the *Saṃçaptakas* were left alive. *Dhṛshṭadyumna* + the *Pāṇḍavas* (and all the kings on their side) & *Karṇa*; *Sātyaki* & *Karṇa*; *Açvatthāman* & *Dhṛshṭadyumna*; *Karṇa* & the *Pāñcālas*, etc. (ψψ); *Dhṛshṭadyumna* was worsted by *Açvatthāman* and rescued by *Arjuna*; *Arjuna* & *Açvatthāman* (abandoning *Dhṛshṭadyumna*); *Dhṛshṭadyumna* was brought away by *Sahadeva* on the latter's chariot; *Açvatthāman* swooned on his chariot and was carried away by his driver. *Arjuna* proceeded towards the *Saṃçaptakas* (VIII, **59**).

Kṛshṇa pointed out to *Arjuna* that *Yudhishṭhira* was being pursued by many *Dhārtarāshṭras*, headed by *Duryodhana*, while the *Pāñcālas* were following in order to rescue him, and that he was in great danger, though the *Kurus* had been checked by *Sātyaki* and *Bhīma*, because *Duryodhana*, etc. (ωω), would break down the very mountains; "*Yudhishṭhira* is exceedingly emaciated in consequence of his fastings; he is endued with *Brāhma* force, but not with much of *kshatriya* might"; he was surrounded by the *Dhārtarāshṭra* warriors with the weapons *Sthūṇākarṇa*, etc. (*aaa*); in the very sight of the twins, etc. (βββ), *Karṇa* was destroying the *Pāṇḍava* division, and rushing against *Bhīmasena*; having vanquished the *Pāñcālas*, etc. (γγγ), he would soon come against *Arjuna*, and he was protected by *Duryodhana*; he should be slain; *Karṇa* was rushing against *Dhṛshṭadyumna* in order to exterminate the *Pāñcālas*; however, *Yudhishṭhira* was living; *Bhīma* (+ *Sṛñjayas* and *Sātyaki*) and the *Pāñcālas* were now conquering the *Kauravas*, who were flying away, *Kṛpa* and *Karṇa*, etc., resisting the *Pāñcālas* (headed by *Dhṛshṭadyumna*); the *Nishāda* prince (coming on his elephant against *Yudhishṭhira*) was slain by *Bhīma*, who had checked three *akshauhiṇīs* of *Duryodhana's* soldiers. *Arjuna* then destroyed the remnant of his foes; the *Saṃçaptakas* fled (VIII, **60**). Requested by *Dhṛtarāshṭra* (δδδ), *Sañjaya* related: *Karṇa*, etc., & *Bhīmasena* + the *Pāṇḍavas*, etc. (εεε); *Çikhaṇḍin* & *Karṇa*; *Dhṛshṭadyumna* & *Duḥçāsana*; *Nakula* & *Vṛshasena* (at the side of his father); *Yudhishṭhira* & *Citrasena*; *Sahadeva* & *Ulūka*; *Sātyaki* & *Çakuni*; the *Draupadeyas* & the other *Kauravas*; *Açvatthāman* & *Arjuna*; *Kṛpa* & *Yudhāmanyu*; *Kṛtavarman* & *Uttamaujas*; *Çikhaṇḍin* was deprived of his chariot by *Karṇa* and retreated; *Dhṛshṭadyumna* (+ many *Pāñcālas*) & *Duḥçāsana*: Si. and Aps., etc., wondered. *Karṇa* endeavours to rally the retreating troops of the *Dhārtarāshṭras*. After *Karṇa* had gone away, *Nakula* proceeded against the *Kauravas*; *Karṇa's* son, avoiding *Nakula*, went to *Karṇa* in order to protect his chariot-wheel. *Ulūka* was made driverless by *Sahadeva* and entered the division of the *Trigartas*. *Çakuni* ascended the chariot of *Ulūka*, who took him away from *Sātyaki*, who then routed the *Kuru* army. *Duryodhana* & *Bhīmasena*, who deprived him of his chariot and bow and made him fly away; the whole *Kuru* army attacked *Bhīmasena*, who scattered them. *Yudhāmanyu* retreated on his chariot, driving it himself. *Uttamaujas* sat down and was taken away by his driver. The whole *Kuru* army attacked *Bhīmasena*; *Duḥçāsana* and *Çakuni* (with an elephant force) & *Bhīmasena*, who made *Duryodhana* fly away, invoked his celestial weapons, and scattered and destroyed them (description) (VIII, **61**). *Arjuna* (with *Kṛshṇa*) appeared. *Duryodhana* (with half his troops in order to seize *Yudhishṭhira*) & *Yudhishṭhira*, whose warriors (ζζζ) then came to rescue him with an *akshauhiṇī*; *Karṇa* checked them all; *Sahadeva* (invoking a celestial weapon) & *Duryodhana*; *Karṇa* began an onslaught on the troops of *Yudhishṭhira* and *Dhṛshṭadyumna*; they fled away; *Karṇa* & *Yudhishṭhira*, who sat down and ordered his driver to retreat; *Duryodhana* and the *Dhārtarāshṭras* pursued him; but 1,700 *Kekaya* troops and a body of *Pāñcāla* troops checked them. *Duryodhana* & *Bhīma* (VIII, **62**). *Karṇa* & the *Kaikayas*, who fled to *Bhīmasena*. *Karṇa* & *Yudhishṭhira* (who was proceeding slowly towards the *Pāṇḍava* encampment with *Nakula* and *Sahadeva*, the protectors of his chariot-wheels, on his two sides); *Nakula* and *Sahadeva* & *Karṇa*, who slew the steeds both of *Yudhishṭhira* and *Nakula*, who both ascended the chariot of *Sahadeva*; *Çalya*, in order to rescue them, exhorted *Karṇa* to fight with *Arjuna*, but in vain; *Yudhishṭhira* turned from the battle; *Çalya* once more reminded *Karṇa* of *Arjuna*, etc. (ηηη), and that *Duryodhana* was in danger from *Bhīmasena*. *Karṇa* then left *Yudhishṭhira* and the twins and rushed to the rescue of *Duryodhana*. *Yudhishṭhira* in shame retreated with the steeds of *Sahadeva*, with the twins, whom he then dispatched to *Bhīma* (VIII, **63**). *Açvatthāman* & *Arjuna*; *Açvatthāman* employed the *Aindra* weapon, which *Arjuna* baffled with a powerful weapon created by *Indra*; *Açvatthāman*, having had his driver slain, himself guided his steeds while he fought with *Arjuna*; then he was brought away by his steeds. The *Pāṇḍavas*, repeatedly charging the *Kauravas*, broke their ranks and caused them to fly away in the very sight of *Dhṛtarāshṭra's* sons, etc. (θθθ). *Duryodhana* caused *Karṇa* to rally the troops; *Karṇa*, employing the *Bhārgava* weapon, harassed the *Pāñcālas*, who, with the *Cedis*, began to lose their senses. The *Sṛñjayas* called upon *Arjuna* and *Vāsudeva*. *Arjuna* spoke to *Kṛshṇa* about *Karṇa*; *Kṛshṇa* reminded him first to seek *Yudhishṭhira* (VIII, **64**). *Arjuna* met with *Bhīma* and asked him to bring intelligence of *Yudhishṭhira*; *Bhīma* feared to incur the reproach of cowardice by leaving the battle; *Arjuna* went to *Yudhishṭhira* in the *Pāṇḍava* camp upon *Bhīma* agreeing to resist the *Saṃçaptakas*. *Arjuna* and *Kṛshṇa* found *Yudhishṭhira* lying on his bed; thinking that *Karṇa* had been slain (VIII, **65**), *Yudhishṭhira* congratulated them (ιιι) (VIII, **66**). *Arjuna* told *Yudhishṭhira* the real motive of his arrival in camp (κκκ), and swore to slay *Karṇa* and all the foes that very day (VIII, **67**). *Yudhishṭhira* censured *Arjuna*, thinking that he had run away from the battle, leaving *Bhīma* unsupported (λλλ), several times invoking him to give up *Gāṇḍīva* to somebody else (VIII, **68**). *Arjuna* drew his sword in order to strike off *Yudhishṭhira's* head in fulfilment of his vow about the person who would tell him to give up *Gāṇḍīva* (μμμ); *Kṛshṇa* addressed *Arjuna* on the nature of truth (ννν), relating the story of *Balāka* (*f*) and of *Kauçika* (*g*); *Arjuna* said he must keep his vow (ξξξ); *Kṛshṇa* suggested that *Arjuna* by insulting *Yudhishṭhira*, by addressing him as "thou," would be regarded as having slain him (οοο) (VIII, **69**). Urged by *Kṛshṇa*, *Arjuna* insulted *Yudhishṭhira* in a long speech (πππ); then he became despondent and desired to strike off his own head; *Kṛshṇa* urged him to utter his own praises, as self-praise is equal to self-destruction. *Arjuna* praised himself (ρρρ), and begged for *Yudhishṭhira's* forgiveness, promising to slay *Karṇa* and rescue *Bhīma*. *Yudhishṭhira* grieved, saying that *Bhīmasena*, not he, ought to be king. *Kṛshṇa* comforted *Yudhishṭhira* and induced him to forgive both himself and *Arjuna* (σσσ) (VIII, **70**). Speeches of *Kṛshṇa*, *Arjuna*, and *Yudhishṭhira* on the same topic (τττ) (VIII, **71**). *Arjuna* proceeded to slay *Karṇa*, having obtained *Yudhishṭhira's* leave; commanded by *Kṛshṇa*, *Dāruka* had equipped the chariot. Auspicious omens. *Kṛshṇa* addressed *Arjuna* in order to raise his spirits (υυυ) (VIII, **72**); continuation (υυυ) (VIII, **73**). *Arjuna's* cheerful reply to *Kṛshṇa* (φφφ) (VIII, **74**). Requested by *Dhṛtarāshṭra* (χχχ), *Sañjaya* related: Description of the battle; *Arjuna* slew many. *Kṛpa* & *Çikhaṇḍin*; *Sātyaki* & *Duryodhana*; *Çrutaçravas* & *Açvatthāman*; *Yudhāmanyu* & *Citrasena*; the *Sṛñjaya* *Uttamaujas* & *Karṇa's* son *Susheṇa*; *Sahadeva* & the *Gāndhāra* king *Çakuni*; *Nakula's* son *Çatānīka* & *Karṇa's* son *Vṛshasena*; *Nakula* & *Kṛtavarman*; the *Pāñcāla* king *Dhṛshṭadyumna* & *Karṇa*; *Duḥçāsana* (with the *Saṃçaptakas* in the *Bharata* army) & *Bhīma*. *Uttamaujas* slew *Susheṇa*. *Karṇa* & *Uttamaujas*, who had his steeds slain, slew the steeds of *Kṛpa*, etc., and ascended the chariot of *Çikhaṇḍin*. *Çikhaṇḍin* did not wish to strike *Kṛpa* while the latter had no chariot: *Açvatthāman* rescued *Kṛpa*. *Bhīma* scorched the *Kuru* troops with his arrows (VIII, **75**). The *Bharata* host fled before *Bhīma*, who said to his charioteer *Viçoka* that he was anxious about *Arjuna* and *Yudhishṭhira*; requested by *Bhīma*, *Viçoka* took an estimate of his weapons. *Bhīma* once more addressed *Viçoka*, saying that he would that day slay all the *Kurus* or himself succumb, etc. (ψψψ). *Viçoka* pointed out to *Bhīma* that *Arjuna* was returning to battle (ωωω). *Bhīma* promised to give *Viçoka* fourteen villages, 100 female slaves, and twenty chariots for this agreeable intelligence (VIII, **76**). *Arjuna* and *Bhīma* attacked the *Kaurava* army with great vigour (description). *Duryodhana* told his troops to slay *Bhīma*, who made a formidable carnage among them (description). *Çakuni* (urged by *Duryodhana*) + his brothers & *Bhīma*; *Çakuni* was brought away by *Duryodhana*, who retreated; the troops fled away to *Karṇa* (VIII, **77**). Requested by *Dhṛtarāshṭra* (α′), *Sañjaya* related: In the afternoon *Karṇa* assailed the *Somakas*, and *Bhīma* the *Dhārtarāshṭra* troops. *Karṇa* assailed the *Pāñcālas*, etc. (β′); the *Pāṇḍavas* encompassed him on all sides; *Çikhaṇḍin*, etc. (γ′), & *Karṇa*, who vanquished them. *Cedis* and *Matsyas* & *Karṇa*, who checked them; D., Si., and Cā. were gratified; the *Pāṇḍava* troops fled, and were attacked by the *Dhārtarāshṭra* archers. *Duryodhana* rejoiced; *Duryodhana*, etc. (δ′), slew the *Pāṇḍava* warriors; similarly the *Pāṇḍava* heroes *Dhṛshṭadyumna*, etc. (ε′), made an onslaught on the *Kurus* (VIII, **78**). *Arjuna* produced a river of blood (description). Requested by *Arjuna* (ζ′), *Kṛshṇa* took him to *Karṇa*, whom *Çalya* informed (η′), and who answered *Çalya* (η′). Requested by *Karṇa*, *Duryodhana*, etc. (θ′), in order to open up a path for *Karṇa* to *Arjuna*, speedily proceeded and attacked *Arjuna*, who caused a great onslaught; *Açvatthāman* & *Kṛpa* and *Kṛtavarman* & *Arjuna*, who vanquished them. *Çikhaṇḍin*, etc. (ι′), proceeding towards *Arjuna*, checked the foes; the *Kurus* and *Sṛñjayas* slew one another (VIII, **79**). *Arjuna* (avoiding *Karṇa*) proceeded to the rescue of *Bhīma* and slew the assailants of *Bhīma*; the *Kurus* fled; *Arjuna* informed *Bhīma* that *Yudhishṭhira* was well, and then proceeded; he was surrounded by ten sons of *Dhṛtarāshṭra* (who were all *Duḥçāsana's* juniors in age), whom he slew (VIII, **80**). *Arjuna* was assailed by ninety *Saṃçaptakas* as he was proceeding towards *Karṇa's* chariot; he slew them. Many *Kauravas* attacked him, whom he destroyed. Then he was attacked by a force of *Mlecchas*, riding 1,300 elephants, commanded by *Duryodhana*. *Arjuna* made a heavy onslaught. Abandoning the small remnant of *Kauravas*, *Bhīmasena* rushed towards *Arjuna* and also destroyed this remnant; then he followed *Arjuna* in his rear; *Karṇa* was deserted by his troops; the sons of *Dhṛtarāshṭra* repaired to *Karṇa*. *Karṇa* attacked the *Pāñcālas* (VIII, **81**); *Karṇa* felled *Janamejaya's* driver and steeds, and cut off the bows of *Çatānīka* and *Sutasoma*; *Karṇa* & *Dhṛshṭadyumna*, etc. (κ′); *Ugrakarman* (the commander of the *Kaikeya* division) & *Karṇa's* son *Prasena*; *Karṇa* slew *Ugrakarman*; *Prasena* & *Sātyaki*, who slew him; *Karṇa* & *Sātyaki* + *Çikhaṇḍin*; *Karṇa* slew *Dhṛshṭadyumna's* son and attacked *Sutasoma*. *Kṛshṇa* urged *Arjuna* to slay *Karṇa*; *Arjuna* proceeded with *Bhīmasena*; *Uttamaujas*, etc. (λ′), & *Karṇa* (grinding the *Somakas*), who vanquished them; they were rescued by the *Draupadeyas*; *Sātyaki* & *Duryodhana* + *Kṛpa*, etc. (μ′); *Duḥçāsana* & *Bhīma* (VIII, **82**). *Bhīma* (addressing *Karṇa*, etc.) (μ′) slew *Duḥçāsana* and drank his blood in the very sight of *Duryodhana* and *Karṇa*; the bystanders, with *Karṇa's* brother *Citrasena*, fled away, thinking *Bhīma* to be a Rā.; *Yudhāmanyu*, etc., pursued *Citrasena*; *Citrasena* (turning back) was slain by him; *Karṇa* (putting the *Pāṇḍava* host to flight) & *Nakula*; *Bhīmasena* took up a little of *Duḥçāsana's* blood and drank it (ν′), addressing *Kṛshṇa* and *Arjuna* and vowing soon to slay *Duryodhana* (VIII, **83**). Ten of *Dhṛtarāshṭra's* sons (ξ′) & *Bhīma*, who slew them. *Karṇa* was afraid, but was encouraged by *Çalya* (ο′). *Karṇa's* son *Vṛshasena* & *Bhīma* + *Nakula*, who had his white steeds of the *Vanāyu* breed slain by him, and sprang upon *Bhīma's* chariot in the sight of *Arjuna*; urged by *Bhīma* and *Nakula*, *Arjuna* proceeded towards *Vṛshasena* (VIII, **84**). Eleven warriors (π′) + the *Kulindas* (upon elephants, born in *Himālayan* regions) & *Kṛtavarman*, etc. (ρ′); the *Kulinda* prince & *Kṛpa*, who slew him; the younger brother of the *Kulinda* prince & *Kṛpa* + the *Gāndhāra* king, who slew the *Kulinda*; the *Kurus* & the *Pāṇḍus* & *Sṛñjayas*; the *Bhoja* chief *Kṛtavarman* & *Çatānīka*; *Açvatthāman* slew three elephants; the third brother of the *Kulinda* chief & *Duryodhana*; the *Kulinda*, mounting another elephant, & *Krātha*, who was slain; *Vṛka* & the same *Kulinda*, whose elephant crushed him; the son of *Babhru* & the same elephant + *Sahadeva's* son; *Babhru* fell down; the same *Kulinda* & *Çakuni* (the *Gāndhāra* chief), who slew him; *Nakula's* son *Çatānīka* (who slew elephants, etc.) & a *Kulinda* warrior [on the *Kaurava* side], who was slain by him; *Karṇa's* son *Vṛshasena* & *Çatānīka* + *Arjuna*, etc. (σ′); *Arjuna*, informing *Karṇa* and all the other *Kurus* headed by *Duryodhana* and *Açvatthāman* that he would slay *Vṛshasena* and then *Karṇa*, as *Bhīma* would slay *Duryodhana*, slew *Vṛshasena*; *Karṇa* & *Arjuna* (+*Kṛshṇa*) (VIII, **85**); *Kṛshṇa* addressed *Arjuna* (τ′); *Arjuna's* reply (υ′) (VIII, **86**); description of *Arjuna* and *Karṇa* (φ′); all the inhabitants of the world were heard to differ amongst themselves: D., Dā., G., Pç., the Snakes, Rā.; As., *Yātudhānas*, Gh., etc., sided with *Karṇa*; the *Vedas*, etc. (χ′), with *Arjuna*; the smaller snakes all sided with *Karṇa*; V., M., Sā., R., V.-D., A., *Agni*, etc. (χ′), sided with *Arjuna*, while all Ā. sided with *Karṇa*; the *Vaiçyas*, etc. (ψ′), sided with *Karṇa*; P., etc. (χ′), with *Arjuna*; the *Pretas*, Pç., Rā., etc., with *Karṇa*; D.-ṛ., B.-ṛ., R.-ṛ. with *Arjuna*, as also G. headed by *Tumburu*. With the *Prādheyas* and *Mauneyas*, G. and Aps., and many wise sages, having for their vehicles wolves, etc., came in order to witness the encounter that was also witnessed by D., Dā., G., N., Y., etc., M.-ṛ., P. (subsisting upon *svadhā*), etc., and *Brahmán* with B.-ṛ. and *Prajāpatis* and *Bhava*. *Indra* wished that *Arjuna* should vanquish *Karṇa*; *Sūrya* that *Karṇa* should vanquish *Arjuna*. The gods urged *Brahmán* that the success of both should be equal, *Indra* that *Arjuna* and *Kṛshṇa* should win; *Brahmán* and *Içāna* (i.e. Çiva) said that the victory of *Arjuna* was certain (ω′); "let *Karṇa* obtain identity with V. or M.; let him with *Droṇa* and *Bhīshma* be worshipped in heaven." *Indra* acquiesced in their words. Description of *Karṇa's* and *Arjuna's* chariots. The ape on *Arjuna's* banner attacked the elephant's rope on *Karṇa's* banner. *Kṛshṇa* and *Çalya* cast keen glances at each other, and so did *Arjuna* and *Karṇa*. *Karṇa* asked *Çalya* what he would do if he was slain; *Çalya* said that then he would slay both *Kṛshṇa* and *Arjuna*; similarly asked by *Arjuna*, *Kṛshṇa* said that *Karṇa* could not slay *Arjuna*; if so, the destruction of the universe would be at hand, and he would himself slay *Karṇa* and *Çalya*. *Arjuna* said that that very day the wives of *Karṇa* would become widows (*aa'*) (VIII, **87**). In the welkin D., N., As., Si., Y., G., Rā., Aps., B.-ṛ., etc., looked on. The battle commenced. *Duryodhana*, etc. (*aβ'*), & *Arjuna* (+*Kṛshṇa*); *Arjuna* defeated all of them; floral showers fell, etc.; *Açvatthāman* told *Duryodhana* to make peace (*aγ'*), but in vain (*aδ'*); *Duryodhana* urged his troops (VIII, **88**); description of the battle between *Arjuna* and *Karṇa*; *Arjuna* employed an *Āgneya* weapon, which was quenched by *Karṇa* with a *Vāruṇa* weapon by means of clouds, which *Arjuna* dispelled by a *Vāyavya* weapon; *Arjuna* employed the *Aindra* weapon (? *astraṃ dayitaṃ devarājñaḥ*), *Karṇa* the *Bhārgava* weapon. The *Pāñcālas* and *Somakas* & *Karṇa*, who slew them. Seeing *Arjuna's* weapons baffled by *Karṇa*, *Bhīma* urged *Arjuna* to put forth his strength (*aε'*), and so did *Kṛshṇa* (*aς'*). *Arjuna* bowed to *Brahmán* and invoked the *Brāhma* weapon, which could be applied by the wind alone; *Karṇa* baffled it; urged by *Bhīma*, *Arjuna* applied a second *Brāhma* weapon, which caused a great carnage among the *Kaurava* troops (description). *Karṇa* & *Bhīmasena*, etc. (*aη'*). *Arjuna* shot at *Karṇa* and *Çalya*, and slew *Sabhāpati*, etc. The *Kauravas* urged *Karṇa* to slay *Arjuna*. *Yudhishṭhira* appeared in order to witness the encounter. *Arjuna's* bowstring broke; *Karṇa* took advantage of the interval to hit *Arjuna*, etc. (*aθ'*). *Karṇa* employed as arrows five snakes that had sided with *Takshaka's* son [i.e. Açvasena, at Khāṇḍava]; they penetrated *Kṛshṇa's* body, entered the earth, and, having bathed [in Bhogavatī], returned to *Karṇa*, but were cut off by *Arjuna*, who then covered *Karṇa's* chariot with showers of arrows and slew 2,000 *Kurus*, who had been urged by *Duryodhana* to fight. The *Kurus* fled, leaving *Karṇa* to fight singly with *Arjuna* (VIII, **89**). *Karṇa* baffled *Arjuna's* weapon; *Karṇa* and *Arjuna* shot at each other dense showers of arrows. The snake *Açvasena*, who was hostile to *Arjuna*, was passing his time in the nether region, having escaped from the conflagration at *Khāṇḍava*; recollecting the death of his mother he now soared up and entered into *Karṇa's* quiver in the shape of an arrow. *Karṇa* and *Arjuna* were fanned and sprinkled with fragrant sandal water by many Aps. staying in the welkin, and *Çakra* and *Sūrya* with their hands gently brushed their faces. *Karṇa* aimed that arrow, born in *Airāvata's* race (i.e. the snake in the shape of an arrow), which he had long kept for *Arjuna's* destruction, and which lay singly in a golden quiver amid sandal dust; omens appeared, and the *Lokapālas* with *Çakra* raised loud wails. *Karṇa* did not know that the snake *Açvasena* had entered his arrow by the aid of his *yoga* powers. *Çalya* in vain exhorted *Karṇa* to take another arrow; *Karṇa* said: "*Karṇa* never aims an arrow twice; persons like us never become crooked warriors." *Kṛshṇa* with his feet pressed *Arjuna's* chariot about a cubit into the earth, and the snake-arrow, failing to strike off *Arjuna's* head, broke his diadem (made by *Svayambhū* for *Indra* > *Arjuna*), incapable of being crushed by *Rudra*, etc. (*aι'*). Celestial flowers were showered upon *Kṛshṇa*, etc. *Açvasena* appeared to *Karṇa* and asked him to shoot the same weapon again; *Karṇa* refused to avail himself of another's help or shoot the same shaft twice. *Açvasena* then, of his own accord, rushed on *Arjuna* in the shape of an arrow; *Kṛshṇa* informed *Arjuna* that it was *Açvasena*, who, as an unborn child, was saved with his mother at *Khāṇḍava*. *Arjuna* cut the snake into pieces, and *Kṛshṇa* with his arms raised the chariot from the earth. Once, when *Karṇa* was stupefied and stood inactive, *Arjuna* was disinclined to slay him in such distress, but he was taught by *Kṛshṇa* never to spare an enemy, however weak. At that time, when the hour of *Karṇa's* death had come, *Kāla*, approaching invisibly, in consequence of the brahman's wrath, said "the earth is swallowing up thy wheel," and the weapon that *Rāma* had given him escaped from his memory, and the earth engulfed his left wheel. *Karṇa* began to rail at righteousness as not always protecting its worshippers. *Karṇa* invoked the *Brāhma* weapon, and *Arjuna* the *Aindra* weapon, which was baffled by *Karṇa*; urged by *Kṛshṇa* to "shoot high weapons," *Arjuna* shot the *Brāhma* weapon. *Karṇa* cut off, one after another, eleven bowstrings of *Arjuna's*, not knowing that *Arjuna* had one hundred strings to his bow; urged by *Kṛshṇa* to strike *Karṇa* with "superior weapons," *Arjuna* then consecrated another celestial weapon with *mantras*, uniting the *Raudra* weapon with it. At that time the earth swallowed up one of *Karṇa's* wheels. Quickly alighting, *Karṇa* seized his sunken wheel with his two arms and endeavoured to lift it up; the earth rose up to the height of four fingers breadth, with her seven islands, etc.; *Karṇa* shed tears from wrath and asked *Arjuna* to wait for a moment till he had lifted his sunken wheel (VIII, **90**). *Kṛshṇa* taunted *Karṇa* for appealing to virtue and the rules of fair fight by reminding him of all the wrongs done to the *Pāṇḍavas* by himself and *Duryodhana* acting according to his counsels (*aκ'*). *Karṇa* dropped his head in shame and gave no answer, and continued to fight. *Kṛshṇa* urged *Arjuna* to pierce *Karṇa* with a celestial weapon; *Arjuna*, remembering the incidents alluded to by *Kṛshṇa*, blazed up with fury; blazing flames of fire seemed to emanate from all the pores of his body, a sight that appeared exceedingly wonderful. Both *Karṇa* and *Arjuna* invoked the *Brāhma* weapon, and *Karṇa* once more made an effort to extricate his chariot. *Arjuna* shot an *Agni* weapon, quenched by *Karṇa* with a *Vāruṇa* weapon, covering all the points of the compass with darkness, which *Arjuna* dispelled with the *Vāyavya* weapon. Pierced by a shaft of *Karṇa's*, while the earth trembled, etc., *Arjuna* began to reel, the *Gāṇḍīva* dropped from his hand, etc. At the interval *Karṇa* fruitlessly endeavoured to extricate his chariot. Recovering his senses, *Arjuna* took up an *añjalika* weapon. Urged by *Kṛshṇa* to cut off the head of *Karṇa*, *Arjuna* cut off his standard, and then, with an *añjalika* weapon (the Ṛ. loudly crying out "peace be to the universe"), struck off *Karṇa's* head before *Karṇa* could mount his chariot. A light issued from *Karṇa's* body and entered the Sun. The *Pāṇḍavas* rejoiced (*aλ'*) (VIII, **91**). *Duryodhana*, etc., grieved; *Bhīma*, uttering loud roars, frightened the *Kauravas*, etc. (*aμ'*). *Çalya* informed *Duryodhana* of *Karṇa's* death (*aν'*). *Duryodhana* became almost deprived of his senses (VIII, **92**). Requested by *Dhṛtarāshṭra*, *Sañjaya* related the state of the *Kaurava* army after *Karṇa's* fall (*aξ'*). *Duryodhana* resolved to make a final stand (*aο'*). *Bhīmasena* and *Dhṛshṭadyumna* (+ four kinds of forces) & *Duryodhana* (+ 25,000 warriors on foot, who were slain); *Arjuna* & the chariot force of the *Kauravas*; *Nakula*, etc. (*aπ'*), & *Çakuni*; the *Kurus* fled away; *Cekitāna*, etc. (*aρ'*), blew their conches. *Duryodhana* challenged all the *Pāṇḍavas* and fought with them with great valour; he rallied the remnants of his troops and exhorted them to fight (*aσ'*); they fled away heedless of his words (VIII, **93**). *Çalya* described to *Duryodhana* the carnage on the field (*aτ'*), and urged the withdrawal of the troops to their nightly quarters.

Having repeatedly comforted *Duryodhana*, they retired headed by *Açvatthāman*. *Karṇa* did not lose his splendour. D., Ṛ., etc., retired. The portents that were seen at *Karṇa's* fall. *Arjuna* and *Kṛshṇa* blew their conches, at which the *Kauravas* left the field, deserting *Çalya* and *Duryodhana*. D., G., men, Cā., M.-ṛ., Y., and M.-U. congratulated *Kṛshṇa* and *Arjuna* (VIII, **94**). Enumeration of the *Kauravas* retiring from the field (αυ'). Urged by *Kṛshṇa* (αφ'), who told *Dhṛshṭadyumna*, etc. (αχ'), to stand there with care, *Arjuna* presented himself to *Yudhishṭhira*, who, rising from his bed, greeted *Arjuna* and *Kṛshṇa*; *Kṛshṇa* congratulated *Yudhishṭhira* (αψ'), who ascribed his success to *Kṛshṇa's* influence (αω'). *Yudhishṭhira*, with *Kṛshṇa* and *Arjuna*, came back to the field to have a look at *Karṇa's* body. The kings, filled with joy, approached *Yudhishṭhira* and gladdened him greatly; so *Nakula*, etc. (βα'). *Dhṛtarāshṭra* and *Gāndhārī* swooned away and were comforted by *Vidura*, *Sañjaya*, and the *Kuru* ladies. The fruits of reciting the *Karṇaparvan*, as also of hearing it recited (VIII, **96**): VIII, **96**, 5046.—§ 795*c* (Mahābhārata): XVIII, **6**, 273.

Karṇaprāvaraṇa, pl. (°*āḥ*), a people. § 284 (Sahadeva): II, **31**, 1170 (in the south, vanquished by Sahadeva on his digvijaya).—§ 295 (Dyūtap.): II, **52**, 1875 (brought tribute to Yudhishṭhira).—§ 578 (Bhīshmavadhap.): VI, **51**τ, 2103 (in the army of Duryodhana).

Karṇaprāvaraṇā, a mātṛ. § 615*u* (Skanda): IX, **46**θ, 2643.

Karṇaputra[1] ("the son of Karṇa") = Vṛshasena: V, 5792 (*V*°); VII, 7527, 7531, 7542; VIII, 2282 (?), 3107, †3813 (*V*°), †4290, †4294, †4302, †4305, †4333; IX, 32 (*V*°). Cf. Karṇasuta, Karṇātmaja, Kārṇi.

Karṇaputra[2] (do.) = Bhānusena: VIII, 2260 (*Bh*°). Cf. Karṇasuta.

Karṇaputra[3] (do.) = Prasena: VIII, †4185 (*P*°). Cf. Karṇātmaja.

Karṇaputra[4] (do.) = Susheṇa: IX, 502, 508, 511 (°*vadhaṃ*). Cf. Karṇātmaja.

Kārṇaputra, dual. (°*au*) and pl. (°*āḥ*). § 608 (Karṇap.): VIII, **48**, 2256 (°*āḥ*); **78**, 4000 (°*au*).—§ 611 (Çalyap.): IX, **8**, 391 (°*āḥ*); **10**, 481 (°*au* . . . *Susheṇaḥ Satyasenaç ca*).—§ 795 (Svargārohanap.): XVIII, **5**λ, 150 (°*āḥ*, in heaven).

[Karṇasambhava] ("the origin of Karṇa"). § 175 (Sambhavap.): Karṇa's birth, etc. Indra's asking for his natural armour (repetition from §§ 131 (v. Kuntī) and 131*b* (v. Karṇa); cf. also § 547) (I, **111**).

Karṇasuta[1] ("the son of Karṇa") = Vṛshasena: VII, 6363 (*V*°), 6408, 7540; VIII, †4329, †4343. Cf. Karṇaputra, Karṇātmaja, Kārṇi.

Karṇasuta[2] (do.) = Bhānusena: VIII, 2262. Cf. Karṇaputra.

Karṇasuta, dual. (°*au*). § 604 (Karṇap.): VIII, **7**, †211.

Karṇāṭa: III, 16352 (read with B. *karṇaṭṭa*°).

Karṇāṭaka, pl. (°*āḥ*), a people. § 574 (Jambūkh.): VI, **9**ν, 366 (in the south).

Karṇātmaja[1] ("the son of Karṇa") = Vṛshasena: VII, 626, 627; VIII, †4281, †4282, †4292, †4336. Cf. Karṇaputra, Karṇasuta, Kārṇi.

Karṇātmaja[2] (do.) = Satyasandha: VIII, †210 (*S*°).

Karṇātmaja[3] (do.) = Susheṇa: VIII, †3816. Cf. Karṇaputra.

Karṇātmaja[4] (do.) = Prasena: VIII, †4183 (*P*°). Cf. Karṇaputra.

Karṇaveshṭa, a prince. § 130 (Aṃçāvat.): I, **67**, 2696 (among the incarnations from the Krodhavaça gaṇa).—§ 554 (Sainyodyogap.): V, **4**γ, 78 (among the princes to whom the Pāṇḍavas ought to send messengers).

Kārṇi ("the son of Karṇa") = Vṛshasena: VIII, †4302. Cf. Karṇaputra, Karṇasuta, Karṇātmaja.

Karṇikā, an Apsaras. § 191 (Arjuna): I, **123**, 4820 (among the Apsarases who sang at the birth of Arjuna).

Karṇikāradhvaja ("having a Karṇikāra flower in his banner") = Abhimanyu: VI, 5365 (*Saubhadraṃ*).

Karṇikāramahāsragvin = Çiva (1000 names[2]).

Karṇikārasrajapriya = Çiva (1000 names[1]).

Karoṭaka, a serpent. § 47 (Sarpanāmak.): I, **35**, 1553 (enumeration).

Karpaṭa, v. Pañcakarpaṭa.

Kārshṇa, adj. ("composed by Kṛshṇa, i.e. Vyāsa"). § 7 (Anukram.): I, **1**, 261 (°*ṃ vedaṃ*, i.e. the Mahābhārata).—§ 72 (Ādivaṃçāvatāraṇap.): I, **62**, 2300 (do.).—§ 795 (Svargārohaṇap.): XVIII, **5**, 188 (do.).

Kārshṇi[1], a Devagandharva. § 191 (Arjuna): I, **123**, 4812 (among the Devagandharvas who sang at the birth of Arjuna).

Kārshṇi[2] ("the son of Kṛshṇa [Vāsudeva]") = Pradyumna: III, †10233, †10270; V, †668 (°*pratimaṃ*, sc. Sātyaki); VII, 4263 (*Makaradhvajaḥ*).

Kārshṇi[3] ("the son of Kṛshṇa [i.e. Arjuna]") = Abhimanyu: VI, 1822, 1826, 1827, †2674, 2682, 2690, 2729, 2763, 3436, 3437, 4552, 4559, 4595, 4596, 4602 (*Mahendrapratimaṃ*), 5379, 5380; VII, 558, 559, 569, 573, 1096 (*Kṛshṇasamaḥ*), 1498, 1637, 1716, 1844, 1894, 1929, 1964 (*Kṛshṇārjunasamaḥ*), 1988 (slain); XI, 570 (*Abhimanyoḥ*), 716 (had fought with [and slain] Bṛhadbala).

Kārshṇi[4] ("the son of Kṛshṇa [i.e. Vyāsa]") = Çuka: XII, 12258, 12264.

Kārtasvara, a Daitya (?). § 673*b* (Bali-Vāsavasaṃv.): XII, **227***a*, 8264 (among the ancient rulers of the earth).

Kārtavīrya ("the son of Kṛtavīrya") = Arjuna, the Haihaya king: I, 444 (°*vadhaḥ*), 4794 (°*samaḥ*, sc. Arjuna Pāṇḍava); II, 321 (in the palace of Yama), 649 (became emperor (*saṃrāj*) by the energy of his asceticism), 877 (among the kings who met with destruction, having disregarded their superiors); III, 141 (had delivered his people by means of tapas), 492 (°*samaḥ*, sc. Bhoja), 8273 (°*ārjuno yathā*), 8465 (°*sya*, sc. *lokān*), 10134 (*Haihayādhipateḥ*), 10142, 10189, 10193, 10197, 10201, 10202 *bis*, 10889 (°*samaṃ yudhe* . . . *Phālgunaṃ*); V, 2377 (*sadṛçaṃ bāhuvīryeṇa K°sya Pāṇḍavaṃ*, i.e. Arjuna), 3157 (*ishvastre sadṛço rājñaḥ K°sya*, sc. Arjuna Pāṇḍava); VII, 2429 (is slain by Rāma Jāmadagnya), 3648, 6032 (°*samo yudhi*, sc. Çūra), 8971 (°*samo vīrye*, sc. Açvatthaman); VIII, 144 (*K°ç ca Rāmeṇa Bhārgaveṇa yathā hataḥ*), 1263 (°*samaṃ vīrye Karṇaṃ*), 4397 (°*samau*, sc. Karṇa and Arjuna Pāṇḍava), 4743 (°*samo yudhi*, sc. Arjuna Pāṇḍava); XII, 1755, 1757, 1762 (*Haihayendreṇa*), 1767 (is slain by Rāma Jāmadagnya), 13879 (°*sutā hatāḥ*), 13880; XIII, 865 (*hato* . . . *cakravartī*), 5662 (among the kings who abstained from meat during the month of Kārttika), 7187 (*Sahasrabhujabhṛt* . . . *Māhishmatyāṃ*); XIV, 817 (°*sya saṃvādaṃ samudrasya*), 818.

Kārtayuga, adj. ("relating to Kṛtayuga"). § 149 (Yayāti): I, **90**, †3600 (°*pradhāna*, sc. Yayāti).—§ 641 (Rājadh.): XII, **69**, 2681 (*dharmān*).—§ 717*b* (Nārāyaṇīya): XII, **341**, 13062 (°*dharma*°).

Kartṛ[1], a Viçvadeva. § 749 (Ānuçāsanik.): XIII, **91**γ, 4360 (enumeration).

Kartṛ[2] = Çiva (1000 names[2]).

Kartṛ[3] = Vishṇu: XIII, 6983 (1000 names), 6990 (do.); 7639.

Kārttika, name of a month. § 277 (Jarāsandhavadhap.): II, **21**, 918 (°*sya tu māsasya . . . prathame 'hani*).—§ 574 (Jambūkh.): VI, **2**, 57 (*paurṇamāsyām K°e*). — § 759 (Ānuçāsanik.): XIII, **106**, 5161 (*māsam*); **109**, 5383 (*dvādaçyām K°e māsi*).—§ 766 (do.): XIII, **132**, 6162 (*māsi*). Cf. Kaumuda.

Kārttikeya = Skanda, q.v.

[Kārttikeyastava] ("the hymn in praise of Kārttikeya" [i.e. Skanda]). § 508 (cf. Mārkaṇḍeyas.): At the request of *Yudhishṭhira*, *Mārkaṇḍeya* enumerated the names of *Skanda* (q.v.). Blessing to the reader.—§ 509 (do.): *Mārkaṇḍeya* praised *Skanda* (q.v.). Blessing to the reader, etc. (III, **232**).

Kārttikī, the day of full moon in the month of Kārttika. § 357 (Pushkara): III, **82**, 4073, 4079.—§ 360 (Tīrthayātrāp.): III, **82**, 5057.—§ 451 (Mārkaṇḍeyas.): III, **182**, 12554.—§ 658*b* (Kṛtaghnop.): XII, **171**, 6376, 6385.—§ 787 (Āçramavāsap.): XV, **11**, 358; **13**, 409; **15**, 429. Cf. Kaumudī.

Karuṇānvita = Sūrya (the Sun): III, 157.

Karūsha, pl. (°*āḥ*), a people. § 190*d* (Arjuna): I, **123**, 4796 (Arjuna shall subjugate *Cedi-Kāçi-Karūshān*).—§ 323*b* (Alarka): III, **25**, †957 (*Alarkam . . . Kāçi-K°rājam*).—§ 561 (Yānasandhip.): V, **62a**, †2415 (among the allies of Yudhishṭhira).—§ 573 (Ambopākhyānap.): V, **196η**, 7623 (*Cedi-Kāçi-K°āṇām netāram*, i.e. Dhṛshṭaketu). — § 574 (Jambūkh.): VI, **9μ**, 348 (*Cedi-Matsya-K°āḥ*). — § 578 (Bhīshmavadhap.): VI, **47δ**, 1811 (*Cedi-Kāçi-K°eshu*).—§ 579 (do.): VI, **54θ**, 2242 (*Cedi-Matsya-K°ās tu Bhīmasena-purogamāḥ*).—§ 580 (do.): VI, **56η**, 2415 (*Cedi-Kāçi-K°aiḥ*, follow Dhṛshṭaketu); **59ξ**, †2640 (*Cedi-Pāñcāla-K°-Matsyāḥ*).—§ 585 (do.): VI, **97λλ**, 4443.—§ 586 (do.): VI, **106ν**, 4819 (*Cedi-Kāçi-K°āṇām sahasrāṇi caturdaça*, slain by Bhīshma).—§ 587 (do.) · VI, **116π**, 5446 (do., do.).—§ 589 (Droṇābhishekap.): VII, **11ν**, 396 (*Vātsya-Gārgya-K°ān*, had formerly been vanquished by Kṛshṇa).—§ 608 (Karṇap.): VIII, **54ιι**, 2625 (resisted by Karṇa); **73**, 3662 (had been slain by Bhīshma in the great battle). Cf. Kārūsha, pl.

Karūsha[1]. § 273 (Rājasūyārambhap.): II, **14**, 577 (*Dantavakraḥ*? BR. proposes to read *Kā°ḥ* ("the king of the Karūshas")).

Karūsha[2], an ancient king. § 761 (Ānuçāsanik.): XIII, **115δ**, 5666 (among the kings who abstained from meat during the month of Kārttika). Cf. Kārūsha[1].

Kārūsha[1], son of Manu Vaivasvata. § 139 (Manu Vaivasvata): I, **75**, 3141 (the sixth son of Manu; read *Ka°*?).

Kārūsha[2] ("the king of the Karūshas"). § 291 (Çiçupālavadhap.): II, **45**, 1540 (Bhadrā Vaiçālī was robbed by Çiçupāla for the sake of *K.*).

Kārūsha[3], the country of the Karūshas. § 295 (Dyūtap.): II, **52**, 1864 (*samudrānte*?).

Kārūsha, pl. (°*āḥ*), a people = Karūsha, pl. § 580 (Bhīshmavadhap.): VI, **56ε**, 2410 (in Bhīshma's (!) array).—§ 589 (Droṇābhishekap.): VII, **9**, 288 (*Cedi-K°aiḥ*, encompassed Droṇa).—§ 592 (Saṃçaptakavadhap.): VII, **21θ**, 877 (*Cedi-K°-Koçalāḥ*), (ι), 883 (vanquished by Droṇa). — § 600 (Ghaṭotkacavadhap.): VII, **156ι**, 6779 (*Cedi-K°-Koçalāḥ*, follow Arjuna and Bhīmasena).—§ 605 (Karṇap.): VIII, **12ββ**, 459; **30ξξ**, 1231 (*Cedi-K°-Matsyānām*, encompassed Karṇa).—§ 608 (do.): VIII, **47κ**, 2226; **49χ**, 2334 (assailed Vasusheṇa); **56μμ**, 2693 (Karṇa slew many *Cedi-K°ān*); **73**, 3639; **78β'**, 3949.

Kārūshādhipati ("the king of the Karūshas"). § 264 (Sabhākriyāp.): II, **4β**, 124 (waited upon Yudhishṭhira).—§ 273 (Rājasūyārambhap.): II, **14**, 576 (*Vakraḥ*?, had joined Jarāsandha). Cf next.

Kārūshādhipati (do.). § 232 (Svayaṃvarap.): I, **186**, 6996 (present at the svayaṃvara of Draupadī). Cf. the prec.

Kārūshaka, adj. ("belonging to the Karūshas"). § 556 (Sañjayayānap.): V, **22**, †669 (*Cedi-K°āḥ . . . bhūmipālāḥ*, had joined Yudhishṭhira). Cf. next.

Kārūshaka, adj. (do.). § 130 (Aṃçāvat.): I, **67**, 2700 (*rājānaḥ*, among the incarnations of the Krodhavaça gaṇa).—§ 554 (Sainyodyogap.): V, **4γ**, 81 (do., among the princes to whom the Pāṇḍavas ought to send messengers).

Karūsharāja ("the king of the Karūshas"). § 556 (Sañjayayānap.): V, **22**, †671 (°*pramukhāḥ*, had honoured Çiçupāla).

Karvaṭa, pl. (°*āḥ*), a people. § 280 (Bhīmasena): II, **30**, 1098 (°*ādhipatim*, in the east, vanquished by Bhīmasena on his digvijaya).

Kārya(m) = Çiva (1000 names[1]).

Kāryātman = Kṛshṇa: XII, 1652.

Kaserumat, a Yavana king. § 317*b* (Kṛshṇa Vāsudeva): III, **12**, 491 (*Yavanaḥ*, had been slain by Kṛshṇa).

Kāshṭha. § 269 (Vaiçravaṇasabhāv.): II, **10**, 415 (a follower of Çiva?, in the palace of Kubera).

***kāshṭhāḥ**[1], pl. ("small divisions of time," personif.). § 615*u* (Skanda): IX, **45γ**, 2517 (came to the investiture of Skanda).

kāshṭhāḥ[2] = Sūrya (the Sun): III, 150.—Do.[3] = Çiva (1000 names[1–2]).

Kaṭakaṭa = Çiva (1000 names[1]).

Kaṭaṅkaṭa = Çiva (1000 names[1]).

Kaṭha, a ṛshi. § 22 (Pramadvarā): I, **8a**, 962.—§ 264 (Sabhākriyāp.): II, **4a**, 113.—§ 717*c* (Uparicara): XII, **337ε**, 12760 (*ādyaḥ*, among the sadasyas at the sacrifice of Vasu Uparicara).

Kaṭhaka, a warrior of Skanda. § 615*u* (Skanda): IX, **45η**, 2569.

Kathita = Vishṇu (1000 names).

Katirā, a mātṛ. § 615*u* (Skanda): IX, **46θ**, 2632.

Kātyāyanī = Durgā (Umā): VI, 798.

Kaubera, adj. ("relating to or belonging to Kubera"). § 305 (Anudyūtap.): II, **78**, 2578 (*visarge*).—§ 334 (Kairātap.): III, **41**, 1705 (*astram*, obtained by Arjuna).—§ 552 (Goharaṇap.): V, **64**, 2058 (°*m*, sc. *astram*).—§ 572 (Rathātirathasaṅkhyānap.): V, **169**, 5870 (*astragrāmaḥ*, sc. Arjuna's).—§ 615*u* (Skanda): IX, **46ι**, 2654 (°*yaḥ*, sc. *mātaraḥ*).—§ 615*x* (Kubera): IX, **47**, 2752 (*tīrtham*), 2755 (*kānanottame*).—§ 731*b* (Ashṭāvakra-Diksaṃv.): XIII, **19**, 1421 (°*ā Yaksha-Gandharva-Kinnarāḥ*).—§ 746 (Ānuçāsanik.): XIII, **79κ**, 3773 (*lokam*).—§ 789 (Putradarçanap.): XV, **33κ**, 903 (do.).

Kauberya, adj. (do.). § 592 (Saṃçaptakavadhap.): VII, **23ρ**, 1041 (sc. *dhanuḥ*, among the bows of the Draupadeyas).

Kauçala (III, 2897), v. Kosala.

Kauçala, pl. (°*āḥ*), (VII, 397), v. Kosala, pl.

Kauçalya, Kauçalya, pl., **Kauçalyā, Kauçalyānandavardhana, Kauçalyānandivardhana, Kauçalyāmatṛ, Kauçalyātmajā**, v. Kaus°.

Kauçija, pl. (°*āḥ*), a people. § 574 (Jambūkh.): VI, **9μ**, 349 (in Bhāratavarsha).

Kauçika[1] ("descendant of Kuçika") = Viçvāmitra: I, 2936, 6695; III, 8120, 8121 (*V°*), 8311 (*V°*), 8313; V, 3722, 3728, 3972 (*reme . . . yathā . . . Haimavatyāñ ca K°aḥ*), 4021, 7354 (°*syāçrame*); IX, 2295, 2384 (*ṛshisattamam*);

XII, 1594 (?), 5352, 5353, 5367, 5410, 7599, ††13205 (?); XIII, 1350, 2897 (*dvijaḥ*), 7116 (*V°*).

Kauçika[2] (do.) = Ashṭaka: V, 4089 (*A°*).

Kauçika[3] ("the son of Kuçika") = Gādhi: IX, 2297; XIII, 2897.

Kauçika[4] = Caṇḍakauçika: II, 760.

Kauçika[5] = Indra: III, 331, 10312, 10711; XII, 1720 (*Gādhir nāma . . . Pākaçāsanaḥ*, incarnate as Gādhi); XIII, 829, 877 (*Devarājaḥ*), 3590, 3600 (read *K°a* with B.), 6950 (*°sya Çacī*).

Kauçika,[6] various brahmans, descendants of Kuçika. § 264 (Sabhākriyāp.): II, **4a**, 107.—§ 277 (Jarāsandhavadhap.): II, **21**, 807 (*°o Maṇimāṃç ca*, had favoured the country of the Māgadhas, = Caṇḍakauçika?, = Viçvāmitra?). — § 479 (Pativratop.): III, **206**, 13652, 13700.—§ 608*g* (Karṇap.): An ascetic *K.* lived near a village where many rivers met. He made a vow always to speak the truth, and became celebrated as a speaker of truth. From fear of robbers, certain persons entered that wood. The robbers came and asked *K.* by which path the men had gone, and he told them the truth; the robbers finding out the persons slew them all. *K.* fell into a grievous hell: VIII, **69**, 3439, 3446, 3448, 3449, 3451, 3452, 3454.—§ 641 (Rājadh.): XII, **109**, 4030 (? Nīl. and PCR. take *kauçikaḥ* in the sense of 'an owl', but this verse seems to allude to VIII, **69**, although the text is in disorder).—§ 662*b* (Jāpakop.): XII, **199**, 7201 (*Paippalādiḥ sa-Kauçikaḥ*).

Kauçika[7], the senāpati of Jarāsandha. § 277 (Jarāsandhavadhap.): II, **22**, 885 (formerly named Haṃsa).

Kauçika[8] (III, 8134), v. Kauçikī.

Kauçika, adj. ("relating to Kuçika or Kauçika"). § 435 (Jaṭāsuravadhap.): III, **157**, 11461 (*khaḍgam*). — § 593 (Abhimanyuvadhap.): VII, **48**, 1920 (*mārgaiḥ K°ādyaiḥ*).—§ 602 (Droṇavadhap.): VII, **191**, 8793 (*sampātam*?).—§ 615 (Gadāyuddhap.): IX, **57**, 3223 (*mārgān*).—§ 745*b* (Cyavanop.): XIII, **52**, 2719 (*vaṃçāt*).

Kauçika, pl. (*°āḥ*) (the descendants of Kuçika or Kauçika). § 225 (Vāsishṭha): I, **176**, 6739.

Kauçikācārya = Ākṛti: II, 1165 (*Ā°*; read *Kaiç°*?).

Kauçikī[1], a river. § 134 (Viçvāmitra): I, **71**, 2924 (created by Viçvāmitra, who named it Pārā).—§ 249 (Arjunavanavāsap.): I, **215**, 7818 (visited by Arjuna). — § 280 (Bhīmasena): II, **30**, 1096 (*°nilayaṃ rajānaṃ Mahaujasaṃ*). § 364 (Tīrthayātrāp.): III, **83**, 6065 (*°yāḥ . . . saṅgame . . . Dṛshadvatyāḥ*). — § 370 (do.): III, **84**, 8110, 8121, 8134 (*Kālikāsaṅgame . . . K°y-Aruṇayor gataḥ*, C. has *Kauçikāruṇayoḥ*).—§ 377 (Dhaumyatīrthak.): III, **87**, 8309 (there Viçvāmitra attained to the state of a brahman).—§ 390 (Tīrthayātrāp.): III, **110**, 9987 (*c*: on *K.* Viçvāmitra practised austerities), 9989. § 392 (Tīrthayātrāp.): III, **114**, 10095.—§ 459 (Mārkaṇḍeyas.): III, **188a**, 12907 (seen by Mārkaṇḍeya in the stomach of Narayaṇa).—§ 494 (Āṅgirasa): III, **222**, 14231 (among the rivers who are mothers of fires).—§ 574 (Jambūkh.): VI, **9**λ, 326, 337.—§ 594 (Mṛtyu): VII, **54**, 2094.—§ 680*c* (Mṛtyu-Prajāpatisaṃv.): XII, **259**, 9207.—§ 721 (Ānuçāsanik.): XIII, **3**, 190.—§ 733 (do.): XIII, **25a**, 1717 (a tīrtha).—§ 751*b* (Çapathavidhi): XIII, **94**, †4552 (*puṇyatīrtham*).—§ 757*m* (Goloka): XIII, **101a**, 4889.—§ 768*b* (Umā-Maheçvarasaṃv.): XIII, **146**δ, 6764.—§ 775 (Ānuçāsanik.): XIII, **166a**, 7653 (enumeration). Cf. Pārā.

Kauçikī[2] = Durgā (Umā): VI, 800.

Kaukulikā, a mātṛ. § 615*u* (Skanda): IX, **46**θ, 2633.

Kaukura, pl. (*°āḥ*), a people = Kukura, pl. § 294 (Dyūtap.): II, **50**, 1804 (*Nīpa-Citraka-K°āḥ*, are living as bondsmen in the palace of Yudhishṭhira).—§ 295 (do.): II, **51**, 1871 (bring tribute to Yudhishṭhira).—§ 793 (Mausalap.): XVI, **5**, 134 (*Vārshṇeyān sa-Bhojāndhaka-K°ān*).

Kaukuṭṭaka, pl. (*°āḥ*), a people. § 574 (Jambūkh.): VI, **9**ν, 367 (in the south).

Kaumāra, adj. ("belonging to Kumāra [i.e. Skanda]"). § 358 (Tīrthayātrāp.): III, **82**, 4086 (by living on vegetables or fruits at *Āgastyaṃ saraḥ* one attains to *K°ṃ padaṃ*).—§ 497 (Skandotpatti): III, **226**, 14351 (*maṅgalāni . . . K°āṇi trayodaça*).—§ 615*u* (Skanda): IX, **46**ι, 2655 (*°yaḥ*, sc. *mātaraḥ*).

Kaumāra, name of a varsha in Çākadvīpa. § 575*b* (Çākadvīpa): VI, **11**β, 426.

Kaumodakī, name of the mace of Kṛshṇa. § 257 (Khāṇḍavadahanap.): I, **225**, 8200 (*e*: capable of slaying every Daitya (*Daityāntakaraṇīm*), given to Kṛshṇa by Varuṇa).—§ 596 (Pratijñāp.): VII, **79**, 2809.

Kaumuda, name of a month = Kārttika. § 562 (Bhagavadyānap.): V, **83**, 2926 (*°e māsi*).—§ 746 (Ānuçāsanik.): XII, **66**, 3370 (*°e çuklapakshe*).—§ 761 (do.): XIII, **115**, 5656 (*°e . . . çuklapakshe*), 5660 (*°ṃ pakshaṃ*), 5670 (*māsaṃ*).

Kaumudī, the day of full moon in the month of Kaumuda [i.e. Kārttika]. § 766 (Ānuçāsanik.): XIII, **130**, 6132.

Kauṇakutsya, a ṛshi. § 22 (Pramadvarā): I, **8a**, 962.

Kauṇapa[1], a serpent. § 63 (Sarpasattra): I, **57**, 2147 (of Vāsuki's race).—Do.[2] pl. = Rākshasa, pl.: I, 6450.

Kauṇapāçana, a serpent. § 47 (Sarpanāmak.): I, **35**, 1559 (enumeration).

Kauṇḍinya, a muni. § 264 (Sabhākriyāp.): II, **4a**, 111 (in the palace of Yudhishṭhira).

Kauṇḍīvṛsha, pl. (*°āḥ*), a people. § 580 (Bhīshmavadhap.): VI, **56**ε, 2410 (in the *gāruḍavyūha* of Bhīshma, only C., B. has *Ku°*).

Kauṅkaṇa, pl. (*°āḥ*), a people. § 574 (Jambūkh.): VI, **9**ν, 367 (in the south, only C., B. has *Koṅ°*).—§ 608 (Karṇap.): VIII, **73**, 3652 (only C., B. has *Taṅgaṇāḥ*).

Kaunteya[1] ("the son of Kuntī") = Arjuna: I, 2275 (*Bībhatsuḥ*), 5234, 5257 (*A°*), 5456, 5468, 5479, 5494, 5741 (*Dhanañjayaḥ*), 6504, 6527, 6537, 6796, 6953, 7756, 7783, 7700, 7701, 7806, 7808, 7813, 7821, 7849, 7888, 7897, 7901, 7937, 7967, 7975, 7978, 8195; II, 2, 1012, 1018, 1026, 1049; III, 1476, 1477, 1478, 1480, 1486, 1514, 1531, 1568, 1600, 1687, 1693, 1733 (*A°*), 1774, 1792, 1793, 3088, 8421 (*Bībhatsuḥ*), 11981, 12004, 12074, 12272, 12292, 12296, 17265, 17268; IV, 8, 39 (*Dhanañjayaḥ*), 1260, 1428, 1441 (*Bībhatsuḥ*), 1445, 1513, 1523, 1588, 1698 (*Bībhatsuḥ . . . Çvetavāhanaḥ*), 1808, 1840, 1884, 1922, 1936, 1947, 1993, 1997 (*Kirīṭamālī*), 2029 (do.), 2039, 2043, 2068 (*Kirīṭamālī*), 2070, 2258, 2368 (*Dhanañjayaḥ*); V, 134 (do.), 2216 (*Bībhatsuḥ*), 2824, 3195 (*Dhanañjayaḥ*), 4812, 5375, 5502, 5522, 5567, 5875; VI, 518, 812, 857, 892, 915, 938, 989, 1057, 1099, 1119, 1147, 1157, 1176, 1179, 1193, 1197, 1201, 1323, 1352, 1359, 1362, 1424, 1502, 1504, 1514, 1999 (*Dhanañjayaḥ*), 2002, 2552, 3212 (*Çvetavāhanaḥ*), 3568, 3740 (*Çvetavāhanaḥ*), 3742, 3744, 4641, 4837, 5431, 5496 (*Çvetavāhanaḥ*), 5512, 5514 (*Çvetavāhanaḥ*), 5618 (only B.); VII, 292 (only C.), 660, 664, 678, 1196, 1989, 2670, 3127 (read *Kaunteye* with B.), 3161, 3276 (*Kirīṭamālī*), 3284, 3365, 3409, 3416, 3442, 3445, 3669, 3726, 3729, 3758, 3831, 3902, 3959 (*Kṛshṇasārathiḥ*), 5813 (*Dhanañjayaḥ*), 5862, 5867,

5954, 6068, 6139, 6199, 6200, 6205, 6206, 6231 (*Pākaçāsaniḥ*), 6305, 6392, 7088 (*Bībhatsuḥ*), 7759, 7809, 8262, 8275 (*A*°), 8431 (do.), 8447, 9083 (*A*°), 9087, 9399, 9520, 9529, 9644; VIII, 1579, 1629, 2164, 2791, 2798, 2824, 2836, 3026, 3029, 3035, 3037, 3282, 3283, 3326, 3331, 3336, 3403 (*Çveta-vāhanaḥ*), 3406, 3408, 3409, 3487, 3701, 4023, 4358, 4739, 4770, 4850, 4985; IX, 142 (*Dhanañjayaḥ*), 1029 (do.), 3478, 3480; X, 442; XII, 579, 600, 793, 1912, 13155, 13161, 13165, 13234, 13298, 13300; XIV, 591, 1468, 2123, 2140, 2227, 2234, 2255, 2323, 2431, 2453, 2470, 2474, 2484, 2577 (*Jishṇuṃ*); XVI, 227 (*A*°); XVII, 4.

Kaunteya[2] (do.) = Bhīmasena: I, 2242, 5021, 5061 (*Bhīmasenaḥ*), 7406; II, 921, 922, 1067, 1084, 1089, 1090, 1103; III, 543 (*Bhīmasenaḥ*), 545, 2051, 10841 (*Vṛkodara*), 10842, 11189, 11257, 11301, 11325, 11360, 11362, 11422, 11424, 11624, 11731, 17280; IV, †236, 518, 528, 602, 631, 632, 633, 640, 720, 746; V, 2022, 2485 (*Bhīmasenaṃ*), 2974, 4746, 5473; VI, 2304, 2799, 3305 (*Bhīmasenaḥ*), 3429, 4343 5708 (*Bhīmasenaṃ*); VII, 940, 3525 (*Bhīmasenaṃ*), 5140, 5155, 5180 (*Bhīmasenaḥ*), 5210, 5213, 5214, 5228, 5244 (*Bhīmasenaḥ*), 5385, 5592, 5601, 5635, 5637, 5759, 5773, 5791, 8046, 8054, 9187, 9271, 9272, 9274; VIII, 2488, 3855, 3944, 4091; IX, 150, 583, 1439 (*Bhīmasenaḥ*), 1914, 1943, 3213, 3218; X, 601 (*Bhīmasenaḥ*), 658, 662; XI, 336; XII, 1377 (*Bhīmaḥ*), 1475 (*Bhīmasenaṃ*); XIV, 2102 (*Bhīmasenaḥ*), 2525.

Kaunteya[3] (do.) = Karṇa: V, 4736, 4753, 4918; VI, 5826, 5840; XVIII, 23 (*K*°), 140 (*Rādheyaḥ*).

Kaunteya[4] (do.) = Yudhishṭhira: I, 5284, 5820 (*Y*°), 5849, 6045 (*Y*°), 7226, 7245, 7249, 7271, 7553, 7568; II, 501, 1211, 1301, 1356, 1429, 1632, 1689, 1720, 1739, 1740, 1764, 1802, 1930, 2141, 2167, 2389, 2581, 2621 (*Dharmaputro Yudhishṭhiraḥ*); III, 128, 211, 677, 750, 801, 815, 817, 843, 874, 899, †919 (*Y*°), 968 (*Y*°), 972, 1225, 1328, 1349, 1352, †1363, 1378, 1399, 1445, 1913 (*Dharmarājaṃ*), 2088, 2130, 2773, 3030, 3081, 8318, 8338, 8340, 8383, 8405, 8411, 8438, 8444, 8458, 8498, 8540, 8630, 8662, 8686, 9968, 9981, 9983, 9986, 10098, 10113, 10123, †10247, 10309, 10311, 10422, 10469, 10516, 10534, 10549, 10588, †10601, †10691, 10698, 10699, 10772, 10793, 10820, 10823, 10829, 10831, 10862, 10863, 10994, 11444, 11445, 11524, 11553, 11739 (*Ajāta-çatruḥ*), 11930, 11946, 12435 (*Y*°), 12444, 12630, 12763, 12796, 13002, 13009 (*Y*°), 13041, 13213 (*Y*°), 14694, 14838 (*Y*°), 15354 (*Y*°), 15356, 15488, 17235 (*Y*°), 17316, 17327, 17431, 17434; IV, 57, 150, 642, 2225, 2348; V, 48, 53, 126, 1972, 2214 (*Y*°), 2288 (*Y*°), 2484 (*Y*°), 2955, 5240, 5415, 5416, 5547, 7581, 7622 (*Y*°); VI, 696, 1574, 1588, 1616, 3698, 3798, 4654, 5189 (*Y*°); VII, 317 (*rājānaṃ*; PCR. wrongly = *Bhīmasena*), 2923, 2932, 2936, 2946, 3529 (*Ajātaçatruṃ*), 3983 (only B., C. has *Kaikeyena*), 4174 (*Ajātaçatruḥ*), 4331, 6484, 6963, 7273, 8317, 9231; VIII, 2356, 2976 (*Dharmarājaṃ Yudhishṭhiraṃ*), 2986, 3187, 3207 (*Y*°), 3308, 5031; IX, 557 (*Ajātaçatruṃ Yudhishṭhiraṃ*), 844, 851, 1012, 1188, 1718 (*Ajātaçatruḥ*), 1759, 1783; X, 551; XI, 230; XII, 384 (*Dharmarāje Yudhishṭhire*), 452, 476, 606, 620, 627, 651 (*Pāṇḍavaḥ*), 663, 698 (*Ajātaçatruṃ*), 703, 732 (*Y*°), 832, 1150, 1158, 1207, 1213, 1225, 1228, 1360, 1409, 1419, 1715, 1729, 1753, 2455, 2458, 2460, 2471 (*Y*°), 2478 (do.), 2480, 2482, 2745, 2857, 3127, 3193, 3229, 3339, 4621, 4714, 4815, 4891, 5420, 5908, 6332, 7558, 9465, 9854, 10085, 10205, 11052, 11070, 11092, 11138, 11172, 11196, 11197, 11203, 12856, 13179; XIII, 17, 979, 1306, 1313, 1862, 1874, 2043, 2254, 2552, 3014, 3056, 3312, 3314, 3364, 3381, 3392, 4620, 4908 (*Y*°), 5117, 5139, 5151, 5175, †5203, 5631, 6219, 6280, 6923, 6927 (*Y*°), 7455, 7703, 7713, 7731 (*Y*°); XIV, 7, 17, 61, 321, 329, 2085, 2560 (*Dharmajaḥ*), 2562, 2570, 2614, 2638; XV, 55, 122, 134, 165, 178, 217, 220, 261, 762; XVII, 57 (*Y*°); XVIII, 51, 128.

Kaunteya, pl. (°*āḥ*) and dual (°*au*) ("the sons of Kuntī"): I, 185, 2250, 5066, 5647, 5688, 5770, 6410, 6517, 7369 [7411 (*ekaikaḥ . . . Kaunteyaḥ*)], 7419, 7424, 7461, 7465, 7544, 7552; II, 1362, 2646; III, 19, 8437, 11066, 11552, 14933; IV, 1131, 1612; V, 51, 195, 569, 597, 4152, 4268, 4678; VI, 535, 2931, 5298 (°*au*, i.e. Arjuna and Bhīmasena), 5301 (do.); VII, 292 (only B., C. has *Kaunteyāt*), 6854, 7673; VIII, 38 (°*rājaputrāḥ*), 311, 343, 1338, 1349, 2850; XI, 374.

Kaurava, adj. ("belonging to Kuru or to the Kurus (Kauravas)"): I, 5457 (°*īṃ camūṃ*); III, 1421 (°*aṃ pakshaṃ*, i.e. the party of Duryodhana); V, 4992 (*vaṃçaṃ*), 5020 (*vaṃçaḥ*), 5072 (*kulasya*); VI, 1558 (*sainyaṃ*, i.e. the army of Duryodhana), 2480 (°*īṃ senāṃ*, do.), 2488 (*sainyaṃ*, do.); VII, 5677 (*sainyaṃ Sindhu-Sauvīra-K°aṃ*, do.), 7147 (°*īṃ senāṃ*, do.), 7350 (*sainyaṃ*, do.), 7728 (°*īṃ senāṃ*, do.); VIII, 914 (°*ī senā*, do.), 2562 (°*ī senā*, do.), 2694 (*sainyaṃ*, do.), 3641 (*balaṃ*, do.), 3845 (°*ī senā*, do.); IX, 521 (°*īṃ senāṃ*, do.), 525 (°*ī . . . camūḥ*, do.), 537 (°*ī . . . pṛtanā*, do.), 1009 (*sainyaṃ*, do.), 1764 (*vaṃçe*).

Kaurava, pl. (°*āḥ*) (the descendants of Kuru or name of a people (= Kuru, pl.); very often it designs only the sons of Dhṛtarāshṭra and their adherents, in opposition to the sons of Pāṇḍu and their adherents): I, 116, 299, 499, 561 (*muninā K°āṇāṃ yaçobhṛtā*, i.e. Vyāsa), 584 (°*āyodhanaṃ*), 1664 (°*vaṃçajaḥ*), 3126, 4378, 4449 (°*āṇāṃ yaçobhṛtā . . . Pāṇḍunā*), 4466, 4958, 5034, 5097, 5099, 5212 (the sons of Dhṛtarāshṭra and the sons of Pāṇḍu), 5214 (do.), 5239 (do.), 5452, 5453, 5457, 5458, 5465, 5524 (°*saṃsadi*), 5712, 5790, 5860, †7084 (°*āgraiḥ*, i.e. the sons of Pāṇḍu), †7337 (°*rāja-putrāḥ*, = do.), †7341 (°*vaṃçavardhanāḥ* = do.), 7531, 7535, 7537, 7556, 7776 (°*āṇāṃ yaçaskaraṃ*, i.e. Arjuna), 7961; II, 2022, 2062 (°*āṇāṃ kulakaraṃ jyeshṭhaṃ Pāṇḍavaṃ acyutaṃ*, i.e. Yudhishṭhira), †2117 (*saṃsadi K°āṇāṃ*), 2211, 2212, †2213, 2255, 2269, 2292, 2293 (°*ārṇavamagnāṃ māṃ*, sc. Draupadī), 2306, 2350, 2351, 2352, †2368, †2379 (°*āṇāṃ guruḥ*, i.e. Droṇa?), 2538, 2653, 2666; III, †220, †252, †255, 311, 598, †962, 1423 (°*sainyasya*), 8513 (i.e. the Pāṇḍavas), 13006 (°*arshabhāḥ*, i.e. the Pāṇḍavas), 14880, 14887, 14889, 14935, 14952, 14954, 14956, 14961, 15011, 15027, 15318 (°*sarva*°), 15338; IV, 206 (°*vāhinīṃ*), 887, 977, 981, 992, 999, 1297, 1428, 1528, 1626 (°*āṇāṃ rājā*, i.e. Duryodhana), 1630, 1708, 1998, 2234; V, †39, 128, 602, †701, †765, 825, 827, 843, 948 (°*āṇāṃ rājā*, i.e. Yūdhishṭhira), †1332 (*medhībhūtaḥ K°āṇāṃ tvaṃ*, sc. Dhṛtarāshṭra), †1333, 1806, †1835, †1847 (°*āṇāṃ pravīre*, i.e. Bhīshma), 2284, †2411 (*saṃsadi K°āṇāṃ*), †2505, 2525, †2577, 2623, 2670, 2711, 3273, 3331, 4181, 4281, 4443, 4851, 4953, 4966 (°*mukhyayoḥ*, i.e. B' īshma and Dhṛtarāshṭra), 5081, 5230, 5269 (the army of D. ryodhana consisting of eleven akshauhiṇīs), 5376, 5717 (°*āṇ n sainapatyaṃ prāpya Gāṅgeyaḥ*, i.e. Bhīshma), 5938 (° *rāṅgadaṃ K°āṇām ādhipatye 'bhyashecayaṃ*, sc. Bhīshma); VI, 4, 26, 28, 126, 635, 1556, 1568, 1584, 1599, 1610, 1613, 2067, 2139 (°*ānīkaṃ*), 2143 (°*āṇāṃ pitāmahaḥ*, i.e. Bhīshma), 2179, 2432, 2577, 2593, 2620 (°*āṇāṃ adhipaḥ*, i.e. Duryodhana), 2883, 2890, 3290, 3299, 3313, 3850, 3921, 3942, 3950, 3951, 4206,

4225, 4319, 4326, 4430 (°*āṇāṃ rājā*, i.e. Duryodhana), 4727, 5310, 5330, 5710 (°*āṇāṃ pitāmahaḥ*, i.e. Bhīshma); VII, 23, 50 (*Bhīshme K°āṇām upāçraye*), 118, 124, 210, 416, 436, 928, 1330, 2000, 2645, 2654, 3078, 3082, 3085, 3735, 3737 (°*endrāṇāṃ*), 4133, 4173, 4192, 4202, 4481, 4729, 4730 (°*sainyasya*), 4734, 4738, 4988, 5259, 5461, 5657, 5856, 5862, 6021, 6104 (°*çreshṭhāḥ*), 6160, 6477, 6481, 6606, 6659, 6986, 7180, 7274, 7296, 7325 (°*āṇām anīkinīṃ*), 7350, 7352, 7655, 7747 (°*saṃkrande*), 7755, 7773, 8358, 8541, 8841, 8900, 8958, 9053 (only in B), 9054, 9170, 9188, 9204, 9234, 9273 (°*nandanāḥ*), 9392 (only in B., C. has *Pauravaiḥ*), 9492, 9495; VIII, 244 (*Yādava-K°ān*), 342, 345, 349, 411, 412, 1077, 1129, 1244, 1255, 1712, 1714, 1947, 2518, 2650, 2685, 2696, 2780, 2903, 3014, 3034, 3079, 3107, †3342, †3348 (*samāgame Sṛñjaya-K°āṇāṃ*), †3352, †3360, †3510, 3637, 3640, 3660, 3749, 3792, 3798, †3846, †3859, †4070, 4121, 4259, 4607, 4893, 4956; IX, 182, 288, 378, 548, 932, 1060, †1076, 1687 (*Pāṇḍu-K°sammardāt*), 1700 (°*āṇāṃ mahārathān*, i.e. Açvatthāman, Kṛpa, and Kṛtavarman), 3504, 3626 (°*āṇāṃ mahārathāḥ*, i.e. Açvatthāman, Kṛpa, and Kṛtavarman); X, 714; XI, 230, 234 (*avigrahe K°āṇāṃ*), 824 (*vaiçasaṃ . . . K°āntakaraṃ*); XII, 1495, 1575 (*Bhīshme K°āṇāṃ dhurandhare*), 1816, 1875 (°*āṇāṃ dhurandhare*, i.e. Bhīshma), 1928 (*Bhīshme K°āṇāṃ dhurandhare*); XIII, 6275 (°*āṇāṃ dhurandhara*, sc. Yudhishṭhira), 7689 (*Bhīshme K°āṇāṃ dhurandhare*), 7781; XIV, 1548, 1550, 1780 (°*endrāṇāṃ*), 2203 (°*āṇāṃ mahāratham*, i.e. Arjuna), 2336 (°*āṇāṃ dhurandhare*, i.e. Arjuna), 2590 (do.); XV, 76, 77 (°*āṇām ādhipatye*), †431 (*striyaḥ K°-Pāṇḍavānāṃ . . . K°rājavaṃçyāḥ*), †439, 872, 1007 (°*yoshitaḥ*).

Kaurava[1] = Arjuna: I, 5409, 6535; III, 1709; VII, 6087.

Kaurava[2] = Babhruvāhana: XIV, 2386.

Kaurava[3] = Bhīmasena: III, 11169 (*Somavaṃçīyaḥ*), 15782; VII, 5660 (only C., B. has *Pāṇḍavaḥ*).

Kaurava[4] = Bhīshma: I, 4120, 4121; II, 1373; III, 8046; V, 5485 (*Gāṅgeyaḥ*), 5728, 5823, 5849, 5972, 7139, 7261; VI, 2495, 3799, 3808, 4933, 5843; VII, 39; XII, 1581, 1949, 1990, 8478, 11178; XIII, 196, 3313, 7741, 7770.

Kaurava[5] = Bhūri: VII, 7361 (*Bh°*), 7399, 7403.

Kaurava[6] = Bhūriçravas: VI, 2814; VII, 5896, 5947, 5953, 6055.

Kaurava[7] = Çatānīka[3]: I, 8044 (*rājarsheḥ*).

Kaurava[8] = Çāntanu: XIII, 2443.

Kaurava[9] = Dhṛtarāshṭra: I, 2744, 7371 (*Dh°*); II, 1971; III, 451, 600, 14823; V, 112, 4122; VI, 2926; VII, 7; VIII, 80; IX, 235, 3574; XI, 347; XII, 1447 (*Dh°*); XV, 61, 89, 122, 365, 373, 385, 734, 801 (°*sya vadhūnāṃ*), 969, 1079 (*rājarsheḥ*).

Kaurava[10] = Duḥçāsana: VI, 5714; VII, 4877, 4938; VIII, 901.

Kaurava[11] = Durmukha: V, 2503 (*D°*); VII, 4036.

Kaurava[12] = Duryodhana: I, 5416, 5732, 7451; III, 14878 (*rājā*), 15125, 15180, 15223 (*D°*), 15274, 15308, 15338, 15517; IV, 1617; V, †1835, 2832, 3037 (*rājā*), 3245 (?), 3248, 3510, 4678, 5228, 5311, 5632, 5671, 5860, 7189, 7198, 7400, 7488, 7621 (*rājā*); VI, 1570, 1585, 1586, 2932, 4117, 4195, 4204, 4241; VII, 1587, 3485, 6535, 6983, 7120, 7123, 7144, 7151, 7445, 7451, 8432, 8923, 8995; VIII, 1387; IX, 2, 340, 812 (?), 1277, 1699, 1740, 3062, 3100, †3242, †3244, 3265 (*rājā Dhārtarāshṭraḥ*), 3336, 3663.

Kaurava[13] = Janamejaya: I, 4081, 5076; II, 513; III, 14865; XIV, 2514; XV, 12.

Kaurava[14] = Pāṇḍu: I, 4445 (*rājā*), 4787 (do.), 4943, †7191.

Kaurava[15] = Somadatta: I, 5707 (*S°*); VII, 6740, 6744, 6926, 7249.

Kaurava[16] = Suhotra: III, 13251.

Kaurava[17] = Vicitravīrya: I, 4125 (*rājā*).

Kaurava[18] = Vidura: V, 3046.

Kaurava[19] = Yudhishṭhira: I, 7581 (°*sya niveçanaṃ*); III, 600, 631, 655, 667, 892, 972 (*Kaunteya*), 2633, 13491, 13600; IV, 1364 (*Dharmarājasya*); V, 7602; VII, 4316; XI, 2 (*rājā Dharmaputraḥ*), 247 (do.); XII, 1496 (*rājā*); XIV, 2092, 2532; XV, 292 (*rājā Kuntīputraḥ*), 734 (*rājā*); XVII, 2 (*rājā*); XVIII, 102.

Kaurava[20] = Yuyutsu: XI, 780 (*Y°*).

Kauravaçārdūla = Janamejaya: III, 1524.

Kauravācāryamukhya = Droṇa: I, 6379 (*Bhāradvājasya*).

Kauravaçreshṭha[1] = Arjuna: XIV, 2252.

Kauravaçreshṭha[2] = Bhīmasena: III, 12412.

Kauravaçreshṭha[3] = Çreṇimat: V, 5919 (so C., but read with B. *K°ṭha*, i.e. Duryodhana).

Kauravaçreshṭha[4] = Dhṛtarāshṭra: VI, 481.

Kauravaçreshṭha[5] = Duryodhana: III, 15286; V, 5919 (only B., C. has by error *K°ṭhaḥ* = Çreṇimat); VII, 7442.

Kauravaçreshṭha[6] = Yudhishṭhira: III, 615, 716, 1963 (*Dharmarājo Yudhishṭhiraḥ*), 13546.

Kauravadāyāda = Bhūriçravas: VI, 3253; VIII, 106 (*Bh°*).

Kauravādhama[1] = Bāhlīka: VII, 7225 (*B°*).

Kauravādhama[2] = Bhīshma: II, 1447.

Kauravāgrya[1] = Bhīshma: XIII, 7710.

Kauravāgrya[2] = Yudhishṭhira: X, †573.

Kauravanandana[1] = Arjuna: I, 6747; VI, 5791; XIV, 2173, 2246.

Kauravanandana[2] = Bhīmasena: III, 11270.

Kauravanandana[3] = Bhīshma: XII, 1964.

Kauravanandana[4] = Dhṛtarāshṭra: XII, 4614; XV, 531 (*rājā*), 785, 962 (*Dh°*).

Kauravanandana[5] = Duryodhana: V, 7290, 7554; IX, 1804.

Kauravanandana[6] = Janamejaya: III, 8407.

Kauravanandana[7] = Pāṇḍu: I, 4424 (*P°*), 4628 (*rājā*).

Kauravanandana[8] = Yudhishṭhira: II, 501; III, 8543; V, 555; XII, 3343, 4349; XIII, 2402, 5689, 5699, 6910; XVI, 1 (*Y°*).

Kauravanandana, pl. (°*āḥ*) = the sons of Pāṇḍu: II, 2021 (*Pāṇḍavāḥ*), III, 10869; IV, 1613.

Kauravanātha = Yudhishṭhira: XIII, 7770 (?).

Kauravarāja = Dhṛtarāshṭra (?): XV, †431 (*striyaḥ . . . K°vaṃçyāḥ*).

Kauravarājapatnī = Draupadī: I, †7211.

Kauravarājaputra = Arjuna: VIII, †4049.

Kauravarshabha[1] = Arjuna: III, 1937.

Kauravarshabha[2] = Pāṇḍu: I, 4410.

Kauravarshabha[3] = Yudhishṭhira: XIV, 2567.

Kauravasattama[1] = Arjuna: VI, †2615.

Kauravasattama[2] = Yudhishṭhira: VI, †2661 (*Dharmarājñā*).

Kauravātmaja = Duryodhana: IV, 2246.

Kauravavaṃçabhṛt = Dhṛtarāshṭra: XV, 640.

Kauravavaṃçavardhana = Yudhishṭhira: IV, †215.

Kauravendra[1] = Bāhlīka: VIII, 180 (*B°*).

Kauravendra[2] = Dhṛtarāshṭra: V, †968; VI, 423; VII, †252, †8139; VIII, †4557; XV, 22, 141, †440, †558, 576.

Kauravendra[3] = Duryodhana: V, †5934, †7233, †7515; VI, 5208 (?), †5799 (*Duryodhanaḥ*), †5813; IX, 3145 (*Suyodhane*), 3311, 3394; XIV, 1785, 1806 (*Suyodhane*).

Kauravendra[4] = Janamejaya: XVIII, 110 (according to C.).
Kauravendra[5] = Yudhishṭhira: III, †12651; VI, 3801; VII, 7025; XII, 11512; XIII, †4588, †7359; XVIII, 110 (according to B., *Y°m*).
Kauraveya, pl. = Kaurava, pl.: I, 5217, 5689, 5690; II, 2349, †2366; III, 313, †14744 (i.e. the Pāṇḍavas); IV, 1136 (do.); V, 126, 601, †1873, 3095, 5407; VI, 2429, 2659, 3956; VII, 3084, 3573, 3835, 5214, †7203, †8176, 8547, 8692; VIII, 48, 2098, 2468; IX, 1190, 1515.
Kauraveya[1] = Arjuna: VII, 5962.
Kauraveya[2] = Bhūriçravas: VII, 5892, 6006, 6026 (*Bh°*).
Kauraveya[3] = Duryodhana: III, 15034, 15194; V, 5268; VII, 7034; IX, 1303, 1764.
Kauraveya[4] = Somadatta: VII, 6739.
Kauraveya, adj. (= Kaurava, adj.): VII, 4857 (*sainyam*, i.e. the army of Duryodhana), 7029 (*sarvasainyāni* = do.).
Kauravī ("daughter of Kauravya") = Ulūpī: XV, 437.
Kauravya, a serpent. § 47 (Sarpanāmak.): I, **35**, 1558 (enumeration).—§ 66 (Sarpasattra): I, **57**, 2153 (*°kulajān nāgān*), 2155 (*°kulajāḥ*, enumeration of the serpents of *K.'s* race who fell into the fire).—§ 248 (Arjunavanavāsap.): I, **214**, 7789 (*°sya nāgasya bhavane*), 7793 (*Airāvatakule jātaḥ K°o nāma pannagaḥ*, father of Ulūpī), 7809 (*°sya niveçanāt*). —§ 564 (Mātalīyop.): V, **103**γ, 3631 (enumeration), 3635 (*°syāryakasya*). — § 785 (Anugītāp.): XIV, **88**, 2604 (*°syātmajā*, i.e. Ulūpī).
Kauravya, pl. (*°āḥ*) = Kaurava, pl.: I, 94 (i.e. Dhṛtarāshṭra, Pāṇḍu, and Vidura), 4914, 5464, 5892 (i.e. the sons of Pāṇḍu); II, 1435; III, 2 (i.e. the Pāṇḍavas); 345, 348, 14705 (i.e. the Pāṇḍavas), 14901, 14903, 15369 (i.e. the Pāṇḍavas); IV, 93 (do.); V, 5348; VI, 362 (so C., but B. has *Kauravya* = Dhṛtarāshṭra), 1569, 1628 (*sutāṃs tava*, i.e. Dhṛtarāshṭra's), 5155 (i.e. the brothers of Duryodhana); VII, 933, 1237, 1549, 5866, 8245, 9110; VIII, 1170, 3012, 3147; XI, 377; XIV, 1794.
Kauravya[1] = Arjuna: I, 6503, 6531; V, 130 (*Kuntīputro Dhanañjayaḥ*); VII, 6321; VIII, 2904; XIV, 391, 398, 2258, 2408; XVI, 139, 205, 244 (*Dhanañjayaḥ*).
Kauravya[2] = Bhīmasena: IV, 718; XIV, 2521; XV, 59.
Kauravya[3] = Bhīshma: I, 4094, 5176, 5187; II, 1478; III, 8249, 8251; V, †692 (*Bh°*), 7067, 7093, 7097, 7256, 7264, 7293, 7366; VI, 2562, 4847, 5318 (?), 5339; VII, 38; XII, 806, 6028, 12045; XIII, 5148, 7721 (*Pitāmaham*), 7769; XIV, 1780 (*Bh°*).
Kauravya[4] = Bhūriçravas: VII, 5880, 6355.
Kauravya[5] = Bṛhadbala: VI, 623 (read *Kausalyaḥ* with B.).
Kauravya[6] = Çāntanu: I, 4126 (*Ç°*), 4148 (*Ç°*).
Kauravya[7] = Dhṛtarāshṭra: I, 4446 (*Dh°*), 5634 (*Dh°*), 5636 (*Dh°*), 5649, 5740 (*Dh°*); II, 1882; III, †224, 339, 351; V, 644, 2459, 2965 (*Dh°*), 3392, 3394, 3396; VI, 321, 362 (only B., C. has *Kauravyāḥ*), 417, 425, 427, 433, 442, 451, 472, 474, 490, 5062; VII, 5, 6, 5006, 5050, 5238, 5248, 5428, 5559, 7834, 8791; VIII, 20, 2362; IX, 70, 779 (so B., C. has *Kauravyo* = Çalya), 1243; X, 36, 363; XI, 339; XV, 34 (*Dh°*), 347, 426 (*rājā*), 737 (do.), 1004.
Kauravya[8] = Duḥçāsana: III, 15105 (*°au*, i.e. Duḥçāsana and Duryodhana); VII, 1685; VIII, 913.
Kauravya[9] = Duryodhana: II, 1721; III, 14867, 14932, 15105 (*°au*, i.e. Duryodhana and Duḥçāsana), 15112; IV, 867 (*rājānaṃ Dhṛtarāshṭrajam*), 882, 946; V, 591, 592, 595, 603 (?), 2469, 5222, 5260, 5679 (*Dhārtarāshṭraṃ Suyodhanam*), 5680, 5998, 7181, 7243, 7355, 7357, 7557 (*rājā Duryodhanaḥ*), 7616; VI, 3467 (*D°*), 5318 (?); VII, 3441, 3860, 6084, 6550, 6559, 6979, 7121 (*pārthivaḥ*), 7126, 8430, 8992, 9008; VIII, 1360; IX, 1275, 1403 (*D°*), 1841, 1951 (*D°*), 3216; X, 506; XII, 119 (*D°*); XIV, 1495 (*Dhṛtarāshṭrajaḥ*).
Kauravya[10] = Janamejaya: I, 2675, 2697, 4636, 4875, 5842, 8429; II, 840; III, 12315, 12557, 14872; IV, 511; VIII, 4; IX, 2281, 2382, 2627, 2639; XIII, 7723, 7759; XIV, 1731, 1903, 2072, 2199, 2231, 2383, 2450, 2484 (read *Kauravya* with B.); XV, 302, 634; XVII, 27, 29; XVIII, 81, 157.
Kauravya[11] = Jayatsena[4]: IX, 1412.
Kauravya[12] = Pāṇḍu: I, 4578, 4782 (*P°*); V, 5006.
Kauravya[13] = Sahadeva: II, 1106, 1158.
Kauravya[14] = Somadatta: I, 6994 (*S°*); II, 1267 (*S°*).
Kauravya[15] = Suhotra: III, 13251, ††13255.
Kauravya[16] = Vicitravīrya: I, 4143.
Kauravya[17] = Yudhishṭhira: I, 5871 (*Y°*); II, 283, 1298, 1338 (?); III, 606, 610, 629, 630, 650, 665, 687, 704, 712, 727, 1320, 1993, 2220, 8311, 8318, 8393, 8595, 8616, 13600, 14241, 14485, 15622 (*rājā Kuntīputro Yudhishṭhiraḥ*); IV, 491, 587 (*Ajātaçatrum*), 1368 (*Y°*), 2230, 2289 (*Y°*); VI, 13, 3794 (*Y°*), 3835 (*Y°*), 5756; VII, 815, 4276; XII, 498, 651, 2009, 2163, 2472, 2650, 2700, 4416, 4441, 5425, 5892, 5897, 5942, 6102, 9552, 10109, 10153, 10161, 10204, 12197, 12199; XIII, 2140, 2247, 2346, 2371, 2375, 3017, 3051, 3429, 3887, 4219, 4329, 6931, 7715, 7737; XIV, 113, 359, 1528 (*Dharmarāje Yudhishṭhire*), 2103; XV, 46, 236, 244, 769 (*Y°*), 1002; XVII, 19 (*rājā K°o Dharmaputro Yudhishṭhiraḥ*); XVIII, 61 (*rājā*), 86 (do).
Kauravya[18] = Yuyutsu: VII, 2951 (*Y°*); XIV, 1805 (*Y°*), 1894 (*Yuyutsuṃ Dhṛtarāshṭrajam*).
Kauravyadāyāda = Pāṇḍu: I, 4918 (*P°*).
Kauravyaduhitṛ ("the daughter of Kauravya [the serpent]") = Ulūpī: XIV, 2425 (? PCR. translates "the daughter(-in-law) of Kuru's house" = Citrāṅgadā).
Kauravyakulanandinī (do.) = Ulūpī: XIV, 2402 (PCR. translates "the daughter-in-law of Kuru's race").
Kauravyamukhya = Bhūriçravas: VII, 5875.
Kauravyapatnī = Kuntī: V, 4914 (*Vārshṇeyī*).
Kausalya[1] (C. Kauç°) ("the king of the Kosalas") = Bṛhadbala: V, 5765 (*B°*); VI, 623 (*B°*, only in B., C. has by error *Kauravyaḥ*), 3534 (*B°*), 3855 (*B°*), 5325 (*B°*), 5408; VII, 1964 (has been slain by Abhimanyu), 2575 (all. to his encounter with Abhimanyu); XI, 790 (his corpse is burnt).
Kausalya[2] (C. Kauç°) (do.) = Bṛhadratha: V, 7612 (*Bṛhadrathaḥ*; read *Bṛhadbalaḥ* ?).
Kausalya[3] (C. Kauç°) (do.) = Vasumanas: XII, 2537 (*V°*), 2541, 2595.
Kausalya[4] (C. Kauç°) (do.) = Kshemadarçin: XII, 3059, 3066, 3123, 3124, 3858, 3874, 3876, 3887, 3922, 3951, 3955.
Kausalya, pl. (C. Kauç°) (*°āḥ*), a people = Kosala, pl. § 608 (Karṇap.): VIII, **47**κ, 2226.
Kausalyā[1] (C. Kauç°), wife of Pūru. § 156 (Pūruvaṃç.): I, **95**, ††3764 (mother of Janamejaya[6]).
Kausalyā[2] (C. Kauç°) = Ambikā: I, 4266, 4267, 4269, 4275, 4286.
Kausalyā[3] (C. Kauç°) = Ambālikā: I, 4471, 4472, 4614, 4912, 4955, 4974.
Kausalyā[4] (C. Kauç°), wife of Daçaratha and mother of Rāma. § 525 (Rāmopākhyānap.): III, **274**, 15879 (*Rāmasya mātā*).—§ 527 (do.): III, **277**, 15962, 15980.
Kausalyā[5] (C. Kauç°), wife of Janaka. § 624 (Rājadh.): XII, **18**, 546.

Kausalyāmātṛ (C. Kauç°) (do.) = Rāma Dāçarathi: III, 16302, 16572.
Kausalyānandavardhana (C. Kauç°) ("the son of Kausalyā" [i.e. Ambālikā]) = Pāṇḍu: I, 4466.
Kausalyānandivardhana (C. Kauç°) ("the son of Kausalyā") = Rāma Dāçarathi: III, 15957.
Kausalyātmajā (C. Kauç°), dual (°e) = Ambikā and Ambālikā: I, 3804.
Kaushika = Mahāpurusha (Mahāpurushastava).
Kaustubha, the jewel of Kṛshṇa (Vishṇu). § 28 (Amṛtamanthana): I, **18**, 1147 (*maṇir divyaḥ*, emerged when the gods churned the milky ocean).—§ 521 (Draupadīharaṇap.): III, **263**, 15533 (°*bhūshaṇa*, sc. Kṛshṇa).—§ 562 (Bhagavadyānap.): V, **94**, 3343 (*maṇim*, worn by Kṛshṇa).—§ 564 (Mātalīyop.): V, **102**, 3613 (*maṇiratnam*, arose at the churning of the [milky] ocean).—§ 608 (Karṇap.): VIII, **46**, 2181 (*atyartham bhrājate Kṛshṇe K°s tu maṇis tataḥ*); **76**, †3855 (*urasi*—sc. Kṛshṇa's—*K°ñ ca jājvalyamānam*).—§ 637 (Rājadh.): XII, **45**ε, 1546 (°*enorasisthena maṇinābhirājitam*, sc. Kṛshṇa). Cf. Kirīṭa-Kaustubhadhara.
Kautsa, a brahman. § 59 (Sarpasattra): I, **53**, 2046 (= Jaimini?, among the priests at the snake-sacrifice of Janamejaya).—§ 767 (Ānuçāsanik.): XIII, **137**, 6270 (Bhagīratha attained to heaven by giving his daughter Haṃsī to *K.*).
Kavacin, a son of Dhṛtarāshṭra. § 130 (Aṃçāvat.): I, **67**, 2738.—§ 182 (Dhṛtarāshṭraputranāmak.): I, **117**, 4550.—§ 608 (Karṇap.): VIII, **51**δδ, 2446 (attacked Bhīmasena); **84**ξ[1], 4262 (do., is slain by Bhīmasena).
Kavasha, a ṛshi. § 665 (Mokshadh.): XII, **208**η, 7596 (one of the ṛshis of the west).
Kāverakā, a river in Çākadvīpa. § 575*b* (Çākadvīpa): VI, **11**γ, 432.
Kāverī, a river. § 268 (Varuṇasabhāv.): II, **9**, 372 (among the rivers present in the palace of Varuṇa).—§ 370 (Tīrthayātrāp.): III, **85**, 8164 (a tīrtha).—§ 459 (Mārkaṇḍeyas.): III, **188***a*, 12910 (among the rivers seen by Mārkaṇḍeya in the stomach of Nārāyaṇa).—§ 494 (Āṅgirasa): III, **222**, 14232 (among the rivers who are mothers of fires).—§ 574 (Jambūkh.): VI, **9**λ, 328 (in Bhāratavarsha).—§ 775 (Ānuçāsanik.): XIII, **166***a*, 7646, 7648.
Kavi[1], a ṛshi. § 121 (Aṃçāvat.): I, **66**, 2606 (son of Bhṛgu and father of Uçanas (Çukra), cf. Nīl. ad. I, 3204).—§ 747*b* (Suvarṇotpatti): XIII, **85**, 4123 (sprang together with Bhṛgu and Aṅgiras from the sacrificial fire (viz. from the extinguished coals) into which the seed of Brahmán had fallen), 4142 (was adopted by Brahmán), 4149 (had eight sons named *Vāruṇāḥ*), 4151 (°*sutāḥ*), 4152, 4153 (adopted by Çiva in the shape of Varuṇa).—§ 751*b* (Çapathavidhi): XIII, **94***a*, †4550, (4578).
Kavi[2] = Çukra (Uçanas): I, 3196 (?).
Kavi[3], a Viçvadeva. § 749 (Ānuçāsanik.): XIII, **91**γ, 4361 (enumeration).
Kavi[4], a son of Kavi[1]. § 747*b* (Suvarṇotpatti): XIII, **85**ι, 4150 (first son of Kavi).
Kavi[5] = Vishṇu (1000 names).
Kavi[6] = Agni: XIII, 7220 (cursed by Aṅgiras).
Kaviputra ("the son of Kavi") = Çukra (Uçanas): I, 3204.
Kavisuta (do.) = Çukra (Uçanas): I, 2606 (*grahaḥ*).
Kāvya[1], a son of Kavi[1]. § 747*b* (Suvarṇotpatti): XIII, **85**ι, 4150 (second son of Kavi[1] = Çukra?).—Do.[2] = Çukra, q.v.

Kāyaçodhana, a tīrtha. § 364 (Tīrthayātrāp.): III, **83**, 6012.
Kāyavya, name of a robber. § 643*b* (Kāyavyacarita): XII, **135**, 4854 (*Naishādiḥ*), (4864), 4874, 4875, 4876 (°*caritam*).
[Kāyavya-carita(m)] ("the history of Kāyavya"): § 643*b* (Āpaddh.): There was a robber *Kāyavya*, born of a *Kshatriya* father and a *Nishāda* mother. *K.* was a practiser of *kshatriya* duties, conversant with the scriptures, free from cruelty, devoted to the *brahmans*, etc. Morning and evening he went deer-hunting; he was well conversant with all the practices of the *Nishādas*, and of all animals living in the forest, etc. Alone he could vanquish many hundreds of soldiers. He worshipped his old, blind, and deaf parents in the forest every day, etc. One day many thousands of robbers made him their leader, promising not to slay women, *brahmans*, etc. By abstaining from sin they obtained great prosperity. *Kāyavya*, though a robber, still succeeded in winning felicity in heaven * (XII, **135**).
Keçarin[1], name of a monkey, v. Kesarin.
Keçarin[2], a mountain in Çākadvīpa. § 575*b* (Çākadvīpa): VI, **11**, 424 (only C., B. has *Kesaraḥ*, q.v.).
Keçava = Kṛshṇa (Vishṇu), q.v.
Keçavāgraja ("the elder brother of Keçava" [i.e. Kṛshṇa]) = Balarāma: IX, 2062, 3135.
Keçavanandana ("the son of Keçava" [i.e. Kṛshṇa]) = Pradyumna: III, 723, 754.
Keçavapūrvaja ("the elder brother of Keçava" [i.e. Kṛshṇa]) = Balarāma: IX, 1965, 2978.
Keçayantrī, a mātṛ. § 615*u* (Skanda): IX, **46**θ, 2635.
Keçihan, Keçihantṛ = Kṛshṇa (Vishṇu), q.v.
Keçin[1], an Asura. § 92 (Aṃçāvat.): I, **65**, 2531 (son of Danu).—§ 495 (Skandotpatti): III, **223**, 14248, (14251), 14252, 14253, 14254; **224**, 14257, 14259 (*mahāsuraḥ*; *K.* had ravished Daityasenā, but was defeated by Indra when he tried to ravish Devasenā).—§ 785 (Anugītāp.): XIV, **69**, 2031 (had been slain by Kṛshṇa).—§ 793 (Mausalap.): XVI, **6**κ, 158 (do.).
Keçin[2]. § 412 (Ashṭāvakrīya): III, **134**, 10670 (?, *trayodaçāhāni sasāra Keçī; agnir vāyuḥ sūryaç ca keçinaḥ iti vaidikaprasiddheḥ*, Nīl.).
Keçinī[1], an Apsaras. § 103 (Aṃçāvat.): I, **65**, 2558 (daughter of Prādhā and Kaçyapa).
Keçinī[2], wife of Ajamīḍha. § 152 (Puruvaṃç.): I, **94**, 3722 (mother of Jahnu, Vrajana, and Rūpin).
Keçinī[3], the maidservant of Damayantī. § 353 (Nalopākhyānap.): III, **74**, 2890, (2895), (2899), (2902), 2906, 2912, 2920; **75**, 2921, 2922, 2924, 2926, (2928), 2940, 2943, 2945, 2948; **76**, 2951, 2952.
Keçinī[4]. § 506 (Skandayuddha): III, **231**, 14562 (followed Pārvatī, i.e. Umā).
Keçinī[5]. § 558 (Virocana): V, **35**, 1185, 1186, 1187, (1188), 1189, (1190), 1193, 1194 (the dispute of Virocana and Sudhanvan on account of *K.*).
Keçinishūdana, Keçisūdana = Kṛshṇa, q.v.
Kedāra[1], a mountain in Çākadvīpa. § 575*b* (Çākadvīpa): VI, **11**, 427 (= Keçarin, v. 424?, B. reads *Kesara* in both passages).
Kedāra(ḥ) Kapilasya, v. Kapilasya kedāra(ḥ).
Kedāra(ḥ) Kapishṭhalasya, v. Kapishṭhalasya kedāra(ḥ).
Kedāra(ḥ) Mataṅgasya, v. Mataṅga.
Kekaya, pl. (°*āḥ*), a people, especially five brothers, princes of the Kekayas, who joined Yudhishṭhira (the rest followed Duryodhana). § 402 (Tīrthayātrāp.): III, **120**, †10284

(? *sa-K°ç Cedipatiḥ*). — § 556 (Sañjayayānap.): V, **30,** †889 (in the army of Duryodhana).—§ 561 (Yānasandhip.): V, **50**γ, 1973 (have joined Yudhishṭhira), 2004 (*bhrātaraḥ pañca*); **53**θ, 2107 (in the army of Yudhishṭhira); **54,** 2137 (*Pāñcālāç ca sa-K°āḥ*); **55**κ, 2145.—§ 569 (Bhagavadyānap.): V, **141**γ, 4780 (*bhrātaraḥ*, had joined Yudhishṭhira).—§ 572 (Rathātirathasaṅkhyānap.): V, **160,** 5417 (*Somakaiḥ sa-K°aiḥ*, follow Yudhishṭhira).—§ 574 (Jambūkh.): VI, **9**μ, 356 (among the peoples in Bhāratavarsha).—§ 578 (Bhīshmavadhap.): VI, **47**ε, 1837 (only B., = the five brothers?, C. has by error *Kaikayaḥ*); **49**μ, 2022 (are slain by Bhīshma); **50,** 2088 (followed Virāṭa).—§ 579 (do.): VI, **52**γ, 2141 (*Prācya-Sauvīra-K°āḥ*, followed Bhīshma).—§ 582 (do.): VI, **74,** 3271 (*dhanurvedaviçāradāḥ*, = the five brothers?, support Arjuna).—§ 583 (do.): VI, **75**δ, 3295 (*Madra-Sauvīra-K°āḥ*, in the *krauñca* array of Bhīshma); **79**ν, 3470, 3501 (*pañca sodarāḥ*), 3503 (*bhrātaraḥ*).—§ 585 (do.): VI, **95**εε, 4271 (the five brothers?), 4308 (do.), (ζζ), 4321 (do.). — § 590 (Droṇābhishekap.): VII, **1***a*, 577 (the five brothers?, C. has *Kaikeyaḥ*).—§ 592 (Saṃçaptakavadhap.): VII, **20**θ, 877 (attack Droṇa); **22**ν, 926 (defeated by Droṇa), (ξ), 942 (follow Bhīmasena); **24**σ, 1052 (had sided with Yudhishṭhira). — § 593 (Abhimanyuvadhap.); VII, **35**ζ, 1528 (follow Abhimanyu); **40**ο, 1691 (applaud Abhimanyu).—§ 599 (Jayadrathavadhap.): VII, **95,** 3498 (resisted by Droṇa).—§ 600 (Ghaṭotkaçavadhap.): VII, **158**τ, 6972 (only C., B. has *Kaikeyaiḥ*), 6980.—§ 603 (Nārāyaṇāstramokshap.): VII, **193**γ, 8919 (fought with Açvatthāman). —§ 605 (Karṇap.): VIII, **13,** 508 (the Kekaya princes Vinda and Anuvinda are slain by Sātyaki).—§ 608 (do.): VIII, **68**λλλ, 3390 (*jetā Madra-Kaliṅga-K°ān*, said of Arjuna in a prophecy).—§ 615 (Gadāyuddhap.): IX, **55**π, 3122. — § 619 (Strīvilāpap.): XI, **22**η, 628 (followed Jayadratha, when he robbed Draupadī; all. to § 522); **25**κ, 720 (*bhrātaraḥ pañca*, had been slain by Droṇa).—§ 620 (Çrāddhap.): XI, **26**β, 791 (i.e. the five brothers?, their corpses are burnt). — § 641 (Rājadh.): XII, **77,** 2889 (*°ānām adhipatiṃ* = Kaikaya[4]).—§ 787*b* (Çatayūpa): XV, **19,** 529 (ruled by Çatayūpa). Cf. the numerous passages, where B. has Kekaya instead of the reading of C.: Kaikaya (q.v.) or Kaikeya (q.v.).

Kekayādhipati = Sahasracitya: XV, 543 (*S*°).

Kekayarājaputra, v. Kaikayarājaputra.

Kelikala = Çiva (1000 names[1]).

Keraka, pl. (*°āḥ*), a people. § 284 (Sahadeva): II, **31,** 1173 (only C., B. has *Keralān*, q.v.).

Keraḷa, pl. (*°āḥ*), a people. § 223 (Vāsishṭha): I, **175,** 6685 (*Hūṇān sa-K°ān*, among the peoples who sprang from the froth of Vasishṭha's cow).—§ 284 (Sahadeva): II, **31,** 1173 (in the south, vanquished by Sahadeva; only B., C. has *Kerakān*), 1174 (*Draviḍāṃç caiva sahitāṃç codra-K°aiḥ*, vanquished by Sahadeva).—§ 574 (Jambūkh.): VI, **9,** [352 (*°aṃ*, error in C. for *kevalaṃ*, B.)], (ν), 366 (in the south).—§ 605 (Karṇap.): VIII, **12**ββ, 455 (*Colāḥ sa-K°āḥ*, in the army of Yudhishṭhira).—§ 607 (do.): VIII, **44**κ, 2066.

Kerala, sg. ("the king of the Keralas"). § 515 (Karṇadigvijaya): III, **254,** 15250 (caused by Karṇa to pay tribute to Duryodhana).

Kesara, a mountain in Çākadvīpa. § 575*b* (Çākadvīpa): VI, **11,** 424 (only B., C. has *Keçarī*), 427 (only B., C. has *Kedārasya*).

Kesarin (*Keç°*, C.), name of a monkey. § 425 (Hanūmad-Bhīmasenasaṃv.): III, **147,** 11193 (Hanūmat was begotten by Vāyu with the wife of *K.*).—§ 608 (Karṇap.): VIII, **68,** †3402 (*°naḥ sutasya*, i.e. Hanūmat, on the banner of Arjuna).

Ketu[1], name of a certain demon (or planet), originally the tail or body of Rāhu. § 608 (Karṇap.): VIII, **87,** 4464 (*Rāhu-K°ū yathā*).

Ketu[2] = Çiva (1000 names[2]).

Ketu, pl. (*°avaḥ*), a kind of ṛshis. § 630 (Rājadh.): XII, **26***a*, 774 (have attained to heaven by means of study).

Ketuçṛṅga, an ancient king. § 6 (Anukram.): I, **1***a*, 230 (in Sañjaya's enumeration of departed kings).

Ketudharman, the younger brother of the Trigarta king Sūryavarman. § 785 (Anugītāp.): XIV, **74,** 2154, 2155, 2156 (is slain by Arjuna).

Ketumāla, a varsha. § 574 (Jambūkh.): VI, **6**δ, 207, 226 (*d:* On the western side of *Meru* is *K.*, there is also *Jambūkhaṇḍa.* There the duration of human life is 100,000 years; the men are all of golden complexion, and the women are like *Apsarases*; all the residents are without sickness or sorrow).

Ketumālā, a tīrtha. § 377 (Dhaumyatīrthak.): III, **89,** 8368 (among the sacred places of the west).

Ketumālin = Çiva (1000 names[2]).

Ketumat[1], an Asura. § 92 (Aṃçāvat.): I, **65,** 2532 (son of Danu).—§ 130 (do.): I, **67,** 2646 (incarnate as king Amitaujas).

Ketumat[2], various princes. § 264 (Sabhākriyāp.): II, **4**β, 122 (waited upon Yudhishṭhira), 127 (the same?, do.).—§ 576 (Bhagavadgītāp.): VI, **17,** 668 (followed the Kaliṅga king), 671, 673 (in the army of Duryodhana). — § 578 (Bhīshmavadhap.): VI, **51,** 2110 (do.).—§ 579 (do.): VI, **54,** 2239 (*Naishādaṃ*, followed Çrutāyus, the Kaliṅga king), 2240, 2310 (is slain by Bhīmasena), 2354.—§ 589 (Droṇābhishekap.): VII, **10,** 349 (*d: yo'vadhīt K°ān vīro rājaputraṃ durāsadaṃ | apakrāntaṃ giridvāre* (*aparāntagi°*, B.); proceeded against Droṇa).

Kevalī, a city? § 515 (Karṇadigvijaya): III, **254,** 15245 (conquered by Karṇa on his digvijaya).

Kha(ṃ) = Sūrya (the Sun): III, 147. —Do.[2] = Kṛshṇa: III, 481.—Do.[3] = Çiva (1000 names[1]).

Khacara = Çiva (1000 names[2]).

Khacārin = Skanda: III, 14635.

Khaça or **Khasa,** pl. (*°āḥ*), a barbarous people. § 223 (Vāsishṭha): I, **175,** 6684 (only B.: *Khasān* instead of *Vaçān*, C., arose from the froth of Vasishṭha's cow).—§ 295 (Dyūtap.): II, **52,** 1859 (*°s°*, brought tribute to Yudhishṭhira).—§ 571 (Ulūkadūtāgamanap.): V, **160**γ, 5510 (*°ç°*, in the army of Duryodhana); **161,** 5555 (do., do.).—§ 589 (Droṇābhishekap.): VII, **11**ν, 399 (*°s°*, C.; *°ç°*, B., had formerly been vanquished by Kṛshṇa).—§ 599 (Jayadrathavadhap): VII, **121**θθ, 4847 (*°ç°*, C.; *°s°*, B., fought with Sātyaki).—§ 605 (Karṇap.): VIII, **20,** 779 (*°s°*, mangled by the Pāṇḍya king).—§ 607 (do.): VIII, **44**λ, 2070 (*°ç°*). —§ 608 (do.): VIII, **73,** 3652 (*°ç°*, had been vanquished by Arjuna).

Khaçira (*Khā°*, B.), pl. (*°āḥ*), a people. § 574 (Jambūkh.): VI, **9**ο, 375.

Khaḍga, a warrior of Skanda. § 615*u* (Skanda): IX, **45**η, 2569.

Khaḍgajihva = Çiva (1000 names[1]).

Khaḍgin = Çiva (1000 names[2]).

[Khaḍgotpattikathana(ṃ)] (the narrative of the origin of the sword). § 656 (cf. Āpaddh.): Nakula (*b*) questioned Bhīshma as to which (the sword or the bow) is really the foremost of weapons, and how the sword was first created and for what purpose, and who was the first instructor in the use of that weapon. Bhīshma related that in ancient times the universe was one vast expanse of water, enveloped in darkness, etc. There *Pitāmaha* (i.e. *Brahmán*) took his birth, he then created wind, fire, etc., and then assuming a visible form he begot *Marīci*, etc. (*a*) [and *Pracetas*; the last begot] *Daksha* (*c*). When *Sarvaloka-pitāmaha* (i.e. *Brahmán*) had called into existence all creatures he promulgated the eternal religion laid down in the *Vedas*. That religion was accepted by the gods with their preceptors and priests, and by Ā., V., R., S., M., A., *Bhṛgu*, *Atri*, *Aṅgiras*, Si., the *Kāçyapas*, *Vasishṭha*, etc. (β); all of them lived in obedience to *Brahmán*. But the foremost of the *Dānavas*, *Hiraṇyakaçipu*, etc. (γ), and many other *Daityas* and *Dānavas*, filled with wrath and covetousness, took delight in all kinds of wicked acts, etc., wielding only the rod of chastisement; those foremost of *Asuras* forsook every kindly intercourse with other creatures. Then *Brahmán* with the *Brahmarshis* proceeded to a delightful summit of *Himavat*, and after 1,000 years he arranged a sacrifice. From the sacrificial fire arose *Asi* ("the sword") (*d*), which *Brahmán* gave to *Rudra* (i.e. *Çiva*) in order to enable him to put down irreligion. *Rudra* (description) with the sword destroyed and dispersed the *Asuras* (*Dānavas*); some of them penetrated into the bowels of the earth, others got under the cover of the mountains, some went upwards, others entered the depths of the sea. *Rudra* then gave the sword to *Vishṇu*, *Vishṇu* to *Marīci*, *Marīci* to the *maharshis*, the *maharshis* to *Vāsava* (i.e. *Indra*), *Mahendra* (i.e. *Indra*) to the *lokapālas*, the *lokapālas* to *Manu* (*e*) the son of *Sūrya*. He gave it to his son *Kshupa*. Thence it passed successively to *Ikshvāku*, etc. (δ), from *Droṇa* to *Kṛpa*, from *Kṛpa* to thee (*Nakula*) and thy brothers. *Kṛttikāḥ* is the *nakshatra* of the sword, *Agni* its deity, *Rohiṇī* its *gotra*, *Rudra* its high preceptor. Its eight mysterious names are *Asi*, etc. (ε). Of all weapons the sword is the foremost; the *Purāṇas* truly declare that it was first wielded by *Maheçvara* (i.e. *Çiva*). *Pṛthu* (*Vainya*) (*f*) created the first bow. Persons skilled in weapons should always worship the sword. Blessing to the reader (XII, **166**).

Khaga[1], a serpent. § 564 (Mātalīyop.): V, **103**γ, 3626.

Khaga[2] = Çiva (1000 names[2]).

Khagama, a brahman. § 25 (Sahasrapād): I, **11**, 995 (cursed Sahasrapād to become a *duṇḍubha*).

Khagarāj = Garuḍa: IX, 922.

Khagoçvara = do.: I, †1255.

Khalin = Çiva (1000 names[2]).

Khalin, pl. (°*āḥ*), a *gaṇa* of Dānavas. § 772*l* (Vasishṭha): XIII, **156**, 7281 (*Dānavāḥ*), 7286, 7288 (*halāç ca Kh°o yatra sa deçaḥ khalino 'bhavat*).

***khanaka** ("miner"): I, 5798, 5813, 5817 (°*sattamāt*).

Khaṇḍakhaṇḍā, a mātṛ. § 615*u* (Skanda): IX, **40**θ, 2638.

Khaṇḍaparaçu = Vishṇu (Kṛshṇa): XII, 13276 (etymology), XIII, 7010 (1000 names).

Khāṇḍava, name of a forest. § 4 (Anukram.): I, **1**, 150 (all. to Khāṇḍavadahanaparvan).—§ 11 (Parvasaṅgr.): I, **2**, 363 (*dahanaṃ Kh°sya*, do.), 403 (°*sya dāhanaṃ*, do.).—§ 17 (Uttaṅka): I, **3**, 802 (Takshaka had formerly dwelt in Kurukshetra and *Kh°*).—§ 71 (Ādivaṃçāvatāraṇap.): I, **61**, 2275 (all. to Khāṇḍavadahanaparvan).—§ 190*d* (Arjuna): I, **123**, 4797 (do., in a prophecy).—§ 254 (Khāṇḍavadahanap.): I, **223**, 8083, 8088 (the abode of Takshaka, and therefore protected by Indra), 8092 (Agni wished to consume *Kh.*).—§ 255 (Agniparābhava): I, **223**, 8094, 8095, 8096, 8097, 8148 (*vanam*), 8151, 8152 (Agni seven times in vain tried to consume *Kh.*).—§ 256 (do.): I, **224**, 8159, 8161, 8162 (Brahmán advises Agni to apply to Arjuna and Kṛshṇa).—§ 256*b* (Khāṇḍavadahanap.): I, **224**, 8166.—§ 257 (do.): I, **225**, 8208 (*dāvaṃ*, Agni began to consume *Kh.*).—§ 258 (do.): I, **226**, 8212 (*pakshiṇaḥ Kh°ālayāḥ*), 8214, 8222, 8227, 8229; **227**, 8234 (*vanaṃ*), 8284 (*prāṇinaḥ Kh°ālayāḥ*); **228**, 8285 (°*ālayāḥ*), 8300, 8305, 8310 (°*ālayāḥ*) (Kṛshṇa and Arjuna prevented the residents of *Kh.* from escaping; Indra and the gods engaged in battle with them, but were vanquished; Açvasena, the son of Takshaka, escaped, and the Asura Maya was spared).—§ 259 (Çārṅgakop.): I, **229**, 8349, 8350, 8362 (*dāvaṃ*), 8363; **231**, 8401; **232**, 8428 (*dāvaṃ*) (the story of the *çārṅgakas* who dwelt in *Kh.*).—§ 260 (Khāṇḍavadahanap.): I, **234**, 8465.—§ 331 (Kairātap.): III, **39**, 1596 (all. to Khāṇḍavadahanap.).—§ 340 (Indralokābhigamanap.): III, **48**, 1927 (do.); **49**, 1953 (do.).—§ 437 (Yakshayuddhap.): III, **160**, 11682 (do.).—§ 549*c* (Arjuna): IV, **2**, 38 (do.).—§ 551 (Kīcakavadhap.): IV, **19**, 571 (do.).—§ 552 (Goharaṇap.): IV, **36**, 1188 (do.); **37**, 1211 (do.), †1229 (do.); **45**, 1431 (do.).—§ 556 (Sañjayayānap.): V, **22**, †657 (do.).—§ 561 (Yānasandhip.): V, **52**, 2094 (thirty-three years had passed since Arjuna gratified Agni in *Kh.*); **60**, 2366 (all. to Khāṇḍavadahanaparvan); **62**, †2418 (do.).—§ 570*e* (Gāṇḍīva): V, **158**, 5356 (do.).—§ 570 (Sainyaniryāṇap.): V, **158**, 5375 (do.).—§ 585 (Bhīshmavadhap.): VI, **98**μμ, 4453 (do.).—§ 589 (Droṇābhishekap.): VII, **11**, 402 (do.).—§ 601 (Droṇavadhap.): VII, **185**γ, 8433 (do.).—§ 607 (Karṇap.): VIII, **42**, †1985 (do.).—§ 608 (Karṇap.): VIII, **46*a***, 2130 (do.); **68**λλλ, †3390 (do.); **79**, †4052 (do.); **87**ω', 4441 (do.); **89***a*ε', †4564 (do.); **90**, †4634 (°*dāhamuktaḥ*, sc. Açvasena, all. to § 258), †4680 (all. to Khāṇḍavadahanap.).—§ 613 (Gadāyuddhap.): IX, **34**ι, 1921 (°*e Agnim ivārjunaḥ*, do.).—§ 615 (do.): IX, **56**ρ, 3145 (°*e Pāvako yathā*, do.).—§ 773*b* (Kṛshṇa Vāsudeva): XIII, **159**, †7378 (all. to Khāṇḍavadahanaparvan).—§ 792 (Nāradāgamanap.): XV, **38*a***, 1067 (do.).—§ 794 (Mahāprasthānikap.): XVII, **1**, 38 (do.).

Khāṇḍavadāha ("the burning of the Khāṇḍava forest"): § 10 (Parvasaṅgr.): I, **2**, 316 (°*ākhyaṃ parva*, i.e. Khāṇḍavadahanaparvan).

[Khāṇḍavadahanaparvan(°va)], the 19th of the minor parvans, in *C.*, including also Mayadarçanaparvan, in all I, **222–34** (cf. Khāṇḍavadāha). § 254: At the instance of Dhṛtarāshṭra and Bhīshma the Pāṇḍavas at Indraprastha began to bring other kings under their sway. All the subjects lived happily. Once, in the summer, Arjuna and Kṛshṇa sported on the banks of the Yamunā with Draupadī and Subhadrā, etc. They were then approached by a brahman, whose complexion was like molten gold (I, **222**). It was Agni. He asked them to help him to consume the forest of Khāṇḍava and the creatures therein; for Indra always prevented him from consuming it, because he was a friend of the Nāga Takshaka, who dwelt there with his followers and family.—§§ 255–6, *a* (Agniparābhava, q.v.): the antecedents of the Khāṇḍavad. (I, **223**, **224**).—§ 256, *b*: Arjuna said that he wanted a stronger bow and inexhaustible arrows, and a resplendent chariot to ride in, and that Kṛshṇa needed a weapon with which he could slay Nāgas and Piçācas (I, **224**).—§ 257: Then Agni thought of Varuṇa (*b*), who presented Arjuna with: (1) the Gāṇḍīva bow (*c*); (2) two inexhaustible quivers; (3) a chariot yoked with horses. Then Agni gave to Kṛshṇa: (1) a discus (Sudarçana) (*d*). Varuṇa, after this, gave to Kṛshṇa: (2) the mace Kaumodakī (*e*). They were then ready to fight, and Agni began to consume the forest (I, **225**).—§ 258: Arjuna and Kṛshṇa prevented the creatures from escaping. Even the gods became afraid and applied to Indra. Indra poured down showers of rain, that were at first dried up in the sky by the heat of the fire (I, **226**). When more rain was poured down, Arjuna dispelled it with a shower of his weapons. Takshaka was not present, having gone to Kurukshetra. But his son Açvasena was there; his mother, a she-snake, attempted to swallow him, but had her head cut off by Arjuna; Indra, raising a violent wind, for a moment deprived Arjuna of his consciousness, during which time Açvasena effected his escape, being cursed by Kṛshṇa, Arjuna, and Agni ("never shalt thou be famous"). Indra assailed Arjuna with clouds, which were dispersed by the Vāyavya weapon, and with a shower of stones, and with a peak from the Mandara, but in vain. Garutmat (Garuḍa) and other birds, and Nāgas, who also assailed Kṛshṇa and Arjuna, were vanquished; and As., G., Y., Rā., and Nāgas were defeated by Arjuna, as were the Dai. and Dā. by Kṛshṇa with his discus. They were also attacked by Yama with his death-dealing mace, Kubera with his spiked club, Varuṇa with his noose and beautiful missile, Skanda with his long lance, the Açvins with resplendent plants, Dhātṛ with his bow, Jaya with a thick club, Tvashṭṛ with a huge mountain, Sūrya with a bright çakti, Mṛtyu with a battle-axe, Aryaman with a bludgeon furnished with sharp spikes, Mitra with a discus sharp as a razor, Pūshan, Bhaga, Savitṛ, R., V., M., V.-D., and S. (I, **227**). With his discus Kṛshṇa slaughtered Pç., N., Rā., Dā., As., etc. The gods retired from the scene. Indra became filled with joy and applauded Kṛshṇa and Arjuna. An incorporeal voice addressed him, saying that Takshaka was in Kurukshetra, and that Kṛshṇa and Arjuna, being the old ṛshis and gods Nara and Nārāyaṇa, were invincible, and that the destruction of the forest of Khāṇḍava had been ordained by fate. Then also Indra went back to heaven. The Vidyādharas, etc., dwelling in that forest, all became frightened. Agni, drinking the nectar-like stream of animal fat, became filled with joy. When the Asura Maya, the brother of Namuci, was about to be slain by Kṛshṇa and burnt by Agni, Arjuna rescued him. Agni burnt the forest for fifteen days, sparing only six of its dwellers: Açvasena, Maya, and four çārṅgakas (a sort of birds, Nīl.) (I, **228**).—§ 259 (Çārṅgakopākhyāna, q.v.): I, **229**, 1–**234**, 4, (8331–8464).—§ 260: When Agni had consumed fat, marrow, and flesh in abundance, and burnt the forest for fifteen days, he became gratified and extinguished himself. Indra, with M., appeared before Kṛshṇa and Arjuna, and granted them a boon. Arjuna asked him to give him all his weapons (both the Āgneya and the Vāyavya), and Indra promised to give them when Mahādeva had been pleased with him. To Kṛshṇa he granted that his friendship with Arjuna should be eternal. Then he ascended to heaven with the celestials. Arjuna, Vāsudeva, and the Dānava Maya, having wandered a little, sat down on the bank of a river (I, **234**).

Khāṇḍavaprastha = Indraprastha, q.v.

Khāṇḍavāyana, pl. (°*āḥ*), a family (?) of brahmans. § 398 (Paraçurāma): III, **117**, 10208 (*tām—sc. vedīm—Kaçyapasyānumate brāhmaṇāḥ khaṇḍaças tadā | vyabhajans te tadā rājan prakhyātāḥ Kh°āḥ*).

Khanīnetra, a king, son of Vivimça and father of Suvarcas. § 778*c* (Saṃvartta-Maruttīya). King *Vivimça* had fifteen sons, all powerful archers, revering brahmans, etc.; the eldest brother *Kh.* oppressed them all, but having conquered the entire kingdom he could not retain it, as the people were not pleased with him; they dethroned him and installed his son *Suvarcas* as king, and then they rejoiced: XIV, **4**, 70, 71.

Khara, a Rākshasa, son of Viçravas. § 526 (Rāmopākhyānap.): III, **275**, 15896 (Rākā bore *Kh.* and Çūrpaṇakhā from Viçravas), 15900 (proficient in archery and hostile to the brahmans), 15907 (*Kh.* and Çūrpaṇakhā attended on Rāvaṇa and Vibhīshaṇa while they were practising austerities).—§ 528 (do.): III, **277**, 15986 (his hostilities with Rāma Dāçarathi on account of Çūrpaṇakhā), 15988 (Rāma slew *Kh.* and Dūshaṇa), 15996.—§ 537 (Rāma-Rāvaṇayuddha): III, **285*a***, 16365 (the same (?), in the army of Rāvaṇa).—§ 599 (Jayadrathavadhap.): VII, **107**, 4040 (*yathā Dāçarathī Rāmaḥ Kh°ṃ hatvā mahābalaṃ*, cf. § 528).

Kharajaṅghā, a mātṛ. § 615*u* (Skanda): IX, **46*θ***, 2640.

Kharakarṇī, a mātṛ. § 615*u* (Skanda): IX, **46*θ***, 2644.

Kharī, a mātṛ. § 615*u* (Skanda): IX, **46*θ***, 2624.

Khaṭṭāṅga, v. Khaṭvāṅga.

Khaṭvāṅga[1], an ancient king. § 61 (Sarpasattra): I, **55**, 2109 (°-*Nābhaga-Dilīpakalpa*, sc. Janamejaya, C. has *Khaṭṭ*°).

Khaṭvāṅga[2] = Dilīpa: VII, 2269 (C. *Khaṭṭ*°).

Khaṭvāṅgadhārin = Çiva: X, 254.

Khaṭvāṅgin = Çiva (1000 names[1]).

***khecara** ("moving in the air") said of the devadūta: I, 972, 974.

Khyātā, a mātṛ. § 615*u* (Skanda): IX, **46*θ***, 2638.

Kīcaka, the senāpati and brother-in-law of Virāṭa. § 11 (Parvasaṅgr.): I, **2**, 483 (*dushṭātmano vadho yatra K°sya Vṛkodarāt*, cf. § 551).—§ 551 (Kīcakavadhap.): IV, **14**, 376 (*senāpatir Virāṭasya*), 377, †383, (384), 416, 424, †429, †430; **15**, 431, (432), 439, 440, 444, 447, 448; **16**, (452), (456), †458, 460, 461, 462, 464, 465, 483, 484, 487, 500, 501; **18**, 527, 529 (*Virāṭasya . . . senānīḥ . . . çyālaḥ*); **21**, 643, 644, 662, 663, 665, 668, 670, 672, 676 (*Virāṭasya . . . sārathiḥ*), 684, 687, 689, 692; **22**, 694, 700, 705, (707), 711, 712, 716, 718, 719, 720, 725, 727, 730, 731, 733, 734, 735, 739, 754, 758, 762, 763, 766, 770, 775, †777, 783, 784, 785, 786, 787, 789 (*vinipātitaṃ*); **23**, 793, 794, 797 (*hataḥ*), 799 (do., the slaughter of *K.* and his relatives by Bhīmasena on account of Draupadī).—§ 552 (Goharaṇap.): IV, **25**, 861, 862, 864, 880 (*b*: *K.* had repeatedly vanquished and slain the Trigartas); **30**, 972 (had several times vanquished the Trigarta king Suçarman), 974; **31**, 1002 (*hataḥ*).—§ 555 (Sainyodyogap.): V, **8**, 223 (all. to § 551).—§ 562 (Bhagavadyānap.): V, **90** *o*, 3151 (°*sya . . . hantā*, i.e. Bhīmasena, cf. § 551).—§ 599 (Jayadrathavadhap.): VII, **139**, 5799 °*o nihato yathā*, all. to § 551).—§ 608 (Karṇap.): VIII, **50**, 2413 (*sagaṇo hataḥ*, do.).—§ 617 (Aishīkap.): X, **11**, 598 (*Virāṭanagare K°ena bhṛçārditām*, sc. Kṛshṇā, do.).—§ 623 (Rājadh.): XII, **16**, 502 (°*ena padā vadhaṃ*, do.).—§ 779 (Açvamedhikap.): XIV, **12*a***, 325 (°*ena padā vadhaḥ*, do.). Cf. Sūtaputra.

Kīcaka, pl. (°*āḥ*), a tribe or family. § 10 (Parvasaṅgr.): I, **2**, 328 (°*ānāṃ vadhaḥ parva*, i.e. Kīcakavadhaparvan).—§ 214 (Hiḍimbavadhap.): I, **156**, 6085 (*Matsyāṃs Trigartān Pañcālān K°ān antareṇa*, the Pāṇḍavas went to Ekacakrā).—§ 551 (Kīcakavadhap.): IV, **22**, 751 (°*ānāṃ mukhyasya*, i.e. Kīcaka), 774 (°*ādhamaṃ*, i.e. Kīcaka); **23**, 801, 811, 827 (105 Kīcakas are slain by Bhīmasena); **24**, 835.—§ 552

(Goharaṇap.): IV, **44,** 1372 (had been slain for the sake of Draupadī).—§ 553 (Vaivāhikap.): IV, **71,** 2293 (*hantā K°ānām,* i.e. Bhīmasena), 2296 (*hatāḥ*). Cf. Sūta, pl., Sūtaputra, pl.

[Kīcakavadhaparvan] ("the slaughter of the Kīcakas"), the 54th of the minor parvans of Mhbhr. § 551: The Pāṇḍavas thus passed ten months in Matsya's city. As the year was about to expire, Kīcaka, the senāpati and brother-in-law of Virāṭa, became enamoured of Kṛshṇā, who rebuked him and warned him of the Gandharvas, her husbands (IV, **14**). Then he caused Sudeshṇā (*Kaikeyī*) to send Kṛshṇā to him to fetch wine. Kṛshṇā adored the Sun, who commanded a Rākshasa to protect her invisibly (IV, **15**). As Kīcaka seized her, she dashed him to the ground and rushed to Yudhishṭhira, followed by Kīcaka, who brought her down and seized her by the hair, but the Rākshasa gave him a push, so that he fell down senseless. Yudhishṭhira, apprehensive of discovery, commanded Bhīmasena to forbear. Kṛshṇā rebuked Virāṭa and was praised by the courtiers, but sent back to Sudeshṇā by Yudhishṭhira: "the Gandharvas will surely dispel thy woe." Sudeshṇā said: "I shall cause Kīcaka to be slain, if thou wishest it." Kṛshṇā answered: "Even others will slay him" (IV, **16**). Kṛshṇā rose up at night and proceeded to Bhīmasena (IV, **17**), and complained of their plight and especially that of Sahadeva (*b*) (IV, **18–21**). Bhīmasena exhorted her to endure a little longer, reminding her of Sukanyā, Indrasenā (*c*), Sītā, Lopāmudrā, and Sāvitrī (IV, **21**), and said: "To-morrow evening you should manage to have a meeting with Kīcaka in the dancing hall, but so that others may not espy thee." Kīcaka came to the rendezvous and was slain by Bhīmasena, and Kṛshṇā said to the keepers of the dancing-hall: "Kīcaka has been slain by my Gandharva husbands" (IV, **22**). Kīcaka's relatives obtained permission from Virāṭa to cremate Kṛshṇā with him, and carried her towards the burning-place. She cried "Jaya", etc. (*a*). Bhīmasena hearing it, came and slew 105 of them with a tree (IV, **23**). Virāṭa got afraid and caused Sudeshṇā to ask Kṛshṇā to leave the country, but she obtained permission to remain for thirteen days (IV, **24**).

Kilakila = Çiva (1000 names[1]).

Kiṃ = Vishṇu (1000 names).

Kiṃjapya, a tīrtha. § 364 (Tīrthayātrāp.): III, **83,** 6049.

Kimpunā, a river. § 268 (Varuṇasabhāv.): II, **9,** 373 (among the rivers present in the palace of Varuṇa).—§ 450 (Mārkaṇḍeyas.): III, **188*a*,** 12910 (seen by Mārkaṇḍeya in the stomach of Narayaṇa).

Kimpurusha, pl. (°*āḥ*), a class of beings. § 113 (Aṃçāvat.): I, **66,** 2572 (among the offspring of Pulaha). — § 279 (Arjuna): II, **28,** 1038 (*deçaṃ K°āvāsaṃ Drumaputreṇa rakshitam,* in the north conquered by Arjuna on his digvijaya). — § 386 (Agastyop.): III, **104,** 8801 (came to see the exploits of Agastya). § 418*c* (Mandara): III, **139,** 10825 (attended upon Māṇibhadra).—§ 423 (Gandhamādanapr.): III, **145,** 11027 (in the north).—§ 432 (Saugandhikāh.): III, **153,** 11359 (at the lotus lake of Kubera). — § 436 (Yakshayuddhap.): III, **158,** 11561 (°*āvāsaṃ . . . Gandhamādanaṃ*), 11620; **159,** 11644 (*kāminaḥ saha kāntābhiḥ*).— § 526 (Rāmopākhyānap.): III, **275,** 15921 (followed Kubera when he settled at Gandhamādana).—§ 533 (Sītā-Rāvaṇas.): III, **281,** 16168 (*deva - Dānava - Gandharva - Yaksha - K°aiḥ*). — § 603 (Nārāyaṇāstramokshap.): VII, **199,** 9196.—§ 638*b* (Kṛtaghnop.): XII, **169,** 6321 (sg. °*o yathā*).—§ 664 (Mokshadh.): XII, **207*ε*,** 7542 (born from a wife of Kaçyapa).—§ 785 (Anugītāp.): XIV, **88,** 2639 (°*saṅkīrṇaḥ,* sc. the açvamedha of Yudhishṭhira).

Kimpurushācārya ("leader of the Kimpurushas") = Druma: II, 1350 (*D*°), 1534 (*D*°).

Kimpurushasiṃha (do.) = Druma: V, 5352.

Kimpurusheça (do.) = Druma: II, 410.

Kindama, a muni. § 183 (Pāṇḍu): I, **118,** 4585 (was slain by Pāṇḍu while he in the shape of a deer had sexual intercourse, therefore he cursed Pāṇḍu).

Kindāna, a tīrtha. § 364 (Tīrthayātrāp.): III, **83** 6049.

Kindatta, a tīrtha. § 364 (Tīrthayātrāp.): III, **83,** 6068 (*kūpaṃ,* C. °*dataṃ*).

Kiṅkara[1], a Rākshasa. § 224 (Kalmāshapāda): I, **176,** 6716 (entered Kalmāshapāda).

Kiṅkara[2], the rod of Mṛtyu or Yama. § 345 (Pativratāmāhātmyap.): III, **298,** 16895 (*Yamaḥ . . . sa-K°aḥ*).— § 608 (Karṇap.): VIII, **50*ββ*,** 2414 (°*odyatadaṇḍena Mṛtyunā*); **56,** 2812 (*yathā kruddho Mṛtyuḥ K°-daṇḍabhṛt*).— § 613 (Gadāyuddhap.): IX, **32,** 1866 (*Vaivasvatam iva K°odyatapāṇim*).—§ 746 (Ānuçāsanik.): XIII, **62*a*,** 3129 (*mṛtyur* [read: *Mṛtyor* ?] *vai K°o daṇḍaḥ*).

Kiṅkara, pl. (°*āḥ*), a tribe of Rākshasas. § 11 (Parvasaṅgr.): I, **2,** 407 (°*āṇāṃ darçanam*). — § 263 (Sabhākriyāp.): II, **3,** 76, 86 (°*ā nāma Rākshasāḥ,* guarded the palace of Yudhishṭhira).—§ 294 (Dyūtap.): II, **48,** 1710 (*Mayenoktāḥ K°ā nāma Rākshasāḥ vahanti tāṃ sabhāṃ,* sc. Yudhishṭhira's, cf. § 263).—§ 785 (Anugītāp.): XIV, **65,** 1918 (Yudhishṭhira offered bali to the *K.*).

Kiṅkiṇikāçrama, a tīrtha. § 733*k* (Vaimānikā): XIII, **25,** 1709.

Kinnara, pl. (*āḥ*), a class of beings. § 28 (Amṛtamanthana): I, **18,** 1113 (°*air Apsarobhiç ca devair api sevitaṃ,* sc. Mandara).—§ 112 (Aṃçāvat.): I, **66,** 2571 (among the offspring of Pulastya).—§ 133 (Dushyanta): I, **70,** 2858 (*matta - vānara - K°ṃ,* sc. *vanaṃ*), 2868 (*nadīṃ . . . sa-K°gaṇāyāsaṃ*). § 222 (Tapatyup.): I, **172,** 6569 (°*odgīta-bhāshinī*). — § 258 (Khāṇḍavadahanap.): I, **228,** 8304 (*Yaksha - Rākshasa - Gandharva - Nara - K°-pannagaiḥ,* worship Kṛshṇa and Arjuna).—§ 264 (Sabhākriyāp.): II, **4,** 132 (*kṛtaniçramāḥ,* sing in the palace of Yudhishṭhira).—§ 269 (Vaiçrāvaṇasabhāv.): II, **10,** 396 (°*ā nāma Gandharvāḥ,* in the palace of Kubera), 409 (*çataçaḥ,* do.).—§ 359 (Vaḍavā): III, **82,** 5036 (at Vaḍava).—§ 370 (Tīrthayātrāp.): III, **84,** 7083 (at Saugandhikavana); **85,** 8168 (at Gokarṇa).— § 377 (Dhaumyatīrthak.): III, **90,** 8391 (*Kirāta-K°āvāsaṃ çailaṃ,* at Gaṅgādvāra).—§ 389 (Gaṅgāvataraṇa); III, **108,** 9929 (on Himavat). § 418*d* (Kailāsa): III, **139,** 10831 (*Yaksha-Rākshasa-K°āḥ,* on Kailāsa).—§ 423 (Gandhamādanapr.): III, **143,** 10968 (°*caritaṃ giriṃ,* i.e. Gandhamādana); **145,** 11027 (*vānara-K°aiḥ*).—§ 424 (Bhīmakadalīkh.): III, **146,** 11083 (*giriṃ . . . K°caritaṃ,* i.e. Gandhamādana). —§ 432 (Saugandhikāh.): III, **153,** 11359 (at Kubera's lotus lake).—§ 436 (Yakshayuddhap.): III, **158,** 11622 (°*sevitāṃ,* sc. *Mahāgaṅgāṃ*).—§ 437 (do.): III, **160,** 11696. —§ 438 (do.): III, **162,** 11813 (followers of Kubera).— § 439 (Ājagarap.): III, **177,** †12339 (*nagottamaṃ prasravaṇair upetaṃ . . . K°pakshibhiḥ*). — § 474 (Mārkaṇḍeyas.): III, **201,** 13485 (*kathāṃ . . . K°āpsarasāṃ*). — § 495 (Skandotpatti): III, **224,** 14264 (*deva-Dānava-Yakshāṇāṃ K°oraga-rakshasāṃ jetā,* i.e. Skanda). — § 526 (Rāmopākhyānap.): III, **275,** 15913 (*sarpa-K°-Bhūtebhyaḥ*). —

§ 542 (Rāvaṇavadha): III, **290,** 16525 (*deva-Dānava-K°āḥ*).—§ 553*b* (Yudhishṭhira): IV, **70,** 2271 (*Gandharva-Yakshapravarāḥ sa-K°mahoragāḥ*). — § 555 (Indravijaya): V, **12,** 369 (*jagat . . . sa-K°mahoragam*); **15,** 464 (*°oraga-Rākshasāḥ*).—§ 596 (Pratijñāp.): VII, **80,** 2848 (*Gaṅgām . . . K°gītanāditām*), 2852 (*Mahā-Mandaram . . . K°aiç caiva çobhitam*).—§ 599 (Jayadrathavadhap.): VII, **111,** 4269 (*pṛthivī . . . sa-K°mahoragā*).—§ 600 (Ghaṭotkacavadhap.): VII, **163,** †7293.—§ 615*u* (Skanda): IX, **46,** 2706.—§ 658*b* (Kṛtaghnop.): XII, **169,** 6323 (*Yaksha-K°sevitam*, sc. *vanam*). — § 674*b* (Çrī-Vāsavas.): XII, **229,** †8425 (*°-Yaksha-Rākshasāḥ*). — § 677 (Mokshadh.): XII, **233,** 8524 (*nara-K°-Rakshāṃsi*).—§ 705 (do.): XII, **303,** 11244 (*trailokye . . . sa-K°mahorage*).—§ 714*b* (Himavat): XII, **328,** 12315 (on Himavat).—§ 717*b* (Nārāyaṇīya): XII, **335,** 12665 (*sa-K°mahoragāḥ*).—§ 730*g* (Upamanyu): XIII, **14,** †643 (*gītaiḥ . . . K°āṇām*, at the hermitage of Upamanyu).—§ 731*b* (Ashṭāvakra-Diks.): XIII, **19,** 1421 (in the palace of Kubera).—§ 746 (Ānuçāsanik.): XIII, **58,** 2998 (*°oraga-Rakshāṃsi*); **83,** 3886 (*°oraga-Rākshasāḥ*).—§ 749 (do.): XIII, **87,** 4224 (*Piçāca-K°āṇām*). — § 757*f* (Nandana): XIII, **102,** †4865 (*°rājajushṭam . . . Nandanam Nāradasya*). — § 768*b* (Umā-Maheçvaras.): XIII, **140***a*, 6344.—§ 782*g* (Guruçishyas.): XIV, **43,** 1183 (*nara-K°-Yakshāṇām . . . īçvaraḥ*); **44,** 1226 (*nara-K°-Yakshāṇām . . . prabhuḥ*).—§ 785 (Anugītāp.): XIV, **63,** 1885; **88,** 2639 (present at the açvamedha of Yudhishṭhira).—§ 786*e* (Agastya): XIV, **92,** 2870 (*Gandharvāç ca sa-K°āḥ*).

Kinnarī (female Kinnara), sg. and pl. § 416 (Yavakrītop.): III, **136,** 10753 (*°īm iva*, sc. the daughter-in-law of Raibhya). — § 436 (Yakshayuddhap.): III, **158,** 11562 (pl., on Gandhamādana).—§ 549 (Pāṇḍavapr.): IV, **9,** 258 (Kṛshṇā is questioned if she is a *K.*, etc.).—§ 757*e* (Meru): XIII, **102,** †4862 (*vanam K° gītajushtam*).

Kirāta, pl. (*°āḥ*), a barbarous people ("hunters"). § 223 (Vāsishṭha): I, **175,** 6684 (among the peoples who sprang from the cow of Vasishṭha).—§ 273 (Rājasūyārambhap.): II, **14,** 584 (*Vaṅga-Puṇḍra-K°eshu*).—§ 279 (Arjuna): II, **26,** 1002 (followed Bhagadatta).—§ 280 (Bhīmasena): II, **30,** 1085 (in the east, seven kings of the *K.* vanquished by Bhīmasena).—§ 285 (Nakula): II, **32,** 1199 (in the west, vanquished by Nakula).—§ 295 (Dyūtap.): II, **52,** 1865 (*carmavāsasaḥ*, brought tribute to Yudhishṭhira). — § 342 (Indralokābhigamanap.): III, **51,** 1990 (present at the rājasūya of Yudhishṭhira).—§ 377 (Dhaumyatīrthak.): III, **90,** 8391 (*°Kinnarāvāsam çailam*, at Gaṅgādvāra).—§ 419 (Gandhamādanapr.): III, **140,** 10864 (*Subāhuvishayam . . . K°-Taṅganākīrṇam*).—§ 555 (Sainyodyogap.): V, **19,** 584 (in the *akshauhiṇī* of Bhagadatta).—§ 561 (Yānasandhip.): V, **64,** 2470, 2475.—§ 573 (Ambopākhyānap.): V, **195**ε, 7609 (in the army of Duryodhana).—§ 574 (Jambūkh.): VI, **9**μ, 358, 364, (ν), 376 (in the north-east).—§ 576 (Bhagavadgītāp.): VI, **20,** †753 (followed Kṛpa).—§ 578 (Bhīshmavadhap.): VI, **50**π, 2080 (in the army of Yudhishṭhira). — § 589 (Droṇābhishekap.): VII, **4**β, 121 (*Himavaddurganilayāḥ*, had been vanquished by Karṇa for Duryodhana).—§ 599 (Jayadrathavadhap.): VII, **112,** 4318, 4320, 4322 (*c*: the *K.* have elephants sprung from the race of *Añjana*, with impenetrable skins, well trained . . . adorned with armour of solid gold, and resembling *Airāvata* and coming from the northern hills, ridden by fierce robbers of strong limbs, the foremost of warriors, cased in steel coats of mail; among them are persons born of the cow, or of the ape, or of various other creatures, and also born of men. That division of the assembled *Mlecchas*, who are all sinful and come from the fastnesses of Himavat, seem at a distance to be of a smoky colour), 4339 (*vishakalpaiḥ prahāribhiḥ*); **119**ββ, 4716 (Sātyaki has vanquished many Çakas, *K.*, etc.), (γγ), 4747 (thousands of *K.*, etc., have been slain by Sātyaki).—§ 608 (Karṇap.): VIII, **73,** 3653 (have been vanquished by Arjuna).—§ 641 (Rājadh.): XII, **65**θ, 2429 (enumeration of barbarous peoples). — § 664 (Mokshadh.): XII, **207**θ, 7560 (among the barbarous peoples of the north).—§ 730*g* (Upamanyu): XIII, **14**η, 732 (*°-Çabarāṇām*, Çiva assumes their form).—§ 739 (Ānuçāsanik.): XIII, **35**ε, 2159 (have been degraded to çūdras).—§ 785 (Anugītāp.): XIV, **73,** 2136 (vanquished by Arjuna, when he followed the sacrificial horse); **83,** 2469 (*Koçalān K°ān atha Taṅganān*).

Kirāta, sg. = Çiva in the shape of a *K.*, when he fought with Arjuna (v. Kairātaparvan): I, †160 (*Devadevam K °rūpam*), 433 (*°vapushā*, sc. *Mahādevena*); III, 1555 (*°veça-saṃchannaḥ*, sc. Çiva), 1561, 1563, 1567, 1572, (1578), 1582, 1586, 1604 (*°rūpī*, sc. Çiva), 1605 (*°samarūpini*, sc. Çiva), 1606, 1607, 1609, 1616, 11956, 11977 (*°rūpam*); IV, 1536 (*°rūpeṇa sthitam Rudram*); VIII, 1251 (*°rūpeṇa sthitam Çarvam*).

Kirātarāja (the king of the Kirātas). § 264 (Sabhākriyāp.): II, **4**β, †119 (*Pulindaḥ?*, waited upon Yudhishṭhira), 120 (*Sumanāḥ?*, do.).—§ 599 (Jayadrathavadhap.): VII, **112,** 4320 (had given elephants to Arjuna).

Kirātarājan (do.) = Subāhu: III, †12349 (*S°*).

Kirīṭabhṛt, Kirīṭamālin, Kirīṭavat = Arjuna, q.v.

Kirīṭakaustubhadhara = Kṛshṇa (Vishṇu Nārāyaṇa): III, 13563; VI, 2994.

Kirīṭin[1] ("having a diadem") = Arjuna, q.v.

Kirīṭin[2] = Nara: I, 1188.

Kirīṭin[3] = Indra: I, 1525 (*devendraḥ*); II, 287; XIII, 765 (Çiva in the shape of Indra), 2276.

Kirīṭin[4] = Çiva: XIII, †981.

Kirīṭin[5], a warrior of Skanda. § 615*u* (Skanda): IX, **45**η, 2573.

Kirīṭitanayātmaja ("the grandson of Kirīṭin [i.e. Arjuna]") = Parikshit: XIV, 1975.

Kirmīra, a Rākshasa. § 11 (Parvasaṅgr.): I, **11,** 425 (*°sya vadhaḥ cātra*, cf. § 316).—§ 315 (Maitreyaçāpa): III, **10,** 368 (*Rakshasaḥ*, had been slain by Bhīmasena), 382, 384 (*°vadha°*). — § 316 (Kirmīravadhap.): III, **11,** 385 (*°sya vadhaḥ*), 407 (*ahaṃ Bakasya vai bhrātā K°a iti viçrutaḥ*), 412, 431, 454 (is slain by Bhīmasena), 460 (*Rakshasāṃ varam*).—§ 600 (Ghaṭotkacavadhap.): VII, **176,** 8007 (kinsman of Alāyudha), 8010 (*Hiḍimba-Baka-K°ā nihatā mama bāndhavāḥ*, says Alāyudha); **180**δδδ, †8211 (*Rākshasendrā Hiḍimba-K°-Bakapradhānāḥ*); **181,** 8235 (*Hiḍimba-Baka-K°ā Bhīmasenena pātitāḥ*).

Kirmīravadha ("the killing of Kirmīra"). § 10 (Parvasaṅgr.): I, **2,** 319 (i.e. Kirmīravadhaparvan).

Kirmīravadhaparvan(°va) ("the section relating to the killing of Kirmīra," the 31st of the minor parvans of Mhbhr.; cf. Kirmīravadha). § 316: *Vidura* had heard it from the *Pāṇḍavas* and now related it to *Dhṛtarāshṭra*. Departing from *Hāstinapura* and travelling for three days and nights the *Pāṇḍavas* reached the *Kāmyaka* wood. At midnight a man-eating *rākshasa*, *Kirmīra*, brother of *Baka* and friend of *Hiḍimba*, obstructed their path with a lighted brand, and would avenge himself on *Bhīma*. *Kṛshṇā* was afraid. *Dhaumya* destroyed his illusion by *rākshasa*-destroying *mantras*. *Arjuna* stringed his bow *Gāṇḍīva*; but *Bhīma*, making him desist, fought with trees, etc., against *Kirmīra*, as the brothers *Vāli* and *Sugrīva* had done of yore for the sake of the same woman. At last *Bhīma* seized him with his arms and whirled him about and killed him. Then placing *Kṛshṇā* in their front they set out for *Dvaitavana*. Having cleared the forest of its pest they began to live there. "Passing through the forest, I saw the body of the *rākshasa*, and heard the story from the brahmans" (III, **11**).

Kīrti ("fame," personif.), a goddess. § 115 (Aṃçāvat.): I, **66,** 2578 (daughter of Daksha and wife of Dharma).—§ 270 (Brahmasabhāv.): II, **11,** 458 (in the palace of Brahmán).—§ 330 (Indradarçana): III, **37,** 1488.

Kīrtimat[1]. § 641 (Rājadh.): XII, **59,** 2211 (son of Virajas and father of Kardama).

Kīrtimat[2], a Viçvadeva. § 749 (Ānuçāsanik.): XIII, **91**γ, 4356 (enumeration).

Kīrtivarman, a Pāṇḍava warrior. § 600 (Ghaṭotkaca-vadhap.): VII, **158**χ, 7009.

Kīrtyāvāsa = Mahāpurusha (Mahāpurushastava).

Kishkindhā, a city. § 281 (Sahadeva): II, **31,** 1122 (at *K.* Sahadeva fought with the monkey-kings Dvivida and Mainda).—§ 531 (Rāmopākhyānap.): III, **280,** 16107 (C. °*dhyāṃ*), 16108 (do.), 16131 (do., the capital of Sugrīva and Vālin).—§ 534 (Hanūmatpratyāgamana): III, **282,** 16201, 16203, 16209.—§ 543 (Rāmābhisheka): III, **291,** 16587, 16588.

Kishkindhyā, v. Kishkindhā.

Kīṭa ("the worm"). § 762*b* (Kīṭop.): XIII, **117–19,** 5728 (*Dvaipāyanasya saṃvādaṃ kīṭasya*), 5729, 5730, (5732), 5735, etc.

Kīṭaka, a prince. § 130 (Aṃçāvat.): I, **67,** 2696 (among the incarnations from the Krodhavaça gaṇa).

Kitava[1] = Çakuni: I, 412 (Ç°); VII, 1504 (*Gāndhārarājaḥ*).

Kitava[2] = Duḥçāsana: I, †156.

Kitava[3] = Ulūka: V, 5694 (the çloka is wanting in B.).

Kitava, pl. (°*āḥ*), a people. § 295 (Dyūtap.): II, **51,** 1832 (brought tribute to Yudhishṭhira).—§ 586 (Bhīshmavadhap.): VI, **106**τ, 4808 (protect Bhīshma).—§ 587 (do.): VI, **119***aa*, 5648 (abandon Bhīshma).—§ 589 (Droṇābhishekap.): VII, **7**ζ, 184 (in the army of Duryodhana).

[Kīṭopākhyāna] ("the episode relating to the worm"). § 762*b* (Anuçāsanik.). *Bhīshma* said: In days of old, when the emancipated (*Brahmabhūtaḥ*) brahman *Vyāsa* roamed over the world, he saw a worm speedily moving on a chariot-road. Asked by *Vyāsa*, who was omniscient and knew the language of every animal, the worm said that it was running away from a large cart, lest it should be killed; every creature, in whatever situation it may be placed, becomes attached to it; "in even this order of being I am happy, I think, and wish to live"; in his former life he was a cruel *Çūdra*, a usurer, etc., never dedicating food to D. and P., etc. (description); he now was filled with repentance and grief; he had, however, worshipped his old mother, and once showed hospitality to a brahman; in consequence thereof the memory had not forsaken him, and he thought he should once more regain happiness (XIII, **117**). *Vyāsa* said: "It is the consequence of a meritorious act of mine that thou art not stupefied; in consequence of my penances I am able to rescue a being of demerit by the simply granting him sight of my person; there is no stronger power than that of penances. Thou mayst again attain to righteousness and merit; the state of a worm is really fraught with great misery. The superior brahman worships the Sun and the Moon uttering *mantras*; when thou hast attained to that state, I shall impart to thee *Bráhman*." The worm remained and was killed by the cart. He was reborn in diverse orders of being, such as a porcupine, Iguana, boar, deer, bird, *Cāṇḍāla*, *Çūdra*, and *Vaiçya*. Born at last as a *Kshatriya* (with *Kāmboja* steeds, *Sūtas* and *Māgadhas*, etc.; description) through the grace of *Vyāsa*, he came and worshipped him. *Vyāsa* said that the sin of his former life had yet not been destroyed; he should become a brahman by giving up his life on the field of battle for the sake of cows or brahmans; performing many sacrifices he should attain to heaven, and after emancipation (*Brahma-bhūtaḥ*) he should enjoy eternal happiness. The ascending order of transmigration is: († v. 5774) animal > *Çūdra* > *Vaiçya* > *Kshatriya* > *Brahman* > *Svarga* (XIII, **118**). He betook himself to severe austerities; *Vyāsa* went to him and said that the penances of the *Kshatriyas* consist in the protection of all creatures; thereby he should attain to the state of a brahman. Then he protected his subjects righteously, and after death became a brahman. *Vyāsa* came and told him not to fear death, but only the loss of righteousness. He caused the earth to be marked with 100 sacrificial stakes, and then obtained a residence in the egion of *Brahmán* himself, and obtained the eternal *Bráhman* by his own acts, according to the words of *Vyāsa*. Also the *Kshatriyas*, who have been slain [on the field of Kurukshetra], have attained to a meritorious end (*gatiṃ puṇyāṃ*); therefore, do not mourn on their account" (XIII, **119**).

Koçā, a river. § 574 (Jambūkh.): VI, **9**λ, 342 (so C., B. has *Koshāṃ*).

Koçala, Koçalā, Koçalarāja, Koçalādhipa, Koçalādhipati, Koçaleçvara, Koçalendra, v. Kos°.

Koçika, pl. (°*āḥ*) (VII, 1052), v. Kāçika, pl.

Kohala, a ṛshi. § 59 (Sarpasattra): I, **53,** 2049 (among the sadasyas at the snake sacrifice of Janamejaya).—§ 767 (Ānuçāsanik.): XIII, **137***a*, 6271 (Bhagīratha attained to blessing by giving a hundred thousand kine to *K.*).—§ 775 (do.): XIII, **166**ζ, 7671 (one of the ṛshis of the north).

Kokamukhā = Durgā (Umā): VI, 800.

Kokāmukha, a tīrtha. § 370 (Tīrthayātrāp.): III, **84,** 8136.—§ 733*x* (Cāṇḍālikāçrama): XIII, **25,** 1738.

Kokanada, pl. (°*āḥ*), a people. § 279 (Arjuna): II, **27,** 1026 (in the north, vanquished by Arjuna on his digvijaya).

Kokanada, various warriors of Skanda. § 615*u* (Skanda): IX, **45**η, 2562, 2563, 2576.

Kokaraka, pl. (°*āḥ*), a people. § 574 (Jambūkh.): VI, **9**ν, 369 (in the south, only C., B. has *Kokabakāḥ*).

Kokila, name of a mouse. § 571 (Ulūkadūtāgamanap.): V, **160,** 5441.

Kokilaka, a warrior of Skanda. § 615*u* (Skanda): IX, **45**η, 2575.

Kolagiri, a mountain. § 284 (Sahadeva): II, **31,** 1171 (in the south, conquered by Sahadeva on his digvijaya).

Kolāhala, a mountain (personif.). § 75 (Vasu): I, **63,** 2367 (C. has by error *Kolālāhalaḥ*), 2368 (when he attacked the River Çuktimatī, Vasu struck him with his foot).

Kolisarpa, pl. (°*āḥ*), a people. § 739 (Ānuçāsanik.): XIII, **33***a*, 2104 (have been degraded to *çūdras*).

Kolvagireya, pl. (°*āḥ*), a people. § 785 (Anugītāp.): XIV, **83,** 2476 (so C., B. has *Kolla*°, vanquished by Arjuna when he followed the sacrificial horse).

Koṅkana, pl., v. Kauṅkana, pl.

Konvaçira, pl. (°āḥ), a people. § 739 (Ânuçāsanik.): XIII, **35**ε, 2158 (have been degraded to *çūdras*).

Kopavega, a muni. § 264 (Sabhākriyāp.): II, **4**a, 111 (waited upon Yudhishṭhira).

Kosala (C. Koç°), pl. (*āḥ*), a people. § 273 (Rājasūyārambhap.): II, **14**, 591 (*pūrvāḥ*, fled before Jarāsandha).—§ 276 (Jarāsandhavadhap.): II, **20**, 795 (*pūrvāṃç ca Koçalān*, only B., C. has *pūrvāṃ ca Koçalāṃ*). — § 280 (Bhīmasena): II, **30**, 1077 (*uttarān*, vanquished by Bhīmasena on his digvijaya).—§ 281 (Sahadeva): II, **31**, 1117 (*prāk-K°ān nṛpān*, so C., B. has *Prākoṭakān nṛpān*, vanquished by Sahadeva on his digvijaya).—§ 347 (Nalopākhyānap.): III, **61**, 2319 (only B., C. has *Koçalāṃ*).—§ 574 (Jambūkh.): VI, **9**μ, 347.—§ 578 (Bhīshmavadhap.): VI, **51**ν, 2105 (in the army of Duryodhana).—§ 589 (Droṇābhishekap.): VII, **11**ν, 397 (*Kāçi-K°ān*, have formerly been vanquished by Kṛshṇa, C. has *-Kauç°*).—§ 592 (Saṃçaptakavadhap.): VII, **21**θ, 877 (*Matsya-Karūsha-K°āḥ*, attack Droṇa); **24**σ, 1052 (have sided with Yudhishṭhira).—§ 593 (Abhimanyuvadhap.): VII, **47**, 1879 (*°ānām adhipaḥ*, i.e. Bṛhadbala), 1881 (*°ānāṃ bhartāram*—B. *adhipaṃ—rājaputraṃ Bṛhadbalaṃ*).—§ 599 (Jayadrathavadhap.): VII, **125**μμ, 5069 (*Kāçi-K°āḥ*, attack Droṇa).—§ 600 (Ghaṭotkacavadhap.): VII, **156**ι, 6779 (*Cedi-Karūsha-K°āḥ*, follow Arjuna against Droṇa).—§ 604 (Karṇap.): VIII, **5**ζ, 110 (*°ānām adhipatiḥ*, i.e. Bṛhadbala has been slain by Abhimanyu, C. has by error *Kailāsānām*); **8**, 236 (*Kāçi-K°ān*, had been vanquished by Karṇa for Duryodhana).—§ 605 (do.): VIII, **12**ββ, 459 (in the army of Yudhishṭhira); **22**ζζ, 864 (attack Dhṛshṭadyumna).—§ 607 (do.): VIII, **44**μ, 2084 (know the eternal religion, *dharmaṃ*); **45**ν, 2105 (*prekshitajñāḥ*).—§ 608 (do.): VIII, **49**χ, 2334 (*Kāçi-K°āḥ*, attack Karṇa); **54**ηη, 2564 (are slain by Arjuna).—§ 619 (Strīvilāpap.): XI, **25**κ, 715 (*°ānām adhipatim Bṛhadbalam*).—§ 641 (Rājadh.): XII, **82**, 3060 (*°ānām ādhipatyaṃ*, ruled by Kshemadarçin).—§ 744 (Ânuçāsanik.): XIII, **44**β, 2441 (had been vanquished by Bhīshma at the svayaṃvara of Ambā, etc.).—§ 785 (Anugītap.): XIV, **82**, 2464 (*Puṇḍrān sa-K°ān*); **83**, 2469 (vanquished by Arjuna when he followed the sacrificial horse). Cf. Kausalya, pl.

Kosala = Ṛtuparṇa: III, 2897 (so B., C. has *Kauçalaḥ*).

Kosalā (C. Koç°) = Ayodhyā. § 276 (Jarāsandhavadhap.): II, **20**, 795 (v. Kosala, pl.).—§ 347 (Nalopākhyānap.): III, **61**, 2319 (v. Kosala, pl.).—§ 353 (do.): III, **76**, 2978 (the residence of king Ṛtuparṇa).—§ 370 (Tīrthayātrāp.): III, **85**, 8152 (*Ṛshabhaṃ tīrtham āsādya K°āyāṃ*), 8153 (*°ān tu samāsādya Kālatīrtham upaspṛçet*).—§ 515 (Karṇadigvijaya): III, **254**, 15246 (conquered by Karṇa on his digvijaya).—§ 530 (Viçvāvasumokshaṇa): III, **279**, 16077 (*°gataṃ*, sc. Rāma Dāçarathi).—§ 615*i* (Saptasārasvata): IX, **38**, 2208 (*uttare K°bhage*, there Uddālaka performed a sacrifice, at which the River Sarasvatī appeared as Manoramā).

Kosalādhipa[1] (C. Koç°) ("the king of the Kosalas") = Kshemadarçin: XII, 3879.

Kosalādhipa[2] (do.) (do.) = Saudāsa (Kalmāshapāda): XIII, 326 (*S°*).

Kosalādhipati[1] (do.) (do.), the king of the Kosalas at the time of Yudhishṭhira. § 232 (Svayaṃvarap.): I, **186**, 7002 (present at the svayaṃvara of Draupadī).—§ 280 (Bhīmasena): II, **30**, 1075 (*Bṛhadbalaṃ*, vanquished by Bhīmasena on his digvijaya).—§ 281 (Sahadeva): II, **31**, 1117 (the same?, vanquished by Sahadeva on his digvijaya).—§ 592 (Saṃçaptakavadhap.): VII, **23**ο, 1004 (*°eḥ putraṃ Sukshatraṃ*). Cf. Bṛhadbala.

Kosalādhipati[2] (do.) (do.) = Ṛtuparṇa: III, 2877.

Kosalaka (C. Koç°), adj. ("belonging to the Kosalas"). § 578 (Bhīshmavadhap.): VI, **44**, 1684 (*rājā*, i.e. Bṛhadbala).

Kosalarāja (C. Koç°) ("the king of the Kosalas") = Bṛhadbala: VII, 1880.

Kosaleçvara (do.) (do.) = Sudāsa: XIII, 7682.

Kosalendra[1] (do.) (do.) = Rāma Dāçarathi: III, 16332, 16344.

Kosalendra[2] (do.) (do.) = Bṛhadbala: VI, 5406, 5407.

Koshā, a river. § 574 (Jambūkh.): VI, **9**λ, 342 (only B., C. has *Koçā*).

Koshthavat, a mountain. § 782*g* (Guruçishyas.): XIV, **43**η, 1174 (among the principal mountains).

Koṭarā, a mātṛ. § 615*u* (Skanda): IX, **46**θ, 2635.

Koṭaraka, a serpent. § 564 (Mātalīyop.): V, **103**γ, 3628 (enumeration).

Koṭiça, a serpent. § 63 (Sarpasattra): I, **57**, 2146 (of Vāsuki's race).

Koṭika = Koṭikāsya: III, 15586, (15615).

Koṭikāsya, a prince, follower of Jayadratha. § 522 (Draupadīharaṇap.): III, **264**, 15582 (*rājānaṃ*), 15587; **265**, (†15588), †15593 (*Surathasya putraḥ*); **266**, 15605 (*Surathasya putraṃ*); **267**, 15612; **271**, 15720, 15739 (is slain by Bhīmasena). Cf. Koṭika.

Koṭitīrtha, name of various tīrthas. § 358 (Tīrthayātrāp.): III, **82**, 4091 (*Mahākālaṃ tato gacchen niyato niyatāçanaḥ* | *K°m upaspṛçya hayamedhaphalaṃ labhet*). — § 362 (do.): III, **83**, 5087 (*tataḥ Pañcanadaṃ gatvā niyataḥ niyatāçanaḥ* | *K°m upaspṛçya hayamedhaphalaṃ labhet*).—§ 368 (do.): III, **83**, 7071 (*abhivādya tato Yakshaṃ dvārapālaṃ Macakrukaṃ* | *K°m upaspṛçya labhed bahusuvarṇakaṃ*).—§ 370 (do.): III, **84**, 8005 (*tatrābhishekaṃ kurvīta*—i.e. at Gaṅgādvāra—*K°e samāhitaḥ* | *puṇḍarīkam avāpnoti kulañ caiva samuddhāret*), 8055 (*°e naraḥ snātvā arcayitvā Guhaṃ nṛpa* | *gosahasraphalaṃ vindyāt tejasvī ca bhaven naraḥ*).—§ 372 (do.): III, **85**, 8204 (*°e naraḥ snātvā gosahasraphalaṃ labhet*).

krama (a certain method of reciting the Vedas): XII, 13261 (*°ākshаravit*), 13262 (*°pāragaḥ*), 13263; XIII, 4107 (*pada-k°vibhūshitaḥ*, sc. *ṛgvedaḥ*).

Krama[1] = Çiva (1000 names[2]). Do.[2] = Vishṇu (1000 names).

Kramajit, a prince. § 264 (Sabhākriyāp.): II, **4**β, 123 (waited upon Yudhishṭhira).

Krami, pl. (V, 2729), v. Kṛmi, pl.

Kratha[1], an Asura. § 130 (Aṃçāvat.): I, **67**, 2665 (*mahāsuraḥ*, incarnate as king Parvatīya; only C., B. has *Kapaṭaḥ*).

Kratha[2], a king. § 130 (Aṃçāvat.): I, **67**, 2697 (among the incarnations from the Krodhavaça gaṇa).

Kratha[3], a king. § 280 (Bhīmasena): II, **30**, 1081 (*Supārçvam abhitaḥ*, vanquished by Bhīmasena on his digvijaya). Cf. Kratha[2].

Kratha[4], a ṛshi. § 562 (Bhagavadyānap.): V, **83**η, 2946 (worshipped Kṛshṇa).

Kratha[5], a Kuru warrior. § 599 (Jayadrathavadhap.): VII, **120**δδ, 4768.

Kratha[6], a warrior of Skanda. § 615*u* (Skanda): IX, **45**ζ, 2572.

Kratha[7], pl. (°*āḥ*), a people. § 273 (Rājasūyārambhap.): II, **14**, 585 (*vidyābalād yo vyajayat Pāṇḍya-K°-Kaiçikān*, sc. Bhīshmaka).

Krātha[1], son of the elder Dhṛtarāshṭra. § 154 (Pūruvaṃç.): I, **94**, 3747.

Krātha[2] ("the king of the Krathas"?), various princes.

§ 130 (Aṃçāvat.): I, **67**, 2676 (incarnation of Rāhu).—§ 233 (Svayaṃvarap.): I, **187**, †7019 (present at the svayaṃvara of Draupadī). — § 317*b* (Kṛshṇa Vāsudeva): III, **12**, 489 (had been slain by Kṛshṇa at Jārūthī).—§ 592 (Saṃçaptakavadhap.): VII, **20**η, 804 (in the army of Duryodhana).—§ 593 (Abhimanyuvadhap.): VII, **37**κ, 1609 (attacked Abhimanyu); **46**υ, 1856 (= *Krāthaputra*, is slain by Abhimanyu). — § 608 (Karṇap.): VIII, **85**ρ', †4307 (°*Devāvṛdhau*), †4319 (is slain by the Kulinda king). Cf. Krāthādhipa, Krāthaputra.

Krātha[3], a monkey. § 535 (Setubandhana): III, **283**β, 16287.

Krātha[4], son of Dhṛtarāshṭra. § 608 (Karṇap.): VIII, **51**δδ, 2446, (εε), 2455 (is slain by Bhīmasena). Cf. Krathana[3].

Krātha[5] = Çiva, VIII, 1448.

Krātha[6], a warrior of Skanda. § 615*u* (Skanda): IX, **45**η, 2572.

Krātha[7], a serpent. § 793 (Mausalap.): XVI, **4**η, †120.

Krāthādhipa = Krātha[2]: VIII, †4320 (is slain by the Kulinda king).

Krathana[1], a Nāga (?) (accord. to Nīl., a Yaksha). § 46 (Garuḍa): I, **32***a*, 1488 (had an encounter with Garuḍa).

Krathana[2], an Asura. § 130 (Aṃçāvat.): I, **67**, 2693 (*mahāsuraḥ*, incarnate as king Sūryāksha).—§ 268 (Varuṇasabhāv.): II, **9**, 366 (among the Asuras in the palace of Varuṇa).

Krathana[3], son of Dhṛtarāshṭra. § 182 (Dhṛtarāshṭraputranāmak.): I, **117**, 4550.

Krathana[4] = Çiva: VIII, 1448.

Krāthaputra, a prince. § 554 (Sainyodyogap.): V, **4**γ, 82 (among the princes to whom the Pāṇḍavas ought to send messengers).—§ 593 (Abhimanyuvadhap.): VII, **46**υ, 1854, 1857 (is slain by Abhimanyu). Cf. Krātha[2].

Kratu[1], a ṛshi, son of Brahmán. § 86 (Aṃçāvat.): I, **65**, 2518 (the sixth of Brahmán's spiritual sons).—§ 109 (do.): I, **66**, 2568 (do.).—§ 114 (do.): I, **66**, 2573 (his sons were the *pataṅgasahacāriṇaḥ* ("companions of the sun"), i.e. the Vālakhilyas, Nīl.).—§ 191 (Arjuna): I, **123**, 4808 (present at the birth of Arjuna).—§ 228 (Aurvop.): I, **181**, 6873 (*mahākratuḥ*, came to the Rākshasa sacrifice of Parāçara to save the Rākshasas).—§ 266 (Çakrasabhāv.): II, **7**, 298 (in the palace of Indra). § 270 (Brahmasabhāv.): II, **11**, 437 (in the palace of Brahmán).—§ 615*u* (Skanda): IX, **45**γ, 2512 (came to the investiture of Skanda).—§ 637 (Rājadh.): XII, **47**η, 1597 (among the ṛshis who surrounded Bhīshma).—§ 656 (Khaḍgotpattik.): XII, **166***a*, 6135 (among the sons of Brahmán).—§ 664 (Mokshadh.): XII, **207**δ, 7534 (do.). — § 665 (do.): XII, **208***a*, 7570 (do.). — § 680*b* (Tulādhāra-Jājalis.): XII, **263***a*, 9380 (among the deities who dwell in the living creatures).—§ 717*b* (Nārāyaṇīya): XII, **335***a*, 12685 (among the twenty-one Prajāpatis).—§ 717*c* (Uparicara): XII, **336**β, 12724 (one of the seven ṛshis).—§ 717*b* (Nārāyaṇīya): XII, **341**ν, 13040 (among the eight prakṛtis), (ξ), 13075 (one of the seven ṛshis).—§ 730 (Ānuçāsanik.): XIII, **14**ββ, 990. — § 734 (do.): XIII, **26***a*, 1761 (came to see Bhīshma).—§ 749 (do.): XIII, **92**δ, 4392 (among the masters of yoga).

Kratu[2] = Kṛshṇa: XII, 1512.—Do.[3] = Vishṇu (1000 names).

Krauñca[1], a mountain. § 496 (Skandotpatti): III, **225**, 14331 (*Himavataḥ sutaṃ*, pierced by Skanda). — § 587 (Bhīshmavadhap.): VI, **111**, 5186 (*Skandaçaktyā yathā K°ḥ*). — § 599 (Jayadrathavadhap.): VII, **139**, 5804 (? *haṃsāḥ K°m ivāviçan*). — § 600 (Ghaṭotkacavadhap.): VII, **156**, 6821 (°*m Agnisuto yathā*, sc. *nihanishyāmi*).—§ 608 (Karṇap.): VIII, **90**, †4696 (°*m ivādrim Agnijaḥ*, sc. *parābhinat*).—§ 611 (Çalyap.): IX, **17**, 914 (°*o yathā Skandahato mahādriḥ*).—§ 615*u* (Skanda): IX, **46**, 2701, 2702 (origin of the name: *krauñcanādanāditaṃ*), 2709, 2712 (the Asura Bāṇa sought refuge at *K.*, then Skanda cleft the mountain in twain). Cf. Krauñcaparvata.

Krauñca[2], a mountain on Krauñcadvīpa. § 575 (Bhūmip.): VII, **12**η, 458, 459, (θ), 462.

krauñca, a kind of battle array. § 578 (Bhīshmavadhap.): VI, **51**, 2091 (i.e. the *krauñcāruṇa vyūha* formed by Dhṛshṭadyumna).—§ 583 (do.): VI, **75**, 3291 (formed by Bhīshma).—§ 589 (Droṇābhishekap.): VII, **7**, 192 (formed by Yudhishṭhira).

Krauñcadvīpa, name of a dvīpa. § 575 (Bhūmip.): VI, **11***a*, 403; **12**, 448 (with the mountain Mahākrauñca), 458 (with the mountain Krauñca).—§ 623 (Rājadh.): XII, **14**, 405 (*adhareṇa Mahāmeroḥ*, ruled by Yudhishṭhira), 406.

Krauñcanisūdaka (B. °*nishūdana*), "Krauñca-splitter," i.e. Skanda. § 370 (Tīrthayātrāp.): III, **84**, 8138 (? it seems to be impossible to take this as a name of Skanda, because it is adj. to *Ṛshabhadvīpaṃ*).

Krauñcapadī, a tīrtha. § 733*s* (Açmapṛshṭha): XIII, **25**, 1728 (C. by error *Kro°*).

Krauñcaparvata = Krauñca[1]: IX, 2700.

Krauñcāruṇa, a kind of battle array. § 578 (Bhīshmavadhap.): VI, **50**, 2072 (formed by Dhṛshṭadyumna).

***kravyāda**, pl. = Rākshasa, pl.: II, 401; VII, 1576, 2694, 2711, 9032; VIII, 4422; X, 458; XIII, 5620.

kravyāda**, pl., one of the three classes of Pitṛs. § 684 (Mokshadh.): XII, **270a*, 9650.

Kriyā[1], daughter of Daksha and wife of Dharma. § 115 (Aṃçāvat.): I, **66**, 2578.

Kriyā[2] = Çiva (1000 names[1]).

Kriyāvastha = Çiva (1000 names[2]).

Kroçanā, a mātṛ. § 615*u* (Skanda): IX, **46**θ, 2635.

Krodha[1] ("Wrath," "Anger," personif.). § 130 (Aṃçāvat.): I, **67**, 2708 (Açvatthāman was produced by a union of Mahādeva, Antaka, Kāma, and *K.*).—§ 223 (Vāsishṭha): I, **174**, 6639 (*Kāma-K°au*, used to shampoo the feet of Vasishṭha).—§ 498 (Skandotpatti): III, **226**, 14363 (*nārī K° sambhavā*).—§ 662*b* (Jāpakop.): XII, **199**, 7316 (*Kāma-K°au*, in the shape of Virūpa and Vikṛta).—§ 717*b* (Nārāyaṇīya): XII, **335***a*, 12680 (among the twenty one Prajāpatis). — § 743 (Ānuçāsanik.): XIII, **40**, 2256 (*Kāmasya . . . sahāyam*, created by Brahmán). — § 786*f* (Jamadagni): XIV, **92**, 2888, 2890, 2894, 2899 (Dharma assumed the shape of *K.*)

Krodha[2], an Asura. § 97 (Aṃçāvat.): I, **65**, 2543 (son of Kalā).

Krodhā, daughter of Daksha. § 87 (Aṃçāvat.): I, **65**, 2520 (= Krūrā, v. 2540, or perhaps = Krodhavaçā, v. 2624).

Krodhaçatru, an Asura. § 97 (Aṃçāvat.): I, **65**, 2543 (son of Kālā; C. prints by error *Krodhaḥ Çatruḥ*).

Krodhahan = Vishṇu (1000 names).

Krodhahantṛ[1], an Asura. § 97 (Aṃçāvat.): I, **65**, 2543 (son of Kālā).—§ 130 (do.): I, **67**, 2681 (*Asuraḥ*, younger brother of the Asura Vṛtra; incarnate as king Daṇḍa).

Krodhahantṛ[2] = Senābindu: V, 5912 (*S°*).

Krodhaja = Çiva: XII, 12737 (*Rudraḥ*), 13300, 13302.

Krodhakṛt = Vishṇu (1000 names).

Krodhana[1], a ṛshi. § 266 (Çakrasabhāv.): II, **7**, 293 (in the palace of Indra).

Krodhana[2] = Çiva: XIV, 203.
Krodhanā, a mātṛ. § 615*u* (Skanda): IX, **46**θ, 2624.
Krodhavaça, pl. (°*āḥ*), a class of Rākshasas. § 432 (Saugandhikāharaṇa): III, **153**, 11361 (°*ā nāma Rākshasāḥ*); **154**, †11385, 11392 (sought in vain to prevent Bhīmasena from gathering saugandhikas, but 100 of them were slain).—§ 553 (Vaivāhikap.): IV, **71**, 2292 (°*ān hatvā parvate Gandhamādane*, sc. Bhīmasena, all. to § 432). — § 561*e* (Bhīmasena): V, **50**, 1990 (*Kṛshṇāyāç caratā prītiṃ yena*—i.e. Bhīmasena—*K°ā hatāḥ*, all. to § 432).—§ 562 (Bhagavadyānap.): V, **90**o, 3151 (*hantā . . . K°ānāṃ*, i.e. Bhīmasena, all. to § 432).—§ 794 (Mahāprasthānikap.): XVII, **3**, †82 (*svarge loke çravatāṃ nāsti dhishṇyam ishṭapūrtaṃ K°ā haranti*), †85 (*çunā dṛshṭaṃ K°ā haranti*).
Krodhavaça, a Rākshasa. § 537 (Rāma-Rāvaṇayuddha): III, **285a**, 16365 (followed Rāvaṇa).
Krodhavaçā (?). § 127 (Aṃçāvat.): I, **66**, 2624 (mother of nine daughters produced from wrath (*krodhasambhavāḥ*) (?), PCR. takes *krodhavaçā(ḥ)* as an adjective to *nārīḥ*; enumeration of her nine daughters and their offspring).
Krodhavaça(ḥ) gaṇa(ḥ). § 95 (Aṃçāvat.): I, **65**, 2540 (the offspring of Krūrā).—§ 130 (do.): I, **67**, 2695 (re-born as the kings Madraka, etc.), 2702.
Krodhavardhana, an Asura. § 130 (Aṃçāvat.): I, **67**, 2682 (incarnate as king Daṇḍadhāra).
Kroñcapadī, v. Krauñcapadī.
Kroryātman = Kṛshṇa: XII, 1653.
Kroshṭṛ, a prince, one of the ancestors of Kṛshṇa. § 768*b* (Kṛshṇa Vāsudeva): XIII, **147**, 6833 (son of Mahāsattva and father of Vṛjinīvat).
Krūrā. § 95 (Aṃçāvat.): I, **65**, 2540 (= Krodhā, v. 2520 (?), her offspring was the Krodhavaça(ḥ) gaṇa(ḥ)).
Kṛcchra = Mahāpurusha (Mahāpurushastava).
Kṛça[1], a son of a ṛshi. § 51 (Parikshit): I, **40**, 1682 (*ṛshiputreṇa*), (1683); **41**, 1691, (1692), (1696).
Kṛça[2], a serpent. § 63 (Sarpasattra): I, **57**, 2152 (of Airāvata's race).
Kṛça[3], a ṛshi. § 734 (Ānuçāsanik.): XIII, **26a**, 1764 (among the ṛshis who came to see Bhīshma).
Kṛça[4] = Çiva: XII, 10365 (1000 names[1]), 10387 (do.); XIV, 194.—Do.[5] = Vishṇu (1000 names).
Kṛçāçva, an ancient king. § 267 (Yamasabhāv.): II, **8**, 328 (in the palace of Yama).—§ 552 (Goharaṇap.): IV, **56**ζ, 1769 (among the kings who came in the chariot of Indra to see the encounter). — § 775 (Ānuçāsanik.): XIII, **166**η, 7675 (enumeration).
Kṛçaka, a serpent. § 564 (Mātalīyop.): V, **103**γ, 3631 (enumeration).
Kṛçanāça, Kṛçāṅga = Çiva (1000 names[1]).
Kṛçānu = Agni: VIII, †3402.
Kṛkaṇeyu, son of Raudrāçva. § 150 (Pūruvaṃç.): I, **94**, 3700 (third son of Raudrāçva and Miçrakeçī).
Kṛmi, pl. (°*ayaḥ*), a people. § 562 (Bhagavadyānap.): V, **74**γ, 2729 (ruled by Vasu; C. has *Kram°*).
Kṛmi, a river. § 574 (Jambūkh.): VI, **9**λ, 324 (only B., cf. Ikshumālavī).
Kṛpa, a brahman, son of Çaradvat and brother of Kṛpī. § 4 (Anukram.): I, **1**, 138, †196.—§ 11 (Parvasaṅgr.): I, **2**, 562 (cf. § 616), 570 (do.).—§ 83 (Ādivāṃçāvatāraṇa): I, **63**, 2436 (*K.* and Kṛpī (*Açvatthāmnaç ca jananī*) were born in a clump of reeds (*çarastambāt*) from the seed of Gautama, i.e. Çaradvat, cf. § 198).—§ 130 (Aṃcāvat.): I, **67**, 2712 (*Brahmarshiḥ*, born from the gaṇa of the Rudras).—[§ 197 (Bhīmasenarasapāna): I, **129**, 5070 (*Gautame*, is appointed by Bhīshma as preceptor of the young princes).]—§ 198 (Çaradvat): I, **130**, 5071 (*K.* and Kṛpī were born from the seed of Çaradvat, which had fallen in a clump of reeds (*çarastambe*), they were reared by Çāntanu; *K.* acquired the Dhanurveda from Çaradvat and then taught it to the sons of Pāṇḍu, those of Dhṛtarāshṭra, the Yādavas, etc.).—§ 202 (Droṇa): I, **131**, 5148, 5159.—§ 208 (Astradarçana): I, **134**, 5313, 5324 (*ācāryasattamaṃ*); **136**, 5384, 5404, 5408 (*Çāradvataḥ*); **137**, 5439 (*Pāṇḍavāḥ saha-K°āḥ*). — § 213 (Jatugṛhap.): I, **142**, 5692 (*Çāradvataḥ*); **143**, 5708; **145**, 5735; **150**, 5860.—§ 234 (Svayaṃvarap.): I, **190**, 7116 (*Çaradvataḥ*).—§ 241 (Vidurāgamanap.): I, **200**, 7373.—§ 244 (Rājyalābhap.): I, **207**, 7557 (*Gautamaṃ*).—§ 286 (Rājasūyikap.): II, **33**, 1259.—§ 287 (do.): II, **34**, 1267 (came to the rājasūya of Yudhishṭhira).—§ 288 (do.): II, **35**, 1292 (appointed to look after the wealth and to distribute dakshiṇās).—§ 289 (Arghāharaṇap.): II, **37**, 1349 (*Bhāratācāryaḥ*).—§ 290 (Çiçupālavadhap.): II, **44**, 1535 (*Bhāratācāryaṃ Çāradvataṃ*).—§ 298 (Dyūtap.): II, **58**, 2014; **60**, 2052; **65**, 2181.—§ 299 (do.): II, **68**, 2264.—§ 305 (Anudyūtap.): II, **78**, 2561; **79**, 2609 (*Bhīshma-Droṇa-K°ādishu*). — § 307 (do.): II, **81**, 2697.—§ 313 (Āraṇyakap.): III, **8**, 316.—§ 318 (Arjunābhigamanap.): III, **13**, 599.—§ 327 (Draupadīparitāpav.): III, **29**, 1111.—§ 328 (Kāmyakavanapr.): III, **36**, 1425.—§ 330 (Indradarçana): III, **37**, 1459 (*Bhīshme Droṇe K°e Karṇe Droṇaputre ca, Bhārata, Dhanurvedaḥ catushpāda eteshv adya pratishṭhitaḥ*).—§ 333*c* (Brahmaçiras): III, **40**, 1645, 1648.—§ 377 (Dhaumyatīrthak.): III, **86**, 8283.—§ 401 (Balarāma): III, **119**, †10245 — § 402 (Tīrthayātrāp.): III, **120**, †10269. — § 446 (Nivātakavacayuddhap.): III, **174**, 12276.—§ 512 (Ghoshayātrāp.): III, **249**, 15084.—§ 513 (do.): III, **252**, 15165 (*Bhīshma-Droṇa-K°ādīṃç ca*, possessed by the Asuras), 15191 (*Bhīshma-Droṇa-K°ādyāç ca*, do.).—§ 515 (Karṇadigvijaya): III, **253**, 15209; **254**, 15261. — § 516 (Duryodhanayajña): III, **256**, 15302; **257**, 15332.—§ 517 (Ghoshayātrāp.): III, **257**, 15350.—§ 547 (Karṇa): III, **307**, 17170 (*Droṇāt K°āc ca Rāmāc ca so 'stragrāmaṃ caturvidhaṃ labdhvā*, sc. Karṇa).—§ 552 (Goharaṇap.): IV, **25**, 867; **29**, 947 (*Çāradvataḥ*); **30**, 986; **35a**, 1150; **36**, 1176; **38**, 1238, 1243; **39**, 1302; **45**δ, 1434; **47**, 1471, 1488; **49**, 1530; **51**, 1583, 1588, 1599; **52**, 1628 (*Çāradvataḥ*); **53**, 1643, 1649; **54**, †1688; **55**, 1733 (*Çāradvataṃ*), 1739 (*lohitāçvaṃ vaiyāghraṃ nīlaṃ patākam āçritya*), 1758; **56**, 1764 (°*ārjunasamāgame*); **57**, 1780 (*Çāradvataḥ*), 1785, 1789 (*Çāradvataḥ*), 1795, 1797, 1802, 1812, 1817, 1818, 1821 (is vanquished by Arjuna); **58**, 1823; **59**, 1908; **63**, 2021, 2024; **66**, †2109, †2131; **68**, 2167, 2203, 2237.—§ 554 (Sainyodyogap.): V, **2**β, †31; **5**, 95 (*ācāryayoḥ sakhāsī*—sc. Drupada—*Droṇasya ca K°sya ca*); **6**, 118.—§ 556 (Sañjayayānap.): V, **22**, †668 (Sātyaki had obtained weapons from Kṛpa, etc.); **23**δ, †694, †703; **25**θ, †733; **27**, †791; **30**ξ, 880.—§ 561 (Yānasandhip.): V, **47**, 1796; **48**, †1916; **51**, 2062 (*Çāradvataḥ*); **55**, 2149, 2159, (λ), 2185, 2189, (μ), 2192 (*ācāryamukhaḥ*, son of Gautama, i.e. Çaradvat), 2196, 2201 (ν), 2205; **57**π, 2268, (ρ), 2281; **58**ι, 2301, (υ), 2304; **60**, 2368 (χ), 2375; **61**ω, 2409; **62**, 2432; **65**δδ, 2493; **66**εε, 2501. — § 562 (Bhagavadyānap.): V, **73**, 2681; **83**ι, 2966; **89**λ, 3103, 3114, (μ), 3117; **90**ρ, 3180; **91**σ, 3271; **92**τ, 3284; **95**υ, 3402.—§ 567 (do.): V, **124**β, 4138, (δ), 4170; **127**, 4246; **128**θ, 4284; **129**λ, 4329, (μ), 4358, 4360; **131**π, 4453, (ρ),

4457.—§ 569 (do.): V, **141,** 4795 (*Droṇaçishyāç ca K°sya Çaradvataḥ*); **142**ε, 4824, (ζ), 4828; **143,** 4874.—§ 570 (Sainyaniryāṇap.): V, **155**θ, 5274; **158**μ, 5372, (ν), 5382. —§ 571 (Ulūkadūtāgamanap.): V, **160,** 5458. —§ 572 (Rathātirathasaṅkhyānap.): V, **165,** 5734 (*Droṇaçishyāç ca K°sya Çaradvataḥ*); **166,** 5767 (*Çāradvataḥ . . . Gautamasya maharsher ya ācāryasya Çaradvataḥ Kārttikeya ivājeyaḥ çarastambāt suto 'bhavat*, among the rathas in the army of Duryodhana); **171,** 5914.—§ 573 (Ambopākhyānap.): V, **193a,** 7562, 7576 (*Çāradvataḥ*).—§ 576 (Bhagavadgītāp.): VI, **14,** 526; **17,** 664, 675 (in the array of Duryodhana); **25**ι, 837.—§ 577 (Bhīshmavadhap.): VI, **43,** 1596, (1598), 1604.—§ 578 (do.): VI, **45**[14], 1720 (*Çāradvataḥ*, attacked Bṛhatkshattra), 1721; **47**[25] γ, 1809, ([26]), 1820, 1826, ([27]), 1841; **48**θ, 1925, (κ), 1963; **49,** 1993; **50**ο, 2070; **51**ρ, 2092, (ψ), 2109 (in the rear of Duryodhana's army).—§ 579 (do.): VI, **52**β, 2134, (δ), 2144, 2147; **55**[15] κ, 2360, ([16]λ), 2364, (μ), 2365.—§ 580 (do.): VI, **56a,** 2405 (in the head of Bhīshma's gāruḍavyūha); **58**[9] λ, 2496, 2497, 2500 (only B.); **59**μ, †2583, (ρ), †2648.—§ 581 (do.): VI, **60**β, †2672; **65,** 2910, (ν), 2928.—§ 582 (do): VI, **71**ε, 3141 (attacked Dhṛshṭadyumna); **72**ζ, 3163.—§ 583 (do.): VI, **75,** 3292 (in the krauñcavyūha of Bhīshma), (θ), 3304; **76**ι, 3329; **79**[12], 3467.—§ 584 (do.): VI, **81**[1], 3562 (attacked by Cekitāna); **84,** 3716 (*Çāradvataḥ*, fought with Cekitāna); **85**ε, †3768; **86**ζ, 3838.—§ 585 (do.): VI, **87,** 3859 (*Çāradvataḥ*); **89,** 3931, (λ), 3933, (π), 3970; **92**χ, 4118, 4129; **94**ω, 4194; **95**γγ, 4244; **96**ηη, 4339; **97**κκ, 4407; **98**νν, 4489.—§ 586 (do.): VI, **99a,** 4501 (in Bhīshma's sarvatobhadra array); **100**η, 4545; **102**ι, 4665; **103**ξ, 4724.—§ 587 (do.): VI, **108,** 5006, (δ), 5050; **110,** 5105 (*Çāradvataḥ*, fought with Sahadeva); **111,** 5167 (do., do.), 5168; **113**ι, 5239, 5243, 5248, 5260, 5270, 5278; **114**κ, 5292, 5296, 5309; **117**σ, 5496, 5497 (deprived by Arjuna of his chariot); **118**τ, 5519; **119,** 5678.—§ 589 (Droṇābhishekap.): VII, **7**δ, 181 (in the left wing of Droṇa's array).—§ 590 (do.): VII, **14,** 527, 528 (fights with Dhṛshtaketu); **16**β, 633.—§ 592 (Saṃçaptakavadhap.): VII, **23**ο, 1017 (the Pāṇḍya king Sāraṅgadhvaja had obtained weapons from Kṛpa, etc.); **25,** 1114 (*Çāradvataḥ*) 1115 (fights with Vārdhakshemi); **32**ω, 1410.—§ 593 (Abhimanyuvadhap.): VII, **34**β, 1501; **37**θ, 1589, (ι), 1600 (*Çāradvataḥ*), (κ), 1609; **39**μ, 1650, 1654, **40**ι, 1660, (υ), 1851, **47**φ, 1864, 1868, 1871, 1878 (*Çāradvataḥ*); **48,** 1901.—§ 596 (Pratijñāp.): VII, **72,** 2525; **73,** 2575, 2589; **74a,** 2619; **75**γ, 2673.—§ 598 (Jayadrathavadhap.): VII, **85**β, 3037 (had not approved of the gambling), (γ), 3043; **87**θ, 3098.—§ 599 (do.): VII, **95,** 3538 (η), 3540; **104**μ, 3894, 3917; **105**ν, 3940 (the standard of *K.* had for its mark a bull); **112,** 4301 (protects Jayadratha), (φ), 4329; **119**ββ, 4720; **135**υυ, 5541; **137**ωω, 5629; **143**ηηη, 5956, (κκκ), 6004; **145**μμμ, 6063, 6074, (οοο), 6097, **146,** 6206, 6227, 6247; **147,** 6298 (*Çāradvataḥ*), 6307 (*Çāradvate*), 6320 (pierced by Arjuna, *K.* swoons away); **150,** 6498; **151**γ′, 6550, 6558.—§ 600 (Ghaṭotkacavadhap.): VII, **155**δ, 6720; **156**κ, 6849; **158**φ, 6981 (*Çāradvataḥ*), (7003), 7019 (*Çāradvataṃ*); **159,** 7051 (read *Kṛpaç* with B.), 7055, 7058, (7059), (ββ), 7087, 7106, 7107; **160**γγ, 7146; **163**ηη, 7281; **165,** 7365 (*Çāradvataḥ*); **169,** 7579 (do.), 7586, 7590 (*Çāradvataḥ*, defeats Çikhaṇḍin); **177**φφ, 8031; **183**ηηη, 8309.—§ 602 (Droṇavadhap.): VII, **187**ι, 8545; **191,** 8801; **192,** 8810, 8851.—§ 603 (Nārāyaṇāstramokshap.): VII **193**δ, (8930); **200aa,** 9308 (*Çāradvataḥ*), 9316; **202**ηη, 9514.—§ 604 (Karṇap.): VIII, **2**γ, 45; **9**θ, 330 (*Çāradvataḥ*).—§ 605 (do.): VIII, **13,** 495 (fights with Dhṛshṭadyumna); **20**γγ, 772; **26,** 1037, 1046 (*Çāradvataḥ*, fights with Dhṛshṭadyumna); **28**μμ, 1126; **30,** 1225; **32**σσ, 1332.—§ 607 (do.): VIII, **41**ε, 1947.—§ 608 (do.): VIII, **46**β, 2133 (*Çāradvataḥ*), 2157 (Yudhishṭhira will fight with Kṛpa); **47**ι, 2225; **48**ο, 2262; **51**ζζ, 2507; **54**θθ, 2610, 2613, 2615, 2616, 2617, 2621, 2626 (*Çāradvataḥ*), 2629 (defeats Çikhaṇḍin); **60,** 3049; **61,** 3121; **66,** 3330; **73,** 3646, 3688, 3693; **75**χχ, †3811, †3818, †3819; **78,** 3941, (δ), 3998 (*Çāradvataḥ*); **79**ζ′, 4012, 4035 (*samānaḥ . . . Kṛpena*, sc. Karṇa), †4065, †4073, †4080, †4081, †4082; **82**μ′, †4204; **83**μ′, †4231; **84**ο′, 4272; **85**ρ′, †4307 (°-*Hṛdikasutau*), †4310; **88**aβ′, †4503; **95**aυ′, 4970 (*Çāradvataḥ*); **96,** 5013.—§ 609 (Çalyop.): IX, **1**δ, 36 (one of the three only remnants of Duryodhana's army); **2**ζ, 72, 124.—§ 610 (do.): IX, **4,** 191, 237 (*Çāradvataḥ*, advises Duryodhana to make peace); **5,** 240 (*Çāradvataṃ*); **6**ξ, 293.—§ 611 (do.): IX, **8a,** 373; **11**μ, 563; **12,** 617, (ξ), 626; **16,** 799, (φ), 840; **17,** †887, 941 (*Çāradvataḥ*); **21,** 1121 (rescues Kṛtavarman); **25**ππ, 1377, 1384, 1398; **27**σσ, 1447, (υυ), 1459.—§ 612 (Hradapraveçap.): IX, **29a,** 1603, 1622 (*Çāradvataṃ*), 1630; **30**δ, 1674, (a), 1681, 1734, 1737, 1741.—§ 615 (Baladevatīrthayātrā): IX, **54**ζ, 3064 (only three of Duryodhana's army are alive, viz. *K.*, Kṛtavarman, and Açvatthāman), 3065.—§ 615 (Gadāyuddhap.): IX, **61,** 3407; **63**ββ, 3548; **64**εε, 3610 (*Çāradvataḥ*); **65,** 3627, 3635, 3647, 3663, 3668 (*Çāradvataḥ*, installed Açvatthāman as generalissimo).—§ 616 (Sauptikap.): X, **1a,** 16, 28, 31, 57 (°-*Bhaujau*, read -*Bhojau* with B.); **2,** (70); **3,** 105; **4,** (141), 148; **5,** (176), 213; **6,** 216, 217, 234; **8,** 319, 323, 425, 427 (participates in the nightly encounter); **9,** 485, (489), 513, 515, (λ), 528 (*Çāradvataḥ*), (ν), 533.—§ 617 (Aishīkap.): X, **10,** 545 (*Gautamena*); **16,** 735 (*Çāradvatāt*, shall become the preceptor of Parikshit).—§ 618 (Jalapradānikap.): XI, **1,** 2 (°*prabhṛtayaḥ . . . trayaḥ*, i.e. *K.*, Kṛtavarman, and Açvatthāman), (γ), 30 (*Çaradvataḥ*); **9**η, 247 (°*prabhṛtayaḥ . . . trayaḥ*); **11,** 289 (*Çāradvataṃ*), (ι), 293 (*Çāradvataḥ*), 306, 309 (*Çāradvataḥ*, went to Hāstinapura).—§ 619 (Strīvilāpap.): XI, **20**ε, 585; **25**κ, 735.—§ 621 (Rājadh.): XII, **5**ζ, 141.—§ 623 (do.): XII, **14a,** 103.—§ 637 (do.): XII, **45**ε, 1539; **47,** 1695.—§ 638 (do.): XII, **48a,** 1698.—§ 639 (do.): XII, **52**ε, 1889 (*Çaradvataḥ*).—§ 640 (do.): XII, **58**γ, 2116, 2120.—§ 656 (Khaḍgotpattik.): XII, **166**δ, 6200 (received the sword from Droṇa, from him it passed over to the Pāṇḍavas).—§ 702 (Mokshadh.): XII, **297**δ, 10874 (among those who attained to their position by means of penances).—§ 785 (Anugītāp.): XIV, **60a,** 1775, (β), 1786, 1805 (°-*Bhojābhyāṃ*, all. to the great battle); **61**γ, 1821 (all. to the battle).—§ 787 (Āçramavāsap.): XV, **1,** 13 (*çyālo Droṇasya*); **3**γ, 79, 119; **4**η, 167; **5**η, 172 (*Çāradvataḥ*); **10**ν, 332; **16,** 445 (did not follow Dhṛtarāshṭra, etc., to the forest).—§ 788 (do.): XV, **23,** 623 (*Gautamaḥ*).—§ 794 (Mahāprasthānikap.): XVII, **1,** 14 (became the preceptor of Parikshit), 27.

Cf. also the following synonyms:—

Acārya, Ācāryasattama, q.v.
Bhāratācārya, q.v.
Brahmarshi, q.v.

Çaradvat: I, 7116 (*K*°); V, 4795 (*K*°), 5734 (*K*°); XI, 30 (*K*°).

Çāradvata ("son of Çaradvat"): I, 138 (*K*°), 1945 (preceptor of Parikshit), 5408 (*K*°), 5692 (do.); II, 1535 (do.); IV, 947 (do.), 986 (do.), 1624, 1628 (*K*°), 1733 (do.), 1780 (do.), 1789 (do.), 1793, 1809, 1819, †2117 (*Ācārya-Ç°yoḥ*, i.e. Droṇa and Kṛpa), 2244; V, †880, †1897, 2062 (*K*°), 5528 (°*mahāmīnaṃ*, sc. *purushodadhiṃ*, i.e. the army of Duryodhana), 5573 (do.), 5767 (*K*°), 7576 (do.); VI, †753 (*Gautamaḥ*), 1595, 1720 (*K*°), 2697, 3716 (*K*°), 3859 (do.), 4458, 4622, 5105 (*K*°), 5167 (do.), 5172; VII, 1114 (*K*°), 1600 (do.), 1878 (do.), 6107, 6140, 6143, 6252, 6298 (*K*°), 6303 (C. has *S*°), 6305, 6307 (*K*°), 6308, 6981 (*K*°), 6993, 7019 (*K*°), 7117, 7365 (*K*°), 7579 (do.), 7590 (do.), 8797, 8904 (fled), 8927, 8928, 9308 (*K*°, C. has *S*°); VIII, †201 (*Gautamaḥ*), 330 (*K*°, C. has *S*°), 1041, 1046 (*K*°), 2133, 2623 (°*rathaṃ*), 2624 (do.), 2626 (*K*°), 2630, 2989 (C. has *S*°), 3998 (*K*°), 4970 (do.); IX, 237 (do.), 240 (do.), 941 (do.), 951, 1185, 1186 (fights with Yudhishṭhira), 1389, 1622 (*K*°), 3610 (do., C. has *S*°), 3668 (*K*°); X, 206, 528 (*K*°, C. has *S*°), 735 (*K*°); XI, 289 (do.), 293 (do.), 309 (do.); XII, 1813, 1889 (*K*°); XV, 172 (do.).

Çaradvatsuta (do.): VIII, †4310.

Gautama, q.v.

Kṛpa[2], an ancient king(?). § 761 (Ānuçāsanik.): XIII, **115**δ, 5666 (only C., B. has *Kshupa*, q.v.).

Kṛpī, sister of Kṛpa, wife of Droṇa, and mother of Açvatthāman. [§ 83 (Ādivaṃçāvatāraṇa): I, **63**, 2436 (*Açvatthāmnaç ca jananī*, with Kṛpa she was born in a clump of reeds from the seed of Çaradvat).]—[§ 198 (Çaradvat): I, **130** (the birth of Kṛpa and *K*. in a clump of reeds from the seed of Çaradvat; Çāntanu reared them and gave them names (etymology, v. 5089)).] — § 201 (Droṇa): I, **130**, 5114 (*Çāradvatīṃ*, married to Droṇa and mother of Açvatthāman).—§ 619 (Strīvilāpap.): XI, **23**, 668, 671, 676. Cf. Çāradvatī, Gautamī.

Kṛshībala, a ṛshi. § 266 (Çakrasabhāv.): II, **7**, 295 (in the palace of Indra).

Kṛshṇa[1] **(Vāsudeva)**, son of Vasudeva and Devakī, husband of Rukmiṇī, etc., and father of Pradyumna, Çāmba, etc., a prince of the Dāçārhas (Vṛshṇis, Mādhavas, Yādavas), considered as an avatāra of Vishṇu (Nārāyaṇa), the supreme god. [§ 2 (Anukram.): I, **1**, 24 (*Vishṇum . . . Hṛshīkeçaṃ*).] —§ 4 (do.): I, **1**, †109 (*mūlaṃ Kṛshṇo Brahma brāhmaṇāç ca*), 172 (°*ārjunau*, identified with Nārāyaṇa and Nara), 173, 179, 194 (-*Pārthau*), 205.—§ 10 (Parvasaṅgr.): I, **2**, 333 (°*sya sabhāpraveçaḥ*, cf. § 562).—§ 11 (do.): I, **2**, 390 (*Rāma-K°au*), 399, 401 (*Devakīnandane*), 409, 427, 428, 494, 496, 506, 507, 510, 511, 523, 524, 538 (°-*Pārthayoḥ*), 571, 576, 582, 587, 606.—§ 61 (Sarpasattra): I, **55**, †2111, (°*o yathā sarvaguṇotpannaḥ*). — § 71 (Ādivaṃçāvatāraṇap.): I, **61**, [2273 (*anujāṃ Vāsudevasya Subhadrāṃ*, ravished by Arjuna, cf. § 252)], 2274 (*Çrīḥ K°eneva*, sc. *yuyuje*).—[§ 82 (cf. Adivaṃçāvatāraṇa): Vishṇu was begotten [as Kṛshṇa] by Vasudeva on Devakī among the Andhakas and the Vṛshṇis: I, **63**, 2428 (*Vishṇuḥ*).] — [§ 83 (Ādivaṃçāvatāraṇa): I, **63**, 2449 (*Abhimanyuḥ . . . svasrīyo Vāsudevasya*).]—[§ 84 (Ādivaṃçāvatāraṇap.): I, **64** (the gods prevailed upon Nārāyaṇa (v. 2505) to become incarnate [as Kṛshṇa]).]—[§ 130*g* (Abhimanyu): I, **67**, 2751 (*Nārāyaṇaḥ*), 2754 (*Nara-Nārāyaṇābhyāṃ*, i.e. Arjuna and *K*.).] — [§ 132 (Aṃçāvat.): I, **67**, 2785 (*Vāsudevaḥ*, born from a portion of Nārāyaṇa).] — [§ 159 (Pūruvaṃç.): I, **95**, ††3830 (*bhaginīṃ Vāsudevasya Subhadrāṃ, Abhimanyuṃ . . . dayitaṃ Vāsudevasya*).] — [§ 160 (do.): I, **95**, ††3835 (*Purushottamasya Vāsudevasya*), ††3836 (*Vāsudevena*, revived Parikshit, cf. § 785).]—[§ 232 (Svayaṃvarap.): I, **186**, 6997 (*Vāsudevaḥ*, present at the svayaṃvara of Draupadī).] — § 233 (do.): I, **187**, †7012 (*Janārdanaḥ*), †7013 (*Yaduvīramukhyaḥ*, recognized the Pāṇḍavas); **188**, 7051 (°*ñ ca manasā kṛtvā jagṛhe cārjuno dhanuḥ*); [**189**, †7079 (*Dāmodaraḥ*)].—§ 234 (do.): I, **190**, 7116 (*Devakīputrāt*), 7121.—§ 235 (do.): I, **191**, †7149, †7150, †7152 (visits the Pāṇḍavas).—§ 238 (Pañcendrop.): I, **197**, †7308 (*Keçavaḥ*, born from the black hair of Vishṇu).—§ 240 (Vaivāhikap.): I, **199**, 7362 (gave precious gifts to the Pāṇḍavas).—§ 241 (Vidurāgamanap.): I, **202**, 7431.—§ 243 (do.): I, **205**, [7507 (*Janārdanaḥ*, counsellor of the Pāṇḍavas)], 7513 (*yataḥ K°s tataḥ sarve yataḥ K°s tato jayaḥ*); [**206**, 7528 (*Vāsudevaṃ*)].—§ 244 (Rājyalābhap.): I, **207**, 7548 (*Rāma-K°au*), 7554, 7571 (°*purogamāḥ*, led the Pāṇḍavas to Khāṇḍavaprastha), [7595 (*Keçavaḥ*, returned to Dvārakā)].—§ 251 (Arjunavanavāsap.): I, **218**, 7888 (°-*Pāṇḍavau*, *K*. and Arjuna met in Prabhāsa), [7889 (*Nara-Nārāyaṇau* = Arjuna and Kṛshṇa)], 7892, 7893, 7905 (°*sya bhavane*, in Dvārakā). — § 252 (Subhadrāharaṇap.): I, **219**, 7920, 7929; **220**, 7932 (with the permission of *K*. Arjuna ravished his sister Subhadrā).—§ 253 (Haraṇāharaṇap.): I, **221**, 7994 (came to the nuptials of Arjuna and Subhadrā), 8006 (gave to the Pāṇḍavas a thousand chariots, etc.), 8031 (performed the rites on the birth of Abhimanyu), 8037 (°*sya sadṛçaṃ çaurye vīrye rūpe tathākṛtau*, sc. Abhimanyu).—§ 254 (Khāṇḍavadahanap.): I, **222**, 8063, 8071 (*Pārtha-K°yoḥ*), 8082 (only C., read *Kṛshṇau* with B.); **223**, 8085 (°-*Pāṇḍavau*; Agni asked *K*. and Arjuna for their assistance when he wished to consume the Khāṇḍava forest). — § 256 (Agniparābhava): I, **224**, [8161 (*Vāsudevaṃ*, Arjuna and *K*. are Nara and Nārāyaṇa born on earth)], 8164 (°-*Pārthau*). — § 256*b* (Khāṇḍavadahanap.): I, **224**, 8171.—§ 257 (do.): I, **225**, 8196 (obtained a cakra (discus) Vajranābha from Agni).— § 258 (do.): I, **227**, 8253 (°-*Pāṇḍavau*), 8257 (°-*Pārthau*), 8259, 8269 (°-*Pārthau*), 8270 (do.); **228**, 8288, 8290, 8292, 8294, 8296, [8302 (*Nara-Nārāyaṇāu etau pūrvadevau viçrutau*, i.e. Arjuna and *K*.)], 8317 (°*ārjuna*°), 8322, 8329 (°-*Pārthābhyāṃ*, *K*. and Arjuna slew the inhabitants of the Khāṇḍava forest and fought with the gods, etc.).— § 260 (do.): I, **234**, 8473 (asked Indra to establish eternal friendship between himself and Arjuna).—§ 261 (Sabhākriyāp.): II, **1**, 2, 7, 9 (*lokanāthaḥ Prajāpatiḥ*), 14, 18.—§ 262 (Bhagadvadyāna): II, **2**, 24 (*Hṛshīkeçaḥ*), 29, [35 (*Çaibya-Sugrīvavāhanaḥ*)], 39, 42, 44 (*Yādavaçreshṭhaṃ*), 47, 49 (returned to Dvārakā).—[§ 263 (Sabhākriyāp.): II, **3**, 73 (*Vāsudevena*, performed sacrifices at Bindusaras), 74 (*Keçavaḥ*, gave yūpas).]—§ 272 (Rājasūyārambhap.): II, **13**, 549 (*Janārdanaṃ*), [550 (*sarvalokāt paraṃ . . . Hariṃ*)], 552 (*Bhūtagurave*), 553, 559, 561 (advises Yudhishṭhira to perform the rājasūya).—§ 273 (do.): II, **14**, (565) (*Çrī*°, tells Yudhishṭhira of the might of Jarāsandha, etc.).—§ 274 (do.): II, **15**, 647, 648 (*Çrī*°); **16**, 660.—§ 275 (do.): II, **17**, 686, (687) (*Çrī*°), (703) (do.), 726 (do.); **18**, (737) (do.); **19**, (741) (do., tells the history of Jarāsandha), 761, 763 (the enmity between Jarāsandha and *K*.). — § 276 (Jarāsandhavadhap.): II, **20**, 786, 787 (*K*., Arjuna, and Bhīmasena go to Girivraja). — § 277 (do.): II, **21**, 823

(°-*Bhīma-Dhanañjayāḥ*), 830, 846, (848) (*Çrī°*); **22**, (860) (do.), 881, 882; **23**, (891) (*Çrī°*), 898, 923; **24**, 925, 926, 927, 935, 936 (when Jarāsandha had been slain by Bhīmasena *K.* set the confined kings free and with Arjuna and Bhīmasena left Girivraja in the chariot of Jarāsandha), 937 (°*sārathiḥ*, sc. the chariot of Jarāsandha, differently Nīl. and PCR.), 938 (°*sārathiḥ . . . rathavaryaḥ* = do.), 939, 942, 943, 945 (Garuḍa came to *K.* and took his seat on his flagstaff), 964, 965, 967, 971, 979, 980 (*Devakinandane*).—[§ 281 (Sahadeva): II, **31**, 1111 (*Jambhakasyātmajam . . . Vāsudevena çeshitam pūrvavairiṇā*).] —[§ 284 (do.): II, **31**, 1168 (*prītipūrvam . . . Vāsudevam avekshya*, sc. Bhīshmaka).]—[§ 285 (Nakula): II, **32**, 1183 (*Vāsudevajitām āçām*, i.e. the west).]—§ 286 (Rājasūyikap.): II, **33**, [1213 (*Hariḥ*, etc.), 1214 (*Keçavaḥ Keçisūdanaḥ*)], 1219, 1221, 1226, 1229, 1230 (came to the rājasūya of Yudhishṭhira).—§ 288 (do.): II, **35**, 1295 (washed the feet of the brahmans). — § 289 (Arghāharaṇap.): II, **36**, [1318 (*Puṇḍarīkākshaṃ . . . Hariṃ*, has become incarnate [as *K.*], cf. § 84)], 1332 (*Vārshṇeyam*), 1334, 1336 (Bhīshma orders Sahadeva to give the argha to *K.*); **37**, 1343, 1345, 1346, 1347, 1348, 1349, 1351, 1353, 1358, 1361 (Çiçupāla could not bear this and depreciated *K.*); **38**, 1372, 1373, 1374 (*lokavṛddhatame*), 1378 (has vanquished many kshatriyas), 1379, [1385 (*Hariḥ*)], 1391, 1393, 1394, 1397, 1399 (Bhīshma praises *K.* and declares him to be the supreme god (v. 1391 foll.)); **39**, 1402, 1408 (*kamalapatrākshaṃ*), 1410, 1417.—§ 290 (Çiçupālavadhap.): II, **41**, 1452; **42**, 1476, 1478 (all. to § 277); **43**, 1512, 1513 (Çiçupāla's mother was the sister of Kṛshṇa's father), 1515, (1515) (*K.* has promised the mother of Çiçupāla to pardon him 100 times); **44**, 1519 (*jagadbhartuḥ*), [1521 (*Hareḥ*)], 1560 (*Yādavasya devasya*); **45**, 1563, 1564, 1565 (enumerates the evil deeds of Çiçupāla), 1577, 1579, 1586 (*kamalapatrākshaṃ*, cut off the head of Çiçupāla with his discus (*cakra*)), 1589, 1593.—§ 291 (Rājasūyikap.): II, **45**, 1625 (°-*Pāṇḍavau*, i.e. *K.* and Yudhishṭhira), 1626 (*Sātvatapravare*, returned to Dvārakā).—§ 294 (Dyūtap.): II, [**47**, 1688 (*Vāsudeva*); **48**, 1705 (do.), 1716 (do.); **49**, 1752 (do.)]; **50**, 1814.—§ 295 (do.): II, **52**, 1889, 1890 (friend of Arjuna), 1891. — § 296 (do.): II, **53**, 1923 (at the end of the rājasūya *K.* had bathed Yudhishṭhira), [1926 (*Keçavaḥ*)].—§ 298 (do.): II, **62**, 2101 (had slain Kaṃsa).—§ 299 (do.): II, **67**, †2229 (*K°ñ ca Jishṇuñ ca Hariṃ Narañ ca*); **68**, 2291 (*Hariḥ*, invoked by Kṛshṇā Draupadī by the names *Govinda*, *Dvārakāvāsin*, etc.), [2292 (*Ramānātha Vrajanātha*)], 2293 (*Janārdana*), 2294 (came from Dvārakā to protect Draupadī), 2295 (*K°ñ ca Vishṇuñ Hariṃ ca Narañ ca*).—[§ 301 (do.): II, **69**, 2349 (*Vāsudevasya sakhī*, i.e. Draupadī).]—§ 305 (Anudyūtap.): II, **79**, 2606 (*Dvārakāvāsin . . . Saṅkarshaṇānuja*).—[§ 307 (do.): II, **81**, 2702 (*Vāsudevena*).]—317*b* (Arjunābhigamanap.): Arjuna enumerates the feats of *K.*: (1) *K.* wandered for 10,000 years on Gandhamādana as a *muni*, who had his home where he happened to be when evening fell; (2) he dwelt for 11,000 years at *Pushkara*, subsisting on water alone; (3) he stood for 100 years at *Badarī* on one leg with arms uplifted, subsisting on air; (4) he performed a twelve years' *sattra* on the banks of the *Sarasvatī*, emaciated and without upper garments; (5) he stood for 100 divine years on one leg at the tīrtha *Prabhāsa*; (6) *Vyāsa* had told that *K.* was the cause of the creation, etc.; (7) he slew *Naraka Bhauma* and took his ear-rings, and then let loose the first sacrificial horse; (8) he slew all the *Daityas* and *Dānavas* and bestowed on *Indra* the sovereignty of the universe; (9) he took birth among men; (10) having been *Nārāyaṇa*, he became *Hari*, *Brahmán*, *Sūrya*, *Dharma*, *Dhātṛ*, *Yama*, *Anala*, *Vāyu*, *Vaiçravaṇa*, *Rudra*, *Kāla*, the firmament (*khaṃ*), the earth, and the ten directions, etc.; (11) in the forest of *Caitraratha* he gratified the highest god with sacrifices and at each sacrifice he offered gold by hundreds of thousands; (12) becoming *Vishṇu*, the son of *Aditi*, and the younger brother of *Indra*, he, even while a child, pervaded, in three steps, the heaven, the firmament, and the earth, and, standing in the abode of the Sun (*Ādityasadane*, B. however has *Ādityasyandane*, i.e. in the chariot of the Sun), outshone him by his splendour; (13) in thousands of incarnations (*prādurbhāveshu*) he slew sinful *Asuras* by hundreds; (14) he cut the bonds of *Muru* (v. BR. s.v. *Maurava*), killed *Nisunda* and *Naraka*, and again rendered safe the road of *Prāgjyotisha*; (15) he slew *Āhvṛti* at *Jārūthī* (a river, BR.; a city, Nīl.), and also *Krātha*, *Çiçupāla* with his adherents, *Jarāsandha*, *Çaibya*, and *Çatadhanvan*; (16) on his chariot, roaring like clouds, he conquered his queen, the daughter of the *Bhoja* king (*Bhojyāṃ*) by defeating in battle *Rukmin*; (17) he slew *Indradyumna* and the *Yavana Kaçerumat*; (18) he slew *Çālva*, the lord of *Saubha*, and destroyed *Saubha*; (19) at Irāvati he slew *Bhoja*, who was equal to *Kārtavīrya* in battle; (20) he slew *Gopati* and *Tālaketu*; (21) he had appropriated to himself the wealthy (*bhogavatīṃ*) and holy *Dvārakā*, beloved by the ṛshis (so PCR., who has read *ṛshikāntāṃ* instead of *rshikāṃ tāṃ*) and will again submerge it within the ocean; (22) at the end of the *yuga* he had contracted all beings and withdrawn the whole universe into his own self; (23) in the beginning of the *yuga* Brahmán sprung from the lotus of his navel; (24) when the Dānavas *Madhu* and *Kaiṭabha* were bent upon slaying *Brahmán*, there sprang from his (i.e. *K.*'s) forehead *Çambhu* (i.e. *Çiva*), the holder of the trident (*Çūlapāṇiḥ*) with three eyes (*Trilocanaḥ*); thus these two foremost deities (i.e. Brahmán and Çiva) had sprung from his body to do his work; this Nārada had told; (25) the deeds he performed when a boy, assisted by *Baladeva*, never had been done nor would be done by others; (26) he dwelt on *Kailāsa* together with brahmans.—*K.* said to Arjuna: "Thou art mine and I am thine, those who are mine are also thine, he who hates thee hates me, and he who follows thee follows me; thou art *Nara* and I am *Hari Nārāyaṇa*; we are the ṛshis *Nara* and *Nārāyaṇa* born in the world [of men] in time (i.e. for a special purpose, PCR.); thou art the same as I and I am the same as thou; there is no difference between us." —Draupadī said: "(1) They say that in the creation of beings thou art the one *Prajāpati*; (2) *Asita Devala* called thee the creator of all worlds; (3) *Jāmadagnya* (so B.) said that thou art *Vishṇu*, the sacrifice, the sacrificer, and he to whom the sacrifice is performed; (4) the ṛshis call thee Forgiveness and Truth; (5) *Kaçyapa* said that thou art sacrifice sprung from truth; (6) *Nārada* called thee the lord of the lords of the *Sādhyas*, gods and *çivas*, the creator and the lord of all things; thou sportest with the hosts of the gods, including *Brahmán*, *Çaṅkara*, and *Çakra*, etc., even as a child with his toys; the firmament is covered by thy head and the earth by thy feet, these worlds are thy womb, thou art the eternal Purusha; thou art the best of the ṛshis, sanctified with Vedic lore, etc. . . . the refuge of the *rājarshis* . . . the supreme Lord of all creatures celestial and human": III, **12**, 471, 472, 474, 475, 477, 482, 485, 487, 501.—§ 317 (Arjunābhigamanap.): III, **12**, 503, 521, 525, 534 (father of Pradyumna), 538, 542, 544, 575, 577,

581, 587, 588, 595 (*Rāma-K°au*).—§ 319 (Saubhavadhop.): III, **13,** 614, (615).—§ 320 (do.): III, **16,** (659); **19,** 773 (*Devakinandanaḥ*), **22,** 869 (*K.* relates the encounters with Çālva (ch. **15-22**), whom he slew).—§ 321 (do.): III, **22,** 895, 896 (returned to Dvārakā).—§ 327 (Draupadīparitāpav.): III, **29,** 1110 (*Devakīputraḥ*); **33,** 1275.—§ 333*b* (Arjuna): III, **40,** [1637 (*Vishṇau . . . Purushottame*)], 1638 (*Çakrābhisheke sumahad dhanur jaladaniḥsvanaṃ pragṛhya Dānavāḥ çastās tvayā*—i.e. by Arjuna—*K°ena ca*).—[§ 339 (Indralokābhigamanap.): III, **47,** 1888 (*Nara-Nārāyaṇau* identified with *Hṛshīkeça-Dhanañjayau*, i.e. *K.* and Arjuna), 1896 (*bhūmigato Vishṇur Madhusūdanaḥ*; *c:* under the name of *Kapila K.* by his glance alone had destroyed the sons of *Sagara*).]—[§ 340 (do.): III, **49,** 1951 (*Janārdanaḥ, Haris Trailokyanāthaḥ*, friend of Arjuna).]—§ 342 (do.): III, **51,** 1977 (*Rāma-K°-praṇītānām Vṛshṇīnām*), 1986, 2009.—§ 343 (Nalopākhyānap.): III, **52,** 2024 will assist the Pāṇḍavas).—[§ 356 (Tīrthayātrāp.): III, **80,** 4018 (*Vāsudevasya*).] — § 370 (do.): III, **83,** 7098 (*Vishṇuḥ*, worshipped Çiva at Suvarṇa). — § 377 (Dhaumyatirthak.): III, **86,** 8287 (*°āniloddhūtaḥ . . . Arjunodīrito meghaḥ*); **88,** 8351 (*Govindaḥ*, etc., resided in Dvārakā, identified with the supreme god (*Devadevaḥ, Hariḥ, Madhusūdanaḥ*)).—[§ 387 (Sagara): III, **107,** 8880 (*Vāsudeva*, identified with Kapila).] —[§ 400 (Tīrthayātrāp.): III, **118,** †10231 (*Janārdanaḥ*, came to the Pāṇḍavas in the tīrtha Prabhāsa).] — § 401 (Balarāma): III, **119,** †10241. — § 402 (Tīrthayātrāp.): III, **120,** †10275, †10285, †10289 (returned home).— § 406 (do.): III, **125,** 10417 (engaged in penances on the Yamunā). —§ 448 (Âjagarap.): III, **176,** †12330 (*Suparṇaketuḥ*).— § 452 (Mārkaṇḍeyas.): III, **183,** 12564 (came to the Pāṇḍavas in the Kāmyaka forest), 12567 (*°sya mahishī*, i.e. Satyabhāmā), †12588.—§ 453 (do.): III, **183,** 12600, (12601). — [§ 458 (do.): III, **188,** 12822 (*Pītavāsā Janārdanaḥ*, identical with Nārāyaṇa (Vishṇu)).] — § 459 (do.): III, **189,** 13003 (*Vārshṇeyaḥ*, identical with Nārāyaṇa (Vishṇu)).—[§ 460 (do.): III, **190,** 13014 (*Vṛshṇiçārdūlam*); **191,** 13140 (*Çārṅgadhanvanā*).] — § 468 (Indradyumnop.): III, **199,** ††13348 (*Devakīputreṇāpi K°ena Narake majjamāno rājarshir Nṛgas tasmāt kṛcchrāt punaḥ samuddhṛtaḥ svargaṃ prāpitaḥ*, cf. § 746).—§ 510 (Draupadī-Satyabhāmāsamv.): III, **233,** 14651 (*°sya mahishī priyā*, i.e. Satyabhāmā), 14656, 14659 (*°sya mahishī priyā*, i.e. Satyabhāmā); **234,** †14713, †14716; **235,** 14738 (*°mahishī*, i.e. Satyabhāmā, *K.*, and Satyabhāmā returned home).—[§ 513 (Ghoshayātrāp.): III, **252,** 15175 (*Keçavārjunau*).]—§ 521 (Draupadīharaṇap.): III, **263,** 15528 (*Kaṃsanisūdanaṃ*, prayed to by Draupadī, who praised *K.* with the hymn v. 15528*b* foll.), 15540, 15546, 15562, (15562) (*Çrī°*) (*K.* came to Draupadī's assistance when Durvāsas, etc., visited the Pāṇḍavas).—§ 524*d* (Vishṇu): III, **272,** 15849 (*Vishṇuḥ*), 15850 (*Çaṅkhacakragadādharaṃ*), 15851.—§ 547 (Karṇa): III, **310,** 17205 (identical with Nārāyaṇa, *yam āhur vedavidvāṃso Vārāham aparājitaṃ*).—[§ 549*f* (Durgā): IV, **6,** 181 (*Vāsudevasya bhaginī*, i.e. Durgā).] — § 549 (Pāṇḍavapraveçap.): IV, **9,** 262 (*Satyabhāmāṃ K°sya mahishīṃ priyāṃ*).—§ 552 (Goharaṇap.): IV, **45** *δ*, 1434 (*Mādhavaṃ*); **48,** 1536 (all. to Subhadrāharaṇaparvan); **53,** 1651 (*Devakīputrāt*); **64,** 2056 (do.). — [§ 553 (Vaivāhikap.): IV, **72,** 2343 (*svasrīyo Vāsudevasya*, i.e. Abhimanyu), 2350 (*Janārdanaṃ*, came to the wedding of Abhimanyu and Uttarā).]—§ 554 (Sainyodyogap.): V, **1,** †8 (†10) (*Çrī°*); **5,** 101 (returned to Dvārakā); **7,** 131, 135, 136, 137, 139, (144), 150, [151 (*Nārāyaṇaṃ amitraghnaṃ kāmāj jātam Ajaṃ nṛshu*)], 153, 162, 165 (*pītāmbaradharo jagatsrashṭā Janārdanaḥ*), 171 (Duryodhana obtained from *K.* the Nārāyaṇas as his allies, Arjuna that *K.* became his charioteer). — § 556 (Sañjayayānap.): V, **20,** 622 (*°sya buddhyā yudhyeta ko naraḥ*); [**21,** 625 (*Dāmodareṇa*)]; **22,** †670, †672 (has slain Çiçupāla), †673, [†674 (*Vishṇoḥ*), †677 (*Vṛshṇivīraç ca Vishṇuḥ*)], †682; [**25** *ζ*, †724 (*Vāsudevaṃ ca Çauriṃ*)]; **28,** †803, †805 (*Vṛshṇy-Andhakā hy Ugrasenādayo vai K°praṇītāḥ*), †806; **29,** (†809) (*Vāsudevaḥ*). — § 561 (Yānasandhip.): V, **48,** †1840 (*°samaḥ*, sc. Abhimanyu), †1876 (*Vāsudevaḥ . . . Sugrīvayuktena rathena*), †1878.— § 561*c* (do.): *K.* having mowed down in battle all the royal warriors of the *Bhoja* race, had in a single chariot carried off *Rukmiṇī* in order to make her his wife; she afterwards bore him *Pradyumna*. Having smashed the *Gāndhāras* and vanquished the sons of *Nagnajit* he forcibly liberated king *Sudarçana* from confinement. He slew the *Pāṇḍya* king by striking his breast (*kapāṭena* (?), v. the note of PCR., p. 174) and mowed down the *Kaliṅgas* in battle. The city of *Vārāṇasī* was burned by *K.* and remained for many years without a king. *Ekalavya*, the king of the *Nishādas*, who could not be defeated by others, always used to challenge *K.* to battle, but slain by him he lay dead like the Asura *Jambha* violently thrashed on a hillock. Having *Baladeva* for his second he slew *Ugrasena's* wicked son (i.e. Kaṃsa) seated in court in the midst of the *Vṛshṇis* and the *Andhakas*, and then gave the kingdom to *Ugrasena*. He fought with *Çālva*, and at the gate of Saubha he with his hands caught the fierce *çataghnī*. The Asuras had a city named *Prāgjyotisha*, which was formidable, inaccessible, etc. It was there that *Naraka Bhauma* kept the ear-rings of Aditi, which he had stolen; the gods with *Çakra* (i.e. Indra) at their head were incapable of conquering him, and therefore employed *K.* to destroy these *Asuras*. At the city of *Nirmocana K.* slew 6,000 *Asuras*, and having cut their *paçāḥ kshurāntāḥ*, he slew *Muru* and crowds of *Rākshasas* (*ogharakshaḥ*, which by Nīl. is taken as a *Rākshasa* named *Ogha*), and then he entered that city. It was there that an encounter took place between *Naraka* and *Vishṇu* (i.e. Kṛshṇa); slain by *K.*, *Naraka* lay lifeless like a *karṇikāra*-tree uprooted by the wind. When he had slain *Naraka* and *Muru* and recovered the ear-rings, *K.* came back and the gods granted him boons: "fatigue will never be thine in fight; neither the firmament nor the waters shall stop thy course, nor shall weapons penetrate thy body": V, **48,** †1884, †1889, †1891 (*Vishṇoḥ*), †1892, †1894. —§ 561 (do.): V, **48,** [†1895 (*Vishṇuṃ*)], †1896 (friend of the Pāṇḍavas).—§ 561*d* (Nara-Nārāyaṇau): V, **49,** 1936 (*K.* is identical with Nārāyaṇa, Arjuna with Nara).—§ 561 (Yānasandhip.): V, [**49,** 1939 (*Çaṅkhacakragadāhastaṃ . . . Keçavaṃ*)]; **50,** 1992 (*°dvitīyo vikramya tushṭyarthaṃ Jātavedasaḥ*, sc. Arjuna; all. to Khāṇḍavadahanaparvan), 2009 (*°sadṛço vīrye*, sc. Abhimanyu); [**52,** 2095 (*Hṛshīkeçaḥ*, charioteer of Arjuna)]; **53,** 2108 (*çreshṭho jagataḥ*); **55,** 2147 (*°pradhānāḥ*, sc. *mahārathāḥ*); **57** *ζ*, 2233 (*mukhyam Andhaka-Vṛshṇīnāṃ*, among the allies of Yudhishṭhira); **59,** 2324 (*°-Dhanañjayau*), 2342; **62,** †2418 (*°dvitīyena Dhanañjayena*); **65** *γγ*, 2489 (*Puṇḍarīkākshaṃ*); **68,** [2523 (*Vāsudevaḥ*; *m: K.* and Arjuna are perfectly equal to each other as to their godlike nature, and they have both taken their births of their own wish. The discus of *K.* occupies a space full 5 cubits in diameter, is capable of being hurled at the foe according to the wish of the wielder himself, and depends on illusion, it is invisible to the Kurus, etc.), 2526 (*Mādhavaḥ*, has slain Naraka, Çambara, Kaṃsa, and Çiçupāla)], 2531 (*yataḥ K°s tato jayaḥ*), [2536 (*Hariḥ*)]; **69**, [2540 (*triyugaṃ Madhusūdanaṃ kartāram akṛtaṃ devaṃ*)], 2549; **70**, [2562 (*Vishṇuḥ*)], 2563 (etymology), [2564 (*Vishṇuḥ*)], 2570, [2571 (*Vishṇuḥ*)] (Sañjaya explained the names of *K.*: Vāsudeva, etc.); [**71**, †2574 (*Vāsudevaṃ*, praised by Dhṛtarāshṭra as *ṛshiṃ sanātanaṃ*, etc. (vv. 2578–80)).]—§ 562 (Bhagavadyānap.): V, **72**, 2586, 2590, 2600, 2609, 2614, 2624, 2629, 2634, 2636, 2644, 2652, 2656, 2659, 2663, 2664, 2670, 2673 (*K.* promised to go to Hāstinapura and try to obtain peace); **74**, 2721, 2736; [**75**, 2740 (*Keçavaḥ*), 2741 (*Rāmānujaḥ Çauriḥ Çārṅgadhanvā*)]; **76**, 2769; **78**, 2807, 2812, 2817; **80**, 2850; **81**, 2864, 2865; **82**, 2879, 2880, 2883, 2885, 2889, 2891, 2893, 2900, 2901, 2902, 2905, 2907; **83**, 2939, 2947 (*Yadusukhāvahaṃ Vāsavānujaṃ*, worshipped by the ṛshis), 2948, [2954 (*Keçavaḥ / īçvaraḥ sarvabhūtānāṃ Devadevaḥ*)], (ι), 2962, 2965, 2968 (*K.* set out for Hāstinapura); [**84**, 2995 (*Dāçārhaḥ Madhusūdanaḥ*, description of his journey from Upaplavya to Vṛkasthala)]; **85**, [3027 (*bhūtānām īçvaraḥ*)], 3029; [**86**, 3040 (*Janārdanaḥ*), 3041 (*Āhukānām adhipatiḥ . . . Janārdanaḥ*), 3042 (*sphītasya Vṛshṇirāshṭrasya bhartā goptā ca Mādhavaḥ / trayāṇām api lokānāṃ bhagavān prapitāmahaḥ*]; **87**, 3066, 3067, 3072; **88**, 3078, 3082, 3093 (Duryodhana wished to imprison *K.*), 3098; **89**, 3101, 3106, [3124 (*antarātmā 'si dehināṃ*, says Vidura to *K.*)] (*K.* the next day set out from Vṛkasthala and came to Hāstinapura, where he stopped in the house of Vidura); **90**, 3129, 3131, 3149, 3156, 3164, 3168, 3182, 3189, 3193, 3196 (*Dharmāya Vedhase?*), 3197, 3231, 3232 (discourse with Kuntī); **91**, 3247, 3276 (*K.* came as an envoy to the palace of Duryodhana, but would not eat there, and took his meal in the house of Vidura); **92**, 3293, 3294, †3302, [3307 (*antarātmā 'si dehināṃ*)] (discourse with Vidura); **93**, 3323 (do.); **94**, 3332, 3336 (*Dāçārhaṃ*), 3337, 3344, 3346, 3347, 3349, 3352, 3358, 3359, 3363 (*Vāsudevasya*), 3367, 3376 (came to the conclave in the palace of Dhṛtarāshṭra); **95**, 3384 (his discourse to Dhṛtarāshṭra).—[§ 563 (do.): V, **96**, 3448 (*Keçavaḥ*), 3494 (*Nārāyaṇaḥ*, friend of Arjuna), 3495 (*Janārdanaḥ*), 3496 (Arjuna and *K.* (Keçava) are identical with Nara-Nārāyaṇau).] — [§ 564 (Mātalīyop.): V, **105**, 3710 (*Cakragadādharaḥ*, identified with Vishṇu).]—§ 565 (Gālavacarita): V, **107**, 3755 (*vibudhaçreshṭhaṃ tribhuvaneçvaraṃ Vishṇuṃ*), 3756; **111**, 3824 (*Nārāyaṇaḥ K°o Jishṇuç caiva narottamaḥ*, in Badarī); [**117**, 3976 (*reme . . . yathā . . . Rukmiṇyāṃ Janārdanaḥ*)].—§ 567 (Bhagavadyānap.): V, **124**, 4122 (*Keçava*), 4123 (spoke to Duryodhana about making peace); **125**, 4187, 4197 (°-*Bhīshmau*), 4200 (°-*Bhīshmayoḥ*), 4201 (*Devakīputro devair api suduḥsahaḥ*), 4210; **127**, 4242, 4245; [**128**, 4259 (*Dāçārhaḥ*, spoke to Duryodhana)]; **129**, 4309, 4311, 4346 (°-*Pāṇḍavau*), 4347 (*Keçavaḥ*); **130**, 4375, [4383 (*Vāsavānujaṃ*)], 4416 (Duryodhana wished to seize *K.*, Vidura enumerated the deeds of *K.* (v. 4407 foll.)); **131**, 4427, 4428 (showed his divine form); [**132**, (4460) (*Vāsudevaḥ*, discourse with Kuntī)].—§ 569 (do.): V, **137**, 4651, 4655 (*Mādhava*), 4668 (Kuntī had asked *K.* to bring word to the Pāṇḍavas); **138**, 4677; [**139**, 4713 (*Vāsudevaḥ*), 4722 (*mantrī Janārdano yasya*, i.e. Yudhishṭhira's)]; **140**, 4728 (*K.*'s conversation with Karṇa); **141**, 4756, 4758, 4765, 4767, 4769, 4770, 4782, 4784, 4799, 4800, 4801 (do.); [**142**, 4813 (*Keçavaḥ*)] (do.); **143**, 4833 (*Madhusūdanaṃ*), 4836, 4842, 4848, 4864, 4870, 4878, 4880, 4881 (do.);

144, 4885, 4887; **146**, 4937 (°*ena sahitāt Dhanañjayāt*); **147**, 4959 (*Dāçārhaṃ*), 4969 (returning to Upaplavya *K.* represented to the Pāṇḍavas what had happened (ch. **146–50**)).—§ 570 (Sainyaniryāṇap.): V, **151**, 5131 (*Dāçārhaḥ*), 5133 (do.), 5134, 5147 (proposed Dhṛshṭadyumna as generalissimo); [**152**, 5174 (*Keçavaḥ*, arranged the camp of the Pāṇḍavas)]; **154**, 5221, (5222) (*Çrī°*); **157**, 5318, (5322) (*Çrī°*), 5345.—§ 570*f* (Çārṅga): V, **158**, 5355 (held the bow Çārṅga).—§ 570*d* (Rukmin): V, **158**, 5364 (ravished Rukmiṇī and vanquished Rukmin).—§ 571 (Ulūkadūtāgamanap.): V, **160**, 5455, 5468; **161**, 5538; **162**, 5585, 5587, 5590, (5636) (*Çrī°*); [**163**, 5644 (*Keçavaṃ*)].—[§ 572 (Rathātirathasaṅkhyānap.): V, **165**, 5715 (*Vāsudevasahāyena Pārthena*); **169**, 5865 (*Guḍākeço Nārāyaṇasahāyavān*).] — [§ 573 (Ambopākhyānap.): V, **193**, 7579 (*Pārthaṃ Vāsudevasamāyuktaṃ*); **194**, 7588 (*Vāsudevaṃ*), 7590 (*Vāsudevasahāyavān*, sc. Arjuna); **196**, 7639 (*Vāsudeva-Dhanañjayau*).]—[§ 574 (Jambūkh.): VI, **1**, 17 (*Vāsudevaḥ*), 18 (*Vāsudeva-Dhanañjayau*).] — § 576 (Bhagavadgītāp.): VI, **21**, 771 (*yataḥ K°s tato jayaḥ*), 772, 773 (*yataḥ K°ḥ tato jayaḥ*), [774 (*Hariḥ*)], 775; [**22**, †786 (*Keçava°*, charioteer of Arjuna)]; **23**, 793, 813 (°*ārjunau ekarathau*), [818 (*Nara-Nārāyaṇau*, identical with Arjuna and *K.*)], 821 (*yato dharmas tato K°ḥ yataḥ K°s tato jayaḥ*); **25**, 859, 862, 871; **29**, 1036; **30**, 1098, 1101, 1103; **35**, †1281, †1287; **41**, 1427; **42**, 1529 (*yogeçvarāt*), 1532 (*yogeçvaraḥ*) (when Arjuna became despondent *K.* expounded to him the eternal religion (i.e. Bhagavadgītā, ch. **25–42**), declaring himself to be the supreme Lord).—§ 577 (Bhīshmavadhap.): VI, **43**, 1551, 1560 (°*ārjunau*), 1588 (= 821), 1621.—§ 578 (do.): VI, **49**, 1998 (°*sahitaḥ Pārthaḥ*); **50**, 2036, 2042 (ξ), 2067.—§ 579 (do.): VI, **52**, 2155 (°*ena sahitaḥ*, sc. Arjuna); **55**, 2374 (°*tulyaparākramaḥ*, sc. Abhimanyu), 2395. — § 580 (do.): VI, **59**[10], 2549, 2572, ([11]), †2597, [†2598 (*Mahendrāvarajaḥ*)], †2600, [†2601 (*Mahendrāvarajaṃ*), †2604 (*Deveça jagannivāsa . . . Çārṅgagadāsipāṇe*)], †2605, †2606, [†2610 (*Hariḥ*), †2611 (*Vishṇuḥ*)], †2613 (*K.* wished to slay Bhīshma, but was restrained by Arjuna).—§ 581 (do.): VI, **65** ξ, 2962, 2967 (*sṛshṭvā*—C. *dṛshṭvā—Saṅkarshaṇaṃ devaṃ svayam ātmānam ātmanā, K°a, tvam ātmanāsrakshīḥ* (C. °*aḥ sākshī*) *Pradyumnaṃ ca* (C. *hy*) *ātmasambhavaṃ*) (in days of yore Brahmán praised the supreme Lord with the hymn vv. 2944–72, asking him to be born on earth [as *K.*]); **66**, 3007 (= 821) (the god consented; asked by the gods Brahmán expounded to them the nature of Vāsudeva (vv. 2978–95); Bhīshma praised Vāsudeva (vv. 2996–3013)); **67**, 3033, 3034 (Bhīshma described the glory of Vāsudeva (π) (vv. 3015–36)); **68**, 3052 (Bhīshma quoted a hymn sung by Brahmán in honour of Vāsudeva (vv. 3038 foll.)).—§ 582 (do.): VI, **73**, 3203.—§ 584 (do.): VI, **82**, 3587.—§ 585 (do.): VI, **96**, 4328; [**99**, 4401 (*jagadgoptā Çaṅkhacakragadādharaḥ*), 4462 (*Vāsudevo 'nantaçaktiḥ sṛshṭisaṃhārakārakaḥ / sarveçvaro Devadevaḥ Paramātmā sanātanaḥ*)].—§ 586 (do.): VI, **106**, 4858, [4864 (*Devadeva*)], 4866 (*K.* wished again to slay Bhīshma, but was restrained by Arjuna); **107**, 4898, 4903, 4904, 4910, 4934, 4971, 4981.—§ 587 (do.): VI, **120**, 5759.—§ 588 (do.): VI, **121**, 5803 (*Devakīputraḥ*), 5806; **122**, 5833 (*sadṛçaḥ K°ena*, sc. Karṇa).—§ 589 (Droṇābhishekap.): VII, [**2**, †82 (*Vāsudevaḥ*, in the army of Yudhishṭhira)]; **3**, 107 (*yathā Vāyur . . . tathā K°ḥ*); [**10**, 380 (*Nārāyaṇaḥ*)]; **11**, 387 (enumeration of the feats of *K.*), 404, 406 (*Īçvaram*), 419 (*Arjunaḥ Keçavasyātmā K°o 'py ātmā Kirīṭinaḥ*), 421

(*Keçavam*), 422 (*Dāçārham*; *Nara - Nārāyaṇau* = Arjuna and *K.*). — § 591 (Saṃçaptakavadhap.): VII, **17**, 676 (°-*Pāṇḍavau*).—§ 592 (do.): VII, **18**, 725; **19**, 756, 760, 773; **23** *o*, 983 (*yam āhur adhyardhaguṇaṃ K°āt Pārthāc ca saṃyuge Abhimanyum*), [1016 (*Keçavena*, had slain the father of the Pāṇḍya king)]; **25**, 1096 (°*samaḥ*, sc. Abhimanyu); **27**, 1196, 1203, 1213 (*Janārdanaḥ*), 1225; **28**, 1226, 1228, 1251; [**29**, 1278 (*Vāsudevaḥ*, baffled the Vaishṇavāstra hurled by Bhagadatta, and then having described his fourfold form, told Arjuna how he formerly had bestowed that weapon on Naraka)].—§ 593 (Abhimanyuvadhap.): VII, [**33**, 1464 (*Viçvasṛṭ . . . Govindaḥ*)]; **34** *a*, 1482 (*sa-K°āḥ Pāṇḍavāḥ*), 1490; **35** *ε*, 1521 (knows how to pierce the cakravyūha); [**36**, 1544 (*Vishṇuṃ mātulaṃ*, sc. Abhimanyu's)]; **49**, [1927 (*Vishṇoḥ svasur nandakaraḥ*, i.e. Abhimanyu)], 1964 (°*ārjunasamaḥ*, sc. Abhimanyu).—§ 596 (Pratijñāp.): VII, **72**, 2486, 2536, 2540, 2543, 2551 (comforted Arjuna); **73**, 2587 (*purushottamam*); [**75**, 2648 (*Vāsudevaḥ*)]; **76**, 2685, 2697, 2705; **77**, [2707 (*Nara-Nārāyaṇau* = Arjuna and *K.*)], 2714 (comforted Subhadrā, etc.); **78**, 2768, 2774 (do.); [**79**, 2772 (*Govindaḥ*), 2783 (*Vishṇuḥ*) (ordered Dāruka to equip his chariot)]; **80**, [2821 (*Garuḍadhvajaḥ*)], 2822, 2824, 2832, 2833, 2836, 2841, 2853, 2855, 2866, [2869 (*Nara-Nārāyaṇau* = Arjuna and *K.*)], (2874) (°*ārjunau*) (*K.* appeared in a dream to Arjuna, then they repaired to the abode of Çiva, whom they praised); **81**, 2888, [2894 (*Nara-Nārāyaṇau* = Arjuna and *K.*)], 2897 (when Arjuna had obtained the Pāçupata weapon from Çiva, he and *K.* returned to the camp).—§ 597 (do.): VII, **82**, 2911; **83**, 2953, 2956, 2960, 2963 (*Devadeveça . . . Vishṇo Jishṇo Hare K°a Vaikuṇṭha Purushottama*) (praised by Yudhishṭhira), (2966) (promised victory to Arjuna); [**84**, 2978 (*Keçavasya prasādajaṃ*, all. to ch. **80–81**), 2984 (*Hṛshīkeçaḥ*, equipped the chariot of Arjuna, who then having *K.* for his charioteer proceeded to slay Jayadratha)].—§ 598 (Jayadrathavadhap.): VII, **85**, 3045; **86**, 3074, 3075, 3082 (°*ārjunau*); **88**, 3141. — § 599 (do.): VII, **89**, 3154 (°-*Dhanañjayau*); **91**, 3218, 3220 (°*samaḥ*, sc. Droṇa), 3227 (°-*Pāṇḍavau*), 3247; **92**, 3285, 3313 (*Çaurim*); **93**, 3353, 3394; **94**, 3428, 3445; [**98**, 3644 (*Dāçārhaḥ*)]; **99**, 3702; **100**, 3740, 3745, 3748 (groomed the horses of Arjuna and caused them to drink); **101**, 3777 (°-*Dhanañjayau*), 3794 (do.), 3800 (°-*Pārthau*), 3804; **102**, 3837 (°-*Pāṇḍavau*); **103**, 3847, 3853, 3854, 3856, 3858, 3868 (°-*Pāṇḍavau*), 3889 (°-*Dhanañjayau*); [**104**, 3901 (*Vāsudeva-Dhanañjayau*), 3923 (*Hareḥ*)]; **110**, 4179 (°*tulyaparākramaḥ*, sc. Sātyaki), 4186, [4222 (*Dāçārhaṃ goptāraṃ jagataḥ patim*)]; **111**, 4298 (°-*Pāṇḍavau*); **114**, 4460 (do.), 4470 (*Dāçārham*), 4480 (°-*Dhanañjayau*), 4489; [**117**, 4653 (*Dāçārhaḥ*); **118**, †4685 (*Keçava-Phālgunābhyām*)]; **122** *θθ*, 4883; **126**, 5138; **127**, 5189; [**128**, 5248 (*Vāsudevaḥ*)]; **129**, 5279, 5308; **130**, 5324 (°-*Dhanañjayau*); **131**, 5373 (do.); **132** *σσ*, 5451 (do.); **135**, 5554; [**136** *ωω*, 5629 (*Keçavārjunau*); **139**, 5802 (*Vṛshṇisiṃhasya*)]; **140** *γγγ*, 5819 (°-*Bhīmābhyām*), 5841; **141**, 5869; **142** *ζζζ*, 5889, 5931; **143**, 5964 (°*sakhaḥ*), 5987 (°-*Dhanañjayau*), (*ιι*), 5998 (ordered Bhūriçravas to go to his (*K.*'s) world and become equal to *K.*), (*κκκ*), 6004; **145**, 6057, 6060, 6141 (°-*Pārthau*); **146**, 6220 (*yogīnām īçvaro Hariḥ*), 6221, 6223 (created darkness; when Arjuna was about to slay Jayadratha *K.* caused him to throw the head of Jayadratha on the lap of Vṛddhakshatra); **147**, 6317, 6337; **148**, 6421, (6423), 6450; **149**, 6453, 6456 (only B., C. has *Kṛshṇau*), 6463 (Yudhishṭhira praised *K.* with the hymn vv. 6455*b*–74*a*); **152** *δ*, 6571 (°*sahāyena Pāṇḍavena*), 6586.—§ 600 (Ghaṭotkacavadhap.): VII, **156** *η*, 6747 (*çape 'haṃ K°caraṇaiḥ*), [6775 (*Govindam*)]; **158** *φ*, 6987, 6998, 7000 (°-*Pāṇḍavau*), 7001, 7005 (°-*Pāṇḍavau*), 7023; **159** *aa*, 7048; [**162**, 7269 (*Vāsudevaḥ*); **167**, 7497 (*Vāsudeva-Dhanañjayau*); **171**, 7724 (do.); **172**, 7757 (*Janārdanaḥ*)]; **173**, 7802, 7817 (despatched Ghaṭotkaca against Karṇa); **177**, 8062; [**178**, 8064 (*Vāsudevaḥ*); **180**, 8179 (do.); **181** *δδδ*, (8214) (do.)]; **182** *εεε*, 8259, 8261, 8262, (*ζζζ*), 8268, (*Vārshṇeyaḥ*), 8269, 8270, 8271, 8277 (*Purushottamaḥ*), 8279; **183** *εεε*, 8300 (*Devakīsutam*), 8302 (*Devakīputre*), 8317, 8319, 8320, 8323, 8333, 8334, 8338.—§ 602 (Droṇavadhap.): VII, **186**, 8464; **190**, 8748 (proposed to tell Droṇa that Açvatthāman was slain); **191**, 8804 (*Keçava*); [**192**, 8866 (*Vāsudevaç ca Vārshṇeyaḥ*)].—§ 603 (Nārāyaṇāstramokshap.): VII, [**195** *θ*, 9007 (*Janārdanaḥ*, does not know the Nārāyaṇāstra)]; **198**, 9133, (*σ*), 9180; **200**, [9270 (*Nara-Nārāyaṇau* = Arjuna and *K.*)], 9275; **201**, 9405.—[§ 603*b* (Nārāyaṇa): VII, **201**, †9459 (*Vāsudevaḥ* = Nārāyaṇa), 9471 (*Vāsudevāya* = do.), 9478 (*Çauriṇā* = do.).] — § 603 (Nārāyaṇāstramokshap.): VII, **201**, 9488 (*sanātanaḥ*); **202**, 9637 (°*ena darçitaḥ*, sc. Çiva, all. to chap. **80–1**).—§ 604 (Karṇap.): VIII, **5** *ζ*, 144 (*yathā K°ena Narako Muraç ca nihato raṇe*). — § 605 (do.): VIII, **16**, [629 (*Nara-Nārāyaṇau* = Arjuna and *K.*)], 635; [**17**, †665 (*Vāsudeve*); **18**, 688 (*Keçavaḥ*), 701 (*Indrānuja*)]; **19**, 734, 763, 765; **21**, 824; **24**, 963 (°-*Phālgunau*); **27**, 1091, 1094; **30**, [†1217 (*Arjuna-Keçavau*), (*νν*), 1227 (pierced by Karṇa)]; **31**, 1307 (*srashṭā jagataḥ*), 1311, 1314; **32** *σσ*, 1342, 1344, 1345, 1385 (*abhyadhikaḥ K°ād açvajñāne*, sc. Çalya).—§ 606 (do.): VIII, **34**, 1576 (°*āt . . . viçishṭaḥ*, sc. Çalya); **35**, 1627, 1628, 1629, (*a*), 1644, 1645, 1659 (*yathā*).—§ 607 (do.): VIII, **36**, 1670 (°*ād abhyadhikaḥ*, sc. Çalya); **40**, 1819, 1824 (*Devakīputrāt*), 1826, 1829 (armed with the cakra).—§ 608 (do.): VIII, **46** *ε*, 2137, 2181 (*etac cakraṃ gadā çārṅgaṃ çaṅkhaṃ K°sya*); **53**, 2582, 2584; **56**, 2776, 2779, 2781 (°-*Pāṇḍavau*), 2815 (°-*Dhanañjayau*), 2824, 2826, 2830; **58**, 2859, [2863 (*Hariḥ*)], 2898, 2900; **59**, 2960 (°-*Dhanañjayau*), 2974; **60**, 2976; [**62**, 3142 (*Nārāyaṇa°*)]; **64**, †3240, †3274, 3275, 3278; [**65**, †3296 (*Nārāyaṇam*)]; **66** *ιι*, 3347; **69** *μμμ*, 3410, (3419) (told Arjuna the tales of Kauçika and of Balāka), (*ξξξ*), 3471 (*paramā gatiḥ*); **70**, †3514, †3520, †3526, 3547 (*Hṛshīkeçam*); **71**, 3553, 3575; **72**, 3597, 3598; [**73**, 3634 (*Keçavaḥ*)]; **74** *φφφ*, 3754, 3756, 3758, 3761, 3763, 3781, 3787, 3791, 3793; **76** *ωωω*, †3855; **79** *ζ'*, 4010, 4014, [4018 (*Hariḥ*)], †4047, †4052 (all. to Khāṇḍavadahanaparvan), †4058, [†4059 (*Keçavena Nārāyaṇena*), †4060 (*Çaṅkhacakrāsipaṇer Vishṇor Jishṇor Vasudevātmajasya*), †4061 (*Nārāyaṇaḥ*)]; **81**, 4125; **82**, 4189; [**83**, 4257 (*Keçavārjunau*)]; [**84**, †4304 (*Keçava°*)]; **85**, †4331, †4335, †4347; **86**, 4364 (*Madhusūdana*), 4368, 4369; **87** *φ'*, 4387, [4451 (*Nara-Nārāyaṇau* = Arjuna and *K.*)], 4476 (*Govindam*), 4479, 4481; [**88**, †4511 (*Janārdanaḥ*)]; **89** *aη'*, †4584, (*aθ'*), †4601, †4615; **90**, †4678, (4680), †4707, 4717, 4731 (*K.* rescued Arjuna from Açvasena by making the chariot sink down into the earth); **91**, †4805 (Karṇa was slain by Arjuna); [**94**, 4956 (*Mādhavasya*)]; **96** *aφ'*, 4990, 4998, [5009 (*Nara-Nārāyaṇau* = Arjuna and *K.*)], 5011, 5016.—[§ 609 (Çalyap.): IX, **1** *δ*, 36 (*Vāsudevaḥ*, among the seven Pāṇḍava warriors who were still alive after the battle).]—§ 610 (do.): IX, **3**, 159 (°*sārathiṃ . . . rathaṃ*, i.e. the chariot of Arjuna); **4** *μ*, 201 (°*netraḥ*, sc. *Arjunaḥ*), 207, 235; **5** *ν*, 246, 248; [**7**, 347 (*Vāsudevaḥ*, advised

Yudhishṭhira to slay Çalya)].—§ 611 (do.): IX, [**11,** 567 (*Keçavārjunau*)]; [**13,** 693 (*Mādhavavacaḥ*, all. to chap. **7**)]; **16,** 798 (°-*Pārthayoḥ*), 811 (*Mādhavaṃ*); [**17,** †900 (*Govindavākyaṃ*, all. to chap. **7**), †901 (*uktam Indrāvarajasya*, do.)]; **19,** 1014, 1022 (*jagato nāthaḥ K°o Janārdanaḥ*); **24**νν, 1301; **27,** 1455, (ττ), 1456, 1457, 1462, 1466, 1467. —[§ 612 (Hradapraveçap.): IX, **30,** 1719 (*Janārdanaṃ*); **31,** 1744 (*Vāsudevaṃ*).]—§ 613 (Gadāyuddhap.): IX, **33,** [1889 (*Vāsudevaḥ*)] (censured Yudhishṭhira for his having given Duryodhana a chance of victory by proposing a single encounter about the kingdom), (ζ), 1906, 1909.—§ 614 (do.): IX, **34,** 1951.—§ 615 (do.): IX, **35,** 1976 (*Purushasattamaḥ*), 1977, 1979, 1980 (when Balarāma could not induce *K.* to join the Kurus he became enraged and set out on a tīrthayātrā, cf. § 570).—§ 615*ee* (Ādityatīrtha): IX, **49,** 2848 (*Madhusūdanaḥ*, present in the Ādityatīrtha). — § 615 (Baladevatīrthayātrā): IX, **54,** 3066 (Balarāma returned).—§ 615 (Gadāyuddhap.): IX, **55**ο, 3121; [**58,** 3246 (*Vāsudevaṃ*, *K.* advised Bhīmasena to vanquish Duryodhana by means of deception; Bhīmasena then fractured the thighs of Duryodhana)]; **60,** (3363) (*Çrī°*) (exculpated Bhīmasena), 3374, 3386; **61,** 3390, (φ), 3410, 3448 (*K.* and Duryodhana upbraided one another); **62**ψ, 3470 (when *K.* descended from the chariot of Arjuna it was reduced to ashes) (ω), 3483, 3486, 3491 (*yato dharmas tato K°o yataḥ K°as tato jayaḥ*); **63***aa*, 3504, 3506, 3523, 3525 (after the death of Duryodhana, *K.* went to Hāstinapura to comfort Gāndhārī and Dhṛtarāshṭra); **65**ηη, 3654.—§ 616 (Sauptikap.): X, **8,** 313 (had adored Çiva), [472 (*asānnidhyāt . . . Keçavasya*)]; **9,** 503, 509 (*Vārshṇeyaṃ*), (λ) [528 (*Vāsudevaḥ*)].—[§ 617 (Aishīkap.): X, **12,** 606 (*Puṇḍarīkākshaḥ*).] — § 617*b* (Brahmaçiras): X, **12,** 618, 641.—§ 617 (Aishīkap.): X, [**13,** 647 (*sarva-Yādavanandanaḥ*, description of his chariot)]; **14,** 670 (*Dāçārhaḥ*); **16,** 728 (promised to revive the fœtus in Uttarā's womb (i.e. Parikshit) after it had been slain by Açvatthāman with the Brahmaçiras weapon), 759; **17,** 761.—§ 618 (Jalapradānikap.): XI, **1**β, 15, (γ), 30; [**12,** 328 (*Hariḥ*), 329 (*Hariḥ*) (substituted an iron statue for Bhīmasena when Dhṛtarāshṭra embraced him)]; **13,** 354 (*Devakīputraṃ*), 356; **15,** 424.—§ 619 (Strīvilāpap.): XI, [**16,** 443 (*Puṇḍarīkākshaṃ . . . Purushottamaṃ*, Gāndhārī in her grief upbraided *K.*)]; **17**β, 503 (*Bhārata* (!)), 508, 511; **18**γ, 528, 541; **19**δ, 554, 555, 559, 563; **20**ε, 570, 572, 576; **22**η, 621, 629 (only B., C. has Kṛshṇā), 631; **23**θ, 639, 649; **24**ι, 702; **25**κ, 735, 739, 744 (Gāndhārī cursed *K.*, declaring that after the slaughter of all his kinsmen he should perish in the wilderness; *K.* declared this to be the will of fate, cf. Mausalaparvan).—[§ 620 (Çrāddhap.): XI, **26,** 761 (*Vāsudevasya*, *K.* censured Gāndhārī).] § 621 (Rājadh.): XII, **1**γ, 13, 16 (*Hariṃ*); **7**η, 187.—§ 630 (do.): XII, **27**β, 820 (*Puṇḍarīkākshaṃ*). —[§ 632 (do.): XII, **29,** (900) (*Vāsudevaḥ*, comforted Yudhishṭhira by telling him Shoḍacarājopākhyāna).] — § 633 (do.): XII, **30,** (1046) (*Çrī°*, told the story of Nārada and Parvata).—§ 635 (do.): XII, **37,** 1369, 1382 (*rathaṃ . . . Çaibya-Sugrīvayojitaṃ . . . samāsthāya*).—§ 637 (do.): XII, [**39,** 1430 (*Devakīputraḥ . . . Janārdanaḥ*, told the story of Cārvāka)]; **40***a*, 1458; **43,** 1500, 1503, 1509, 1514, 1515 (praised by Yudhishṭhira as Vishṇu (Nārāyaṇa) with the hymn vv. 1500–14); **45**ε, 1544; **46,** [1562 (*Vāsavānujaḥ*), 1579 (*kartā lokānāṃ*)], 1584 (*Keçavasya*); **47,** 1601, [1602 (*yogeçvaraṃ Padmanābhaṃ Vishṇuṃ Jishṇuṃ Jagatpatiṃ*)], 1604, 1680, 1681, 1683, 1689, [1690 (*Hariḥ*)] (Bhīshma praised *K.* as Vishṇu (Nārāyaṇa) with the hymn vv. 1604–88; *K.* bestowed divine knowledge on Bhīshma).—§ 638 (do.): XII, **48,** 1712 (*Vāsavānuja*); [**49,** (1715) (*Vāsudevaḥ*, told the story of Rāma Jāmadāgnya)].—§ 639 (do.): XII, **50**β, 1813; **51**δ, 1845 (*Hṛshīkeça*, praised by Bhīshma with the hymn vv. 1845–52); **52,** 1862, [1863 (*Lokanātha Mahābāho Çiva Nārāyaṇācyuta*)], 1874, 1883; **53,** [1898 (*Viçvakarmāṇaṃ Vāsudevaṃ Prajāpatiṃ*)], 1904, 1906, 1908, 1914, 1915.—§ 640 (do.): XII, **54***a*, 1929 (through the favour of *K.* Bhīshma had become competent to discourse on dharma); **55,** 1978; **56,** 1996 (*Vedhase*); [**58**γ, 2116 (*Vāsudevaḥ*)]. — § 641 (do.): XII, **60,** 2273 (*Vedhase*); **81,** 3036 (*Vārshṇeya*), 3040, 3050 (discourse between *K.* and Nārada); [**110,** 4077 (*Pītavāsaḥ . . . Acyutaḥ*), 4078 (*Govindaḥ Purushottamaḥ*, identified with Nārāyaṇa (Hari))].—§ 664 (Mokshadh.): XII, **207,** 7548 (= Vishṇu (Nārāyaṇa), performed the creation, etc.), 7565. — § 666 (do.): XII, **209,** 7604 (*avyayam īçvaraṃ*), 7636 (= Vishṇu (Nārāyaṇa)). —[§ 667 (do.): XII, **210,** 7650 (*Vāsudevaḥ* = Vishṇu (Nārāyaṇa)), 7654 (*Vārshṇeyaṃ*, adj.).] — [§ 676 (do.): XII, **231,** 8455 (*Keçavaḥ*), (8457) (*Vāsudevaḥ*) (discourse between *K.* and Ugrasena).]—[§ 692 (do.): XII, **281,** 10086 (*Janārdanaḥ*, identified with the supreme Lord), 10088 (*Keçavam Acyutaṃ*, the eighth part of the supreme Lord).]—§ 717*b* (Nārāyaṇīya): XII, **335,** 12658 (one of the forms of Nārāyaṇa born as son of Dharma), 12667 (do.); [**340,** 12968 (*Sātvataḥ*, ninth avatāra of Vishṇu); [**342** (*K.* = Vishṇu (Nārāyaṇa) explained his names to Arjuna)]; **343**φ, 13238 (etymology) (do., *K.* expounded the power of Agni and Soma; *K.* has been born from Dharma as the ṛshis Nara and Nārāyaṇa); **347,** 13443 (*çṛṇvatoḥ K°-Bhīshmayoḥ*, Nārada had recited the Nārāyaṇīya (?)); **349,** 13557 (do., Nārada discoursed on the dharma of Nārāyaṇa), 13611 (do., Vyāsa repeated the discourse of Nārada), 13636 (*lokānāṃ bhāvanaḥ*). –§ 725 (Ānuçāsanik.): XIII, **9,** 421 (°*sya . . . kathāṃ*) (? = Vyāsa, Nīl.).—[§ 727 (do.): XIII, **11,** †508 (*Devakīputrasannidhau*), †511 (*Garuḍadhvajasya*, the discourse between Rukmiṇī and Çrī).]—§ 730 (do.): XIII, **14,** 597 (had in Badarī gratified Çiva), 600 (gratifies Çiva in every yuga), [602 (*Harir Acyutaḥ*), 606 (*Surāsuraguro deva Vishṇo*)], 658, 678 (in order to get a son by the favour of Çiva *K.* set out and came to the hermitage of Upamanyu).—§ 730*g* (Upamanyu): XIII, **14,** 721, 768, 863, 929, 957 (Upamanyu told *K.* about his relations to Çiva). § 730 (Ānuçāsanik.): XIII, **14,** 958, [(971), (*Çrī-Vishṇuḥ*)], 999, [(1002) (*Vishṇuḥ*)], 1023, 1024 (*Yādavaçārdūla*); **15,** (1025) (*Çrī°*); [**16,** 1110 (*Yādaveçvara*)]; **17,** 1126, 1131 (Çiva granted *K.* the boon that he should get a son), 1283 (read *K°a* with B., C. by error *K°aḥ*); **18**κκ, 1327, 1357, 1367, [(†1368) (*Vishṇuḥ*)].—§ 737 (do.): XIII, **31,** 2032 (discourse between *K.* and Nārada).—[§ 739 (do.): XIII, **34,** 2129 foll. (discourse between *K.* and the Earth).]—§ 746 (do.): XIII, **70,** 3457, 3461, 3479, 3480 (rescued Nṛga, who in consequence of a curse had been transformed into a lizard); **72,** 3544 (do.).—§ 753 (do.): XIII, **97,** 4671 (discourse between *K.* and the Earth).—[§ 759 (do.): XIII, **109** (the twelve names under which *K.* (*Vishṇu*) is to be worshipped).] — § 768 (do.): XIII, **139,** 6297, 6303, 6332 (*K.* (Vishṇu, Nārāyaṇa, Hari) observed a vrata for twelve years; then fire issued from his mouth; it was his soul that repaired to Brahmán and obtained the boon that a half of Çiva should be born as the son of *K.*).—§ 768*b* (do.): Çiva said: *Hari* has ten arms, a curl of hair on his breast, curly locks, *Brahmán* has risen from his abdomen, I (Çiva) from his head, the gods and Asuras from the hairs of his body, the ṛshis, etc., from his body; assuming a human form, he will cause all the kings on earth to be slain in battle in order to achieve the purposes of the gods; he is identical with Brahmán (*brahmabhūtasya satataṃ*) and the refuge of the *Devarshis*, and the abode of Brahmán, Çiva, and of all the gods; he is armed with the cakra and the çaṅkha, has Garuḍa for his standard, his illusive power depends upon yoga, and he has a thousand eyes; he will take birth in the race of Prajāpati Manu as Kṛshṇa (Vāsudeva). The stem of genealogy will be the following: *Manu* > *Aṅga* > *Antardhāman* > *Havirdhāman* (*Prajāpatir aninditaḥ*) > *Prācīnabarhis* > *Pracetas* (+ nine other sons) > *Daksha Prajāpati* > *Dākshāyanī* > *Āditya* > *Manu* > *Ilā* (= *Sudyumna*) ↔ *Budha* > *Purūravas* > *Āyu* > *Nahusha* > *Yayāti* > *Yadu* > *Kroshṭṛ* > *Vṛjinīvat* > *Ṛshadgu* (B. *Ushaṅgu*) > *Citraratha* > *Çūra* (younger son) > *Vasudeva Ānakadundubhi* > [Kṛshṇa] *Vāsudeva*. *K.* will have four arms, love and be beloved by the brahmans; he will liberate the kings confined by the *Magadha* king *Jarāsandha*; he will be the king of all kings on earth; grown up among the *Çūrasenas* and residing at *Dvārakā* he will conquer and protect the whole earth, conversant [as he is] with policy (*nayavit sadā*); he who wishes to see me (Çiva) or *Brahmán* should first see *Vāsudeva*; then we are seen; that person with whom the lotus-eyed *Vāsudeva* becomes gratified, with him all the gods, headed by Brahmán, become gratified; he will be an instructor in *dharmas*; he, for the sake of righteousness, created millions of ṛshis, who are now headed by Sanatkumāra, residing on Gandhamādana, engaged in penances; in him [are] the three [great gods] (*tṛtayaṃ*); his elder brother will be Balarāma (*c*), the bearer of the plough (*halī*), capable of lifting the whole earth (XIII, **147**); XIII, **147**, 6807 (*Hariḥ*).—§ 768*b* (Umā-Maheçvarasaṃv.): XIII, **148**, 6876.—§ 768 (Ānuçāsanik.): XIII, **148**, 6978 (*Devakinandanaḥ*), 6879, 6885, [6888 (*Nārāyaṇaḥ*), 6892 (*Vishṇuh*), 6896 (*Nārāyaṇaḥ*)], 6897, [6898 (*Hari-Gāṇḍīvivigrahaṃ*)], 6903, 6904, 6912, 6932.—§ 769*b* (Vishṇu's 1000 names): XIII, **149**, 6956, 7008.—§ 769 (Ānuçāsanik): XIII, **149**, 7071 (= Vishṇu).—§ 773*b* (do.): Bhīshma praised *K.* as the supreme god, mentioning his incarnation as a boar, and that *Brahmán* sprang from the lotus which appeared in his navel; he existed in the *Kṛta* age in the form of Righteousness, in the *Tretā* in that of Knowledge, in the *Dvāpara* in that of Might, in the *Kali* in that of Unrighteousness; he slew the *Daityas*, he ruled [as *Bali*] the *Asuras*; he is always accompanied by hundreds of *Gandharvas* and *Apsarases*, and hymned by the very *Rākshasas*; he is praised by the *Sāman* singers by reciting the *Rathantara*; he was hymned by the gods [when he lifted up the *Govardhana* mountain] in order to protect the cowherds [of Vṛndāvana] (? *taṃ ghoshārthe gīrbhir Indrāḥ stuvanti*, v. 7370, **159**, v. 18); he lifted up the earth, agitating all the *Dānavas* and *Asuras*; he caused the seed of the [two] gods [Mitra and Varuṇa] to fall into a jar, whence they say that the *Ṛshi* Vasishṭha has arisen; he is *Mātariçvan*, etc.; he [is the soul] of gods, men, and *Pitṛs*; vanquishing the *Rākshasas* and *Uragas*; he offers everything up in *Agni*, who (so C., B. has *sa*) was gratified in the Khāṇḍava forest; he gave white horses to [*Arjuna*] *Pārtha*; he crossed the streams to slay Indra and paralysed him when he was about to hurl the vajra; he is *Mahendra* who is praised by the brahmans in great sacrifices with 1,000 old *Ṛc* verses; he alone could keep *Durvāsas* as a guest in his house; he is the one ancient *Ṛshi*; the *Rudras*, the *Ādityas*, the *Vasus*, the *Açvins*, the *Sādhyas*, the *Viçvedevas*, the *Maruts*, *Prajāpati*, the mother of the gods, *Diti* and the seven Ṛshis [have] all [sprung] from *K.*; when he becomes *jīva* he is called *Saṅkarshaṇa*; then he becomes *Pradyumna*, and then *Aniruddha*; in this way he displays himself in fourfold form; he created the gods, the *Asuras*, men, the worlds, the *Ṛshis*, etc.; he is *Nārāyaṇa* (XIII, **159**): XIII, **159**, †7358, †7359, †7360, †7363, †7365, †7377, †7387, †7397, [†7400 (*Nārāyaṇaḥ*)].—§ 773*c* (Durvāsas): XIII, **160**, 7422, 7447 (had 16,000 wives, Rukmiṇī being the first) (Durvāsas put *K.* and Rukmiṇī to the test, and granted him that he should be invulnerable except on the soles of his feet).—[§ 773 (Ānuçāsanik.): XIII, **161–2** (recited the Çatarudriya to Yudhishṭhira).]—§ 774 (do.): XIII, **163**, 7532 (*Devakinandane*).—§ 776 (do.): XIII, **167**, 7695.—§ 777 (Svargārohaṇik. p.): XIII, **168**, [7742 (*Devadeveça*, etc.), 7743 (*Vāsudevo hiraṇyātmā Purushaḥ*, etc.)], 7745, 7746 (*yato K°s tato dharmo yato dharmas tato jayaḥ*), [7750 (*Nara-Nārāyaṇau* = Arjuna and *K.*)], 7751 (granted Bhīshma leave to quit his body and promised him that he would attain to the status of the Vasus); **169**β, 7778, 7795, 7796 (°*mukhāḥ*).—[§ 778 (Açvamedhikap.): XIV, **2**, 20 (*Keçavaḥ*, consoled Yudhishṭhira).]—[§ 779 (do.): XIV, **11–13** (discoursed on the encounter between Indra and Vṛtra, etc.).]—§ 780 (do.): XIV, **14**, 366 (°-*Phālgunau*).—§ 781 (do.): XIV, **15**, 376 (°-*Pāṇḍavau*).—§ 782 (Anugītāp.): XIV, **16**, 408, 410, 414, 423; **18**, 584; **34**, 932; **51**, 1470 (requested by Arjuna *K.* recited the Anugītā (ch. **16–51**), identifying himself with Kshetrajña (v. 934)), 1476.—§ 783 (do.): XIV, **52**, 1478, 1481 (°-*Pāṇḍavau*), [1491 (*Ātmā ca Paramātmā ca*, praised by Arjuna)], 1511, 1512.—§ 784 (do.): XIV, **53**, 1538 (returned to Dvārakā).—§ 784*b* (Uttaṅka): XIV, **53**, 1554, 1556 (Uttaṅka wished to curse Kṛshṇa); [**54**, (*K.* expounded his divine nature to Uttaṅka)]; **55**, [1591 (*Vishṇoḥ*) (Uttaṅka saw the divine form of *K.*), 1592 (*Parameçvaraṃ*), 1593 (*Viçvakarman*, etc.)], 1597, 1598, 1609, 1623 (*K.* granted Uttaṅka the boon ever to have water); [**56**, 1625 (*Vishṇave*)].—§ 785 (Anugītāp.): XIV, **59**, 1765; [**60**, (1778) (*Vāsudevaḥ*) (returning to Dvārakā *K.* recounted the events of the battle)]; **61**, 1812, 1814, 1820 (related the fall of Abhimanyu); **62**, 1853 (performed the obsequial rites for Abhimanyu), 1865 (*Vṛshṇivīreṇa*); **66**, 1942 (came to Hāstinapura), 1946, 1949, 1957; **67**, 1971, 1972, 1973, 1982; **68**, 1994, 2002, 2003, 2004, 2007; **69**, 2024; **70**, 2033, 2042 (*K.* gave life to the stillborn Parikshit); **71**, 2064 (*Devakinandanaṃ*), 2069; **72**, 2083; **86**, 2566 (came to the açvamedha of Yudhishṭhira); **87**, 2574, 2578, 2583, 2584, 2597 (*Yadunandanaḥ*); **88**, 2610, 2611; [**89**, 2661 (*Vāsudevaḥ*), 2680 (*Govindaṃ*, returned to Dvārakā)].—§ 787 (Āçramavāsap.): XV, **7**, 255; [**16**, 462 (*Vāsudevāt*, all. to § 568); **17**, 49, (*Vāsudevaṃ*, do.)].—§ 788 (do.): XV, **25**γ, 667 (*paspardha K°ena sadā yo nṛpaḥ*, sc. the father-in-law of Bhīmasena).—§ 789 (Putradarçanap.): XV, **29**, 784 (*Subhadrā K°bhaginī*), 807 (°*sya bhaginī*, i.e. Subhadrā); [**31**η, 854 (*Hṛshīkeçam*, identical with Nārāyaṇa)].—§ 793 (Mausalap.): XVI, **1**, 21 (*Jarā K°ṃ mahātmānaṃ çayānaṃ bhuvi bhetsyati*, cf. ch. **4**); [**2** (observed the bad omens and remembered the curse of Gāndhārī, then he caused the Vṛshṇis to go to Prabhāsa)]; **3**, 60, [68 (*Hariḥ*)], 72, 91, 93 (caused the destruction of the Vṛshṇis in Prabhāsa); **4**, †106, †110, †114, †125, [†130 (*Nārāyaṇaḥ*)], †131 (having been pierced at the heel by Jaras, *K.* ascended to heaven and attained to his own region); **5**, 139, 142, 144 (left 16,000 widows); **6**, 156, 175; **7**, 214 (his grandson Vajra was installed as king in Indraprastha), 250 (some of his widows ascended his funeral pyre), [251 (*Hari-*)]; **8**ν, 261, 266, 268, [277 (*Vishṇuṃ*)], (ξ), 280, 283.—§ 794 (Mahāprasthānikap.): XVII, **1**, 1 (*divaṅ gate*), [12 (*Hariṃ*)], (*a*) 40 (his cakra had disappeared). —[§ 795 (Svargārohaṇap.): XVIII, **4**, 126 (*Govindaṃ Brāhmeṇa vapushā sthitaṃ*, in heaven); **5**, 171 (*Vāsudevaḥ*, was a portion of Nārāyaṇa, into whom he entered, his 16,000 wives were incarnate Apsarases).]

Cf. Kṛshṇa (dual.), Nārāyaṇa, Vishṇu, and the following synonyms:—

Acyuta, Adhideva, Adhokshaja, Ādideva, q.v.

Āhukānām adhipati(ḥ) ("the king of the Āhukas"): V, 3041.

Aja, q.v.

Amadhya, Anādi, Anādimadhyaparyanta, Anādinidhana, Anādya, Ananta, v. Vishṇu.

Andhaka-Vṛshṇinātha ("the lord of the Andhakas and the Vṛshṇis"): VI, 2606.

Asita ("the black one"): IX, 3351 (*pītāsitau Yaduvarau*, i.e. Balarāma and Kṛshṇa).

Atman, Avyakta, Avyaya, q.v.

Bhojarājanyavardhana ("enhancing the glory of the Bhoja princes"): XIV, 2581.

Bhūtānām īçvara(ḥ), Bhūtapati, Bhūtātman, Bhūteça, q.v.

Cakradhara ("discus-bearer"): I, 6257 (i.e. Vishṇu?); VII, †5833 (°*prabhāvaḥ*, sc. Sātyaki).

Cakradhārin (do.): XIII, 6868.

Cakragadābhṛt ("bearing discus and mace"): V, 2933.

Cakragadādhara (do.): II, 1560 (*K*°); V, 3251, 3740; XI, 747; XIV, 30, 2610; XVI, 282.

Cakragadāpāṇi (do.): I, 2506 (i.e. Vishṇu).

Cakrapāṇi ("discus-handed"): VI, 1900 (°*r ivāsurān*, i.e. Vishṇu).

Cakrāyudha ("whose weapon is a discus"): I, 1163 (i.e. Vishṇu); V, 56; XV, †665.

Çaibya-Sugrīvavāhana ("having Çaibya and Sugrīva for his horses"), q.v.

Çambhu, q.v.

Çaṅkhacakragadādhara ("bearing conch, discus, and mace"): III, 743, 12989 (i.e. Nārāyaṇa (Vishṇu)), 15850 (*K*°); VI, 4461; VII, 2962; XIII, 7742; XIV, 1609; XVI, 273.

Çaṅkhacakragadāhasta (do.): V, 1939.

Çaṅkhacakragadāpāṇi (do.): VIII, 1630.

Çaṅkhacakrāsipāṇi ("holding conch, discus, and sword"): VIII, †4060.

Çārṅgacakragadādhara ("bearing bow, discus, and mace"): II, 1599; VI, 2986; XVI, 102.

Çārṅgacakrāsipāṇi ("holding bow, discus, and sword"): XII, 1514.

Çārṅgadhanurdhara ("bearing the bow Çārṅga"): VI, 2947.

Çārṅgadhanvan (do.): III, 178, 10264, 13140; V, 2741, 4675; VI, 2937; VII, 379; VIII, 233; X, 653, 656; XII, 7523; XIII, 7056 (Vishṇu's 1000 names); XIV, 1541; XVI, 10, 268.

Çārṅgagadāpāṇi ("holding bow and mace"): VIII, 2182.

Çārṅgagadāsipāṇi ("holding bow, mace, and sword"): VI, †2604.

Çārṅgiṇ ("having the bow Çārṅga"): VII, 2964; XVII, 13.

Çauri ("descendant of Çūra"): I, 7989; II, 48, 50, 622 (*Çāmbaḥ Ç°samaḥ*), 781, 878 (*Hṛshīkeçaḥ*), 887, 1380, 1599; III, 12559, 14739; V, †724 (*Vāsudevaṃ*), 2741, 2940, 3220, 3236, 3344, 3351, 3360, 3380, 4209, 4408, 4414, 4421, 4444, 4448, 4456, 4957; VI, 2137, †2616; VII, 3313, 3743, 3795, 7016, 7018, 9478 (= Nārāyaṇa); VIII, 1308 (*sadṛçaḥ Ç°eḥ*, sc. Çalya), †1963, 3216; XI, 743; XII, 898, 1530; XIV, 380 (*Janārdanaḥ*), 1545.

Çūlabhṛt, Çūlin, q.v.

Dāçārha: I, 7551, 8012 (*Janārdanaḥ*), 8207, 8328; II, 961, 1223, 1225, 1342; III, 494, 897, 12566; IV, 38 (all. to Khāṇḍavadahanap.); V, 2582, 2628, 2765, 2863, 2871, 2876, 2879, 2886, 2889, 2969, 2985, 2995, 3019, 3026, 3029, 3039, 3044, 3053, 3066, 3076, 3113, 3123, 3127, 3241, 3256, 3259, 3274, 3334, 3336, 3340, 3345, 3350, 3353, 3365, 3370, 3371, 3381, 4259, 4280, 4291 (*Pushkarekshaṇaḥ*), 4650, 4670, 4693 (°*pramukhā nṛpāḥ*), 4959 (*K*°), 5131 (*K*°), 5133 (*K*°), 5195, 5197, 5582; VI, 3456 (all. to Bhagavadyānap.); VII, 422 (*K*°), 1231, 1257 (°-*Pāṇḍavau*, i.e. *K.* and Arjuna), 3033, 3149, 3644, 3671, 3700, 3749, 3757, 3834, 4222, 4470 (*K*°), 4489, 4653, 6776, 7819, 8272, 9231; VIII, 1305, 1312, 2813, 2860, 2975, †3475, 3702 (*Vāsudevaṃ*), 4349, 4982, 5005; IX, 1322, 1325, 1469; X, 619 (C. °*s*°), 653, 654, 670, 745, 760; XI, 315, 568, 755; XII, 1454, 1457, 1499 (*Puṇḍarīkākshaṃ*), 1902 (*Acyutaḥ*); XIV, 1855 (*Vāsudevaḥ*), 1955, 1958, 2025 (*Acyutaḥ*), 2076; XVI, 103.

Daçārhabhartṛ: III, †12579.

Daçārhādhipati: III, †903.

Dāçārhakulavardhana: XII, 1870.

Dāçārhanandana: I, 8076 (*Kuru-D°au*, i.e. Arjuna and *K.*).

Daçārhanātha: VIII, †679.

Daçārhasiṃha: III, †12578.

Dāçārhavīra: V, †3303.

Dāmodara ("having a rope round his waist"): I, †7079; II, 1510; III, 1953; V, 625, 2566 (etymology); XII, 1505, 13172 (etymology); XIII, 5383, 6989 (Vishṇu's 1000 names), 7788.

Devadeva, Devadeveça, Devadeveçvara, q.v.

Devakīmātṛ ("the son of Devakī"): VII, 726; VIII, 3309; XIV, 411.

Devakīnandana (do.): I, 401 (*K*°); II, 954, 980 (*K.*); III, 773 (*K*°); VII, 8293; VIII, 5006; XIII, 6878, 7532 (*K*°); XIV, 1498, 2061 (*K*°).

Devakīnandana (do.): III, 15528 (*K*°).

Devakīputra (do.): I, 7116 (*K*°); III, 1110 (*K*°), 12563, 12612, ††13348 (*K*°); V, 2545, 4201 (*K*°), 5239; VI, 5548, 5803; VII, 1259, 1260, 6326, 8302 (*K*°); VIII, 1387, 1648, 1824 (*K*°); IX, 1286, 1444; X, 740; XI, 354 (*K*°); XII, 1430 (*Janārdanaḥ*), 1936; XIII, 508, †7384.

Devakīsuta (do.): II, 50 (*Çauriḥ*), 1222; IV, 1651 (*K*°), 2056 (*K*°); VII, 68, 2946, 8296, 8300; XIII, 6856, 6949 (Vishṇu's 1000 names).

Devakītanaya (do.): XIII, 6300.

Gadāgraja ("the elder brother of Gada"): III, 733, †12570; VI, 1617, 4979; XII, 1713; XIV, †1530, †1531; XV, 82.

Gadapūrvaja (do.): V, †27.

Kapila, q.v.

Kaustubhabhūshaṇa ("adorned with the Kaustubha"): III, 15533.

Keçava: I, †174, †175, †213, 393, 621 (*Rāma-K°au*), 2276, 2315, †7308, 7532, 7553, 7595, 7959, 7986, 7998, 8000, 8025 (*°sya priyā svasā*, i.e. Subhadrā), 8290, 8298 (*°ārjunau*), 8309 (do.), 8467; II, 23, 39, 43, 47, 54, 74, 644 1214 (*Keçisūdanaḥ*), 1387, 1396, 1402 (*Keçihantāraṃ*), 1437, 1447, 1475, 1509 (*Rāma-K°au*), 1524, 1536, 1537, 1540, 1543, 1592, 1598, 1618, 1926, 2292; III, 464, 469, 476, 479, 507, 587, 596, 731 (*°syāgrajaḥ . . . Baladevaḥ*), 830, 870, 1999, 2001, 5038 (*Vishṇoḥ*, worshipped at Vaḍavā), 5039 (= do.), 5067 (worshipped at Sarasvatī on the fourteenth day of the bright fortnight of Caitra), 8038 (*na devaḥ K°āt paraḥ*), 10286, 11257 (i.e. Vishṇu, becomes black—*kṛshṇaḥ*—in the Kaliyuga), 12562, †12593, †12594, †12595, †12596, 12601, 13567 (i.e. Vishṇu), 13575 (= do., slew Madhu and Kaiṭabha), 14723, 14735, 15175 (*°ārjunau*), 15538, 15544, 15565; IV, 918 (*°ānugatāḥ*, sc. the Pāṇḍavas), 1403 (*°enāpi saṅgrāme . . . samaṃ*, sc. Arjuna); V, 150, 159, †653, †654, †672, †674, †732, †804, †808, †1810, †1859, †1888, 1939, 2132 (*çreshṭhaḥ . . . sarvabhūtānāṃ*), 2329, 2341, 2358, †2419, 2437, 2491, †2519 (*°-Pārthayoḥ*), 2537, 2540, 2544, 2545, 2559, 2561, 2643, 2674, 2740, 2848, 2855, 2878, 2890, 2894, 2898, 2914, 2921, 2933, 2954, 2964, 2968, 2976, 2979, 2987, 3012, 3021, 3037, 3049, 3050, 3054, 3075, 3080, 3085, 3112, 3135, 3137, 3156, 3242, 3247, 3275, 3278, 3288, 3333, 3357, 3448, 3496 (*°ārjunau*), 4122, 4186, 4188, 4189, 4192, 4195, 4211, 4213, 4234, 4238, 4254, 4257, 4258, 4347, 4371, 4376, 4386, 4402, 4403, 4406, 4418, 4421, 4430, 4450, 4451, 4463, 4644, 4670, 4755, 4805, 4808, 4812, 4813, 4833, 4846, 4849, 4873, 4882, 4884, 4892, 4956, 4967, 5097, 5098, 5130, 5174, 5177, 5178, 5333, 5346, 5374, 5500, 5525, 5545, 5569, 5581, 5584, 5644, 5697 (*°ārjunayoḥ*); VI, 446 (i.e. Nārāyaṇa), †759, †786, 932, 951, 1218, †1281, 1322, 1530 (*°ārjunayoḥ*), 1558, 1620, 2041, 2046, 2575, †2613, †2614, 3031, 3033, 3036, 3047, 3048, 3049, 3566, 4322 (*°ārjunau*), 4335, 4867, 4872, 4873, 4909, 5759; VII, 343, 411, 419, 420, 421, 671, 736, 770, 1016, 1273, 1274, 1292, 1456 (*°ārjunayoḥ*), 2480, 2501, 2502, 2510, 2537 (*°ārjunayoḥ*), 2686, 2693, 2704, 2732, 2750, 2830, 2834, 2842, 2844, 2909 (*Arjuna-K°au*), 2978, 3032, 3151, 3247, 3317, 3349, 3357, 3400, 3401, [illegible], [illegible], 3704, 3705, 3841, 3856, 3866, 3881, 3902, 3908, 4179, 4193, †4685 (*°-Phālgunābhyāṃ*), 5557, 5613, 5629 (*°ārjunau*), 5803, 5854, 5867, 5868, 5873, 5876, 5883 (*°ārjunau*), 5930 (*°ārjunayoḥ*), 6219, 6226, 6287, 6328, 6343, 6381, 6401, 6419, 6474, 7760 (*°ārjunau*), 7834, 8182, 8275, 8298, 8303, 8468, 8702, 8804, 9396 (*saha°*), 9429 (*°ārjunau*), 9430, 9433 (*°ārjunau*), 9444 (do.), 9486 (*Rudrasambhavaḥ*), 9490; VIII, 30 (all. to Bhagavadyānaparvan), 157, 627 (*°ārjunayoḥ*), 628 (*°ārjunau*), 636, 639, 641 (*Arjuna-K°au*), †666, 686 (*°ārjunau*), 688, †1217 (*°ārjunau*), 1271 (*Pārthān . . . saha-K°ān*), 1630, 1665, 1774 (*°ārjunau*), 1952 (*prabhāvaḥ . . . paurāṇaḥ K°sya*), 1960 (*Arjuna-K°au*), 2016 (*Pārthān sa-K°ān*), 2111 (*°ārjunau*), 2138, 2161 (*°ārjunau*), 2577, 2578, 2581, 2782, 2784 (*°ārjunau*), 2959, 3282, 3298, 3307 (*°ārjunau*), †3397, †3398, 3404, †3476, †3477, †3515, 3576, 3634, 3751, 3752, 3766, 3783, 3786, 3791, †3853, 4017, †4059, †4085, 4257 (*°ārjunau*), †4304, †4572, †4951 (*°-Pāṇḍunandanau*), 4963 (i.e. Vishṇu; *iva Sureça-K°au*), 4989, 5005, 5008 (*°ārjunau*); IX, 250, 362, 363, 567 (*°ārjunau*), †1564, 1661, 1862, 1949, 1969, 1970, 3266, †3318, 3350, 3352, 3365, 3467, 3479, 3533, 3534, 3535, 3539, 3568, 3569, 3571, 3573, 3576 (*Keçisūdanaṃ*); X, 472, 643, 673, 727, 747 (*saha°*); XI, 357, 360 (*saha°*), 469, 484, 485, 504, 568, 650, 666, 670, 688, 733; XII, 30 (*saha°*), 897, 1090, 1133, 1513, 1584, 1692 (*Purushottomaṃ*), 1694, 1817, 1889, 1891, 1938 (*Acyutaḥ*), 1945, 1980, †2120, 3048, 4491 (i.e. Vishṇu), 7519 (i.e. Vishṇu (Nārāyaṇa)), 7522 (= do.), 7549 (= do.), 7566 (= do.), 7656 (= do.), 8455, 10088 (*Acyutaṃ*, is the eighth part of the Supreme god), 13132, 13135, 13177 (etymology), 13184, 13185, 13542 (i.e. Vishṇu); XIII, 665, 669, 690, 879, 1361 (*°tvaṃ*, sc. *Rudraḥ prayacchati*), 1365, 2010, 2029, 5372, 6846, 6952 (Vishṇu's 1000 names), 7018 (do.), 7059 (i.e. Vishṇu), 7356, †7359, †7389, †7397, †7399, †7400, 7447, 7448, 7449, 7704; XVI, 20, 379, 407 (*°ārjunau*), 412, 1522, 1527, 1546, 1548, 1563, 1821, 1951, 1968, 1980, 2002, 2006, 2034, 2598; XVI, 23, 56, 78, 80, 84, 92, †105, †108, †109, †115, †116, †126, 135, 190 (*°sya niveçane*); XVIII, 299.

Keçihan ("the slayer of Keçin"): XII, †1697; XIII, 7018; XIV, 1984, 2585.

Keçihantṛ (do.): II, 1402 (*Keçavaṃ*).

Keçinishūdana ("the destroyer of Keçin"): VI, 1455.

Keçisūdana (do.): II, 1214 (*Keçavaḥ*); IX, 3576 (*Keçavaṃ*); XVI, 52.

Kirīṭa-Kaustubhadhara, q.v.

Kshetrajña, q.v.

Lokabhāvana, Lokakartṛ, Lokakṛt, Lokanātha, Lokasākshin, Lokayoni, q.v.

Mādhava, Mādhavarshabha, q.v.

Madhughātin, Madhu-(Kaiṭabha)han, Madhunihan, Madhupravīra, Madhusūdana, q.v.

Mahābāhu: V, 2567 (etymology); XII, 1863.

Mahāvarāha, q.v.

Maheçvara, q.v.

Mahendrāvaraja, v. Vishṇu.

Padmanābha, q.v.

Paramātman, Parameçvara, Parameshṭhin, q.v.

Pinākaçūlahasta, q.v.

Pītavāsas ("dressed in yellow"): I, 2506 (i.e. Vishṇu); III, 12882, 12900 (i.e. Nārāyaṇa), 12934 (do.), 13005 (*Vishṇuṃ*); V, 3382; XII, 4077.

Prabhu, q.v.

Prajāpati, Prajāpatipati, q.v.

Puṇḍarīkāksha, Puṇḍarīkekshaṇa, q.v.

Purusha, Purushaçreshṭha, Purushasattama, Purushottama, q.v.

Pushkarāksha, Pushkarekshaṇa, q.v.

Ramānātha ("the husband of Ramā"): II, 2292.

Rāmānuja ("the younger brother of [Balarāma]"): V, 2741.

Sanātana, q.v.

Saṅkarshaṇānuja ("the younger brother of Saṅkarshaṇa [i.e. Balarāma]"): II, 2606; V, 5329.

Sarva, Sarvabhūtādi, Sarvabhūtapitāmaha, Sarvabhūtātman, Sarvabhūteça, Sarvabhūteçvara, q.v.

Sarvadāçārhabhartṛ ("the Lord of all the Dāçārhas"): VI, †2591.

Sarvajña, q.v.

Sarvalokaguru, Sarvalokakṛt, Sarvalokapitāmaha, Sarvalokeçvara, q.v.

Sarvanāgaripudhvaja ("having the enemy of all the serpents [i.e. Garuḍa] on his standard"): XIII, 6820.

(1853), (1875), 1898 (*Viçvakarmāṇaṃ . . . Prajāpatiṃ*), 1907, 1917, 1918 (*hayā V°sya Dārukena pracoditāḥ*), (1939), (1949), (1975), 1995, 2116, 3025 (*saṃvādaṃ V°sya surarsher Nāradasya ca*), (3026), (3043), 7650 (*param idaṃ viçvasya Brahmaṇo mukhaṃ*, i.e. Vishṇu), (8457), ††12864 (= Mahāpurusha), 12889 (*paramātmā*, i.e. Vishṇu), 12896 (*ekaṃ Purushaṃ V°ṃ sanātanaṃ*, do.), 12897 (*sarvabhūtātmabhūtaḥ*, do.), 12904 (*Kshetrajñaḥ*, do.), 12990 (*a-V°bhaktāya*, do.), 13169 (etymology), 13323 (°*sahāyaḥ*, i.e. Arjuna), 13388 (*Kshetrajñam*, i.e. Vishṇu), 13389 (= do.), 13544 (*sarvabhūtakṛtāvāsaḥ*, = do.); XIII, 605, (610), (614), (961), (1033), (*Çrī°*), (1114), 1325, (1358), 2009 (*Nāradasya ca saṃvādaṃ V°sya cobhayoḥ*), 2129 (*saṃvādaṃ V°sya Pṛthyāç ca*), (2130), †3458, 3476, 3481 (a çloka of his is quoted), 4652 (°*sya saṃvādaṃ Pṛthivyāç caiva*), 4653, (4654), 4675, (6317), 6806, 6838 (*caturbāhuḥ*), 6844, 6923, 6925 (*triyugau puṇḍarīkākshau V°-Dhanañjayau*), 6985 (Vishṇu's 1000 names), 7023 (do.), 7025 (do.), 7061 (i.e. Vishṇu), 7066 (do.), 7067 (°*bhaktān*, do.), 7070 (= do.), 7072 (°*ātmakāni* = do.), †7392 (*viçvāvāsaṃ*), (7402), (7460), (7502), 7726, 7741, 7743, 7747, (7752), 7763 (°*purogamāḥ*); XIV, 293, (296), (314), (331), 372 (°-*Dhanañjayau*), 373 (do.), (383), (415), (454), (586), (599), (935), (946), (1468), (1471), 1482, 1528 (*varaḥ puṃsāṃ*), (1564), (1599), (1778), 1809, 1840, 1851, 1855 (*Dāçārhaḥ*), 1861, 1936, 1947, 1950, 1963 (*svasrīyo V°sya*, i.e. Abhimanyu), 2032, 2055, 2063, 2073, (2078), 2661; XV, 78, 462 (all to § 568), 491 (do.), 990 (°*parigrahāt*); XVI, 8, 10, 12, 19 (°*sya dāyādaḥ Çāmbaḥ*), 55, †121, 138 (*shoḍaçastrīsahasrāṇi V°parigrahaḥ*), 207, 214 (°*āvarodhanaṃ*), 282 (*purāṇarshiḥ . . . caturbhujaḥ*); XVII, 10; XVIII, 171 (*shoḍaçastrīsahasrāṇi V°parigrahaḥ*), 173.

Vasudevaputra (do.): VI, †2596.

Vasudevasuta (do.): III, 621; VI, 5842.

Vasudevātmaja (do.): VIII, †4060 (*Vishṇoḥ*).

Vedhas, Vibhu, q.v.

Viçva, Viçvakarman, Viçvakṛt, Viçvaksena, Viçvarūpa, Viçvasambhava, Viçvasṛj, Viçvātman, Viçvāvāsa, Viçvāvasu, Viçvayoni, Viçveça, Viçveçvara, q.v.

Virāj, Viriñci, q.v.

Vishvaksena, q.v.

Vrajanātha ("lord of the herds"): II, 2292.

Vṛsha, Vṛshabha, Vṛshadarbha, Vṛshākapi, q.v.

Vṛshṇiçārdūla, Vṛshṇiçreshṭha, Vṛshṇikulodvaha, Vṛshṇinandana, Vṛshṇipati, Vṛshṇipravara, Vṛshṇipravīra, Vṛshṇipuṅgava, Vṛshṇisattama, Vṛshṇisiṃha, Vṛshṇivīra, Vṛshṇyandhakapati, Vṛshṇyandhakottama, q.v.

Yādava, Yādavaçārdūla, Yādavaçreshṭha, Yādavāgrya, Yādavanandana, Yādaveçvara, q.v.

Yaduçārdūla, Yaduçreshṭha, Yadūdvaha, Yadukulaçresṭha, Yadukulanandana, Yadukulodvaha, Yadunandana, Yadupravīra, Yadupuṅgava, Yadusukhāvaha, Yadūttama, Yaduvaṃçavivardhana, Yaduvara (dual), **Yaduvīra, Yaduvīramukhya**, q.v.

Yogeçvara, Yogīça, Yogīçvara, Yogin, q.v.

[*Remarks.*—Besides the above synonyms numerous epithets of Kṛshṇa of minor importance are found in hymns or descriptions of him scattered about in the Mhbhr., cf. especially the following passages: I, 22-4, 2429-32; II, 1213-15, 2291-3; III, 470, 510-20, 8350-3, 12821-4, 13001-6, 15528-35; V, 2560-80; VI, 2944-72, 2978-95, 2996-3013, 3015-36, 3038-44; VII, 6457-74; XII, 1502-14, 1604-88, 1845-52, 1863-74, 13129 foll., 13224 foll.; XIII, 6807 foll., 7359-400; XIV, 1485-94, 1563 foll., 1593-4.]

Kṛshṇa[2] = Vyāsa: I, 60, 614 (*ṛsheḥ*), †2103 (*Satyavatyāḥ sutasya*), 2220 (*pitāmahāya*), 2324, 4234, 4365, 7252, 7254; II, 1633, 2573 (*Dvaipāyanena*); VII, 8881 (*Satyavatyāḥ sutasya*); IX, 3531 (*pitāmahaḥ*), 3538; XI, 429 (*maharsheḥ*); XII, 12182, 12573; XIII, 421 (? so Nīl.), 1338, 5797, 5798; XIV, 355 (*Dvaipāyanena*), 1875 (*Vyāsaḥ*), 2659 (*Dvaipāyanaḥ*); XVIII, 183.

Kṛshṇa[3], a serpent. § 268 (Varuṇasabhāv.): II, **9**, 360 (among the serpents in the palace of Varuṇa).

Kṛshṇa[4] = Arjuna Pāṇḍava: II, 1814 (? so PCR.); IV, 1376 (enumeration of the ten names of Arjuna), 1378, 1389 (etymology); XIV, 2228.

Kṛshṇa[5], a mountain. § 575 (Bhūmip.): VI, **12**, 445 (in the western dvīpa, dear to Nārāyaṇa).

Kṛshṇa[6], a warrior of Skanda. § 615*u* (Skanda); IX, **45**η, 2559.

Kṛshṇa[7], a ṛshi. § 637 (Rājadh.): XII, **47**η, 1599 (among the ṛshis who surrounded Bhīshma on his arrow-bed).

Kṛshṇa[8] = Çiva: XII, 10409 (1000 names[1]); XIII, 1158 (1000 names[2]); XIV, 203.

Kṛshṇa[1], dual (°*au*) = Kṛshṇa Vāsudeva and Arjuna Pāṇḍava. § 11 (Parvasaṅgr.): I, **2**, 402.—§ 254 (Khāṇḍavadahanap.): I, **222**, 8077, 8082 (only B., C. has *Kṛshṇaḥ*).—§ 258 (do.): I, **227**, 8252; **228**, 8287.—§ 260 (do.): I, **234**, 8465.—§ 276 (Jarāsandhavadhap.): II, **20**, 781, 791.—§ 377 (Dhaumyatīrthak.): III, **86**, 8279.—§ 522 (Draupadīharaṇap.): III, **268**, †15652.—§ 556 (Sañjayayānap.): V, **22**, †675 (*ekarathe sametau*).—§ 561 (Yānasandhip.): V, **49**, 1940 (*ekarathe sthitau*); **52**, 2096 (*ekarathe*); **59**, 2326.—§ 567 (Bhagavadyānap.): V, **126**, 4215.—§ 580 (Bhīshmavadhap.): VI, **59**, 2570.—§ 582 (do.): VI, **73**, 3208.—§ 584 (do.): VI, **81**, 3570, 3571.—§ 592 (Saṃçaptakavadhap.): VII, **19**, 771; **29**, 1258; **30**, 1316.—§ 593 (Abhimanyuvadhap.): VII, **38**, 1637; **39**, 1669.—§ 596 (Pratijñāp.): VII, **81**, 2892.—§ 599 (Jayadrathavadhap.); VII, **100**, 3762; **101**, 3768, 3774, 3779, 3780, 3787, 3791, 3802; **102**, 3838; **103**, 3867, 3890; **111**, 4270; **126**, 5143; **127**, 5144; **139**, 5796; **143**, 5988; **147**, 6340, 6373 (°*ayoḥ sadṛço vīrye Sātyakiḥ*); **149**, 6454, 6456 (only C., B. has *Kṛshṇa*).—§ 600 (Ghaṭotkacavadhap.): VII, **158**, 7003; **170**, 7672.—§ 603 (Nārāyaṇāstramokshap.): VII, **200**, 9269; **201**, 9441.—§ 605 (Karṇap.): VIII, **16**, 630; **17**, 664.—§ 607 (do.): VIII, **38**, 1773; **39**, 1785, 1810; **40**, 1833, 1834, 1871; **41**, 1953; **42**, †1964.—§ 608 (do.): VIII, **56**, 2819; **63**, 3197; **64**, 3218, 3243; **65**, 3303; **79**, 4034, 4045, †4060, †4061; †4064; **87**, 4439 (*pūrvaṃ bhagavatā proktaṃ K°ayor vijayo dhruvaḥ*, 4450 (*srashṭārau jagataḥ*), 4454; **89**, †4557, †4606; **92**, †4829; **93**$a\sigma'$, 4887; **96**, 5033.—§ 610 (Çalyap.): IX, **3**λ, 177; **4**μ, 212; **5**ν, 249; **7**ρ, 322.—§ 611 (do.): IX, **14**, 710; **19**, 1054.—§ 614 (Gadāyuddhap.): IX, **34**, 1955.

Kṛshṇa[2], dual = Nakula and Sahadeva (?): V, 199 (*Bhīmārjunau K°au svasrīyau ca yamāv ubhau*).

Kṛshṇā[1] = Draupadī: I, 125, 148, 167, 384, 430, 2259, 2289 (*D°*), 2438, 6323, 6325, 6402, 6407 (origin of the name),

6434 (*Pārshatī*), 6942, 6952, 6977, †6979, †7007, †7009, †7015, †7024, †7059, 7125, †7132, 7142, †7164, †7167, †7169, †7171, †7174, †7177, †7179, †7181, †7182, †7183, †7198, †7203, †7205, †7211, 7221, 7227, 7235, 7239, 7243, 7263, 7326 (*Pārshatī*), †7331, †7332, †7333, †7334, †7339, 7349, 7384, 7404, 7411, 7422, 7423, 7521, 7541 (*Pāñcālīṃ*), 7544, 7555, 7598, 7599, 7600, 7607, 7611, 7744, 7754, 7979, 7984, 8045; II, 27, 976, 2172, 2189, 2217, †2220, †2223, †2227, †2229, †2231, †2239, †2240, †2242, 2274, 2278, 2280, 2281, 2337, 2338, 2388, †2405 (*Pāñcālīṃ*), 2417, 2451, 2502, 2584, 2604, 2615, 2626, 2688, 2690, 2698, 2700; III, 10, 400, 440, 453, 582, 591, †903, †943, †950, 989, 990, 1078, 1093, 1099, 1105, 1162, 1164, 1182, 1189, 1191, 1199, 1201, 1403, 1479, (1479), 1492, 1933, 1945, 2003, 2014, 2015, 3070, 4021, 8293, 8415, 8481, 8651, †10219, †10229, †10282, 10417, †10837, †10838, 10842, 10849, 10859, 10860, 10869, 10976, 10997, 11004, 11007, 11019, 11021, 11052, 11058, 11067. 11403, 11406, 11412, 11430, 11453, 11494, 11558, 11629, 11679, 11740, 11786, †11907, 11935, 12315, 12557, †12571, †12576, †12578, †12579 (*Yājñasenīṃ*), †12580, †12581, †12582, †12584, 14708, 14725, 14730, 14738, †14746, †14751, †14753, 14792, 14803, 15019, 15493, 15521, 15537, 15540, 15541, 15542, 15543, †15606, 15611, 15615 (*D*°), 15619, 15636, 15637, †15648, †15649, †15663, †15681, †15683, †15697, 15747, 15762, 15766, 15783, 15859, 15860, 16611 (*D*°). 16617, †17219, 17221, 17222, 17224, 17243, 17476; IV, 74 (*D*°), 81, 90, 146, 245, 263 (*bhāryāṃ Kurūṇāṃ*), 279, 335, 337, 383, 434, 451, 464, 485, 487, 490, 497, 503, 504, 508, 521, 636, 644, 690, 711, 738, 773, 780, 786, 796, 801, 803, 807, 822, 839, 846, 876, 1182, 1370, 1537, 1566, 1576, 2292, †2305, 2367; V, 201, 222, 689 (*D*°), †847, †849, †850, †854, †928, †931, 1990, 2326, 2329, 2349, 2871, 2912, 2914, 2919, 3177, 3185, 3211, 3217, 3228, 3442, 4655, 4662, 4665, 4666, 5478, 5489, 5495, 5497, 5519, 5541, 5564; VI, 4090 (*D*°), 4907; VII, 1684, 3818, 3825, 5425, 5428, 5656, 5658, 6543, 9166, 9226; VIII, 7, 308, 310, †3346, 3716, 3717, 3770, 4489, †4562, 4754, 4755, 4756, 5002; IX, 248, 255, 257, 259, 3433; X, 577, 579, 582, 589 (*Yājñasenī*), 594, 746 (*D*°), 759; XI, 628, 629 (read *Kṛshṇa* with B.); XII, 499, 1384, 1398, 1456 (*Drupadātmajāṃ*); XIV, 322, 356, 1505, 2584 (*D*°), 2604; XV, †437 (*D*°), 654, †664, 806 (*D*°); XVII, 24, 51, 58, 77, †86; XVIII, 97, 119.

Kṛshṇā[2] = Durgā (Umā): IV, 184, 187; VI, 801.

Kṛshṇā[3], a river. § 574 (Jambūkh.): VI, **9**λ, 340 (in Bhāratavarsha).

Kṛshṇā[4], a mātṛ. § 615*u* (Skanda): IX, **46**θ, 2640.

Kṛshṇacchavisamā = Durgā (Umā): IV, 187.

Kṛshṇa-Dvaipāyana = Vyāsa, q.v.

Kṛshṇā Gaṅgā, a river. § 757*m* (Goloka): XIII, **102a**. 4888.

Kṛshṇagati = Agni: IX, 1334.

Kṛshṇājinottarīya = Çiva (1000 names[1]).

Kṛshṇakeça, a warrior of Skanda. § 615*u* (Skanda): IX, **45**η, 2563.

Kṛshṇanetra = Çiva: XIV, 200.

Kṛshṇānubhautika, a ṛshi. § 637 (Rājadh.): XII, **47**η, 1598 (among the ṛshis who surrounded Bhīshma).

Kṛshṇapiṅgala = Çiva (1000 names[2]).

Kṛshṇapiṅgalā = Durgā (Umā): VI, 796.

Kṛshṇaraktekshaṇa = Çiva (1000 names[1]).

Kṛshṇasārathi ("having Kṛshṇa for his charioteer") = Arjuna: I, 2292 (*Pāṇḍavaḥ*); V, 4818 (*Çvetāçvaṃ*); VI, 4315 (*Pāṇḍavaḥ*), 5070 (*Çvetāçvaḥ*), 5451 (*Çvetāçvaṃ*), 5470 (*Çvetāçvāt*); VII, 3919 (*Çvetāçvaḥ*), 3959 (*Kaunteyaḥ*), 4712 (*Çvetāçvaṃ*), 5262 (*Çvetāçvaḥ*), 6589 (do.); VIII, 1578 (*Çvetāçvaṃ*), 2163 (*Çvetāçvaḥ*), 2192 (*Çvetāçvaṃ*), 2600 (*Çvetāçvaḥ*), 4021 (*Çvetāçvaṃ*), 4022 (*Çvetāçvaḥ*), 4867; IX, 1364 (*Çvetāçvaḥ*).

Kṛshṇasya sabhāpraveça(ḥ) ("*K.*'s arrival at the assembly of the Kurus"). § 10 (Parvasaṅgr.): I, **1**, 333 (cf. V, chap. **94**).

Kṛshṇātreya, a ṛshi. § 667 (Mokshadh.): XII, **210**, 7663 (*cikitsaṃ veda*).

Kṛshṇavarṇa = Çiva (1000 names[2]).

Kṛshṇavarṇā, a mātṛ. § 615*u* (Skanda): IX, **46**θ, 2642.

Kṛshṇavartman[1] = Agni, q.v. Do.[2] = Kṛshṇa: XII, 1509.

Kṛshṇavenā, a river. § 268 (Varuṇasabhāv.): II, **9**, 372 (°*ṇvā*, C., among the rivers in the palace of Varuṇa).—§ 370 (Tīrthayātrāp.): III, **85**, 8180 (*Devahrade 'raṇye K°jalodbhave*).—§ 459 (Mārkaṇḍeyas.): III, **188a**, 12909 (seen by Mārkaṇḍeya in the stomach of Nārāyaṇa).—§ 494 (Āṅgirasa): III, **222**, 14233 (among the rivers who are mothers of fires).—§ 574 (Jambūkh.): VI, **9**λ, 323 (C. °*ṇī*), 335.—§ 775 (Ānuçāsanik.): XIII, **166a**, 7648.

Kṛshṇaveṇī, Kṛshṇaveṇvā, *v.* **Kṛshṇaveṇā.**

Kṛta, a Viçvadeva. § 749 (Ānuçāsanik.): XIII, **91**γ, 4356.

Kṛta(ṃ)[1], name of a yuga = Kṛtayuga. § 173 (Pāṇḍurājyābhisheka): I, **109**, 4341 (*yugaṃ*).—§ 310*b* (Sūrya): III, **3**, 150 (among the names of the sun, besides the names of the other yugas).—§ 426 (Hanūmad-Bhīmasenasaṃv.): III, **149**, 11234 (*yugaṃ*), 11235.—§ 426*b* (Kṛtayuga): III, **149**, 11242 (*yuge*), 11246 (do.).—§ 458 (Mārkaṇḍeyas.): III, **188**, 12826 (*yugaṃ*, consists of 4000 [celestial] years), 12831 (*yugaṃ*, follows each Kaliyuga).—§ 460 (do.): III, **190**, 13013, 13017; **191**, 13109 (will be restored by Kalkin), 13113, 13115 (*yuge*).—§ 567 (Bhagavadyānap.): V, **132**, 4476 (the king creates the *K.*, etc.).—§ 569 (do.): V, **142**, 4819 (*na tadā bhavitā Tretā na K°ṃ Dvāparaṃ na ca*), 4821 (do.), 4823 (do.), 4825 (do.).—§ 574 (Jambūkh.): VI, **10**π, 387.—§ 611 (Rājadh.): XII, **65**, 2441 (*yuge*); **69**, 2694; **91**μ, 3408.—§ 649 (Āpaddharmap.): XII, **141a**, 5328.—§ 677 (Mokshadh.): XII, **232**, 8496, 8497 (*yugaṃ*), 8500 (*yuge*), 8502; **233**, 8542 (*yuge*), 8547 (do.); **239**, 8719 (*yuge*), 8720. — § 717*b* (Nārāyaṇīya): XII, **335**, 12658 (*yuge*); **340**, 12969 (*yuge*); **349**, 13588 (°*ādau*).—§ 730 (Ānuçāsanik.): XIII, **14**ζ, 692 (*yuge*); **16**, 1037.—§ 766 (do.): XIII, **133**, 6178 (*yuge*).—§ 770 (do.): XIII, **151**, 7128 (do.).—§ 773*b* (Kṛshṇa Vāsudeva): XIII, **159**, 7363 (do.). — § 782*g* (Guruçishyas.): XIV, **44**, 1220 (*ādir yugānāṃ*). Cf. Kṛtayuga.

Kṛta(ṃ)[2], a term of dice. § 552 (Goharaṇap.): IV, **50**, 1578 (*nākshān kshipati Gāṇḍīvaṃ na K°ṃ Dvāparaṃ na ca*).

Kṛtabandhu (°v°, C.), an ancient king. § 6 (Anukramaṇik.): I, **1a**, 231 (in Sañjaya's enumeration).

Kṛtacetas, a brahman. § 324 (Dvaitavanapr.): III, **26a**, 985 (among the brahmans who worshipped Yudhishṭhira).

Kṛtaçauca, a tīrtha. § 362 (Tīrthayātrāp.): III, **83**, 5091 (°*ṃ samāsādya tīrthasevī, narādhipa, puṇḍarīkam avāpnoti kṛtaçauco bhavec ca saḥ*).

Kṛtaçrama, a muni. § 264 (Sabhākriyāp.): II, **4a**, 109 (among the munis who waited upon Yudhishṭhira).

Kṛtāgama = Vishṇu (1000 names).

[Kṛtaghnopākhyāna(ṃ)] ("the episode about an ungrateful person"). § 658*b* (Āpaddh.): *Bhīshma* related: *Gautama*, a brahman, belonging to the middle country, devoid of *Vedic* learning, entered a village desirous of obtaining charity. In that village lived a robber (*dasyu*), possessed of great wealth, devoted to the *brahmans*, etc. He gave to *Gautama* a piece of new cloth, a widowed (*bhartrā virahitām*) young woman, and a house. *Gautama* lived happily in that village of aborigines (*çabarālaye*) for many years, helping the relatives of his wife, the female slave (*dāsī*). He began to practise archery, and went into the woods and killed wild cranes (*cakrāṅgān*), etc., in abundance, and became like one of the robbers. One day a *brahman*, devoted to the study of the *Vedas*, etc., and who did never accept any food if given by a *Çūdra*, came to the house of his ancient friend *Gautama*. Seeing *Gautama*, who resembled a cannibal, he exhorted him to abandon his sinful mode of life. *Gautama*, repenting, agreed to leave this village next morning with his guest, who passed the night there, refraining touching anything (though hungry) (XII, **168**). Next morning, when the guest had left the house, *Gautama* proceeded towards the sea, having met with a caravan of merchants. The caravan was assailed by an infuriated elephant, but *Gautama* managed to escape, and fled towards the north, not knowing whither he proceeded, wandering alone in the forest like a *kimpurusha*. At last he reached a delightful forest, resembling the very woods of *Nandana*, and inhabited by *Y.* and *K.*, adorned with *Çālas*, etc., with *Bhāruṇḍas* (having faces resembling those of human beings), *Bhūliṅgas*, etc. Under a delightful banyan tree (description) he fell asleep; when the sun had set, the king of cranes, *Nāḍījaṅgha* or *Rājadharman*, *Kaçyapa's* son, the child of a celestial maiden (*devakanyāsutaḥ*), one of the daughters of *Daksha* (v. 6343), and possessed of great wisdom and a friend of *Brahmán*, came home from *Brahmaloka*. Exhausted with hunger and thirst, *Gautama* thought of slaying him. *Nāḍījaṅgha* welcomed *Gautama*, and asked him to stay with him till the next morning (XII, **169**). He, who equalled *Yama* himself in his knowledge of duties, made for him a bed of the *çāla* flowers, and offered him large fishes from the *Bhāgīrathī*, etc. Learning that he was desirous of going to the sea in order to earn wealth, he, quoting *Bṛhaspati* as to the fourfold means of earning wealth, directed him in the morning to his friend, the chief of the *Rākshasas*, *Virūpāksha*, about 3 *yojanas* away. *Gautama* reached the city of *Meruvraja* (description), and was welcomed by *Virūpāksha* (XII, **170**). Though not satisfied with *Gautama's* antecedents, *Virūpāksha*, because *Gautama* was a brahman, and for the sake of *Rājadharman*, entertained him with the 1,000 *brahmans* that were to be entertained in his house on the day of full moon of the *Kārttika* month (description). Some amongst them were selected to represent the V.-D., P., and the deities of fire. This he did every year on the *Āshāḍhī* and *Māghī*, and especially on the *Kārttikī*, after the expiry of the autumn, giving away gold, jewels, etc.; on this one day there was no fear of *Rā.* *Gautama* came away with much wealth, and returned to *Rājadharman*, who welcomed him. Having no food to live on by the way, he thought of slaying *Rājadharman* (XII, **171**). This he did; having plucked off the feathers and the down, he roasted the flesh, and taking it up together with the gold he had brought, he quickly fled from the spot. The next day *Virūpāksha* became anxious because he had not for two mornings and two nights seen *Rājadharman*, who when returning from *Brahmaloka* every morning never went home without paying him a visit; he suspected that *Gautama* had slain him, and sent his son with other Rā. to inquire after him. *Gautama* was caught and brought to *Meruvraja*; as the Rā. refused to eat the flesh of that great sinner, he was hacked into pieces, which were given away to the robbers. But the very robbers, though cannibals, refused to eat the flesh of that vile man (XII, **172**). *Virūpāksha* caused a funeral pyre, etc., to be made for *Rājadharman*. At that time the goddess *Surabhi*, the daughter of *Daksha*, appeared in the sky above the pyre; from her mouth froth mixed with milk fell upon the funeral pyre, and *Rājadharman* became revived. *Indra* came and related that once *Rājadharman* had absented himself from *Brahmaloka* and was cursed by *Brahmán*, who said that he should not die soon; "therefore he has come back to life." Asked by *Rājadharman* on behalf of his "dear friend *Gautama*", *Indra* sprinkled *amṛta* over *Gautama*, and restored him to life. *Rājadharman* embraced him with great joy, dismissed him with his wealth, and returned home. At the due hour he repaired to *Brahmaloka* and was honoured by *Brahmán*. *Gautama* begot many sinful children upon his *Çūdrā* wife. According to a heavy curse denounced upon him by the gods, he afterwards had to sink into a terrible hell for many years. "All this was recited to me formerly by Nārada."

Kṛtajña, Kṛtakarman, Kṛtākṛta = Vishṇu (1000 names).

Kṛtakshaṇa, a prince. § 264 (Sabhākriyāp.): II, **4**β, 122 (among the princes who waited upon Yudhishṭhira).

Kṛtalakshaṇa = Vishṇu (1000 names).

***kṛtānta** ("destiny, death" (personif. = Yama)): II, 2430 (*yugāntakāle samprāpte K°syeva rūpiṇaḥ*); III, 12635 (°*vidhi*°); VII, 900 (°*vat*); IX, 3641; XI, 235; XII, 1174 (°*vidhi*°), 1206 (°*bala*°), 5687 (°*vihite*), 5724, 6542, 7907, 10541 (°*vaçyāni*).

Kṛtāntakṛt = Vishṇu (1000 names).

Kṛtāstra, a prince. § 264 (Sabhākriyāp.): II, **4**β, 127 (among the princes who waited upon Yudhishṭhira).

Kṛtavāc, a brahman. § 324 (Dvaitavanapr.): III, **26***a*, 987 (waited upon Yudhishṭhira).

Kṛtavandhu, v. Kṛtabandhu.

Kṛtavarman, a Vṛshṇi prince, son of Hṛdika. § 4 (Anukram.): I, **1**, †196, †204.—§ 11 (Parvasaṅgr.): I, **2**, 562, 570.—§ 83 (Ādivaṃçāvatāraṇa): I, **63**, 2433 (*Sātyakiḥ K°ā ca Nārāyaṇam anuvratau*, son of Hṛdika). —§ 130 (Aṃçāvat.): I, **67**, 2716 (born from the Maruts).—§ 232 (Svayaṃvarap.): I, **186**, 6998 (*Hārdikyaḥ*, came to the svayaṃvara of Draupadī).—§ 253 (Haraṇāharaṇap.): I, **221**, 7991 (*Sātvataḥ*, came to the wedding of Arjuna and Subhadrā). —§ 264 (Sabhākriyāp.): II, **4**β, 125 (waited upon Yudhishṭhira).—§ 273 (Rājasūyārambhap.): II, **14**, 623 (one of the seven mahārathas of the Vṛshṇis).—§ 320 (Saubhavadhop.): III, **18**, 741 (desisted from fighting with Çāl a in order that Kṛshṇa might slay the latter).—§ 553 (Vaivāhikap.): IV, **72**, 2357 (*Hārdikyaḥ*, came to the wedding of Abhimanyu and Uttarā).—§ 554 (Sainyodyogap.): V, **7**, 163 (gave one akshauhiṇī of troops to Duryodhana).—§ 555 (do.): V, **19**θ, 586 (*Hārdikyaḥ . . . Bhojāndha-Kukuraiḥ saha*, sided with Duryodhana with one akshauhiṇī of troops).—§ 561 (Yānasandhip.): V, **47***a*, 1796; **57**, 2252 (*Bhojam*, Sātyaki will fight *K.*).—§ 562 (Bhagavadyānap.): V, **94**, 3347 (followed Kṛshṇa), 3363, 3377.—§ 567 (do.): V, **130**, 4374 (arrayed the troops in order to protect Kṛshṇa); **131**, 4447 (*Hārdikyaḥ*).—§ 568 (do.): V, **143**, 4874 (*Sātvataḥ*, in the army of Duryodhana).—§ 570 (Sainyaniryāṇap.): V, **155**θ, 5274 (commanded one akshauhiṇī of Duryodhana's army).—§ 571 (Ulūkadūtāgamanap.): V, **164**ε, 5707 (Çaibya is pitted against *K.*).—§ 572 (Rathātirathasaṅkhyānap.): V,

165, 5737 (*Bhojaḥ*, among the atirathas in Duryodhana's army).—§ 573 (Ambopākhyānap.): V, **195**ζ, 7611.—§ 576 (Bhagavadgītāp.): VI, **16***a*, 623 (*Sātvataḥ*, commanded one akshauhiṇī of Duryodhana's army).—§ 578 (Bhīshmavadhap.): VI, **45**^{2}, 1680 (fought with Sātyaki), 1681; **47**^{25} γ, 1809 (^{26}), 1817 (pierced by Abhimanyu), 1826, (^{27}), 1841 (^{28}), 1849; **48**^{34} θ, 1925; **49**^{36}, 2010 (followed Çalya); **51**ψ, 2109 (*Sātvataḥ*, in the rear of the army of Duryodhana).—§ 580 (do.): VI, **56**^{1} *a*, 2404 (*Sātvataḥ*); **59**^{10} μ, †2583.—§ 581 (do.): VI, **61**ε, 2698; **65**ν, 2928 (*Hārdikyaḥ*).—§ 582 (do.); VI, **71**, 3141.—§ 583 (do.): VI, **75**γ, 3293 (*sahitaḥ Kāmbojavara-Bāhlikaiḥ*, in the head of Bhīshma's krauñcāruṇavyūha); **76**ι, 3329.—§ 584 (do.): VI, **81***a*, 3532 (*Sātvataḥ*); **82,** 3632 (fought with Bhīmasena), 3633; **86**^{13}ζ, 3838 (*Sātvataḥ*).—§ 585 (do.): VI, **89**π, 3970; **95**γγ, 4244 (*Sātvataḥ*).—§ 586 (do.): VI, **99***a*, 4501 (in the sarvatobhadra array of Bhīshma); **104,** 4744 (pierced by Sātyaki), 4755.—§ 587 (do.): VI, **108,** 5006; **110,** 5102 (resisted Dhṛshtadyumna); **113,** 5239, 5243, 5247, 5260, 5271, 5273; **114**κ, 5293, 5309; **119**ψ, 5583.—§ 589 (Droṇābhishekap.): VII, **7**δ, 181.—§ 590 (do.): VII, **14,** 529 (pierced by Sātyaki); **15,** 611, 613 (rescued Çalya).—§ 592 (Saṃçaptakavadhap.): VII, **20,** 797 (in the eye of Droṇa's gāruḍavyūha); **25,** 1073 (fought with Sātyaki), 1074 (read *Kshatravarmā* with B.).—§ 593 (Abhimanyuvadhap.): VII, **37**θ, 1589, 1601 (pierced Abhimanyu), (κ), 1616; **46**τ, 1838, (υ), 1852 (*Hārdikyaḥ*); **47**φ, 1864 (*Hārdikyaḥ*), 1868, 1878 (fought with Abhimanyu).—§ 596 (Pratijñāp.): VII, **73,** 2575 (among the six chariot warriors who had surrounded Abhimanyu in order to slay him).—§ 598 (Jayadrathavadhap.): VII, **87**θ, 3111 (at the mouth of Droṇa's sūcī array).—§ 599 (do.): VII, **91***a*, 3253 (*Sātvataḥ*); **92,** 3277, 3282, 3284, 3285, 3286, 3288, 3289 (*Bhojaḥ*), 3293, 3295 (fought with Arjuna, etc.); **97,** 3574 (attacked by Yudhishṭhira); **111**υ, 4285; **113,** 4417, 4419, 4420, 4423, 4425, 4427 (*Hārdikyaṃ*), 4437 (fought with Sātyaki); **114,** 4454 (*°mahāhradaṃ*, sc. the ocean, with which the army of Duryodhana is compared), 4497, (ψ), 4500, 4502, 4504, 4508, 4511, 4512, 4522, 4524, 4533, 4538, 4539 (fought with the Pāṇḍavas and Çikhaṇḍin); **115,** 4545, 4546 (*Hārdikyaḥ*), 4547, 4552 (was vanquished by Sātyaki); **116,** 4627, 4630, 4633, 4640, 4644 (was vanquished by Sātyaki); **121,** 4814; **130,** 5337; **141**δδδ, 5857; **144,** 6025; **147,** 6371.—§ 600 (Ghaṭotkacavadhap.): VII, **156**κ, 6850; **165,** 7360 (*Hārdikyaḥ*, fought with Yudhishṭhira), 7378 (do., do.), 7380, 7395, 7396; **171,** 7702; **183,** 8337 (had slain the steeds of Abhimanyu).—§ 602 (Droṇavadhap.): VII, **187**ι, 8545; **189,** 8633 (*Hārdikyaḥ*, assisted by three brothers he opposed Dhṛshṭadyumna).—§ 603 (Nārāyaṇāstramokshap.): VII, **193***a*, 8905 (*Bhojānīkena çishṭena Kaliṅgāraṭṭa-Bāhlikaiḥ . . . vṛtaḥ*); **200***aa*, 9308.—§ 604 (Karṇap.): VIII, **2**γ, 45 (*Bhojasya*); **7,** †197 (*Ānarttavāsī Hṛdikātmajaḥ . . . Sātvatānāṃ varishṭhaḥ . . . Bhojaḥ*); **9,** 326 (*Sātvatānāṃ mahārathaḥ*).—§ 605 (do.): VIII, **11**ρ, 416 (*Nārāyaṇabalair yukto Gopālaiḥ*); **13,** 495 (attacked by Çikhaṇḍin); **26,** 1059, 1064, 1065, 1070 (fought with Çikhaṇḍin); **29,** 1202, 1203.—§ 608 (do.): VIII, **46**β, 2133 (*Sātvataḥ*, in the right wing of Droṇa's array); **47**ι, 2225; **51**ζζ, 2507; **54**θθ, 2610, 2622, 2640, 2643, 2646, 2648 (was vanquished by Dhṛshṭadyumna); **61,** 3080 (proceeded against Uttamaujas), 3125 (pierced Uttamaujas); **73,** 3646, 3688, 3694; **75,** †3814 (attacked by Nakula); **78,** 3941 (δ′), 3999; **79**ζ′, 4012, †4083 (his horses were slain by Arjuna); **80,** 4100; **83**μ′, †4231; **85,** †4315; **95,** 4968, *Nārāyaṇāvaçeshaiḥ*, sc. *vṛtaḥ*).—§ 609 (Çalyap.): IX, **1**δ, 36 (among the three only remnants of Duryodhana's army); **2,** 124 (do.).—§ 610 (do.): IX, **6**ξ, 293 (*Sātvataḥ*).—§ 611 (do.): IX, **8***a*, 373, (β), 392 (*Traigartaiḥ parivāritaḥ*, on the left side of Çalya's array); **11**μ, 563, 565, 575; **12**ξ, 626; **15,** 759; **16,** 799, (φ), 840; **17,** 942 (deprived of his chariot by Sātyaki), 949; **21,** 1094, 1108, 1109, 1112, 1113, 1114, 1118, 1120, 1122 (was vanquished by Sātyaki); **22,** 1160; **23,** 1185; **25**ππ, 1377 (*Sātvataḥ*), 1384, (ππ), 1398 (*Sātvataḥ*); **27**σσ, 1447, (υυ), 1459 (*Sātvataḥ*).—§ 612 (Hradapraveçap.): IX, **29***a*, 1602 (among the three only remnants of Duryodhana's army), 1623 (*Bhojaṃ*, do.); **30**δ, 1674, 1681 (*Sātvataḥ*), (*a*), 1734.—§ 615 (Baladevatīrthayātrā): IX, **54**ξ, 3064.—§ 615 (Gadāyuddhap.): IX, **64**εε, 3589, 3609 (*Sātvataḥ*); **65,** 3627 (do.).—§ 616 (Sauptikap.): X, **1,** 16, 28; **4**γ, 143 (*Sātvataḥ*), 148, 152, 157, 158; **5,** 213 (*Sātvataḥ*); **6,** 217; **8,** 323, 425 (took part in the nightly encounter); **9,** 485 (*Sātvataḥ*, came to the dying Duryodhana), 513, 528.—§ 617 (Aishīkap.): X, **10,** 545, 548.—§ 618 (Jalapradānikap.): XI, **11,** 289, 306 (returned to his own country).—§ 619 (Strīvilāpap.): XI, **25**κ, 736.—§ 785 (Anugītāp.): XIV, **66**θ, 1938 (accompanied Kṛshṇa); **86**τ, 2557 (do.).—§ 793 (Mausalap.): XVI, **3**γ, 72, 73, 76, 83, 84 (Sātyaki slew him); [**7,** 245 (the son of K. (*Hārdikyatanayaṃ*) was installed as king of Mārttikāvata)].—§ 795 (Svargārohaṇap.): XVIII, **4,** 159 (*Hārdikyaḥ*, after death he entered the gaṇa of the Maruts).

Cf. also the following synonyms:—

Ānarttavāsin: VIII, †197.

Bhoja, Bhojarāja, q.v.

Hārdikya ("the son of Hṛdika"): I, 302 (*Drauṇi-H°-Gautamāḥ*, all. to Sauptikaparvan), 6998 (*K°*), 7916; III, 781; IV, 2357 (*K°*); V, 586 (*K°*), 4373, 4441, 4447 (*K°*), 5531; VI, 2928 (*K°*), 3558, 3972 (*Sātvataḥ*), 4340, 4362, 5180, 5181; VII, 549, 1850 (*K°*), 1864 (do.), 3287, 3291, 3437 (*Bhojaḥ*), 3774, 3786, 4427, 4428, 4436, 4498, 4499, 4501, 4503, 4507, 4513, 4515, 4525, 4535, 4536, 4540, 4541, 4542, 4543, 4546, 4647, †4684, 4708, 4766, 5240, 6485, 7087, 7146, 7338, 7360 (*K°*), 7378 (do.), 7379, 7381, 7388, 7391, 7394, 7523, 8633 (*K°*); VIII, 327 (do.), 1058, 1061, 1074, 1226, 2157, 2262, 2642, 2647, 3123; IX, 216, 398, 934, 935, 938, 940, 948, 950, 1101, 1105, 1129, 1186; X, 427; XI, 309; XVI, 74, 75, 157; XVIII, 159 (*K°*).

Hṛdikasuta (do.): VIII, †4307.

Hṛdikātmaja (do.): III, 742, 779; VII, 4527; VIII, †197, 2642; IX, 1107.

Mādhava, q.v.

Sātvata, q.v.

Vārshṇeya, Vṛshṇi, Vṛshṇisiṃha, q.v.

Kṛtavega, an ancient king (?). § 267 (Yamasabhāv.): II, **8,** 320 (in the palace of Yama).

Kṛtavīrya, an ancient king. § 6 (Anukram.): I, **1***a*, 221 *bis* (in Sañjaya's enumeration).—§ 227 (Aurvop.): I, **178,** 6802 (was the yājya of the Bhṛgus).—§ 267 (Yamasabhāv.): II, **8,** 319 (in the palace of Yama).

Kṛtavīryaduhitṛ ("the daughter of Kṛtavīrya") = Bhānumatī, the wife of Ahaṃyāti: I, †3768 (*Bh°*).

Kṛtavīryātmaja ("the son of Kṛtavīrya") = Arjuna Kārtavīrya: XII, 1750 (*Arjunaḥ . . . Haihayādhipaḥ*), XIII, 7190.

Kṛtayuga, name of the first yuga. § 84 (Ādivaṃçāvatāraṇap.): I, **64,** 2480.—§ 374 (Tīrthayātrāp.): III, **85,** 8232 (*sarvaṃ K°e puṇyam*).—§ 384 (Agastyop.): III, **100,** 8691.—§ 422 *bis* (Varāhāvatāra.): III, **142,** 10933 (*purā K°e*).—§ 426 (Hanūmad-Bhīmasenas.): III, **149,** 11230, 11236, 11237, 11246 (*b:* In the *K.* there were no gods, Dānavas, Gandharvas, Yakshas, or Pannagas, nor buying or selling, nor Sāma-, Ṛg-, or Yajur-veda, nor castes, nor labour; there was only one Veda and one occupation for the four castes; Nārāyaṇa was white, etc.).—§ 438 (Yakshayuddhap.): III, **162,** 11804 (*d:* In the *K.* men were patient and efficient in their respective occupations, and knew how to display prowess).—§ 459 (Mārkaṇḍeyas.): III, **189,** 12981 (in the *K.* Nārāyaṇa is white).—§ 460 (do.): III, **191,** 13120.—§ 567 (Bhagavadyānap.): V, **132,** 4473, 4475 (*°srashṭā,* sc. the king).—§ 574 (Jambūkh.): VI, **10,** 388, 389, 393.—§ 594 (Akampana): VII, **52,** 2029 (*purā K°e*).—§ 606 (Tripurākhyāna): VIII, **34,** 1474 (became the yoke of the chariot of Çiva).—§ 615 (Baladevatīrthayātrā): IX, **37,** 2159 (*°e*); **40,** 2287.—§ 615*v* (Varuṇa): IX, **47,** 2732.—§ 636 (Rājadh.): XII, **39,** 1432.—§ 641 (do.): XII, **59,** 2134; **69,** 2675, 2676, 2693.—§ 664 (Mokshadh.): XII, **207,** 7562 (*°e,* then the barbarians did not exist).—§ 677 (do.): XII, **232,** 8504 (*°e*), 8505 (do.).—§ 678*b* (Anukampaka): XII, **257,** 9150 (*purā K°e*).—§ 679 (Mokshadh.): XII, **261,** 9264.—§ 681 (do.): XII, **268*a*,** 9591 (*°e*).—§ 717*c* (Uparicara): XII, **337,** 12769, 12807; **338,** 12822.—§ 717*b* (Nārāyaṇīya): XII, **341,** 13088; **349,** 13563, 13575, 13580, 13610 (*°prāptiḥ*).—§ 730*g* (Upamanyu): XIII, **14,** 701.—§ 778*b* (Saṃvartta-Maruttīya): XIV, **4,** 65. Cf. Devayuga, Kṛta(m).

Kṛti[1], an ancient king (?). § 267 (Yamasabhāv.): II, **8,** 320 (in the palace of Yama).

Kṛti[2], a Viçvadeva. § 749 (Ānuçāsanik.): XIII, **91,** 4360.

Kṛti[3] = Vishṇu (1000 names).

Kṛtin, a king. § 295 (Dyūtap.): II, **52,** 1882 (*rājā . . . Çūkarāṇām,* brought tribute to Yudhishṭhira).

Kṛtīsuta ("son of Kṛtī") = Ruciparvan: VII, 1177 (*R°*).

Kṛttikā, pl. (*°āḥ*), the six wives of the seven ṛshis, name of a constellation (the Pleiads). § 116 (Vasu, pl.): I, **66,** 2588 (*°ābhyupapatteç ca Kārttikeya iti smṛtaḥ,* sc. Skanda).—§ 370 (Tīrthayatrāp.): III, **84,** 0020 (*° Maghayoç caiva tīrtham*).—§ 412 (Ashṭāvakrīya): III, **134,** †10663 (*shaṭ*).—§ 488 (Āṅgirasa): III, **217,** 14103 (*Rudraç ca sambhūto Gaṅgāyāṃ K°āsu ca,* sc. Skanda).—§ 501 (Skandopākhyāna): III, **229,** 14429 (*Pāvakasyendriyaṃ Çvete K°ābhiḥ kṛtaṃ nage*).—§ 502 (Manushyagrahak.): III, **230,** 14464 (when Svāhā had assumed the forms of the six wives of the saptarshis and cohabited with Agni, and Skanda was born, their husbands divorced them; then they adopted Skanda, rose to the sky, and became a nakshatra—*tridivaṃ K°ā gatā nakshatraṃ saptaçīrshābhaṃ bhāti tad Vahnidaivatam*).—§ 509 (Kārttikeyastava): III, **232,** 14642 (*Svāhā-Mahī-K°ānām,* sc. *sutaḥ,* i.e. Skanda). — § 574 (Jambūkh.): VI, **3,** 96 (sg. *°āṃ pīḍayaṃs tīkshṇair nakshatram,* sc. Ṛāhu, omens).—§ 592 (Saṃçaptakavadhap.): VII, **20,** 809 (*°yogayuktena paurṇamāsyāṃ ivendunā*).—§ 615*u* (Skanda): IX, **44,** 2459, 2462 (reared Skanda); **46,** 2717 (*°ānām,* sc. *sutaḥ,* i.e. Skanda).—§ 656 (Khaḍgotpattik.): XII, **166,** 6201 (*°ās tasya nakshatram Aser Agniç ca daivatam*).—§ 733*f* (Mahāgaṅgā): XIII, **25,** 1708 (*°āṅgārake,* name of a tīrtha ?, at the conjunction of the Kṛttikās and Aṅgāraka, i.e. the planet Mars, BR.).—§ 733*k* (Vaimānika): XIII, **25,** 1711 (*°ānām āçrame,* a tīrtha).—§ 733*u* (Punarāvartanandā): XIII, **25,** 1732 (*°yoge*).—§ 746 (Ānuçāsanik.): XIII, **64,** 3256 (merit of gifts of food made under the nakshatra *K.*).—§ 747*b* (Suvarṇotpatti): XIII, **85,** 4097 (reared Skanda, who therefore was called Kārttikeya).—§ 748*b* (Tārakavadhop.): XIII, **86,** 4190, 4193, 4195 (reared Skanda), 4198.—§ 749 (Ānuçāsanik.): XIII, **89*a*,** 4256 (*°yoge*).—§ 759 (do.): XIII, **90,** 5390 (description of the candravrata).

Kṛttikāputra = Skanda: I, 5431; III, 14617.

Kṛttikāsuta = Skanda: III, 14568.

Kṛttivāsas = Çiva, q.v.

Kṛtya = Çiva (1000 names[1]).

Kṛtyā, a river. § 574 (Jambūkh.): VI, **9** λ, 326 (in Bhāratavarsha).

***kṛtyā** ("sorceress"): III, 10704, 15149, 15151, 15183; XII, 13258; XIII, 4453 foll., 4474 foll.

Kshama, Kshāma = Vishṇu (1000 names).

Kshamākshame = Çiva (1000 names[1]).

Kshamiṇāṃ vara(ḥ) = Vishṇu (1000 names).

Kshaṇa = Sūrya (the Sun): III, 150.—Do.,[2] pl. (*°āḥ*) = Çiva (1000 names[2]).

Kshaṇabhojin, a prince. § 604 (Karṇap.): VIII, **7,** †207 (? among the remnants of Duryodhana's army).

Kshānta = Çiva (1000 names[1]).

Kshapā = Sūrya (the Sun): III, 150.—Do.,[2] pl. (*°āḥ*) = Çiva (1000 names[2]).

Kshapācara, pl. ("night-walkers") = Rākshasa, pl.: III, 16506.—Do. sg.: III, 16497 (= Rāvaṇa); V, 7539 (= Sthūṇa).

***kshapaṇaka,** a religious mendicant: I, ††789, ††790.

Kshara = Vishṇu (Kṛshṇa): XII, 13115; XIII, 7000 (1000 names).

Kshatradeva, son of Çikhaṇḍin. § 561 (Yānasandhip.): V, **57***o*, 2263 (has joined the Pāṇḍavas).—§ 572 (Rathātirathasaṅkhyānap.): V, **171,** 5902 (among the rathas of the army of the Pāṇḍavas).—§ 573 (Ambopākhyānap.): V, **196** χ, 7646.—§ 585 (Bhīshmavadhap.): VI, **93** ψ, 4152 (followed Bhīmasena); **95** δδ, 4254, (εε), 4271, 4309 (Bhagadatta pierced his right arm).—§ 589 (Droṇābhishekap.): VII, **10** λ, 358.—§ 590 (do.): VII, **14,** 543 (fought with Lakshmaṇa).—§ 592 (Saṃçaptakavadhap.): VII, **21** κ, 904 (fought with Droṇa), 910; **23** *o*, 955 (*Çaikhaṇḍiḥ,* description of his horses), 974 (*Çikhaṇḍinaḥ putraṃ,* description of his horses).—§ 604 (Karṇap.): VIII, **6,** 176 (*Çikhaṇḍitanayaḥ,* has been slain by Lakshmaṇa). Cf. Çaikhaṇḍi, Çikhaṇḍitanaya.

Kshatradharman, son of Dhṛshṭadyumna. § 572 (Rathātirathasaṅkhyānap.): V, **171,** 5899 (*Dhṛshṭadyumnasya tanayaḥ,* is a half ratha).—§ 585 (Bhīshmavadhap.): VI, **93** ψ, 4152.—§ 592 (Saṃçaptakavadhap.): VII, **21** κ, 903 (attacked Droṇa); **23** *o*, 954 (*çoṇāçvaḥ*).—§ 593 (Abhimanyuvadhap.): VII, **35** δ, 1509 (proceeded against Droṇa).—§ 598 (Jayadrathavadhap.): VII, **85** δ, 3049 (*Saumakiḥ*).—§ 599 (do.): VII, **125,** 5079, 5082 (is slain by Droṇa).—§ 604 (Karṇap.): VIII, **6,** 175 (had been slain by Droṇa). Cf. Dhṛshṭadyumnasuta, Kshatravarman, Saumaki.

Kshatrahan, a Pāṇḍava warrior. § 573 (Ambopākhyānap.) V, **196,** 7646 (*°hā Kshatradevaç ca,* C.; but B. has *Kshatradeva-Brahmadevau,* in the rear of the army of the Pāṇḍavas).

Kshatrañjaya, a Pāṇḍava warrior. § 589 (Droṇābhishekap.): VII, **10** λ, 358 (son of Dhṛshṭadyumna ?, attacked Droṇa).

Kshatravarman = Kshatradharman (?). § 589 (Droṇābhishekap.): VII, **10** λ, 358 (attacked Droṇa). — § 592 (Saṃçaptakavadhap.): VII, **25,** 1073, 1074 (only B., C. has by error *Kṛtav°*), 1076 (fought with Jayadratha).

Kshatriyāḥ (pl.) = Çiva (1000 names[1]).
Kshattṛ = Vidura, q.v.
Kshaudra, name of a caste: XIII, 2584.
Kshaya = Çiva: VIII, 1448; XII, 10368 (1000 names[1]).
Kshema, a prince. § 130 (Aṃçāvat.): I, **67**, 2701 (among the incarnations from the Krodhavaça gaṇa).—§ 592 (Saṃçaptakavadhap.): VII, **21**, 907 (is slain by Droṇa).
Kshemā, an Apsaras. § 191 (Arjuna): I, **123**, 4818 (among the Apsarases who sang at the birth of Arjuna).
Kshemaçarman, a Kuru warrior. § 592 (Saṃçaptakavadhap.): VII, **20**γ, 797 (in the neck of Droṇa's gāruḍavyūha).
Kshemadarçin, king of the Kosalas. § 641 (Rājadh.): XII, **82**, 3060 (*Kosalānām ādhipatyam samprāptam*), 3070 (instructed by Kālakavṛkshīya, whom he then made his purohita); **104**, 3849 (do.). Cf. Kausalya, Kosalādhipa.
Kshemadarçīya, adj. ("relating to Kshemadarçin"). § 641 (Rājadh.): XII, **104**, 3848 (*itihāsaḥ*).
Kshemadhanvan, a Kuru warrior. § 576 (Bhagavadgītāp.): VI, **17**, 662 (in the van of Duryodhana's army).—§ 620 (Çrāddhap.): XI, **26**β, 788 (*rājānam*, among the fallen warriors whose corpses were cremated).
Kshemadhūrti, one or more princes. § 130 (Aṃçāvat.): I, **67**, 2700 (among the incarnations from the Krodhavaça gaṇa).—§ 554 (Sainyodyogap.): V, **4**γ, 81 (among the princes to whom the Pāṇḍavas ought to send messengers).—§ 592 (Saṃçaptakavadhap.): VII, **25**, 1110 (°-*Bṛhantau bhrātarau*, fought with Sātyaki).—§ 599 (Jayadrathavadhap.): VII, **95**ζ, 3526 (supported three sons of Dhṛtarāshṭra); **106**, 3972 (rushed against Bṛhatkshattra); **107**, 4013, 4015, 4017 (Bṛhatkshattra cut off the head of *K.*).—§ 604 (Karṇap.): VIII, **5**ζ, 133 (had been slain by Bhīmasena).—§ 605 (do.): VIII, **12**, 465, 472, 479, 481, 483 (king of the Kulūtas, slain by Bhīmasena).
Kshemaka[1], a serpent. § 47 (Sarpanāmak.): I, **35**, 1556 (enumeration).
Kshemaka[2], a prince. § 264 (Sabhākriyāp.): II, **4**β, 117 (waited upon Yudhishṭhira).—§ 554 (Sainyodyogap.): V, **4**γ, 86 (among the princes to whom the Pāṇḍavas ought to send messengers).
Kshemakīrti, a Kuru warrior. § 611 (Çalyap.): IX, **21**, 1100 (slain by Sātyaki).
Kshemakṛt = Vishṇu (1000 names).
Kshemamūrti, a son of Dhṛtarāshṭra. § 130 (Aṃçāvat.): I, **67**, 2735 (enumeration).
Kshemaṅkara, a Trigarta king, follower of Jayadratha. § 522 (Draupadīharaṇap.): III, **271**, 15731 (°-*Mahāmukhau*, slain by Nakula). Cf. Traigarta, Trigartarāja.
Kshemavāha, a warrior of Skanda. § 615*u* (Skanda): IX, **45**η, 2568.
Kshemavarman, a Pāṇḍava warrior. § 592 (Saṃçaptakavadhap.): VII, **21**κ, 910 (pierced by Droṇa).
Kshemavṛddhi, the generalissimo of Çālva. § 320 (Saubhavadhop.): III, **16**, 669 (*camūpatim*), 671, 672, 674 (defeated by Çāmba he fled).
Kshemi, a Pāṇḍava warrior. § 592 (Saṃçaptakavadhap.): VII, **23**o, 1005 (*yuddhe satyadhṛtim K°m*, description of his horses; PCR. takes Satyadhṛti as the name).
Kshemya = Çiva: XIV, 194.
***Ksetrajña**, the supreme soul in the form of the individual soul, often identified with Kṛshṇa (Vishṇu): I, 3018, †3612, †3653, †3664, †3669; III, 476 (= Kṛshṇa), 8353 (= Kṛshṇa), 13979; V, 1070; VI. 1322, 1323, 1324 (= Kṛshṇa), 1347; XII, 1641 (*kshetre k°m āsīnam*, i.e. Kṛshṇa), 6923, 8821, 11619, 11649, 12680 (= Purusha), 12691, 12864 (= Mahāpurusha), 12892, 12901 (*Vāsudevaḥ*), 13081, 13388 (*Vāsudevam*), 13604 (*Hariḥ*), 13745 (= Purusha); XIII, 6951 (= Vishṇu, 1000 names); XIV, 933 (= Kṛshṇa), 1205 (= Purusha).
Kshetrātman = Kṛshṇa: XII, 1641.
Kshīranidhi ("the ocean of milk"). § 564 (Mātalīyop.): V, **102**, 3605 (*yasyāḥ*—i.e. Surabhi's—*kshīrasya dhārāyā nipatantyā mahītale | hradaḥ kṛtaḥ K°ḥ*).
Kshīrapā = Çiva (1000 names[1]).
Kshīravatī, a tīrtha. § 370 (Tīrthayātrāp.): III, **84**, 8046.
Kshīroda[1] ("the ocean of milk"). § 11 (Parvasaṅgr.): I, **2**, 366 (°*manthanam*, cf. § 28 (Amṛtamanthana)).—§ 535 (Setubandhana): III, **283**, 16289 (*sāgaram*).—§ 575 (Bhūmip.): VI, **11**, 410 (*sāgaraḥ*).—§ 717*c* (Uparicara): XII, **337**, 12774 (*Meror uttarabhāge K°syānukūlataḥ*, there Ekata, Dvita, and Trita performed austerities).—§ 717*b* (Nārāyaṇīya): XII, **340**, 13001 (*amṛtāçayam*); **341**, 13032 (°*syānukūlataḥ*, there Vyāsa performed austerities), 13051 (°*syottaram kūlam*).—§ 717*d* (Brahma-Rudrasamv.): XII, **351**, 13721 (°*samudrasya madhye*, there the mountain Vaijayanta is situated).—§ 730*g* (Upamanyu): XIII, **14**, 832 (*sāgaram*), 917 (*sāgarāṇām*, i.e. Çiva), 951 (*sāgaraḥ*). Cf. Kshīrodadhi.
Kshīroda[2] = Çiva (1000 names[1]).
Kshīrodadhi ("the ocean of milk"). § 717*b* (Nārāyaṇīya): XII, **336**, †12703 (°*er uttarato hi dvīpaḥ Çvetaḥ*).—§ 717*c* (Uparicara): XII, **337**, 12778 (°*er uttarato Çvetadvīpaḥ*). Cf. Kshīroda[1].
***Kshiti** ("Earth," personif.): VII, 1286.
Kshitīça = Vishṇu (1000 names).
Kshitikampana, a warrior of Skanda. § 615*u* (Skanda): IX, **45**η, 2561.
Kshitimukha = Çiva: X, 258.
Kshitipati = Çiva: XIV, 213.
Kshobhaṇa[1] = Çiva (1000 names[1]).—Do.[2] = Vishṇu (1000 names).
Kshubhā. § 310*b* (Sūrya): III, **3**, 199 (°*ayā sahitā Maitrī; Kshubhā-Maitryau nigrahānugrahakartryau devate*, Nīl.).
Kshubdha = Çiva (1000 names[1]).
Kshudra[1], name of a caste: XIII, 2587.
Kshudra[2] = Çiva (1000 names[1]).
Kshudraka, pl. (°*āḥ*), a people. § 295 (Dyūtap.): II, **52**, 1871 (°-*Mālavaiḥ*, bring tribute to Yudhishṭhira).—§ 578 (Bhīshmavadhap.): VI, **51**ν, 2106 (do., in the army of Duryodhana).—§ 580 (do.): VI, **59**μ, †2584 (°-*Mālavāḥ*), †2646 (do., had been slain).—§ 585 (do.): VI, **87**, 3853 (°-*Mālavaiḥ*, followed Bhīshma).—§ 595 (Shoḍaçarāj., v. Rāma Jāmadagnya): VII, **70**β, 2435 (*Kunti-K°-Mālavān*, had formerly been slain by Rāma).—§ 604 (Karṇap.): VIII, **5**ζ, 137 (had been slain by Arjuna).
Kshudralubdha = Çiva (1000 names[1]).
Kshupa, a ṛshi. § 267 (Yamasabhāv.): II, **8**, 323 (in the palace of Yama).—§ 641 (Rājadh.): XII, **102**, 4485 (*Prajāpatiḥ*, son of Brahmán; the fœtus fell from the head of Brahmán when he sneezed—*kshuvataḥ*), 4503, 4506 (received the rod of chastisement from the Lokapālas), 4507 (made it over to Manu (Vaivasvata)).—§ 656 (Khaḍgotpattik.): XII, **166**δ, 6192 (son of Manu, received the sword), 6193 (gave it to Ikshvāku).—§ 761 (Ānuçāsanik.): XIII, **115**δ, 5669 (among the kings who did not eat meat during the month of Kārttika).—§ 775 (do.): XIII, **166**η, 7682 (*rājarshiḥ*).—

§ 778*b* (Saṃvartta-Maruttīya): XIV, **4,** 66 (son of Prasandhi and father of Ikshvāku). Cf. Prajānām adhipaḥ, Prajāpati.

Kshura = Çiva (1000 names[1]).

Kshurakarṇī, a mātṛ. § 615*u* (Skanda): IX, **46*θ*,** 2643.

Kshuta = Çiva (1000 names[1]).

Kubalāçva, v. Kuvalāçva.

Kubera, the lord of riches, regent of the northern quarter, king of the Guhyakas, Rākshasas, and Yakshas, husband of Ṛddhi (Bhadrā). § 155 (Çakuntalop.): I, **74,** 3072 (°*sya*, sc. *bhavanaṃ*).—§ 185 (Pāṇḍu): I, **120,** 4650 (*uttarāṃ* ... *K°sya*, in the north).—§ 221 (Caitrarathap.): I, **170,** 6448 (°*sya priyaḥ sakhā*, i.e. the Gandharva Citraratha).—§ 238 (Pañcendrop.): I, **197,** 7277.—[§ 258 (Khāṇḍavadahanap.): I, **227,** 8264 (in the encounter between the gods and Arjuna + Kṛshṇa, Vaiçravaṇa, i.e. *K.*, hurled his mace against Kṛshṇa).]—§ 265 (Lokapālasabhākhyānap.): II, **6,** 281.—§ 268 (Varuṇasabhāv.): II, **9,** 382 (°*sya sabhāṃ*).—[§ 269 (Vaiçravaṇasabhāv.): II, **10** (description of the palace of *K.*, Bhava, i.e. Çiva made friendship with Paulastya, i.e. *K.* (v. 417)).]—§ 298 (Dyūtap.): II, **58,** 1994 (°*bhavanopamaṃ*, sc. the palace (*rājagṛha*) of Yudhishṭhira).—§ 329 (Kāmyakavanapr.): III, **36,** 1442 (will give weapons to Arjuna).—§ 334 (Kairātap.): III, **41,** 1671 (*Yakshair anugataḥ*, came to see Arjuna), [1697 (*Dhanādhyakshaḥ*, gave his weapon Antardhāna to Arjuna)].—§ 356 (Tīrthayātrāp.): III, **80,** 3095 (°*ena yathā hīnaṃ vanaṃ Caitrarathaṃ yatha*).—§ 377 (Dhaumyatīrthayātrāp.): III, **89,** 8358 (*jajñe Dhanapatir yatra*—i.e. on the Narmadā—*Kubero Naravāhanaḥ*).—§ 378 (Tīrthayātrāp.): III, **91,** 8419 (Arjuna had obtained weapons from *K.*).—§ 418*c* (Mandara): III, **139,** 10824 (*Yaksharāṭ*, on Mandara).—§ 418 (Tīrthayātrāp.): III, **139,** 10829 (°*sacivāḥ* . . . *Rākshasāḥ*).—§ 418*d* (Kailāsa): III, **139,** 10831 (°*sadanaṃ*, on Kailāsa).—§ 420 (Gandhamādanapr.): III, **141,** 10894 (°*nalinīṃ ramyāṃ Rākshasair abhisevitāṃ*).—§ 432 (Saugandhikāharaṇap.): III, **153,** 11352 (°*nalinīṃ* . . . *K°bhavanābhyāse jātāṃ parvatanirjhare*), 11358 (*ākrīḍaṃ Rājarājasya K°sya*); **154,** 11370 (*ākrīḍo 'yaṃ K°sya*), 11378 (*bhavanaṃ K°sya*, Bhīmasena slew many of the Krodhavaças, the rest fled to the abode of *K.*).—§ 433 (do.): III, **155,** 11416 (°*sya nalinyāḥ*), 11428 (the Pāṇḍavas lived for some time at the lotus-tank of *K.*, with the permission of *K.*).—[§ 434*c* (do.): III, **156,** 11441 (*Vaiçravaṇāvāsaṃ*, inhabited by Siddhas).]—§ 438 (Yakshayuddhap.): III, **161,** 11747 (°*sadanaṃ*), 11758 (do.), 11769 (*Yaksharakshogaṇavṛtaṃ*), 11770, 11780 (Bhīmasena slew the Yakshas).—[§ 438*c* (Agastya): III, **161** (*K.* had been cursed by Agastya, but was freed by Bhīmasena).]—§ 438 (Yakshayuddhap.): III, **162,** 11830, 11836 (°*sadanaṃ prati*, the Pāṇḍavas lived there for some time).—§ 443 (Nivātakavacayuddhap.): III, **168,** 12004 (*Naravāhanaḥ*, repetition of § 334).—§ 448 (Ājagarāp.): III, **176,** †12328.—§ 449 (do.): III, **177,** †12340 (*Kailāsaṃ* . . . *K°kāntaṃ*), †12347 (°*kāntāṃ nalinīṃ; c:* frequented by gods and Siddhas).—§ 512 (Ghoshayātrāp.): III, **240,** 14869 (Citrasena came from *K°bhavanāt*).—[§ 525 (Rāmopākhyānap.): III, **274,** 15883 foll. (*Vaiçravaṇaḥ*, son of Pulastya and a cow; he deserted his father, who then assumed the form of Viçravas. Brahmán made *K.* a god, Dhaneça ("lord of wealth") and one of the Lokapālas, and he obtained the friendship of Çiva, a son named Nalakūbara, the vimāna Pushpaka, the sovereignty of the Yakshas, and the state of Rājarāja).]—§ 526 (do.): III, **275,** 15890 (*Rākshaseçvaraḥ*, resided in Laṅkā); [**276** (Rāvaṇa conquered Laṅkā and the vimāna of *K.* (Pushpaka); *K.* repaired to the Gandhamādana)].—§ 541 (Indrajidvadha): III, **289,** 16474 (a Guhyaka came to Vibhīshaṇa from *K.* from the mountain Çveta).—[§ 543 (Rāmābhishekap.): III, **291,** 16600 (*Vaiçravaṇāya*, having vanquished and slain Rāvaṇa, Rāma returned the vimāna Pushpaka to *K.*).]—§ 552 (Goharaṇap.): IV, **56*ζ*,** 1770 (came to see the encounter).—§ 555 (Indravijaya): V, **16,** †511 (*Lokapālaḥ*), †515, 518 (*g:* Indra bestowed the sovereignty of the Yakshas and all the wealth of the world on *K.*); **18,** 545.—§ 556 (Sañjayayānap.): V, **29,** †824 (*Vaiçravaṇaḥ*).—§ 561 (Yānasandhip.): V, **64,** 2473 (*madhupītakamākshikaṃ* . . . *K°dayitaṃ*).—§ 569 (Bhagavadyānap.): V, **139,** 4718 (°*sadanaṃ prāpya*, sc. the Pāṇḍavas, all. to §§ 433 or 438).—§ 570 (Sainyaniryāṇap.): V, **156,** 5289 (°*a iva Yakshāṇāṃ*, sc. *senāpatiḥ*).—§ 571 (Ulūkadūtāgamanap.): V, **162,** 5604.—§ 573 (Ambopākhyānap.): V, **192,** 7519 (*Naravāhanaḥ*, cursed Sthūṇa).—§ 574 (Jambūkh.): VI, **6,** 217 (enjoys only the fourth part of all wealth).—§ 574*e* (Gandhamādana): VI, **6,** 229 (*Guhyakādhipaḥ*, together with the Rākshasas on Gandhamādana).—§ 578 (Bhīshmavadhap.): VI, **50,** 2039 (*gadādharaḥ*).—§ 589 (Droṇābhishekap.): VII, **6,** 159 (°*a iva Yakshāṇāṃ*, sc. *senāpatiḥ*).—§ 595 (Shoḍaçarāj., v. Rantideva): VII, **67,** 2370 (°*sadaneshv api*).—§ 595 (Sṛñjaya): VII, **71,** 2459 (°*tanayopamaḥ*, sc. the son of Sṛñjaya).—§ 596 (Pratijñāp.): VII, **76*δ*,** 2691; **80,** 2846 (°*sya vihāre ca nalinīṃ padmabhūshitāṃ*, passed by Kṛshṇa and Arjuna on their way to the abode of Çiva).—§ 600 (Ghaṭotkacavadhap.): VII, **180*δδ*,** 8194.—§ 607 (Karṇap.): VIII, **37,** †1737 (*Yama-Varuṇa-K°-Vāsavā vā yadi*).—§ 608 (do.): VIII, **92,** †4831 (°-*Vaivasvata-Vāsavānāṃ tulyaprabhāvāḥ*).—§ 615*x* (Baladevatīrthayātrā): In days of yore, *Kubera*, the chief of the Yakshas, practised austerities there (i.e. in Kaubera-tīrtha) and obtained many boons: the lordship of all treasures, the friendship of Rudra, the state of a god (*suratvaṃ*), the state of a Lokapāla, and a son, Nalakūbara. The Maruts installed him. He also obtained a celestial chariot, fleet as thought, yoked with haṃsas, the vimāna Pushpaka, and the lordship of the *Nairṛtas* (i.e. Rākshasas): IX, **47,** 2756 (*Yaksharājñā*).—§ 621 (Rājadh.): XII, **5*ζ*,** 141 (Arjuna had obtained weapons from *K.*).—§ 637 (do.): XII, **44,** 1525 (°*bhavanaprakhyaṃ*, sc. the palace of Durmarshaṇa).—§ 641 (do.): XII, **67,** 2521 (°*a iva Nairṛtān*, sc. *sukho dhāsyati*); [**74,** (discourse with Mucukunda, who had vanquished his troops)]; **122,** 4496 (*dhanānāṃ Rākshasānāñ ca K°m api ceçvaraṃ*).—§ 647*b* (Brahmadatta-Pūjanīsaṃv.): XII, **139,** 5239 (°*a iva kamadaḥ*).—§ 730*g* (Upamanyu): XIII, **14,** 912 (*sarvayakshāṇāṃ*, sc. Çiva).—[§ 731*b* (Ashṭāvakra-Diksaṃv.): XIII, **19** (visited by Ashṭāvakra).]—§ 746 (Ānuçāsanik.): XIII, **61,** 3101 (°*m iva Rakshāṃsi*).—§ 778*f* (Muñjavat): XIV, **8,** 183, 186 (°*ānucaraiḥ*), 190 (°*sya sahāyaiḥ*), 191.—§ 782*g* (Guruçishyasaṃv.): XIV, **40*θ*,** 1180 (*sarvaratnānāṃ rājā*).—§ 785 (Anugītāp.): XIV, **65,** 1918 (*Yakshendrāya*).—§ 787 (Āçramavāsap.): XV, **20,** 570 (after death Dhṛtarāshṭra will go to *K°bhavanaṃ*).—§ 795 (Svargārohaṇap.): XVIII, **5,** 175 (°*sya bhavanaṃ*).

Cf. also the following synonyms:—

Alakādhipa, q.v.

Dhanada ("wealth-giving"): II, 395, 401, 405, 415, 466, 986, 1011 (*uttarāṃ diçaṃ* . . . *Dh°pālitāṃ*); III, 11287 (°*odyānaṃ*), 11322, 11445, 11656, 11666, 11773, 11803, 11829, 11888, †12364; V, 3570, 3831 (on the mountain

Kailāsa), 3899, 7532; VII, 1223, 9628; VIII, †678 (°*endrakalpau*), †3392 (°*sya lakshmyā*, sc. *tulyaḥ*); IX, 2657 (*ṛddhyā Dh°opamāḥ*, sc. *mātaraḥ*); XII, 1528 (*Kailāsaṃ Dh°o yathā*, sc. *labdhvā*), (2816), 10052 (Vishṇu identified with *Dh.*), 10666 (*Yaksharakshodhipaḥ*), 10668; XIII, 1396 (?), 1412 (*Mandākinīñ ca nalinīṃ Dh°sya*), 1422, 1441.

Dhanadeçvara ("wealth-giving lord"): II, 410 (C. by error *Da°*).

Dhanādhigoptṛ ("guardian of treasures"): V, 7521.

Dhanādhipa ("lord of treasures"): III, 11766, 11776, 11779; XIII, 1432.

Dhanādhipati (do.): III, 11768, 11837, 11838; IX, 2757.

Dhanādhyaksha ("overseer of treasures"): I, 6837, 7581 (*Kauravasya niveçanaṃ Dh°kshayopamam*); III, 1697, 11831, 16177; X, 498 (°*opamaṃ*); XIV, 1923.

Dhanānām īçvaraḥ ("lord of treasures"): I, 408, 409, 414; II, 1672.

Dhanapati (do.): I, 7853 (*ishṭā Dh°eḥ*, sc. Vargā); II, 417 (°*eḥ sakhā*, i.e. Çiva), 481, 991 (*diçaṃ Dh°eḥ*); III, 8358 (*K°*); V, 3898 (?); VIII, 1998 (*sagadāt . . . api*); XII, 10667.

Dhaneça (do.): III, 14546, 15886 (°*tvaṃ*); VII, 2522; XVIII, 160 (°*sya lokān*).

Dhaneçvara (do.): I, †7010, 8264 (hurled his mace against Kṛshṇa); II, 407, 417, 418; III, 770 (*devagaṇāḥ . . . saha-Dh°āḥ*), 10224, 11372, 11375, 11392, 11394, 11722, 11757, 11761, 11772, 11775, (11792), 11799, 11933 (°*gṛha°*), †15590, 15920, 15925, 16189; IV, 2281 (°*am ivāmarāḥ*); V, 545 (*K°*), 3968 (*reme . . . yathā carddhyāṃ Dh°aḥ*), 7481 (°*syānucaraḥ*, sc. Sthūṇa); VI, 4902 (*sagadaḥ*); VII, 1844 (°*sutopamaṃ*, sc. Abhimanyu), 5464 (*iva*); XII, 2819, 7552 (*Nidhipaṃ*); XIII, 1059 (Çiva identified with *Dh.*), 1431, 7117 (°*sya guravaḥ saptaite uttarāçritāḥ*, sc. Atri, etc.), 7637 (*saharddhyā ca Dh° aḥ*).

Draviṇapati ("lord of wealth"): III, 11702 (°*eḥ puraṃ*).

Gadādhara ("bearing a mace"): VI, 2039.

Guhyakādhipa, Guhyakādhipati, q.v.

Kailāsanilaya ("having his abode on the Kailāsa"): II, 275; III, 1697; XII, 10216.

Naravāhana ("borne by men"): III, 8358 (*K°*), 11653, 11781, 12004 (*K°*), 14546 (rides on Pushpaka), 15902 (*Vaiçravaṇaṃ*); V, 7519 (*K°*); XII, 2240 (*Yaksha-Rākshasabhartā*).

Nidhipa ("guardian of treasures"): XII, 7552.

Paulastya, Rājarāja, Rājarājan, Rākshasādhipati, Rākshaseçvara, q.v.

Vaiçravaṇa ("son of Viçravas"): I, †164, 468 (*samāgamaḥ Pāṇḍavānāṃ yatra V°ena ca*), †2100 (*yajñas tathā V°sya rājñaḥ*, comparison), 7352 (*yathā V°e Bhadrā . . . bhava bhartṛshu*, says Kuntī to Draupadī); II, 384 (had obtained his sabhā by means of tapas), 690 (°*opamaḥ*, sc. the Māgadha king Bṛhadratha); III, 481 (Kṛshṇa identified with *V.*), 2554 (*yathā Yakshādhipaḥ . . . V°ḥ*), 11359, 11378 (*K°*), 11441 (°*āvāsaṃ*), 11442 (°*āçramāt*), 11653, 11655, 11665, 11697 (°*āvāsaṃ*), 11720 (*sakhā V°sya*, i.e. the Rākshasa Maṇimat), 11722 (°*āvāsaṃ*), 11754 (°*ālayaṃ*), 11845 (*Indra-V°au*), 11846 (°*sya . . . sadma*, sc. the mountain Mandara), 11901 (°*sya*, sc. *astram*, obtained by Arjuna), †12319, †12332 (°*ādhivāsaṃ*), 12954 (Nārāyaṇa identifies himself with *V.*), 15883, 15885, 15886, 15889, 15902 (*Naravāhanaṃ*), 15922, 16600; IV, 363 (*pradadau vittaṃ bahu . . . yathā V°ḥ*), 1433, 2274 (*dhanaiḥ sañcayaiḥ Çakra-V°opamaḥ*, sc. Yudhishṭhira); V, †824 (*K°*), 4467–8 (gave the earth to Mucukunda), 5381, 7535, 7542; VI, 236 (together with the Guhyakas on Kailāsa), 4703 (*ṛddhyā V°ñ cāti*), 5741 (*diçaṃ V°ākrāntāṃ*, i.e. the north); VII, 346 (*Yama-V°āditya-Mahendra-Varuṇopamaṃ*, sc. Uttamaujas), 991 (*Yama-V°opamāḥ*), 2417 (when the *puṇyajanāḥ* milked the earth, *V.* acted as their milker), 3676, 9535 (*yasya*—i.e. Çiva's—*V°aḥ sakhā*); VIII, 241 (*rājñāṃ V°o varaḥ*), 1782 (*yathā*), †3498 (*V°āntakopamaḥ*, sc. Bhīmasena), 4421 (sided with Arjuna in the encounter between Arjuna and Karṇa); IX, 3106 (°*sya . . . sadṛçau*, sc. Duryodhana and Bhīmasena); XII, 440 (among those who are slaughterers), 2064 (*Yama-V°opamaḥ*), 2576, 2581, 2810 (*Mucukundasya saṃvādaṃ rājño V°sya ca*), 2812 (*rājā*), 2815 (do.), 2823, 2827, 5236, 5831, 10216 (°*o rājā Guhyakair abhisaṃvṛtaḥ Yakshāṇām īçvaraḥ çrīmān Kailāsanilayaḥ prabhuḥ*); XIII, 1415 (*rājā*), 1417, 1428 (*rājā*), 1431, 2803 (*yathā*), †4860 (*Mandākinī V°sya rājñaḥ*), 6750 (*Ṛddhir V°sya*, sc. *sādhvī*); XIV, 2051 (°*syeva nivāsaḥ*), 2576 (*yathā*); XV, 334 (do.).

Vittagoptṛ ("guardian of wealth"): VIII, †4661.

Vittānām patiḥ ("lord of riches"): VIII, 1485 (*Surāmbupretavittānāṃ patīn*).

Vittapati (do.): VII, 8444.

Vitteça (do.): VI, 1227 (°*o Yaksha-Rakshasāṃ*, sc. *asmi*, says Kṛshṇa); VII, 37 (*Pitṛ-Vittāmbudeveçān*); XIV, †289 (*iva*).

Yakshādhipa, Yakshādhipati, Yakshapati, Yakshapravara, Yaksharāj, Yaksharāja, Yaksharājan, Yaksha - Rākshasabhartṛ, Yaksharakshodhipa, q.v.

Kubjāmraka, a tīrtha. § 370 (Tīrthayātrāp.): III, **84**, 8018.

Kucīrā, a river. § 574 (Jambūkh.): VI, **9**λ, 334 (in Bhāratavarsha).

Kuçabindu (C. °*vi*°), pl. (°*avaḥ*), a people. § 574 (Jambūkh.): VI, **9**μ, 363 (among the peoples of Bhāratavarsha).

Kuçacīrā, a river. § 574 (Jambūkh.): VI, **9**λ, 330 (in Bhāratavarsha).

Kuçadhārā, a river. § 574 (Jambūkh.): VI, **9**λ, 332 (in Bhāratavarsha).

Kuçadvīpa, one of the seven dvīpas. § 575 (Bhūmip.): VI, **11**, 402; **12**, 447 (with a clump of kuça grass—*kuçastamba*, so B., C. has °*stambha*), 450 (with a mountain of the same name (?) and five other mountains).—§ 730*e* (Vidyutprabha): XIII, **14**, 673 (Çiva gave *K.* to the Dānava Vidyutprabha).

Kuçādya, pl. (°*āḥ*), a people. § 574 (Jambūkh.): VI, **9**μ, 352 (only B., C. has *Kulādyāḥ*).

Kuçala[1], a region in Krauñcadvīpa. § 575 (Bhūmip.): VI, **12**θ, 462.

Kuçala[2], pl. (°*āḥ*), a people. § 574 (Jambūkh.): VI, **9**μ, 359 (in Bhāratavarsha).

Kuçalya, pl. (°*āḥ*), a people. § 574 (Jambūkh.): VI, **9**μ, 347 (only B., C. has *Sukutyāḥ*).

Kuçāmba, son of Vasu Uparicara. § 74 (Vasu): I, **63**, 2363 (*yam āhur Maṇivāhanaṃ*).

Kuçaplavana, a tīrtha. § 370 (Tīrthayātrāp.): III, **85**, 8179.

Kuçastamba, a tīrtha. § 733*l* (Çarastamba): XIII, **25**, 1714.

Kuçasthala, a village. § 556 (Sañjayayānap.): V, **31**, 934

(B. *Avisthalam*, one of the five villages for which Yudhishṭhira asked Duryodhana). Cf. Avisthala.

Kuçasthalī = Dvārakā. § 273 (Rājasūyārambhap.): II, **14**, 614 (*Raivatenopaçobhitām*, the Vṛshṇis fled from Mathurā and took up their abode in *K.*).—§ 717*b* (Nārāyaṇīya): XII, **340**, 12955 (°*īṃ karishyāmi niveçaṃ Dvārakāṃ purīṃ*, says Nārāyaṇa, sc. incarnate as Kṛshṇa), 12957.

Kuçāvarta, a tīrtha. § 733*f* (Gaṅgādvāra): XIII, **25**, 1700.

Kuçavat, a lake. § 410 (Plakshāvataraṇag.): III, **130**, 10553 (*hradaḥ K°ān esha yatra padmaṃ kuçeçayam*).

Kuçavatī, a city (?). § 438 (Yakshayuddhap.): III, **161**, 11792 (°*yāṃ* (*Kuçasthalīsañjñe deçaviçeshe*, Nīl.)).

Kuçavindu, pl., v. Kuçabindu, pl.

Kuçeçaya[1], a mountain in Kuçadvīpa. § 575 (Bhūmip.): VI, **12**ε, 452.

Kuçeçaya[2] = Mahāpurusha (Mahāpurushastava).

Kuçika, an ancient king. § 22 (Pramadvarā): I, **8***a*, 961.—§ 223 (Vāsishṭha): I, **175**, 6651 (father of king Gādhi in Kānyakubja and grandfather of Viçvāmitra).—§ 267 (Yamasabhāv.): II, **8**, 321 (in the palace of Yama).—§ 370 (Tīrthayātrāp.): III, **84**, 8109 (°*syāçramam*, a tīrtha).—§ 562 (Bhagavadyānap.): V, **83**η, 2946 (among the ṛshis who worshipped Kṛshṇa).—§ 574 (Jambūkh.): VI, **9***aa*, 315.—§ 638*b* (Rāmopākhyāna): XII, **49**, 1717 (son of Balākaçva and father of Gādhi).—§ 721*b* (Viçvāmitrop.): XIII, **4**, 204 (son of Vallabha and grandson of Balākāçva), 205 (father of Gādhi).—§ 745*c* (Cyavana-Kuçikasaṃv.): XIII, **52**, 2722 (*Cyavanasya ca saṃvādaṃ K°sya ca*), 2725, (2726), 2728, 2734, 2738, 2741, 2747; **53**, 2768, 2769, 2780, 2813, 2818, 2821; **54**, 2827, 2848, 2849, (2863); **55**, (2868), (2901); **56**, 2919 (the relations of Cyavana and *K.*). Cf. Kuçikarshi.

Kuçika, pl. (°*āḥ*), a family, the descendants of Kuçika. § 152 (Pūruvaṃç.): I, **94**, 3723 (descended from Jahnu).—§ 223 (Vāsishṭha): I, **174**, 6639 (the family of Viçvāmitra).—§ 745*c* (Cyavana-Kuçikasaṃv.): XIII, **52**, 2724 (*kulaṃ* . . . *K°ānāṃ*); **55**, 2879 (*cikīrshan K°occhedaṃ*, sc. Cyavana); **56**, 2924 (*Bhṛgūnāṃ K°ānāñ ca abhisambandhakāraṇaṃ*).

Kuçikanandana ("the son of Kuçika") = Gādhin: XII, 1745 (*G°*).

Kuçikarshi = Kuçika (?): XIII, 3323.

Kuçikavaṃça ("the race of Kuçika"). § 721 (Ānuçasanik.): XIII, **3***a*, 184 (*brahmarshiçatasaṅkulaḥ*, i.e. the descendants of Viçvāmitra).

Kuçikottama ("the uppermost of the Kuçikas") = Indra: XIII, 800.

Kūçm°, v. Kushm°.

Kuhana. § 522 (Draupadīharaṇap.): III, **265**, †15598 (one of the standard-bearers of Jayadratha).

Kuhara[1], a king. § 130 (Aṃçāvat.): I, **67**, 2701 (among the incarnations from the Krodhavaça gaṇa).

Kuhara[2], a serpent. § 564 (Mātalīyop.): V, **103**γ, 3631.

Kuhū[1] ("the new moon"). § 489 (Āṅgirasa): III, **218**, 14129 (the eighth daughter of Aṅgiras).—§ 615*u* (Skanda): IX, **45**γ, 2515 (came to the investiture of Skanda).

Kuhū[2] = Devasenā: III, 14451.

Kukkura, a muni. § 264 (Sabhākriyāp.): II, **4***a*, 113 (waited upon Yudhishṭhira).

Kukkura, pl. (°*āḥ*), a people. § 295 (Dyūtap.): II, **52**, 1872 (brought tribute to Yudhishṭhira).—§ 574 (Jambūkh.): VI, **9**ν, 368 (°*āṅgāramārishāḥ*, in the south). — § 578 (Bhīshmavadhap.): VI, **51***a*, 2097 (protected Bhīshma). Cf. Kukura, pl.

Kukkuṭikā, a mātṛ. § 615*u* (Skanda): IX, **46**θ, 2633.

Kukshi[1], a Dānava. § 130 (Aṃçāvat.): I, **67**, 2692 (*Dānavānāṃ mahābalaḥ*, incarnate as king Parvatīya).

Kukshi[2]. § 717*b* (Nārāyaṇīya): XII, **349**, V), 13589 (*diçāṃ pālāya*, son of Raibhya).

Kukuna, a serpent. § 564 (Mātalīyop.): V, **103**γ, 3626.

Kukura[1], a serpent. § 564 (Mātalīyop.): V, **103**γ, 3626.

Kukura[2], an ancient king. § 775 (Ānuçāsanik.): XIII, **166**η, 7679.

Kukura, pl. (°*āḥ*), a people (a tribe of the Yādavas). § 275 (Rājasūyārambhap.): II, **19**, 767 (°*āndhakaiḥ*). — § 452 (Mārkaṇḍeyas.): III, **183**, |12588 (°*āndhakāḥ*). — § 555 (Sainyodyogap.): V, **19**, 586 (*Bhojāndha-K°aiḥ*, followed Kṛtavarman).—§ 556 (Sañjayayānap.): V, **29**, 804 (followed Kṛshṇa).—§ 574 (Jambūkh.): VI, **9**μ, 350.—§ 641 (Rājadh.): XII, **81**λ, 3052.—§ 793 (Mausalap.): XVI, **3**, 98 (°*āndhakāḥ*, were exterminated). Cf. Kukkura, pl.

Kukurādhipa ("the king of the Kukuras") = Ugrasena: XII, 8457.

Kulādya, pl., v. Kuçādya, pl.

Kulahārin, Kulakartṛ = Çiva (1000 names[2]).

Kulampuna, a tīrtha. § 364 (Tīrthayātrāp.): III, **83**, 6074 (°*e naraḥ snātvā punāti svakulam*).

Kulampunā, a river. § 775 (Ānuçāsanik.): XIII, **166***a*, 7646.

Kulattha, pl. (°*āḥ*), a people. § 574 (Jambūkh.): VI, **9**ξ, 373 (in the north).

Kulika, a serpent. § 100 (Aṃçāvat.): I, **65**, 2549 (son of Kadrū).

Kulinda, pl. (°*āḥ*), a people. § 273 (Rājasūyārambhap.): II, **14**, 590 (fled from fear of Jarāsandha).—§ 279 (Arjuna): II, **26**, 996 (in the north, vanquished by Arjuna on his digvijaya), 997.—§ 295 (Dyūtap.): II, **52**, 1859 (brought tribute to Yudhishṭhira).—§ 419 (Gandhamādanapr.): III, **140**, 10866 (°*ānām īçvaraḥ*, i.e. Subāhu).—§ 574 (Jambūkh.): VI, **9**ν, 370 (in the north).—§ 599 (Jayadrathavadhap.): VII, **121**εε, 4819 (followed Duryodhana, only in B., C. has *Kuliṅgāḥ*).—§ 604 (Karṇap.): VIII, **8**, 236 (had formerly been vanquished by Karṇa).—§ 608 (do.): VIII, **85**, †4308, †4312, †4324 (fought with the army of Duryodhana).

Kulinda ("the king of the Kulindas") = Subāhu (?). § 449 (Ājagarap.): III, **177**, †12350 (*deçān* . . . *K°sya*).

Kulindādhipati (do.). § 419 (Gandhamādanapr.): III, **140**, 10868 (= Subāhu). § 522 (Draupadīharaṇap.): III, **265**, 15594 (*putraḥ K°eḥ*, followed Jayadratha).

Kulindaja = Kulindaputra[2]: VIII, †4323 (slain by Çakuni).

Kulindaputra[1] ("son of the Kulinda king"). § 608 (Karṇap.): VIII, **85**, †4310 (slain by Kṛpa), †4311 (°*āvarajaḥ*, slain by Çakuni).

Kulindaputra[2] (do.). § 608 (Karṇap.): VIII, **85**, †4319 (slain by Çakuni)

Kulindaputra[3] (do.). § 608 (Karṇap.): VIII, **85**, †4328 (slain by Çatānīka).

Kulindarājāvaraja = Kulindaputra[2]: VIII, †4317.

Kulindopatyaka, pl. (°*āḥ*), a people. § 574 (Jambūkh.): VI, **9**μ, 363.

Kuliṅga, pl., v. Kulinda, pl.

Kulūta, pl. (°*āḥ*), a people. § 605 (Karṇap.): VIII, **12**, 485 (*nṛpatiṃ* . . . *Kulūtānāṃ*, i.e. Kshemadhūrti, slain by Bhīmasena).

Kulūtādhipati = Kshemadhūrti: VIII, 475.

Kulyā, a tīrtha. § 733*y* (Ujjānaka): XIII, **25**, 1742.

Kumāra[1] = Skanda, q.v.

Kumāra[2], a prince. § 554 (Sainyodyogap.): V, **4**γ, 87 (among the princes to whom the Pāṇḍavas ought to send messengers).

Kumāra[3], a Suparṇa, son of Garuḍa. § 564 (Mātalīyop.): V, **101**β, 3598 (enumeration).

Kumāra[4], a Pāñcāla prince. § 590 (Droṇābhishekap.): VII, **16**, 639 (*Pāñcālānāṃ yaçaskaraḥ*, the cakraraksha of Yudhishṭhira), 640, 641, 642, 643 (slain by Droṇa).

Kumāra[5] = Sanatkumāra: V, 1566, 1569; XII, 1355 (*Pitāmahasutaṃ jyeshṭhaṃ*).

Kumāra[6], pl. (°*āḥ*), a people. § 280 (Bhīmasena): II, **30**, 1075 (°*vishaye Çreṇimantaṃ*, vanquished by Bhīmasena on his digvijaya).—§ 295 (Dyūtap.): II, **52**, 1870 (brought tribute to Yudhishṭhira).

Kumāra[7], pl. (°*āḥ*), a class of demons. § 500 (Skandop.): III, **228**, 14390 (sons (?) of Skanda).—§ 502 (Manushyagrahak.): III, **230**, 14484.

Kumāradhārā, a tīrtha. § 370 (Tīrthayātrāp.): III, **84**, 8127.

Kumāraka, a serpent. § 65 (Sarpasattra): I, **57**, 2154 (of Kauravya's race).

Kumāraka, pl. (°*āḥ*) = Kumāra[7], pl.: III, 14387.

Kumārakoṭi, a tīrtha. § 360 (Tīrthayātrāp.): III, **82**, 5058.

Kumārapitṛ[1] = Skanda: III, 14391 (only B., C. has *Kumāraṃ pitaraṃ*).

Kumārapitṛ[2] = Çiva: VIII, 1450; X, 259.

Kumārasū ("father of Kumāra [i.e. Skanda]") = Agni: II, 1148.

Kumārī[1], wife of the elder Bhīmasena. § 156 (Pūruvaṃç.): I, **95**, ††3796 (*Kaikeyīṃ*, mother of Pratiçravas).

Kumārī[2], wife of Dhanañjaya. § 565 (Gālavacarita): V, **117**, 3976 (*reme . . . yathā . . . K°yāñ ca Dhanañjayaḥ*).

Kumārī[3], a river. § 574 (Jambūkh.): VI, **9**λ, 343 (in Bhāratavarsha).

Kumārī[4], a river in Çākadvīpa. § 575*b* (Çākadvīpa): VI, **11**γ, 432.

Kumārī[5] = Durgā (Umā): IV, 184; VI, 796.

Kumārī[6], pl. (°*yaḥ*), name of a tīrtha. § 377 (Dhaumyatīrthak.): III, **88**, 8339 (in the country of the Pāṇḍyas).

Kumārī[7], pl. (°*yaḥ*), a class of demons. § 502 (Manushyagrahak.): III, **230**, 14484.

Kumārikā, pl. (°*āḥ*), a country (?). § 358 (Tīrthayātrāp.): III, **82**, 5023 (°*ānāṃ Çakrasya tīrthaṃ*).

Kumbha[1], an Asura. § 90 (Aṃçāvat.): I, **65**, 2527 (the second son of Prahlāda).

Kumbha[2] = Vishṇu (1000 names).

Kumbhaka, a warrior of Skanda. § 615*u* (Skanda): IX, **45**η, 2577.

Kumbhakarṇa[1], a Rākshasa, brother of Rāvaṇa. § 478 (Dhundhumārop.): III, **204**, 13610 (°*m ivāparaṃ*, sc. *Dhundhuṃ*).—§ 526 (Rāmopākhyānap.): III, **275**, 15895 (Pushpotkaṭā bore *K.* and Daçagrīva (i.e. Rāvaṇa) to Viçravas), 15899 (most powerful in battle and master in illusive power), (β), 15905 (performed austerities with the head downwards, etc.) (γ), 15916 (Brahmán granted him long lasting sleep).—§ 532 (Sītāsāntvana): III, **280**, 16157 (°*ādayaç ceme nagnāḥ*, etc., seen by Trijaṭā).—§ 538 (Kumbhakarṇaraṇagamana): III, **286**, 16397, 16398, 16400 (Rāvaṇa awaked the sleeping *K.*), 16406, 16408 (sent against Rāma).—§ 539 (Kumbhakarṇādivadha): III, **287**, 16409, 16414 (*Rakshasaḥ*), 16416, 16417, 16419, 16421, 16423, 16428 (*Vṛtrasaṅkāçaṃ*, slain by Lakshmaṇa with the Brahmāstra).—§ 540 (Indrajidvadha): III, **288**, 16438 (*hataṃ*), 16443. Cf. Rakshas, Rākshaseçvara (dual), Rākshasendra.

Kumbhakarṇa[2] = Çiva (1000 names[1]).

Kumbhakarṇāçrama, a tīrtha. § 370 (Tīrthayātrāp.): III, **84**, 8135.

[**Kumbhakarṇādivadha** ("the slaughter of Kumbhakarṇa, etc.").] § 539: Kumbhakarṇa ate Bala, Caṇḍabala, Vajrabāhu, and other monkeys, then he fought with Sugrīva and Lakshmaṇa; when his arms were cut off double the number of arms appeared; at last Lakshmaṇa killed him with the Brahmāstra. The Rākshasas fled. Lakshmaṇa fought with Vajravega and Pramāthin; Hanūmat killed Vajravega, and Nala killed Pramāthin (III, **287**).

[**Kumbhakarṇaraṇagamana** ("the march of Kumbhakarṇa to battle").] § 538: Prahasta was killed by Vibhīshaṇa and Dhūmrāksha by Hanūmat. The Rākshasas fled and informed Rāvaṇa, who roused Kumbhakarṇa and sent him out with Vajravega and Pramāthin (III, **286**).

Kumbhāṇḍaka, a warrior of Skanda. § 615*u* (Skanda): IX, **45**η, 2571.

Kumbharetas, a fire. § 490 (Āṅgirasa): III, **219**, 14139 (*havishā yo dvitīyena Somena saha yujyate Rathaprabhū Rathādhvānaḥ Kumbharetāḥ sa ucyate*).

Kumbhasambhava ("born in a water-jar") = Droṇa: VII, 6956, 8823.

Kumbhavaktra, a warrior of Skanda. § 615*u* (Skanda): IX, **45**η, 2577.

Kumbhayoni[1], an Apsaras. § 336 (Indralokābhigamanap.): III, **43***a*, 1785 (among the Apsarases who danced in the palace of Indra).

Kumbhayoni[2] ("born in a water-jar") = Agastya: III, 8596; XII, ††13216 (*Agastyaḥ . . . Maitrāvaruṇiḥ*).

Kumbhayoni[3] (do.) = Droṇa: VII, 6947, 6956, 8364, 8367, 8371, 8820.

Kumbhikā, a mātṛ. § 615*u* (Skanda); IX, **46**θ, 2633.

Kumbhīnasi, an Asura (?). § 742 (Ānuçāsanik.): XIII, **39**, 2238 (*māyā . . . K°eḥ*).

Kumbhīnasī, the wife of the Gandharva Citraratha. § 221 (Caitrarathap.): I, **170**, 6469, 6470 (*Gandharvī*, asked Yudhishṭhira to spare Citraratha).

Kumuda[1], a serpent. § 47 (Sarpanāmak.): I, **35**, 1560 (enumeration).—§ 564 (Mātalīyop.): V, **103**γ, 3629 (do.).—§ 793 (Mausalap.): XVI, **4**η, †119.

Kumuda[2], a monkey. § 541 (Indrajidvadha): III, **289***a*, 16468 (follower of Sugrīva).

Kumuda[3], an elephant. § 564 (Mātalīyop.): V, **99**, 3561 (of Supratīka's race).

Kumuda[4], a Suparṇa, son of Garuḍa. § 564 (Mātalīyop.): V, **101**β, 3597.

Kumuda[5], a mountain in Kuçadvīpa. § 575 (Bhūmip.): VI, **12**ε, 451.

Kumuda[6], a companion of Skanda. § 615*u* (Skanda): IX, **45**ζ, 2541 (given to Skanda by Dhātṛ).

Kumuda[7], a warrior of Skanda. § 615*u* (Skanda): IX, **45**η, 2558.

Kumuda[8] = Vishṇu (1000 names).

Kumudāksha, a serpent. § 47 (Sarpanāmak.): I, **35**, 1560 (enumeration).

Kumudamālin, a companion of Skanda. § 615*u* (Skanda): IX, **45**, 2527 (given to Skanda by Brahmán).

Kumudottara, a varsha (?) in Çākadvīpa. § 575*b* (Çākadvīpa): VI, **11**β, 425.

Kunādika, a warrior of Skanda. § 615*u* (Skanda): IX, **45**η, 2560.

Kunda[1], a companion of Skanda. § 615*u* (Skanda): IX, **45**ζ, 2541 (given to Skanda by Dhātṛ).

Kunda[2] = Vishṇu (1000 names).

Kuṇḍa[1], a son of Dhṛtarāshṭra. § 182 (Dhṛtarāshṭraputranāmak.): I, **117**, 4550 (enumeration).

Kuṇḍa[2], a serpent. § 191 (Arjuna): I, **123***a*, 4828 (present at the birth of Arjuna).

Kuṇḍa[3] = Çiva (1000 names[1]).

Kuṇḍabheda, a son of Dhṛtarāshṭra. § 585 (Bhīshmavadhap.): VI, **96**$\theta\theta$, 4349 (among other sons of Dhṛtarāshṭra, who are slain by Bhīmasena). Cf. next.

Kuṇḍabhedin, a son of Dhṛtarāshṭra. § 130 (Aṃçāvat.): I, **67**, 2739 (enumeration).—§ 182 (Dhṛtarāshṭraputranāmak.): I, **117**, 4552 (do.).—§ 593 (Abhimanyuvadhap.): VII, **37**κ, 1610, 1615 (°*iṃ*, acc., is slain by Abhimanyu).—§ 599 (Jayadrathavadhap.): VII, **127**$\nu\nu$, 5176 (attacked Bhīmasena), ($\xi\xi$), 5203 (is slain by Bhīmasena).—§ 600 (Ghaṭotkacavadhap.): VII, **156**κ, 6850 (the same?).

Kuṇḍaçāyin, a son of Dhṛtarāshṭra. § 182 (Dhṛtarāshṭraputranāmak.): I, **117**, 4549 (enumeration).

Kuṇḍāçin, a son of Dhṛtarāshṭra. § 182 (Dhṛtarāshṭraputranāmak.): I, **117**, 4553.

Kuṇḍadhāra[1], a son of Dhṛtarāshṭra. § 182 (Dhṛtarāshṭraputranāmak.): I, **117**, 4546, 4550 (the same?).—§ 585 (Bhīshmavadhap.): VI, **88**ι, 3901, 3904, 3909 (among seven sons of Dhṛtarāshṭra, who were slain by Bhīmasena).

Kuṇḍadhāra[2], name of two serpents. § 268 (Varuṇasabhāv.): II, **9**, 361, 362 (in the palace of Varuṇa).

Kuṇḍadhāra[3], name of a cloud (according to Nīl.). § 685 (Mokshadh.): XII, **272**, 9756, 9760 (*meghaṃ K°ṃ nāmataḥ*, Nīl.), 9767, 9771, 9772, (9773), 9774, 9777, (9778), 9782, 9795, 9796, 9797, (9799), (9802), 9806, 9807 (discourse between *K.* and a brahman).

Kuṇḍadhāra[4], a ṛshi. § 702 (Mokshadh.): XII, **293***a*, 10762 (worshipped Vishṇu).

Kuṇḍaja, a son of Dhṛtarāshṭra. § 130 (Aṃçāvat.): I, **67**, 2740 (enumeration).

Kuṇḍajathara, a ṛshi. § 59 (Sarpasattra): I, **53**, 2048 (*Ātreyaḥ* (?), among the sadasyas at the snake-sacrifice of Janamejaya; B., however, has *Kuṇḍajatharau*). — § 376 (Tīrthayātrāp.): III, **85**, 8263 (*Ātreyaḥ*?, among the ṛshis who expected Yudhishṭhira on his tīrthayātrā).

Kuṇḍaka, a son of Dhṛtarāshṭra. § 232 (Svayaṃvarap.): I, **186**, 6983 (present at the svayaṃvara of Draupadī). Cf. Kuṇḍa[1].

Kuṇḍala, a serpent. § 66 (Sarpasattra): I, **57**, 2154 (of Kauravya's race).

Kuṇḍala, pl. (°*āḥ*), a people. § 574 (Jambūkh.): VI, **9**ν, 370 (in the south, only B., C. has *Kunthakāḥ*).

Kuṇḍalā, a river. § 574 (Jambūkh.): VI, **9**λ, 329 (only C., B. has *Kuṇḍalīṃ*).

Kuṇḍalāharaṇa ("the taking away of the ear-rings"). § 10 (Parvasaṅgr.): I, **2**, 327 (*parva*, i.e. Kuṇḍalāharaṇaparvan).

[**Kuṇḍalāharaṇaparvan** ("the section relating to the taking away of the ear-rings")], the fiftieth of the minor parvans of Mhbhr.—§ 546: Asked by Janamejaya, Vaiçampāyana related how Indra removed Yudhishṭhira's fear of Karṇa, as he had promised to Yudhishṭhira through Lomaça: In the thirteenth year of the exile of the Pāṇḍavas, Indra resolved, in the guise of a brahman, to ask Karṇa for his ear-rings (sprung from amṛta) and mail for the benefit of Arjuna. Sūrya then came to Karṇa in a dream and dissuaded him from giving them. "There is beside some mystery which you will understand in time." Karṇa refused to break his vow always to give to brahmans and confided in the weapons which he had obtained from Rāma Jāmadagnya and Droṇa. Sūrya then prevailed upon him to beseech Indra to give him a dart (III, **300–2**).—§ 547: Karṇa (q.v.).

Kuṇḍalī, v. Kuṇḍalā.

Kuṇḍalin[1], a Suparṇa, son of Garuḍa. § 564 (Mātalīyop.): V, **101**β, 3594.

Kuṇḍalin[2], a son of Dhṛtarāshṭra. § 585 (Bhīshmavadhap.): VI, **96**$\theta\theta$, 4346 (is slain by Bhīmasena).

Kuṇḍalin[3] = Vishṇu (1000 names).

Kundara = Vishṇu (1000 names).

Kundārikā, a mātṛ. § 615*u* (Skanda): IX, **46**θ, 2633.

Kuṇḍika, son of Dhṛtarāshṭra[4]. § 154 (Pūruvaṃç.): I, **94**, 3747 (eldest son of Dhṛtarāshṭra).

Kuṇḍin = Çiva (1000 names[2]).

Kuṇḍina[1], son of Dhṛtarāshṭra[4]. § 154 (Pūruvaṃç.): I, **94**, 3747 (fifth son of Dhṛtarāshṭra).

Kuṇḍina[2], the capital of the Vidarbhas. § 346 (Nalopākhyānap.): III, **60**, 2290.—§ 353 (do.): III, **73**, 2853 (*puraṃ*), 2872; **77**, 3029 (*nagare*).—§ 570 (Sainyaniryāṇap.): V, **158**, 5363 (Rukmin being vanquished by Kṛshṇa would not return to his city *K.*, but built Bhojakaṭa).

Kuṇḍīvisha, pl. (°*āḥ*), a people. § 578 (Bhīshmavadhap.): VI, **50**π, 2083 (in the krauñcavyūha of Dhṛshṭadyumna).

Kuṇḍīvṛsha, pl. (°*āḥ*) v. Kauṇḍīvṛsha, pl.

Kuṇḍoda, a mountain. § 377 (Dhaumyatīrthak.): III, **87**, 8321 (°*aḥ parvato ramyo bahumūlaphalodakaḥ* | *Naishadas*—i.e. Nala, Nīl.—*tṛshito yatra jalaṃ çarma ca labdhavān*).

Kuṇḍodara[1], a serpent. § 47 (Sarpanāmak.): I, **35**, 1561 (°*Mahodarau*, enumeration).

Kuṇḍodara[2], a son of Dhṛtarāshṭra[1]. § 130 (Aṃçāvat.): I, **67**, 2732.

Kuṇḍodara[3], son of Janamejaya[5]. § 154 (Pūruvaṃç.): I, **94**, 3746 (sixth son of Janamejaya).

Kuṇi = Garga: IX, 2982 (*G°*), 2983 (*G°*).

Kuñjala, a warrior of Skanda. § 615*u* (Skanda): IX, **45**η, 2578.

Kuñjara[1], a serpent. § 47 (Sarpanāmak.): I, **35**, 1561 (enumeration).—§ 793 (Mausalap.): XVI, **4**η, †119.

Kuñjara[2], a prince. § 522 (Draupadīharaṇap.): III, **265**, †15597 (one of the standard bearers of Jayadratha).

Kuñjaraketana ("having an elephant for his device") = Bhoja[3]: VII, 1892 (*Bh°*).

Kuntala (the king of the Kuntalas). § 287 (Rājasūyikap.): II, **34**, 1270 (came to the rājasūya of Yudhishṭhira).

Kuntala, pl. (°*āḥ*), a people. § 569 (Bhagavadyānap.): V, **140**β, 4751.—§ 574 (Jambūkh.): VI, **9**μ, 347 (only C., B. has *Kuntayaḥ*), 359 (ν), 367 (in the south).—§ 578 (Bhīshmavadhap.): VI, **51**τ, 2102 (followed Droṇa).—§ 605 (Karṇap.): VIII, **20**$\delta\delta$, 779 (followed Karṇa, attacked by the Pāṇḍya king).

Kunṭhaka, pl. (°*āḥ*), a people. § 574 (Jambūkh.): VI, **9**ν, 370 (only C., B. has *Kuṇḍalāḥ*, in the south).

Kunti[1] ("the king of the Kuntis"). § 264 (Sabhākriyāp.): II, **4**β, 119 (waited upon Yudhishṭhira). Cf. Kuntibhoja.

Kunti[2], a Vṛshṇi. § 273 (Rājasūyārambhap.): II, **14**, 623 (one of the seven atirathas of the Vṛshṇis).

Kunti, pl. (°*ayaḥ*), a people. § 273 (Rājasūyārambhap.): II, **14**, 590 (fled from fear of Jarāsandha).—§ 549 (Pāṇḍavapraveçap.): IV, **1***a*, 12 (°*rāshṭraṃ*).—§ 574 (Jambūkh.): VI,

9μ, 347 (only B., C. has *Kuntalāḥ*), 350.—§ 595 (Shoḍaçarāj., v. Rāma Jāmadagnya): VII, **70β**, 2435 (°-*Kshudraka-Mālavān*, had been slain by Rāma Jāmadagnya).—§ 604 (Karṇap.): VIII, **6**, 152 (slain by Bhīshma in the great battle).

Kuntī ("the daughter of the Kunti king"), daughter of Çūra, adopted by Kuntibhoja, by Sūrya mother of Karṇa, wife of Pāṇḍu, and mother of Yudhishṭhira, Bhīmasena, and Arjuna; her proper name was Pṛthā (P.).—§ 3 (Anukram.): I, **1**, 99, 124, 151.—[§ 4 (do.): I, **1**, 175 (P.).]—§ 11 (Parvasaṅgr.): I, **2**, 589 (*gūḍhotpannasya cākhyānaṃ Karṇasya Pṛthayātmanaḥ*), 612 (P.).—§ 131 (cf. Aṃçāvataraṇap.): Çūra (the Yadu, father of Vasudeva) gave his daughter Pṛthā as daughter to Kuntibhoja, the son of his paternal aunt, who was without offspring. Durvāsas, satisfied with her worshipful attentions, gave her a mantra by which she could summon whatever deity she liked and obtain children. Thus by Arka (the Sun) she brought forth in secrecy a child who was born with ear-rings and a coat of mail. Kuntī (=Pṛthā) threw him (i.e. Karṇa (*b*)) into the water (cf. § 547): I, **67**, [2764 (P.)], 2774.—[§ 131*b* (Karṇa): I, **67**, 2783 (*Pṛthāyāḥ prathamaḥ sutaḥ*, i.e. Karṇa).] — § 132 (Aṃçāvat.): I, **67**, 2794 (incarnation of the goddess Siddhi).—§ 157 (Pūruvaṃç.): I, **95**, ††3811 (*Pṛthā*, wife of Pāṇḍu), ††3814 (*putrān utpādayām āsa Dharmād Yudhishṭhiraṃ Mārutād Bhīmasenaṃ Çakrād Arjunam iti*, cf. § 190), ††3816, ††3818, ††3819 (cf. §§ 192 ff.).—[§ 160 (do.): I, **95**, †3835 (P., cf. § 785).] —§ 175 (Karṇasaṃbhava): I, **111**, [4382 (P., daughter of Çūra, adopted by Kuntibhoja)], 4388, (4391), [4397 (*Kuntirājasutām*), 4401 (*Vārshṇeyī*)], 4402 (bore Karṇa from Sūrya, cf. § 547).—§ 176 (Kuntīvivāha): I, **112**, [4412 (*Pṛthā duhitā Kuntibhojasya*), 4417 (*Kuntibhojasutā*)], 4418, 4419, 4421, 4424 (married to Pāṇḍu).—§ 177 (Pāṇḍudigvijaya): I, **113**, 4444.—§ 178 (Pāṇḍu): I, **114**, 4474, 4477.—§ 180 (Gāndhārīputrotpatti): I, **115**, 4484.—§ 184 (do.): I, **119**, 4613, 4616 (followed Pāṇḍu to the wood).—§ 185 (do.): I, **120**, 4666, 4667, [4671 (P.), 4675 (P.)], 4677.—§ 186 (do.): I, **121**, 4680, (4710).—§ 187 (do.): I, **122**, 4717.—§ 189 (do.): I, **122**, 4746 (told Pāṇḍu of the mantra she had acquired (cf. § 131)).—§ 190 (Pāṇḍavotpatti): I, **123**, 4759, 4762, 4765, 4770, 4774, 4782, 4787, 4793, 4794, 4799 (requested by Pāṇḍu, she by her mantra summoned Dharma, Vāyu, and Indra, by whom she bore Yudhishṭhira, Bhīmasena, and Arjuna).—§ 191 (Arjuna): I, **123**, 4803.—§ 191 (Pāṇḍavotpatti): I, **123**, 4833 (refused to have more children).—§ 192 (do.): I, **124**, 4839, [4840 (*Kuntirājasutā*), 4841 (*Kuntisutām*)], 4844, 4859, [4860 (P.)] (communicated the mantra to Mādrī).—§ 193 (Pāṇḍu): I, **125**, 4880, 4882, (4888), 4893 (Pāṇḍu's death).—§ 194 (do.): I, **126**, 4921 (*Puruhūtād ayaṃ jajñe Kuntyām eva Dhanañjayaḥ*).—§ 195 (do.): I, **127**, 4934 (Pāṇḍu and Mādrī are cremated), 4957.—§ 196 (Vyāsa): I, **128**, 4964.—§ 197 (Bhīmasenarasapāna): I, [**128**, 5026 (*Āryakena . . . Pṛthāyā āryakena*)]; **129**, 5038, 5043, 5045, 5051.—§ 208 (Astradarçana): I, **134**, 5326; **135**, 5359, [5363 (*Pṛthāraṇīsamudbhūtaiḥ*, sc. Bhīmasena and Arjuna)]; **136**, [5381 (*kanyāgarbhaḥ . . . Pṛthāyāḥ*, i.e. Karṇa)], [5405 (*Kuntibhojasutā*)], 5406, [5409 (*Pṛthāyās tanayaḥ kanīyān*, i.e. Arjuna)]; **137**, 5441 (rejoiced at seeing Karṇa installed as king of the Aṅgas).—§ 213 (Jatugṛhap.): I, **141**, 5636, 5638, 5639, 5642; **142**, 5686; **144**, 5727; **145**, 5762; **148**, 5823, [5824 (*Mādhavīm*)]; **150**, [5867 (*Kuntirājasutām*)], 5869, 5872; **151**, 5897, 5905 (*Kuntirājasutām*) (*K.* and her sons escaped from the lac house).—§ 214 (Hiḍimbavadhap.): I, [**152**, 5941 (P.)]; **154**, 6008; **155**, 6045; **156**, 6086, 6094.—§ 215 (Bakavadhap.): I, **157**, 6107, [6110 (P.)], 6111, 6112, [6113 (P.)], 6120; **159**, 6204; **160**, (6205); **161**, (6222), (6233), [6239 (P.)], 6240; **162**, (6244), (6252).—§ 216 (Caitrarathap.): I, **165**, 6320.—§ 219 (do.): I, **168**, 6411, (6412), 6419, 6420.—§ 220 (do.): I, **169**, 6436.—[§ 234 (Svayaṃvarap.): I, **189**, †7083 (P.), †7084 (P.).]—§ 235 (do.): I, [**196**, 7129 (P.)]; **191**, [†7131 (P.)], †7132, †7133, (†7134), †7136 (when the Pāṇḍavas had won Draupadī, *K.* said: "Enjoy ye all").—§ 236 (do.): I, **192**, †7159, †7164.—§ 237 (Vaivāhikap.): I, **194**, †7205, †7211; **195**, 7227, 7235, 7249; **196**, (7269), 7273.—§ 240 (do.): I, **199**, 7348, [7350 (P.)].—§ 241 (Vidurāgamanap.): I, **200**, 7370; **203**, [7453 (P.)], 7455; **204**, 7467.—§ 243 (do.): I, **206**, [7522 (P.)], 7531, [7540 (P.)], 7544.—§ 244 (Rājyalābhap.): I, **207**, 7555.—§ 253 (Haraṇāharaṇap.): I, **221**, 7982 (*Pṛthām*), 7986.—[§ 262 (Bhagavadyāna): II, **2**, 22 (P.).]—§ 275 (Rājasūyārambhap.): II, **17**, 676 (°*yāḥ sutasya*).—[§ 277 (Jarāsandhavadhap.): II, **24**, 976 (P.).]—[§ 292 (Rājasūyikap.): II, **45**, 1616 (P.).]—§ 305 (Anudyūtap.): II, [**78**, 2564 (P.)]; **79**, [2584 (P.)], 2586, [2593 (P.)], (2596), 2613, 2614.—§ 330 (Indradarçana): III, **37**, 1479.—§ 337 (Indralokābhigamanap.): III, **44**, †1799.—§ 338 (do.): III, **46**, 1854 (*yathā*), 1862 (do.), [1871 (P.)].—§ 339 (do.): III, **47**, 1886.—§ 424 (Bhīmakadalīkhaṇḍapr.): III, **147**, 11169 (°*yā garbheṇa dhāritaḥ*, sc. Bhīmasena).—§ 432 (Saugandhikāharaṇa): III, **154**, †11386 (*Vātena K°yāṃ balavān sujātaḥ*, sc. Bhīmasena).—§ 452 (Mārkaṇḍeyas.): III, **183**, 12583.—§ 510 (Draupadī-Satyabhāmasaṃv.): III, **233**, 14688, [14689 (P.)].—§ 522 (Draupadīharaṇap.): III, **270**, †15713 (°*yāḥ prāṇair ishṭatamaḥ*, sc. Sahadeva).—§ 547 (Karṇa): III, [**303**, 17007 (P.), 17009 (P.), 17019 (P.), 17024 (P.), 17025 (P.); **304**, 17039 (P.), 17046 (P.)]; **305**, [17051 (P.), 17058 (P.)], (17061), [17069 (P.)]; **306**, 17079, (17081), †17094; **307**, (17105), (17114), (17116), (17119), 17120, [17124 (*Kuntirājātmajā*)]; **308**, [17126 (P.)], 17134, [17147 (P.), 17148 (P.)]; **309**, [17167 (P.)], 17173 (*Sūryasambhavaḥ Karṇaḥ K°yāṃ*) (Pṛthā (i.e. Kuntī), the daughter of Çūra, was adopted by Kuntibhoja; she attended on a brahman, who gave her a mantra by which she might summon whatever god she liked. She summoned Sūrya (the Sun), who begot Karṇa on her, the child she threw into the water).—§ 548 (Āraṇeyap.): III, **313**, 17295, 17416, 17417. — § 549 (Pāṇḍavapraveçap.): IV, **4**, 134.—§ 551 (Kīcakavadhap.): IV, **19**, 581, 596; **20**, 634.—§ 556 (Sañjayayānap.): V, **31**, 931.—§ 562 (Bhagavadyānap.): V, **90**, [3128 (P.), 3130 (P.), 3220 (P.)], 3230, (3231); [**91**, 3236 (P.)].—§ 567 (do.): V, **132**, (4463) (told Kṛshṇa to urge Yudhishṭhira to battle).—§ 568 (Vidulāputraçāsana): V, **133**, (4494); **136**, (4637) (asked Kṛshṇa to tell Yudhishṭhira Vidulāputraçāsana).—§ 569 (do.): V, **137**, (4644), 4645 (sent Kṛshṇa with a message to the Pāṇḍavas); **138**, 4676, 4677; **140**, 4753; **141**, 4758, 4775 (°*yāḥ prathamajaṃ*, i.e. Karṇa); **144**, [4885 (P.)], 4894, 4910, [4912 (P.)], [4914 (*Kauravyapatnī Vārshṇeyī*)], 4915, 4916; **145**, (4918); **146**, [4930 (P.)], 4952, [4955 (P.)] (Kṛshṇa told Karṇa that he was the son of *K.*, Kuntī disclosed to Karṇa that she is his mother and solicited him to make peace with the Pāṇḍavas, Karṇa promised to save the Pāṇḍavas except Arjuna).—§ 570 (Sainyaniryāṇap.): V, **154**, 5219, 5239.—§ 583 (Bhīshmavadhap.): VI, **79μ**, 3453 (°*yāḥ parikleçam*).—§ 588 (do.): VI, **122**, 5841 (*avakīrṇas tv ahaṃ K°yā*, says Karṇa).—

§ 599 (Jayadrathavadhap.): VII, **127,** 5166; **131,** 5364, 5377 (*°yāḥ putrasya sadṛçaṃ nedam*); **132** σσ, 5425 (*saputrām*, all. to § 213); **139,** 5783 (*°yā vacaḥ smaran*, sc. Karṇa, cf. § 569).—§ 600 (Ghaṭotkacavadhap.): VII, **167,** 7481 (*°yāḥ smṛtvā vacaḥ*, sc. Karṇa, cf. § 569).—§ 605 (Karṇap.): VIII, **24,** 964 (*smṛtvā K°yā vacaḥ*, sc. Karṇa, cf. § 569).—§ 608 (do.): VIII, **49,** 2352 (*°vākyañ ca so 'smarat*, sc. Karṇa, cf. § 569); **68,** [†3382 (*Pṛthāyā garbham*), †3389 (read *Pṛthām* with B.)], †3393 (a celestial voice came to *K.* at the birth of Arjuna); [†3400 (*garbhe . . . Pṛthāyāḥ*)]; **69** ννν, †3433; **70** ρρρ, †3528; **87,** 4488.—§ 613 (Gadāyuddhap.): IX, **33** ε, 1903 (*Pāṇḍoḥ K°yāç ca santatiḥ*).—§ 618 (Jalapradānikap.): XI, **10,** 270, 272 (came to see the battle-field); **14,** 374 (*yathā*); [**15,** 414 (P.), 415 (P.), 419 (P.)].—§ 620 (Çrāddhap.): XI, **27** γ, 805 (disclosed to the Pāṇḍavas that Karṇa was her son).—§ 621 (Rājadh.): XII, I, **18,** 21 (*gūḍhotpannaḥ sutaḥ K°yāḥ*, i.e. Karṇa), 22, 24 (*jyeshṭhaputraḥ K°yāḥ*, sc. Karṇa), [26 (P.), 27 (P.), 31 (P.), 35 (P.), 36 (P.), 38 (P.)], 42 (*Pṛthāyāḥ*); **4,** 139 (*°yāç ca varadānena*, Karṇa was slain on account of the boon he had granted to *K.*, cf. § 569); **5,** 146.—§ 635 (do.): XII, **37,** 1384.—[§ 637 (do.): XII, **40,** 1446 (P.).]—§ 641 (do.): XII, **75,** 2853 (*na hy etām āçishaṃ Pāṇḍur na ca K°ī na tv ayācata*), 2854.—[§ 777 (Svargārohaṇik. p.): XIII, **168,** 7714 (P.).]—[§ 781 (Açvamedhikap.): XIV, **15** *a*, 388 (P.).]—[§ 783 (Anugītāp.): XIV, **52** γ, 1505 (P.), 1507 (P.).]—§ 785 (do.): XIV, **61,** [1839 (P.)], 1844, [1846 (*Vārshṇeyī*)], 1848 (consoled Uttarā); **62,** [(1859 (P.); **63** ζ, 1893 (P.)]; **66** ι, [1940 (P.)], 1949 (*Bhojasutā*, prevailed upon Kṛshṇa to revive Parikshit), [1962 (P.)], 1964; **67** ν, [1965 (P.), 1973 (P.)]; **69,** 2010; **70** ο, 2038; **71** π, 2061; **87,** 2602; **88** φ, [2604 (P.)], 2607; **89,** 2671, [2672 (P.)].—§ 787 (Āçramavāsap.): XV, **1,** [8 (*Kuntibhojasutā*)], 11 (*a*), 23; **3** β, 73, (δ), 111, 138; **5** η, 174; **10** ξ, 348; **11** π, 373; **15** τ, 436; **16,** 447, 449 (450), 465, 466; **17,** (474); **18,** 495, 496, [497 (P.)], 503, 504, 509, 515 (followed Dhṛtarāshṭra and Gāndhārī to the forest); **19,** [525 (*Kuntibhojajā*, P.)], 534; **20,** 540.—§ 788 (do.): XV, **21** *a*, 578 (*Pṛthā*), 580; **22,** [596 (P.)], 602, 604, [606 (P.)], 608; **24,** [643 (P.), 646 (P.)], 654; **25** γ, 663; **27** δ, 731; **28,** 746.—§ 789 (Putradarçanap.): XV, **29,** 766, (β), 778 (γ), 783, 801, 814, 817; **30,** (819), 841; **31** ζ, 844, [845 (P.)].—§ 791 (do.): XV, **36,** 983, 995, 998.—§ 792 (Nāradāgamanap.): XV, **37,** [1017 (P.)], 1021, 1024, [1027 (P.)], 1039, [1041 (P.), 1045 (P.), 1054 (P.); **38,** 1063 (P.), 1072 (P.); **39,** 1090 (P.), 1095 (P.)] (*K.* was burnt in a forest fire).—§ 795 (Svargārohaṇap.): XVIII, **5,** 144 (together with Pāṇḍu in heaven).

Kuntibhoja ("the king of the Kuntis (and the Bhojas?)"), name of the adoptive father of Kuntī, and of the [adoptive] brother of Kuntī (= Purujit (?)). § 131 (Kuntī): I, **67,** 2766 (cousin of Çūra, who gave him his daughter Pṛthā (afterwards named Kuntī) as a daughter).—§ 175 (Karṇasambhava): I, **111,** 4383 (repetition of § 131).—§ 176 (Kuntīvivāha): I, **112,** 4412 (*duhitā K°sya Pṛthā*, i.e. Kuntī), 4414, 4420 (*°sya duhitrā*, i.e. Kuntī), 4421.—§ 281 (Sahadeva): II, **31,** 1110 (in the south, vanquished by Sahadeva on his digvijaya).—§ 287 (Rājasūyikap.): II, **34,** 1271 (came to the rājasūya of Yudhishṭhira).—§ 547 (Karṇa): III, **303,** 17001, 17003, 17006; **304,** 17039; **305,** 17057, 17067 (C. by error *°tībh°*) (*K.*, the adoptive father of Kuntī, ordered her to wait upon a brahman).—§ 562 (Bhagavadyānap.): V, **90,** 3191, 3192 (Kuntī was given to *K.* by Çūra).—§ 569 (do.): V, **141** γ, 4781 (*mātulaḥ Bhīmasenasya*, among the allies of Yudhishṭhira); **144,** 4904 ([adoptive] father of Kuntī).—§ 570 (Sainyaniryāṇap.): V, **151,** 5163 (sided with Yudhishṭhira).—§ 572 (Rathātirathasaṅkhyānap.): V, **172,** 5922 (*mātulo Bhīmasenasya*, in B. his name is Purujit (? = C. *ripujit*); among the atirathas in Yudhishṭhira's army).—§ 576 (Bhagavadgītap.): VI, **25** θ, 834 (in Yudhishṭhira's army).—§ 578 (Bhīshmavadhap.): VI, **45**[21], 1740, 1742, 1743 (*K.* and his son fought with Vinda and Anuvinda); **50** π, 2079 (*K.* and Çaibya in the eye section of Dhṛshṭadyumna's krauñcavyūha).—§ 583 (do.): VI, **75,** 3287 (*K.* and Çatānīka in the foot section of Dhṛshṭadyumna's makaravyūha).—§ 585 (do.): VI, **89** ν, 3948.—§ 586 (do.): VI, **99** ζ, 4511.—§ 587 (do.): VI, **110** ζ, 5098; **118** υ, 5554.—§ 592 (Saṃçaptakavadhap.): VII, **23** ο, 995 (*Purujit* (C. *purajit*) *mātulaḥ Savyasācinaḥ*, description of his horses).—§ 593 (Abhimanyuvadhap.): VII, **35** δ, 1508.—§ 599 (Jayadrathavadhap.): VII, **95,** 3537 (fought with Alambusha); **96,** 3559, 3560 (do.); **111** υ, 4284.—§ 600 (Ghaṭotkacavadhap.): VII, **156,** 6912 (*°sutān*, ten of *K.*'s sons are slain by Açvatthāman); **157,** 6922 (*°sutān . . . nihatān*).—§ 604 (Karṇap.): VIII, **6,** 172 (*Purujit K°aç ca mātulau* (!) *Savyasācinaḥ*, slain by Droṇa; read *mātulaḥ*?).—§ 609 (Çalyap.): IX, **2** ζ, 79. Cf. Kunti, Kuntirāja, Purujit.

Kuntibhojajā ("the daughter of Kuntibhoja") = Kuntī: XV, 525 (*Pṛthā*).

Kuntibhojasutā (do.) = Kuntī: I, 4417, 5405; XV, 8.

Kuntibhojasutāsuta, pl. (*°āḥ*) ("the grandsons of Kuntibhoja") = Kaunteya, pl.: I, 7454.

Kuntibhojātmajāputra ("the grandson of Kuntibhoja") = Arjuna: I, 7969.

Kuntikanyā ("the daughter of the Kunti king") = Kuntī: I, 2427.

Kuntīmātṛ[1] ("son of Kuntī") = Arjuna: I, 8065; II, 1009; III, 1707.

Kuntīmātṛ[2] (do.) = Bhīmasena: III, 12451.

Kuntīnandana[1] (do.) = Arjuna: XIV, 2579.

Kuntīnandana[2] (do.) = Yudhishṭhira: V, 5852 (*rājā*).

Kuntīputra[1] (do.) = Arjuna (Dhanañjaya): I, 6518 (*Dh°*), 7753 (do.), 7762 (do.), 7790 (do.), 7822 (do.), 7829 (do.), 7848 (do.), 7851 (do.), 7900; II, 1011 (*Dh°*), 2634 (*A°*); III, 1710 (*Dh°*), 14972 (do.), 14989 (do.), 14996, 14998; IV, 1211 (*Dh°*), 1571 (do.), 1822 (do.), 2080 (do.), 2045 (do.); V, 130 (*Dh°*), 150 (do.), 2500 (do.), 3496 (do.), 4691 (do.), 5295 (do.), 5370 (do.); VI, 1541 (*Dh°*), 5647 (do.), 5736; VII, 460 (*Dh°*), 760 (do.), 1238, 1322 (*Dh°*), 2820 (do.), 2824, 6142 (*Dh°*), 6234, 6302 (*Dh°*), 8283 (do.), 8471 (do.), 8602, 8706 (*Dh°*), 8873 (do.), 8945 (do.), 9390 (do.), 9495 (do.); VIII, 61 (*Dh°*), 1955, †1976, †1982, 3273 (*Dh°*), 4473 (do.); IX, 1286 (*Dh°*), 1444 (do.), 1477 (*Pārtho Dh°h*); XI, 647; XII, 1913; XIV, 2123 (*Dh°*).

Kuntīputra[2] (do.) = Bhīmasena (Vṛkodara): I, 4000 (*V°*), 6280 (do.); III, 11504 (*V°*, C. has by error *Kuntīputrau*); IV, 1104 (*V°*); V, 1988 (*V°*), 1989 (do.), 2173 (do.), 5595 (do.); VI, 4353; VII, 5764, 9249.

Kuntīputra[3] (do.) = Yudhishṭhira: I, 5158 (*Y°*), 5519 (do.), 5804 (do.), 7145 (do.), 7219, 7233, 7234 (*Y°*), 7401 (do.), 7547 (do.), 8002 (do.), 8029 (do.); II, 128, 1247 (*Y°*), 1623 (do.), 1746, 1907, 1967 (*Y°*), 1991 (do.), 2623 (do.); III, 48 (*Y°*), 131 (do.), 1411 (do.), 1449, 11481 (*Y°*), 11752 (do.), 11926 (do.), 11932 (do.), 12273 (do.), 14697, 15020 (*Y°*), 15034 (do.), 15378 (do.), 15622 (do.), 15630 (do.), 17225 (do.), 17250 (do.), 17255 (do.), 17261 (do.), 17274 (do.); IV, 169 (*Y*°), 729 (do.), 1077 (do.), 1099 (do.), 2289 (do.), 2314 (do.), 2347 (do.), 2370 (do.); V, 113 (*Y*°), 114, 186, 566 (*Y*°), †677 (*Ajātaçatruḥ*), †682, 686 (*Y*°), 1971 (do.), 2949 (do.), 4281, 4689 (*Y*°), 4745 (do.), 4820 (do.), 5155 (do.), 5172 (do.), 5702 (do.), 7654; VI, 7 (*Y*°), 719 (do.), 760 (do.), 845 (do.), 1615 (do.), 1623 (do.), 1698 (do.), 2116 (do.); VII, 647 (*Y*°), 900 (?), 2003 (*Y*°), 2022 (do.), 3067 (do.), 4012 (do.), 5125 (do.), 6961 (do.), 7269 (do.), 8736 (do.), 9199 (do.); VIII, 2986 (*Y*°), 3146 (do.), 3148 (do.), 3279 (*rājā*), 5029 (*Y*°); IX, 549 (*Y*°), 648 (do.), 802 (do.), 843 (do.), 1191 (do.), 3087 (do.); X, 549 (*Y*°), 606 (do.); XI, 779 (*Y*°), 813 (do.); XII, 1374 (*Y*°), 1457 (do.), 1535 (do.); XIII, 7729; XV, 72 (*Y*°), 176, 292 (*Y*°), 323, 344, 380 (*Y*°), 384 (do.), 419, 737.

Kuntīputra, dual (°*au*): III, 11504 (read °*o Vṛkodaraḥ* with B.), 17299 (= Bhīmasena and Arjuna).

Kuntīputra, pl. (°*āḥ*) ("the sons of Kuntī") = Kaunteya, pl.: I, 4836, 4854, 6103, 6104, 7399, 7519; IV, 1002; V, 1979, 1981, 5884 (?); VII, 2801; XV, 350.

Kuntirāja ("the king of the Kuntis") = Kuntibhoja: V, 4919.

Kuntirājasutā ("the daughter of the king of the Kuntis") = Kuntī: I, 4397, 4840, 5867, 5905 (*K*°).

Kuntirājātmajā (do.) = Kuntī: III, †17124.

Kuntīsuta[1] ("son of Kuntī") = Arjuna: I, 5357 (*madhyamaḥ Pāṇḍavaḥ*), 7033, 7059, 7837; III, 1725, †15707; IV, 1802, †2092 (*Jishṇuṃ*); VI, 4849; VII, 1213, 2799 (*A*°), 2969 (do.); VIII, 2179 (*Bībhatsuṃ*).

Kuntīsuta[2] (do.) = Bhīmasena: III, 11355; VIII, 2202 (*Bhīmaṃ*).

Kuntīsuta[3] (do.) = Karṇa: XI, 819 (*K*°).

Kuntīsuta[4] (do.) = Yudhishṭhira: I, 4492, 4497 (*jyeshṭhaṃ*), †7150; II, 1697, †2245, †2400 (*Dharmarājaḥ*); III, 223, 8457, 17282 (*rājā*); V, †33, †47; VII, 441 (*rājā*), 445 (do.), 448; VIII, 3764, 3765 (*rājā*); IX, 893; XII, †892, 1443; XIII, 6910, 7706 (*rājā*); XIV, 2605; XV, 30 (*rājā*), 275 (*rājñaḥ*); XVIII, 41.

Kuntīsuta, dual (°*au*): I, 7121 (= Bhīmasena and Arjuna).

Kuntīsuta, pl. (°*āḥ*) ("the sons of Kuntī") = Kaunteya, pl.: I, 7217, †7312, 7442, 7563; II, 2305; V, †18, †28, 5941; VII, 8012, 8702.

Kuntisutā ("the daughter of the Kunti king") = Kuntī: I, 4841.

Kuntivardhana ("propagator of the Kuntis") = Purujit: II, 581 (*P*°).

[Kuntīvivāha] ("the marriage of Kuntī"). § 176 (cf. Sambhavap.): At her svayaṃvara Pṛthā (i.e. Kuntī) chose Pāṇḍu for her husband (I, **112**).

Kūpa[1], a tīrtha. § 368 (Tīrthayātrāp.): III, **83,** 7043.

Kūpa[2] = Çiva (1000 names[2]).

Kupaṭa, an Asura. § 92 (Aṃçāvat.): I, **65,** 2534 (among the sons of Danu).

Kupatha, an Asura. § 130 (Aṃçāvat.): I, **67,** 2664 (*mahāsuraḥ*, incarnate as king Supārçva).

Kuraṅga, name of a country (or mountain?). § 733*e* (Indratoyā): XIII, **25,** 1699 (*Karatoyāṃ K°e ca trirātro-poshito naraḥ açvamedham avāpnoti*).

Kūrcāmukha, a son of Viçvāmitra. § 721*b* (Viçvāmitrop.): XIII, **4**β, 252.

Kūrma, a serpent. § 100 (Aṃçāvat.): I, **65,** 2549 (son of Kadrū).

Kūrmarājan ("the king of the tortoises"). § 28 (Amṛta-manthana): I, **18,** 1122 [1123 (*kūrmeṇa*)] (held the mountain Mandara on his back, while the gods churned the ocean).

Kuru[1], an ancient king, the son of Saṃvaraṇa and the ancestor of the Kurus. § 6 (Anukram.): I, **1*a*,** 225 (in Sañjaya's enumeration of deceased kings).—§ 136 (Yayātyup.): I, **75,** 3126.—§ 154 (Pūruvaṃç.): I, **94,** 3738 (son of Saṃvaraṇa and Tapatī).—§ 156 (do.): I, **95,** ††3791 (do.), ††3792 (married the Daçārha princess Çubhāṅgī).—§ 222 (Tapatyup.): I, **173,** 6633 (son of Saṃvaraṇa and Tapatī).—§ 409 (Plakshā-vataraṇag.): III, **129,** 10535 (*Kuror vai yajñaçīlasya kshetram etad mahātmanaḥ*, sc. Kurukshetra).—§ 615*i* (Saptasārasvata): IX, **38,** 2211 (at the sacrifice of *K.* in Kurukshetra, the River Sarasvatī appeared there as the River Oghavatī).—§ 615*kk* (Kurukshetrak.): IX, **53,** †3009 (*rājarshivareṇa*), 3010, 3011, 3013, 3021 (tilled Kurukshetra, regarding which he obtained boons from Indra).—§ 637 (Rājadh.): XII, **47**η, 1595.—§ 775 (Ānuçāsanik.): XIII, **166**η, 7679.—§ 787 (Āçramavāsap.): XV, **10,** 325 (°-*Saṃvaraṇādīnāṃ*).

Kuru[2] = Duryodhana: VII, 8647 (°*Mādhavau*, i.e. Duryodhana and Sātyaki).

Kuru[3] = Karṇa: VIII, 438 (error in C., B. has *Karṇa*°).

Kuru, pl. (°*avaḥ*) (the descendants of Kuru or name of a people; very often it denotes only the sons of Dhṛtarāshṭra and their adherents as opposed to the sons of Pāṇḍu and their adherents): I, 13, †173, 282 (°-*Pāṇḍavasenayoḥ*), 298 (do.), 300 (°*vāhinīm*), 334 (°-*Pāṇḍavānāṃ*), 349, 487, 488, 552 (°*mukhyānāṃ*), 1705 (°*ūnām ayaçaskaraṃ*, sc. Parikshit), 1762 (°*kulotpannaṃ Parīkshitaṃ*), 1946 (*parikshīṇeshu K°shu sottarayām ajījanat*, sc. Parikshit), 1950 (*rājyaṃ K°kulāgataṃ*), 2224, 2228, 2230 (?), 2234 (?), 2237, 2283 (*Mahābhāratam ākhyānaṃ K°ūṇāṃ caritaṃ*), 2312 (°*ūṇāṃ vaṃçaṃ*), 2454, 2711 (*Bhīshmaḥ K°ūṇām abhayaṅkaraḥ*), 2722 (°*ūṇām ayaçaskaraḥ*, sc. Duryodhana), 2800, 3978 (*Hāstinapure ramye K°ūṇāṃ puṭabhedane*), 3985 (°*patiçreshṭhe*, sc. Çāntanu), 4078 (°*rājye*), 4129, 4145 (°*puṅgavāḥ*), 4276 (do.), 4284 (°*ūṇāṃ nṛpatiḥ*), 4336, 4337, 4346 (*uttaraiḥ Kurubhiḥ sārdhaṃ dakshiṇāḥ K°as tathā | vispardhamānā vyacaraṃs tathā Devarshi-Cāraṇaiḥ*), 4347, 4352 (°*mukhyānāṃ*), 4380, 4446 (°*sattamān*), 4453, 4455, 4462 (°*rāshṭraṃ*; °*dhanāni*), 4511, 4680 (°*ūṇām ṛshabhaṃ*, sc. Pāṇḍu), 4738, 4756, 4796, 4856 (°*sattamāḥ Pāṇḍuputrāḥ*), 4930, 4959, 4965, 5001, 5006, 5095, 5100, 5176 (°*mukhyānāṃ nagaraṃ nāgasāhvayaṃ*, i.e. Hāstinapura), 5206, 5209, 5211 (°*veçmani*), 5246 (°-*Pāṇḍavāḥ*), 5357, 5500, 5536, 5539 (°*rāshṭraṃ*), 5736, 5738 (°*puṅgavāḥ*), 5791 (do.), 6343 (°*mukhyānāṃ nagaraṃ nāgasāhvayaṃ*, i.e. Hāstinapura; 6500 (*Dharmaṃ Vāyuñ ca Çakrañ ca vijanāmy Açvinau tathā | Pāṇḍuñ ca . . . shaḍ etān K°vardhanān*), 6515 (°*ūṇāṃ vaṃçavardhana*, sc. Arjuna), 6527 (°*ūnāṃ vṛshabhaḥ . . . Saṃvaraṇaḥ*), 6562 (°*ūṇāṃ kulakaraṃ*, sc. Saṃvaraṇa), 6611 (do.), 6957, 7127 (°*puṅgavāḥ*, i.e. the Pāṇḍavas), 7135 (°*ūṇām ṛshabha*, sc. Yudhishṭhira), †7148 (°*pravīrān*, sc. the Pāṇḍavas), †7151 (i.e. the Pāṇḍavas), 7164 (°*sattamānāṃ*, do.), †7165 (°*puṅgavān*, do.), †7205 (°*puṅgavāḥ*, do.), †7206 (°*ūttamānāṃ*, do.), 7381, 7443, 7444 (°*ūttamānāṃ*), 7487, 7539, 7541 (°*vīrastriyaḥ*), 7746, 8019 (°-*Vṛshṇy-Andhakottamāḥ*, = the Pāṇḍavas), 8020 (°-*Vṛshṇayaḥ* = do.), 8021 (do.), 8022 (°*sattamāḥ*, = the Pāṇḍavas); II, 261 (°*ūṇām ṛshabhaḥ*, i.e. Yudhishṭhira), 518 (do.), 793, 1007 (°*ūṇām ṛshabhaḥ*, i.e. Yudhishṭhira), 1365, 1632, 1794 (°*ūṇāṃ pravaraḥ*, i.e. Vidura), 1999, 2017 (?), 2027 (°*puṅgavāḥ*), 2103, †2195, †2197, †2219 (= the Pāṇḍavas?), †2223, †2235 (°*vīramadhye*), †2236, †2248, 2293, 2341, 2347, 2356, †2396, †2397, †2398, †2400, †2404 (°*puṅgavānāṃ*), 2419 (°*madhye*), 2446, 2508, †2525, 2532,

2589, 2616, 2642, 2643 (°*vṛddhānāṃ*), 2652, 2688, 2706; III, 143 (°*ūṇām ṛshabhaḥ . . . Yudhishṭhiraḥ*), †227, 347, 355, 365, 522 (°*saṃsadi*), 607, †909 (°*ūṇām ṛshabhaḥ*, i.e. Yudhishṭhira), †911 (°*ūṇām adhipaḥ*, i.e. Yudhishṭhira), †946 (*ṛshabhaḥ K°ūṇāṃ*, i.e. Yudhishṭhira), 997, 1011, 1063, 1339, †1364 (°*saṃsadi*), †1365, †1367, †1372, †2011, 4009, 8259 (*Bhīshmaḥ K°ūṇāṃ pravaraḥ*), †10268, †10269 (°*yodhapramukhyān*), 10281 (°*ūṇām ṛshabhaḥ*, i.e. Yudhishṭhira), †11394 (°*ūṇāṃ pravaraṃ*, sc. Bhīmasena), 11428 (°*puṅgavāḥ*, i.e. the Pāṇḍavas), 11631 (°*çreshṭhān*, sc. *Pāṇḍoḥ putrān*), 11632 (°*ūṇām ṛshabhaṃ Yudhishṭhiraṃ*), 11824 (°*ūṇāṃ kīrtivardhanaḥ*, sc. Arjuna), †11913 (°*puṅgavānāṃ*, i.e. the Pāṇḍavas), †12327 (*rājyaṃ K°puṅgavānāṃ*), †12336 (*patiḥ K°ūṇāṃ*, i.e. Yudhishṭhira), †12351 (*vṛshabhāḥ K°ūṇāṃ*, i.e. the Pāṇḍavas), †12358 (i.e. the Pāṇḍavas), †12563 (°*sattamān*, do.), †12577, 13127 (°*ūṇāṃ pravaro Yudhishṭhiraḥ*), 13136, ††13249, 14651 (*kathāḥ K° - Yadūtthitāḥ*), 14729 (°*striyaḥ*), †14769, 14782, 14885 (°*sainikāḥ*), 15029, 15060 (°*dāreshu*), †15660 (°*pravīraiḥ*, i.e. the Pāṇḍavas), †15674, †15678 (°*puṅgavānāṃ*, i.e. the Pāṇḍavas), †15696 (do.), 17227 (°*sattamāḥ*, i.e. the Pāṇḍavas), 17293 (°*ūṇāṃ kīrtivardhana*, sc. Bhīmasena); IV, 11 (*paritaḥ K°ūn*), 212, 263 (*Kṛshṇāṃ . . . K°ūṇām ekasundarīṃ*), †284 (°*puṅgavānāṃ*, i.e. the Pāṇḍavas), 615, 646, 1029 (°*puṅgavāḥ*, i.e. the Pāṇḍavas), 1153, 1158, 1162, 1167, 1175, 1178, 1179, 1192, 1203, 1207, 1213, 1224 (*Bhīshma-Droṇamukhān*), 1227, 1229, 1230, 1231, 1234, 1240, 1241 (°*sainyaṃ*), 1245, 1251, 1255, 1256, 1262, 1270, 1281, 1282, 1286, 1399, 1426, 1529, 1535, 1538, 1640, 1647 (°*puṅgavāḥ*), †1661 (°*pravīrāḥ*), †1663 (°*siṃhavṛndaṃ*), 1667 (°*puṅgavānāṃ*), †1671, †1682, †1686, †1692 (*pravaraḥ K°ūṇāṃ*, sc. Arjuna), 1726 (°*senāçarīrāṇi*), 1728, 1765, 1772, 1779, 1783 (°*senāyāḥ*), 1784, 1787, 1913, 1926 (°*madhye*), 1930, 1954, 1969, 1972, 1979, 1980, 1985, 2029, 2047, 2054, †2112 (°*puṅgavānāṃ*), †2115 (°*pravīrāḥ*), †2116, †2123 (do.), †2126, †2130 (°*pravīrān*), †2131, †2134, †2135, 2136, 2137 (°*sainikāḥ*), †2142, †2143, †2145, †2147, †2149 (°*ūttamānāṃ*, i.e. the Pāṇḍavas), †2152, †2159, 2166, 2170, 2176, 2178, 2179, 2180, 2198, 2239, 2243, 2250, 2252, 2275 (°*ūṇām ṛshabho Dharmarājaḥ*, i.e. Yudhishṭhira), 2278, 2280, 2309; V, †1 (°*pravīrāḥ*, i.e. the Pāṇḍavas), †30 (°-*Pāṇḍavānāṃ*), 92 (°-*Pāṇḍushu*), 97 (°-*Pāṇḍūnāṃ*), 103 (°*siṃhānāṃ*, i.e. the Pāṇḍavas), 105 (°*Pāṇḍavakāraṇāt*), 108, 583, 614 (°*puṅgavāḥ*), 616, 618, 638 (°*çreshthān*), †676, †695, †703, †704, †713 (do.), †725, †730, †731, †733, †736 (°-*Sṛñjayānāṃ*), †745, †750, †753, †754, †756 (do.), †759, †760, †768, †839, †840, †844, †845, †846, †856, †857, †882 (*pranetā K°ūṇāṃ*, i.e. Bhīshma), †884 (*çūratamaḥ K°ūṇāṃ . . . Duḥçāsanaḥ*), †887 (*arhattamaḥ K°ūṇāṃ Saumadattiḥ*), †888 (°*mukhyāḥ*), †893 (*vṛndārakaṃ . . . Kurumadhyeshu amūḍhaṃ*, sc. Yuyutsu), †905, †914, 919, 920, 926 (*Viduraṃ . . . K°ūṇāṃ mantradhāriṇaṃ*), 927, 928, 929, 930, 936, 937 (°-*Pāñcālān*), †959 (°*kshayaḥ*), †960, †966, †969, †970, †1095, 1098, †1331, †1332 (°*kulaṃ*), †1811, †1822, †1903, †1904, †1916, †1941, 1957, 1966, 1976 (°*saṃsadi*), 1977 (do.), 1980 (do.), 2003, 2024 (°*ūṇām ṛshabho Vṛkodaraḥ*, i.e. Bhīmasena), 2056, 2074, 2082, 2118, 2127 (*sa-Jāṅgalāḥ*), 2146, 2152, 2289 (*sa-Bāhlīkān*), 2298, 2302, 2322, 2362, 2366, 2379, 2380, 2381, †2424, 2493, 2660 (°*saṃsadaṃ*), 2662 (°-*Sṛñjayān*), 2663, 2668, 2671, 2686 (°*mukhyānāṃ*), 2708, 2710, 2717, 2725, 2734, 2737, 2798, 2808, 2809, 2822, 2854 (°*madhye*), 2863, 2908, 2920, 2924, 2948, 2967 (*Viduraṃ . . . K°ūṇāṃ mantradhāriṇaṃ*), 2988, 3039 (°*sadma*, i.e. Hāstinapura), 3075, 3120, 3122 (°*saṃsadi*), 3149 (*çreshṭhaḥ K°ushu sarveshu*, sc. Ajātaçatru, i.e. Yudhishṭhira), 3159, 3179, 3180, 3185, 3195, 3212 (°*mukhyānāṃ*), 3239, 3246, 3247, 3271, 3272, 3274, 3315, 3316, 3323 (°*Pāṇḍavān*), †3326, †3327, 3328 (°*pārthivāḥ*), 3337, 3344, 3354 (*puraṃ K°ūṇāṃ*, i.e. Hāstinapura), 3356, 3362, 3369, 3386, 3389, 3391, 3394, 3405 (°-*Pāṇḍavaiḥ*), 3414, 3450 (°*saṃsadi*), 3501, 3508, 4233 (do.), 4259, 4268 (do.), 4280 (do.), 4292 (°*vṛddhānāṃ*), 4359, 4381 (°*saṃsadi*), 4450, 4452, 4454 (do.), 4458, 4459, 4646, 4647, 4666 (°*vīrāṇāṃ*), 4669 (°*puṅgavān*), 4670, 4725 (°*vṛddhaye*), 4836, 4842, 4885, 4892, 4893, 4925, 4966 (°*mukhyayoḥ*, i.e. Bhīshma and Dhṛtarāshṭra; °*saṃsadi*), 4970, 5004 (*rājā K°ūṇāṃ*, sc. Pāṇḍu), 5005 (°*ūṇāṃ vaṃçavardhanaḥ*, i.e. Pāṇḍu), 5023, 5029, †5033 (*rājyaṃ K°ūṇāṃ*), †5039 (do.), 5042 (*Somaḥ Prajāpatiḥ pūrvaṃ K°ūṇāṃ vaṃçavardhanaḥ*), 5083 (°*saṃsadi*), 5095 (do.), 5098 (do.), 5194, 5380, 5391, 5393 (°-*Pāṇḍavasenayoḥ*), 5414, 5415, 5455 (°*saṃsadi*), †5510 (°-*Madhyadeçyaiḥ*), 5540 (°*virāṇām*), †5555 (°-*Madhyadeçyaiḥ*), 5600, 5610, †5652, 5749, 5821, 5844, 7227, 7586 (°*saṃsadi*); VI, 2 (°-*Pāṇḍava-Somakāḥ*), 3 (do.), 27 (do.), 34 (do.), 46, 49 (°*ūṇāṃ prapitāmahaḥ*, i.e. Vyāsa), 79, 91, 120, 130, 346 (°-*Pāñcālāḥ*, among the peoples of Bhāratavarsha), 382, 508 (°*ūṇām ṛshabho Bhīshmaḥ*), 511 (do.), 547, 586 (°-*Pāṇḍavasenayoḥ*), 600, 611 (do.), 630 (°-*Pāṇḍavāḥ*), 653 (°*camūpatiḥ*, i.e. Bhīshma), 684, 704 (*Duryodhanapurogamāḥ*), 708, †745 (*Dhārtarāshṭrāḥ*), †747, 855, 1638, 1662 (°-*Pāṇḍavasene te*), 1671 (°*ūṇāṃ Sṛñjayānāñ ca*), 1759, 1804, 1868, 1892, 1897, 1979, 2074, 2120 (°-*Pāṇḍavāḥ*), 2379, †2592, †2602, †2614, †2617 (°*pravīrāḥ*), †2618, †2639, †2640 (°*vīrayodhān*), †2643, †2645, †2650, †2656, †2679 (°-*Sṛñjayāḥ*), 2713, 2809 (°*puṅgavān*), 2889, 3101, 3173, 3176, 3208 (°*sattamāḥ*), 3237, 3247 (°*ūṇāṃ kīrtivardhanaḥ*, sc. Bhūriçravas), 3274, 3276, 3277 (°-*Pāṇḍavāḥ*), †3382, 3444, †3786, 3841, 3847, 3883 (°-*Pāṇḍavasainikāḥ*), 3958, 4325, 4401 (°-*Pāṇḍavāḥ*), 4402 (do.), 4430, 4725, 4743, 4766, 4878, 4894, 5004, 5054, 5336, 5337, 5340, 5376, 5501, 5635 (°*vīrāṇāṃ*), 5646 (°*sainyānāṃ*), 5651, 5676 (°*ūṇāṃ çṛṅge Bhīshme*), 5678, 5681, 5690, 5698 (°*ūṇāṃ samitiñjaye*, sc. Bhīshma), 5700, 5709, 5713, 5716, 5720, 5751, 5767 (°-*Pāṇḍavāḥ*), 5787 (*Bhīshmaṃ K°ūṇām ṛshabhaṃ*), 5789, 5830 (°*saṃsadi*); VII, 10, 11, 13 (*Devavrate . . . K°ūṇāṃ ṛshabhe*, i.e. Bhīshma), 25 (°*vāhinī*), 32, †52, †54, †58, †64, †66 (°*vṛshabhān*, i.e. the Pāṇḍavas), †73, †86, 100, 101, 102 (°*kshayaṃ*), 103, 104, 125, 128, 131, 133, 187, 209 (°-*Pāṇḍavasenānāṃ*), 217, 415, 418, 428, 440 (°*ūṇām ācāryaḥ*, i.e. Droṇa), 484, 583, 591, 631 (°-*Pāṇḍavāḥ*), 662, 895 (°-*Sṛñjayavāhinīṃ*), 917, 944 (°*puṅgavaḥ*, i.e. the Pāṇḍavas), 979 (*pure K°ūṇām Udayendunamni*), 1349, 1350, 1362 (°*vāhinīm*), 1417, 1418, 1422, 1872 (°*ūṇāṃ kīrtivardhanaṃ*, sc. *Vṛkshārakaṃ*—*Vṛndā°*, B.), 1938 (°*ūṇāṃ kīrtivardhanaḥ*, sc. *Dauḥçāsaniḥ*), 2613, 2913, 3011, 3023 (°-*Pāṇḍava-Sātvataiḥ*), 3069, 3086, 3117, †3238 (°*pravīrān*), 3488, 3542, 3576, 3744 (°*bala çreshṭhāḥ*), 3748, 3836, 3888 (?°-*Pāndavayor bale*), 3899 (°*yodhavarāḥ*), 3953, 3962 (°*ūṇām ṛshabhe 'rjune*), 3965, 3966, 3968, 4217, 4251 (*Dronaṃ K°shu çreshṭhasammataṃ*), 4335 (°*vīrābhirakshitāḥ*), 4458, 4471, 4492, 4599 (°*puṅgavāḥ*), 4600, 4836, 4986, 5166, 5204 (*Vṛndārakaṃ . . . K°ūṇāṃ kīrtivardhanaṃ*), 5228, 5328 (°*saṃsadi*), 5330, 5551, 5569, 5630 (°-*Pāṇḍavapravarāḥ*), 5714 (*sa-K°-Sauvīra-Sindhuvīrabalakshayaṃ*), 5768, †5836, 5863 (°*sainyāt*), 5904 (°-*Vṛshṇiyaçaskarau*, i.e. Bhūriçravas and Sātyaki), 5906 (do.), 5924 (°-*Sātvatapuṅgavau*, = do.), 5945 (°*ūṇāṃ kīrtivardhanaḥ*, sc. Bhūriçravas), 6059 (°*senāmahārathaiḥ*), †6145, †6147, †6149 (°*pravīrān*), 6191, 6311 (°*mukhyānāṃ*), 6504, 6530, 6547,

6569 (°-*Sṛñjayāḥ*), 6612, 6694, 6826 (°*ūṇāṃ vipule kule*), †6958 (*patiḥ K°ūṇāṃ*, sc. Droṇa), 7039, 7233 (°-*Vṛshṇiyaçaskarau*, sc. Somadatta and Sātyaki), 7479, 7666 (°*puṅgavāḥ*), 7856 (°*sainyaṃ*), 7863, 7864, 7951 (°*puṅgavāḥ*), 8026, †8135, †8154, †8156, †8162, †8177, 8305, 8374, 8389, 8457, 8460 (°-*Pāṇḍuyodhāḥ*), 8462, 8623, 8691, 8882, 8893, 8912, 8931, 9036, 9039, 9049 (°*sāgare*), 9051, 9056 (°*ūṇām abhayaṅkaraṃ*, sc. Açvatthāman), 9203 (°*Pāṇḍavasenayoḥ*), 9206, 9207, 9245; VIII, 14, 15, 92, 308, 829, 846 (-*Pāñcāla-Pāṇḍushu*), 918, 1008 (°*ūṇāṃ kīrtivardhanau*, i.e. Çrutakarman and Çatānīka), 1167, 1704, †1722, †1743, 1949 (°*vīrāṇāṃ*), 2054 (°*saṃsadi*), 2062 (do.), 2084 (*saha-Pāñcālāḥ*, know the eternal religion—*dharmaṃ*), †2086 (°-*Pāñcāladeçyāḥ*), †2100, 2106 (°-*Pāñcālāḥ*), †2144, 2229 (°*pravīraiḥ*), 2233, 2299, 2361, 2393, 2508, 2514, 2772, 2836, †2851 (°-*Sṛñjayānāṃ*), 2909 (°-*Sṛñjayāḥ*), 3068, 3081, 3218, †3346 (°*vīramadhye*), †3358 (°*sainyeshu*), †3361 (*Ācāryaputraḥ pravīraḥ K°ūṇāṃ*, i.e. Açvatthāman), †3390, †3482, 3654, 3801, †3823, †3841, 3943, 4039, †4088 (°*pravīrāḥ*), 4091, 4094, 4111, 4112, 4123, 4129, 4131, 4163, 4165, 4166, 4170, 4175, †4180, †4300 (°*pravīrāḥ*), †4313, †4325, †4330, 4381, †4494 (°-*Pāṇḍavānāṃ*), †4502, (°-*Pāṇḍavāçrayāḥ*), †4566, †4590, †4591, †4608, †4619 (°*pravīrān*; *ṛshabhaḥ K°ūṇāṃ*, i.e. Arjuna), †4620, †4621, †4622, †4624, †4628, †4637, †4786, †4816, †4823, †4834 (°-*Sṛñjayānāṃ*), †4905, †4921, †4958, 4964, 4976, 4977, 4979; IX, 1, 9 (°-*Pāṇḍavasenayoḥ*), 34, 42 (°*yoshitaḥ*), 126, 392 (°*puṅgavaiḥ*), 402, 413, 444 (°-*Sṛñjaya°*), 466, 798, 825 (°*puṅgavāḥ*, i.e. the army of Yudhishṭhira; PCR. seems to read °*puṅgavaṃ* = Çalya), †881 (*ṛshabhaṃ K°ūṇāṃ*, i.e. Yudhishṭhira), †904 (*pravaraḥ K°ūṇāṃ*, i.e. Yudhishṭhira), †905, †931, 1096, 1192, 1193, 1223 (°-*Pāṇḍavāḥ*), 1441, 1562, 1646, 1656 (°*kshaye*), 1786 (*rājyaṃ K°ūṇāṃ*), 1891, 1913, 1978, 1984, 1989, 3056, 3057 (°*saṅkshayaṃ*), 3256, 3326 (°*ūṇām adhipaṃ*, i.e. Duryodhana); X, 29 (°-*Pāṇḍavayoḥ kshayaṃ*), 391 (°-*Pāṇḍavasenayoḥ*), 540 (do.), †568 (*rājā K°ūṇāṃ*, i.e. Yudhishṭhira), 724 (*parikshīṇeshu*); XI, 209 (°*ūṇāṃ vaiçase*), 275 (°*veçmasu*), 286 (°*saṅkshaye*), 288 (do.), 360 (°-*Pāṇḍavāḥ*, but read °*puṅgavāḥ* (= the Pāṇḍavas) with PCR.), 375 (°*saṅkshaye*), 427 (°*ūṇām avakartanaṃ*), 436 (°*striyaḥ*), 441 (*Pāñcāla-K°yoshāṇāṃ*), 443 (°*ūṇāṃ vaiçasaṃ*), 452, 470 (°*striyaḥ*), 471 (°*yoshitāṃ*), 659, 660 (°*ūṇāṃ dvijasattamaṃ Droṇaṃ*), 663, 680 (°*saṅkrandanaṃ*), 746, 748 (°-*Pāṇḍavāḥ*), 802 (°*striyaḥ*), 822; XII, 160, 176, 1382, 1384 (°*striyaḥ*), 1967, 2866 (°*ūṇāṃ rājā*, i.e. Yudhishṭhira), 6264 (°*ūṇāṃ prītivardhanaḥ*, i.e. Bhīshma), 8428 (°*ūṇāṃ vara*, i.e. Yudhishṭhira), 13554 (°-*Pāṇḍavayoḥ*), 13680 (*Bhāratāḥ*); XIII, 371 (°*puṅgavāḥ*), 2245 (°*ūṇāṃ vaṃçavardhana*, i.e. Bhīshma), 2929, †3692 (*rājyaṃ K°ūṇāṃ*), 6930, 7155, 7777 (°*ūdvahāḥ*; °*ūttamāḥ*), 7782 (°*vṛddhānāṃ*); XIV, 369 (*Bhīshma-Karṇapurogānāṃ*), †404 (°*ūṇām adhipaḥ*, i.e. Yudhishṭhira), 1484 (°*sāgaraṃ*), 1534 (°*rāshṭravardhanān*), 1545 (°-*Pāṇḍavasadma*), 1556 (°*puṅgavāḥ*), 1558 (°*çreshṭhāḥ*), 1583, 1777 (°*vīrāṇāṃ*), 1782, 1834 (°*yoshitaḥ*), 1866, 1875, 1966 (*parikshīṇeshu*), 2053 (*dakshiṇottarān*), 2079 (°*vīrāṇāṃ*), 2178 (°*ūṇām ṛshabhaḥ*, i.e. Arjuna), 2351, 2586, 2600, 2601, 2605 (°*yoshitaḥ*); XV, 76 (°*kshayaḥ*), 273, 329, 331, 337 (°*çreshṭhāḥ*), 485, 489 (only C.), 505 (°*striyaḥ*), 631 (°*puṅgavāḥ*, i.e. the Pāṇḍavas), 637 (°*mukhyānāṃ*), 659 (°*striyaḥ*), 873 (°-*Pāṇḍavasenayoḥ*), 895, 896, 906; XVI, †106, †107, †123 (°*kshayaṃ*), 133; XVII, 38 (°*çreshṭhāḥ*, i.e. the Pāṇḍavas); XVIII, 125 (°*puṅgavāḥ*), 177. Cf. Kaurava, pl., Kurūdvaha, pl., Kurujāṅgala, pl., Kurukula, Kuruvaṃça, and Uttarāḥ Kuravaḥ.

Kurubhūta = Çiva (1000 names[2]).

Kuruçārdūla[1] = Arjuna: I, 6500; VI, 1679 (°*au*, i.e. Arjuna and Bhīshma); XII, 13266, 13588; XIV, 403; XVI, 156, 279.

Kuruçārdūla[2] = Bhīmasena: II, 1522.

Kuruçārdūla[3] = Bhīshma: V, 6089 (*Bh°*); VI, 1679 (°*au*, i.e. Arjuna and Bhīshma); XIII, 4270, 7727, 7792 (*Bh°*).

Kuruçārdūla[4] = Dauḥçāsani: V, 5763 (°*au*, i.e. Dauḥçasani and Lakshmaṇa).

Kuruçārdūla[5] = Dhṛtarāshṭra: IX, 3554.

Kuruçārdūla[6] = Duḥçāsana: VII, 1666.

Kuruçārdūla[7] = Janamejaya: XII, 1589.

Kuruçārdūla[8] = Lakshmaṇa (the son of Duryodhana): V, 5763 (°*au*, i.e. Dauḥçāsani and Lakshmaṇa).

Kuruçārdūla[9] = Yudhishṭhira: II, 617, 1423; III, 645, 827, 8378; V, 219; XII, 10117; XIV, 7; XV, 131.

Kuruçreshṭha[1] = Arjuna: III, 10879; IV, 2345 (*Dhanañjaye*); VI, 1223, 5730; VII, 1227, 6271; VIII, 5027 (*Arjunaṃ*); XIV, 1864, 2121 (*Dhanañjayaṃ*), 2313, 2481.

Kuruçreshṭha[2] = Bhīmasena: I, 7111; III, 11286, 11322; IX, 3115 (°*au*, i.e. Bhīmasena and Duryodhana).

Kuruçreshṭha[3] = Bhīshma: III, 4045, 8160; V, 5727, 5974, 7014 (*Bh°*), 7168; VI, 3581 (*Bh°*), 4843 (only B., C. has °*ṭha*, i.e. Dhṛtarāshṭra), 5729, 5822; XII, 3463, 4628, 4915; XIII, 2245, 2613, 3430, 7777.

Kuruçreshṭha[4] = Bhūriçravas: VII, 5937.

Kuruçreshṭha[5] = Dhṛtarāshṭra: VI, 484, 2558, 3645, 4843 (only C., B. has °*ṭhaḥ*, i.e. Bhīshma), 4891; VIII, 5008; IX, 1743, 3574; XV, 175, 406, 1000.

Kuruçreshṭha[6] = Duryodhana: II, †2368; III, 15170, 15280; V, 4142, 7550, 7565; VII, 6086; IX, 3115 (°*au*, i.e. Bhīmasena and Duryodhana); X, 497, 520.

Kuruçreshṭha[7] = Janamejaya: IX, 2175, 2954.

Kuruçreshṭha[8] = Nakula: II, 1200 (*N°*).

Kuruçreshṭha[9] = Parikshit: I, 1980 (*rājā . . . Parīkshin nāma*).

Kuruçreshṭha[10] = Senābindu(!): VIII, 182 (PCR. omits this half-çloka).

Kuruçreshṭha[11] = Yudhishṭhira: II, 102, 1354; III, 46, 464, 611, 651, 907, 969, 8357, 8370, 9987, 10123, 11006, 11635, 16614; V, †713; VII, 5129; VIII, †3297; X, 616; XII, 1998, 2031, 2180, 4757, 5925, 7562; XIII, 3324, 5678, 7705; XIV, 1926, 2588, 2662; XV, 216, 254, 496.

Kuruçreshṭhatama = Yudhishṭhira: III, †15701 (*Yudhishṭhiraṃ Dharmasutaṃ*).

Kurūdvaha[1] = Arjuna: III, 1844, 12022, 12057; VIII, 3487; XIV, 387.

Kurūdvaha[2] = Bāhlīka: XV, 809 (*B°*).

Kurūdvaha[3] = Bhīshma: I, 4429; III, 5078, 6011, 6021, 6069, 6079, 7018, 7036, 8057, 8227, 8230; V, 7114, 7305; XII, 5963.

Kurūdvaha[4] = Bhūriçravas: VII, 6007.

Kurūdvaha[5] = Dhṛtarāshṭra: I, 5631; VII, 1208, 8259; VIII, 2437 (only B., C. has °*vahaḥ* = Karṇa); XV, 30, 52, 121, 530, 968, 1017.

Kurūdvaha[6] = Duryodhana: V, 7253, 7272; VII, 6599; XII, 4570.

Kurūdvaha[7] = Janamejaya: II, 1140, 1678; XV, 797, 939.

Kurūdvaha[8] = Karṇa: VIII, 2437 (error in C., B. has °*vaha* = Dhṛtarāshṭra).

Kurūdvaha[9] = Pāṇḍu: I, 4692.

Kurūdvaha[10] = Yudhishṭhira: III, 10512; XII, 1994,

2472, 3069, 5888, 6014; XIII, 3452, 3495, 7627 (*Y*°); XV, 46, 196, 207, 455.

Kurūdvaha, pl. (°*āḥ*): I, 5013 (*Pāṇḍavā Dhārtarāshṭrāç ça*); III, 391 (i.e. the Pāṇḍavas), 11066 (do.), 11428 (do.), 11560 (do.), 15206 (i.e. the Dhārtarāshṭras), 17436 (i.e. the Pāṇḍavas); VI, 778 (*Pāṇḍavāḥ*); XIII, 7777; XIV, 1509, 1878 (only B., = Bhīmasena, Arjuna, Nakula, and Sahadeva, C. has °*ha*), 1935, 2065.

Kurujāṅgala, name of a country. § 154 (Pūruvaṃç.): I, **95**, 3739 (named after Kuru).—§ 173 (Pāṇḍurājyābhisheka): I, **109**, 4337, 4360.—§ 194 (Pāṇḍu): I, **126**, 4905.—§ 240 (Vaivāhikap.): I, **199**, 7355 (°*mukhyeshu rāshṭreshu*).—§ 276 (Jarāsandhavadhap.): II, **20**, 793 (on their way to Girivraja, Kṛshṇa, Arjuna, and Bhīmasena passed from the Kurus to *K.*).—§ 315 (Āraṇyakap.): III, **10**, 354 (only C., B. has °*ān*).—§ 555 (Sainyodyogap.): V, **19**, 598 (covered by the armies).—§ 570 (Sainyaniryāṇap.): V, **153**, 5191.—§ 574 (Jambūkh.): VI, **4**, 160.—§ 595 (Shoḍaçarāj. v. Suhotra): VII, **56**, 2192 (Suhotra performed sacrifices in *K.*).—§ 604 (Karṇap.): VIII, **1**, 17 (i.e. the battle-field).—§ 607 (do.): VIII, **44**, 2038, 2040.—§ 632*b* (Shoḍaçarāj. v. Suhotra, cf. § 595): XII, **29**, 921 (Suhotra performed a sacrifice in *K.*).—§ 635 (Rājadh.): XII, **37**, 1366 (i.e. the kingdom of Yudhishṭhira).

Kurujāṅgala, pl. (°*āḥ*), the inhabitants of Kurujāṅgala.—§ 315 (Āraṇyakap.): III, **10**, 354 (only B., C. has °*āt*), 356.—§ 322 (Dvaitavanapr.): III, **23**, 907, 908.—§ 452 (Mārkāṇḍeyas.): III, **183**, †12576.—§ 777 (Svargārohanik. p.): XIII, **168**, 7727.—§ 787 (Āçramavāsap.): XIV, **8**, 269, 280; **10**, 307. Cf. Jāṅgala, pl., Kuru, pl.

Kurukartṛ = Çiva (1000 names [2]).

Kurukshetra ("the country of the Kurus"). § 12 (Paushyap.): I, **3**, 661 (Janamejaya performed a sacrifice at *K.*).—§ 17 (Uttaṅka): I, **3**, 802, 803 (Takshaka lived in *K.* in Ikshumatī).—§ 154 (Pūruv.): I, **95**, 3739 (°*ṃ sa*—i.e. Kuru—*tapasā puṇyaṃ cakre mahātapāḥ*).—§ 166 (Citrāṅgadop.): I, **101**, 4074 (in *K.* Citrāṅgada fought with the Gandharva of the same name).—§ 173 (Pāṇḍurājyābhisheka): I, **109**, 4337 (*Kurujāṅgalaṃ Kuravo K*°*ṃ*).—§ 246 (Sundopasundop.): I, **210**, 7678 (Sunda and Upasunda took up their abode in *K.*).—§ 258 (Khāṇḍavadahanap.): I, **227**, 8236 (Takshaka had gone from Khāṇḍava to *K.*); **228**, 8300 (do.).—§ 312 (Āraṇyakap.): III, **5**, 240 (the Pāṇḍavas went from the bank of the Gaṅgā to *K.*).—§ 361 (cf. Tīrthayātrāp.): At the sight of *K.* (*Brahmakshetra*, v. 5076) all creatures are freed from sin, as also he who constantly says "I will live in *K.*" has his sins destroyed and goes to *Brahmaloka*; the mere dust of *K.* leads even a sinful man to bliss (*paramāṃ gatiṃ*); it lies to the south of the Sarasvatī and to the north of the Dṛshadvatī; there one should reside for a month on the Sarasvatī, where the gods headed by Brahmán, the ṛshis, the Siddhas, the Cāraṇas, the Gandharvas, the Apsarases, the Yakshas, and the Pannagas repair to the highly sacred *Brahmakshetra*; a visit there ensures the merit of the rājasūya and the horse-sacrifice: III, **83**, 5071, 5072, 5073, 5077, 5078.—§ 362 (Tīrthayātrāp.): III, **83**, 5094 (°*sya tad dvāraṃ*, sc. Yakshiṇī).—§ 364 (do.): III, **83**, 6080 (the ṛshis had gone from the Naimisha forest to *K.*).—§ 367 (Pṛthūdaka): III, **83**, 7015 (*puṇyaṃ*).—§ 369 (cf. Tīrthayātrāp.): Naimisha is the foremost tīrtha with regard to merit on earth, Pushkara with regard to merit in the firmament, *K.* with regard to merit in the three worlds (so Nīl. and PCR.; Nīl. takes *K.* in this çloka to be another name of Kāçī, cf. also the note of PCR.); the mere dust of *K.* leads even a sinful man to bliss (*paramāṃ gatiṃ*); they who reside in *K.*, which lies to the south of the Sarasvatī and to the north of the Dṛshadvatī, really reside in heaven (*Tripishṭape*). He who merely expresses the wish to go to *K.* becomes cleansed of his sins. *K.* is the altar of Brahmán (*Brahmavedī*) worshipped by the Brahmarshis; the country between *Tarantuka* and *Arantuka* and *Rāma's* lakes and *Macakruka*, that *Kurukshetra-Samantapañcaka* is styled the northern altar (*uttaravediḥ*) of *Pitāmaha*: III, **83**, 7073, 7074, 7075, 7076, 7077, †7078 (*Tarantukārantukayor yad antaraṃ Rāmahradānāñ ca Macakrukasya ca | etat Kurukshetra-Samantapañcakaṃ Pitāmahasyottaravedir ucyate*).—§ 375 (Tīrthayātrāp.): III, **85**, 8230 (°*samā Gaṅgā*), 8233 (*Dvāpare 'pi*, sc. *puṇyaṃ*), 8234.—§ 407 (Māndhātrup.): III, **126**, 10467 (Māndhātṛ performed a sacrifice, *K*°*sya madhyataḥ*).—§ 409 (Plakshāvataraṇag.): III, **129**, 10523 (*dvāram etad . . . K*°*sya*).—§ 520 (Mudgala): III, **260**, 15407 (Mudgala lived in *K.*).—§ 549 (Pāṇḍavapraveçap.): IV, **5**, 161.—§ 569 (Bhagavadyānap.): V, **141**, 4808 (*puṇyatame*); **150**, 5079, 5095 (the great battle shall be fought in *K.*).—§ 570 (Sainyaniryāṇap.): V, **151**, 5165, 5166 (the Pāṇḍava forces marched to *K.*); **152**, 5176 (*saritaṃ puṇyāṃ K*°*e Hiraṇvatīṃ*); **153**, 5188, 5201; **156**, 5311 (the army of Duryodhana marched to *K.*); **159**, 5391.—§ 571 (Ulūkadūtāgamanap.): V, **160**, 5500; **161**, 5545.—§ 573 (Ambopākhyānap.): V, **178**, 7048, 7083, 7085, 7093, 7099, 7106, 7108 (Rāma Jāmadagnya challenged Bhīshma to an encounter which took place in *K.*); **195**, 7613.—§ 574 (Jambūkh.): VI, **1**, 3 (*tapaḥkshetre*), 4, 24 (the battle-field).—§ 576 (Bhagavadgītāp.): VI, **25**, 830 (*Dharmakshetre*).—§ 607 (Karṇap.): VIII, **44**η, 2029 (*bahishkṛtā . . . Sarasvatyā Yamunayā K*°*ena*, sc. the Bāhīkas).—§ 611 (Çalyap.): IX, **23**, 1203 (the battle-field).—§ 615 (Gadāyuddhap.): IX, **35**, 2005.—§ 615 (Baladevatīrthay.): IX, **37**, 2175.—§ 615*i* (Saptasārasvata): IX, **38**, 2211, 2213 (the river Sarasvatī appeared in *K.* as the Oghavatī).—§ 615 (Baladevatīrthay.): IX, **52**, 3006, 3007.—§ 615*kk* (Kurukshetrakathana): IX, **53**, 3009 (named after Kuru, also named Samantapañcaka), 3029 (its sanctity), 3032 (*Tarantukārantukayor yad antaraṃ Rāmahradānāñ ca* (C. *tu*) *Macakrukasya* (C °*kra*°) *ca | etat Kurukshetra-Samantapañcakaṃ Prajāpater uttaravedir ucyate*).—§ 615 (Baladevatīrthay.): IX, **54**, 3035 (visited by Balarāma).—§ 615 (Gadāyuddhap.): IX, **55**, 3083, 3092 (the encounter between Bhīmasena and Duryodhana took place in *K.*).—§ 618 (Jalapradānikap.): XI, **8**ζ, 219 (the battle-field).—§ 619 (Strīvilāpap.): XI, **16**, 437 (do.).—§ 630 (Rājadh.): XII, **27**, 806 (in *K.* Bhīshma had encountered Rāma Jāmadagnya, cf. § 573).—§ 638 (do.): XII, **48**, 1699, 1700, 1703, 1711 (Bhīshma lay on his arrow-bed in *K.*).—§ 639 (do.): XII, **53**, 1919 (do.).—§ 641 (do.): XII, **59**, 2123 (do.).—§ 652*b* (Indrota-Pārīkshitīya): XII, **152***a*, 5645 (a sacred place).—§ 720*b* (Sudarçanop.): XIII, **2**, 124 (Sudarçana lived with his wife in *K.*).—§ 766 (Ānuçāsanik.): XIII, **125**β, 5967 (a tīrtha).—§ 775 (do.): XIII, **166***a*, 7650.—§ 777 (Svargārohaṇik. p.): XIII, **168**, 7717.—§ 786*b* (Nakulākhyāna): XIV, **90**, 2695 (*uñchavṛtter vadānasya K*°*nivāsinaḥ*), 2709 (do.), 2712 (*Dharmakshetre*).—§ 787 (Āçramavāsap.): XV, **19**, 527 (Dhṛtarāshṭra, etc., repaired to *K.*).—§ 788 (do.): XV, **22**, 612 (°*āçramaṃ*); **23**, 633; **27**, 735 (°*nivāsinaḥ*).—§ 789 (Putradarçanap.): XV, **31**, 849 (the battle-field).—§ 790 (Nāradāgamanap.): XV, **37**, 1020.—§ 793 (Mausalap.): XVI, **7**, 243.

Cf. Brahmakshetra, Brahmavedī, Dharmakshetra, Samantapañcaka.

Kurukshetrakathana(ṃ) ("relation of Kurukshetra") § 615*kk* (Baladevat.): The R̥. said to *Bala-Rāma*: This *Samantapañcaka* is said to be the eternal northern altar of *Prajāpati*; there, in days of yore, the gods performed a great sacrifice. The R.-r̥. *Kuru* had cultivated this field for many years; hence it came to be called *Kurukeshetra* ("the field of Kuru"). Requested by *Bala-Rāma*, the R̥. related: In days of yore *Kuru* was engaged in perseveringly tilling this field; requested by *Indra*, he said: "Those that will die upon this plain, shall proceed to regions of bliss after being cleansed of their sins." *Çakra*, ridiculing this, went back to heaven. This happened repeatedly. *Indra* summoned the gods, who asked him to stop *Kuru* by granting him a boon; "if men, by only dying there, were to come to heaven, without having performed sacrifices to us, our very existence would be endangered." *Indra* then came, and they agreed that *Kuru* should not toil any more; but those that would die there, having abstained from food, with all their senses awake, and those that would perish there in battle, should go straight to heaven. It was sanctioned by all the principal gods, headed by *Brahmán*, that on earth there should be no more sacred spot than this; those men that performed austere penances here would all, after laying down their bodies, go to *Brahmán's* abode; those who gave away their wealth here would soon have their wealth doubled; those who would reside constantly here would never have to behold the region of *Yama*; those kings that would perform great sacrifices here would reside as long in heaven as earth would last. *Indra* had himself composed a verse here and sang it: "The very dust of *Kurukshetra* . . . shall cleanse persons of wicked acts and carry them to heaven." The principal gods, *brahmans*, kings as *Nr̥ga*, etc., having performed costly sacrifices here, have, after abandoning their bodies, proceeded to heaven. The space between *Tarantuka* and *Arantuka* and the lakes of *Rāma* (*Rāmahradānāṃ*) and *Macakruka* (C. °*kra*°), this *Kurukshetra-Samantapañcaka* is called the northern altar of *Prajāpati*. All that *Çakra* said was approved by *Brahmán*, *Vishṇu*, and *Maheçvara* (IX, **53**).

Kurukula ("the race of Kuru"): I, 1762, 1950 (*rājyaṃ K°āgataṃ*); V, †1332; XV, 981.

Kurukulaçreshṭha [1] = Arjuna: XIV, 948, 2595.

Kurukulaçreshṭha [2] = Bhīshma: III, 4042 (*Bh°*), 6051.

Kurukulaçreshṭha [3] = Dhr̥tarāshṭra: VII, 8297; XV, 342.

Kurukulaçreshṭha [4] = Duryodhana: IX, 3231.

Kurukulaçreshṭha [5] = Janamejaya: XV, 950.

Kurukulaçreshṭha [6] = Yudhishṭhira: XIII, 4263, 4393; XV, 359.

Kurukulādhama [1] = Bhīshma: II, 1444; III, 15228 (*Bh°*).

Kurukulādhama [2] = Duryodhana: IV, 1641; IX, 3146.

Kurukulādhama [3] = Parikshit: I, 1709.

Kurukulodvaha [1] = Arjuna: III, 1506; XIV, 1469, 1472, 2287.

Kurukulodvaha [2] = Bhīmasena: III, 11232.

Kurukulodvaha [3] = Bhīshma: III, 7024; V, 7040 (*Bh°*); VI, 5667 (*Bh°*); XII, 11219; XIII, 1940, 4189, 7773 (*Bh°*).

Kurukulodvaha [4] = Dhr̥tarāshṭra: VI, 434, 462; VII, 9439; XV, 43.

Kurukulodvaha [5] = Janamejaya: IX, 2765; XIV, 1880.

Kurukulodvaha [6] = Pāṇḍu: I, 4929 (*P°*).

Kurukulodvaha [7] = Vicitravīrya: V, 4977 (*V°*).

Kurukulodvaha [8] = Yudhishṭhira: II, 1632; III, 700, 851, 13070, 14112; XIV, 2104; XV, 133; XVII, 97.

Kurumukhya [1] = Arjuna: XIV, 2367.

Kurumukhya [2] = Bhīmasena: VI, 1688 (°*au* = Bhīmasena and Duryodhana); IX, 3246 (°*ayoḥ* = do.).

Kurumukhya [3] = Bhīshma: I, 4038; V, 2345 (*Bh°*), †5037 (*Devavrataḥ*); VI, 4992, 5551 (°*ānāṃ r̥shabhaḥ*).

Kurumukhya [4] = Citrāṅgada: I, 4074.

Kurumukhya [5] = Dhr̥tarāshṭra: II, 1724.

Kurumukhya [6] = Durmukha: VII, 822 (*Pāñcālya-K°yoḥ*, i.e. Dhr̥shṭadyumna and Durmukha).

Kurumukhya [7] = Duryodhana: VI, 1688 (°*au* = Bhīmasena and Duryodhana); IX, 3246 (°*ayoḥ* = do.).

Kurumukhya [8] = Yudhishṭhira: VIII, 1261; XIV, 2349.

Kurunandana [1] = Abhimanyu: VI, 4608.

Kurunandana [2] = Arjuna: I, 6643, 6786, 7156 (°*au* = Bhīmasena and Arjuna), 7237 (*A°*), 7795, 7844, 7845, 7978, 8076, 8471 (*Kuru-Dāçārhanandanau* = Arjuna and Kr̥shṇa); II, 62, 1027, 1029 (*Kirīṭī*), 1041; III, 1602, 1640, 1684, 1705 (*A°*), 1733 (do.), 1744, 1770, 12310, 14995; IV, 39; V, 135 (°*au* = Arjuna and Duryodhana), 5115; VI, 919, 1107, 1368, 5114 (according to B.); VII, 6232, 6254; VIII, 4131; XIV, 1865, 2335, 2351.

Kurunandana [3] = Bhīmasena: I, 5060, 7156 (*au* = Bhīmasena and Arjuna); II, 924, 1068; III, 11221, 14950.

Kurunandana [4] = Bhīshma: II, 1331, 1345, 1346; III, 4063, 5009, 5068, 6046, 8051, 8151, 8159; V, 7067, 7127; XII, 11215; XIII, 2234, 5143, 7794.

Kurunandana [5] = Dhr̥tarāshṭra: I, 7497; II, 1972; III, 362; V, 3416, 4436, 5299; VI, 188, 408, 409, 485, 1547, 1897, 4532, 5086, 5114 (according to C.); X, 472; XV, 328.

Kurunandana [6] = Duryodhana: I, 7457; II, 1663, 2140; III, 14854, 15032, 15047; IV, 900, 1622; V, 135 (°*au* = Duryodhana and Arjuna), 158, 164, 3024 (?), 3719, 5752, 7188, 7399, 7532; VII, 2663; VIII, 1359; IX, 3390.

Kurunandana [7] = Janamejaya: I, 4244, 4245; II, 1318; III, 1690; V, 585; XII, 13609, 13632.

Kurunandana [8] = Pāṇḍu: I, 4420, 4443 (*rājā*), 4630, 4683, 4838, 4877 (*P°*), 5744 (do.).

Kurunandana [9] = Parikshit: I, 1747.

Kurunandana [10] = Pratīpa: I, 3881.

Kurunandana [11] = Sahadeva: II, 1128, 1157 (*S°*); IV, 282; V, 5104.

Kurunandana [12] = Vidura: III, 278.

Kurunandana [13] = Yudhishṭhira: I, 6414, 7244; II, 633, 1348, 1611; III, 628, 834, 1306, 1343, 2825, 2912, 2943, 8261, 8419, 8440, 8539, 10496, 10520, 11867, 11946, 12221, 12793, 15957, 17240; V, 200; VI, 1569, 1571, 1577 (*Y°*), 4937; VII, 2523, 2938; IX, 354, †915, 1744, 1786, 3171; XII, 288, 704, 1475, 1722, 2006, 2601, 2620, 2658, 2660, 2738, 4478, 9837, 10157, 10203, 10225, 11830; XIII, 1524, 2347, 2524, 2534, 2547, 2551, 2750, 2768, 2967, 3314, 3481, 3933, 4419, 4630, 5600, 5602, 7403; XIV, 2619; XV, 93, 116, 148, 177, 1020; XVII, 105; XVIII, 130, 133.

Kurunandana, pl. (°*āḥ*) = the sons of Pāṇḍu: IV, 18, 22, 325, 326; V, 626.

Kuru-Pāṇḍavāgrya = Yudhishṭhira: II, 2247.

Kuru-Pāṇḍavasattama = Arjuna: III, 1753.

Kurupati [1] = Bhīshma: VI, 1988.

Kurupati [2] = Duryodhana: VI, 3464; VIII, 2726.

Kurupati [3] = Pāṇḍu: XV, 657 (°*eḥ putrān Pāṇḍavān*).

Kurupati [4] = Yudhishṭhira: II, 37; XI, 827 (*Y°*); XIV, 2527, 2630.

Kurupitāmaha = Bhīshma: I, 4372 (*Bh*°); II, 1419 (do.), 1422 (do.), 1556 (do.); III, 15220 (do.); V, 3084 (do.); VI, 498, 640, 1867, 2129, 2142, 2403, 2555, 4234 (*Bh*°), 4841 (do.), 4939, 4944 (*Bh*°), 4949, 4975 (*Bh*°), 5536, 5611, (*Bh*°), 5663 (do.), 5665 (do.), 5696 (do.); VII, 6479 (do.), 9168 (do.); XII, 1349 (do.), 10659; XIII, 5387; XIV, 1492.

Kurupravīra[1] = Arjuna: VI, †1294; VIII, †3294, †4786.

Kurupravīra[2] = Bhīshma: V, †31 (*Bh*°); XII, †1857.

Kurupravīra[3] = Dhṛtarāshṭra: II, 1933; VIII, †202.

Kurupravīra[4] = Duryodhana: IV, 2099, 2126; VIII, †4065.

Kurupravīra[5] = Janamejaya: I, †1807 (*J*°), †1810.

Kurupravīra[6] = Pāṇḍu (?): I, †7173 (*Vicitravīryasya sutasya*).

Kurupravīra[7] = Purumitra: VIII, †203 (*P*°).

Kurupravīra[8] = Vikarṇa: IV, 1668.

Kurupravīra[9] = Yudhishṭhira: I, †7136, †7152; III, †910, 13210, 14637; V, †35; XII, 6261.

Kurupravīra, pl. (°*āḥ*) = Kuru, pl. (q.v.).

Kurupṛtanāpati ("the commander of the Kurus") = Karṇa: VIII, 1747.

Kurupuṅgava[1] = Abhimanyu: VI, 2486 (*Çaineya-K°au*, i.e. Sātyaki and Abhimanyu).

Kurupuṅgava[2] = Arjuna: I, 5529; IV, 159, 1919; XIV, 1515 (*Vārshṇeya-K°au*, i.e. Kṛshṇa and Arjuna), 2265 (*A*°); XVI, 148, 285.

Kurupuṅgava[3] = Bhīmasena: I, 5055.

Kurupuṅgava[4] = Bhīshma: II, 1343; VII, †62; XIII, 2970, 3003.

Kurupuṅgava[5] = Bhūriçravas: VII, 5924 (*Kuru-Sātvata-puṅgavau*), 5934.

Kurupuṅgava[6] = Dhṛtarāshṭra: II, †2224 (*vṛddhasya rājñaḥ*); VII, 7772.

Kurupuṅgava[7] = Duryodhana: V, 97, 5889, 7547; VI, 5383; VII, 6982, †7294 (?).

Kurupuṅgava[8] = Somadatta: VII, 6756, 7230.

Kurupuṅgava[9] = Yudhishṭhira: II, 1343; VII, 7269; VIII, 5003; IX, †884, 953; XII, 1097; XIII, 5721.

Kurupuṅgava, pl. (°*āḥ*) = Kuru, pl. (q.v.).

Kurupuṅgavāgraja = Janamejaya: I, †1808.

Kurupuṅgavāgrya = Sātyaki: VII, †4684 (C. °*aḥ*, but read with B. °*u* = Dhṛtarāshṭra).

Kururāja[1] = Çāntanu: IX, 3153 (?).

Kururāja[2] = Dhṛtarāshṭra: II, †1998; VII, 6054; XV, 307, 561, 771, 1044.

Kururāja[3] = Duryodhana: I, 5347, 5348, II, †2367; V, 1799 (*D*°), 5214 (?); VI, 3215, 5834 (?); VII, 1668, 4613, 4615, 4624, 5338, 5882 (*Suyodhanaṃ*), 7043; VIII, 212, 4852, 4879; IX, 144, 170, 318, 3090, 3135, 3152, 3442, 3466; X, 494, 535; XI, 516.

Kururāja[4] = Parikshit: X, 736; XVII, 8.

Kururāja[5] = Yudhishṭhira: I, 322 (°*tīrthayātrā*), 599 (*Y*°), 6472 (do.); II, 1596; III, †12322, 12609 (*Pāṇḍavaḥ*); IV, 64, 291 (*Y*°), 2216, †2301; VII, 1031 (*Pāṇḍavasya*); VIII, 4985; IX, 828; X, 652 (*Y*°); XI, 799 (do.); XIII, 6917, 7694 (*Y*°); XIV, 401, 1796 (*Y*°), 2072 (do.), 2479, 2664, 2679 (*Y*°), 2803; XV, 18 (*Y*°), 624 (do.), †660, 758 (*Y*°), 775 (do.), 1012; XVI, 7 (*Y*°); XVII, 99; XVIII, 19 (*Y*°), 82 (do.), 123 (do.).

Kururājan[1] = Duryodhana: XIV, 2287.

Kururājan[2] = Yudhishṭhira: XV, 622.

Kururājaputra, dual (°*au*) and pl. (°*āḥ*): I, 7075 (°*au Arjuna-Bhīmasenau*): III, 11910 (i.e. the Pāṇḍavas).

Kururājarshisattama = Bhīshma: XII, 11852.

Kurusattama[1] = Arjuna: I, 6635, 6714, 7814, 7817; VI, 1024; VII, 3278, 6218; VIII, 4129 (*Phālgunaṃ*); XII, 199.

Kurusattama[2] = Bhīmasena: III, 11786; IX, 3128 (°*au* = Bhīmasena and Duryodhana), 3195 (do., do.).

Kurusattama[3] = Bhīshma: I, 5650 (*Bh*°), 7489 (do.); II, 1493; III, 14810 (*Bh*°); V, †881 (do.), 2163; VI, 5763; VII, 100; VIII, 191 (°*au* = Bhīshma and Droṇa); XII, 1353, 11037; XIII, 1771 (*Gāṅgeyaṃ*), 2503.

Kurusattama[4] = Citrāṅgada: I, 4075.

Kurusattama[5] = Çāntanu: I, 3883.

Kurusattama[6] = Dhṛtarāshṭra: I, 5314, 5547; II, 2107; III, †14745, 14819; V, 2151, 2169, 3391; VI, 389; VII, 7948, 8818; VIII, 2573, 4977; IX, 3283; XI, 53, 68, 193, 259.

Kurusattama[7] = Droṇa: VIII, 191 (°*au* = Bhīshma and Droṇa).

Kurusattama[8] = Duryodhana: II, 1730 (*D*°); III, 15167, 15307; V, 4129; VI, 5806; VII, 6638, 7052 (only in B.), 7147, 7154; VIII, 1315; IX, 3128 (°*au* = Bhīmasena and Duryodhana), 3195 (do., do.), 3224, †3321, 3332; XII, 4618.

Kurusattama[9] = Janamejaya: I, 4309, 4422, 5997; II, 1235; III, 14864, 17230; IV, 1237; IX, 2463; XV, 5.

Kurusattama[10] = Yudhishṭhira: III, 997, 4024, †10279, 11862, 12621; V, 280; VIII, †3289 (*rājñaḥ*); XII, 5, 706, 1112, 1986, 2115, 2118, 2866, 9255, 9991, 9992, 12170; XIII, 396, 3030, 3385, 7402; XIV, 369; XV, 219.

Kurusattama, pl. (°*āḥ*) = Kuru, pl. (q.v.).

Kurusiṃha, pl. (°*āḥ*) = Kuru, pl. (q.v.).

Kurusiṃha[1] = Bhīshma: VI, 5693.

Kurusiṃha[2] = Duryodhana: VII, 8662.

Kurutīrtha, name of a tīrtha. § 368 (Tīrthayātrāp.): III, **83**, 7036, 7037.

Kurūttama[1] = Arjuna: VII, 3891 (*Vṛshṇy-Andhaka-K°au* = Kṛshṇa and Arjuna).

Kurūttama[2] = Bhīshma: II, 1470.

Kurūttama[3] = Duryodhana: VII, 6079.

Kurūttama[4] = Yudhishṭhira: III, 14314; VI, †784; XIII, 387.

Kurūttama, pl. (°*āḥ*) = Kuru, pl. (q.v.).

Kuruvaṃça ("the race of Kuru"): I, 46, 99, 3542 (*vardhanaḥ K°sya*, i.e. Yayāti), 4285, 4304, 6496; V, 5090; IX, 2453; XI, 658; XII, 11218 (°*pradīpaḥ*); XIV, 2040.

Kuruvaṃçakara = Vyāsa: XIII, 1339.

Kuruvaṃçaketu = Bhīshma: VI, †791.

Kuruvaṃçavivardhana = Dhṛtarāshṭra: I, 2718 (*Dh*°).

Kuruvaṃçavivardhana, pl. (°*āḥ*): I, 4304 (i.e. Dhṛtarāshṭra, Pāṇḍu, and Vidura), 4862 (*Pāṇḍoḥ sutāḥ pañca*), 4865 (*pañca çatāni caiva*, i.e. the sons of Pāṇḍu and Dhṛtarāshṭra).

Kuruvaraçreshṭha = Bhīshma: III, 5013, 5019, 8010.

Kuruvardhana[1] = Durjaya: VI, 3435 (°*au* = Durjaya and Vikarṇa).

Kuruvardhana[2] = Duryodhana: I, 7416; VI, 387.

Kuruvardhana[3] = Parikshit: I, 1739.

Kuruvardhana[4] = Vikarṇa: VI, 3435 (°*au* = Durjaya and Vikarṇa).

Kuruvardhana[5] = Yudhishṭhira: III, 607; XIV, 403, 2529.

Kuruvarṇaka, pl. (°*āḥ*), a people. § 574 (Jambūkh.): VI, **9**μ, 364 (in Bhāratavarsha).

Kuruvāsin = Çiva (1000 names[2]).

Kuruvinda, pl. (°*āḥ*), a people. § 585 (Bhīshmavadhap.): VI, **87**ε, 3855 (only B.).

Kuruvīra[1] = Arjuna: XIV, 2160, 2365.

Kuruvīra[2] = Bhīmasena: III, 11170.

Kuruvīra[3] = Dhṛtarāshṭra: XV, 37, 514.

Kuruvīra[4] = Karṇa: VIII, 4435 (*Kuru-Pāṇḍavavīrau*, i.e. Karṇa and Arjuna).

Kuruvīra[5] = Yudhishṭhira: V, 980.

Kuruvīramukhya, dual (°*au*) = Arjuna and Karṇa: VIII, †4925.

Kuruvṛddha[1] = Bhīshma: IV, 986; V, 4713, 4962 (*Pitāmahaḥ*), †5654 (*Bh*°), 5718; VI, 841 (*Pitāmahaḥ*), 2112 (do.), 2348, 4915 (*Pitāmahaṃ*), 4977 (*Pitāmahena*), 5217, 5766 (*Pitāmahaṃ*), 5823; VII, 115 (*Pitāmahaḥ*); XI, 29 (*Bh*°).

Kuruvṛddha[2] = Dhṛtarāshṭra: V, †691.

Kuruvṛddhatama, dual (°*au*) = Bhīshma and Dhṛtarāshṭra: II, 2263.

Kuruvṛddhavarya = Dhṛtarāshṭra: XV, 673.

Kuruvṛsha = Bhīmasena: II, 1071 (*Kuru - Cedivṛshau* = Bhīmasena and Çiçupāla).

Kuruvṛshabha = Yudhishṭhira: III, †949 (*Y*°).

Kuruyodha = Karṇa: VIII, 4436 (*Kuru-Pāṇḍavayodhau* = Karṇa and Arjuna).

Kusasthalī, v. Kuçasthalī.

Kushmāṇḍa (B. *Kūçm*°), name of a mantra: XIII, 6236, 6242.

Kushmāṇḍaka (B. *Kūçm*°), a serpent. § 47 (Sarpanāmak.): I, **35**, 1556.

Kustumbaru, a Yaksha. § 269 (Vaiçravaṇasabhāv.): II, **10**, 397 (among the Yakshas in the palace of Kubera).

Kusuma, a companion of Skanda. § 615*u* (Skanda): IX, **45**ζ, 2541 (given to Skanda by Dhātṛ).

Kūṭamohana = Skanda: III, 14632.

Kuṭara, a serpent. § 47 (Sarpanāmak.): I, **35**, 1560.

Kuṭhāra, a serpent. § 67 (Sarpasattra): I, **57**, 2156 (of Dhṛtarāshṭra's race).

Kuṭīmukha, a follower of Çiva (?). § 269 (Vaiçravaṇasabhāv.): II, **10**, 415 (in the palace of Kubera).

Kuṭṭāparanta, pl. (°*āḥ*), a people. § 574 (Jambūkh.): VI, **9**μ, 356 (only C., B. has *Kuṇḍā*°).

Kuvalāçva (C. *Kub*°), a king of Ayodhyā, the slayer of Dhundhu. § 474 (Mārkaṇḍeyas.): III, **201**, 13486 (*Ikshvākuḥ* . . . *Dhundhumāratvam āgataḥ*), 13487.—§ 474*b* (Dhundhumārop.): III, **201**, 13490 (*Ikshvākuḥ* . . . *Dhundhumāratvam agamat*), 13513 (son of Bṛhadaçva).—§ 475 (do.): III, **202**, 13519 (do., father of 21,000 sons).—§ 476 (do.): III, **202**, 13520; **203**, 13547.—§ 478 (do.): III, **204**, 13592, 13593, 13599, 13601, 13604, 13610 (his sons are consumed by Dhundhu), 13613 (*rājarshiḥ*), 13614 (slew Dhundhu with the Brahmāstra and was therefore called Dhundhumāra), 13622, 13623 (had three sons left, Dṛḍhāçva, Kapilāçva, and Candrāçva). Cf. Dhundhumāra, Ikshvāku.

Kuvaleçaya = Vishṇu (1000 names).

L

Labdhalaksha, a Pāṇḍava warrior. § 600 (Ghaṭotkacavadhap.): VII, **158**χ, 7012 (brother of Virāṭa?).

Laḍaka, pl. (°*āḥ*), a people. § 578 (Bhīshmavadhap.): VI, **50**π, 2083 (in the army of Yudhishṭhira; only in C., B. has *Dhenukāḥ*).

Laghantī, a river. § 268 (Varuṇasabhāv.): II, **9**, 375 (among the rivers present in the palace of Varuṇa; only in C., B has *Laṅghatī*).

***laghiman** ("lightness"). § 705 (Mokshadh.): XII, **303**, 11229 (attributes of Çambhu).—§ 707 (do.): XII, **313**, 11602 (attributes of Çambhu Prajāpati).—§ 730 (Ānuçāsanik.): XIII, **14**εε, 1015 (= Çiva).

Laghu = Çiva (1000 names[2]).

Lajjā ("shame," personif.). § 115 (Aṃçāvat.): I, **66**, 2579 (daughter of Daksha and wife of Dharma).

Lakshaṇā, an Apsaras. § 191 (Arjuna): I, **123**, 4818 (dancing at the birth of Arjuna).

Lakshmaṇa[1], son of Daçaratha and Sumitrā and brother of Rāma. § 267 (Yamasabhāv.): II, **8**, 329 (in the palace of Yama).—§ 323 (Dvaitavanapr.): III, **25**, †953 (accompanied Rāma to the forest, cf. § 527).—§ 525 (Rāmopākhyānap.): III, **274**, 15878 (son of Daçaratha), 15879 (Sumitrā was the mother of *L.* and Çatrughna).—§ 527 (do.): III, **277**, 15945 (*Rāma-L°au*), 15973 (when Rāma was banished by his father, *L.* accompanied him), 15976 (*Rāma-L°au*), 15982.—§ 528 (Sītāharaṇa): III, **278**, 16019, 16023, 16024, 16025, 16029, 16031 (*L.* was sent by Sītā to rescue Rāma, then Sītā was ravished by Rāvaṇa).—§ 530 (Viçvāvasumokshaṇa): III, **279**, 16057 (C. has by error *Laksha*°), 16060 (do.), 16061, 16063, 16064 (*Rāma-L°au*), 16074, 16079, 16083, 16092 (*Rāma-L°au*, *L.* was seized by Kabandha, who was slain by Rāma).—§ 531 (Rāmopakhyānap.): III, **280**, 16099, 16100 (*Rāma-L°au*), 16114 (the meeting with Sugrīva, etc.).—§ 532 (Sītāsāntvana): III, **280**, 16149 (*Rāmo L°ānugataḥ*), 16161.—§ 534 (Hanūmatpratyāg.): III, **282**, 16200, 16201, 16204, 16208, 16212, 16213, 16217 (sent by Rāma to Sugrīva), 16227 (*Rāma-L°sannidhau*), 16229, 16259 (*Rāma-L°au*).—§ 535 (Setubandhana): III, **283**, 16317 (Vibhīshaṇa was made the friend of *L.*).—§ 536 (Laṅkāpraveça): III, **284**, 16346 (attacked the southern gate of the city of Laṅkā).—§ 537 (Rāma-Rāvaṇayuddha): III, **285**β, 16371, 16376 (fought with Indrajit, the son of Rāvaṇa).—§ 539 (Kumbhakarṇādivadha): III, **287**, 16421 (slew Kumbhakarṇa with the Brahmāstra), 16431 (fought with Pramāthin and Vajravega).—§ 540 (Indrajidyuddha): III, **288**, 16439, 16442 (*Rāma-L°-Sugrīvāḥ*), 16446 (*çubhalakshmaṇaṃ*), 16447, 16453, 16459 (fought with Indrajit), 16460 (*Rāma-L°au*), 16463 (do.).—§ 541 (Indrajidvadha): III, **289**, 16465 (*Rāma-L°au*), 16476, 16481, 16484 (slew Indrajit).—§ 542 (Rāvaṇavadha): III, **290**, 16505.—§ 543 (Rāmābhishekap.): III, **291**, 16546 (C. has by error *Laksha*°).—§ 599 (Jayadrathavadhap.): VII, **108**, 4065 (°*ṃ Rāvaṇir*—i.e. Indrajit—*yathā*, sc. *yodhayām āsa*); **142**, 5888 (*yathā Rāmānujenājau Rāvaṇir*—i.e. Indrajit—*L°ena*, sc. *nihataḥ*, all. to § 541).—§ 746 (Ānuçāsanik.): XIII, **74**, 3617 (Rāma Dāçarathi imparted Brahmán's discourse on kine to *L.*, who while living in the forest imparted it to the ṛshis).

Cf. also the following synonyms:—

Ikshvākunandana: III, 16507.

Kākutstha: III, 16207.

Rāghava: III, 16285 (°*au* = Rāma and *L.*).

Rāmānuja: VII, 5888 (*L*°).

Saumitri ("the son of Sumitrā"): III, 16071, 16074, 16082, 16095, 16114, 16129, 16153, 16197, 16211, 16260, 16284, 16300, 16362, 16376, 16410, 16420, 16423, 16425, 16426, 16429, 16430, 16433, 16450, 16480, 16483, 16484, 16485, 16507, 16531, 16581, 16589, 16594.

Lakshmaṇa[2], son of Duryodhana Dhārtarāshṭra. § 572 (Rathātirathasaṅkhyānap.): V, **166,** 5761 (*tava*—i.e. Duryodhana's—*putrakaḥ*, in the army of Duryodhana).—§ 579 (Bhīshmavadhap.): VI, **55,** 2366 (*tava*—i.e. Dhṛtarāshṭra's—*pautraḥ*, fought with Abhimanyu), 2369.—§ 582 (do.): VI, **73**[12], 3228 (*pautras tava*, fought with Abhimanyu), 3229, 3230, 3231, 3232, 3234.—§ 586 (do.): VI, **104,** 4755 (Bālhīka ascended the chariot of *L.*).—§ 590 (Droṇābhishekap.): VII, **14,** 543 (fought with Kshatradeva).—§ 592 (Saṃçaptakavadhap.): VII, **25,** 1098, 1099 (fought with Paṭaccarahantṛ).—§ 593 (Abhimanyuvadhap.): VII, **34,** 1499 (*pautraṃ tava*, at the head of Droṇa's cakravyūha); **46,** 1840 (attacked Abhimanyu), 1843 (*pautraṃ tava*), 1845, 1849, 1850 (is slain by Abhimanyu).—§ 604 (Karṇap.): VIII, **6,** 161 (had slain Ambashṭha's son (the slayer of the Paṭaccaras, PCR., but B. and C. have *sapatnānāṃ nihantā*)), 177 (had slain Kshatradeva, the son of Çikhaṇḍin).—§ 610 (Çalyap.): IX, **4,** 198 (*tava*—i.e. Duryodhana's—*putre*, sc. *nihate*).—§ 615 (Gadāyuddhap.): IX, **64**εε, 3615.—§ 619 (Strīvilāpap.): XI, **20**ε, 602; **25,** 732 (*putraḥ pitaram anvagacchat* | *Duryodhanaṃ . . . L°aḥ*).—§ 620 (Çrāddhap.): XI, **26**β, 787 (his corpse is burnt).—§ 789 (Putradarçanap.): XV, **32**θ, 878 (among the dead warriors who, summoned by Vyāsa, arose from the Gaṅgā). Cf. Duryodhanasuta, Kuruçārdūla.

Lakshmaṇāgraja ("elder brother of Lakshmaṇa[1]") = Rāma Dāçarathi: VII, 2226.

Lakshmaṇamātṛ ("mother of Lakshmaṇa[2]") = the wife of Duryodhana: IX, 3618; XI, 511, 524.

***Lakshmī**[1] (the goddess of beauty and prosperity (=Çrī), wife of Vishṇu (Nārāyaṇa)). § 28 (Amṛtamanthana): I, **18,** 1155 (the Asuras fought with the gods in order to obtain the amṛta and *L.*).—§ 115 (Aṃçāvat.): I, **66,** 2578 (daughter of Daksha and wife of Dharma).—§ 123 (do.): I, **66,** 2615 (daughter of Brahmán and sister of Dhātṛ and Vidhātṛ; her spiritual sons are sky-ranging horses).—§ 238 (Pañcendrop.): I, **197,** †7310 (incarnate as Draupadī).—§ 240 (Vaivāhikap.): I, **199,** 7352 (*yathā Nārāyaṇe L°ḥ*, wife of Nārāyaṇa).—§ 266 (Çakrasabhāv.): II, **7,** 286 (with Mahendrāṇī and Çrī in the palace of Indra).—§ 269 (Vaiçravaṇasabhāv.): II, **10,** 400 (in the palace of Kubera).—§ 270 (Brahmasabhāv.): II, **11,** 458 (in the palace of Brahmán). § 310*b* (Sūrya): III, **3,** 194.—§ 330 (Indradarçana): III, **37,** 1488 (Draupadī's blessing upon Arjuna).—§ 459 (Mārkaṇḍeyas.): III, **188,** 12000 (*sākshāl L°ya ivāvāsaḥ*).—§ 501 (Skandopākhyāna): III, **229,** 14452 (came to Skanda).—§ 551 (Kīcakavadhap.): IV, **14,** 388 (*padmālayā*, Kīcaka asks Draupadī if she is *L.*, etc.).—§ 553 (Vaivāhikap.): IV, **71,** †2305 (*mūrtimatīva L°īḥ*, sc. Kṛshṇā).—§ 564 (Mātalīyop.): V, **102,** 3613 (with Vāruṇī and amṛta she arose at the churning of the ocean).—§ 565 (Galavacarita): V, **117,** 3960 (*rome . . . yathā Nārāyaṇo L°yā*, wife of Nārāyaṇa).—§ 568 (Vidulāputraçāsana): V, **135,** 4612 (*abhivartati*).—§ 599 (Jayadrathavadhap.): VII, **94**ε, 3452 (Droṇa's blessing upon Duryodhana).—§ 615*u* (Skanda): IX, **46**κ, 2682 (proceeded in the van of Skanda's army).—§ 641 (Rājadh.): XII, **121,** 4432 (*Brahmakanyā*, etc. = Nīti, the wife of Chastisement).—§ 671*b* (Bali-Vāsavasaṃv.): XII, **225,** 8155 (=Çrī), 8167 (do.).—§ 674*b* (Çrī-Vāsavasaṃv.): XII, **229*a*,** 8354 (= Çrī), 8420 (*°sahitam āsīnaṃ Maghavantaṃ*).—§ 717*b* (Nārāyaṇīya): XII, **348**κκ, 13536 (*Nārāyaṇaparā . . . L°īç ca devatā*).—§ 737 (Ānuçāsanik.): XIII, **31*a*,** 2013.—§ 788 (Āçramavāsap.): XV, **25,** 664 (*mūrtimatīva L°īḥ*, sc. Kṛshṇā). Cf. Çrī.

Lakshmī[2] = Devasenā: III, 14451.—Do.[3] = Vishṇu (1000 names).

Lakshmīvat = Vishṇu (1000 names).

Lakshmyāvāsa = Mahāpurusha (Mahāpurushastava).

Lalāṭāksha ("having an eye in the forehead") = Çiva: III, 1628; XIII, 1264 (1000 names[2]).

Lalita = Skanda: III, 14634.

Lalitaka, v. Lalitika.

Lalitika, a tīrtha. § 370 (Tīrthayātrāp.): III, **84,** 8012 (*Çāntanos tīrthaṃ*, B. has *Lalitakaṃ*).

Lalītika, a tīrtha. § 370 (Tīrthayātrāp.): III, **84,** 8142 (this çloka is omitted in B.). Cf. the prec.

Lalittha, pl. (*°āḥ*), a people. § 591 (Saṃçaptakavadhap.): VII, **17**β, 692 (among the Saṃçaptakas).—§ 592 (do.): VII, **19**β, 768 (crushed by Arjuna).—§ 599 (Jayadrathavadhap.): VII, **91**β, 3255 (attacked Arjuna).—§ 604 (Karṇap.): VIII, **5**ζ, 137 (have been slain by Arjuna).

Lalittha, sg. ("the king of the Lalitthas"). § 593 (Abhimanyuvadhap.): VII, **37**κ, 1610 (attacked Abhimanyu).

Lambā, a mātṛ. § 615*u* (Skanda): IX, **46**θ, 2636.

Lambana = Çiva (1000 names[2]).

Lambapayodharā, a mātṛ. § 615*u* (Skanda): IX, **46**θ, 2639.

Lambinī, a mātṛ. § 615*u* (Skanda): IX, **46**θ, 2636.

Lambitoshṭha = Çiva (1000 names[2]).

Lambodaraçarīra = Kṛshṇa: XII, 1667.

Lambodaraçarīrin = Çiva (1000 names[2]).

Lampāka, pl. (*°āḥ*), a people. § 599 (Jayadrathavadhap.): VII, **121**θθ, 4847 (attacked Sātyaki).

Lāṅgaladhārin, Lāṅgaladhvaja, Lāṅgalin = Balarāma, q.v.

Lāṅgalī, a river. § 268 (Varuṇasabhāv.): II, **9,** 374 (among the rivers present in the palace of Varuṇa).

Laṅghatī, v. Laghantī.

Laṅkā, the city of Rāvaṇa, formerly belonging to Kubera. § 342 (Indralokābhigamanap.): III, **51,** 1989 (*°nivāsinaḥ*, present at the rājasūya of Yudhishṭhira).—§ 425 (Hanūmad-Bhīmasaṃv.): III, **148,** 11209 (when Hanūmat had found the ravished Sītā in *L.*, he burnt the whole city, cf. § 534), 11213 (after the death of Rāvaṇa, Vibhīshaṇa was installed as king of *L.*, cf. § 543).—§ 430 (do.): III, **150,** 11279.—§ 525 (Rāmopākhyānap.): III, **274,** 15874, 15887 (*Rākshasagaṇasevitaṃ*, given by Brahmán to Kubera as residence).—§ 526 (do.): III, **275,** 15891 (abode of Kubera), 15920 (Rāvaṇa conquered *L.* from Kubera), 15921.—§ 528 (Rāvaṇagamana): III, **277,** 15989 (residence of Rāvaṇa).—§ 529 (Sītāharaṇa): III, **278,** 16035 (*purī*, on the other side of the sea).—§ 530 (Viçvāvasumokshaṇa): III, **279,** 16056 (Rāvaṇa carried Sītā to *L.*), 16087 (*Rāvaṇena . . . L°ādhivāsinā*).—§ 532 (Sītāsāntvana): III, **280,** 16133 (*purīṃ*).—§ 534 (Hanūmatpratyāgamana): III, **282,** 16252 (*d*: on the other side of the sea in a valley of the mountain Trikūṭa).—§ 535 (Setubandhana): III, **283,** 16319 (Rāma and his followers devastated the gardens of *L.*).—§ 536 (Laṅkāpraveça): III, **284,** 16324 (strongly fortified), 16329 (Aṅgada was sent as a messenger to *L.*), 16343 (*purīṃ*), 16345, 16347 (Rāma and his followers broke down the ramparts and attacked the city), 16353, 16361, 16363.—§ 538 (Kumbakarṇaraṇagamana): III, **286,** 16394.—§ 541 (Indrajidvadha): III, **289,** 16489.—§ 543 (Rāmābhisheka): III, **291,** 16535 (when Rāvaṇa had been slain Rāma bestowed *L.* on Vibhīshaṇa), 16582.

Laṅkāpraveça ("the entry into Laṅkā"). § 536 (cf. Rāmopākhyānap.). Rāvaṇa made Laṅkā yet more strong and armed his warriors. Rāma sent the monkey Aṅgada as messenger to Rāvaṇa. Aṅgada delivered the message of Rāma: "Release Sītā." Rāvaṇa became furious. Aṅgada leaped up with four Rākshasas and then let them fall; then he leaped over the walls of Laṅkā and informed Rāma. Rāma, Lakshmaṇa, Vibhīshaṇa, and Jāmbavat with monkeys and bears attacked Laṅkā and pulled down the fortifications. Then the host of the Rākshasas set out at the command of Rāvaṇa. A great battle ensued; at last Rāma withdrew his troops (III, **284**).

Laṅkeçavanāri ("destroyer of the forests of the king of Laṅkā [i.e. Rāvaṇa]") = Hanūmat: IV, 1294 (*°ketuḥ*, i.e. Arjuna).

Lapeṭikā, a tīrtha. § 370 (Tīrthayātrāp.): III, **85**, 8157.

Lapitā, the second wife of Mandapāla. § 259 (Çārṅgakop.): I, **229**, 8347, 8348, 8350; **233**, 8430, 8435, 8453.

Latā, an Apsaras. § 250 (Arjunavanavāsap.): I, **216**, 7858 (among five Apsarases who according to the curse of a brahman became crocodiles, but were delivered by Arjuna).—§ 269 (Vaiçravaṇasabhāv.): II, **10**, 394 (in the palace of Kubera).

Lāṭa, pl. (*°āḥ*), a people. § 739 (Ānuçāsanik.): XIII, **34**ε, 2158 (have been degraded from kshatriyas to çūdras).

Latāḥ = Çiva (1000 names[1]).

Lauhitya[1] ("the bloody one"), name of an ocean. § 11 (Parvasaṅgr.): I, **2**, 630 (*sāgaram*, cf. § 794).—§ 794 (Mahāprasthānikap.): XVII, **1**, 33 (*salilārṇavam*, Arjuna threw the Gāṇḍīva [which belonged to Varuṇa] into *L.*). Cf. Lohita(ḥ) udadhi(ḥ).

Lauhitya[2], a river, the present Brahmaputra. § 268 (Varuṇasabhāv.): II, **9**, 374 (*mahānadaḥ*, among the rivers present in the palace of Varuṇa).—§ 280 (Bhīmasena): II, **30**, 1100 (in the east; = the ocean, BR.).—§ 295 (Dyūtap.): II, **52**, 1864 (*L°am abhitaç ca ye*; name of a mountain, Nīl.). Cf. Lohita, Lohityā.

Lauhitya[3], a tīrtha. § 370 (Tīrthayātrāp.): III, **85**, 8144. — § 733*u* (Punarāvartanandā): XIII, **25**, 1732. Cf. Lauhitya[2].

Laumaharshaṇi = Ugraçravas, q.v.

Lavāḥ, pl. = Çiva (1000 names[2]).

Lavaṇa[1], an Asura (according to Nīl.). § 39 (Rāmaṇīyaka): I, **27**, 1305 (had been seen on the island Rāmaṇīyaka).

Lavaṇa[2], a Rākshasa. § 730*g* (Upamanyu): XIII, **14**σ, 861 (*°sya rakshasaḥ*, had been slain by Māndhātṛ with the çūla of Çiva).

Lavaṇa[3] = Çiva (1000 names[2]).

Lavaṇāçva, a ṛshi. § 324 (Dvaitavanapr.): III, **26***a*, 986 (waited upon Yudhishṭhira).

***lavaṇajala** ("the sea of salt water"): I, 660, 1186 (*sāgaram*); cf. VI, 190, 406.

***lavaṇāmbhas** (do.): I, 619, 1131, 1168; III, 12787, 16239; XVII, 44.

Laya = Çiva (1000 names[2]).

Lekha, pl. (*°āḥ*), a class of gods. § 730 (Ānuçāsanik.): XIII, **18**λλ, 1371 (only B., C. has *Lokāḥ*).

Lelihāna = Çiva: XIV, 198.

Likhita, an ancient ṛshi, brother of Çaṅkha. § 266 (Çakrasabhāv.): II, **7**, 292 (*Çaṅkhaç ca Likhitaç ca*, in the palace of Indra).—§ 628 (Rājadh.): XII, **23**, 668, 670, 671, 678, 679, 686, 690, (693) (the story of *L.*'s being punished).—§ 746 (Ānuçāsanik.): XIII, **56**, 3320 (*Çaṅkhaç ca L°as tathā*, ascended to heaven by making gifts of sesame seed).—§ 767 (do.): XIII, **137***a*, 6263 (king Sudyumna attained to blessed regions by having caused *L.* to be punished, cf. § 628). Cf. Brahmarshi.

Lilādhya, a son of Viçvāmitra. § 721*b* (Viçvāmitrop.): XIII, **4**β, 252.

Līlāyudha, v. Nīlāyudha.

***liṅga**, the Phallus of Çiva. VII, 9485, 9486, 9489, 9616, 9617, 9625, 9631; X, 780, 782; XIII, 824 (?), 1255 (Çiva's 1000 names[2]), 7512, 7516, 7517, 7518.

Liṅgādhyaksha = Çiva (1000 names[2]).

Lobha = Çiva (1000 names[1]).

Loha, pl. (*°āḥ*), a people. § 279 (Arjuna): II, **27**, 1033 (in the north, vanquished by Arjuna on his digvijaya).

Lohajaṅgha, pl. (*°āḥ*), a people. § 294 (Dyūtap.): II, **50**, 1804 (living in the palace of Yudhishṭhira as bondsmen).

Lohājavaktra, a warrior of Skanda. § 615*u* (Skanda): IX, **45**η, 2577.

Lohamekhalā, a matṛ. § 615*u* (Skanda): IX, **46**θ, 2636, 2639 (also B.).

Lohatāriṇī, a river. § 574 (Jambūkh.): VI, **9**λ, 326 (so C., B. has *Lohi[a]tāraṇīm*).

Lohita[1], a serpent. § 268 (Varuṇasabhāv.): II, **9**, 360 (in the palace of Varuṇa).

Lohita[2] (a country, BR.; a king, PCR.). § 279 (Arjuna): II, **27**, 1025 (in the north, conquered by Arjuna on his digvijaya).

Lohita[3], a river (= Brahmaputra?). § 775 (Ānuçāsanik.): XIII, **166***a*, 7647 (*mahānadaḥ*). Cf. Lauhitya, Lohityā.

Lohita(ḥ) udadhi(ḥ) ("the bloody ocean"). § 498 (Skandotpatti): III, **226**, 14366 (*lohitasyodadheḥ kanyā*, nursed Skanda).—§ 502 (Manushyagrahak.): III, **230**, 14494 (do., named Lohitāyani and worshipped on kadamba trees). Cf. III, 14269 (*lohitodo Varuṇālayaḥ*), 14524 (*lohitode*).

Lohitāksha[1], name of a sūta. § 62 (Sarpasattra): I, **56**, †2119 (*Paurāṇikaḥ*).—§ 68 (Āstīka): I, **58**, 2177 (*sūtāya sthapataye*, had announced that a brahman, viz. Āstīka, would interrupt the sacrifice, cf. I, 2029). Cf. Sūta.

Lohitāksha[2], a companion of Skanda. § 615*u* (Skanda): IX, **45**, 2526 (given to Skanda by Brahmán).

Lohitāksha[3] = Çiva (1000 names[2]). — Do.[4] = Vishṇu (1000 names).

Lohitākshī, a mātṛ. § 615*u* (Skanda): IX, **46**θ, 2640, 2642.

Lohitāṅga[1] ("the red-limbed," i.e. the planet Mars [Aṅgāraka]). § 574 (Jambūkh.): VI, **3**, 86 (*Brahmarāçiṃ samāvṛtya L°o vyavasthitaḥ*, omens).—§ 600 (Ghaṭotkacavadhap.): VII, **166**, 7408 (? *nipapāta L°a ivākāçād dīptaraçmir yadṛcchayā*, = the Sun, PCR.).

Lohitāṅga[2] = Sūrya (the sun): VII, 8877; IX, 3113 (? *°āv iva*).

Lohitāntargatā dṛshṭiḥ = Çiva (1000 names[1]).

Lohitāraṇī, v. Lohatāriṇī.

Lohitāyani ("daughter of the bloody [ocean]"). § 502 (Manushyagrahak.): III, **230**, 14494 (*Lohitasyodadheḥ kanyā dhātrī Skandasya sā smṛtā | L°ir ity evaṃ kadambe sā hi pūjyate*).

Lohityā, a river. § 574 (Jambūkh.): VI, **9**λ, 343 (in Bhāratavarsha). Cf. Lohita, Lauhitya.

Loka = Çiva (1000 names[2]).

Loka, pl. (*°āḥ*), a class of gods. § 730 (Ānuçāsanik.): XIII, **18**λλ, 1371 (only C., B. has *Lekhāḥ*).

Lokabandhu = Vishṇu (1000 names).

Lokabhāvana[1] = Agni: III, 14112; IX, 2744.

Lokabhāvana[2] = Brahmán: I, 7710; III, 15943; V, 3710, 4300; IX, 2671; XIII, 791 (*B*°); XIV, 1365.

Lokabhāvana[3] = Çiva: I, 8129 (*Çaṅkaraḥ*); III, 1594.

Lokabhāvana[4] = Kṛshṇa (Vishṇu): III, 10959 (Vishṇu as the boar); XII, 13226.

***lokabhāvana,** adj.: IX, 2945 (*Sārasvataḥ*), 2957 (sc. Dadhīca).

Lokabhāvanabhāvajña = Kṛshṇa: VI, 3038.

Lokacārin = Çiva (1000 names [2]).

Lokadhāman = Vishṇu: XII, 13489.

Lokadhātṛ[1] = Brahmán: VIII, 1574.—Do.[2] = Çiva (1000 names [2]).

Lokādhipati = Indra: XIV, †259.

Lokādhishṭhāna(m) = Vishṇu (1000 names).

Lokādhyaksha[1] = Brahmán: XII, 12925 (°*tvaṃ*).—Do.[2] = Vishṇu (1000 names).

Lokādikartṛ = Brahmán (?): XII, 2410.

Lokādinidhaneçvara = Brahmán: VII, 2068.

Lokādya = Vishṇu: XII, 13487.

Lokaguru[1] = Brahmán: I, 57, †7278; III, 12811 (?), 13560; IX, 2439; X, 779; XII, 13058 (*B*°), 13083; XIII, 4136 (*B*°), 6401 (?).

Lokaguru[2] = Çiva: X, 783; XII, 10122 (*Tryakshaḥ*).

Lokaguru[3] = Daksha: IX, 2045.

Lokaguru[4] = Kṛshṇa (Vishṇu): VI, †2603.

lokaguru, said of Duryodhana: IX, 3644.

Lokahita = Vishṇu (1000 names).

Lokakārin = Brahmán: XII, 13595.

Lokakartṛ[1] = Brahmán: I, 2494; III, 10004 (*B*°); XII, 13100.

Lokakartṛ[2] = Kṛshṇa (Vishṇu): III, 13556, 13558; VII, 6468; XII, 1874, 12716.

Lokakartṛ[3] = Çiva (1000 names [2]).

Lokakṛt[1] = Brahmán: VII, 2061; XII, 6920 (*B*°), 11390 (?); XIII, 1103.

Lokakṛt[2] = Kṛshṇa (Vishṇu): XII, 13146.

Lokāloka ("world and non-world"): IX, 2741 (°*vināçe* = Agni?); XIII, 802 (°*āntareshu*), 816 (°*āntakāraṇaṃ*, i.e. Çiva).

Lokānāṃ kīrtivardhanaḥ = Vishṇu (1000 names).

Lokānāṃ mātaraḥ, i.e. the kine: XIII, 5981.

Lokānāṃ patiḥ = Çiva: VII, 9534.

Lokanātha[1] = Brahmán: XIII, †4918, †4941.

Lokanātha[2] = Çiva: VII, 9580; XIII, 930.

Lokanātha[3] = Kṛshṇa (Vishṇu): II, 9; III, 470; VI, †2605; VII, 380 (*Nārāyaṇaḥ*); XII, 1863, †12698 (?), 13609 (*Nārāyaṇāt*); XIII, 6942 (Vishṇu's 1000 names), 7027 (do.); XIV, 2021; XVI, 137.

Lokanātha[4] = Skanda: III, 14646.

***lokanātha,** said of princes: IX, 86 (i.e. Bhīshma); XII, 1976 (i.e. Yudhishṭhira).

Lokanātha, dual (°*au*) = Nara and Nārāyaṇa: XII, 12660.

Lokapa ("world-protector"), pl. (°*āḥ*): I, 3651 (°*ā Brahmaṇo ye*).

Lokapāla (do.), pl. (°*āḥ*): I, 433, 8176 (*caturthaṃ L°ānāṃ*, i.e. Varuṇa); II, 446; III, 518, 1444, 1680 (i.e. Varuṇa, Kubera, Yama, and Indra), 1710 (gave weapons to Arjuna), 1711, 1714, 2127 (*sāgnikāḥ*, set out for the svayaṃvara of Damayantī), 2132 (i.e. Indra, Agni, Varuṇa, and Yama), 2164, 2171, 2180, 2182, 2211, 2225, 2239, 2249 (°*same*), 2367, 8213, 11746 (*iva*), 11996 (*Vaivasvatādibhiḥ*), 12024, 12286, 12305, 14653 (°*opamān*), 14964 (*iva*), 15807, 15894 (°*opamān*), 16188 (°*samaḥ*); V, †513 (i.e. Kubera, Yama, Soma, and Varuṇa), 520, 1994, 4061 (°*opameshu*), 4423, 7560 (°*samaiḥ*); VI, 3324 (°*opamaiḥ*); VII, 4448 (°*opamaiḥ*), 8219; VIII, †4056, †4646 (*sa-Çakrāḥ*); IX, 3453 (*api*); XII, 4506, 6187, 7191 (*caturṇāṃ*), 7338, 12174, 12202 (*Çakrapurogāḥ*), 12318 (*catvāraḥ*); XIII, 6351, 7177, †7384 (*trayaḥ*, identified with Kṛshṇa); XV, 294 (°*samāḥ*), 618 (°*opamaiḥ*); XVIII, 215.

Lokapāla (do.), sg. Names of single Lokapālas:—

Agni: I, 8352, 8438.

Kubera: I, 7854 (°*niveçanaṃ*); III, 15886 (°*tvaṃ*); V, †511 (*K*°); IX, 2757 (°*tvaṃ*).

Varuṇa: V, 3527 (*Apāṃ patiḥ*); XIII, 7249.

Yama: VII, 2107 (*Y*°); XII, 4721.

Lokapāla[1] = Çiva (1000 names [2]).—Do.[2] = Skanda: III, 14640.

Lokapālasabhākhyāna(m) ("description of the palaces of the Lokapālas"). § 11 (Parvasaṅgr.): I, **2**, 408 (i.e. Lokapālasabhākhyānaparvan).

[Lokapālasabhākhyānaparvan] ("the section containing the description of the palaces of the Lokapālas," the 21st of the minor parvans of the Mahābhārata). (Cf. Lokapālasabhākhyāna.)—§ 265: While the *Pāṇḍavas* were sitting in that palace, with the great *Gandharvas*, there came unto them the *devarshi Nārada* (his accomplishments are enumerated at great length), having wandered over the different worlds, accompanied by the *ṛshis Pārijāta, Raivata, Sumukta*, and *Saumya*. *Nārada* informed *Yudhishṭhira* about religion, pleasure, and profit, in the form of questions about his conduct. By following his advice *Yudhishṭhira* conquered the whole earth (II, **5**). *Yudhishṭhira* answered that he observed all those rules. Then he asked *Nārada* if he had ever seen a palace like his. *Nārada* (*Brahmarshiḥ*, v. 281) replied that no palace among men was like his, but that he would describe unto him the palaces of *Pitṛrāja* (i.e. *Yama*), *Varuṇa, Indra*, the dweller on *Kailāsa* (i.e. *Kubera*), and *Brahmán*, always worshipped by gods, *Pitṛs* and *Sādhyas*, etc. (II, **6**).—§ 266: *Çakrasabhāvarṇana* (q.v.).—§ 267: *Yamasabhāvarṇana* (q.v.).—§ 268: *Varuṇasabhāvarṇana* (q.v.).—§ 269: *Vaiçravaṇasabhāvarṇana* (q.v.).—§ 270: *Brahmasabhāvarṇana* (q.v.).—§ 271: *Yudhishṭhira* said: It appears that almost all the monarchs are in the sabhā of *Yama*—the *Nāgas, Daityas*, rivers, and oceans in that of *Varuṇa*—the *Yakshas, Guhyakas, Rākshasas, Gandharvas, Apsarases*, and *Çiva* in that of *Kubera*—the great *ṛshis*, and gods, and *çāstras* in that of *Pitāmaha* (i.e. *Brahmán*); and in that of *Çakra* (i.e. *Indra*) gods, *Gandharvas* and various *ṛshis*, but only one king, the *rājarshi Hariçcandra* (*b*); this is explained by *Nārada*. *Pāṇḍu*, beholding the good fortune of *Hariçcandra*, had asked *Nārada* to tell *Yudhishṭhira* to subjugate the whole earth and then perform a *rājasūya*. Thereby also *Pāṇḍu* and his ancestors would go to the region of *Indra*. *Brahmarakshases*, that destroy the sacrifices, always look for opportunities of obstructing it. Then *Nārada* went away to the city of the *Dāçārhas*, accompanied by the *ṛshis* with whom he had come (II, **12**).

Lokaparāyaṇa = Kṛshṇa: XII, 1553.

Lokapati = Brahmán: I, 3593 (*Prajāpatiḥ*).

Lokapitāmaha[1] = Brahmán, q v.

Lokapitāmaha[2] = Daksha: I, 3130.

lokapitaraḥ, said of the seven ṛshis: XII, 12748.

Lokapradhāna = Vishṇu (1000 names).

Lokasākshin[1] = Mahāpurusha (Mahāpurushastava).
Lokasākshin[2] = Kṛshṇa (Vishṇu): XII, 13249, †13447.
Lokasambhava = Brahmán: XIII, 940 (*B*°).
Lokasāraṅga, Lokasvāmin = Vishṇu (1000 names).
Lokasrashṭṛ = Brahmán: VIII, 1531 (*Pitāmahaḥ*).—Do.[2] = Çiva: VIII, 1573 (*Maheçvaraḥ*).
Lokasyādhipati(ḥ) = Çiva: XII, 10464.
Lokātman = Kṛshṇa (Vishṇu): XII, 1657 [13433 (*ātmā lokasya*)].
Lokatrayāçraya = Vishṇu (1000 names).
Lokatrayeça = Indra: I, 811 (*Purandarāya*).
Lokatrayeçvara = Çiva: VII, 9566.
***lokayajña**, a kind of sacrifice: X, 790, 791 (pl.).
Lokayoni = Kṛshṇa (Vishṇu): XII, †13448.
Lokeça[1] = Agni: I, 930.
Lokeça[2] = Brahmán: VII, 2086, 3754 (?); XII, 9199, 10192, 10194.
Lokeça[3] = Çiva: VIII, 1458; XII, 12174; XIII, 3997.
Lokeçvara[1] = Brahmán: III, 10113 (= Viçvakarman); XI, 47 (? °*parā gatiḥ*, or read: *lokeçvara* (voc.) = Dhṛtarashṭra).
Lokeçvara[2] = Çiva: VIII, 1567.
Lokeçvara[3] = Sūrya (the sun): III, 16951.
Lokeçvara, pl. (°*āḥ*): VIII, 1485 (= *lokapālāḥ* ?).
Lokeçvareçvara[1] = Brahmán: XII, 9175.
Lokeçvareçvara[2] = Indra: XII, 1720 (*Pākaçāsanaḥ*).
Lokoddhāra, a tīrtha. § 364 (Tīrthayātrāp.): III, **83**, 6015.
Lomaça[1], a ṛshi. § 11 (Parvasaṅgr.): I, **2**, 437, 438.—§ 327 (Draupadīparitāpav.): III, **31**, 1171.—§ 339 (Indralokābhigamanap.): III, **47**, 1879 (*maharshiḥ*, saw Arjuna in the abode of Indra), 1884, 1910 (is ordered by Indra to accompany the Pāṇḍavas on their tīrthayātrā), 1912.—§ 376 (Tīrthayātrāp.): III, **85**, 8266 (*maharshiḥ*, do.).—§ 378 (do.): III, **91**, 8407 (*ṛshiḥ*, came to the Pāṇḍavas), 8431 (*maharshiḥ*), **92**, (8432), 8449, 8457; **93**, 8459 (*ṛshinā*), 8471, 8472, 8474, 8482; **94**, 8488, (8489).—§ 382 (Tīrthayātrāp., Agastyop.): III, **96**, 8541 (*L.* accompanied the Pāṇḍavas and pointed out to them the different tīrthas, and told their various legends), (8543); **97**, (8570); **98**, (8595), (8599), (8604), (8610), (8614); **98**, (8615).—§ 383 (do., Paraçurāma): III, **99**, (8649), 8654, (8656), (8670).—§ 384 (do., Agastyop.): III, **100**, (8690); **101**, (8714); **102**, (8737).—§ 385 (do., Vindhya): III, **104**, (8782).—§ 386 (do., Agastyop.): III, **105**, (8805); **106**, (8825).—§ 387 (do., Sagara): III, **106**, (8831); **107**, (8849).—§ 388 (do., Asamañjas): III, **107**, (8888).—§ 389 (do., Gaṅgāvataraṇa): III, **108**, (9920), (9940); **109**, (9947).—§ 390 (Tīrthayātrāp.): III, **110**, 9974, (9974), (9989).—§ 391 (do., Ṛshyaçṛṅga): III, **110**, (9999); **111**, (10027), (10040).—§ 392 (do., Mahendrācalagamana): III, **114**, (10098), 10108, (10110).—§ 393 (do., Paraçurāma): III, **115**, 10126.—§ 400 (Tīrthayātrāp.): III, **118**, †10229.—§ 402 (do.): III, **120**, †10289. —§ 403 (do.): III, **121**, (10291).—§ 404 (do.): III, **121**, 10307 (*ṛshiḥ*), (10309).—§ 405 (Tīrthayātrāp., Sukanyop.): III, **122**, (10316), (10341); **123**, (10345); **124**, (10371), (10383); **125**, (10396).—§ 407 (do., Māndhātrup.): III, **126**, (10426), 10469 (*maharshiṃ*).—§ 408 (do., Jantūp.): III, **127**, (10471); **128**, (10492), (10508).—§ 409 (do., Plakshāvataraṇag.): III, **129**, (10513), 10531, (10532).—§ 410 (do., do.): III, **130**, (10536).—§ 411 (Tīrthayātrāp., Çyenakapotīya): III, **131**, (10587).—§ 412 (do., Ashṭāvakrīya): III, **132**, 10603, (10603); **134**, (†10657), (†10670), (10682), (†10687).—§ 413 (Tīrthayātrāp.): III, **135**, (10692).—§ 414 (do., Yavakrītop.): III, **135**, (10703), (10714), (10720), (10732).—§ 416 (do., do.): III, **135**, (10751); **136**, (10752); **137**, (10772), (10790).—§ 417 (do., do.): III, **138**, (10791), (10801), (10801), (10809), (10818).—§ 418 (Tīrthayātrāp.): III, **139**, (10820), †10837.—§ 419 (do., Gandhamādanapr.): III, **140**, 10845, (10861).—§ 421 (do., do.): III, **142**, (10899), 10909.—§ 422 (do., do.): III, **142**, 10912.—§ 422 *bis* (do., Varāhāvatāra): III, **142**, 10932, (10961).—§ 423 (Tīrthayātrāp., Gandhamādanapr.): III, **143**, 10978; **145**, 11022.—§ 433 (do., Saugandhikāharaṇa): III, **155**, 11417, 11426 (*maharshiṃ*).—§ 434 (do., do.): III, **156**, 11440.—§ 435 (Jaṭāsuravadhap.): III, **157**, 11458 (°*prabhṛtīn . . . maharshīn*). — § 436 (Yakshayuddhap.): III, **158**, 11537, 11558 (*mahān ṛshiḥ*).—§ 437 (do.): III, **160**, 11671.—§ 448 (Ājagarap.): III, **176**, 12337 (took his leave from the Pāṇḍavas and went to heaven).—§ 546 (Kuṇḍalāharaṇap.): III, **300**, 16919.—§ 620 (Çrāddhap.): XI, **26**, 776 (*Devarshiḥ*, had given spiritual vision—*divyaṃ cakshuḥ*—to Yudhishṭhira).—§ 637 (Rājadh.): XII, **47**η, 1594 (among the ṛshis who surrounded Bhīshma on his arrow-bed).—§ 766 (Ānuçāsanik.): XIII, **129**, (6087).—§ 770 (do.): XIII, **151**κ, 7121.—§ 775 (do.): XIII, **166**ζ, 7672 (one of the ṛshis of the north). Cf. Brahmarshi, Devarshi.
Lomaça[2], name of a cat. § 646*b* (Mārjāramūshikasaṃv.): XII, **138**, 4934 (*mārjāraḥ*), 4978, 4987, 5010, 5012, 5025, 5026, 5034, 5036, 5047, 5086, (5096).
Lomaharshaṇa, a Sūta, father of Ugraçravas. § 26 (Āstīkap.): I, **13**, 1026 (*pitā me*—i.e. Ugraçravas's—*L°ḥ* | *çishyo Vyāsasya*, had related the history of Āstīka to the ṛshis in the Naimisha forest).—§ 264 (Sabhākriyāp.): II, **4a**, 107 (*sasutaḥ*, among the munis who waited upon Yudhishṭhira).—§ 775 (Ānuçāsanik.): XIII, **166**ζ, 7672 (one of the ṛshis of the north). Cf. Sūta.
Lomaharshaṇaputra = Ugraçravas, q.v.
Lomapāda, king of the Aṅgas and father of Çāntā. § 378 (Tīrthayātrāp.): III, **93**, 8465 (*rājarsher L°sya . . . lokān*).—§ 390*d* (Ṛshyaçṛṅga): III, **110**, 9993, 9994 (gave his daughter Çāntā to Ṛshyaçṛṅga, cf. § 391).—§ 391 (Tīrthayātrāp.): III, **110**, 9997 (*rājarshiḥ*).—§ 391 (Ṛshyaçṛṅga): III, **110**, 10009 (*sakhā Daçarathasya . . . Aṅgānām īçvaraḥ*); **113**, 10080 (when there was a drought in the country of the Aṅgas *L.* caused Ṛshyaçṛṅga to come, then it rained, and *L.* gave his daughter Çāntā in marriage to Ṛshyaçṛṅga).—§ 677 (Mokshadh.): XII, **235**, 8609 (*rājarshiḥ*, obtained the fruition of all wishes by giving his daughter Çāntā to Ṛshyaçṛṅga).—§ 767 (Ānuçāsanik.): XIII, **137**, 6269 (do.). Cf. Aṅgādhipati, Aṅgapati, Aṅgarāja (see Aṅga, pl.).
Lopāmudrā, daughter of the Vidarbha king and wife of Agastya. § 11 (Parvasaṅgr.): I, **2**, 442.—§ 382 (Agastyop.): III, **96**, 8563 (created by Agastya as the daughter of the Vidarbha king); **97**, 8571, 8574, 8576, 8577, 8582 (married to Agastya), 8589, (8590), (8592); **99**, 8633, (8634), (8637) (mother of Dṛḍhasyu or Idhmavāha).—§ 391 (Ṛshyaçṛṅga): III, **110**, 10092 (*L°ā vā yathā hy Agastyam*).—§ 410 (Plakshāvataraṇag.): III, **130**, 10541 (*etat Sindhor mahātīrthaṃ yatrāgastyam arindama* | *L°ā samāgamya bhartāram avṛṇīta vai*, cf. § 382).—§ 551 (Kīçakavadhap.): IV, **21**, 654 (°*ā tathā bhīru vayorūpasamanvitā* | *Agastyam anvayād dhitvā kāmān sarvān amānushān*). Cf. Vaidarbhī.
Lubdha = Çiva (1000 names[1]).

M

Macakruka, name of a Yaksha and of a tīrtha belonging to him. § 362 (Tīrthayātrāp.): III, **83**, 5079 (*dvārapālaṃ . . . Yakshaṃ samabhivādya*, only B., C. has *Maṅkanakaṃ*).—§ 368 (do.): III, **83**, 7070 (*abhivādya tato Yakshaṃ dvārapālaṃ M°ṃ*, at Koṭitīrtha (?)).—§ 369 (Kurukshetra): III, **83**, †7078 (v. Arantuka).—§ 615*kk* (Kuruksketrak.): IX, **53**, †3032 (do., C. has by error °*krak*°).

Maçaka, pl. (°*āḥ*), a people in Çākadvīpa. § 575*b* (Çākadvīpa): VI, **11**δ, 436, 437 (are kshatriyas).

Mada ("intoxication," personif.), an Asura. § 405 (Sukanyop.): III, **124**, 10389 (*kṛtyā . . . mahāsuraḥ*, created by Cyavana, description); **125**, 10396 (frightened Indra), 10403 (was distributed in drinks, women, dice, and hunting), 10404.—§ 772*n* (Cyavana): XIII, **157**, 7317 (*o: Cyavana* created *M.* (description) as an enemy of Indra), 7320, 7322 (was distributed in dice, hunting, drinks, and women).—§ 772*p* (Kapa, pl.): XIII, **158**, 7327, 7329.—§ 778*b* (Samvartta-Maruttīya): XIV, **9**, †251 (*Asuraṃ*, description, all. to § 405). Cf. Asura, Dānava.

Madadhāra, a king (?). § 280 (Bhīmasena): II, **30**, 1083 (*mahīdharaṃ* (a mountain ?), vanquished by Bhīmasena on his digvijaya in the east). Cf. Mahīdhara.

Maḍaka, pl. (°*āḥ*), a people. § 578 (Bhīshmavadhap.): VI, **50**π, 2083 (in the army of Yudhishṭhira, only in C., B. has *Mārutāḥ*).

***Madana**[1] = Kāma: I, 951; III, 1829, 10324.

Madana[2] = Çiva (1000 names[2]).

Madayantī, wife of king Kalmāshapāda (Mitrasaha, Saudāsa). § 188*b* (Pāṇḍu): Commanded by her husband, *M.*, the wife of Saudāsa Kalmāshapāda obtained from the ṛshi Vasishṭha the son Açmaka (cf. § 229): I, **122**, 4736.—§ 229 (Vasishṭhop.): I, **182**, 6910 (on account of his being himself cursed, Kalmāshapāda caused *M.* to go to Vasishṭha, who begat a son on her, cf. § 188*b*).—§ 677 (Mokshadh.): XII, **235**, 8604 (having given *M.* to Vasishṭha, Mitrasaha ascended to heaven; C. has by error *Damayantīṃ*).—§ 767 (Ānuçāsanik.): XIII, **137***a*, 6262 (do.).—§ 784*b* (Uttaṅka): XIV, **57**, 1680; **58**, 1695, 1708 (Uttaṅka obtained the ear-rings of *M.*).

Madgura ("pearl-fisher"), name of a caste: XIII, 2583 (*dāsaṃ nāvopajīvanaṃ*).

Mādhava[1] ("belonging to the tribe of the Madhus") = Balarama: V, 44, 131 (*Baladeve*); IX, 2126, 2131, 2269, 2725, 3006, 3068, 3069.

Mādhava[2] (do.) = Kṛshṇa Vāsudeva: I, †171, †197, 546, 7360, 7888, 7984 (*svasāraṃ M°sya*, i.e. Subhadrā), 7994, 8078 (*Pārtha-M°au*), 8171, 8199, 8275; II, 643, 1216, 1223, 1362, 1431, 1559; III, 733, 13006; IV, 1434 (*K*°); V, †9, 133, 141, 2526, 2539 (*sarvalokamaheçvaraṃ*), 2563, 2583, 2622, 2655, 2657, 2665, 2766, 2820, 2844, 2845, 2856, 2959, 2988, 2990, 3027, 3042 (*Vṛshṇirāshṭrasya bhartā goptā ca*), 3116, 3122, 3187, 3198, 3202, 3250, 3291, 3296, 3306, 3335, 3368, 3385, 4197, 4247, 4249, 4255, 4406, 4433, 4452, 4655, 4760, 4763, 4778, 4786, 4804, 4844, 4854, 4861, 4874, 4882, 5382 (?); VI, 772, 843, 868, 2048, 2172, 2556, 3566, 3741, 4334, 4841, 4855, 4859, 4872, 4875, 4926, 4929, 4931, 4936, 4977, 4993 (? *saha-M°āḥ*), 5755; VII, 112, 395, 1222, 2490, 2527 (*svasrīyo M°sya*, i.e. Abhimanyu), 2715, 2778, 2832, 2943, 2959, 2964, 3280 (*Vāsudevaṃ*), 3703, 3825, 3859, 5249, 5873, 5948, 6342, 6472, 7765 (*Pāṇḍava-M°au*, i.e. Arjuna and Kṛshṇa), 8330, 8462, 8463; VIII, 634, 645 (°-*Pāṇḍavau*), 1091, 1092, 2816 (°-*Pāṇḍavau*), 2899, 2955, 3549 (*Govinda*), 3574, 3578, 3794, 3796, 4475 (°-*Pāṇḍavau*), 4483, 4489, †4652, 4654, 4956, 5017 (°-*Phālgunau*), 5021 (°-*Pāṇḍavau*); IX, 345, 346, 693 (°*vacaḥ*), 811 (*K*°), 1290, 1291, 1292, 1312, 1317, 1318, 1321, 1455, 1460, 1747, 1907, 1953, 3458, 3525, 3528, 3535, 3572; XI, 355, 444, 496, 509, 516, 519, 532, 538, 547, 550, 560, 602, 611, 654, 659, 661, 665, 673, 677, 691, 717, 722, 738; XII, 10, 894, 1557, 1577, 1580, 1690, 1897, 1903, 1948, 3053, 13359 (*devaḥ*), 13709; XIII, 599, 698, 702, 706, 711, 968, 1122, 1290, 2030, 2138, †3459, 4655, 4662, 5374, 6349, 6895, 6911, 6957 (= Vishṇu, 1000 names), 6967 (do.), 7027 (do.); XIV, 413, 424, 576, †1533, 1544, 1558, 1953, 1974, 2563; XVI, 100, 101.

Mādhava[3] (do.) = Kṛtavarman: VII, 7382, 7390; IX, 1116.

Mādhava[4] (do.) = Sātyaki: III, †10281, †10286; V, †1858, 2316 (*Çaineyaḥ*), 5882 (*S*°); VI, 3614, 3619, 3621, 4624, 4633, 4765, 4805, 5141, 5142, 5143, 5145, 5146, 5148, 5153; VII, 3619, 4146, 4188, 4200, 4229, 4249, 4254, 4255, 4258, 4278, 4365, 4402, 4477 (°-*Pārthābhyāṃ*, i.e. *S.* and Arjuna), 4583, 4606, 4615, 4628, 4661, 4667, 4670, 4797, 4852, 4942, 4984 (°-*Pāṇḍavau*, i.e. *S.* and Arjuna), 5015, 5100, 5110, 5889, 5891, 6418, 7231, 7238, 7668, 7683, 7686, 7694, 7701, 8647 (*Kuru-M°au*, i.e. Duryodhana and *S.*), 8675, 9151, 9179; IX, 873, 1393 (°*ānīkaṃ*).

Mādhava[5] = Jalasandha: V, 5793 (*J*°; read *Māgadhaḥ*).

Mādhava[6] (VIII, 688), v. Māgadha (= Daṇḍadhāra).

Mādhava[7], name of a month (= Caitra, PCR.; = Vaiçākha, Nīl.). § 371 (Ṛshyaçṛṅga): III, **112**, †10058 (°*māsi*).—§ 416 (Yavakrītop.): III, **136**, 10752 (°*e māsi*).

Mādhava[8], a weapon of Indra. § 444 (Nivātakavaca-yuddhap.): III, **170**, 12122 (*astraṃ . . . dayitaṃ Devarājasya M°ṃ nāma*, employed by Arjuna against the Asuras).

Mādhava, pl. (°*āḥ*), a tribe = Madhu, pl. § 273 (Rāja-sūyārambhap.): II, **14**, 617.

Mādhavāgrya = Sātyaki: VII, †5827, †5828.

Mādhavarshabha = Kṛshṇa: VI, 4862.

Mādhavasiṃha = Sātyaki: VII, 8662 (*Kuru-M°yoḥ*, i.e. Duryodhana and *S.*).

Mādhavī[1] ("belonging to the tribe of the Madhus") = Subhadra: I, 449.

Mādhavī[2] (do.) = Anantā, the wife of Janamejaya[6]: I, ††3765 (*A*°).

Mādhavī[3] (do.) = Sampriyā, the wife of Vidūratha: I, ††3793 (*S*°).

Mādhavī[4] (do.) = Kuntī: I, 5824.

Mādhavī[5], daughter of Yayāti. § 565 (Gālavacarita): V, **115**, 3930 (Yayāti gave *M.* to Gālava); **116**, 3957, 3958 (mother of Vasumanas); **117**, 3977 (mother of Pratardana); **118**, 3981 (mother of Çibi); **119**, 4010 (mother of Ashṭaka); **120**, 4027.—§ 566 (Yayāti): V, **121**, 4068, 4070, 4072 (her penances). Cf. Yayātijā.

Mādhavī[6], a mātṛ. § 615*u* (Skanda): IX, **46**θ, 2625.

Mādhavīsuta (the son of Mādhavī[5]) = Ashṭaka: V, 4089 (*Kauçikaḥ*).

Mādhavottama[1] = Balarāma: IX, 2726, 3342 (*Baladevaḥ*).

Mādhavottama[2] = Sātyaki: VII, 4049, 4589.

Madhu[1], an ancient king. § 267 (Yamasabhāv.): II, **8**, 327 (in the palace of Yama).

Madhu[2], an Asura, slain by Kṛshṇa (Vishṇu). § 317*b* (Kṛshṇa Vāsudeva): III, **12**, 498 (°-*Kaiṭabhau*, tried to slay

Brahmán).—§ 476 (Dhundhumārop.): III, **202**, 13532 (°-*Kaiṭabhayoḥ putro Dhundhur nāma*).—§ 477 (do.): III, **203**, 13562 (°*uç ca Kaiṭabhaç ca*), 13565 (°-*Kaiṭabhayoḥ*), (13573) (°-*Kaiṭabhau*), (13580) (°-*Kaiṭabhayoḥ*, *M.* and Kaiṭabha terrified Brahmán, but were slain by Madhusūdana, i.e. Kṛshṇa (Vishṇu)).—§ 478 (do.): III, **204**, 13590 (°-*Kaiṭabhayoḥ putro Dhundhuḥ*), 13623 (°-*Kaiṭabhayoḥ sutaḥ*, i.e. Dhundhu).—§ 567 (Bhagavadyānap.): V, **130**ζ, 4414 (*ekārṇave ca svapatā*—sc. *Kṛshṇena—nihatau M°-Kaiṭabhau*, cf. § 477).—§ 581 (Bhīshmavadhap.): VI, **67**, 3025 (*karṇasrotodbhavañ ca M°ṃ nāma mahāsuraṃ . . . Brahmaṇo 'pacitiṃ kurvāñjaghāna Purushottamaḥ*, i.e. Kṛshṇa, therefore Kṛshṇa is called Madhusūdana, cf. § 477 and § 664).—§ 615*ee* (Ādityatīrtha): IX, **49**, 2850 (°-*Kaiṭabhau*, had been slain by Vishṇu, cf. § 477).—§ 615 (Gadāyuddhap.): IX, **55**, 3106 (*sadṛçau tau*—i.e. Bhīmasena and Duryodhana —*M°-Kaiṭabhayor yudhi*).—§ 664 (Mokshadh.): XII, **207**, 7531 (*mahāsuraḥ; b:* After Brahmán had sprung from the primeval lotus, *M.* was born from the attribute of darkness (*tamasā pūrvajaḥ*). In order to gratify Brahmán (*Brahmaṇo 'pacitiṃ kurvan*), Kṛshṇa (*Purushottamaḥ*) slew *M.* engaged even then in the fierce act [of slaying Brahmán]. Therefore all gods, Dānavas, and men call Kṛshṇa Madhusūdana (cf. § 581)).—§ 673*b* (Bali-Vāsavasaṃv.): XII, **227***a*, 8265 (among the Daityas and Dānavas who had ruled the earth).—§ 717*b* (Nārāyaṇīya): XII, **348**, 13474 (sprung from a drop in the primeval lotus; originated from *tamas*), 13509 (°-*Kaiṭabhau*, had robbed the Vedas which Vishṇu recovered), 13519 (*rajastamovishṭatanū tāv ubhau M°-Kaiṭabhau* | *Brahmaṇo 'pacitiṃ kurvan jaghāna Madhusūdanaḥ*). Cf. Asura, Asurendra, dual, Dānava, dual, Dānavendra, dual, Kaiṭabha.

Madhu[3] = Çiva (1000 names[2]).—Do.[4] = Vishṇu (1000 names).

Madhu, pl. (°*avaḥ*), a people = the Vṛshṇis. § 277 (Jarāsandhavadhap.): II, **22**, 888 (*avadhyaṃ M°bhiḥ*, sc. *Jarāsandhaṃ*).—§ 452 (Mārkaṇḍeyas.): III, **183**, †12589 (°*ūnāṃ senā*, will assist the Pāṇḍavas).

Madhucchanda, a brahman. § 677 (Mokshadh.): XII, **245**β, 8899 (had observed renunciation).—§ 721*b* (Viçvāmitrop.): XIII, **4**β, 249 (son of Viçvāmitra).

Madhuçcyutānām agrapā(ḥ) = Çiva (1000 names[1]).

Madhūdvaha = Sātyaki: VII, 8804.

Madhughātin ("the slayer of Madhu") = Kṛshṇa (Vishṇu): X, 750.

Madhuhan (do.) = do.: III, †12571; V, 2563; VII, 8257; XIII, 6814; XIV, 1996.

Madhu-Kaiṭabhahan ("the slayer of Madhu and Kaiṭabha") = Vishṇu (Nārāyaṇa, Kṛshṇa): XII, 13445.

Madhukalocana = Çiva (1000 names[2]).

Madhukumbhā, a mātṛ. § 615*u* (Skanda): IX, **46**θ, 2637.

Madhulikā, a mātṛ. § 615*u* (Skanda): IX, **46**θ, 2637.

Madhumatta, pl. (°*āḥ*), a people. § 574 (Jambūkh.): VI, **9**μ, 360 (in Bhāratavarsha).

Madhunihan ("the slayer of Madhu") = Kṛshṇa (Vishṇu): III, 740 (*Hariḥ*).

Madhunisūdana ("the destroyer of Madhu") = Kṛshṇa (Vishṇu): III, 1896 (*Vishṇuḥ*).

Madhuparka, a Suparṇa, son of Garuḍa. § 564 (Mātalīyop.): V, **101**β, 3599 (enumeration).

Madhupravīra[1] = Balarāma: V, †40.—Do.[2] = Kṛshṇa: V, †2509.

Madhura, a warrior of Skanda. § 615*u* (Skanda): IX, **45**η, 2573.

Madhurā (XII, 3737), *v.* Mathurā.

Madhurasvanā, an Apsaras. § 336 (Indralokābhigamanap.): III, **43***a*, 1785 (danced in the palace of Indra).

Madhusrava, a tīrtha. § 368 (Tīrthayātrāp.): III, **83**, 7020.

Madhusūdana ("the destroyer of Madhu") = Kṛshṇa (Vishṇu): I, 7364, 7887, 8064, 8197, 8323; II, 45, 889, 953, 1354, 1355, 1366, 1578, 1580; III, 473, 482, 494, 496, 511, 520, 524, 537, 539, 576, 581, 585, 593, 892, 1900, 1982, 1985, 4076 (*surāṇāṃ sarveshām ādiḥ*), 8349 (in Dvāravatī), 8353 (*Hariḥ*, do.), 8755 (i.e. Vishṇu (Nārāyaṇa)), 8761 (do.), 13497 (do.), 13569 (do.), 13579 (do.), 13580 (do., slew Madhu and Kaiṭabha); V, 139, 141, 2144, 2261, 2541 (*triyugaṃ*), 2542 (do.), 2563, 2573, 2594, 2620, 2646, 2657, 2717, 2726, 2727, 2780, 2814, 2874, 2882, 2908, 2944, 2967, 2982, 2984, 2995, 3015, 3022, 3026, 3056, 3125, 3143, 3151, 3159, 3165, 3217, 3231, 3242, 3256, 3257, 3272, 3273, 3276, 3286, 3290, 4235, 4239, 4240, 4246, 4438, 4441, 4726, 4730, 4759, 4773, 4774, 4776, 4790, 4807, 4833, 4838, 4841, 4847, 4859, 4860, 5342, 5343, 5349; VI, 865, 878, 882, 1097, 1143, 2171, 3027 (origin of the name), 3045, 4326, 4330, 4333, 4907, 4932, 5547; VII, 1197, 1229 (only B.), 2680, 2684, 2947, 2954, 2957, 3050, 3693, 3857, 6421, 6458, 7804, 7808, 8183, 8187, 8941; VIII, 3608, 3768, 3783, 3784, 3789, 4117, 4364, 4487, †4656, †4678; IX, 1905, 1973, 1980, 1983, 2848 (*K°*), 3405; XI, 343, 452, 455, 480, 548, 557, 618, 668, 705, 711, 726, 731, 746, 749; XII, 16 (*Hariṃ*), 1583, 1601, 1867, 1872, 1896, 1937, 7533 (*Purushottamaḥ*, i.e. Vishṇu, origin of the name), 7546 (= do.), 13129, 13188, 13522 (i.e. Vishṇu, slew Madhu and Kaiṭabha), 13620, 13672 (i.e. Vishṇu); XIII, 622, 689, 722, 2138, 2140, 3469, 4657, 4658, 5377, 6315, 6333, 6359, 6879, 6894, 6957 (= Vishṇu, 1000 names), 7401, 7404, 7443, 7458; XIV, 424, 569, 1484, 1486, 1488, 1521, 1544, 1557, 1961, 1992 (*purāṇarshiḥ*), 2004, 2559; XV, 259; XVI, 23, 79, 100, 160; XVIII, 128.

Madhuvāhinī, a river. § 574 (Jambūkh.): VI, **9**λ, 334.

Madhuvana, name of a forest. § 534 (Hanūmatpratyāgamana): III, **282**, 16223 (*b: M.* was guarded by Vālin and afterwards by Sugrīva, but was pillaged by Hanūmat, etc.).

Madhuvarna, a warrior of Skanda. § 615*u* (Skanda): IX, **45**η, 2574.

Madhuvaṭī, a tīrtha. § 364 (Tīrthayātrāp.): III, **83**, 6064.

Madhuvilā, a river. § 413 (Tīrthayātrāp.): III, **135**, 10692 (= Samaṅgā).

***Madhyadeça** ("the midland country"): XII, 6310, 6372; XIII, 3397.

Madhyadeçīya, adj. ("living in the midland country"): XII, 6294 (*brāhmaṇaḥ*).

Madhyadeçya, pl. (°*āḥ*) (do.). § 571 (Ulūkadūtāgamanap.): V, **160**, †5510 (in the army of Duryodhana); **161**, †5555 (do.).

Madhyama = Çiva: XIII, 1166 (1000 names[2]); XIV, 199.

Madhyamakeya, pl. (°*āḥ*), a people. § 285 (Nakula): II, **32**, 1190 (in the west, vanquished by Nakula on his digvijaya).

Madirā, one of the wives of Vasudeva. § 793 (Mausalap.): XVI, **7**, 194.

Madirāçva[1] = Madirāksha, the brother of Virāṭa. § 561 (Yānasandhip.): V, **57**ζ, 2237 (°*purogamāḥ*, have joined

Yudhishṭhira, only C., B. has *Madirāksha°*).—§ 572 (Rathātirathasaṅkhyānap.): V, **171**, 5907 (among the rathas of the Pāṇḍavas).—§ 604 (Karṇap.): VIII, **6**, 184 (slain).

Madirāçva[2], an ancient king. § 677 (Mokshadh.): XII, **235**, 8608 (*rājarshiḥ*, by having given his daughter to Hiraṇyahasta, *M.* went to regions praised by the very gods).—§ 720*b* (Sudarçanop.): XIII, **2**, 91 (son of Daçāçva), 92 (father of Dyutimat).—§ 767 (Ānuçāsanik.): **137*a***, 6268 (= XII, 8608).

Madirāksha, brother of Virāṭa. § 552 (Goharaṇap.): IV, **31**, 1012 (*Çatānīkād avarajaḥ*); **32**, 1057 (in the rear of the army of Virāṭa); **33**, 1106. Cf. Madirāçva.

Madra[1], pl. (°*āḥ*), a people. § 190*d* (Arjuna): I, **123**, 4796 (will be vanquished by Arjuna).—§ 234 (Svayaṃvarap.): I, **190**, 7092 (*Çalyo M°āṇām īçvaraḥ*).—§ 285 (Nakula): II, **32**, 1196 (*Çākalaṃ . . . M°āṇāṃ puṭabhedanaṃ*).—§ 295 (Dyūtap.): II, **52**, 1870 (°-*Kaikayāḥ*, brought tribute to Yudhishṭhira, B. has *Bh°*).—§ 545 (Pativratāmāhātmyap.): III, **293**, 16620 (ruled by Açvapati).—§ 581 (Bhīshmavadhap.): VI, **61**$^{3}\delta$, 2691 (*saha Kaikayaiḥ*, in the army of Duryodhana, attack Arjuna and Abhimanyu). — § 582 (do.): VI, **71**$^{10}\gamma$, 3132 (°-*Sauvīra-Gāndhāraiḥ*, supported Çakuni), (δ), 3138 (°*āṇām ṛshabheṇa*, sc. *Çalyena*).—§ 583 (do.): VI, **75**δ, 3295 (-*Sauvīra-Kekayaiḥ*, followed Bhagadatta).—§ 589 (Droṇābhishekap.): VII, **7**ζ, 183 (in the rear of Droṇa's array).—§ 590 (do.): VII, **15**, 613 (°*āṇām adhipaṃ*, i.e. Çalya).—§ 592 (Saṃçaptakavadhap.): VII, **20**γ, 799 (°-*Kaikayāḥ*, in the neck of Droṇa's gāruḍavyūha).—§ 599 (Jayadrathavadhap.): VII, **95**, 3529 (°*āṇām īçvaro Çalyaḥ*).—§ 603 (Nārāyaṇāstramokshap.): VII, **193**, 8903 (do.).—§ 604 (Karṇap.): VIII, **9**, 331 (°*āṇām adhipaḥ*, i.e. Çalya).—§ 605 (do.): VIII, **11**, 418 (*Çalyaḥ . . . mahatyā senayā sārdhaṃ M°deçasamutthayā*). **22**$\zeta\zeta$, 864 (attacked the Pāñcālas).—§ 607 (do.): VIII, **44**λ, 2070 (°-*Gāndhārāḥ*, among the peoples who have blameable practices); **45**, 2086 (sg.), 2093 (°*striyaḥ*, are the most debased of women).—§ 608 (do.): VIII, **46**, 2143 (°-*Kaikeyaiḥ*, protected Duryodhana); **47**λ, 2229 (supported Duryodhana); **50**, 2404 (°*āṇām īçvaraḥ*, i.e. Çalya), 2408 (°*āṇām īçvare*, i.e. Çalya); **56**$\rho\rho$, 2762 (°-*Saindhavān*, attacked by Bhīmasena). — § 610 (Çalyap.): IX, **7**, 332 (°*āṇām adhipaḥ*, i.e. Çalya).—§ 611 (do.): IX, **12**, 617 (°*āṇāṃ vṛshabhaṃ Çalyaṃ*); **13**, 674 (°*āṇām adhipaṃ*, i.e. Çalya); **15**, 782 (do.), 784 (°*āṇām adhipasya*, i.e. Çalya); **18**, 957, 973, 984 (attack Yudhishṭhira after the slaughter of Çalya, but are slain by the Pāṇḍavas); **23**, 1205 (°*yodhāḥ*). Cf. Madraka, pl., Mādreya, pl.

Madra[2], pl. (°*āḥ*). § 186 (Vyushitāçvop.): I, **121**, 4714 (the dead Vyushitāçva begat on Bhadrā three Çālvas and four *M.*).

Madrādhipa[1] ("king of the Madras") = Açvapati: III, 16658, 16914 (*A°*).

Madrādhipa[2] (do.) = Çalya, q.v.

Madrādhipati (do.), **Madraja, Madrajanādhipa, Madrajaneçvara** = Çalya, q.v.

Madraka, a prince. § 130 (Aṃçāvat.): I, **67**, 2696 (reborn from the Krodhavaça gaṇa).—Do.[2] = Çalya, q.v.

Madraka, pl. (°*āḥ*), a people = Madra, pl. § 264 (Sabhākriyāp.): II, **4**β, 119 (°*āṇāṃ rājā*, = Çalya?, waited upon Yudhishṭhira).—§ 578 (Bhīshmavadhap.): VI, **51**σ, 2097 (protected Bhīshma).—§ 581 (do.): VI, **61**ϵ, 2695 (°*ānīkān Kekayāṃç ca*), 2698 (pierced by Dhṛshṭadyumna).—§ 607 (Karṇap.): VIII, **40**, 1836, 1838 (sg.), 1839 (sg.), 1840, 1844 (pl., sg.), 1845 (sg., pl.), 1847, 1848 (sg.), 1851 (sg.), 1857 (description of their evil practices); **45**, 2078 (*Gāndhāra-M°āḥ*), 2096, 2108, 2109 (sg.) (description of their evil practices).—§ 610 (Çalyap.): IX, **7**σ, 329.—§ 611 (do.): IX, **8**, 391 (followed Çalya); **18**, 960 (*Madrarājapriye yuktair M°āṇāṃ mahārathaiḥ*).—§ 641 (Rājadh.): XII, **65**θ, 2429 (*Āndhra-M°āḥ*, enumeration of low peoples).—§ 664 (Mokshadh.): XII, **207**η, 7559 (in the south).

Madrakādhama, Madrakādhipa, Madrakeçvara = Çalya, q.v.

Madranābha, pl. (°*āḥ*), name of a caste: XIII, 2585.

Madrāṇām adhipa(ḥ), Madrāṇām īçvara(ḥ), Madrāṇām ṛshabha(ḥ), Madrāṇāṃ vṛshabha(ḥ) = Çalya, q.v.

Madranṛpānuja ("the younger brother of the king of the Madras" [i.e. Çalya]) = Çalyānuja.—§ 611 (Çalyap.): IX, **17**, 930. Cf. Madrarājānuja.

Madrapa, Madrapati, Madrarāj = Çalya, q.v.

Madrarāja[1], = Dyutimat: I, ††3832 (D°). — Do.[2] = Çalya, q.v.—Do.[3] = Açvapati: III, 16628.

Madrarājānuja = Madranṛpānuja: IX, 924 (*yuvā*).

Madrarājasutā ("the daughter of the king of the Madras") = Mādrī: I, 4896.

Madrarājātmaja ("the son of the king of the Madras") = Rukmaratha (?).—§ 604 (Karṇap.): VIII, **5**ζ, 112 (had been slain by Abhimanyu).

Madrarājeçvarātmaja = Çalya, q.v.

Mādravatī[1], wife of Parikshit.—§ 160 (Pūruv.): I, **95**, ††3837 (wife of Parikshit and mother of Janamejaya[1]).

Mādravatī[2] = Mādrī: XIV, 1969 (°*yāḥ sutau*, i.e. Nakula and Sahadeva).

Mādravatīputra ("the son of Mādravatī [i.e. Mādrī]") = Sahadeva: XVII, 55.

Mādravatīputra (do.), dual (°*au*) = Nakula and Sahadeva: XIV, 389.

Mādravatīsuta[1] (do.) = Nakula: III, 15732, 15738; V, 2254 (*N°*); XII, 6204; XV, †669 (*jyeshṭhasya*).

Mādravatīsuta[2] (do.) = Sahadeva: II, 1176, 2550 (*S°*); VII, 7475; XV, †668 (*yavīyasaḥ*), 1075.

Mādravatīsuta (do.), dual (°*au*) = Nakula and Sahadeva: III, 16607; V, †5, †18, †724; IX, 814, 3318; XIV, †1533, 2081.

Madroça = Çalya, q.v.

Madreçvara[1] ("the king of the Madras") = the father of Mādrī [and Çalya]: I, 4367 (°*sya*, sc. *sutā*, i.e. Mādrī).

Madreçvara[2] = Çalya, q.v.

Madreçvarasuta (the son of Madreçvara [i.e. Çalya]) = Rukmaratha: VII, 1811 (*R°*).

Mādreya[1] ("son of Mādrī") = Nakula: III, 17246, 17253; VIII, 963; XII, 6129, 6207.

Mādreya[2] (do.) = Sahadeva: II, 1155, 1161, 2611; III, 11486; V, 2253 (*S°*); VII, 4032, 7478, 7479, 7481; VIII, 908; IX, 768 (*S°*).

Mādreya (do.), dual (°*au*) = Nakula and Sahadeva: I, 5647; III, 1123.

Mādreya, pl. (°*āḥ*), a people = Madra, pl.—§ 574 (Jambūkh.): VI, **9**μ, 346 (°-*Jāṅgalāḥ*).

Mādrī[1] ("the daughter of the Madra king"), the wife of Pāṇḍu and mother of Nakula and Sahadeva. § 132 (Aṃçāvat.): I, **67**, 2794 (incarnation of the goddess Dhṛti). — § 157 (Pūruvaṃç.): I, **95**, ††3811 (wife of Pāṇḍu), ††3816,

††3817 (by the Açvins mother of Nakula and Sahadeva), †3818 (all. to § 192 foll.).—§ 177 (Pāṇḍudigvijaya): I, **113**, 4430 (sister of Çalya), 4441, 4442, 4444 (Pāṇḍu married *M.*).—§ 178 (Pāṇḍu): I, **114**, 4474, 4477 (Pāṇḍu went to the wood with his wives).—§ 180 (Gāndhārīputrotpatti): I, **115**, 4484.—§ 184 (Pāṇḍu): I, **119**, 4613, 4616 (cursed by Kindama, Pāṇḍu retired to the wood with his wives).—§ 192 (Pāṇḍavotpatti): I, **124**, 4849, 4850 (at the wish of Pāṇḍu *M.* learnt the mantra from Kuntī and invoked the Açvins, who on her begat Nakula and Sahadeva), 4859.—§ 193 (Pāṇḍu): I, **125**, 4870, 4874, 4878, 4880, 4882, 4884, (4887), 4888, (4890) (Pāṇḍu's death).—§ 194 (do.): I, **126**, 4922 (by the Açvins mother of Nakula and Sahadeva), 4926 (had ascended the funeral pyre of Pāṇḍu).—§ 195 (do.): I, **127**, 4932, 4933, 4934 (the pretakārya of Pāṇḍu and *M.* was performed), 4940, 4953.—§ 214 (Hiḍimbavadhap.): I, **156**, 6097 (°*yāḥ*, sc. *putrau*, i.e. Nakula and Sahadeva).—§ 305 (Anudyūtap.): II, **79**, 2602. — § 338 (Indralokābhigamanap.): III, **46**, 1862 (*yathā*).—§ 522 (Draupadīharaṇap.): III, **266**, †15607 (°*yāḥ putrau*, i.e. Nakula and Sahadeva).—§ 548 (Āraṇeyap.): III, **313**, 17416 (wife of Pāṇḍu), 17417.—§ 611 (Çalyap.): IX, **17**, †871 (°*yāç ca putrau*, i.e. Nakula and Sahadeva). — § 618 (Jalapradānikap.): XI, **13**, †359 (do., do.).— § 795 (Svargārohaṇap.): XVIII, **4**, 144 (with Pāṇḍu in heaven). Cf. Madrarājasutā, Mādravatī.

Mādrī[2] (do.) = Vijayā, the wife of Sahadeva: I, ††3832 (*V*°).

Mādrikā, pl. (°*āḥ*) ("Madra women").—§ 607 (Karṇap.): VIII, **40**, 1853 (sg.), 1855 (pl.).

Mādrinandana[1] ("son of Mādrī") = Nakula: IX, 764, (*N*°).

Mādrinandana[2] (do.) = Sahadeva: II, 1116.

Mādrinandana (do.), dual (°*au*) = Nakula and Sahadeva: III, 19 (°*ān* (!)).

Mādrīnandanaka (do.), dual (°*au*) = Nakula and Sahadeva: III, 10856.

Mādrīnandikara (do.) = Sahadeva: V, 2000.

Mādrīputra[1] (do.) = Nakula: III, 1020 (*N*°); IV, 165, 1359; V, 1997; VI, 3168 (*N*°); VII, 7567, 7578, 8568; VIII, 930, 3188, †3814 (*N*°); IX, 489; XII, 6126.

Mādrīputra[2] (do.) = Sahadeva: I, †7163 (*S*°); II, 2624 (*S*°); III, 15749; IV, 1354 (*S*°); V, †708 (*S*°), 3166 (*S*°); VI, 5168, 5171, 5401 (*S*°); VII, 3532, 7465, 8582; VIII, 496 (*S*°); IX, 773, †891 (*S*°), 1140, 1544.

Mādrīputra[3] (do.), dual (°*au*) = Nakula and Sahadeva: I, 4855, 4879, 5742, 7399, 7465; II, 2157, 2621; III, 11503, 11739, 14987, †15658, 17225; IV, 2294, 2319; V, †653, †660, †711, 3207, 4426, 4657, 4791, 4826, 5152, 5854; VI, 711, 2068, 2473, 2733, 2744, 2746, 3694, 3865, 4508, 4669, 4782, 4799, 4912, 5074, 5228, 5559; VII, 1380, 1509, 3562, 3566, 6626, 8805 (C. by error °*aṃ*), 8811; VIII, 1638, 1690, 2360, 2709, 2710, 3183, 3194, 3206, 3210, 4864, 4872, 4991, 4999; IX, 156, 164, 400, 453, 516, 550, 646, 652, 656, 779, 832, 961, 1019, 1021, 1026, 1064, 1373; 1725, 1956, 3481; X, 550; XII, 1379, 1396, 1464, 6231; XIII, 7772.

Mādrīsuta[1] (do.) = Nakula: I, †200 (*N*°); II, 1202; V, †709, 2229 (*N*°); VI, 1691; VIII, †4298, †4331 (*N*°); X, †569, †570.

Mādrīsuta[2] (do.) = Sahadeva: II, 1163; V, 2868; VI, 5169; VII, 517, 7471, 8575; IX, †1558 (*S*°), †1559 (slew Çakuni).

Mādrīsuta (do.), dual (°*au*) = Nakula and Sahadeva: I, †109, 2290; III, 1275, †2009, †10283, †11907, †11916; V, †718, †861, †868, 5115; VI, 3764; VIII, 3204; IX, †873.

Mādrītanūja (do.), dual (°*au*) = Nakula and Sahadeva: V, †688.

Magadha, pl. (°*āḥ*), a people.—§ 130 (Amçāvat.): I, **67**, 2683 (°*eshu Jayatsenas teshām āsīt pārthivaḥ*, incarnation of the first of the Kāleyas).—§ 177 (Pāṇḍudigvijaya): I, **113**, 4451 (*goptā M°rāshṭrasya Dīrgho Rājagṛhe*, slain by Pāṇḍu on his digvijaya).—§ 275 (Rājasūyārambhap.): II, **18**, 738 (°*eshu*, Bṛhadratha established a feast in honour of the Rākshasī Jarā among the *M.*).—§ 295 (Dyūtap.): II, **52**, 1874 (brought tribute to Yudhishṭhira).—§ 375 (Tīrthayātrāp.): III, **85**, 8234 (°*eshu*, the holiness of the country).—§ 561*e* (Bhīmasena): V, **50**, 1986 (*Kāçi-Vaṅga-M°ān*, had been vanquished by Bhīmasena).—§ 561*g* (Sahadeva): V, **50**, 1997 (*Kāçīn Aṅga-M°ān*, had been vanquished by Sahadeva).—§ 561 (Yānasandhip.): V, **53**θ, 2107 (among the allies of Yudhishṭhira).—§ 574 (Jambūkh.): VI, **9**μ, 357 (only B., C. has *Mā*°, among the peoples of Bhāratavarsha). Cf. Māgadha, pl.

Magadha (VIII, 186), v. Māgadha[9].

Magadha = the country of the Magadhas. § 641*f* (Pṛthu Vainya): XII, **59**, 2234 (bestowed by Pṛthu Vainya on Māgadha [i.e. the ancestor of the Māgadhas]).

Māgadha[1] ("king of the Magadhas") = Bṛhadratha: II, 744.

Māgadha[2] (do.) = Daṇḍadhāra: VIII, 688 (only B., C. has by error *Mādhavaḥ*).

Māgadha[3] (do.) = Jalasandha: VII, 4573, 4578, 4583.

Māgadha[4] (do.) = Jarāsandha: II, 586, 610 (*nṛpam*), 647, 657, 754, 762, 770, 788 (the country?), 876, 879, 892 (*Jarāsandho rājā*), 919; VIII, 243 (*rājā*, having obtained the friendship of Karṇa he confined the kings of the earth); XII, 129 (*rājā . . . Jarāsandhaḥ*); XIII, 6839 (°*samruddhān*, sc. *rājñaḥ*, liberated by Kṛshṇa, all. to Jarāsandhavadhaparvan).

Māgadha[5] (do.) = Jayasena: II, 121 (*J*°). Cf. next.

Māgadha[6] (do.) = Jayatsena, son of Jarāsandha: II, 1538 (*J*°); V, 577 (*Jayatseno Jārāsandhiḥ*); VI, 5007 (*J*°), 5317, 5321; VIII, 120 (*Jayatseno Jārāsandhiḥ*, had been slain by Abhimanyu). Cf. the prec. and Māgadha[9].

Māgadha[7] (do.) = Meghasandhi, the son of Sahadeva: XIV, 2448, 2449, 2450, 2460, 2466.

Māgadha[8] (do.) = Sahadeva, son of Jarāsandha: V, 5325 (*S*°). Cf. next.

Māgadha[9] (do.), one or more Magadha kings at the time of Yudhishṭhira = Jayatsena or Sahadeva (?).—§ 296 (Dyūtap.): II, **53**, 1914 (waited upon Yudhishṭhira).—§ 561 (Yānasandhip.): V, **57**, 2239 (*Jārāsandhiḥ*, had joined Yudhishṭhira).—§ 576 (Bhagavadgītāp.): VI, **17**, 663 (in the army of Duryodhana); **18**, 691 (*nṛpatiḥ*, do.).—§ 581 (Bhīshmavadhap.): VI, **62**, 2750, 2761, 2762 (fought with Abhimanyu).—§ 584 (do.): VI, **81**, 3533 (in Duryodhana's army).—§ 587 (do.): VI, **108**δ, 5051 (do.). — § 593 (Abhimanyuvadhap.): VII, **48**, 1891 (°*sya putram*, slain by Abhimanyu).—§ 599 (Jayadrathavadhap.): VII, **107**, 4045 (°*sya sute*, i.e. Vyāghradatta, slain by Sātyaki). — § 604 (Karṇap.): VIII, **6**, 186 (had been slain by Bhīshma, C. has by error *Ma*°).—§ 609 (Çalyap.): IX, **2**, 73 (had joined Duryodhana), 92 (had been slain).

Māgadha[10] (adj.) ("belonging to the Magadhas").—§ 273 (Rājasūyārambhap.): II, **14**, 617 (*girimukhyaṃ* ?).—§ 276

(Jarāsandhavadhap.): II, **20**, 797 (*puram*, i.e. Girivraja).—§ 277 (do.): II, **21**, 798 (*niveçaḥ* = do.), 809 (*puram* = do.); **22**, 873 (*sainyaiḥ*).—§ 581 (Bhīshmavadhap.): VI, **62**, 2749 (*anīkam*).—§ 607 (Karṇap.): VIII, **38**, 1770 (*dāsīnām M°īnām*).—§ 619 (Strīvilāpap.): XI, **25**, 712 (*°yaḥ . . . yoshitaḥ*).

Māgadha[1], the ancestor of the Māgadhas (tribe and caste).—§ 641*f* (Pṛthu Vainya): XII, **59**, 2233 (*Sūta-M°au*, became the bards of Pṛthu Vainya), 2234 (Pṛthu Vainya gave *M.* the country of Magadha).

Māgadha, pl. (*°āḥ*), a people = Magadha, pl. — § 4 (Anukram.): I, **1**, †153 (*°ānām varishṭham Jarāsandham*).—§ 74 (Vasu Uparicara): I, **63**, 2363 (*mahāratho M°ānām viçruto yo Bṛhadrathaḥ*).—§ 242 (Ambuvīca): I, **204**, 7476 (*Ambuvīca itīçvaraḥ* | *āsīd Rājagṛhe M°ānām mahīkshitām*).—§ 275 (Rājasūyārambhap.): II, **19**, 741 (ruled by Bṛhadratha).—§ 276 (Jarāsandhavadhap.): II, **20**, 796 (*°kshetram*, the realm of Jarāsandha).—§ 277 (do.); II, **21**, 807 (*aparihāryā meghānām M°ā Manunā kṛtāḥ*), 815 (*°ānām suruciram Caityakam*), 827; **24**, 932, 933, 942 (after the slaughter of Jarāsandha his son Sahadeva became king of the *M.*).—§ 280 (Bhīmasena): II, **30**, 1090 (ruled by Daṇḍa and Daṇḍadhāra (?), vanquished by Bhīmasena, accompanied Bhīmasena when he vanquished the son of Jarāsandha in Girivraja).—§ 515 (Karṇadigvijaya): III, **254**, 15244 (vanquished by Karṇa on his digvijaya).—§ 574 (Jambūkh.): VI, **9**μ, 353 (among the peoples of Bhāratavarsha), 357 (do., only C., B. has *Ma°*).—§ 578 (Bhīshmavadhap.): VI, **51**τ, 2102 (followed Bhīshma).—§ 580 (do.): VI, **56**δ, 2409 (on the right wing of Bhīshma's gāruḍavyūha).—§ 585 (do.): VI, **87**δ, 3854 (followed Bhagadatta).—§ 589 (Droṇābhishekap.): VII, **11**ν, 397 (formerly vanquished by Kṛshṇa).—§ 592 (Saṃçaptakavadhap.): VII, **20**ζ, 802 (in the back of Droṇa's gāruḍavyūha).—§ 599 (Jayadrathavadhap.): VII, **107**, 4045, 4048 (attacked Sātyaki after the slaughter of Vyāghradatta, the son of the Magadha king).—§ 605 (Karṇap.): VIII, **12**ββ, 459 (in the army of Yudhishṭhira?); **18**, †690 (*°ānām pravaraḥ*, i.e. Daṇḍadhāra); **22**ζζ, 863 (attacked the Pāñcālas).—§ 607 (do.): VIII, **45**μ, 2084, (ν), 2101, 2105.—§ 608 (do.): VIII, **46**β, 2133 (on the right wing of the Kaurava array); **70**πππ, †3500; **73**, 3657 (*°ānām adhipatir Jayatsenaḥ*, had been slain by Abhimanyu).—§ 613 (Gadāyuddhap.): IX, **33**η, 1913 (have been slain).—§ 619 (Strīvilāpap.): XI, **25**, 712 (*°ānām adhipatiṃ Jayatsenam*), 714 (*°yaḥ*, fem.).—§ 711 (Ānuçāsanik.): XIII, **44**β, 2441 (vanquished by Bhīshma at the svayaṃvara of Ambā, etc.).—§ 793 (Mausalap.): XVI, **6**κ, 159 (had been vanquished by Kṛshṇa).

***Māgadha**, pl., name of a caste (bards): I, 6940 (*sūta-m°āḥ*); III, †14750 (*°-sūtapūgaiḥ*); IV, 541 (*sūta-m°āḥ*), †2180; V, †1314, 3333 (*sūta-m°āḥ*); VI, 4433; VII, 176 (*sūta-m°-vandināṃ*), 2739 (*sūta-m°-vandibhiḥ*); VIII, 12 (do.); XII, 1386, 10868 (*sūta-m°āḥ*); XIII, 2573 (sg., son of a vaiçya and a kshatriya wife), 2581, 2584 (*°ī*, fem.), 2622, 5768; XIV, 1896 (*sūta-m°-vandibhiḥ*), 2040 (*sūta-m°-saṅghāḥ*); XV, 624 (*sūta-m°-vandibhiḥ*), 1061 (*sūta-m°-saṅghaiḥ*).

Magadhādhipa ("king of the Magadhas") = Jarāsandha: XV, 668 (*°sya sutā Jarāsandha iti çrutasya*, i.e. the wife of Sahadeva).

Magadhādhipati (do.) = Bṛhadratha: II, 688 (*B°*), 740 (*°eḥ sutaḥ*, i.e. Jarāsandha), 756.

Magadheçvara (do.) = Meghasandhi: XIV, 2444.

Māgadhendra (do.) = Jarāsandha: V, 2056 (*J°*).

Māgadhī ("daughter of the Magadha king") = Amṛtā, wife of Anaçvan: I, ††3794.

Maghā, mostly pl. (*°āḥ*), name of a nakshatra (v. Su. Si.).—§ 246 (Sundopasundop.): I, **210**, 7653 (*°āsu*).—§ 370 (Tīrthayātrāp.): III, **84**, 8029 (*Kṛttikā-M°yoḥ . . . tīrtham*).—§ 574 (Jambūkh.): VI, **3**, 81 (*°āsv Aṅgārako vakraḥ*, omens).—§ 576 (Bhagavadgītāp.): VI, **17**, 637 (*°vishayago somaḥ*).—§ 746 (Ānuçāsanik.): XIII, **64**, 3263 (*°āsu*, the merit of making gifts under the constellation of *M.*).—§ 749 (do.): XIII, **88**, 4251 (*°āsu*), 4252 (do.); **89***a*, 4259 (*°āsu*, the merit of performing a çrāddha under the constellation of *M.*).—§ 759 (do.): XIII, **110**, 5394 (*°āṃ*, sg., description of the cāndravrata, cf. Açleshāḥ).—§ 766 (do.): XIII, **126**, 6040 (sg., a çrāddha should be performed under the constellation of *M.*).

Māgha, name of a month. § 587 (Bhīshmavadhap.): VI, **119**, 5632 (*°māse gavā iva*, but B. reads *māghamāṃ segavā iva*, cf. the explanation of Nīl.).—§ 733*p* (Gaṅgā-Yamunayos tīrtham): XIII, **25**, 1724 (*°māse*, then one should bathe in Prayāga).—§ 746 (Ānuçāsanik.): XIII, **66**, 3316 (*°māse*, the merit of gifts of seeds in the month of *M.*).—§ 759 (do.): XIII, **106**β, 5152 (*°māsaṃ*, the merit of fasting during *M.*); **109**, 5374 (*dvādaçyāṃ M°māse*, then one should worship Kṛshṇa as Mādhava).—§ 777 (Svargārohanik. p.): XIII, **168**, 7733 (*māsaḥ*, the month in which Bhīshma died).—§ 785 (Anugītāp.): XIV, **85**, 2513 (*dvādaçīṃ M°pākshikīṃ*; *°māsikīṃ*, B.).

Maghavan, Maghavat = Indra, q.v.

Maghavātman = Çiva: XII, 790.

Māghī, the day of full moon in the month of Māgha. § 658*b* (Kṛtaghnop.): XII, **171**, 6384 (on this day the Rākshasa king entertained brahmans).—§ 733*p* (Gaṅgā-Yamunayos tīrtham): XIII, **25**, 1723 (on this day 30,010,000 tīrthas are assembled in Prayāga).—§ 751*b* (Çapathavidhi): XIII, **94**, 4552 (on this day Çukra, etc., came to Kauçikī).—§ 785 (Anugītāp.): XIV, **85**, 2517 (*paurṇamāsī*).

Mahābāhu[1], two sons of Dhṛtarāshṭra. § 130 (Aṃçāvat.): I, **67**, 2733, 2740.—§ 182 (Dhṛtarāshṭraputranāmak.): I, **117**, 4545, 4553.—§ 600 (Ghaṭotkacavadhap.): VII, **157**ο, 6938 (among ten sons of Dhṛtarāshṭra who are slain by Bhīmasena).

Mahābāhu[2] = Kṛshṇa (Vishṇu): V, 2567.

Mahābala[1] = Çiva (1000 names[2]).—Do.[2] = Vishṇu (1000 names).

Mahābalā, name of two mātṛs. § 615*u* (Skanda): IX, **46**ο, 2627, 2644.

Mahābhāga = Vishṇu (1000 names).

Mahābhārata, the poem of Vyāsa. § 1 (Anukram.): I, **1**, 11 (*°saṃçritāḥ kathāḥ*). The *M.* had been composed by Vyāsa and was originally recited by Vaiçampāyana to Janamejaya, afterwards by Ugraçravas to Çaunaka).—§ 7 (do.): I, **1**, 265, 266 (etymology).—§ 11 (Parvasaṅgr.): I, **2**, 656 (*°m ākhyāya*), 657 (do.).—§ 70 (Ādivaṃçāvatāraṇap.): I, **59**, 2203 (*ākhyānam*, recited at the sacrifice of Janamejaya); 2206 (recited by Sauti, i.e. Ugraçravas).—§ 72 (do.): I, **62**, 2283 (*ākhyānam*), 2319 (*°ākhyānam*), 2320 (etymology), 2322, 2333 (*tribhir varshair . . . Kṛshṇa-Dvaipāyano . . . M°m ākhyānaṃ kṛtavān*).—§ 78 (Vyāsa): I, **63**, 2418 (Vyāsa taught his disciples *Vedān M°pañcamān*).—§ 717*b* (Nārāyaṇīya): XII, **341**, 13027 (do. do.); **347**, 13438 (*°kṛt*, i.e. Vyāsa).—§ 795*c* (Svargārohaṇap.): Sauti said: "The race of the *Bharatas* is the topic [of the *M.*]. Therefore it is called Bhārata, and on account of this and of its greatness it is called *M.* (v. 192); this history is called Jaya, it should be heard by everyone who desires emancipation," etc. Blessing to the reader. *Vyāsa* made an abstract of the *Bhārata* from love of righteousness; he made another compilation (*saṃhitāṃ*) of six millions of verses; three millions of these verses are placed in *Devaloka*, 1,500,000 among the Pitṛs, 1,400,000 among the Yakshas, and 100,000 among men. *Nārada* recited it to the gods, *Asita Devala* to the *Pitṛs*, *Çuka* to the *Rākshasas* and *Yakshas*; *Vaiçampāyana* to men; it is equal to the *Vedas*; blessing to the reader; the *Sāvitrī* of the *Bhārata* (i.e. vv. 203*b*–207) is quoted; "what need has that man of a sprinkling of the waters of Pushkara who attentively listens to this Bhārata . . . ?" (v. 211 + one verse in *B.*) (XVII, **5**).—Asked by *Janamejaya* according to what rites one should listen to the Bhārata, etc., Vaiçampāyana expounded what gods, etc., are found in the Mahābhārata (*ξ*); çrāddha offerings should be made after the hearing of it, likewise gifts to the brahmans (specification); one should appoint as reciter one who is pure, etc.; the reciter, seated at his ease, free from all bodily complaints, with rapt attention should recite the text without too much slowness, etc.; (*o*) the merit won at the conclusion of each *pāraṇa* (*π*); the gifts that should be made at the conclusion of each parvan (*ρ*), its topic (*σ*) and fruits (*τ*) (XVIII, **6**): XVIII, **5**, 190, 191, 192 (etymology); **6**, 299 (°*ākhyanaṃ*). Cf. Bhārata[18], Jaya[14].

Mahābhāsura = Mahāpurusha (Mahāpurushastava).

Mahābhauma, a prince. § 156 (Pūruvaṃç.): I, **95**, ††3772 (son of Ariha), ††3773 (husband of Suyajñā and father of Ayutanāyin).

Mahābhaya ("great fear"). § 125 (Aṃçāvat.): I, **66**, 2619 (son of Adharma and Nirṛti).

Mahābhīmā = Umā: XII, 10304.

Mahābhisha, a king. § 161 (Mahābhishop.): I, **96**, 3843 (*Ikshvākuvaṃçaprabhavaḥ*), 3845, 3847, 3848, 3850 (cursed to be reborn on earth).—§ 162 (Çāntanūp.): I, **97**, 3882 (reborn as Çāntanu).—§ 376 (Tīrthayātrāp.): III, **85**, 8268 (*yathā rājā M°ḥ*).—§ 706 (Mokshadh.): XII, **310**, 11540 (*rājarshir adhṛtiḥ svargāt patito hi M°ḥ*, all. to § 161).—§ 775 (Ānuçāsanik.): XIII, **166***η*, 7681 (enumeration).

[Mahābhishopākhyāna(ṃ)] ("episode relating to king Mahābhisha"). § 161 (Sambhavap.): The *rājarshi Mahābhisha*, of the race of *Ikshvāku*, had gratified *Indra* by 1,000 horse sacrifices and 100 *rājasūyas* and attained to *Svarga*. One day, when the gods and *rājarshis* were worshipping *Brahmán*, the *Wind* loosened the garments of *Gaṅgā*. The gods bent down their heads, but *Mahābhisha* rudely stared at her, and for this *Brahmán* cursed him, saying that he should be reborn on earth, [as should also *Gaṅgā*, but when his wrath should be provoked by her he should again attain to heaven] (the words in brackets are only to be found in B.). He then wished to be born as a son of *Pratīpa*. The *Vasus* had been cursed by the ṛshi *Vasishṭha*, whom they had crossed when he was engaged in his twilight adorations, that they should be born among men. They chose to be born of *Gaṅgā* as sons to *Çāntanu*, who should be borne to *Pratīpa*, and *Gaṅgā* promised that she would throw them into the water as soon as they were born, except one, upon whom they would each contribute one-eighth of their energies, but who should be childless (I, **96**). (For continuation v. Çāntanūpākhyāna.)

Mahābhoga, Mahābhūta = Vishṇu (1000 names).

***mahābhūta**, pl. (°*āni*) ("the elements"): III, 13913 (°*ātmakaṃ Brahma*), 13914 (enumerated), 13921 (*pañca*, do.); VI, 178 (do., do.), 182 (*pañcasu*), 1327; XII, 6821, 6823, 7071, 7072, 7073 (*pañca*), 7077, 7525 (enumerated), 7725, 8739, 8976 (do.), 8979 (*pañca*), 9877 (do.); XIII, 7074; XIV, 983 (*pañca*), 1092 (do., enumerated); XV, 924. Cf. Bhūta, pl.

Mahābhūtādhipati = Vishṇu (Nārāyaṇa, Kṛshṇa): XII, 13110.

Mahābīja = Çiva (1000 names[2]).

Mahābuddhi = Vishṇu (1000 names).

Mahācūḍā, a mātṛ. § 615*u* (Skanda): IX, **46***θ*, 2623.

Mahāçakti, Mahāçana = Vishṇu (1000 names).

Mahāçaṅkha, name of a tree (thus Nīl.) in Çaṅkhatīrtha. § 615*f* (Çaṅkhatīrtha): IX, **37**, 2138 (*nagaṃ*).

Mahāçiras[1], a muni. § 264 (Sabhākriyāp.): II, **4***a*, 105 (waited upon Yudhishṭhira).

Mahāçiras[2], an Asura. § 268 (Varuṇasabhāv.): II, **9**, 366 (among the Daityas and Dānavas in the palace of Varuṇa).

Mahāçoṇa, a river. § 276 (Jarāsandhavadhap.): II, **20**, 794 (crossed by Kṛshṇa, Arjuna, and Bhīmasena on their journey from Indraprastha to Girivraja). Cf. Çoṇa.

Mahāçrama, a tīrtha. § 370 (Tīrthayātrāp.): III, **84**, 8031.—§ 733*g* (Saptagaṅga): XIII, **25**, 1704 (result of bathing there).

Mahāçṛṅga = Vishṇu (1000 names).

Mahāçva, an ancient king. § 267 (Yamasabhāv.): II, **8**, 330 (in the palace of Yama).

Mahādaṃshṭra = Çiva (1000 names[1-2]).

Mahādanta = Çiva (1000 names[2]).

Mahādbhuta, name of a fire (= Adbhuta?). § 493 (Āṅgirasa): III, **222**, 14212.

Mahad bhūta(ṃ) = Vishṇu (1000 names).

Mahādeva[1] ("the great god") = Çiva, q.v.

Mahādeva[2] (do.) = Brahmán: XII, 9176, 13047.

Mahādeva[3] (do.) = Vishṇu (Kṛshṇa): III, 8125 (*Vishṇuṃ*); V, 298; VI, 3036 (= Kṛshṇa); XII, 4490, 10087; XIII, 7001 (1000 names).

Mahādevapura ("the city of Mahādeva"). § 322 (Dvaitavanapr.): III, **23**, †913 (*puraṃ M°prakāçaṃ*).

[Mahādevasahasranāmastotra(ṃ)] (the hymn containing the 1,008 names of Mahādeva, i.e. Çiva), v. Çiva.

[Mahādevastava(ḥ)] ("the praising of Mahādeva, i.e. Çiva"). § 332 (cf. Kairātap.): Arjuna enumerated the names of Çiva, Kapardin, etc. (III, v. 1624*b*–1633).

Mahādevī[1] ("the great goddess") = Aditi: XIII, 3905.

Mahādevī[2] (do.) = Umā: III, 8129 (*Gauryāḥ*); IV, 200; VI, 805; XII, 10333; XIII, 4069; XIV, 1184 (*Pārvatī*). Cf. Devī.

Mahādhana = Vishṇu (1000 names).

Mahādhanu(s), Mahādhātu = Çiva (1000 names[2]).

Mahādridhṛk = Vishṇu (1000 names).

Mahadyuman, name of a tīrtha or of the sun (Nīl.). § 17 (Uttaṅka): I, **3**, 804 (*avasad yo*—i.e. Çrutasena—*Mahadyumni prārthayan nāgamukhyatāṃ*).

Mahādyuti[1] = Vishṇu (1000 names).

Mahādyuti[2] = Çiva: XIV, 201, 206 (°*te*, dat.).

Mahāgaṇapati = Çiva: X, 254.

Mahāgaṅgā, name of a tīrtha. § 733*j* (Ānuçāsanik.): By fasting and bathing in *M.* at the conjunction of the Kṛttikās and Aṅgāraka (so BR., PCR. takes *Kṛttikāṅgārake* as the name of a tīrtha) one becomes cleansed of his sins and ascends to heaven: XIII, **25**, 1708.

Mahāgarbha, Mahāgarbhaparāyaṇa = Çiva (1000 names[2]).
Mahāgarta = Vishṇu (1000 names).
Mahāgaurī, a river. § 574 (Jambūkh.): VI, **9**λ, 341 (in Bhāratavarsha).
Mahāghora = Çiva (1000 names[2]).
Mahāgiri ("the great mountain") = Himavat: III, 8004.
Mahāgīta, Mahāgrīva = Çiva (1000 names[2]).
Mahāhaṃsa = Mahāpurusha (Mahāpurushastava).
Mahāhanu[1], a serpent. § 64 (Sarpasattra): I, **57**, 2151 (of Takshaka's race).
Mahāhanu[2], a serpent. § 67 (Sarpasattra): I, **57**, 2158 (of Dhṛtarāshṭra's race).
Mahāhanu[3] = Çiva (1000 names[2]).
Mahāharsha, Mahāhasta = Çiva (1000 names[2]).
Mahāhavis = Vishṇu (1000 names).
Mahāhrada[1], one or more tīrthas. § 370 (Tīrthayātrāp.): III, **84**, 8122 (*sarvatīrthavare*).—§ 391 (Ṛshyaçṛṅga): III, **110**, 10001 (Ṛshyaçṛṅga lived at *M.*); **113**, 10094 (do.).—§ 733*g* (Saptagaṅga): XIII, **25**, 1705 (*°e upaspṛçya Bhṛgutuṅge*).—§ 733*v* (Rāmahrada): XIII, **25**, 1734.—§ 757*m* (Goloka): XIII, **102a**, 4888.
Mahāhrada[2] = Vishṇu (1000 names).
Mahājānu, a ṛshi. § 22 (Pramadvarā): I, **8a**, 961.
Mahājaṭa, Mahājatru = Çiva (1000 names[2]).
Mahājavā, name of two mātṛs. § 615*u* (Skanda): IX, **46**θ, 2634 (only C., B. has *Manojavā*), 2640.
Mahājaya, a serpent. § 615*u* (Skanda): IX, **45**, 2554 (given to Skanda by Vāsuki).
Mahājihva, Mahājvāla = Çiva (1000 names[2]).
Mahākāça, a varsha (?) on Çākadvīpa. § 575*b* (Çākadvīpa): VI, **11**β, 425.
Mahākāla[1], name of a form of Çiva. § 358 (Tīrthayātrāp.): III, **82**, 4090 (name of a tīrtha? or of the god worshipped there (in Ujjayinī?)).—§ 696*b* (Dakshaprokta-Çivasahasranāmastotra): XII, **285**, 10392 (Çiva's 1000 names[1]).
Mahākāla[2], followers of Çiva. § 91 (Aṃçāvat.): I, **65**, 2529 (= Bāṇa; *Rudrasyānucaraḥ*).—§ 269 (Vaiçravaṇasabhāv.): II, **10**, 414 (in the palace of Kubera).
Mahākālī = Umā: IV, 195; VI, 797; XII, 10304.
Mahākalpa, Mahākambu = Çiva (1000 names[2]).
Mahākarman[1] = Çiva (1000 names[2]).—Do.[2] = Vishṇu (1000 names).
Mahākarṇa = Çiva (1000 names[1-2]).
Mahākarṇī, the minister of king Ambuvīca. § 242 (Ambuvīca): I, **204**, 7478.
Mahākarṇī, a mātṛ. § 615*u* (Skanda): IX, **46**θ, 2644.
Mahākartṛ = Çiva (1000 names[2]).
Mahākāya = Çiva: VII, 9532; XIII, 1148 (1000 names), 1168 (do.), 1199 (do.).
Mahākāyā, a mātṛ. § 615*u* (Skanda): IX, 46θ, 2642.
Mahākeça, Mahāketu = Çiva (1000 names[2]).
Mahākoça, Mahākrama, Mahākratu = Vishṇu (1000 names).
Mahākrauñca, a mountain in Krauñcadvīpa. § 575 (Bhūmip.): VI, **12**, 448. Cf. Krauñca.
Mahākrodha = Çiva (1000 names[2]).
Mahākṛcchra = Mahāpurusha (Mahāpurushastava).
Mahāksha[1] = Çiva (1000 names[2]). — Do.[2] = Vishṇu (1000 names).
Mahālaya, a tīrtha. § 370 (Tīrthayātrāp.): III, **84**, 8032.—§ 375 (do.): III, **85**, 8233.
Mahāliṅga = Çiva (1000 names[2]).

Mahāmakha = Vishṇu (1000 names).
Mahāmāla = Çiva (1000 names[2]).
Mahāmanas = Vishṇu (1000 names).
Mahāmatī, a daughter of Aṅgiras. § 489 (Āṅgirasa): III, **218**, 14128 (*mahāmakhesv Āṅgirasī dīptamatsu mahāmate | M°īti vikhyātā saptamī kathyate sutā*). Cf. Āṅgirasī.
Mahāmātra = Çiva (1000 names[2]).
Mahāmāya[1] = Çiva (1000 names[2]). — Do.[2] = Vishṇu (1000 names).
Mahāmāyādhara = Mahāpurusha (Mahāpurushastava).
Mahāmegha, a Kuru warrior. § 593 (Abhimanyuvadhap.): VII, **48**χ, 1899 (slain by Abhimanyu).
Mahāmeghacayaprakhya = Çiva (1000 names[1]).
Mahāmeghanivāsin = Çiva (1000 names[2]).
Mahāmeru[1-2] = Meru[1-2], q.v.
Mahāmukha[1], a warrior of Jayadratha. § 522 (Draupadīharaṇap.): III, **271**, 15371 (*Kshemaṅkara-M°au*, slain by Nakula).
Mahāmukha[2], **Mahāmuni, Mahāmūrdhan** = Çiva (1000 names[2]).
Māhāmūrti[1] = Çiva (1000 names[1]).—Do.[2] = Mahāpurusha (Mahāpurushastava).—Do.[3] = Vishṇu (1000 names).
Mahānada[1] ("the great river") = Sindhu: XIII, 1695.—Do.[2] = Çiva (1000 names[2]).
Mahānadī[1], one or more rivers. § 249 (Arjunavanavāsap.): I, **215**, 7818 (visited by Arjuna).—§ 370 (Tīrthayātrāp.): III, **84**, 8062.—§ 377 (Dhaumyatīrthak.): III, **87**, 8307 (near Gayā).—§ 379 (Tīrthayātrāp.): III, **95**, 8519 (do.).—§ 459 (Mārkaṇḍeyas.): III, **188a**, 12909 (among the rivers seen by Mārkaṇḍeya in the stomach of Nārāyaṇa).—§ 606 (Tripurākhyāna): VIII, **34**, 1473 (became the jaṅghā of Çiva's chariot).—§ 775 (Ānuçāsanik.): XIII, **166a**, 7646.
Mahānadī[2], a river in Çākadvīpa. § 575*b* (Çākadvīpa): VI, **11**γ, 433.
Mahānadīsuta ("the son of the great river [i.e. Gaṅgā]") = Bhīshma: XII, † 2120.
Mahānāgahana, Mahānakha, Mahānana = Çiva (1000 names[2]).
Mahānandā, a tīrtha. § 733*u* (Punarāvartanandā): XIII, **25**, 1731.
Mahānāsa, Mahānetra, Mahāṅga = Çiva (1000 names[2]).
Mahānidhi = Vishṇu (1000 names).
Mahāniyama = Mahāpurusha (Mahāpurushastava). Cf. XII, 13052.
Mahānṛtya, Mahāntaka, Mahāpāda = Çiva (1000 names[2]).
Mahāpadma[1], an elephant. § 581 (Bhīshmavadhap.): VI, **64**μ, 2866 (one of the world's elephants, followed Ghaṭotkaca).—§ 599 (Jayadrathavadhap.): VII, **121**ζζ, 4830 (*°kule*, sc. *jātā nāgāḥ*).
Mahāpadma[2], a city. § 718*b* (Uñchavṛttyup.): XII, **354**, 13775 (*purottame Gaṅgāyā dakshiṇe tīre*).
Mahāpārçva[1], an Asura. § 268 (Varuṇasabhāv.): II, **9**, 366 (among the Daityas and Dānavas in the palace of Varuṇa).
Mahāpārçva[2] = Çiva (1000 names[1]).
Mahāpārishadeçvara, a warrior of Skanda. § 615*u* (Skanda): IX, **45**η, 2568.
Mahāpatha = Çiva (1000 names[2]).
Mahāpavitra, Mahāprajāpati = Mahāpurusha (Mahāpurushastava).
Mahāprasāda = Çiva (1000 names[2]).

Mahāprasthānika(m) [parva(n)] ("[the section] relating to the great journey [to the other world]," i.e. Mahāprasthānikaparvan).—§ 10 (Parvasaṅgr.): I, **2**, 356 (°*aṃ parva*).—§ 11 (do.): I, **2**, 629 (C. has °*prā*°), 633 (°*aṃ parva*, C. has °*prā*°).—§ 795*c* (Mahābhārata): XVIII, **6**, 279 (°*e*).

[Mahāprasthānikaparvan] ("the section relating to the great journey to the other world," the 17th of the great and the 99th of the minor parvans of Mhbhr.; cf. Mahāprasthānika(ṃ) parva(n)).—§ 794: *Janamejaya* said: Having heard of the battle with iron clubs between the *Vṛshṇis* and *Andhakas*, and of *Kṛshṇa's* ascension to heaven, what did the *Pāṇḍavas* do? *Vaiçampāyana* said: Having heard the particulars of the great slaughter of the *Vṛshṇis*, *Yudhishṭhira* set his heart on leaving the world, saying to his brothers that it is Time that ripens every creature, of which they approved. He made the kingdom over to *Yuyutsu* and installed *Parikshit* as king in *Hāstinapura*, while *Vajra* ruled in *Indraprastha*. Then he offered oblations of water to *Kṛshṇa*, *Rāma*, and *Vasudeva*, etc., and *çrāddhas* to his deceased kinsmen, and fed *Vyāsa*, *Nārada*, *Mārkaṇḍeya*, and *Yājñavalkya*, and gave jewels, etc. (specification) to brahmans in honour of *Kṛshṇa*. *Kṛpa* was installed as the preceptor of *Parikshit*. Then he summoned his subjects and informed them of his intentions; they tried in vain to dissuade him. He and his brothers and *Draupadī* removed their ornaments and wore barks of trees; then they threw their sacred fires into the water. Then they set out on their journey: the five *Pāṇḍavas*, *Draupadī*, and a dog. *Kṛpa*, etc., stood around *Yuyutsu*; *Ulūpī* entered the waters of *Gaṅgā*; *Citrāṅgada* set out for *Maṇipūra*; the grandmothers of *Parikshit* surrounded him. *Yudhishṭhira*, etc., set out with their faces turned towards the east, devoting themselves to *yoga*, resolved to observe the religion of renunciation; *Yudhishṭhira* first, then the other *Pāṇḍavas* in the order of their birth, behind them all *Draupadī*; a dog followed them. They reached the sea of red water. *Agni* came, and mentioning the *Khāṇḍava* forest, etc. (*a*), he caused *Arjuna* to throw the *Gāṇḍīva* and his inexhaustible quivers into the water to be given back to *Varuṇa*. Then *Agni* disappeared. They now proceeded towards the south; then, by the northern coast of the salt sea, to the south-west; then towards the west, where they saw *Dvārakā* covered by the ocean; then to the north, observant of *yoga*, desirous of making a round of the whole earth (XVII, **1**). They crossed *Himavat*, and beheld a vast desert of sand, and then *Meru*. *Kṛshṇā* dropped down; asked by *Bhīmasena*, *Yudhishṭhira* said that this was the consequence of her partiality for *Arjuna*. Then *Sahadeva* fell down; asked by *Bhīmasena*, *Yudhishṭhira* said it was because he never thought anybody his equal in wisdom. They went on. *Nakula* fell; asked by *Bhīmasena*, *Yudhishṭhira* said it was because he thought that nobody equalled him in beauty, though his righteousness was without blemish. *Arjuna* fell down; asked by *Bhīmasena*, *Yudhishṭhira* said that it was because *Arjuna* had said that he would consume all the foes in a single day, but did not accomplish it. *Bhīmasena* fell down; *Yudhishṭhira* told him it was because he was a great eater, and used to boast of his strength. *Yudhishṭhira* went on with the dog (XVII, **2**). *Indra* came with a chariot, and asked *Yudhishṭhira* to ascend it for going to Heaven; *Yudhishṭhira* wanted to take *Draupadī* and his fallen brothers with him; *Indra* said they have already reached Heaven, where he will see them; *Yudhishṭhira* would have the dog to accompany him; † as *Indra* said there is no place in Heaven for persons with dogs, as the *Krodhavaças* take away all the merits of such persons, *Yudhishṭhira* refused to ascend the chariot. Then [the dog, transformed into] *Dharma*, said to *Yudhishṭhira* (†vv. 80–9) that he had formerly tested him in the *Dvaitavana*, where he had chosen the revival of *Nakula*, disregarding *Bhīmasena* and *Arjuna*, for doing good to his [step]mother; "there is no one in Heaven that is equal to thee." Then *Dharma*, *Indra*, M., A., D., D.-ṛ., causing *Yudhishṭhira* to ascend the chariot, proceeded to Heaven on their respective chariots. *Nārada* said that *Yudhishṭhira* was superior to all the R.-ṛ. there. *Yudhishṭhira* wished to proceed to where his brothers were; *Indra*, saying that his brothers had won regions of felicity, tried to persuade him to stay, beholding D.-ṛ. and Si.; *Yudhishṭhira* wished to be united with his brothers and *Draupadī* (XVII, **3**).

Mahāpuṃs, a varsha (?) in Çākadvīpa. § 575*b* (Çākadvīpa): VI, **11**β, 427.

Mahāpura, a tīrtha. § 733*k* (Vaimānika): XIII, **25**, 1712.

Mahāpurāṇasambhāvya, an ancient king. — § 6 (Anukram.): I, **1***a*, 232 (in Sañjaya's enumeration).

Mahāpurusha ("the great Spirit")=Vishṇu (Nārāyaṇa, Kṛshṇa). § 717*c* (Uparicara): XII; **337**, 12795.—§ 717*b* (Nārāyaṇīya): XII, **339**, ††12864 (praised by Nārada with the Mahāpurushastava, q.v.); **341**, 13035, 13050; **348**, 13455.—§ 717*d* (Brahma-Rudrasaṃv.): XII, **352**, 13748.

[Mahāpurushastava] ("the praise of the great Spirit"). § 717*b* (Nārāyaṇīya): XII, **339**, ††12864 (recited by Nārada at Çvetadvīpa). The names (Devadeveça, etc., numbers 1–200), alphabetically arranged, are the following: *Abhagnaparisaṅkhyāna* (119), *Abhagnayoga* (118), *Abhāsura* (41), *Acala* (172), *Ādideva* (20), *Agni* (90), *Agrāhya* (171), *Āhuti* (92), *Aja* (168), *Ākhaṇḍala* (123), *Amadhya* (134), *Amṛta* (13), *Amṛtāksha* (14), *Amṛteçaya* (80), *Anādi* (133), *Ananta* (7, 132), *Anantabhoga* (131), *Anantagati* (130), *Anantākhya* (15), *Aparājita* (69), *Aparimita* (54), *Aparinindita* (53), *Aparinirmita* (51), *Apratarkya* (179), *Atharvaçiras* (113), *Atikṛcchra* (160), *Avaçavartin* (56), *Avijñeya* (180), *Avyaktamadhya* (so B., C. only *Avyakta*, 135), *Avyaktanidhana* (136), *Bāndhava* (197), *Bhaktavatsala* (198), *Brahmāgrya* (181), *Brahmakāyika* (38), *Brāhmaṇapriya* (194), *Brāhmaṇarūpa* (193), *Brāhmaṇyadeva* (199), *Brahmapurohita* (37), *Brahmeçaya* (84), *Bṛhat* (178), *Cakshurājya(ṃ)* (99), *Candramas* (98), *Cāturmahārājika* (40), *Chinnasaṃçaya* (190), *Chinnatṛshṇa* (189), *Citraçikhaṇḍin* (185), *Çrīvāsa* (145), *Dayāvāsa* (141), *Devadeveça* (1), *Deveçaya* (82), *Dhanaprada* (154), *Diçāṃ gaja(ḥ)* (101), *Digbhānu* (102), *Dikpati* (34), *Divaspati* (30), *Ekāntadarçana* (200), *Gatādhvara* (188), *Guhya* (36), *Haṃsa* (74), *Harihaya* (149), *Harimedha* (150, 155), *Hayaçiras* (104), *Hiraṇmaya* (so C., B. has *Hiraṇyamaya*, 177), *Hiraṇyeçaya* (81), *Jagadanvaya* (88), *Jagatpati* (28), *Jagatprakṛti* (89), *Kaushika* (*Kauç*° B., 125), *Kīrtyāvāsa* (144), *Kṛcchra* (159), *Kshetrajña* (5), *Kuçeçaya* (83), *Lakshmyāvāsa* (142), *Lokasākshin* (4), *Mahābhāsura* (42), *Mahāhaṃsa* (76), *Mahākṛcchra* (161), *Mahāmāyādhara* (184), *Mahāmūrti* (196), *Mahāniyama* (158), *Mahāpavitra* (176), *Mahāprajāpati* (25), *Mahāpurusha* (9), *Mahārājika* (39), *Māhātmyaçarīra* (174), *Mahātushita* (48), *Mahāvibhūti* (173), *Mahāyajña* (58), *Mahāyajñabhāgahara* (151), *Mahāyāmya* (45), *Manas* (97), *Mānasika* (70), *Manaspati* (29), *Marutpati* (31), *Māsikavratadhara* (112), *Nāmanāmika* (71), *Nirguṇa* (3), *Nishkriya* (2), *Nivṛttabhrama* (164), *Nivṛttarūpa* (192), *Niyama* (157), *Niyamadhara* (163),

Oṃkāra (95), *Padmeçaya* (85), *Pañcāgni* (107), *Pañcakālakartṛpati* (66), *Pañcamahākalpa* (114), *Pañcarātrika* (67), *Pañcayajña* (65), *Parāmahaṃsa* (75), *Paramayajñika* (77), *Parasvāmin* (72), *Parinirmita* (50), *Pavitra* (175), *Phenapācārya* (115), *Pracīnagarbha* (124), *Pradhāna* (12), *Prāgjyotishajyeshṭha* (110), *Prajānidhanakara* (183), *Prajāpati* (22), *Prajāsargakara* (182), *Pramardana* (49), *Prathamatrisauparṇa* (105), *Pravacanagata* (165), *Pravṛttavedakriya* (167), *Pṛçnigarbhapravṛtta* (only B., 166), *Pṛthivīpati* (33), *Puroḍāçabhāgahara* (187), *Puruhūta* (127), *Purusha* (8), *Purushottama* (6, 10), *Purushṭuta* (126), *Pūrvanivāsa* (35), *Ṛtadhāman* (19), *Sadasadvyaktāvyakta* (18), *Salilapati* (32), *Sāmaga* (111), *Samudrādhivāsa* (138), *Sanātana* (17), *Sañjñāsañjña* (46), *Sāṅkhyamūrti* (79), *Sāṅkhyayoga* (78), *Saptamahābhāga* (43), *Sārathi* (93), *Sarvacchandaka* (148), *Sarvadarçin* (170), *Sarvagati* (169), *Sarvakṛcchra* (162), *Sarvatovṛtta* (191), *Sarvāvāsa* (146), *Shaḍaṅganidhāna* (109), *Sukhaprada* (153), *Suprajāpati* (23), *Sūrya* (100), *Susnāta* (73), *Tapas* (96), *Tapovāsa* (140), *Triguṇa* (11), *Trināciketa* (108), *Tushita* (47), *Ūrjaspati* (26), *Vācaspati* (27), *Vaçavartin* (52, 55), *Vaḍavāmukho'gniḥ* (91), *Vaikhānasa* (117), *Vaikuṇṭha* (68), *Vālakhilya* (116), *Vanaspati* (24), *Varaprada* (152, 186), *Varṇadhara* (106), *Vashaṭkāra* (94), *Vāsudeva* (147), *Vasuvrada* (21), *Viçvakṛt* (128), *Viçvaksena* (87), *Viçvamūrti* (195), *Viçvarūpa* (129), *Viçveçvara* (86), *Vidigbhānu* (103), *Vidyāvāsa* (143), *Vratāvāsa* (137), *Vyoman* (16), *Yaçovāsa* (139), *Yajña* (57), *Yajñabhāgahara* (64), *Yajñagarbha* (61), *Yajñahṛdaya* (62), *Yajñasambhava* (59), *Yajñastuta* (63), *Yajñayoni* (60), *Yama* (156), *Yāmya* (44), *Yugādi* (120), *Yugamadhya* (121), *Yuganidhana* (122).

Mahārājika = Mahāpurusha (Mahāpurushastava).

Mahāratha[1], an ancient king. § 5 (Anukram.): I, **1***a*, 223 (in Nārada's enumeration).

Mahāratha[2] = Çiva (1000 names[2]).

Mahāraudra, a Rākshasa. § 585 (Bhīshmavadhap.): VI, **91***v*, 4083 (slain by Duryodhana).

Maharddhi = Vishṇu (1000 names).

Mahāretas = Çiva (1000 names[2]).

Mahārha = Vishṇu (1000 names).

Mahārṇavanipānavid, Mahāroman = Çiva (1000 names[2]).

Maharshayaḥ sapta = Saptarshi, pl.: I, 4807 (*sapta 'va maharshayaḥ*, enumerated); VI, 1210 [1229 (*maharshīṇām Bhṛgur aham*, sc. Kṛshṇa)].

Maharshi[1] = Çiva (1000 names[2]).—Do.[2] = Vishṇu (1000 names).

Mahārūpa = Çiva (1000 names[2]).

Mahāsaras, a tīrtha. § 652*b* (Indrota-Pārīkshitīya): XII, **152***β*, 5646, (*γ*), 5662. Cf. Mahatsaras.

Mahāsattva = Agni, q.v.

Mahāsena[1] = Skanda, q.v.—Do.[2] = Çiva (1000 names[2]).

Mahāsura, v. Asura.

Mahāsurī ("the great female Asura") = Kālakā: III, 12203 (*K.*).

Mahāsvana = Vishṇu (1000 names).

Mahat[1], a prince. § 150 (Pūruvaṃç.): I, **94**, 3704 (the second of the four sons of Matināra).

Mahat[2] = Hiraṇyagarbha: XII, 11231.

Mahat[3] = Çiva: XIII, 1150 (1000 names[2]), 1157 (do.), 1243 (do.); XIV, 197.

Mahat[4] = Vishṇu (1000 names).

Mahātapas[1] = Çiva (1000 names[2]).—Do.[2] = Vishṇu (1000 names).

Mahātejas[1] = Çiva (1000 names[2]).—Do.[2] = Vishṇu (1000 names).

Mahātman = Çiva (1000 names[2]).

Māhātmyaçarīra = Mahāpurusha (Mahāpurushastava).

Mahatsaras, a tīrtha. § 757*m* (Goloka): XIII, **102***α*, 4887. Cf. Mahāsaras.

Mahattara, a fire (?). § 491 (Aṅgirasa): III, 14164 (son of the pitṛ Kāçyapa (C. *Ka°*)).

Mahātushita = Mahāpurusha (Mahāpurushastava).

Mahaujas[1], one or more princes. § 130 (Aṃçāvat.): I, **67**, 2688 (incarnation of the fifth of the Kāleyas).—§ 280 (Bhīmasena): II, **30**, 1096 (*Kauçikīnilayam*, vanquished by Bhīmasena on his digvijaya).—§ 554 (Sainyodyogap.): V, **4***γ*, 85 (among the princes to whom the Pāṇḍavas ought to send messengers).

Mahaujas[2] = Çiva: XIV, 202, 207.

Mahaujas, pl. (°*asaḥ*), a people. § 562 (Bhagavadyānap.): V, **74***γ*, 2731 (*Varayuç ca M°āṃ*).

Mahaushadha, Mahāvakshas = Çiva (1000 names[2]).

Mahāvāc = Samāçvāsa (a fire): III, 14155.

Mahāvaktra = Çiva (1000 names[1]).

Mahāvarāha = Vishṇu (Kṛshṇa): XIII, 6858, 7007 (1000 names).

Mahāvega = Çiva (1000 names[2]).

Mahāvegā, a mātṛ. § 615*u* (Skanda): IX, **46***θ*, 2634.

Mahāvibhūti = Mahāpurusha (Mahāpurushastava).

Mahāvīra, a prince. § 130 (Aṃçāvat.): I, **67**, 2696 (among the incarnations from the Krodhavaça gaṇa).

Mahāvīrya = Vishṇu (1000 names).

Mahāvrata = Bhīshma, q.v.

Mahāyaças = Çiva (1000 names[2]).

Mahāyajña[1] = Mahāpurusha (Mahāpurushastava). — Do.[2] = Vishṇu (1000 names).

Mahāyajñabhāgahara = Mahāpurusha (Mahāpurushastava).

Mahāyajvan = Vishṇu (1000 names).

Mahāyāmya = Mahāpurusha (Mahāpurushastava).

mahāyogeçvara, pl. ("great masters of yoga"): XIII, 4393 (= Brahmán, etc.).

Mahāyogin = Çiva: XIV, 206.

Mahāyudha = Çiva (1000 names[2]).

Maheça ("the great Lord") = Çiva: XIII, 780.

Maheçvara[1] (do.) = Çiva, q.v.

Maheçvara[2] (do.) = Vishṇu (Kṛshṇa): XII, 13064; XIII, 6813.

Maheçvara[3], a Rudra. § 770 (Ānuçāsanik.): XIII, **151***β*, 7090 (enumeration).

Māheçvara, adj. ("belonging to Maheçvara [i.e. Çiva]"): VII, 9572 (*sthānam*, C. by error *Ma°*); IX, 2455 (*tejaḥ*); XII, 10265 (*tejo Jvaro nāma*), 10678 (*koshṭham*); XIII, 604 (*vibhūtim*), 815 (*padam*), 825 (*pūjā*).

Maheçvarapada, a tīrtha. § 370 (Tīrthayātrāp.): III, **84**, 8097.

Maheçvarapura, a tīrtha. § 370 (Tīrthayātrāp.): III, **84**, 8107 (there Vṛshadhvaja, i.e. Çiva, is to be worshipped).

Maheçvarasakha ("the friend of Maheçvara" [i.e. Çiva]) = Kubera: IX, 583 (*Alakādhipam*).

Maheçvarī = Umā: XII, 10304.

Māheçvarī = Umā: XIV, 1184 (*Pārvatī*).

Māheçvarī dhārā a tīrtha. § 370 (Tīrthayātrāp.): III, **84**, 8095.

Mahejya = Vishṇu (1000 names).

Mahendra[1] = Indra, q.v.

Mahendra[2], a mountain, the abode of Rāma Jāmadagnya. § 84 (Ādivaṃçāvatāraṇap.): I, **64**, 2459 (*parvatottame*).—§ 201 (Droṇa): I, **130**, 5120, 5121.—§ 249 (Arjunavanavāsap.): I, **215**, 7824 (°*parvatam*, visited by Arjuna Pāṇḍava).—§ 252 (Subhadrāharaṇap.): I, **219**, 7907 (only C., but read with B. *mahe tasya* instead of *Mahendrasya*). — § 269 (Vaiçravaṇasabhāv.): II, **10**, 412 (present in the palace of Kubera).—§ 370 (Tīrthayātrāp.): III, **85**, 8158 (*Jāmadagnyanishevitam*) — § 377 (Dhaumyatīrthak.): III, **87**, 8318 (°*o nāma Bhārgavasya*, in the east).—§ 378 (Tīrthayātrāp.): III, **93**, 8467 (°*ādīṃç ca parvatān*).—§ 383 (Paraçurāma): III, **99**, 8681.—§ 392 (Tīrthayātrāp.): III, **114**, †10124 (visited by Yudhishṭhira, etc., on their tīrthayātrā).—§ 398 (Paraçurāma): III, **117**, 10209 (*çailendre*).—§ 399 (Mahendrācalagamana): III, **117**, 10213.—§ 459 (Mārkaṇḍeyas.): III, **188**, 12919 (seen by Mārkaṇḍeya in the stomach of Nārāyaṇa).—§ 573 (Ambopākhyānap.): V, **176**, 6054; **186**, 7338.—§ 574 (Jambūkh.): VI, **9**κ, 318 (among the *kulaparvatāḥ* of Bhāratavarsha).— § 595 (Shoḍaçarāj., v. Rāma Jāmadagnya): VII, **70**, 2447 (*parvatottamam*, having given the earth to Kaçyapa, Rāma took his abode on *M.*). — § 621 (Rājadh.): XII, **2**, 59 (*parvatam*), 62 (*svargasammite*).—§ 775 (Ānuçāsanik.): XIII, **166**a, 7657 (enumeration). — § 782g (Guruçishyasaṃv.): XIV, **43**η, 1174 (do.).

Mahendra[3] = Rāvaṇa (?): II, 410 (*Rākshasādhipatiḥ*, but the text seems to be in disorder, cf. v. 412).

Mahendra[4] = Vishṇu (1000 names).

Mahendrā, a river. § 574 (Jambūkh.): VI, **9**λ, 330 (in Bhāratavarsha).

Māhendra, adj. ("belonging to Mahendra [i.e. Indra]"). § 568 (Vidulāputraçāsana): V, **134**, 4562 (*pragraham*, C.; *ca graham*, B.).—§ 570 (Sainyaniryāṇap.): V, **158**, 5353 (*dhanuḥ*, i.e. Vijaya), 5354 (*dhanur Vijayam*). — § 572 (Rathātirathasaṅkhyānap.): V, **169**, 5870 (*astragrāmaḥ*, acquired by Arjuna).—§ 580 (Bhīshmavadhap.): VI, **59**, †2624 (*astram*, employed by Arjuna).—§ 592 (Saṃçaptakavadhap.): VII, **23**ρ, 1038 (*dhanuḥ*, held by Yudhishṭhira).— § 600 (Ghaṭotkacavadhap.): VII, **157**, †6958 (*astram*, employed by Yudhishṭhira).—§ 601 (Droṇavadhap.): VII, **184**, 8408 (°*ī dik*).—§ 615u (Skanda): IX, **46**ι, 2655 (°*yaḥ*, sc. *mātaraḥ*).—§ 635 (Rājadh.): XII, **38**, 1428 (°*āçaninirdagdhaḥ*, but B. has *Ma°*).

[Mahendrācalagamana(m)] ("the going to the Mahendra mountain"). § 399 (cf. Tīrthayātrāp.): On the fourteenth day of the moon *Rāma* showed himself and was worshipped by the Pāṇḍavas. *Rāma* praised them, and at his direction *Yudhishṭhira* spent the night on *Mahendra*, and then started for the south (III, **117**).

Mahendraloka = Indraloka: I, 434 (°*gamanam*, all. to Indralokābhigamanaparvan).

Mahendrāṇī = Çacī, q.v.

Mahendrasūnu ("the son of the great Indra") = Arjuna: VIII, †4540, †4799.

Mahendratanaya (do.) = Arjuna: VI, 5470.

Mahendravāṇī, a river. § 775 (Ānuçāsanik.): XIII, **166**a, 7654 (enumeration).

Mahendrāvaraja ("younger brother of Mahendra") = Kṛshṇa (Vishṇu), q.v.

Maheshvāsa = Vishṇu (1000 names).

Mahettha, name of a country. § 285 (Nakula): II, **32**, 1188 (in the west, conquered by Nakula on his digvijaya).

Māheya, pl. (°*āḥ*), a people. § 574 (Jambūkh.): VI, **9**μ, 356 (in Bhāratavarsha).

***Mahī**[1] ("the Earth," personif.): I, 2491, 2492, 2493, 2501; II, 438; III, 10113, 14642; VII, 2406 foll.; XIII, 7232 (*Brahmaṇaḥ sutām*).

Mahī[2], a river. § 494 (Āṅgirasa): III, **222**, 14230 (among the rivers who are mothers of fires).

Mahībhartṛ = Vishṇu (1000 names).

Mahīcārin = Çiva (1000 names[2]).

Mahīdhara[1], a king (? PCR.). § 280 (Bhīmasena): II, **30**, 1083 (vanquished by Bhīmasena on his digvijaya), cf. Madadhāra.

Mahīdhara[2], a tīrtha (?). § 379 (Tīrthayātrāp.): III, **95**, 8508 (near Gayā, consecrated by Gaya).

Mahīdhara[3] = Vishṇu (1000 names).

Māhika, pl. (°*aḥ*), a people. § 574 (Jambūkh.): VI, **9**μ, 354 (in Bhāratavarsha).

Mahisha, an Asura. § 507 (Skandayuddha): III, **231**, 14595 (*Dānavaḥ*), 14596, 14599, 14600-2, 14604, 14605, 14609, 14610 (slain by Skanda), 14619, 14620 (°*tulyānām Dānavānām*).—§ 600 (Ghaṭotkacavadhap.): VII, **166**, 7412 (°*m Shaṇmukho*—i.e. Skanda—*yathā*, sc. *nihanishyāmi*).—§ 604 (Karṇap.): VIII, **5**, 146 (*yathā Skandena M°ḥ*, sc. *hataḥ*, so B.).—§ 615u (Skanda): IX, **46**λ, 2692 (slain by Skanda). —§ 730g (Upamanyu): XIII, **14**λ, 805. Cf. Dānava.

Mahishaghna ("the slayer of Mahisha") = Çiva: XIII, 905.

Māhishaka (B. mostly *Ma°*), pl. (°*āḥ*), a people. § 574 (Jambūkh.): VI, **9**ν, 366 (*Ma°*, B., in the south).—§ 607 (Karṇap.): VIII, **44**κ, 2066 (destitute of religion).—§ 739 (Ānuçāsanik.): XIII, **33**a, 2104 (*Ma°*, B., degraded to çūdras).—§ 785 (Anugītāp.): XIV, **83**, 2476 (*Ma°*, B., vanquished by Arjuna).

Mahishānanā, a mātṛ. § 615u (Skanda): IX, **46**θ, 2643.

Mahishārdana ("the destroyer of Mahisha") = Skanda: III, 14630.

Mahishāsuranāçinī ("destroyer of the Asura Mahisha") = Durgā (Umā): IV, 193.

Mahishmatī, daughter of Aṅgiras. § 489 (Āṅgirasa): III, **218**, 14127 (the sixth daughter of Aṅgiras).

Māhishmatī, a city. § 282 (Sahadeva): II, **31**, 1124 (on his digvijaya Sahadeva came to *M.*, the capital of king *Nīla*, and fought with *Nīla*, who was assisted by *Agni*).— § 282b (do.): *Agni* had become enamoured of *Nīla's* daughter and would not blaze up till agitated by the breath of her lips; one day when he enjoyed her love, disguised as a brahman, he was discovered by *Nīla*, who ordered the brahman to be punished according to the law, but as *Agni* flamed up in wrath, the king bestowed his daughter upon him and was granted the boon that his army should have no fear from enemies, and from that time those monarchs who attacked *Nīla* were consumed by *Agni*. The wives of *M.* were granted sexual liberty, and were not confined to a particular husband. From that time the monarchs avoid *M.* from fear of *Agni*: II, **31**, 1130 (°*vāsī bhagavān Havyavāhanaḥ*), 1140.—§ 555 (Sainyodyogap.): V, **19**, 592 (°*vāsī Nīlaḥ*).—§ 572 (Rathātirathasaṅkhyānap.): V, **166**, 5751 (*Nīlo M°vāsī*).—§ 720b (Sudarçanop.): XIII, **2**, 89 (the capital of Daçāçva), 116 (all. to § 282 foll., the capital of Duryodhana[2], who bestowed his daughter Sudarçanā on *Agni*).—§ 772b (Pavanārjunasaṃv.): XIII, **153**, 7187 (the capital of Arjuna Kārtavīrya).

Mahitā, a river. § 574 (Jambūkh.): VI, **9**λ, 328 (only C., B. has *Ahitām*).

Mahodadhi = Çiva (1000 names[1]).

Mahodadhiçaya = Vishṇu (1000 names).

Mahodara[1], a serpent. § 47 (Sarpanāmak.): I, **35**, 1561 (*Kuṇḍodara-M°au*, enumeration).

Mahodara[2], an Asura. § 92 (Aṃçāvat.): I, **65**, 2533 (only C., B. has *Harāharau*, among the sons of Danu).

Mahodara[3], a son of Dhṛtarāshṭra. § 130 (Aṃçāvat.): I, **67**, 2732 (*Kuṇḍodara-M°au*).—§ 182 (Dhṛtarāshṭraputranāmak.): I, **117**, 4546 (*Kuṇḍodaro M°ḥ*).—§ 585 (Bhīshmavadhap.): VI, **88**, 3901, 3903, 3913 (slain by Bhīmasena).

Mahodara[4], a muni. § 615 (Baladevatīrthayātrā): IX, **39**, 2250.—§ 615*k* (do.): Formerly *Rāma* [Dāçarathi] lived in the forest of *Daṇḍaka* from desire of slaying Rākshasas. In *Janasthāna* he cut off the head of a Rākshasa, which coursing at will fell upon the thigh of the brahman *M.* (who wandered through the woods) and piercing it, it stuck to it and remained there. *M.* in vain visited all the other tīrthas and spoke to many ṛshis; at last upon his having bathed in the tīrtha *Auçanasa*, the head of the Rākshasa fell off and was lost in the waters. *M.*, with purified soul and all his sins washed away, returned to his hermitage; the ṛshis on account of this event called the tīrtha by the name of *Kapālamocana*. The great ṛshi *M.*, repairing once more to that tīrtha, drank its water and was crowned with great ascetic success: IX, **39**, 2257, 2266.

Mahodara[5] =| Çiva: VII, 9532; XII, 10416 (1000 names[1]).

Mahodaya (B. °*rya*), a prince. § 775 (Ānuçāsanik.): XIII, **166**η, 7678 (enumeration; P.C.R. translates "highly fortunate").

Mahopamā, a river. § 574 (Jambūkh.): VI. **9**λ, 336 (only C., B. has *mahāpagām*).

Mahopanishad or **Mahopanishada** ("great upanishad"): VI, 5688 (°*am* . . . *japan*); VII, 5986 (*dhyāyan m°aṃ*); XII, 12976 (*idaṃ m°aṃ* . . . *Pañcarātrānuçabditaṃ*).

***Mahoraga** ("great serpents"), mostly pl. (°*āḥ*): I, 248, 7011; III, 1841 (°*gaṇeshu*), 7083, 8168, 8804 (*sa-Gandharva-M°āḥ*), 11646 (°*gaṇāḥ*), 12817 (*samutsanna-M°e*), 13498 (*devāsura-M°āḥ*); IV, 1762 (*deva-Yaksha-Gandharva M°samākulam*), 2271 (*sa-Kinnara-M°āḥ*); V, 332 (*Yaksha-Raksho-M°āḥ*), 369 (*jagat* . . . *sa-Kinnara-Mahoragam*); VII, 3612 (sg. °*a iva çvasan*), 3642 (*Vidyādhara-M°āḥ*), 4269 (*pṛthivī* . . . *sa-Kinnara-M°ā*), 4656 (*yathā kruddhā M°āḥ*), 4953 (*iva*), 5527 (do.), 5618 (sg. *çvasan iva M°āḥ*), 9473 *devāsura-M°āḥ*); VIII, 558 (sg *iva*), †1742 (*Asurasura-M°āḥ*), |4078 (sg., i.e. Açvasena), †4687 (do.), †4962 (*Yaksha-M°aiḥ*); XII, 1607 (*Siddha-M°āḥ*), 1623 (*ṛshi M°āh*), 5890, 6138, 6932 (*Daityāsura-M°āḥ*), 11244 (*trailokye* . . . *sa-Kinnara-M°e*), 12665 (*sa-Kinnara-M°āḥ*); XIII, 3908 (*sarshi-M°āḥ*), 6359 (°*samākulam*), †7088 (sg., i.e. Ananta).

Mahoraga = Vishṇu (1000 names).

Mahoragapati = Çiva (1000 names[1]).

Mahoraska, Mahoshṭha = Çiva (1000 names[1]).

Mahotsaha[1], an ancient king. § 6 (Anukram.): I, **1***a*, 229 (in Sañjaya's enumeration).

Mahotsaha[2] = Vishṇu (1000 names).

Mahya (B. Sahya). § 3 (Anukram.): I, **1**, 43 (son of Vivasvat? (cf. Āçāvaha[1]), father of Devabhrāj; acc. to Nīl. Sahya is = Manu).

Mahyuttara, pl. (°*āḥ*), a people. § 574 (Jambūkh.): VI, **9**μ, 358 (only C., B. has *Samantarāḥ*).

Maināka[1], a mountain. § 30*b* (Samudra): I, **21**, 1219 (*vajrapātasantrasta-M°syābhayapradam*, sc. the ocean).—§ 263 (Sabhākriyāp.): II, **3**, 59 (*uttareṇa tu Kailāsaṃ M°ṃ parvataṃ prati*), 66 (*uttareṇa Kailāsān M°ṃ parvataṃ prati*, there Hiraṇyaçṛṅga, Bindusaras, etc., are situated).—§ 316 (Kirmīravadhap.): III, **11**, 399 (°*a iva parvataḥ*, sc. *āvṛṇot*).—§ 377 (Dhaumyatīrthak.): III, **89**, 8364 (in the west).—§ 412 (Ashṭāvakrīya): III, **134**, 10655 (°*syeva parvatāḥ*, sc. *nikṛshṭabhūtāḥ*). — § 413 (Tīrthayātrāp.): III, **135**, 10694 (*etad vinaçanaṃ kukshau M°sya*).—§ 418 (do.): III, **139**, 10820 (passed by by the Pāṇḍavas). — § 423 (Gandhamādanapr.): III, **145**, 11057 (near Bindusaras and Hiraṇyaçikhara).—§ 430 (Hanūmad - Bhīmasaṃv.): III, **150**, 11278 (°*m iva parvataṃ*).—§ 436 (Yakshayuddhap.): III, **158**, 11540 (*parvataṃ*, passed by by the Pāṇḍavas).—§ 574 (Jambūkh.): VI, **6**, 237 (*abhyuttareṇa Kailāsaṃ M°ṃ parvataṃ prati*, there Hiraṇyaçṛṅga, Bindusaras, etc., are situated). — § 578 (Bhīshmavadhap.): VI, **45**, 1736 (*nākampayata vai M°m iva parvataṃ*); **47**, 1826 (*nākampayat* . . . *M°m iva parvataṃ*).—§ 585 (do.): VI, **92**, 4121 (*nākampata* . . . *M°a iva parvataḥ*).—§ 589 (Droṇap.): VII, **3**, 92 (*Mahendreṇeva M°m asahyaṃ bhuvi pātitaṃ*).—§ 593 (Abhimanyuvadhap.): VII, **47**, 1875 (*nākampayat* . . . *M°m iva parvataṃ*). — § 599 (Jayadrathavadhap.): VII, **92**, 3277 (*abhyayāt* . . . *M°m iva parvataṃ*); **99**, 3693 (*nākampayat* . . . *M°m iva parvataṃ*); **123**, 4936 (do.). — § 600 (Ghaṭotkacavadhap.): VII, **175**, 7952 (*vyadrçyata* . . . *M°a iva parvataḥ*).—§ 611 (Çalyap.): IX, **19**, 1041 (*na cacāla tataḥ sthānān M°a iva parvataḥ*).—§ 733*y* (Ujjānaka): XIII, **25**, 1745 (*parvate*, a tīrtha).

Maināka[2], a mountain in Krauñcadvīpa. § 575 (Bhūmip.): VI, **12**η, 459, 460.

Mainākaparvata. § 606 (Tripurākhyāna): VIII, **34**, 1490 (so C., but read with B. *kanakaparvataḥ* as apposition to *Meruḥ*).

Mainda, a monkey king. § 281 (Sahadeva): II, **31**, 1122 (*vānararājābhyāṃ M°ena Dvividhena ca*, at Kishkindhā, vanquished by Sahadeva on his digvijaya).—§ 531 (Rāmopākhyānap.): III, **280**, 16115 (°*aç ca Dvividhaç cāpi*, among the counsellors of Sugrīva).—§ 535 (Setubandhana): III, **283**β, 16287 (°*M°-Dvividha*°, in the army of Sugrīva).—§ 541 (Indrajidvadha): III, **289***a*, 16468 (*Susheṇa-M°-Dvividhaiḥ*, do.) (β), 16477 (*M°-Dvividha-Nīlāḥ*).—§ 542 (Rāvaṇavadha): III, **290***a*, 16500.

Maireyaka, pl. (°*āḥ*), name of a caste: XIII, 2582.

Maithila = Janaka, q.v.

Maithilī = Sītā, q.v.

Maitra, adj. ("belonging to Mitra"). § 562 (Bhagavadyānap.): V, **83**, 2925 (*muhūrte*) —§ 615 (Gadāyuddhap.): IX, **35**, 1982 (Baladeva set out on his tīrthayātra *M°nakshatrayogena*, i.e under the constellation of Anurādhā?).—§ 707 (Mokshadh.): XII, **318**, 11705 (*sthānam*).—§ 747*b* (Suvarṇotpatti): XIII, **85**, 4130 (*Raudraṃ lohitam*—sc. Agni's—*ity āhur loh itāt kanakaṃ smṛtaṃ* | *tan Maitram iti vijñeyaṃ*; the text is not clear and Nīl. is silent)

maitra ("friendly"?), said of brahmans: XII, 2279 (*maitro brāhmaṇa ucyate*), 8725 (do.); XIII, 1877 (do.): 6455 (*maitra esha smṛto dvijaḥ*).

Maitrāvaruṇi[1] ("the son of Mitra and Varuṇa") = Agastya: III, 8776, 8797, 8807; XII, ††13216 (*Kumbhayonir Agastya* (*Ā*°, C.) *ṛshivaraḥ*); XIII, 4771 (*A*°), 4786.

Maitrāvaruṇi[2] (do.) = Vasishṭha: I, 6801; IX, 2386; XII, 11222.

maitrāyaṇa ("benevolence," cf. Nīl.): III, 13993 (°*gatiḥ*, C.; °*gataḥ*, B.); XII, 5952 (°*gatiḥ*, both B. and C.), 6961 (°*gataḥ*), 9971, 12439 (do.). Cf. Hopkins, *Great Epic*, p. 43.

Maitreya[1], one or more ṛshis. § 264 (Sabhākriyāp.): II,

4a, 105 (waited upon Yudhishṭhira).—§ 315 (Maitreyaçāpa): III, **10,** 349 (*ṛshiḥ*), 352, (356), 363, (364), 373, 376, 378, (381), 382, (383), 384 (cursed Duryodhana, who had slighted him, to have his thigh smashed by Bhīmasena).—§ 615 (Gadāyuddhap.): IX, **60,** 3357 (°*eṇābhiçaptaç ca pūrvam eva maharshiṇā*, all. to § 315).—§ 637 (Rājadh.): XII, **47η,** 1593 (among the ṛshis who surrounded Bhīshma).—§ 763b (Maitreyabhikshā): XIII, **120,** 5794 (°*sya ca saṃvādaṃ Kṛshṇa-Dvaipāyanasya ca*), 5795, 5796, 5798; **121,** 5821, (5822), 5823, (5824); **122,** 5838, 5853, 5856, 5857 (discourse with Vyāsa).

Maitreya[2] = Sūrya: III, 157.

Maitreya-bhikshā] ("the alms of Maitreya"). § 763b (Ānuçāsanik.): *Bhīshma* said: Once *Vyāsa*, while wandering in disguise, waited at *Vārāṇasī* upon *Maitreya* in the house of a loose woman (*svairiṇīkule*; so BR.; quite otherwise Nīl. and PCR.), and was fed by him with excellent food. As he smiled, *Maitreya* said that he did not see much difference between one that behaved as an ordinary person [such as Vyāsa] [and himself], [or generally] between one who is unemancipated and one who is emancipated, especially when [the latter, such as Maitreya] was distinguished by birth (*pṛthag ācaratas tāta pṛthagātmasukhātmanoḥ | alpāntaram ahaṃ manye, viçishṭam api cānvayāt*; cf. Nīl. and PCR.). *Vyāsa* said that he wondered that the *Vedas* should [seemingly] contain an untruth; for even a small gift (as, for instance, a little water given to a thirsty man) produces great results, and *Maitreya* had, by feeding *Vyāsa*, conquered many high regions of felicity, as one does [according to the *Vedas*, only] by great sacrifices. Gift is more auspicious than all sacred acts (XIII, **120**). *Maitreya*, approving of the words of *Vyāsa*, praised the brahmans as the root of righteousness: "if the brahman be gratified, D. and P. also are gratified," referring to Ṛ. (XIII, **121**). *Vyāsa*, saying that even the most atrocious sins are washed off by (gifts and) penances, recommended to him the duties of householders (XIII, **123**).

[Maitreya-çāpa(ḥ)] ("the curse of Maitreya"). § 315 (Āraṇyak.). *Vyāsa* said that the *ṛshi Maitreya* would admonish *Duryodhana*. *Maitreya* came, having on a *tīrthayātrā* arrived at *Kurujāṅgala*, and having visited *Yudhishṭhira* in the *Kāmyaka* wood. As *Maitreya* advised *Duryodhana* to make peace with the *Pāṇḍavas* now that *Bhīma* had slain *Kirmīra*, etc., *Duryodhana* gave him a slight by slapping his thigh and scratching the ground with his foot. Therefore *Maitreya* cursed him, saying that *Bhīma* should smash that thigh of his with his mace; this curse, however, should not take effect if he made peace with the *Pāṇḍavas*. *Dhṛtarāshṭra* wished to hear about the death of *Kirmīra*, but *Maitreya* would not speak again to him, because his words were not regarded by *Duryodhana*; saying that *Vidura* would relate it to him, he went away. *Duryodhana* went out perturbed. (III, **10**.)

Maitrī ("benevolence," personif.). § 310b (Sūrya): III, **3,** 199.

Majjala, a warrior of Skanda. § 615u (Skanda): IX, **45η,** 2572 (only C., B. has *Majjānaḥ*)

Majjāna, v. Majjala.

Mākandī[1], a region in the country of the Pāñcālas. § 209 (Drupadaçāsana): I, **138,** 5512 (°*m atha Gaṅgāyās tīre janapadāyutāṃ so 'dhyāvasad dīnamanāḥ Kāmpilyañ ca purottamaṃ*, sc. Drupada).

Mākandī[2], a city. § 556 (Sañjayayānap.): V, **31,** 934 (among the five villages which the Pāṇḍavas wished to have from Duryodhana).—§ 562 (Bhagavadyānap.): V, **72β,** 2595 (do.); **82ζ,** 2877 (do.).

Makara[1] = Çiva (1000 names[2]).

Makara[2], a vyūha: VI, 3059 (*vyūhaṃ*), 3068, 3280 (*vyūhaṃ*), 3288, †3516 (*vyūhaṃ*); VIII, 413 (*vyūhaṃ*).

makara[3] (the device of Pradyumna): III, 693.

Makaradhvaja[1] ("having a makara on his banner") = Kāma: III, 16192.

Makaradhvaja[2] (do.) = Pradyumna: VII, 4263 (*Kārshṇiḥ*); XIII, 509 (°*sya mātā*, i.e. Rukmiṇī).

Makaraketumat (do.) = Pradyumna: III, 727.

Makarī, a river. § 574 (Jambūkh.): VI, **9λ,** 331 (in Bhāratavarsha).

Māla, pl. (°*āḥ*), a people. § 574 (Jambūkh.): VI, **9μ,** 347 (in Bhāratavarsha).

Mālā, a river. § 276 (Jarāsandhavadhap.): II, **20,** 795 (crossed by Kṛshṇa, Bhīmasena, and Arjuna on their way from Indraprastha to Girivraja).

Malada, pl. (°*āḥ*), a people. § 280 (Bhīmasena): II, **30,** 1082 (in the east, vanquished by Bhīmasena on his digvijaya).—§ 589 (Droṇābhishekap.): VII, **7ζ,** 183 (followed Duryodhana and Karṇa).

Malaja, pl. (°*āḥ*), a people. § 574 (Jambūkh.): VI, **9μ,** 353 (only B., C. has *Malayāḥ*).

Mālatikā, a mātṛ. § 615u (Skanda): IX, **46θ,** 2622.

Mālava, pl. (°*āḥ*), a people. § 285 (Nakula): II, **32,** 1189 (in the west, vanquished by Nakula on his digvijaya).—§ 287 (Rājasūyikap.): II, **34,** 1270 (came to the rājasūya of Yudhishṭhira).—§ 295 (Dyūtap.): II, **52,** 1871 (brought tribute to Yudhishṭhira, *Kshudraka-M°āḥ*).—§ 342 (Indralokābhigamanap.): III, **51,** 1991 (had been present at the rājasūya of Yudhishṭhira).—§ 515 (Karṇadigvijaya): III, **254,** 15256 (vanquished by Karṇa on his digvijaya).—§ 545 (Pativratāmāhātmyap.): III, **297,** 16807 (hundred *M.* shall be begotten by Açvapati on his wife Mālavī).—§ 561 (Yānasandhip.): V, **57,** 2249 (the *M.* and the Çālvakas are assigned to the Kekayas as their matches in the battle).—§ 574 (Jambūkh.): VI, **9ν,** 367 (only B., C. has *Mālavānakāḥ*), 370 (in the south).—§ 578 (Bhīshmavadhap.): VI, **51ν,** 2106 (*Kshudraka-M°aiḥ*, in the army of Duryodhana).—§ 580 (do.): VI, **59μ,** †2584 (*Kshudraka-M°āḥ*, attacked Arjuna) (π), †2646 (*Kshudraka-M°āḥ*, defeated by Arjuna).—§ 585 (do.): VI, **87β,** 3852 (in the van of the army of Duryodhana), (γ), 3853 (*Kshudraka-M°āḥ*).—§ 586 (do.): VI, **106c,** 4808 (defended Bhīshma, cf. v. 5649).—§ 587 (do.): VI, **117ρ,** 5484 (attacked Arjuna); **119aa,** 5649 (*saṃgrāmeṇa jahur Bhīshmaṃ*, B.; *saṃgrāme nājahuḥ*, etc., C.).—§ 589 (Droṇābhishekap.): VII, **7ζ,** 183 (followed Duryodhana and Karṇa); **11ν,** 398 (formerly vanquished by Kṛshṇa).—§ 592 (Saṃçaptakavadhap.): VII, **19β,** 768 (among the Saṃçaptakas who are slain by Arjuna).—§ 595 (Shoḍaçarāj., v. Rāma Jāmadagnya): VII, **70β,** 2435 (*Kshudraka-M°ān*, had been slain by Rāma Jāmadagnya).—§ 600 (Ghaṭotkacavadhap.): VII, **157β,** 6948, 6950 (slain by Yudhishṭhira); **161δδ,** 7206 (do.) (ζζ), 7208 (slain by Arjuna).—§ 604 (Karṇap.): VIII, **5ζ,** 137 (among the slain of Duryodhana's army).

Mālava[1] ("the king of the Mālavas"). § 591 (Saṃçaptakavadhap.): VII, **17β,** 691 (among the Saṃçaptakas). Cf. the two next.

Mālava[2] (do.) = Indravarman: VII, 8708 (*Indravarmaṇah*, of the Pāṇḍava army, his elephant named Açvatthāman is slain by Bhīmasena), 8744 (do., do.), 8949 (do., do.).

Mālava[3] (do.) = Sudarçana: VII, 9330 (*Sudarçanaḥ*, attacked Açvatthāman), 9334, †9337, 9343 (slain by Açvatthāman), 9400 (*Sudarçane . . . hate*).

Mālavā, a river. § 775 (Ānuçāsanik.): XIII, **166a**, 7651 (enumeration).

Mālavānaka, pl. (°*āḥ*), a people. § 574 (Jambūkh.): VI, **9ν**, 367 (only C., B. has *Mālavā narāḥ*).

Mālavī, wife of the Madra king Açvapati. § 545 (Pativratāmāhātmyap.): III, **293**, 16637 (read so instead of *Mānavī*); **297**, 16807 (Yama promised that *M.* should bear 100 Mālavas to Açvapati); **299**, 16914 (the 100 sons are born).

Malaya[1], a mountain. § 39 (Rāmaṇīyaka): I, **27**, 1309 (*vṛkshair M°jaiḥ*, i.e. sandal-trees, BR.).—§ 269 (Vaiçravaṇasabhāv.): II, **10**, 412 (present in the palace of Kubera).—§ 295 (Dyūtap.): II, **52**, 1892 (the Cola king and the Pāṇḍya king brought as tribute sandal juice from *M.* and sandal and aloe tree from Dardura).—§ 375 (Tīrthayātrāp.): III, **85**, 8234 (on *M.* one should ascend the funeral pyre).—§ 459 (Mārkaṇḍeyas.): III, **188**, 12920 (seen by Mārkaṇḍeya in the stomach of Nārāyaṇa).—§ 531 (Rāmopākhyānap.): III, **280**, 16126 (*çrīmān iva mahāçailo M°o meghamālayā*).—§ 534 (Hanūmatpratyāgamana): III, **282**, 16239 (*Sahya-M°au Darduraṅ ca mahāgirim*), 16240 (crossed by the monkeys on their way to Laṅkā).—§ 548 (Āraṇeyap.): III, **313**, †17318 (four mountains enumerated).—§ 555 (Indravijaya): V, **11a**, 353.—§ 574 (Jambūkh.): VI, **6**, 252 (°*parvataḥ*); **9κ**, 318 (among the *kulaparvatāḥ* of Bhāratavarsha).—§ 594 (Mṛtyu): VII, **54**, 2098 (Mṛtyu performed austerities on *M.*).—§ 603*d* (Tripura): VII, **202**, 9564 (Çiva made *M.* the yūpa (i.e. *yuga* [yoke], Nīl.) of his chariot).—§ 605*b* (Pāṇḍya): VIII, **20**, 803 (°*pratimam*, sc. the standard of the Pāṇḍya king (Malayadhvaja)).—§ 716 (Çukābhipatana): XII, **333**, 12597 (*parvatam*, there Urvaçī and Pūrvacitti always dwell).—§ 775 (Ānuçāsanik.): XIII, **166a**, 7657 (enumeration).

Malaya[2], a mountain in Çākadvīpa. § 575*b* (Çākadvīpa) VI, **11**, 416 (*parvataḥ*). Cf. Jalada.

Malaya[3], a Suparṇa, son of Garuḍa. § 564 (Mātalīyop.) V, **101β**, 3599 (only C., B. has *Mā°*).

Malaya, pl. (°*āḥ*), a people. § 574 (Jambūkh.): VI, **9μ**, 353 (only C., B. has *Malajāḥ*).

Mālaya, v. Malaya[3].

Malayadhvaja, name of a Pāṇḍya king. § 605 (Karṇap.): VIII, **20**, 789, †809 (slain by Açvatthāman). Cf. Pāṇḍya.

Mālin = Çiva (1000 names[2]).

Mālinī[1], a river. § 133 (Dushyanta): I, **70**, 2864 (flowed by the hermitage of Kaṇva), 2872.—§ 134 (Viçvāmitra): I, **72**, 2946 (*prasthe Himavato ramye M°īm abhito nadīm*, there Menakā bore Çakuntalā).

Mālinī[2], one of the mothers of Çiçu. § 500 (Skandop.): III, **228a**, 14396.

Mālinī[3], a Rākshasī. § 526 (Rāmopākhyānap.): III, **275**, 15893, 15896 (by Viçravas, mother of Vibhīshaṇa).

Mālinī[4], a goddess. § 549 (Pāṇḍavapraveçap.): IV, **9**, 259 (Draupadī is asked if she is *M.*).

Mālinī[5]. § 549 (Pāṇḍavapraveçap.): IV, **9**, 264 (the name which Draupadī assumed at the court of Virāṭa).

Mālinī[6], a city (according to Harivaṃça, v. 1699, identical with Campā). § 621 (Rājadh.): XII, **5**, 134 (given to Karṇa by Jarāsandha).

Malla, pl. (°*āḥ*), a people. § 280 (Bhīmasena): II, **30**, 1077 (°*ānām adhipam*, vanquished by Bhīmasena, in the east), 1086 (*dakshiṇa-M°ān*, in the east, vanquished by Bhīmasena).—§ 549 (Pāṇḍavapraveçap.): IV, **1a**, 12.—§ 574 (Jambūkh.): VI, **9μ**, 354. Cf. Mallarāshṭra.

malla, pl. (°*āḥ*) ("athletes"): II, 102; IV, 339 foll.; IX, 1231; XIV, 2039.

Mallarāshṭra ("the kingdom of the Mallas"). § 574 (Jambūkh.): VI, **9μ**, 352. Cf. Malla, pl.

Mallava, pl. (°*āḥ*), a people. § 574 (Jambūkh.): VI, **9ν**, 370 (only C., B. has *Ballavāḥ*).

Mālyapiṇḍaka, a serpent. § 564 (Mātalīyop.): V, **103γ**, 3629 (enumeration).

Mālyavat, one or more mountains. § 436 (Yakshayuddhap.): III, **158**, 11560 (*mahāgirim*, in the north, passed by by the Pāṇḍavas on their way to Gandhamādana).—§ 531 (Rāmopākhyānap.): III, **280**, 16118 (°*o 'bhyāse*, the abode of Sugrīva, in the south), 16132 (*pṛshṭhe M°aḥ*, there Rāma dwelt for four months).—§ 534 (Hanūmatpratyāgamana): III, **282**, 16197, 16218.—§ 574 (Jambūkh.): VI, **6**, 203 (south of Nīla and north of Nishadha); **7**, 253 (*parvatam*).—§ 574*j* (do.): On the summit of *M.* is always seen the fire called *Saṃvartaka*, which blazes forth at the end of the yuga for the destruction of the universe. On the summit of *M.* towards the east there are many small mountains; *M.* measures 11,000 yojanas. The men there are of the complexion of gold; they have fallen from the *Brahmaloka* and are good, and given to severe ascetic austerities and sexual abstinence (*ūrdhvaretasaḥ*); in order to protect the creatures they enter the sun; heated with the sun's rays for 66,000 years, they then enter the lunar disc: VI, **7**, 281, 282.—§ 782*g* (Guruçishyasaṃv.): XIV, **43η**, 1174.

Mamatā, the wife of Utathya. § 170 (Dīrghatamas): I, **104**, 4179, 4180, 4188 (mother of Dīrghatamas, q.v.).

māṃsa, name of a caste (?): XIII, 2584.

Mānada[1], son of Dhṛshṭadyumna. § 589 (Droṇābhishekap.): VII, **10λ**, 358.

Mānada[2] = Vishṇu (1000 names).

Manaḥsuparṇa = Sūrya (the Sun): III, 155.

Manas ("mind," personif.). § 270 (Brahmasabhāv.): II, **11**, 438 (in the palace of Brahmán).

Mānasa[1], name of two serpents. § 63 (Sarpasattra): I, **57**, 2146 (of Vāsuki's race).—§ 67 (do.): I, **57**, 2157 (of Dhṛtarāshṭra's race).

Mānasa[2], a sacred lake, the present Manasarovara (or Mansaraur). § 279 (Arjuna): II, **28**, 1041 (*sara uttamam*, in the region Hāṭaka), 1042 (*saraḥ*).—§ 410 (Plakshāvataraṇag.): III, **130**, 10547 (°*sya dvāram*).—§ 587 (Bhīshmavadhap.): VI, **119**, 5665 (*haṃsaḥ . . . M°aukasaḥ*).—§ 607 (Haṃsakākīyop.): VIII, **41**, 1894 (do.).—§ 608 (Karṇap.): VIII, **60**, 3048 (°*ād etya haṃsair Gaṅgeva*).—§ 652*b* (Indrota-Pārikshitīya): XII, **152**, 5647 (PCR. is hardly right in connecting *Mānasaḥ saraḥ* with *Sarasvatī-Dṛshadvatyoḥ saṅgamaḥ*).—§ 717*b* (Nārāyaṇīya): XII, **343**, VII), ††13213 (°*sarogatām nalinīm*), ††13215 (*saraḥ*).—§ 772*l* (Vasishṭha): XIII, **156**, 7280 (*saraḥ*, only B., C. has *Vaikhānasam*). Cf. Mānasa(m) tīrtha(m), Uttaramānasa

Mānasa[3], a mountain. § 495 (Skandotpatti): III, **223**, 14246 (*çailam*); **224**, 14258.

Mānasa[4], a name of the primeval being. § 660*b* (Bhṛgu-Bharadvājasaṃv.): XII, **182**, 6775, 6798, 6802; **183**, 6805; **187**, 6920.

mānasa, adj. ("belonging to the mind"). § 660*b* (Bhṛgu-Bharadvājasaṃv.): XII, **188**, 6949 (*sṛshṭir m°ī*).—§ 717*b* (Nārāyaṇīya): XII, **348ηη**, 13489 (*janma*, sc. *Brahmaṇaḥ*); **349**, I), 13559 (do.).

Mānasa, pl. (°*āḥ*). § 575*b* (Çākadvīpa): VI, **11***δ*, 436, 438 (i.e. the vaiçyas of Çākadvīpa).

Manasaḥ paramā yoniḥ = Çiva (1000 names[1]).

Mānasa(m) tīrtha(m). § 757*m* (Goloka): XIII, **102***a*, 4887. Cf. Mānasa[2].

mānasa(m) tīrtha(m) ("tīrtha of mind," metaph.): XIII, 5351.

Mānasika, Manaspati = Mahāpurusha (Mahāpurushastava).

Manasvinī. § 116 (Vasu, pl.): I, **66**, 2583 (wife of Prajāpati and mother of Soma (the moon)).

Manasyu, a prince. § 150 (Pūruvaṃç.): I, **94**, 3696 (son of Pravīra and Çūrasenī), 3697 (husband of Sauvīrī, with whom he had three sons, Çakta, Saṃhana, and Vāgmin).

***Mānava**, pl. (°*āḥ*) ("descendants of Manu"). § 139 (Manu Vaivasvata): I, **75**, 3139 (i.e. the men), 3140 (*brāhmaṇāḥ*).

Mānava, adj. ("belonging to Manu or to the Mānavas"). § 277 (Jarāsandhavadhap.): II, **21**, 803 (*vaṃçam*).—§ 603 (Nārāyaṇāstramokshap.): VII, **194***ζ*, 8965 (sc. *astram*).—§ 768*b* (Kṛshṇa Vāsudeva): XIII, **147**, 6827 (*Prājāpatye çubhe mārge M°e dharmasaṃhite*, sc. *vaṃçe*?). — § 770 (Ânuçāsanik.): XIII, **151**, 7107 (*ṛshisattamān*, i.e. Yavakrīta, etc.).

Mānavarjaka, pl. (°*āḥ*), a people. § 574 (Jambūkh.): VI, **9***μ*, 357 (in Bhāratavarsha).

Mānavī[1] (III, 16637), v. Mālavī.

Mānavī[2], a river. § 574 (Jambūkh.): VI, **9***λ*, 339 (only B., C. has *Tāmasī*).

Mandaga, pl. (°*āḥ*). § 575*b* (Çākadvīpa): VI, **11***δ*, 436, 439 (i.e. the çūdras of Çākadvīpa).

Mandagā, a river. § 574 (Jambūkh.): VI, **9***λ*, 340 (in Bhāratavarsha).

Mandaka, pl. (°*āḥ*), a people. § 574 (Jambūkh.): VI, **9***μ*, 351 (in Bhāratavarsha).

Mandākinī, name of more rivers. § 372 (Tīrthayātrāp.): III, **85**, 8201 (near Citrakūṭa).—§ 565 (Gālavac.): V, **111**, 3832 (in the north).—§ 574 (Jambūkh.): VI, **9***λ*, 342, 344.—§ 716 (Çukābhipatana): XII, **334**, 12623, 12635 (°*tīre*).—§ 731*b* (Ashṭāvakra-Diksaṃv.): XIII, **19***a*, 1412 (near Kubera's lake), 1443 (*nadīm*).—§ 733*m* (Citrakūṭa): XIII, **25**, 1715 (°*jale*, near Citrakūṭa).—§ 757*d* (Hastikūṭa): Gautama said: The blessed *M.* of king *Vaiçravaṇa* [Kubera] is accessible to those who are devoted to enjoyments (*bhogijanapraveçyā*) [and is] pleasing to *Gandharvas, Yakshas*, and *Apsarases*. *Dhṛtarāshṭra* said: Those who regard hospitality as a vow, who are observant of good vows, who give shelter to brahmans, and who feed on remnants, adorn the *M.*: XIII, **102**, †4860, †4861.—§ 775 (Ânuçāsanik.): XIII, **166***a*, 7648 (enumeration).

Maṇḍala, name of a vyūha: VI, 3551 (*mahāvyūhaḥ*), 3552 (*vyūham*).

Maṇḍalaka, a serpent. § 64 (Sarpasattra): I, **57**, 2149 (of Takshaka's race).

Mandapāla, a ṛshi. § 11 (Parvasaṅgr.): I, **2**, 404 (*maharsher M°sya çārṅgyāṃ tanayasambhavaḥ*, cf. § 259).—§ 259 (Çārṅgakop.): I, **229**, 8335 (*maharshiḥ*). (8339), 8345, 8350, (8353), 8361, 8362; **231**, 8402; **232**, 8409 (°*sya putrakāḥ*), 8423, 8425; **233**, 8429, 8435, 8442, 8448, (8450), (8454); **234**, (8461), 8464 (the story of *M.* and his two wives and his sons, the çārṅgakas). Cf. Viprarshi.

Mandara[1], a mountain. § 28 (Amṛtamanthana): I, **18**, 1112 (*parvatavaram*), 1116, 1121, 1124, 1130, 1134, 1143 (the gods made *M.* their churning staff, when they churned the ocean in search of *amṛta*); **19**, †1187 (returned to its own place).—§ 133 (Dushyanta): I, **68**, 2810 (*udyamya M°m dorbhyāṃ vahet savanakānanam*, sc. Dushyanta).—§ 244 (Rājyalābhap.): I, **207**, 7576 (*gopurair M°opamaiḥ*).—§ 258 (Khāṇḍavadahanap.): I, **227**, 8281 (Indra tore a peak from *M.* and hurled it against Arjuna).—§ 269 (Vaiçravaṇasabhāv.): II, **10**, 412 (present in the palace of Kubera).—§ 295 (Dyūtap.): II, **52**, 1858 (*Meru-M°yor madhye Çailodām abhito nadīm*).—§ 335*b* (Indralokābhigamanap.): *M.* is the refuge of heaven-seeking *munis*; by its grace brahmans, kshatriyas, and vaiçyas attain to heaven; there many tīrthas are seen, and there *Arjuna* had lived happily; it resounds with notes of *Apsarases* and the chanting of the *Vedas*: III, **42**, 1734 (*çailarājam*, Arjuna came to *M.* and praised it).—§ 384 (Agastyop.): III, **101**, †8728 (*yathā mahāçailavaraḥ purastāt sa M°o Vishṇukarād vimuktaḥ*).—§ 418*c* (Tīrthayātrāp.): On *M.* lives the Yaksha Māṇivara and the *Yaksha* king (*Yaksharāṭ*) Kubera and 88,000 *Gandharvas*, and four times as many (*caturguṇaḥ*) *Kimpurushas* and *Yakshas* surround the *Yakshendra Māṇibhadra*: III, **139**, 10824 (*parvatam*).—§ 421*b* (Gandhamādanapr.): *M.* is the dwelling-place of the celestial ṛshis: III, **142**, 10900 (*parvatam*).—§ 439 (Yakshayuddhap.): III, **163**, 11844 (*asau sāgaraparyantām bhūmim āvṛtya tishṭhati çailarājo, mahārāja, M°o 'tivirājate*), 11873 (*evam esha*—i.e. the moon—*hy atikramya Mahāmerum atandritaḥ | bhāvayan sarvabhūtāni punar gacchati M°m*).—§ 459 (Mārkaṇḍeyas.): III, **188**, 12918 (seen by Mārkaṇḍeya in the stomach of Nārāyaṇa); **189**, 12959 (*catuḥsamudraparyantām Meru-M°bhūshaṇām*, sc. *bhūmim*) —§ 505 (Skandayuddha): III, **231**, 14536 (*iva*).—§ 549 (Durgā): IV, **6**, 191 (*vibhrājase cābaddhena bhogenevehā M°ḥ*). — § 555 (Indravijaya): V, **9**, 289 (*upavishṭā M°āgre*, sc. the gods); **11***a*, 353. — § 564 (Mātalīyop.): V, **102**, 3612 (*manthānam M°m kṛtvā*, all. to § 28).—§ 565 (Gālavac.): V, **110**, 3809 (*atra*—i.e. in the west—*mūlam Himavato M°m yāti çāçvatam*); **111**, 3832 (in the north).—§ 574 (Jambūkh.): VI, **3**, 104 (*Kailāsa-M°ābhyām*).—§ 596 (Pratijñāp.): VII, **80**, 2848 (°*sya pradeçāc ca*), 2852 (*mahā-M°m*, seen by Kṛshṇa and Arjuna on their way to Çiva's abode).—§ 599*c* (Vṛtra): VII, **94**, 3464 (the abode of Çiva).—§ 603*d* (Tripura): VII, **202**, 9568 (Çiva made *M.* his bow).—§ 606 (Tripurākhyāna): VIII, **34**, 1473 (*parvataḥ*, became the *aksha* of Çiva's chariot). — § 607 (Karṇap.): VIII, **36**, 1685 (°*stha ivāṃçumān*).—§ 611 (Çalyap.): IX, **11**, 584 (? *mandarārthe*, C.; *nadan Pārtho*, B.; PCR. seems to have read *mandārārthe*, "for the sake of procuring *mandāra* flowers").—§ 731*b* (Ashṭāvakra-Diksaṃv.): XIII, **19**, 1434 (crossed by Ashṭāvakra on his way to the north).—§ 775 (Ânuçāsanik.): XIII, **166***a*, 7658. Cf. Parvatarājan.

Mandara[2], v. Mandāra.

Mandāra (so B.; Mandara, C.), son of Hiraṇyakaçipu. § 730*c* (Hiraṇyakaçipu): *M.* succeeded, through the boon he had obtained from Çiva, in fighting Indra for a million of years; neither the thunderbolt of Indra nor the discus of Vishṇu could make the slightest impression in his body: XIII, **14**, 663.

Mandaravāsinī ("dwelling on Mandara") = Durgā (Umā): VI, 796.

Mandavāhinī, a river. § 574 (Jambūkh.): VI, **9***λ*. 340 (in Bhāratavarsha).

Māṇḍavya, a ṛshi (= Aṇīmāṇḍavya). § 171 (Vicitravīryasutotpatti): I, **106**, 4302 (*Dharmo Vidurarūpeṇa çāpāt tasya* *mahātmanaḥ* | *M°sya*, cf. § 172).—§ 172 (Aṇīmāṇḍavyop.): I, **107,** 4306 (why *M.* was called Aṇīmāṇḍavya, q.v., his cursing Dharma to be born as Vidura). — § 573 (Ambopākhyānap.): V, **186,** 7355 (*°syāçrame*, there Ambā performed austerities).—§ 637 (Rājadh.): XII, **47**η, 1598 (among the ṛshis who surrounded Bhīshma on his arrow-bed).—§ 689 (Mokshadh.): **XII, 277,** 9916, 9927 (his discourse with Janaka).—§ 730 (Ānuçāsanik.): XIII, **18**κκ, (1343) (being impaled, cf. § 172, *M.* had adored Çiva, who promised his deliverance).—§ 788 (Āçramavāsap.): XV, **28,** 752 (*°çāpād dhi sa vai Dharmo Viduratām gataḥ*), 754 (*°enarshiṇā Dharmo hy abhibhūtaḥ*, cf § 172) Cf. Aṇīmāṇḍavya.

Māndhātṛ[1], an ancient king, son of Yuvanāçva. § 11 (Parvasaṅgr.): I, **2,** 446 (*°uç cāpy upākhyānam rājñaḥ*, cf. Māndhātrupākhyāna).—§ 61 (Sarpasattra): I, **55,** 2109 (*Yayāti-M°-samaprabhāva*, sc. Janamejaya).—§ 267 (Yamasabhāv.): II, **8,** 319 (in the palace of Yama).—§ 335 (Indralokābhigamanap.): III, **42,** 1754 (*vyarocata yathā pūrvam M°ā pārthivasattamaḥ*, sc. Arjuna).—§ 377 (Dhaumyatīrthak.): III, **94,** 8507 (*yathā*).—§ 407 (Māndhātrup.): III, **126,** 10423 (*Yauvanāçvaḥ*), 10425, 10427, 10453 (origin of the name), 10468 (the history of *M.*).—§ 516 (Duryodhanayajña): III, **257,** 15329 (among the princes who had attained to heaven by performing the Vaishṇava sacrifice).—§ 562 (Bhagavadyānap.): V, **90**ν, 3146.—§ 576 (Bhagavadgītāp.): VI, **17**β, 645.—§ 595 (Shoḍaçarāj.): King *M. Yauvanāçva* vanquished the gods, the Asuras, and men; the *Açvins* took him out from his father's womb by a surgical operation, as *Yuvanāçva*, when a-hunting, had drunk the sacrificial butter from a sacrifice and become quick with child. Then *Indra* let him suck milk from his fingers (whence the name of *M.*); in twelve days he became 12 cubits in stature. He conquered the whole earth and vanquished the kings *Janamejaya*, etc. (*a*), in a single day; all the lands lying between the mountain where the sun rises and the mountain where he sets are known to this day as the dominions of *M.* Having performed a hundred horse-sacrifices and a hundred *rājasūyas*, he gave to the brahmans some *rohita* fishes of gold, 10 *yojanas* in length and 1 *yojana* in breadth. The gods, the Asuras, men, the Yakshas, the Gandharvas, the Uragas, the birds, the brahmans, and the *ṛshis* came to his sacrifices. At last he repaired to the regions of the righteous (C. *puṇyakṛtāl lokān*; B. *°ām lo°*) (VII, **62**): VII, **62,** 2272 (*Yauvanāçvaḥ*), 2278, 2282, 2283 (*Yauvanāçvasya*).—§ 621 (Rājadh.): XII, **8**θ, 238 (among the princes to whom the earth has belonged).—§ 623 (do.): XII, **14,** 421 (*yathā*).—§ 632*b* (Shoḍaçarāj., cf. § 595): XII, **29,** 974 (*Yauvanāçvam . . . yam devā Maruto garbham pituḥ pārçvad apaharan*), 977 (origin of the name), 981, 983 (*Yauvanāçvam*) (repetition from § 595).—§ 641 (Rājadh.): XII, **64,** 2397, 2398 (†2405); **65,** (2429), (2439) (discourse between *M.* and Vishṇu in the shape of Indra about the duties of the kshatriyas); **90,** 3362 (*Yauvanāçvāya*), 3364, 3383, 3387, 3390; **91,** 3441, 3444, 3456, 3461, 3462 (discourse of Utathya to *M.*); **122,** 4474, 4475, 4478, (4479) (Vasuhoma instructed *M.* about the origin of Chastisement); **124,** 4564 (had conquered the earth in course of one night).—§ 718*b* (Uñchavṛttyup.): XII, **356,** 13802 (in Naimisha *M.* had neglected Indra).—§ 730*g* (Upamanyu): XIII, **14,** 860 (*Yauvanāçvo hato yena*, i.e. by the çūla of Çiva, *M°ā sabalaḥ purā*).—§ 746 (Ānuçāsanik.): XIII, **76,** 3668 (instructed by Bṛhaspati about kine), (ι), †3689 (*Yauvanāçvaḥ*, attained to heaven by gifts of kine), †3691, †3693; **81**λ, 3806 (*Yauvanāçvaḥ*, used to give kine in thousands).—§ 761 (do.): XIII, **115**γ, 5663 (among the princes who abstained from meat during the month of Kārttika).—§ 775 (do.): XIII, **166**η, 7679 (enumeration). — § 787 (Āçramavāsap.): XV, **20,** 549 (*°ur api cātmajaḥ Purukutsaḥ*).—§ 795 (Svargārohaṇap.): XVIII, **4**θ, 107 (*rājarshiḥ*, in heaven).

Cf. the following synonyms:—

Yauvanāçva ("the son of Yuvanāçva"): II, 1929; III, 10423 (*M°*); VII, 2272 (*M°*), 2279, 2283 (*M°*); XII, 974 (*M°*), 978, 982, 983 (*M°*), 3362 (*M°*); XIII, 860 (*M°*), †3689 (*M°*), 3806 (*M°*), 7675 (so both C. and B., but as *M.* is mentioned v. 7679, we have perhaps to read *Yuvanāçvaḥ*).

Yauvanāçvi (do.): II, 649.

Māndhātṛ[2] = Çiva (1000 names[2]).

[Māndhātrupākhyāna(m)] (episode relating to Māndhātṛ.) (cf. *Māndhātuḥ . . . upākhyānam*, I, 446).—§ 407 (Tīrthay.): Questioned by *Yudhishṭhira*, *Lomaça* said: King (*rājarshi*, v. 10429) *Yuvanāçva Saudyumni*, of *Ikshvāku's* race, performed besides other sacrifices 1,000 horse-sacrifices. As he had no sons, he made over the duties of the state to his ministers, and retired to the woods. Having once observed a fast, he entered the hermitage of *Bhṛgu*, while the great ṛshis were asleep, and drank a jar of water, which the son of *Bhṛgu* (*maharshiḥ*), after having performed severe austerities, had destined to be drunk by *Yuvanāçva's* queen in order that she should bear him a son, who by his bravery might send even *Indra* to the abode of *Yama*. A sacrifice was then performed for him; after 100 years a son pierced *Yuvanāçva's* left side (nor did *Yuvanāçva* die). *Indra* came, and put the boy's forefinger into his mouth, saying "me he shall suck" (*mām ayam dhāsyati*, whence the boy was called *Māndhātṛ*). Thereby *Māndhātṛ* became very strong, and grew 13 cubits (*kishkūn*), and acquired the whole of the *Vedas* including the *Dhanurveda* by his thought alone, and on the same day he obtained the bow *Ājagava* and a number of shafts made of horn, and an impenetrable coat of mail. He was placed on the throne by *Indra* himself, and conquered the three worlds in a righteous way; the gems of their own accord came into his possession, and he performed a number of sacrifices with abundant gratuities, and sat at *Indra's* side. His sacrificial grounds (*caityaiḥ*) were to be found all over the earth, and he is said to have given away to the Brahmans 10,000 *padmas* of kine. After twelve years' drought he caused rain to come down, paying no heed to *Indra*. He slew the *Gāndhāra* king of the lunar dynasty. Here, in the midst of *Kurukshetra*, is the spot where he sacrificed to the gods (III, **126**).

Maṇḍika, pl. (*°āḥ*), a people. § 515 (Karṇadigvijaya): III, **254,** 15243 (only C., B. has *Çuṇḍikān*, in the east, vanquished by Karṇa on his digvijaya).

Mandodarī[1], wife of Rāvaṇa. § 533 (Sītā-Rāvaṇasaṃv.): III, **281,** 16181 (*bhāryā me bhava . . . yathā M°ī*, says Rāvaṇa to Sītā).

Mandodarī[2], a mātṛ. § 615*u* (Skanda): IX, **46**θ, 2635.

***maṇḍūka**[1], pl. ("frogs"): III, ††13165, ††13166, ††13168, ††13169, ††13170, ††13172.

maṇḍūka[2], pl. (*°āḥ*), a kind of horse: II, 1043 (*tittirikalmāshān m°ākhyān hayottamān*).

Maṇḍūkarāj ("king of the frogs") = Āyu(s): III, ††13167.

Maṇḍūkarāja (do.) = Āyu(s): III, ††13173 (*Ā°*), ††13178.

Maṅga, pl. (*°āḥ*), a people: VI, 436–7 (only B.; Mṛga, C.).

Maṅgala(m)[1] = Çiva (1000 names[1]). — Do.[2] = Vishṇu (1000 names).

Maṇi[1], a ṛshi (?). § 270 (Brahmasabhāv.): II, **11**, 442 (in the palace of Brahmán).

Maṇi[2], a serpent. § 67 (Sarpasattra): I, **57**, 2160 (only B., C. has *Maṇiskandhaḥ* instead of *Maṇiḥ Skandhaḥ*).—§ 564 (Mātalīyop.): V, **103**γ, 3626 (*ṅāgaḥ*, enumeration).

Maṇi[3], a companion of Skanda. § 615*u* (Skanda): IX, **45**, 2534 (together with Sumaṇi *M.* is given to Skanda by Soma).

Maṇibhadra (C. often Mā°), a Yaksha. § 269 (Vaiçravaṇasabhāv.): II, **10**, 397 (among the Yakshas in the palace of Kubera). — § 347 (Nalopākhyānap.): III, **64**, 2529 (*Yaksharāḍ adya M°ḥ prasīdatu*); **65**, 2553 (*nūnaṃ na pūjito 'smābhir M°o mahāyaçāḥ*, *M.* is the tutelary deity of travellers and caravans).—§ 418*c* (Mandara): III, **139**, 10826 (*Yakshendraṃ*, on Mandara, *Mā°* both C. and B.).—§ 685 (Mokshadh.): XII, **272**, 9769 (*Mā°*, C.), 9772 (do.), 9774 (do.), 9775 (do.), (9781) (do.), (9783) (do.).—§ 731*b* (Ashṭāvakra-Diksaṃv.): XIII, **19**, 1413 (*°purogamāḥ*, sc. *Rākshasāḥ*, C. *Mā°*), 1421 (do., do.).—§ 785 (Anugītāp.): XIV, **65**, 1918 (oblations are given to Kubera and *M.*). Cf. Yaksharāj, Yakshendra.

Maṇibhadraka, pl. (*°āḥ*), a people. § 578 (Bhīshmavadhap.): VI, **51**σ, 2099 (in the army of Duryodhana, only C., B. has *Pāribhadrakaiḥ*).

Maṇibiddha, v. Maṇividdha.

Maṇijalā, a river in Çākadvīpa. § 575*b* (Çākadvīpa): VI, **11**γ, 433.

Maṇika, a serpent (?). § 608 (Karṇap.): VIII, **87**χ', 4414 (sided with Arjuna in the encounter between Karṇa and Arjuna).

Maṇikāñcana, a varsha (?) in Çākadvīpa. § 575*b* (Çākadvīpa): VI, **11**β, 426 (*Çyāmasya*).

Maṇikuṭṭikā, a mātṛ. § 615*u* (Skanda): IX, **46** θ, 2638.

Maṇimantha, a mountain. § 730 (Ānuçāsanik.): XIII, **18**κκ, 1328 (*çaile*, in a former existence Kṛshṇa had worshipped Çiva on *M.*).

Maṇimat[1], a Yaksha or Rākshasa. § 11 (Parvasaṅgr.): I, **2**, 454 (*Rākshasaiḥ . . . Yakshaiḥ . . . M°pramukhaiḥ*, all to § 432, where however *M.* is not mentioned), 457 (*Yakshaiḥ . . . M°pramukhaiḥ*, all. to § 437).—§ 437 (Yakshayuddhap.): III, **160**, 11720 (*sakhā Vaiçravaṇasya . . . Rākshasaḥ*), 11724 (fights with Bhīmasena), 11732, 11733 (slain by Bhīmasena).—§ 438 (do.): III, **161**, 11759 (*te*—i.e. Kubera's —*sakhā*), 11796 (had disregarded Agastya and been cursed by him to be slain by a mortal). Cf. Rākshasa, Rākshasādhipati.

Maṇimat[2], one or more kings. § 130 (Aṃçāvat.): I, **67**, 2680 (*rājarshiḥ*, incarnation of the Asura Vṛtra).—§ 232 (Svayaṃvarap.): I, **186**, 6987 (present at the svayaṃvara of Draupadī).—§ 280 (Bhīmasena): II, **30**, 1085 (*bhūmipālāṃç ca M°pramukhān*, in the east, vanquished by Bhīmasena).—§ 554 (Sainyodyogap.): V, **4**γ, 83.—§ 592 (Saṃçaptakavadhap.): VII, **25**, 1116 (*rājānaṃ*, fights with Bhūriçravas (Saumadatti)).—§ 604 (Karṇap.): VIII, **6**, 163 (*M.* and Daṇḍadhāra had been slain by Droṇa in the battle).

Maṇimat[3], a serpent. § 268 (Varuṇasabhāv.): II, **9**, 361 (in the palace of Varuṇa).

Maṇimat[4], a ṛshi (?). § 277 (Jarāsandhavadhap.): II, **21**, 807 (*Kauçiko M°āñ ca*, have favoured the Magadhas).

Maṇimat[5], a tīrtha. § 360 (Tīrthayātrāp.): III, **82**, 5043.

Maṇimat[6], a mountain. § 596 (Pratijñāp.): VII, **80**, 2843 (*parvataṃ*, description, reached by Kṛshṇa and Arjuna on their way to the abode of Çiva).

Maṇimatī, a city. § 382 (Agastyop.): III, **96**, 8540 (the abode of Ilvala; = *Durjayā*, Nīl.)

Maṇināga[1], a serpent. § 47 (Sarpanāmak.): I, **35**, 1551 (enumeration). — § 277 (Jarāsandhavadhap.): II, **21**, 806 (resides near Girivraja).

Maṇināga[2], a tīrtha (presumably named after Maṇināga[1]). § 370 (Tīrthayātrāp.): III, **84**, 8084. 8085 (*tairthikaṃ bhuñjate yas tu M°sya, Bhārata | dashṭasyāçīvisheṇāpi na tasya kramate vishaṃ*).

Maṇiṅgā, a river. § 574 (Jambūkh.): VI, **9**λ, 342 (only C., B. has *Anaṅgāṃ*).

Maṇipūra, the capital of Citravāhana (later of Babhruvāhana). § 249 (Arjunavanavāsap.): I, **215**, 7824.—§ 250 (do.): I, **217**, 7883.—§ 794 (Mahāprasthānikap.): XVII, **1**, 28 (*Maṇipūrapuraṃ*).

Maṇipūrapati ("the lord of Maṇipūra") = Babhruvāhana: XIV, 2301, 2340 (*°er mātā*, i.e. Citrāṅgadā), 2401, 2402 (*°er mātuḥ*, i.e. Citrāṅgadā), 2424, 2571.

Maṇipūreçvara[1] (do.) = Citravāhana: I, 7826.

Maṇipūreçvara[2] (do.) = Babhruvāhana: XIV, 2303, 2381, 2419.

Maṇipushpaka, the conch of Sahadeva. § 576 (Bhagavadgītāp.): VI, **25**κ, 845.—§ 578 (Bhīshmavadhap.): VI, **51** *aa*, 2116

Maṇiskandha, a serpent. § 67 (Sarpasattra): I, **57**, 2160 (only C., B. has *Maṇiḥ Skandhaḥ*, of Dhṛtarāshṭra's race).

Maṇivāhana = Kuçamba: I, 2363.

Māṇivara, a Yaksha. § 418*c* (Mandara): III, **139**, 10824 (*Yakshaṃ*, resides on Mandara).

Maṇividdha (C. *°bi°*) = Çiva (1000 names[2]).

Mañjulā, a river. § 574 (Jambūkh.): VI, **9**λ, 341 (in Bhāratavarsha).

Maṅkaṇaka[1] (III, 5079), v. Macakruka.

Maṅkaṇaka[2], a ṛshi. § 365 (cf. Tīrthayātrāp.): At the tīrtha *Saptasārasvata* the great *ṛshi M.* became perfect (*siddhaḥ*), so that when he had cut his hand with the pointed blade of a *kuça* grass, there flew from his wound vegetable juice, at which he began to dance, and the animate and inanimate creation also began to dance together with him. Then the gods, headed by Brahman and the ṛshis, asked *Mahādeva* (i.e. Çiva) to prevent him from dancing. The god then in the presence of *M.* pressed his thumb with the tip of his own finger, and from the wound there came ashes, white as snow. Then *M.* became ashamed and adored *Rudra*, saying that he was the refuge of the world, including the gods and the Asuras, that he had created the three worlds, and swallows everything at the end of the *yuga*, that he cannot be fathomed by the gods themselves, that all the gods headed by *Brahmán* are to be seen in him, etc. At his request *Çiva* said to the *Brahmarshi* that his asceticism (*tapas*) should through the grace of *Çiva* increase a thousandfold, that he would dwell with him in the āçrama, and that those who bathe in *Saptasārasvata* and worship *Çiva* should be able to obtain everything here and hereafter, and go to the *Sārasvata loka*; then *Mahādeva* disappeared: III, **83**, 6086.—§ 615 (Baladevatīrthayātrā): IX, **37**, 2185 (*siddhaḥ . . . mahāmuniḥ*, had performed austerities at Saptasārasvata); **38**, 2186.—§ 615*j* (do.): *M.* had from his youth led the life of a *brahmacārin*. Once, when performing his ablutions in the river *Sarasvatī*, he beheld a woman bathing in the river; at this sight his seed dropped and fell into the *Sarasvatī*; he took it up and placed it in his earthen pot; then it became divided into seven parts, whence were born seven *ṛshis*: *Vāyuvega*, etc. (β), who were the progenitors of the *Maruts*. (Then the same story as in § 365 is related.) *M.* was the son of *Mātariçvan* and *Sukanyā*: IX, **38**, 2217, 2224, 2244.—§ 615 (do.): IX, **39**, 2246. Cf. Brahmarshi.

Maṅki, name of a man. § 659 (Mokshadh.): XII, **177**, 6589 (*itihāsaṃ purātanaṃ M°nā gītaṃ*, i.e. vv. 6594–6638), 6590, 6593, 6638, 6639 (how *M.* lost his two bulls, his discourse about desire; freed from attachment, *M.* attained to Brahma); **180a**, 6692.

Manmatha = Kāma, q.v.

Manmathakara, a warrior of Skanda. § 615*u* (Skanda): IX, **45**η, 2574.

Manobhava = Kāma, q.v.

Manogati = Agni: V, 477.

Manohara = Vishṇu (1000 names).

Manoharā. § 116 (Vasu, pl.): I, **66**, 2586 (wife of Varcas (? otherwise, BR.), mother of Varcasvin (?, adj. to *Varcāḥ*?), Çiçira, Prāṇa, and Ramaṇa).

Manojava[1], son of the Vasu Anila and Çivā. § 116 (Vasu, pl.): I, **66**, 2589.

Manojava[2], a tīrtha. § 364 (Tīrthayātrāp.): III, **83**, 6063.

Manojava[3] = Çiva (1000 names[2]).—Do.[4] = Vishṇu (1000 names).

Manojavā, a mātṛ. § 615*u* (Skanda): IX, **46** θ, 2634 (only B., C. has *Mahājavā*).

Manonuga, a region in Krauñcadvīpa. § 575 (Bhūmip.): VI, **12** θ, 462.

Manoramā[1], an Apsaras. § 103 (Aṃçāvat.): I, **65**, 2558 (among the Apsarases, who were daughters of Prādhā).—§ 191 (Arjuna): I, **123**, 4818 (danced at the birth of Arjuna).

Manoramā[2], a river, one of the seven Sarasvatīs. § 615*i* (Saptasārasvata): IX, **37a**, 2189 (C. has by error *Manau°*), 2210 (arose at the sacrifice of Auddālaka, in the northern part of Kosala).

Manovega = Çiva (1000 names[2]).

Manovirudh, pl. (*°aḥ*), a class of gods. § 730 (Ānuçāsanik.): XIII, **18**, 1372.

Manthāna = Çiva (1000 names[2]).

Mantharā, the maid of Kaikeyī. § 526 (Rāmopākhyānap.): III, **276**, 15938 (the Gandharvī Dundubhī was born as the hunchbacked *M.*), 15943 (*g*: instructed by Brahmán she went hither and thither always engaged in fomenting quarrels). — § 527 (do.): III, **277**, 15960 (instigated Kaikeyī)

Manthinī, a mātṛ. § 615*u* (Skanda): IX, **46** θ, 2647.

Mantra[1] ("sacred text," personif.). § 270 (Brahmasabhāv.): II, **11**, 447 (in the palace of Brahmán).

Mantra[2] = Çiva (1000 names[1-3]).—Do.[3] = Vishṇu (1000 names).

Mantrakāra = Çiva (1000 names[2]).

Mantramūrti = Çiva: I, 1154.

Mantraparvan ("the section treating of the counsel"). § 10 (Anukram.): I, **2**, 317 (entered among the parvans of the second book of Mhbhr., but not found there, presumably another name of Rājasūyārambhaparvan).

Mantrastuta = Skanda: III, 14639

Mantravid = Çiva (1000 names[2]).

Manu[1], father of the human race, one or more Prajāpatis. § 3 (Anukram.): I, **1**, 32 (issued from the primordial egg).—§ 4 (do.): I, **1**, 52 (*°ādi Bhārataṃ kecit*, sc. *adhīyate*; Nīl., however, takes *manu* = *mantra*, sc. the initial çloka *Nārāyanaṃ namaskṛtya*, etc.).—§ 5 (do.): I, **1a**, 220 *bis* (in Nārada's enumeration of deceased kings).—§ 51 (Parikshit): I, **41**, 1722 (*ity evaṃ M°r abravīt*, quotation).—§ 116 (Vasu, pl.): I, **66**, 2581 (*Paitāmaho M°r devas tasya putraḥ Prajāpatiḥ*, so C., but B. has *muniḥ*).—§ 122 (Aṃçāvat.): I, **66**, 2610 (*Ārushī tu Manoḥ kanyā*, wife of Cyavana).—§ 123 (do.): I, **66**, 2614.—§ 135 (Çakuntalop.): I, **74**, 3091 (*°r abravīt*, quotation).—§ 221*o* (Cākshushī): I, **170**, 6478 (communicated the science Cākshushī to Soma).—§ 277 (Jarāsandhavadhap.): II, **21**, 807 (granted to the Magadhas, that they should never have a drought).—§ 296 (Dyūtap.): II, **53**, 1929 (had not obtained such prosperity as Yudhishṭhira had by his rājasūya).—§ 327 (Draupadīparitāpav.): III, **32**, 1240 (*°or esha niçcayaḥ*, quotation); **35**, 1396 (*yathā vai M°r abravīt*, quotation).—§ 344 (Nalopākhyānap.): III, **53**, 2075 (*sākshād iva M°ḥ svayam*).—§ 370 (Tīrthayātrāp.): III, **84**, 8115 (*°oḥ Prajāpater lokaṃ*).—§ 376 (do.): III, **85**, 8270 (*yathā*).—§ 378 (do.): III, **92**, 8441 (*rājarshibhiḥ . . . M°ādibhiḥ*, had made a tīrthayātrā).—§ 552 (Goharaṇap.): IV, **56**, 1769 (came to see the encounter).—§ 553*b* (Yudhishṭhira): IV, **70**, 2274 (*yathā*).—§ 559 (Prajāgarap.): V, **40**, 1543 (*°r abravīt*, quotation).—§ 565 (Gālavacarita): V, **117**, 3973 (*reme . . . Sarasvatyāṃ yathā M°ḥ*) —§ 574*f* (Bindusaras): VI, **6**, 241 (performs sacrifices at Bindusaras).—§ 615*u* (Skanda): IX, **45**γ, 2512 (came to the investiture of Skanda).—§ 640 (Rājadh.): XII, **55**, 1983 (*°r abravīt*, quotation); **56**, 2009 (*°nā . . . gītau çlokau mahātmanā dharmeshu sveshu*, sc. v. 2010–11).—§ 641 (do.): XII, **67**, 2516, (2517) (appointed as the lord of men); **78**, 2947 (*°r abravīt*, quotation); **88**, 3317 (*iti vyavasthā bhūtānāṃ purastād M°nā kṛtā*, quotation); **112**, 4190 (*°r abravīt*, quotation), 4192 (do., do.); **121**, 4418 (*°unā proktaṃ*, sc. v. 4419, quotation), 4420 (*yathoktaṃ M°nā* = do.), 4430 (*Rudratanayo jyeshṭho M°ḥ*, identified with Chastisement (*daṇḍa*)).—§ 647 (Āpaddh.): XII, **139**, 5236 (*°r āha Prajāpatiḥ*, quotation).—§ 652*b* (Indrota-Pārīkshitīya): XII, **152**, 5648 (*°r abravīt*, quotation), 5665 (do., do.)—§ 663 (Mokshadh.): XII, **201**, 7366 (*°oḥ Prajāpateḥ saṃvādaṃ maharsheç ca Bṛhaspateḥ*), (†7375), (†7379); **202**, (7394); **203**, (†7417); **204**, (7440); **205**, (7460); **206**, (7486) (discourse between *M.* and Bṛhaspati).—§ 665 (do.): XII, **208**, 7587 (*Prajāpatiḥ*, father of the Vasus?).—§ 681 (do.): XII, **266**, 9471 (*°r abravīt*; quotation).—§ 717*b* (Nārāyaṇīya): XII, **335a**, 12685 (among the twenty-one Prajāpatis); **343**, XI), ††13219 (married ten daughters of Daksha); **350**, 13692 (*Çanaiçcaraḥ Sūryaputro bhavishyati M°uḥ* (C. *°oḥ*)), 13693 (*°ādigaṇapūrvakaḥ*, sc. Vyāsa). — § 730 (Ānuçāsanik.): XIII, **14**, 1003 (Çiva identified with *M.*); **16**ηη, 1045 (*°oḥ . . . gatiṃ*, i.e. Çiva), 1059 (Çiva identified with *M.*).—§ 744 (do.): XIII, **44**, 2421 (*taṃ dharmaṃ M°r abravīt*, quotation), 2426 (*°r evaṃ praçaṃsati*, quotation); **46**, 2491 (*striyaḥ puṃsāṃ paridade M°r jigamishur divaṃ*); **47**, 2534 (*°unābhihitaṃ çāstraṃ*).—§ 746 (do.): XIII, **61**, 3000 (*°oḥ çrutvānuçāsanaṃ*, quotation); **65**γ, 3291 (*°r abravīt*, quotation); **67**, 3394 (*ity abravīd M°ḥ*, quotation); **68**, 3426 (*dharmaṃ taṃ M°ḥ prāha dharmavit*, quotation).—§ 749 (do.): XIII, **88**, 4243 (*°r abravīt*, quotation).—§ 761 (do.): XIII, **115**, 5646 (do.).—§ 768*b* (Kṛshṇa Vāsudeva): XII, **147**, 6828 (*°or vaṃçe*, father of Aṅga).—§ 775 (Ānuçāsanik.): XIII, **166**η, 7683 (*Prajāpatiḥ*). Cf. Manu[2,7] and Prajāpati, Prajeçvara.

Manu[2], Cākshusha. § 730 (Ānuçāsanik.): XIII, **18**kk, 1315 (*Varishṭho nāma Cākshushasya M°oḥ sutaḥ*).

Manu[3], Prācetasa. § 640 (Rājadh.): XII, **57**, 2089

(*Prācetasena M°nā çlokau cemau udāhṛtau rājadharmeshu,* sc. vv. 2090–2091); **58**β, 2093 (*Prācetasaḥ*).

Manu[4], Sāvarṇa. § 730 (Ânuçāsanik.): XIII, **18**κκ, 1339 (*Sāvarṇasyà M°oḥ sarge saptarshiç ca bhavishyasi,* sc. Parāçara).

Manu[5], Svārocisha. § 717b (Nārāyaṇīya): XII, **349**, IV), 13582 (*Svārocisham*, learnt the religion of Nārāyaṇa from Brahmán, and imparted the knowledge of it to his son Çaṅkhapada).

Manu[6], Svāyambhuva. § 135 (Çakuntalop.): I, **73**, 2963 (*teshām—sc. vivāhānām—dharmāny athā M°ḥ Svāyambhuvo 'bravīt,* quotation). § 185 (Pāṇḍu): I, **120**, 4675 (*M°ḥ Svāyambhuvo 'bravīt,* quotation (b)).—§ 450 (Âjagarap.): III, **180**, 12485 (*M°ḥ Svāyambhuvo 'bravīt,* quotation).—§ 559 (Prajāgarap.): V, **37**, 1334 (*M°ḥ Svāyambhuvo 'bravīt,* quotation).—§ 595 (Shoḍaçarāj., v. Pṛthu Vainya): VII, **69**, 2414 (*Svāyambhuvaḥ*, C. has *muniḥ* instead of *Manuḥ*; acted as the calf when the men milked the earth).—§ 626 (Rājadh.): XII, **21**, 626 (*M°ḥ Svāyambhuvo 'bravīt,* quotation).—§ 635 (do.): XII, **36**, 1293 (*Siddhānāñ caiva saṃvādaṃ M°oç caiva Prajāpateḥ*), 1296 (*Svāyambhuvaḥ*, discourse between *M.* and the Siddhas).—§ 683 (Mokshadh.): XII, **268**, 9595 (*M°ḥ Svāyambhuvo 'bravīt,* quotation).—§ 717c (Uparicara): XII, **336**, 12740 (*M°ḥ Svāyambhuvaḥ*, will declare law according to the çāstra of the seven ṛshis).—§ 717b (Nārāyaṇīya): XII, **341**, 13040 (*M°ḥ Svāyambhuvaḥ*, among the eight *prakṛtis*); **350**, 13678 (*M°oḥ Svāyambhuve 'ntare*).—§ 754 (Ânuçāsanik.): XIII, **98**, 4678 (*°oḥ Prajāpater vādaṃ Suvarṇasya ca*), 4681, 4684 (*Svāyambhuvam*), (4686), 4741 (discourse between *M.* and Suvarṇa).—§ 761 (do.): XIII, **115**, 5605 (*M°ḥ Svāyambhuvo 'bravīt,* quotation). Cf. Svāyambhuva.

Manu[7], Vaivasvata. § 136 (Yayātyup.): I, **75**, 3126 (*M°or Vaivasvatasya,* sc. *vaṃçam*).—§ 139 (cf. Sambhavap.): Kaçyapa, the son of Marīci (*Māricaḥ*), begat upon [Aditi] the daughter of Daksha (*Dākshāyaṇī*) the Âdityas (among whom Indra was the first) and Vivasvat (also called Mārttāṇḍa). Vivasvat begat Manu [Vaivasvata] and Yama Vaivasvata. Manu begat sixty sons; the names of ten were the following: Vena, Dhṛshṇu, Narishya(n)t(a), Nābhāga, Ikshvāku, Kārusha, Çaryāti, Ilā, Pṛshadhra, Nābhāgārishṭa; the rest perished quarrelling with each other: I, **75**, 3137, 3138, 3142.—§ 155 (Pūruvaṃç.): I, **94**, 3753 (*°or anvāye*).—§ 156 (do.): I, **95**, 3756 (*Prajāpatito M°oḥ*), ††3760 (son of Vivasvat and father of Ilā).—§ 457 (Vaivasvatop.): III, **187**, 12746 (*Vaivasvatasya*), 12748, 12755 (*Vaivasvataḥ*), 12756 (do.), 12757, 12759–61, 12763, 12766, 12767, 12769–71, 12781, 12783, 12784, 12786, 12791, 12798, 12800 (*Vaivasvataḥ*), 12802, 12803 (the story of *M.* and the fish). — § 574 (Jambūkh.): VI, **9**αα, 313 (*Vaivasvatasya*).—§ 576 (Bhagavadgītāp.): VI, **28**, 994 (Vivasvat declared the system of yoga to *M.*, who again declared it to Ikshvāku).—§ 641 (Rājadh.): XII, **122**, 4507 (*Âdityatanayaḥ . . . Çrāddhadevaḥ*), 4510 (*Sūryaputraḥ*). — § 656f (Khaḍgotpattik.): When the *Lokapālas* gave the sword to *M.* the son of Sūrya, they said: "Thou art the Lord of all men; protect all creatures with this sword containing religion within its womb (*dharmagarbhena*); . . . they should be punished essentially with wordy rebukes, and with fines and forfeitures (*durvācā nigraho daṇḍo hiraṇyabahulas tathā*); loss of limbs (*vyaṅgatā tu çarīrasya*) or death should only be inflicted for grave reasons (*analpakāraṇāt*)." *M.* gave the sword to his son Kshupa for the protection of the creatures: XII, **166**, 6187 (*Sūryaputrāya*), 6192.—§ 717b (Nārāyaṇīya): XII, **349**, VII), 13597, 13598 (learnt the religion of Nārāyaṇa from Vivasvat, and imparted the knowledge of it to Ikshvāku).—§ 720b (Sudarçanop.): XIII, **2**, 88 (*Prajāpateḥ*, father of Ikshvāku). — § 730 (Ânuçāsanik.): XIII, **17**, 1290 (*Vaivasvatāya*, learnt the 1,000 names of Çiva from Gautama, and taught them to Nārāyaṇa).—§ 736b (Vītahavyop.): XIII, **30**, 1945 (father of Çaryāti).—§ 767 (Ânuçāsanik.): XIII, **137**a, 6263 (father of Sudyumna).—§ 768b (Kṛshṇa Vāsudeva): XIII, **147**, 6831 (father of Ilā = Sudyumna).—§ 778b (Saṃvartta-Maruttīya): XIV, **4**, 65 (*daṇḍadharaḥ*, father of Prasandhi and grandfather of Kshupa, whose son was Ikshvāku). Cf. Âdityatanaya, Sūryaputra, Vaivasvata.

Manu[8] = Vishṇu (1000 names).

Manu[9], name of a fire. § 493 (Âṅgirasa): III, **221**, 14180 (one of the five *ūrjaskara* fires, son of the fire Tapas), 14183 (= Bhānu), 14191 (only B., C. has *Bhānoḥ*, husband of Niçā and father of one daughter, Agnī-Shomau, and five fires), 14193 (*Viçvapatir nāma dvitīyo vai M°oḥ sutaḥ*).

Manu[10], a daughter of Prādhā and Kaçyapa. § 102 (Aṃçāvat.): I, **65**, 2553.

manu ("mantra," Nīl.): I, 52 (?); XIII, 362 (*Manuṃ*, read *maruṃ*, cf. 2939).

Manu, pl. (°*avaḥ*). § 310b (Sūrya): III, **3**, 186 (*°ūnāṃ . . . īçvaraḥ*, sc. Sūrya).—§ 576 (Bhagavadgītāp.): VI, **34**, 1210 (*catvāraḥ*).—§ 730g (Upamanyu): XIII, **14**a, 873 (*Svāyambhuvādyāḥ*).—§ 730 (Ânuçāsanik.): XIII, **14**ββ, 991 (*sapta*).

Manuputra, pl. (°*āḥ*) ("the sons of Manu"). § 310b (Sūrya): III, **3**, 186 (*°ūnāṃ . . . īçvaraḥ*, sc. Sūrya).

Mānusha, a tīrtha. § 364 (Tīrthayātrāp.): III, **45**, 6035, 6037.

[**Manushyagrahakathana(ṃ)**] ("on the demons that possess mankind"). § 502 (cf. Skandop.). The six divorced wives of the *ṛshis*, together with *Vinatā*, obtained permission from *Skanda* to become his mothers. At the request of *Indra* the *Kṛttikās* (i.e. the six wives of the *ṛshis*) (together with *Vinatā*, see v. 14464 and Nīl.) are placed among the *nakshatras* (and presided over by *Agni*) instead of *Abhijit*, the younger sister of *Rohiṇī*, who from jealousy had repaired to the woods. *Brahmán* ordered that time should be reckoned from *Dhanishṭhā*, while it had formerly been reckoned from *Rohiṇī* (so Nīl.). Then (these seven) mothers asked *Skanda* that they might become the mothers of the worlds instead of the old mothers (*Brāhmī*, *Māheçvarī*, etc.; Nīl.) and devour the progeny of those old mothers, because they had slandered them before their husbands, and always dwell with *Skanda*. *Skanda* granted that until the age of 16 years they should have the power of afflicting the human kind, and he loosed from his body his *Raudra* nature, under the name of *Skandāpasmāra*, that they might dwell with him. Enumeration of several grahas (the number 18 in v. 14490 is difficult to explain), among others (*a*) the male and female children of *Skanda* (the males are the husbands of the females); they are all named *Skandagrahas*; they are propitiated with offerings, ablutions, unguents, etc., and particularly by the worship of *Skanda*; and when they are propitiated they bestow good on men. Then are mentioned the *grahas*, that afflict men from the 16th to the 70th year; after the 70th year fever takes the place of the *grahas*. These evil spirits always avoid those who have subdued their senses, etc., and those who are devoted to *Maheçvara* (III, **230**).

***manvantara** ("the period of a Manu"): III, 186 (°*ūnāṃ*

sarveshum īçvarāṇāṃ tvam īçvaraḥ, sc. Sūrya); XII, 2236 (pl.), ††13206 (sg., *pūrve Svāyambhuve*), 13679 (pl.), 13693 (sg.); XIII, 626 (pl.).

Mānya[1] = Çiva (1000 names[2]).—Do.[2] = Vishṇu (1000 names).

Manyantī, a fire. § 490 (Āṅgirasa): III, **219**, 14151 (= Svāhā; only in C., B. has *manyetāṃ* instead of *Manyantīṃ*).

Manyu, name of a fire (?). § 490 (Āṅgirasa): III, **219**, 14151 (*yaḥ praçānteshu bhūteshu Manyur bhavati pāvakaḥ*; Nil. takes *pāvakaḥ* = Bṛhaspati and *manyuḥ* = *krodharūpī*).

Manyumat, a fire. § 493 (Āṅgirasa): III, **221**, 14187 (*yaḥ praçānteshu bhūteshu manyur bhavati dāruṇaḥ* || *agniḥ sa M°ān nāma dvitīyo Bhānutaḥ sutaḥ*)

Mārdamarshi, v. Mārgamarshi.

Mārga[1] = Çiva (1000 names[1]).—Do.[2] = Vishṇu (1000 names).

Mārgaçīrsha, name of a month. § 576 (Bhagavadgītāp.): VI, **34**, 1239 (*māsānāṃ M°o 'haṃ*, sc. *asmi*, says Kṛshṇa).—§ 759 (Ānuçāsanik.): XIII, **106**β, 5149 (*māsaṃ*); **109**, 5372 (*dvādaçyāṃ M°e*, then one should worship Kṛshṇa as Keçava); **110**, 5389 (*māsasya*, description of the cāndravrata).

Mārgaçīrshī, the day of full moon in the month of Mārgaçīrsha). § 378 (Tīrthayātrāp.): III, **93**, 8484 (°*yām atītāyāṃ Pushyeṇa prayayuḥ*, sc. the Pāṇḍavas on their tīrthayātrā).—§ 641 (Rājadh.): XII, **100**, 3691 (*Caitryāṃ vā M°yāṃ vā senāyogaḥ praçasyate*).

Mārgamarshi, a son of Viçvāmitra. § 721*b* (Viçvāmitrop.): XIII, **4**β, 256 (only C., B. has *Mārdamarshiḥ*).

Mārgaṇapriyā, one of the daughters of Pradhā. § 102 (Aṃçāvat.): I, **65**, 2553.

Mārīca[1], a Rākshasa, friend of Rāvaṇa. § 425 (Hanūmad-Bhīmasaṃvāda): III, **147**, 11200 (all. to § 529).—§ 528*b* (Rāvaṇagamana): From fear of Rāma *M.* adopted an ascetic mode of life: III, **277**, 16000.—§ 529 (Sītāharaṇa): III, **278**, 16001, 16006, 16009, 16010, 16014, 16017 (in order to assist Rāvaṇa in robbing Sītā, *M.* transformed himself into a deer which Rāma pursued). Cf. Raksh°.

Mārīca[2] ("son of Marīci") = Kaçyapa: V, 3819 (*maharsheḥ K°sya*); VII, 2445; XII, 7538 (*K°*, C. by error *Kā°*); XIII, 2561 (*K°*), 4124 (*K°*), 7643 (*K°*).

Marīci[1], a ṛshi, son of Brahmán and father of Kaçyapa. § 86 (Aṃçāvat.): I, **65**, 2518 (the first of Brahmán's six mind-born sons), 2519 (father of Kaçyapa).—§ 109 (do.): I, **66**, 2568 (the first of Brahmán's six sons).—§ 118 (do.): I, **66**, 2598 (father of Kaçyapa).—§ 191 (Arjuna): I, **123**, 4808 (present at the birth of Arjuna).—§ 266 (Çakrasabhāv.): II, **7**, 208 (in the palace of Indra).—§ 270 (Brahmasabhāv.): II, **11**, 436 (among the *prajānāṃ patayaḥ* in the palace of Brahmán).—§ 421*e* (Ākāçagaṅgā): III, **142**, 10904 (at Ākāçagaṅgā).—§ 524*e* (Vishṇu): III, **272**, 15822 (°*pramukhān maharshīn asṛjan nava*, sc. Brahmán).—§ 576 (Bhagavadgītāp.): VI, **34**, 1225 (°*r Marutām asmi*, says Kṛshṇa).—615*u* (Skanda): IX, **45**γ, 2512 (came to the investiture of Skanda).—§ 637 (Rājadh.): XII, **47**η, 1597 (among the ṛshis who surrounded Bhīshma as he lay on his arrow-bed).—641 (do.): XII, **122**, 4505 (Aṅgiras gave the rod of chastisement to Indra and *M.*; *M.* again gave it to Bhṛgu).—§ 656 (Khaḍgotpattik.): XII, **166***a*, 6135 (*ṛshiṃ*, the first of Brahmán's sons), 6186 (Vishṇu gave the sword to *M.*, from *M.* it passed over to the maharshis).—§ 664*i* (Mokshadh.): XII, **207**δ, 7534 (the first of Brahmán's sons), 7535 (father of Kaçyapa), 7536.—§ 665 (do.): XII, **208***a*, 7570 (the first of Brahmán's sons), 7574 (father of Kaçyapa).—§ 717*b* (Nārāyaṇīya): XII, **335***a*, 12685 (among the twenty-one Prajāpatis).—§ 717*c* (Uparicara): XII, **336**, 12724 (one of the seven ṛshis, also called Citraçikhaṇḍins).—§ 717*b* (Nārāyaṇīya): XII, **341**ν, 13040 (the first of the eight prakṛtis), (ξ), 13075 (the first of Brahmán's seven mind-born sons).—§ 730*g* (Upamanyu): XIII, **14**ββ, 990.—§ 747*b* (Suvarṇotpatti): XIII, **85**ζ, 4124 (sprung from the rays—*marīcibhyaḥ*—of the sacrificial fire, father of Kaçyapa), 4160 (the first offspring of Brahmán).

Marīci[2], an Apsaras. § 191 (Arjuna): I, **123**, 4818 (danced at the birth of Arjuna).

Marīci[3] = Vishṇu (1000 names).

Marīcin ("having rays") = Sūrya (the Sun): V, 1335.

Marīcipa**, pl. (°*āḥ*) ("drinking rays"), a kind of ṛshis.—§ 43 (Garuḍa): I, **30**, 1398 (?, adj. to *Vālakhilyāḥ* ?).—§ 246 (Sundopasundop.): I, **211**, 7683.—§ 270 (Brahmasabhāv.): II, **11**, 437 (in the palace of Brahmán).—§ 310*b* (Sūrya): III, **3**, 174.—§ 602 (Droṇavadhap.): VII, **190**ν, 8728.—§ 615*u* (Skanda): IX, **45**γ, 2510 (came to the investiture of Skanda).—§ 656 (Khaḍgotpattik.): XII, **166**β, 6143 (*Vaiçvānara - M°āḥ*).—§ 761 (Ānuçāsanik.): XIII, **115a*, 5604.—§ 786*e* (Agastya): XIV, **92**, 2851.

Mārisha, pl. (°*āḥ*), a people. § 574 (Jambūkh.): VI, **9**ν, 368 (in the south).

Mārishā, a river. § 574 (Jambūkh.): VI, **9**λ, 343 (in Bhāratavarsha).

Mārjalīya = Çiva: III, 1628.

Mārjāra - mūshika - saṃvāda(ḥ) ("the discourse between a cat and a mouse"). § 646*b* (Āpaddh.): There was a large banyan in the midst of a forest, with various kinds of birds, etc. A wise mouse, *Palita*, lived at the foot of that tree, having made a hole there with 100 outlets. On the branches lived a cat *Lomaça*. A *Cāṇḍāla* came and built a hut, setting his traps of leather strings every evening after sunset. One day he caught the cat. *Palita* began to eat the flesh in the trap, but beheld the mongoose *Harita* and the owl *Candraka*. He resolved upon saving the cat, though an enemy, in order to escape from them; having made peace with the cat, he crouched beneath it; the mongoose and owl left the spot; the mouse began to cut the strings slowly, notwithstanding the cat's impatience. At morning the *Cāṇḍāla Parigha* appeared (description), accompanied by a pack of dogs. Then the mouse quickly cut the remaining string; the cat got upon the banyan, *Palita* entered his hole. The hunter took up his net and left the spot. *Palita* would not conclude friendship with the cat, and entered another hole.

Mārkaṇḍeya, a Brahmarshi. § 264 (Sabhākriyāp.): II, **4***a*, 110 (*mahāmuniḥ*, waited upon Yudhishṭhira).—§ 270 (Brahmasabhāv.): II, **11**, 439 (in the palace of Yudhishṭhira).—§ 323 (Dvaitavanapr.): III, **25**, †948 (came to the Pāṇḍavas in the wood), (†952) (consoled Yudhishṭhira by relating the banishment of Rāma Dāçarathi).—§ 327 (Draupadīparitāp.): III, **31**, 1170 (*dharmeṇa cirajīvitā*; all. to § 323).—§ 370 (Tīrthayātrāp.): III, **84**, 8058 (°*sya* . . . *tīrthaṃ* . . . *Gomatī-Gaṅgayoç caiva saṅgame*).—§ 376 (do.): III, **85**, 8263 (among the ṛshis who expected Yudhishṭhira).—§ 377 (Dhaumyatīrthak.): III, **88**, 8330 (at Payoshṇī *M.* sang a genealogical verse (*anuvaṃçyāṃ* . . . *gāthāṃ*) about king Nṛga).—§ 452 (Mārkaṇḍeyas.): III, **183**, 12561 (*bahuvatsarajīvī*, will come to the Pāṇḍavas).—§ 453 (do.): III, **183**, 12598 (*b*: *M.* had lived many thousand years, but looked like a youth of twenty-five years old and was immortal), 12603, 12606, 12607, (12617) (*M.* came to the Pāṇḍavas and discoursed upon various topics: ch. **184–232**).—§ 454 (do.,

Brāhmaṇamāhātmya): III, **184**, 12652, (12654).—§ 455 (do., do.): III, **185**, (12677), (12695), (12700), (12709).—§ 456 (do., Sarasvatī-Tārkshyasaṃv.): III, **186**, (12715), (†12718). — § 457 (do., Vaivasvatop.): III, **187**, 12746, (12747).—§ 458 (Mārkaṇḍeyas.): III, **188**, 12805, (12821). —§ 459 (do.): III, **188**, 12902 (*Bhārgava*), 12935 (had lived during the cataclysm, and then entered the stomach of Nārāyaṇa); **189**, (12999).—§ 460 (do.): III, **190**, 13009, (13015); **191**, (13107), 13127, (13129), 13139, 13141.—§ 461 (do., Vāmadevacarita): III, **192**, 13142-4, (††13145), (†13196), (†13203), (†13210).—§ 462 (do., Baka-Çakrasaṃv.): III, **193**, ††13212, (13216).—§ 463 (do., Çibi): III, **194**, ††13248. — § 464 (do., Yayāti): III, **195**, (††13256).—§ 465 (Mārkaṇḍeyas.): III, **196**, ††13262.—§ 466 (do., Çibi): III, **197**, (††13274) (only B.).—§ 467 (do., Rājanyamahābhāgya): III, **198**, ††13301.—§ 468 (do., Indradyumnop.): III, **199**, ††13331, ††13347.—§ 469 (Mārkaṇḍeyas.): III, **200**, 13349, (13352), (13361).—§ 470 (do., Yamaloka): III, **200**, 13392, (13394).—§ 471 (Mārkaṇḍeyas.): III, **200**, (13414).—§ 472 (do.): III, **200**, (13431).—§ 473 (do.): III, **200**, (13470).—§ 474 (do.): III, **201**, 13482, 13488, (13489).—§ 475 (do., Dhundhumārop.): III, **202**, (13515).—§ 476 (do., do.): III, **202**, (13523); **203**, (13546).—§ 477 (do., do.): III, **203**, (13554).—§ 478 (do., do.): III, **204**, (13582).—§ 479 (do., Pativratop.): III, **205**, 13628, (13643); **206**, (13652), (13658), (13670), (13700).—§ 480 (do., do.): III, **207**, (13701), (13717), (13760); **208**, (13802); **209**, (13842).—§ 481 (do., do.): III, **210**, (13898).—§ 483 (do., do.): III, **211**, (13920).—§ 484 (do., do.): III, **212**, (13947).—§ 485 (do., do.): III, **213**, (13960).—§ 486 (do., do.): III, **214**, (14000), (14004), (14017); **215**, (14030).—§ 487 (do., do.): III, **216**, (14094).—§ 488 (do., Āngirasa): III, **217**, 14100, (14105), (14117).—§ 489 (do., do.): III, **218**, (14122).—§ 490 (do., do.): III, **219**, (14130).—§ 491 (do., do.): III, **220**, (14156).—§ 493 (do., do.): III, **221**, (14176); **222**, (14208).—§ 495 (do., Skandotpatti): III, **223**, (14241).—§ 496 (do., do.): III, **224**, (14292); **225**, (14299), (14308).—§ 497 (do., do.): III, **226**, (14339).—§ 498 (do., do.): III, **226**, (14355).—§ 499 (do., Çakra-Skandasaṃv.): III, **227**, (14368).—§ 500 (do., Skandop.): III, **228**, (14387).—§ 501 (do., do.): III, **229**, (14402), (14424). — § 502 (do., Manushyagrahak.): III, **230**, (14454), (14460), (14467), (14477). — § 506 (do., Skandayuddha): III, **231**, (14514), (14520).—§ 504 (do., do.): III, **231**, (14527).—§ 506 (do., do.): III, **231**, (14541).—§ 507 (do., do.): III, **231**, (14572).—§ 508 (do., Kārttikeyastava): III, **232**, 14629, (14630).—§ 509 (do., do.): III, **232**, (14637).—§ 511 (Draupadī-Satyabhāmasaṃv.): III, **235**, 14722.—§ 522 (Draupadīharaṇap.): III, **271**, 15763. — § 525 (Rāmopākhyānap.): III, **273**, 15861; **274**, (15872), (15877) (told the story of Rāma Dāçarathi: ch. **274-91**).—§ 526 (do.): III, **275**, (15889), (15915), (15920); **276**, (15929), (15934).—§ 527 (do.): III, **277**, (15947). — § 529 (do., Sītāharaṇa): III, **278**, (16001).—§ 530 (do., Viçvāvasumoksh.): III, **279**, (16045).—§ 531 (Rāmopākhyānap.): III, **280**, (16093).—§ 533 (do., Rāvaṇa-Sītāsaṃv.): III, **281**, (16166). — § 534 (do., Hanūmatpratyāg.): III, **282**, (16197).—§ 535 (do., Setubandhana): III, **283**, (16269).—§ 536 (do., Lankāpraveça): III, **284**, (16323). — § 537 (do., Rāma-Rāvaṇayuddha): III, **285**, (16364). — § 538 (do., Kumbhakarṇaraṇag.): III, **286**, (16379).—§ 539 (do., Kumbhakarṇādivadha): III, **287**, (16409).—§ 540 (do., Indrajidyuddha): III, **288**, (16438).—§ 541 (do., Indrajidvadha): III, **289**, (16465). — § 542 (do., Rāvaṇavadha): III, **290**, (16498). — § 543 (do., Rāmābhisheka): III, **291**, (16531), (16568).—§ 544 (do., Yudhishṭhirāçvāsa): III, **292**, (16602), 16615. — § 545 (Pativratāmāhātmyap.): III, **293**, (16619), (16634), (16652); **294**, (16658), (16663), (16690); **295**, (16691); **296**, (16714), (16721), (16731), (16736), (16742); **297**, (16747), (16761), (16802), (16815), (16842), (16848); **298**, (16858), (16877), (†16901); **299**, (16902) (told the story of Sāvitrī). —§ 547 (Karṇa): III, **310**, †17219.—§ 581 (Bhīshmavadhap.): VI, **66**o, 2999 (Bhīshma had heard of the glory of Kṛshṇa from *M.*); **67**π, 3016 (praised Kṛshṇa); **68**ρ, 3039 (do.).—§ 606 (Karṇap., Tripurākhyāna): VIII, **33**, 1392 (*mahān ṛshiḥ*, had related the Tripurākhyāna to Dhṛtarāshṭra). —§ 635 (Rājadh.): XII, **37**, 1356 (°*mukhāt kṛtsnaṃ yatidharmam avāptavān*, sc. Bhīshma).—§ 637 (do.): XII, **47**η, 1598 (among the ṛshis who surrounded Bhīshma). § 664 (Mokshadh.): XII, **207**β, 7521 (had spoken of the glory of Kṛshṇa).—§ 666 (do.): XII, **209**, 7607 (°*āçrame*). —§ 712 (Çukotpatti): XII, **324**, 12181 (*sa devacaritānīha kathayām āsa*). — § 730 (Ānuçāsanik.): XIII, **17**, 1292 (Nāciketa communicated the 1,000 names of Çiva to *M.*, who communicated them to Upamanyu). — § 732 (do.): XIII, **22**, 1537 (°*aḥ purā prāha*) (*a*), 1540 (*mataṃ . . . M°sya*), (1544) (a sentence of his is quoted).—§ 734 (do.): XIII, **26***a*, 1763 (among the ṛshis who surrounded Bhīshma). § 743 (do.): XIII, **43**, 2394 (*mahāmuniḥ*, had told Bhīshma the story of Vipula). — § 761 (do.): XIII, **115**, 5631 (discoursed on the demerits of eating meat).—§ 768*b* (Umā-Maheçvarasaṃv.): XIII, **146**γ, 6750 (Dhūmorṇā is his wife).—§ 770 (Ānuçāsanik.): XIII, **151**λ, 7122 (enumeration). — § 777 (Svargārohanik. p.): XIII, **168**, 7753 (°*a ivāparaḥ*).—§ 794 (Mahāprasthānikap.): XVII, **1**, 12. Cf. Bhārgava, Bhārgavasattama, Bhṛgukulaçreshṭha, Bhṛgunandana, Brahmarshi, Viprarshi.

Mārkaṇḍeyasamāsyā ("the [Pāṇḍavas'] enjoying the company of Mārkaṇḍeya"). § 10 (Parvasaṅgr.): I, **2**, 323 (*parva*, i.e. Mārkaṇḍeyasamāsyāp.).—§ 11 (do.): I, **2**, 466, 468 (*purāṇam* = do.).

[Mārkaṇḍeyasamāsyāparvan(°va)] ("section relating to the [Pāṇḍavas'] enjoying the company of Mārkaṇḍeya," the 41st of the minor parvans of Mhbhr.). (Cf. Mārkaṇḍeyasamāsyā.) § 451: When the *Pāṇḍavas* were dwelling at that very place (cf. v. 12547: *caratāṃ marudhanvasu*, "roaming about in deserts"), there set in the season of the rains (description). Then in the autumn (description) they spent the holiest night, that of the full moon in the month of *Kārttika*, on the *Sarasvatī* with the ascetics. As soon as the dark fortnight set in, they with their charioteers and cooks entered the *Kāmyaka* forest (III, **182**).—§ 452: In the *Kāmyaka* wood many *brahmans* came to them, and one of them said that *Kṛshṇa* and *Mārkaṇḍeya* would come to see them. Immediately *Kṛshṇa* arrived with *Satyabhāmā* on his chariot that was yoked with *Çaibya* and *Sugrīva*. He told *Kṛshṇā* that her sons, though her father and brothers proffered them a kingdom and territories, found no joy in the house of *Drupada*, but that in the town of the *Vṛshṇis* they were directed by *Subhadrā* and received instruction from *Raukmiṇeya* even as *Aniruddha*, *Abhimanyu*, *Sunītha*, and *Bhānu*, and were instructed by the young *Abhimanyu* in the use of arms. Then he suggested to *Yudhishṭhira* with the *Daçārhas*, *Kukuras*, and *Andhakas*, to kill *Duryodhana*, etc. *Yudhishṭhira* said they would stand by their promise, and after the thirteen years take refuge in

Kṛshṇa.—§ 453: While they were thus talking, the *brahmarshi* *Mārkaṇḍeya* (*b*) appeared. When they had taken their seats, the *devarshi Nārada* also came to visit them. *Yudhishṭhira*, mentioning the happiness of the impious *Dhārtarāshṭras*, asked *Mārkaṇḍeya* about the results of men's acts. *Mārkaṇḍeya*, after having described the *Kṛta* age and the subsequent deterioration, answered the question (III, **183**).—§§ 454–5: *Brāhmaṇamāhātmya - kathana* (q.v.). — § 456: *Sarasvatī-Tārkshya-saṃvāda* (q.v.).—§ 457: *Vaivasvatopākhyāna* (q.v.). —§ 458: *Yudhishṭhira*, saying that *Mārkaṇḍeya* alone worships *Brahmán* at the time of the great dissolution, when he sleeps in a lotus flower, and when he awakes to recreate the world, asked him to explain the causes of things. *Mārkaṇḍeya* said: *Janārdana* attired in yellow robes is the great creator of everything. After the dissolution, creation again comes to life. *Kṛta yuga* = 4,000 years + dawn 400 years + eve 400 years; *Tretā yuga* = 3,000 + 300 + 300; *Dvāpara yuga* = 2,000 + 200 + 200; *Kali yuga* = 1,000 + 100 + 100; altogether a cycle of *yugas* = 12,000 years. After the *Kali yuga* is over, the *Kṛta yuga* comes again. One thousand cycles constitute a day of *Brahmán*. Description of *Kali yuga* (*b*). Then comes a long drought, and seven suns drink up all water and reduce wood and grass to ashes. Then the *Samvartaka* fire with wind penetrates into *Rasātala* and terrifies the gods, *Dānavas*, and *Yakshas*, and consumes this world with gods, *Asuras*, *Gandharvas*, *Yakshas*, *Uragas*, and *Rākshasas*. And there rise in the sky deep masses of clouds flooding the entire surface of the earth and showering incessantly for twelve years. Then *Svayambhū*, dwelling in the lotus, drinks this terrible wind and goes to sleep.—§ 459: When all has become water, I (i.e. *Mārkaṇḍeya*) alone wander in affliction and become fatigued, and find no resting-place. Then I behold a vast banyan-tree, and on a couch attached to a bough of that tree a fair boy with yellow robes, with the mark of *Çrīvatsa*. He caused me to enter his body through the mouth, and then I beheld the whole earth with cities and kingdoms, *Gaṅgā*, *Çatadru*, etc. (enumeration) (*α*), gods, *Sādhyas*, *Rudras*, *Ādityas*, etc. (enumeration) (*β*). At last I was suddenly projected through his open mouth by a gust of wind. Within that very moment I acquired a new sight and beheld myself emancipated (*nirmuktaṃ*). I wished to know his self. Then he spoke to me (III, **188**): "The gods even do not know me truly. I am *Nārāyaṇa* (v. 12952: "in ancient times I called the waters *nārā*, and because the waters have ever been my *ayana* [home], therefore I have been called *Nārāyaṇa*"), the eternal and unchangeable source of all things, the Creator and Destroyer of all; I am *Vishṇu*, *Brahmán*, *Çakra*, etc.; in the form of *Çesha* I support this earth, in the form of a boar I raised it when sunk in water; I am the *Vaḍavāvaktra* fire; from my mouth, arms, thighs, and feet sprang *brahmans*, *kshatriyas*, *vaiçyas*, and *çūdras*; from me spring the *Ṛg.-*, *Sāma-*, *Yajur-*, and *Atharva-veda*; I am the *Samvartaka* fire, the *Samvartaka* wind, the *Samvartaka* sun, and the *Samvartaka* fire (!) (v. 12966 foll.); the stars are the pores of my skin, etc. When virtue and morality decrease, I create myself into new forms; in the *Kṛta* age I become white, etc. (see §§ 426*b*, 427, 428, 429). When the end comes, I alone in the form of *Kāla* destroy the three worlds, etc. The grandsire of all creatures (*Sarvalokapitāmaha*) is half of my body. I am the bearer of the conch-shell, the discus, and the mace. For a period of 1,000 cycles of *yugas* I sleep, overwhelming all creatures in insensibility, and I stay here, in the form of a boy though I am old, until *Brahmán* wakes up; under the form of *Brahmán* I have repeatedly granted thee boons When *Brahmán* (*Sarvalokapitāmaha*) awakes, I will then alone create all creatures." Then he disappeared, and I (*Mārkaṇḍeya*) beheld this creation start into life. And that deity is *Kṛshṇa*, thy relative. In consequence of the boon granted by him memory does not fail me, my life is long, and death is under my control (v. 13002). Then all bowed down unto *Janārdana* (i.e. *Kṛshṇa*), who comforted them (III, **189**).—§ 460: *Yudhishṭhira* asked him about the future cause of the government (*sāmrājya*) of the earth. *Mārkaṇḍeya*, having given a short description of the other *yugas*, described in detail the *Kali-yuga* (*b*); "in the new *Kṛta-yuga*, *Kalkin* (*c*) will arise." Then *Mārkaṇḍeya* gave *Yudhishṭhira* some moral precepts and exhortations (III, **190–1**).—§ 461: *Vāmadevacarita* (q.v.).—§ 462: *Baka-Çakra-saṃvāda* (q.v.). § 463: *Çibi* (q.v.).—§ 464: *Nāhusha-carita* (v. *Yayāti*).— § 465, on the same topic: There were two learned and able kings, *Vṛshadarbha* and *Seduka*. *Seduka* knew that *Vṛshadarbha* had from his boyhood an unuttered vow, that he would give no other metal to *brahmans* than gold and silver. He once sent a *brahman*, who asked him for 1,000 horses for his preceptor, to *Vṛshadarbha*, who whipped him and then gave him a day's tribute (which was more than the value of 1,000 horses), "because he had whipped him" (III, **196**). —§ 466: *Çibi* (q.v.).—§ 467: *Rājanyamahābhāgya* (q.v.).— § 468: *Indradyumnopākhyāna* (q.v.).—§ 469: Asked by *Yudhishṭhira* in what condition (age) a man should practise charity, *Mārkaṇḍeya* enumerated four kinds of futile life and sixteen kinds of futile charity. The *brahmans* save others and themselves by *japa*, *mantra*, and *homa*. He next enumerated the *brahmans* that should be excluded from *çrāddhas*, and gave other moral precepts (of offerings to the gods of flowers and sandals and pastes, entertainment of guests); then he enumerated the persons to whom one should make gifts; the effects of various gifts to *brahmans* (food is the best).— § 470: *Yamaloka* (q.v.).—§ 471: Precepts about gifts, washing the feet of *brahmans*, etc. Blessing upon the reader.— § 472: Three kinds of purity (speech, deed, water): by adoring *sandhyā* and reciting *Gāyatrī* one is protected against sin and evil results from gifts, against inauspicious stars, and against *Rākshasas*. Greatness of the *brahmans*. The carrying of three staves, etc., are useless if the heart be not pure. They who do not commit sin in *manas*, word, deed, and *buddhi* do really practise austerities (v. 13468: by *tapas* one may attain *Svarga*, by charity enjoyment, by knowledge salvation (*moksha*), by bathing in *tīrthas* purgation from sins).— § 473: On the effects of various gifts at various times (v. 13480: the first offspring of fire is gold, earth springs from *Vishṇu*, and the cows from the sun; he, therefore, that gives away gold, land, and kine, has given the three worlds [of *Agni*, *Vishṇu*, and the Sun]) (III, **200**).—§ 474: Having heard the history of *Indradyumna*, *Yudhishṭhira*, saying that *Mārkaṇḍeya* knew the gods, *Dānavas*, *Rākshasas*, the royal genealogies and the genealogies of the *ṛshis*, and *Gandharvas*, *Yakshas*, *Kinnaras*, and *Apsarases*, asked him about *Kuvalāçva Ikshvāku*. *Mārkaṇḍeya* related: *Dhundhumāropākhyāna* (q.v.).—§§ 479–87: *Pativratopākhyāna* (q.v.).—§§ 488–94: *Āṅgirasa* (q.v.).—§§ 495–8: *Skandotpatti* (q.v.).—§ 499: *Skanda-Çakra-samāgama* (q.v.).—§§ 500–1: *Skandopākhyāna* (q.v.).—§ 502: *Manushyagrahakathana* (q.v.).—§§ 503–7: *Skandayuddha* (q.v.).—§§ 508–9: *Kārttikeyastava* (q.v.)

Mārtaṇḍa = Vivasvat (Sūrya), q.v.

Mārttikāvata[1] ("belonging to the city of Mṛttikāvatī"), a country. § 320 (Saubhavadhop.): III, **20**, 791 (i.e. the kingdom of Çālva[5]).

Mārttikāvata[2] (do.), pl. (°*āḥ*), a people. § 595 (Shoḍaçarāj. v. Rāma Jāmadagnya): VII, **70**β, 2436 (slain by Rāma Jāmadagnya).

Mārttikāvata[3] (do.), adj. § 793 (Mausalap.): XVI, **7**, 245 (*nagaraṃ M°ṃ*, there the son of Kṛtavarman is established as king of the remnant of the women of the Bhoja king).

Mārttikāvataka (do.), adj. § 319 (Saubhavadhop.): III, **14**, 629 (°*o nṛpaḥ*, i.e. Çālva[5]).—§ 396 (Jamadagni): III, **116**, 10176 (*Citrarathaṃ nāma M°ṃ nṛpaṃ*).

Mārttikāvatika (do.), adj. § 593 (Abhimanyuvadhap.): VII, **48**, 1892 (*Bhojaṃ kuñjaraketanaṃ*).

Maru (XII, 12956), v. Muru.

Marubhūmi, a country. § 285 (Nakula): II, **32**, 1187 (in the west, conquered by Nakula on his digvijaya).—§ 518 (Mṛgasvapnodbhavap.): III, **258**, 15365 (°*eḥ çirahsthānaṃ*, sc. the Kāmyaka forest).—§ 555 (Sainyodyogap.): V, **19**, 599 (among the countries which were overspread with the army of the Kurus).

Marudgaṇa, name of a tīrtha. § 733*q* (Ānuçāsanik.): By bathing in the tīrtha *M.*, in the retreat of the *Pitṛs*, and in the tīrtha of *Vaivasvata* one becomes cleansed. By bathing in the tīrtha *Brahmasaras* on the *Bhāgīrathī* one attains to the region of *Soma*: XIII, **25a**, 1725.

Mārudha, a country. § 281 (Sahadeva): II, **31**, 1118 (in the south, conquered by Sahadeva on his digvijaya).

Marukaccha (II, 1830), v. Bharukaccha.

Marut = Vāyu (the Wind), q.v.: XII, 5831.

Marut, pl., a class of gods ("the winds"), followers of Indra. § 19 (Bhṛgu): I, **5**, 867 (*devaiḥ . . . sarshi-M°gaṇaiḥ*).—§ 44 (Garuḍa): I, **30**, 1417 (*Sādhyānāṃ M°āñ caiva ye cānye devatāgaṇāḥ*).—§ 106 (Aṃçāvat.): I, **65**, 2562.—§ 120 *bis* (do.): I, **66**, 2602 (°*āṃ*, sc. *pakshaḥ*).—§ 130 (do.): I, **67**, 2714 (Sātyaki was born from the paksha of the *M.*), 2717 (Virāṭa was born from the gaṇa of the *M.*).—§ 149 (Yayāti): I, **87**, 3551.—§ 191 (Arjuna): I, **123a**, 4827 (present at the birth of Arjuna).—§ 233 (Svayaṃvarap.): I, **187**, †7010 (came to see the svayaṃvara of Draupadī).—§ 248 (Arjunavanavāsap.): I, **214**, 7779 (°*bhir iva Vāsavaḥ*, sc. *vṛtaḥ*). — § 258 (Khāṇḍavadahanap.): I, **227**, 8269 (among the gods who fought with Kṛshṇa and Arjuna).—§ 260 (do.): I, **234**, 8467 (°*gaṇair vṛtaḥ*, sc. Indra).—§ 266 (Çakrasabhāv.): II, **7**, 288 (in the palace of Indra).—§ 270 (Brahmasabhāv.): II, **11**, 448 (in the palace of Brahmán), 460 (do.).—§ 298 (Dyūtap.): II, **62**, 2110 (°*bhiḥ sahitaḥ . . . Marutpatiḥ*).—§ 310*b* (Sūrya): III, **3**, 174 (worship the Sun).—§ 327 (Draupadīparitāp.): III, **33**, 1349 (°*bhir iva Vṛtrahā*, sc. *parivṛtaḥ*).—§ 330 (Indradarçana): III, **37**, 1490 (°*gaṇān*).—§ 336 (Indralokābhigamanap.): III, **43**, 1768 (in the world of Indra). — § 347 (Nalopākhyānop.): III, **62**, 2356 (*Açvinau sa-M°gaṇau*).—§ 357 (Pushkara): III, **82**, 4064 (°*gaṇāḥ*, in Pushkara).—§ 364 (Tīrthayātrāp.): III, **83**, 6075 (°*āṃ tīrthaṃ*).—§ 375 (do.): III, **85**, 8248 (°-*Açvibhiḥ*, bathe in the tīrthas).—§ 377 (Dhaumyatīrthak.): III, **90**, 8404 (do., visit the tīrthas).—§ 383 (Paraçurāma): III, **99**, 8673 (°*gaṇān*, seen in the body of Rāma Dāçarathi).—§ 400 (Tīrthayātrāp.): III, **118**, †10224 (°*gaṇānāṃ*, sc. *āyatanaṃ*, visited by Yudhishṭhira, etc.).—§ 406 (do.): III, **125**, 10411 (°*āṃ sthānaṃ*, sc. Ārcīkaparvata). — § 418 (do.): III, **139**, 10834 (*sahāçvibhyāṃ*).—§ 421*c* (Ākāçagaṅgā): III, **142**, 10905 (*āhnikaṃ suraçreshṭho*—i.e. Indra—*japate sa-M°gaṇaḥ*, sc. on Ākāçagaṅgā). — § 435 (Jaṭāsuravadhap.): III, **157**, 11523.—§ 440 (Yakshayuddhap.): III, **165**, †11885 (*divaṃ . . . M°gaṇānāṃ*).—§ 443 (Nivātakavacayuddhap.): III, **168**, 12002 (°*āñ ca gaṇāḥ*), 12020 (°*gaṇāt*, Arjuna obtained weapons from the *M.*), 12043 (°*gaṇān*).—§ 445 (do.): III, **173**, 12268 (°*bhiḥ sahitaḥ*, sc. *Purandaraḥ*, i.e. Indra).—§ 456 (Sarasvatī-Tārkshyasaṃv.): III, **186**, 12745 (*devāḥ sahendrāḥ saha-M°gaṇāḥ*). — § 507 (Skandayuddha): III, **231**, 14586.—§ 509 (Kārttikeyastava): III, **232**, †14643 (Skanda is identified with the *M.*).—§ 512 (Ghoshayātrāp.): III, **237**, 14782 (°*bhir iva Vāsavaḥ*, sc. *vṛtaḥ*); **249**, 15093 (°*o Vṛtrahā yathā*, sc. *pālaya*).—§ 522 (Draupadīharaṇap.): III, **265**, †15600 (°*gaṇair Indra ivābhiguptaḥ*). — § 544 (Yudhishṭhirāçvāsa): III, **292**, 16605 (*nihato Vṛtro M°bhir Vajrapāṇinā*), 16608 (*Vajriṇaḥ senāṃ . . . sa-M°gaṇāṃ*).—§ 547 (Karṇa): III, **308**, 17139.—§ 548 (Āraṇeyap.): III, **313**, 17317; **314**, 17421.—§ 552 (Goharaṇap.): IV, **56**, 1762 (*Viçvāçvi-M°āṃ gaṇāḥ*, came to see the battle); **68**, 2204 (°*gaṇaiḥ parivṛtaḥ . . . Marutpatiḥ*, i.e. Indra).—§ 553 (Vaivāhikap.): IV, **70**, 2265 (°*gaṇair upāsīnaṃ Tridaçānāṃ iveçvaraṃ*, i.e. Indra). — § 561*d* (Nara-Nārāyaṇau): V, **49**, 1918 (*Mahendreṇa . . . saha*).—§ 561 (Yānasandhip.): V, **61**, 2399 (°*bhiḥ saha Vṛtrahā*).—§ 562 (Bhagavadyānap.): V, **91**, 3277 (*anuyāyibhiḥ sārdhaṃ M°bhir iva Vāsavaḥ*).—§ 565 (Gālavacarita): V, **110**, 3808 (°*gaṇaḥ*, their origin, cf. Diti).—§ 567 (Bhagavadyānap.): V, **131**o, 4424 (°*aç ca sahendreṇa*, issue from the mouth of Kṛshṇa).—§ 570 (Sainyaniryāṇap.): V, **157**, 5332 (°*bhir iva Vāsavaḥ*, sc. *abhiguptaḥ*).—§ 576 (Bhagavadgītāp.): VI, **34**, 1225 (*Marīcir M°ām asmi*, says Kṛshṇa); **35**, 1252 (seen in the body of Kṛshṇa), †1268.—§ 593 (Abhimanyuvadhap.): VII, **35**, 1536 (*Sādhya-Rudra-M°kalpaiḥ*, sc. the warriors of Droṇa).—§ 595 (Shoḍaçarāj., v. Marutta): VII, **55**, 2176 (the *M.* acted as distributors of food in the palace of Marutta). — § 596 (Pratijñāp.): VII, **76**, 2682 (°*aç ca sahendreṇa*).—§ 599 (Jayadrathavadhap.): VII, **108**, 4096 (*yathā Çakraṃ M°gaṇāḥ*, sc. *apūjayan*).—§ 600 (Ghaṭotkacavadhap.): VII, **175**, 7971 (°*bhir iva Vāsavaṃ*, sc. *vṛtaṃ*); **179**, †8177 (*pūjyamāno yathā Çakro Vṛtravadhe M°bhiḥ*).—§ 605 (Karṇap.): VIII, **19**, 718 (°*bhiḥ preritā meghāḥ . . . iva*); **31**, 1262 (°*gaṇasamaṃ bale*, sc. Karṇa). — § 606 (Tripurākhyāna): VIII, **33**, 1426 (*Çakro M°vṛtaḥ*).—§ 608 (Karṇap.): VIII, **82**, †4206 (°*gaṇāḥ Çakram iva*, sc. *jugupuḥ*); **87**χ', 4418 (sided with Arjuna), 4455 (*samalokatvaṃ M°āṃ*).—§ 615*j* (Maṅkanaka): IX, **38**, 2221 (°*āṃ gaṇāḥ*), 2222 (sprang from the seven sons of Maṅkanaka).—§ 615*u* (Skanda): IX, **44**, 2478; **45**γ, 2508 (came to the investiture of Skanda).—§ 615*x* (Kubera): IX, **47**, 2758 (*samāgamya M°gaṇaiḥ*, sc. Kubera).—§ 615*ee* (Ādityatīrtha): IX, **49**, 2848 (*Viçvedevāḥ sa-M°aḥ*, in Ādityatīrtha).—§ 623 (Rājadh.): XII, **15**β, 440 (are destroyers of life).—§ 632*b* (Shoḍaçarāj., cf. § 595): XII, **29**, 915 (at the sacrifice of Marutta the *M.* acted as distributors of food and the *M°gaṇāḥ* drank *soma*), 974 (*Māndhātāraṃ . . . yaṃ devā M°garbhaṃ pituḥ pārçvād apāharan*).—§ 635 (Rājadh.): XII, **33**, 1198 (°*bhiḥ saha jitvārīn bhagavān Pākaçāsanaḥ*), 1199 (°*gaṇair vṛtaḥ Çakraḥ*). — § 641 (do.): XII, **64**η, †2395 (°*āṃ gaṇaḥ*, observe kshatriya duties); **65**, 2448 (°*gaṇavṛtaḥ*, sc. Vishṇu in the shape of Indra). — § 656 (Khaḍgotpattik.): XII, **166**β, 6141 (°-*Açvinaḥ*).—§ 660*b* (Bhṛgu-Bharadvājasaṃv.): XII, **186**, 6886 (°*gaṇaiḥ*, i.e. the winds).—§ 661 (Mokshadh.): XII, **198a**, 7191 (°*āṃ*, sc. *sthānaṃ*).—§ 662*b* (Jāpakop.): XII, **200**δ, 7339.—§ 665 (Mokshadh.): XII, **208,** 7588 (*Ṛbhavo Marutaç caiva devānāñ cādito gaṇāḥ*), 7589 (are vaiçyas—*viçaḥ*).—§ 673*b* (Bali-Vāsavasaṃv.): XII, **227,** 8289 (had formerly been vanquished by Bali).—§ 695*b* (Dakshayajñavināça): XII, **285***a*, 10279 (°*gaṇaiḥ*).—§ 702 (Mokshadh.): XII, **297**β, 10837 (°*gaṇāḥ*).—§ 704 (do.): XII, **302**β, 11104 (°*āṃ vishayān*), 11172 (*saptānāṃ M°āṃ*—i.e. the winds?—*çreshṭhaḥ*).—§ 707 (do.): XII, **318,** 11706 (if the soul (*jīva*) escapes through the flanks one attains to the *M.*).—§ 712 (Çukotpatti): XII, **324,** 12175.—§ 717*b* (Nārāyaṇīya): XII, **341**π, 13111 (°*āṃ pataye*, i.e. Vishṇu (Nārāyaṇa)).—§ 730*g* (Upamanyu): XIII, **14**χ, 915 (*Çakro 'si M°āṃ*, sc. Çiva).—§ 730 (Ânuçāsanik.): XIII, **16,** 1045 (*Indrāgni-M°āṃ . . . gatiṃ*, sc. Çiva).—§ 744 (do.): XIII, **44,** 2438 (*kanyāvaraḥ purā datto M°bhir iti naḥ çrutam*).—§ 746 (do.): XIII, **75,** 3653 (*satyena M°o vānti*); **79**κ, 3778 (°*āṃ lokaṃ*).—§ 747*b* (Suvarṇotpatti): XIII, **84,** 4011.—§ 753 (Ânuçāsanik.): XIII, **97,** 4663 (*bali* should be offered to the *M.* in the interior of the house).—§ 759 (do.): XIII, **107**ε, 5238 (°*āṃ lokaṃ*), 5299 (°*āṃ*, sc. *lokaṃ*), 5315 (*saptānāṃ M°āṃ lokaṃ*), 5330 (°*āṃ lokaṃ*).—§ 766 (do.): XIII, **125,** 5988 (*devatāḥ, sa-M°gaṇāḥ*); **134**γ, 6187.—§ 768*b* (Umā-Maheçvarasaṃv.): XIII, **140***a*, 6351.—§ 773*b* (Kṛshṇa Vāsudeva): XIII, 159, †7387 (°*āṃ gaṇāḥ*, have sprung from Kṛshṇa).—§ 775 (Ânuçāsanik.): XIII, **166***a*, 7638 (°*gaṇaḥ*).—§ 778*f* (Muñjavat): XIV, **8,** 185 (worship Çiva on Muñjavat).—§ 782*g* (Guruçishyasaṃv.): XIV, **43**θ, 1175 (*gaṇānāṃ M°aḥ*, sc. are the foremost, only B.; C. by error has *mahatāṃ*), 1176 ((°*ām Indraḥ*, sc. *rājā*).—§ 789 (Putradarçanap.): XV, **31**η, 851 (Pāṇḍu had been born from the gaṇa of the *M.*—*M°gaṇāt*), 853 (Bhīmasena had been born from the gaṇa of the *M.*—*M°gaṇāt*).—§ 794 (Mahāprasthānikap.): XVII, **3,** 95.—§ 795 (Svargārohaṇap.): XVIII, **3,** 87; **4,** 125 (*sarshi-M°gaṇaiḥ*), (κ), 131 (°*gaṇavṛtaṃ*, sc. *Bhīmasenaṃ*, in heaven), 141 (°*āṃ gaṇeshu*); **5**μ, 159 (°*gaṇān*, Kṛtavarman entered the *M.*). Cf. Māruta, pl., and Marutvat, pl.

Maruta, a prince (= Marutta). § 562 (Bhagavadyānap.): V, **83**η, 2946 (?, among the ṛshis who worshipped Kṛshṇa).—§ 677 (Mokshadh.): XII, **235,** 8602 (*Karandhamasya putraḥ*, read *pautraḥ*; attained to heaven by giving his daughter to Aṅgiras, cf. XIII, 6260).

Māruta = Vayu (the Wind), q.v.

Māruta, adj. ("bolonging to tho wind"). § 569 (Bhagavadyānap.): V, **142,** 4818 (*Agni-M°e*, sc. *astre*, will be employed by Arjuna).

***Māruta**[1], pl. (°*āḥ*) (the winds). § 575 (Bhūmip.): VI, **12,** 479 (*çvasadbhir muñcamānās tu diggajair iha mārutāḥ*).—§ 695*b* (Dakshayajñavināça): XII, **285,** 10311.—§ 714 (Çukakṛtya): XII, **329,** 12417 (*Diteḥ putrāḥ*, i.e. Saṃvaha, etc.). Cf. Marut, pl.

Māruta[2], pl. (°*āḥ*), the warriors of the gods. § 506 (Skandayuddha): III, 14569, 14570 (*saptamaṃ M°skandhaṃ raksha nityam atandritaḥ*, says Çiva to Skanda).

Māruta[3], pl. (°*āḥ*), a people. § 578 (Bhīshmavadhap.): VI, **50**π, 2083 (in the army of Yudhishṭhira, only B.; C. has *Madakāḥ*).

Mārutāçana, a warrior of Skanda. § 615*u* (Skanda): IX, **45**η, 2564.

Mārutantavya, a son of Viçvāmitra. § 721*b* (Viçvāmitrop.): XIII, **4**β, 253.

Mārutātmaja[1] ("the son of the Wind") = Bhīmasena, q.v.

Mārutātmaja[2] (do.) = Hanūmat, q.v.

Māruti (do.) = Bhīmasena, q.v. (add. VII, 4071, 4091, 4096, 4110, 4509; VIII, 2435, 2500, 3051).

Marutpati[1] ("the lord of the Maruts") = Indra, q.v.—Do.[2] (do.) = Mahāpurusha (Mahāpurushastava).—Do.[3] (do.) = Çiva (1000 names[1]).

Marutsuta ("the son of the Wind") = Bhīmasena: VIII, †4600.

Marutta, an ancient king, son of Avikshit. § 5 (Anukram.): I, **1***a*, 220 *bis* (in Nārada's enumeration).—§ 266 (Çakrasabhāv.): II, **7,** 298 (the same?, among the ṛshis in the palace of Indra).—§ 267 (Yamasabhāv.): II, **8,** 321, 327 (among the kings in the palace of Yama).—§ 274 (Rājasūyārambhap.): II, **15,** 650 (among the five emperors (*samrājaḥ*) of yore).—§ 378 (Tīrthayātrāp.): III, **94,** 8507 (*yathā*).—§ 409 (Plakshāvataraṇag.): III, **129,** 10528 (had performed sacrifices with Saṃvarta as his priest).—§ 565 (Gālavac.): V, **111,** 3842 (performed sacrifices in the north).—§ 573 (Ambopākhyānap.): V, **178,** 7073 (*ayañ cāpi . . . Purāṇe çrūyate . . . M°ena . . . gītaḥ çlokaḥ*, i.e. v. 7074).—§ 595 (Shoḍaçarāj.): VII, **55**: M., the son of Avikshit, in order to compete with Bṛhaspati (*spardhayā vai Bṛhaspateḥ*), caused Saṃvarta (C. *Saṃvartaṃ*; B. °*to*) to officiate at his sacrifice. Çiva had given him wealth. The sacrifice took place on the golden base of Himavat (read *haime Himavataḥ pāde* in accordance with XIV, 89; C. and B. *haimaṃ . . . pādaṃ*); the gods with *Indra* and *Bṛhaspati* used to come to him (description of his riches and sacrifices); the *Maruts* used to become distributors of food (*pariveshṭāraḥ*) in his palace; the *Viçvedevas* were his courtiers (*sabhāsadaḥ*); the gods yielded copious showers of rain; he gratified the ṛshis, the Pitṛs, and the gods, he reigned for 1,000 years, and then repaired to the eternal regions of bliss acquired by his merits (*jitāl lokān gataḥ puṇyaduho 'kshayān*): VII, **55,** 2170 (*Âvikshitaṃ*), 2176, 2182.—§ 626 (Rājadh.): XII, **20,** †613 (*Âvikshitaḥ pārthivo 'sau M°a ṛddhyā Çakraṃ yojayed* (B. *yo 'jayad*) *Devarājaṃ*).—§ 632*b* (Shoḍaçarājikop., cf. § 595): XII, **29,** 910 (*Âvikshitaṃ*), 915 (repetition from § 595), 981 (vanquished by Māndhātṛ).—§ 634*b* (Rāmopākhyana): XII, **49,** 1798 (°*syānvāye rakshitāḥ kshatriyātmajāḥ*, sc. from Rāma Jāmadagnya).—§ 640 (Rājadh.): XII, **57,** 2052 (°*ena hi rājñā vai gītaḥ çlokaḥ purātanaḥ | rājādhikāre rājendra Bṛhaspatimate purā*, sc. v. 2053).—§ 656 (Khaḍgotpattik.): XII, **166,** 6197 (received the sword from Mucukunda, from *M.* it passed over to Raivata).—§ 767 (Ânuçāsanik.): XIII, **137***a*, 6260 (*Karandhamasya pautras tu M°o 'vikshitaḥ* (C. *vi*°) *sutaḥ*, attained to heaven by giving his daughter to Aṅgiras, cf. XII, 8602).—§ 775 (do.): XIII, **166**η, 7678 (enumeration).—§ 778 (Açvamedhikap.): XIV, **3,** 61, 62 (much gold was left behind at Himavat by the brahmans at the sacrifice of *M.*); **4,** 64 (*rājarsheḥ*).—§ 778*b* (Saṃvartta-Maruttīya): XIV, **4,** 86, 91 (son of Avikshit, held a sacrifice on the north of Himavat near Meru on the golden base of the mountain (? *kāñcanaḥ sumahān pādaḥ*); there thousands of golden vessels were prepared); **5,** 105–7, 109–12, 116 (surpassed Indra, who prevailed upon Bṛhaspati not to assist at the sacrifice of *M.*); **6,** 120, 121,–126, 127, 129, 133, (134), (139) (Nārada then told *M.* to apply to Saṃvarta); **7,** (155), (157), 159, (165), 166, (174) (Saṃvarta from hatred of his brother Bṛhaspati undertook the sacrifice); **8,** 215 (worshipped Çiva on Muñjavat); **9,** †222, †225–7, (229), (†231), †233, †234, †237, †239, †240, †244; **10,** †257, (†261), (†265), (†271), (†273), †276, (†278), †283 (Saṃvarta completed the sacrifice, Indra became gratified).—§ 785 (Anugītāp.): XIV, **63**, 1872 (*ratnañ ca yad M°ena nihitam*), 1879 (°*sya dhanam*, Yudhishṭhira obtained the wealth of *M.*); **89**, 2664 (°*syānukurvatā*, sc. Yudhishṭhira). Cf. Āvikshita, Maruta.

Marutvat = Indra, q.v.

Marutvat, pl. (°*antaḥ*), a class of gods (=Marut, pl.?). § 266 (Çakrasabhāv.): II, **7**, 289 (in the palace of Indra).—§ 664 (Mokshadh.): XII, **207**, 7540 (sons of Dharma [and a daughter of Daksha]). Cf. Marut, pl.

Maryādā[1], a Vidarbha princess. § 156 (Pūruvaṃç.): I, **95**, ††3771 (*Vaidarbhīm*, wife of Avācīna and mother of Ariha[1]).

Maryādā[2], a Videha princess. § 156 (Pūruvaṃç.): I, **95**, ††3776 (*Vaidehīm*, wife of Devātithi and mother of Ariha[2]).

Māsa[1] = Skanda: III, 14639 (°*ārdhamāsau*).—Do.[2] = Çiva (1000 names[1-2]).

māsa, pl. (°*āḥ*) ("the months," personif.): IX, 2517.

Māsārdha(m) = Çiva (1000 names[1]).

Māsikavratadhara = Mahāpurusha (Mahāpurushastava).

Masīra, pl. (°*āḥ*), a people. § 574 (Jambūkh.): VI, **9**μ, 360 (in Bhāratavarsha, only B.; C. has *Samīrāḥ*).

Mātali, the charioteer of Indra. § 11 (Parvasaṅgr.): I, **2**, 508 (*varānveshaṇam . . . M°eḥ*).—§ 334 (Kairātap.): III, **41**, 1709 (*ratho M°saṃyuktaḥ*, sc. Indra's).—§ 335 (Indralokābhigamanap.): III, **42**, 1715 (do.), 1723, (1724), 1728, 1732 (*Çakrasārathiḥ*), 1751 (conveyed Arjuna to the abode of Indra).—§ 351 (Nalopākhyānap.): III, **71**, 2797 (*kiṃ nu syād M°r ayaṃ Devarājasya sārathiḥ*, thought Ṛtuparṇa about Nala).—§ 441 (Nivātakavacayuddhap.): III, **165**, †11904 (°*saṃgṛhītaḥ*, sc. the chariot of Indra), †11910, †11911 (conveyed Arjuna from the abode of Indra to the Pāṇḍavas). § 443 (do.): III, **168**, 12023, 12024, 12026, 12028, 12032, 12036 (*Çakrasārathiḥ*, repetition from § 335), 12065 (°*saṃyuktaṃ rathaṃ*, was given to Arjuna for the battle with the Nivātakavacas).—§ 444 (do.): III, **169**, 12085, 12095; **170**, 12109–11, 12115, 12117 (*Çakrasārathiḥ*), 12125, 12126; **171**, 12145, 12154, 12159; **172**, 12172, 12173, 12180, 12181, 12183, 12187, 12189, 12196 (charioteer of Arjuna on the chariot of Indra).—§ 445 (do.): III, **173**, 12202, (12203), 12213, 12215, 12228, 12255 (*Çakrasārathiḥ*), 12263, 12265 (continuation of § 444).—§ 542 (Rāvaṇavadha): III, **290**, 16509, (16510), 16512 (*M.* came with the chariot of Indra to Rāma Dāçarathi, who ascended it and thus fought with Rāvaṇa).—§ 552 (Goharaṇap.): IV, **45**, 1412 (*yathā Çakrasya M°iḥ*, sc. *sārathiḥ*).—§ 564 (Mātalīyop.): V, **97**, 3511, 3512 (*Trilokarājasya sārathiḥ*), 3514, 3519; **98**, 3522, 3524, 3526–8, 3536–8, 3546; **99**, 3562, 3565, 3566; **100**, 3572, 3574, 3582, 3583; **101**, 3588, 3592, 3601; **102**, 3607, 3608, 3610, 3611, 3613; **103**, 3633, 3634, 3638, 3640, 3641; **104**, 3643 (*sutaḥ . . . Çakrasya dayitaḥ suhṛt*), 3654, 3661, 3666, 3668 (accompanied by Nārada, *M.* in all worlds sought a husband for his daughter Guṇakeçī; he chose Sumukha, who through the intervention of Vishṇu was not eaten by Garuḍa).—§ 597 (Pratijñāp.): VII, **84**, 2992 (*iva*).—§ 599 (Jayadrathavadhap.): VII, **112**, 4351 (*iva*).—§ 606 (Karṇap.): VIII, **35**, 1668 (°*vat*).—§ 607 (do.): VIII, **36**, 1670 (*yantā Deveçasyeva M°ḥ*), 1671 (*yathā*).

Cf. the following synonyms:—

Çakrasārathi ("the charioteer of Indra"): III, 1732 (*M*°), 12036 (*M*°), 12117 (*M*°), 12255 (*M*°), 16509 (*M*°), 16577.

Devasārathi (do.): III, 12254.

Mātalīya, adj. ("relating to Mātali"). § 10 (Parvasaṅgr.): I, **2**, 331 (°*am upākhyānam*, i.e. Mātalīyopākhyāna).

[Mātalīyopākhyāna(m)] ("the episode relating to Mātali"). (Cf. Mātalīyam upākhyānam.) § 564 (Bhagavady.). The holy *Ṛshi* (*bhagavān ṛshiḥ*) *Kaṇva* said to *Duryodhana* in the assembly of the *Kurus*: *Brahmán*, the grandsire of the universe (*Lokapitāmahaḥ*), is indestructible and eternal. The holy *Ṛshis* (*bhagavantāv ṛshī*) *Nara* and *Nārāyaṇa* are of the same character. Of all the sons of *Aditi*, *Vishṇu* alone is eternal . . . In this connection is cited an old story: *Mātali*, the charioteer of *Indra*, had, by his wife *Sudharmā*, one beautiful daughter, *Guṇakeçī*. As he found no suitable husband for her amongst D., Dai., G., or men and Ṛ., *Mātali* set out for the *Nāgaloka* (V, **97**). On the way *Nārada*, proceeding to visit *Varuṇa*, followed *Mātali*, and first showed him the abode of *Varuṇa*, surrounded by his sons and grandsons. *Varuṇa's* son *Pushkara* had been chosen as husband by *Soma's* daughter *Jyotsnākālī* (who had [before] chosen (so PCR.) the eldest and foremost of *Aditi's* sons (i.e. Sūrya, Nīl.)). He then showed him the abode, entirely made of gold, of the liquor (*Vāruṇyam*): to the possession of that liquor (*surā*) the gods owe their being *Surāḥ*. He showed him also the weapons that had belonged to the *Daityas* and had been obtained by the gods as a booty of war; when hurled at the foe they always return into the hand that hurls them. Here dwelt in days of yore many tribes of Rā. and Dai. Here is that fire of blazing flames and the discus of *Vishṇu*; and that knotty bow that was created for the destruction of the world; it is always protected with great vigilance by the gods, and it is from this bow that the one wielded by *Arjuna* has taken its name; it is endued with the strength of 100,000 bows; it punishes all wicked (*rakshobandhushu*) kings; it was first created by *Brahmán* and praised by *Çukra* (B. *Cakreṇa*); it is held by the sons of the Lord of waters. He showed him also *Varuṇa's* umbrella in the umbrella-house, always dropping water that cannot be seen. Innumerable are the wonders to be seen here (V, **98**). In the very centre of the *Nāgaloka* is the city *Pātāla* with *Daityas* and *Dānavas*, the *Asura* fire, fed by water; here the gods, having first vanquished their foes, quaffed the *amṛta* and deposited the residue; the *Āditya Hayaçiras*; from here *Airāvata* takes up water in order to impart it to the clouds, and it is that water which *Indra* pours down as rain; aquatic animals, the *timi*, etc., which subsist on the rays of the moon; here *Mahādeva* practised ascetic austerities for the benefit of all creatures; *maharshis* addicted to the vow of *go* (*govratinaḥ*); here in the race of the celebrated elephant *Supratīka* were born the elephants *Airāvaṇa* (the king of his tribe), *Vāmana*, *Kumuda*, and *Añjana*; an egg in the waters from the commencement of the creation, whence, when the end of the world comes, a fire bursts forth and consumes the three worlds, etc. *Mātali* said: "No one here seems to be eligible" (V, **99**). In *Pātāla* is *Hiraṇyapura*, built by the *Dānava* (so PCR.; B. and C. *Viçvakarmaṇā*) *Maya*, belonging to the *Daityas* and *Dānavas*, who in days of yore lived here having obtained boons, exhibiting 1,000 different kinds of illusion, incapable of being vanquished by *Çakra*, *Yama*, *Varuṇa*, or *Kubera*, etc. The *Kālakhañjas* (*Asuras*, who sprang from *Vishṇu* (?), so PCR.: *Asurāḥ Kālakhañjāç ca tathā Vishṇupadodbhavāḥ*; C. *Kālaka*°) and the *Yātudhānas* (*Rākshasas*, who sprang from the feet of *Brahmán* (?), so PCR.: *Nairṛtā Yātudhānāç ca Brahmapadodbhavāç ca ye*) (description); the *Nivātakavacas* (*Dānavas*); "many times,

O *Mātali*! thou with thy son *Gomukha* and *Indra* hadst to retreat before them"; description of their abodes (the gems *arkasphaṭika*, *vajrasāra*, *padmarāga*, etc.). *Mātali* would not choose a son-in-law among the *Dānavas*, the enemies of the gods; "as regards thyself (i.e. Nārada), I know that thy heart is ever set on fomenting quarrels (*hiṃsātmakaṃ*)" (V, **100**). Then the world of the *Suparṇas*, who subsist on snakes and have sprung from the six sons of *Garuḍa*: *Sumukha*, etc. (*a*), of *Kaçyapa's* and *Vinatā's* race, adorned with the *Çrīvatsa*, belonging to the *kshatriya* order, for they never attain to brahmanhood (*brāhmaṇyaṃ*) in consequence of their preying upon their kinsmen; they are shown favour by *Vishṇu*, and adore *Vishṇu*. The names of the principal are: *Suvarṇacūḍa*, etc. (*β*) (V, **101**). *Rasātala* is the seventh stratum below the earth; here dwells *Surabhī*, the mother of kine, born of the *amṛta*; her milk springs from the essence of the six different kinds of tastes; she sprang of old from the mouth of *Brahmán*, who was gratified with drinking the *amṛta* and vomited the best of things (i.e. the cow and the brahman, PCR.). A jet of her milk created the Milky Ocean (*kshīraṇidhi*), covered with white foam that is the food of the ascetics (*munisattamāḥ*) *Phenapāḥ* ("Foam-drinkers"); the very gods fear them because of their austerities. From *Surabhī* are born the four kine that support the quarters (*diçāṃ pālyaḥ*): in the East *Surūpā*, in the South *Haṃsikā*, in the West *Subhadrā*, in the North (*dharmyām Ailavilasañjñitāṃ*) *Sarvakāmadughā*. The gods and the *Asuras*, making *Mandara* their pole, churned the Ocean, and obtained *Vāruṇī*, *Lakshmī*, *amṛta*, *Uccaiḥçravas*, and *Kaustubha*. *Surabhī* milks *sudhā* to those who live on *sudhā* (i.e. the Nāgas, PCR.), *svadhā* to those who live on *svadhā* (i.e. the Pitṛs, PCR.), and *amṛta* to those who live on *amṛta* (i.e. the gods, PCR.). The *gāthā* that was sung by the dwellers of *Rasātala* in days of old is still heard to be recited in the world by persons of learning: "Neither in the *Nāga-loka*, nor in *Svarga*, nor in a *vimāna*, nor in heaven (*Tripishṭape*) is residence so happy as in *Rasātala*" (V, **102**). The city of *Bhogavatī* resembles *Indra's* city *Amarāvatī*; it is ruled over by *Vāsuki*, the king of the *Nāgas*; here dwells *Çesha* (*b*); here dwell the innumerable *Nāgas* (description), the sons of *Surasā*, wearing *svastika*, etc. The principal are *Vāsuki*, etc. (*γ*). *Mātali* wished to get for his son-in-law the *Nāga Sumukha* of *Airāvata's* race, the son of *Cikura* (who had been not long before slain by *Garuḍa*), and the grandson of *Āryaka Kauravya* and the daughter's son of *Vamana* (V, **103**). *Nārada* introduced *Mātali* to *Āryaka* as the friend and charioteer of *Indra*, who drives his chariot drawn by 1,000 steeds, and thereby has vanquished the enemies of the gods. *Āryaka* objected that *Garuḍa*, who had slain *Cikura*, when he left these regions had said that after a month he would devour *Sumukha* also. According to a proposal of *Mātali*, they all visited *Indra* and *Vishṇu*; *Vishṇu* proposed to give *amṛta* to *Sumukha*; but *Indra* disagreed on account of the prowess of *Garuḍa*; instead he gave him an excellent lease of life, and having married *Mātali's* daughter he returned home (V, **104**). *Garuḍa* made remonstrances to *Indra*, saying that he, like him, can without any fatigue bear the weight of the three worlds; that he had slain the *Daityas Çrutaçrī*, etc. (*δ*); that he not only perches on *Vishṇu's* flagstaff, but sometimes carries him with all his friends on his back, and he can carry *Vishṇu* without fatigue on only one of his feathers. *Vishṇu* shows him that he cannot bear the weight of his one right arm; then he threw *Sumukha* with the toe of his foot upon *Garuḍa's* breast. And from that time *Garuḍa* has ever lived (in friendship?) with that snake. *Kaṇva* continued: "In the same way, O *Duryodhana*! thou canst note ncounter *Bhīma*, etc. (*ε*)." *Duryodhana*, fixing his eyes on *Karṇa*, burst into laughter, saying: "I am precisely what the creator has made me" (V, **105**).

Mataṅga[1], an ancient king. § 134 (Viçvāmitra): I, **71**, 2925 (*rājarshiḥ*, lived as a hunter [in consequence of his father's curse] and maintained the wife of Viçvāmitra), 2927 (Viçvāmitra became his priest). Cf. the story of Satyavrata (Triçaṅku) in Harivaṃça (v. 717 foll.).

Mataṅga[2], one or more ṛshis. § 267 (Yamasabhāv.): II, **8**, 340 (in the palace of Yama).—§ 370 (Tīrthayātrāp.): III, **84**, 8079 (°*syāçramaṃ*, a tīrtha); **85**, 8159 (°*sya tu kedāraḥ*, a tīrtha).—§ 377 (Dhaumyatīrthak.): III, **87**, 8321 (*kedāraç ca M°sya*, a tīrtha in the east). — § 702 (Mokshadh.): XII, **297***δ*, 10875 (had obtained his status by way of penances).—§ 721 (Ānuçāsanik.): XIII, **3**, 198, 199 (*sthāne M°o brāhmaṇyaṃ nālabhad, Bharatārshabha* | *caṇḍālayonau jāto hi*, cf. § 735).—§ 735 (do.): XIII, **27**, 1872 (°*sya saṃvādaṃ gardabhyāç ca*), 1873, 1879, 1883, (1885), 1888, 1889, (1891), 1892; **28**, 1896, 1898, 1900, 1902, 1911; **29**, 1913, (1915), 1917, 1920, 1922, (1926), 1934, 1938 (*M.*, the son of a brāhmaṇī was informed by a she-ass that he was in reality a caṇḍāla, and in vain tried by way of penances to become a brahman; at last he succeeded in becoming *Chandodeva*).

Mātaṅga, a ṛshi. § 567 (Bhagavadyānap.): V, **127**, 4252 (°*vacanaṃ*, a sentence of his (i.e. v. 4251) is quoted).

***mātaṅga**,′ pl. (°*āḥ*) ("elephants"). § 127 (Aṃçāvat.): I, **66**, 2630 (the offspring of Mātaṅgī).

mātaṅga, name of a caste (= caṇḍāla): XII, 5368 (sg.), 5410 (sg.); XIV, 1602 ff. (sg.).

Mataṅgavāpī, a tīrtha. § 733 (Ānuçāsanik.): XIII, **25***a*, 1718.

Mātaṅgī, daughter of Krodhavaçā, mother of the elephants. § 127 (Aṃçāvat.): I, **66**, 2625, 2630.

Mātariçvan[1] = Vāyu (the Wind), q.v.

Mātariçvan[2], a Suparṇa, son of Garuḍa. § 564 (Mātalīyop.): V, **101***β*, 3599 (enumeration).

Māṭhara, a follower of Sūrya (the Sun). § 310*b* (Sūrya): III, **3**, 198 (*anucarāḥ . . . M°aruṇadaṇḍādyāḥ*) — § 377 (Dhaumyatīrthak.): III, **88**, 8335 (°*sya vanaṃ*, a sacred place in the south) —§ 702 (Mokshadh.): XII, **293**, 10754 (*sa-M°ṃ*, i.e. Sūrya, worshipped by Çaibya).

Māṭhara, pl. (VIII, 3652), v. Rāmaṭha, pl.

Mathurā, a city, the present Muthra. § 273 (Rājasūyārambhap.): II, **14**, 609 (the city of the Yādavas, from which they fled from fear of Jarāsandha), 632 (°*ṃ samparityajya*, sc. the Yādavas).—§ 275 (do.): II, **19**, 763, 764 (Jarāsandha hurled a mace toward *M.*; the place near *M.* where it fell down is named *Gadāvasāna*).—§ 641 (Rājadh.): XII, **101**, 3737 (°*m abhitaç ca ye*, are skilful in fighting with the bare arms).—§ 717*b* (Nārāyaṇīya): XII, **340**, 12954 (Nārāyaṇa will take birth as Kṛshṇa in *M.*).

Māthuradeçya, adj. ("originating from the country of Mathurā"). § 253 (Haraṇāharaṇap.): I, **221**, 8006 (*dogdhrīṇāṃ*).

Mati[1] ("thought"), a goddess. § 115 (Aṃçāvat.): I, **66**, 2579 (daughter of Daksha and wife of Dharma).—§ 132 (do.): I, **67**, 2794 (incarnate as Gāndhārī).

Mati[2] = Çiva: XIV, 200.

Matimat[1], a king. § 130 (Amçāvat.): I, **67**, 2701 (among the incarnations from the Krodhavaça gaṇa).

Matimat[2] = Çiva (1000 names[2]).

Matināra, an ancient king. § 150 (Pūruvaṃç.): I, **94**, 3703 (son of Anādhṛshṭi, performed a rājasūya and an açvamedha), 3704 (father of four sons, Taṃsu, etc.).—§ 156 (do.): I, **95**, ††3778 (son of Ṛksha and Jvālā), ††3779 (performed a twelve years sacrifice on the river Sarasvatī, who then became his wife and bore Taṃsu), 3780 (a çloka relating to *M.* is quoted). Cf. Anādhṛshṭisuta.

Matkulikā, v. Matkuṇikā.

Matkuṇikā, a mātṛ. § 615*u* (Skanda): IX, **46***θ*, 2637 (only C., B. has *Matkulikā*).

Mātrāḥ, pl. = Çiva (1000 names[2]).

Mātṛ = Çiva (1000 names[2]).

***Mātṛ**, pl. (°*araḥ*) ("mothers"): III, 14359 (*lokasya mātaraḥ*), 14364 (°*gaṇena*), 14368, 14369 (°*gaṇaiḥ*), 14395 (seven mothers of Çiçu enumerated), 14399 (°*gaṇa*°), 14467 (°*gaṇaḥ* . . . *lokasya mātaraḥ*), 14468 (?), (14469), (14472), (14474), 14497 (°*gaṇāḥ*); VII, 9539 (°*ṝṇāṃ patiḥ*, i.e. Çiva); IX, 2461 (i.e. the Kṛttikās), 2478 (*sapta M°gaṇāḥ*), 2619 (°*gaṇān Kumārānucarān*), 2620 (enumeration), 2648, 2672; XII, 7551 (*Bhūta-M°gaṇādhyaksham Virūpāksham*); XIII, 874 (*vividhāḥ*), 5981 (*lokānāṃ mātaraç caiva gāvaḥ sṛshṭāḥ Svayambhuvā*); XIV, 199 (°*bhaktaḥ*).

Mātṛtīrtha, a tīrtha. § 364 (Tīrthayātrāp.): III, **83**, 6028.

Mātṛvatsala = Skanda: III, 14633.

Matsa (IV, 145), v. Matsya[2].

Matsya[1], a king, son of Vasu Uparicara. § 76 (cf. Ādivaṃçāvatāraṇa): When *Girikā's* season came, the pitṛs of *Vasu* (q.v.) asked him to slay deer; when he in the forest was longing for *Girikā*, he gave his semen, enveloped by an açoka leaf, to a hawk in order that it should be carried to *Girikā*; persecuted by another hawk, the hawk let the semen fall into the *Yamunā*, where it was swallowed by the Apsaras *Adrikā*, who had by the curse of a brahman been transformed into a fish. In the tenth month the fish was caught, and out of its womb came a boy, who was given to *Uparicara* and afterwards became the king *Matsya*, and a girl, *Satyavatī*, who was of a fishy smell, and was retained by the fisherman. When killed, *Adrikā* assumed her own celestial shape and went away to the regions of the *Siddhas*, the *Ṛshis*, and the *Cāraṇas*: I, **63**, 2393 (*rājā*).—§ 267 (Yamasabhāv.): II, **8**, 320 (in the palace of Yama). Cf. next.

Matsya[2] ("king of the Matsyas") = Virāṭa: II, 1883 (*V°*), 1915 (waited upon Yudhishṭhira); IV, 16 (*V°*), 18, 145 (°*sya vishayaṃ*, C. has by error *Matsa*°), †226, 326 (°*sya nagare*, i.e. Upaplavya), 331, 373 (°*sya nagare*), 471, 483, 484, 547, 586, 591, 600, 635, 729, 880 (*sūtena rājño M°sya Kīcakena*), 972 (*sūtena caiva M°sya Kīcakena*), 993 (°*sya vishayaṃ*), 1018, 1019, 1061, †1073, 1142, 1143, 1145, 1147, 1157 (*Bhumiñjayaṃ nāma putraṃ M°sya*), 1159, †1195 (°*sya rājño duhitā*, i.e. Uttarā), 1482–4, 1486, 1582, 1625, †1662 (°*sya putraṃ*, i.e. Uttara), 1964 (°*sya kule*), †2143 (°*sya putraṃ*), 2198, 2200 (*rājā*), 2230, 2259 (*putreṇa M°sya*), 2265, 2324, 2354, 2363; V, †4, 103 (°-*Pāñcālayoḥ*), †784 (*rājā*), 5107 (*V°*); VI, 3162 (*V°*), 3555 (attacked by Droṇa), 3590 (pierced by Droṇa), 5419 (fights with Jayadratha); VII, 227, 375 (*V°*), 646 (pierced by Droṇa), 879 (°*ād avarajaḥ Çatānīkaḥ*), 965, 1083 (*V°*), 3533 (*V°*), 6764 (*V°*).

Matsya[3] ("belonging to the Matsya tribe") = Uttara: IV, 1784, †2149.

Matsya[4], the country of the Matsyas.—§ 549 (Pāṇḍavapraveçap.): IV, **12**, †324.—§ 552 (Goharaṇap.): IV, **31**, 1013 (°*sya rājā*, only C.; B. has *Matsyānāṃ rājā*).

Matsya[5] = Çiva (1000 names[1]).

Matsya[1], pl. (°*āḥ*), a people. § 214 (Hiḍimbavadhap.): I, **156**, 6085 (among the countries visited by the Pāṇḍavas).—§ 273 (Rājasūyārambhap.): II, **14**, 592 (among the peoples who fled from fear of Jarāsandha).—§ 280 (Bhīmasena): II, **30**, 1082 (vanquished by Bhīmasena on his digvijaya in the east). — § 281 (Sahadeva): II, **31**, 1108 (*apara-M°ān*, vanquished by Sahadeva on his digvijaya in the south).—§ 549 (Pāṇḍavapraveçap.): IV, **1***a*, 11; **7**, †225 (ruled by Virāṭa); **11**, †304.—§ 550 (Samayapālanap.): IV, **13**, 328, 338, 360.—§ 551 (Kīcakavadhap.): IV, **16**, 485 (*rājānaṃ M°ānāṃ*, i.e. Virāṭa), 494; **21**, 644; **22**, 702 (°*ānāṃ rājā*, i.e. Virāṭa), 728.—§ 552 (Goharaṇap.): IV, **30**, 972 (°-*Çālveyakāḥ*, had followed Kīcaka); **31**, 1008 (*senāṃ M°ānāṃ*), 1013 (°*ānāṃ rājā*, only B., C. has *Matsyasya rājā*), 1033; **32**, 1036, 1037; **33**, 1076; **34**, 1135 (°*ānām īçvaraḥ*); **35**, 1152; **38**, 1256; **47**, 1478, 1480, 1481, 1486 (*rājā M°ānāṃ*); **48**, 1508 (do.); **54**, †1661; **68**, 2164 (*rājā M°ānāṃ Virāṭaḥ*), 2173 (do.); **71**, 2325 (*Bhārata-M°yoḥ*); **72**, 2347, (*M°-Pārthayoḥ*), 2365.—§ 555 (Sainyodyogap.): V, **19**, 581 (*rājā M°ānāṃ Virāṭaḥ*, joined Yudhishṭhira together with one akshauhiṇī of troops).—§ 556 (Sañjayayānap.): V, **21**, 634; **22**, †663 (°*ānām adhipo Virāṭaḥ*).—§ 561 (Yānasandhip.): V, **48**, †1845 (*Virāṭaḥ* . . . *M°aiḥ sārdhaṃ*); **50***γ*, 1973 (wait upon Yudhishṭhira); **53***θ*, 2107 (among the allies of Yudhishṭhira); **54***ι*, 2137 (disregard Duryodhana); **57**, 2243 (*Virāṭo* . . . *sārdhaṃ M°aiḥ*, will support Çikhaṇḍin) (*o*), 2264; **61***ψ*, 2406; **62***aa*, †2415.—§ 562 (Bhagavadyānap.): V, **72***a*, 2594 (among the allies of Yudhishṭhira); **74***γ*, 2732 (*Sahajaç Cedi-M°ānāṃ*).—§ 571 (Ulūkadūtāgamanap.): V, **160***γ*, †5510 (in the army of Duryodhana (!)); **161**, 5538 (in the army of Yudhishṭhira), †5555 (in the army of Duryodhana).—§ 574 (Jambūkh.): VI, **9***μ*, 347 (among the peoples in Bhāratavarsha), 348 (*Cedi-M°-Karūshāḥ*, do.). § 576 (Bhagavadgītāp.): VI, **18***δ*, 688 (protected Bhīshma); **20**, †752 (in Bhīshma's division).—§ 578 (Bhīshmavadhap.): VI, **49***μ*, 2022 (are slain by Bhīshma).—§ 579 (do.): VI, **52***a*, 2129 (*Cedi-M°eshu*, attacked by Bhīshma); **54***θ*, 2242 (*Cedi-M°-Karūshās tu Bhīmasenapurogamāḥ*), 2352 (praise Bhīmasena).—§ 580 (do.): VI, **56***a*, 2405 (°-*Kaikeyaiḥ*, only C., in the head of Bhīshma's gāruḍavyūha); **59***ξ*, †2640 (*Cedi-Pāñcāla-Karūsha-M°āḥ*).—§ 582 (do.): VI, **71***ε*, 3140 (attack Duryodhana and Çakuni); **74**, 3271 (°*āḥ Kekayāç ca*, surround Arjuna). — § 587 (do.): VI, **118**, 5537, 5565 (°-*Pāñcāla-Cedīnāṃ*).—§ 589 (Droṇābhishekap.): VII, **9**, 288 (attack Droṇa).—§ 590 (do.): VII, **14**, 532 (*Virāṭaḥ saha M°aiḥ*); **16**, 629.—§ 592 (Saṃçaptakavadhap.): VII, **21***θ*, 877, 882, 883 (defeated by Droṇa the *M.* fled), (*λ*), 915 (°-*Kaikayān*), 919; **22***ν*, 926 (*ξ*), 942; **25**, 1085 (°*ānāṃ Kaikayaiḥ sārdham abhītāçvarathadvipaṃ*). — § 593 (Abhimanyuvadhap.): VII, **35***ζ*, 1528 (follow Abhimanyu); **40***o*, 1695 (°-*Pāñcāla-Sṛñjayāḥ*); **42***π*, 1744; **43***σ*, 1780 (°-*Pāñcāla-Kaikayāḥ*).—§ 596 (Pratijñāp.): VII, **78***ε*, 2744.—§ 599 (Jayadrathavadhap.): VII, **98***κ*, 3662; **110***ρ*, 4165; **122***ιι*, 4892.—§ 600 (Ghaṭotkacavadhap.): VII, **154***β*, 6651 (proceeded against Droṇa); **156***ι*, 6779; **157***σ*, 6967; **158***τ*, 6972; **161***ηη*, 7218; **166***ιι*, 7459.—§ 602 (Droṇavadhap.): VII, **186**, 8491 (defeated by Droṇa), 8500 (slain by Droṇa); **189**, 8683; **190**, 8725 (five hundred *M.* slain by Droṇa).—§ 603 (Nārāyaṇāstramokshap.): VII, **193** δ, 8934; **195** ι, 9018 (°-*Kaikayān*); **201**, 9392. — § 604 (Karṇap.): VIII, **8** η, 235 (had formerly been vanquished by Karṇa).—§ 605 (do.): VIII, **30** ξξ, 1231 (*Cedi-Kārūsha-M°ānām*).—§ 607 (do.): VIII, **45** μ, 2084 (know the eternal religion), †2086, (ν), †2098 (perform sacrifices), †2100.— § 608 (do.): VIII, **47** κ, 2226 (*Kāçya-M°aiḥ*); **48** ξ, 2254; **49** χ, 2334; **56** ρρ, 2762; **73**, 3639, 3662 (°-*Kaikayān*); **78**, 3966 (*Cedi-M°āḥ*).—§ 611 (Çalyap.): IX, **16** τ, 822; **20** ιι, †1087 (*Pāñcāla-M°āḥ*).—§ 616 (Sauptikap.): X, **8**, 477 (the remaining of the *M.* are slain by Açvatthāman); **9**, 529 (do.).—§ 791 (Putradarçanap.): XV, **36**, 990.

Matsya[2], pl. ("Matsya kings (?)"). § 267 (Yamasabhāv.): II, **8**, 333 (*nṛpatayaḥ*, 100 *M.* in the palace of Yama).

Matsyā = Satyavatī: I, 2396.

Mātsya[1] ("the son of the Matsya king") = Uttara: V, †1846 (*jyeshṭhaṃ Virāṭaputraṃ*).

Mātsya[2], a ṛshi. § 702 (Mokshadh.): XII, **297** δ, 10875 (had attained to his status by way of penances).

Mātsyaka, adj. ("relating to the fish"). § 457 (Vaivasvatop.): III, **187**, 12802 (°*ṃ nāma purāṇam*, i.e. Vaivasvatopākhyāna).

Matsyanagara ("the city of the Matsyas") = Upaplavya: IV, 325; VII, 5260.

Matsyapati ("the king of the Matsyas") = Virāṭa: IV, 1168 (°*eḥ sutaḥ*, i.e. Uttara); V, †2 (*sabhā . . . M°eḥ*); XIV, 2023 (°*eḥ sutā*, i.e. Uttarā).

Matsyaputra ("the son of the Matsya king") = Uttara: IV, 1233 (°-*Dhanañjayau*), 1640, †2116, †2134.

Matsyarāj ("the king of the Matsyas") = Virāṭa; IV, †308, †313, 343, 2163.

Matsyarāja (do.) = Virāṭa: II, 1106 ("vanquished by Sahadeva on his digvijaya in the south"); IV, †232, 696, 1065 (fights with Suçarman), 1070, 1078, 1087, 1138, 1139, 1316 (*dāyādaṃ M°sya*, i.e. Uttara); †2144, 2190, 2215, 2310, 2318, 2376 (*nagaraṃ M°sya*, i.e. Upaplavya); V, 1981 (°*gṛhāvāsanirodhenāvakarshitān*, sc. the Pāṇḍavas), 2480; VII, 7010 (*sahānujaḥ*); XI, 597 (°*kulastriyaḥ*).

Matsyarājan (do.) = Virāṭa: I, †169; III, 2009; IV, 527, 974, 1064, 1074; VII, 964.

Matsyavīra = Uttara: IV, †2158.

Matsyopākhyāna ("the episode relating to the fish"). § 11 (Parvasaṅgr.): I, **2**, 467 (i.e. Vaivasvatopākhyāna).

Mattamayūraka, pl. (°*āḥ*), a people. § 285 (Nakula): II, **32**, 1187 (*çūraiḥ*, in the west, vanquished by Nakula on his digvijaya).

Maudākin, v. Modākin.

Maudgalya ("descendant of Mudgala"), one or more ṛshis. § 59 (Sarpasattra): I, **53**, 2049 (among the sadasyas at the snake-sacrifice of Janamejaya). — § 520 (Mudgala): III, **261**, 15446, 15453, 15464 (C. *Mo*°), 15472, 15477 (= Mudgala, q.v.). — § 637 (Rājadh.): XII, **47** η, 1596 (among the ṛshis who surrounded Bhīshma on his arrow-bed).—§ 767 (Ānuçāsanik.): XIII, **137**, 6265 (king Çatadyumna ascended to heaven by giving a golden mansion to *M.*).

maudgalya, adj. (?), said of a caste: XIII, 2571 (*Vaidehikañ cāpi maudgalyaṃ*).

Mauleya, pl. (°*āḥ*), a people. § 295 (Dyūtap.): II, **52**, 1871 (bring tribute to Yudhishṭhira).

Mauneya, pl. (°*āḥ*) ("sons of Muni"), a family of Devagandharvas. § 101 (Aṃçāvat.): I, **65**, 2552 (*Devagandharvāḥ*).

§ 608 (Karṇap.): VIII, **87**, 4424 (came to see the encounter between Karṇa and Arjuna).

Mauñjāyana, a muni. § 264 (Sabhākriyāp.): II, **4** *a*, 108 (among the munis who waited upon Yudhishṭhira).

Maurava, adj. ("belonging to Muru"). § 317*b* (Kṛshṇa Vāsudeva): III, **12**[14], 488 (*sāditā M°āḥ pāçā Nisunda-Narakau hatau | kṛtaḥ kshemaḥ punaḥ panthāḥ puraṃ Prāgjyotishaṃ prati*, sc. by Kṛshṇa).—§ 570*f* (Çārṅga): V, **158**, 5357 (*sañchidya M°ān pāçān*, sc. Kṛshṇa). Cf. Muru.

Mausala[1] ("[battle] performed with clubs"). § 793 (Mausalap.): XVI, **1**, 7, 11; **2**, 133; **8**, 262.—§ 794 (Mahāprasthānikap.): XVII, **1**, 1 (°*m āhavaṃ*).

Mausala[2] ("[the section] relating to the battle with clubs") = Mausalaparvan. § 4 (Anukram.): I, **1**, 91 (°*çrutisaṅkshepaḥ . . . Bhāratadrumaḥ*).—§ 10 (Parvasaṅgr.): I, **2**, 356 (°*aṃ parva*).—§ 11 (do.): I, **2**, 619 (do., C. °*sha*°), 628 (do., C. °*sha*°). — § 795*c* (Mahābhārata): XVIII, **6**, 279 (°*e sārvaguṇikam gandhamālyānulepanaṃ*).

[Mausalaparvan] ("the section relating to the battle with clubs," the 16th of the great and the 98th of the minor parvans of Mhbhr.; cf. Mausala). § 793: *Vaiçampāyana* said: When the 36th year [after the great battle] was reached, *Yudhishṭhira* beheld many unusual portents (specification). A little while afterwards he heard of the wholesale carnage of the *Vṛshṇis* in a battle with clubs, where only *Kṛshṇa* and *Rāma* had escaped with life; he summoned his brothers and took counsel with them; they were filled with grief; the death of *Kṛshṇa* they could not believe. *Janamejaya* inquired about the particulars of the destruction of the *Vṛshṇis* and *Andhakas*. *Vaiçampāyana* said: ** When the 36th year . . . (cf. above). Asked by *Janamejaya*, cursed by whom the *Vṛshṇis*, etc. (*a*), met with destruction, *Vaiçampāyana* said: *Sāraṇa*, etc., saw *Viçvāmitra*, *Kaṇva*, and *Nārada* arrived at *Dvārakā*; they disguised *Çāmba* as a woman, calling her the wife of *Babhru*, and asked the ascetics what [sort of child] this one would bring forth. The ascetics answered: "This *Çāmba* will bring forth a terrible iron club for the destruction of the *Vṛshṇis* and *Andhakas*, except *Rāma* (who will enter the ocean) and *Kṛshṇa* (whom *Jarā* will pierce while lying on the ground)." Then they went to *Kṛshṇa*. Informed of what had taken place, *Kṛshṇa* summoned all the *Vṛshṇis* and told them of it, but did not try to annul the curse. The next day *Çāmba* actually brought forth an iron club. The fact was reported to the king [*Ugrasena*], who caused it to be reduced into powder and thrown into the sea. At the command of *Āhuka*, etc. (*β*), the manufacture of spirits was forbidden among all the *Vṛshṇis* and *Andhakas*, under the penance of being impaled alive with all one's kinsmen. All the citizens (knowing that it was the command of Rāma also) bound themselves by the rule (XVI, 1). [The embodied form of] Time every day wandered about their houses, like a man of terrible and fierce aspect, bald head, black and tawny of complexion; they shot innumerable arrows at him, without being able to pierce him. Also other dreadful portents of calamity were daily seen by the *Vṛshṇis* throughout the city (description). They showed disregard for brahmans, P., and D., etc., except *Rāma* and *Kṛshṇa*, etc. When the *Pāñcajanya* was blown in their houses, asses brayed aloud from every direction. *Kṛshṇa*, seeing that the day of the new moon coincided with the 13th [and 14th] lunation, summoned the *Yādavas* and said: The 14th lunation has been made the 15th by *Rāhu* once more, as at the time of the great battle of the *Bharatas* (v. the note of PCR. on p. 5). He understood that the 36th year had come according to the curse of *Gāndhārī*, and that the omens were similar to those which *Yudhishṭhira* had noticed when the two armies were arrayed in order of battle. He endeavoured to bring about those occurrences which would make *Gāndhārī's* words true. He commanded the *Vṛshṇis* to make a pilgrimage to some sacred water, and caused the messengers to proclaim a journey to the sea-coast (XVI, **2**). At that time the *Vṛshṇi* ladies dreamt every night that a black woman with white teeth, entering their abodes, laughed aloud and ran through *Dvārakā* stealing [from them]; the men dreamt of vultures that devoured the *Vṛshṇis* and *Andhakas* in the houses and fire-chambers; their ornaments, etc., were taken away by Rā. The iron discus of *Kṛshṇa*, given by *Agni*, with a nave of adamant, ascended to heaven. *Kṛshṇa's* chariot was dragged away by his four steeds over the ocean; *Kṛshṇa's* and *Baladeva's* standards (resp. *Garuḍa* and a palmyra), which were reverently worshipped by those two heroes, were taken away by Aps., who day and night called upon the *Vṛshṇis* and *Andhakas* to set out on a pilgrimage to some sacred water. They prepared various kinds of edibles and spirits, and set out to *Prabhāsa*. *Uddhava* took leave of them and *Kṛshṇa* before departing [from the world]. The *Vṛshṇis*, mixing with spirits the food that had been cooked for the brahmans, gave it to apes, and began revels with drinking, so also *Rāma*, etc. (γ); *Yuyudhāna* blamed *Kṛtavarman* for the nightly slaughter, and was applauded by *Pradyumna*, but was rebuked by *Kṛtavarman* with having killed *Bhūriçravas* while sitting in *prāya*; *Kṛshṇa* cast an angry glance [at *Kṛtavarman*], and *Sātyaki* informed him of the story of the gem *Syamantaka*, which was *Satrājit's*; *Satyabhāmā*, weeping, approached *Kṛshṇa*, and sitting on his lap enhanced his anger; *Sātyaki* swore that he would cause *Kṛtavarman* to follow the five sons of *Draupadī*, etc (δ), whom he had slain with the help of *Açvatthāman*, and he severed his head in the very sight of *Kṛshṇa* and began to strike down others; *Kṛshṇa* rushed forward to prevent him from doing further mischief, and the *Bhojas* and *Andhakas* all assailed him; *Kṛshṇa* did not interfere; they struck *Yuyudhāna* with the pots from which they had been eating; *Pradyumna* rushed forward to rescue *Yuyudhāna*; they were both slain. *Kṛshṇa* in wrath took up a handful of *erakā* grass, which became a terrible iron club, with which *Kṛshṇa* slew all that came before him. The *Andhakas*, etc. (ε), also took up blades of the *erakā* grass, which were converted into iron clubs, and struck one another in consequence of the curse of the brahmans; son killed father and vice versa, inebriated with spirits. Beholding that *Çāmba*, etc. (ζ), were slain, *Kṛshṇa* exterminated the *Vṛshṇis* and the *Andhakas*. *Babhru* and *Dāruka* told him now to go to *Rāma* (XVI, **3**). *Dāruka*, *Kṛshṇa*, and *Babhru*, seeking *Rāma*, saw him sitting thoughtfully, reclining his back against a tree. *Kṛshṇa* sent *Dāruka* to inform *Arjuna* and tell him to come quickly, and he also dispatched *Babhru* to protect the ladies against robbers; but as soon as *Babhru* had proceeded to a distance, an iron club attached to the mallet of a hunter came and slew him *Kṛshṇa* then, entering *Dvāravatī*, told his father to protect the ladies till *Arjuna* came, saying that he would practise penances with *Rāma*. When he came to *Rāma*, the latter had applied himself to *yoga*, and from his mouth issued a huge white *Nāga* with 1,000 heads and red eyes, who proceeded to the ocean, and was received by the ocean and many celestial snakes (and many sacred rivers): *Karkoṭaka*, etc. (η). After *Rāma's* death *Kṛshṇa* wandered for some time, and then sat down, thinking of *Gāndhārī* (§ 619) and *Durvāsas* (§ 773c), and the destruction of the *Vṛshṇis*, *Andhakas*, and *Kurus*, whence he concluded that the hour [of his death] had come; he then restrained his senses [in *yoga*]; though he was the Supreme Deity, he wished to die in order to dispel all doubts, etc., and to make the words of *Durvāsas* true. The hunter *Jarā*, mistaking *Kṛshṇa* for a deer, pierced him at the heel with an arrow; coming up, he beheld a man dressed in yellow robes, rapt in *yoga*, with many arms; he became filled with fear; *Kṛshṇa* comforted him and then ascended upwards, and was received in heaven by *Indra*, etc. (θ) (XVI, **4**). Meanwhile *Dāruka* came and informed the *Pāṇḍavas* of the slaughter of the *Vṛshṇis*, etc. (ι). *Arjuna* with *Dāruka* proceeded to *Dvārakā*; when *Kṛshṇa's* 16,000 wives saw *Arjuna*, they uttered a loud cry; the city seemed to *Arjuna* to be the fierce river *Vaitaraṇī*; *Arjuna*, *Satyā* (the daughter of *Satrājit*), and *Rukmiṇī* fell down and wailed; then praising *Kṛshṇa* and comforting the ladies, *Arjuna* went to *Vasudeva* (XVI, **5**), whom he found lying on the ground and burning with grief; *Vasudeva* lamented (κ) and said he would die by abstaining from food (XVI, **6**). *Arjuna* said that the hour had come for the *Pāṇḍavas* also for departing [from the world] (λ); he would, however, first remove to *Indraprastha* the women, the children, and the aged of the *Vṛshṇis*. Saying to *Dāruka* that he wished to see the chief officers of the *Vṛshṇis*, *Arjuna* entered the hall of the *Yādavas* called *Sudharmā*, where he said to the citizens and ministers that he would take away with him the remnants of the *Vṛshṇis* and *Andhakas*, as the sea would soon engulf the city; *Vajra* would be their king at *Indraprastha*; they would set out on the seventh day at sunrise. *Arjuna* passed that night in the mansion of *Kṛshṇa*. At dawn *Vasudeva* by *yoga* attained to the highest goal; the ladies were in despair. His four wives, *Devakī*, *Bhadrā*, *Rohiṇī*, and *Madirā*, ascended the funeral pyre, and attained to the regions of *Vasudeva*. When *Arjuna* had caused *Vasudeva* and his four wives to be burnt (under immense tokens of sympathy from the women), the boys (headed by *Vajra*) and the ladies offered oblations of water to *Vasudeva*. Then *Arjuna* visited the spot where the *Vṛshṇis* had been killed and caused the last rites to be performed, and caused *Rāma* and *Kṛshṇa* to be cremated. On the seventh day he set out, mounting his chariot, with the ladies and children, the *Yādava* troops, and other inhabitants, with *Kṛshṇa's* 16,000 wives and *Vajra*; they numbered many millions in all. Then the ocean flooded *Dvārakā*. They proceeded in slow marches. When they had planted their encampment at *Pañcanada*, the *Ābhīras* (*Mlecchas*) conspired to rob the cavalcade. *Arjuna* succeeded only with great difficulty in stringing his bow; his celestial weapons would not come to his mind; the *Vṛshṇi* warriors failed to rescue the women, who were snatched away by the robbers; *Arjuna's* shafts soon became exhausted; formerly they had been inexhaustible. *Arjuna* became very cheerless; he escorted the remnant of the cavalcade to *Kurukshetra*; he established the son of *Kṛtavarman* in the city of *Mārttikāvata* with the remnant of the women of the *Bhoja* king; the remainder, with children and old men and women, at *Indraprastha*, with *Vajra* as their ruler; the son of *Yuyudhāna* (with old men, etc.) on the banks of the *Sarasvatī*; the widows of *Akrūra*, notwithstanding the entreaties of *Vajra*, entered the woods; *Rukmiṇī*, etc. (μ), ascended the funeral pyre; *Satyabhāmā* and the other wives of *Kṛshṇa* entered the woods in order to practise penances in the contemplation of *Hari*; going beyond *Himavat*, they took up their abode in *Kalāpa-grāma*. Then *Arjuna* entered the retreat of *Vyāsa* (XVI, **7**). Asked by *Vyāsa* ("Hast thou been sprinkled with water from anybody's nails or hair, etc.?"), *Arjuna* informed him of what had passed (ν) ("500,000 warriors have thus been laid down"). *Vyāsa* said that the *Vṛshṇis* and *Andhakas* had been consumed by the brahman's curse; it was destiny: "*Kṛshṇa*, as also the *Pāṇḍavas*, have finished their work; the time has come for your departure from the world," etc. (ξ). *Arjuna* entered *Hāstinapura* and informed *Yudhishṭhira* of what had taken place (XVI, **8**).

Māvelaka, pl., v. Māvellaka, pl.

Māvella ("king of the Māvella[ka]s"?). § 74 (Vasu): I, **63**, 2364 (the fourth son of Vasu Uparicara).—§ 287 (Rājasūyikap.): II, **34**, 1272 (came to the rājasūya of Yudhishṭhira).

Māvellaka, pl. (°*āḥ*), a people. § 591 (Saṃçaptakavadhap.): VII, **17**β, 692 (among the Saṃçaptakas, C. has *Māvelakaiḥ*).—§ 592 (do.): VII, **19**β, 768 (slain by Arjuna).—§ 599 (Jayadrathavadhap.): VII, **91**β, 3255 (attacked Arjuna).—§ 604 (Karṇap.): VIII, **5**ζ, 138 (mentioned among the slain, C. has *Māvelvakāḥ*).

Māvelvaka, pl., v. Māvellaka, pl.

Maya, an Asura. § 4 (Anukram.): I, **1**, 133 (°*ena sukṛtāṃ sabhāṃ*, cf. § 263).—§ 10 (Parvasaṅgr.): I, **2**, 316 (°*darçanam*, i.e. I, **228–34**).—§ 11 (do.): I, **2**, 364 (°*sya darçanam*, do.), 403 (°*sya mokshaḥ*, all. to § 258).—§ 71 (Ādivaṃçāvataraṇap.): I, **61**, 2278 (*mahāsuram*, all. to § 258).—§ 258 (Khāṇḍavadahanap.): I, **228**, 8323 (*Asuram*), 8326, 8328 (*Namucer bhrātaram*), 8330 (is rescued from the flagration of the *Khāṇḍava* forest).—§ 259 (Çārṅgakop.): I, **229**, 8332 (*Dānavasya*).—§ 260 (Khāṇḍavadahanap.): I, **234**, 8478 (*Dānavaḥ*).—§ 261 (Sabhākriyāp.): II, **1**, 1, (4), 8, 12–15.—§ 263 (do.): II, **2**, v. 36 (B., this çloka is wanting in C.); **3**, 58, 76, 85, 87, 95 (*M.* fetched a mace for Bhīmasena from Bindusaras and built the palace of Yudhishṭhira).—§ 294 (Dyūtap.): II, **48**, 1709–10 (all. to §§ 258 ff.); **50**, 1809 (*kṛtāṃ . . . M°ena*, sc. the palace of Yudhishṭhira).—§ 322 (Dvaitavanapr.): III, **23**, †914 (*cakāra yāṃ . . . sabhāṃ M°ḥ*, cf. § 263).—§ 534 (Hanūmatpratyāg.): III, **280**, 16237 (°*sya . . . Daityasya . . . veçma*, seen by Hanumat, etc., on their way from Kishkindhā to Laṅkā; the abode of the female ascetic Prabhāvatī).—§ 564 (Mātalīyop.): V, **100**, 3568 (*Hiraṇyapuram . . . nirmitam viçvakarmaṇā M°ena manasā kṛtam*).—§ 586 (Bhīshmavadhap.): VI, **100**, 4549 (°*ṃ jitveva Vāsavaḥ*); **101**, 4605 (°*ṃ Çakra ivāhave*).—§ 587 (do.): VI, **110**, 5123 (°*-Çakrau yathā purā*).—§ 600 (Ghaṭotkacavadhap.): VII, **174**, 7879 (°*ṃ Vishṇur ivāhave*, sc. *nyavadhīt*).—§ 606 (Tripurākhyāna): VIII, **33**, 1406 (*mahāsuraṃ viçvakarmāṇaṃ ajaraṃ Daitya-Dānavapūjitam*), 1407 (built three cities for the Asuras), 1415 (*sarvayogavahaḥ*), 1417.—§ 641 (Rājadh.): XII, **82**, 3086 (error in C. instead of *Yamaḥ*, B.).—§ 673*b* (Bali-Vāsavasaṃv.): XII, **227***a*, 8261 (among the ancient rulers of the earth).—§ 743 (Ānuçāsanik.): XIII, **40**, 2250 (*māyāç ca M°jāḥ*). Cf. Asura, Daitya, Daiteya, Dānava.

Māya = Çiva: XIII, 909.

Māyā (?). § 10 (Parvasaṅgr.): I, **2**, 352 (see Durvāsaḥ-saṃvāda, but cf. also Umā-Maheçvara-saṃvāda: XIII, **140** ff.).

Māyātman = Kṛshṇa: XII, 1646.

Māyāvin = Çiva (1000 names[2]).

Mayūra, an Asura. § 130 (Aṃçāvat.): I, **67**, 2671 (*mahāsuraḥ*, incarnate as king Viçva).

Mayūraketu ("having a peacock for emblem") = Skanda: III, 14630.

Mecaka = Çiva (1000 names[1]).

Meda[1], a serpent. § 65 (Sarpasattra): I, **57**, 2152 (of Airāvata's race).

Meda[2], name of a caste: XIII, 1552.

Medhā ("intelligence"), a goddess. § 115 (Aṃçāvat.): I, **66**, 2578 (daughter of Daksha and wife of Dharma).—§ 266 (Çakrasabhāv.): II, **7**, 300 (in the palace of Indra).

Medhaja, Medhas = Vishṇu (1000 names).

Medhātithi[1], a ṛshi. § 266 (Çakrasabhāv.): II, **7**, 298 (in the palace of Indra).—§ 665 (Mokshadh.): XII, **208**ε, 7593 (*ṛshir M°eḥ putraḥ Kaṇvaḥ*, among the ṛshis of the east).—§ 677 (Mokshadh.): XII, **245**β, 8900 (had attained to his status by way of penances).—§ 682 (do.): XII, **267**, 9525 (*Gautamaḥ* [husband of Ahalyā, Nīl.] and father of Cirakārin, v. Gautama[1]).—§ 717*c* (Uparicara): XII, **337**ε, 12758 (*ṛshiḥ*, among the sadasyas at the sacrifice of Vasu Uparicara).—§ 734 (Ānuçāsanik.): XIII, **26***a*, 1764 (among the ṛshis who had come to see Bhīshma on his arrow-bed).—§ 770 (do.): XIII, **151**ζ, 7109 (*ṛshir M°iḥ* (°*eḥ*, B.) *putraḥ Kaṇvaḥ*, among the seven gurus of Indra [in the east]).—§ 775 (do.): XIII, **166**γ, 7664 (among the ṛshis of the east).

Medhātithi[2], a river. § 494 (Āṅgirasa): III, **222**, 14230 (among the rivers who are mothers of fires).

Medhāvikā, a tīrtha. § 372 (Tīrthayātrāp.): III, **85**, 8197.

Medhāvin[1], son of Bāladhi. § 415 (Tīrthayātrāp.): In ancient times the muni *Bāladhi* practised austerities in order to have an immortal son. He obtained a son *Medhāvin* of a very irritable temper, but the gods did not make him immortal; they only granted the boon that he should live as long as the mountains existed. *Medhāvin* grew haughty, and insulted the munis. The learned *Dhanushākṣha* then cursed him, saying, "Be thou reduced to ashes." When, however, *Medhāvin* was not reduced to ashes, *Dhanushāksha* caused the mountains to be scattered by buffaloes, and then *Medhāvin* perished. As his father bewailed him, the munis quoted the following gāthā: "A mortal on no condition can overcome what has been ordained by fate," etc.: III, **135**, 10740, 10742–3.

Medhāvin[2], a brahman. § 659 (Mokshadh.): XII, **175**, 6524 (discourse between him and his father).—§ 600 (do.): XII, **278**, 9930 (do.).

Medhāvin[3] = Vishṇu (1000 names).

Medhraja = Çiva (1000 names[2]).

Medhyā, a river. § 377 (Dhaumyatīrthak.): III, **89**, 8368 (in the west).—§ 494 (Āṅgirasa): III, **222**, 14230 (among the rivers who are mothers of fires).—§ 775 (Ānuçāsanik.): XIII, **166***a*, 7652 (enumeration).

Medhyāraṇya, a forest. § 545 (Pativratā-māhātmyap.): III, **295**, 16693.

***Medinī** ("the earth," personif.): XIII, 2140. Cf. Pṛthivī.

Medinīpati = Vishṇu (1000 names).

Meghahṛt, v. Meshahṛt.

Meghakāla = Çiva (1000 names[1]).

Meghamālā, a mātṛ. § 615*u* (Skanda): IX, **46**θ, 2648.

Meghamālin, a companion of Skanda. § 615*u* (Skanda): IX, **45**, 2549 (together with Kāñcana given to Skanda by Meru).

Meghanāda, a warrior of Skanda. § 615*u* (Skanda): IX, **45**η, 2564.

Meghapushpa, one of Kṛshṇa's horses. § 552 (Goharaṇap.): IV, **45**, 1414 (°*sya javane sadṛçam*, sc. the one of Uttara's horses).—§ 562 (Bhagavadyānap.): V, **83**, 2938 (*vājibhiḥ Çaibya-Sugrīva-M°-Balāhakaiḥ*, yoked to the chariot of Kṛshṇa).—§ 596 (Pratijñāp.): VII, **79**ζ, 2812.—§ 599 (Jayadrathavadhap.): VII, **147**ρρ, 6344 (*kāmagaiḥ Çaibya-Sugrīva-M°Balāhakaiḥ . . . yuktam*, sc. the chariot of Kṛshṇa).—§ 617 (Aishīkap.): X, **13**, 649 (*pārshṇivāhau . . . M°-Balāhakau*).—§ 639 (Rājadh.): XII, **53**η, 1917.

Megharavā, a mātṛ. § 615*u* (Skanda): IX, **46**θ, 2648.

Meghasandhi[1], a king. § 232 (Svayaṃvarap.): I, **186**, 6988 (only B.; C. has by error *Meshasandhiḥ*, came to the svayaṃvara of Draupadī).

Meghasandhi[2], king [of the Magadhas] in Rājagṛha, son of Sahadeva. § 785 (Anugītāp.): XIV, **82**, 2438, 2439 (vanquished by Arjuna when he followed the sacrificial horse). Cf. Māgadha, Magadheçvara, Sahadevaja, Sahadevātmaja.

Meghasaṅghāḥ = Çiva (1000 names[1]).

Meghasvanā, a mātṛ. § 615*u* (Skanda): IX, **46**θ, 2626.

Meghavāhana, a king. § 273 (Rājasūyārambhap.): II, **14**, 577 (among the allies of Jarāsandha).

Meghavāhinī, v. Meshavāhinī.

Meghāvarta = Çiva (1000 names[1]).

Meghavāsas, an Asura. § 268 (Varuṇasabhāv.): II, **9**, 367 (in the palace of Varuṇa).

Mekala, pl. (°*āḥ*), a people. § 574 (Jambūkh.): VI, **9**μ, 348 (°*āç cotkalaiḥ saha*, among the peoples of Bhāratavarsha).—§ 578 (Bhīshmavadhap.): VI, **51**τ, 2103 (followed Bhīshma; C. has by error *Melakaiḥ*).—§ 585 (do.): VI, **87**ε, 3855 (follow Bṛhadbala, the Kosala king; C. has by error *Melakaiḥ*).—§ 589 (Droṇābhishekap.): VII, **4**β, 122 (*Utkalā M°āḥ*, had formerly been vanquished by Karṇa).—§ 605 (Karṇap.): VIII, **22**ζζ, 864 (attack the Pāñcālas), (θθ), 882 (*M°otkala Kāliṅgāḥ*, attack Nakula).—§ 739 (Ānuçāsanik.): XIII, **35**ε, 2158 (among the kshatriyas who have been degraded to çūdras).

Melaka, pl. (°*āḥ*) (VI, 2103, 3855), v. Mekala.

Menā, a river. § 574 (Jambūkh.): VI, **9**λ, 331 (in Bhāratavarsha).

Menakā, an Apsaras. § 21 (Pramadvarā): I, **8**, 943, 944 (*Apsarāḥ*), 945 (do., with the Gandharva king Viçvāvasu the mother of Pramadvarā, whom she dropped near the hermitage of Sthūlakeça).—§ 134 (Viçvāmitra): I, **71**, 2915, 2916, 2918, (2921); **72**, 2937, 2938, 2945 (*M.* was sent by Indra to tempt Viçvāmitra; on her Viçvāmitra begot Çakuntalā).—§ 135 (Çakuntalop.): I, **74**, 3055 (among the foremost Apsarases), 3056 (*Brahmayonivarā*, mother of Çakuntalā), 3061, 3063 (*Apsarasām çreshṭhā*), 3065, 3067, 3070.—§ 191 (Arjuna): I, **123**, 4820 (sung at the birth of Arjuna).—§ 269 (Vaiçravaṇasabhāv.): II, **10**, 392 (in the palace of Kubera).—§ 336 (Indralokābhigamanap.): III, **43***a*, 1784 (danced in the palace of Indra).—§ 565 (Gālavac.): V, **117**, 3975 (*reme . . . M°āyām yathorṇāyuḥ*).—§ 775 (Ānuçāsanik.): XIII, **166**β, 7641 (enumeration).

Menakātmajā ("the daughter of Menakā") = Çakuntalā: I, 2948.

Meru[1], a mountain. § 28 (Amṛtamanthana): I, **17**, 1098 (description, the gods held counsel there).—§ 72 (Ādivaṃçāvatāraṇap.): I, **62**, 2328 (*yathā M°r mahāgiriḥ*).—§ 134 (Viçvāmitra): I, **71**, 2930 (*saṃkshiped mahā-M°m*, sc. Viçvāmitra).—§ 135 (Çakuntalop.): I, **74**, 3071 (*antaram . . . M°sarshapayor iva*).—§ 148 (Yayāti): I, **85**, 3508 (°*çṛṅge tathottare*, there Yayāti sported with Viçvācī).—§ 164 (Āpavop.): I, **99**, 3925 (°*oḥ pārçve nagendrasya*, there the hermitage of Vasishṭha was situated).—§ 208 (Astradarçana): I, **134**, 5327 (*harshād āruruhur mañcān M°ṃ devastriyo yathā*).—§ 225 (Vāsishṭha): I, **176**, 6740 (Vasishṭha precipitated himself from the summit of *M.* in order to commit suicide).—§ 257 (Khāṇḍavadahanap.): I, **225**, 8210 (°*or iva nagendrasya*).—§ 258 (do.): I, **227**, 8265 (°*r ivācalaḥ*).—§ 269 (Vaiçravaṇasabhāv.): II, **10**, 413 (among the mountains who are present in the palace of Kubera).—§ 275 (Rājasūyārambhap.): II, **18**, 736 (°*ṃ vā khāditum çaktā*, sc. *asmi*, says Jarā).—§ 289 (Arghāharaṇap.): II, **38**, 1395 (*parvatānāṃ mukhaṃ M°ḥ*).—§ 295 (Dyūtap.): II, **52**, 1858 (°*-Mandarayor madhye Çailodām abhito nadīm*).—§ 327 (Draupadīparitāpav.): III, **35**, 1404 (°*or iva nigūhanaṃ*).—§ 328 (Kāmyakavanaprav.): III, **36**, 1413 (°*or iva vimardanaṃ*).—§ 331 (Kairātap.): III, **39**, 1552 (*girir M°r ivāparaḥ*).—§ 334 (do.): III, **41**, 1704 (°*pratimagaurava*, sc. Arjuna).—§ 356 (Tīrthayātrāp.): III, **81**, 4025 (*na jahau . . . M°m arkaprabhā yathā*).—§ 360 (do.): III, **82**, 5053 (*gacchaty antarhitā yatra M°pṛshṭhe Sarasvatī*).—§ 385 (Vindhya): III, **104**, 8782 (*adrirājaṃ mahāçailaṃ M°ṃ kanakaparvataṃ*, the sun revolves round Meru), 8783 (*yathā*). — § 422 (Gandhamādanapr.): III, **142**, 10911 (°*sannibhaṃ*).—§ 439 (Yakshayuddhap.): III, **163**, 11852 (*mahā-M°ḥ*, the abode of the seven ṛshis, the spiritual sons of Brahmán), 11856 (the abode of Brahmán), 11860 (the abode of Vishṇu lies to the west of *M.*), 11867 (the Sun and the Moon every day round Meru, *pradakshiṇam upāvṛtya*), 11871 (°*m anuvṛttaḥ*, sc. the Sun), 11873 (*atikramya mahā-M°m*, sc. the Moon).—§ 459 (Mārkaṇḍeyas.): III, **188**, 12919 (*kanakaparvataṃ*, seen by Mārkaṇḍeya in the stomach of Nārāyaṇa); **189**, 12959 (°*-Mandarabhūshaṇām*, sc. the earth).—§ 496 (Skandotpatti): III, **225**, 14332 (*parvataṃ*, why swans and vultures go to the mountain of *M.*).—§ 520 (Mudgala): III, **261**, 15448 (°*ḥ parvatarāḍ yatra hiraṇmayaḥ*, extends over 33,000 yojanas).—§ 561 (Yānasandhip.): V, **65**, 2486 (*çreshṭhaṃ M°ṃ çikhariṇām iva*).—§ 562 (Bhagavadyānap.): V, **83**, 2940 (°*çikharaprakhyaṃ*, sc. *rathaṃ*).—§ 570 (Sainyaniryāṇap.): V, **156**, 5290 (*parvatānāṃ yathā M°ḥ*, sc. *senāpatir bhava*).—§ 571 (Ulūkadūtāgamanap.): V, **160**, 5505 (*na hi çuçruma vātena M°m unmathitaṃ giriṃ*), 5506 (*anilo vā vahed M°ṃ*); **161**, 5550 (= v. 5505), 5551 (= v. 5506).—§ 574 (Jambūkh.): VI, **6**, 204 (*parimaṇḍalaḥ . . . kanakaparvataḥ*, between Gandhamādana and Mālyavat, description), 209, 226 (°*oḥ paçcime pārçve Ketumālaḥ*); **7**, 253 (°*or apy antaraṃ pārçve pūrvaṃ*, C.; °*or athottaraṃ pārçvaṃ pūrvaṃ ca*, B.).—§ 574*g* (Uttara-Kuru, pl.): VI, **7**, 254 (°*oḥ pārçve tathottare*).—§ 574*h* (Bhadrāçva): VI, **7**, 267 (°*oḥ pārçvaṃ . . . pūrvaṃ*).—§ 574*i* (Jambū): VI, **7**, 278 (the juice from the Jambū flows round the *M.* to the Uttara-Kurus).—§ 576 (Bhagavadgītāp.): VI, **34**, 1227 (°*uḥ çikhariṇām ahaṃ*, sc. *asmi*, says Kṛshṇa).—§ 578 (Bhīshmavadhap.): VI, **46**, 1807 (*babhau . . . candramā iva M°ṇā*); **48**, 1898 (*girir M°r ivācalaḥ*).—§ 581 (do.): VI, **63**, 2787 (do.).—§ 583 (do.): VI, **78**, 3437 (°*r iva sthitaḥ*); **79**, 3473 (*giriṃ M°ṃ ivāmbudāḥ*).—§ 584 (do.): VI, **82**, 3603 (*çikharaiḥ kāñcanamayair M°s tribhir ivocchritaiḥ*); **83**, 3670 (*pracchādayām āsa giriṃ M°m ivāmbudāḥ*).—§ 587 (do.): VI, **109**, 5092 (*mahā-M°r çailo meghair ivāvṛtaḥ*); **110**, 5128 (*yathā M°ḥ . . . çṛṅgair atyartham ucchritaiḥ*).—§ 589 (Droṇābhishekap.): VII, **9**, 272 (°*or iva visarpaṇaṃ*).—§ 593 (Abhimanyuvadhap.): VII, **34**, 1503 (°*r ivācalaḥ*).—§ 594 (Mṛtyu): VII, **54**, 2096 (*mahā-M°ṃ*).—

§ 595 (Shoḍaçarāj., v. Çibi Auçīnara): VII, **58**, 2215 (*yāvan M°oḥ mahopalāḥ*); (do., v. Pṛthu Vainya): VII, **69**, 2411 (when the mountains milked the earth, *M.* was their milker).—§ 597 (Pratijñāp.): VII, **83**, 2990 (°*or* (B. °*āv*) *iva divākaraḥ*).—§ 599 (Jayadrathavadhap.): VII, **120**, 4761 (°*çṛṅgam ivābabhau*); **144**, 6052 (*api M°ṃ vahet*).—§ 600 (Ghaṭotkacavadhap.): VII, **156**, 6810 (*babhau . . . girir M°r ivārditaḥ*); **166**, 7410 (*abhyavarshat . . . M°ṃ vṛshṭyā yathāmbudaḥ*); **174**, 7864 (*abhyavarshan megho M°m ivācalaṃ*); **180**, 8187 (°*or iva visarpaṇaṃ*).—§ 603 (Nārāyaṇāstramokshap.): VII, **193**, 8899 (*viparyāsaṃ yathā M°oḥ*).—§ 603*d* (Tripura): VII, **202**, 9569 (Çiva made *M.* his standard when he proceeded against Tripura).—§ 604 (Karṇap.): VIII, **8**, 220 (°*oḥ saṃsarpaṇaṃ yathā*).—§ 606 (Tripurākhyāna): VIII, **34**, 1491 (became the flagstaff of Çiva).—§ 607 (Karṇap.): VIII, **40**, 1823 (*nirbhindyāṃ . . . api M°ṃ mahāgiriṃ*, says Karṇa).—§ 608 (do.): VIII, **46**, 2202 (°*m ivāparaṃ*); **68**, †3392 (*sthairyeṇa M°oḥ*); **88**, †4521 (*mahāgiriṃ M°m ivogramārutāḥ*, sc. *prasahet*).—§ 610 (Çalyap.): IX, **6**ο, 299 (°*gauravaṃ*, sc. Açvatthāman).—§ 615*f* (Çaṅkhatīrtha): IX, **37**, 2138 (*mahā-M°m ivocchritaṃ*).—§ 615*u* (Skanda): IX, **45**γ, 2516 (*anekaçṛṅgavān*), 2550 (gave to Skanda two companions named Kāñcana and Meghamālin).—§ 623 (Rājadh.): XII, **14**, 405 (*Krauñcadvīpaḥ . . . uttareṇa mahā-M°oḥ*), 406 (*Çākadvīpaḥ . . . pūrveṇa ca mahā-M°oḥ*), 407 (*uttareṇa mahā-M°oḥ . . . Bhadrāçvaḥ*).—§ 635 (do.): XII, **35**, 1257 (°*prapātaṃ prapatan*, only C.; B. has *maru*°).—§ 641*f* (Pṛthu Vainya): XII, **59**, 2240 (*mahā-M°ḥ svayaṃ kanakaparvataḥ*, gave heaps of gold to Pṛthu).—§ 641 (Rājadh.): XII, **122**, 4471 (*çṛṅge Himavato M°au* (!) *kanakaparvate*), 4496 (*M.* was made the lord of the mountains).—§ 648 (Āpaddh.): XII, **140**, 5267 (°*oḥ . . . yat çreyas tat samācaret*).—§ 654 (do.): XII, **154**, 5820 (°*vat*).—§ 678*c* (Mṛtyu-Prajāpatisaṃv.): XII, **259**, 9208.—§ 694*b* (Jvarotpatti): XII, **284**, 10212 (°*oḥ çṛṅgaṃ Jyotishkaṃ nāma Sāvitraṃ*).—§ 712 (Çukotpatti): XII, **324**, 12168 (°*çṛṅge*, Çiva resided on *M.*); **325**, 12198 (°*pṛshṭhe*, Çuka was bathed on *M.*).—§ 713 (Çukakṛti): XII, **326**, 12228 (°*or Hareç ca dve varshe*).—§ 716 (Çukābhipatana): XII, **334**, 12615 (*sa çṛṅge . . . Himavan-M°sambhave | saṃçlishṭe çvetapīte dve rukmarūpyamaye || çatayojanavistāre*, rent in twain by Çuka); **335**, 12662 (*mahā-M°oḥ çṛṅgāt*).—§ 717*b* (Nārāyaṇīya): XII, **336**, †12702, 12704 (Çvetadvīpa is situated in a distance of 32,000 yojanas from *M.*).—§ 717 (Uparicara): XII, **336**, 12723 (on *M.* the seven ṛshis composed a çāstra); **337**, 12774 (°*or uttarabhāge Kshīrodasyānukūlataḥ*, Çvetadvīpa is situated).—§ 717*b* (Nārāyaṇīya): XII, **340**, 12986 (°*au samāgatā devāḥ*), **341**, 13028 (*girivare*, Vyāsa with his disciples lived on *M.*); **343**, XII), ††13221 (Sthūlaçiras practised austerities, *M°oḥ prāguttare*), XIII), ††13222 (Vaḍavāmukha practised austerities on *M.*); **344**, 13334, 13336.—§ 730*b* (Hiraṇyakaçipu): XIII, **14**, 662 (°*kampanaḥ*, sc. Hiraṇyakaçipu).—§ 730*g* (Upamanyu): XIII, **14**ι, 802 (°*oç ca vibhaveshv antareshu ca*), (χ), 912 (*parvatānāṃ bhavān M°ḥ*, sc. *asi*, i.e. Çiva).—§ 730 (Ānuçāsanik.): XIII, **18**, 1297 (Vyāsa had performed austerities on *M.*).—§ 734 (do.): XIII, **26**, †1856 (°*oḥ samudrasya ca sarvaratnaiḥ* (B. *sarvayatnaiḥ*) *saṅkhyopalānām udakasya vāpi* [*na*] *çakyaṃ vaktuṃ*).—§ 747*b* (Suvarṇotpatti): XIII, **85**, 4083 (Gaṅgā dropped the semen of Rudra on Meru).—§ 749 (Ānuçāsanik.): XIII, **92**, 4378 (°*çṛṅge samāsīnaṃ Pitāmahaṃ*).—§ 752*b* (Chattropānahotpatti): XIII, **96**a, 4638 (*prabhāṃ M°oḥ*).—§ 754 (Ānuçāsanik.): XIII, **98**, 4682 (*kāñcanaparvate*).—§ 757*e* (Hastikūṭa): *Gautama* said: The delightful wood, decked with flowers, graced with the song of *Kinnarīs*, with the beautiful high *Jambū* on the summit of *M.* Dhṛtarāshṭra said: Mild, truthful, learned, compassionate brahmans who study the Purāṇa and the Itihāsas and offer [libations of] honey to the brahmans attain to this region (*loka*): XIII, **102**, †4862.—§ 775 (Ānuçāsanik.): XIII, **166**a, 7657.—§ 778*b* (Saṃvartta-Maruttīya): XIV, **4**, 88 (at *M.—Himavatpārçva uttare*—Marutta caused golden vessels, etc., to be made and performed a sacrifice).—§ 782*g* (Guruçishyas.): XIV, **44**ι, 1224 (*parvatānāṃ mahā-M°ḥ sarveshām agrajaḥ smṛtaḥ*).—§ 785 (Anugītāp.): XIV, **59**, 1759 (°*r muniganair iva*).—§ 794 (Mahāprasthānikap.): XVII, **2**, 48 (*mahāçailaṃ M°ṃ çikhariṇāṃ varaṃ*). Cf. Sumeru.

Meru[2], a mountain in Çākadvīpa. § 575*b* (Çākadvīpa): VI, **11**, 415, (β) 425 (*mahā-M°ḥ*).

Merubhūta, pl. (°*āḥ*), a people. § 574 (Jambūkh.): VI, **9**μ, 355 (in Bhāratavarsha).

Merudhāman = Çiva (1000 names[2]).

Merusāvarṇa, a ṛshi. § 770 (Ānuçāsanik.): XIII, **151**λ, 7122.

Merusāvarṇi, a ṛshi. § 305 (Anudyūtap.): II, **78**, 2573 (had instructed Yudhishṭhira on Himavat).

Meruvraja, the city of the Rākshasa king Virūpāksha. § 658*b* (Kṛtaghnop.): XII, **170**, 6360 (*nagaraṃ*); **172**, 6416.

Mesha, a warrior of Skanda. § 615*u* (Skanda): IX, **45**η, 2566 (only B., C. has *Meshapravāhaḥ*).

Meshahṛt, a Suparṇa, son of Garuḍa. § 564 (Mātalīyop.): V, **101**β, 3597 (only B., C. has *Meghahṛt*).

Meshapravāha, a warrior of Skanda. § 615*u* (Skanda): IX, **45**η, 2566 (only C., B. has *Meshaḥ Pravāhaḥ*).

Meshasandhi, v. Meghasandhi.

Meshavāhinī, a mātṛ. § 615*u* (Skanda): IX, **46**θ, 2636 (only C., B. has *Meghavāhinī*).

Miçraka, name of a tīrtha. § 364 (Tīrthayātrāp.): III, **83**, 6061, 6062.

Miçrakeçī, an Apsaras. § 103 (Aṃçāvat.): I, **65**, 2557 (among the daughters of Prādhā).—§ 150 (Pūruvaṃç.): I, **94**, 3698 (*Apsarasi*, wife of Raudrāçva and mother of ten sons: Ṛceyu, etc.).—§ 191 (Arjuna): I, **123**, 4817 (danced at the birth of Arjuna).—§ 269 (Vaiçravaṇasabhāv.): II, **10**, 392 (in the palace of Kubera).—§ 336 (Indralokābhigamanap.): III, **43**a, 1784 (danced in the palace of Indra).—§ 549 (Pāṇḍavapraveçap.): IV, **9**, 259 (Sudeshṇa asks Draupadī if she is *M.*, etc.).—§ 731*b* (Ashṭāvakra-Diks.): XIII, **19**β, 1424 (danced in the abode of Kubera).—§ 775 (Ānuçāsanik.): XIII, **166**β, 7641 (enumeration).

Miçrin, a serpent. § 793 (Mausalap.): XVI, **4**η, †119.

Mīḍhvas = Çiva, q.v.

Mihira = Sūrya (the Sun): III, 191.

Mīlīmilin = Çiva (1000 names[1]).

Miñjikāmiñjika (i.e. Miñjikā and Miñjika). § 504 (Skandayuddha): III, **231**, 14523 (arose from the semen of Rudra, i.e. Çiva), 14528 (*mithunaṃ Rudrasambhavaṃ namaskāryaṃ sadaiveha bālānāṃ hitam icchatā*).

Mithilā, the capital of the Videhas. § 177 (Pāṇḍudigvijaya): I, **113**, 4452 (Pāṇḍu went to *M.* and vanquished the Videhas).—§ 276 (Jarāsandhavadhap.): II, **20**, 795 (on their way from Indraprastha to Rājagṛha, Kṛshṇa, etc., came to *M.*).—§ 479 (Pativratop.): III, **206**, 13695, 13696 (the abode of the virtuous fowler); **207**, 13702, 13705, 13706 (*Janakena surakshitāṃ*), 13714.—§ 486 (do.): III,

215, 14031.—§ 623 (Rājadh.): XII, **17**, 529 (*°āyām pradīptāyām na me dahyati kiñcana*, a sentence of Janaka).—§ 659 (Mokshadh.): XII, **178**, 6641 (do.). — § 668*b* (Pañcaçikhavākya): XII, **218**, 7883 (*Janako janadevas tu M°āyām janādhipaḥ*), 7886.—§ 689 (Mokshadh.): XII, **277**, 9917 (= v. 529).—§ 709*b* (Sulabhā-Janakasaṃv.): XII, **321**, 11863 (*Videhānām purīm*).—§ 713 (Çukakṛti): XII, **326**, 12221, 12226, 12236 (*°opavanam*), 12238 (Çuka went to Janaka in *M.*).—§ 782*f* (Janaka): XIV, **32**, 895.

Mithila, pl. (*°āḥ*) ("the inhabitants of Mithilā"). § 515 (Karṇadigvijaya): III, **254**, 15243 (vanquished by Karṇa on his digvijaya).

Mithilādhipa, Mithilādhipati, Mithileçvara = Janaka, q.v.

Mitra ("friend"), one of the Ādityas. § 88 (Aṃçāvat.): I, **65**, 2523 (the second of the Ādityas). — § 171 (Vicitravīryasutotpatti): I, **105**, 4260 (*putrān . . . M°ā-Varuṇayoḥ samān*).—§ 191 (Arjuna): I, **123**, 4822 (the third of the Ādityas, present at the birth of Arjuna).—§ 258 (Khāṇḍavadahanap.): I, **227**, 8268 (armed with a discus he partook in the battle between the gods and Arjuna+Kṛshṇa); **229**, 8360 (Agni identified with *M.*).—§ 266 (Çakrasabhāv.): II, **7**, 302 (in the palace of Indra).—§ 310*b* (Sūrya): III, **3**, 191 (Sūrya identified with *M.*).—§ 370 (Tīrthayātrāp.): III, **84**, 8113 (*°ā-Varuṇayor lokān*).—§ 392 (do.): III, **114***a*, †10121. — § 600 (Ghaṭotkacavadhap.): VII, **155**, 6718 (*yathāmbupati-M°au Tārakam Daityasattamam*, sc. *adhāvatām*).—§ 615*u* (Skanda): IX, **45**γ, 2507 (came to the investiture of Skanda), (δ), 2543 (gave Skanda two companions, Suvrata and Satyasandha). — § 615*ff* (Asita Devala): IX, **50**μ, 2892 (*°ā-Varuṇayor lokān*). — § 615 (Baladevatīrthayātrā): IX, **54**, 3048 (*°ā-Varuṇayor . . . āçramam*).—§ 665 (Mokshadh.): XII, **208**β, 7581 (the fourth of the Ādityas), (η), 7595 (*°ā-Varuṇayoḥ putraḥ . . . Agastyaḥ*). — § 682 (do.): XII, **281**β, 10052 (Vishṇu identified with *M.*). — § 707 (do.): XII, **314**, 11608 (*pāyur adhyātmam ity āhur yathā tattvārthadarçinaḥ | visargam adhibhūtañ ca M°s tatrādhidaivatam*); **319**, 11751 (*°m Varuṇam eva ca*), 11762 (= Purusha).—§ 719 (Gautamī-lubdhaka-vyāla-Mṛtyu-Kālas.): XIII, **1***a*, 55.—§ 730 (Mahādevasahasranāmas.): XIII, **17**, 1218 (= Çiva, 1000 names [2]).—§ 748*b* (Tārakavadhop.): XIII, **86***a*, 4201 (came to see Skanda).—§ 770 (Ānuçāsanik.): XIII, **151**γ, 7092 (the third of the Ādityas), (η), 7113 (*°ā-Varuṇayoḥ putraḥ . . . Agastyaḥ*).—§ 775 (do.): XIII, **166**δ, 7666 (do.).—§ 782*b* (Brāhmaṇagītā): XIV, **21**, 631.—§ 782*g* (Guruçishyas.): XIV, **42**, 1127 (*avāggatir apānaç ca pāyur adhyātmam ucyate | adhibhūtam visargaç ca M°as tatrādhidaivatam*), 1167 (= the Supreme spirit).—§ 785 (Anugītāp.): XIV, **60**β, 1787 (*gupto . . . M°eṇa Varuṇo yathā*).

Mitrā, an Apsaras. § 731*b* (Ashṭāvakra-Diks.): XIII, **19**β, 1424 (danced in the abode of Kubera, only C.; B. has *Citrā*).

Mitrabhānu, a king. § 775 (Ānuçāsanik.): XIII, **166**η, 7680 (enumeration).

Mitradeva, a Kuru warrior. § 605 (Karṇap.): VIII, **27**λλ, 1078 (attacked Arjuna), 1084, 1087 (pierced by Arjuna).

Mitradharman, a god. § 492 (Āṅgirasa): III, **220**, 14167 (among the fifteen *yajñamushaḥ*).

Mitrajña, a god. § 492 (Āṅgirasa): III, **220**, 14167 (among the fifteen *yajñamushaḥ*).

Mitrasaha, the proper name of Kalmāshapāda Saudāsa (q.v.): I, 6720 (only B., *rājarshiḥ*); XII, 8604 (*rājā*); XIII, 6262 (*rājā*); XIV, 1690.

Mitrasāhvayā, a goddess. § 506 (Skandayuddha): III, **231**, 14562 (followed Umā).

Mitrasena, a Kuru warrior. § 605 (Karṇap.): VIII, **27**, 1101 (Arjuna cut off his head).

Mitravardhana, a god. § 492 (Āṅgirasa): III, **220**, 14167 (among the fifteen *yajñamushaḥ*).

Mitravarman [1], a Pāñcāla warrior. § 604 (Karṇap.): VIII, **6**, 175 (*Pāñcālyaḥ*, had been slain by Droṇa).

Mitravarman [2], a Kuru warrior. § 605 (Karṇap.): VIII, **27**λλ, 1078 (attacked Arjuna), 1084, 1087 (pierced by Arjuna), 1098 (Arjuna cut off his head).

Mitrāvaruṇayoḥ putraḥ ("the son of Mitra and Varuṇa") = Agastya: XII, 7595 (*A*°); XIII, 7113 (*A*°), 7666 (*A*°).

Mitravat, a god. § 492 (Āṅgirasa): III, **220**, 14167 (among the fifteen *yajñamushaḥ*).

Mitravinda, a fire. § 493 (Āṅgirasa): III, **220**, 14174 (*Rathantaraç ca Tapasaḥ putro 'gniḥ paripaṭhyate | M°āya vai tasmai havir adhvaryavo viduḥ*).

Mleccha, pl. (*°āḥ*) ("non-Aryan"). § 11 (Parvasaṅgr.): I, **2**, 378 (*hitopadeçaḥ . . . Vidureṇa kṛtaḥ . . . M°bhāshayā*, cf. § 213).—§ 133 (Dushyanta): I, **68**, 2803 (*deçān . . . ā-M°āvadhikān*).—§ 148*c* (Turvasu): I, **84**, 3480 (*gurudāraprasakteshu tiryagyonigateshu ca paçudharmishu pāpeshu M°eshu tvam bhavishyasi*, sc. *rājā*, sc. Turvasu).—§ 148*e* (Anu): I, **85**, 3533 (*Anos*—sc. *sutāḥ*—*tu M°jātayaḥ*).—§ 213 (Jatugṛhap.): I, **141**, 5645 (*°ādhamaḥ . . . Purocanaḥ*); **148**, 5803 (*Vidureṇokto M°vācā 'si*, sc. Yudhishṭhira).—§ 223 (Vāsishṭha): I, **175**, 6685 (*°ān bahuvidhān*, arose from the foam of Vasishṭha's cow), 6686 (*nānā-M°gaṇaiḥ*, defeated the army of Viçvāmitra).—§ 246 (Sundopasundop.): I, **210**, 7659 (*samudravāsinīḥ sarvā M°jātīḥ*, vanquished by Sunda and Upasunda).—§ 280 (Bhīmasena); II, **30**, 1099 (*sarvān M°gaṇān*, in the east, vanquished by Bhīmasena), 1101 (*°nṛpatīn sāgarānūpavāsinaḥ*, vanquished by Bhīmasena).—§ 284 (Sahadeva): II, **31**, 1170 (*nṛpatīn M°yonijān*, in the south, vanquished by Sahadeva).—§ 285 (Nakula): II, **32**, 1198 (*sāgarakukshisthān M°ān*, in the west, vanquished by Nakula). — § 287 (Rājasūyikap.): II, **34**, 1269 (*°aiḥ sāgarānūpavāsibhiḥ*, followed Bhagadatta).—§ 295 (Dyūtap.): II, **51**, 1834 (*Prāgjyotishādhipaḥ . . . Mlecchānām adhipaḥ*, i.e. Bhagadatta); **52**, 1897 (*sarve M°āḥ*, waited upon Yudhishṭhira).—§ 342 (Indralokābhigamanap.): III, **51**, 1989 (had been present at the rājasūya of Yudhishṭhira).—§ 347 (Nalopākhyānap.): III, **64**, 2402 (*vanam . . . M°taskarasevitam*).—§ 423 (Gandhamādanapr.): III, **145**, 11026 (*deçān M°janākīrṇān*, in the north). — § 458*b* (Kaliyuga): III, **188**, 12838 (*°rājānaḥ*, will rule in the Kaliyuga).—§ 460*b* (do.): III, **190**, 13037 (*°bhūtam jagat sarvam*, sc. in the Kaliyuga), 13046 (*°ībhūtam jagat sarvam*, do.), 13054 (do., do.), 13061 (*°ācārāḥ . . . manushyāḥ*, do.), 13080 (*mahī M°janākīrṇā bhavishyati*, do.).—§ 460*c* (Kalkin): III, **190**, 13106 (*sarva-M°gaṇān.*, will be exterminated by Kalkin).—§ 515 (Karṇadigvijaya): III, **254**, 15255 (*sa-M°āṭavikān*, vanquished by Karṇa on his digvijaya).—§ 556 (Sañjayayānap.): V, **22**, †666 (have joined Yudhishṭhira).—§ 561*f* (Nakula): V, **50**, †1995 (*pratīcīm diçam . . . M°gaṇāyutām*, conquered by Nakula).—§ 571 (Ulūkadūtāgamanap.): V, **160**γ, †5510 (in the army of Duryodhana); **161**, †5555 (do.).—§ 574 (Jambūkh.): VI, **9**, 321 (*Āryā M°āç ca*), (ξ), 372 (in the north), 373 (*°jātayaḥ*).—§ 575 (Bhūmip.): VI, **12**, 456 (*M°jātyaḥ*, are not found in the varshas of Kuçadvīpa).—§ 577 (Bhīshmavadhap.): VI, **43**,

1636 (*M°āç cāryāç ca*).—§ 595 (Shoḍaçarāj., v. Suhotra): VII, **56**, 2188 (*vasumatīm M°āṭavikavarjitām*). — § 599 (Jayadrathavadhap.): VII, **93**, 3374 (*gajapṛshṭhagāḥ*), (δ), 3379 (*goyoniprabhavāḥ*), 3381 (*nānāyuddhaviçāradāḥ*), 3384, 3385 (defeated and slain by Arjuna); **94**, 3438 (*°āç cāyutaço hatāḥ*, sc. by Arjuna); **112**, 4307 (*āsthitā bahubhir M°aiḥ*, sc. *nāgāḥ*, in the army of Duryodhana), 4328 (*pāpakartṝṇāṃ himadurganivāsināṃ*); **119**, 4716, (ββ), 4723 (have been vanquished by Sātyaki), 4745 (*hanyamānāḥ . . . Sātyakinā*); **122**θθ, 4889 (*sainyena mahatā yukto M°ānāṃ*, sc. Duḥçāsana); **128**oo, 5243 (*°gaṇān*).—§ 602 (Droṇavadhap.): VII, **192**, 8847 (*°gaṇān*, had been slain by Droṇa).—§ 605 (Karṇap.): VIII, **22**, 871 (*°aiḥ preshitā nāgāḥ*, attacked by Nakula, etc.).—§ 607 (do.): VIII, **40**, 1858 (*pāpadeçodbhavā M°āḥ*, i.e. the Madrakas, etc.); **45**, 2095 (*manushyānāṃ malaṃ M°āḥ M°ānām aushṭrikā malaṃ*), (ν), 2107 (*svasañjñāniyatāḥ*). —§ 608 (do.): VIII, **46**, 2145 (*mātangāḥ çūrair M°aiḥ samanvitāḥ*, in the army of Duryodhana); **73**, 3653 (have been vanquished by Arjuna); **81**, 4133 (*°āḥ sthitā mattais trayodaçaçatair gajaiḥ*, attacked Arjuna).—§ 609 (Çalyap.): IX, **1**γ, 27 (have been slain); **2**, 74 (had taken up arms for Duryodhana), 96 (have been slain).—§ 611 (do.): IX, **20**, 1066 (*Çālvo M°gaṇādhipaḥ*).—§ 613 (Gadāyuddhap.): IX, **32**, 1820 (*iyañ ca pṛthivī sarvā sa-M°āṭavikā*).—§ 621 (Rājadh.): XII, **4**ε, 115 (*°ācāryāç* [!] *ca rājānaḥ*).—§ 641*d* (Vena): XII, **59**, 2218 (*Vindhyanilayāḥ*).—§ 658*b* (Kṛtaghnop.): XII, **168**, 6293.—§ 660*b* (Bhṛgu-Bharadvājas.): XII, **188**, 6947 (*°jātayaḥ*).—§ 759 (Ānuçāsanik.): XIII, **106**, 5133.—§ 760 (do.): XIII, **111**, 5525 (*asaṃvāsāḥ*).—§ 785 (Anugītāp.): XIV, **73**, 2137 (vanquished by Arjuna when he followed the sacrificial horse); **82**, 2465 (*°sainyāni*, do., in the east?); **89**, 2669 (*°jātayaḥ*, present at the açvamedha of Yudhishṭhira).—§ 793 (Mausalap.): XVI, **7**, 239 (i.e. the Ābhīras).

Mleccha, sg. (do.), said of two Anga princes. § 592 (Saṃçaptakavadhap.): VII, **26**, 1145 (slain by Bhīmasena; [*Angaḥ* v. 1142]). — § 605 (Karṇap.): VIII, **22**, 880 (*Angaputre*, slain by Nakula).

Modāgiri, a mountain (?). § 280 (Bhīmasena): II, **30**, 1095 (at *M.*—in the east—Bhīmasena slew the king).

Modākin, a varsha in Çākadvīpa. § 575*b* (Çākadvīpa): VI, **11**β, 427 (only C., B. has *Maud°*).

Modāpura, a city. § 279 (Arjuna): II, **27**, 1020 (in the north, subjugated by Arjuna on his digvijaya).

Moha = Çiva (1000 names¹).

Mohana, a city (?) § 515 (Karṇadigvijaya): III, **254**, 15246 (subjugated by Karṇa on his digvijaya).

Mohanāstra. § 583 (Bhīshmavadhap.): VI, **77**, 3389 (employed by Dhṛshṭadyumna).

Mohanī, name of a particular spell. § 785 (Anugītāp.): XIV, **80**, 2385 (*°ī nāma māyā*).

Mohātman = ṛshṇa: XII, 1665.

***mokshaçāstra** ("the doctrine of emancipation"): I, 2305 (sg.): XII, 4911 (pl.), 11856 (sg.), 11890 (*°vidaḥ*), 12225 (*°viçāradaḥ*), 12291 (*°viçāradaiḥ*).

Mokshadharma ("the rule of emancipation") = Mokshadharmaparvan. § 10 (Parvasangr.): I, **2**, 351.—§ 11 (do.): I, **2**, 596 (pl.).

***mokshadharma** (do.): IX, 2909, 2917; XII, 1990, 5736 (*°āçritaiḥ*), 6525 (*°ārthakuçalaḥ*), 8430, 8734 (*°ārthasaṃyuktaṃ*), 9931, 9968 (pl.), 10961 (do.), †10995, 11336, 11650, 11876 (*trividhe*), 11911, 12036 (pl.), 12214 (*°ānudarçinaḥ*), 12216 (pl.), 12219 (*°viçāradaṃ*), 12270 (*°ārthakovidaḥ*), 12648 (*°opasaṃhitaṃ*), 13015, 13080 (*°pravartakāḥ*), 13112 (*°ānubhāshiṇe*), 13764 (*°āçritāḥ*); XIII, 6480; XIV, 36 (pl.), 423, 570, 586 (*°āçritaḥ*), 944 (*°ārthakuçalaḥ*).

[Mokshadharmaparvan] ("the section containing the rule for attaining to emancipation from transmigration," the 90th of the minor parvans of Mhbhr.; cf. Mokshadharma). § 659: *Yudhishṭhira* inquired about the duties in the four stages of life; *Bhīshma* indicated the attainment of emancipation as the highest of all duties. *Yudhishṭhira* asked *Bhīshma* how grief might be overcome; *Bhīshma* related the old story of the conversation between a *brahman* and king *Senajit*, burning with sorrow on account of the death of his son; dissociation from the world is the grand method of overcoming grief. The *brahman* cited the verses sung by *Pingalā* (a fallen woman who was denied the company of her lover through an accident) about the manner in which she had acquired eternal merit; freedom from hope and desire is felicity. King *Senajit* experienced delight and became very happy (XII, **174**). *Yudhishṭhira* inquired of *Bhīshma* as to what constitutes the highest good that man should seek in view of the transient character of time; *Bhīshma* related the old narrative of a discourse between a *brahman*, who was devoted to the study of the *Vedas*, and his son *Medhāvin*, who was well conversant with the religion of emancipation, and acquainted also with the affairs of the world, on the uncertainty of life and the mutability of all things save *Bráhman* (XII, **175**). *Yudhishṭhira* asked how happiness and misery come to the rich and the poor; *Bhīshma* related the old narrative of what was sung by *Çampāka*, who had achieved emancipation, told in former times by a poor *brahman* rendered miserable by a bad wife, etc.; the faults of prosperity; in renunciation is the highest good of men (XII, **176**). *Yudhishṭhira* asked what a man must do to find happiness if he be poor. *Bhīshma* explained who is a happy man, and related the old narrative of what *Manki* had sung when freed from attachments; *Manki* found that he was assiduously doomed to disappointments; at last, with a remnant of his property, he purchased a couple of young bulls with a yoke; a camel ran away with them upon its neck; *Manki's* observations, quoting *Çuka*: desire is fraught with sorrow (XII, **177**). In this connection reference is made to the old verses sung by the *Videha* king *Janaka*, who had attained to tranquillity of soul: "even if the whole of *Mithilā* be consumed in a conflagration I shall incur no loss." Discourse between king *Nahusha* (i.e. Yayāti) and Ṛ. *Bodhya* about freedom from attachment; *Bodhya's* six preceptors (*Pingalā*, etc.) (XII, **178**). *Yudhishṭhira* wished to know by what conduct a person may succeed in this world and attain to an excellent end. *Bhīshma* related the old story of the discourse between king *Prahlāda* and a sage who had adopted the *Ājagara* vow: the indifference of the latter to all worldly objects in view of the inevitability of death (XII, **179**). *Yudhishṭhira* asked which of these, viz. kinsmen, or acts, or wealth, or wisdom, should be the refuge of man. *Bhīshma* answered that wisdom should be the refuge, instancing *Bali*, etc. (*a*), and related the old story of the discourse between *Indra* and *Kāçyapa*, a Ṛ.'s son, who was brought to the ground by a *vaiçya* negligently driving his chariot, and who in despair resolved to end his life; *Indra* appeared to him in the form of a jackal and proved to him the superiority of his status as a human being and a brahman; not to yield to the instigation of the senses constitutes happiness; "thou dost not regret (*smarasi*) wine (*Vāruṇī*) nor the *latvāka* fowls; there is no drink and no food more delicious than these; . . . the vilest *Pukkasa* or *Cāṇḍāla* never wishes to give up his life." *Kāçyapa* gave up the desire of ending his life; he knew the jackal to be *Indra*, worshipped him, and returned home (XII, **180**). *Yudhishṭhira* asked whether gifts, sacrifices, penances, and dutiful services to preceptors are productive of merit. *Bhīshma's* discourse on righteousness and sin and their respective consequences on life (XII, **181**).—§ 660: *Yudhishṭhira* inquired about him who has created the universe and to whom it returns when dissolution comes. *Bhīshma* related the old narrative of the sacred words that M.-ṛ. *Bhṛgu* uttered in reply to the questions of *Bharadvāja*, on the *Kailāsa* summit, explaining to him the cosmogony, i.e. *Bhṛgu-Bharadvāja-saṃvāda* (*b*) (XII,**182–192**).—§ 661: *Yudhishṭhira* asked *Bhīshma* about the ordinances about conduct. *Bhīshma's* discourse on the characteristics of the wicked and the good ("*Sūrya* should always be worshipped," etc.), and the duties that all men should practise, quoting D.-ṛ. *Nārada*; "one who has abstained from meat should not take meat even if it be sanctified with *mantras* from the *Yajurveda*" (XII, **193**). Asked by *Yudhishṭhira*, *Bhīshma* discoursed on *adhyātma*; the nature of the three attributes of Goodness, Passion, and Darkness; the distinction between matter (*sattva*) and soul (*kshetrajña*); the highest end to be obtained is emancipation (XII, **194**). *Bhīshma* discoursed on the four kinds of *yoga*; "M.-ṛ., obtaining a knowledge of the same, attain to eternal success (*siddhiṃ*) even here" (XII, **195**). *Yudhishṭhira* inquired after the fruits of the silent recitation of sacred *mantras*; *Bhīshma* wanted to recite the old narrative of the discourse between *Yama*, a *brahman*, and Time (v. *infra*, ch. **199**); on *Sāṅkhya*, "otherwise called the *Vedānta*," and *Yoga*, *Bráhman*, etc. (XII, **196**). *Yudhishṭhira* inquired about the other aims of silent reciters; *Bhīshma* indicated the different aims realized by different kinds of reciters (XII, **197**); the nature of the hell into which reciters may sink; the regions of Lp., etc. (**a**), are hells compared to the region of the Supreme Soul, i.e. to emancipation (XII, **198**).—§ 662: *Yudhishṭhira* wished to hear in full the dispute between Time, *Mṛtyu*, *Yama*, *Sūrya's* son *Ikshvāku*, and a *brahman*, referred to above (v. ch. **196**); *Bhīshma* related this old story, i.e. *Jāpakopākhyāna* (*b*) (XII, **199–200**).—§ 663: *Yudhishṭhira* inquired about the results of the *yoga* of knowledge, of all the *Vedas*, and of observances and vows; *Bhīshma* related the old discourse between *Manu Prajāpati* and his disciple M.-ṛ. *Bṛhaspati* (the foremost of D.-ṛ.), in days of old, who had studied the *Ṛcs*, etc. (**a**); *Bṛhaspati* asked how an embodied being departs from one body and attains to another; acts result from the desire of obtaining happiness and avoiding misery; the efforts for the acquisition of knowledge arise from the desire of avoiding both happiness and misery; it is by avoiding acts that one succeeds in entering into *Bráhman*; the nature of *Bráhman* (XII, **201**); continuation of *Manu's* discourse on the nature of emancipation and the soul; the soul takes its character from the body; how the soul leaving one body enters into another (XII, **202**); though invisible, the soul exists (XII, **203**); continuation of *Manu's* discourse, explaining how the soul may be seen (XII, **204**); continuation of *Manu's* discourse, explaining how grief may be avoided; how *Bráhman* may be attained (XII, **205**); abstention from acts is the highest religion (XII, **206**).—§ 664: *Yudhishṭhira* asked *Bhīshma* about the nature of the Supreme Deity (*Vishṇu*, *Nārāyaṇa*, etc. (**a**)). *Bhīshma's* discourse, which he had heard from *Rāma Jāmadagnya*, etc. (*β*), on the nature of *Nārāyaṇa* or *Govinda*, etc. (*γ*); the *Asura Madhu* (*b*); *Brahmán's* seven will-born sons (*δ*), etc. (*ε*). *Madhusūdana* (*Kṛshṇa*) created day and night, etc. (*ζ*); then from his mouth he created 100 *brahmans*, from his arms 100 *kshatriyas*, from his thighs 100 *vaiçyas*, and from his feet 100 *çūdras*, and then he made *Dhātṛ* (i.e. *Brahmán*, PCR.) the lord and ruler of all created beings; *Brahmán* also became the expositor of the knowledge of the *Vedas*; *Virūpāksha* he made the ruler of the spirits and ghosts and *Mātṛs*; *Yama* the ruler of P. [and] all sinful men; *Kubera* the lord of all treasures; *Varuṇa* the lord of the waters and of all aquatic animals; *Indra* the lord of the gods. In those times men lived as long as they chose, without any fear of *Yama*; offspring was begotten by a fiat of the will. In the *Tretā* age children ~~were~~ begotten by touch alone. In the *Dvāpara* age sexual intercourse originated. In the *Kali* age men have come to marry and live in pairs. The sinful creatures of the earth, born in the southern region and called *Andhrakas*, etc. (*η*); in the northern region, the *Yaunas*, etc. (*θ*); their practices are similar to those of *Cāṇḍālas* and ravens and vultures; in the *Kṛta* age they were nowhere on earth; it is from the *Tretā* that they have had their origin; when the terrible interval [between the *Tretā* and the *Dvāpara*] came, the *kshatriyas* engaged in battle. D.-ṛ. *Nārada*, that observer of all the worlds, has said that *Kṛshṇa* is the supreme god (XII, **207**).—§ 665: *Yudhishṭhira* asked who are the first *Prajāpatis*, and who the great *Ṛshis*, and in which direction they dwell. *Bhīshma* enumerated *Brahmán's* seven sons (**a**), mentioned in the *Purāṇas* as seven *Brahmáns*. The *Prajāpatis* that came after these are: (*a*) in *Atri's* race: *Prācīnabarhis* (*Brahmayoniḥ sanātanaḥ*) > the ten *Prācetasaḥ* > *Prajāpati Daksha* or *Ka*; (*b*) *Marīci* had one son *Kaçyapa* or *Arishṭanemi*. *Atri* had another son born of his loins, the handsome and princely *Soma*; he performed penances for 1,000 celestial *yugas*. *Aryaman* and his sons were rulers and creators of all creatures. *Çaçabindu* had 10,000 wives, and begot upon each of them 1,000 sons, who would call none *Prajāpati* save themselves; the ancient (*purāṇāḥ*) brahmans call creatures (*prajāṃ*) *Çāçabindavī*; this race became the progenitor of the *Vṛshṇi* race. "These that I have named are the illustrious *Prajāpatis*." The deities are: the twelve *Ādityas* (all sprung from *Kaçyapa*) (*β*); the *Açvins* (*γ*) (the sons of *Mārtaṇḍa—ashṭamasya*); these were first called the gods and the two classes of Pitṛs (? *te ca pūrvaṃ surāç ceti dvividhāḥ pitaraḥ smṛtāḥ*). *Tvashṭṛ's* son was the handsome *Viçvarūpa*; *Ajaikapād*, etc. (*δ*) [are the eleven *Rudras*]; these were reckoned as gods at the time of the *Prajāpati Manu*; the *Siddhas* and *Sādhyas*, different as to perfect conduct and youth; the *Ṛbhus* and the *Maruts* were also classes of gods (C. *devānāṃ cādito gaṇāḥ*; B. *codito gaṇaḥ*); thus are enumerated the *Viçvedevās* and the *Açvins*. Amongst them the *Ādityas* are *kshatriyas*, the *Maruts* *vaiçyas*, the *Açvins* (engaged in penances) *çūdras*; the gods [called] *Aṅgirasaḥ* are *brahmans*. The person who at morn recites the names of these deities becomes cleansed of all his sins. *Yavakrīta*, etc. (*ε*), and *Kaṇva*, etc. (*ζ*), all reside in the east; *Unmuca*, etc. (*η*), in the south; *Ushaṅgu*, etc. (*θ*), in the west; *Ātreya*, etc. (*ι*), in the north. These are the witnesses [of the universe] and the creators of all the worlds. By reciting these names one is cleansed of all one's sins; by sojourning to these points a person becomes cleansed of all his sins and succeeds in returning home in safety (XII, **208**).—§ 666: *Yudhishṭhira* inquired about the reason of *Kṛshṇa's* assuming the form of an animal. *Bhīshma* said that formerly, while hunting, he arrived at the hermitage of *Mārkaṇḍeya*, where he was honoured by Ṛ., and M.-ṛ. *Kaçyapa* related: In former days Dā. and As. *Naraka*, etc., oppressed D. and D.-ṛ.; the earth seemed to be oppressed with a heavy weight. The *Ādityas* repaired to *Brahmán*, who said that *Vishṇu* in the form of a boar would slay the As. Some time afterwards *Vishṇu* (having *yoga* for his soul, etc.) penetrated into the earth (into *Rasātala*) in the form of a boar, and uttering tremendous roars (*nādena*), at which even D. with *Indra* became terror-stricken, pierced the As. with his hoofs, etc., whence he came to be called *Sanātana*. *Brahmán* explained to the gods that he was *Kṛshṇa*, the Creator of all things, the foremost of *yogins*, etc., he from whose navel the primeval lotus had sprung, etc. (XII, **209**).—§ 667: *Yudhishṭhira* inquired about the nature of that high *yoga* by which emancipation may be attained. *Bhīshma* related the old narrative of a discourse between a preceptor (the foremost of Ṛ.) and his disciple on emancipation; on *adhyātma* (undisclosed in the very *Vedas*); *Vāsudeva* is the supreme [cause] of the universe; he is the origin of the *Vedas* (*viçvasya brahmano mukham*), etc.; he created P., D., Ṛ., Y., Rā., N., As., and men, etc.; having reduced everything into non-existence, he once more, in the beginning of a *yuga*, creates *Prakṛti*; at the end of every *yuga* the *Vedas* and all other scriptures disappear; in consequence of the grace of *Svayambhū*, M.-ṛ., through their penances, first re-acquire the *Vedas* and *Itihāsas*; *Svayambhū* knows the *Vedas*, *Bṛhaspati* their *Aṅgas*, *Bhārgava* (i.e. Çukra) the *Nītiçāstra* (science of morality, etc.), *Nārada* the *Gāndharva* (the science of music), *Bharadvāja* the science of arms (*Dhanurgrahaṃ*), *Gārgya* the history of the celestial Ṛshis (*devarshicaritaṃ*), *Kṛshṇātreya* medicine, diverse other teachers the philosophical systems (*Nyāyatantrāṇi*, cf. Nīl.). Neither D. nor Ṛ. were [originally] able to apprehend *Bráhman*; only *Nārāyaṇa* knew it; from him Ṛ., the foremost D., As., and R.-ṛ. of old learnt it. Etymology of *Purusha* (*navadvāraṃ puraṃ vyāpya çete*, v. 7679) (XII, **210**). Continuation of *Bhīshma's* discourse explaining how the inclinations and instincts of a past life run towards the soul in a new life (XII, **211**). Continuation of *Bhīshma's* discourse on abstention from acts and the nature of knowledge. Asked by *Yudhishṭhira*, *Bhīshma* discoursed on the faults that should be got rid of in order to attain to emancipation (XII, **212**). Continuation of *Bhīshma's* discourse (XII, **213**). *Bhīshma's* discourse on the means of conquering the senses (XII, **214**). *Bhīshma's* discourse on the consequences of attachment to the objects of the senses (XII, **215**). *Bhīshma's* discourse on the nature and causes of dreams. Darkness has been adopted by the *Asuras*; *Bráhman* is difficult of attainment by either the gods or the *Asuras*; goodness, passion, and darkness belong to the deities and the *Asuras*; goodness is the attribute of the deities, while the two others belong to the *Asuras*; *Bráhman* transcends all those attributes; it is pure knowledge, and is obtainable only by withdrawing the mind and the senses from all external objects (XII, **216**). Who may be said to know *Bráhman*; the distinction between *pravṛtti* and *nivṛtti*; the respective nature of *prakṛti* and *purusha*; the nature and consequences of *yoga* (XII, **217**).—§ 668: *Yudhishṭhira* inquired about the conduct by which *Janaka* the king of Mithilā attained to emancipation. *Bhīshma* recited the old narrative of the conversation between *Pañcaçikha* and *Janaka* of Mithilā, i.e. *Pañcaçikhavākya* (*b*) (XII, **218–219**).—§ 669: *Yudhishṭhira* asked what leads to happiness and what to misery and what to freedom from fear; *Bhīshma's* discourse on self-restraint (XII, **220**). *Yudhishṭhira's* question about the merits of subsisting upon the remnants of sacrifices, and whether fasting be really a penance (*tapas*); *Bhīshma* explained that though fasting is generally regarded as a penance, it is not so in reality, being rather an impediment to the acquisition of the knowledge of soul; living upon sacrificial remnants is regarded as fasting of the highest merit (XII, **221**).—§ 670: *Yudhishṭhira* asked whether man should be regarded as the real doer of acts. *Bhīshma* related the old narrative of a discourse between the *Daitya* king *Prahlāda*, who was unattached to worldly objects, etc., and *Indra*, who questioned *Prahlāda* about the best means by which knowledge of the soul can be attained, etc., and was instructed by him. *Indra* became filled with wonder, and, having worshipped the *Daitya* king, proceeded to his own abode (XII, **222**).—§ 671: *Yudhishṭhira* inquired about the kind of intelligence by adopting which a king deprived of kingdom and prosperity may still live on earth. *Bhīshma* related the old narrative of the discourse between *Indra* and *Virocana's* son *Bali*, i.e. Bali-Vāsava-saṃvāda (*b*) (XII, **223–225**).—§ 672: *Bhīshma* related the old narrative of the discourse between *Indra* and the *Asura Namuci*, i.e. Çakra-Namuci-saṃvāda (*b*) (XII, **226**).—§ 673: *Yudhishṭhira* asked as to what is good for a man sunk into dire distress. *Bhīshma* discoursed on fortitude, quoting the old narrative of the discourse between *Bali* and *Vāsava* (Indra), i.e. Bali-Vāsava-saṃvāda (*b*) (XII, **227**).—§ 674: *Yudhishṭhira* inquired about the indications of future greatness and future fall. *Bhīshma* related the old story of the discourse between *Çrī* and *Çakra*, i.e. Çrī-Vāsava-saṃvāda (*b*) (XII, **229**).—§ 675: *Yudhishṭhira* inquired about the practices that lead to the attainment of *Bráhman*. *Bhīshma* said that one engaged in the religion of *nivṛtti*, etc., can attain to *Bráhman*, quoting the old narrative of the discourse between the wise *Jaigīshavya* and *Asita Devala*, who was instructed by *Jaigīshavya* to behave indifferently towards praise and blame, etc., "D., G., Pç., and Ra. cannot reach the rank which is his who has attained to the highest end" (XII, **230**).—§ 676: Requested by *Yudhishṭhira* about the man that is dear to all, *Bhīshma* quoted the words that *Kṛshṇa*, asked by *Ugrasena*, said to him on a former occasion on the subject of D.-ṛ. *Nārada's* qualifications (XII, **231**).—§ 677: *Yudhishṭhira* inquired about the origin and the end of all creatures, the nature of their thoughts and acts, of the divisions of time, and of the allotted periods of life in the respective epochs or *yugas*; having heard the discourse of *Bhṛgu* to B.-ṛ. *Bharadvāja*, he had become attached to *yoga*. *Bhīshma* recited the old narrative of what the divine *Vyāsa* said to his son *Çuka* (who had studied the *Vedas* with all their branches, and the *Upanishads*, and was desirous of leading the life of *brahmacarya*) about these very questions. *Vyāsa* said: Only *Bráhman* is without beginning and without end. Ṛ. have measured time thus: 15 winks of the eye = 1 *kāshṭhā*; 30 *kāshṭhās* = 1 *kalā*; $30\frac{1}{10}$ *kalās* = 1 *muhūrta*; 30 *muhūrtas* = 1 day and night; 30 days and nights = 1 month (= 1 day and night of the *Pitṛs*, the lighted fortnight being their day and the dark fortnight their night); 12 months = 2 *ayanas* = 1 year = 1 day and night of the gods (*udagayana*, i.e. from winter solstice to summer solstice = the day; *dakshiṇāyana*, i.e. from the latter to the former = the night). Moreover, there are the day and night of *Brahmán* and his years also. Of the *Kṛta-yuga* the duration is 4,000 [celestial] years, with a morning (*sandhyā*) of 400 years and an evening (*sandhyāṃça*) of 400; the other *yugas* gradually decrease by a quarter. In the *Kṛta* age all duties exist in their entirety, and all live for 400 years (free from disease, etc.); in the other *yugas* duty, etc., decrease by a quarter. The duties for the several *yugas* are different. In *Kṛta* penance is foremost, in *Tretā* knowledge, in *Dvāpara* sacrifice, in *Kali* gift. These 12,000 [celestial!] years constitute a *yuga*; 1,000 *yugas* = 1 day of *Brahmán* (when the universe starts into life) = 1 night of *Brahmán* (= universal dissolution, the Creator being asleep, having taken recourse to *yoga*, meditation). *Brahmán*, waking up, modifies the indestructible *Bráhman*, etc. (XII, **232**). *Vyāsa* explained the creation, etc. (XII, **233**). *Vyāsa* told how the *Supreme Lord* merges everything into his soul (XII, **234**). *Vyāsa* discoursed on the duties of a brahman; "they that are good deserve to have even *Uccaiḥçravas*"; *Satyasandha*, having offered his life to save a brahman, ascended to heaven; likewise *Saṅkṛti's* son *Rantideva*, having given tepid water to *Vasishṭha*; *Ātreya Indradamana*, having given wealth to a deserving person; *Çibi Auçīnara*, having given his limbs and son for the sake of a brahman; the *Kāçi* king *Pratardana*, having given his eyes to a brahman; king *Devāvṛdha*, having given a costly umbrella (with all the people of his kingdom); *Sāṅkṛti Ātreya*, having given instructions to his disciples on *Bráhman*; *Ambarīsha*, having given eleven *arbudas* of kine to the brahmans (with all the people of his kingdom); *Sāvitrī* [i.e. Sāvitra = Karṇa, cf. XIII, 6253], by giving away the ear-rings; *Janamejaya*, by giving away his own body; *Yuvanāçva Vṛshādarbhi*, by giving gems, a mansion, and beautiful women; the *Videha* king *Nimi* gave away his kingdom, *Jāmadagnya* (*Paraçu-Rāma*) the whole earth, *Gaya* the earth with her towns (to the brahmans); *Vasishṭha*, when the clouds ceased to pour rain, kept alive all creatures; *Karandhama's* son *Maruta*, by giving away his daughter to *Aṅgiras*, ascended to heaven; king *Brahmadatta Pāñcālya*, by giving the jewel *Çaṅkha* (to brahmans); king *Mitrasaha*, by giving his dear wife *Madayantī* to *Vasishṭha* (with that wife of his); R.-r. *Sahasrajit*, having given his life for the sake of a brahman; king *Çatadyumna*, having given to *Mudgala* a house made of gold, etc.; the *Çālva* king *Dyutimat*, having given unto *Ṛcīka* his kingdom; R.-ṛ. *Lomapāda*, having given his daughter *Çāntā* to *Ṛshyaçṛṅga* (obtained all his wishes); R.-ṛ. *Madirāçva*, by giving his daughter to *Hiraṇyahasta*; king *Prasenajit*, by giving 100,000 cows with calves; etc. (XII, **235**). Continuation of *Vyāsa's* discourse on the duties of a brahman: the knowledge that should be acquired (*a*); knowledge is necessary for emancipation (XII, **236**). The different stages of a *yogin's* progress (XII, **237**). Asked by *Çuka*, *Vyāsa* discoursed on the character of that knowledge which leads to emancipation (XII, **238**). *Vyāsa's* discourse on whether acts are obligatory or optional; "the men of the *Tretā*, *Dvāpara*, and *Kali yugas* are inspired with doubts; the men of the *Kṛta yuga* are devoted to penances, etc. In the beginning of the *Tretā*, the *Vedas* and sacrifices and the divisions of caste and the several modes of life exist in their entirety; in consequence, however, of the duration of life having decreased in *Dvāpara*, all these things likewise decline; in the *Dvāpara* age, and even in the *Kali*, the *Vedas* are overtaken with perplexity; towards the close of the *Kali* again it is doubtful if they ever become even visible to the eye" (XII, **239**). Asked by *Çuka*, *Vyāsa* discoursed on the import of those duties that lead to emancipation; "in the feet [of living creatures] is *Vishṇu*; in their arms *Indra*; within the stomach *Agni*; in the ears are the quarters; in the tongue is speech which is *Sarasvatī*"; success cannot be attained to without knowledge, penances, subjugation of the senses, and renunciation; the doctrine of knowledge as expounded in the *Sāṅkhya* system (XII, **240**). The doctrine of *Yoga* (XII, **241**). Asked by *Çuka*, *Vyāsa* reconciled the declarations of the *Veda* about acts and abstention from acts (XII, **242**). *Çuka* inquired about how emancipation may be acquired without violating the ordinance about the obligatory character of acts; *Vyāsa's* discourse on the duties of *brahmacārins* (XII, **243**). *Vyāsa's* discourse on the duties of the householder (XII, **244**). The duties of the forest stage of life. "The fourth stage [of life] is based upon the *Upanishads*; the duties laid down for it [i.e. renunciation] may be observed in all the stages of life equally; this stage differing from the others comes after domestic and forest life; in this very *yuga* many learned brahmans have been known to observe this stage; *Agastya*, etc. (*β*), were the authors of this course of duties, and themselves observing them have all proceeded to heaven; and so also *Sudivātaṇḍi* (*yathāvāso 'kṛtaçramaḥ*, i.e. who had no fixed residence), and the numerous *Yāyāvaras*, etc. (*γ*); freed from fear and not being counted among the stars and planets (*anakshatrāḥ*), [these] are to be seen in the firmament [as] hosts of luminous bodies (*jyotishāṃ gaṇāḥ*)" (XII, **245**). *Çuka* inquired how one leading the forest mode of life should act wishing to achieve emancipation; *Vyāsa's* answer about the necessity, after having passed through the first and the second stages, of having recourse to *yoga* in order to attain to emancipation; the duties to be observed by such a man (XII, **246**). *Vyāsa's* observations on the soul (*jīva*) and the Supreme Soul (XII, **247**). *Çuka* asked what is *adhyātma* and whence it comes; *Vyāsa's* explanation of *adhyātma*; *Çuka* asked how one may succeed in understanding the unequal distribution of the five elements in different objects, and which among those elements represents which sense, etc.; *Vyāsa's* observations on the nature of mind, understanding, and the soul (XII, **248**). Continuation (XII, **249**). Do. (XII, **250**). *Çuka* inquired about what constitutes the highest duty; *Vyāsa's* discourse on duties (XII, **251**). Continuation (XII, **252**). The relation of the senses and their objects to the five primal elements (XII, **253**). Persons conversant with the scriptures succeed in beholding the soul, etc.; . . . the practice of *yoga* has been recommended by *Çāṇḍilya* (XII, **254**). The tree of desire, its seed and roots and branches and leaves and fruit (XII, **255**). *Bhīshma* recapitulated the substance of *Vyāsa's* discourse on the respective attributes of the elements (XII, **256**).—§ 678: *Yudhishṭhira* lamented the carnage caused on the field of *Kurukshetra*. *Bhīshma* recited the story of *Anukampaka* (*b*) with Mṛtyu-Prajāpati-saṃvāda (*c*) (XII, **257–259**).—§ 679: *Yudhishṭhira* asked what is righteousness and whether righteousness is for this world or for the next or for both. *Bhīshma's* answer: the practices of the good, the *Smṛtis,* and the *Vedas,* etc., according to Ṛ. of old (XII, **260**). Continuation (XII, **261**).—§ 680: Inquired of by *Yudhishṭhira* about righteousness (XII, **262**) *Bhīshma* related the old narrative of the conversation of *Tulādhāra* with *Jājali* on the topic of righteousness, i.e. Tulādhāra-Jājali-saṃvāda (*b*) (XII, **263-265**).—§ 681: *Bhīshma* related an old narrative of what was recited by king *Vicakhyu* (B. °*khn*°) through compassion for all creatures, in condemnation of animal slaughter when he saw the mangled body of a bull and heard the painful groans of the kine in a cow sacrifice, and observed the cruel brahmans gathered there to assist at the ceremonies. "*Manu* has applauded harmlessness in all acts. . . . The true brahmans realize the presence of *Vishṇu* in every sacrifice." Asked by *Yudhishṭhira, Bhīshma* said that one should acquire merit and act in such a way that one's body may not languish and suffer pain, and that death may not come (XII, **266**).—§ 682: *Yudhishṭhira* asked whether one should act speedily or with delay. *Bhīshma* told the old story of what occurred with respect to the wise *Cirakārin,* the son of *Medhātithi Gautama* of the race of *Aṅgiras* (*Āṅgirase kule*), who came to be called thus because he used to reflect long upon all matters, etc., and was regarded as an idle and foolish person. Once M.-ṛ. *Gautama* (the foremost of practisers of *yoga*), witnessing an act of grave misconduct in his wife *Ahalyā,* in wrath commanded *Cirakārin* to slay her, and then departed for the woods. *Cirakārin* began to think for a long while (description), remembering that the father is the performer of *garbhādhāna* and *sīmantonnayana,* etc., and that the mother is the son's *dhātrī,* etc. (etymology of several names of the mother and of the father), etc.; he thought that his mother was not to blame, as *Indra* had come to her in the form of her husband, etc. When many days had expired *Gautama* returned, shedding tears of repentance and thinking that the fault committed was due to his own carelessness (etymology of two names of the wife), and now became filled with great joy, and from that time, dwelling in his hermitage, did not live separately from his spouse or his son. He said: "Blessed be thou, O *Cirakārika*! do thou always reflect long before acting," uttering some verses upon the merits of reflecting long. *Gautama* at last ascended to heaven with his son (XII, **267**).—§ 683: *Yudhishṭhira* asked how a king should protect his subjects without injuring anybody. *Bhīshma* related the old narrative of the conversation between *Dyumatsena* and his son king *Satyavat,* and the words spoken by the latter in behalf of some individuals who had been brought out for execution at the command of his father ("the killing of individuals can never be a righteous act"), quoting the instructions he had received from their grandsires of olden days, as to how kings should rule their subjects in the different ages (*a*); "when the *Kali* age sets in . . . fifteen parts of even that one-fourth of righteousness disappear, one-sixteenth thereof being all that then remains of it," and quoting *Manu Svāyambhuva* (XII, **268**).—§ 684: *Yudhishṭhira* inquired about the relative superiority of domestic life and *yoga*. *Bhīshma* recited the old narrative of the discourse between the *Yati Kapila* and *Syūmaraçmi* on animal sacrifices, the obligatory character of acts, and the merits of *yoga* and renunciation. In days of old when *Tvashṭṛ* came to king *Nahusha,* the latter was on the point of killing a cow in order to show him hospitality; *Kapila* said, "Alas! ye *Vedas*"; Ṛ. *Syūmaraçmi,* entering the cow, blamed this saying of *Kapila,* etc. (XII, **269**); the three classes of *Pitṛs* (*a*), etc. (XII, **270**). Continuation (XII, **271**).—§ 685: *Yudhishṭhira* asked which among the three, viz. religion, profit, and pleasure, is superior. *Bhīshma* recited the ancient narrative of the benefit that the cloud *Kuṇḍadhāra* (not yet adored by other men) in days of old had conferred upon a poor brahman that was devoted to him, and who had failed to obtain wealth by worshipping the gods. The brahman worshipped the cloud with *dhūpas,* etc.; the cloud became pleased and said to the brahman that the wise have ordained expiation for brahmanicide, drinking spirits, stealing, etc., but not for one that is ungrateful; "Expectation has a child named Iniquity, Wrath is a child of Envy, Cupidity of Deceit, Ingratitude is barren." After that the brahman, on a bed of *kuça*-grass and penetrated with the energy of *Kuṇḍadhāra,* beheld all living beings in a dream, and *Maṇibhadra* in the midst of the gods employed in giving his orders; the gods were engaged in bestowing kingdoms, etc., upon men, etc.; *Kuṇḍadhāra* prostrated himself before the gods in the presence of all Y. and prayed for some favour in behalf of the brahman; *Maṇibhadra* first offered to give him wealth, but was prevailed upon by *Kuṇḍadhāra* to give virtue alone. The brahman became disgusted with the world and entered the woods and practised severe penances (description), and his mind was firmly set upon virtue; his strength did not diminish, and after a long time he acquired spiritual vision, etc. *Kuṇḍadhāra* then paid him a visit and caused him to see the end that is attained by kings; he beheld thousands of kings sunk in hell, and many living in this world embracing lust and wrath, etc. *Kuṇḍadhāra* said: "With these [vices] all human beings are enchained; the gods are afraid of men; these vices, at the command of the gods, mar and disconcert on every side; no man can become virtuous unless permitted by the gods. . . ." The brahman confessed that he had not appreciated *Kuṇḍadhāra's* favour as he ought to do; *Kuṇḍadhāra* forgave him and disappeared. The brahman roamed through all the worlds, having attained to ascetic success (*siddhiṃ*) through the grace of *Kuṇḍadhāra*. D., *brahmans,* Y., good men, and Cā. always adore only the virtuous (XII, **272**).—§ 686: *Yudhishṭhira* asked what that sacrifice is which is ordained for the sake of virtue alone and not for the acquisition of heaven or wealth. *Bhīshma* related the history, formerly recited by *Nārada,* of a brahman named *Satya,* who in order to perform sacrifices lived according to the *uñcha* vow (description); his wife *Pushkaradhāriṇī* did not approve of his conduct (i.e. his cruel sacrifices), but at his command she (clad in plumes of peacocks) joined a sacrifice where he was the *hotṛ*. His neighbour the virtuous *Parṇāda* at the command of *Çukra* (or, according to a various reading, of *Çukra's* race, so B., the text of C. is in disorder) addressed him in the shape of a deer, telling him to slay him and sacrifice with him, and *Sāvitrī* also told him to do so, but in vain; *Sāvitrī* then entered the sacrificial fire; but the deer (who was *Dharma*), causing the brahman through spiritual vision to behold Aps. and G., at first made him desire to slay the deer (at which his *tapas* diminished greatly), but then won him over to the *ahiṃsā* religion, and himself assisted him in his sacrifice; "the injury of living creatures forms no part of sacrifice (leading only to heaven)" (XII, **273**).—§ 687: *Yudhishṭhira* inquired about how one becomes sinful, or virtuous, by what one attains to renunciation, and by what one wins emancipation, whereafter he was instructed by *Bhīshma* (XII, **274**). Asked by *Yudhishṭhira*, *Bhīshma* expounded the means for attaining to emancipation (XII, **275**).—§ 688: Continuation of *Bhīshma's* discourse, quoting the old narrative of the discourse between *Nārada* and *Asita Devala*, whom *Nārada* questioned about the origin and destruction of all creatures (XII, **276**).—§ 689: *Yudhishṭhira* inquired after the means for removing desire. *Bhīshma* related the old narrative of what was said by the *Videha* king to the inquiring *Māṇḍavya*: "Even if the whole of *Mithilā* burn in a conflagration, nothing of mine will be burnt down." The brahman *Māṇḍavya* became filled with joy and betook himself to the path of emancipation (XII, **277**).—§ 690: *Yudhishṭhira* inquired about the good which one should pursue in view of the transient character of time. *Bhīshma* related the old narrative of a discourse between a father, who was devoted only to the study of the *Vedas*, and his son *Medhāvin*, who was conversant with the religion of emancipation. The father acted in the way pointed out [by his son] (XII, **278**).—§ 691: Asked by *Yudhishṭhira*, *Bhīshma* explained of what behaviour a man should be, of what acts, of what kind of knowledge, etc., in order to be able to attain to *Bráhman* (XII, **279**).—§ 692: *Yudhishṭhira* asked when he should succeed in abandoning sovereignty for adopting renunciation. *Bhīshma's* answer stating the certainty of *Yudhishṭhira's* acquisition of emancipation, and quoting that discourse which was sung in days of old, viz. the conversation between Dai. (As.) *Vṛtra*, after he became divested of all his prosperity, and [his preceptor] *Uçanas*; *Vṛtra* said: "Desirous of fighting *Indra*, I beheld in that battle *Hari* = *Nārāyaṇa*, etc. (*a*)" (XII, **280**); while *Uçanas* instructed him about *Vishṇu* whose head is the infinite place [i.e. emancipation], *Sanatkumāra* came there and, asked by *Uçanas*, instructed *Vṛtra*; "*Vishṇu* is *Brahmán*, etc." (*β*); the six colours; the four higher regions (*γ*); the indestructible and infinite some say is the region of *Mahādeva*, etc. (*δ*). *Vṛtra* became free from sorrow, gave up his life-breaths, and attained to the highest station. *Yudhishṭhira* asked whether *Kṛshṇa* is identical with the Supreme Deity; *Bhīshma* answered in the affirmative. *Yudhishṭhira's* applause of *Vṛtra*. *Bhīshma* said that the *Pāṇḍavas* would in the end be numbered among the *Siddhas* (XII, **281**).—§ 693: *Yudhishṭhira* asked how *Vṛtra*, whose virtue and devotion to *Vishṇu* and comprehension of the *Upanishads* and the *Vedānta* were so great, was vanquished by *Indra*, and how the battle took place. *Bhīshma* described the battle, i.e. Vṛtra-vadha (*b*) (XII, **282–283**).—§ 694: *Yudhishṭhira* inquired about the origin of fever. *Bhīshma* narrated the Jvarotpatti (*b*) (XII, **284**).—§ 695: *Janamejaya* (!) inquired how the horse-sacrifice of *Prajāpati Daksha Prācetasa* was destroyed during the age of *Manu Vaivasvata* by *Çiva* in consequence of *Umā's* rage and grief, and how *Daksha* was enabled to reunite the divided limbs of that sacrifice. *Vaiçampāyana* (!) narrated the Dakshayajña-vināça (*b*).—§ 696: Asked by *Yudhishṭhira*, *Bhīshma* told the 1,008 names by which *Daksha* adored *Çiva*, i.e. Daksha-prokta-Çiva-sahasra-nāma-stotra (*b*) (XII, **285**).—§ 697: *Yudhishṭhira* again inquired about *adhyātma*, and had it explained by *Bhīshma* (XII, **286**).—§ 698: *Yudhishṭhira* inquired how sorrow and death may be avoided. *Bhīshma* related the old narrative of the discourse between *Nārada* and *Samaṅga* (XII, **287**).—§ 699: *Yudhishṭhira* asked what is beneficial for one who is not conversant with the scriptures, etc. *Bhīshma* related the old narrative of the discourse between *Gālava* and D.-ṛ. *Nārada* (devoted to *yoga*) about the *āçramas*, etc. (XII, **288**).—§ 700: *Yudhishṭhira* inquired how a king should behave in view of the great object of acquisition, and what attributes he should have for freeing himself from attachments. *Bhīshma* recited the old narrative that was uttered by *Tārkshya Arishṭanemi* to *Sagara*, who asked his counsel. *Sagara* acquired those virtues which are productive of emancipation and continued, with their aid, to rule his subjects (XII, **289**).—§ 701: *Yudhishṭhira* asked why D.-ṛ. *Uçanas Kāvya* (*Bhārgavadāyāda*) sided with the *Asuras* and not with the gods, and whence he came to be called *Çukra*; whence he got such superior excellence, and why he does not succeed in travelling to the centre of the firmament. *Bhīshma* related the Bhava-Bhārgava-samāgama (*b*) (XII, **290**).—§ 702: *Yudhishṭhira* inquired about the acts by performing which one wins the highest good both here and hereafter. *Bhīshma* narrated what king *Janaka* in days of yore had inquired of *Parāçara* about the duties of life. "The sceptic argues: the deities, G., and Dā. have become what they are in consequence of their own nature" (XII, **291**). Continuation (XII, **292**). "*Rantideva* obtained success in all the worlds by worshipping the ascetics with offerings of only roots and fruits and leaves. The royal son of *Çibi* won the highest regions of bliss by gratifying *Sūrya* along with his companion with offerings of the same kind. . . . *Ṛcīka's* son became the son of *Viçvāmitra* by adoring the gods with *Ṛcs*. *Uçanas* became *Çukra* by gratifying the god of gods, and by hymning *Devī* he sports in the firmament. M.-ṛ. *Asita*, etc. (*a*), by adoring *Vishṇu* with *Ṛcs* and by penances attained to success" (XII, **293**). Continuation. "*Svayambhū* first created *Dhātṛ*; *Dhātṛ* created a son who was engaged in upholding all the worlds" (v. the note of PCR., p. 539) (XII, **294**). Continuation. "The *Asuras* could not bear that righteousness that prevailed in the world; multiplying they [in the form of Lust and Wrath, PCR.] entered the bodies of men; then was pride generated in men . . .; at that time the gods repaired to *Çiva* and imparted to him their conjoined energy, and he felled to earth with a single shaft those three *Asuras*, viz. *Desire*, *Wrath*, and *Cupidity*, who were staying in the firmament, along with their very habitations, and also the chief of those *Asuras* (i.e. *Mahāmoha*, PCR.); the men again obtained their proper natures and began once more to study the *Vedas*, etc. Then the seven Ṛ. came forward and installed *Indra* as the chief of the gods, and took upon themselves the task of holding the rod of chastisement over mankind. After the seven Ṛ. came king *Viprthu*, etc., of the *kshatriya* order; but there were certain elderly men from whose minds all wicked feelings did not fly away" (XII, **295**). Continuation. "*Brahmán* by penances created all existent objects; Ā., V., etc. (*β*), have all been crowned with success through their penances" (XII, **296**). Asked by *Janaka*, *Parāçara* expounded the reason of the difference of colour in men; "originally sprung from *Brahmán*, all the inhabitants of the earth should have been *brahmans*." Various kinds of *kshatriyas*, etc. (*γ*), have sprung from the four original orders by intermixture. *Janaka* asked how those born in pure wombs and those in impure ones all became *brahmans*.

Parāçara said that it was by cleansing their souls by penances, instancing *Vasishṭha*, etc. (δ). "Originally only four *gotras* arose: *Angiras*, *Kaçyapa*, *Vasishṭha*, and *Bhṛgu*; the others have been due to the penances of those that have founded them" (XII, **297**). Continuation. "Repairing to the *Sarasvatī*, etc. (ε) one should make gifts, etc." (XII, **298**). Continuation of *Parāçara's* discourse on duties. *Janaka* heard everything the Ṛ. said and obtained great happiness from it (XII, **299**).—§ 703: *Yudhishṭhira* asked what opinion should be entertained about the virtues of truth, self-restraint, forgiveness, and wisdom. *Bhīshma* recited the old narrative of the discourse between the *Sādhyas* and a Swan (*haṃsa*), who was *Brahmán* wandering through the three worlds, and having come upon the *Sādhyas* instructing them about the religion of emancipation; at last the *Sādhyas* put a series of detached questions, which were answered by the Swan (XII, **300**).—§ 704: Asked by *Yudhishṭhira*, *Bhīshma* discoursed on the difference between the *Sāṅkhya* and the *Yoga* [systems of philosophy]; what the kinds of diet are by taking which and what the things are by conquering which a *yogin* acquires *yoga* power; "the *yogin* can at his will enter into and emerge from *Brahmán*, etc. (*a*) . . .; the *yogin* has *Nārāyaṇa* for his soul; prevailing over all things, he is capable of creating all things" (XII, **301**). Asked by *Yudhishṭhira*, *Bhīshma* discoursed on the principles of the *Sāṅkhya* [philosophy]; these principles have been established by all the puissant *Yatis*, *Kapila*, etc.; with the objects are engaged men, Pç., etc. (β); "*Vishṇu* is attached to [the organs of] motion, *Indra* to [those of] strength, *Agni* to the stomach, etc.; . . . *Sattva* is attached to the soul; the soul has *Nārāyaṇa* for its refuge, and he has emancipation for his refuge; emancipation is independent of all refuge; . . . the *Prajāpatis*, etc. (γ), fall away from their puissance in course of many long ages; . . . the miseries endured by those that fall into the river *Vaitaraṇī* in the realms of *Yama* . . . the swallowing up of the moon and the sun by *Rāhu*, the falling of stars from their fixed positions and the diversions of constellations from their orbits . . . lead the *Sāṅkhyas* to seek emancipation"; the faults attaching to one's body; "the knowledge of *Vedānta* is the island of the ocean of life; . . . *Sattva* carries the *Yatis* to *Nārāyaṇa*; *Nārāyaṇa* carries them to the Supreme Soul (*paramātmānaṃ*)." *Yudhishṭhira* inquired whether there is any consciousness in the emancipate state; *Bhīshma's* answer. Praise of the *Sāṅkhya* philosophy (XII, **302**).—§ 705: *Yudhishṭhira* inquired about what does deteriorate and what does not. *Bhīshma* related the old narrative of the discourse between Ṛ. *Vasishṭha* and king *Karāla-Janaka*, who asked for his instruction. "At the end of *Brahmán's* night (differently Nīl. and PCR., cf. note, p. 589), *Çambhu* of formless soul, etc., awakes, and once more creates that first or eldest of all creatures; the eldest-born being is called *Hiraṇyagarbha* = *Buddhi* = *Mahat* (*Yogeshu*) = *Viriñci* = the unborn; in the *Sāṅkhya* scriptures (*Sāṅkhye çāstre*) he has many names . . ."; the creations of knowledge and of ignorance; "bodies are possessed by all bodiless creatures, D., etc. (*a*); . . . transcending the twenty-four topics already adverted to is the twenty-fifth called *Vishṇu*." "There are three colours in all: white, red, and dark" (XII, **303**). Continuation (XII, **304**). Do. (XII, **305**). Do. "That which the *Yogins* behold is precisely that to which the *Sāṅkhyas* strive to attain" (XII, **306**).

Continuation (XII, **307**). *Vasishṭha's* discourse on what is *Vidyā* and what is *Avidyā*. "*Yogins* have great regard for the *Sāṅkhya* system, as also for the *Vedas*; in the *Sāṅkhya* system no principle transcending the twenty-fifth is admitted; in the *Yoga* it is said that *Bráhman* . . . becomes the personal soul (*jīva*) only when invested with ignorance; in the *Yoga* scriptures, therefore, both *Bráhman* and *jīva* are spoken of" (PCR.) (XII, **308**). *Vasishṭha's* discourse on *buddha* and *abuddha*. "I had acquired this knowledge from the eternal *Hiraṇyagarbha* himself, who communicated it to me for my having carefully gratified that great Being of very superior Soul . . .; it has been imparted to thee exactly as I had it from *Brahmán* himself." *Bhīshma* said, "This knowledge was obtained by *Vasishṭha* from *Hiraṇyagarbha*, from *Vasishṭha* it was handed over to *Nārada*, and from this to me" (XII, **309**).—§ 706: *Bhīshma* recited the conversation between king *Vasumat*, son of *Janaka*, and a brahman and Ṛ. of *Bhṛgu's* race, whom *Vasumat* saw in the forests when in pursuit of deer, and by whom he was instructed. "R.-ṛ. *Mahābhisha*, through want of firmness, fell from heaven; *Yayāti*, though his merits had become exhausted, succeeded in regaining regions of bliss through his firmness." King *Vasumat*, withdrawing his mind from the pursuit of desire, set it upon the acquisition of righteousness (XII, **310**).—§ 707: Asked by *Yudhishṭhira*, *Bhīshma* discoursed on that which is freed from duty and its reverse by reciting the old narrative of the discourse between Ṛ. *Yājñavalkya* and king *Daivarāti Janaka*, who got instruction from *Yājñavalkya*. The nine kinds of creation (XII, **311**). *Yājñavalkya's* discourse on the creation of the universe; "10,000 *kalpas* are said to constitute a single day of the unmanifest one; the duration of his night is equal; when his night expires he awakes, and first creates herbs and plants; he then creates *Brahmán* or *Prajāpati*, who springs from a golden egg . . .; 7,500 *kalpas* measure the day of *Brahmán*, and his night is of equal duration; *Brahmán* (*mahān ṛshiḥ*) then creates *Ahaṅkāra* (i.e. consciousness; *bhūtaṃ divyātmakaṃ*), etc." (XII, **312**). *Yājñavalkya's* discourse on the destruction of the universe: "*Brahmán*, who is eternal and undecaying, and who is without beginning and without end, repeatedly creates and destroys all created objects; when his day expires and night comes he becomes desirous of sleep; at such a time the unmanifest and holy one urges the Being called *Mahā-Rudra* (*ahaṃkṛtaṃ naraṃ*, i.e. *Ahaṅkārābhimāninaṃ*, Nīl.), who assumes the form of *Sūrya* and divides himself into twelve portions, etc.; . . . Consciousness (*Ahaṅkāraḥ Prajāpatiḥ*) in his turn is swallowed up by the Great Soul (*mahān ātmā*; v. 11601: the reading of B. is different), who (*viçvaṃ*) is again swallowed up by *Çambhu Prajāpati*, [who is] *Aṇiman*, etc. (*a*) . . . " (XII, **313**). *Yājñavalkya's* discourse on *adhyātma* ("the two feet," etc.), *adhibhūta* ("the act of walking," etc.), and *adhidaivata* ("*Vishṇu*," etc.) (XII, **314**). *Yājñavalkya's* discourse on *sattva*, *rajas*, and *tamas* (XII, **315**). *Yājñavalkya's* discourse of what is possessed of attributes and what is not possessed of them (XII, **316**). *Yājñavalkya's* discourse on the *Yoga* philosophy, "conferring eight kinds of puissance and possessed of eight limbs" (XII, **317**). *Yājñavalkya's* discourse on the diverse ends that people attain to as depending on the manner in which the soul (*jīva*) escapes from its mortal frame (XII, **318**). The story of *Yājñavalkya's* acquisition of the *Yajurveda*, as a boon from *Sūrya,* who had been gratified with his penances; *Sūrya* had said: "Made up of the essence of speech, the goddess *Sarasvatī* will enter into thy body"; "he then commanded me to open my mouth; *Sarasvatī* then entered into my body and I began to burn, and plunged into a stream, angry with *Sūrya,* who told me that the burning would soon cease, and then the whole *Veda* with its appendix and the *Upanishads* would appear in me by inward light, and I should edit the entire *Çatapatha,* and then turn to the path of emancipation, coveted both by *Sāṅkhyas* and by *Yogins. Sūrya* then went to the *Asta* hills. *Sarasvatī* appeared before me (description). I taught the *Çatapathabrāhmaṇa,* etc., to 100 good disciples and thereby did what was disagreeable to my maternal uncle [*Vaiçampāyana*]. I undertook the management of the sacrifice of thy father; there a dispute arose between me and my maternal uncle as to who should be permitted to appropriate the *dakshiṇā* for the recitation of the *Vedas*; in the very presence of *Devala* I took half of that *dakshiṇā*; thy father and *Sumantu* and *Paila* and *Jaimini,* etc., all acquiesced in that arrangement. I had thus got from *Sūrya* the fifteen *Yajushes,* and likewise *Romaharsha* learned the *Purāṇas* (differently PCR.). Aided by *Sarasvatī* and *Sūrya* I then set myself to compile the *Çatapathabrāhmaṇa.* . . . G. *Viçvāvasu* (*Kāçyapa,* v. 11777), conversant with the *Vedānta,* once put me twenty-four questions relating to the *Vedas,* and then a twenty-fifth (*ānvīkshikīṃ*) (*a*); having thought of *Sarasvatī* I answered them properly, having expounded to him the fourth science that treats of emancipation, and which is based upon the twenty-fifth principle, i.e. *jīva.*" (The answers to the questions.) The personal soul (*jīva*) and the Supreme Soul should be regarded as one and the same. This *Viçvāvasu* thought difficult to understand, quoting *Jaigīshavya,* etc. (*β*); "M.-ṛ. in *Brahmaloka* say that *Āditya* (the sun) himself is thy preceptor." *Yājñavalkya* instructed him of the relation of the twenty-fifth (*jīva*) to the twenty-sixth (the Supreme Soul). "*Viçvāvasu* proceeded towards heaven, and inculcated the science he had obtained from me to the gods in *Brahmaloka,* etc." Honoured by *Daivarāti, Yājñavalkya* left his court; the king gave a million of kine, etc., to a number of brahmans; installing his son in the sovereignty of the *Videhas,* he adopted the practices of the *Yatis,* and began to study the science of the *Sāṅkhyas* and *Yogins.* "They who wait upon *Mahat* attain to the regions of *Mahat*; they who wait upon Consciousness attain to the spot that belongs to Consciousness, etc." "I (*Bhīshma*) got all this knowledge from *Janaka,* who had obtained it from *Yājñavalkya*" (XII, **319**).—§ 708: *Yudhishṭhira* asked how one may avoid decrepitude and death. *Bhīshma* related the old narrative of the *Bhikshu* M.-ṛ. *Pañcaçikha* and king *Janaka Vaideha,* who put him that same question and was instructed by him (XII, **320**).—§ 709: Asked by *Yudhishṭhira* as to how it is possible for a householder to attain to emancipation, *Bhīshma* recited the Sulabhā-Janakasaṃvāda (*b*) (XII, **321**).—§ 710: *Yudhishṭhira* inquired how in days of old *Çuka Vaiyāsaki* was won over to renunciation (*nirvedam āpannaḥ*). *Bhīshma* recited the discourse of *Vyāsa* to *Çuka* expounding the vanity of worldly attachments. "That sinful wretch who transgresses the ten boundaries that have been fixed by *Svayambhū* himself is obliged to pass his time in great affliction in the wild wastes in the dominions of the king of the *Pitṛs*; that man who is tainted with cupidity . . . has to go to deep hells . . . and is forced to bathe in the broad river *Vaitaraṇī,* whose waters are scalding, etc. (description of hell). . . . Very soon the wind of *Yama* will blow before thee. . . . By performing the duties of the domestic life men attain to the region of *Prajāpati* or *Bṛhaspati* or *Indra.*" *Çuka,* leaving his father, proceeded to seek a preceptor that could teach him the religion of emancipation (XII, **322**).—§ 711: Asked by *Yudhishṭhira, Bhīshma* discoursed on the efficacy of gifts, sacrifices, penances, services to preceptors, etc. (XII, **323**).—§ 712: Çukotpatti (q.v.).—§ 713: Çukakṛti (q.v.).—§ 714: Çukakṛtya (q.v.).—§ 715: Çuka-Nārada-saṃvāda (q.v.).—§ 716: Çukābhipatana (q.v.) (XII, **324-334**).—§ 717: *Yudhishṭhira* asked who the Supreme Deity is, etc. *Bhīshma* recited the old story of the discourse between *Nārada* and Ṛ. *Nārāyaṇa* in the hermitage of *Badarī,* i.e. Nārāyaṇīya (*b*), including the story of *Uparicara* (*c*) and Brahma-Rudra-saṃvāda (*d*) (XII, **335-352**).—§ 718: Asked by *Yudhishṭhira* about the foremost duties of men belonging to the different modes of life, *Bhīshma* related the discourse on this topic in days of yore between D.-ṛ. *Nārada* and *Indra,* i.e. Uñchavṛtty-upākhyāna (*b*) (XII, **353-356**).

Mokshadvāra(ṃ) = Sūrya (the sun): III, 156 (*Trivishṭhapaṃ*).—Do.[2] = Çiva (1000 names[2]).

Mokshātman = Kṛshṇa: XII, 1644.

Mṛdu = Çiva: XIII, 1185 (1000 names[2]); XIV, 203.

Mṛga, pl. (°*āḥ*), the brahmans in Çākadvīpa. § 575*b* (Çākadvīpa): VI, **11,** 436, 437 (*brāhmaṇabhūyishṭhāḥ*; only C., B. has *Maṅgāḥ*).

mṛga, pl. (°*āḥ*) ("deer"). § 127 (Aṃçāvat.): I, **66,** 2626 (the offspring of Mṛgī). Do.[2] = Çiva (1000 names[1]) (°*pakshiṇaḥ*).

Mṛgabāṇārpaṇa = Çiva (1000 names[2]).

Mṛgaçiras, name of a nakshatra, v. Su. Si. § 759 (Ānuçāsanik.): XIII, **110,** 5394 (description of the cāndravrata). Cf. Mṛgottama.

Mṛgadhūma, a tīrtha. § 364 (Tīrthayātrāp.): III, **83,** 6071.

Mṛgāksha = Çiva: VIII, 1447.

Mṛgālaya = Çiva (1000 names[2]).

Mṛgamandā, daughter of Krodhavaçā. § 127 (Aṃçāvat.): I, **64,** 2624, 2626 (mother of the bears and the *sṛmaras*).

Mṛgasvapnanidarçana ("the dream of the deer"). § 11 (Parvasaṅgr.): I, **2,** 471 (*Dharmarājasya cātraiva m°ṃ,* i.e. Mṛgasvapnodbhavaparvan).

Mṛgasvapnodbhava ("the dream of the deer"). § 10 (Parvasaṅgr.): I, **2,** 324 (i.e. Mṛgasvapnodbhavaparvan).

Mṛgasvapnodbhavaparvan ("the dream of the deer," the 44th of the minor parvans of Mhbhr.). (Cf. Mṛgasvapnanidarçana, Mṛgasvapnodbhava.) § 518: In consequence of a dream of *Yudhishṭhira,* in which the still remnant deer of *Dvaitavana* entreated him to spare them by changing his residence, the *Pāṇḍavas* with *Indrasena,* etc., and the *brahmans* removed to the *Kāmyaka* forest, situated at the head of the desert, near lake *Tṛṇabindu.* They had then dwelt in *Dvaitavana* during a year and eight months (III, **258**).

Mṛgavāṇārpaṇa, v. Mṛgabāṇārpaṇa.

Mṛgavyādha[1], a Rudra. § 108 (Aṃçāvat.): I, **66,** 2566 (son of Sthāṇu).—§ 191 (Arjuna): I, **123,** 4825 (among the Rudras present at the birth of Arjuna).

Mṛgavyādha[2] = Çiva: XIV, 197.

Mṛgī ("hind"). § 127 (Aṃçāvat.): I, **66,** 2624 (daughter of Krodhavaçā), 2626 (mother of the deer (*mṛgāḥ*)).

Mṛgottama, a nakshatra (= Mṛgaçiras, PCR.). § 749 (Ānuçāsanik.): XIII, **89a,** 4257.

Mṛta = Çiva (1000 names [2]).

Mṛtapā, an Asura. § 130 (Aṃçāvat.): I, **67,** 2669 (*Asurottamaḥ*, incarnate as Paçcimānūpaka ("the king of the western shore"?)). Cf. Amṛtapa.

Mṛttikāvatī, a city. § 515 (Karṇadigvijaya): III, **254,** 15245 (conquered by Karṇa on his digvijaya).

***Mṛtyu** [1] ("Death"), masc., sometimes identified with Antaka and Yama (Dharma): I, 2619 (*Antakaḥ*, son of Adharma), 5641 (*°pāçāt*), 6764 (*°ur ivogreṇa daṇḍena*), 8267 (*devaḥ*, armed with an axe he partook in the encounter between the gods and Kṛshṇa + Arjuna); II, 340 (*Kālaḥ*?); III, †12356 (*°m ivograrūpaṃ*), 14550 (followed Yama); IV, 1580; V, †1580 (*na vai M°r vyāghra ivātti jantūn*), †1841 (*°m ivāpatantaṃ*), 2044 (*nararūpeṇa*, sc. Bhīmasena), 2463 (*°pāçavaçānugau*), 2662 (*°pāçāt*), 4671 (*°pāçavaçīkṛtā*), 5616 (*°pāçavaçaṅgatāḥ*), 7274 (*°saṅkāçaṃ bāṇaṃ*); VI, 1238 (Kṛshṇa identified with *M.*), 1946 (*°or daṇḍasamaprabhām*, sc. *çaktiṃ*), 2202 (*°daṇḍam ivāparaṃ*), 2797 (*°or āgārasannibhaṃ*), 2800 (*°m ivāyāntaṃ*), 2831 (*Kāla-M°samaprabhaṃ*), 2874 (*Kāla-M°samau*), 3406 (*preshayām āsa M°ave*), 3516 (*çarair M°daṇḍaprakāçaiḥ*), 3675 (*preshayām āsa M°ave*), 3793 (*°or āsyam anuprāptaṃ*), 3959 (*preshayām āsa M°ave*), 4359 (do.), 4758 (*°kalpāṃ*, sc. *mahāçaktiṃ*), 4800 (*°or āsyayutaṃ yathā*), 5312 (*preshayām āsa M°ave*), 5380 (*°or ghorām iva svasām*); VII, 23 (*°nāhūtāḥ*), †68 (*°mukhād iva*), 272 (*°nā hataḥ*), 421 (*°pāçapuraskṛtaḥ*), 656 (*°ur ivāntakaḥ*), 1071 (*kruddho M°r ivāhave*), 2020, 2025, 2039, 3012 (*kruddhaṃ M°m ivāntakaṃ*), 3135 (*°ḥ Kālena coditaḥ*), 3257 (*kruddhaṃ M°m ivāntakaṃ*), 3838 (*preshayishyāmi M°ave*), 4459 (*grastān M°nā saṅgatān*), 5808 (?*praishīd m°m ivāntakaḥ*), 6167 (*°ur vigrahavān iva*), 6179 (*°or āghātalalitaṃ*), 7450 (*°or iva svasāraṃ*, sc. *çaktiṃ*), 7637 (*°or āsyam anuprāptaṃ*), †8168 (*°or svasāraṃ jvalamānām iva*, sc. *çaktiṃ*), 8288 (*°or āsyāntarān muktān*), 8935 (*preshayām āsa M°ave*), 9596 (Çiva identified with *M.*); VIII, †666 (*api*), 909 (*çaraṃ . . . M°-Kālāntakopamaṃ*), †1722 (*°m ivograrūpiṇaṃ*), †1972 (*°mukhaṃ nayishe*), 2309 (*nāçakat tān atikrāntuṃ M°r brahmavido yathā*), 2414 (*Kiṅkarodyatadaṇḍena M°nāpi*), 2470 (*°daṇḍam ivāparaṃ*, sc. *parighaṃ*), 2480 (*preshayām āsa M°ave*), 2629 (*āpanno M°or āsyam ivāturaḥ*), 2709 (*°or upāntikaṃ prāptau*), 2812 (*antakale yathā kruddho M°ḥ Kiṅkaradaṇḍabhṛt*), 2922 (*çaram . . . M°daṇḍam ivāparaṃ*), 2936 (*preshayishyāmi M°ave*), 2957 (*°or āsyagataṃ yathā*), 2986 (*°or mukhagataṃ yathā*), †3370 (*prahinon M°sadma*), †3808 (?), †3809 (*°vaçaṃ ināya*), †3810 (*°vaçaṃ . . . ninye*), †4222 (*çaktiṃ . . . M°rūpāṃ*), †4669 (*aprāpya M°vaçaṃ*), †4795 (*api*); IX, 870 (*°m ivāntakaṃ*), 947 (*martyā M°m ivāgataṃ*), 2519 (*Kālo Yamaçca M°çca*, came to the investiture of Skanda), 3108 (*°oḥ*, sc. *samau*, sc. Bhīmasena and Duryodhana); XI, 114 (*°ṃ . . . yacchati*), 336 (*°or daṃshṭrāntaraṃ gataḥ*), 506 (*°vaçaṃ gataḥ*), 541 (*°pāça-*); XII, 168 (*°yānaṃ*), 347 (*°pāçena kaṇṭhe badhnāti Mṛtyurāṭ*), 380 (*°or āsye sa vartate*), 440 (among those who are slayers), 481 (*°mukhāni*, read *°mukhaṃ* with B.), 526 (*°or vishayaṃ gatāḥ*), 2214 (*°or duhitā . . . Sunīthā nāma*), 2576 (= Antaka), 2585 (*iva*), 2982 (*°padaṃ*), 4497 (*prāṇeçvaraṃ*), 4501 (*caturvibhāgasya*, see PCR.), 6550 (*°senāṃ*), 7198 (*Kāla-M°-Yamānāṃ*), 7200, 7213, 7226, 7227, (7230), 7230, 7231, 7251, 7317, 7332, 7843 (*°mukhaṃ*), 9149 (fem.?), 11061, 12413 (*°-Vaivasvatau*); XIII, 16 (*saṃvādaṃ M°-Gautamyoḥ Kāla-lubdhakapannagaiḥ*), 23 (*°or lokaṃ*), 35, 49, (50), 58, 60, 61, 62, 63, 64, (65), 66, (67), 69, 70, 76, 78, 79, 80, 86, 87, 124, 131, 142 (*raudrabhāvena*), 150 (*kūṭamudgarahastaḥ*), 164 (= Dharma), 170, 174, 178, 1288 (learnt the 1000 names of Çiva from Çakra and taught them to the Rudras), 2230, 3129, 3177, 6905 (*°oḥ panthānaṃ*), 7098, †7397 (Kṛshṇa identified with *M.*), 7497 (Rudra (Çiva) identified with *M.*), 7521 (do.); XIV, 296 (*°padaṃ*), 337 (*°or āsye*), 1489.

Mṛtyu [2] = Sūrya (the sun): III, 146.—Do. [3] = Çiva (1000 names [1]).

Mṛtyu [4] ("Death"), fem. § 594 (Akampana): Nārada said to Akampana: In the beginning the Grandsire *Brahmán* created all creatures. As the creation bore no sign of decay, he began to think about the destruction of the universe. Failing to find any means of destruction, he became angry, and in consequence of his anger a fire sprang from the apertures of his body (*khebhyaḥ*) and destroyed all creatures. Then *Çiva* (the lord of all the wanderers at night) appealed to *Brahmán* (the greatest of ascetics), who said, "Thou hast been born out of our wish" (*kāmāt*) (VII, **52**), and that the Earth, afflicted with the heavy weight of creatures, had asked him to destroy them. *Çiva*, saying that he had been appointed by *Brahmán* the protector of creatures, prevailed upon *Brahmán* to keep his wrath within his own inner self and extinguish the fire. Then *Brahmán* expounded the doctrine of *pravṛtti* and *nivṛtti*. From his organs of sense (*gobhyaḥ*, cf. *khebhyaḥ* in a parallel passage, XII, 9179) then issued a female who was dark, etc., and set out for the southern quarter; *Brahmán* called her Death (*Mṛtyu*) and told her to slay the creatures. She wept, but *Brahmán* caught her tears with his two hands and implored her (VII, **53**)—who wished to go to the hermitage of *Dhenuka* to perform austerities—to slay the creatures. Soon *Brahmán* smiled, the creatures continued to live as before, and *Mṛtyu* proceeded to *Dhenuka*, where she practised austere vows during twenty-one times ten billions of years, and then she wandered 10,000 billions of years with the creatures. Next she repaired to *Nandā* and there passed 8,000 years, and became purified from all her sins. Then she went to *Kauçikī*, where she lived upon air and water only. Then she repaired to *Pañcagaṅgā* and next to *Vetasaka* (C. *Ce°*), then to the *Gaṅgā* and thence to *Meru*, motionless and suspending her life-breaths. Thence to the top of *Himavat* (where the gods had performed sacrifices) for a billion of years standing on the toe only of her feet. Then to *Pushkara*, and *Gokarṇa*, and *Naimisha*, and *Malaya*, with steady devotion to the Grandsire without acknowledging any other god. *Brahmán* was gratified with her and said that in slaying the creatures she should be without sin; *Yama* and the diseases should become her helpmates. She prevailed upon him that the passions, covetousness, etc., should tear the bodies of the creatures before she slew them. Her tears which were in his hands should become diseases springing from the creatures themselves and kill men; she should be the virtue of living creatures and the goddess of this virtue. Sin would slay those who were of wicked behaviour; "it will be thy work to sink them in their sins that are wicked." Nārada further expounded the nature of death and told Akampana not to grieve for his dead son: VII, **53,** 2068, 2070 (*kamalalocanā*); **54,** (2074), 2082, 2088, 2101, 2105, 2112, †2117, †2118, †2122 (*devasṛshṭā*), †2123 (*daṇḍapāṇiḥ*).—§ 595 (Abhimanyuvadhap.): VII, **55,** 2134 (*°samutpattiṃ*, all. to § 594); **71,** 2471 (*sambhavo M°oḥ*, do.).—§ 678b (Mṛtyu-Prajāpatisaṃv.): XII, **258,** 9182, 9185;

259, 9195, 9197, 9201, 9204, 9212, 9214, 9219, †9220, †9223, †9224, †9228 (repetition from § 594).

Mṛtyuloka ("the world of Mṛtyu [i.e. Death]"). § 561 (Yānasandhip.): V, **48,** †1912 (°ṃ *nayeyam*). — § 579 (Bhīshmavadhap.): VI, **54,** 2315 (*prahiṇot M°āya*).— § 585 (do.): VI, **88,** 3909 (*prahiṇon M°āya*). — § 587 (do.): VI, **113,** 5254 (do.).—§ 592 (Saṃçaptakavadhap.): VII, **28,** 1255 (do.).—§ 599 (Jayadrathavadhap.): VII, **93,** 3391 (do.).—§ 600 (Ghaṭotkacavadhap.): VII, **157,** 6948 (do.); **161,** 7209 (do.).—§ 608 (Karṇap.): VIII, **73,** 3661 (°ṃ *gatāḥ*), **76,** †3839 (°*ena tulyaṃ*, sc. *āhavaṃ*).—§ 616 (Sauptikap.): X, **8,** 398 (*prahiṇon M°āya*).

Mṛtyupā = Çiva (1000 names[1]).

[Mṛtyu-Prajāpatisamvāda(ḥ)] ("the conversation between Death and Prajāpati [i.e. *Brahmán*]"). § 678*c* (Anukampaka): substantially the same as § 594 (Mṛtyu (q.v.): VII, ch. **52** foll.), but told to Anukampaka (XII, **257-259**).

Mucukunda, an ancient king. § 267 (Yamasabhāv.): II, **8,** 332 (in the palace of Yama).—§ 378 (Tīrthayātrāp.): III, **94,** 8507 (*yathā*).—§ 567*b* (Bhagavadyānap.): In days of yore *Vaiçravaṇa*, having been gratified, made a gift of this earth to the *rājarshi M.* The latter did not accept the gift, but said, "I desire to enjoy a sovereignty which is won by prowess of arms." At this *Vaiçravaṇa* was highly delighted. *M.* ruled the earth, having conquered it by prowess (cf. § 641*g*): V, **132,** 4467 (*rājarsheḥ*), 4469.— § 641*g* (Mucukundop.): XII, **74,** 2810 (°*sya saṃvādaṃ rājño Vaiçravaṇasya ca*), 2811, 2812, 2813, 2815, 2819, 2825, (2826), 2827, 2828 (the conversation between *M.* and *Vaiçravaṇa* [i.e. Kubera]).—§ 651 (Āpaddh.): XII, **143,** 5464, 5465 (*Bhārgava* told *M.* Kapotalubdhakasaṃvāda).— § 656 (Khaḍgotpattik.): XII, **166,** 6196, 6197 (received the sword from Kāmboja, from *M.* it passed over to Marutta). — § 746 (Ānuçāsanik.): XIII, **76**ι, †3689 (among the kings who attained to heaven by making gifts of kine).—§ 761 (do.): XIII, **115**γ, 5663 (among the kings who abstained from meat during the month of Kārttika). — § 775 (do.): XIII, **166**η, 7680 (*rājarshiḥ*, enumeration).

Mucukundopākhyāna(ṃ) ("the episode relating to Mucukunda"). § 641*g* (Rājadh.). King *Mucukunda*, having subjugated the whole earth, repaired to *Kubera* in order to test his strength. *Kubera* created a large force of Rā., who annihilated the forces of *Mucukunda*. *Mucukunda* rebuked his priest *Vasishṭha*, who then by penances caused those Rā. to be slain. *Kubera's* haughty address and *Mucukunda's* manly answer.

Mudāvarta (V, 2729), v. Udāvarta.

Mudgala, a ṛshi. § 391 (Ṛshyaçṛṅga): III, **113,** 10093 (*Nārāyaṇīvendrasenā*, i.e. the wife of *M.*,*babhūva vaçyā nityaṃ M°sya*).—§ 520 (Vrīhidrauṇikap.): III, **260,** 15404.— § 520 (cf. Vrīhidrauṇikap.): Vyāsa said: There lived in *Kurukshetra* a virtuous sage named *Mudgala*, who lived by picking up ears of corn and grain, collecting a *droṇa* of corn during one fortnight and eating it together with his son and wife the other fortnight; yet he celebrated the *sattra* called *ishṭīkṛta* and the *darça-* and *paurṇamāsa*-sacrifices, where *Indra* himself and the gods partook of the food offered, and entertained his guests with food, for the remainder of the *droṇa* of corn increased as soon as a guest appeared, so that hundreds of brahmans were fed with it; he lived himself on the food that remained after the gods and the guests had eaten. Having heard of *M.*, *Durvāsas*, naked and frantic, came to him uttering insulting words, and during six seasons ate up all his food, without perceiving any agitation in *M.'s* heart. *Durvāsas* then told *M.* that in reward he should go to heaven even in his own body. Immediately a celestial messenger (*devadūta*) appeared upon a chariot yoked with swans and cranes, etc., and invited *M.* to ascend it. *M.* first asked the *devadūta* to tell him about the advantages and disadvantages of heaven (III, **260**). The *devadūta* then described heaven (*Svarga*) (atheists and untruthful persons and those who have not practised ascetic austerities and those who have not performed great sacrifices cannot repair thither), with its advantages: myriads of beautiful worlds owned by the gods, the *Sādhyas*, the *Viçve*, the *maharshis*, the *Yāmas*, the *Dhāmas*, the *Gandharvas*, and the *Apsarases*; *Meru* extending over 33,000 yojanas; the gardens of the celestials; *Nandana*, etc.; no grief, etc., no sweat, stench, excreta, nor urine, nor dust; the foremost regions are the regions of Brahmán (*Brāhmaṇāḥ . . . lokāḥ*); thither repair sanctified *ṛshis* and there dwell the *Ṛbhus*, the gods of the gods themselves, who suffer no pangs from women, do not possess wealth, etc., do not subsist on oblations nor *amṛta*, and cannot be perceived by the senses, nor do they change at the revolution of a *kalpa*; for them there is neither ecstasy, nor joy, nor happiness, nor misery, etc.; they are thirty-three in number, to their regions repair wise men after having observed excellent vows, and also *M.* had acquired that success by his charity. Its disadvantages: while reaping the fruit of his acts a person cannot be engaged in any others, for this world is one of acts, the other one of fruition; after one has entirely exhausted his merit, he is subject to fall; he is then stupefied and agitated by emotions, and when the garlands of those who are to fall fade away, fear invades their hearts; but by reason of their merits they take birth among men, and then they attain to high fortune and happiness, while, if one cannot acquire knowledge here, he comes by an inferior birth. As *M.* did not desire to go to heaven, but asked a region where people have not to lament nor to be pained nor agitated, the *devadūta* described to him the supreme seat of Vishṇu, which is called the highest *Bráhman* and lies above the abode of *Brahmán*; thither only those who are free from selfishness, etc., and those who are given to contemplation and *yoga*, can repair. Then *M.* bade farewell to the *devadūta*, and being always engaged in meditation, etc., he at last attained to that supreme state of perfection (*jagāma çāçvatāṃ siddhiṃ parāṃ nirvāṇalakshaṇām*). "Therefore," *Vyāsa* continued, "you also, O son of *Kuntī*, ought not to grieve; after the thirteenth year you will get back your kingdom." Having said this *Vyāsa* returned to his hermitage to practise austerities (III, **261**): III, **260,** 15407, 15415, 15418, 15420, 15427, 15434; **261,** 15443, 15448, 15469, 15476, (15481).—§ 677 (Mokshadh.): XII, **235,** 8606 (Çatadyumna went to heaven after having given a mansion to *M.*).—§ 721*b* (Viçvāmitrop.): XIII, **4**β, 250 (the same?, son of Viçvāmitra). Cf. Maudgalya.

Mudgala, pl. (°*āḥ*), a people. § 589 (Droṇābhishekap.): VII, **11**ν, 397 (*Piçācāṃç ca sa-M°ān*, had formerly been vanquished by Kṛshṇa).

Mudgara, a serpent. § 64 (Sarpasattra): I, **57,** 2151 (of Takshaka's race).

Mudgaraparṇaka, a serpent. § 564 (Mātalīyop.): V, **103**γ, 3629 (so B., C. has by error *Muharaparṇakaḥ*).

Mudgarapiṇḍaka, a serpent. § 47 (Sarpanāmak.): I, **35,** 1554 (enumeration).
Mudita = Çiva (1000 names [2]).
Muditā, wife of Saha. § 493 (Āṅgirasa): III, **222,** 14208 (*Āpasya Muditā*—so B., C. has *duhitā—bhāryā Sahasya paramā priyā*).
Muharaparṇaka, v. Mudgaraparṇaka.
Muhūrta [1], pl. (°*āḥ*) = Sūrya (the sun): III, 150.—Do.[2] = Çiva (1000 names [2]) (°*āhāḥ*).
Mūka [1], a serpent. § 64 (Sarpasattra): I, **57,** 2150 (of Takshaka's race).
Mūka [2], an Asura (?). § 331 (Kairātap.): III, **39,** 1557 (°*ṃ nāma Danoḥ putraṃ*, assumed the shape of a boar), 1564 (slain by Arjuna and the Kirāta, i.e. Çiva). Cf. Rākshasa.
Mukhamaṇḍikā, a female demon. § 502 (Manushyagrahak.): III, **230,** 14483 (= Diti, q.v.).
Mukhara, a serpent. § 564 (Mātalīyop.): V, **103**γ, 3632 (enumeration).
Mukhavāditravādin = Çiva (1000 names [1]).
Mukhya = Çiva (1000 names [2]).
Muktānāṃ paramā gatiḥ = Vishṇu (1000 names).
Muktatejas = Çiva (1000 names [2]).
Muktimatī, v. Çuktimatī.
Mukunda = Vishṇu (1000 names).
Mukuṭa, pl. (°*āḥ*), a people. § 562 (Bhagavadyānap.): V, **74**γ, 2732 (°*ānāṃ Vigāhanaḥ*).
Mukuṭā, a mātṛ. § 615*u* (Skanda): IX, **46**θ, 2641.
Mukuṭin ("wearing a diadem") = Indra: XIII, 2276.
Mukuṭṭa, pl. (°*āḥ*), a people. § 273 (Rājasūyārambhap.): II, **14,** 590 (fled from fear of Jarāsandha, only in C., B. has *Sukuṭṭāḥ*).
Mūla(ṃ) = Çiva (1000 names [2]).
Mumucu, a ṛshi. § 775 (Ānuçāsanik.): XIII, **166,** 7665 (among the ṛshis of the south).
Muṇḍa = Çiva: XII, 10366 (1000 names [1]), 10420 (do.); XIII, 1159 (1000 names [2]), 1244 (do.); XIV, 194.
Muṇḍa, pl. (°*āḥ*), a people. § 342 (Indralokābhigamanap.): III, **51,** 1991 (have been present at the rājasūya of Yudhishṭhira, B. only, C. has *Hūṇān*).—§ 580 (Bhīshmavadhap.): VI, **56**ε, 2410 (with Bṛhadbala in the left wing of Bhīshma's gāruḍavyūha). — § 599 (Jayadrathavadhap.): VII, **119,** 4728, 4730 (°*ānīke*).
Muṇḍavedāṅga, a serpent. § 67 (Sarpasattra): I, **57,** 2158 (of Dhṛtarāshṭra's race).
Muṇḍī, a mātṛ. § 615*u* (Skanda): IX, **46**θ, 2635.
Muṇḍin = Çiva: XIII, 609, 1171 (1000 names [2]).
Muni [1] (?), son of Ahar. § 116 (Vasu, pl.): I, **66,** 2587 (*çāntas tathā muniḥ* ?).
Muni [2], son of Kuru. § 154 (Pūruvaṃç.): I, **94,** 3740 (fourth son of Kuru).
Muni [3] = Çiva (1000 names [2]).
Muni [4], fem., mother of the Devagandharvas Mauneyas. § 87 (Aṃçāvat.): I, **65,** 2520 (daughter of Daksha and wife of Kaçyapa).
Munideça, a region in Krauñcadvīpa. § 575 (Bhūmip.): VI, **12**θ, 463, 464.
Muniloka ("the world of ascetics"). § 370 (Tīrthayātrāp.): III, **84,** 7082.
Munīndra ("the great ascetic") = Çiva: XIII, 887.
Munivīrya, a Viçvadeva. § 749 (Ānuçāsanik.): XIII, **91**γ, 4356 (enumeration).
Muñja, a brahman. § 324 (Dvaitavanapr.): III, **26***a*, 986 (waited upon Yudhishṭhira).
Muñjagrāma, a city. § 281 (Sahadeva): II, **31,** 1118 (in the south, conquered by Sahadeva on his digvijaya; C. only, B. has Ramyagrāma).
Muñjakeça [1], a prince. § 130 (Aṃçāvat.): I, **67,** 2662 (incarnation of the Asura Nicandra).—§ 554 (Sainyodyogap.): V, **4**γ, 77 (among the princes to whom the Pāṇḍavas ought to send messengers).
Muñjakeça [2] = Çiva (1000 names [1]). — Do.[3] = Vishṇu: XII, 10019.
Muñjakeçavat = Kṛshṇa (Vishṇu, Nārāyaṇa): XII, 13271 (etymology).
Muñjakeçin = Vishṇu (Nārāyaṇa): XII, 13112.
Muñjaketu, a king. § 264 (Sabhākriyāp.): II, **4**β, 116 (among the princes who waited upon Yudhishṭhira).
Muñjapṛshṭha, name of a place. § 641 (Rājadh.): XII, **122,** 4470 (*çṛṅge Himavataḥ*), 4472 (*deço Rudrasevitaḥ*). Cf. Muñjāvaṭa.
Muñjavāsas = Çiva: VII, 9527.
Muñjavat, a mountain. § 617 (Aishīkap.): X, **17,** 785 (*girer M°aḥ padaṃ*, Çiva repaired to *M.*).—§ 778*f* (Saṃvartta-Maruttīya): A peak in *Himavat* where Çiva is constantly engaged in contemplation, accompanied by Umā, armed with his trident, surrounded by diverse hosts of Bh., and adored by R., Sā., V.-D., V., *Yama, Varuṇa, Kubera*, etc., Bh. and Pç., A., G., Aps., Y., D.-ṛ., Ā., M., and *Yātudhānas*; it looks resplendent like the morning sun; there is neither heat nor cold, nor sun or wind, nor age, nor hunger, nor thirst, nor death, nor fear; on all sides there are gold-mines protected by the attendants of Kubera, etc.: XIV, **8,** 180 (°*vān nāma parvataḥ*).
Muñjavaṭa, a tīrtha. § 362 (Tīrthayātrāp.): III, **83,** 5092 (*Sthāṇoḥ sthānaṃ*).—§ 372 (do.): III, **85,** 8210 (*sthānaṃ devasya*, i.e. Çiva's, PCR. has Mayūravaṭa).
Muñjāvaṭa = Muñjapṛshṭha: XII, 4471 ("under a well-known banyan," PCR.).
Mura, v. Muru.
Mūrdhaga = Çiva (1000 names [2]).
Murmurā, a river. § 494 (Āṅgirasa): III, **222,** 14232 (among the rivers who are mothers of fires).
Mūrtau hi te . . . sarve vai devatāḥ = Çiva (1000 names [1]).
mūrtiçāstra ("the science of entities endowed with form"): XII, 9090 (°*vidhānavit*).
Mūrtija = Çiva (1000 names [2]).
Muru, an Asura, slain by Kṛshṇa (C. mostly Mura): § 273 (Rājasūyārambhap.): II, **14,** 578 (*Muruñ ca Narakañ ca çāsti yo Yavanādhipatiḥ*, i.e. Bhagadatta; name of a country ?).—§ 561*c* (Kṛshṇa Vāsudeva): V, **48,** †1890 (*Nirmocane shaṭ sahasrāṇi hatvā sañchidya pāçān sahasā kshurāntān* | *Muraṃ hatvā vinihatyaugharaksho Nirmocanaṃ cāpi jagāma vīraḥ*, sc. Kṛshṇa; *Muraṃ* also B.); †1892 (*hatvā Bhaumaṃ Narakaṃ Murañ ca*, sc. Kṛshṇa; *Muraṃ* also B.).—§ 570*f* (Çārṅga): V, **158,** 5357 (*sañchidya Mauravān pāçān, nihatya Muram*—B. *Murum—ojasā* | *nirjitya Narakaṃ Bhaumaṃ*, sc. Kṛshṇa).—§ 589 (Droṇābhishekap.): VII, **11**μ, 386 (C. *Muraṃ*, B. *Muruṃ*, had been slain by Kṛshṇa).—§ 604 (Karṇap.): VIII, **5,** 144 (*yathā Kṛshṇena Narako Muraç*—B. *Muruç—ca nihataḥ*). — § 717*b* (Nārāyaṇīya): XII, **341,** 12956 (*hanishye Narakaṃ Bhaumaṃ Muruṃ*—B. *Muruṃ—Pīthañ ca Dānavaṃ* (sc. incarnate as Kṛshṇa), says Nārāyaṇa). Cf. Hariv., ch. **121** foll.
Mūshaka, pl. (°*āḥ*), a people. § 574 (Jambūkh.): VI, **9**ν, 366, 371 (in the south).

Mūshakāda, a serpent. § 47 (Sarpanāmak.): I, **35**, 1557 (enumeration). Cf. Mūshikāda.

Mushala, son of Viçvāmitra. § 721*b* (Viçvāmitrop.): XIII, **4***β*, 252.

Mushalāyudha ("club-armed") = Balarāma: IX, 2065, 2834.

Mūshika, pl. (°*āḥ*), a people. § 574 (Jambūkh.): VI, **9***ν*, 366 (in the south; only C., B. has *Bhūshikāḥ*).

Mūshikāda, a serpent. § 268 (Varuṇasabhāv.): II, **9**, 372 (in the palace of Varuṇa).—§ 564 (Mātalīyop.): V, **103***γ*, 3630 (enumeration). Cf. Mūshakāda.

N

Nābha = Çiva (1000 names[1]).

Nābhāga[1], one or more ancient kings. § 61 (Sarpasattra): I, **55**, †2109 (*Khaṭvāṅga-N°-Dilīpakalpa*, sc. Janamejaya).—§ 139 (Manu Vaivasvata): I, **75**, 3140 (son of Manu Vaivasvata).—§ 267 (Yamasabhāv.): II, **8**, 330 (°-*Sagarau*, in the palace of Yama).—§ 296 (Dyūtap.): II, **53**, 1929.—§ 323 (Dvaitavanapr.): III, **25**, †956 (*nṛpāç ca N°-Bhagīrathādayaḥ*, have conquered the earth).—§ 576 (Bhagavadgītāp.): VI, **17***β*, 645.—§ 641 (Rājadh.): XII, **96**, 3578 (*sarājakāṇi rāshṭrāṇi N°o dakshiṇām dadau*); **124**, 4564 (conquered the earth in the course of seven nights).—§ 751*b* (Çapathavidhi): XIII, **74***β*, (4577).—§ 761 (Ānuçāsanik.): XIII, **115***γ*, 5661 (? *Ambarīsheṇa*? among the kings who abstained from meat during the month of Kārttika).

Nābhāga[2] ("son of Nābhāga") = Ambarīsha: III, 10514 (*A*°); VII, 2303 (*A*°), 2313; XII, 993 (only B., C. has *Nābhāgiṃ*); XIII, 5661 (?). Cf. Nābhāgi.

Nābhāgārishṭa, son of Manu Vaivasvata. § 139 (Manu Vaivasvata): I, **75**, 3147 (the tenth son of Manu).

Nābhāgi ("son of Nābhāga") = Ambarīsha: XII, 993 (*A*°, only C., B. has *Nābhāgam*), 995 (*A*°), 3615 (*A*°). Cf. Nābhāga[2].

Nabhaḥsthala, Nabhas, Nābhi = Çiva (1000 names[2]).

Nabhoda, a Viçvadeva. § 749 (Ānuçāsanik.): XIII, **91***γ*, 4359 (enumeration).

Nābhya = Çiva (1000 names[1]).

Nācika, a son of Viçvāmitra. § 721*b* (Viçvāmitrop.): XIII, **4***β*, 257 (enumeration).

Nāciketa, a ṛshi, son of Uddālaki. § 730 (Ānuçāsanik.): XIII, **17**, 1291, 1292 (Yama communicated the 1000 names of Çiva to *N.*; *N.* again taught them to Mārkaṇḍeya).—§ 746 (do.): XIII, **71**, 3486 (*ṛsher Uddālaker vākyam N°sya cobhayoḥ*), 3487 (son of Uddālaki), 3493, 3495, (3521) (cursed by his father, *N.* went for a time to the abode of Yama, who instructed him about the merit of making gifts of kine); **72**, 3542 (all. to chap. **71**).—§ 747 (do.): XIII, **84**, 3934 (*gavām uktam pradānam . . . ṛshiṇā N° ena*, cf. § 746).—§ 775 (do.): XIII, **166***ζ*, 7672 (among the ṛshis of the north). Cf. the next.

Nāciketu, a muni. § 264 (Sabhākriyāp.): II, **4***a*, 112 (waited upon Yudhishṭhira). Cf. the prec.

Nācīna, pl. (°*āḥ*), a people. § 281 (Sahadeva): II, **31**, 1119 (*rājānaḥ*?, vanquished by Sahadeva on his digvijaya in the south).

Nadija = Bhīshma, q.v.

Nāḍījaṅgha, a crane (= Rājadharman), son of Kaçyapa. § 468 (Indradyumnop.): III, **199**, ††13337.—§ 658*b* (Kṛtaghnop.): XII, **169**, 6336 (*Brahmaṇaḥ sakhā bakarājo mahāprājñaḥ Kaçyapasyātmasambhavaḥ*).

Nadīsuta ("the son of the river [i.e. Gangā]") = Bhīshma: XII, 807; XIII, 7696.

Nādyopahāralubdha = Çiva (1000 names[1]).

Nāga, pl. (°*āḥ*) ("Serpents"), sons of Kaçyapa and Kadrū (or Surasā). § 11 (Anukram.): I, **2**, 365 (*sarva-N°ānām . . . sambhavaḥ*), 369 (°*ānām . . . samudbhavaḥ*).—§ 17 (Uttaṅka): I, **3**, 797 (*Airāvatarājānaḥ sarpāḥ*), 799 (*bahūni N°veçmāni Gaṅgāyās tīra uttare*), 804 (*prārthayan N°mukhyatām*, sc. Çrutasena), ††806, ††813, ††830 (°*bhavane*, the adventures of Uttaṅka in the world of the *N.*).—§ 26 (Jaratkāru): I, **15**, 1063 (all. to § 68).—§ 27 (Kaçyapa): I, **16**, 1076 (°*sahasraṃ*, sons of Kaçyapa and Kadrū).—[§ 29 (Kadrū): I, **20** (Kadrū cursed her sons, that they should be consumed by the fire at the snake-sacrifice of Janamejaya).]—§ 30*b* (Samudra): I, **21**, 1210 (°*ānām ālayam*, i.e. the ocean).—§ 31 (Kadrū): I, **22**, 1223.—§ 31*b* (Samudradarçana): I, **22**, 1230 (do.).—§ 32*b* (Garuḍa): I, **23**, 1247 (°*kshayakaraḥ*, i.e. Garuḍa).—§ 36 (Kadrū): I, **25**, 1282 (°*ānām ālayaḥ*, i.e. the ocean).—§ 38 (do.): I, **26**, 1301.—§ 39 (Rāmaṇīyaka): I, **27**, 1304, 1310.—§ 40 (Garuḍa): I, **28**, 1332.—§ 47 (Sarpanāmak.): I, **35**, 1562 (enumeration of the principal serpents).—§ 49 (Vāsuki): I, **37**, 1606, 1608, 1614; **38**, 1637, 1640; **39**, 1641 (consultation of the serpents about the means of being delivered from the curse of Kadrū).—§ 51 (Parikshit): I, **43**, 1792, 1795.—§ 58*b* foll. (Sarpasattra): I, **53**, 2052, 2053, 2059 (the snake-sacrifice of Janamejaya, Āstīka obtained from Janamejaya the boon that the sacrifice might be ended).—§ 63 (do.): I, **57**, 2148 (enumeration of the serpents of Vāsuki's race who had fallen into the fire).—§ 64 (do.): I, **57**, 2151 (do., of Takshaka's race).—§ 65 (do.): I, **57**, 2153 (do., of Airāvata's race).—§ 66 (do.): I, **57**, 2155 (do., of Dhṛtarāshṭra's race), 2160.—[§ 68 (Āstīka): I, **58** (thus Āstīka had delivered the serpents from the curse of Kadrū).]—§ 129 (Aṃçāvat.): I, **66**, 2634 (sons of Surasā, the pannagas being sons of Kadrū).—§ 191 (Arjuna): I, **123**, 4829 (present at the birth of Arjuna, enumeration).—§ 197 (Bhīmasenarasap.): I, **128**, 5018 (°*bhavane*, °*kumārakān*), 5025, 5031, 5033; **129**, 5057, 5058, 5060 (Bhīmasena was rescued by the Nāgas and dwelt for some time in the world of the Nāgas).—§ 233 (Svayaṃvarap.): I, **187**, 7017 (*Suparṇa-N°āsura-Siddhajushṭam*, sc. *antarīksham*).—§ 244 (Rājyalābhap.): I, **207**, 7575 (°*air Bhogavatī yathā*), 7594 (do.).—§ 246 (Sundopasundop.): I, **210**, 7659 (*antarbhūmigatān*, vanquished by Sunda and Upasunda); **212**, 7712 (Sunda and Upasunda robbed the jewels of the *N.*).—§ 247 (Arjunavanavāsap.): I, **213**, 7745 (°*air iva Sarasvatī*).—§ 256*b* (Khāṇḍavadahanap.): I, **224**, 8171.—§ 257*d* (Sudarçana): I, **225**, 8198 (°*ānām adhikaḥ*, sc. Kṛshṇa).—§ 258 (Khāṇḍavadahanap.): I, **228**, 8285, 8318 (slain at the conflagration of the Khāṇḍava forest).—§ 267 (Yamasabhāv.): II, **8**, 335 (*çataṃ*, in the palace of Yama).—[§ 268 (Varuṇasabhāv.): II, **9**, 363 (*sarpāḥ*, enumeration).]—§ 270 (Brahmasabhāv.): II, **11**, 465 (worship Brahmán), 472 (come to the palace of Brahmán).—§ 271 (Lokapālasabhākh.): II, **12**, 480 (in the palace of Varuṇa).—§ 314 (Āraṇyakap.): III, **9**, 330.—§ 345 (Nalopākhyānap.): III, **57**, 2195 (°*air Bhogavatīm iva*).—§ 362 (Tīrthayātrāp.): III, **83**, 5084 (*Sarpadevīṃ . . . N°ānāṃ tīrtham*).—§ 373 (Prayāga): III, **85**, 8214 (in Prayāga).—§ 418*d* (Kailāsa): III, **139**, 10831 (on the mountain of Kailāsa).—§ 437 (Yakshayuddhap.): III, **160,** 11696 (°-*mahānāga*-°). — § 445 (Nivātakavacayuddhap.): III, **173,** 12262 (*hatanāgam iva hradam*).— § 459 (Mārkaṇḍeyas.): III, **188,** 12924, 12942 (seen by Mārkaṇḍeya in the stomach of Nārāyaṇa). — § 460*b* (Kaliyuga): III, **190,** 13075 (°*ānām ālayeshu*), 13093.— § 476 (Dhundhumārop.): III, **202,** 13535 (°*ānām* . . . *varam*).—§ 549*d* (Dhṛtarāshṭra): IV, **2,** 44 (*Dhṛtarāshṭraç ca N°ānām*, sc. *varah*).—§ 552 (Goharaṇap.): IV, **26,** 887 (*iva N°endrāḥ*?, "elephants" PCR.).—§ 561 (Yānasandhip.): V, **71,**†2580 (°-*Rakshasām*, sc. *janitram*, i.e. Kṛshṇa (Vishṇu).— § 564 (Mātaliyop.): V, **97,** 3520 (*M.* would seek a husband for his daughter among the *N.*); **103,** 3620 (*Surasāyāḥ sutāḥ*), 3624 (enumeration of the principal Nāgas).—§ 565 (Gālavacarita): V, **120,** 4028 (°-*Yaksha-manushyānām samāgamaḥ*).—§ 573 (Ambopākhyānap.): V, **179,** 7152 (*ksharanto rudhiram N°ā iva*).—§ 574 (Jambūkh.): VI, **6**θ, 246 (*sarpā N°āç ca*, on the mountain Nishada).—§ 576 (Bhagavadgītāp.): VI, **34,** 1233 (*Anantaç cāsmi N°ānām*, says Kṛshṇa).— § 586 (Bhīshmavadhap.): VI, **104,** 4758 (*mahāçaktim* . . . *Nāgakanyopamām*).—§ 600 (Ghaṭotkacavadhap.): VII, **156,** †6921 (applauded Açvatthāman); **163,** †7293. — § 601 (Droṇavadhap.): VII, **185**γ, 8434 (had been slain by Arjuna in the Khāṇḍava forest, cf. § 258).—§ 603*b* (Nārāyaṇa): VII, **201**ζζ, †9465 (° *Rakshaḥ-Piçācān*, 9475. — § 605 (Karṇap.): VIII, **24,** 925 (*āçīvishā yathā N°ā bhittvā gām salilam yayuḥ*), 975 (only C., read *nagāḥ* ("mountains") with B.). — § 606 (Tripurākhyāna): VIII, **34,** 1483 (enumeration, became the *vālabandhanāḥ* of the horses of Çiva).—§ 608 (Karṇap.): VIII, **87**χ', 4415 (sided with Arjuna), 4426 (°-*Yakshāḥ*); **88,** †4490 (*deva-N°āsura-Siddha-Yakshāḥ*).—§ 611 (Çalyap.): IX, **10,** 498 (*lelihānām iva* . . . *Nāgakanyām*, sc. *çaktim*).—§ 615 (Gadāyuddhap.): IX, **58,** 3271 (*Garutmantau yathā N°āmishaishiṇau*); **62,** 3464 (*hṛtanāgam iva hradam*).—§ 616 (Sauptikap.): X, **6,** 219 (°-*yajñopavītinam*, sc. Açvatthāman).—§ 617 (Aishīkap.): X, **15,** 715.—§ 618 (Jalapradānik.): XI, **5,** 133 (*pañcaçīrshadharaiḥ*). — § 637 (Rājadh.): XII, **47,** 1636 (*paryaṅke N°bhūshite*, sc. Kṛshṇa's).—§ 641*f* (Pṛthu Vainya): XII, **59,** 2245 (*Yaksha-Rākshasa-N°aiḥ*). — § 660*b* (Bhṛgu-Bharadvājasamv.): XII, **188,** 6932 (*Yaksha - Rākshasa-N°āḥ*).—§ 662*b* (Jāpakop.): XII, **200**δ, 7341.—§ 667 (Mokshadh.): XII, **210,** 7657.—§ 704 (do.): XII, **301,** †11097.—§ 717*b* (Nārāyaṇīya): XII, **341**γγ, 13366 — § 718*b* (Uñchavṛttyup.): XII, **361,** 13966 (*Saurabheyāḥ*, read *Sauraseyāḥ*).—§ 723 (Ānuçāsanik.): XIII, **6**α, 308.— § 730*g* (Upamanyu): XIII, **14**η, 746 (*nāgamauñjī*, etc., sc. Çiva).—§ 734 (do.): XIII, **26,** 1807 (*sudhā yathā ca N°ānām*).—§ 746 (do.): XIII, **67,** 3388 (°*ānāñ ca sudhā tathā*, sc. *annam*).—§ 747 (do.): XIII, **84**γ, 3978 (*kuñjarāḥ smṛtā N°āḥ*).—§ 747*b* (Suvarṇotpatti): XIII, **85,** 4023.— § 754 (Ānuçāsanik.): XIII, **98,** 4705 (*Gandharva-N°-Yakshebhyaḥ*), 4711, 4738 (°*ānām dayitā nityam padmotpalavimiçritāḥ*, sc. *balayaḥ*).—§ 759 (do.): XIII, **107**ζ, 5261 (°*vīthīsamākūlam*, sc. *vimānam*). — § 766 (do.): XIII, **132,** 6163 (*Baladevaprabhṛtayaḥ*), 6171. — § 768*b* (Umā-Maheçvaras.): XIII, **140**α, 6351; **142,** 6544.—§ 768*c* (Balarāma): XIII, **147,** 6862.—§ 782*b* (Brāhmaṇagītā): XIV, **26,** 752.—§ 782*g* (Guruçishyas.): XIV, **43**θ, 1183 (*deva-Dānava-N°ānām* . . . *īçvaraḥ*, i.e. Vishṇu).—§ 784*b* (Uttaṅka): XIV, **54,** 1566, 1581 (°*yonau*, °*vat*); **57,** 1685 (*deva-Rākshasa-N°ānām*); **58,** 1740 (*Vāsukipramukhānām*), 1744, 1746, 1748 (*Vāsukipramukhānām*) (Uttaṅka's adventures in the world of the *N.*).—§ 793 (Mausalap): XVI, **4,** †118 (the *N.* (enumeration) welcomed the serpent who after the death of Balarāma issued from his body). Cf. Kādraveya, pl., Kadrūja, pl., and also pannaga, pl., sarpa, pl.—Names of single Nāgas:—

Açvasena: I, 8242; VIII, †4633 (*A*°), †4676, †4677 (°-*rāja*), †4679.
Açvatara: II, 361 (*Kambalāçvatarau nāgau*).
Airāvaṇa: II, 360 (*A*°).
Airāvata: V, 3627 (*A*°).
Akarkara: I, 1561 (*Karkarākarkarau nāgau*).
Anīla: I, 1552 (*Nīlānīlau nāgau*).
Apūraṇa: I, 1551.
Āryaka: I, 5028, 5031.
Atishaṇḍa: XVI, †120 (*Cakramandātishaṇḍau*).
Bahumūlaka: I, 1561 (*B*°).
Baladeva: XVI, †117.
Cakramanda: XVI, †120 (*Cakramandātishaṇḍau*).
Cikura: V, 3640 (*C*°).
Çaṅkhamukha: I, 1556 (*Ç*°).
Çesha: I, 1586, 1587, 2786; III, 13557 (*Ç*°), 13562 (°*bhoge*); V, 3618 (*Ç*°); VII, 9563 (°*endra*, *Ç*°).
Dhṛtarāshṭra: XVI, †119 (*D*°).
Elāpatra: I, 1648 (*E*°).
Jaya: IX, 2554 (*J*°).
Kalaçapotaka: I, 1552.
Kālīyaka: I, 1555 (*K*°).
Kambala: II, 361 (*Kambalāçvatarau nāgau*).
Kapila: III, 8010 (°-*rāja*, *K*°).
Kardama: I, 1561 (*K*°).
Karkara: I, 1561 (*Karkarākarkarau nāgau*).
Karkoṭaka: III, 2610 (°*rājan*), 2614 (*K*°), 2616 (°*endra*), 2617 (*K*°), 2620, 2621 (*K*°), 2633 (°*rāja*), 2634, 2843 (do.), 2997 (do.), 3072 (*K*°).
Kauravya: I, 7788 (°*rājasya kanyayā*, i.e. Ulūpī), 7789 (*K*°), 7791 (°*rājasutā*, i.e. Ulūpī), 7809 (°*bhavane*); XIV, 2371 (*nāgottamasutā*, i.e. Ulūpī), 2383 (°*rājapateḥ sutā*, i.e. Ulūpī), 2399 (°*endraduhitar*, i.e. Ulūpī), 2420 (°*endra*).
Kshemaka: I, 1556 (*K*°).
Mahājaya: IX, 2554 (*M*°).
Maṇi: V, 3626.
Nahusha°: III, 12402 (*N.* as ajagara), 12471 (°*endra*), 12486 (do.).
Nīla: I (*Nīlānīlau nāgau*).
Padma: XII, 13803 (*padmanābho mahanāgaḥ Padma ity eva viçrutaḥ*), 13807, 13823, 13824, 13825 (°*patnī*), 13827, (13829) (°*bhāryā*), 13836, 13844, (13852), 13854 (°*endra*), 13857 (do.), 13862 (do.), (13864), (13868) (°*bhāryā*), (13876), 13885 (°*endra*), 13888, (13891), 13892, (13901), (13927).
Piṇḍāraka: I, 1556 (*P*°).
Piñjaraka: I, 1551.
Prabhākara: I, 1560.
Reṇuka: XIII, 6156 (*R*°).
Sumukha: V, 3639 (*S*°), 3642, 3674.
Takshaka: I, ††774 (°*rāja*, *T*°), ††775 (do.), 802 (do.), 1760 (°*endra*, *T*°), 1768 (°*endra*), 1769 (do.), 1771, 1789 (*T*°), 1803, 1979 (°*endra*, *T*°), 1983, 1987, 2054 (°*endra*, *T*°), 2056 (°*endra*), 2123, 2133, 2134 (do., *T*°), 2167, 8236 (°*rāja*, *T*°); III, 5032 (*T*°); V, 3798 (*T*°).
Vāsuki: I, 1125 (°*rājo*, C., but read with B. °*rājño*), 1126, 1127 (*V*°), 1644 (*V*°), 1647 (°*rāj*), 1649 (°*endra*), 1652 (do.), 1865 (do.), 1866 (do.), 1872, 1878 (*svasā N°pateḥ*,

i.e. Jaratkāru), 1924 (do.), 2078 (°*rāja*), 2085, 2088 (°*endra*), 5023 (do.), 5027 (do., *V*°), 5029 (do.), 5056; IX, 2518 (°*rāja*, *V*°).

Vegavat: I, 2158 (*V*°).

Nāga, adj. ("belonging to the Serpents"). § 608 (Karṇap.): VII, **53**, 2586 (°*m astraṃ*, employed by Arjuna).

Nāgaçata, a mountain. § 184 (Pāṇḍu): I, **119**, 4636 (*giriṃ*, in the north, visited by Pāṇḍu).

Nāgāçin, a Suparṇa, son of Garuḍa. § 564 (Mātalīyop.): V, **101** β, 3594 (enumeration).

Nāgadatta, a son of Dhṛtarāshṭra. § 130 (Aṃçāvat.): I, **67**, 2737.—§ 182 (Dhṛtarāshṭraputranāmak.): I, **117**, 4550.—§ 600 (Ghaṭotkacavadhap.): VII, **157** o, 6938 (among ten sons of Dhṛtarāshṭra who are slain by Bhīmasena).

Nāgadhanvan (Nāgavatman, C.), a tīrtha on the Sarasvatī. § 615g (Baladevatīrthayātrā): *N.* is swarming with numerous snakes, it was the abode of Vāsuki and of 14,000 *Ṛshis*; there is no fear of snakes. There the gods had installed Vāsuki as king of all the snakes: IX, **37**, 2148.

Nāgadvīpa, a region. § 574 (Jambūkh.): VI, **6**, 251.

Nāgāhvaya[1] ("named after the elephant") = Hāstinapura: VII, 8 (*puraṃ*); XIV, 1933 (*puraṃ*), 2510 (*puraṃ*).

Nāgāhvaya[2], a city of the Nāgas (Serpents) on the Gomatī. § 718b (Uñchavṛttyup.): XII, **356**, 13801 (*puraṃ*).

Nāgaloka ("the world of the Nāgas (Serpents)"). § 17 (Uttaṅka): I, **3**, ††793, ††796, ††815, ††823.—§ 197 (Bhīmasenarasapāna): I, **129**, 5059, 5065.—§ 360 (Tīrthayātrāp.): III, **82**, 5055.—§ 362 (do.): III, **83**, 5085.—§ 458 (Mārkaṇḍeyas.): III, **188**, 12875.—§ 524c (Vishṇu): III, **272**, 15810 (pl.).—§ 564 (Mātalīyop.): V, **97**, 3519; **98**, 3529; **99**, 3547 (°*sya nābhishṭhāne . . . Pātālam*); **102**, 3616, 3620.—§ 585b (Irāvat): VI, **90**, 3980 (°*e saṃvṛddhaḥ*, sc. Irāvat).—§ 784c (Uttaṅka): The *N.* extended thousand of yojanas on all sides, and had many walls of pure gold, and was decked with jewels and gems; there were many fine tanks of water with flights of staircases made of pure crystal, and many rivers of clear and transparent water; Uttaṅka also saw many trees with diverse species of birds; the gate was five yojanas high and 100 yojanas in width: XIV, **58**, 1719, 1722, 1723, 1725, 1726, 1730, 1738, 1739.

Nāgapati, pl. (°*ayaḥ*) ("lords of the Serpents"). § 606 (Tripurākhyāna): VIII, **34**, 1481 (*daça N°īn . . . Dhṛtarāshṭramukhān*, Çiva made them the *īshā* of his chariot).

Nāgapura, name of a town = Hāstinapura: I, 4464 (°*ālayāt*), 4632, 4907, 5147, 5207; III, 8456, †12591, †12592; V, 4960, 4961; VI, †781 (only B.); VIII, 17, 25; IX, 1465; XIV, †1531.

Nāgapurādhipa ("lord of Nāgapura") = Pāṇḍu: I, 4459.

Nāgapurasiṃha (do.) = Pāṇḍu: I, 4462.

Nāgasāhvaya ("named after the elephant") = Hāstinapura: I, 506 (*nagaraṃ*), 1786 (do.), 2249 (*nagarāt*), 5146 (*nagaraṃ*), 6343 (do.); II, 1663 (*nagare*); III, 35 (do.), 890, 15258, 15265 (do.); V, 127 (*nagaraṃ*), 129 (do.), 5674 (*pure*); IX, 3499, 3536; XI, 313: XII, 128 (*nagaraṃ*), 1386 (do.); XIII, 7703 (do.); XIV, 1856 (*nagare*), 2047, 2065 (*nagaraṃ*); XVI, 291 (do.).

Nāgatīrtha, a tīrtha. § 370 (Tīrthayātrāp.): III, **84**, 8011.

Nagātmajā ("daughter of the Mountain [i.e. Himavat]") = Umā: XIII, 6382.

Nāgavatmān, v. Nāgadhanvan.

Nāgendra = Çiva (1000 names[1]).

***nāgī** ("female serpent"): I, 8239 (= the wife of Takshaka and mother of Açvasena); XII, 13834 (= the wife of Padma).

Nagnajit, a king [of the Gandhāras ?]. § 83 (Ādivaṃçāvatāraṇa): I, **63**, 2455 (*Prahlādaçishyo N°t Subalaç cābhavat tataḥ*, is not *N.* another name of Subala?).—§ 130 (Aṃçāvat.): I, **67**, 2657 (incarnation of the Asura Ishupa (Ishupad, B.)).—§ 515 (Karṇadigvijaya): III, **254**, 15257 (°*pramukhān gaṇān*, vanquished by Karṇa on his digvijaya).—§ 561c (Kṛshṇa Vāsudeva): V, **48**, 1882 (*ayaṃ*—i.e. Kṛshṇa—*Gāndhārāṃs tarasā sampramathya jitvā putrān N°aḥ samagrān | baddhaṃ mumoca vinadantaṃ prasahya Sudarçanaṃ vai devatānāṃ lalāmam*).—§ 589 (Droṇābhishekap.): VII, **4** β, 120 (°*pramukhā nṛpāḥ*, had been vanquished by Karṇa).

Nagnajita, pl. (°*āḥ*), a people or a family ("the sons of Nagnajit"?). § 608 (Karṇap.): VIII, **79**, 4040 (had been vanquished by Karṇa, BR. conjectures *Nā*°).

Nāgodbheda, a tīrtha. § 360 (Tīrthayātrāp.): III, **82**, 5053, 5055 (there the Sarasvatī reappears).

Nahusha[1], a serpent. § 47 (Sarpanāmak.): I, **35**, 1554 (enumeration).—§ 564 (Mātalīyop.): V, **103** γ, 3625 (do.).—§ 606 (Tripurākhyāna): VIII, **34**, 1483 (among the serpents who became the *vālabandhanāḥ* of the horses of Çiva). Cf. Nahusha[2].

Nahusha[2], an ancient king, son of Āyus and father of Yayāti, etc., for some time king of the gods, but cursed and born as a serpent (*ajagara*). § 141 (Purūravas): I, **75**, 3150 (eldest son of Āyus and Svarbhānavī). — § 142 (cf. Purūravas): *N.* protected the *Pitṛs*, gods, *Ṛshis*, brahmans, *Gandharvas*, *Uragas*, *Rākshasas*, etc.; having slain the Dasyus, he made the Ṛshis pay tribute and carry him on their back like beasts of burden, and having conquered the gods, he became *Indra*: I, **75**, 3151 (*Āyushaḥ putraḥ*), 3152. — § 143: *N.* had six sons: *Yati*, *Yayāti*, *Saṃyāti*, *Āyāti*, *Ayati*, and *Dhruva*. *Yati* betaking himself to asceticism, *Yayāti* became the successor of *N.* and begot with *Devayānī*, *Yadu* and *Turvasu*, and with *Çarmishṭhā*, *Druhyu*, *Anu*, and *Pūru*: I, **75**, 3155. — § 149 (Yayāti): I, **88**, †3564 (°*sya putra*, i.e. Yayāti), †3577 (*Yayātir N°sya putraḥ*); **93**, †3684 (*Yayātiḥ . . . N°sya putraḥ*).—§ 156 (Pūruvaṃç.): I, **95**, ††3760 (son of Āyus and father of Yayāti). — § 267 (Yamasabhāv.): II, **8**, 319 (in the palace of Yama).—§ 296 (Dyūtap.): II, **53**, 1930.—§ 310 (Āraṇyakap.): III, **3**, 141.—§ 384 (Agastyop.): III, **103**, 8777 (had oppressed the gods who were rescued by Agastya, cf. § 555). — § 450 (Ājagarap.): III, **179**, 12408 (*rājarshiḥ*), **180**, 12453 (do.); 12460 (*rājā*); **181**, 12533 (*nṛpatiḥ*, cursed by Agastya (cf. § 555), *N.* became a serpent (*ajagara*), but was liberated by Yudhishṭhira). — § 516 (Duryodhanayajña): III, **257**, 15329 (had performed the *Vaishṇava* sacrifice). — § 552 (Goharaṇap.): IV, **56** ζ, 1768 (came to see the encounter).—§ 555 (Indravijaya): V, **11**, 342, 344, 354, 357, 361, 366, 367; **12**, 368, 379, 380, 382, 392, 393, 397, 398, 399, 400; **13**, 401 (*Devarāj*), 402, 404 (*Devarājaṃ*), 406, (407), 408, 415, 421; **14**, 441, 444; **15**, 446, 448, 450, 451, 461, 470, 472; **16**, 505, 506, †508, †509, †510, †513, †514, †515, †516; **17**, 520, 522, 526, 527, 528, 529, 530, 542 (*N.* became the king of the gods, but cursed by Agastya he fell down and became a serpent for 10,000 years).—§ 555 (Sainyodyogap.): V, **17**, 556.—§ 562 (Bhagavadyānap.): V, **90** ν, 3146 (worshipped Kṛshṇa).—§ 576 (Bhagavadgītāp.): VI, **17** β, 645.—§ 599e (Çini): VII, **144**, 6029 (son of Āyus and father of Yayāti).—§ 621 (Rājadh.): XII, **8**, 211 (a sentence of his is quoted), (θ), 238 (the earth had belonged to *N.*):—

§ 656 (Khadgotpattik.): XII, **166**, 6193, 6194 (received the sword from Āyus, from *N.* it passed over to Yayāti).—§ 680*b* (Tulādhāra-Jājalisaṃv.): XII, **263**, 9388, 9389, 9390 (*N.* had slain a cow and a bull and was rebuked by the ṛshis, who however distributed the sin incurred among the creatures in the form of diseases).—§ 684 (Mokshadh): XII, **269**, 9601 (*āmnāyam anupaçyan hi purāṇaṃ çāçvataṃ dhruvaṃ* | *N°ḥ pūrvam ālebhe Tvashṭur gāṃ*, cf. § 680*b*). — § 717*b* (Nārāyaṇīya): XII, **343**, VII), ††13214 (*Āyushaḥ putraṃ*), ††13216 (repetition from § 555).— § 745 (Ānuçāsanik.): XIII, **50**, 2642 (*°sya saṃvādaṃ maharsheç Cyavanasya ca*).—§ 745*b* (Cyavanop.): XIII, **50**, 2667; **51**, 2668, (2671), (2673), (2675), (2677), (2679), 2681, 2682, (2685), 2688, 2690, (2692), 2708, 2710, 2713 (how Cyavana was purchased by *N.* at the price of a cow).—§ 746 (Ānuçāsanik.): XIII, **81**λ, 3806 (had made gifts of kine).—§ 751*b* (Çapathavidhi): XIII, **94*a***, 4551, (4574).—§ 755*b* (Nahushop.): XIII, **99**, 4745 (*°sya ca saṃvādam Agastyasya Bhṛgos tathā*), 4746, 4747, 4757 (*Devendrasya*), 4764, 4770; **100**, 4782, 4790, 4792, 4795, 4797, 4803, 4804, 4805, 4809, 4810 (the story of *N.*'s becoming the king of the gods and falling from that place (somewhat different from the narration § 555) and allusion to § 450).—§ 761 (Ānuçāsanik.): XIII, **115**γ, 5662 (abstained from meat during the month of Kārttika).—§ 768*b* (Kṛshna Vāsudeva): XIII, **147**, 6832 (son of Āyus and father of Yayāti).—§ 775 (Ānuçāsanik.): XIII, **166**η, 7674 (enumeration).

Cf. also the following synonyms:—

Devarāj ("king of the gods"): V, 401; XIII, 4765, 4788, 4793.

Devarāja (do.): V, 354 (*N°*), 369, 371, 380 (*N°*), 404 (*N°*), 455.

Devarājan (do.): V, 368.

Devendra (do.): V, 356; XIII, 4757 (*N°*), 4767 (*ku°*), 4775 (do.).

Jagatpati, q.v.

Nāga, Nāgendra, v. Nāga, pl.

Surādhipa ("lord of the gods"): V, 372, 454, 457; XIII, 4790.

Surapati (do.): XIII, 4789.

Sureçvara (do.), q.v.

Surendra (do.): V, 461; XIII, 4782 (*°tvaṃ*), 4784.

Nahusha[2] = Kṛshṇa (Vishṇu): XII, 1511; XIII, 6983 (Vishṇu's 1000 names).

Nāhusha, Nahushātmaja = Yayāti, q.v.

[Nahushopākhyāna] ("the episode relating to Nahusha"). § 755*b* (Ānuçāsanik.): *Nahusha*, having acquired the sovereignty of heaven, performed both human and celestial acts, for instance *bali* and offering of incense and of light, etc.; and although he had become the chief of the gods, he yet worshipped the gods as in days of yore. But then he was filled with pride in consequence of the boon he had received from all the gods, and he ceased to perform religious actions; for a very long time he used to employ the Ṛ. by turns as the bearers of his vehicles; but in consequence of his abstention from religious acts his energy began to diminish; when it was *Agastya*'s turn to carry the vehicle, *Bhṛgu* came to the hermitage of *Agastya* (*Maitrāvaruṇi*), and when the latter, mentioning *Brahmán*'s boon to *Nahusha* (that whoever would come within the range of his eyesight would, deprived of all energy, be within his sway), and that *Brahmán* had given him *amṛta* to drink, despaired of being able to curse him, *Bhṛgu* said that he had come at the command of *Brahmán*, and that he would curse *Nahusha* to be a snake, when he insulted *Agastya* by a kick, and this very day he would hurl him down and re-establish *Indra*. *Agastya* became highly gratified (XIII, **99**). Asked by *Yudhishṭhira*, *Bhīshma* continued [referring to and developing the beginning of XIII, **99**: *Nahusha*'s sacrificial rites and presents were obstructed by Rā.]: *Nahusha* ordered Ṛ. *Agastya* to carry the vehicle from the banks of *Sarasvatī*. *Bhṛgu*, telling *Agastya* to close his eyes, had entered the matted locks of *Agastya*, taking care not to cast his eyes upon *Nahusha*. *Nahusha* urged *Agastya* on with his goad and then struck him on the head with his left foot. Then *Nahusha* was cursed by *Bhṛgu* and transformed into a snake, but, in consequence of his gifts, etc., he retained his memory, and, assisted by *Agastya*, pacified *Bhṛgu*, who said that *Yudhishṭhira* would rescue him, and then went to the abode of *Brahmán* and informed him, while *Agastya* returned to his own hermitage. *Brahmán* once more installed (caused the gods to instal) *Indra* in the sovereignty of heaven. "Thou hast, O king, rescued *Nahusha* from *Bhṛgu*'s curse; he ascended to the abode of *Brahmán* before thy eyes; in consequence of the merits he had acquired through acts of the kind I have mentioned, he succeeded in once more regaining his lost position. Hence, when evening comes, persons leading the domestic mode of life, should give lamps" (XIII, **100**).

Naigameya, a god associated to or a form of Skanda. § 116 (Vasu, pl.): I, **66**, 2588 (son (?) (brother, PCR.) of Skanda, *tasya Çākho Viçākhaç ca N°ç ca pṛshṭhajaḥ*).—§ 498 (Skandotpatti): III, **226**, 14367 (*Agnir bhūtvā N°ç chāgavaktro bahuprajo ramayām āsa çailastham*—sc. Skanda—*bālaṃ krīḍanakair iva*).—§ 508 (Kārttikeyastava): III, **232**, 14634 (among the names of Skanda).—§ 615*u* (Skanda): IX, **44**, 2487 (one of the four forms of Skanda, *tasya Çākho Viçakhaç ca N°aç ca pṛshṭhataḥ*), 2489 (*kumāro pāvakaprabhuḥ*).

Naighaṇṭuka, a collection of Vedic words. § 717 (Nārāyaṇīya): XII, **343**, 13247 (*°padākhyāne*; so B., C. has *Nirghaṇṭaka°*).

Naika, Naikaçṛnga = Vishṇu (1000 names).

Naikadṛç, son of Viçvāmitra. § 721*b* (Viçvāmitrop.): XIII, **4**β, 253.

Naikaja, Naikakarmakṛt, Naikamāya = Vishṇu (1000 names).

Naikapṛshtha, pl. (*āḥ*). § 574 (Jambūkh.): VI, **9**μ, 349 (in Bhāratavarsha; C. has by error *°shṭāḥ*).

Naikarūpa = Vishṇu (1000 names).

Naikasānucara = Çiva (1000 names[2]).

Naikātman = Çiva (1000 names[2]).—Do.[2] = Vishṇu (1000 names).

Naimisha, a sacred forest. § 249 (Arjunavanavāsap.): I, **215**, 7817 (*ramyam araṇyaṃ*, visited by Arjuna). § 360 (Kurukshetra): I, **83**, 7073 (*tīrthaṃ*).—§ 370 (Tīrthayātrāp.): III, **84**, 8037, 8038, 8039, 8041, 8042 (description).—§ 377 (Dhaumyatīrthak.): III, **87**, 8302 (in the east).—§ 594 (Mṛtyu): VII, **54**, 2098 (visited by Mṛtyu).—§ 607 (Karṇap.): VIII, **45**, 2086.—[§ 615*h* (Baladevatīrthayātrā): Requested by *Janamejaya*, Vaiçampāyana related: In the *Kṛta*-age, the ascetics who dwelt in *Naimisha* (*Naimisheyās tapasvinaḥ*, IX, 2159) were engaged in a grand sacrifice (extending over twelve years); many Ṛ. came there; after the completion of the twelve years' sacrifice they set out in large numbers to sojourn at the tīrthas; the tīrthas on the southern bank of the *Sarasvatī* looked like towns and cities, they took up their abodes on the bank up to *Samantapañcaka,* the whole region resounded with *Vedic* recitations, there were present many sorts of ascetics: *Vālakhilyas, Açmakuṭṭas, Dantolūkhalins, Prasaṅkhyānas,* such as lived on air, such as lived on water, such as lived on leaves, such as lay on the earth instead of in beds, etc. (cf. the note of PCR. p. 150); they made the *Sarasvatī* beautiful as the gods beautify the *Gaṅgā.* Not finding sufficient room on the banks of the Sarasvatī they measured out small plots of land with their sacred threads. For their sake the Sarasvatī appeared and made many abodes (*kuñjāḥ*) in that spot, and then once more flowed in a western direction, therefore this receptacle of water (*kuñjaḥ*) is named after the ṛshis of Naimisha (*Naimishīya iti smṛtaḥ,* v. 2175).]—§ 615*i* (Saptasārasvata): IX, **38,** 2201, 2204 (the river Sarasvatī appeared in *N.* as the river Kāñcanākshī).—§ 653 (Āpaddh.): XII, **153,** 5676.—§ 702 (Mokshadh.): XII, **298**ε, 10937 (°*Pushkareshu*).—§ 718*b* (Uñchavṛttyup.): XII, **356,** 13801 (°*e Gomatītīre tatra Nāgāhvayaṃ puraṃ*).—§ 733*c* (Pushkara): XIII, **25,** 1696.—§ 733*n* (Mataṅgavāpī): XIII, **25,** 1719.—§ 757*o* (Goloka): XIII, **102a,** 4887.—§ 758 (Ānuçāsanik.): XIII, **103**β, 4944.—§ 775 (do.): XIII, **166a,** 7649 (enumeration). Cf. Naimishāraṇya.

Naimisha, pl. (°*āḥ*), a people ("the inhabitants of Naimisha"). § 607 (Karṇap.): VIII, **45**μ, 2084, (ν), 2100.

Naimishakuñja, a tīrtha. § 364 (Tīrthayātrāp.): III, **83,** 6079 (on the Sarasvatī, cf. *kuñjaḥ . . . Naimishīyaḥ,* IX, 2175).

Naimishāraṇya = Naimisha[1]. § 1 (Anukram.): I, **1,** 1 (there Çaunaka held his twelve years' sacrifice), 3 (°*vāsināṃ*).—§ 11 (Parvasaṅgr.): I, **2,** 359 (in *N.* the eighteen parvans of the Mhbhr. were recited).—§ 18 (Paulomap.): I, **4,** 851 (there Çaunaka held his twelve years' sacrifice).—§ 26 (Āstīkap.): I, **13,** 1025 (°*vāsibhiḥ*).—§ 238 (Pañcendrop.): I, **197,** 7275 (the gods held a sacrifice in *N.*).—§ 379 (Tīrthayātrāp.): III, **95,** 8510 (visited by Yudhishṭhira on his tīrthayātrā).—§ 471 (Mārkaṇḍeyas.): III, **200,** 13428 (°*vāsinaḥ*).—§ 615*o* (Baka Dālbhya): IX, **41,** 2344.—§ 717*b* (Nārāyaṇīya): XII, **340,** 13004 (°*vāsinaḥ,* i.e. Çaunaka, etc.); **347,** 13442 (*Çaunakādyeshu N°vāsishu*). Cf. Naimisha[1].

Naimisheya, adj. ("belonging to the Naimisha forest"). § 364 (Tīrthayātrāp.): III, **83,** 6079 (*ṛshayaḥ*).—§ 615 (Baladevatīrthayātrā): IX, **37,** 2155 (*ṛshīṇāṃ,* C. by error °*bhi*°).—§ 615*h* (Naimisha): IX, **37,** 2159 (*tapasvinaḥ*). Cf. next.

Naimishīya, adj. (do.). § 615*h* (Naimisha): IX, **37,** 2161 (*sattre*), 2175 (*kuñjaḥ,* cf. Naimishakuñja).—§ 615*o* (Baka Dālbhya): IX, **41,** 2320 (°*ānāṃ sattre dvādaçavarshike*). Cf. prec.

Nairṛta[1], pl. (°*āḥ*) ("the sons of Nirṛti") = Rākshasa, pl. § 125 (Aṃçāvat.): I, **66,** 2618 (*Rākshasāḥ,* son of Nirṛti and Adharma).—§ 445 (Nivātakavacayuddhap.): III, **173,** 12247.—§ 539 (Kumbhakarṇādivadha): III, **287,** 16437 (the followers of Rāvaṇa).—§ 564 (Mātalīyop.): V, **100,** 3571 (*Yātudhānāḥ?*).—§ 565 (Gālavacarita): V, **109,** 3786 (°*ānāṃ sahasrāṇi,* in the south); **111,** 3832 (*atra,* i.e. in the north, *Saugandhikavanaṃ N°air api rakshyate*).—§ 615*u* (Skanda): IX, **45,** 2530 (*senāṃ N°saṅkulāṃ,* given to Skanda by the gods); **46,** 2721 (*dadau N°mukhyebhyas trailokyaṃ Pāvakātmajaḥ,* i.e. Skanda).—§ 615*x* (Kubera): IX, **47,** 2759 (°*aiçvaryaṃ,* sc. Kubera's).—§ 641 (Rājadharm.): XII, **67,** 2521 (*sukhe dhāsyasi naḥ Kubera iva N°ān*); **74,** 2812 (created (?) by Kubera and dispatched against the troops of Mucukunda).—§ 673*b* (Bali-Vāsavasaṃv.): **227,** 8266.

Nairṛta[2], pl. (°*āḥ*), a people. § 574 (Jambūkh.): VI, **9**μ, 359 (*Ānartta-N°āḥ,* among the peoples of Bhāratavarsha).

Nairṛta, adj. ("belonging to Nirṛti or to the Nairṛtas). § 306 (Anudyūtap.): II, **80,** 2641 (°*ān darbhān,* i.e. pointing to the south-west?).—§ 443 (Nivātakavacayuddhap.): III, **168,** 12021 (°*āni,* sc. *astrāṇi*).—§ 600 (Ghaṭotkacavadhap.): VII, **156,** 6864 (*akshauhiṇīṃ . . . N°īṃ*).—§ 615*u* (Skanda): IX, **46,** 2673 (°*ī senā,* i.e. the army of Skanda).—§ 655 (Āpaddh.): XII, **165,** 6090 (°*īṃ diçaṃ,* i.e. the south-west).—§ 656 (Khaḍgotpattik.): XII, **166,** 6132 (*bhūmiñ ca N°īṃ,* created by Brahmán).

Nairṛti, an Asura. § 673*b* (Bali-Vāsavasaṃv.): XII, **227a,** 8264 (among the ancient rulers of the earth).

Naishāda, adj. (pl. said about the practices of the Nishādas). § 643*b* (Kāyavyacarita): XII, **135,** 4855 (°*ānāṃ kovidaḥ,* sc. Kāyavya).

Naishadha, pl. (°*āḥ*), a people = Nishadha, pl. § 347 (Nalopākhyānap.): III, **61,** 2315; **64,** 2413 (°*ānāṃ janādhipa,* i.e. Nala).

Naishadha[1] = Nala, q.v.

Naishadha[2], the king of the Nishadhas at the time of Yudhishṭhira. § 592 (Saṃçaptakavadhap.): VII, **20**η, 804 (in Droṇa's gāruḍavyūha); **32**δδ, 1437 (*Bṛhatkshattraṃ ca N°aṃ,* slain by Dhṛshṭadyumna).

Naishadhya, adj. ("originating from the Nishadhas"). § 552 (Goharaṇap.): IV, **42,** 1338 (sc. *khaḍgaḥ*).

Naishādi[1] ("prince of the Nishādas") = Ekalavya: I, 5242, 5248, 5260, 5268; VII, 8214, 8229, 8230.

Naishādi[2] (do.) = Ekalavyasuta: XIV, 2475; XVI, 159 (E°).

Naishādi[3] (do.) = Kāyavya: XII, 4854 (K°).

Naishādi[4] (do.) = Ketumat: VI, 2239.

Naishādi[5] (do.), a Kuru warrior. § 608 (Karṇap.): VIII, **60,** 3055 (slain by Bhīmasena).

naiyāyika ("logician"): I, 450 (°*ānāṃ mukhyena Varuṇasyātmajena,* i.e. Bandin).

Nāka, name of a weapon. § 563 (Bhagavadyānap.): V, **96**φ, 3490 (will be employed by Arjuna).

***Nakshatra**[1], mostly pl. (°*āṇi*) ("lunar mansions"): I, 2581 (°*yoginyaḥ,* sc. the twenty-seven wives of Soma, the daughters of Daksha), 2928 (*cakārānyañca lokaṃ vai kruddho n°sampadā | Pratiçravaṇapūrvāṇi n°āṇi cakāra yaḥ,* sc. Viçvāmitra); II, 443 (in the palace of Brahmán), 986 (sg.), 1322 (°*āṇām ivoḍurāṭ*), 1395 (°*āṇāṃ mukhaṃ candraḥ*); III, 13100 (*çubhāni*), 15235 (sg.), 16198 (*çaçalakshaṇaṃ graha-n°-tārābhir anuyātaṃ*); IV, 1383 (*uttarābhyāṃ Phalgunībhyāṃ n°ābhyāṃ*); V, †818 (°*yogān*), †1905 (°*yogeshu*), 4753 (°*air iva candramāḥ,* sc. *parivṛtaḥ*); VI, 211 (*candramāç ca san°aḥ*), 297 (do.); VII, 161 (°*āṇām iva çaçī*), 2343 (°*dakshiṇāḥ*); VIII, 3894 (°*air iva candramāḥ,* sc. *parivṛtaḥ*); IX, 1834 (°*āṇīva sarvāṇi Savitā* (C. *sahitā*) *rātrīsaṅkshaye . . . nāçayishyāmi*), 1967 (°*gaṇaiḥ parikīrṇo niçācaraḥ*), 2014 (°*yoganiratāḥ,* the twenty-seven wives of Soma, the daughters of Daksha), 2017 (°*ākhyāḥ* = do.), 3126 (°*air iva sampūrṇo vṛto niçākaraḥ*); XII, 1373 (°*air iva candramāḥ,* sc. *parivṛtaḥ*), 1922 (do.), 2261 (*vaṃçaç ca n°āṇāṃ*), 3707 (*tithin°pūjitaḥ*), 4499 (*īçaṃ . . . n°āṇāṃ niçākaraṃ*), 4586 (°*āṇīva candramāḥ,* sc. *adhitishṭhāmi*), 6734 (sg.), 6735 (*āsureshu*), †7372 (°*gatiṃ*), 10048 (°*çakraṃ*), 10923 (sg.), ††13219 (°*ākhyāṃ gatāsu,* sc. the twenty-seven wives of Soma, daughters of Daksha);

XIII, 912 (*°āṇāñ ca candramāḥ*, sc. *asi*, sc. Çiva), 1528 (*°vidhiyogena*), 2173 (*°āṇīva candramāḥ*, sc. *adhitishṭhāmi*), 3252 (*°yogasya . . . dānakalpam*), 3288 (*°yogataḥ*), 5018 (*yogena*), 5082 (sg.), 6052 (*yogena*), 6162 (do.), 7386 (*°yogāḥ*; identified with Kṛshṇa), 7499 (identified with Çiva); XIV, 1175 (*adhipaḥ . . . n°āṇāñ ca candramāḥ*), 1906 (sg.), †1910 (do.), 2513 (do.); XVI, 48 (sg.).—Do.[2] = Çiva (1000 names[1]).

Nakshatranemi = Vishṇu (1000 names).

Nakshatrapati = Soma (the Moon): XII, 6383 (pl., *yathā*).

Nakshatrarāj = do.: III, 14782.

Nakshatrarāja = do.: XII, 1024 (C. *°je*, but read *°jam* with B.).

Nakshatrasādhaka, Nakshatravigrahamati = Çiva (1000 names[2]).

Nakshatriṇ = Vishṇu (1000 names).

Nakta(m), Naktañcara[1] = Çiva (1000 names[2]).—Do.[2] pl. ("nocturnal demons"): I, 6508; III, 16822. Cf. Bhūta, pl.

Nakula, Pāṇḍava. § 4 (Anukram.): I, **1**, †200 (*Mādrīsutam*).—§ 71 (Ādivaṃçāvatāraṇap.): I, **61**, 2267 (conquered the western region, cf. § 285).—§ 83 (Ādivaṃçāvatāraṇa): I, **63**, 2445 (*Yamau . . . N°ḥ Sahadevaç ca*, born from the Açvins, cf. § 192).—§ 130 (Aṃçāvat.): I, **67**, 2747 (*N.* and Sahadeva are portions of the Açvins).—§ 157 (Pūruvaṃç.): I, **95**, ††3816 (*N.* and Sahadeva are born by Mādrī from the Açvins, cf. § 192).—§ 159 (do.): I, **95**, ††3827 (with Draupadī, father of Çatānīka), ††3831 (married to Kareṇumatī and father of Niramitra).—§ 192 (Pāṇḍavotpatti): I, **124**, 4851 (*N.* and Sahadeva are born by Mādrī (the wife of Pāṇḍu) from the Açvins), 4854 (the elder of the twins).—[§ 205*c* (Droṇa): *N.* and Sahadeva excelled everyone in handling the sword: I, **132**, 5271 (*Yamajau*).]—§ 210*e* (Sambhavap.): Taught by *Droṇa*, *N.* became an *atiratha*: I, **139**, 5533.—§ 214 (Hiḍimbavadhap.): I, **154**, 6019, 6025.—§ 235 (Svayaṃvarap.): I, **191**, †7139 (elder than Sahadeva).—§ 253 (Haraṇāharaṇap.): I, **221**, 8044 (with Draupadī, father of Çatānīka).—§ 272 (Rājasūyārambhap.): II, **13**, 524.—§ 278 (Digvijayap.): II, **25**, 992 (conquered the western region, cf. § 285).—§ 285 (do.): *N.* assailed *Rohītaka* and vanquished there the *Mattamayūrakas*, etc.; *Vāsudeva* and *Çalya* accepted his sway, etc.; 10,000 camels carried with difficulty the treasures he had earned when he returned to *Indraprastha* (II, **32**): II, **32**, 1183, 1200 (*Kuruçreshṭhaḥ*), 1202.—§ 286 (Rājasūyikap.): II, **33**, 1258 (*Pāṇḍavam*).—§ 287 (do.): II, **34**, 1260 (*Pāṇḍavaḥ*).—§ 288 (do.): II, **35**, 1201. § 292 (do.): II, **45***a*, 1608 (accompanied Subala and his son). § 294 (Dyūtap.): II, **48**, 1716.—§ 298 (do.): II, **65**, †2152, †2153 (lost by Yudhishṭhira at the game).—§ 301 (do.): II, **70**, †2363; **71**, †2383.—§ 302 (Anudyūtap.): II, **74**, 2465.—§ 304 (do.): II, **77**, 2555, (2556) (promised to slay the Dhārtarāshṭras).—§ 305 (do.): II, **78**, 2569 (*arthasaṅgrahī*).—§ 306 (do.): II, **80**, 2625, (*a*), 2637 (had gone away, staining himself with dust, that he might not steal the hearts of the ladies).—§ 325 (Draupadīparitāpav.): III, **27**, 1020, 1021.—§ 327 (do.): III, **35**, 1389, 1402.—§ 342 (Indralokābhigamanap.): III, **51**, 1971 (*devaputrau . . . N°ḥ Sahadevaç ca*).—§ 356 (Tīrthayātrāp.): III, **80**, 4012 (*Pāṇḍunandanaḥ*), (4013).—§ 419 (Gandhamādanapr.): III, **140**, 10845, 10862.—§ 420 (do.): III, **141**, 10875 (*°āt pūrvajam*, i.e. Arjuna).—§ 423 (do.): III, **143**, 10978, 10990, (10991).—§ 424 (Bhīmakadalīkhaṇḍapr.): III, **146**, 11102.—§ 433 (Saugandhikāharaṇa): III, **155**, 11426.—§ 435 (Jaṭāsuravadhap.): III, **157**, 11478 (carried off by Jaṭāsura).—§ 438 (Yakshayuddhap.): III, **161**, 11774.—§ 450 (Ājagarap.): III, **179**, 12432 (*N°aḥ Sahadevaç ca Yamau*), 12443.—§ 522 (Draupadīharaṇap.): III, **270**, †15709 (*yasyottamam rūpam āhuḥ pṛthivyām*, v. 15708); **271**, 15725, 15731 (slew Kshemaṅkara and Mahāmukha), 15734, 15735, 15736 (slew Suratha).—§ 548 (Āraṇeyap.): III, **311**, 17240; **312**, 17246, 17248, 17251, 17254, 17255, 17257, 17274; **313**, 17408, 17409, 17410, 17412, 17414, 17415, 17417 (when the four Pāṇḍavas had been slain by the Yaksha, Yudhishṭhira chose that *N.* should revive); **315**, 17472.—§ 549 (Pāṇḍavapraveçap.): IV, **3**, 61, (62) (will under the name of Granthika serve Virāṭa as horse-keeper); **5**, 166 (etymology of the name: *kule nāsti samo rūpe yasyeti N°ḥ smṛtaḥ*), 170; **12**, (317) (became under the name Granthika the horse-keeper of Virāṭa).—§ 550 (Samayapālanap.): IV, **13**, 334, 368.—§ 552 (Goharaṇap.): IV, **31**, 1024 (the four Pāṇḍavas in disguise mounted chariots and partook in the encounter with the Trigartas); **33**, 1100 (slew 700 Trigartas); **43**, 1353 (*°syaitad āyudham*), 1358 (*°sya kalāpaḥ*), 1365 (*°syaisha nistriṃçaḥ*); **44**, 1368, 1372 (*açvabandhaḥ*); **50**, 1564.—§ 553 (Vaivāhikap.): IV, **71***a*, 2290, (*β*), 2294 (*açvabandhaḥ*).—§ 556*e* (Sañjayayānap.): Yudhishṭhira said to Sañjaya: "*N.* was formerly sent under your eye to conquer the *Çibis* and the *Trigartas*, and brought the western region under my power": V, **23**, †709.—§ 556 (do.): V, **26**, †763; **29**, †854 (all. to Dyūtap.).—§ 561 (Yānasandhip.): V, **48**, †1832, †1833.—§ 561*f* (do.): *N.* had vanquished the whole western region teeming with Mlecchas: V, **50**, 1996.—§ 561*l* (do.): *N.* was borne by excellent steeds presented by Mahendra, and like to the Wind (*Vāyu*) in might and speed: V, **56**, †2229 (*Mādrīsutam*).—§ 561 (do.): V, **57**, 2254 (*Mādravatīsutaḥ*, will have Ulūka, etc., for his matches in the battle), (*o*), 2262.—§ 562 (Bhagavadyānap.): V, **80**, (2844); **90**, 3168, 3169, 3170.—§ 567 (do.): V, **126**, 4220.—§ 569 (do.): V, **138**, 4681; **140**, 4748; **141***γ*, 4778, 4791 (*N°ḥ Sahadevaç ca Mādrīputrau . . . çamitram . . . karishyataḥ*); **143***ι*, 4871.—§ 570 (Sainyaniryāṇap.): V, **151**, 5108 (proposed to elect Drupada to be generalissimo).—§ 571 (Ulūkadūtāgamanap.): V, **160**, 5476; **163**, 5679, 5696; **164***ε*, 5707 (is pitted against Kṛtavarman).—§ 573 (Ambopākhyānap.): V, **196***ν*, 7635.—§ 576 (Bhagavadgītāp.): VI, **19***ε*, 709 (among the leaders of the Pāṇḍava army); **25***κ*, 845 (blew his conch Sughosha).—§ 577 (Bhishmavadhap.): VI, **43**, (1545), 1555.—§ 578 (do.): VI, **44***β*, 1655; **45**[5], 1690, 1693 (fought with Duḥçāsana and got his horses slain); **50***π*, 2085 (in the left wing of the Pāṇḍava array); **51***aa*, 2116 (= v. 845).—§ 581 (do.): VI, **62***θ*, 2755 (followed Bhīmasena).—§ 582 (do.): VI, **72***ε*, 3168 (*Mādrīputraḥ*, engaged in battle with the Trigartas).—§ 583 (do.): VI, **75***a*, 3282 (*N.* and Sahadeva stationed in the eyes of the makaravyūha).—§ 584 (do.): VI, **81**[1], 3556 (*N.* and Sahadeva proceeded against Çalya); **83**[4], 3684 (*N.* and Sahadeva fought with Çalya); **86**, 3802 (*ratham . . . N°sya*).—§ 585 (do.): VI, **89**, 3962 (*N.* and Sahadeva attacked the cavalry).—§ 586 (do.): VI, **99***ε*, 4508 (*N°ḥ Sahadevaç ca Mādrīputrau*); **101***θ*, 4586, 4589; **105***o*, 4776, (*ρ*), 4797 (pierced Çalya); **106***σ*, 4803 (pierced by Bhīshma), 4805 (pierced Bhīshma).—§ 587 (do.): VI, **108***β*, 5013; **110***ζ*, 5099 (attacked Bhīshma), 5104 (resisted by Vikarṇa); **111**, 5173, 5174 (fought with Vikarṇa).—§ 588 (do.): VI, **121***γ*, 5809.—§ 589 (Droṇābhishekap.): VII, **10***κ*, 335 (proceeded against Droṇa).—§ 590 (do.): VII, **14**, 525 (*svasrīyam*, sc. Çalya's), 526 (fought with Çalya); **16**γ, 645 (pierced by Droṇa).—§ 592 (Saṃçaptakavadhap.): VII, **23**ο, 956 (description of his horses), (π), 1033 (*çarabhaṃ pṛshṭhasauvarṇaṃ N°sya mahādhvajaṃ*), (ρ), 1040 (held [the bow] Vaishṇava); **32**ζζ, 1443 (protected Sātyaki).—§ 593 (Abhimanyuvadhap.): VII, **34a**, 1487 (is praised by Sañjaya), 1491; **39**ν, 1657.—§ 599 (Jayadrathavadhap.): VII, **98**κ, 3661 (protected Sātyaki); **106**, 3976 (attacked by Vikarṇa); **107**, 4042 (defeated Vikarṇa); **109**π, 4111, 4113 (partook in the encounter with Alambusha); **111**ν, 4284; **114**ψ, 4501 (pierced Kṛtavarman); **124**κκ, 4983; **143**ιι, 5997.—§ 600 (Ghaṭotkacavadhap.): VII, **154**β, 6650 (proceeded against Droṇa); **156**θ, 6763 (pierced by Droṇa); **165**, 7364 (resisted by Çakuni); **168**, 7522 (*°sya sutaḥ*, i.e. Çatānīka); **169**, 7559, 7561, 7568, 7570 (*Pāṇḍunandanaḥ*), 7573 (do., fought with Çakuni, whom he defeated and wounded), 7577; **170**νν, 7672; **177**ψψ, 8060; **178**ωω, 8080 (pierced the Rākshasas, who were followers of Alāyudha), (**aaa**), 8084 (do.).—§ 601 (Droṇavadhap.): VII, **184a**, 8367.—§ 602 (do.): VII, **187**, 8567, 8571, 8572 (fought with Duryodhana, whom he defeated); **188**, 8596 (*°sya . . . rathaṃ*).—§ 604 (Karṇap.): VIII, **5**ζ, 118 (had slain the son of Bhagadatta).—§ 605 (do.): VIII, **11aa**, 427 (in the ardhacandravyūha of the Pāṇḍavas); **13**, 491 (proceeded against Karṇa); **22**ηη, 870, 877, 879 (slew the Aṅga king), 881, 883, 888; **24**, 915, 916, 919, 923, 927, 929 *bis*, 931, 932, 940, 944, 958 (fought with Karṇa and was defeated; Karṇa, however, spared his life, remembering his promise to Kuntī).—§ 608 (do.): VIII, **46**, 2156 (proceeded against Vṛshasena), (η), 2205; **48**, 2267, 2268, 2270, 2273, (π), 2281; **54**, 2624 (checked by Duryodhana); **56**, 2698, 2700 (fought with Duryodhana), (ππ), 2756; **61**, 3078 (proceeded against Vṛshasena), 3102, 3103 (fought with Vṛshasena), 3107; **62**ζζζ, 3148; **63**, 3184, 3188 (fought with Karṇa), 3212; **73**, 3732; **75**, †3814 (*Mādrīputraḥ*, attacked Kṛtavarman); **78**, 3955, 3958 (pierced Karṇa); **79**η', 4029; **83**, †4247; **84**, †4281 (fought with Vṛshasena), †4282, †4283, †4285, †4287, †4288, †4289, †4291, †4293, †4294, †4297, †4302, †4303, †4304 (Vṛshasena slew his horses and defeated him); **85**, †4305, †4329, †4331 (*Mādrīsutaṃ*); **96**βa', 5030.—§ 611 (Çalyap.): IX, **10**, 468 (fought with Citrasena, the son of Karṇa), 472 (slew Citrasena), 475, 477, 486 (fought with Susheṇa and Satyasena, sons of Karṇa), 491, 494, 496 (slew Satyasena), 502, 503, 507, 510 (slew Susheṇa), 511; **11**, 561 (pierced Çalya); **13**ο, 661 (do.), 663 (pierced by Çalya), 677 (attacked Çalya), 680 (*°preritāṃ çaktiṃ*), 688; **15**, 764 (*Mādrīnandanaḥ*, rushed against Çalya), 765, 767, 771; **16**, 800; **17**, 893 (Çalya cut off the shaft of *N.*'s chariot—*ratheshāṃ*); **22**λλ, 1139 (pierced by Duryodhana), 1142 (pierced Duryodhana), 1157, 1158 (fought with Ulūka); **27**σσ, 1446; **28**, 1527 (pierced by Çakuni).—§ 613 (Gadāyuddhap.): IX, **32**β, 1882; **33**ϵ, 1890, 1900.—§ 617 (Aishīkap.): X, **10**, †568 (*N.* is sent to bring Draupadī to the camp); **11**, 577, 602.—§ 618 (Jalapradānikap.): XI, **14**ξ, 376; **15**ο, 393 (*hatāçve N°e Vṛshasenena*, all. to VIII, ch. **84**), 397 (*hatāçvaṃ N°ṃ Vṛshasenena*, do.).—§ 619 (Strīvilāpap.): XI, **18**γ, 540 (all. to Dyūtaparvan); **23**θ, 635 (*°mātulaḥ*, sc. Çalya).—§ 623 (Rājadh.): XII, **11**, 333, (335).—§ 637 (do.): XII, **40**, 1446; **41**, 1478 (appointed to supervise the army); **44**, 1526 (got the palace of Durmarshaṇa).—§ 656 (Khaḍgotpattik.): XII, **166**, 6120 (*b: N.* was an accomplished swordsman), (6121), 6128 (*b: N.* was the disciple of Droṇa), 6231, (6232) (*°-Sahadevau*).—§ 780 (Açvamedhikap.): XIV, **14**β, 356.—§ 783 (Anugītāp.): XIV, **52**ϵ, 1524.—§ 785 (do.): XIV, **66**μ, 1954; **72**, 2102, 2108 (together with Bhīma he protected the city during the horse-sacrifice); **85**, 2514.—§ 787 (Āçramavāsap.): XV, **16**, 455; **17**χ, 481.—§ 788 (do.): XV, **24**β, 646.—§ 793 (Mausalap.): XVI, **7**λ, 179.—§ 794 (Mahāprasthānikap.): XVII, **2**, 58, 59, 60, 61, 63 (on the Pāṇḍavas' mahāprasthāna *N.* fell down on account of his having boasted of his beauty); **3**, 92 (all. to § 548).—§ 795 (Svargārohaṇap.): XVIII, **2**ϵ, 67; **4**κ, 133 (in heaven). Cf. Āçvineya (dual), Açvinīsuta (dual), Açvisuta (dual), Ājamīḍha[3], Bhārata, Bharataçreshṭha, Bharatarshabha, Dāmagranthi, Granthika, Kuruçreshṭha, Mādravatīputra (dual), Mādravatīsuta (sg. and dual), Mādreya (sg. and dual), Mādrinandana (sg. and dual), Mādrinandanaka (dual), Mādrīputra (sg. and dual), Mādrīsuta (sg. and dual), Mādrītanūja (dual), Pāṇḍava (sg. and dual), Pāṇḍaveya, Pāṇḍunandana, Pāṇḍuputra, Pāṇḍusuta, Yama (dual), Yamaja (dual).

Nākula, pl. (*°āḥ*), a people. § 578 (Bhīshmavadhap.): VI, **50**π, 2084 (in the army of Yudhishṭhira).

Nakuladāyāda = Çatānīka, q.v.

Nakulākhyāna ("the narrative of the mungoose"). § 11 (Parvasaṅgr.): I, **2**, 609.—§ 786*b* (Anugītāparvan): At the conclusion of *Yudhishṭhira's* horse-sacrifice, after everybody had been gratified, a blue-eyed mungoose, with one side of its body changed into gold, came and said, in voice as loud and deep as thunder, that this great sacrifice was not equal to a *prastha* of powdered barley given away by a liberal brahman of *Kurukshetra*, who was observing the *uñcha-* (or the pigeon-)vow. Asked by the brahmans the mungoose related: The brahman named lived with his wife, son, and daughter-in-law, and practised penances; he used to eat every day at the sixth division; during a famine he had nothing to eat day after day; one day in the month of *Jyaishṭha*, while the sun was in the meridian, he was picking up grains of corn, but got nothing; one day, after the sixth division had come, he obtained a *prastha* of barley, which they reduced to powder for making *saktu*; having finished their recitations and libations, etc., they divided the powdered barley among themselves, so that each got a *kuḍava*; then came a guest, who ate all the portions, the wife, son, and daughter-in-law with difficulty prevailing upon the brahman to give their portions as well. The guest turned out to be *Dharma*; flowers were rained down from heaven; D.-ṛ, D., G., *Devadūtas*, etc., and B.-ṛ. standing in *vimānas* and dwelling in *Brahmaloka* were struck with wonder; "I have been rescued, and others who have not yet come (*anāgatāḥ*) have been rescued for countless *yugas*; he that gives away 100 having 1,000, 10 having 100, and a handful of water having no wealth, are equal in merit," citing *Rantideva* (*c*), *Nṛga* (*d*), and *Çibi Auçīnara*; "thou hast conquered *Brahmaloka*." The brahman, with his wife, son, and daughter-in-law, proceeded to heaven on a celestial chariot. The mungoose continued: "I came out of my hole, and by the contact with the powder of barley, etc., my head and half of my body became gold; in order to convert the rest of my body into gold I repeatedly repair to the hermitages of ascetics and to the sacrifices of kings; I came hither with high hopes, but I have not been made into gold." Then the mungoose disappeared (XIV, **90**).—That mungoose was *Dharma*, who having injured *Jamadagni* (*f*) had been cursed by the *Pitṛs*, but became freed from the curse by disparaging himself in the form of *Yudhishṭhira* (XIV, **92**).

Nakulānuja ("the younger brother of Nakula") = Sahadeva: II, 1121.

Nakulasya suta(ḥ), Nakulātmaja, Nākuli = Çatānīka, q.v.

Nala[1], king of the Nishadhas, son of Vīrasena, and husband of Damayantī. § 5 (Anukram.): I, **1a**, 224 (in Nārada's enumeration).—§ 6 (do.): I, **1a**, 229 (the same? in Sañjaya's enumeration).—§ 11 (Parvasaṅgr.): I, **2**, 436 (°*sya caritam*, i.e. Nalopākhyānaparvan).—§ 240 (Vaivāhikap.): I, **199**, 7351 (*Damayantī yathā N°e*).—§ 267 (Yamasabhāv.): II, **8**, 322 (in the palace of Yama).—§ 343 (Nalopākhyānap.): III, **52**, 2068 (son of the Nishadha king Vīrasena), 2071.—§ 344 (do.): III, **53**, 2072 (*Vīrasenasutaḥ*), 2086, 2087 (*Naishadhasya*), 2089, 2091, 2098, 2101, 2102.—§ 345 (do.): III, **54**, 2130, 2131, 2134; **55**, 2135, 2141, 2150, 2153, (2156); **56**, 2160, 2164, 2177, 2181, (2184); **57**, 2201, 2202, 2203, 2210, 2220, 2225, 2231, 2236 (in his marriage with Damayantī *N.* had the children Indrasena and Indrasenā).—§ 346 (do.): III, **58**, 2242, 2245, 2246, 2249, 2250, 2252; **59**, 2257, 2258, 2260, 2262, 2271; **60**, 2274, 2276, 2277, 2280, 2281, 2286, 2290, 2292 (°*sārathiḥ*, i.e. Vārshṇeya), 2295.—§ 347 (do.): III, **61**, 2301, 2304, 2308, 2311, 2320, (2326); **62**, (2333), 2335, 2340, 2349, 2350, 2357, 2358, 2360; **63**, 2362; **64**, 2410, 2419, 2429, 2430, 2433 (*Nishadhādhipateḥ*), 2434, 2435, 2450 (*Puṇyaçlokaḥ*), 2453, 2455, 2477 (*Nishadhādhipatiḥ*), 2480, 2485, 2487, 2488, 2492, 2495, 2504, 2513 (°*patnī*, i.e. Damayantī), 2524 (*Naishadhaḥ*), 2525, 2527; **65**, 2573.—§ 348 (do.): III, **66**, 2608, 2609, 2610, 2611, 2613, 2616, 2620, 2622, 2633.—§ 349 (do.): III, **67**, 2634 (*Naishadhaḥ*), 2641, 2645.—§ 350 (do.): III, **68**, 2654, 2655, 2657, 2659, 2673; **69**, 2695 (*Vīrasenasutaḥ*), 2722, 2727, 2741, 2742.—§ 351 (do.): III, **70**, 2745 (*Naishadham*), 2761, 2762, 2769; **71**, 2773, 2790, 2793, 2799, 2800, 2801, 2804.—§ 352 (do.): III, **72**, 2810, 2812, 2813, 2837, 2840 (*Nishadhādhipatiḥ*), 2845, 2850, 2851.—§ 353 (do.): III, **73**, 2854, 2855, 2856, 2860, 2886, 2887, 2888; **74**, 2892, 2900, 2902, 2903, 2904, 2905, 2912, 2919; **75**, 2921, 2939, 2944; **76**, 2952, 2953, 2956, 2957, 2958, 2961 (*Puṇyaçlokam*), 2975, 2991, 2996, 2999, 3002, 3003, 3005; **77**, 3009, 3010, 3012, 3014, 3016, 3017, (3022), 3028.—§ 354 (do.): III, **78**, 3033, 3046, 3047, 3048, 3055; **79**, 3065.—§ 355 (do.): III, **79**, 3068, 3069, 3072, 3077 (°*sya caritam*, i.e. Nalopākhyānaparvan (III, ch. **53-79**)).—§ 391 (Ṛshyaçṛṅga): III, **113**, 10092 (°*sya vai Damayantī yathā*).—§ 552 (Goharaṇap.): IV, **56**ζ, 1769 (came in Indra's chariot to see the encounter).—§ 565 (Gālavacarita): V, **117**, 3974 (*reme . . . yathā . . . Damayantyāṃ N°ḥ*).—§ 608 (Karṇap.): VIII, **91**, †4761 (all. to Nalopākhyānaparvan; C. has by error *Nelā* instead of *Nalo*).—§ 761 (Ānuçāsanik.): XIII, **115**δ, 5666 (among the kings who abstained from meat during the month of Kārttika).—§ 775 (do.): XIII, **166**η, 7083 (enumeration).

Cf. also the following synonyms:—

Naishadha ("king of the Nishadhas"): I, 229 (*N°*); III, 2087, 2092, 2133, 2137, 2143, 2144, 2149, 2172, 2189, 2207, 2213, 2216, 2217, 2225, 2226, 2227, 2228, 2232, 2239, 2254 (*rājā*), 2256, 2266, 2267, 2288, 2303, 2321, 2363, 2370, 2377, 2383, 2385, 2386, 2399, 2458, 2492, 2524 (*N°*), 2618, 2634 (*N°*), 2652 (*rājā*), 2659, 2676, 2678, 2695 (*rājā . . . Vīrasenasuto Nalaḥ*), 2745, 2846, 2847 (*rājā*), 2862, 2866, 2886, 2888, 2889, 2903, 2947, 2979, 3018, 3019, 3020, 3026, 3030, 3040, 3041, 3043, 3056, 8322; XIII, 3689.

Nishadhādhipa (do.): III, 2209, 2337, 2352, 2427, 2656, 2976, 3061.

Nishadhādhipati (do.): III, 2309, 2433 (°*er bhāryāṃ*, i.e. Damayantī), 2477 (*N°*), 2840 (*N°*), 3027.

Nishadharājendra (do.): III, 2134.

Nishadheçvara (do.): III, 2628.

Puṇyaçloka: III, 2212, 2215, 2233, 2271, 2272, 2280, 2300, 2313, 2450 (*N°*), 2609 (*N°*), 2695, 2726, 2805 (°*sya sārathiḥ*, i.e. Vārshṇeya), 2868, 2900 (°*sya vai suto Vārshṇeya iti viçrutaḥ*), 2939, 2951, 2961, 2998, 3056.

Vīrasenasuta ("the son of Vīrasena"): III, 601, 2072 (*N°*), 2220, 2466, 2695 (*Naishadhaḥ . . . N°ḥ*), 3033 (*N°*).

Nala[2], a monkey. § 535 (Setubandhana): III, **283**β, 16287 (among the allies of Rāma Dāçarathi), 16309 (son of Tvashṭṛ), 16311 (Rāma caused him to construct a bridge to Laṅkā), 16313 (°*setuḥ*).—§ 537 (Rāma-Rāvaṇayuddha): III, **285**β, 16372 (fought with the Rākshasa Tuṇḍa).—§ 541 (Indrajidvadha): III, **289a**, 16468.—§ 542 (Rāvaṇavadha): III, **290a**, 16500.

Nālā, a river. § 574 (Jambūkh.): VI, **9**λ, 339 (so C., but B. has *Nīlāṃ*).

Nalakānana, pl. (°*āḥ*), a people. § 574 (Jambūkh.): VI, **9**ν, 367 (in the south).

Nalakūbara (C. °*kūv*°), a son of Kubera. § 269 (Vaiçravaṇasabhāv.): II, **10**, 400 (in the palace of Kubera).—§ 525 (Rāmopākhyānap.): III, **274**, 15887 (son of Kubera).—§ 532*b* (cf. Sītāsāntvana). *N.* cursed Rāvaṇa, who had ravished Rambhā, the spouse of *N.*, that he should never be able to violate an unwilling woman: III, **280**, 16151 (°*çāpena*). — § 543 (Rāmābhisheka): III, **291**, 16563 (°*çāpena*, cf. § 532*b*).—§ 615*x* (Kubera): IX, **47**, 2757 (son of Kubera).

Nalinī, a river. § 459 (Mārkaṇḍeyas.): III, **188a**, 12908 (among the rivers seen in the stomach of Nārāyaṇa).—§ 574*f* (Bindusaras): VI, **6**η, 243 (one of the seven rivers into which the Gaṅgā divided herself). Cf. next.

nalinī, said of Kubera's lotus-tank. I, 453; III, 11351, 12347-8; VII, 2846; XIII, 1412. Cf. the prec.

Nalopākhyāna ("the episode relating to Nala"), i.e. Nalopākhyānaparvan.—§ 10 (Parvasaṅgr.): I, **2**, 321.—§ 11 (do.): I, **2**, 436.

[Nalopakhyānaparvan(°va)] ("the episode relating to Nala," the 35th of the minor parvans of the Mahābhārata; cf. Nalopākhyāna).—§ 343: One day, when the *Pāṇḍavas* were grieving for *Arjuna*, *Bhīma* asked *Yudhishṭhira* to permit him to go and slay *Duryodhana*, interpreting the time to be complete ("as in the *Veda* a day is often equivalent to a year, when passed in suffering") (*kṛcchrataḥ*), but he did not prevail upon *Yudhishṭhira*. While they were conversing the great *ṛshi Bṛhadaçva* came before them, and, asked by *Yudhishṭhira* if there was on earth a king more unfortunate than himself, he said that he would narrate a history of a prince more miserable than *Yudhishṭhira*, viz. *Nala* (the son of the *Nishadha* king *Vīrasena*), who, defeated deceitfully by *Pushkara* (the brother of *Nala*, v. 2296), dwelt in the woods with his spouse, having neither slaves nor chariots nor brothers nor friends with him (III, **52**).—§ 344: *Bṛhadaçva* said: The *Nishadha* king *Nala*, the son of *Vīrasena*, was above all kings, etc., and fond of dice.

The *Vidarbha* king *Bhīma* was granted by the *Brahmarshi Damana* a daughter, *Damayantī*, and three excellent sons, *Dama*, *Dānta*, and *Damana*. Both *Nala* and *Damayantī* had not their equals in beauty, and, continually hearing of each other's virtues, they conceived attachment to each other, though they had never seen each other. Once *Nala* in his garden saw a number of golden-winged swans and caught one of them, but let it loose, as it promised to speak well of him before *Damayantī*. The swans having arrived at the *Vidarbha* country, the one who had been caught by *Nala* led *Damayantī* to a secluded spot and fulfilled its mission. *Damayantī* caused it to speak to *Nala* of her (III, **53**).—§ 345: As *Damayantī* became sick of love, her father invited all the kings to her *svayaṃvara*. At this time the *ṛshis* of the gods *Nārada* and *Parvata*, having arrived in course of their wanderings at the regions of *Indra*, told him that the kings did not now come to him because they were intent on the *svayaṃvara* of *Damayantī*. Hearing this, the *Lokapālas* set out on their vehicles for the *svayaṃvara*, but seeing *Nala* on the way and filled with astonishment at his beauty, they left their chariots in the sky and asked *Nala* to be their messenger (III, **54**). *Nala* promised to do so, but when *Indra* told him to go to *Damayantī* and tell her that *Indra*, *Agni*, *Varuṇa*, and *Yama* desired her to choose one of them for her lord, he asked them to spare him as he had come with the same object; but, as they insisted that he should stand by his promise, he by their power entered without being perceived by the guardians into the apartments of *Damayantī*, and, saying his name, fulfilled his mission (III, **55**). *Damayantī* declared that if she did not become the wife of *Nala* himself she would resort to poison, or fire, or water, or the rope. *Nala* advised her to choose one of the gods, maintaining that having come in a different mission he dared not seek his own interest. *Damayantī* then told him to come to her *svayaṃvara* in company with the gods, then she would choose him, at which no blame would be his, and *Nala* returned to the *Lokapālas* and told them what had happened (III, **56**). At the sacred hour of the holy lunar day of the auspicious season *Bhīma* summoned the kings to the *svayaṃvara*, and that assembly of kings resembled the *Bhogavatī* swarming with *Nāgas*. *Damayantī*, beholding five persons all alike in appearance, and recollecting the marks of the celestials, of which she had heard from old people, was unable to distinguish which of them was *Nala*. Filled with grief, she then decided upon seeking the protection of the gods themselves, and prevailed upon them that they assumed their true shapes. Thereupon she beheld the gods unmoistened with perspiration, with unwinking eyes and unfading garlands, not stained with dust, and staying without touching the ground, while *Nala* was revealed by his shadow, his fading garlands, and by his being stained with dust and sweat, and resting on the ground with winking eyes. She then chose *Nala*, seizing the hem of his garment and placing a floral wreath round his neck. *Nala* promised *Damayantī* that he would remain hers as long as he lived, and she spoke words of like import to him. The *Lokapālas* bestowed each a couple of boons on *Nala*: *Indra*, that he should be able to behold his divine nature in sacrifices, and blessed regions thereafter (*gatim anuttamāṃ*); *Agni*, his own presence wherever he wished and regions as bright as himself; *Yama*, subtle taste in food and pre-eminence in virtue; *Varuṇa*, water wherever he desired and garlands of celestial fragrance. Then the gods went to heaven and the kings returned home. *Nala*, after the wedding, stayed there for a time, returned home, ruled righteously, and celebrated the horse-sacrifice, etc. He begat the son *Indrasena* and the daughter *Indrasenā* upon *Damayantī* (III, **57**).—§ 346: When the *Lokapālas* were returning they met *Dvāpara* with *Kali* going to the *svayaṃvara*, and *Indra* told *Kali* that *Damayantī* had already chosen *Nala*. As *Kali* threatened to avenge himself he was rebuked by the *Lokapālas*, as *Nala* had studied the four *Vedas* with the *Ākhyāna* as the fifth, etc. When the gods had gone to heaven, *Kali* said that he would take possession of *Nala* and deprive him of his kingdom, and asked *Dvāpara* to enter the dice (III, **58**). *Kali* then went to the country of the *Nishadhas* and always watched for an opportunity. At last, in the twelfth year, when *Nala*, after answering a call of nature, touching water had said his twilight prayers without having washed his feet, *Kali* entered his person. Then *Kali* becoming *Vṛsha* ("*vṛsho gavāṃ*," the principal die, Nīl.) (PCR. thinks we ought to read that "*Dvāpara* also approached *Pushkara* becoming *Vṛsha*") prevailed upon *Pushkara*, that he challenged *Nala* to a match of dice in order to acquire his kingdom. *Nala* and *Pushkara* gambled together for many months, *Nala* being always worsted; no one amongst his friends could succeed in dissuading him from the play; at last they came in a body, which was told by the *sūta* to *Damayantī*, who in vain represented it to *Nala*; he uttered not a word in reply (III, **59**). Seeing that *Nala* had lost everything, *Damayantī* told her nurse and maidservant *Bṛhatsenā* to summon the councillors in the name of *Nala* and tell them what had been lost; the councillors approached *Nala*, and *Damayantī* informed him that the citizens had come again in a body, but he regarded her not. She then caused *Bṛhatsenā* to summon the *sūta Vārshṇeya*, who at her request yoked *Nala's* favourite horses and brought her two children to *Kuṇḍina* (the city of *Bhīma*, Nīl.). There he left the children, the chariot, and the horses, and went to *Ayodhyā*, where he entered the service of king *Ṛtuparṇa* (the king of *Koçala*, v. 2877) as a charioteer (III, **60**).—§ 347: At last, when *Pushkara* had won all *Nala's* wealth and his kingdom, he proposed to him to stake *Damayantī*. But *Nala*, feeling as if his heart would burst and gazing at *Pushkara* in anguish without speaking a word, took all the ornaments off his body, and attired in a single piece of cloth left the city accompanied by *Damayantī*. They stayed for three nights in the outskirts of the city, living on water alone. Nobody showed him hospitable regards, as *Pushkara* had proclaimed through the city that he that should show any attention to *Nala* would be put to death. After many days *Nala* saw some birds of golden hue and covered them with his cloth in order to catch them, but they rose up to the sky taking away that garment of his, and then told him they were the dice that had come hither to take away even his cloth. *Nala* proposed to *Damayantī* to leave him, pointing out to her the roads to *Avantī*, *Ṛkshavat*, *Vindhya*, *Payoshṇī*, *Vidarbha*, *Koçala* (C. *Koçalāṃ*, B. and Bopp *Koçalān*), and the south. But she would not leave him, but suggested that they should go to *Vidarbha* (III, **61**). *Nala* refused to appear before *Bhīma* in his state of misery. They went on attired in the same piece of cloth. Once when *Damayantī* had fallen into a profound slumber in a shed for travellers (*sabhā*), *Nala*, influenced by *Kali*, resolved upon deserting *Damayantī*, as separated from him she might perchance wander to her relatives. With a sword that he found near the shed he cut off one half of the cloth and throwing the instrument away departed, having first returned again and again, dragged away by *Kali*, but drawn back by love (III, **62**). When *Damayantī* awoke, she lamented and cursed the being through whose imprecation *Nala* suffered woe, saying that it should lead a still more miserable life. Thereupon, wandering on, she was seized by a gigantic serpent and rescued by a hunter; as the hunter, after comforting her, tried to force her to love him, he was cursed by her and fell down lifeless upon the ground (III, **63**). Description of the forest, *Damayantī's* lamentations. She went in a northerly direction for three days and nights, then she came to an asylum of ascetics, who told her that she should again become happy together with *Nala*. Then the asylum disappeared. Sometime afterwards, having proceeded a long way, she met with a body of merchants landing on the banks of a river; its leader was *Çuci* (v. 2529, "so help us now, *Maṇibhadra*, the king of *Yakshas*"), and it was bound for the city of the *Cedi* king *Subāhu* (III, **64**). *Damayantī* followed the caravan. Once, at midnight, the caravan was destroyed by wild elephants and many men were trodden to death, which some ascribed to their not having worshipped *Maṇibhadra* or *Vaiçravaṇa*, the kings of *Yakshas*, others to their having received *Damayantī*, whom they thought to be a *Rākshasa* or *Piçāca* or *Yaksha* woman, and resolved upon killing her when they saw her. Hearing this *Damayantī* fled. The next day the remnant of the caravan left the place. *Damayantī*, with the brahmans that had survived the slaughter of the caravan, came towards evening to the city of the *Cedi* king *Subāhu*. The boys began to follow her; when she came before the palace of the king, the queen-mother let the nurse take her in. *Damayantī* agreed to stay there on the conditions that she should not eat remnants, not wash anyone's feet, nor speak with other men, but be protected against all aspirations. The queen gave her as a *sairindhrī* to her daughter *Sunandā* (III, **65**).—§ 348: *Nala*, having deserted *Damayantī*, saw a conflagration in the forest and therefrom heard a voice calling him by name and saw the *Nāga Karkoṭaka*, who, unable to stir, told him that he had deceived the great ṛshi *Narada* and been cursed by him with the words: "Stay thou here immobile until *Nala* takes thee hence, then thou shalt be freed from my curse," and asked him to deliver him and promised to instruct him in respect of his welfare. The snake then became as small as a thumb, and *Nala* taking him up went to a spot free from fire. *Karkoṭaka* let him proceed yet counting his steps, and bit him at the tenth step (*adaçad daçame pade*) (see Nīl. and PCR.). Then the form of *Nala* was changed, in order that people might not recognize him, and *Karkoṭaka* assumed his own form, and said that *Kali* dwelling in *Nala* should be tortured by his venom, and that *Nala* should have no fear from animals with fangs, from enemies, and from men versed in the Veda (*brahmavidbhyaḥ*), and told him to go to *Ayodhyā* and present himself as a *sūta Bāhuka* before *Ṛtuparṇa* (of the race of *Ikshvāku*), who would give *Nala* his skill in dice (*akshahṛdaya*) in exchange for *Nala's* knowledge of horses (*açvahṛdaya*), and when he had become an adept at dice he should have prosperity and meet with his wife and children and regain his kingdom. The *Nāga* king then gave *Nala* two pieces of celestial cloth, saying that when he desired to get back his own form he should remember him and wear this garment. Then he disappeared (III, **66**).—§ 349: On the tenth day *Nala* entered the city of *Ṛtuparṇa*; he approached the king and named himself *Bāhuka*, and said that he surpassed everybody in managing steeds and might be consulted in matters of difficulty (*arthakṛcchreshu*) and affairs of skill (*naipuṇeshu*), and that he was versed in the art of cooking. Then he was appointed superintendent of *Ṛtuparṇa's* horses on a pay of 10,000, and *Vārshṇeya* and *Jīvala* should be under his direction. Every evening he recited the çloka, "Where lies that helpless one (*tapasvinī*) afflicted with hunger and thirst and worn with toil (*çrāntā*), or upon whom does she now wait (*upatishṭhati*)?" Once *Jīvala* asked him who she was, and *Nala* related to him the main features of his story without naming her or himself (III, **67**).—§ 350: *Bhīma* sent out brahmans in all directions to search for *Nala* and *Damayantī*, promising 1,000 kine, etc., to him that should find them. At length the brahman *Sudeva*, the friend of *Damayantī's* brother, recognized *Damayantī* in the city of the *Cedis*, seated with *Sunandā* during the time of the king's prayers (*puṇyāhavācane rājñaḥ*), and told her who he was and that her relatives and children were well. Beholding *Damayantī* weeping and conversing in private with *Sudeva*, *Sunandā* caused her mother to question *Sudeva* (III, **68**). *Sudeva* told the story of *Damayantī*, and that he had recognized her by a mole between her eyebrows, which was now almost covered with dust as her whole body. Then *Sunandā* washed away the dust and the queen-mother recognized her by the mole as the daughter of her sister, as she and *Damayantī's* mother were both daughters of the *Daçārṇa* king *Sudāman*, and she herself had been bestowed on *Vīrabāhu* and her sister on *Bhīma*; she had witnessed *Damayantī's* birth in the palace of her father in the Daçārṇa country. At her own request *Damayantī* was brought in a litter carried by men and protected by a large escort to the city of *Bhīma*, and was received with respect and worshipped the gods and brahmans. *Bhīma* gave unto *Sudeva* 1,000 kine, etc. The next day *Damayantī* let her mother cause *Bhīma* to send brahmans out in all directions to seek for *Nala*. *Damayantī* ordered them everywhere to recite the *çlokas*: "O beloved gambler, where hast thou gone, cutting off half of my garment," etc., but to take care that no one knew that it was on her command (III, **69**).—§ 351: After a long time the brahman *Parṇāda* told that he had in *Ayodhyā* visited *Bhaṅgāsuri* (i.e. *Ṛtuparṇa*), and that *Bāhuka* had been affected by hearing his *çloka*, and had said to him: "Chaste women, though overtaken by calamity, yet protect themselves," etc. *Damayantī* then thanked *Parṇāda* and promised him great wealth and consulted with her mother, and, without *Bhīma's* knowing it, sent *Sudeva*, who told *Ṛtuparṇa* that to-morrow *Damayantī* would hold another *svayamvara* (III, **70**) When ordered by *Ṛtuparṇa* to conduct him to the *svayaṃvara* of *Damayantī*, *Bāhuka* felt his heart bursting with grief, but promised to go there in a single day; he yoked four horses born in *Sindhu* (description of their marks), made *Vārshṇeya* sit on the chariot, and set out with so great speed that *Vārshṇeya* thought he must be *Mātali* or *Çālihotra*, who had taken a human shape, or *Nala* (III, **71**).—§ 352: As the chariot was coursing thus, *Ṛtuparṇa* lost his upper garment, and *Nala* declared that it was impossible to recover it, as they had already travelled one *yojana* thence. As *Ṛtuparṇa* rightly indicated the number of fruits of a *vibhītaka*-tree (*Terminalia bellerica*), and said he was skilled in dice as in numbers, *Nala* prevailed upon him to teach him the science and in future receive instead his science of horses. Then *Kali* came out from the body of *Nala*, vomiting the poison of *Karkoṭaka*, and assumed his own shape, as the fire of *Damayantī's* curse had left him, but remained invisible to others except *Nala*. *Kali* prevailed upon *Nala* that he should not curse him, promising that those men who would attentively recite his history should be free from fear of him, and entered the *vibhītaka*-tree till *Nala* had gone far away. Then *Kali* returned to his abode. From the touch of *Kali* the *vibhītaka*-tree from that hour fell into disrepute. *Nala* now became free from calamity, though he did not assume his original form (III, **72**).—§ 353: At night they arrived at *Kuṇḍina*, having passed 100 *yojanas*. The steeds of *Nala* that were in that city, and peacocks and elephants and *Damayantī* recognized the sound of *Nala's* chariot; *Damayantī* ascended the terrace with the desire of seeing *Nala*. The *Koçala* king (*Ṛtuparṇa*) wondered, as he did not hear any talk of the *svayaṃvara*, etc., and *Bhīma* thought that he had come simply to pay his respects. When *Ṛtuparṇa* had gone to his appointed quarters with *Vārshṇeya*, and *Bāhuka*, having tended the horses, was sitting at the side of the chariot, *Damayantī* sent a female messenger in search of *Nala* (III, **73**). The female messenger *Keçinī* asked *Bāhuka* about *Vārshṇeya* and himself; he said that *Vārshṇeya* was the charioteer of *Nala*, that nobody knew *Nala* except *Nala* himself and his wife, as he did not discover his marks of identity anywhere, and that he himself was the charioteer and cook of king *Ṛtuparṇa*; at last she repeated the *çloka* of *Parṇāda*: "O beloved gambler," etc., and said that *Damayantī* wished again to hear the reply he had given *Parṇāda*; then *Bāhuka*, weeping, said: "Chaste women, though overtaken by calamity," etc., and *Keçinī* went to *Damayantī* and acquainted her with everything (III, **74**). *Damayantī* again sent *Keçinī* to stay in silence at *Bāhuka's* side and mark his conduct; she related that low passages grew in height so that he might pass through them easily, that when he approached narrow holes opened wide, that only by his looking upon them the vessels became filled with water, that when he held a handful of grass in the sun the fire blazed up all of a sudden, that he touched fire and was not hurt, that water falling at his will flowed in a stream, and that flowers pressed with his hands became gayer and more fragrant than before. *Damayantī* then caused *Keçinī* without *Bāhuka's* knowledge to bring her some meat that had been boiled and dressed by him, from the kitchen, and recognized the taste. She then sent her two children with *Keçinī*. *Bāhuka* embraced them crying aloud, saying they were like his own children, and sent *Keçinī* away lest people might think "evil" (III, **75**). Having obtained the consent both of her father and mother, *Damayantī* caused *Nala* to be brought to her apartments; it came to an explication; *Damayantī* declared that she had feigned to hold a second *svayaṃvara* because no one except *Nala* could in one day manage 100 *yojanas* with horses, and swore by the Air, Sun, and Moon ("who dwells as a witness within every creature," v. 2989), who had been her protector for these three years, and *Vāyu* bore witness to the truth of her words. Then a floral shower fell there, and the celestial kettledrum began to play. *Nala* then wore the garment he had received from the serpent king and regained his old form. Thus *Nala* in the fourth year was reunited with his wife (III, **76**). The next day they presented themselves before *Bhīma*. The citizens were in great joy and adorned (*arcitāni*) the temples (*devatāyatanāni*), etc. *Ṛtuparṇa* asked *Nala's* forgiveness, and *Nala* also asked *Ṛtuparṇa's* forgiveness, and made over to him his horse-lore, having obtained from him the mystery of dice. Then *Ṛtuparṇa* went away to his own city, employing another person as his charioteer (III, **77**).—§ 354: Having dwelt for a month at *Kuṇḍina*, *Nala* set out for the *Nishadha* country with a single white chariot, sixteen elephants, fifty horses, and 600 infantry, and proposed to *Pushkara* that they should gamble again, as *Nala* had won great wealth; the stake should be *Damayantī*, wealth and kingdom, and their lives; if not, he proposed a single combat. *Pushkara*, hoping to win *Damayantī*, whom he loved, gladly consented to gamble, and lost at a single throw. *Nala*, declaring that it was *Kali* who had done it all, forgave his brother and granted him his portion, and after a month let him go to his own town. All the citizens and subjects rejoiced at *Nala's* return (III, **78**). Then *Nala* with a large force brought *Damayantī* and his children home, and passed his days in joy and performed numerous sacrifices with abundant gifts to brahmans.—§ 355: "So thou also, O *Yudhishṭhira*, wilt blaze forth in effulgence soon. They that will repeatedly recite this history of *Nala* and they that will hear it recited will never be touched by adversity." As *Yudhishṭhira* feared that some one skilled in dice might summon him, *Bṛhadaçva* taught him the science of dice (*akshahṛdaya*) and then went to *Açvaçiras* for a bathe. *Yudhishṭhira* then learnt from brahmans and ascetics from various directions that *Arjuna* was still engaged in ascetic penances, and *Yudhishṭhira* grieved for him (III, **79**).

Nāmanāmika = Mahāpurusha (Mahāpurushastava).

Namas, Namaskāra = Çiva (1000 names[1]).

Namuci, an Asura, slain by Indra. § 17 (Uttaṅka): I, **3**, 810 (°*er nihantā*, i.e. Indra).—§ 92 (Aṃçāvat.): I, **65**, 2530 (son of Danu).—§ 258 (Khāṇḍavadahanap.): I, **228**, 8328 (°*er bhrātaraṃ Mayaṃ*).—§ 297 (Dyūtap.): II, **55**, 1957 (*adrohasamayaṃ kṛtvā ciccheda N°eḥ çiras Çakraḥ*, cf. § 615*s*). § 323 (Dvaitavanapraveçap.): III, **25**, †954 (°*eç ca hantā*, i.e. Indra ?).—§ 441 (Nivātakavacayuddhap.): III, **165**, †11909 (°*er nihantā*, i.e. Indra).—§ 443 (do.): III, **168**, 12073 (had been defeated by Indra). — § 544 (Yudhishṭhirāçvāsa): III, **292**, 16605 (had been slain by Indra).—§ 555 (Indravijaya): V, **16**, 497 (*mahāsuro hataḥ, Çakra, N°ir dāruṇo tvayā*).—§ 584 (Bhīshmavadhap.): VI, **83**, 3678 (*prādravad bhayāt yathendrasya raṇāt pūrvaṃ N°ir Daityasattamaḥ*).—§ 585 (do.): VI, **88**, 3903 (*vivyādha . . . N°ṃ Vṛtrahā yathā*).—§ 605 (Karṇap.): VIII, **26**, 1057 (*trāsayām āsa Mahendro N°ṃ yathā*).—§ 608 (do.): VIII, **85**, †4333 (*yathā Mahendraṃ N°iḥ purā*, sc. *abhyāpatat*), †4334 (*viddhveva Çakraṃ N°iḥ*); **86**, 4363 (*jahi . . . N°ṃ Vṛtrahā yathā*); **89**, †4569 (*Çakro Namucer ivāreḥ*); **90**, †4700 (°*iṃ yathā Hariḥ*, sc. *vidhya*).—§ 610 (Çalyap.): IX, **7**, 358 (*jahi . . . Vāsavo N°iṃ yathā*).—§ 611 (do.): IX, **17**, †885 (*vivyādha . . . yathā Mahendro N°iṃ*).—§ 615*s* (Indra): IX, **43**, 2433, 2434, 2437, 2445 (Indra broke his agreement with *N.* and slew him).—§ 641 (Rājadh.): XII, **98**ξ, 3661 (had been slain by Indra).—§ 656 (Khaḍgotpattik.): XII, **166**γ, 6146 (among the foremost of the Dānavas).—§ 659 (Mokshadh.): XII, **180***a*, 6692.—§ 672*b* (Çakra-Namucisaṃv.): XII, **226**, 8187 (*Çatakratoç ca saṃvādaṃ*

N°eç ca), 8189, (8190) (discourse between Indra and *N.*).—§ 673*b* (Bali-Vāsavasaṃv.): XII, **227*a*,** 8262 (among the ancient rulers of the earth).—§ 742 (Ānuçāsanik.): XIII, **39*a*,** 2237 (*māyā N°eḥ*).—§ 778*b* (Saṃvartta-Maruttīya): XIV, **5,** 114 (*°eḥ . . . nihantā*, i.e. Indra). Cf. Asura, Asuraçreshṭha, Daityasattama.

Namucighna ("the slayer of Namuci") = Indra: I, 1286.

Namucihan (do.) = Indra: I, 8231.

Nanda[1], a son of Dhṛtarāshṭra. § 130 (Aṃçāvat.): I, **67,** 2731 (*°opanandakau*, enumeration).—§ 182 (Dhṛtarāshṭra-putranāmak.): I, **117,** 4544 (do., do.).—§ 578 (Bhīshmavadhap.): VI, **51***σ*, 2098 (*°opanandakaiḥ*).—§ 608 (Karṇap.): VIII, **51** *δδ*, 2446 (*°opanandakau*, among several sons of Dhṛtarāshṭra who attacked Bhīmasena), 2458 (*°opanandau*, slain by Bhīmasena). Cf. Nandaka[1].

Nanda[2], a drum in Yudhishṭhira's standard. § 522 (Draupadīharaṇap.): III, **270,** †15700 (*mṛdaṅgau N°opanandau*).—§ 592 (Saṃçaptakavadhap.): VII, **23***π*, 1032 (*mṛdaṅgau . . . N°opanandakau*).

Nanda[3], a cowherd. § 549*f* (Durgā): IV, **6,** 179 (*°gopālakule jātām*, sc. Durgā (Umā)).—§ 576 (Bhagavadgītāp.): VI, **23,** 799 (*°gopākulodbhave*, sc. Durgā (Umā)).

Nanda[4], a serpent. § 564 (Mātalīyop.): V, **103***γ*, 3628 (*°opanandakau*, enumeration).

Nanda[5], two warriors of Skanda. § 615*u* (Skanda): IX, **45***η*, 2566, 2567.

Nanda[6] = Vishṇu (1000 names).

Nandā[1] ("joy"), wife of Harsha. § 117 (Aṃçāvat.): I, **66,** 2597.

Nandā[2], a river. § 249 (Arjunavanavāsap.): I, **215,** 7818 (*°m Aparanandāñ ca*, visited by Arjuna).—§ 370 (Tīrthayātrāp.): III, **84,** 8137 (only C., B has *Prānnadīm*).—§ 377 (Dhaumyatīrthak.): III, **87,** 8323 (in the east).—§ 390 (Tīrthayātrāp.): III, **110,** 9968 (*°m Aparanandāñ ca*, visited by Yudhishṭhira, etc.).—§ 390*b* (Hemakūṭa): III, **110,** 9979.—§ 390 (Tīrthayātrāp.): III, **110,** 9987.—§ 594 (Mṛtyu): VII, **54,** 2092, 2093 (visited by Mṛtyu).—§ 775 (Ānuçāsanik.): XIII, **166*a*,** 7654 (enumeration).

Nandāçrama, a sacred place. § 573 (Ambopākhyānap.): V, **186*a*,** 7353 (visited by Ambā).

Nandaka[1], a son of Dhṛtarāshṭra. § 232 (Svayaṃvarap.): I, **186,** 6983 (present at the svayaṃvara of Draupadī).—§ 581 (Bhīshmavadhap.): VI, **64**[12], 2818 (*tava*—i.e. Dhṛtarāshṭra's—*putraḥ*, attacked Bhīmasena), 2821 (pierced by Bhīmasena). § 600 (Ghaṭotkacavadhap.): VII, **166,** 7455 (*ratham . . . N°sya*). Cf. Nanda[1].

Nandaka[2], a serpent. § 564 (Mātalīyop.): V, **103***γ*, 3627 (enumeration).

Nandaka[3], the sword of Kṛshṇa (v. BR.). § 567 (Bhagavadyānap.): V, **131,** 4427.

Nandaka[4], a warrior of Skanda. § 615*u* (Skanda): IX, **45***η*, 2570.

Nandakin ("armed with the sword Nandaka") = Vishṇu (1000 names).

Nandana[1], a celestial forest. § 133 (Dushyanta): I, **69,** 2830 (*°pratimaṃ vanam*); **70,** 2877 (*vanaṃ N°prakhyam*).—§ 148 (Yayāti): I, **85,** 3508 (*vane*, Yayāti sported with Viçvācī in *N.*).—§ 149 (do.): I, **89,** †3595 (Yayāti lived for a hundred ayutas of years in *N.*), †3597; **90,** †3600.—§ 269 (Vaiçravaṇasabhāv.): II, **10,** 390 (*°sya vanasya*, sc. *gandham*, in the palace of Kubera).—§ 336 (Indralokābhigamanap.): III, **43,** 1758 (*°ñ ca vanaṃ divyam Apsarogaṇasevitam*, Arjuna came to *N.*).—§ 354 (Nalopākhyānap.): III, **79,** 3065 (*Devarāḍ iva N°e*).—§ 422*bis* (Varāhāvatāra): III, **142,** 10958 (Vishṇu dwelt in *N.*).—§ 436*b* (Gandhamādana): III, **158,** 11563 (*Gandhamādanavanaṃ tan N°vanopamam*).—§ 443 (Nivātakavacayuddhap.): III, **168,** 12035 (*°ādīni devānāṃ vanāni*).—§ 449 (Ājagarap.): III, **177,** 12348 (*remire N°vāsam etya dvijarshayo vītamalā yathaiva*).—§ 520 (Mudgala): III, **261,** 15449 (*°ādīni puṇyāni vihārāḥ puṇyakarmaṇām*).—§ 532 (Sītāsāntvana): III, **280,** 16133 (*bharane N°opame*).—§ 555 (Indravijaya): V, **11*a*,** 352 (*°opavaneshu ca*, there Nahusha sported).—§ 594 (Akampana): VII, **54,** 2127 (Nārada went to *N.*).—§ 658*b* (Kṛtaghnop.): XII, **169,** 6323 (*°oddeçasadṛçam*, sc. *vanam*).—§ 717*b* (Nārāyaṇīya): XII, **343,** VII), ††13209 (*°vanam*, Viçvarūpa dwelt there).—§ 733*u* (Punarāvartanandā): XIII, **25*a*,** 1731 (having bathed in Punarāvartanandā, etc., one after death repairs to *N.*).—§ 757*f* (Hastikūṭa): *Gautama* said: The flowering forest *N.* (differently PCR.) is favoured by the *Kinnara* king and always dear to *Nārada*, the *Gandharvas*, and the *Apsarases*. Dhṛtarāshṭra said: This region (*lokaḥ*) is for those who never solicit alms, who cultivate music and dancing, and rove about together: XIII, **102,** 4865 (*vanam*).—§ 768*b* (Umā-Maheçvarasaṃv.): XIII, **145,** 6688 (*°ādishu*).—§ 781 (Açvamedhikap.): XIV, **15,** 375 (*Açvināv iva N°e*).

Nandana[2], a companion of Skanda. § 615*u* (Skanda): IX, **45***c*, 2540 (given to Skanda by the Açvins).

Nandana[3] = Çiva (1000 names[2]).

Nandana[4] = Vishṇu (1000 names).

Nandi[1], a Devagandharva. § 191 (Arjuna): I, **123,** 4812 (sung at the birth of Arjuna).

Nandi[2], a follower of Çiva. § 730*g* (Upamanyu): XIII, **14,** 872 (*purastāc ca devasya . . . dvitīyam iva Çaṅkaram*). Cf. Nandīçvara, Nandin.

Nandi[3] = Çiva (1000 names[2]).

Nandi[4] = Vishṇu (1000 names).

Nandīçvara[1], a follower of Çiva. § 269 (Vaiçravaṇasabhāv.): II, **10,** 414 (in the palace of Kubera). Cf. Nandi, Nandin.

Nandīçvara[2] = Çiva, q.v.

Nandigrāma, a city. § 527 (Rāmopākhyānap.): III, **277,** 15983 (there Bharata, the son of Daçaratha, kept the realm for his brother Rāma).—§ 543 (Rāmābhisheka): III, **291,** 16592 (do.).

Nandikara = Çiva (1000 names[2]).

Nandikuṇḍa, a tīrtha. § 733 (Kālodaka): XIII, **25,** 1746.

Nandimukha = Çiva (1000 names[1]).

Nandin[1], a follower of Çiva. § 601 (Jvarotpatti): XII, **284,** 10223, 10239. Cf. Nandi, Nandīçvara.

Nandin[2] = Çiva (1000 names[2]).

Nandin[3] = Vishṇu (1000 names).

Nandinī[1], the cow of Vasishṭha: § 164 (Āpavop.): I, **99,** 3933 (daughter of Surabhi and Kaçyapa).—§ 223 (Vāsishṭha): I, **175,** 6663, 6664, 6665, 6669, 6670, 6672, 6673, 6675, (6677).

Nandinī[2], a tīrtha. § 370 (Tīrthayātrāp.): III, **84,** 8133 (bathing there one acquires the merit of a human sacrifice).

Nandinī[3], a mātṛ. § 615*u* (Skanda): IX, **46***θ*, 2623.

Nandisena, a companion of Skanda. § 615*u* (Skanda): IX, **45,** 2526 (given to Skanda by Brahmán).

Nandivardhana = Çiva (1000 names[2]).

Nandivega, pl. (*°āḥ*), a people. § 562 (Bhagavadyānap.): V, **74***γ*, 2733 (*Samaç ca N°ānām*).

Naptṛ, a Viçvadeva. § 749 (Ānuçāsanik.): XIII, **91***γ*, 4362 (enumeration).

Napumsaka(m) = Çiva (1000 names [1]).

Nara [1], a god or ṛshi (commonly connected with Nārāyaṇa) with whom Arjuna Pāṇḍava is identified. § 4 (Anukram.): I, **1**, 172 (°-*Nārāyaṇau tau Kṛshṇārjunau*).—§ 28 (Amṛtamanthana): I, **19**, 1159 (*Vishṇuḥ . . . N°eṇa sahitaḥ*, took away the amṛta from the Asuras), 1176 (°-*Nārāyaṇau*, fought with the Asuras), 1177 (armed with a celestial bow), †1185 [†1188 (*Kirīṭine*, the gods made over the amṛta to *N.* that he might guard it)].—§ 130*g* (Abhimanyu): I, **67**, 2751 (will be born as the son of Indra (*Aindriḥ*), i.e. Arjuna), 2754 (°-*Nārāyaṇau* = Arjuna and Kṛshṇa).—§ 133 (Dushyanta): I, **70**, 2872 (°-*Nārāyaṇasthānam*—i.e. Badarī—*Gaṅgayevopaçobhitam*).—§ 251 (Arjunavanavāsap.): I, **218**, 7889 (°-*Nārāyaṇāv ṛshī* = Arjuna and Kṛshṇa).—§ 256 (Agniparābhava): I, **224**, 8160 (°-*Nārāyaṇau yau tau pūrvadevau . . . samprāptau mānushe loke*, sc. as Arjuna and Kṛshṇa).—§ 258 (Khāṇḍavadahanap.): I, **228**, 8302 (°-*Nārāyaṇāv etau pūrvadevau viçrutau*, sc. Arjuna and Kṛshṇa)).—§ 263 (Sabhākriyāp.): II, **3**, 72 (°-*Nārāyaṇau* (C. by error °*ṇo*), performed sacrifices at Bindusaras).—§ 299 (Dyūtap.): II, **67**, †2229 (*Kṛshṇañ ca Jishṇuñ ca Hariṃ N°ñ ca*, invoked by Draupadī); **68**, †2295 (*Kṛshṇañ ca Vishṇuñ* (read *Ji*° ?) *ca Hariṃ N°ñ ca*, invoked by Draupadī).—§ 317*b* (Kṛshṇa Vāsudeva): III, **12**, 505 (= Arjuna), 506 (°-*Nārāyaṇāv ṛshī*, = Arjuna and Kṛshṇa).—§ 333*b* (Arjuna): III, **40**, 1636 (*Nārāyaṇasahāyavān*, in Badarī, = Arjuna).—§ 334 (Kairātap.): III, **41**, 1681 (*pūrvarshiḥ* = Arjuna).—§ 339 (Indralokābhigamanap.): III, **47**, 1888 (°-*Nārāyaṇau yau tau purāṇau ṛshisattamau . . . Hṛshīkeça-Dhananjayau*), 1889 (°-*Nārayaṇāv ṛshī*).—§ 377 (Dhaumyatīrthak.): III, **86**, 8281 (*Vāsudeva-Dhanañjayau . . . N°-Nārāyaṇāv ṛshī*).—§ 406 (Tīrthayātrāp.): III, **125**, 10415 (°-*Nārāyaṇau cobhau sthānaṃ prāptāḥ sanātanaṃ*).—§ 420 (Gandhamādanapr.): III, **141**, 10893 (*viçālā Badarī yatra N°-Nārāyaṇāçramaḥ*).—§ 423 (do.): III, **145**, 11031 (°-*Nārāyaṇāçramaḥ*, i.e. Badarī), 11039 (*āçramaṃ . . . N°-Nārāyaṇāçritaṃ*, do.), 11054 (°-*Nārāyaṇasthānaṃ Bhāgirathyopaçobhitaṃ*).—§ 434 (Saugandhikaharaṇa): III, **156**, 11439 (*viçālā Badarī . . . N°-Nārāyaṇāçramaḥ*), 11443 (°-*Nārāyaṇasthānaṃ Badarīty abhiviçrutaṃ*), 11449 (°-*Nārāyaṇāçramaṃ*, = Badarī).—§ 524*b* (Arjuna): III, **272**, 15805 (*Sureçvaraṃ*, had performed austerities in Badarī, = Arjuna).—§ 561*d* (Nara-Nārāyaṇau): V, **49**, 1921 (*pūrvadevau . . . N°-Nārāyaṇāv ṛshī*), 1924 (°-*Nārāyaṇau*), 1927 (do.), 1930 (had vanquished the Paulomas and the Kālakhañjas, sc. as Arjuna, cf. Nivātakavacayuddhaparvan), 1935 (°-*Nārāyaṇau devau pūrvadevāv iti çrutiḥ*), 1936 (*Phālgunaḥ*, i.e. Arjuna).—§ 563 (Dambhodbhavop.): V, **96**, 3461 (°*o Nārāyaṇaç caiva tāpasau*), 3462 (°-*Nārāyaṇau*), (3469), (do.), 3473, 3482 (*N.* and Nārāyaṇa humiliated Dambhodbhava).—§ 563 (Bhagavadyānap.): V, **96**, 3488, 3496 (°-*Nārāyaṇau . . . Arjuna-Keçavau*). — § 564 (Mātalīyop.): V, **97**, 3502 (°-*Nārāyaṇāv ṛshī*).—§ 565 (Gālavacarita): V, **111**, 3826 (°-*Nārāyaṇau*), 3840 (*Jishṇuṃ*).—§ 574*f* (Bindusaras): VI, **6**, 241 (°-*Nārāyaṇau*, at Bindusaras).—§ 574 (Jambūkh.): VI, **8**, 307 (°*o Nārāyaṇaç caiva*).—§ 576 (Bhagavadgītāp.): VI, **23**, 810 (°*s tvam asi*, sc. Arjuna), 818 (°-*Nārāyaṇau*, = Arjuna and Kṛshṇa), 819 (error in C., B. has *tathānaghaḥ* instead of *tathā Naraḥ*).—§ 581 (Bhīshmavadhap.): VI, **66**, 2982 (Nārāyaṇa will be born among men together with *N.*), 2983 (°-*Nārāyaṇau purāṇāv ṛshisattamau*), 2984 (°-*Nārāyaṇāv ṛshī*), 3004 (°-*Nārāyaṇau devau*, = Arjuna and Kṛshṇa); **68**, 3050 (°-*Nārāyaṇau*), 3053 (°-*Nārāyaṇau devau*, = Arjuna and Kṛshṇa).—§ 589 (Droṇābhishekap.): VII, **11**, 422 (*pūrvadevau . . . N°-Nārāyaṇau*, = Arjuna and Kṛshṇa).—§ 596 (Pratijñāp.): VII, **77**, 2707 (°-*Nārāyaṇau*, do.); **80**, 2869 (do., do.); **81**, 2894 (°-*Nārāyaṇāv ṛshī*, do.).—§ 598 (Jayadrathavadhap.): VII, **88**, 3139 (*Nārāyaṇānugaḥ* = Arjuna).—§ 603*b* (Nārāyaṇa): VII, **201**, 9479 (born by means of the tapas of Nārāyaṇa, = Arjuna).—§ 605 (Karṇap.): VIII, **16**, 629 (°-*Nārāyaṇau*, = Arjuna and Kṛshṇa).—§ 608 (do.): VIII, **87***ω'*, 4451 (°-*Nārāyaṇāv . . . etau purāṇāv ṛshisattamau*, do.); **96**, 5009 (°-*Nārāyaṇau devau*, do.).—§ 641 (Rājadh.): XII, **127**, 4661 (°-*Nārāyaṇāçramaṃ*, i.e. Badarī), 4664 (°-*Nārāyaṇāv ṛshī*, in Badarī).—§ 692 (Mokshadh.): XII, **281***δ*, 10076 (°*sya*, sc. *sthānaṃ*).—§ 707 (do.): XII, **318**, 11707 (*muniçreshṭhaṃ*, if the soul (*jīva*) issues through the neck, one goes to *N.*).—§ 717*b* (Nārāyaṇīya): XII, **335**, 12658 (read *Naro*, among the four sons of Dharma born from Nārāyaṇa, viz. *N.*, Nārāyaṇa, Hari, and Kṛshṇa), 12659 (*Nārāyaṇa-N°au*, in Badarī), 12667 (°-*Nārāyaṇābhyāṃ*, discourse between Nārada and *N.* and Nārāyaṇa); **340**, 12964 (°-*Nārāyaṇāv ṛshī*, = Arjuna and Kṛshṇa), 12975 (°-*Nārāyaṇau*, in Badarī); **342**, 13165 (°-*Nārāyaṇau*, = Arjuna and Kṛshṇa), 13168 (*āpo vai N°sūnavaḥ*); **343**, 13266 (°-*Nārāyaṇau*), 13274 (*N.* and Nārāyaṇa fought with Rudra); (*αα*), 13286 (°*o Nārāyaṇaç caiva Dharmakulodvahau devaçreshṭhau*); **344**, 13310 (°-*Nārāyaṇau devasattamau*), (*ββ*), 13329 (°-*Nārāyaṇau*), 13332 (°-*Nārāyaṇāv ṛshī*), (13350) (°-*Nārāyaṇau*, discourse between them and Nārada); **345**, (13371) (°-*Nārāyaṇau*), 13397 (°-*Nārāyaṇāçramaṃ*), 13398 (°-*Nārāyaṇau*, continuation); **346**, (13410) (°-*Nārāyaṇau*) (continuation); **347**, 13427 (°-*Nārāyaṇa*°), 13428 (°-*Nārāyaṇāçrame*), 13429 (°-*Nārāyaṇāv ṛshī*); **348**, 13449 (*janma Dharmagṛhe . . . N°-Nārāyaṇātmakaṃ*).—§ 777 (Svargārohaṇik. p.): XIII, **168**, 7749 (in Badarī), 7750 (°-*Nārāyaṇāv etau sambhūtau manushyeshu*, = Arjuna and Kṛshṇa).—§ 789 (Putradarçanap.): XV, **31***η*, 853 (*ṛshim imaṃ Pārthaṃ Dhanañjayaṃ*, i.e. Arjuna).—§ 795*c* (Mahābhārata): XVIII, **6***o*, 232 (cf. the introductory çlokas of books I–XVIII), 287 (°-*Nārāyaṇau*). Cf. Kirīṭin, Sureçvara.

Nara [2] = Çiva (1000 names [2]).—Do. [3] = Vishṇu (1000 names).

Nara, pl. (°*āḥ*), a class of Gandharvas. § 269 (Vaiçravaṇasabhāv.): II, **10**, 396 (in the palace of Kubera).

Nārada [1], a Devarshi, son of Parameshṭhin, often mentioned together with Gandharvas and therefore presumably himself a Gandharva. Cf. Nārada [2]. § 4 (Anukram.): I, **1**, 106 (recited the Mahābhārata to the gods); †172 (*vadato N°sya*, all. to § 561*d*).—§ 5 (do.): I, **1**, 221, 223*bis* (*surarshiṇā*, enumerated to Çaibya (Çvaitya, B.), twenty-four kings who have died).—§ 11 (Parvasaṅgr.): I, **2**, 394, 408, 440 (*maharshiṇā*), 462 (*surarshiṇā*), 616.—§ 59 (Sarpasattra): I, **53**, 2048 (°*aḥ Parvatas tathā*, among the sadasyas at the snake sacrifice of Janamejaya).—§ 138 (Daksha Prācetasa): I, **75**, 3132 (taught the sons of Daksha *sāṅkhyajñānaṃ*).—§ 221 (Caitrarathap.): I, **170**, 6497 (°*prabhṛtīnāṃ devarshīṇāṃ*).—§ 233 (Svayaṃvarap.): I, **187**, †7011 (*Viçvāvasur N°-Parvatau*, present at the svayaṃvara of Draupadī).—§ 245 (Rājyalābhap.): I, **208**, 7604 (*devarshiḥ*), 7608, 7610, (7612).—§ 246 (Sundopasundop.): I, **209**, (7619), (7644); **210**, (7652); **211**, (7679), (7700); **212**, (7711), (7736), 7739, 7740 (*devarshiḥ*), 7741, 7742 (*N.* related to Yudhishṭhira the Sundopasundopākhyāna and caused the Pāṇḍavas to establish a rule among themselves with regard to Draupadī).—§ 250 (Arjunavanavāsap.): I, **217**, 7874 (*devarshim*, directed *Vargā*, etc., to go to Nārītīrthāni and prophesied their deliverance by Arjuna). — § 265 (Lokapālasabhākhyānap.): II, **5**, 144, 147 (*ṛshim*), (151), (247), 248 (*muniḥ*), (249), 261, (263) (questioned Yudhishṭhira about his government); **6**, 269, 273, (274), 278, 282.—§ 266-70 (do.): II, **7**, (283); **8**, (311); **9**, (353); **10**, (383); **11**, (420) (described the different *sabhās* of the gods).—§ 271 (do.): II, **12**, (488) (told Yudhishṭhira that Pāṇḍu wished that he should perform a rājasūya), 512, 513. — § 289 (Arghāharaṇap.): II, **36**, 1308 (*maharshayaḥ . . . N°pramukhāḥ*), 1315, 1316, 1318, 1325 (knew that Kṛshṇa was Nārāyaṇa); **39**, 1407 (praised Kṛshṇa).—§ 293 (Dyūtap.): II, **46**, 1635 (a saying of his about the rājasūya is quoted).—§ 296 (do.): II, **53**, 1917 (at the rājasūya *N.* sprinkled water over Yudhishṭhira).—§ 305 (Anudyūtap.): II, **78**, 2575 (would become the instructor of Yudhishṭhira).—§ 306 (do.): II, **80**, 2652 (foretold the great battle). — § 310*b* (Sūrya): III, **3**, 209 (learnt the hymn to the Sun from Çakra and taught it to Dhaumya).—§ 317*b* (Kṛshṇa Vāsudeva): III, **12**, 500 (had told Arjuna about the nature of Kṛshṇa), 513 (a saying of his about Kṛshṇa is quoted). — § 320 (Saubhavadhop.): III, **19**, 770 (the gods sent *N.* and the Wind as messengers to Kṛshṇa).—§ 322 (Dvaitāvanapraveça): III, **24**, 924 (wanders over all the worlds, waited upon Yudhishṭhira).—§ 324 (do.): III, **26*a***, 985 (waited upon Yudhishṭhira). — § 327 (Draupadīparitāpav.): III, **31**, 1171. — § 336 (Indralokābhigamanap.): III, **43**, 1769 (*Tumburur N°ç caiva*, in the abode of Indra).—§ 345 (Nalopākhyānap.): III, **54**, 2117 (*°ḥ Parvataç caiva*), 2119, 2120, 2123, 2128 (told Indra about the svayaṃvara of Damayantī).—§ 348 (do.): III, **66**, 2612 (*maharshiḥ*, had cursed Karkoṭaka).—§ 356 (Tīrthayātrāp.): III, **81**, 4022 (*devarshim*), 4026 (*ṛshiḥ*), (4032) (repeated the description of tīrthas delivered by Pulastya to Bhīshma). — § 364 (do.): III, **83**, 6051 (*°sya . . . tīrtham . . . Ambājanma*), 6052.—§ 376 (do.): III, **85**, (8255), 8274 (*ṛshiḥ*, having completed the description of tīrthas, *N.* disappeared).—§ 377 (Dhaumyatīrthak.): III, **86**, 8276, 8280 (knew Kṛshṇa and Arjuna to be Nārāyaṇa and Nara); **88**, 8347 (*devarshiṇā*, a çloka of his about Ujjayanta is cited).—§ 378 (Tīrthayātrāp.): III, **93**, 8470 (all. to § 356 foll.), 8475 (*Parvata-N°au*, came to Yudhishṭhira), 8483.—§ 387 (Sagara): III, **107**, 8882 (informed Sagara of the death of his sons).—§ 412 (Ashṭāvakrīya): III, **134**, †10659 (*dvau devarshī N°-Parvatau*). — § 447 (Nivātakavacayuddhap.): III, **175**, 12308 (sent by the gods to prevent Arjuna from discharging the celestial weapons).—§ 453 (Mārkaṇḍeyas.): III, **183**, 12603 (*devarshiḥ*, came to Yudhishṭhira), 12605 (do.). — § 463 (Çibi): III, **194**, ††13249, ††13249 *bis*, ††13250 (quoted three çlokas in order to settle the dispute between Çibi and Suhotra), ††13254, ††13255. — § 467 (Rājanyamahābhāgya): III, **198**, ††13302, ††13303 (*surarshim*), ††13312, ††13318 (instructed Çibi, etc.).—§ 545 (Pativratāmāhātmyap.): III, **294**, 16660, (16661), (16668), (16672), (16674), (16679), (16682), (16686), (16689), 16690 (foretold that Satyavat would die within a year); **295**, 16713 (all. to ch. **294**); **296**, 16715 (do.), 16727 (do.); **297**, 16753 (do.); **298**, 16894 (do.).—§ 555 (Indravijaya): V, **11**, 356 (*Viçvāvasur N°ç ca*, attended upon Nahusha as Indra).—§ 561*d* (Nara-Nārāyaṇau): V, **49**, 1938 (had told the Vṛshṇis that Kṛshṇa was Nārāyaṇa, and Arjuna Nara).—§ 561 (Yānasandhip.): V, **61**, 2385 (*kathām akathayat purā*).—§ 562 (Bhagavadyānap.): V, **83*γ***, 2946 (worshipped Kṛshṇa); **94**, 3371 (*°pramukhān ṛshīn*, came to the conclave of the Kurus).—564 (Mātalīyop.): V, **98**, 3522 (*maharshiṇā*), 3523, 3524 (only B., C. by error *Varuṇam*), 3527, 3528, 3530, (3531); **99**, (3547), 3566; **100**, (3567); **101**, (3586); **102**, (3602); **103**, (3617), 3634, (3639); **104**, (3643), 3655, 3662, 3666, 3668, 3673; **105**, 3710 (when Mātali sought in all worlds for a husband for his daughter he was accompanied by *N.*).—§ 565 (Gālavacarita): V, **106**, 3717, (3718); **107**, (3741); **112**, (3854), (3869); **113**, (3873); **114**, (3896); **115**, (3917); **116**, (3938); **117**, (3962), 3974 (*reme . . . yathā . . . Satyavatyāñ ca N°ḥ*); **118**, (3981); **119**, (4002); **120**, (4026) (related the Gālavacarita). — § 566 (Yayāti); V, **121**, (4048), (4068); **122**, (4078); **123**, (4097), (4116) (related the history of Yayāti).—§ 567 (Bhagavadyānap.): V, **124**, 4121; **131**, 4442 (*ṛshayaḥ . . . N°ādayaḥ*, disappeared).—§ 571 (Ulūkadūtāgamanap.): V, **160**, 5421 (had related the story of the wicked cat). — § 573 (Ambopākhyānap.): V, **185**, 7291 (prevented Bhīshma from discharging the Prasvāpa weapon against Rāma), 7295, 7313, 7316 (*munayaḥ . . . N°mukhāḥ*); **186**, 7344; **188**, 7398, 7408 (informed Bhīshma of Çikhaṇḍin's birth, etc.).—§ 574 (Jambūkh.): VI, **6**, 214 (*Tumburur N°ç caiva*, on Meru).—§ 576 (Bhagavadgītāp.): VI, **21**, 767 (*ṛshiḥ*), 771 (a saying of his about Kṛshṇa is quoted); **23**, 819 (all. to §§ 565–6); **34**, 1217 (*devarshiḥ*, declared Kṛshṇa to be the supreme god), 1230 (*devarshīṇāñ ca N°ḥ*, sc. *asmi*, says Kṛshṇa).—§ 581 (Bhīshmavadhap.): VI, **66*ο***, 2999; **68*ρ***, 3038 (a saying of his about Kṛshṇa is quoted).—§ 585 (do.): VI, **98**, 4463 (had described the glory of Kṛshṇa).—§ 588 (do.): VI, **121**, 5792 (had spoken of Arjuna as an ancient ṛshi (i.e. Nara)); **122**, 5826 (had told Bhīshma the secret that Karṇa was the son of Kuntī).—§ 594 (Abhimanyuvadhap.): VII, **52**, 2023 (*Akampanasya kathitam N°ena purā*); do. (Akampana): VII, **52**, 2034 (*devarshiḥ*), 2039; do. (Mṛtyu): VII, **52**, (2040); **53**, (2063); **54**, (2073), (2084), (†2117); do. (Akampana): VII, **54**, 2125, 2127 (comforted Akampana). — § 595 (Sṛñjaya): VII, **55**, 2138, 2145, 2146, 2148 (rivalling one another with the daughter of Sṛñjaya, *N* and Parvata cursed one another), 1628, 2169 (*N.* granted Sṛñjaya the son Suvarṇashṭhīvin).—§ 595 (Shoḍaçarāj.): VII, **56**, (2184); **57**, (2196); **58**, (2209); **59**, (2224); **60**, (2249); **61**, (2263); **62**, (2272); **63**, (2292); **64**, (2303); **65**, (2321); **66**, (2331); **67**, (2356); **68**, (2377); **69**, (2394); **70**, (2427) (*N.* related the Shodaçarājika to Sṛñjaya).—§ 595 (Sṛñjaya): VII, **71**, 2452, (2456), (2458) (revived Suvarṇashṭhīvin). — § 597 (Pratijñāp.): VII, **83**, 2964 (had described Kṛshṇa as Nārāyaṇa). — § 599 (Jayadrathavadhap.): VII, **99**, 3728 (*°muniḥ*, came to see the lake made by Arjuna).—§ 600 (Ghaṭotkacavadhap.): VII, **163**, †7294 (*°-Parvatābhyām*, brought lamps). — § 604 (Karṇap.): VIII, **2*γ***, 31 (all. to §§ 565–6). — § 615*ii* (Vṛddhakanyā): IX, **52**, 2989, 2991.—§ 615 (Baladevatīrthayātrā): IX, **54**, 3051 (*ṛshiḥ*, description (*ll*): with matted locks and attired in golden rays, he bore in his hand a staff made of gold and a waterpot of gold, he was accomplished in song and dance and adored by gods and brahmans, he had with him a beautiful *vīṇā* of melodious notes, made of tortoise-shell; he was wont to provoke quarrels and fond of quarrel), 3056, 3057, (3060), 3070 (informed Balarāma about the battle).—§ 617 (Aishīkap.):

X, **14**, 681 (*sarvabhūtatmā*); **16**, 743 (*mahāmuniḥ*).—§ 618 (Jalapradānikap.): XI, **1β**, 14 (*devarshiḥ*, all. to §§ 565–6) (γ), 30; **8**, 214 (°*pramukhāç ca devarshayaḥ*), 226, 229 (had foretold the battle), 231.—§ 621 (Rājadh.): XII, **1β**, 4 (came to Yudhishṭhira), 9, (γ), 18; **2**, 46 (*muniḥ*), (47) (related the history of Karṇa); **3**, (75) (continuation); **4**, (108) (do.); **5**, (129) (do.); **6**, 144 (*devarshiḥ*).—§ 632 (do.): XII, **29**, 906 (related the Shoḍaçarājikopākhyāna to Sṛñjaya, cf. § 595), †1039, †1040 (*maharshe*), (1042) (revived Suvarṇashṭhīvin, cf. § 595).—§ 633*b* (Nārada-Parvatop.): XII, **30**, 1046 (°*ḥ Parvataç caiva dvāv ṛshī*), 1048 (the maternal uncle of Parvata), 1059, 1062, 1068, 1072, 1073, 1074 (*devarshim*), 1077, 1078, 1082, 1084 (*ṛshiḥ*), 1086, 1087 (*N.* and Parvata cursed one another, cf. § 595).—§ 634 (Rājadh.): XII, **31**, 1088, 1089 (*muniḥ*), (1090) (*N.* granted Sṛñjaya the son Suvarṇashṭhīvin, cf. § 595).—§ 635 (do.): XII, **37**, 1348 (*sarvajñānāṃ purātanam*).—§ 637 (do.): XII, **47η**, 1592 (*surarshiṇā*, among the ṛshis who surrounded Bhīshma).—§ 640 (do.): XII, **54a**, 1928 (*siddhā N°pramukhāḥ*), 1931 (*devadarçanaḥ*), 1935.—§ 641 (do.): XII, **81**, 3025 (*saṃvādaṃ Vāsudevasya surarsher N°sya ca*), 3026, 3027, 3030, 3031, 3035, (3036), (3044) (discourse between Kṛshṇa and *N.*); **124**, 4567 (*itihāsaṃ purātanaṃ N°ena purā proktam*).—§ 654*b* (Pavanaçālmalisaṃv.): XII, **154**, 5809; **155**, 5822, 5827, (5830); **156**, 5841, (5842), 5845, 5846, 5855, 5856; **157**, 5867 (discourse between *N.* and the çālmali).—§ 656 (Khaḍgotpattik.): XII, **166β**, 6142 (°-*Parvatau*).—§ 658*b* (Kṛtaghnop.): XII, **173**, 6448 (had related the Kṛtaghnopākhyāna to Bhīshma).—§ 661 (Mokshadh.): XII, **193**, 7038 (*devarshiḥ*, a sentence of his is quoted).—§ 662*b* (Jāpakop.): XII, **200δ**, 7340 (°*ḥ Parvataç caiva*).—§ 664 (Mokshadh.): XII, **207β**, 7520 (*devarsheḥ*), 7564 (*devarshiḥ*, declared Kṛshṇa to be the supreme god), 7565.—§ 667 (do.): XII, **210**, 7662 (*Gāndharvaṃ N°o veda*).—§ 674*b* (Bali-Vāsavasaṃv.): XII, **229**, 8337, 8348 (*devarshim*), 8349, 8418 (*devarshiḥ*), †8422.—§ 676 (Mokshadh.): XII, **231**, 8455, 8456, 8457, 8459, 8460 (description of the virtues of *N.*).—§ 678*b* (Anukampaka): XII, **257**, 9152, 9154, 9155; **258**, (9177), (9187) (told the story of Mṛtyu to Anukampaka, cf. § 594).—§ 686 (Mokshadh.): XII, **273**, 9812, 9813 (told the story of the brahman Satya).—§ 688 (do.): XII, **276**, 9874 (°*sya ca saṃvādaṃ Devalasyāsitasya ca*), 9875 (9876), 9879 (discourse between *N.* and Asita Devala).—§ 694*b* (Jvarotpatti): XII, **284a**, 10218 (°-*Parvatau*, came to the sacrifice of Daksha).—§ 695*b* (Dakshayajñavināça): XII, **285a**, 10278 (*Tumburu-N°au*), 10287 (sat beside Umā).—§ 698 (Mokshadh.): XII, **287**, 10533 (°*sya ca saṃvādaṃ Samaṅgasya ca*), (10534), 10538, †10541, 10552 (discourse between *N.* and Samaṅga).—§ 699 (do.): XII, **288**, 10555 (*Gālavasya ca saṃvādaṃ devarsher N°sya ca*), 10556, (10564) (discourse between *N.* and Gālava).—§ 702 (do.): XII, **293a**, 10761 (°-*Parvatau*).—§ 705 (do.): XII, **309**, 11511, 11512 (obtained the knowledge of the supreme soul from Vasishṭha and taught it to Bhīshma).—§ 707 (do.): XII, **319β**, 11784 (had instructed Viçvāvasu).—§ 712 (Çukotpatti): XII, **324**, 12176 (°-*Parvatau*, beside Çiva on Meru); **325**, 12201 (*Tumburu-N°au*).—§ 714 (Çukakṛtya): XII, **328**, 12314 (*devarshiḥ*); **329**, 12375, 12380, (12384), 12386 (came to the hermitage of Vyāsa).—§ 715 (Çuka-Nāradasaṃv.): XII, **330**, 12422, 12423 (*devarshim*), 12424, 12425, (12426); **331**, (12482); **332**, (12512) (discourse between *N.* and Çuka).—§ 716 (Çukābhipatana): XII, **332**, 12557, 12572 (*ṛshim*); **333**, 12583 (*devarshim*), 12585; **334**, 12647 (*devarshiḥ*).—§ 717*b* (Nārāyaṇīya): XII, **335**, 12656 (°*sya ca saṃvādam ṛsher Nārāyaṇasya ca*), 12663 (*sumahadbhūtam*), 12672 (*ṛshiḥ*), (12674), 12695 (came to Badarī and worshipped Nara and Nārāyaṇa); **336**, (†12697), †12701 (*Parameshṭhiputraḥ*, repaired to Çvetadvīpa); **338**, 12859 (*ṛshiḥ*, do.); **339**, 12861 (do., do.), (††12864) (worshipped Nārāyaṇa); **340**, 12865, 12874 (*dvijasattamaḥ*), (12880), 12882 (*Parameshṭhinam*, Nārāyaṇa showed himself to *N.* and described his own nature), 12890, 12906, 12909, 12920, 12946, 12975 (returned to Badarī), 12977 (described in the abode of Brahman his meeting with Nārāyaṇa), 12998, 13002 · (°*oktam*); **344**, 13308, 13309, 13313 (*surarshiṇā*), 13326 (*Parameshṭhijaḥ*), 13327 (*ṛshim avyayam*), 13329, 13330 (*Parameshṭhijaḥ*), 13334, 13342, 13347, 13349, (13351) (discourse with Nārāyaṇa and Nara); **345**, 13372, 13396, 13398 (*ṛshiḥ*) (do.); **346**, 13399 (*Parameshṭhijaḥ*), (13402), 13413 (do.); **347**, 13427 (returned to his own hermitage on Himavat), 13436, 13443 (recited the Nārāyaṇīya); **349**, 13557 (discoursed on the dharma of Nārāyaṇa), 13558, VII), 13600 (instructed by Nārāyaṇa), 13612, 13633 (instructed Vyāsa).—§ 718*b* (Uñchavṛttyup.): XII, **353**, 13767 (*maharshiṇā*), 13768 (*maharshiḥ*), 13773 (related the Uñchavṛttyupākhyāna to Indra); **366**, 13937, 13938 (do.).—§ 730 (Ānuçāsanik.): XIII, **14ζ**, 696 (attends on Çiva with song and music).—§ 734 (do.): XIII, **26a**, 1764 (°*ḥ Parvataç caiva*, came to see Bhīshma).—§ 737 (do.): XIII, **31**, 2009 (°*sya ca saṃvādaṃ Vāsudevasya cobhayoḥ*), 2010, (2012) (discourse between *N.* and Kṛshṇa).—§ 739 (do.): XIII, **34**, 2133 (a saying of his is quoted.)—§ 742 (do.): XIII, **38**, 2203 (°*sya ca saṃvādaṃ puṃçcalyā Pañcacūḍayā*), 2204 (*devarshiḥ*), 2206, (2207), 2212, 2231 (discourse between *N.* and Pañcacūḍā).—§ 746 (do.): XIII, **63**, 3203 (*devadarçanaḥ*), (3204), 3242 (discoursed to Bhīshma on gifts of food); **64**, 3253 (*Devakyāç ca saṃvādaṃ maharsher N°sya ca*), 3254 (*devadarçanam*), 3255 (*devarshiḥ*), (3256), 3288 (discourse between Devakī and *N.*); **83ξ**, 3887 (°*ḥ Parvataç caiva*, sung).—§ 751*b* (Çapathavidhi): XIII, **94a**, †4550 (°-*Parvatau*), (4576).—§ 754 (Ānuçāsanik.): XIII, **98**, 4741, 4742 (discoursed to Bhīshma).—§ 757*f* (Nandana): XIII, **102**, †4865 (*Nandanaṃ N°sya*).—§ 761 (Ānuçāsanik.): XIII, **115β**, 5607 (a saying of his is quoted).—§ 766 (do.): XIII, **126**, †6043 (worshipped the kine).—§ 768 (do.): XIII, **139a**, 6297 (°-*Parvatau*, came to Kṛshṇa), 6334, 6337 (*devarshiḥ*); **140**, 6338 (*Nārāyaṇasuhṛt*).—§ 768*b* (Umā-Maheçvarasaṃv.): XIII, **140**, (6339); **141**, (6413); **146**, (6747); **148**, (6870) (related the discourse between Çiva and Umā).—§ 768 (Ānuçāsanik.): XIII, **148**, 6912, 6922, 6925, 6933 (*ṛshayaḥ . . . N°pramukhāḥ*).—§ 770 (do.): XIII, **151λ**, 7123 (*Sāṅkhyayogaḥ?*).—§ 772γ (Utathya): XIII, **155**, 7248, 7250, 7252, 7254 (sent by Utathya to Varuṇa).—§ 772*p* (Kapa, pl.): XIII, **158**, 7346, 7347.—§ 775 (Ānuçāsanik.): XIII, **166a**, 7639 (enumeration).—§ 777 (Svargārohaṇik. p.): XIII, **168**, 7718, 7750 (had told Bhīshma that Kṛshṇa was Nārāyaṇa); **169β**, 7778.—§ 778 (Açvamedhikap.): XIV, **2**, 24 (had instructed Yudhishṭhira).—§ 778*b* (Saṃvartta-Maruttīya): XIV, **6**, 129, 130 (*devarshiṇā*), 133 (*maharshiṇā*), 135, 136, (137), 139, (141), 144, 146, 147 (directed Marutta to seek Saṃvartta for his *ṛtvij*); **7**, 155, 156.—§ 780 (Açvamedhikap.): XIV, **14β**, 356 (had comforted Yudhishṭhira), 360, 364 (*devarshiṇā*). — § 782*b* (Brāhmaṇagītā): XIV, **24,** 711 (°*sya ca saṃvādam ṛsher Devamatasya ca*), (715) (discourse between *N.* and Devamata). — § 783 (Anugītāp.): XIV, **52a,** 1492 (had taught Arjuna that Kṛshṇa was the supreme god).—§ 785 (do.): XIV, **88ψ,** 2641 (present at the açvamedha of Yudhishṭhira).—§ 787 (Āçramavāsap.): XV, **20ββ,** 538 (°*ḥ Parvataç caiva*), 542 (*devarshiḥ*), (543), 558, 559, 560, 566 (*divyadarçī*), (567) (told Dhṛtarāshṭra that only three years of life were left for him).—§ 789 (Putradarçanap.): XV, **29a,** 774 (°*ḥ Parvataç caiva*).— § 791 (do.): XV, **36,** 964 (all. to ch. **20**). — § 792 (Nāradāgamanap.): XV, **37,** 1011 (*devarshiḥ*), (1015), (1019); **39,** (1078), (1101) (reported the death of Dhṛtarāshṭra, Gāndhārī, and Kuntī).—§ 793 (Mausalap.): XVI, **1,** 15 (cursed Çāmba, etc.); **6κ,** 161 (knew Kṛshṇa to be Vishṇu).—§ 794 (Mahāprasthānikap.): XVII, **1,** 12; **3,** 98 (praised Yudhishṭhira), 101 (°*sya vacaḥ*). — § 795 (Svargārohaṇap.): XVIII, **1β,** 11, 19, 25, 26 (in heaven). — § 795*c* (Mahābhārata): XVIII, **5,** 199 (recited the Mahābhārata to the gods). Cf. Brahmarshi, Devarshi, Parameshṭhija, Parameshṭhin, Parameshṭhiputra, Surarshi.

Nārada[2], a Devagandharva (probably originally identical with Nārada[1]). § 101 (Aṃçāvat.), I, **65,** 2552 (son of Muni). — § 191 (Arjuna): I, **123,** 4813 (among the Devagandharvas present at the birth of Arjuna).—§ 615*u* (Skanda): IX, **44,** 2480 (°*pramukhāç cāpi Devagandharva-sattamāḥ*).

Nārada[3], a son of Viçvāmitra. § 721*b* (Viçvāmitrop.): XIII, **4β,** 252 (enumeration).

Nāradāgamana ("the arrival of Nārada"). § 10 (Parva-saṅgr.): I, **2,** 355 (°*ṃ parva*, i.e. Nāradāgamanaparvan).

[Nāradāgamanaparvan] ("the section containing the arrival of Nārada," the ninety-seventh of the minor parvans of Mahābhārata; cf. Nāradāgamana).—§ 792: *Vaiçampāyana* said: Two years after their return from the retreat of *Dhṛtarāshṭra* the *Pāṇḍavas* were visited by D.-ṛ. *Nārada*. *Yudhishṭhira* inquired after *Dhṛtarāshṭra*, etc. *Nārada* said: After thy return from *Kurukshetra*, *Dhṛtarāshṭra* proceeded towards *Gaṅgādvāra* with the sacrificial fire and *Gāndhārī*, *Kuntī*, *Sañjaya*, and all the *yājakas*. They themselves took to severe austerities (description), while the sacred fire was duly worshipped by the *yājakas*. They wandered about, *Sañjaya* acting as a guide, *Pṛthā* becoming the eye of *Gāndhārī*. Once *Dhṛtarāshṭra* bathed in the *Gaṅgā*, and was returning to his retreat. A violent forest conflagration set in; *Dhṛtarāshṭra* dismissed *Sañjaya* and sat down, facing the east, with *Gāndhārī* and *Kuntī*; they concentrated their soul, and were burnt by the conflagration. *Sañjaya* escaped and was seen by me (*Nārada*) on the banks of the *Gaṅgā* in the midst of ascetics; he bade them farewell and started for *Himavat*. In the course of my wanderings I saw the three bodies. The ascetics, from whom I heard all the details, did not at all grieve for them. *Vaiçampāyana* said: The *Pāṇḍavas* and the citizens felt great grief (XV, **37**). *Yudhishṭhira* lamented (*a*) (XV, **38**). *Nārada* comforted *Yudhishṭhira* by informing him of the sacred character of the fire that had burnt *Dhṛtarāshṭra* and the two queens. When *Dhṛtarāshṭra* entered the woods he caused his sacrificial fires to be duly ignited; having performed his sacred rites with them he abandoned them all; then the *Yājakas* had left them in a solitary part of the wood and gone away; the fires thus left to themselves produced a general conflagration; "this is what I have heard from the ascetics on the *Gaṅgā*." *Vaiçampāyana* said: Headed by *Yuyutsu* the *Pāṇḍavas* and the citizens all proceeded to the *Gaṅgā* in order to offer oblations of water to the deceased king and queens. Then they came back, taking up their residence outside the city. *Yudhishṭhira* sent a number of men to the retreat to cremate the remains of his uncle, aunt, and mother in due form. On the twelfth day he performed the *çrāddhas* with gifts in abundance (description). Then all returned to *Hāstinapura*. The great Ṛ. *Nārada*, having comforted *Yudhishṭhira*, went away. *Dhṛtarāshṭra* had passed three years in the forest and fifteen years in the city. *Yudhishṭhira* was plunged in grief [*; not in B.] (XV, **39**).

[Nārada-Parvatopākhyāna(m)] ("the episode relating to Nārada and Parvata"). § 633*b* (Rājadh.): Ṛ. *Nārada* and his sister's son *Parvata* had in days of old left heaven for a pleasant ramble on earth in order to taste clarified butter and rice. They wandered under a compact of telling each other their inmost thoughts. They arrived at the court of *Sṛñjaya* (*Çvaitya*). *Nārada* was taken with the charms of *Sṛñjaya's* daughter *Sukumārī*; but shamefulness prevented him from disclosing his love to *Parvata*, who then cursed him for his reticence, saying that *Sukumārī* should become his wife, but then she and every man should behold him in the shape of an ape. *Nārada* cursed *Parvata* in return, saying that he should not succeed in proceeding to heaven. *Parvata* began to wander over the earth. *Sukumārī* beheld *Nārada* as an ape, but devoted herself entirely to him, and did not desire any D., Mu., or Y. for a husband. *Nārada* and *Parvata*, after some time, became reconciled and withdrew their mutual curses. *Sukumārī* fled, thinking *Nārada* to be somebody else, but was informed by *Parvata*. *Parvata* proceeded to heaven and *Nārada* to his home. *Kṛshṇa* continued: "Ṛ. *Nārada* is here; he will tell thee everything that happened" (XII, **30**).

Nāradin, a son of Viçvāmitra. § 721*b* (Viçvāmitrop.): XIII, **4β,** 258 (*mahān ṛshiḥ*).

nārāḥ (pl.) = *āpaḥ* ("the waters"): III, 12952, 15819; XII, 13167.

Naraka[1], an Asura, son of Bhūmi (the Earth) and slain by Kṛshṇa (Vishṇu). § 93 (Aṃçāvat.): I, **65,** 2537 (among the sons of Danu (!)).—§ 268 (Varuṇasabhāv.): II, **9,** 364 (*pṛthiviñjayaḥ*, in the palace of Varuṇa).—§ 273 (Rājasūyārambhap.): II, **14,** 578 (? *Muruñ ca Narakañ caiva çāsti yo Yavanādhipaḥ* (i.e. Bhagadatta), name of a country ?). — § 317*b* (Kṛshṇa Vāsudeva): III, **12,** 177 (*Bhaumaṃ*, Kṛshna slew *N.* and recovered the ear-rings [of Aditi]), 488 (*Nisunda-N°au hatau*, destroying the bonds of Muru, Kṛshṇa slew Nisunda and *N.* and made safe the way to Prāgjyotisha; cf. Harivaṃça, v. 6791 foll.).—§ 422 (Gandhamādanapr.): III, **142,** 10914 (*asthīni Daityasya N°sya*, in the north).— § 422*b* (do.): Lomaça told: *N.* aspired to the position of Indra (*Aindram . . . sthānaṃ*) by practising austerities during 10,000 years and by learning. Indra became afraid and thought of Vishṇu, who then slew *N.* with his hand: III, **142,** 10923 (*Daityendrāt*).—§ 443 (Nivātakavacayuddhap.): III, **168,** 12073 (*Prahlāda-N°au*, have been defeated by Indra).—§ 513 (Ghoshayātrāp.): III, **252,** 15174 (*hatasya N°syātmā Karṇamūrtim upāçṛtya*, possessed Karṇa), 15189 (*Karṇo 'py āvishṭacittātmā N°syāntarātmanā*, do.).—§ 561*c* (Kṛshṇa Vāsudeva): V, **48,** †1887 (*Bhaumaḥ*, robbed the ear-rings of Aditi, cf. § 317*b*), †1892 (*Bhaumaṃ*, slain by Kṛshṇa, do.).—§ 561 (Yānasandhip.): V, **68ζζ,** 2526 (had been defeated by Kṛshṇa). — § 567 (Bhagavadyānap.):

V, **130**, 4407 (°*aḥ saha Dānavaiḥ*, cf. § 317*b*).—§ 570*f* (Çārṅga): V, **168**, 5357 (*nirjitya N°m Bhaumam āhṛtya maṇikuṇḍale*, cf. § 317*b*).—§ 589 (Droṇābhishekap.): VII, **11**μ, 386 (had been slain by Kṛshṇa).—§ 592*c* (Vaishṇavāstra): VII, **29**, 1283, 1286, 1288 (Bhūmi (the Earth), the mother of *N.* asked the Vaishṇava weapon for her son, from him it passed over to Bhagadatta).—§ 592 (Saṃçaptakavadhap.): VII, **29**, 1291 (had been slain by Kṛshṇa).—§ 604 (Karṇap.): VIII, **5**ζ, 144 (*yathā Kṛshṇena N°o Muraç ca nihataḥ*, cf. § 317*b*).—§ 637 (Rājadh.): XII, **47**θ, 1682 (°*santrāsarakshamaṇḍalakāriṇe Vishṇave*, i.e. Kṛshṇa).—§ 666 (Mokshadh.): XII, **209**, 7610 (*Dānavamukhyāḥ . . . N°ādyā mahāsurāḥ*).—§ 673*b* (Bali-Vāsavas.): XII, **227a**, 8261 (among the ancient rulers of the earth).—§ 717*b* (Nārāyaṇīya): XII, **340**, 12956 (*Bhaumaṃ*, will be slain by Nārāyaṇa, incarnate as Kṛshṇa). Cf. Bhauma, Daitya, Daityendra, Dānava.

Naraka[2], a tīrtha. § 368 (Tīrthayātrāp.): III, **83**, 7039 (only C., B. has *Anarakaṃ*).

***naraka** ("hell"): I, 636, 1841, 3026 (*Punnāmno n°āt*), 3092 (*trāyante n°āj jātāḥ putrā dharmaplavāḥ pitṝn*), †3603 (*imaṃ bhaumaṃ n°ṃ*), †3605 (*bhaumaṃ*), †3606 (*imaṃ bhaumaṃ n°aṃ*), †3651 (do.), 3673, 4706, 6125, 8344 (*Punnāmno n°āt*); II, †2195, 2262, 2518; III, 1144, 1178, 1385, 2251, 10501, 10504 (°*āgninā*), 10506, 11493, †12728 (*tīvrāndhakāre*), ††13348, 13874, 13938, 13939, 14046, 17388, 17389, 17390, 17391; V, †853 (figur.), 1036, 1589 (figur.), 1723 (°*pratishṭhāḥ*), 2613, 2614, 3988, 4471, 4478; VI, 872, 875, 1418, 1423, 4839; VII, 2166, 2458, 3766, 5427, 5658, 6319, 6736, 9080; VIII, †3388 (figur.), †3400 (do.), 3455, †3519, 3557, 3717 (figur.), 4756; IX, 1393, 2094, 3320, 3339 (°*saṃjñaṃ* (C. °*ñā*) *vai duḥkham*); X, 189; XII, 91, 92, 521, 886, 1170, 1193, 2555, 2574, 2586, 2696, 2921, 3217, 3365, 3478, 3652, 3666, 3668 (pl.), 3669, 5608, 5667 (*pāralokye*), 6061, 6084, 6086, 6451, 6518 (*dhūrtā n°rūpiṇaḥ*), 6970, 6981, 7806, 10006, 10008, 10010, †10062, 10548, 10906, 11108, 11851, 13432; XIII, 1131, 1804, 2121, 2929, †2956, 3176, 3272 (°*ādīn saṃkleçān*), 3316, 3353, 3361, 3483, 3664, 4818, 4819, 4827, 4975, 5398, 5412, 5560, 5640 (°*bhāk*), 5995, 6036, 6074, 6139, 7560, 7633; XIV, 2377, 2736 (pl.), 2789; XVIII, 72, 92, 94 (°*bhāk*), 96, 97, 116 (°*ārhāḥ*), 117 (pl.), 118 (°*ārhāḥ*), 119 (do.).

***naramedha** ("human sacrifice"): III, 8133; IX, 2889; XIII, 4942 (pl.); XIV, 48.

Nārāṇām patiḥ = Çiva: VII, 9539.

Nara-Nārāyaṇau. § 561*d* (Yānasandhip.): Once *Bṛhaspati* and *Uçanas* went to *Brahmán*, and also the *Maruts* with Indra, the *Vasus* with *Agni*, the *Ādityas*, the *Sādhyas*, the seven ṛshis (*saptarshayaḥ*), the *Gandharva Viçvāvasu*, the *gaṇas* of Apsarases, and having bowed down to Brahmán they sat around him. Just then the two ancient deities (*pūrvadevau*), the Ṛshis *Nara* and *Nārāyaṇa*, left the place. *Bṛhaspati* said to *Brahmán*: "Who are these two that leave the place without worshipping thee?" Brahmán said that they were *Nara* and *Nārāyaṇa* who had come from the world of men to the world of *Brahmán* (so Nīl.); "worshipped by the gods and the *Gandharvas* they exist only for the destruction of the Asuras." Indra went to the spot where those two were practising austerities, accompanied by all the gods headed by *Bṛhaspati.* At that time the gods had been very much alarmed in consequence of a war with the *Asuras. Indra* obtained the boon that *Nara* and *Nārāyaṇa* (i.e. *Arjuna* and *Kṛshṇa*) assisted him in the battle (cf. Arjuna). Both of them, by their acts, enjoy numerous eternal and celestial regions, and are repeatedly born in the times of war. Even this is what *Nārada*, conversant with the *Vedas*, had said to the Vṛshṇis.

Narārāshṭra, v. Navarāshṭra.

Nararshabha = Çiva (1000 names[2]).

Narasiṃha ("man-lion"). § 717*b* (Nārāyaṇīya): XII, **340**, 12968 (the fifth of Nārāyaṇa's (i.e. Vishṇu's) avatāras).

Nārasiṃha, adj. ("belonging to the man-lion"). § 384*c* (Vishṇu): III, **102**, 8758 (°*ṃ vapuḥ kṛtvā*, sc. Vishṇu, when he slew Hiraṇyakaçipu).—§ 524*d* (do.): III, **272**, 15837 (°*ena vapushā*, sc. Vishṇu, when he slew Hiraṇyakaçipu). § 717*b* (Nārāyaṇīya): XII, **340**κ, 12942 (°*ṃ vapuḥ kṛtvā*, in this form Nārāyaṇa (i.e. Vishṇu) will slay Hiraṇyakaçipu); **350**, 13673 (sc. *rūpaṃ*, i.e. Vishṇu's).

Nārasiṃhavapus = Vishṇu (1000 names).

Naravāhana = Kubera, q.v.

Nārāyaṇa, name of an ancient god or ṛshi, the son of Dharma, commonly connected with Nara (q.v.), but also the name of the Supreme God (Vishṇu, Kṛshṇa), from whom the son of Dharma was born. § 1 (Anukram.): I, **1** (introductory çloka).—§ 4 (do.): I, **1**, 172 (*Nara-N°au tau . . . Kṛshṇārjunau*).—§ 11 (Parvasaṅgr.): I, **2**, 451 (°*āçrame*, i.e. Badarī).—§ 28 (Amṛtamanthana): I, **17**, 1109 (*devaḥ*); **18**, 1118, 1126 (*ananto bhagavān devaḥ*), 1141, 1142, 1144, 1147 (*Kaustubhaḥ . . . N°a urogataḥ*), 1156 (disguised as a woman, *N.* took away the amṛta from the Asuras); **19**, 1176 (*Nara-N°au devau*, fought with the Asuras).—§ 46 (Garuḍa): I, **33**, 1506 (*Vishṇunā*), 1508, 1511 (made Garuḍa his vehicle and emblem).—§ 61 (Sarpasattra): I, **55**, †2110 (°*vat*).—§ 82 (Kṛshṇa Vāsudeva): I, **63**, 2431 (= Vishṇu, incarnate as Kṛshṇa).—§ 83 (Ādivaṃçāvatāraṇa): I, **63**, 2433 (i.e. Kṛshṇa, followed by Sātyaki and Kṛtavarman).—§ 84 (Ādivaṃçāvatāraṇap.): I, **64**, 2505 (*Vaikuṇṭhaṃ*, i.e. Vishṇu).—§ 85 (Aṃçāvat.): I, **65**, 2509, 2510 (= Vishṇu, became incarnate with a part of himself).—§ 130*g* (Abhimanyu): I, **67**, 2751 (= Kṛshṇa, friend of Nara (= Arjuna)), 2754 (*Nara-N°au* = Arjuna and Kṛshṇa).—§ 132 (Aṃçāvat.): I, **67**, 2785 (Kṛshṇa was an incarnation of a part of *N.*).—§ 133 (Dushyanta): I, **70**, 2872 (*Nara-N°sthānam*, i.e. Badarī, *Gaṅgayevopaçobhitaṃ*).—§ 238 (Pañcendrop.): I, **197**, 7306 (a black and a white hair of his was born as Kṛshṇa and Balarāma).—§ 240 (Vaivāhikap.): I, **199**, 7352 (*yathā N°e Lakshmīḥ*.)—§ 251 (Arjunavanavāsap.): I, **218**, 7889 (*Nara-N°āv ṛshī* = Arjuna and Kṛshṇa).—§ 256 (Agniparābhava): I, **224**, 8160 (*Nara-N°au yau tau pūrvadevau . . . samprāptau mānushe loke*, sc. as Arjuna and Kṛshṇa).—§ 258 (Khāṇḍavadahanap.): I, **228**, 8302 (*Nara-N°āv etau pūrvadevau viçrutau*, = Arjuna and Kṛshṇa).—§ 261 (Sabhākriyāp.): II, **1** (introductory çloka).—§ 263 (do.): II, **3**, 72 (*Nara-N°au* (C. °*o* by error), perform sacrifices at Bindusaras).—§ 270 (Brahmasabhāv.): II, **11**, 468 (*devaḥ*, in the palace of Brahman).—§ 289 (Arghāharaṇap.): II, **36**, 1319 (= Vishṇu), 1321 (do.), 1325 (*Hariṃ*, do. born as Kṛshṇa).—§ 308 (Āraṇyakap.): III, **1** (introductory çloka).—§ 317*b* (Kṛshṇa Vāsudeva): III, **12**, 480 (= Kṛshṇa), 500 (do.).—§ 317 (Arjunābhigamanap.): III, **12**, 505 (*Harir N°ḥ* = Kṛshṇa), 506 (*Nara-N°āv ṛshī*, = Arjuna and Kṛshṇa).—§ 329*b* (Arjuna): III, **36**, 1443 (°*sahāyavān*, sc. Arjuna).—§ 333*b* (do.): III, **40**, 1636 (*Naraḥ* (= Arjuna) . . . *N°sahāyavān*).—§ 339 (Indralokābhigamanap.): III, **47**, 1888 (*Nara-N°au yau tau purāṇāv ṛshisattamau . . . Hṛshīkeça-Dhanañjayau*), 1889 (*Nara-N°āv ṛshī*).—§ 368

(Tīrthayātrāp.): III, **83**, 7040 (*devaiḥ* . . . *N°purogamaiḥ*, in the tīrtha Naraka), 7043 (*Padmanābham*, = Vishṇu).—§ 370 (do.): III, **84**, 8100 (*sthānam N°sya*, a tīrtha = Çālagrāma?).—§ 371 (Tuṅgaka): III, **85**, 8192 (*Hariḥ*, in Tuṅgaka). — § 377 (Dhaumyatīrthak.): III, **86**, 8281 *Vāsudeva-Dhanañjayau* . . . *Nara-N°āv ṛshī*); **90**, 8395 (*Vishṇuḥ*, in Badarī), 8398 (*devam*), 8399 (*devaḥ*).—§ 384 (Agastyop.): III, **100**, 8701 (= Vishṇu); **101**, 8722 (do.); **102**, 8754 (*c*: enumeration of the incarnations of *N.* (v. Vishṇu)).—§ 406 (Tīrthayātrāp.): III, **125**, 10415 (*Nara-N°au cobhau sthānam prāptāḥ sanātanam*).—§ 409 (Plakshāvataraṇag.): III, **129**, 10518 (*°āçramam*).—§ 420 (Gandhamādanapr.): III, **141**, 10893 (*viçālā Badarī yatra Nara-N°āçramaḥ*).—§ 422, *bis* (Varāhāvatāra): III, **142**, 10939 (*devam* = Vishṇu, became incarnate as a boar).—§ 423 (Gandhamādanapr.): III, **145**, 11031 (*Nara-N°āçramam*, i.e. Badarī), 11039 (*āçramam* . . . *Nara-N°āçritam*, do.), 11054 (*Nara-N°sthānam Bhāgīrathyopaçobhitam*).—§ 426*b* (Kṛtayuga): III, **149**, 11244 (= Vishṇu, is white in the Kṛtayuga).—§ 434 (Saugandhikāharaṇa): III, **156**, 11439 (*viçālā Badarī* . . . *Nara-N°āçramaḥ*), 11443 (*Nara-N°āçramam Badarīty abhiviçrutam*), 11449 (*Nara-N°āçramam*, i.e. Badarī).—§ 436 (Yakshayuddhap.): III, **158**, 11524 (*°āçramam*, i.e. Badarī).—§ 439 (do.): III, **163**, 11857 (*anādinidhanam devam prabhum*, — Vishṇu), 11860 (*°sthānam*, east of Meru, do.), 11863 (*Harim*, do.).—§ 449 (Ājagarap.): III, **177**, †12347 (*°sthāna°*, i.e. Badarī) —§ 458 (Mārkaṇḍeyas.): III, **188**, 12813 (*°āṅkaprakhyas tvam*, sc. Mārkaṇḍeya).—§ 459 (do.): III, **189**, 12952 (etymology), 12953, 12989 (*Çaṅkhacakragadādharaḥ*, during the cataclysm Mārkaṇḍeya saw *N.*, who expounded to him his own nature. Mārkaṇḍeya entered the stomach of *N.*).—§ 478 (Dhundhumārop.): III, **204**, 13600 (= Vishṇu, filled Kuvalāçva with his own energy).—§ 524*b* (Arjuna): III, **272**, 15806 (*°sahāyakam*, sc. *Naram*, i.e. Arjuna).—§ 524*c* (Vishṇu): III, **272**, 15814 (*°ākhyaḥ*, = Vishṇu), 15818 (= do.), 15819 (= do., etymology).—§ 547 (Karṇa): III, **310**, 17205 (Kṛshṇa is *N.*).—§ 549 (Pāṇḍavapr.): IV, **1** (introductory çloka).—§ 549*f* (Durgā): IV, **6**, 179 (*°varapriyām*, sc. *Durgām*), 186 (*yathā Padmā N°parigrahaḥ*).—§ 554 (Sainyodyogap.): V, **1** (introductory çloka); **7**, 151 (= Kṛshṇa).—§ 561*d* (Nara-Narayaṇau): V, **49**, 1921 (*pūrvadevau Nara-N°āv ṛshī*), 1924 (*Nara-N°au*), 1927 (do.), 1934 (had slain Asuras), 1935 (*Nara-N°au devau purvadevav iti çrutiḥ*), 1936 (= Kṛshṇa).—§ 561 (Yānasandhip.): V, **70**, 2568 (= Kṛshṇa, etymology). — § 563 (Dambhodbhavop.): V, **96**, 3461 (*Naro N°ç caiva tāpasau*), 3462 (*Nara-N°au*), (3469), (*Nara-N°au*) (Nara and *N.* humiliated Dambhodbhava).—§ 563 (Bhagavadyānap.); V, **96**, 3489, 3494 (*yasya*—sc. Arjuna's —*N°o* [i.e. *Kṛshṇa*] *bandhuḥ*), 3496 (*Nara-N°au* . . . *Arjuna-Keçavau*).—§ 564 (Mātalīyop.): V, **97**, 3502 (*Nara-N°āv ṛshī*).—§ 565 (Gālavacarita): V, **111**, 3824 (*Kṛshṇaḥ*, in Badarī), 3826 (*Nara-N°au*), 3840 (*°m devam Naram vā Jishṇum*); **117**, 3966 (*reme* . . . *yathā N°o Lakshmyām*).—§ 572 (Rathātirathasaṅkhyānap.): V, **169**, 5865 (*Guḍākeço N°sahāyavān*, = Kṛshṇa).—§ 574 (Jambūkh.): VI, **1**, 1 (introductory çloka).—§ 574*f* (Bindusaras): VI, **6**, 241 (*Nara-N°au*, at Bindusaras).—§ 574 (Jambūkh.): VI, **8**, 307 (*Naro N°ç caiva sarvajñaḥ sarvabhūtakṛt*).—§ 575 (Bhūmip.): VI, **12**, 445 (*°sakhaḥ*, sc. the mountain Kṛshṇa), 450 (*Hariḥ*, resides on the mountain Gomanda (B. Gomanta)). —§ 576 (Bhagavadgītāp.): VI, **23**, 810 (*Naraḥ* (i.e. Arjuna) . . . *N°sahāyavān*, = Kṛshṇa), 818 (*Nara-N°āvṛshī*, = Arjuna and Kṛshṇa).—§ 580 (Bhīshmavadhap.): VI, **59**, †2600 (*ādipadmam* . . . *N°nābhijātam*), †2601 (= Kṛshṇa).—§ 581 (do.): VI, **65**ξ, 2947 (= Vishṇu, praised by Brahmán, who prevailed upon him to become incarnate [as Kṛshṇa]); **66**, 2983 (*Nara-N°au purāṇāv ṛshisattamau*), 2984 (*Nara-N°āv ṛshī*), 3004 (*Nara-N°au devau*, = Arjuna and Kṛshṇa); **68**, 3050 (*Nara-N°au*), 3053 (*Nara-N°au devau*, = Arjuna and Kṛshṇa).—§ 589 (Droṇābhishekap.): VII, **1**, 1 (introductory çloka); **10**, 380 (= Kṛshṇa); **11**, 422 (*pūrvadevau* . . . *Nara-N°au*, = Arjuna and Kṛshṇa).—§ 594 (Akampana): VII, **52**, 2030 (*°samaḥ*, sc. Hari, the son of Akampana).—§ 596 (Pratijñāp.): VII, **76**, 2703 (*°e jayaḥ*, = Kṛshṇa?); **77**, 2707 (*Nara-N°au*, = Arjuna and Kṛshṇa); **80**, 2869 (do., do.); **81**, 2894 (*Nara-N°āv ṛshī*, do.).—§ 598 (Jayadrathavadhap.): VII, **88**, 3139 (*Naro* (i.e. Arjuna) *N°ānugaḥ*, = Kṛshṇa).—§ 599 (do.): VII, **110**, 4227 (*astre N°samaḥ*, sc. Sātyaki).—§ 603 (Nārāyaṇāstramokshap.): VII, **195**, 9009, 9019 (gave the Nārāyaṇa weapon to Droṇa).—§ 603*b* (do.): *N.* is older than the oldest ones. For some purpose that creator of the universe took his birth as the son of *Dharma*. On Himavat he underwent austerities for 66,000 years (description) and then for twice that period, and thus he became *Bráhman* (*brahmabhūtaḥ*) and beheld the supreme deity Çiva (*c*). The lotus-eyed *N.* recited a hymn to *Mahādeva* (i.e. Çiva) (given in full) (ζζ). Çiva then granted him boons, that neither gods nor the Asuras, the mahoragas, the Piçācas, the Gandharvas, men, the Rākshasas, the birds, the Nāgas, nor any creatures in the universe should ever be able to withstand his prowess, "thou shalt be superior to myself if thou ever goest to battle with me." Even that god then walked over the earth (as Kṛshṇa Vāsudeva), beguiling the universe by his illusive power. From the austerities of *N.* was born a great *muni Nara*, who was equal to *N.* himself. Arjuna was none else than that *Nara*. The two ṛshis who are said to be older than the oldest gods, take their births in every yuga for the benefit of the world: VII, **201**, 9447, 9460, (9464), 9472.—§ 604 (Karṇap.): VIII, **1** (introductory çloka).—§ 605 (do.): VIII, **16**, 629 (*Nara-N°au*, = Arjuna and Kṛshṇa).—§ 606 (Tripurākhyāna): VIII, **34**, 1556 (= Vishṇu, in the arrow of Çiva).—§ 608 (Karṇap.): VIII, **62**, 3142 (= Kṛshṇa); **65**, †3296 (do.); **79**, †4059 (*Keçavena*, do.), †4061 (= Kṛshṇa); **87**ω', 4451 (*Nara-N°āv etau purāṇāv ṛshisattamau*, = Arjuna and Kṛshṇa); **91**, †4790 (*Pināka-N°cakrasannibham* . . . *khacaram*); **96**, 5009 (*Nara-N°āv ṛshī*, = Arjuna and Kṛshṇa).—§ 609 (Çalyap.): IX, **1** (introductory çloka).—§ 616 (Sauptikap.): X, **1** (introductory çloka).—§ 618 (Jalapradanikap.): XI, **1** (introductory çloka).—§ 621 (Rājadh.): XII, **1** (introductory çloka).—§ 637 (Rājadh.): XII, **47**θ, 1606 (*Hariḥ*, = Kṛshṇa), 1607 (= do.), 1612 (= do.), 1625 (*Harim* = do.), 1688 (*N°param Brahma N°param tapaḥ N°paro devaḥ sarvam N°aḥ sadā*).—§ 639 (do.): XII, **52**, 1860 (= Kṛshṇa). —§ 641 (do.): XII, **59**, 2209 (*devaḥ*, father of Virajas); **61**, †2336 (*°gītam*, a sentence of his (v. †2337) quoted); **64**, 2393 (*Vishṇum* . . . *sarvabhūteçvaram*), 2398 (*anādimadhyanidhanam*, i.e. Vishṇu), †2402 (*Ādidevam*, i.e. Vishṇu, showed himself in the form of Indra to Māndhātṛ); **110**, 4076 (*bhaktā N°m devam*), 4080 (*bhaktā N°m Harim*); **121**, 4431 (*daṇḍo hi bhagavān Vishṇur daṇḍo N°ḥ prabhuḥ*); **127**, 4661 (*Nara-N°āçramam*, i.e. Badarī), 4664 (*Nara-N°āv ṛshī*, in Badarī).—§ 664 (Mokshadh.): XII, **207**, 7519 (*Hṛshīkeçam*, etc., = Vishṇu (Kṛshṇa)).—§ 667 (do.): XII, **217**, 7843 (*ṛshir N°ḥ*, described the religion of *pravṛtti*),

7880 (do.). — § 678*b* (Anukampaka): XII, **257,** 9151 (°*samaḥ*, sc. Hari the son of Anukampaka). — § 692 (Mokshadh.): XII, **280*a*,** 10018 (*Hariḥ*, i.e. Vishṇu); **281,** 10043 (do., do.), 10048 (°*ātmakam*, description of the nature of the Supreme God), †10081 (= do.).—§ 704 (do.): XII, **301,** †11098 (*yogī* . . . *N°ātmā*); **302,** 11120 (*deve*, i.e. the Supreme God), 11174 (= do.), 11193 (°*ātmānaṃ*, = do.), †11211 (= do.), 11212 (= do.).—§ 717*b* (Nārāyaṇīya): XII, **335,** 12656 (*Nāradasya ca saṃvādam ṛsher N°sya ca*), 12657 (*viçvātmā caturmūrtiḥ sanātanaḥ*), 12658 (the eternal *N.* (i.e. the Supreme God) was born as the son of Dharma in a fourfold form, viz. as Nara, *N.*, Hari, and Kṛshṇa), 12659 (*Nara-N°au*, in Badarī), 12667 (*Nara-N°ābhyāṃ*), 12670, 12673 (i.e. the son of Dharma, Nārada came to Nara and Nārāyaṇa in Badarī); **336,** †12696 (*uttamapūrushena*, i.e. the son of Dharma), †12700 (= do.).— § 717*c* (Uparicara): XII, **336,** 12712 (*Hariṃ*), 12713, 12717, 12729 (*devaṃ Hariṃ*), 12730 (through the grace of *N.* (i.e. Vishṇu) the seven ṛshis composed a treatise on duties); **337,** 12775 (*devaṃ N°ātmakaṃ*), 12776 (*devaṃ*), 12779 (°*parāḥ*, Ekata, Dvita, and Trita repaired to Çvetadvīpa, but in vain attempted to get a sight of *N.*), 12811 (*viçvasṛg havyakavyabhuk*), 12815 (°*paro bhūtvā N°japaṃ japan*, sc. Vasu Uparicara); **338,** 12835, 12847 (*japyaṃ N°mukhodgataṃ*), 12848 (*Hariḥ*, sent Garuḍa to bring Vasu Uparicara to heaven).—§ 717*b* (Nārāyaṇīya): XII, [**339** (Nārada repaired to Çvetadvīpa and hymned *N.* (v. Mahāpurushastava)]; **340,** 12872 (*Hariḥ*, showed himself to Nārada and expounded his own nature and future feats and incarnations), 12964 (*Nara-N°āv ṛshī*, = Arjuna and Kṛshṇa), 12975 (Nārada returned to *Nara* and *N.* in Badarī), 12977 (*mahopanishadaṃ* . . . *Pañcarātrānuçabditaṃ N°mukhodgītaṃ*), 12998 (°*parāḥ*, sc. Yudhishṭhira, etc.), 13000; **341,** 13010 (°*kathāḥ*), 13032 (bestowed omniscience on Vyāsa) [13050 (*Mahāpurushaṃ*, worshipped by the gods, etc. [in Çvetadvīpa])]; **342***ρ*, 13140 (the Supreme God, identified with Kṛshṇa), 13150 (°*ātmakaḥ*, sc. Rudra), 13151 (*devaḥ*), 13155 (*Rudro N°ç caiva sattvam ekaṃ dvidhākṛtaṃ*), 13159 (*devaṃ N°ṃ Hariṃ*), 13165 (*Nara-N°au*, = Arjuna and Kṛshṇa), 13168 (etymology); **343,** I) ††13192 (°*guṇāçrayāt* . . . *tamasaḥ*), ††13205 (°*mukhodgataḥ* . . . *brāhmaṇāḥ*), V) ††13206 (seized Rudra in the throat which became blue (*nīla*)), XIII), ††13222 (born as the ṛshi Vaḍavāmukha), (*φ*), 13243 (granted a boon to Gālava), (*ω*), 13263 (seized the throat of Rudra), 13266 (*Nara-N°au*), 13270 (°*orasi*), 13271, 13272, 13274 (*viçvātmā*), (***aa***), 13278, 13286 (*Naro-N°aç caiva* . . . *Dharmakulodvahau*), 13290 (*devaṃ*), 13296 (encounter between Rudra and Nara + *N.*); **344,** 13305 (°*kathā*), 13306 (*kathāṃ* . . . *N°āçrayāṃ*), 13308 (*devaṃ N°ṃ Hariṃ*), 13310 (*devasattamau Nara-N°au*, in Badarī), (*ββ*), 13317 (°*kathāçrayaṃ*), 13321 (°*kathā*), 13329 (*Nara-N°au*), 13332 (*Nara-N°āv ṛshī*), 13333 (°*kathāṃ*), 13349 (i.e. the ṛshi), (13350) (*Nara-N°au*) (discourse between Nārada and Nara and *N.*); **345,** (13371) (*Nara-N°au*), 13396 (*Nāradaḥ* . . . *N°parāyaṇaḥ*), 13397 (*mantrān N°gatān* . . . *Nara-N°āçrame*), 13398 (*Nara-N°au*) (continuation); **346,** 13405 (°*vidhau*), (13410) (*Nara-N°au*), 13426 (*sarvātmā*, = Vishṇu) (continuation); **347,** 13427 (*Nara-N°eritaṃ*), 13428 (*Nara-N°āçrame*), 13429 (*Nara-N°āv ṛshī*), 13433 (*devaṃ N°ṃ Hariṃ*, i.e. Vishṇu), 13436 (Vyāsa was an incarnation of *N.*); **348,** 13449 (*janma Dharmagṛhe Nara-Nārayaṇātmakaṃ*), 13461 (*Īçvaraḥ* . . . *Virāṭ*), 13473 (°*kṛtau bindau*), 13474 (Madhu and Kaiṭabha were born from two drops created by *N.*, i.e Vishṇu), [13489 foll. (Brahmán's births)], 13519 (when Madhu and Kaiṭabha robbed the Vedas *N.* recovered them, having assumed a horse's head, afterwards he slew Madhu and Kaiṭabha), (*κκ*), 13530, 13531, 13532, 13533, 13534, 13535, 13536, 13537, 13540 (*Hariḥ*); **349,** 13550 (°*priyaḥ*), 13556, I), 13559 (*mānasaṃ janma N°mukhodgataṃ Brahmaṇaḥ*), II), 13563 (°*ātmakaḥ*, sc. *dharmaḥ*), III), 13565, 13570, IV), 13572 (*Hariḥ*), 13577 (°*mukhodbhavaṃ*, sc. *dharmaṃ*), 13581 (*Deveçaṃ Hariṃ*), V), 13586 (*devo Hariḥ*), 13590, VI), 13591 (°*mukhāt*), VII), 1359[illegible], 13599, 13601 (Brahmán's births from *N.* (i.e. Vishṇu), and the promulgations of the religion (*dharma*) of *N.* in the different kalpas), 13613 (°*parāyaṇaḥ*), 13617 (°*paraḥ*), 13618 (°*parāyaṇaḥ*), 13621 (°*ātmake mokshe*), 13622, 13630 (*dharmo N°ātmakaḥ*), 13631; **350,** †13640 (°*syāmçajam ekaputraṃ Dvaipāyanaṃ*, i.e. Vyāsa), †13641 (created Vyāsa), 13643 (°*sutaṃ*, i.e. Vyāsa), 13644 (*janma N°odbhavaṃ*, sc. Vyāsa's), 13650, 13651, 13698 (*janma* . . . *N°āmçajaṃ*, sc. Vyāsa's, who had before been the ṛshi Apāntaratamas, sprung from the speech of *N.*), 13707, 13708 (*ṛshiṃ*), †13711. — § 717*d* (Brahma-Rudrasaṃv.): XII, **352,** 13754 (*sarvātmā Purushaḥ*).—§ 719 (Ānuçāsanik.): XIII, **1** (introductory çloka).—§ 727 (do.): XIII, **11,** †509 (= Kṛshṇa, °*syāṅkagatāṃ* . . . *Çriyaṃ*), †526 (°*e* . . . *vasāmi* . . . *çarīrabhūtā*, sc. Çrī).—§ 730 (do.): XIII, **14,** 596 (*Çaṅkhacakragadādharāt*, = Kṛshṇa).—§ 730*g* (Upamanyu): XIII, **14***ν*, 870 (*Vainateyaṃ samāruhya Çaṅkhacakragadādharaḥ*, = Kṛshṇa), 876 (= do.), 877 (= do.). — § 730 (Ānuçāsanik.): XIII, **17,** 1290 (*sādhyāya*), 1291 (*sādhyaḥ*, learnt the 1,000 names of Çiva from Manu and taught them to Yama).—§ 759 (do.): XIII, **109,** 5373 (merit of worshipping Kṛshṇa as *N.* in the month of Pausha).—§ 766 (do.): XIII, **125,** 5932 (*svayaṃ*); **132,** 6165 (= Vishṇu, raised the submerged earth).—§ 768 (do.): XIII, **139,** 6292 (= Kṛshṇa), 6303 (do.), 6310 (do.); **140,** 6338 (°*suhṛd Nāradaḥ*). — § 768*b* (Kṛshṇa Vāsudeva): XIII, **147,** 6851 (*Hariḥ*, = Kṛshṇa). — § 768 (Ānuçāsanik.): XIII, **148,** 6888 (= Kṛshṇa), 6896 (do.).—§ 769 (do.): XIII, **149,** 6975 (Vishṇu's 1,000 names), 7074 (°*odbhavaṃ jagat*).—§ 773 (do.): XIII, **159,** 7400 (= Kṛshṇa).—§ 775 (do.): XIII, **166*a*,** 7635 (*Vishṇuḥ*).—§ 777 (Svargārohaṇik. p.): XIII, **168,** 7750 (*Nara N°au*, = Arjuna and Kṛshṇa).— § 778 (Açvamedhikap.): XIV, **1** (introductory çloka).— § 782*b* (Brāhmaṇagītāp.): XIV, **25,** 744 (°*vidaḥ*, *devāya*), 745 (*Sarvātmānaṃ*).—§ 787 (Āçramavāsap.): XV, **1** (introductory çloka).—§ 789 (Putradarçanap.): XV, **31***η*, 854 (Kṛshṇa (*Hṛshīkeçaṃ*) identical with *N.*).—§ 793 (Mausalap.): XVI, **1** (introductory çloka); **4,** 130 (= Kṛshṇa).—§ 794 (Mahāprasthānikap.): XVII, **1** (introductory çloka), 38 (= Kṛshṇa).—§ 795 (Svargārohaṇap.): XVIII, **1** (introductory çloka); **5,** 170 (*Devadevaḥ*, after death Kṛshṇa entered into *N.*).—§ 795*c* (Mahābhārata): XVIII, **6***o*, 232 (= the introductory çloka of books I–XVIII), 287 (*Nara-N°au*). Cf. Kṛshṇa Vāsudeva, Mahāpurusha, Vishṇu.

Nārāyaṇa, pl. (°*āḥ*), a tribe of cowherds. § 554 (Sainyodyogap.): V, **7,** 147 (*gopānāṃ arbudaṃ mahat N°ā iti khyātāḥ*, chosen as allies by Duryodhana).—§ 592 (Saṃçaptakavadhap.): VII, **18,** 752 (*gopālāḥ*), 759 (attacked Arjuna); **31,** 1372 (°*balasya*).—§ 599 (Jayadrathavadhap.) : VII, **91***β*, 3255 (*gopālāḥ*, attacked Arjuna).—§ 604 (Karṇap.): VIII, **6,** 153 (had been slain by Bhīshma (!)).—§ 605 (do.): VIII, **11***ρ*, 416 (°*balaiḥ* . . . *gopālaiḥ*, followed Kṛtavarman); **27***λλ*, 1077 (°*balaṃ*, attacked Arjuna).—§ 608 (do.): VIII,

53 ηη, 2564 (*°balasya*, fought with Arjuna); **95**, 4968 (*°āvaçeshāḥ*, followed Kṛtavarman).—§ 609 (Çalyap.): IX, **2** ζ, 95 (*gopālāḥ*, have been slain in the battle).

Nārāyaṇa, adj. ("belonging to Nārāyaṇa"). § 4 (Anukram.): I, **1**, †201 (*°m divyam astram*, all. to § 603).—§ 11 (Parvasaṅgr.): I, **2**, 537 (*astram . . . N°m*, all. to § 603).—§ 603 (Nārāyaṇāstramokshap.): VII, **194**, 8965 (sc. *astram*, known by Droṇa); **195**, 9010 (*paramam astram N°m*, given to Droṇa by Nārāyaṇa, from him it passed over to Açvatthāman); **196**, 9028 (*astre*); **197**, 9029 (*astre prādurbhūte*, sc. by Açvatthāman); **199**, 9209 (*prāduçcakre astram N°am*, sc. Açvatthāman), 9216 (*astreṇa*).—§ 717*b* (Nārāyaṇīya): XII, **344**, 13318 (*tejaḥ*).—§ 730*g* (Upamanyu): XIII, **14**, 854 (sc. *astrāt*).

Nārāyaṇāstra ("the weapon belonging to Nārāyaṇa"). § 10 (Parvasaṅgr): I, **2**, 345 (*moksho N°sya parva*, i.e. Nārāyaṇāstramokshap.).—§ 603 (Nārāyaṇāstramokshap.): VII, **195**, 9022 (known by Açvatthāman); **199**, 9245 (employed by Açvatthāman), 9247; **200**, 9270, 9276, 9290 (was neutralized).—§ 604 (Karṇap.): VIII, **2**, 43 (*°e hate*, all. to § 603). Cf. Nārāyaṇa, adj.

[Nārāyaṇāstramokshaparvan(°va)] ("the section including the hurling of the Nārāyaṇa weapon"), the 78th of the minor parvans of the Mbhbr. § 603. THE LAST PART OF THE 15TH DAY. After the fall of *Droṇa*, the *Kurus*, even *Duryodhana*, etc. (**a**), fled away, *Kṛtavarman* with the remnant of his *Bhoja* troops, etc. (β), *Suçarman* with the remnant of the *Saṃçaptakas*. Only *Açvatthāman* did not flee: *Açvatthāman* & *Çikhaṇḍin*, etc. (γ). *Açvatthāman* asked *Duryodhana* why the troops were fleeing away, even *Karṇa's* troops; *Duryodhana* caused *Kṛpa* to inform *Açvatthāman* of the truth (δ), at which *Açvatthāman* was filled with rage (VII, **193**). *Dhṛtarāshṭra* asked *Sañjaya* what *Açvatthāman* said (ε), he who knew the weapons of men and *Varuṇa*, etc. (ζ) (VII, **194**). *Sañjaya* related: *Açvatthāman* complained before *Duryodhana* that his father has been killed (η), and vowed to destroy the *Pāñcālas* and the *Pāṇḍavas*; neither D., nor G., As., U., Rā., etc., were able to vanquish him; there were none equal to him and *Arjuna* in knowledge of weapons; he had á weapon (the *Nārāyaṇa* weapon) that neither *Arjuna*, etc. (θ) knew, given by *Nārāyaṇa* to his father as a boon, with the promise that no man should ever be his equal in battle; only, this weapon must never be used in haste, etc., and never be hurled upon persons that abandon their chariots or weapons in battle, etc.; with this he would rout and slay the *Pāṇḍavas*, etc. (ι). The *Kuru* army rallied; many blew their conches, etc.; the *Pāṇḍavas* took counsel of one another; *Açvatthāman* touched water and invoked the *Nārāyana* weapon (VII, **195**). Fierce omens in nature appeared. D., Dā., and G. became inspired with fear. *Dhṛtarāshṭra* asked *Sañjaya* what counsel was adopted by the *Pāṇḍavas* in order to protect *Dhṛshṭadyumna* on seeing the retreating *Kauravas* once more advance to battle, rallied by *Açvatthāman*. *Sañjaya* related: *Yudhishṭhira* spoke about the matter to *Arjuna* (κ), fearing that it was *Indra* himself who was approaching for the sake of the *Kauravas*. *Arjuna* in reply described the prowess of *Açvatthāman* and the unrighteousness of the *Pāṇḍavas* in slaying *Droṇa* (λ); "all of us have passed the greater part of our lives; the days that remain to us are few; this exceedingly unrighteous act has stained that remnant"; "I did not interfere, as he was about to be slain; for this fault I have already sunk into hell, overcome with shame" (VII, **196**). *Bhīmasena*, reproaching *Arjuna*, vindicated the deed (μ); "I can, with my arrows, rout the united D. with *Indra* at their head, and As., U., and men." Then *Dhṛshṭadyumna* spoke in justification of his conduct (ν) (VII, **197**). Asked by *Dhṛtarāshṭra* (ξ), *Sañjaya* related: All the other persons present remained silent; *Arjuna*, glancing obliquely towards *Dhṛshṭadyumna*, seemed to reproach him with tears and sighs; *Yudhishṭhira*, etc. (ο) stood ashamed; *Sātyaki* wrathfully rebuked *Dhṛshṭadyumna* (π). *Dhṛshṭadyumna* in reply taunted *Sātyaki* with the slaughter of *Bhūriçravas* (ρ). *Sātyaki* rushed towards *Dhṛshṭadyumna* in order to slay him; *Bhīma*, urged by *Kṛshṇa*, held him back; *Sahadeva* endeavoured to bring about a reconciliation (σ); *Dhṛshṭadyumna* asked *Bhīma* to let him slay *Sātyaki* (τ); then he or *Arjuna* would slay the enemies. *Kṛshṇa* and *Yudhishṭhira* restored peace with great difficulty, and all the warriors proceeded to battle (VII, **198**). *Açvatthāman* caused a great carnage among the *Pāṇḍava* troops (description); before *Duryodhana* he repeated his vow (υ). *Duryodhana* rallied his troops. *Açvatthāman* invoked the *Nārāyaṇa* weapon (description). The *Pāṇḍavas*, etc. (φ), became exceedingly agitated. *Yudhishṭhira*, relying on *Kṛshṇa*, advised *Dhṛshṭadyumna* to flee away with his *Pāñcālas*, and *Sātyaki* with the *Vṛshṇis* and *Andhakas*; he and his brothers would ascend a funeral pile (χ). *Kṛshṇa* prevailed upon the troops to lay down their weapons and alight from their chariots. *Bhīmasena* alone refused to do so, and dissuaded the others (ψ). *Arjuna* said that his vow was that the *Gāṇḍīva* should not be used against the *Nārāyaṇa* weapon, kine, and brahmans. *Bhīma* attacked *Açvatthāman*, but was overwhelmed by the energy of the *Nārāyaṇa* weapon (VII, **199**). *Arjuna* covered *Bhīmasena* with the *Vāruṇa* weapon; *Arjuna* and *Kṛshṇa*, alighting from their chariot, proceeded on foot towards *Bhīma* and forcibly brought him down from his chariot, making him abandon his weapons. Then the *Nārāyaṇa* weapon became neutralized; all the quarters became clear, etc. The *Pāṇḍava* host stood arrayed once more. *Duryodhana* urged *Açvatthāman* to use the same weapon once more; *Açvatthāman* said that it could not be used twice; if brought back it would without doubt slay himself. *Duryodhana* then urged him to slay the enemies with other weapons. *Dhṛtarāshṭra* asked, what then came to pass (ω); *Sañjaya* related: *Dhṛshṭadyumna* & *Açvatthāman*, who deprived *Dhṛshṭadyumna* of his steeds, driver, and chariot; the *Pāñcālas* fled away. *Sātyaki* & *Açvatthāman*, who was worsted by him. *Duryodhana*, etc. (**aa**), & *Sātyaki*, who made them flee away deprived of their chariots. *Açvatthāman* (upon another chariot) & *Sātyaki*, who once more deprived him of his chariot and caused him to retreat; the *Pāṇḍavas* blew their conches, and *Sātyaki* slew 300 of *Vṛshasena's* division, etc. (**aa**). *Açvatthāman* (upon another chariot) & *Sātyaki*; *Açvatthāman* repeated his vow (ββ); *Sātyaki* was carried away by his driver. *Açvatthāman* & *Dhṛshṭadyumna*, who was much afflicted; *Arjuna*, etc. (γγ), & *Açvatthāman*, who slew *Sudarçana* (the *Mālava* king), *Paurava* (*Bṛhatkshattra*), and the young *Cedi* prince. *Bhīma* & *Açvatthāman*; *Bhīma* was carried away by his steeds; the *Pāñcālas* fled away (VII, **200**). *Arjuna* (+ *Kṛshṇa*) (rallying his troops) & *Açvatthāman* (+ the *Kauravas*); *Arjuna* addressed *Açvatthāman* in harsh words (δδ). *Dhṛtarāshṭra* asked *Sañjaya* about the cause of this, as *Arjuna* and *Açvatthāman* loved each other. *Sañjaya* said that it was in consequence of his grief (εε). *Açvatthāman* became angry with *Arjuna* and especially with *Kṛshṇa*, touched water, and made use of the *Āgneya* weapon, from which dire omens in nature appeared, and a great slaughter in the *Pāṇḍava* army resulted; Rā. and Pç. uttered fierce cries, etc. (description). *Arjuna* invoked the *Brāhma* weapon: the darkness was dispelled, etc.; a full *akshauhiṇī* of the *Pāṇḍava* troops had been killed; *Kṛshṇa* and *Arjuna* were unwounded; the *Pāṇḍavas* rejoiced, the *Kauravas* wondered, *Açvatthāman* was disconsolate, and ran away from the fight; he met *Vyāsa*, and asked him the reason; "neither As., nor G., Pç., Rā., U., Y., and birds, nor men can baffle this weapon." *Vyāsa* told him the story of *Nārāyaṇa* (*b*); *Nara* and *Nārāyaṇa* are *Arjuna* and *Kṛshṇa*; even *Açvatthāman* has been born as a portion of *Rudra*, and was [in a former birth] endued with great wisdom, regarding the universe to consist only of *Mahādeva*, etc., and *Çiva* had granted him numerous boons, and he had, in every *Yuga*, adored the great god in his *Phallic* form. *Kṛshṇa* had sprung from *Rudra* himself, and always worshipped him, regarding his *Phallic* emblem as the origin of the universe, and he viewed the identity of *Bráhman* with the universe; D., Si., and M.-ṛ. adore *Kṛshṇa* in order to attain to *Mahādeva*; *Kṛshṇa* is the Creator of everything; the eternal *Kṛshṇa* should be adored with sacrifices, etc. *Açvatthāman* bowed unto *Rudra*, regarded *Kṛshṇa* as worthy of the highest regards, and became filled with delight, the marks whereof appeared on his body. Bowing to *Vyāsa*, he caused the army to be withdrawn, and so did also the *Pāṇḍavas*. Having fought for five days . . . , *Droṇa* repaired to *Brahmaloka* (VII, **201**). *Arjuna* met with *Vyāsa* and inquired of him about the invisible person who aided him in the battle; *Vyāsa* said that it was *Mahādeva* himself, and recited a long enumeration of his attributes ($\eta\eta$); if *Mahādeva* becomes angry, neither D., nor As., G., Rā., even if they hide themselves in deep caves, can have peace. In days of yore *Mahādeva* destroyed the sacrifice of *Daksha*; the *Sacrifice* fled away, and D. and As. fell down and submitted to *Mahādeva*, the *Nāgas* and Ṛ. became agitated, etc.; *Pūshan* was eating the *puroḍāça*: *Çiva* tore out his teeth; the gods assigned to *Rudra* a substantial share in sacrifices; he then re-established the sacrifice. Then *Vyāsa* related the destruction of *Tripura* (*d*). He [*Çiva*] is *Rudra*, etc. ($\iota\iota$). Explanation of some of the names of *Mahādeva* ($\kappa\kappa$). Blessings upon the reader, especially the readers of the *Çatarudriya* ($\lambda\lambda$) (VII, **202**).

Nārāyaṇī ("the daughter of Nārāyaṇa"?) = Indrasenā[2]: III, 10093 (*I*°); IV, 651 (*I*°).

Nārāyaṇīya, adj. ("relating to Nārāyaṇa"). § 717*b* (Nārāyaṇīya): XII, **347,** 13442 (°*m ākhyānam*, i.e. Nārāyaṇīya).

[Nārāyaṇīya(ṃ)] ("the section treating of Nārāyaṇa"): § 717*b* (Mokshadh.). *Bhīshma* said: "I heard it from my father that in the *Kṛta* age, during the epoch of *Manu Svāyambhuva*, the eternal *Nārāyaṇa*, the Soul of the universe, took birth as the son of *Dharma* in a quadruple form: as *Nara*, *Nārāyaṇa*, *Hari*, and the Self-existent (*Svayambhuvaḥ*!) *Kṛshṇa*. Amongst them all, *Nārāyaṇa* and *Nara* practised the several austerities, repairing to the *Himālayan* hermitage *Badarī* and riding in their golden chariot (description; v. the note of PCR., p. 740). *Nārada* dropped down on *Gandhamādana* from a summit of *Meru* and wandered over all the world, and at last repaired to *Badarī* at the hour of *Nara's* and *Nārāyaṇa's* performing their daily rites. He said to himself: this is truly the abode of that Being in whom are established all the worlds including D., As., G., K., and M.-U.; in this spot *Kṛshṇa* and *Hari* dwelt formerly; what is that deity whom these two worship? who are these *Pitṛs* whom these two *Pitṛs* of all beings adore?" Ṛ. *Nārada*, bowing unto *Mahādeva*, praised *Nārāyaṇa* ("sung in the *Vedas*, *Purāṇas*, *Aṅgas*, and *Upāṅgas*"), and asked what god or *Pitṛ* he was sacrificing to. *Nārāyaṇa* said that about this topic nothing should be said, as it was an ancient mystery; but because of his devotion he instructed him about *Kshetrajña*, etc. The twenty-one *Prajāpatis*: *Brahmán*, etc. (*a*) were first born, and obeyed the eternal law of the Supreme God (XII, **335**). *Nārada* (*Pārameshṭhya*) proceeded to *Çvetadvīpa* ("White Island") to behold *Nārāyaṇa* in his original shape; by *yoga* he soared into the firmament, rested for a short while on a summit of *Meru*, then he directed his eyes towards the north-west, and north of the milky ocean he saw the large island *Çvetadvīpa*, more than 32,000 *yojanas* from *Meru*; the inhabitants of that realm have no senses, etc. (description); they are white and free from every sin, etc. *Yudhishṭhira* asked for further information about this people. *Bhīshma* related the story of *Uparicara* (*c*), "the essence of all narratives," which he had heard from his father (XII, **336–8**). Arrived at *Çvetadvīpa*, *Nārada* stood in *yoga* and hymned *Nārāyaṇa* (ζ) [i.e. Mahāpurushastava] (XII, **339**). *Nārāyaṇa* showed himself to *Nārada*, bearing all forms (*viçvarūpadhṛk*; enumeration), uttering with his mouths *Gāyatrī*, *oṃ*, and the *Āraṇyaka*, and the four Vedas; he mentioned *Ekata*, *Dvita*, and *Trita*, and instructed *Nārada* (η). *Vāsudeva* = *Soul* = *Jīva* = *Çesha* = *Saṅkarshaṇa* (when he takes birth as *Jīva*) = *Kshetrajña*; > *Sanatkumāra* = *Mind* = *Pradyumna*; > *the Creator* = *Aniruddha* = *Īçāna* = *Īçvara* = *Ahaṅkāra*. "I am known as *Purusha*; without acts I am the 25th. *Hiraṇyagarbha*, etc. (θ), are in me." *Nārāyaṇa's* boons to *Brahmán* in days of yore. "I am *Kapila*, etc. (ι). *Brahmán* springs from *Aniruddha's* navel." The feats that *Nārāyaṇa* will perform (those that he will slay; his incarnations) (κ); "in the *Tretā* age I shall take birth as Rāma of *Bhṛgu's* race . . . ; in the twilight (*sandhyāṃçe*) between *Tretā* and *Dvāpara* I shall take birth as *Rāma Dāçarathi*; at that time *Ekata* and *Dvita* (in consequence of their injury to *Trita*) will have to take birth as apes; all those apes shall become my allies . . . ; in the period (*sandhau*) joining the *Dvāpara* and the *Kali* I shall take birth in *Mathurā* in order to slay *Kaṃsa*, and take up my residence in *Kuçasthalī* [at] *Dvārakā*; I shall transplant *Prāgjyotisha* to *Dvārakā*, and subjugate *Maheçvara* and *Mahāsena* (i.e. Skanda), who will help Dā. *Bāṇa* (with 1,000 arms); . . . *Brahmán* himself never obtained a sight of me in this shape of mine, which thou hast seen to-day." *Hari* then disappeared; *Nārada* returned to *Badarī*, to behold *Nara* and *Nārāyaṇa*. This great *Upanishad*, consistent with the four *Vedas* and with *Sāṅkhya-Yoga*, and called *Pāñcarātra*, and recited by *Nārāyaṇa* himself, was repeated by *Nārada* in the abode of *Brahmán*. *Yudhishṭhira* asked: "Was not *Brahmán* acquainted with this wonderful narrative of the glory of *Nārāyaṇa*?" *Bhīshma* said that it was only to Ṛ. in the abode of *Brahmán* that *Nārada* recited his narrative. The propagation of the narrative: Ṛ. > *Sūrya* > 66,000 Ṛ. in *Sūrya's* train, etc., > D. on *Meru* > *Asita* > the *Pitṛs*; "I heard it from my father *Çāntanu*; it is a *Purāṇa*, and should not be communicated to anyone that is not a worshipper of *Vāsudeva*; it is really the essence of the hundreds of other narratives thou hast heard from me; in days of yore, D. and As., uniting together, churned the ocean for the *amṛta*; after the same manner, the brahmans in days of yore, uniting together, churned all the scriptures and raised this narrative." He who reads this becomes an inhabitant of *Çvetadvīpa*, etc.—*Vaiçampāyana* said: *Yudhishṭhira* and all his brothers became devoted to *Nārāyaṇa*; *Vyāsa* visited (through the sky) the ocean of milk (which is always the abode of nectar), and worshipping the great God there, he came back to his own hermitage.—*Bhīshma* said: "I have now repeated the narrative that was recited to *Nārada*; that narrative has descended from person to person from very ancient times; I heard it from my father."—*Sūta* said: "I have now told you all that *Vaiçampāyana* recited to *Janamejaya*. King *Janamejaya* properly discharged all his duties according to the scriptures. You have all undergone severe penances, etc.; residing in this sacred *Naimisha* forest, ye are . . . conversant with the *Vedas*, . . . ye have come to this sacrifice of *Çaunaka*; do ye all adore . . . *Nārāyaṇa*. I heard this excellent narrative, that has descended from generation to generation, from my father in former times" (XII, **340**).—*Çaunaka* asked about *pravṛtti* and *nivṛtti*, etc. *Sauti* recited the discourse of *Vaiçampāyana* to *Janamejaya*. *Janamejaya* said that the whole world with *Brahmán*, D., As., and men are deeply attached to acts; *Brahmán*, etc. (λ), have adopted the religion of *pravṛtti*. *Vaiçampāyana* said that this question related to a deep mystery, and that it required penances and acquaintance with the *Purāṇas*; he recited what M.-ṛ. *Vyāsa* said to his disciples *Sumantu*, etc. (μ) (as he used to teach them the four *Vedas* and *Mahābhārata* as the fifth), on *Meru* (inhabited by Si. and Cā.); *Nārāyaṇa* had been gratified by his penances on the shore of the ocean of milk, and he had, with the eye of knowledge, beheld all that occurred in the beginning of the *Kalpa*: *Mahā-Purusha* or *Paramātmā* (according to both *Sāṅkhya* and *Yoga*) > *Avyakta* (*Pradhāna*) > *Aniruddha* (*mahān ātmā, Ahaṅkāra*) > *Pitāmaha* (i.e. Brahmán); from *Ahaṅkāra* have sprung the five elements (*mahābhūtāni*); *Marīci*, etc. (ν), are the eight *Prakṛtis*, upon whom all the worlds depend; *Brahmán* created them with the *Vedas*, *Vedāṅgas*, etc.; *Rudra* (from the principle of wrath) > ten *Rudras*: these eleven *Rudras* = *Vikārapurushāḥ* . . . *Brahmán* with the R., *Prakṛtis*, and D.-ṛ. repaired to the northern shore of the ocean of milk and practised the penances named *mahāniyama* (declared by *Brahmán* in the *Vedas*) for 1,000 celestial years (description); then *Hari* spoke to them, saying that he would invest them with *pravṛtti*. They performed a sacrifice in honour of *Vishṇu* according to the ordinances laid down for the *Kṛta* age. The great god was pleased and said that their *pravṛtti* should be fraught with ends whence there will be return; "*Marīci*, etc. (ξ), the seven Ṛ. who are *mānasāḥ* (spiritual sons of *Brahmán*) will become the preceptors of the *Vedas*, wedded to the religion of *pravṛtti*, and created for procreating offspring (*Prājāpatye*); . . . *Sana*, etc. (ο), these seven Ṛ. who are spiritual (*mānasāḥ*) sons of *Brahmán*, and whose knowledge comes to them of itself, are wedded to the religion of *nivṛtti*, conversant with *Yoga* and *Sāṅkhya*, and cause the religion of *nivṛtti* to flow in the worlds. *Kshetrajña* is myself . . . *Brahmán's* son *Rudra* has sprung from his brow at his command . . . In the *Kṛta-yuga* living creatures should not be slain in the sacrifices; in the *Tretā-yuga* animals, dedicated with *mantras*, will be slain in the sacrifices; then comes the mixed (*miçraḥ*) *yuga Dvāpara*; then *Tishya* with *Kali* in the van." *Vyāsa* continued: D. and Ṛ. went away. Only *Brahmán* remained, desirous of beholding the great god, then residing in the form of *Aniruddha*; the god then showed himself to *Brahmán* with a vast equine head, etc. (description), saying that at times he would appear in incarnate forms. Then he disappeared, and *Brahmán* proceeded to his own region. "Do you bow to him who is the lord of the *Rudras*, etc. (π)." Blessing upon the reader (XII, **341**). *Janamejaya* inquired of the meaning of the different names of *Nārāyaṇa*; *Vaiçampāyana* related what *Keçava* (Kṛshṇa) had said to *Phālguna* (Arjuna), when the latter asked him about the signification of his names mentioned by M.-ṛ. in the *Vedas* and the *Purāṇas*. *Kṛshṇa* said: In the *Ṛgveda*, etc. (ρ), many are the names that have been mentioned by M.-ṛ.; "from *Nārāyaṇa's* [as *Aniruddha*] grace has arisen *Brahmán*, and from his wrath has arisen *Rudra*"; description of *Rudra* (σ); "I adored in days of yore the ancient *Rudra* for obtaining the boon of a son; *Brahmán*, etc. (τ), adore *Hari Nārāyaṇa* (*Vishṇu*)." Etymology of *Nārāyaṇa*, etc. (υ); "Ṛ *Trita*, the eldest (*ādyaḥ*) son of *Brahmán*, when thrown into a well by *Ekata* and *Dvita*, invoked me as *Pṛçnigarbha* and was rescued from the pit; *Dīrghatamas* (§ 170) invoked me as *Keçava*, became cured of his blindness, and then came to be called *Gotama* (v. Nīl.); *Agni* and *Soma*, blending together, became transfused in one and the same substance (*ekayonitvam āgataḥ*) . . . , in the *Purāṇa* this is said, and further that the gods have *Agni* for their mouth" (XII, **342**). Asked by *Arjuna* about the unity of nature of *Agni* and *Soma*, *Kṛshṇa* related this ancient story: I) When only the infinite water (quotation of the *çruti*) exists (called *tamas*), *Bráhman* > *Purusha* > *Brahmán*, who caused *Agni* (the *kshatra*) and *Soma* (*bráhman*, i.e. the *brahmans*) to spring from his own eyes (quotation of the *çruti* relating to *Agni*); *Agni* is the *hotṛ* and the *brahmán* of the sacrifice; he who offers food in the mouth of a *brahman* is said to pour libations into the sacred fire for gratifying the deities (quotation from Çatapatha-brāhmaṇa); in this way *brahmans* have come to be regarded as *Agni*. *Agni* is again *Vishṇu* (quoting *Sanatkumāra*). II) By *Gautama's* curse (for his assault on *Ahalyā*), *Indra* got a green beard; through the curse of *Kauçika*, *Indra* lost his testicles and got those of a ram.—III) As *Indra* with uplifted thunderbolt would prevent the *Açvins* from receiving a share in sacrifice (*graha-*), *Cyavana* paralysed his arms.—IV) Incensed at the destruction of his sacrifice, *Daksha* by his austerities caused a third eye to appear on the forehead of *Rudra*.—V) When *Rudra* would destroy *Tripura*, *Uçanas* tore a matted lock from his head and hurled it at *Rudra*, whence serpents began to bite *Rudra*, whose throat became blue, just as in the *Svāyambhuva Manvantara*, when *Nārāyaṇa* seized *Rudra* by the throat.—VI) When *Aṅgiras Bṛhaspati* sat [on the shores of the ocean] to make preparation for the churning in order to raise the *amṛta* and touched water (*upaspṛçataḥ*), the water was not clear (*na prasādaṃ gatavatyaḥ*); he became angry and [cursed] the ocean, saying: "From this day thou shalt be tainted with fishes, etc."—VII) *Viçvarūpa Triçiras Tvāshṭra* was the *purohita* of the gods; he was the sister-son of the *Asuras*; while publicly offering to the deities he secretly offered shares to the *Asuras*; the *Asuras* with

Hiraṇyakaçipu at their head prevailed upon him through his mother, that he (who had come to the *Nandana* wood) should aid *Hiraṇyakaçipu*, who was cursed by *Hairaṇyagarbha Vasishṭha*, saying: "Since thou hast chosen another *hotṛ*, thy sacrifice shall not be completed, and thou shalt be slain by a hitherto unknown kind of being." *Viçvarūpa* performed austere *tapas*; *Indra* sent *Apsarases*, of whom *Viçvarūpa* became enamoured, and he promised to destroy *Indra* and the gods; he uttered *mantras* by which he grew; with one mouth he drank all the *soma* that was offered to the gods by the brahmans in all the worlds; with one [he ate] food; with one [he drank the energy of all] the gods, including *Indra*. These repaired to *Brahmán* (so B.; *Brāhmaṇaṃ*, C.), and according to his counsel they prevailed upon Ṛ. *Bhārgava Dadhīca*, that he should abandon his body by his *yoga* power; his bones *Dhātṛ* shaped into a thunderbolt (*vajra*), which was pervaded by the energy of *Vishṇu*; with this *vajra Indra* struck *Viçvarūpa*, and severed the heads from the body. By the pressing (*mathana*) of his limbs *Vṛtra* came into existence, whom *Indra* slew. Terrified with the double brahmanicide, *Indra* abandoned the sovereignty of the gods; he entered a cool lotus-stalk in the *Mānasa* lake, and becoming very minute (*aṇumātraḥ*) by his *yoga* power (*aiçvarya-yogāt*) he entered the fibres of that lotus-stalk. Now *rajas* and *tamas* assailed the deities; the *mantras* of M.-ṛ. lost their efficacy (*na prāvartanta*), Rā. appeared; the *Vedas* (*Brahma*) were about to disappear (*utsādanaṃ jagāma*); without an *Indra*, the worlds lost their strength and became easy to overwhelm. Then the gods and *Ṛshis* crowned *Āyus*' son *Nahusha* as king of the gods. *Nahusha* ruled over heaven with 500 luminaries on his forehead, which had the virtue of robbing the energy of every creature. Then follows, somewhat abbreviated, the contents of § 555 (Indra) = V, **11** foll.—VIII) In days of yore, when M.-ṛ. *Bharadvāja* was saying his prayers (*upāspṛçat*) on the shore of the celestial *Gaṅgā*, he was approached by *Vishṇu*, who was taking his three strides; *Vishṇu*, struck with water by *Bharadvāja* on the breast, received a mark [i.e. Çrīvatsa] on his breast.—IX) Cursed by M.-ṛ. *Bhṛgu*, *Agni* was obliged to become a devourer of all things.—X) *Aditi* cooked food for the gods to strengthen them so that they might slay the *Asuras*; there *Budha* [i.e. the planet Mercury], after completing a vow (*vratacaryā*-), came and asked for alms of *Aditi*; but she, intending that only the gods should eat it first, gave him no alms. At this *Budha* (*Brahmabhūtaḥ*) cursed *Aditi*, saying that she would have a pain (*vyathā*) in her womb; in the second birth (as an egg) of *Vivasvat*, the egg of [his] mother *Aditi* [was] killed (so B.); [therefore] *Vivasvat Çrāddhadeva* [became] *Mārtaṇḍa*.—XI) *Daksha* had sixty daughters, of whom he gave thirteen to *Kaçyapa*, ten to *Dharma*, ten to *Manu*, and twenty-seven (the *Nakshatras*) to *Soma*; although the latter were all alike in respect of beauty, etc., yet *Soma* became more attached to *Rohiṇī*, and was cursed by *Daksha*, etc., cf. § 615 (Prabhāsotpattikathana) = IX, **35**; *Prabhāsa* in the western ocean was originally called *Hiraṇyasaras*; from this curse also have come the dark spots in the disc of the moon, exhibiting the mark of a hare.—XII) M.-ṛ. *Sthūlaçiras* practised austerities on the north-eastern side of *Meru*; a breeze, charged with all delicious perfumes, gratified him; the trees around him [from jealousy] put forth their flowers to make a display; he cursed them, saying that they should not have flowers at all times.—XIII) *Nārāyaṇa*, in days of yore, for the good of the world, became M.-ṛ. *Vaḍavāmukha*; practising austerities on *Meru*, he summoned the ocean; but it did not come; he then, with the heat of his body, evaporated its water and caused it to become as saltish in taste as the human sweat; it should cease to be drinkable; only to *Vaḍavāmukha* it should be sweet, when he drinks it; therefore, to this day, the water from the ocean is drunk only by *Vaḍavāmukha*, who lives within it (*anuvartinā*).—XIV) *Umā*, the daughter of the mountain *Himavat*, was desired in marriage by *Rudra*; M.-ṛ. *Bhṛgu*, was refused, and therefore he brought about that *Himavat* ceased to abound with jewels and gems. Even such is the glory of the brahman. [Almost the whole of the preceding part of this chapter is in prose.]—Etymologies of *Hṛshīkeça*, etc. (ϕ); Ṛ. *Yāska*, having adored me by the name of *Çipivishṭa*, succeeded in restoring (*abhijagmivān*) the *Nirukta*, which had disappeared into the nether regions (*adho nashṭam*). Other identifications with *Nārāyaṇa* (χ); Ṛ. *Pāñcāla*, etc. (ψ), aided by *Nārāyaṇa*; etymology of *Dharmaja*, etc. (ω).—Asked by *Arjuna* about that battle between *Rudra* and *Nārāyaṇa*, *Kṛshṇa* related: All the universe became suddenly filled with anxiety, etc. (*aa*); peace was brought about by *Brahmán*; the mark made by *Rudra's* lance on *Nārāyaṇa's* cheek should assume the form of a beautiful whirl, and *Rudra* should be called *Çrīkaṇṭha* from the mark of *Nārāyaṇa's* hand on his throat.—The two Ṛ. *Nara* and *Nārāyaṇa* then made friends with *Rudra*, and, dismissing the gods, once more set themselves to penances. "In this way, O son of *Kuntī*! assuming diverse forms do I rove at will through the earth, *Brahmaloka*, and the high and eternal region of felicity called *Goloka*. That being, whom, at the time of all thy battles, thou beheldest stalking in thy van, is no other than *Rudra*; . . . those foes whom thou hast slain, were all, in the first instance, slain by him" (XII, **343**). *Çaunaka* asked, why *Nārada*, having seen the Supreme Lord in the form of *Aniruddha*, again proceeded so quickly to *Nara* and *Nārāyaṇa*. *Sauti* said: At an interval in his snake-sacrifice, *Janamejaya* addressed his great-grandfather *Vyāsa*, asking him this same question, etc. ($\beta\beta$). *Vaiçampāyana* answered: Leaving *Çvetadvīpa*, *Nārada* quickly proceeded to *Meru*, full of wonder, thence to *Gandhamādana*, and, traversing the sky, to *Badarī*, where he saw the Ṛ. [*Nara* and *Nārāyaṇa*], engaged in penances, both with *Çrīvatsa* and matted locks, both with "the swan's foot" on their palms, etc., each of them with four *mushkas* (v. the note of PCR., p. 822), sixty teeth, and four arms, etc. (description), and told them what he had seen at *Çvetadvīpa*, and that the marks of *Nara* and *Nārāyaṇa* were the same that he had seen on the Supreme Soul; "that realm, where he resides, the Sun warms not, etc.; having constructed an altar, measuring eight fingers' breadth, he is practising penances there, standing on one foot, etc.; whatever libations . . . are poured on the sacrificial fire by Ṛ., etc. ($\gamma\gamma$), all reach the feet of that great deity" (XII, **344**). Discourse of *Nara* and *Nārāyaṇa* to *Nārada* about *Nārāyaṇa*; "*Sūrya* is said to be the door [through which the emancipate must pass]; entering *Sūrya*, their bodies are consumed by his fire; they then become invisible . . . ; reduced to invisible atoms they then enter into *Nārāyaṇa* [who resides in the centre of *Sūrya*] > *Aniruddha* > (losing all physical attributes and transformed into mind alone) *Pradyumna* > *Saṅkarshaṇa* (*Jīva*) (both those conversant with *Sāṅkhya* and those that are devoted to the Supreme deity) > *Kshetrajña* (= *Vāsudeva*) divested of *sattva*, *rajas*, and *tamas*; . . . thou wert beheld by us in *Çvetadvīpa*." D.-ṛ. *Nārada* became entirely devoted to *Nārāyaṇa*, and dwelt in *Badarī* for 1,000 celestial years (XII, **345**). *Vaiçampāyana* related the discourse between *Nara* and *Nārāyaṇa* on one side and *Nārada* on the other about the rites in honour of the *Pitṛs*. *Nārada*, the son of *Daksha*, was originally the son of *Brahmán*, created before all others by a fiat of his will. On one occasion the deities taught their children [the *Pitṛs*] the *çrutis*, and, having lost their knowledge, had to acquire it again from those sons (v. the note of PCR., p. 829); the gods and the *Pitṛs*, placing three *piṇḍas* on some blades of *kuça*-grass, worshipped each other. Then *Nārada* asked why the *Pitṛs* in days of yore acquired the name of *piṇḍas*. *Nara* and *Nārāyaṇa* said: The earth, in days of yore, disappeared, and was raised up by *Govinda* (*Vṛshākapi*) in the shape of a gigantic boar; when the hour came for his morning prayers, he, suddenly shaking off three balls of mud from his tusk, placed them upon the earth and dedicated them to his own self, saying that he was resolved to create those that were to be called *Pitṛs*; seeing that the three balls of mud had fallen towards the south, he declared that these should be known henceforth by the name of *Pitṛs*. Having then offered those *piṇḍas* on the *Varāha* mountain, worshipping his own self, he disappeared. Therefore those who sacrifice to the *Pitṛs*, etc., sacrifice, etc., to *Vishṇu* himself (XII, **346**). *Vaiçampāyana* continued: D.-ṛ. *Nārada*, after 1,000 years, repaired to his own retreat on *Himavat*, while *Nara* and *Nārāyaṇa* remained in *Badarī*, engaged in austerities; "the ancestors of that person who hates *Nārāyaṇa*, sink into hell for ever"; glorification of *Nārāyaṇa*, citing *Vyāsa* and referring to *Harigītā* (i.e. Bhagavadgītā); "*Vyāsa* is *Nārāyaṇa* on earth; who else could compile such a treatise as the *Mahābhārata*? Having listened to the diverse kinds of duties and resolved upon a horse-sacrifice, let thy great sacrifice go on."—*Sauti* continued: Formerly *Nārada* had recited the discourse about *Nārāyaṇa* to my preceptor in the hearing of many Ṛ. and the *Pāṇḍavas* and *Kṛshṇa* and *Bhīshma*. *Sauti's* eulogium on *Nārāyaṇa* (δδ) (XII, **347**). *Çaunaka* said: "I have heard from thee the glory of the Supreme Soul, etc. (εε); the form of *Vishṇu* with the equine head, that appeared in the great ocean on the north-east was beheld by *Brahmán Parameshṭhin*." *Çaunaka* then inquired why *Hari* had appeared, in the form of *Aniruddha* with the horse-head, to *Brahmán*. *Sauti* said he would recite that which *Vaiçampāyana* recited to *Janamejaya* (in the Snake-sacrifice), who put the same question to *Vaiçampāyana*. *Janamejaya* put the question to *Vaiçampāyana*. *Vaiçampāyana* expounded how the destruction is brought about of all things; then "from the primeval darkness (fraught with immortality) arises *Bráhman* > *Purusha* = *Aniruddha* = *Pradhāna* (divested of sex) = *Avyakta* = *Viçvaksena Hari*, who, yielding to *yoga*-sleep (*nidrāyogam*), lays himself down on the waters thinking of the creation; > *Ahaṅkāra* = *Brahmán*, etc. = *Hiraṇyagarbha*, who takes birth within the lotus [that springs] from *Aniruddha*. Adopting the attribute of *sattva* (*sattvasthaḥ*), *Brahmán* commenced to create the universe. In the primeval lotus two drops of water had been deposited by *Nārāyaṇa*: one like honey (*madhu*) which became *Madhu* made up of *tamas*; the other hard (*kaṭhina*) which became *Kaiṭabha* made up of *rajas*; these two *Asuras* (*Dānavas*), armed with maces, beheld within the lotus *Brahmán* creating the four *Vedas*, seized them, and dived to *Rasā*[-*tala*] in the north-eastern ocean." *Brahmán* complained before *Īçāna* (ζζ); then he hymned *Hari* (ηη): "my first birth from thee was due to a fiat of thy will; my second birth in days of yore was from thy eyes; my third birth was from thy speech; my fourth birth was from thy ears; my fifth birth was from thy nose; my sixth birth was from an egg; this is my seventh birth, in this lotus." *Purusha* rose from his slumber and assumed an equine head, he who was the abode of the *Vedas*; the firmament became the crown of his head, etc. (θθ); then he disappeared and proceeded to *Rasā*[-*tala*]; there he set himself to *yoga*, and adopting a voice according to the *çikshā* he began to loudly utter Vedic mantras. The two *Asuras*, making an appointment with the *Vedas* as to the time of their return, threw them down to *Rasātala* and ran after the sound. Meanwhile *Hari* took up all the *Vedas* and gave them to *Brahmán*; he placed the horse-head in the north-eastern ocean, [which horse-head], moreover, [was] the abode (*ālayaṃ*) of the *Vedas*, and thence he was called (*babhūva*) *Açvaçiras* ("horse-headed"). Returning to the lotus, *Madhu* and *Kaiṭabha* saw him in the form of *Aniruddha* in *yoga*-sleep on the water, white, endued with stainless *sattva*, on the hood of a snake surrounded with a garland of flames. They awakened him and were slain by him; thence he came to be called *Madhusūdana*. Aided then by *Hari* and assisted by the *Vedas*, *Brahmán* created all the worlds. Then *Hari* disappeared. Once more, however, he assumed the same form for the sake of the religion of *pravṛtti* (*pravṛttidharmārthaṃ* B.; C. °*ttiṃ dha*°). The brahman who frequently (*nityaṃ*) hears or mentally recites (*dhārayīta*) this story, will never forget his [Vedic or other] lore. Having adored with austere penances the god with the equine head, Ṛ. *Pañcala* [i.e. *Gālava*, PCR.] acquired [the science of] *Krama* proceeding along the path pointed out by the deity [i.e. *Rudra*, PCR.; cf. XII, **343**, 13261–63]. *Hari* is the receptacle (*nidhiḥ*) of the *Vedas*, and of penances, and *yoga*, etc. (ιι); *ṛta*, etc. (κκ), has *Nārāyaṇa* for its soul; the Supreme Being is the cause of all this as *Purusha* and as *Pradhāna*; he is the agent, etc.; the thoughts of all, including *Brahmán*, etc. (λλ), are known to *Keçava*; but none of these can know what his thoughts are, etc.; he is called *Vāsudeva* because of his being the abode of all creatures; he is the eternal highest M.-ṛ., etc.; only the M.-ṛ. that have knowledge for their souls behold the eternal *Purusha* who transcends all attributes (*guṇādhikaṃ*) (XII, **348**). *Janamejaya* said that the *ekāntins* [i.e. those who are devoted to *Nārāyaṇa* with their whole souls] at once attain to the fourth or highest end (i.e. *Purushottama*) without going through the three [i.e. *Aniruddha, Pradyumna*, and *Saṅkarshaṇa*; PCR.], and this end is better than that attained to by brahmans studying the *Vedas* with the *Upanishads*, etc., and by *Yatis*; and he asked who first promulgated the religion of Devotion.—*Vaiçampāyana* said: When the *Pāṇḍava* and the *Kuru* armies were drawn up in array for the battle, and *Arjuna* became cheerless, *Kṛshṇa* himself explained this religion [sc. in the Bhagavadgītā]. Having created this religion in the *Kṛta* age, it is borne by *Nārāyaṇa* himself. *Nārada* was questioned about it by *Arjuna* in the midst of Ṛ. and in the presence of *Kṛshṇa* and *Bhīshma*. My preceptor *Vyāsa* heard what D.-ṛ. *Nārada* said, and imparted it to me.—I) In that *Kalpa*, when *Brahmán* took his birth in (A) the mind of *Nārāyaṇa* (*mānasaṃ janma*) and issued from the latter's mouth, *Nārāyaṇa* himself performed the rites of this religion. From him it passed to Ṛ. *Phenapāḥ* (froth-drinking)

> *Vaikhānasāḥ* > *Soma*; then it disappeared.—II) A: the eyes of *Nārāyaṇa* (*cākshusaṃ janma*): *Soma* > *Brahmán* > *Rudra* > R. *Vālakhilyāḥ* (in the *Kṛta* age); then it once more disappeared through the illusive power of that god [*Nārāyaṇa*, PCR.].—III) A: the speech of *Nārāyaṇa* (*vācikaṃ*): *Nārāyaṇa* > R. *Suparṇa* (who recited it thrice [a day, PCR.]—*triḥ parikrāntavān*—whence it came to be called *Trisauparṇa*, referred to in the *Ṛgveda*) > *Vāyu* > R. *Vighasāçinaḥ* [i.e. who subsist on remains of sacrifices after feeding guests, etc.], > the ocean (*mahodadhiḥ*); it once more disappeared and became merged (*-samāhitaḥ*) into *Nārāyaṇa*.—IV) A: the ear of *Nārāyaṇa* (*çravaṇajā sṛshṭiḥ*): *Nārāyaṇa* > *Brahmán* (". . . together with the *Āraṇyakas*") > *Manu Svārocisha* > his son *Çaṅkhapada* > his son *Suvarṇābha* (*diçāṃ pālaṃ*); when the *Tretā yuga* came it once more disappeared.—V) A: the nose of *Nārāyaṇa* (*nāsatye janmani*): *Nārāyaṇa* > *Brahmán* > *Sanatkumāra* > *Prajāpati Vīraṇa* (in the beginning of the *Kṛta* age) > the *muni Raibhya* > his son *Kukshi* (*diçām pālaya*); then it disappeared.—VI) A: an egg [that sprang from *Hari*, PCR.] (*aṇḍaje janmani*): *Nārāyaṇa* > *Brahmán* > Mu. *Barhishads* > *Jyeshṭha* (a brahman who had mastered the whole *Sāmaveda*) > king *Avikalpana* (B. °*kampa*°); then it disappeared.—VII) A: the lotus that sprang from the navel of *Nārāyaṇa* (this seventh birth, *padmajaṃ*): *Nārāyaṇa* > *Brahmán* > *Daksha* > his eldest daughter's son *Āditya* (elder brother of *Savitṛ*) > *Vivasvat* > *Manu* (in the beginning of the *Tretā yuga*) > his son *Ikshvāku* > the whole world; when the universal destruction comes (*kshayānte*) it will once more return to *Nārāyaṇa*.—The religion of the *Yatis* has been narrated to thee in the *Harigītā*. *Nārada* got it from *Nārāyaṇa* himself. *Nārāyaṇa* is adored (*dṛçyate*) as of one form (*ekavyūhavibhāgaḥ* [i.e. as *Aniruddha*, PCR.]), or of two [do. + *Pradyumna*], or three [do. + *Saṅkarshaṇa*] or four [do. + *Vāsudeva*].—*Janamejaya* asked why all persons do not follow the religion of Devotion. *Vaiçampāyana* pointed to *sattva*, *rajas*, and *tamas*. *Hari* casts a kind eye upon the person endued with *sattva*; only *Brahmán* looks kindly upon him who is overwhelmed with *rajas* and *tamas*; D. and R. are given to *sattva*, but [the deities] not in its subtle form.—Asked by *Janamejaya* how one may attain to the Supreme Being (*Purushottama*), and about *pravṛtti*, *Vaiçampāyana* said that the *Sāṅkhya-Yoga*, the *Veda* and *Āraṇyakas* (*Vedāraṇyakaṃ*), and the *Pañcarātra* are parts of one whole (*parasparāṅgāni*), and even this is the religion of the *Ekāntins*, the *Sāttvika* religion, the *Ekāntagati* of the Yatis of Çvetadvīpa (v. *Çveta*, pl.; differently PCR., v. the note, p. 852). *Vyāsa* imparted this religion to *Yudhishṭhira* (XII, **349**).—*Janamejaya* asked whether the *Sāṅkhya*, *Pañcarātra* (B. *Pā*°), and *Vedāraṇyaka* are *ekanishṭha* ("preaching the same course of duties," PCR.) or *pṛthaṅnishṭha* ("preaching courses of duties different from one another," PCR.), and about *pravṛtti*. M.-ṛ. *Vaiçampāyana* said: "I bow to M.-ṛ. [*Vyāsa*] (cf. § 77 = I, **63**), the sixth in the series beginning with *Pitāmaha* (Brahmán), sprung from a portion of *Nārāyaṇa*, the only son [of his parents], whom *Nārāyaṇa* in the first ages (*ādikāleshu*) created as his son, the unborn and ancient (*ajaṃ purāṇaṃ*), the great receptacle of the *Vedas*. *Janamejaya* said: When *Vasishṭha* > *Çaktri* > *Parāçara* > *Vyāsa*, how can *Vyāsa* be the son of *Nārāyaṇa*? *Vaiçampāyana* said: *Vyāsa* dwelt for some time on the *Himavat*; he became tired of his penances owing to the great work of composing the Mahābhārata (*Bhāratam ākhyānaṃ*), waited upon by his disciples, *Sumantu*, etc. (μμ), recapitulating (*āvartayan*) the *Vedas*, etc. (νν); asked by us, *Vyāsa* related: This narrative, belonging to the early times (*ādikālodbhavaṃ*), has become known to me through my penances. In the seventh creation, that from the lotus (*prajāvisarge vai saptame padmasambhave*), *Brahmán* being hesitating on account of the difficulty of creating, *Nārāyaṇa* caused Intelligence (*Buddhi*) to enter *Brahmán*, who now created Dai., Dā., G., and Rā., etc.; seeing that many of these would afflict D. and R., *Nārāyaṇa* resolved upon incarnations (as boar, man-lion, dwarf, man), and upon upholding the earth as a snake in *Pātāla*. Then uttering the syllable *bho*, he, from the voice (*Sarasvatī*) created *Sārasvata Apāntaratamas*, whom he caused to distribute the *Vedas* in the [*Manv*]*antara* of *Manu Svāyambhuva*, saying that he should do thus in each *Manvantara*, and, when *Tishya* (i.e. Kali-yuga) had set in, he should become the father of the *Kauravas*, etc., and distribute the *Vedas* into diverse classes, and be of a dark complexion, born from M.-ṛ. *Parāçara* in *Vasishṭha's* (the mind-born son of *Brahmán*) line by a maiden; he should know the past, the present, and the future; not he, but his son, should be freed from passion (*rāgāt*); he should see *Kṛshṇa*; *Sūrya's* son *Çanaiçcara* [i.e. the planet Saturn] will be a great *Manu* [read with B. *Manur* = Manu Sāvarṇi? during his Manvantara Vyāsa will be one of the seven Ṛshis]; during that *Manvantara* thou shalt be the foremost of the class beginning with *Manu* (*Manv-ādi-gaṇa-pūrvakaḥ* [i.e. of the Manu, gods, Ṛshis, etc., in the respective Manvantara])." *Vyāsa* said: "I am he that was born as *Apāntaratamas*; I underwent, in days of yore, the austerest penances."—*Vaiçampāyana* said: the preceptors (*vaktṛ*, *vettṛ*) of the diverse systems (*jñānāni*) are: 1) of *Sāṅkhya*: the great R. *Kapila*; 2) of *Yoga* (read *yogasya* with B.): the primeval (*purātanaḥ*) *Hiraṇyagarbha*; 3) of the *Vedas*: R. *Apāntaratamas*, by some called *Prācīnagarbha*; 4) of *Pāçupata*: *Çiva* (the son of *Brahmán*); 5) of *Pañcarātra* (B. *Pā*°): *Bhagavat* [i.e. Nārāyaṇa], and he may be seen in all the systems. The *Sāṅkhya*, *Yoga*, and *Vedas* are eternal; those conversant with the *Pañcarātra* (B. *Pā*°) enter *Nārāyaṇa*; all acts spring from R. *Nārāyaṇa* (XII, **350**).—*Janamejaya* asked whether there are many *Purushas* or only one, etc. *Vaiçampāyana* said that in the *Sāṅkhya* and *Yoga* many *Purushas* are spoken of; but as the many *Purushas* have only one origin (*yoniḥ*), so the one *Purusha* is the universe (*viçvaṃ*) above the qualities (*guṇādhikaṃ*), citing the *Vedas*, etc. (ξξ), and the old narrative of the discourse between *Brahmán* and *Tryambaka* (Çiva), i.e. Brahma-Rudra-saṃvāda (*d*) (XII, **351-2**).

Narishyanta or **Narishyat**, son of Manu Vaivasvata. § 139 (Manu Vaivasvata): I, **75**, 3140 (third son of Manu).

Nārītīrthāni, pl., name of five tīrthas. § 250 (Arjunavanavāsap.): I, **217**, 7871 (i.e. Agastyatīrtha, Saubhadra, Pauloma, Kārandhama, and Bhāradvājasya tīrthaṃ (v. 7841 foll.), assigned by Nārada to five Apsarases (Vargā, etc.), who had been cursed to become crocodiles; at his visit at *N.* Arjuna liberated the Apsarases from the curse).—§ 400 (Tīrthayātrāp.): III, **118**, †10217 (visited by Yudhishṭhira, etc.; all. to § 250).

Narmadā, a river, the present Nerbudda. § 268 (Varuṇasabhāv.): II, **9**, 371 (among the rivers present in the palace of Varuṇa).—§ 281 (Sahadeva): II, **31**, 1114 (in the south).—§ 358 (Tīrthayātrāp.): III, **82**, 4094 (a tīrtha).—§ 370 (do.): III, **85**, 8151 (*Çoṇasya N°āyāç ca prabhave* (°*bhede*, B.) . . . *Vaṃçagulme*).—§ 377 (Dhaumyatīrthak.):

III, **89**, 8355, 8357 (in the west).—§ 404 (Tīrthayātrāp.): III, **121**, 10306 (visited by Yudhishṭhira, etc.), 10310 (merit of bathing in the *N.*).—§ 434 (Saugandhikāharaṇa): III, **156**, 11437.—§ 459 (Mārkaṇḍeyas.): III, **188***a*, 12908 (seen by Mārkaṇḍeya in the stomach of Nārāyaṇa).—§ 494 (Āṅgirasa): III, **222**, 14231 (among the rivers who are mothers of fires).—§ 574 (Jambūkh.): VI, **9**λ, 322.—§ 639 (Rājadh.): XII, **52**, †1893 (*yathā mahānadī tam Ṛkshavantaṃ giriṃ etyā N°ā*).—§ 720*b* (Sudarçanop.).—XIII, **2**, 101 (*devanadī*, wife of Duryodhana the king of Māhishmatī and mother of Sudarçanā). — § 733*w* (Ānuçāsanik.): By bathing in Narmadā and in the tīrtha Çūrpāraka, observing a fast during a fortnight, one becomes born as a prince: XIII, **25**, 1736.—§ 775 (do.): XIII, **166***a*, 7646 (enumeration).—§ 787 (Āçramavāsap.): XV, **20**γγ, 550 (*saritāṃ varā*, wife of Purukutsa).

Nartaka[1], name of a weapon. § 563 (Bhagavadyānap.): V, **96**φ, 3491 (will be employed by Arjuna).

Nartaka[2]=Çiva (1000 names[2]).

Nartanaçīla = Çiva (1000 names[1]).

Nāsatya, name of one of the two Açvins. § 15 (Upamanyu): I, **3**, ††723 (°-*Dasrau*).—§ 608 (Karṇap.): VIII, **89**, †4594 (°-*Dasrātrisutodbhavādyaiḥ*, among the surgeons of Indra, only in C.).—§ 665 (Mokshadh.): XII, **208**γ, 7583 (*N°ç caiva Dasraç ca smṛtau dvāv Açvināv api*).—§ 717*b* (Nārāyaṇīya): XII, **340**, 12917 (*°añ caiva Dasrañ ca bhishajau*). —§ 770 (Anuçāsanik.): XIII, **151**, 7095 (*°ç cāpi Dasraç ca smṛtau dvāv Açvināv api*).

Nāsatya, dual (°*au*) = Açvin, dual: I, 445, 731 (*A°*), 1487; III, 10315, 10346 (*A°*), 10367, 10379; XIV, 184 (*A°*).

Nāsatya, adj. ("relating to the Açvins," viz. one of Brahmán's births). § 717*b* (Nārāyaṇīya): XII, **348**ηη, 13491 (*°añ ca . . . janma*, the fifth birth of Brahmán, *Açvidaivatyaghrāṇajaṃ*, Nīl.); **349**, V), 13585 (*°e janmani . . . Brahmaṇaḥ*).

***nāstika,** mostly pl. (°*āḥ*) ("atheists"): I, 5600; III, 13771, 15443, 17382 (sg.), 17383 (sg.); V, †801 (sg.), 991 (*a°*, sg.), 1228 (sg.), 1507, 1520 (sg.), 4710 (sg.); VII, 706, 3766; VIII, 1863; XII, 296, 331 (*a°*), 337 (*bhṛça°*), 416, 456, 1287, 2703 (sg. only C., B. has *cāstikaḥ*), 4539 (*°tā*), 4828 (sg.), 6228, 6271 (sg.), 6738 (sg.), 6749, 7908, 8411, 9399 (sg.), 9401, 9470, 12053 (*bhṛça°*), 12059 (sg.), 12118, 12142; XIV, 1369.

***nāstikya** ("atheism"): II, 241; III, 1160, 1165, 1200; XII, 358, 8402, 9398, 9705; XIV, 999.

Nāṭakeya, pl. (°*āḥ*), a people. § 281 (Sahadeva): II, **31**, 1118 (in the south, vanquished by Sahadeva on his digvijaya).

Naubandhana. § 457 (Vaivasvatop.): III, **187**, 12795 (a peak of Himavat where Manu Vaivasvata tied his ship).

Naukarṇī, a mātṛ. § 615*u* (Skanda): IX, **46**θ, 2647.

Navacakrāṅga = Çiva (1000 names[1]).

Navarāshṭra, name of a country. § 281 (Sahadeva): II, **31**, 1110 (in the south, conquered by Sahadeva. B. has *Nara°*).

Navarāshṭra, pl. (°*āḥ*), a people ("the inhabitants of Navarāshṭra"). § 549 (Pāṇḍavapr.): IV, **1***a*, 12 (also B.).

Navatantu, son of Viçvāmitra. § 721*b* (Viçvāmitrop.): XIII, **4**β, 257 (enumeration).

Nāvyāçrama ("floating hermitage"), name of a place (?). § 391 (Ṛshyaçṛṅga): III, **113**, 10078 (*vanaṃ*? cf. v. 10027 and 10029).

Naya = Vishṇu (1000 names).

Netṛ[1]=Skanda: III, 14634.—Do.[2]=Çiva (1000 names[1]).—Do.[3]= Vishṇu (1000 names).

Neya = Vishṇu (1000 names).

Nibiḍa, v. Niviḍa.

Nicandra, an Asura. § 92 (Aṃçāvat.): I, **65**, 2534 (son of Danu).—§ 130 (do.): I, **67**, 266 (*Asurottamaḥ*, incarnate as king Muñjakeça).

Nicita, a river. § 574 (Jambūkh.): VI, **9**λ, 326 (among the rivers of Bhāratavarsha).

Niçā[1], wife of the fire Bhānu (B. Manu). § 493 (Āṅgirasa): III, **221**, 14190.

Niçā[2]=Upaçruti (?): V, 425.

***Niçācara,** pl. (°*āḥ*) ("night-wanderers") = Rākshasa, pl. I, 8291; II, 411; III, 159, 11369, 11738, 16321 (dual), 16354, 16358, 16395; VI, 4080, 4085; VII, †6443 (*°çvavṛkapiçācamodanaṃ*); VIII, †4946; X, 451 (adj.); XI, 438 (adj.?); XII, 6423, 6424, 11244 (*trailokye sadevarshi-n°e*); XIII, 4664 (adj.?), 6142 (*aparoksha-n°āḥ*), 6144.

***Niçācara,** sg. (do.): III, 16021 (= Mārīca), 16047 (=Rāvaṇa), 16155 (do.), 16182 (do.), 16337 (do.), 16517 (do.), 16541 (do.); VI, 4110 (= Ghaṭotkaca), 4578 (= Alambusha), 4597 (do.); VII, 4127 (do.); VIII, 2094 (i.e. Kalmāshapāda).

Niçācara=Çiva (1000 names[2]).

Niçācarapati ("lord of Rākshasas") = Çiva: VII, 2046.

Niçācarendra (do.)=Rāvaṇa: III, 11212 (R°).

Niçācarī ("a female night-wanderer"): III, 14481 (sg.= Çītapūtanā); XIII, 7207 (sg.=Gāyatrī? cf. Nīl.).

Niçācarin = Çiva (1000 names[2]).

Niçākara[1] = Soma (the Moon), q.v.

Niçākara[2], a Suparṇa, son of Garuḍa. § 564 (Mātalīyop.): V, **101**β, 3599 (enumeration).

Niçākara[3] = Çiva (1000 names[2]).

Niçālaya = Çiva (1000 names[2]).

Niçaṭha[1], a Vṛshṇi prince (son of Balarāma and Revatī according to Harivaṃça, v. 1953). § 252 (Subhadrāharaṇap.): I, **219**, 7915.—§ 253 (Haraṇāharaṇap.): I, **221**, 7992 (came to the wedding of Arjuna and Subhadrā).—§ 262 (Bhagavadyāna): II, **2**, 56 (*Pradyumna-Çāmba-N°ān*).—§ 287 (Rājasūyikap.): II, **34**, 1275 (came to the rājasūya of Yudhishṭhira).—§ 402 (Tīrthayātrāp.): III, **120**, †10277 (among the Vṛshṇis who will assist the Pāṇḍavas).—§ 553 (Vaivāhikap.): IV, **72**, 2537 (came to the wedding of Abhimanyu and Uttara, C. has by error *Nish°*).—§ 589 (Droṇābhishekap.); VII, **11**ξ, 409.—§ 785 (Anugītāp.): XIV, **66***a*, 1989 (accompanied Kṛshṇa); **86**τ, 2557 (do.).—§ 795 (Svargārohaṇap.): XVIII, **5**λ, 162 (among those who after death entered the deities).

Niçaṭha[2], an ancient king. § 267 (Yamasabhāv.): II, **8**, 322 (in the palace of Yama).

Niçcirā, v. Nirvīra.

Niçcitā, a river. § 574 (Jambūkh.): VI, **9**λ, 326 (only C., B. *Tridivāṃ*).

Niçcyavana, a fire. § 490 (Āṅgirasa): III, **219**, 14141.

***nidhi,** pl. (°*ayaḥ*) ("treasures"): VIII, 4413 (personif.); XIV, 1924 (*Çaṅkhādīṃç ca nidhīn*).

Nidhi[1]=Çiva (1000 names[2]).—Do.[2]=Vishṇu (1000 names[1]).

Nidhipa = Kubera: XII, 7552 (*Dhaneçvaraṃ*).

nidhipāla, pl. (°*āḥ*): XIV, 1924.

Nidrātman = Kṛshṇa: XII, 1637.

Nigraha[1] = Çiva (1000 names[2]). — Do.[2] = Vishṇu (1000 names).

Nihantṛ, Nija = Çiva (1000 names[6]).

Nikharvaṭa, a Rākshasa. § 537 (Rāma-Rāvaṇayuddha): III, **285** β, 16372 (fought with Tāra).

Nikumbha[1], name of several Asuras. § 90 (Aṃçāvat.): I, **65**, 2527 (son of Prahlāda).—§ 92 (do.): I, **65**, 2534 (another, son of Danu).—§ 130 (do.): I, **67**, 2662 (incarnate as king Devādhipa).—§ 246 (Sundopasundop.): I, **209**, 7620 (*Daityendraḥ*, father of Sunda and Upasunda).

Nikumbha[2], a Kuru warrior. § 600 (Ghaṭotkaçavadhap.): VII, **156** κ, 6850.

Nikumbha[3], a warrior of Skanda. § 615u (Skanda): IX, **45** η, 2558.

Nīla[1], a serpent. § 47 (Sarpanāmak.): I, **35**, 1552 (°*ānīlau*).

Nīla[2], king of Māhishmatī. § 130 (Aṃçāvat.): I, **67**, 2697 (*bhūmipaḥ*, among the incarnations from the Krodhavaça gaṇa).—§ 232 (Svayaṃvarap.): I, **186**, 6990 (present at the svayaṃvara of Draupadī).—§ 282 (Sahadeva): II, **31**, 1124 (on his digvijaya Sahadeva fought with *N.*, who was assisted by Agni).—§ 282b (Māhishmatī): II, **31** [1131 (°*rājño-duhitā*)], 1133 (Agni married the daughter of *N.*).—§ 284 (Sahadeva): II, **31**, 1160 (°*sya kule*), 1162 (paid tribute to Sahadeva).—§ 515 (Karṇadigvijaya): III, **254**, 15250 (*mahīpatiṃ*, vanquished by Karṇa on his digvijaya).—§ 554 (Sainyodyogap.): V, **4** γ, 79.—§ 555 (do.): V, **19**, 592 (*Māhishmatīvāsī N°o Nīlāyudhaiḥ saha*, came with troops to Duryodhana).—§ 572 (Rathātirathasaṅkhyānap.): V, **166**, 5751 (*Māhishmatīvāsī nīlavarmā*, among the rathas in Duryodhana's army).—§ 580 (Bhīshmavadhap.): VI, **56**, 2414 (*Nīlāyudhaiḥ saha*, in the army of Yudhishṭhira), 2415. — § 585 (do.): VI, **93** ψ, 4153 (*Anūpādhipatiḥ*, followed Ghaṭotkaca); **94**, 4210 (*Anūpādhipatiḥ*), 4213, 4215, 4216, 4217 (fought with Açvatthāman, was defeated and swooned).—§ 592 (Saṃçaptakavadhap.): VII, **23** o, 1012 (proceeded against Droṇa, description of his horses, etc.); **25**, 1109 (fought with the sons of Dhṛtarāshṭra); **31**, 1362, 1364, 1365, 1367, 1370 (slain by Açvatthāman).—§ 604 (Karṇap.): VIII, **6**, 166 (*Anūpavāsī*, had been slain by Açvatthāman).—§ 621 (Rājadh.): XII, **4** ε, 113 (present at the svayaṃvara of the daughter of the Kaliṅga king Citrāṅgada). Cf. Nīlarājan.

Nīla[3], a mountain. § 459 (Mārkaṇḍeyas.): III, **188**, 12918 (seen by Mārkaṇḍeya in the stomach of Nārāyaṇa).—§ 574 (Jambūkh.): VI, **6** β, 198 (*vaidūryaparvataḥ*, among the varshaparvatas of Jambūdvīpa), 202 (*dakshiṇena tu N°sya Nishadhasyottareṇa*, there lies Mālyavat) (γ), 232 (north of Nīla lies the [varsha] Çveta), 247 (the abode of Brahmarshis).—§ 574g (Uttara-Kuru, pl.): VI, **7**, 254 (*dakshiṇena tu N°sya Meror pārçve tathottare*, there the Uttara Kurus live).—§ 574i (Jambū): VI, **7**, 272 (*dakshiṇena tu N°sya Nishadhasyottareṇa tu*, there the Jambū tree is situated).—§ 574 (Jambūkh.): VI, **8**, 290 (*dakshineṇa tu Nīlasya Nishadhasyottarena tu*, there lies the varsha Hiraṇmaya).—§ 775 (Ānuçāsanik.): XIII, **166a**, 7658 (enumeration).—§ 782g (Guruçishyasaṃv.): XIV, **43** η, 1174 (enumeration).—§ 785 (Anugītāp.): XIV, **76**, 2201 (? *çailaṃ N°m ivāmbudaḥ*). Cf. Nīlaparvata.

Nīla[4], a monkey. § 535 (Setubandhana): III, **283**, 16287 (in the army of the monkeys).—§ 539 (Kumbhakarṇādivadha): III, **287**, 16435 (fought with the Rākshasa Pramāthin).—§ 541 (Indrajidvadha): III, **289a**, 16468, (β), 16477.—§ 542 (Rāvaṇavadha): III, **290a**, 16500.

Nīla[5], a Pāṇḍava warrior. § 572 (Rathātirathasaṅkhyānap.): V, **171**, 5907 (among the rathas in the army of Yudhishṭhira). Cf. Nīla[2].

Nīla[6], a Kuru warrior. § 600 (Ghaṭotkacavadhap.): VII, **156** κ, 6849.

Nīla[7] = Çiva (1000 names[1-2]).

Nīlā, a river. § 574 (Jambūkh.): VI, **9** λ, 339 (only B., C. has *Nālāṃ*).

Nīlaçikhaṇḍa = Çiva: VII, 2878.

Nīlagrīva, Nīlakaṇṭha, Nīlalohita = Çiva, q.v.

Nīlamauli = Çiva (1000 names[2]).

Nīlaparvata, a mountain. § 733f (Gaṅgādvāra): XIII, **25**, 1700. Cf. Nīla[3].

Nīlarājan = Nīla[2]: II, 1137.

Nīlavāsas ("dressed in dark clothes") = Balarāma: I, 7950; IX, 2137, 3126.

Nilaya = Çiva (1000 names[2]).

Nīlāyudha, pl. (°*āḥ*), a people (= the followers of Nīla?). § 555 (Sainyodyogap.): V, **19**, 592 (C. has by error *Lī°*).—§ 580 (Bhīshmavadhap.): VI, **56**, 2414.

Nīlī, wife of Ajamīḍha. § 152 (Pūruvaṃç.): I, **94**, 3722 (second wife of Ajamīḍha and mother of Dushyanta and Parameshṭhin).

Nīlikā, a river. § 775 (Ānuçāsanik.): XIII, **166**, 7654.

Nimesha[1], a Nāga (?), accord. to Nīl., a Yaksha. § 46 (Garuḍa): I, **32**, 1489 (fought with Garuḍa).

Nimesha[2], **Nimeshāḥ** (pl.), **Nimeshonmesha-karman** = Çiva (1000 names[1]).

Nimi[1], an ancient king of the Videhas. § 6 (Anukram.): I, **1a**, 227 (in Sañjaya's enumeration).—§ 267 (Yamasabhāv.): II, **8**, 320 (in the palace of Yama).—§ 677 (Mokshadh.): XII, **235**, 8600 (*Vaidehaḥ*, gave his kingdom to the brahmans).—§ 761 (Ānuçāsanik.): XIII, **115** δ, 5667 (among the kings who did not eat meat during the month of Kārttika).—§ 767 (do.): XIII, **137a**, 6255 (gave his kingdom [to the brahmans], cf. XII, 8600; PCR. is wrong in connecting *Vaidarbhiḥ* with *Nimiḥ*).—§ 775 (do.): XIII, **166** η, 7681 (*rājā*, enumeration). Cf. Vaideha.

Nimi[2], son of Dattātreya and father of Çrīmat. § 749 (Ānuçāsanik.): XIII, **91**, 4330 (*Dattātreyasya putraḥ*, father of Çrīmat), 4332, 4345 (was the first who performed a çrāddha), **92**, 4372.

Nimisha[1], a Suparṇa, son of Garuḍa. § 564 (Mātalīyop.): V, **101** β, 3595 (enumeration).

Nimisha = Vishṇu (1000 names).

Nimitta(m), Nimittastha = Çiva (1000 names[2]).

Nimnagāsuta ("son of the river") = Bhīshma: XIII, 7723.

Nīpa, pl. (°*āḥ*), a tribe or family. § 267 (Yamasabhāv.): II, **8**, 333 (100 *N.* in the palace of Yama).—§ 294 (Dyūtap.): II, **50**, 1804 (among those who lived in the palace of Yudhishṭhira as his bondsmen).—§ 295 (do.): II, **51**, 1844 (waited upon Yudhishṭhira). — § 562 (Bhagavadyānap.): V, **74** γ, 2729 (°*ānāṃ Janamejayaḥ*).—§ 739 (Ānuçāsanik.): XIII, **34** γ, 2126 (vanquished by the Āṅgirases (? *Āṅgiraso*, B.; *Āṅgirajo*, C.)).

Nipātin, Nīraja = Çiva (1000 names[2]).

Nirāmarda, an ancient king. § 6 (Anukram.): I, **1a**, 230 (in Sañjaya's enumeration).

Nirāmaya[1], an ancient king. § 6 (Anukram.): I, **1a**, 231 (in Sañjaya's enumeration).

Nirāmaya[2] = Çiva (1000 names[2]).

Niramitra[1], son of Nakula. § 159 (Pūruvaṃç.): I, **95**, ††3831 (son of Nakula and Kareṇumatī).

Niramitra[2], a Trigarta prince. § 599 (Jayadrathavadhap.): VII, **107**, 4037, 4038, 4039 (*Trigartarājasya sutaḥ*), 4041 (*rājaputraṃ*, slain by Sahadeva).

Niravagraha = Çiva (1000 names[2]).

Niravinda, a sacred mountain. § 733*s* (Açmapṛshṭha): XIII, **25**, 1728 (*parvate*, a tīrtha near Gāyā).

***Niraya** ("hell"): I, 1825, 5671; III, 8556, 12419, 12626; IV, 547, 569; V, †729, †1339; VII, 6319; VIII, †3508; XII, 95, †2801, 6447, 7175 (pl.), 7176–8, 7182–4, 7186–7, 7192 (pl.), 7196–7, 7211, 7328, 9798, †10066, 10851, 11260, 11302, 11304–5, 11672, †12122, 13875; XIII, 1385, 1551, 1631–55, 2479, 3611, 4965, 5534, 5674, 6576, 6674–5, 6695, 6703, 6716; XIV, 443, 1370, 2412; XVIII, 93.

Nirghaṇṭaka, v. Naighaṇṭuka.

Nirguṇa[1] = Mahāpurusha (Mahāpurushastava). — Do.[2] = Vishṇu (1000 names).

Nirjīva = Çiva (1000 names[2]).

Nirmāṇarata, pl. (°*āḥ*), a class of gods. § 730 (Ānuçāsanik.): XIII, **18**λλ, †1372 (? "capable of assuming diverse forms," PCR.).

Nirmocana, name of a city (Nīl.). § 561*c* (Kṛshṇa Vāsudeva): V, **48**, 1890 (there Kṛshṇa slew 60,000 Asuras, etc.).—§ 567 (Bhagavadyānap.): V, **130**, 4407 (cf. v. 1890).

Nirṛti[1], a Rudra. § 108 (Aṃçāvat.): I, **66**, 2566 (enumeration of the eleven Rudras, sons of Sthānu).—§ 191 (Arjuna): I, **123**, 4825 (among the Rudras present at the birth of Arjuna).

Nirṛti[2] ("destruction"), a goddess. § 125 (Aṃçāvat.): I, **66**, 2618 (wife of Adharma and mother of the Nairṛtas). —§ 641 (Rājadh.): XII, **122**, 4514 (*devī*).

Niruddha (I, 6999), error in C. instead of Aniruddha, q.v.

***nirukta** (the etymological work of Yāska): XII, 7372, †8944, 13232; XIII, 4108.

Niruktaga = Brahmán: XII, 12914 (*B*°), 13283 [probably for Aniruktaga, cf. PCR. and Hopkins, Gr. Ep., p. 14].

***nirvāṇa** ("final emancipation"): III, 1185, 10439 (?), 13502 (*padaṃ*), 15487 (*siddhim parāṃ n°lakshaṇāṃ*); VI, 950 (*brahman*°), 1059 (*brahman*°), 1060 (*brahman*°), 1061 (do.), 1079 (*çāntiṃ n°paramāṃ*); XII, 631, 783, †6258 (°*parāḥ*), 6966, 7130 (°*gatamānasāḥ*), 7150, 13014 (*paramaṃ sukhaṃ*), 13239 (*paramaṃ Brahma*); XIII, 1051 (°*da*); XIV, 543.

Nirvāṇa(ṃ) = Çiva (1000 names[2]).—Do.[2] = Vishṇu (1000 names)

Nirvīra, a tīrtha. § 370 (Tīrthayātrāp.): III, **84**, 8116 (PCR. reads *Niçcirā*, cf. next).

Nirvīrāsaṅgama, a tīrtha. § 370 (Tīrthayātrāp.): III, **84**, 8117 ("the confluence of Niçc(h)irā," PCR.).

Niryāṇa(ṃ) ("marching out," cf. Sainyaniryāṇa). § 10 (Parvasaṅgr.): I, **2**, 334 (°*ṃ Kuru-Pāṇḍavasenayoḥ*, i.e. Sainyaniryāṇaparvan).

Nishada (II, 326), v. Nishadha[2].

Nishāda, pl. (°*āḥ*), name of low-caste tribes. § 10 (Garuḍa): I, **28**, 1321 (*b*: the *N.* lived in a remote region in the midst of the ocean), †1335, ‡1336, †1337 (Garuḍa devoured the *N.* (*matsyajīvinaḥ*, v. 1339)); **29**, 1350.—§ 281 (Sahadeva): II, **31**, 1109 (°*bhūmiṃ*, conquered by Sahadeva).—§ 284 (do.): II, **31**, 1170 (vanquished by Sahadeva).—§ 410 (Plakshāvataraṇag.): III, **130**, 10539 (*dvāraṃ N°rāshṭrasya*, sc. Vinaçana, where the Sarasvatī disappears from hatred of the *N.*).—§ 574 (Jambūkh.): VI, **9**μ, 350 (among the peoples of Bhāratavarsha).—§ 578 (Bhīshmavadhap.): VI, **50**π, 2081 (in the army of Yudhishṭhira).—§ 579 (do.): VI, **54**, 2241 (followed Ketumat and proceeded against Bhīmasena), 2243, 2249.—§ 587 (do.): VI, **117**ρ, 5484 (attacked Arjuna).—§ 589 (Droṇābhishekap.): VII, **4**β, 122 (had been vanquished by Karṇa).—§ 593 (Abhimanyuvadhap.): VII, **46**ρ, 1854 (fought with Abhimanyu).—§ 603 (Nārāyaṇāstramokshap.): VII, **197**, 9118 (°*vishaye*).—§ 604 (Karṇap.): VIII, **8**, 236 (among the peoples whom Karṇa had vanquished and caused to pay tribute to Duryodhana).— § 605 (do.): VIII, **17**, †671 (*Kaliṅga-Vaṅgāṅga-N°vīrāḥ*, attacked Arjuna); **20**δδ, 779 (*Pulinda-Khasa-Bāhlīka-N°āndhraka-Kuntalān*, slain by Pāṇḍya); **22**ζζ, 864 (attacked the Pāñcālas) (θθ), 882 (attacked Nahula).—§ 608 (do.): VIII, **49**τ, 2304 (attacked Karṇa); **70**, 3500 (°-*Māgadhān*, slain by Bhīmasena).—§ 641*e* (Vena): The *N.* are wicked tribes who reside in hills and forests: XII, **59**, 2218 (origin of the *N.*).—§ 702 (Mokshadh.): XII, **297**γ, 10868 (enumeration of the different castes).—§ 714 (Çukakṛtya): XII, **329**, 12378 (°*ānām ivālayaḥ*).—§ 744 (Ānuçāsanik.): XIII, **48**, 2574 (sg. *matsyaghnaḥ*, son of a çūdra and a kshatriya wife), 2583 (sg.), 2585 (sg.), 2589 (sg.) (description of different castes and their intermixture).—§ 745*b* (Cyavanop.): XIII, **50**, 2652 (*matsyoddharaṇaniçcayāḥ*), (2664), 2667, 2673, 2675, 2677, 2679; **51**, (2702), 2707, 2713 (some *N.* caught Cyavana in their net and sold him to Nahusha for a cow, then they ascended to heaven).—§ 785 (Anugītāp.): XIV, **83**, 2473 (vanquished by Arjuna when he followed the sacrificial horse).

Nishāda[1], sg. ("king of the Nishādas"). § 554 (Sainyodyogap.): V, **4**γ, 84 (among the princes to whom the Pāṇḍavas ought to send messengers).—Do.[2] = Ekalavya: VII, †8210 (*E*°).

Nishādādhipati ("king of the Nishādas"). § 130 (Aṃçāvat.): I, **67**, 2686 (incarnation of the third of the Kāleyas).—§ 280 (Bhīmasena): II, **30**, 1085 (in the east, vanquished by Bhīmasena on his digvijaya.).—Do.[2] = Hiraṇyadhanus: I, 5255 (°*er* . . . *Hiraṇyadhanushaḥ sutaṃ*, i.e. Ekalavya), 5259 (°*eḥ sutaṃ*, i.e. Ekalavya).

nishadaḥ (pl., a kind of sacred texts): XII, 1613 (°*tsūpanishatsu*).

Nishādaja ("son of the Nishāda king") = Ekalavya: I, 5263; VII, 8217 (cf. Nishāda, v. 8210).

Nishādarāja[1] ("king of the Nishādas") = Hiraṇyadhanus: I, 5241 (°*sya Hiraṇyadhanushaḥ sutaḥ* / *Ekalavyaḥ*).

Nishādarāja[2] (do.) = Ekalavya: V, †1884 (*E*°).

Nishādarājan (do.)—the son of Ekalavya: XIV, 2472 (°*jño vishayaṃ*., C. has by error *Vishā*°).

Nishadha[1], son of the elder Janamejaya. § 154 (Pūruvaṃç.): I, **94**, 3745.

Nishadha[2], an ancient king ("king of the Nishadhas"). § 267 (Yamasabhāv.): II, **8**, 326 (in the palace of Yama; C. has by error *Nishadaḥ*).

Nishadha[3], a mountain. § 459 (Mārkaṇḍeyas.): III, **188**, 12917 (seen by Mārkaṇḍeya in the stomach of Nārāyaṇa).—§ 548*d* (Indra): III, **315**, 17460 (Indra went to *N.* and dwelt there in disguise).—§ 574 (Jambūkh.): VI, **6**β, 198 (among the *varshaparvatāḥ* of Jambūdvīpa), 202 (*dakshiṇena tu Nīlasya N°syottareṇa tu*, there lies Mālyavat), (θ) 246 (inhabited by *sarpāḥ* and *nāgāḥ*).—§ 574*i* (Jambū): VI, **7**, 272 (*dakshiṇena tu Nīlasya N°syottareṇa tu*, the Jambū is situated).—§ 574 (Jambūkh.): VI, **8**, 288 (*dakshiṇena tu Çvetasya N°ottareṇa tu*, there the varsha Ramaṇaka is situated), 290 (*dakshiṇena tu Nīlasya N°syottarena tu*, there lies the varsha Hiraṇmaya, but the text seems to be in disorder in this passage).—§ 775 (Ānuçāsanik.): XIII, **166a**, 7658 (enumeration).

Nishadha, pl. (*°āḥ*), a people and country. § 343 (Nalopākhyānap.): III, **52**, 2067 (*°eshu mahīpālo Vīrasenaḥ*).—§ 344 (do.): III, **54**, 2074 (ruled by Nala), 2098 (*Nalo nāma N°eshu mahīpatiḥ*), 2103.—§ 346 (do.): III, **59**, 2255, 2258.—§ 347 (do.): III, **64**, 2448, 2455 (*°ānām adhipatiḥ . . . Nalaḥ*), 2478 (*? goptā N°vamçasya*), 2487 *Nalaḥ . . . N°ānāṃ janādhipaḥ*), 2492 (*°ānām adhipatiṃ Nalaṃ*), 2504 (*Nalaṃ N°ānām adhipatiṃ*).—§ 354 (do.): III, **78**, 3030.—§ 574 (Jambūkh.): VI, **9**μ, 359 (among the peoples of Bhāratavarsha).

Nishadhādhipa, Nishadhādhipati, Nishadharājendra, Nishadheçvara = Nala, q.v.

Nishādī ("Nishāda wife"). *a*) the *N.* who was burnt with the lac house: I, 379, 5644, 5825, 5862.—*b*) the wife of a brahman who was devoured by Garuḍa: I, 1342, 1343, 1344.—*c*) the mother of Kāyavya: XII, 4854.—*d*) in general: XIII, 2588, 2590.

Nishaṅgin, a son of Dhṛtarāshṭra. § 130 (Aṃçāvat.): I, **67**, 2738 (enumeration).—§ 182 (Dhṛtarāshṭraputranāmak.): I, **117**, 4547 (do.).—§ 608 (Karṇap.): VIII, **51**δδ, 2446 (among [twenty] sons of Dhṛtarāshṭra who attacked Bhīmasena); **84**, 4262 (among ten sons of Dhṛtarāshṭra who were slain by Bhīmasena).

Nishaṭha (IV, 2537), v. Niçaṭha.

Nishkampa = Çiva (1000 names[1]).

Nishkriya = Mahāpurusha (Mahāpurushastava).—Do.[2] = Vishṇu: XII, 12888, 12895, 12907.

Nishkṛti, name of a fire. § 490 (Āṅgirasa): III, **219**, 14143.

Nishkuṭa, a mountain (?). § 279 (Arjuna): II, **27**, 1037 (*Himavantaṃ sa-Nishkuṭaṃ*, conquered by Arjuna on his digvijaya).

Nishkuṭikā, a mātṛ. § 615*u* (Skanda): IX, **46**θ, 2630.

Nishṭhā = Vishṇu (1000 names).

Nishṭhānaka, a serpent. § 47 (Sarpanāmak.): I, **35**, 1554.

Nishṭhurika, a serpent. § 564 (Mātalīyop.): V, **103**γ, 3628.

Nisunda, an Asura. § 317*b* (Kṛshṇa Vāsudeva): III, **12**, 488 (*°-Narakau*, had been slain by Kṛshṇa, cf. Harivaṃça, v. 6858).

Nitambhū, a ṛshi. § 734 (Ānuçāsanik.): XIII, **26a**, 1765 (among the ṛshis who came to see Bhīshma).

Nītha, a Vṛshṇi. § 402 (Tīrthayātrāp.): III, **120**, †10277 (*Bāhuka-Bhānu-N°āḥ*, will assist the Pāṇḍavas).

Nīti[1] ("policy," personif.). § 641 (Rājadh.): XII, **122**, 4493 (= Sarasvatī), cf. v. 4432.

Nīti[2] = Çiva (1000 names[2]).

nītiçāstra ("treatise of political ethics"): I, 1948 (*°vidūttamaḥ*), 4355 (pl.), 5119 (sg.), 5567 (*°ārthadarçinaḥ*), 5754 (*°ānusariṇīṃ*), 6087 (sg.); II, 765 (*°viçāradau*); V, 128 (*°ārthakovidaḥ*); XII, 2195 (sg.), 4155 (*°vit*), 4951 (*°viçāradaḥ*), 4954 (sg.), 5107 (pl.), 7662 (*Bhārgavo n°n tu jagāda*), 9567 (sg.); XIII, 7603 (pl.); XIV, 1959 (sg.).

Nitya, Nityanarta = Çiva (1000 names[2]).

Nivārā, a river. § 574 (Jambūkh.): VI, **9**λ, 328 (in Bhāratavarsha).

Nivātakavaca, pl. (*°āḥ*), a tribe of Asuras. § 10 (Parvasaṅgr.): I, **2**, 323 (*°air yuddhaṃ parva*, i.e. Nivātakavacayuddhaparvan).—§ 11 (do.): I, **2**, 459 (*°air yuddhaṃ Hiraṇyapuravāsibhiḥ* (?), cf. Nivātakavacayuddhaparvan), 460 (*Dānavaiḥ suraçatrubhiḥ*, do.).—§ 190*d* (Arjuna): I, **123**, 4801 (*°ā nāma Daityāḥ*, would be defeated by Arjuna).—§ 334 (Kairātap.): III, **41**, 1684 (*Dānavāḥ*, do.).—§ 339 (Indralokābhigamanap.): III, **47**, 1893 (*Asurāḥ*), 1899 (do.).—§ 443 (Nivātakavacayuddhap.): III, **168**, 12063 (*°ā nāma Dānavā mama* (i.e. Indra's) *çatravaḥ/samudrakukshim āçritya*), 12071, 12074.—§ 444 (do.): III, **169**, 12092, 12100 (*samprahāraḥ . . . N°āntakaḥ*); **170**, 12103, 12107, 12119, 12127, 12131; **171**, 12160, 12161 (*yuddhe N°āntake*); **172**, 12164, 12168, 12176, 12179, 12183 (*°striyaḥ*), 12189 (slain by Arjuna).—§ 445 (do.): III, **173**, 12265 (*nihatya ca mahāsurān/N°ān*), 12267 (*°ānāñ ca vadhaṃ*); **174**, 12288 (*hatāḥ*), 12289 (*nipātitāḥ*).—§ 552 (Goharaṇap.): IV, **45**γ, 1431 (all. to Nivātakavacayuddhaparvan); **50**ε, 1539 (do.).—§ 561*d* (Nara-Nārāyaṇau): V, **49**, 1932 (do.).—§ 564 (Mātalīyop.): V, **100**, 3573 (*°ā nāma Dānavāḥ*, in Pātāla).—§ 569 (Bhagavadyānap.): V, **138**, 4683 (*Dānavāḥ*, all. to Nivātakavacayuddhaparvan).—§ 570 (Sainyaniryāṇap.): V, **158**μ, 5379 (all. to Nivātakavacayuddhaparvan).—§ 585 (Bhīshmavadhap.): VI, **98**, 4460 (*Vāsavena api durjayān*, all. to Nivātakavacayuddhaparvan).—§ 593 (Abhimanyuvadhap.): VII, **51**, 1997 (all. to Nivātakavacayuddhaparvan).—§ 599 (Jayadrathavadhap.): VII, **128**ππ, 5258 (do.).—§ 601 (Droṇavadhap.): VII, **185**γ, 8436 (do.).—§ 605 (Karṇap.): VIII, **31**οο, 1251 (do.).—§ 608 (do.): VIII, **47**, 2220 (*yādṛk N°aiḥ saha*, sc. *samprahāraḥ*).—§ 730*g* (Upamanyu): XIII, **14**λ, 806.

Nivātakavacāntaka ("the destroyer of the Nivātakavacas) = Arjuna: VII, 3137; XIV, 2098, 2229.

[Nivātakavacayuddhaparvan(°va).] ("Arjuna's combat with the Nivātakavacas," the 39th of the minor parvans of Mhbhr.) § 441: One day, when the Pārthas were thinking of *Arjuna*, they saw *Indra's* chariot (in which *Indra* had slain seven phalanxes of *Diti's* sons), driven by *Mātali*, illuminating the sky, and *Arjuna* descended and saluted each of them; *Mātali* also greeted and instructed them, and then returned in the chariot to *Indra*. *Arjuna* then gave to *Draupadī* precious gems, etc., presented to him by *Indra*. Then he related all as it had happened, and slept that night with the two sons of *Mādrī* (III, **165**). The next morning *Indra* visited them under the sound of musical instruments, etc., and blessed *Yudhishṭhira*, and advised him to repair to *Kāmyaka*. Blessing upon the reader (III, **166**).—§ 442: When *Indra* had gone, *Arjuna* related his journey from *Kāmyaka* (see §§ 330–3), etc. (of mountains he mentioned only *Bhṛgutuṅga*, where he spent one night and subsequently saw the brahman; then *Himavat*, where the meeting with the *Kirāta* took place on the first day of the fifth month after the beginning of his penances; the *Kirāta* multiplied a hundredfold and a thousandfold, and was transformed in various manners; *Arjuna* in vain employed the *Vāyavya*, *Sthūṇākarṇa* (see Nīl.), *Jāla* (i.e. *Vāruṇa*, Nīl.), and the *Çalabhāstra*, and showers of shafts and stones, as the *Kirāta* swallowed them up all; *Arjuna* in vain discharged the *Brahmāstra*) (III, **167**).—§ 443: *Arjuna* continued his narrative (see §§ 334–7): he passed the night after the meeting with the *Kirāta* at that place, and in the morning he saw again the same brahman (= *Indra*), and in the evening he had the visit of the *Lokapālas*; the weapons that *Indra* promised to teach him were: those of *Vāyu*, *Agni*, the *Vasus*, *Varuṇa*, the *Maruts*, the *Sādhya* and *Paitāmaha* weapons, those of the *Gandharvas*, *Uragas* (i.e. Snakes), and *Rākshasas*, and all the *Vaishṇava* and *Nairṛta* weapons [v. 12020 foll.]; in the chariot of *Indra*, *Mātali* wondered that *Arjuna* was not jerked, though *Indra* always himself gets jerked at the first pull by the steeds [v. 12030]; when he had learnt the weapons, *Indra* said that now even the gods could not conquer him (v. 12054); he had received knowledge of fifteen weapons with five modes of using them, viz. *prayoga* [discharge], *upasaṃhāra* [withdrawal], *āvṛtti* [redischarge], *prāyaçcitta* [revival of harmless beings slain by any weapon, PCR., Nīl.], and *pratighāta* [revival of weapons baffled by those of the enemies, PCR., Nīl.] (vv. 12058–9); *Indra* asked him, as his fee, to slay the *Nivātakavacas*, who were thirty millions (*tisraḥ koṭyaḥ*) in number and dwelt in the ocean, and gave him the chariot (conducted by *Mātali*), upon which he (*Indra*) had vanquished *Bali* (*Baliṃ Vairocaniṃ*, v. 12068), *Çambara*, *Bala*, *Vṛtra*, *Prahlāda*, and *Naraka*, and millions of *Daityas*, and "this" diadem, and ornaments like his own, and the impenetrable mail, and fastened "this" durable (*ajarām*) string to the *Gāṇḍīva*, and the gods gave him the shell *Devadatta*, through which *Indra* had conquered the worlds (cf. § 446)(III, **168**).—§ 444: *Arjuna* continued: When he came to the ocean, he saw at a short distance the *Daitya* city filled with *Dānavas*. *Mātali* drove the chariot with force, and the *Dānavas* shut the gates. Then *Arjuna* blew the *Devadatta*, and the *Nivātakavacas* appeared with iron javelins, maces, clubs, hatchets, sabres, discs, *çataghnīs*, *bhuçuṇḍīs*, and swords, and sounded dissonant musical instruments. The *Devarshis*, the *Dānavarshis*, the *Brahmarshis*, and the *Siddhas* came to the battle (III, **169**). With arrows inspired with *mantras* relating to the *Brahman*-weapon (*Brahmāstraparimantritaiḥ*), then with the *Mādhava* (PCR. Māghava) weapon and the *Gāṇḍīva Arjuna* killed innumerable *Nivātakavacas*, and the 10,000 horses yoked at the chariot conducted by *Mātali* trampled upon them (III, **170**). *Arjuna* reduced a shower of crags to powder by the *Mahendra* weapon, then dried up showers of water by the weapon *Viçoshana*, that he had acquired from *Indra*; then he annihilated fire by the water weapon (*salilāstra*), and by the stone weapon (*çailena mahāstreṇa*) he repeatedly resisted the wind. Then darkness enveloped the world; the steeds turned away, *Mātali* fell off, and the golden lash fell from his hand; as *Mātali* was stupefied, a terrible fear seized *Arjuna*; *Mātali* said that he had conducted *Indra's* chariot in the battle for the sake of nectar, and in the battles with *Çambara*, *Vṛtra*, *Vairocani*, etc., but never had he lost his senses before. *Arjuna* comforted *Mātali* and repeatedly frustrated the magic of the enemy, and *Mātali* again conducted the chariot. Then on a sudden *Arjuna* did not see the *Dānavas*, who had become hidden by illusion (*māyā*) (III, **171**). *Arjuna* then fought with invisible weapons. Then they withdrew the illusion and entered their city. The fallen and their weapons covered the ground so that the horses had to proceed in the sky. The *Nivātakavacas* remaining invisible, covered the welkin with crags; others, entering into the earth, seized the legs of the horses and the wheels of the chariot. *Arjuna* became distressed, but being advised by *Mātali*, he applied the thunderbolt, inspiring the *Gāṇḍīva* with *mantras*, so that the arrows sent by the thunderbolt, becoming thunderbolts, penetrated the illusions and killed the *Nivātakavacas*. While the wives of *Dānavas* were bewailing and at last fled to their palaces, *Arjuna* and *Mātali* entered the city, that was superior to that of the gods (to that of *Indra*, v. 12188). *Mātali* told him that this was originally the city of *Indra*, but the gods had been driven away from it by the *Nivātakavacas*, who had through austerities gratified *Pitāmaha* and obtained from him the boons, that they might reside here and be free from danger from the gods. When *Indra* applied to *Svayambhū*, he was told that he himself in another body should destroy them. As the gods were unable to slay them, *Indra* had given those weapons to *Arjuna*, so that he might destroy them. Then *Arjuna* and *Mātali* again went to the abode of the gods (III, **172**).—§ 445: While returning he beheld a celestial city, moving at will, with trees of gems, etc., with four gates, etc., and *Mātali* told him it was *Hiraṇyapura*, made by *Brahmán* himself for the great *Asuras*, the *Paulomas*, and *Kālakañjas*, as the *Daiteyī Pulomā* and the *Mahāsurī Kālakā* had by practising austerities for 1,000 celestial years obtained from *Svayambhū* that their offspring should suffer little misfortune, be incapable of being killed by gods, and obtain an aërial, etc., city, invincible even by the gods, *Maharshis*, *Yakshas*, *Gandharvas*, *Pannagas*, *Asuras*, and *Rākshasas*. *Brahmán* had destined that *Arjuna*, a mortal, should kill them. "Therefore destroy them with the thunderbolt." A battle ensued; the *Asuras* resorted to illusion; the city now entered into the earth, and now it rose upwards, etc. Shot with the iron shafts of *Arjuna* the city fell down. Then they environed him in 60,000 chariots, etc. *Arjuna* applied to *Rudra*, and seeing a man with three heads, nine eyes, etc., he applied the *Raudra* weapon to the *Gāṇḍīva*; when it had been hurled, there appeared forms of deer, lions, tigers, *Garuḍas*, *Gandharvas*, *Yakshas*, *Asuras*, *Guhyakas*, *Nairṛtas*, *Yātudhānas*, etc., by thousands. The *Dānavas*, some of whom had three heads, some four tusks, etc., were destroyed. *Arjuna* again worshipped *Tripuraghna* (i.e. Çiva). *Mātali* rejoiced and praised *Arjuna*. The wives of the *Dānavas* came out of the city bewailing the slain. *Mātali* took *Arjuna* to the abode of *Indra*, and related in detail to *Indra Arjuna's* achievement, and *Indra* with the *Maruts* (v. 12269: the gods) praised him, and said that gods, *Dānavas*, *Rākshasas*, *Yakshas*, *Asuras*, *Gandharvas*, birds, and serpents should not be able to resist him in fight, etc. (III, **173**).—§ 446: *Indra* said that on the battlefield *Bhīshma*, *Droṇa*, *Kṛpa*, *Karṇa*, *Çakuni*, etc., should not amount to $\frac{1}{16}$ part of *Arjuna*. Then *Indra* gave him "this" golden garland, the shell *Devadatta*, etc. (see § 443). Then *Indra* told him to depart, "and thus after five years I come to you on the summit of this lower range of *Gandhamadana* (*Gandhamādanapādasya*)." Having promised that he should in the next morning show *Yudhishṭhira* all the celestial weapons, *Arjuna* passed that night there with all his brothers (III, **174**).—§ 447: The next morning, when *Arjuna* was about to show the celestial weapons to *Yudhishṭhira*, the earth trembled, etc. The *Brahmarshis*, *Siddhas*, *Maharshis*, *Devarshis*, gods, *Yakshas*, *Rākshasas*, *Gandharvas*, etc., *Pitāmaha*, the *Lokapālas*, and *Mahādeva* with his *gaṇas* appeared; *Vayu* threw celestial garlands, sent by the gods, on *Arjuna*, the *Gandharvas* chanted ballads, and *Apsarases* danced; and sent by the gods *Nārada* came and prevailed upon *Arjuna* not to use the celestial weapons without necessity, as they would destroy the three worlds. Then the gods, etc., went whence they had come, and the *Pāṇḍavas* pleasantly dwelt in that same forest with *Kṛshṇā* (III, **175**).

Nivedana = Çiva (1000 names [2]).

Niviḍa (Nib°, B.), a mountain in Krauñcadvīpa. § 575 (Bhūmip.): VI, **12**η, 460 (*parvataḥ*).

Nivṛttabhrama = Mahāpurusha (Mahāpurushastava).
Nivṛttarūpa = Mahāpurusha (Mahāpurushastava).
Nivṛttātman = Vishṇu (1000 names).
Nivṛtti = Çiva (1000 names[2]).
Niyama[1] = Mahāpurusha (Mahāpurushastava). — Do.[2] = Çiva (1000 names[2]).—Do.[3] = Vishṇu (1000 names).
Niyamāçrita = Çiva (1000 names[2]).
Niyamadhara = Mahāpurusha (Mahāpurushastava).
Niyamendriyavardhana = Çiva (1000 names[2]).
Niyantṛ[1] = Çiva: VIII, 1449.—Do.[2] = Vishṇu (1000 names).
Niyata[1], name of a fire. § 493 (Āṅgirasa): III, **222**, 14213, 14214 (according to Nīl. the same as the fire Bharata).
Niyata[2] = Çiva (1000 names[2]).
Niyatāyus, a Kuru warrior. § 599 (Jayadrathavadhap.): VII, **93**, 3364 (*N.* and Dīrghāyus, the sons of Çrutāyus and Acyutāyus, are slain by Arjuna).
Niyati ("self-restraint"), a goddess. § 270 (Brahmasabhāv.): II, **11**, 459 (in the palace of Brahmán).
Nṛçaṃsa = Çiva: XIV, 203.
Nṛga, an ancient king. § 61 (Sarpasattra): I, **55**, †2101 (°*sya yajñaḥ*, comparison). —§ 267 (Yamasabhāv.): II, **8**, 319 (in the palace of Yama).— § 377 (Dhaumyatīrthak.): III, **88**, 8329 (*sarin N°sya*, i.e Payoshṇī), 8330 (Mārkaṇḍeya sung a gāthā in honour of *N.*), 8331 (performed a sacrifice, at the tīrtha Vārāha on the Payoshṇī).—§ 378 (Tīrthayātrāp.): III, **94**, 8503 (*yathaiva hi N°o rājā*).—§ 403*b* (Payoshṇī): III, **121**, 10291 (description of *N*'*s* sacrifice on the Payoshṇī). —§ 468 (Indradyumnop.): III, **199**, ††13348 (*nanu Devakīputreṇāpi Kṛshṇena Narake majjamāno rājarshir N°s tasmāt kṛcchrāt punaḥ samuddhṛtya svargaṃ prāpitaḥ*, cf. § 746).— § 574 (Jambūkh.): VI, **9*aa***, 315.—§ 576 (Bhagavadgītāp.): VI, **17*β***, 645 (obtained the highest regions). — § 595 (Shoḍaçarāj., v. Māndhātṛ): VIII, **62*a***, 2282 (vanquished by Māndhātṛ).—§ 615*kk* (Kurukshetrak.): IX, **53**, †3031 (°*ādyā naradevamukhyāḥ*, performed sacrifices in Kurukshetra). —§ 621 (Rājadh.): XII, **8*θ***, 238 (had ruled the earth).— § 720*b* (Sudarçanop.): XIII, **2**, 121 (grandson of Oghavat). —§ 723 (Ānuçāsanik.): XIII, **6*a***, 332 (had been transformed into a lizard (*kṛkalāsa*, cf. § 746).—§ 746 (do.): XIII, **70**, 3452 (°*ena sumahat kṛcchraṃ yad avāptam*), 3458, 3461, 3481, 3482, 3483 (on account of his giving away a cow who did not belong to him *N.* was reborn as a lizard (*kṛkalāsa*) but was rescued by Kṛshṇa); **72**, 3453 (all. to chap. **70**); **76*c***, †3689 (had made gifts of kine).—§ 747 (do.): XIII, **84**, 3934 (do.).—§ 761 (do.): XIII, **115*γ***, 5662 (abstained from meat during the month of Kārttika).—§ 775 (do.): XIII, **166*η***, 7674 (enumeration).—§ 786*d* (Nakulākhyāna): King *N.* made gifts of thousands of cows to the twice born, by giving away only one cow which did not belong to him he fell into hell: XIV, **90**, 2789.
***nṛparshi**, pl. (°*ayaḥ*) ("royal sages"): VIII, 4423; XIII, 4589.
Nṛsiṃha ("man-lion"). § 524*d* (Vishṇu): III, **272**, 15836 (Vishṇu in this avatāra slew Hiraṇyakaçipu). Cf. Narasiṃha, Nārasiṃha, adj.
Nṛtyapriya = Çiva (1000 names[2]).
Nṛtyapriyā, a mātṛ. § 615*u* (Skanda): IX, **46*θ***, 2628.
***nṛyajña**, a kind of sacrifice: X, 790, 791.
Nyagrodha[1] = Çiva (1000 names[2]). — Do.[2] = Vishṇu (1000 names).
Nyagrodhākhya, a tīrtha (?). § 377 (Dhaumyatīrthak.): III, **90**, 8382.
Nyagrodharūpa = Çiva (1000 names[2]).
***Nyāya** ("logic"): I, 67 (°*çikshā*), 2885; II, 137 (°*vid*); XII, 2262, 9702 (°*çāstreṇa*).
Nyāya = Vishṇu (1000 names).
Nyāyanirvapaṇa = Çiva: XIII, 1239.

O

Oḍra, pl. (°*āḥ*), a people. § 295 (Dyūtap.): II, **51**, 1843 (waited upon Yudhishṭhira). Cf. Uḍra, pl.
Ogharakshas. § 561*c* (Kṛshṇa Vāsudeva): V, **48**, 1890 (*nihatyaugharaksho Nirmocanaṃ cāpi jagāma*, sc. Kṛshṇa; *Oghasaṃjñaṃ rakshaḥ*, Nīl.).
Ogharatha, son of Oghavat[2]. § 720*b* (Sudarçanop.): XIII, **2**, 122.
Oghavat[1], a Kuru warrior. § 604 (Karṇap.): VIII, **5*ζ***, 132 (had been slain in the battle).
Oghavat[2], a king. § 720*b* (Sudarçanop.): XIII, **2**, 121 (*nṛpaḥ*, grandfather of Nṛga), 122 (father of Ogharatha and Oghavatī).
Oghavatī[1], a river. § 574 (Jambūkh.): VI, **9*λ***, 329.— § 615*i* (Saptasārasvata): IX, **38*a***, 2189 (one of the seven Sarasvatīs), 2212 (at the sacrifice of Kuru the river Sarasvatī appeared in Kurukshetra as the river *O.*).—§ 615 (Gadāyuddhap.): IX, **62**, 3498.—§ 639 (Rājadh.): XII, **50**, 1812 (*nadīṃ*. Bhīshma lay on his arrow bed on the bank of the river *O.*). Cf. next.
Oghavatī[2], daughter of Oghavat[2] and wife of Sudarçana. § 720*b* (Sudarçanop.): XIII, **2**, 122, 124 (dwelt in Kurukshetra), 125, 130, 133, 136, 143 (together with her husband Sudarçana put to the test by Dharma), 168 (with half her body she became the river of the same name). Cf. prec.
Ojas = Vishṇu (1000 names).
Oṃkāra[1] = Mahāpurusha (Mahāpurushastava). — Do.[2] = Çiva (1000 names[1]).
Oshadhi, pl. (°*yaḥ*) ("plants," personif. as a class of gods). § 120 *bis* (Aṃçāvat.): I, **66**, 2604.—Do.[2] = Çiva (1000 names[1]).
Oshadhīpati = Soma (the Moon): III, 137.

P

Pacapaca = Çiva (1000 names[1]).
Pāça = Çiva (1000 names[2]).
Pāçāçinī, v. Palāçinī.
Pāççimānūpaka ("inhabiting the western marshy country," name of a prince and his people). § 130 (Aṃçāvat.): I, **67**, 2670 (incarnation of the Asura Mṛtapā). Cf. V, 81 (*Paççimānūpakāḥ*).
Pāçin, a son of Dhṛtarāshṭra. § 182 (Dhṛtarāshṭraputranāmak.): I, **117**, 4547.—§ 608 (Karṇap.): VIII, **51*δδ***, 2446 (attacked Bhīmasena); **84*ξ***, 4262 (among ten sons of Dhṛtarāshṭra slain by Bhīmasena).
Pāçivāṭa, pl. (°*āḥ*), a people. § 574 (Jambūkh.): VI, **9*ν***, 371 (in the south).
Paçu = Çiva: XIV, 204.

Paçu[1], pl. (°*avaḥ*), a people. § 574 (Jambūkh.): VI, **9**o, 375 (only B., C. has *Pattibhiḥ*).

***paçu**[2], pl.(°*avaḥ*) ("beasts"): I, 2604; II, 465.—Do.[3] = Çiva (1000 names[1]).

Paçubhartṛ = Çiva: IX, 2414; XII, 10291; XIII, 620.

Paçubhūmi, a country. § 280 (Bhīmasena): II, **30**, 1083 (in the east, conquered by Bhīmasena).

Paçūnāṃ pati(ḥ) = Çiva: XII, 10356 (1000 names[1]); XIV, 199.

Pāçupata, adj. ("belonging to Paçupati [i.e. Çiva]"). § 4 (Anukram.): I, **1**, 67 (sc. *jñānaṃ*?), 160 (*mahāstraṃ*, cf. § 333).—§ 190*d* (Arjuna): I, **123**, 4800 (*astraṃ P°ṃ nāma*, all. to § 333).—§ 333 (Kairātap.): III, **40**, 1643 (*astraṃ*, i.e. Brahmaçiras), 1650 (do. do., obtained by Arjuna from Çiva).—§ 440 (Yakshayuddhap.): III, **164**, 11900 (sc. *astraṃ*, among the weapons obtained by Arjuna from Indra).—§ 442 (Nivātakavacayuddhap.): III, **167**, 11985 (*astraṃ*, all. to § 333).—§ 524 (Jayadrathavimokshanap.): III, **272**, 15807 (*çaraṃ*, do.).—§ 561 (Yānasandhip.): V, **48**, †1913 (*mahāstraṃ*, known by Arjuna).—§ 569 (Bhagavadyānap.): V, **141**δ, 4786 (sc. *astraṃ*, do.).—§ 588 (Bhīshmavadhap.): VI, **121**β, 5802 (do., do.).—§ 596 (Pratijñāp.): VII, **80**, 2838 (°*ṃ nāma paramāstraṃ*).—§ 602 (Droṇavadhap.): VII, **188**λ, 8604 (sc. *astraṃ*, employed by Droṇa).—§ 608 (Karṇap.): VIII, **60**aaa, 2998 (sc. *astreṇa*); **79**, †4055 (*mahāstraṃ*, all. to § 333).—§ 696*b* (Dakshaprokta-Çiva-sahasranāmastotra): XII, **285**, 10470 (*vrataṃ*).—§ 717*b* (Nārāyaṇīya): XII, **350**, 13702 (sc. *jñānaṃ*?), 13705 (*jñānaṃ*, taught by Çiva).—§ 730*g* (Upamanyu): XIII, **14**, 851 (*astraṃ*, description).

Pāçupatāstra ("the Pāçupata weapon"). § 606 (Tripurākh.): VIII, **34**, 1562 (employed by Çiva). Cf. the prec.

Paçupati = Çiva, q.v.

Paçusakha, name of a çūdra. § 750*b* (Bisastainyop.): XIII, **93**, 4417 (*çūdraḥ*, the husband of Gaṇḍā), (4447), 4475, (4501), (4532).

pada (a certain method of reciting the Vedas): I, 2880 (°-*kramaiḥ*), 2883 (do.); XIII, 4107 (°*kramavibhūshitaḥ*, sc. *ṛgvedaḥ*).

Pāda(ḥ) = Çiva (1000 names[2]).

Pada(m) anuttama(m) = Vishṇu (1000 names).

Pādāṅga = Kṛshṇa: XII, 1634.

pādapa, pl. (°*āh*) ("trees," personif.): IX, 2514.

Padāti, son of the elder Janamejaya. § 154 (Pūruvaṃç.): I, **94**, 3746 (seventh son of Janamejaya).

Padma[1], name of several serpents. § 47 (Sarpanāmak): I, **35**, 1555 (*nāgau dvau*, two serpents of that name).—§ 268 (Varuṇasabhāv.): II, **9**, 360 (in the palace of Varuṇa).—§ 564 (Mātalīyop.): V, **103**γ, 3629 (*dvau*, two serpents of that name).—§ 718*b* (Uñchavṛttyup.): XII, **356**, 13803 (*Padmanābho mahānāgaḥ P°a iti viçrutaḥ*).

Padma[2], an ancient king (?). § 267 (Yamasabhāv.): II, **8**, 332 (in the palace of Yama).

Padma[3], a treasure. § 269 (Vaiçravaṇasabhāv.): II, **10**, 418 (*nidhipravaramukhau Çaṅkha-P°au*, in the palace of Kubera).

Padma[4], a warrior of Skanda. § 615*u* (Skanda): IX, **45**η, 2558.

padma, name of a vyūha: VII, 3110.

Padmā = Çrī: II, 2294 (? B. reads *padbhyām*); IV, 186 (*yathā P°ā Nārāyaṇaparigrahaḥ*); XII, 8347 (Ç°), 8353 (do.); XIII, 507 (do.); XIV, 1489.

Padmagarbha[1] = Çiva (1000 names[2]). Do.[2] = Vishṇu (1000 names).

Padmaja, adj. ("originating from the lotus," viz. one of Brahmán's births). — § 717*b* (Nārāyaṇīya): XII, **349**, VII), 13594 (*janma saptamaṃ Brahmaṇaḥ*). Cf. next.

Padmajanman ("the birth from the lotus," viz. Brahmán's). § 717*b* (Nārāyaṇīya): XII, **348**, 13492 (*saptamaṃ janma P°eti*). Cf. the prec.

Padmaketana, a Suparṇa, son of Garuḍa. § 564 (Mātalīyop.): V, **101**β, 3596.

Padmāksha = Vishṇu (Nārāyaṇa): VII, 9463.

Padmālaya = Brahmán: III, 12890.

Padmalocana = Vishṇu: I, 1117.

Padmanābha[1] = Vishṇu: I, 1218, 2506; III, 7043 (*Nārāyaṇam*); VI, 2946; XII, 1602 (i.e. Kṛshṇa), 7638 (do.), 13105; XIII, 5382 (i.e. Kṛshṇa), 6324 (?), 6955 (1000 names), 6970 (do.), 6987 (do.).

Padmanābha[2], a son of Dhṛtarāshṭra. § 130 (Aṃçāvat.): I, **67**, 2731. Cf. Sunābha.

Padmanābha[3] = Padma[1]: XII, 13803 (*P°*), 13888.

Padmanābha[4], **Padmanālāgra** = Çiva (1000 names[2]).

Padmanibhekshaṇa = Vishṇu (1000 names).

Padmasambhava = Brahmán, q.v.

Padmasambhava, adj. ("originating from the lotus"). § 717*b* (Nārāyaṇīya): XII, **350**, 13653 (*prajāvisarge saptame*, i.e. when Brahmán had been born from the lotus; cf. Padmaja, Padmajanman).

Padmasaras, name of a place. § 276 (Jarāsandhavadhap.): II, **20**, 793 (passed by Kṛshṇa, etc., on the way from Indraprastha to Girivraja).

Padmātman = Kṛshṇa: XII, 1647.

Padmāvatī = a mātṛ. § 615*u* (Skanda): IX, **46**θ, 2627.

Padmayoni = Brahmán, q.v.

Padmeçaya = Mahāpurusha (Mahāpurushastava).

Padmin = Vishṇu (1000 names).

Padmodbhava = Brahmán, q.v.

Pahlava, pl. (°*āḥ*), a people ("the Parths").—§ 223 (Vāsishṭha): I, **175**, 6683 (sprung from the tail of the cow of Vasishṭha).—§ 285 (Nakula): II, **32**, 1199 (in the west, vanquished by Nakula).—§ 292 (Dyūtap.): II, **52**, 1871 (brought tribute to Yudhishṭhira).—§ 342 (Indralokābhigamanap.): III, **51**, 1990 (only B., C. has *Pallavān*, present at the rājasūya of Yudhishṭhira).—§ 554 (Sainyodyogap.): V, **4**γ, 78 (*Çakānāṃ P°ānāñ ca Daradānāñ ca nṛpāḥ*).—§ 574 (Jambūkh.): VI, **9**υ, 375 (among the peoples of the north-east).—§ 641 (Rājadh.): XII, **65**θ, 2429 (enumeration of low and barbarous peoples).

Pahnava, pl. (°*āḥ*), a people. § 574 (Jambūkh.): VI, **9**μ, 355 (only C., probably error for *Pahl°*, but B. has *Pañcālāḥ*).

Paiçāca, adj. ("belonging to the Piçācas"). — § 135 (Çakuntalop.): I, **73**, 2962 (sc. *vivāhaḥ*), 2965 (do.).—§ 502 (Manushyagrahak.): III, **230**, 14506 (*adhirohanti yaṃ nityaṃ Piçācāḥ purushaṃ prati | unmādyati sa tu kshipraṃ grahaḥ P°a eva saḥ*). § 587*b* (Bhīshma). VI, **108**, 5009 (sc. *vyūhān*).—§ 704 (Mokshadh.): XII, **302**β, 11102 (*vishayān*).—§ 731*b* (Ashṭāvakra-Diksaṃv.): XIII, **19**, 1397 (sc. *pārçvadaiḥ*, in the palace of Kubera).—§ 744 (Ānuçāsanik.): XIII, **44**, 2412 (sc. *vidhiḥ* or *vivāhaḥ*).

Paiçāca, pl. (°*āḥ*), a people. § 599 (Jayadrathavadhap.): VII, **121**εε, 4819 (attacked Sātyaki). Cf. Piçāca, pl.

Paijavana, name of a çūdra. § 641 (Rājadh.): XII, **60**, 2306 (*çūdraḥ P°o nāma*, gave 100,000 *pūrṇapātras* as dakshiṇā).

Paila, a ṛshi. § 78 (Vyāsa): I, **63**, 2418 (disciple of Vyāsa).—§ 264 (Sabhākriyāp.): II, **4**a, 106 (waited upon

Yudhishṭhira).—§ 286 (Rājasūyikap.): II, **33**, 1239 (*Vasoḥ putraḥ*, acted as hotṛ at the rājasūya of Yudhishṭhira).—§ 637 (Rājadh.): XII, **47***a*, 1593 (among the ṛshis who surrounded Bhīshma).—§ 707 (Mokshadh.): XII, **319**, 11743.—§ 714*b* (Himavat): XII, **328**, 12338 (disciple of Vyāsa).—§ 717*b* (Nārāyaṇīya): XII, **341**μ, 13025 (do.): **350**μμ, 13647 (do.).—§ 785 (Anugītāp.): XIV, **72**, 2085.

Pailagarga, a ṛshi. § 573 (Ambopākhyānap.): V, **186**, 7355 (°*sya āçrame*, there Ambā performed austerities).

Paiṅga, a muni. § 264 (Sabhākriyāp.): II, **4***a*, 112 (waited upon Yudhishṭhira).

Paippalādi, a brahman. § 662*b* (Jāpakop.): XII, **199**, 7201 (*sa-Kauçikaḥ*, was a reciter, the dispute between Kāla, Mṛtyu, Yama, Ikshvāku, and *P.*).

Paitāmaha, adj. ("belonging to Pitāmaha [i.e. Brahman]"). § 443 (Nivātakavacayuddhap.): III, **168**, 12021 (sc. *astraṃ*).—§ 615*u* (Skanda): IX, **45**, 2579 (*mahāpārishadāḥ*).—§ 655 (Āpaddh.): XII, **160**, 5957 (°*ṃ sthānaṃ Brahmarāçisamudbhavaṃ guhāyāṃ pihitaṃ nityaṃ*).

Paitāmaha = Manu (?): I, 2581 (*Manuḥ*, so C., B. has *muniḥ*).

***Paitra**, adj. ("belonging to the pitṛs"): VII, †9466 (*karma*).

***Paitrya**, adj. (do.): XIII, 6029 (°*aṃ*, the offerings to the pitṛs).

***Paitṛka**, adj. (do.): XIII, 1573 (°*aṃ kuryād aparāhne*, i.e. the rites for the pitṛs).

Pāka, an Asura. § 641 (Rājadh.): XII, **98**ξ, 3660 (had been slain by Indra).

Pākaçāsana = Indra, q.v.

Pākaçāsanadāyāda ("the son of Pākaçāsana [i.e. Indra]") = Arjuna: II, 1004.

Pākaçāsananandana (do.) = Arjuna: II, 1044.

Pākaçāsani (do.) = Arjuna: I, 5386, 5477, 8280; II, 991, 1028, 1031, 1033, 1040; IV, 1388, 1594; V, 5356; VII, 1263, 2714, 3149, 3186, 5816 (*Pārthaḥ*), 6231, 6232; XI, 623; XII, 5875 (*Pāṇḍavena*); XIV, 2158 (only B.), 2211, 2433, 2475; XVI, 238.

Pākātman = Kṛshṇa: XII, 1661.

Paksha = Çiva (1000 names[1-2]).

Pakshālikā, a mātṛ. § 615*u* (Skanda): IX, **46**θ, 2637.

Paksharūpa = Çiva (1000 names[2]).

Pakshin, sg. and pl. = Çiva (1000 names[1-2]).

Pakshirāj[1] ("king of birds") = Garuḍa: I, 1337, 1437, 1472, 1481, 1484, 1488, 1516, 4119 (*iva*); III, 10574 (*Suparṇaḥ*); VI, 291; VII, 1920 (*iva*), 5229 (*Suparṇaḥ*).—Do.[2] = Sampāti: III, 16251.

Pakshirāja[1] (do.) = Garuḍa: V, 3589; XII, 12317 (*Garutmān*).—Do.[2] = Suruc: V, 3588.

Paktṛ, Pakvāmamāṃsalubdha, Pakvabhuj = Çiva (1000 names[1])

Pāla, a serpent. § 63 (Sarpasattra): I, **57**, 2146 (of Vāsuki's race).

Palāça, pl. (°*āḥ*), a family (?). § 267 (Yamasabhāv.): II, **8**, 336 (100 *P.* in the palace of Yama).

Palāçinī, a river. § 574 (Jambūkh.): VI, **9**λ, 330 (only C., B. has *Pāçāçinīṃ*).

Palālā, one of the mothers of Çiçu. § 500 (Skandop.): III, **228***a*, 14396.

Palita, name of a mouse. § 646*b* (Marjāramūshikasaṃv.): XII, **138**, 4933, 4938, 4975, 4983, 4987, 4988, 5000, 5002, 5004, 5034, 5036, 5094, 5112, 5113.

Pālitā, a mātṛ. § 615*u* (Skanda): IX, **46**θ, 2621.

Pallava, pl. (III, 1990), v. Pahlava, pl.

Palvalāni, pl. = Çiva (1000 names[1]).

Pāṃçurāshṭra, a country. § 295 (Dyūtap.): II, **52**, 1884 (from *P.* Vasudāna brought elephants as tribute).

Pāṃçurāshṭra, pl. (°*āḥ*), a people. § 574 (Jambūkh.): VI, **9**μ, 351 (only C., B. has *Pāṇḍu°*).

Pāṃçurāshṭrādhipa ("the king of Pāṃçurāshṭra") = Vasudāna? § 554 (Sainyodyogap.): V, **4**γ, 83.

Pampā, name of a lake (?). § 530 (Viçvāvasumoksh.): III, **279**, 16088 (*taḍākinī*, near the mountain Ṛshyamūka).—§ 531 (Rāmopākhyānap.): III, **280**, 16093 (*nalinīṃ*), 16100 (*vāri P°āyāḥ*).—§ 757*m* (Goloka): XIII, **102***a*, 4889.

Paṇa = Vishṇu (1000 names).

Panasa, a monkey chief. § 535 (Setubandhana): III, **283***a*, 16274 (came with 52 crores (*koṭi*) of monkeys to Rāma).—§ 537 (Rāma-Rāvaṇayuddha): III, **285**β, 16372 (fought with Paṭuça).

Panavin = Çiva (1000 names[2]).

Pañcacūḍā, an Apsaras. § 412 (Ashṭāvakrīya): III, **134**, †10662 (? *dṛshṭā Vede P°āpsarāḥ*).—§ 716 (Çukābhipatana): XII, **333**, 12595 (°*prabhṛtayaḥ*).—§ 742 (Ānuçāsanik.): XIII, **38**, 2203 (*Nāradasya saṃvādaṃ puṃçcalyā P°ayā*), 2204 (*Apsarasaṃ Brāhmīṃ*) (2212) (discourse between *P.* and Nārada).—§ 775 (do.): XIII, **166**β, 7641. Cf. Rambhā.

Pañcaçikha, a muni. § 668*b* (Pañcaçikhavākya): XII, **218**, 7886 (*Kāpileyo mahāmuniḥ*), 7892, 7895 (disciple of Āsuri, sucked Kapilā, therefore he was called Kāpileya); **219**, 7934, †7982 (instructed Janaka).—§ 707 (Mokshadh.): XII, **319**β, 11783 (had instructed Viçvāvasu).—§ 708 (do.): XII, **320**, 11839 (°*syeha saṃvādaṃ Janakasya ca*), 11840 (*maharshiṃ*, instructed Janaka).—§ 709*b* (Sulabhā-Janakasaṃv.): XII, **321**, 11875 (*Parāçaragotrasya . . . bhikshoḥ P°syāhaṃ çishyaḥ*, sc. Janaka), 12015. Cf. Kāpileya.

[Pañcaçikha-vākya(ṃ)] ("the discourse of Pañcaçikha"). § 668*b* (Mokshadh.): *Bhīshma* said: The *Mithilā* king Janaka was always engaged in reflecting upon the courses of conduct that might lead to the attainment of *Brâhman*. One hundred preceptors always used to live in his palace. Given to the study of the *Vedas*, he was not very well satisfied with the speculations of his instructors on the character of the soul and their doctrines of extinction upon the dissolution of the body or of rebirth after death. Once the great ascetic *Pañcaçikha Kāpileya* came to *Mithilā*, having roamed over the earth. He seemed to have assumed the form of that great *Ṛ.* [and] *Prajāpati*, whom the *Sāṅkhyas* call *Kapila*; they say he was the first disciple of *Āsuri* [and] long-living. He was performing a mental sacrifice for 1,000 years (cf. Pañcasrotas). He was fully conversant with the *Pañcarātra* (i.e. "the sacrifice that leads to the state of *Vishṇu*", Nīl.) and the five sheaths that cover the soul, etc. He had approached one day a large concourse [of *Ṛ.*] following the *Sāṅkhya* doctrine (*Kāpilaṃ*), and instructed them about the Unmanifest; *Āsuri* had inquired of his preceptor (? so Nīl. and PCR.) and understood the distinction between the body and the soul, and had acquired celestial vision. For that assembly of *Ṛ.*, *Āsuri* made his exposition of *Brâhman*. *Pañcaçikha* became a disciple of *Āsuri*; he lived on human milk; he was accepted as a son by the *brāhmaṇī Kapilā*, the wife of *Āsuri*, and used to suck her breasts. This was said to me by the holy one [i.e. Mārkaṇḍeya or Sanatkumāra, Nīl.]. *Janaka*, abandoning his 100 preceptors, began to follow *Kāpileya* (i.e. *Pañcaçikha*) upon the religion of emancipation which is explained in *Sāṅkhya* treatises. "Some say that, when ignorance is destroyed by knowledge, the destruction of existence itself follows [this opinion also is erroneous]." The king became filled with wonder (XII, **218**). Continuation of the discourse between *Pañcaçikha* and the king on the topic of existence and non-existence after death. The *Mithilā* king (*Maithilena*), beholding his city burning in a conflagration, himself proclaimed (*gītam*), "in this conflagration nothing of mine is burning." The king gave up his sorrows, etc. He who reads this discourse attains to emancipation (XII, **219**).

Pañcagaṅga (B. °*gā*), pl., name of a tīrtha. § 594 (Mṛtyu): VII, **54**, 2095 (C. °*eshu*; B. °*āsu*, visited by Mṛtyu).

Pañcāgni = Mahāpurusha (Mahāpurushastava).

Pañcajana [1], an Asura. § 589 (Droṇābhishekap.): VII, **11**, 401 (*Pātālavāsinam*, slain by Kṛshṇa, who thus obtained the conch Pāñcajanya).

Pañcajana [2] (XVI, 270), v. Pañcanada.

Pāñcajanya [1], the conch of Kṛshṇa. § 30*b* (Samudra): I, **21**, 1215 (°*sya jananam*, sc. the ocean).—§ 319 (Saubhavadhop.): III, **14**, 633 (*jalajam*).—§ 320 (do.): III, **20**, 789 (*çaṅkhapravaram*), 808 (*jalajam*).—§ 561 (Yānasandhip.): V, **48**, †1872 (*divyam çaṅkham*).—§ 570 (Sainyaniryāṇap.): V, **151**, 5167 (°*sya nirghosham*).—§ 574 (Jambūkh.): VI, **1**, 19 (do.).—§ 576 (Bhagavadgītāp.): VI, **25**κ, 844 (blown by Kṛshṇa).—§ 578 (Bhīshmavadhap.): VI, **51**, 2115 (do.).—§ 580 (do.): VI, **59**, †2616 (°*sya raveṇa*).—§ 582 (do.): VI, **71**, 3120 (°*sya nirghoshaṃ*).—§ 587 (do.): VI, **112**η, 5211 (°*sya nirghoshaḥ*).—§ 589 (Droṇābhishekap.): VII, **3**, 108 (*nadataḥ P°sya*); **11**, 401 (v. Pañcajana [1]).—§ 596 (Pratijñāp.): VII, **73**, 2610 (blown by Kṛshṇa), †2611; **79**, 2813 (°*sya nirghosham*).—§ 598 (Jayadrathavadhap.): VII, **88**, 3141 (*çaṅkhapravaram*).—§ 599 (do.): VII. **90**, 3197 (°*svanena*); **100**, 3757 (blown by Kṛshṇa); **103**, 3881 (do.); **104**, 3902 (do.), 3903; **110**, 4169 (°*sya niḥsvanam*); **126**, 5130 (*çaṅkhasya nirghoshaḥ P°sya*); **127**, 5163 (°*ravaḥ*); **148**, 6450 (blown by Kṛshṇa).—§ 608 (Karṇap.): VIII, **53**, 2584; **76**, †3855 (*Kṛshṇasya . . . P°m . . . dvijarājavarṇam*); **94**, 4955 (°*sya nirghoshaḥ*).—§ 610 (Çalyap.): IX, **4**, 203 (°*svanena*).—§ 615 (Gadāyuddhap.): IX, **61**, 3458 (blown by Kṛshṇa).—§ 637 (Rājadh.): XII, **40**, 1459 (°*ābhishiktaḥ*, sc. Yudhishṭhira).—§ 793 (Mausalap.): XVII, **2**, 49.

Pāñcajanya [2], name of a fire. § 491 (Āṅgirasa): III, **120**, 14160 (its origin and offspring). Cf. Tapas.

Pañcaka, a companion of Skanda. § 615*u* (Skanda): IX, **45**, 2537 (given to Skanda by Indra).

Pañcakālakartṛpati = Mahāpurusha (Mahāpurushastava).

Pañcakarpaṭa, pl. (°*āḥ*), a people. § 285 (Nakula): II, **32**, 1189 (in the west, vanquished by Nakula; C. prints *pañca karpaṭān* in two words).

Pañcāla, pl. (°*āḥ*), a people. § 280 (Bhīmasena): II, **29**, 1061 (°*ānāṃ puram*, i.e. Kāmpilya?), 1062 (conciliated by Bhīmasena on his digvijaya).—§ 549 (Pāṇḍavapraveçap.): IV, **4**, 86 (the servants of the Pāṇḍavas repaired to the *P.* during the thirteenth year of the exile); **5**, 144 (*uttareṇa Daçārṇān . . . P°ān dakshiṇena*, there the Pāṇḍavas passed by on their way to the country of the Matsyas).—§ 556 (Sainyaniryāṇap.): V, **21**, 634; **25**, †725 (°*ānām adhipam caiva vṛddham*, i.e. Drupada), †735 (do.).—§ 572 (Rathātirathasaṅkhyānap.): V, **165**, 5735; **171**, 5895 (*Prabhadrakāḥ?*).—§ 609 (Çalyap.): IX, **1**, 31 (have been slain).—§ 610 (do.): IX, **3**, 161 (°*ānāṃ mahārathāḥ*, so C., but read with B. °*thaḥ*, i.e. Dhṛshṭadyumna). Cf. Pāñcāla, pl.

Pañcāla, sg.[1] (III, 462), v. Pāñcāla, sg.[2] (= Drupada).—Do.[2] = Gālava (?): XII, 13527 (°*ena kramaḥ prāpto devena pathi deçite*). Cf. Pāñcāla, sg.[4]—Do.[3] = Çiva (1000 names [1]).

Pāñcāla, pl. (°*āḥ*) (B. mostly *Pa°*), a people = Pañcāla, pl. § 4 (Anukram.): I, **1**, †152, †210.—§ 11 (Parvasaṅgr.): I, **2**, 385, 387, 425, 564 (*sarva-P°ān Dhṛshṭadyumnapurogamān*, slain), 567, 570, 572.—§ 71 (Ādivaṃçāvatāraṇap.): I, **61**, 2259 (*Kṛshṇāṃ P°eshu svayaṃvarām*, cf. § 231 foll.).—§ 152 (Pūruvaṃç.): I, **94**, 3723 (*sarva-P°āḥ*, descended from Dushyanta and Parameshṭhin).—§ 201*b* (Drupada): I, **130**, 5111 (Drupada became king of the northern (*uttareshu*) *P.*)—§ 209 (Drupadaçāsana): I, **138**, 5448, 5460, 5469, 5476, 5478, 5497 (*sarva-P°āḥ*), 5513 (*dakshiṇān*) (assisted by his pupils, Droṇa vanquished Drupada, but restored him to the half of the kingdom, viz. that part which lay on the southern side of the Gaṅgā and the southern *P.* as far as the Carmaṇvatī).—§ 214 (Hiḍimbavadhap.): I, **156**, 6085.—§ 216 (Caitrarathap.): I, **165**, 6322 (°*eshu adbhutākāram Yājnasenyāḥ svayaṃvaram*; cf. § 231 foll.).—§ 218 (Draupadīsambhava): I, **167**, 6395, 6396, 6404 (*sarva-P°āḥ*) (the birth of Draupadī and Dhṛshṭadyumna).—§ 219 (Caitrarathap.): I, **168**, 6415, 6416.—§ 231 (Svayaṃvarap.): I, **184**, 6929; **185**, 6945 (*rājñā dakshiṇa-P°ān Drupadenābhirakshitān*), 6949 (the svayaṃvara of Draupadī).—§ 273 (Rājasūyārambhap.): II, **14**, 591 (*dakshiṇāḥ*), 593 (*sarva-P°āḥ*, fled from fear of Jarāsandha).—§ 295 (Dyūtap.): II, **52**, 1907 (*Pā°* also B., related to the Pāṇḍavas by marriage).—§ 307 (Anudyūtap.): II, **81**, 2702, 2703.—§ 317 (Arjunābhigamanap.): III, **12**, 524.—§ 342 (Indralokābhigamanap.): III, **51**, 1975.—§ 343 (Nalopākhyānap.): III, **52**, 2019.—§ 356 (Tīrthayātrap.): III, **80**, 4009.—§ 377 (Dhaumyatīrthak.): III, **87**, 8311 (°*eshu kathayanty Utpalāvanam*).—§ 549 (Pāṇḍavapraveçap.): IV, **1***a*, 11; **4**, 139 (Dhaumya repaired to the *P.* during the thirteenth year of the exile); **5**, 162 (*Pā°* also B., had formerly been vanquished by Bhīmasena).—§ 551 (Kīcākavadhap.): IV, **20**, 615.—§ 556 (Sañjayayānap.): V, **31**, 936 (*Pā°* also B.), 937 (do.).—§ 561 (Yānasandhip.): V. **50**, 1970 (do.), 1971 (do.), 1972 (do.), 1973 (do.); **53**θ, 2107; **54**ι, 2137; **57**ο, 2264 (*Pā°* also B.), 2273 (do.), 2282 (do.); **61**ψ, 2406 (do.); **62***aa*, 2415 (do.).—§ 562 (Bhagavadyānap.): V, **72***a*, 2594 (do., among the allies of Yudhishṭhira); **82**, 2895.—§ 569 (do.): V, **140***a*, 4743, 4748; **144**λ, 4887 (*Pā°* also B.), (ν) 4896.—§ 570 (Sainyaniryāṇap.): V, **151**γ, 5153 (*Prabhadrakāḥ?*).—§ 572 (Rathātirathasaṅkhyānap.): V, **167**, 5789; **168**, 5830; **171**, 5903 (°*sattamāḥ*, *Pā°* also B.).—§ 573 (Ambopākhyānap.): V, **173**, 5943; **190**, 7441.—§ 574 (Jambūkh.): VI, **1**, 16; **9**μ, 346 (*Kuru P°āḥ*, in Bhāratavarsha, *Pā°* also B., 349.—§ 576 (Bhagavadgītāp.): VI, **14**, 524 (only C., *Pāṇḍavānāṃ* B.), 535 (*sa-Sṛñjayān*, *Pā°* also B.).—§ 578 (Bhīshmavadhap.): VI, **47**δ, 1811; **49**, 1985 (μ), 2022.—§ 579 (do.): VI, **52**, 2135; **53**, 2206.—§ 580 (do.): VI, **56**θ, 2416 (*Prabhadrakāḥ?*); **59**, 2509, (ζ), 2640 (*Pā°* also B.).—§ 581 (do.): VI, **64**, 2881, 2885.—§ 582 (do.): VI, **72**, 3193.—§ 583 (do.): VI, **79**, 3509.—§ 584 (do.): VI, **86**, 3829 (*sarva-P°ān*).—§ 585 (do.): VI, **88**, 3889, 3890; **93**, 4147; **95**ζζ, 4321; **97**λλ, 4443; **98**, 4466.—§ 586 (do.): VI, **103**, 4695 (B. by error *Pāñcālyam*); **105**, 4770.—§ 587 (do.): VI, **108**γ, 5022; **109**, 5063, 5087; **115**ν, 5349, (ο), 5360 (*sa°*); **118**, 5537 (φ), 5565 (*Pā°* also B.); **119**ββ, 5683 (*sa°*); **120**, 5696.—§ 589 (Droṇābhishekap.): VII, **7**, 213 (*Pā°* also B.), 215 (*Dhṛshṭadyumnapurogamāḥ*); **8**, 243, 255; **10**, 345.—§ 590 (do.): VII, **16**, 629, 639 (°*ānāṃ yaçaskaraḥ*, sc. Kumāra), (ε) 670.—§ 592 (Saṃçaptakavadhap.): VII, **21,** 876 (°*ānāṃ mahārathe*, sc. Satyajit), (θ), 877, (ι), 883, 914 (°*ānāṃ rājaputre* = ?), (λ), 915, 919; **22,** 920, (ν), 926, 930, (ξ), 942; **23**ο, 969 (followed Çikhaṇḍin), 989 (°*senānīḥ*, i.e. Dhṛshṭadyumna; *Pā*° also B.), 998 (°*ānāṃ naravyāghraḥ . . . Janamejayaḥ*); **26,** 1160, 1174; **31,** 1349, 1351; **32,** 1411, (αα), 1412.—§ 593 (Abhimanyuvadhap.): VII, **35,** 1516, (ζ), 1528; **39,** 1667; **40**ο, 1691, 1695 (°-*Sṛñjayāḥ*); **43**σ, 1780.—§ 596 (Pratijñāp.): VII, **72,** 2556 (*Pāṇḍu-P°ān*); **78,** 2740, (ε), 2743.—§ 598 (Jayadrathavadhap.): VII, **86,** 3070.—§ 599 (do.): VII, **95,** 3498, 3499, 3517; **106,** 3965, 3966, 3967, 3968, 3969; **108**ο, 4087; **110,** 4162, 4163, (ρ), 4165, 4167; **111**υ, 4284; **113,** 4436; **114,** 4483, (ω), 4539; **117,** 4682 (*Pā*° also B.), 4683; **121,** 4858; **122,** 4869, 4890, (ιι), 4892 (*Pā*° also B.), 4896, 4902, 4911, 4930, 4932, 4933; **124,** 5000, 5010; **125,** 5040, 5065, 5067, 5068, 5070, 5073, 5088; **126,** 5096, 5098; **127,** 5175; **130,** 5335, 5354 (°*ānān tu mukhyau tau rājaputrau*, i.e. Uttamaujas and Yudhāmanyu); **135**νν, 5557; **150**β′, 6506 (follow Çikhaṇḍin, B. has *Pāñcālyaiḥ*), 6519; **151,** 6554, 6562 (*sarva-P°ān*).—§ 600 (Ghaṭotkacavadhap.): VII, **153,** 6606, 6612, 6621, 6626, 6635 (°-*Pāñcālya*° B.), 6638; **154,** 6646, 6647, (β), 6651, 6653 (*Prabhadrakāḥ*?); **155**γ, 6684, 6688; **156**ι, 6779; **157,** 6964, 6967; **158**τ, 6972, 6973, 6975, (υ), 6980; **159,** 7060, 7063, 7088, 7111 (*Parthaṃ* (°*ān*, B.) *sa P°aṃ* (°*ān*, B)), 7133, 7134, 7137, 7138, 7139, 7142; **160**δδ, 7155, 7156, 7158, 7161, 7165, 7166, 7184 (*sarva-P°senābhiḥ*, *Pā*° also B.), 7196, 7198 (°*ānāṃ mahārathaḥ* = Dhṛshṭadyumna (?)), 7199, 7200; **161,** 7214, 7217; **162,** 7278 (*Pāṇḍu-P°ān*); **164,** 7331, 7332, 7352 (*Pā*° also B.); **165,** 7356, 7358; **166,** 7430, (ιι), 7459; **168,** 7536 (°*ānāṃ mahārathe*, i.e. Drupada); 7541 (not in B.); **169,** 7592 (protect Çikhaṇḍin); **170,** 7611; **171,** 7696; **172**ππ, 7749, 7757, 7758, 7764; **173,** 7784, 7786, 7787, 7792, 7796, (ττ), 7825; **177,** 8030, 8056; **178,** 8082, 8085, 8107; **179,** 8117; **182,** 8267; **183**ηηη, 8306, (ιι), 8347.—§ 601 (Droṇavadhap.): VII, **185**γ, 8430 (*sarva-P°ān*).—§ 602 (do.): VII, **186,** 8461, 8486, 8500, 8504, 8506; **187,** 8542, 8547; **189,** 8683, 8691, 8692 (*Dhṛshṭadyumnapurogamān*); **190,** 8694 (C. by error *Pāçe*°), 8696, 8697, 8698, 8715, 8717 (°*ānāṃ mahārathaḥ* = Dhṛshṭadyumna (?)), 8718, 8720, 8723.—§ 603 (Nārāyaṇāstramokshap.): VII, **193,** 8919 (*Prabhadrakaiḥ*?), (δ), 8930, 8934, 8937; **195,** 8993, 8995, 9018, 9023 (°*āpasadaḥ*, sc. Dhṛshṭadyumna; *Pā*° also B.); **198**π, 9145, (σ), 9179, 9181; **199**υ, 9204, 9209, 9214, 9220 (*Pā*° also B.), (χ), 9228 (*Satyajidmukhāḥ*); **200,** 9282, 9301, 9321 (*sarva-P°ān*), 9386.—§ 604 (Karṇap.): VIII, **3**δ, 70, 72; **5**ζ, 94; **6,** 155 (many have been slain); **8**η, 236 (had formerly been vanquished by Karṇa and caused to pay tribute to Duryodhana); **9,** 253.—§ 605 (do.): VIII, **10**κ, 378, 379; **12**ββ, 459; **21,** 838 (°*vīrāṇāṃ*), 844, 846; **22,** 865, 868, 884; **24,** 967, 968, 971, 990; **25,** 1004; **28,** 1129, 1166 (slain by Karṇa); **32**σσ, 1349.—§ 607 (do.): VIII, **37**γ, †1729; **45**μ, 2084 (*Kuravaḥ saha-P°āḥ*, know the eternal religion), †2086 (*Kuru-P°deçyāḥ*), (ν), 2098 (*brāhmaṃ P°āḥ*), †2100 (*Pā*° also B.), 2106 (*ardhoktāḥ Kuru-P°āḥ*).—§ 608 (do.): VIII, **46**ζ, 2178; **47**θ, 2214, (μ), 2229; **48,** 2236, 2237, 2244, 2246, 2247, (ν), 2248 (five *P.* slain by Karṇa), 2249, 2250, (ξ), 2254; **49**ι, 2307, 2309, (ω), 2359; **55**κκ, 2662; **56,** 2695, 2696, 2732, 2733, (οο), 2748, 2749, 2751, 2753, (ππ), 2754, 2758, 2837; **58**χχ, 2902; **59,** 2936 (°*āpasada*, sc. Dhṛshṭadyumna), (ψψ), 2945, 2972; **60,** 2978, 2999, (ββ), 3002, 3009, (γγ), 3010, 3031, 3032, 3035, 3041, 3042, 3043, 3044, 3048, 3050; **61,** 3100; **62,** 3174; **64,** 3254, 3258, 3263, 3267; **66**ιι, 3319; **67**κκκ, †3369; **73,** 3662, 3668, 3691, 3730, 3731, 3733, 3734, 3735, 3737, 3738, 3739, 3740, 3744, 3746; **74**φφφ, 3755, 3796; **75,** †3814 (°*ānām adhipo Yājñaseniḥ*, i.e. Dhṛshṭadyumna); **78,** 3947, 3948, (β′), 3949, 3951, 3965, 3973, 3987, 3990, 3992, 3997; **79**ζ′, 4011, 4012; **81,** 4176, 4178, 4179; **82,** †4196 (°*rathapravīrāḥ*, five enumerated, attacked Karṇa), †4206 (°*mahārathāḥ*); **83,** †4226; **86**ι′, 4357; **89,** †4552, †4553, †4554, †4556, †4560, †4592, †4604 (°*varāḥ*); **93,** 4869 (°*ānāṃ mahārathaḥ*, i.e. Dhṛshṭadyumna); **94,** 4936; **96**βα′, 5031.—§ 609 (Çalyap.): IX, **1,** 13 (C. °*sainikān*; B. °-*Somakān*); **2**ζ, 78, 123 (*nihatāḥ*).—§ 610 (do.): IX, **6,** 317; **7**ι, 333, 335, 363, 364.—§ 611 (do.): IX, **8,** 410; **13,** 686; **14,** 741 (°*ānāṃ mahārathaḥ*, sc. Suratha); **16**ι, 822, 824; **17,** 870 (*Pāṇḍu-P°-Somakāḥ*); **18**ββ, 962, 968; **19,** 1007, 1009; **20**ιι, †1087 (C. °-*Matsyāḥ*, B. °*putrāḥ*); **21,** 1099 (read *P°ān* with B.), 1103, (κκ), 1126 (°*ānāñ ca ye gaṇāḥ*); **23,** 1193, 1214.—§ 612 (Hradapraveçap.): IX, **30,** 1695 (Açvatthāman will slay all the *P.*), 1720, (ε), 1726; **31,** 1788 (°-*Pāṇḍūnāṃ*).—§ 613 (Gadāyuddhap.): IX, **32**β, 1830, (γ), 1848, 1859 (*sarva-P°āḥ*), 1860, 1863 (*sa*°); **33**θ, 1917.—§ 615*a* (Baka Dālbhya): IX, **41,** 2321.—§ 615 (Gadāyuddhap.): IX, **55**π, 3122; **58,** 3305; **60**ν, 3370; **61,** 3390, 3404, 3458; **65,** 3661 (Açvatthāman will slay all the *P.*).—§ 616 (Sauptikap.): X, **1,** 56, 62; **3,** 129, 133, 134, 135 (*sarva-P°ān*), 136 (*sarva-P°aiḥ*), 137, 139 (°-*Pāṇḍūnāṃ*), 140 (°*senāṃ*, *Pā*° also B.); **4**γ, 144, 156 (°*anāṃ varūthinīṃ*), 159, 166, 167; **5,** 188, 201, 202; **7,** 314, 315; **8,** 322, 467, 476 (all the *P.* are slain by Açvatthāman, etc., in the nightly encounter); **9,** 479 (*hatvā sarva-P°ān*, sc. Açvatthāman), 529 (*nihatāḥ*).—§ 618 (Jalapradānikap.): XI, **11**ι, 300 (°*ā nihatāḥ sarve Dhṛshṭadyumnapurogamāḥ*); **12**κ, 316 (°*yoshidbhiḥ*).—§ 619 (Strīvilāpap.): XI, **16,** 441 (°-*Kuruyoshāṇāṃ*), 452 (°*ānāṃ vināçe*); **20,** 587.—§ 620 (Çrāddhap.): XI, **27,** 822 (°*ānāṃ ca nāçena*).—§ 621 (Rājadh.): XII, **7,** 176 (*hatāḥ*).—§ 791 (Putradarçanap.): XV, **36**α, 988 (*subhṛçaṃ kshīṇāḥ*). Cf. Pañcāla, pl., Pāñcālya, pl., Prabhadhraka, pl., Somaka, pl., Sṛñjaya, pl.

Pāñcāla, sg.[1] (do.) = Dhṛshṭadyumna: VII, 484 (so C., °*lya* B.), 1361 (so B., C. has °*lya*), 9191; VIII, 888; IX, 1389 (°*sya balena*), 1574 (only C., B. has °*lyaṃ*); X, 810 (°*sya padānugāḥ*).

Pāñcāla, sg.[2] (do.) = Drupada: I, 5452 (only B., C. has °*lyaḥ*), 5455 (do., do), 5481, 5483, 5495, 5496 (°*rathaṃ*), 5509, 7270; III, 462 (°*sya dāyādāḥ*, so B., C. has by error *Pa*°); V, 103 (*Matsya-P°yoḥ*, i.e. Virāṭa and *D.*), 2001 (°*sya sutā*, i.e. Çikhaṇḍin[ī]), 7442 (*nṛpatiṃ*); VII, †251.

Pāñcāla, sg.[3] (do.) = Satyajit: I, 5484, 5486, 5489.

Pāñcāla, sg.[4] = Gālava (?). § 717*b* (Nārāyaṇīya): XII, **343,** 13262 (°*ena kramaḥ prāptaḥ*). Cf. Pañcāla, sg.[2].

Pāñcāladāyada [1] = Çikhaṇḍin (?): VI, 5232.—Do.[2] = Dhṛshṭadyumna: VI, 2361, 2362, 2707 (only B., C. has *Pāñcālyaputraḥ*).

Pāñcālaja = Yudhāmanyu: VIII, †4245.

Pañcālaka = Drupada: V, 7504 (*rājā*, so C., but B. has *Pā*°).

Pāñcālaka = Dhṛshṭadyumna: VII, 9148.

Pāñcālaka, adj. ("belonging to the Pāñcālas"). § 209 (Drupadaçāsana): I, **138,** 5482 (*bale*).—§ 241 (Vidurāgamanap.): I, **202,** 7427 (*pakshaḥ*).

Pāñcālakulanandana = Vīraketu: VII, 4900, 4901.
Pāñcālakulavardhana = Dhṛshṭadyumna: VI, 2697.
Pāñcālamukhya (B. *Pa°*) = Dhṛshṭadyumna: VII, 7777 (*Dh°*).
Pāñcālanagara ("the city of the Pāñcālas") = Kāmpilya (?): I, 388, 3825, 6435.
Pāñcālanṛpa ("king of the Pāñcālas") = Drupada: I, †7346.
Pāñcālapati (B. *Pa°*) (do.) = Drupada: III, †10284.
Pāñcālaputra[1] = Dhṛshṭadyumna: VI, 5420; VII, 265, 3578, 7636 (so C., B. *Pāñcālyaputram*); IX, †1076 (*senāpatiḥ Pāṇḍava-Sṛñjayānām*), †1078, †1088.
Pāñcālaputra[2] = Vīraketu: VII, 4893 (*V°*).
Pāñcālaputra, pl. (*°āḥ*): III, 2009 (so C., B. *Pa°*); VII, 9143; VIII, †4180; IX, †1087 (only B.).
Pāñcālaputrī = Draupadī: XV, 377.
Pañcālarāja ("king of the Pāñcālas") = Drupada: I, †7135 (*°sya sutām*, i.e. Draupadī), †7140, †7167 (*°sya sutaḥ*, i.e. Dhṛshṭadyumna), †7201; V, 602 (B. *Pā°*), †680 (B. *Pā°*), 5893 (*°sya sutaḥ*, i.e. Çikhaṇḍin), 7424 (*°sya sutām*, i.e. Çikhaṇḍin[ī]), 7500 (*D°*); VII, †247. Cf. next.
Pāñcālarāja[1] (do.) = Drupada (B. often *Pa°*): I, 5446 (*D°*, B. *Pa°*), 5480, 6971 (B. *Pa°*), †7169 (do.), †7189 (do.), †7190 (do.), †7196 (do.), †7202 (do.), †7204 (do.); II, †2362 (*°sya sutām*, i.e. Draupadī), 2700 (*°sya sutā*, i.e. Draupadī); III, 10991, (do. do., B. *Pa°*); V, †4, 7446; VI, †2629 (*D°*), 2710 (*putraḥ P°sya*, i.e. Dhṛshṭadyumna), 5552 (B. *Pa°*), 5576 (do.); VII, 953 (*°sya suto Dhṛshṭadyumnaḥ*), 2491, 4373 (*°sya sutaḥ* = do.), 7168 (*putraḥ P°sya Dhṛshṭadyumnaḥ*, B. *Pa°*), 7480 (B. has *Pañcāla-Pāṇḍūnām* instead of *P° sya* in C.), 7663 (*°sya putraḥ*, i.e. Dhṛshṭadyumna), 8755 (*°sya suto Dhṛshṭadyumnaḥ*, B. *Pa°*), 8954 (*°sya sutaḥ* = do.), 9104 (*°sya putraḥ* = do.), 9185 (*°sya sutaḥ* = do.); VIII, 4870 (*putraḥ P°sya Dhṛshṭadyumnaḥ*); IX, 162 (do., B. *Pa°*), †1081 (*°sya sutam* = do., but B. has *Pañcālarājasya ratham*, thus *P.* = *Dhṛshṭadyumna*), †1084 (*°sya sutam*, i.e. Dhṛshṭadyumna, B. *Pa°*), †1089 (*°sya sutaḥ* = do., B. *Pa°*), 1376 (*putraḥ P°sya* = do., B. *Pa°*); X, 210 (*putram P°sya* = do.), 339 (*sutaḥ P°sya* = do., B. *Pa°*), †566 (B. *Pa°*), †570 (do.). Cf. the prec.
Pāñcālarāja[2] (do.) = Dhṛshṭadyumna (B. mostly *Pa°*): VI, 2328; VII, 9299 (*Pā°* also B.); VIII, 845 (do.); IX, †1081 (*°sya ratham*, according to B.), 1384; X, 138 (*Dh°*).
Pañcālarājan (do.) = Drupada (B. also *Pā°*): V, 7441; VII, 520 (B. *Pā°*); XI, 723
Pāñcālarājan (do.) = Dhṛshṭadyumna (B. *Pa°*): X, 351.
Pañcālasutā ("the daughter of the Pāñcāla king") = Çikhaṇḍinī (B. *Pā°*): V, 7436.
Pāñcālatanaya ("the son of the Pāñcāla king") = Dhṛshṭadyumna: VII, 7176.
Pāñcāleya ("son of Pāñcālī, i.e. Draupadī") = Çatānīka: VIII, †3813.
Pāñcālī ("daughter of the Pāñcāla king") = Draupadī: I, 314 (*svayaṃvaro devyāḥ P°yāḥ*), 361, 427, 456, 483, 2450 (*D°*), 6398, 6920, 6924 (*°yāḥ . . . svayaṃvaram*), 7123, 7141, 7144, 7541, 7612, 8038, 8040; II, 2172 (*Kṛshṇā*), 2179, 2209, 2216, 2223, 2261, 2358, †2364, 2374, 2405, 2406, 2418, 2523, 2683, 2686, 2698, 2701; III, 202, 509, 583, 592, 2001, 2005, 4000, 10855, 10858, 10871, 10987, 11003, 11015, 11071, 11368, 11404, 11450, 12442, 14656, 14708, 14709; IV, 148, 375, 512, 513, 515, 595, 735, 781, 783, 823, 842, 1181, 1184, 1370 (*D°*), 1432; V, 2864, 2897, 4659, 5157 (*D°*); VII, 2766, 2770, 5656, 8324; VIII, 308, 3773; XI, 352, 386, 417, 539, 540; XII, 413, 1397; XIV, 2020; XV, 348, 495; XVIII, 9 (*D°*), 37, 69, 134.
Pāñcālya[1] = Āruṇi: I, ††685 (*Ā°*), ††686 (do.), ††689 (do.), ††691 (do.).
Pāñcālya[2] = Brahmadatta: XII, 8603 (*B°ḥ P°o rājā*); XIII, 6261 (*B°*).
Pāñcālya[3] = Çikhaṇḍin: V, 2002, 4803 (*°au* = Ç. and Dhṛshṭadyumna), 5325 (*Ç°*), 5936 (do.), 7496 (do.); VI, 503, 527 (*Ç°*), 4989, 5055 (*Ç°*), 5214, 5340 (? *Arjunaṃ sa-P°aṃ*), 5451 (*Ç°*), 5563, 5695 (*Ç°*); VII, 2 (do.), 968 (do.); IX, 801 (do.); XI, 789 (do.); XII, 809 (do.); XVIII, 26 (do.).
Pāñcālya[4] = Drupada: I, 5135, 5146, 5174 (*rājaputraç ca Yajñasenaḥ*), 5178, 5452 (only C., B. has *Pāñcālaḥ*), 5455 (do. do.), 6343, 6352, 6354, 6953, 7218, 7225, 7252, 7424, 7429 (*rājā*), 7430 (*°sadanam*), 7537; II, †2384 (*°sya Drupadasyātmajām*, i.e. Draupadī); III, 8455; V, 107, 2235, 7439 (*pārthivam*), 7501 (*nṛpādhamam*), 7546; VI, 720 (*Yajñasenaḥ*), 2023 (*D°*), 2118 (only C., B. has *Pāncālyāḥ*), 2703 (*putram P°sya*, i.e. Dhṛshṭadyumna), 4695 (only B. by error); VII, 961 (*rājā P°o Drupadaḥ*), 999 (?); XI, 724 (*rājānam*).
Pāñcālya[5] = Dhṛshṭadyumna: I, 6408 (*Dh°*), 7156; V, 2110 (*Dh°*), 2487 (do.), 4779 (do.), 4803 (*°au* = Çikhaṇḍin and *Dh.*), 5193 (*Dh°*), 5324 (do.), 5482 (do.), 5705 (do.); VI, 712 (do.), 1701, 1838, 2151, 2193, 2194 (*Pārshataḥ*), 2232, 2360, 2693, 2700, 2712, 3400, 3819 (*Dh°*), 3825, 4499, 5364; VII, 285, 484 (only B., C. has *°Pāñcāla°*), 822 (*°-Kurumukhyayoḥ*, i.e. *Dh.* and Durmukha), 1351, 1361 (B. *°Pāñcāla°*), 1438, 3535 (*Dh°*), 3579, 3605, 4148 (*Dh°*), 4913, 4915, 4987, 7372 (*Dh°*), 7614, 7625, 8503, 8513 (*Dh°*), 8544 (?), 8631, 8645, 8758, 8780, 8834, 8835, 8977 (*Yajñasenasutaḥ*), 9061, 9130, 9173, 9174, 9183, 9200, 9297, 9328, 9396; VIII, 2692 (?), 2712, 2713, 2714, 2963; IX, 832, 1242 (*Dh°*), 1353 (do.), 1354, 1448 (?), 1452, 1574 (only B.), 1725 (*Dh°*); X, 211, 331, 336.
Pāñcalya[6] = Janamejaya: VII, 7483 (*J°*); VIII, 2335 (*J°*).
Pāñcālya[7] = Mitravarman: VIII, 175 (*M°*).
Pāñcālya[8] = Satyajit: VII, 716, 859, 872, 874.
Pāñcālya[9] = Siṃhasena: VII, 997 (*S°*).
Pāñcālya[10] = Sudhanvan: VII, 1002 (*S°*).
Pāñcālya[11] = Uttamaujas: V, 2263 (*U°*); VII, 2951 (do.), 3048 (do.), 5346 (do.).
Pāñcālya[12] = Vīraketu: VII, 4895.
Pāñcālya[13] = Vṛka: VII, 867 (*V°*, only B, the çloka wanting in C.).
Pāñcālya[14] = Vyāghradatta: VII, 650 (*V°*), 652 (do.).
Pāñcālya[15] ("the king of the Pāñcālas"). § 153 (Pūruvaṃç.): I, **94**, 3728 (vanquished Saṃvaraṇa).
Pāñcālya[16], a Pāñcāla prince. § 592 (Saṃçaptakavadhap.): VII, **21**, 912 (slain by Droṇa).
Pāñcālya[17], name of a tīrtha (?). § 377 (Dhaumyatīrthak.): III, **90**, 0082 (twice in B., in the second place C. has *Puṇyākhya*).
Pāñcālya, dual (*°au*) = Yudhāmanyu and Uttamaujas: V, 7624 (*Yudhāmanyūttamaujasau*), 7638 (do.); VI, 714 (do.); VII, 3252 (do.), 3287, 5336 (*Yudhāmanyūttamaujasau*), 5350, 6325, 6335 (*cakrarakshau*); VIII, 428 (*Yudhāmanyūttamaujasau*).—Do.[2] = Candradeva and Daṇḍadhāra: VIII, 2327.
Pāñcālya, pl. (*āḥ*), a people = Pāñcāla, pl. § 578 (Bhīshmavadhap.): VI, **51aa**, 2118 (only B., C. has *Pāñcālyaḥ*).—§ 579 (do.): VI, **54**[14], 2352.—§ 587 (do.): VI, **108**, 4999 (so C., B. has *Pañcālaiḥ*).—§ 589 (Droṇābhishekap.):

VII, **9,** 287 (°*āpasadaḥ*, sc. Dhṛshṭadyumna).—§ 592 (Saṃçaptakavadhap.): VII, **26,** 1158 (*sa-P°aḥ*, sc. Yudhishṭhira). — § 599 (Jayadrathavadhap.): VII, **97,** 3607 (*rathāḥ*?); **149,** 6483; **150**β', 6506 (only B., *Pāñcālaiḥ* C.).—§ 600 (Ghaṭotkacavadhap.): VII, **153,** 6635 (only B., C. has *Pāñcāla*°); **170,** 7679 (so C., B. has *Pañcālaiḥ*). —§ 608 (Karṇap.): VIII, **56,** 2753 (sg.); **82,** †4189 (*a-P°ṃ kriyate*).

Pāñcālyaputra = Dhṛshṭadyumna: VI, 2707 (so C., B. has *Pāñcāladāyadaḥ*); VII, 7636 (only B., *Pāñcālaputraṃ* C.).

Pañcamī, a river. § 574 (Jambūkh.): VI, **9**λ, 333 (in Bhāratavarsha).

Pañcanābhi = Kṛshṇa: XIII, 7380.

Pañcanada ("the country of the five rivers," i.e. Pañjāb). § 285 (Nakula): II, **32,** 1193 (*kṛtsnaṃ*, conquered by Nakula).—§ 358 (Tīrthayātrāp.): III, **82,** 5025.—§ 362 (do.): III, **83,** 5086 (the same?).—§ 412 (Ashṭāvakrīya): III, **134,** †10662 (*loke sthānaṃ P°ṃ puṇyaṃ*). — § 494 (Āṅgirasa): III, **222,** 14229 (? the five rivers?).—§ 555 (Sainyodyogap.): V, **19,** 598 (*kṛtsnaṃ*).—§ 757*m* (Goloka): XIII, **102***a*, 4888 (a tīrtha).—§ 785 (Anugītāp.): XIV, **83,** 2483.—§ 793 (Mausalap.): XVI, **7,** 221; **8,** 270 (°*ālayaiḥ*, sc. *Ābhīraiḥ*, only B., C. has by error *Pañcajanā*°).

Pañcanada, adj. ("belonging to Pañcanada"). § 544 (Sainyodyogap.): V, **4**γ, 82 (*nṛpāḥ*).

Pañcanada, pl. (°*āḥ*), a people ("the inhabitants of Pañcanada"). § 576 (Bhagavadgītāp.): VI, **20,** †750 (in the army of Duryodhana).—§ 580 (Bhīshmavadhap.): VI, **56**β, 2406 (do.).—§ 607 (Karṇap.): VIII, **45,** 2100, 2110. Cf. next.

Pāñcanada, pl. (°*āḥ*), a people = Pañcanada, pl. § 607 (Karṇap.): VIII, **45,** †2086.

Pāñcanada, adj. ("belonging to the Pañcanadas"). § 607 (Karṇap.): VIII, **45,** 2089 (*dharmaṃ*), 2091 (do.).

Pañcarātra (B. mostly *Pā*°), a literary work. § 668*b* (Pañcaçikhavākya): XII, **218,** 7891 (°*viçāradaḥ*, sc. Pañcaçikha; cf. Nīl.).—§ 717*c* (Uparicara): XII, **336,** 12720 (°*vidaḥ*, B. *Pā*°).—§ 717*b* (Nārāyaṇīya): XII, **340,** 12976 (*idaṃ mahopanishadaṃ caturvedasamanvitaṃ Sāṅkhyayogakṛtaṃ tena P°ānuçabditaṃ* | *Nārāyaṇa-mukhodgītaṃ Nārado çravayat punaḥ* | *Brahmaṇaḥ sadane tāta yathā dṛshṭaṃ yathā çrutaṃ*); **350,** 13702 (the third of the five *jñānāni*, B. *Pā*°), 13706 (°*sya kṛtsnasya vettā bhagavān svayaṃ*, sc. Nārāyaṇa, B. *Pā*°), 13710 (°*vidaḥ*; B. *Pā*°).

Pañcarātrika = Mahāpurusha (Mahāpurushastava).

Pañcasrotas, name of a place (?) (= *manasi*, Nīl.). § 668*b* (Pañcaçikhavākya): XII, **218,** 7890 (°*i yaḥ sattram āste varshasahasrikaṃ*, sc. Pañcaçikha), 7891 (°*i nishṇātaḥ*, sc. Pañcaçikha).

Pañcavaktra, a warrior of Skanda. § 615*u* (Skanda): IX, **45**η, 2578.

Pañcavaṭī, a tīrtha. § 368 (Tīrthayātrāp.): III, **83,** 7033.

Pañcavīrya, a Viçvadeva. § 749 (Ānuçāsanik.): XIII, **91**γ, 4361 (enumeration).

Pañcayajña = Mahāpurusha (Mahāpurushastava).

Pañcayakshā, a tīrtha. § 370 (Tīrthayātrāp.): III, **84,** 7088.

[Pañcendropākhyāna(ṃ)] ("episode relating to the five Indras"). § 238 (cf. Vaivāhikap.): *Vyāsa* said to *Drupada*: In days of yore, when the gods were celebrating a great sacrifice in the forest of *Naimisha*, *Yama*, holding the office of *çamitṛ*, did not slay the creatures, so that their numbers increased very greatly. *Soma*, *Çakra*, *Varuṇa*, *Kubera*, the *Sādhyas*, the *Rudras*, the *Vasus*, the *Açvins*, etc., complained thereof to *Prajāpati*, who comforted them, saying that when the sacrifice was over *Yama* would again sweep away the inhabitants of the earth. The gods then returned to the place of the sacrifice, and saw a golden lotus carried along the *Bhāgīrathī*. *Indra* proceeded to the spot where the *Gaṅgā* issues, and saw a beautiful woman (it was *Çrī*), whose tears were being transformed into golden lotuses. She led him to *Mahādeva*, who as a handsome youth was seated with a young lady on a throne on one of the peaks of the *Himavat*, playing dice. When *Indra* spoke haughtily of himself, *Mahadeva* caused *Çrī* to paralyse him and lead him into a hole, where four *Indras* of old were confined in order to be reborn in the world of men, there to slay a large number of men, and then to regain the region of *Indra*. Their fathers should be *Dharma*, *Vāyu*, *Maghavat*, and the *Açvins*, *Indra* creating a person from himself to be the fifth among them. Their names were *Viçvabhuj*, *Bhūtadhāman*, *Çibi*, *Çānti*, and *Tejasvin*. The weeping woman (*Çrī*) was appointed to be their common wife in the world of men. *Nārāyaṇa*, to whom *Īçāna* (i.e. *Çiva*) and the five *Indras* repaired, approved of everything. The five *Indras* were reborn as the *Pāṇḍavas*, and *Çrī* as *Draupadī*. A white hair of *Nārāyaṇa's* became *Baladeva*, and a black *Kṛshṇa*, after having entered the wombs of *Devakī* and *Rohiṇī*. Having related this to *Drupada*, *Vyāsa* granted him celestial sight, so that he beheld the *Pāṇḍavas* endued with their former bodies.—§ 239: *Vyāsa* then related to *Drupada* the story of the damsel (= *Çrī* = *Kṛshṇā*) whom *Çaṅkara*, i.e. *Çiva*, appointed to be in a future birth the wife of five husbands (see § 220) (I, **197**).

Pāṇḍara, a serpent. § 65 (Sarpasattra): I, **57,** 2152 (of Airāvata's race).

Pāṇḍaravāsinī ("dressed in white") = Çrī: I, 1146 (Ç°).

Pāṇḍava, pl. (°*āḥ*), the five sons of Pāṇḍu, viz. Yudhishṭhira, Bhīmasena, and Arjuna (born by Kuntī), Nakula and Sahadeva (born by Mādrī), husbands of Draupadī; sometimes, especially in books V–IX, the name seems to denote all the adherents of Yudhishṭhira: I, 13, 100, 115, 116, 122, 132, 133, 145, †158, †171, †186, †201, †208, †215, 282 (*Kuru-P°senayoḥ*), 298 (do.), 334 (do.), 376, 377, 380, 390, 393, 407, 409, 414, 418, 422, 438, 440, 465, 470, 478, 482, 484, 485, 487, 493, 497, 498, 499, 501, 502, 512, 515, 564, 572, 575 (*a-P°āya*), 578, 629, 1763 (°*ānāṃ kulakaraṃ*, sc. Parikshit), 2203 (*Mahābhārataṃ* . . . *P°ānāṃ yaçaskaraṃ*), 2209 (°*ānāṃ pitāmahaṃ*, i.e. Vyāsa), 2224, 2228, 2230 (*Kuru-P°yoḥ*), 2237, 2239, 2245, 2248, 2255, 2269, 2282, 2286, 2310, ††3819, ††3820, ††3834 (their eleven sons), ††3839, 4295 (*pañca*), 4559, 4832 (the birth of the five *P.*), 4902, 4947, 4959, 4960, 4961, 4962, 4963, 4977, 4998, 5001, 5006, 5012, 5034, 5069, 5093, 5097, 5099, 5214, 5222, 5246 (*Kuru-P°āḥ*), 5247, 5251, 5253, 5256, 5294, 5346 (°*āraṇiḥ*, sc. Kuntī), 5363 (*Pṛthāraṇisamudbhūtais tribhiḥ P°vahnibhiḥ*), 5439, 5444, 5465, 5466, 5540, 5545, 5631, 5638, 5643, 5648, 5650, 5651, 5653, 5655, 5656, 5661 (°*jyeshṭhaṃ*, i.e. Yudhishṭhira), 5675, 5685, 5693, 5701, 5712, 5720, 5726, 5731, 5734, 5761, 5775, 5798, 5799, 5800, 5802, 5836, 5837, 5842, 5855, 5858, 5861, 5862, 5869, 5873, 5874, 5894 (*pañcānāṃ*), 5941, 5962, 6038, 6080, 6103, 6241, 6309, 6316, 6320, (6325), 6347, 6421, 6436, 6437, 6442, 6917, 6918, 6920, 6925 (*pañca*), 6927, 6945, 6946, 6950, 6971, †7154, †7169, 7252, 7273, †7309 (incarnations of the five Indras), †7310, 7327 (Çrī was born as Draupadī for the sake of the *P.*),

†7346 (married Draupadī), 7347, 7366, 7372, 7376, 7380, 7385, 7388, 7402, 7404, 7416, 7425, 7431, 7434, 7435, 7445, 7456, 7467, 7468, 7469, 7470, 7485, 7524, 7525, 7528, 7531, 7539, 7543, 7548, 7554, 7560, 7564, 7571, 7592, 7593, 7595, 7596, 7600, 7608, 7611, 7741, 7743, 7746, 7748, 7749, 7754, 8049, 8062; II, 17, 45, 94, 104, 135, 146, 150, 776, 809 (dual = Arjuna and Bhīmasena), 837 (°-*Yādavān*, i.e. Arjuna, Bhīmasena, and Kṛshṇa), 878 (dual = Arjuna and Bhīmasena), 949 (do.), 968 (do.), 975, 979 (*Yudhishṭhira-mukhāḥ*), 981, 1340, 1411 (*Vṛshṇi-P°ān*), 1451, 1480, 1562 (*sarva°*), 1563, 1565, 1606, 1658, 1677 (°*çrī*°), 1679, 1687, 1702, 1786, 1899, 1926, 1934, 1964, 1965, 1971, †1978, †1992, 2021 (*catvāraḥ*), 2022, 2103, 2107, 2108, †2115, †2119, 2141, †2186, †2199, †2200 (*mahishīṃ P°ānāṃ*, i.e. Draupadī), 2218, †2226, †2238, 2255, 2261, 2273, 2283, 2287, 2288, 2289, 2339, 2346, 2452, 2456, 2460 (°*dhanaiḥ*), 2462, 2468, 2471, 2475, 2478, 2490, 2511, 2519, †2521, †2522, †2523, 2526, †2527, †2536, (2566), 2585 (°*āntaḥpure*), 2613, 2628, 2657, 2659, 2660, 2663, 2671, 2674, 2675, 2677 (°*ānāṃ priyāṃ bhāryāṃ Draupadīṃ*), 2686, 2698, 2701, 2706, 2707; III, 10, 17, 19, 40, 41, 42, 218, †219, †231, †235, †236, 240, 262, 263, 273, 278, 290, 294, 296, 304, 307, 312, 314, 318, 319, 320, 345, 349, 354, 365, 372, 387, 399, 402 (*pañca*), 461, 526, 531, 547, 555, 572, 580 (°*ānāṃ priyā bhāryā*, i.e. Draupadī), 590, 892, 895, 898, 899, 900, 931, 934, †944 (*pañcabhiḥ*), †947, †948, 964, 1432 (dual = Bhīmasena and Yudhishṭhira), 1433, 1753 (*Kuru-P°sattamaḥ*, i.e. Arjuna), 1920, 1933, 1940, 1955, 1982, 1985, †2011, †2012, 2013, 3090, 3094, 3096, 8297, 8410, 8434, 8481, 8486, 8511, 8523, 10107, †10237, †10238, †10239, 10869, 10900, 10909, 10910, 10912, 10986, 10998, 11002, 11011, 11021, 11039, 11055, 11058, 11061, 11062, 11068, 11331, 11401, 11416, 11451, 11542, 11544, 11549, 11551, 11554, 11598, 11630, 11658 (°*çreshṭhāḥ*), 11670, 11673, 11677, 11769, 11772, 11773, 11829, 11840, 11841, 11933, 12315, †12320, 12537, 12538, 12549, 12555, 12556, 12567, 12568, †12594, 12600, 12601, 12604, 12607, 12608, 13014, 13140, 13142, ††13248, ††13331, ††13347, ††13348, 14649, 14652, 14654, 14666, 14701, 14722, 14773, 14775, 14783, 14784, 14787, 14797, 14798, 14838, 14839, 14921, 14922, 14947, 14960, 14964 (*caturaḥ*), 14977, 14978, 14980 (*catvāraḥ*), 15007, 15028, 15037, 15038, 15058, 15061, 15068, 15073, 15074, 15090, 15108, 15111, 15115, 15116, 15119, 15130, 15132, 15171 (*pañca*), 15181, 15188, 15213, 15215, 15216, 15217, 15223, 15226, 15227 (*caturbhiḥ*), 15263, 15305, 15306, 15315, 15339, 15343, 15345, 15366, 15370, 15378, 15492, 15521, 15552, 15554, 15557, 15559, 15568, 15570, 15573, 15576 (*bhāryaṃ P°ānāṃ . . . Draupadīṃ*), 15665, †15680, †15697, †15708, †15711 (*jaghanyajaḥ P°ānāṃ*, i.e. Sahadeva), 15804, 15854 (*caturaḥ*), 15858, 15859, 16929, †17216, †17218, 17221, 17224, 17234, 17237, 17239, 17412, 17419, 17444, 17448, 17476 (*pañca*); IV, 16, 87, 80, 144, 155, 172, 211, †324, 332, 333, 334, 869, 873, 878, 879, 884, 886, 893, 919, 920, 921, 938, 947, 960, 961, 962, 963, 969, 988, 1000, 1005, 1030, 1098, 1130, 1187, 1212, 1475, 1493, 1496, 1615, 1621, 2160, 2260 (*pañca*), 2265, 2272, 2299, 2306 (*pañca*), 2312, 2318, 2322, 2349 (*pañca*); V, †9, †30, (*Kuru-P°ānāṃ*), 92, 96, 105 (*Kuru-P°kāraṇāt*), 113, 128, 132, 172, 196, 576, 581, 583, 616, 626, 628, 638, 642, 643, 644, †647, †652, †657, †661, †662, †663, †665, †666, †667, †668, †671, †682, †683, 685, †703, †721, †723, †726, †761, †764, †782, †809, †810, †830, †840, †842, †845 (*bhāryāṃ Draupadīṃ P°ānāṃ*), †850, †856, 864, 866, †889, †896, 920, 929, †943, †946, †982, 1177, 1258, †1331 (*Pāṇḍoḥ sutāḥ*), †1354, †1375, 1377 (*pañca*), †1397, 1443, 1466, 1471, 1563, 1803, 1806, 1808, †1812, †1814, †1818, †1846, †1896, †1898, †1899, †1906, 1948, 1952, 1955, 1963, 1965, 1970, 1971, 1975, 1982, 1984, 1986, 1989, 1992, 1995, 1997, 1998, 2004, 2006, 2009, 2010, 2011, 2012, 2013, 2016, 2066, 2069, 2106, 2108, 2117 (°*āgniṃ*), 2130, 2142, 2150, 2159, 2167, 2170, 2186, 2212, 2232, 2234, 2240, 2241, 2259, 2261 (dual, *Savyasāci-Vṛkodarau*, i.e. Arjuna and Bhīmasena), 2267, 2269, 2270, 2271, 2273, 2275, 2277, 2282, 2309, 2311, 2312, 2314, 2321, 2362, 2367, 2381, 2406, 2434 (*pañca*), 2437, †2505 (°*āgnau*), 2515, †2516, 2525, 2528, 2533, 2584, 2662, 2684, 2690, 2719, 2773, 2808, 2809, 2820, 2821, 2822, 2863, 2867, 2874, 2881, 2884, 2889, 2898, 2960, 3026, 3069 (*pañca*), 3070, 3076, 3087, 3090, 3091, 3127, 3135, 3137, 3160, 3162, 3172, 3189, 3190, 3228, 3229, 3262, 3264, 3289, †3301, †3303, 3306, 3320, 3323 (*Kuru-P°āṇ*), 3326, 3386, 3398, 3400, 3401, 3405 (*Kuru-P°aiḥ*), 3409, 3412, 3413, 3414, 3420, 3423, 3437, 3498, 3508, 3510, 4118, 4136, 4142, 4152, 4163 (°*arshabhān*), 4165, 4166, 4168, 4184, 4218, 4230, 4239, 4240, 4242, 4243, 4246, 4257, 4258, 4261, 4262, 4272, 4273, 4274, 4276, 4281, 4282, 4306 (read °*vebhyaḥ* with B.), 4308, 4345, 4354, 4361, 4369, 4371, 4389, 4420, 4451, 4461, 4666, 4685, 4718, 4720, 4736, 4737, 4738, 4742 (*pañca*), 4750, 4752, 4754, 4769, 4773, 4800, †4815, 4836, 4848, 4850, 4852, 4885, 4892, 4896, 4900, 4901, 4902, 4938, 4956, 4958, 5028, 5029, 5091, 5151, 5166, 5178, 5186, 5192, 5194, 5197, 5269, 5293, 5342, 5344, 5348, 5359, 5366, 5393 (*Kuru-P°senayoḥ*), 5401, 5407, 5412, 5414, 5453, 5459, 5466, 5482, 5538, 5579, 5589, 5605, 5630, †5653, 5713, 5723, 5736 (only B.), 5741, 5744, 5746, 5747, 5770, 5810, 5829, 5830, 5834, 5850, 5851, 5885, 5902, 5904, 5910, 5912, 5917, 5918, 5919, 5921, 7568, 7574, 7603; VI, 2 (*Kuru-P°-Somakāḥ*), 3 (do.), 4, 17, 27 (*Kuru-P°-Somakāḥ*), 34 (do.), 47, 91, 126, 130, 311, 382 (*Kuru-P°āḥ*), 504, 516, 520, 524 (only B., C. has *Pāñcālānāṃ*), 531, 546, 548, 553, 560, 572, 586 (*Kuru-P°senayoḥ*), 591, 600, 611 (*Kuru-P°senayoḥ*), 612, 630 (*Kuru-P°āḥ*), 633, 679, 708, 720, 730, 738, †741, †745, †746, †759, 778, 830, 831 (°*ānīkaṃ*), 1241 (°*ānāṃ Dhanañjayaḥ*, sc. *asmi*, says Kṛshṇa), 1534, 1617, 1621, 1632, 1638, 1640, 1643 (°-*Dhārtarāshṭrayoḥ*), 1662 (*Kuru-P°sene*), 1676, 1729, 1759, 1804, 1810, 1836, 1902, 1903, 1908, 1909, 1910 (°*ānīkaṃ*), 1921, 1945, 1964, 1979, 1985, 1989, 1990, 1996, 2004, 2027, 2030 (°*rathān*), 2056, 2058 (*sarva-*°), 2071, 2089 (only B.), 2120 (*Kuru-P°āḥ*), 2124, 2131, 2161, 2187, 2206, 2337, 2420, 2427, 2428, 2429, 2453, 2458, 2459, 2497, 2499, 2503, 2507, 2511, 2512, 2513, 2521, 2528 (°*rathān*), 2530, 2578, 2579, †2613, 2706, 2713, 2717, 2719, 2721, 2757, 2816, 2833, 2875, 2881, 2885, 2886, 2888, 2880, 2901, 2903, 2913, 2919, 2923, 2924, 2930, 2933, 2937, 3003, 3009, 3048, 3051, 3052, 3058, 3059, 3062, 3075, 3076 (°*ānīkaṃ*), 3088, 3091, 3101, 3114, 3117, 3118, 3135, 3172, 3236, 3238, 3269, 3274, 3276, 3277 (*Kuru-P°āḥ*), 3289, 3299, 3313, 3339, 3441, 3444, 3449, 3455, 3510, †3515, †3520, †3523, 3538, 3540, 3588, 3601, 3666, 3667, 3750, 3830, 3840, 3841, 3847, 3850, 3868, 3883 (*Kuru-P°sainikāḥ*), 3885, 3887, 3896, 3930, 3940, 3951, 3958, 3971, 3972, 4055, 4058, 4090, 4188, 4191, 4194, 4196, 4209, 4229, 4235, 4237, 4253, 4270, 4277, 4281, 4304, 4306, 4320 (°*balaṃ*), 4325, 4337, 4401 (*Kuru-P°āḥ*), 4402 (do.), 4409, 4413, 4415, 4416, 4445, 4465, 4479, 4486, 4491, 4505,

4513, 4515, 4517, †4528 (°-*Dhārtarāshṭrayoḥ*), 4541, 4557, 4561, 4563, 4564, 4580, 4621, 4623, 4683, 4722, 4725, 4740, 4742, 4743, 4764, 4766, 4767, 4769, 4770, 4777, 4790, 4810, 4811, 4878, 4879 (°*sainyāni*), 4882, 4892, 4893, 4895, 4943, 4956, 4993, 4994, 4995, 4996, 5003, 5004, 5014, 5016, 5018, 5019 (°-*Sṛñjayaiḥ*), 5020, 5022, 5023, 5027, 5039, 5056 (°*ānīke*), 5057, 5063, 5065, 5082, 5084, 5085, 5112, 5116 (read °*vānām* with B.), 5119, 5156, 5268, 5283 (dual = Arjuna and Bhīmasena), 5326, 5333, 5335, 5336, 5337, 5344 (°*vāhinīm*), 5355, 5376, 5460, 5461, 5465, 5469, 5476, 5478, 5501, 5520, 5529, 5562, 5569, 5577 (°*ānīkinīm*), 5586, 5599 (*sarva*°), 5600, 5622, 5634, 5640, 5676, 5680, 5682, 5690, 5700, 5706, 5716, 5720, 5751, 5754, 5762, 5767 (*Kuru-P°āḥ*), 5810, †5813, 5828, 5837, 5842, 5846; VII, 4, 12, 29, 40, 102, †114 (°*yuddhaçauṇḍam*, but read with B. °*m yu* °*m*, i.e. Arjuna), 170, 172, 177, 188, 209 (*Kuru-P°senānām*), 210, 211, 212, 214 (°-*Sṛñjayān*), 220 (°-*Sṛñjayāḥ*), 221, 224, 230, 231 (°*ānīkam*), 243, 254, 255, 259, 261 (°-*Sṛñjayāḥ*), 280, 283, 348, 361, 414, 415, 444, 450, 463, 480, 481, 484, 495 (°*ānīke*), 583, 591, 616, 631 (*Kuru-P°āḥ*), 637 (°*ānīkam*), 656, 794, 867, 891 (°*ānīke*), 915, 920, †926, 935 (°-*Sṛñjayaiḥ*), 938, 939, 942, 949, 984, 1069, 1076, 1157, 1174, 1183 (°*yodhāḥ*), 1200 (°*balam*), 1203 (°*vāhinī*), 1350, 1353, 1371, 1383, 1407, 1408, 1411, 1417 (°*yugāntārkaḥ*, sc. Arjuna), 1460, 1473, 1482 (*pañca*), 1489, 1515, 1540, 1549, 1691 (pl. B., dual C. by error), 1696, 1700, 1749, 1760, 1778, 1780, 2494, 2622, 2624, 2643, 2740, 2784, 2806, 2962, 2999, 3023 (*Kuru-P°-Sātvataiḥ*), 3031, 3039, 3041, 3042, 3046, 3070, 3078, 3086, 3101, 3128, 3419, 3421, 3423 (°*nigrahe*), 3487, 3488, 3496, 3498, 3500, 3504, 3511, 3515, 3517, 3520, 3542, 3573, 3576, 3702, 3807, 3809, 3888 (*Kuru-P°yor bale*), 3969, 4084 (°*sainyānam*), 4088, 4095, 4106, 4119, 4120, 4135, 4154, 4160, 4167, 4179, 4329, 4374 (°*ānīke*), 4487, 4490, 4491, 4500 (*sarva*°), 4526, 4540, 4647, 4737, 4812, 4858, 4869, 4871, 4881, 4882, 4883, 4884, 4885, 4886, 4890, 4891, 4934, 4981, 4992, 5012, 5066, 5088, 5096, 5132, 5323, 5366, 5462, 5463, 5465, 5553, 5630 (*Kuru-P°pravarāḥ*), 5658, 5659, 6021 (*P°-Kauravāḥ*), 6293, 6493, 6500, 6545, 6547, 6561, 6569 (°-*Sṛñjayān*), 6603, 6617, 6620, 6622, 6642, 6654, 6675 (*Droṇa-P°*), 6687, 6692, 6695, 6699, 6760, 6761 (°*ānīkam*), 6769, 6820 (°*ānīkam*), 6826, 6855, 6970, 6972, 6973, 6979 (*sarva*-°), 6984, 6987 (*sarva*-°), 7020, 7028, 7033, 7037, 7039, 7040, 7056, 7060, 7062, 7063, 7072, 7140, 7145, 7148, 7149, 7205, 7258, 7287, †7296 (°-*Kauraveyāḥ*), †7316, 7340, 7344 (only B.), 7347, 7356, 7611, 7676, 7733, 7752, 7760, 7763 (*Somaka-P°aiḥ*), 7768, 7773, 7821, 7822, 7823, 7831, 7850, 7854, 7859, 8013, †8024 (°*vāhinīm*), †8025 (°*yodhavīrāḥ*), 8072, 8107, †8155 (read °*ārthe* with B.), †8175, 8178, 8179, 8248 (*Sṛñjaya-P°āḥ*), 8255, 8256, 8262, †8273 (*Yadukula-P°nandanaḥ*, i.e. Kṛshṇa), 8284, 8305, 8339, 8347, 8371, 8372, 8374, 8389 (*Kuru-P°āḥ*), 8421, 8450, 8457, 8461 (*Somaka-P°ān*), 8481, 8511, 8547, 8552, 8623 (*Kuru-P°sainyayoḥ*), 8641, 8698, 8704, 8739 (*nish-P°ām urvīm*), 8752, 8852, 8882 (*Kuru-P°-Sṛñjayāḥ*), 8886, 8892, 8934, 8943, 9000, 9004, 9018, 9022, 9026, 9036, 9135, 9166, 9181 (°-*Vṛshṇayaḥ*), 9203 (*Kuru-P°senayoḥ*), 9206 (*Kuru-P°āḥ*), 9207 (*Kuru-P°sainikāḥ*), 9210, 9215, 9257, 9280, 9314, 9329 (°*taḥ*), 9432, 9492, 9494; VIII, 6, 13, 14, 15 (*Kuru-P°senayoḥ*), 72, 82, 93 (°*yodhān*), 115, 151, 182, 189, 240, 266, 275, 284, 286, 307, 316, 321, 325, 337, 341, 347, 362, 377, 379, 381, 383, 384, 413, 430, 431, 487, 488 (C. has by error *Vāṇḍavāḥ*), 562, 610, 611, 806, 824, 829 (*Kuru-P°āḥ*), 830, 968, 1033 (°*ānīkam*), 1167 (*Kuru-P°senayoḥ*), 1246, 1247, 1267, 1276, 1280, 1318, 1339, 1641, 1696, 1697, 1714, †1729, †1744, †1751, 1752, 1861, 2126, 2190, 2210, 2229, 2243 (°*balam*), 2296, 2299 (*Kuru-P°āḥ*), 2324, 2338, 2339 (°*vanam*), 2359 (*Cedi-P°-Pāñcālāḥ*), 2364, 2391, 2441, 2508, 2514, 2518, 2731, 2758 (*Cedi-Pāñcāla-P°ān*), 2761, 2772, 2843, 2850, 2902, 2910, 2912, 2945, 2999, 3003, 3071, 3072, 3075, 3189 (dual = Yudhishṭhira and Nakula), 3247, 3248, 3252, 3256, 3266, †3346, 3624 (°*dveshī*, sc. Karṇa), 3638, 3639, 3640 (read *Pāṇḍavān* . . . *mahārathān* with B.), 3657, 3661, 3668, 3672, 3695, 3717, 3730, 3746, 3773, 3776, †3804 (°-*Sṛñjayānām*), 3953 (°*balam*), 3954, 3974, 3976, 3978, 3985, 4000, 4001, 4002, 4044, 4168, †4226, †4247, 4273, 4277, 4382, 4401, 4405, 4448, †4494 (*Kuru-P°ānām*), †4502 (*Kuru-P°āçrayāḥ*), †4510, †4511, †4517, 4756, 4761 (°*a* C., but read °*ā*(*ḥ*) with B.), 4776, †4804, †4830, 4880, 4884, 4888, 4936, 4971; IX, 2, 9 (*Kuru-P°senayoḥ*), 17, 34, 35 (*sapta P°taḥ çeshāḥ*), 59, 81, 82, 85, 88, 92, 112, 121, 124, 126, 171, 174, 177, 178, 184, 186, 230, 242, 256, 261, 267, 308, 317, 324, 333, 338, 362, 364, 374, 375, 377, 395, 401, 408, 409, 410, 454, 456, 457, 464, 465, 522, 523, 524, 528, 534 (°*sainikān*), 537, 539, 540, 548, 556, 576 (*Somaka-P°ān*), 624, 625, 632, 686, 689, 694, 699, 700, 702, 761 (*sa-Sātyaki-Vṛkodarān*), 763, 781, 798, 804, 808, †896, †898 (°*yodhamukhyaiḥ*), 932, 946, 959, 963, 970, 982, 995, 1007, 1009, 1030, 1041, 1054, 1055, 1062, 1066, †1072, †1076 (°-*Sṛñjayānām*), 1096, 1103, 1132, 1179, 1180, 1192, 1193, 1194, 1204, 1210 (°*ānīkam*), 1219, 1223 (*Kuru-P°āḥ*), 1238 (°*ānīkam*), 1263, 1264, 1267, 1272, 1283, 1305, 1351 (°*ānīkam*), 1353, 1362, 1368, 1375, 1383, 1386, 1396, 1397, 1454, 1466, 1472, 1489, 1498, 1515, 1523, 1525, 1533, 1543, 1566, 1574, 1576, 1579 (°*ānīkāt*), 1583, 1586, 1590, 1597, 1617, 1619, 1645, 1680, 1709, 1720, 1735, 1739, 1740, 1742, 1835, 1861, 1862, 1863, 1866, 1881, 1927, 1928, 1939, 1944, 1946, 1947, 1949, 1951 (*Kṛshṇam sa-P°am*), 1960, 1973, 1977, 1983, 3005, 3066, 3088, 3090, 3174, 3226 (*Somaka-P°āḥ*), †3240, 3305, 3309, †3319, 3354, 3358, 3370, 3377 (so C., but read *Pāṇḍavaḥ* (i.e. Bhīmasena) with B.), 3388, 3390, 3404, 3429, 3430, 3447, 3457, 3461, 3466, 3496, 3497, 3499, 3502, 3532, 3543, 3551, 3554, 3555, 3556, 3566, 3570, 3575, 3577, 3580, 3592, 3593, 3610; X, 4, 8, 28 (*Kuru-P°yoḥ*), 46, 52, 59, 66, 96, 174, 321 (*Somaka-P°ān*), 391 (*Kuru-P°senayoḥ*), 450, 474, 510, 527 (*sapta P° taḥ çeshāḥ*, sc. the five brothers, Sātyaki, and Kṛshṇa), 530, 540 (*Kuru-P°senayoḥ*), 588, 667 (*a-P°āya*), 702, 711, 713, 714, 742, 743, 747; XI, 22, 228, 230, 231, 239, 298, 302, 323, 347, 360 (*Kuru-P°āḥ*), 362, 542, 562, 606, 630, 633, 657, 663, 703, 735, 744, 748 (*Kuru-P°āḥ*), 755, 807, 812; XII, 415 (*sarva*°), 1167, 1417, 1473, 1534, 1698 (*catvāraḥ*), 1813 (do.), 1884 (*sa-P°āḥ*), 1889 (*saha-P°aḥ*), 1891, 1915, 1926, 1931, 2122 (°-*Yādavāḥ*), †2714 (°*mukhyasamvṛtaḥ*, sc. Yudhishṭhira), 10096, 13430 (°*ānām kulodvaha*, sc. Janamejaya), 13443, 13554 (*Kuru-P°yor mṛdhe*); XIII, 334, 1769, 1771, 1772, 1774, 2968, 2969, 6891, 7689, 7747, 7754, 7769; XIV, 5, 373 (only B.), 1484, 1545 (*Kuru-P°sadma*), 1553 (*pañca*), 1585, 1775, 1782, 1787, 1795, 1800 (*pañca*), 1804 (do.), 1805, 1856, 1861, 1877, 1888, 1955, 1970, 2011, 2046, 2055, 2056, 2059, 2131, 2182, 2564 (°*ānām balāgraṇīḥ*, sc. Arjuna), 2603, 2608 (*Bhīmādīn*), 2674; XV, 1, 4, 6, 9 (°*striyaḥ*), 20, 29, 44, 48 (*rajā* . . . *P°ānām dhurandharaḥ*, i.e. Yudhishṭhira), 175, 341, 342, 428, †431 (*Kaurava-P°ānām*), †439, 473, 495, 497, 507, 509, 576, 583, 592, 636, 638, 639, 650, 657 (*Kurupateḥ putrān*), 717, 733

(*Bhīmasenādayaḥ*), 741, 771, 792, 863, 865, 869, 872, 873 (*Kuru-P°senayoḥ*), 892, 893, 960, 1011, 1050, 1076 (*pañca*), 1087 (°*ānāṃ dhurandharaḥ*, i.e. Yudhishṭhira); XVI, 9, 11, 134; XVII, 1, 29, 33, 36, 43; XVIII, 1, 124, 177, 186. Cf. Pāṇḍaveya, pl., Pāṇḍu, pl., Pāṇḍudāyada, pl., Pāṇḍukumāra, pl., Pāṇḍunandana, pl., Pāṇḍuputra, pl., Pāṇḍusuta, pl., Pāṇḍutanaya, pl.

Pāṇḍava, dual (°*au*) ("sons of Pāṇḍu") = Nakula and Sahadeva: I, 4879 (*Mādrīputrau*), 7399 (do.); II, 2621 (do.); III, 1971 (*Nakulaḥ Sahadevaç ca*), †15646 (*jaghanyajābhyāṃ*), 17225 (*Mādrīputrau*); IV, 2319 (do.); V, 2949 (do.); VI, 2473 (do.), 2733 (do.), 3865 (do.), 4782 (do.), 5074 (do.), 5228 (do.), 5559 (do.); VII, 1380 (do.), 8811 (do.); VIII, 2360 (do.), 3194 (do.), 3206 (do.), 3211, 4999 (*Mādrīputrau*); IX, 516 (do.), 550 (do.), 652 (do.), 656 (do.), 832 (do.), 961 (do.), 1021 (do.), 1373 (do.), 1725 (do.), 3481 (do.); X, 550 (do.); XII, 1396 (do.), 1464 (do.); XIV, 1504 (do.).

Pāṇḍava, sg.[1] ("son of Pāṇḍu") = Arjuna: I, †193, 524 (*Gāṇḍīvadhanvā*), 607, 2274 (*A*°), 2292 (*Kṛshṇasārathiḥ*), 4825, 5223, 5235, 5297, 5298, 5303, 5357 (*madhyama-P*°), 5474, 5477, 5492, 5531 (*Dhanañjayaḥ*), 6461 (do.), 6466, 6741, 6952 (*Kirīṭine*), 7103 (*Kirīṭinaḥ*), 7115 (do.), †7309 (*Savyasācī*), 7503 (*Savyasācī Dhanañjayaḥ*), 7753 (*Dhanañjayaḥ*), 7755, 7765, 7789, 7821, 7829 (*Dhanañjayah*), 7836, 7843, 7884, 7888 (*Kṛshṇa-P°au*), 7890, 7892 (*Kṛshṇa-P°au*), 7894, 7895, 7930, 7965, 7967, 8085 (*Kṛshṇa-P°au*), 8194, 8233 (*Bībhatsuḥ*), 8234, 8240, 8241, 8242, 8253 (*Kṛshṇa-P°au*), 8254, 8296 (*Kṛshṇa-P°au*), 8470; II, 5, 781, 1001, 1017, 1025, 1042, 1044, †2163 (*Savyasācī*), 2370 (*Bībhatsuḥ*); III, 503, 1492, 1606, 1607, 1609, 1614, 1650, 1659, 1747, 1764, 1790, 1792, 1869, 1880, 3093, 8291, †11931, 11936, 11938, 11985, 12012, 12016, 12151, 12293 (*Dhanañjayaḥ*), 12301, 12306, 14969, 14993, 15000, 15016, 15066, 15067, 15072, 16983 (*Phālgunaṃ*); IV, †310, 367 (*Bībhatsuḥ*), 1183, 1194, 1218, 1271, 1520 (°*āgniṃ*), 1521, 1569, 1575, 1576, 1624, †1665, †1679, †1682, †1695, 1731, 1809, 1834, 1868 (*Droṇa-P°yoḥ*), 1876, 1895, 1896, 1915, 1943, 2002, 2012, 2042, 2044, 2045, 2047 (*Bhīshma-P°yoḥ*), 2051, 2053, 2066, 2068, 2069, †2104, 2255, 2345, 2350; V, 1964, 2293 (*Savyasācī*), 2353, 2377, 2491 (*ātmā yasya*—i.e. Kṛshṇa's—*P°ḥ*), 2822, 2839, 2973, 3157, 3160, 3209 (*A*°), 4175, 4346 (*Kṛshṇa-P°au*), †4815 (°*sya samucchrito vānaraketuḥ*), 5296, 5370, 5372, 5488, 5497, 5649, 5806, 7630 (*Dhanañjayaṃ*); VI, 700, 810, 843, 849, 1028, 1066, 1250, 1001, 1377, 1407, 1680, 2023 (*Savyasācinaṃ*), 2139, 2146, 2151, 2163, 2195, 2196, 2197, †2619, 3001 (*Dhanañjayaṃ*), 3282 (*Dhanañjayaḥ*), 3577, 3976 (°*sya sutuḥ*, i.e. Irāvat), 3984, 4315 (*Kṛshṇasārathiḥ*), 4317, 4319 (*Çvetavāhanaḥ*), 4358 (*A*°), 4453, 4461, 4643 (*Dhanañjayaḥ*), 4644, 4657, 4970 (*Dhanañjayaḥ*), 4971 (*Dhanañjayāt*), 5069, 5071, 5121, 5124, 5127, 5129, 5136, 5219, 5221, 5356 (*Dhanañjayaṃ*), 5366 (do.), 5432, 5434, 5430, 5481(?), 5527 (*Dhanañjaye*), 5551, 5577 (*Dhanañjayaṃ*), 5585, 5592, 5725 (*Dhanañjayaṃ*), 5737, 5740, 5778, 5784, 5804; VII, 114 (read with B. °*aṃ yuddhaçauṇḍaṃ*), 200 (*Karṇa-P°au*), 422 (*A*°), 482 (?), 662, 676 (*Kṛshṇa-P°au*), 740, 762, 765 (°*Yādavau*), 1211, 1231, 1239, 1256, 1257 (*Dāçārha-P°au*), 1267, 1270, 1272, 1297, 1311, 2787, 2888, 2903, 2992, 3173, 3227 (*Kṛshṇa-P°āu*), 3228, 3237, †3238 (°*ādityaçarāṃçu*°), 3245 (*Droṇa-P°yoḥ*), 3249, 3325, 3331, 3340, 3350, 3351, 3368, 3381, 3395 (°*āgniḥ*), 3439, 3670, 3682, 3687, 3731, 3754, 3756, 3765, 3794 (*Kṛshṇa-P°au*), 3818, 3834 (*Dhanañjayaḥ*), 3837 (*Kṛshṇa-P°au*), 3868 (do.), 3912, 3916, 4189 (?), 4215 (*Guḍākeçaḥ*), 4265, 4295, 4298 (*Kṛshṇa-P°au*), 4301, 4323, 4367, 4460 (*Kṛshṇa-P°au*), 4729, 4984 (*Mādhava-P°au*), 5106 (*Dhanañjayaḥ*), 5807 (*Savyasācinaṃ*), 5859, 5935 (*Dhanañjaye*), 5944, 5949, 5953, 5968, 6072 (*Kirīṭinā*), 6125, 6156, 6161, 6169, 6191, 6193, 6199, 6201, 6202, 6214, 6248, 6253, 6276, 6299, 6329, 6455 (*Dhanañjayaṃ*), 6474 (*Keçava-P°au*), 6571 (*Kirīṭinā*), 6576, 6590, 6974, 7000 (*Kṛshṇa-P°au*), 7023, 7086, 7093, 7095, 7102 (*Karṇa-P°yoḥ*), 7221, 7509, 7510, 7656, 7719, 7762, 7765 (°*Mādhavau*), 7817 (*Dhanañjayaṃ*), 8059, 8061, †8167, 8180, 8208, 8240, 8244, 8286 (*Çvetavāhane*), 8322 (*Çvetavāhanaṃ*), 8368 (*Dhanañjayaḥ*), 8454, 8455, 8504, 8601 (*Droṇa P°yoḥ*), 8603, 8605, 8616, 8618, 8626 (*Droṇa-P°yoḥ*), 9120, 9424 (*Savyasācī*), †9648 (°-*Vṛshṇisiṃhayoḥ*); VIII, 42 (*Dhanañjayena*), 425 (*Çvetavāhanaḥ*), 427 (*Dhanañjayaḥ*), 617, 630, 638, 641, 645 (*Mādhava-P°au*), 646, 649, 659, 660, †671, †698, †702, 714, 822 (read *sa P*°), 827, 1082, 1083, 1114, 1225, 1270 (?), 1285, 1297, 1304, 1307, 1331, 1351, †1737, 1802, 1820, 1955 (*Kuntīputraṃ*), 1956 (*Dhanañjayaṃ*), †1963, †1978, †1988, †1990, †1995 (°-*Vāsudevau*), 2564, 2574, 2586, 2587, 2609 (*Kirīṭinā*), 2780, 2781 (*Kṛshṇa-P°au*), 2796 (read °*aḥ*), 2816 (*Mādhava-P°au*), 2821, 2823 (*Droṇa-P°yoḥ*), 2900, 2975, 2977, 2987, 3055, 3220, 3235, †3240, 3242, 3420, 3432, †3481, †3490, 3554 (?), 3582, 3599, 3602, 3606, 3618, 3620, 3660, 3871, 4018, 4020, 4041, †4052 (*Savyasācī*), †4061 (°-*Vāsudevau*), †4063, †4074, 4132, 4142, 4172, †4193, 4267, 4350, 4356, 4370, 4371, 4423, 4475 (*Mādhava-P°au*), †4501 (*Karṇa-P°au*), 4539, †4550, †4584, †4598, †4599, †4688, †4689, †4692, †4698, 4728, 4740, 4742, 4746, 4769, 4875 (*Savyasācī*), 4886, 5011 (*Dhanañjayaḥ*), 5021 (*Mādhava-P°au*); IX, 127, 167 (*Savyasācī*), 211, 219, 225 (?), 725, 726, 737 (*A*°), 739, 1469, 3257; X, 671, 673, 696 (*A*°), 710; XI, 589, 662 (*Bībhatsuḥ*); XII, 773, 893 (*Guḍākeçaḥ*), 5875 (*Pākaçāsaninā*); XIV, 376 (*Kṛshṇa-P°au*), 388, 401, 410 (*A*°), 417, 596, 1479, 1481 (*Kṛshṇa-P°au*), 2132, 2153, 2154, 2189, 2199, 2200, 2205, 2214, 2220, 2270, 2276, 2301 (*saha*°), 2330, 2331, 2335, 2390 (*Pārthaṃ*), 2442, 2444, 2466 (*Çvetavāhanaḥ*), 2490, 2494; XV, 362 (*Guḍākeçaḥ*); XVI, 147, 170 (*Bībhatsuḥ*), 175, 208, 246; XVII, 64 (*Çvetavāhanaḥ*).

Pāṇḍava, sg.[2] (do.) = Bhīmasena (Bhīma): I, 2258 (*Bh*°), 4980, 5018 (read °*vo* with B.), 5032, 5052, 5053, 5058, 5060, 5065, 5472, 5520 (*Vṛkodaraḥ*), 5828, 6002, 6043, 6064, 6071, 6270 (*Bh*°), 6271, 6279 (*Vṛkodaraḥ*), 6285 (*Bh*°), 6287, 6289, 6293, 7117 (*Vṛkodarāt*), 7241 (*Bh*°); II, 923, 931, 1062, 1070, 1080, 1089, 1005, 1103, 1920 (*Bh*°), 2623 (*Bh*°); III, 426, 431, 445, 2048, 10888, 11099, 11117, 11130, 11137, 11169 (*Vāyutanayo Bh°ḥ*), 11355, 11367 (*Bh*°), 11372, 11409, 11520, 11689, 11693, 11708, 11714, 11723, 11790, 12398 (*Bh*°), 14806 (*Bh*°), 15741; IV, †237, 552, 597, 618, 623, 638, 721, 750, 701, 764 (*Sūta-P°au*), 1112 (*Bh*°), 1368 (*Bh*°); V, †1824 (*Bh*°), 2022, 2035, 2038 (*madhyamaḥ*), 2009, †2084 (*gadāhastaḥ*), 2748, 2784, 2792, 2796, 3150, 3153, 3155 (*madhyamaḥ*), 4802 (will drink the blood of Duḥçāsana); VI, 2251, 2253, 2266, 2284, 2296, 2316, 2357, 2477 (*Bh*°), 2747 (do.), 2764 (do.), 2785, 2792, 2801, 2836, 2841, 2845 (*Bh*°), 2850, 3348, 3352, 3357, †3373 (*Bh*°), 3902, 3921, 4183, 4208, 4508 (*Bh*°), 4589 (do.), 4673, 5188, 5245, 5247, 5257, 5266, 5318 (*Bh*°), 5553 (do.), 5809 (do.); VII, 1140, 1141, 1148, 1150, 1657 (*Bh*°), 3660 (do.), 4074, 4090, 5001 (*Bh*°), 5118 (do.), 5143, 5187, 5203, 5207, 5216, 5219, 5233, 5254, 5287, 5310, 5381, 5390, 5416, 5440, 5457, 5493, 5500, 5506, 5519,

5535, 5555, 5564, 5586, 5594, 5598, 5600, 5611 (*Bh°*), 5617, 5625, 5626, 5627, 5637, 5645, 5652, 5660 (only B., C. has *Kauravaḥ*), 5666, 5677 (*Karṇa-P°yoḥ*), 5685, 5697, 5704, 5708, 5709, 5742, 5745 (*Karṇa-P°yoḥ*), 5751, 5752, 5771, 5775, 5779, 5787, 6402, 6649 (*Bh°*), 6706, 6711, 6720, 6936, 7204 (*Bh°*), 7672 (do.), 7732 (*Vṛkodaraḥ*), 7835 (*Bh°*), 8504, 8678 (*Bh°*), 8890, 9176, 9238 (*Bh°*), 9264 (only B.), 9343, 9354, 9356, 9359, 9360, 9377, 9386 (*Bh°*); VIII, 88, 475, 476, 569, 570, 571, 574, 575, 584, 588, 609, 2425 (*Karṇa-P°yoḥ*), 2426, 2433, 2460, 2462 (*Karṇa-P°yoḥ*), 2467, 2473 (*Karṇa-P°yoḥ*), 2479, 2480, 2489, 2507 (*Karṇa-P°yoḥ*), 2857 (*Bh°*), 3127, †3849, 3912, 3922, 4149 (read *°aḥ* with B.), †4279, †4300, 4999 (*Vṛkodaraḥ*), 5030 (do.); IX, 29 (slayer of Duryodhana), 252 (*madhyamaḥ . . . Bh°ḥ*), 779 (*Bh°*), 1423, 1432, 1438, 1497, 1715 (*Bh°*), 1917, 1921, 3173 (*Vṛkodaraḥ*), 3188, 3218 (*Bh°*), †3241, 3268, 3285 (*Bh°*), 3291, 3364, 3366, 3377 (only B., C. has *Pāṇḍavāḥ*), 3480 (*Bh°*); XI, 357 (*madhyamam*), 366; XII, 1464 (*Bh°*); XIV, 2555; XV, 86.

Pāṇḍava, sg.[3] ("descendant of Pāṇḍu") = Janamejaya: I, 2221 (*J°*).

Pāṇḍava, sg.[4] ("son of Pāṇḍu") = Nakula: II, 1195, 1258, 1260; IV, 165 (*Mādrīputraḥ*), 312; V, 3167, 5900 (?*Dhṛṣṭaketuḥ . . . sambandhī P°sya*); VI, 3168 (*N°*); VII, 334; VIII, 879, 924, 942 (*Karṇa-P°yoḥ*), 947, 948, 962, 965, †4282; IX, 470, 479, 482, 484, 488, 489, 490, 506.

Pāṇḍava, sg.[5] (do.): Sahadeva: I, †206 (*Saubalaṃ P°ena hataṃ*); II, 1125, 1160; III, 11460 (*S°*), 11485 (do.); IV, 333 (do.); V, 5479; VI, 5172; VII, 4031 (*S°*), 7362 (do.); IX, 1213, 1218, 1540, 1561 (slew Çakuni and Ulūka); XI, 700; XVI, 179 (*S°*); XVII, 58 (do.).

Pāṇḍava, sg.[6] (do.) = Yudhishṭhira: I, 144 (*rājasūye . . . P°sya*), 419, 638, 5467 (*Y°*), 5666, 5669, 5741, 5760, 5803, 6259, †7155, 7232, 7506 (*jyeshṭhe*); II, 13 (*°sya . . . sabhāṃ*), 44 (*Y°*), 61 (*sabhāṃ . . . P°sya*), 103, 220, 270, 273, 282, 301, 312, 422, 449, 470, 506, 540, 551, 973, 1230, 1231, 1257, 1263 (*Dharmarājam*), 1339 (?), 1594, 1625 (*Kṛshṇa-P°au*), 1690, 1762, 1856, 2011, 2013, 2062 (*jyeshṭham*), †2118 (*Ajātaçatruḥ*), †2163, †2203 (*Ajātaçatruḥ*), †2244, 2492, 2496, 2576, 2583 (*Y°*), 2631 (*rājā*); III, 200, 212, †260, 410 (*Dharmarājaḥ*), 1326, 1442, 2064, 2217, 3070, 3083, 3088, 8300, 8365, 8374, 8444, 8449, 8460, 8476, 8500, 8651, 8652, 9973, 10095, 10116, †10121, †10122, 10135, 10167, 10317, 10418, 10707, 11052, 11533, 11782, 11823, 11845, 11862, 11871, 11881, 11929, 12464, †12572, †12576, †12590, 12610, 12746, 13020, 13121, ††13261, ††13301, 13405, †14764, 14837 (*jyeshṭhaḥ*), 15033, 15278 (*rājasūyam P°sya*), 15314, 15356, 15374, 15416, 16917, 17443; IV, 20, 58, 65, 204, 217, †319 (*Y°*), †322, 329, 552, 2191, 2198, 2200, 2226, 2287, 2311, 2316; V, 60, 62, 90 (*rājñaḥ*), 113 (*Kuntīputro Y°ḥ*), 177, 192, 193, 217, 220, 269, †677 (*Kuntīputraḥ P°o 'jātaçatruḥ*), †713, †714, †719, †767, †769, †780, †786, †787, †811, †812, †849, †867, 939, †950, †951, †1818, †1819, †1820, †1822 (*jyeshṭhaḥ*), 1967 (*rājā Dharmaputraḥ*), 1973, 2115, †2292, 2295, 2930, 4687, 4716, 4721, 4722, 4723, 5096, 5233, 5330, 5335 (*rājā*), 5375 (*Dharmarājam*), 5535, 5543, 5544, 5736 (?only C., B. has *Pāṇḍavān*), 5852 (*rājā*), 5928, 5929, 7597, 7635, 7637; VI, 14, 695, 697, 761, 767, 1555, 1562, 1566, 1993 (*Dharmarājaḥ*), 2052, 2089 (only C., B. has *Pāṇḍavāḥ*), 2091, 2326 (*Dharmarājaḥ*), 2412, 2481 (*Dharmaputraḥ*), 2577, 3700, 3702, 3704, 3706, 3795, 4776 (*Dharmarājam*), 4796, 4913, 4915, 4961, 5346, 5350, 5351 (*Y°*); VII, 195, 229, 234, 464, 473, 659, 680, 682, 936 (?), 1031 (*Kururājasya*), 2132, 2792, 2928, 3074 (*rājānam*), 3985, 3999, 4006, 4172 (*rājā*), 4256, 4983 (*Dharmarājaḥ*), 5154 (*rājānam*), 6288, †6445 (*Ajātaçatrum*), 6480, 6492, 6631 (*jyeshṭhaḥ*), 6637 (*rājānam*), 6953, 7003 (*Dharmarājam*), 7264, 7268, 7278, 7385, 7386, 7387, 7390 (*jyeshṭhaḥ*), 8360, 8361, 8370, 8738, 8866 (*Dharmarājaḥ*), 8991, 9059, 9064, 9125 (*jyeshṭhaḥ*), 9165 (*Y°*); VIII, 148, 438 (C. *Kuru-P°au*, but read *Karṇa-P°au* with B.), 1175 (*rājā*), †1728 (*rājā*), 2326, 2347, 2354, 2659 (*Dharmarājaḥ*), 2687, 2709, 2984, 2994 (*Y°*), 3145, 3171 (*rājānam*), †3372, 3432 (*Y°*), 3473 (*Dharmarājam Y°m*), †3478, †3509, †3533 (*Dharmarājaḥ*), 3567, 4489 (*Dharmarājam*), 5000; IX, 81, 235, 284, 641, 645, 650, 653, 809 (*Dharmarājo Y°ḥ*), 845 (*jyeshṭhaḥ*), 851, 855, 925, 1018 (*jyeshṭhasya*), 1282 (?), 1704, 1758, 3145, 3588 (*jyeshṭham*); X, 582, 589 (*Y°m . . . Dharmarājam*), 590 (*rājarshiḥ*), 594, 607, 712 (*rājarshiḥ*), 807; XI, 324, 763; XII, 11, 651 (*Kaunteyaḥ*), 720, 1143, 1172, 1192, 1429, 1458, 1463, 1492, 1515 (*jyeshṭham*), 1536, 1570, 1804, 1938, 1948, 1953, 1967, 1968, 1969, 1970, 1971, 1972, 1973, 1974, 2008, 2032, 2162, 2168, 2210, 2238, 2242, 2253, 2265, 2349, 2366, 2374, 2386, 2458, 2494, 2608, 2739, 2746, 3361, 4401, 5128, 12164; XIII, 421, 1334, 1355, 1356, 1775, 3634, 5195, 5550, 5879, 5921, 6922, 6934, 7627; XIV, †292 (*rājā*), 1898 (so B., C. has by error *Pāṇḍavāḥ*), 1901 (*rājā*), 1933, 2089 (*pṛthivīpatiḥ*); XV, 127, 129, 135, 136, 141, 209, 247, 343, 474, 616, 704 (*Dharmarājaḥ*), 736, 761, 1048, 1093; XVI, 8; XVII, 95, 100; XVIII, 58 (*Dharmaja rājarshe*), 64, 146.

Pāṇḍava, adj. ("belonging to the Pāṇḍavas"): VI, 2016 (*senā*), 3193 (*senām*), 3303 (*senā*), 3308 (*senām*), 3680 (do.), 4781 (*camūḥ*); VII, 486 (*senām*), 1120 (*camūm*), 1370 (*senā*), 2537 (*balam*), 3521 (*sainyam*), 4999 (*pṛtanā*), 6623 (*senā*), 6625 (do.), 6773 (do.), 7147 (*senām*), 7197 (*senā*), 7747 (*camūm*), 7753 (*senā*), 8329 (*sainyam*), 9422 (*senām*); VIII, 432 (do.), 489 (*camūm*), 1036 (*senām*), 1075 (*senā*), 2125 (*senām*), 2242 (do.), 2358 (do.), 2813 (*camūḥ*), 2859 (*camūm*), 3263 (*senā*), 3669 (*senām*), 3735 (do.), 3977 (*sainyam*), 3988 (*senām*), 3999 (do.), †4809 (do.); IX, 525 (*senā*), 1074 (*mahācamūḥ*); XIV, 1803 (*sainyam*), 2006 (*çriyam*); XV, 630.

Pāṇḍavaçārdūla = Sahadeva: II, 1123.

Pāṇḍavaçreshṭha[1] = Arjuna: I, 7815, 7881, 7987; II, 1039; III, 1616, 1655, 10532 (*Çvetavāhanam*); IV, 1427, 2326; V, 7308 (*A°*).

Pāṇḍavaçreshṭha[2] = Bhīmasena: II, 1076, 1093.

Pāṇḍavaçreshṭha[3] = Yudhishṭhira: I, 5921 (*Y°*), 6100; II, 147; III, 825, 4000, 8474, 10531; VII, 453, 1078 (*Y°*), 1081; VIII, 2991; XII, 695, 2493; XIII, 7083.

Pāṇḍavadāyāda = Abhimanyu: XV, 856.

Pāṇḍavāgraja = Yudhishṭhira: II, 1289, 2281; III, 8408; VI, 1622; XII, 1381; XIII, 1307; XVII, 7.

Pāṇḍavāgrya[1] = Arjuna: V, 688; VIII, 1388, 1649.

Pāṇḍavāgrya[2] = Yudhishṭhira: VIII, †3291.

Pāṇḍavamukhya[1] = Arjuna: VII, 4709, 4731, 6082.

Pāṇḍavamukhya[2] = Yudhishṭhira: V, †2716.

Pāṇḍavānām praveça(ḥ) ("the entrance of the Pāṇḍavas"). § 10 (Parvasaṅgr.): I, **2**, 327 (i.e. Pāṇḍavapraveçaparvan).

Pāṇḍavanandana[1] = Arjuna: II, 1004 (only C., *Kauravanandana* B.); VI, 5595; XII, 13156.

Pāṇḍavanandana[2] = Bhīmasena: III, 11092, 11335, 11789; VII, 5377.

Pāṇḍavanandana[3] = Janamejaya: XV, 951.

Pāṇḍavanandana[4] = Yudhishṭhira: III, 11456, 11950, 15380, 15491.

Pāṇḍavapraveçaparvan ("the section relating to the entrance of the Pāṇḍavas"). § 549: Questioned by *Janamejaya, Vaiçampāyana* related: Having obtained boons from *Dharma, Yudhishṭhira* returned to the hermitage and restored to the brahman his *araṇī* and *mantha.* Then he asked *Arjuna* to select some spot where they might dwell undiscovered. *Arjuna* mentioned some countries surrounding the kingdom of the *Kurus* (*a*). *Yudhishṭhira* chose the city of king *Virāṭa,* who was attached to the *Pāṇḍavas. Yudhishṭhira* would introduce himself as a brahman named *Kaṅka,* who was skilled in dice and had been the friend of *Yudhishṭhira* (IV, **1**). *Bhīmasena* as a cook and wrestler named *Vallava,* who had served *Yudhishṭhira*; *Arjuna* (*b–e*) as a hermaphrodite, *Bṛhannalā* by name, who had served *Kṛshṇā* as a waiting-maid (IV, **2**). *Nakula* as a keeper of horses, named *Granthika,* who had formerly been employed by *Yudhishṭhira*; *Sahadeva* as a cowherd, named *Tantripāla*; *Kṛshṇā* would serve *Sudeshṇā* (the queen of *Virāṭa*) as a *sairindhrī,* skilled in dressing hair, who had waited upon *Kṛshṇā* (IV, **3**). *Yudhishṭhira* said: "Let our priest, with our charioteers and cooks, repair to the abode of *Drupada* and there maintain our *agnihotra* fires, and *Indrasena,* etc., with the empty chariots proceed to *Dvāravatī,* and the maid-servants go to the *Pāñcālas,* together with the charioteers and the cooks. Let all of them say that the *Pāṇḍavas* had left them at the *Dvaitavana* lake." *Dhaumya* advised the *Pāṇḍavas* as to how they should behave at court and performed the rites ordained in respect of departure, and then set out for the *Pāñcālas,* taking with him their sacred fires; *Indrasena,* etc., proceeded to the *Yādavas* (IV, **4**). The *Pāṇḍavas* then proceeded in the direction of the southern bank of the river *Kālindī* and passed through the countries of the *Yakṛllomas* and the *Çūrasenas,* leaving behind on the right the country of the *Pāñcālas* and on the left that of the *Daçārṇas. Arjuna* carried *Kṛshṇā.* When they had reached the capital of *Virāṭa, Arjuna,* as *Gāṇḍīva* was known to all men, caused them to stow away their weapons in a *çamī*-tree near a cemetery. Nakula ascended the tree and tied the weapons fast. In the tree they hung up a corpse and said to the inquirers: "This is our mother, aged 180 years." They kept for themselves the names *Jaya, Jayanta, Vijaya, Jayatsena, Jayadbala* (IV, **5**). *Yudhishṭhira* praised *Durgā* (*f*), who then showed herself to him and promised him victory, etc. (IV, **6**). They then entered the city and were successively received by *Virāṭa. Yudhishṭhira* (naming himself *Kaṅka Vaiyāghrapadya*) was accepted as a courtier (IV, **7**). *Bhīmasena* (naming himself *Vallava*) was accepted as a cook and a wrestler (IV, **8**). *Kṛshṇā* was seen by the queen *Sudeshṇā Kaikeyī* and accepted as a *sairindhrī*; she said: "My five husbands, who are *Gandharvas* and sons of a *Gandharva* king, always protect me" (IV, **9**). *Sahadeva* came clad in a cowherd's dress and speaking the dialect of cowherds, and said that he was a *vaiçya* named *Arishṭanemi.* He was accepted as the king's head cowherd (IV, **10**). Then *Arjuna* appeared dressed as an eunuch and naming himself *Bṛhannalā,* and was accepted as a dancing master (IV, **11**). *Nakula,* who named himself *Granthika,* likewise was accepted as the king's head horsekeeper (IV, **12**).

Pāṇḍavarshabha[1] = Arjuna: I, 7786; II, 1029 (*Kirīṭī*); III, 15007; IV, 1206, 1214; VII, 4455; VIII, †4080; XIV, 2222, 2233, 2450.

Pāṇḍavarshabha[2] = Bhīmasena: II, 1082; VI, 4674; VII, 5437.

Pāṇḍavarshabha[3] = Yudhishṭhira: II, 424; III, 8473; IV, 2315; VII, 2975; XII, 1193; XIV, 370.

Pāṇḍavavīra = Arjuna: VIII, 4435 (*Kuru-Pāṇḍavavīrau,* i.e. Karṇa and *A.*).

Pāṇḍavayodha = Arjuna: VIII, 4436 (*Kuru-Pāṇḍavayodhau,* i.e. Karṇa and A.).

Pāṇḍaveya, pl. (°*āḥ*) = Pāṇḍava, pl. (also = the partisans of Yudhishṭhira): I, †152, †167, †181, †214, 429, 2234 (*Kuru-P°yoḥ*), 2450, 5727, 5817, †7153, †7333, 7386, 7426, 7430, 7446, 7498, 7985; II, 788 (dual = Arjuna and Bhīmasena), 1676 (?), 1821, 1885, †2120, 2516; III, †249, 3093, 11454, †12595, †12596; IV, 616; V, 58 (*pañca*), 608, †859, 2488 (°*hite*), 3263, 4462, 5368, 5389, 5535, 5735, 5878; VI, 12 (sg., i.e. one belonging to the party of the Pāṇḍavas), 823, 1868, 2190, 2433, 2509, 2533, 2890, 3173, †3517, 4062, 5090, 5091, 5200, 5547, 5555; VII, 15, 39, 492, 617, 1064, 1190, 1757, 2621, 2631, 4030, 5058, 5063, 6070, 6615, 6693, 6881, 7155, 7979, 8108, 8424, 8699, 9169, 9322; VIII, 47, 57, 151, †198 (*svasrīyān,* sc. Çalya's), 1353, †3627, 3716, 3969, 3972, 3985, †4299 (dual = Nakula and Bhīmasena), †4301 (dual = Bhīmasena and Arjuna), †4832, 4883; IX, 80, 366 (°*ānāṃ sainyam*), 402, 1260, 1497, 1499, †1565, 1822, 1860, 1877 (*pañcānām*), 1917, 1978, 1984; X, 67, 394 (*çibiraṃ P°ānāṃ*), 655 (dual = Arjuna and Yudhishṭhira), 703, 718 (*garbheshu P°ānām*), 720 (do.); XI, 587; XII, 4561; XIII, 7745; XIV, 372.

Pāṇḍaveya, sg.[1] = Abhimanyu: VII, 1904.

Pāṇḍaveya, sg.[2] = Arjuna: I, 7799, 7878 (*Dhanañjayaḥ*); II, 1006; III, 1572, 1698; V, 5759 (*Bhīmasenānujena*); VII, 3298, 6307, 7069 (?); VIII, 36 (protected Çikhaṇḍin), †1972, †3400, 4019, †4050, 4745, 4772; IX, 3255; XII, 13150.

Pāṇḍaveya, sg.[3] = Bhīmasena: VII, 5114 (*Bh°*); VIII, †3837, 3906, 3942.

Pāṇḍaveya, sg.[4] = Janamejaya: I, 1062, 1196 (*J°*), 1623 (do.), 2041 (do.), 2175 (*Pārīkshitasya*), 4528.

Pāṇḍaveya, sg.[5] = Nakula: XII, 6203.

Pāṇḍaveya, sg.[6] = Parikshit: I, 1784.

Pāṇḍaveya, sg.[7] = Yudhishṭhira: II, 1246, 1274; III, 10169, 10554, 10700, ††13143, 14629; IV, 2190 (*Y°*); V, 7559; VI, 2020 (?), 2106; VII, 42, 490; VIII, 2907; IX, 3505; X, 11, 12; XII, 705, †1813.

Pāṇḍaveya, adj. ("belonging to the Pāṇḍavas"): III, 15118 (*ratnani*); VIII, 1634 (*sainyāni*), 3008 (*mahābalam*); XIV, 373 (*rāshṭre*; instead of *Pāṇḍaveye tu* B. has *Pāṇḍavai rājan*).

Pāṇḍavīya, adj. (do.): V, 123 (*parikleçān*).

[Pāṇḍavotpatti(ḥ)] ("the birth of the Pāṇḍavas"). § 190: When *Gāndhārī* had been with child a full year *Kuntī* invoked *Dharma,* who came seated on his chariot. She brought forth *Yudhishṭhira* (*b*). Similarly the birth of *Bhīmasena* (*c*) and *Arjuna* (*d*) are related in full (cf. § 157) — § 191: Then *Kuntī* refused to have any more sons (I, **123**). —§ 192: Birth of *Nakula* and *Sahadeva* (cf. § 157); celestial voice. The *ṛshis* on *Çataçṛṅga* gave the sons of *Pāṇḍu* names. They were born at intervals of one year from one another. They became great favourites of the *ṛshis* and their wives, dwelling on *Çataçṛṅga* (cf. v. 4864: *Haimavate girau*). *Kuntī* refused to help *Mādrī* to get more children, as she had been deceived by her having two sons at once (I, **124**).

Paṇḍita[1], a son of Dhṛtarāshṭra. § 585: (Bhīshmavadhap.): VI, **88**, 3910, 3911 (slain by Bhīmasena). Cf. Paṇḍitaka.

Paṇḍita[2] = Çiva (1000 names[2]).

Paṇḍitaka, a son of Dhṛtarāshṭra = Paṇḍita. § 130 (Aṃçāvat.): I, **67**, 2736 (enumeration).—§ 585 (Bhīshmavadhap.): VI, **88**ι, 3901 (attacked Bhīmasena), 3906.

Pāṇḍodrarājau (II, †119), v. Pāṇḍyarāja.

Pāṇḍu, son of Vyāsa by Ambālikā, the widow of Vicitravīrya; husband of Kuntī and Mādrī and father of the five Pāṇḍavas. § 4 (Anukram.): I, **1**, 95 (son of Vyāsa), 110, 117, 118.—§ 11 (Parvasaṅgr.): I, **2**, 376.—§ 51 (Parikshit): I, **40**, 1665 (*yathā*, great-grandfather of Parikshit).—§ 56 (do.): I, **49**, 1955 (*yathā*).—§ 70 (Ādivaṃçāvatāraṇap.): I, **60**, 2213 (begotten by Vyāsa).—§ 83 (Ādivaṃçāvatāraṇa): I, **63**, 2441 (do.), 2443 (his five sons), 2449 (grandfather of Abhimanyu).—§ 130 (Aṃçāvat.): I, **67**, 2721 (younger brother of Dhṛtarāshṭra), 2751 (°*oḥ putraḥ*, sc. Arjuna).—§ 157 (Pūruvaṃç.): I, **95**, ††3808 (son of Vyāsa), ††3811 (husband of Kuntī and Mādrī), ††3812, ††3813, ††3815 (his five sons), ††3817 (his death).—§ 171 (Vicitravīryasutotpatti): I, **106**, 4291 (? his birth from Ambālikā, the widow of Vicitravīrya, by Vyāsa), 4301 (brother of Vidura).—§ 173 (Pāṇḍurājyābhisheka): I, **109**, 4353, 4357, 4361 (became king).—§ 176 (Kuntīvivāha): I, **112**, 4415 (*Bharatasattamam*), 4417, 4419, 4423, 4424 (*Kauravanandanaḥ*, married Kuntī).—§ 177 (Pāṇḍudigvijaya): I, **113**, 4425, 4430, 4442 (married Mādrī), 4445, 4449 (*Kauravāṇām yaçobhṛtā*), 4452, 4455, 4460, 4461, 4462 (his digvijaya).—§ 178 (cf. Sambhavap.): *P.* then at the command of *Dhṛtarāshṭra* offered his wealth to *Bhīshma*, *Satyavatī*, *Kausalyā*, *Vidura*, etc., and with the wealth acquired by him *Dhṛtarāshṭra* performed 100 horse sacrifices. With Kuntī and Mādrī he became a permanent inhabitant of the woods, addicted to hunting on the southern slope of the *Himālaya*, supplied with every object of pleasure and enjoyment at the command of *Dhṛtarāshṭra*: I, **114**, 4470, 4474, 4477.—§ 180 (Gāndhārīputrotpatti): I, **115**, 4484 (his five sons), 4487.—§ 183 (cf. Sambhavap.): The muni Kindama inflicted a curse on *P.*, cf. Agastya (*b*) (I, **118**): I, **118**, 4562 (*rājā*), 4563, (4569), (4574), 4591.—§ 184 (do.): *P.* declared that he would lead the life of a *brahmacārin* according to the *āraṇyaçāstras*, and send his attendants to *Hāstinapura* to inform *Bhīshma*, etc. (*Dhṛtarāshṭra* wept), and with his wives, protected by *mahābhūtas*, *Siddhas*, and *paramarshis*, he traversed the mountain of *Nāgaçata*, *Caitraratha*, *Kālakūṭa*, *Himavat*, *Gandhamādana*, *Indradyumnasaras*, and *Haṃsakūṭa*; then he practised ascetic austerities on *Çataçṛṅga* (I, **119**): I, **119**, 4593, 4615, (4621), 4629, 4630, 4634, 4636.—§ 185 (do.): *P.* became dear to the *Siddhas*, *Cāraṇas*, and *ṛshis*, and like to a *brahmarshi*. On the new-moon day when the *maharshis* assembled in order to partake of a great gathering of gods, *ṛshis*, and *pitṛs* in the abode of *Brahmán*, *P.* wanted to accompany them with his wives from *Çataçṛṅga* to the north, but they told him that the princesses could not ascend the king of mountains (*çailarāja*), where they had seen the retreats of gods, *Gandharvas*, and *Apsarases*, and the gardens of *Kubera*, where only *Vāyu* and the *Siddhas* and the *paramarshis* could go. As he complained of being childless, they told him to let somebody else raise offspring for him. *P.'s* conversation with *Kuntī*. *P.* quoted the words of *Manu Svāyambhuva* (*b*) and the example of *Çāradaṇḍāyanī* (*c*) (I, **120**): I, **120**, 4643, 4645, 4647, (4654), 4665.—§ 186 (do.): *Kuntī* in reply alleged the Paurāṇic narrative of *Vyushitāçva* (q.v.) and entreated *Pāṇḍu* to beget children by his ascetic power (I, **121**): I, **121**, 4680.—§ 187 (do.): *P.* said that women formerly were not bound to adhere faithfully to their husband, and were not regarded sinful when yielding to their desire; that practice was applauded by the *maharshis*, and even now prevailed among birds and beasts and among the *Uttara-Kurus*. It was the muni *Çvetaketu* (*b*) who established the now existing practice (§ 188). *P.* further alleged the example of *Madayantī* (*b*) and of *Vyāsa*: I, **122** (4717).—§ 189 (do.): *Kuntī* related to *Pāṇḍu* how she had obtained the mantra from *Durvāsas* (cf. § 131); *P.* told her to invoke *Dharma* (I, **122**): I, **122**, 4746, (4754).—§ 190 (Pāṇḍavotpatti): I, **123**, 4767 (*Yudhishṭhiraḥ* . . . *P°oḥ prathamajaḥ sutaḥ*), 4768, 4776, 4777, 4782 (*Kuntī* gave birth by *Dharma* to *Yudhishṭhira*, by *Vāyu* to *Bhīmasena*, by *Indra* to *Arjuna*).—§ 191 (do.): I, **123**, 4833.—§ 192 (do.): I, **124**, 4836, (4842), 4844, 4857, 4859 (by the *Açvins Mādrī* gave birth to *Nakula* and *Sahadeva*), 4862 (°*oḥ sutāḥ pañca*).—§ 193 (cf. Sambhavap.): *P.* died in accordance with the curse inflicted on him by *Kindama* (cf. § 183). *Kuntī* wished to be burnt together with him, but this *Mādrī* did not allow, and herself ascended the funeral pyre (I, **125**): I, **125**, 4866, 4869, 4877 (*Kurunandanaḥ*), 4882.—§ 194 (do.): The ascetics took *Kuntī*, the children, and the two corpses to *Hāstinapura*. Hearing of the arrival of thousands of *Cāraṇas* (*Guhyakas*, v. 4930; *Siddhas*, v. 4931) and munis, people soon after sunrise began to come out from the city to see, together with *Bhīshma*, *Somadatta*, *Bāhlika*, the blind *rājarshi* (i.e. *Dhṛtarāshṭra*), the kshattṛ *Vidura*, *Satyavatī*, *Kausalyā*, *Gāndhārī*, accompanied by the other ladies of the royal household (*rājadāraiḥ*), and the sons of *Dhṛtarāshṭra*. It was seventeen days after the death of *P.* (v. 4925). The *ṛshis*, etc., suddenly disappeared like a fata morgana (*Gandharvanagara*) (I, **126**): I, **126**, 4899, 4901 (°*oḥ putrān*), 4903 (°*or darāṃç ca putrāṃç ca*), 4918 (*Kauravyadāyādaḥ*), 4923, 4925, 4929 (*Kurukulodvahaḥ*).—§ 195 (do.): *Dhṛtarāshṭra* caused *Vidura* (in consultation with *Bhīshma*) to celebrate the funeral ceremonies (*pretakāryāṇi*) of *P.* and *Mādrī* on the bank of the *Gaṅgā* (I, **127**); I, **127**, 4932, 4933, 4935, 4936, 4937, 4942, 4948.—§ 196 (Vyāsa): I, **128**, 4964.—§ 211 (Sambhavap.): I, **139**, 5535.—§ 213 (Jatugṛhap.): I, **141**, 5668; **142**, 5677, 5679, 5681, 5682; **145**, 5744 (*Kurunandanaḥ*); **150**, 5866; **151**, 5906 (*bhāryām P°oḥ*, i.e. Kuntī).—§ 221 (Caitrarathap.): I, **170**, 6500.—§ 235 (Svayaṃvarap.): I, **191**, †7147 (°*os tanayāḥ*).—§ 237 (Vaivāhikap.): I, **193**, †7191 (°*r hi rājā Drupadasya rājñaḥ priyaḥ sakhā*).—§ 241 (Vidurāgamanap.): I, **200**, 7387 (°*ḥ putrāḥ*); **203**, 7441.—§ 243 (do.): I, **206**, 7519 (sc. *putrāḥ*).—§ 244 (Rājyalābhap.): I, **207**, 7562 (*iva*).—§ 267 (Yamasabhāv.): II, **8**, 336 (in the palace of Yama).—§ 271 (Lokapālasabhākhyānap.): II, **12**, 486, 501, 506 (wished that Yudhishṭhira should perform the rājasūya, that he might himself ascend to the world of Indra).—§ 289 (Arghāharaṇap.): II, **37**, 1350 (*Bhīshmake* . . . *P°vat kṛtalakshaṇe*, otherwise PCR.).—§ 297 (Dyūtap.): II, **54**, 1943 (°*oḥ sutān*).—§ 305 (Anudyūtap.): II, **79**, 2600 (*mṛte*, all. to § 193), 2610.—§ 311 (Āraṇyakap.): III, **4**, †222 (°*oḥ sutān*), †232 (°*oḥ putram*, sc. Yudhishṭhira).—§ 313 (do.): III, **6**, 285 (°*oḥ sutāḥ*).—§ 314 (do.): III, **9**, 342 (*yādṛçaḥ*), 343 (sc. *putrāḥ*).—§ 317 (Arjunābhigamanap.): III, **12**, 580 (*snushā P°oḥ*, i.e. Draupadī).—§ 325 (Draupadīparitāpav.): III, **27**, 1022 (*snushām P°oḥ*, i.e. Draupadī).—

§ 436 (Yakshayuddhap.): III, **159,** 11631 (°*oḥ putrān*).—§ 437 (do.): III, **160,** 11661 (°*oḥ putrāḥ*).—§ 438 (do.): III, **161,** 11770 (°*oḥ putrān*).—§ 449 (Ājagarap.): III, **177,** †12348 (°*oḥ sutāḥ*).—§ 525 (Rāmopākhyānap.): III, **273,** 15863 (*snushā P°oḥ*, i.e. Draupadī).—§ 554 (Sainyodyogap.): V, **1,** †11 (°*oḥ sutaiḥ*).—§ 556 (Sañjayayānap.): V, **20,** 606; **24,** †720 (°*oḥ sutāḥ*).—§ 557 (Prajāgarap.): V, **33,** †1092 (*rājñaḥ P°oḥ putrāḥ pañca*).—§ 559 (do.): V, **36,** †1331 (°*oḥ sutāḥ*).—§ 562 (Bhagavadyānap.): V, **82,** 2892 (*snushā P°oḥ*, i.e. Draupadī).—§ 567 (do.): V, **132,** 4481.—§ 569 (do.): V, **137,** 4655 (*snushāṃ P°oḥ*, i.e. Draupadī); **140,** 4734 (°*oḥ putro 'si dharmataḥ*, sc. Karṇa); **141,** 4756 (°*oḥ putro 'smi dharmataḥ*, says Karṇa), 4758 (do.); **147,** 4997; **148,** 5008, 5009, †5036 (*rājyam P°oḥ*); **149,** 5068, 5069.—§ 570 (Sainyaniryāṇap.): V, **156,** 5298 (°*oḥ putrāḥ*); **158,** 5376 (°*oḥ putraḥ*, sc. Arjuna).—§ 586 (Bhīshmavadhap.): VI, **104,** 4764 (°*pūrvajaṃ*, sc. *Bhīshmaṃ* C.; °*pūrvajāḥ*, sc. *Pāṇḍavāḥ* B.; but read °*pūrvaja*, i.e. *Dhṛtarāshṭra* with PCR.); **107,** 4941 (°*pūrvajaṃ*, sc. *Bhīshmaṃ*, B. and C.; read °*pūrvaja*), 4954 (°*pūrvajaḥ*, sc. *Bhīshmaḥ*, B. and C.; read °*pūrvaja*), 4979.—§ 587 (do.): VI, **108,** 5020 (read with B. °*pūrvaja*, C. °*pūrvajaṃ*); **109,** 5065 (do., do.); **116,** 5432 (°*pūrvaja* = Dhṛtarāshṭra).—§ 593 (Abhimanyuvadhap.): VII, **39,** 1670 (°*oḥ kshetrodbhavāḥ sutāḥ*).—§ 596 (Pratijñāp.): VII, **74,** 2616 (°*oḥ khila kshetre jātaḥ Çakreṇa*, sc. Arjuna).—§ 599 (Jayadrathavadhap.): VII, **102,** 3840.—§ 608 (Karṇap.): VIII, **61,** 3100 (°*pūrvaja*, i.e. Dhṛtarāshṭra).—§ 611 (Çalyap.): IX, **13,** 694 (do.).—§ 613 (Gadāyuddhap.): IX, **33**ε, 1903 (°*oḥ Kuntyāç ca santatiḥ*).—§ 641 (Rājadh.): XII, **75,** 2853.—§ 777 (Svargārohaṇik. p.): XIII, **168,** 7738 (*yathā P°oḥ sutāḥ*).—§ 785 (Anugītāp.): XIV, **66,** 1955 (°*oç ca piṇḍaḥ*).—§ 787 (Āçramavāsap.): XV, **4,** 160; **9**λ, 284; **10,** 321; **17**χ, 476 (°*oḥ . . . santatiḥ*), 488 (°*oḥ putrāḥ*); **20,** 554 (*Balahantur samīpataḥ*), 567 (in the abode of Indra).—§ 789 (Putradarçanap.): XV, **31**η, 851 (*Marudgaṇād dhi viçishṭatamaṃ*).—§ 795 (Svargārohaṇap.): XVIII, **4,** 144; **5,** 161 (*Mahendrasadanaṃ yayau*). Cf. Bhārata, Bharatarshabha, Bharatasattama, Kaurava, Kauravanandana, Kauravarshabha, Kauravya, Kauravyadāyāda, Kausalyānandavardhana, Kurūdvaha, Kurukulodvaha, Kurunandana, Kurupati, Kurupravīra, Nāgapurādhipa, Nāgapurasiṃha.

Pāṇḍu[2], son of the elder Janamejaya. § 154 (Pūruvaṃç.): I, **94,** 3745 (second son of Janamejaya).

Pāṇḍu, pl. = Pāṇḍava, pl. (also = the party of Yudhishṭhira). I, 444, 458, 462, 5541, 5728, 7359, 7556, 7782 (°*ūnāṃ pravaraḥ*, i.e. Arjuna), 8017 (°*sāgaraṃ*); II, †2349; III, 244, 11021, 15071, 15186, 15792, 16023; IV, 213, 263 (*Kṛshṇāṃ ca bhāryāṃ P°ūnāṃ*); V, 52, 92 (*Kuru-P°shu*), 97 (*Kuru-P°ūnāṃ*), 582, 2271, 2366 (*Kuru-P°samāgame*), 2896, 5925, 7583; VI, 2028 (°*sainyeshu*), 2066, 2324, 2716 (°*sainyena*), 2918, 2935, 3639, 3669 (°*ūnāṃ . . . sainyeshu*), 3884, 3969, 4256, 4292, 4365 (°*sainyaṃ*), 4696 (°*senāḥ*), †4885 (°*senāṃ*), 5002 (°*sainyasya*), 5468 (°*senāṃ*), 5521 (°*senā*), 5600, 5817, VII, 413, 434 (°-*Sṛñjayaiḥ*), 489 (°-*Sṛñjayāḥ*), 494 (°*vāhinīṃ*), 669 (°-*Sṛñjayāḥ*), 883, 1066, 1160 (°-*Pāñcālān*), 1175, 1359, 1412, 1414, 1692, 1763, 1779, 1782, 2556 (°-*Pāñcālān*), 2612, 2613, 3078, 3513 (°-*Sṛñjayaiḥ*), 3939, 3959 (°*ūnāṃ ṛshabhasya*, i.e. Arjuna), 4010, 4011 (°*sainyasya*), 4163, 4435 (°*sainye*), 4482, 4497, 4498 (°*sainyam*), 4682 (°-*Pāñcāla*-), 4683 (°-*Pāñcālān*), 4892 (°-*Pāñcāla-Matsyānāṃ*), 4933 (°-*Pāñcālān*), 5018, 5098, 5307 (°*senā*), 5335 (°-*Sṛñjayaiḥ*), 6519, 6521, 6605 (°*senāṃ*), 6622 (°*sainikāḥ*), 6625 (°*senāṃ*), 6641, 6679 (°-*Sṛñjayāḥ*), 6770 (°*sainyāni*), 7352 (°-*Pāñcālasainyānāṃ*), 7480 (only B.), 7738, 8267 (°-*Pāñcālān*), 8268, 8269, 8271, 8308 (°-*Sṛñjayāḥ*), 8391, 8392, †8460 (*Kuru-P°yodhāḥ*), 8919, 8939, 9159, 9204 (°-*Pāñcālāḥ*), 9209, 9214 (°-*Pāñcāla-Sṛñjayāḥ*), 9217, 9245 (*Kuru-P°shu*), 9254 (°*sainyam*), 9266, 9388 (°*vāhinīṃ*); VIII, 307, 687, 839, 844 (°-*Sṛñjaya-Pāñcālān*), 846 (*Kuru-Pāñcāla-P°shu*), 868 (°-*Pāñcālāḥ*), 884 (°-*Pāñcāla-Somakāḥ*), 889 (°*yodhān*), 890 (°*rathakuñjarāḥ*), 1236, 1281, 2285, 2307 (°-*Pāñcālāḥ*), 2309 (°-*Pāñcāla-Kaikayaiḥ*), 2312, 2332, 2682, 3010 (°-*Sṛñjayān*), 3012, 3013, 3067 (°-*Sṛñjayaiḥ*), 3090 (°*sainyāni*), 3258, 3891 (°*sainyaṃ*), 3951 (°-*Pāñcālāḥ*), 4018 (°*sainyāni*), †4313 (°-*Sṛñjayaiḥ*), †4325 (do.), †4492 (*Kuru-P°yodhāḥ*), †4592 (°-*Pāñcālagaṇān*), 5031 (°-*Pāñcāla-Sṛñjayāḥ*); IX, 339, 538 (°*camūṃ*), 619 (°*senāṃ*), 870 (°-*Pāñcāla-Somakāḥ*), 958, 965, 976 (°*vāhinīṃ*), 1032, 1097 (°*senāṃ*), 1125, 1211, 1239, 1581 (°-*Sṛñjayaiḥ*), 1687 (°-*Kauravasaṃmardāt*), 1713, 1788 (*Pāñcāla-P°ūnāṃ*), 3209, 3408, 3583; X, 56, 139 (*Pāñcāla-P°ūnāṃ*), 158, 159, 398 (°-*Sṛñjayān*); XI, 299 (°*ūnāṃ kadanaṃ*), 353, 628; XII, †1895 (*Yaduvṛsha-P°avaḥ*); XIV, 1974 (*garbhān . . . P°ūnāṃ*).

Pāṇḍudāyāda, pl. = Pāṇḍava, pl.: I, 5833, 5859; II, 2644.

Pāṇḍudāyāda, sg. = Bhīmasena: VII, 5209.

[Pāṇḍu-digvijaya(ḥ)] ("subjection of the earth by Pāṇḍu"). § 177 (Sambhavap.): After some time *Bhīshma* went to the capital of the *Madra* king *Çalya* ("the bull of the *Bāhlīkas*"), and, according to the custom observed in that family and ordained by *Svayambhū* himself, he obtained his sister *Mādrī* for *Pāṇḍu* by giving great riches, and took her to *Hāstinapura*, where the nuptials were celebrated on an auspicious day and *muhūrta*. After thirty days *Pāṇḍu* started on his conquest of the world, and conquered the *Daçārṇas* (*āgaskṛtaḥ*), slew the *Magadha* king *Dīrgha* (who had offended against numerous kings) in *Rājagṛha*; then going into *Mithilā* he defeated the *Videhas*; then the *Kāçis*, *Suhmas*, and *Puṇḍras*, etc., and after having made all kings the vassals of the *Kurus*, he returned laden with much wealth to *Hāstinapura*, where people said: "They who before robbed the *Kurus* of both territory and wealth, have been made to pay tribute" by *Pāṇḍu* (I, **113**).

Pāṇḍukumāra, pl. (°*āḥ*) ("the sons of Pāṇḍu") = Pāṇḍava, pl.: VI, 2898.

Pāṇḍunandana[1], pl. (°*āḥ*) (do.) = Pāṇḍava, pl.: I, 5713, 5829, 5856, 5877, 6439, 6495, 6949, 7141, 7309, 7530, 7602; II, 2044; III, 10912, 12558, 15210, 15518; IV, 133; V, 5159; VI, 525, 3001 (dual = Nakula and Sahadeva); VII, 1759 (*caturaḥ*), 5466, 7150, 7675, 9124; IX, 621, 1014; XII, 1, 2; XIV, 1892; XV, 38 (*pañca bhrātaraḥ*), 596.

Pāṇḍunandana[2] ("(grand)son of Pāṇḍu") = Abhimanyu: VII, 1863.

Pāṇḍunandana[3] ("son of Pāṇḍu") = Arjuna: I, 5235, 5262 (*Phālgunaḥ*), 5409, 7779, 8201; II, 1031 (*Phālgunaḥ*); III, 1512, 1541; IV, 1225, 1232, 1421, 1436, 1779; V, 134 (*Dhanañjayaḥ*); VI, 2564; VII, 3688, 6228, 7105, 7764, 9603; VIII, 2405, 2588, 2791, 3004, 3604, †4951 (*Keçava-P°au*), 5025 (*Gāṇḍīvadhanvā*); IX, 521 (*Kapidhvajaḥ*), 1481; XII, 13151, 13189, 13225 (C. has by error °*aḥ*, read °*a* with B.), 13282; XIV, 2492, 2577; XVI, 201.

Pāṇḍunandana[4] (do.) = Bhīmasena: I, 5016, 5033, 6038; III, 448, 11107, 11350; IV, 513 (*madhyamaṃ*), 775; VII, 5202, 5212, 5245, 5295, 5302, 5649, 5778, 5781, 6712, 9272; VIII, 4154; IX, 569, 574, 1913.

Pāṇḍunandana[5] (do.) = Nakula: II, 1189; III, 4012 (*N*°); VII, 7570 (do.), 7573 (do.); IX, 494, 501.
Pāṇḍunandana[6] (do.) = Sahadeva: II, 1119; VIII, 913.
Pāṇḍunandana[7] (do.) = Yudhishṭhira: III, 611, 638, 691, 1910, 8415, 8654, 8687, 15861; V, 2113, 7629; VII, 2563 (*jyeshṭhāt*), 2929, 6955; VIII, 2351, 3580; XII, 1372, 1392; XIII, 386, 976, 1029, 1298, 2400, 3041; XIV, 106, 2111 (*Dharmarājaḥ*); XV, 43, 178, 245.
Pāṇḍunṛpātmaja ("the Pāṇḍu king's son" = Yudhishṭhira): XIII, 1303.
Pāṇḍupūrvaja, v. Pāṇḍu[1].
Pāṇḍuputra, pl. (°*āḥ*) ("the sons of Pāṇḍu") = Pāṇḍava, pl.: I, 139, †154, 421, 431, 4856, 4990 (*madhyamaḥ P°āṇām*, i.e. Bhīmasena), 5312, 5632, 5694, 5715, 5769, 5865, 5870, 5886, 5930, †7026, 7074 (dual = Arjuna and Bhīmasena), †7165, 7441, 7520, 7532, 7539, 7542, 7552; II, 16, 133, 1688, 1942, 1969, †2193, 2417, 2418, 2419, 2659; III, †225, †233, †249, 289, 398, 404, 524, 581 (*pañcānām*), 1956, 1957, 2018, †14742, 14785, 14962, 14983, 15191, 15353, 15616 (*pañcānām P°āṇām mahishīm*), 15634, †15649, †15714, 16944, 16948; IV, 288 (°*āṇām pañcānām jyeshṭho bhrātā Yudhishṭhiraḥ*), 317 (do.), 614 (*mahishī P°āṇām*, i.e. Draupadī), 909, 1117, 1168, 1306; V, 104, 607, †645, 862, †1333, 2140, 2255, 2297, 2298, 2310, †2420, 2483 (*pañcānām*), 2759, 2892, 2894, 2895, 3125, 4267 (*mahishī P°āṇām*, i.e. Draupadī), 4352, 4355, 5016, 5187, 5369, 5713, 5857; VI, 310, 575, 641, 832, 1628, 1633, 1636, 2095, 2545, 2548, 2891, 2902, 3069, 4721, 4830, 4917; VII, 73, 630, 1667, 3565 (dual = Nakula and Sahadeva), 5657, 6528, 6601, 7069, 7128, 7142, 7150, 7164, 7373, 8452, 8690, 8941, 9031, 9188; VIII, 65, 66, 230, 369, 1826, 2705 (dual = Nakula and Sahadeva), †3629, 3775; IX, 230, 525, 545, 682, 1673, 1676, 1821, 1970, 3553; XI, 232, 310, 312, 358, 435, 637; XII, 499; XIV, 322, 1781, 1792, 1982, 2049 (°*priyepsayā*); XV, 50, 81, 333 (*caturbhiḥ*), 767, 777.
Pāṇḍuputra[2] ("the son of Pāṇḍu") = Arjuna: III, 1832 (*Phālgunasya*), 1877 (*Dhanañjayaḥ*); IV, 1638 (do.), 1810, 2041; V, 2355; VII, 112, 732, 1344, 2837, 3171, 6002, 6226, 8439; VIII, 125 (*Savyasācinā*), 1117, †1736, 2611, †4371, 4773; IX, 734, 3420, 3469 (*Dhanañjayaḥ*); XIV, 2138, 2176, 2379 (*Dhanañjayaḥ*); XVI, 210 (*Dhanañjayam*).
Pāṇḍuputra[3] (do.) = Bhīmasena: V, 2057 (had slain Jarāsandha); VI, 1554 (*Vṛkodare*); VII, 5482, 6709; IX, 1401 (?), 1702, 1703, 3596 (*Vṛkodaraḥ*).
Pāṇḍuputra[4] (do.) = Nakula: VIII, 922, 928, 945.
Pāṇḍuputra[5] (do.) = Sahadeva: VIII, 895; IX, †1562.
Pāṇḍuputra[6] (do.) = Yudhishṭhira: I, 530 (*Dharmarājasya*), 5517 (*Y*°), 5712, 6242 (*Y*°), 7553 (do.); II, 1277 (°*sya rājasūyam*), 1747 (*yajñe P°sya*), 1759 (do.), 1761 (°*sya çriyam*), 1767, 1966 (*Y*°), 2272; III, 8410, †10215, 15026, 16919 (*Y*°); V, 633 (do.), †946 (do.), †949, †1561, 2244 (*jyeshṭhasya*), 5782, 5933, 7573; VI, 2546, 2574, 4831, 4833, 4854, 5191; VII, 238, 4084, 6766; VIII, 891, 1691, 2350 (*Y*°), 3207 (do.); IX, 461 (do.), 649; XII, 833 (*jyeshṭhasya*), 1836 (do.), 1936 (*Y*°), †2364; XIV, 1929; XVIII, 79.
Pāṇḍura, a warrior of Skanda. § 615*u* (Skanda): IX, **45**η, 2575.
[Pāṇḍurājyābhisheka] ("anointing of Pāṇḍu as a king"). § 173 (Sambhavap.): Upon the birth of those three children (§ 171), *Kurujāñgala*, *Kurukshetra*, and the *Kurus* grew in prosperity, etc. The southern *Kurus*, in virtuous rivalry with the northern *Kurus*, walked about in the company of gods, *ṛshis*, and *Cāraṇas*. Virtuously ruled by *Bhīshma*, the kingdom was adorned with hundreds of *caityas* and *yūpas*. *Dhṛtarāshṭra*, *Pāṇḍu*, and *Vidura* were brought up by *Bhīshma* as if they were his own children, and became well exercised in archery, etc., and well read in the *Itihāsas* and *Purāṇas* and various sciences, and the *Vedas* and *Vedāngas*. *Pāṇḍu* excelled all men in archery, *Dhṛtarāshṭra* in personal strength, *Vidura* in devotion to virtue. *Hāstinapura* was the foremost among cities. Because of *Dhṛtarāshṭra's* blindness and *Vidura's* being a *pārasava* (son of a *brahman* with a *çūdra* woman), *Pāṇḍu* became king. One day *Bhīshma* addressed *Vidura* [about the marriage of the two princes] (I, **109**).
Pāṇḍurāshṭra, pl. (°*āḥ*) (VI, 351, B.), v. Pāṃçurāshṭra, pl.
Pāṇḍusaupāka, name of a caste. XIII, 2588 (*tvaksāravyavahāravān*).
Pāṇḍusūnu[1] ("the son of Pāṇḍu") = Arjuna: VII, †6145.
Pāṇḍusūnu[2] (do.) = Yudhishṭhira: VI, 3698.
Pāṇḍusuta[1], pl. (°*āḥ*) ("the sons of Pāṇḍu") = Pāṇḍava, pl.: I, 142, 437, 5543, 5657, 5739, 6349 (*pañca*), †7083, †7187, 7492; III, 8413, 8516, †10232, †10234, †12652, 14786, 14804; IV, 337; V, †17, 197, 1378, 1396, 1531, 3706; VI, 515, 2180, 2498, 2505, 2576, 2904, 3008, 3075, 3640, 3644, †3765, 4405, 4441, 4442, 4727, 5288 (dual = Arjuna and Bhīmasena), 5330, 5522; VII, 189, 4541, 5462, 5539, 6984, 6998, 7001, 7020, 7739; VIII, 276, 1127, 1270, 1272, 1319, 2128; IX, 335, †907, †1069, 1453, 1629, 3474; X, 135, 703; XI, 370; XII, 1468; XIV, 1547 (*pañca*), 1889; XVII, 36.
Pāṇḍusuta[2] ("the son of Pāṇḍu") = Arjuna: V, 629 (*Dhanañjayam*); VI, 2155, 2395, 4454, 4664, 5070 (*Çvetāçvaḥ Kṛshṇasārathiḥ*), 5451 (*Çvetāçvam Kṛshṇasārathim*); VII, †672; VIII, 274, 2605.
Pāṇḍusuta[3] (do.) = Bhīmasena: III, 11119; VII, 5546.
Pāṇḍusuta[4] (do.) = Nakula: VIII, †4292.
Pāṇḍusuta[5] (do.) = Sahadeva: VIII, 908.
Pāṇḍusuta[6] (do.) = Yudhishṭhira: I, 5658 (*jyeshṭham*); III, †10218, 15060 (*jyeshṭhaḥ*); V, 63 (*Y*°); VI, †3781 (*Y*°), 4792 (*jyeshṭhaḥ*), 5109 (*jyeshṭham*); VII, 7014, †7309; VIII, 2314; XII, 1088 (*rājā*); XIII, 1313 (*nṛpam*), 7707 (*nṛpaḥ*); XV, 166 (*rājā*).
Pāṇḍutanaya[1], pl. (°*āḥ*) ("the sons of Pāṇḍu") = Pāṇḍava, pl.: III, 11564; VII, 6975.
Pāṇḍutanaya[2] ("the son of Pāṇḍu") = Arjuna: VII, 5990 (*Phālgunaḥ*).
Pāṇḍuvīra = Yudhishṭhira: IX, †898 (*Madrapa-P°yoḥ*).
Pāṇḍya[1], pl. (°*āḥ*), a people and their country. § 273 (Rājasūyārambhap.): II, **14**, 585 (*sa-P°-Kratha-Kaiçikān*, vanquished by Bhīshmaka).—§ 284 (Sahadeva): II, **31**, 1174 (vanquished by Sahadeva on his digvijaya).—§ 377 (Dhaumyatīrthak.): III, **88**, 8339 (*Agastyatīrtham P°eshu*; *Kumāryaḥ kathitāḥ . . . P°eshu*).—§ 578 (Bhīshmavadhap.): VI, **50**π, 2084 (in the army of Yudhishṭhira).—§ 589 (Droṇābhishekap.): VII, **11**ν, 398 (had been vanquished by Kṛshṇa).—§ 592 (Saṃçaptakavadhap.): VII, **23**ο, 1016 (*bhinne kapāṭe P°ānām*, then Kṛshṇa had slain their king, the father of Sāraṅgadhvaja (B. *Sāgaradhvaja*), cf. V, 1883).—§ 605 (Karṇap.): VIII, **12**ββ, 455.
Pāṇḍya[2] ("the king of the Pāṇḍyas"), two or more kings. § 11 (Parvasaṅgr.): I, **2**, 544 (*vadhaḥ P°sya*, cf. § 608).—§ 233 (Svayaṃvarap.): I, **187**, †7020 (*Kaliṅga-Vāṅgādhipa-P°-Pauṇḍrāḥ*, present at the svayaṃvara of Draupadī).—§ 290 (Çiçupālavadhap.): II, **44***a*, 1539.—§ 295 (Dyūtap.): II, **52**, 1893 (*Cola-P°au*, brought tribute to Yudhishṭhira).—

§ 555 (Sainyodyogap.): V, **19**γ, 578 (came with troops to Yudhishṭhira).—§ 556 (Sañjayayānap.): V, **22**, †667 (*rājā*, among the allies of Yudhishṭhira).—§ 561*c* (Kṛshṇa Vāsudeva): V, **48**, †1883 (Kṛshṇa slew *P.* (*kapāṭena*, cf. VII, 1016)).—§ 592 (Saṃçaptakavadhap.): VII, **23**, 1019 (*Sāraṅgadhvajaḥ* (B. *Sāgaradhvajaḥ*), proceeded against Droṇa; his father had been slain by Kṛshṇa, cf. V, 1883), 1021 (°*ānuyāyinām* . . . *rathamukhyānām*); **25**, 1120 (fought with Vṛshasena).—§ 605 (Karṇap.): VIII, **19**, 766, 769; **20**, 775, 776, 777, 781, [789 (*Malayadhvajaḥ*)], 790, 792, 793, 796, 802 (*b: P.*'s standard, smeared with sandal-paste, etc., had for its device the Malaya mountain (*Malayapratimam*)), 808, [809 (*Malayadhvajaḥ*)], †819 (slain by Açvatthāman); **21**, 821 (*hate*), 824 (do.).—§ 608 (do.): VIII, **46**, 2157 (shall proceed against Açvatthāman, only in C., B. has *Dhṛshṭadyumnaḥ*); **49**χ, 2333 (attacked Karṇa).—§ 609 (Çalyap.): IX, **2**ζ, 91 (among the slain). Cf. Pāṇḍyarāja, Pāṇḍyarāshṭrādhipa.

Pāṇḍya[3], the country of the Pāṇḍyas. § 370 (Tīrthayātrāp.): III, **85**, 8163 (only B., there the mountain Ṛshabha is situated).

Pāṇḍya[4], adj. ("belonging to the Pāṇḍyas"). § 515 (Karṇadigvijaya): III, **254**, 15250 (°*m çailam*, i.e. Çrī, Nīl.).

Pāṇḍyarāja ("the king of the Pāṇḍyas") = Pāṇḍya[2]. § 264 (Sabhākriyāp.): II, **4**β, †119 (°*oḍra-rājau*, C. by error *Pāṇḍo°*).—§ 281 (Sahadeva): II, **31**, 1121 (vanquished by Sahadeva).—§ 572 (Rathātirathasaṅkhyānap.): V, **171**, 5918 (among the rathas in the army of Yudhishṭhira).—§ 605 (Karṇap.): VIII, **20**, 815 (°*ānucarān*).

Pāṇḍyarāshṭrādhipa (do.) = Pāṇḍya[2]. § 130 (Aṃçāvat.): I, **67**, 2678 (incarnation of an Asura who was the younger brother of Vikshara).

Pāṇika, a companion of Skanda. § 615*u* (Skanda): IX, **45**, 2545 (given to Skanda by Pūshan).

Pāṇikarna = Çiva (1000 names[1]).

Pāṇikhāta, name of a tīrtha. § 364 (Tīrthayātrāp.): III, **83**, 6059.

Pāṇikūrcan, a warrior of Skanda. § 615*u* (Skanda): IX, **45**η, 2578.

Pāṇimat (II, 362, B.), v. Aṇimat.

Pāṇītaka, a companion of Skanda. § 615*u* (Skanda): IX, **45**, 2545 (given to Skanda by Pūshan).

Paṅkadigdhāṅga, a warrior of Skanda. § 615*u* (Skanda): IX, **45**η, 2570.

Paṅkajit, a Suparṇa, son of Garuḍa. § 564 (Mātalīyop.): V, **101**β, 3595 (enumeration).

Pannaga[1], pl. (°*āḥ*) ("serpents," generally synonymous with Nāga, pl.): I, 799, 1015, 1004, 1092 (°*bhojanaḥ*, sc. Garuḍa), 1283, 1284, 1313, 1537, 1548, 1510, 1504, 1618, 1625 (°*sattamāḥ*), 1626 (do.), 1627 (°*çreshṭhāḥ*), 1630, 1632, 1651, 1652, 1661, 1864, 1914, 1932, 1998 (°*antakarīṃ matiṃ*), 2038, 2042, 2071, 2079, 2144, 2173, 2184, 2189, 2492, 2513, 2514, 2634 (sons of Kadrū, different from the Nāgas), 2637, 7577 (*iva*), 8256, 8304; II, 946 (*Garutmān °āçanaḥ*); III, 170, 1566, 1646, 1674, 2409, 5076, 8168, 11236, 12205, 12206, 12243, 12272, 12400, 12522, 14589 (*iva*), 16579; IV, 40 (all. to Khāṇḍavadahanaparvan), 1522 (*iva*), 1914 (do.); V, 3586 (*Suparṇānāṃ* . . . °*āçināṃ*), 3855 (°*āçana*, sc. Garuḍa), 3865 (do.), 4025 (*Suparṇaṃ °āçanaṃ*, i.e. Garuḍa), 4175, 4326, †7212; VI, 2961, 3478 (*iva*), 3495 (do.), 3592 (do.), 4045, 4279 (*iva*), 5494 (do.); VII, 1340 (do.), 1565 (do.), 2731, 4086, 4119, 4139 (*iva*), 5590 (*iva*), 5603 (dual), 5672 (*iva*), 5685 (do.), 5702 (do.), 6803 (do.), 7384 (do.), 7742 (dual, *iva*), 7933 (*iva*), 8401 (°*bhogābhaiṛ hastaiḥ*), 9210 (*iva*), 9251 (do.), 9354 (do.); VIII, 740 (*iva*), 1082 (*iva*), 2545 (do.), 2716 (do.), 2758 (do.), 2868 (do.), 2962 (do.), 4170 (do.); IX, 792 (*iva*), 922 (do.), 2149, 2151, 2496, 2509, 2703; XI, 159; XII, †741, 1608, 6793 (°*ādhipāḥ*), 13922; XIII, 993, †1373, 4734, 7147, 7467, 7644 (*Kadrūjāḥ*); XIV, †747, †750, 751 (*Prajāpatau P°ānāṃ Devarshīṇāñ ca saṃvidam*), 1684, 1745, 2382 (*sañjīvanaṃ maṇiṃ* . . . *P°ānāṃ parāyaṇaṃ*), 2389 (°*endrān*), 2446 (*iva*).

Pannaga, sg. ("serpent-demon"): I, 1703, 1706 (*çava-pannagam*); II, 2182 (*iva*), 2551 (do.); III, 2615, 8647 (°*endravadhūr iva*), 11734 (*iva*); IV, 1519 (do.); V, 4326 (do.); VI, 3612 (do.), 4097 (do.), 4323 (*yathā*); VII, 1294 (*iva*), 1613 (do.), 1687 (do.), 4124 (*yathā*), 4640 (*iva*), 5952 (*iva*), 7516 (do.); VIII, 911 (do.), 966 (do.), 2477 (do.), 2955 (*iva p° ottamaṃ*), 3882 (*yathā*), 4468 (do.); IX, 676 (do.); XI, 814 (*iva*); XII, 10972 (*yathā*), 13918; XIII, 16, 19 (°*ādhamaḥ*), †26, †27, †31, 34, 37, 38, 39, 44, 47 (°*ādhama*), 49, 50, 56, 66, 69, 70, 79, 80, 849; XIV, 2160 (*iva*), 2323 (*iva*).

Names of single Pannagas:—

Arbuda: II, 806.

Çakravāpin: II, 806.

Çesha: I, 1579 (°*ottama*); VII, 3456 (°*çreshṭhaḥ*).

Çrīvaha: I, 1558.

Kauravya: I, 7793.

Nahusha: III, 12397, 12400 (°*sattama*), 12451 (°*ottamaḥ*), 12505 (°*sattama*).

Padma: XII, 13828 (°*āçramam*), 13845, 13849.

Sumukha: V, 3662, 3671.

Takshaka: I, 840, 848 (°*ādhamaḥ*), 1709 (°*ottamaḥ*), 1758 (°*çreshṭhaḥ*), 1762 (do.), 1769 (°*ottamaḥ*), 1770, 1804 (°*çreshṭham*), 1978 (°*ottamāt*), 1995 (°*ādhamaḥ*), 2001, 2018, 2020, 2126, 2170 (°*ottamam*), 8089, 8202.

Vāsuki: I, 1059 (°*ottamaḥ*), 1589 (do.), 1617 (°*ottamam*), 1865, 1925 (°*ottamaḥ*), 2060 (°*ottamam*), 2080 (°*ottamaḥ*), 2084 (°*ottama*), 2090 (do.); IX, 2150 (°*ottamam*).

Pannaganandinī ("daughter of a Pannaga") = Ulūpī: XIV, 2347.

Pannagapati = Padma[1]: XII, 13884.

Pannagarāja[1] = Çesha (Ananta): V, 3818 (*A°*).

Pannagarāja[2] = Vāsuki: I, 1931; IX, 2148 (*V°*).

Pannagarājan = Vāsuki: IX, 2150 (*V°*).

Pannagasutā ("daughter of a Pannaga") = Ulūpī: XIV, 2342 (*U°*), 2358.

Pannagātmajā (do.) = Ulūpī: XIV, 2309 (*U°*), 2312 (*U°*), 2348 (*U°*).

Pannageçvara[1] ("serpent-king") = Takshaka: I, 1704 (*T°*), 1801 (*T°*).

Pannageçvara[2] (do.) = Vāsuki: I, 1919 (*V°*); IX, 2555 (*V°*); XIII, 7104 (? read with B. *patageçvaraḥ*).

Pannageçvarakanyā ("the serpent-king's daughter") = Ulūpī: I, 7808.

Pannagendra[1] = Takshaka: I, 1759, 1761, 1763, 1772, 1773, 1998, 1999, †2133; IX, 3423 (°*sutasya Açvasenasya*).

Pannagendra[2] = Vāsuki: I, 1874.

Pannagī[1] ("serpent-maid"): I, 3895; VII, 3997 (*yathā*), 5048 (*iva*). Do.[2] = Ulūpī: I. 7793 (*U°*).

Pāpahan = Agni, q.v.

Pāpaharā, a river. § 574 (Jambūkh.): VI, **9**λ, 330 (in Bhāratavarsha).

Pāpanāçana = Vishṇu (1000 names).

Para, an ancient king. § 6 (Anukram.): I, **1***a*, 227 (in Sañjaya's enumeration).

Para(ḥ) = Çiva (1000 names[2]).

Para(ṃ) = Çiva (1000 names[2]).—Do.[2] = Vishṇu (1000 names).

Parā[1], a goddess. § 270 (Brahmasabhāv.): II, **11**, 458 (in the palace of Brahmán).

Parā[2], a river. § 574 (Jambūkh.): VI, **9**λ, 327 (only C., B. has *Veṇām*).

Pārā, another name of the river Kauçikī. § 134 (Viçvāmitra): I, **71**, 2926 (Viçvāmitra changed the name of the river into *P.*).

Parāçara[1], a ṛshi, son of Çakt(r)i and Adṛçyantī, and father of Vyāsa. § 70 (Ādivaṃçāvatāraṇap.): I, **60**, 2209 (*janayām āsa yaṃ Kālī Çaktreḥ putrāt P°āt*, sc. Vyāsa).—§ 77 (Vyāsa): I, **63**, 2399, 2415 (begot Vyāsa on Satyavatī).—§ 156 (Pūruvaṃç.): I, **95**, ††3802 (do.). — § 171 (Vicitravīryasutotpatti): I, **105**, 4229 (*paramarshiḥ*, do.).—§ 226 (cf. Vāsishṭha): Then *Adṛçyantī* (the widow of Cakt(r)i) in the hermitage of *Vasishṭha* brought forth a son, *Parāçara* (so named because he had hindered *Vasishṭha*, when he was *parāsu* (i.e. resolved upon self-destruction)), who knew *Vasishṭha* as his father. *Adṛçyantī*, however, told him that his father had been devoured by a *Rākshasa*. *P.* then in his anger resolved to destroy the whole creation, but was restrained by *Vasishṭha* (*Maitrāvāruṇi*): I, **178**, 6794.—§ 227 (Aurvop.): I, **180**, 6864 (Vasishṭha told *P.* the story of Aurva).—§ 228 (do.): I, **181**, 6866 (*Çāktreyaḥ*), 6874, 6877, 6881 (*P.* then controlled his wrath, but performed a *Rākshasa* sacrifice; Pulastya prevailed upon him to make an end of it).—§ 266 (Çakrasabhāv.): II, **7**, 292 (in the palace of Indra).—§ 637 (Rājadh.): XII, **47**η, 1597 (among the ṛshis who surrounded Bhīshma). — § 638*b* (Rāmopākhyāna): XII, **49**, 1792 (protected the son of Saudāsa).—§ 702 (Mokshadh.): XII, **291**, 10699 (10702); **292**, (10728); **293**, (10747); **294**, (10770); **295**, (10791); **296**, (10822); **297**, (10863), (10872), (10880), (10892), (10896); **298**, (†10900); **299**, 10942, (10944) (instructed Janaka).—§ 707 (do.): XII, **319**β, 11782 (*viprarsheḥ*, had instructed Viçvāvasu). — § 709*b* (Sulabhā-Janakasaṃv.): XII, **321**, 11875 (*°sagotrasya . . . Pañcaçikhasya*).—§ 717*b* (Nārāyaṇīya): XII, **350**, 13639 (begot Vyāsa on Satyavatī), 13642 (*Çaktriputraḥ*), 13643 (*°sya dāyādaḥ Kṛshṇa-Dvaipāyano muniḥ*), †13687 (*maharshiḥ*).—§ 730 (Ānuçāsanik.): XIII, **18**, (1336), 1341 (obtained the son Vyāsa by gratifying Çiva).—§ 746 (do.): XIII, **66**, 3369 (*āha*, a sentence of his is quoted).—§ 770 (do.): XIII, **151***a*, †7088 (*Vedanidhim*), 7153 (*°matam*, about the Sāvitrī mantras). Cf. Çāktra, Çaktreḥ putraḥ, Çāktreya, Çaktrija, Çaktriputra.

Parāçara[2], a serpent. § 67 (Sarpasattra): I, **57**, 2160 (of Dhṛtarāshṭra's race).

Parāçaraçarīraja ("the son of Parāçara") = Vyāsa: XIII, 1679.

Parāçarasuta (do.) = Vyāsa: II, 1637 (*Kṛshṇa-Dvaipāyano Vyāsaḥ*); VII, 9645; XII, 8806, 10484 (*V°*), 12369, 12421, 13030 (*V°*); XIII, 680 (*Vedavyāsaḥ*).

Parāçarātmaja (do.) = Vyāsa: I, 55; XII, 12353 (*V°*).

Pārāçarya[1] (do.) = Vyāsa: I, 541 (*muninā*), 2414, 4235 (*mahān ṛshiḥ*); III, 1438; VI, 594 (*pitus tava*, sc. Dhṛtarāshṭra's); XII, 12336 (*V°*), 12344 (*mahāmuniḥ*); XIII, 7670 (one of the ṛshis of the north), 7718 (*V°*); XVIII, 157 (*muniḥ*).

Pārāçarya[2], one or two ṛshis of Parāçara's race. § 264 (Sabhākriyāp.): II, **4***a*, 108 (*Sārikaḥ*?).—§ 266 (Çakrasabhāv.): II, **7**, 295 (*Kṛshībalaḥ*?, in the palace of Çakra).

pāraçava, name of a caste: XIII, †2566 (son of a brahman and a çūdra woman). Cf. pārasava.

Paraçu, an ancient king. § 6 (Anukram.): I, **1***a*, 228 (in Sañjaya's enumeration).

[Paraçu-]Rāma, v. Rāma[1].

Paraçuvana, name of a hell (?). § 710 (Mokshadh.): XII, **322**, †12075 (*°çayo nipātitaḥ*).

Paraçvadhāyudha = Çiva (1000 names[2]).

Pārada, pl. (*°āḥ*), a people. § 295 (Dyūtap.): II, **51**, 1832; **52**, 1859, 1869 (brought tribute to Yudhishṭhira).—§ 585 (Bhīshmavadhap.): VI, **87**, 3853 (in the army of Duryodhana, followed Droṇa).—§ 599 (Jayadrathavadhap.): VII, **93**δ, 3379 (attacked Arjuna); **121**εε, 4818 (attacked Sātyaki).

Parā gati(ḥ) = Çiva (1000 names[2]).

Parahan, an ancient king. § 6 (Anukram.): I, **1***a*, 232 (in Sañjaya's enumeration).

Parākrama, a Kuru warrior. § 600 (Ghaṭotkacavadhap.): VII, **156**κ, 6850.

Parakrāthin, a Kuru warrior. § 600 (Ghaṭotkacavadhap.): VII, **156**κ, 6852.

Paramahaṃsa = Mahāpurusha (Mahāpurushastava).

Paramakrodhin, a Viçvadeva. § 749 (Ānuçāsanik.): XIII, **91**γ, 4357 (enumeration).

Paramaṃ brahma = Çiva (1000 names[2]).

Paramaṃ haviḥ = Agni: I, 8416.—Do.[2] = Skanda: III, †14640.

Paramaṃ padaṃ = Kṛshṇa: XII, 1626.

Paramaṃ pavitraṃ = Skanda: III, †14639.

Paramaṃ tapaḥ = Çiva (1000 names[2]).

Paramaspashṭa = Vishṇu (1000 names).

Paramatigmāṃçu = Sūrya (the Sun): III, 16977.

Paramātman ("the Supreme Soul," often identified with Brahmán, Çiva, or Vishṇu (Kṛshṇa, Nārāyaṇa)): III, 10915 (*Vishṇunā*), 10931 (= Vishṇu), 10955 (*Vishṇunā*), 11174 (*nirguṇaḥ*); V, †1675; VI, 1343, 1352, 1399 (*uttamaḥ purushaḥ*), 4462 (= Kṛshṇa); VII, 6466 (do.); XII, 6921 (= Brahmán?), 7108, 7192 (*sthānasya P °naḥ*), †7400 (*°kārī*), 7743, 8822, †8943 (*°tāṃ*), †8949, 11174, 11175, 11194, 11720, 12889 (*Vāsudevaḥ*, = Nārāyaṇa (Kṛshṇa)), 12982 (= do.), 12989 (= do.), 13012 (*dehināṃ*, = do.), 13034 (= do.), 13139 (= do.), 13335 (= do.), 13350 (= do.), 13354 (= do.), 13358 (= do.), 13369 (= do.), 13374 (= do., *°aḥ sthānasya*), 13387 (= do.), 13402 (= do.), 13449 (= do.), 13684, 13753, 13754 (*Nārāyaṇaḥ*): XIII, 1252 (= Çiva (1000 names[2])), 4104 (*Brahmaṇaḥ*), 6865 (= Kṛshṇa), 6951 (Vishṇu's 1000 names), 7743 (= Kṛshṇa); XIV, 1491 (do.)

Parameçvara ("the Supreme Lord", often identified with Brahmán, Çiva, or Vishṇu (Kṛshṇa, Nārāyaṇa): III, 8353 (*Kshetrajñaḥ* = Kṛshṇa); V, 3870 (= Kāla); VI, 1348, 2941 (= Kṛshṇa); XII, 2398 (*Nārāyaṇam*), 12875 (= Nārāyaṇa), 13005 (do); XIII, 595 (= Çiva), 792 (do.), 795 (do.), 797 (do.), 842 (do.), 913 (do.), 922 (do.), 1119 (do.), 1360 (do.), 3621 (*Brahmā*), 6908 (identified with Kāla), 6990 (Vishṇu's 1000 names); XIV, 1320, 1592 (= Kṛshṇa).

Paramayajñika = Mahāpurusha (Mahāpurushastava).

Pārameshṭha ("son of Parameshṭhin [i.e. Brahmán]") = Nārada: XII, 12700 (B. *Pārameshṭhya*).

Parameshṭhija (do.) = Nārada: XII, 13326 (*N.*), 13330 (*N.*), 13399 (*N°*).

Parameshṭhin[1] = Brahmán (Prajāpati): I, 32, 61, 935,

1249 (Garuḍa identified with *P.* Prajāpati), 2497, 8150 (°*mukhāt*); III, 8694, 8708, 12897 (*B*°), 12810, 12815 (?); V, 4299 (*Prajāpatiḥ*), 4303 (do.), 4304; VI, 546 (? *sarvalokeçvarasyeva Parameshṭhī Prajāpateḥ*); VII, 2046 (*B*°); XII, 5826 (?), 7320 (*B*°), 8803 (°*sāmyatā*), 11578 (= *ahaṅkāra*), 12686 (?, one of the twenty-one Prajāpatis), 13404 (father of Nārada, so Nīl. and PCR., cf. Hariv., vv. 123 foll.), 13452 (*B*°), 13472, 13665 (*B*°).

Parameshṭhin[2] = Çiva: III, 1514; VII, 9508.

Parameshṭhin[3] = Vishṇu (Nārāyaṇa, Kṛshṇa): III, 8774, 12885; XII, 1605 (= Kṛshṇa); XIII, 6994 (1000 names).

Parameshṭhin[4] = Nārada: XII, 12882 (*N*°, read °*ijaṃ* instead of °*inaṃ*?).

Parameshṭhin[5], son of Ajamīḍha. § 152 (Pūruvaṃç.): I, **94,** 3722 (*Dushyanta-P°au*, sons of Ajamīḍha and Nīlī), 3723 (*Dushyanta-P°oḥ*, the Pañcālas are their offspring).

Parameshṭhiputra ("the son of Parameshṭhin [i.e. Brahmán]") = Nārada: XII, †12701.

Pārameshṭhya, adj. ("belonging to Parameshṭhin"). § 246 (Sundopasundop.): I, **211,** 7682 (*ṛshayaḥ*, i.e. the Brahmarshis).—§ 440 (Yakshayuddhap.): III, **164,** 11900 (sc. *astraṃ*, acquired by Arjuna).—§ 588 (Bhīshmavadhap.): VI, **121,** 5802 (sc. *astraṃ*, known to Arjuna). Cf. Pārameshṭha.

Paramo mantraḥ = Çiva (1000 names[2]).

Parānta, pl. (°*āḥ*), a people. § 574 (Jambūkh.): VI, **9**μ, 355 (in Bhāratavarsha).

Pararddhi = Vishṇu (1000 names).

pārasava (name of a caste), said of Vidura: I, 4361. Cf. pāraçava.

pārasavī ("woman of the pārasava caste"), said of the wife of Vidura, the daughter of king Devaka: I, 4480.

Pārasika, pl. (°*āḥ*), a people. § 574 (Jambūkh.): VI, **9**ζ, 373 (in the north).

Parasvāmin = Mahāpurusha (Mahāpurushastava).

Parataṅgana, pl. (°*āḥ*), a people. § 295 (Dyūtap.): II, **52,** 1859 (*Taṅgaṇāḥ P°āḥ*).

Parāvaha, name of a wind. § 714*n* (Çukakṛtya): The wind which takes away the lives of the creatures, whose track is followed by Mṛtyu and [Yama] Vaivasvata, which leads yogins to immortality, by whose aid the ten thousand sons of Daksha (otherwise PCR.) attained to the ends of the universe, by whose touch one becomes emancipated and never returns [to this world], that wind is called by the name of *P.*: XII, **329,** 12416.

Parāvara = Skanda: III, 14645.

Parāvarajña = Skanda: III, 14645.

Parāvasu, a brahman, son of Raibhya and brother of Arvāvasu. § 414 (Yavakrītop.): III, **135,** 10704 (*Arvāvasu-P°ū*, sons of Raibhya).—§ 416 (do.): III, **136,** 10757 (*bhāryāṃ . . . P°oḥ*); **137,** 10789.—§ 417 (do.): III, **138,** 10792 (*Arvāvasu-P°ū*, performed a sacrifice for Bṛhaddyumna), 10793 (*bhāryāṃ P°oḥ*), 10794, 10802, 10810 (*P.* killed his father by a mistake, threw suspicion on Arvāvasu, etc.).—§ 638*b* (Rāmopākhyāna): XII, **49,** 1771 (*Viçvāmitrasya pautraḥ . . . Raibhyaputraḥ*, censured Rāma Jāmadagnya), 1775.—§ 665 (Mokshadh.): XII, **208,** 7592 (*Arvāvasu-P°ū*, among the ṛshis of the east).—§ 717*c* (Uparicara): XII, **337**ε, 12752 (do., among the sadasyas at the sacrifice of Vasu Uparicara).—§ 770 (Ānuçāsanik.): XIII, **151,** 7108 (do., among the seven *Mahendrasya guravaḥ* in the east).

Pārāvata, a serpent. § 65 (Sarpasattra): I, **57,** 2152 (of Airāvata's race).

Parāyaṇa(m) = Sūrya (the Sun): III, 147.—Do.[2] = Vishṇu (1000 names).

pārçvada (B. *pārshada*) = pārishada: IX, 2546; XIII, 1397, 1399.

Pāribarha (B. *Pa*°), a Suparṇa, son of Garuḍa. § 564 (Mātalīyop.): V, **101**β, 3598 (enumeration).

Pāribhadraka, pl. (°*āḥ*), a people. § 578 (Bhīshmavadhap.): VI, **51***a*, 2099 (in the army of Duryodhana, only B., C. has *Maṇibh*°).

pariçesha ("supplement"): XII, 11739 (*Çatapathaṃ . . . sa-p°ṃ*), 11757.

Pariçruta, name of two warriors of Skanda. § 615*u* (Skanda): IX, **45**η, 2562, 2563.

Paridhīpatikhecara = Çiva (1000 names[2]).

Paridvīpa, v. Sariddvīpa.

Parigha[1], a companion of Skanda. § 615*u* (Skanda): IX, **45**δ, 2536 (given to Skanda by Aṃça).

Parigha[2], name of a caṇḍāla. § 646*b* (Mārjāramūshikasaṃv.): XII, **138,** 5028.

Parigraha = Vishṇu (1000 names).

Pārijāta[1], a serpent. § 65 (Sarpasattra): I, **57,** 2152 (of Airāvata's race).

Pārijāta[2], a ṛshi. § 265 (Lokapālasabhākh.): II, **5,** 145 (accompanied Nārada).

***pārijāta**[3], pl. (°*āḥ*) ("coral-trees"): III, 14537 (°*vanaiḥ*); IX, 2181.—Do.[4] (the celestial pārijāta): § 567 (Bhagavadyānap.): V, **130**ξ, 4413 (robbed by Kṛshṇa from heaven).—§ 589 (Droṇābhishekap.): VII, **11,** 403 (do., from the abode of Mahendra).

Pārijātaka, a muni. § 264 (Sabhākriyāp.): II, **4***a*, 109 (waited upon Yudhishṭhira).

Parikshit or **Parīkshit** (C. has in book I °*rī*°, in books X–XVII °*ri*°; B. mostly °*ri*°), son of Abhimanyu and Uttarā, and father of Janamejaya. § 11 (Parvasaṅgr.): I, **2,** 606 (°*aḥ . . . janma*, °*rī*° also B.).—§ 51 (cf. Āstīkap.): One day king *P.*, the son of *Abhimanyu*, when hunting, having pierced a deer lost sight of it. He then asked the muni *Çamīka*, but received no answer as the muni was then observing the vow of silence; in anger the king then placed upon the muni's shoulder a dead snake and returned to his capital *Hāstinapura*. Of this the muni's son *Çṛṅgin* was informed in a quarrel by his companion *Kṛça* (I, **40**), and then cursed *P.*, saying that within seven nights he should be stung to death by *Takshaka*. The muni was not pleased with the curse, as *P.* properly protected his subjects (I, **41**). Therefore he sent his disciple *Gauramukha* to inform *P.*, who became very repentant and sorrowful. A mansion was erected upon a solitary column and well guarded. The seventh day the brahman *Kāçyapa* was coming desirous of curing the king. *Takshaka* in the shape of an old brahman met with *Kāçyapa* (I, **42**). As *Kāçyapa* revived a banyan which had been reduced to ashes by being bitten by *Takshaka*, *Takshaka* gave to *Kāçyapa* more wealth than what he expected from *P.*, and having ascertained by means of *yoga* that *P.*'s span of life was at an end, *Kāçyapa* retired. *Takshaka* went to *Hāstinapura*, and hearing that *P.* was protected by poison-neutralizing *mantras* and medicines, he caused some serpents in the guise of ascetics to present the king with *kuça*-grass, water, and fruits, in one of which he himself was concealed as a tiny ugly insect. As such he appeared when *P.* was eating the fruit. *P.* said: "The sun is setting, to-day I have no more fear from poison; therefore let this insect becoming *Takshaka* bite me so that the words of the ascetic may be rendered true." Then he placed the insect on his neck and was bitten by *Takshaka*, who coiled round his neck and uttered a tremendous roar (I, **43**): I, **40**, 1664 (*Kauravavamçajaḥ*), 1670, 1673 (*rājā . . . Abhimanyujaḥ*, °*rī*° also B.); **41**, 1692, 1696 (*rājā . . . Abhimanyujaḥ*), 1709, 1716; **42**, 1737, 1762 (*nṛpaṃ Kurukulotpannaṃ*).—§ 56 (do.): The ministers of *Janamejaya* told him about *P.*, that he was virtuous, a pupil of *Çāradvata* (i.e. *Kṛpa*) in the science of arms and dear to *Govinda* (i.e. *Kṛshṇa*), and that he had got his name because he was born by *Uttarā*, "*parikshīṇeshu Kurushu*," and that he ruled sixty years; that being addicted to hunting he made over all affairs of state to his ministers; then how he insulted *Çamīka*, and his death (cf. § 51); they also mentioned that *Takshaka* had insulted the *ṛshi Uttaṅka*: I, **49**, 1934, 1947 (*Saubhadrasyātmajaḥ*); **50**, 1980 (*rājā Kuruçreshṭhaḥ*). — § 160 (Pūruvaṃç.): I, **95**, ††3836 (*parikshīṇe kule jātaḥ*), ††3837 (married Mādravatī).—§ 617 (Aishīkap.); X, **16**, 724 (*parikshīṇeshu Kurushu putras tava bhavishyati | etad asya P°tvaṃ*), 725, 734, 737 (being still a fœtus *P.* was slain by Açvatthāman, but Kṛshṇa promised to revive him).—§ 785 (Anugītāp.): XIV, **66**, 1943 (was still-born); **70**, 2044 (was revived by Kṛshṇa; *parikshīṇe kule yasmād jāto 'yam Abhimanyujaḥ | P°d iti nāmāsya bhavishyati*); **78**, 2288 (*Abhimanyor yathā jātaḥ*).—§ 788 (Āçramavāsap.): XV, **21**, 591 (*Vairāṭyās tanayaṃ . . . pitaraṃ te*, i.e. Janamejaya's).—§ 790 (Putradarçanap.): XV, **35**, 944 (Janamejaya wished to see *P.*, Vyāsa then summoned him from the other world).—§ 791 (Mahāprasthānikap.): XVII, **1**, 7, 9, 15, 28 (when the Pāṇḍavas left this world *P.* was installed as king in Hāstinapura. Kṛpa became his preceptor). Cf. Abhimanyoḥ sutaḥ, Abhimanyuja, Bharataçreshṭha, Kirīṭitanayātmaja, Kuruçreshṭha, Kurukulādhama, Kurunandana, Kururāja, Kuruvardhana, Pāṇḍaveya.

Parikshit[2] or **Parīkshit**, son of Avikshit. § 154 (Pūruvaṃç.): I, **94**, 3741 (son of Avikshit; °*rī*° both C. and B.), 3743 (father of Janamejaya[5], etc.; °*rī*° both C. and B.).

Parikshit[3] (C.) or **Parīkshit** (B.), a king of Ayodhyā. § 461 (Vāmadevac.): III, **192**, ††13145 (*Ayodhyāyām Ikshvākuḥ*, married the daughter of the frog king, etc.).

Parīkshit, son of Anaçvan. § 156 (Pūruvaṃç.): I, **95**, 3794 (son of Anaçvan), 3795 (husband of Suyaçā Bāhudā, and father of Bhīmasena[3]).

Pārīkshit (B. °*ri*°) = Janamejaya[10]; XII, 5596 (*J*°).

Pārikshita or **Pārīkshita** = Janamejaya[1], q.v.

Parinirmita = Mahāpurusha (Mahāpurushastava).

Pāripātra (C.) or **Pāriyātra** (B.), a mountain. § 269 (Vaiçravaṇasabhāv.): II, **10**, 412 (among the mountains present in the palace of Kubera).—§ 459 (Mārkaṇḍeyas.): III, **188**, 12920 (seen by Mārkaṇḍeya in the stomach of Nārāyaṇa).—§ 548 (Āraṇeyap.): III, **313**, 17295 (*uttare*; *b*: there the beings had sung that Arjuna should be invincible), 17318.—§ 574 (Jambūkh.): VI, **9**κ, 319 (one of the *kulaparvatāḥ* of Bhāratavarsha).—§ 641 (Rājadh.): XII, **129**, 4719 (*giriṃ*, there Gotama had his hermitage).—§ 643*b* (Kāyavyac.): XII, **135**, 4856 (°*caraḥ*, sc. Kāyavya; °*yā*°, both C. and B.).—§ 782*g* (Guruçishyas.): XIV, **43**η, 1173 (enumeration of the principal mountains).

Pāriplava, a tīrtha. § 362 (Tīrthayātrāp.): III, **83**, 5082.

***pārishada**, mostly pl. (°*āḥ*), said of the followers of Çiva and Skanda: II, 414 (surround Çiva in the palace of Kubera), 416 (do.); III, 9949 (sc. Çiva's), 14330 (sc. Skanda's), 14387 (*Skanda-°ān*), 15856 (sc. Çiva's); VII, 9511 (do.); VIII, 1542 (do.); IX, 2526 (*mahā*°, sc. Skanda's), 2552 (dual, do.), 2553 (*mahā*°, dual, do.), 2579 (*mahā*°, do.), 2580 (do.), 2606 (do.), 2610 (do.), 2614 (*mahā*°, do.), 2615 (do.), 2672 (do.); X, 283 (sc. Çiva's).

Pārishadapriya = Çiva: X, 258.

Parivaha, name of a wind. § 714*m* (Çukakṛtya): The wind who bears the celestial waters and supports the celestial Gaṅgā, who causes the Sun with its thousand rays to appear as a luminous body of only one ray, and who causes the Moon to increase after his waning, that wind is named *P.*; XII, **329**, 12412.

Parivyādha, a ṛshi. § 665 (Mokshadh.): XII, **208**θ, 7596 (one of the ṛshis of the west).—§ 770 (Ānuçāsanik.): XIII, **151**θ, 7114 (one of the seven *Varuṇasya ṛtvijaḥ* in the west).—§ 775 (do.): XIII, **166**ε, 7667 (among the ṛshis of the west).

Pāriyātra, v. Pāripātra.

Parjanya[1], the god of rain = Indra, q.v.

Parjanya[2], a Devagandharva. § 101 (Aṃçāvat.): I, **65**, 2552 (the fourteenth son of Muni).—§ 191 (Arjuna): I, **123***a*, 4812 (*caturdaçaḥ*, among the Devagandharvas present at the birth of Arjuna).

Parjanya[3] = Vishṇu (1000 names).

Pārjanya, adj. ("belonging to Parjanya"). § 208 (Astradarçana): I, **135**, 5365 (°*enāsṛjad* [sc. °*astreṇa*] *ghanān*, sc. Arjuna). Cf. next.

Pārjanyāstra ("the Parjanya-weapon"). § 588 (Bhīshmavadhap.): VI, **121**, 5784 (employed by Arjuna in order to get water).

Parṇacīrapaṭa = Çiva (1000 names[1]).

Parṇāçā, a river. § 268 (Varuṇasabhāv.): II, **9**, 373 (among the rivers present in the palace of Varuṇa).—§ 298 (Dyūtap.): II, **65**, †2146 (*yat kiṃcid anu P°āṃ prāk Sindhoḥ*, sc. *gavāçvaṃ*, belongs to Yudhishṭhira).—§ 574 (Jambūkh.): VI, **9**λ, 339 (C. has by error *Pūrṇāçaṃ*).—§ 599*b* (Çrutāyudha): VII, **92**, 3305 (*mahānadī*, by Varuṇa, mother of Çrutāyudha).—§ 599 (Jayadrathavadhap.): VII, **92**, 3319 (°*āyāḥ priyaḥ sutaḥ*, i.e. Çrutāyudha).—§ 775 (Ānuçāsanik.): XIII, **166***a*, 7647 (enumeration).

Parṇaçālā, name of a village. § 746 (Ānuçāsanik.): XIII, **68**, 3398 (between the Gaṅgā and the Yamunā, at the foot of the mountain Yāmuna, inhabited by brahmans).

Parṇāda, name of one or more brahmans. § 264 (Sabhākriyāp.): II, **4***a*, 108 (waited upon Yudhishṭhira).—§ 351 (Nalopākhyānap.): III, **70**, 2744 (*dvijaḥ*), 2757, 2761 (sent to seek for Nala).—§ 353 (do.): III, **74**, 2893; **76**, 2978 (*brāhmaṇaḥ*, the same).—§ 686 (Mokshadh.): XII, **273**, 9818 (only B., *Çukrasya punar ājñābhiḥ P°o nāma—cāpadhyānāt tu punar ājñāti*, C.—*dharmavit*).

pārshada, v. parçvada.

Pārshata[1] ("the son of Pṛshata") = Drupada: I, 5462, 5474, 6334, 6348 (*Drupado nāma*), 7255; V, 7398, 7405, 7411, 7443.

Pārshata[2] ("the grandson of Pṛshata") = Dhṛshṭadyumna: I, 7273 (*Dh*°); II, 2349 (°*sya svasā*, i.e. Draupadī), 2665; III, 897 (*Dh*°); V, 57 (do.), †725 (*Dh°ṃ . . . Yājñasenim*), †732, 2262 (*Dh*°), 4220 (do.), 5152 (do.), 5175 (do.), 7548 (do.), 7598 (do.); VI, 1655 (do.), 1837 (do.), 1866 (do.), 1962 (do.), 2060 (do.), 2062 (do.), 2064, 2071, 2072, 2082 (*Dh*°), 2128 (do.), 2149 (do.), 2194 (*Pāñcālyaḥ*), 2202, 2213, 2226, 2228, 2229, 2327, 2329, 2334, 2340 (*Dh*°), 2481, 2499, 2706 (*Dh*°), 2714, 2715, 2724, 2733 (*Dh*°), 2742, 2755 (*Dh*°), 2760, 2788 (*Dh*°), 3063 (do.), 3353 (do.), 3362 (do.), 3373,

3374, 3390, 3391, 3400, 3403, 3404, 3408, 3431, 3556 (attacked by Duryodhana), 3629, 3631, 3822, 3823, 3824, 3839 (*Dh°*), 3861 (*pṛtanāpatim*), 3862, 3863, 4057, 5180 (fought with Kṛtavarman), 5181, 5236 (*rājānaṃ*), 5326 (*Dh°*), 5353 (*vāhinīpatiḥ*), 5421, 5422, 5425, 5426, 5427, 5553 (*Dh°*), 5558 (do.), 5578 (do.), 5587 (do.); VII, 171, 217, 218, 219, 226, 254, 263, 266, 286, 298, 494, 633, 812, 819, 820, 821, 1054, 1508 (*Dh°*), 3128 (do.), 3491, 3500, 3501, 3504, 3522, 3523, 3596, 3600, 4149, 4282, 4287, 4914, 4927, 5148, 6762, 6898, 6909, 6923 (*Dh°*), 7175, 7182, 7183, 7184, 7187, 7194, 7281, 7664 (*Dh°*), 7665, 7754, 7758, 7774, 7781, 7783, 8630, 8632, 8714, 8760, 8785, 8788, 8791, 8793, 8821, 8822, 8829, 8835, 8840, 8870 (slew Droṇa), 8887 (*Dh°*), 8888, 8889, 8956, 8989, 9008, 9060, 9068, 9069, 9132, 9150, 9184, 9291, 9395, 9494, 9495; VIII, 862 (*Dh°*), 866 (only B., C. has *pārçvato*), 1038, 1045, 1047, 1048, 1057, 1231, 2214, 2215, 2398 (*Dh°*), 2400, 2641 (fought with Kṛtavarman), 2643, 2646, 2648, 2710, 2725, 2731, 2917, 2920, 2928, 2930, 2931, 2932, 2934, 2942, 2944, 2948, 2954, 2956, 2957, 2965, 2972, 3096, 3148 (*Dh°*), 3157, 3955 (*Dh°*), 4028 (do.), †4195, 4854 (*Dh°*), 4855, 4856; IX, 146 (*Dh°*), 147, 148, 753 (*Dh°*), 755, 757, 946 (*Dh°*), 1020 (do.), 1037 (do.), 1125 (do.); XI, 789 (do.); XIV, 1789 (*Droṇa-P°saṅgare*).—Do.[3] = Çikhaṇḍin: VIII, 1070.

Pārshata, pl. (*°āḥ*), the sons of Drupada. § 243 (Vidurāgamanap.): I, **205**, 7508.—§ 315 (Maitreyaçāpa): III, **10**, 371.

Pārshatātmaja ("the son of Pārshata [i.e. Drupada]") = Dhṛshṭadyumna: VIII, †4200 (*Somaka-P°au*, i.e. Janamejaya[8] and Dhṛshṭadyumna).

Pārshatī[1] ("daughter-in-law of Pṛshata"?), the queen of Drupada. § 218 (Draupadīsambhava): I, **167**, 6405. Cf. Pṛshatī.

Pārshatī[2] ("daughter of Pārshata [i.e. Drupada]") = Draupadī: I, 6434 (*Kṛshṇā*), 7326 (do.); III, 215 (*Dr°*); V, 5520, 5565.

Pārshṇikshemasamūha, a Viçvadeva. § 749 (Ānuçāsanik.): XIII, **91**γ, 4355 (enumeration).

Pārtha[1], pl. (*°āḥ*) ("the sons of Pṛthā [i.e. Kuntī]") = Yudhishṭhira, Bhīmasena, and Arjuna (also often incl. Nakula and Sahadeva, the sons of Mādrī); in some passages = the adherents of Yudhishṭhira: I, 111, 120, †151 (*pañca*), †164 (*Bhīmam anyāṃç ca P°ān*), 562, 571 (*pañca*), 2254, 2265, 2290 (dual = Bhīmasena and Arjuna), 5376, 5534 (*Arjunapramukhāḥ*), 5839 (dual = Yudhishṭhira and Arjuna), 5844, 6315, 6345, 6423, 6436, 6922, †7016, †7131 (dual = Bhīmasena and Arjuna), †7185, †7186, 7378, 7403, 7453, 7515, 7522, 7744; II, 18, 21, 48, 512, 965 (dual = Bhīmasena and Arjuna), 967 (do., do.), 995, 1678, 1699, 1888, 2030, 2110, †2119, †2194, †2381, 2417, 2484, 2514, 2518, †2523, †2527, 2565, 2663 (*Dhṛshṭadyumnaḥ P°ānāṃ çyālaḥ*), 2672, 2701, 2705; III, 3, 9, †239, 291, 344, 463, 468, 521 (*bhāryā P°ānāṃ*, i.e. Draupadī), †963, 967, 980, 1522, 1944, 1976, 1982, 1984, 1986, 4025, †10234, †10245, †10262, 11004, 11454, 11534, 11558, 11596, 11745, †11894, †11909, †11911, †11922, 12286, †12316, †12338, †12355, †12596, 13007 (*Yamau ca*), †14741, 14923, 15129, 15131, 15198, 15208, 15210, 15272, 15334, 15563, 15566, †15607, 15616, 15632, †15659, †15667, †15679, †15682, †15715, 17171, †17217; IV, 175, †285, 373, 871, 876, 963, 1024, 1028, 1029, 1367, 1614, †2144, 2161 (*saha-P°aḥ*), 2162, 2290, 2300, †2306, 2362 (*Matsya-P°yoḥ*?), 2363; V, 119, 643, †648, †649, †650, †664, †727, †731, †735, †740, †782, †827, 865, †1332, 1793, 2123, 2126, 2128, 2144, 2145, 2219, 2369, 2381, 2383, 2387, 2400, †2415, †2416, 2429, 2432, 2885, 3078, 3134, 3224, 3225, 3263, 3285, 3445, 4184, 4235, 4241, 4357, 4391, 4735, 4753, 4937, 5196, 5465, 5633, 5637, 5756, 5757, 5760; VI, 573, 601, 640, †745, 1805, 1984, 2032, 2100, 2157, †2640, 2914, 2916, 3194 (*Dhṛshṭadyumnamukhāḥ*), 3808, 3927, 4060, 4064, 4407, 4412, 4443, 4446, 4480, 4514, 4802, 4957, 4975, 5011, 5017, 5031, 5062, 5328 (*Yudhishṭhiramukhāḥ*), 5329, 5339, 5359, 5465, 5480, 5536, 5542, 5544, 5812; VII, 190, 294, 365 (*Dhṛshṭadyumnaṃ P°ānāṃ mantradhāriṇaṃ*), 377, 379, 1129, 1507, 1656, 1713, 1747, 1751, 3076, 3077, 3081, 3430, 3490 (*Dhṛshṭadyumnamukhāḥ*), 3491, 3544, 3926, 4020, 4127, 4496 (*Bhīmasenamukhāḥ*), 4499, 4537, 4538, 4539, 4881, 5008, 5095, 5096, 5427, 5430, 5459, 5461, 5557, 5679, 6596, 6694, 6909, 6977, 7021, 7022, 7027, 7067, 7112, 7113, 7139, 7180, †7306, 7341, 7576, 7674, 7740, 7743, 7744, 7833 (*Dhṛshṭadyumnapurogamaiḥ*), 7851, †8163, 9130, 9138, 9290, 9434; VIII, 254, 314, 372, 392, 453 (*Vṛkodarapurogamāḥ*), 825, 829, 1230, 1244, 1268, 1271, 1337, 1653, 1672, 1731, 2122, 2234, 2235, 2236, 2300 (*Yudhishṭhiramukhāḥ*), 2903, 2909 (*Yudhishṭhiramukhāḥ*), 3700, 3702, 4016, †4512, †4534, 4753 (all. to Jatugṛhaparvan); IX, 68, 78, 236, 324, 337, 342, 384, 386, 388, 403, 462, 562, 591, 780, 787, 796, 797, 946, 953, 991, 1052, 1063, 1137, 1575, 1643, 1682, 1785, 1826, 1867, 1933, 3463; X, 9, 327 (*°ānāṃ çibiraṃ*), 441, 472, 597, 704, 712; XI, 41, (*°pāvakaḥ*), 590; XII, 1393; XIV, 2332 (*°ānām ṛshabhaḥ*, i.e. Arjuna); XV, 506; XVI, 133. Cf. Pṛthātmaja, pl., Kaunteya, pl., Kuntīputra, pl., Kuntīsuta, pl.

Pārtha[2] ("the son of Pṛthā") = Arjuna: I, †182, †189, †194 (*Kṛshṇa-P°au*), †203, 397, 399, 432, 462, 488 (*Kirīṭinā*), 521, 525, 530, 533, 534, 538 (*Kṛshṇa-P°yoḥ*), 548, 631, 2276, 2277, 4806, 5222, 5229, 5293, 5296, 5304, 5353, 5362 (*Phālgunaḥ*), 5387, 5390, 5393, 5395, 5399, 5404, 5411, 5424, 5454, 5476, 5481, 5483, 5485, 5486, 5488, 5489, 5493, 5496 (*Dhanañjayaḥ*), 5516, 5536 (defeated the Sauvīra king Vipula), 6023, 6500, 6502, 6506, 6508, 6519, 6533, 6536, 6538, 6632, 6646, 6650, 6669, 6671, 6696, 6711, 6718, 6722, 6746, 6760, 6874, 7035, †7054, 7057, †7059, †7077, †7172, †7173, 7241, 7569, 7766, 7804, 7875, 7918, 7920, 7926, 7940, 7946, 7956, 7968, 7970, 7972, 7973, 7977, 7980, 8015, 8066 (*°-Govindau*), 8068 (*Vārshṇeya-P°yoḥ*), 8071 (*°-Kṛshṇayoḥ*), 8078 (*°-Mādhavau*), 8084 (*Vārshṇeya-P°au*), 8164 (*Kṛshṇa-P°au*), 8178, 8191, 8221, 8255, 8257 (*Kṛshṇa-P°au*), 8269 (do.), 8270 (do.), 8327, 8328, 8320 (*Kṛshṇa-P°ābhyām*), 8467, 8469, 8473; II, 1, 14, 29, 40, 58 (*A°*), 66, 647 (*Dhanañjaye*), 665, 781, 798, 805, 830 (*°-Bhīmayoḥ*), 983, 989, 1034, 1046, 1058, 1889 (*Dhanañjayaḥ*), 1891, 2428, 2550, 2704; III, 504, 506, 527, 538, 576, 930, 1015, 1315, 1387 (*Bībhatsuḥ*), 1439 (*Dhanañjayaḥ*), 1464, 1477, 1484, 1485, 1516, 1522, 1525, 1543, 1544, 1557, 1604, 1616, 1624, 1635, 1639, 1640, 1654, 1656, 1668, 1690, 1692, 1706, 1714, 1722, 1751, 1765, 1767, 1771, 1777, 1788, 1793, 1795, 1800, 1817, 1821, 1835, 1844, 1849, 1864, 1866, 1882, 1898, 1914, 1915, 1916, 1923, 1929, 1935, 1949, 1950, 1954, 1987, 2013, 2014, 2028, 3084 (*Savyasācinaṃ*), 3086, 3087 (*Dhanañjayaḥ*), 3090, 8283, 8413, 8414, 8416, 8419, 8429, †10235, †10265, 10875, 10881 (*Yamayoḥ pūrvajaḥ . . . Çvetāçvaḥ*), 11451, 11531, 11823, 11826, 12058, 12148, 12189, 12211, 12270, 12308, 12313, 12314, †12320, †12569 (*Dhanañjayena*), 14969, 14976 (*Savyasācī Dhanañjayaḥ*), 14999, 15175, 15187, 15723, 15775, 15776, 15852, 16853, 17269, 17270, 17272, 17273 (*Savyasācī Dhanañjayaḥ*); IV, 160, 571, 584, 586, 620

(*Dhanañjayaḥ*), 1179 (*A*°), 1186, 1189, †1197, †1199, 1211, 1225, 1239, 1267 (*A*°), 1278, 1284, 1293, 1295 (*Savyasācī*), 1297 (all. to Kairātaparvan), 1300, 1303, 1308, 1317, 1343, 1345, 1349 (*Çvetavāhanaḥ*), 1368 (*A*°), 1371 (do.), 1373, 1390, 1391 (*Dhanañjaya*), 1420, 1421, 1429, 1468, 1499, 1510, 1518, 1519, 1522, 1528, 1534, 1537, 1541, 1547, 1548, 1549, 1551, 1573, 1601, 1633, 1637, 1639, 1652, 1654, 1655, †1668, †1670, †1674, †1682, †1688, †1690, †1695, 1699, 1701, 1705, 1707, 1710, 1724, 1725, 1726, 1727, 1736, 1737, 1779, 1793, 1794, 1795, 1796, 1797, 1798, 1800, 1804, 1806, 1807, 1812, 1813, 1820, 1834, 1838 (*Droṇa-P°au*), 1839, 1843, 1844, 1845, 1854, 1857 (*Dhanañjayaḥ*), 1860, 1881, 1888, 1889, 1891, 1892, 1897, 1898, 1899, 1901, 1906, 1909, 1910, 1915, 1918, 1920, 1931, 1932, 1935, 1944, 1950, 1952, 1990, 1994, 2001, 2011, 2019, 2040, 2046, 2049, 2055, 2060, 2074, 2080 (°-*Bhīshmasamāgamam*), †2091, †2094, †2097, †2099, †2102 (*tṛtīyaḥ*), †2107, †2108, †2110 (*Dhanañjayaḥ*), †2111, †2114, †2115, †2116, †2121, †2123, †2126, †2130, (*Dhanañjayaḥ*), †2132, †2135, 2139, †2143, †2150, 2256, 2297 (*A*°), 2311, 2324 (*Dhanañjayam*), 2346, 2347 (*Matsya-P°yoḥ*), 2362 (do.?), 2370 (?); V, †16, 144 (*Dhanañjayaḥ*), 146 (do.), 149, 160 (?), 170, 171, 629 (*Kirīṭī*), 639, †704, †961, †1875 (*Savyasācin*), 2090, 2129, 2187 (*Dhanañjayam*), 2247 (*A*°), 2330, 2331, 2341, 2356, 2357, 2376, †2411, †2508 (*Dhanañjayaḥ*), †2519 (*Keçava-P°yoḥ*), 2830, 2835, 2839, 2840, 2901, 3220 (°*sakhaḥ*, i.e. Kṛshṇa), 3495, 4178, 4682, 4691 (*Dhanañjayaḥ*), 4701, 4772, 5174, 5241, 5466 (*Savyasācinā*), 5499, 5503, 5507, 5512, 5521, 5564 (*sa-Gāṇḍīvāt*), 5566, †5576, 5588, 5589, 5590, 5642, 5710, 5715, 5716, 5785, 5786, 5845, 5868, 5880, 5932, 7578; VI, 607, 718, 795, 809, 812, 855, 856, 881, 899, 910, 917, 920, 933, 950, 966, 972, 973, 1004, 1026, 1104, 1112, 1121, 1149, 1155, 1160, 1163, 1168, 1182, 1202, 1228, 1251, 1255, 1308, 1406, 1408, 1452, 1454, 1484, 1485, 1486, 1487, 1488, 1489, 1526, 1528, 1532, 1679, 1998 (*Kṛshṇasahitaḥ*), 2078, 2155, 2159, 2162, 2165, 2169, 2180, 2186, 2392, 2426, 2466, 2488, 2542, 2549, 2557, 2561, 2564, 2566, 2572, 2581, †2591, †2610, †2612, †2619, †2626, †2627, †2632, †2648, †2675, 2683, 3064, 3120, 3201, 3207, 3270, 3272, 3443, 3574, 3575, 3579, †3754, †3755, †3759, †3760, †3767, 3977 (father of Irāvat), 3980, 4335, 4460, 4495, 4555, 4619, 4642, 4644, 4646, 4648, 4649, 4652, 4656, 4660, 4667, 4730, 4732, 4834 (*Bībhatsum*), 4843, 4846, 4850, 4853, 4856, 4867, 4868, 4920, 4921, 4922, 4923, 4982 (read °*a* with B.), 4983, 4984, 5067, 5096, 5097, 5120, 5126, 5129, 5131, 5133, 5134, 5136, 5138, 5196, 5201, 5214, 5217 (only B.), 5230, 5295, 5299, 5307, 5312, 5314, 5318, 5349, 5366, 5383, 5406, 5439, 5458, 5463, 5486, 5492, 5499, 5523, 5524, 5622, 5634, 5646, 5731, 5785, 5786, 5787, 5793, 5800, 5806 (?); VII, 107, 195, 196, 285, 326, 341 (°*ena samam*, sc. *Sātyaki*), 402, 448, 454, 457, 669, 676, 719, 734, 735, 747, 769, 773, 783, 788, 793, 982 (°*samam*, sc. Çrutakīrti), 983, 1130, 1195, 1213, 1214, 1216, 1222, 1223, 1225, 1226, 1233, 1242, 1244, 1245, 1251, 1252 (*Acyuta-P°yoḥ*), 1256, 1261, 1271, 1273, 1278, 1289, 1290, 1292, 1293, 1302, 1305, 1310, 1324, 1330, 1338, 1343, 1420, 1431, 1433, 1486 (*Gāṇḍīvadhanvanaḥ*), 1533, 1758 (*Dhanañjayam*), 2542, 2551, 2552 (read °*aḥ* with B.), 2618, 2638, 2639, 2646, 2648, 2668 (all. to Kairātaparvan), 2676, 2724, 2730, 2743, 2773, 2777, 2778, 2780, 2782, 2791 (*Dhanañjayaḥ*), 2795, 2797, 2824, 2825, 2836, 2838, 2844, 2853, 2856, 2862, 2886, 2889, 2897, 2901 (only C., but read *pārçvād* with B.), 2966 (*Dhanañjayaḥ*), 2986, 2991, 2993, 2997, 3008, 3058, 3141, 3153, 3155, 3163, 3164, 3169, 3170, 3195, 3203, 3208, 3230, 3246, 3247, 3261, 3271, 3274, 3280, 3283, 3285, 3296, 3297, 3304, 3322, 3324, 3325, 3329, 3335, 3338, 3341, 3351, 3353, 3358, 3359, 3363, 3367, 3376, 3399, 3400, 3404, 3408, 3418, 3434 (*Dhanañjayaḥ*), 3486 (°-*Vārshṇeyayoḥ*), 3698, 3704, 3709, 3711, 3718, 3724, 3725, 3730, 3732, 3733, 3734, 3735, 3736 (°-*Govindau*), 3745, 3760, 3795, 3800 (*Kṛshṇa-P°au*), 3807, 3809, 3813, 3814, 3817, 3820, 3821, 3823, 3833, 3839, 3840, 3845, 3848, 3851, 3852, 3870, 3884, 3896, 3918, 3919, 3956, 3962, 4172, 4230, 4234, 4242, 4269, 4291, 4302, 4476 (*Sātyaki-P°ābhyām*), 5100, 5247, 5249, 5259, 5260, 5261, 5262, 5308, 5376, 5613, 5802, 5803, 5816 (*Pākaçāsaniḥ*), 5852 (*Dhanañjayam*), 5854, 5860, 5861, 5863, 5864, 5885 (*Dhanañjayaḥ*), 5889, 5947, 5950, 5953, 5956, 5959, 5961, 5965, 5966, 5995, 5996, 6004, 6006, 6017, 6071, 6076, 6078, 6086, 6093, 6098, 6103, 6106, 6115, 6117, 6122 (*Dhanañjayaḥ*), 6126, 6130, 6141, 6143, †6150, 6155 (*Dhanañjayaḥ*), 6167, 6179, 6214, 6221, 6237, 6285, 6287, 6298, 6299 (*Phālgunam*), 6308, 6325, 6330, 6368, 6370, 6422, 6440, 6451, 6499, 6574, 6648, 6683, 6733, 6736 (*Jishṇunā*), 6767, 6964, 6974, 6986, 6990, 6993, 7087, 7094, 7103, 7105, 7110, 7111, 7114, 7119, 7121, 7123 (only B.), 7126, 7127, 7215, 7508, 7657, 7667, 7719, 7800, 7801, 7802, 7816, †8163, 8181, 8219, 8226, 8231, †8247, 8259, 8260, 8261, 8268, 8277, 8283 (*Dhanañjayāt*), 8290 (*Dhanañjayam*), 8291 (do.), 8300, 8302 (*Çakrakalpe*), 8330, 8397, 8464, 8606, 8609, 8613, 8621, 8624, 8692, 8797, 8865 (*Dhanañjayaḥ*), 9084, 9101, 9104, 9106, 9108, 9116, 9122, 9142, 9158, 9219, 9334, 9336, †9338, 9404, 9405, 9408, 9503, 9512, 9514, 9515, 9547, 9571, 9636, 9639; VIII, 115 (had slain Çrutāyus), 129 (had slain the Çreṇis, the Saṃçaptakas, etc.), 141, 231, 274, 382, 422, 613, 635, 638, 658, †669, †672, †682, 689, †696, †699, †705, 712, 726, 727, 732, 733, 738, 823, 1093 (*Dhanañjayaḥ*), 1096 (do.), 1118 (*Jishṇuḥ*), 1227, 1250, 1286, 1287, 1288, 1304, 1311, 1328, 1342, 1343, 1345, 1347, 1385, 1629, 1630, 1659, 1665, 1669, †1716, †1795, †1799, 1800 (*Dhanañjayam*), 1801, 1805 (*Dhanañjayam*), 1815, 1826, 1947, 1952, 1958, †1977, †1979, †1981, †1996, 2000, 2016, 2180, 2187, 2191, 2197, 2199, 2210, 2217, 2222, 2565, 2566, 2567, 2568, 2569, 2578, 2579, 2590, 2591, 2599, 2696, 2793, 2797, 2798, 2826, 2830, 2866, 2899, 2900, 2938, 2956, 2961, 2964, 2967, 2970, 2974 (*Dhanañjayaḥ*), 2976, 2980, 2995, 2998, 3001, 3003, 3004, 3006, 3011, 3016, 3020, 3024, 3032, 3059, 3065, 3191 (*Phālgunena*), 3192, 3193, 3197, 3215, 3216, 3224, 3226, 3228, 3229, 3232, 3236, †3238, †3239, 3278, 3280, †3295, 3328, †3345, †3347, †3382, †3384, 3397, 3404, 3418, 3419, 3421, 3423, 3425, 3430, 3431, 3469, †3481, 3486, †3491, †3492, †3516, †3517, †3519, †3520, †3527, †3529, †3534, 3542, 3543, 3552, 3553, 3554, 3556, 3576, 3582, 3583, 3593, 3607, 3609, 3616, 3618, 3629, 3633, 3637, 3643, 3644, 3645, 3660, 3661, 3681, 3683, 3684, 3686, 3745, 3748, 3750, †3810, †3848, †3856, †3865, 3872, 3877, 3881, 3883, 3884, 4027, 4030, †4048, †4061, †4071, †4081, †4082, 4119, 4133, 4134, 4141, 4166, 4168, 4174, 4175, †4189, †4333, †4334, †4335, †4344, 4362, 4363, 4368, 4369, 4402, 4403, 4417, 4434, 4447, 4466, 4474, 4476, †4533, †4535, †4538, †4565, †4571, †4586, †4597, †4601, †4607, †4609, †4610, †4623, †4627, †4630 (*Kirīṭī*), †4632, †4635, †4637, †4642, †4643, †4644, †4662, †4664, †4666 (*çyāmaḥ*), †4673, †4676, †4677, †4678, †4695, †4707, †4713, 4717, 4722, 4724, 4731, 4737, 4738, 4764, 4769, †4780, †4787, †4790, †4799, †4806, †4826, †4830, 4836, 4847, 4849, 4933, 4934, 4936, 4982, 4989, 4993, 5007, 5012, 5028; IX, 128, 140, 141, 160, 189, 708 (*A*°), 713, 715,

716, 717 (°*pāvakaḥ*), 721, 723, 725 (*Dhanañjayaḥ*), 735, 736, 738, 739, 798 (*Kṛshṇa-P°yoḥ*), 820 (*Dhanañjayaḥ*), 960, 1028, 1331, 1332, 1333, 1449, 1477 (*Dhanañjayaḥ*), 1478, 1483 (slays Suçarman), 1484, 3422, 3489; X, 443 (*Dhanañjayaḥ*), 634, 705 (*Dhanañjayaḥ*); XI, 603 (had slain Karṇa), 646, 647 (*Dhanañjayam*), 695 (had slain Bhūriçravas); XII, 25 (*Çvetavāhanaḥ*), 37 (had slain Karṇa), 200 (*kanīyān*), 584, 599, 769, 777, 778, 784, 803 (had slain Bhīshma), 6219, 13151, 13165, 13170, 13171, 13189, 13237, 13260, 13265, 13270, 13296, 13557 (?); XIII, †7379 (Kṛshṇa gave him white horses); XIV, 379, 380, 387, 390, 400, †404, †405, 408, 415, 422, 586, 587, 588, 589, 592, 594, 598, 599, †748 (!), 938, 947, 1480, 1538, 1793, 1827, 1966 (*pautram P°sya*, i.e. Parikshit), 2129, 2147, 2151, 2161, 2173, 2179, 2182, 2223 (*Bhīmasenād anantarāt*), 2226, 2232, 2243, 2244, 2245, 2247, 2273, 2278, 2279, 2286, 2292, 2297, 2300, 2317, 2318, 2329, 2390 (*Pāṇḍavam*), 2391, 2410, 2426, 2448, 2488, 2489, 2491, 2495, 2497, 2500, 2501, 2510, 2566, 2576, 2592, 2607; XV, 379, 408 (*Dhanañjayaḥ*), †666 (°*sya bhāryā*, i.e. Ulūpī), 853 (*Dhanañjayam*, = Nara), 855 (read with B. °*ād udbhūtaḥ*, sc. Abhimanyu, C. by error has °*a*), 1069; XVI, †106, 137, 144, 149, 154, 158, 175, 176, 185, 189, 190, 195, 211, 213, 216, 222, 234, 236 (*Dhanañjayaḥ*), 239, 242, 245, 252, 257, 260, 291; XVII, 41 (°*kāraṇāt*); XVIII, 96.

Pārtha[3] (do.) = Bhīmasena: I, 5470 (*Bhīmaḥ*), 5784, 6025, †7077; II, 1814 (according to PCR.), 2534 (*Vṛkodaraḥ*); III, 2050, 10897, 11075, 11081 (*atmajam Mātariçvanaḥ*), 11314, 11608, 11610, 11620, 11695 (*ātmajam Mātariçvanaḥ*), 11750, 15789 (*Vṛkodaraḥ*), 17278 (do.); IV, 619, 730, 1111, 1121 (*Vṛkodaraḥ*), 1351; V, 2180 (*Vṛkodaraḥ*), 2755, 2758, 4217 (*Bhīmasenaḥ*), 5334 (*Vṛkodaraḥ*), 5471; VI, 2308 (*Bhīmaḥ*), 2334, 2823, 3347, 4021, 4670 (*Vṛkodaraḥ*), 4677; VII, 977 (father of Sutasoma; = Arjuna, PCR. by error), 1133, 4075, 4366, 5109 (*Vṛkodaram*), 5142, 5153, 5168, 5391, 5457, 5505, 5508, 5620, 5627, 5776, 7459 (*Vṛkodaraḥ*), 9251; VIII, †3836, 4266, 4856 (°-*Pārshatayoḥ*); IX, 148, 1830 (*Vṛkodarāt*), 1894 (do.), 1916, 3134, 3236, 3280; X, 599; XI, 376 (*Vṛkodaraḥ*); XVII, 71.

Pārtha[4] (do.) = Karṇa: V, 4928.

Pārtha[5] (do.) = Yudhishṭhira: I, 5038, 6254, 7619 (*Y°*), 8060; II, 189, 194, 223, 286, 291, 311, 345, 350, 513, 547, 554, 555, 655, 1596, 1684 (*yajñam P°sya*), 1931, †1999, 2011, 2037, 2078, †2384, 2491 (*Y°*), 2496, 2507, 2513; III, 40, 145, †910, †953, †901, 969, 972, 1026, 1127, 1128, 1156, 1202, 1218, 1315, 1319, 1400, 1402, 1403, 8250, 8381, †10244, 10410, 10828, 10832, †10836, 11445, 11633, 11634, 11637, 11638, 11641, 11645, 11652, 11781, 11806, 11826, 11880, †12571 (?), †12575, 12769, 12834, 13371, 13441, 14374, 15729, 16431, 16456, 16472, 16883, 16885, 17327; IV, 906, 910, 943, 2209, 2258 (*Y°*), 2322 (?), 2370 (?); V, 160, 199, †713, †767, †771, †778, †788, †791, †854, †918 (*Ajātaçatrum*), 1974, 2138, 2238, 2316, 2669, 4278, 4706 (?), 4710, 5540, 5893; VI, 14, 765 (*Y°*), 1567, 2057, 2069, 2072, 3281, 3701, 3806; VII, 823, 1053, 1773, 4169, 4275, 5149, 5151 (*Y°*), 5464 (?), 5467, 6962 (*Droṇa-P°au*), 7261, 7267, 7383, 7388, 8737; VIII, 345, 2344, 2348, 2349, 2357, 2689, 2977, 2992, 3183, †3380, †3490, 3690, 5008; IX, 71, 246 (?°*hite rataḥ*, sc. Kṛshṇa), 358, 640, 647, 854, †875, †882, 923, 1013, 1024 (*Y°*); X, 584, 586; XII, 65, 342, 343, 344, †369, †370, 389, 510, 605, 656, 700, 826, 1184, 1383 (*jyeshṭhaḥ pitā P°sya*, sc. Dhṛtarāshṭra), 1388, 1572, 1705, 2461, 2471 (*Y°*), 2474, 2959, 2981, 3141, 3298, 3781, 5465, †6262, 6524, 7068, 7129, 7131, 9599, 9930, 10202, 11060, 11176, 11191 (*Y°*), †11208, †11209; XIII, 200, 1019, 1295, 1321, †1378, 1540, 2141, 2395, 2558, 3045, 3453, 3483, †3692, †3730, 4807, 4844, 5184, 5345, 5402 (°-*Gāṅgeyayoḥ*), 5660, 5790, 6895, †7358, †7362, †7363, †7366, †7377, †7386, †7393, 7491, 7699; XIV, 33, 59, 60, 63, 295, 321, 325, 337, 2676; XVII, 73; XVIII, 60, 81 (*Dharmarāje Y°e*), 106, 112, 116.

Parvaṇa, a Rākshasa. § 537 (Rāma-Rāvaṇayuddha); III, **285a**, 16365 (followed Rāvaṇa).

Parvānukramaṇī ("table of contents of the greater sections"), the first of the minor parvans of the Mhbhr. (= Anukramaṇikāparvan). § 10 (Parvasaṅgr.): I, **2**, 311. Cf. Anukramaṇī.

Parvasaṅgraha ("outlines of the greater sections"): I, 311, 360, 644, 659.—Do.[2] = Parvasaṅgrahaparvan. § 10 (Parvasaṅgr.): I, **2**, 311.

[Parvasaṅgrahaparvan(°va)], the second of the minor parvans; cf. Parvasaṅgraha. § 8: Sauti related: Rāma (Jāmadagnya), having in the intervals between the Tretā and Dvāpara yugas repeatedly destroyed the warrior caste, formed five lakes of blood at Samantapañcaka, where he offered oblations of blood to the manes of his ancestors, until those pacified him, and his lakes became holy *tīrthas* (places of pilgrimage).—§ 9: Sauti explained the term *akshauhiṇī* (an army) and its subdivisions. Eighteen *akshauhiṇīs* partook of the battle; *Bhīshma* holding the command for ten days, *Droṇa* for five, *Karṇa* for two, *Çalya* for half a day, the combat between *Bhīma* and *Duryodhana* lasting half a day, and the nightly assault of *Drauṇi* (i.e. *Açvatthāman*), *Hārdikya* (i.e. *Kṛtavarman*), and *Gautama* (i.e. *Kṛpa*) on *Yudhishṭhira's* army taking place at the end of the same day.—§ 10: *Sauti* enumerated the 100 smaller parvans, or greater chapters, together with the three parvans of *Harivaṃça* (together 103). —§ 11: *Sauti* enumerated the eighteen books or greater parvans, with *Harivaṃça* as the nineteenth, with a summary of their contents, a computation of the number of verses, and renewed praises (I, **2**).

Parvata[1], a Devarshi, son of Nārada's sister, often mentioned together with Gandharvas (cf. Parvata[2]). § 59 (Sarpasattra): I, **53**, 2048 (Nārada and *P.* among the sadasyas at the snake-sacrifice of Janamejaya).—§ 233 (Svayaṃvarap.): I, **187**, †7011 (*Nārada-P°au*, present at the svayaṃvara of Draupadī). —§ 264 (Sabhākriyāp.): II, **4a**, 110 (waited upon Yudhishṭhira).—§ 265 (Lokapālasabhākhyānap.): II, **5**, 145 (only B., C. has *Raivatena*, accompanied Nārada). § 266 (Çakrasabhāv.): II, **7**, 292 (in the palace of Indra).—§ 345 (Nalopākhyānap.): III, **54**, 2117 (Nārada and *P.* came to Indra).—§ 378 (Tīrthayātrāp.): III, **93**, 8475 (°-*Nāradau*, came to Yudhishṭhira), 8483 (*devarsheḥ*).—§ 412 (Ashṭāvakrīya): III, **134**, †10659 (*dvau devarshī Nārada-P°au*).—§ 595 (Sṛñjaya): VII, **55**, 2138 (*ṛshī Nārada-P°au*), 2142, 2146 (contending about the daughter of Sṛñjaya, Nārada and *P.* cursed one another).—§ 600 (Ghaṭotkacavadhap.): VII, **163**, †7294 (*Narāda-P°ābhyām*, brought lamps).—§ 632 (Rājadh.): XII, **29**, †1042 (had granted Sṛñjaya the son Suvarṇashṭhīvin).—§ 633*b* (Nārada-Parvatop.): XII, **30**, 1043, 1046 (*Nāradaḥ P°ç caiva dvāv ṛshī*), 1048 (the sister-son of Nārada), 1060, 1061, 1068, 1071, 1076, 1077, 1078, 1083, 1085, 1086 (Nārada and *P.* cursed one another, cf. § 595).—§ 634*b* (Suvarṇashṭhīvisambhavop.): XII, **31**, 1091 (*svasrīyo me*, sc. Nārada's), 1093, 1095, 1097, 1101, (1103), 1105, 1106, 1115 (granted Sṛñjaya the son Suvarṇashṭhīvin). —§ 656 (Khaḍgotpattik.): XII, **166β**, 6142 (*Nārada-P°au*).

—§ 662*b* (Jāpakop.): XII, **200**δ, 7340 (*Nāradaḥ P°ç caiva*).—§ 694*b* (Jvarotpatti): XII, **284*a***, 10218 (*Nārada-P°au*, came to the sacrifice of Daksha).—§ 702 (Mokshadh.): XII, **293*a***, 10761 (*Nārada-P°au*).—§ 712 (Çukotpatti): XII, **324**, 12176 (do. with Çiva on Meru).—§ 734 (Ānuçāsanik.): XIII, **26*a***, 1764 (*Nāradaḥ P°ç caiva*, came to see Bhīshma).—§ 746 (do.): XIII, **83**ξ, 3887 (*Nāradaḥ P°ç caiva*, sung).—§ 751*b* (Çapathavidhi): XIII, **94*a***, †4550 (*Nārada-P°au*), (4580).—§ 768 (Ānuçāsanik.): XIII, **139*a***, 6297 (*Nārada-P°au*, came to Kṛshṇa).—§ 775 (do.): XIII, **166*a***, 7639 (*Nāradaḥ P°ç caiva*).—§ 787 (Āçramavāsap.): XV, **20**ββ, 538 (do.).—§ 789 (Putradarçanap.): XV, **29*a***, 774 (do.). Cf. next.

Parvata[2], a Gandharva (probably originally identical with Parvata[1]). § 269 (Vaiçravaṇasabhāv.): II, **10**, 406 (among the Gandharvas in the palace of Kubera).

Pārvata, adj. ("mountainous"). § 208 (Astradarçana): I, **135**, 5366 (sc. *astreṇa*, employed by Arjuna).

Parvataja ("born on the mountains") = Kulindaputra[2]: VIII, †4320.

Parvatapati ("lord of the mountains") = Bhagadatta (acc. to PCR.): VII, 1179.

Parvatarāja-kanyā ("daughter of the great mountain, i.e. Himavat") = Umā: I, 7008.

Parvatarājan ("mountain-king") = Mandara: I, 1119.

Parvatavāsin, pl. (°*āḥ*) ("living in mountains"), a people (= Pārvatīya, pl.?). § 515 (Karṇadigvijaya): III, **254**, 15255 (vanquished by Karṇa on his digvijaya).

Parvateçvara[1] ("lord of the mountains") = Bṛhanta[2]: II, 1018.—Do.[2] = Bhagadatta: VII, 1266.

Pārvateya ("belonging to the mountaineers"), a king. § 130 (Aṃçāvat.): I, **67**, 2665 (incarnation of the Asura Kratha (B. Kapaṭha)).

Pārvatī = Umā, q.v.

***Pārvatīya**[1], pl. (°*āḥ*) ("Mountaineers"), a people. § 295 (Dyūtap.): II, **52**, 1863 (brought tribute to Yudhishṭhira).—§ 556 (Sañjayayānap.): V, **30**, †890 (in the army of Duryodhana).—§ 574 (Jambūkh.): VI, **9**μ, 365.—§ 589 (Droṇābhishekap.): VII, **11**ν, 397 (had formerly been vanquished by Kṛshṇa).—§ 591 (Saṃçaptakavadhap.): VII, **20**ζ, 802 (in the gāruḍavyūha of Droṇa).—§ 599 (Jayadrathavadhap.): VII, **121**εε, 4819 (attacked Sātyaki), 4835 (*çūrān*, adj.?), 4841.—§ 607 (Karṇap.): VIII, **45**ν, 2106 (are stupid).—§ 608 (do.): VIII, **46**γ, 2135 (followed Çakuni and Ulūka); **73**, 3653 (in the army of Duryodhana).—§ 609 (Çalyap.); IX, **1**γ, 27 (have been slain).

Pārvatīya**[2], adj. ("belonging to the Pārvatīyas"). § 287 (Rājasūyikap.): II, **34**, 1269 (*rājānaḥ*, came to the rājasūya of Yudhishṭhira).—§ 292 (do.): II, **45*a, 1609.—§ 522 (Draupadīharaṇap.): III, **271**, 15723 (*mahārathān*, follow Jayadratha, are slain by Arjuna).—§ 554 (Sainyodyogap.): V, **4**γ, 82 (*nṛpāḥ*).—§ 573 (Ambopākhyānap.): V, **195**ε, 7608 (*nṛpāḥ*, in the army of Duryodhana).—§ 593 (Abhimanyuvadhap.): VII, **37**η, 1574 (sc. *hayān*). — § 599 (Jayadrathavadhap.): VII, **121**ηη, 4831 (sc. *hayavarān*), 4837 (*rājānaḥ*).—§ 604 (Karṇap.): VIII, **7**, †200 (sc. *hayāḥ*?, otherwise PCR.).

Pārvatīya[3] ("king of the Mountaineers"), a prince. § 130 (Aṃçāvat.): I, **67**, 2692 (incarnation of the Asura Kukshi).

Pārvatīya[4] = Çakuni: II, †2120; III, †1357 (*C°*); V, †895 (*Ç°*).

Pārvatīya[5] = Janamejaya[9]: VIII, 169 (*J°*).

Paryavasthita = Vishṇu (1000 names).

Paryaya = Çiva (1000 names[2]).

Pāshāṇatīrtha, name of a vedi. § 377 (Dhaumyatīrthak.): III, **88**, 8338 (the first of Jamadagni's two vedis in Çūrpāraka).

Paṭaccara, pl. (°*āḥ*), a people. § 273 (Rājasūyārambhap.): II, **14**, 590 (among the peoples who fled from fear of Jarāsandha). — § 281 (Sahadeva): II, **31**, 1108 (in the south, vanquished by Sahadeva).—§ 549 (Pāṇḍavapraveçap.): IV, **1*a***, 11.—§ 578 (Bhīshmavadhap.): VI, **50**π, 2081 (in the army of Yudhishṭhira).

Paṭaccarahantṛ, name of a prince. § 592 (Saṃçaptakavadhap.): VII, **23**ο, 1010 (proceeded against Droṇa); **25**, 1098 (fought with Lakshmaṇa). Cf. next.

Paṭaccaranihantṛ, name of a prince. § 232 (Svayaṃvarap.): I, **186**, 6996 (present at the svayaṃvara of Draupadī). Cf. the prec.

Patagaçreshṭha ("Lord of birds") = Garuḍa: I, 1492; VIII, 1803.

Patagapati (do.) = Garuḍa: I, †1545.

Patagarāja (do.) = Garuḍa: VII, 4953.

Patageçvara (do.) = Garuḍa: I, 1093, 1249, 1313, 1407 (*G°*); VI, 5794; XIII, 7104 (only B.).

Patagendra (do.) = Garuḍa: I, 1474, 1486; V, 2939, 3884.

Patagottama (do.) = Garuḍa: I, 1316; VI, 291.

Patākin, a Kuru warrior. § 600 (Ghaṭotkacavadhap.): VII, **156**κ, 6851.

Pātāla, a region under the earth, the abode of the Asuras in the world of the Nāgas. § 28 (Amṛtamanthana): I, **18**, 1132 (°*talavāsini*, sc. *bhutāni*).—§ 30*b* (Samudra): I, **21**, 1211 (°*jvalanāvāsaṃ*, sc. the ocean), 1217 (°*talam avyayaṃ*).—§ 31*b* (Samudradarçana): I, **22**, 1231 (°*jvalanāvāsaṃ*, sc. the ocean), †1234 (°*jvalanaçikhāvidīpitāṅgaṃ*, sc. the ocean).—§ 246 (Sundopasundop.): I, **212**, 7731 (the Daityas fled to *P.*).—§ 339 (Indralokābh.): III, **47**, 1895 (°*vāsino raudrā Danoḥ putrāḥ*).—§ 386 (Agastyop.): III, **105**, 8816 (°*talam āsthitāḥ*, sc. the Kāleyas).—§ 422 *bis* (Varāhāvatāra): III, **142**, 10927 (*nashṭā vasumatī kṛtsnā P°e caiva majjitā*).—§ 513 (Ghoshayātrāp.): III, **251**, 15145 (°*vāsino raudrāḥ*, sc. *Daiteya-Dānavāḥ*). — § 522 (Draupadīharaṇap.): III, **268**, †15642 (?°*mukhe patantaṃ*; "pit," PCR.); **271**, 15757 (°*talasaṃstho 'pi yadi Çakro 'sya sārathiḥ*).—§ 524*c* (Vishṇu): III, **272**, 15810 (*nāgalokāṃç ca P°talacāriṇaḥ*).—§ 564 (Mātaliyop.): V, **99**, 3547 (*puraṃ . . . Daitya-Dānavasevitaṃ*, in the world of the Nāgas), 3552 (etymology of the name), 3555 (°*talam āçritāḥ*); **100**, 3568 (°*talam āçritam*, sc. Hiraṇyapura).—§ 565 (Gālavacar.): V, **108**, 3772 (°*m āçritya Varuṇaḥ*, in the west).—§ 576 (Bhagavadgītāp.): VI, **23**, 806 (*nityaṃ vasasi P°e*, sc. Durgā).—§ 578 (Bhīshmavadhap.): VI, **49**, 1992 (only C.).—§ 589 (Droṇābhishekap.): VII, **1**, 31 (°*a iva majjantaḥ*); **11**, 401 (°*talavāsinaṃ Pañcajanyaṃ*).—§ 599 (Jayadrathavadhap.): VII, **103**, 3887 (*vasundharā . . . sa-P°ā*); **114**, 4454 (*Droṇagambhīrapātālaṃ*, sc. the army of Duryodhana, compared to an ocean).—§ 608 (Karṇap.): VIII, **47**, 2222 (°*talasannibhe*, sc. *sainyamahāvarte*); **60**, 3000 (?*majjantam iva P°e*; "a bottomless ocean," PCR.); **66**, 3315 (°*m iva gambhīram*, sc. Karṇa); **73**, 3689 (*urvīṃ . . . sākāçajala-P°āṃ*); **90**, †4633 (°*tale çayāno nāgo 'çvasenaḥ*).—§ 610 (Çalyap.): IX, **7**, 360 (*Bhīshma-Droṇārṇavaṃ . . . Karṇa-P° sambhavaṃ*).—§ 654*b* (Pavanaçalmalīsaṃv.): XII, **154**, 5815 (*çoshayaty eva P°ṃ vahad gandhavahaḥ çuciḥ*, sc. Vāyu (the wind)).—§ 659 (Mokshadh.): XII, **177**, 6624 (°*a iva dushpūraḥ*, sc. desire).—§ 677 (do.): XII, **251**, 9052 (*nadīṃ . . . saṃsārasāgaragamāṃ yoni-P°dustarāṃ* [sic !]).—§ 717*b* (Nārāyaṇīya): XII, **340,** 12947 (*Baliñ caiva karishyāmi P°vāsinaṃ,* says Nārāyaṇa); **348***θθ*, 13499 (*ākāça-P°e,* the ears of Nārāyaṇa); **350,** 13671 (*°sthena bhoginā,* i.e. Çesha).—§ 723 (Ānuçāsanik.): XIII, **6***a*, 329 (*Baliḥ . . . Vishnoḥ purushakārena . . . P°sadanaḥ kṛtaḥ*).—§ 742 (do.): XIII, **38,** 2230.

Paṭalāvatī, a river. § 574 (Jambūkh.): VI, **9**λ, 330.

Patana, a Rākshasa. § 537 (Rāma-Rāvaṇayuddha): III, **285***a*, 16365 (followed Rāvaṇa).

Pataṅga[1] = Sūrya (the Sun) (Nīl.): I, 2573 (*°sahacārinaḥ,* sc. the sons of Kratu, q.v.).

Pataṅga[2] = Kṛshṇa: XII, 1510.

Pataṅgarāja ("king of birds") = Garuḍa: V, 3933.

Patatrivara = Garuḍa: VII, 632 (*°-bhoginām*).

Paṭavāsaka, a serpent. § 67 (Sarpasattra): I, **57,** 2159 (*Samṛddha-P°au,* of Dhṛtarāshṭra's race; C. has by error *Paṭha°*).

Paṭhavāsaka, v. Paṭavāsaka.

Pathikṛt, name of a fire. § 493 (Āṅgirasa): III, **221,** 14206.

Paṭhyase çrutibhiç caiva vedopanishadāṃ gaṇaiḥ = Çiva (1000 names[1]).

Pati = Çiva: XIII, 1233 (1000 names[2]); XIV, 204.

Patitri, a Kuru warrior. § 608 (Karṇap.): VIII, **48***o*, 2263 (brother of Ulūka, PCR.).

Pativratānāṃ lokā(ḥ) ("the worlds of the faithful wives"): IX, 2896.

[Pativratāmāhātmyaparvan] ("the section about the greatness of the faithful wife") (cf. Pativratāyā māhātmyaṃ Sāvitryāḥ). § 545: Asked by *Yudhishṭhira, Mārkaṇḍeya* related, on account of *Kṛshṇā*: The *Madra* king *Açvapati,* the husband of *Mālavī,* was old and childless. After eighteen years of vows and offerings to *Sāvitrī, Sāvitrī* granted him a boon; he asked for many sons, but was promised a daughter. She was called *Sāvitrī.* As nobody asked her in marriage, she was sent to look for a husband herself (III, **293**). She chose *Satyavat,* the son of the *Çālva* king *Dyumatsena* (the husband of *Çaibyā*), who had been blinded and deprived of his kingdom and lived as an ascetic in the forest. *Satyavat* equalled *Rantideva Sāṅkṛti, Çibi Auçīnara, Yayāti,* etc., but *Nārada* said: "Within a year of this day he will die"; then *Nārada* went to heaven (III, **294**). After her marriage *Sāvitrī* dressed in bark garments, etc. (III, **295**). She counted the days, and having ascertained that her husband would die on the fourth day following, she observed a *trirātra* vow; on the fourth day all the ascetics uttered benedictions that she should never suffer widowhood; she would not eat before the sun set. She followed *Satyavat* as he, taking his axe, set out for the woods (III, **296**). He fell ill and slept with his head on her lap. *Yama* himself—and not his emissary—came with a noose in his hand and pulled out of the body of *Satyavat* a person of the size of a thumb, bound it in the noose and proceeded in a southern direction. *Sāvitrī* followed him and was granted five boons: (1) that her father-in-law should attain his eyesight and be strong; (2) that her father-in-law should regain his kingdom and never fall off from his duties; (3) that her father should have 100 sons; (4) that she and *Satyavat* should have 100 sons "begotten from both of us"; (5) that *Satyavat* should be restored to life and live 400 years. *Yama* untied the noose; she went back to the corpse and placed his head on her lap. *Satyavat* regained his consciousness. He was anxious about his parents, and they returned to the hermitage (III, **297**). Meanwhile *Dyumatsena* had regained his sight, but was anxious at not finding *Satyavat.* He was comforted by the brahmans *Suvarcas, Gautama, Bharadvāja, Dālbhya, Āpastamba,* and *Dhaumya.* A little while afterwards *Satyavat* and *Sāvitrī* reached the hermitage. *Sāvitrī* narrated everything that had happened and was praised by the ṛshis (III, **298**). Meanwhile the enemy of *Dyumatsena* had been slain by his minister, and *Dyumatsena* then again became king of the *Çālvas.* *Sāvitrī* after a long time gave birth to 100 sons, and her father also got 100 sons by *Mālavī.* "So also *Kṛshṇā* will rescue ye all." *Yudhishṭhira* and his brothers continued to live in the *Kāmyaka* forest (III, **299**).

Pativratāyā ākhyāna(ṃ) ("the story of the faithful wife"). § 11 (Parvasaṅgr.): I, **2,** 469 (i.e. Pativratopākhyāna).

Pativratāyā māhātmya(ṃ) Sāvitryāḥ ("the greatness of the faithful wife Sāvitrī"). § 10 (Parvasaṅgr.): I, **2,** 326 (i.e. Pativratāmāhātmyaparvan).

[Pativratopākhyāna] ("the story of the faithful wife") and **[Brāhmaṇavyādhasaṃvāda]** ("a conversation between a brahman and a hunter") (cf. Pativratāyā ākhyānaṃ). § 479 (Mārkaṇḍ.): Questioned by *Yudhishṭhira* about the virtue of women, *Mārkaṇḍeya,* saying that the work of a mother is more difficult than that of a father, and that for women neither sacrifices nor *çrāddhas* nor fasts are of any efficacy, but that they can win heaven only by serving their husbands (III, **205**), related: When the *brahman Kauçika,* who had studied the Vedas and the Upanishads, was reciting the Vedas under a tree, a female crane befouled his body, and looked upon with anger by *Kauçika* fell to the ground. *Kauçika* regretted his angry deed. When he had entered a village in order to procure alms, in a certain house the wife first served her husband, who came home tired and hungry, with food, etc. (description), and then began to conciliate the angry *Kauçika,* who blamed her for exalting her husband above the *brahmans.* She said that she was no she-crane, that she knew that the ocean had been made brackish and undrinkable by the wrath of the *brahmans,* that the fire of their wrath had not to this day been extinguished in the forest of *Daṇḍaka,* but that she regarded her husband as her supreme god, and deserved forgiveness, that anger is a foe to men within themselves, and that the gods know him to be a *brahman* who has abandoned anger and passion, etc., and who, though himself injured, never returns the injury, etc., that virtue (*dharma*) is difficult to understand, but must be based on truth; the ancients have declared that virtue depends on *çruti,* but it is variously defined (*bahudhā dṛçyate*) and subtle to be understood (*sūkshma*); "thou art cognisant of virtue and studiest the Vedas; but I think, however, that thou dost not know what virtue really is; a fowler (*vyādha*) in *Mithilā* will discourse to thee on virtue." *Kauçika* blessed her, and returned to his abode, reproaching himself (III, **206**).—§ 480: He set out for *Mithilā* (description), ruled over by *Janaka,* and found out the fowler, who was seated in a butcher's yard, selling venison and buffalo meat to a large crowd of buyers; but he at once went to *Kauçika,* and proving that he knew why he had come, he led him to his abode, where he honoured him duly, and explained to him that, notwithstanding his cruel trade, which he had inherited from his sires and grandsires, and which belonged to his caste by birth, he led a virtuous life, serving his superiors and old people, speaking truth, never envying others, giving to the best of his power, etc. In the kingdom of *Janaka* there did not exist a single subject that did not follow the duties of his caste. He did not slay the boars and buffaloes himself, nor did he eat meat himself; he fasted during the day and ate in the night; "even though the behaviour of his order be bad, a person may yet be himself of good behaviour; so also a person may become virtuous, although he may by profession be a slayer of animals." It is the fault of the kings when the subjects decay, and monsters, dwarfs, etc., are produced, but *Janaka* ruled justly. If one repents a wrong done by him, he is delivered from his sin (v. 13751). If a man seeks redemption (*kalyāṇam abhipadyate*) after having committed a sin, he becomes purified of all his sins (v. 13756). It is temptation (*lobha*) that constitutes the basis of sin. Then he gave some advice as to what is virtuous conduct (v. 13794 foll.: "these three are said to constitute the perfect way (*padaṃ*) of the virtuous: a man must not do wrong to anybody, he must give alms, and must always be truthful"); (v. 13797 foll.: "freedom from malice, forbearance, peace of mind, contentment, pleasant speech, renunciation of desires and anger, virtuous conduct, and actions regulated according to the ordinances of the sacred texts, constitute the perfect way (*mārgaṃ*) of the virtuous") (III, **207**). The fowler and the animals slain by him are driven by their *karman* in a former life. In days of yore 2,000 animals and 2,000 cows used to be killed every day in the kitchen of king *Rantideva*; at the *cāturmāsya* animals are sacrificed; the *çruti* says, "The fires are fond of meat" (v. 13812), and at the sacrifices animals are killed by the regenerate, and these animals are purged of sin, and by *mantras* go to heaven. Regarding animal food this rule has been laid down by *munis*: Whoever partakes of animal food after having first offered it duly and respectfully (*yathāvidhi yathāçrāddhaṃ*) to the gods and the *Pitṛs*, is not polluted by the act. The *çruti* says, "Such a man is not one who partakes of animal food," and a *brahman* who has intercourse with his wife during her season is a *brahmacārin*. King *Saudāsa*, under the influence of a curse, ate human flesh. Agriculture is considered to be praiseworthy, though the plough destroys many creatures. Seeds of rice, etc., are all living creatures. As to hunting and the cutting of trees and herbs, many creatures live in trees and fruits and water. The earth and the air are all swarming with living organisms, which are unconsciously destroyed by men from mere ignorance (III, **208**). When life is at stake and in the matter of marriage, it is justified to tell an untruth. Whichever conduces most to the good of all creatures is considered to be truth (*satyaṃ*) (v. 13845; cf. v. 13990). The fowler discoursed upon the influence of *karman* upon metempsychosis and salvation (*moksha*; *Brahmaṇaḥ padaṃ*, v. 13895) (III, **209**).—§ 481: Questioned by *Kauçika* about the senses, the fowler discoursed about the sinful (in thought, word, and action (v. 13906); the evolution of sin is this: First *manas* is bent on *vijñāna*; thence successively originate *kāma, rosha, karman, rāga, dvesha, lobha, moha, vyāja, adharma, pāpa*). The virtuous man discerns these evils by means of his spiritual insight (v. 13908).—§ 482: Then he shortly enumerated the elements of the *brāhmī vidyā* (the universe, consisting of the five great elements, space, wind, fire, water, and earth, is *Bráhman* [neuter]; their qualities: sound, touch, form, flavour, and taste; *manas, buddhi, ahaṅkāra*; the five senses, *ātman, rajas, sattva, tamas*; the last seventeen are "*rāçir avyaktasañjñakaḥ*", in all (with the objects of senses and the manifest and the unmanifest) twenty-four (*caturviṃçaka ity esha vyaktāvyaktamayo guṇaḥ*) [read *gaṇah*, cf. Hopkins, Great Epic, p. 34] (III, **210**).—§ 483: A somewhat more detailed explanation of the five elements and their qualities. The terms *vyakta* and *avyakta* (v. 13931). Salvation, etc., are dependent on self-discipline (*tapas*), that is impossible without subduing the senses. The body is like a chariot, the coachman being the soul, and the horses the six senses (III, **211**).—§ 484: The three qualities *sattva, rajas*, and *tamas* (III, **212**).—§ 485: The five vital airs (*prāṇa, samāna, apāna, udāna, vyāna*), that are all seated (*pratishṭhitāḥ*, v. 13973) in the navel, and by whose collision the internal fire is generated that digests the food. The arteries (*nāḍyaḥ*), issuing from the heart in all directions, carry the essence of food (*annarasān*) acted upon by the ten *prāṇas*. The perception of the internal spirit, purification of the heart, destroys the good and evil effects of actions and leads to eternal beatitude. That state of peace and purification of heart (*prasādasya*, v. 13984) is likened to the state of a person who in a cheerful state of mind (*tṛptaḥ*) sleeps soundly (*sukhaṃ*), or to a lamp shining on a windless spot, well kindled. Community with *Bráhman* cannot be taught to us even by the *guru* (v. 13992) (III, **213**).—§ 486: Saying "Thou shalt see by what means I have attained to this blissful state", the fowler introduced *Kauçika* to his parents, whom he honoured together with his wife and children like gods (description; v. 14025: "I do what is agreeable to them, even though it be not strictly justifiable") (III, **214**).—The fowler said: "Thou hast wronged thy father and thy mother, for thou hast left home without their permission, for the purpose of learning the *Vedas*, and they have become blind from grief at thy loss. Thereby thy ascetic merit, etc., have become useless to thee. Do return home this very day." *Kauçika* acknowledged that the fowler had rescued him when he was on the point of falling into hell, and that he did not consider him to be a *çūdra*, as it was very difficult for a *çūdra* to learn the eternal religion (*dharmaḥ*); his being a *çūdra* must surely be due to any action in a former birth; this *Kauçika* wished to learn.—§ 487: The fowler told: "I was formerly a *brahman*, son of an eminent *brahman*, and versed in the *Vedas* and the *Vedāṅgas*, and friend of a king, who was accomplished in the *Dhanurveda*, and thence skilled in archery myself; one day, when I accompanied the king on a hunting expedition, I killed a *ṛshi*, whom I took for a deer, and was cursed by him to be born as a fowler in the *çūdra* caste (III, **215**); but I prevailed upon him to grant me that I should remain a pious man and honour my parents, and thereby attain great perfection (*siddhiṃ*), remember my past life, and again become a *brahman*. I took the *ṛshi* to the hermitage, and he did not die."—*Kauçika* saluted him respectfully, and having returned home he honoured his old parents (III, **216**).

Patrorṇa, pl. (°*āḥ*), a people. § 295 (Dyūtap.): II, **52**, 1874 (brought tribute to Yudhishṭhira).

Pattana, name of a city. § 515 (Karṇadigvijaya): III, **254**, 15246 (conquered by Karṇa on his digvijaya).

Pattanādhipati ("the king of Pattana"?). § 232 (Svayaṃvarap.): I, **186**, 6993 (a king present at the svayaṃvara of Draupadī).

Patti, pl. (°*ayaḥ*), a people. § 574 (Jambūkh.): VI, **9**$_{ɑ}$, 375 (only C., B. has *Paçubhiḥ*).

Paṭṭiçin = Çiva (1000 names[2]).

Paṭuça, a Rākshasa. § 537 (Rāma-Rāvaṇayuddha): III, **285**β, 16372 (fought with the monkey Panasa).

Paudanya, a city. § 225 (Vāsishṭha): I, **177**, 6791 (founded by Açmaka).

Paulastya[1] ("son of Pulastya") = Kubera: II, 417; III, †12364 (*Dhanadaṃ*); V, 7543.

Paulastya[2] (do.) = Rāvaṇa: III, 16331; V, 3790 (*Rākshasarājena*); VII, 2228.

Paulastya[3] (do.) = Vibhīshaṇa: II, 1177 (*V*°); III, 16598 (*V*°).

Paulastya[4], pl. (°*āḥ*) ("sons or descendants of Pulastya"). § 130 (Aṃçāvat.): I, **67**, 2724, 2726 (i.e. Rākshasas, reborn as the sons of Dhṛtarāshṭra).—§ 532 (Sītāsāntvana): III, **280**, 16154 (°*kulaghātinaḥ*, sc. Rāvaṇa).—§ 535 (Setubandhana): III, **283**, 16304 (°*pāṃsanaṃ*, sc. Rāvaṇa).—§ 600 (Ghaṭotkacavadhap.): VII, **156**, 6842 (°*air Yātudhānaiç ca*, a class of Rākshasas).

Paulastya[5], adj. ("belonging to Pulastya"?). § 592 (Saṃçaptakavadhap.): VII, **23**ρ, 1040 (*dhanuḥ*, held by Ghaṭotkaca).

Paulastyatanaya = Rāvaṇa: IX, 1752 (*R*°).

Pauloma[1], adj. ("relating to Pulomā or Puloman," sc. parvan) = Paulomaparvan. § 4 (Anukram.): I, **1**, 88 (°*āstīkamūlavān*, sc. *Bhāratadrumaḥ*).—§ 10 (Parvasaṅgr.): I, **2**, 304, 312.—§ 11 (do.): I, **2**, 360, 365.

Pauloma[2], a tīrtha. § 250 (Arjunavanavāsap.): I, **216**, 7841 (*tīrthaṃ*, one of the five Nārītīrthāni).

Pauloma[3], pl. (°*āḥ*), a tribe of Asuras. § 11 (Parvasaṅgr.): I, **2**, 460 (°*aiḥ Kālakeyaiç ca yatra yuddhaṃ Kirīṭinaḥ*, cf. § 445).—§ 445 (Nivātakavacayuddhap.): III, **173**, 12198 (°*aiḥ Kālakañjaiç ca*, in Hiraṇyapura), 12208 (the offspring of Pulomā, in Hiraṇyapura), 12209 (*mahāsuraiḥ*, destroyed by Arjuna).—§ 552 (Goharaṇap.): IV, **45**, 1431 (defeated by Arjuna, all. to § 445).—§ 552*d* (Arjuna): IV, **61**, 1976 (°*ān Kālakañjāṃç ca*, vanquished by Arjuna, all. to § 445).—§ 561*d* (Nara-Nārāyaṇau): V, **49**, 1930 (do., slain by Nara (i.e. Arjuna), all. to § 445).—§ 593 (Abhimanyuvadhap.): VII, **51**, 1998 (*Hiraṇyapuravāsinaḥ . . . P°āḥ saganā hatāḥ*, sc. by Arjuna, all. to § 445). Cf. next.

Pauloman, pl. = Pauloma, pl.: I, †162.

[Paulomaparvan], the fourth of the minor parvans. (Cf. Pauloma[1].) § 18: *Sauti's* conversation, in the forest of *Naimisha*, with the ṛshis at the twelve years' sacrifice of *Çaunaka* (I, **4**).—§ 19: *Çaunaka's* lineage from *Brahmán* through *Bhṛgu*, *Cyavana*, *Pramati*, *Ruru*, and *Çunaka* was related to him by *Sauti*.—§ 20: *Pulomā*.—§§ 21–3: *Pramadvarā*.—§§ 24–5: From this time *Ruru* made a vow to destroy the serpents, and whenever he saw a serpent he always killed it. *Sahasrapad* (q.v.) directed *Ruru* to ascertain the facts about the serpent sacrifice of *Janamejaya* and the deliverance of the serpents by *Āstīka*; *Ruru*, having come home, asked his father, who related all about the story (I, **9–12**).

Paulomī = Çacī, q.v. (add. X, 599).

Pauṇḍra[1] ("king of the Puṇḍras or Pauṇḍras"). § 233 (Svayaṃvarap.); I, **187**, †7020 (*Kaliṅga-Vangādhipa-Pāṇḍya-P°āḥ*, present at the svayaṃvara of Draupadī).—§ 554 (Sainyodyogap.): V, **4**γ, 84 (only C., B. has *Tuṇḍaḥ*).

Pauṇḍra[2], the conch-shell of Bhīmasena. § 576 (Bhagavadgītāp.): VI, **25**κ, 844 (*mahāçaṅkhaṃ*).—§ 578 (Bhīshmavadhap.): VI, **51**αα, 2115 (do.).

Pauṇḍra[3], pl. (°*āḥ*), a people. § 223 (Vāsishṭha): I, **175**, 6684 (arose from the froth of Vasishṭha's cow).—§ 342 (Indralokābhigamanap.): III, **51**, 1988 (*sa-P°oḍrān*, had been present at the rājasūya).—§ 574 (Jambūkh.): VI, **9**μ, 365 (only C.).—§ 578 (Bhīshmavadhap.): VI, **50**π, 2081 (only B., C. has *Huṇḍāḥ*), 2083 (only C., B. has *Puṇḍrāḥ*, in the army of Yudhishṭhira).—§ 589 (Droṇābhishekap.): VII, **4**β, 122 (had formerly been vanquished by Karṇa); **11**ν, 396 (had formerly been vanquished by Kṛshṇa).—§ 592 (Saṃçaptakavadhap.): VII, **20**ς, 802 (°-*Matsyakāḥ*, in the army of Duryodhana).—§ 607 (Karṇap.): VIII, **45**μ, 2084 (*Kāça-P°āḥ*).—§ 641 (Rājadh.): XII, **65**θ, 2430 (enumeration of barbarous and low peoples).—§ 739 (Ānuçāsanik.): XIII, **35**ε, 2158 (degraded to çūdras). Cf. Pauṇḍrika, pl., Puṇḍra, pl.

Pauṇḍraka (king of the Puṇḍras) = Vāsudeva[3]. I, 6992 (*V*°); II, 584 (*V*°), 1270 (*V*°). Cf. Pauṇḍra, Puṇḍrādhipa.

Pauṇḍramātsyaka, a king. § 130 (Aṃçāvat.): I, **67**, 2679 (incarnation of the Asura Balīna).

Pauṇḍrika, pl. (°*āḥ*), a people = Pauṇḍra, pl. § 295 (Dyūtap.): II, **52**, 1872 (brought tribute to Yudhishṭhira).

***Paurāṇa**, adj. ("mentioned in the Purāṇa, traditional, ancient"). I, 543 (*Tripurasya nipātanaṃ*), 3024 (*kavayaḥ*), 4685 (*kathāṃ*), 4721 (*dharmaṃ*), 8097 (do.), 8098 (*rājā*); IV, 2076 (*mahāstrāṇāṃ*); V, 3615 (*gāthā*), 3773 (*Vasishṭhasya*), 7087; VIII, 1952 (*prabhāvaḥ Pārthasya p°ḥ Keçavasya ca*); XII, 13525 (*rūpaṃ*, sc. Vishṇu's form with the horse-head); XIII, †7370 (*brahmaguhāṃ*); XV, 677 (*vṛttiṃ*).

Paurandara, adj. ("belonging to Purandara [i.e. Indra]"). § 178 (Pāṇḍu): I, **114**, 4477 (*gajaḥ*).—§ 234 (Svayaṃvarap.): I, **190**, 7105 (sc. *astre*).

Paurāṇika, adj. ("conversant with the Purāṇa"): I, 2 (*Ugraçravāḥ Sautiḥ*), ††851 (do.), ††852 (= do.), 2021 (pl.), 2029 (*sūtaḥ*), 2119 (do.), 7777 (*sūtāḥ*); VI, 483 (pl.); XII, 3202 (*sūtaṃ*).

Paurava[1], pl. (°*āḥ*) ("the descendants of Pūru," also name of a people). § 133 (Dushyanta): I, **68**, 2801 (°*āṇāṃ vaṃçakaro Dushyantaḥ*).—§ 135 (Çakuntalop.): I, **73**, 2968 (°*çreshṭha* = Dushyanta), 2987.—§ 156 (Pūruvaṃç.): I, **95**, 3763 (descended from Pūru).—§ 165 (Satyavatīlābhop.): I, **100**, 4008, 4009 (ruled by Çāntanu).—§ 183 (Pāṇḍu): I, **118**, 4578 (°*āṇāṃ . . . vaṃçe jātasya*, sc. Pāṇḍu).—§ 338 (Indralokābhigamanap.): III, **46**, 1856 (°*vaṃçasya jananī*, sc. Urvaçī).—§ 580 (Bhīshmavadhap.): VI, **56**η, 2415 (followed Dhṛshṭaketu).—§ 599 (Jayadrathavadhap.): VII, **111**ι, 4266 (*Saindhava-P°āḥ*, attacked Arjuna). § 603 (Nārāyaṇāstramokshap.): VII, **201**, 9392 (only C.). Cf. Pauravaka, pl.

Paurava[2] ("descendant of Pūru" or "king of the Pauravas") = Bṛhatkshattra[2]: VII, 9330 (*B*°), 9334, †9337, †9341, 9343, 9400 (*B.*). Cf. Paurava[7].

Paurava[3] (do.) = Çāntanu: I, 4007.

Paurava[4] (do.) = Dushyanta: I, 3047, 3105, 3107 (*rājā*).

Paurava[5] (do.) = Janamejaya[1]: IX, 2151.

Paurava[6] (do.) = Saṃvaraṇa: I, 3735.

Paurava[7] (do.), one or more kings at the time of Yudhishṭhira. § 130 (Aṃçāvat.): I, **67**, 2664 (incarnation of the Asura Çarabha).—§ 232 (Svayaṃvarap.): I, **186**, 6995 (*Dṛḍhadhanvā*?).—§ 279 (Arjuna): II, **27**, 1023, 1024 (king of the Pārvatīyas?), 1025 (defeated by Arjuna).—§ 554 (Sainyodyogap.): V, **4**γ, 77.—§ 572 (Rathātirathasaṅkhyānap.): V, **167**, 5788 (a mahāratha in the army of Duryodhana).—§ 576 (Bhagavadgītāp.): VI, **17**, 662 (°-*Kāliṅgāḥ*, in the army of Duryodhana).—§ 581 (Bhīshmavadhap.): VI, **61**ε, 2699 (*Damanañ cāpi dāyādaṃ P°sya*).—§ 587 (do.): VI,

115o, 5361 (Dhṛshṭaketu fought *P.*); **116,** 5388, 5390, 5391, 5397, 5398, 5400 (do.).—§ 590 (Droṇābhishekap.): VII, **14,** 544, 546, 547, 548, 553, 556, 558 (defeated by Abhimanyu).—§ 593 (Abhimanyuvadhap.): VII, **37**θ, 1590 (attacked Abhimanyu).—§ 604 (Karṇap.): VIII, **5**ζ, 125 (had been slain by Arjuna in the great battle).—§ 609 (Çalyap.): IX, **2,** 90 (sc. *hataḥ, Jalasandhaḥ*?).—§ 611 (do.): IX, **24,** 1297 (sc. *hate, Jalasandhe*?). Cf. Paurava[2], Pauraveçvara.

Paurava[3], an ancient king of the Aṅgas (= Bṛhadratha[7]). § 595 (Shoḍacarāj.): King *P.* (*Aṅga*, v. 2206) also had died; description of his horse-sacrifices and his gifts to brahmans versed in *çikshā* and *akshara*, whom he diverted by actors and dancers and singers; *gāthās* in praise of *P.* are sung by those who are acquainted with the history of the past (*Purāṇavidaḥ*) (VII, **57**): VII, **57,** 2196. Cf. Bṛhadratha[7], Aṅga[4].

Paurava[3], adj. ("belonging to Pūru [or to the Pauravas]"). § 144 (Yayāti): I, **75,** 3170 (*vayasā*), 3180 (*vaṃçaḥ*).—§ 188 (do.): I, **85,** 3500 (*vayasā*), 3534 (*vaṃçaḥ*).—§ 150 (Pūruvaṃç.): I, **94,** 3705 (*vaṃçam*).

Pauravadāyāda = Vidūrathasuta: XII, 1791 (*V°*).

Pauravaka, pl. (*°āḥ*), a people = Paurava, pl. § 578 (Bhīshmavadhap.): VI, **50**π, 2081 (in the army of Yudhishṭhira).

Pauravanandana[1] = Bharata: I, 3713.

Pauravanandana[2] = Çāntanu: I, 3935.

Pauravanandana[3] = Saṃvaraṇa: I, 6529.

Pauravanandana[4] = Vasu Uparicara: I, 2325 (*V°*).

Pauraveçvara ("the king of the Pauravas"). § 284 (Sahadeva): II, **31,** 1164 (in the south, vanquished by Sahadeva).

Paurika ("the king of Purikā"), a prince. § 641 (Rājadh.): XII, **111,** 4085.

Paurukutsa ("son of Purukutsa") = Trasadasyu: III, 8606 (*T°*).

Paurūravasa, adj. ("belonging to Purūravas"). § 607 (Karṇap.): VIII, **50,** 1866 (*vṛttam*).

***Paurusha**, adj. ("belonging to Purusha"). § 524*c* (Vishṇu): III, **272,** 15824 (*°ī tanuḥ*).—§ 717*b* (Nārāyaṇīya); XII, **348,** 13466 (*°īṃ tanuṃ*).

Pausha ("named after the nakshatra Pushya," name of a certain month). § 759 (Ānuçāsanik.): XIII, **106,** 5151 (*°māsam*, merit of eating only one meal during the month of *P.*); **109,** 5373 (merit of fasting on the twelfth day in the month of *P.*, worshipping Kṛshṇa as Nārāyaṇa).—§ 766 (do.): XIII, **126,** 6052 (*°-māsasya çukle*, merit of performing a çrāddha under the constellation of Rohiṇī in the light fortnight of the month of *P.*).

Paushṭī, wife of Pūru. § 150 (Pūruvaṃç.): I, **94,** 3495 (wife of Pūru and mother of Pravīra, etc.).

Paushya[1], a kshatriya. § 16 (Veda): I, **3,** ††746 (*P.* and Janamejaya appointed Veda as their *upādhyāya*).—§ 17 (Uttaṅka): I, **3,** ††759 (*rājānaṃ*), ††765, ††766, ††768, ††769, ††770, ††771, ††776, ††779, ††780, ††781, ††785 (Uttaṅka got the ear-rings of the queen of *P.* to the wife of his preceptor).

Paushya[2] (adj. "relating to Paushya", sc. parvan) = Paushyaparvan. § 10 (Parvasaṅgr.): I, **2,** 304, 312 (C. has by error *Paushpaṃ*).—§ 11 (do.): I, **2,** 360, 364 (*parvaṇi*).

Paushya[3], adj. ("relating to the nakshatra Pushya"). § 240 (Vaivāhikap.): I, **198,** 7333 (*yogam*, Nīl. explains *paushyaṃ* as "*pushyaty anena*", "as Pushya is not fit for marriages", and mentions the various reading *paushpaṃ*).

[Paushyaparvan] ("the section treating of Paushya"), the third of the minor parvans of Mhbhr. (Cf. Paushya[2].) § 12: When *Janamejaya*, the son of *Parikshit*, with his brothers *Çrutasena, Ugrasena*, and *Bhīmasena* was attending his long sacrifice at *Kurukshetra*, his brothers beat an offspring of *Saramā*. *Saramā* then cursed them, saying that evil should come upon them unexpectedly. § 13: *Janamejaya* then returned to *Hāstinapura* and began to search for a purohita who might neutralize the curse; one day when hunting he obtained for this purpose *Somaçravas*, son of the *ṛshi Çrutaçravas* and a serpent; *Somaçravas* would grant to any brahman whatever might be demanded of him. *Janamejaya* then conquered *Takshaçilā*.—§ 14: About this time there was a *ṛshi* named *Āyoda Dhaumya*, with three disciples; *Upamanyu, Āruṇi Pāñcālya* (q.v.), and *Veda*.—§ 15: Upamanyu (q.v.).—§ 16: Veda (q.v.).—§ 17: Ut(t)aṅka (q.v.) (I, **3**).

Pāvaka[1] = Agni, q.v.

Pāvaka[2], pl. (*°āḥ*), a class of ṛshis (?). § 406 (Tīrthayātrāp.): III, **125,** 10413.

Pāvakāçani, v. Pākaçāsani.

Pāvakasuta ("the son of Pāvaka [i.e. Agni]") = Sudarçaṇa: XIII, 125.

Pāvakātmaja (do.) = Skanda: III, 14374, 14380, 14433; IX, 2721.

Pāvakātmajā ("the daughter of Pāvaka [i.e. Agni]") = Draupadī: IV, 1181.

Pāvaki[1] ("the son of Pāvaka [i.e. Agni]") = Skanda: III, 1576, 10552 (*Ujjānakaḥ . . . P°r yatra çāntavān*), 14378, 14442, 14541; V, 5292 (*devānām iva P°ḥ*); VII, 163 (do.), 6854 (*jahi . . . Asurān iva P°ḥ*), 6976 (*iva*), 7673 (*jahi . . . Asurān iva P°ḥ*); IX, 320 (*abhishicyasva . . . devānām iva P°ḥ*), 2709, 2711; XII, 12324; XIII, 4027, 4217 (*hiraṇyamūrtiḥ . . . Kumāraḥ*).

Pāvaki[2] (do.) = Sudarçana: XIII, 141, 148.

Pavana[1] = Vāyū (the Wind), q.v.

Pavana[2] = Çiva (1000 names[1]). — Do.[3] = Vishṇu (1000 names).

Pāvana[1], a tīrtha. § 368 (Tīrthayātrāp.): III, **83,** 7046.

Pāvana[2], a Viçvadeva. § 749 (Ānuçāsanik.): XIII, **91**γ, 4335 (enumeration).

Pāvana[3] = Vishṇu (1000 names).

[Pavana-çālmali-saṃvāda(ḥ)] ("the discourse between the Wind-god and the *çālmali*-tree"). § 654*b* (Āpaddh.): *Bhīshma* said: There was a lordly *çālmali*-tree on the *Himavat*. One day *Nārada* praised it, saying that *Pavana* must be its friend and protector, since he spared it, though he eradicates the tallest and strongest trees (XII, **154**). The *çālmali* said that the Wind was not its friend, but that it was stronger itself than the Wind. *Nārada* warned him, saying that the Wind was stronger than even *Indra*, etc. (*a*) (XII, **155**). Informed by *Nārada*, the Wind came and rebuked the *çālmali*-tree, saying that he had spared it because *Brahmán*, while creating the world, had for a time rested under it. The *çālmali* laughed and challenged the Wind to show his power, which the Wind threatened to do next day. When night came the *çālmali* reflected that all that it had said to *Nārada* was false, that it was in reality weaker than other trees, and inferior in might to the Wind; "but in intelligence no tree is my equal" (XII, **156**). The *çālmali* then caused all its branches to be cut off. The Wind smiled; the *çālmali* felt great shame, and, remembering the words of *Nārada*, repented greatly of his folly.

[Pavan-Ārjuna-saṃvāda] ("conversation between the

Wind and Arjuna Kārtavīrya"). § 772*b* (Ānuçāsanik.): *Bhīshma* said: The *Haihaya* king *Arjuna Kārtavīrya*, with 1,000 arms, became the lord of the whole of this world (i.e. the earth) [residing] in *Māhishmatī*; he gave large gifts to *Dattātreya*, who granted him four boons: that he should have 1,000 arms in battle, but only two at home; that he should subjugate the whole earth righteously, and sway her with vigilance; and that whenever he might happen to go wrong, the righteous should set him right. *A.* now regarded himself as having no equal. A celestial voice said that the brahman is superior to the *kshatriya*; *A.* maintained that the brahmans take refuge with the *kshatriyas*; what the virgin *Gāyatrī* had said from the sky was not true (*asatyaṃ*, so B. and Nīl.). "I shall bring the skin-clad brahmans under my subjection." At these words of *A.* the invisible goddess (*Gāyatrī*) became agitated (*vitrastā 'bhūn niçācarī*; cf. Nīl.). Then *Vāyu* (wind) warned *A.*, addressing him from the air. Asked by *A.* what kind of earthly creature the brahman is, if he resembles the wind, water, fire, sun, or sky (XIII, **153**), *Vāyu* praised the brahmans above all, citing *Kaçyapa* (*c*), *Aṅgiras* (*d*), *Gautama* (*e*), [*Kapila*] (*f*), *Aurva* (*g*), and *Dattātreya*; even *Agni* (*h*) and *Brahmán* (*i*) are brahmans; the large kingdom of the *Daṇḍakas* was destroyed by a brahman; the ocean, that was full of crystal water, cursed by the brahmans, became saline in taste. *Arjuna* remained silent (XIII, **154**). *Vāyu* repeated the story of *Kaçyapa* in detail, and asked *Arjuna* if he knew a *kshatriya* superior to *Kaçyapa*. *Arjuna* remained silent. Then *Vāyu* related the story of *Utathya* (*j*) (XIII, **155**). *Arjuna* remained silent. *Vāyu* then described the greatness of *Agastya* (*k*). *Arjuna* remained silent. *Vāyu* related a feat of *Vasishṭha's* (*l*) (XIII, **156**). *Arjuna* remained silent. *Vāyu* related a feat of *Atri's* (*m*). *Arjuna* remained silent. *Vāyu* related a feat of *Cyavana's* (*n*) (XIII, **157**). *Arjuna* remained silent. *Vāyu* related the history of the *Kapas* (*p*). *Arjuna* praised the brahmans, mentioning *Dattātreya*. *Vāyu* told him always to protect them; "a terrible danger threatens thee from the *Bhṛgus*; that will take place after a time" (XIII, **158**).

Pavanasya hrada(ḥ) ("the lake of the Wind-god"), a tīrtha. § 364 (Tīrthayātrāp.): III, **83**, 6075.

Pavanātmaja[1] = Bhīmasena, q.v. (add. II, 1100; III, 11479; VII, 1135, 5184).

Pavanātmaja[2] = Hanūmat, q.v.

Pavitra(ḥ) = Skanda: III, 14633.—Do.[2] = Mahāpurusha (Mahāpurushastava).

Pavitrā, a river. § 574 (Jambūkh.): VI, **9**λ, 329 (in Bhāratavarsha).

Pavitra(m)[1] = Çiva (1000 names [1-2]).—Do.[2] = Kṛshṇa: XII, 1513.—Do.[3] = Vishṇu (1000 names).

Pavitrapāṇi, a ṛshi. § 264 (Sabhākriyāp.): II, **4***a*, 110 (waited upon Yudhishṭhira).—§ 200 (Çakrasabhāv.); II, **7**, 293 (in the palace of Indra).

Payasya, son of Aṅgiras. § 747*b* (Suvarṇotpatti): XIII, **85**θ, 4147 (the third of Aṅgiras' eight sons).

Payodā, a mātṛ. § 615*u* (Skanda): IX, **46**θ, 2646.

Payonidhi = Çiva (1000 names[2]).

Payoshṇī, a river. § 347 (Nalopākhyānap.): III, **61**, 2318 (*samudragā*).—§ 370 (Tīrthayātrāp.): III, **85**, 8182 (*saritāṃ varāṃ*).—§ 377 (Dhaumyatīrthak.): III, **88**, 8329 (*ramya-tīrthā*, in the south), 8332, 8333, 8335 (king Nṛga performed a sacrifice in the tīrtha Vārāha on the *P.*, description).—§ 402*c* (Tīrthayātrāp.): The river *P.* was adorned (? *upacitāṃ*) by the Vidarbha king, and its waters were mixed with *soma* juice (see Nīl.); III, **120**, †10289 (visited by Yudhishṭhira, etc., on his *tīrthayātrā*), †10290.—§ 403*b* (do.): Here (i.e. on the river *P.*) king *Nṛga* gratified *Indra* by offering *soma*. Here the gods with *Indra* and the *Prajāpatis* performed sacrifices. Here king *Gaya Āmūrtarāyasa* satisfied *Indra* with *soma* in seven horse-sacrifices, where all the articles, which else are made of wood or earth, were of gold. Seven sets of these articles were prepared by him, and at the top of each sacrificial stake seven rings were fastened; the gods themselves with *Indra* erected the sacrificial stakes. *Indra* became delighted with *soma* and the brahmans with the *dakshiṇās*, which were innumerable as the sand-grains, the stars, or the raindrops. *Gaya* presented the brahmans with golden cows (otherwise PCR.) made by *Viçvakarman*, so numerous were his caityas that but little space was left on the earth. Thus *Gaya* attained to the worlds of *Indra* (*lokān . . . Aindrān*); he who bathes in the *P.* attains to the same: III, **121**, 10304.—§ 403 (do.): III, **121**, 10306 (visited by Yudhishṭhira, etc., on his *tīrthayātrā*).—§ 574 (Jambūkh.): VI, **9**λ, 324, 327.

Peçala = Vishṇu (1000 names).

Phalakaksha, a Yaksha. § 269 (Vaiçravaṇasabhāv.): II, **10**, 398 (among the Yakshas in the palace of Kubera).

Phalakīvana, a tīrtha. § 364 (Tīrthayātrāp.): III, **83**, 6056.

Phalgu, name of a tīrtha or of a river. § 370 (Tīrthayātrāp.): III, **84**, 8076 (at Gayā).—§ 377 (Dhaumyatīrthak.): III, **87**, 8308 (°*nāmā mahānadī*, do. (?), in the east). Cf. Phalgutīrtha.

Phālguna[1] = Arjuna, q.v.

Phālguna[2] ("named after the nakshatra Phalgunī," name of a certain month). § 213 (Jatugṛhap.): I, **145**, 5767 (*ashṭame 'hani Rohiṇyāṃ . . . P°sya*).—§ 759 (Ānuçāsanik.): XIII, **109**, 5375 (*māse*).

Phālgunātmaja ("the son of Phālguna [i.e. Arjuna]") = Abhimanyu: VII, 1710.

Phālguni[1] (do.) = Abhimanyu: VI, 4535, 4536, 4594, 4611, 5408, 5410; VII, 1568, 1794, 1815, 1828, 1870, 1881, 1885; XIV, 2008.

Phālguni[2] (do.) = Irāvat: VI, 1739.

Phalgunī, sg., dual, or pl., name of two nakshatras (*pūrvā* and *uttarā*) (v. Su. Si.). § 552 (Goharaṇap.): IV, **44**, 1383 (*uttarābhyāṃ P°ībhyāṃ nakshatrābhyām ahaṃ divā jāto Himavataḥ pṛshṭhe tena māṃ Phālgunaṃ viduḥ*). § 746 (Ānuçāsanik.): XIII, **64**, 3264 (°*pūrvasamaye . . . uttarā-vishaye*, merit of making gifts under the *P°s*).—§ 749 (do.): XIII, **89***a*, 4260 (°*īshu . . . uttarāshu*, merit of a çrāddha under this constellation).—§ 759 (do.): XIII, **110**, 5390 (sg., description of the *cāndravrata*).

Phalgutīrtha, name of a tīrtha. § 775 (Ānuçasanik.): XIII, **166***a*, 7655 (enumeration). Cf. Phalgu.

Phalodaka, a Yaksha. § 269 (Vaiçravaṇasabhāv.): II, **10**, 398 (among the Yakshas in the palace of Kubera).

Phaṇīndra ("serpent-king") = Ananta (Çesha): I, 1177.

***phenapa**, subst. and adj. ("foam-drinking"): II, 341 (*pitaraḥ?*); V, 3606 (*munisattamāḥ*), 3607 (pl. subst.); XII, 13560 (*ṛshayaḥ*), 13561 (pl. subst.); XIII, 647 (do.), 6488 (do.).

Phenapācārya = Mahāpurusha (Mahāpurushastava).

Picchala, a serpent. § 63 (Sarpasattra): I, **53**, 2147 (of Vāsuki's race).

Picchalā, a river. § 574 (Jambūkh.): VI, **9**λ, 336.

Piçâca, pl. (°*āḥ*), a class of beings ("goblins"), also name of a people. § 3 (Anukram.): I, **1**, 35 (issued from the primordial egg).—§ 28 (Amṛtamanthana): I, **19**, †1181 (*papau raṇe rudhiram atho P°vat*).—§ 221 (Caitrarathap.): I, **170**, 6496 (°*oraga-Dānavāḥ*).—§ 256*b* (Khāṇḍavadahanap.): I, **224**, 8171.—§ 257*d* (Sudarçana): I, **225**, 8198 (*Rakshaḥ-P°-Daityānām*).—§ 258 (Khāṇḍavadahanap.): I, **228**, 8293, 8295 (°*oraga-Rākshasān*).—§ 266 (Çakrasabhāv.): II, **7**, 295 (°*oraga-Rākshasān*, in the palace of Indra).—§ 269 (Vaiçravaṇasabhāv.): II, **10**, 415 (worship Kubera in his palace).—§ 270 (Brahmasabhāv.): II, **11**, 465 (worship Brahmán in his palace).—§ 333*c* (Brahmaçiras): III, **40**, 1646.—§ 333 (Kairātap.): III, **40**, †1662 (*Ditija-P°sūdanam . . . Gāṇḍīvam*).—§ 347 (Nalopākhyānap.): III, **64**, 2407 (°*oraga-Rākshasān*).—§ 370 (Tīrthayātrāp.): III, **85**, 8168 (*Bhūta-Yaksha-P°āç ca*, worship Çiva at Gokarṇa). — § 445 (Nivātakavacayuddhap.): III, **173**, 12246. — § 450 (Ājagarap.): III, **179**, 12400. — § 496 (Skandotpatti): III, **225**, 14310 (on the mountain Çveta). —§ 501 (Skandopākhyāna): III, **229**, 14441 (°*ānāṃ gaṇaiḥ*, surround Skanda).—§ 502 (Manushyagrahak.): III, **230**, 14506 (v. Paiçāca[2]).—§ 504 (Skandayuddha): III, **231**, 14530 (°*ānāṃ asaṅkhyeyā gaṇāḥ*.) — § 505 (do.): III, **231**, 14534 (°*ānāṃ gaṇaiḥ*, surround Skanda).—§ 524 (Jayadrathavimokshaṇap.): III, **272**, 15823 (°*oraga-mānushān*, created by the maharshis).—§ 526 (Rāmopākhyānap.): III, **275**, 15926 (*Rākshasāḥ purushādāç ca P°āç ca*, made Rāvaṇa their king).—§ 533 (Sītā-Rāvaṇas.): III, **281**, 16176 (*caturdaça P°ānāṃ kanyāḥ*, wives of Rāvaṇa).—§ 537 (Rāma-Rāvaṇayuddha): III, **285**, 16364 (*gaṇān . . . P°-kshudra-Rakshasām*), 16368 (°*ānām*, sc. *balaiḥ*, follow Rāvaṇa). —§ 576 (Bhagavadgītāp.): VI, **23**, 814 (*Yaksha-Rakshaḥ-P°ebhyaḥ*).—§ 578 (Bhīshmavadhap.): VI, **48**, 1975 (°*oraga-Rākshasāḥ*); **50**, 2083 (a people in the army of Yudhishṭhira).—§ 580 (do.): VI, **58**, 2467 (°*oraga-Rākshasāḥ*, praise Arjuna).—§ 581 (do.): VI, **65**ζ, 2961.—§ 584 (do.): VI, **86**[13], 3833 (*Rākshasāç ca P°āç cānye piçitāçanāḥ*.)— § 585 (do.): VI, **87**δ, 3854 (a people in the army of Duryodhana).—§ 589 (Droṇābhishekap.): VII, **11**ν, 398 (a people that had been vanquished by Kṛshṇa).—§ 593 (Abhimanyuvadhap.): VII, **50**, †1975 (°*saṅghāḥ*), †1979 (drink blood).—§ 596 (Pratijñāp.): VII, **77**, 2731; **79**, 2806 (°*oraga-Rākshasāḥ*).—§ 599 (Jayadrathavadhap.): VII, **146**, 6188 (*nṛtyat-preta-P°ādyair Bhūtākīrṇām*, sc. *nadīm*); **148**, †6443 (*niçācara-çva-vṛka-P°modanam mahītalam*, i.e. the battle-field).—§ 600 (Ghaṭotkacavadhap.): VII, **156**, †6921 (*Siddha-Gandharva-P°saṅghāḥ*, praised Açvatthāman); **158**, 7021 (°*oraga-Rākshasaiḥ*); **167**, 7499 (*ghoradarçanaiḥ*, yoked to the chariot of Alambusha); **175**, 7983 (*yuktam gajanibhair vāhaiḥ P°vadanaiḥ kharaiḥ*, sc. the chariot of Ghaṭotkaca), 7997 (assisted Ghaṭotkaca).—§ 603 (Nārāyaṇāstramokshap.): VII, **201**, 9410, 9442.—§ 603*b* (Nārāyaṇa): VII, **201**ζζ, †9465 (*Nāga-Rakshaḥ-P°ān*), 9473.—§ 605 (Karṇap.): VIII, **30**, 1248 (*Rakshaḥ-P°āç ca*, on the battle-field).—§ 607 (do.): VIII, **37**, †1742 (*Garuḍa-P°sayaksha-Rākshasān*, vanquished by Arjuna in the Khāṇḍava forest); **45**, 2104 (*Rakshaḥ-P°āç ca*, protect Himavat).—§ 608 (do.): VIII, **46**, 2135 (*iva*); **87**, 4409 (°*oraga-Rākshasāḥ*, present at the encounter between Karṇa and Arjuna), 4422 (sided with Karṇa). — § 615*f* (Çaṅkhatīrtha): IX, **37**, 2140 (in Çaṅkhatīrtha). — § 615*ee* (Ādityatīrtha): IX, **49**, 2849 (in Ādityatīrtha).—§ 615 (Gadāyuddhap.): IX, **58**, 3297 (°*ānāṃ . . . antarīkshe mahānadaḥ*).—§ 616 (Sauptikap.): X, **8**, 452 (*Rakshāṃsi P°āç ca . . . khādanto naramāṃsāni pibantaḥ çoṇitāni ca*).—§ 619 (Strīvilāpap.): XI, **16**, 438.— § 641 (Rājadh.): XII, **121**, 4409 (*Yaksha-Rakshaḥ-P°ānām*).—§ 659 (Mokshadh.): XII, **175**, 6555 (°*vat*).— § 660 (do.): XII, **188**β, 6932, 6947.—§ 675 (do.): XII, **230**, 8453.—§ 680*b* (Tulādhāra-Jājalisaṃv.): XII, **262**, 9283.—§ 683 (Mokshadh.); XII, **268**, 9581 (sg. = *piçācopahata*, Nīl.).—§ 690 (do.): XII, **278**, 9960 (°*vat*).— § 694*b* (Jvarotpatti): XII, **284**, 10222.—§ 695*b* (Dakshayajñavināça): XII, **285**, 10278 (°*oraga-Rākshasāḥ*), 10336 (°*oraga-Rākshasaiḥ*). — § 696*b* (Dakshaprokta-Çivasahasranāmastotra): XII, **285**, 10477.—§ 705 (Mokshadh.): XII, **303*a***, 11244 (*sa-Cāraṇa-P°e*, sc. *trailokye*).—§ 716 (Çukābhipatana): XII, **332**, 12570 (°*oraga-Rākshasān*).—§ 730 (Ānuçāsanik.): XIII, **14**, 591 (*Brahmādayaḥ Piçācāntāḥ . . . devāḥ*).—§ 730*g* (Upamanyu): XIII, **14**η, 732 (*Preta-P°yoḥ*). —§ 730 (Ānuçāsanik.): XIII, **14**ζζ, †1020; **17**, 1294; **18**, 1373 (*Suparṇa-Gandharva-P°-Dānavāḥ*).—§ 739 (do.): XIII, **33**, 2098.—§ 746 (do.): XIII, **82**, 3865 (°*oraga-Rākshasāḥ*).—§ 747 (do.): XIII, **84**, 3981.—§ 749 (do.): XIII, **87**, 4224 (°-*Kinnarāṇāṃ*); **90**, 4292 (*Yātudhānāḥ P°āç ca lumpanti tad dhaviḥ*), 4316 (°*dakshiṇā*).—§ 761 (do.): XIII, **116**ε, 5704.—§ 768*b* (Umā-Maheçvarasaṃv.): XIII, **140*a***, 6351 (on Himavat).—§ 770 (Ānuçāsanik.): XIII, **151**, 7148 (sg.).—§ 778*f* (Muñjavat): XIV, **8**, 184 (worship Çiva on Muñjavat).—§ 782*g* (Guruçishyasaṃv.): XIV, **42**, †1169; **44**, 1226 (°*oraga-Rakshasām . . . Īçvaraḥ prabhuḥ*); **51**, 1434 (°*āsura-Rākshasāḥ*).—§ 789 (Putradarçanap.): XV, **31**ζ, 848 (had been reborn as warriors of the great battle); **33**, 904.

Piçâca[2], name of a Yaksha. § 269 (Vaiçravaṇasabhāv.): II, **10**, 397 (among the Yakshas in the palace of Kubera).

Piçâcaka (= Piçāca), dual (°*au*) = Bahi and Hīka: VIII, 2064.

Piçâcî ("female Piçāca"). § 347 (Nalopākhyānap.): III, **65**, 2558 (Damayantī is supposed to be a *P.*).—§ 409 (Plakshāvataraṇagamana): III, **129**, 10520 (*atrānuvaṃçaṃ paṭhataḥ çṛṇu me Kurunandana | ulūkhalair ābharaṇaiḥ P°ī yad abhāshata*). — § 502 (Manushyagrahak.): III, **230**, 14811 (*Çīta-Pūtanā*).—§ 532 (Sītāsāntvana): III, **280**, 16139 (pl., in the palace of Rāvaṇa), 16165 (do.).

Piçaṅga, a serpent. § 67 (Sarpasattra): I, **57**, 2158 (of Dhṛtarāshṭra's race).

***piçitâça** ("flesh-eating"), pl. = Rākshasa, pl.: VII, 899, 3585; XIII, 6152.

piçitâçana (do.), sg. = Ghaṭotkaca: VI, 4100.

***piçitâçin** (do.), pl. = Rākshasa, pl.: III, 13435; VI, 3833.

Pinâka, the staff or bow of Çiva. § 581 (Bhīshmavadhap.): VI, **62**, 2776 (°*m iva Rudrasya*, sc. the mace of Bhīmasena): **63**, 2797 (do.).—§ 608 (Karṇap.): VIII, **90**, †4661 (*Harāmbupākhaṇḍalavittagoptṛbhiḥ P°pāçāçanisāyakottamaiḥ | surottamair apy avishahyam arditum*, sc. the diadem of Arjuna); **91**, †4790 (*añjalikam . . . P°-Nārāyaṇacakrasannibham*).— § 701*b* (Bhava - Bhārgavasamāgama): XII, **290**, 10676 (*ānatenātha çūlena pāṇinā 'mitatejasā P°m iti covāca çūlam Ugrāyudhaḥ* (i.e. Çiva) *prabhuḥ*).—§ 730*g* (Upamanyu): XIII, **14**π, 849 (*dhanuḥ P°m iti vikhyātam*).—§ 768*b* (Umā-Maheçvarasaṃv.): XIII, **140**, 6386; **141**, 6396.

Pinâkaçûlahasta = Kṛshṇa: XII, 1670.

Pinâkadhṛk, Pinâkagoptṛ, Pinâkapâṇi = Çiva, q.v.

Pinâkin[1], a Rudra. § 108 (Aṃçāvat.): I, **66**, 2566 (among the sons of Sthāṇu).—§ 191 (Arjuna): I, **123*a***, 4826 (present at the birth of Arjuna).—§ 665 (Mokshadh.): XII, **208**δ, 7586.—§ 770 (Ānuçāsanik.): XIII, **151**β, 7090.

Pinākin[2] = Çiva, q.v.

Piṇḍāra, a serpent. § 564 (Mātalīyop.): V, **103**γ, 3630 (enumeration). Cf. next.

Piṇḍāraka[1], a serpent. § 47 (Sarpanāmak.): I, **35**, 1556 (enumeration). — § 67 (Sarpasattra): I, **57**, 2158 (of Dhṛtarāshṭra's race).

Piṇḍāraka[2], a Vṛshṇi. § 232 (Svayaṃvarap.): I, **186**, 7000 (among the Vṛshṇis present at the svayaṃvara of Draupadī).

Piṇḍāraka[3], a tīrtha. § 358 (Tīrthayātrap.): III, **82**, 50071 (at Dvāravatī).—§ 377 (Dhaumyatīrthak.): III, **88**, 8346 (in the country of the Surāshṭras).—§ 733*y* (Ujjānaka): XIII, **25**, 1743.

Piṇḍasektṛ, a serpent. § 64 (Sarpasattra): I, **57**, 2149 (of Takshaka's race).

Piṅga = Çiva: X, 259.

Piṅgākshī, names of two mātṛs. § 615*u* (Skanda): IX, **46**θ, 2636, 2639.

Piṅgala[1], a serpent. § 47 (Sarpanāmak.): I, **35**, 1554 (enumeration).

Piṅgala[2], names of two brahmans. § 52 (Sarpasattra); I, **53**, 2046 (acted as adhvaryu at the snake-sacrifice of Janamejaya), 2047 (among the sadasyas at the sacrifice).

Piṅgala[3], a Yaksha king. § 506 (Skandayuddha): III, **231**, 14565 (*vyāpṛtas tu çmaçāne yo nityaṃ Rudrasya vai sakhā* (C. ç°) *P°o nama Yakshendraḥ*).

Piṅgala[4] = Çiva: XIII, 882.

Piṅgalā, a courtesan. § 659 (Mokshadh.): XII, **174**, 6513 (°*āyā gītā gāthāḥ*), 6514 (*veçyā*), (6516), 6520 (some gāthās sung by *P.* are quoted); **178**, 6646, 6647 (all. to ch. **174**).

Piṅgalaka, a Yaksha. § 269 (Vaiçravaṇasabhāv.): II, **10**, 399 (among the Yakshas in the palace of Kubera).

Piṅgatīrtha, a tīrtha. § 358 (Tīrthayātrāp.); III, **82**, 4099.

Piṅgāyā(ḥ) āçrama(ḥ), a tīrtha. § 733*y* (Ujjānaka): XIII, **25**, 1741 (B. °*āç cāçrame*, C. by error °*āñ cā*°).

Piṅgeça = Agni, q.v.

Piñjalā, a river. § 574 (Jambūkh.): VI, **9**λ, 335.

Piñjaraka, a serpent. § 47 (Sarpanāmak.): I, **35**, 1551 (enumeration).—§ 564 (Mātalīyop.): V, **103**γ, 3627 (do.).

Pippalāda, a ṛshi. § 637 (Rājadh.): XII, **47**η, 1596 (among the ṛshis who surrounded Bhīshma).

Pītakauçeyavāsas = Kṛshṇa. III, 13563 (= Vishṇu), 15851.

Pitāmaha[1] = Bhīshma, q.v.

Pitāmaha[2] = Brahmán, q.v. (add. IX, 2190, 2196, 2198, 2199, 2200 (his sacrifice at Pushkara), 2311, 2438, 2492, 2511).

Pitāmaha[3] = Çiva: III, 14567; XIII, 1190, 1256.

***pitāmaha**, pl. (°*āḥ*) = *pitṛ*, pl.: I, 1033 (i.e. Rāma Jāmadagnya's), 1034 (do.), 1041 (do.), 1049 (do.), 1066 (do.), 1007 (do.), 7787; V, 4493, 7311; XIII, 4387, 5958, 6100; XIV, 836 (i.e. Rāma Jāmadagnya's), 872 (do.), 2701.

Pitāmahasaras ("the lake of the Grandsire"), name of one or more tīrthas. § 370 (Tīrthayātrāp.): III, **84**, 8126 (near Çailarāja [i.e. Himavat]).—§ 377 (Dhaumyatīrthak.): III, **89**, 8369 (= Pushkara). Cf. next.

Pitāmahasya saras (do.), name of one or more tīrthas. § 370 (Tīrthayātrāp.): III, **84**, 8127 (thence comes the Kumāradhārā).—§ 615*q* (Sarasvatī): IX, [illegible] 2387 (thence comes the Sarasvatī; = Mānasa, PCR.). C[illegible] the prec.

Pitāmahasuta[1] ("the son of Pitāmaha [i.e. Brahmán]") = Atri: XIII, 3289 (*A*°).

Pitāmahasuta[2] (do.) = Sanatkumāra: IX, 2716 (*S*°); XII, 1355 (*Kumāraṃ*).

Pitā, mātā, pitāmaha(ḥ) = Sūrya (the Sun): III, 156.

Pītātman = Çiva (1000 names[2]).

Pītavāsas = Kṛshṇa, q.v.

Pītavāsinī = Durgā (Umā): VI, 800.

Pīṭha, an Asura. § 589 (Droṇābhishekap.): VII, **11**μ, 386 (had been slain by Kṛshṇa).—§ 717*b* (Nārāyaṇīya): XII, **340**, 12956 (*Dānavaṃ*, will be slain by Kṛshṇa, in a prophecy).

Piṭhara, an Asura. § 268 (Varuṇasabhāv.): II, **9**, 366 (in the palace of Varuṇa).

Piṭharaka, a serpent. § 47 (Sarpanāmak.): I, **35**, 1559 (enumeration). — § 67 (Sarpasattra): I, **57**, 2156 (of Dhṛtarāshṭra's race).—§ 564 (Mātalīyop.): V, **103**γ, 3630 (enumeration).

Pitṛ[1] = Çiva (1000 names[2]).—Do.[2] = Vishṇu (1000 names).

***Pitṛ**, pl. (°*araḥ*) ("the Manes"): I, 35, 106, 259, 274 (i.e. Rāma Jāmadagnya's), 275 (do.), 276 (do.), 277 (do.), 279 (do.), 860, 917, 918, 919, 920, 921, (1036) (i.e. Jaratkāru's), 1041 (do.), (1042) (do.), 1050 (do.), 1052 (do.), 1064 (do.), 1066 (do.), 1815 (do.), (1824) (do.), 1834 (do.), 1846 (do.), 1847 (do.), (1849) (do.), 1850 (do.), 1855 (do.), 1856 (do.), 1857 (do.), 1858 (do.), 1860 (do.), 1861 (do.), 2318, 2372 (i.e. Vasu Uparicara's), 2373 (do.), 3090, 3092, 3152, 3157, 3502, 3546, 3983, 4625, 4646, 4655, 4656, 4658, 4929 (°*medhaṃ*), 5113 (?), 5180, 6137, 6188, 6198, 6457, 6832 (i.e. Aurva's) (6833) (do.), 6842 (do.), 6848 (do.), 6853 (do.), 7676 (°*kāryaṃ*), 8314; II, 277 (°*gaṇaiḥ*), 341 (*Agnishvāttāḥ*, etc.), 449, 460, 461 (°*ṝṇāñ ca gaṇān viddhi sapta vai*, enumerated), 462, 463, 464, 1659, 2393; III, 129, †159, 173 (°*gaṇāḥ sapta ye divyā ye ca mānushāḥ*, worship the Sun), 1127, 1455, 1673, 1734, 4035, 4044, 4069, 4082, 4085, 4088, 4094, 5004, 5011, 5019, 5031, 5035, 5036, 5059, 5095, 5098 (i.e. Rāma Jāmadagnya's), 5099 (do.), 6000 (do.), 6001 (do.), 6002 (do.), 6004 (do.), 6005 (do.), 6007 (do.), 6008 (do.), 6009 (do.), 6016, 6017, 6019, 6025, 6039, 6040, 6048, 6064, 7013, 7031, 7046, 7086, 7090, 8007, 8027, 8044, 8047, 8061, 8062, 8078, 8131, 8150, 8183, 8197, 8201, 8206, 8213, 8308, 8512, 8553 (i.e. Agastya's) 8555 (do.), 8557 (do.), 8644 (do.), 8653, 8674, 8683 (i.e. Rāma Jāmadagnya's), (8683) (do.), 9903 (i.e. the sons of Sagara), 9916 (do.), 9921 (do.), 9939 (do.), 9944 (do.), 9946 (do.), 10107, †10216, †10225 (°*ṝṇāṃ*, sc. *āyatanaṃ*), †10229, 10246, 10407, 10415, †10658 (°*ṝṇām īçaḥ* . . *Yamaḥ*), †10666 (°*ṝṇāṃ tathā prāhur navayogaṃ visargaṃ*), 11435, 11465, 11639, 11824, 11827, 12924, 13130, 13242, 13285, 13363, 13416, 13417, 13806, 13815, 13911 (?), 14161 (?), 14163 (?), 14502 (v. Pitṛgraha), 10100, 16896 (*diçaṃ P°nishevitāṃ*, i.e. the south), 17343, 17390 (°*dharmeshu*); IV, 1707; V, 344, 348, †507, 519 (°*ṝṇāṃ* . . . *ādhipatyaṃ*, given to Yama), 540, 1005, 1045, 1291, 1635, †2511 (*diçaṃ P°ṝṇāṃ*, i.e. the south), 2619, 3780 (°*pakshaḥ*), 3781 (in the south), 3987 (i.e. Uçīnara's), 5451, 7248, (7299), (i.e. Rāma Jāmadagnya's), 7310 (do.), 7321 (do.); VI, 873, 1195, 1233 (°*ṝṇām Aryamā cāsmi*, says Kṛshṇa), 1536, 5687; VII, 37, 160 (°*ṝṇām iva Dharmendraḥ*), 258, 709 (°*jushṭāṃ diçaṃ*, i.e. the south), †1622, 2178, 2242, 2255, 2375, 2404, 2419 (when the *P.* milked the earth, Yama was their calf and Antaka their milker), †2607, 2683, 4167, †6921, 7005, 9170 (°*niveçanaṃ*); VIII, †819, 1454,

1594, 2057, 2102 (in the south), 3904 (°*sādanam*), 4420, 4426; IX, 268, 276, 2124, 2478, 2481 (*jagataḥ çreshṭhā devānām api devatāḥ*), 2508, 2531, 2555, 2911, 2941, 2964, 2984, 2987, 3047; X, 428 (°*nandanaḥ*, sc. Açvatthāman); XI, 88 (°*vanam*, i.e. the crematorium, PCR.), 119 (do.), 794 (°*medhāḥ*); XII, 174, 252, 298, 321 (°*vaṃçān*), 323 (do.), 328, 349, 364 (°*svadhāṃ*), 543, 544, 654, 689, 694, 703, 875, 888, 1009 (*tarpayāmāsa . . . P°ṝn svadhābhiḥ*), 1131, 1268, 1326, 1341, 1627, 1705 (i.e. Rāma Jāmadagnya's), 2375 (°*yajñaiḥ*), 2435 (°*yajñāḥ*), 2461 (°*yajñān*), 2768, 2769, 2777(?), 2855, 3220, 3360 (°*gaṇāḥ*), 3372, 3460, 3620, 4016, 4091 (°*vane*, i.e. the cemetery), 4409, 4470, 4495 (*Yamaṃ Vaivasvatañ cāpi P°ṝṇām akarot prabhuṃ*), 4663, 4866, 4882, 5417, 5544, 5608 (°*vaṃçaṃ*, sc. Janamejaya's), 5726 (°*ṝṇāṃ vaṃçakartāraṃ*), 5740 (°*piṇḍadaṃ*), 5901, 5974, 5977, 5999, 6039 (°*kārya*°), 6137 (°*gaṇāḥ*), 6382 (*Viçvedevāḥ sa-P°aḥ*), †6527, †6996, 7552, 7584 (*te ca pūrvaṃ surāç ceti vividhāḥ P°aḥ smṛtāḥ*), 7587 (do.), 7656, 8018, 8020, 8116, 8362, 8375, 8389, 8523, 8587, 9580, 9650 (*arcishmanto barhishadāḥ kravyādāḥ*), 9651, †9933, 10281, 10570, 10755, 10756, 10837, †11096, 11104, 11576 (°*ṝṇāṃ pitaraḥ*), 11577 (*devāḥ P°ṝṇāṃ sutāḥ*), 11708, 11786, †12073 (°*vishaya*°), 12275, 12653, 12669, 12677 (sg.), 12715, 12921 (°*gaṇān caturaḥ*), 12922 (°*kāryaṃ*), 12923, 12928, 12987, 13405, 13406 (°*yajñeshu*), 13409, 13416 (°*kāryavidhīn*), 13417, 13418, 13423 (*piṇḍasaṃjñitāḥ*), 13424, 13432, 13501 (*somapāḥ*); XIII, †340 (°*vana*°), 431, 459 (°*kāryaṃ*), 465 (°*kārye*), 487 (do.), 625, 916 (°*ṝṇāṃ Havyavāḍ asi*, sc. Çiva), 1020, 1603, 1606, 1643 (°*ijyāḥ*), 1711, 1807 (°*ṝṇāṃ ca yathā svadhā*), 1820 (*saptāvarān sapta parān*), 1823, 1832 (°*ṝṇāñ caiva candramāḥ*, sc. *yathā*), 1922, 2040, 2043, 2097, 2098, 2116, 2117, 2120, 2200, 2404, 2977, 2994, 2995 (°*vaṃçe*), 2997, 3061, 3130 (*ṝn . . . Pitṛlokasthān*), 3197, 3214, 3219, 3271, 3275, 3284, 3290, 3315 (°*pakshaḥ*), 3317, 3342, 3343, 3389 (*annaṃ . . . P°ṝṇāñ ca svadhā*), 3422, 3423, 3440 (°*sadmāni*), 3653, 3927 (°*kāryeshu*), 3952, 3954, 3958 (*mat*°, sc. Bhīshma's). 4223 (°*yajñaṃ*), 4224, 4225, 4226, 4229, 4240, 4242, 4244 (°*gaṇasya*), 4245, 4247, 4249, 4250 (*gāthāḥ . . . P°gītāḥ*), 4254, 4261, 4282, 4286, 4311, †4316, †4317, 4345 (°*yajñāḥ*), 4349 (*Viçve devāḥ . . . saha P°bhiḥ gocarāḥ*), 4352, 4353, (*saptakaḥ P°vaṃçaḥ*), 4368, 4372 (°*yajñaṃ*), 4374, 4375, 4376, 4378, (4379), 4382, 4386 (°*mateti*), 4388, 4390, 4391, 4393, 4410, 4412, 4545, 4655, 4659, 4666, 4667, 4701, 4735, 4781, 5365, 5482 (°*kāryaṃ*), 5543, 5594, 5645, 5653, 5701 (°*yajñeshu*), 5744 (°*yajñārthaṃ*), 5828, 5867, 5924, 5930, 5937, 5940, (5941), 5945, 5947, 5948, 5949, (5952), 5953 (°*kārya*°), 5954, 5957, 5959, 5960 (°*tvaṃ*), 5966, 5989, (5992), 5993, 5996, (5998), 5998, 5999, 6003, 6026, 6030, 6031, 6034, 6039, 6058, 6059, 6061, 6068, 6078, 6082, 6085, 6087, 6089, 6097, 6100, 6101, 6102, 6112, 6135, 6140, 6141, 6160, 6172, 6193, 6194, 6231, 6233, 6496, 6500, 6511, 6606 (°*daḥ*), 7074, 7098 (°*gaṇāḥ*), 7144, 7170, 7266 (°*ṝṇāṃ svadhā*), †7374, 7395, 7408, 7584 (*ashṭakāḥ P°daivatyāḥ*), 7642, 7699, 7774 (°*medham*); XIV, 22, (838) (i.e. Rāma Jāmadagnya's), (839) (do.), 910, †1169, 1176 (*Yamaḥ P°ṝṇām adhipaḥ*), 1443, 2735, 2760, 2776, 2895, 2896; XV, 14, 33, 424 (?), 680; XVI, 42, 199 (°*medhaṃ*); XVIII, 189, 199, 311.

Pitṛgraha, the Pitṛ-demon. § 502 (Manushyagrahak.): III, **230**, 14502 (*āsīnaç ca çayānaç ca yaḥ paçyati naraḥ pitṝn / unmādyati sa tu kshipraṃ sa jñeyaḥ P°ḥ*).

Pitṛloka ("the world of the Pitṛs"): I, 2292, 4925, 6832, 8337; II, 486; III, 6026, †10248, 11639; V, 1581; VII, 101, 512, 6697; IX, 445, 2881 (different from Yama's world); XI, 250, 593; XII, 11788; XIII, 3130, 3471, 3774, 6101, 6494; XIV, 2776.

Pitṛlokarshi, pl. (°*ayaḥ*) ("the Ṛshis of Pitṛloka"): V, 3783.

Pitṝṇām āçrama(ḥ), name of a tīrtha. § 733*q* (Marudgaṇa): XIII, **25**, 1725.

Pitṛpati, Pitṛrāja, Pitṛrājan = Yama, q.v.

Pitṛrūpa, a Rudra. § 770 (Ānuçāsanik.): XIII, **151β**, 7090 (enumeration).

Pitrya ("belonging to the Pitṛs"), adj.: I, 105 (*loke*), 4655 (*ṛṇāt*), 4660 (do.); III, †947 (°*āni*); XII, 5414 (*karma*), 8493 (*rātryahanī = māsaḥ*), 12651, 12671, 12682, 12688, 13399, 13400, 13413, 13542, 13560; XIII, 1572, 1579, 1583, 1615, 1620, 1675, 4271 (*karmaṇi*), 5060 (°*āni*), 5065, 5075 (°*āni*), 5081, 7144; XIV, 109 (*karma*); XVIII, 198 (*loke*).

Pitṛyāna ("the path leading to the Pitṛs"): III, 122 (°*pathe*); XII, 525, 12394; XIII, 1082 (°*ānāṃ candramā dvāram ucyate*).

plakshajāta, adj. ("rising from the fig-tree"), said of the river Sarasvatī: I, 6455 (*S*°).

Plakshā = Sarasvatī: III, 7085.

Plakshaprasravaṇa, name of a tīrtha. § 615 (Baladevatīrthayātrā); IX, **54**, 3045 (*prabhāvaṃ Sarasvatyāḥ*), 3071.

plaksharāja ("the great fig-tree"): IX, †2449 (in Somatīrtha).

Plakshāvataraṇa, a tīrtha. § 377 (Dhaumyatīrthak.): III, **90**, 8375 (on Yamunā).—§ 409*d* (Plakshāvataraṇag.): *P.* is situated on the *Yamunā*, and is the entrance to the region of heaven; there the *paramarshis* had performed sacrifices of the *Sārasvata* kind; their king *Bharata* let loose the horse for his horse-sacrifice; there *Marutta*, assisted by the *ṛshi Saṃvarta*, performed excellent sacrifices: III, **129**, 10525.

Plakshāvataraṇagamana(ṃ) ("going to Plakshāvataraṇa"). § 409 (Tīrthay.): *Lomaça* pointed out to *Yudhishṭhira* the spots where sacrifices had been performed by *Prajāpati* (*Ishṭākṛta*, lasting 1,000 years), *Ambarīsha Nābhāga* (*b*), the *sārvabhauma Yayāti Nāhusha* (*c*); the door of *Kurukshetra*; the *çamī*-tree, which had got only a single leaf; the lakes of *Paraçu-Rāma*; the hermitage of *Nārāyaṇa*; the path of *Ṛcīka's* son (when he roamed over the earth, practising the *yoga* rites) in the river *Raupyā*; further, that a *Piçāca* woman with pestles for her ornaments had said: "Having eaten curd in *Yugandhara*, and lived in *Acyutasthala*, and bathed in *Bhūtilaya*, thou shouldst live with thy sons," etc.; the tīrtha *Plakshāvataraṇa* (*d*). "Having taken his bath on this spot one becomes able to behold all the worlds and is purified from his evil deeds." The *Pāṇḍavas* having bathed, *Yudhishṭhira* beheld all the worlds and *Arjuna* (*Çvetavāhana*) (III, **129**).—§ 410: *Daksha*, when engaged in a sacrifice there, had blessed the spot, saying: "Those men that die on this spot shall win a place in heaven." *Lomaça* pointed out to *Yudhishṭhira* the *Sarasvatī*, the *Oghavatī*, *Vinaçana* (*b*), *Camasodbheda* (*c*), the tīrtha of *Sindhu* (*d*), *Prabhāsa* (*e*), *Vishṇupada*, *Vipāçā* (*f*), *Kāçmīramaṇḍala* (*g*), the gate of *Mānasa*, a gap (? see Nīl.) opened by *Rāma* in the midst "of this mountain" *Vātikakhaṇḍa* (B. °*sh*°), on the north of *Videha*, "yonder lake," where people propitiate *Çiva* with *sattras* in the month of *Caitra*, and become free from sins, *Ujjānaka*, the lake *Kuçavat* with a lotus in the kuça grass, and the hermitage of *Rukmiṇī*, *Bhṛgutuṅga*, *Vitastā*, the holy rivers *Jalā* and

Upajalā, where *Indra* and *Agni* tested king *Uçīnara* (v. *Çyenakapotīya*, § 411).

Plakshavatī, a river. § 775 (Ānuçāsanik.): XIII, **166a**, 7651 (= Sarasvatī ?).

Plavaṅga = Agni, q.v.

Potaka, a serpent. § 564 (Mātalīyop.): V, **103**γ, 3627 (enumeration).

Potimatsaka, a king. § 554 (Sainyodyogap.): V, **4**γ, 83 (only C., B. has *Yo*°). Cf. Pauṇḍramātsyaka.

Potṛ = Çiva: VII, 2878.

Prabāhu, a Kuru warrior. § 593 (Abhimanyuvadhap.): VII, **37**κ, 1610 (attacked Abhimanyu).

Prabālaka, v. Pravālaka.

Prabhā[1] ("splendour," personif.), a goddess. § 270 (Brahmasabhāv.): II, **11**, 457 (in the palace of Brahmán).

Prabhā[2], an Apsaras. § 731*b* (Ashṭāvakra-Diksaṃv.): XIII, **19**β, 1425 (in the abode of Kubera).

Prabhadraka, pl. (°*āḥ*) ("the beautiful ones"), mostly said of a division of the Pāñcālas. § 561 (Yānasandhip.): V, **48**, †1842 (*yuvānaḥ*); **57**ο, 2264 (*Pāñcālāç ca P°āḥ*, among the allies of Yudhishṭhira).—§ 570 (Sainyaniryāṇap.): V, **151**γ, 5153 (°*āç ca Pāñcālā Bhīmasenamukhāḥ*).—§ 576 (Bhagavadgītāp.): VI, **19**, 712 (followed Dhṛshṭadyumna).—§ 578 (Bhīshmavadhap.): VI, **49**μ, 2022.—§ 580 (do.): VI, **56**θ, 2416 (*Pāñcālāç ca P°āḥ*, followed Dhṛshṭadyumna and Çikhaṇḍin).—§ 592 (Saṃçaptakavadhap.): VII, **23**ο, 992 (*Kāmbojāḥ* ?, followed Dhṛshṭadyumna); 1026 (followed Bhīmasena).—§ 593 (Abhimanyuvadhap.): VII, **35**ζ, 1528.—§ 599 (Jayadrathavadhap.): VII, **95**, 3535 (followed Dhṛshṭadyumna).—§ 600 (Ghaṭotkacavadhap.): VII, **162**, 7258; **183**ιι, 8345 (followed Çikhaṇḍin).—§ 601 (Droṇavadhap.): VII, **184a**, 8367.—§ 603 (Nārāyaṇāstramokshap.): VII, **193**γ, 8919 (°*aiç ca Pāñcālaiḥ*).—§ 605 (Karṇap.): VIII, **12**ββ, 454; **22**ηη, 870 (κκ), 888; **30**ξξ, 1230.—§ 608 (do.): VIII, **48**, 2243 (°*ānāṃ pravarān adahat saptasaptatiṃ*, sc. Karṇa), (ξ), 2253; **49**χ, 2333; **56**ππ, 2756; **67**, †3370, †3376.—§ 609 (Çalyap.): IX, **1**γ, 31 (had been slain, cf. § 616).—§ 610 (do.): IX, **7**τ, 336.—§ 611 (do.): IX, **11**μ, 552 (many *P.* slain by Çalya); **15**, 759 (supported Çikhaṇḍin); **27**σσ, 1448.—§ 616 (Sauptikap.): X, **8**, 367, 381 (C. has by error *Sa*°), 384 (slain by Açvatthāman).

***Prabhākara**[1] = Sūrya (the Sun): III, 146.

Prabhākara[2], name of a varsha in Kuçadvīpa. § 575 (Bhūmip.): VI, **12**, 454.—Do.[3], see Prabhāraka.

Prabhañjana, a king. § 249 (Arjunavanavāsap.): I, **215**, 7830 (ancestor of king Citravāhana of Maṇipūra).—Do.[2] = Vāyu (the Wind), q.v.

Prabhañjanasuta ("the son of Prabhañjana [i.e. Vāyu (the Wind)]") = Bhīmasena: IV, 822.

Prabhañjanasutānuja ("younger brother of the son of the Wind") = Arjuna: VII, 6268.

Prabhāraka, a serpent. § 47 (Sarpanāmak.): I, **35**, 1500 (B. has *Prabhākara*).

Prabhāsa[1], one of the Vasus. § 116 (Vasu, pl.): I, **66**, 2582 (the eighth of the Vasus), 2584 (son of Prajāpati[2] and Prabhātā), 2591 (his wife was the sister of Bṛhaspati; their son was Viçvakarman).—§ 770 (Ānuçāsanik.): XIII, **151**δ, 7095 (the eighth of the Vasus).

Prabhāsa[2], a tīrtha. § 251 (Arjunavanavāsap.): I, **218**, 7886 (on the western ocean), 7887 (°*deçam*), 7888, 7892 (Arjuna met Kṛshṇa in *P.*).—§ 317*b* (Kṛshṇa Vāsudeva): III, **12**, 475 (there Kṛshṇa had performed austerities).—§ 358 (Tīrthayātrāp.): III, **82**, 5000 (*tīrtham uttamam*, there Hutāçana, i.e. Agni, dwells).—§ 377 (Dhaumyatīrthak.): III, **88**, 8346 (*tīrthaṃ*, in the country of the Surāshṭras on the ocean).—§ 378 (Tīrthayātrāp.): III, **93**, 8467 (°*ādīni tīrthāni*).—§ 400 (do.): III, **118**, †10228 (*tīrthaṃ*, the Pāṇḍavas came to *P.*).—§ 410*e* (Plakshāvataraṇag.): *P.* is the favoured spot of Indra and removes all sins: III, **130**, 10542 (*tīrthaṃ*).—§ 615 (Baladevatīrthayātrā): IX, **35**, 2009 (origin of the name), 2010 (etymology). — § 615 (Prabhāsotpattik.); IX, **35**, 2051 (*prathamaṃ tīrthaṃ Sarasvatyāḥ*), 2053, 2057, 2058, 2059 (origin of the name).—§ 652*b* (Indrota-Pārikshitīya): XII, **152**β, 5646 (°*ottaramānase*), (γ), 5662 (do.).—§ 717*b* (Nārāyaṇīya): XII, **343**, XI), ††13221, (*tīrthaṃ*, = Hiraṇyasaras, origin of the name, cf. § 615).—§ 733*c* (Pushkara): XIII, **25**, 1696.—§ 733*x* (Cāṇḍālikāçrama): XIII, **25**, 1740.—§ 751*b* (Çapathavidhi): XIII, **94**, 4549 (in the west).—§ 757*m* (Goloka): XIII, **102a**, 4887.—§ 766 (Ānuçāsanik.): XIII, **125**β, 5967.—§ 775 (do.): XIII, **166a**, 7645, 7649.—§ 785 (Anugītāp.): XIV, **83**, 2478 (near Dvāravatī).—§ 793 (Mausalap.): XVI, **3**, 66, 71 (there the Vṛshṇis met with destruction): **8**, 262. Cf. Hiraṇyasaras, Prabhāsatīrtha.

Prabhāsa[3], a warrior of Skanda. § 615*u* (Skanda): IX, **45**η, 2571.

Prabhāsa[4], pl. (°*āḥ*), a sort of ṛshis. § 656 (Khaḍgotpattik.): XII, **166**β, 6143.

Prabhāsatīrtha = Prabhāsa[2]: I, 399, 444; III, †10237.

Prabhāsotpattikathana(m) ("on the origin of Prabhāsa"). § 615 (Baladevat.): *Daksha* had twenty-seven daughters, married to *Soma*, connected with the several constellations serving to help men in calculating time, all beautiful; *Rohiṇī*, however, was the foremost in beauty. As *Soma* lived long with *Rohiṇī*, his other wives complained to *Daksha*, who got them reconciled. As *Soma*, however, still continued to live with *Rohiṇī* exclusively, his other wives once more approached *Daksha*, who now threatened to curse him. His threats were not, however, heeded, and when the wives complained a third time, *Daksha* cursed *Soma*, so that he was affected with phthisis. His sacrifices, etc., were in vain; the herbs became tasteless and failed to grow, etc. The gods prevailed upon *Daksha* to withdraw the curse on condition that *Soma* should behave equally towards all his wives, and bathe in the *tīrtha* (sc. *Prabhāsa*) where the *Sarasvatī* mingles with the ocean, and adore *Mahādeva* there, then he should during the one half of the month wane every day and during the other wax every day. Bathing there on the day of new moon, he was restored. *Daksha* told *Soma* not to disregard women and brahmans. *Prabhāsa* became the foremost of all *tīrthas*; *Soma* bathes there on every recurring day of the new moon and regains his form and beauty; thence comes its name *Prabhāsa*, because *Soma* there regained his effulgence (*prabhā*).

Prabhātā (wife of Prajāpati[2] and mother of the Vasus Pratyūsha and Prabhāsa). § 116 (Vasu, pl.): I, **66**, 2584.

Prabhava = Vishṇu (1000 names).

Prabhāva = Çiva (1000 names[2]).

Prabhavaḥ sarvabhūtānām = Brahmán: I, 2499.—Do.[2] = Çiva: XIV, 208.

Prabhāvatī[1], name of a female ascetic. § 534 (Hanūmatpratyāgamana): III, **282**, 16237 (*tāpasī*, performed austerities in the abode of the Asura Maya, received Hanūmat, etc.).

Prabhāvatī[2], the wife of Sūrya (the Sun). § 565 (Gālavac.): V, **117**, 3967 (*reme . . . P°yāṃ yathā Raviḥ*).

Prabhāvatī[3], a mātṛ. § 615*u* (Skanda): IX, **46**θ, 2621.

Prabhāvatī[4], a princess. § 743b (Vipulop.): XIII, **42**, 2351 (sister of Ruci and wife of the Aṅga king Citraratha).
Prabhāvātman = Çiva (1000 names[2]).
Prabhu[1], an ancient king. § 6 (Anukram.): I, **1a**, 229 (in Sañjaya's enumeration).
Prabhu[2], = Brahmán: XII, 6153, 6800 (*B°*), 6931, †6977 (*B°*); XIII, 7227 (*B°*).
Prabhu[3] = Çiva (1000 names[1–2]).
Prabhu[4] = Kubera (?): III, 15344 (*yathā Caitraratham prabhuḥ*, sc. *praviveça*).
Prabhu[5] = Skanda: III, 14634, 14641.
Prabhu[6] = Sūrya (the Sun): III, 190.
Prabhu[7] = Vishṇu (Kṛshṇa): I, 2429–31 (=*K.*); III, 13004 (=*K.*), 15826, 15832, 15838; VI, 302, 3027 (=*K.*); XII, 1625 (*Harim Nārāyaṇam*=*K.*); 11174 (*Nārāyaṇam*=*K.*), 13290 (*Nārāyaṇam*); XIII, 6953 (1000 names), 6981 (do.).
Prabhuḥ prabhūṇām = Skanda: III, 14644.
Prabhūta = Vishṇu (1000 names).
Pracaṇḍa = Skanda: III, 14641.
Pracetas[1], a ṛshi or Prajāpati. § 266 (Çakrasabhāv.): II, **7**, 297 (in the palace of Indra).—§ 270 (Brahmasabhāv.): II, **11**, 436 (in the palace of Brahmán).—§ 615u (Skanda): IX, **45**γ, 2512 (came to the investiture of Skanda).—§ 768b (Kṛshṇa Vāsudeva): XIII, **147**, 6830 (the eldest of Prācīnabarhis' ten sons and father of Daksha). Cf. Pracetas, pl. Prācetas[1–2].
Pracetas[2] = Çiva: VII, 9454.
Pracetas[3], pl. (*°asaḥ*). § 237 (Vaivāhikap.): I, **196**, 7266 (ten brothers of the same name, *P.* married a *vārkshī*; cf. Harivaṃça, v. 66 foll.).
Prācetas[1] (the father of the ten Pracetasaḥ). § 137 (Daksha Prācetasa): I, **75**, 3129 (*daça P°saḥ putrāḥ*, fathers of Daksha; is perhaps the form Prācetasaḥ, nom. pl. (so BR.) = Pracetas, pl. ?).
Prācetas[2], pl. (*°asaḥ*) = Pracetas, pl. § 137 (Daksha Prācetasa): I, **75**, 3129 (v. Prācetas[1]).—§ 665 (Mokshadh.): XII, **208**, 7572 (*daça*, fathers of Daksha).
Prācetasa[1] ("son of the ten Pracetasaḥ") = Daksha: I, 33 (*D°*), 3130 (*D°*), 3131 (*D°*); XII, 666 (*D°*), 695 (*D°*), 6136 (*D°*), 10272 (*D°*); XIII, 2484 (? *°sya vacanam*), 6830 (C. has by error *Pra°*).
Prācetasa[2] (do.) = Manu[3]: XII, 2089 (*M°*), 2093 (*M°*).
Prācinvat, an ancient king. § 156 (Pūruvaṃç.): I, **95**, ††3765 (son of Janamejaya and Anantā, conquered the east—*prācīm diçam*), ††3766 (husband of Açmakī and father of Saṃyāti).
Prācīnabarhis, a Prajāpati. § 665 (Mokshadh.): XII, **208**, 7572 (*Brahmayoniḥ*, born in the race of Atri, father of the ten Prācetases).—§ 768b (Kṛshṇa Vāsudeva): XIII, **147**, 6829 (son of Havirdhāman and father of ten sons, Pracetas, etc.).—§ 775 (Ānuçāsanik.): XIII, **166**η, 7684.
Prācīnagarbha[1] = Mahāpurusha (Mahāpurushastava).
Prācīnagarbha[2] = Apāntaratamas: XII, 13704.
Prācya, pl. (*°āḥ*) ("the Easterners"), a people. § 211 (Sambhavap.): I, **139**, 5538 (vanquished by Arjuna).—§ 556 (Sañjayayānap.): V, **30**, †890 (*°odīcyāḥ*, in the army of Duryodhana).—§ 561 (Yānasandhip.): V, **57**, 2245 (assigned to Bhīmasena as his matches in the battle).—§ 571 (Ulūkadūtāgamanap.): V, **160**γ, †5510 (in the army of Duryodhana); **161**, †5555 (do.).—§ 573 (Ambopākhyānap.); V, **195**ε, 7609 (*°odīcyāḥ*, do.).—§ 574 (Jambūkh.); VI, **9**ν, 366 (in the south (!)).—§ 576 (Bhagavadgītāp.): VI, **15**, 604 (protected Bhīshma).—§ 579 (Bhīshmavadhap.): VI, **52**γ, 2141 (*°-Sauvīra-Kekayaiḥ*, do.).—§ 580 (do.): VI, **59**μ, †2584 (attacked Arjuna), †2646 (defeated by Arjuna).—§ 586 (do.): VI, **106**τ, 4808 (protected Bhīshma).—§ 587 (do.): VI, **119**αα, 5648 (abandoned Bhīshma).—§ 589 (Droṇābhishekap.): VII, **7**ζ, 184.—§ 592 (Saṃçaptakavadhap.); VII, **20**γ, 798 (ζ), 802.—§ 599 (Jayadrathavadhap.): VII, **93**, 3369 (*nṛpāḥ*, attacked Arjuna).—§ 604 (Karṇap.): VIII, **5**ζ, 138 (*°odīcyāḥ*, had been slain by Arjuna).—§ 605 (do.): VIII, **22**ζζ, 863 (attacked the Pāñcālas).—§ 607 (do.): VIII, **45**, 2098 (*dāsāḥ*).—§ 608 (do.): VIII, **70**, †3511 (had been slain), †3524 (do.); **73**, 3650 (do.)—§ 609 (Çalyap.): IX, **1**γ, 28 (do.).—§ 613 (Gadāyuddhap.): IX, **33**η, 1913 (do.).—§ 641 (Rājadh.): XII, **101**ο, 3736 (skilled in fighting from the backs of elephants).
Praçamī, an Apsaras. § 731b (Ashṭāvakra-Diksaṃv.): XIII, **19**β, 1425 (in the palace of Kubera).
Praçānta = Çiva: XIV, 196.
Praçāntātman = Sūrya (the Sun): III, 157.—Do.[2] = Skanda: III, 14632.—Do.[3] = Çiva (1000 names[2]).
Praçastā, a river. § 400 (Tīrthayātrāp.): III, **118**, †10215 (visited by Yudhishṭhira on his tīrthayātrā).
Praçni, v. Pṛçni.
Pradakshiṇāvartaçikha = Agni: I, 2106.
Pradara, pl. (*°āḥ*), a people. § 295 (Dyūtap.): II, **52**, 1859 (brought tribute of gold to Yudhishṭhira).
Pradātṛ, a Viçvadeva. § 749 (Ānuçāsanik.): XIII, **91**γ, 4357 (enumeration).
Prādhā, daughter of Daksha and wife of Kaçyapa. § 87 (Aṃçāvat.): I, **65**, 2520 (enumeration of the daughters of Daksha, wives of Kaçyapa, C. has *Pra°*).—§ 102 (do.): I, **65**, 2554 (mother of eight Apsarases and ten Devagandharvas).—§ 103 (do.): I, **65**, 2557 (mother of thirteen Apsarases by the Devarshi, i.e. Kaçyapa (and of the four Gandharvasattamāḥ (§ 104)?)).
Pradhāna, a rājarshi. § 709b (Sulabhā-Janakasaṃv.): XII, **321**, 12034 (*rājarshiḥ*, ancestor of Sulabhā).
***pradhāna** = prakṛti: I, 2429 (i.e. Kṛshṇa); XII, 7484, 9105, 9115, 11635, 13035, 13466 (identified with Aniruddha), 13537, 13758; XIII, 1009, 1090; XIV, 522, 529, 1080, 1325, 1399, 1400.—Do.[2] = Mahāpurusha (Mahāpurushastava).
Pradhānadhṛk = Çiva (1000 names[2]).
Pradhānapurusha = Çiva: III, 15808; XIII, 939.
Pradhānapurusheçvara = Vishṇu (1000 names).
Prādheya, pl. (*°āḥ*), ("the sons of Prādhā"), a family of Devagandharvas. § 102 (Aṃçāvat.): I, **65**, 2556 (*Devagandharvāḥ*, i.e. Siddha, etc.).—§ 608 (Karṇap.): VIII, **87**χ′, 4424 (came to see the encounter between Karṇa and Arjuna).
Pradveshī, wife of Dīrghatamas. § 170 (Dīrghatamas): I, **104**, 4193 (mother of Gautama, etc.), (4199), 4200, (4201).
Pradyota, a Yaksha. § 269 (Vaiçravaṇasabhāv.): II, **10**, 397 (among the Yakshas in the palace of Kubera).
Pradyumna, son of Kṛshṇa and Rukmiṇī. § 132 (Aṃçāvat.): I, **67**, 2786 (incarnation of Sanatkumāra).—§ 253 (Haraṇāharaṇap.): I, **221**, 7992 (came to the marriage of Arjuna and Subhadrā).—§ 262 (Bhagavadyāna): II, **2**, 56 (*°-Çāmba-Niçathāṃç ca*).—§ 287 (Rājasūyikap.): II, **34**, 1275 (*Gada-P°-Çāmbāç ca*, came to the rājasūya of Yudhishṭhira).—§ 317 (Arjunābhigamanap.): III, **12**, 534 (*°o yādṛçaḥ*).—§ 320 (Saubhavadhop.): III, **16**, 667, 687, 691; **17**, 699, 700, 701, 704, 705, 712, 713, 716; **18**, 717, 718, (728), 738; **19**, 750, 761, 765, 774, 775 (*P.*'s encounter with Çālva, whom he defeated).—§ 342 (Indralokābhigamanap.):

III, **51**, 1994 (will assist the Pāṇḍavas), 2009 (°-*Sāmbau*, do.).—§ 402 (Tīrthayātrāp.): III, **120**, †10262 (°-*Çāmbau*, do.), †10269 (°*muktān niçitān*).—§ 510 (Draupadī-Satyabhāmāsaṃv.): III, **234**, †14719 (°-*Çāmbau*).—§ 511 (do.): III, **235**, 14735 (°*jananī*, i.e. Rukmiṇī), 14737.—§ 554 (Sainyodyogap.): V, **1***a*, †5 (°-*Çāmbau*); **3**, 59 (*Gada-P°-Çāmbāṃç ca Kālavajrānalopamān*).—§ 561*g* (Sahadeva): V, **50**, 1999.—§ 562 (Bhagavadyānap.): V, **90**, 3218.—§ 567 (do.): V, **131***o*, 4426 (*Vṛshṇayaḥ . . . P°mukhāḥ*).—§ 581 (Bhīshmavadhap.): VI, **65**, 2967 (Kṛshṇa created himself as *P.*, born from his own self), 2968 (from *P.* Kṛshṇa created Aniruddha).—§ 589 (Droṇābhishekap.): VII, **11***ξ*, 408.—§ 593 (Abhimanyuvadhap.): VII, **35***ε*, 1521.—§ 596 (Pratijñāp.): VII, **72**, 2510 (°*sya priyaṃ*, sc. Abhimanyu).—§ 597 (do.): VII, **84**, 3005.—§ 599 (Jayadrathavadhap.): VII, **110***σ*, 4193, 4227 (is an atiratha): **111**, 4250, [4263 (*b*: *Kārshṇiḥ . . . Makaradhvajaḥ*)]. —§ 600 (Ghaṭotkacavadhap.): VII, **156***ζ*, 6732.—§ 602 (Droṇavadhap.): VII, **191***ξ*, 8798 (°-*Yuyudhānābhyāṃ*).—§ 617*b* (Brahmaçiras): X, **12**, 636 (*Sanatkumāraḥ*, son of Kṛshṇa and Rukmiṇī).—§ 641 (Rājadh.): XII, **81**, 3030 (*rūpena mattaḥ P°ḥ*).—§ 717*b* (Nārāyaṇīya): XII, **340**, 12902 (*P.* is the manas of all creatures, which springing from Saṅkarshaṇa becomes Sanatkumāra), 12905 (*P.* = manas sprang from Saṅkarshaṇa, from *P.* sprang Aniruddha), 12937 (Saṅkarshaṇa begot *P.*, from *P.* sprang Aniruddha); **345**, 13386 (*manobhūtāḥ . . . P°ṃ praviçanti*).—§ 730 (Ānuçāsanik.): XIII, **14**, 617 (°-*Cārudeshṇādīn Rukmiṇyāḥ . . . putrakān*), (*a*), 621.—§ 769 (do.): XIII, **149**, 7017 (Vishṇu's 1000 names).—§ 773*b* (Kṛshṇa Vāsudeva): XIII, **159**, 7392 (considered as [the third] form of Kṛshṇa); **160**, 7403, 7406.—§ 785 (Anugītāp.): XIV, **86***τ*, 2557 (accompanied Kṛshṇa); **88**, 2611 (*iva*); **89***ω*, 2680 (*Vṛshṇivīrāṃç ca P°ādyān*).—§ 793 (Mausalap.): XVI, **3**, 75 (*ζ*), 101 (is slain); **6**, 155.—§ 795 (Svargārohaṇap.): XVIII, **5***μ*, 160 (after death *P.* entered Sanatkumāra).

Cf. also the following synonyms:—
Jānardani: III, 723.
Kārshṇi, q.v.
Makaradhvaja, Makaraketumat, q.v.
Raukmiṇeya ("the son of Rukmiṇī"): I, 6997, 7914; II, 129; III, 683, 692, 726, 751, 764, 768, 771, 836, †12584, †12586; V, †1881, 5331; VII, 4260; XIII, 616 (had slain Çambara), 7407, 7409, 7454; XIV, 1938; XVI, 157.
Rukmiṇīnandana (do.): III, 708, 711, 760, XVI, 89.
Sātvatamukhya, Vṛshṇipravīra, q.v.

Prādyumni ("the son of Pradyumna") = Aniruddha: I, 6997.

Prāgdakshiṇa = Çiva (1000 names[1]).

Praghasa, a Rākshasa. § 537 (Rāma-Rāvaṇayuddha): III, **285***a*, 16365 (followed Rāvaṇa).

Praghasā, a mātṛ. § 615*u* (Skanda): IX, **46***θ*, 2634.

Prāgjyotisha[1], name of a city. § 279 (Arjuna): II, **26**, 1000 (the capital of Bhagadatta; Arjuna came to *P.* on his digvijaya).—§ 291 (Çiçupālavadhap.): II, **45**, 1567 (°*puraṃ*, the Vṛshṇis had gone to *P.*, meantime Çiçupāla burnt Dvārakā).—§ 317*b* (Kṛshṇa Vāsudeva): III, **12**, 488 (*kṛtaḥ kshemaḥ punaḥ panthāḥ puraṃ P°ṃ prati*, sc. by Kṛshṇa; the capital of Naraka).—§ 320 (Saubhavadhop.): III, **22**, 857 (?).—§ 561*c* (Kṛshṇa Vāsudeva); V, **48**, †1887 (*durgaṃ puraṃ ghoram Asurāṇāṃ*, the capital of Naraka, conquered by Kṛshṇa).—§ 567 (Bhagavadyānap.): V, **130**, 4408 (Çauri, i.e. Kṛshṇa, went to *P.*, cf. § 561*c*).—§ 717*b* (Nārāyaṇīya): XII, **340**, 12956 (Kṛshṇa will transplant *P.* to Dvārakā after having slain Naraka).—§ 782 (Anugītāp.): XIV, **75**, 2175 (the capital of Vajradatta).

Prāgjyotisha[2] ("the king of Prāgjyotisha") = Bhagadatta: II, 1002, 1268 (*nṛpatir Bhagadattaḥ*); VI, 2856 (°*gajaḥ*); 3295, 3559, 3664 (*rājā*), 3675, 3676 (°*gajaṃ*), 4277, 4297 (*nṛpaḥ*), 4316, 5147, 5148 (*rājā*), 5269, 5292, 5432; VII, 808, 1147, 1162, 1169 (*rājā*), 1176, 1197 (*rājā*), 1239, 1251 (*rājā*), 1256, 1257, 1265, 1289, 1302 (is slain by Arjuna).

Prāgjyotishādhipa[1] (do.) = Bhagadatta: II, 1834 (*Bh°*), 1836 (*Bh°*); V, 2186, 2206, 5804 (*Bh°*); VII, 1201.

Prāgjyotishādhipa[2] (do.) = Vajradatta: XIV, 2210.

Prāgjyotishajyeshṭha = Mahāpurusha (Mahāpurushastava).

Prāgjyotishapati ("the king of Prāgjyotisha") = Bhagadatta: VII, 1164.

Pragraha, Prāgvaṃça = Vishṇu (1000 names).

Prahartṛ = Çiva (1000 names[1]).

Prahāsa[1], a serpent. § 67 (Sarpasattra): I, **57**, 2157 (of Dhṛtarāshṭra's race).

Prahāsa[2], a warrior of Skanda. § 615*u* (Skanda): IX, **45***η*, 2570.

Prahasta, a Rākshasa. § 537 (Rāma-Rāvaṇayuddha): III, **285***β*, 16377 (fought with Vibhīshaṇa).—§ 538 (Kumbhakarṇaraṇag.): III, **286**, 16379, 16383 (slain by Vibhīshaṇa), 16396 (*nihataṃ*), 16403 (°*ādiḥ . . . svajano hataḥ*).—§ 540 (Indrajidvadha): III, **288**, 16438 (sc. *hataṃ*), 16443. Cf. Rākshasa.

Prahlāda[1], an Asura (= Prahrāda) (B. has mostly Prahrāda). § 89 (Aṃçāvat.): I, **65**, 2526 (eldest son of Hiraṇyakaçipu).—§ 90 (do.): I, **65**, 2527 (father of Virocana, Kumbha, and Nikumbha).—§ 130 (do.): I, **67**, 2642 (*Saṃhlādaḥ . . . P°syānujaḥ*).—§ 270 (Brahmasabhāv.): II, **11**, 437 (among the *prajānāṃ patayaḥ* in the palace of Brahmán). § 299 (Dyūtap.): II, **68**, 2314 (°*sya ca saṃvādaṃ muner Āṅgirasasya ca*; °*hl°* also B.).—§ 300 (do.): *Virocana*, the son of the king of the *Daityas P.*, for the sake of obtaining a bride, quarrelled with *Sudhanvan Āṅgirasa*, and they mutually wagered their lives as to who was superior, and made *P.* the arbitrator between them. As *P.* was frightened, *Sudhanvan* threatened him saying that if he answered falsely or did not answer, *Indra* would split his head into 100 pieces with his thunderbolt. *P.* then asked *Kaçyapa* what regions were obtainable by those who, upon being asked a question, answered it not or answered it falsely. *Kaçyapa* said that they cast 1,000 *Vāruṇa* pāças upon themselves, each of which could not be loosened in less than a full year, etc. *P.* then declared *Sudhanvan* to be superior to *Virocana*, as *Aṅgiras* was to himself, and the mother of *Sudhanvan* to the mother of *Virocana*. *Sudhanvan*, because *P.* had spoken truth, granted that *Virocana* should live 100 years; II, **68**, 2315 (*Daityendraḥ*, °*hl°* also B.), 2317 (°*hl°* also B.), 2319 (do.), (2321) (do.), 2329 (do.), 2334 (do.).—§ 326 (Draupadīparitāpav.): III, **28**, 1029 (°*sya ca saṃvādaṃ Baler Vairocanasya ca*), 1030 (*Asurendraṃ . . . Daityendraṃ*), (1034) (discourse between *P.* and [his grandson] Bali).—§ 443 (Nivātakavacayuddhap.): III, **168**, 12073 (had been defeated by Indra).—§ 538 (Kumbhakarṇaraṇagamana): III, **286**, 16390 (*Indra-P°yor iva*, sc. *yuddhaṃ*; °*hl°*, also B.).—§ 541 (Indrajidvadha): III, **289**, 16482 (*Çakra-P°yor iva*, sc. *yuddhaṃ*; °*hl°*, also B.).—§ 571 (Ulūkadūtāgamanap.): V, **160**, 5419 (a çloka sung by *P.* is quoted).—§ 576 (Bhagavadgītāp.): VI, **34,** 1234 (°*ç cāsmi Daityānām*, says Kṛshṇa).—§ 599 (Jayadrathavadhap.): VII, **108,** 4096 (°*aṃ samare jitvā yathā Çakraṃ*); **122,** 4925 (*Çakra-P°yor iva*, sc. *yuddhaṃ*; °*hl*°, also B.).—§ 600 (Ghaṭotkacavadhap.): VII, **156,** 6856 (do., do.); **166,** 7426 (do., do.).—§ 647*b* (Brahmadatta-Pūjanīsaṃv.): XII, **139,** 5203 (Uçanas recited two gāthās to *P.*; °*hl*°, also B.).—§ 656 (Khaḍgotpattik.): XII, **166**γ, 6146.—§ 714*f* (cf. Himavat): *P.*, the son of *Hiranyakaçipu*, could not raise the dart of Skanda, but fell down in a swoon: XII, **328,** 12328. — § 778*b* (Saṃvartta-Maruttīya): XIV, **9,** †248 (*divaḥ P°ṃ avasānam ānayaṃ*, says Indra; °*hl*°, also B.). Cf. Asurādhipa, Asurendra, Daiteya, Daitya, Daityapati, Daityendra, Dānava.

Prahlāda[2], a Bāhlīka prince. § 130 (Aṃçāvat.): I, **67,** 2667 (*Bāhlīkaḥ*, incarnation of the Asura Çalabha).

Prahlāda[3], a serpent. § 268 (Varuṇasabhāv.): II, **9,** 362 (in the palace of Varuṇa).

Prahlāda, pl. (°*āḥ*), a people. § 574 (Jambūkh.): VI, **9**μ, 354.

Prahrāda, an Asura, = Prahlāda (q.v.). § 83 (Ādivaṃçāvataraṇa): I, **63,** 2439 (°*çishyo Nagnajit*).—§ 558 (Virocana): V, **35,** 1202, 1203, (1204), 1206, (1207), 1208, (1210), (1212), (1217), 1219, 1220 (cf. § 300 (v. Prahlāda)).—§ 600 (Ghaṭotkacavadhap.): VII, **173,** 7843 (*Çakra-P°yor iva*, sc. *yuddhaṃ*; B. °*hl*°).—§ 615 (Gadāyuddhap.): IX, **57,** 3177 (*Indra-P°yor iva*, sc. *yuddhaṃ*; B. °*hl*°).—§ 641 (Rājadh.): XII, **98**ξ, 3662 (had been slain by Indra); **124,** 4568 (*Daityena*), 4575, 4576, 4577, 4579, 4582, (4583), 4588 (*Daityendraḥ*), 4590 (*Daityendraṃ*), 4593, 4594, 4596, 4599, 4601, 4607, 4615 (disguised as a brāhmaṇa Indra acquired *P.*'s nature, *P.* having conquered the three worlds from Indra; then Prosperity, etc., left *P.*).—§ 659 (Mokshadh.): XII, **179,** 6654 (°*sya saṃvādaṃ muner Ājagarasya*), 6655 (*rājā*), (6656), 6661, 6662, 6664 (discourse between *P.* and the Ājagara muni); **180***a*, 6692.—§ 670 (do.): XII, **222,** 8023 (°*sya saṃvādam Indrasya ca*), 8028, 8031, 8032 (*Daiteya*), (8034), 8053, (8054) (discourse between *P.* and Indra). § 673*b* (Bali-Vāsavasaṃv.): XII, **227***a*, 8262 (among the ancient rulers of the earth). For synonyms v. Prahlāda.

Prāhrāda (son of Prahrāda) = Virocana: V, 1195 (only C.).

Prāhrādi[1] (do.) = Vātāpi: III, 8645.—Do.[2] (do.) = Virocana: V, 1193, 1195 (only B.).

Prahuta = Çiva (1000 names[1]).

Prajābhāva = Vishṇu (1000 names).

Prajābija (C. °*vī*°) = Çiva (1000 names[2]).

Prajādhyaksha = Sūrya (the Sun): III, 151.

Prajādvāra = Çiva (1000 names[2]).

Prajāgara[1] ("sleeplessness," sc. Dhṛtarāshṭrasya, cf. Prajāgaraparvan). § 10 (Parvasaṅgr.): I, **2,** 330 (°*ḥ parva*, i.e. Prajāgaraparvan).—§ 11 (do.): I, **2,** 502.

Prajāgara[2] = Vishṇu (1000 names).

Prajāgarā, an Apsaras. § 336 (Indralokābhigamanap.): III, **43***a*, 1785 (in the palace of Indra).

[Prajāgaraparvan(°va)] ("section relating to the sleeplessness of Dhṛtarāshṭra," the 59th of the minor parvans of Mhbhr.; cf. Prajāgara). § 557: *Dhṛtarāshṭra*, after *Sañjaya* had left him, requested *Vidura* to tell him what may be good for a person that is sleepless and burning. *Vidura* said that *Yudhishṭhira* was worthy of being the sovereign over the three worlds, while the qualities of *Dhṛtarāshṭra* were the very reverse of those; *Dhṛtarāshṭra* had no right to a share in the kingdom owing to his being blind; *Vidura* blamed him for having bestowed on *Duryodhana*, *Çakuni*, *Karṇa*, and *Duḥçāsana* the management of the empire. Then he explained the marks of a wise man and of a fool, quoting *Bṛhaspati's* answer to *Indra*, and alluding to the conversation between *Sudhanvan* and *Asurendra* [i.e. *Prahlāda*] in relation to the son of the latter (V, **33**). Continuation of *Vidura's* discourse (V, **34**).—§ 558: *Vidura* said that as long as a man's good deeds are spoken of in this world, so long he is glorified in heaven, and cited the old story about the conversation between *Virocana* (q.v.) and *Sudhanvan*, both suitors for *Keçinī's* hand. "Entrusting the cares of thy kingdom to *Duryodhana*, *Çakuni*, the foolish *Duḥçāsana*, and to *Karṇa*, how canst thou hope for prosperity? Possessed of every virtue, the *Pāṇḍavas* depend on thee as their father; oh, confide thou in them as thy sons" (V, **35**).—§ 559: *Vidura* related the old history of the discourse between *Ātreya* and the *Sādhyas*, who received instruction from *Ātreya* when he was wandering as a beggar (". . . One should not return the slanders or reproaches of others, for the pain that is felt by him who suffers silently, consumes the slanderer; and he that endures, succeeds also in appropriating the virtues of the slanderer—the slanderer's merits become his . . . The very gods desire company of that man who, when abused, does not himself return the abuse nor cause others to return it, or who, when beaten, does not himself return the blow nor cause others to do it, and who wishes not the slightest injury to him that injures him . . ."). Then he explained what are those families that are called high (". . . let none in our race serve a king as minister") (V, **36**). *Vidura* spoke of the seven and ten kinds of foolish men according to *Manu Svāyambhuva*; of the reasons why not all men attain the allotted period of life (100 years according to the *Veda*), etc. But *Dhṛtarāshṭra* could not abandon his son (V, **37–40**).

prajānām adhipa(ḥ) ("lord of creatures") = Kshupa: XII, 4503 (*K*°), 6192.

Prajānām īçvareçvara(ḥ) = Brahmán: VII, 2085.

Prajānāṃ patayaḥ = Prajāpati, pl. § 3 (Anukram.): I, **1***a*, 33 (twenty-one in number they issued from the primordial egg).—§ 191 (Arjuna): I, **123***a*, 4807 (present at the birth of Arjuna).—§ 270 (Brahmasabhāv.): II, **11,** 435 (i.e. Daksha, etc., in the palace of Brahmán).—§ 665 (Mokshadh.): XII, **208,** 7567, 7568, 7580.—§ 746 (Ānuçāsanik.): XIII, **83,** 3886.—§ 747*b* (Suvarṇotpatti): XIII, **85**ζ, 4127 (origin from the ears of Agni), 4144 (*trayaḥ*, i.e. Bhṛgu, Aṅgiras, and Kavi), 4156 (= do.).

Prajānāṃ patiḥ[1] ("lord of creatures") = Brahmán: XIII, 4660.

Prajānāṃ patiḥ[2] = Çiva: VII, 9530.

Prajānāṃ patiḥ[3] = Daksha: XII, 10232.

Prajānāṃ patiḥ[4]: III, 12703 (among the honourable appellations of the king).

Prajānidhanakara = Mahāpurusha (Mahāpurushastava).

Prajāpati[1] ("lord of creatures"), mostly identified or identifiable with Brahmán.—§ 3 (Anukram.): I, **1,** 32 (*Brahmā*, issued from the primordial egg).—§ 26 (Jaratkāru): I, **13,** 1028 (°*samaḥ* . . . *Jaratkāruḥ*).—§ 27 (Kaçyapa): I, **16,** 1074 (°*samaḥ*, sc. Kaçyapa).—§ 33 (Garuḍa): I, **23,** 1249 (Garuḍa identified with *P.*).—§ 48 (Çesha): I, **36,** †1583 (i.e. Brahmán).—§ 56 (Parikshit): I, **49,** 1942 (*iva*).—§ 61 (Sarpasattra): I, **55,** 2097 (had performed sacrifices in Prayāga).—§ 84 (Ādivaṃçāvatāraṇap.): I, **64,** 2499 (*Īçaḥ Çambhuḥ P°iḥ*, = Brahmán), 2507 (°*patiḥ*, i.e. Vishṇu

Nārāyaṇa).—§ 149 (Yayāti): I, **89**, †3593 (°*er lokam*).—§ 238 (Pañcendrop.): I, **197**, †7277 (i.e. Brahmán).—§ 254 (Khāṇḍavadahanap.): I, **222**, 8057 (*iva*).—§ 270 (Brahmasabhāv.): II, **11**, 459 (= Brahmán), 464 (do.).—§ 296 (Dyūtap.): II, **53**, 1921 (gave a çaṅkha to Indra).—§ 310*b* (Sūrya): III, **3**, 190 (Sūrya (the Sun) identified with *P.*).—§ 317 (Arjunābhigamanap.): III, **12**, 470 (°*pater Vishṇoḥ*).—§ 327 (Draupadīparitāpav.): III, **32**, 1202 (*Īçvaraṃ*).—§ 370 (Tīrthayātrāp.): III, **85**, 8145 (°*kṛto vidhiḥ*). — § 371 (Tuṅgaka): III, **85**, 8191 (in Tuṅgaka).—§ 373 (Prayāga): III, **85**, 8215 (in Prayāga), 8219 (*vedir eshā P°eḥ*, sc. Prayāga, etc.), 8220.—§ 377 (Dhaumyatīrthak.): III, **89**, 8370 (sung a gāthā at Pushkara).—§ 379 (Tīrthayātrāp.): III, **95**, 8516 (*vedīṃ P°eḥ*, i.e. Prayāga).—§ 391 (Ṛshyaçṛṅga): III, **110**, 10000 (°*samadyuteḥ*, sc. Vibhāṇḍaka).—§ 409 (Plakshāvataraṇag.): III, **129**, 10513 (performed a sacrifice lasting 1,000 years), 10535 (*vedir eshā P°eḥ*, sc. Kurukshetra).—§ 440 (Yakshayuddhap.): III, **164**, 11900 (°*eḥ*, sc. *astraṃ*, obtained by Arjuna).—§ 453 (Mārkaṇḍeyas.): III, **183**, 12620 (*sasarja dharmatantrāṇi*).—§ 455 (Brāhmaṇamāhātmyak.): III, **185**, 12704 (among the honourable appellations of the king).—§ 457 (Vaivasvatop.): III, **187**, 12747 (°*samadyutiḥ*, sc. Manu Vaivasvata), 12797 (*Brahmā*, in the shape of a fish).—§ 459 (Mārkaṇḍeyas.): III, **189**, 13001 (°*patiḥ* . . . *Govindaḥ*).—§ 469 (do.): III, **200**, 13386 (*annaṃ P°ç coktaḥ sa ca saṃvatsaro mataḥ*).—§ 471 (do.): III, **200**, 13417.—§ 504 (Skandayuddha): III, **231**, 14521 (*Brahmā*).—§ 524*c* (Vishṇu): III, **272**, 15824 (*sṛjate Brahmamūrtis tu, rakshate Paurushī tanuḥ | Raudrībhāvena çamayet tisro 'vasthāḥ Prajāpateḥ*). — § 525 (Rāmopākhyānap.): III, **274**, 15882 (father of Pulastya, grandfather of Rāvaṇa and Kubera).—§ 534 (Sītā-Rāvaṇasaṃv.): III, **281**, 16187 (°*samaḥ*, sc. the father of Rāvaṇa).—§ 579 (Pāṇḍavapraveçap.): IV, **9**, 259 (*Dhātuḥ*?, Draupadī is supposed to be the wife of *P.*).—§ 554*c* (Gāṇḍīva): IV, **43**, 1347 (had the Gāṇḍīva for 503 years, different from Brahmán).—§ 554 (Goharaṇap.): IV, **56**, 1770 (°*eḥ*, sc. *vimānaṃ*).—§ 554*d* (Arjuna): IV, **61**, 1977 (preceptor of Arjuna, different from Brahmán ?).—§ 561 (Yānasandhip.): V, **48**, †1871 (*P°eḥ karma yathā 'rthanishṭhitaṃ*).—§ 562 (Bhagavadyānap.): V, **78**, 2808 (*yatha*).—§ 565 (Gālavacarita): V, **113*a***, 3880.—§ 567 (Bhagavadyānap.): V, **128**, 4299 (*Parameshṭhī*), 4303 (do., ordered Dharma to bind the Asuras).—§ 568 (Vidulāputraçāsana): V, **134**, 4575 (°*vinirmitaṃ*, sc. *kshatrahṛdayaṃ*).—§ 569 (Bhagavadyānap.): V, **148**, 5025 (°*ḥ prajāḥ sṛshṭvā yathā saṃharate tathā*).—§ 570 (Sainyaniryāṇap.): V, **157**, 5316 (°*im ivaudārye*, sc. Bhīshma).—§ 575 (Bhūmip.): VI, **12**, 466 (on the mountain Pushkara in Pushkaradvīpa); 470 (*Īçvaraḥ*).—§ 576 (Bhagavadgītāp.): VI, **14**, 546 (*sarvalokeçvarasya*); **27**, 900 (*sahayajñāḥ prajāḥ sṛshṭvā*); **35**, †1285 (Kṛshṇa identified with *P.*).—§ 581 (Bhīshmavadhap.): VI, **65**, 2940 (i.e. Brahmán), 2955 (°*pate*, i.e. Vishṇu (Kṛshṇa)).—§ 587 (do.): VI, **120**, 5719 (°*m ivāmarāḥ*).—§ 588 (do.): VI, **121**, 5802 (°*eḥ*, sc. *astraṃ*, known to Arjuna).—§ 594 (Mṛtyu): VII, **54**, 2073 (i.e. Brahmán).—§ 595 (Shoḍaçarāj., v. Çibi Auçīnara): VII, **58**, 2216.—§ 603*d* (Tripura): VII, **202**, 9586 (*devāḥ* . . . *sa-P°ayaḥ*, i.e. Brahmán).—§ 606 (Tripurākhyāna): VIII, **33**, 1413; **34**, 1573 (°*mukhāḥ surāḥ*).—§ 607 (Karṇap.): VIII, **44**, 2065 (*naishā sṛshṭiḥ P°eḥ*, sc. the Bāhīkas), 2068 (*tulyakālāḥ P°eḥ*, sc. *brāhmaṇāpasadāḥ*).—§ 608 (do.): VIII, **87**, 4435 (*Svayambhuvaṃ*, i.e. Brahmán).—§ 615*b* (Udapāna): IX, **36**, 2072 (°*samāḥ*, sc. Ekata, Dvita, and Trita).—§ 615*kk* (Kurukshetrak.): IX, **53**, †3008 (°*er uttaravedir ucyate* . . . *Samantapañcakaṃ*), †3032 (*etat Kurukshetra-Samantapañcakaṃ P°er uttaravedir ucyate*). — § 615 (Gadāyuddhap.): IX, **55**, †3085 (*Samantapañcakaṃ* . . . *uttaravediḥ* . . . *P°eḥ*).—§ 616 (Sauptikap.): X, **3**, 122 (*prajāḥ sṛshṭvā karma tāsu vidhāya ca*).—§ 617 (Aishīkap.): X, **17**, 775 (created by Brahmán and father of Daksha, etc.).—§ 619 (Strīvilāpap.): XI, **23*θ***, 666 (*Vedā yasmāc ca catvāraḥ sarvāstrāṇi ca* . . . *anapetāni vai çūrād yathaivādau P°eḥ*, all. to Brahmán's loss of the Vedas).—§ 623 (Rājadh.): XII, **12**, 351 (*asṛjad vai prajāḥ*).—§ 632 (Shoḍaçarāj., v. Çibi Auçīnara, cf. § 595); XII, **29**, 935 (cf. VII, 2216).—§ 641 (Rājadh.): XII, **60**, 2290 (created the domestic animals), 2295 (°*r hi varṇānāṃ dāsaṃ çūdram akalpayat*); **65**, 2446 (*sarvañ caivāsṛjad jagat*); **91**, 3407 (metaphorically of the king); **108**, 4014; **121**, 4449 (among the names of Chastisement), 4465 (*Brahmā*); **122**, 4511, 4512 (different from Brahmán?). — § 655 (Āpaddh.): XII, **161**, 5961 (*idaṃ sarvaṃ tapasaivāsṛjat*).—§ 660*b* (Bhṛgu-Bharadvājasaṃv.): XII, **182**, 6800 (*Brahmā*); **187**, 6929 (*sṛshṭiḥ P°er eshā*); **190**, 6982; **191**, 6996; **192**, 7023 (attained to Brahmaloka).—§ 662*b* (Jāpakop.): XII, **200**, 7341 (*Devadevaḥ*).—§ 665 (Mokshadh.): XII, **208**, 7578 (?).—§ 667 (do.): XII, **217**, 7845 (described the religion of pravṛtti).—§ 671*b* (Bali-Vāsavasaṃv.): XII, **224**, 8139 (Kāla (Time) identified with *P.*). — § 677 (Mokshadh.); XII, **233**, 8522 (*ādikartā sa bhūtānāṃ*); **235**, 8601 (*jīvayām āsa P°r iva prajāḥ*); **237**, 8667 (*iva*).—§ 678*c* (Mṛtyu-Prajāpatisaṃv.): XII, **258**, (9167) (i.e. Brahmán). — § 680*b* (Tulādhāra-Jājalisaṃv.): XII, **263**, 9338 (= *vṛshabha* (the bull)); **265**, 9453.—§ 684 (Mokshadh.): XII, **269**, 9616.—§ 702 (do.): XII, **296**, 10836 (*prajāḥ pūrvam asṛjat tapasā*); **297**, 10865 (*sṛjataḥ P°er lokān*).—§ 703 (do.): XII, **300**, 10994 (assumed the form of a golden swan).—§ 705 (do.): XII, **303**, 11234 (*Ahaṅkāraṃ*, created from Hiraṇyagarbha).—§ 707 (do.): XII, **311**, 11572 (came out of the golden egg and created heaven and earth); **313**, 11601 (*bhūtātmā so Ahaṅkāraḥ P°ḥ*), 11602 (*Çambhuḥ*); **314**, 11609 (the adhidaivata of the organ of generation); **318**, 11705 (when the soul (*jīva*) escapes through the thighs, one attains to *P.*).—§ 710 (do.): XII, **322**, 12104 (°*eḥ salokatāṃ*). — § 717*b* (Nārāyaṇīya): XII, **339**, 12864 (= Mahāpurusha); **343**, 13253 (*Viriñcaḥ*, Kṛshṇa identified with *P.*) —§ 717*d* (Brahma-Rudrasaṃv.): XII, **351**, 13726 (i.e. Brahmán).—§ 724 (Ānuçāsanik.): XIII, **7**, 368 (*yena prīṇāti pitaraṃ tena prīṇāti P°ṃ*).—§ 730 (do.): XIII, **14**, 998 (*sa-P°-Çakrāntaṃ jagat*); **16**, 1083 (praised Çiva).—§ 731*b* (Ashṭāvakra-Diksaṃv.): XIII, **19**, 1475 (*abhāshata*, a sentence of his quoted); **20**, 1498 (°*mataṃ*).—§ 743 (Ānuçāsanik.): XIII, **40**, 2255 (*sargat Prajapateḥ*), 2259 (Brahmán's creating of the women).—§ 744 (do.): XIII, **44**, 2420; **48**, 2564 (*asṛjat*).—§ 746 (do.): XIII, **63**, 3230 (*āha*, a sentence of his quoted); **67**, 3381 (do., do.); **79*κ***, 3780 (°*er lokaṃ*).—§ 747 (do.): XIII, **84**, 3954, 3990 (told the story Suvarṇotpatti).—§ 747*b* (Suvarṇotpatti): XIII, **85**, 4112 (Çiva identified with *P.*), 4164 (Agni identified with *P.*).—§ 753 (Ānuçāsanik.): XIII, **97**, 4662.—§ 767 (do.): XIII, **138**, 6287 (*āha*, a sentence of his quoted).—§ 770 (do.): XIII, **151**, 7100 (°*kṛtān etān lokān*).—§ 772*i* (Brahmán): XIII, **154**, 7227 (*Brahmā*).—§ 773*b* (Kṛshṇa Vāsudeva): XIII, **159*β***, †7387 (created from Kṛshṇa).—§ 773 (Ānuçāsanik.): XIII, **161**, 7462 (composed the Çatarudriya).—§ 773*d* (Çiva): XIII, **161**, 749 (*devāḥ* sa-P°ayaḥ, i.e Brahmán).—§ 778b (Saṃvartta-Maruttīya): XIV, **9,** †236 (lokāḥ . . . P°eḥ), †241 (°eḥ . . . lokāḥ).—§ 782 (Anugītāp.): XIV, **18,** 524 (asṛjat sarvabhūtāni pūrvadṛshṭaḥ).—§ 782b (Brāhmaṇagītā): XIV, **21,** 631, 647; **23,** 707 (Brahmā), 708; **26,** 751 (°au pannagānāṃ Devarshīnāṃ saṃvidam), 752.—§ 782g (Guruçishyasaṃv.): XIV, **35**δ, 960 (read Bṛhaspati° with PCR.?), 969, 976; **42,** 1128 (the presiding deity of the organ of generation), (ε), 1167 (= mahān ātmā); **43,** 1180 (bhūtādhipaḥ sargaḥ prajānāṃ); **44,** 1216 (devatānām ādiḥ); **51,** 1438 (°r idaṃ sarvaṃ manasaivāsṛjat), 1445 (sakāçe P°eḥ).—§ 785 (Anugītāp.): XIV, **71,** 2077 (Kṛshṇa identified with P.); **73,** 2114 (iva).—§ 786 (do.): XIV, **91,** 2832 (Svayambhuvaṃ).—§ 787 (Āçramavāsap.): XV, **8,** 263 (°samaṃ, sc. Dhṛtarāshṭra). Cf. Prajānāṃ pati(ḥ).

Prajāpati[2] (do.), the father of the Vasus. § 116 (Vasu, pl.): I, **66,** 2581 (Paitāmaho Manur (B. munir) devas tasya putraḥ P°ḥ | tasyāshṭau Vasavaḥ putrāḥ, = Daksha?, = Dharma?).

Prajāpati[3] (do.) = Çiva: XII, 4520 (Mahādevaḥ), 10344 (Tryakshaḥ); XIII, 594 (Brahmāṇam asṛjat tasmād Devadevaḥ P°ḥ), 1173 (1000 names[2]). Cf. Prajāpati[1].

Prajāpati[4] (do.) = Vishṇu (Kṛshṇa): II, 9; III, 510; XII, 1605, 1619, 1898 (Vāsudevaṃ), 2208 (Vishṇuṃ); XIII, 6957 (Vishṇu's 1000 names), 6970 (do.). Cf. Prajāpati[1].

Prajāpati[5-22] (do.), said of different ṛshis, etc.:—

Agni: XIII, 4102.
Bharata (the fire): III, 14137.
Çaçabindu: XII, 7579.
Çukra: XII, 1677 (only C.).
Daksha: I, 2576, 3126 (D°), 3132, 3183 (? = Brahman?), 4808 (D°); V, 3040 (D°, identified with Kṛshṇa (Vishṇu)); IX, 2018, 2046, 2054; XII, 7536 (D°), 7537, 7539 (D°), 7573 (D°), 10226 (D°), 10272 (Prācetasasya D°sya), 10277, 10323 (D°), 10331 (D°), 10340 (D°), 10346 (D°), 10461, 10463, 12415 (D°, read P°eḥ); XIII, 3711, 3718, 3722, 6830 (D°), 7468 (D°); XIV, 94 (D°), 2634 (D°). Cf. Prajānāṃ patiḥ.
Havirdhāman: XIII, 6829.
Indra: III, 12691 (Mahendraḥ), 12692 (I°).
Kaçyapa: I, 1204, 1440 (K°), 1451 (K°), 1452, 1456, 1457, 1465; III, 12955 (read Ka° with B., Nārayaṇa identified with K.), 14257 (°eḥ kanyā Devasenā), 14258; VI, 215 (K°); XII, 13248 (K°).
Kapila: XII, 7889 (K°).
Kardama: XII, 2212 (K°).'
Kshupa: XII, 4485 (K°). Cf. Prajānām adhipa(ḥ).
Manu: I, 3756 (M°); III, 8115 (Manoḥ P°er lokam); XII, 1293 (M°), 1294, 1295, 5236 (M°), 7366 (M°), 7367, 7587 (M°); XIII, 88 (M°), 4678 (M°), 7683 (M°).
Pṛthu Vainya: XIII, 7126.
Soma (the Moon): V, 5042 (S°).
Svishṭakṛt (the fire): III, 14194.
Tvashṭṛ: V, 229 (T°), 272 (T°).
Viçvakarman: I, 8186 (Bhaumanaḥ).
Vīraṇa: XII, 13587 (V°).

Prajāpati, pl. (°ayaḥ) (do.). § 403b (Payoshṇī): III, **121,** 10292 (the gods with Indra and the P. performed sacrifices at the river Payoshṇī).—§ 603 (Nārāyaṇāstramokshap.): VII, **202**ηη, 9502 (°īnāṃ prathamaṃ, sc. Çiva).—§ 606 (Tripurākhyāna): VIII, **34aa,** 1446 (°ibhir ījyate, sc. Çiva).—§ 608 (Karṇap.): VIII, **87,** 4428 (came to see the battle).—§ 617 (Aishīkap.): X, **17,** 774 (sapta Dakshādīṃs tu P°īn | yair imaṃ vyakarot sarvaṃ bhūtagrāmaṃ caturvidhaṃ).—§ 660b (Bhṛgu-Bharadvājasaṃv.): XII, **188,** 6930 (arsṛjad brāhmaṇān evaṃ pūrvaṃ Brahmā P°īn).—§ 665 (Mokshadh.): XII, **208,** 7571.—§ 704 (do.): XII, **301,** 11060; **302**β, 11106 (°īnāṃ vishayān), (γ), (11125).—§ 717b (Nārāyaṇīya): XII, **335a,** 12687 (twenty-one in number, enumerated); **340**θ, 12917.—§ 747b (Suvarṇotpatti): XIII, **85,** 4067 (°gaṇān), 4151 (i.e. the eight sons of Kavi).—§ 782g (Guruçishyasaṃv.): XIV, **44**ι, 1223 (ahaṃ P°īnāñ ca, sc. ādiḥ, says Brahmán). Cf. Prajānāṃ patayaḥ.

Prajāpatimakhaghna ("destroyer of the sacrifice of the Prajāpati [i.e. Daksha]") = Çiva: VIII, 1446.

Prajāpatipati ("lord of the Prajāpatis") = Vishṇu (Kṛshṇa): I, 2507; III, 470 (Vishṇoḥ), 13004; VI, 2955; XII, 13130 (Hareḥ).

Prajāpatisuta ("the son of Prajāpati [i.e. Brahmán]") = Bhṛgu: IX, 2957.—Do.[2] (do.), pl. (°āḥ) = Ekata, Dvita, and Trita: XII, 12757 (Ekataç ca Dvitaç caiva Tritaç caiva maharshayaḥ), 12950 (dual = Ekata and Dvita).

Prajāpatisutā, dual (°e), (the daughters of the Prajāpati [i.e. Daksha]) = Kadrū and Vinatā: I, 1073.

Prājāpatya, adj. ("relating to the Prajāpati or the Prajāpatis"). § 135 (Çakuntalop.): I, **73,** 2962 (sc. vivāhaḥ).—§ 493 (Āṅgirasa): III, **221,** 14180 (sc. karma?).—§ 552 (Goharaṇap.): IV, **64,** 2058 (sc. astraṃ).—§ 556 (Sañjayayānap.): V, **28,** 802 (sc. lokaṃ).—§ 569 (Bhagavadyānap.): V, **143**θ, 4840 (nakshatraṃ, i.e. Rohiṇī, Nīl.).—§ 573 (Ambopākhyānap.): V, **183,** 7259 (Prasvāpaṃ).—§ 600 (Ghaṭotkacavadhap.): VII, **157,** 6957 (sc. astraṃ).—§ 606b (Tripurākhyāna): VIII, **34,** 1455 (padaṃ).—§ 641 (Mokshadh.): XII, **60,** 2312 (upadravaḥ); **112,** 4176 (°yuge, i.e. the Kṛtayuga).—§ 655 (Āpaddh.): XII, **165,** 6062 (açvaṃ).—§ 677 (Mokshadh.): XII, **244,** 8870 (sc. loke)—§ 680b (Tulādhāra-Jājalisaṃv.): XII, **262,** 9299 (vidhinā).—§ 717b (Nārāyaṇīya): XII, **341,** 13076 (°e—sc. karmaṇi?—ca kalpitāḥ, sc. the seven sons of Brahmán, Marīci, etc.).—§ 731 (Ānuçāsanik.): XIII, **19,** 1382 (dharmaḥ).—§ 741 (do.): XIII, **76,** 3674 (arthavādāḥ); **81,** 3834 (sc. mantraṃ?).—§ 759 (do.): XIII, **107,** 5212 (devastrīṇām adhivāse).—§ 768b (Kṛshṇa Vāsudeva): XIII, **147,** 6827 (mārge . . . Mānave).

Prājāpatya, pl. (°āḥ) ("sons or descendants of the Prajāpati"). § 558 (Virocana): V, **35,** 1189.—§ 673b (Bali-Vāsavasaṃv.): XII, **227,** 8274 (Dākshāyaṇīputrāḥ).—§ 747b (Suvarṇotpatti): XIII, **85,** 4158 (maharshayaḥ).

Prājāpatyā(ḥ) lokā(ḥ) ("the worlds of the Prajāpatis"). § 757l (Hastikūṭa): Gautama said: "Above heaven (nākasya pṛshṭhe) are the great P. l., happy and free from sorrow, coveted by all, belonging to them from whom all the worlds have sprung." Dhṛtarāshṭra said: "These regions (lokāḥ) are for the kings who are anointed (abhishiktāḥ) after the rājasūya sacrifice, righteous protectors of their subjects, who have bathed after the horse sacrifice": XIII, **102,** †4882.

Prājāpatyaka = Agni: III, 14116.

Prajāsargakara = Mahāpurusha (Mahāpurushastava).

Prajeçvara[1] ("lord of creatures") = Brahmán, VII, 2079.—Do.[2] = Daksha: IX, 2019.—Do.[3] = Manu: XIII, 4685.—Do.[4] = Yama II, 351.

Prajñāstra, name of a celestial weapon. § 541 (Indrajidvadha): III, **289,** 16469 (by means of the P. Vibhīshaṇa roused Rāma and Lakshmaṇa from insensibility).—§ 583

(Bhīshmavadhap.): VI, **77**[7], 3389 (by means of the *P.* Droṇa neutralized the Pramohana weapon).

Prakāça[1], a ṛshi. § 736*b* (Vītahavyop.): XIII, **30**, 2002 (son of Tamas), 2003 (father of Vāgindra).

Prakāça[2] = Çiva (1000 names[2]).

Prakāçakarman, Prakāçakartṛ, q.v. = Sūrya.

Prakāçana, Prakāçātman = Vishṇu (1000 names).

Prakālana, a serpent. § 63 (Sarpasattra): I, **57**, 2147 (of Vāsuki's race).

Prākçṛṅgavat, a ṛshi. § 615*ii* (Vṛddhakanyā): IX, **52**, 2993 (*Gālavasambhavaḥ*, married the old daughter of Kuṇi Garga). Cf. Gālavasambhava. Gālavi.

Prākkoçala, pl., v. Kosala, pl.

Prākkoṭaka, pl. (°*āḥ*), a people (?). § 281 (Sahadeva): II, **31**, 1117 (misprint in B. *Prākoṭ°*, C. *Prākkoçalān*).

Prakṛshṭāri = Çiva (1000 names[2]).

***prakṛti** ("the original substance"): I, 2430 (= Kṛshṇa); VI, 977, 1179, 1322, 1341–2, 1355; XII, 7481–3, 7666, 7668, 11335, 11354, 11646, 13044.—Do. personif.: V, **111**, 3825 (°*yā Purushaḥ sārdhaṃ*, on the top of Himavat); XII, **341**, 13044; XIII, 593.

prakṛti (do.), pl. (°*ayaḥ*). XII, 7670 (*mūla°*), 11552 (*ashṭau*), 11554 (do.), 12725 (*sapta*, i.e. the seven ṛshis, Manu is the eighth), 12737 (=do.), 13041 (*ashṭau*, i.e. the seven ṛshis (Marīci, etc.) and Manu), 13042 (*ashṭābhyaḥ*); XIII, 1060, 1091 (*ashṭau*), 1100 (°*īnāṃ layānāñ ca sā gatis tvaṃ*, sc. Çiva).

Pralamba, an Asura. § 93 (Aṃçāvat.): I, **65**, 2537 (son of Danu).—§ 589 (Droṇābhishekap.): VII, **11**μ, 386 (had been slain by Kṛshṇa).

Pralambahan ("the slayer of Pralamba") = Balarāma: IX, 2740, 3358.

Pramadvarā, wife of Ruru. § 19 (Paulomap.): I, **5**, 872 (wife of Ruru and mother of Çunaka).—§ 21 (cf. Paulomap.): *Menakā* dropped her child by *Viçvāvasu*, *P.* near the hermitage of *Sthūlakeça*, who took it up and reared it. *P.* was betrothed to *Ruru*, but a few days before the nuptials she was killed by a snake: I, **8**, 940, 950, 951, 953.—§ 22 (do.): Svastyātreya, etc. (*a*), (the inhabitants of the forest) came to see her (I, **8**).—§ 23 (do.): *Ruru* retired into a deep wood and, weeping aloud, cried to the gods to resuscitate *P.* A *devadūta* (messenger of the gods) told him to resign to her half of his own life, which he did. Then the king of the *Gandharvas* (i.e. Viçvāvasu) and the *devadūta* obtained from Dharma the favour that *P.* revived endued with a moiety of Ruru's life; then they were married and became happy: I, **9**, 965, 968, 972, 974, 976, 977, 978.—§ 736*b* (Vītahavyop.): XIII, **30**, 2004 (mother of Çunaka).

Pramāṇa, name of a banyan-tree. § 308 (Āraṇyakap.): III, **1**, 41 (°*ākhyam mahāvaṭam*, on the banks of the Gaṅgā).

Pramāṇa(ṃ) = Çiva (1000 names[2]).—Do.[2] = Vishṇu (1000 names).

Pramāṇakoṭi, name of a place. § 71 (Ādivaṃçāvatāraṇap.): I, **61**, 2241 (all. to § 197).—§ 197 (Bhīmasenarasapāna): I, **128**, 4996, 5015 (there Duryodhana poured poison into the food of Bhīmasena).—§ 317 (Arjunābhigamanap.): III, **12**, 542 (all. to § 197, Nīl.: *Pramāṇākhyo Gaṅgātīrastho vaṭaviçeshas tatpradeçe*).—§ 608 (Karṇap.): VIII, **83**, 4251 (all. to § 197). — § 615 (Gadāyuddhap.): IX, **56**, 3149 (do.).

Pramardana = Mahāpurusha (Mahāpurashastava).

Pramataka, a ṛshi. § 59 (Sarpasattra): I, **53**, 2047 (among the sadasyas at the snake-sacrifice of Janamejaya).

Pramatha, a son of Dhṛtarāshṭra. § 182 (Dhṛtarāshṭraputranāmak.): I, **117**, 4552 (enumeration).

Pramatha, pl. (°*āḥ*), a kind of Rākshasas, followers of Çiva. § 730 (Ānuçāsanik.): XIII, **14**, 983 (°*ānāṃ gaṇaiḥ* . . . *parivāritaṃ*, sc. Çiva).—§ 766 (do.): XIII, **125***a*, 5924; **130**, 6141, (6145).

Pramātha[1], a companion of Skanda. § 615*u* (Skanda): IX, **45**, 2532 (given to Skanda by Yama).

Pramātha[2] (VII, 6938), v. Pramāthin[1].

Pramathanātha = Çiva (1000 names[1]).

Pramāthin[1], a son of Dhṛtarashṭra. § 182 (Dhṛtarāshṭraputranāmak.): I, **117**, 4552.—§ 600 (Ghaṭotkacavadhap.): VII, **157**o, 6938 (C. has °*thaç cograyāyy api*, but read with B. °*thy Ugro 'nuyāyy api*).

Pramāthin[2], a Rākshasa, brother of Dūshaṇa and Vajravega. § 538 (Kumbhakarṇaraṇagamana): III, **286**, 16405 *Dūshaṇāvarajau Vajravega-P°au*), 16407 (*Vajravega-P°au*).—§ 539 (Kumbhakarṇādivadha): III, **287**, 16430, 16433, 16435 (*Dūshaṇāvarajaṃ*, slain by the monkey Nala).

Pramāthin[3], a Rākshasa. § 585 (Bhīshmavadhap.): VI, **91**v, 4083 (slain by Duryodhana).

Pramāthinī, an Apsaras. § 191 (Arjuna): I, **123**, 4819 (danced at the birth of Arjuna).

Pramati, a ṛshi, father of Ruru. § 19 (Paulomap.): I, **5**, 871 (son of Cyavana and father of Ruru).—§ 21 (Pramadvarā): I, **8**, 939 (son of Cyavana and Sukanyā), 940 (begot Ruru on Ghṛtācī), 952 (demanded Pramadvarā as wife for Ruru).—§ 22 (do.): I, **8***a*, 963.—§ 25 (Sahasrapad): I, **11**, 1004 (*Rurur nāma P°er ātmajaḥ*), 1005 (*Ruruḥ khyātaḥ P°er ātmajaḥ*).—§ 35 (Āstīkap., Aruṇa): I, **24**, (1266), (1277).—§ 69 (Āstīkap., Sarpasattra): I, **58**, 2195 (told Ruru the Āstīkaparvan).—§ 734 (Ānuçāsanik.): XIII, **26***a*, 1762 (among the ṛshis who came to see Bhīshma).—§ 736*b* (Vītahavyop.): XIII, **30**, 2003 (son of Vāgindra and father of Ruru). Cf. Bhārgava.

Prāṃçu = Vishṇu (1000 names).

Pramlocā, an Apsaras. § 191 (Arjuna): I, **123**, 4821 (sang at the birth of Arjuna).—§ 269 (Vaiçravaṇasabhāv.): II, **10**, 393 (in the palace of Kubera).

Pramoda[1], a serpent. § 65 (Sarpasattra): I, **57**, 2152 (of Airāvata's race).

Pramoda[2], a warrior of Skanda. § 615*u* (Skanda): IX, **45**η, 2567.

Pramodana = Vishṇu (1000 names).

Pramohanāstra, name of a weapon. § 583 (Bhīshmavadhap.): VI, **77**[5], †3380, †3381, ('), 3386 (employed by Dhṛshṭadyumna).

Pramuca, a ṛshi. § 665 (Mokshadh.): XII, **208**, 7595 (one of the ṛshis of the south). Cf. next.

Pramucu, a ṛshi. § 770 (Ānuçāsanik.): XIII, **151**η, 7112 (one of the seven Dharmarājartvijaḥ).—§ 775 (do.): XIII, **166**δ, 7665 (one of the ṛshis of the south). Cf. the prec.

Prāṇa[1] ("breath"). § 116 (Vasu, pl.): I, **66**, 2586 (son of Varcas (or of Varcasvin, BR.) and Manoharā). § 270 (Brahmasabhāv.): II, **11**, 443 (in the palace of Brahmán).

Prāṇa[2] (do.), name of fires. § 491 (Āṅgirasa): III, **220**, 14156 (*Prāṇaḥ Prāṇaputrakaḥ*), 14165 (father of Anudātta).

***Prāṇa**[3], one of the five vital breaths. § 485 (Pativratop.): III, **213**, 13961, 13962, 13964, 13970, 13972, 13976 (the whole exposition is nearly identical with § 660*c*).—§ 560 (Sanatsujātap.): V, **46**, 1757, 1760.—§ 579 (Bhagavadgītāp.): VI, **29**, 1062 (*prāṇāpānau*).—§ 595 (Shoḍaçarāj., v. Rāma Dāçarathi): VII, **59**, 2237 (*prāṇāpānasamānāḥ*).—

§ 603 (Nārāyaṇāstramokshap.): VII, **202**κκ, 9630.—§ 660*b* (Bhṛgu-Bharadvājasaṃv.): XII, **184**, 6844 (°*āt praṇīyate prāṇī*), **189**, 6965.—§ 660*c* (do.): The wind or breath called *Prāṇa* residing within the head, and the heat that is there, cause all kinds of exertion. That *Prāṇa* is the living creature, the universal soul, the eternal Being, and the Mind, Intellect, and Consciousness of all living creatures, etc. Thus the living being is, in every respect, caused by *Prāna* to move about and exert . . . That heat, residing between *Apāna* and *Prāṇa*, in the region of the navel, operates, with the aid of those two breaths, in digesting all food that is taken by a living creature. There is a duct beginning from the mouth down to the anal canal. Its extremity is called the anus. From this main duct (*srotas*) numerous subsidiary ones branch out in the bodies of all living creatures. In consequence of the rush of the several breaths (*Prāṇa*, *Samāna*, etc.) those breaths mingle together. The heat (*agniḥ*) [that dwells in *Prāṇa*, PCR.] is called *Ūshman*. It is this heat that causes digestion . . . The breath called *Prāṇa*, the bearer of a current of heat, descends [from the head, PCR.] downwards to the extremity of the anal canal and thence is pushed upwards again. Coming back to its seat in the head it once more sends back the heat it bears. Below the navel is the region of digested matter, and above it that for the food not yet digested. The navel is the depositary of all the forces of life, which sustain the body. Urged by the ten kinds of breaths the ducts (*nāḍyaḥ*), branching out from the heart, convey the liquid juices that food yields upwards, downwards, and in transverse directions. The main duct leading from the mouth to the anus is the path by which *yogins* succeed in attaining to *Bráhman* by holding the soul within the brain. Even thus heat is planted in the breaths called *Prāṇa* and *Apāna* of all embodied creatures. That heat is always burning there like fire in any vessel: XII, **185**, 6868, 6870, 6878, 6882.—§ 662*b* (Jāpakop.): XII, **200**є, 7346.—§ 667 (Mokshadh.): XII, **213**, 7758.—§ 668 (Pañcaçikha-v.): XII, **219**, 7939 (*prāṇāpānau*).—§ 677 (Mokshadh.): XII, **240**, 8740 (do.); **253**, 9091 (do.).—§ 695*b* (Dakshayajñavināça): XII, **285**, 10337 (do.).—§ 704 (Mokshadh.): XII, **302**, 11124.—§ 714*g* (Samāna): XII, **329**, 12397 (son of Apāna), 12398, 12399.—§ 782*b* (Brāhmaṇagītā): XIV, **20***a*, 612, 613, 614; **21**, 646, 647, 653; **23**, 685, 687, (691), 692, 693, 694, 696, 697, 699, 705 (the contention of the vital breaths about superiority); **24**, 712, 716, 719, 722; **25**, 742; **28**, 789.—§ 782*g* (Guruçishyasaṃv.): XIV, **42**, 1109.

Prāṇa[4] = Çiva (1000 names[1]).—Do.[2] = Vishṇu (1000 names).

***prāṇa**, pl. (*āḥ*) ("vital breaths"): III, 13969, 13971, 13973, 13974 (10 (!) in number); XII, 6877, 6879, 6880 (10 (!) in number), 12413.

Prāṇabhagna = Çiva (1000 names[1]).

Prāṇabhṛt, Prāṇada = Vishṇu (1000 names).

Prāṇadhāraṇa[1] = Sūrya (the Sun): III, 155.—Do.[2] = Çiva (1000 names[2]).

Prāṇaghaṇṭa = Çiva (1000 names[1]).

Prāṇajīvaṇa, Prāṇanilaya = Vishṇu (1000 names).

Prāṇātman = Kṛshṇa: XII, 1660.

Praṇava = Vishṇu (1000 names); cf. VI, 1119; XIII, 2178.

Praṇidhi, name of a fire (?). § 491 (Āṅgirasa): III, **220**, 14164 (son of Bṛhadratha).

Prāṅnadī, a tīrtha. § 370 (Tīrthayātrāp.): III, **84**, 8137 (only B., C. has *sakṛn Nandām*).

Prapitāmaha[1] ("great-grandfather") = Bhīshma, q.v.

Prapitāmaha[2] (do.) = Brahmán: I, 7733; III, 1152 (*Svayambhūḥ*); V, 3042 (Kṛshṇa identified with *P.*); VI, †1285 (do.); VIII, 1626; IX, 2192; XII, 7351, 9161; XIII, 1126; XIV, 966.—Do.[3] = Vishṇu (1000 names).

Prāpti[1], wife of Çama. § 117 (Aṃçāvat.): I, **66**, 2597.

Prāpti[2], daughter of Jarāsandha and wife of Kaṃsa. § 273 (Rājasūyārambhap.): II, **14**, 595 (*Astiḥ Prāptiç ca nāmnā te Sahadevānuje*).

***prāpti**[3] (the power of obtaining everything). § 705 (Mokshadh.): XII, **303**, 11229 (among the attributes of Çambhu).—§ 707 (do.): XII, **313**, 11602 (among the attributes of Çambhu Prajāpati).—§ 730 (Ānuçāsanik.): XIII, **14**єє, 1015 (= Çiva).

Praruja[1], a Nāga (?) (according to Nīl. a Yaksha). § 46 (Garuḍa): I, **32***a*, 1489 (had an encounter with Garuḍa).

Praruja[2], a Rākshasa. § 537 (Rāma-Rāvaṇayuddha): III, **285***a*, 16365 (followed Rāvaṇa).

Prasāda = Çiva (1000 names[2]).

Prāsānāṃ prabhavo 'vyayaḥ = Çiva (1000 names[2]).

Prasandhi, son of Manu. § 778*b* (Saṃvartta-Maruttīya): XIV, **3**, 65, 66 (father of Kshupa).

Prasaṅkhyāṇa, pl. (°*āḥ*), a class of ṛshis. § 615*h* (Naimisha): IX, **37**, 2166.

Prasanna = Çiva (1000 names[2]).

Prasannātman = Vishṇu (1000 names).

Prasena, son of Karṇa. § 608 (Karṇap.): VIII, **82**κ', †4183 (*Karṇātmajam*), †4185 (*Karṇaputraḥ*, slain by Sātyaki).

Prasenajit, an ancient king. § 267 (Yamasabhāv.): II, **8**, 332 (in the palace of Yama).—§ 396 (Jamadagni): III, **116**, 10172 (father of Reṇukā, the wife of Jamadagni).—§ 655 (Āpaddh.): XII, **159***a*, 5924 (attained to heaven).—§ 677 (Mokshadh.): XII, **235**, 8610 (attained to heaven by making gifts of kine).

Prāsenajitī ("daughter of Prasenajit") = Suyajñā, the wife of Mahābhauma: I, ††3773 (*S*°).

Praskandana = Çiva (1000 names[2]).

Prasravaṇam Indrasya, a tīrtha. § 406 (Tīrthayātrāp.): III, **125**, 10418.

Prasthala, pl. (°*āḥ*), a people, a clan of the Trigartas. § 607 (Karṇap.): VIII, **44**λ, 2070 (among the peoples of blameable behaviour).

Prasthalādhipa ("king of the Prasthalas") = Suçarman, the Trigarta king; VI, 3296 (*S*°), 3856 (*Traigartaḥ*), 5289 (do.); VII, 691 (*Suçarmā . . . Trigartaḥ*).

Prasthalādhipati (do.) = Suçarman: IX, 1485.

Prastuta, a Daitya. § 564 (Mātalīyop.): V, **105**, 3685 (had been slain by Garuḍa).

Prasuhma, pl. (°*āḥ*), a people. § 280 (Bhīmasena): II, **30**, 1090 (in the east, vanquished by Bhīmasena on his digvijaya). Cf. Suhma, pl.

Prasvāpa, name of a weapon. § 573 (Ambopākhyānap.): V, **183**, 7259 (*ástram . . . Prājāpatyaṃ Viçvakṛtaṃ P°aṃ nāma*, acquired by Bhīshma), 7265; **184**, 7289 (*astram*), **185**, 7290, 7291 (*astram*), 7292 (Nārada forebade Bhīshma to employ the *P.* against Rāma Jāmadagnya).

Pratāpa, a Sauvīra prince, one of the standard-bearers of Jayadratha. § 522 (Draupadīharaṇap.): III, **265**, †15598.

Pratāpana = Vishṇu (1000 names).

Prātara, a serpent. § 66 (Sarpasattra): I, **57**, 2154 (°*ātakau*, of Kauravya's race).

Pratardana[1], king of the Kāçis, son of Divodāsa. § 149 (Yayāti): I, **86**, 3539; **92**, (†3658), (†3660); **93**, †3688 (when Yayāti fell down from heaven his daughter's sons,

Pratardana, etc., offered him their worlds, but he would not accept them; then they all (Yayāti, *P.*, etc.) ascended to heaven).—§ 267 (Yamasabhāv.): II, **8,** 320 (in the palace of Yama), 329 (do., the same?).—§ 467 (Rājanyamahābhāgya): III, **198,** ††13302, ††13307 (Nārada described the merits of *P.*).—§ 565 (Gālavacarita); V, **117,** 3977 (born of Mādhavī, the daughter of Yayāti to Divodāsa).—§ 566 (Yayāti): V, **121,** 4057; **122,** 4083 (the daughter-sons of Yayāti, viz. *P.*, etc., caused him again to ascend to heaven by means of their good deeds).—§ 638*b* (Rāmopākhyāna): XII, **49,** 1773 (*ye te Yayātipatane yajñe santaḥ samāgatāḥ P°prabhṛtayaḥ*, cf. § 149 and § 566), 1795 (father of Vatsa). —§ 641 (Rājadh.): XII, **96,** 3576; **99,** 3664 (battle between *P.* and Janaka). —§ 656 (Khaḍgotpattik.): XII, **166**δ, 6199, 6200 (received the sword from Çibi, from *P.* it passed over to Ashṭaka).—§ 677 (Mokshadh.): XII, **235,** 8594 (*Kāçipatiḥ*, gave his eyes to a brahman).—§ 736*b* (Vītahavyop.): XIII, **30,** 1969 (son of Divodāsa), 1975, 1976, 1979, 1981, 1985, 1992 (the wars between *P.* and Vītahavya).—§ 767 (Ānuçāsanik.): XIII, **137*a*,** 6249 (*Kāçipatiḥ*, gave his son to a brahman, cf. XII, § 594).—§ 775 (do.): XIII, **166**η, 7682 (enumeration). Cf. Divodāsātmaja, Kāçipati.

Pratardana[2], a Kuru warrior. § 593 (Abhimanyuvadhap.): VII, **37**κ, 1610 (attacked Abhimanyu).

Pratardana[3] = Vishṇu (1000 names).

Prathamatrisauparṇa = Mahāpurusha (Mahāpurushastava).

Pratīcya, pl. (°*āḥ*) ("the Westerners"). § 512 (Ghoshayātrāp.): III, **237,** 14774 (°*odīcyavāsinaḥ*).—§ 556 (Sañjayayānap.): V, **30,** †890 (in the army of Duryodhana).—§ 571 (Ulūkadūtāgamanap.): V, **160**γ, †5510 (do.); **161,** †5555 (do.).—§ 573 (Ambopākhyānap.): V, **195**ε, 7608 (do.).—§ 576 (Bhagavadgītāp.): VI, **15,** 604 (shall protect Bhīshma). —§ 586 (Bhīshmavadhap.): VI, **106**τ, 4808 (protect Bhīshma).—§ 587 (do.): VI, **117**ρ, 5484 (attacked Arjuna); **119*aa*,** 5648 (abandoned Bhīshma).—§ 589 (Droṇābhishekap.): VII, **7**ζ, 183 (in the rear of Duryodhana's army).—§ 604 (Karṇap.): VIII, **5**ζ, 138 (had been slain).—§ 608 (do.): VIII, **70**πππ, †3511 (do.), †3524 (do.).—§ 609 (Çalyap.): IX, **1**γ, 28.

Pratīcya, adj. ("belonging to the west") § 285 (Nakula): II, **32,** 1104 (*nṛpāḥ*, vanquished by Nakula).

Pratīcyā, the wife of Pulastya. § 565 (Gālavacarita): V, **117,** 3975 (*reme . . . yathā . . . Pulastyaç ca P°ayā*).

Pratiçravaṇa, a nakshatra. § 134 (Viçvāmitra): I, **71,** 2928 (*cakārāñyañ ca lokaṃ vai kruddho nakshatrasampadā* | *P°pūrvāṇi nakshatrāṇi cakāra yaḥ*, sc. Viçvāmitra; named *P.* in opposition to Çravaṇa).

Pratiçravas, an ancient king. § 156 (Pūruvaṃç.): I, **95,** ††3796 (son of Bhīmasena and Kaikeyī), ††3797 (father of Pratīpa).

Prathita = Vishṇu (1000 names).

Prathu = Vishṇu (1000 names, only C.; B. has *Pṛthu*).

Pratijñāparvan(°va) ("the section including the vow of Arjuna," the 74th of the minor parvans of Mhbhr.).—§ 10 (Parvas.): I, **2,** 339.—§ 596: In the evening, when *Arjuna*, having slain large numbers of *Saṃçaptakas*, proceeded towards his tent, he said to *Kṛshṇa* that his heart was affrighted; he noticed indications of disaster; *Abhimanyu* did not come out with smiles to receive him, etc. He remembered that *Droṇa* had this day formed the circular army, which none save *Abhimanyu* could break, but he had not taught him how to come out of it, after having pierced it; he had heard the leonine shouts of the *Dhārtarāshṭras*, and *Kṛshṇa* had heard *Yuyutsu* censuring them for having slain a child instead of *Arjuna*, and then *Yuyutsu* had thrown away his weapons afflicted with rage and grief. *Kṛshṇa* consoled *Arjuna*, referring to the *kshatriya* duties and heaven. None save *Kṛshṇa* and *Yudhishṭhira* (who were always acceptable to him) could address *Arjuna*. *Yudhishṭhira*, addressing him, told (VII, **72**) him the particulars of *Abhimanyu's* heroism and fall. *Arjuna* vowed to slay *Jayadratha* before the setting of the morrow's sun (his oath); even as to *As.*, *D.*, men, birds, snakes, *P.*, wanderers of the night, *B.-ṛ.*, *D.-ṛ.*, etc., he said that they would not succeed in protecting him, even if he entered *Rasātala*, or ascended the firmament, or repaired to the city of the gods (*Devapuraṃ*) or the city of *Diti* (*Diteḥ puraṃ*); if the sun set before he had slain him, he would himself ascend the pyre. *Arjuna* bent the *Gāṇḍīva*, *Kṛshṇa* blew the *Pāñcajanya*, *Arjuna* the *Devadatta* (VII, **73**). Having been informed by spies, *Jayadratha* was overwhelmed with sorrow and fear, thinking that not even *Droṇa*, etc. (*a*), not even *D.*, *G.*, *As.*, *U.*, *Rā.*, can protect him against *Arjuna*; he wished to return home. *Duryodhana* comforted him, saying that he, *Karṇa*, etc. (β), would protect him. *Jayadratha*, accompanied by *Duryodhana*, repaired that very night to *Droṇa* and questioned him about the difference between himself and *Arjuna*. *Droṇa* said they had got the same instruction, but *Arjuna* was superior to *Jayadratha* in consequence of *yoga* and the hard life led by *Arjuna*; *Droṇa* would, however, protect him, forming an impenetrable array; and, moreover, death ought not to be an object of terror to him (VII, **74**). *Kṛshṇa* remonstrated with *Arjuna* for his rash vow; the *Kurus* had expected an attack by *Arjuna*; now they will protect *Jayadratha* (who had mentioned *Arjuna's* encounter with *Çiva*, *Hiraṇyapura*, etc.); *Karṇa*, etc. (γ) would be in *Jayadratha's* van; *Droṇa's* army would be half a *çakaṭa* and half a lotus with a needle-mouthed array in the middle (VII, **75**). *Arjuna* assured *Kṛshṇa* of his competence to accomplish his vow, notwithstanding *Droṇa*, *Sā.*, *R.*, *V.*, *A.*, *M.*, with *Indra*, *V.-D.*, *D.*, *P.*, *G.*, *Garuḍa*, etc., by the means of *Gāṇḍīva* and the weapons he had obtained from *Yama*, etc. (δ), and the *Brāhma* weapon (VII, **76**). The gods with *Indra* became very anxious. Sinister omens appeared in nature. *Kṛshṇa* went to *Arjuna's* abode and comforted *Subhadrā* (with the *kshatriya* duties, etc., and revenge) (VII, **77**). *Subhadrā* lamented over *Abhimanyu*, and said "fie on *Bhīmasena*, etc." (ε), because they had not protected him. *Draupadī* and *Uttarā* came to her, lamenting. *Kṛshṇa* said that *Abhimanyu* had obtained the most laudable and enviable goal. Then he returned to *Arjuna* (VII, **78**). *Arjuna* performed his usual nightly sacrifice to *Çiva*. *Kṛshṇa* with *Dāruka* repaired to his own tent. None in the *Pāṇḍava* camp slept that night, thinking of *Arjuna*. In the middle of the night *Kṛshṇa* said to *Dāruka* that he had resolved to fight to-morrow [if necessary]; he should equip his chariot, placing on it *Kaumodakī*, etc., making room for *Garuḍa*, and yoking thereto *Balāhaka*, etc. (ζ); when hearing *Pāñcajanya* emitting the shrill *Ṛshabha* note, he should come to *Kṛshṇa* (VII, **79**). *Arjuna* in a dream saw *Kṛshṇa*, who told him not to grieve, and mentioned the *Pāçupata* weapon (with which *Çiva* slew all the *Daityas* in battle); if he remembered it now, he would be able to slay *Jayadratha* to-morrow; otherwise he should pray to *Çiva*. At the *Brāhma* hour,

Arjuna saw himself sojourning through the sky (*Himavat*); *Maṇimat*, frequented by *Si.* and *Cā.*, etc. (η) with *Kṛshṇa*, to where *Çiva* was seated with *Pārvatī* (description) (δ); *Kṛshṇa* and *Arjuna* hymned *Mahādeva* (VII, **80**). *Arjuna* saw that the offerings he had made every night to *Kṛshṇa* had come to *Çiva*, and he mentally worshipped both *Kṛshṇa* and *Çiva*. *Çiva* then told *Kṛshṇa* and *Arjuna* where to fetch his bow and arrow from a lake of *amṛta*. In the lake they saw two terrible snakes; when they had uttered the *Brahma Çatarudriya*, the snakes assumed the forms of a bow and arrow. From *Çiva's* body there came out a *brahmacārin* of blue throat and red locks, and having showed *Arjuna* the use of the bow and arrow, and the *mantras*, he sped these weapons to that same lake. Having thus once more obtained the *Pāçupata* weapon, *Arjuna* with *Kṛshṇa* came back to their own camp (VII, **81**).—§ 597: THE FOURTEENTH DAY. *Yudhishṭhira* underwent his morning rites (very copious description); *Kṛshṇa* visited *Yudhishṭhira* (VII, **82**). Then also *Virāṭa*, etc., came (*a*). *Yudhishṭhira* asked *Kṛshṇa* to rescue the *Pāṇḍavas*, quoting *Nārada*. *Kṛshṇa* assured *Yudhishṭhira* of *Arjuna's* success (VII, **83**). *Arjuna* came and acquainted *Yudhishṭhira* of his dream. Then he and *Kṛshṇa* and *Yuyudhāna* (these two in one chariot) set out to *Arjuna's* pavilion. *Kṛshṇa* equipped *Arjuna's* chariot (which had previously been sanctified by *mantras*), which *Arjuna* circumambulated, bow and arrows in hand. *Arjuna*, *Yuyudhāna*, and *Kṛshṇa* mounted the chariot. Many auspicious omens appeared. *Arjuna* charged *Yuyudhāna* to protect *Yudhishṭhira* in his absence (only he or *Pradyumna* is able to do it). *Yuyudhāna* proceeded to *Yudhishṭhira* (VII, **84**).

prātikāmin ("servant," or "messenger", esp. said of that *sūta* who was sent to bring Draupadī to the assembly): II, †2198 (°*īṃ. acc.*), †2199, †2200 (C. by error °*kakā*°), (†2201), †2202, (†2203), 2210 (*sūtaḥ*), (†2211), †2219 (*sūtaṃ*), 2491, 2678 (*sūtaputraṃ*); III, 17243; IV, 524; IX, 1937, 3163. Cf. Sūta, Sūtaja, Sūtaputra.

Pratimāsya (C.) or **Pratimatsya** (B.), pl. (°*āḥ*), a people. § 574 (Jambūkh.): VI, **9**μ, 359. Cf. Potimatsaka.

Pratīpa, an ancient king. § 155 (Pūruvaṃç.): I, **94**, 3749 (son of the elder Dhṛtarāshṭra (so B.) or of Kuṇḍika (so C.)), 3750 (father of Devāpi, Çāntanu, and Bālhīka).—§ 156 (do.): I, **95**, ††3797 (son of Pratiçravas, husband of Sunandā Çaibyā, and father of Devāpi, Çāntanu, and Bālhīka).—§ 161 (Mahābhishop.): I, **96**, 3849, 3858 (°*sya sutaḥ . . . Çāntanuḥ*, Mahābhisha chose to be born as Çāntanu, the son of *P.*).—§ 162 (Çāntanūp.): I, **97**, 3865, 3868, 3870, 3872, 3881, 3884, 3887 (accepted Gaṅgā for his daughter-in-law, birth of his son Çāntanu).—§ 569 (Bhagavadyānap.): V, **147**, 4988 (°*rakshitaṃ rāshṭraṃ*); **149**, 5053 (*pitur mama pitāmahaḥ*, says Dhṛtarāshtra; father of Devāpi, Çāntanu, and Bālhīka). — § 775 (Ānuçāsanik.): XIII, **166**η, 7683 (enumeration). Cf. Kurunandana.

Prātīpa ("son of Pratīpa") = Çāntanu: V, 5003 (*Ç*°).

Prātīpeya[1] (do.) = Çāntanu: I, 5088.

Prātīpeya[2] (do.) = Bālhīka: V, †693 (*B*°); XI, 621 (*B*°).

Prātīpeya (pl.) (°*āḥ*) ("descendants of Pratīpa"). § 298 (Dyūtap.): II, **63**, 2112, †2117.—§ 561 (Yānasandhip.): V, **57**, 2289.

Prātīpīya ("son of Pratīpa") = Bālhīka: VII, 6934.

Pratirūpa, an Asura (?). § 673*b* (Bali-Vāsavasamv.): XII, **227*a***, 8265 (among the ancient rulers of the earth).

Pratiskandha, a warrior of Skanda. § 615*u* (Skanda): IX, **45**η, 2559.

Pratishṭhā, a mātṛ. § 615*u* (Skanda): IX, **46**θ, 2647.

Pratishṭhāna, a city (on the Gaṅgā, near the confluence of the Gaṅgā and the Yamunā). § 373 (Prayāga): III, **85**, 8219 (a tīrtha near Prayāga).—§ 376 (Tīrthayātrāp.): III, **85**, 8257 (there Bhīshma ended (*pratishṭhitā*) his tīrthayātrā). —§ 565 (Gālavac.): V, **114**, 3905 (the capital of Yayāti).

Pratishṭhita = Vishṇu (1000 names).

Pratismṛti, name of a science. § 11 (Parvasaṅgr.): I, **2**, 431 (*vidyayā*, cf. § 329).—§ 329 (Kāmyakavanapr.): III, **36**, 1440 (*vidyāṃ P°ṃ nāma*, communicated by Vyāsa to Yudhishṭhira and by him to Arjuna).

Pratīta, a Viçvadeva. § 749 (Ānuçāsanik.): XIII, **91**γ, 4357 (enumeration).

Prativindhya[1], son of Yudhishṭhira and Draupadī. § 83 (Ādivaṃçāvatāraṇa): I, **63**β, 2451 (°*o Yudhishṭhirāt*, cf. § 253).—§ 130 (Aṃçāvat.): I, **67**, 2763 (the sons of Draupadī were incarnations of the Viçvadevas). — § 159 (Pūruvaṃç.): I, **95**, ††3827 (enumeration of the sons of the Pāṇḍavas).—§ 253 (Haraṇāharaṇap.): I, **221**, 8039 (his birth), 8041 (origin of his name).—§ 301 (Dyūtap.): II, **71**, 2408 (*mamātmajaṃ*, says Draupadī).—§ 317 (Arjunābhigamanap.): III, **12**, 533 (°*o Yudhishṭhirāt*, all. to § 253). —§ 511 (Draupadī-Satyabhāmāsaṃv.): III, **235**, 14731.—§ 578 (Bhīshmavadhap.): VI, **45**[18], 1731, 1733 (fights with Çakuni).—§ 586 (do.): VI, **100**, 4568 (fights with Alambusha).—§ 592 (Saṃçaptakavadhap.): VII, **23**ο, 976 (description of his horses); **25**, 1092, 1093 (fights with Açvatthāman). — § 600 (Ghaṭotkacavadhap.): VII, **165**, 7366 (resisted by Duḥçāsana); **168**, 7545, 7547, 7549, 7550 (°*hayān*, *P.* fights with Duḥçāsana, his horses are felled).—§ 605 (Karṇap.): VIII, **13**, 493 (attacked Citra); **14**, 545, 547, 549, 550, 551, 554, 555, 556, 560 (slew Citra); **25**, 1009 (°*rathaṃ*).—§ 608 (do.): VIII, **55**λλ, 2664 (pierced Açvatthāman).—§ 616 (Sauptikap.): X, **8**, 372 (slain by Açvatthāman at the nightly encounter). Cf. Yaudhishṭhira, Yaudhishṭhiri.

Prativindhya[2], one or more kings. § 130 (Aṃçāvat.): I, **67**, 2658 (incarnation of the Asura Ekacakra).—§ 279 (Arjuna): II, **26**, 998 (in the north, vanquished by Arjuna on his digvijaya).—§ 554 (Sainyodyogap.): V, **4**γ, 76.

Prativindhya, pl. (°*āḥ*). § 267 (Yamasabhāv.): II, **8**, 335 (100 *P.* in the palace of Yama).

Pratyagraha, son of Vasu Uparicara. § 74 (Vasu): I, **63**, 2363 (second son of Vasu).

Pratyakshadharman = Yama: III, 15406.

Pratyaṅga, an ancient king. § 6 (Anukram.): I, **1*a***, 232 (in Sañjaya's enumeration).

Pratyaya[1] = Çiva (1000 names[2]).—Do[2] = Vishṇu (1000 names).

Pratyūsha, name of one of the Vasus. § 116 (Vasu, pl.): I, **66**, 2582 (enumeration), 2584 (son of Prabhātā [and Prajāpati]), 2590 (father of the ṛshi Devala).—§ 770 (Ānuçāsanik.): XIII, **151**δ, 7095 (the seventh of the Vasus).

Praushṭhapada ("named after the nakshatra Proshṭhapadā"), name of a month. § 759 (Ānuçāsanik.): XIII, **106**β, 5159.

Praushṭhapadā (VI, 82), v. Proshṭhapadā.

Pravacanagata = Mahāpurusha (Mahāpurushastava).

Pravaha, name of a certain wind. § 704 (Mokshadh.): XII, **302**, 11124 (*anilaṃ*), 11170 (*vāyuḥ*).—§ 714*h* (Çukakṛtya). The wind which urges masses of clouds born of smoke and heat, is the first of the winds and named *P.*: XII, **329**, 12400 (*anilaḥ*).

Pravāha, a warrior of Skanda. § 615*u* (Skanda): IX, **45**η, 2566 (only B.), 2572.
Pravālaka (C. °*abā*°), a Yaksha. § 269 (Vaiçravaṇasabhāv.): II, **10,** 399 (in the palace of Kubera).
Pravara = Çiva (1000 names[2]).
Pravarā, a river. § 574 (Jambūkh.): VI, **9**λ, 331 (in Bhāratavarsha).
Pravara(ḥ) surāṇām = Skanda: III, 14644.
Prāvāra, a region on Krauñcadvīpa. § 575 (Bhūmip.): VI, **12**θ, 463. Cf. next.
Prāvāraka = Prāvāra: VI, 463.
Prāvārakarṇa, name of an old owl. § 468 (Indradyumnop.): III, **199,** ††13334 (°*o nāmolūkaḥ*), ††13347 (*ulūkam*).
Pravasu, son of Īlina. § 150 (Pūruvaṃç.): I, **94,** 3708 (fifth son of Īlina).
Praveṇī, a river. § 377 (Dhaumyatīrthak.): III, **88,** 8336 (°*yuttaramārge tu puṇye Kaṇvāçrame tathā* | *tāpasānām araṇyāni kīrtitāni*, in the south).
Pravepana, a serpent. § 64 (Sarpasattra): I, **57,** 2150 (of Takshaka's race).
Pravīra, son of Pūru. § 150 (Pūruvaṃç.): I, **94,** 3694 (second son of Pūru and Paushṭī).
Pravīra, pl. (°*āḥ*), a people. § 562 (Bhagavadyānap.): V, **74**γ, 2732 (°*āṇāṃ Vṛshabhadhvajaḥ*).
Prāvṛsheya, pl. (°*āḥ*), a people. § 574 (Jambūkh.): VI, **9**μ, 358.
Pravṛttavedakriya = Mahāpurusha (Mahāpurushastava).
Pravṛtti = Çiva (1000 names[2]).
Prayāga, a tīrtha at the confluence of the Gaṅgā and the Yamunā. § 61 (Sarpasattra): I, **55,** 2097 (there Soma, Varuṇa, and Prajāpati had performed sacrifices).—§ 373 (cf. Tīrthayātrāp.): At *P.*, whose praise has been sung by *ṛshis*, the gods dwell with *Brahmán* at their head, further the quarters with their presiding deities (*sadigīçvarāḥ*), the *Lokapālas*, the *Sādhyas*, the *Pitṛs*, the great *ṛshis* (*paramarshayaḥ*) *Sanatkumāra*, etc., the stainless *Brahmarshis*, *Aṅgiras*, etc., the *Nāgas*, the *Suparṇas*, the *Siddhas*, the *cakracaras* (i.e. the Sun, etc., Nīl., cf. BR., "Snakes," PCR.), the rivers, the seas, the *Gandharvas*, the *Apsarases*, and *Hari* with *Prajāpati*. There are three fire caverns (*agnikuṇḍāni*) between which the Gaṅgā, that foremost of *tīrthas*, rolls rapidly. There the world-purifying daughter of the Sun (*Tapanasya*) *Yamunā* unites with the Gaṅgā. The country between the Gaṅgā and the Yamunā is regarded as the mons Veneris (*jaghanaṃ*) of the Earth, and the ṛshis regard *P.* as its genitals (*upasthaṃ*). *P.* with *Pratishṭhāna*, *Kambala*, and *Açvatara* and the *tīrtha Bhogavatī* constitute the altar (*vediḥ*) of Prajāpati. There the *Vedas* and the sacrifices in their embodied forms and the ṛshis adore *Prajāpati*; there the gods and rulers of territories (*cakradharāḥ*) perform their sacrifices; therefore *P.* is the most sacred in the three worlds and the foremost of all *tīrthas*. By going thither, by praising it, etc., one is cleansed from sin, etc., and he who bathes there obtains the merit of a *rājasūya* and an *açvamedha*. "Let not the words of the *Vedas* nor the words of men dissuade thy mind from the desire of dying at *P.*" There are 600,010,000 *tīrthas* at *P.* By only bathing there one acquires the merits of the four kinds of knowledge (*cāturvidye*, i.e. the three Vedas and the *ātmavidyā*, Nīl.) and of the truthful (*satyavādishu*): III, **85,** 8212, 8218, 8219 (*sa-Pratishṭhānāṃ*), 8222, 8226 (°*maraṇaṃ*).—§ 375 (Tīrthayātrāp.): III, **85,** 8231.—§ 377 (Dhaumyatīrthak.): III, **87,** 8315 (*Gaṅgā-Yamunayor vīra saṅgamaṃ lokaviçrutaṃ* | *yatrāyajata bhūtātmā pūrvam eva Pitāmahaḥ* | *P°m iti vikhyātaṃ*).—§ 379 (Tīrthayātrāp.): III, **95,** 8514 (*devayajane . . . Gaṅgā-Yamunayoç caiva saṅgame*).—§ 573 (Ambopākhyānap.): V, **186,** 7354 (*devayajane*, there Ambā performed ablutions).—§ 733*p* (Gaṅgā-Yamunayos tīrthaṃ): XIII, **25,** 1723, 1724.—§ 775 (Ānuçāsanik.): XIII, **166*a*,** 7649.
Prayāga, pl. (°*āḥ*), a people (the inhabitants of Prayāga, BR.). § 578 (Bhīshmavadhap.): VI, **50**π, 2080 (in the army of Yudhishṭhira).
Prayatātman = Çiva (1000 names[2]).
Prayuta, a Devagandharva. § 101 (Aṃçāvat.): I, **65,** 2551 (among the Devagandharvas, sons of Muni).
***preta,** pl. (°*āḥ*) ("ghosts"): III, 12245, 12650 (°*gaṇān*); VI, 1775; VII, 6188; VIII, 1485 (*surāmbupretavittānāṃ patīn*, i.e. Indra, Varuṇa, Yama, and Kubera), 4422; X, 389; XII, 5773, 6947; XIII, 732 (°-*Piçācayoḥ*), 4318, 4394; XVIII, 46 (*Vindhyaçailopamaiḥ*). Cf. Pitṛ, pl.
Pretacārin = Çiva (1000 names[2]).
Pretādhipa ("lord of the dead") = Yama: III, 12954 (*Y*°).
Pretaloka ("the world of the dead"): I, 2073, 4588; III, 13406; VI, 4028; VII, 1669, 6696, 7179; XIII, 6117, 6124, 6128, 6139.
Pretarāj ("king of the dead") = Yama: VIII, 542 (*yathā*). Cf. next.
Pretarāja (do.) = Yama: I, 2063, 2757, 4589, 6626; III, 11849; VI, 4533, 4719, 4729, 5449; VII, 3356, 5444, 5548, 7252; VIII, 2554, 3272; IX, 3662; XII, 1108; XV, 795.
Prītivardhana = Vishṇu (1000 names).
Priya[1] = Skanda: III, 14632, 14636.—Do.[2] = Çiva (1000 names[1-2]).
Priyā, wife of the fire Adbhuta. § 494 (Āṅgirasa): III, **222,** 14234 (*Adbhutasya P°ā bhāryā*, so PCR.).
Priyabhṛtya, an ancient king. § 6 (Anukram.): I, **1*a*,** 230 (in Sañjaya's enumeration).
Priyadarçana, a warrior of Skanda. § 615*u* (Skanda): IX, **45**η, 2561.
Priyadattā = Pṛthivī (the earth): XIII, 3114 (*nāma guhyaṃ devyāḥ*).
Priyaka, a warrior of Skanda. § 615*u* (Skanda): IX, **45**η, 2567.
Priyakṛt[1] = Skanda: III, 14636.—Do.[2] = Vishṇu (1000 names).
Priyamālyānulepana, a warrior of Skanda. § 615*u* (Skanda): IX, **45**η, 2562.
Priyaṅkara, an ancient king. § 775 (Ānuçāsanik.): XIII, **166**η, 7680.
Priyārha = Vishṇu (1000 names).
Proshaka, pl. (°*āḥ*), a people. § 574 (Jambūkh.): VI, **9**ο, 376 (in the north-east).
Proshṭha, pl. (°*āḥ*), a people. § 574 (Jambūkh.): VI, **9**ν, 369 (in the south).
Proshṭhapadā, dual and pl., name of a double nakshatra (= Bhādrapadā). § 565 (Gālavacarita): V, **114,** 3898 (°*ābhyāṃ*).—§ 574 (Jambūkh.): VI, **3,** 82 (*Çukraḥ P°e pūrve samāruhya virocate uttare tu parikramya sahitaḥ samudīkshyate* (omens); = *Pūrvabhādrapadānakshatraṃ* and *Uttarabhādrapadānakshatram*, Nīl., C. by error has *Prau*°).—§ 749 (Ānuçāsanik.): XIII, **89*a*,** 4267 (*pūrva-P° āḥ . . . uttarāsu*, merit of performing çrāddhas under the constellation of *P.*).—§ 759 (do.): XIII, **104,** 5082 (°*ayoḥ*, no çrāddha should be performed under the constellation of *P.*). Cf. Bhādrapadā.
Pṛçni, pl. (°*ayaḥ*), a class of ṛshis. § 602 (Droṇavadhap.):

VII, **190**ν, 8728.—§ 630 (Rājadh.): XII, **26**a, 774 (C. by error *Pra°*).—§ 656 (Khaḍgotpattik.): XII, **166**β, 6144 (do.).

Pṛçnigarbha = Kṛshṇa (Vishṇu): XII, 1504, 13173 (etymology), 13174, 13175.

Pṛçnigarbhapravṛtta = Mahāpurusha (Mahāpurushastava (not in C.)).

Pṛshadaçva, an ancient king. § 267 (Yamasabhāv.): II, **8**, 323 (in the palace of Yama).—§ 656 (Khaḍgotpattik.): XII, **166**δ, 6200 (received the sword from Ashṭaka, from *P.* it passed over to Bharadvāja).

Pṛshaddhra, an ancient king. § 775 (Ānuçāsanik.): XIII, **166**η, 7683. Cf. next.

Pṛshadhra, one or more ancient kings. § 139 (Manu Vaivasvata): I, **75**, 3141 (ninth son of Manu Vaivasvata).—§ 787 (Āçramavāsap.): XV, **20**, 548 (*Vajradharopamaḥ*, ascended to heaven). Cf. the prec.

Pṛshadhru (B. *°a*), a Pāṇḍava warrior. § 600 (Ghaṭotkacavadhap.): VII, **156**ν, 6912 (slain by Açvatthāman).

Pṛshata, king of the Pāñcālas, father of Drupada).—§ 201*b* (Drupada): I, **130**, 5109 (friend of Bharadvāja), 5111 (father of Drupada).—§ 217 (Caitrarathap.): I, **166**, 6333 (friend of Bharadvāja (C. *Bhā°*) and father of Drupada), 6335 (succeeded by Drupada).

Pṛshatātmaja ("the son of Pṛshata") = Drupada: V, 7415.

Pṛshatī = Pārshatī[1]: I, 6390.

Pṛshṭaja, a son or form of Skanda. § 116 (Vasu, pl.): I, **66**, 2588 (cf. Naigameya).

Pṛthā = Kuntī (q.v.): I, 175, 589, 612, 2764, 2783, ††3811, ††3835, 4382, 4412, 4671, 4675, 4860, 5026, 5363, 5381, 5409, 5941, 6110, 6113, 6239, †7083, †7084, 7129, †7131, 7350, 7453, 7522, 7540, 7982; II, 22, 976, 1616, 2564, 2584, 2593; III, 1871, 14689, 17007, 17009, 17019, 17024, 17025, 17039, 17046, 17051, 17058, 17069, 17126, 17147, 17148, 17167; V, 3128, 3130, 3220, 3236, 4885, 4912, 4930, 4955; VIII, 3382, †3389 (so B.), †3400; XI, 414, 415, 419; XII, 26, 27, 31, 35, 36, 38, 42, 1446; XIII, 7714; XIV, 388, 1505, 1507, 1839, 1859, 1893, 1940, 1962, 1965, 1973, 2604, 2672; XV, 497, 525, 578, 596, 606, 643, 646, 845, 1017, 1027, 1041, 1045, 1054, 1063, 1072, 1090, 1095.

Pṛthāçva, an ancient king. § 267 (Yamasabhāv.): II, **8**, 330 (in the palace of Yama).

Pṛthātmaja, pl. (*°āḥ*) ("the sons of Pṛthā [i.e. Kuntī]") = Pārtha, pl.: VIII, †4521.

***Pṛthivī** ("Earth," personified): II, 458; III, 147 (identified with Sūrya (the sun)), 481 (identified with Kṛshṇa), (10939); VII, 1283; IX, 2514; XI, 214, 217; XII, 421 (*devīṃ*), 1788, (1790), 1803, 2238, 13424 (*mātaraṃ*); XIII, 369 (*prīṇāti mātaraṃ yena P°ī tena pūjitā*), 1540, (1541), 1545, (2131), 4096 (*devī . . . Vasumatī*), 4350 (*Vaishṇavī Kāçyapī*), 4652 (*Vāsudevasya saṃvādaṃ P°yāç caiva*); 4653, (4655), 7235, 7238 (*Kāçyapī*). Cf. Pṛthvī.

Pṛthiviñjaya = Uttara: IV, 2167, 2220. Cf. Bhūmiñjaya.

Pṛthivīpati = Mahāpurusha (Mahāpurushastava).

Pṛthivītīrtha, a tīrtha. § 362 (Tīrthayātrāp.): III, **83**, 5083.

Pṛthu[1], name of a Vasu. § 164 (Āpavop.): I, **99**, 3930 (*°vādyā Vasavaḥ*), 3945 (*°vādyair bhrātṛbhiḥ . . . Dyauḥ*). Cf. Dhara.

Pṛthu[2], a Vṛshṇi. § 232 (Svayaṃvarap.): I, **186**, 6998 (came to the svayaṃvara of Draupadī).—§ 252 (Subhadrāharaṇap.): I, **219**, 7915.—§ 589 (Droṇābhishekap.): VII, **11**ξ, 409.

Pṛthu[3], a king of Ayodhyā. § 475 (Dhundhumārop.): III, **202**, 13516 (son of Anenas), 13517 (father of Viçvagaçva).

Pṛthu[4], = Çiva: XIV, 210.—Do.[5] = Vishṇu (1000 names; only B., C. has *Prathu*).

Pṛthu Vainya (C. sometimes Vaiṇya), a mythical king. § 11 (Parvasaṅgr.): I, **2**, 466 (*°or Vainyasya yatroktam ākhyānaṃ paramarshiṇā* (i.e. Mārkaṇḍeya); in the third book of Mhbhr., however, the narrative alluded to is not found).—§ 296 (Dyūtap.): II, **53**, 1929 (*Vainyaḥ*).—§ 574 (Jambūkh.): VI, **9**aa, 314 (*Vainyasya*).—§ 595 (Shoḍaçarāj.): King *Pṛthu Vainya* in his rājasūya was installed by M.-ṛ. as emperor (*sāmrājye*); (etymology of *Pṛthu*, *kshatriya*, and *rājan*). During his time the earth yielded crops in sufficiency, etc.; the *kuça* blades were all of gold, etc.; when king *P.* went to the sea, the waves became solid; the very mountains used to open before him that he might pass through them. Once the trees, the mountains, the gods, the Asuras, the men, the Uragas, the seven ṛshis, the Yakshas, the Apsarases, and the Pitṛs came to *P.* and calling him their emperor (*samrāṭ*), etc., asked boons from him. Taking his *Ājagava* bow, *P.* caused them to milk the Earth (whom he made his daughter) by means of a calf (A), a milker (B), and vessels (C) for various kinds of milk (D): (1) [the trees]: the çāla-tree (A), the fig-tree (*plakshaḥ*) (B.), a vessel of udumbara wood (C), torn buds (*chinnaprarohaṇaṃ*) (D). (2) [The mountains]: the eastern hill (*Udayaḥ parvataḥ*) (A), Meru (B), a stone (*açmamayaṃ*) vessel (C), gems and herbs (D). (3) [The gods]: a god (Indra?) (B), things capable of bestowing strength (D). (4) The Asuras: *Virocana* (A), *Dvimūrdhan* (B), an unbaked pot (C), wine (*madyaṃ*) (D). (5) Men: *Manu Svāyambhuva* (A), *Pṛthu* (B), cultivation and crops (D). (6) The serpents: *Takshaka* (A), *Dhṛtarāshṭra* (B), a gourd (C), poison (D). (7) The seven ṛshis: *Soma* (A), *Bṛhaspati* (B), *chandas* (C), the Vedas (D). (8) The Yakshas: *Vṛshadhvaja* (A), *Vaiçravaṇa* (i.e. Kubera) (B), an unbaked pot (C), the power of disappearing at will (*antardhānaṃ*) (D). (9) The Gandharvas and the Apsarases: *Citraratha* (A), *Viçvaruci* (B), a lotus (C), perfumes (D). (10) The Pitṛs: *Yama Vaivasvata* (A), *Antaka* (B), silvern vessels (C), *svadhā* (D). "To this day the creatures exist in the same way." *P.* caused golden images to be made of every article on earth and bestowed them all on the brahmans at his great horse-sacrifice, also 66,000 elephants of gold; also the whole world (VII, **69**): VII, **69**, 2394 (*Vaiṇyaṃ*), 2395, 2396 (*Vaiṇyaṃ*), 2406 (*Vaiṇyaḥ*), 2408, 2414, 2421 (*Vaiṇyaḥ*).—§ 632*b* (Shoḍaçarāj., cf. § 595): XII, **29**, 1030 (*Vainyaṃ*), 1031, 1032 (*Vainyaṃ*, repetition from § 595).—§ 641*f* (cf. Vena). When *P.* had sprung from the right hand of Vena, the M.-ṛ., R., and the gods told him to observe righteousness and punish the wicked, etc. *Çukra* became his priest, the *Vālakhilyas* his counsellors, the *Sārasvatas* his companions (*Sārasvatyo gaṇas tathā*), the M.-ṛ. *Garga* became his astrologer (*sāṃvatsaraḥ*); *Sūta* and *Māgadha* (who came into existence before *P.*) became his panegyrists, he gave to *Sūta* the land lying on the sea-coast (*Anūpadeçaṃ*), to *Māgadha Magadha*. *P.* made the earth even (in every manvantara the earth becomes uneven), removing the rocks lying around with the horn of his bow; by this means the hills and the mountains became enlarged. Then *Vishṇu*, etc. (δ) crowned *P.* and gave him rich gifts; steeds, chariots, etc., came into existence as soon as *P.* thought of them.

At this time there was neither decrepitude nor famine, etc., nobody had any fear from reptiles and thieves, etc.; when he proceeded to the sea, the waters used to be solidified, the mountains granted him passage, etc. He drew from the earth as a milker from a cow seventeen kinds of crops for the *Y.*, *Rā.*, and *N.*, etc. He caused all creatures to regard righteousness as the foremost of all things; he was called *rājan* (etymology) and *kshatriya* (etymology), etymology of the name Pṛthivī. *Vishṇu* confirmed his power and entered his body in consequence of his penances; for this reason the entire universe bows to the king as to a god. At this time a gold lotus was born from *Vishṇu's* brow, from that lotus was born the goddess *Çrī*, who became the spouse of *Dharma* ("righteousness"); their son was *Artha* ("profit"); all the three were established in sovereignty. The king is really a portion of Vishṇu on earth. He who once beheld his (*P.'s* ?) amiable face became (becomes ?) obedient to him: XII, **59**, 2234 (*Vainyaḥ*).—§ 656*f* (Khaḍgotpattik.): It was Pṛthu Vainya who first created the bow; he also milked the earth for very many [sorts of] grain (*çasyāni*) and protected the earth virtuously as before: XII, **166**, 6205.—§ 673*b* (Bali-Vāsavasaṃv.): XII, **227**, 8261 (among the ancient rulers of the earth).—§ 761 (Ānuçāsanik.): XIII, **115**δ, 5667 (did not eat meat during the month of Kārttika).—§ 770 (do.): XIII, **151**μ, 7125 (*Vainyaṃ nṛpavaraṃ Pṛthvī yasyābhavat sutā | Prajāpatiṃ sarvabhaumaṃ*).—§ 795 (do.): XIII, **166**η, 7680 (*ādirājaḥ P°ur Vainyaḥ*). Cf. Prajāpati, Vainya.

Pṛthuçravas[1], one or more ancient kings. § 156 (Pūruvaṃç.): I, **95**, ††3774 (father of Kāmā, the wife of Ayutanāyin).—§ 267 (Yamasabhāv.): II, **8**, 323 (in the palace of Yama).

Pṛthuçravas[2], a brahman. § 324 (Dvaitavanapraveça): III, **26***a*, 985 (worshipped Yudhishṭhira).

Pṛthuçravas[3], a warrior of Skanda. § 615*u* (Skanda): IX, **45**η, 2564.

Pṛthuçravas[4], a serpent. § 793 (Mausalap.): XVI, **4**η, †119.

Pṛthūdaka, a tīrtha on the Sarasvatī. § 366 (Tīrthayātrāp.): III, **83**, 7012.—§ 367 (do.): They say that *Kurukshetra* is holy, that *Sarasvatī* is holier than *Kurukshetra*, that the (united) tīrthas are holier than *Sarasvatī*, and *P.* holier than the (united) tīrthas. It has been sung by *Sanatkumāra* and *Vyāsa* that he who, reciting prayer (*japyaparaḥ*), gives up his body in *P.* shall not die (B. has: "him death to-morrow will not afflict"). Even the sinful attain to heaven by bathing in *P.*: III, **83**, 7016, 7017, 7018, 7020.—§ 615*l* (Rushaṅgu): IX, **39**, 2275, 2279 (Rushaṅgu bathed in *P.* and uttered a benediction on it (v. 2279, cf. III, 7016*b*–7017*a*)).—§ 652*b* (Indrota-Pārīkshitīya): XII, **152***a*, 5645 (= III, 7015*b*–7016*a*).

Pṛthuhara = Çiva: XIV, 210 (C. *Pṛthu°*).

Pṛthulāçva, an ancient king. § 267 (Yamasabhāv.): II, **8**, 333 (in the palace of Yama).

Pṛthulāksha, an ancient king. § 267 (Yamasabhāv.): II, **8**, 320 (in the palace of Yama).

Pṛthuvaktrā, a mātṛ. § 615*u* (Skanda): IX, **46**θ, 2637.

Pṛthuvega, an ancient king. § 267 (Yamasabhāv.): II, **8**, 323 (in the palace of Yama).

***Pṛthvī** = Pṛthivī (the Earth): XIII, 2129 (*saṃvādaṃ Vāsudevasya P°vyāç ca*, C. by error *°thyā°*), 7125 (daughter of Pṛthu Vainya).

Pucchāṇḍaka, a serpent. § 64 (Sarpasattra): I, **57**, 2149 (of Takshaka's race).

Pudgala = Çiva (1000 names [1]).

Pūjanī, name of a bird. § 647*b* (Brahmadatta-Pūjanīsaṃv.): XII, **139**, 5136 (*°yā saha saṃvādaṃ Brahmadattasya bhūpateḥ*), 5137 (*çakuniḥ*), 5140, 5146, 5147, 5152, 5155, 5156, (5157), 5168, (5169), (5171), (5175), 5186, (5187), (5209), 5246 (discourse between Brahmadatta and *P.*, the child of the latter having been killed by the son of Brahmadatta).

Pukkaça or **Pukkasa** (B. *Pulkasa*), name of a caste: XII, 6727, 10868, 11245 (*trailokye . . . sa-P°se*); XIII, 1552 (*°sānam*, read *°sānāṃ*), 1901, 1902, 2586 (*P.°sañ cāpi kharāçvagajabhojinaṃ mṛtacailapraticchannaṃ bhinnabhājanabhojinaṃ*), 6705 (*çvapāka-P°sādināṃ*).

Pulaha, a ṛshi, one of the mind-born sons of Brahmán. § 86 (Aṃçāvat.): I, **65**, 2518 (the fifth of Brahmán's six mind-born sons).—§ 109 (do.): I, **66**, 2568 (do., one of the six maharshis).—§ 113 (do.): I, **66**, 2572 (his offspring were the çalabhas, the lions, the Kimpurushas, the tigers, the Yakshas (PCR. 'bears', *ṛkshā(ḥ)* being the original reading), and the wolves).—§ 191 (Arjuna): I, **123***a*, 4808 (present at the birth of Arjuna).—§ 228 (Aurvop.): I, **181**, 6873 (came to the sacrifice of Parāçara to save the Rākshasas).—§ 266 (Çakrasabhāv.); II, **7**, 298 (in the palace of Indra).—§ 270 (Brahmasabhāv.): II, **11**, 436 (in the palace of Brahmán).—§ 421 (Gandhamādanapr.): III, **142**, 10904 (among the ṛshis who sang *sāmans* on the Gaṅgā).—§ 615*u* (Skanda): IX, **45**γ, 2511 (came to the investiture of Skanda).—§ 637 (Rājadh.): XII, **47**η, 1596 (among the ṛshis who surrounded Bhīshma).—§ 656 (Khaḍgotpattik.): XII, **166***a*, 6135 (fourth son of Brahmán). — § 664 (Mokshadh.): XII, **207**δ, 7534 (the fifth of Brahmán's seven mind-born sons).—§ 665 (do.): XII, **208***a*, 7570 (the fifth of Brahmán's seven sons—*brahmāṇaḥ*).—§ 717*b* (Nārāyaṇīya): XII, **335***a*, 12685 (among the twenty-one Prajāpatis).—§ 717*c* (Uparicara): XII, **336**β, 12724 (one of the seven ṛshis (Citraçikhaṇḍins)).—§ 717*b* (Nārāyaṇīya): XII, **341**, 13040 (one of the eight *prakṛtis*), 13075 (one of the seven ṛshis).—§ 730 (Ānuçāsanik.): XIII, **14**ββ, 990.—§ 734 (do.): XIII, **26***a*, 1761 (among the ṛshis who came to see Bhīshma).—§ 749 (do.): XIII, **92**δ, 4392.

Pulastya, a ṛshi, one of the mind-born sons of Brahmán. § 86 (Aṃçavat.): I, **65**, 2518 (the fourth of Brahmán's six mind-born sons).—§ 109 (do.): I, **66**, 2568 (do., one of the six maharshis).—§ 112 (do.): I, **66**, 2571 (his offspring were the Rākshasas, the monkeys, the Kinnaras, and the Yakshas).—§ 191 (Arjuna): I, **123***a*, 4808 (present at the birth of Arjuna).—§ 228 (Aurvop.): I, **181**, 6873, 6874, 6885 (prevailed upon Parāçara to make an end to his Rākshasa sacrifice).—§ 266 (Çakrasabhāv.): II, **7**, 298 (in the palace of Indra).—§ 270 (Brahmasabhāv.): II, **11**, 437 (in the palace of Brahmán).—§§ 356–376 (Tīrthayātrāp.): III, **81**, 4032, 4036 (*ṛshisattamaṃ*); **82**, (4043), (4050); **83**, (5071); **84**, (7079); **85**, (8143), 8255 (*ṛshiḥ*), 8256 (*P.* enumerated to Bhīshma the various tīrthas and the merits of visiting them).—§ 525 (Rāmopākhyānap.): III, **274**, 15883 (mind-born son of Brahmán, father of Kubera).—§ 526 (do.): III, **275**, 15889 (v. Viçravas).—§ 565 (Gālavacarita): V, **117**, 3970 (*reme . . . P°ḥ Sandhyayā yātha*), 3975 (*reme . . . P°ç ca Pratīcyayā*).—§ 615*u* (Skanda): IX, **45**γ, 2511 (came to the investiture of Skanda).—§ 637 (Rājadh.): XII, **47**η, 1597 (among the ṛshis who surrounded Bhīshma).—§ 656 (Khaḍgotpattik.): XII, **166***a*, 6135 (third son of

Brahmán).—§ 664 (Mokshadh.): XII, **207**δ, 7534 (the fourth of Brahmán's seven mind-born sons).—§ 665 (do.): XII, **208***a*, 7570 (the fourth of Brahmán's seven sons—*brahmāṇaḥ*).—§ 707 (do.): XII, **319**β, 11784 (had instructed Viçvāvasu).—§ 717*b* (Nārāyaṇīya): XII, **335***a*, 12685 (among the twenty-one Prajāpatis).—§ 717*c* (Uparicara): XII, **336**β, 12724 (one of the seven ṛshis (Citraçikhaṇḍins)).—§ 717*b* (Nārāyaṇīya): XII, **340,** 12952 (°*kulapāṃsanaṃ*, sc. Rāvaṇa); **341,** 13040 (one of the eight prakṛtis), 13075 (one of the seven ṛshis).—§ 730 (Ānuçāsanik.): XIII, **14**ββ, 990.—§ 734 (do.): XIII, **26***a*, 1761 (among the ṛshis who came to see Bhīshma).—§ 749 (do.): XIII, **92**δ, 4392. Cf. Brahmarshi, Brahmayoni, Viprarshi.

Pulastyatīrthayātrā (Pulastya's description of the tīrthas). § 11 (Parvasaṅgr.): I, **2,** 440 (i.e. III, chap. **81–85**).

Pulina, a Nāga (?) (according to Nīl. a Yaksha). § 46 (Garuḍa): I, **32***a*, 1489 (had an encounter with Garuḍa).

Pulinda, pl. (°*āḥ*), a barbarous people. § 223 (Vāsishṭha): I, **175,** 6685 (created from the froth of Vasishṭha's cow).—§ 280 (Bhīmasena): II, **29,** 1068 (°*nagaraṃ*, there Bhīmasena vanquished Sukumāra and Sumitra?).—§ 281 (Sahadeva): II, **31,** 1120 (vanquished by Sahadeva, in the south).—§ 419 (Gandhamādanapr.): III, **140,** 10864 (*Subāhuvishayaṃ . . . P°çatasaṅkulaṃ*, but read *Kulinda°*).—§ 458*b* (Kaliyuga): III, **188,** 12839 (among the barbarous peoples who will rule the world in the Kaliyuga).—§ 571 (Ulūkadūtāgamanap.): V, **160**γ, †5510 (in the army of Duryodhana); **161,** †5555 (do.).—§ 574 (Jambūkh.): VI, **9**μ, 347 (only B., C. has *Kaliṅgāḥ*); (ν), 369 (in the south).—§ 585 (Bhīshmavadhap.): VI, **87**γ, 3853 (followed Droṇa).—§ 599 (Jayadrathavadhap.): VII, **121**θθ, 4847 (attacked Sātyaki).—§ 605 (Karṇap.): VIII, **20**δδ, 779 (°-*Khasa-Bāhlīka*-°, fought with the Pāṇḍya king).—§ 608 (do.): VIII, **73,** 3653 (have been slain).—§ 641 (Rājadh.): XII, **65**θ, 2430 (enumeration of low and barbarous peoples).—§ 652*b* (Indrota-Pārīkshitīya): XII, **151,** 5620 (°-*Çabarā iva*).—§ 664 (Mokshadh.): XII, **207**η, 7559 (in the south).—§ 739 (Ānuçāsanik.): XIII, **23***a*, 2104 (have been degraded to çūdras from want of brahmans). Cf. Pulindaka, pl.

Pulinda, sg. ("the king of the Pulindas"). § 264 (Sabhākriyāp.): II, **4**β, 119 (waited upon Yudhishṭhira).

Pulindaka, pl. (°*āḥ*), a people. § 574 (Jambūkh.); VI, **9**μ, 348 (*Sindhu-P°āḥ*). Cf. Pulinda, pl.

Pulkasa, v. Pukkaça.

Pulomā[1], the wife of Bhṛgu. § 20 (cf. Paulomap.): *P.*, the wife of *Bhṛgu*, had first been betrothed to the *Rākshasa Puloman*, who one day when *Bhṛgu* was absent came to carry her away, and asked the sacrificial fire whether she was rightly his or *Bhṛgu's* wife. The Fire (*Agni*) answered that she was *Bhṛgu's*, by whom she had been taken with holy rites and invocations (I, **5**). When *Puloman* began to carry her away *Cyavana* dropped from her womb, and *Puloman* instantly was converted to ashes. Of her tears *Brahmán* formed the river *Vadhūsarā*. *Bhṛgu* cursed *Agni* (*b*) (I, **6–7**): I, **5,** 875, 876, 879, 893, 894; **6,** 900, 905, (908), 910.—§ 565 (Gālavacarita): V, **117,** 3971 (*reme . . . yathā Bhṛguḥ P°yāṃ*).

Pulomā[2], a female Asura. § 445 (Nivātakavacayuddhap.): III, **173,** 12203 (*Daiteyī*, obtained boons from Brahmán for her offspring, the great Asuras, viz. the Paulomas).

Puloman, a Rākshasa, or Asura. § 20 (Pulomā): I, **5,** 877 (*rakshaḥ*), 881 (carried away Pulomā, but was burnt to ashes, when she in her terror gave birth to Cyavana); **7,** 938.—§ 92 (Aṃçāvat.): I, **65,** 2530 (fourth son of Danu).—§ 673*b* (Bali-Vāsavas.): XII, **227***a*, 8262 (among the ancient rulers of the earth). Cf. Dānava, Dānavanandana, Rakshas.

Puṃs = Çiva (1000 names[1]).

Punaçcandrā: § 377 (Dhaumyatīrthak.): III, **88,** 8338 (a vedī in Çūrpāraka, belonging to Jamadagni).

Punarāvartanandā, name of a tīrtha. § 733*u* (Ānuçāsanik.): By bathing in *P.*, as also in Mahānandā, one attains to Nandana. By bathing in the tīrtha *Urvaçī* on the river *Lohitya* on the day of full moon of the month of *Kārttika* one obtains the merits of a puṇḍarīka sacrifice: XIII, **25,** 1731.

Punarvasu[1], name of a nakshatra (v. Sū. Si.). § 608 (Karṇap.): VIII, **49,** 2328 (*rathābhyāse cakāçete candrasyeva P°ḥ*, B. *P°vasū*, dual).—§ 746 (Ānuçāsanik.): XIII, **64,** 3260 (merit of making gifts under the constellation of *P.*).—§ 749 (do.): XIII, **89***a*, 4258 (merit of performing a çrāddha under the constellation of *P.*).—§ 759 (do.): XIII, **110,** 5392 (description of the cāndravrata).

Punarvasu[2] = Kṛshṇa (Vishṇu): XII, 1511; XIII, 6965 (Vishṇu's 1000 names).

Puṇḍarīka[1], an ancient king. § 267 (Yamasabhāv.): II, **8,** 325 (in the palace of Yama).

Puṇḍarīka[2], a tīrtha. § 364 (Tīrthayātrāp.): III, **83,** 6053.

Puṇḍarīka[3], a serpent. § 564 (Mātalīyop.): V, **103**γ, 3622 (enumeration).—§ 793 (Mausalap.): XVI, **4**η, †119.

Puṇḍarīkā, an Apsaras. § 191 (Arjuna): I, **123***a*, 4819 (danced at the birth of Arjuna).—§ 549 (Pāṇḍavapr.): IV, **9,** 259 (Sudeshṇā asks Draupadī if she is *P.*).

Puṇḍarīkāksha[1] ("lotus-eyed") = Kṛshṇa (Vishṇu): I, 7986; II, 35 (*Çaibya-Sugrīvavāhanaḥ*). 1318 (*Hariṃ*), 1339, 1621, 1623; III, 502, 509, 743 (*purushaṃ*), 8352 (*Devadevaḥ*), 12568, 12944 (i.e. Nārāyaṇa (Vishṇu)), 15838 (i.e. Vishṇu incarnate as the dwarf), 15852; V, 2489 (*Kṛshṇaṃ*), 2560, 2564 (etymology), 2899, 2905, 2906, 2922, 3111, 4379, 4382, 4399, 4434, 4809, 4960, 5136; VI, 3015, 3028, 4863, 4864; VII, 399, 405, 1275, 2769, 2775, 2782, 2954, 2965, 3800; VIII, 4471; X, 606 (*Yadūnāṃ ṛshabhaḥ*), 727; XI, 443 (*purushottamaṃ*), 444, 533, 576, 723; XII, 820 (*Kṛshṇaṃ*), 1499 (*Dāçārhaṃ*), 1501, 1686, 1852, 7518 (*Vishṇuṃ*), 7566, 7640 (i.e. Vishṇu incarnate as the boar), 12795 (i.e. Nārāyaṇa), 13493 (= do.); XIII, 655, 964, 5384, 6819 (*devaḥ*), 6845, 6925 (°*au Vāsudeva-Dhanañjayau*, i.e. Kṛshṇa and Arjuna), 6926, 6943, 6961 (Vishṇu's 1000 names), 7744; XIV, 1521, 1754, 1777, 1815, 1818, 1966, 1995, 1998, 2023.

Puṇḍarīkāksha[2] = Çiva (1000 names[1]).

Puṇḍarīkavanālaya = Çiva (1000 names[1]).

Puṇḍarīkekshaṇa ("lotus-eyed") = Kṛshṇa: II, 951; XII, 896.

Puṇḍarīyaka, a Viçvadeva. § 749 (Ānuçāsanik.): XIII, **91**γ, 4359.

Pundra (I, 288), v. Puṇḍra[1].

Puṇḍra[1], an ancient king. § 6 (Anukram.): I, **1***a*, 228 (only B., C. by error has *Pundraḥ*; in Sañjaya's enumeration).—§ 170 (Dīrghatamas): I, **104,** 4219 (the fourth son of Sudeshṇā, the wife of Bali, born by the touch of Dīrghatamas), 4221 (from him the Puṇḍras descended).

Puṇḍra[2] ("the king of the Puṇḍras"). § 605 (Karṇap.): VIII, **22,** 875 (°*sya nāgaṃ*, at the time of the great battle).

Puṇḍra, pl. (°*āḥ*), a people. § 170 (Dīrghatamas): I, **104,**

4221 (descended from Puṇḍra[1]).—§ 177 (Pāṇḍudigvijaya): I, **113**, 4453 (vanquished by Pāṇḍu).—§ 273 (Rājasūyārambhap.): II, **14**, 584 (*Vaṅga-P°-Kirāteshu rājā . . . Pauṇḍrako Vāsudeveti yo 'sau loke 'bhiviçrutaḥ*). — § 295 (Dyūtap.): II, **52**, 1872 (paid tribute to Yudhishṭhira).—§ 574 (Jambūkh.): VI, **9**μ, 358.—§ 578 (Bhīshmavadhap.): VI, **50**π, 2083 (only B., C. has *Pauṇḍrāḥ*, in the army of Yudhishṭhira).—§ 599 (Jayadrathavadhap.): VII, **93**δ, 3380 (attacked Arjuna). — § 604 (Karṇap.): VIII, **9**, 236 (°-*Cīnakān*, had formerly been vanquished by Karṇa).—§ 605 (do.): VIII, **22**ζζ, 863.—§ 782*e* (Arjuna Kārtavīrya): XIV, **29**γ, 832 (*vṛshalatvaṃ parigatāḥ*).—§ 785 (Anugītāp.): XIV, **82**, 2464 (°*ān sa-Koçalān*, vanquished by Arjuna). Cf. Pauṇḍra, pl., Pauṇḍrika, pl., Puṇḍraka, pl.

Puṇḍrādhipa ("the king of the Puṇḍras") = Vāsudeva (Pauṇḍraka): II, 1096 (*V*°).

Puṇḍraka ("the king of the Puṇḍra(ka)s"). § 264 (Sabhākriyāp.): II, **4**β, 119 (waited upon Yudhishṭhira).

Puṇḍraka, pl. = **Puṇḍra**, pl. § 295 (Dyūtap.): II, **52**, 1874 (*Tāmraliptāḥ sa-P°āḥ*, so C., but B. reads *supuṇḍrakāḥ*).

Puñjikasthalā, an Apsaras. § 191 (Arjuna): I, **123***a*, 4820 (sung at the birth of Arjuna).—§ 269 (Vaiçravaṇasabhāv.): II, **10**, 393 (in the palace of Kubera).

Puṇya[1], name of a lake. § 377 (Dhaumyatīrthak.): III, **89**, 8364 (*hradaḥ*, in the west). Cf. Puṇyākhya[2].

Puṇya[2] = Vishṇu (1000 names).

Puṇyā, a river. § 574 (Jambūkh.): VI, **9**λ, 344 (so C., B. *Supuṇyā*).

Puṇyacañcu = Çiva (1000 names[2]).

Puṇyaçloka = Nala, q.v.

Puṇyaçravaṇakīrtana = Vishṇu (1000 names).

Puṇyajana, pl. ("good people"), a designation of certain supernatural beings, as Yakshas or Rākshasas: III, 475 (?); VII, 2403, 2417; XV, 848; XVIII, 146.

Puṇyākhya[1], name of one or more hermitages. § 377 (Dhaumyatīrthak.): III, **90**, 8382 (in the west; only C., B. has *Pāñcālyāḥ*).—§ 390 (Tīrthayātrāp.): III, **110**, 9990 (*āçramaç caiva P°ḥ Kāçyapasya*, i.e. Vibhāṇḍaka's).—Do.[2], name of a lake. § 413 (Tīrthayātrāp.): III, **135**, 10698 (*apāṃ hradañ ca P°ṃ*).

Puṇyakīrti = Vishṇu (1000 names).

Puṇyakṛt, a Viçvadeva. § 749 (Ānuçāsanik.): XIII, **91**γ, 4355.

Puṇyanāman, a warrior of Skanda. § 615*u* (Skanda): IX, **45**η, 2561.

Puṇyodakā, a river. § 766 (Ānuçāsanik.): XIII, **100**, 6125 (*nadī*, in the realm of death).

Puramālinī, a river. § 574 (Jambūkh.): VI, **9**λ, 329.

Purāṇa ("ancient tale or tradition"), sg. and pl.: I, 16 (°*saṃçritāḥ puṇyaḥ kathāḥ*), 17 (*Dvaipāyanena yat proktaṃ P°ṃ*, i.e. the Mhbhr.), 63 (*itihāsa-P°ānāṃ unmeshaṃ nirmitañ ca yat*), 65 (°*anāṃ ca kṛtsnaçaḥ*), 86 (°*pūrṇacandrena*), 235 (sg.), 246 (sg.), 260 (*itihāsa-P°ābhyāṃ*), 357 (*Harivaṃçaḥ . . . P°ṃ*), 468 (*Mārkaṇḍeyasamāsyā ca P°ṃ*), 649 (*asyākhyānasya*—i.e. the Mhbhr.—*vishaye P°ṃ vartate*), 852 (*Paurāṇikaḥ P°e kṛtaçramaḥ*), 863 (°*m akhilaṃ pitā te*—i.e. Lomaharshaṇa — *'dhītavān purā*), 864 (sg.), 869 (°*āçrayasaṃyutaṃ*, sc. *vaṃçaṃ*), 1025 (*itihāsam imaṃ viprāḥ P°aṃ paricakshate*), 1438 (°*e yadi paṭhyate*), 1439 (*vishayo 'yaṃ P°sya*), 2020 (*sarpasattraṃ . . . P°e paripaṭhyate*), †2120 (sg.), 2298 (°*m ṛshisaṃstutaṃ*, i.e. the Mhbhr.), 2546 (*vaṃçaprabhavaḥ . . . P°ṇe saṃçrutaḥ*), 2560 (*apatyaṃ Kapilāyās tu P°e parikīrtitaṃ*), 4034 (? pl.), 4356 (*itihāsa-P°eshu*), 4692 (°*vidaḥ*), 6650 (*Vāçishṭham ākhyānaṃ P°ṃ paricakshate*), 7265 (*çrūyate hi P°e Jaṭilā*); II, 136 (*itihāsa-P°jñaḥ*, sc. Nārada), 1472 (°*vidaḥ*); III, †958 (? *Dhātrā vidhir yo vihitaḥ P°aiḥ*), 12802 (*Mātsyakaṃ nāma P°ṃ*, i.e. Matsyopākhyāna (Vaivasvatopākhyāna)), 13122 (*Vāyuproktam anusmṛtya P°m ṛshisaṃstutaṃ*), 13141 (sg.); IV, 1593 (pl. °*āni*); V, 7073 (°*e çrūyate . . . Maruttena . . . gītaḥ çlokaḥ*); VI, †2589 (? *kathitaḥ P°aiḥ*), 2938 (°*gītaṃ* ?); VII, 2203 (°*vidaḥ*), 2369 (do.), 9601 (°*ādhyatmaniçcayāḥ*); VIII, 1498 (pl. °*āḥ*); XI, 344 (pl. °*āni*); XII, 1619 (°*e Purushaṃ proktaṃ*, sc. Kṛshṇa), 1841 (*itihāsa-P°ārthāḥ*), 1898 (*stuti-P°jñāḥ*), 2260 (? *āyamaḥ P°ānāṃ*), 5595, 6205 (*Maheçvarapraṇītaç ca*—sc. the sword—*P°e niçcayaṃ gataḥ*), 6207 (? *ārshaṃ*), †7370 (sg.), 7524 (°*vidaḥ*), 7571 (*sapta brahmāṇa ity ete P°e niçcayaṃ gatāḥ*), 10798 (*çrūyate hi P°eshu prajā dhigdaṇḍaçāsanāḥ*), †11205 (*yac cāpi dṛshṭaṃ dvividhaṃ P°e Sāṅkhyāgataṃ*), 11744 (*Romaharshena P°m avadhāritaṃ*), 12674 (*Vedeshu sa-P°eshu*), 12970 (*atikrāntāḥ P°eshu çrutāḥ te yadi*, sc. the Vedas), 12983 (°*ṃ Vedasammitaṃ*), 12989 (*idaṃ*), 13024 (*a-P°vidā*), 13134 (*Vedeshu sa-P°eshu*), 13136 (°*e . . . mama*—i.e. Kṛshṇa's—*nāmāni kīrtitāni*), ††13187 (*api hi P°e bhavati*), 13189 (sg.), ††13205 (*Veda-P°etihāsa*°), 13457 (°*ṃ Vedasammitaṃ*), 13528 (do.); XIII, 1054 (°*jñaiḥ surarshibhiḥ*), 1102 (*Veda-çāstra-P°oktaḥ*), 1542 (sg.), 3990 (*çrutaṃ . . . P°e*), 4304 (sg.), 4863 (*setihasaṃ*), 5104 (sg.), 6902 (do.), 7358 (do.); XVIII, 304 (*ashṭādaça P°ānāṃ*).

Purāṇa(ḥ) = Çiva (1000 names[2]).

Pūraṇa, a ṛshi. § 637 (Rājadh.); XII, **47**η, 1599 (among the ṛshis who surrounded Bhīshma).

Purandara[1] = Indra, q.v. Do.[2] = Vishṇu (1000 names).

Purandarasuta ("the son of Purandara [i.e. Indra]") = Arjuna: V, 7308.

Purañjaya, a Kuru warrior. § 600 (Ghaṭotkacavadhap.): VII, **156**κ, 6851 (will follow Çakuni).

Purātana = Vishṇu (1000 names).

Purāvatī, a river. § 574 (Jambūkh.): VI, **9**λ, 331.

Pūrayitṛ = Vishṇu (1000 names).

Purikā, name of a city. § 641 (Rājadh.): XII, **111**, 4085 (°*āyāṃ puri . . . Pauriko nṛpaḥ*).

Pūrṇa[1], a serpent. § 63 (Sarpasattra): I, **57**, 2146 (of Vāsuki's race).

Pūrṇa[2], a Devagandharva. § 102 (Aṃçāvat.): I, **65**, 2554 (son of Prādhā).

Pūrṇa[3] = Vishṇu (1000 names).

Pūrṇabhadra, a serpent. § 47 (Sarpanāmak.): I, **35**, 1557 (enumeration).

Pūrṇāçā, v. Parṇāçā.

Pūrṇamukha, a serpent. § 67 (Sarpasattra): I, **57**, 2157 (of Dhṛtarāshṭra's race).

Pūrṇāṅgada, a serpent. § 67 (Sarpasattra): I, **57**, 2157 (of Dhṛtarāshṭra's race).

Pūrṇāyus, a Devagandharva. § 102 (Aṃçāvat.): I, **65**, 2554 (son of Prādhā).

Purocana, name of a man, a confidant and helper of Duryodhana. § 11 (Parvasaṅgr.): I, **2**, 380 (°*sya . . . dahanaṃ*, cf. § 213).—§ 71 (Ādivaṃçāvatāraṇap.): I, **61**, 2252.—§ 213 (Jatugṛhap.): I, **141**, 5645; **144**, 5716, 5717, 5732, 5733; **146**, 5775, 5776, 5778, 5779, 5783, 5788, 5789, 5797; **147**, 5801, 5807, 5812, 5815, 5817; **148**, 5819, 5820, 5821, 5822, 5828; **150**, 5857, 5864, 5879 (constructed the lac house and set fire to it in order to burn the five Pāṇḍavas and Kuntī, but was himself burned).—§ 215 (Bakavadhap.):

I, **162**, 6249 (*nihataḥ*, all. to § 213).—§ 241 (Vidurāgamanap.): I, **200**, 737 (all. to § 213), 7377 (do.); **203**, 7453 (do.), 7455 (do.).—§ 243 (do.): I, **205**, 7510 (do.); **206**, 7523 (do.).

Puroḍāçabhāgahara = Mahāpurusha (Mahāpurushastava).

Puroravas, v. Purūravas.

Puru[1], v. Pūru[1].

Puru[2], a king at the time of Yudhishṭhira. § 264 (Sabhākriyāp.): II, **4**β, 122 (waited upon Yudhishthira).

Puru[3], the charioteer of Arjuna. § 286 (Rājasūyikap.): III, **33**, 1234 (*Arjunasārathiḥ*, B. *Pū°*).

Puru[4], a mountain. § 377 (Dhaumyatīrthak.): III, **90**, 8393 (*parvataç ca P°r nāma yatra yātaḥ Purūravaḥ*).

Pūru[1], an ancient king, son of Yayāti. § 6 (Anukram.): I, **1**a, 225 (in Sañjaya's enumeration, C. has *Pu°*).—§ 136 (Yayātyup.): I, **75**, 3126.—§ 143 (Nahusha): I, **75**, 3160 (son of Yayāti and Çarmishṭhā).—§ 144 (Yayāti): I, **75**, 3162, 3167, 3181 (accepted the decrepitude of Yayāti, and was installed on the throne, cf. § 148).—§ 147 (Devayānī): I, **83**, 3433 (son of Yayāti and Çarmishṭhā). — § 148 (Yayāti): I, **84**, 3492, 3493, 3495, 3498, 3499 (accepted the decrepitude of Yayāti); **85**, 3509, 3516, 3517, 3518, 3519, 3520, 3526, 3527, 3528, 3530, 3531, 3532 (passing over his elder sons Yayāti installed *P.* on the throne).—§ 148*f* (do.): From *P.* the Pauravas descended (among them Janamejaya Pārikshita was born); I, **85**, 3534.—§ 149 (do.): I, **86**, 3544; **87**, †3554; **89**, †3577 (*Yayātiḥ . . . P°oḥ pita*); **93**, †3684 (do.).—§ 150 (Pūruvaṃç.): I, **94**, 3691 (*°or vaṃçakarān nṛpān*), 3694 (*°or vaṃcadharān vīrān*), 8695 (by Paushṭī, father of Pravīra, Īcvara, and Raudrāçva).—§ 156 (do.): I, **95**, 3762 (son of Yayāti and Çarmishṭhā), ††3763 (from *P.* the Pauravas descended), ††3764 (husband of Kauçalyā and father of Janamejaya[6]).—§ 160 (do.): I, **95**, ††3839 (*°or vaṃçaḥ*).—§ 186 (Vyushitāçvop.): I, **121**, 4686 (*Vyushitāçvaḥ . . . P°vaṃçavivardhanaḥ*). — § 267 (Yamasabhāv.): II, **8**, 319 (in the palace of Yama).—§ 338 (Indralokābhigamanap.): III, **46**, 1859 (*°or vaṃçe*).—§ 376 (Tīrthayātrāp.): III, **85**, 8270 (*yathā*).—§ 378 (do.): III, **94**, 8504 (*yathā*).—§ 552 (Goharaṇap.): IV, **56**ζ, 1769 (came from heaven to see the encounter).—§ 565 (Gālavacarita): V, **120**, 4027 (C. *Pu°*), 4038 (C. *Pu°*).—§ 569 (Bhagavadyānap.): V, **149**, 5044 (son of Yayāti and Çarmishṭhā, and ancestor of Dhṛtarāshṭra).—§ 595 (Shoḍaçarāj., v. Yayāti): VII, **63**, 2301 (succeeded Yayāti).—§ 632*b* (Shoḍaçarāj., cf. § 595): XII, **29**, 991 (do.).—§ 656 (Khaḍgotpattik.): XII, **166**δ, 6194 (received the sword from Yayāti, from *P.* it passed over to Amūrtarayas).—§ 751*b* (Çapathavidhi): XIII, **94**a, †4551, (4569).—§ 761 (Ānuçāsanik.): XIII, **115**γ, 5661 (abstained from meat during the month of Kārttika). — § 775 (do.): XIII, **166**η, 7674 (enumeration).

Pūru[2], v. Puru[3].

Pūru[3], a prince. § 595 (Shoḍaçarāj., v. Māndhātṛ): VII, **62**a, 2281 (only B., C. has *Çūnaṃ*, vanquished by Māndhātṛ).

Puruhūta = Indra, q.v.—Do.[2] = Mahāpurusha (Mahāpurushastava).

Purujit[1], an ancient king. § 267 (Yamasabhāv.): II, **8**, 331 (in the palace of Yama).

Purujit[2], a Kunti prince. [*P.* seems in the most passages (except only VIII, 172) to be another name of Kuntibhoja.] —§ 273 (Rājasūyārambhap.): II, **14**, 581 (*mātulo bhavataḥ* (i.e. Yudhishṭhira's) . . . *P°t Kuntivardhanaḥ*).—§ 572 (Rathātirathas.): V, **172**, 5922 (*P°t* (so B., C. *ripujit*) *Kuntibhojaç ca . . . mātulo Bhīmasenasya*).—§ 576 (Bhagavadgītāp.): VI, **25**θ, 834 (*P°t Kuntibhojaç ca*). — § 592 (Saṃçaptakavadhap.): VII, **23**o, 995 (*Kuntibhojaḥ . . . P°t* (C. *Pura°*) *mātulaḥ Savyasācinaḥ*, description of his horses); **25**, 1103 (fought with Durmukha). — § 604 (Karṇap.): VIII, **6**, 172 (*P°t Kuntibhojaç ca mātulau Savyasācinaḥ* | *saṅgrāmanirjitān lokān gamitau Droṇasāyakaiḥ*).—Cf. Kuntibhoja, Kuntivardhana[1].

Purujit[3] = Vishṇu (1000 names).

Purukutsa, an ancient king, son of Māndhātṛ. § 267 (Yamasabhāv.): II, **8**, 324 (in the palace of Yama).— § 787 (Āçramavāsap.): XV, **20**, 549 (Nārada said: King *P.*, the son of *Māndhātṛ*, here attained to high success; the river *Narmadā* became his wife; having undergone penances here, he proceeded to heaven).

Purumīḍha, a prince. § 152 (Pūruvaṃç.): I, **94**, 3720 (son of Suhotra and Aikshvākī, and brother of Ajamīḍha and Sumīḍha).

Purumitra, a son of Dhṛtarāshṭra. § 83 (Ādivaṃçāvatāraṇa): I, **63**a, 2448 (among eleven sons of Dhṛtarāshṭra who are mahārathas).—§ 298 (Dyūtap.): II, **58**, †2004 (present at the gambling).—§ 561 (Yānasandhip.): V, **55**ν, 2207 (among the chief warriors of Duryodhana); **58**τ, 2301, (ν), 2305; **66**εε, 2502.—§ 571 (Ulūkadūtāgamanap.): V, **160**, 5532 (*°gādhaṃ*, sc. *puroshodadhiṃ*, i.e. the army of Duryodhana); **161**, 5575 (do.).—§ 576 (Bhagavadgītāp.): VI, **17**, 657 (followed Açvatthāman); **18**δ, 687 (protected Bhīshma); **20**, †752.—§ 578 (Bhīshmavadhap.): VI, **44**a, 1653 (attacked Bhīmasena).—§ 580 (do.): VI, **57**ι, 2452.— § 581 (do.): VI, **62**ζ, 2732 (protected Çalya), 2743.— § 582 (do.): VI, **73**θ, 3220, 3222 (pierced by Abhimanyu). —§ 596 (Pratijñāp.): VII, **74**β, 2628.—§ 598 (Jayadrathavadhap.): VII, **85**β, 3036.—§ 600 (Ghaṭotkacavadhap.): VII, **156**κ, 6850 (*°sutāḥ*).—§ 604 (Karṇap.): VIII, **7**, †203 (*sutas te*, still alive). Cf. Kurupravīra.

Purūravas, an ancient king, son of Ilā [and Budha], and husband of Urvaçī. § 52 (Janamejaya): I, **44**, †1811 (*yathorvaçīṃ prāpya purā P°āḥ*).—§ 140 (cf. Sambhavap.): *P.* was born of *Ilā*, who was both his father and mother. *P.* held sway over thirteen dvīpas, and though a human being he was always surrounded with beings who were not human. He robbed the brahmans of their wealth. *Sanatkumāra* then came from *Brahmaloka* and gave him good advice, which he rejected. Then *P.*, who intoxicated with power had lost his reason, was destroyed by the curse of the *maharshis*. Accompanied by *Urvaçī*, he, for sacrificial purposes, brought the fires from the *Gandharvaloka* duly arranged in three places (*yathāvad vihitāṃs tridhā*); I, **75**, 3143, 3144, 3145.—§ 141 (do.): *P.* (*Aila*) had from *Urvaçī* six sons: *Āyus*, *Dhīmat*, *Amāvasu*, *Dṛḍhāyus*, *Vanāyus*, and *Çatāyus*. *Āyus* married *Svarbhānavī*, and had from her the sons *Nahusha*, *Vṛddhaçarman*, *Rāji*, *Gaya*, and *Anenas*.—§ 156 (Pūruvaṃç.): I, **95**, ††3760 (son of Ilā and father of Āyus).—§ 305 (Anudyūtap.): II, **78**, 2576 (*°am Ailaṃ tvaṃ buddhyā jayasi*).—§ 376 (Tīrthayātrāp.): III, **85**, 8268 (*yathā*).— § 377 (Dhaumyatīrthak.): III, **90**, 8393 (*parvataç ca Purur nāma yatra yātaḥ P°āḥ*).—§ 378 (Tīrthayātrāp.): III, **94**, 8504 (*yathā*, C. has by error *Puroravāḥ*).—§ 562 (Bhagavadyānap.): V, **74**γ, 2731 (*Dīptākshāṇāṃ P°āḥ*, among the princes who annihilated their kinsmen, etc., the same?).— § 565 (Gālavacarita): V, **117**, 3973 (*reme . . . yathā . . . Urvaçyāṅ ca P°āḥ*).—§ 599*e* (Çini): VII, **144**, 6028 (son of Budha), 6029 (father of Āyus).—§ 641 (Rājadh.): XII,

72, 2750 (°*sa Ailasya saṃvādaṃ Mātariçvanaḥ*), (2751) (discourse between *P.* and the Wind).—§ 656 (Khaḍgotpattik.): XII, **166***δ*, 6193 (received the sword from Ikshvāku, from *P.* it passed over to Āyus).—§ 723 (Ānuçāsanik.): XIII, **6***a*, 325 (*rājarshiḥ . . . Ailaḥ*, attained to heaven).—§ 746 (do.): XIII, **76***ι*, †3690 (made gifts of kine).—§ 768*b* (Kṛshṇa Vāsudeva): XIII, **147**, 6832 (son of Budha and father of Āyus).—§ 770 (Ānuçāsanik.); XIII, **151***μ*, 7127 (*Ailaṃ Budhasya putraṃ*). Cf. Aila.

Purusattama = Vishṇu (1000 names).

***Purusha** ("Spirit," especially the Supreme Spirit, often identified with Kṛshṇa (Vishṇu, Nārāyaṇa), also with Çiva and Brahmán): I, 22 (*ādyaṃ P°ṃ . . . Vishṇuṃ*), 34 (°*ç cāprameyātmā yaṃ sarve ṛshayo viduḥ*, issued from the primordial egg), 2430, 2432 (*sa vibhuḥ kartā sarvabhūtapitāmahaḥ*, incarnate as Kṛshṇa); III, 151 (Sūrya identified with *P.*), 515 (°*o asi sanātanaḥ*, sc. Kṛshṇa), 743 (*Çaṅkhacakragadādharaṃ*, i.e. Kṛshṇa), 12821 (*Svayambhuve P°āya purāṇāya*, i.e. Kṛshṇa), 12825 (*yady esha P°o veda vedā api na taṃ viduḥ*), 13005 (*ādidevam ajaṃ Vishṇum P°ṃ pītavāsasaṃ*, i.e. Kṛshṇa), 13505 (*Hariṃ P°ṃ çāçvataṃ*, i.e. Vishṇu), 15531 (*purāṇa P°a* (C. in one word) in an invocation of Kṛshṇa), 15815 (*sahasraçīrshaṃ*, i.e. Vishṇu, incarnate as Kṛshṇa); V, †2579 (i.e. Kṛshṇa), 3825 (*Himavatpṛshṭhe nityam āste Maheçvaraḥ* | *Prakṛtyā P°ḥ sārdhaṃ yugāntāgnisamaprabhaḥ*); VI, 1145 (*adhidaivataṃ*), 1149 (*paramaṃ*), †1151 (*paraṃ*), 1216 (*çāçvataṃ*, i.e. Kṛshṇa), †1264 (*sanātanas tvaṃ P°o mato me*, sc. Kṛshṇa), †1284 (*tvam ādidevaḥ P°ḥ purāṇaḥ*, sc. Kṛshṇa), 1322, 1341, 1342, 1343, 1344, †1386 (*ādyaṃ*), 1398 (dual), 2941 (i.e. Kṛshṇa (Vishṇu)), 2988 (°*saṃjñaḥ*), 3043 (i.e. Kṛshṇa); VII, 6469 (*paraṃ purāṇaṃ P°ṃ*, i.e. Kṛshṇa), 8858 (*purāṇaṃ P°ṃ Vishṇuṃ*), 9522 (i.e. Çiva); XII, 1502 (*tvām*, i.e. Kṛshṇa—*ekam āhuḥ P°ṃ*), 1506 (i.e. Kṛshṇa), 1619 (*Purāṇe P°ṃ proktaṃ*, sc. Kṛshṇa), 1628 (*mahataḥ tamasaḥ pāre P°ṃ*, sc. Kṛshṇa), 1677 (°*o 'si sanātanaḥ*, sc. Kṛshṇa), 7483, 7522 (i.e. Kṛshṇa), 7651 (°*ṃ sanātanaṃ Vishṇum yan taṃ vedavido viduḥ*, i.e. Kṛshṇa), 7666 (°*ādhishṭhitān bhāvān*), 7701 (°*ādhishṭhitāḥ*), 7847 (*avyakta-P°ābhyāṃ*), 7879 (*sanātanaṃ*), 7892 (°*āvastham avyaktaṃ*), 10437 (= Çiva, 1000 names[1]), 11405, 11622, 11658, 11691, 11762 (Mitra and Varuṇa = *P.* and Prakṛti), 11763, 11764, 11765, 11766, 11767, 11769, 12680, 12784 (= Nārāyaṇa Vishṇu), 12857 (*Harir Īçvaraḥ*, do.), ††12864 (= Mahāpurusha (Mahāpurushastava)), 12888 (*pañcaviṃçakaḥ*, sc. in the Sāṅkhya system, = Nārāyaṇa Vishṇu), 12895 (*nishkriye* = do.), 12890 (*Vāsudevaṃ*), 12907 (*ahaṃ hi P°o jñeyo nishkriyaḥ pañcaviṃçakaḥ*, says Nārāyaṇa), 12999 (i.e. Nārāyaṇa Vishṇu), 13068 (*ādityavarṇam . . . Īçānaṃ*, = do.), 13143 (*purāṇaḥ*, = do.), ††13192 (*Harir avyayaḥ*, = do.), ††13194 (= do.), 13351 (*viçvarūpadharo 'vyayaḥ*, = do.), 13447 (*purāṇaṃ*, = do.), 13464 (= do.), 13494 (= do.), 13512 (*adikaraṃ*, = do.), 13516 (*çvetaḥ*, = do.), 13537 (= do.), †13546 (*guṇādhikaṃ*, = do.), 13572 (created from Hari, = Brahmán?), 13573 (*Brahmā*), 13607 (*avyayaḥ*, i.e. Nārāyaṇa Vishṇu), 13616 (do.), 13617 (= do.), 13628 (= do., *pañcaviṃçakaḥ*), 13713 (pl. and sg.), 13715 (pl. and sg.), 13717 (°*sūktaṃ*), 13719 (°*aikatvaṃ*), 13734 (*Virāṭ*), 13735 (pl. and sg., = *Virāṭ*), 13737 (pl.), 13738 (pl.), 13739 (*paramaṃ*), 13740 (*çāçvataḥ*), 13747 (*sanātanaṃ*), 13748, †13750, 13752, 13754 (*Nārāyaṇaḥ . . . sarvātmā*), 13756 (*bahuvidhaḥ*, = do.), 13762 (= do); XIII, 592 (°*sya ca yaḥ paraḥ*, sc. Çiva), 593 (*Prakṛtiṃ P°añ caiva kshobhayitrā*, sc. Çiva), 910 (*Sāṅkhye P°a ucyate*, sc. Çiva), 1015 (i.e. Çiva), 1017 (do.), 1040 (do.), 1050 (°*ākhyaḥ*, do.), 6807 (*Hariḥ*, i.e. Kṛshṇa), 6939 (= Vishṇu), 6940 (do.), 6951 (do., 1000 names), 6993 (do.), 7743 (i.e. Kṛshṇa); XIV, 194 (= Çiva), 1088 (= *mahān ātmā*), 1096 (do.), 1207, 1340, 1342, 1374, 1379, 1382, 1422, 1455, 1456.

Pūrusha = Purusha: XII, 11335 (*Prakṛti-P°au*).

***Purushaçreshṭha** = Kṛshṇa: VII, 8058.

***Purushasattama** = Kṛshṇa: II, 28; V, 2849; IX, 1976 (*K*°); XII, 1848.

Purushavara = Vishṇu = I, 1180.

Purushottama ("the highest being") = Kṛshṇa (Vishṇu): I, 2508 (i.e. Vishṇu), ††3835 (*Vāsudevasya*), 7551 (*Dāçārhaḥ*), 7998; II, 964, 1588; III, 481, 541, 892, 1637 (*Vishṇau*), 8395 (*Nārāyaṇaḥ prabhur Vishṇuḥ çāçvataḥ P°aḥ*, in Badarī), 8758 (i.e. Vishṇu), 12593, 13500 (i.e. Vishṇu), 13573 (do.); V, 2527, 2560, 2569 (etymology), 2847, 2868, 2941, 3208, 3218, 3257, 4124, 4386 (*Acyutaḥ*), 4658, 4673; VI, 1142, 1219, 1249, 1400, 1401, 3016 (*bhūtātmā*), 3018 (do.), 3026 (slew Madhu and Kaiṭabha), 3045, 4869; VII, 2587 (*K*°), 2963 (*Vishṇo . . . Kṛshṇa*), 6472, 8277 (*K*°); VIII, †4613, †4683; IX, 3528; X, 741, 752; XI, 443 (*Puṇḍarīkākshaṃ*); XII, 1503 (*Vishṇo Jishṇo Hare Kṛshṇa*), 1560, 1604 (*K*°), 1692 (*Keçavaṃ*), 1693, 4078 (*Govindaḥ*, i.e. Vishṇu), 4079 (= do.), 7525 (*bhūtātmā*), 7526, 7532, †10084 (i.e. Vishṇu), 12325 (do.), 12734 (i.e. Nārāyaṇa (Vishṇu)), 12747 (do.), 12779 (do.), ††12864 (= Mahāpurusha), 12997 (i.e. Nārāyaṇa (Vishṇu)), 13357 (do.), 13372 (do.), 13379 (do.), 13411 (do.), 13518 (do.), 13521 (do.), 13549 (do.), 13566 (do.), 13618 (do.), 13627 (do.), 13736 (= ?), 13909 (= ?); XIII, 965, 6939 (i.e. Vishṇu), 6952 (do., 1000 names), 7065 (i.e. Vishṇu), 7069 (do.), 7745; XIV, 1597, 1942 (*K*°), 1973 (*K*°). Cf. Uttamapūrusha.

***Purushottama**[2], said of various men: II, 582 (*Cedishu*, i.e. Çiçupāla?), 583 (i.e. Pauṇḍraka Vāsudeva?); III, 1641 (i.e. Arjuna).—Do.[2], dual (°*au*) = Nara and Nārāyaṇa: XII, 13343.

Purushṭuta = Mahāpurusha (Mahāpurushastava).

[Pūruvaṃçānukīrtana(ṃ)] ("genealogy of the Pūrus"), a section of Sambhavaparvan (I, **94–95**). (Cf. LIA, I, Anhang III.) § 150:

Pūru ∼ Paushṭī.
|
(1) Pravīra (∼Çūrasenī), (2) Īçvara, (3) Raudrāçva (∼Apsaras Miçrakeçī).

Pravīra →
Manasyu (∼Sauvīrī).
|
Çakta + 2 others (β).

Raudrāçva →
(1) Ṛceyu + 9 others (α).
|
Matināra.
|
(1) Taṃsu, (2) Mahat, (3) Atiratha, (4) Druhyu.

Taṃsu →
Īlina ∼ Rathantarī.
|
(1) Dushyanta ∼ Çakuntalā, (2) Çūra, (3) Bhīma, (4) Pravasu, (5) Vasu.

Dushyanta →
Bharata.

§ 151: Bharata (q.v.) obtained from Bharadvāja a son of the name Bhumanyu, who became his heir apparent.

§ 152:

Bharata.
|
Bhumanyu (∼Pushkariṇī).
|
(1) Diviratha, (2) Suhotra (∼Aikshvākī), (3) Suhotṛ, (4) Suhavis, (5) Suyajus, (6) Ṛcīka.

Suhotra →
(1) Ajamīḍha (∼(*a*) Dhūminī, (*b*) Nīlī, (*c*) Keçinī) + 2 others (α).

Ajamīḍha →
(*a*) Ṛksha, (*b*, 2–3), (2) Dushyanta, (3) Parameshṭhin, (*c*, 4–6), (4) Jahnu + 2 others (β).

Ṛksha → Saṃvaraṇa.
Dushyanta, Parameshṭhin → Pāñcālāḥ.
Jahnu → Kuçikāḥ.

§ 153 : Saṃvaraṇa (q.v.).
§ 154:

Saṃvaraṇa∼Tapatī Saurī.
Kuru (∼Vāhinī).
Avikshit + 4 others (α).
Parikshit + 7 others (β).
Janamejaya + 6 others (γ).
(1) Dhṛtarāshṭra, (2) Pāṇḍu, (3) Bāhlīka + 5 others (δ).
(1) Kuṇḍika, (2) Hastin + 6 others (ε).

§ 155 : Among the grandsons (B, sons) of Dhṛtarāshṭra three became famous: Pratīpa, Dharmanetra, and Sunetra.—Pratīpa had three sons: Devāpi, Çāntanu, and Bāhlīka. Devāpi adopted an ascetic life; Çāntanu and Bāhlīka became kings.—There were many other kings like to the Devarshis, in the race of Bharata and Manu, who adorned the Aila dynasty (I, **94**).

§ 156 : Janamejaya wished to hear the same more in full, commencing from Manu.

Daksha.
Aditi.
Vivasvat.
Manu.
Ilā.
Purūravas.
Āyus.
Nahusha. Uçanas. Vṛshaparvan.
Yayāti.∼(a) Devayānī. (b) Çarmishṭhā.
(a, 1–2), (1) Yadu, (2) Turvasu, (b, 3–5), (3) Druhyu, (4) Anu, (5) Pūru (∼Kauçalyā).
Yādavāḥ. Janamejaya (∼Anantā Mādhavī).
Prācinvat (∼Açmakī Yādavī).
Saṃyāti (∼Varāṅgī, daughter of Dṛshadvat).
Ahaṃyāti (∼Bhānumatī, daughter of Kṛtavīrya).
Sārvabhauma (∼Sunandā Kaikeyī).
Jayatsena (∼Suçravā Vaidarbhī).
Avācīna (∼Maryādā Vaidarbhī).
Ariha (∼Āṅgī).
Mahābhauma (∼Suyajñā Prāsenajitī).
Ayutanāyin (∼Kāmā, daughter of Pṛthuçravas).
Akrodhana (∼Karambhā Kāliṅgī).
Devātithi (∼Maryādā Vaidehī).
Ariha (∼Sudevā Āṅgeyī).
Ṛksha (∼Jvālā, daughter of Takshaka).
Matināra (∼Sarasvatī).
Taṃsu (∼Kāliṅgī).
Īlina (∼Rathantarī).

Īlina (∼Rathantarī).
Dushyanta (∼Çakuntalā, daughter of Viçvāmitra) + 4 other sons.
Bharata (∼Sunandā Sārvasenī Kāçeyī).
Bhumanyu (∼Vijayā Dāçārhī).
Suhotra (∼Suvarṇā Ikshvāku-kanyā).
Hastin (∼Yaçodharā Traigartī).
Vikuṇṭhana (∼Sudevā Dāçārhī).
Ajamīḍha (∼(a) Kaikeyī, (b) Gāndhārī, (c) Viçālā, (d) Ṛkshā)
Saṃvaraṇa (∼Tapatī Vaivasvatī) + 123 other sons.
Kuru (∼Çubhāṅgī Dāçārhī).
Vidūratha (B. Vidūra) (∼Sampriyā Mādhavī).
Anaçvan (∼Amṛtā Māgadhī).
Parīkshit (∼Suyaçā Bāhudā).
Bhīmasena (∼Kumārī Kaikeyī).
Pratiçravas.
Pratīpa (∼Sunandā Çaibyā).
(1) Devāpi, (2) Çāntanu (∼(a) Gaṅgā Bhāgīrathī, (b) Satyavatī), (3) Bāhlīka.
(a, 1) Devavrata or Bhīshma, (b, 2–3) (2) Vicitravīrya (∼Ambikā and Ambālikā, Kausalyātmaje, daughters of the king of Kāçi), (3) Citrāṅgada.

§ 157 : *Vicitravīrya* died without leaving a child. Then *Satyavatī* began to think how the dynasty of *Dushyanta* might be perpetuated, and she recollected the ṛshi *Dvaipāyana* and prevailed upon him to beget three children for *Vicitravīrya*: *Dhṛtarāshṭra, Pāṇḍu, Vidura.*—In consequence of a boon granted by *Dvaipāyana, Dhṛtarāshṭra* had 100 sons by *Gāndhārī*, of whom the most celebrated were *Duryodhana, Duḥçāsana, Vikarṇa*, and *Citrasena.*—*Pāṇḍu* had two wives: *Kuntī* or *Pṛthā*, and *Mādrī*. One day, when hunting, he with his arrow pierced a ṛshi cohabiting with [his wife in the shape of] a deer. The ṛshi cursed him, saying that he should also die when in such a state. *Pāṇḍu* then prevailed upon *Kuntī* to raise offspring for him, and by *Dharma* she had *Yudhishṭhira*, by *Māruta* (i.e. the Wind) *Bhīmasena*, and by *Çakra* (i.e. Indra) *Arjuna*. He then caused her to impart on *Mādrī* the *vidyā* (i.e. the mantra of invocation), and *Mādrī* by the *Açvins* had *Nakula* and *Sahadeva*. One day when *Pāṇḍu*, filled with desire, touched *Mādrī*, he immediately died, and *Mādrī* ascended the funeral pyre with him, after having recommended her twins to *Kuntī*. Then the *Pāṇḍavas* with *Kuntī* were taken by the ascetics to *Hāstinapura* and introduced to *Bhīshma* and *Vidura*, whereafter the ascetics disappeared from sight, while flames poured down upon the earth and the drums of the gods were heard. They then performed the obsequial rites for their father. As they were being brought up there *Duryodhana* became exceedingly jealous of them.—§ 158: Brief mention of *Duryodhana's* efforts against the *Pāṇḍavas*; how they are sent by *Dhṛtarāshṭra* to *Vāraṇāvata* to be burnt in a lac-house, but are rescued by *Vidura*; killing of *Hiḍimba*; they go to *Ekacakrā*; kill the *Rākshasa Baka*; go to *Pāñcālanagara*, obtain *Draupadī*, and return home.—§ 159: The eleven sons of the *Pāṇḍavas*: (1) *Prativindhya* (son of *Yudhishṭhira*); (2) *Sutasoma* (of *Vṛkodara*, i.e. *Bhīmasena*); (3) *Çrutakīrti* (of *Arjuna*); (4) *Çatānīka* (of *Nakula*):

(5) *Çrutakarman* (of *Sahadeva*); (6) *Yaudheya* (of *Yudhishṭhira*⁀*Devikā*, daughter of *Govāsana Çaibya*); (7) *Sarvaga* (of *Bhīmasena*⁀*Balandharā Kāçyā*); (8) *Abhimanyu* (of (*Arjuna*⁀*Subhadrā*, sister of *Vāsudeva*, i.e. *Kṛshṇa*, from Dvāravatī); (9) *Niramitra* (of *Nakula*⁀*Kareṇumatī Caidyā*); (10) *Suhotra* (of *Sahadeva*⁀*Vijayā Mādrī*, daughter of the Madra king *Dyutimat*); (11) the *Rākshasa Ghaṭotkaca* (of *Bhīmasena* ⁀ *Hiḍimbā*). *Abhimanyu* was the perpetuator of the family.—§ 160: *Abhimanyu* married *Uttarā*, daughter of *Virāṭa*; she brought forth a dead child (of six months, burnt by the "weapon"), whom *Kuntī* took up on her lap at the command of *Vāsudeva Purushottama*, i.e. *Kṛshṇa*, who revived him and called him *Parīkshit*, because he was born in an extinct race (*parikshīṇe kule*). "*Parīkshit* married *Mādravatī*, thy mother *Janamejaya*! thou hast begotten two sons on thy wife *Vapushṭamā*, named *Çatānīka* and *Çaṅkukarṇa*; and *Çatānīka* has on *Vaidehī* begot a son *Açvamedhadatta*."—Blessings upon the readers (of all four castes) (I, **95**).

***pūrvā**, sc. diç.: V, 3768 (etymology), 3769.

Pūrvābhirāmā, a river. § 574 (Jambūkh.): VI, **9**λ, 329.

Pūrvacitti, an Apsaras. § 135 (Çakuntalop.): I, **74**, 3055 (among the principal Apsarases).—§ 191 (Arjuna): I, **123**, 4821 (sung at the birth of Arjuna).—§ 336 (Indralokābhigamanap.); III, **43***a*, 1784 (in the palace of Indra).—§ 716 (Çukābhipatana): XII, **333**, 12597 (Urvaçī and *P.* dwell on Malaya).

Pūrvadeva = Kṛshṇa: XIII, 7364 (origin of the name).—Do. = Arjuna: III, 1699.—Do., dual = Nara-Nārāyaṇau: I, 8160, 8302; V, 1921, 1935.—Do. = Asura (Nīl.); II, 16.

Pūrvanivāsa = Mahāpurusha (Mahāpurushastava).

Pūrvapālin, a king. § 554 (Sainyodyogap.); V, **4**γ, 80 (among the princes to whom the Pāṇḍavas ought to send messengers).

Pūrvapūrvānugaṇḍikā, name of a place. § 574*j* (Mālyavat): VI, **7**, 282 (so BR., "towards the east are many small mountains [sc. on the summit of Mālyavat]," PCR.).

Pūshan, a god, one of the Ādityas. § 88 (Aṃçāvat.): I, **65**, 2523 (the ninth of the Ādityas).—§ 191 (Arjuna): I, **123**, 4824 (do., present at the birth of Arjuna).—§ 258 (Khāṇḍavadahanap.): I, **227**, 8268 (fought with Kṛshṇa and Arjuna).—§ 310*b* (Sūrya): III, **3**, 146 (the fifth name of Sūrya in Dhaumya's enumeration), 191 (=Sūrya, in Yudhishṭhira's hymn).—§ 573 (Ambop.): V, **179**, 7162 (=Sūrya).—§ 603 (Nārāyaṇāstramokshap.): VII, **202**, 9550 (Çiva tore out the teeth of *P.* while he was eating the *puroḍāça* at the sacrifice of Daksha).—§ 615*u* (Skanda). IX, **45**γ, 2507 (came to the investiture of Skanda), 2546 (gave two companions to Skanda).—§ 617 (Aishīkap.): X, **18**, 801 (°*aç ca daçanān*, torn out by Çiva, cf. § 603), 807 (do., restored by Çiva).—§ 623 (Rājadh.): XII, **15**, 441 (*na* . . . *P°āṇaṃ*, sc. *namasyanti janāḥ*).—§ 664 (Mokshadh.): XII, **207**β, 7582 (the tenth of the Ādityas).—§ 746 (Ānuçāsanik.): XIII, **65**δ, 3295 (becomes gratified by ghee); **81**, 3833 (*etān lokān avāpnoti gān datvā* . . . *yeshām adhipatiḥ P°ā*).—§ 747*b* (Suvarṇotpatti); XIII, **85**, 4116.—§ 770 (Ānuçāsanik.): XIII, **151**γ, 7093 (the tenth of the Ādityas).—§ 773*d* (Çiva): XIII, **161**, 7476 (Çiva tore out the teeth of *P.*, cf. § 603).

Pūshaṇā, a mātṛ. § 615*u* (Skanda): IX, **46**θ, 2638.

Pūshānuja = Indra: VIII, 798 (only B., C. has by error *Pūshātmaja*).

Pūshātmaja[1] ("the son of Sūrya") = Karṇa: VIII, †4600.

Pūshātmaja[2] = Indra, v. Pūshānuja.

Pushkara[1], sg. and pl. (°*āṇi*), name of a group of tīrthas. § 11 (Parvasaṅgr.): I, **2**, 655 (°*jalaiḥ*).—§ 253 (Haraṇāharaṇap.): I, **221**, 7976 (sg.) —§ 317*b* (Kṛshṇa Vāsudeva): III, **12**, 472 (°*eshu*, there Kṛshṇa had performed austerities).—§ 357 (cf. Tīrthayātrāp.): *P.* is the tīrtha of the god of the gods (*Devadevasya*), where the *Ādityas*, the *Vasus*, the *Rudras*, the *Sādhyas*, the *Marudgaṇas*, the *Gandharvas*, and the *Apsarases* are ever present, and where the gods, the *Daityas*, and the *Brahmarshis* have obtained great merit by ascetic devotions. The bathing there is equal to the bathing in all tīrthas together and to horse-sacrifices, and frees even *çūdras* from rebirth; especially the visiting of *P.* on the day of the full-moon in the month of Kārttika is equal in merit to the performing of *agnihotras* during a hundred years, and leads to the worlds of Brahmán; dwelling twelve years purely at *P.* gives the merit of all sacrifices and leads to the abode of Brahmán. "There are three white hillocks (*çṛṅgāṇi*) and three springs (*praçravaṇāni*), known from the remotest times—we do not know why—by the name of *P.*"; it is difficult to go to *P.*, etc.; III, **82**, 4062 (sg., *Devadevasya tīrthaṃ*), 4063 (sg.), 4066 (pl.), 4068 (pl.), 4073 (sg.), 4074 (pl.), 4076 (sg.), 4077 (sg.), 4080 (pl. and sg.), 4081 (sg.).—§ 362 (Tīrthayātrāp.): III, **83**, 5095 (*sammitaṃ P°āṇāṃ*, sc. Yakshiṇī).—§ 369 (Kurukshetra): III, **83**, 7073 (*antarīkshe ca P°ṃ*, sc. *viçishyate*).—§ 375 (Tīrthayātrāp.): III, **85**, 8232 (*Tretāyāṃ P°ṃ smṛtaṃ*, sc. *puṇyaṃ*), 8233 (sg.), 8234 (°*e tu tapas tapyet*).—§ 377 (Dhaumyatīrthak.): III, **89**, 8369 (*Pitāmahasaraḥ P°ṃ nāma*, in the west), 8370 (pl.), 8371 (pl.).—§ 406 (Tīrthayātrāp.): III, **125**, 10480 (°*eshu* . . . *sarveshu*; "holy lakes," PCR.).—§ 594 (Mṛtyu): VII, **54**, 2098 (pl., there Mṛtyu performed austerities).—§ 615*i* (Saptasārasvata): IX, **38**, 2196 (°*sthe Pitāmahe*), 2198 (pl.), 2200 (do., the river Sarasvatī appeared at *P.* as the river Suprabhā).—§ 652*b* (Indrota-Pārīkshitīya): XII, **152**β, 5646 (pl.), (γ), 5662 (pl.).—§ 702 (Mokshadh.): XII, **298**ε, †10937 (*Naimisha-P°eshu*).—§ 733*c* (Ānuçāsanik.): By bathing in *P.* and *Prabhāsa* and *Naimisha*, and the ocean and *Devikā* and *Indramārga*, and *Svarṇabindu*, one attains to heaven: XIII, **25**, 1696 (sg.).—§ 757*m* (Goloka): XIII, **102***a*, 4887 (pl.).—§ 758 (Ānuçāsanik.): XIII, **103***a*, 4916 (pl.).—§ 766 (do.): XIII, **125**β, 5967 (pl.); **127**, 6064 (pl.); **130**, 6119 (sg., there one should make the gift of a *kapilā* cow), 6100 (do.).—§ 775 (do.): XIII, **166***a*, 7645 (pl.).—§ 795*c* (Mahābhārata): XVIII, **5**, 211 (°*jalaiḥ*).

Pushkara[2], son of Varuṇa. § 268 (Varuṇasabhāv.): II, **9**, 381 (in the palace of Varuṇa).—§ 564 (Mātalīyop.): V, **98**, 3533 (*asya*—i.e. Varuṇa's—*putraḥ*).

Pushkara[3], brother of Nala. § 343 (Nalopākhyānap.): III, **52**, 2068.—§ 346 (do.): III, **59**, 2257, 2259, 2260, 2271: **60**, 2285, 2286 (*P.* vanquished Nala at dice).—§ 347 (do.): III, **61**, 2297, 2298, 2300, 2301, 2304, 2305 *P.* won from Nala his kingdom, etc.).—§ 351 (do.): III, **78**, 3033, 3034, 3039, 3040, 3047, 3049, 3054, 3056, 3058, 3060 (Nala vanquished *P.* at dice and recovered his kingdom, etc.).—§ 608 (Karṇap.): VIII, **91**, †4761 (all. to Nalopākhyānaparvan).

Pushkara[4], name of a dvīpa. § 575 (Bhūmip.): VI, **12**, 465.

Pushkara[5], name of a mountain in the dvīpa Pushkara. § 575 (Bhūmip.): VI, **12**, 465 (*parvataḥ*).

Pushkara[6] = Kṛshṇa: XII, 1512.

Pushkaradhāriṇī, wife of the brahman Satya. § 686 (Mokshadh.): XII, **273**, 9816.

Pushkarāksha ("lotus-eyed") = Kṛshṇa (Vishṇu): V,

3124; XII, †1515, 1647; XIII, 6954 (Vishṇu's 1000 names), 7008 (do.), 7078 (i.e. Vishṇu).—Do.² = Skanda: III, 14640.

Pushkaramālinī¹, the sabhā of Indra. § 266 (Çakrasabhāv.): II, **7**, 310. Do.², the sabhā of Varuṇa. § 267 (Yamasabhāv.): II, **8**, 352.

Pushkarāraṇya, name of a forest in the tīrtha Pushkara. § 48 (Çesha): I, **36**, 1567 (there Çesha performed austerities).—§ 285 (Nakula): II, **32**, 1190 (°*vāsinaḥ*, in the west, vanquished by Nakula).—§ 357 (Pushkara): III, **82**, 4070 (at Pushkara). Cf. Pushkara¹.

Pushkarasthapati = Çiva (1000 names²).

Pushkarekshaṇa ("lotus-eyed") = Kṛshṇa (Vishṇu): I, 8010; III, 8756 (i.e. Vishṇu), 10240; V, 4291 (*Dāçārhaḥ*); VII, 386, 391, 2837, 3739.—Do.² = Indra: XIII, 3922.

Pushkariṇī, wife of Bhumanyu. § 152 (Pūruvaṃç.): I, **94**, 3714 (mother of Diviratha, Suhotra, etc.).

Pūshṇo dantabhid ("destroyer of Pūshan's teeth") = Çiva: XIV, 193.

Pūshṇo dantavināça(ḥ) (do.) = Çiva: VII, 9541.

Pūshṇo dantavināçana(ḥ) (do.) = Çiva: XII, 10423 (1000 names¹); XIII, 6565 (B. °*nipātana*).

Pushpa, a serpent. § 564 (Mātalīyop.): V, **103**, 3629 (enumeration). Cf. the two next.

Pushpadaṃshṭra, a serpent. § 47 (Sarpanāmak.): I, **35**, 1557 (enumeration). Cf. the next.

Pushpadanta¹, a serpent (?). § 603*d* (Tripura): VII, **202**, 9564 (Çiva made Elapatra and *P.* the two pins of his chariot).

Pushpadanta², a companion of Skanda. § 615*u* (Skanda): IX, **45**, 2553 (given to Skanda by Pārvatī).

Pushpadhāraṇa = Kṛshṇa: XII, 1512.

Pushpahāsa = Vishṇu (1000 names).

Pushpaka, the *vimāna* of Kubera. § 438*b* (Yakshayuddhap.): *P.* was constructed by Viçvakarman: III, **161**, 11775 (°-*āsanavaraṃ*).—§ 506 (Skandayuddha): III, **231**, 14546 (*āsthāya ruciraṃ yāti P°ṃ Naravāhanaḥ*).—§ 525 (Rāmopākhyānap.): III, **274**, 15888 (*vimānaṃ . . . kāmagaṃ*, given to Kubera by Brahmán).—§ 526 (do.): III, **275**, 15922 (*vimānaṃ*, robbed by Rāvaṇa). — § 543 (Rāmābhisheka); III, **291**, 16583 (*vimānena khecareṇa virājatā kāmagena*), 16588 (*vimānaṃ*), 16599 (do., having slain Rāvaṇa, Rāma gave *P.* back to Kubera).—§ 615*x* (Kubera): IX, **47**, 2759.

Pushpaketu ("flower-marked") = Kāma: III, 16172.

Pushpāmbhas, a tīrtha. § 360 (Tīrthayātrāp.): III, **82**, 5048.

Pushpānana, a Yaksha. § 269 (Vaiçravaṇasabhāv.): II, **10**, 399 (in the palace of Kubera).

Pushpavat¹, a mountain on Kuçadvīpa. § 575 (Bhūmip.): VI, **12**ε, 452.

Pushpavat², an Asura (?). § 673*b* (Bali-Vāsavasaṃv.): XII, **227*a***, 8263 (among the ancient rulers of the earth).

Pushpavatī, a tīrtha. § 370 (Tīrthayātrāp.): III, **85**, 8154.

Pushpaveṇī, a river. § 574 (Jambūkh.): VI, **9**λ, 342.

Pushpodakā, a river. § 470 (Yamaloka): III, **200**, 13407 (*nadī*, in the region of Yama).

Pushpotkaṭā, name of a female Rākshasa. § 526 (Rāmopākhyānap.): III, **275*a***, 15893, 15895 (by Viçravas mother of Kumbhakarṇa and Rāvaṇa).

Pushṭa = Vishṇu (1000 names).

Pushṭi ("thriving," personif.), a goddess. § 115 (Aṃçāvat.): I, **66**, 2578 (daughter of Daksha and wife of Dharma).—§ 270 (Brahmasabhāv.): II, **11**, 459 (in the palace of Brahmán).—§ 330 (Indradarçana): III, **37**, 1488 (in Draupadī's blessing of Arjuna).

Pushṭimati, a fire. § 493 (Āṅgirasa): III, **221**, 14176 (the same as Bharata?).

Pushya, name of a nakshatra = Tishya, also = the time of the moon's conjunction with Pushya. § 378 (Tīrthayātrāp.): III, **93**, 8484 (°*eṇa prayayuḥ*).—§ 527 (Rāmopākhyānap.): III, **277**, 15959 (*adya P°o niçi . . . puṇyaṃ yogam upaishyati*).—§ 554 (Sainyodyogap.): V, **6**, 125 (°*yogena muhūrtena Jayena ca*).—§ 569 (Bhagavadyānap.): V, **150**, 5079 (°*o 'dyeti*).—§ 574 (Jambūkh.): VI, **3**, 80 (*Dhūmaketur mahāghoraḥ P°ñ cākramya tishṭhati*, omens).—§ 614 (Gadāyuddhap.): IX, **34**, 1952 (°*eṇa samprayāto 'smi Çravaṇe punar āgataḥ*, sc. Balarāma).—§ 615 (do.): IX, **35**, 1978 (*nirgacchadhvaṃ, Pāṇḍaveyāḥ, P°eṇa*), 1983 (*Rauhiṇeye* —i.e. *Balarāma—gate . . . P°eṇa*).—§ 746 (Ānuçāsanik.): XIII, **64**, 3261 (merit of making a gift of gold under the constellation *P.*)—§ 749 (do.): XIII, **89**, 4258 (merit of performing a çrāddha under the constellation *P.*).—§ 759 (do.): XIII, **110**, 5393 (description of the cāndravrata, v. Āçleshā). Cf. Tishya.

Put, name of a hell. § 135 (Çakuntalop.): I, **74**, 3026 (°*n-nāmno narakād yasmāt pitaraṃ trāyate sutaḥ | tasmāt putra iti proktaḥ*).—§ 259 (Çārṅgakop.): I, **229**, 8344 (°*n-nāmno narakāt putras trāyate pitaraṃ çrutiḥ*). Cf. XIV, 2752.

Pūtanā¹, a female demon (in the shape of a bird). § 290 (Çiçupālavadhap.): II, **41**, 1436 (had been slain by Kṛshṇa). —§ 502 (Manushyagrahak.): III, **230**, 14480 (°*m Rākshasīṃ prāhus taṃ vidyāt Pūtanāgrahaṃ*). — § 567 (Bhagavadyānap.): V, **130**, 4409 (*çakunī*, had been slain by Kṛshṇa).

Pūtanā², a mātṛ. § 615*u* (Skanda): IX, **46**θ, 2634.

Pūtātman = Vishṇu (1000 names).

Putradarçana ("the seeing of the sons"). § 10 (Parvasaṅgr.): I, **2**, 355 (i.e. Putradarçanaparvan).

[Putradarçanaparvan] ("the section relating to the seeing of the sons," the 96th of the minor parvans of Mhbhr.; cf. Putradarçana). § 789: *Janamejaya* said: Tell me what that wonderful feat was which M.-ṛ. *Vyāsa* accomplished after his promise to *Dhṛtarāshṭra* when he had taken up his abode in the forest with *Gāndhārī* and *Kuntī*, and after *Vidura* had left his body and entered into *Yudhishṭhira*, and when all the *Pāṇḍavas* were in the ascetic retreat; for how many days did *Yudhishṭhira* stay with his men in the woods; on what food did the *Pāṇḍavas* support themselves with their men and wives? *Vaiçampāyana* said: The *Pāṇḍavas* passed about a month in that forest, supporting themselves on diverse kinds of food and drink. Then *Vyāsa* came there and *Nārada*, etc. (*a*); they sat down on sacred seats [of *kuça* grass] and on seats of peacock feathers; *Gāndhārī*, etc. (β) also sat down; they spoke of Ṛ., D., and As. Then *Vyāsa* said that he knew that burning grief in the heart of *Dhṛtarāshṭra*, etc. (γ); "let D., G., and M.-ṛ. to-day behold the energy of my penances; therefore tell me what wish of thine I shall grant to-day." *Dhṛtarāshṭra* wished to see his dead children and kinsmen, mentioning *Duryodhana* and the slaughter of *Bhīshma* and *Droṇa*. Hearing this the grief of *Gāndhārī*, etc. (δ) became fresh; *Gāndhārī* said that for sixteen years *Dhṛtarāshṭra* never had slept for grief; and also *Kṛshṇā*, etc. (ε) grieved exceedingly. *Vyāsa* then asked *Kuntī* to tell what she wished (XV, **29**). *Kuntī* told the story of *Karṇa's* birth (mentioning *Durvāsas*, etc.); *Vyāsa* promised to show her

Karṇa, and said that she had no fault in what had happened about the birth of *Karṇa*; "the gods beget after five methods (thought, word, sight, touch, and sexual union)" (XV, **30**). *Vyāsa* promised to show everyone the persons whom they wished to see and who were in the other world (ζ); "they were all portions of D.; both G., Aps., Pç., Gh., Rā., *Puṇyajanāḥ*, Si., D.-ṛ., D., and Dā. met with death on the battlefield of *Kurukshetra*"; he explained who among the dead, etc., was what: *Dhṛtarāshṭra* was the *Gandharva* king *Dhṛtarāshṭra*, etc. (η). They all, *Dhṛtarāshṭra* with his ministers and the *Pāṇḍavas* and Ṛ. and G., proceeded towards the Bhāgīrathī and waited for the advent of night; at sunset they bathed and finished their evening rites (XV, **31**). When night came, *Vyāsa* plunged into the Bhāgīrathī for a bath, and summoned all the deceased warriors, who all rose up from the water with a loud uproar, everyone presenting the same aspect that he did when clad for battle; there were *Bhīshma*, etc. (θ); all of them were now robed in celestial vestments and had brilliant earrings; they were free from all animosity, etc.; G. sang their praises, etc.; each of them was waited upon by bands of Aps. *Vyāsa* gave *Dhṛtarāshṭra* celestial vision; endued with celestial knowledge, *Gāndhārī* saw all the slain; *Dhṛtarāshṭra* became full of joy (XV, **32**). Divested of wrath and malice, the spirits of the dead mingled with the living in happy converse (ι). Having sported with one another for that night they, taking leave from each other, returned to the places they had come from (κ), *Vyāsa* dismissing them within the twinkling of an eye; of Rā. and Pç. some proceeded to the *Uttarakurus*, others to the gods. With *Vyāsa's* permission, many widows plunged into the waters of the Bhāgīrathī in order to accompany their deceased lords, and proceeded to those regions where their husbands had found their abodes. *Vyāsa* granted to all the men there assembled the fruition of their wishes. People of diverse realms, hearing of this meeting between the dead and living, became highly delighted (XV, **33**).—§ 790: *Sauti* said: *Janamejaya* filled with joy asked *Vaiçampāyana*, how it is possible for persons whose bodies have been destroyed to reappear in those very forms. *Vaiçampāyana* said: Acts are never destroyed; bodies are born of acts; so also are features, etc., quoting a *çruti* in the horse-sacrifice (XV, **34**). *Dhṛtarāshṭra* had never beheld his own sons, but got spiritual vision from *Vyāsa*, he had learnt all the royal duties, as also the *Vedas* and *Upanishads*; *Vidura* attained to high success through penances. *Janamejaya* said: If *Vyāsa* shows me my father as he was when he died I may then believe all that thou hast told me. *Sauti* said: Then *Vyāsa* brought *Parikshit* [from the other world], and *Çamīka* and his son *Çṛṅgin*; all the counsellors and ministers of the king beheld them. *Janamejaya*, performing the final bath in his sacrifice, highly rejoiced; he poured the sacred water over his father, as also over himself; then he said to *Āstīka* that this his sacrifice was fraught with many wonderful incidents; *Āstīka* praised *Vyāsa* and the snake-sacrifice, from which *Takshaka* had with difficulty escaped, the worship of Ṛ., etc. *Janamejaya* honoured *Āstīka*, and then asked Ṛ. *Vaiçampāyana* about *Dhṛtarāshṭra's* further residence in the woods (XV, **35**).—§ 791: *Janamejaya* said: Having seen his sons, etc., what did *Dhṛtarāshṭra*, and king *Yudhishṭhira* also, do? *Vaiçampāyana* said: Beholding that wonderful sight, the reappearance of his children, R.-ṛ. *Dhṛtarāshṭra* became relieved of his grief and returned to his retreat; the people and Ṛ., dismissed by *Dhṛtarāshṭra*, returned home. *Vyāsa* came and asked *Dhṛtarāshṭra* to dismiss the *Pāṇḍavas* ("thou hast heard discourses from Ṛ., the mysteries of D. from *Nārada*, etc."), who now had passed more than a month in the woods. *Dhṛtarāshṭra* addressed *Yudhishṭhira* affectionately, and dismissed him and his brothers. *Yudhishṭhira* offered to wait upon his uncle and his two mothers; *Gāndhārī* dissuaded him from that step. *Yudhishṭhira* said that his mind was wholly set upon penances, as the whole earth were empty now, etc. (*a*) *Sahadeva*, saying that he dared not leave his mother, urged *Yudhishṭhira* to return to the capital; he would himself remain, engaged in penances and in serving the old king and his mothers. *Kuntī* affectionately dissuaded her sons from remaining with her and thereby obstructing her penances. They then took leave of their mother and *Dhṛtarāshṭra*, who blessed and comforted *Yudhishṭhira*, etc. (β), and embraced them one after another. Then *Gāndhārī* blessed them, and *Kuntī* kissed them on their heads, etc. *Gāndhārī* and *Kuntī* embraced *Draupadī*, etc., and instructed them. *Yudhishṭhira* with his wives and troops and kinsmen set out for *Hāstinapura* (XV, **36**).

R

Rabheṇaka, a serpent. § 64 (Sarpasattra): I, **57**, 2149 (of Takshaka's race).

Raçmivat, a Viçvadeva. § 749 (Ānuçāsanik.): XIII, **91**γ, 4361 (enumeration).

Rādhā, wife of Adhiratha, foster-mother of Karṇa. § 131*b* (Karṇa): I, **67**, 2775 (*°āyāḥ kalpayām āsa putraṃ* [sc. Karṇa] *so 'dhirathaḥ*, cf. § 547).—§ 547 (do.): III, **309**, 17154, 17162, 17163 (Adhiratha and *R.* found Karṇa, whom they adopted).—§ 569 (Bhagavadyānap.); V, **141**, 4759, 4760 (reared Karṇa, cf. § 547).

Rādhābhartṛ ("the husband of Rādhā") = Adhiratha: I, 2775, 4403.

Rādhāsuta, Rādhātmaja, Rādheya = Karṇa, q.v.

Rāga = Çiva (1000 names [1]).

Rāgā, name of a daughter of Aṅgiras. § 489 (Āṅgirasa): III, **218**, 14125 (*rāgād R°eti yāṃ āhur dvitīyā 'ṅgirasaḥ sutāṃ* [read *sutā* with B.]).

Rāghava ("descendant of Raghu") = Rāma Dāçarathi: III, 8665, 11201, 11208 (*Vaidehīṃ R°priyāṃ*), 11284, 11320, 15970, 15987, 15988, 16021, 16029 (*Lakshmaṇaḥ priya-R°ḥ*), 16030, 16036, 16067, 16082, 16099, 16144, 16150, 16163, 16197, 16237, 16283, 16286, 16300, 16301, 16316, 16332 (*Koçalendraḥ*), 16344, 16363, 16370, 16375, 16512, 16547, 16557, 16559, 16585, 16594, 16599; IX, 2255; XIII, 3617.

Rāghava, dual (*°au*) (do.) = Rāma and Lakshmaṇa: III, 16285.

Rāghava, pl. (*°āḥ*) (do.). § 770 (Ānuçāsanik.): XIII, **151**, 7155 (*Somādityānvayāḥ sarve R°āḥ Kuravas tathā*).

Raghu, an ancient king. § 6 (Anukram.): I, **1***a*, 226 (in Sañjaya's enumeration). § 552ᵘ (Goharaṇap.): IV, **56**ζ, 1769 (came on the chariot of Indra to see the encounter).—§ 656 (Khaḍgotpattik.): XII, **166**δ, 6197 (received the sword from Yuvanāçva, from him it passed over to Hariṇāçva).—§ 761 (Ānuçāsanik.): XIII, **115**γ, 5661 (abstained from meat during the month of Kārttika).—§ 770 (do.): XIII, **151**ξ, 7160 (*saṃgrāmajid bhavati caiva R°ṃ namasyan*). § 775 (do.): XIII, **166**η, 7677 (enumeration).

Raghukulodvaha ("propagator of the Raghu family") = Lakshmaṇa: III, 16203.

Raghunandana ("descendant of Raghu") = Rāma Dāçarathi: III, 11215, 16038, 16345, 16558, 16600.

Rahasyā, a river. § 574 (Jambūkh.): VI, **9**λ, 326.

Rāhu, an Asura, the demon (planet) who causes eclipses. § 28 (Amṛtamanthana): I, **19**, 1161 (*Dānavaḥ*), 1166 (°*mukhena*; disguised as a god *R.* drank *amṛta*, but was discovered by Sūrya and Soma, Nārāyaṇa cut off *R.'s* head, which to this day swallows Sūrya and Soma [at the eclipses]). —§ 35 (Aruṇa): I, **24**, 1266 (*Candrādityair yadā R°r ākhyāto hy amṛtaṃ pivan* | *vairānubandhaṃ kṛtavān candrāditye tadā*, cf. § 28), 1267 (swallows the sun).—§ 72 (Ādivaṃçāvatāraṇap.): I, **62**, 2302 (*mucyate . . . R°ṇā candramā yathā*).—§ 94 (Aṃçāvat.): I, **65**, 2539 (*Candrārkamardanaṃ*, son of Siṃhikā).—§ 270 (Brahmasabhāv.): II, **11**, 447 (among the planets in the palace of Brahmán).—§ 307 (Anudyūtap.): II, **81**, 2693 (°*ç cārkam upāgrasat*, i.e. caused an eclipse).—§ 350 (Nalopākhyānap.): III, **68**, 2667 (*paurṇamāsīm iva niçāṃ R°grastaniçākarāṃ*).—§ 368 (Tīrthayātrāp.): III, **83**, 7062 (°*graste divākare*), 7067 (do.).— § 460*b* (Kaliyuga): III, **190**, 13091 (*aparvaṇi . . . Sūryaṁ Rāhur upaishyati*, at the end of the yuga).—§ 473 (Mārkaṇḍeyas.): III, **200**, †13477 (*dinasya R°oḥ*).—§ 512 (Ghoshayātrāp.): III, **247**, 15045 (*upaplutaṃ yathā Somaṃ R°ṇā rātrisaṅkshaye*).—§ 569 (Bhagavadyānap.): V, **143**, 4843 (°*r arkam upaiti*, omens).—§ 574 (Jambūkh.): VI, **3**, 78 (*arkaṃ R°r upaiti*, omens).—§ 575 (Bhūmip.): VI, **11***a*, 403; **12** [482 (*b*: The planet *R.* (*Svarbhānuḥ*) is globular, its diameter is 12,000 yojanas (therefore he can envelop both the sun and the moon), and its circumference 42,000 yojanas)], 488 (*chādayaty etau*, i.e. the sun and the moon, *yathākālaṃ*). § 586 (Bhīshmavadhap.): VI, **101**, 4627 (°*ḥ khe çaçinaṃ yathā*, sc. *abhyadravat*), 4638 (*grastaṃ R°ṇeva niçākaraṃ*).— § 587 (do.): VI, **110**, 5130 (*parvaṇīva susaṃkruddho R°ḥ pūrṇaṃ niçākaraṃ*, sc. *pīḍayām āsa*).—§ 593 (Abhimanyuvadhap.): VII, **39**, 1668 (*yathā R°r divākaraṃ*, sc. *grasishyāmi*). —§ 599 (Jayadrathavadhap.): VII, **101**, 3767 (°*or āsyān muktau prabhākarau*); **110**, 4147 (*grasyate . . . bhānumān iva R°ṇā*); **116**, 4627 (*grasyamānaṃ . . . khe Somam iva R°ṇā*).—§ 600 (Ghaṭotkacavadhap.): VII, **179**, †8131 (*divīva R°raṃçumator pradīptaṃ*).—§ 608 (Karṇap.): VIII, **87**, 4464 (°-*Ketū yathākāçe uditau*); **89**, †4596 (°*or vimuktam . . . candraṃ yathā*).—§ 615 (Gadāyuddhap.): IX, **56**ρ, 3138 (°*ç cāgrasad ādityam aparvaṇi*).—§ 660*b* (Bhṛgu-Bharadvājasaṃv.): XII, **190**, 6975 (°*grastasya Somasya yathā*).—§ 661 (Mokshadh.): XII, **193**, 7061 (°*r yathā candram upaiti*).—§ 663 (do.): XII, **203**, 7438 (*yathā candrārkanirmuktaḥ sa R°r nopalabhyate*).—§ 696*b* (Daksha-prokta-Çiva-sahasranāmastotra): XII, **285**, 10448 (*praviçya vadanaṃ Rāhor yaḥ somaṃ pivate*, sc. Çiva).—§ 766 (Ānuçāsanik.): XIII, **125**, 5968 (*mucyeta . . . R°ṇā candramā yathā*).—§ 773*b* (Kṛshṇa Vāsudeva): XIII, **159**, 7366 (Kṛshṇa identified with *R.*).—§ 775 (Ānuçāsanik.): XIII, **166***a*, 7643 (enumeration of the planets).—§ 785 (Anugītāp.): XIV, **77**, 2235 (*agrasad ādityaṃ yugapat somam eva ca*).— § 793 (Mausalap.): XVI, **2**, 51. Cf. Daitya, Dānava, Graha, Svarbhānu.

Raibhya, a brahman, father of Arvāvasu and Parāvasu. § 11 (Parvasaṅgr.): I, **2**, 451 (*ākhyānaṃ R°sya*, cf. § 414 foll.).—§ 264 (Sabhākriyāp.): II, **4***a*, 111 (waited upon Yudhishṭhira).—§ 413*b* (Tīrthayātrāp.): At the hermitage of *R.* the *kavi Yavakrīta Bhāradvāja* perished (cf. § 416): III, **135**, 10700 (°*āçramaḥ*).—§ 414 (Yavakrītop.): III, **135**, 10703 (friend of Bharadvāja), 10704 (father of Arvāvasu and Parāvasu), 10705, 10706.—§ 416 (do.): III, **135**, 10748, 10749, 10750; **136**, 10752 (°*āçramapadaṃ*), 10755, 10756, 10759, 10762, 10771; **137**, 10777; 10783, 10785, 10786 (Yavakrīta, the son of Bharadvāja, attempted to seduce the daughter-in-law of *R.*; *R.* by a spell created a rakshas who slew Yavakrīta; then Bharadvāja cursed *R.*, that he should be killed by his eldest son).—§ 417 (do.): III, **138**, 10791 (°*yājyaḥ*, i.e. Bṛhaddyumna), 10792 (°*sya vai putrau Arvāvasu-Parāvasū*), 10815 (*R.* was by a mistake killed by Parāvasu, but afterwards revived).— § 665 (Mokshadh.): XII, **208**ε, 7592 (one of the ṛshis of the east).—§ 717*c* (Uparicara): XII, **337**ε, 12758 (among the sadasyas at the sacrifice of Vasu Uparicara).—§ 717*b* (Nārāyaṇīya): XII, **349** (IV), 13588 (*munaye*), 13589 (learnt the religion of Nārāyaṇa from Vīraṇa and made it over to his son Kukshi).—§ 734 (Ānuçāsanik.): XIII, **26***a*, 1763 (among the ṛshis who came to see Bhīshma).—§ 770 (do.): XIII, **151**ζ, 7108 (among the seven *Mahendrasya guravaḥ* in the east; only B., C. has by error *Vaidyaḥ*).—§ 775 (do.): XIII, **166**γ, 7663 (one of the ṛshis of the east).

Raibhyaputra ("the son of Raibhya"): Parāvasu: XII, 1771 (*Viçvāmitrasya pautraḥ*).

Raivata[1], a mountain near Dvārakā. § 252 (Subhadrāharaṇap.): I, **220**, 7936 (*çailendraṃ*).—§ 273 (Rājasūyārambhap.): II, **14**, 614 (*Kuçasthalīṃ purīṃ . . . R°opaçobhitām*). Cf. Raivataka.

Raivata[2], a ṛshi. § 265 (Lokapālasabhākh.). II, **5**, 145 (accompanied Nārada, only C., B. *Parvata*).

Raivata[3], a graha (sickness-demon): § 502 (Manushyagrahak.): III, **230**, 14482 (*Aditiṃ Revatīṃ prāhur grahas tasyās tu R°ḥ*).

Raivata[4], an ancient king. § 565 (Gālavacarita): V, **109**, 3788 (*atra*—i.e. in the south—*sāmāni gāthābhiḥ çrutvā gītāni R°aḥ* | *gatadāro gatāmatyo gatarājyo vanaṃ gataḥ*, i.e. while *R.* listened to the sāmans, he did not know how long time had passed, but when he returned he found his wife dead, etc. (Nīl.), cf. Harivaṃça v. 645 foll. PCR. erroneously a Daitya).—§ 656 (Khaḍgotpattik.): XII, **166**δ, 6197 (received the sword from Marutta, from *R.* it passed over to Yuvanāçva)—§ 761 (Ānuçāsanik.): XIII, **115**δ, 5665 (abstained from meat during the month of Kārttika).— § 775 (do.): XIII, **166**η, 7679 (C. has by error *Re°*).

Raivata[5], a Rudra. § 665 (Mokshadh.): XII, **208**δ, 7585.

Raivata[6], adj ("relating to Revatī"). § 767 (Ānuçāsanik.): XIII, 136, 6236 (*ishṭiṃ*, otherwise Nīl.), 6242 (do., C. has by error *Re°*).

Raivataka[1], a mountain (= Raivata). § 251 (Arjunavanavāsap.): I, **218**, 7892.—§ 252 (Subhadrāharaṇap.): I, **219**, 7906 (*girau*), 7917; **220**, 7931.—§ 291 (Çiçupālavadhap.): II, **45**, 1567 (*krīḍato Bhojarājasya . . . R°e girau*, then Çiçupāla burnt Dvārakā).—§ 785 (Anugītāp.): XIV, **59**, 1754 (°*sya mahe*), 1764 (do.).

Raivataka[2], a mountain in Çākadvīpa. § 575*b* (Çākadvīpa): VI, **11**, 418 (the constellation Revatī is permanently placed over *R.*).

Raja, a warrior of Skanda. § 615*u* (Skanda): IX, **45**η, 2575.

Rājadharman = Nāḍījaṅgha: XII, 6337, (6340), 6342, (6343), 6396 (*khagottamaḥ*), 6407 (do.), 6412, 6414, 6416, 6417, 6421, 6433, 6436, 6440, 6443. Cf. Dharmarāj.

Rājadharmānuçāsana ("the teaching of the duties of

kings"). § 10 (Parvasaṅgr.): I, **2**, 351 (i.e. Rājadharmānuçāsanaparvan).

[Rājadharmānuçāsanaparvan(°va)] ("the section containing the teaching of the duties of kings," the 88th of the minor parvans of Mhbhr.; cf. Rājadharmānuçāsana). § 621: After the completion of the water rites by the *Pāṇḍavas*, etc. (*a*), many *Brahmarshis*, etc. (*β*), came to *Yudhishṭhira*. *Nārada* congratulated *Yudhishṭhira* upon his success. *Yudhishṭhira* lamented the loss of his kinsmen (*γ*); *Yudhishṭhira* at the match of dice had wondered seeing that *Karṇa's* feet resembled the feet of *Kuntī*; he inquired of *Nārada*, why the earth had swallowed up the wheels of *Karṇa's* chariot (XII, **1**). *Nārada* recited to *Yudhishṭhira* the story of *Karṇa's* pupilage with *Droṇa* and *Rāma* (among G., Rā., Y., and D.) and the curse called down upon him by a brahman whose cow *Karṇa* had inadvertently slain (*δ*) (XII, **2**); then the story of *Karṇa's* extraordinary powers of endurance, in consequence of which his real caste became known to *Rāma* (who had taught him the *Brāhma* weapon), who thereupon cursed him for his deceit; the worm *Alarka* was an Asura named *Daṃça*, who in the *Kṛta* age had ravished the spouse of *Bhṛgu* and been cursed by him, until he should be liberated by *Paraçu-Rāma*. *Karṇa*, arriving before *Duryodhana*, told him: "I have mastered every weapon" (XII, **3**). *Nārada* said: "To a self-choice at *Rājapura*, the capital of the *Kāliṅga* king *Citrāṅgada Duryodhana* (with *Karṇa*), *Çiçupāla*, etc. (*ε*), repaired; the maiden (who was accompanied by her nurse and a guard of eunuchs) passed by *Duryodhana*, who then (relying upon *Bhīshma* and *Droṇa*) took her up on his chariot and abducted her by force. *Karṇa*, riding on his chariot, proceeded in *Duryodhana's* rear. The kings pursued *Karṇa* and *Duryodhana*; but *Karṇa* made them all turn away, and *Duryodhana* reached *Hāstinapura* with the maiden" (XII, **4**). *Nārada* said: "The *Māgadha* king *Jarāsandha* challenged *Karṇa* to a single combat; at last they fought with bare arms, and *Karṇa* was about to sever the two portions of *Jarāsandha's* body that had been united together by *Jarā*; then *Jarāsandha* gave up all desire of hostility and gave unto *Karṇa* the town *Mālinī* (i.e. *Campā*). From that time he ruled over *Campā* and the *Aṅgas* agreeably to the wishes of *Duryodhana*." Allusions to XII, **2**, **3**, etc. (*ζ*) (XII, **5**). D.-ṛ. *Nārada* became silent; *Yudhishṭhira* grieved; *Kuntī* comforted *Yudhishṭhira* by telling him that neither she nor *Sūrya* could dissuade *Karṇa* from fighting the *Pāṇḍavas* (XII, **6**). *Yudhishṭhira's* lament (*η*) before *Arjuna*; he wished to renounce the sovereignty (XII, **7**). *Arjuna* addressed *Yudhishṭhira*, justifying war and approving of the acquisition of wealth, quoting *Nahusha* (who cried fie on the state of poverty, in which he had done many wicked acts, and which is for recluses and *R*.), and citing the conduct of the gods and Dā., which is sanctioned by the *Vedas*; "this earth formerly belonged to king *Dilīpa*, etc. (*θ*); she now belongs to thee; a great sacrifice awaits thee; if thou dost not perform this sacrifice, the sins of this kingdom shall all be thine; those subjects whose king performs a horse-sacrifice . . . all become pure," as shown by the example of *Mahādeva* (*Çiva* (*b*)); "this is the great path called *Dāçaratha* (affording place for ten waggons, i.e. the sacrifice [Nīl.])" (XII, **8**). Unmoved by *Arjuna's* words, *Yudhishṭhira* desired to lead the life of a religious recluse (XII, **9**). *Bhīma's* address to *Yudhishṭhira* commending sovereignty (XII, **10**).—§ 622: *Arjuna* recited the story of the discourse between *Çakra* (in the shape of a golden bird) and certain youths (Ṛ.) desirous of leading a forest life (XII, **11**). —§ 623: *Nakula* addressed *Yudhishṭhira*, blaming renunciation and commending the life of a householder (XII, **12**). *Sahadeva* recommended to *Yudhishṭhira* a life of action with the soul free from attachments (XII, **13**). *Draupadī* reminded *Yudhishṭhira* of his former counsels (*a*) (XII, **14**). *Arjuna* praised him who wields the rod of chastisement; "*Indra*, by the slaughter of *Vṛtra*, became the great *Indra*; those among the gods that are given to slaughtering others are adored much more by men; *Rudra*, etc. (*β*) are all slaughterers; all people bend to these gods, but not to *Brahmán* or *Dhātṛ* or *Pūshan* at any time, except a few men of noble disposition" (XII, **15**). *Bhīma's* second address to *Yudhishṭhira* (*γ*), urging him to subdue his grief (XII, **16**). *Yudhishṭhira* exposed the folly of earthly enjoyments quoting *Janaka* (observant of the religion of *moksha*): "my treasures are immense; yet I possess nothing; if again the whole of *Mithilā* were burnt, nothing of mine will be burnt" (XII, **17**).—§ 624: *Arjuna* recited the story of the discourse between the *Videha* king *Janaka* (who had shaved his head) and his queen (the princess of *Koçala*), in which the latter explained the claims of a life of poverty and renunciation (XII, **18**).—§ 625: *Yudhishṭhira's* reply to *Arjuna* on the vanity of wealth (XII, **19**). —§ 626: *Devasthāna* pointed out to *Yudhishṭhira* that the period had not come when he could retire into the woods (*a*) (XII, **20**), and recommended the assumption of sovereignty with his soul freed from attachment, quoting a discourse which *Bṛhaspati* delivered to *Indra*; the Ṛ., etc., adopt the religion of Exertion (not Emancipation), and attain to heaven through their acts (XII, **21**).—§ 627: *Arjuna* justified before *Yudhishṭhira* the slaughter of foes in battle: "*Indra*, himself, though a brahman, became a *kshatriya* in his acts, and battled with his sinful kinsfolk 810 times" (XII, **22**).—§ 628: *Vyāsa* dissuaded *Yudhishṭhira* from a life of retirement and commended a life of domesticity, quoting a verse of *Bṛhaspati* ("like a snake devouring mice, the Earth devours a king that is inclined to peace and a *brahman* that is exceedingly attached to domesticity"), and reciting the story of R.-ṛ. *Sudyumna*: the brothers *Çaṅkha* and *Likhita* dwelled in two separate dwellings on the banks of *Bāhudā*; once, when *Çaṅkha* had gone out, *Likhita* came to his asylum and ate many ripe fruits. *Çaṅkha* told him to confess to the king and ask him to inflict on him the punishment of a thief. King *Sudyumna* would pardon him; but *Likhita* would not; *Sudyumna* then caused his hands to be cut off; *Likhita*, having asked pardon of *Çaṅkha*, was told by him to gratify D., R., and P. at *Bāhudā*, upon which two hands grew out. *Çaṅkha* said that he was not his chastiser, "but the king has been himself purified, as also thyself, along with P." That king became eminent by this act and obtained the highest success (XII, **23**). *Vyāsa* exhorted *Yudhishṭhira* to grant the wishes of his brothers, perform sacrifices, and imitate the great monarchs of old, especially *Hayagrīva* (*b*) (XII, **24**).—§ 629: Hearing the words of *Vyāsa* and seeing *Arjuna* angry, *Yudhishṭhira* declared to *Vyāsa* that earthly rule could give him no delight. *Vyāsa* answered, pointing out the virtues of Time, quoting "the old story recited by king *Senajit* in grief". "Engaging in battle has been said to be the sacrifice for a king; a due observance of the science of chastisement is his *yoga*; and the gift of wealth in sacrifices in the shape of *dakshiṇā* is his renunciation; all this should be regarded as acts that sanctify him" (XII, **25**).—§ 630: *Yudhishṭhira's* reply to *Arjuna* recommending a life of *yoga* and austerities;

this is the practice of R̥., regarded by D. as *brahmans*; this is the opinion of the *Vaikhānasas*; the *Ajāḥ*, etc. (*a*) have all gone to heaven by means of *Vedic* study; by performing the acts indicated in the *Vedas*, battle, sacrifices, study of the *Vedas*, restrainment of passion, one goes to heaven by the southern path of the Sun; the northern path is travelled by those devoted to *yoga*, and is much applauded by those conversant with the *Purāṇas*; "one acquires heaven through contentment," citing the discourse of *Yayāti* of old (XII, **26**). *Yudhishṭhira* censured himself for his cupidity and for the slaughter he caused of his kinsmen (β); *Bhīshma* had, by the energy of his weapons, burnt *Ugrāyudha*, etc.; *Vyāsa* comforted *Yudhishṭhira* by explaining the action of Destiny, and exhorted him to work (XII, **27**).—§ 631: *Vyāsa* recited "the old story, that is known by the name of *Açman's* discourse": the *Videha* king *Janaka*, filled with sorrow, questioned the wise *brahman Açman* as to how a man should behave upon occasions of the accession and the destruction of both kinsmen and wealth. *Açman* said that Destiny and Time are inevitable; "no person can see either heaven or hell; the scriptures, however, are the eyes of the virtuous; frame thy conduct according to the scriptures." *Janaka* became freed from grief; "enjoy the earth, O son of *Kuntī*!" (XII, **28**).—§ 632: *Arjuna* asked *Kr̥shṇa* (who from his earliest years was dearer to *Yudhishṭhira* than even *Arjuna* himself) to dispel *Yudhishṭhira's* grief. *Kr̥shṇa* asked *Yudhishṭhira* not to grieve for men who died heroically in battle in the observance of *kshatriya* duties, quoting the *Shoḍaçarājopākhyāna* (*b*), i.e. the old discourse of *Nārada* before *Sr̥ñjaya* when the latter was deeply afflicted with grief on account of the death of his son. *Sr̥ñjaya* was freed from grief, and *Nārada* gave back to him his son *Suvarṇashṭhīvin*, whom *Parvata* had given him, and who had been bereft of life; that child should live 1,000 years (XII, **29**).—§ 633: Requested by *Yudhishṭhira*, *Kr̥shṇa* told *Nārada-Parvatopākhyāna* (*b*) (XII, **30**).—§ 634: Thereafter *Nārada* told *Suvarṇasṭhīvisambhavopākhyāna* (*b*) (XII, **31**).—§ 635: *Vyāsa* exhorted *Yudhishṭhira* to shake off his grief and assume the reins of sovereignty. *Yudhishṭhira* feared that the guilt of slaughter had stained him; *Vyāsa* repeated his observations on Destiny (XII, **32**); as *Yudhishṭhira* still was remorseful (*a*), *Vyāsa* repeated his observations on Time, and pointed to expiatory rites, illustrating the case by the war of 32,000 years, by which the gods, having slain Dai., gained possession of heaven, and slew 88,000 brahmans called *Çālāvr̥kāḥ* who had joined the Dā.; "thou hast only followed the path formerly trodden by the very gods; men like you never go to hell." He recommended a horse-sacrifice as an expiation, mentioning that *Indra*, assisted by the *Maruts*, gradually performed 100 sacrifices and became *Çatakratu*, and is adored in the heavens by Aps., R̥., and D. (XII, **33**). *Vyāsa* discoursed on expiation and indicated the acts for which there should be expiation, citing the sage *Uddālaka*, who caused his son *Çvetaketu* to be begotten by a disciple, etc. (XII, **34**), and declared that by penances, religious rites, and gifts one may wash off sins if one does not commit them anew, and indicated diverse kinds of expiation for diverse kinds of sins (XII, **35**). Asked by *Yudhishṭhira*, *Vyāsa* declared what food is clean and what is unclean (XII, **36**). *Yudhishṭhira* desired to hear of the duties of kings and of the four different orders. *Vyāsa*, casting his eyes on *Nārada*, directed *Yudhishṭhira* to apply to *Bhīshma* for discourses on kingly duties, as *Bhīshma*, having gratified D.-r̥. with Br̥h. at their head, had acquired a knowledge of the duties of kings, and of that science, with its interpretations, that *Uçanas* and *Br̥haspati* know; and a knowledge of all the *Vedas* with their branches, from *Vasishṭha* and *Cyavana* of *Bhr̥gu's* race; in olden days he studied under *Sanatkumāra* (the eldest-born son of *Brahmán*); he learned the duties of the *Yatis* from *Mārkaṇḍeya*; and obtained all weapons from *Rāma* and *Indra*; although childless, yet he has many regions of bliss before himself; B.-r̥. were always his courtiers. *Yudhishṭhira* was ashamed to approach *Bhīshma*. *Kr̥shṇa* exhorted *Yudhishṭhira* to rise up, shaking off his grief (β). Thus addressed by *Kr̥shṇa*, etc. (γ), *Yudhishṭhira* gave up his grief and anxiety, and with his brothers and the other kings, headed by *Dhr̥tarāshṭra*, set out for *Hāstinapura*. The procession described (δ) (XII, **37**). The citizens welcomed *Yudhishṭhira* and *Draupadī*, etc. (ε). *Yudhishṭhira* entered the palace with *Dhaumya* and *Dhr̥tarāshṭra*, and was blessed by the *brahmans*, but cursed by *Cārvāka*, a Rā. who had disguised himself as a *brahman*, and a friend of *Duryodhana*; the *brahmans* killed *Cārvāka* by uttering the mere sound *huṃ* (XII, **38**).—§ 636: *Kr̥shṇa* related: In the *Kr̥ta* age Rā. *Cārvāka* performed penances in *Badarī*; at last he solicited from *Brahmán* the boon of immunity from fear at the hands of every being in the universe, which *Brahmán* granted him, only with the limitation that he should be careful not to offend *brahmans*. Then he began to cause trouble to the gods; *Brahmán* predicted *Cārvāka's* friendship with *Duryodhana*, and that he would insult the *brahmans* (XII, **39**).—§ 637: The ceremony of *Yudhishṭhira's* installation on the throne described (*a*); he made gifts to the *brahmans*, who all blessed him and his brothers (XII, **40**). *Yudhishṭhira* answered and enjoined respect for his aged uncle, disposed of the high appointments of state (β) (XII, **41**), and caused the obsequial rites (*çrāddha*) to be performed in honour of the slaughtered heroes (γ), and performed acts of kindness to the ladies, widowed in the battle, the destitute, the blind, and helpless (XII, **42**). Then he adored *Kr̥shṇa* (XII, **43**), and assigned to his brothers proper residences from among the palaces of the *Kuru* princes slain in battle (δ). They passed a happy night in their respective abodes, and in the morning presented themselves before king *Yudhishṭhira* (XII, **44**). *Yudhishṭhira's* gifts to diverse persons (ε). Then he addressed *Kr̥shṇa* (with the *Kaustubha*), whom he found rapt in meditation (XII, **45**); he uttered a hymn to *Kr̥shṇa*, who awoke and praised *Bhīshma* (ζ), asking *Yudhishṭhira* to resort to *Bhīshma* for instruction. *Yudhishṭhira* requested *Kr̥shṇa* to grant *Bhīshma* the sight of his divine person. *Kr̥shṇa* caused *Sātyaki* to let *Dāruka* yoke his chariot with *Sugrīva* and *Çaibya*, etc. (XII, **46**). Description of the bed of arrows on which *Bhīshma* lay, surrounded by R̥. *Vyāsa*, etc. (η). *Bhīshma* hymned *Kr̥shṇa* (θ). *Kr̥shṇa* moved by *Bhīshma's* adorations, bestowed upon him heavenly knowledge compassing the Past, the Present, and the Future, and went away. Those holy brahmans adored *Bhīshma* and *Kr̥shṇa*. Seeing the devotion of *Bhīshma*, *Kr̥shṇa* suddenly rose from his seat and ascended his chariot with *Sātyaki*; *Yudhishṭhira* and *Arjuna* mounted another; *Bhīmasena* and the twins a third; *Kr̥pa*, *Yuyutsu*, and *Sañjaya* on their respective chariots (XII, **47**).—§ 638: Then *Kr̥shṇa*, etc. (*a*), proceeded to *Kurukshetra* (description). *Kr̥shṇa* pointed out to *Yudhishṭhira* the five lakes of *Rāma Bhārgava*. Requested by *Yudhishṭhira* (XII, **48**), *Kr̥shṇa* related: *Rāmopākhyāna* (*b*). Then he proceeded quietly in his chariot (XII, **49**).—§ 639: *Yudhishṭhira's* eulogy of *Rāma* (*a*).

Beholding from a distance the spot on which *Bhīshma* lay (on the banks of the river *Oghavatī*), *Yudhishṭhira*, etc. (β), descended from their chariots and approached and saluted the Ṛ. (headed by *Vyāsa*). Seeing *Bhīshma* on the point of death, *Kṛshṇa* addressed him kindly (γ), and eulogized him ("competent to subjugate D., G., As., Y., and Rā.; spoken of by *brahmans* as the ninth of the *Vasus*; knowing the knowledge of the *cāturhotra* — v. BR. — and the *Sāṅkhya* and *Yoga*, etc., the *Vedas* and the *Purāṇas*") (XII, **50**). *Bhīshma* saluted *Kṛshṇa* (δ), and beheld his eternal form. *Kṛshṇa* said that it was owing to *Bhīshma's* devotion that he had displayed his celestial form to him; "those regions, O king! are ready for thee whence there is no return; fifty-six days still remain for thee to live; when *Sūrya* turns to his northerly course, you shall go there; D. and V., riding on their chariots, are waiting for thee invisibly." *Kṛshṇa* asked *Bhīshma* to instruct *Yudhishṭhira*, etc.; "when thou wilt leave this world for that, all knowledge will expire with thee" (XII, **51**). *Bhīshma* alleged physical weakness and mental darkness as reasons for his inability to obey *Kṛshṇa*, and he also hesitated to speak in *Kṛshṇa's* presence. *Kṛshṇa* removed *Bhīshma's* pain and granted him power to recollect everything and behold the universe like a fish in a limpid stream. M.-ṛ. with *Vyāsa* adored *Kṛshṇa* with words, accompanied by *Ṛc*, *Yajus*, and *Sāman* verses; celestial flowers fell, and Aps. sang, etc. At sunset the M.-ṛ., rising up, saluted *Kṛshṇa*, *Bhīshma*, and *Yudhishṭhira*. Upon this, *Kṛshṇa* (etc.) (ε), returned to *Hāstinapura*, after having saluted *Bhīshma*, saying that they would return next day (description) (XII, **52**). *Kṛshṇa* passed the night happily, performed his morning rites, and was welcomed with music and song at early dawn; asked by *Kṛshṇa*, *Sātyaki* saw *Yudhishṭhira* and apprised him of *Kṛshṇa's* readiness to accompany him into the presence of *Bhīshma*. *Yudhishṭhira* asked *Arjuna* to see that his chariot was made ready; then he, with the twins, etc. (ζ), proceeded to *Kṛshṇa's* abode. *Kṛshṇa*, accompanied by *Sātyaki*, mounted his chariot, yoked with *Balāhaka*, etc. (η), urged by *Dāruka*. The princes set out. Arrived near *Bhīshma* (surrounded by M.-ṛ.), *Kṛshṇa*, etc. (θ), alighting from their chariots, saluted Ṛ. by raising their right hands. *Yudhishṭhira* approached *Bhīshma*, eying him timidly (XII, **53**).—§ 640: Many Ṛ. and Sā., etc. (*a*), came to *Bhīshma*. *Nārada* urged the *Pāṇḍavas* to take advantage of the short span of life still left to *Bhīshma* for soliciting him to discourse on morality. *Yudhishṭhira* requested *Kṛshṇa* to put questions to *Bhīshma*. *Bhīshma's* cheerful answer. He enquired of *Kṛshṇa* why he was desired to discourse on morality and the duties of kings, *Kṛshṇa's* divine self being best fitted to do so; *Kṛshṇa* explained that his motive was only the enhancement of *Bhīshma's* glory; "thou hast always worshipped Ṛ. and D." (XII, **54**). *Bhīshma* consented to discourse on morality and duty, and desired *Yudhishṭhira* to question him. *Kṛshṇa* introduced *Yudhishṭhira* to *Bhīshma*, who comforted *Yudhishṭhira*, saying that what he had done he had done in observance of *kshatriya* duties. *Yudhishṭhira* humbly approached *Bhīshma* and touched his feet; *Bhīshma*, kissing his head, asked him to take a seat and question him without anxiety (XII, **55**). *Yudhishṭhira* solicited *Bhīshma* to discourse on kingly duties which are regarded as the root of all other duties in the world. *Bhīshma*, bowing to *Dharma*, *Kṛshṇa* (who is *Bráhman* in full), and the *brahmans*, set forth the general duties of kings ("as regards Ṛ. also, truth is their great wealth"); he quoted two *çlokas* of *Manu*: "fire has sprung from water, the *kshatriya* from the *brahmán*, and iron from stone; these three can exert their force on every other thing; but on their origins (*yonishu*), it is extinguished (*çāmyati*)"; and two *çlokas* of M.-ṛ. *Uçanas* (a *brahman* who rushes to battle may be chastised by a *kshatriya*); and a *çloka* of *Bṛhaspati* (according to B.) (a king should not always be mild, nor always fierce) (XII, **56**). Continuation of *Bhīshma's* discourse, enjoining readiness for action on kings; quoting a *çloka* sung by *Uçanas* ("like a snake swallowing up mice"; cf. ch. **23**); and one by king *Marutta*, agreeably to *Bṛhaspati's* opinion; *Bāhu's* son, king *Sagara*, who exiled his eldest son *Asamañjas*, who used to drown the children of the citizens in the *Sarayū*; Ṛ. *Uddālaka* who cast off his favourite son *Çvetaketu*, because the latter used to invite *brahmans* with deceptive promises of entertainment. The king should administer justice like *Yama* and amass wealth like *Kubera*. He quoted a verse sung in days of old by *Bhārgava* [i.e. *Vālmīki* (cf. Hopkins, p. 61)], in the narrative called *Rāmacarita*, on king[ly duties] ("one should first select a king; then should he select a wife, and then earn wealth; if there be no king, what would become of his wife and acquisitions?" (XII, **57**). Continuation of *Bhīshma's* discourse, inculcating that protection is the very essence of kingly duties, quoting *Bṛhaspati*, etc. (β), and verses sung by *Bṛhaspati* ("by exertion the *amṛta* was obtained, by exertion the *Asuras* were slain," etc.). *Vyāsa*, etc. (γ), expressed their delight with the discourse. Ṛ. and the princes left *Bhīshma* for the night and ascended their chariots; then they bathed in the *Dṛshadvatī*, offered oblations of water to their ancestors, etc., and entered *Hāstinapura* (XII, **58**).—§ 641: The next morning the *Pāṇḍavas* and the *Yādavas* set out to *Kurukshetra*, approached *Bhīshma* and saluted the Ṛ.; *Yudhishṭhira* enquired about the origin of the word *rājan* ("king"). *Bhīshma's* answer: In the *Kṛta* age sovereignty first began; the population of the earth became sinful; the *Vedas*, etc., were lost; D. applied to *Brahmán*, who composed a treatise of 100,000 lessons, on virtue, profit, and pleasure, and emancipation, etc. (description). *Brahmán*, addressing the gods, said that his work, aided by Chastisement (*Daṇḍanīti*), would protect the world. *Çiva* studied the great work and abridged it (then called *Vaiçālāksha*, in 10,000 lessons) for *Indra*, who abridged it further to 5,000 lessons, and called it *Bāhudantaka*; *Bṛhaspati* further abridged it to 3,000 lessons, and called it *Bārhaspatya*; *Kāvya* [i.e. *Uçanas*] (the preceptor of *yoga*) further abridged it to 1,000 lessons. Thus, in view of the period of men's lives and [the general] decrease, that science (*çāstra*) was abridged by M.-ṛ. Asked by the gods, who deserved to have superiority among men, *Vishṇu* created by his will a son, *Virajas*; but he inclined to renunciation; and so did *Virajas'* son *Kīrtimat* and the latter's son *Kardama*. *Kardama's* son *Anaṅga* became a protector of creatures, fully conversant with the science of chastisement.

Anaṅga — *Mṛtyu*
| |
Atibala (*b*) ~ *Sunīthā* (*c*)
|
Vena (*d*)

Then follows the history of *Pṛthu Vainya* (*f*). Thus the tales of all past events (*āgamaç ca Purāṇānām*), the origin of M.-ṛ., etc. (ε) were all treated of in this treatise of *Brahmán* (*Paitāmahe çāstre*) (XII, **59**). Requested by *Yudhishṭhira*, *Bhīshma* discoursed on the general duties of the four orders and the special duties of each of the orders. Sacrifice has been laid down for the *çūdra* also, but without *svāhā* and *vashaṭkāra* or any other *mantra*; he should perform *pākayajñas*, where the *dakshiṇā* is *pūrṇapātra* (v. the note of PCR., p. 195); in days of old a *çūdra* of the name of *Paijavana* gave a *dakshiṇā* of 100,000 *pūrṇapātras* according to the ordinance called *Aindrāgnya* (B. *Aindrāgna*). Devotion cleanses all sacrifices. The members of the three other classes have all sprung from the *brahmans*; the *brahmans* are the gods of the very gods. The *çūdra*, who is without *Ṛc*, *Yajus*, and *Sāman*, has *Prajāpati* for his god, and devotion for his sacrifice. A verse sung in praise of sacrifice by the *Vaikhānasa munis*. The *homas* called *skanna* and *askanna* (XII, **60**). The four modes of life specified (ζ). M.-r. cite a verse sung by *Nārāyaṇa* (XII, **61**). The four stages of life have been laid down for the *brahman*; the other three orders do not adopt them. What duties are improper for a *brahman* (XII, **62**). Continuation. The duties in the four stages of life stated more specifically. A *kshatriya*, for leading the life of Ṛ., may adopt the *bhikshu* mode of life; [but] a life of mendicancy is not obligatory upon the three orders (XII, **63**). The nature of kingly duties. "It has been told to you how, in days of old, many kings repaired to *Vishṇu* (*Nārāyaṇa*) for the sake of the science of chastisement. S., etc. (η) are all observant of *kshatriya* duties. In days of old when Dā. had multiplied, *Māndhātṛ* became king and performed a great sacrifice from desire of beholding *Nārāyaṇa* (*Vishṇu*), who, in the form of *Indra*, had a discourse with him touching *Vishṇu*, extolling the *kshatriya* duties above all other duties, and citing the example of *Vishṇu* himself, who for the sake of D. and Ṛ. and *Brahmán* and the *brahmans*, slew all his foes among the As. (XII, **64**). *Indra* extolled the *kshatriya* duties. Asked by *Māndhātṛ*, he set forth the duties of the *Yavanas*, etc. (θ). Then *Nārāyaṇa* (in the form of *Indra*), accompanied by M., repaired to his eternal abode (XII, **65**). Asked by *Yudhishṭhira*, *Bhīshma* discoursed in detail on the four stages of life (XII, **66**). What should be the characteristics of kingdoms. In days of old, in consequence of anarchy, men met with destruction; they made certain compacts, but soon repaired to *Brahmán* to get a king; *Manu* was prevailed upon to accept the kingdom, against getting one-fiftieth of their animals, one-tenth of their grain, one-quarter of their merit, etc. *Manu* then made his round through the world, checking everywhere all acts of wickedness. Men desiring happiness must choose a king (XII, **67**). Why the king is regarded as a god on earth. *Bhīshma* recited the discourse between *Bṛhaspati* (the son of *Aṅgiras*) and *Vasumanas* (king of *Koçala*); *Bṛhaspati* described the evils of anarchy; the king becomes *Agni*, etc. (ι). *Vasumanas* thenceforth began to protect his subjects (XII, **68**). The special duties of a king; the duties of a king in case of an invasion by a stronger monarch, quoting *Bṛhaspati* (v. 2619) and two verses (v. 2667–8) sung by *Aṅgiras* (i.e. *Bṛhaspati*). The blessedness of chastisement; the king causes the *Kṛta* age, etc. (κ), to set in (XII, **69**). The thirty-six virtues that a king should possess. Hearing the words of *Bhīshma*, king *Yudhishṭhira*, protected by *Bhīma*, etc., worshipped *Bhīshma*, and from that time began to rule according to his teaching (XII, **70**). Asked by *Yudhishṭhira*, *Bhīshma* explained the way in which the king should discharge the duty of protection (XII, **71**). The qualifications of the king's priest: *Bhīshma* recited the old story about the discourse between *Aila's* son *Purūravas* and *Mātariçvan*, explaining the order of birth of the four classes (from *Brahmán's* mouth, arms, thighs, and feet, respectively) and their duties, the right of dominion appertaining to the *brahman*; therefore a king should appoint a priest; D., men, P., G., Us., and Rā. all depend upon sacrifices for their support, and sacrifices depend upon the king, who is *Indra*, *Yama*, and *Dharma* (XII, **72**). The effects of a disunion between *brahmans* and *kshatriyas*: the old story about the discourse of *Aila's* son and *Kaçyapa*; the *brahman* and the *kshatriya* are said to be the progenitors of all men; in consequence of the sins perpetrated by sinful men, the god *Rudra* appears in the kingdom. Asked by *Aila*, *Kaçyapa* explained who *Rudra* is and what his acts are (*Rudra* exists in the hearts of men; his shape is like that of the wind-gods). Then follows a discussion of the following question: "If chastisement touches the wicked and the good equally, why should the good yet abstain from acts of wickedness" (XII, **73**). The preservation and growth of the king rest upon the king's priest: *Mucukundopākhyāna* (*g*), the old narrative about the discourse between king *Mucukunda* and king *Vaiçravaṇa* (the lord of *Alakā*, Kubera) (XII, **74**). The conduct by which a king aggrandises his subjects and wins regions of felicity hereafter. *Yudhishṭhira* did not see any merit in sovereignty and wished to retire into the woods. *Bhīshma* urged *Yudhishṭhira* to put forth manliness and exertion (XII, **75**). The difference between *brahmans* engaged in their own duties and those amongst them that are not so engaged (XII, **76**). The king is the lord of all wealth except what belongs to the *brahmans*. The old narrative of the speech made by the *Kaikeya* king unto a Rā., who was about to abduct him, but at last left him (XII, **77**). Whether a *brahman*, in seasons of distress, can practise, as a means of livelihood, the duties of a *vaiçya*; what articles, in this case, he may sell; how the king should behave when he is opposed by all the orders of men; if *kshatriyas* become hostile to *brahmans*, how the latter should be protected; *Yudhishṭhira* inquired whether, upon an anarchy happening, any man that protects and rules acquires merit; *Bhīshma* answered in the affirmative; a king that does not or cannot protect is useless (XII, **78**). The kind of persons that are eligible as royal priests; the limits or measure of the *dakshiṇā* (XII, **79**). Who should and who should not be trusted by the king (XII, **80**). How the king should conduct himself for winning over kinsmen and friends: the old story of a discourse between *Kṛshṇa* and *Nārada*: *Kṛshṇa* said: "My heart is worried through the cruel speeches of my kinsmen; might resides in *Saṅkarshaṇa*, mildness in *Gada*; and as regards *Pradyumna*, he surpasses even myself in beauty of person; [but] many others of the *Andhakas* and the *Vṛshṇis* are possessed of great prosperity and might. What can be more painful than [my relation to] *Āhuka* and *Akrūra* (v. the note of PCR., p. 260)?" *Nārada* said that the calamity was due to Kṛshṇa himself; "the kingdom cannot be taken back from *Babhru* and *Ugrasena*, employ soft words, etc.; the *Yādavas*, etc. (λ) are dependent on thee; Ṛ. always pray for thy advancement; thou art the lord of all creatures, etc." (XII, **81**). The second means by which a king may win kinsmen and friends; an old story is cited of what the sage (*brahmarshi*) *Kālakavṛkshīya* had said to the *Koçala* king *Kshemadarçin*; *Kālakavṛkshīya* travelled through the country with a crow in a cage and observed the misdeeds of all the officers of the king, saying that it was the crow that told him all this, and related it to the king; the crow then was found pierced with a shaft within the cage; he quoted *Yama* as to the painful lot of those that serve the king; "this thy kingdom is like the river *Sīlā*, boats sink in it; thy father regarded me lovingly as his friend; when distress overtook this kingdom during the reign of thy father I performed many penances." *Kshemadarçin* then took a minister from the *kshatriya* order, and appointed *Kālakavṛkshīya* as his *purohita*, and subjugated the whole earth (XII, **82**). The qualifications of legislators, ministers, courtiers, and counsellors (XII, **83**). The merits of agreeableness of speech; the old account of a conversation between *Bṛhaspati* and *Çakra* (i.e. Indra) (XII, **84**). Which are the affairs of state that a king has to deal with, and by which persons ought they to be executed? (XII, **85**). The kind of city which a king should have (XII, **86**). How a kingdom should be consolidated and how it should be protected (XII, **87**). How a king should behave if he wishes for wealth (XII, **88**). A king should not cut down trees yielding edible fruits. How one man acquires superiority over the rest; the gifts made by thee in this world support D., P., men, N., Rā., birds, and animals (XII, **89**). The duties of kings (*kshatradharmān*) explained by *Añgiras Utathya* to *Māndhātṛ Yauvanāçva*, about the king's power being only a trust for the good of his people and not for the gratification of his own caprices; the Ṛ. made the king, intending that he should be the embodiment of righteousness on earth; he is called *rājan* ("king") in whom righteousness shines (*rājeta*); he in whom there is no righteousness is called a *vṛshala* (*yasmin vilīyate dharmaḥ* (= *vṛshaḥ*)); *dharma* ("righteousness") comes (*sravati*) from *dhana* ("wealth") or from *dhāraṇa* ("restraining"); *Svayambhū* (Brahmán) created *Dharma* for the advancement and growth of creatures; in consequence of his malice towards the brahmans *Çrī* deserted *Bali Vairocana* and repaired to *Indra*, and *Bali* indulged in many vain regrets. The *çrutis* declare that Unrighteousness (*Adharma*) begat a son named Pride (*Darpa*) upon *Çrī*; Pride led many D. and As. to ruin, and many R.-r.; when the king does not restrain vice, sinful Rā., and persons of neutral sex, etc., begin to take birth even in respectable families, etc. (XII, **90**). Continuation of *Utathya's* discourse. "The ages *Kṛta*, etc. (μ), are all dependent on the conduct of the king. It is said that the Creator (*Dhātṛ*) created power for the object of protecting the weak; weakness is indeed a great being, for everything depends upon it. The king is *Yama* himself. This is the way in which *Indra*, etc. (ν) have acted. D., R., P., and G. sing the praises, both here and hereafter, of that king whose conduct is righteous." Thus addressed by *Utathya*, *Māndhātṛ* did as he was directed, and became the sole lord of the wide earth (XII, **91**). How a righteous king desirous of acting righteously should behave: the old story of what M.-ṛ. *Vāmadeva* sang in ancient times to king *Vasumanas* (XII, **92**); the consequences that result from the king's acting unrighteously. "*Yayāti Nāhusha*, thus having propounded the king's lore (*rājopanishadam*), said that a king should slay even contemptible foes" (XII, **93**). Continuation of *Vāmadeva's* discourse. Thus addressed by *Vāmadeva*, king *Vasumanas* did as he was directed (XII, **94**). How a *kshatriya* should act who desires to subjugate another (XII, **95**). A king should never desire to subjugate the earth by unrighteous means. It was by such behaviour that *Indra* got the sovereignty of the world. King *Pratardana*, subjugating his foes in great battle, took all their wealth, including their very grain and medicinal herbs, but left their land untouched. King *Divodāsa*, after subjugating his foes, brought away the very remnants of their sacrificial fires, their clarified butter, and their food; for this reason he was deprived of the merit of his conquest. King *Nābhāga* gave away whole kingdoms with their rulers as sacrificial presents to the *brahmans*, excepting the wealth of learned *brahmans* and ascetics (XII, **96**). *Yudhishṭhira's* condemnation of *kshatriya* practices. *Bhīshma* pointed out that by chastening the wicked, protecting the good, performing sacrifices, etc., a king cleanses himself, and ultimately obtains a residence in *Indra's* heaven (XII, **97**). The regions of felicity acquired by heroes killed in battle: the old story of the discourse between *Ambarīsha* and *Indra*. *Ambarīsha*, the son of *Nābhāga*, having repaired to heaven, beheld his own generalissimo *Sudeva* in the company of *Indra*, and going to regions still higher. *Indra* explained to *Ambarīsha* the sacrifice of battle. "That warrior who, having slain the commander of the hostile army, mounts the vehicle of his fallen antagonist, comes to be regarded as possessed of the powers of *Vishṇu* and the intelligence of *Bṛhaspati* . . . thousands of Aps. covet him for their lord; having slain *Jambha*, etc. (ξ), I myself have become the chief of the celestials" (XII, **98**). The old story of the battle between *Pratardana* and king *Janaka*, who cheered his troops by showing them both heaven (full of G.-girls, etc.) and hell; his warriors vanquished their foes in battle (XII, **99**). How kings should lead their troops to battle. "It is proper to set the troops in motion on *Caitrī* or *Mārgaçīrshī*. Keeping *Saptarshayaḥ* (Ursa major) behind them, the troops should fight; the wind, the sun, and *Çukra* (Venus) should blow and shine from behind them; the wind is superior to the sun, the sun to *Çukra*. When a small number of troops is to fight with a great many, the array called *Sūcīmukha* should be formed" (XII, **100**). How the troops should be accoutred, armed, and disposed for battle. The *Gāndhāras*, etc. (o), fight best with their curved knives (*nakhara*) and lances. The *Uçīnaras* are possessed of great strength and skilled in all kinds of weapons. The *Prācyas* are skilled in fighting from the backs of elephants and conversant with stratagems (*kūṭayodhinaḥ*). The *Yavanas*, etc. (π), are well skilled in fighting with bare arms. The *Dākshiṇātyas* are skilled in fighting sword in hand. Indications of courage (XII, **101**). What the indications are of the future success of an army. "*Çambara* has said that having afflicted a foe first, forgiveness should be shown afterwards" (XII, **102**). How a king should behave towards a foe that is mild, towards one that is fierce, and towards one that has many allies: the old narrative of the discourse between *Bṛhaspati* and *Indra*; *Bṛhaspati* recommended conciliation or lulling a foe into security; other means; a king should never slay a large number of the defeated troops, etc.; the indications of wicked persons. *Indra*, in subduing his foes, acted strictly according to the words of *Bṛhaspati*, and reduced all his enemies to subjection (XII, **103**). How a righteous king deprived of his kingdom should act; the discourse between *Kshemadarçin* and *Kālakavṛkshīya* in days of old, when prince (*nṛpasutaḥ*) *Kshemadarçin* had become weak and fallen into great distress; "only a fool, deprived of former prosperity, censures the Supreme Ordainer (*Dhātṛ*)" (XII, **104**). Continuation of the discourse; "do thou serve the *Mithilā* king *Janaka* . . .; cause thy enemy to perform the great sacrifice called *viçvajit* and divest him by that means of all his possessions, and cause an ascetic conversant with *yoga* to make thy foe desire to adopt renunciation" (XII, **105**). The king's reply discountenancing deceit and fraud. Asked by *Kālakavṛkshīya*, the *Videha* king *Janaka* made friends with the *Koçala* prince *Kshemadarçin*, took him to *Mithilā*, and bestowed upon him his own daughter, etc. (XII, **106**). How the king should behave towards the aristocracy (XII, **107**). Important duties in brief; the relative superiority of parents and preceptors (XII, **108**). Characteristics of truth and falsehood; "even a person that is disrespectable . . . may succeed in earning great merit as the hunter *Balāka* by slaying the blind [beast]"; *Kauçika* again, on the banks of the *Gaṅgā*, obtained great merit (*sic*! cf. PCR., p. 352, and Kauçika[6]); a deceitful person always wishes to betake himself to the practice of As. (PCR. *amānavaṃ dharmaṃ*) (XII, **109**). How many creatures avoid difficulties? "they that worship with devotion the god *Nārāyaṇa* (*Kṛshṇa*), that Supreme Lord of all creatures . . . succeed in overcoming all difficulties. He is always engaged in doing what is agreeable to *Arjuna*, and also to *Yudhishṭhira*." Blessing upon the reader (XII, **110**). How may good and wicked men be recognized? the old story of the discourse between a tiger and a jackal: in ancient times, in a rich city called *Purikā*, there was a cruel king *Paurika*, who was reborn as a jackal; remembering his former prosperity he became filled with grief and abstained from meat, and became compassionate and truthful, etc., and lived upon fruit that had dropped from the trees; he dwelt in a vast crematorium, his birth-place. The other jackals in vain endeavoured to make him eat carrion, promising to give him food. He consented to become the minister of a tiger, on the condition that the latter should always meet with him alone and in secret, etc. The old servants of the king (i.e. the tiger) first in vain tried to bribe him; then they secretly placed the meat intended for the king in the house of the jackal. The king ordered the jackal to be slain. The mother of the king dissuaded him ("the firmament seems to be like the solid base of a vessel, the fire-fly seems to be like the actual spark of fire; in reality, however, the sky has no base, and there is no fire in the fire-fly; there is necessity for secreting"). A righteous agent of the jackal discovered everything about the false accusation. Notwithstanding the entreaties of the king, the jackal retired to the forest, gave up his body by sitting in *prāya*, and proceeded to heaven (XII, **111**). A king should not behave after the manner disclosed in the history of a camel: There was, in the *Kṛta* age, a huge camel who had recollection of all the acts of his former life; he practised severe austerities in the forest; *Brahmán* granted him the boon that he should have a neck so long that he could seize any food at even the end of 100 *yojanas*. He became idle. One day a great storm arose. The camel placed his head and a portion of his neck within the cave of a mountain; it began to pour in torrents; a jackal with his wife entered the cave for shelter and began to eat of the camel's neck, and thus the camel met with his death because of his idleness. "*Manu* has said that victory depends upon intelligence" (XII, **112**). The old story of the discourse between the Ocean and the Rivers. The Ocean (the refuge of the foes of the gods) asked the Rivers why the latter never washed away a cane; *Gaṅgā* replied that the reason is that the cane bends (XII, **113**). How a man of worth should behave when insulted with harsh words in an assembly (XII, **114**). The qualifications of persons that may be employed by the king. "Criminal laws should be duly administered, even after the manner of *Çaṅkha* and *Likhita*" (XII, **115**). *Bhīshma* related the story of the dog who by favour of the Ṛ. became a *çarabha* and was, for misconduct, retransformed into his own canine form; *Bhīshma* had heard the tale in the hermitage of *Rāma Jāmadagnya*, recited by many Ṛ.; the dog first was transformed into a leopard, then into a tiger subsisting upon the other animals of the forest (XII, **116**); then into an elephant > a lion > a *çarabha* (having eight legs and eyes on the forehead); one day, eagerly thirsting for blood, he wished to slay the sage, who then retransformed him into a dog (XII, **117**); the dog became very cheerless, and was driven by Ṛ. from his hermitage. Continuation of *Bhīshma's* discourse on the qualifications of servants (XII, **118**). The lessons to be drawn from the story of the dog that was transformed into a *çarabha* (XII, **119**). How a king should exercise the duty of protection; "the human body is the residence of *Indra*, etc. (ρ)" (XII, **120**). Asked by *Yudhishṭhira*, *Bhīshma* discoursed about the origin and character of chastisement ("the foremost of all beings among D., Ṛ., P., Y., Rā., Pç., Sā., As., etc."), quoting *Manu* and *Brahmán* ("the first word": *prāgvacanaṃ*); some of the names of chastisement (σ); "beggars, principal judges, astrologers, performers of propitiatory and *Atharvan* rites, treasury, allies, grain, etc., constitute the body, composed of seven attributes and eight limbs, of a kingdom; chastisement is another powerful limb of a kingdom"; it springs from *Brahmán* (the creator of the universe with D., As., Rā., etc.) and the *Veda*; several kinds of *vyavahāra*; *Brahmán* has laid down: "neither mother nor father, nor brother, nor wife, nor priest, is unpunishable with that king who rules agreeably to his duty" (XII, **121**). The discourse between the *Aṅga* king *Vasuhoma* (who was pious and, with his spouse, always practised penances) and *Indra's* friend king *Māndhātṛ*, at *Muñjapṛshṭha* (esteemed by P. and D.-ṛ.) on that peak of *Himavat* (near *Meru*) (*yatra Muñjāvaṭe Ramo jaṭāharaṇam ādiçat*; Nīl. is silent) a favourite haunt of *Rudra*, where *Vasuhoma* came to be regarded as a D.-r. Asked by *Māndhātṛ* about the origin of chastisement, *Vasuhoma* (who knew the doctrines of *Bṛhaspati* and *Uçanas*) related: Once *Brahmán*, desiring to perform a sacrifice, failed to find a priest; he conceived in his brain; after 1,000 years he sneezed; the fœtus, *Kshupa*, fell from his head; he became a lord of creatures and a priest in the sacrifice of *Brahmán*. Chastisement disappeared; a great confusion set in; *Brahmán* repaired to *Vishṇu* (armed with an enormous *çūla*), who created his own self into the form of chastisement (having righteousness for its legs); from that form the goddess *Sarasvatī* created the Science of Chastisement (*daṇḍanīti*); after this *Vishṇu* (*çūlavarāyudhaḥ*) made *Indra* the ruler of D., *Yama Vaivasvata* of P., *Kubera* of treasures and Rā., *Meru* of the mountains, the Ocean of the rivers, *Varuṇa* of the waters and As., Death of life and all living things, Fire of all things possessed of energy, *Mahādeva* of R., *Vasishṭha* of the *brahmans*, *Jātavedas* of V., *Sūrya* of all luminous bodies, the Moon of Stars and constellations, *Aṃçumat* of herbs, *Skanda* (of twelve arms) of spirits and ghostly beings; Time of all creatures and the fourfold death (v. PCR.) and of grief and joy. Upon the completion of that sacrifice, *Mahādeva* made over chastisement to *Vishṇu* > *Aṅgiras* > *Indra* and *Marīci* > *Bhṛgu* > all Ṛ.> Lp. > *Kshupa* > *Manu Vaivasvata* (*çrāddhadeva*) > his sons. Chastisement remains awake, protecting all creatures, being in the hands of successive holders: *Indra* > *Agni* > *Varuṇa* > *Prajāpati* > righteousness > the son of *Brahmán*, i.e. Law > energy > the herbs > the mountains > the juices > *Nirṛti* > the planets and the luminous bodies in heaven > the *Vedas* > the form of *Vishṇu* with equine head > *Brahmán* > *Mahādeva* > *Viçvedevāḥ* > Ṛ. > *Soma* > D. > the *brahmans* > the *kshatriyas*. Several names of *Mahādeva* (τ). Blessing upon the reader (XII, **122**). *Bhīshma's* discourse on Virtue, Wealth, and Pleasure. The narrative of the discourse in olden times between Ṛ. *Kāmanda*[*ka*] and king *Āngarishṭha* (XII, **123**). How may one acquire a virtuous behaviour? *Bhīshma* recited the discourse of *Dhṛtarāshṭra* to *Duryodhana*; as the latter was burning with envy at the sight of the prosperity of *Yudhishṭhira* and his brothers at *Indraprastha* and his mistakes in the palace he, accompanied by *Karṇa*, went to *Dhṛtarāshṭra* with the same question; "10,000 *snātakas* eat at *Yudhishṭhira's* palace off plates of gold; his steeds are of the *Tittiri* and the *Kalmāsha* breeds (? so PCR.; *açvāṃs tittiri-kalmāshān*), etc." *Dhṛtarāshṭra* said: "*Māndhātṛ* conquered the whole world in only one night, *Janamejaya* in the course of three, *Nābhāga* in seven," and he related the story of *Indra's* taking away from Dai. *Prahlāda* the latter's prosperity; *Prahlādá* in days of yore, by the merit of his behaviour, snatched from *Indra* his sovereignty and reduced the three worlds to subjection. *Indra* repaired for knowledge to *Bṛhaspati*, who caused him to repair to *Bhārgava* (Uçanas), who said that *Prahlāda* had better knowledge. *Indra*, in the shape of a *brahman*, repaired to *Prahlāda*, who said that he was ever obedient to the teachings of *Çukra*, etc. *Prahlāda* granted him a boon, and *Indra* wished him to acquire *Prahlāda's* nature (*çīla*). *Prahlāda* was filled with fear, but granted the boon. A flame of light issued out of his body: it was the embodiment of his nature, which was going away and entered the body of *Indra*. Then a similar apparition issued out: it was Righteousness; then Truth; then Good Deeds; then Might; then Prosperity, that informed him that the brahman was *Çakra*. Asked by *Duryodhana*, *Dhṛtarāshṭra* told him how moral conduct (*çīla*) might be acquired (XII, **124**). The characteristics of Hope; "*Duryodhana* destroyed the hope I had cherished," said *Yudhishṭhira*. The discourse between R.-ṛ. *Sumitra* (of the *Haihaya* race) and *Ṛshabha*. *Sumitra*, when hunting, was led away by a deer that he had pierced with an arrow; he shot at it again, but in vain (XII, **125**); arrived at an asylum he asked Ṛ. about Hope (XII, **126**); *Ṛshabha* told him that he had visited *Badarī*, the asylum of *Nara* and *Nārāyaṇa*, where the sage *Açvaçiras* reads the *Vedas*; "having performed my ablutions in the lake and offered oblations of water to P. and D., I entered the asylum; not far from that spot I entered another retreat, where I beheld a very tall and emaciated Ṛ., *Tanu*, exceedingly feeble; he began to discourse in the midst of Ṛ.; a king came with his forces and ladies on a chariot drawn by fleet steeds; the name of this king was *Vīradyumna*; his son and only child *Bhūridyumna* had been missing, and *Vīradyumna* came there in course of his wanderings amidst the forest in pursuit of the missing one. *Tanu* said that a Ṛ. had been insulted by *Bhūridyumna*, who, asked by him for a golden jar and vegetable barks, contemptuously had refused to gratify the ascetic, who became disappointed (XII, **127**). *Tanu* hung down his head; in former days he had been disappointed by the king, and he had practised penances for a long time, and determined to drive away hope from his mind. He then discoursed about the slenderness of Hope. Then he caused the lost prince to be brought thither, rebuked the king, and displayed himself to be the god of righteousness." Thus addressed by *Ṛshabha*, king *Sumitra* gave up his hope (XII, **128**). *Bhīshma* cited the old narrative of the discourse between *Gautama* and *Yama*. *Gautama* owned a wide retreat on the *Pāripātra* hills; for 60,000 years he underwent ascetic austerities there. One day Lp. *Yama* (*Dharma*) came and spoke about truth, etc. (XII, **129**). How may a king in great danger and distress left by his friends behave? (XII, **130**).

Rājagṛha, the metropolis of the Māgadhas (= Girivraja). § 177 (Pāṇḍudigvijaya): I, **113**, 4451 (the capital of king Dīrgha).—§ 242 (Ambuvīca): I, **204**, 7476 (the capital of king Ambuvīca).—§ 277 (Jarāsandhavadhap.): II, **21**, 832 (? the capital of Jarāsandha).—§ 370 (Tīrthayātrāp.): III, **84**, 8082 (a tīrtha).—§ 785 (Anugītāp.): XIV, **82**, 2436 (the capital of Meghasandhi). Cf. Girivraja.

rājan, pl. (°*ānaḥ*) = Yaksha, pl. (?): V, 4717; VII, †5828 (*rājavara*, i.e. the rākshasa Alambusha).

Rājanī, a river. § 574 (Jambūkh.): VI, **9**Λ, 329.

[Rājanyamahābhāgya(m)] ("the grandeur of the kshatriyas"). § 467 (Mārk.): To the horse-sacrifice of king *Ashṭaka Vaiçvāmitri* all kings repaired, also his brothers *Pratardana*, *Vasumanas*, and *Çibi Auçīnara*. After the sacrifice was completed, these four took *Nārada* on their chariot and asked him who of them (as they were all blessed with long life and virtuous) should first fall from Heaven? *Nārada* answered that *Ashṭaka* should first come down, because he had praised himself for having given away thousands of kine; then *Pratardana*, because he, though he had given to *brahmans* successively the four horses yoked to his chariot, and then had drawn the chariot himself, had done so with detraction (*asūyati*); then *Vasumanas*, because he, though he had twice at the *svastivācana* for the sake of a flowery chariot (*pushparathasya*, v. 13313, see the note of PCR., p. 601) given the chariot to *Nārada*, because he praised it, had not done so on a third occasion; *Nārada* himself would come down before *Çibi*, because *Çibi*, at the request of *Vidhātṛ* in the disguise of a *brahman*, who was desirous of trying *Çibi*, had cooked his son *Bṛhadgarbha* as food for the *brahman* without being angry, though the *brahman* meanwhile had set fire to *Çibi's* abode and treasury and arsenal, and when the *brahman* ordered *Çibi* himself to eat his son's body *Çibi* was willing to do it; but the *brahman* said, "Thou hast conquered wrath, there is nothing that thou canst not give to the *brahmans*," and withdrew his hand, and then *Çibi* beheld his son like a child of the gods, while the *brahman* disappeared; and that *Çibi* had not done this for fame or wealth, etc., but because this is not practised by the sinful (III, **198**).

Rājapura, a city of the Kāmbojas. § 589 (Droṇābhishekap.): VII, **4**, 119 (Karṇa proceeded to *R.* and vanquished the Kāmbojas).

Rājarāja[1] ("king of Yakshas"?) = Kubera: III, 11358 (*K*°), 11765, 15888 (°*tvaṃ*), 15891, 16473; XV, 570.

Rājarāja[2] = Çiva: XII, 4502 (*Çūlapāṇiḥ*); XIII, 1263 (1000 names[2]).

Rājarājan ("king of Yakshas"?) = Kubera: III, 16188.

Rajas = Çiva (1000 names[1]).

[Rājasūyārambhaparvan(°va)] ("the beginning of the rājasūya sacrifice," the 22nd of the minor parvans of Mhbhr.). (Cf. Rājasūyasya ārambhaḥ.)—§ 272: *Yudhishṭhira* consulted his counsellors, brothers, *ṛtvijes*, ministers,

Dhaumya, Draipāyana, etc., as to the *rājasūya* ("in which *ṛshis* of austere vows establish six fires singing *mantras* of the *Sāmaveda*; at the conclusion thereof the performer, when installed in the sovereignty, is rewarded with the fruit of all sacrifices, including the *darvīhomas*"). They all encouraged him to perform it. All people lived happily under his sway and loved him (therefore he was called *Ajātaçatru*); *Bhīma* ruled over all men justly, *Arjuna* protected the people from enemies, *Sahadeva* administered justice impartially, *Nakula* behaved towards everybody with humility. There was no extortion, disease, etc. *Yudhishṭhira* sent a messenger to *Kṛshṇa* in *Dvāravatī*, and *Kṛshṇa* came to *Indraprastha* accompanied by *Indrasena*, and was consulted by *Yudhishṭhira* (II, **13**). — § 273: *Kṛshṇa* said that *Yudhishṭhira*, in order to become *samrāj*, ought to slay the *Magadha* king *Jarāsandha*, and deliver the princes whom *Jarāsandha* held shut up in a mountain hole in order to sacrifice them to *Mahādeva* (i.e. Çiva). "The now existing *kshatriyas* are descended from the remnants of those who were exterminated by *Rāma*. They represent themselves to be the descendants of *Aila* and *Ikshvāku*; of those there are 100 families. The *Bhojas*, descendants of *Yayāti*, are great and scattered all over the earth; but now *Jarāsandha*, ruling the middle land (i.e. Mathurā, Nīl.), has overpowered them. His allies are (1) *Çiçupāla*, who has become his *senāpati*; (2) the *Karūsha* king *Vakra*, who fights by illusion (*māyāyodhin*); (3–4) *Haṃsa* and *Ḍimbhaka* (see below); (5–8) *Dantavakra, Karūsha, Karabha, Meghavāhana*; (9) *Bhagadatta*, the *Yavana* king, the ruler of the west, who bears on his head the most wonderful gem on earth, the old friend of thy father, and who chastises *Muru* and *Naraka*; he obeys *Jarāsandha*, but in his heart he is tied by affection to thee; (10) the king of *Aṅga, Vaṅga, Puṇḍra*, and of the *Kirātas, Pauṇḍraka Vāsudeva*, who among the *Cedis* is called *Purushottama*, and always bears, from foolishness, the distinctive signs of *Kṛshṇa*; (11) *Bhīshmaka*, king of the *Bhojas*, the friend of *Indra*, who governs a fourth part of the world, who by his learning has conquered the *Pāṇḍyas, Krathas*, and *Kaiçikas*, and whose brother *Ākṛti* is like to *Rāma Jāmadagnya*, has placed himself under *Jarāsandha*, though *Kṛshṇa*, etc., his relatives, are engaged every day in doing what is agreeable to him. Only *Yudhishṭhira's* maternal uncle, the *Kunti* king *Purujit*, who has his dominions in the west and the south, regards *Yudhishṭhira* with affection. The following peoples have fled for fear of *Jarāsandha*: (1) the eighteen tribes of the northern *Bhojas* have fled towards the west; (2–10) the *Çūrasenas, Bhadrakāras, Bodhas, Çālvas, Paṭaccaras, Susthalas, Mukuṭṭas* (B. Su°), *Kulindas*, and *Kuntis*; (11–13) the *Çālvāyana* kings with their brethren and followers, the southern *Pañcālas*, and the eastern *Koçalas*, have all fled to the *Kuntis* (?); (14–15) the *Matsyas* and the *Sannyastapādas* (? so B.; C. Sanya°) have left their dominions in the north and fled into the southern country; (16) all the *Pañcālas* have fled in all directions." *Jarāsandha's* relations to the *Yādavas* were the following: *Kaṃsa*, having persecuted the *Yādavas*, married *Asti* and *Prāpti*, daughters of *Jarāsandha* and sisters of *Sahadeva*, and began also to oppress the old chiefs of the *Bhojas*, who sought the help of *Kṛshṇa*, etc.; *Kṛshṇa* bestowed upon *Akrūra* the daughter of *Āhuka*, and with *Saṅkarshaṇa* (i.e. Balarāma) he slew *Kaṃsa* and *Sunāman*. Then *Jarāsandha* took up arms, and the eighteen tribes (*kulair ashṭādaçāvaraiḥ* (?), differently Nīl.) thought they would be unable to check him even in 300 years. His friends *Haṃsa* and *Ḍimbhaka* were incapable of being slain by weapons. Some other king, named *Haṃsa* (differently Nīl.), was slain by *Rāma* in the battle of the eighteen tribes (*ashṭādaçāvare* ?); then *Ḍimbhaka*, thinking that he could not live without *Haṃsa*, killed himself in the *Yamunā*, and *Haṃsa*, hearing that, also jumped into the *Yamunā*; then *Jarāsandha* returned to his kingdom, and the *Yādavas* continued to live at *Mathurā*. But the widow of *Kaṃsa* (PCR. *Haṃsa*), the daughter of *Jarāsandha*, urging him to revenge the death of her husband, the *Yādavas* fled from *Mathurā*, and took up their abode in *Kuçasthalī* (i.e. *Dvāravatī*), adorned by *Raivata*, and strongly fortified the *Gomanta* mountains, three *yojanas* in length. "In the race of *Kṛshṇa* there are 8,000 brothers [and cousins, PCR.]. *Āhuka* has 100 sons. *Cārudeshṇa* with his brother, *Cakradeva, Sātyaki, Kṛshṇa, Rauhiṇeya* (i.e. *Balarāma*), and *Çāmba* (like *Çauri* in battle) are seven heroes (*rathāḥ*); *Kṛtavarman, Anādhṛshṭi, Çamīka, Samitiñjaya, Kaṅka, Çaṅku*, and *Kunti* are seven *mahārathas*; then there are also two sons of *Andhakabhoja* and himself; all these heroes, remembering the middle country, are now living among the *Vṛshṇis*" (II, **14**).—§ 274: *Yudhishṭhira* had some scruples, which were opposed by *Bhīma* and *Kṛshṇa*, who cited from the *Kṛta* age five kings, who had become emperors (*samrāj*): *Yauvanāçvi* (i.e. *Māndhātṛ*) by the remission of taxes (B. *jitvā jayyān*, "by victories"), *Bhagīratha* by protection, [Arjuna-]*Kārtavīrya* by asceticism, *Bharata* by strength, and *Marutta* by prosperity; 100 families of kings have been unable to oppose *Jarāsandha*; he has already brought eighty-six kings to the house of *Paçupati* (i.e. Çiva); when he has fourteen more he will offer them as sacrifices (II, **15**).—Some further objections of *Yudhishṭhira* are refuted by *Arjuna* (II, **16**).—§ 275: The origin of *Jarāsandha* was the following: The *Magadha* king *Bṛhadratha*, who had three akshauhiṇīs of troops, married the two twin daughters of the king of *Kāçi*, making an engagement never to show a preference for either. As he was childless he repaired to the ṛshi *Caṇḍa-Kauçika*, the son of *Kākshīvat Gautama*, who was sitting under a mango-tree. He gave a mango fruit to the king, who gave it to his queens. They then brought forth each one half of a child, which were thrown away, but, found and laid together by the *rākshasī Jarā*, became one living child (II, **17**).—*Jarā* had been created by *Svayambhū* for the destruction of the *Dānavas* and named *Gṛhadevī* (*gṛhe gṛhe manushyāṇāṃ nityaṃ tishṭhāmi rākshasī*, v. 730), and always lived in the king's house and did him good, because there was on the walls a likeness of her endued with youth and in the midst of children, and she was daily worshipped with scents, etc. The king ordered a great festival to be held in *Magadha* in honour of *Jarā*, and named the boy *Jarāsandha* (*Jarayā sandhito*, v. 739) (II, **18**). Some time after *Caṇḍa-Kauçika* again came to *Magadha*, and foretold the greatness of *Jarāsandha*, that weapons should not hurt him, and that he should see *Rudra*. After having installed *Jarāsandha, Bṛhadratha* with his two wives retired to the woods and, after practising ascetic penances, ascended to heaven. When king *Kaṃsa* was slain by *Vāsudeva* (i.e. Kṛshṇa), *Jarāsandha*, from *Girivraja*, whirling a mace ninety-nine times, hurled it towards *Mathurā*, where *Kṛshṇa* was residing at that time; the mace fell at *Gadāvasāna*, near *Mathurā*, at a distance of ninety-nine *yojanas* [from Girivraja, PCR.]. He, with *Haṃsa* and *Ḍimbhaka* (who were skilled in the *nītiçāstra*, v. 765), were more than a match for the three worlds; therefore, from policy, the *Kukuras, Andhakas,* and *Vṛshṇis*, chose not to fight with him (II, **19**).

Rājasūyasya ārambha(ḥ) ("the beginning of the rājasūya sacrifice"). § 11 (Parvasaṅgr.): I, **2**, 408 (*rājasūyasya cārambhaḥ*, i.e. Rājasūyārambhaparvan).

Rājasūyika(ṃ) parva[n] ("the section relating to the Rājasūya sacrifice"). § 10 (Parvas.): I, **2**, 318 (*parva . . . R°ṃ*, i.e. Rājasūyikaparvan).

[Rājasūyikaparvan(°va)] ("the section relating to the Rājasūya sacrifice," the 25th of the minor parvans of Mhbhr.). (Cf. Rājasūyikaṃ parva.) § 286: Under *Yudhishṭhira's* rule the people were very happy, and great riches filled the treasury. Then *Yudhishṭhira* resolved upon the celebration of the *rājasūya. Kṛshṇa* came there, having appointed *Ānakadundubhi* to the command of the army. Then *Yudhishṭhira*, sitting with *Dhaumya, Kṛshṇa-Dvaipāyana*, his brothers, etc., asked *Kṛshṇa* to install himself in that sacrifice or to permit the *Pāṇḍavas* to be installed in it. *Kṛshṇa* said that *Yudhishṭhira* ought to perform it and employ himself (i.e. *Kṛshṇa*) in some office. Then *Yudhishṭhira* caused his minister (*mantrin*) *Sahadeva* to get the articles together that *Dhaumya* might order as required for the sacrifice, and to let *Indrasena* and *Viçoka* and *Puru*, with *Arjuna* for his charioteer, engage in collecting food. *Dvaipāyana* himself became the *brahman* and appointed learned brahmans as *ṛtvijes*; *Susāman* ("the bull of the *Dhanañjayas*") became the *sāmaga*, *Yajñavalkya* the *adhvaryu*, *Paila* (the son of *Vasu*) the *hotṛ* accompanied by *Dhaumya*, and their disciples and sons the *hotragas* (see BR.) who uttered benedictions, etc. Then *Yudhishṭhira* caused *Sahadeva* to dispatch messengers, who invited men of the four castes. Then the brahmans installed (*dīkshayāñ cakrire*) *Yudhishṭhira* in the *rājasūya* sacrifice, the guests arrived, the artificers erected habitations, etc. Then *Yudhishṭhira* despatched *Nakula* to *Hāstinapura* in order to fetch *Bhīshma* and *Droṇa, Dhṛtarāshṭra, Vidura, Kṛpa*, etc. (II, **33**). Enumeration of kings who came to *Yudhishṭhira's rājasūya* (II, **34**).—§ 288: *Yudhishṭhira* saluted *Kṛshṇa-Dvaipāyana*, etc. (*a*), and appointed *Duḥçāsana* to attend to the food, etc., *Açvatthāman* to the brahmans, *Sañjaya* to the kings, *Bhīshma* and *Droṇa* to see what was done and what left undone, *Kṛpa* to attend to the diamonds, etc., and the dakshiṇās; *Vidura* became the disburser, *Duryodhana* the receiver of the tributes (*arhaṇāni*). *Kṛshṇa* washed the feet of the brahmans. *Yudhishṭhira* performed the sacrifice with six fires (II, **35**).—§ 292 (cf. Çiçupālavadhaparvan): Then the sacrifice was completed, watched by *Kṛshṇa*. When the kings departed, the *Pāṇḍavas*, commanded by *Yudhishṭhira*, followed them to the confines of his dominions, one after another (*a*). *Kṛshṇa* asked leave to go to *Dvārakā*, being thanked by *Yudhishṭhira* for his co-operation, and having bidden farewell to *Pṛthā*, etc. (*β*), and having performed his ablutions, etc., he walked round the *Garuḍa*-bannered chariot, which *Dāruka* had fetched, and ascending it set out for *Dvāravatī*, followed on foot by the *Pāṇḍavas*, till they took leave. Now *Duryodhana* alone, with king *Subala's* son *Çakuni*, remained in the assembly house (II, **45**).

Rāji (B., more correctly Raji), a prince. § 141 (Purūravas): I, **75**, 3150 (third son of Āyus and Svarbhānavī).

Rājñām āgamana(ṃ) ("arrival of the kings"). § 11 (Parvasaṅgr.): I, **2**, 410 (cf. Rājasūyikaparvan).

Rājoparicara = Vasu Uparicara: XII, 12838.

Rājyalābha ("the Pāṇḍavas' getting half of the kingdom"). § 10 (Parvasaṅgr.): I, **2**, 315 (B. *°lambha*, i.e. Rājyalābhaparvan). Cf. Rājyalambha.

[Rājyalābhaparvan(°va)] ("on the Pāṇḍavas' getting half of the kingdom," the 15th of the minor parvans of Mhbhr.). (Cf. Rājyalābha, Rājyalambha.) § 244: The *Pāṇḍavas* with *Kuntī* and *Kṛshṇā* journeyed towards *Hāstinapura. Dhṛtarāshṭra* despatched *Vikarṇa, Citrasena, Droṇa*, and *Kṛpa* to receive them. The inhabitants were filled with joy. In order to prevent any difference between them and their cousins, *Dhṛtarāshṭra* caused them, with *Kṛshṇa* in the van, to repair to *Khāṇḍavaprastha*, taking half the kingdom. With *Dvaipāyana's* assistance they measured out a piece of land for their city, which was very beautiful, and came to be called *Indraprastha*. Having settled the *Pāṇḍavas* there, *Kṛshṇa* came back with *Rāma* to *Dvāravatī* (I, **207**).—§ 245: When the *Pāṇḍavas* were dwelling in happiness at *Khāṇḍavaprastha*, one day the *Devarshi Nārada* came to them, and recommended them to make an arrangement so that disunion might not arise among them for the sake of their common wife, mentioning how *Sunda* and *Upasunda* had killed each other for the sake of *Tilottamā*. *Yudhishṭhira* asked who those *Asuras* were, and who this *Tilottamā* was (I, **208**).—§ 246: *Sundopasundopākhyāna* (q.v.). The arrangement the *Pāṇḍavas* made was, that if one of them should be sitting with *Draupadī*, and one of the other ones should happen to see it, he would have to retire into the forest for twelve years and live as a *brahmacārin*. Then *Nārada* went away (I, **212**).

Rājyalambha = Rājyalābha. § 11 (Parvasaṅgr.): I, **2**, 362.

Rākā[1], a female Rākshasa. § 525 (Rāmopākhyānap.): III, **274*a***, 15893, 15896 (by Viçravas, mother of Khara and Çūrpanakhā).

Rākā[2] ("the day of the full moon," personif.). § 615*u* (Skanda): IX, **45*γ***, 2516 (came to the investiture of Skanda).

Rakshaṇa = Vishṇu (1000 names).

Rakshas, pl. (°*āṃsi*), a kind of being = Rākshasa, pl.: I, 106 (*Gandharvoraga-Yaksha-R°āṃsi*), 1247 (*ahito Daitya-R°āṃ*, sc. Garuḍa), 2515 (*Yaksha-R°āṃ . . . sambhavaṃ*), 2637 (*Gandharvoraga-R°āṃ . . . sambhavaṃ*), 2781 (*Gandharvoraga-R°āṃ*), 2798 (*aṃçāvataraṇaṃ deva-Gandharva-R°āṃ*), 2799 (*deva-Dānava-R°āṃ aṃçāvataraṇam*), 4410 (*Gandharvoraga-R°āṃ*), 5966 (°*obalānvitā*, sc. Hiḍimbā), 5987 (°*āṃ vai yaçohara*, sc. Hiḍimba), 6028 (*Raudre muhurte R°āṃsi prabalāni bhavanty uta*), 6042, 6082 (°*āṃ çreshṭhaḥ*, sc. Ghaṭotkaca), 6299, 6300, 6444 (*Yaksha Gandharva-R°aṃ*), 6868, 6873, 6874, 6875, 6883, 6887 (Parāçara performed a Rākshasa sacrifice), 7128, 7658 (*Yaksha-R°ogaṇāḥ*), 7712 (*nāga-pārthiva-R°āṃ*), 8198 (°*-Piçāca-Daityānāṃ*); II, 76 (*Kiṅkaraiḥ*), 258 (*roga-R°obhayāt*); III, 367 (*Hiḍimba-Baka-mukhyānāṃ*), 388, 403 (°*ghnaiḥ . . . mantraiḥ*), 460 (*Kirmīraṃ R°aṃ varaṃ*), 1686 (*aṃçāḥ kshitisamprāptā deva-Dānava-R°āṃ*), 8260 (°*gaṇavikīrṇāni tīrthāni*), 8391 (*Gandharva-Yaksha-R°obhiḥ*, at Gaṅgādvāra), 8436, 8470 (*tīrthāni . . . anukīrṇāni R°obhiḥ*), 8873 (*Asuroraga-R°āṃsi*), †10070, 11001 (°*ghnān . . . mantrān*), †11393, 11452, 11463, 11465 (*Gandharvoraga-R°āṃ*), 11654 (*adhipaṃ Yaksha-R°āṃ*, i.e. Kubera), 11682 (*Gandharvoraga-R°āṃsi*, all. to Khāṇḍavadahanaparvan), 11712, 11713 (*Yaksha-R°āṃ*), 11714 (Bhīmasena slew many *R.*, among them Maṇimat), 11769 (*Kuberaṃ . . . Yaksha-R°gaṇavṛtaṃ*), 11784 (*Yaksha-R°āṃ*), 11787 (do.), 11838, 12021 (*Gandharvoraga-R°āṃ*), 13534 (*avadhyaḥ . . .*

R°āṃ, sc. Dhundhu), 13584 (*sarpa-Gandharva-R°āṃ*), 14264 (*Kinnaroraga-R°āṃ*), 14548 (*Yaksha-R°bhiḥ*, followed Rudra), 15172 (*Daitya-R°gaṇāḥ*, reborn as warriors in the great battle), †15640 (*Yaksha-R°āṃ*), 15887 (*Laṅkāṃ . . . R°gaṇānvitāṃ*), 15921 (°-*Kimpurushaiḥ*, followed Kubera to Gandhamādana), 15989 (*hateshu*, sc. by Rāma Dāçarathi), 16086 (*prāptaḥ . . . yoniṃ R°sevitāṃ*, sc. Viçvāvasu), 16176 (*purushādānāṃ*, Rāvaṇa ruled over 28 *koṭis* of R.), 16359, 16364, 17277 (*Yaksha-R°āṃ*); V, 348, 457, †1911, 4424 (*rūpāṇi Yaksha-Gandharva-R°āṃ*); VI, 246 (*θ*) (reside on Himavat), 814 (*Yaksha-R°-Piçācebhyaḥ | na bhayaṃ vidyate*), 1227 (*Vitteço*—i.e. Kubera—*Yaksha-R°āṃ*, sc. *asmi*, says Kṛshṇa), 4061 (*āvishṭā iva . . . R°-bhūtaiḥ*), 4525 (*purushādānāṃ*), 5509 (*nadatsu*, on the battle-field); VII, 1125 (°*grāmaṇimukhyayoḥ*, i.e. Ghaṭotkaca and Alambusha), 1321 (*vividhāni*), †1451 (*çvāpada-pakshi-R°āṃ*), †1975 (°*āṃ gaṇāḥ*, on the battle-field), 2241, 2242 (slain by Rāma Dāçarathi at Janasthāna), 4087 (*nadīṃ . . . R°gaṇasamākulāṃ*), 4099 (°*grāmaṇimukhyayoḥ*, i.e. Ghaṭotkaca and Alambusha), 4131 (*Ghaṭotkacaḥ . . . R°balavatāṃ varaḥ*), 6790 (°*āṃ ghorarūpāṇām akshauhiṇyā samāvṛtaḥ*, sc. Ghaṭotkaca), 6827 (°*ām adhirājo 'haṃ*, says Ghaṭotkaca), 6862 (*yūthaṃ R°āṃ*), 6866 (°*āṃ camūṃ*), 6876 (*yūthaṃ R°āṃ*), †6921 (°*gaṇāḥ*), 7851 (°*ghnaṃ*, sc. *karma*), 7877 (°*āṃ pravarau*, i.e. Ghaṭotkaca and Alambusha), 7925 (°*āṃ ghorarūpāṇāṃ . . . senayā vṛtaḥ*, sc. Ghaṭotkaca), 7976 (*yūthaṃ R°āṃ pīnavakshasāṃ*), 8078 (dual, i.e. Ghaṭotkaca and Alāyudha), †8148 (°*gaṇān*), 8444 (*nāsuroraga-R°āṃsi*), 9410 (°*āṃsi Piçācāç ca vineduḥ*), †9465 (*nāga-R°-Piçācān*); VIII, 1248 (-*Piçācāḥ*), 2097 (°*opasṛshṭeshu*), 2104 ((*ξ*) °-*Piçācāḥ*, on Himavat); IX, 2127 (*chāyāḥ . . . deva-Gandharva-R°āṃ*), 2396 (*çoṇitam . . . R°grāmaṇisammataṃ*), 2406, 2424, 2426 (*bhāgāḥ . . . R°āṃ*), 2491 (*deva-Dānava-R°āṃ*), 2496 (*deva-Gandharva-R°āṃ*), 2531 (*Yaksha-R°āṃsi*); X, 318 (followed Açvatthāman), 411, 438 (*Yaksha-R°samākīrṇe*), 440, 444, 452, 455, 459, 716 (°*gaṇabhayaṃ*); XI, 434 (*purushādānāṃ*), 438; XII, 63 (*deva-Dānava-R°āṃ*), 1703 (°*gaṇasevitaṃ . . . Kurukshetraṃ*), 2814 (forwarded by Kubera, but slain by Mucukunda), 2912, 3360 (*mānushoraga-R°āṃsi*), 3395 (*pāpa-R°āṃsi*), 4409 (*Yaksha-R°-Piçācānāṃ*), 6137, 6413, 6416, 8524 (*nara-Kinnara-R°āṃsi*), 9283, 9286, 10666 (*Dhanadaḥ*—i.e. Kubera— . . . *Yaksha-R°odhipaḥ*), 12385, 12944 (*sa-devāsura-R°āṃ*), 12952 (°*patiṃ*, i.e. Rāvaṇa), ††13214, 13666 (*Daitya-Dānava-Gandharva-R°gaṇasamākulā*); XIII, 804 (*devānāṃ sa - Yakshoraga - R°āṃ*), 806 (*yajñendrabala - R°su*), 1020 (°*gaṇāḥ*), 1129 (°*ghnaṃ*, sc. the 1,000 names of Çiva), 1574 (*bhāgaṃ R°āṃ*), 2097 (*manushyoraga-R°āṃ*), 2998 (*Kinnaroraga-R°āṃsi*), 3101 (*Kuberam iva R°āṃsi*, sc. *anujīvanti*), 3197 (°*āṃ bhāgaḥ*), 3299, 4020, 4224 (*Gandharvoraga-R°āṃ*), 4281, 4384, 4701, 4731, 4737 (*Yaksha-R°āṃ*), 4785, 5646 (°*vat*), 5680 (*mahā-R°gaṇā iva*), 6143 (°*ghnāni*), 6153 (do.), 6217 (°*āṃ kulavardhanaḥ*), 6344 (-*Bhūtagaṇaiḥ*); XIV, 607, †1169 (°*gaṇāḥ*), 1183 (*Gandharvoraga-R°āṃ*), 1226 (*Piçācoraga-R°āṃ . . . Īçvaraḥ prabhuḥ*), 2034 (*neduḥ*); XV, 14 (*kathāḥ . . . Devarshi-pitṛ-R°āṃ*), 572 (*lokān . . . deva-Gandharva-R°āṃ*); XVI, 59; XVIII, 199 (°-*Yakshān Çuko 'çrāvayat*, sc. the Mhbhr.).—Do., sg.: I, 7632 (*çūlahastena*); III, 10762 (created by Raibhya for the destruction of Yavakrīta), 10768 (= do.), 10778 (= do.), 10779 (= do.), 11469; IV, 450 (protected Draupadī at the injunction of Sūrya), 462 (= do., °*balasamāhataḥ*, sc. Kīcaka); VI, 4149 (only C., but read *rakshasva* with B.); VIII, 4243; X, 354; XII, 2888 (seized Kaikeyarāja), 2889 (= do.); XIII, 5883, 5884, 5886, 5887, 5889, 5918 (a pale and lean *R.* who seized a brahman but instructed by him set him free).

Names of single Rakshases:—

Alambusha: VI, 3621, 4038 (= Ārshyaçṛṅgi), 4047, 4559 (= Ārshyaçṛṅgi), 4561–4, 4568, 4604, 4605, 4610, 4611, 5144; VII, 3560, 4068, 4130, 7854 (son of Jaṭāsura), 7857 (*A*°).

Alāyudha: VII, 8050, 8068 (*nara-R°soḥ*, i.e. Bhīma and *A.*), 8074, 8075, 8108 (*pātite*), 8115 (*A*°).

Baka: I, 6209 (°*bala*°), 6212, 6220, 6222, 6224, 6271, 6288, 6291, 6294, 6296.

Cārvāka: I, 349 (*C*°); XII, 1420, 1436.

Dhūmrāksha: III, 16391.

Ghaṭotkaca: VI, 4113; VII, 6785 (*Bhaimaseniḥ*), 7816, 7845, 7891, 7958, 7993, 7994, 8002, †8162, †8165 (only C.), †8169, †8175, 8239, 8355, 8356; XII, 1489 (*Haiḍimbasya*).

Hiḍimba: I, 2253 (*H*°), 5951, 5993, 6024, 6027 (*pāpa*°), 6029, 6031, 6044; III, 567.

Jaṭāsura: III, 11448, 11506 (°-*Vṛkodarau*), 11507 (*Bhīma-R°oḥ*), 11518.

Kiṅkara: I, 6715, 6717, 6718, 6726, 6732, 6733, 6736, 6762, 6767, 6772, 6798.

Kirmīra: III, 368 (*K*°), 385, 390, 406, 425, 429, 442.

Lavaṇa: XIII, 861.

Maṇimat: III, 11736.

Mārīca: III, 11200 (*M*°), 16059 (*mṛgarūpadhareṇa*).

Ogha: V, 1890 (*Ogharakshaḥ*, v. Nīl.).

Puloman: I, 877 (*P*°), 879, 880, 884, 888, 897, 899, 906, 908, 909.

Rāvaṇa: III, 15872, 16031 (*R*°), 16521 (*Daçagrīvasya*), 16524, 16541 (°*veçmani*); IV, 653 (all. to Rāmopākhyānaparvan).

Vajravega: III, 16434 (*V*°).

Rākshasa, pl. (°*āḥ*), a class of beings = Rakshas, pl.: I, 454, 1396 (*deva-Dānava-R°āḥ*), 2513 (incarnate and slain by the incarnations of the gods), 2514 (do.), 2571 (the offspring of Pulastya), 2618 (*Nairṛtāḥ*, the offspring of Nirṛti and Adharma), 2795 (*aṃçāvataraṇaṃ . . . R°ānaṃ*), 3152 (*Gandharvoraga-R°ān*), †3607 (*bhaumā R°ās tīkshṇadaṃshṭrāḥ*), †3608 (do.), 5950 (*vanaṃ R°sevitaṃ*), 5960, 5969 (*sarva-R°āḥ*), 5992 (*karishyāmīdaṃ vanam a-R°m*, says Bhīmasena), 5994 (°*pāṃsana*, i.e. Hiḍimba), 6075, 6173, 6236 (*nihatāḥ*, sc. by Bhīmasena), 6445, 6496 (*Yaksha-R°-Gandharvāḥ*), 6866 (°*sattreṇa*, Parāçara performed a Rākshasa sacrifice), 6867, 6886 (*sarva-R°sattrāya*), 8256 (*Yaksha-R°-Pannagāḥ*), 8285, 8295 (*Piçācoraga-R°ān*), 8304 (*Yaksha-R°-Gandharva - nara - Kinnara - Pannagāḥ*), 8318; II, 86 (*Kiṅkarā nāma*), 415 (in the palace of Kubera), 465 (in the palace of Brahmán), 481, 1171 (*ye ca Kālamukhā nāma nara-R°yonayaḥ*, vanquished by Sahadeva), 1710 (*Kiṅkarā nāma*); III, 420 (°*kaṇṭhakaṃ*, sc. Bhīmasena), 435 (°*ānāṃ mukhyasya*, i.e. Kirmīra), 878, 1188 (*Gandharvāsura-R°āḥ*), 1646, 1909 (§ 339*d*: The *R.* live in inaccessible mountains and rugged countries), 2100 (*deva-Gandharva-manushyoraga-R°ān*), 2407 (*Piçācoraga-R°ān*), 5037 (in the tīrtha Vaḍavā), 8437, 8438 (*Yātudhānāḥ*), 8674 (seen in the body of Rāma Dāçarathi, the incarnate Vishṇu), 8854 (*Gandharva-R°ān*), 10829 (*Kuberasacivāç ca . . . raudrā maitrāç ca R°āḥ*), 10831 (*Yaksha-R°-Kinnarāḥ*, on Kailāsa), 10851 (*çaile 'smin R°ākīrṇe*), 10894 (*Kuberanalinīṃ . . . R°air abhisheritāṃ*), 11023,

11025, 11038 (°*skandhataḥ*), 11211, 11212 (*sa-R°gaṇaṃ Rāvaṇaṃ*), 11236 (did not exist in the Kṛtayuga), 11287 (*Dhanadodyānaṃ rakshitaṃ Yaksha-R°aiḥ*), 11351 (*nalinīṃ R°air abhirakshitāṃ*), 11359, 11361 (*Krodhavaçā nāma*), 11367, (11370), 11375, 11379, 11381 (many *R.* slain by Bhīmasena at the lotus-tank of Kubera), 11411, 11464 (*dharmasya R°ā mūlaṃ dharmaṃ te viduḥ*), 11499 (*nihatāḥ*, sc. by Bhīmasena), 11537, 11538, 11652, 11672, 11684 (*sarva*°), 11696, 11708 (*Yaksha-R°-Gandharvāḥ*), 11709 (*Yaksha-R°bāhubhiḥ*), 11711, 11713, 11717 (*sarva*°, Bhīmasena slew many *R.*, among them Maṇimat), 11743, 11747, 11753, 11777, 11779, 11835, 11840, 11990 (*sura-Dānava-R°aiḥ*), 12205 (*sura-R°-Pannagaiḥ*), 12271 (*deva-Dānava-R°aiḥ*), 12301 (*Yaksha-R°-Gandharvāḥ*), 12425 (*Himavān . . . Yaksha-R°saṅkulaḥ*), 12427 (*deva-Gandharva-R°aiḥ*), 12522 (*Brahmarshi-deva-Gandharva-Yaksha-R°-Pannagāḥ*), 12877 (*sa-Yakshoraga-R°aṃ*), 12891 (*Yaksha-R°varjite*), 12942 (*deva-Dānava-R°āḥ*), 12979 (*Gandharvoraga-R°ān*), 15178 (reborn as the Saṃçaptakas), 15196 (*Saṃçaptakāḥ . . . R°āvishṭacetasaḥ*), 15823 (*Yaksha-R°-Bhūtāni*), 15913 (*Yaksha-R°taḥ*), 15919 (°*yonau te jātasya*, sc. Vibhīshaṇa), 15925 (*Yaksha-R°senayoḥ*), 15926, 15987 (slain by Rāma Dāçarathi), 16317 (Rāma installed Vibhīshaṇa as king of all the *R.*), 16330 (°*koṭīnāṃ*), 16338 (*a-R°m imaṃ lokaṃ kartāsmi*), 16351, 16355 (*kāmarūpinaḥ*), 16360 (*vānara-R°āḥ*), 16362, 16368, 16390 (*hari-R°-vīrayoḥ*, i.e. Hanūmat and Dhūmrāksha), 16394, 16428, 16432 (dual, = Pramathin and Vajravega), 16499, 16503, 16504, 16508, 16579 (*Yaksha-R°-Pannagāḥ*), 17319; IV, 40 (*hatvā Pannaga-R°ān*, sc. Arjuna, all. to Khāṇḍavadahanaparvan), 1571, 1767, 2271; V, 464 (*Kinnaroraga-R°āḥ*), 540, 2033 (*yena*—i.e. by Bhīmasena—*bhīmabalā Yakshā R°āç ca purā hatāḥ*), 2401, 3830 (*atra*—i.e. in the north—*R°-Yaksha-Gandharvāṇāñ ca . . . ādhipatyena Kailāse Dhanado*—i.e. Kubera—*abhishecitaḥ*), 5803 (°*sainyaṃ*), 5867, 5927 (*asya*—i.e. Ghaṭotkaca's—*sacivāḥ*); VI, 100 (*çoṇitair vaktrasampūrṇā ātṛptās tatra R°āḥ*, omens), 212 (*Gandharvāsura-R°āḥ*, on Meru), 229 (*Kuberaḥ saha R°aiḥ*, on Gandhamādana), 1975 (*Piçācoraga-R°āḥ*), 2467 (do.), 2867 (followers of Ghaṭotkaca), 2869, 2961 (*Yaksha-R°-Pannagāḥ*), 2981 (*Daitya-Dānava-R°āḥ*, reborn as warriors in the great battle), 3704 (*deva-Gandharva-R°āḥ*), 3833, 4027, [4035 (§ 585*c*: illusion is natural with the *R.* and their age and form are dependent on their will)], 4070 (°*puṅgavaiḥ*, followed Ghaṭotkaca), 4076 (= do.), 4077 (= do.), 4080 (= do.), 4082 (four enumeratod, slain by Duryodhana), 4123 (°*ānaṃ mukhyasya*, i.e. Ghaṭotkaca), 4219, 4220 (attacked Açvatthāman), 5624 (*deva-Dānava-R°āḥ*); VII, 540 (dual, *Hiḍimbālambushau*), 1463 (*sa-Yakshoraga-R°āḥ . . . lokāḥ*), †1976 (*prakarshamāṇāḥ kuṇapāni*), 2226 (slain by Rāma Dāçarathi at Janasthāna), 2623 (*Asuroraga-R°āḥ*), 2661 (do.), 2806 (*Piçācoraga-R°āḥ*), 3444 (*sa-Yakshoraga-R°āḥ . . . lokāḥ*), 4098 (°*siṃhayoḥ*, i.e. Ghatotkaca and Alambusha), 1269 (*pṛthivī . . . sa-R°gaṇā*), 6048 (*Yakshoraga-R°āḥ*), 6339 (do.), 6797, 6840 (followed Ghaṭotkaca), 6843, 6863, 6867, 6872, 6875, 6880 (°*ānīkaṃ*), 6898 (*akshauhiṇīm R°ānāṃ*), 6908, 6922, 7015 (*jagat . . . sa-Yaksha-R°gaṇaṃ*), 7021 (*Piçācoraga-R°aiḥ*), 7832, 7928, 7969 (followed Ghaṭotkaca), 7976, 7977, 7997, 8005, 8009 (*Hiḍimba-Baka-Kirmīrā nihatāḥ*, sc. by Bhīmasena), 8011, 8045 (*Bhīmaḥ . . . R°āntakaraḥ*), 8047, 8049 (followed Alāyudha), 8055, 8057, 8061, 8063, 8079, 8084, †8172, 8231 (*sa-R°oragāḥ*), 8432, 8611 (*Yaksha-R°-saṅkulaṃ*), 9001 (*nāsuroraga-R°āḥ*), 9101 (*devān . . . sa-R°gaṇān*), 9442, 9474, 9543; VIII, †819 (°*bhojanān*), †1742 (*Garuḍa-Piçāca-sa-Yaksha-R°ān*), 4409 (*Piçācoraga-R°āḥ*), 4422 (sided with Karṇa), †4567 (had been slain by Arjuna yuga after yuga); IX, 1757, 2139 (in Çaṅkhatīrtha), 2255 (slain by Rāma Dāçarathi in the Daṇḍaka forest), 2301, 2401 (drank blood from the Sarasvatī), 2407, 2417, 2421, 2422 (the cause of men's becoming *R.*), 2427 (°*ānnaṃ*; § 615*r*: The food over which one has sneezed, that in which there are worms and insects, that which may be mixed with any leavings of dishes, that which is mixed with hair, that which is trodden upon, that which is mixed with tears, shall form the share of the *R.* Knowing this the learned man shall carefully avoid these kinds of food. He who takes such food shall be regarded as eating the food of *R.*), 2428, 2429 (went to heaven having bathed in the Aruṇā), 2448 (battle between the gods and the Dānavas, the Daiteyas, and the *R.*), 2509 (*Yaksha-R°-Pannagaiḥ*), 2685 (defeated by Skanda), 2849 (in Ādityatīrtha), 3297; X, 441; XII, 62, 1608 (*Yaksha-R°-Pannagāḥ*), 1830 (*Yaksha-R°ān*), 2240 (*Yaksha-R°-bhartā . . . Naravāhanaḥ*, i.e. Kubera), 2245 (*Yaksha-R°-Nāgaiḥ*), 2768 (*Gandharvoraga-R°āḥ*), 2812 (forwarded by Vaiçravaṇa—i.e. Kubera—but slain by Mucukunda), †2907, †2908, 4496 (°*ānāñ ca Kuberam api ceçvaraṃ*), 5436 (*iva*), 5773 (*Yaksha-R°sevitaḥ*), 6392, 6393, 6415, 6421, 6425, 6932 (*Yaksha-R°-Nāgāç ca*), 6947, 7656 (*Yaksha-R°ān*), 8116 (had been under the sway of Bali), †8425 (*Kinnara-Yaksha-R°āḥ*), 8453, 10222 (*mahāraudrāḥ*), 10278 (*Piçācoraga-R°āḥ*), 10336 (*Piçācoraga-R°aiḥ*), 10477, 10838 (*Yaksha-R°-Gandharvāḥ*), 12323 (*devagaṇaṃ . . . sāsura-R°aṃ*), 12333 (*Yaksha-R°-Dānavāḥ*, on Ādityaparvata), 12622 (*Yaksha-R°saṅghaiḥ*), 13365 (*Daitya-Dānava-R°āḥ*), 13667 (do.); XIII, 184 (forwarded by Viçvāmitra), 734 (Çiva assumes the forms of the *R.*, etc.), 996, 1294 (*Yaksha-R°āḥ*), 1413 (*Māṇibhadra-purogamāḥ*, protect the lotus-lake of Kubera), 1414, 1415, 2098, 2977 (*pitaroraga-R°āḥ*), †3687, 3865 (*Piçācoraga-R°āḥ*), 3886 (*Kinnaroraga-R°āḥ*), 3979 (*kukkuṭāç ca varāhaç ca R°āḥ*), 3981 (*Gandharvoraga-R°āḥ*), 4023 (*deva-Dānava-R°ān*), 4207 (presented Skanda with a boar and a buffalo), 4211 (°*āsura-saṅghāḥ*), 4711 (*Yaksha-R°āḥ*), 4717 (*Yaksha-R°-bhoginām*), 4725, 4732 (*yeshāṃ nāgrabhujo viprā devatātithibālakāḥ*), 4734 (*Yaksha-R°-Pannagāḥ*), 5704, 6741 (°*opamāḥ*), 7071 (*sa-Yakshoraga-R°aṃ . . . jagat*), †7368 (praise Kṛshṇa), †7378 (had been defeated by Kṛshṇa), 7677 (*Rāmo R°ha*); XIV, 1434 (*Piçācāsura-R°āḥ*), 1566 (*Yaksha-Gandharva R°ān*), 1581 (*Yaksha-R°-yonyoḥ*), 1685 (*deva-R°-Nāgānāṃ*), 1989 (°*ghnāni . . . dravyāṇi*), 2034; XV, 848 (*Guhyaka-R°āḥ*, have been incarnatod as warriors in the battle), 852 (= Duḥçāsana, etc.), 904; XVIII, 174 (= the followers of Duryodhana). Cf. Brahmarākshasa, pl.—Do., sg.: I, 568 (cf. X, chap. 6), 2761 (incarnate as Çikhaṇḍin), 6706 (°*vat*), 6708 (do.), 6880; III, 10765 (created by Raibhya for the destruction of Yavakrīta), 10770 (= do.), 10771 (= do.), 10777 (= do.), 16063, 16262; IV, 462 (protected Kṛshṇā at the injunction of Sūrya); V, 4063 (Yayāti is questioned if he is a *R.*); VI, 3003 (said of Duryodhana); IX, 2250 (slain by Rāma Dāçarathi), 2256 (= do.); X, 350 (Açvatthāman is believed to be a *R.*), 364 (do.); XII, (2911) (seized Kaikeyarāja), 8164; XIII, 7148; XV, 857 (incarnate as Çikhaṇḍin).

Names of single Rākshasas:—

Alambusha: VI, 1712, †2808 (*A*°), 3561 (*A*°), 3615 (*A*°), 4018 (*Ārshyaçṛṅgaṃ*), 4022, 4025, 4026, 4030, 4033,

4036, 4038, 4041, 4044, 4046, 4048 (slew Irāvat), 4560, 4566, 4567 (°*ottamaḥ*), 4569 (do.), 4576, 4578, 4579, 4593, 4599, 4612, 5052 (*Ārshyaçṛṅgiṃ*), 5141, 5142, 5143, 5145, 5147; VII, 1124 (*A*°), 3981, 4066, 4070, 4078, 4083, 4093, 4094, 4112, 4113, 4116, 7502, 7503.

Alāyudha: VII, 3568 (*A*°), 8039, 8092, 8105; IX, 76 (*A*°), 94 (*A*°), 1299 (*A*°); XV, 879 (*A*°).

Baka: I, ††3825 (*B*°), 6202, 6207 (*B*°), 6221, 6234, 6235, 6272, 6275, 6277, 6279, 6281, 6282, 6304, 6316 (*Baka-R*°*ṃ*), 6317; VII, 4076 (°*pravaraḥ*).

Cārvāka: XII, 1414 (*C*°), 1425 (*C*°), 1427 (*pāpa*°), 1432 (*C*°), 1435, 1440 (*C*°).

Daṃça: XII, 89.

Dhūmrāksha: III, 16389, 16390 (°*vīra-*), 16391.

Ghaṭotkaca: I, †197 (*Gh*°), ††3833 (*Gh*°); III, 11010 (*Gh*°), 11013 (do.); V, 5591 (do.); VI, 2454 (do.), 2458 (do.), 2864, 2874, 3170 (*Gh*°), 3283 (do.), 3671, 3673, 3867 (*Gh*°), 4065 (*Bhaimasenir Gh*°*ḥ*), 4069, 4102, 4114, 4116, 4121 (°*sattamaḥ*), 4139, 4145, 4146, 4219, 4221, 4239 (°*āpasadam*), 4245, 4249, 4254 (*Gh*°), 4300, 4303, 4307, 4510 (*Gh*°), 4586 (do.), 5075 (do.), 5106 (*Bhaimasenim*), 5587 (*Gh*°); VII, 376 (*māyāvī*), 1124, 3536 (*Gh*°), 4116, 4118, 4283 (*Gh*°), 6652 (*Gh*°), 6828, 6856 (*Drauṇi-R*°*yoḥ*), 6886, 6916, 7013 (*Gh*°), 7367 (*Bhaimasenim*), 7413, 7425 (*Drauṇi-R*°*yoḥ*), 7427, 7433, 7810 (*Gh*°), 7834 (do.), 7840, 7843 (*Karṇa-R*°*yoḥ*), 7847, 7848, 7854, 7864, 7870, 7883, 7889, 7890 (*Gh*°), 7904, 7914 (*Karṇa-R*°*yoḥ*), 7921 (do.), 7953, 7972, 7985, 8029 (*Karṇa-R*°*yoḥ*), 8041, 8092, 8133, 8134, †8135, †8158 (*māyāṃ . . . R*°*sya*), †8159, †8164, †8165 (only C.), †8168, †8171, †8176 (*nihataṃ*), 8292, 8312 (*Gh*°), 8331, 8333; VIII, 2406 (*Gh*°); IX, 79 (do.); XV, 875 (do.).

Hiḍimba: I, 5927 (*H*°), 5954, 5957 (°*bhojanam*), 5958, 5972 (?), 5973, 5977, 5983, 5990, 6002, 6011 (*H*°), 6018, 6023, 6025, 6033, 6034; III, 561 (°*ādhamaḥ*), (562), 564, 565, 569.

Indrajit: III, 16457, 16462.

Jaṭāsura: I, 455 (*J*°); III, 11454, 11465, 11468, 11476, 11479, 11480, 11484, 11485, 11488, 11490, 11493, 11497, 11501, 11504, 11505, 11517, 11524 (*nihate*); VII, 7850 (*J*°*o . . R*°*āgryaḥ*).

Kalmāshapāda: VIII, 2092 (read *Kalmāshapādaḥ sarasi* with B.).

Kiṅkara: I, 6716 (*K*°), 6764 (?), 6766, 6767 (?).

Kirmīra: III, 423, 436, 437, 448, 449 (°*ādhamam*), 452, 457.

Maṇimat: III, 11720 (*M*°), 11722, 11729, 11737.

Mārīca: III, 16002, 16020.

Mūka: III, 1570, 1577.

Prahasta: III, 16382.

Rāvaṇa: III, 11283 (°*ādhamaḥ*), 11284 (°*ādhamam*), 16051, 16200 (°*veçmani*), 16513 (*māyeshā . . . R*°*sya*), 16612 (*Daçagrīvam*); VII, 2227 (*R*°); IX, 1752 (*R*°).

Virūpāksha: VII, 7905 (the charioteer of Ghaṭotkaca); XII, (6371), 6430.

Rākshasa, adj. ("belonging to the Rākshasas"). I, 2962 (sc. *virāhaḥ*), 2964 (do.), 2966 (*Gāndharva-R*°*au*, sc. *vivāhau*), ††3821 (°*īṃ buddhim āçritaḥ*, sc. Duryodhana); III, 393 (*māyāṃ*), 403 (do.), 1566 (*rūpaṃ*), 16321 (do.); VI, 1181 (*prakṛtiṃ mohinīṃ*), 3617 (*māyāṃ*), 3619 (do.), 4228 (*māyeshā R*°*ī*), 5009 (*vyūhān*); VII, 6348 (*nāsuroraga-R*°*aṃ*, sc. *yuddhaṃ*), 6879 (*senāṃ*), 7815 (*astrāṇi*), 7821 (*māyā*), 7924 (*māyāṃ*), 7978 (*senāṃ*), 8000 (*māyāṃ*), 8090 (do.) †8138 (do.), †8147 (*vṛshṭiṃ*), 8614 (*yuddhaṃ*); VIII, 2097 (*bhaishajaṃ*); XII, 11103 (*vishayān*); XIII, 2411 (*vidhiḥ*), 5694 (do.).

Rākshasaçreshṭha[1] ("the best of the Rākshasas") = Alambusha: VI, 4034, 4554, 4594 (*māyāvī*), 4601.

Rākshasaçreshṭha[2] (do.) = Rāvaṇa: III, 16527.

Rākshasādhipa[1] ("king of the Rākshasas") = Ghaṭotkaca: VI, 4137, 4223 (*māyāvī*).

Rākshasādhipa[2] (do.) = Rāvaṇa: III, 16399, 16502 (*R*°).

Rākshasādhipa[3] (do.) = Virūpāksha: XII, 6423.

Rākshasādhipati[1] (do.) = Kubera: III, 11705.

Rākshasādhipati[2] (do.) = Maṇimat: III, 11796.

Rākshasādhipati[3] (do.) = Rāvaṇa: II, 410.

Rākshasādhipati[4] (do.) = Virūpāksha: XII, 6356 (*V*°), 6365 (*V*°).

Rākshasamaheçvara ("the great lord of the Rākshasas") = Rāvaṇa: III, 16194.

Rākshasapati ("lord of the Rākshasas") = Rāvaṇa: III, 16406.

Rākshasapuṅgava[1] ("chief of the Rākshasas") = Alambusha: VI, 4045.

Rākshasapuṅgava[2] (do.) = Alāyudha: VII, 8016.

Rākshasapuṅgava[3] (do.) = Avindhya: III, 16148 (*A*°).

Rākshasapuṅgava[4] (do.) = Ghaṭotkaca: III, 11014; VI, 4098, 4147, 4251.

Rākshasapuṅgava[5] (do.) = Indrajit: III, 16446.

Rākshasapuṅgava[6] (do.) = Rāvaṇa: III, 15898 (*Daçagrīvaḥ*), 16034.

Rākshasarāja[1] ("king of the Rākshasas") = Baka: I, 6286 (*nara-R*°*yoḥ*, i.e. Bhīma and *B.*).

Rākshasarāja[2] (do.) = Rāvaṇa: III, 16035 (*R*°); V, 3790 (*R*°).

Rākshaseçvara[1] ("lord of the Rākshasas") = Ghaṭotkaca: V, 5926 (*Haiḍimbaḥ*); VI, 3559 (do.); VII, 7924, 8257.

Rākshaseçvara[2] (do.) = Hiḍimba: I, 5962 (*H*°).

Rākshaseçvara[3] (do.) = Kubera: III, 15890 (*K*°).

Rākshaseçvara[4] (do.) = Rāvaṇa: III, 16004, 16010, 16046 (*R*°), 16056, 16184.

Rākshaseçvara (do.), dual (°*au*) = Kumbhakarṇa and Rāvaṇa: III, 15895.

Rākshasendra[1] ("king of the Rākshasas") = Alambusha: V, 5802 (*A*°); VI, 3616, 3622, 4555, 4571, 4588, 4598, 4609; VII, 3537 (*A*°), 4067 (*Ārshyaçṛṅgiṃ*), 4095, 4106 (*A*°), 4117, 4122 (°*rathaṃ*), 4128, 7371 (*A*°), 7498 (*A*°), 7508, 7879 (*A*°); VIII, 135 (*A*°); XI, 792 (*A*°).

Rākshasendra[2] (do.) = Alāyudha: VII, 8004 (*A*°), 8028 (*A*°), 8033 (*A*°), 8045, 8052, 8054, 8056, 8058, 8064, 8067, 8076 (*A*°), 8077 (*Bakabhrātrā*).

Rākshasendra[3] (do.) = Ghaṭotkaca: III, 11023; VI, 2811, 3633 (*Haiḍimbaḥ*), 3672, 3676, 4127, 4154 (*Gh*°), 4246; VII, 6794 (*Gh*°), 6882 (*Gh*°), 7417 (*Gh*°), 7434, 7436 (*Gh*°), 7980 (*Gh*°); VIII, 299 (*Gh*°); XI, 792 (*Gh*°).

Rākshasendra[4] (do.) = Hiḍimba: I, 2254, 6012.

Rākshasendra[5] (do.) = Kumbhakarṇa: III, 16413.

Rākshasendra[6] (do.) = Rāvaṇa: III, 11199 (*R*°), 15873 (*R*°), 16048, 16145, 16314 (*bhrātā R*°*sya*, i.e. Vibhīshaṇa), 16329, 16507 (°*sya māyāṃ*), 16531 (*R*°).

Rākshasendra[7] (do.) = Virūpāksha: XII, 6361, 6362, 6367, 6368, 6380, 6390, 6392, 6414 (*putraḥ R*°*sya*), 6423, 6424, 6431.

Rākshasendra[8], mostly pl. (°*āḥ*): I, 5979 (*pūrveshāṃ*); III, 11758 (*pravarā R*°*āṇāṃ*, slain by Bhīmasena); VII,

4102 (dual = Ghaṭotkaca and Alambusha), 8040 (dual = Ghaṭotkaca and Alāyudha), †8211 (*nihatā R°ā Hiḍimba-Kirmīra-Bakapradhānāḥ*).

Rākshasī [1] ("female Rākshasa"), pl. (°*yaḥ*): I, 6077 (*sadyo hi garbhān R°yo labhante prasavanti ca*); III, 15891 (*tisraḥ*, i.e. Pushpotkaṭā, Rākā, and Mālinī), 16136, 16145, 16195 (waited upon Sītā).

Rākshasī [2] (do.), sg.: I, 6523, 6553; III, 2519 (Damayantī is asked if she is a *R.*), 2558 (Damayantī is supposed to be a *R.*); IV, 260; VIII, 2048 (in Çākala), 2067.

Names of single Rākshasīs:—

Çūrpanakhā: III, 15990.

Dīrghajihvā: III, 16605 (*D*°).

Hiḍimbā: I, 5940 (*H*°), 5942, 5956, (5958), 5959, 6041, 6060, 6062 (*H*°), 6072; III, 554 (*H*°).

Jarā: II, 715 (*J*°), 716, 718, 722, (725), 727, (729), 729 (*J*°), 730, 738; VII, 8224 (*J*°), 8226.

Trijaṭā: III, 16146 (*T*°), 16571 (*T*°).

Rakshitā, an Apsaras. § 103 (Aṃçāvat.): I, **65**, 2558 (daughter of Prādhā).

Rakshovaha, pl. (°*āḥ*), a people. § 595 (Shoḍaçarāj., v. Rāma Jāmadagnya): VII, **70**β, 2436 (slain by Rāma Jāmadagnya).

Rakta, Raktamālyāmbaradhara = Çiva (1000 names [1]).

Raktāṅga [1], a serpent. § 67 (Sarpasattra): I, **57**, 2159 (of Dhṛtarāshṭra's race).

Raktāṅga [2] = Çiva (1000 names [2]).

Raktavirakta = Çiva (1000 names [1]).

Rāma [1], son of Jamadagni and Reṇukā, otherwise called Paraçu-Rāma, which name, however, does not occur in the text of the Mbhbr.; generally he is only named Rāma; passages where he is mentioned only by synonyms are put within square brackets; note the following abbreviations: Bh. = Bhārgava, J. = Jāmadagnya. § 8 (Parvasaṅgr.): I, **2**, 272 (*çastrabhṛtāṃ varaḥ*; at the interval of the *Tretā* and the *Dvāparayuga R.* repeatedly slew the kshatriyas of the whole earth), 275 (Bh.), 277 (formed five lakes of blood in Samantapañcaka, cf. § 363).—§ 11 (do.): I, **2**, 443 (J.).—§ 61 (Sarpasattra): I, **55**, 2112 (°*o yathā çāstravid astravic ca*, sc. Janamejaya).—[§ 84 (Ādivaṃçāvatāraṇap.): I, **64**, 2459 (J.; twenty-one times he deprived the earth of the *kshatriyas*, then he performed austerities on the mountain Mahendra), 2460 (Bh.).]—§ 122 (Aṃçāvat.): I, **66**, 2612 (*sarvaçāstreshu kuçalaḥ kshatriyāntakaraḥ*, the youngest of Jamadagni's four sons).—§ 130*b* (Bhīshma): I, **67**, 2712 (J., Bh., encounter with Bhīshma, all. to § 573).—§ 165 (Satyavatīlābhop.): I, **100**, [4004 (J.)], 4005 (*yad astram R°o veda*).—§ 169 (cf. Bhīshma-Satyavatī-saṃvāda); *Bhīshma* told *Satyavatī*: When *Rāma Jāmadagnya*, angry at the slaughter of his father, had slain with his battle-axe the *Haihaya* king *Arjuna*, he exterminated the *kshatriyas* twenty one times, but the *kshatriya* race was restored by the *kshatriya* ladies, cohabiting with the brahmans: I, **104**, 4172 (J.), [4175 (Bh.)].—[§ 190*d* (Arjuna): I, **123**, 4799 (*Jāmadagnyasamaḥ*, sc. Arjuna).]—§ 201 (Droṇa): I, **130**, [5118 (J.)], 5119 (°*sya Dhanurvedam*), [5121 (*Bhṛgūdvaham*), 5123 (J.)], 5126 (*praharatāṃ çreshṭham*), (5127), [5131 (Bh.), 5132 (Bh.)] (communicated his weapons and the whole Dhanurveda to Droṇa, cf. § 217).—§ 217 (Caitrarathap.): I, **166**, 6335, 6336, (6337), [6339 (*Bhṛgunandanaḥ*)], 6340 (Droṇa acquired weapons from *R.*, especially the Brahmāstra, cf. § 201). — [§ 218 (Draupadīsambhava): I, **167**, 6382 (*kshatrocchedāya vihito Jāmadagnya ivāsthitaḥ*, sc. Droṇa).]—§ 233 (Svayaṃvarap.): I, **188**, 7047 (J., had vanquished the *kshatriyas*).—§ 234 (do.): I, **190**, 7101, 7104, 7115 (?).—§ 267 (Yamasabhāv.): II, **8**, 330 (J., in the palace of Yama).—§ 273 (Rājasūyārambhap.): II, **14**, 566 (J., left a part of the *kshatriyas* unslain), [586 (*Jāmadagnyasamaḥ*, sc. Ākṛti)].—[§ 289 (Arghāharaṇap.): II, **37**, 1352 (*Jāmadagnyasya dayitaḥ çishyaḥ*, sc. Karṇa).]—[§ 296 (Dyūtap.): II, **53**, 1918 (J., present at the rājasūya of Yudhishṭhira).]—§ 305 (do.): II, **78**, 2574 (had on Bhṛgutuṅga instructed Yudhishṭhira).—[§ 317*b* (Kṛshṇa Vāsudeva): III, **12**, 511 (J., praised Kṛshṇa, C. has by error *Yā*°).] — [§ 324 (Dvaitavanapraveça): III, **26***a*, 985 (J., waited upon Yudhishṭhira)]. — § 362 (Tīrthayātrāp.): III, **83**, 5095 (J., had made the tīrtha Yakshiṇī).—§ 363 (Rāmahradāḥ): III, **83**, 5097, 5099 (Bh.), 6001, 6004, 6009 (Bh.), 6010 (Bh.), 6011 (made five lakes of blood, which afterwards became tīrthas, in Kurukshetra).—§ 370 (Tīrthayātrāp.): III, **85**, 8144 (made Lauhitya a tīrtha), [8158 (*Mahendraṃ . . . Jāmadagnyanishevitaṃ*), 8185 (*Çūrpārakam . . . Jāmadagnyanishevitam*)].—[§ 377 (Dhaumyatīrthak.): III, **87**, 8318 (*Mahendraḥ . . . Bhārgavasya*).]—§ 383*c* (Bhṛgos tīrthaṃ): III, **99**, 8650 (regained his energy by bathing in *Bhṛgos tīrtham*).—§ 383 (Tīrthayātrāp.): III, **99**, 8652, 8655. — § 383 (cf. do.): For the destruction of *Rāvaṇa Vishṇu* corporeally took his birth as the son of king Daçaratha. I (sc. Lomaça) saw him in Ayodhyā when he had been born. Then Rāma Bhārgava, the [grand]son of *Ṛcīka* and the son of *Reṇukā*, went to *Ayodhyā* with his bow with which he had destroyed the *kshatriyas*, to see Rāma Dāçarathi. *Daçaratha* sent *Rāma* to receive him. *Rāma Dāçarathi* stringed *Rāma Bhārgava's* bow without exertion and enabled him to see him in his true form and to behold, in his body, the *Adityas*, the *Vasus*, the *Rudras*, the *Sādhyas*, the *gaṇas* of the *Maruts*, the *Pitṛs*, *Hutāçana* (i.e. Agni), the *nakshatras* and planets, the *Gandharvas*, the *Rākshasas*, the *Yakshas*, the rivers and *tīrthas*, the eternal *ṛshis* named *Vālakhilyas*, who had become identical with *Brahmán*, the *Devarshis*, the seas and mountains, the *Vedas* with the *Upanishads*, the *vashaṭkāras*, and the sacrifices, the Sāmans in their living form (*cetamanti*), the Dhanurveda, the clouds, rains, and lightnings; then he shot a celestial shaft presented to him by *Rāma Bhārgava*; at this the earth was filled with sounds of thunder, etc., and began to quake. *Rāma Bhārgava* was for a time deprived of his senses, and the shaft came blazing back into *Rāma Dāçarathi's* hands. *Rāma Bhārgava* proceeded to the *Mahendra* mountain, where he dwelt in terror and shame till after a year his *pitṛs*, beholding him deprived of energy, caused him to bathe in the sacred river *Vadhūsara*, especially in the tīrtha *Dīptoda*, where *Bhṛgu* had practised austerities in the *devayuga*; by this *R.* regained his energy (III, **99**): III, **99**, 8656 (Bh.), 8658 (*Ṛcīkanandano Rāmo Bhārgavo Reṇukāsutaḥ*), 8659, 8661, 8662, 8665, 8666, 8668, 8669 (J.), [8671 (Bh.)], 8673 (Bh.), 8679, 8681, 8683, 8686, 8687.—§ 393 (Tīrthayātrap.): III, **115**, 10127, 10128 (Bh.), 10129, 10130 (*R.* appeared to the ascetics on the fourteenth and the eighth [days of the lunar month]).—§ 394 (Arjuna Kārtavīrya): III, **115**, 10131 (J.), 10132 (°*eṇa nirjitāḥ . . . kshatriyāḥ*), 10134 (J.), 10135 (slew Arjuna the king of the Haihayas).—§ 396 (Jamadagni): III, **116**, 10174 (fifth son of Jamadagni and Reṇukā), 10183, 10184 (ordered by Jamadagni, *R.* slew his mother with his axe, but then solicited that she might be restored to life).—§ 397 (do.): III, **116**, 10192, [10193 (Bh.)], 10195, 10196, 10197, [10199 (*Bhṛgunandanaḥ*)] (slew Arjuna Kārtavīrya, who had injured Jamadagni, then the kinsmen of Arjuna slew Jamadagni).—§ 398 (cf. Jamadagni): After having lamented and cremated his father, *R.* vowed to slay the entire *kshatriya* caste, he then killed the sons of *Arjuna Kārtavīrya*, and the *kshatriyas* who followed them, and twenty-one times he made the earth devoid of *kshatriyas*; then he made five lakes of blood in *Samantapañcaka*, where he offered libations (*tarpayām āsa*) to the *Bhṛgus*, and *Ṛcīka* appeared to him and gave him advice. At a sacrifice *R.* satisfied *Indra* and gave the earth to the *ṛtvijes*, and a golden altar, 10 vyāmas in breadth and 9 in height, to Kaçyapa, which Kaçyapa allowed the brahmans to divide in shares (thence they were named *Khāṇḍavāyanāḥ*). After having given the earth to Kaçyapa. *R.* dwelt on the *Mahendra* mountain: III, **117**, 10195, (10201), 10201 *bis*, 10203, 10205 (*Bhṛgukulodvahaḥ*), [10206 (J.)], 10210.—§ 399 (Mahendrācalag.): III, **117**, 10211, [10213 (J.)] (the Pāṇḍavas worshipped *R.* on Mahendra).—§ 410 (Plakshāvataraṇag.): III, **130**, 10547 (had made a varsha (?) in the midst of the mountain).—§ 486 (Pativratop. Brāhmaṇavyādhasaṃv.): III, **214**, 14012 (J., *yathā*).—[§ 546 (Kuṇḍalāharaṇap.): III, **302**, 16985 (J., had been the preceptor of Karṇa in arms).]—§ 547 (Karṇa): III, **309**, 17170 (Karṇa had acquired weapons from *R.*).—[§ 552 (Goharaṇap.): IV, **48**, 1524 (J., do.); **51**, 1593 (J.).]—§ 561 (Yānasandhip.): V, **49**, 1944 (had cursed Karṇa, cf. § 621); **55**, 2197 (*anujñātaç ca R°eṇa matsamo 'sīti*, sc. Karṇa); **61**, 2385 (J., *kathām akathayat purā*); **62**, †2412 (under the pretence that he was a brahman Karṇa acquired the Brahmāstra from *R.*, Rāma cursed Karṇa, cf. § 621), †2427.—[§ 562 (Bhagavadyānap.): V, **83**, 2984 (J., waited upon Kṛshṇa).]—§ 563 (do., Dambhodbhavop.): V, **96**, [3450 (J.)], (3472), 3477 (told Duryodhana the Dambhodbhavopākhyāna). — [§ 564 (Mātalīyop.): V, **97**, 3501 (J.). — § 567 (Bhagavadyānap.): V, **125**, 4201 (*yathoktaṃ Jāmadagnyena*, cf. § 563).] — § 569 (do.); V, **147**, 4980, 4981 (Bhīshma's encounter with *R.*, all. to § 573).—§ 570 (Sainyaniryāṇap.): V, **151**, 5123 (do. do.), 5127 (*rūpaṃ ... R°syeva*).—§ 572 (Rathātirathasaṅkhyānap.): V, **168**, 5813 (had cursed Karṇa, cf. § 621), 5840 (J., all. to § 573).—§ 573 (Ambopākhyānap.): V, **176**, 6047 (J.), [6048 (*Bhārgavaçreshṭham*), 6051 (Bh.)], 6053 (J.), 6054 (on Mahendra), 6056, 6057 (*Jamadagnisutaḥ*), 6058, 6062 (*çreshṭhaṃ maharshīṇāṃ*), [6063 (J.)], 6064, 6065, 6082; **177**, 6084, 6085 (Bh.), 6092, 6093, 6098, [7001 (Bh.), 7002 (J.)], 7003 (*Bhṛguçreshṭhaṃ*), 7004, 7005, (7008), 7010, 7011 (*Bhṛgūdvahaḥ*), 7012 (Bh.), [7013 (J.)], (7014), [7019 (*Bhṛgunandana*), 7021 (*Bhṛguçārdūla*), 7022 (Bh.)], 7024; **178**, 7025, (7030), 7031, 7033 (*°āmbayoḥ*), 7034, [7035 (*Bhṛgunandana*), 7038 (Bh.)], 7040 (Bh.) [7041 (*Bhṛgunandana*)], (7042), 7046, 7048, [7049 (*Bhṛguçreshṭha°*), 7053 (J.)], (7054), 7061, 7062, [7063 (*Bhṛguçārdūlaṃ*), 7065 (Bh.)], 7069 (*Brahmarshe*), [7070 (J.)], 7081, [7082 (*Bhṛgunandana*), 7086 (Bh.)], 7087, 7088, 7091, 7092, 7098, 7099, 7108, 7109, [7112 (Bh.), 7114 (J.), 7115 (J.)], 7116, 7118, 7119 (Bh.), [7123 (*Bhṛguçreshṭhaḥ*)]; **179**, 7125, 7126, 7128, [7129 (J.), 7132 (Bh.), 7133 (Bh.)], 7134, 7136, 7137, (7138), 7148, 7153, 7154, 7155, 7157, 7158, [7161 (J.)]; **180**, 7165, 7166, [7167 (J.), 7169 (J.), 7171 (J.)], 7173 (J.), 7174, 7175, 7176 (J.), 7178, 7179, 7180, 7182, 7183, 7184, 7185 (J.), 7186, 7187, 7190, 7192, 7194, 7198; **181**, 7201, [†7205 (J.)], †7207, [†7210 (J.), †7211 (J.), †7212 (*Haihayeçapramāthī*)], †7216; **182**, [7217 (Bh.)], 7218, 7221, 7222, [7223 (Bh.)], 7225, 7226, [7235 (J.)], 7236, 7237, 7242, 7243, 7244, [7245 (Bh.)]; **183**, [7250 (J.)], 7251 (J.), [7252 (J.)], 7257 (J.), 7259, 7261, [7262 (J.)], 7265; **184**, [7269 (Bh.)], 7273, [7274 (J.), 7278 (J.)], 7281, 7283; **185**, [7291 (*Bhṛgunandane*)], 7293, †7297, [†7298 (J.), 7300 (Bh.), 7303 (Bh.)], 7305, [7308 (Bh.)], 7310, 7318 (*Bhṛgunandanaṃ*), 7319 (Bh.), [7320 (Bh.), 7321 (*Bhṛgunandanaṃ*)], 7323, 7324, 7325, [7326 (Bh.)]; **186**, (7328), 7332, [7336 (*Bhṛgūdvaha*), 7338 (*Bhṛgusattamaḥ*)], 7358 (Ambā sought the protection of *R.*, who engaged in fight with Bhīshma, his former disciple. The encounter lasted for twenty-three days, at last *R.* declared himself to be vanquished and the Ṛshis and the Pitṛs brought about peace).—§ 576 (Bhagavadgītāp.): VI, **13**, 501 (J., all. to § 573); **14**, [528 (J., do.)], 554 (J., do.), 556 (J., do.), [557 (Bh.)]; **23**, 819 (all. to § 563); **34**, 1235 (*°aḥ çastrabhṛtām ahaṃ*, sc. *asmi*, says Kṛshṇa).—§ 578 (Bhīshmavadhap.): VI, **49**, 1995, (J., all. to § 563).—§ 581 (do.): VI, **66**o, 2999 (J., had praised Kṛshṇa).—§ 587 (do.): VI, [**108**, 5038 (J., all. to § 573)]; **118**, 5534 (had been the preceptor of Bhīshma in arms); [**120**, 5694 (J., all. to § 573)].—§ 589 (Droṇābhishekap.): VII, [**1**, 45 (J., had been the preceptor of Karṇa in arms, cf. § 621)]; **3**, 113 (vanquished by Bhīshma, all. to § 573).—§ 589*b* (Sātyaki): VII, **10**, 342 (*°eṇa samam astreshu*, sc. Sātyaki).—§ 592 (Saṃçaptakavadhap.): VII, **23**o, 1017 (the Pāṇḍya king Sāraṅgadhvaja acquired weapons from *R.*).—§ 593 (Abhimanyuvadhap.): VII, [**34***a*, 1485 (J.)]; **40**, 1706 (*°çishyaḥ*, sc. Karṇa).—§ 595 (cf. Shoḍaçarāj.): also Rāma Jāmadagnya will die without being satiated. The calf having been stolen and his father slain by the *kshatriyas* he slew the invincible *Kārtavīrya*. With his bow he slew 640,000 *kshatriyas*, among them 14,000 brahman-hating *kshatriyas*, and [the king of] Dantakrūra (so Nīl.); of the Haihayas he slew 1,000 with his club, 1,000 with his sword, 1,000 by hanging (*udbandhanāt*) [some more details in B., especially: *Guṇāvatīm uttareṇa Khāṇḍavād dakshiṇena ca*], etc.; he proceeded against the Kāçmīras, etc. (*β*), and slew them all; bringing all the eighteen *dvīpas* of the earth under his subjection, he performed 100 sacrifices, his sacrificial altar (18 nalas high, of gold, etc.) and the earth he gave as *dakshiṇā* to *Kaçyapa*, etc.; having divested the earth of *kshatriyas* for twenty-one times, he gave the earth to the brahmans, and it was Kaçyapa who accepted it with its seven dvīpas. Then *Kaçyapa* told *R.* to go out of the earth; *R.* with his arrows caused the ocean to stand aside, and repairing to the *Mahendra* mountain he continued to live there (VII, **70**): VII, **70**, 2427 (J.), [2433 (J.)], 2434, 2435, [2437 (J.), 2439 (Bh.)], 2442 (J., C. by error *Yā°*), 2443, 2445, [2448 (J.)].—§ 599 (Jayadrathavadhap.): VII, **98**ι, 3648; [**119**, 4719 (*api . . . Jāmadagnyaḥ*)].—§ 600 (Ghaṭotkacavadhap.): VII, **181**, 8230 (*°a ivāparaḥ*).—§ 603 (Nārāyaṇāstramokshap.): VII, **194**, 8967 (Droṇa had acquired the Dhanurveda from *R.*), 8971 (*°syānumataḥ saṅkhye*, sc. Açvatthāman).—§ 604 (Karṇap.): VIII, **2**, 37 (*Bhārgavaḥ pradadau yasmai paramāstraṃ*, sc. Bhīshma; *sākshād Rāmeṇa yo bālye Dhanurveda upākṛtaḥ*, do.); **5**ς, 144 (*Kārtavīryaç ca R°eṇa Bhārgavena yathā hataḥ*); [**8**, 221 (*cittamoham ivāyuktaṃ Bhārgavasya*); **9**, 295 (J., had taught Karṇa the use of the

Brahmāstra)].—§ 605*b* (Vijaya): VIII, **31**, [1294 (Bh., obtained the bow Vijaya from Indra and gave it to Karṇa)], 1296 (*dhanur ghoraṃ R°dattaṃ*, sc. the Vijaya).—§ 605 (Karṇap.): VIII, **31**, 1297 (Bh.).—§ 606*b* (do.): In the race of the *Bhṛgus* was *Jamadagni*. His son *Rāma* by ascetic penances gratified *Bhava* (i.e. Çiva) in order to obtain weapons; *Çiva* showed himself to him and promised him all weapons when he would become pure; those weapons burn a person who is not deserving of them. With penances, etc., and *homa* performed with *mantras Rāma* adored *Çiva* for many years. Gratified with him *Çiva* repeatedly proclaimed his virtues in the presence of D. and Ṛ. Meanwhile the *Daityas* became very mighty and afflicted the gods, who, having failed to vanquish them, repaired to *Çiva*. *Çiva* summoned *Rāma* and prevailed upon him to slay the *Dānavas*. Then touched by *Çiva*, his wounds were immediately healed, and *Çiva* gave him all the celestial weapons and granted him boons: VIII, **34**, 1584, 1587, [1588 (Bh.), 1589 (J.), 1592 (Bh.)], 1593, 1598 (Bh.), [1599 (Bh.)], (1601), 1603, [1605 (Bh.), 1606 (Bh.), 1608 (Bh.), 1610 (*Bhṛgunandana*)], 1611. — § 606 (Karṇap.): VIII, **34**, [1613 (Bh.), 1614 (*Bhṛgunandanaḥ*)], 1619 (°*çishyaḥ*, i.e. Karṇa). — § 607 (do.): VIII, **37**, †1733 (gave Karṇa an excellent chariot with excellent horses); **40**, 1865 (*yā gatir guruṇā proktā purā Rāmeṇa*, says Karṇa); **41**ε, 1952 (*punaḥ prabhāvaḥ Pārthasya paurāṇaḥ Keçavasya ca kathitaḥ . . . R°eṇa sabhāyāṃ rājasaṃsadi*, all. to § 563); **42**, †1964, †1965 (had cursed Karṇa, cf. § 621).—§ 608 (do.): VIII, **66**, 3312 (*anujñātaṃ R°eṇāstre*, sc. Karṇa), 3332 (°*tulyaḥ . . . astreṇa*, sc. Karṇa); **73**, 3741 (Bh., Karṇa had acquired a weapon from him); **90**, †4625 (°*ād upāttena mahāmahimnā hy Atharvaṇena*, employed by Karṇa), [4710 (Bh.)], 4712 (according to the curse of *R.* Karṇa forgot the [Brāhma] weapon he had acquired from him). —[§ 611 (Çalyap.): IX, **24**, 1314 (*çrutvā vacaḥ pathyaṃ Jāmadagnyāt*, all. to § 563).]—§ 615*cc* (Rāmatīrtha): IX, **49**, 2836 (Bh., performed in Rāmatīrtha a sacrifice where he gave the earth as *dakshiṇā* to Kaçyapa).—[§ 618 (Jalapradānikap.): XI, **1**β, 14 (*vākyaṃ Jāmadagnyasya*, all. to § 563).]—[§ 619 (Strīvilāpap.): XI, **21**, 613 (*Ācāryaçāpaḥ*, cf. § 621).]—§ 621 (Rājadh.): XII, **2**, 59 (on Mahendra), 60 (Bh.), 61, [63 (*Bhṛguçreshṭhāt*)], 74; **3**, [75 (*Bhṛguçārdūlaḥ*)], 78, [79 (J.), 83 (Bh.), 84 (*Bhṛgūdvahaḥ*)], 86, 88, 90 (*Bhṛguçārdūla*), [92 (J.)], 96 (Bh.), 98 [100 (Bh.), 101 (Bh.), 102 (Bh.), 103, (*Bhṛguçreshṭhaḥ*)], 107 (under the false pretence of being a brahman, Karṇa acquired the Brahmāstra from *R.* Having discovered the untruth (at the time of the deliverance of Daṃça from a curse) *R.* cursed Karṇa, that he should forget the Brahmāstra); [**4**, 108 (*Bhārgavanandanāt*)]; **5**, 139 (*çāpena R°sya*). — [§ 630 (Rājadh.): XII, **27**, 806 (Bh., all. to § 573).]—§ 635 (do.): XII, **37**, 1356 (Bhīshma had acquired weapons from *R.*) — § 637 (do.): XII, **46**, 1566 (Bh., all. to § 573), 1570 (J., Bhīshma was the disciple of *R.*); **47**η, 1596 (Bh., among the ṛshis who surrounded Bhīshma).—§ 638 (Rājadh.): XII, **48**, [1704 (J.)], 1706 (made the earth devoid of kshatriyas twenty-one times), 1707, 1708, 1709, 1711 (Bh.).—§ 638*b* (Rāmopākhyāna): XII, **49**, 1715, [1716 (J.)], 1747 (*kshatriyahantāraṃ*), 1758, 1763 (J.), 1766, [1767 (*Bhṛguçārdūlaḥ*), 1769 (Bh.)], 1773, [1775 (Bh.)], 1781, [1782 (J.)], 1801 (the story of *R.* anew related, cf. especially §§ 394–398).—§ 639 (Rājadh.): XII, **50**, 1806, 1807, 1808.—§ 641 (do.): XII, **116**, 4255 (J.); **122**, 4471 (*tatra çṛṅge Himavato Merau kanakaparvate | yatra R°o Muñjāvaṭe jaṭāharaṇam ādiçat*).—[§ 651 (Āpaddh.): XII, **143**, 5464 (Bh.), 5465 (Bh.), 5466 (Bh.) (?, told Mucukunda the Kapotalubdhakasaṃvāda).] — § 664 (Mokshadh.): XII, **207**β, 7520 (J., praised Kṛshṇa).—[§ 677 (do.): XII, **235**, 8600 (J., gave the earth to the brahmans)].—§ 702 (do.): XII, **293***a*, 10761 (J.).—§ 717*b* (Nārāyaṇīya): XII, **340**, 12948 (*Bhṛgukulodvahaḥ*, in the Tretāyuga Vishṇu incarnate as *R.* will exterminate the kshatriyas), 12968 (seventh incarnation of Vishṇu).—§ 718*b* (Uñchavṛttyup.): XII, **361**, 13879, 13880 (J., had slain Arjuna Kārtavīrya and his sons); **366**, 13940 (all. to § 573).—§ 723 (Ānuçāsanik.): XIII, **6***a*, 327 (*Açvatthāmā ca Rāmaç ca muniputrau dhanurdharau na gacchataḥ svargalokaṃ svakṛteneha karmaṇā*).—§ 730*g* (Upamanyu): XIII, **14**τ, 864 (the axe with which *R.* slew [Arjuna] Kārtavīrya, had been given to him by Çiva), 866 (exterminated the kshatriyas twenty-one times). — § 734 (Ānuçāsanik.): XIII, **26***a*, 1765 (J., among the ṛshis who came to see Bhīshma).—§ 745*b* (Cyavanop.): XIII, **52***a*, 2717 (J.), 2718–2720. — § 745*c* (Cyavana-Kuçikasaṃv.): XIII, **56**, 2925.—[§ 746 (Ānuçāsanik.): XIII, **62**, 3136 (J., had given the earth to Kaçyapa).] — § 747 (do.): XIII, **84**, 3960 (J.), 3961, [3964 (J.), 3965 (Bh.)], 3967, [3969 (*Bhṛgunandana*), 3972 (do., Bh.)], 3975, [3979 (*Bhṛgunandana*), 3982 (*Bhṛgūttama*), 3990 (*Bhṛgunandana*)] (after the slaughter of the kshatriyas *R.* consulted the ṛshis about means of purifying himself).—§ 747*b* (Suvarṇotpatti): XIII, [**84**, 3991 (*Bhṛgukulodvaha*), 3992 (*Bhṛgunandana*), 3994 (*Bhṛgūdvaha*), 4007 (do.)]; **85**, [4035 (*Bhṛgūttama*), 4044 (do.), 4049 (*Bhṛgūdvaha*), 4050 (do.), 4052 (*Bhṛgukulaçreshṭha*), 4061 (Bh.), 4085 (*Bhṛgūdvaha*)], 4104, 4105, [4118 (*Bhṛgunandana*; C. by error °*aḥ*), 4165 (*Jāmadagnyaḥ*, both B. and C., one that knows the identity of gold with fire, PCR.; Nīl. is silent, but we have only to read Jāmadagnya, voc.), 4170 (Bh.), 4180 (*Bhṛgūdvaha*), 4183 (J.)] (Vasishṭha told *R.* the story named Brahmadarçana, *R.* purified himself by making gifts of gold). — § 748*b* (Tārakavadhop.): XIII, **86**, 4219, 4220 (Vasishṭha told *R.* the Tārakavadhopākhyāna; Rāma purified himself by making gifts of gold and finally went to heaven).—§ 767 (Ānuçāsanik.): XIII, **137**, 6256 (J., gave the earth to a brahman [Kaçyapa] and attained to heaven).—§ 770 (do.): XIII, **151**κ, 7121 (?).—§ 775 (do.): XIII, **166**ζ, 7671 (only B., C. has *Vāmaḥ*).—§ 777 (Svargārohaṇik. p.): XIII, **169**, 7783 (J., all. to § 573), [7787 (J., all. to § 573)].—§ 782*c* (Arjuna Kārtavīrya): XIV, **29**, 824, 825, 826, 827, [828 (Bh.)], 829, [830 (J.)] (slew Arjuna Kārtavīrya and his kinsmen).—§ 782*d* (do.): Having slain Arjuna Kārtavīrya and destroyed his troops he afterwards repeatedly destroyed the *kshatriyas* begotten by brahmans upon *kshatriya* women, who had lost their children, twenty one times. Then a bodiless voice from heaven which was heard by all people told him to desist, and as he refused, being unable to forgive the slaughter of his father, his Pitṛs (XIV, **29**) told him the old story of king Alarka(*e*) and caused him to practise penances, by which he attained to high success (XIV, **80**): XIV, **29**, [833 (J.)], 834, 835; **30**, 871 [872 (J.)].

Rāma[2] Dāçarathi, king of Ayodhyā, son of Daçaratha and husband of Sītā. § 5 (Anukram.): I, **1***a*, 221 *bis* (*Dāçarathiṃ*, in Nārada's enumeration).—§ 11 (Parvasaṅgr.): I, **2**, 475.—§ 243 (Vidurāgamanap.): I, **205**, 7493 (*anavarau . . . R°ād Dāçaratheḥ*). — § 267 (Yamasabhāv.): II, **8**, 329 (*Dāçarathiḥ*, in the palace of Yama).—§ 303 (Anudyūtap.):

II, **76**, 2495 (all. to § 529).—§ 323 (Dvaitavanapr.): III, **25**, †950, †952 (*Dāçarathim*, all. to Rāmopākhyānaparvan). —§ 370 (Tīrthayātrāp.): III, **84**, 8048 (? went to heaven having bathed in Gopratāra on the Sarayū), 8050.—§ 372 (do.): III, **85**, 8208 (*Dāçarathiḥ*, crossed the Gaṅgā at Çṛṅgaverapura).—§ 376 (do.): III, **85**, 8269 (? *yathā*).—§ 383 (Paraçu-Rāma): III, **99**, 8656 (*Daçarathasya putraḥ*, incarnation of Vishṇu), 8658 (*Dāçaratheḥ*), 8660 (do.), 8661, 8666 (*Dāçarathiḥ*), 8668 (do.), 8670, 8673 (°*çarīre*), 8680 (humiliated Rāma Jāmadagnya by showing him his celestial power).—§ 424 (Hanūmad-Bhīmasaṃv.): III, **147**, 11178 (°*patnī*, i.e. Sītā).—§ 425 (do.): III, **147**, 11197 (*Dāçarathiḥ*); **148**, 11210, 11211, 11214, 11216, 11217 (°*kathā*), 11219 (the history of *R.* briefly narrated, cf. Rāmopākhyānap.).—§ 430 (do.): III, **150**, 11279 (all. to § 425).—§ 431 (Saugandhikāharaṇa): III, **151**, 11324 (*Rāghavaṃ R°ābhidhānaṃ Vishṇuṃ*). — § 525 (Rāmopākhyānap.): III, **274**, 15872, 15874, 15875, 15876, 15878 ([eldest] son of Daçaratha), 15879 (son of Kausalyā), 15880 (married Sītā, the daughter of Janaka), 15881.—§ 527 (do.): III, **277**, 15945 (°*ādīnāṃ*), 15946 (*Dāçarathī . . . R°-Lakshmaṇau*), 15950 (*jyeshṭhaḥ*), 15952 (anointed *yuvarājā*), 15958, 15959, 15970 (°*ārthaṃ*), 15972, 15974, 15975, 15976 (°-*Lakshmaṇau*), 15979, 15981, 15982 (*saha-Lakshmaṇaṃ*), 15983 (*R.* was banished by his father and went to Citrakūṭa, accompanied by Sītā and Lakshmaṇa; after the death of Daçaratha Bharata reigned in the name of *R.*). — § 528 (Rāvaṇagamaṇa): III, **277**, 15984, 15986, 15996, 16000 (at Janasthāna *R.* slew the Rākshasas Khara, Dūshaṇa, etc.). —§ 529 (Sītāharaṇa): III, **278**, 16006, 16012, 16015 (*āçramaṃ R°sya*), 16018, 16020, 16021, 16022, 16024, 16025, 16028, 16030, 16044 (while Rāma was pursuing a golden deer, Rāvaṇa ravished Sītā).—§ 530 (Viçvāvasumokshaṇa): III, **279**, 16050, 16057, 10060, 16062, 16064 (°-*Lakshmaṇau*), 16071 (*Saumitriṇā saha*), 16075, 16081, 16085, 16092 (°-*Lakshmaṇau*, *R.* and Lakshmaṇa delivered Viçvāvasu, who directed them to the monkey-king Sugrīva on Ṛshyamūka).—§ 531 (Rāmopākhyānap.): III, **280**, 16093, 16100 (°-*Lakshmaṇau*), 16103, 16105, 16113 (*Daçarathātmajaḥ*), 16116, 16120, 16127, 16129 (*Saumitriṇā saha*), 16132 (Rāma and Lakshmaṇa assisted Sugrīva against Vālin).—§ 532 (Sītāsāntvana): III, **280**, 16148, 16149 (*bhartā te*—i.e. Sītā's—*kuçalī R°o Lakshmaṇānugataḥ*), 16160 (°*syāstreṇa*). —§ 533 (Sītā-Rāvaṇasaṃv.): III, **281**, 16194.—§ 534 (Hanūmatpratyāgamana): III, **282**, 16211, 16216, 16218, 16220, 16226, 16227 (°-*Lakshmaṇa-sannidhau*), 16228, 16229, 16230, 16233, 16249, 16258 (°*sya dūtaḥ*, i.e. Hanūmat), 16259 (°-*Lakshmaṇau*), 16260, 16267 (Hanūmat announced to *R.* that he had found Sītā).—§ 535 (Setubandhana): III, **283**, 16269, 16270, 16277, 16294, 16303, 16306, 16307, 16311, 16313, 16315, 16321 (followed by the monkeys, etc., *R.* started for Laṅkā, *R.* prayed to the ocean, Nala built a bridge over the ocean). — § 536 (Laṅkāpraveça): III, **284**, 16331, 16361 (Laṅkā was attacked). — § 537 (Rāma-Rāvaṇayuddha): III, **285**β, 16371, 16375 (the battle began, encounter between *R.* and Rāvaṇa).—§ 538 (Kumbhakarṇaraṇagamana): III, **286**, 16387 (°-*Rāvaṇasainyānāṃ*), 16401, 16405 (°*ādīn*, continuation of the battle). —§ 539 (Kumbhakarṇādivadha): III, **287**, 16410, 16436 (°-*Rāvaṇasainyānāṃ*) (continuation of the battle).—§ 540 (Indrajidyuddha): III, **288**, 16439, 16442 (°-*Lakshmaṇa-Sugrīvāḥ*), 16458, 16463 (°-*Lakshmaṇau*), (continuation of the battle).—§ 541 (Indrajidvadha): III, **289**, 16465 (°-*Lakshmaṇau*), 16472 (*Ikshvākunandanaṃ*), 16476, 16491 (continuation of the battle).—§ 542 (Rāvaṇavadha): III, **290**, 16499, 16504, 16505, 16506, 16507, 16509, 16517, 16518, 16520, 16523, 16525, 16526, 16528 (*R.* slew Rāvaṇa). —§ 543 (Rāmābhisheka): III, **291**, 16531, 16533, 16534, 16535, 16540, 16546, 16551, 16567, 16568, 16572, 16575 (°*kīrtyā samaṃ putra jīvitaṃ te*—i.e. Hanūmat's—*bhavishyati*), 16577, 16580, 16581, 16587, 16588, 16589 (*R.* would first not accept Sītā, but the gods, etc., attested her innocence; *R.* returned to Ayodhyā and was anointed king).—§ 544 (Yudhishṭhirāçvāsa): III, **292**, 16612 (°*eṇa Vaidehī punar āhṛtā*).—§ 551 (Kīcakavadhap.): IV, **21**, 653–4 (*Rāmasya mahishī*—i.e. Sītā—*Rāmam evānupadyata*).—§ 565 (Gālavacarita): V, **117**, 3976 (*reme . . . Vaidehyāṃ yathā R°ḥ*).—§ 595 (Shoḍaçarāj.): *R.*, of countless virtues, the elder brother of *Lakshmaṇa*, lived for fourteen years in the woods together with his wife, at the command of his father; in order to protect the ascetics he at *Janasthāna* slew 14,000 *Rā.* *Rāvaṇa* (incapable of being slain by D. and As.) ravished his wife, the princess of *Videha*; *R.* slew him with all his kinsmen and followers. D. and Ṛ. applauded *R.*; he performed 100 horse-sacrifices, etc.; when *R.* ruled his kingdom, Ṛ., D., and men lived together on earth, nobody died in youth, etc. (description), men were each blessed with 1,000 children and lived for 1,000 years; *R.* reigned 11,000 years and then went to heaven, having established his line in eight dynasties (VII, **59**): VII, **59**, 2224 (*Dāçarathim*), 2228, 2234, 2235 (*Dāçarathiḥ*), 2236, 2237, 2245, 2246.—§ 599 (Jayadrathavadhap.): VII, **96**, 3569 (*yādṛçaṃ . . . R°-Rāvaṇayor mṛdhe*); **106**, 3981 (*yādṛk . . . vṛttaṃ R°-Rāvaṇayoḥ*); **107**, 4040 (*yathā Dāçarathī R°o Kharaṃ hatvā mahābalaṃ*).—§ 603 (Nārāyaṇāstramokshap.): VII, **194**, 8975 (°*o Dāçarathir yathā*); **196**, 9063 (°*o Vālivadhād yadvat*).—§ 604 (Karṇap.): VIII, **5**ζ, 143 (*yathā R°eṇa Rāvaṇaḥ*, sc. *hataḥ*).—§ 612 (Hradapraveçap.): IX, **31**ζ, 1753 (had slain Rāvaṇa).—§ 615 (Baladevatīrthayātrā): IX, **39**, 2250 (*Rākshasasya . . . R°çishṭasya vai purā*).—[§ 615*k* (Mahodara): IX, **39**, 2255 (*Rāghaveṇa*, slew Rākshasas).] — § 615 (Gadāyuddhap.): IX, **55**, 3107 (*sadṛçau . . . R°-Rāvaṇayoḥ*).—§ 632*b* (Shoḍaçarāj., cf. § 595): XII, **29**, 944 (*Dāçarathim*), 945, 946, 947, 948, 949, 950, 951, 954 (repetition from § 595).—§ 653*b* (Gṛdhragomāyusaṃv.): XII, **153**, 5742 (*çrūyate Çambuke* (B. *Ja°*), *çūdre hate brāhmaṇadārako jīvito dharmam āsadya R°āt satyaparākramāt*).—§ 717*b* (Nārāyaṇīya): XII, **340**, 12949 (*Dāçarathiḥ*, incarnation of Vishṇu, *sandhyāṃçe samanuprāpte Tretāyā(ṃ) Dvāparasya ca*, will slay Rāvaṇa), 12968 (*Dāçarathiḥ*, eighth incarnation of Vishṇu).—§ 718*b* (Uñchavṛttyup.): XII, **361**, 13878 (*Daçagrīvaḥ*—i.e. Rāvaṇa— . . . *hato R°eṇa*).—§ 746 (Ānuçāsanik.): XIII, **74**, 3616 (communicated the discourse between Brahmán and Indra to Lakshmaṇa); **76**ι, 3690 (*Dāçarathiḥ*, attained to heaven by means of gifts of kine).—§ 761 (do.): XIII, **115**δ, 5666 (among the kings who did not eat meat during the month of Kārttika).—§ 767 (do.): XIII, **137**, 6258 (*Dāçarathiḥ*, attained to heaven by making gifts of wealth at the sacrifices). —§ 775 (do.): XIII, **166**η, 7677 (*Rākshasahā*, enumeration). —§ 778 (Açvamedhik.): XIV, **3**, 49 (°*o Dāçarathir yathā*, sc. *yajasva vājimedhena*).

Cf. also the following synonyms:—

Ayodhyādhipati ("the king of Ayodhyā"): XII, 954.

Daçarathasya putra(ḥ) ("the son of Daçaratha"): III, 8656.

Daçarathātmaja (do.): III, 16113 (*R*°).

Dāçarathi (do.): I, 221 (*R*°), 2101 (*yathā yajño D°eḥ*), 7493 (*R*°); II, 329 (*R*°); III, †952 (*R*°), †954, 8208 (*R*°), 8657, 8658 (*R*°), 8660 (*R*°), 8666 (*R*°), 8668 (*R*°), 11197 (*R*°), 11338, 16291; VII, 2224 (*R*°), 2235 (*R*°), 4040 (*R*°), 6937 (*°eḥ samāḥ*), 8975 (*R*°); VIII, 4397 (*°eḥ samau*, sc. Karṇa and Arjuna); XII, 944 (*R*°), 12949 (*R*°), 12968 (*R*°); XIII, 3690 (*R*°), 6258 (*R*°); XIV, 49.

Ikshvākunandana, Kākutstha, Kausalyānandivardhana, Kausalyāmātṛ, Kosalendra, Lakshmaṇāgraja (VII, 2226), **Rāghava**, q.v.

Rāma[3] (i.e. Bala-Rāma, q.v.): I, 390, 596, 621, 624, 7014, 7507, 7548, 7595, 7955, 7987, 7998, 8000, 8015, 8022; II, 598, 643, 1274, 1509; III, 595, 1977, 1993, †2009, 10231, 10233, 10240, †10259, †10260, †10261, †10262, †10267, 14736; V, 3, 2855, 3218, 4926, 5349; VI, †5797; VII, 412, 1042, 4193; VIII, 31, 1952; IX, 598, 1948, 1950, 1951, 1959, 1960, 1965, 1969, 1971, 1972, 1984, †2004, 2176, 2246, 2248, 2314, 2316, 2760, 2762, 3006, 3008, (3010), 3011, 3038, 3052, 3055, 3064, 3067, 3068, 3072, 3078, 3079, 3081, 3106 (?), 3121, 3344, 3365, 3370; X, 505, 638; XII, 4471 (?); XIII, 630, 6867; XVI, 8, 20, 29, 32, 43, 62, 72, 104, 105, 111, 112, 114, 116, 142, 172, 207, 261; XVII, 10.

Rāma[4] = Vishṇu (1000 names).

Rāmacarita ("Rāma's exploits"; name of a poetical work). § 640 (Rājadh.): XII, **57**, 2086 (*çlokaç cāyaṃ* (i.e. v. 2087) *purā gīto Bhārgaveṇa mahātmanā ākhyāne* (B. *ākhyāte*) *R°e nṛpatiṃ prati*; PCR. takes Bhārgava = Uçanas, but Bhārgava is probably = Vālmīki, and the Rāmāyaṇa is meant).

Rāmahrada[1], pl. (*°āḥ*) (the lakes of Rāma[1]). § 363 (Tīrthayātrāp.): The *R.* had been dug by *Rāma Jāmadagnya* and filled with the blood of the *kshatriyas* in order to gratify his father and forefathers, who therefore granted him the boon that his ascetic merit should again be increased (*tapa āpyāyanaṃ*), that he should be freed from his sin of having exterminated the *kshatriya* race, and that his lakes should be *tīrthas* celebrated over the world. Then they disappeared. To him who bathing there offers oblations to the *Pitṛs*, they will grant his desires and eternal heaven (*Svargalokaṃ*), etc.: III, **83**, 5096, 6010.—§ 369 (Kurukshetra): III, **83**, 7078 (*Tarantukārantukayor antaraṃ R°ānāṃ ca Macakrukasya etat Kurukshetraṃ Samantapañcakaṃ*).—§ 409 (Plakshāvataraṇag.): III, **129**, 10518.—§ 615*kk* (Kurukshetrak.): IX, **53**, 3032 (= III, 7078, with *tu* for *ca* and *°kra°* for *°kru°*).—§ 638 (Rājadh.): XII, **48**, 1705 (*pañca*, made by Rāma Jāmadagnya).—Do.[2], sg. (do.): § 573 (Ambopākhyānap.): V, **186**, 7355 (there Ambā performed austerities).—§ 733*v* (Ānuçāsanik.): By bathing in the *R.* and offering water to the *Pitṛs* in the *Vipāçā* one is cleansed from his sins. By bathing in the *Mahāhrada* one attains to the end of *Jamadagni*, etc.: XIII, **25**, 1733.

Rāmaka, a mountain. § 284 (Sahadeva): II, **31**, 1172 (*parvataṃ*, in the south, conquered by Sahadeva).

Ramaṇa[1]. § 116 (Vasu, pl.): I, **66**, 2586 (son of Varcas (or of Varcasvin) and Manoharā).

Ramaṇa[2], pl. (*°āḥ*), a people. § 574 (Jambūkh.): VI, **9ζ**, 374 (in the north).

Ramaṇaka, name of a varsha. § 574*i* (Jambūkh.): On the south of Çveta and the north of Nishadha is the varsha *Ramaṇaka*. The men there are white, of good parentage and handsome, without enemies, living for 11,500 years, ever cheerful: VI, **8**, 288 (*varshaṃ*).

Ramānātha ("the husband of Ramā, i.e. Lakshmī") = Kṛshṇa: II, 2292.

Rāmaṇīyaka, name of an island. § 38 (Kadrū): I, **26**, 1303.—§ 39 (cf. Āstīkap.): Description of *R.*: by Viçvakarman it had been made the abode of the makaras, there the serpents first saw the terrible *Lavaṇa* [the *Asura*, Nīl.]; it is adorned with many trees which grow only on the hills of Malaya, and is dear to the Gandharvas (I, **27**).

Rāmānuja[1] ("younger brother of Rāma[1]") = Kṛshṇa: V, 2741 (*Çauriḥ*).

Rāmānuja[2] ("younger brother of Rāma[2]") = Lakshmaṇa: VII, 5888 (*L*°).

Rāma[rājy]ābhisheka ("the anointing of Rāma"). § 543: Having slain *Rāvaṇa*, *Rāma* was worshipped by D., R., and G. uttering *jaya*; he gave *Laṅkā* to *Vibhīshaṇa*, *Avindhya* came with *Sītā*, whom *Rāma* repudiated. *Lakshmaṇa* and the monkeys were sorrowful; *Brahmán* appeared on his chariot, etc. (*a*); *Sītā* swore by *Mātariçvan*, etc. (β), that she was innocent. A celestial voice was heard, *Vāyu*, etc. (γ) attested her innocence. *Brahmán* said that it was by his grace that *Rāvaṇa* (the enemy of D., G., N., Y., Dā., M.-ṛ.) had been unslayable; but *Sītā* had been protected by the curse of *Nalakūbara*. *Daçaratha* commanded him to take back his wife and rule his kingdom at *Ayodhyā*, his exile of fourteen years was over. *Rāma* gave boons to *Avindhya* and *Trijaṭā*. *Brahmán* and the gods, headed by *Indra*, granted *Rāma* adherence to virtue and invincibility, and the monkeys were restored to life. *Sītā* granted to *Hanūmat*, that his life might last as long as the fame of *Rāma*, and gave him celestial wines and drinks. *Mātali* said: "Thou hast dispelled the sorrows of D., G., Y., As., N., and men, and therefore all creatures with D., As., G., Y., Rā., and Pn. will always speak of thee." Having made arrangements for the protection of *Laṅkā*, *Rāma*, etc. (δ) recrossed the bridge riding on *Pushpaka*, at the seashore he dismissed the monkeys with presents, then he re-entered *Kishkindhyā*, where he installed *Aṅgada* as *yuvarāja*. Having reached *Ayodhyā* he dispatched *Hanūmat* as envoy to *Bharata*. Then he entered *Nandigrāma* and saw *Bharata* and *Çatrughna*, *Bharata* made the kingdom over to him. *Vasishṭha* and *Vāmadeva* installed him in the sovereignty under the *nakshatra* which belongs to *Vishṇu* (*Vaishṇave*, i.e. *Çravaṇa*, Nīl.). Then he dismissed *Sugrīva*, *Vibhīshaṇa*, etc., and gave *Pushpaka* back to *Kubera*. He then performed ten *jārūthya* horse-sacrifices on the *Gomatī* (III, **291**).

Rāma-Rāvaṇa-yuddha ("the combat between *Rāma* and *Rāvaṇa*"). § 537: Headed by *Rāvaṇa* many small *Rākshasas* and *Piçācas*, viz. *Parvaṇa*, etc. (*a*), invisible penetrated among the monkeys. *Vibhīshaṇa* broke the spell of their invisibility, and they were all slain. *Ravaṇa* with the *Rākshasas* and *Piçācas* formed the array named after *Uçanas* (*Auçanasaṃ vyūhaṃ*). *Rāma* disposed his troops after the rule of *Bṛhaspati* (*Bārhaspatyaṃ vidhiṃ*). *Rāvaṇa* fought with *Rāma*, etc. (β), then an encounter came about with celestial weapons of great force (III, **285**).

Ramaṭa, pl., v. Rāmaṭha, pl.

Ramaṭha, pl. (*°āḥ*). § 641 (Rājadh.): XII, **65**θ, 2430 (enumeration of low or barbarous peoples). Cf. next.

Rāmaṭha, pl. (*°āḥ*), a people. § 285 (Nakula): II, **32**, 1194 (in the west, vanquished by Nakula).—§ 342 (Indralokābhigamanap.): III, **51**, 1991 (only B., C. has *Ramaṭāḥ*, present at the *rājasūya* of Yudhishṭhira).—§ 608 (Karṇap.): VIII, **73**, 3652 (°-*Kauṅkaṇāḥ*, only C., B. has *Māṭhara-Taṅgaṇāḥ*, had been slain by Arjuna).

Rāmatīrtha, name of several tīrthas. § 370 (Tīrthayātrāp.): III, **84**, 8051 (on the Gomatī); **85**, 8159 (near Mahendra), 8186 (at Çūrpāraka).—§ 615*cc* (Baladevatīrthayātrā): *Rāma Bhārgava* having repeatedly subjugated the earth and slain all the foremost of *kshatriyas* in that *tīrtha* performed a *vājapeya* and 100 horse-sacrifices through the assistance of his preceptor the *muni* Kaçyapa whom he gave as sacrificial fee the earth with the oceans. Having duly bathed there and made presents to the *brahmans*, etc., *Rāma* retired into the woods: IX, **49**, 2835 (on the Sarasvatī).

Rāmāyaṇa, the well-known work of Vālmīki. § 424 (Bhīmakadalīkhaṇḍapr.): III, **147**, 11177 (°*e ativikhyātaḥ çrīmān vānarapuṅgavaḥ*, sc. Hanūmat). — § 795*c* (Mahābhārata): XVIII, **6**, 300 (°*e* . . . *Hariḥ sarvatra gīyate*). Cf. Rāmacarita.

Rāmāyaṇa(m) upākhyāna(m) ("the episode relating to Rāma [Dāçarathi]"). § 11 (Parvasaṅgr.): I, **2**, 475 (i.e. Rāmopākhyānaparvan). Cf. Rāmopākhyāna [1].

Rambhā [1], an Apsaras. § 103 (Aṃçāvat.): I, **65**, 2558 (daughter of Prādhā).—§ 191 (Arjuna): I, **123**, 4818 (danced at the birth of Arjuna).—§ 269 (Vaiçravaṇasabhāv.): II, **10**, 392 (in the palace of Kubera).—§ 336 (Indralokābhigamanap.): III, **43***a*, 1784 (danced in the palace of Indra).—§ 565 (Gālavacarita): V, **117**, 3975 (*reme* . . . *yāthā* . . . *Tumburuç caiva R°ayā*).—§ 721 (Ānuçāsanik.): XIII, **3**, 191 (*pañcacūḍā* . . . *Apsarāḥ*, transformed into a rock by Viçvāmitra).—§ 731*b* (Ashṭāvakra-Diksaṃv.): XIII, **19**β, 1424 (danced in the palace of Kubera).—§ 775 (Ānuçāsanik.): XIII, **166**β, 7641 (enumeration).

Rambhā [2]: § 532 (Sītāsāntvana): III, **282**, 16152 (*vadhūṃ*, wife of Nalakūbara?, Rāvaṇa violated her and was therefore cursed by Nalakūbara).

Raṃhas = Çiva: XIV, 195, 212.

Rāmopākhyāna [1] ("the episode relating to Rāma [Dāçarathi]"). § 10 (Parvasaṅgr.): I, **2**, 326 (*parva*, i.e. Rāmopākhyānaparvan). Cf. Rāmāyaṇa(m) upākhyāna(m).

Rāmopākhyāna [2] ("the episode relating to Rāma Jāmadagnya"). § 638*b* (Rājadh.): *Jahnu* > *Aja* > *Balākāçva* > *Kuçika*, who performed penances in order to get a son; *Indra* became his son:

Gādhi. *Bhṛgu*.
(2) *Viçvāmitra*. (1) *Satyavatī* ∼ *Ṛcīka*.
Jamadagni.
Paraçu-Rāma.

Ṛcīka destined a certain portion of the sacrificial food (wherein had been placed the *brahman* energy) for *Satyavatī*, which would give her a son of great wisdom, the foremost of *brahmans*; and another (wherein had been placed the sum total of *kshatriya* energy) for her mother, which would give her for a son an invincible *kshatriya*. Then *Ṛcīka* proceeded to the woods to practise penances. King *Gādhi*, on a *tīrthayātrā*, arrived at *Ṛcīka's* retreat with his queen. There the mother of *Satyavatī*, from ignorance, exchanged the two portions of the food. *Ṛcīka* predicted that the son of *Satyavatī* would become a terrible *kshatriya*, but asked by *Satyavatī*, he granted that not her son (*Jamadagni*) but her grandson (*Paraçu-Rāma*) would become such; her mother would give birth to a brahman (*Viçvāmitra*). Besides the other sciences, *Rāma* mastered the *Dhanurveda*; gratifying *Mahādeva* on *Gandhamādana*, he asked him for weapons, especially the axe, which made him unrivalled on earth. Meanwhile the virtuous *kshatriya*, the *Haihaya* king *Arjuna Kārtavīrya*, who had got 1,000 arms through the grace of *Dattātreya*, having subjugated the whole earth with its mountains and seven islands, became a powerful emperor, and gave away the earth to the *brahmans* at a horse-sacrifice. Once, solicited by *Agni*, he gave alms to that deity: springing from the points of his shafts, *Agni* burnt villages, etc., and also the retreat of *Āpava* (i.e. *Vasishṭha*, Nīl.), who cursed *Arjuna*, saying that *Rāma* should lop off his arms. *Arjuna*, always devoted to peace, always regardful of *brahmans*, etc., did not think of that curse. His sons, always haughty and cruel, seized and brought away the calf of *Jamadagni's homa*-cow, without the knowledge of *Arjuna*; *Rāma* lopped off the arms of *Arjuna* and brought back the calf; the sons of *Arjuna* came and slew *Jamadagni*, in the absence of *Rāma*, who vowed to free the earth of *kshatriyas*, and slaughtered all the sons and grandsons of *Arjuna*, and thousands of *Haihayas*, and annihilated all *kshatriyas*, and then, filled with compassion, retired into the woods. After some thousands of years, the grandson of *Viçvāmitra* and son of *Raibhya*, *Parāvasu* said to *Rāma* in public: "were not *Pratardana*, etc., who were assembled at a sacrifice at the time of *Yayāti's* fall, *kshatriyas* by birth; thou art not true of thy vow; through fear of *kshatriya* heroes thou hast betaken thyself to the mountains." *Rāma* once more slew *kshatriyas* by hundreds. Those *kshatriyas*, however, that he spared, counted by hundreds, multiplied and became mighty monarchs on earth. *Rāma* once more slaughtered them, not sparing the very children. Some *kshatriya* ladies, however, succeeded in protecting their children. Having made the earth destitute of *kshatriyas* twenty-one times, *Rāma*, at the completion of a horse-sacrifice, gave away the earth as a sacrificial present to *Kaçyapa*. In order to preserve the remnant of the *kshatriyas*, *Kaçyapa* told *Rāma* to repair to the shores of the southern ocean and not to reside within his dominion. The ocean suddenly created *Çūrpāraka* for *Rāma*. *Kaçyapa* gave the earth to the *brahmans* and then entered the great forest. Then *çūdras* and *vaiçyas* began to cohabit with the wives of *brahmans*; unprotected duly by *kshatriyas*, the earth quickly sank, and was held by *Kaçyapa* on his lap (*ūru*), whence she was called *Urvī*. For protection's sake she asked *Kaçyapa* for a king, saying that she had concealed some *Haihaya kshatriyas* among women; [further] *Paurava* (son of *Vidūratha*), brought up among bears in the *Ṛkshavat* mountain; [further] a son of *Saudāsa*, protected through compassion by *Parāçara*, and named *Sarvakarman* (etymology); *Çibi's* son *Gopati*, brought up in the forest among kine; *Pratardana's* son *Vatsa*, brought up among calves in a cow-pen; *Dadhivāhana's* grandson and *Diviratha's* son, concealed on the banks of *Gaṅgā* by *Gautama*; *Bṛhadratha*, protected by apes (? *golāṅgūlaiḥ*, cf. BR.; PCR.: wolves) on *Gṛdhrakūṭa*; many *kshatriyas* belonging to the race of *Marutta* have been brought up by the ocean; they are living among artisans and goldsmiths; "their fathers and grandfathers have been slain for my sake by *Rāma*; it is my duty to see that their funeral rites are duly performed." *Kaçyapa*, seeking out those *kshatriyas*, installed them duly as kings in days of yore.

Those *kshatriya* races that are now extant are the progeny of those princes.

Rāmopākhyānaparvan ("the episode relating to Rāma[2]," i.e. the subject-matter of the Rāmāyaṇa; it is the 48th of the minor parvans of Mhbhr.). (Cf. Rāmopākhyāna, Rāmāyaṇa.) § 525: As *Yudhishṭhira* asked *Mārkaṇḍeya* if he knew any one more unfortunate than he was (III, **273**), *Mārkaṇḍeya* related the story of *Rāma Dāçarathi*: King *Aja* of *Ikshvāku's* race had a son *Daçaratha*, who had four virtuous sons: *Rāma* (son of *Kausalyā*), *Lakshmaṇa* and *Çatrughna* (sons of *Sumitrā*), and *Bharata* (son of *Kaikeyī*). *Sītā*, the daughter of the *Videha* king *Janaka*, was created by *Tvashṭṛ* himself to become the wife of *Rāma*. *Prajāpati* (*Pitāmaha*, *Svayambhū*, the Creator of all the worlds) had a mind-born son *Pulastya*, who with a cow begat a son *Vaiçravaṇa* (i.e. *Kubera*). Leaving his father, *Vaiçravaṇa* went to his grandfather, and angered at this, his father with half of his own self became born as *Viçravas* for wreaking vengeance on *Vaiçravaṇa*. But *Pitāmaha*, pleased with *Vaiçravaṇa*, gave him immortality and made him the sovereign of wealth (*Dhaneça*), a *lokapāla* and friend of *Īçāna*, and gave him a son *Nalakūbara*, and *Laṅkā* for his capital, guarded by hosts of *Rākshasas*, and the *vimāna Pushpaka* capable of going everywhere, and the kingship of the *Yakshas*, etc. (III, **274**).—§ 526: The *muni Viçravas* was greatly enraged against *Vaiçravaṇa*. *Kubera* (*Naravāhana*), the king of the *Rākshasas*, always sought to please his father, and, living in *Laṅkā*, sent three *Rākshasa* women (*a*) skilled in singing and dancing to wait upon him. *Pulastya* granted them boons: to *Pushpotkaṭā* two sons: *Kumbhakarṇa* and *Daçagrīva* (= *Rāvaṇa*); *Mālinī* bore one son, *Vibhīshaṇa*; *Rākā* became the mother of the twins *Khara* and *Çūrpaṇakhā*. *Vibhīshaṇa* surpassed everybody in beauty and was very pious; *Daçagrīva* was energetic and strong; *Kumbhakarṇa* was the most powerful in battle and a master of illusion; *Khara* was proficient in archery and hostile to *brahmans*; *Çūrpaṇakhā* troubled the ascetics (*siddhavighnakarī*). Learned in the *Vedas*, they lived with their father on *Gandhamādana*. And there they beheld *Vaiçravaṇa* seated with their father, and seized with jealousy, they gratified *Brahmán* with severe penances (β), while *Khara* and *Çūrpaṇakhā* protected and attended on them. After 1,000 years *Daçagrīva*, cutting off his head (i.e. heads), offered it (i.e. them) in the fire, and *Brahmán* appeared and made them desist from their austerities, granting them boons (γ) except immortality. Now *Daçagrīva* defeated *Kubera* in battle and drove him from *Lankā*; *Kubera* then, followed by *Gandharvas*, *Yakshas*, *Rākshasas*, and *Kinnaras*, went to live on *Gandhamādana*. *Rāvaṇa* took from him *Pushpaka*, upon which *Vaiçravaṇa* cursed him saying: "This chariot shall never carry thee, but him who will slay thee in battle, and as thou hast insulted thy elder brother thou shalt soon die." *Vibhīshaṇa* followed *Kubera*, who invested him with the command of the *Yaksha* and *Rākshasa* hosts. On the other hand, the man-eating *Rākshasas* and *Piçācas* anointed *Daçagrīva* as their sovereign. *Daçagrīva* deprived the gods and *Daityas* of their valuable possessions, and because he terrified (*rāvayām āsa*, v. 15928) all creatures, he was called *Rāvaṇa* (III, **275**). The *Brahmarshis*, *Siddhas*, and *Devarshis*, with *Agni* as their spokesman, sought the protection of *Brahmán*, who said that the four-armed *Vishṇu* had already been incarnate for this object, and caused *Indra* and the gods, *Gandharvas*, and *Dānavas* to beget strong sons, capable of assuming any form at will, on monkeys and bears; and the *Gandharvī Dundubhī* he caused to be born on earth as the hunchbacked *Mantharā*, who, instructed by *Brahmán*, went hither and thither ever engaged in fomenting quarrels (III, **276**).—§ 527: Asked by *Yudhishṭhira*, *Mārkaṇḍeya* related: The sons of *Daçaratha* were conversant with the *Vedas* and the *Dhanurveda*. *Rāma* equalled *Indra* and *Bṛhaspati*. At night, the *Pushya* being in a lucky conjuncture, *Rāma* was to be invested as *yuvarāja*. *Mantharā* aroused the jealousy of *Kaikeyī* against *Kausalyā*, *Kaikeyī* prevailed upon *Daçaratha* that *Bharata* should be anointed and *Rāma* be in exile in the forest of *Daṇḍaka* for fourteen years. *Rāma* was accompanied by *Lakshmaṇa* and *Sītā*. *Daçaratha* died. *Bharata* rebuked *Kaikeyī* and set off to find *Rāma*, accompanied by *Kausalyā*, *Sumitrā*, *Kaikeyī*, *Çatrughna*, *Vasishṭha*, *Vāmadeva*, etc. He saw *Rāma* and *Lakshmaṇa* on the mountain *Citrakūṭa*, but *Rāma* would adhere to the order of his father. *Bharata* then ruled in Nandigrāma, keeping before him the shoes of *Rāma*.—§ 528: *Rāvaṇagamana* (q.v.).—§ 529: *Sītāharaṇa* (q.v.).—§ 530: *Viçvāvasumokshaṇa* (q.v.).—§ 531: Having bathed in the lake *Pampā*, *Rāma* and *Lakshmaṇa* on the mountain *Ṛshyamūka* beheld the monkey-king *Sugrīva* (whom his brother *Vālin* had deprived of his wife *Tārā* and his kingdom) and his four counsellors, *Hanūmat* (equalling *Himavat*), etc. *Sugrīva* showed *Rāma* a piece of cloth that had been dropped by *Sītā*. *Sugrīva* promised to bring back *Sītā*. *Rāma* installed *Sugrīva* as king of all the monkeys and promised to slay *Vālin*. Then they all repaired to *Kishkindhyā*. *Vālin* came out; *Tārā* (who understood the voice of every creature) told him that it was *Rāma*, *Lakshmaṇa*, *Mainda*, *Dvivida*, *Hanūmat*, *Jāmbavat* (the king of the bears), and *Sugrīva* who had come to destroy him. *Vālin* suspected *Tārā*. Near the mountain *Mālyavat* he had an encounter with *Sugrīva*. *Hanūmat* placed a garland round *Sugrīva's* neck (so that he shone like the mountain Malaya), and *Rāma* recognized *Sugrīva* by that sign and killed *Vālin* with an arrow. *Sugrīva* thus regained *Kishkindhyā* and *Tārā*. *Rāma* dwelt on Mālyavat for four months.—§ 532: *Sītāsāntvana* (q.v.).—§ 533: *Sītā-Rāvaṇasaṃvāda* (q.v.). — § 534: *Hanūmatpratyāgamana* (q.v.).—§ 535: *Setubandhana* (q.v.).—§ 536: *Laṅkāpraveça* (q.v.).—§ 537: *Rāma-Rāvaṇayuddha* (q.v.).—§ 538: *Kumbhakarṇanirgamana* (q.v.). § 539: *Kumbhakarṇādivadha* (q.v.).—§ 540: *Indrajidyuddha* (q.v.).—§ 541: *Indrajidvadha* (q.v.).—§ 542: *Rāvaṇavadha* (q.v.).—§ 543: *Rāmābhisheka* (q.v.).—§ 544: *Yudhishṭhirāçvāsa* (q.v.).

Ramyagrāma, name of a city. § 281 (Sahadeva): II, **31**, 1118 (only B., C. has *Muñjagrāma*; in the south, conquered by Sahadeva).

Raṇapriya = Vishṇu (1000 names).

Raṇeshv agnimukha(ḥ) = Çiva (1000 names[1]).

Raṇotkaṭa, a warrior of Skanda. § 615*u* (Skanda): IX, **45**η, 2570.

Rantideva, an ancient king, son of Saṅkṛti. § 5 (Anukram.): I, **1***a*, 224 (in Nārada's enumeration).—§ 61 (Sarpasattra): I, **55**, †2099 (*yathā yajño R°sya*). — § 296 (Dyūtap.): II, **53**, 1929. — § 358 (Tīrthayātrāp.): III, **82**, 4096 (*Carmaṇvatīṃ samāsādya niyato niyatāçanaḥ* | *R°ābhyanujñāto* (B. °*am*) *agnishṭomaphalaṃ labhet*). — § 480 (Pativratop. Brāhmaṇavyādhasaṃv.): III, **208**, 13809, 13810 (description of his gifts of food).—§ 545 (Pativratāmāhātmyap.): III, **294**, 16674 (*Sāṃkṛte R°sya svaçaktyā dānataḥ samaḥ*, sc. Satyavat). — § 595 (Shoḍaçarāj.): *R. Sāṅkṛti* had

200,000 cooks to distribute food to the brahmans, etc.; countless numbers of animals desirous of going to heaven used to come to him of their own accord; the number of animals sacrificed in his agnihotras was so large that the secretions from the heaps of skins formed a veritable river, which came to be called *Carmaṇvatī* (now Chambal); even when he had on a single day given away to the brahmans a crore of *nishkas* he thought he had given away very little, etc., etc. People who are acquainted with ancient history (*purāṇavido janāḥ*) quote *gāthās* regarding *R.* (VII, **67**): VII, **67**, 2356 (*Sāṅkṛtiṃ*), 2368, 2369, 2371, 2373.—§ 632*b* (Shoḍaçarāj., cf. § 595): XII, **29**, 1013 (*Sāṅkṛtyaṃ*), 1015, 1019, 1020 (*Sāṅkṛteḥ*), (repetition from § 595).—§ 677 (Mokshadh.): XII, **235**, 8591 (*Sāṃkṛtyaḥ*, ascended to heaven by giving lukewarm water to Vasishṭha).—§ 702 (do.): XII, **293**, 1075 (obtained his success by giving roots, and fruits, and leaves to the ascetics).—§ 746 (Ānuçāsanik.): XIII, **66**, 3351 (performed a great sacrifice, the juice from the skins of the slaughtered animals formed the river Carmaṇvatī), 3365 (went to heaven by gifts of foods).—§ 760 (do.): XIII, **112**, 5544 (*b*: do.).—§ 761 (do.): XIII, **115**, 5665 (among the kings who abstained from meat during the month of Kārttika).—§ 767 (do.): XIII, **137**, 6250 (*Sāṅkṛtyaḥ*, attained to heaven by making gifts (*arghyaṃ*) to Vasishṭha).—§ 770 (do.): XIII, **151**μ, 7129 (*gavām ayena yajñena yeneshṭaṃ vai Kṛtayuge | R°ṃ mahādevaṃ* (?) *kīrtayet*). — § 786*c* (Nakulākhyāna): King *R.*, when divested of all his wealth, gave a small quantity of water with a pure heart, by this gift he went to heaven: XIV, **90**, 2787. Cf. Sāṅkṛti, Sāṅkṛtya.

Rasa ("essence," personif.). § 270 (Brahmasabhāv.): II, **11**, 438 (in the palace of Brahmán).

Rasā = Rasātala: XII, 13479, 13503, 13504, 13511 (*°nāmālayāt*, or *Rasānām ālayāt* ?).

Rasāhara. § 491 (Āṅgirasa): III, **220**, 14162.

Rasātala, the nether world. § 392*c* (Svayambhuvo vanaṃ): III, **114**, 10114 (*yāsyāmi R°ṃ*, says the earth).—§ 458 (Mārkaṇḍeyas.): III, **188**, 12874 (*bhittvā pṛthivīṃ praviçya ca R°ṃ*, sc. the Saṃvartaka fire).—§ 513 (Ghoshayātrāp.): III, **251**, 15152 (Duryodhana was carried to *R.* by a kṛtyā).—§ 564 (Mātalīyop.): V, **102**, 3602 (*idaṃ R°ṃ nāma saptamaṃ pṛthivītalaṃ*), 3615 (*°nivāsibhiḥ*), 3616 (*°tale*).—§ 571 (Ulūkadūtāgamanap.): V, **160**, 5462. — § 596 (Pratijñāp.): VII, **73**, †2608 (*yadi viçate R°ṃ*).—§ 603 (Nārāyaṇāstramokshap.): VII, **199**, 9236 (*nihanishyati . . . sarvān R°gatān api*).—§ 637 (Rājadh.): XII, **47**θ, 1663 (*°gataḥ . . . Anantaḥ*, identified with Kṛshṇa).—§ 638*b* (Rāmopākhyāna): XII, **49**, 1786 (*praviveça R°ṃ*, sc. the earth).—§ 660*b* (Bhṛgu-Bharadvājasaṃv.): XII, **182**, 6793 (*°ānte salilaṃ jalānte pannagādhipāḥ*).—§ 666 (Mokshadh.): XII, **209**, 7629 (*°gataḥ*, sc. Vishṇu in the form of a boar).—§ 686 (do.): XII, **273**, 9822 (Sāvitrī went to *R.*).—§ 696*b* (Dakshaprokta-Çivasahasranāmastotra): XII, **285**, 10455 (*°gatāḥ*, sc. the Rudras).—§ 717*b* (Nārāyaṇīya): XII, **348**, 13506, 13507 (*°gato Hariḥ*, Vishṇu went to *R.* to recover the Vedas).—§ 723 (Ānuçāsanik.): XIII, **6**, 328 (*°talaṅgataḥ*, sc. Vasu Uparicara).—§ 747*b* (Suvarṇotpatti): XIII, **85**, 4037 (*maṇḍūko R°talotthitaḥ*), 4038 (*°tale*), 4060 (*āpo R°e*).—§ 766 (Ānuçāsanik.): XIII, **132**, 6156 (*nāgo R°caraḥ*).—§ 786 (Anugītāp.): XIV, **91**, 2831 (Vasu Uparicara had to go to *R.*).—§ 795 (Svargārohaṇap.): XVIII, **5**, 169 (Ananta entered *R.*).

Ratā, wife of Prajāpati[2] and mother of the Vasu Ahar. § 116 (Vasu, pl.): I, **66**, 2584.

Rathacakrabhṛt = Vishṇu: V, 3691.

Rathacitrā, a river. § 574 (Jambūkh.): VI, **9**λ, 334.

Rathādhvana = Kumbharetas: III, 14139.

Rathāksha, a warrior of Skanda. § 615*u* (Skanda): IX, **45**η, 2565.

Rathāṅgapāṇī = Vishṇu (1000 names).

Rathantara[1], name of a sāman. § 270 (Brahmasabhāv.): II, **11**, 447 (in the palace of Brahmán).—§ 491 (Āṅgirasa): III, **220**, 14162 (*Bṛhad-R°ṃ*, created from the head of Pāñcajanya).—§ 560 (Sanatsujātap.): V, **44**, †1711 (*R°e Bārhadrathe vā*).—§ 637 (Rājadh.): XII, **47**θ, 1633 (*R°ṃ Bṛhatsāma*, = Kṛshṇa).—§ 693*b* (Vṛtravadha): XII, **282**, 10118 (Vasishṭha restored Indra to his senses with the *R.*, cf. XIV, 311).—§ 695*b* (Dakshayajñavināça): XII, **285**β, †10299 (*°ṃ sāmagāç copagānti*). — § 730*g* (Upamanyu): XIII, **14**ϕ, 875 (*Brahmā . . . R°m udīrayan*). — § 730 (Ānuçāsanik.): XIII, **14**ω, 989 (*°ṃ sāma īrayanti*); **18**, 1317 (*sāmni*).—§ 757*o* (Somapīthin, pl.): XIII, **102**, †4896 (*R°ṃ yatra Bṛhac ca gīyate*).—§ 773*b* (Kṛshṇa Vāsudeva): XIII, **159**, †7369 (*°e sāmagāç ca stuvanti*, sc. *Kṛshṇam*).—§ 779*b* (Vṛtra): XIV, **11**, 311 (Vasishṭha restored Indra to his senses with the *R.*, cf. XII, 10118).

Rathantara[2], name of a fire (?). § 492 (Āṅgirasa): III, **220**, 14174 (son of Tapas).

Rathantarī, wife of Īlina. § 150 (Pūruvaṃç.): I, **94**, 3707 (mother of Dushyanta, etc.).—§ 156 (do.): I, **95**, ††3781 (do.).

Rathaprabhu = Kumbharetas: III, 14139.

Rathasena, a Pāṇḍava warrior. § 592 (Saṃçaptakavadhap.): VII, **23**o, 1009 (proceeded against Droṇa, description of his horses).

Rathasthā, a river. § 221*b* (Gaṅgā): I, **170**, 6455.

Rathātirathasaṅkhyā ("enumeration of the rathas and the great rathas"). § 10 (Parvasaṅgr.): I, **2**, 335 (*parva*, i.e. Rathātirathasaṅkhyānaparvan). — § 589 (Droṇābhishekap.): VII, **1**, 37 (all. to § 572). Cf. next.

Rathātirathasaṅkhyāna (do.). § 11 (Parvasaṅgr.): I, **2**, 516 (i.e. Rathātirathasaṅkhyānaparvan).

[Rathātirathasaṅkhyānaparvan(va)] ("section relating to the enumeration of the *rathas* and the *atirathas*"; the 65th of the minor parvans of the Mhbhr.; cf. Rathātirathasaṅkhyāna). § 572: When *Bhīshma* had obtained the command, he said to *Duryodhana* that he would command worshipping *Kumāra*. He said that he was as well versed in military affairs as *Bṛhaspati*, etc. At the request of *Duryodhana* he enumerated the principal *rathas* and *atirathas* in *Duryodhana's* army (*a*) (V, **165**); continuation (V, **166**); continuation (V, **167**); *Karṇa* he considered only half a *ratha*, at which *Karṇa* was enraged, and said he would not fight before *Bhīshma* was slain. *Bhīshma* rebuked him, but was pacified by *Duryodhana* (V, **168**). At the request of *Duryodhana*, *Bhīshma* enumerated the *rathas* and *atirathas* of the *Pāṇḍavas* (β) (V, **169**). Continuation (V, **170**). Continuation (V, **171**). Continuation. *Bhīshma* would not slay *Çikhaṇḍin* (mentioning the time when *Vicitravīrya* was installed *yuvarāja*, and his own vow not to slay a woman or one who had been a woman), for *Çikhaṇḍin* was formerly a woman; nor would he be able to slay the sons of *Kuntī* (V, **172**).

Rathavāhana, a Pāṇḍava warrior. § 600 (Ghaṭotkacavadhap.): VII, **158**χ, 7012 (brother of Virāṭa?).

Rathāvarta, name of a tīrtha. § 370 (Tīrthayātrāp.): III, **84**, 8001.

Rathayogin = Çiva (1000 names[2]).

Rathin, an ancient king. § 267 (Yamasabhāv.): II, **8**, 324 (in the palace of Yama).

Rathyavirathya = Çiva (1000 names[1]).

Rati[1] ("Delight, Lust," personif.), a goddess, wife of Kāma. § 117 (Aṃçāvat.): I, **66**, 2597 (wife of Kāma).—§ 270 (Brahmasabhāv.): II, **11**, 459 (in the palace of Brahmán).—§ 350 (Nalopākhyānap.): III, **68**, 2665 (*Manmathasya R°īm iva*).

Rati[2], an Apsaras. § 731*b* (Ashṭāvakra-Diksaṃv.): XIII, **19**β, 1425 (danced in the palace of Kubera).

Rati[3] = Çiva (1000 names[2]).

Ratiguṇa, a Devagandharva. § 102 (Aṃçāvat.): I, **65**, 2555 (sixth son of Prādhā).

Ratnagarbha, Ratnanābha = Vishṇu (1000 names).

Ratnaprabhūta = Çiva (1000 names[2]).

Rātri ("Night," personif.). § 135 (Çakuntalop.): I, **74**, 3017.—§ 555 (Indravijaya): V, **13**, 425 (*devīṃ*).—§ 615*u* (Skanda): IX, **45**γ, 2517 (*°y-ahanī*, came to the investiture of Skanda). Cf. Niçā[2].

Raudra[1] ("son of Rudra") = Skanda: I, 5431; III, 14632.

Raudra[2] (do. ?) = Açvatthāman: VII, 9481.

Raudra[3] = Çiva: XIV, 210.

Raudra[4], son of Çukra. § 98 (Aṃçāvat.): I, **65**, 2545 (? *dvau anyau Raudrakarmiṇau*, enumeration of the sons of Çukra).

* **Raudra**[5], adj. ("belonging to Rudra (i.e. Çiva) or to the Rudras"). § 214 (Hiḍimbavadhap.): I, **154**, 6028 (*muhūrte*).—§ 442 (Nivātakavacayuddhap.): III, **167**, 11985 (*mahāstraṃ*, given to Arjuna by Çiva).—§ 445 (do.): III, **173**, 12238 (*mahāstraṃ*, employed by Arjuna), 12240 (*astraṃ*).—§ 496 (Skandotpatti): III, **224**, 14268 (*muhūrte*).—§ 506 (Skandayuddha): III, **231**, 14554 (*chattraṃ*).—§ 524*c* (Vishṇu): III, **272**, 15824 (*sṛjate Brahmamūrtis tu rakshate Paurushī tanuḥ | Raudrībhāvena çamayet tisro 'vasthāḥ Prajāpateḥ*).—§ 552*d* (Arjuna): IV, **61**, 1982 (*astraṃ*, obtained by Arjuna from Çiva).—§ 569 (Bhagavadyānap.): V, **138**, 4683 (*astraṃ*, all. to Nivātakavacay.).—§ 572 (Rathātirathasaṅkhyānap.): V, **169**, 5870 (*astragrāmaḥ*, sc. Arjuna's).—§ 592 (Saṃçaptakavadhap.): VII, **23**ρ, 1041 (sc. *dhanūratnaṃ*), 1042 (*dhanuḥ*, owned by Abhimanyu, who got it from Balarāma). § 598 (Jayadrathavadhap.): VII, **88**, 3123 (*muhūrte*). —§ 603*d* (Tripura): VII, **202**, 9561 (*°ā bhavishyanti paçavaḥ*).—§ 608 (Karṇap.): VIII, **64**, 3237 (*astravegena*, B. *Aindreṇa* for *Raudreṇa*); **82**, †4192 (*muhūrte*); **89**, †4611 (do.); **90**, 4708 (*°mahāstrasambhṛtaṃ*, sc. *mahāçaraṃ*), 4733 (*astraṃ*, employed by Arjuna); **94**, 4920 (*muhūrte*).—§ 615*u* (Skanda): IX, **46**ι, 2654 (*°yaḥ*, sc. *mātaraḥ*).—§ 746 (Ānuçāsanik.): XIII, **77**, 3716 (*tejas*).—§ 747*b* (Suvarṇotpatti): XIII, **85**ζ, 4130 (*°ṃ lohitaṃ*, "the blood of Agni is regarded as the source of the Rudras," PCR.).—§ 773*d* (Çiva): XIII, **161**, 7484 (*°ā bhavishyanti paçavaḥ*).

Raudra, pl., name of a people (BR.). § 785 (Anugītāp.): XIV, **83**, 2476 (*-Andhrairaudrair-*). Cf. Audra, pl.

Raudrāçva, a prince. § 150 (Pūruvaṃç.): I, **94**, 3695 (son of Pūru and Paushṭi), 3698 (begat on Miçrakeçī ten sons, Ṛceyu, etc.).

Raudrakarman, a son of Dhṛtarāshṭra. § 130 (Aṃçāvat.): I, **67**, 2739.—§ 182 (Dhṛtarāshṭraputranāmak.): I, **117**, 4551.—§ 599 (Jayadrathavadhap.): VII, **127**νν, 5178 (attacked Bhīmasena), (ξξ), 5205 (slain by Bhīmasena).

Raudrarūpa = Çiva (1000 names[2]).

Raudrāstra ("the weapon of Rudra"). § 445 (Nivātakavacayuddhap.): III, **173**, 12254 (employed by Arjuna). Cf. Raudra, adj.

Rauhiṇeya ("the son of Rohiṇī[3]") = Balarāma: I, †7148 (*saha-R°*), †7151; II, 622; III, †10268; V, †4 (*saha-R°*), 155, 5338, 5388 (*Vārshṇeyaḥ*); VII, 8220; IX, 1957, 1959, 1964, 1979, 1983, 1994, †2978 (*Keçavapūrvajaḥ*), 3057, 3061, 3104 (*ubhau çishyau gadāyuddhe R°sya*, sc. Duryodhana and Bhīmasena, C. has by error *Ro°*), 3343, 3369.

Rauhiṇinandana (VII, 8222), v. Rohiṇinandana.

Raukmiṇeya = Pradyumna, q.v.

Raumya, pl. (*°āḥ*), a class of beings. § 695*b* (Dakshayajñavināça): XII, **285**, 10308 (*°ān nāma gaṇeçvarān*, created by Çiva from the pores of his body—*romakūpebhyaḥ*).

Raupyā, name of a river. § 409 (Plakshāvataraṇagamana): III, **129**, 10519 (there Jamadagni practised austerities).

Raurava, name of a hell. § 756 (Ānuçāsanik.): XIII, **101**, 4825.

Rāvaṇa, king of the Rākshasas on Laṅkā, son of Viçravas (Pulastya) (originally named Daçagrīva). § 11 (Parvasaṅgr.): I, **2**, 475 (*Rāmeṇa . . . nihato R°aḥ*, cf. Rāmopākhyānaparvan).—§ 383 (Paraçu-Rāma): III, **99**, 8657 (Vishṇu was born as Rāma Dāçarathi in order to slay *R.*).—§ 425 (Hanūmad-Bhīmasenasaṃv.): III, **147**, 11199 (*Rākshasendreṇa*, had ravished Sītā); **148**, 11205, 11208, 11212 (*lokarāvaṇaḥ*, the contents of Rāmopākhyānaparvan briefly narrated).—§ 430 (do.): III, **150**, 11279, 11281, 11283.—§ 525 (Rāmopākhyānap.): III, **274**, 15873 (*Rākshasendreṇa*, had ravished Sītā), 15875, 15881, 15882 (grandson of Brahmán and son of Pulastya (in the form of Viçravas)).—§ 526 (do.): III, **275**, [15895 (*Rākshasendrau Kumbhakarṇa-Daçagrīvau*, sons of Viçravas and Pushpotkaṭā), 15898 (*Daçagrīvaḥ . . . Rākshasendraḥ*), (β), 15904 (*Daçagrīvaḥ*, lived upon air alone amidst five fires, standing on one leg during 1,000 years)], (γ), (15913) (Brahmán gave back to *R.* his heads which he had cut off and offered to the fire and granted him that he should be able to assume any form at will and never experience defeat at the hands of *Gandharvas*, gods, *Kinnaras*, *Asuras*, *Yakshas*, *Rākshasas*, Serpents, and *Bhūtas* (but only from men whom he despised)), 15922 (defeated Kubera and obtained the sovereignty of Laṅkā and the *vimāna* of Kubera, named Pushpaka; Kubera cursed *R.*), 15928 (installed as king of the Rākshasas and the Piçācas, etymology of the name *R.*).—§ 528 (Rāvaṇagamana): III, **277**, 15990, 15991 (Çūrpaṇakhā excited Rāvaṇa to take vengeance on Rāma Dāçarathi, *R.* sought the assistance of Mārīca).—§ 529 (Sītāharaṇa): III, **278**, 16001, 16005, 16006, 16008, 16015, 16016, 16031, 16035 (*Rākshasarājaḥ*), 16042 (in the shape of a mendicant *R.* ravished Sītā).—§ 530 (Viçvāvasumokshaṇa): III, **279**, 16046 (*Rākshaseçvaraṃ*, slew Jaṭāyus), 16066, 16067, 16087 (*Laṅkānivāsinā*), 16091.—§ 531 (Rāmopākhyānap.): III, **280**, 16097.—§ 532 (Sītāsāntvana): III, **280**, 16133, 16151 (*b*: *R.* had been cursed by *Nalakūbara* for having violated *Rambhā*: he would not be able to violate any woman by force).—§ 533 (Sītā-Rāvaṇasaṃv.): III, **281**, 16167 (*b*: *R.* was the conqueror of the gods, *Dānavas*, *Gandharvas*, *Yakshas*, and *Kimpurushas*, he looked like the *kalpavṛksha* of *Indra* and like *Çanaiçcara* when approaching *Rohiṇī*. He possessed many daughters of the gods and the *Gandharvas*, of the *Dānavas* and the *Daityas*. He ruled 140 millions of *Piçācas*, twice as many man-eating *Rākshasas* and thrice as many *Yakshas* (some are under the sway of *Kubera*), in his drinking-hall *Gandharvas* and *Apsarases* wait upon him (as upon *Kubera*), he was the son of the ṛshi *Viçravas*, his queen was *Mandodarī*), 16191.—§ 534 (Hanūmatpratyāgamana): III, **282**, 16220, 16252, 16256.—§ 535 (Setubandhana): III, **283**, 16320 (°*āmatyau* . . . *Çuka-Sāraṇau*), 16322.—§ 536 (Laṅkāpraveça): III, **284**, 16324 (fortified Laṅkā), 16339.—§ 537 (Rāma-Rāvaṇayuddha): III, **285**, 16364 (*R°ānugāḥ*), 16368, 16371, 16375 (fought with Rāma Dāçarathi).—§ 538 (Kumbhakarṇaraṇagamana): III, **286**, 16387 (*Rāma-R°-sainyānāṃ*), 16395, 16396 (roused his brother Kumbhakarṇa and caused him to set out for battle).—§ 540 (Indrajidyuddha): III, **288**, 16439 (father of Indrajit).—§ 541 (Indrajidvadha): III, **289**, 16489, 16490, 16496 (Indrajit is slain).—§ 542 (Rāvaṇavadha): III, **290**, 16502, 16512, 16513 (*māyā* . . . *Rāvaṇasya*), 16515, 16526 (°*āntakaraṃ*, sc. *çaraṃ*), 16528 (*nihataṃ*, Rāma slew *R.*).—§ 543 (Rāmarājyābhisheka): III, **291**, 16531 (*hatvā R°ṃ Rākshasendraṃ*, sc. *Rāmaḥ*).—§ 565 (Gālavacarita): V, **109**, 3790 (*atra*—i.e. in the south—*Rākshasarājena Paulastyena mahātmanā R°ena tapaç cartvā surebhyo 'maratā vṛtā*).—§ 592 (Saṃçaptakavadhap.): VII, **23**π, 1037 (*açvāç ca kāmagās tasya R°sya yathā purā*).—§ 595 (Shoḍaçarāj., v. Rāma Dāçarathi): VII, **59**, 2227 (*Rākshasaḥ*, all. to Rāmopākhyānaparvan).—§ 599 (Jayadrathavadhap.): VII, **96**, 3569 (*yādṛçaṃ* . . . *Rāma-R°yor mṛdhe*); **106**, 3981 (*yādṛk* . . . *purā vṛttaṃ Rāma-R°yoḥ*).—§ 600 (Ghaṭotkacavadhap.): VII, **181**, 8236 (°*ena samaprāṇāḥ*, sc. *Hiḍimba-Baka-Kirmīrāḥ*).—§ 604 (Karṇap.): VIII, **5**ζ, 143 (*yathā Rāmeṇa R°ḥ*, sc. *nihataḥ*).—§ 612 (Hradapraveçap.): IX, **31**, 1752 (*Paulastyatanayo R°o nāma Rākshasaḥ Rāmeṇa nihataḥ*).—§ 615 (Gadāyuddhap.): IX, **55**, 3107 (*sadṛçakarmāṇau* . . . *Rāma-R°yoḥ*, sc. Bhimasena and Duryodhana).—§ 717*b* (Nārāyaṇīya): XII, **340**, 12953 (*tato Rakshaḥpatiṃ ghoraṃ Pulastyakulapāṃsanaṃ hanishye*—sc. incarnate as Rāma Dāçarathi—*R°ṃ raudraṃ sagaṇam lokakaṇṭakaṃ*, says Nārāyaṇa).

Cf. also the following synonyms:—

Daçagrīva ("having ten necks"): III, 15895 (*Kumbhakarṇa-D°au*), 15898, 15904, 15915, 15920, 15927, 15928, 15930, 16011, 16304, 16400, 16498, 16501, 16515, 16519, 16521, 16532, 16535, 16612, 17467; VII, 6827 (°*samaḥ*, sc. Ghaṭotkaca); XII, 13878.

Daçakandhara (do.): III, 16516.

Daçānana ("having ten faces"): III, 15908, 15999, 16000, 16370, 16505.

Daçāsya (do.): III, 11324.

Paulastya, Paulastyatanaya, q.v.

Rakshaḥpati ("lord of the Rakshases"): XII, 12952.

Rakshas, Rākshasa, Rākshasādhipa, Rākshasādhipati, Rākshasaçreshṭha, Rākshasamaheçvara, Rākshasapati, Rākshasapuṅgava, Rākshasarāja, Rākshaseçvara, Rākshasendra, q.v.

Rāvaṇagamana ("the expedition of Rāvaṇa"). § 528: Fearing intrusion by the people of Ayodhyā, *Rāma Dāçarathi* went away to the wood and visited the hermitage of *Çarabhaṅga*; then he entered the forest of *Daṇḍaka* (*Daṇḍakāraṇyaṃ*) on the river *Godāvarī*, where he, on account of *Çūrpaṇakhā*, had hostilities with *Khara*, and then dwelling in *Janasthāna* slew 14,000 Rākshasas together with *Khara* and *Dūshaṇa*. *Çūrpaṇakhā* with mutilated nose and lips repaired to *Rāvaṇa* on *Laṅkā*. *Rāvaṇa* crossed the *Trikūṭa* and *Kāla* mountains and arrived at *Gokarṇa* (the favourite resort of *Çiva*) where he met *Mārīca* (*b*) (III, **277**).

Ravaṇātmaja ("the son of Rāvaṇa") = Indrajit: III, 16453, 16457.

Rāvaṇavadha ("the killing of Rāvaṇa"). § 542: *Rāvaṇa* with the *Rākshasas* rushed towards *Rāma* and the monkeys (*a*); *Rāvaṇa* from his body created thousands of *Rākshasas*, whom *Rāma* slew with a celestial weapon. Then *Rāvaṇa* produced *Rākshasas*, resembling *Rāma* and *Lakshmaṇa*, whom *Rāma* slew. *Mātali* came with the chariot of *Indra*, *Rāma* thought it to be an illusion, but was reassured by *Vibhīshaṇa*, and riding in that chariot he killed *Rāvaṇa* with an arrow which he had consecrated with mantras as a *Brahmāstra*. The gods, the *Gandharvas*, *Indra*, the *Dānavas*, the *Kinnaras*, and the *Cāraṇas* rejoiced (III, **290**).

Rāvaṇi ("the son of Rāvaṇa") = Indrajit: III, 16449, 16460, 16463, 16465, 16484; VII, 4065 (*yodhayām āsa* . . . *Lakshmaṇaṃ R°r yathā*), 5888 (*yathā Rāmānujenājau R°ir Lakshmaṇena ha*, sc. *nihataḥ*).

***Ravi** [1] = Sūrya ("the Sun"): I, 42 (a form or son of Vivasvat, cf. Āçāvaha), 419, 1274; II, 790 (°-*Somāgnivapushāṃ*); III, 136, 138, 146 (Sūrya's 108 names), 192, 8437 (*yathā cāpy Angirā R°ṃ tathā rakshasva*); VI, 4566 (*dudruvuḥ* . . . . *grahāḥ pañca R°ṃ yathā*); XII, 440, 11732; XV, 826; XVIII, 167 (after death Karṇa entered *R.*).

Ravi [2], one of the standard-bearers of Jayadratha. § 522 (Draupadīharaṇap.): III, **265**, 15598.

Ravi [3], a son of Dhṛtarāshṭra. § 611 (Çalyap.): IX, **26**ρρ, 1404, 1414 (among eleven sons of Dhṛtarāshṭra, who are slain by Bhimasena).

Ravi [4] = Çiva (1000 names [2]). Do. [5] = Vishṇu (1000 names).

Ravilocana = Vishṇu (1000 names).

Ravisūnu ("the son of Ravi [i.e. the Sun]") = Karṇa, q.v.

Ravitanaya (do.) = Karṇa: VIII, †1213.

Recaka, pl. (°*āḥ*), a people. § 578 (Bhīshmavadhap.): VI, **51**π, 2097 (only C., B. has *Ārocakāḥ*, in the army of Duryodhana).

Reṇuka [1], a Nāga (?) (according to Nīl., a Yaksha). § 46 (Garuḍa): I, **32**, 1488 (had an encounter with Garuḍa).

Reṇuka [2], name of an elephant (?). § 766 (Ānuçāsanik.): XIII, **132**, 6156 (*nāgo Rasātalacaraḥ*), 6158, 6159, (6160), 6172 (questioned the *diggajas*).

Reṇukā, wife of Jamadagni. § 396 (Jamadagni): III, **116**, 10172 (daughter of Prasenajit), 10173, 10175, 10176, 10177 (mother of five sons, of whom Rāma was the youngest; fell in love with Citraratha, therefore Jamadagni ordered his sons to slay her; Rāma cut off her head with his axe, but afterwards she was revived).—§ 565 (Gālavacarita): V, **117**, 3972 (*reme* . . . *R°āyāṃ yathārcīkaḥ*, i.e. Jamadagni).—§ 762*b* (Chattropānahotpatti): XIII, **95**, 4607, 4610, 4615, (4616), 4618 (Sūrya gave to Jamadagni an umbrella and a pair of sandals for the use of *R.*).

Reṇukāsuta ("the son of Reṇukā") = Rāma Jāmadagnya: III, 8658 (*R°*).

Reṇukātīrtha, name of a tīrtha. § 368 (Tīrthayātrāp.): III, **83**, 7030. Cf. next.

Reṇukāyās tīrtha(m), name of a tīrtha. § 358 (Tīrthayātrāp.): III, **82**, 5024. Cf. the prec.

Reṇupa, pl. (°*āḥ*), a people. § 569 (Bhagavadyānap.): V, **140**β, 4751 (only C., B. has *Veṇupāḥ*).

Revata[1], a mountain (?) in Çākadvīpa. § 575*b* (Çākadvīpa): VI, **11**β, 426 (= Raivataka (v. 418)?).

Revata[2], an ancient king. § 775 (Ānuçāsanik.): XIII, **166**η, 7679 (only C., B. has *Raivataḥ*).

Revata[3], adj., v. Raivata.

Revatī[1], wife of Balarāma. § 252 (Subhadrāharaṇap.): I, **219**, 7912 (*Haladharaḥ . . . R°sahitaḥ*).

Revatī[2], name of a demon of disease. § 502 (Manushyagrahak.): III, **230**, 14482 (= *Aditi*, from *R.* originates the graha Raivata).

Revatī[3], name of a nakshatra (v. Su. Si.). § 562 (Bhagavadyānap.): V, **83**, 2926 (°*yām*).—§ 575*b* (Çākadvīpa): VI, **11**, 419 (placed over the mountain Raivataka).—§ 746 (Ānuçāsanik.): XIII, **64***a*, 3284 (result of making gifts under the constellation of *R.*).—§ 749 (do.): XIII, **89***a*, 4268 (result of performing çrāddhas under the constellation of *R.*).—§ 759 (do.); XIII, **110**, 5391 (description of the cāndravrata).

Revatīsuta ("the son of Revatī[2]") = Skanda: III, 14633.

Rishṭa, an ancient king. § 267 (Yamasabhāv.): II, **8**, 326 (in the palace of Yama).

Rocamāna[1], name of several princes. § 130 (Aṃçāvat.): I, **67**, 2654 (incarnation of the Asura Açvagrīva).—§ 232 (Svayaṃvarap.): I, **186**, 6990 (present at the svayaṃvara of Draupadī).—§ 279 (Arjuna): II, **27**, 1027 (*Urugāvāsinam*, in the north, vanquished by Arjuna).—§ 280 (Bhīmasena): II, **29**, 1066 (*Açvamedheçvaram*, in the east, vanquished by Bhīmasena).—§ 554 (Sainyodyogap.): V, **4**γ, 75 (among the princes to whom the Pāṇḍavas ought to send messengers).—§ 572 (Rathātirathasaṅkhyānap.): V, **172**, 5921 (a mahāratha in the army of Yudhishṭhira).—§ 592 (Saṃçaptakavadhap.): VII, **23**ο, 996 (proceeded against Droṇa, description of his horses), 1014 (°*sya sutam*, do.).—§ 608 (Karṇap.): VIII, **56**νν, 2736, 2740 (a Pāñcāla, slain by Karṇa).

Rocamāna[2], dual (°*au*). § 604 (Karṇap.): VIII, **6**, 170 (have been slain by Droṇa).

Rocamānā, a mātṛ. § 615*u* (Skanda): IX, **46**θ, 2647.

Rocanāmukha, a Daitya. § 564 (Mātalīyop.): V, **105**δ, 3685 (had been slain by Garuḍa).

Rohī, a river. § 574 (Jambūkh.): VI, **9**λ, 338.

Rohiṇeya, v. Rauhiṇeya.

Rohiṇī[1]. § 127 (Aṃçāvat.): I, **66**, 2631 (daughter of Surabhi), 2632 (mother of the kine).

Rohiṇī[2], daughter of Daksha and wife of Soma (the Moon), also name of a nakshatra (v. Sū. Si.). § 210 (Jatugṛhap.): I, **145**, 5767 (°*yām*, i.e. the nakshatra).—§ 240 (Vaivāhikap.): I, **199**, 7351 (°*ī ca yathā Some*).—§ 298 (Dyūtap.): II, **58**, 2019 (*saṃvṛtām . . . tārābhir iva R°m*).—§ 350 (Nalopākhyānap.): III, **68**, 2676 (°*ī Çaçino yathā*).—§ 382 (Agastyop.): III, **96**, 8566 (°*īva divi prabhā*).—§ 391 (Ṛshyaçṛnga): III, **113**, †10091 (°*ī Somam ivānukūlā*).—§ 502 (Manushyagrahak.): III, **230**, 14461 (*Abhijit . . . R°yāḥ kanīyasī svasā*), 14463 (*Dhanishṭhādis tathā kālo Brahmaṇā parikalpitaḥ | R°ī hy abhavat pūrvam, evam saṃkhyā samā 'bhavat*).—§ 533 (Sītā-Rāvaṇasaṃv.): III, **281**, 16171 (°*īm etya Çanaiçcara iva grahaḥ*).—§ 549 (Pāṇḍavapraveçap.): IV, **9**, 258 (Sudeshṇā asks Draupadī if she is *R.*).—§ 565 (Gālavacarita): V, **117**, 3968 (*reme . . . yathā Candraç ca R°yām*).—§ 574 (Jambūkh.): VI, **2**, 66 (°*īm pīḍayann esha sthitaḥ . . . Çanaiçcaraḥ*, omens); **3**, 84 (°*īm pīḍayantau . . . Çaçi-Bhāskarau*, omens).—§ 608 (Karṇap.): VIII, **94**, †4945 (*Bṛhaspatiḥ samparivārya R°m*, omens).—§ 615 (Prabhāsotpattik.): IX, **35**, 2015, 2017, 2018, 2023, 2026, 2028 (the most beautiful of the twenty-seven daughters of Daksha, whom Soma married. As Soma stayed a long time with *R.*, his other wives complained to Daksha, who then cursed Soma).—§ 656 (Khaḍgotpattik.): XII, **166**, 6202 (°*īm gotram āsthāpya*, sc. of the sword).—§ 717*b* (Nārāyaṇīya): XII, **343**, XI), ††13219 (cf. § 615).—§ 746 (Ānuçāsanik.): XIII, **64***a*, 3257 (results of making gifts under the constellation of *R.*).—§ 749 (do.): XIII, **89***a*, 4257 (result of performing çrāddhas under the constellation of *R.*).—§ 759 (do.): XIII, **110**, 5389 (description of the cāndravrata).—§ 766 (do.): XIII, **126**, 6052 (*yadā yujyeta R°ī*).—§ 768*b* (Umā-Maheçvarasaṃv.): XIII, **146**γ, 6751 (*Çaçinaḥ sādhvī*).

Rohiṇī[3], wife of Vasudeva. § 238 (Pañcendrop.): I, **197**, 7308 (Vishṇu's white hair was born by Rohiṇī as Balarāma).—§ 793 (Mausalap.): XVI, **7**, 194 (together with the other wives of Vasudeva she ascended his funeral pyre).

Rohiṇī[4], daughter of Hiraṇyakaçipu. § 493 (Āṅgirasa): III, **221**, 14194 (*Hiraṇyakaçipoḥ sutā*; PCR. follows Nīl., who seems to take Hiraṇyakaçipu = Manu (the fire), who marries his own daughter *R.* = Svishṭakṛt).

Rohiṇinandana ("the son of Rohiṇī[3]") = Balarāma: VII, 8222 (C. by error *Rauh°*).

Rohiṇīsuta (do.) = Balarāma: VII, 1042; IX, 2128.

Rohita[1] = Çiva (1000 names[1]). — Do.[2] = Vishṇu (1000 names).

Rohitaka, name of a country (?).—§ 285 (Nakula): II, **32**, 1186 (*Kārttikeyasya dayitam*, in the west, conquered by Nakula).

Rohitaka, pl. (°*āḥ*), a people. § 515 (Karṇadigvijaya): III, **254**, 15256 (vanquished by Karṇa on his *digvijaya*).

Rohitakāraṇya, name of a forest. § 555 (Sainyodyogap.): V, **19**, 599 (covered by the army of the Kurus).

Romaça, pl. (°*āḥ*), a people. § 295 (Dyūtap.): II, **51**, 1850 (brought tribute to Yudhishṭhira).

Romaharsha = Lomaharshaṇa. § 707 (Mokshadh.): XII, **319**, 11744 (°*eṇa Purāṇam avadhāritam*).

Romaka, pl. (°*āḥ*), a people. § 295 (Dyūtap.): II, **51**, 1837 (brought tribute to Yudhishṭhira).

Roman, pl. (°*āṇaḥ*), a people. § 574 (Jambūkh.): VI, **9**μ, 363 (in Bhāratavarsha).

Rosha ("Wrath," personif.). § 565 (Gālavacarita): V, **111**, 3830 (in the north).

Ruci[1], a son of Viçvāmitra. § 721*b* (Viçvāmitrop.): XIII, **4**β, 251 (only C., B. has *ṛshiḥ*).

Ruci[2], an Apsaras. § 731*b* (Ashṭavakra-Dikṣaṃv.): XIII, **19**β, 1121 (danced in the palace of Kubera).

Ruci[3], wife of Devaçarman. § 743*b* (Vipulop.): XIII, **40**, 2263, 2269, 2286, 2291; **41**, 2310; **42**, 2347 (°*yā bhaginyā*), 2350, 2352, 2354, 2373; **43**, 2378 (Vipula protected *R.* against Indra).

Ruciparvan, a Pāṇḍava warrior, son of Kṛti(n). § 592 (Saṃçaptakavadhap.): VII, **26**, 1177 (*Kṛtīsutaḥ*), 1178 (slain by Bhagadatta).

Ruciprabha, a Daitya (?). § 673*b* (Bali-Vāsavasaṃv.): XII, **227**, 8264 (among the ancient rulers of the earth).

Rucirāṅgada = Vishṇu (1000 names).

Rudra, pl. (°*āḥ*), a class of gods, followers of Çiva (Rudra). § 44 (Garuḍa): I, **30**, 1416.—§ 46 (do.): I, **32**, 1486.—§ 106 (Aṃçāvat.): I, **65**, 2562 (°*āṇām*, sc. *sambhavaḥ*).—§ 108 (do.): I, **66**, 2567 (eleven sons of Sthāṇu, viz. *Mṛgavyādha, Sarpa, Nirṛti, Ajaikapād, Ahirbudhnya, Pinākin, Dahana, Īçvara, Kapālin, Sthāṇu, Bhaga*).—§ 120 *bis* (do.):

I, **66,** 2602 (°*āṇām pakshaḥ*).—§ 130 (do.): I, **67,** 2712 (°*āṇām gaṇāt*, Kṛpa was born from the *R.*).—§ 191 (Arjuna): I, **123,** 4826 (present at the birth of Arjuna, their names as in § 108).—§ 233 (Svayamvarap.): I, **187,** 7010 (°*ādityāḥ*, present at the svayaṃvara of Draupadī).—§ 238 (Pañcendrop.): I, **197,** †7277, †7315.—§ 258 (Khāṇḍavadahanap.): I, **227,** 8269 (fought with Kṛshṇa and Arjuna).—§ 270 (Brahmasabhāv.): II, **11,** 460 (in the palace of Brahmán).—§ 309 (Āraṇyakap.): III, **2,** 127.—§ 310*b* (Sūrya): III, **3,** 174 (worship the Sun), 190 (Sūrya identified with the *R.*).—§ 330 (Indradarçanap.): III, **37,** 1490.—§ 331 (Kairātap.): III, **39,** 1590 (sg., = Çiva?). — § 336 (Indralokābhigamanap.): III, **43,** 1768.—§ 338 (do.): III, **46,** 1840.—§ 347 (Nalopākhyānap.): III, **62,** 2356.—§ 357 (Pushkara): III, **82,** 4064 (in Pushkara).—§ 359 (Vaḍavā): III, **82,** 5037 (worshipped Kṛshṇa at Vaḍavā).—§ 360 (Tīrthayātrāp.): III, **82,** 5063 (?in Rudrakoṭi Çiva had multiplied himself into a *koṭi* of forms—*koṭīti R°āṇām*—for the sake of the munis).—§ 370 (do.): III, **84,** 8102 (adore Janārdana at *sthānaṃ Nārāyaṇasya*).—§ 383 (Paraçu-Rāma): III, **99,** 8673 (seen in the body of Rāma Dāçarathi, the incarnate Vishṇu).—§ 412 (Ashṭāvakrīya): III, **134,** †10668 (eleven in number).—§ 443 (Nivātakavacayuddhap.): III, **168,** 12043.—§ 459 (Mārkaṇḍeyas.): III, **188,** 12924 (seen in the body of Nārāyaṇa).—§ 506 (Skandayuddha): III, **231,** 14549.—§ 512 (Ghoshayātrāp.): III, **237,** 14782 (°*air iva Yamaḥ* (sic!), sc. *vṛtaḥ*).—§ 547 (Karṇa): III, **308,** 17139.—§ 548 (Āraṇeyap.): III, **313,** 17317; **314,** 17421.—§ 549*c* (Arjuna): IV, **2,** 48 (*dvādaçaṃ R°āṇām*, sc. Arjuna).—§ 556 (Sañjayayānap.): V, **29,** †823 (°*ādityāḥ*).—§ 562 (Bhagavadyānap.): V, **86,** 3043 (*yathā*).—§ 567 (do.): V, **128***ι*, 4301; **131,** 4420.—§ 572 (Rathātirathasaṅkhyānap.): V, **169,** 5865 (°*vat*).—§ 576 (Bhagavadgītāp.): VI, **34,** 1227 (°*āṇāṃ Çaṅkaraç cāsmi*, says Kṛshṇa); **35,** 1252 (seen in Kṛshṇa), †1268 (do.).—§ 589 (Droṇābhishekap.): VII, **6,** 159 (°*āṇām iva Kāpālī*, sc. *senāpatiḥ*).—§ 592 (Saṃçaptakavadhap.): VII, **23***o*, 1007 (*Samudrasenaputram R°tejasaṃ*, sg.?); **35,** 1536 (*Sādhya - R° - Marutkalpaiḥ*). — § 596 (Pratijñāp.): VII, **76,** 2682 (in Arjuna's oath).—§ 605 (Karṇap.): VIII, **15,** 597 (°*au dvāv iva*).—§ 608 (do.): VIII, **87***χ*, 4418 (sided with Arjuna).—§ 615*u* (Skanda): IX, **44,** 2479 (°*ādityāḥ*); **45***γ*, 2508 (came to the investiture of Skanda), 2555 (made gifts to Skanda).—§ 615*ff* (Asita Devala): IX, **50,** 2893 (°*āṇāṃ . . . sthānaṃ*).—§ 626 (Rājadh.): XII, **21***β*, 634.—§ 641 (do.): XII, **64***η*, 2395 (observe kshatriya duties); **122,** 4498 (°*āṇām api ceçānaṃ*—i.e. Çiva—*goptāraṃ*), 4502 (*īçvaraḥ . . . sarveshām eva R°āṇāṃ Çūlapāṇiḥ*, i.e. Çiva).—§ 656 (Khaḍgotpattik.): XII, **166***β*, 6141.—§ 661 (Mokshadh.): XII, **198***a*, 7192 (°*āditya-Vasūnāṃ*, sc. *sthānāni*).—§ 664 (do.): XII, **207***ε*, 7540 (sons of Dharma?).—[§ 665 (do.): XII, **208,** 7585 foll. (The names here enumerated, viz. *Ajaikapād, Ahirbradhna, Virūpāksha, Raivata, Hara, Bahurūpa, Tryambaka, Sureçvara, Sāvitra, Jayanta, Pinākin*, seem to be quoted in order to give a list of the Rudras.)]—§ 673*b* (Bali-Vāsavasaṃv.): XII, **227,** 8220 (accompanied Indra), 8288 (had been vanquished by Bali).—§ 695*b* (Dakshayajñavināça): XII, **285***a*, 10279 (present at Daksha's sacrifice), 10292 (*çūlahastāḥ kapardinaḥ* | *ekādaçasthānagatāḥ*). — § 696*b* (Dakshaprokta-Çivasahasranāmastotra): XII, **285,** 10456 (description).—§ 702 (Mokshadh.): XII, **296***β*, 10837.—§ 712 (Çukotpatti): XII, **324,** 12175.—§ 717*b* (Nārāyaṇīya): XII, **340***θ*, 12915 (*ekādaça*), **341,** 13043 (*ekādaçaite R°ās tu vikārāḥ purushāḥ smṛtāḥ*), 13044, 13110 (°*āṇāṃ pataye*, sc. Vishṇu).—§ 730*g* (Upamanyu): XIII, **14***η*, 731 (°*ādityāçvinām*), 910 (°*āṇāṃ Nīlalohitaḥ*, sc. Çiva).—§ 730 (Ānuçāsanik.): XIII, **14,** 984 (*ekādaça çatāni*, surround Çiva); **17,** 1141 (°*āṇām api yo Rudraḥ*, i.e. Çiva), 1288 (learnt the 1000 names of Çiva from Mṛtyu and communicated them to Taṇḍi(n)); **18***λλ*, †1368.—§ 747*b* (Suvarṇotpatti): XIII, **84,** 4011; **85***ζ*, 4131 (together with the Ādityas the *R.* sprung from the flames of Agni).—§ 759 (Ānuçāsanik.): XIII, **107***ε*, 5257 (°*āṇāṃ tam adhīvāsaṃ*), (*ζ*), 5331 (°*āṇāṃ lokaṃ*).—§ 766 (do.): XIII, **134***γ*, 6186.—§ 770 (do.): XIII, **151***β*, 7091 (*ekādaça*, their names are the following: *Ajaikapād, Ahirbradhna, Pinākin, Ṛta, Pitṛrūpa, Tryambaka, Maheçvara, Vṛshākapi, Çambhu, Havana*, and *Īçvara*).—§ 773*b* (Kṛshṇa Vāsudeva): XIII, **159***β*, 7387 (°*ādityāḥ*).—§ 775 (Ānuçāsanik.): XIII, **166***a*, 7642.—§ 778*f* (Muñjavat): XIV, **8,** 183 (worship Çiva on Muñjavat).—§ 784*b* (Uttaṅka): XIV, **54,** 1564.—§ 793 (Mausalap.): XVI, **4***θ*, 129 (°*ādityāḥ*, received Kṛshṇa in heaven).—§ 795 (Svargārohaṇap.): XVIII, **3,** 88.

Rudra[2] = Çiva, q.v.—Do.[3] = Sūrya: III, 148.—Do.[4] = Vishṇu (1000 names).

Rudragarbha = Agni, q.v.

Rudraja ("born from Rudra") = Açvatthāman: XV, 858 (*Drauṇiṃ*).

Rudrakoṭi, name of two tīrthas. § 360 (Tīrthayātrāp.): III, **82,** 5060, 5066.—§ 364 (do.): III, **83,** 6047.

Rudraloka ("the world of the Rudras or of Rudra [i.e. Çiva]"). § 368 (Tīrthayātrāp.): III, **83,** 7050 (by bathing in Sthāṇuvaṭa one attains to *R.*).—§ 603 (Nārāyaṇāstramokshap.): VII, **202,** 9641 (one attains to *R.* by hearing the *Çatarudriya*).—§ 759 (Ānuçāsanik.): XIII, **107***ζ*, 5304.

Rudramārga, name of a tīrtha. § 368 (Tīrthayātrāp.): III, **83,** 7052 (only B., C. has *Indramārgaṃ*).

Rudra(m) pada(m), name of a tīrtha. § 360 (Tīrthayātrāp.): III, **82,** 5042 (PCR. *Raudrapada*).

Rudrāṇī = Umā, q.v.

Rudrapatnī ("the wife of Rudra (Çiva)") = Umā: III, 7041.

Rudraromā, a mātṛ. § 615*u* (Skanda): IX, **46***θ*, 2625.

Rudrasena, a Pāṇḍava warrior. § 600 (Ghaṭotkacavadhap.): VII, **158***χ*, 7009.

Rudrāstra ("the weapon of Rudra (Çiva)"). § 616 (Sauptikap.): X, **8,** 352 (Açvatthāman slew the Pāñcālas with the *R.*).

Rudrasūnu ("the son of Rudra (Çiva)") = Skanda: III, 14428, 14430, 14431, 14432.

Rudrasya tīrthaṃ ("the tīrtha of Rudra"). § 360 (Tīrthayātrāp.): III, **82,** 5047 (*Kāmākhyaṃ*).

Rudrātman = Kṛshṇa: XII, 1669.

Rudrāvarta, name of a tīrtha. § 370 (Tīrthayātrāp.): III, **84,** 8015.

Rudravaṭa, name of a tīrtha. § 358 (Tīrthayātrāp.): III, **82,** 4092 (only C., B. has *Bhadravaṭaṃ*).

Rukma, a prince. § 233 (Svayaṃvarap.): I, **188,** †7051. Cf. the foll.

Rukmāṅgada, a prince. § 232 (Svayaṃvarap.); I, **186,** 6994 (son of Çalya(?), present at the svayaṃvara of Draupadī).—§ 599 (Jayadrathavadhap.): VII, **116***aa*, 4610 (fought with Sātyaki).

Rukmaratha[1], son of Çalya. § 232 (Svayaṃvarap.): I, **186,** 6994 (?present at the svayaṃvara of Draupadī).—§ 578 (Bhīshmavadhap.): VI, **47,** 1857 (only B., C. has

Çvetaratham), 1858 (fought with Çveta).—§ 593 (Abhimanyu-vadhap.): VII, **45**, 1811 (*Madreçvarasutaḥ*), 1816 (*putraṃ Çalyasya*, slain by Abhimanyu).—§ 604 (Karṇap.): VIII, **5**ζ, 116 (*Çalyaputraḥ*, had been slain by Sahadeva).

Rukmaratha[2] ("having a golden chariot") = Droṇa: IV, 1824; VII, 253, 256, 268, [279], 283, 488, 496, 4675, 8901, 8911; VIII, 94 (*D*°).—Do.[3] (do.) = Suçarman: IV, 1059; VII, 4554 (?).—Do.[4] (do.) = Virāṭa: V, †784.

Rukmaratha, pl. (°*āḥ*), a host of Kuru warriors. § 599 (Jayadrathavadhap.): VII, **112**, 4310 (*mahārathāḥ*, commanded by Karṇa).

Rukmavāhana ("having a golden chariot") = Droṇa: VII, 8943.

Rukmin, king of Bhojakaṭa, son of Bhīshmaka, and brother of Rukmiṇī. § 130 (Aṃçāvat.): I, **67**, 2698 (incarnation of the Krodhavaça gaṇa). — § 284 (Sahadeva): II, **31**, 1168 (*rājñe Bhojakaṭasya*, Sahadeva caused *R.* to pay tribute to Yudhishṭhira).—§ 289 (Arghāharaṇap.): II, **37**, 1351.—§ 290 (Çiçupālavadhap.): II, **44***a*, 1536 (*purushottamam*).—§ 317*b* (Kṛshṇa Vāsudeva): III, **12**, 490 (*avāpsīr mahishīṃ Bhojyāṃ*—i.e. Rukmiṇī—*raṇe nirjitya R°am*, sc. Kṛshṇa, cf. § 570*d*). — § 515 (Karṇadigvijaya): III, **254**, 15247 (*Dākshiṇātyeshu*), 15248, 15250 (vanquished by Karṇa on his digvijaya).—§ 554 (Sainyodyogap.): V, **4**γ, 79 (among the princes to whom the Pāṇḍavas ought to send messengers).—§ 561*g* (Sahadeva): V, **50**, 1999 (equal to Sahadeva in strength).—§ 570*d* (cf. Sainyaniryāṇap.): *R.* was a disciple of *Druma*, that lion among the *Kimpurushas* on the mountain of *Gandhamādana*. He had obtained from his preceptor the whole fourfold (*catushpādam*) *Dhanurveda* and the celestial bow *Vijaya*, belonging to the great *Indra*, and equal to the *Gāṇḍīva* (*e*) and the *Çārṅga* (*f*). When he obtained *Vijaya* from *Druma*, *R.* came to the *Pāṇḍavas*. Formerly when *Kṛshṇa* had ravished his sister *Rukmiṇī*, he set out in pursuit having sworn that he would not return without having slain *Kṛshṇa*. But he was vanquished and did not return to [his city] *Kuṇḍina*; on the spot where he was vanquished he built the city of *Bhojakaṭa*: V, **158**, 5351 (*Āhukānām adhipatiḥ Bhojasya yaçasvinaḥ* | *Dākshiṇātyapateḥ sutaḥ*), 5356, 5359.—§ 570 (Sainyaniryāṇap.): V, **158**, 5385, 5388 (rejected by Arjuna and by Duryodhana he did not take part in the battle).—§ 592 (Saṃçaptakavadhap.): VII, **23**ο, 1017 (*astraiḥ samatvaṃ samprāpya R°-Karṇārjunācyutaiḥ*, sc. the Pāṇḍya king Sāraṅgadhvaja).—§ 621 (Rājadh.): XII, **4**ε, 113 (came to the *svayaṃvara* of the daughter of the Kaliṅga king Citrāṅgada).

Rukmiṇī, sister of Rukmin, wife of Kṛshṇa, and mother of Pradyumna, etc. § 132 (Aṃçāvat.): I, **67**, 2790 (*Bhīshmakasya kule*, incarnation of a portion of Çrī). — § 262 (Bhagavadyāna): II, **2**, 57. — § 291 (Çiçupālavadhap.): II, **45**, 1574, 1577 (ravished by Kṛshṇa, although she had been intended for Çiçupāla).—§ 317 (Arjunābhigamanap.): III, **12**, 575 (*yathā tvayā jitā, Kṛshṇa, R°ī Bhīshmakātmajā*).—§ 410 (Plakshāvataraṇag.): III, **130**, 10554 (*āçramaç caiva R°yāḥ*, the same?).—§ 521 (Draupadīharaṇap.): III, **263**, 15538 (*pārçvasthāṃ çayane tyaktvā R°ṃ Keçavaḥ*).—§ 561*c* (Kṛshṇa Vāsudeva): V, **48**, †1881 (*yo R°ṃ ekarathena Bhojān utsādya rājñaḥ samare prasahya*-| *uvāha bhāryāṃ yaçasā jvalantīṃ yasyāṃ jajñe Raukmiṇeyo* (i.e. Pradyumna) *mahātmā*, sc. Kṛshṇa).—§ 565 (Gālavacarita): V, **117**, 3976 (*reme . . . yathā . . . R°yāṃ Janārdanaḥ*).—§ 570*d* (Rukmin): V, **158**, 5360 (°*yā haraṇaṃ*, ravished by Kṛshṇa).—§ 617*b* (Brahmaçiras): X, **12**, 636 (°*yāṃ yo anvajāyata . . . Pradyumnaḥ*).—§ 727 (Ānuçāsanik.): XIII, **11**, 508 (discourse between *R.* and Çrī).—§ 730 (do.): XIII, **14**, 617 (*Pradyumna-Cārudeshṇādīn . . . R°yāḥ putrakān*), 620, 622 (enumeration of *R.*'s sons with Kṛshṇa).—§ 768 (do.): XIII, **148**, 6889 (mother of Pradyumna).—§ 773*c* (Durvāsas): XIII, **160**, 7429, 7434, 7445 (gratified Durvāsas).—§ 793 (Mausalap.): XVI, **5**, 145; **7**μ, 249 (when the corpse of Kṛshṇa was burnt, *R.*, etc., ascended the funeral pyre). Cf. Bhīshmakātmajā, Bhojyā.

Rukmiṇīnandana = Pradyumna, q.v.

Rumaṇvat, son of Jamadagni. § 396 (Jamadagni): III, **116**, 10180 (*jyeshṭho Jāmadagnyaḥ*, ordered by Jamadagni to slay his mother Reṇukā *R.* did not obey, and was therefore cursed by Jamadagni).

Ruṇā, a river. § 368 (Tīrthayātrāp.): III, **83**, 7022 (*Sarasvatyā Ruṇāyāç ca saṅgamam*, probably an irregular contraction from °*tyā Aru*°?, PCR. *Aruṇā*).

Rūpa ("form," personif.). § 270 (Brahmasabhāv.): II, **11**, 438 (in the palace of Brahmán).

Rūpavāhika, pl. (°*āḥ*), a people. § 574 (Jambūkh.): VI, **9**μ, 351.

Rūpiṇa, son of Ajamīḍha and Keçinī. § 152 (Pūruvaṃç.): I, **94**, 3722 (*Vrajana-Rūpiṇau*), 3724 (*Vrajana-R°ayoḥ*).

Ruru, a brahman. § 19 (Bhṛgu): I, **5**, 871 (son of Pramati and Ghṛtācī), 872 (husband of Pramadvarā and father of Çunaka).—§ 21 (Pramadvarā): I, **8**, 940 (do.), 941, 951, 953.—§ 22 (do.): I, **8**, 963.—§ 23 (do.): I, **9**, 964, 969, (972), 974, (974), 976 (°*or bhāryā*, i.e. Pramadvarā), 977 (do.), 978, 979 (when Pramadvarā had been bitten by a serpent and died, *R.* granted her half his life, Pramadvarā then was restored to life).—§ 24 (Sahasrapad): I, **9**, 983; **10**, (987), 991, 992, 994.—§ 25 (do.): I, **11**, 1004, 1005, 1007, 1011; **12**, (1014), 1016, 1017, 1019 (*R.* afterwards killed all serpents he met. Ruru's meeting with Sahasrapad, who told his story and directed *R.* to Pramati to hear the story of Āstīka).—§ 35 (Āstīkap.): I, **24** (1265) (Pramati told the story of Āstīka to *R.*).—§ 69 (do.): I, **58**, 2195 (do.).—§ 736*b* (Vītahavyop.): XIII, **30**, 2004 (son of Ghṛtācī and Pramati (of Vītahavya's race), husband of Pramadvarā and father of Çunaka). Cf. Bhṛgunandana.

Rushadgu (II, 324), v. Vṛshadgu.

Rushaṅgu, a brahman. § 615*l* (Baladevatīrthayātrā): *R.* was an old brahman always devoted to ascetic penances. Resolved to give up his body he told his sons to take him to *Pṛthūdaka* on the *Sarasvatī* (with hundreds of tīrthas and on whose banks dwelt *ṛshis* unconnected with the world). There *R.* bathed according to due rites and then said to his sons: "He who would abandon his body in *Pṛthūdaka* on the northern bank of the *Sarasvatī* while employed in mentally reciting sacred mantras (*japyaparaḥ*) would never again be afflicted with death" (*nainaṃ çvo maraṇaṃ tapet*, v. Nīl.): IX, **39**, 2270, 2273, 2275.

Rushardika, a king § 562 (Bhagavadyānap.): V, **74**γ, 2730 (*Surāshṭrāṇāṃ*, among the wicked kings who annihilated their kinsmen and relatives).

Ṛ

Ṛbhu, pl. (°*avaḥ*), a class of gods. § 520 (Mudgala): III, **261**, 15459 (in heaven, PCR. seems to be wrong in referring the following description (v. 15459*b*–15465) to the *R.*).—§ 665 (Mokshadh.): XII, **208**, 7588 (*Ṛbhavo Marutaç caiva devānāṃ cādito gaṇāḥ*—*codito gaṇaḥ*, B.).

ṛc, mostly pl. (°*aḥ*) ("the verses of the Ṛgveda"): I, 66, ††721 (some *R.* quoted by Upamanyu), 1374, 2880 (°*o bahvṛcamukhyaiç ca preryamāṇaḥ padakramaiḥ*); III, 966, 1773 (°-*yajuḥ-sāmasambhavaiḥ*), 5038, 11237 (*sāma-ṛg-yajurvarṇāḥ*, did not exist in the Kṛtayuga), 11252 (*anṛcaḥ*), 17339 (sg.); V, 1623, 1624, 1662 (*anṛcaḥ*), †1711 (read with B. *navarkshu*); VI, 1187 (sg.?); IX, 2098; XI, 795; XII, 1883 (°-*yajuḥ-sāmasahitair vacobhiḥ*), 2311 (°*yajuḥ-sāmavid*), 2312 (*anṛgyajuḥ*), †2315 (sg.), 2871 (°-*yajuḥ-sāmasampannān*), 7372 (°-*sāmasaṅghān*), 7501, 7503, 8398 (*anṛcaḥ*), 8543 (°-*samāni*), 8613 (°-*sāmavarṇākshārataḥ*), [8650 (*anṛco dvijaḥ*)], 8720 (°-*sāmasu*), 8964 (°*sahasrāṇi*), 9065, 9621, 9632, 10759, 10763, 11532 (°-*yajuḥ-sāmagaḥ*), 12736 (*yajur-ṛg-sāmabhiḥ*), 13120 (*caturvedodgatābhiḥ*); XIII, 1084 (*ṛgbhir anuçāsanti . . . bahvṛcaḥ*), 4520, 6333 (*vāgbhir ṛgbhūshitārthābhiḥ*), 6413 (*vāgbhir ṛgbhūshitābhiḥ*); XIV, 744; XVI, †132. Cf. Ṛgveda.— Do.[2], pl. (°*aḥ*) = Çiva (1000 names[1]).

Ṛceyu, a prince. § 150 (Pūruvaṃç.): I, **94**, 3700 (first son of Raudrāçva), 3702 (= Anādhṛshti (?), became king, father of Matināra). (According to v. 3698 *R.* seems to be identical with Anvagbhānu, q.v.) Cf. Ṛksha[2].

Ṛcīka[1], a form or son of Vivasvat (the Sun). § 3 (Anukram.): I, **1**, 42 (*sa Ṛcīkaḥ*, v. Āçāvaha).

Ṛcīka[2], a ṛshi, son or descendant of Bhṛgu, and father of Jamadagni and Çunaḥçepha. § 8 (Parvasaṅgr.): I, **2**, 275 (°*ādayaḥ . . . pitaro*, sc. Rāma Jāmadagnya's).—§ 122 (Aṃçāvat.): I, **66**, 2611 (son of Aurva and father of Jamadagni). — § 395 (Jamadagni): III, **115**, 10146 (*Bhārgavaḥ*), (10149), 10154 (*R.* married Satyavatī, having given as a dowry 1,000 horses which he obtained from Varuṇa; birth of Jamadagni).—§ 398 (Paraçurāma): III, **117**, 10205 (among the pitṛs of Rāma Jāmadagnya).—§ 565 (Gālavacarita): V, **117**, 3973 (*reme . . . yathā . . . R°ḥ Satyavatyāñ ca*); **119**, 4005, 4007 (had given 1000 horses as a dowry for Satyavatī, cf. § 395).—§ 573 (Ambopākhyānap.): V, **185**, 7312 (*munayo . . . R°mukhāḥ*, the pitṛs of Rāma Jāmadagnya, headed by *R.* caused Rāma to desist from the battle with Bhīshma).—§ 638*b* (Rāmopākhyāna): XII, **49**, 1721 (*Bhṛguputrāya*), 1723 (*Bhārgavaḥ*), 1726 (*Bhṛgunandanaḥ*), 1727, 1731 (*Bhṛguçārdūlaḥ*), (1738), (1740), (1743), 1746 (the story of the birth of Jamadagni (and Viçvāmitra) once more related, deviating a little from § 395).—§ 665 (Mokshadh.): XII, **208***ι*, 7599 (*putraḥ . . . R°sya . . . Jamadagniḥ*).—§ 677 (do.): XII, **235**, 8607 (Dyutimat gave his kingdom to *R.* and thus attained to heaven).—§ 721 (Ānuçāsanik.): XIII, **3***a*, 186 (°*syātmajaç caiva Çunaḥçephaḥ*).—§ 721*b* (Viçvāmitrop.): XIII, **4**, 207 (*Bhārgavaḥ . . . Cyavanasyātmasambhavaḥ*), 208, (210), 215, 217, 223, 228, 260 (*R.* married Satyavatī, having given as a dowry 1,000 horses which he obtained from Varuṇa; birth of Jamadagni (and Viçvāmitra), cf. § 395 and § 638*b*).—§ 745*c* (Cyavana-Kuçikasaṃv.): XIII, **56**, 2910 (*Bhṛgunandanam*, Cyavana prophesied that *R.* would be born from Ūrva, and marry the daughter of Gādhi [i.e. Satyavatī]). — § 767 (Ānuçāsanik.): XIII, **137***a*, 6267 (Dyutimat gave his kingdom to *R.* and thus attained to heaven).—§ 771 (do.): XIII, **151**, 7158 (°*tanayaiḥ*).—§ 782*d* (Paraçurāma): XIV, **29**, 836 (°*pramukhāḥ . . . pitāmahāḥ*, told Rāma Jāmadagnya to desist from slaughtering the kshatriyas). Cf. Bhārgava, Bhārgavarshabha, Bhṛguçārdūla, Bhṛgunandana, Bhṛguputra, Bhṛgusattama, Bhṛgusuta, Brahmarshi, Viprarshi.

Ṛcīka[3], son of Bhūmanyu. § 152 (Pūruvaṃç.): I, **94**, 3714 (sixth son of Bhūmanyu and Pushkariṇī).

Ṛcīkanandana, "[grand]son of Ṛcīka" = Rāma Jāmadagnya: III, 8657.

Ṛcīkaputra ("son of Ṛcīka") = Jamadagni: III, †10223 (?), 10519 (?); XIII, 7671 (*J°*).

Ṛcīkatanaya[1] (do.) = Çunaḥçepha: XII, 10759 (cf. XIII, 186).

Ṛcīkatanaya[2] (do.) = Jamadagni: XIII, 7117 (*J°*).

Ṛçyaçṛṅga, v. Ṛshyaçṛṅga.

Ṛddha = Vishṇu (1000 names).

Ṛddhi ("prosperity," personif.), a goddess, wife of Kubera. § 565 (Gālavacarita): V, **117**, 3968 (*reme . . . yathā carddhyāṃ Dhaneçvaraḥ*). — § 768*b* (Umā-Maheçvarasaṃv.): XIII, **146***γ*, 6750 (*Vaiçravaṇasya*, sc. *sādhvī*).—§ 775 (Ānuçāsanik.): XIII, **166***a*, 7637 (*saharddhyā ca Dhaneçvaraḥ*).

Ṛgveda. § 270 (Brahmasabhāv.): II, **11**, 449 (in the palace of Brahmán).—§ 459 (Mārkaṇḍeyas.): III, **189**, 12963 (springs from Nārāyaṇa).—§ 606 (Tripurākhyāna): VIII, **34**, 1498 (forerunner of Çiva's chariot).—§ 717*b* (Nārāyaṇīya): XII, **342**, 13136 (in *R.* the names of Kṛshṇa are enumerated); **343**, 13256 (*ekaviṃçatisāhasram*, identified with Kṛshṇa); **349**, III), 13568 (°*pāṭhapaṭhitaṃ vratam*).— § 736*b* (Vītahavyop.): XIII, **30**, 1998 (°*e vartate cāgryā çrutir yasya* — sc. Gṛtsamada's — *mahātmanaḥ*). — § 747*b* (Suvarṇotpatti): XIII, **85***ε*, 4107 (*padakramavibhūsitaḥ*). Cf. ṛc, pl.

Ṛgyajuḥsāmadhāman = Kṛshṇa: XII, 1630.

Ṛksahasrāmitekshaṇa = Çiva (1000 names[2]).

Ṛksha[1], a prince, son of Ajamīḍha. § 152 (Pūruvaṃç.): I, **94**, 3722, 3724 (son of Ajamīḍha and Dhūminī; father of Saṃvaraṇa).

Ṛksha[2], a prince, son of Ariha. § 156 (Pūruvaṃç.): I, **95**, 3777 (son of Ariha and Āṅgeyī), 3778 (husband of Jvālā and father of Matināra).

***ṛksha**, pl. (°*āḥ*) ("bears"). § 127 (Aṃçāvat.): I, **66**, 2626 (offspring of Mṛgamandā).

***ṛksha**, pl. (°*āṇi*) ("constellations"). XIII, 625; XIV, 1213 (*Çravaṇādīni*).

Ṛkshā[1], wife of Ajamīḍha. § 156 (Pūruvaṃç.): I, **95**, 3790 (fourth wife of Ajamīḍha).

Ṛkshā[2], a mātṛ. § 615*u* (Skanda): IX, **46***θ*, 2630.

Ṛkshaputra ("the son of Ṛksha[1]") = Saṃvaraṇa: I, 6527.

Ṛkshavat, name of a mountain. § 347 (Nalopākhyānap.): III, **61**, 2317 (*parvatāṃ*, towards the south). — § 574 (Jambūkh.): VI, **9***κ*, 318 (only B., C. has *Gandhamādanam*, among the *kulaparvatāḥ* of Bhāratavarsha).—§ 638*b* (Rāmopākhyāna): XII, **49**, 1791 (*Pauravadāyādo Vidūrathasutaḥ . . . ṛkshaiḥ saṃvardhitaḥ . . . R°y atha parvate*).—§ 639 (Rājadh.): XII, **52**, †1893 (*yathā mahānadī taṃ R°antaṃ girim etya Narmadā*, sc. *puraç ca paçcāc ca*).

Ṛṅmaya = Çiva (1000 names[1]).

Ṛshabha[1], a serpent. § 67 (Sarpasattra): I, **57**, 2168 (of Dhṛtarāshṭra's race).

Ṛshabha[2], one or more ṛshis. § 270 (Brahmasabhāv.): II, **11**, 442 (in the palace of Brahmán).—§ 390*b* (Hemakūṭa): III, **110**, 9975 (*tāpasaḥ*, on Ṛshabhakūṭa).—§ 641 (Rājadh.): XII, **125**, 4629 (*Sumitrasya nirvṛttaṃ R°sya ca*); **127**, 4660 (*viprarshiḥ*); **128**, (4689), 4713 (discourse between *R.* and Sumitra).

Ṛshabha[3], name of a certain cannibal. § 277 (Jarāsandhavadhap.): II, **21**, 812 (*māṃsādam*, in Girivraja, slain by Bṛhadratha).

Ṛshabha[4], a tīrtha. § 370 (Tīrthayātrāp.): III, **85**, 8152 (*tīrthaṃ . . . Koçalāyāṃ*).

Ṛshabha[5], one or more mountains. § 370 (Tīrthayātrāp.): III, **85**, 8163 (*parvataṃ*).—§ 565 (Gālavacarita): V, **112**, 3872 (*°o nāma parvataḥ sāgarāntike*); **113**, 3873 (*°sya . . . çṛṅgaṃ*, there Çāṇḍilī dwelt).

Ṛshabha[6], an ancient king. § 574 (Jambūkh.): VI, **9aa**, 315 (*priyaṃ . . . Ṛ°sya*, sc. Bhāratavarsha). — § 673*b* (Bali-Vāsavasaṃv.): XII, **227a**, 8263 (among the ancient rulers of the earth, an Asura?).

Ṛshabha[7], a prince. § 592 (Saṃçaptakavadhap.): VII, **20**η, 804 (only B., in Droṇa's *gāruḍavyūha*).

Ṛshabha[8] = Çiva: VII, 9453.

Ṛshabha[9], a dvīpa. § 615*i* (Saptasārasvata): IX, **38**, 2211 (*dvīpe*, with the river Sureṇu, q.v.). Cf. next.

Ṛshabhadvīpa, name of a place. § 370 (Tīrthayātrāp.): III, **84**, 8138 (*krauñcanisūdakaṃ* (*°nishūdanaṃ*, B.)).

Ṛshabhaketu ("having a bull in his banner") = Çiva: XII, 6164 (*Rudrāya*).

Ṛshabhakūṭa = Hemakūṭa: III, 9975.

Ṛshadgu, a prince. § 768*b* (Kṛshṇa-Vāsudeva): XIII, **147**, 6834 (son of Vṛjinīvat and father of Citraratha[5]; B. reads *Ushaṅgu*).

ṛshayaḥ sapta, v. Saptarshi, pl.

Ṛshigiri, name of a mountain. § 277 (Jarāsandhavadhap.): II, **21**, 799 (one of the five hills near Girivraja).

Ṛshika, a king. § 130 (Aṃçāvat.): I, **67**, 2669 (incarnation of the Asura Arka).

Ṛshika, pl. (*°āḥ*), a people. § 279 (Arjuna): II, **27**, 1033 (*uttarān*), 1034, 1035 (in the north, vanquished by Arjuna on his digvijaya). — § 554 (Sainyodyogap.): V, **4**γ, 81 (*rājānaḥ*, adj.?).—§ 574 (Jambūkh.): VI, **9**ν, 372 (only B., in the south).—§ 604 (Karṇap.): VIII, **8**, 237 (had formerly been vanquished by Karṇa and caused to pay tribute to Duryodhana).

Ṛshikulyā, pl. (*°āḥ*) and sg., name of several sacred waters. § 279 (Arjuna): II, **28**, 1041 (pl., in the north).—§ 370 (Tīrthayātrāp.): III, **84**, 8026, 8027 (sg., a tīrtha).—§ 574 (Jambūkh.): VI, **9**λ, 343 (sg., a river in Bhāratavarsha).—§ 775 (Ānuçāsanik.): XIII, **166a**, 7652 (pl.).

Ṛshiloka ("the world of the ṛshis"). § 364 (Tīrthayātrāp.): III, **83**, 6060 (by bathing in Pāṇikhāta one attains to *Ṛ*.).—§ 370 (do.): III, **84**, 8027 (by bathing in Ṛshikulyā one attains to *Ṛ*.).—§ 758 (Ānuçāsanik.): XIII, **103**, 4910.

Ṛshyaçṛṅga (B. *Ṛçya°*), a muni, son of Vibhāṇḍaka. § 11 (Parvasaṅgr.): I, **2**, 443 (*°sya caritraṃ*, cf. § 391).—§ 270 (Brahmasabhāv.): II, **11**, 440 (in the palace of Brahmán).—§ 390*d* (Tīrthayātrāp.): *Ṛ*., the son of *Kāçyapa* (i.e. Vibhāṇḍaka) born by a hind, caused *Indra* to rain during a drought in the territory of Lomapāda, who gave him his daughter Çāntā: III, **110**, 9991.—§ 391 (do.): III, **110**, 9994.—§ 391 (cf. do.). The *viprarshi Vibhāṇḍaka Kāçyapa* practising austerities near a great lake saw the *Apsaras Urvaçī*, whence his semen fell into the water and was lapped up by a hind, that was drinking. That hind was a daughter of the gods (*devakanyā*). Brahmán had transformed her into a hind, and when she had given birth to a *muni* she would be freed. She now gave birth to a son, who was named *Ṛshyaçṛṅga*, because there was a horn on his head. He passed his days in the forest, devoted to brahmacarya, and he had never seen any human being except his father. At that time the king of the *Aṅgas*, *Lomapāda*, a friend of *Daçaratha*, had been shunned by the brahmans and was without a *purohita*, because he had been guilty of falsehood towards a brahman and therefore *Indra* did not give rain in his territory. At the advice of a wise brahman he did atonement for his sins and appeased the brahmans. Thereafter he assembled his ministers in order to discuss means for bringing *Ṛ*. to his land. According to their counsel a courtezan with a number of women, etc., was sent to *Ṛ*. (III, **110**). She had constructed a floating hermitage which she moored at a short distance from *Vibhāṇḍaka's* hermitage, and then sent her daughter, a courtezan, to Ṛshyaçṛṅga. She refused the fruits, foot-washing, etc., saying that her religious vows consisted in not receiving such things, but implied that she might embrace him. By giving him unsuitable food, garlands, beautiful garments, and drinks, and by playing and clasping him in her arms, she made him overpowered with love, and as she went away under the pretext of performing the *agnihotra*, he became sad. When Vibhāṇḍaka (*b*) returned he wondered that *Ṛ*. was not splitting the logs for fuel, etc., and asked who had been there (III, **111**). *Ṛ*. said that a religious student (*brahmacārin*) had come to him; he had a mass of hair (*jaṭilaḥ*) and a pair of ornaments upon his wrist like his rosary (*akshamālā*); his matted hair (*jaṭāḥ*) was neatly tied up and adhered to the forehead and was divided in two, etc. He (*Ṛ*.) wished to go to him and see him every day (III, **112**). *Vibhāṇḍaka* declared that it was a *Rākshasa*, and in vain spent three days in searching for this one. When Vibhāṇḍaka had gone out to collect fruits the courtezans allured *Ṛ*. to enter the bark, which they unmoored, and in this way they brought him to *Lomapāda*, who prepared a beautiful forest named *Nāvyāçrama* ("Floating hermitage") and kept *Ṛ*. in the female apartments. Suddenly rain poured down. Lomapāda gave his daughter *Çāntā* to *Ṛ*. When *Vibhāṇḍaka* was going to *Campā* in order to burn the king, the city, and his whole territory, the king let kine be placed and fields ploughed along the road, and ordered the cowherds to honour *Vibhāṇḍaka* with hospitality when he was fatigued and hungry, and to say that all this belonged to his son and that they were his slaves. Thus *Vibhāṇḍaka* was appeased. According to the command of his father *Ṛ*., as soon as a son had been born to him, returned to his father in the wood, and *Çāntā* followed and obeyed him, as *Indrasenā Nārāyaṇī* was ever obedient to *Mudgala*, etc. (III, **113**): III, **110**, 9999, 10000, 10006, 10007 (origin of the name), 10014, 10018, 10021, 10024 (*ṛsheḥ sutaṃ*); III, †10034, (†10035), (†10039), †10041, †10043, †10044, †10045; **112**, (†10051); **113**, †10075 (*muniṃ*), †10076, †10080, †10091, †10093. — § 677 (Mokshadh.): XII, **235**, 8609 (*Lomapādaç ca rājarshiḥ Çāntāṃ dattvā sutāṃ prabhuḥ | Ṛ°āya vipulaiḥ sarvakāmair ayujyata*, all. to § 391).—§ 702 (do.): XII, **297**δ, 10874 (*Kāçyapaḥ*? (so B., C. has *Ka°*)).—§ 767 (Ānuçāsanik.): XIII, **137a**, 6269 (= XII, 8609, with a slight variation). Cf. Kāçyapa, Kāçyapaputra, Kāçyapātmaja.

Ṛshyamuka, name of a mountain. § 323 (Dvaitavanapr.): III, **25**, †953 (Mārkaṇḍeya had seen Rāma Dāçarathi on *Ṛ*.). — § 425 (Hanūmad-Bhīmasaṃv.): III, **147**, 11196 (the abode of Sugrīva, when deprived of his kingdom, there Rāma met him).—§ 530 (Viçvāvasumoksh.): III, **279**, 16088 (*çailasya*, near [the lake] Pampā).—§ 531 (Rāmopākhyānap.): III, **280**, 16101 (*giryagre*, on *Ṛ*. *Rāma* made alliance with Sugrīva).

Ṛta, name of a Rudra. § 770 (Ānuçāsanik.): XIII, **151**β, 7090.

Ṛta(ṃ) = Kṛshṇa: XII, 1622.

Ṛtā = Sarasvatī (?): XII, 13234 (*Brahmasutā devī Sarasvatī*)
Ṛtadhāman[1] = Mahāpurusha (Mahāpurushastava).—Do.[2] = Kṛshṇa (Nārāyaṇa): XII, 13228 (etym.).
Ṛtasya kartṛ = Skanda: III, 14644.
Ṛtavaḥ shaṭ = Skanda: III, 14639.
Ṛteyu, a ṛshi. § 770 (Ānuçāsanik.): XIII, **151θ**, 7114 (the second of the seven *Varuṇasyartvijaḥ*).
Ṛtu[1] = Çiva (1000 names[2]).—Do.[2] = Vishṇu (1000 names).—Do.[3], pl. (°*avaḥ*), personif.; IX, 2513, 2517.—Do.[4], pl. (°*avaḥ*) = Çiva (1000 names[1]).
Ṛtuparṇa, king of Ayodhyā. § 346 (Nalopākhyānap.): III, **60**, 2296 (Vārshṇeya, the charioteer of Nala, became the charioteer of *Ṛ*.).—§ 348 (do.): III, **66**, 2628 (will teach Nala the science of dice).—§ 349 (do.): III, **67**, 2634 (°*sya nagaraṃ*), 2637, (2638), 2641 (°*sya nagare*) (Nala is appointed as superintendent of *Ṛ.'s* stables).—§ 35 (do.): III, **70**, 2746, 2747, 2748, 2766, 2770 (is invited to the second svayaṃvara of Damayantī); **71**, 2771, 2778, 2782, 2789, 2806 (with Nala as his charioteer *Ṛ*. proceeds to Vidarbhā).—§ 352 (do.): III, **72**, 2825, 2835, 2837 (teaches Nala the science of dice).—§ 353 (do.): III, **73**, 2852, 2868, 2870, 2872, 2875, 2883, 2888; **74**, 2901; **75**, 2931; **76**, 2978 (*Koçalāyāṃ Ṛ°niveçane*); **77**, 3016, 3026 (learnt the horse lore from Nala), 3028.—§ 355 (do.): III, **79**, 3072 (°*sya rājarsheḥ kīrttitaṃ kalināçanaṃ*). Cf. Bhaṅgāsuri, Kosala (C. *Kauç*°), Kosalādhipati.
Ṛtusthalā, an Apsaras. § 191 (Arjuna): I, **123**, 4821 (danced at the birth of Arjuna).
ṛtvābṛhattva (I, 4813, according to B.), v. *satvārṛhattvā*.

S

(*What is not found under S should be sought for under Ç.*)

Sabhā = Sabhāparvan. § 4 (Anukram.): I, **1**, 88 (°*āraṇyaviṭaṅkarān*, sc. *Bhāratadrumaḥ*).
Sabhadraka, pl. (X, 381), v. Prabhadraka, pl.
Sabhākriyā ("building of the palace"). § 11 (Parvasaṅgr.): I, **2**, 407 (*Pāṇḍavānāṃ*, i.e. Sabhākriyāparvan).
Sabhākriyāparvan ("the section relating to the building of the palace," the 20th of the minor parvans of the Mhbhr. Cf. Sabhākriyā). § 261: *Maya* said he was a great artist (*mahākavi*), the *Viçvakarman* of the *Dānavas*, and asked *Arjuna* to tell him what he was to do for him, because he had been rescued by him. *Arjuna* told him to do something for *Kṛshṇa* (*lokanāthaḥ Prajāpatiḥ*, v. 9), who asked him to build a palace for *Yudhishṭhira*. *Maya* was introduced to *Yudhishṭhira*, and recited the history of the Asura (*pūrvadeva-caritaṃ*), i.e. of Vṛshaparvan (so Nīl.). Then on an auspicious day, after the initiatory rites, and having gratified thousands of *brahmans*, he measured out a piece of land 10,000 *kishkus* square (II, **1**).—§ 262: Kṛshṇa departed for *Dvārakā* (v. *Bhagavadyāna*).—§ 263: To the north of *Kailāsa*, near *Maināka*, there is a huge mountain named *Hiraṇyaçṛṅga*, consisting of jewels. Near this mountain is situated the lake *Bindusaras*, where King *Bhagīratha* had dwelt for many years, desiring to behold the *Gaṅgā*. There the lord of all beings (i.e. *Prajāpati*, Nīl) had performed 100 sacrifices, where, for the sake of embellishment, though not according to rule (*dṛshṭāntataḥ*), the sacrificial stakes were made of gems and the altars (*caityāḥ*) of gold. There the 1,000-eyed *Çacīpati* had become perfect (*siddhiṃ gataḥ*) by sacrifice. There *Bhūtapati* (= *Mahādeva*, Nīl.) took up his abode after having created all the worlds, and there he dwells, worshipped by thousands of spirits (*bhūtaiḥ*). There *Nara* and *Nārāyaṇa*, *Brahmán*, *Yama*, and *Sthāṇu* perform their sacrifices at the expiration of 1,000 *yugas*. There *Vāsudeva* has performed *sattras* for many years, and placed thousands and tens of thousands of sacrificial stakes adorned with golden garlands and altars of great splendour. There *Maya*, when the *Dānavas* wished to perform a sacrifice on the bank of the *Bindusaras*, had made utensils of gems from the house of *Vṛshaparvan*. That wealth, which was guarded by *Yakshas* and *Rākshasas*, he brought away, and thereof constructed the palace of *Yudhishṭhira*. A club with which *Vṛshaparvan* had slain all foes in battle, and which had been placed in *Bindusaras*, *Maya* gave to *Bhīmasena*; the conch-shell *Devadatta*, that came from *Varuṇa*, and was also there, he gave to *Arjuna*; at its sound all creatures trembled in awe. The palace surpassed the *Sudharmā* of *Kṛshṇa* and the palace of *Brahmán*, and covered an area of 10,000 *kishkus* square. Eight thousand *Rākshasas*, called *Kiṅkaras*, guarded and supported the palace. In it was a tank, whose lotuses were of dark-coloured gems, etc.; many kings mistook it for solid ground, and fell into it. The palace was constructed in seventeen months (II, **3**).—§ 264: Enumeration of *ṛshis* (*α*) and kings (*β*) from various countries, who were present when *Yudhishṭhira*, after having fed 10,000 brahmans. etc., entered the palace. Also *Tumburu*, the friend of *Dhanañjaya*, and the *Gandharva Citrasena* with his ministers, and many other *Gandharvas* and *Apsarases* and *Kinnaras* came there (II, **4**).
Sabhāparvan ("the section relating to the palace"), the second of the eighteen great parvans of the Mhbhr. § 10 (Parvasaṅgr.): I, **2**, 317.—§ 11 (do.): I, **2**, 407, 415 (stated to contain 2,500 çlokas).—§ 795*c* (Mahābhārata): XVIII, **6**, 267. Cf. Sabhā.
Sabhāpati[1] = Bhūtakarman: VII, 1085 (*Bh*°, slain by Çatānīka).
Sabhāpati[2], a Kuru warrior. § 608 (Karṇap.): VIII, **89**, †4587 (slain by Arjuna).
Sabhāvana = Çiva (1000 names[2]).
Sāçva, an ancient king. § 267 (Yamasabhāv.): II, **8**, 328 (in the palace of Yama).
Sada, a son of Dhṛtarāshṭra. § 182 (Dhṛtarāshṭraputranāmak.): I, **117**, 4548 (read *Sadaḥsuvāc* as one name?).
Sadaçva, an ancient king. § 267 (Yamasabhāv.): II, **8**, 323 (in the palace of Yama).
Sadaçvormi, an ancient king. § 267 (Yamasabhāv.): II, **8**, 321 (in the palace of Yama; only C, B. has *Sadasyormiḥ*).
Sadākāntā, a river. § 574 (Jambūkh.): VI, **9**λ, 332 (in Bhāratavarsha).
Sadākshapriya = Çiva (1000 names[1]).
Sadāmarshin = Vishṇu (1000 names).
Sadānīrā, a river. § 276 (Jarāsandhavadhap.): II, **20**, 794 (crossed by Kṛshṇa, etc., on their way from Indraprastha to Girivraja).—§ 574 (Jambūkh.): VI, **9**λ, 332 (in Bhāratavarsha).
Sadānīrāmayā, a river. § 574 (Jambūkh.): VI, **9**λ, 340 (in Bhāratavarsha).
Sadasadvyaktāvyakta = Mahāpurusha (Mahāpurushastava).
Sadasatoḥ para(m) = Kṛshṇa: XII, 1622 (*brahma*).

Sadasatpati = Çiva: XIII, 1282.
Sadasyormi, v. Sadaçvormi.
Sadāyogin, Sadbhūti = Vishṇu (1000 names).
sadbhūtotpādaka, said of the abode of Nārāyaṇa: XII, 13382 (°*m nāma tat sthānam*).
Sadgati, Sādhu = Vishṇu (1000 names).
Sādhya, pl. (°*āḥ*), a class of gods. § 3 (Anukram.): I, **1a**, 35 (issued from the primeval egg).—§ 44 (Garuḍa): I, **30**, 1417 (°*ānām*, sc. *praharaṇam*).—§ 46 (do.): I, **32**, 1486 (fled before Garuḍa).—§ 120 *bis* (Aṃçāvat.): I, **66**, 2602 (°*ānām*, sc. *pakshaḥ*).—§ 134 (Viçvāmitra): I, **71**, 2933 (afraid of the penances of Viçvāmitra).—§ 149 (Yayāti): I, **87**, 3551 (*pūjitas tridaçaiḥ S°aiḥ*, etc., sc. Yayāti).—§ 191 (Arjuna): I, **123a**, 4827 (present at the birth of Arjuna).—§ 233 (Svayaṃvarap.): I, **187**, 7010 (present at the svayaṃvara of Draupadī).—§ 238 (Pañcendrop.): I, **197**, †7277 (present at the sacrifice of the gods in the Naimisha forest).—§ 258 (Khāṇḍavadahanap.): I, **227**, 8270 (fought with Kṛshṇa and Arjuna).—§ 265 (Lokapālasabhākhyānap.): II, **6**, 277 (worship the palace of Brahmán).—§ 266 (Çakrasabhāv.): II, **7**, 289 (in the palace of Indra), 303 (do.).—§ 270 (Brahmasabhāv.): II, **11**, 460 (in the palace of Brahmán).—§ 309 (Āraṇyakap.): III, **2**, 127 (rule the creatures by virtue of yoga).—§ 310*b* (Sūrya): III, **3**, 174 (worship Sūrya).—§ 317*b* (Kṛshṇa Vāsudeva): III, **12**, 513 (°*ānām api devānām çivānām īçvareçvara*, sc. Kṛshṇa).—§ 330 (Indradarçana): III, **37**, 1490 (mentioned in a blessing to Arjuna).—§ 334 (Kairātap.): III, **41**, 1669 (accompany Varuṇa).—§ 336 (Indralokābhigamanap.): III, **43**, 1768 (on the *suravīthī*).—§ 357 (Pushkara): III, **82**, 4064 (dwell in Pushkara).—§ 373 (Prayāga): III, **85**, 8213 (dwell at Prayāga).—§ 375 (Tīrthayātrāp.): III, **85**, 8248 (C. has by error °*ṛddh*°).—§ 377 (Dhaumyatīrthak.): III, **90**, 8404 (worship the tīrthas).—§ 383 (Paraçurāma): III, **99**, 8673 (seen by Rāma Jāmadagnya in the body of Rāma Dāçarathi).—§ 400 (Tīrthayātrāp.): III, **118**, †10225 (°*gaṇasya*, sc. *āyatanam*, visited by Yudhishṭhira).—§ 421 (Gandhamādanapr.): III, **142**, 10905 (attend on Indra).—§ 439 (Yakshayuddhap.): III, **163**, 11847 (worship the rising sun).—§ 443 (Nivātakavacayuddhap.): III, **168**, 12043 (in Amarāvatī).—§ 459 (Mārkaṇḍeyas.): III, **188**, 12924 (seen in the body of Nārāyaṇa).—§ 507 (Skandayuddha): III, **231**, 14587 (fought with the Dānavas).—§ 520 (Mudgala): III, **261**, 15446 (their world).—§ 547 (Karṇa): III, **308**, 17139 (mentioned in a blessing to Karṇa).—§ 559 (Prajāgarap.): V, **36**, 1260, 1261 (*devāḥ*), (1262), 1262 (*devāḥ*, discourse between Ātreya and the *S.*).—§ 561*d* (Nara-Nārāyaṇau): V, **49**, 1919.—§ 565 (Gālavacarita): V, **108**, 3763 (*yatra*—i.e. in the east—*sandhyāyāṃ S°ānāṃ vartate tapaḥ*).—§ 567 (Bhagavadyānap.): V, **131o**, 4423 (seen in the body of Kṛshṇa).—§ 576 (Bhagavadgītāp.): VI, **35**, 1268 (became amazed at beholding Kṛshṇa).—§ 581 (Bhīshmavadhap.): VI, **68ρ**, 3038 (°*ānām api devānāṃ devadeveçvaraḥ prabhuḥ*, sc. Kṛshṇa).—§ 593 (Abhimanyuvadhap.): VII, **35**, 1536 (°-*Rudra-Marutkalpaiḥ*).—§ 596 (Pratijñāp.): VII, **76**, 2682 (mentioned in the oath of Arjuna).—§ 608 (Karṇap.): VIII, **87χ′**, 4418 (sided with Arjuna).—§ 615*u* (Skanda): IX, **44**, 2478 (came to see Skanda); **45γ**, 2508 (do.), 2555 (gave commanders of forces to Skanda).—§ 623 (Rājadh.): XII, **15β**, 440 (are slaughterers).—§ 626 (do.): XII, **21β**, 634.—§ 632*b* (Shoḍaçarāj., v. Marutta): XII, **29**, 915 (present at the sacrifices of Marutta).—§ 641 (Rājadh.): XII, **64η**, 2395 (*devāḥ*, observe *kshatriya* duties); **121**, 4409.—§ 655 (Āpaddh.): XII, **165**, 6054.—§ 656 (Khaḍgotpattik.): XII, **166β**, 6141.—§ 661 (Mokshadh.): XII, **198a**, 7191 (°*ānām*, sc. *vimānāni? sabhāḥ?*).—§ 662*b* (Jāpakop.): XII, **200δ**, 7339.—§ 664 (Mokshadh.): XII, **207ε**, 7540 (sons of Dharma and a daughter of Daksha)—§ 665 (do.): XII, **208**, 7588 (*Siddha-S°yoḥ*).—§ 673*b* (Bali-Vāsavasaṃv.): XII, **227**, 8288 (had been vanquished by Bali)—§ 692 (Mokshadh.): XII, **281**, 10093 (sg.).—§ 695*b* (Dakshayajñavināça): XII, **285a**, 10279 (present at the sacrifice of Daksha)—§ 702 (Mokshadh.): XII, **296β**, 10837.—§ 703 (do.): XII, **300**, 10993 (°*ānāṃ saṃvādaṃ haṃsasya ca*), 10994, (†10995), †10995 (*devāḥ*), (†11030), (†11032), (11034), 11036 (discourse between Prajāpati in the shape of a swan and the *S.*).—§ 707 (do.): XII, **318**, 11704 (*devān*; if the soul issues through the knees one attains to [the world of] the *S.*).—§ 712 (Çukotpatti): XII, **324**, 12174.—§ 714*g* (Samāna): XII, **329**, 12396 (*devagaṇāḥ*, fathers of Samāna).—§ 730 (Ānuçāsanik.): XIII, **14**, 985 (praised Çiva); **18λλ**, †1368.—§ 741 (do.): XIII, **79κ**, 3777 (°*ānāṃ lokaṃ*)—§ 747*b* (Suvarṇotpatti): XIII, **84**, 4012 (afflicted by Tāraka).—§ 748*b* (Tārakavadhop.): XIII, **86a**, 4201 (came to see Skanda).—§ 759 (Ānuçāsanik.): XIII, **107ζ**, 5330 (°*ānāṃ*, sc. *lokaṃ*).—§ 766 (do.): XIII, **134γ**, 6186.—§ 768*b* (Umā-Maheçvarasaṃv.): XIII, **140a**, 6351.—§ 773*b* (Kṛshṇa Vāsudeva): XIII, **159β**, 7387.—§ 778*f* (Muñjavat): XIV, **8**, 183 (worship Çiva on Muñjavat).—§ 793 (Mausalap.): XVI, **4θ**, †131 (receive Kṛshṇa in heaven).—§ 795 (Svargārohaṇap.): XVIII, **1**, 5; **3**, 88; **4**, 141.—§ 795*c* (Mahābhārata): XVIII, **6**, 215 (in one of two çlokas inserted in B.).
Sādhya = Nārāyaṇa: XIII, 1290 (*N*°), 1291 (*N*°).
Sādhya, adj. ("belonging to the Sādhyas"). § 443 (Nivātakavacayuddhap.): III, **168**, 12021 (sc. *astram*).
Sādhyarshi = Çiva (1000 names[2]).
Sadvṛtta = Çiva: XIV, 193.
Sadvṛtti = Devasenā: III, 14451.
sādyaṣka, a sacrifice performed with soma bought on the same day: III, 10663 (*shaṭ s°āḥ sarvavedeshu dṛshṭāḥ*), 14864 (*yajñena*); V, 1041 (*catvāry āha . . . s°āni Bṛhaspatiḥ*); XII, 8908 (*yajñān*); XIII, 4934 (°*ānām ayutaiḥ*, C. has by error *sa*°)
sadyaskāra, adj. (do.): XII, 8906 (*ishṭim*).
Sagaṇa = Çiva (1000 names[2]).
Sagara[1], an ancient king of Ayodhyā. § 6 (Anukram.): I, **1a**, 227 (in Sañjaya's enumeration).—§ 267 (Yamasabhāv.): II, **8**, 330 (in the palace of Yama).—§ 339 (Indralokābhigamanap.): III, **47**, 1897 (*Kapilaḥ . . . yena pūrvaṃ mahātmānaḥ khanamānā Rasātalaṃ | darçanād eva nihatāḥ S°syātmajāḥ*, all. to § 387).—§ 387 (Tīrthayātrāp.): At the request of *Yudhishṭhira*, *Lomaça* said: King *S.* of the family of the *Ikshvākus* had no sons. He subdued the *Haihayas* and the *Tālajaṅghas*. His wives were *Vaidarbhī* and *Çaibyā*. With them he on *Kailāsa* practised ascetic austerities in order to obtain a son, and practising yoga he succeeded in seeing *Çiva*, who said that owing to the *muhūrta* at which *S.* had addressed his prayers to him, one of the wives of *S.* would have 60,000 sons of exceeding pride, who should perish altogether, and the other wife would have one valorous son, who would perpetuate the race of *S.* Then *Çiva* disappeared and *S.* and his wives went home. *Vaidarbhī* after some time brought forth a gourd and *Çaibyā* a beautiful son. As *S.* was about to throw away the gourd, a voice from the sky told him

to take out the seeds and preserve them in steaming vessels partly filled with clarified butter, as they would become 60,000 sons (III, **106**). The *rājarshi S.* did as he was told, and provided a nurse for every receptacle. When they were born their acts were ruthless, they were able to roam about in the sky and harassed the gods, the *Gandharvas*, the *Rākshasas*, and all beings. The gods, etc., went to Brahmán, who dismissed them saying that in a short time the sons of *S.* would be destroyed. When after some time they were protecting *S.'s* sacrificial horse who roamed over the world, the horse suddenly disappeared when it had come to the waterless sea. Having told *S.* that the horse had been stolen, they were commanded to search for it, but they did not find it. *S.* then filled with wrath forbade them to return without the horse. They then began to dig the sea with spades, etc., and killed *Asuras*, *Uragas* (snakes), *Rākshasas*, and other beings by hundreds and thousands. After a long time they dug down to *Pātāla* in the north-eastern region, and seeing the horse there they ran after it without heeding *Kapila* ("whom they say is Vāsudeva," v. 8880), who was present there. *Kapila* then burnt them to ashes. *Nārada* told it to *S.*, who sent for *Aṃçumat*, the son of his son *Asamañjas*, whom he had abandoned according to his duty and for the good of the citizens: III, **106**, 8830, 8831 (*Ikshvākūṇāṃ kule jātaḥ*), 8841; **107**, 8859 (*rājā*), 8869 (°*ātmajāḥ*), 8871 (do.), 8876 (do.), 8882 (°*āntikaṃ*).—§ 388 (Asamañjas): III, **107**, 8887, 8888 (*Asamañjāḥ . . . S°sya sutaḥ*), 8890 (abandoned his son Asamañjas).—§ 389 (Gaṅgāvataraṇa): III, **107**, 8895, (8896), 8898, 8905, 8907, 8909, 8911, 8912 (asked by *S.*, Aṃçumat repaired to Kapila, who granted him the horse and that his grandson should bring the Gaṅgā down from heaven. *S.* made the ocean his son and was succeeded on the throne by Aṃçumat); **108**, 8939 (°*ātmajān*; Bhagīratha, the grandson of Aṃçumat, by the favour of Mahādeva brought down the Gaṅgā, that she might besprinkle the bodies of the sons of *S.*).—§ 478 (Dhundhumārop.): III, **204**, 13609 (*pureva Kapilaḥ . . . S°ātmajān*, sc. *adahat*, all. to § 387).—§ 552 (Goharaṇap.): IV, **56**ξ, 1769 (came from heaven to see the encounter).—§ 565 (Gālavacarita): V, **109**, 3796 (*vidur yaṃ Kapilaṃ devaṃ yenārttāḥ Sagarātmajāḥ*, all. to § 387).—§ 632*b* (Shoḍaçarāj.): XII, **29**, 1023 (*Aikshvākuṃ*): Also *S.* of Ikshvāku's race fell a prey to death. Sixty thousand sons walked behind him. He performed 1,000 horse sacrifices and gave precious gifts to the brahmans (description). Through anger he caused the earth to be excavated, and thus she came to have the ocean on her bosom, for this the ocean has come to be called Sāgara after the name of *S.*—§ 640 (Rājadh.): XII, **57**, 2054 (*Bāhoḥ putreṇa . . . S°ena . . . Asamañjāḥ . . . tyaktaḥ*, all. to § 388).—§ 700 (Mokshadh.): XII, **289**, 10613 (*itihāsaṃ purātanaṃ Arishṭaneminā proktaṃ S°āyānupṛcchate*), (10614) (instructed by Arishṭanemi). — § 734 (Ānuçāsanik.): XIII, **26**, 1838 (*putrān S°syeto bhashmākhyān anayad divaṃ*, sc. *Gaṅgā*, all. to § 389).—§ 761 (do.): XIII, **115**δ, 5668 (did not eat meat during the month of Kārttika). —§ 770 (do.): XIII, **151**, 7130 (*Sagarasyātmajā* (C. by error *Sā° jo*) *yena plāvitās tāritās tathā*, sc. Bhagīratha, all. to § 389. As stated under Çveta, PCR. before this inserts a passage (omitted in both C. and B.), of which the last çloka (mentioning Bhagīratha) ought to be connected with this).—§ 775 (do.): XIII, **166**η, 7675 (C. has by error *Sā°*).—§ 785 (Anugītāp.): XIV, **87**, 2594 (°*ādayaḥ*, had not performed the horse sacrifice). Cf. Aikshvāku.

***Sāgara**[2] ("the son of Sagara," cf. III, 9912) = the Ocean (personif.): III, 16301; XII, 4197 ff.—Do., pl. (°*āḥ*): IX, 2556.

Sāgara[3] = Sūrya: III, 152.

Sāgara[4] (XIII, 7130, 7675), v. Sagara.

Sāgara, pl. ("the sons of Sagara"). § 387 (Sagara): III, **107**, 8855, 8857, 8861, 8864, 8872, 8873, 8881 (reduced to ashes by Kapila).—§ 389 (Gaṅgāvataraṇa): III, **107**, 9905, 9906, 9910; **108**, 9936, 9938 (their bodies besprinkled by the Gaṅgā).

Sāgaradhvaja, v. Sāraṅgadhvaja.

Sāgaragāsuta ("the son of the river") = Bhīshma: V, 7577; VI, 4938.

Sāgaraka, pl. (°*āḥ*), a people. § 295 (Dyūtap.): II, **52**, 1874 (brought tribute to Yudhishṭhira).

Sāgarālaya ("dwelling in the ocean") = Varuṇa: IX, 2736 (*V°*).

Sāgarānūpaka, pl. (°*āḥ*), a people. § 342 (Indralokābhigamanap.): III, **51**, 1989 (had been present at the rājasūya of Yudhishṭhira).

Sāgarodaka, a tīrtha. § 733*c* (Pushkara): XIII, **25**, 1696 ("the Ocean," PCR.).

Saha[1], a son of Dhṛtarāshṭra. § 182 (Dhṛtarāshṭraputranāmak.): I, **117**, 4541.—§ 232 (Svayaṃvarap.): I, **186**, 6981 (came to the svayaṃvara of Draupadī). — § 608 (Karṇap.): VIII, **51**δδ, 2447 (attacked Bhīmasena), 2455 (only B. erroneously); **84**ξ', 4263 (slain by Bhīmasena).

Saha[2], name of a fire? father of Adbhuta. § 493 (Āṅgirasa): III, **222**, 14208 (*Āpasya duhitā*—B. *Muditā—Sahasya bhāryā*; Nīl. takes *Āpasya* as an epithet to *Sahasya*. According to the reading *duhitā*, Āpa may be the father of Saha's wife. The following story of the Fire's disappearance is by Nīl. referred to *S.*).

Saha[3] = Çiva (1000 names[2]).—Do.[4] = Vishṇu (1000 names).

Sahā, an Apsaras. § 336 (Indralokābhigamanap.): III, **43***a*, 1785 (in the abode of Indra).

Sahadeva[1], Pāṇḍava. § 4 (Anukram.): I, **1**, 206 (*Saubalaṃ Pāṇḍavena hataṃ . . . S°ena*, cf. § 611).—§ 11 (Parvasaṅgr.): I, **2**, 553 (*Çakuneç ca vadhaḥ . . . S°ena*, do.).—§ 71 (Ādivaṃçāvataraṇap.): I, **61**, 2268 (conquered the southern region, cf. § 281 foll.).—§ 83 (Ādivaṃçāvatāraṇa): I, **63**, 2445 (Nakula and *S.* sons of the Açvins), 2452 (father of Çrutasena).—§ 130 (Aṃçāvat.): I, **67**, 2747 (Nakula and *S.* incarnate portions of the Açvins—*Açvinoḥ . . . aṃçau*).—§ 157 (Pūruvaṃç.): I, **95**, ††3816 (*Mādryāṃ Açvibhyāṃ Nakula-S°au*).—§ 159 (do.): I, **95**, ††3827 (had with Draupadī the son Çrutakarman), ††3832 (husband of Vijayā, daughter of the Madra king Dyutimat, by her he had the son Suhotra).—§ 192 (Pāṇḍavotpatti): I, **124**, 4851 (Nakula and Sahadeva are born by Mādrī from the Açvins), 4855 (the younger of the twins).—[§ 205*c* (Droṇa): Nakula and *S.* excelled every one in handling the sword: I, **132**, 5271 (*Yamajau*).]—§ 210 (Drupadaçāsana): I, **139**, 5532 (*d*: learnt the whole science of morality from the chief of the gods (*vibudhādhipateḥ*), i.e. Bṛhaspati (PCR.)).—§ 214 (Hiḍimbavadhap.): I, **154**, 6019, 6025.—§ 235 (Svayaṃvarap.): I, **191**, †7139.—§ 236 (do.): I, **192**, †7163 (the Pāṇḍavas won Draupadī). — § 253 (Haraṇāharaṇap.): I, **221**, 8040 (begat Çrutasena on Draupadī), 8045 (do.).—§ 272 (Rājasūyārambhap.): II, **13**, 524 (°*sya dharmāṇāṃ anuçāsanāt*).—§ 278 (Digvijayap.): II, **25**, 992 (*dakshiṇāṃ*—sc. *diçaṃ—vyajayata*).—§ 281 (do.): *S.* proceeded against the south and vanquished the *Çūrasenas*

(C. *Sū°*,), etc. (*a*), then the son of *Jambhaka* (*b*), etc. (*β*), then *Bhīshmaka* (*c*), etc. Coming to *Kishkindhā* he for seven days fought with the monkey-kings *Mainda* and *Dvivida*, who then paid tribute: II, **31**, 1105, 1112, 1123.—§ 282 (do.): From *Kishkindhā S.* marched towards *Māhishmatī* (*b*) and fought with king *Nīla*, but was exposed to great risk, as Agni assisted *Nīla*, so that the army of *S.* all appeared to be on fire: II, **31**, 1125, 1127, 1129.—§ 283 (do.): *S.* was not afraid, but purifying himself by touching water he praised *Agni* (*b*) saying that his exertion was for *Agni* (viz. for a sacrifice), etc.: II, **31**, 1143 (1145).—§ 284 (do.): Then *S.* spread some *kuça* grass, and sat down in front of his troops. And *Agni* did not pass over him, but said that he had only been trying him, and though he should protect this city as long as there was a descendant in *Nīla's* line, he nevertheless would accomplish the desire of *S.* When *Agni* had disappeared, *Nīla* came at the command of that deity and paid tribute. Then *S.* went further towards the south and vanquished the king of Tripura, etc. (*a*), and then returned to Yudhishṭhira (II, **31**): II, **31**, (1155), 1158, 1163, 1180.—§ 286 (Rājasūyikap.): II, **33**, 1231, 1236, 1243 (acted as mantrin at the rājasūya of Yudhishṭhira).—§ 289 (Arghāharaṇap.): II, **36**, 1335 (presents the first argha to Kṛshṇa); **39**, 1401, 1406, 1409.—§ 292 (Rājasūyikap.): II, **45a**, 1608 (accompanied Droṇa and his son).—§ 294 (Dyūtap.): II, **48**, 1716; **50**, 1818.—§ 298 (do.): II, **65**, 2155 (*ayaṃ dharmān S°o 'nuçāsti*; is staked and lost by Yudhishṭhira).—§ 299 (do.): II, **68**, 2256.—§ 301 (do.): II, **70**, 2363; **71**, 2383 (*°Ārjunau*). — § 302 (Anudyūtap.): II, **74**, 2465.—§ 304 (do.): II, **77**, 2539 (will slay Çakuni), 2550 (*Mādravatīsutaḥ*), (2552), 2555.—§ 305 (do.): II, **78**, 2570; **79**, 2591, 2611.—§ 306 (do.): II, **80a**, 2624 (went away to the forest besmearing his face that none might recognize him).—§ 325 (Draupadīparitāpav.): III, **27**, 1021—§ 327 (do.): III, **35**, 1389, 1402.—§ 342 (Indralokābhigamanap.): III, **51**, 1971 (*devaputrau . . . devarājasamadyutī Nakulaḥ S°ç ca Pāṇḍavau*) —§ 356 (Tīrthayātrāp.): III, **80**, (4017) (proposes to remove from the Kāmyaka forest).—§ 401 (Balarāma): III, **119**, †10254 (*yaḥ Sindhukūle vyajayan nṛdevān samāgatān Dākshiṇātyān*, cf. § 281 foll.).—§ 419 (Gandhamādanapr.): III, **140**, 10843, 10849, 10852, 10862.—§ 423 (do.): III, **143**, 10977; **144**, 10993.—§ 424 (Bhīmakadalīkh.): III, **146**, 11102.—§ 433 (Saugandhikāharaṇa): III, **155**, 11426.—§ 435 (Jaṭāsuravadhap.): III, **157**, 11460 (*Paṇḍavaḥ*), 11480, 11485 (*Pāṇḍavaḥ*), 11488 (carried away by Jaṭāsura, snatched the sword Kauçika (?)).—§ 438 (Yakshayuddhap.): III, **161**, 11774.—§ 450 (Ājagarap.): III, **179**, 12432 (*Nakulaḥ S°ç ca Yamau*), 12443. — § 511 (Draupadī-Satyabhāmāsamv.): III, **235**, 14732 (father of Çrutasena by Draupadī, cf. § 159).—§ 521 (Draupadīharaṇap.): III, **263**, 15546, 15547, 15557 (in all three passages only B., C. has *Bhīmasena* instead). — § 522 (do.): III, **270**, †15709 (*dhīmān*). †15712; **271**, 15726, 15730 (Yudhishṭhira ascends the chariot of *S.* and causes Draupadī to be taken upon it).—§ 548 (Āraṇeyap.): III, **312**, (17245), 17257, 17260, 17274 (slain by the Yaksha, but restored to life).—§ 549 (Pāṇḍavapraveçap.): IV, **3**, 66, (67) (as a teller of kine, under the name of Tantipāla, he will serve Virāṭa); **5**, 167 (had vanquished the south, hid his weapons); **10**, †280, †288 (calls himself a vaiçya named Arishṭanemi (also called Tantipāla), and is charged with the supervision of Virāṭa's cattle).—§ 550 (Samayapālanap.): IV, **13**, 333 (*gopānāṃ veçam āsthāya*), 369 (gives his brothers curds, milk, and ghee).—§ 551 (Kīcakavadhap.): IV, **19**, 588 (*yavīyasaṃ; gavāṃ patiṃ*), 589, 590, 593 (*b*: the weeping Kuntī embraced *S.* when he set out to the forest and said: "he is my favourite child"), 597.—§ 552 (Goharaṇap.): IV, **31**, 1024 (disguised as Tantipāla *S.* follows Virāṭa against the Trigartas); **33**, 1100 (protected the wheel of Bhīmasena); **43**, 1354, 1360, 1366; **44**, 1368, 1372; **50**, 1564.—§ 553 (Vaivāhikap.): IV, **71a**, 2290, 2294 (*gosaṅkhyaḥ*).—§ 556*d* (Sañjayayānap.): *S.* in *Dantakūra* conquered the *Kaliṅgas*, shooting arrows by both the left and the right hand: V, **23**, †708 (*Mādrīputraḥ*).—§ 556 (do.): V, **26**, †763.—§ 561 (Yānasandhip.): V, **48**, †1836 (description of his chariot), †1838.—§ 561*g* (do.): *S.* had vanquished the *Kāçis*, the *Aṅgas*, the *Magadhas*, and the *Kaliṅgas*. Only four men are his equals in strength, viz. *Açvatthāman*, *Dhṛshṭaketu*, *Rukmin*, and *Pradyumna*: V, **50**, 1998, 1999.—§ 561*k* (do.): Steeds of sable bodies and backs variegated like the wings of the *tittiri* bird, all presented by his gratified brother *Phālguna* (i.e. Arjuna), and superior to those of *Phālguna* himself, cheerfully carried *S.*: V, **56**, †2229.—§ 561 (do.): V, **57**, 2253 (*Mādreyaḥ*, chose Çakuni for his match in the battle) (*o*), 2262.—§ 562 (Bhagavadyānap.): V, **80**ε, 2855; **81**, (2862), 2866; **82**, 2872; **90**π, 3164, 3165 (*°sya bhrātaraḥ*), 3166.—§ 567 (do.): V, **126**, 4220.—§ 569 (do.): V, **138**, 4681; **140a**, 4748; **141**γ, 4778, 4791 (*Nakulaḥ S°ç ca Mādrīputrau . . . çāmitrāṃ . . . karishyataḥ*); **143**ι, 4871.—§ 570 (Sainyaniryāṇap.): V, **151**, 5104, (*β*), (5106), 5108.—§ 571 (Ulūkadūtāgamanap.): V, **160**, 5478; **162**, 5608, 5614; **163**, 5681, 5697; **164**ε, 5709 (pitted against Çakuni). — § 572 (Rathātirathasaṅkhyānap.): V, **166**, 5752 (had vanquished Nīla, cf. § 284).—§ 573 (Ambopākhyānap.): V, **196**ι, 7635.—§ 576 (Bhagavadgītāp.): VI, **19**ε, 709; **25**κ, 845 (blew the çaṅkha Maṇipushpaka).—§ 577 (Bhīshmavadhap.): VI, **43a**, (1546), 1555.—§ 578 (do.): VI, **44**β, 1655; **45**[6], 1694, 1695 (fought with Durmukha), ([19]), 1735 (read with B. *Sā°iṃ*, i.e. Çrutakarman); **50**π, 2085 (in the army of Yudhishṭhira); **51aa**, 2116 (blew the çaṅkha Maṇipushpaka).—§ 581 (do.): VI, **62**θ, 2755.—§ 582 (do.): VI, **71**δ, 3139 (fought with Vikarṇa); **72**ε, 3166 (attacked Çakuni and Ulūka).—§ 583 (do.): VI, **75**, 3282 (on the one eye of the makaravyūha).—§ 584 (do.): VI, **81**[1], 3556 (Nakula and *S.* attacked Çalya); **83**, 3682, 3689 (encounter with Çalya). § 585 (do.): VI, **89**, 3962.—§ 586 (do.): VI, **99**ε, 4508 (*Nakulaḥ S°ç ca Mādrīputrau*); **101**θ, 4586, 4589; **105**ο, 4776, (ρ), 4797 (pierced Çalya); **106**σ, 4803.—§ 587 (do.): VI, **108**β, 5013; **110**ζ, 5099, 5105 (resisted by Kṛpa); **111**, 5167 (pierced Kṛpa); **116**, 5401 (rescued Dhṛshṭaketu). — § 588 (do.): VI, **121**γ, 5809. — § 589 (Droṇābhishekap.): VII, **10**, 337.—§ 590 (do.): VII, **14**, 516 (fought with Çakuni); **16**γ, 645.—§ 592 (Saṃçaptakavadhap.): VII, **23**ο, 958 (description of his horses), (ν), 1031 (on his standard there was a beautiful swan of silver), (ρ), 1040 (held the bow Āçvina); **32**ζζ, 1443. — § 593 (Abhimanyuvadhap.): VII, **34a**, 1488 (*sadṛço devayoḥ . . . Açvinoḥ*), 1491 (*vinayāt S°sya sadṛçaḥ*, sc. Abhimanyu); **39**ν, 1657.—§ 599 (Jayadrathavadhap.): VII, **98**κ, 3661; **106**, 3977 (attacked by Durmukha), 4011 (*°rathaṃ*, carried away Yudhishṭhira); **107**, 4031, 4033 (fought with Durmukha), 4036, 4038 (slew Niramitra), 4040; **109**π, 4110, 4112; **111**υ, 4284; **124**κκ, 4983; **143**ιι, 5997.—§ 600 (Ghaṭotkacavadhap.): VII, **154**β, 6650; **156**θ, 6763; **165**, 7362 (pierced by Droṇa); **167**, 7462 (pierced Karṇa), 7463, 7467, 7469, 7470, 7473, 7476, 7477, 7482 (defeated by Karṇa); **170**νν, 7672; **177**ψψ, 8060; **178**ωω, 8080, 8084; **183**, 8326.—§ 601 (Droṇavadhap.): VII, **184a**, 8367.—§ 602 (do.): VII, **188**, 8574, 8576, 8580 (encounter with Duḥçāsana).—§ 603 (Nārāyaṇāstramokshap.): VII, **198**, 9178, 9185 (pacified Sātyaki).—§ 604 (Karṇap.): VIII, **5**ζ, 116 (had slain his cousin Rukmaratha); **9**, 297 (had been vanquished by Karṇa, cf. § 600).—§ 605 (do.): VIII, **11aa**, 427; **13**, 496 (attacked Duḥçāsana); **22**ηη, 876, 877, 887 (fought with the Angas, etc.); **23**, 893, 896, 897, 898, 900, 903, 904, 905, 909 (encounter with Duhçāsana).—§ 608 (do.): VIII, **46**, 2156 (proceeded against Çakuni), (η), 2205; **48**π, 2273, (ρ), 2280; **54**, 2624; **56**, 2699 (°*sya dhvajaṃ kāñcanaṃ*), 2700, (ππ), 2756; **59**, 2965 (bore away Dhṛshṭadyumna); **61**, 3078 (proceeded against Ulūka), 3108, 3109 (encounter with Ulūka); **62**ζζζ, 3148, 3154 (pierced Duryodhana); **63**, 3184, 3189 (°*rathaṃ*; bore away Yudhishṭhira), 3208, 3212; **73**, 3732; **75**χχχ, †3812 (attacked Çakuni); **78**γ', 3955 (pierced Karṇa), 3958, 3963; **79**η', 4029; **96**βa', 5030.—§ 611 (Çalyap.): IX, **11**, 561 (attacked Çalya), 570, 571 (slew [Rukmaratha] the son of Çalya); **13**o, 661, 664, 665, 667, 681, 688 (fought with Çalya); **15**ρ, 768 (*Mādreyaḥ*), 771 (pierced by Çalya), 774 (pierced Çalya); **16**, 800 (checked Çakuni); **17**χ, 866 (pierced by Çalya), 891; **22**λλ, 1138 (pierced by Duryodhana), 1140, 1154 (carried away Yudhishṭhira); **23**, 1212, 1216, 1243; **27**σσ, 1446, (φφ), 1471, 1474, 1475, 1476 (fought with Duryodhana); **28**, 1501, 1502, 1503, 1506, 1516, 1517, 1525, 1528, 1530, 1531, 1532 (slew Ulūka), 1535, 1536, 1537, 1539, 1541, 1546, 1547, 1553, 1554, 1556, 1557, 1558, 1565 (slew Çakuni).—§ 612 (Hradapraveçap.): IX, **29**, 1568, 1569.—§ 613 (Gadāyuddhap.): IX, **32**β, 1882; **33**ε, 1890, 1900.—§ 618 (Jalapradānikap.): XI, **14**, 376.—§ 619 (Strīvilāpap.): XI, **18**γ, 540; **24**, 698 (*Çakuniḥ . . . nihataḥ S°ena*).—§ 623 (Rājadh.): XII, **13**, (371).—§ 637 (do.): XII, **40a**, 1446; **41**β, 1481; **44**δ, 1528 (got the palace of Durmukha).—§ 657 (Āpaddh.): XII, **167**, 6231, (6232) (*Nakula-S°au*).—§ 720*b* (Sudarçanop.): XIII, **2**, 116 (*dṛshṭaṃ . . . S°ena vijayatā*, sc. *sānnidhyaṃ . . . Vibhāvasoḥ*, i.e. Agni, all. to § 282 foll.).—§ 780 (Açvamedhikap.): XIV, **14**β, 356.—§ 783 (Anugītāp.): XIV, **52**ε, 1524.—§ 785 (do.): XIV, **60**β, 1797 (had slain Çakuni); **66**μ, 1954; **72**, 2103, 2109 (waited upon the guests at the açvamedha); **85**σ, 2514.—§ 787 (Āçramavāsap.): XV, **16**, 450; **17**χ, 481.—§ 788 (do.): XV, **22**, 600, 605; **24**, 643, 645.—§ 791 (Putradarçanap.): XV, **36**, 992 (*yudhāṃ patiḥ*), 999.—§ 792 (Nāradāgamanap.): XV, **38a**, 1074 (the darling of Kuntī).—§ 793 (Mausalap.): XVI, **7**, 179 (*Pāṇḍavaḥ*).—§ 794 (Mahāprasthānikap.): XVII, **2**, 54, 57, 58 (*Pāṇḍavaṃ*, on the mahāprasthāna of the Pāṇḍavas *S.* fell down, because he thought nobody his equal in wisdom).—§ 795 (Svargārohaṇap.): XVIII, **2**ε, 67; **4**κ, 133 (in heaven). Cf. Āçvineya, sg. and dual, Açviṇīsuta, dual, Açvisuta, dual, Bharataçreshṭha, dual, Bharatarshabha, Bharatasattama, Kauravya, Kurunandana, Mādravatīputra, sg. and dual, Mādravatīsuta, sg. and dual, Mādreya, sg. and dual, Mādrinandana, sg. and dual, Mādrīnandanaka, dual, Mādrīnandakara, Mādrīputra, sg. and dual, Mādrīsuta, sg. and dual, Mādrītanūja, dual, Nakulānuja, Pāṇḍava, sg. and dual, Pāṇḍunandana, Pāṇḍuputra, Pāṇḍusuta, Tantipāla, Yama, dual, Yāmaja, dual.

Sahadeva[2], king of the Magadhas, son of Jarāsandha. § 232 (Svayaṃvarap.): I, **186**, 6988 (°-*Jayatsenau*, present at the svayaṃvara of Draupadī).—§ 273 (Rājasūyārambhap.): II, **14**, 595 (son of Jarāsandha and brother of Asti and Prāpti).—§ 277 (Jarāsandhavadhap.): II, **22**, 884 (installed by Jarāsandha as king of the Magadhas); **24**, 962 (*Jarāsandhātmajaḥ*, do.), 963.—§ 561 (Yānasandhip.): V, **50**η, 2014 (*Jārāsandhiḥ*, among the allies of Yudhishṭhira).—§ 570 (Sainyaniryāṇap.): V, **157**, 5325 (*Māgadhaṃ*, commander of one division of Yudhishṭhira's troops).—Cf. Jarāsandhasuta, Jarāsandhātmaja, Jārāsandhi, Māgadha.

Sahadeva[3], a ṛshi(?). § 266 (Çakrasabhāv.): II, **7**, 297 (in the palace of Indra).

Sahadeva[4], an ancient king [of the Pañcālas]. § 267 (Yamasabhāv.): II, **8**, 328 (in the place of Yama).—§ 377 (Dhaumyatīrthâk.): III, **90**, 8376 (performed a sacrifice at Agniçiras), 8378 (do., on the Yamunā).

Sahadevaja ("the son of Sahadeva[2]") = Meghasandhi: XIV, 2463.

Sahadevasūnu ("the son of Sahadeva[1]") = Çrutakarman (Çrutasena): VIII, †4322.

Sahadevātmaja ("the son of Sahadeva[2]") = Meghasandhi: XIV, 2437.

Sāhadevi[1] ("the son of Sahadeva[4]") = Somaka: III, 10422.

Sāhadevi[2] ("the son of Sahadeva[1]") = Çrutakarman (Çrutasena): VI, 1735 (only B., C. has *Sahadevaṃ*); VII, 4062.

Sahaja, a king. § 562 (Bhagavadyānap.): V, **74**γ, 2732 (*Cedi-Matsyānāṃ*, among the wicked kings who annihilated their kinsmen and relatives).

Sahajanyā, an Apsaras. § 135 (Çakuntalop.): I, **74**, 3055 (among the principal Apsarases)—§ 191 (Arjuna): I, **123**, 4820 (sang at the birth of Arjuna).—§ 269 (Vaiçravaṇasabhāv.): II, **10**, 393 (in the palace of Kubera).—§ 336 (Indralokābhigamanap.): III, **43a**, 1785 (in the abode of Indra).

Sahasrabāhu[1], a warrior of Skanda. § 615*u* (Skanda): IX., **45**η, 2561.—Do.[2] = Skanda: III, 14640.—Do.[3] = Çiva: VII, 9528; XIII, 1246 (1000 names[2]).

Sahasrabāhumukuṭa = Kṛshṇa: XII, 1611.

Sahasrabhū = Skanda: III, 14641.

Sahasrabhuj = Skanda: III, 14641.

Sahasrabhujamanyu = Çiva: VII, 2883 (so C., B. has °*mṛtyu*).

Sahasracaraṇa[1] = Çiva: VII, 9528; XII, 10382 (1000 names[1]); XIV, 205.—Do.[2] = Vishṇu: V, 3827.

Sahasracaraṇekshaṇa = Kṛshṇa: XII, 1611.

Sahasracitya[1], a prince. § 767 (Ānuçāsanik.): XIII, **137a**, 6264 (attained to excellent regions by sacrificing his life for the sake of a brahman). Cf. next and Sahasrajit[1].

Sahasracitya[2], a Kaikeya king. § 787 (Āçramavāsap.): Nārada said: The Kekaya king *S.* was the grandfather of *Çatayūpa*, resigning his kingdom to his eldest son, he retired into the woods and after great penances attained to the region of Indra (*Purandarasya*), where I have often seen him: XV, **20**, 543 (*Kekayādhipatiḥ . . . Çatayūpapitāmahaḥ*), 544.

Sahasraçiras[1] = Çiva: VII, 2883; XIV, 205.—Do.[2] = Kṛshṇa: XII, 1611, 1647.

Sahasraçirasa = Vishṇu: V, 3827.

Sahasraçīrsha[1] = Çiva: XII, 10382 (1000 names[1]); XIII, 7089.—Do.[2] = Skanda: III, 14642.—Do.[3] = Vishṇu (Kṛshṇa): III, 15815; V, †2579; XII, 7343 (*V*°).

Sahasrada = Çiva (1000 names[2]).

Sahasrādhmātaghaṇṭa = Çiva (1000 names[1]).

Sahasradṛç = Indra, q.v.
Sahasrahasta = Çiva (1000 names[2]).
Sahasrajit[1], a king. § 677 (Mokshadh.): XII, **235,** 8605 (attained to excellent regions by sacrificing his life for the sake of a brahman). Cf. Sahasracitya[1].
Sahasrajit[2] = Vishṇu (1000 names).
Sahasrajyotis. § 3 (Anukram.): I, **1**β, 44 (son of Subhrāj and father of 1,000,000 sons).
Sāhasraka, a tīrtha. § 368 (Tīrthayātrāp.): III, **83,** 7029.
Sahasrakiraṇa = Sūrya (the Sun): XIII, 428.
Sahasrāksha[1] = Indra, q.v.—Do.[2] = Çiva: XII, 10349 (1000 names[1]); XIII, 763, 1151 (1000 names[2]), 7514; XIV, 195.—Do.[3] = Vishṇu (Kṛshṇa): III, 15814; V, 3827; XIII, 6823 (i.e. Kṛshṇa), 6973 (1000 names).
Sahasralocana = Indra, q.v.
Sahasrāṃçu = Sūrya (the Sun), q.v.—Do.[2] = Vishṇu (1000 names).
Sahasramūrdhan[1] = Çiva (1000 names[1]).—Do.[2] = Vishṇu (1000 names).
Sahasranāma = Vishṇu: XIII, 7089.
Sahasranayana[1] = Indra, q.v.—Do.[2] = Çiva: VII, 9528; XII, 10383 (1000 names[1]).
Sahasranetra = Indra, q.v.
Sahasranetrapāda = Çiva: VII, 2883.
Sahasrapad[1], a ṛshi. § 24 (cf. Paulomap.): One day *Ruru* in consequence of his vote for the destruction of the serpents was about to kill an old *ḍuṇḍubha*, but this objected that he had done him no harm (I, **9**). He told that he was formerly a ṛshi, named *S.*, who had been metamorphosed by the curse of a brahman (I, **10**): I, **10,** 993.—§ 25 (do.): The *ḍuṇḍubha* said: "I had a friend named *Khagama*; one day, when he was engaged in the *agnihotra*, I made a mock-snake of blades of grass in order to frighten him, and he went into a swoon; then he cursed me saying that I should be turned into a venomless serpent, until I had seen *Ruru*." *S.* then recovered his original form, and told *Ruru* that a brāhmaṇa never should take life which was the duty of the kshatriya. Cf. Uraga.
Sahasrapad[2], a brahman. § 324 (Dvaitavanapr.): III, **26**α, 985 (worshipped Yudhishṭhira). Cf. the prec.
Sahasrapad[3] = Çiva (1000 names[2]).—Do.[4] = Skanda: III, 14642.—Do.[5] = Vishṇu: III, 15814; XIII, 6973 (1000 names).
Sahasraraçmi = Sūrya: III, 192.
Sahasrārcis = Vishṇu (1000 names).
Sahasrasūryapratima = Çiva (1000 names[1]).
Sahasratushṭi = Skanda: III, 14641.
Sahasravāc, a son of Dhṛtarāshṭra. § 130 (Aṃçāvat.): I, **67,** 2735 (enumeration).
Sahasravadanojjvala = Kṛshṇa: XII, 1611.
Sahasravaktra = Skanda: III, 14640.
Sahasrodyataçūla = Çiva (1000 names[1]).
Sahāya = Çiva (1000 names[2]).
Sahishṇu = Vishṇu (1000 names).
Sahma (II, 1029) v. Suhma, pl.
Sahya[1]. § 3 (Anukram.): I, **1,** 43 (so B. for Mahya (q.v.) and cf. Āçāvaha).
Sahya[2], a mountain. § 534 (Hanūmatprātyāg.): III, **282,** 16239 (°-*Malayau*, on their way to Laṅkā, Hanūmat, etc., came to *S.* on the shore of the sea).—§ 555 (Indravijaya): V, **11**α, 353.—§ 574¦(Jambūkh.): VI, **9**κ, 318 (among the kulaparvatas of Bhāratavarsha).—§ 782*g* (Guruçishyasaṃv.): XIV, **43**γ, 1173.

Saikata, pl. (°*āḥ*), a class of ṛshis. § 677 (Mokshadh.): XII, **245**γ, 8903. Cf. Sikata, pl.
Saindhava[1] ("king of the Sindhus") = Jayadratha: I, †190, †191, †196, 7001 (*J*°); II, 1267 (*J*°, C. has by error *Drayadrathaḥ*); III, 15637, 15716 (*rājā*, adj.?), 15719, 15758, 15760 (°*āpasadaḥ*), 15762, 15768, 15770, 15771, 15775, 16610 (all. to Draupadīharaṇap.), †17219 (all. to Jayadrathavimokshaṇap.); IV, 164 (all. to Draupadīharaṇap. and Jayadrathavimokshaṇap.), 526 (all. to Draupadīharaṇap.); V, 2246 (*J*°), 2504, 3403, 4824 (*J*°), 5274 (*J*°), 5708 (Sātyaki is pitted against Jayadratha), 7608 (*J*°); VI, 1723 (*J*°), 2141 (pl.? °*pramukhaiḥ*), 2452 (*J*°), †2648 (°*Bāhlikau*), 3138, 3164, †3761 (°*ādīn rājñaḥ*), 4092 (all. to Draupadīharaṇap.), 4195, 4501, 4545, 5050 (*J*°), 5240 (*J*°), 5244, 5250, 5253, 5256, 5258, 5277 (*rājā*, adj.?), 5292 (*J*°), 5309 (*J*°), 5417 (*rājā*, adj.?), 5418, 5419, 5583 (*J*°); VII, 179, 558, 1073, 1075, 1723, 1749, 1750, 1762, 1779, 1780, 1781, 1782, 1853, 1865, 2007, 2615, 2631, 2632, 2633, 2646 (*rājā*, adj. ?), 2649, 2653 (*sa-S°āḥ*, only B.), 2665 (*rājā*, adj.?), 2687, 2692, 2694, 2696, 2723, 2725, 2789, 2831, 2833, 2837, 2973, 2994, 3002, 3006, 3015 (°*sya niveçane*), 3101, 3426, 3538, 3539, 3541, 3668, 3699, 3701, 3754, 3756, 3778, 3796, 3797, 3884, 3922, 3965, 4170, 4213 (pl.?, °*ānīkaṃ*), 4253, 4255, 4303, 4323, 4367, 4467, 4713, 4865, 5133, 5150, 5246, 5264, 5311, 5325, 5326, 5331, 5332, 5333, 5395, 5820, 5822, 5870, 5871, 5948, 6005, 6063, 6068, 6075, 6082, 6084, 6094, 6097, 6099, 6104, 6106, 6114, 6143, 6201 (pl. ? °*ābhimukhaṃ*), 6207, 6211, 6215, 6216, 6228, 6257, 6258 (*Vṛddhakshatraḥ S°sya pitā*), 6259, 6274, 6275, 6286 (slain by Arjuna), 6290, 6293, 6295 (*nṛpaṃ*, adj.?), 6297 (*nihate*), 6298 (*nihataṃ*), 6324 (do.), 6334 (*nipātite*), 6451 (*hate*), 6456 (*nihataḥ*), 6494 (*nihate*), 6499, 6550, 6557 (*ahanyata*), 6576 (*hatrā S°ṃ*); 6578, 6592 (*nihataḥ*), 6616 (°*sya vadhaṃ*), 6648 (°*ṃ hatvā*), 7737, 8281 (*sa*-°), 8307 (°*sya*, sc. *vadhāt*), 8335, 8339, 8342, 9227; VIII, 3647, 3682 (*nihataḥ . . . S°o rājā*); IX, 3614 (*J*°); X, 137, 524; XI, 736; XII, 501 (all. to Draupadīharaṇap.); XIV, 324 (do.), 1497 (°*sya vadhopāyaḥ*, all. to Jayadratha-vadhap.), 2229 (*hantāraṃ S°sya*, i.e. Arjuna); XV, 361 (°*āpasadasya*, sc. *çrāddhaṃ*).
Saindhava[2] (do.) = Vṛddhakshatra: VII, 1747 (°*sya putraḥ . . . Jayadrathaḥ*).
Saindhava[3], pl. (°*āḥ*), a people = Sindhu, pl. § 342 (Indralokābhigamanap.): III, **51,** 1991 (had been present at the rājasūya of Yudhishṭhira).—§ 522 (Draupadīharaṇap.); III, **271,** 15722 (°*dhvajinīmukhe*, i.e. the followers of Jayadratha), 15743, 15751 (°*sainikān*).—§ 568 (Vidulāputraçāsana): V, **134,** 4570 (°*kanyānām avasannaḥ*, sc. Sañjaya[4]), **135,** 4601 (*sarva-S°ān*, Sañjaya had been defeated by the *S.*).—§ 584 (Bhīshmavadhap.): VI, **81**α, 3532 (only C., follow Somadatta).—§ 599 (Jayadratha-vadhap.): VII, **111**γ, 4266 (° *Pauravāḥ*)—§ 600 (Ghaṭotkaca-vadhap.): VII, **179,** †8159 (applauded Karṇa).—§ 608 (Karṇap.): VIII, **56**ρρ, 2762.—§ 785 (Anugītāp.): XIV, **77,** 2221, 2242, 2248 (*yodhāḥ*), 2249, 2250; **78,** 2254 (*yodhāḥ*), 2262, 2266, 2269 (*nṛpāḥ*, adj.?), 2298 (recollecting the slaughter of Jayadratha, the *S.* fought with Arjuna, but were defeated).
Saindhava[4], adj. ("belonging to or originating from [the country of] the Sindhus"). § 522 (Draupadīharaṇap.): III, **269,** †15672 (*vājibhiḥ*).—§ 525 (Rāmopākhyānap.): III, **273,** 15867 (*balaṃ*, i.e. the army of Jayadratha).—§ 561 (Yānasandhip.): V, **47,** 1804 (*sādhuvāhibhiḥ*).—§ 589

(Droṇābhishekap.): VII, **9,** 276 (*sādhuvāhinaḥ*).—§ 592 (Saṃçaptakavadhap.): VII, **23**o, 973 (*hayottamāḥ*); **26,** 1171 (*açvān*).—§ 593 (Abhimanyuvadhap.): VII, **43,** 1764 (*açvāḥ*). — § 598 (Jayadrathavadhap.): VII, **87,** 3104 (*hayāḥ*).—§ 599 (do.): VII, **104,** 3898 (*hayottamāḥ*); **112,** 4358 (*vājinaḥ*); **116,** 4635 (*vāhān*); **140,** †5837 (*sadaçvāḥ*). —§ 600 (Ghaṭotkacavadhap.): VII, **162,** 7226 (*turangamān*): **173,** 7786 (*sādhuvāhinaḥ*).—§ 604 (Karṇap.): VIII, **7,** †200 (sc. *açvaiḥ* ?).—§ 611 (Çalyap.): IX, **8,** 389 (sc. *açvān*).

Saindhavaka, adj. (do.).—§ 522 (Draupadīharaṇap.): III, **271,** 15757 (°*o nṛpaḥ*, i.e. Jayadratha).—§ 578 (Bhīshmavadhap.): VI, **45**[15], 1724 (°*o rājā* = do.). — § 596 (Pratijñāp.): VII, **73,** 2574 (do. = do.); **76,** 2695 (do. = do.).—§ 597 (do.): VII, **84,** 3001 (°*o nṛpaḥ* = do.). —§ 599 (Jayadrathavadhap.): VII, **118,** 5266–7 (°*o rājā* = do.); **145,** 6073 (°*aṃ nṛpaṃ* = do.).

Saindhavāraṇya, name of a forest. § 377 (Dhaumyatīrthak.): III, **89,** 8368 (in the west).—§ 406 (Tīrthayātrāp.): III, **125,** 10408 (°*m āsādya kulyānāṃ kuru darçanaṃ*).

Saindhavāyana, a son of Viçvāmitra. § 721*b* (Viçvāmitrop.): XIII, **4**β, 250.

Sainyaniryāṇa(m) ("the marching out of the troops"). § 10 (Parvasangr.): I, **2,** 333 (i.e. Sainyaniryāṇaparvan).

[Sainyaniryāṇaparvan(°va)] ("the section relating to the marching out of the troops," the 63rd of the minor parvans of Mhbhr.; cf. Sainyaniryāṇa). § 570: The *Pāṇḍavas* had seven *akshauhiṇīs* led by *Drupada*, etc. (**a**). *Yudhishṭhira* consulted with his brothers about the election of a generalissimo, who might also withstand *Bhīshma*. *Sahadeva*, etc., proposed *Virāṭa*, etc. (β). *Kṛshṇa* named *Dhṛshṭadyumna*, who was elected. Then they marched out to *Kurukshetra* (description), with *Bhīma* in the van, etc. (γ). *Draupadī* with her ladies, etc., remained at *Upaplavya*. The *Kekaya* princes, etc. (δ) marched behind *Yudhishṭhira*, keeping him in their centre. In the rear were *Virāṭa*, etc. (ε), 40,000 chariots, etc. *Anādhṛshṭi*, etc. (ζ) marched surrounding *Kṛshṇa* and *Arjuna*. Entering *Kurukshetra*, they blew their conches, also *Kṛshṇa* and *Arjuna*; *Pāñcajanya* filled them with joy (V, **152**). *Yudhishṭhira* encamped on *Kurukshetra*. *Kṛshṇa*, etc. (η) each did some special work. At the holy *Hiraṇvatī* (an excellent *tīrtha*, with sacred water, without pointed pebbles and mire), *Kṛshṇa* caused a moat to be excavated. There were assembled hundreds upon hundreds of skilled mechanics in receipt of regular wages, and surgeons and physicians, etc. Then their allies began to march thither (V, **152**). When *Kṛshṇa* had departed, *Duryodhana* urged *Karṇa*, *Duḥçāsana*, and *Çakuni* to make preparations for battle, which was fixed to commence the next morning (I, **153**). At the request of *Yudhishṭhira*, *Kṛshṇa* related *Duryodhana's*, etc., project of imprisoning him; "neither *Bhīshma* nor *Droṇa* said anything on that subject; indeed, all of them follow *Duryodhana*, except *Vidura*. . . . War is that which should now take place." *Yudhishṭhira* gave order to array the troops, but then he complained that he should slay his preceptors, etc. *Arjuna* reminded him of what *Kuntī* and *Vidura* had said through *Kṛshṇa*, and *Kṛshṇa* affirmed it. The *Pāṇḍavas* and their soldiers passed the night in great happiness (V, **154**). After that night had passed away, *Duryodhana* arranged his eleven *akshauhiṇīs* (description), under *Kṛpa*, etc. (θ) (V, **155**). Referring to a contest between the *brahmans*, whom also the *vaiçyas* and the *çūdras* followed, and the *kshatriyas* among the *Haihayas* (*b*), *Duryodhana* urged *Bhīshma* to become their generalissimo. *Bhīshma* said that he did not see upon earth the warrior that was equal to him, except *Arjuna*; but *Arjuna* would never openly fight with him; *Bhīshma* said he could, in a trice, destroy the universe with D., As., Rā., and men; but the *Pāṇḍavas* he could not exterminate; but he would slay every day 10,000; and either *Karṇa* or *Bhīshma* should fight first. *Karṇa* declared he would not fight before *Bhīshma* was slain; then he would fight with *Arjuna*. Then *Bhīshma* was solemnly installed, under a bloody shower, etc. Then they marched out to *Kurukshetra*, and *Duryodhana* and *Karṇa* caused the camps to be measured out on a level part of the plain (V, **156**). When *Yudhishṭhira* heard that *Bhīshma* had been installed in the command of the *Kuru* army, he summoned his brothers and *Vāsudeva*, and selected seven leaders for his seven *akshauhiṇīs*: *Drupada*, etc. (ι) (cf. **a**!), and above them all *Dhṛshṭadyumna*; and *Dhanañjaya* (i.e. *Arjuna*) of curly hair was made the leader of all those leaders; and *Kṛshṇa* the leader of *Arjuna* and driver of his steeds. *Halāyudha* (i.e. *Balarāma*), etc. (κ) came there, and *Yudhishṭhira*, etc. (λ) rose from their seats and offered worship to *Halāyudha*. *Halāyudha* said that a fierce slaughter was inevitable, that the *Pāṇḍavas* would certainly win because of the help of *Kṛshṇa*, that he had repeatedly tried to prevail upon *Kṛshṇa* to remain neuter; that he would himself do; but as he could not be without *Kṛshṇa*, he would repair to the *tīrthas* of the *Sarasvatī*. Then he set out for his *tīrthayātrā* (V, **157**). About this time there came to the *Pāṇḍava* camp *Bhīshmaka's* (*c*) son *Rukmin* (*d*). He entered the camp with an *akshauhiṇī* of troops, from desire of doing what was agreeable to *Vāsudeva*. He offered *Arjuna* his assistance, if he was afraid. He would slay everyone: *Droṇa*, etc. (μ). *Arjuna*, mentioning his exploits against the *G.*, at *Khāṇḍava*, against the *Nivātakavacas* and *Kālakeyas*, at *Virāṭa's* city, and that he had paid his respects for battle's sake to *Rudra*, etc. (ν), would not say he was afraid. *Rukmin* then went to *Duryodhana*, saying the same words, and was rejected in the same way. Then the *Pāṇḍavas* again consulted, presided over by *Yudhishṭhira* (V, **158**). *Dhṛtarāshṭra* asked *Sañjaya* to tell him all that had happened in the matter of encamping, and complained that though he understood the defects, he could not withstand *Duryodhana*. *Sañjaya* said that he ought not to impute the fault only to *Duryodhana*: "as to our acts, some say that everything is ordained by God; some that they are the result of free-will; others that they are the result of those of our past lives" (V, **159**).

[Sainyodyogaparvan(°va)] ("the section relating to the preparations before warfare," the 57th of the minor parvans of Mhbhr.). § 554: After the nuptials of *Abhimanyu* the *Kurus*, etc. (**a**) next morning assembled in the presence chamber of *Virāṭa*. *Kṛshṇa* spoke about the affairs of the *Pāṇḍavas*, and proposed to send an ambassador to *Duryodhana*, etc., in order to induce them to give half the kingdom to *Yudhishṭhira* (V, **1**). *Baladeva* approved of it, and said that the ambassador ought to salute *Bhīshma*, etc. (β), that *Yudhishṭhira* had been wrong in challenging *Çakuni*, and that *Duryodhana* only ought to be addressed in a conciliatory tone, that war might be avoided (V, **2**). *Sātyaki* severely blamed *Baladeva*, and asserted that it was *Y dhishṭhira* who had been challenged in the game at dice, that he could not have declined according to the rules of the Kshatriya caste, and that *Çakuni* had won by a trick; the *Kauravas* had not obeyed *Bhīshma* and *Droṇa*; they ought to be besought by sharp arrows; they could not withstand *Yuyudhāna*, etc. (ββ) (V, **3**). *Drupada* approved of what had been said by *Baladeva*, except that *Duryodhana* should not be addressed mildly, and they ought also to send messengers to *Çalya*, etc. (γ) to collect an army; his own *purohita* ought to be sent to *Dhṛtarāshṭra*, *Duryodhana*, *Bhīshma*, and *Droṇa* (V, **4**). Having approved of *Drupada's* words, *Kṛshṇa* set out for *Dvārakā*, and the *Pāṇḍavas* and the *Dhārtarāshṭras* began to make preparations for war, and collect troops; and *Drupada* despatched his *purohita* to the *Kurus* (V, **5**). *Drupada* gave instructions to his *purohita* (cf. Pushya, § 554), who set out for *Hāstinapura* with a following of disciples (V, **6**). After *Kṛshṇa*, etc. (γγ) had set out for *Dvārakā*, *Arjuna* and *Duryodhana* come thither, while *Kṛshṇa* was asleep; *Duryodhana* sat down at the head of the bed; after him *Arjuna* came and stood at the back of the bed. And when *Kṛshṇa* awoke, he first saw *Arjuna*. *Arjuna* chose for his partner *Kṛshṇa* himself, who was not to fight; *Duryodhana* selected for himself *Kṛshṇa's* ten crores of *Nārāyaṇa* cowherds. *Balarāma* said he would fight neither for *Kuntī's* sons nor for *Duryodhana*. *Kṛtavarman* gave an *akshauhiṇī* to *Duryodhana*. *Kṛshṇa* promised to become *Arjuna's* charioteer; *Arjuna* came back to *Yudhishṭhira* with *Kṛshṇa* and the flower of the *Daçārha* race (V, **7**).—§ 555: *Çalya* with his sons and troops (description) was advancing in order to join the *Pāṇḍavas*; but *Duryodhana* caused fine palaces of entertainment to be constructed at different spots for his reception; *Çalya* first thought this had been arranged by *Yudhishṭhira*, until *Duryodhana* came forward and showed himself; then he promised *Duryodhana* to become the leader of his army. *Çalya*, however, first proceeded to the *Pāṇḍavas* at *Upaplavya*, and told them about the matter. He promised *Yudhishṭhira* that when he became *Karṇa's* charioteer he would act so that *Karṇa* might be dispirited; and in order to comfort *Yudhishṭhira* he reminded him that *Çakra* (*Indra*) had to endure, together with his wife, very great misery (V, **8**). At the request of *Yudhishṭhira*, *Çalya* related the ancient story (*itihāsaṃ purātanaṃ*) of the great misery endured by *Indra* and his queen (v. Indravijaya) (V, **9-17**). So *Yudhishṭhira* should also regain his kingdom. This story of the victory of *Indra*, equal to the *Veda*, should be listened to by a king desirous of victory; he who reads it with a heart full of religious faith is purified from his sins, etc. *Çalya* repeated his promise to damp the spirits of *Karṇa*, and went with his army to *Duryodhana* (V, **18**). *Yuyudhāna*, etc. (γ) came to *Yudhishṭhira* with troops (description). For the *Pāṇḍavas* there were thus assembled seven *akshauhiṇīs* of troops from various directions. In the same way king *Bhagadatta* (with an *akshauhiṇī* crowded with *Cīnas* and *Kirātas*), etc. (δ) came to the *Dhārtarāshṭras*. And thus *Duryodhana* had a force which numbered eleven *akshauhiṇīs*, so that there was no room for them in the city of *Hāstinapura*; but the *Pañcanada*, the whole *Kurujāṅgala*, etc. (ε), full of abundant corn and wealth, was entirely overspread with the army of the *Kauravas*. And this army was beheld by the *purohita* who had been sent by the *Pāñcāla* king to the *Kurus* (V, **19**).

Sairandhrī (B.) or **Sairindhrī** (C.) ("a woman of the Sairandhra caste"): IV, 77 (pl.); XIII, 2581.—Do. said of Damayantī: III, 2586, 2604, 2687.—Do. said of Draupadī: IV, 78, 246, 247, 251, 260, 412, 416, (425), 432, 439, 440, (441), (448), 491, 494, 495, (496), 502, (509), 530, 565, 566, 604, 665, 713, 748, 776, 800, 808, 819, 831, 832, 833, 836, 837, 848, 849, (850), 850, 851, 856, (859), 1190, 1193, 1205, 1212, 1254, 1255, 1372, 2191, 2221, 2296.

Saisikata, pl. (°*āḥ*), a people. § 574 (Jambūkh.): VII, **9**μ, 365 (only C., B. has *Saisiridhrāḥ*).

Saisiridhra, pl., v. Saisikata, pl.

Sakala = Çiva (1000 names[2]).

Sakṛdgrāha (B. °*graha*), pl. (°*āḥ*), a people. § 574 (Jambūkh.): VI, **9**ξ, 373.

Sakṛnnandā (?), name of a river (BR.): III, 8137 (°*āṃ samāsādya*, read *sakṛn Nandāṃ samāsādya*; B. has *Prāṇnadīṃ ca samāsādya*).

Sākshin = Vishṇu (1000 names).

Sālaṅghāyana, a son of Viçvāmitra. § 721*b* (Viçvāmitrop.): XIII, **4**β, 251.

Salilapati = Mahāpurusha (Mahāpurushastava).

Salilarāja ("king of the waters") = Varuṇa: III, 5004 (*tīrthe S°sya*), 5010 (do.); V, 3543 (*putrāḥ S°sya*), 3544 (°*sya cchatraṃ*), 3801 (*V°*).

Salilāstra ("the watery weapon"). § 444 (Nivātakavacayuddhap.): III, **171**, 12141 (employed by Arjuna).

Salileça ("lord of the waters") = Varuṇa: V, 3525.

Salileçvara (do.) = Varuṇa: III, 14552 (*V°*), 17137 (*V°*); XIII, 7255.

Sama[1], a son of Dhṛtarāshṭra. § 130 (Aṃçāvat.): I, **67**, 2731 (enumeration).—§ 182 (Dhṛtarāshṭraputranāmak.): I, **117**, 4541 (do.).—§ 581 (Bhīshmavadhap.): VI, **64**κ, 2838 (attacked Bhīmasena).—§ 608 (Karṇap.): VIII, **51**δδ, 2446, 2455 (slain by Bhīmasena).

Sama[2] (V, 2733), v. Çama.

Sama[3] = Vishṇu (1000 names).

Samā (°*āḥ*, pl. C.), a region. § 575*c* (Bhūmip.): After these regions is seen a habitation of the name *Samā*. It is of a starry shape with four corners and thirty-three *maṇḍalas*. There dwell the four world-elephants (*diggajāḥ*), *Vāmana*, *Airāvata*, etc., and also *Supratīka*, whose dimensions have for ever remained unascertained; there winds blow from all directions and are seized by the elephants with the tips of their trunks and let out over the earth; in consequence thereof people draw breath and live: VI, **12**, 473 (°*ā nāma dṛçyate* (C. °*ante*) *lokasaṃsthitiḥ* (C. °*te*)).

Samāçvāsa, name of a fire (?) § 490 (Āṅgirasa): III, **219**, 14155 (= Mahāvāc).

Sāmaga[1] = Mahāpurusha (Mahāpurushastava). — Do.[2] = Vishṇu (1000 names).

Sāmagāyana = Vishṇu (1000 names).

Samakarṇa = Çiva (1000 names[1]).

Samāmnāya = Çiva (1000 names[2]).

sāman, mostly, pl. ("verses from the Sāmaveda"): I, 66, 1374, 2881 (°*gītaiḥ*), 2883 (*pūrrayajñiya-sāmagāḥ*); II, 536 (sg.), 1238 (°*gaḥ*), 2627 (*yāmyāni sāmāni raudrāṇi ca*), 2641 (*yāmyāni*), 2642; III, 966, 1773 (*ṛgyajuḥsāmasambhavaiḥ*), 1783 (sg.), 8676, 8702 (°*gaiḥ*), †10686 (sg.), 10904 (sg., °*gāḥ*), 11237 (°*ṛgyajurvarṇāḥ*, did not exist in the Kṛtayuga), 11621, 11656 (*gīta-sāmasvanaḥ*), 17338 (sg.), 17339 (sg.); V, †1624, †1711, 3788; VI, 1187 (sg.), 1239 (*Bṛhatsāma tathā sāmnāṃ*); IX, 2098; XI, 672 (*trīṇi samāni sāmagāḥ*), 675 (*tribhiḥ*), 794, 795; XII, 1614, 1883 (*ṛgyajuḥsāmasahitaiḥ*), 2311 (*ṛgyajuḥsāmavid*), 2312 (*anṛgyajuḥsāmā*), †2315 (*ekaṃ*), 2871 (*ṛgyajuḥsāmasampannāḥ*), 2963 (*chandaḥ sāmādi*), 3634 (°*āni sāmagāḥ*), †7372 (*ṛksāmasaṅghāṃç ca yajūṃshi*), 7501, 7503, 8543 (*ṛksāmāni yajūṃshi ca*), 8613 (*ṛksāmavarṇākṣharato yajusho 'tharvaṇas tathā*), 8720 (*ṛks°su yajuḥsu*), 9065, 9621, 9632, †10299 (*°gāḥ*), 10399 (*°gāḥ*), 11532 (*ṛgyajuḥsāmagaḥ*), 12737 (*yajurṛksāmabhiḥ*), 13136, 13256 (*sahasraçākham*, identified with Kṛshṇa (Nārāyaṇa)); XIII, 643 (*°gānām*), 986 (sg., *Rathantaram*), 1085 (*°bhir . . . sāmagāḥ*), 1316 (sg.), 4107 (*mūrtimanti*), †7369 (*°gāḥ*), 7774 (*jaguḥ sāmāni sāmagāḥ*); XIV, 745; XVI, 202 (*°gānām*).

Sāman = Vishṇu (1000 names).—Do.[2], pl. (*°āni*) = Çiva (1000 names[1]).

Samāna[1], name of one of the life-breaths. § 485 (Pativratop., Brāhmaṇavyādhasaṃv.): III, **213**, 13964 (description), 13970 (*°odānayor madhye*).—§ 595 (Shoḍaçarāj. v. Rāma Dāçarathi): VII, **59**, 2237 (*Prāṇāpāna-S°āç ca Rāme rājyaṃ praçāsati*).—§ 660*b* (Bhṛgu-Bharadvājasaṃv.): XII, **184**, 6844 (within the heart); **185**, 6870 (*d*: In consequence of *S*. every one of the senses is made to act as it does), 6874 (*d*: There is heat (*agniḥ*) in the bodies of living creatures (*dhātushu*), circulated by *S*.; residing thus in the body that breath operates (*vartayan*) upon all watery (*rasān*) and other elementary substances (*dhātūn*) and all bad humours (*doshān*)).—§ 662*b* (Jāpakop.): XII, **200**ϵ, 7346.—§ 667 (Mokshadh.): XII, **213**, 7759.—§ 704 (do.): XII, **302**, 11124.—§ 714*g* (Çukakṛtya): The host of gods named the *Sādhyas* had the son *Samāna*, his son was *Udāna*, his son was *Vyāna*, from him arose *Apāna*, and from *Apāna Prāṇa*. *Prāṇa* was childless. This wind (*vāyuḥ*) is the cause of the functions of all living creatures, and from this (*prāṇanāt*) he is called *Prāṇa*: XII, **329**, 12396.—§ 782*b* (Brāhmaṇagītā): XIV, **20**, 612, 614; **21**, 654; **23**, 685, 688 (*vāyuḥ*), 692, 699, 700, 703, 705 (the contention among the life-breaths about superiority); **24**, 712, 718, 719, 722, 726.—§ 782*g* (Guruçishyasaṃv.): XIV, **42**, 1109.

Samāna[2] = Çiva (1000 names[1]).

Samaṅga[1], name of a herdsman. § 512 (Ghoshayātrāp.): III, **239**, 14821 (*vallavaḥ*).

Samaṅga[2], a ṛshi (?). § 698 (Mokshadh.): XII, **287**, 10533 (*Nāradasya ca saṃvādaṃ S°sya ca*), (10536) (discourse between Nārada and *S*.).

Samaṅga, pl. (*°āḥ*), a people. § 574 (Jambūkh.): VI, **9**ν, 368 (in the south).

Samaṅgā, a river. § 412 (Ashṭāvakrīya): III, **134**, †10689, †10690 (Ashṭāvakra bathed in the river and his limbs became straight (*samair aṅgaiḥ*); from that time the river is called *S*.).—§ 413 (Tīrthayātrāp.): III, **135**, 10692 (formerly named Madhuvilā), 10693.

Samantapañcaka, name of a place = Kurukshetra. § 1 (Anukram.): I, **1**, 12 (the place of the battle between the Kurus and the Pāṇḍavas).—§ 8 (Parvasaṅgr.): I, **2**, 270, 271 (*°ākhyam*), 273 (there Rāma Jāmadagnya dug five lakes which were filled with the blood of the kshatriyas whom he slew), 278 (the lakes became tīrthas), 282 (*°e yuddhaṃ Kuru-Pāṇḍavasenayoḥ*).—§ 398 (Paraçurāma): III, **117**, 10204 (Rāma Jāmadagnya made five lakes in *S*.).—§ 574 (Jambūkh.): VI, **1**, 7 (C. by error *Sya°*).—§ 596 (Pratijñāp.): VII, **77**, 2725 (do.).—§ 615 (Baladevatīrthayātrā): IX, **37**, 2163 (on the Sarasvatī).—§ 615*u* (Skanda): IX, **44**, 2501 (*°e yā vai trishu lokeshu viçrutā*, sc. Sarasvatī).—§ 615 (Baladevatīrthay.): IX, **52**, 3006 (*°dvārā*) (B. *°āt*)).—§ 615*kk* (Kurukshetrak.): IX, **53**, †3008 (*Prajāpater uttaravedir ucyate*), 3032 (*etat Kurukshetra-S°m Prajāpater uttaravedir ucyate*).—§ 615 (Gadāyuddhap.): IX, **55**, 3085 (*uttaravedī . . . Prajāpateḥ*), 3087; **64**, 3620 (*puṇye*, there Duryodhana died).

Samantara, pl. (*°āḥ*), a people. § 574 (Jambūkh.): VI, **9**μ, 358 (only B., C. has *Mahyuttarāḥ*).

Samaramardana = Çiva (1000 names[2]).

Samasaurabha, a brahman. § 59 (Sarpasattra): I, **53**, 2049 (among the sadasyas at the snake-sacrifice of Janamejaya).

Samāsya = Çiva (1000 names[2]).

Samātman, Samāvarta = Vishṇu (1000 names).

Sāmaveda. § 270 (Brahmasabhāv.): II, **11**, 449 (in the palace of Brahmán).—§ 459 (Mārkaṇḍeyas.): III, **189**, 12963 (had sprung from Nārāyaṇa).—§ 560 (Sanatsujātap.): V, **43**, 1623.—§ 576 (Bhagavadgītāp.): VI, **34**, 1226 (*Vedānāṃ S°o 'smi*, says Kṛshṇa).—§ 606 (Tripurākhyāna): VIII, **34**, 1498 (among those works which became the *puraḥsarāḥ* of Çiva).—§ 717*b* (Nārāyaṇīya): XII, **349**, 13556 (*sammitaḥ S°ena*, sc. *dharmaḥ*); VI), 13592 (*°āntagaṃ dvijam*).—§ 730*g* (Upamanyu): XIII, **14**, 915 (*°aç ca Vedānāṃ*, sc. Çiva). Cf. *sāman*, pl.

Samavegavaça, pl. (*°āḥ*), a people. § 574 (Jambūkh.): VI, **9**ν, 369 (in the south).

Samayajña = Vishṇu (1000 names).

Samayapālanaparvan ("the section about the keeping of the agreement"). § 550: Asked by *Janamejaya*, *Vaiçampāyana* related: By the grace of *Tṛṇabindu* and *Dharma*, the *Pāṇḍavas* continued to live unrecognized in the city of *Virāṭa*. *Yudhishṭhira* distributed the wealth he won from *Virāṭa* among his brothers. In the fourth month the great festival in honour of *Brahmán*, which was celebrated with pomp in the country of the *Matsyas*, came about; urged by *Virāṭa*, *Bhīmasena* there killed the athlete *Jīmūta* and numerous other athletes; the king also made him fight with tigers, lions, and elephants. So also *Arjuna*, *Nakula*, and *Sahadeva* pleased the king in their respective occupations (IV, **13**).

Samayasya pālana(m) ("the keeping of the agreement"). § 10 (Parvasaṅgr.): I, **2**, 327 (i.e. Samayapālanaparvan).

Sāmba, Sambara, Sambarahan, v. Ç°.

Sambaraṇa, Sambartta, Sambarttaka, v. Saṃv°.

Sambhagna = Çiva (1000 names[2]).

Sambhalagrāma, name of a city. § 460*c* (Kalkin): III, **190**, 13102 (the birthplace of Kalkin).

Sambhava[1] = Sambhavaparvan. § 4 (Anukram.): I, **1**, 88 (*°skandhavistāraḥ*, sc. *Bhāratadrumaḥ*).

Sambhava[2] = Vishṇu (1000 names).

Sambhavaparvan(°va) ("the section relating to the origins," the 7th of the minor parvans of Mhbhr.).—§ 10 (Parvas.): I, **2**, (312). — § 11 (do.): I, **2**, (367).—§§ 85–132: Aṃçāvataraṇa (q.v.). — §§ 133–5: Çakuntalopākhyāna (q.v.). —§§ 136–48: Yayātyupākhyāna (q.v.).—§ 149: Uttara-Yayātyupākhyāna (v. Yayāti).—§§ 150–60: Pūru-vaṃçānukīrtana (q.v.).—§ 161: Mahābhishopākhyāna (q.v.).—§ 162: Çāntanūpākhyāna (q.v.).—§ 163: Bhīshmotpatti (q.v.).—§ 164: Āpavopākhyāna (q.v.).—§ 165: Satyavatīlābhopākhyāna.—§ 166: Citrāṅgadopākhyāna (q.v.).—§ 167: Vicitravīryoparama (q.v.).—§§ 168–71: Bhīshma-Satyavatī-saṃvāda (q.v.).—§ 172: Aṇīmāṇḍavyopākhyāna (q.v.).—§ 173: Pāṇḍurājyābhisheka (q.v.).—§ 174: Dhṛtarāshṭravivāha (q.v.).—§ 175: Karṇasambhava (q.v.).—§ 176: Kuntī-vivāha (q.v.).—§ 177: Pāṇḍu-digvijaya (q.v.).—§ 178: Pāṇḍu (q.v.). — § 179: Viduraparinaya (q.v.). — § 180: Gāndhārī-putrotpatti (q.v.).—§ 181: Duḥçalotpatti (q.v.).—§ 182: Dhṛtarāshṭraputranāmakathana (q.v.).—§§ 183–5: Pāṇḍu (q.v.).—§ 186: Vyushitāçvopākhyāna (q.v.).—§ 187:

Pāṇḍu (q.v.).—§ 188: Madayantī (q.v.).—§ 189: Pāṇḍu (q.v.).—§§ 190–2: Pāṇḍavotpatti (q.v.).—§§ 193–5: Pāṇḍu (q.v.).—§ 196: Vyāsa (q.v.).—§ 197: Bhīmasena-rasapāna (q.v.).—§ 198: Çaradvat (q.v.).—§ 199–203: Droṇa (q.v.).—§ 204: Ekalavya (q.v.).—§§ 205–7: Droṇa (q.v.).—§ 208: Astradarçana (q.v.).—§ 209: Drupadaçāsana (q.v.).—§ 210: After a year *Dhṛtarāshṭra* installed *Yudhishṭhira* as heir apparent. For continuation see *Bhīmasena* (*b*), *Arjuna* (*c*), *Sahadeva* (*d*), *Nakula* (*e*). § 211: The *Pāṇḍavas*, headed by *Arjuna*, in war slew *Sauvīra*, who had performed a three years' sacrifice, notwithstanding the invasion of the *Gandharvas*. The *Yavana* king, whom even *Pāṇḍu* had failed to subject, was subdued by *Arjuna*; likewise the *Sauvīra Vitula* (B. has *Vipula*), who had always shown a disregard for the *Kurus*; and the Sauvīra *Sumitra*, called *Dattāmitra* (see LIA. i, pp. 656–804, n. 2). Then, assisted by *Bhīma*, *Arjuna* with only a single chariot subjugated all the kings of the East (*prācyāḥ*) backed by 10,000 chariots; and in the same way those of the South. *Dhṛtarāshṭra's* sentiments suddenly became poisoned against the *Pāṇḍavas*, and from anxiety he could not sleep (I, **139**).—§ 212: Kaṇikavākya (q.v.).

Sambhinna = Çiva (1000 names[1]).

Sambodhana, name of a weapon. § 573 (Ambopākhyānap.): V, **183**, 7263 (*astreṇa*).

Saṃçaptaka, pl. (°*āḥ*) ("sworn together"), a host of Kuru warriors. § 4 (Anukram.): I, **1**, †187 (C. °*sa*°).—§ 11 (Parvasaṅgr.): I, **2**, 530 (do.), 535 (do.).—§ 513 (Ghoshayātrāp.): III, **252**, 15178 (do.), 15187 (do.), 15190 (do., some Rākshasas will be incarnate as the *S*. with the wish to slay Arjuna).—§ 561 (Yānasandhip.): V, **55**, 2201 (°*ānāṃ vṛndāni*, have taken oaths, cf. § 591); **57**, 2249 (*Trigartānāñ ca mukhyau . . . S°au*).—§ 576 (Bhagavadgītāp.): VI, **20**, †754.—[§ 591 (Saṃçaptakavadhap.): VII, **17*a*-β**, 689 foll. (enumeration of the Trigarta princes and others who took oaths either to slay Arjuna or to be slain themselves)].—§ 592 (do.), VII, **18**, 722, 730 (°*varūthinī*), 752 (°*gaṇāḥ*, fought with Arjuna); **19**, 753 (°*gaṇān*), 754 (do.), 775 (°*vrātān*, defeated and slain by Arjuna); **20**, 793 (°*gaṇaiḥ . . .* °*vadhaṃ*); **26**, 1130; **27**, 1204, 1208 (°*vadhe*), 1212 (°*mahārathāḥ*), 1224 (do.), 1225 (slain by Arjuna); **28**, 1229, 1230 (i.e. Suçarman and his brothers); **31**, 1372 (°*āvaçeshasya*); **32**, 1414, 1415, 1417 (slain by Arjuna).—§ 593 (Abhimanyuvadhap.): VII, **33**, 1468 (°*gaṇāḥ*, fought with Arjuna).—§ 596 (Pratijñāp.): VII, **72**, 2478 (*hatvā S°vrātān*, sc. Arjuna); **73**, 2566.—§ 599 (Jayadrathavadhap.): VII, **121**, 1817; **123**, 4947.—§ 603 (Nārāyaṇāstramokshap.): VII, **193**, 8910 (°*gaṇān . . . hataçeshān*, followed Suçarman).—§ 604 (Karṇap.): VIII, **2γ**, 42 (°*ānāñ ca balaṃ*, slain by Arjuna); **5ζ**, 129 (°*gaṇāḥ*, do.); **9**, 300 (only B.).—§ 605 (do.): VIII, **13**, 494 (°*gaṇān*, slain by Arjuna); **16**, 610, 613, 639, 649, 656, 660 (slain by Arjuna); **17**, †667 (°*sainyaṃ*), 686 (slain by Arjuna); **18**, 689, †710 (°*saṅghahā*, i.e. Arjuna); **19**, 711, 733, 734 (fought with Arjuna); **27** λλ, 1077 (attack Arjuna), 1099 (°*gaṇān*), 1102, 1118 (°*gaṇān*, slain by Arjuna).—§ 608 (do.): VIII, **46** δ, 2136, 2195, 2196 (attack Arjuna), **47**, 2210, 2216, 2217, 2223 (do.); **53**, 2564, 2565, 2568, 2582 (°*gaṇān*), 2585 (°*varūthinī*), 2603 (°*gaṇānāṃ*), 2607 (fought with Arjuna); **56**, 2696, 2773 (°*gaṇān*), 2775 (*mahārathāḥ*), 2788 (°*gaṇān*), 2793, 2798, 2836 (defeated by Arjuna); **59**, 2911, 2974; **60**, 3064 (°*gaṇān*, fled); **65**, †3293, †3294, †3295 (°*ānīkaṃ*); **67** κκκ, †3358; **70**, †3525; **75**, 3815 (followed Duḥçāsana), **81**, 4124, 4126 (°*rathāḥ*, ninety in number, attacked Arjuna); **95**, 4972 (°*āvaçishṭena balena*, followed Açvatthāman).—§ 609 (Çalyap.): IX, **1**γ, 27 (*hatāḥ*); **2**ζ, 94 (slain).—§ 611 (do.): IX, **8**, 398 (°*gaṇān*, attacked by Arjuna); **10**, 521 (slain by Arjuna); **14**, 749 (°*vṛtaḥ*, sc. Açvatthāman).—§ 615 (Gadāyuddhap.): IX, **62**, 3489 (°*gaṇā jitāḥ*).—§ 785 (Anugītāp.): XIV, **61**, 1827 (all. to the battle).

Saṃçaptakanihantṛ ("the slayer of the Saṃçaptakas") = Arjuna: XIV, 2229.

Saṃçaptakanis(h)ūdana ("the destroyer of the Saṃçaptakas") = Arjuna: XIV, 2172.

Saṃçaptakavadha(ḥ) (C. °*sa*°) ("the slaughter of the Saṃçaptakas"). § 10 (Parvasaṅgr.): I, **2**, 338 (i.e. Saṃçaptakavadhaparvan).

[Saṃçaptakavadhaparvan(°va)] ("the section relating to the slaughter of the Saṃçaptakas," the 72nd of the minor parvans of the Mhbhr.; cf. Saṃçaptakavadha). § 591: *Droṇa* confessed his inability to seize *Yudhishṭhira* if *Arjuna* were by. The *Trigarta* king said that *Arjuna* had always injured them, and took an oath that either *Arjuna* or the *Trigartas* should be slain. This oath was taken by the five brothers *Satyaratha*, etc., (*a*) with their 10,000 chariots, and by the *Mālava* king, etc. (β). Then they summoned *Arjuna* towards the southern part of the field. *Arjuna* told *Satyajit* to guard *Yudhishṭhira*, and went out against the *Trigartas* (VII, **17**).—§ 592: THE TWELFTH DAY'S BATTLE. The *Saṃçaptakas* rejoiced at the prospect of fighting *Arjuna*, who addressed Kṛshṇa about this ill-timed joy, and terrified them with the sound of *Devadatta*, and attacked them. *Subāhu* & *Arjuna*; *Suçarman*, etc. (*a*) & *Arjuna*; they fled to *Duryodhana*; but urged by the *Trigarta* king, they once more returned to the field with the *Nārāyaṇa* cowherds (VII, **18**). *Kṛshṇa* conveyed *Arjuna* to the *Saṃçaptakas*. The *Nārāyaṇas* & *Arjuna* (+ *Kṛshṇa*); *Arjuna* blew *Devadatta* and employed the *Tvāshṭra* weapon, that confounded the foes, who began to fight each other; *Arjuna* crushed the *Lalitthas*, etc. (β), and with the *Vāyavya* weapon he dispersed the arrows shot by his foes, and *Vāyu* blew away crowds of *Saṃçaptakas* with their steeds, etc. Meanwhile *Droṇa* attacked *Yudhishṭhira* (VII, **19**). *Droṇa* had arrayed his troops in the shape of a *garuḍa*: *Droṇa* in the mouth; *Duryodhana* and his brothers = the head; *Kṛtavarman* and *Kṛpa* = the two eyes; *Bhūtaçarman*, etc. (γ), in its neck; *Bhūriçravas*, etc. (δ), in the right wing; *Vindu*, etc. (ε), in the left wing before *Açvatthāman*; in the back the *Kaliṅgas*, etc. (ζ); in the tail *Karna* with his sons, etc.; *Jayadratha*, etc. (η), in the bosom; in the midst the *Prāgjyotisha* king. *Yudhishṭhira* disposed his troops in the shape of a semicircle. *Dhṛshṭadyumna* & *Droṇa* + *Durmukha Dhārtarāshṭra*; *Droṇa* dispersed *Yudhishṭhira's* host (VII, **20**). *Droṇa* & *Yudhishṭhira* + *Satyajit* + *Vṛka*; *Satyajit* was slain by *Droṇa*; *Yudhishṭhira* fled. The *Pāñcālas*, etc. (θ), attacked *Droṇa*, and were consumed; *Çatānīka* (younger brother of the *Matsya* king) & *Droṇa*, who slew him; the *Matsyas* fled. *Droṇa* defeated the *Cedis*, etc. (ι). *Yudhishṭhira* & *Droṇa*; *Çikhaṇḍin*, etc. (κ), & *Droṇa*; *Droṇa* slew *Kshema*. *Yudhishṭhira* fled away. *Droṇa* slew *Pāñcālya* (*Pāñcālyanāmnā*, Nīl.). *Droṇa* crushed the *Pāñcālas*, etc. (λ), and, supported by the *Kurus*, he vanquished *Sātyaki*, etc. (μ). The *Pāṇḍavas* fled away in all directions (VII, **21**). *Duryodhana* addressed *Karṇa* in joy, beholding the *Pāñcālas*, etc. (ν), broken by *Droṇa*, and *Bhīmasena* abandoned by the *Pāṇḍavas* and the *Sṛñjayas*. *Karṇa* said that *Bhīmasena*, followed by *Sātyaki*, etc. (ξ), would never leave the fight; *Duryodhana* proceeded to *Droṇa's* chariot, where a deafening noise was heard of *Pāṇḍava* warriors returning to the fight (VII, **22**). At the request of *Dhṛtarāshṭra*, *Sañjaya* described the steeds of *Bhīmasena*, etc. (*o*), especially mentioning *Bṛhanta* (*b*); the standards of *Droṇa*, etc. (π), and the bows of *Yudhishṭhira*, etc. (ρ) (VII, **23**). The despondency of *Dhṛtarāshṭra*, mentioning *Bhīma*, etc. (σ) (VII, **24**). When the *Pāṇḍavas* returned to fight and attacked *Droṇa*, the *Kurus* were afraid. *Duryodhana* urged his troops against them. *Durmarshaṇa Dhārtarāshṭra* & *Bhīma*; *Kṛtavarman* & *Yuyudhāna*; the *Sindhu* king & *Kshatravarman*; *Subāhu* & *Yuyutsu*, who cut off the two arms of *Subāhu*; *Çalya* & *Yudhishṭhira*; *Bāhlīka* & *Drupada*; *Vinda* and *Anuvinda* & *Virāṭa*; that encounter between the *Matsyas* and the *Kekayas* resembled that between D. and As. in days of old; *Bhūtakarman Sabhāpati* & *Nakula's* son *Çatānīka*; *Bhūtakarman* was slain by *Çatānīka*; *Viviṃçati* & *Sutasoma*; *Bhīmaratha* (*Dhārtarāshṭra*) slew *Çālva*; *Citrasena's* son & *Çrutakarman*; *Prativindhya* & *Açvatthāman*; the son of *Duḥçāsana* & *Çrutakīrti* (the son of *Arjuna* by *Draupadī*); *Lakshmaṇa* (son of *Duryodhana*) & *Paṭaccarahantṛ*; *Vikarṇa* (*Dhārtarāshṭra*) & *Çikhaṇḍin*; *Aṅgada* & *Uttamaujas*; *Durmukha* & *Purujit*; *Karṇa* & the five *Kekaya* brothers; *Durjaya* + *Jaya* + *Vijaya* (*Dhārtarāshṭrāḥ*) & *Nīla* + the *Kāçi* king + *Jayatsena*; *Kshemadhūrti* + *Bṛhanta* & *Sātyaki*; the *Cedi* king & *Ambashṭha*; *Kṛpa* & *Vārdhakshemi*; *Somadatta's* son & *Maṇimat*; *Vṛshasena* (the son of *Karṇa*) & *Pāṇḍya*; *Ghaṭotkaca* & *Alambusha* (VII, **25**); *Duryodhana* & *Bhīmasena*; the *Aṅga* king (Mleccha king) & do.; *Bhīma* slew him, and his divisions fled; the *Prāgjyotisha* king (upon his elephant *Supratīka*) & *Bhīma* (who knew the *añjalikāvedha*); *Bhīma* escaped from the elephant, but was supposed to have been slain; *Yudhishṭhira* (+ the *Pāñcālas*) & *Bhagadatta* (upon *Supratīka*); the *Daçārṇa* king (upon his elephant) & *Bhagadatta*; *Bhagadatta* & *Yuyudhāna*; *Bhagadatta* destroyed the *Pāṇḍava* troops; *Bhīma* & *Bhagadatta*, whose elephant frightened *Bhīma's* steeds, that bore *Bhīma* away; *Ruciparvan* (*Kṛtī-sutaḥ*) & *Bhagadatta*, who slew him; *Abhimanyu*, etc. (τ), & *Bhagadatta's* elephant; *Yuyutsu* had his steeds and charioteer trod down and fled; *Duryodhana* (?) & *Abhimanyu*; *Arjuna*, etc. (υ) & *Bhagadatta*; the *Pāṇḍava* troops fled (VII, **26**). Urged by *Arjuna*, *Kṛshṇa* began to proceed against *Bhagadatta*; the *Saṃçaptakas* (10,000 *Trigartas* and 4,000 *Nārāyaṇāḥ* (*Vāsudevasyānugāḥ*)) challenged *Arjuna*, and he encountered them, shot the *Brāhma* weapon, defeated and slew them, and then turned against *Bhagadatta* (VII, **27**); but as *Suçarman* with his brothers followed him from behind, he again attacked *Suçarman*, and then again *Bhagadatta* (VII, **28**); *Bhagadatta*, at last, by means of *mantras* changed his hook into the *Vaishṇava* weapon, which, received by *Kṛshṇa* on his breast, became a garland. As *Arjuna* taxed *Kṛshṇa* for his taking part in the battle, *Kṛshṇa* related the history of the *Vaishṇavāstra* (*c*). "The great *Asura* has now been divested of that supreme weapon; now slay *Bhagadatta*, that enemy of the gods, even as I formerly for the benefit of the worlds slew the *Asura Naraka*." *Arjuna* then slew both *Bhagadatta* (who was ever the favourite and friend of *Indra*, v. 1302), and the elephant (VII, **29**). Then *Arjuna* slew the two brothers *Vṛsha*[*ka*] and *Acala* (sons of the *Gāndhāra* king *Subala*). *Dhṛtarāshṭra's* sons attacked *Arjuna*, and *Çakuni* created illusions in order to confound him and *Kṛshṇa*: clubs, etc., and asses, etc., which *Arjuna* slew with celestial weapons; then darkness, whence proceeded harsh voices; this *Arjuna* dispelled with the weapon *Jyotishka*; then waves of water, dried up with the *Āditya* weapon; *Çakuni* fled. *Arjuna* slaughtered the *Kuru* army: one stream proceeded towards *Droṇa*, one towards *Duryodhana*; a fierce battle took place on the southern side between *Arjuna* and the *Kurus*. The various divisions of *Yudhishṭhira's* force smote the foe on every part of the field (VII, **30**). *Droṇa* + the *Kurus* & *Yudhishṭhira*, etc. (φ), + the *Pāṇḍavas*; *Nīla* & *Açvatthāman*, who slew him; the *Pāṇḍavas* regretted that *Arjuna* was engaged in the southern part of the field in slaughtering the *Saṃçaptakas* and the *Nārāyaṇa* force (VII, **31**). *Bhīmasena* & *Bāhlīka* + *Karṇa*; *Droṇa*, etc. (χ) & *Bhīma*; *Yudhishṭhira* despatched *Nakula*, etc. (ψ), to the rescue of *Bhīma*; *Bhīma*, etc., & *Droṇa*; the *Pāṇḍavas*, etc. (ω) & *Droṇa*, etc. (**aa**). *Arjuna*, having slain the *Saṃçaptakas*, & *Droṇa* + the *Kurus* + *Arjuna*, who employed the *Āgneya* weapon; *Dhṛshṭadyumna*, etc. (ββ) & *Karṇa*; *Arjuna* slew three of *Karṇa's* brothers (γγ); *Bhīma* slew fifteen of *Karṇa's* combatants; *Dhṛshṭadyumna* slew *Candravarman*, etc. (δδ); *Duryodhana*, etc. (εε) & *Sātyaki*, rescuing *Karṇa*; *Dhṛshṭadyumna*, etc. (ζζ) protected *Sātyaki*. At sunset the armies retired (VII, **32**).

Samedī, a matṛ. § 615*u* (Skanda): IX, **46**θ, 2631.

Saṃgraha, etc., see below under **Saṅg°**.

Saṃhanana, son of Manasyu. § 150 (Pūruvaṃç.): I, **94**, 3697 (third son of Manasyu).

Saṃhatāpana, a serpent. § 65 (Sarpasattra): I, **57**, 2152 (of Airāvata's race).

***Saṃhitā** ("vedic text"): I, 2883 (*padakramāyutām*), 6363 (*°ādhyayane*); III, 13425; XII, 7166, 7167, 7203, 7279, 7314, 7320 (*°ādhyāyin*).

Saṃhlāda, an Asura (*Saṃhrāda*, B.). § 89 (Aṃçāvat.): I, **65**, 2526 (second son of Hiraṇyakaçipu).—§ 130 (do.): I, **67**, 2642 (*Prahlādasyānujaḥ*, incarnate as king Çalya). Cf. next.

Saṃhrāda, an Asura. § 268 (Varuṇasabhāv.): II, **9**, 365 (among the Daityas and Dānavas in the palace of Varuṇa); 367 (do., the same?). Cf. the prec.

Saṃhṛshṭa = Çiva (1000 names[1]).

Samīcī, an Apsaras. § 250 (Arjunavanavāsap.): I, **216**, 7858 (one of the five Apsarases who were delivered by Arjuna).—§ 269 (Vaiçravaṇasabhāv.): II, **10**, 394 (in the palace of Kubera).

Samīhana = Vishṇu (1000 names).

Samīka, v. Çamīka.

Samīra, pl. (°*āḥ*), a people. § 574 (Jambūkh.): VI, **9**μ, 360 (only C., B. has *Masīrāḥ*).

Samīraṇa[1] = Vāyu (the wind), q.v. — Do.[2] = Vishṇu (1000 names).

Samitiñjaya[1], a Vṛshṇi. § 273 (Rājasūyārambhap.): II, **14**, 623 (one of the seven *mahārathas* of the Vṛshṇis).—Do.[2] = Vishṇu (1000 names).

Saṃkalpa, etc., see below under **Saṅk°**.

Sammita = Vishṇu (1000 names).

Sammohana, name of a weapon. § 552 (Goharaṇap.): IV, **66**, 2112 (*astram*, employed by Arjuna).

Saṃnyāsakṛt = Vishṇu (1000 names).

Sampanna = Çiva (1000 names[2]).

Sampāti[1], a vulture, brother of Jaṭāyus. § 128 (Aṃçāvat.): I, **66**, 2634 (with Jaṭāyus son of Aruṇa and Çyenī).—§ 425 (Hanūmad-Bhīmasaṃv.): III, **148**, 11205 (all. to § 534).—§ 530 (Viçvāvasumokshaṇa): III, **279**, 16045 (brother of Jaṭāyus).—§ 534 (Hanūmatpratyāg.): III, **282**, 16245, 16248 (directed Hanūmat, etc., to Laṅkā).

Sampāti[2], a Kuru warrior. § 592 (Saṃçaptakavadhap.): VII, **20**ε, 804 (in the bosom of Droṇa's gāruḍa vyūha).

Sampratardana = Vishṇu (1000 names).

Sampravartaka = Çiva (1000 names[1]).

Sampriyā, Mādhavī, a princess. § 156 (Pūruvaṃç.): I, **95**, 3793 (wife of Vidūratha (B., Vidura), and mother of Anaçvan).

Saṃrāj = Kṛshṇa: XII, 1509.

Saṃṛddha, a serpent. § 67 (Sarpasattra): I, **57**, 2159 (°-*Paṭhavāsakau*, of Dhṛtarāshṭra's race).

Saṃsaptaka, pl., **Saṃsaptakavadha**, v. Saṃç°.

Saṃskṛti = Kṛshṇa: XII, 1507.

Saṃsthāna, pl. (°*āḥ*), a people. § 578 (Bhīshmavadhap.): VII, **51**σ, 2097 (in the army of Duryodhana).

Saṃsthāna = Vishṇu (1000 names).

***Samudra**("the Ocean") (selected passages, mostly personif.). § 28 (Amṛtamanthana): I, **18**, 1120, 1139, 1145 (the churning of the Ocean).—§ 30*b* (cf. Kadrū): The Ocean is the home of *Varuṇa*, the charming abode of the Serpents (*Nāgānām ālayaṃ ramyaṃ*), of the subterranean fire (i.e. *Vāḍavāgniḥ*, Nīl.) (*Pātālajvalanāvāsaṃ*), the asylum of the *Asuras* (*Asurānāṃ ca bāndhavaṃ*, i.e. *çaraṇaṃ*, Nīl.), the parent of *Pāñcajanya*; formerly it was agitated by *Govinda* (*gāṃ vindatā Govindena*) in the shape of a wild boar; *Atri* could not fathom its bottom in 100 years, it is the bed of Vishṇu at the dawn of every yuga and the refuge of the mountain *Maināka* under the fear of the falling thunderbolt, it offers waters as sacrificial butter to the fire issuing from the mouth of Vaḍavā: I, **21**, 1207.—§ 31*b* (Samudradarçana): I, **22**, 1217 (repetition from § 30*b*).—§ 615*u* (Skanda): IX, **45**, 2552 (gave two companions to Skanda).—§ 638*b* (Rāmopākhyāna): XII, **49**, 1798 (protected the descendants of Marutta).—§ 639 (Rājadh.): XII, **50**, 1808 (all. to § 638*b*). Cf. Sāgara, Udadhi.—Do.[2] = Çiva (1000 names[2]).

Samudra, pl. (°*āḥ*) ("Oceans," personif.). § 615*u* (Skanda): IX, **45**η, 2514 (came to see Skanda).—§ 716 (Çukābhipatana): XII, **333**, 12606.—Do.[2] = Çiva (1000 names[1]).

Sāmudra = Citrasena[6]: VIII, 165 (*C*°).

[Samudradarçana(ṃ)] ("the seeing of the Ocean"). § 31*b* (cf. Kadrū): Repetition from I, **21** (§ 30*b* (Samudra)) (I, **22**).

Samudrādhivāsa = Mahāpurusha (Mahāpurushastava).

Sāmudraka, a tīrtha. § 370 (Tīrthayātrāp.): III, **84**, 8019.

Samudrāmbarasannibha = Çiva (1000 names[1]).

Samudramahishī ("the spouse of the ocean") = Gaṅgā: III, 8618.

Sāmudranishkuṭa, pl. (°*āḥ*), a people. § 574 (Jambūkh.): VI, **9**μ, 356.

Samudrasena, a king. § 130 (Aṃçāvat.): I, **67**, 2690 (incarnation of the seventh of the Kāleyas).—§ 280 (Bhīmasena): II, **30**, 1098 (in the east, with Candrasena vanquished by Bhīmasena).—§ 554 (Sainyodyogap.): V, **4**γ, 85 (*rājā . . . saha putreṇa*).—§ 604 (Karṇap.): VIII, **6**, 166 (in the army of Duryodhana, had slain Citrasena Sāmudra).

Samudrasenaputra ("the son of Samudrasena") = Candrasena: I, 6991 (*C*°); VII, 1007 (*C*°).

Samudravega, a warrior of Skanda. § 615*u* (Skanda): IX, **45**η, 2565.

Samudronnādana, a warrior of Skanda. § 615*u* (Skanda): IX, **45**η, 2570.

Saṃvaha, name of a wind. § 714*k* (Çukakṛtya): "The wind which supports the clouds and divides them into diverse portions, which melts them for pouring rain, and once more solidifies them, which is perceived as the sound of the roaring clouds, etc., this fourth wind is called *S*.": XII, **329**, 12407.

Saṃvaraṇa (*Samb*° *C*.), a king, son of Ṛksha, husband of Tapatī, and father of Kuru. § 152 (Pūruvaṃç.): I, **94**, 3724 (son of Ṛksha).—§ 153 (cf. do.): During the reign of *S*. the kingdom suffered much from famine, pestilence, drought, and disease. The king of the *Pāñcālas* invaded the *Bhāratas* with ten *akshauhiṇīs* and defeated them. *S*. with his relatives took shelter in the forests on the banks of the *Sindhu*, where the *Bhāratas* lived for 1,000 years within their fort. Then they made Vasishṭha their *purohita*, who appointed *S*. to be sovereign (*sāṃrājye*) of the whole kshatriya race. *S*. then retook the ancient capital of Bharata and once more made the monarchs pay tribute to him: I, **94**, 3725 (*Ārkshe*), 3728, 3729 (*rājā*).—§ 154 (Pūruvaṃç.): I, **94**, 3738 (husband of Tapatī, the daughter of the Sun (*Saurī*), and father of Kuru).—§ 156 (do.): I, **95**, ††3790 (son of Ajamīḍha), ††3791 (husband of Tapatī Vaivasvatī and father of Kuru).—§ 222 (Tapatyup.): I, **171**, 6527 (*Ṛkshaputraḥ*), 6530, 6532, 6533, 6548; **173**, 6596, 6605, 6606, 6608, 6609, 6615, 6633 (*S*. fell in love with Tapatī and with the assistance of Vasishṭha got her for his wife. *S*. begat Kuru).—§ 775 (Ānuçāsanik.): XIII, **166**η, 7679.—§ 787 (Āçramavāsap.): XV, **10**, 325 (*Kuru-S°ādīnāṃ*). Cf. Ājamīḍha, Ārksha (v. additions), Paurava, Pauravanandana, Ṛkshaputra.

Saṃvarta[1] (C. Sambartta or Saṃvartta), a Brahmarshi, son of Aṅgiras. § 110 (Aṃçāvat.): I, **66**, 2569 (third son of Aṅgiras).—§ 266 (Çakrasabhāv.): II, **7**, 300 (in the palace of Indra).—§ 270 (Brahmasabhāv.): II, **11**, 440 (in the palace of Brahmán).—§ 370 (Tīrthayātrāp.): III, **85**, 8174 (°*sya tu viprarsher vāpīṃ*, a tīrtha).—§ 409 (Plakshāvataraṇag.): III, **129**, 10529 (*atraiva . . . Maruttaḥ sattram uttamaṃ | prāpa caivarshimukhyena S°enābhipālitaḥ*, cf. § 778*b*).—§ 595 (Shoḍaçarāj., v. Marutta): VII, **55**, 2171 (read *Saṃvarto* with B., performed sacrifices for Marutta, cf. § 778*b*).—§ 632*b* (Shoḍaçarāj., cf. § 595): XII, **29**, 913 (younger brother of Bṛhaspati, performed sacrifices for Marutta, cf. § 778*b*).—§ 637 (Rājadh.): XII, **47**η, 1596 (among the ṛshis who surrounded Bhīshma).—§ 734 (Ānuçāsanik.): XIII, **26**α, 1762 (among the ṛshis who came to see Bhīshma).—§ 747*b* (Suvarṇotpatti): XIII, **85**θ, 4148 (the seventh of Aṅgiras' eight sons).—§ 770 (Ānuçāsanik.): XIII, **151**λ, 7122.—§ 778*b* (Saṃvartta-Maruttīya): XIV, **5**, 95 (son of Aṅgiras and brother of Bṛhaspati), 96; **6**, 137 (*Aṅgirasaḥ putraḥ*), 138, 139 (*Sav*° C. by error), 142, 144, 149, 151, 152; **7**, (153), (156), 158, 165, (171), (176); **8**, (180), 217; **9**, †222, †223, †225, †234, (†237), †240, †243, †255; **10**, †257, †262, †264, (†267), (†272), (†274), (†277), (†280), 287 (*S*. performed a sacrifice for Marutta). Cf. Āṅgirasa, Viprarshi.

Saṃvarta[2] (C. °*rtta*) = Çiva (1000 names[1]).

Saṃvartāgni (C. Sambarttāgni), the fire of dissolution: VIII, 2317.

Saṃvartaka[1] (C. mostly Sambarttaka), adj. ("relating to the dissolution"): III, 12873 (*vahniḥ*), 12877 (*analaḥ*), 12966 (*vahniḥ . . . anilaḥ*), 12967 (*sūryaḥ*); VI, 4290 (*analaḥ*); VII, 6880 (*analaḥ*), 9422 (*analaḥ*); VIII, 1482 (°-*balāhakān*); XIII, 838 (*analaḥ*), 942 (*analaḥ*), 6974 (*vahniḥ*; *Saṃvartta*° C.).—Do.[2] subst. ("the fire of dissolution"): III, 13607 (*pāvakaṃ . . . S°samaṃ*); VI, 281

(°o nāma kālāgniḥ); XII, 10338 (°opamaḥ, sc. Çiva).—Do. [3]: Sūrya (the Sun): III, 153.—Do. [4], a serpent. § 47 (Sarpanāmak.): I, **35,** 1555 (read with B. *Vṛttasaṃvartakau*; C. has °*saṃvartako*).

Saṃvartakāgni (*Sambartta*°, C.) = Sūrya (the Sun): III, 187.

Sāṃvartakāgni (*Sambartta*°, C.) ("the fire of dissolution"): IX, 907 (°*pratimam*).

Saṃvartabalāhaka (*Sambartta*°, C.) = Çiva (1000 names[1]).

Saṃvarta-Maruttīya (*Sambartta*°, C.), adj. ("relating to Saṃvarta and Marutta").—§ 11 (Parvasaṅgr.): I, **2,** 606 (*ākhyānam*, i.e. Saṃvartta-Maruttīya).

Saṃvartavāta, the wind of dissolution: II, 1418 (only B.).

[Saṃvar(t)ta-Maruttīya] ("the tale of Saṃvartta and Marutta"): § 778*b* (Açvamedh.).** *Vyāsa* said: In the *Kṛta* age *Manu* was the ruler; > *Prasandhi* > *Kshupa* > *Ikshvāku* > *Viṃça* (the model bowman, the eldest of 100 brothers, all kings) > *Viviṃça* > *Khanīnetra* (*c*) > *Suvarcas* (*d*) *Karandhama* > *Avikshit* (*e*) *Kārandhama* > *Marutta* (who surpassed his father, had the strength of 10,000 elephants, and was equal to *Vishṇu*). Desirous of performing a sacrifice, *Marutta*, coming to *Meru*, on the northern side of *Himavat*, caused thousands of gold vessels to be forged; there on a huge golden hill he performed the rites along with other princes (XIV, **4**). Asked by *Yudhishṭhira*, *Vyāsa* said: As the offspring of *Prajāpati Daksha*, D. and As., challenged each other, so did *Aṅgiras*' sons *Bṛhaspati* and *Saṃvarta*; troubled by his elder brother *Saṃvarta* went naked to the woods. *Indra*, having vanquished the As., appointed Bṛh. as his priest. Formerly (read *pūrvam* with B.) *Aṅgiras* was the family priest of king *Karandhama* (see *d*); so also of his son *Avikshit* (equal to *Yayāti*). His son *Marutta* used to defy *Indra*, and *Indra* used to defy *Marutta*, but could not prevail over him. Then *Indra* took the promise from Bṛh. that he would not perform priestly offices for *Marutta* ("thou hast destroyed *Namuci*, *Viçvarūpa*, and *Bala*," said Bṛh.). *Vaiçampāyana* said: Then *Indra* was cured for his envy and went home (XIV, **5**). *Vyāsa* said: The ancient tale of the discourse between Bṛh. and *Marutta* is cited in this connection. *Marutta* in vain tried to persuade Bṛh. to officiate at his sacrifice (which Bṛh. had himself formerly proposed); D.-ṛ. (M.-ṛ.) *Nārada* told him to apply to *Saṃvarta*, who now, desirous of seeing *Maheçvara*, wandered about in *Vārāṇasī* in the garb of a madman; "having reached the gate of that city, thou must place a dead body somewhere near it, and the man who shall turn away on seeing the corpse, do thou know that man to be *Saṃvarta*; if he should ask thee to follow me," said *Nārada*, "thou mayst even tell him without hesitation that I have ascended the pyre." *Vyāsa* said: "By acting thus, *Marutta* found *Saṃvarta* in a lonely place; *Saṃvarta* covered him with mud and ashes and phlegm and spittle. At last he sat down under a *nyagrodha* tree" (XIV, **6**). *Marutta* told him the matter (also that *Nārada* had mounted the pyre); *Saṃvarta* then, as a lunatic, scolding *Marutta* repeatedly with harsh words, told him to go to Bṛh. first (as his elder brother), and taking Bṛh.'s permission he might come back. As *Marutta* said that he had already been repulsed by Bṛh., and that he now desired to sacrifice even with all his goods in order to outstrip *Indra*, *Saṃvarta* consented, if *Marutta* would agree to do all that *Saṃvarta* would ask him to do, as Bṛh. and *Indra* were certain to do all they could to injure *Marutta*. *Marutta* took an oath to this. *Saṃvarta* said that *Marutta* would surpass *Indra*, D., and G.; he himself had no desire for wealth, but would only do what was disagreeable to *Indra* and Bṛh. (XIV, **7**). *Saṃvarta* said: There is a peak *Muñjavat* (*f*) on the *Himālaya*, where *Çiva* is constantly engaged in austerities; go thither and appease *Çiva*, whose names are *Çarva*, etc. (*a*); then thou shalt acquire that gold. *Marutta* acted accordingly; Bṛh. became sick from envy; *Indra* with D. came (XIV, **8**) and was told about the matter ("prosperity of a rival is always painful, and for this reason thou with D. persecutest As. and kills them"). He despatched *Agni* (*g*) to *Marutta*, asking him to let Bṛh. officiate as his priest instead of *Saṃvarta*, promising him the greatest rewards ("such as the highest regions created by *Prajāpati* and even the whole kingdom of the gods"); *Saṃvarta* threatened to burn *Agni* with his fearful eye, if he ever came again on such an errand. *Agni* was frightened and returned to *Indra* and Bṛh. and said that *Marutta* had refused and did not care for his promises. *Indra* asked *Agni* to return to *Marutta*, and threatened him with *Indra's* thunderbolt if he did not obey; *Agni*, afraid of *Saṃvarta*, suggested that the G. king should go; *Indra* said that nobody could burn *Agni*; *Agni* asked why then *Vṛtra* could deprive *Indra* of the sovereignty of Heaven; *Indra*, mentioning his victories over the *Kālakeyas*, Dā., and *Prahlāda*, said that it was because he did not accept *soma* from a foe, nor strike the weak with his thunderbolt; *Agni* reminded him of *Cyavana* at *Çaryāti's* sacrifice and the creation of *Mada* (description): "the might of brahmans is greater than that of kshatriyas" (XIV, **9**). Then *Indra* sent G. *Dhṛtarāshṭra* on the same errand, but in vain. *Vyāsa* said: As the clouds indicated that *Indra* must be near, *Marutta* repaired to *Saṃvarta*, who comforted him, saying that *Agni* would protect him, and that he would himself dispel the thunder by the winds, and granted him the boon that *Indra* should come in person to his sacrifice and accept the oblations offered to him, and so should all the gods. And so it happened by the power of *Saṃvarta's* incantations. Requested by *Saṃvarta*, *Indra* himself gave directions to all the gods to erect a hall of assembly: 1,000 well-furnished rooms with a durable staircase for the ascent of G. and Aps., and to furnish that portion of the sacrificial ground reserved for the dance of Aps., like unto the palace of *Indra* in heaven; *Indra* said that *Marutta's* ancestors and the gods had been highly pleased, and told him to offer a red bull to *Agni*, and a blue bull with a variegated skin to V.-D. Then *Indra* and the gods returned home. *Marutta* placed heaps of gold on various spots and distributed immense wealth to the brahmans.

Saṃvatsara [1] = Skanda: III, 14639.—Do. [2] = Çiva (1000 names [1-2]).—Do. [3] = Vishṇu (1000 names).

Saṃvatsarakara = Çiva (1000 names[2]).

Saṃvatsarakaro 'çvattha(ḥ) = Sūrya (the Sun): III, 151.

Saṃvedya, a tīrtha. § 370 (Tīrthayātrāp.): III, **85,** 8143.

Saṃvibhāgapriya = Çiva (1000 names[1]).

Saṃvṛta = Vishṇu (1000 names).

Saṃvṛtta, a serpent. § 564 (Mātalīyop.): V, **103**γ, 3630.

Saṃvṛtti, a goddess. § 270 (Brahmasabhāv.): II, **11,** 459 (in the palace of Brahmán).

Saṃyamana, the abode of Yama. § 439 (Yakshayuddhap.): III, **163,** 11849 (*Pretarājasya bhavanam*). Cf. Saṃyamanī.

Sāṃyamani, a Kuru warrior. § 581 (Bhīshmavadhap.): VI, **61**γ, 2680 (*putraḥ S°eḥ*, attacked Abhimanyu), 2687 (*dhvajam S°eḥ*), 2690 (*Çalaḥ?*) 2700 (°*eḥ putraḥ*), 2703 (*putraṃ S°eḥ*), 2708 (Dhṛshṭadyumna smashed the head of [the son of] *S.* (*Sāṃyamaneḥ*, C., B. has *senāpatiḥ*), 2712 (enraged at the slaughter of his son), 2714.

Saṃyamanī, the residence of Yama. § 596 (Pratijñāp.): VII, **72**, 2520 (*sadā sukṛtināṃ gatiḥ*).—§ 599 (Jayadrathavadhap.): VII, **119**, 4725 (°*īṃ gantuṃ*); **142**, 5888 (°*īṃ yātā . . . nihataḥ*). — § 757*c* (Yamaloka): XIII, **102**, †4858 (*Vaivasvatī S°ī janānāṃ*). Cf. Saṃyamana.

Saṃyata = Çiva (1000 names [2]).

Saṃyāti [1], son of Nahusha. § 143 (Nahusha): I, **75**, 3155 (third son of Nahusha).

Saṃyāti [2], a king § 156 (Pūruvaṃç.): I, **95**, ††3766 (son of Prācinvat and Açmakī), ††3767 (husband of Varāṅgī and father of Ahaṃyāti).

Saṃyoga, Saṃyugāpīḍavāhana = Çiva (1000 names[2]).

Sana, a mind-born son of Brahmán. § 717*b* (Nārāyaṇīya): XII, **341***o*, 13078.

Sanaka, a mind-born son of Brahmán. § 717*b* (Nārāyaṇīya): XII, **341***o*, 13078.

Sanandana, a mind-born son of Brahmán. § 717*b* (Nārāyaṇīya): XII, **341***o*, 13078.

Sanātana [1], a muni. § 264 (Sabhākriyāp.): II, **4***a*, 111 (waited upon Yudhishṭhira).

Sanātana [2], a mind-born son of Brahmán. § 717*b* (Nārāyaṇīya): XII, **341***o*, 13078.

Sanātana [3] = Sūrya (the Sun): III, 151.

Sanātana [4] = Mahāpurusha (Mahāpurushastava).

Sanātana [5] = Kṛshṇa (Vishṇu): XII, 1624, 7630 (etymology), 7651, 13350 (*Paramātmā*), 13402 (do.); XIII, 7743.

Sanātana [6]: Hiraṇyagarbha [i.e. Brahmán]: XII, 13471.

Sanātanānām api çāçvataḥ = Skanda: III, 14644.

Sanatkumāra, a ṛshi, son of Brahmán. § 132 (Aṃçāvat.): I, **67**, 2786 (incarnate as Pradyumna).—§ 140 (Purūravas): I, **75**, 3146 (came from Brahmaloka to give Purūravas counsel which was rejected). — § 270 (Brahmasabhāv.): II, **11**, 441 (*yogācāryaḥ*, in the palace of Brahmán).—§ 367 (Pṛthūdaka): III, **83**, 7017 (had praised the tīrtha Pṛthūdaka).—§ 373 (Prayāga): III, **85**, 8213 (°*pramukhāḥ . . . paramarshayaḥ*, in Prayāga).—§ 377 (Dhaumyatīrthak.): III, **90**, 8393 (praises Gaṅgādvāra).—§ 413 (Tīrthayātrāp.): III, **135**, 10697 (had obtained success on the Gaṅgā).—§ 455 (Brāhmaṇamāhātmyak.): III, **185**, 12700 (12702) (instructed some munis).—§ 581 (Bhīshmavadhap.): VI, **68***ρ*, 3046 (°*pramukhaiḥ*, praise Hari, i.e. Kṛshṇa).—§ 615*u* (Skanda): IX, **46**, 2716 (*Pitāmahasutaṃ prabhuṃ S°ṃ sarveshāṃ Brahmayoniṃ tam agrajaṃ*, by some identified with Skanda).—§ 617*b* (Brahmaçiras): X, **12**, 636 (incarnate as Pradyumna).—§ 637 (Rājadh.): XII, **47***η*, 1595 (among the ṛshis who surrounded Bhīshma).—§ 692 (Mokshadh.): XII, **281**, 10027 (*mahāmuniḥ*), 10030, 10086 (discourse with Vṛtra about emancipation and Vishṇu). — § 694*b* (Jvarotpatti): XII, **284***a*, 10217 (°*pramukhāḥ . . . maharshayaḥ*).—§ 707 (Mokshadh.): XII, **319***β*, 11784 (had instructed Viçvāvasu).—§ 715 (Çuka-Nāradasaṃv.): XII, **330**, 12426 (a saying of his quoted).—§ 717*b* (Nārāyaṇīya): XII, **340**, 12901 (°*tvaṃ labhet*, sc. Pradyumna (= manas)); **341***o*, 13078 (the fifth of the mind-born sons of Brahmán); **343**, 13200 (°*gītāḥ çlokāḥ*, some çlokas of his are quoted); **349**, V), 13587 (studied the religion [of Nārāyaṇa] and communicated it to Vīraṇa).—§ 730*g* (Upamanyu): XIII, **14***χ*, 916 (°*o yoginām asi*, sc. Çiva).—§ 730 (Ānuçāsanik.): XIII, **14***ββ*, 990.—§ 749 (do.): XIII, **88**, 4250 (*gāthāḥ . . . S°o mayyapi abhāshata*, some verses sung by him are quoted).—§ 768*b* (Kṛshṇa Vāsudeva): XIII, **147**, 6850 (°*pramukhāḥ*, sc. *ṛshayaḥ*).—§ 795 (Svargārohaṇap.): XVIII, **5***μ*, 160 (after death Pradyumna entered *S.*). Cf. Brahmayoni, Kumāra, Pitāmahasuta.

Sanāt sanātanatama(ḥ) = Vishṇu (1000 names).

Sanatsujāta, a ṛshi. § 11 (Parvasaṅgr.): I, **2**, 504 (cf. § 560).—§ 560 (Sanatsujātap.): V, **41**, 1566 (*kumāro vai yaḥ purāṇaḥ sanātanaḥ*); **42**, †1578, (†1579), (†1593), (†1595), (†1598), (1602), **43**, (†1622), (†1624), (†1627), (1632), 1634, (1635), (1663); **44**, †1684, (†1685), (†1687), (†1689), (†1709); **45**, (1715), **46**, (1737) (instructed Dhṛtarāshṭra).—§ 561 (Yānasandhip.): V, **47**, 1791 (all. to § 560): § 717*b* (Nārāyaṇīya): XII, **341***o*, 13078 (the second of the mind-born sons of Brahmán).

Sānatsujāta, adj. ("relating to Sanatsujāta"). § 10 (Parvasaṅgr.): I, **2**, 330 (*parva S°ṃ*, i.e. Sanatsujātaparvan).

[Sanatsujātaparvan(°va)] ("the section relating to Sanatsujāta," the 60th of the minor parvans of the Mbhbr.; cf. Sānatsujāta). § 560: As *Dhṛtarāshṭra* wished to hear more, *Vidura*, as he was born in the *Çūdra* order, did not venture to say more himself, but he thought of that ancient and eternal *Ṛshi* who, leading a life of perpetual celibacy, had said that there is no death. The *Ṛshi* came (V, **41**), was questioned by *Dhṛtarāshṭra*, and discoursed upon death, the efficacy of religious acts, etc. (V, **42–46**).

Sañcāraka, a warrior of Skanda. § 615*u* (Skanda): IX, **45***η*, 2576.

Saṇḍa, pl. (°*āḥ*), a people. § 574 (Jambūkh.): VI, **9***μ*, 351 (only B., C. has *Shaṇḍāḥ*).

Sandhātṛ [1] = Çiva (1000 names [1]).—Do. [2] = Vishṇu (1000 names).

Sandhimat = Vishṇu (1000 names).

Sandhiparvan = Kṛshṇa: XII, 1634.

Sandhyā [1], a river. § 268 (Varuṇasabhāv.): II, **9**, 375 (present in the palace of Varuṇa).

Sandhyā [2] ("twilight," personif.). § 565 (Gālavacarita): V, **117**, 3970 (wife of Pulastya).

Sandhyārāga = Çiva (1000 names [1]).

Sāṅgarevas (I, 2046), v. Çārṅgarava.

Saṅgraha [1], a companion of Skanda. § 615*u* (Skanda): IX, **45**, 2552 (given to Skanda by the Ocean).—Do. [2] = Çiva (1000 names [2]).—Do. [3] = Vishṇu (1000 names).

Saṅgrahādhyāya(ḥ) ("outline chapter") = Parvasaṅgraha: § 4 (Anukram.): I, **1**, 88 (°*bījaḥ*, sc. *Bhāratadrumaḥ*).

Saṅgrāmajit [1], a prince. § 264 (Sabhākriyāp.): II, **4***β*, 116 (waited upon Yudhishṭhira).

Saṅgrāmajit [2], brother of Karṇa. § 552 (Goharaṇap.): IV, **54**, 1666, 1678 (slain by Arjuna).

Sanīya, pl. (°*āḥ*), a people. § 574 (Jambūkh.): VI, **9***ν*, 371 (in the south, only C., B. has *Sanīpāḥ*).

Sañjaya [1], a Sūta, son of Gavalgaṇa. § 4 (Anukram.): I, **1**, 81, 140, 146, 148–212, 217, 218 (Dhṛtarāshṭra's complaint to *S.*).—§ 5 (do.): I, **1**, (220) (comforted Dhṛtarāshṭra). § 11 (Parvasaṅgr.): I, **2**, 501, 505, 520, 615 (*Gāvalgaṇiḥ*). —§ 81 (Ādivaṃçāvatāraṇa): The *muni*-like Sūta *S.* was born of Gavalgaṇa: I, **63**, 2426.—§ 288 (Rājasūyikap.): II, **35**, 129 (present at the rājasūya).—§ 305 (Anudyūtap.): II, **78**, 2562.—§ 307 (do.): II, **81**, 2673, (2674), (2676), 2689, 2696 (rebuked Dhṛtarāshṭra)—§ 313 (Āraṇyakap.): III, **6**, 265, 268, 269, 271, 272, 275, 276, (277) (sent by Dhṛtarāshṭra to bring Vidura back).—§ 327 (Draupadīparitāpav.): III, **29**, 1111 (*Kṛpaç ca S°ç caiva çamam eva vadishyataḥ*). — § 340 (Indralokābhigamanap.): III, **48**,

1915; **49,** (1932), 1952 (discourse with Dhṛtarāshṭra).—§ 342 (do.): III, **51,** 1968 (*Sūtam*), 1974, 1981 (told Dhṛtarāshṭra how the princes promised to assist Yudhishṭhira).—§ 512 (Ghoshayātrāp.): III, **249,** 15084.—§ 556 (Sañjayayānap.): V, **21,** 643, 644; **22,** †645, †646, †647, †674 (*Gāvalgaṇe*), †676, †680, †684; **23,** 685, †687 (*Gāvalgaṇiḥ . . . Sūtaḥ*), †690, †691, †695, †699, †709, †712; **24,** (†713); **25,** (†724); **26,** †738, †739, †748, †752, †753, †764, †765; **27,** (†767); **28,** †794, †796, †797, †798, †799, †802; **29,** †809, †810, †811, †812, †816, †825, †830, †839, †841, †843, †855, †862, 864; **30,** (†867), †869, †870, †873, †880, †882, †883, †884, †885, †887, †898, †899, †900, †902, †903, †914; **31,** 916, 922, 935, 938; **32,** 939, 941, †943, †944, (†946), †948, (†949) (*S.* was sent as an ambassador to the Pāṇḍavas).—§ 557 (Prajāgarap.): V, **33,** 979, †982 (*S.* returned).—§ 561 (Yānasandhip.): V, **47,** (1806); **48,** †1809, (†1810); **49,** 1963; **50,** (1970), 1975, 1978, 1979, 1980, (1981); **51,** 2032, 2034, 2053, 2054, 2059, 2067, 2070, 2081; **52,** 2098; **53,** 2112; **54,** (2121); **55,** 2212; **56,** 2214, (2215), 2218, (2220); **57,** 2232, (2233), 2266, 2274, 2276, (2278); **58***т*, 2300, (*v*) 2304, 2323; **59,** (2324), 2345; **60,** 2359; **61,** 2410; **66,** 2498, 2499, (2500), 2501, †2506, †2507; **67,** 2514, †2517, (†2518), 2521, †2522; **68,** (2523); **69,** 2538, (2540), (2543), 2544, 2549, 2554, (2555); **70,** 2560, (2561); **71,** †2574 (*S.* gave an account of his ambassade and praised Kṛshṇa).—§ 562 (Bhagavadyānap.): V, **72,** 2581, 2586; **73,** 2675; **82,** 2876; **85***κ*, 3023.—§ 567 (do.): V, **124***β*, 4138; **131,** 4432.—§ 569 (do.): V, **140,** 4726, 4728, (4729); **142,** (4813); **143,** (4833), (4882) (related the discourse of Karṇa and Kṛshṇa).—§ 570 (Sainyaniryāṇap.): V, **159,** 5392, 5393, 5397, (5398) (Dhṛtarāshṭra asked *S.* to tell all what happened).—§ 571 (Ulūkadutāgamanap.): V, **160,** (5407), 5414, 5465; **161,** (5535); **162,** (5578); **163,** (5643); **164,** (5702).—§ 572 (Rathātirathasaṅkhyānap.): V, **165,** 5718, (5719).—§ 573 (Ambopākhyānap.): V, **193,** (7558), (7572).—§ 574 (Jambūkh.): VI, **2,** 43, 44, 45 (Vyāsa bestowed celestial vision upon *S.*, that he might relate all events of the battle to Dhṛtarāshṭra); **4,** 156, 157, 159, 161, (163); **5,** 176, 177, (178); **6,** 194, 196, (197); **7,** 253, (254); **8,** 287, (288), 305; **9,** (311); **10,** 386, (387) (*S.* described the earth, etc., to Dhṛtarāshṭra).—§ 575 (Bhūmip.): VI, **11,** 401, 402, (404), 413 (only B.), (414), 421, (422); **12,** (442), 480, (481), (continuation).—§ 576 (Bhagavadgītāp.): VI, **13,** (497) (*S.* began his narration of the events of the battle (ad X, **9** incl.)); **14,** 509, 512, 516, 525, 529, 530, 531, 540, 543, 544, 546, 547, 560, 562, 564, 568, 569, 570, 573, 576, 580, 582, 584, 585; **15,** (588); **16,** (608); **17,** (636); **18,** (676); **19,** 696, (697); **20,** †741, (†743); **21,** (760); **22,** (777); **23,** (793), (795), (809); **24,** 822, 823, (825); **25,** 830, (831), (854), (878); **26,** (879), (887); **35,** (1255), (†1281), (†1296); **42,** (1528),—§ 577 (Bhīshmavadhap.): VI, **43,** (1533), (1547), (1595), (1602), (1616), (1621) (only B.), (1628).—§ 578 (do.): VI, **44,** (1639); **45,** (1670); **46,** (1757); **47,** (1808); **48,** 1868, (1870); **49,** 1987, 1991, 1993, 1995, 1997, 2003, 2006, (2007); **50,** (2033); **51,** (2091).—§ 579 (do.): VI, **52,** (2122); **53,** 2194, 2195, 2196, (2197); **54,** (2237); **55,** (2359).—§ 580 (do.): VI, **56,** (2402); **57,** (2423); **58,** (2462); **59,** 2509, (2510).—§ 581 (do.): VI, **60,** (†2651); **61,** (2680); **62,** 2716, 2718, 2721, (2722); **63,** (2780); **64,** (2813); **65,** 2898, 2899, 2900, 2905, 2908, 2911, (2912); **68,** (3048).—§ 582 (do.): VI, **69,** (3056); **70,** (3090); **71,** (3119); **72,** (3162); **73,** (3197); **74,** (3240).—§ 583 (do.): VI, **75,** (3277); **76,** 3314, 3332, 3333, 3336; **77,** (3337); **78,** (3413), (3430) (only C.); **79,** (3450); **80,** (3512).—§ 584 (do.): VI, **81,** (3531); **82,** (3577); **83,** 3639, 3640, (3642); **84,** (3696); **85,** (†3751); **86,** (3791).—§ 585 (do.): VI, **87,** (3847); **88,** (3887), (3925); **89,** 3931, 3932, (3939); **90,** (3971); **91,** 4064, (4065); **92,** (4096); **93,** (4139); **94,** (4182); **95,** (4232); **96,** (4323); **97,** (4404); **98,** (4448).—§ 586 (do.): VI, **99,** (4500); **100,** (4530); **101,** 4584 (only B., C. has by error Bhārata), 4587, (4588); **102,** 4644, (4646); **103,** (4682); **104,** (4729); **105,** (4767); **106,** (4802), 4836 (all. to Sañjayayānaparvan); **107,** (4886), (4937), (4975).—§ 587 (do.): VI, **108,** 4994, (4995), 5017, (5019), (5043); **109,** (5059); **110,** (5094); **111,** (5140); **112,** (5198); **113,** (5239); **114,** (5291); **115,** 5335, (5337); **116,** (5378); **117,** (5452); **118,** (5515); **119,** (5569); **120,** 5692, (5696), (5728), (5745).—§ 588 (do.): VI, **121,** (5762), †5797 (*°enāpi coktam*), (5817); **122,** (5818), (5856).—§ 589 (Droṇābhishekap.): VII, **1,** 8, 12, 13, (14), 47; **2,** (†52), (†59), (†85); **3,** (89); **5,** (134); **6,** (155), (166); **7,** (173), (178); **8,** (224); **9,** 269, 297, 303, 305; **10,** 378; **11,** 382, 383, 398, 405, 407, 413, 414, 427.—§ 590 (do.): VII, **12,** (434), (462); **13,** (465), (480); **15,** 582, (585); **16,** (619).—§ 591 (Saṃçaptakavadhap.): VII, **17,** (673), (683), (718).—§ 592 (do.): VII, **18,** (722); **19,** (753); **20,** (792), (816); **21,** (856); **22,** 925, (926), (948); **23,** 950, (951); **24,** 1060, 1064; **25,** (1066); **26,** 1130, (1131); **27,** (1195); **28,** (1226): **29,** (1257); **30,** (1302); **31,** 1344, 1345, (1346); **32,** (1373).—§ 593 (Abhimanyuvadhap.): VII, **33,** (1453), 1475, 1478, (1479); **34,** (1482), (1493); **35,** (1507), (1537); **36,** (1538); **37,** (1585); **38,** (1624); **39,** 1646, (1648); **40,** (1677); **41,** (1714); **42,** (1743); 1749, (1752); **43,** (1763); **44,** (1782); **46,** (1836); **47,** (1863); **48,** (1885); **49,** (1927); **50,** (1967); **51,** (1982).—§ 594 (do.): VII, **52,** (2003), (2010), (2022).—§ 595 (do.): VII, **55,** (2134).—§ 596 (Pratijñāp.): VII, **72,** (2477), (2484), (2494), (2542); **74,** (2613), (2633); **75,** (2648); **76,** (2704); **77,** (2706); **78,** (2732); **79,** (2775); **80,** (2820), (2885); **81,** (2886).—§ 597 (do.): VII, **82,** (2911); **83,** (2946); **84,** (2974).—§ 598 (Jayadrathavadhap.): VII, **85,** 3014, 3018, 3037, 3058, 3061, 3063; **86,** (3064); **87,** (3087); **88,** (3121).—§ 599 (do.): VII, **89,** (3151); **90,** (3185); **91,** (3217), (3223), (3251); **92,** (3261); **93,** (3338); **94,** (3409), (3447), (3478); **95,** (3486); **96,** (3542); **97,** (3573); **98,** 3609, (3611); **99,** (3666), (3706); **100,** (3726); **101,** (3763); **102,** (3823); **103,** (3843), (3864); **104,** (3891); **105,** 3926, (3927); **106,** 3965, (3966); **107,** (4013); **108,** (4053); **109,** (4097); **110,** 4134, (4135); **111,** (4239); **112,** (4291), (4344); **113,** (4372), (4406); **114,** 4440, 4456, 4460, 4463, 4466, 4482, 4485, (4486); **115,** (4543); **116,** (4602); **117,** (4648); **118,** (†4684); **119,** (4702), (4739); **120,** (4758); **121,** 4806, 4809, 4812, (4816); **122,** (4864); **123,** (4935); **124,** 4975, (4976), (4998); **125,** (5017); **126,** (5096); **127,** (5146); **128,** (5219); **129,** 5273, 5280, (5281); **130,** (5311); **131,** (5355), 5362, 5372, (5373); **132,** 5413, (5416); **133,** 5457, 5461, 5469, (5470); **134,** (5500); **135,** 5542, 5547, 5552, 5554, (5559); **136,** (5575); **137,** (5615); **138,** 5667, 5668, 5669, (5670); **139,** (5696); **140,** 5817, 5822, 5824, (†5825); **141,** (5842); **142,** (5879); **143,** (5951), (5984), (6001), (6021); **144,** (6027); **145,** 6055, (6056); **146,** (†6153); **147,** 6297, (6298), 6335, (6336),

6377, (6378); **148,** 6388, (6389), (6450); **149,** (6451); **150,** (6494); **151,** 6530, (6531); **152,** (6570), 6603.—§ 600 (Ghaṭotkacavadhap.): VII, **153,** (6605); **154,** (6648); **155,** 6694, (6695); **156,** (6729), (6824), (6848), 6851 (the same?); **157,** (6922); **158,** (6970), (6981), (7019); **159,** (7042), (7051), (7057), (7060), (7093); **160,** (7143); **161,** (7204); **162,** (7224); **163,** (7279), 7288, (7289); **164,** (7317), 7334, (7336); **165,** (7355); **166,** (7397); **167,** (7462), (7484); **168,** (7512); **169,** (7559); **170,** (7609); **171,** (7680); **172,** (7735), (7766); **173,** (7774), (7834), (7841); **174,** (7844); **175,** 7893, (7894); **176,** (8004); **177,** (8026); **178,** (8074); **179,** (8115), (8132), (8134), (†8135); **180,** (8178); **182,** 8250, (8257), (8266), (8279), (8293); **183,** 8296, (8297), 8310, (8312).—§ 601 (Droṇavadhap.): VII, **184,** (8362); **185,** (8419), (8427), (8440).—§ 602 (do.): VII, **186,** (8457), (8468); **187,** (8518); **188,** (8574); **189,** (8628), (8657); **190,** (8694); **191,** (8755); **192,** (8809).—§ 603 (Nārāyaṇāstramokshap.); VII, **193,** (8893), (8961); **194,** 8970; **195,** (8979); **196,** (9029), 9036, (9037); **197,** (9082); **198,** 9130, (9131), (9171); **199,** (9195); **200,** (9258), (9277), (9291); **201,** (9390), 9398, (9400), (9490); **202,** (9495), (9645).—§ 604 (Karṇap.): VIII, **1,** 17; **2,** 29, 34, 46, (48), 50; **3,** (51), (68); **4,** 78, 85, 86; **5,** 90 (*Sūtam*), (93); **6,** 151, (152); **7,** 190, 193, (†195), 215; **8,** 227, 246, 249; **9,** (250), 256, 259, 261, 263, 277, 278, 282, 285, 289, 315, 329, 333, 334, 335, 339, 342.—§ 605 (do.): VIII, **10,** (344), (353), (381), (385); **11,** 401, (402); **12,** (441): **13,** (487); **14,** (526); **15,** (566); **16,** 611, (612); **17,** (661); **18,** (687); **19,** (711); **20,** 770, (772); **21,** 821, 823, (824); **22,** (862); **23,** (893); **24,** (915); **25,** (993); **26,** (1037); **27,** (1076); **28,** (1119); **29,** 1169, 1172, (1173); **30,** (1205); **31,** (1254), 1267, 1274, 1275, (1278), (1320), (1323); **32,** (1324), (1354), (1376), (1390).—§ 606 (do.): VIII, **35,** (1632), (1651), (1661).—§ 607 (do.): VIII, **36,** (1673), (1703); **37,** (1704), (†1738), (†1747), (1749); **38,** (1752); **39,** (1793); **40,** (1816); **41,** (1873); **42,** (†1962); **43,** (2014); **44,** (2025); **45,** (2119).—§ 608 (do.): VIII, **46,** (2122), 2126, 2127, (2132), (2159); **47,** 2210, (2212); **48,** 2234, (2236); **49,** (2301); **50,** (2391), (2408), (2422); **51,** 2440, (2443); **52,** (2520); **53,** (2563); **54,** (2610); **55,** (2652); **56,** (2692): **57,** (2840); **58,** (2857); **59,** (2909); **60,** (2970), (3000), **61,** 3060, (3060); **62,** (3142); **63,** (3176); **64,** (3215); **65,** (†3285), (†3299), (†3306); **67,** (†3357); **68,** (†3380); **69,** (3403), (3418); **70,** (†3492), (†3513), (†3529); **71,** (3552), (3584), (†3591); **72,** (3593); **73,** (3634); **74,** (3751); **75,** (†3805); **76,** (†3821); **77,** (3861); **78,** 3940, 3944, (3946); **79,** (4004); **80,** (4091); **81,** (4123); **82,** (†4180); **83,** (†4216); **84,** (4261); **85,** (†4305); **86,** (4348); **87,** (4372), (4476); **88,** (†4490); **89,** (†4524); **90,** (†4622), (†4682); **91,** (†4748), (4763); **92,** (†4818); **93,** (4835), (4894); **94,** (†4895); **95,** (4964); **96,** (4982), (5005), (5028), 5037 (C. has *Sṛñ°*).—§ 609 (Çalyap.): IX, **1,** 14, 18, 25, 50, 55; **2,** 61, 98, 101, 104, 121, 125.—§ 610 (do): IX, **3,** (126); **4,** (187); **5,** (239); **6,** (292); **7,** (321), (341).—§ 611 (do.); IX, **8,** (367), 381, (382), 403, (404); **9,** (413); **10,** (460); **11,** (529); **12,** (593); **13,** (656); **14,** (705); **15,** (753); **16,** (796); **17,** (864); **18,** (955); **19,** (996); **20,** (1066); **21,** (1093); **22,** (1130); **23,** (1179), (1238); **24,** (1272); (1322); **25,** (1338); **26,** (1401); **27,** (1443), 1445; **28,** (1501).—§ 612 (Hradapraveçap.): IX, **29,** (1566), 1587, (1589), 1606 (set free by Sātyaki), 1607, 1616, 1617, 1624, 1625; **30,** 1673, (1675), (1692); **31,** (1742), (1758), (1779), (1796).—§ 613 (Gadāyuddhap.): IX, **32,** 1820, 1822, (1823), (1852), (1864), (1879); **33,** (1889), (1910).—§ 614 (do.): IX, **34,** (1947).—§ 615 (do.): IX, **55,** 3078, (3079); **56,** 3133, (3134); **57,** (3175); **58,** (3246); **59,** (3309), (3341); **60,** 3343, (3344), (3365), (3378); **61,** 3388, (3389), (3442); **62,** (3460); **64,** 3582, (3584), 3598, 3599, 3600; **65,** (3626).—§ 616 (Sauptikap.): X, **1,** (1), 7, 8, 10, 12, 13, 14, 15, 16, (17); **3,** (105); **5,** (205); **6,** 216, (217); **7,** (251); **8,** 322, (323), (472); **9,** (479), (497), (526) (having lost his celestial vision at the death of Duryodhana, *S.* here concluded his narrative).—§ 618 (Jalapradānikap.): XI, **1,** 3, 5, 18, 23, 45 (comforted Dhṛtarāshṭra); **8**ε, 195; **9,** 248, 249 (*vigataprājñaḥ*), (250), 253 (related to Dhṛtarāshṭra that the Kurus had been slain); **13**μ, 346.—§ 620 (Çrāddhap.): XI, **20**a, 779 (*Sūtaḥ*), 782 (do.)—§ 637 (Rājadh.): XII, **40**a, 1448; **41,** 1477, 1483 (appointed supervisor of finances); **44**δ, 1529; **47,** 1695 (*Sūtaḥ*).—§ 639 (do.): XII, **52**ε, 1889.—§ 640 (do.): XII, **58**γ, 2116.—§ 785 (Anugītāp.): XIV, **60,** 1806.—§ 787 (Āçramavāsap.): XV, **1,** 5, 12; **3,** 80, 119; **4**η, 168; **5**η, 172 (*Sūtaḥ*); **8,** 259; **15**τ, †435; **16,** 444 (*Sūto Gāvalgaṇiḥ*); **18**ψ, 513; **19,** 537; **20,** 557 (*svargam avāpsyati*; *S.* accompanied Dhṛtarāshṭra, etc., when he retired to the forest).—§ 788 (do.): XV, **25,** 659 (*Sutaḥ*), (γ) (660) (shows the Pāṇḍavas and their wives to the ascetics); **26,** 690.—§ 792 (Nāradāgamanap.): XV, **37,** 1017 (*Sūtaputraḥ*), 1021 (*Sūtena*), 1024, 1026, 1027, 1033 (*Sūtam*), 1034, 1036, 1038, 1039, 1042, 1044 (after the death of Dhṛtarāshṭra, etc., *S.* went to the Himavat).

Cf. also the following synonyms:—

Gāvalgaṇi ("the son of Gavalgaṇa"): I, 220, 245 (*Sūtaḥ*), 615 (*S°*); II, 2709; V, †674 (*S°*), †687 (*S°*), †690 (*S°*), †723, †755 (*Sūta*), 919, †1914, 1976, †2516, 2542; VI, 46, 403, 495; VII, 7, 311 (*Sūtam*), 1477, 1647, 8265; VIII, 25, 47, 84 (*Sūtam . . . S°m*); IX, 110 (*Sūtam*), 118; X, 9; XI, 332 (*Sūtaḥ*), XV, 444 (*Sūtaḥ*), 581.

Sauti, Sūta, Sūtanandana, Sūtaputra, q.v.

Sañjaya[2], an ancient king. § 6 (Anukram.): I, **1**a, 223 (in Sañjaya's enumeration).

Sañjaya[3], one of the standard-bearers of Jayadratha. § 522 (Draupadīharaṇap.): III, **265,** †15597 (only B., C. has *Sṛñjayaḥ*).

Sañjaya[4], a Sauvīra king, son of Vidulā. § 568 (Vidulāputraçāsana): V, **133,** 4523, 4536; **134,** 4545, 4549, 4554, 4578; **135,** 4584, 4586, 4592; **136,** 4629, 4631 (*S.* was defeated by the Sindhu king, Vidulā by her exhortations prevailed upon him to exert himself to regain his kingdom).

Sañjayantī, a city. § 284 (Sahadeva): II, **31,** 1173 (*nagarīm*, in the south, conquered by Sahadeva).

Sañjayayāna(m) ("the mission of Sañjaya"). § 10 (Parvasaṅgr.): I, **2,** 329 (*°ākhyam parva*, i.e. Sañjayayānaparvan).

[Sañjayayānaparvan(°va)] ("the section relating to the mission of Sañjaya," the 58th of the minor parvans of Mhbhr.; cf. Sañjayayāna). § 556: *Drupada's purohita* was honoured by *Dhṛtarāshṭra*, *Bhīshma*, and *Vidura.* He mentioned the eternal duties of kings; the *Pāṇḍavas* had not obtained their share of the paternal wealth; the murderous contrivances of the *Dhārtarāshṭras*; the deceitful game; the indignities in the council-hall; the exile for thirteen years; the *Pāṇḍavas* desired nothing but a peaceful settlement; the *Pāṇḍavas* were more powerful; men like *Sātyaki*, *Bhīmasena*, and the twins were equal in might to 1,000 *akshauhiṇīs*; *Arjuna* and *Kṛshṇa* nobody could fight (V, **20**). *Bhīshma* approved of his speech; but *Karṇa* wrathfully interrupted him. *Dhṛtarāshṭra* pacified *Bhīshma*, rebuked *Karṇa*, sent *Drupada's purohita* back to the *Pāṇḍavas*, and summoned *Sañjaya* to the council-hall (V, **21**). *Dhṛtarāshṭra* gave instructions to *Sañjaya*, praising the *Pāṇḍavas* (*a*) and *Kṛshṇa* and some of their adherents (β), mentioning the killing of *Çiçupāla* (*b*), blaming *Duryodhana* and *Karṇa*, and ordered him to go to *Upaplavya* to salute them and the five sons of *Draupadī*, and tell them that *Dhṛtarāshṭra* was desirous of peace with the *Pāṇḍavas* (V, **22**). *Sañjaya* came to *Upaplavya* and saluted *Yudhishṭhira* and enquired about *Bhīmasena*, etc. (γ). *Yudhishṭhira* inquired about *Dhṛtarāshṭra*, etc. (δ), and mentioned the prowess of *Arjuna* (*c*), *Sahadeva* (*d*), *Nakula* (*e*), and the *Ghoshayātrā* (V, **23**). *Sañjaya* delivered his message and answered *Yudhishṭhira's* questions (V, **24**). In the presence of the *Pāṇḍavas*, etc. (ε), *Sañjaya* greeted *Yudhishṭhira*, etc. (ζ), and recommended peace, "for what, in sooth, is life after having killed all your kinsfolk?"; he mentioned *Kṛshṇa*, etc. (η) on the side of the *Pāṇḍavas*, and *Droṇa*, etc. (θ), on the side of the *Kauravas* (V, **25**). *Yudhishṭhira* said that peace was preferable to war, but complained that *Duryodhana* had disregarded the words of *Vidura*, and *Dhṛtarāshṭra* had been desirous solely of satisfying his sons; that *Duryodhana's* counsellors were now *Duḥçāsana*, *Çakuni*, and *Karṇa*. He compared *Arjuna*, *Bhīma*, *Nakula*, and *Sahadeva* with *Karṇa* and *Duryodhana*. He claimed *Indraprastha* for his kingdom (V, **26**). *Sañjaya* declared that if, without war, the *Kurus* would not yield his share to *Yudhishṭhira*, then it would be far better for him to live upon alms in the kingdom of the *Andhakas* and the *Vṛshṇis* than to obtain sovereignty by war (V, **27**). *Yudhishṭhira* said that virtue and vice, which are both eternal and absolute, exchange their aspects during seasons of distress; he would not seek even what belongs to *Prajāpati*, or heaven, or *Brahmaloka* (*Prājāpatyaṃ tridivaṃ Brahmalokaṃ*) by unrighteous means; but he would be guided by *Kṛshṇa*, as did *Sātyaki*, etc. (ι); *Kṛshṇa* was the great judge of the propriety or otherwise of all acts (V, **28**). *Kṛshṇa* said he wished prosperity for both the *Pāṇḍavas* and *Dhṛtarāshṭra*; therefore he desired peace; but when *Dhṛtarāshṭra* and his sons were so covetous, war was inevitable; "some say that work should be shunned and that salvation is attainable by knowledge; but the brahmans know this, that though one may have a knowledge of eatable things, yet the hunger will not be appeased unless one actually eats; such branches of knowledge as are of use in doing works bear fruit, but not the other ones. In the other world it is by virtue of work that the gods, etc. (κ) flourish. *Yudhishṭhira* is constantly engaged in the study of the *Veda*; he is bent on the horse-sacrifice and the *rājasūya*; he rides horses and elephants, etc.; if the *Pāṇḍavas* could see a course of action not involving the slaughter of the sons of *Kuru*, they would adopt it. But we must take into consideration the division into four castes and the respective duties allotted to each (specification). War and weapons were invented by *Indra* for putting the *Dasyus* to death." *Kṛshṇa* alluded to the game and the role of *Çakuni* there, to the indignities undergone by *Kṛshṇā* from *Duḥçāsana* and *Karṇa*, while the *Kurus* with *Bhīshma* at their head did not interfere, and only *Vidura* took her part; and that *Duḥçāsana* had called the *Pāṇḍavas* eunuchs at their departure. He would go in person to the *Kurus*. He compared the evil passions of *Duryodhana*, etc. (λ), with the righteousness of *Yudhishṭhira*, etc. (μ). "King *Dhṛtarāshṭra* with his sons constitute a forest, while the *Pāṇḍavas* are its tigers; do not cut down the forest with its tigers, and let not the tigers be driven away from the forest; the tiger out of the wood is easily slain; the wood also that is without a tiger is easily cut down." Similarly the *Dhārtarāshṭras* are as creepers, the *Pāṇḍavas* are *Çāla*-trees, and the creepers cannot dispense with a large tree round which it can twine (V, **29**). *Sañjaya* then bade farewell to *Yudhishṭhira*, etc. (ν). *Yudhishṭhira* spoke approvingly of *Sañjaya's* agreeable speech and excellent conduct as an ambassador, and compared him to *Vidura*, and declared him to be as dear to them as *Dhanañjaya* (i.e. Arjuna). He recommended the *brahmans* to him, and told him to salute *Droṇa*, etc. (ξ), and the aged, middle-aged, and young ladies, "the daughters of our house," and the maidservants and manservants, and the many humpbacked and lame ones among them, and those that were defective in limb, or imbecile, and the dwarfs to whom *Dhṛtarāshṭra* gave food and raiment from motives of humanity, the blind, the aged, the many that had the use only of their hands, being destitute of legs, the masterless and weak, those that vainly strived to earn a living, the ignorant, in fact, all those that were in pitiable circumstances, all the ambassadors arrived from all sides, etc. He concluded with this message to *Duryodhana*: "give me back my own *Indraprastha* (*Çakrapurīṃ*), or fight with me" (V, **30**). *Yudhishṭhira* said that the Creator (*Dhātṛ*) gives and takes according to his will. He told *Sañjaya* especially to salute *Dhṛtarāshṭra*, *Bhīshma*, and *Vidura*, and recommend the *Pāṇḍavas* to them, that they might counsel peace; and to say to *Duryodhana* that the *Pāṇḍavas* were willing to forgive his insults to *Draupadī* (*Kṛshṇā*) and *Duḥçāsana's* dragging her, disregarding *Kuntī*; but they must have their proper share of the kingdom; "give us even a single province of the empire; give us even *Kuçasthala* (B. *Avi°*), *Vṛkasthala*, *Mākandī*, *Vāraṇāvata*, and in the fifth place any other village that thou likest; even this will end the quarrel." He said that to see the *Kurus* and the *Pāñçālas* live happily united was what he desired (V, **31**). Having returned to *Hāstinapura*, *Sañjaya* addressed *Dhṛtarāshṭra* at night; he praised *Yudhishṭhira*, "who shines in his natural perfection, leaving his load of sins to be borne by thee," while *Dhṛtarāshṭra's* acts were contrary to both religion and profit. In delivering the message from *Yudhishṭhira* he did not mention the alternative of giving them the five villages. He alluded to *Arjuna's* ascending to the very heavens and being honoured there. King *Bali*, not finding a primary cause (*pāraṃ*), regarded time (*kālaḥ*) to be the cause of everything. "To-morrow morning the *Kurus*, assembled together in the council-hall, will hear the words of *Ajātaçatru* (i.e. *Yudhishṭhira*)" (V, **32**).

Sañjīvana ("making alive"), name of a jewel. § 785 (Anugītāp.): XIV, **80**, 2382 (*maṇiṃ Pannagānāṃ parāyaṇaṃ*, Ulupī revived Arjuna by means of the *S.*).

Sañjīvinī (do.), name of a science. § 145 (Kaca): I, **76**, 3192 (*vidyāṃ*), 3215 (*vidyāṃ*, C. has °*va*°), †3253 (obtained by Kaca from Çukra).

Sañjña = Mahāpurusha (Mahāpurushastava).

Sañjñā, wife of Vivasvat and mother of the Açvins. § 770 (Ānuçāsanik.): XIII, **151**, 7096 (°*nāsāvinirgatau*, sc. *Açvinau*).

Saṅkalpa ("the Will," personif.). § 775 (Ānuçāsanik.): XIII, **166***a*, 7638.
Saṅkalpaja = Kāma: I, †7007.
Sāṅkāçya, a rājarshi. § 267 (Çakrasabhāv.): II, **8**, 321 (in the palace of Indra).
Saṇkarshaṇa[1] = Balarāma (q.v.), identified with Çesha, and as jīva (the soul) considered as a form of Kṛshṇa (Purushottama). § 210*b* (Bhīmasena): I, **139**, 5520 (preceptor of Bhīmasena).—§ 232 (Svayaṃvarap.): I, **186***a*, 6997 (present at the svayaṃvara of Draupadī).—§ 233 (do.): I, **189**, 7080.—§ 273 (Rājasūyārambhap.): II, **14**, 598 (°*dvitīyena*, sc. Kṛshṇa).—§ 290 (Çiçupālavadhap.): II, **43**, 1508 (°-*Yādavau*).—§ 420 (Gandhamādanapr.): III, **141**, 10890.—§ 549*f* (Durgā): IV, **6**, 187 (°*samānanā*, sc. Durgā, C. has by error Ç°).—§ 561 (Yānasandhip.): V, **55**, 2177. —§ 567 (Bhagavadyānap.): V, **131***o*, 4425.—§ 581 (Bhīshmavadhap.): VI, **65**ζ, 2967 (*dṛshṭvā* [read with B. *sṛshṭvā*], *S°ṃ devaṃ*, sc. Kṛshṇa); **66**, 3012 (*gītaḥ S°ena*, sc. Kṛshṇa); **67**, 3023 (*agrajaṃ sarvabhūtānāṃ*, created by Kṛshṇa).— § 599 (Jayadrathavadhap.): VII, **110**, 4227 (°*samo bale*, sc. Sātyaki).—§ 637 (Rājadh.): XII, **47**θ, 1620 (*kshaye S°ṃ proktaṃ*, sc. Kṛshṇa).—§ 641 (do.): XII, **81**, 3030 (*balaṃ S°e*).—§ 664 (Mokshadh.): XII, **207**, 7529 (*agrajaṃ sarvabhūtānāṃ*, created by Kṛshṇa (*Purushottamaḥ*)).—§ 717*b* (Nārāyaṇīya): XII, **340**, 12900, 12904 (i.e. Vāsudeva (Kṛshṇa) in the form of jīva), 12905 (from *S.* sprang Pradyumna [i.e. the Mind]), 12937 (= Çesha, creates *Pradyumna*); **345**, 13386 (= *jīva*). — § 773*b* (Kṛshṇa Vāsudeva): XIII, **159**, 7392 (i.e. Vāsudeva (Kṛshṇa) in the form of jīva).—Do.[2] = Vishṇu (1000 names).
Saṅkarshaṇānuja ("the younger brother of Saṅkarshaṇa") = Kṛshṇa: II, 2206; V, 5329.
Saṅkoca, a Daitya (?). § 673*b* (Bali-Vāsavasaṃv.): XII, **227***a*, 8264 (among the ancient rulers of the earth).
Sāṅkhya(ṃ), a system of philosophy, propounded by Kapila. § 138 (Daksha Prācetasa): I, **75**, 3132 (°*jñānaṃ*, Nārada taught the sons of Daksha the *S.*).—§ 265 (Lokapālasabhākriyāp.): II, **5**, 141 (°-*Yogavibhāgajñaḥ*, sc. Nārada). —§ 308 (Āraṇyakap.): III, **2**, 61 (*Yoge S°e ca kuçalaḥ*, sc. Çaunaka).—§ 493 (Āṅgirasa): III, **221**, 14197 (°-*Yogapravartakaḥ*, sc. Kapila).—§ 576 (Bhagavadgītāp.): VI, **26**, 917; **29**, 1039 (°-*Yogau*); **37**, 1345; **42**, 1467.—§ 602 (Droṇavadhap.): VII, **192**, 8857 (*paramaṃ S°m āsthitaḥ*). —§ 639 (Rājadh.): XII, **50**, 1838 (*Yoge S°e ca niyatā ye ca dharmaḥ*).—§ 661 (Mokshadh.): XII, **190**, 7154 (°-*Yogakriyāvidhiḥ*); 7157 (°-*Yogau*), 7158 (*do.*).—§ 668*b* (Pañcaçikhavākya): XII, **210**, 7900 (*abravīt paramaṃ mokshaṃ yat tat S°e 'bhidhīyate*, sc. Pañcaçikha).—§ 677 (Mokshadh.): XII, **237**, 8673, 8674 (*Yoge S°e pi ca*); **240**, 8736; **241**, 8768 (°*jñānena*).—§ 688 (do.): XII, **276**, 9912 (°*jñānaṃ*). —§ 696*b* (Dakshaproktа-Çivasahasranāmastotra): XII, **285**, 10467 (°-*Yogāt*).—§ 704 (Mokshadh.): XII, **301**, 11037 (°*e Yoge ca*), 11038, 11041; **302**, 11099, 11110 (°*jñāne*), 11198, (*jñānaṃ*, adj. ?), 11203, †11206, †11207, †11209, †11211 (the doctrines of the *S.* briefly expounded).—§ 705 (do.): XII, **303**, 11232 (*çāstre*, adj. ?); **306**, 11347 (*ekaṃ S°ñ ca Yogañ ca*), 11361 (°-*Yoge ca kuçalāḥ*); **307**, 11372 11393 (°*jñānaṃ*), 11397, 11409 (°*darçanaṃ*); **308**, 11418 (°*darçanaṃ*), 11420, 11461 (°-*Yogau*); **309**, 11483 (°*çrutinidarçanāt*).—§ 707 (do.): [**314**, 11610 (*saṅkhyānadarçinaḥ*)]; **315**, 11653 (°*jñānaṃ*); **316**, 11673 (°*darçanaṃ*); **317**, 11675 (°*jñānaṃ*), 11676 (°*samaṃ*), 11678; **318**, 11722 (*sa-S°dhāraṇaṃ*); **319**, 11735 (°-*Yogepsitaṃ*), 11790 (°*jñānaṃ*), 11810 (°*dharme*), 11822 (°*jñānaṃ*). — § 709*b* (Sulabhā-Janakasaṃv.): XII, **321**, 11876 (°*jñāne*), 11931 (°*kramau*). —§ 717*b* (Nārāyaṇīya): XII, **340**, 12932 (°*niçcitaniçcayāḥ*), 12976 (°-*Yogakṛtaṃ* . . . *Pañcarātrānuçabditaṃ*); **341**, 13080 (°*jñānaviçāradāḥ*); **342**, 13137; **348***ι*, 13530, 13537; **349**, 13621 (°-*Yogena*), 13629 (°-*Yogaṃ*); **350**, 13637, (°-*Yogaṃ*), 13702, 13703 (°*sya vaktā Kapilaḥ*), †13711; **351**, 13714 (°-*Yogavicāraṇe*).—§ 717*d* (Brahma-Rudrasaṃv.): XII, **352**, 13746 (*vidhinā*, adj. ?), 13763 (°*jñāne*).—§ 726 (Ānuçāsanik.): XIII, **10***a*, 470.—§ 730*g* (Upamanyu): XIII, **14**, 789 (°-*Yogārthadaṃ*, sc. Çiva), 910 (°*e Purusha ucyate*, sc. Çiva).—§ 730 (Ānuçāsanik.): XIII, **18**, †1374. —§ 732 (do.): XIII, **22**, 1542.—§ 746 (do.): XIII, **75**, 3645 (°*çūrāḥ*).—§ 769 (do.): XIII, **149**, 7075.—§ 771 (do.): XIII, **151**, 7132.—§ 795*b* (Janamejaya): XVIII, **5**, 185 (°-*Yogavatā*, sc. Vyāsa).
Sāṅkhya, pl. (°*āḥ*), the followers of the Sāṅkhya system. § 310*b* (Sūrya): III, **3**, 167 (*tvaṃ gatiḥ sarva-S°ānāṃ*, sc. Sūrya).—§ 576 (Bhagavadgītāp.): VI, **27**, 953; **29**, 1040. —§ 637 (Rājadh.): XII, **47**θ, 1642 (*yaṃ prāhuḥ saptadaçaṃ S°āḥ*, sc. Kṛshṇa).—§ 668*b* (Pañcaçikhavākya): XII, **218**, 7889 (*yam āhur Kapilaṃ S°āḥ paramarshiṃ Prajāpatiṃ*).— § 677 (Mokshadh.): XII, **237**, 8679, 8685 (sg.).—§ 704 (do.): XII, **301**, 11038, 11040, 11043; **302**, 11100, 11133, 11151 (*Kāpilāḥ*), 11158, 11169, 11197, 11202, †11205 (?), †11208, 11209. — § 705 (do.): XII, **306**, 11346, 11347, 11359 (°-*Yogāḥ*): **307**, 11409, 11410, 11462, 11464.—§ 707 (do.): XII, **311**, 11550; **316**, 11673, 11678; **319**, 11780, 11794 (°-*Yogāḥ*), 11802, 11810, 11825. — § 709*b* (Sulabhā-Janakasaṃv.): XII, **321**, 11878 (°*mukhyena*, i.e. Pañcaçikha).—§ 717*b* (Nārāyaṇīya): XII, **341**, 13034; **344**, 13254 (*niçcitaniçcayāḥ*); **345**, 13387; **347**, 13448 (°-*Yogibhiḥ*); **348**ηη, 13487 (°-*Yoganidhe*, sc. Vishṇu), 13541. — § 730*g* (Upamanyu): XIII, **14**, 916 (°*ānāṃ Kapilo hy asi*, sc. Çiva). — § 730 (Ānuçāsanik.): XIII, **16**ηη, 1040, 1062 (*gatiḥ S°-Yogānāṃ*), 1079 (°*āḥ* . . . *S°çāstraviçāradāḥ*); **17**, 1286 (*gatiḥ S°-Yogānāṃ*).—Do.[2] sg. = Çiva: XII, 10388 (1000 names[1]), XIII, 901.—Do.[3], a ṛshi. —§ 770 (Ānuçāsanik.): XIII, **151**λ, 7123 (read *Sāṅkhya-Yogau* with B., C. has *Sāṅkhyayogaḥ*).
Sāṅkhyamukhya = Çiva (1000 names[1]).
Sāṅkhyamūrti = Mahāpurusha (Mahāpurushastava).
Sāṅkhyaprasāda, Saṅkhyāsamāpana = Çiva (1000 names[2]).
Sāṅkhyayoga[1] = Mahāpurusha (Mahāpurushastava). — Do.[2], a ṛshi, v. Sāṅkhya[3].
Sāṅkhyayoganidhi = Vishṇu: XII, 13487.
Sāṅkhyayogapravartin = Çiva (1000 names[1]).
Sāṅkhyātman = Kṛshṇa: XII, 1642.
Sāṅkhyarshi = Kapila: XIII, 1299.
Saṅkrama, a companion of Skanda. § 615*u* (Skanda): IX, **45**ε, 2539 (given to Skanda by Vishṇu).
Saṅkṛti, an ancient king. § 6 (Anukram.): I, **1***a*, 227 (in Sañjaya's enumeration).
Sāṅkṛti[1], one or more ṛshis. § 677 (Mokshadh.): XII, **235**, 8596 (*Ātreyaḥ*, but cf. XIII, 6247, where we have *satkṛtaḥ* instead of Sāṅkṛtiḥ); **245**β, 8900.
Sāṅkṛti[2] ("the son of Saṅkṛti") = Rantideva: II, 321 (?); III, 16674 (*R*°); VII, 2356 (*R*°), 2371 (*R*°); XII, 1020 (*R*°), 8596, 8900.
Sāṅkṛtya (do.) = Rantideva: XII, 1013 (*R*°), 8591 (*R*°); XIII, 6250 (*R*°).
Saṅksheptṛ = Vishṇu (1000 names).

Sannateyu, son of Raudrāçva. § 150 (Pūruvaṃç.): I, **94**, 3701 (tenth son of Raudrāçva).

Sannihata, name of a fire. § 493 (Āṅgirasa): III, **221**, 14195.

Sannihatī or **Sannihityā**, name of a tīrtha. § 368 (Tīrthayātrāp.): III, **83**, 7061, 7062, 7065, 7066.

Sannivāsa = Vishṇu (1000 names).

Sannyastapāda, pl. (°*āḥ*), a people. § 273 (Rājasūyārambhap.): II, **14**, 592 (so B., C. has *Sanya*°, fled from fear of Jarāsandha).

Santa, a brahman. § 736*b* (Vītahavyop.): XIII, **30**, 2001 (son of Satya and father of Çravas).

Santāna, name of a weapon. § 563 (Bhagavadyānap.): V, **96**ϕ, 3491 (will be employed by Arjuna).

santānaka, adj. ("like to the Santāna tree of Indra's heaven"): III, 14536 (°*vanaiḥ*); V, 3833 (*nagāḥ*), XIII, 3825 (°*vanaiḥ*).

Santānikā, a mātṛ. § 615*u* (Skanda): IX, **46**θ, 2627.

Santāpitṛ = Çiva (1000 names[1]).

Santarjana, a warrior of Skanda. § 615*u* (Skanda): IX, **45**η, 2620.

Sanyastapāda, pl. v. Sannyastapāda.

Saphalodaya = Çiva (1000 names[2]).

Saptacaru, a tīrtha (= Vaḍavā). § 359 (Vaḍavā): III, **82**, 5040 (origin of the name).

Saptadaça = Kṛshṇa: XII, 1642 (*yaṃ prāhuḥ s°aṃ Sāṅkhyāḥ*).

Saptagaṅga, a tīrtha. § 370 (Tīrthayātrāp.): III, **84**, 8007.—§ 733*g* (Ānuçāsanik.): By giving oblations of water to one's pitṛs at *S.* and *Trigaṅga* and *Indramārga* one obtains *amṛta*, etc.: XIII, **25**, 1703.

Saptagodāvara, a tīrtha. § 370 (Tīrthayātrāp.): III, **85**, 8186.

Saptaidhas, Saptajihva = Vishṇu (1000 names).

Saptakṛt, a Viçvadeva. § 749 (Ānuçāsanik.): XIII, **91**γ, 4361 (enumeration).

Saptamahābhāga = Mahāpurusha (Mahāpurushastava).

Saptapāla, a muni. § 264 (Sabhākriyāp.): II, **4***a*, 109 (only B., C. has *Satyapālaḥ*).

Saptarāva, a Suparṇa, son of Garuḍa. § 564 (Mātalīyop.): V, **101**β, 3596 (so B., C. has *Saptavārāḥ*).

Saptārcis = Agni, q.v. (add. XVII, 36).

Saptarshi, pl. (°*ayaḥ*) ("the seven ṛshis," also name of a constellation (Ursa major), sometimes confounded with the seven mindborn sons of Brahmán). [§ 191 (Arjuna): I, **123***a*, 4807 (*sapta . . . maharshayaḥ*, i.e. Bharadvāja, Kaçyapa, Gautama, Viçvāmitra, Jamadagni, Vasishṭha, and Atri)].—§ 259*b* (Arundhatī): I, **233**, 8457 (°*madhyagaṃ*, i.e. Vasishṭha).—§ 266 (Çakrasabhāv.): II, **7**, 309 (in the palace of Indra).—§ 296 (Dyūtap.): II, **53**, 1919 (*Mahendram iva Devendraṃ divi S°ayo yathā*, sc. *abhijagmuḥ*).—§ 323 (Dvaitavanapr.): III, **25**, †958 (*divi prabhānti*).—§ 412 (Ashṭāvakrīya): III, **134**, †10664 (*sapta*).—[§ 439 (Yakshayuddhap.): III, **163**, 11855 (*sapta devarshayaḥ . . . Vasishṭhapramukhāḥ*)].—§ 457 (Vaivasvatop.): III, **187**, 12776 (ascend the ship together with Manu Vaivasvata), 12791.—§496 (Skandotpatti): III, **224**, 14297 (°*patnīnāṃ*); **225**, 14303 (°*īṇāṃ priyāḥ striyaḥ*), 14312 (*saptānāṃ*) (Agni fell in love with the wives of the *S.*, Svāhā assumed the form of the six of the wives and cohabited with Agni).—§ 497 (do.): III, **226**, 14343 (*patnibhiḥ S°īṇāṃ*), 14346 (dismissed their wives), 14347, 14348.—§ 502 (Manushyagrahak.): III, **230**, 14454 (°*patnyaḥ shaṭ*, the six dismissed wives (i.e. the seven with exception of Arundhatī) became the Kṛttikāḥ).—§ 543 (Rāmābhisheka): III, **291***a*, 16548.—§ 555 (Indravijaya): V, **15**, 466.—§ 561*d* (Nara-Nārāyaṇau): V, **49**, 1919.—§ 565 (Gālavacarita): V, **106**, 3722 (°*īṇām anyatamaṃ vesham* [sc. Vasishṭha's] *āsthāya*, sc. Dharma).—§ 574 (Jambūkh.): VI, **3**, 94 (°*īṇāṃ . . . prabhā*, omens); **6**, 215 (repair to Meru on every *parvan*).—§ 595 (Shoḍaçarāj., v. Pṛthu Vainya): VII, **69**, 2403, 2416 (milked *bráhman*, i.e. the Vedas from the earth, Bṛhaspati was their calf).—§ 606 (Tripurākhyāna): VIII, **34**, 1477 (°*maṇḍalaṃ*, became the parishkara of Çiva's chariot).—§ 615*z* (Arundhatī): IX, **48**, 2795, 2811 (°*saṃsadi*), 2814.—§ 641 (Rājadh.): XII, **100**, 3700 (°*īn pṛshṭataḥ kṛtvā*); **127**, 4685 (°*aya iva Dhruvaṃ*, sc. *upāviçan*).—§ 665 (Mokshadh.): XII, **208**ϵ, 7594 (?in the east?).—[§ 677 (do.): XII, **245**β, 8899 (*sapta ṛshayaḥ*)].—§ 702 (do.): XII, **295**, 10809 (installed Vāsava as king of the gods), 10810 (ruled over mankind, and were succeeded by Vipṛthu, etc.).—§ 704 (do.): XII, **302**γ, 11126.—[§ 717*b* (Nārāyaṇīya): XII, **336**, 12722 (*ṛshayaḥ . . . sapta Citraçikhaṇḍinaḥ*, i.e. the [mindborn] sons of Brahmán: Marīci, Atri, Aṅgiras, Pulaha, Kratu, Pulastya, Vasishṭha; probably referring to their position as the seven ṛshis of the first Manvantara (cf. Harivaṃça v. 413)?); **340**θ, 12917 (*sapta ṛshīn*)].—§ 730 (Ānuçāsanik.): XIII, **16**, 1089 (identified with Çiva); [**18**$\lambda\lambda$, †1370 (*munayaç ca sapta*)].—§ 750*b* (Bisastainyop.): XIII, **93**, 4415 (*Vṛshādarbheç ca saṃvādaṃ S°īṇāṃ ca*; their names are: Kaçyapa, Atri, Vasishṭha, Bharadvāja, Gautama, Viçvāmitra, and Jamadagni), [4455 (*ṛshīṇām . . . saptānāṃ*)].—§ 759 (Ānuçāsanik.): XIII, **107**ϵ, 5222 (°*īṇāṃ . . . loke*).—§ 761 (do.): XIII, **115***a*, 5604.—[§ 766 (do.): XIII, **126**, 6046 (*sapta . . . ṛshayo . . . Vasishṭhapramukhāḥ*)].—§ 770 (Ānuçāsanik.): XIII, **151**, 7156.—[§ 773*b* (Kṛshṇa Vāsudeva): XIII, **159**β, 7387 (*ṛshayaç caiva sapta*)].—§ 782*b* (Brāhmaṇagītā): XIV, **26**, †748 (*divi prabhānti*); **27**, 781 (? *sapta saptarshayaḥ siddhā Vasishṭhapramukhaiḥ saha*; read °*pramukhās tathā*?).—§ 785 (Anugītāp.): XIV, **77**, 2237, 2244; **88**, 2633 (*Mahendrānugatā devā yathā S°bhir divi*). Cf. Maharshi, pl., Ṛshi, pl.

Saptarshi[2], sg. ("one of the seven ṛshis"). § 730 (Ānuçāsanik.): XIII, **18**$\kappa\kappa$, 1339 (in the manvantara of Manu Sāvarṇa, Kṛshṇa [i.e. Vyāsa] will become one of the *S.*).

Saptarshikuṇḍa, pl. (°*āni*), a tīrtha. § 364 (Tīrthayātrāp.): III, **83**, 6042.

Saptasapti = Sūrya (the Sun): III, 193; VIII, 473.

Saptasārasvata, a tīrtha on the Sarasvatī. § 365 (Maṅkaṇaka): III, **85**, 6085 (there Maṅkaṇaka won ascetic success), 7003.—§ 615 (Baladevatīrthayātrā): IX, **37**, 2184 (*tīrthaṃ*, visited by Balarāma); **38**, 2186 (*tīrthaṃ*).—§ 615*i* (do.): The seven *Sarasvatīs* cover this universe. Whithersoever the *Sarasvatī* was summoned, thither she made her appearance. Her seven forms are *Suprabhā*, etc. (*a*). I) *Pitāmaha* [i.e. Brahmán] was once performing a sacrifice at *Pushkara*; whatever he thought of, immediately appeared, the *Gandharvas* sung, the *Apsarases* danced. The *ṛshis* missed *Sarasvatī*, *Brahmán* thought of her and she appeared there at *Pushkara* under the name of *Suprabhā*. II) At *Naimisha* many *munis* were assembled, performing sacrifices and talking about the *Vedas*, they thought of *Sarasvatī*, who made her appearance and came to be called *Kāñcanākshī*. III) Similarly she came to the sacrifice of *Gaya* in the country of the *Gayas* (*Gayeshu*), where she flowed from the slopes of

Himavat and was called *Viçālā*. IV) At the sacrifice of *Auddālaki* in the northern part of *Kosalā* (*uttare Koçalābhāge*), having been previously thought of by *Uddālaka* when sacrificing, she was mentally called *Manoramā* by the *ṛshis*. V) At *Kuru's* sacrifice at *Kurukshetra*, she was summoned by *Vasishṭha*, and named *Oghavatī*. VI) At *Daksha's* sacrifice at *Gaṅgādvāra* she appeared under the name of *Sureṇu* (see the note of PCR. pag. 154). VII) At *Brahmán's* sacrifice on the *Himavat*, as *Vimalodā*. All these seven forms then came and mingled together in the tīrtha, which from this is known by the name of *Saptasārasvata*. "Thus I have told thee of the seven Sarasvatīs by their names and of the tīrtha *S.*; listen now to a great feat of *Maṅkaṇaka*": IX, **38,** 2216, 2217.—§ 615*j* (Maṅkaṇaka): IX, **38,** 2243 (there Maṅkaṇaka dwelt, from his seed which fell in the Sarasvatī seven ṛshis were born; the ascetic success of Maṅkaṇaka, cf. § 365).

Saptatantu = Kṛshṇa: XII, 1631.

Saptavāhana = Vishṇu (1000 names).

Saptavāra, v. Saptarāva.

Sāragrīva = Çiva (1000 names [2]).

Saraka, a tīrtha. § 364 (Tīrthayātrāp.): III, **83,** 6045, 6046, 6051. Cf. III, 10518.

Saramā, the bitch of the gods. § 12 (Paushyap.): I, **3,** ††668, ††671 (*devaçunyā*, cursed Janamejaya and his brothers). —§ 270 (Brahmasabhāv.): II, **11,** 457 (in the palace of Brahmán).—§ 502 (Manushyagrahak.): III, **230,** 14487 (*mātā çunām*, a demon).

Sārameya, mostly pl. (°*āḥ*) ("sons of Saramā," i.e. dogs): I, ††662 (sg.); XI, 109 (*upagacchanti s°ā ivāmisham*); XII, 4223 (*varjyam s°āmisham yathā*), 4489 (*vilumpanti s°ā yathāmisham*).

Sarāṃsi (pl.) = Çiva (1000 names [1]).

Sāraṇa, a Vṛshṇi, son of Vasudeva. § 252 (Subhadrāharaṇap.): I, **219,** 7915, 7922 (°*sya sahodarā*, i.e. Subhadrā). —§ 253 (Haraṇāharaṇap.): I, **221,** 7992 (came to the wedding of Arjuna and Subhadrā).—§ 264 (Sabhākriyāp.): II, **4***β*, 125 (waited upon Yudhishṭhira).—§ 287 (Rājasūyikap.): II, **34,** 1274 (*saha-S°ḥ*, came to the rājasūya).— § 320 (Saubhavadhop.): III, **18,** 736 (*Gada-S°au*).—§ 402 (Tīrthayātrāp.): III, **120,** †10277 (°-*Cārudeshṇau*).—§ 589 (Droṇābhishekap.): VII, **11***ξ*, 408 (*sa-S°āḥ*).—§ 599 (Jayadrathavadhap.): VII, **110***σ*, 4194. — § 785 (Anugītāp.): XIV, **66***θ*, 1939. — § 793 (Mausalap.): XVI, **1,** 15 (°*pramukhā vīrāḥ*, tried to deceive Viçvāmitra, etc., and were cursed by them).

Sāraṇa[2], a counsellor of Rāvaṇa. § 535 (Setubandhana): III, **283,** 16320 (*Rāvaṇāmatyau mantriṇau Çuka-S°au*).

Sāraṅga = Çiva (1000 names [2]).

Sāraṅgadhvaja = Pāṇḍya: VII, 1019 (only C., B. has *Sāgaradhvajaḥ*).

Sārasa, a Suparṇa, son of Garuḍa. § 564 (Mātalīyop.): V, **101***β*, 3596.

Sārasvata, a ṛshi, son of Dadhīca and Sarasvatī. § 368 (Tīrthayātrāp.): III, **83,** 7058 (*yatra*—i.e. in Dadhīca's tīrtha—*S°o yātaḥ* [read *jātaḥ* with PCR.] *so 'ṅgirās tapaso nidhiḥ*, cf. § 615*gg*).—§ 371 (Tuṅgaka): III, **85,** 8189 (*Aṅgirasaḥ sutaḥ*, when the Vedas had been lost, *S.* taught them to the ascetics, cf. § 615*gg*).—§ 615 (Baladevatīrthayātrā): IX, **51,** 2926 (°*sya munes tīrtham*), 2927 (*muniḥ*, during a drought of twelve years he taught the Vedas to the brahmans), 2928 (*muniḥ*).—§ 615*gg* (do.): In days of yore the *muni Dadhīca*, living as a *brahmacārin*, had by his austerities afflicted *Indra* with fear. As he could not be turned away even by diverse kinds of rewards, *Indra* despatched to him the *Apsaras Alambushā* on the banks of the *Sarasvatī*. At the sight of her his seed fell into the *Sarasvatī*, the river held it in her womb and brought forth a son whom she brought to the *ṛshis*, who granted her a boon, saying that the *Viçvadevas*, the *ṛshis*, the *Gandharvas*, and the *Apsarases* would henceforth derive great happiness when oblations of her water were presented to them, and praised her as having sprung from the lake of *Brahmán*, etc., and said that the child should be named *S.*, and during a drought of twelve years teach the *Vedas* to many brahmans, and that she should become the foremost of all sacred rivers. The river took the child with her. Meanwhile, on the occasion of a war between the gods and the *Dānavas*, *Indra* wandered through the three worlds in search of weapons, but failed to find such weapons as were fit to slay the enemies of the gods, until *Dadhīca* (*hh*), solicited by the gods, gave up his life (and obtained many regions of inexhaustible merit) and Indra from his bones caused many kinds of weapons (thunderbolts, discs, maces, clubs, and bludgeons) to be made. With the thunderbolt born of *Brāhma* energy and inspired with *mantras*, *Indra* made a loud noise when he hurled it and slew ninety-nine heroes among the *Daityas*. After a long time a twelve years' drought occurred, and the ṛshis fled away; only *S.* was retained by the *Sarasvatī*, who supplied him with food, giving him large fishes, and he offered oblations to the *ṛshis* and the gods. While wandering with famished stomachs, the ṛshis had lost the knowledge of the *Vedas* and solicited one another to lecture on the *Vedas*. Then they learnt them from *S.*, becoming his disciples, 60,000 in number, though he was but a boy: IX, **51,** 2945, 2946, 2947, 2962, 2967, 2968, 2970 (*muniçreshṭham*), 2976 (*viprarsheḥ*).

Sārasvata[2], a ṛshi, son of Atri. § 665 (Mokshadh.): XII, **208***θ*, 7597 (one of the ṛshis of the west, *Atreḥ putraḥ*).— § 770 (Ānuçāsanik.): XIII, **151***θ*, 7115 (*Atreḥ putraḥ*, one of seven *Varuṇasya ṛtvijaḥ* in the west).—§ 775 (do.): XIII, **166***ε*, 7669 (*Atreḥ putraḥ*, one of the ṛshis of the west).

Sārasvata[3] ("son of Sarasvatī [2]") = Apāntaratama(s): XII, 13675 (*A°*), 13695 (*A°*).

Sārasvata[4], adj. ("belonging to Sarasvatī [1-2]"). § 365 (Maṅkaṇaka): III, **83,** 7004 (*lokam*).—§ 370 (Tīrthayātrāp.): III, **84,** 8044 (*lokeshu*). — § 377 (Dhaumyatīrthak.): III, **90,** 8375 (*avabhṛtaiḥ*).—§ 409 (Plakshāvataraṇag.): III, **129,** 10526 (*yajñaiḥ*), 10534 (do.).—§ 561 (Yānasandhip.): V, **57,** 2254 (*gaṇāḥ*, follow Ulūka?).—§ 615 (Gadāyuddhap.): IX, **35,** 2006 (*tīrthānām*).—§ 615*j* (Maṅkaṇaka): IX, **38,** 2244 (*lokam*).—§ 615*p* (Vasishṭhāpavāha): IX, **42,** 2365 (*tīrthe*, i.e. Sthāṇutīrtha).

Sārasvata(m) parva ("the section treating of the Sarasvatī"). § 10 (Parvasaṅgr.): I, **2,** 347 (i.e. Baladevatīrthayātrā).

Sarasvatī[1], a sacred river. § 11 (Parvasaṅgr.): I, **2,** 557 (°*yās tīrthānām puṇyatā*, cf. Baladevatīrthayātrā). — § 156 (Pūruvaṃç.): I, **95,** ††3779 (wife of Matināra and mother of Taṃsu), 3780 (do.).—§ 166 (Citrāṅgadop.): I, **101,** 4074 (*nadyās tīre S°yāḥ*). — § 221*b* (Gaṅgā): I, **170,** 6455 (*plakshajātām*?).—§ 247 (Arjunavanavāsap.): I, **213,** 7745 (*paramaprītā nāgair iva S°ī*).—§ 268 (Varuṇasabhāv.): II, **9,** 371 (present in the palace of Varuṇa).—§ 285 (Nakula): II, **32,** 1192 (*Çūdrābhīragaṇāç caiva ye cāçritya S°īm*, in the west).—§ 312 (Āraṇyakap.): III, **5**, 241 (°-*Dṛçadvatyau*), 242 (°*tīre*).—§ 317*b* (Kṛshṇa Vāsudeva): III, **12**, 474 (Kṛshṇa performed a sacrifice on the *S.*).—§ 323 (Dvaitavanapr.): III, **25**, †945 (°*çālavaneshu*, the Pāṇḍavas dwelt [in Dvaitavana] on the *S.*).—§ 329 (Kāmyakavanapr.): III, **36**, 1451 (°*kūle*, there the Kāmyaka forest is situated).—§ 358 (Tīrthayātrāp.): III, **82**, 5002 (°*yāḥ sāgarasya ca saṅgame*). — § 360 (do.): III, **82**, 5053 (*Vinaçanaṃ . . . gacchaty antarhitā Merupṛshṭhe* (!) *S°ī* | *Camase ca Çivodbhede Nāgodbhede ca dṛçyate*), 5056 (with the tīrtha Çaçayāna), 5067 (*saṅgamaṃ . . . S°yāḥ*).—§ 361 (Kurukshetra): III, **83**, 5074 (*dakshiṇena S°yā Dṛshadvatyuttareṇa ca . . . Kurukshetre*), 5075.—§ 364 (Tīrthayātrāp.): III, **83**, 6022 (with the tīrtha [of] Arantuka (Taraṇḍaka)), 6078 (with the tīrtha Çrīkuñja), 6080 (with the tīrtha Naimishakuñja) —§ 367 (Pṛthūdaka): III, **83**, 7015–7016 (*puṇyam āhuḥ Kurukshetraṃ Kurukshetrāt S°ī* | *S°yāç ca tīrthāni tīrthebhyaç ca Pṛthūdakam*). — § 368 (Tīrthayātrāp.): III, **83**, 7021 (°*tyāruṇāyāç ca saṅgamaḥ*).—§ 369 (Kurukshetra): III, **83**, 7075 (*uttareṇa Dṛshadvatyā dakshiṇena S°īṃ*, sc. Kurukshetra).—§ 370 (Tīrthayātrāp.): III, **84**, 7085 (*Plakshā devī smṛtā*), 8016 (*Gaṅgāyāç ca . . . S°yāç ca saṅgame*), 8044, 8139 (the same ?, near Ṛshabhadvīpa). — § 377 (Dhaumyatīrthak.): III, **90**, 8374 (in the north), 8381 (there the Vālakhilyas performed sacrifices). — § 384 (Agastyop.): III, **100**, 8701 (the hermitage of Dadhīca was situated on the bank of the *S.*). — § 409 (Plakshāvataraṇag.): III, **129**, 10533.—§ 410 (do.): III, **130**, 10538, 10539, 10540 (disappears at Vinaçana from hatred of the Nishādas, but reappears at Camasodbheda). — § 434 (Saugandhikāharaṇa): III, **156**, 11437.—§ 449 (Ājagarap.): III, **177**, †12359, †12361 (°*tīra*°), †12362 (*d*: pleasing to *Yakshas, Gandharvas*, and *maharshis*).—§ 451 (Mārkaṇḍeyas.): III, **182**, 12552 (*puṇyatīrthām*), 12553.—§ 459 (do.): III, **188*a***, 12907 (seen by Mārkaṇḍeya in the stomach of Nārāyaṇa).—§ 494 (Āṅgirasa): III, **222**, 14229 (among the rivers who are mothers of fires).—§ 570 (Sainyaniryāṇap.): V, **157**, 5347 (*tīrthāni S°yāḥ*, Balarāma set out to visit the tīrthas of the *S.*, cf. § 615).—§ 574*f* (Bindusaras): VI, **6**η, 243 (among the seven streams into which the Gaṅgā divided herself), 245 (*dṛçyā cādṛçyā*).—§ 574 (Jambūkh.): VI, **9**λ, 321, 343 (the same ?).—§ 595 (Shoḍaçarāj., v. Bharata): VII, **68**, 2384 (Bharata performed sacrifices on the *S.*).—§ 606 (Tripurākhyāna): VIII, **34**, 1477.—§ 607 (Karṇap.): VIII, **44**η, 2029 (*bahishkṛtāḥ . . . S°yāḥ*, sc. the Bāhīkas).—§ 610 (Çalyap.): IX, **5**, 289 (*āruṇām*, read *aruṇāṃ* with B.).—§ 615 (Gadāyuddhap.): IX, **35**, 1981 (*tīrthayātrāṃ . . . S°yāḥ*), 1987, 1989 (°*īṃ pratisrotas*), 2005 (°*tīrthavareshu*, Baladeva's journey to the tīrthas of the *S.* with tales of the different tīrthas, their holiness and origins (ch. **35–54**)).—§ 615 (Prabhāsotpattik.): IX, **35**, 2048, 2050 (°*abdhisaṅgamaṃ*), 2051 (with the tīrtha Prabhāsa).—§ 615*b* (Udapāna): IX, **35**, 2063 (*nashṭāṃ*); **36**, 2088, 2111 (appeared at Udapāna).—§ 615 (Baladevatīrthayātrā): IX, **37**, 2119 (disappears at Vinaçana from contempt of the Çūdras and the Ābhīras), 2120.—§ 615*c* (Subhūmika): IX, **37**, 2121, 2126 (with the tīrtha Subhūmika).—§ 615*e* (Gargasrotas): IX, **37**, 2134 (with the tīrtha Gargasrotas).—§ 615*f* (Çaṅkhatīrtha): IX, **37**, 2139, 2143 (with the Çaṅkhatīrtha).—§ 615 (Baladevatīrthayātrā): IX, **37**, 2147, 2154 (*yatra bhūyaḥ S°ī prāṅmukhaṃ vai nivavṛte*).—§ 615*h* (Naimisha): IX, **37**, 2157, 2162, 2171, 2173, 2176 (for the sake of the ṛshis the *S.* turned her course and made many *kuñjas*, then she again flowed in a westerly direction).—§ 615 (Baladevatīrthayātrā): IX, **37**, 2179 (°*tīrthavaraṃ*, i.e. Saptasārasvata), 2180.—§ 615*i* (Saptasārasvata): IX, **38**, 2188, 2189 (?), 2197, 2198, 2199, 2200, 2202, 2204, 2209, 2212, 2213 (invoked at sacrifices the *S.* appeared at seven different places under various names).—§ 615*j* (Maṅkaṇaka): IX, **38**, 2219 (Maṅkaṇaka's seed fell into the *S.*, from that seed was born seven ṛshis).—§ 615*k* (Mahodara): IX, **39**, 2262 (°*yās tīrthavaraṃ . . . Auçanasaṃ*).—§ 615*l* (Rushaṅgu): IX, **39**, 2276, 2279 (°-*uttare tīre . . . Pṛthūdake*).—§ 615*n* (Viçvāmitra): IX, **40**, 2307 (*tīrthavare S°yāḥ*).—§ 615*o* (Baka): IX, **41**, 2329 (°*yās tīrthe*), 2339.—§ 615 (Baladevatīrthayātrā): IX, **41**, 2350 (at the sacrifice of Yayāti the *S.* produced milk and clarified butter [in the Yāyāta tīrtha]). —§ 615*p* (Vasishṭhāpavāha): IX, **42**, 2363, 2368, 2372, 2384, 2386, 2387 (*q*: Vasishṭha's praise of the *S.*: "From the *Mānasa* lake (*Pitāmahasya sarasaḥ*) thou hast taken thy rise; the whole universe is filled with thy waters. Going through the firmament thou impartest thy waters to the clouds. Through thee we read the Vedas (*adhīmahi*). Thou art *Pushṭi* (growth), *Dyuti* (splendour), *Kīrtti* (fame), *Siddhi* (success), *Buddhi* (intellect), *Umā*, *Vāṇī* (speech), and *Svāhā*. This whole universe is dependent upon thee. It is thou who dwellest in all creatures in four forms"), 2390, 2392, 2396, 2398; **43**, 2403, 2406, 2407, 2412, 2414, 2415, 2416 (according to the curse of Viçvāmitra, the waters of the *S.* became mixed with blood, but she was delivered from the curse by some munis and then formed the river Aruṇā).—§ 615*t* (Aruṇā): IX, **43**, 2441 (°*yāruṇāyāç ca . . . saṅgamaḥ*), 2443.—§ 615 (Baladevatīrthayātrā): IX, **44**, 2450. — § 615*u* (Skanda): IX, **44**, 2501 (*Haimavatīṃ devīṃ*), 2502; **45**, 2522; **46**, 2719 (°*yās tīrthavaryasya*).—§ 615*ee* (Ādityatīrtha): IX, **49**, 2850 (*tīrthe S°yāḥ*, sc. Ādityatīrtha).—§ 615*gg* (Sārasvata): IX, **51**, 2932, 2933, 2941, 2948, 2963 (from Dadhīca *S.* became the mother of Sārasvata[1]).—§ 615 (Baladevatīrthayātrā): IX, **54**, 3045 (*prabhāvaṃ* (!) *ca S°yāḥ Plakshaprasravaṇaṃ*), †3073, †3074, 3075.—§ 615 (Gadāyuddhap.): IX, **55**, 3094 (*dakshiṇena S°yāḥ*, there Bhīmasena and Duryodhana fought with each other).—§ 632*b* (Shoḍaçarāj. v. Bharata, cf. § 595): XII, **29**, 939. — § 652*b* (Indrota-Pārīkshitīya): XII, **152*a***, 5645 (= III, 7015*b*–7016*a*, but with °*īṃ* instead of °*ī*), 5647 (°-*Dṛshadvatyoḥ saṅgamaḥ*).—§ 702 (Mokshadh.): XII, **298**ε, 10937.—§ 717*b* (Nārāyaṇīya): XII, **348**δδ, 13500 (Gaṅgā and *S.* became the hips of Nārāyaṇa). — § 730 (Ānuçāsanik.): XIII, **18**κκ, 1334 (°*yās taṭe*, there Çiva was gratified with Garga, cf. Gargasrotas).—§ 755*b* (Nahushop.): XIII, **100**, 4786 (°*kūlāt*).—§ 757*m* (Goloka): XIII, **102**, 4889 (°-*Dṛçadvatyau*). — § 768*b* (Umā-Maheçvarasaṃv.): XIII, **146*a***, 6763 (*nadīnām uttamā*).—§ 772*j* (Utathya): XIII, **155**, 7258 (at the injunction of Utathya the *S.* became invisible (*adṛçyā*) and went into the desert).—§ 776 (Ānuçāsanik.): XIII, **166*a***, 7645, 7654 (the same ?).—§ 793 (Mausalap.): XVI, **7**, 247 (the son of Sātyaki was established on the *S.*).—§ 795 (Svargārohaṇap.): XVIII, **5**, 172 (the 16,000 wives of Kṛshṇa plunged into the *S.*). Cf. Plakshā, plakshajātā, Plakshavatī (?).

Sarasvatī[2], the goddess of Speech. § 1 (Anukram.): I, **1** (introductory çloka). — § 11 (Parvasaṅgr.): I, **2**, 467 (*saṃvādaḥ S°yās Tārkshyarsheḥ*, i.e. Sarasvatī-Tārkshyasaṃvāda).—§ 262 (Sabhākriyāp.): II, **1** (introductory çloka). —§ 266 (Çakrasabhāv.): II, **7**, 300 (in the palace of Indra).

—§ 308 (Āraṇyakap.): III, **1** (introductory çloka).—§ 330 (Indradarçana): III, **37**, 1488 (mentioned in a blessing on Arjuna).—§ 400 (Tīrthayātrāp.): III, **118**, †10226 (°*yāḥ*, sc. *āyatanam*).—§ 412 (Ashṭāvakrīya): III, **132**, 10598 (Çvetaketu saw *S.* in a human form).—§ 456 (Sarasvatī-Tārkshyasaṃv.): III, **186**, †12715 (°*yā gītaṃ*), †12718, (†12719), (†12732), (†12736), (†12738), (†12741) (discourse between *S.* and Tārkshya).—§ 549 (Pāṇḍavapraveçap.): IV, **1** (introductory çloka).—§ 554 (Sainyodyogap.): V, **1** (do.).—§ 565 (Gālavacarita): V, **117**, 3973 (*reme* . . . *S°yāṃ yathā Manuḥ*).—§ 574 (Jambūkh.): VI, **1**, 1 (introductory çloka).—§ 576 (Bhagavadgītāp.): VI, **23**, 804 (identified with Durgā).—§ 581 (Bhīshmavadhap.): VI, **65**ξ, 2958 (*devī jihvā S°ī*, sc. Kṛshṇa's), **67**, 3019.—§ 589 (Droṇābhishekap.): VII, **1**, 1 (introductory çloka).—§ 603 (Nārāyaṇāstramokshap.): VII, **201**, 9438 (°*yā vāsaṃ Vyāsaṃ*).—§ 604 (Karṇap.): VIII, **1** (introductory çloka).—§ 606 (Tripurākhyāna): VIII, **34**, 1487 (became the *parirathyā* of Çiva's chariot).—§ 609 (Çalyap.): IX, **1** (introductory çloka).—§ 615*u* (Skanda): IX, **45**γ, 2515.—§ 616 (Sauptikap.): X, **1** (introductory çloka).—§ 618 (Jalapradānikap.): XI, **1** (do.).—§ 621 (Rājadh.): XII, **1** (do.)—§ 641 (Rājadh.): XII, **120**ρ, †4397; **121**σ, 4432 (= Lakshmī), 4493 (from Vishṇu in the form of chastisement *S.* created the *daṇḍanīti*).—§ 662*b* (Jāpakop.): XII, **199**, 7268; **200**, 7340.—§ 667 (Mokshadh.): XII, **240**, 8741 (*jihvāyāṃ vāk S°ī*).—§ 707 (do.): XII, **319**, 11729 (*vāg bhūtā*), 11730, 11736, 11737 (*devī*), 11738, 11745 (*devīṃ*), 11756 (do.).—§ 717*c* (Uparicara): XII, **336**, 12730 (*devī*).—§ 717*b* (Nārāyaṇīya): XII, **340**θ, 12920 (*Vedānāṃ mātaraṃ* . . . *devīṃ*), **343**φ, 13234 (*Ṛtā Brahmasutā devī*); **350**, 13675 (from the speech (*S.*) of Nārāyaṇa arose Apāntaratamas).—§ 719 (Ānuçāsanik.): XIII, **1** (introductory çloka).—§ 737 (do.): XIII, **31***a*, 2014.—§ 746 (do.): XIII, **69**, 3433, 3434 (*Brāhmīṃ*).—§ 778 (Açvamedhikap.): XIV, **1** (introductory çloka).—§ 782*b* (Brāhmaṇagītā): XIV, **21**, 642 (*vāg*), 645, 652.—§ 787 (Āçramavāsap.): XV, **1** (introductory çloka).—§ 793 (Mausalap.): XVI, **1** (do.).—§ 794 (Mahāprasthānikap.): XVII, **1** (do.).—§ 795 (Svargārohanap.): XVIII, **1** (do.).—§ 795*c* (Mahābhārata): XVIII, **6**o, 232 (= the introductory çloka of books I–XVIII), 299. Cf. Vāc, Vāṇī.—Do.[3] = Çiva (1000 names[1]).—Do.[4], appellative ("speech, voice"): III, |10028, XII, 2197 (*navanītaṃ s°yaḥ*), 2764, 6811 (*vāṇī*), 6944 (*Brāhmī*), 12999; XIII, 4045 (*bahuvidhāṃ*), 5207.

Sarasvatī, pl. (rivers named *S.*).—§ 615*i* (Saptasārasvata): IX, **38**, 2188 (*sapta*), 2216 (do.).—§ 680*b* (Tulādhāra-Jājalisaṃv.): XII, **264**, 9439 (*sarvā nadyaḥ S°yaḥ*).—§ 746 (Ānuçāsanik.): XIII, **76**, †3676 (*nadyaḥ iva*, Nīl.).

[Sarasvatī-Tārkshya-saṃvāda(ḥ)] ("conversation between Sarasvatī and Tārkshya"). § 456 (Mārk.): *Mārkaṇḍeya* related how *Sarasvatī* instructed *Tārkshya* about the celestial regions, and especially about the efficiency of different presents to *brahmans*. Then she spoke of the *agnihotra*; she said she had come from the *agnihotra* to clear away the doubts of the *brahmarshis*, and that she was nourished by sacrifice. *Tārkshya* asked her about the salvation (*moksha*) taught by *Sāṅkhya* and *Yoga*; she again mentioned the *Vedic* sacrifice; [this (v. 12732–12745) is wanting in PCR.] (III, **186**).

Sārasvatya, adj. ("belonging to Sarasvatī"). § 641*f* (Pṛthu Vainya): XII, **59**, 2232 (°*o gaṇaḥ*, among the mantrins of Pṛthu Vainya).

Sārathi = Mahāpurusha (Mahāpurushastava).

Sarayū, a river (the present Sarju). § 221*b* (Gaṅgā): I, **170**, 6455 (C. has *Ç°*).—§ 268 (Varuṇasabhāv.): II, **9**, 374 (present in the palace of Varuṇa).—§ 276 (Jarāsandhavadhap.): II, **20**, 795 (crossed by Kṛshṇa, etc., on their way from Indraprastha to Girivraja).—§ 370 (Tīrthayātrāp.): III, **84**, 8048 (with the tīrtha Gopratāra).—§ 490 (Āṅgirasa): III, **219**, 14140 (wife of the five Kumbharetas, C. *Ç°*).—§ 494 (do.): III, **222**, 14230 (among the rivers who are mothers of fires, *Ç°*).—§ 574 (Jambūkh.): VI, **9**λ, 326.—§ 591 (Saṃçaptakavadhap.): VII, **17**, 721 (*Gaṅgā-S°rau vegena pravṛshīvolvaṇodake*).—§ 640 (Rājadh.): XII, **57**, 2055 (Asamañjas drowned children in the *S.*).—§ 758 (Ānuçāsanik.): XIII, **103**β, 4944.—§ 772*b* (Vasishṭha): XIII, **156**, 7288 (origin of the *S.*).—§ 775 (Ānuçāsanik.): XIII, **166***a*, 7647.

Sarga[1] = Çiva (1000 names[2]).—Do.[2] = Vishṇu (1000 names).

Sariddvīpa, v. Paridvīpa.

Saridvarāsuta ("son of the best of rivers (Gaṅgā)") = Bhīshma: XII, 6263.

Sārika, a muni. § 264 (Sabhākriyāp.): II, **4***a*, 108 (waited upon Yudhishṭhira).

Sārisṛkka (B.) or **Sārisṛkva** (C.), a çārṅgaka, son of Mandapāla. § 259 (Çārṅgakop.): I, **230**, 8372; **232**, (8406), (8412); **233**, 8434.

Saritaḥ (pl.)[1] ("rivers," personif.): IX, 2513 (*mūrtimatyaḥ*), 2556; XII, 4197 foll., 12175, 12606.—Do.[2] = Çiva (1000 names[1]).

Saritpati ("lord of rivers") = Samudra (the Ocean): I, 1220.

Sarpa, one of the Rudras. § 108 (Aṃçāvat.): I, **66**, 2566 (son of Sthāṇu).—§ 191 (Arjuna): I, **123**, 4825.

***Sarpa**, mostly pl. (°*āḥ*) ("serpents"): I, 369, 797 (*Airāvatarājānaḥ*), 800, 957 (sg.), 959, 998 (sg.), 1012, 1014, 1020, 1063, 1198, 1202, 1204, 1286, 1306, 1315, 1316, 1317, 1319, 1320, 1349, 1536, 1539, 1540, 1541, 1542, †1543, 1596, 1622, 1675 (sg.), 1699 (sg.), 1742 (sg.), 1962 (sg.), 1963 (sg.), 1967 (sg.), 1973 (sg.), 1981 (sg.), 2034, 2035, 2142, 2188, 2190 (sg.), 2191 (sg.), 2194, 2243, 3381 (sg.), 5019; II, 363, 1958 (sg.); III, 544, 545, 1016, 1049 (sg.), †10267, 12384, 12924, 13584, 14660 (sg.), †14753 (sg. *iva*), 15913; IV, 42, 1355, 1509 (°*tāṃ*), 1767, 1807 (sg. *iva*); V, 536, †953 (sg. *iva*), 1023 (sg.), 1390, 1392 (sg.) †1776 (*iva*), 2701 (sg.), 4273, 4617 (sg. *iva*), 7156, 7274; VI, 246 (on the mountain Nishadha), 814, 1202 (°*āṇāṃ asmi Vāsukiḥ*, says Kṛshṇa), 1126 (*iva*), 4602 (°*yiçur yathā*), 5473; VII, 3627 (*iva*), 5032 (*kṛshṇa-* °*o yathā*), 5052 (*iva*), 5129 (*kṛshṇa-* °*a iva*), 5784 (sg.), 8972, 9172 (sg. *yathā*), 9191 (°*vat*), 9442; VIII, 899 (sg. *iva*), 1801 (*kṛshṇa-* °*ṃ*), 3411 (sg. *iva*), 4036 (sg. *yathā*), †4295 (sg. *iva*), 4415, 4416, †4687 (sg. *iva*), †4708; IX, 2511; X, 33 (sg. *iva*), 220 (*mahā°*), 280, 281 (*mahā°*); XI, 544 (sg. *iva*); XII, 665 (sg.), 2049 (sg.), 4224 (sg. *iva*), 6707 (sg.), 6749, 9456 (sg. *iva*), 11187 (sg. *iva*); XIII, 734; XIV, 754, 756; XV, 951.—Do. sg. said of Karkoṭaka: I, 4828 (*K°*).—Do., said of Nahusha: III, 12396, 12397 (*mahā°*), 12406 (°*rūpaṃ*), 12419 (°*yoniṃ*), 12420 (*mahā°*), 12450, (12455), (12460), 12467, (12469), 12471, (12472), 12476, 12478, 12479, (12480), 12481 (*mahā°*), 12487 (do.), (12488), (12490), 12491, (12492), 12496, (12497), 12504, (12506), (12513), (12518), 12525 (?); V, 543; XII, ††13216; XIII, 4796.—Do. said of Sumukha: V, 3704. Cf. Nāga, Pannaga.

Sarpaçīranivāsana = Çiva (1000 names[2]).
Sarpadevī, name of a tīrtha. § 362 (Tīrthayātrāp.): III, **83**, 5084 (*nāgānāṃ tīrtham uttamaṃ*).
Sarpamālin, a muni. § 264 (Sabhākriyāp.): II, **4a**, 105 (so C., B. has *Sarpim°*).
Sarpamātṛ ("the mother of the serpents") = Kadrū: I, 1283.
[Sarpanāmakathana] ("enumeration of the names of the snakes"). § 47 (Āstīkap.): Questioned by Çaunaka, Sauti enumerated the names of the principal snakes: Çesha, etc. (I, **35**).
Sarpānta, a Suparṇa, son of Garuḍa. § 564 (Mātalīyop.): V, **101**β, 3597.
Sarparāja ("king of the serpents") = Nahusha: III, 12469.—Do.[2] = Vāsuki: I, 1637 (*V°*); IV, 41.
Sarparājan (do.) = Vāsuki: I, 5022.
Sarpasattra ("snake sacrifice"): I, 9, 366, 845, 1013, 1020, 1022, 1031, 1062, 1196, 1603, 1605, 1915, 2015, 2020, 2027, 2032, 2041, 2042, 2043, 2051, 2056, 2142, 2177, 2189, 2193, 2200, 2208; XVIII, 182.
Sarpasattra(m) ("the snake-sacrifice"). — § 58*b* (cf. Āstīkap. and Janam.). Compelled by the *mantras* innumerable snakes fell into the fire (I, **52**).—§ 59: *Caṇḍabhārgava* (of the race of *Cyavana*) was the *hotṛ* at the snake sacrifice, the old *Kautsa* (*Jaimini*) the udgātṛ, *Çārṅgarava* (C. *Sāṅgarava*) the brahman, and *Piṅgala* the adhvaryu. *Vyāsa*, etc. (**a**), were the *Sadasyas*.—§ 60: *Takshaka* repaired to *Indra*, who comforted him saying: "*Brahmán* was pacified by me for thy sake." *Vāsuki* summoned his sister (I, **53**), who told the matter to *Āstīka*; *Āstīka* comforted *Vāsuki* and went to the Snake-Sacrifice, but was not at first admitted by the door-keepers, wherefore he gratified them; then he began to adore the king, etc. (I, **54**).—§ 61: Comparing his sacrifice to *Soma's*, *Varuṇa's*, and *Prajāpati's* in *Prayāga* of old, and to *Indra's*, etc. (**a**), he praised *Janamejaya's* protection of his subjects, and his abstinence, and said that he was either *Varuṇa* or *Yama*, and compared him with *Indra*, *Khaṭvāṅga* (a king, BR.; = Çiva?), etc. (β) (I, **55**).—§ 62: *Janamejaya* was inclined to confer a boon on *Āstīka*; but the *hotṛ* declared that *Takshaka* was not yet burnt, and the *ṛtvij'es* declared from the *çāstras*, and the *Sūta Lohitāksha* (v. § 58) confirmed it from the *Purāṇas*, that *Takshaka* was now hiding in the dwelling of *Indra*. As the *hotṛ* with *mantras* began to pour clarified butter into the fire, *Indra* appeared in his *vimāna* with the gods, *Vidyādharas* and *Apsarases*, and *Takshaka* hid himself in the upper garment of *Indra*. *Janamejaya* ordered to throw *Indra* himself into the fire together with *Takshaka*. Shaking off *Takshaka*, *Indra* quickly returned to his own abode. *Takshaka* was now falling from heaven, and *Janamejaya* promised to grant to *Āstīka* what he might desire. *Āstīka* said: "Let no more snakes fall into the fire," and refused to ask for any other boon (I, **56**). —§ 63: Enumeration of the principal snakes of *Vāsuki's* race that fell into the fire; (§ 64) of *Takshaka's* race; (§ 65) of *Airāvata's* race; (§ 66) of *Kauravya's* race; (§ 67) of *Dhṛtarāshṭra's* race (I, **57**).—§ 68: *Janamejaya* let the sacrifice come to an end; he bestowed wealth unto *Lohitāksha*, etc.
Sarpī ("female serpent"), sg.: I, 677.
Sarpimālin, v. Sarpamālin.
Sarva[1] = Çiva, q.v.—Do.[2] = Kṛshṇa (Vishṇu): VI, †1286; XII, 1616; XIII, 6953 (Vishṇu's 1000 names).
Sarvā, a river. § 574 (Jambūkh.): VI, **9**λ, 344 (only B., C. has *Sarvagaṅgāṃ*).

Sarvabandhavimocana = Çiva (1000 names[2]).
Sarvabhaksha (C. *°kshya*) = Çiva (1000 names[1]).
Sarvabhauma, a prince. § 156 (Pūruvaṃç.): I, **95**, ††3768 (son of Ahaṃyāti and Bhānumatī), ††3769 (husband of Sunandā and father of Jayatsena).
Sarvabhāvakara = Çiva (1000 names[2]).
Sarvabhāvana[1] = Kṛshṇa: XII, 1616. — Do.[2] = Çiva (1000 names[2]).
Sarvabhūtabhavodbhava = Vishṇu (1000 names).
Sarvabhūtāçraya = Çiva: X, 309.
Sarvabhūtādi = Kṛshṇa: XII, 7640.
Sarvabhūtaguru = Çiva: XIII, 790.
Sarvabhūtahara = Çiva (1000 names[2]).
Sarvabhūtakara = Çiva (1000 names[1]).
Sarvabhūtamaheçvara = Çiva: III, 1629; V, 3558 (*Bhūtapatiḥ*).
Sarvabhutānām antarātman = Vishṇu: XII, 13488.
Sarvabhūtāntarātman = Çiva: XII, 10 63 (1000 names[1]), 10457.
Sarvabhūtapati = Çiva: XII, 10457.
Sarvabhūtapitāmaha[1] = Brahmán, q.v.—Do.[2] = Kṛshṇa (Vishṇu): I, 2432, XII, 10019.
Sarvabhūtātman ("the soul of all beings"): I, 8295 (= Kṛshṇa); III, 13963 (*purushaḥ sa sanātanaḥ*, sc. *prāṇa*); X, 681 (= Nārada); XII, 1670 (*°bhūtāya*, sc. Kṛshṇa), 6780 (*°bhūtakṛt* = Brahmán), 6785 (*°bhūtasthaḥ* = Vishṇu), 6869 (= III, 13963), 7112 (*°bhūḥ*), 7552 (= Kṛshṇa), 7677 (*°bhūtasthaṃ*), 7766 (*°bhūtāḥ*), 7835 (*°bhūtasthaṃ*), 8756 (*°bhūtasya*), 9018 (do.), 9372 (do.), 9657 (do.), 9668 (*°bhūtaḥ*), 12897 (do. = Vāsudeva), 13318 (*°bhāvanaḥ* = Nārāyaṇa); XIII, 1149 (= Çiva, 1000 names), 2031 (*°yonīn*), 5570 (*°bhūtasya*), 5660 (*°bhūtasthaiḥ*), 6533 (*°bhūtaḥ*), †7390 (*°yoniḥ* = Kṛshṇa).
Sarvabhūteça[1] = Brahmán, q.v. (add III, 12818).—Do.[2] = Çiva: VII, 3465; XIII, 6378, 6409, 6525, 6624.—Do.[3] = Dharma: IV, 14.—Do.[4] = Kṛshṇa: XII, 7655.
Sarvabhūteçvara[1] = Dhātṛ: V, 3677.—Do.[2] = Kṛshṇa (Vishṇu): XII, 2394 (*Nārāyaṇaṃ*), 7526, 7636.
Sarvacārin = Çiva (1000 names[2]).
Sarvacchandaka = Mahāpurusha (Mahāpurushastava).
Sarvaçastrabhṛtāṃ vara(ḥ) = Vishṇu (1000 names).
Sarvāçaya = Çiva (1000 names[2]).
Sarvaçilpapravartaka = Çiva (1000 names[1]).
Sarvāçraya, Sarvaçubhaṅkara = Çiva (1000 names[2]).
Sarvada = Çiva (1000 names[1-2]).
Sarvadāçārhabhartṛ = Kṛshṇa: VI, †2591.
Sarvadamana = Bharata: I, 2995.
Sarvadānavasūdana = Indra: X, 156
Sarvadaṇḍadhara = Çiva: XIV, 196.
Sarvadarçana = Vishṇu (1000 names).
Sarvadarçin = Mahāpurusha (Mahāpurushastava). — Do.[2] = Vishṇu (1000 names).
Sarvadeva = Çiva: XII, 4502 (*Çūlapāṇiḥ*); XIII, 1262 (1000 names[2]).
Sarvadevamaya = Çiva (1000 names[2]).
Sarvadevānāṃ tīrtha(m), name of a tīrtha. § 364 (Tīrthayātrāp.): III, **83**, 6058.
Sarvadevānāṃ tīrthāni (pl.), name of certain tīrthas. § 368 (Tīrthayātrāp.): III, **83**, 7044.
Sarvadeveça[1] = Indra: I, 1285.—Do.[2] = Çiva: III, 1624, 1936; VII, 9452 (*Īçvaraṃ*, only C.). — Do.[3] = Vishṇu: V, 296.
Sarvadeveçvara = Çiva: XII, 10253.
Sarvadhārin = Çiva (1000 names[2]).

Sarvadharmajña = Vishṇu (1000 names).
Sarvadhātunishecitṛ = Sūrya (the Sun): III, 154.
Sarvādi, Sarvadṛç = Vishṇu (1000 names).
Sarvaga[1], § 159 (Pūruvaṃç.): I, **95**, ††3829 (son of Bhīmasena Pāṇḍava and Balandharā).
Sarvaga[2] = (1000 names[2]).—Do.[3] = Vishṇu (1000 names).
Sarvagandhasukhāvaha = Çiva (1000 names[2]).
Sarvagati = Mahāpurusha (Mahāpurushastava).
Sarvaghna = Çiva (1000 names[1]).
Sarvahrada, a tīrtha. § 370 (Tuṅgaka): III, **85,** 8182.
Sarvajña[1] = Kṛshṇa (Vishṇu): XII, 1616; XIII, 6997, 7036 (1000 names).—Do.[2] = Çiva (1000 names[2]).
Sarvakāçīça ("lord of all Kāçis") = Yayāti: V, 3918.
Sarvakālaprasāda, Sarvakāma = Çiva (1000 names[2]).
Sarvakāmada[1] = Kṛshṇa (Vishṇu): XII, 1621; XIII, 7040 (Vishṇu's 1000 names).—Do.[2] = Çiva (1000 names[2]).
Sarvakāmadughā, name of a cow. § 564 (Mātalīyop.): V, **102,** 3611 (*°ā nāma dhenur dhārayate diçam uttarāṃ*).
Sarvakāmaguṇāvaha, Sarvakāmavara, Sarvakara = Çiva (1000 names[2]).
Sarvakarman[1], a prince. § 638*b* (Rāmop.): XII, **49,** 1793 (son of Saudāsa, protected by Parāçara).
Sarvakarman[2] = Çiva (1000 names[2]).
Sarvakurūttama ("the foremost of all Kurus") = Arjuna: VIII, †4701.—Do.[2] (do.) = Bhīshma: II, 1434.
Sarvalakshaṇalakshaṇya = Vishṇu (1000 names).
Sarvalakshaṇalakshita, Sarvalālasa, Sarvalocana = Çiva (1000 names[2]).
Sarvalokaguru = Kṛshṇa: VII, 6458; VIII, 4364.
Sarvalokakṛt[1] = Brahmán, q.v. = Do.[2] = Kṛshṇa (Vishṇu): XII, 13253.—Do.[3] = Çiva (1000 names[2]).
Sarvalokamaheçvara = Kṛshṇa (Vishṇu): III, 13556 (*Vishṇuṃ*); V, 2538; VI, 1064, 2985; XIII, 6941 (1000 names).
Sarvalokāmara = Indra: XIV, †748 (*Çakro gataḥ S°tvaṃ*).
Sarvalokanamaskṛta = Sūrya (the Sun): III, 153.
Sarvalokānāṃ pati(ḥ) = Çiva: XIII, 6377.
Sarvalokapati = Manu Svārocisha: XII, 13583.
Sarvalokapitāmaha[1] = Brahmán, q.v. — Do.[2] = Çiva: XIII, 6321.—Do.[3] = Kṛshṇa: VI, 3031; XIII, 6858.
Sarvalokaprajāpati = Çiva (1000 names[2]).
Sarvalokeçvara[1] = Balarāma: XIII, 6862. — Do.[2] = Brahmán: VI, 546; VIII, 1401; XII, 10169.—Do.[3] = Çiva: VII, 9502, 9577, 9585; XIII, 762.—Do.[4] = Kṛshṇa (Vishṇu): VI, 3017; VII, 4492, 7702; XII, 13380.
Sarvalokeçvareçvara = Çiva: VII, 9508.
Sarvam āvṛtya tishṭhasi = Çiva (1000 names[1]).
***sarvamedha,** a sacrifice: IX, 2890; XII, 241, 359, 704; XIII, 1775, 4942, 5260; XIV, 48.
Sarvanāgaripudhvaja = Kṛshṇa: XIII, 6820.
Sarvāṅga, Sarvāṅgarūpa, Sarvapārçvamukha, Sarvapāvana = Çiva (1000 names[2]).
Sarvapitṛ = Kṛshṇa: VII, 413.
Sarvapraharaṇāyudha = Vishṇu (1000 names).
Sarvaprāṇishu nityastha(ḥ) = Agni (q.v.).
Sarvapūjita, Sarvaratnavid, Sarvasādhana, Sarvasādhunishevita = Çiva (1000 names[2]).
Sarvasaha = Vishṇu (1000 names).
Sarvasaṅgā, a river. § 574 (Jambūkh.): VI, **9λ,** 344 (*only* C., B. has *Sarvāṃ Gaṅgāṃ*).
Sarvasāraṅga, a serpent. § 67 (Sarpasattra): I, **57,** 2159 (of Dhṛtarāshṭra's race).
Sārvasenī ("daughter of Sarvasena") = Sunandā, wife of Bharata: I, ††3785.
Sarvasūkshma = Kṛshṇa: XII, 1512.
Sarvāsunilaya(ḥ) = Vishṇu (1000 names).
Sarvasurapravīra = Skanda: III, 14646.
Sarvasureça = Çiva: XIII, 903 (B. *Surāsureçāya*).
Sarvasyādi(ḥ) = Sūrya (the Sun): III, 153.
Sarvataçcakshus = Vishṇu (1000 names).
Sarvataḥ çrutimāṃl loke, Sarvataḥpāṇipādānta = Çiva (1000 names[1]).
Sarvātman[1] = Çiva: VIII, 1438; XIII, 1145 (1000 names[2]).—Do.[2] = Kṛshṇa (Vishṇu): XII, 1605, 1616, 1672, 13426, 13754 (*Nārāyaṇaḥ*).
sarvatobhadra, name of a battle array. § 586 (Bhīshmavadhap.): VI, **99,** 4500 (*vyūhaṃ,* formed by Bhīshma).—§ 611 (Çalyap.): IX, **8,** 387 (*vyūhaṃ,* formed by Çalya).
Sarvātodyaparigraha = Çiva (1000 names[2]).
Sarvato 'kshiçiromukha = Çiva (1000 names[1]).
Sarvatomukha = Kṛshṇa (Vishṇu): III, 15534; XII, 13496 (*Purushaḥ*); XIII, 7036 (1000 names).—Do.[2] = Çiva (1000 names[2]).—Do.[3] = Sūrya: III, 154 (so B., °*su* °C.).
Sarvato vṛtta(ḥ) = Mahāpurusha (Mahāpurushastava).
Sarvatūryaninādin = Çiva (1000 names[2]).
Sarvavāc = Vishṇu (1000 names).
Sarvavarishṭha = Çiva (1000 names[1]).
Sarvavāsa[1] = Mahāpurusha (Mahāpurushastava).—Do.[2] = Çiva (1000 names[2]).
Sarvavāsin = Çiva (1000 names[2]).
Sarvavid[1] = Çiva: VII, 9594; XIII, 7498.—Do.[2] = Kṛshṇa (Vishṇu): XII, 1616; XIII, 6963 (1000 names), 7034 (do.).
Sarvavigraha, Sarvavikhyāta = Çiva (1000 names[2]).
Sarvayādavanandana = Kṛshṇa: V, 3344, 4673; X, 647; XII, 1704.
***sarvayajña,** name of a sacrifice: XII, †612.
Sarvayogeçvareçvara = Çiva: XII, 10240.
Sarvayogavinihsṛta = Vishṇu (1000 names).
Sarvayogin, Sarvāyudha = Çiva (1000 names[2]).
Sarveça = Kṛshṇa: VII, 2957.—Do.[2] = Çiva: VII, 9519 (only B.); XIV, 198 (do.).
Sarveçvara = Vishṇu (Kṛshṇa): VI, 4462; XIII, 6960 (1000 names).
Sarveshāṃ prāṇinām pati(ḥ) = Çiva (1000 names[2]).
Saryāti, v. Çaryāti.
Sat[1] = Çiva (1000 names[2]).—Do.[2] = Vishṇu (1000 names).
Satāṃ gatiḥ = Vishṇu (1000 names).
Satīrtha = Çiva: XIV, 195 (read with B. *Sutīrthāya*).
Satkartṛ, Satkīrti = Vishṇu (1000 names).
Satkṛta = Çiva (1000 names[2]).—Do.[2] = Vishṇu (1000 names).
Satkṛti, Satparāyaṇa, Satpathācāra = Vishṇu (1000 names).
Satrājit, a Vṛshṇi prince. § 793 (Mausalap.): XVI, **3,** 79 (had owned the jewel Syamantaka).
Sātrājitī ("daughter of Satrājit") = Satyabhamā, wife of Kṛshṇa: III, 14652; XVI, 145 (*Satyā*).
Sattā, Sattra = Vishṇu (1000 names).
Sattva, a son of Dhṛtarāshṭra. § 182 (Dhṛtarāshṭraputranāmak.): I, **117,** 4543.
Sattva(ṃ) = Çiva (1000 names).
Sattvastha = Kṛshṇa (Vishṇu): XII, 1614; XIII, 7001 (Vishṇu's 1000 names).
Sattvat, Sāttvat, Sāttvata, v. Satva°, Sātva°.
Sattvavat, Sāttvika = Vishṇu (1000 names).
Satuṅga, v. Sutuṅga.

Satvan, v. Satvāvṛhattvā.
Satvat (C. *Sātt°*), pl., a people = Sātvata, pl.: VII, 7662 (*°āṃ varaḥ*, i.e. Sātyaki); XII, 13237 (the worshippers of Kṛshṇa).
Sātvat (C. often *Sātt°*), pl. = Sātvata, pl.: V, 2581 (*ṛshabhaṃ sarva-S°āṃ*, i.e. Kṛshṇa), 3041 (*purogaḥ sarva-S°āṃ*, i.e. Kṛshṇa), 3334 (*ṛshabhaḥ sarva-S°āṃ*, i.e. Kṛshṇa), 3360 (do., do.), 4370 (*ṛshabhe sarva S°āṃ*, do.); VII, 3649 (*°āṃ vare*, i.e. Sātyaki); VIII, 1639 (*Sātyakiḥ S°āṃ varaḥ*), 2208 (do.); IX, 3502 (*°āṃ varaḥ*, i.e. Kṛshṇa), 3532 (*°āṃ çreshṭha*, do.); X, 726 (*°āṃ pravaraṃ*, do.); XII, 1502 (*°āṃ gatiḥ*, do.), 1614 (*°āṃ patiḥ*, do.), 7533 (*ṛshabhaṃ sarva-S°āṃ*, = do.).
Sātvata (C. often *Sātt°*), adj. ("belonging to the Sātvatas or to Sātvata = Kṛshṇa"). § 581 (Bhīshmavadhap.): VI, **66**, 3012 (*vidhiṃ*).—§ 602 (Droṇavadhap.): VII, **191**, 8793 (*sampātaṃ?*).—§ 641 (Rājadh.): XII, **64**, †2412 (*dharmāḥ*, *only* C., B. has *çāçvatāḥ*).—§ 717*c* (Uparicara): XII, **336**, 12714 (*vidhiṃ*), 12719 (*vidhiṃ*).—§ 717*b* (Nārāyaṇīya): XII, **349**, IV), 13575 (*dharmaṃ*; only B., C. has *çāçvataṃ*), 13580 (*dharmaṃ*), 13632 (*dharmaḥ*).
Sātvata (C. often *Sātt°*), pl. (*°āḥ*), a people (a tribe of the Yādavas; sometimes it designs the worshippers of Sātvata, i.e. Kṛshṇa). § 253 (Haraṇāharaṇap.): I, **221**, 7965.—§ 291 (Çiçupālavadhap.): II, **45**, 1566 (*°ānāṃ nṛçaṃsātmā*, sc. Çiçupāla).—§ 402 (Tīrthayātrāp.): III, **120**, †10278 (*sa-Vṛshṇi-Bhojāndhakayodhamukhyā . . . . S°çūrasenā*).—§ 555 (Sainyodyogap.): V, **19**, 570 (*Yuyudhānaḥ . . . S°ānāṃ mahārathaḥ*).—§ 598 (Jayadrathavadhap.): VII, **85*a***, 3023 (*Kuru-Pāṇḍu-S°aiḥ*).—§ 599 (do.): VII, **121**, 4853 (*°ānāṃ mahārathaḥ*), i.e. Sātyaki); **140**, †5839 (*pravaraḥ S°ānāṃ*, i.e. Sātyaki).—§ 600 (Ghaṭotkacavadhap.): VII, **157**, 6967.—§ 604 (Karṇap.): VIII, **7**, †197 (*°ānāṃ varishṭhaḥ*, sc. Kṛtavarman); **9**, 326 (*Kṛtavarmā . . . S°ānāṃ mahārathaḥ*).—§ 606 (do.): VIII, **35**, 1644.—§ 717*b* (Nārāyaṇīya): XII, **340**, 12965 (*sarva-S°mukhyānāṃ*); **343**, 13237 (*°jñāna°*, the worshippers of Kṛshṇa); **349**, 13602 (= do.). Cf. Satvat, pl., Sātvat, pl.
Sātvata[1] = Balarāma: IX, 3035.
Sātvata[2] (C. *Sātt°*) = Cekitāna: VI, 3718, 3720.
Sātvata[3] (C. sometimes *Sātt°*) = Kṛshṇa: I, 7896, 8083 (*Vāsudevaṃ*); III, 1954 (do.); V, 2563 (*K°*), 2565 (etymology), †2576; IX, 124 (*°au* = Sātyaki and Kṛshṇa); XII, 12968 (ninth avatāra of Vishṇu), 13237 (etymology); XIV, 381, 1526.
Sātvata[4] (C. sometimes *Sātt°*) = Kṛtavarman: I, 7991 (*K°*); V, 4874 (*K°*); VI, 623 (*K°*), 2109 (*K°*), 2404 (*K°*), 3532 (*K°*), 3634, 3838 (*K°*), 3972 (*Hārdikyaḥ*), 4244 (*K°*), 5270; VII, 3253 (*K°*), 3279, 4520; VIII, 2133 (*K°*); IX, 293 (*K°*), 1095, 1097, 1102 (*°au*, i.e. Sātyaki and Kṛtavarman), 1377, 1398 (*K°*), 1459 (*K°*), 1681 (*K°*), 3609 (*K°*), 3627 (*K°*); X, 143 (*K°*), 150, 213 (*K°*), 485 (*K°*).
Sātvata[5] (C. often *Sātt°*) = Sātyaki: II, 50 (so PCR.); VI, †2592, †2593, 4058 (only C., B. has *Sātyakasya*), 4694 (*S°*), 5387; VII, 343, 1110, 3006, 3608, 3624, 4050, 4142, 4174, 4227, 4238, 4378, 4391, 4420, 4456, 4471, 4480, 4558, 4562, 4567, 4586, 4593, 4595, 4600, 4614, 4635, 4642, 4649, 4658, 4680, 4751, 4788, 4811, 4839, 4876, 4964, 5016, 5107, 5111, 5118, 5119, 5120, 5136, 5138, 5143, 5151, 5168, 5279, 5311 (?), 5317 (?), 5459 (*sa-S°ān*), 5868, 5879, 5887, 5926, 5939, 5941, 5978, 6045 (*na ca çakyo raṇe jetuṃ S°o manujarshabhaiḥ*), 6094, 6115, 6328, 6332, 6365, 6386, 6496, 6628, 6730, 6732, 6735, 6755, 6784, 6926, 6927, 6930, 6933, 6998 (*saha-S°ān*), 7001 (*sa-S°ān*), 7228, 7243, 7247, 7248, 7256, 7281, 7405, 7406, 7639, 7651, 7676, 7681, 7837, 8290, 8653, 8657, 8663, 8807, 8811, 9150, 9169, 9307, 9323; VIII, 518, 2983 (?); IX, 124 (*°au* i.e. Sātyaki and Kṛshṇa), 351, 787, †1092, 1102 (*°au*, i.e. Sātyaki and Kṛtavarman), 1116.
Sātvataçreshṭha[1] = Kṛshṇa: VI, 4865.—Do.[2] = Sātyaki: VII, 5945.
Sātvatāgrya = Sātyaki: VI, 780.
Sātvatāṃ patiḥ = Vishṇu (1000 names).
Sātvatamukhya[1] = Kṛshṇa: II, 1686. — Do.[2] = Pradyumna: III, 754.—Do.[3] = Sātyaki: VII, †4691 (C. *Sātt°*).
Sātvatapravara[1] = Kṛshṇa: II, 1626 (*K°*). — Do.[2] = Sātyaki: VII, 5937 (C. *Sātt°*).
Sātvatapuṅgava = Sātyaki: VII, 5924 (C. *Sātt°*).
Sātvatarshabha = Sātyaki: VII, 6330 (C. *Sātt°*).
Sātvatātmajā = Subhadrā: I, 7978.
Sātvatī = Subhadrā: I, 8028 (C. *Sātt°*); XIV, 2020; XV, 23, 348, 437, 778.
Sātvatīputra[1] = Abhimanyu: VI, 3228; VII, 1665, 2573.
Sātvatīputra[2] = Kṛshṇa: II, 1376.
Sātvatīsuta = Çiçupāla: II, 1566.
satvāvṛhattvā: I, 4813 (so C., B. reads *ṛtvābṛhattvā*, the text is presumably corrupted, one or two names [of Devagandharvas] are expected here (perhaps *Satvan* (or *Ṛtvan*) and *Bṛhatvan*); cf. I, 2554, where is read *Siddhaḥ Pūrṇaç ca*).
Satya[1], name of one or more brahmans. § 264 (Sabhākriyāp.): II, **4*a***, 105 (waited upon Yudhishṭhira).—§ 686 (Mokshadh.): XII, **273**, 9816, 9819, 9823.—§ 736*b* (Vītahavyop.): XIII, **30**, 2001 (son of Vitatya and father of Santa).
Satya[2], name of a fire. § 490 (Āṅgirasa): III, **219**, 14142 (= Nishkṛti, son of the fire Niçcyavana).
Satya[3], a Kuru warrior. § 579 (Bhīshmavadhap.): VI, **54**[12], 2309 (a Kaliṅga?, slain by Bhīmasena).
Satya[4] = Çiva: VII, 2877.—Do.[5] = Kṛshṇa (Vishṇu): XII, 1507, 1614; XIII, 6961 (Vishṇu's 1000 names), 6972 (do.), 7042 (do.).
Satya(ṃ) = Çiva (1000 names[1]).
Satyā[1] = Satyavatī[1]: I, 4287, 4292.
Satyā[2] = Satyabhāmā: III, 14658, 14706, 14708, †14711, †14716, 14723; V, 2329; XVI, 145 (*Sātrājitī*).
Satyā[3], wife of the fire Çaṃyu. § 490 (Āṅgirasa): III, **219**, 14133.
Satyabhāmā, daughter of Satrājit, wife of Kṛshṇa Vāsudeva. § 10 (Parvasaṅgr.): I, **2**, 324 (*saṃvādas tataḥ parva Draupadī-S°yoḥ*, i.e. Draupadī-Satyabhāmāsaṃv.).—§ 11 (do.): I, **2**, 469 (*Draupadyāḥ . . . saṃvādaḥ S°ayā*, do.). — § 452 (Mārkaṇḍeyas.): III, **183**, 12563 (*sahitaḥ S°ayā*, sc. Kṛshṇa), 12567.—§ 453 (do.): III, **183**, 12602.—§ 510 (Draupadī-Satyabhāmasaṃv.): III, **233**, 14649, 14651, 14657, 14666 (conversation between Draupadī and Satyabhāmā).—§ 511 (do.): III, **235**, 14724, 14739 (do.).—§ 549 (Pāṇḍavapraveçap.): IV, **9**, 262 (*Kṛshṇasya mahishīṃ priyāṃ*).—§ 561 (Yānasandhip.): V, **59**, 2326.—§ 793 (Mausalap.): XVI, **3**, 80; **7**, 250 (after the death of Kṛshṇa, *S.*, etc. entered the forest). Cf. Sātrājitī, Satyā.
Satyaçravas, a Kuru warrior. § 572 (Rathātirathasaṅkhyānap.): V, **167**, 5790 (*bṛhadbalaḥ*, a ratha in the army of Duryodhana, Nīl. takes *satyaçravāḥ* as an adj. and Bṛhadbala as the name, but Bṛhadbala is mentioned v. 5765).—§ 593 (Abhimanyuvadhap.): VII, **45**, 1805, 1806 (seized by Abhimanyu).
Satyadeva, a Kuru warrior. § 579 (Bhīshmavadhap.): VI, **54**[12], 2309 (a Kaliṅga (?), slain by Bhīmasena).
Satyadharman[1], a Pāñcāla prince. § 569 (Bhaga-

vadyānap.): V, **141**γ, 4779 (*Saumakiḥ*, PCR. takes *satya-dharmā* as an adj. to *Saumakiḥ* = Yudhāmanyu).

Satyadharman[2] = Vishṇu (1000 names).

Satyadharmaparākrama, Satyadharmaparāyaṇa = Vishṇu (1000 names).

Satyadhṛti, one or more princes. § 232 (Svayaṃvarap.): I, **186,** 6990 (present at the svayaṃvara of Draupadī).—§ 572 (Rathātirathasaṅkhyānap.): V, **171,** 5910 (among the mahārathas of the Pāṇḍavas).—§ 573 (Ambopākhyānap.): V, **196**μ, 7649 (*Saucittiḥ*, in the army of Yudhishṭhira).—§ 585 (Bhīshmavadhap.): VI, **93**ψ, 4151 (*Saucittiḥ*); **95**δδ, 4254.—§ 592 (Saṃçaptakavadhap.): VII, **23**ο, 988, 990 (*Saucittiḥ*).—§ 604 (Karṇap.): VIII, **6,** 181 (has been slain), 184.

Satyajit, a Pāñcāla, son of Drupada. § 209 (Drupadaçāsana): I, **138,** 5480, 5483, 5485, 5487, 5488, 5491 (took part in the battle when Droṇa, etc., assailed Drupada).—§ 561 (Yānasandhip.): V, **57**ζ, 2235 (*°pramukhaiḥ*, sc. the sons of Drupada).—§ 572 (Rathātirathasaṅkhyānap.): V, **171,** 5903 (among the Pāñcālas in the army of Yudhishṭhira), 5916 (*Drupadātmajaḥ*).—§ 591 (Saṃçaptakavadhap.): VII, **17,** 716, 717 (protected Yudhishṭhira).—§ 592 (do.): VII, **21,** 858, 860, 865, 867, 870, 871, 875 (do., slain by Droṇa).—§ 603 (Nārāyaṇāstramokshap.): VII, **199**χ, 9228 (*yena*, i.e. by Droṇa, *Pāñcālāḥ S°mukhāḥ . . . vinipātitāḥ*).—§ 604 (Karṇap.): VIII, **6,** 154 (had been slain by Droṇa).—§ 795 (Svargārohaṇap.): XVIII, **5**λ, 149. Cf. Pāñcāla, Pāñcālya.

Satyaka, a Vṛshṇi, son of Çini and father of Sātyaki (Yuyudhāna). § 83 (Ādivaṃçāvatāraṇa): I, **63,** 2434 (father of Sātyaki).—§ 252 (Subhadrāharaṇap.): I, **219,** 7916 (*S°aḥ Sātyakiç caiva*).—§ 253 (Haraṇāharaṇap.): I, **221,** 7991 (do.).—§ 264 (Sabhākriyāp.): II, **4**β, 125 (*Çineḥ sutaḥ*).—§ 785 (Anugītap.): XIV, **62**ε, 1855. Cf. Çineḥ suta(ḥ) (II, 125).

Sātyaka = Sātyaki, q.v.

Satyakarman[1], a Trigarta prince. § 591 (Saṃçaptakavadhap.): VII, **17***a*, 689 (among five Trigarta brothers who belonged to the Saṃçaptakas).—§ 611 (Çalyap.): IX, **27,** 1480 (slain by Arjuna).

Satyakarman[2] = Kṛshṇa: XII, 1614.

Sātyaki ("the son of Satyaka"), a Vṛshṇi, properly named Yuyudhāna, son of Satyaka and grandson of Çini. [§ 4 (Anukram.): I, **1,** †194 (*Yuyudhānam*)].—§ 11 (Parvasaṅgr.): I, **2,** 534, 571.—§ 83 (Ādivaṃçāvatāraṇa): I, **63,** 2433 (*S°ḥ Kṛtavarmā ca Nārāyaṇam anuvratau*, son of Satyaka).=§ 130 (Aṃçāvat.): I, **67,** 2714 (*Vṛshṇikulodvahaḥ*, born from the paksha of the Maruts).—§ 232 (Svayaṃvarap.): I, **186,** 6998 (present at the svayaṃvara of Draupadī).—§ 243 (Vidurāgamanap.): I, **205,** 7507 (partisan of the Pāṇḍavas).—§ 252 (Subhadrāharaṇap.): I, **219,** 7916.—§ 253 (Haraṇāharaṇap.): I, **221,** 7991 (came to the wedding of Arjuna and Subhadrā).—§ 264 (Sabhākriyāp.): II, **4,** 120 (*Yuyudhānaḥ*, instructed by Arjuna in the science of arms).—§ 273 (Rājasūyārambhap.): II, **14,** 621 (among the seven *atirathas* of the Vṛshṇis).—§ 296 (Dyūtap.): II, **53,** 1920 (held the umbrella for Yudhishṭhira at the rājasūya), 1926.—[§ 318 (Arjunābhigamanap.): III, **13,** 611 (*Yuyudhānaḥ*, told Kṛshṇa of the gambling)].—§ 320 (Saubhavadhop.): III, **18** [735 (*Çiner naptā*)], 744 (*°ṃ Baladevañ ca ye cānye 'ndhaka-Vṛshṇayaḥ*); **21,** 833, 836.—[§ 342 (Indralokābhigamanap.): III, **51,** 2009 (*Yuyudhāna-Bhīmau*)].—§ 343 (Nalopākhyānap.): III, **52,** 2019.—§ 400 (Tīrthayātrāp.): III, **118,** †10233 (*Çineḥ . . . pautraṃ*, came to Yudhishṭhira in Prabhāsa)].—§ 402 (do.): III, **120** (†10259), [†10286 (*Çinipravīra*)].—[§ 448 (Ājagarap.): III, **176,** †12330 (*Çineḥ . . . naptā*)].—§ 553 (Vaivāhikap.): IV, **72,** 2357 (*Yuyudhānaḥ*, came to the wedding of Abhimanyu and Uttarā).—§ 554 (Sainyodyogap.): V, [**1,** †4 (*Çinipravīraḥ*), †40 (do.)]; **2,** (41) (only B.), [†55 (*Yuyudhānasya*)].—[§ 555 (do.): V, **19**γ, 570 (*Yuyudhānaḥ*, came to Yudhishṭhira with an army)].—§ 556 (Sañjayayānap.): V, **20,** 619 (in the army of Yudhishṭhira); **22,** [†653 (*Sātyakaḥ*)], †668; **25**η, 732; [**27,** †783 (*Yuyudhānaḥ*); **28**ι, †804 (*Çaineyaḥ*)]; **30**ν, †868.—§ 561 (Yānasandhip.): V, **48,** [1817 (*Çaineyena*)], †1852 (*Çiner naptāraṃ*), †1858 (*Mādhavasya*); [**50,** 2006 (*Yuyudhānena Vṛshṇivīreṇa*)]; **53,** 2109; **55,** 2204; **57**ξ, 2233 (*Yuyudhānam*), [2252 (*Yuyudhānaḥ*, will fight with Kṛtavarman); **58**φ, 2315 (*Yuyudhānena*)]; **61**ψ, 2406; **65**γγ, 2488 (*sammato 'ndhaka-Vṛshṇīnāṃ*).—§ 562 (Bhagavadyānap.): V, **80**ε, 2856; **81,** (2866), **82,** 2872; **83,** 2930 (*Çiner naptāraṃ*), 2941 (accompanied Kṛshṇa); **94,** 3347, 3362, 3377; **95**υ, 3404.—§ 567 (do.): V, **130,** 4373, 4380 (discovered the plan of seizing Kṛshṇa); **131,** 4441.—§ 569 (do.): V, **137,** 4669; **141**γ, 4779, 4797; **143**ι, 4871, 4884 (*Keçavaḥ saha-S°iḥ*).—§ 570 (Sainyaniryāṇap.): V, **151***a*, 5101 (among the seven leaders of Yudhishṭhira's troops), [5143 (*Yuyudhānadvitīyam Dhṛshṭadyumnaṃ*)], (ζ), 5164; **152**η, 5175 (*Yuyudhānaḥ*); [**157,** 5324 (*Çinipuṅgavam*)].—§ 571 (Ulūkadūtāgamanap.): V, **162,** 5591; [**164**ε, 5708 (*Vārshṇeyaṃ Yuyudhānaṃ*, pitted against Jayadratha)].—§ 572 (Rathātirathasaṅkhyānap.): V, **170,** 5882 (*Mādhavaḥ*, among the heroes in the army of Yudhishṭhira).—§ 573 (Ambopākhyānap.): V, [**194**γ, 7598 (*Yuyudhānaḥ*), 7600 (*Çaineyaḥ*)]; **196,** [(η), 7622 (*Yuyudhānaṃ*), 7630 (do.)], (λ), 7645 (*Vṛshṇīnāṃ pravaraḥ*).—§ 576 (Bhagavadgītāp.): VI, [**19**ε, 714 (*Yuyudhānaḥ*); **22,** 780 (*Yuyudhānena*)]; **25**θ, [833 (*Yuyudhānaḥ*)], (κ), 846.—§ 578 (Bhīshmavadhap.): VI, **45**[2], 1680 (attacked Kṛtavarman), 1681; **47**ε, 1837, 1838 (pierced by Bhīshma), [1865 (*Sātyake*)]; **48**κ, 1962, 1972 (pierced by Bhīshma); **50**ν, 2060, (π), 2082; **51***aa*, 2117.—§ 579 (do.): VI, **52**ζ, 2149; **54**[13], 2333, 2340, 2352, 2353 (assisted Bhīma and Dhṛshṭadyumna).—§ 580 (do.): VI, **56**θ, 2417; **57**κ, 2454, 2460; **58,** 2468, 2470 (fought with the Gāndhāras), 2499; [**59,** †2587 (*Çinipravīraḥ*), †2589 (do., came to the aid of Arjuna), †2592 (*Çaineyam*, *Çinipravīra*), †2594 (*Çaineya*)].—§ 581 (do.): VI, **63**[9], †2806 (*Çinipravīraḥ*, attacked Bhīshma), †2812 (attacked by Bhūriçravas); **64,** 2813, 2814, 2816 (encounter with Bhūriçravas).—§ 582 (do.): VI, **69***a*, 3064, (³), 3076 (checked Droṇa), (⁴), 3079; **71**ε, 3140; **72**η, 3169, 3187 (the charioteer of *S.* slain by Bhīshma); **74**[15], 3240, 3245, 3249, 3250, 3266 (encounter with Bhūriçravas who slew ten sons of *S.*).—§ 583 (do.): VI, **75***a*, 3284.—§ 584 (do.): VI, **81,** 3560 (attacked by Alambusha); **82,** 3615, 3621, 3623 (encounter with Alambusha); **86**[8], 3819, (⁹), 3825, (ζ), 3839.—§ 585 (do.): VI, **87,** 3861 (at the horn of the *çṛṅgaṭaka vyūha*); **89**ν, 3946; **96,** 4340 (attacked by Kṛtavarman and Bāhlīka).—§ 586 (do.): VI, **99**ζ, 4509; **101**θ, 4586, 4623 (pierced Kṛpa), 4637 (fought with Droṇa), 4640 (fought with Droṇa); **103**ν, 4694 (*Sātvataḥ*, attacked Bhīshma); **104,** 4744 (pierced Kṛtavarman), 4755, 4763 (pierced by Bhīshma); **106**σ, 4803, 4806 (pierced by Droṇa).—§ 587 (do.): VI, **108,** 4999, (β), 5013; **109**ε, 5074; **110,** 5107 (fought with Duryodhana); **111,** 5140, 5144, 5152 (fought with Alambusha and Bhagadatta); **112**θ, 5234; [**115,** 5361 (*Çiner naptā*, fought with Açvatthāman)]; **116,**

5384, 5386 (fought with Açvatthāman); **118**ν, 5554, 5558; **119**χ, 5577, (ω), 5587.—§ 589 (Droṇābhishekap.): VII, **2**α, †68, †82; **8**η, 228, [†248 (*Çineh . . . naptā*), †251 (*Çaineya*)]; [**10**, 339 (*Yuyudhāne*; *b*: Having crushed the host of the *Sauvīra* king, Yuyudhāna took for his wife the beautiful *Bhoja* maiden (*Bhojāṃ kanyāṃ*). In battle he is equal to *Vāsudeva*, and has, through the instruction of *Arjuna*, become foremost in the use of arrows and equal to *Arjuna* himself in weapons; he is equal to *Rāma* in prowess, etc., and in knowledge of the *Brahmāstra*)].—§ 590 (do.): VII, **14**, 529 (pierced Kṛtavarman), (α), 577; **16**, [(β), 633 (°-*Sātyakaiḥ*)], (γ), 646 (pierced by Droṇa), (δ), 650.—§ 592 (Saṃçaptakavadhap.): VII, **21**κ, 904, 911, (μ), 916; **22**, 942 (°*pramukhā rathāḥ*); [**23**ο, 951 (*Çaineyaḥ*, description of his horses); **25**, 1073 (*Çineḥ pautraṃ*, checked by Kṛtavarman)]; **26**, 1171 (attacked by Bhagadatta); **31**φ, 1348; **32**, [(φ), 1380 (*Yuyudhānaprabhṛtayaḥ*)], (ββ), 1427, [1439 (*Çaineyaḥ*, pierced Karṇa), 1441 (*Sātyakārṇavāt*)], 1443. — § 593 (Abhimanyuvadhap.): VII, **35**δ, 1508, (ζ), 1528; **40**ο, 1695; **42**π, 1743; **43**ρ, 1769, 1776.—§ 597 (Pratijñāp.): VII, **83**α, 2949; **84**, 3008 (Arjuna exhorted *S.* to protect Yudhishṭhira).—§ 598 (Jayadrathavadhap.): VII, **85**δ, 3047 (*Vṛshṇivīraḥ*), [3056 (*Çaineyena*)]; **86**, 3082, 3083.—§ 599 (do.): VII, **95**, 3530 (attacked by Duḥçāsana); **96**, 3555, 3556 (fought with Duḥçāsana); **97**, 3603, 3605 (*Çinipuṅgavaḥ*, rescued Dhṛshṭadyumna); **98**, 3644, 3646, 3653, 3655, 3661 (encounter with Droṇa); **106**, 3978 (attacked by Vyāghradatta); **107**, 4047 (slew Vyāghradatta, the son of the Māgadha king), 4052; **110**, 4136 (*Yuyudhānena*), 4137, 4141, 4143, 4147 (*Vṛshṇivaraḥ*), 4148, 4152, 4177, 4186, 4229 (fought with Droṇa and was rescued by Yudhishṭhira, etc.); **111**, 4240 (*Çinipuṅgavaḥ*); **112**, 4293, 4360 (read *sa S°iḥ* with B.), 4361, 4364, 4370 (at the injunction of Yudhishṭhira *S.* set out to assist Arjuna); **113**, 4375, 4382, 4392, 4393 (*Yuyudhānaḥ*), 4395, 4397, (4404), 4416, 4417, 4418, 4419, 4421, 4424, 4425, 4426, 4427, 4431, 4433 (encounter with Kṛtavarman, etc.); **114**, 4468. 4476; **115**, 4546, 4549, 4550 (fought with Kṛtavarman and the elephant division headed by Rukmaratha), 4574, 4577, 4583, 4584, 4590, 4592 (slew Jalasandha), 4600; **116**, 4610, 4613, 4618, 4620, 4627, 4639, 4643, 4644 (fought with Droṇa, etc.; vanquished Kṛtavarman); **117**, 4659, 4663, 4665, 4672, 4675, 4679 (encounter with Droṇa); **118**, †4689, †4692, †4694 (slew Sudarçana); **119**, 4702 (*Vṛshṇipuṅgavaḥ*), (4728), 4741, 4742, 4745, 4755 (praised by his charioteer, vanquished the Yavanas, the Kāmbojas, etc.); **120**, 4767, 4769, 4776, 4778, 4782, 4787, 4789, 4791, 4796, 4797, 4799, 4802, 4804 (fought with Duryodhana, etc.); **121**, 4808, 4823, 4832, 4835, 4837, 4841, 4845, 4847, 4860 (vanquished the Saṃçaptakas, Mlecchas, etc.); **122**, 4869, 4879, 4886, 4887, 4888 (continuation); **123**, 4936, 4938, 4941, 4942, 4957, 4960, 4961, 4962, 4963; 4970 (encounter with Duḥçāsana, whom he defeated but did not slay); **124**, 4972, 4974, 4991; **126**, 5102 (*Vṛshṇīnāṃ pravaraṃ*), 5105 (*Çaineyaḥ*), 5106, 5109 (*Vārshṇeyaṃ*), 5121, 5140, 5141, 5143 (*Sātvataṃ*); **128**οο, 5243, 5255; **130**, 5314, 5316, [5326 (*Yuyudhāna-Vṛkodarau*)]; **134**, 5557 (*Keçava-S°ī*); **136**ψψ, 5613: **137**ωω, 5629; **139**, 5806; **140**γγγ, †5828, †5831 (slew Alambusha), [†5839 (*Çaineyaṃ*)], **141**, 5845, 5856, 5857, 5858, 5859, 5860, 5861, 5862, 5863, 5864, 5865, 5866, 5867, 5871, 5874, 5876, 5877 (defeated the Trigartas and proceeded to where Arjuna was); **142**, 5899, 5901, 5903, 5908, 5929, 5932, 5936, 5943 (*Vārshṇeyaṃ*), 5946 (*pravaraṃ Vṛshṇivīrāṇāṃ*) (defeated by Bhūriçravas); **143**, 5953, 5971, 5974, 5980, 5982, 6002, 6006, 6007, 6011, (6012) (slew Bhūriçravas when the latter was sitting in prāya); [**144**, 6027 (*Çaineyasya*)].—[§ 599*e* (*Çini*): VII, **144**, 6041 (*Çineḥ sutaṃ*), 6043 (do.)].—§ 599 (Jayadrathavadhap.): VII, **147**, 6325 (rushed at Karṇa), 6327, 6335, 6337, 6341, 6354 (*Yuyudhānaḥ*), 6364, 6368, 6371, 6373, 6375, 6376 (fought with Karṇa, etc.); **149**, 6482, 6484 (*Bhīma-S°ī*), [6492 (*Yuyudhāna-Vṛkodarau*)]; **150**, 6514 (had slain Jalasandha, cf. chap. **115**).—§ 600 (Ghaṭotkacavadhap.): VII, **154**β, 6648; **156**, 6729, 6731 (only B.), 6738, 6753, 6756, (θ), 6762, (ι), 6782, 6783 (encounter with Somadatta, etc.); **157**, 6924, 6929 (encounter with Somadatta); **162**, 7224, 7230, 7231, 7240, 7241, 7245, 7246, 7251 (encounter with Somadatta, whom he slew); [**165**, 7361 (*Çaineyaṃ*, attacked by Bhūri)]; **166**, 7398, 7406, 7407, 7410 (encounter with Bhūri, whom he slew); **170**, 7638, 7640, 7641, 7642, 7643, 7646, 7647, 7649, 7662 (*Sātvatāṃ varaḥ*), 7664, 7666, 7667, 7677 (encounter with Karṇa, etc.); **171**, 7683, 7685 (encounter with Duryodhana), [(ξξ), 7732 (*Yuyudhānaḥ*)]; **172**, [7743 (*Çaineyapramukhān*), (ππ), 7745 (*Çinipuṅgavaṃ*), 7747 (*Çaineyaṃ*)], (σσ), 7758; **173**, 7835, 7836 (protected Ghaṭotkaca); [**177** ψψ, 8060 (*Yuyudhānaḥ*)]; **178**, (ωω), 8080 (*Yuyudhānaḥ*)], (ααα), 8084; **179** βββ, 8119; **182**, 8279, 8293 (questioned Kṛshṇa about the dart of Karṇa).—§ 601 (Droṇavadhap.): VII, **184**α, 8368.—§ 602 (do.); VII, **187**ι, 8544; **189**, 8646, 8649, 8660, 8664, 8665, 8667, 8668, 8670, 8671 (encounter with Duryodhana); **191**, 8801, 8805, 8806 (rescued Dhṛshṭadyumna); [**192**, 8809 (*Çaineyasya*), 8810 (*Çaineyaṃ*), 8812 (do.), 8813 (*Çaineyasya*)]. —§ 603 (Nārāyaṇāstramokshap.): VII, **195**θ, 9008; **198**, 9133, 9150, 9156, 9165, 9171, 9176, 9191 (quarrelled with Dhṛshṭadyumna); **199**, 9220; **200**, 9310, 9314, 9315, 9317 (encounter with Açvatthāman); **201** εε, 9401. — § 604 (Karṇap.): VIII, **5**ζ, 106 (had slain Bhūriçravas), 134 (had slain Jalasandha).—§ 605 (do.): VIII, **12**ββ, 454; **13**, 492, 497, 499, 500, 506, 510, 511, 513, 519, 524 (slew the Kaikeya princes Vinda and Anuvinda); [**21**εε, 845 (*Yuyudhānaḥ*, proceeded against Karṇa)]; **22**ηη, 870, 873, 875 (killed the elephant of the Aṅga king and its rider), [(κκ), 888 (*Pāñcāla-Çaineyau*)]; **30**, [†1211 (*Çiniputraṃ*), †1213 (*Çinipravīraṃ*), †1214 (*Çinivṛshabhaḥ*), †1215 (*Çinivṛshabha-*, fought with Karṇa, etc.)], (νν), 1227, 1229.—§ 606 (do.): VIII, **35**, 1639 (*Sātvatāṃ varaḥ*, had been vanquished by Karṇa).—§ 607 (do.): VIII, **37**γ, †1728.—§ 608 (do.): VIII, **46**, [2157 (*Çinipuṅgavaḥ*, shall proceed against Kṛtavarman)], (η), 2208 (*Sātvatāṃ varaḥ*); [**47**μ, 2229 (*Sātyakena*)]; **48**ξ, 2253, 2274, 2277 (defeated Vṛshasena and fought with Duḥçāsana), (σ), 2296; **49**τ, 2304, (χ), 2333, (ω), 2359, 2387 (°*pramukhāḥ*); **50**, 2398 (protected Yudhishṭhira); **51**, 2502 (attacked Karṇa); **55**, 2659, (κκ), 2662, 2663 (λλ), 2666, 2673 (fought with Açvatthāman); **56**, 2728 (defeated by Karṇa), [(ππ), 2756 (*Çiner naptā*)]; **59**, 2924 (fought with Karṇa), (ψψ), 2946; **60**ββ, 3001, [3034 (*Çaineyena*)]; **61**, 3079 (proceeded against Çakuni), 3111, 3113 (encounter with Çakuni whom he defeated), 3116; **63**ηηη, 3200; [**66**ιιι, 3318 (*Yuyudhānasya*)]; **67**κκκ, 3373 (*Çaineyaḥ*); **73**ννν, 3732; [**74**, φφφ, 3794 (*Çaineyasya*), 3796 (*Sātyakasya*)]; **75**χχχ, †3811; **78**γ', 3955, 3956, 3961 (fought with Karṇa); **79**, 4028, [(ι'), 4087 (-*Çaineya*-)]; **82**, †4182 (his horses slain by Karṇa), [†4185 (*Çaineya*°, slew Prasena)], †4205; [**83**π', †4306 (*Çaineya*°)]; **93**, 4864, 4872; **96**, [4991 (*Yuyudhānam*)], (βα'), 5030 (*Vṛshṇīnāṃ pravaro rathaḥ*).—§ 609 (Çalyap.): IX, **1**δ, 36 (among the seven who are left of Yudhishṭhira's army after the nightly encounter); **2**ζ, 79.—§ 610 (do.): IX, **3**ι, 156 (attacked Çakuni), 164; **4**μ, 223 (°*eḥ . . . vegaḥ*); **7**τ, 335.—§ 611 (do.): IX, **8**ζ, 396; **10**κ, 516, [**11**λ, 550 (*Çaineyam*)]; **12**o, 646, 652; **13**, 656, (o), 660, 663, 667, 673, 674, 675, 679, 683, 688 (fought with Çalya); **15**, 761, (ρ), 768, 771, 775, 776, 778, 781, 784, 785, 786 (do.); **16**, [σ, 819 (*Çaineyaḥ*)], (υ), 832; **17**χ, 866 [†871 (*Çineḥ . . . naptā*), †894 (do.)], 933 (*Çiner naptā*), 935, 937 (defeated Kṛtavarman); **18**ββ, 962, [967 (*Çaineyaḥ*), 969 (*Yuyudhānaḥ*)]; **19**δδ, 1020, (εε), 1026, (ηη), 1064; [**20**θθ, †1084 (*Çineḥ . . . naptā*), †1091 (*Çinipravīraḥ*, slew Çālva)]; **21**, 1099 (*Çiner naptā*, slew Kshemakīrti), 1109, 1118 (fought with Kṛtavarman); **22**λλ, 1139, 1143 [1160 (*Çaineyaḥ*, do.)]; **25**, 1391, 1394 (made Sañjaya captive); [**27**σσ, 1445 (*Çinipuṅgavaḥ*, do.)].—§ 612 (Hradapraveçap.): IX, **29**, 1603 (at the injunction of Vyāsa *S.* set Sañjaya free); **30**ε, 1726.—§ 613 (Gadāyuddhap.): IX, [**32**β, 1831 (*Yuyudhānāt*)]; **33**θ, 1917.—§ 614 (do.): IX, **34**a, 1962.—§ 615 (do.): IX, [**35**, 1983 (*Yuyudhānena*, had sided the Pāṇḍavas); **61**, 3422 (*Çaineyena*, had slain Bhūriçravas)]; **62**ψ, 3461, 3496, 3497 (the Pāṇḍavas and *S.* passed the night outside the camp).—§ 616 (Sauptikap.): X, [**5**, 197 (*Yuyudhānena*, had slain Bhūriçravas)]; **8**, 473 (absent when the nightly encounter took place); **9**, 528 (among the seven survivers of the Pāṇḍava army).—§ 617 (Aishīkap.): X, **10**, 550.—[§ 618 (Jalapradānikap.): XI, **12**κ, 315 (*Yuyudhānena*)].—§ 619 (Strīvilāpap.): XI, **23**θ, 660 (*ācāryam S°eḥ . . . Droṇam*); **24**ι, [677 (*Yuyudhānena*, had slain Bhūriçravas), 678 (*Yuyudhānena*)], 687 (had slain Bhūriçravas), 690.—§ 635 (Rājadh.): XII, **37**, 1382 (accompanied Kṛshṇa).—§ 637 (do.): XII, **40**a, 1444; **44**δ, 1530; **46**, 1583, 1584, 1585; **47**, 1694 (in the same chariot as Kṛshṇa).—§ 639 (do.): XII, **50**, 1815; **52**ε, 1889; **53**, 1904, 1906, (θ), 1921.—§ 640 (do.): XII, **58**γ, 2116.—[§ 777 (Svargārohaṇik. p.): XIII, **168**, 7715 (*Yuyudhānena*, accompanied Yudhishṭhira)].—§ 783 (Anugītāp.): XIV, **52**, †1533, †1534 (accompanied Kṛshṇa).—§ 785 (do.): XIV, **59**, 1752 (do.), 1767; [**60**, 1804 (*Yuyudhānasahāyena*, sc. Kṛshṇa)]; **61**, 1840; **62**ε, 1855; [**66**θ, 1938 (*Yuyudhānena*, accompanied Kṛshṇa), 1946 (*Yuyudhānadvitīyena*, sc. Kṛshṇa); **86**τ, 2557 (*Yuyudhānena*, accompanied Kṛshṇa)].—[§ 787 (Āçramavāsap.): XV, **10**ν, 332 (*Yuyudhānena*)].—§ 793 (Mausalap.): XVI, **3**, 81, 90 (slew Kṛtavarman and was himself slain); [**6**κ, 155 (*Yuyudhānaḥ*), 157 (*Çaineyam*)]; **7**, 247 (*Yauyudhānim . . . putram S°eḥ*).—§ 795 (Svargārohaṇap.): XVIII, **1**δ, 24; **4**, 142 (°*pramukhān vīrān*, after death among the Sādhyas, etc.).

Cf. also the following synonyms:—

Ānartta ("belonging to the Ānartta tribe"): IX, 947.

Çaineya ("grandson of Çini"): V, †804, †1817, 2100, 2316, 2670, 7600; VI, 2334, 2486 (*Kurupuṅgavau*, i.e. Sātyaki and Abhimanyu), †2592, †2594, 3078, 3617, 3622, 4625, 4627, 4632, 4636, 4638, 5143, 5147, 5157, 5385; VII, †251 (°-*Bhīmārjunavāhinīçam*), 530, 951 (C. *Sai°*), 1073 (only B.), 1439, 3056, 3616, 3620 (*Droṇa-Ç°au*), 3624 (*Droṇa-Ç°yoḥ*), 4175, 4176, 4183, 4195, 4199, 4203, 4205, 4232, 4289, 4406, 4465, 4545, 4546, 4547, 4550, 4574, 4580, 4587, 4599, 4605, 4625, 4633, 4648, 4668, 4682, 4748, 4783 (°*velām*), 4793, 4806, 4807, 4809 (C. by error *Sai°*), 4820, 4822, 4824, 4833, 4838, 4861, 4935, 4951, 4958, 4968, 4975, 5104, 5105, †5839, 5847, 5854, 5870, 5900, 6001, 6027 (*utpattim Ç°sya*), 6348, 6353 (*Karṇa-Ç°yoḥ*), 6356, 6363, 6374, 6381, 6784, 7229, 7242, 7255, 7361, 7397, 7399, 7403, 7409, 7411, 7644, 7684, 7695, 7697, 7699, 7700, 7703, 7743 (°*pramukhān Pārthān*), 7747, 8809, 8810, 8812, 8813, 9185, 9302, 9318, 9320; VIII, 501, 509, 521, 522, 888 (*Pāñcāla-Ç°au*), 2277, 2283, 2652, 2675, 2676, 2729, 2923, 2925, 2927 (*Karṇa-Ç°yoḥ*), 3034, 3113, 3117, †3373, 3794, †4087 (*Çikhaṇḍi-Ç°-Yamāḥ*), †4185, †4186, †4306 (*Drupadasutavarishṭhāḥ . . . Ç°shashṭāḥ*); IX, 550, 682, 819, 967, 1110 (*Çinipuṅgavaḥ*), 1122, 1160, 3422 (had slain Bhūriçravas); XII, 1905, 1915; XIV, 86, 89, 91 (slain), 157.

Çaineyanandana ("delighter of the Çaineyas"): VII, 5111.

Çauri, q.v.

Çineḥ pautra(ḥ) ("grandson of Çini"): III, †10233; VII, 1073, 1170, 3606, 3610, 4576, 4636, 4650, 4669, 4780, 4787, 6344, 6355, 6359, 9186.

Çineḥ putra(ḥ) ("son of Çini"): VII, 4378.

Çineḥ suta(ḥ) ("son of Çini"): VII, 6041, 6043; XVI, 89.

Çiner naptā ("grandson of Çini"): III, 735, †12330; V, †1852 (*S°*), †1853, 2930 (*S°*); VI, 2356, 2808, 5361; VII, †248, †4696, 4815, †5833, †5840; VIII, 2756; IX, †871, †894, 933 (*S°*), †1084, 1099 (*S°*), 1604, 1606.

Çinīnām adhipa(ḥ), Çinīnām pravaro ratha(ḥ), Çinīnām ṛshabha(ḥ), v. Çini, pl.

Çinipravara ("the hero of the Çini race"); VII, 4949.

Çinipravīra (do.); III, †10286; V, †4, †40; VI, †2587, †2589, †2592, †2806 (*S°*); VII, †4684, †4697, †5825; VIII, †1213, †4185, †4206; IX, †1091; XIV, †1535.

Çinipuṅgava (do.); V, 5324; VI, 2485, 5142; VII, 3001, 3605, 4175, 4177, 4233, 4240, 4291, 4646, 4654, †4686, †4691, 4770, 4790, 4795, 4842, †5830, 5875, 5880, 5902, 7253 (only B.), 7745, 8285, 8651, 8655, 8799, 9177, 9183; VIII, 2157; IX, 938, 1101, 1105 (*Hārdikya-Ç°au*), 1110, 1113, 1115, 1121, 1445.

Çiniputra ("son of Çini"): VIII, †1211.

Çinivīra ("the hero of the Çini race"): VII, 4563.

Çinivṛshabha (do.): VIII, †1214, 1215.

Dāçārha ("belonging to the Daçārhas"): VII, 4233 (v. Dāçārha, pl.), 5882, 7638 (C. *Dās°*), 8671.

Mādhava, Mādhavāgrya, Mādhavasiṃha, Mādhavottama, Madhūdvaha, q.v.

Sātvata, Sātvataçreshṭha, Sātvatāgrya, Sātvatamukhya, Sātvatapravara, Sātvatarshabha, q.v.

Sātyaka ("son of Satyaka"): V, †653; VI, 1865, 2328, 2348, 4058 (only B.), 4695, 5155; VII, 633, 1441 (°*ārṇavāt*), 7281 (only B.); VIII, 2229, 3796.

Vārshṇeya, Vṛshṇi, Vṛshṇiçārdūla, Vṛshṇikulodvaha, Vṛshṇipravīra, Vṛshṇipuṅgava, Vṛshṇisiṃha, Vṛshṇivara, Vṛshṇivīra, Vṛshṇy-Andhakapravīra, Vṛshṇy-Andhakavyāghra, q.v.

Yādava, Yadūdvaha, Yadūttama, Yaduvīra, Yaduvyāghra, q.v.

Yuyudhāna, the proper name of Sātyaki: I, †194 (*Vārshṇeyam*); II, 129 (*S°*); III, 611, 2009 (-*Bhīmau*); IV, 2357 (*S°*); V, 55, 570 (*Sātvatānām mahārathaḥ*), †683, †723, †724, †783, 2006 (*Vṛshṇivīreṇa*), 2233 (*S°*), 2252, 2315, 2869, 4887 (°-*Yamaiḥ*), 5143 (°*dvitīyam*, sc. Dhṛshṭadyumna), 5175 (*S°*), 5708 (*Vārshṇeyam*), 7598, 7624, 7630; VI, 714, 780, 833, 3192 (°*ratham*), 3247, 3251 (°*sya sutāḥ*); VII, 339, 1169 (°*ratham*), 1170, 1380 (°*prabhṛtayaḥ*), 2953, 2982, 2983 (°-*Janārdanau*), 2991 (do.), 3000, 3609, 3612,

3641, 3648, 3651, 3657, 4045, 4049, 4134, 4135 (°*purogamaiḥ*), 4136, 4138, 4141, 4144, 4150, 4151 (°*ratham*), 4153, 4192, 4372, 4373, 4377 (°*ratham*), 4393 (*S*°), 4394, 4396, 4398, 4400, 4415, 4432, 4434, 4435, 4455, 4568, 4599, 4602, 4630, 4651, 4655, 4657, 4660, 4673, 4740, 4752, 4758, 4786, 4812, 4814, 4839, 4851 (°*ratham*), 4854, 4861, 4945 (°*ratham*), 4946, 4952, 5108, 5326 (°-*Vṛkodarau*), 5853, 5892, 5984, 6354 (*S*°), 6397, 6492 (°-*Vṛkodarau*), 6758, 6923, 7227, 7257, 7645 (*Vṛshṇīnāṃ pravaraḥ*), 7650, 7652, 7680 (°*ratham*), 7688, 7690, 7692 (°*ratham*), 7693, 7732, 8060, 8080, 8291, 8798, 9319; VIII, 845, 2276, 2280, 2286, 3318, †3813 (only C., read *yuvā yuvānaṃ* with B.), 4991; IX, 969, 1117, 1831, 1983; X, 197; XI, 315, 677 (had slain Bhūriçravas), 678; XIII, 7715; XIV, 1754 (°*ānugaḥ*, sc. Kṛshṇa), 1804 (°*sahāyena*, do.), 1938, 1946 (°*dvitīyaḥ*, sc. Kṛshṇa), 2557; XV, 332; XVI, 72, 73, 75, 85, 88, 155.

Satyaloka ("the world of truth"): XIII, 1073 (*satyakāmānāṃ S°aḥ*, said of Çiva).

Satyamedhas = Vishṇu (1000 names).

Satyapāla, a muni. § 264 (Sabhākriyāp.): II, **4***a*, 109 (only C., B. has *Saptapālaḥ*).

Satyaparākrama = Vishṇu (1000 names).

Satyaratha, a Trigarta prince. § 572 (Rathātirathasaṅkhyānap.): V, **166**, 5758 (the leader among five brothers of the Trigarta race, among the rathas of Duryodhana).—§ 591 (Saṃçaptakavadhap.): VII, **17***a*, 689 (with his four brothers among the Saṃçaptakas).

Satyasandha[1], son of Dhṛtarāshṭra. § 130 (Aṃçāvat.): I, **67**, 2735 (enumeration). — § 182 (Dhṛtarāshṭraputranāmak.): I, **117**, 4548.

Satyasandha[2], a Kuru warrior. § 556 (Sañjayayānap.): V, **23***θ*, 694 (= Bhūri?).

Satyasandha[3] = Bhīshma, q.v.

Satyasandha[4], son of Karṇa (if not a mere adj.?). § 604 (Karṇap.): VIII, **7**, †210 (*Karṇātmajaḥ*).

Satyasandha[5], a companion of Skanda. § 615*u* (Skanda): IX, **45**, 2543 (given to Skanda by Mitra).

Satyasandha[6] = Vishṇu (1000 names).

Satyasena[1], various Kuru warriors. § 604 (Karṇap.): VIII, **7**, †206 (the son of Dhṛtarāshṭra?, or the son of Karṇa?).—§ 605 (do.): VIII, **27***λλ*, 1078, 1083, 1086, 1090, 1094, 1096, 1097 (among the Saṃçaptakas, slain by Arjuna).

Satyasena[2], a son of Karṇa. § 608 (Karṇap.): VIII, **48**, 2251 (*Karṇasya putrau*, sc. *S.* and Susheṇa, guarded the wheels of Karṇa); **49**, 2329 (pierced by Yudhishṭhira).—§ 611 (Çalyap.): IX, **10**, 481 (*Karṇaputrau . . . Susheṇaḥ S°aç ca*), 487, 488, 489, 492, 495, 496, 499 (together with Susheṇa slain by Nakula).

Satyātman = Kṛshṇa: XII, 1638.

Satyavāc[1], a Devagandharva. § 100 (Aṃçāvat.): I, **65**, 2551 (the eighth of the sons of Muni).

Satyavāc[2] = Çāntanu: I, 3968. — Do.[3] = Skanda: III, 14631.

Satyavādin ("speaking the truth") = Kauçika[6]: VIII, 3449.

Satyavarman, a Kuru warrior (a Trigarta prince). § 591 (Saṃçaptakavadhap.): VII, **17***a*, 689 (among five brothers among the Saṃçaptakas).

Satyavat[1], son of Dyumatsena and husband of Sāvitrī. § 545 (Pativratop.): III, **294**, 16667, 16668, 16669, 16671, 16673, 16680, 16687; **295**, 16697, 16702 (*bhāryāṃ S°aḥ*, sc. Sāvitrī), 16707; **296**, 16714, (16733), (16735), 16741, 16744; **297**, (16749), 16755, 16759, 16763, †16778, †16784, †16792, †16799, †16801, 16805, (16812), 16815, (16824), (16829), (16846), 16849, (16853); **298**, 16861, 16868, 16871, 16872, 16873, 16874, 16875, 16876, 16877, 16878, 16883, (16887), 16898 (married Sāvitrī; when Yama came to fetch *S.*, Sāvitrī followed him and obtained several boons, among these the life of *S.*).—§ 551 (Kīcakavadhap.): IV, **21**, 655 (*Dyumatsenasutaṃ vīraṃ S°ntam aninditā Sāvitry anucacāraikā Yamalokaṃ manasvinī*, cf. § 545). — § 565 (Gālavacarita): V, **117**, 3971 (*reme . . . Sāvitryāṃ S°ān yathā*). — § 652*b* (Indrota-Pārīkshitīya): XII, **152**, 5649 (some gāthās of his are quoted).—§ 683 (Mokshadh.): XII, **268**, 9560 (*Dyumatsenasya saṃvādaṃ rājñā S°tā saha*), 9561, 9563, (9565), (9582), 9594 (!) (discourse between Dyumatsena and *S.*).—§ 744 (Ānuçāsanik.): XIII, **44**, 2451, 2454 (some çlokas of his in answer of a question about marriage are quoted).—§ 775 (do.): XIII, **166***η*, 7675 (enumeration). Cf. Citrāçva, Dyumatsenasuta.

Satyavat[2], a Kuru warrior. § 572 (Rathātirathasaṅkhyānap.): V, **167**, 5799 (*senāpatiḥ*, a mahāratha in the army of Duryodhana).

Satyavatī[1], daughter of Vasu and Adrikā, by Parāçara mother of Vyāsa, wife of Çāntanu and mother of Citrāṅgada and Vicitravīrya). — § 61 (Sarpasattra): I, **55**, †2103 (*Kṛshṇasya . . . S°yāḥ sutasya*, i.e. Vyāsa).—§ 76 (Matsya): I, **63**, 2398 (Matsya and *S.* were born by Adrikā from the seed of Vasu, *S.* had a fishy smell and was reared by a fisherman).—§ 77 (Vyāsa): I, **63**, (2405), 2413, 2415 (by Parāçara mother of Vyāsa, by the grace of Parāçara she remained a virgin and emitted a sweet scent extending over a yojana, thence she was named Gandhavatī or Yojanagandhā (v. 2411–12)).—§ 156 (Pūruvaṃç.): I, **95**, 3801 (by Çāntanu mother of Citrāṅgada and Vicitravīrya, formerly she had born Vyāsa).—§ 157 (do.): I, **95**, 3805 (appointed Vyāsa to beget children, cf. § 171).—§ 165 (Satyavatīlābhop.): I, **100**, 4043, 4044, 4045, 4055 (Çāntanu's receiving *S.* as his wife).—§ 166 (Citrāṅgadop.): I, **101**, 4069, 4071 (mother of Citrāṅgada and Vicitravīrya).—§ 167 (Vicitravīryop.): I, **102**, †4132, 4145.—§ 168 (Bhīshma-Satyavatī-saṃv.): I, **103**, 4146, 4159, 4164 (Bhīshma consulted with *S.*).—§ 171 (Vicitravīryasutotpatti): I, **105**, 4225, 4251, 4258, (4262), 4267; **106**, 4274, 4302 (asked by *S.* Vyāsa begat children on the widows of Vicitravīrya).—§ 174 (Dhṛtarāshṭravivāha): I, **110**, 4365.—§ 178 (Pāṇḍu): I, **114**, 4469, 4471.—§ 184 (do.): I, **119**, 4614.—§ 194 (do.): I, **126**, 4912.—§ 196 (Vyāsa): I, **128**, 4975 (retired to the forest with her daughters-in-law).—§ 238 (Pañcendrop.): I, **197**, 7318 (°*yāḥ sutaḥ*, i.e. Vyāsa).—§ 573 (Ambopākhyānap.): V, **173**, 5947, 5965; **174**, 5968, 5969; **176**, 6072, 6075 (repetition from § 166 foll.); **178**, 7099; **186**, 7339.—§ 602 (Droṇavadhap.): VII, **192**, 8881 (*ṛsheḥ . . . Kṛshṇasya S°yāḥ sutasya*).—§ 717*b* (Nārāyaṇīya): XII, **350**, 13639 (bore Vyāsa from Parāçara).—§ 778 (Açvamedhikap.): XIV, **10**, †292 (°*yāḥ sutasya*, i.e. Vyāsa). Cf. Dāçeyī, Gandhakālī, Gandhavatī (I, 2411; V, 5976; XII, 8835 (°*yāḥ sutaḥ*, i.e. Vyāsa)), Kālī, Satyā, Vāsavī, Yojanagandhā.

Satyavatī[2], daughter of Gādhi and wife of Ṛcīka. § 395 (Jamadagni): III, **115**, 10153 (married to Ṛcīka), 10163 (mother of Jamadagni).—§ 565 (Gālavacarita): V, **117**, 3973 (*reme . . . yathā . . . Ṛcīkaḥ S°yāñ ca*), **119**, 4005 (*Gādheḥ sutāṃ*, married to Ṛcīka).—§ 638*b* (Rāmopākhyāna): XII, **49**, 1721, 1728, 1730, 1735, (1739), 1742, 1744 (married to Ṛcīka, birth of Jamadagni).—§ 721*b* (Viçvāmitrop.): XIII,

4, 206, 228, 229, 234, 235, 241 (do., do.). Cf. Gādheyī, Gādhisutā.

Satyavatī[3], wife of Nārada. § 565 (Gālavacarita): V, **117**, 3974 (*reme . . . yathā S°yāñ ca Nāradaḥ*).

[Satyavatīlābhopākhyāna(m)] ("the episode relating how Çāntanu got Satyavatī"). § 165 (cf. Āpavop.): Description of *Çāntanu*, the princes anointed him as "King of Kings" (*rājarājyē*, v. 3974); he ruled the earth from *Hāstinapura*, the town (*puṭabhedana*) of the *Kurus* (v. 3978); there was no killing of deer, boars, etc., under his reign (cf. § 162!) except for the sacrifices to the gods, *ṛshis*, and *pitṛs*. For thirty-six years he, without enjoying the love of women, roamed about in the woods, and his son, *Gāṅgeya Devavrata*, the *Vasu*, was equal to him. One day, when pursuing a deer he had wounded along the banks of the *Gaṅgā*, he saw a youth who, with a heavenly weapon, checked the flow of the *Gaṅgā*. It was his son who, knowing him, but not known by him, and clouding his perception by illusion (*māyā*), suddenly disappeared. On *Çāntanu's* prayer, *Gangā* appeared holding the boy, and having told him that he was his son, and that he had studied all the *Vedas* and their *Aṅgas* with *Vasishṭha* and knew all *çāstras* that were known by *Uçanas* and *Bṛhaspati* (adored by the gods and *Asuras*), and by the *ṛshi Rāma Jāmadagnya*, and also the *rājadharmas*, she let him take him to his capital, where he was installed as heir-apparent. After four years *Çāntanu* met with *Satyavatī* in the wood on the banks of *Yamunā*, and demanded her hand from her father, the king of the fishermen (*dāçarāja*), who would not consent unless *Çāntanu* would promise that his son by *Satyavatī* should become his successor on the throne. *Çāntanu* would not grant the boon, but returned to *Hāstinapura* and passed his time in sorrow until *Devavrata*, having learned from the old minister the cause of his grief, by declaring that he would adopt the vow of *brahmacarya* (including celibacy), prevailed upon the fisherman (who had formerly rejected the *Devarshi Asita*, because *Parāçara* had pointed out to him *Çāntanu* as a suitable husband for her), that he gave *Satyavatī* to *Çāntanu*, while the gods and *ṛshis* showered flowers upon *Devavrata*, calling him *Bhīshma*. *Bhīshma* then took the maiden to *Hāstinapura* on his chariot, and *Çāntanu* bestowed upon him the boon of death at choice (I, **100**). (For continuation v. Citrāṅgadop.)

Satyavatīputra, Satyavatīsuta, Satyavatyātmaja = Vyāsa, q.v.

Satyavrata[1], an ancient king. § 6 (Anukram.): I, **1***a*, 229 (in Sañjaya's enumeration).

Satyavrata[2], a son of Dhṛtarāshṭra. § 100 (Aṃçāvat.). I, **67**, 2448 (enumeration).—§ 298 (Dyūtap.): II, **58**, †2004.—§ 561 (Yānasandhip.): V, **58**τ, 2301, (*v*), 2305.—§ 576 (Bhagavadgītap.): VI, **18**δ, 687.—§ 581 (Bhīshmavadhap.): VI, **62**ζ, 2732 (protected Çalya), 2743 (pierced by Abhimanyu).—§ 582 (do.): VI, **73**θ, 3221 (do.), 3222 (pierced Abhimanyu).—§ 596 (Pratijñāp.): VII, **74**β, 2628.—§ 599 (Jayadrathavadhap.): VII, **116** *aa*, 4609 (pierced by Sātyaki).—§ 604 (Karṇap.): VIII, **7**, †208.

Satyavrata[3], a Trigarta prince. § 591 (Saṃçaptakavadhap.): VII, **17** *a*, 689 (with four brothers among the Saṃçaptakas).

Satyavrata[4] = Çiva (1000 names[2]).

Satyepsu, an Asura (?). § 673*b* (Bali-Vāsavasaṃv.): XII, **227** *a*, 8263 (B. °*eshu*, among the ancient rulers of the earth).

Satyeshu, a Trigarta prince. § 591 (Saṃçaptakavadhap.): VII, **17** *a*, 689 (with his four brothers among the Saṃçaptakas).—§ 611 (Çalyap.): IX, **27**, 1482 (only B., slain by Arjuna).

Satyeyu, a prince. § 150 (Pūruvaṃç): I, **94**, 3701 (eighth son of Raudrāçva).

Saubala[1] = Çakuni, q.v.

Saubala[2], pl. (°*āḥ*) ("the sons of Subala"). § 585 (Bhīshmavadhap.): VI, **90**, 4010 (i.e. Gaja, etc.; cf. v. 3997), 4012. Cf. Subalalātmaja, pl.

Saubala[3], adj. ("belonging to Saubala [i.e. Çakuni]"). § 580 (Bhīshmavadhap.): VI, **58**, 2485 (°*īṃ senāṃ*).

Saubalaka = Çakuni, q.v.

Saubalaka, pl. (°*āḥ*), the followers of Çakuni. § 580 (Bhīshmavadhap.): VI, **58**[4], 2469 (*çūrāḥ*, attacked Sātyaki; cf. *Gāndhārāḥ*, v. 2468).

Saubaleya = Çakuni, q.v.

Saubaleyī, Saubalī = Gāndhārī, q.v.

Saubalya, pl. (°*āḥ*), a people. § 574 (Jambūkh.): VI, **9**μ, 347 (only C., B. has *Sauçalyāḥ*).

Saubha, the aerial city of Çālva[5]. § 317*b* (Kṛshṇa): III, **12**, 491 (*pātitaṃ*, sc. by Kṛshṇa; cf. § 319).—§ 319 (Saubhavadhap.): III, **14**, 615 (*Çālvasya nagaraṃ*), 619 (*kāmagaṃ*), 628 (*kāmagena*); **16**, 685 (do.), 688, 690; **17**, 695 (°*nivāsinaḥ*); **19**, 776; **20**, 786 (°*nagaraṃ*), 792, 793, 802, 805 (°*madhye*); **21**, 835, 840, †847; **22**, 849, 851, 857 (*kāmagamaṃ*), 875, 880, 882 (*nagaraṃ*), 883 (destroyed by Kṛshṇa), 884, 889.—§ 561*c* (Kṛshṇa Vāsudeva): V, **48**, 1886 (°*dvāri pratyagṛhṇāc chataghnīṃ dorbhyāṃ*, sc. Kṛshṇa). — § 567 (Bhagavadyānap.): V, **130**, 4405 (°*dvāre*, there the monkey Dvivida covered Kṛshṇa with a shower of stones).—§ 589 (Droṇābhishekap.): VII, **11**, 395 (*Daityapuraṃ khasthaṃ Çālvaguptaṃ*, destroyed by Kṛshṇa; cf. § 319).—§ 717*b* (Nārāyaṇīya): XII, **340**, 12959 (°*nivāsinaḥ*, will be destroyed by Kṛshṇa, in a prophecy).

Saubha[2] ("lord of the Saubha") = Çālva[5]: III, 632, 636, 654; V, †1886 (*Çālvarājaṃ*).

Saubhādhipati (do.) = Çālva[5]: III, †12590.

Saubhadra ("the son of Subhadrā") = Abhimanyu: I, †188, 489 (*A*°), 1947 (°*syātmajaḥ*, i.e. Parikshit), 8025, 8034; II, 1609; IV, 2369, 2371; V, 59, †1841 (*Indrapratimaṃ*), 2231 (°*ādīn*), 2250 (selected Bṛhadbala as his match in the battle), 4737, 4787, 5152, 5710 (pitted against Vṛshasena, etc.); VI, 835, 847, 1655, 1684 (B. *Abhimanyor*), 1685, 1832, 1833, 1835, 1865, 2128, 2363, 2366, 2367, 2370, 2375, 2485, †2675, 2680, 2685, 2755, 2761, 2762, 2771 (°*pramukhā rathāḥ*), 3066, 3169, 3220, 3227, 3230, 3231, 3232, 3283, 3391 (°*pramukhā vīrāḥ*), 3472, 3477, 3480 (°*pramukhān rathān*), 3735, 4361, 4362, 4363, 4364, 4531, 4534, 4537, 4544, 4554, 4585, 4588, 4604, 4614, 4749, 4998, 5007, 5365 (*Karṇikāradhvajaṃ*), 5383, 5405, 5407, 5551; VII, 227, †251, 355, 544, 546, 547, 550, 566, 571, 575, 579, 581, 584, 587, 588, 1042 (Balarāma gave him the bow Raudra), 1179, 1443, 1473, 1474 (*nihate*), 1478, 1479, 1492 (*A*°), 1518, 1535, 1538, 1580, 1585, 1586, 1590, 1592, 1596, 1608, 1619, 1625, 1635, 1646, 1652, 1653, 1656, 1668, 1669, 1672, 1674 (*A*°), 1690, 1693, 1700, 1702, 1705, 1707, 1712, 1713, 1719, 1724, 1727, 1735, 1779, 1784, 1791, 1793, 1813, 1816, 1819, 1829, 1834, 1835, 1839, 1845, 1848, 1857, 1866, 1867, 1883, 1889, 1906, 1907, 1932, 1939, 1940, 1954, 1960, 1982 (*nihate*), 1983, 1989, 2005 (*nihataḥ*), 2006, 2492, 2495, 2497, 2499, 2555, 2570, 2575, 6403 (*nihataḥ*), 7665 (°*vat*), 8338, 9167 (*vinipātitaḥ*), 9225 (*ghātitaḥ*); VIII, 102 (had slain the son of Duryodhana), 110 (had slain Bṛhadbala), 112 (had slain the son of Çalya), 120 (had slain the Māgadha king Jayatsena), 160 (slain by Dauḥçāsani), 296, 3705 (*nihataṃ*), 3709, 3711; X, 584; XI, 418 (*āryaputrāḥ . . .*

S°sahitāḥ), 573, 595; XII, 15; XIV, 1812 (*°vadham*), 1960; XV, 807 (*°vadha-*), 844, 856 (incarnation of Soma), 875, 892; XVIII, 143 (*A°*).

Saubhadra[2], name of a tīrtha. § 250 (Arjunavanavāsap.): I, **216**, 7841, 7847 (*maharshes tīrtham uttamam*, one of the five Nārītīrthāni, q.v.).

Saubhapati ("lord of the Saubha") = Çālva[5]: III, 491 (*Ç°*), 659, 689, 711, 808 (C. by error *Çau°*), 869 (*Ç°*).—Do.[2] = Çālva[4]: I, 4133 (chosen by Ambā to become her husband); V, 6076 (*Ç°*), 6084.

Saubhara, name of a fire, son of Varcas. § 491 (Āṅgirasa): III, **220**, 14164 (*putro Varcasya*).

Saubharāj[1] ("king of the Saubha") = Çālva[5]: III, 624, 690, 706, 761, 763, 765.—Do.[2] = Çālva[4]: V, 7018.

Saubhavadhākhyāna ("the story of the destruction of Saubha"). § 71 (Parvasaṅgr.): I, **2**, 428 (i.e. Saubhavadhopākhyāna).

[Saubhavadhopākhyāna(m)] ("the episode relating to the destruction of Saubha"; cf. Saubhavadhākhyāna). § 319 (cf. Arjunābh.). *Kṛshṇa* related: When *Çiçupāla*, the son of *Damaghosha*, had been slain, his brother, the *Mārttikāvata*-king *Çālva*, in order to avenge him, came to *Dvārakā* in the *Saubha*, who moved at will and slew many of the *Vṛshṇis*, and sought for *Kṛshṇa* desiring to kill him. *Kṛshṇa* was in *Indraprastha* at the *rājasūya* of Yudhishṭhira, and when he learnt this on returning home, he set out to slay him, and found him in an island in the ocean (see Nīl. and PCR.; BR. "a bay"), and blowing his conch *Pāñcajanya*, slew numerous *Dānavas*. Then, as soon as he heard of the game at dice, he had come to the *Pāṇḍavas* (III, **14**).—§ 320. Copious description of the combats with *Çālva*: When *Çālva* attacked *Dvārakā* it was well furnished and strongly fortified (description of fortifications and measures taken to defend the city by *Ugrasena*, *Uddhava*, etc.) and defended by *Gada*, *Çāmba*, etc. (III, **15**). *Cārudeshṇa* (son of *Kṛshṇa* and *Rukmiṇī*), *Çāmba* (son of *Kṛshṇa* and *Jāmbavatī*), and *Pradyumna* (son of *Kṛshṇa* and *Rukmiṇī*) rushed out against him. They on both sides fought by means of *māyā*. *Çāmba* put *Kshemavṛddhi*, the commander of *Çālva's* troops, to flight by a shower of arrows, and slew a *Daiteya* named *Vegavat* with his mace. *Cārudeshṇa* slew the *Dānava Vivindhya* with a consecrated arrow. Then *Çālva*, riding on *Saubha*, encountered *Pradyumna* (III, **16**). Riding on his chariot with a gaping *makara* in its standard, *Pradyumna* with showers of arrows slew the *Dānavas* and pierced the heart of *Çālva* so that he fell in a swoon, but he rose again and wounded *Pradyumna* about his throat so that he became senseless (III, **17**). *Pradyumna's* charioteer *Dāruki*, a *sūta*, carried him off the field by the help of his fleet steeds, but when *Pradyumna* had regained his senses, he ordered him to turn the chariot, reminding him of the customs of the *Vṛshṇis* in battle, and saying that he had restrained *Kṛtavarman*, the son of *Hṛdika*, from sallying out, as he would himself resist *Çālva* (III, **18**). As Çālva used his *māyā* of the *Asuras*, *Pradyumna* shot him down with the *Brahmāstra*, and was about to aim another arrow at him, capable of killing any person, when all the hosts of the gods, with *Indra* and *Dhaneçvara* (i.e. Kubera), sent *Nārada* and *Çvasana* (i.e. the Wind), who ordered him to desist as the creator (*Dhātṛ*) had destined *Kṛshṇa*, the son of *Devakī*, to slay him. *Çālva* then mounted *Saubha* and went away through the skies leaving *Dvārakā* (III, **19**). When *Çālva* had left *Dvārakā*, *Kṛshṇa* returned from the *rājasūya*, and found *Dvārakā* deprived of its splendour, etc. He learnt from *Hārdikya* (i.e. Kṛtavarman) about the invasion of *Çālva*, committed the city to the charge of king *Āhuka* and *Ānakadundubhi* (i.e. Vasudeva), etc., bowed to *Bhava* (i.e. Çiva), and set out on his chariot yoked with *Çaibya* and *Sugrīva* and with *Dāruka* for his charioteer, blowing the *Pāñcajanya*, till he arrived at *Mārttikāvata*, and pursued *Çālva* (*Daiteyāpasadaḥ*, v. 796), who, staying in *Saubha*, remained in the sky above the midst of the ocean a *kroça* off, so that *Kṛshṇa's* soldiers could not see it, but were obliged to stand as mere spectators. After a long battle with arrows, in which *Kṛshṇa* killed numerous *Dānavas*, they took to fight by means of illusion, whirling maces, ploughshares, etc., and then mountain peaks. As none could ascertain whether it was day or night, or distinguish the points of the horizon, *Kṛshṇa*, becoming bewildered, made use of the *Prajñāstra*, by which he regained light (III, **20**). *Dāruka* was covered all over with shafts. Then a messenger of *Āhuka* came from *Dvārakā*, saying that *Çālva* had come to *Dvārakā* and had slain *Vasudeva*. *Kṛshṇa* thought that then *Sātyaki*, *Baladeva*, *Pradyumna*, *Cārudeshṇa*, *Çāmba*, etc., must necessarily have been killed first. Now he saw *Vasudeva* falling from *Saubha*, and swooned away; but, as he, after regaining consciousness, saw neither *Saubha*, nor *Çālva*, nor *Vasudeva*, he concluded that it was illusion (III, **21**). Though *Kṛshṇa* could not see *Saubha*, which had vanished through illusion, he discharged many arrows from the *Çārṅga*. The *Dānavas* set up a loud howl, and when *Kṛshṇa*, making use of a weapon that pierced the foe following the sound, killed them at one place, the yell ceased at that place and started from another quarter. Then *Saubha* reappeared at *Prāgjyotisha*. *Kṛshṇa*, *Dāruka*, and the horses were covered by torrents of rocks that concealed them, and the *Vṛshṇis* fled in all directions. *Kṛshṇa* then destroyed the crags with *Indra's* thunderbolt, *Dāruka* pointed at *Çālva* and exhorted *Kṛshṇa* to slay him. *Kṛshṇa* made use of his *Āgneya* weapon and hurled his discus *Sudarçana* (*b*) against the city of *Saubha*, that fell cut in twain like the city of *Tripura* by the shafts of *Maheçvara*. Then the discus came back into his hands and was hurled against *Çālva* and cut him in twain. The remaining *Dānavas* fled in fear. *Kṛshṇa* returned to the *Ānarttas*. It was for this reason that he could not come to *Hāstinapura* and prevent the gambling.—§ 321: Then *Kṛshṇa* took leave of *Yudhishṭhira*, etc., and set out for *Dvārakā* in his chariot yoked with *Çaibya* and *Sugrīva*, taking with him *Subhadrā* and *Abhimanyu*. Then *Dhṛshṭadyumna* set out for his own city, taking with him the *Draupadeyas*. And the *Cedi* king, *Dhṛshṭaketu* (*Çiçupāla's* son, Nīl.), set out for his beautiful city of *Çuktimatī*, taking with him his sister [*Kareṇumatī*, the wife of *Nakula*; Nīl., v. I, 3831]. Also the Kaikeyas (B. *Kekayāḥ*; *Sahadevaçyālāḥ*, Nīl.) went away. But the brahmans, *vaiçyas*, and inhabitants of the country would not leave the *Pāṇḍavas*. *Yudhishṭhira* in due time ordered his men to make the chariots ready (III, **22**). (For continuation v. Dvaitavanaprav.).

Saucitti, a prince (probably patron. of Satyadhṛti). § 573 (Ambopākhyānap.): V, **196**μ, 7649 (*Satyadhṛtiḥ*).—§ 585 (Bhīshmavadhap.): VI, **93**ψ, 4151 (*Satyadhṛtiḥ*).—§ 592 (Saṃçaptakavadhap.): VII, **23**o, 986 (different from Satyadhṛti), 990 (*Satyadhṛtiḥ*).

Sauçalya, pl., v. Saubalya, pl.

Sauçruti, a Kuru warrior. § 605 (Karṇap.): VIII, **27**$\lambda\lambda$, 1078, 1084, 1086, 1088 (among the Saṃçaptakas, slain by Arjuna).

Saudāsa ("the son of Sudāsa") = Kalmāshapāda (Mitrasaha):

I, 4736, 6774; III, 13817; XII, 1792 (*dāyādaḥ S°sya . . . Sarvakarmā*); XIII, 326 (*Koçalādhipaḥ*), 3732 (*Ikshvākuvamçajo rājā*), 3734; XIV, 1654, 1656 (*purushādam*), (1672), (1674), (1679), 1681, (1691), (1694), (1700), (1704).

Saudeva ("the son of Sudeva") = Divodāsa: XIII, 1954 (*D°*), 1967.

Saudyumni ("the son of Sudyumna") = Yuvanāçva: III, 10432, 10435.

saugandha, name of a caste: XIII, 2584.

[Saugandhikāharaṇam] ("the bringing of the fragrant lotuses"; cf. Tīrthayātrāp.). § 431: When *Bhīma* was embraced by *Hanumat* his fatigue went off. *Hanumat* asked him not to tell anyone that he dwelt there; this was the time of the arrival of the gods and of the *Gandharvas* (cf. v. 11220); he declared himself willing if *Bhīma* might wish it to go to *Hāstinapura* and slay the *Dhārtarāshṭras*, etc., and dive into the army of his foes, giving leonine roars and remaining on the flagstaff of *Arjuna's* chariot. Then *Hanumat* vanished (III, **151**).—§ 432: Description of the proceeding of *Bhīma* along the *Gandhamādana* till he found the lotuses (III, **152**). Description of the lotus-lake, near *Kailāsa*, guarded by hundreds of thousands of *Rākshasas* (called *Krodhavaçāḥ*), sprung from a cascade near the abode of *Kubera*, the sporting place of *Kubera*, frequented by *Gandharvas*, *Apsarases*, gods, divine *ṛshis*, *Yakshas*, *Kimpurushas*, *Rākshasas*, and *Kinnaras*. *Bhīma* drank of the water (III, **153**). The *Krodhavaças* ordered *Bhīma* to ask the permission of *Kubera* before he entered the lake; but *Bhīma* plunged into the water, and as the *Rākshasas* attacked him, he slew 100 of them with his mace, inlaid with golden plates, and then drank of the water, by which his strength was fully restored, and gathered *saugandhika*-lotuses, while the *Krodhavaças* fled through the sky to the peaks of *Kailāsa* and gave account to *Kubera*, who said: "Let *Bhīma* take as many lotuses as he likes." The *Rākshasas* then returned to *Bhīma* (III, **154**).—§ 433: As there arose a violent wind with gravel, meteors, thunder, darkness, earthquake, dust, and evil omens, *Yudhishṭhira*, having learned from *Kṛshṇā* the depart of *Bhīma*, and alleging that *Bhīma* had not formerly done any wrong to the *Siddhas* (*siddhānām brahmavādinām*, v. 11415), resolved to find out *Bhīma* and let *Ghaṭotkaca* carry *Kṛshṇā*, while other *Rākshasas* carried the *Pāṇḍavas* and the brahmans, and so they proceeded with *Lomaça* to the lake, where the slaughtered *Yakshas* were lying, and *Yudhishṭhira* entreated *Bhīma* never again to offend the gods; the *Pāṇḍavas* began to sport in the lake, and the warders (i.e. the Rākshasas), with rocks for weapons, bowed down in humility. There they dwelt for a short time on the slopes of *Gandhamādana*, expecting *Arjuna* (III, **155**).—§ 434: One day when *Yudhishṭhira*, remembering the tīrthas, rivers (*Ilā*, etc.), etc., that they had visited, consulted with *Bhīma* how they should repair to the abode of *Vaiçravaṇa* (*b*), a voice from the sky said that they must first return to *Badarī* and thence to the hermitage of *Vṛshaparvan* (*c*) and that of *Ārshṭishena*. There came a shower of blossoms. According to the counsel of *Dhaumya*, they all returned to the hermitage of *Nara* and *Nārāyaṇa* (III, **156**).

Saugandhikavana, name of a place. § 370 (Tīrthayātrāp.): III, **84**, 7082 (a tīrtha).—§ 430 (Hanūmad-Bhīmasamv.): III, **150**, 11286.—§ 432 (Saugandhikāharaṇa): III, **152**, 11339, 11349.—§ 565 (Gālavacarita): V, **111**, 3832 (in the north, guarded by Nairṛtas).

Sauhṛda, pl. (°āḥ), a people. § 574 (Jambūkh.): VI, **9**ν, 367 (in the south).

Saukanya(m) ākhyāna(m) ("the episode relating to Sukanyā"). § 11 (Parvasaṅgr.): I, **2**, 445 (i.e. Sukanyopākhyāna).

Saumadatti[1] ("the son of Somadatta") = Bhūriçravas: I, 536 (C. by error *So°*); II, 1713; III, 15084; V, †791, †887, 4171 (*Bh°*), 5530 (*°timiṅgilam*, sc. *purushodadhim*, i.e. the army of Duryodhana), 5573 (do.), 5742 (*Bh°*); VI, 837, 1653, 1705, 2092, 2108 (only B., C. has *Somadattaḥ*), †2672, 2688, †2811 (*Bh°*), 2815, 3261, 3298, 3730, 3731, 3934, 4244, 4407, 5052, 5103, 5184 (*Bh°*), 5187, 5188; VII, 537 (*°-Çikhaṇḍinau*), 539, 1116, 1117, 1650, 3027, 3098, 3540 (*°purogamāḥ*), 3921, 3947 (*°eḥ punar yūpo yajñaçīlasya dhīmataḥ / dhvajaḥ sūrya ivābhāti somaç cātra pradṛçyate*), 3948, 4329, 5900, 5901, 5908, 5931, 5942, 6001, 6043, 6328, 6337 (only B.), 6526 (*hataḥ*), 6783 (*°vadhāt*), 8307 (*°er vadhāt*), 9158 (*hataḥ*); VIII, 3646; XI, 686 (*Yūpaketoḥ*).

Saumadatti[2] (do.) = Çala(?): VII, 3979, 4053, 4055, 4056, 4060, 4064 (fought against the Draupadeyas and was slain by the son of Sahadeva).

Saumaki[1] ("king of the Somakas" or "descendant of Somaka") = Drupada: I, 5192, †7198 (*rājā*), †7345; II, 126 (*Yajñasenaḥ*), †2523 (do.).

Saumaki[2] ("descendant of Somaka") = Satyadharman: V, 4779 (*S°*).

Saumaki[3] (do.) = Dhṛshṭadyumna or Çikhaṇḍin: V, 5162 (*Yājñaseniḥ*).

Saumaki[4] (do.) = Kshatradharman: VII, 3049 (*K°*).

Saumitri = Lakshmaṇa,[1] q.v.

Saumya[1], a ṛshi. § 265 (Lokapālasabhākhyānap.): II, **5**, 145 (accompanied Nārada).

Saumya[2] = Kṛshṇa: VI, 2946; XI, 556.

***Saumya**, adj. ("belonging to Soma (the Moon)"). § 305 (Dyūtap.): II, **78**, 2578 (*ātmapradānam saumyam tvam*, B. *saumyatvam*).—§ 440 (Yakshayuddhap.): III, **164**, 11900 (sc. *astram*).—§ 512 (Ghoshayātrāp.): III, **245**, 14995 (do.).—§ 588 (Bhīshmavadhap.): VI, **121**β, 5801 (do.).—§ 603*b* (Nārāyaṇa): VII, **201**ζ, 9466 (*karma*).—§ 615*u* (Skanda): IX, **46**, 2654 (sc. *mātaraḥ*).—§ 616 (Sauptikap.): X, **7**, 304 (*mantreṇa*).—§ 746 (Ānuçāsanik.): XIII, **76**, †3675 (*gāvaḥ*).

saupāka, name of a caste: XIII, 2589 (read with B. *saupākaḥ*).

Sauparṇa, adj. ("belonging to Suparṇa, i.e. Garuḍa"). § 585 (Bhīshmavadhap.): VI, **90**, 4045 (*rūpam*).—§ 608 (Karṇap.): VIII, **53**, 2592 (*astram*).

Sauptika(m) ("the nightly encounter"). § 10 (Parvasaṅgr.): I, **2**, 347 (*°m parva*, i.e. Sauptikaparvan).—§ 11 (do.): I, **2**, 561 (do., do.), 579 (*parva*, i.e. the tenth book of Mhbhr.), 581 (*°-Aishīkasambaddhe parvaṇi*).—§ 793 (Mausalap.): XVI, **3**, 82 (all. to § 616).

[Sauptikaparvan(°va)] ("the section including the nightly attack"): (*a*) the 10th of the greater parvans of Mhbhr., including the 83rd and the 84th of the minor parvans; (*b*) the 83rd of the minor parvans; cf. Sauptika). § 616: *Açvatthāman*, etc. proceeded towards the south. At the hour of sunset they reached a spot near the encampment. Hearing the shouts in the *Pāṇḍava* camp, they proceeded farther and reached a dense forest. *Dhṛtarāshṭra* interrupted *Sañjaya* by expressing his grief for *Duryodhana*, and then inquired about the acts of the three survivors (*a*). *Sañjaya* continued: *Açvatthāman*, etc., laid themselves down for rest under a huge banyan; *Kṛpa* and *Kṛtavarman* fell asleep;

Açvatthāman was kept awake by wrath and the desire of vengeance. He saw a fierce owl coming to that banyan and slaying a large number of crows roosting on its branches; at this sight he formed the resolution of slaying the *Pāṇḍava* army while buried in sleep; he roused *Kṛpa* and *Kṛtavarman*, unfolded his project before them, and asked for their advice (X, **1**); *Kṛpa* dissuaded him from executing his wicked design; "Let us repair to *Dhṛtarāshṭra*, *Gāndhārī*, and *Vidura*, and ask them as to what we should do" (X, **2**); *Açvatthāman* tried to refute *Kṛpa's* arguments (β) (X, **3**). *Kṛpa* promised to aid *Açvatthāman* if the latter would fight the foe the next morning during daylight (γ); *Açvatthāman's* answer: he would not desist (δ) (X, **4**). *Kṛpa* earnestly remonstrated with *Açvatthāman*, who declared his resolution to be unaltered (ε), yoked his steeds to his chariot, and proceeded alone, saying that he would avenge his father (ζ); *Kṛpa* and *Kṛtavarman* followed him. Approaching the *Pāṇḍava* camp, *Açvatthāman* stopped at the gate (X, **5**). He beheld a being of gigantic frame (description; hundreds and thousands of *Hṛshīkeças* issued from its flames) ready to resist him, and fearlessly fought it; it devoured all the weapons of *Açvatthāman*, who repented of his rash deed, and resolved to seek the protection of *Mahādeva* (X, **6**), to whom he recited a hymn (η). A golden altar appeared before him with a blazing fire on it; many mighty beings of extraordinary appearance came there (description), worshippers of *Mahādeva*. *Açvatthāman* felt no fear at the sight; he offered himself to *Mahādeva* as a libation on the fire; *Mahādeva* appeared and declared that the period of life of everybody in the camp had ran out; he gave a sword to *Açvatthāman* and filled him with his own energy; many invisible beings and Rā. proceeded to his right and left as he set out (X, **7**). He asked *Kṛpa* and *Kṛtavarman* to stand at the gate and slay everybody who would seek to escape; he entered the *Pāṇḍava* camp like a thief and slew *Dhṛshṭadyumna*, etc. (θ) (description; he employed the *Rudra* weapon); Rā. uttered loud roars in joy; also Y. came there; *Kṛpa* and *Kṛtavarman* set fire to the *Pāṇḍava* camp in three places; "*Arjuna* is incapable of being vanquished by D., As., G., Y., and Rā." Before midnight the vast host of the *Pāṇḍavas* was slain by *Açvatthāman*; the camp was invaded by Rā. and Pç. that gorge upon blood and flesh. *Açvatthāman* forgot his grief for his father; when morning dawned he issued from the camp and joined *Kṛpa* and *Kṛtavarman*. *Dhṛtarāshṭra* asked why *Açvatthāman* did not achieve such a feat before; *Sañjaya* answered that the absence of the *Pāṇḍavas* with *Kṛshṇa*, as also the sleep, was the cause of *Açvatthāman's* success. They congratulated each other and resolved to give notice of the slaughter to *Duryodhana* (X, **8**). They beheld *Duryodhana* still living, surrounded by wolves, hyenas, etc. They lamented and informed him (ι); *Açvatthāman* asked him, when he came to heaven, to inform *Droṇa* and embrace *Bāhlīka*, etc. (κ), and informed him who were yet alive (λ) and who had been slain (μ). *Duryodhana* regained his senses and praised *Açvatthāman*, etc. (ν). Saying "we shall all meet again in heaven", he gave up his life-breaths; his soul ascended to heaven. At early dawn *Sañjaya* came to the city and lost his spiritual sight. *Açvatthāman*, etc., ascended their chariots. *Dhṛtarāshṭra* breathed long and hot sighs (X, **9**).

***Saura**, adj. ("belonging to Sūrya (the Sun)"). § 417 (Yavakrītop.): III, **138**, 10812 (*vedasya*, learnt by Arvāvasu).—§ 512 (Ghoshayātrāp.): III, **245**, 14995 (sc. *astraṃ*, employed by Arjuna).—§ 586 (Bhīshmavadhap.): VI, **101**, 4608 (*astraṃ*, employed by Abhimanyu, only C.)—§ 615*u* (Skanda): IX, **46**, 2656 (sc. *mātaraḥ*).—Do.², pl. ("worshippers of the sun"): VII, 2926.

Saurabheya, mostly pl. (°*āḥ*) ("sons of Surabhi," i.e. cattle, sg. bull): I, 4195 (sg.) = *Kāmadhenuputraḥ*, Nīl.); V, 5262 (°*ā ivarshabhaṃ*); VII, 163 (do.); VIII, 4416 (pl.); XII, 10261 (*khorakaḥ S°ānāṃ*), 13866 (*nāgāḥ*, read *Sauraseyāḥ*); XIII, 842 (°*gataṃ*, sc. Çiva).

Saurabheyī, an Apsaras. § 250 (Arjunavanavāsap.): I, **213**, 7858 (among the five Apsarases who were delivered from a curse by Arjuna).—§ 269 (Varuṇasabhāv.): II, **10**, 394 (in the palace of Varuṇa).

Saurabheyī, mostly pl. (°*yyaḥ*) ("daughters of Surabhi," i.e. kine): XIII, 1370 (sg.), 3713, 3754.

Saurabhī ("daughter of Surabhi," i.e. cow): I, 6120 (*iva*); V, 3609 (*Surūpā nāma*).

Sauratha, pl. (°*āḥ*), a tribe or family among the Çibis. § 466 (Çibi): III, **197**, ††13300 (*Kapotaromāṇaṃ . . . ṛshabhaṃ S°ānāṃ*).

Sauratheya = Çibi¹: III, †13297.

Saurī ("daughter of Sūrya (the Sun)") = Tapatī: I, 3738 (*T°*).

Saurya, adj. (= Saura): XIII, †3675 (*gāvaḥ*).

Sauti¹ ("son of the Sūta [i.e. Lomaharshaṇa]") = Ugraçravas, the reciter of the Mhbhr.—§ 1 (Anukram.): I, **1**, 1 (*Lomaharshaṇaputra Ugraçravāḥ*), 7, (9).—§ 2 (do.): I, **1**, (22).—§ 4 (do.): I, **1**, (74), (93) (only B., C. has *Sūtaḥ*), (217).—§ 5 (do.): I, **1**, (219).—§ 7 (do.): I, **1**, (245).—§ 8 (Parvasaṅgr.): I, **2**, (271).—§ 9 (do.): I, **2**, (289).—§ 12 (Paushyap.): I, **3**, (661).—§ 17 (do., Uttaṅka): I, **3**, (837), (839), (848).—§ 18 (Paulomap.): I, **4**, ††851 (*Lomaharshaṇaputra Ugraçravāḥ*), 856, (859).—§ 20 (do., Pulomā): I, **5**, (875), (888); **6**, (897) (only B.); **7**, (911), (922), (935).—§ 23 (do., Pramadvarā): I, **9**, (964), (978).—§ 24 (do., Sahasrapad): I, **10**, (991).—§ 25 (do., do.): I, **12**, (1017).—§ 26 (Āstīkap., Jaratkāru): I, **13**, 1021, (1023), (1025); **14**, (1051); **15**, (1058).—§ 27 (do., Kaçyapa): I, **16**, 1069, (1072), (1082).—§ 28 (do., Amṛtamanthana): I, **17**, (1098); **18**, (1112), (1117); **19**, (1158).—§ 29 (do., Kadrū): I, **20**, (1189), (1193).—§ 30 (do., do.): I, **21**, (1205).—§ 31 (do., do.): I, **22**, (1223).—§ 34 (do., Garuḍa): I, **24**, (1263).—§ 36 (do., Kadrū): I, **25**, (1279).—§ 38 (do., do.): I, **26**, (1296).—§ 39 (do., Ramaṇīyaka): I, **27**, (1304).—§ 40 (do., Garuḍa): I, **27**, (1318); **28**, (1320), (†1335); **29**, (1340), (1344).—§ 42 (do., do.): I, **29**, (1371).—§ 43 (do., do.): I, **30**, (1384), (1399), (1401).—§ 44 (do., do.): I, **30**, (1426).—§ 45 (do., Vālakhilya): I, **31**, (1439), (1458).—§ 46 (do., Garuḍa): I, **32**, (1471); **33**, (1496); **34**, (1525), (1531).—§ 47 (do., Sarpanāmakathana): I, **35**, (1549).—§ 48 (do., Çesha): I, **36**, (1585), (1587).—§ 49 (do., Vāsuki): I, **37**, (1589) (C. by error *So°*), (1597); **38**, (1622); **39**, (1641), (1652).—§ 50 (do., Jaratkāru): I, **40**, (1657).—§ 51 (do., Parikshit): I, **40**, (1661); **41**, (1690), (1701), (1706); **42**, (1737); **43**, (1769), (1772), (1783), (1787) (only B., C. has *Sūtaḥ*), (1790).—§ 53 (do., Jaratkāru): I, **46**, (1846); **47**, (1869), (1872).—§ 55 (do., Āstīka): I, **48**, (1912), (1924).—§ 56 (do., Parikshit): I, **49**, (1934), (1937), (1953).—§ 57 (do., Janamejaya): I, **50**, (1992).—§ 58 (do., do.): I, **51**, (2015), (2022).—§ 58 bis (do., Sarpasattra): I, **52**, (2032).—§ 59 (do., do.): I, **53**, (2044).—§ 60 (do., do.): I, **53**, (2058); **54**, (2067), (2070), (2083), (2092).—§ 61 (do., do.): I, **55**, (†2113).—§ 62 (do., do.): I, **56**, (†2116), (2126), (2134), (2139) (C. by error *So°*).—

§ 63 (do., do.): I, **57**, (2143).—§ 68 (do., Āstika): I, **58**, (2166), (2170), (†2184), (2192) (only B., C. has *Sūtaḥ*).—§ 70 (Ādivaṃçāvatāraṇap.): I, **59**, 2198, 2201, (2202), (2206); **60**, (2208), (2227).—§ 294 (Dyūtap.): II, **50**, 1788/89 (only B.).—§ 717*b* (Nārāyaṇīya): XII, **341**, (13011); **344**, 13304, 13305; **347**, (13441).—§ 790 (Putradarçanap.): XV, **34**, (920); **35**, (944), (955).—§ 795 (Svargārohaṇap.): XVIII, **5**, (154).—§ 795*b* (Janamejaya): XVIII, **5**, (178). Cf. Sūta (instead of which B. generally reads *Sauti*).

Sauti[2] = Sañjaya: I, 147.

Sauti[3] = Dāruki: III, 721, 722, (723), 728, 732, 745, 747.

Sauti[4] = Bandin: III, 10688.

Sauti[5] ("the son of the Sūta" [i.e. Adhiratha]) = Karṇa: V, 215; VII, †8169, 8275; VIII, 3630, †4571, †4573; XIV, 1793.

sautrāmaṇi, name of a sacrifice: IX, 2890; XIII, 5381.

Sauvīra[1] ("king of the Sauvīras"). § 211 (Sambhavap.): I, **139**, 5534.

Sauvīra[2] (do.) = Vipula (C. Vitula): I, 5536 (*V*°).

Sauvīra[3] (do.) = Sumitra: I, 5537 (*S*°).

Sauvīra[4] (do.) = Jayadratha: III, 15617, 15723.

Sauvīra[5] (do.) = Çalya: VIII, 331 (*Madrāṇām adhipaḥ*).

Sauvīra, pl. (°*āḥ*), a people = Suvīra, pl. § 291 (Çiçupālavadhap.): II, **45**, 1569.—§ 522 (Draupadīharaṇap.): III, **265**, †15600 (°*vīrāḥ*); **267**, 15617 (°*ābhimukhaḥ*), 15618 (*patiḥ S°-Sindhūnāṃ*, i.e. Jayadratha), 15621, 15635 (*Sindhu-S°ān*); **271**, 15718 (*Çibi-S°-Sindhūnāṃ*), 15742 (*dvādaçānāṃ*, i.e. the twelve standard-bearers of Jayadratha; slain by Arjuna), 15765 (*Sindhu-S°ān*).—§ 555 (Sainyodyogap.): V, **19**δ, 588 (*Sindhu-S°vāsinaḥ*, followed Jayadratha).—§ 568 (Vīdulāputraçāsana): V, **134**, 4570 (°*kanyābhiḥ*).—§ 574 (Jambūkh.): VI, **9**μ, 361 (*Sindhu-S°āḥ*, among the peoples of Bhāratavarsha).—§ 576 (Bhagavadgītāp.): VI, **18**δ, 689 (in the army of Duryodhana, protect Bhīshma); **20**ζ, †750 (do.).—§ 578 (Bhīshmavadhap.): VI, **51**σ, 2104 (*Sindhu-S°āḥ*, follow Bhīshma).—§ 579 (do.): V, **52**γ, 2141 (*Prācya-S°-Kekayaiḥ*).—§ 580 (do.): VI, **56**β, 2406 (*Sindhu-S°āḥ*, in the neck of Bhīshma's gāruḍavyūha); **59**μ, †2584 (°*gaṇāḥ*, attack Arjuna) (π), †2646 (do., slain).—§ 582 (do.): VI, **71**γ, 3132 (*Madra-S°-Gāndhāraiḥ*).—§ 583 (do.): VI, **75**δ, 3295 (*Madra-S°-Kekayaiḥ*, follow Bhagadatta).—§ 586 (do.): VI, **106**τ, 4808.—§ 587 (do.): VI, **117**ρ, 5484 (attack Arjuna); **119**αα, 5648.—§ 589 (Droṇābhishekap.): VII, **7**ζ, 184.—§ 596 (Pratijñāp.): VII, **75**, 2658 (*Sauvīra-Sindhūnāṃ īçvaraḥ*, i.e. Jayadratha).—§ 599 (Jayadrathavadhap.): VII, **95**, 3535 (follow Āvantya); **110**, 4208 (*Sindhu-S°air nakharaprāsayodhibhiḥ*); **138**, 5677 (*sainyaṃ Sindhu-S°-Kauravaṃ*); **139**, 5714 (*sa-Kuru-S°-Sindhuvīrabalakshayaṃ*).—§ 607 (Karṇap.): VIII, **40**, 1857 (*Sindhu-S°āḥ*, do not know dharma); **44**λ, 2070 (*Vasāti-Sindhu-S°āḥ*, blameable in their practises).—§ 641 (Rājadh.): XII, **101**ρ, 3735 (*Sindhu-S°āḥ*).—§ 649*b* (Kaṇikopadeça): XII, **142**, 5250 (*rājā Catruñjayo nāma S°eshu mahārathaḥ*).

Sauvīraka = Jayadratha: III, 15612.

Sauvīraka, adj. ("belonging to the Sauvīras"). § 522 (Draupadīharaṇap.): III, **265**, †15596* (°*ā dvādaça rājaputrāḥ*, i.e. the standard-bearers of Jayadratha).—§ 599 (Jayadrathavadhap.): VII, **111**, 4266 (°*ā yodhāḥ*).

Sauvīrarāja ("the king of the Sauvīras"). § 589*b* (Sātyaki): VII, **10**, 338 (°*sya . . . mahatīṃ camūṃ*, had been vanquished by Sātyaki).—Do.[2] (Jayadratha): III, †15599 (J°), †15650, †15651.

Sauvīrī ("daughter of the Sauvīra king"). § 150 (Pūruvaṃç.): I, **94**, 3697 (°*tanayās trayaḥ*, wife of Manasyu).

Sava = Vishṇu (1000 names).

Savana, a son of Bhṛgu. § 747*b* (Suvarṇotpatti): XIII, **85**η, 4146 (seventh son of Bhṛgu).

Sāvarṇa, a ṛshi or a Manu. § 264 (Sabhākriyāp.): II, **4**a, 110 (waited upon Yudhishṭhira).—§ 730 (Ānuçāsanik.): XIII, **18**κκ, 1339 (°*sya Manor sarge*, then Vyāsa will be one of the Saptarshis). Cf. next.

Sāvarṇi, a ṛshi or a Manu. § 266 (Çakrasabhāv.): II, **7**, 292 (in the palace of Indra), 293 (the same?, do.).—§ 565 (Gālavacarita): V, **109**, 3789 (*atra*—i.e. in the south—*S°ṇā caiva Yavakrītātmajena ca maryādā sthāpitā, brahman, yāṃ sūryo nātivartate*).—§ 730 (Ānuçāsanik.): XIII, **14**ζ, 692 (*ṛshiḥ*, gratified Çiva in the Kṛta age). Cf. the prec.

Sāvitra[1] ("the son of Savitṛ [i.e. Sūrya]") = Karṇa: I, 5386; XIII, 6253 (°*ḥ kuṇḍalaṃ devyaṃ . . . dattvā gato lokān anuttamān*, cf. XII, 8598). Cf. Sāvitrin.

Sāvitra[2], a Rudra. § 665 (Mokshadh.): XII, **208**δ, 7586 (enumeration).

Sāvitra[3], a Vasu. § 775 (Ānuçāsanik.): XIII, **151**δ, 7094 (enumeration).

Sāvitra, adj. ("belonging to Savitṛ"). § 600 (Ghaṭotkacavadhap.): VII, **157**, 6954 (sc. *astraṃ*, employed by Droṇa). § 694*b* (Jvarotpatti): XII, **284**, 10212 (*Meroḥ çṛṅgaṃ . . . Jyotishkaṃ nāma S°ṃ*).—§ 759 (Ānuçāsanik.): XIII, **104**, 5014 (°*āṇi*, sc. *mantrāṇi*?).

Sāvitra(ṃ)[1], name of a nakshatra ("belonging to Savitṛ") = Hasta. § 208 (Astradarçana): I, **135**, 5376 (*pañcatāreṇa saṃyuktaḥ S°eṇeva candramāḥ*).

Sāvitra(ṃ)[2] (sc. upākhyāna(ṃ)). § 10 (Parvasaṅgr.): I, **2**, 332 (in the enumeration of parvans, entered among the parvans of the fifth book, but not found there).

Sāvitrī[1], daughter of Açvapati and wife of Satyavat. § 10 (Parvasaṅgr.): I, **2**, 326 (*pativratāyā māhātmyaṃ S°yāḥ*, i.e. Pativratāmāhātmyaparvan).—§ 11 (do.): I, **2**, 476 (°*yāç cāpy upākhyānaṃ*, do.).—§ 545 (Pativratop.): III, **293**, 16640 (named *S.* because she was bestowed by the goddess Sāvitrī); **294**, (16664), 16668, 16681, (16683), 16686, 16689; **295**, 16698, 16713; **296**, 16715, 16717, (16719), 16721, 16722, 16725, 16726, (16730), 16731, 16732, (16734), 16740, 16744; **297**, 16750, 16752, (16757), 16758, (16760), 16765, 16766, (16767), (†16774), (†16778), (†16779), (†16781), (†16785), (†16787), (†16792), (†16794), (†16799), 16802, 16808, 16809, 16811, (16813), 16820, (16825), 16843, 16846, 16848, 16850; **298**, 16861, 16867, 16872, 16873, 16874, 16878, 16880, 16883, 16887, 16891, 16892, (16893); **299**, 16903, 16911, 16913, 16916, 16918 (°*ākhyānaṃ*) (*S.* choose Satyavat for her husband; when Yama came to fetch Satyavat, *S.* followed him and obtained several boons, among these the life of Satyavat).—§ 551 (Kīcakavadhap.): IV, **21**, 656 (*Satyavantaṃ . . . S°y anucacāraikā Yamalokaṃ*, all. to § 545).—§ 565 (Gālavacarita): V, **117**, 3971 (*reme . . . S°yāṃ Satyavān yathā*).—§ 744 (Ānuçāsanik.): XIII, **45**, 2464 (*svayaṃ vṛttena S°ī pitrā vai pratyapadyata*, all. to § 545, but the text of B. runs: *svayaṃvṛtena sājñaptā pitrā*, etc.).

Sāvitrī[2], name of a certain mantra (named after Savitṛ), also a goddess (daughter of Savitṛ), wife of Brahmán. § 270 (Brahmasabhāv.): II, **11**, 471 (in the palace of Brahmán).—§ 356 (Tīrthayātrāp.): III, **81**, 4025 (*yathā ca Vedān S°ī*, sc. *na jahau*).—§ 370 (do.): III, **84**, 8071 (°*yās tu padaṃ* *tatra dṛçyate*, sc. on the mountain Udyanta); **85**, 8173 (*abrāhmaṇasya S°īṃ paṭhataḥ*).—§ 390 (do.): III, **110**, 9994 (*dadau . . . S°īṃ Savitā yathā*).—§ 450 (Ājagarap.): III, **180**, 12484 (*mātā S°ī . . . ucyate*).—§ 506 (Skandayuddha): III, **231**, 14562 (followed Umā).—§ 545 (Pativratāmāhātmyap.): III, **293**, 16624, 16625, (16627), (16631), 16634, 16635, 16639 (Açvapati performed sacrifices to *S.*, who bestowed the daughter Sāvitrī upon him).—§ 565 (Gālavacarita): V, **108**, 3770 (*atraivoktā*—sc. in the east—*Savitrāsīt S°ī*).—§ 576 (Bhagavadgītāp.): VI, **23**, 804 (*Vedamātā*, identified with Durgā), 807 (identified with Durgā).—§ 603*d* (Tripura): VII, **202**, 9567 (Çiva made Gāyatrī and *S.* his reins).—§ 606 (Tripurākhyāna): VIII, **34**, 1490 (became the bow-string of Çiva).—§ 635 (Rājadh.): XII, **35**, 1277 (*°īm . . . adhīyīta*).—§ 662*b* (Jāpakop.): XII, **200**, (7208).—§ 680*b* (Tulādhāra-Jājalisaṃv.): XII, **265**, 9449 (*Çraddhā Vaivasvatī seyam Sūryasya duhitā . . . Sāvitrī* (sā avatrī, Nīl.)).—§ 686 (Mokshadh.): XII, **273**, 9821 (*°ī sākshāt taṃ sannyamantrayat*).—§ 717*b*(Nārāyaṇīya): XII, **340**, 12871 (*udgiran . . . S°īṃ*, sc. Nārāyaṇa).—§ 730 (Ānuçāsanik.): XIII, **14**β, 627.—§ 732 (do.): XIII, **23**, 1595 (*°jñāḥ*), 1598 (*°īṃ japet*).—§ 746 (do.): XIII, **67**, 3381 (*°yāḥ . . . vacanaṃ*).—§ 747*b* (Suvarṇotpatti): XIII, **85**ε, 4109.—§ 749 (Ānuçāsanik.): XIII, **92**, 4385 (*brūyāc çrāddhe S°īṃ*).—§ 767 (do.): XIII, **136**, 6223, 6228, 6236, 6242.—§ 768*b* (Umā-Maheçvarasaṃv.): XIII, **146**γ, 6750 (*Brahmaṇaḥ*, sc. *satī*).—§ 770 (Ānuçāsanik.): XIII, **151**, 7082 (*mantraṃ . . . S°yā vihitaṃ*), 7146 (*°īṃ . . . paṭhan*), 7147 (*°ī yatra paṭhyate*), 7149 (*°īṃ . . . paṭhan*), 7155 (*paṭhanti . . . S°īṃ*), 7158 (*°īm adhigamya*), 7161 (*Brahma*).—773*d* (Çiva): XIII, **161**, 7486 (became the bow-string of Çiva).—§ 775 (Ānuçāsanik.): XIII, **166***a*, 7635 (*Brahmaṇaḥ satī*).—§ 782*g* (Guruçishyasaṃv.): XIV, **44**ι, 1216 (*sarvavidyānāṃ*, sc. *ādiḥ*), 1217 (*yad asmin niyataṃ loke sarvaṃ S°ir* [sic! perhaps a wrong reading instead of *sāvitram*, adj.] *ucyate*).—§ 795*c* (Mahābhārata): XVIII, **5**, 208 (*Bhārata-s°īṃ.*). Cf. Devī.

Sāvitrin ("the son of Savitṛ [i.e. Sūrya]") = Karṇa: XII, 8598 (*°ī kuṇḍale divye . . . brāhmaṇārthe parityajya jagmatur lokam uttamaṃ*, cf. XIII, 6253). Cf. Sāvitra.

Sāvitrīputraka, pl. (*°āḥ*), a people. § 604 (Karṇap.): VIII, **5**ζ, 138 (had been slain in the battle).

Sāvitryavarajā ("the younger sister of Sāvitrī[2]") = Tapatī: I, 6522, 6605 (*T°*).

Savitṛ ("impeller"), one of the Ādityas, sometimes identical with Vivasvat (Sūrya, the Sun, personified). § 3 (Anukram.): I, **1**, 42 (a son or form of Vivasvat, cf. Āçāvaha).—§ 35 (Aruṇa): I, **24**, 1277 (got Aruṇa for his charioteer).—§ 88 (Aṃçāvat.): I, **65**, 2523 (the tenth of the Ādityas).—§ 119 (do.): I, **66**, 2599 (husband of Tvāshṭrī and father of the Açvins).—§ 191 (Arjuna): I, **123**, 4824 (the tenth of the Ādityas).—§ 222 (Tapatyup.): I, **172**, 6583 (father of Tapatī).—§ 258 (Khāṇḍavadahanap.): I, **227**, 8268 (fought against Kṛshṇa and Arjuna).—§ 266 (Çakrasabhāv.): II, **7**, 302 (in the palace of Çakra).—§ 310*b* (Sūrya): III, **3**, 135 (i.e. Sūrya).—§ 310 (Āraṇyakap.): III, **3**, 146 (among the 108 names of Sūrya).—§ 310*b* (Sūrya): III, **3**, 191 (identified with Sūrya).—§ 390 (Tīrthayātrāp.): III, **110**, 9994 (*dadau . . . Sāvitrīṃ S°ā yathā*).—§ 400 (Tīrthayātrāp.): III, **118**, 10224 (*°uḥ*, sc. *āyatanaṃ*).—§ 439 (Yakshayuddhap.): III, **163**, 11850 (i.e. Sūrya), 11871 (do., description of the course of the Sun), 11880 (do.).—§ 440 (do.): III, **164**, 11901 (*°uḥ*, sc. *astraṃ*).—§ 522 (Draupadīharaṇap.): III, **264**, †15591 (*°uḥ*, sc. *sadanāt*).—§ 565 (Gālavacarita): V, **108**, 3770 (*atraivoktā*—sc. in the east—*S°trāsīt Sāvitrī*).—§ 588 (Bhīshmavadhap.): VII, **121**β, 5802 (*°uḥ*, sc. *astraṃ*).—§ 617 (Aishīkap.): X, **18**, 801, 807 (Rudra broke the arms of *S.*).—§ 665 (Mokshadh.): XII, **208**β, 7581 (the sixth of the Ādityas).—§ 717*b* (Nārāyaṇīya): XII, **349**, VII), 13597 (*Āditye S°ur jyeshṭhe*).—§ 730 (Ānuçāsanik.): XIII, **14**β, 626; **16**, 1058 (Çiva identified with *S.*).—§ 772*m* (Atri): XIII, **157**, 7297, 7302.—§ 773*b* (Kṛshṇa Vāsudeva): XIII, **159**, †7373 (*raçmivān*, Kṛshṇa identified with *S.*).—§ 777 (Svargārohaṇik. p.): XIII, **168**, 7743 (Kṛshṇa identified with *S.*).—Do.[2] (a mere appellative designing the sun): I, 1797, 1883, 8411; III, 1334, 2933, 10052 (*iva*), †10639; V, 772 (*iva*), 1741, 2751, 3763; VI, 1899, 3818; VII, 1639, 2835, 9241; VIII, 1750 (*yathā*), 2342, 4943; IX, †1069 (*yathā*); XII, 2119, 6340, 7425, 7452; XIII, 428 (*sahasrakiraṇasya*), 7357; XIV, 190 (*raçmayo s°ur yathā*).

Savitṛ[3] = Çiva (1000 names[2]).—Do.[4] = Vishṇu (1000 names).

Savyacārin = Arjuna: XIII, 6901 (only C., read with B. *Savyasācī*).

Savyasācin = Arjuna, q.v.

Sayana, son of Viçvāmitra. § 721*b* (Viçvāmitrop.): XIII, **4**β, 257 (B. *Seyanaḥ*).

Seduka, name of a king. § 465 (Mārkaṇḍeyas.): III, **196**, ††13262 (*Vṛshadarbha-S°nāmānau rājānau*), ††13263, ††13264, ††13265, ††13271.

Seka, pl. (*°āḥ*), a people. § 281 (Sahadeva): II, **31**, 1113 (*S°ān apara-S°ān ca*, in the south, vanquished by Sahadeva).

Senābindu[1] (C. Senāvindu), one or more kings. § 130 (Aṃçāvat.): I, **67**, 2656 (incarnation of the Asura Tuhuṇḍa).—§ 232 (Svayaṃvarap.): I, **186**, 6989 (present at the svayaṃvara of Draupadī).—§ 279 (Arjuna): II, **27**, 1019, 1022 (*Devaprasthaṃ . . . S°oḥ puraṃ*, vanquished by Arjuna).—§ 554 (Sainyodyogap.): V, **4**γ, 76.—§ 572 (Rathātirathasaṅkhyānap.): V, **171**, 5912 (*Krodhahantā ca nāmataḥ*, a ratha among the Pāṇḍavas).—§ 592 (Saṃçaptakavadhap.): VII, **21**μ, 916; **23**ο, 975 (description of his horses).—§ 604 (Karṇap.): VIII, **7**, 179 (*°sutaḥ çreshṭhaḥ*, so both B. and C., but PCR. seems to have read *°ḥ sūtaçreshṭhaḥ*, had been slain by Bālhīka), 182 (*Kuruçreshṭhaḥ* (!), the half-çloka omitted by PCR.).

Senābindu[2], a Pāñcāla prince. § 608 (Karṇap.): VIII, **48**ν, 2248 (slain by Karṇa).

Senādhipati = Skanda: III, 14641.

Senājit, name of one or more kings. § 554 (Sainyodyogap.): V, **4**γ, 76 (at the time of Yudhishṭhira).—§ 629 (Rājadh.): XII, **25**, 744 (*itihāsaṃ purātanaṃ . . . gītaṃ rājñā S°tā*, some çlokas of his quoted), 760.—§ 659 (Mokshadh.): XII, **174**, 6464, (6468), 6521 (*S.'s* discourse with a brahman on account of the loss of a son).

Senākālpa = Çiva (1000 names[2]).

Senānī[1], a son of Dhṛtarāshṭra. § 182 (Dhṛtarāshṭraputranāmak.): I, **117**, 4548. Cf. Senāpati.[1]

Senānī[2] = Çiva: XIV, 199.—Do.[3] = Skanda: V, 5720.

Senāpati[1], a son of Dhṛtarāshṭra. § 130 (Aṃçāvat.): I, **67**, 2732.—§ 581 (Bhīshmavadhap.): VI, **64**κ, 2837, 2841 (slain by Bhīmasena). Cf. Senānī[1].

Senāpati[2] = Çiva (1000 names[2]).

Setubandhana(ṃ) ("the building of the bridge"). § 535 (cf. Rāmopākhyānap.): The monkey chiefs (*a*) began to flock together to *Rāma* and *Sugrīva* on *Mālyavat*. On a lucky day the army set out. *Hanūmat* was in the van, *Lakshmaṇa* in the rear, the army was protected by *Nala*, etc. (β).

Arriving at the shore of the milky ocean (*kshīrodaṃ . . . sāgaraṃ*, v. 16289), *Rāma* thought of means of crossing it. He and *Lakshmaṇa* lay down on the seashore, the Ocean appeared to him in a vision and said: "I also have sprung from the race of Ikshvāku; the monkey *Nala* is a son of *Tvashṭṛ*, whatever he will throw into my waters I will support." *Nala* then built a bridge, which to this day is known as *Nalasetu*. At this time *Vibhīshaṇa* with four of his counsellors came to *Rāma*. *Sugrīva* suspected him to be a spy, but *Rāma* installed him in the sovereignty of all the *Rākshasas* and made him his own counsellor and the friend of *Lakshmaṇa*. It was under the guidance of *Vibhīshaṇa* that the army crossed the bridge in a month. *Rāma* then caused the gardens of *Laṅkā* to be devastated by his monkeys. *Rāvaṇa's* counsellors *Çuka* and *Sāraṇa* came as spies and were seized by *Vibhīshaṇa*, but dismissed by *Rāma*. *Rāma* then sent *Aṅgada* as his envoy to *Rāvaṇa* (III, **283**).

Seyana, see Sayana.

Shaḍānana ("six-faced") = Skanda: III, 14637; XII, †11094; XIII, 4203.

Shaḍaṅganidhāna = Mahāpurusha (Mahāpurushastava).

Shaḍarcis = Skanda: III, 14639.

Shaḍvaktra ("six-faced") = Skanda: III, 14352.

Shaṇḍa, a son of Dhṛtarāshṭra. § 608 (Karṇap.): VIII, **84**ξ, 4263 (attacked Bhīmasena).

Shaṇḍa, pl. (°*āḥ*), a people. § 574 (Jambūkh.): VI, **9**μ, 351 (only C., B. has *Saṇḍāḥ*).

Shanmukha ("six-faced") = Skanda: III, †14643; VII, 3454, 7412 (*Mahishaṃ S°o yathā*, sc. *nihanishyāmi*, C. has by error °*mū*°).

Shashṭī, a goddess. § 270 (Brahmasabhāv.): II, **11**, 458 (in the palace of Brahmán).—§ 501 (Skandop.): III, **229**, 14451 (among the names of Devasenā).

Shashṭibhāga = Çiva (1000 names[2]).

Shashṭihrada, a tīrtha. § 733*p* (Gaṅgā-Yamunayos tīrthaṃ): XIII, **25**, 1722.

Shashṭīpriya ("dear to Shashṭī") = Skanda: III, 14633.

Shaṭkarmatushṭa = Çiva (1000 names[1]).

Shoḍaçarājaka(ṃ) parva. § 10 (Parvasaṅgr.): I, **2**, 332 (*p°. S°ṃ*, i.e. Shoḍaçarājika, in the enumeration of parvans erroneously entered among those of the fifth book).

[Shoḍaçarājika(ṃ)] ("the section relating to the sixteen kings"). § 595 (cf. Sṛñjaya). Nārada told Sṛñjaya the stories of the following kings: 1) *Marutta* (q.v.) (VII, **55**); 2) *Suhotra* (q.v.) (VII, **56**); 3) *Paurava* (q.v.) (VII, **57**); 4) *Çibi* (q.v.) (VII, **58**); 5) *Rāma Dāçarathi* (q.v.) (VII, **59**); 6) *Bhagīratha* (q.v.) (VII, **60**); 7) *Dilīpa* (q.v.) (VII. **61**); 8) *Māndhātṛ* (q.v.) (VII, **62**); 9) *Yayāti* (q.v.) (VII, **63**); 10) *Ambarīsha* (q.v.) (VII, **64**); 11) *Çaçabindu* (q.v.) (VII, **65**); 12) *Gaya* (q.v.) (VII, **66**); 13) *Rantideva* (q.v.) (VII, **67**); 14) *Bharata Daushmanti* (q.v.) (VII, **68**); 15) *Pṛthu Vainya* (q.v.) (VII, **69**); 16) *Rāma Jāmadagnya* (q.v.) (VII, **70**).

[Shoḍaçarājopākhyāna(ṃ)] ("the episode relating to the sixteen kings," XII, **29**). § 632*b* (Rājadh.). The histories of the same sixteen kings as in Shoḍaçarājika (§ 595), except that Paurava is here named Bṛhadratha ("the Aṅga king") and Rāma Jāmadagnya is replaced by Sagara (q.v.).

Siddha[1], a Devagandharva. § 102 (Aṃçāvat.): I, **65**, 2554 (son of Prādhā).

Siddha[2], an ancient king. § 267 (Yamasabhāv.): II, **8**, 320 (in the palace of Yama).

Siddha[3] = Çiva: XIV, 196.—Do.[4] = Vishṇu (1000 names).

***Siddha**[5], pl. (°*āḥ*) ("the perfect ones," i.e. who have acquired supernatural powers by penances), a class of beings, commonly occurring together with the Cāraṇas, etc.: I, 2396, 2400, 2858, †3577 (*surasiddharshilokāt*), 3889, 4640, 4931, †7017 (*suparṇa-nāgāsura-siddhajushṭaṃ*, sc. *antarīkshaṃ*); II, 289 (in the palace of Indra), 340 (in the palace of Yama); III, 159 (*Asura-niçācara-siddhavanditaṃ*, sc. the Sun), 170, 174 (*Vālakhilyādayaḥ*), †938 (°*ṛshigaṇān*), †940, 1530, 1756, 1786, 1830, 1841, 1891, 5023, 5024, 5036, 5075, 6038, 7083, 8024, 8035, 8037, 8094, 8168, 8176, 8214, 8357 (°*ṛshi-Cāraṇaiḥ*), 8369, 8402, 10226 (°*gaṇasya*, sc. *āyatanaṃ*), 10968 (*ṛshi-siddhāmarayutaṃ . . . giriṃ*), 11022 (°*mārgeṇa*), 11190 (sg.), 11231, 11415 (*brahmavādināṃ*), 11439, 11441, 11444, 11465, 11561, 11655 (*deva-Dānava-siddhānāṃ*), 11847, 12101, †12347, 12368, 14503 (*avamanyati yaḥ Siddhān kruddhāç cāpi çapanti yaṃ / unmādyati sa tu kshipraṃ jñeyaḥ Siddhagrahas tu saḥ*); IV, †2176 (*devāsura-siddha-Yakshān*); V, 2471, 3826 (*Gandharva-Yaksha-S°aiḥ*), 3833 (*svairacāriṇāṃ*), 4052 (°*āç cāpsarasaḥ*), 5126, 7095, 7351; VI, 199, 254, 269, 273, 407, 429, 464, 808, †1267, †1268, †1282, 1536, 1753, 5704; VII, †1622, 2843, 3118, 3642, 3652, 3728, 4025, 5692, 5746, 6008, 6132, 6340, †6921, 7138 (?), 7188, †7312, †7313, 8611, 8614, 8807; VIII, 592, 598, 599, 626, 1018, 2817, 3098, 3970, 4128 (*apatanta . . . savimānā yathā S°āḥ svargāt puṇyakshaye*), 4400, 4413, †4490; IX, 337, 658, 990 (*gaganāt pracyutāḥ S°āḥ puṇyānām iva saṃkshaye*), 1157, 1269 (*vimānebhyo divo bhrashṭāḥ S°āḥ puṇyakshayād iva*, sc. *petuḥ*), 1315, 2140, 2479, 2481 (*Bṛhaspatipurogamāḥ*), 2762, 2812, 2879, 2898, 2902 (*brahmasattriṇāṃ*), 2903, 2905, 3050, 3307, 3444; XII, 1607 (°-*mahoragāḥ*), 1623, †2395, 5587 (*Yaksha-Gandharva-S°ānāṃ madhye*), 6142, 6788 (*ākāçaṃ S°daivata-sevitaṃ*), 6797, 7341, 7588 (°-*Sādhyayoḥ*), 8221 (accompanied Indra), †10097 (*saṃyāsi S°saṅkhyāṃ*), 10114 (riding in vimānas), 10220, 10275 (*deçe ṛshi-S°nishevite*), 10838, 12176, 12314 (*Himavantaṃ S°-Cāraṇasevitaṃ*), 12576, 12982, 13028 (*Merau . . . S°-Cāraṇasevite*), 13366; XIII, 439, 741 (°-*Cāraṇarūpadhṛk*, sc. Çiva), 800 (°-*Gandharva-devaiḥ*), 813 (*ṛshi-Gandharva-S°aiḥ*), 958, 1396, 1407, 1748, 6111, 6339, 6350 (*ūrdhvaretasaḥ*), 7766; XIV, 402, 429 (*antarhitaiḥ*), 958; XV, 575 (°*gatim āsthitāḥ*), 655, 848 (had been incarnate); XVI, †129, †131; XVII, 96 (riding in vimānas), 106; XVIII, 88, 216.

Siddha[6], pl. (°*āḥ*), a people. § 574 (Jambūkh.): VI, **9**μ, 364.

Siddhabhūtārtha = Çiva (1000 names[2]).

Siddhagraha, name of a demon. § 502 (Manushyagrahak.): III, **230**, 14503 (v. Siddha, pl.).

Siddhakshetra ("the blessed land," said of sacred regions): III, 8270 (*Gaṅgātīrasamāçritaṃ*).

Siddhaloka ("the world of the Siddhas"): XII, 10078 (*cyutāḥ S°āt*).

Siddhamantra = Çiva: XIV, 197, 198.

***siddhānta** ("scientific result or treatise"): I, 2887; XII, 8676.

Siddhapātra, a warrior of Skanda. § 615*u* (Skanda): IX, **45**η, 2568.

Siddhārtha[1], a king. § 130 (Aṃçāvat.): I, **67**, 2696 (among the incarnations from the Krodhavaça gaṇa).

Siddhārtha[2], a warrior of Skanda. § 615*u* (Skanda): IX, **45**η, 2566.

Siddhārtha[3] = Çiva (1000 names[2]).—Do.[4] = Vishṇu (1000 names).

Siddhārthakārin, Siddhasādhaka = Çiva (1000 names[2]).
Siddhasankalpa = Vishṇu (1000 names).
Siddhasenānī = Durgā (Umā): VI, 796.
Siddhayogin = Çiva (1000 names[2]).
Siddhi[1] ("success," personif.). § 132 (Aṃçāvat.): I, **67,** 2794 (incarnate as Kuntī).—§ 615*q* (Sarasvatī): IX, **42,** 2389 (the river Sarasvatī is identified with *S.*).—§ 615*u* (Skanda): IX, **46**κ, 2689.—§ 704 (Mokshadh.): XII, **301***a*, †11095 (*devīṃ Varuṇasya patnīṃ*).
Siddhi[2], a fire. § 490 (Āṅgirasa): III, **219,** 14140.
Siddhi[3] = Çiva (1000 names[2]).—Do.[4] = Vishṇu (1000 names).
Siddhida = Vishṇu (1000 names).
***siddhikshetra** ("field of success," said of a tīrtha): IX, 2262 (*Kapilamocanaṃ*).
Siddhisādhana = Vishṇu (1000 names).
Sikata, pl. (°*āḥ*), a class of ṛshis. § 602 (Droṇavadhap.): VII, **190**ν, 8728.—§ 630 (Rājadh.): XII, **26***a*, 774.—§ 656 (Khaḍgotpattik.): XII, **166**β, 6143.
Sikatāksha, name of a place. § 406 (Tīrthayātrāp.): III, **125,** 10407.
Silībāka, a muni. § 264 (Sabhākriyāp.): II, **4***a*, 109 (so C., B. has *Sinīvākaḥ*).
Siṃha ("lion") = Vishṇu (Kṛshṇa): VI, 3027; XIII, 6971 (1000 names), 7001 (do.).
***siṃha,** pl. (°*āḥ*) ("lions"). § 113 (Aṃçāvat.): I, **66,** 2572 (among the offspring of Pulaha).—§ 127 (do.): I, **66,** 2629 (among the offspring of Çārdūlī).
Siṃhacandra, a Pāṇḍava warrior. § 600 (Ghaṭotkacavadhap.): VII, **158**χ, 7009.
Siṃhaçārdūlarūpa, Siṃhadamshtra, Siṃhaga = Çiva (1000 names[2]).
Siṃhagrīva = Açvatthāman: V, 5780.
Siṃhaketu[1] ("having a lion in his banner") = Bṛhadbala: VI, 5365 (read *S°r* with B.).
Siṃhaketu[2], a Pāṇḍava warrior. § 608 (Karṇap.): VIII, **56**νν, 2740 (slain by Karṇa).
Siṃhala, pl. (°*āḥ*), a people. § 223 (Vāsishṭha): I, **175,** 6684 (among the barbarous people who arose from the cow of Vasishṭha).—§ 287 (Rājasūyikap.): II, **34,** 1271 (present at the rājasūya).—§ 295 (Dyūtap.): II, **52,** 1894 (brought tribute to Yudhishṭhira).—§ 342 (Indralokābhigamanap.): III, **51,** 1989 (had been present at the rājasūya).—§ 592 (Saṃçaptakavadhap.): VII, **20**γ, 798 (in Droṇa's gāruḍavyūha).
Siṃhalāṅgūlaketana, Siṃhalāṅgūlaketu, Siṃhalāṅgūlalakshman ("having a lion's tail [or an ape (?), cf. VII, 3928 foll.] in his banner") = Açvatthāman: VII, 9291, 9393; VII, 6102; VII, 1094.
Siṃhanāda = Çiva (1000 names[2]).
Siṃhapura, a city. § 279 (Arjuna): II, **27,** 1028 (in the north, vanquished by Arjuna).
Siṃhasena[1], a Pāṇḍava warrior. § 590 (Droṇābhishekap.): VII, **16**κ, 650, 653, 655 (slain by Droṇa).
Siṃhasena[2], a Pāñcālya. § 592 (Saṃçaptakavadhap.): VII, **23**ο, 997 (*Pāñcālyaṃ Gopateḥ putraṃ*, proceeded against Droṇa, description of his horses).—§ 608 (Karṇap.): VIII, **56**νν, 2736 (fought with Karṇa).
Siṃhavāhana = Çiva (1000 names[2]).
Siṃhikā, daughter of Daksha. § 87 (Aṃçāvat.): I, **65,** 2520 (wife of Kaçyapa).—§ 94 (do.): I, **65,** 2539 (mother of four sons, viz. Rāhu, etc.).—§ 130 (do.): I, **67,** 2676 (mother of Graha, i.e. Rāhu).
Siṃhikātanaya, pl. (°*āḥ*) ("the sons of Siṃhikā"), a family of Asuras. § 459 (Mārkaṇḍeyas.): III, **188,** 12926 (seen by Mārkaṇḍeya in the stomach of Nārāyaṇa).
Sindhu, the river Indus (sometimes another river seems to be meant). § 153 (Pūruvaṃç.): I, **94,** 3730 (*nadasya mahato nikuñje*, there Saṃvaraṇa dwelt when defeated).—§ 268 (Varuṇasabhāv.): II, **9,** 372 (among the rivers in the palace of Varuṇa).—§ 285 (Nakula): II, **32,** 1191 (°*kūlāçritā ye ca grāmaṇīyāḥ*, vanquished by Nakula).—§ 295 (Dyūtap.): II, **51,** 1831 (*pāre-Sindhu*).—§ 298 (do.): II, **65,** 2146 (*yat kiṃcid anu Parṇāçāṃ prāk Sindhor api*).—§ 358 (Tīrthayātrāp.): III, **82,** 4095 (*dakshiṇaṃ*, in the south), 5010 (*sāgarasya ca S°oç ca saṅgamaṃ*).—§ 370 (do.): III, **84,** 8024 (°*oç ca prabhavaṃ*, a tīrtha).—§ 401 (Balarāma): III, **119,** †10254 (*yaḥ S°kūle vyajayan nṛdevān samāgatān Dākshiṇātyān mahīpān*, sc. Sahadeva; in the south?).—§ 410 (Plakshāvataraṇag.): III, **130,** 10541 (°*or mahātīrthaṃ*, in the south?; *d*: there *Lopāmudrā* accepted *Agastya* as her lord).—§ 459 (Mārkaṇḍeyas.): III, **188***a*, 12908 (seen by Mārkaṇḍeya in the stomach of Nārāyaṇa).—§ 494 (Āṅgirasa): III, **222,** 14229 (among the rivers who are mothers of fires).—§ 496 (Skandotpatti): III, **224,** 14274 (°*r apīyaṃ tu pratyasṛgvāhinī bhṛçaṃ*, omens).—§ 562 (Bhagavadyānap.): V, **84,** 2998 (*pratyag ūhur mahānadyaḥ prāṅmukhāḥ S°saptamāḥ*).—§ 574*f* (Bindusaras): VI, **6**η, 243 (among the seven streams into which the *Gaṅgā* divides herself).—§ 574 (Jambūkh.): VI, **9**λ, 321, 329 (the same?).—§ 599 (Jayadrathavadhap.): VII, **101,** 3790 (*bāhubhyām iva saṃtīrṇau S°shashṭāḥ samudragāḥ*).—§ 606 (Tripurākhyāna): VIII, **34,** 1477.—§ 607 (Karṇap.): VIII, **44,** 2030 (*pañcānāṃ S°shashṭānāṃ nadīnāṃ*), 2055 (°*shashṭāḥ*).—§ 733*b* (Candrabhāgā): XIII, **25,** 1695.—§ 768*b* (Umā-Maheçvarasaṃv.): XIII, **146**δ, 6764 (among the rivers who came to Umā).—§ 775 (Ānuçāsanik.): XIII, **166***a*, 7645.
Sindhu[2], the country of the Sindhus on the river Indus. § 555 (Sainyodyogap.): V, **19**δ, 588 (*Jayadrathamukhāḥ . . . S°-Sauvīravāsinaḥ*).—§ 576 (Bhagavadgītāp.): VI, **20,** †750 (*ye ca S°oḥ*).
Sindhu[3] = Kṛshṇa: XII, 1508.
Sindhu, pl. (°*avaḥ*), a people = Saindhava, pl. § 522 (Draupadīharaṇap.): III, **264,** 15576 (*rājā S°ūnāṃ Vārddhakshatriḥ*, i.e. Jayadratha), 15581 (*rājā S°ūnāṃ Vārddhakshatrir Jayadrathaḥ*); **267,** 15618 (*patiḥ Sauvīra-S°ūnāṃ . . . Jayadrathaḥ*), 15621, 15635 (°*-Sauvīrān*); **271,** 15718 (*Çibi-Sauvīra-S°ūnāṃ*), 15765 (°*-Sauvīrān*).—§ 574 (Jambūkh.): VI, **9**μ, 348 (°*-Pulindakāḥ*), 361 (°*-Sauvīrāḥ*).—§ 578 (Bhīshmavadhap.): VI, **51**σ, 2104 (°*-Sauvīrāḥ*, follow Bhīshma).—§ 580 (do.): VI, **56**β, 2406 (°*-Sauvīrāḥ*, in the neck of Bhīshma's gāruḍavyūha).—§ 583 (do.): VI, **79,** 3466 (*rājā S°ūnāṃ*, i.e. Jayadratha).—§ 596 (Pratijñāp.): VII, **75,** 2658 (*Sauvīra-S°ūnām īçvaraḥ*, do.).—§ 599 (Jayadrathavadhap.): VII, **110,** 4208 (°*-Sauvīrair nakharaprāsayodhibhiḥ*); **138,** 5677 (*sainyaṃ S°-Sauvīra-Kauravaṃ*); **139,** 5714 (*sa-Kuru-Sauvīra-S°vīrabalakshayaṃ*).—§ 604 (Karṇap.): VIII, **5**ζ, 100 (°*rāshṭramukhāni daça rāshṭrāṇi*, ruled by Jayadratha).—§ 607 (do.): VIII, **40,** 1857 (°*-Sauvīrāḥ*, do not know dharma).—§ 641 (Rājadh.): XII, **101**υ, 3735.
Sindhudvīpa, an ancient king, son of Jahnu. § 615 (Baladevatīrthayātrā): IX, **39,** 2282 (*rājarshiḥ*, became a brahman); **40,** 2285, 2294 (in the Kṛta age, do.).—§ 721*b* (Viçvāmitrop.): XIII, **4,** 203 (son of Jahnu, from him sprang Balākāçva).—§ 786 (Anugītāp.): XIV, **91***a*, 2843 (obtained high success).

Sindhuja, adj. ("born in the country of the Sindhus"). § 351 (Nalopākhyānap.): III, **71**, 2784 (sc. *açvān*).—§ 585 (Bhīshmavadhap.): VI, **90**ρ, 3973 (*vājinām*).

Sindhupati[1] ("king of the Sindhus") = Jayadratha: III, 15825; VI, 667; VII, 1074, 3423, 3424, 6224, 6268; IX, 3060 (sc. *hataḥ*).

Sindhupati[2] (do.) = Vṛddhakshatra: VII, 1755 (°*eḥ sutam*, i.e. Jayadratha).

Sindhurāj (do.) = Jayadratha: VII, 2675, 6217.

Sindhurāja[1] (do.). § 568 (Vidulāputraçāsana): V, **133**, 4497 (vanquished Sañjaya, the son of Vidulā); **134**, 4542.

Sindhūrāja[2] (do.) = Jayadratha: I, 2744 (married Duḥçalā); III, 15636, †15694, 15747 (*J*°); V, 1988 (only B., C. has by error *Sindhurājño*), 2186 (*J*°), 5743 (*dviguṇo rathaḥ*); VI, †3784, 5261; VII, 567, 571, 1503, 1505, 1756 (*J*°), 1763, 1777, 2648 (°*vadhe*), 2652 (do.), 2681, 2684, †2731, 2785 (°*sya vadho Gāṇḍīvadhanvanā*), 2790, 3102 (*J*°), 3107, 3217, 3409, 3753, 3773, 3776, 3780, 3794, 3798, 3803, 3945, 4329, 4457, 4485 (°*vadham*), 5315, 5321, 5821, 6141, 6213 (*varāhaḥ S*°*sya*), 6223, 6247, 6263, 6275 (only B.), 6279, 6285 (*vinihate*), 6286 (*J*°, only C.), 6474 (only B.), 6529 (*hate*), 6549, 6551, 6555, 6558, 6578 (only B.), 6580, 8311 (°*vadhena*), 9637 (°*vadha*°-); XIV, 2231 (*vadham* . . . *S*°*sya*).

Sindhurājan (do.) = Jayadratha: V, 1988 (only C., read with B. *Sindhurājo*); VI, 4134; VII, 3222.

Sindhu-Sauvīrabhartṛ = Jayadratha: XI, 625 (*J*°), 627.

Sindhūttama, name of a tīrtha. § 358 (Tīrthayātrāp.): III, **82**, 5021.—§ 775 (Ânuçāsanik.): XIII, **166a**, 7650.

Sinīvāka v. Silībāka.

Sinīvālī, a goddess (the first day of new moon). § 489 (Āṅgirasa): III, **218**, 14126 (*Kapardisutā*, third daughter of Aṅgiras).—§ 500 (Skandopākhyāna): III, **229**, 14451 (Devasenā identified with *S.*).—§ 606 (Tripurākhyāna): VIII, **34**, 1486 (among the auspicious days who became the *yoktrāṇi* of Çiva's chariot).—§ 615*u* (Skanda): IX, **45**γ, 2515 (came to the investiture of Skanda).

Sīrabhṛt ("plough-holder") = Balarāma: IX, 3359.

Sita[1], a warrior of Skanda. § 615*u* (Skanda): IX, **45**η, 2571.

Sita[2] ("white") = Balarāma: IX, 3351 (°*āsitau*, i.e. Balarāma and Kṛshṇa).

Sītā[1], daughter of Janaka, the Videha king and wife of Rāma Dāçarathi. § 425 (Hanūmad-Bhīmasaṃv.): III, **148**, 11203 (had been carried away by Rāvaṇa, cf. § 529), 11205, 11207 (*sutāṃ Janakarājasya*), 11218 (°*prasādāc ca mām-ihastham, arindama, upatishṭhanti me divyā bhogā, Bhīma, yathepsitāḥ*, says Hanūmat).—§ 430 (do.): III, **150**, 11285 (*ānītā svapurīṃ*, sc. by Rāma, cf. § 542).—§ 431 (Saugandhikā-haraṇa): III, **151**, 11324 (°*vaktrāravindārkam*, sc. Rāma).—§ 525 (Rāmopākhyānap.): III, **274**, 15880 (daughter of Janaka and wife of Rāma), 15881.—§ 527 (do.): III, **277**, 15973 (*Vaidehī Janakātmajā*, followed Rāma to the forest).—§ 529 (Sītāharaṇa): III, **278**, 16011, 16012, 16013, 16023, 16035 (carried away by Rāvaṇa).—§ 530 (Viçvāvasumokshaṇa): III, **279**, 16046, 16051, 16056 (taken to Laṅkā), 16066, 16087 (*Rāvaṇena hṛtā*).—§ 531 (Rāmopākhyānap.): III, **280**, 16093 (°*haraṇaduḥkhārttaḥ*, sc. Rāma).—§ 532 (Sītāsāntvana): III, **280**, 16133, 16138, 16147, 16149, 16163 (comforted by Trijaṭā).—§ 533 (Sītā-Rāvaṇasaṃv.): III, **281**, 16173, 16189, 16192 (conversation between *S.* and Rāvaṇa).—§ 534 (Hanūmatpratyāg.): III, **282**, 16200 (*ruddhāṃ* . . . *Rākshasaveçmani*), 16213, 16228, 16249, 16256, 16257, 16258, 16260, 16262, 16264 (found out by Hanūmat).—§ 536 (Laṅkāpraveça): III, **284**, 16334 (°*m āharatā balāt*, sc. Rāvaṇa), 16338 (*Jānakī*).—§ 538 (Kumbhakarṇaraṇag.): III, **286**, 16402 (*mayā tv apahṛtā bhāryā S*°*ā nāmāsya Jānakī*, says Rāvaṇa).—§ 542 (Rāmābhisheka): III, **291**, 16536 (after the death of Rāvaṇa, *S.* was given back to Rāma), 16538, 16563 (Rāma did not accept her until the gods attested her innocence), 16574 (granted Hanūmat a boon), 16581. — § 551 (Kīcakavadhap.): IV, **21**, 653 (*duhitā Janakasyāpi Vaidehī yadi te çrutā / patim anvacarat S*°*ā mahāraṇyanivāsinaṃ / Rakshasā nigrahaṃ prāpya Rāmasya mahishī priyā / kliçyamānāpi suçroṇī Rāmam evānvapadyata*).

Cf. also the following synonyms:—

Janakātmajā ("the daughter of Janaka"): III, 15973, 16033, 16231.

Jānakī (do.): III, 15872, 16037, 16091, 16233, 16265, 16338 (*S*°), 16402 (*S*°), 16537, 16577.

Maithilī ("daughter of the king of Mithilā"): III, 15946, 16047, 16226, 16543, 16557, 16558, 16559.

Vaidehī, q.v.

Sītā[2], a goddess (the goddess presiding of corn, PCR.). § 599*b* (Çalya): VII, **105**ν, 3945 (*sītā bhrājate* . . . *sarvabījaviruddheva yathā Sītā Çriyā vṛtā*).

Sītā[3], one or more rivers. § 423 (Gandhamādanapr.): III, **145**, 11063 (only B., C. has *çītā* as an adj. to Bhāgīrathī, "cool" PCR.).—§ 459 (Mārkaṇḍeyas.): III, **188a**, 12907 (among the rivers seen by Mārkaṇḍeya in the stomach of Nārāyaṇa).—§ 574*f* (Bindusaras): VI, **6**η, 243 (among the seven streams into which Gaṅgā divides herself).—§ 575*b* (Çākadvīpa): VI, **11**γ, 432 (in Çākadvīpa; reading of B.: *Çītāçī Veṇikā* or *Çītā Çīveṇikā*?).—§ 641 (Rājadh.): XII, **82**, 3099 (°*ā nāma nadī, rājan, yatra plavo nimajjati*).

Sitāçva ("having white horses") = Arjuna: III, †11898.

Sītāharaṇa(m) ("the carrying away of Sītā"). § 529 (cf. Rāmopākhyānap.). *Rāvaṇa* caused *Mārīca* to entice away *Rāma* by assuming the shape of a deer with golden horns and a golden skin. Seeing this deer *Rāma* pursued it, like *Rudra* pursuing the stellar deer (*tārāmṛgaṃ*) in days of yore; struck with *Rāma's* arrow *Mārīca*, imitating *Rāma's* voice cried out, calling upon *Sītā* and *Lakshmaṇa*. *Lakshmaṇa*, thinking that nobody was able to slay *Rāma*, at first inclined to stay there and protect *Sītā*, but as she suspected him, he set out on the track of *Rāma*. Then *Rāvaṇa*, in the guise of an ascetic, with shaven head and with a *kuṇḍala* and a triple staff, came to the hermitage and began to carry away *Sītā* to *Laṅkā*; on his way he was seen by the vulture *Jaṭāyu* (III, **278**).

Sitāṅga = Çiva (1000 names[1]).

Sītā-Rāvaṇasaṃvāda ("discourse between Sītā and Rāvaṇa"). § 533 (cf. Rāmopākhyānap.). While *Sītā* in *Laṅkā* was grieving for *Rāma* and was waited on by *Rākshasīs*, *Rāvaṇa*, afflicted by the shafts of *Kāma*, asked her to accept him as her lord, but was rejected. *Sītā* continued to dwell there, treated with tenderness by *Trijaṭā* (III, **281**).

Sītāsāntvana ("the consoling of Sītā"). § 532 (cf. Rāmopākhyānap.). In *Laṅkā Rāvaṇa* placed *Sītā* in an abode equal to *Nandana* and caused *Rākshasīs* and *Piçācīs* to guard her. The *Rākshasī Trijaṭā* told her of the *Rākshasa Avindhya* who had told her of *Rāma's* and *Lakshmaṇa's* meeting with *Sugrīva* and of the curse of *Nalakūbara* (*b*) which prevented *Rāvaṇa* from violating *Sītā*, and of a dream of evil omens about *Rāvaṇa*, *Kumbhakarṇa*, etc., running towards a southern direction, but of good omens about *Vibhīshaṇa* and his four counsellors (ascending the mountain *Çveta*), and *Rāma*,

Lakshmaṇa, and *Sītā* (running to a northern direction) (III, **280**).

Sītavana, name of a tīrtha. § 364 (Tīrthayātrāp.): III, **83**, 6029 (so B., C. has *Çī*°).

Skanda[1], the senāpati of the gods, son of Agni and Svāhā, reared by the Kṛttikās, armed with a dart (*çakti*) and having a peacock (*mayūra*) for his device. [§ 72 (Ādivaṃçāvatāraṇap.): I, **62**, 2316 (*anekajanano yatra*—i.e. in the Mhbhr. —*Kārttikeyasya sambhavaḥ*)].—[§ 116*b* (Vasu, pl.): *Kumāra* (i.e. *S*.), the son of *Agni* (*Anala*) was born in the forest of reeds (*çaravanālayaḥ*), and was called *Kārttikeya* because he was reared by the *Kṛttikāḥ*. He was father of *Çākha*, *Viçākha*, *Naigameya* and *Pṛshṭaja* (v. 2588, cf. BR. s.v. pṛshṭaja, PCR. translates differently): I, **66**, 2587 (*Agneḥ putraḥ Kumāras tu çrīmān çaravanālayaḥ*), 2588 (*Kārttikeyaḥ*)].—[§ 208 (Astradarçana): I, **137**, 5431 (*Āgneyaḥ Kṛttikāputro Raudro Gāṅgeya ity api çrūyate bhagavān devaḥ sarvaguhyamayo Guhaḥ*)].—§ 258 (Khāṇḍavadahanap.): I, **227**, 8265 (*çaktiṃ samādāya tasthau Merur ivācalaḥ*, in the encounter between the gods and Arjuna and Kṛshṇa).—[§ 368 (Tīrthayātrāp.): III, **83**, 7036 (*Guhaḥ*, anointed as senāpati of the gods in the tīrtha Taijasa)].—[§ 488 (Āṅgirasa): III, **217**, 14103 (*Kumāraç ca yathotpanno yathā cāgneḥ suto 'bhavat / yathā Rudrāc ca sambhūto Gaṅgāyāṃ Kṛttikāsu ca*, cf. §§ 495 foll.)].—[§ 495 (Skandotpatti): III, **223**, 14241 (*janma . . . Kārttikeyasya*)]. — § 496 (do.): III, 14315 (°*tām*, etymology), 14337-8 (assuming the forms of six of the wives of the seven ṛshis Svāhā cohabited with Agni; the semen of Agni she threw on the mountain Çveta, where it developed to *S*. with six heads, etc. The feats of *S*.: his rending asunder the mountain Krauñca, etc.).—§ 497 (do.): III, **226**, 14345 (Viçvāmitra performed the rites of childhood to *S*.).—§ 498 (do.): III, **226**, 14355, 14356, 14359, 14365 (the mothers of the worlds adopted *S*. as their son).—§ 499 (Skanda-Çakrasamāgama): III, **227**, 14370, 14381, 14382, 14383, 14385 (defeated the gods headed by Indra; from his side Viçākha sprang forth).—§ 500 (Skandopākhyāna): III, **228**, 14387, 14391 (*tataḥ Kumāraṃ Pitaraṃ Skandam āhur janā bhuvi; Kumārapitaraṃ, B.*), 14393, 14395, 14397 (°*prasādajaḥ putraḥ*, i.e. Çiçu), 14398 (*vīrāshṭakaḥ . . . S°mātṛgaṇodbhavaḥ* = do.), 14399 (*shashṭaṃ chāgamayaṃ vaktraṃ S°sya*) (the followers (*pārishadāḥ*) and the different forms (sons) of *S*.).—§ 501 (do.): III, **229**, 14402, 14406, (14409), (14415), (14420), 14422, (14423), 14431 (*Rudrasūnuḥ*, why he was so called), 14432 (do., do.), 14438, 14445, 14447, 14450, 14452, 14453 (as *S*. refused to become Indra, he was anointed as senāpati of the gods and married Devasenā).—§ 502 (Manushyagrahak.): III, **230**, (14459), 14460, 14462, 14465, (14466), 14467, (14468), (14471), (14473), 14474, 14475, (14475), (the Kṛttikās and Vinatā considered as mothers of Skanda), 14477, 14479 (Skandāpasmara sprung from *S*.), 14484 (*kumārāç ca kumāryaç ça . . . S°sambhavāḥ*), 14494 (*Lohitasyodadheḥ kanyā dhātrī S°sya*), [14495 (*Āryā mātā Kumārasya*)], 14497 (°*grahāḥ*), 14498.—§ 503 (Skandayuddha): III, **231**, 14514, 14515, (14518), 14520.—[§ 504 (do.): III, **231**, 14521 (*Mahāsenaṃ*, considered as son of Rudra and Umā)].—§ 505 (do.): III, **231**, 14532 (description), 14541.—§ 506 (do.): III, **231**, (14570) (took the command of the seventh army corps of the gods).—§ 507 (do.): III, **231**, 14572, 14604, 14613, 14614 (°*pārishadaiḥ*), 14616, 14618, 14619, 14625 (in the battle with the Daityas *S*. slew Mahisha, etc.), 14627 (°*sālokyatāṃ*). —§ 508 (Kārttikeyastava): III, **232**, 14630 (the 51 names of *S*. v. below).—§ 509 (do.): III, **232**, 14648 (°*sālokyaṃ*) (praised by Mārkaṇḍeya; for the names enumerated v. below). — § 576 (Bhagavadgītāp.): VI, **34**, 1228 (*senānīnām ahaṃ S°ḥ*, sc. *asmi*, says Kṛshṇa).—§ 587 (Bhīshmavadhap.): VI, **111**, 5186 (°*çaktyā yathā Krauñcaḥ purā*, sc. *babhau*).—§ 589 (Droṇābhishekap.): VII, **7**, 174 (*saināpatye yathā S°ṃ Çakramukhāḥ surāḥ*, sc. *abhishishicuḥ*). —§ 593 (Abhimanyuvadhap.): VII, **36**, 1581 (°*enevāsurīṃ camūṃ*, sc. *viprahatāṃ*); **39**, 1647 (°*syevāsuraiḥ saha*, sc. *vikrīḍitaṃ*).—§ 599 (Jayadrathavadhap.): VII, **105**ν, 3943 (*yathā S°sya, rājendra, mayūreṇa virājatā*, sc. *rathaḥ*).—§ 600 (Ghaṭotkacavadhap.): VII, **173**, 7837 (*yathendras Tārakaṃ pūrvaṃ Skandena saha jaghnivān*).—§ 604 (Karṇap.): VIII, **5**ζ, 146 (*yathā S°ena Mahishaḥ*, sc. *hataḥ*).—§ 605 (do.): VIII, **10**, 376 (*devatānāṃ yathā S°ḥ senānīḥ*), 386 (*senāpatyena* [read *sai*° with B.] *S°m ivāmarāḥ*, sc. *abhishishicuḥ*), 399 (*devair api yathā S°ḥ saṅgrāme Tārakāmaye*, sc. *vṛtaḥ*).—§ 610 (Çalyap.): IX, **6**, 312 (*devaiḥ S°m ivājitaṃ*), 319 (°*o devān ivāhave*, sc. *pāhi*).—§ 611 (do.): IX, **17**, †914 (*Krauñco yathā S°hato mahādriḥ*). — § 615*p* (Vasishṭhāpavāha): IX, **42**, 2364 (*surārinibarhaṇaṃ*, in Sthāṇutīrtha installed as senāpati).—§ 615 (Baladevatīrthayātrā): IX, **43**, †2448 (*yatra*—i.e. in *Somasya tīrtham*—*Tārakākhyaṃ jaghāna*), [†2449 (*Mahāsenaḥ*, *Kārttikeyaḥ*, *Kumāraḥ*, was anointed in the *Somasya tīrthaṃ*, there he always dwells)]; **44**, 2452. — § 615*u* (do.): In days of yore the seed of *Maheçvara* dropped and fell into a blazing fire; *Agni* could not burn it, and at the command of Brahmán threw it into the *Gaṅgā*, who, unable to bear it, washed it away on Mount *Himavat*, where it, on a clump of reeds, developed into *S*. (Kārttikeya, Gāṅgeya), who was seen by the *Kṛttikāḥ*, and having assumed six mouths, sucked them all. *Himavat* was transformed into gold, and from this reason mountains became producers of gold. Lying on that golden clump of reeds he was praised by *G*., etc. *Gaṅgā* waited upon him, and Earth held him; the celestial priest *Bṛhaspati* performed the usual rites (*jātakarmādikāḥ kriyāḥ*); the *Veda* in a fourfold form (*caturmūrtiḥ*) and the fourfold (*catushpādaḥ*) *Dhanurveda* and all weapons (*çastragrāmaḥ sasaṅgrahaḥ*) approached him. One day he saw *Çiva* and *Umā* amid a swarm of ghastly creatures (description). Also the seven *Mātṛs* were present there, and S., V.-D., M., V., P., R., Ā., Si., Serpents, Dā., the birds, *Brahmán* with his two sons, and *Vishṇu* and *Indra*, and D.-G. headed by *Nārada* and D.-ṛ., and Si. headed by *Bṛhaspati*, and the fathers of the universe who are the gods of even the gods, and the *Yāmas* and *Dhāmas*. *Çiva*, *Umā*, *Gaṅgā*, and *Agni* each thought: "he will come to me," therefore he by his yoga power assumed four forms; *Skanda* went to *Rudra*, *Viçākha* to *Umā*, *Çākha* (which is his *Vāyu*-form) to *Agni*, *Naigameya* to *Gaṅgā*. D., Dā., and Rā. made a loud noise. *Rudra*, *Umā*, *Agni*, and *Gaṅgā* prevailed upon *Brahmán*, who had formerly given away the sovereignties of D., G., Rā., Bh., Y., birds, and Pn., that he gave him the state of a generalissimo (*saināpatya*) among all creatures; and *Brahmán* ordered the kings of the hosts of the gods to wait upon him. Then the gods headed by *Brahmán*, taking *Skanda* with them, came together to *Himavat* for his instalment on the bank of the *Sarasvatī* (*puṇyāṃ Haimavatīṃ devīṃ*), which at *Samantapañcaka* is celebrated over the three worlds; there D. and G. cheerfully took their seats (IX, **44**). Collecting all articles for the investiture according to the scriptures, *Bṛhaspati* duly poured libations into the fire; *Himavat* gave a seat adorned with gems, on which *Kārttikeya* was seated; *Indra*, etc. (γ) there came together; *Brahmán*, *Kāçyapa*, etc., poured water from the *Sarasvatī* upon *Skanda*, even as the gods had poured water on the head of *Varuṇa*, the lord of the waters, in order to invest him with sovereignty. *Brahmán* gave to *Skanda* four mighty companions (*mahāpārishadān*) with speed like the wind, and crowned with ascetic success (*siddhān*): *Nandisena*, *Lohitāksha*, *Ghaṇṭākarṇa*, and *Kumudamālin*. *Sthāṇu* gave to *Skanda* a mighty companion (*pārishadam*) capable of producing 100 illusions, and who, in the great battle between the gods and the Asuras, slew with his hands alone 14 millions (*prayutāni caturdaça*). Then the gods made over to *Skanda* an army consisting of *Nairṛtas* of a form like that of *Vishṇu*. Then D. with I., G., Y., Rā., Mu. and P. shouted "victory" (*jayaçabdam*). Then *Yama* gave him two companions (*anucarau*), both of whom resembled Death (read *Yamaḥ Kālopamau* with C., B. has *Yama-Kālopamau*): *Unmātha* and *Pramātha*. *Sūrya* gave him two of his followers, *Subhrāja* and *Bhāsvara*; *Soma* gave him two companions (*anucarau*): *Maṇi* and *Sumaṇi*, both like summits of *Kailāsa*, with white garlands and white unguents. *Agni* gave to his son (i.e. Skanda) the heroic *Jvālājihva* and *Jyotis*. *Aṃça* gave him five companions: *Parigha*, etc. (δ). *Indra* gave him two companions: *Utkroça* and *Pañcaka*, armed with thunderbolt and club respectively, and who had in battle slain innumerable enemies of *Indra*. *Vishṇu* gave him three companions: *Cakra*, etc. (ϵ). The *Açvins* gave him *Vardhana* and *Nandana*, who had mastered all the sciences. *Dhātṛ* gave him five companions: *Kunda*, etc. (ζ). *Tvashṭṛ* gave him *Cakra* and *Anucakra*, both capable of producing illusions (*mahāmāyau*), etc. *Mitra* gave him *Suvrata* and *Satyasandha* of great learning and ascetic merits (*tapovidyādharau*), and capable of granting boons. *Vidhātṛ* gave him *Suprabha* and *Çubhakarman*. *Pūshan* gave him two companions (*pārshadau*): *Pāṇītaka* and *Kālika*, with great powers of illusion (*mahāmāyāvinau*). *Vāyu* gave him *Bala* and *Atibala*, with great mouths. *Varuṇa* gave him *Yama* and *Atiyama* (PCR.: *Ghasa* and *Atighasa*), with mouths like that of the *timi*. *Himavat* gave him *Suvarcas* and *Ativarcas*. *Meru* gave him *Kāñcana* and *Meghamālin*. *Manu* gave him *Sthira* and *Atisthira*. *Vindhya* gave him *Ucchṛṅga* and *Atiçṛṅga* (PCR.: *Ucchrita* and *Agniçṛṅga*) who fought with large stones. *Samudra* (the ocean) gave him *Saṅgraha* and *Vigraha*, armed with maces. *Pārvatī* gave him *Unmāda*, *Çaṅkukarṇa*, and *Pushpadanta*. *Vāsuki* gave him the snakes *Jaya* and *Mahājaya*. Similarly S., R., V., P., etc. gave commanders of forces armed with lances, etc. Moreover, there were several other combatants: *Çaṅkukarṇa*, etc. (η). Besides, *Brahmán* gave him thousands upon thousands of mighty companions, devoted to ascetic austerities and regardful of brahmans, of different ages and with different kinds of faces (*extremely fanciful description*; the faces of some resembled that of *Garuḍa*, etc.), they spoke various kinds of languages (*nānābhāshāḥ; kuçalā deçabhāshāsu*) (IX, **45**). Also the large bands of the Mothers (*Mātṛgaṇān*), those slayers of foes, by whom the universe is pervaded, became the companions of *Kumāra*; the names of the *Mātṛs* are: *Prabhāvatī*, etc. (θ) (description), some of them partook of the nature of *Yama*, some of that of *Rudra*, etc. (ι); they were beautiful like Aps., in voice they resembled the *kokila*, in prosperity *Kubera*, in battle their energy resembled that of *Indra*, etc., they have their abodes on trees and open spots and crossings of four roads, also in caves, crematoriums, mountains, and springs; they speak different languages. *Indra* gave to *Guha* (i.e. Skanda) a dart for the destruction of the enemies of the gods (description), and a banner. *Çiva* gave him a large army named *Dhanañjayā*, protected by 30,000 warriors equal to Rudra himself. *Vishṇu* gave him a triumphal garland that enhanced the power of the wearer. *Umā* gave him two pieces of cloth, of effulgence like that of the sun. *Gaṅgā* a celestial waterpot produced from amṛta. *Garuḍa* gave him his favourite son *Citrabarhin*, a peacock. *Aruṇa* gave a cock of sharp talons. *Varuṇa* gave a snake of great energy. *Brahmán* gave him, as devoted to the *Bráhman* (*brahmaṇyāya*), a black deerskin and (*Lokabhāvanaḥ*, presumably = Brahmán) victory in all battles. (Description of Skanda's army.) The gods with *Indra* praised *Kumāra*. The D-G. sung, and Aps. danced. *Skanda* granted a boon to all the gods, saying: "I shall slay all your foes." He then, with that vast host, set out for the destruction of the *Daityas*, having Exertion (*Vyavasāya*), etc. (κ) in the van. All Dai., Rā., and Dā. fled, pursued by the gods. Millions of darts issued from *Skanda's* dart. He at last slew *Tāraka* (the chief of the *Daityas*), etc. (λ); the foes were consumed with flames, produced by *Skanda*; many were killed by his roars alone, etc. (description). *Bali's* son, the *Daiteya Bāṇa*, took shelter within the *Krauñca* mountain (named after its sound, resembling the cry of a *krauñca* bird) which *Kārttikeya* (i.e. *Skanda*) pierced with that dart given to him by Agni (! v. the note of PCR., page 186) (description); Vd. soared into the air; K. became very anxious; Dai. came out and were slain together with that son of the *Daitya*-chief and his younger brother. Repeatedly hurled from *Skanda's* hand, the dart repeatedly came back to him. The gods, G. and M-ṛ (*yajvānaḥ*) honoured *Skanda* (*yoginām īçvaram*), the celestial ladies showered plenty of flowers upon him. Some speak of him as *Sanatkumāra* (the eldest son of *Brahmán*), some as the son of *Maheçvara*, and some as that of *Agni*, or of *Umā*, or of the *Kṛttikās*, or of *Gaṅgā*. That tīrtha on the *Sarasvatī* then became a second heaven; staying there *Skanda* gave to everybody various kinds of dominion and bestowed the three worlds on the foremost of the *Nairṛtas* (*Nairṛtamukhyebhyaḥ*, so both B. and C.; "the foremost ones of the celestials," PCR.): IX, **44**, 2488; **45**, 2528, 2537, 2539, 2540, 2542, 2557 (°*sya sainikāḥ*), 2617 (°*syānucarāḥ*); **46**, 2671, 2686, 2688, 2697.—§ 615 (Baladevatīrthayātrā): IX, **46**, 2724, 2727 (*abhishiktaḥ*, all. to § 615*u*).—§ 619 (Strīvilāpap.): XI, **23**, 652 (*çete . . . S°ḥ çaravanaṃ yathā*). — § 623 (Rājadh.): XII, **15** β, 439 (among those who are slaughterers). —§ 641 (do.): XII, **122**, 4500 (*Kumāraṃ dvādaçabhujam*, made the chief of the Bhūtas).—[§ 653*b* (Gṛdhragomāyusaṃv.): XII, **153** *a*, 5752 (*Kumāraḥ*)]. — [§ 696*b* (Dakshaprokta Çiva-sahasranāmastotra): XII, **285**, 10481 (*Guhasya*)]. — [§ 704 (Mokshadh.): XII, **301** *a*, †11094 (*Shaḍānanam*)].—§ 714*d* (Himavat): *Skanda* (*Kumara*) threw his dart on the *Himavat* and challenged all beings to draw it up or at least to shake it: XII, **328**, [12319 (*Kumārena*)], 12320.—[§ 714*e* (Vishṇu): XII, **328**, 12324 (*Pāvakiṃ*), 12327 (*Skandarājasya*, C. has by error Skandha°) (from respect of Skanda Vishṇu only shook that dart though he was capable of drawing it up)].—[§ 714*f* (Prahlāda): **XII, 328**, 12328 (*vīryaṃ Kumārasya*)].—[§ 717*b* (Nārāyaṇīya): XII, **340**, 12957 (*Maheçvara-Mahāsenau Bāṇapriyahitaishiṇau*, will be defeated by Kṛshṇa)].—§ 730*g* (Upamanyu): XIII, **14** ν, 871 (°*o mayūram āsthāya sthito Devyāḥ samīpataḥ çaktighaṇṭe* (C. *s*°) *samādāya dvitīya iva Pāvakaḥ*).—§ 730

(Ânuçâsanik.): XIII, **16**, 1058 (°*endrau*, Çiva identified with *S.*, etc.).—§ 737 (do.): XIII, **31***a*, 2013 (C. has by error *Skā*°).—§ 747*b* (Suvarṇotpatti): XIII, **85**, [4027 (*Pāvakiḥ*), 4098 (*Kārttikeyatvaṃ*, origin of the name Kārttikeya)], 4099 (°*tāṃ*, etymology), [4179 (*Kārttikeyasya*), 4180 (*Kārttikeyaḥ*)] (Skanda arose from the semen of Rudra which had fallen into fire and was reared by the Kṛttikās and became the generalissimo of the gods).—§ 748*b* (Tārakavadhop.): XIII, **86**, 4199 (°*tāṃ*, origin of the name; *Kārttikeyaḥ*, origin of the name), 4216 (*senāpatiḥ*) (the birth of *S.*, the different gifts bestowed on him by the gods; *S.* slew Tāraka).—§ 766 (Ânuçâsanik.): XIII, **134**, (6182).—§ 770 (do.): XIII, **151***e*, 7106.—§ 775 (do.): XIII, **166***a*, 7636 (*senāpatiḥ*).

Cf. also the following synonyms:—

Āgneya, q.v.
Agnidāyāda ("the son of Agni"): III, 14323.
Agnija (do.): VIII, †4696.
Agniputra, Agnisuta (do.), q.v.
Analaputra (do.): IX, 2538.
Analasūnu (do.): IX, 2690.
Analātmaja (do.): IX, 2460.
Bhadraçākha, Brahmaṇya, Chāgavaktra, Çākha, Çaktidhara, q.v.
Çaktidhṛk: III, 14383.
Çaktipāṇi: V, 5720.
Çaravaṇālaya, Devasenāpati, Gāṅgeya, q.v.
Guha: I, 5431; III, 7036 (invested in Taijasa), 8055 (to be worshipped in Koṭitīrtha), 8203 (*Mahāsenaḥ*, in Bhartṛsthāna), †12569 (*babhau yathā Bhūtapatiḥ* . . . *sametya* . . . *G°ena*), 14317, 14376, 14430 (*Rudrasūnuṃ tataḥ prāhur G°ṃ*), 14532, †14637; IX, 2663, 2684; XII, 10481; XIII, †1850, 4099 (etymology, identified with gold), 4199 (etymology), 4214.
Hutāçanasuta ("the son of Agni"), **Jvalanasūnu** (do.), **Jvalanātmaja** (do.), q.v.
Kārttikeya ("the [adopted] son of the Kṛttikās"): I, 2316 (*anekajanano* . . . *K°sya sambhavaḥ*), 2588, †7083 (*yau tau Kumārau iva K°au*); II, 1186 (°*sya dayitaṃ* . . . *Rohītakaṃ*); III, 7006 (present in the tīrtha Auçanasa), 7012 (*Pṛthūdakaṃ* . . . *K°sya*), 14241 (*janma* . . . *K°sya*), 14375, 14533 (*patākā K°sya*), 14636; V, 5768 (°*a ivājeyaḥ çarastambāt suto 'bhavat*); VI, 2066 (°*o yathā nityaṃ devānām abhavat purā*, sc. *senāpatiḥ*), 5820 (*çaratalpagataṃ* . . . *janmaçayyāgataṃ vīraṃ K°m iva*); VII, 154 (*senāpatiṃ kuru* / *jigīshanto 'surān saṅkhye K°m ivāmarāḥ*), 3454 (*Shaṇmukhaḥ*), 7084 (°*samuddhūtām Āsurīm iva tāṃ camūṃ*), 8191 (°*m ivāhave*); IX, †2449 (dwells in Somasya tīrtha(ṃ)), 2465, 2493, 2533, 2545, 2546, 2547, 2548, 2616, 2649 (°*ānuyāyinyaḥ*, sc. *mātaraḥ*), 2699, 2701, 2702, 2719; XIII, 4098 (°*tvaṃ*, origin of the name), 4179, 4180, 4199 (origin of the name), 4218 (*suvarṇaṃ* . . . *sahajaṃ K°sya Vishṇos tejaḥ paraṃ*).
Kṛttikāputra (do.): I, 5431; III, 14617.
Kṛttikāsuta (do.): III, 14568.
Kumāra: I, 2587; III, 8123 (*Vīrāçramavāsinaṃ*), 14103, 14316, 14350 (?), 14353, 14373, 14495 (*Āryā mātā K°sya*); V, 5290 (°*a iva Bhūtānāṃ*, sc. *senāpatiḥ*), 5720 (*senānye Çaktipāṇaye*); IX, †2449 (*Kārttikeyaḥ*, dwells in *Somasya tīrthaṃ*), 2450 (°*syābhishekaṃ*), 2454, 2465 (*Kārttikeyaḥ*), [2480 (*kumāravaraṃ*)], 2489 (*Naigameyaḥ?*), 2500, 2520 (°*ābhishekārthaṃ*), 2523 (read *Kumāraṃ* with B., C. has *k°ān*), 2543, 2580, 2619 (*mātṛgaṇān K°ānucarān*), 2668, 2677, 2695 (°*ānucarāḥ*), 2708 (do.), 2720, 2728 (*abhishekaṃ K°sya*), 2730 (do.); XII, 4500 (*dvādaçabhujaṃ Skandaṃ*), 5752, 12319, 12328; XIII, 4202 (*Jvalanātmajaṃ*), 4203 (*Shaḍānanaṃ*), 4215, 4217 (*Pāvakiḥ*).
Kumārapitṛ, q.v.
Mahāsena: II, 467 (in the palace of Brahmán), 1486 (*jagrāha* . . . *M°m iveçvaraḥ*); III, 8203 (*Guhaḥ*), 14326, 14339, 14350, 14363, 14364, 14366, 14369, 14371, 14442, 14454 (*Devasenāpatiṃ*), 14521, 14526, 14534, 14569, 14606, 14609, 14613, 14618, 14624; IX, 311 (*iva*), †2449, 2678, 2681, 2682, 2691, 2701; XII, 12957.
Naigameya, Pāvakātmaja ("the son of Agni"), **Pāvaki** (do.), **Pṛshṭhaja, Raudra** ("the son of Rudra"), **Rudrasūnu** (do.), **Senānī, Shaḍānana, Shaḍvaktra, Shaṇmukha, Skandarāja, Vahninandana** ("the son of Agni"), **Vibudhasattama, Viçākha**, q.v.

Skanda, names of, found in the **Kārttikeyastava** (III, **232**): *a*) The fifty-one names of Skanda (vv. 14630–14636*a*): *Āgneya*, 14630, *Amogha*, 14632, *Anagha*, 14632, *Anāmaya*, 14630, *Bālakrīḍanapriya*, 14634, *Bhadrakṛt*, 14632, *Bhūteça*, 14630, *Bhuvaneçvara*, 14631, *Brahmacārin*, 14635, *Caṇḍa*, 14631, *Candrānana*, 14632, *Çaravaṇodbhava*, 14635, *Çiçu*, 14631, *Çīghra*, 14631, *Çubhānana*, 14631, *Çuci*, 14631, *Çūra*, 14635, *Devasenāpriya*, 14635, *Dharmātman*, 14630, 14633, *Dīptaçakti*, 14632, *Dīptakīrti*, 14630, *Dīptavarṇa*, 14631, *Kāmada*, 14631, *Kāmajit*, 14631, *Kānta*, 14631, *Kanyābhartṛ*, 14633, *Khacārin*, 14635, *Kūṭamohana*, 14632, *Lalita*, 14634, *Mahishārdana*, 14630, *Mātṛvatsala*, 14633, *Mayūraketu*, 14630, *Naigameya*, 14634, *Netṛ*, 14634, *Pavitra(ḥ)*, 14633, *Prabhu*, 14634, *Praçāntātman*, 14632, *Priya*, 14632, 14636, *Priyakṛt*, 14636, *Raudra*, 14632, *Revatīsuta*, 14633, *Satyavāc*, 14631, *Shashṭīpriya*, 14633, *Skanda*, 14630, *Suduçcara*, 14634, *Suvrata*, 14634, *Svāheya*, 14633, *Vāsudevapriya*, 14636, *Vibhakta*, 14633, *Viçākha*, 14634, *Viçvāmitrapriya*, 14635.—*b*) The names occurring in Mārkaṇḍeya's praise of Skanda (v. †14637–†14646): *Acalendra*, 14643, *Anantarūpa*, 14642, *Aprameya*, 14637, *Ardhamāsa*, 14639, *Aravindavaktra*, 14640, *Ayana(ṃ)*, 14639, *Bhāvana*, 14640, *Brahmaja*, 14638, *Brahmajña*, 14638, *Brāhmaṇānāṃ netṛ*, 14638, *Brāhmaṇasavratin*, 14638, *Brahmaṇya*, 14638, *Brahmapriya*, 14638, *Brahmavratāṃ varishṭha(ḥ)*, 14638, *Brahmavid*, 14638, *Brahmeçaya*, 14638, *Çaktidhara*, 14637, *Çatrujetṛ*, 14641, *Daksha*, 14643, *Dharaṇī*, 14641, *Dharma*, 14643, *Diçaḥ* (pl.), 14639, *Ditijāntaka*, 14644, *Dvādaçanetrabāhu*, 14646, *Gaṅgāsuta*, 14642, *Guruçaktidhārin*, 14642, *Indra*, 14643, *Jetṛ ripūnāṃ*, 14644, *Lokanātha*, 14646, *Lokapāla*, 14640, *Mantrastuta*, 14639, *Māsa*, 14639, *Parama(ṃ) havis*, 14640, *Parama(ṃ) pavitra(ṃ)*. 14639, *Parāvara*, 14645, *Parāvarajña*, 14645, *Prabhu*, 14641, *Prabhu(ḥ) prabhūṇāṃ*, 14644, *Pracaṇḍa*, 14641, *Pravara(ḥ) surāṇāṃ*, 14644, *Pushkarāksha*, 14640, *Ṛtasya kartṛ*, 14644, *Ṛtavaḥ shaṭ*, 14639, *Sahasrabāhu*, 14640, *Sahasrabhū*, 14641, *Sahasrabhuj*, 14641, *Sahasraçīrsha*, 14642, *Sahasrapad*, 14642, *Sahasratushṭi*, 14641, *Sahasravaktra*, 14640, *Saṃvatsara*, 14639, *Sarvasurapravīra*, 14646, *Senādhipati*, 14641, *Shaḍānana*, 14637, *Shaḍarcis*, 14639 (*prathitaḥ*), *Shaṇmukha*, 14643, *Soma*, 14643, *Sūkshmaṃ tapas tatparaṃ*, 14645, *Suvīra*, 14637, *Svadhā*, 14639, *Svāhā*, 14639, *Svāhāsuta*, 14632, *Ugradhanvan*, 14644, *Vāyu*, 14643, *Vibhu*, 14641.

Skanda[2] = Sūrya (the Sun): III, 148.—Do.[3] = Çiva (1000 names[2]). Do.[4] = Vishṇu (1000 names).

Skānda (XIII, 2013), v. Skanda[1].

[Skanda-Çakra-samāgama(ḥ)] ("meeting of Skanda with Indra").—§ 499 (cf. Skandotp.). The planets (*grahāḥ*) and *upagrahas* (see BR.), *Mātṛs* and the *gaṇas* of the *parishads* preceded by Fire and other terrible gods waited on *Skanda*. *Indra*, with the hosts of the gods approached, mounted on *Airāvata*, in order to kill him. But *Skanda* defeated them by flames, and when *Indra* pierced his right side with his thunderbolt, thence sprang forth an armed youth *Viçākha* (*vajra-viçanād jāto*, v. 14384), and *Indra* and the gods sought and obtained the protection of *Skanda* (III, **227**).

Skandadhara = Vishṇu (1000 names).

Skandamātṛ ("the mother of Skanda") = Durgā (Umā): VI, 803.

Skandāpasmara, name of a demon. § 502 (Manushyagrahak.): III, **230**, 14479.

Skandarāja = Skanda: XII, 12327 (C. has *Skandha°*).

Skandaviçākha = Çiva: XIII, 907 (C. has *Skandha°*).

[Skandayuddha(ṃ)] ("the combat of Skanda"). § 503 (cf. Manushyagr.). Then *Svāhā*, the daughter of *Daksha*, who had in vain loved *Agni* from her childhood, prevailed upon *Skanda* that she should live for ever with *Agni*, in so far as offerings with *mantras* to the gods and *pitṛs* (*havyaṃ kavyañ ca*) should always be coupled with the name of *Svāhā*. —§ 504. Then *Skanda* was sent by *Brahmán* to his father *Rudra*; for *Rudra* and *Umā* had entered *Agni* and *Svāhā*, and from this combination *Skanda* had sprung; *Rudra's* semen had been thrown back upon the hill, whence sprang forth *Miñjikā* and *Miñjika*, and portions of it fell into the Blood Sea, into the rays of the sun, upon the earth, and upon the trees, whence sprang forth the various troops of his *pārishadas*, living on flesh. These five classes of spirits should be honoured with sun-flowers (*arkapushpaiḥ*: Calotropis gigantea) for the sake of wealth and healing of diseases; *Miñjikā* and *Miñjika* must be honoured for the welfare of children; the females, named *Vṛddhikās*, who were produced in the trees and live on human flesh, must be worshipped by persons who desire to have children. These are the innumerable *gaṇas* of *Piçācas*.—§ 505. *Airāvata* had two bells named *Vaijayantī*; *Indra* gave one of them to *Viçākha* and the other one to *Skanda*; the standards of *Skanda* and *Viçākha* were red. *Skanda*, surrounded by troops of *Piçācas* and gods, sat on the golden mountain with the toys that had been given to him by the gods. Description of the *Çveta* mountain.—§ 506. Then *Çiva*, with *Pārvatī*, rode in their shining chariot, yoked with 1,000 lions and managed by *Kāla*, to *Bhadravaṭa*; they were preceded by *Kubera* (riding in *Pushpaka*) with the *Guhyakas*, and followed by *Indra* (riding on *Airāvata*) and the gods; in the right wing of his army was the great *Yaksha Amogha*, with the *Jṛmbhakas*, *Yakshas*, *Rakshases*, *Vasus*, *Rudras*, etc.; there was also *Yama*, with *Mṛtyu*, surrounded by hundreds of terrible diseases; behind *Yama* the trident of *Çiva*, named *Vijaya*, surrounded by *Varuṇa*, with various aquatic animals; the *paṭṭiça* of *Rudra* surrounded by clubs, etc., and followed by the umbrella of *Rudra*, and after this the water-vessel, worshipped by the troops and maharshis, and on the right side of this the sceptre (*daṇḍaḥ*), with *Bhṛgus*, *Aṅgirases*, and gods. Behind these rode *Rudra* in his white chariot, followed by rivers, etc.; *Apsarases*, *nakshatras*, planets, the children of the gods, etc., and *Parjanya*. *Soma* held a white umbrella over his head, and *Agni* and *Vāyu* held the two fans. Behind him came *Indra* and the *rājarshis*, and *Gaurī*, *Vidyā*, etc., and the sciences (*vidyāgaṇāḥ*). In the front the *Rākshasā graha* advanced, holding the standard. The foremost of *Yakshas*, *Piṅgala*, the friend of *Rudra*, who is always busy in places where corpses are burned, at one time was ahead of the army and at another behind it. *Rudra* is worshipped by mortals with virtuous actions in various forms. At the request of *Çiva*, *Skanda* took the command of the seventh army corps (*skandhasya*) and was advised always to look up to *Çiva*, then he should attain great welfare.—§ 507. Omens frightened *Çiva*, *Pārvatī*, the gods, and the *Dānavas* (*Asuras*, *Daityas*); *Indra* encouraged the gods when about to flee; the *Dānava Mahisha* crushed 10,000 of the gods with a mountain, put *Indra* and the gods to flight, and seized the pole of *Rudra's* chariot, while heaven and earth groaned, etc., and the *maharshis* lost their senses, but (as *Rudra* did not choose to kill him himself) *Skanda* killed him, cutting off his head that barred the entrance of sixteen *yojanas* [to the *Uttara-Kurus*, Nīl.], though the *Uttara-Kurus* at present pass easily by that gate. The *Dānavas* fell in large numbers from the lance and arrows of *Skanda*; the lance always returned to his hand again after killing thousands of enemies; the *pārishadas* of *Skanda* devoured them and drank their blood. When the *Dānavas* were defeated, *Skanda* went to *Çiva* and was embraced and praised by *Indra*, Then *Indra*, with the gods, took leave from *Çiva* and left the place, and *Rudra* returned to *Bhadravaṭa*, after having recommended to the gods to render allegiance to *Skanda* just as to himself. In one day *Skanda* had killed the *Dānavas* and conquered the three worlds* (ch. **231**).

Skandāksha, a warrior of Skanda. § 615*u* (Skanda): IX, **45***η*, 2562.

Skandha, a serpent. § 67 (Sarpasattra): I, **57**, 2160 (only B., C. has *Maṇiskandhaḥ* instead of *Maṇiḥ Skandhaḥ*).

Skandharāja, v. Skandarāja.

Skandhaviçākha, v. Skandaviçākha.

[Skandopākhyāna(ṃ)] ("episode of Skanda").—§ 500 (cf. Skanda-Çakra-samāg.). The *Pārishadas* of *Skanda*: When *Skanda* was struck with the thunderbolt, a number of male children were produced, who steal little children, whether born or in the womb, as also a number of female children. They adopted *Viçākha* as their father. *Bhadraçākha* (form of *Skanda*, cf. v. 14400), with a face like that of a goat, in the battle protected his sons and daughters, in the presence of the mothers. Therefore they call *Skanda Kumārapitṛ* (so B., C. has *Kumāraṃ pitaraṃ*), and those who desire to have sons worship *Rudra* as *Agni*, and *Umā* as *Svāhā* (so C., B. has *Agnimukhāṃ* instead of *Agnim Umāṃ*). The daughters of the *Tapa* fire obtained from *Skanda* that they became the mothers of the whole world; some of them should be good (*çivāḥ*) and some evil (*açivāḥ*). Having adopted *Skanda* as their son, the host of the mothers departed. *Kākī*, *Halimā*, etc. (in all seven) (*a*) had, by the grace of *Skanda*, a terrible son *Çiçu*, who is named *vīrāshṭaka* (i.e. consisting of eight men) or, when the goat's head is included, *navaka* (i.e. consisting of nine). The sixth face of *Skanda* is that of a goat, the best of the six, honoured by the mothers, that by which *Bhadraçākha* created the divine energy (? *çaktiṃ yenāsṛjad divyāṃ*). This happened on the fifth day of the bright half of the month, and on the sixth a terrific battle took place (III, **228**).—§ 501. Description of *Skanda*. *Çrī*, embodied and looking like a lotus, rendered her allegiance to him. The *brahmans* and *maharshis* praised him, saying: "*Hiraṇyagarbha*! thou who wast born only six nights ago, do thou become *Indra*," and at his request they explained to him the offices of *Indra* (*b*). Even *Indra* besought him to become the lord of the gods. But, at the request of *Skanda*, *Indra* retained his sovereignty, and, with all the gods, anointed *Skanda* as the leader of the celestial forces, and fastened the celestial wreath of gold, of *Viçvakarman's* manufacture, round his neck. *Rudra* came with *Pārvatī* and honoured him. *Skanda* is called the son of *Rudra* because *Agni* is called *Rudra* by *brahmans*, and because he was produced by *Rudra* entering Fire, and because he was honoured by *Rudra* before all the gods, and because the *Çveta* mountain, where he was reared by the *Kṛttikās*, was formed of *Rudra's* semen virile. The red cock, given him by *Agni*, formed the ensign of *Skanda*, perched on the top of his chariot. The power (*çakti*) which conduces to the victory of the gods, advanced before him. An innate armour entered into his body, and always manifests itself on the battle-field. Under the recitation of holy texts he was honoured by D., G., Aps., Pç., etc. Then he married *Devasenā* (names v. 14451), Bṛh. performing the necessary prayers and oblations. Then *Lakshmī* began to serve him. Therefore the fifth lunar day is called *Çrī-pañcamī*, and the sixth "a great tithi" (*mahātithiḥ*) (III, **229**).

[Skandotpatti(ḥ)] ("origin of Skanda").—§ 495 (Mārk.). *Mārkaṇḍeya* promised to tell the story of *Kārttikeya*, the son of *Adbhuta*, begotten of the wives of the *Brahmarshis*. Formerly, when the *Asuras* always defeated the gods, *Indra*, anxious to find out a leader for the celestial host, repaired to the *Mānasa* mountain, and, hearing a woman crying for protection, rescued her from the *Asura Keçin*, whom he wounded and put to flight (III, **223**). She told *Indra* that she was *Devasenā*, daughter of *Prajāpati*, and that her sister *Daityasenā* had let herself be taken away by *Keçin* from the *Mānasa* mountain, where they used to sport with their female friends with the permission of *Prajāpati*. *Indra* said that she was a sister's daughter of his mother *Dākshāyaṇī*. She asked *Indra* to select a husband for her, who was able to conquer the gods, *Dānavas*, *Yakshas*, *Kinnaras*, *Uragas*, *Rakshas*, and *Daityas*. *Indra* was grieved, thinking there was no such husband for her.—§ 496. Then *Indra* perceived the Sun rising from the *Udaya* hill, and *Soma* (the Moon) entering the Sun on the *amāvasyā* (new-moon day) at the *Raudra muhūrta*, and the gods and *Asuras* fighting on the *Udaya* mountain, the morning twilight tinged with red clouds, the Sea blood-red; *Bhṛgus* and *Aṅgirases* offered oblations, and *Agni* took the oblations and entered the Sun, whilst the Sun was entering the twenty-fourth *parvan*, and *Sindhu* was flowing with a current of fresh blood, etc. *Indra* thought that, if now *Soma* or *Agni* gave birth to a son, this son might become the husband of *Devasenā*. Then he repaired with *Devasenā* to the world of *Brahmán*, who promised that it should be as *Indra* had thought. Then *Indra*, with *Devasenā*, repaired to the place where the *devarshis Vasishṭha*, etc. lived, and the gods also came thither to drink *soma* and receive their shares of offerings, and the *Adbhuta* fire came from the solar disc to the *āhavanīya* and made over the offerings to the gods. He, (Adbhuta), then saw the wives of the *ṛshis* sleeping in their *āçramas* and fell in love. In order to look at them daily, he entered the *gārhapatya* fire, and dwelt there for a long time, and at last, from despair, repaired to a forest in order to do away with himself. *Svāhā*, daughter of *Daksha*, who had in vain loved *Adbhuta*, now resolved upon assuming the guise of the wives of the seven *ṛshis* (III, **224**). *Svāhā* first gratified her desire in the guise of *Çivā*, the wife of *Aṅgiras*, and then, lest somebody should unduly suspect the brāhmaṇa ladies, she went out of the forest in the guise of a bird (*garuḍī*, *suparṇī*), and on the *Çveta* mountain, that was covered with clumps of reeds and guarded with seven-headed poisonous serpents, *rākshasas*, *Piçācas*, etc., she threw the semen, which she held in her hand, into a golden basin. Then, assuming successively the form of five of the others, she did the same on the first lunar day (*pratipadi*). Only the form of *Arundhatī* she was unable to assume because of her ascetic merit and devotion to her husband. The semen produced a child, whom the *ṛshis* called *Skanda* (etymology v. 14315), with six heads, etc. On the second day it first assumed a form, on the 3rd it looked like a little child, on the fourth the limbs were developed. Seizing the bow used by the destroyer of *Tripura*, *Skanda* uttered a terrible roar, so that the great *nāgas Citra* and *Airāvata* sprang up. But *Skanda* seized them with two of his hands, and holding a dart in one hand, a cock in another, etc., and blowing a conch-shell, he terrified the creatures with his roars. The persons of various orders, who then sought the protection of *Skanda*, are called his followers by the brahmans (*pārishadān brāhmaṇān*, read *brāhmaṇāḥ*). Discharging his arrows in the direction of the *Çveta* mountain, he rent asunder the mountain *Krauñca*, the son of *Himavat*; therefore the swans and vultures go to the mountain *Meru*. The other mountains also screamed aloud. Then, with his lance, he rent in twain one of the peaks of the *Çveta* mountain. Mount *Çveta* and the other mountains left the Earth and fled; the Earth was torn asunder on all sides; she went to *Skanda* and regained her power; the mountains bowed down to *Skanda* and came back to the Earth, and all creatures worshipped *Skanda* on the fifth day of the lunar month (III, **225**).—§ 497. Terrific prodigies were seen everywhere. The *ṛshis* tried to restore tranquillity to the universe. The inhabitants of the *Caitraratha* forest accused the wives of the six *ṛshis*, other ones the fowl (*garuḍī*) of being the cause thereof; but nobody suspected *Svāhā*. The seven *ṛshis* divorced their wives with the exception of *Arundhatī*, though *Svāhā* claimed the child as hers. *Viçvāmitra*, having concluded the sacrifice of the seven *ṛshis*, had secretly followed the god of fire, and knew everything as it had happened. He sought the protection of *Skanda*, and performed for him the thirteen auspicious rites of childhood (*maṅgalāni kaumārāṇi*): the *jātakarman*, etc., etc. Though *Viçvāmitra* informed the seven *ṛshis* of the innocence of their wives, yet they abandoned them unconditionally.—§ 498. The gods asked *Indra* to kill *Skanda*, but he dared not attack him, saying that *Skanda* was able to destroy even the Creator of the world. Then they let the Mothers of the world approach in order to kill *Skanda*, but they adopted him as their son and let him suck their breasts, especially the daughter of *Krodha* with a spike in her hand, and the daughter of the Red Sea, who lived on blood; and his father *Agni* came and, transformed into *Naigameya* (see BR.) with a goat's mouth, gratified him with toys (III, **226**).

***Smara** = Kāma: VII, †8410.

Smṛti ("tradition," personif.). § 615*u* (Skanda): IX, **46**κ, 2682.

Snehana = Çiva (1000 names[2]).

Sodha, pl. (°*āḥ*), a people. § 574 (Jambūkh.): VI, **9**μ, 349 (only C., B. has *Godhāḥ*).

***Soma**[1], originally the soma juice, generally identified with the Moon. § 28 (Amṛtamanthana): **I, 18,** 1145 (*Çatasahas-*

rāṃçuḥ, Çītāṃçuḥ, arose at the churning of the ocean), 1148; [**19**, 1162 (*Candra-Sūryābhyām*, 1166 (do.) (*S.* and Sūrya discovered Rāhu drinking *amṛta*; Rāhu was slain but his head yet swallows *S.* and Sūrya at the eclipses)]. — § 37 (Indra): I, **25**, 1291 (Indra identified with *S.*).—§ 61 (Sarpasattra): I, **55**, †2097 (°*sya yajñaḥ*).—§ 115 (Aṃçāvat.): I, **65**, [2577 (*Indave*, Daksha gave twenty-seven of his daughters as wives to Soma)], 2580 (*saptaviṃçatiḥ S°sya patnyaḥ kālasya nayane yuktāḥ S°patnyaḥ*).—§ 116 (Vasu pl.): I, **65**, 2582 (among the Vasus), [2583 (*Candramāḥ*, do., son of Manasvinī)], 2586 (father of Varcas).—§ 130*g* (Abhimanyu): I, **67**, 2748, 2759 (let his son Varcas become incarnate as Abhimanyu).—§ 134 (Viçvāmitra): I, **71**, 2933 (fears Viçvāmitra).—[§ 138 (Daksha Prācetasa): I, **75**, 3134 (*Indave*, Daksha gave twenty-seven of his daughters (*kalasya nayane yuktāḥ*) as wives to *S.*)]—§ 147 (Devayānī): I, **82**, 3408 (°*sya . . . gṛhe . . . striyam*).—§ 221*b* (Cākshushī): I, **170**, 6478 (learnt the science Cākshushī from Manu and communicated it to Viçvāvasu).—§ 238 (Pañcendrop.): I, **197**, †7277. —§ 240 (Vaivāhikap.): I, **199**, 7351 (*Rohiṇī ca yathā S°e tvaṃ bhava bhartṛshu*).—[§ 246 (Sundopasundop.): I, **211**, 7682 (*Candrādityau*, in the abode of Brahmán)].—§ 257*c* (Gāṇḍīva): I, **225**, 8177 (*rājñā*, had possessed the bow (i.e. Gāṇḍīva), the quivers, and the chariot which Varuṇa gave to Arjuna).—§ 257 (Khāṇḍavadahanap.): I, **225**, 8186 (*yaṃ sma S°ḥ samāruhya Dānavān ajayat prabhuḥ*, sc. the chariot of Arjuna).—§ 259 (Çārṅgakop.): I, **229**, 8360 (Agni identified with *S.*).—§ 263 (Sabhākriyāp.): II, **3**, 80 (°*sya ca yathā sabhā*).—§ 270 (Brahmasabhāv.): II, **11**, 464 (*etair*, i.e. the *pitṛs*, *āpyāyitaiḥ pūrvaṃ S°a āpyāyate punaḥ*) —[§ 310*b* (Sūrya): III, **3**, 137 (*Oshadhīpatiḥ . . . janayām-āsa*, sc. *oshadhīḥ*), 138 (*Candra°*)]. — § 317*b* (Kṛshṇa Vāsudeva): III, **12**, 480 (Kṛshṇa becomes *S.*, etc.).—[§ 350 (Nalopākhyānap.): III, **68**, 2676 (*bhartuḥ samāgamāt sādhvī Rohiṇī Çaçino yathā*)]. — § 391 (Ṛshyaçṛṅga): III, **114**, †10091 (*khe Rohiṇī S°m ivānukūlā*).—[§ 400 (Tīrthayātrāp.): III, **118**, †10225 (*Candrasya*, sc. *āyatanaṃ*, visited by Yudhishṭhira, etc.)].—[§ 421*c* (Ākāça-Gaṅgā): III, **142**, 10906 (*Candramāḥ*, among the luminous bodies which resort to the Ākāça-Gaṅgā)]. — § 439 (Yakshayuddhap.): III, **163**, [11867 (*Sūrya - Candramasau*, go round Meru)], 11872 (*nakshatraiḥ saha*).—§ 450 (Ājagarap.): III, **180**, 12461 (*puñcamaḥ Somād Āyoḥ putraḥ*, i.e. Nahusha). § 450 (Mārkaṇḍeyas.): III, **189**, 12955 (identified with Nārāyaṇa). —§ 474*b* (Dhundhumārop.): III, **201**, 13498 (*Indra-S°āgni-Varuṇāḥ*, worship Vishṇu).—§ 490 (Āngirasa): III, **219**, 14138, 14139 (*Somena saha yujyate*, sc. the fire Vīra, so Nīl.). —§ 493 (do.): III, **221**, 14190 (*Agnī-Shomau*, sons of Niçā). —§ 496 (Skandotpatti): III, **224**, 14267, 14271, 14275 (°*sya Vahni-Sūryābhyām . . . samāgamaḥ*), 14276. — § 506 (Skandayuddha): III, **231**, 14560 (held a white umbrella over the head of Skanda). § 509 (Kārttikeyaçr.): III, **232**, †14643 (Skanda identified with *S.*).—§ 512 (Ghoshayātrāp.): III, **247**, 15045 (*upaplutaṃ yathā S°ṃ Rāhuṇā*).—§ 522 (Draupadīharaṇap.): III, **265**, †15590 (°*sya*, sc. *patnī*).—§ 552*c* (Gāṇḍīva): IV, **43**, 1348 (held Gāṇḍīva for 500 years). — § 552 (Goharaṇap.): IV, **56**, 1770 (°*sya*, sc. *vimānaṃ*). — § 555 (Indravijaya): V, **16**, †511 (*purāṇo devaḥ*?).—§ 560 (Sanatsujātap.): V, **46**, 1757.—§ 565 (Gālavacarita): V, **108**, 3771 (*atra*—i.e. in the east—*labdhavaraḥ S°ḥ suraiḥ kratubhiḥ pīyate*), [**111**, 3828 (*atra*—i.e. in the north—*rājyena viprāṇāṃ Candramāç cābhyashicata*); **117**, 3968 (*reme . . . yathā Candraç ca Rohiṇyām*)].—§ 569*b* (Yayāti): V, **149**, 5042 (°*ḥ Prajāpatiḥ pūrvaṃ Kurūṇāṃ vaṃçavardhanaḥ / S°ād babhūva shashṭo 'yaṃ Yayātiḥ*).—[§ 575 (Bhūmip.): VI, **11**, 403 (°*ārkayoḥ*)].—[§ 575*e* (do.): the diameter of the moon is 11,000 yojanas, its circumference 38,900 yojanas; VI, **12**, 484 (*Candramāḥ*), 485 (*Çītaraçmeḥ*)]. —§ 576 (Bhagavadgītāp.): VI, **17**, 637 (*Maghāvishayagaḥ S°ḥ*); **39**, 1395 (*pushṇāmi caushadhīḥ sarvāḥ S°o bhūtvā rasātmakaḥ*, says Kṛshṇa). — § 592 (Saṃçaptakavadhap.): VII, **23**ο, 977 (*Sutasomaṃ tu yaṃ Pārthaḥ, S°ād* — B. *saumyam*—*putram ayācata*—B. *ajījanat*).—§ 595 (Shoḍaçarāj., v. Gaya): VII, **66**, 2343 (*īje . . . yathā S°ḥ*); (do. v. Pṛthu Vainya): VII, **69**, 2416 (°*rāṭ*, acted as calf when the Saptarshis milked the earth).—§ 599 (Jayadrathavadhap.): VII, **98**, 3641 (*devā Brahma-S°purogamāḥ*, came to see the encounter between Droṇa and Sātyaki); **116**, 4627 (*grasyamānaṃ . . . khe S°m iva Rāhuṇā*); **137**, 5636 (*prajāsaṃharaṇe . . . S°ṃ sapta grahā iva*, sc. *apīḍayan*).—§ 599*e* (Çini): VII, **144**, 6028 (son of Atri and father of Budha).—§ 603*d* (Tripura): VII, **202**, 9574 (*çaraṃ . . . Vishṇu-S°samāyutaṃ*, employed by Çiva).—§ 603 (Nārāyaṇāstramokshap.): VII, **202** κκ, 9632 (*Somārdhaṃ*, B. *Somo'rdhaṃ*, sc. the one half of the body of Çiva).—§ 606 (Tripurākhyāna): VIII, **34**, 1471 (became the *bhalla* of Çiva's chariot), 1502, 1503 (*agnī-Somaṃ jagat*, so C., B. has *Agnī-Shomau jagat*), 1510 (°-*Vishṇvagnisaṃbhavaṃ*, sc. *bāṇaṃ*), 1533 (*ishuṃ . . . Vishṇu-S°āgnisaṃbhavaṃ*), 1555 (°*agni-Vishṇūnāṃ*) —§ 607 (Karṇap.): VIII, **42**, 2005 (°*rājānaḥ*, having *S.* for their king, scil. the brahmans; differently PCR.); **45**ζ, 2103 (with the brahmans he protects the north).—[§ 608*b* (Arjuna): VIII, **46**, 2160 (*Induḥ*, had been one of the horses of the chariot of Arjuna)].—§ 608 (Karṇap.): VIII, **87**λ, 4418 (sided with Arjuna); [**89**, †4595 (*Atrisutodbhava°*)]; **94**, †4943 (*grahaḥ S°sya putraḥ*, i.e. Budha); [**96**, 5042 (*Agny-anilendubhānavaḥ*)].—§ 615 (Baladevatīrthayātrā): IX, **35**, [2009 (*Uḍurāj*)], 2011.—§ 615 (Prabhāsotpattik.): IX, **35**, 2013, 2014, 2017, 2018, 2020, 2022, 2024, 2025, 2027, 2029, 2030, 2032, 2039, 2043, 2049, 2051, 2053, 2054 (*S.* married twenty-seven daughters of Daksha, on account of his predilection for Rohiṇī, the other wives complained to Daksha who cursed *S.* so that he was affected by phthisis. Soma bathed in Prabhāsa and thus recovered his effulgence, and so he does on every new-moon day).—§ 615 (Baladevatīrthayātrā): IX, **13**, †9116 (°*sya mahat sutīrthaṃ*), 2447 (performed a rājasūya).—§ 615*u* (Skanda): IX, **45** [(γ) 2506 (*Sūrya - Candramasau*)], 2534 (gave two companions to Skanda).—§ 615*v* (Varuṇa): IX, **47***v*, 2735 (°*ena sārdhaṃ hānirṛddhī*).—§ 615 (Baladevatīrthayātrā): IX, **50**, 2924 (°*sya mahat sutīrthaṃ*, there *S.* performed a rājasūya, cf. v. 2447); [**51**, 2925 (*Uḍupatiḥ*, do., do.)].—§ 641 (Rājadh.): XII, **122**, [4499 (*Niçākaram*, made lord of the nakshatras)], 4517.—§ 660*b* (Bhṛgu-Bharadvājasaṃv.): XII, **182**, 6783 (*Agnī Shomau*). § 661 (Mokshadh.): XII, **207**ε, 7541 (married twenty-seven daughters of Daksha).—§ 665 (do.): XII, **208**, 7575 (*rājā*, son of Atri).—§ 693*b* (Vṛtravadha): XII, **282***a*, 10120.—§ 700 (Mokshadh.): XII, **289**, 10644 (*Agnī-Shomau*).—[§ 707 (do.): XII, **314**, 11617 (*Candramāḥ*, the *adhidaivata* of *manas*)]. — [§ 712 (Çukotpatti): XII, **324**, 12175 (*Divākara-Niçākarau*, on the Meru)].—§ 717*b* (Nārāyaṇīya): XII, **335***a*, 12686 (among the twenty-one Prajāpatis); [**341**λ, 13017 (*Tārādhipaḥ*)]; **342**, 13186 (*Agnī-Shomamayam . . . jagat*), ††13187 (*Agnī-Shomau*); **343**, 13188 (do.), ††13194 (do., XI), ††13219 (*rājānaṃ*), ††13220, ††13221 (repetition from § 615), 13225 (*Agnī-*

Shomakṛtaiḥ . . . karmabhiḥ); **349,** I), 13561 (obtained the religion of Nārāyaṇa from the Vaikhānasas), II), 13562 (imparted it to Brahmán).—§ 730*g* (Upamanyu): XIII, **14,** 889 (identified with Çiva).—§ 730 (Ānuçās.): XIII, **14***aa*, 991.—§ 739 (do.): XIII, **34,** 2110 (*°rājānaḥ*, scil. *brāhmaṇāḥ*). —§ 740 (do.): XIII, **36,** (2177), 2182 (discoursed on siddhi). —§ 746 (do.): XIII, **62**β, 3150 (applauds the giver of earth); **63,** 3239 (*Agnī-Shomau*); **67,** 3386 (*nīrajātaḥ . . . S°o grahagaṇeçvaraḥ*); **82,** 3857.—§ 747*b* (Suvarṇotpatti): XIII, **84,** 3977 (*Agnī-Shomātmakaṃ suvarṇaṃ*); **85,** 4103 (*Agnī-Shomātmakaṃ jātarūpaṃ*), 4173 (*Brahma-Vāyv-Agni-Somānāṃ sālokyaṃ*). — [§ 748*b* (Tārakavadhop.): XIII, **86,** 4208 (*Candramāḥ*, gave a sheep to Skanda)].—§ 749 (Ānuçāsanik.): XIII, **91**β, 4348, 4351; **92,** 4375, 4376, 4377, 4378 (questioned about çrāddhas), 4386.—§ 753 (do.): XIII, **97,** 4662 (to *S.* bali is to be offered in the north).—§ 757*h* (Somaloka): XIII, **102,** †4871 (*°sya rājñaḥ sadane*).— § 757*o* (Somapīthin, pl.): XIII, **102,** 4896 (*°vīthīṃ*, differently B.).—§ 759 (Ānuçāsanik.): XIII, **107,** 5279 (*°kanyānivāseshu*).—[§ 764 (do.): XIII, **123,** 5861 (*sutā Tārādhipasyeva*)].—[§ 768*b* (Umā-Maheçvarasaṃv.): XIII, **146**γ, 6751 (*Rohiṇī Çaçinaḥ sādhvī*)] —§ 770 (Ānuçāsanik.): XIII, **151**δ, 7094 (the third of the Vasus), 7155 (*°ādityānvayāḥ*).—§ 772*j* (Utathya): XIII, **155,** 7241 (*Bhadrā S°sya duhitā*), 7250 (had bestowed his daughter Bhadrā on Utathya, then she was ravished by Varuṇa).—§ 772*m* (Atri): XIII, **157,** 7292 (*°-Bhāskarau*, pierced by Rāhu), 7299.—§ 773*b* (Kṛshṇa Vāsudeva): XIII, **159,** 7366 (identified with Kṛshṇa).—§ 773 (Ānuçās.): XIII, **160,** 7408 (*°rājānaḥ*, scil. *brāhmaṇāḥ*).—§ 782*b* (Brāhmaṇagītā): XIV, **20,** 608 (*°o sahāgninā*, in the abode of the soul).—§ 782*g* (Guruçishyasaṃv.): XIV, **43**δ, 1178 (*aushadhīnāṃ patiḥ*), 1179 (*viprāṇāṃ rājā*).—§ 789 (Putradarçanap.): XV, **31**η, 856 (*°a iva (!) Saubhadraḥ*). — § 795 (Svargārohaṇap.): XVIII, **4,** 143 (*°ena sahitaṃ . . . Abhimanyuṃ*); **5,** 166 (after death Abhimanyu entered *S.*).

Cf. also the following synonyms:—

Atrisuta ("the son of Atri"): VIII, 4594 (*Nāsatya-Dasrātrisutodbhavādyair ashṭāṅgavidyāsanam udvahadbhiḥ*).

Aṃçumat: I, 5531 (*sāṅgāraka ivā °ān*); XII, 4500 (*vīrudhām A°ntam*, sc. *īçam*).

***Candra:** I, 1162 (*°-Sūryābhyāṃ*), 1166 (do.), 7682; III, 138 (*°tejobhiḥ*), †10225 (*°sya*, sc. *āyatanam*); V, 3968 (*reme . . . yathā C°ç ca Rohiṇyām*); VII, 9594 (identified with Çiva); IX, 2011; XII, 10438 (*°ādityau cakshushī te*, sc. Çiva's, 1000 names[1]); XIII, 3682 (*Vaishṇavāç C°lokāḥ*), 7295 (*°ādityau*), 7636 (do.).

***Candramas:** I, 2535 (*devānāṃ Sūrya-C°au*), 2583 (son of Manasvinī), 5376 (*pañcatāreṇa saṃyuktaḥ Sāvitreṇeva C°āḥ*), 8234 (*iva*); III, 5024 (*nirmalaç C°ā yathā*), 10906; V, 3828 (was anointed), 4753 (*nakshatrair iva C°āḥ*, sc. *parivṛtaḥ*); VI, 484, 4567 (*pīḍitaḥ . . . yathā yugakshaye ghore C°āḥ pañcabhir grahaiḥ*); VII, 9595 (identified with Çiva), 9600 (do.); IX, 302 (*kāntirūpamukhaiçvaryais tribhiç C°sā samaṃ*), 805 (*°so 'bhyāse Çanaiçcara iva grahaḥ*), 2021, 2028, 2043, 2059, 2506 (*Sūrya-Ç°au*); XII, 11617 (*adhidaivataṃ*, sc. of the *manas*), 12864 (= Mahāpurusha, Mahāpurushastava); XIII, 2014, 4208 (gave a sheep to Skanda), 5968 (*mucyate . . . Rāhuṇā C°ā yathā*), 7497 (identified with Çiva).

***Çaçalakshaṇa** ("hare-marked"): III, 16198 (C. has by error *°lakshmaṇaṃ*); VI, 195 (?); IX, 2041, 2048, 2058.

***Çaçāṅka** (do.): VI, 1285 (identified with Kṛshṇa); VIII, 3392 (*kāntyā Ç°sya*).

***Çaçin** (do.): III, 2676 (*sādhvī Rohiṇī Ç°no yathā*); VII, 161 (*nakshatrāṇāṃ iva Ç°ī*, sc. *senāpatiḥ*), 2993 (*tamo vighnan yathā Ç°ī*); IX, 2012, 2026, 2030, 2047; XII, 318 (*Āditya-Ç°-tārakaṃ*); XIII, 6751 (*Rohiṇī Ç°naḥ sādhvī*).

***Çatasahasrāṃçu** ("having 100,000 rays"): I, 1145 (*S°*).

***Çītāṃçu** ("cool-rayed"): I, 1145 (*S°*), 4162 (*°tāṃ*); III, 3008, 15100 (*°tāṃ*); IX, 2022, 2052.

***Çītaraçmi** (do.): VI, 485; XIII, 2645 (*iva*).

Grahagaṇeçvara, Grahapati, q.v.

***Indu:** I, 2577 (married twenty-seven daughters of Daksha), 3134 (do.); VIII, 2160 (*saptitām gataḥ*), †5042 (*Agny-anilendu-Bhānavaḥ*); XII, 13219; XIII, 1059 (*Varuṇendū*, identified with Çiva).

Kumudanātha ("lord of the lotuses"): VII, †8408.

Nakshatrapati, Nakshatrarāj, Nakshatrarāja, q.v.

***Niçākara** ("night-maker"): III, 2667 (*niçāṃ Rāhugrastam °āṃ*), 2704 (*iva*); VI, 5130 (*pīḍayām āsa . . . parvaṇīva susaṃkruddho Rāhuḥ pūrṇaṃ N°ṃ*); IX, 1967 (*divīva nakshatragaṇaiḥ parikīrṇo N°ḥ*), 2016, 2031, 2039, 2057, 3126 (*nakshatrair iva saṃpūrṇo vṛto niçi N°aḥ*); XII, 4499 (*nakshatrāṇām īçaḥ*), 12175 (*Divākara-N°au*); XIII, 2176.

Oshadhīpati ("lord of herbs"): III, 137.

Prajāpati, Tārādhipa, Tārakārāja, Tārāpati, Uḍupa, Uḍupati, Uḍurāj, Virocana, q.v.

Soma[2] = Sūrya: III, 147.—Do.[3] = Skanda: III, 14643.—Do.[4] = Çiva (1000 names[1-2]).—Do.[5] = Vishṇu (1000 names).

Somā, an Apsaras. § 191 (Arjuna): I, **123,** 4817 (danced at the birth of Arjuna).

Somabhojana, a Suparṇa, son of Garuḍa. § 564 (Mātalīyop.): V, **101**β, 3597.

Somāçrama ("the hermitage of Soma"), a tīrtha. § 370 (Tīrthayātrāp.): III, **84,** 8135.

Somaçravas, a brahman, son of Çrutaçravas. § 13 (Paushyap.): I, **3,** 674 (born by a serpent, became the purohita of Janamejaya Pārikshita).

Somāçrāyāyaṇa, a tīrtha. § 221 (Caitrarathap.): I, **170,** 6438 (visited by the Pāṇḍavas).

Somadatta, a prince (according to Harivaṃça v. 1821, son of Bālhīka and father of Bhūri, Bhūriçravas, and Çala). § 194 (Pāṇḍu): I, **126,** 4911.—§ 208 (Astradarçana): I, **134,** 5313.—§ 213 (Jatugṛhap.): I, **143,** 5707 (*Kauravaṃ*). —§ 232 (Svayaṃvarap.): I, **186,** 6994 (*Kauravyaḥ . . . putraç cāsya*, present at the svayaṃvara of Draupadī).—§ 287 (Rājasūyikap.): II, **34,** 1267 (*Kauravyaḥ*).—§ 288 (do.): II, **35,** 1293.—§ 298 (Dyūtap.): II, **58,** 2015.—§ 302 (Anudyūtap.): II, **74,** 2476.—§ 305 (do.): II, **78,** 2560 (*rājānaṃ*).—§ 307 (do.): II, **81,** 2697.—§ 327 (Draupadīparitāpav.): III, **29,** 1112.—§ 402 (Tīrthayātrāp.): III, **120,** †10274 (*sutair vṛtaṃ*).—§ 514 (Ghoshayātrāp.): III, **252,** 15205.—§ 552 (Goharaṇap.): IV, **38,** 1243.—§ 556 (Sañjayayānap.): V, **30,** †886.—§ 561 (Yānasandhip.): V, **47,** 1796; **55**ν, 2206; **57,** 2252 (Cekitāna will fight with *S.*), (π), 2268; **58**τ, 2301; **66**εε, 2502.—§ 562 (Bhagavadyānap.): V, **83**ι, 2966; **89,** 3114, (μ), 3117; **90**ρ, 3180; **95,** 3402.—§ 567 (do.): V, **124**β, 4138; **128**δ, 4284.— § 578 (Bhīshmavadhap.): VI, **51**χ, 2108 (on the right flank of Bhīshma's array, B. has *Saumadattiḥ*).—§ 581 (do.): VI, **63,** †2811 (*°sya putraṃ*, i.e. Bhūriçravas).—§ 584 (do.):

VI, **81***a*, 3532 (followed by the Saindhavas, only C., B. has *Bhagadatto 'tha Saubalaḥ*).—§ 585 (do.): VI, **92**χ, 4118, 4128 (his standard is overthrown by Ghaṭotkaca): **94,** 4193 (°*purogamāḥ*, attacked the Pāṇḍavas).—§ 586 (do.): VI, **99**γ, 4504 (on the left wing of the sarvatobhadra array).—§ 592 (Saṃçaptakavadhap.): VII, **20**δ, 800 (in Droṇa's gāruḍavyūha). — § 593 (Abhimanyuvadhap.): VII, **37**κ, 1609.—§ 598 (Jayadrathavadhap.): VII, **85,** 3018 (*niveçane . . . S°sya*) (γ), 3042.—§ 599*e* (Çini): VII, **144,** 6035, 6037, 6039, 6042 (*S.* had formerly been defeated by Çini, who then struck him with his foot. Çiva granted *S.* that he should have a son who should in like manner strike the son of Çini; this also happened in the encounter between Bhūriçravas and Sātyaki). — § 600 (Ghaṭotkacavadhap.): VII, **155**δ, 6720; **156,** 6729, 6737, 6738, 6750, 6752, 6755, 6758 (enraged at the slaughter of his son Bhūriçravas, *S.* attacked Sātyaki and was defeated); **157,** 6924 (only B., C. has by error °*sutaḥ*), 6926, 6929, 6930, 6931 (fought once more with Sātyaki); **158**ψ, 7031; **162,** 7224, 7228, 7231, 7238, 7240, 7242, 7243, 7245, 7246, 7247, 7248, 7251, 7256, 7257 (fought once more with Sātyaki and was slain by him).—§ 604 (Karṇap.): VIII, **1,** 22 (had been slain).—§ 609 (Çalyap.): IX, **2**ζ, 72 (among those who had sided with Duryodhana), 88 (*hataḥ*).—§ 611 (do.): IX, **24**νν, 1299 (*hate*).—§ 615 (Gadāyuddhap.): IX, **63**ββ, 3548; **64**εε, 3614.—§ 616 (Sauptikap.): X, **9**κ, 524 (had been slain).—§ 619 (Strīvilāpap.): XI, **24**ι, 678 (*putraçokābhisantaptaḥ*, all. to VII, ch. **156**), 679; **25**κ, 736.—§ 620 (Çrāddhap.): XI, **26**β, 788 (his body is burnt).—§ 787 (Āçramavāsap.): XV, **11**ο, 360 (his çrāddha), (π), 372 (do.), 378; **14**σ, 414 (do.).—§ 789 (Putradarçanap.): XV, **29,** 809 (*nihataḥ . . . pitrā saha*), 813 (°*prabhṛtayaḥ*); **32**δ, 879 (among those who, summoned by Vyāsa, arose from the Gaṅgā). Cf. Bālhika, Bālhikātmaja, Kaurava, Kauraveya, Kauravya, Kurupuṅgava.

Somadattasuta = Bhūriçravas: XI, 677. Cf. Somadatta, VII, 6924.

Somadatti (I, 536) v. Saumadatti.

Somadheya, pl. (°*āḥ*), a people. § 280 (Bhīmasena): II, **30,** 1084 (in the east, vanquished by Bhīmasena).

Somagiri, a mountain. § 775 (Ānuçāsanik.): XIII, **166***a*, 7659.

Somaka, an ancient king (of the Pāñcālas), son of Sahadeva. § 11 (Parvasaṅgr.): I, **2,** 447 (*yatra putreṇa S°ḥ putrārtham ayajat*, cf. § 408) —§ 267 (Yamasabhāv.): II, **8,** 319 (in the palace of Yama).—§ 406 (Tīrthayātrāp.): III, **125,** 10422 (*Sāhadeviḥ*, performed sacrifices on the Yamunā).—§ 407 (do.): III, **126,** 10469.—§ 408 (Jantūp.): III, **127,** 10470, 10471 (*nṛpatiḥ*), 10479, 10481, 10486, (10487); **128,** (10491), 10497, 10500 (°*sya guruḥ*), (10505) (in order to get 100 sons *S.* caused his son Jantu to be sacrificed, on account of this his purohita was grilled in hell. *Somaka* then wished to be tormented in the same manner).—§ 574 (Jambūkh.): VI, **9***aa*, 316.—§ 746 (Ānuçāsanik.): XIII, **76**ι, †3689 (among the kings who attained to heaven by means of gifts of kine).—§ 761 (do.): XIII, **115**δ, 5665 (among the kings who did not eat meat during the month of Kārttika). Cf. Sāhadevi.

Somaka, pl. (°*āḥ*), a tribe or family of the Pāñcālas, often used synonymous with these, but also mentioned together with them. § 4 (Anukram.): I, **1,** †183.—§ 190*d* (Arjuna): I, **123,** 4796 (Arjuna will bring the Kurus and the Somakas, etc. under his sway).—§ 231 (Svayaṃvarap.): I, **185,** 6975 (*purohitaḥ S°ānām*).—§ 237 (Vaivāhikap.): I, **193,** †7174 (*Dhṛshtadyumnaḥ S°ānāṃ prabarhaḥ*). — § 554 (Sainyodyogap.): V, **5,** 90 (°*ānāṃ dhurandhare*, sc. Drupada).—§ 566 (Sañjayayānap.): V, **22,** †662 (°*ānāṃ prabarhaḥ*, i.e. Dhṛshṭadyumna).—§ 561 (Yānasandhip.): V, **48,** 1851 (do., do.?); **50,** 1975 (°*ānāṃ balena*).—§ 567 (Bhagavadyānap.): V, **130,** 4371 (*Pāṇḍavāḥ S°aiḥ saha*).—§ 571 (Ulūkadūtāgamanap.): V, **160,** 5412 (*Pāṇḍavān saha-S°ān*), 5417.—§ 573 (Ambopākhyānap.): V, **173,** 5943 (*Pāñcālān saha-S°aiḥ*).—§ 574 (do.): VI, **1,** 2 (*Kuru-Pāṇḍava-S°āḥ*), 3 (do.), 4 (*Pāṇḍavāḥ saha-S°āḥ*), 27 (*Kuru-Pāṇḍava-S°āḥ*), 34 (do.).—§ 576 (Bhagavadgītāp.): VI, **15,** 601 (*Somakāṃç ca sa-Sṛñjayān*).—§ 577 (Bhīshmavadhap.): VI, **43,** 1534 (only B., C. has *Sṛñjayāḥ*).—§ 579 (do.): VI, **52**², 2151 (*Pāñcālyaḥ saha S°aiḥ*).—§ 580 (do.): VI, **59,** 2577.—§ 582 (do.): VI, **72,** 3193 (*Pāñcālāḥ S°aiḥ saha*, slain by Bhīshma).—§ 583 (do.): VI, **75**β, 3288 (*Çikhaṇḍī . . . S°aiḥ samvṛtaḥ*); **77,** 3385 (*sarva-S°āḥ*).—§ 585 (do.): VI, **88,** 3889 (°*ān saha-Sṛñjayān*), 3890 (*Pāñcālāḥ S°aiḥ saha*); **89**ν, 3947 (*Drupadaḥ . . . sahitaḥ sarva-S°aiḥ*), 3952 (°*ān Sṛñjayaiḥ saha*); **97,** 4412 (*Pārthān . . . sahitān sarva-S°aiḥ*), (λλ), 4442 (Bhīshma had promised to slay the *S.*), 4444; **98**μμ, 4466, 4474.—§ 586 (do.): VI, **103,** 4682 (*saṅgrāmaḥ . . . Bhīshmasya saha-S°aiḥ*); **107,** 4889 (*jitān*).—§ 587 (do.): **108,** 5018 (*vinighnan S°ān*, sc. Bhīshma); **116,** 5439 (slain by Bhīshma), 5448; **118,** 5532 (attacked Bhīshma); **119,** 5683 (*sa-Pāñcālāḥ*).—§ 589 (Droṇābhishekap.): VII, **7,** 172 (*sarva-S°ān*).—§ 599 (Jayadrathavadhap.): VII, **110,** 4168 (*Droṇaṃ nighnantaṃ S°ān*); **118,** †4690; **125,** 5017 (*saṅgrāmaḥ . . . Droṇasya S°aiḥ*); **126,** 5096 (*Pāñcālāḥ saha S°aiḥ*); **127,** 5175 (*Pāñcālāḥ saha-S°āḥ*); **146,** 6292 (*Droṇasya S°aiḥ sārdhaṃ saṅgrāmaḥ*); **151,** 6563.—§ 600 (Ghaṭotkacavadhap.): VII, **155**γ, 6695 (*Pāṇḍavāḥ saha S°aiḥ*); **159,** 7133, 7134, 7140 (do.): **160**δδ, 7155, 7157, 7158 (*Pāñcālān saha S°aiḥ*), 7165, 7166 (do.); **161**ηη, 7218; **164,** 7341 (*Pārthān sa-S°ān*), 7344; **165,** 7356 (*Pāñcālān sa-S°ān*), 7358 (*Pāñcālāḥ S°āḥ tathā*); **168,** 7534 (*sarva*°), 7541 (*Pāñcālāḥ S°aiḥ saha*), 7544; **169,** 7592; **172**ππ, 7748, 7763 (*Bhīmaḥ . . . vṛtaḥ Pāṇḍava-S°aiḥ*); **173,** 7784 (*Pāñcālāḥ saha S°aiḥ*).—§ 602 (Droṇavadhap.): VII, **186,** 8461 (°-*Pāṇḍavān*); **190,** 8719 (*Droṇo vinighnan sarva-S°ān*).—§ 603 (Nārāyaṇāstramokshap.): VII, **193**δ, 8931 (*Kuru-S°āḥ*); **200**ββ, 9322; **201,** 9392 (follow Arjuna).—§ 605 (Karṇap.): VIII, **22**π, 884 (*Pāṇḍu-Pāñcāla-S°aiḥ*); **24,** 939 (fought with Karṇa).—§ 608 (do.): VIII, **74,** 3793 (°*ānāṃ mahārathāḥ*); **78,** 3946 (are slain by Karṇa), 3997 (°*ān hatvā* sc. Karṇa); **79**ζ', 4013; **82,** †4194 (slain by Karṇa); **89,** †4533, †4553, †4601 (*Pārthānugān*); **90,** †4628 (*Kuravaḥ S°āç caiva*), †4637; **91,** †4762 (read *sa-Somakāḥ*, sc. *Pāṇḍavāḥ*—with B.), †4805, †4825.—§ 609 (Çalyap.): IX, **1,** 13 (*Pāñcāla-Somakān*, only B., C. has *Pāñcālasainikān*). § 610 (Çalyap.): IX, **7**ρ, 321, 332 (°-*Sṛñjayāḥ*), 363.—§ 611 (do.): IX, **8**η, 399; **11**λ, 552, (ν), 576 (*Çalyaḥ . . . nighnan S° Pāṇḍavān*); **16**τ, 822, **17**ψ, 870 (*Pāṇḍu-Pāñcāla-S°āḥ*); **18**ββ, 962; **20,** †1072; **21**κκ, 1126.—§ 612 (Hradapraveçap.): IX, **30**δ, 1693 (Açvatthāman had promised to slay the *S.*), 1722.—§ 615 (Gadāyuddhap.): IX, **56**ρ, 3170; **57,** 3209 (*Pāṇḍūn sa-S°ān*), 3226 (°-*Pāṇḍavāḥ*); **59,** 3310, †3321 (°*ānāṃ prabarhāḥ*).—§ 616 (Sauptikap.): X, **8,** 321 (°-*Pāṇḍavān*), 365, 468 (°*ānāṃ janakshaye*), 477 (are slain by Açvatthāman).

Somaka, sg. = Janamejaya the Pāñcāla (so PCR.): VIII, †4200 (°-*Pārshatātmajau*).

Somakīrti, a son of Dhṛtarāshṭra. § 130 (Aṃçāvat.): I, **67,** 2734.—§ 182 (Dhṛtarāshṭraputranāmak.): I, **117,** 4547.

Somakula ("the race of Soma"). § 407 (Māndhātrup.): III, **126**, 10465 (*°otpanno Gāndhārādhipatiḥ*).
Somaloka ("the world of Soma"). § 364 (Tīrthayātrāp.): III, **83**, 6085.—§ 368 (do.): III, **83**, 7056.—§ 370 (do.): III, **84**, 8021, 8066, 8090.—§ 615*ff.* (Asita Devala): IX, **50**μ, 2882.—§ 733*n* (Marudgaṇa): XIII, **25**, 1726.—§ 746 (Ānuçāsanik.): XIII, **79**κ, 3767. — [§ 757*h* (Hastikūṭa): *Gautama* said: Next [to *Uttarāḥ Kuravaḥ*] blaze the eternal redolent regions (*lokāḥ*) in the abode of king *Soma*, which are free from passions and sorrow. *Dhṛtarāshṭra* said: This region (*lokaḥ*) is for those who always make gifts and never receive gifts, who never take anything from others, who give away all their wealth to a deserving person, who are hospitable to everybody, inclined to grace and forgiving, who never speak ill of others, who feed others (*sattrībhūtāḥ*, so BR., otherwise Nīl. and PCR.), and who always are of righteous behaviour (*puṇyaçīlāḥ*): XIII, **102**, 4871 (*lokāḥ . . . Somasya rājñaḥ sadane*)].—§ 759 (Ānuçāsanik.): XIII, **109**, 5375, 5377.—§ 766 (do.): XIII, **125**, 5999 (*pitaraḥ . . . gacchanti S°ṃ*).—§ 768*b* (Umā-Maheçvarasaṃv.): XIII, **141**, 6493; **142**, 6523.
Somānvaya ("the race of Soma"). § 565 (Gālavacarita): V, **114**, 3902 (*°e . . . jātaḥ*, sc. Yayāti).—§ 718*b* (Uñchavṛttyup.): XII, **354**, 13776. Cf. Somakula, Somavaṃça.
Somapa[1], a warrior of Skanda. § 615*u* (Skanda): IX, **45**η, 2572.
Somapa[2], a Viçvadeva. § 749 (Ānuçāsanik.): XIII, **91**γ, 4359.
Somapa[3] = Vishṇu (1000 names).
Somapā = Çiva (1000 names[1]).
***Somapāḥ** (pl.) ("soma-drinkers"), a class of pitṛs or ṛshis. § 270 (Brahmasabhāv.): II, **11**, 463 (a class of pitṛs).—§ 656 (Khaḍgotpattik.): XII, **166**β, 6143 (sc. *ṛshayaḥ*, only C., B. reads *Somavāyavyāḥ*).—§ 695*b* (Dakshayajñavināça): XII, **285**a, 10280.—§ 717*b* (Nārāyaṇīya): XII, **348**$\delta\delta$, 13501 (*pitaraḥ*).—§ 730 (Ānuçāsanik.): XIII, **18**$\lambda\lambda$, †1371.—§ 768*b* (Umā-Maheçvarasaṃv.): XIII, **141**, 6495.
Somapada, a tīrtha. § 370 (Tīrthayātrāp.): III, **84**, 8097.
Somapīthin ("drinker of soma"). § 757*o* (Hastikūṭa): *Gautama* said: There where [the sāmans] *Rathantara* and *Bṛhat* are sung, where one strews the altar [C. *vedīṃ*, B. *vedī*] for *puṇḍarīkas* (sacrifices? so PCR.), where the drinker of soma comes (so B.) with [golden-hued] steeds (*haribhiḥ*): XIII, **102**, †4896 (only B., instead of *upayāti . . . somapīthī*, C. reads *upāyānti . . . Somavīthīṃ*).
Somapura ("the city of Soma"). § 565 (Gālavacarita): V, **119**, 4021 (*puraṃ . . . S° prabhaṃ*).
Somaputra ("the son of Soma (the Moon)") = Varcas: I, 2747 (*V°*); XVIII, 165 (*V°*).
Somaputrī ("the daughter of Soma (the Moon)") = Jyotsnākālī: V, 3533.
Somasūnu ("the son of Soma (the Moon)") = Abhimanyu: VII, 2132.
Somatīrtha, name of various tīrthas. § 362 (Tīrthayātrāp.): III, **83**, 5089.—§ 364 (do.): III, **83**, 6084.—§ 368 (do.): III, **83**, 7056.
Somātman = Kṛshṇa: XII, 1628.
Somavaktra = Çiva; XIV, 197 (C. by error Voma°).
Somavaṃça ("the race of Soma (the Moon)"). § 717*b* (Nārāyaṇīya): XII, **343**, VII) ††13214 (*°odbhavaḥ*, sc. Nahusha).
Somavaṃçīya ("belonging to the lunar-race") = Bhīmasena: III, 11169.

Somavarcas, a Viçvadeva. § 749 (Ānuçāsanik.): XIII, **91**γ, 4358, 4361 (C. by error *°aḥ* instead of *°āḥ*).
Somavāyavyāḥ, pl. (*°āḥ*), a class of ṛshis: XII, **166**β, 6143 (only B., C. has *somapā ṛṣayaḥ*).
Somavīthī, v. Somapīthin.
Sparça ("touch", personif.). § 270 (Brahmasabhāv.): II, **11**, 438 (*Çabda-S°au*, in the palace of Brahmán).
Sparçāçana, pl. (*°āḥ*), a class of gods. § 730 (Ānuçāsanik.): XIII, **18**$\lambda\lambda$, †1372.
Spashṭākshara = Vishṇu (1000 names).
Sphoṭana = Çiva (1000 names[1]).
Sragvin = Vishṇu (1000 names).
Sraja, a Viçvadeva. § 749 (Ānuçāsanik.): XIII, **91**γ, 4358.
Srashṭṛ[1] = Sūrya: III, 153.—Do.[2] = Kṛshṇa (Vishṇu): III, 481; XIII, 7012 (1000 names), 7055 (do.).
Sruvahasta = Çiva: XIII, 1157 (1000 names[2]); XIV, 200.
Sṛñjaya[1], one or more ancient kings. § 5 (Anukram.): I, **1**a, 223 (in Nārada's enumeration).—§ 267 (Yamasabhāv.): II, **8**, 326 (in the palace of Yama). Cf. Sṛñjaya.
Sṛñjaya[2], one of the standard bearers of Jayadratha. § 522 (Draupadīharaṇap.): III, **265**, †15597 (*°-Supravṛddhau*, only C., B. has *Sañjaya°*).
Sṛñjaya[3], father of Suvarṇashṭhīvin. § 595 (Abhimanyuvadhap.): There was a king of the name *Çaibya* (C. *°vya*), his son was *S.*; the ṛshis *Nārada* and *Parvata* were the friends of *S.* Seeing the daughter of *S.*, *Parvata* asked if she was Çrī, etc. (*a*). *Nārada* obtained her as his wife. *Parvata* cursed *Nārada*, saying that he should not go to heaven at his will, and *Nārada* (enumerating what constitutes a marriage) cursed *Parvata*, saying that he should not go to heaven without him. Meanwhile, king *S.*, desirous of a son, prevailed upon the brahmans to ask *Nārada* on his behalf, and, urged by *Nārada*, he prayed for a son possessed of every accomplishment, and whose urine, etc. should be of gold. This son was named *Suvarṇashṭhīvin* ("gold-spitter"), and increased the wealth [of his father] beyond all limits (description). Some robbers seized the prince and slew him, and cut his body into fragments but without finding any gold. The robbers then slew one another and sank into an unimaginably awful hell. To *Sṛñjaya*, who was afflicted with deep sorrow, the D.-ṛ. *Nārada* told the *Shoḍaçarājika* (q.v.), i.e., the histories of sixteen kings who had died (except the last, viz. *Rāma Jāmadagnya*), ending each narrative with the words: "as he died who was superior to thee and to thy son, thou shouldst not grieve for the latter who performed no sacrifice and made no sacrificial present." (Each narrative then ends with the words: *Çvaityeti vyāharan* [read *vyāharat*]; Nīl. takes Çvaitya (i.e. son of Çvitya) as a name of *S.*, cf. also XII, 1052) (VII, **55-70**). The grief of Sṛñjaya was dispelled and Nārada restored his son to life: VII, **55**, 2138 (*Çaibyasya . . . putraḥ*), 2140, 2144 (*nṛpatiḥ*), 2146, 2154, 2169, 2170, 2182; **56**, 2184, 2194; **57**, 2196, 2207; **58**, 2209, 2222; **59**, 2224, 2247; **60**, 2249, 2261; **61**, 2263, 2270; **62**, 2272, 2290; **63**, 2292, 2301; **64**, 2303, 2319; **65**, 2321, 2332; **66**, 2334, 2354; **67**, 2356, 2375; **68**, 2377, 2392; **69**, 2394, 2425; **70**, 2450; **71**, 2451 (2457), 2459.—§ 595 (Abhimanyuvadhap.): VII, **71**, 2472 (*°sya putram*, i.e. Suvarṇashṭhīvin).—§ 618 (Jalapradānikap.): XI, **1**γ, 25 (*putraçokārtte*, all. to § 595).—§ 632 (Rājadh.): XII, **29**, 906 (*°ṃ putraçokārttam*), 910, 916, 917, 922, 924, 931, 932, 935, 937, 938, 943, 944, 955, 956, 963, 964, 973, 974, 986, 987, 992, 993, 997, 998, 1003, 1004, 1012, 1013, 1022, 1023,

1029, 1030, 1037, †1038 (†1039) (Nārada told Sṛñjaya the Shoḍaçarājopākhyāna, cf. § 595).—§ 633 (do.): XII, **30,** 1043 (*Kāñcanashṭhīvī S°sya sutaḥ*), 1044 (*°sya sutaḥ* = do).—§ 633*b* (Nārada-Parvatākhyāna): XII, **30,** 1052 (*Çvaityam*), 1072 (*°ātmajām*, Nārada married the daughter of *S.*, cf. § 595).—§ 634*b* (Suvarṇashṭhīvisambhavop.): XII, **31,** 1091, 1097, (1100), (1102), 1105, 1109, 1110 (*rājarsheḥ*), 1115 (*°sya sutaḥ*, i.e. Suvarṇashṭhīvin), 1117, 1125 (*rājā*) (the birth of Suvarṇashṭhīvin, cf. § 595).—§ 761 (Ānuçāsanik.): XIII, **115**δ, 5665 (among the kings who abstained from meat during the month of Kārttika). Cf. Çvaitya.

Sṛñjaya[4] ("king of the Sṛñjayas"?) = Hotravāhana: V, 6059 (*H°*), 6064, 6080 (*H*), 6086, 6099 (*nṛpam*), 7002, 7008.

Sṛñjaya[5] = Uttamaujas: VIII, †3812 (*U°*).

Sṛñjaya[6] (VIII, 5037), vide Sañjaya (so B.).

Sṛñjaya, pl. (*°āḥ*), a tribe or family among the Pāñcālas, often used synonymous with these, but also mentioned together with them. § 327 (Draupadīparitāpav.): III, **33,** 1275, 1352; **35,** 1390.—§ 556 (Sañjayayānap.): V, **22,** †653, †683; **24,** †721; **25**ε, †723, †736 (*Kuru-S°ānām*); **26,** †756 (do.); **28**ι, †804.—§ 561 (Yānasandhip.): V, **48,** †1814, †1849 (*dṛshṭvā S°ānām anīke Dhṛshṭadyumnam*), †1906 (*kshayam . . . Kuru-S°ānām*); **57**ο, 2264 (among the allies of Yudhishṭhira); **71,** †2575.—§ 562 (Bhagavadyānap.): V, **72,** 2662 (*Kuru-S°ān*); **82,** 2881 (*Pāṇḍavāḥ S°aiḥ saha*), 2884 (*Pāṇḍavaiḥ saha S°aiḥ*), 2889 (*sainikaiḥ*); **93,** 3315 (*Kurūṇām S°ānāñ ca saṅgrāme*).—§ 567 (do.): V, **127,** 4243 (*Pāṇḍavāḥ S°aiḥ saha*).—§ 571 (Ulūkadūtāg.): V, **161,** 5538; **162,** 5585; **163,** †5652 (*°ānām anīkam*).—§ 572 (Rathātirathasaṅkhyānap.): V, **167,** 5784.—§ 576 (Bhagavadgītāp.): VI, **14,** 535 (*Kaunteyān . . . sa-S°ān*), 543; **15,** 601 (*Somakāmç ca sa-S°ān*); **16,** 631 (*Dhṛshṭadyumnapurogamāḥ*).—§ 577 (Bhīshmavadhap.): VI, **43,** 1534 (B. *Somakāḥ*).—§ 578 (do.): VI, **45,** 1671 (*Kurūṇām S°ānāñ ca saṅgrāme*).—§ 580 (do.): VI, **59,** 2530 (*Pāṇḍavāḥ S°aiḥ saha*).—§ 581 (do.): VI, **60,** †2679 (*Kuru-S°āḥ*).—§ 582 (do.): VI, **72,** 3176 (*°āḥ Kurubhiḥ saha*); **73,** 3237 (do.); **74,** 3276 (*Pāṇḍavāḥ S°aiḥ sārdham*).—§ 583 (do.): VI, **75**[2], 3309 (*°āḥ Kaikayaiḥ saha*).—§ 584 (do.): VI, **86,** 3793, 3816, 3817.—§ 585 (do.): VI, **88,** 3889 (*Somakān sa-S°ān*); **89,** 3952 (*Somakān S°aiḥ saha*), 3953; **91,** 4053; **95**ζζ, 4321; **98,** 4465 (*Pāṇḍavaiḥ saha S°aiḥ*).—§ 586 (do.): VI, **107,** 4893 (*Pāṇḍavān saha-S°ān*), 4895.—§ 587 (do.): VI, **108,** 5016 (*Pāṇḍavaiḥ saha-S°aiḥ*), 5019 (*Pāṇḍava-S°aiḥ*), (γ), 5022; **109,** 5057 (*Pāṇḍavaiḥ saha S°aiḥ*), 5091; **114,** 5328 (*Pārthāḥ . . . sahitāḥ sarva-S°aiḥ*); **115,** 5335 (*Pāṇḍavaiḥ saha S°aiḥ*), (ν), 5349, 5350, 5354; **118,** 5532 (*Somakāḥ S°āç ca*), 5534; **119,** 5572 (*sarva-S°āḥ*) (ββ), 5676.—§ 589 (Droṇābhishekap.): VII, **2**α, †82; **7,** 212 (*Pāṇḍavāḥ saha S°aiḥ*), 214 (*Pāṇḍava-S°ān*), 220 (*Pāṇḍava-S°āḥ*); **9,** 261 (do.).—§ 590 (do.): VII, **12,** 434 (*Pāṇḍu-S°aiḥ*, attack Droṇa); **13,** 485, 489 (*Pāṇḍu-S°āḥ*); **14,** 496; **16,** 629, 669 (*Pāṇḍu-S°āḥ*).—§ 592 (Saṃçaptakavadhap.): VII, **21**ι, 883, 884, 895 (*Kuru-S°vāhinīm*), (λ), 915; **22**ν, †926, 935 (*Pāṇḍava-S°āḥ*).—§ 593 (Abhimanyuvadhap.): VII, **35**δ, 1511, 1516 (*Pāñcālāḥ S°aiḥ saha*); **40**ο, 1695 (*Matsya-Pāñcāla-S°āḥ*).—§ 596 (Pratijñāp.): VII, **78**ε, 2744.—§ 599 (Jayadrathavadhap.): VII; **95,** 3513 (*Pāṇḍu-S°aiḥ*); **97,** 3606; **108**ο, 4087 (*Cedi-Pāñcāla-S°ān*); **110,** 4154, 4160, (ρ), 4165; **111**υ, 4284; **114**ω, 4539; **122,** 4932; **125**μμ, 5069, 5088 (*Cedi-Pāñcāla-S°ān*); **130,** 5335 (*Pāṇḍu-S°aiḥ*); **151,** 6561, 6568 (*Kuru-S°āḥ*), 6569 (*Pāṇḍava-S°ān*).—§ 600 (Ghaṭotkacavadhap.): VII, **154,** 6662, 6679 (*Pāṇḍu-S°āḥ*); **155**γ, 6682; **156**ι, 6779; **157**σ, 6967; **160,** 7200 (*Pāñcālāḥ saha S°aiḥ*); **161**ηη, 7217; **164,** 7344, 7345 (*nihateshu*), 7351; **166,** 7430, (ι), 7459; **173,** 7792 (*Pāñcālāḥ S°aiḥ saha*); **177,** 8056; **182**εεε, 8248 (*°-Pāṇḍavaḥ*), (ηηη), 8284 (*Pāṇḍavāḥ S°aiḥ saha*); **183**ηηη, 8306 (*°āḥ saha Pāñcālaiḥ*), 8308 (*Pāṇḍu-S°āḥ*).—§ 602 (Droṇavadhap.): VII, **186**η, 8490 (*Cedi-Kaikeya-S°ān*); **190,** 8696, 8725; **192,** 8823, 8882 (*Kuru-Pāṇḍava-S°āḥ*).—§ 603 (Nārāyaṇāstramokshap.): VII, **199,** 9214 (*Pāṇḍu-Pāñcāla-S°āḥ*).—§ 604 (Karṇap.): VIII, **3,** 70 (*°ānām . . . kadanam*); **5**ζ, 92.—§ 605 (do.): VIII, **10,** 379 (*Pāñcālāḥ S°āç ca*); **21,** 825 (*hatāḥ Karṇena*), 844 (*Pāṇḍu-S°-Pāñcālān*); **24,** 988 (*vadhyamānāḥ samare Sūtaputreṇa*); **25,** 1004; **31**ππ, 1268 (*Pārthān sa-S°ān*); **32,** 1349 (*Kaunteyāḥ . . . sa-Sṛñjayāḥ*).—§ 606 (do.): VIII, **35,** 1640 (*Dhṛshṭadyumnapurogamāḥ*).—§ 607 (do.): VIII, **37,** †1728, †1729.—§ 608 (do.): VIII, **47**δ, 2224, 2233 (*saṅgrāmaḥ . . . Kuru-S°ānām*, C. has by error *Ç°*); **51**γγ, 2441 (*Pāṇḍavān S°aiḥ saha*); **54**θθ, 2613, 2625; **56**μμ, 2693, 2695, (οο), 2751 (*dagdhāḥ*), 2776; **57,** †2851 (*janakshayaḥ . . . Kuru-S°ānām*); **58,** 2864 (*mahārathāḥ*) (χχ), 2902 (*Pāñcāla-S°ānām*), 2905; **59,** 2909 (*Kuru-S°āḥ*); **60**γγγ, 3010 (*Pāṇḍu-S°ān*), 3012, 3014, 3034 (*°sainyena*); **61**δδδ, 3067 (*Pāṇḍu-S°aiḥ*); **64,** 3271 (*vadhyamānāḥ samare Sūtaputreṇa*); **66,** †3348 (*samāgame S°-Kauravāṇām*); **67**κκκ, †3373; **73,** 3638, 3671, 3672, 3745, 3746; **75,** †3804 (*Pāṇḍava-S°ānām*); **79,** 4016, †4088; **85,** †4313 (*Pāṇḍu-S°aiḥ*), †4325 (do.); **92**αμ', 4825; **93,** 4834 (*Kuru-S°ānām*); **94,** 4905 (do.); **96,** 5031 (*Pāṇḍu-Pāñcāla-S°āḥ*).—§ 610 (Çalyap.): IX, **6**σ, 332 (*Somaka-S°ān*).—§ 611 (do.): IX, **9,** 413 (*yuddham Kurūṇām . . . S°aiḥ saha*), 444 (*Kuru-S°saṅkulā*, sc. *nadī*); **13,** 686 (*nihatān*); **20,** †1076 (*senāpatiḥ Pāṇḍava-S°ānām*, i.e. Dhṛshṭadyumna), †1087; **21**κκ, 1126.—§ 612 (Hradapraveçap.): IX, **29,** 1581 (*Pāṇḍu-S°aiḥ*).—§ 613 (Gadāyuddhap.): IX, **32,** 1848; **33,** 1919 (follow Yudhishṭhira), 1944 (*Pāṇḍavāḥ saha-S°āḥ*).—§ 614 (do.): IX, **34,** 1960.—§ 615 (do.): IX, **55**π, 3122; **57,** 3232; **59,** †3318; **61,** 3388, 3390, 3407 (so both C. and B., PCR. has Sañjaya, which seems to be the correct reading).—§ 616 (Sauptikap.): X, **8,** 398 (*Pāṇḍu-S°ān*), 467 (are slain by Açvatthāman).—§ 620 (Çrāddhap.): XI, **26**β, 788 (their bodies are burnt).

Sṛshṭi ("procreation"), a goddess. § 270 (Brahmasabhāv.): II, **11,** 459 (in the palace of Brahmán).

Sṛshṭikṛt ("creator") = Brahmán: I, 1204.

Stambamitra, a çārṅgaka, son of Mandapāla and Jaritā. § 259 (Çārṅgakop.): I, **230,** 8373; **232,** (8407), (8415); **233,** 8434.

Stanakuṇḍa, sg. and pl., name of a tīrtha. § 370 (Tīrthayātrāp.): III, **84,** 8130.

Stanaposhika (so B.) or **Stanayoshika** (so C.), pl. (*°āḥ*), a people. § 571 (Jambūkh.): VI, **9**ο, 376 (in the north-east).

Stavapriya = Vishṇu (1000 names).

stavarāja ("chief-hymn"): XIII, 1135 (i.e. the 1000 names of Çiva), 1136 (do.), 1379.

Stavya = Vishṇu (1000 names).

Stena, pl. (*°āḥ*) ("thieves"), name of a caste: XII, 10868 (C. has by error *tenā(ḥ)*).

Sthānada = Vishṇu (1000 names).

Sthaṇḍileyu, a prince. § 150 (Pūruvaṃç.): I, **94,** 3700 (fourth son of Raudrāçva).

Sthāṇu[1], name of a Rudra. § 108 (Aṃçāvat.): I, **66,** 2567 (among the Rudras, sons of Sthāṇu, i.e. Çiva).—§ 191 (Arjuna): I, **123**, 4826.

Sthāṇu[2] = Çiva, q.v.—Do.[3] = Vishṇu (1000 names).

Sthāṇutīrtha, name of a tīrtha. § 615*p* (Vasishṭāpavāha): IX, **42**, 2361 (the residence of Vasishṭha; there Sthāṇu had performed austerities), 2363.

Sthāṇuvaṭa, a tīrtha. § 368 (Tīrthayātrap.): III, **83**, 7049.

Sthāvara = Vishṇu (1000 names).

Sthāvarāṇāṃ patiḥ = Çiva (1000 names[2]).

Sthavira[1] = Çiva (1000 names[1]).—Do.[2] = Vishṇu (1000 names).

Sthavishṭha = Vishṇu (1000 names).

Sthavishṭhaḥ sthavīyasāṃ = Kṛshṇa: XII, 1612.

Sthira[1], a companion of Skanda. § 615*u* (Skanda): IX, **45**, 2550 (given to Skanda by Meru).

Sthira[2] = Çiva (1000 names[1–2]). — Do.[3] = Vishṇu (1000 names).

Sthita = Çiva (1000 names[1]).

Sthūla[1] = Çiva (1000 names[1]). — Do.[2] = Vishṇu (1000 names).

Sthūlabāluka v. Sthūlavāluka.

Sthūlaçiras, a ṛshi. § 264 (Sabhākriyāp.): II, **4***a*, 106 (waited upon Yudhishṭhira).—§ 413 (Tīrthayātrāp.): III, **135**, 10699 (*āçramaḥ S°aḥ*, a tīrtha).—§ 717*b* (Nārāyaṇīya): **343**, XII) ††13221 (*maharshiḥ*, cursed the trees, saying that they should not put forth flowers at all times).—§ 734 (Ānuçāsanik.): XIII, **26***a*, 1762 (v.l. *Sthūlagirāḥ*, B.; came to see Bhīshma).

Sthūlajīrṇāṅgajaṭila = Çiva (1000 names[1]).

Sthūlakarṇa, Sthūlākarṇa, v. *Sthūṇ°*.

Sthūlakeça, a ṛshi. § 21 (Pramadvarā): I, **8**, 942 (*ṛshiḥ*), 944 (*°āçramaṃ*), 947, 949 (*ṛshiḥ*), 952 (reared Pramadvarā).

Sthūlāksha, a ṛshi. § 734 (Ānuçāsanik.): XIII, **26***a*, 1764 (came to see Bhīshma).

Sthūlavālukā (C., *°bā°*), a river. § 574 (Jambukh.): VI, **9**λ, 323.—§ 757*m* (Goloka): XIII, **102***a*, 4888 (a tīrtha).

Sthūṇa[1], name of a Yaksha. § 83 (Ādivaṃçāvatāraṇa): I, **63**, 2453 (*Yakshaḥ*, all. to § 573).—§ 573 (Ambopākhyānap.): V, **191**, 7477 (*°bhavanaṃ*), 7479 (*Yakshaḥ*); **192**, 7495, 7520, †7521 (*Yakshasya*), 7525, 7529, 7535, 7537 (*Yakshaḥ*), 7539, 7540, 7544 (*°-yaksheṇa*) (*S.* gave his manhood to Çikhaṇḍinī). Cf. Sthūṇākarṇa.

Sthūṇa[2], a son of Viçvāmitra. § 721*b* (Viçvāmitrop.): XIII, **4**β, 250.

Sthūṇakarṇa (Sthūla°, C.), a brahman. § 324 (Dvaitavanapraveçap.): III, **26***a*, 986 (worshipped Yudhishṭhira).

Sthūṇākarṇa, name of a weapon. § 442 (Nivātakavacayuddhap.): III, **167**, 11967 (employed by Arjuna; cf. the explanation of Nīl.).—§ 512 (Ghoshayātrāp.): III, **245**, 14995 (employed by Arjuna, C. has *Sthūlā°*).—§ 569 (Bhagavadyānap.): V, **141**δ, 4786 (employed by Arjuna).—§ 600 (Ghaṭotkacavadhap.): VII, **181**, 8222 (employed by Balarāma), 8226. — § 608 (Karṇap.): VIII, **60***aaa*, 2998 (*°endrajālena*, employed by the Dhartarāshṭras).

Sthūṇākarṇa[2] = Sthūṇa[1]: V, 7476, 7482.

Stobha, name of a certain sacrificial exclamation: II, 304 (pl. *°-āḥ*, personified, only B., C. has *tārāḥ*; cf. graha[1] (v. additions)); XII, 7268, 7340, 9632; XIII, 625, 4108 (only B.).

Stotra(m) = Vishṇu (1000 names).

Stotrātman = Kṛshṇa: XII, 1633.

Stotṛ = Vishṇu (1000 names).

Strī = Çiva (1000 names[1]).

Strīparvan, the 11th book of the Mhbhr. § 4 (Anukram.): I, **1**, 90 (*°aishīkaviçrāmaḥ*, sc. *Bhāratadrumaḥ*). — § 11 (Parvasaṅgr.): I, **2**, 581.—§ 795*c* (Mahābhārata): XVIII, **6**, 276.

Strīrājya, sg. (B.) name of a country ("the kingdom of females"), or pl. (*āḥ*) (C.) a people ("the inhabitants of do.").—§ 342 (Indralokābhigamanap.): III, **51**, 1991.

Strīrājyādhipati ("king of Strīrājya") = Çṛgāla (?): XII, 114 (*Ç°*).

Strīvilāpa ("the lament of the women"). § 10 (Parvasaṅgr.): I, **2**, 348 (i.e. Strīvilāpaparvan).

[Strīvilāpaparvan(°va)] ("the section containing the lament of the women", the 86th of the minor parvans of the Mhbhr.; cf. Strīvilāpa). § 619: Aided by the spiritual sight granted by *Vyāsa*, *Gāndhārī* beheld the field of battle, though distant, from the spot where she stood (description), with Rā., Pç., jackals, etc. *Dhṛtarāshṭra*, at the command of *Vyāsa*, with the *Pāṇḍavas* (headed by *Yudhishṭhira*), with *Kṛshṇa* and all the *Kuru* ladies, proceeded to the field of battle. The *Pāñcāla* and the *Kuru* ladies were plunged into unutterable distress (description), described by the daughter of *Subala*, i.e. *Gāndhārī*, to *Kṛshṇa*, mentioning *Bhīshma*, etc. (*a*); then her eyes fell upon *Duryodhana* (XI, **16**). *Gāndhārī's* lament at the sight of *Duryodhana* (β) (XI, **17**); do. of her sons and daughters-in-law, etc., especially *Duḥçāsana* (γ) (XI, **18**); do. of *Vikarṇa*, etc. (δ) (XI, **19**); do. of *Abhimanyu*, etc., directing *Kṛshṇa's* attention to the laments of *Uttarā* (ε) (XI, **20**); do. of *Karṇa* (ζ) (XI, **21**); do. of the lord of the *Avantis*, etc. (η), *Jayadratha*, and *Duḥçalā* (XI, **22**); do. of *Çalya*, *Bhīshma*, etc., (θ) and *Droṇa*, whose disciples, with *Kṛpī*, were burning his body on the bank of the *Gaṅgā* (XI, **23**); do. of *Somadatta* and *Bhūriçravas*, and the mother and wives of *Bhūriçravas*, and *Çakuni* (ι) (XI, **24**); do. of the *Kāmboja*-king, etc. (κ). Then *Gāndhārī* cursed *Kṛshṇa* for not having prevented the slaughter of the *Kurus* and the *Pāṇḍavas*, saying: "on the thirty-sixth year from this thou shalt, after causing the slaughter of thy kinsmen, etc., perish in a disgraceful way within the wilderness, etc." *Kṛshṇa* said: "there is none in the world, save myself, who is capable of exterminating the *Vṛshṇis*; I am endeavouring to bring it about; in proclaiming this curse, thou hast aided me in the accomplishment of that task." The *Pāṇḍavas* became stupefied (XI, **25**).

Stubha, name of a fire. § 493 (Āṅgirasa): III, **221**, 14190 (only B., C. has *Tubhaḥ*, which seems to suggest a reading *anvayas tu saḥ*).

Stuta = Çiva: X, 256; XII, 10363 (1000 names[1]); XIII, 1174 (1000 names[2]).

Stuti = Vishṇu (1000 names).

***stutiçāstra**, pl. (*°āṇi*): II, 452 (read with B. *stutiçastrāṇi*, "praise and invocations").

Stutya = Çiva: X, 256; XII, 10363 (1000 names[1]).

Stūyamāna = Çiva: X, 256; XII, 10363 (1000 names[1]).

Subabhru = Kṛshṇa: XII, 1511.

Subāhu[1], a serpent. § 47 (Sarpasattra): I, **35**, 1559 (enumeration).—§ 564 (Mātalīyop.): V, **103**γ, 3632 (do.).

Subāhu[2], an Apsaras. § 103 (Aṃçāvat.): I, **65**, 2558 (daughter of Prādhā).—§ 191 (Arjuna): I, **123**, 4819 (among the Apsarases who danced at the birth of Arjuna).

Subāhu[3], various kings at the time of Yudhishṭhira. § 130 (Aṃçāvat.): I, **67**, 2660 (incarnation of the Asura Hara),

2696 (among the incarnations from the Krodhavaça gaṇa).—§ 554 (Sainyodyogap.): V, **4**γ, 77. Cf. Subāhu[5], Subāhu[8-9].

Subāhu[4], son of Dhṛtarāshṭra. § 130 (Aṃçāvat.): I, **67**, 2729.—§ 182 (Dhṛtarāshṭraputranāmak.): I, **117**, 4542.—§ 209 (Drupadaçāsana): I, **138**, 5461.—§ 585 (Bhīshmavadhap.): VI, **96**θθ, 4349 (among other sons of Dhṛtarāshṭra defeated by Bhīmasena).—§ 592 (Saṃçaptakavadhap.): VII, **25**, 1077 (protected Droṇa against his brother Yuyutsu).—§ 596 (Pratijñāp.): VII, **74**β, 2629 (?).—§ 600 (Ghaṭotkacavadhap.): VII, **170**μμ, 7671.—§ 608 (Karṇap.): VIII, **51**δδ, 2447 (among twenty sons of Dhṛtarāshṭra who attacked Bhīmasena).

Subāhu[5], a Kāçi king. § 280 (Bhīmasena): II, **30**, 1080 (*Kāçirājam*, vanquished by Bhīmasena on his digvijaya).

Subāhu[6], a Cedi king at the time of Nala. § 347 (Nalopākhyānap.): III, **64**, 2531 (*Cedīrājasya*); **65**, 2576 (do.). Cf. Cedipati, Cedirāja.

Subāhu[7], king of the Kulindas. § 419 (Gandhamādanapr.): III, **140**, 10863 (°*vishayam*, on Himavat, description), 10865 (*Kulindānām īçvaraḥ*).—§ 449 (Ājagarap.): III, **177**, †12349 (*Kirātarājño vishayam S°oḥ*), †12351 (°*vishaye*), †12352. Cf. Kirātarājan, Kulindādhipati.

Subāhu[8], a Kuru warrior. § 592 (Saṃçaptakavadhap.): VII, **18**, 738, 740, 741 (among the Saṃçaptakas, fought with Arjuna).—§ 609 (Çalyap.): IX, **2**ζ, 76 (had sided with Duryodhana).

Subāhu[9], a Pāṇḍava warrior. § 597 (Pratijñāp.): VII, **83**a, 2951.

Subāhu[10], a warrior of Skanda. § 615u (Skanda): IX, **45**η, 2575.

Subāhu[11], an ancient king. § 761 (Ānuçāsanik.): XIII, **115**δ, 5668 (among the kings who abstained from meat during the month of Kārttika).

Subandhanavimocana, Subāndhava = Çiva (1000 names[2]).

Subala[1], an ancient king. § 6 (Anukram.): I, **1**a, 229 (in Sañjaya's enumeration).

Subala[2], king of the Gāndhāras and father of Çakuni and Gāndhārī. § 83 (Ādivaṃçāvatāraṇa): I, **63**, 2439 (*Nagnajit?*, disciple of Prahrāda).—§ 174 (Dhṛtarāshṭravivāha): I, **110**, 4367 (°*syātmajā*, i.e. Gāndhārī), 4373 (*Gāndhārarājasya*, gave his daughter Gāndhārī in marriage to Dhṛtarāshṭra).—§ 287 (Rājasūyikap.): II, **34**, 1265 (*Gāndhārarājaḥ*, came to the rājasūya of Yudhishṭhira).—§ 292 (do.): II, **45**a, 1608 (accompanied by Nakula).—§ 327 (Draupadīparitāpav.): III, **34**, †1356 (°*sya putraḥ*, i.e. Çakuni).—§ 569 (Bhagavadyānap.): V, **148**, †5031 (°*sya putrī*, i.e. Gāndhārī).—§ 585 (Bhīshmavadhap.): VI, **90**, 4004 (°*syātmajāḥ*, i.e. Gaja, etc.), 4009 (°*syātmajān* = do.).—§ 611 (Çalyap.): IX, **22**, 1153 (°*sya sutaḥ*, i.e. Çakuni); **28**, 1558 (°*sya putraḥ*, i.e. Çakuni), †1561 (do., do.).—§ 612 (Hradapraveçap.): IX, **29**, 1600 (°*sya hate putre*, i.e. Çakuni). Cf. Gāndhārarāja.

Subala[3], a king. § 522 (Draupadīharaṇap.): III, **265**, †15596 (*Ikshvākurājñaḥ S° sya putraḥ*, followed Jayadratha, only C., B. has *Subhavasya*).

Subala[4], a Suparṇa, son of Garuḍa. § 564 (Mātalīyop.): V, **101**a, 3588 (enumeration).

Subala[5] = Çiva (1000 names[2]).

Subaladāyāda ("the son of Subala") = Kālikeya: VII, 1933 (*K*°).

Subalaja = Çakuni, q.v.

Subalajā = Gāndhārī, q.v.

Subalaputra, Subalātmaja = Çakuni, q.v.

Subalātmajā = Gāndhārī, q.v.

Subalātmaja, pl. (°*āḥ*) ("the sons of Subala[2]"). § 585 (Bhīshmavadhap.): VI, **90**, 4011 (i.e. Gaja, Gavāksha, Vṛshabha, Carmavat, Ārjava, and Çuka), 4013 (do., except Vṛshabha they are slain by Irāvat).

Subhā, wife of Aṅgiras. § 489 (Āṅgirasa): III, **218**, 14122 (only B., C. has *Çubhā*).

Subhadra, name of a place. § 607 (Karṇap.): VIII, **44**, 2013 ((°*m nāma catvaram*, in the country of the Bāhīkas; Nīl. explains: *S°m catvaram surābhāṇḍāçrayabhūtam*).

Subhadrā[1], daughter of Vasudeva, wife of Arjuna, and mother of Abhimanyu. § 4 (Anukram.): I, **1**, †149.—§ 11 (Parvasaṅgr.): I, **2**, 400, 401, 428.—§ 71 (Ādivaṃçāvatāraṇap.): I, **61**, 2273 (*anujām Vāsudevasya*), 2274 (all. to § 252).—§ 83 (Ādivaṃçāvatāraṇa): I, **63**, 2449 (*Abhimanyuḥ S°āyām Arjunād abhyajāyata*, cf. § 253).—§ 159 (Pūruvaṃç.): I, **95**, ††3830 (*bhaginīṃ Vāsudevasya*, by Arjuna, mother of Abhimanyu).—§ 252 (Subhadrāharaṇap.): I, **219**, 7919 (only C., B. has *Bhadrām*), 7922 (*Sāraṇasya sahodarā*); **220**, 7936, 7938, 7939, 7959 (*S.* is ravished by Arjuna).—§ 253 (Haraṇāharaṇap.): I, **221**, 7968, 7980, 8004 (the nuptials of Arjuna and *S.*), 8025 (*Keçavasya priyā svasā*, mother of Abhimanyu (*Saubhadram*)), 8026.—§ 254 (Khāṇḍavadahanap.): I, **222**, 8072.—§ 262 (Bhagavadyāna): II, **2**, 25 (*Bhadrām*).—§ 277 (Jarāsandhavadhap.): II, **24**, 977.—§ 292 (Rājasūyikap.): II, **45**, 1618.—§ 321 (Saubhavadhap.): III, **22**, 895 (Kṛshṇa brought *S.* and Abhimanyu to Dvārakā).—§ 356 (Tīrthayātrāp.): III, **80**, 4018 (all. to § 252).—§ 452 (Mārkaṇḍeyas.): III, **183**, †12570, †12583.—§ 511 (Draupadī-Satyabhāmāsaṃv.): III, **235**, 14733.—§ 552 (Arjuna): IV, **49**ε, 1536 (all. to § 252).—§ 593 (Abhimanyuvadhap.): VII, **35**, 1533 (*jātaḥ S°ayā*, sc. Abhimanyu); **51**, 1989, 1991 (Abhimanyu is slain).—§ 596 (Pratijñāp.): VII, **72**, 2501 (°*āyāḥ priyaṃ putram*, i.e. Abhimanyu), 2528 (°*āyāñ ca sambhūtaḥ* = do.), 2532, 2533; **77**, 2714 (consoled by Kṛshṇa); **78**, 2732, 2766, 2770 (do.).—§ 599 (Jayadrathavadhap.): VII, **127**, 5167; **143**, 6013 (°*āyāḥ sutaḥ*, i.e. Abhimanyu).—§ 619 (Strīvilāpap.): XI, **20**ε, 582.—§ 783 (Anugītāp.): XIV, **52**γ, 1505 (°*ādayaḥ . . . Bharatānāṃ striyaḥ*), †1532 (accompanied Kṛshṇa to Dvārakā).—§ 785 (do.): XIV, **61**, 1812, 1818, 1832 (*svasā mama*), 1840, 1848 (*S.*'s grief); **66**θ, 1939 (accompanied Kṛshṇa) (λ), 1948, (μ), 1953; **67**, 1965; **70**ο, 2038; **88**φ, 2605, 2606.—§ 787 (Āçramavāsap.): XV, **1**, 9.—§ 788 (do.): XV, **21**, 500 (*hataputrā*).—§ 789 (Putradarçanap.): XV, **29**γ, 784 (*Kṛshṇabhaginī*), (δ), 801, (ε), 807 (*Kṛshṇasya bhaginī*).—§ 794 (Mahāprasthānikap.): XVII, **1**, 7.

Cf. also the following synonyms:—

Abhimanyujananī (the mother of Abhimanyu): VIII, 4488.

Bhadrā: I, 7919 (only B., C. has *Subhadrām*), 7982 (read °*ā* with B.), 7983, 7985; II, 25 (*S*°); VIII, 1250 (all. to § 252); XV, 471.

Mādhavī, Sātvatātmajā, Sātvatī, Vārshṇeyī, Vāsudevasahodarā, Vasudevasutā, Yādavī, Yadunandanī, q.v.

Subhadrā[2], name of a cow. § 564 (Mātalīyop.): V, **102**, 3610 (*paçcimā Vāruṇī dik ca dhāryate vai S°ayā*).

Subhadrāharaṇa(m) ("the carrying away of Subhadrā")

§ 10 (Parvasaṅgr.): I, **2**, 315 (i.e. Subhadrāharaṇaparvan), 316 (do.).—§ 11 (do.): I, **2**, 363 (do.).

[Subhadrāharaṇaparvan(°va)] ("Arjuna's carrying away Subhadrā", the 17th of the minor parvans of Mhbhr.). (Cf. Subhadrāharaṇa.) § 252: Some days afterwards a mountain festival of the *Bhojas, Vṛshṇis,* and *Andhakas* was held on the *Raivataka* mountain; there *Haladhara* (i.e. Balarāma) with *Revatī,* followed by *Gandharvas,* king *Ugrasena,* with his 1000 wives, *Raukmiṇeya, Çāmba, Akrūra, Sāraṇa, Gada, Babhru, Vidūratha, Niçaṭha, Cārudeshṇa, Pṛthu, Vipṛthu, Satyaka, Sātyaki, Bhaṅgakāra, Mahārava, Hārdikya, Uddhava,* etc., were present; *Arjuna* fell in love with *Subhadrā,* the favourite daughter of *Vasudeva,* the sister of *Kṛshṇa,* and uterine sister of *Sāraṇa. Kṛshṇa* told him to carry her away by force, as the result of a *svayaṃvara* was doubtful. They sent a courier to *Yudhishṭhira* at *Indraprastha,* and obtained his assent (I, **219**). *Arjuna* set out as for a hunting expedition in his chariot, yoked with *Çaibya* and *Sugrīva,* and carried away *Subhadrā* towards *Indraprastha.* The soldiers ran to *Dvārakā* to the *sabhā,* named *Sudharmā,* and informed the *sābhāpāla,* who, by blowing the drum of alarm (*bherīṃ sānnāhikīṃ*) caused the *Vṛshṇis, Andhakas,* and *Bhojas* to assemble at the *sabhā.* While they made a loud uproar, *Baladeva* restored silence by saying that they ought first to hear what *Kṛshṇa* purposed. Then, seeing *Kṛshṇa* sitting silent, he spoke angrily about this deed of *Arjuna* (I, **220**).

Subhaga, brother of Çakuni. § 600 (Ghaṭotkacavadhap.): VII, **157**π, v. 24*b* (a half çloka inserted in B. between v. 6944 and 6945).

Subhagā, an Apsaras, daughter of Prādhā. § 102 (Aṃçāvat.): I, **65**, 2554.

Subhagā, a mātṛ. § 615*u* (Skanda): IX, **46**θ, 2636.

Subhava, a king. § 522 (Draupadīharaṇap.): III, **265**, †15596 (*Ikshvākurājñaḥ S°sya putraḥ,* followed Jayadratha, only B., C. has *Subalasya*).

Subhīma, a god. § 492 (Āṅgirasa): III, **220**, 14166 (one of the fifteen *yajñamushaḥ*).

Subhrāj. § 3 (Anukram.); I, **1**β, 43 (son of Devabhrāj), 44 (father of Daçajyotis, Çatajyotis, and Sahasrajyotis).

Subhrāja, a companion of Skanda. § 615*u* (Skanda): IX, **45**, 2533 (given to Skanda by Sūrya).

Subhrū, a mātṛ. § 615*u* (Skanda): IX, **46**θ, 2626.

Subhuja = Vishṇu (1000 names).

Subhūmika(m), a tīrtha on the Sarasvatī. § 615*c* (Baladevatīrthayātrā): In that tīrtha many Aps. are sporting (therefore it is called *S.*); D. and G. repair thither every month; it is the resort of *Brahmán* himself; G. and diverse tribes of Aps. are to be seen there, passing the time happily; D. and P. sport there in joy, sacred flowers being strewn over them; *Baladeva* heard the sound of those celestial songs and musical instruments, and saw many shadows of D., G., and Rā.; IX, **37**, 2121.

Subhūmikā = Subhūmika: IX, 2126 (°*eti vikhyātā*).

Subīja = Çiva (1000 names[2]).

Sucakra, a warrior of Skanda. § 615*u* (Skanda): IX, **45**η, 2561.

Sucandra[1], an Asura. § 94 (Aṃçāvat.): I, **65**, 2539 (son of Siṃhikā).

Sucandra[2], a Devagandharva. § 102 (Aṃçāvat.): I, **66**, 2555 (tenth son of Prādhā).—§ 191 (Arjuna): I, **123**, 4814 (present at the birth of Arjuna).

Sucāru[1], son of Kṛshṇa and Rukmiṇī. § 730 (Ānuçāsanik.): XIII, **14***a*, 621.

Sucāru[2], son of Dhṛtarāshṭra (?). § 583 (Bhīshmavadhap.): VI, **79**, 3470/71 (only B.).

Sucetas, a brahman, son of Gṛtsamada. § 736*b* (Vītahavyap.): XIII, **30**, 2000 (*Gṛtsamadasya putraḥ,* in the second half-çloka the name is read Sutejas).

Suchattra = Çiva (1000 names[2]).

sūcī ("needle"), name of a vyūha: VII, 2674, 3110 (ç°, C.), 3111 (do.), 3114 (do.).

sūcīmukha ("pointed as a needle"), name of a vyūha: VI, 699, 3395; XII, 3729 (*anīkam*).

Sūcīroman = Çiva (1000 names[1]).

Sucitra[1], a serpent. § 66 (Sarpasattra): I, **57**, 2159 (of Dhṛtarāshṭra's race).

Sucitra[2], one or more kings. § 232 (Svayaṃvarap.): I, **186**, 6990 (present at the svayaṃvara of Draupadī).—§ 604 (Karṇap.): VIII, **6**, 1771 (°*ç Citravarmā ca pitāputrau,* slain by Droṇa).

Sucitra[3], son of Dhṛtarāshṭra (?). § 583 (Bhīshmavadhap.): VI, **79**, 3470/71 (only B.).

Sūcīvaktra, a warrior of Skanda. § 615*u* (Skanda): IX, **45**η, 2574.

Suçānta = Çiva: VII, 9524.

Suçārada = Çiva (1000 names[2]).

Suçarman[1], king of the Trigartas. § 232 (Svayaṃvarap.): I, **186**, 6989 (present at the svayaṃvara of Draupadī).—§ 552 (Goharaṇap.): IV, **30**, 971 (*rājā Trigartānām*), 984, 992, 998; **31**, 1003; **32**, 1059 (*rukmarathaḥ*), 1060 (*rājā Trigartānām*), 1063, 1064; **33**, 1070 (*Traigartaḥ*), †1073 (*Trigartādhipatiḥ*), 1075, 1078 (*Trigartena*), 1089, 1090, 1092 (*bhrātṛbhiḥ saha*), 1094, 1096, 1101, 1102, 1103, 1105, 1107, 1111, 1112, 1114, 1118, 1123, 1124; **34**, 1129, 1130, 1131 (headed by *S.*, the Trigartas carry away the cattle of Virāṭa; a great battle ensues; at last *S.* is defeated and made captive by Bhīmasena, but set free by Yudhishṭhira).—§ 554 (Sainyodyogap.): V, **4**γ, 83.—§ 578 (Bhīshmavadhap.): VI, **45**[17], 1728, 1729, 1730 (fought with Cekitāna); **51**χ, 2108 (in the army of Duryodhana).—§ 583 (do.): VI, **75**δ, 3296 (*Prasthalādhipaḥ,* in the krauñcavyūha of Bhīshma).—§ 584 (do.): VI, **82**[2], 3577, 3580; **84**, 3744, 3747 (engaged in battle with Arjuna); **86**, 3834 (°*ādīn rājñaḥ,* defeated by Arjuna).—§ 585 (do.): VI, **96**ηη, 4339 (attacked Arjuna).—§ 586 (do.): VI, **102**, 4651; **104**, 4730, 4731, 4736 (pierced Arjuna and Kṛshṇa).—§ 587 (do.): VI, **108***a*, 5008 (°*pramukhā nṛpāḥ,* in the rear of Duryodhana's army); **113**, 5287, 5288 (attacked Bhīmasena and Arjuna); **114**, 5292, 5299, 5324 (defeated by Arjuna).—§ 590 (Droṇābhishekap.): VI, **14**, 531 (fought with Senāpati [i.e. Dhṛshṭadyumna?]).—§ 591 (Saṃçaptakavadhap.): VII, **17**β, 691 (*Trigartaḥ Prasthalādhipaḥ,* with his brothers among the Saṃçaptakas who swore either to slay Arjuna or die themselves), 712 (*bhrātṛbhiḥ sārdham*).—§ 592 (do.): VII, **28**, 1227 (do.), 1228 (do.), 1232, 1234, 1235 (encounter with Arjuna).—§ 603 (Nārāyaṇāstramokshap.): VII, **193***a*, 8910 (when Droṇa had fallen *S.* fled with the Saṃçaptakas).—§ 605 (Karṇap.): VIII, **27**λλ, 1079 (*Trigartarājaḥ*), 1085, 1087, 1101 (among the Saṃçaptakas, fought with Arjuna and was wounded).—§ 608 (do.): VIII, **53**ηη, 2567, 2569, 2592 (employed the Sauparṇa weapon), 2597 (Arjuna's encounter with the Saṃçaptakas); **95***av*, 4972 (*Saṃçaptakāvaçishṭena balena mahatā vṛtaḥ*).—§ 611 (Çalyap.): IX, **27**φφ, 1473, 1483, 1487, 1488, 1489 (is slain by Arjuna). Cf. Prasthalādhipa, Prasthalādhipati, Rukmaratha, Traigarta, Trigarta, Trigartādhipati, Trigartarāj, Trigartarāja, Trigartarājan.

Suçarman[2], a Pāṇḍava warrior. § 570 (Sainyaniryāṇap.): V, **151** ε, 5163 (in the army of Yudhishṭhira, B. has *Sudharmā*). —§ 587 (Bhīshmavadhap.): VI, **116,** 5402, 5403 (fought with Citrasena); **118** υ, 5555. Cf. next.

Suçarman[3], a Pāñcāla prince. § 608 (Karṇap.): VIII, **56** νν, 2735 (attacked by Karṇa).

Suçobhanā, daughter of the frog king Āyu(s) and wife of king Parikshit of Ayodhyā. § 461 (Vāmadevacarita): III, **162,** ††13173.

Suçravā, daughter of a Vidarbha king. § 156 (Pūruvaṃç.): I, **95,** ††3770 (*Vaidarbhīm*, wife of Jayatsena).

Suçruta, a son of Viçvāmitra. § 721*b* (Viçvāmitrop.): XIII, **4** β, 254.

Sudakshiṇa[1], a Kāmboja prince. § 232 (Svayaṃvarap.): I, **186,** 6995 (*Kāmbojaḥ*, present at the svayaṃvara of Draupadī).—§ 555 (Sainyodyogap.): V, **19** δ, 590 (*Kāmbojaḥ*, accompanied by Yavanas and Çakas *S.* came to Duryodhana with one akshauhiṇī of troops).—§ 562 (Bhagavadyānap.): V, **95** ν, 3403 (*Kāmbojaḥ*, in the army of Duryodhana).— § 570 (Sainyaniryāṇap.): V, **155** θ, 5274 (*Kāmbojam*, do.). —§ 572 (Rathātirathasaṅkhyānap.): V, **166,** 5748 (*Kāmbojaḥ*, a ratha in the army of Duryodhana).—§ 576 (Bhagavadgītāp.): VI, **16** α, 622 (*Kāmbojaḥ*, had an akshauhiṇī of troops); **17,** 622 (*Kāmbojāḥ sa-S°āḥ*).—§ 578 (Bhīshmavadhap.): VI, **45**[19], 1734 (*Kāmbojānāṃ mahāratham*), 1735 (fought with Çrutakarman the son of Sahadeva); **51** χ, 2108 (*Kāmbojaḥ*, on the right flank of Bhīshma's krauñcavyūha).—§ 580 (do.): VI, **59** μ, †2594.—§ 581 (do.): VI, **65** ν, 2928 (*Kāmbojaḥ*). —§ 586 (do.): VI, **99** ά, 4501 (do., in the van of Bhīshma's sarvatobhadra array); **102** ι, 4666 (*Kāmbojaḥ*).—§ 587 (do.): VI, **108** α, 5007 (*Kāmbojarājaḥ*), (δ), 5051 (*Kāmbojam*); **110,** 5108 (*Kāmbojaḥ*, resisted Abhimanyu); **111,** 5159. — § 589 (Droṇābhishekap.): VII, **7** ζ, 182 (*Kāmbojāḥ S°purahsarāḥ*).—§ 592 (Saṃçaptakavadhap.): VII, **20** ε, 801 (*Kāmbojaḥ*, in the left wing of Droṇa's gāruḍavyūha).— § 596 (Pratijñāp.): VII, **74** β, 2628 (*Kāmbojaḥ*, will protect Jayadratha).—§ 599 (Jayadrathavadhap.): VII, **92,** 3277 (*Kāmbojam*), 3321 (*Kāmbojarājasya putraḥ*), 3326, 3330, 3334, 3337 (*Kāmbojam*, is slain by Arjuna); **93,** 3338 (*hate*); **94,** 3410 (*Kāmbojasya dāyāde hate*), 3438 (*nihataḥ*, sc. by Arjuna).—§ 600 (Ghaṭotkacavadhap.): VII, **158** ω, 7036 (among the slain).—§ 604 (Karṇap.): VIII, **5** ζ, 109 (*nihataḥ Savyasācinā*).—§ 608 (do.): VIII, **56,** 2802 (*°ād avarajaḥ*), 2804 (*°ād avarajaṃ Kāmbojam*, the younger brother of *S.* attacked Arjuna but was slain by him); **72** υυυ, 3612 (*Kāmbojam*).—§ 609 (Çalyap.): IX, **2,** 74 (*Kāmbojaḥ*, had sided with Duryodhana), 90 (*hataḥ*).—§ 611 (do.). IX, **24** νν, 1300 (*Kāmboje*, sc. *hate*).—§ 619 (Strīvilāpap.): XI, **20,** 601 (*Kāmbojam*). Cf. Kāmboja, Kāmbojarāja.

Sudakshiṇa[2], a Pāṇḍava warrior. § 592 (Saṃçaptakavadhap.): VII, **21** κ, 910 (pierced by Droṇa).

Sudāmā, name of two mātṛs. § 615*a* (Skanda): IX, **46** θ, 2623 (only C., B. has *Dāmā*), 2628.

Sudāman[1], a king. § 279 (Arjuna): II, **27,** 1020 (in the north, vanquished by Arjuna on his digvijaya). — § 592 (Saṃçaptakavadhap.): VII, **23** ο, 996/7 (only B.).

Sudāman[2], king of the Daçārṇas. § 350 (Nalopākhyānap.): III, **69,** 2707 (*sute Daçārṇādhipateḥ S°naḥ*, i.e. the wives of the Vidarbha king Bhīma and the Cedi king Vīrabāhu).

Sūdāman, pl. (*°mānaḥ*), a people. § 574 (Jambūkh.): VI, **9** μ, 362.

Sudarça[1], a Kuru warrior. § 604 (Karṇap.): VIII, **7,** †207 (? adj. ? among those who were still alive). Cf. next.

Sudarça[2], a son of Dhṛtarāshṭra (= Sudarçana). § 611 (Çalyap.): IX, **27,** 1443 (only B., C. has Durdharsha; *S.* and Duryodhana were the only two of Dhṛtarāshṭra's sons who were yet unslain). Cf: the prec.

Sudarçana[1], the discus (cakra) of Vishṇu (Kṛshṇa). § 28 (Amṛtamanthana): I, **19,** †1178, †1186 (employed by Nārāyaṇa).—[§ 257 (Khāṇḍavadahanap.): I, **225,** 8196 (*cakram*), given to Kṛshṇa by Agni, *d:* having a hard nave (? *vajranābham*), and being a fiery weapon (*Āgneyam astram*), through it Kṛshṇa should be superior in battle to men, gods, Rākshasas, Piçācas, Daityas, and Nāgas, and it would always return into his hand.] — § 320 (Saubhavadhop.): III, **22,** 881 (*b: S.* burns Yakshas, Rākshasas, and Dānavas), 883 (Kṛshṇa cut Saubha in twain by means of the *S.*).— § 561 (Yānasandhip.): V, **54,** 2132 (*cakrāṇām*, sc. *varam*).— § 580 (Bhīshmavadhap.): VI, **59,** †2599 (in the hand of Kṛshṇa).—§ 589 (Droṇābhishekap.): VII, **7,** 197 (*cakrāṇām*, sc. *varam*).—§ 600 (Ghaṭotkacavadhap.): VII, **175** δδδ, 8195 (*cakram*, held by Kṛshṇa) —§ 608 (Karṇap.): VIII, **89** ζ[1], †4569.—§ 730*d* (Mandāra): Kṛshṇa's discus was given to him by *Mahādeva* (i.e. Çiva) when the latter had slain a Daitya who lived in the water. Originally it was created by *Vṛshāñka* (i.e. Çiva). Only *Pinākin* (i.e. Çiva) can gaze at it. *Bhava* (i.e. Çiva) gave it the name *Sudarçana*: XIII, **14,** 668. Cf. Cakra (add the foll.: III, 178 (*sunābham*); V, 2524 (*Vāsudevasya*); VI, 2596 (*sunābham*); X, 625 (do.)).

Sudarçana[2], a prince. § 264 (Sabhākriyāp.): II, **4** β, 123 (? PCR. takes this as an adj. ("handsome") to *Kramajit*).

Sudarçana[3], the chariot (?) of Indra. § 552 (Goharaṇap.): IV, **56,** 1761 (*Çakraḥ . . . samāruhya S°m*).

Sudarçana[4], a prince (so Nīl.). § 561*c* (Kṛshṇa Vāsudeva): V, **48,** †1882 (having vanquished the Gāndhāras and the sons of Nagnajit Kṛshṇa liberated *S.*, *devatānāṃ lalāmam*).

Sudarçana[5], name of a dvīpa = Jambudvīpa. § 574 (Jambūkh.): VI, **5,** 188 (*dvīpam*), 191 (*°dvīpaḥ*).

Sudarçana[6], the Jambu tree on Meru. § 574ι (Jambū): VI, **7,** 273 (*jambūvṛkshaḥ*). Cf. Sudarçanā[2].

Sudarçana[7], son of Dhṛtarāshṭra. § 583 (Bhīshmavadhap.): VI, **77** κ, 3343.—§ 599 (Jayadrathavadhap.): VII, **127** νν, 5177 (among several sons of Dhṛtarāshṭra who attacked Bhīmasena), (ζζ), 5210 (slain by Bhīmasena). — § 600 (Ghaṭotkacavadhap.): VII, **156** κ, 6852 (the same ?).

Sudarçana[8], a Kuru warrior. § 599 (Jayadrathavadhap.): VII, **118,** †4689 (*rājavaraḥ*), †4691, †4692, †4693, †1696, †4697 (slain by Sātyaki); **119,** 4702 (*°m nihatya*).

Sudarçana[9], a Pāṇḍava warrior. § 600 (Ghaṭotkacavadhap.): VII, **158** χ, 7011 (brother of Virāṭa ?).

Sudarçana[10], a Mālava king. § 603 (Nārāyaṇāstramokshap.): VII, **200** γγ, 9330 (*Mālavaḥ*, attacked Açvatthāman), †9340 (Açvatthāman cut off his head); **201,** 9400 (*ishvastravidhisampanne Mālave*, sc. *hate*). Cf. Mālava.

Sudarçana[11], son of Agni and Sudarçanā. § 720*b* (Sudarçanop.): XIII, **2,** 120 (*Āgneyaḥ*), 123 (married Oghavatī), 131, 132 (*Agniputre*), 145, 147, 151, 180 (*°caritam*), (in the shape of a brahman Dharma put *S.* to the test). Cf. Āgneya, Agniputra, Pāvakasuta, Pāvaki.

Sudarçana[12] = Çiva (1000 names[2]).—Do.[13] = Vishṇu (1000 names).

Sudarçanā[1], daughter of king Duryodhana of Māhishmatī and the river Narmadā. § 720*b* (Sudarçanop.): XIII, **2,** 104 (*rājakanyām*), 106, 118 (married to Agni to whom she bore Sudarçana[11], cf. II, **30**). Cf. Duryodhanasutā.

Sudarçanā[2] = Sudarçana[6] (the Jambu tree): XIII, †4862 (*jambūḥ*).

[Sudarçanopākhyāna(m)] ("the episode relating to Sudarçana"). § 720*b* (Ânuçāsanik.). *Bhīshma* said: *Prajāpati Manu* > *Ikshvāku* > 100 sons; the tenth of those, *Daçāçva*, became the king of *Māhishmatī*; *Daçāçva's* son was the pious *Madirāçva* > *Dyutimat* > *Suvīra* > *Sudurjaya* > R-ṛ *Duryodhana*, in whose kingdom there was no miser, etc., and who was learned in the *Vedas* and *Vedānta*. *Duryodhana* begat the beautiful *Sudarçanā* upon the river *Narmadā*; *Agni*, taking the shape of a brahman, demanded her hand from the king, who would not give her to him; then *Agni* vanished from his great sacrifice. *Duryodhana* repaired to the brahmans, who became informed of the matter by *Agni*; then the king consented, and *Agni* gave, as a marriage-dower, the boon to the king that he would always remain there, and *Agni* has always been present there to this day, and was seen by *Sahadeva* on his digvijaya. She bore to *Agni* the beautiful *Sudarçana*, who, even in his childhood, knew *Brâhman*. *Sudarçana* married *Oghavatī*, the daughter of king *Oghavat* and the sister of *Ogharatha*, and dwelt in *Kurukshetra*; he took the vow of conquering death by leading the life of a householder. He instructed *Oghavatī* that, for pleasing a guest, she must not spare even her own person. One day, when *Sudarçana* went out to fetch firewood, a graceful brahman came to *Oghavatī* and required and obtained her own person. *Mṛtyu*, with his iron club, was always at the side of *Sudarçana*, watching him in order to find out his flaws. When *Sudarçana* came home he showed no anger. The brahman turned out to be *Dharma*, who was pleased with *Sudarçana*, and said: "you have conquered *Mṛtyu*"; *Oghavatī* has been protected from defilement by your virtue and by her own chastity; you will attain to all the worlds in this your body, and, as *yoga* is in the control of *Oghavatī*, she will follow you with half her corporeal self, being with the other half [the river] *Oghavatī*. Then *Indra* came, riding in a fine chariot, and approached that brahman.

Sudāsa, king of the Koçalas [in Ayodhyā]. § 775 (Ânuçāsanik.): XIII, **166**η, 7682 (*Koçaleçvaraḥ*).

Sudella, pl., v. Sudeshṇa, pl.

Sudeshṇa, pl. (°*āḥ*), a people. § 574 (Jambūkh.): VI, **9**μ, 354 (only B., C. has *Sudellāḥ*).

Sudeshṇā[1], wife of the Aṅga king Bali. § 170 (Dīrghatamas): I, **104**, 4211, 4216, 4217 (by Dīrghatamas, mother of Aṅga, Vaṅga, Kaliṅga, Puṇḍra, and Suhma).

Sudeshṇā[2], wife of Virāṭa. § 549 (Pāṇḍavapraveçap.): IV, **3**, 80 (*rājabhāryām*); **9**, (252), 264, (265), (278) (Draupadī served *S.* as a sairindhrī).—§ 551 (Kīcakavadhap.): IV, **14**, 374, 375, 378, †383; **15**, 431, 432, 434, (435), 439, (440), (446); **16**, 491, 497, (499), (501); **20**, 604, 630, 631; **24**, 836, 855 (how Kīcaka (the brother of *S.*, v. 437), fell in love with Draupadī and was slain).—§ 553 (Vaivāhikap.); IV, **72**, 2365. Cf. Kaikeyī.

Sudeshṭa, pl. (°*āḥ*), a people. § 574 (Jambūkh.): VI, **9**μ, 358 (only C., B. has *Sudṛshṭāḥ*).

Sudeva[1], a brahman. § 350 (Nalopākhyānap.): III, **68**, 2660 (*dvijaḥ*), (2663), 2681, 2684, 2686, 2687, 2689, 2692; **69**, (2694), 2703, 2720 (discovered Damayantī).—§ 351 (do.): III, **70**, 2758 (*dvijasattamam*), 2760, 2765, 2766, 2770 (sent to Ayodhyā to invite Ṛtuparṇa to Kuṇḍina); **71**, 2771.

Sudeva[2], the generalissimo of Ambarīsha. § 641 (Rājadh.): XII, **98**, 3617, 3622 (*senāpatiḥ*), 3623.

Sudeva[3], king of the Kāçis. § 736*b* (Vītahavyop.): XIII, **30**, 1952 (*Kāçirājaḥ*, son of Haryaçva and father of Divodāsa). Cf. Kāçinandana, Kāçirāja.

Sudevā[1], an Aṅga princess. § 156 (Pūruvaṃç.): I, **95**, ††3777 (*Āṅgeyīm*, wife of Ariha).

Sudevā[2], a Dāçārha princess. § 156 (Pūruvaṃç.): I, **95**, ††3789 (*Dāçārhīm*, wife of Vikuṇṭhana).

Sudevatanaya ("the son of Sudeva[3]") = Divodāsa: XIII, 1974.

***sudhā**, a delicious drink or nectarlike substance: I, 8322; III, ††13158, ††13161; V, 3614; XIII, 1704, 1807 (*nāgānām*), 2030, 3387, 3388 (*nāgānām*), 5287, 5302, 5313, 5332.

Sudhanus, a Kuru warrior. § 592 (Saṃçaptakavadhap.): VII, **18**, 741 (among the Saṃçaptakas who attacked Arjuna).

Sudhanvan[1], a brahman of Aṅgiras' race. § 300 (Prahlāda): II, **68**, 2315 (*Āṅgirasam*), 2318, 2320, 2335, (2336) (his rivalry with Virocana [on account of Keçinī], cf. § 558).—§ 557 (Prajāgarap.): V, **33**, 1073 (*itihāsam purātanam putrārtham Asurendreṇa* (i.e. Prahlāda) *gītañ caiva S°nā*, cf. § 558).—§ 558 (Virocana): V, **35**, 1185 (*Virocanasya saṃvādam Keçinyarthe S°nā*), 1188, 1190, 1191, 1192, 1193, (1195), 1196, 1197, 1199, (1200), (1202), 1203 (*Virocana-S°au*), 1205, 1206, 1207 (*brahman*), (1208), (1211), 1212, (1213), 1217, 1218, (1219), (his rivalry with Virocana on account of Keçinī, cf. § 300).—§ 734 (Ânuçāsanik.): XIII, **26***a*, 1764 (the same?, among the ṛshis who came to see Bhīshma).—§ 747*b* (Suvarṇotpatti): XIII, **85**θ, 4148 (the eighth of the eight sons of Aṅgiras).—§ 748*b* (Tārakavadhap.): XIII, **86**, 4209 (the same?, gave to Skanda a car and a chariot). Cf. Āṅgirasa.

Sudhanvan[2], a Kuru warrior. § 592 (Saṃçaptakavadhap.): VII, **18**, 743 (among the Saṃçaptakas, slain by Arjuna). Cf. Sudhanus.

Sudhanvan[3], a Pāñcāla prince. § 592 (Saṃçaptakavadhap.): VII, **23**o, 1002 (*Pāñcālyam*, proceeded against Droṇa, description of his horses).—§ 599 (Jayadrathavadhap.): VII, **122**u, 4903 (among the brothers of the Pāñcāla prince Vīraketu; attacked Droṇa). Cf. Pāñcālya.

Sudhanvan[4], an ancient king. § 595 (Shoḍaçarāj. v. Māndhātṛ): VII, **62***a*, 2281 (vanquished by Māndhātṛ).

Sudhanvan[5] = Vishṇu (1000 names).

Sudharmā[1], the sabhā of the Daçārhas (Yādavas), [originally belonging to the gods, but given to Kṛshṇa, v. Harivaṃça v. 6565 foll.]. § 252 (Subhadrāharaṇap.): I, **220**, 7940 (*sabhām*).—§ 263 (Sabhākriyāp.): II, **3**, 84 (*Dāçārhī*).—§ 793 (Mausalap.): XVI, **7**, 183 (*Yādavīm sabhām*).

Sudharmā[2], wife of Mātalī. § 564 (Mātalīyop.): V, **97**, 3519, 3521.

Sudharman[1], a Vṛshṇi prince. § 264 (Sabhākriyāp.): II, **4***a*, 123 (waited upon Yudhishṭhira), 130 (do., among the Vṛshṇi princes who received instruction in the use of weapons from Arjuna).

Sudharman[2], king of the Daçārṇas. § 280 (Bhīmasena): II, **29**, 1063 (*Dāçārṇako rājā*, in the east, vanquished by Bhīmasena on his digvijaya).

Sudharman[3], a Kuru warrior. § 592 (Saṃçaptakavadhap.): VII, **18***a*, 741 (among the Saṃçaptakas).

Sudharman[4], a Pāṇḍava warrior. § 608 (Karṇap.): VIII, **73**, 3732.

Sudharman[5] (according to Nīl. the purohita of Duryodhana). § 620 (Çrāddhap.): XI, **26***a*, 779, 782.—§ 637 (Rājadh.): XII, **40**, 1447; **44**, 1529.

Sudharman[6], v. Suçarman[2].

Sudhāvat, v. Svadhāvat.

Sudina, a tīrtha. § 364 (Tīrthayātrāp.): III, **83,** 6070.

Sudivātaṇḍi, a ṛshi. § 677 (Mokshadh.): XII, **245**β, 8900 (has proceeded to heaven).

Sudṛshṭa, pl. (°*āḥ*), a people. § 574 (Jambūkh.): VI, **9**μ, 358 (only B., C. has *Sudeshṭāḥ*).

Suduçcara = Skanda: III, 14634.

Sudurjaya, king of Māhishmatī, (= Durjaya). § 720*b* (Sudarçanop.): XIII, **2,** 95 (son of Suvīra and father of Duryodhana). Cf. Durjaya.

Sudyumna, an ancient king, son of Manu Vaivasvata. § 267 (Yamasabhāv.): II, **8,** 327 (in the palace of Yama), 333 (the same? do.).—§ 628 (Rājadh.): XII, **23,** 666 (*rājarshiḥ*), 667, 678, 679, 681 (683) (his justice, punishment of Likhita).—§ 767 (Ānuçāsanik.): XIII, **137***a*, 6263 (*Manoḥ putraḥ S°o Likhitāya mahātmane daṇḍam uddhṛtya dharmeṇa gato lokān anuttamān*, cf. § 628).—§ 768*b* (Kṛshṇa Vāsudeva): XIII, **147,** 6831 (*Manoç ca vaṃçaja Ilā S°o ca bhavishyati*; Ilā was changed into a man, viz. Sudyumna, cf. Harivaṃça, v. 630).

Sugaṇā, a mātṛ. § 615*u* (Skanda): IX, **46**θ, 2645.

Sugandha, name of a tīrtha. § 370 (Tīrthayātrāp.): III, **84,** 8014.

Sugandhā[1], an Apsaras. § 191 (Arjuna): I, **123,** 4819 (danced at the birth of Arjuna).

Sugandhā[2], a tīrtha. § 370 (Tīrthayātrāp.): III, **84,** 7088.

Sugāndhāra = Çiva (1000 names[2]).

Sughosha, the conch of Nakula. § 576 (Bhagavadgītāp.): VI, **25**κ, 845.—§ 578 (Bhīshmavadhap.): VI, **51***aa*, 2116.

Sughosha[2] = Vishṇu (1000 names).

Sugoptṛ, a Viçvadeva. § 749 (Ānuçāsanik.): XIII, **91**γ, 4362 (enumeration).

Sugrīva[1], one of Kṛshṇa's horses. § 252 (Subhadrāharaṇap.): I, **220,** 7933 (*Çaibya-S°yuktena*, sc. *rathena*). — § 320 (Saubhavadhop.): III, **20,** 789 (*Çaibya-S°yuktena rathena*).—§ 321 (do.): III, **22,** 896 (do.).—§ 452 (Mārkaṇḍeyas.): III, **183,** 12562 (do.).—§ 552 (Goharaṇap.): IV, **45,** 1413 (°*samaḥ*, sc. one of the horses of Uttara).—§ 556 (Sañjayayānap.): V, **22,** †672 (°*yuktena rathena*).—§ 561 (Yānasandhip.): V, **48,** †1876 (do.).—§ 562 (Bhagavadyānap.): V, **83,** 2938 (*Çaibya-S°-Meghapushpa-Balāhakaiḥ*).—§ 567 (do.): V, **131,** 4446 (*Çaibya-S°yuktena*, sc. *rathena*).—§ 596 (Pratijñāp.): VII, **79**ζ, 2812. § 590 (Jayadrathavadhap.): VII, **147,** 6344 (*Çaibya-S°-Meghapushpa-Balāhakaiḥ / hayodagraiḥ*).—§ 617 (Aishikap.): X, **13,** 649 (description of Kṛshṇa's chariot). — § 635 (Rājadh.): XII, **37,** 1382 (*Çaibya-S°yojitaṃ*, sc. *rathaṃ*). — § 637 (do.): XII, **46,** †1587 (*Çaibyapramukhair varāçvaiḥ*). — § 639 (do.): XII, **53**η, 1917. — § 641 (do.): XII, **101,** 3749 (? cf. Nīl.). Cf. also Çaibya-Sugrīvavāhana (= Kṛshṇa).

Sugrīva[2], a monkey chief in Kishkindhā, brother of Vālin. § 316 (Kirmīravadhap.): III, **11,** 432 (*Vāli-S°yor bhrātror yathā strīkāṅkshiṇoḥ purā*).—§ 425 (Hanūmad-Bhīmasenasaṃv.): III, **147,** 11194 (*Sūryaputraṃ*), 11195, 11196; **148,** 11201, 11202, 11203 (short repetition from Rāmopākhyānaparvan).—§ 435 (Jaṭāsuravadhap.): III, **157,** 11510 (*Vāli-S°yor bhrātroḥ purā strīkāṅkshiṇor yathā*). — § 525 (Rāmopākhyānap.): III, **274,** 15874 (°*balam āçritaḥ*, sc. *Rāmaḥ*).—§ 530 (Viçvāvasumokshaṇa): III, **279,** 16087, 16089 (*bhrātā vānararājasya Vālinaḥ*, had taken his abode at Pampā). — § 531 (Rāmopākhyānap.): III, **280,** 16098 (*haripuṅgavaṃ*), 16102, 16103, 16105 (*plavagādhipaṃ*), 16106, 16108, 16109, 16113, 16115 (°*sacivāḥ*), 16117, 16118, 16120, 16122 (*Vāli-S°au*), 16125, 16127, 16131, 16132 (Vālin had deprived *S.* of his kingdom and his wife Tārā; *S.* made friends with Rāma Dāçarathi; *S.* and Vālin engaged in an encounter under which Rāma killed Vālin with an arrow; *S.* thus regained his kingdom and his wife). — § 532 (Sītāsāntvana): III, **281,** 16153.—§ 534 (Hanūmatpratyāgamana): III, **282,** 16197, 16210 (*plavagādhipaḥ*), 16212 (*vānarādhipaḥ*), 16217 (*vānarendreṇa*), 16218, 16222, 16229, 16260 (*sarvaçākhāmṛgendreṇa*), 16261, 16264 (*S.* despatched spies to find Sītā).—§ 535 (Setubandhana): III, **283,** 16269, 16281, 16283, 16291, 16315 (followed by a great many of monkeys *S.* accompanied Rāma on his expedition to Laṅkā). —§ 537 (Rāma-Rāvaṇayuddha): III, **285**β, 16372 (fo ght with Virūpāksha). — § 539 (Kumbhakarṇādivadha): III, **287,** 16416, 16418, 16419 (fought with Kumbhakarṇa).— § 540 (Indrajidyuddha): III, **288,** 16439, 16442 (*Rāma-Lakshmaṇa-S°āḥ*).—§ 541 (Indrajidvadha): III, **289,** 16467, 16470, 16477 (°-*Jāmbavantau*).—§ 543 (Rāmābhisheka): III, **291**δ, 16582 (°*pramukhaiḥ sarvavānaraiḥ*), 16587, 16597 (*kapiçreshṭhaṃ*). — § 551 (Kīcakavadhap.): IV, **22,** 752 (*Vāli-S°yor bhrātroḥ pureva kapisiṃhayoḥ*, sc. *bāhuyuddhaṃ*). —§ 600 (Ghaṭotkacavadhap.): VII, **178,** 8102 (*yuddhaṃ . . . harīndrayor yathā, rājan, Vāli-S°yoḥ purā*). — § 615 (Gadāyuddhap.): IX, **55,** 3107 (*sadṛçakarmāṇau . . . Vāli-S°yor yathā*, sc. Bhīmasena and Duryodhana). Cf. Sūryaputra.

Suhanu, an Asura. § 268 (Varuṇasabhāv.): II, **9,** 365 (among the Daityas and Dānavas in the palace of Varuṇa).

Suhara, an Asura. § 130 (Aṃçāvat.): I, **67,** 2660 (only C., B. has *Aharaḥ*, incarnate as king Bāhlīka).

Suhasta, son of Dhṛtarāshṭra. § 130 (Aṃçāvat.): I, **67,** 2737.—§ 182 (Dhṛtarāshṭraputranāmak.): I, **117,** 4549.— § 599 (Jayadrathavadhap.): VII, **127**νν, 5178 (among several sons of Dhṛtarāshṭra who attacked Bhīmasena). — § 600 (Ghaṭotkacavadhap.): VII, **157**ο, 6938 (among ten sons of Dhṛtarāshṭra who were slain by Bhīmasena).

Suhavis, son of Bhumanyu. § 152 (Pūruvaṃç.): I, **94,** 3714 (son of Bhumanyu and Pushkariṇī).

Suhçala (I, 4541), v. Duhçala.

Suhma, a prince. § 170 (Dīrghatamas): I, **104,** 4219 (son of Dīrghatamas and king Bali's wife Sudeshṇā), 4221 (the Suhmas are named after *S.*).

Suhma, pl. (°*āḥ*), a people. § 170 (Dīrghatamas): I, **104,** 4221 (named after Suhma).—§ 177 (Paṇḍudigvijaya): I, **113,** 4453 (vanquished by Pāṇḍu on his digvijaya).—§ 279 (Arjuna): II, **27,** 1029 (only B., C. has *Sahmam ca* for *Suhmāṃç ca*).—§ 280 (Bhīmasena): II, **30,** 1090 (°*ān Prasuhmāṃç ca*, in the east, vanquished by Bhīmasena), 1099 (°*ānām adhipaṃ*, vanquished by Bhīmasena). — § 604 (Karṇap.): VIII, **8,** 236 (had been caused by Karṇa to pay tribute to Duryodhana).

Suhotra[1], an ancient king, son of Bhumanyu. § 5 (Anukram.): I, **1***a*, 224 (in Nārada's enumeration). — § 152 (Pūruvaṃç.): I, **94,** 3714 (son of Bhumanyu and Pushkariṇī), 3715, 3716, 3718, 3719 (husband of Aikshvākī and father of Ajamīḍha, Sumīḍha, and Purumīḍha). — § 156 (do.): I, **95,** ††3786 (son of Bhumanyu and Vijayā), ††3787 (husband of Suvarṇā, the daughter of Ikshvāku, and father of Hastin).—§ 595 (Shoḍaçarāj.): King *S.* was invincible in battle, etc., the very gods used to come to see him; he freed the earth from Mlecchas and forest thieves (*vasumatīṃ Mlecchāṭavikavarjitāṃ*); Parjanya showered gold to him from year's end to year's end; the rivers were gold in those olden days and were open to the use of everybody (see the note of PCR., p. 167); his tanks (*vāpyaḥ*) were a kroça in extension; that unlimited wealth of gold the rājarshi *S.* gave away to the brahmans at a sacrifice at Kurujāṅgala; he performed 100 horse-sacrifices, 100 *rājasūyas*, many *kshatriya* sacrifices, etc., and attained to a desirable end (*ishṭām gatim*) (VII, **56**): VII, **56**, 2184, 2186.—§ 632*b* (Shoḍaçarāj., cf. § 595): XII, **29**, 917 (*Atithinam*, repetition from § 595). Cf. Atithin.

Suhotra[2], son of Sahadeva Pāṇḍava. § 159 (Pūruvaṃç.): I, **95**, ††3832 (son of Sahadeva and Vijayā, daughter of the Madra king Dyutimat).

Suhotra[3], a brahman. § 324 (Dvaitavanaprav.): III, **26*a***, 987 (waited upon Yudhishṭhira).

Suhotra[4], a Kuru king. § 463 (Çibi): III, **194**, ††13249 (*Kurūṇām anyatamaḥ*, meeting with Çibi). Cf. Kaurava, Kauravya.

Suhotra[5], a Daitya (?). § 673*b* (Bali-Vāsavasaṃv.): XII, **227*a***, 8263 (among the ancient rulers of the earth).

Suhotṛ, son of Bhumanyu. § 152 (Pūruvaṃç.): I, **94**, 3714 (son of Bhumanyu and Pushkariṇī).

Suhṛd = Vishṇu (1000 names).

Suhṛda = Çiva (1000 names[2]).

Sujāta, son of Dhṛtarāshṭra. § 611 (Çalyap.): IX, **26***ρρ*, 1405 (among 11 sons of Dhṛtarāshṭra who attacked Bhīmasena), 1418 (slain by Bhīmasena).

Sujātā, daughter of Uddālaka, wife of Kahoḍa, and mother of Ashṭāvakra. § 412 (Ashṭāvakrīya): III, **132**, †10605, †10609, †10613, †10617.

Sukandaka, pl. (*°āḥ*), a people. § 574 (Jambūkh.): VI, **9***μ*, 360.

Sukanyā[1], daughter of Çaryāti and wife of Cyavana. § 21 (Pramadvarā): I, **8**, 939 (by Cyavana, mother of Pramati).—§ 404 (Tīrthayātrāp.): III, **121**, 10313 (all. to § 405).—§ 405 (Sukanyop.): III, **122**, 10321, 10327, 10335, 10343; **123**, 10345, 10348, 10355, 10370; **124**, 10372; **125**, 10401, 10406.—§ 547 (Karṇa): III, **304**, 17035 (*Cyavano yadvat S°yāḥ kṛte*, all. to § 405).—§ 551 (Kīcakavadhap.): IV, **21**, 650 (*purā S°ā bhāryā ca Bhārgavaṃ Cyavanaṃ vane / valmīkabhūtaṃ çāmyantam anvapadyata*, cf. § 405).—§ 565 (Gālavacarita): V, **117**, 3970 (*reme . . . yathā . . . Cyavanaç ca S°āyāṃ*). Cf. Çaryātitanayā.

Sukanyā[2], wife of Mātariçvan. § 615*j* (Maṅkanaka): IX, **38**, 2245 (mother of Maṅkanaka).

[Sukanyopākhyāna(ṃ)] ("the episode relating to Sukanyā"). § 405 (Tīrthay.). *Lomaça* related: When *Cyavana*, the son of the *maharshi Bhṛgu* practised austerities by the side of this lake, and, assuming the posture *vīrasthāna*, had been enveloped by an anthill, king *Çaryāti* came to the lake with his 4,000 wives and his only daughter *Sukanyā*. The *viprarshi Cyavana*, seeing *Sukanyā*, was gladdened and spoke to her, but she did not hear him. Then *Sukanyā*, seeing his eyes in the anthill, pierced them with thorns from curiosity. He, becoming very angry, obstructed the excrements and urine of *Çaryāti's* soldiers, and *Çaryāti* at last discovered the cause of their distress, and only obtained deliverance therefrom by bestowing *Sukanyā* upon *Cyavana*. Then *Çaryāti*, with his troops, went to his city, and *Sukanyā* remained with *Cyavana* (III, **122**). Once, when the *Açvins* had seen *Sukanyā*, after she had bathed, they asked her to choose one of them for her husband, and as she refused, they entered the water together with *Cyavana*, and when they all came out of the tank young and beautiful they asked her to choose one of them and she choose *Cyavana*. *Cyavana* promised them to make them drinkers of *soma* in the presence of *Indra*. Then the *Açvins*, highly delighted, ascended to heaven (III, **123**). When *Çaryāti* heard that *Cyavana* had been turned into a youth, he came with his wife and troops to see him, and became very glad. *Cyavana* caused him to perform a sacrifice with *Cyavana* as his priest. When *Cyavana* was about to take up *soma* in order to offer it to the *Açvins*, *Indra* forbade it, saying, that they were physicians and servants, assumed forms at pleasure, and roamed about in the world of mortals, and as *Cyavana* did not obey he prepared to hurl his thunderbolt at him, but *Cyavana* paralysed his arm and fulfilled his intention. Then he created a *kṛtyā*, a great *Asura* named *Mada* (description); this rushed forth to devour *Indra* (III, **124**), who only was delivered when he had sanctioned that the *Açvins* should henceforth be entitled to the *soma* juice, saying that he had only intended to spread the fame of *Cyavana* and *Çaryāti*. *Cyavana* distributed *Mada* (who had been created repeatedly before) in drinks, women, gambling, and hunting.

Sukarman, a prince. § 264 (Sabhākriyāp.): II, **4*a***, 122 (waited upon Yudhishṭhira).

Sukeçī, an Apsaras. § 731*b* (Ashṭāvakra-Diksaṃv.): XIII, **19***β*, 1425 (in the abode of Kubera).

Suketu[1], a prince. § 232 (Svayaṃvarap.): I, **186**, 6989 (with his sons Sunāman and Suvarcas present at the svayaṃvara of Draupadī).

Suketu[2], son of Çiçupāla. § 604 (Karṇap.): VIII, **6**, 183 (*Çiçupālasya sutaḥ*, had been slain by Droṇa).

Suketu[3], son of Citraketu. § 608 (Karṇap.): VIII, **54**, 2630 (*Citraketusutaḥ*), 2633, 2635 (slain by Kṛpa).

Sukhada = Vishṇu (1000 names).

Sukhadā, a mātṛ. § 615*u* (Skanda): IX, **46***θ*, 2646.

Sukhājāta = Çiva (1000 names[2]).

Sukhaprada = Mahāpurusha (Mahāpurushastava).

Sukhapradā = Devasenā: III, 14451.

Sukhāsakta = Çiva (1000 names[2]).

Sukhasecaka, a serpent. § 67 (Sarpasattra): I, **57**, 2156 (B. *Mukha-°*; of Dhṛtarāshṭra's race).

Sukṛatu[1], an ancient king. § 6 (Anukram.): I, **1*a***, 229 (in Sañjaya's enumeration).

Sukratu[2], a prince. § 744 (Ānuçāsanik.): XIII, **45**, 2466 (*naptā Videharājasya Janakasya*, some çlokas of his are quoted).

Sukshatra, son of the Kosala king. § 592 (Saṃçaptakavadhap.): VII, **23***o*, 1004 (*Koçalādhipateh putram*, proceeded against Droṇa; description of his horses).

Sūkshma[1], an Asura. § 92 (Aṃçāvat.): I, **65**, 2533 (son of Danu).—§ 130 (do.): I, **67**, 2654 (incarnate as king Bṛhadratha).

Sūkshma[2] = Çiva (1000 names[2]). — Do.[3] = Vishṇu (1000 names).

Sūkshmaṃ tapas tatparamaṃ = Skanda: III, †14645.

Sūkshmātman[1]—Sūrya: III, 157.—Do.[2]=Kṛshṇa: XII, 1663.—Do.[3] = Çiva (1000 names[2]).

Sukumāra[1], a serpent. § 64 (Sarpasattra): I, **57**, 2150 (of Takshaka's race).

Sukumāra[2], one or more princes. § 232 (Svayaṃvarap.): I, **186**, 6990 (present at the svayaṃvara of Draupadī).—§ 280 (Bhīmasena): II, **29**, 1069 (vanquished by Bhīmasena on his digvijaya).—§ 281 (Sahadeva): II, **31**, 1108 (vanquished by Sahadeva on his digvijaya).

Sukumāra[3], a Kāçi prince (cf. Harivaṃça, v. 1595 and

v. 1751). § 572 (Rathātirathasaṅkhyānap.): V, **171**, 5907 (*Kāçikaḥ?*, a ratha in the army of Yudhishṭhira).—§ 592 (Saṃçaptakavadhap.): VII, **23**o, 976 (*Kāçyasyābhimukham —°ābhibhuvaḥ*, B.—*putram S°m*, PCR. takes it as an adj.).

Sukumāra[4], a varsha (?) in Çākadvīpa. § 575b (Çākadvīpa): VI, **11**β, 426.

Sukumārī[1], a river in Çākadvīpa. § 575b (Çākadvīpa): VI, **11**γ, 432.

Sukumārī[2], daughter of Sṛñjaya. § 633b (Nārada-Parvatop.): XII, **30**, 1056, 1065, 1067, 1073, 1074, 1082 (married Nārada, cf. VII, **55**).

Sukuṇḍala, a son of Dhṛtarāshṭra. § 130 (Aṃçāvat.): I, **67**, 2733.

Sukusumā, a mātṛ. § 615u (Skanda): IX, **46**θ, 2642.

Sukuṭṭa, pl. (°āḥ), a people. § 273 (Rājasūyārambhap.): II, **14**, 590 (only B., C. has *Mu°*).

Sukuṭya, pl. (°āḥ), a people. § 574 (Jambūkh.): VI, **9**μ, 347 (only C., B. has *Kuçalyāḥ*).

Sulabha = Vishṇu (1000 names).

Sulabhā, a female mendicant. § 709b (Sulabhā-Janakasaṃv.): XII, **321**, 11854 (*Janakasya saṃvādaṃ S°āyāç ca*), 11858 (*bhikshukī*), 11867, 11928, 11929, (11930), 12034 (discourse between *S.* and Janaka).

Sulabhā - Janaka - saṃvāda(ḥ) ("the conversation between Sulabhā and Janaka"). § 709b (Mokshadh.). Bhīshma related the old narrative of the discourse in days of yore, in *Dharma-yuga*, between king *Janaka Maithila Dharmadhvaja* (devoted to renunciation, conversant with the Veda, the *moksha-çāstra*, etc.), whom many wise men desired to imitate, and the female mendicant *Sulabhā*, who practised *Yoga* and wandered over the Earth, and had heard from many *tridaṇḍins* about *Janaka*. By her *Yoga*-power she assumed a beautiful form and instantly repaired to *Mithilā*, and, on pretence of begging alms, presented herself before the king, who was surrounded by his ministers and learned scholars. By *Yoga* she entered the king's consciousness by her own consciousness (*sattvaṃ sattvena*). Then they conversed upon emancipation. The king said he was a disciple of the *bhikshu Pañcaçikhā* of *Parāçara's* race, and fully conversant with *Sāṅkhya* and *Yoga*, etc.; *Pañcaçikha* had dwelt with him for four months in the rainy season. *Sulabhā* enumerated thirty principles. *Sulabhā* was the daughter of R-ṛ *Pradhāna*; in the sacrifices of her ancestors *Indra* used to come with *Droṇa*, etc. (*a*); no suitable husband could be obtained for her; therefore, she wandered over the earth alone, observant of the practices of asceticism. *Sulabhā* dwelt this one night in his person like a mendicant in an empty house (XII, **321**).

Sulocana[1], a son of Dhṛtarāshṭra. § 130 (Aṃçāvat.): I, **67**, 2729.—§ 182 (Dhṛtarāshṭraputranāmak.): I, **117**, 4543.—§ 209 (Drupadaçāsana): I, **138**, 5449.—§ 581 (Bhīshmavadhap.): VI, **64**κ, 2837 (among 14 sons of Dhṛtarāshṭra who attacked Bhīmasena), (λ), 2846 (slain by Bhīmasena).

Sulocana[2] = Vishṇu (1000 names).

Sumahābala, an ancient king. § 267 (Yamasabhāv.): II, **8**, 323 (in the palace of Yama).

Sumahāsvana = Çiva (1000 names[2]).

Sumāla, pl. (°āḥ), a people. § 279 (Arjuna): II, **27**, 1029 (only C., B. has *Colān*, vanquished by Arjuna on his digvijaya).

Sumallika, pl. (°āḥ), a people. § 574 (Jambūkh.): VI, **9**μ, 362 (in Bhāratavarsha).

Sumana, a Gandharva (?). § 266 (Çakrasabhāv.): II, **7**, 303 (in the palace of Indra).

Sumanā, a Kaikeyī. § 764 (Ānuçāsanik.): XIII, **123**, 5859 (*Kaikeyī*), 5864, 5878 (discourse with Çāṇḍilī).

Sumanas[1], a king. § 264 (Sabhākriyāp.): II, **4**β, 120 (*Kirātarājaḥ?*, waited upon Yudhishṭhira).

Sumanas[2], an ancient king. § 267 (Yamasabhāv.): II, **8**, 322 (in the palace of Yama).

Sumanas[3], an Asura. § 268 (Varuṇasabhāv.): II, **9**, 365 (among the Daityas and Dānavas in the palace of Varuṇa).

Sumaṇḍala, a king. § 279 (Arjuna): II, **26**, 997 (in the north, vanquished by Arjuna on his digvijaya).

Sumaṅgalā, a mātṛ. § 615u (Skanda): IX, **46**θ, 2630.

Sumani, a companion of Skanda. § 615u (Skanda): IX, **45**, 2534 (given to Skanda by Soma).

Sumanomukha, a serpent. § 564 (Mātalīyop.): V, **103**γ, 3628.

Sumantu, a ṛshi, disciple of Vyāsa. § 78 (Vyāsa): I, **63**, 2418 (Vyāsa taught his disciples the Vedas and the Mhbhr. as the fifth).—§ 264 (Sabhākriyāp.): II, **4**a, 106 (among the munis who waited upon Yudhishṭhira).—§ 637 (Rājādh.): XII, **47**η, 1592 (*Açmaka-S°unā* (!), among the ṛshis who surrounded Bhīshma on his arrow-bed).—§ 707 (Mokshadh.): XII, **319**, 11743.—§ 714 (Çukakṛtya): XII, **328**, 12337.—§ 717b (Nārāyaṇīya): XII, **341**μ, 13025; **350**μμ, 13647.

Sumanyu[1], a Devagandharva. § 191 (Arjuna): I, **123**a, 4814 (present at the birth of Arjuna; only C., B. has *Bhumanyuḥ*).

Sumanyu[2] (XIII, 6266), v. Bhūmanyu.

Sumati[1], an Asura. § 268 (Varuṇasabhāv.): II, **9**, 365 (among the Daityas and Dānavas in the palace of Varuṇa).

Sumati[2], a ṛshi. § 734 (Ānuçāsanik.): XIII, **26**a, 1761 (came to see Bhīshma).

Sumedhas = Vishṇu (1000 names).

Sumeru = Meru: VI, 2078 (*°r iva Bhānunā*, se *paramopetaḥ*, only B., C. has *Svayambhur*).

Sumīḍha, a prince. § 152 (Pūruvaṃç.): I, **94**, 3720 (second son of Suhotra).

Sumitra[1], an ancient king. § 6 (Anukram.): I, **1**a, 229 (in Sañjaya's enumeration).

Sumitra[2], one or more kings at the time of Yudhishṭhira. § 130 (Aṃçāvat.): I, **67**, 2699 (among the incarnations from the Krodhavaça gaṇa).—§ 211 (Sambhavap.): I, **139**, 5537 (*Sauvīraṃ*, also named Dattāmitra, vanquished by Arjuna).—§ 264 (Sabhākriyāp.): II, **4**β, 120 (waited upon Yudhishṭhira).—§ 280 (Bhīmasena): II, **29**, 1069 (vanquished by Bhīmasena on his digvijaya).—§ 281 (Sahadeva): II, **31**, 1105 (vanquished by Sahadeva on his digvijaya).

Sumitra[3], a muni. § 264 (Sabhākriyāp.): II, **4**a, 105 (waited upon Yudhishṭhira).

Sumitra[4], a god. § 492 (Āṅgirasa): III, **220**, 14167 (among the 15 yajñamushaḥ).

Sumitra[5], the charioteer of Abhimanyu. § 593 (Abhimanyuvadhap.): VII, **35**, 1537; **36**, 1547. Cf. Sūtaja.

Sumitra[6], a Haihaya king. § 641 (Rājadh.): XII, **125**, 4629 (*itihāsaṃ S°sya nirvṛttam Ṛshabhasya ca*), 4630 (*rājarshir Haihayaḥ*); **126**, 4648 (*Haihayānāṃ kule jātaḥ*); **128**, 4713 (instructed by Ṛshabha).

Sumitrā, wife of Daçaratha. § 525 (Rāmopākhyānap.): III, **274**, 15879 (mother of Lakshmaṇa and Çatrughna).—§ 527 (do.): III, **277**, 15980.

Sumukha[1], a serpent. § 47 (Sarpanāmak.): I, **35**, 1559.—§ 564 (Mātalīyop.): V, **103**, 3639 (*Nāgarāṭ*, of Airāvata's race, grandson of Āryaka, daughter's son of Vāmana, and son of Cikura); **104**, 3648, 3653, 3659, 3664, 3665, 3668 (married

Guṇakeçī; on account of his being destined to be eaten by Garuḍa, Indra bestowed on him length of days); **105**, 3704 (Vishṇu threw *S.* upon the breast of Garuḍa).

Sumukha[2], one or more Suparṇas, sons (grandsons) of Garuḍa. § 564 (Mātalīyop.): V, **101** *a*, 3587; (*β*), 3597.—§ 574*b* (Jambūkh.): The bird *S.*, the son of Suparṇa (i.e. Garuḍa) beholding that all the birds on *Meru* were of golden plumage, resolved to leave that mountain as there was no difference there between good, middling, and bad birds: VI, **6**, 208 (*Suparṇasyātmajaḥ*).

Sumukha[3], a ṛshi. § 265 (Lokapālasabhākhyānap.): II, **5**, 145 (accompanied Nārada).

Sumukha[4], son of Dhṛtarāshṭra. § 599 (Jayadrathavadhap.): VII, **127** *νν*, 5177.

Sumukha[5] = Çiva (1000 names[1-2]).—Do.[6] = Vishṇu (1000 names).

Sumukhī, an Apsaras. § 731*b* (Ashṭāvakra-Dikṣaṃvāda): XIII, **19** *β*, 1425 (danced in the abode of Kubera).

Sunābha[1], a son of Dhṛtarāshṭra. § 182 (Dhṛtarāshṭra-putranāmak.): I, **117**, 4544.—§ 585 (Bhīshmavadhap.): VI, **88**, 3899 (slain by Bhīmasena).

Sunābha[2], a counsellor of Varuṇa. § 268 (Varuṇasabhāv.): II, **9**, 380 (*Varuṇaç ca tathā mantrī*, in the palace of Varuṇa).

Sunābha[3], a mountain. § 269 (Vaiçravaṇasabhāv.): II, **10**, 413 (*Indrakīlaḥ S°ç ca tathā divyau ca parvatau*, in the palace of Kubera).

Sunakshatrā, a mātṛ. § 615*u* (Skanda): IX, **46** *θ*, 2627.

Sunāman[1], son of Suketu. § 232 (Svayaṃvarap.): I, **186**, 6989 (*Suketuḥ saha putreṇa S°nā*, present at the svayaṃvara of Draupadī).

Sunāman[2], brother of Kaṃsa. § 273 (Jarāsandhavadhap.): II, **14**, 598 (*hatau Kaṃsa-S°au mayā*, i.e. by Kṛshṇa, *Rāmena cāpy uta*).—§ 589 (Droṇābhishekap.): VII, **11**, 388 (*°ā . . . Bhojarājasya madhyastho bhrātā Kaṃsasya . . . Baladevadvitīyena Kṛshṇena . . . dagdhaḥ . . . Çūrasenarāṭ*).

Sunāman[3], a Suparṇa, son of Garuḍa. § 564 (Mātalīyop.): V, **101** *a*, 3587

Sunāman[4], a warrior of Skanda. § 615*u* (Skanda): IX, **45** *η*, 2561.

Sunandā[1], wife of Sarvabhauma. § 156 (Pūruvaṃç.): I, **95**, ††3769 (*Kaikeyīṃ*).

Sunandā[2], daughter of Sarvasena, wife of Bharata. § 156 (Pūruvaṃç.): I, **95**, ††3785 (*Kāçeyīṃ . . . Sārvasenīṃ*).

Sunandā[3], wife of Pratīpa. § 156 (Pūruvaṃç.): I, **95**, ††3797 (*Çaibyāṃ*). Cf. Çaibyā.

Sunandā[4], sister of the Cedi king Subāhu. § 347 (Nalopākhyānap.): III, **65**, 2604, 2606.—§ 350 (do.): III, **68**, 2661, 2686; **69**, 2705.

Sunasā, a river. § 574 (Jambūkh.): VI, **9** *λ*, 338.

Sunaya, pl. (°*āḥ*), a people. § 574 (Jambūkh.): VI, **9** *ν*, 371 (in the south).

Sunda[1], an Asura, brother of Upasunda. § 11 (Parvasaṅgr.): I, **2**, 395 (°*opasundayoḥ . . . ākhyānaṃ*, i.e. Sundopasundopākhyāna).—§ 245 (Rājyalābhap.): I, **208**, 7613 (°*opasundau bhrātarau*), 7616 (°*opasundāv Asurau*). — § 246 (Sundopasundop.): I, **209**, 7621 (°*opasundau Daityendrau*, sons of Nikumbha), 7636 (°*opasundau bhrātarau*), (7642) (°*opasundau*); **210**, 7677 (°*opasundayoḥ*); **211**, 7684 (do.), 7698 (°*opasundābhyām Asurābhyāṃ*); **212**, 7723, 7726 (the story of *S.* and Upasunda). — § 612 (Hradapraveçap.): IX, **31** *ζ*, 1755 (°*opasundāv Asurau kriyayaiva nisūditau*, cf. § 246).—§ 615 (Gadāyuddhap.): IX, **55**, 3107 (*sadṛçakarmāṇau tathā S°opasundayoḥ*, sc. Bhīmasena and Duryodhana). Cf. Asura, Daitya (dual), Daityendra (dual).

Sunda[2] = Vishṇu (1000 names).

Sundara = Vishṇu (1000 names).

Sundaravaṃça, pl. (°*āḥ*), a people. § 562 (Bhagavadyānap.): V, **74** *γ*, 2731 (*Bāhuḥ S°ānāṃ*).

Sundarikāhrada, a tīrtha. § 773*i* (Devikā): XIII, **25**, 1707. Cf. next.

Sundarikātīrtha, name of a tīrtha. § 370 (Tīrthayātrāp.): III, **84**, 8035.

[Sundopasundapākhyāna(m)] ("the episode relating to Sunda and Upasunda"). § 246 (Rājyalābhap.). *Nārada* related: In days of yore the *Daitya Nikumbha* of the race of *Hiraṇyakaçipu* had two sons, *Sunda* and *Upasunda*, who always shared with each other happiness as well as woe, and never went anywhere unless together. Desirous of subjugating the three worlds, they practised terrible penances on the mountain *Vindhya*, which, by the power of their austerities at last began to emit vapour. In vain the gods repeatedly tempted them by means of every precious possession and beautiful girls, and by illusion, causing their sisters, mothers, wives, etc., to appear pursued by a *rākshasa* and imploring their help. When *Brahmán* granted them a boon, they asked to become immortal, which he refused, granting them instead that they should not need to be afraid of anything except each other, etc. They now desisted from their asceticism and returned to their abode, where they lived happy, causing even the moon to rise over their city every night, even out of season (I, **209**). They set out to conquer the three worlds in the night under the constellation of *Maghāḥ*, with a large *Daitya* force cased in mail, etc. The gods sought refuge in *Brahmaloka*, and the *Daityas* subjugated *Indraloka*, and vanquished the tribes of the *Yakshas* and *Rakshases*, and the *Khecaras*, and the *Nāgas* in the earth, and the tribes of the *Mlecchas* dwelling in the ocean. In order to extinguish the sacrifices that strengthened the gods, they slew those that were performing sacrifices and the assistant *brahmans*, etc. Then they took up their abode in *Kurukshetra* (I, **210**). The *Devarshis* and *Siddhas* and *ṛshis* were affected with great grief, and went to the abode of *Pitāmaha*, seated with the gods, the *Siddhas*, and the *Brahmarshis*, *Mahādeva*, *Agni*, *Vāyu*, the sun and moon, *Çakra*, the *Pārameshṭhya ṛshis*, the *Vaikhānasas*, the *Vālakhilyas*, the *Vānaprasthas*, the *Marīcipas*, the *Ajas*, the *Avimūḍhas*, etc. *Brahmán* sent *Tilottamā* (*b*) to them (I, **211**). She came to *Sunda* and *Upasunda* as they were sporting in the *Vindhya* mountains, and from jealousy they struck each other to death with their maces. And *Pitāmaha* then came there with the gods and the great *ṛshis*, and granted to *Tilottamā* that she should roam in the region of the *Ādityas*. Then, bestowing the three worlds on *Indra* as before, he returned to his own region.

Sunetra[1], a prince. § 155 (Pūruvaṃç.): I, **94**, 3749 (son of the elder Dhṛtarāshṭra (so B.) or of Dhṛtarāshṭra's son [Kuṇḍika] (so C.)).

Sunetra[2], a Suparṇa, son of Garuḍa. § 564 (Mātalīyop.): VI, **101** *a*, 3587.

Suniçcala = Çiva (1000 names[2]).

Sunītha[1], name of a mantra (according to Nīl.). § 68 (Āstīkap.): I, **58**, 2188 (*Asitaṃ cārttimantañ ca Sunīthaṃ cāpi yaḥ smaret / divā vā yadi* [*vā*] *rātrau nāsya sarpabhayaṃ bhavet*).

Sunītha[2] = Çiçupāla. I, †7019, †7051; II, 1410, 1413 (°*pramukhā gaṇāḥ*), 1913 (?).

Sunītha[3], an ancient ṛshi. § 266 (Çakrasabhāv.): II, **7**, 297 (in the palace of Indra).

Sunītha[4], name of two ancient kings. § 267 (Yamasabhāv.): II, **8**, 322 (in the palace of Yama), 326 (do.).

Sunītha[5], son of Kṛshṇa and Jāmbavatī (according to Hariv. v. 9186). § 452 (Mārkaṇḍeyas.): III, **183**, †12584 (*yathā S°sya*).

Sunīthā, daughter of Mṛtyu. § 641 (Rājadh.): XII, **59**, 2214 (*c*: *S.* was the spiritual daughter of Mṛtyu and celebrated over the three worlds; *S.* became the wife of Atibala).

Supārçva[1], one or more kings at the time of Yudhishṭhira. § 130 (Aṃçāvat.): I, **67**, 2665 (incarnation of the Asura Kupatha).—§ 280 (Bhīmasena): II, **30**, 1081 (in the east, vanquished by Bhīmasena on his digvijaya).—§ 554 (Sainyodyogap.): V, **4**γ, 77.

Supārçva[2], son of Dhṛtarāshṭra. § 600 (Ghaṭotkacavadhap.): VII, **164**δδ, 7337.

Suparṇa[1] ("having beautiful wings") = Garuḍa: I, †724 (*grastāṃ S°sya balena varttikām*), 1260 (C. by error *Suv°*), 1261, (1262), 1304, 1306, 1313 (*patageçvaram*), 1502, 1518 (origin of the name) 1535, †1544, 1588, 8252 (? *°ādyāḥ patatriṇaḥ*, fight with Kṛshṇa and Arjuna); III, 10574 (*pakshirāṭ*), 10958 (?), 11676 (*mahānāgaṃ . . . sahasāharat*), 11680 (*°ānilavegena*), †15671 (*saraḥ S°ena hṛtoragaṃ yathā*); V, †2578 (*Garuḍaṃ*, identified with Kṛshṇa), 3660, 3663, 3675, (3761), (3779), (3801), (3821), 3850, 3874, 3876, 3880, 3884, 3894, 3896, 3917, 4004, 4112, 4022, 4025 (*pannagāçanam*), 5290 (*°ḥ pakshiṇāṃ yathā*, sc. *senāpatir bhava*); VI, 152 (G°), 208 (*Sumukhaḥ . . . S°syātmajaḥ*), 3978, 3991 (*°patane yathā*, sc. *çabdaḥ*); VII, 2572 (*°a iva sāgaraṃ*, sc. *prāviçat*), 2683, 5229 (*°a iva vegena pakshirāṭ*), 5532 (*°vegaiḥ . . . patatribhiḥ*), 6343 (*rathaṃ . . . S°occhritaketanam*, i.e. Kṛshṇa's); VIII, 1803 (*°ṃ patagaçreshṭhaṃ Vainateyaṃ . . . bhogīvāhvayase pāte*), 1938 (*°vat*), †3857 (*mahāvanānīva S°vāyunā*, sc. *patanti*), †4327 (*°vātaprahatā yathoragāḥ*); X, 38 (*°m iva vegitaṃ*); XII, 8345 (*°ārkaracitaṃ . . . Vaishṇavaṃ padaṃ*); XIII, 682 (*somahartāram*), 4206 (*°sya putraṃ*, but read with B. *S°o 'sya putraṃ*, and cf. IX, 2669), 6864 (*Kaçyapātmajaḥ*), 7104 (*pannageçvaraḥ*, but read *patageçvaraḥ* with B.); XVI, †62 (the banner (*dhvaja*) of Kṛshṇa).

Suparṇa[2], name of two Devagandharvas. § 101 (Aṃçāvat.): I, **65**, 2550 (son of Muni). § 102 (do.): I, **65**, 2555 (son of Prādhā).

Suparṇa[3], an Asura. § 130 (Aṃçāvat.): I, **67**, 2672 (incarnate as king Kālakīrti).

Suparṇa[4] = Sūrya: III, 155.

Suparṇa[5], name of a yajus. § 637 (Rājadh.): XII, **47**θ, 1632 (*°o yajur nāma*, identified with Kṛshṇa; otherwise Nīl. and PCR.).

Suparṇa[6], a ṛshi. § 717*b* (Nārāyaṇīya): XII, **349**, 111), 13566 (*ṛshiḥ*), 13567, 13568 (learnt the religion (*dharma*) [of Nārāyaṇa] from Nārāyaṇa himself, and recited it thrice a day, hence it was named *trisauparṇa*).

Suparṇa[7] = Vishṇu (1000 names).

Suparṇa[8], name of a vyūha. VII, 795 (*vyūḍhaṃ*), 796. Cf. Garuḍa[2].

***Suparṇa**, pl. (*°āḥ*), birds of Garuḍa's race. I, †722 (dual, said of the Açvins), 2562, †7011, †7017 (*°nāgāsurasiddhajushṭaṃ*, sc. *antarīkshaṃ*), 8252 (? *°ādyāḥ patatriṇaḥ*, fought with Kṛshṇa and Arjuna); II, 465 (in the palace of Brahmán), 472 (do.); III, 8214, 10831, 11646, 12924; V, 3586 (*lokaḥ S°ānāṃ pakshiṇāṃ pannagāçināṃ*, enumeration of the *S.*, sons of Garuḍa); VII, 5641 (*°ā iva khecarāḥ*), †6921, †9465, 9475; VIII, 2593 (*bhakshayanto bhujaṅgamān*), †4490 (*Brahmarshi-rājarshi-S°jushṭaṃ*, sc. *viyat*); XI, 453, 778; XII, †1892 (*hayaiḥ S°air iva cāçugāmibhiḥ*), 13366; XIII, †1373 (*°-Gandharva-Piçāca-Dānavāḥ*), 3886 (*devāsura-S°āḥ*). Cf. Garuḍa, pl.

Suparṇaketu ("having Garuḍa in his banner") = Kṛshṇa: III, †12330.

suparṇī, said of Svāhā: III, 14308, 14345.

Suparvaṇa = Çiva: XIII, 1233 (*divi*, 1000 names[2]).

Suprabhā[1], a river, one of the seven Sarasvatīs. § 615*i* (Saptasārasvata): IX, **38***a*, 2189, 2198 (summoned by Brahmán, the Sarasvatī appeared in Pushkara as *S.*).

Suprabhā[2], a mātṛ. § 615*u* (Skanda): IX, **46**θ, 2628.

Suprabhā[3], daughter of Vadānya. § 731*b* (Ashṭāvakra-Diks.): XIII, **19**, 1392 (married to Ashṭāvakra when he had made a journey to the north).

Suprajā, wife of the fire Bhānu. § 493 (Āṅgirasa): III, **221**, 14184 (*Bhānor bhāryā*).

Suprajāpati = Mahāpurusha (Mahāpurushastava).

Suprasāda[1], a warrior of Skanda. § 615*u* (Skanda): IX, **45**η, 2573.

Suprasāda[2] = Vishṇu (1000 names).

Suprasādā, a mātṛ. § 615 (Skanda): IX, **46**δ, 2631.

Supratardana, an ancient king. § 552 (Goharaṇap.): IV, **56**ζ, 1768 (came from heaven to see the encounter, BR. proposes to read *sa-Pratardanaḥ*).

Supratīka[1], an ancient king. § 61 (Anukram.): I, **1***a*, 228 (in Sañjaya's enumeration).

Supratīka[2], the elephant of Bhagadatta. § 11 (Parvasaṅgr.): I, **2**, 531.—§ 585 (Bhīshmavadhap.): VI, **95**, 4255, 4265, 4276.—§ 592 (Saṃçaptakavadhap.): VII, **26**, 1152.

Supratīka[3], a ṛshi, brother of Vibhāvasu. § 41*b* (Garuḍa): When the ṛshi *S.* wished to separate from his elder brother *Vibhāvasu* and make a partition of their patrimony he was cursed by *Vibhāvasu*, who said: "Thou shalt become an elephant," and he himself cursed *Vibhāvasu*, saying: "Thou shalt become a tortoise." In these forms they continued their hostilities in a lake; the elephant being 6 yojanas in height and 12 in circumference, and the tortoise 3 and 10 respectively (I, **29**); I, **29**, 1354 (*mahātapāḥ*), 1355, 1356, 1361, 1362 (*°-Vibhāvasū*).—§ 42–43 (do.): I, **29–30** (both the elephant and the tortoise were seized and afterwards eaten by Garuḍa).

Supratīka[4], one of the elephants of the quarters. § 564 (Mātalīyop.): V, **99**, 3561 (Airāvaṇa, Vāmana, Kumuda, and Añjana were born in the race of *S.*).—§ 575*o* (Samā): VI, **12**, 475 (description). — § 599 (Jayadrathavadhap.): VII, **121**, 4830 (*°kule jātāḥ*, sc. elephants).

Supratima, an ancient king. § 6 (Anukram.): I, **1***a*, 228 (in Sañjaya's enumeration).

Supratishṭhā, a mātṛ. § 615*u* (Skanda): IX, **40**δ, 2647.

Supravṛddha, one of the standard-bearers of Jayadratha. § 522 (Draupadīharaṇap.): III, **265**, †15597.

Suprayogā, a river. § 494 (Āṅgirasa): III, **222**, 14232 (among the rivers who are mothers of fires). — § 574 (Jambūkh.): VI, **9**λ, 328.

Supriyā, an Apsaras. § 104 (Aṃçāvat.): I, **65**, 2559 (daughter of Prādhā). — § 191 (Arjuna): I, **123**, 4819 (among the Apsarases who danced at the birth of Arjuna).

Supuṇḍraka, v. Puṇḍraka.

Supuṇyā, v. Puṇyā.

sura, mostly pl. (°*āḥ*) ("gods"). I, 17, 264, 534, 639 (°*gaṇaiḥ*), 1107, 1109, 1120, 1122 (°*āsurāḥ*), 1128, 1129 (°*āsuragaṇān*), 1130 (°*āsuraiḥ*), 1138, 1162, 1168, †1182, †1187, †1188, †1256, 1267, 1431 (°*ottamāḥ*), 1433 (°*gaṇāḥ*), 1434, 1435, 1472, 1480 (°*gaṇaiḥ*), 1484, 1915, 2076, 2077, 2498 (*sa-s°āsura-lokānāṃ*), 2509, 2517, 2546, 2598 (°*āsurāḥ*), 2607, 2616 (°-*nandinī*, sc. *Surā*), 2748, 2750, 2754, 3004 (°*opamaḥ*), 3187, 3190, 3191, 3577, †3597, 3845, 3847 (°*gaṇāḥ*), 3895 (°*garbhābhe*), 4002, 4003 (°*āsura*°), 4073, 4256 (°*sutopame*), 4297 (°*sutopamā*), 4580 (°*saṅkāça*), 4935 (°*sutopamāḥ*), 6009 (°*garbhābhe*), 6403, 6882, 7657, 8202 (°*āsuraiḥ*), 8262, 8263, 8274, 8297, 8304 (°*āsuraiḥ*), 8305, 8310; II, 136 (°*gaṇa*°), 141 (°*āsurān*), 769 (°*āsuraiḥ*), 1323; III, †159 (°*gaṇa*°), †949 (°*ṛshi-mānavārcitaṃ*), 1442, 1590 (sg.), 1677 (°*gaṇaiḥ*), 1845, 1890, 1894, 1950, 2116, 2159 (°*sattamaiḥ*), 2166 (°*ottamān*), 2187 (°*ottamāḥ*), 2188, 2946 (°*sutopamau*), 4010, 4076, 6089, 6091, 6099, 7000, 8424, 8492, 8692, 8694, 8708, †8709 (°*ottamān*), 8710, †8730, 8768, 8777 (°*aiçvaryāt*), †8788, 8791, 8796, †8811, 8822, 8857, †10051, 10153, 10156 (°*gaṇa*-), †10216, †10222, †10257, 10355 (dual), 10370 (do., *iva*), 10390 (°*āsuraiḥ*), 10506 (°*ālaye*), †10656 (*yathā Mahendraḥ pravaraḥ surāṇāṃ*), 10710 (°*gaṇa*°), 10739 (°*sattamāḥ*), 11089 (*Yaksha-Gandharva-s°-Brahmarshigaṇa*-), 11207 (°*sutopamāṃ*), 11530 (°*āsura*-), 11784, †11915, 11990 (°-*Dānava-Rākshasaiḥ*), 12007, 12008 (°*ṛshabhān*), 12039, 12040 (? °*veçmani*), 12054 (°*gaṇaiḥ*), 12148 (°*āṇām Asurāṇāñ ca saṅgrāmaḥ*), 12189, 12193, 12205 (°-*Rākshasa-pannagaiḥ*), 12212 (°*āsuraiḥ*), 12256 (do.), 12257 (do.), 12307, 12308, †12347 (°*siddhajushṭāṃ*, sc. *nalinīṃ*), 12642 (°*ālayaṃ*), †12649, 12977 (°*sattamaiḥ*), 12995 (°*āsuraiḥ*), 13494 (*sa-s°āsura-mānavāḥ*), 14226, 14262 (°*āsura*-), 14376, 14547, 14599, 14623, †14640 (*bhāvanaḥ sarva-s°āsurāṇāṃ*, sc. Skanda), †14644 (*pravaraḥ s°āṇāṃ*, sc. Skanda), †14646 (*sarva-s°pravīra*, sc. Skanda), 15017 (°*ālayaṃ*), 15939 (°*sattamāḥ*), 16604 (*sendrā api s°āsurāḥ*), 17089 (°*gaṇān*), 17140; IV, 321 (°*opama*, sc. Nakula), 1295 (°*āsuraiḥ*), 1350, 1761 (°*gaṇaiḥ*), 1777, 2206 (*sa-s°āsuramānavān*), †2305 (°*devateva*); V, †14 284, 303 (°*ottamāḥ*), 385 (do.), 390 (°*çreshṭhāḥ*), 393, 398 (°*aiçvaryaṃ*), 417 (°*gaṇāḥ*), 1800 (*yathā*), 1936 (°*āsuraiḥ*), 2095, 2808 (°*āṇām Asurāṇañ ca . . . Prajāpatiḥ*, sc. *suhṛt*), 3535, 3537, 3550, 3756 (°*āsurān*), 3767, 3768, 3771, 3790, 3853, 3927 (°*sutaprakhyā*), 4172 (°*āsuraiḥ*), 5297 (*sa-s°āsura-Rākshasaṃ*); VI, 774 (°*āsurāṇāṃ*), 775, †886, 1206 (°*gaṇāḥ*), †1267 (°*saṅghāḥ*), †2653 (*iva*), 2939, 2956, 2986 (°*sattamāḥ*), 2990 (°*āsuraiḥ*), 2995 (°*ottamāḥ*), †3013 (°*martyalokaṃ*), 3643 (°*nadī*), †3780, 4440 (°*āsurān*), 4960 (°*āsuraiḥ*), 4961 (do.), 5804 (do.); VII, 174 (*yathā*), 461 (°*āsuraiḥ*), 634 (*yathā*), 891 (°*āsuranamaskṛtaḥ*, sc. Vishṇu), 1277 (*sa-s°āsuramānushān*), 1463 (*sa-s°āsura-Gandharvāḥ*), †1622 (*pitṛ-s°-cāraṇa-siddha-saṅghaiḥ*), 1915 (°*āsuraiḥ*), 1928, †2002, 2229 (°*āsuraiḥ*), 2257 (°*gaṇaiḥ*), †2607 (*asura-sura-manushyāḥ*), 2731 (°*āsurāḥ*), 3444 (*sāsuras°āḥ*), 3457 (°*sattamāḥ*), 3460 (°*sattamān*), 3813 (*sa-s°āsuramānushāḥ*), 4218, 4268 (*pṛthivī . . . sa-s°āsura-mānushā*), 5818, 5999 (°*vṛshabhaiḥ*), 6518, †6726 (*yathā*), 6761 (*iva*), †6921, 7033, 7048 (°*āsurāḥ*), †7312 (°-*siddha-saṅghāḥ*), †7314 (°*āsuravyūhasamaṃ*), 7814 (°*parākramaḥ*), 7988, 8219 (°*vāhinīṃ*), 8234 (°*āsuraiḥ*), 8284 (*iva*), 8425 (*sa-s°āsura-Gandharvān . . . lokān*), 8437, †9465 (°*āsurān*), 9543, 9545, 9547 (°*āsurāḥ*), 9553, 9555, 9558, 9571, 9576, 9578, 9582 (°*ottamān*), 9592; VIII, †1211 (°*sūnusannibhāḥ*), 1319 (°*āsurāḥ*), 1414, 1422, 1476 (°*ottamāḥ*, C. by error °*ottamaḥ*), 1575, †1742 (*Asurā-s°-mahoragān*), †1978 (°*āsurān*), 2103, 2199 (°*āsuraiḥ*), †3629 (do.), 3641 (*sa-s°āsuramānushān*), †3800, †4207 (*yathā*), 4348, †4494 (*yathā*), †4498 (°*āsurāḥ*), †4507, †4573, †4661 (°*ottamaiḥ*), 4775, †4947; IX, 276 (°*saṃsadi*), 323 (*pṛthivīṃ . . . sa-s°āsuramānavāṃ*), 331 (*sa-s°āsuramānavān*), 2103, 2226, 2228, 2239, 2314 (°*opamaḥ*) 2364, 2598 (°*sattamaiḥ*), 2673 (°*puṅgavān*), 2722, 2723 (°*gaṇaiḥ*), 2731, 2742, 2757 (°*tvaṃ*), 2951, 2952 (°*sattamāḥ*), 3023, †3031 (°*ṛshabhāḥ*); X, 800; XII, 1623 (°*āsura-Gandharvāḥ*), 2149 (°*ṛshabhāḥ*), †2404, 4411 (*lokaṃ . . . sa-s°āsura-mānushaṃ*), 4466 (*lokānāṃ . . . sa-s°āsura-Rakshasāṃ*), †5667 (°*āsurāḥ*), 6162 (*maharshi-s°-Gandharvān*), 6331 (°*gṛhaprakhyaṃ*), 6446 (°*gaṇaiḥ*), 6791 (*api*), 7584, 7587, 7618 (°*sattamāḥ*), 7638 (do.), 7693 (°*āsurāḥ*), 7773, 8421, 10234, 10235, 10253, 10320 (°*sainyāni*), 10321 (°*yoshitaḥ*), 10660, 10661 (°*sattamaiḥ*), 10665, 12565 (°*gaṇaiḥ*), 12661 (*api*), 12666, 12767, 12808, 12833 (°*pakshaḥ*), 12916 (°*ottamān*), 12927 (°*āsuragaṇānāṃ*), 12929, 12943, 12952, 12989, 12992 (°*āsuraiḥ*), 13013 (*lokāḥ sa-s°āsuramānavāḥ*), 13067, 13087 (°*ottamāḥ*), 13089, 13095 (°*ottamāḥ*), 13103, ††13205 (°*āsura*-), †13249, 13307, 13319, 13391, 13408, 13668 (°*gaṇāḥ*), 13732 (°*āsuraiḥ*), 13866 (°*āsuragaṇānāṃ*); XIII, 190, 671 (°*endrān*), 708 (°*nandinī*, sc. *gauḥ*), 804, 814 (°*āsuraiḥ*), 822, 823, 875, 929, 931, 1001, 1020 (°*āsurāḥ*), 1066 (only C., B. *muneḥ*), 1121, 1807, 1823, 3333 (°*ṛshabhāḥ*), 3605, 4006, 4015, 4018 (°*sattamāḥ*), 4022 (°*ottamāḥ*), 4034, 4041, 4065, 4377, 4806, 6302, 6492, 6624 (only C.), 6757, 6778 (°*sundarī*), 6815, 6857 (°*sattamāḥ*), 6890, 6894, 7071 (°*āsura*-), 7275, 7309 (dual = the Açvins), 7313, †7365, †7372, 7467, 7470, 7471 (°*āsurāḥ*), 7493, 7655, 7742; XIV, 46, 47, 110; XV, 664 (°*devateva*), 847; XVIII, 14 (°*samāḥ*), 33, 38 (°*sattamāḥ*). Cf. Suraçatru, etc.

Sūra, pl., v. Çūra[8].

Surā ("spirituous liquor", personif.), a goddess. § 28 (Amṛtamanthana): I, **18**, 1146 (°*devī*, arose at the churning of the ocean), 1148. — § 124 (Aṃçāvat.): I, **66**, 2616 (*suranandinīṃ*, daughter of Varuṇa and Devī, the daughter of Çukra).—§ 270 (Brahmasabhāv.): II, **11**, 459 (*devī*, in the palace of Brahmán).

Surabhi or **Surabhī**, the celestial cow, mother of kine. § 127 (Aṃçāvat.): I, **66**, 2625 (daughter of Krodhavaçā), 2631 (mother of Rohiṇī, Gandharvī, Vimalā, and Analā).— § 164 (Āpavop.): I, **99**, 3927 (*Dakshasya duhitā . . . devī*, by Kaçyapa, mother of Nandinī, the *homa* cow of Vasishṭha, (°*ī*)).—§ 270 (Brahmasabhāv.): II, **11**, 457 (*devī*?, in the palace of Brahmán, (°*ī*)).—§ 314 (Āraṇyakap.): III, **9**, 327, 328, (331), (338), 339 (°*ī*) (discourse between *S.* and Indra). —§ 502 (Manushyagrahak.): III, **230**, 14486 (*gavāṃ mātā*, a sickness demon (?) mounted by the demon Çakuni).— § 564 (Mātalīyop.): V, **102**, 3602 (*mātā gavām amṛtasambhavā*, in Pātāla), 3614 (°*ī ksharate payaḥ*). — § 565 (Gālavac.): V, **110**, 3810 (°*iḥ ksharate payaḥ*, in the west). —§ 668*b* (Kṛtaghnop.): XII, **173**, 6432 (*devī Dākshāyaṇī . . . payasvinī*). — § 730*g* (Upamanyu): XIII, **14**, 715 (°*īgotravarjite*, sc. *araṇye*). — § 746 (Ānuçāsanik.): XIII, **77**, 3712 (*mukhajāṃ sutāṃ*, sc. Daksha's, (°*ī*)), 3713 (mother of the saurabheyīs (cows)); **83**, 3906 (*Dakshasya duhitā devī*, (°*ī*)), (3912) (°*ī*), 3913 (°*ī*) (*S.* performed austerities).— § 751*b* (Çapathavidhi): XIII, **94**, (4587).—§ 768*b* (Umā-Maheçvarasaṃv.): XIII, **141**, 6399 (*devadhenuṃ*, created by Brahmán, (°*ī*)).—§ 775 (Ānuçāsanik.): XIII, **166*a***, 7638 (*saumyā gauḥ S°ir devī*). Cf. Dākshāyaṇi.—Do. pl. ("cows"): XIII, 3754, 3902.

Surabhi = Çiva (1000 names[2]).

Surabhimat, name of a fire. § 493 (Āṅgirasa): III, **221,** 14204 (only B., C. has *Suramat*).
Surabhīpaṭṭana, a city. § 284 (Sahadeva): II, **31,** 1171 (in the south, conquered by Sahadeva on his digvijaya).
Surabhyākhyāna ("the history of Surabhi"). § 11 (Parvasaṅgr.): I, **2,** 423 (i.e. § 314: III, ch. **9**).
Suraçatru, pl. (°*avaḥ*) ("enemies of the gods") = Asura, pl.: I, 460; III, 12926; VIII, 1553; IX, 2720; XIII, 4024. — Do. sg.: III, 13614 (i.e. Dhundhu); IX, 2701 (i.e. Bāṇa).
Suraçreshṭha[1] = Brahmán: VII, 3459; XII, 13074 (only C., B. had *Suraçreshṭhāḥ*).
Suraçreshṭha[2] = Çiva: XII, 10399 (1000 names[1]), 10435 (do.); XIV, 1889 (*Maheçvaram*).
Suraçreshṭha[3] = Indra: I, 2932; III, 8422, 10905 (*samarudgaṇaḥ*); IX, 2791; XIII, 3180.
Suraçreshṭha[4] = Nārāyaṇa (Vishṇu): XII, 13159 (*N°m Harim*).
Suraçreshṭha[5] = Skanda: III, 14432 (*S°*).
Suraçreshṭha[6] = Sūrya: III, 16986.
Suraçreshṭhā = Durgā (Umā): IV, 193.
Surādevī, v. Surā.
Surādhipa[1] = Indra, q.v.—Do.[2] = Nahusha, q.v.—Do.[3] pl.: XII, 8251.
Surādhyaksha[1] = Çiva (1000 names[2]). — Do.[2] = Vishṇu (1000 names).
***Suradvish**[1], pl. (°*aḥ*) ("enemies of the gods") = Asura, pl.: I, †3230; III, 12214, 12246; VII, 8234, 9560; VIII, 1432 (*Asurāḥ*), 1459; IX, 2663, 2697, 2699; XII, 6163, 6356.—Do.[2] sg.: III, 16531 (i.e. Rāvaṇa); VII, 1291 (i.e. Bhagadatta).
Suragaṇa = Çiva (1000 names[2]).
Suragaṇaçreshṭha = Vishṇu: V, 413.
Suragaṇeçvara = Indra, q.v.
Suraghātin ("slayer of the gods") = Vṛtra: VII, 3472 (only B.).
Suraguru[1] = Brahmán: I, 32 (?), 2504.
Suraguru[2] = Bṛhaspati: VII, 5648 (only B.); XIII, 5574.
Suraguru[3] = Vishṇu (Kṛshṇa): III, 15808 (V°); VII, 6468 (?).
Surajā, an Apsaras. § 103 (Aṃçāvat.): I, **65,** 2558 (daughter of Prādhā).
Sūrakṛt (B., Su°), son of Viçvāmitra. § 721*b* (Viçvāmitrop.): XIII, **4**β, 256.
Suraloka ("the gods' world"): [I, †3577 (*surasiddhaishi-lokāt*); VI, 3013 (*suramartyalokam*)]; XII, 3615 (°*otham*); XIII, 3336 (°*sthaḥ*), †4556, 4910, 6252.
Suramat, name of a fire. § 493 (Āṅgirasa): III, **221,** 14204 (only C., B. has *Surabhimat*).
Surāmukha, a serpent. § 47 (Sarpanāmak.): I, **35,** 1553.
Suranadī ("river of the gods") = Gaṅgā: VI, 3643 (*G°*).
Surāṇāṃ hantṛ, a god. § 492 (Āṅgirasa): III, **220,** 14168 (among the 15 yajñamushaḥ).
[**Surāṇāṁ pati(ḥ)**] = Indra: VIII, 1485 (*Surāmbupreta-vittānāṃ patīn*).
Surānanda = Vishṇu (1000 names).
Suranātha = Vishṇu (Nārāyaṇa): I, 2507.
Surapati[1] = Indra, q.v. — Do.[2] = Nahusha, q.v. — Do.[3] = Vishṇu: XII, 12848.
Surapravīra, a god. § 492 (Āṅgirasa): III, **220,** 14168 (among the 15 yajnamushaḥ).
Surapuṅgava = Indra, q.v.
Surapura ("city of the gods"). § 639 (Rājadh.): XII, **52,** †1895 (*puraṃ S°sammitadyutim*).
Surarāj = Indra, q.v. (add VII, †88 (*iva*)).
Surarāja[1] = Indra, q.v.—Do.[2] = Kṛshṇa: XII, 1509.
Surarājaputra = Arjuna: VIII, †3514.
Surāri, a king. § 554 (Sainyodyogap.): V, **4**γ, 78.
Surāri, pl. (°*ayaḥ*) ("enemies of the gods") = Asura, pl. III, 14319; IX, 2364 (°-*nibarhaṇa*, said of Skanda), 2528 (do., said of Kāma); XII, 4198 (°*nilayaḥ*, i.e. the ocean), 13674; XIII, 905 (°-*mālāya*, i.e. Çiva).—Do., sg.: III, †8712 (i.e. Vṛtra), 15834 (i.e. Hiraṇyakaçipu).
Surārighna = Vishṇu (Nārāyaṇa): I, 2506; III, 10139 (*Devadevaṃ . . . Vishṇum*).
Surārihan[1] = Indra, q.v.—Do.[2] = Çiva (1000 names[2]).— Do.[3] = Vishṇu (1000 names).
Surarsharbha[1] = Indra: XII, 4572, 8421.—Do.[2] = Çiva: XII, 10137.—Do.[3] = Skanda: III, 14470.
Surarshi, pl. (°*ayaḥ*) = Devarshi, pl.: I, †3567 (°-*Gandharva-narāvamānāt*, sc. Yayāti's); III, 10534, 12034, †13299; V, 2231 (°*gaṇasevitaḥ*, sc. Rāma Dāçarathi), †7292 (*devarshi-Gandharva-surarshisaṅghāḥ*); VIII, †4924 (°*saṅghāḥ*); XII, 6148 (*spardhamānāḥ s°bhiḥ*), 10225, 11126, 13044; XIII, 1054 (*Purāṇajñaiḥ*), 1109, 1572 (*vihitaṃ yat s°bhiḥ*), 1972, 4017 (°*gaṇabādhitā*, sc. Tāraka), 5530 (°*īnāṃ çrutam*); XIV, 2774 (°*devagandharvāḥ*). — Do.[2] sg. = Nārada: I, 223 bis (*N°*), 462 (do.); III, ††13303 (do.); XII, 1592 (do.), 3025 (do.), 13313 (do.).
Surasa, a serpent. § 564 (Mātalīyop.): V, **103**γ, 3632.
Surasā[1], the mother of the serpents. § 127 (Aṃçāvat.): I, **66,** 2625 (daughter of Krodhavaçā).—§ 129 (do.): I, **66,** 2634 (mother of the nāgas).—§ 270 (Brahmasabhāv.): II, **11,** 456 (in the palace of Brahmán).—§ 564 (Mātalīyop.): V, **103,** 3620 (°*āyāḥ sutā nāgāḥ*).
Surasā[2], an Apsaras. § 191 (Arjuna): I, **123,** 4819 (danced at the birth of Arjuna).
Surasattama[1] = Brahmán: XIV, 1361.
Surasattama[2] = Çiva: XII, 10668; XIII, 946, 1338, 4001.
Surasattama[3] = Garuḍa: I, 1251 (°*a*, C., but read with B. °*aḥ* = Vishṇu).
Surasattama[4] = Indra: V, 432; XII, 957 (*Pākaçāsanaḥ*), 3845; XIII, 799 (Çiva in the shape of I.), 3902.
Surasattama[5] = Vishṇu: I, 1251 (°*aḥ*, only B., C. has °*a* = Garuḍa), III, 13577.
Sūrasena, pl., v. Çūrasena.
Surāshṭra, pl. (°*āḥ*), a people. § 284 (Sahadeva): II, **31,** 1166 (°*vishayasthaḥ*, sc. Sahadeva, the king of the *S.* had been vanquished by Sahadeva).—§ 377 (Dhaumyatīrthak.): III, **88,** 8344 (Dhaumya describes the tīrthas in the country of the *S.*). — § 549 (Pāṇḍavapraveçap.): IV, **1***a*, 12 (°*āvantayaḥ*). — § 562 (Bhagavadyānap.): V, **74**γ, 2730 (°*aṇaṃ Rushardhikaḥ*). — § 607 (Karṇap.): VIII, **45**ν, †2098 (*saṅkarāḥ*).—§ 785 (Anugītāp.): XIV, **85,** 2477.
Surāshṭrādhipati ("the Surashṭra king") = Ākṛti: II, 1165.
Surāshṭraka, pl. = Surāshṭra, pl.: VI, **20,** 753–54 (only B.).
Surasūnu = Arjuna: III, 8282.
Surāsura, adj. ("belonging to gods and Asuras"): III, 6097 (*jagataḥ*); IX, 2236 (do.); XVIII, 218 (*jagat*). Cf. Devāsura.
Surāsuraguru[1] = Çiva: XIII, 589 (*Çaṅkare*), 773, 807, 936.—Do.[2] = Kṛshṇa (Vishṇu): XII, 12839 (i.e. Nārāyaṇa); XIII, 606.

Surāsurapati = Brahmán (?): V, 2984 (°*eḥ sakhā*, i.e. Rāma Jāmadagnya).

Surāsureça = Çiva: XIII, 903 (only B., C. *sarvasureçāya*).

Suratā, an Apsaras. § 103 (Aṃçāvat.): I, **65**, 2558 (daughter of Prādhā).

Suratha[1], a prince. § 130 (Aṃçāvat.): I, **67**, 2697 (among the incarnations from the Krodhavaça gaṇa).

Suratha[2], an ancient king. § 267 (Yamasabhāv.): II, **8**, 322 (in the palace of Yama).

Suratha[3], the father of Koṭikāsya. § 522 (Draupadīharaṇap.): III, **265**, †15593 (°*sya putraḥ*, i.e. Koṭikāsya), †15605 (°*sya putram*).

Suratha[4], a Trigarta king, follower of Jayadratha. § 522 (Draupadīharaṇap.): III, **271**, 15733 (*Trigartarājaḥ*), 15735 (fought with Nakula and was slain).

Suratha[5], a Kuru warrior. § 592 (Saṃçaptakavadhap.): VII, **18***a*, 741 (among the Saṃçaptakas, fought with Arjuna).

Suratha[6], a son of Drupada. § 600 (Ghaṭotkacavadhap.): VII, **156**, 6910 (*Drupadasya sutaṃ . . . Çatruñjayaṃ S°syā-nujaṃ*, slain by Açvatthāman).

Suratha[7], a Pañcāla prince. § 611 (Çalyap.): IX, **14**, 740, 741 (*Pañcālānāṃ mahārathaḥ*), 743, 745 (slain by Açvatthāman).

Suratha[8], son of Jayadratha. § 785 (Anugītāp.): XIV, **78**, 2276 (°*sya sutaṃ*, i.e. the grandson of Jayadratha and Duḥçalā), 2288 (had died when he heard of the arrival of Arjuna).

Surathākāra, a varsha in Kuçadvīpa. § 575 (Bhūmip.): VI, **12**ζ, 454.

Surāva, name of a horse. § 382 (Agastyop.): III, **99**, 8631 (given to Agastya by Ilvala).

Suravara = Çiva: VII, 9537.

Suravarcas, a god. § 492 (Āṅgirasa): III, **220**, 14168 (among the 15 yajñamushaḥ).

Suravarottama = Vishṇu: III, 13576.

Suravidvish, pl. (°*aḥ*) ("enemies of the gods") = Asura, pl.: III, †8798 (*Kāleyasañjñān*).

Suravīthī ("way of the gods"). § 336 (Indralokābhig.): III, **43**, 1767 (*nakshatramārgaṃ vipulaṃ S°īti viçrutaṃ*).

Sureça[1] = Agni: II, 1147.

Sureça[2] = Brahmán: XIII, †4941.

Sureça[3] = Çiva: VII, 9535; XII, 10245.

Sureça[4] = Indra: III, 1848; VII, 2233 (?), †4665 (°*ātma-samudbhavena*, i.e. Arjuna), 6464 (°*tvaṃ gataḥ Çakraḥ*); VIII, †4528 (°-*Vairocanayor yathā*, sc. *sannipātaḥ*), †4594 (*yathā S° Ditijaiḥ kshatāṅgaḥ*), †4963 (*Baliṃ* (*Balaṃ*, B.) *niyamyeva S°-Keçavau*); XIII, 591, 819 (Çiva in the shape of *I.*).

Sureça[5] = Vishṇu: III, 10928; XIII, 6959 (1000 names).

Sureça[6] = Yama: III, 16776.

Sureça[7], a Viçvadeva. § 749 (Ānuçāsanik.): XIII, **91**γ, 4360 (enumeration).

Sureça[8], v. Suveça.

Sureçvara[1] = Agni: II, 1150.

Sureçvara[2] = Çiva: I, 8123; XIII, 790 (?), 945, 6339 (*Vṛshabhāṅkaḥ*).

Sureçvara[3] = Indra: I, 2927, 5076, 8228 (*pravavarsha*); III, 1526 (*Çakraṃ*), 8411, 12257, 13597 (*vavarsha*), 14370, 14409, 14410, 14971, 15014, 16971; V, 4058, 4982 (*na va-varsha*); VI, 213 (*Çakraḥ*); VII, 3472, 8433; VIII, †4660; XII, 2432, 6440, 8192, 8257, 10133, 10135; XIII, 532 (*I°*), 2269, 3569, 7309; XVII, 75.

Sureçvara[4] = Nahusha: V, 370, 376, 404; XIII, 4751.

Sureçvara[5] = Nara: III, 15805 (*N°*).

Sureçvara[6] = Vishṇu: V, 420 (?); XIII, 6980 (1000 names).

Sureçvara[7], a Rudra. § 665 (Mokshadh.): XII, **208***δ*, 7585.

Sureçvarī = Durga (Umā): IV, 202.

Surendra[1] = Indra, q.v.—Do.[2] = Nahusha, q.v.—Do.[3] = Çiva: XIII, 887.

Surendraloka = Indraloka: VI, †1190.

Sureṇu, a river, one of the seven Sarasvatīs. § 615*i* (Saptasārasvata): IX, **38***a*, 2189, 2211, 2214 (arose at the sacrifice of Daksha at Gaṅgādvāra).

Suretara, pl. (°*āḥ*) ("others than Suras") = Asura, pl.: VIII, 1429, 1435 (C. by error '*s*°).

Surocanā, a mātṛ. § 615*u* (Skanda): IX, **46***θ*, 2647.

Suroman, a serpent. § 64 (Sarpasattra): I, **57**, 2151 (of Takshakā's race).

Surottama[1] = Brahmán: VII, 2077; VIII, 1334.

Surottama[2] = Indra: I, 1290; XII, 3575, 3817, 3825; XIII, 283 (B. *Surādhipa*).

Surottama[3] = Kṛshṇa (Vishṇu): III, 13570; XII, 1686, 1852; XIII, 723.

Surottama[4] = Skanda: III, 14408, 14447.

Surottama[5] = Vāyu: I, 4771.

Surottama, dual (°*au*) = the Açvins: III, 10348.

Suruc, a Suparṇa, son of Garuḍa. § 564 (Mātalīyop.): V, **101***a*, 3588.

Suruci = Vishṇu (1000 names).

Surūpa = Çiva: XIII, 1157 (1000 names[2]); XIV, 192 (B. *Purushāya*).

Surūpā, name of a cow. § 564 (Mātalīyop.): V, **102**, 3609 (*Saurabhī*, supporting the eastern quarter).

Sūrya**[1] (the sun), identified with Savitṛ and Vivasvat, and = Āditya. [§ 3 (Anukram.): I, **1**, 42 (the twelve forms (sons) of Vivasvat (cf. Āçāvaha) seem to be forms of the sun)].—§ 4 (do.): I, **1**, †185 (*yadā Vāyuḥ Çakra-Sūryau ca yuktau Kaunteyānām anulomā jayāya*).—[§ 11 (Parvasaṅgr.): I, **2**, 419 (*Raveḥ*), 420 (*Tigmāṃçuṃ*), (all. to § 310)].—§ 28 (Amṛtamanthana): I, **19**, 1162 (*Candra-S°ābhyāṃ*), 1166 (do., Rāhu swallows up the sun and the moon [at the eclipses] because they discovered him drinking amṛta).—§ 33 (Garuḍa): I, **23**, 1249 (*Tapanaḥ*, Garuḍa is identified with *S.*).—§ 34 (do.): I, **24**, 1264 (*S.* would burn the world).—§ 35 (Aruṇa): I, **24**, 1270 (Aruṇa was placed before *S.* as his charioteer and took away his energy (*tejaḥ*)).—§ 81 (Karṇa): I, **63**, 2427 (father of Karṇa, cf. § 131, etc.).—§ 92 (Aṃçāvat.): I, **65**, 2535 (*devānāṃ Sūryā-Candra-masau*, different from the Dānavas of the same names).—[§ 131 (Kuntī): I, **67**, 2771 (*Arkaṃ*, begat Karṇa on Kuntī, cf. § 175 and § 547)]. —[§ 131*b* (Karṇa): I, **67**, 2784 (*Divākarasya . . . aṃçaṃ*, sc. Karṇa)].—§ 175 (Karṇa-sambhava): I, **111**, (4393) (begat Karṇa on Kuntī, cf. § 131 and § 547).—[§ 208 (Astradarçana): I, **136**, 5381 (*Bhāska-rasya . . . aṃçaḥ Karṇaḥ*), 5383 (*Bhāskarasyātmasambhavaḥ* = do.), 5402 (*Bhāskaraḥ*, assisted Karṇa by dispersing the clouds)].—§ 222 (Tapatyup.): I, **171**, 6527, 6530; **173**, 6595 (bestowed his daughter Tapatī on Saṃvaraṇa).—[§ 246 (Sundopasundop.): I, **211**, 7682 (*Candrādityau*)].—§ 270 (Brahmasabhāv.): II, **11**, 429 (took Nārada with him to the palace of Brahmán). — § 310 (Āraṇyakap.): III, **3**, 146 (having described the activity of the sun (*b*: from compassion with the hungry creatures the sun during his northern course draws up water, and during his southern course he enters the earth with his heat. The moon, the lord of the plants (*Oshadhīpatiḥ*) converts that water into clouds of rain, which he pours down; thus [from the combination of water and heat] the plants are produced. Thus, the vegetables of the six tastes (*shaḍrasāḥ*) which constitute the food of all creatures, have their origin from the sun) *Dhaumya* then enumerated the 108 names of *Sūrya* (**a**), 158.—§ 310*b* (do.): Yudhishṭhira praised *S.* saying: "Thou art the eye of the universe, and the soul of all corporeal existences. Thou art the origin of all creatures, and the embodiment of acts of religious men. Thou art the goal of all the *Sāṅkhyas* and the final end of the *Yogins*. Thou art a door not fastened through bolts and the goal of those who desire emancipation. Thou sustainest, discoverest, sanctifiest, and supportest the world. *Brahmans* versed in the *Vedas* adore thee with different hymns. Thou art adored by the *ṛshis*. *Siddhas, Cāraṇas, Gandharvas, Yakshas, Guhyakas*, and *Pannagas* follow thy chariot through the sky, the thirty-three gods, the hosts of *Vaimānikas*, with *Upendra* (i.e. Vishṇu) and *Mahendra*, the principal *Vidyādharas*, the *Guhyas*, the seven divine and human *Pitṛgaṇas*, the *Vasus*, the *Maruts*, the *Rudras*, the *Sādhyas*, the *Marīcipas*, the *Vālakhilyas*, and other *Siddhas*, have obtained success by adoring thee. *Çārṅgadhanvan's* discus by which he humbles the *Asuras*, has been forged by *Viçvakarman* through thy energy. Thou illuminest the whole earth with her 13 dvipas; thou art the beginning and the end of the day of *Brahmán*, which consists of 1000 yugas; thou art the lord of the *Manus* and of their sons, of the manvantaras and of their lords; at the time of universal destruction the *Saṃvartaka* fire is born from thy wrath; then clouds, begotten of thy rays, bring about the appointed deluge; dividing thyself into twelve suns thou then drinkest up the ocean with thy rays. Thou art *Indra, Vishṇu, Brahmán, Prajāpati, Agni*, the subtle mind, etc.; he who adores thee on the sixth and seventh lunar day with humility and tranquillity of mind obtains the grace of *Lakshmī*; I bow also to thy followers: *Māṭhara, Aruṇa, Daṇḍa*, etc., who whirl thunderbolts (so Nīl.), and to the celestial mātṛs: *Kshubhā, Maitrī*, etc. (enumerated by Nīl.). (He who recites this hymn, concentrating his mind, obtains from the sun what he asks for, etc.; *Brahmán* had communicated it to *Çakra*, and *Çakra* to *Nārada*, and *Nārada* to *Dhaumya*, and *Dhaumya* to *Yudhishṭhira*; it leads the reciter to the *Sūryaloka* (v. 200–10)): III, **3**, 192.—[§ 310 (do.): III, **3**, 200 (*Bhāskaraḥ*), (201) (*Vivasvān*), 216 (*Divākarāt*), (gave to Yudhishṭhira a copper vessel, the food cooked in which became inexhaustible)].—§ 317*b* (Kṛshṇa Vāsudeva): III, **12**, 480 (Kṛshṇa becomes *S.*, etc.).—§ 332 (Mahādevastava): III, **39**, 1628 (among the names of Çiva).—[§ 373 (Prayāga): III, **85**, 8217 (*Tapanasya sutā . . . Yamunā*)].—[§ 384 (Agastyop.): III, **103**, 8778 (*Bhāskarasya nagottamaḥ*, i.e. Vindhya)].—§ 385 (Vindhya): III, **104**, 8783, 8784 (*Bhāskara*), 8786 (°*ā-Candramasor mārgam*), 8789 (do.), (Vindhya's asking *S.* to circumambulate it).—[§ 400 (Tīrthayātrāp.): III, **118**, †10225 (*Divākarasya*, sc. *āyatanam*)].—§ 417 (Yavakrītop.): III, **138**, 10808 (*rahasyavedam . . . S°sya*, applied by Arvāvasu).—§ 421 (Gandhamādanapr.): III, **142**, 10906.—§ 439 (Yakshayuddhap.): III, **163**, 11867 (°*ā-Candramasau*, go round Meru).—§ 473 (Mārkaṇḍeyas.): III, **200**, †13479 (°*sutāç ca gāvaḥ*).—[§ 493 (Āṅgirasa): III, **221**, 14182 (*Gavāṃ patiḥ*)].—§ 521 (Draupadīharaṇap.): III, **262**, 15493 (°*dattākshayānnena*, cf. § 310); [**263**, 15541 (*sthālyāṃ Bhāskaradattāyāṃ*, do.)].—§ 546 (Kuṇḍalāharaṇap.): III, **300**, 16924, 16927 (*yogarddhirūpavān*); **301**, (16958); **302**, (16987), 16994, 16996 (*S.* appeared to Karṇa in a dream and warned him against Indra, and advised him at any rate to ask for the *çakti* of Indra).—§ 547 (Karṇa): III, **303**, 17013; **306**, (17082), 17083, †17091, (†17094); **307**, (17109), (17115), (17118), 17121, (17122), 17123; **309**, 17173; [**310**, 17195 (*Raveḥ*)] (the story of Karṇa's birth, etc., cf. § 131 and § 175).—§ 551 (Kīcakavadhap.): IV, **15**, 449 (appointed a Rākshasa to protect Draupadī); [**16**, 462 (*Arkena*, do.)].—§ 565 (Gālavacarita): V, **108**, 3771 (*atra*—i.e. in the east—*dattāni S°ena yajūṃshi*, *S.* gave the Yajurveda [to Yajñavālkya]); **109**, 3789 (Sāvarṇi and the son of Yavakrīta set in the south a limit which *S.* cannot overstep), 3795 (the ṛshi Cakradhanus was born from *S.*); **110**, 3813 (ordered Dhvajavatī to stop in the sky); [**117**, 3967 (*reme . . . Prabhāvatyāṃ yathā Raviḥ*)]. — § 569 (Bhagavadyānap.): V, [**141**, 4757 (*Bhāskarāt*, father of Karṇa); **145**, 4920 (*Tapanaḥ*, do.)]; **146**, 4929 (*S.* declared that he was the father of Karṇa).—[§ 575 (Bhūmip.): VI, **11**, 403 (*Somārkayoḥ*)].—§ 575*f* (do.): The diameter of Sūrya (the Sun) is 10,000 yojanas, his circumference 35,800 yojanas; VI, **12**, 485.—§ 603*c* (Çiva): VII, **201**, †9457 (°*-Candrau*, identified with Çiva). — § 603 (Nārāyaṇāstramokshap.): VII, **202u*, 9595 (identified with Çiva).—§ 605 (Karṇap.): VIII, **32**, 1347 (*Aruṇena yathā sārdhaṃ tamaḥ S°o vyapohati*), 1348 (dual, *yathā*), 1349 (°*āruṇau yathā*).—§ 608 (do.): VIII, **68**, †3392 (°*sya bhāsā*); **87**, 4430, 4431 (wished that Karṇa might vanquish Arjuna).—§ 615*u* (Skanda): IX, **45**γ, 2506 (came to the investiture of Skanda), 2533 (gave two companions to Skanda).—[§ 620 (Çrāddhap.): XI, **27**γ, 811 (*Bhāskarāt*, father of Karṇa)]. — [§ 621 (Rājadh.): XII, **6**, 148 (*Bhāskarena*, all. to § 569), 149 (*Divākarena*, do.), 150 (*Bhānuḥ*)].—§ 641 (do.): XII, **78**, 2922 (identified with the horse); [**122**, 4499 (*Bhāskaram*, was made lord of all luminous bodies (*tejasāṃ*))].—§ 680*b* (Tulādhāra-Jājalisaṃv.): XII, **265**, 9449 (*Çraddhā Vaivasvatī . . . S°sya duhitā*).—[§ 702 (Mokshadh.): XII, **293**, 10754 (*sa-Māṭharaṃ*, gratified by Çaibya)].—§ 707 (do.): XII, **314**, 11612 (the adhidaivata of the eye); **319**, 11726, 11745 (Yajñavālkya obtained the Yajurveda, the Çatapatha Brāhmaṇa, etc. from *S.*) (**a**), 11752.—[§ 712 (Çukotpatti): XII, **324**, 12175 (*Divākara-Niçākarau*)].—§ 717*c* (Uparicara): XII, **336**, 12714 (*Satvataṃ vidhiṃ . . . prāk Sūryamukhaniḥsṛtam*).—§ 717*b* (Nārāyaṇīya): XII, **340**, 12983, 12985, 12986 (°*anugāmibhiḥ*, *S.* repeated the description of the glory of Nārāyaṇa to the ṛshis who followed him); **341**λ, 13017.—§ 718*b* (Uñchavṛttyup.): XII, **363**, 13916, 13917 (°*a ivāparaḥ*); **364**, (13918), 13924. — [§ 731*b* (Ashṭāvakra-Diksaṃv.): XIII, **20**, 1492 (*Sahasrāṃçuṃ*, worshipped by Ashṭāvakra)].—§ 747 (Ānuçāsanik.): XIII, **84**γ, 3978 (identified with the horse).—§ 752*b* (Chattropanahotpatti): XIII, **95**, 4600 (*Jamadagneç ca saṃvādaṃ S°sya ca*), 4618–21, 4628; **96**, 4631, 4632, 4634 (4635), 4636, 4641, (4642) (when Renukā was afflicted by the rays of the sun, Jamadagni would pierce *S.*, who then, disguised as a brahman, gave him an umbrella and a pair of sandals).—§ 768*b* (Umā-Maheçvarasaṃv.): XIII, **146**γ, 6751 (°*sya ca Suvarcalā*, sc. *sādhvī*).—[§ 768*b* (Kṛshṇa Vāsudeva): XIII, **147**, 6831 (*Dakshāyaṇyaḥ . . . Ādityaḥ*, father of Manu)].—§ 772*m* (Atri): XIII, **157**, 7299 (Svarbhānu pierced the Sun and Moon, then Atri assumed their forms).—§ 773*d* (Çiva): XIII, **161**δ, 7497 (identified with Çiva). — [§ 789 (Putradarçanap.): XV, **30**, 826 (*Divākaram*), 827 (*Sahasrāṃçuḥ*), 830 (*Tigmāṃçuḥ*) (*S.* begot Karṇa)].

Cf. Savitṛ, Vivasvat, and the following synonyms:—

Āditya, q.v.

***Aṃçumat** ("radiant"): I, 6529; III, 2234 (? *iva*); VII, †8131 (? *Rāhv-A°toḥ*).

***Arka**, q.v. (add. I, 3572, 4396; II, 80 (°*sya*, sc. *sabhā*); III, 175; IV, 462; V, 4909).

***Bhānu**, q.v. (add. III, 166, 1664, 8782, 16996, 17074, 17141; V, 4931; VIII, †5042).

***Bhānumat**, q.v. (add. I, 6604; III, 17175).

***Bhāskara**, q.v. (add. I, 1469 (*Aruṇaḥ* . . . *Bh°sya purahsaraḥ*), 4389, 5402, 6600; III, 159, 437 (*paryadhāvata* . . . *Svarbhānur iva Bh°m*), 486, 8778, 8784, 10641, 15541, 16979, 16984; V, 4757, 4929; VII, 1502, 9600 (identified with Çiva).

Çukra, q.v.

Dākshāyaṇya, ***Dīptāṃçu**, q.v.

***Divākara** ("day-maker"): I, †1254, 2784 (°*sya* . . . *aṃçam*, sc. Karṇa), 6607; II, 427; III, 163, 193, 200, 216, 7062 (*Rāhugraste*), 10225, 10808, 13945, 17077, 17175; IX, 1173 (°*patham*); X, 24; XII, 149, 12175; XV, 826.

Gavāṃ patiḥ ("lord of rays"): III, 192, 14182.

Gopati, Lokeçvara, Marīçin, Pataṅga, q.v.

Prakāçakarman ("light-maker"): V, 4920 (*Tapanaḥ*).

Prakāçakartṛ (do.): I, 2772, 4398.

***Raçmivat** ("radiant"): III, 16926.

***Ravi**: I, 42, 419, 1274, 1246; III, 192, 205, 2132, 8437, 17195; V, 3967 (*reme* . . . *Prabhāvatyāṃ yathā R°iḥ*); XVIII, 167.

***Sahasrakiraṇa** ("thousand-rayed"): XIII, 428.

***Sahasrāṃçu** (do.): I, 6601; II, 427; III, 16940, 16994, 17098; XIII, 1492; XV, 827.

Suraçreshṭha, Svarbhānuçatru, Svarbhānusūdana, Tamoghna, q.v.

***Tapana** ("warming"): I, 1249, 4398, 6535, 6609; III, 192, 8217 (°*sya sutā* . . . *Yamunā*), 17138; V, 4920.

Tapishṇu, Tigmāṃçu, Ushṇaraçmi, Vibhāvasu, Vibudhaçreshṭha, Vihaṅgama, Virocana, q.v.

[*Remark.*—Besides the above synonyms, other epithets of the Sun are found in hymns, esp. III, 166–199.]

Sūrya's 108 names (III, 146–157). The names are the following (according to Nīl.): *Açvattha* (v. Saṃvatsarakaro 'çvatthaḥ), *Ādidevo 'diteḥ sutaḥ*, 155; *Aindhana*, 149; *Aja*, 146; *Alolupa*, 156; *Aṃça*, 152; *Ananta*, 154; *Aṅgāraka*, 147; *Āpaḥ*, 147; *Aravindāksha*, 156; *Arihan*, 152; *Arka*, 146; *Aryaman*, 146; *Bhaga*, 146; *Bhānu*, 154; *Bhūtādi*, 155; *Bhūtapati*, 153; *Bhūtāçraya*, 153; *Brahmán*, 148; *Bṛhaspati*, 147; *Budha*, 147; *Carācarātman*, 157; *Çāçvata*, 151; *Çanaiçcara*, 148; *Çauri*, 148; *Çaya* (B., *Jaya*, C.), 154; *Çīghraga*, 155; *Çuci*, 148; *Çukra*, 147; *Dehakartṛ*, 159; *Dhanvantari*, 155; *Dharmadhvaja*, 149; *Dhātṛ*, 146; *Dhūmaketu*, 155; *Dīptāṃçu*, 148; *Dvādaçātman*, 156; *Dvāpara*, 150; *Gabhastimat*, 146; *Indra*, 148; *Jāṭharo 'gniḥ*, 149; *Jaya* (C., *Çaya*, B.), 154; *Jīmūta*, 152; *Jīvana*, 152; *Kalā*, 150; *Kāla*, 146; *Kālacakro vibhāvasuḥ*, 151; *Kālādhyaksha*, 152; *Kaliḥ sarvamalāçrayaḥ*, 150; *Kāmada*, 154; *Kapila*, 154; *Karuṇānvita*, 157; *Kāshṭhā*, 150; *Kha(ṃ)*, 147; *Kṛta(ṃ)*, 150; *Kshapā*, 150; *Kshaṇa*, 150; *Maitreya*, 157; *Manaḥ suparṇaḥ*, 155; *Mokshadvāraṃ Trivishṭapa(ṃ)*, 156; *Mṛtyu*, 146; *Muhūrtāḥ*, 150; *Parāyaṇa(ṃ)*, 147; *Pitā, matā, pitāmahaḥ*, 156; *Prabhākara*, 146; *Praçāntātman*, 157; *Prajādhyaksha*, 152; *Prāṇadhāraṇa*, 155; *Pṛthivī*, 147; *Purusha*, 151; *Pūshan*, 146; *Ravi*, 146; *Rudra*, 148; *Sāgara*, 152; *Sanātana*, 151; *Saṃvartako vahniḥ*, 153; *Saṃvatsarakaro 'çvatthaḥ*, 151; *Sarvadhātunishecitṛ*, 154; *Sarvalokanamaskṛta*, 153; *Sarvasyādi(ḥ)*, 153; *Sarvatomukha* (°*su*° C.), 154; *Savitṛ*, 146; *Skanda*, 148; *Soma*, 147; *Srashṭṛ*, 153; *Sūkshmātman*, 157; *Sūrya*, 146; *Svargadvāraṃ prajādvāraṃ*, 156; *Tamonuda*, 152; *Tejas*, 147; *Tejasāṃ patiḥ*, 149; *Tretā*, 150; *Tvashṭṛ*, 146; *Vaidyuto 'gniḥ*, 149; *Varada*, 154; *Varuṇa*, 148, 152; *Vāyu*, 147; *Vedakartṛ*, 149; *Vedāṅga*, 149; *Vedavāhana*, 149; *Viçāla*, 154; *Viçvakarman*, 152; *Viçvātman*, 157; *Viçvatomukha*, 157; *Vishṇu*, 148; *Vivasvat*, 148; *Vyaktāvyakta(ḥ)*, 151; *Yama*, 148; *Yāma*, 150; *Yogin*, 151.

Sūrya[2], an Asura. § 92 (Aṃçāvat.): I, **65**, 2534 (°*ā-Candramasau*, sons of Danu), 2535 (do., not to be confounded with the gods of the same name).—§ 130 (do.): I, **67**, 2694 (*mahāsuraḥ*, incarnate as king Darada). Cf. Asura.

Sūrya[3] = Mahāpurusha (Mahāpurushastava).—Do.[4] = Çiva (1000 names[1–2]).—Do.[5] = Vishṇu (1000 names).

Sūryabhāsa, a Kuru warrior. § 593 (Abhimanyuvadhap.): VII, **48**χ, 1900 (slain by Abhimanyu).

Sūryaçrī, a Viçvadeva. § 749 (Ānuçāsanik.): XIII, **91**γ, 4358.

Sūryāda ("devourer of the sun") = Rāhu (?): XII, 11752.

Sūryadatta, a follower of Virāṭa. § 552 (Goharaṇap.): IV, **31**, 1014 (description of his coat of mail); **32**, 1057.—§ 561 (Yānasandhip.): V, **57**ξ, 2237 (°*ādibhir vīraiḥ*, follow Virāṭa).—§ 572 (Rathātirathasaṅkhyānap.): V, **171**, 5907 (a ratha in the army of Yudhishṭhira).—§ 600 (Ghaṭotkacavadhap.): VII, **158**χ, 7011 (only B.).—§ 604 (Karṇap.): VIII, **6**, 184 (had been slain by Droṇa).

Sūryadhvaja, a prince. § 232 (Svayaṃvarap.): I, **186**, 6990 (present at the svayaṃvara of Draupadī).

Sūryadhvajapatākin = Çiva (1000 names[1]).

Sūryaja ("the son of Sūrya (the Sun)") = Karṇa: VI, 5826 (only B.); XII, 22, 64, 82; XV, 452, 453, 454; XVIII, 35.

Sūryajā ("the daughter of Sūrya (the Sun)") = Bṛhadbhāsā: III, 14184 (*B°*).

Sūryāksha, a king. § 130 (Aṃçāvat.): I, **67**, 2693 (incarnation of the Asura Krathana).

Sūryaloka ("the world of Sūrya"). § 310*b* (Sūrya): III, **3**, 210 (°*ṃ sa gacchati*, sc. by reciting the hymn to the Sun). —§ 364 (Tīrthayātrāp.): III, **83**, 6019 (°*ñ ca gacchati*), 6070 (°*m avāpnuyāt*).—§ 370 (do.): III, **84**, 8091 (°*ñ ca gacchati*). — § 456 (Sarasvatī-Tārkshyasaṃv.): III, **186**, †12722. — § 746 (Ānuçāsanik.): XIII, **79**κ, 3766 (°*e mahīyate*).—[§ 757*i* (Hastikūṭa): *Gautama* said: Next (read *tato* with B.) [to Somaloka] other eternal regions (*lokāḥ*) blaze free from passion and darkness and sorrow, the place of the sungod (*Ādityadevasya*). *Dhṛtarāshṭra* said: This region is for those who are attentive to the study of the *Vedas*, devoted to the service of their preceptors, observant of penances and excellent vows, firm in truth, never gainsaying their preceptors, always alert, ever ready in the service of their *gurus*, pure, of restrained speech, well versed in the *Vedas*: XIII, **102**, 4874 (*lokāḥ* (C. has by error *kolāḥ*) . . . *Ādityadevasya pade* (B., °*aṃ*))].

Sūryamāla = Çiva (1000 names[1]).

Sūryanetra, a Suparṇa, son of Garuḍa. § 564 (Mātalīyop.): V, **101**β, 3598.

Sūryaputra[1] ("the son of Sūrya (the Sun)") = Çanaiçcara (the planet Saturn): VI, 81 (*Bhagaṃ nakshatram ākramya S°eṇa pīḍyate,* omens); XII, 13692 (*Ç°*).

Sūryaputra[2] (do.) = Karṇa: XVIII, 140 (*Kaunteyaḥ . . . Rādheyaḥ,* only C., B. has *Sūtaputrāgrajaḥ*).

Sūryaputra[3] (do.) = Manu Vaivasvata: XII, 4510 (*M°*), 6187 (*M°*).

Sūryaputra[4] (do.) = Sugrīva (the monkey king): III, 11194 (*S°*).

Sūryaputra[5], (do.) = Yama: XII, 7199, 7231.

Sūryaputra, dual (*°au*) = the Açvins: XIII, 7309 (*Açvinau*).

Sūryasambhava ("the son of Sūrya (the Sun)") = Karṇa: III, 17173 (*K°*).

Sūryasāvitra, a Viçvadeva. § 749 (Ānuçāsanik.): XIII, **91**γ, 4359.

Sūryatīrtha, a tīrtha. § 364 (Tīrthayātrāp.): III, **83,** 6018.

Sūryavarcas, a Devagandharva. § 101 (Aṃçāvat.): I, **65,** 2550 (among the Devagandharvas, sons of Muni).—§ 191 (Arjuna): I, **123,** 4811 (present at the birth of Arjuna).

Sūryavarman, a Trigarta king. § 785 (Anugītāp.): XIV, **74,** 2149 (*Trigartarājānaṃ*), 2151 (vanquished by Arjuna).

Susaha = Çiva (1000 names[2]).

Susāman, a brahman. § 286 (Rājasūyikap.): II, **33,** 1238 (*Dhanañjayānām ṛshabhaḥ,* acted as sāmaga at the rājasūya of Yudhishṭhira).

Susaṅkshepa = Çiva (1000 names[2]).

Susaṅkula, a king. § 279 (Arjuna): II, **27,** 1020 (vanquished by Arjuna on his digvijaya).

Susaraṇa, Sushāḍha = Çiva (1000 names[2]).

Susheṇa[1], a serpent. § 67 (Sarpasattra): I, **57,** 2157 (of Dhṛtarāshṭra's race).

Susheṇa[2], a son of Dhṛtarāshṭra. § 130 (Aṃçāvat.): I, **67,** 2732.—§ 182 (Dhṛtarāshṭraputranāmak.): I, **117**a, 4546.—§ 571 (Ulūkadūtāgamanap.): V, **160,** †5531 (the same?, °-*Çitrāyudhanāganakraṃ,* sc. *purushodadhiṃ,* i.e. the army of Duryodhana); **161,** †5574-75 (repetition of v. 5531, omitted in C.).—§ 581 (Bhīshmavadhap.): VI, **64**κ, 2837 (among fourteen sons of Dhṛtarāshṭra who attacked Bhīmasena), 2843 (slain by Bhīmasena). — § 599 (Jayadrathavadhap.): VII, **127**νν, 5178 (attacked Bhīmasena), 5204 (slain by Bhīmasena).—§ 604 (Karṇap.): VIII, **7,** †206 (*tavatmajaḥ,* i.e. Dhṛtarāshṭra's, still alive). Cf. Susheṇa[7].

Susheṇa[3], son of the elder Parikshit. § 154 (Pūruvaṃç.): I, **94,** 3744.

Susheṇa[4], a prince. § 232 (Svayaṃvarap.): I, **186,** 6996 (present at the svayaṃvara of Draupadī).

Susheṇa[5], son of Jamadagni. § 396 (Jamadagni): III, **116,** 10180.

Susheṇa[6], a monkey. § 535 (Setubandhana): III, **283**a, 16270 (the father-in-law of Vālin, came to Rāma with a crore of monkeys).—§ 541 (Indrajidvadha): III, **289**a, 16468.

Susheṇa[7], various Kuru warriors. § 593 (Abhimanyuvadhap.): VII, **37**a, 1610, 1614 (slain by Abhimanyu).—§ 605 (Karṇap.): VIII, **11**υ, 419 (in the makar-avyūha of Karṇa).—§ 610 (Çalyap.): IX, **6**ζ, 294.

Susheṇa[8], son of Karṇa. § 608 (Karṇap.): VIII, **48,** 2251 (*Karṇasya putrau . . . S°ḥ Satyasenaç ca*), 2257, 2264, 2265, 2267, 2269, 2270, 2271, 2272 (fought with Bhīmasena and Nakula); **49,** 2329 (*°ṃ Satyasenañ ca,* pierced by Yudhishṭhira); **66**ι, 3311 (protected Karṇa); **75,** †3812 (*Karṇasya putraṃ*), †3817 (Uttamaujas cut off the head of *S.*).—§ 611 (Çalyap.): IX, **10,** 481 (*Karṇaputrau . . . S°ḥ Satyasenaç ca*), 489, 490, 492, 495, 500, 504, 506 (fought with Nakula who slew him). Cf. Karṇaputra, Karṇātmaja.

Susheṇa[9] = Kṛshṇa: XII, 1511. — Do.[10] = Vishṇu (1000 names).

Susheṇamātṛ ("the mother of Susheṇa[8]"). § 619 (Strīvilāpap.): XI, **21,** †614 (i.e. the wife of Karṇa).

Susnāta = Mahāpurusha (Mahāpurushastava).

Susthala, pl. (*°āḥ*), a people. § 273 (Rājasūyārambhap.): II, **14,** 590 (among the people who fled from fear of Jarāsandha).

Susvapna = Çiva (1000 names[2]).

Susvara, a Suparṇa, son of Garuḍa. § 564 (Mātalīyop.): V, **101**β, 3599.

Sūta[1], the ancestor of the Sūtas. § 641 (Pṛthu Vainya): XII, **59,** 2233 (°-*Māgadhau,* the eulogists of Pṛthu Vainya), 2234 (Pṛthu Vainya gave *S.* Anūpadeça).

Sūta[2], a ṛshi. § 637 (Rājadh.): XII, **47**η, 1599 (among those who surrounded Bhīshma).

Sūta[3], son of Viçvāmitra. § 721*b* (Viçvāmitrop.): XIII, **4**β, 256.

Sūta[4] ("belonging to the Sūta caste or tribe") = Adhiratha: III, 17151 (*°vishayaṃ*), 17153 (*A°*), 17157 (*A°*), 17160, 17167; V, 4762 (*A°*); VI, 5841.

Sūta[5] (do.) = Bandin: III, †10613.

Sūta[6] (do.) = Karṇa: I, †7026, †7027; IV, 1567; VII, 7047 (*°ādhama*), 7049; VIII, 1784, †1968 (?), †1969, 2010, 3170, †3528 (*°mātā*), 3881 (*°ānīkaṃ*), 4760; XII, 100.

Sūta[7] (do.) = Kīcaka: IV, 451, 764, 767, 880, 972.

Sūta[8] (do.) = Lohitāksha: I, 2119 (*L°*), 2173, 2177 (*L°*).

Sūta[9] (do.) = Lomaharshaṇa: I, 1026 (*L°*).

Sūta[10] (do.) = Sañjaya: I, †166, †205, 216, 245 (*Gāvalganiḥ*), 2426 (*jajñe S°o Gavalganāt*); III, 1916, 1945, 1968 (*S°*), 1969, †2012; V, †679, †682, †691, †698, †738, †754, †755, †763, †764, †809, †824, †871, †888, †890, †895, †912, 1792, †1812, †1834, †1915, 1968, 1977, 2094 (only C., but read with B. *samāhūya* instead of *samāḥ Sūta*), 2289, 2346; VI, 385, 2717, 2908, 3641; VII, 311 (*Gāvalganiṃ*), 429, 1053, 1057, 1492, 1833, 3023, 3031, 3046, 4995, 5366, 5459, 5538, 5558, 5667, 6686, 6694, 7090, 7092, 8264; VIII, 84 (*Gāvalganiṃ*), 85, 87, 90 (*S°*), 248, 261, 271, 1170, 1253, 1205, 2441; IX, 15, 21, 25, 50, 84, 98, 110, 1586; XI, 332 (*Gāvalganiḥ*), 779 (*S°*), 782 (*S°*); XII, 1695 (*S°*); XV, 444 (*Gāvalganiḥ*).

Sūta[11] (do.) = Ugraçravas (B. has generally Sauti): I, (93), (866), (892), (910), (939), (975), (1094), (1144), (1235), (1566), 1660 (also B.), (1747), (1787), (1802), (1813), (1856), (2001), 2169 (also B.), (2192); XII, (13003), 13010 (also B.), (13311), (13457).

***Sūta,** mostly pl. (*°āḥ*), name of a caste [or tribe]: I, 2029 (sg. *Paurāṇikaḥ*), 2783 (*°kule,* sc. Karṇa), 6940 (°-*māgadhāḥ*), 7056 (°-*māgadhasaṅghāḥ*), 7777 (*Paurāṇikāḥ*); II, 102, †2200 (sg. = the prātikāmin), 2208 (do., do.), 2210 (do., do.), †2214 (do., do.), †2219 (do., do.), †2220 (do., do.); III, †14750 (*māgadha-s°pūgaiḥ*), 15325, 17173 (*°kule,* sc. Karṇa); IV, 541 (°-*māgadhāḥ*), †2189, 2279, 2365; V, †1314, 3144 (*bandimāgadhasūtaiḥ*), 3333 (°-*māgadhāḥ*), 4768 (a people), 4918 (*°kule,* sc. Karṇa), 7620 (°-*māgadhabandinaḥ*); VI, 4433; VII, 176 (°-*māgadhabandināṃ*), 177 (only C.), 2517 (°-*māgadhabandibhiḥ*), 2739 (do.), 2912, 2938 (only B.),

2996, 3016; VIII, 12 (°-*māgadhabandibhiḥ*), 1372, 1615 (°*kule*, sc. Karṇa), 1616 (°*kulodbhavaḥ*, sc. Karṇa), 4419; XII, 100 (*brahmakshatrāntare jātaṃ s°ṃ*, sc. Karṇa), 1386 (°*air Māgadhaiç ca*), 3202 (sg., *Paurāṇikaṃ*), 10878 (°*māgadhaiḥ*); XIII, 2571 (sg. son of a brāhmaṇī and a kshatriya), 5768; XV, 624.—Do. pl. = Kīcaka, pl.; IV, 800, 812, 815, 817, 827 (°*shaṭçataṃ*), 830, 834, 848.

Sūtaja[1] ("son of the Sūta") = Karṇa: III, 307, 15247, 15248, 15269, 15278, 17202; V, 5838, 5839, 7594; VI, 5840; VII, 5296, 5364, 5468, 5545, 5747, 6364, 6400, 6988, 7003, 7017, 7842, 8084, 8271; VIII, 300 (only B.), 310 (all. to Dyūtap.), 922, 955, 1267, 1669, †1746, 1921, 2303, 2330, 3106, 3187, 3395/96 (only B.), 3546, 3625, 3798, 4167, †4332, †4345, 4358, †4505, †4658, †4697, †4700; XII, 46.

Sūtaja[2] (do.) = Ugraçravas: I, 1436, 2043, 2142, 2205; XII, 13308.

sūtaja (do.), said of various charioteers (sūtāḥ) [of the Sūta caste?]: III, 741 (i.e. Dāruki); VII, 1544 (i.e. Sumitra).—Do., said of the prātikāmin: II, 2204, 2205. Cf. Sūta, pl.

Sūtanandana[1] (do.) = Adhiratha: I, 4403.

Sūtanandana[2] (do.) = Karṇa: I, 7438; III, 14893, 15252, 15257; VI, 5828/29 (only B.); VII, 5477, 5592, 5782, 6984, 7473, 7978, 8354; VIII, 919, 969, 2438, 4038, 5031 (*nihate*).

Sūtanandana[3] (do.) = Sañjaya: III, 1977.

Sūtanandana[4] (do.) = Ugraçravas: I, 2, 270, 286, 1546, 1655, 2199.

Sutañjaya, a Kuru warrior. § 605 (Karṇap.): VIII, **27**λλ, 1078. Cf. Çatruñjaya.

Sutanu, daughter of Āhuka (cf. Harivaṃça v. 2029). § 273 (Rājasūyārambhap.): II, **14**, 597 (*Āhukasutāṃ*, given in marriage to Akrūra).

Sutantu, Sutapas = Vishṇu (1000 names).

Sūtaputra[1] = Bandin: III, †10671.

Sūtaputra[2] = Karṇa: I, †198, 5221 (*Rādheyaḥ*), 5222, 5423, 5424; II, 1712 (*Rādheyaḥ*), †2386; III, †233, 1430, 1648, 8285 (*K*°), †10280, †14761, 14894, 14909, 14911, 15214, 15215, 15273, 15333, 15346, 15350 (*K*°), 15374, 17166 (°*tvaṃ*), †17217, 17244; IV, 1629 (*K*°), †1664, †1678 (*Vaikartanaḥ*), †1694, 2244; V, †31, 217, 222, †755, †850, †1812, 1944, 1953, 1958, 2290, †2425, 2829, 4357, 4727, 4928, 5301, 5502, 5547, 5599, 5663, 5706, 7577; VI, †1272, 1614, 4404, 4406, 4410, 4455 (*Rādheye*); VII, 34 (*Rādheyaṃ*), 48 (do.), †52, 184, 533, 1434, 1439, 3539, 4412 (°*purogamāḥ*), 5298, 5361, 5363, 5365, 5369, 5371, 5378, 5382, 5387, 5392, 5408, 5436, 5451, 5479, 5508, 5510, 5517, 5524, 5525, 5531, 5573, 5580, 5586, 5589, 5600, 5601, 5627, 5633, 5697, 5700, 5702, 5703, 5712, 5713, 5716, 5717, 5737, 5742, 5749, 5753, 5759, 5762, 5780, 5803, 6116, 6118, 6120, 6125, 6395 (*K*°), 6981, 6989, 7042, 7054, 7066, 7069, 7070, 7076, 7085, 7086, 7087, 7097, 7100, 7643, 7654, 7676, 7761, 7784, 7793, 7811, 7812, 7825, 7826, 7839, 7844, 7932, 7934, 7935, 7939, 7946, 7949, 7956, 7957, 7965, 7984, 7985, 7990, †8137, †8158, †8167, 8217, 8249, †8256, 8280, 8332, 8341 (*sānugaḥ*), 8342, 8343, 8348, 8350, 8355, 8363, 8682, 8889, 8902; VIII, 5, 33, 136 (*Rādheyaḥ*), †199 (*vadhaṃ S°sya*), 262 (*hate*), 335, 382, 408, 431, 491, 829 (°*mukhāḥ*), 923, 944, 945, 948, 965, 966, 983, 988, 991, 1264, 1374, 1629, 1697, 1713, 1775, 1781, †1795, †1798, †1799, 1961, 2138, 2288, 2300 (°*mukhāḥ*), 2311, 2315, 2316, 2320, 2404, 2418, 2428, 2430, 2433, 2437, 2443 (*Rādheyam*), 2459, 2610, 2695, 2738, 2746, 2753, 2772, 2779, 2909 (°*mukhāḥ*), 2945, 3007 (*hastikakshāṃ . . . S°sya ketuṃ*), 3030, 3069, 3085, 3158, 3159, 3181, 3185, 3251, 3259, 3270, 3271, 3275, 3330, †3338, †3339, †3340, †3352, †3353, †3356, †3371, †3375, †3376, †3382, †3479, †3491 (*K*°), †3526, †3532, 3559 (°*rathaṃ*), 3593, 3596, †3628, †3629, 3678 (°*mukhān*), 3769, 3770, 3774 (*K*°), 3946, 3967, 3968, 3995, 4004, 4010, 4013, 4014 (°*rathaṃ*), 4092, 4179, †4180, †4182, 4267, 4410, 4473, †4524 (*Vaikartanaḥ*), †4536, †4539, †4552, †4553, 4554, †4565, †4570, †4599, †4602, †4603, †4646, †4649, †4673, †4711, 4773, 4776, †4787, 4813, †4820 (*balaṃ . . . hata-S°ṃ*), 4839 (*hate*), 4841 (do.), 4846 (do.), 4929, 4931, 5001 (*Vaikartanaḥ*), 5002; IX, 6 (°*vadhaṃ*), 111 (*pātitaṃ*), 114 (*K*°), 127 (*nihate*), 131 (*hate*), 134 (do.), 139 (*nihate*), 216, 340, 366 (°*sya nidhane*), 383 (*pātite*), 1001 (*nihate*), 1296 (*pātite*); XI, 807 (*Rādheyaṃ*); XII, 23 (*Rādheyaṃ*), 50 (°*tvam āgataḥ*).

Sūtaputra[3] = Kīcaka: IV, 412, 425, 456, 473, 474, 475, 476, 477, 479, 503, 671, 673, 720 (*K*°), 721, 738, 798.

Sūtaputra[4] = Sañjaya: V, 686, †693, †723, †911, †945, †970, 1803; VI, 306, 421; VII, 306; VIII, 33.

Sūtaputra[5] = Ugraçravas: I, 359 (*Laumaharshaṇinā*), 861, 874.

Sūtaputra[6], said of various charioteers (sūtas) [of the Sūta caste?]: III, 748 (i.e. Dāruki), 750 (do.); III, 2885 (i.e. Vārshṇeya); VII, †77 (i.e. the charioteer of Karṇa).—Do.[7] = the prātikāmin: II, †2221, 2678 (*prātikāminaṃ*).

Sūtaputra, pl. (*āḥ*) = Kīcaka pl.: IV, 796, 803, 804, 806, 808, 829, 839.—Do. = the brothers of Karṇa: VIII, 88.

Sutasoma, son of Bhīmasena (Pāṇḍava) and Draupadī. § 83 (Ādivaṃçāvataraṇa): I, **63**, 2451 (enumeration of the sons of the Pāṇḍavas, C. has by error *Sū*°).—§ 130 (Aṃçāvat.): I, **67**, 2763 (do., C. has by error *Sutā*°).—§ 159 (Pūruvaṃç.): I, **95**, ††3827 (do.).—§ 253 (Haraṇāharaṇap.): I, **221**, 8039 (do.), 8042 (origin of the name).—§ 317 (Arjunābhigamanap.): III, **12**, 533 (enumeration of the sons of Draupadī).—§ 511 (Draupadī-Satyabhāmasaṃv.): III, **235**, 14731.—§ 578 (Bhīshmavadhap.): VI, **45**[16], 1726 (C. has by error *Çruta*°, fights with Vikarṇa), 1727 (do., do.), 1728 (do., do.).—§ 583 (do.): VI, **79**, 3486 (rescued Çrutakarman).—§ 592 (Saṃçaptakavadhap.): VII, **23**o, 977 (born in the city Udayendu, description of his horses), 979 (origin of the name); **25**, 1087, 1088 (fights with Viviṃçati).—§ 600 (Ghaṭotkacavadhap.): VII, **168**, 7556 (C. has *Çruta*°).—§ 605 (Karṇap.): VIII, **25**, 1010, 1011, 1013, 1019, 1022, 1026, 1030, 1032 (fights with Çakuni).—§ 608 (do.): VIII, **55**λλ, 2665, 2667 (fights with Açvatthāman); **82**, †4181, †4188.—§ 611 (Çalyap.): IX, **10**, 503 (*Draupadeyaḥ*), 506.—§ 616 (Sauptikap.): X, **8**, 373, 374 (slain by Açvatthāman). Cf. Draupadeya, sg. and pl.

Sutasomamātṛ ("the mother of Sutasoma") = Draupadī: III, †11913 (C. has by error °*motra* instead of °*mātre*).

Sūtasūnu[1] = Karṇa: VII, 5369; VIII, †3367.—Do.[2] = Sañjaya: V, †687.

Sūtasuta (do.) = Karṇa: VIII, 3765, †4201, †4509, †4542.

Sūtatanaya (do.) = Karṇa: VII, 5359, 5368, 5370.

Sūtātmaja (do.) = Karṇa: VII, 7053, 7059, 8247; VIII, †4560, †4563, †4630, †4825.

Sutejana, a Pāṇḍava warrior. § 600 (Ghaṭotkacavadhap.): VII, **158**χ, 7009.

Sutejas = Sucetas. § 736*b* (Vītahavyop.): XIII, **30**, 2000 (father of Varcas).

Sūti, son of Viçvāmitra. § 721*b* (Viçvāmitrop.): XIII, **4**β, 256 (so C., B. has *Bhūtiḥ*).

Sutīkshṇadaçana = Çiva (1000 names[2]).

Sutīrtha = Çiva: VII, 9523; XIII, 1158 (1000 names[2]); XIV, 195 (so B., C. has *Sa*-°).

Sutīrthaka, a tīrtha. § 364 (Tīrthayātrāp.): III, **83**, 6024, 6026 (on the Ambumatī ?).

Sutuṅga, a mountain. § 596 (Pratijñāp.): VII, **80**, 2851 (only C., B. has *Satuṅgam*).

Suvāc[1], v. Sadaḥsuvāc.

Suvāc[2], a brahman. § 324 (Dvaitavanapr.): III, **26** *a*, 987 (waited upon Yudhishṭhira).

Suvāha, a warrior of Skanda. § 615*u* (Skanda): IX, **45** *η*, 2568.

Suvāhu, v. Subāhu.

Suvaktra[1], a warrior of Skanda. § 615*u* (Skanda): IX, **45** *η*, 2575.

Suvaktra[2] = Çiva: XIII, 1158 (1000 names[2]); XIV, 195.

Suvāmā, a river. § 574 (Jambūkh.): VI, **9** *λ*, 336.

Suvapus = Çiva: XIV, 206.

Suvarcalā, the wife of Sūrya (the Sun). § 768*b* (Umā-Māheçvarasaṃv.): XIII, **146** *γ*, 6751 (*Sūryasya*, sc. *sādhvī*).

Suvarcas[1], son of Dhṛtarāshṭra. § 130 (Āṃçāvat.): I, **67**, 2737 ((*Vātavega-S°au*).—§ 182 (Dhṛtarāshṭraputranāmak.): I, **117**, 4549 (do.).—§ 232 (Svayaṃvarap.): I, **186**, 6983 (present at the svayaṃvara of Draupadī).—§ 608 (Karṇap.): VIII, **51** *δδ*, 2447 (*Vātavega-S°au*, attacked Bhīmasena); **84**, 4263 (do., slain by Bhīmasena).

Suvarcas[2], a prince. § 232 (Svayaṃvarap.): I, **186**, 6989 (son of Suketu[2], present at the svayaṃvara of Draupadī).

Suvarcas[3], a brahman. § 545 (Pativratāmāhātmyap.): III, **298**, (16867).

Suvarcas[4], a Suparṇa, son of Garuḍa. § 564 (Mātalīyop.): V, **101** *a*, 3587.

Suvarcas[5], a Pāṇḍava warrior. § 592 (Saṃçaptakavadhap.): VII, **21** *μ*, 916.

Suvarcas[6], a Kuru warrior. § 593 (Abhimanyuvadhap.): VII, **48** *χ*, 1899 (slain by Abhimanyu).

Suvarcas[7], a companion of Skanda. § 615*u* (Skanda): IX, **45**, 2548 (given to Skanda by Himavat).

Suvarcas[8] = Karandhama, son of Khanīnetra. § 778 *d* (Saṃvartta-Maruttīya). Seeing the reverses sustained by his father (Khanīnetra) *S.* devoted all his energy to increase the welfare of the people. He was pious, and his subjects were well pleased with him; but as he was constantly engaged in virtuous deeds, his treasures and vehicles became greatly reduced, and the feudatory princes troubled him, so that he came in great distress, but they could not slay him, for his power was established in righteousness; at last he blew into his hand (*pradadhmau karam*), and from that there appeared a supply of forces (read *balam* with B.); then he vanquished all his foes and was called *Karandhama*. His son *Avikshit* lived in the beginning of the *Tretāyuga*: XIV, **4**, 72; [**5**, 99, *Karandhamaḥ*, *d*: Formerly (read *pūrvam* with B. instead of *putram*) *Aṅgiras* was the family priest of *Karandhama*. *S.* was powerful as *Indra*, etc.; he had a chariot, and warriors, and friends, and costly bedsteads, etc., produced through meditation by the breath of his mouth; he had brought all the princes under his sway, and having lived as long as he desired he ascended heaven with his body]. Cf. Karandhama.

Suvarcas[9] = Çiva: XIV, 192.

Suvarcasa, Suvarcasin = Çiva (1000 names[2]).

Suvarman[1], son of Dhṛtarāshṭra. § 130 (Aṃçāvat.): I, **67**, 2732.—§ 182 (Dhṛtarāshṭraputranāmak.): I, **117**, 4545.—§ 585 (Bhīshmavadhap.): VI, **77** *κ*, 3344.—§ 599 (Jayadrathavadhap.): VII, **127** *νν*, 5178, 5209 (slain by Bhīmasena).

Suvarman[2], a Kuru warrior. § 605 (Karṇap.): VIII, **27** *λλ*, 1079 (attacked Arjuna).

Suvarṇa[1], a Devagandharva. § 191 (Arjuna): I, **123**, 4814 (present at the birth of Arjuna). Cf. Suparṇa[2].

Suvarṇa[2], a ṛshi. § 754 (Ānuçāsanik.): XIII, **98**, 4678 (*Manoḥ Prajāpater vādam S°sya ca*), 4679, 4684, 4741 (discourse between Manu and *S.*).

Suvarṇa[3] = Çiva (1000 names[1-2]).

Suvarṇā, daughter of Ikshvāku. § 156 (Pūruvaṃç.): I, **95**, ††3787 (*Ikshvākukanyām*, wife of Suhotra). Cf. Aikshvākī.

Suvarṇābha, son of Çaṅkhapada. § 717*b* (Nārāyaṇīya): XII, **349**, IV), 13584 (*diçām pālam*), learnt the religion of Nārāyaṇa from Çaṅkhapada).

Suvarṇabindu = Vishṇu (1000 names).

Suvarṇacūḍa, a Suparṇa, son of Garuḍa. § 564 (Mātalīyop.): V, **101** *β*, 3594.

Suvarṇaçiras, a ṛshi. § 565 (Gālavacarita): V, **110**, 3812 (*°so 'py atra*—i.e. in the west—*hariromṇaḥ pragāyataḥ*).

Suvarṇadhārin = Kapila: XIII, 7221.

Suvarṇākhya[1] ("named Suvarṇa"), a tīrtha. § 370 (Tīrthayātrāp.): III, **84**, 7096 (*atra Vishṇuḥ prasādārtham Rudram adhārayat purā*).—Do.[2], name of a locality. § 564 (Mātalīyop.): V, **99**, 3551 (*atra* (i.e. in Pātāla) *Ādityo Hayaçirāḥ* (i.e. Vishṇu) *kāle parvaṇi parvaṇi / uttishṭati S°m vāgbhir āpūrayañ jagat*, cf. Nīl.).

Suvarṇakoshaprāpti ("discovery of the gold-treasure"). § 11 (Parvasaṅgr.): I, **2**, 606 (i.e. XIV, ch. **63-65**, see Anugītāp.).

Suvarṇāksha = Çiva: XIII, 599, 1326.

Suvarṇamukuṭa = Çiva: XIV, 202.

Suvarṇanāma, Suvarṇapriya = Çiva (1000 names[1]).

Suvarṇaretas = Çiva (1000 names[2]).

Suvarṇashṭhīvin, son of Sṛñjaya. § 595 (Sṛñjaya): VII, **55**, 2157, 2163 (Sṛñjaya from the grace of Nārada obtained a son whose excreta were gold; *S.* was slain by some robbers but afterwards revived by Nārada).—[§ 632 (Rājadh.): XII, **29**, †1042 (*Suvarṇashṭhīvī*, *S.'s* death and revival).]—§ 633 (do.): XII, **30**, [1043 (*Kāñcana-shṭhīvī*)], 1045.—§ 634*b* (Suvarṇashṭhīvisambhavop.): XII, **31**, 1088, 1089, 1104 (the story of *S.'s* birth, death, and revival, cf. § 595). Cf. Kāñcanashṭhīvin, Svarṇashṭhīvin.

[Suvarṇashṭhīvi-sambhavopākhyāna(m)] ("the episode relating to the origin of Suvarṇashṭhīvin"). § 634*b* (Rājadh.): *Parvata*, after having taken counsel with *Nārada*, granted a boon to *Sṛñjaya* in the form of a son (*Suvarṇa shṭhīvin*), but *Indra* would not let him be long-lived, and *Parvata* would not destine otherwise from partiality to *Indra*, but *Nārada* told *Sṛñjaya* to think of him. *Nārada* and *Parvata* left *Sṛñjaya's* presence. *Indra* slew *Suvarṇashṭhīvin*, causing his *vajra* to assume the form of a tiger, on the shores of the *Bhāgīrathī*. *Sṛñjaya*, in his distress, thought of *Nārada*, who recited to him the Shoḍaçarājop. (§ 632*b*), and brought the child back to life, with *Indra's* permission; *Suvarṇashṭhīvin* ruled for 1100 years, gratifying D. and P., and procreated many sons ere he died (XII, **31**).

Suvarṇavarman, a Kāçi king. § 52 (Janamejaya): I, **44**, †1809 (*Kāçipam*, father of Vapushṭamā, the wife of Janamejaya Pārikshita).

Suvarṇavarṇa = Vishṇu (1000 names).

[Suvarṇotpatti] ("the origin of gold"). § 747*b* (Anuçāsanik.). *Vasishṭha* told to *Rāma Jāmadagnya* (and again *Bhīshma* to *Yudhishṭhira*): After the wedding of *Rudra* and *Devī* on *Himavat*, all the gods, fearing that *Rudra's* offspring would consume the worlds, prevailed upon him to withdraw his vital seed (whence he is called *Ūrdhvaretas*); *Umā* cursed the gods, saying that they should become sonless; but *Agni* was not present. A small quantity of *Rudra's* seed, however, leaped into *fire* and began to develop; meanwhile, the gods, with *Indra*, were scorched by As. *Tāraka*; Ā., V., R., M., A., and Sā. all became afflicted; all the regions of the deities, etc., and the retreats of R̥. were snatched away by As.; D. and R̥. repaired to *Brahmán* (XIII, **84**), who had granted *Tāraka* the boon that he should not be killed by D., As., or Rā., and *Umā* had cursed D.; *Brahmán* said that *Agni* was not there; therefore his offspring, transcending D., Dā., Rā., even G., N., and birds, will with his dart destroy *Tāraka*; *Kāma* is eternal, and in order to slay the enemies of the gods *Agni* will throw *Rudra's* seed into the *Gaṅgā*. The gods failed to find out *Agni*; a frog, having been scorched by the energy of *Agni*, appeared on the surface of the water, and said to the gods that *Agni* was now under the water; *Agni*, leaving the spot, cursed the frogs, saying that they should be without taste; the gods granted them boons (enumeration). An elephant revealed to the gods that *Agni* was now residing within a certain *açvattha* tree; *Agni*, entering the heart of the *çamī* tree, cursed all the elephants, saying that their tongues should be bent back; the gods granted that they should be able to eat everything and utter indistinct cries. *Agni* was then revealed by a parrot, and cursed the parrots, saying that they should be deprived of the power of speech; the gods granted them to speak the letter k, and made *çamī*-wood a sacred resting-place of fire. The waters in the nethermost regions had come into contact with *Agni*, and those heated waters are vomited forth by the mountain springs. The gods asked *Agni* to rescue D., *Prajāpatis*, and R̥. from *Tāraka* by begetting a heroic son. *Agni* united himself spiritually with *Gaṅgā*; an *Asura* uttered a frightful roar; *Gaṅgā* became agitated and unable to bear the seed, and threw it off on *Meru*; the fœtus had the complexion of gold, etc.; therefore R̥. and D. called *Agni* by the name of *Hiraṇyaretas* ("having gold for his vital seed"), and the earth *Vasumatī* ("endued with wealth"). That fœtus, having fallen in a thicket of reeds, assumed a wonderful form; the *Kr̥ttikāḥ* reared it as their son, whence it came to be called *Kārttikeya*; he was also called *Skanda* and *Guha* (etymology). It was in this way that gold came into existence as the offspring of *Agni* (*Jātavedas*), and hence gold was called *jātarūpa*; gold is truly the illustrious *Agni*, the lord of all things, and the foremost of all *Prajāpatis*; the most sacred of all sacred things is gold; it has for its essence *Agni* and *Soma*.—*Vasishṭha* continued: This tale (*Brahmadarçana*) was also heard by me in days of yore about *Brahmán Paramātman* ("the Supreme Soul"): In days of yore (*lokādau*, v. 4163), *Rudra*, who is *Brahmán*, etc. (δ), having assumed the form of *Varuṇa* (cf. v. 4133, *Varuṇaḥ Pāvanātmakaḥ*), performed a sacrifice, to which came the *munis* and all the deities with *Agni*, etc. (ε); *Çiva* (i.e. *Rudra*) then himself poured libations into his own self. At the sight of the celestial damsels the seed (endued with *sattva*, *rajas*, and *tamas*) of *Brahmán* fell upon the Earth; *Pūshan* took it up, and it was taken with the sacrificial ladle and poured as an oblation into the fire; thence *Brahmán* caused the orders of beings to spring into existence; further *Bhr̥gu*, etc. (ζ); for this reason *Agni* is said to be all the deities. *Bhr̥gu* was reckoned the offspring of *Varuṇa*, *Aṅgiras* that of *Agni*, *Kavi* that of *Brahmán*; *Bhr̥gu*, *Aṅgiras*, and *Kavi* were all of them *prajānāṃ patayaḥ*; their offspring (v. 4144–4152) (*Bhr̥gu's*: η; *Aṅgiras'*: θ; *Kavi's*: ι) are called *Vāruṇāḥ*, and *Kavi* and *Bhr̥gu Vāruṇau*. *Agni* is *Brahmán*, *Paçupati*, etc. (κ); gold is the offspring of *Agni* (v. 4146); when fire is not obtainable gold is used as a substitute, oh *Jāmadagnya!* (B. and C. wrongly read *Jāmadagnyaḥ*, which PCR. translates "one that knows the identity of gold with fire") by one who is conversant with the vedic authorities (v. 4165), etc. (v. 4166–7); *Agni* sprang from *Brahmán*, and from *Agni* sprang gold (v. 4168); those persons observant of righteousness who make gifts of gold are regarded as giving away all the deities (v. 4169), etc.; he who makes a gift of gold at the second twilight succeeds in attaining to residence with (*sālokyaṃ*) *Brahmán*, *Vāyu*, *Agni*, and *Soma* (v. 4173), and to the regions of *Indra* (v. 4174), etc.; he has never to fall down from the regions to which he attains (v. 4176). After a long time *Kārttikeya* grew up, and was chosen as generalissimo by all the gods with *Indra*; he slew Dai. *Tāraka* and many other *Asuras*. *Bhīshma* continued: "Thus addressed by *Vasishṭha* [Rāma] *Jāmadagnya* made gifts of gold to the brahmans and became cleansed of his sins" (XIII, **85**). [For continuation v. *Tārakavadhopākhyāna* (§ 748).]

Suvāsa = Çiva (1000 names[2]).

Suvāsas = Çiva: VII, 9535.

Suvāstu (*Suvastrā*, B.), a river. § 574 (Jambūkh.): VI, **9**λ, 333.

Suvāstuka, a prince. § 554 (Sainyodyogap.): V, **4**γ, 76.

Suveça, a god (B. probably more correctly *Sureça*). § 492 (Āṅgirasa): III, **220**, 14168 (among the 15 *yajñamushaḥ*).

Suveṇā, a river. § 459 (Mārkaṇḍeyas.): III, **188*a***, 12909 (seen by Mārkaṇḍeya in the stomach of Nārāyaṇa).

Suviçālā, a mātr̥. § 615*u* (Skanda): IX, **46**θ, 2646.

Suvijñeya = Çiva (1000 names[2]).

Suvīra, pl. (°*āḥ*), a people. § 522 (Draupadīharaṇap.): III, **271**, 15724 (°*āṇāṃ . . . çataṃ*, followers of Jayadratha).—§ 562 (Bhagavadyānap.): V, **74**γ, 2730 (*Ajabinduḥ S°āṇaṃ*). Cf. Sauvīra pl.

Suvīra[1] ("king of the Suvīras"?), a prince. § 130 (Aṃçāvat.): I, **67**, 2696 (among the incarnations from the Krodhavaça gaṇa).

Suvīra[2] (do.) = Jayadratha: III, †15641. Cf. Suvīra, etc.

Suvīra[3], a prince. § 720*b* (Sudarçanop.): XIII, **2**, 93 (son of Dyutimat), 94 (father of Sudurjaya).

Suvīra[4] = Skanda: III, 14637.—Do.[5] = Vishṇu (1000 names).

Suvīrarāshṭrapa[1] ("king of the Suvīras") = Jayadratha: III, †15639.—Do.[2] = Çatruñjaya[7]: XII, †5318.

Suvrata[1], name of two warriors of Skanda. § 615*u* (Skanda): IX, **45**η, 2543, 2544.

Suvrata[2] = Skanda: III, 14634.—Do.[3] = Çiva: VII, 9535.—Do.[4] = Vishṇu (1000 names).

Suyaçā, a princess. § 156 (Pūruvaṃç.): I, **95**, ††3795 (*Bāhudāṃ*, wife of the elder Parikshit).

Suyajñā, a princess, daughter of Prasenajit. § 156 (Pūruvaṃç.): I, **95**, ††3773 (*Prāsenajitīṃ*, wife of Mahābhauma).

Suyajus, son of Bhumanyu. § 152 (Pūruvaṃç.): I, **94**, 3714.

Suyāma, pl. (°*āḥ*), a class of gods. § 730 (Ānuçāsanik.): XIII, **18**λλ, †1371.

Suyāmuna = Vishṇu (1000 names).

Suyodhana = Duryodhana, q.v.

Suyukta = Çiva (1000 names[2]).

Svābhāvya = Vishṇu (1000 names).

***svadhā**[1], the food offered to the pitr̥s: I, 923, 4964; III,

1127 (pl.); V, 3614, 4483; VII, 2241, 2419, 3452 (personif.); VIII, †819, 4426; XII, 364 (*pitṛ°*), 1009 (pl.), 3372, 3620, 9630, 10602; XIII, 1807, 3387, 3389, 5620, 7266; XIV, 22, 1296 (*°vṛttiḥ*).—Different deities identified with the *s.*: Çiva: XII, 10423 (1000 names[1]); Çrī: XII, 8355; Durgā (Umā): VI, 804; Kṛshṇa: VI, 1186; XII, 1513; Skanda: III, †14639.—Do.[2], a ritual exclamation: XIII, 1606; XIV, 1032 (*°kāra*), 1326 (do.).

Svadhāsvarūpa = Çiva: XIV, 205 (only B., C. has *Tripuravighnāya*).

Svadhāvat (B., *Sudhā°*) pl. (*°antaḥ*), a class of pitṛs. § 267 (Yamasabhāv.): II, **8**, 341 (in the palace of Yama).

Svadhṛta = Vishṇu (1000 names).

Svādukāra, name of a caste: XIII, 2584 (sg.).

Svāhā (originally a ritual exclamation: I, 923; III, 14518; V, 4483; XII, 9630, 10602; XIII, 5620), personified as a daughter of Daksha, wife of Agni. § 240 (Vaivāhikap.): I, **199**, 7351 (*yathā . . . S°ā caiva Vibhāvasau*). — § 270 (Brahmasabhāv.): II, **11**, 458 (in the palace of Brahmán).— § 490 (Āṅgirasa): III, **219**, 14152 (a fire = Manyantī?, according to Nīl. daughter of Bṛhaspati).—§ 496 (Skandotpatti): III, **224**, 14295 (*Dakshaduhitā*); **225**, 14314 (*S.* assumed the form of the six wives of the Saptarshis and cohabited with Agni; then she, in the shape of a bird (suparṇī), carried away the semen of Agni, from which Skanda arose).—§ 497 (do.): III, **226**, 14344, 14347, 14354. — § 500 (Skandop.): III, **228**, 14391 (*Rudram Agnim Umām* (B., *Agnimukhām*) *S°ām . . . yajanti putrakāmāç ca putriṇaç ca sadā janāḥ*).—§ 501 (do.): III, **229**, 14432.—§ 503 (Skandayuddhap.): III, **231**, 14514, 14516, 14520, 14522 (Skanda granted *S.* companionship with Agni, so far as offerings should be performed with her name (*svāhety uktvā*, v. 14518)).—§ 509 (Kārttikeyastava): III, **232**, †14642 (*°-Mahī-Kṛttikānām*, sc. *sutaḥ*, i.e. Skanda).— § 565 (Gālavacarita): V, **117**, 3967 (*reme . . . Svāhāyāñ ca yathā Vahniḥ*).—§ 599 (Jayadrathavadhap.): VII, **94**ε, 3452 (mentioned in a benediction to Duryodhana).—§ 615*u* (Skanda): IX, **45**γ, 2515 (came to the investiture of Skanda).—§ 768*b* (Umā-Maheçvarasaṃv.): XIII, **146**γ, 6751 (*Vibhāvasoḥ*, sc. *sādhvī*).—Different deities identified with the *s.*: Çiva: XII, 10423 (1000 names[1]); Çrī: XII, 8355; Kṛshṇa: XII, 1513; Sarasvatī: IX, 2389; Skanda: III, †14639.

Svāhākāra[1], the exclamation *svāhā*: III, 1127: XII, 2305; XIII, 2690, 6738; XIV, 1030.—Do.[2] = Durgā (Umā): VI, 804.

Svāheya ("the son of Svāhā") = Skanda: III, 14633.

Svaksha, pl. (*°āḥ*), a people. § 574 (Jambūkh.): VI, **9**μ, 353.

Svaksha = Vishṇu (1000 names).

Svana, name of a fire. § 490 (Āṅgirasa): III, **219**, 14144.

Svaṅga, Svāṅga, Svāpana = Vishṇu (1000 names).

***Svar**[1] ("heaven"): XIV, 2840 (*svar yānti dhārmikaḥ*); mostly occurring in compounds, e.g. °-*gamana* (VIII, †4088), °-*gata* (I, 355), °-*gati* (I, 263), °-*netṛ* (III, 12705), °-*nivāsa* (I, 3537), °-*yāta* (I, 3807).—Do.[2] = Çiva (1000 names[1]).— Do.[3] = Vishṇu (1000 names).

Svarāj = Kṛshṇa: XII, 1509.

Svarāshtra, a people. § 574 (Jambūkh.): VI, **9**μ, 356.

Svaravyañjanabhūshaṇa = Kṛshṇa: XII, 1634.

Svarbhānavī ("the daughter of Svarbhānu"), wife of Āyus. § 141 (Purūravas): I, **75**, 3150 (*°sutān*, i.e. Nahusha, etc.).

Svarbhānu, an Asura, commonly the demon who causes eclipses (= Rāhu). § 92 (Aṃçāvat.): I, **65**, 2532 (son of Danu, different from Rāhu (son of Siṃhikā, v. 2539)).— § 130 (do.): I, **67**, 2648 (do., incarnate as king Ugrasena). —§ 316 (Kirmīravadhap.): III, **11**, 437 (*°r iva Bhāskaraṃ*, sc. *paryadhāvata*).—§ 565 (Gālavacarita): V, **110**, 3811 (*kabandhaḥ . . . S°oh Sūryakalpasya Soma-Sūryau jighaṃsataḥ*).—§ 573 (Ambopākhyānap.): V, **182**, 7239 (*Arkaṃ . . . S°r abhisaṃvṛṇot*).—§ 575*d* (Rāhu): VI, **12**, 481, 482. —§ 586 (Bhīshmavadhap.): VI, **101**, 4619 (*°r iva Bhāskaraṃ*, sc. *āsasāda*).—§ 600 (Ghaṭotkacavadhap.): VII, **156**, 6808 (*°r iva Bhāskaraṃ*, sc. *prācchādayad bāṇaiḥ*); **174**, 7874 (*°-Bhāskarau*); **175**, 7938 (*°r iva Bhāskaraṃ*, sc. *prācchādayad bāṇaiḥ*).—§ 673*b* (Bali-Vāsavasaṃv.): XII, **227***a*, 8262 (among the ancient rulers of the earth).—§ 696*b* (Dakshaprokta-Çiva-sahasranāmast.): XII, **285**, 10448 (*grasaty arkaṃ S°r bhūtvā*, sc. Çiva).—§ 772*m* (Atri): XIII, **157**, 7292 (*avidhyat . . . Soma-Bhāskarau*). Cf. Asura, Rāhu.—Do.[2] = Çiva (1000 names[1-2]).

Svarbhānuçatru ("enemy of Rāhu") = Sūrya (the Sun): III, 17120.

Svarbhānusūdana ("destroyer of Rāhu") = Sūrya (the Sun): III, 16996.

***Svarga** ("heaven", or "heavenly bliss"): I, 437, etc.; II, 685, etc.; III, 841, etc.; IV, 2247; V, †387, etc.; VI, 126, etc.; VII, 40, etc.; VIII, 447, etc.; IX, 182, etc.; X, 159, etc.; XI, 59, etc.; XII, 49, etc.; XIII, 307, etc., 1057 (identified with Çiva), 6628 (*°gāminaḥ*), etc.; XIV, 26, etc., 1274 (only B., C. has *sarvaṃ*), etc.; XV, 253, etc.; XVII, 75, etc.; XVIII, 1, etc., passim.

Svargadvāra[1], name of a tīrtha. § 368 (Tīrthayātrāp.): III, **83**, 7038.

Svargadvāra[2] = Çiva (1000 names[2]).

Svargadvāraṃ prajādvāraṃ = Sūrya (the Sun): III, 156.

Svargadvārasprça = Agni, q.v.

***Svargaloka** ("the celestial world") = Svarga: I, †3589; II, 1890; III, 1755, 5003, etc.; V, 1184, 1381; VI, 1191; VII, 2130, 2581; XII, 330, †722, 2746 (pl.), etc.; XIII, 327, etc.; XIV, 421; XVIII, 255.

Svargamārga, a tīrtha. § 733*z* (Kālodaka). XIII, **25**, 1747.

Svargaparvan ("the section relating to heaven") = Svargārohaṇaparvan. § 11 (Parvasaṅgr.): I, **2**, 634.—§ 795*c* (Mahābhārata): XVIII, **6**, 280.

[Svargārohaṇaparvan or **°haṇikap°]** ("the section relating to the ascension to heaven", the 18th of the greater and the 100th of the minor parvans of Mhbhr.; cf. Svargaparvan, Svàrgārohaṇika(ṃ)[parva(n)]. § 795. *Janamejaya* said: "Having attained to Heaven, what regions were respectively reached by my grandfathers, the *Pāṇḍavas* and the *Dhārtarāshṭras*? Thou hast been taught everything by M-ṛ *Vyāsa*." *Vaiçampāyana* said: "Having arrived in Heaven, *Yudhishṭhira* beheld *Duryodhana* blazing with effulgence and seated in the midst of Sā.; he expressed his indignation (*a*) and wished to come to his brothers; *Nārada* solicited him to desist from his wrath (*β*); *Yudhishṭhira* indignantly (*γ*) asked for his brothers and *Karṇa*, etc. (*δ*) (XVIII, **1**); *Karṇa* especially lay to him at heart, since his mother had ordered him to offer oblations of water unto *Karṇa*, and he had noticed the resemblance between the feet of his mother and those of *Karṇa*; he would not stay in Heaven if his brothers were not there. The gods ordered a celestial messenger to lead *Yudhishṭhira* to the region reached by his brothers. The path was enveloped in darkness and stench, etc. (description); as he was about to turn back, he heard voices uttering piteous lamentations, calling him by name, and giving evidence to the happiness felt by his presence, and they turned out to come from *Karṇa* and his brothers, etc. (ε); he could not understand this perverse order of things (ζ); he censured the gods and *Dharma*, and declared that he would stay in Hell in order to comfort his relatives. The messenger returned and represented this to *Indra* (XVIII, **2**). All the gods: M. with *Indra*, V., A., Sā., R., Ā., Si., M-ṛ. and *Dharma* came to *Yudhishṭhira*; the illusions of Hell (the river *Vaitaraṇī*, etc.) disappeared; *Indra* informed him that Hell should be seen by every king; he who first endures Hell must afterwards enjoy Heaven, and vice versa; *Yudhishṭhira* must see Hell because he had deceived *Droṇa* in the matter of his son; similarly *Bhīma*, etc. (η) had been shown Hell; but they have all been cleansed of their sins, and they had, as also *Karṇa*, attained to regions of felicity; D., G., and Aps. should wait upon *Yudhishṭhira*; his regions are far above those of kings and equal to those of *Hariçcandra*, etc. (θ). *Dharma* said that this was the third test to which he had put him (ι). Having bathed in the celestial *Gaṅgā*, he left his human body and assumed a celestial form, and became divested of all his enmities and grief. Accompanied by *Dharma* and praised by M-ṛ, he reached that place where the *Pāṇḍavas* and the *Dhārtarāshṭras*, freed from wrath, were enjoying each his respective status (XVIII, **3**). *Yudhishṭhira*, praised by D., M., and Ṛ., proceeded to that place where the foremost ones of the *Kurus* were; he beheld *Govinda* (Kṛshṇa) in his *Brāhma*-form (description), adored by *Arjuna*; in another place *Karṇa* in the company of *Sūrya*, etc. (κ); as *Yudhishṭhira* wished to question *Draupadī*, *Indra* declared that she was *Çrī*, created for the *Pāṇḍavas* by *Çiva*; her five sons are G.; G-king *Dhṛtarāshṭra* was his uncle *Dhṛtarāshṭra*; *Pāṇḍu* frequently comes to *Indra* in his excellent chariot; *Bhīshma* is now in the midst of V.; others walk with G. and Y., etc., or Gh. (XVIII, **4**). *Janamejaya* asked for what period *Bhīshma*, etc. (λ) remained in Heaven, and what became of them when the effect of their actions were exhausted. *Sauti* said: Thus questioned B-ṛ *Vaiçampāyana* with the permission of *Vyāsa* said: Everyone is not capable of returning to his own nature [i.e. final Emancipation, PCR.] when his deeds cease to work [the meaning seems to be that some persons lose their individuality by being absorbed into some deity before final Emancipation, but the text itself is corrupt]; this is a mystery of the gods, explained by *Vyāsa*, who is omniscient; *Bhīshma* attained to the state of V. [absorbed in V., not as a separate individual: *sāyujya*, not *sālokya*, PCR.]; therefore, now eight *Vasus* are seen; etc. (μ). *Sauti* then related the conclusion of *Janamejaya's* (*b*) snake-sacrifice. "I have now told thee everything that *Vaiçampāyana* narrated, at the command of *Vyāsa*, unto the king at his snake-sacrifice. It is a sacred tale, etc., composed by *Vyāsa*" (eulogy of *Vyāsa*) (ν), *; eulogy, etc., of *Mahābhārata* (*c*) (XVIII, **5-6**).

Svargārohaṇika(m) [parva] ("[the section] relating to the ascension to heaven"). § 10 (Parvasaṅgr.): I, **2**, 356 (°*am*, sc. *parva*, i.e. Svargārohaṇaparvan).

Svargārohaṇika(m) parva(n) ("Bhīshma's ascension to Heaven"), the 92nd of the minor parvans of Mhbhr. § 10 (Pārvas.): I, **2**, 353.—§ 777. *Vaiçampāyana* said: When *Yudhishṭhira* had taken leave of the citizens, etc., he comforted the widows, whose husbands had been slain, with abundant gifts, and being duly installed on the throne, he reassured all his subjects [by acts of goodwill], etc. After fifty days, seeing that the sun had begun its northern course, he set out to see *Bhīshma*, taking with him what was necessary for the latter's cremation, accompanied by *Dhṛtarāshṭra*, *Gāndhārī*, *Kuntī*, his brothers, *Kṛshṇa*, *Vidura*, *Yuyutsu*, *Yuyudhāna*, and his other relatives and a great retinue, and his priests. He beheld *Bhīshma* surrounded by Ṛ *Vyāsa*, *Nārada*, *Asita Devala*, and by the remnant of unslain kings from various parts of the country, guarded by the warriors appointed for that duty; all the inhabitants of *Kurujāṅgala* were also there. When *Yudhishṭhira* had told his errand, *Bhīshma* opened his eyes and saw all the *Bharatas* assembled. He seized the hand of *Yudhishṭhira* and welcomed him; he had now been lying there for fifty-eight nights, which he had felt to be as long as a century; now it was the bright fortnight of *Māgha*, and of this one-fourth had passed away. Then he reminded *Dhṛtarāshṭra* of the instructions he had received from *Vyāsa*, and that he should regard the *Pāṇḍavas* and especially *Yudhishṭhira* as his own sons. Then he praised *Kṛshṇa* as the Supreme God, and asked him to grant him leave to die, and that he should ever protect the *Pāṇḍavas*; he complained that *Duryodhana* had never been willing to follow his counsels; he said that he knew from *Nārada* and *Vyāsa*, that *Kṛshṇa* and *Arjuna* were Ṛ *Nārāyaṇa* and *Nara*, who had lived for a long time in *Badarī*. *Kṛshṇa* then gave *Bhīshma* leave to die and come to the *Vasus*, comparing him to *Mārkaṇḍeya*. Having given some few admonitions to *Dhṛtarāshṭra*, etc. (XIII, **168**), *Bhīshma* successively caused his life-breaths to leave his body, and the parts of his body became successively free from wounds and arrows, at which the bystanders became filled with wonder. His soul passed through the crown of his head, ascended to heaven like a meteor, and soon became invisible, while the celestial kettle-drums began to play, a rain of flowers fell down, and Si. and B-ṛ. applauded. Then the *Pāṇḍavas*, etc. (*a*) cremated the corpse. Then, accompanied by Ṛ., etc. (β), they proceeded to *Bhāgīrathī* (Gaṅgā), where they offered oblations of water to *Bhīshma*. Then *Bhāgīrathī* appeared and, weeping, praised *Bhīshma* (γ). *Kṛshṇa* comforted her, mentioning the present felicity of *Bhīshma* as one of the *Vasus*, and declared that he had not been slain by *Çikhaṇḍin*, but by *Arjuna*. *Gaṅgā* gave up her grief; all the kings, headed by *Kṛshṇa*, obtained her permission to depart, and all returned [to the city] (XIII, **169**).

[Svargārohaṇikaparvan] = [Svargārohaṇaparvan], q.v.

Svargatīrtha, name of a tīrtha. § 733*n* (Mataṅgavāpī): XIII, **25**, 1719.

Svarloka ("the world of heaven"): III, 8777, 15442; XII, 8599, 10277 (°*vāsinaḥ*); XIII, 3547 (°*vāsinām*), 3663, 4170.

Svarṇagrīva, a warrior of Skanda. § 615*u* (Skanda): IX, **45**η, 2577.

Svarṇakeça = Çiva: VII, 9541.

Svarṇashṭhīvin = Suvarṇashṭhīvin: XII, †1042, 1129.

Svarṇabindu (C., °*vi*°), a tīrtha. § 733*c* (Pushkara): XIII, **25**, 1696.

Svārocisha = Manu[5]: XII, 13582 (*M*°), 13583 (*sarvalokapatiḥ*).

Svarūpa, an Asura. § 268 (Varuṇasabhāv.): II, **9**, 366 (among the Daityas and Dānavas in the palace of Varuṇa).

Svaryāti: VII, 2991 (v. Çaryāti).

Svasti = Vishṇu (1000 names).

Svastibhāva = Çiva (1000 names[2]).

Svastibhuj = Vishṇu (1000 names).

Svastida[1] = Çiva (1000 names[2]).—Do.[2] = Vishṇu (1000 names).

Svastidakshiṇa = Vishṇu (1000 names).

Svastika[1], a serpent. § 277 (Jarāsandhavadhap.): II, **21**, 806 (*°syālayaç cātra*—i.e. near Girivraja).

Svastika[2], a warrior of Skanda. § 615*u* (Skanda): IX, **45**η, 2567.

Svastikṛt = Vishṇu (1000 names).

Svastimatī, a mātṛ. § 615*u* (Skanda): IX, **46**θ, 2630.

Svastipura, a tīrtha. § 368 (Tīrthayātrāp.): III, **83**, 7045.

Svastyātreya, a ṛshi. § 22 (Pramadvarā): I, **8***a*, 961.—§ 665 (Mokshadh.): XII, **208**η, 7594 (one of the ṛshis of the south). — § 770 (Ānuçāsanik.): XIII, **151**η, 7112 (among the ṛtvijes of Dharmarāja—i.e. Yama).—§ 775 (do.): XIII, **166**δ, 7665 (among the ṛshis of the south).

Svāsya = Vishṇu (1000 names).

Svāti, name of a nakshatra (v. Sū. Si.). § 565 (Gālavacarita): V, **111**, 3835 (*atra*—i.e. in the north—*tishṭhati vai S°r atrāsyā udayaḥ smṛtaḥ*). — § 574 (Jambūkh.): VI, **3**, 85 (*Citrā-Svātyantare caiva dhishṭhitaḥ parushagrahaḥ*, omens).—§ 746 (Ānuçāsanik.): XIII, **64**, 3269 (merit of gifts under the constellation *S.*).—§ 749 (do.): XIII, **89***a*, 4261 (*°yoge*, merit of performing a çrāddha under the constellation *S.*).—§ 759 (do.): XIII, **110**, 5393 (description of the cāndravrata).

Svavaça = Vishṇu (1000 names).

Svayambhū or **Svayambhu** ("self-existent") = Brahmán: I, 869 (*B°*), 2458, 2497, 2517, 2579 (*vihitāni S°vā*), 2607 (*°vā niyuktaḥ*), 3026 (*proktaḥ svayam eva S°vā*, quotation), 3316 (*tushṭenoktaḥ S°vā*, sc. *īçvaraḥ*, i.e. Çukra), 4436 (*dharmaḥ . . . svayam uktaḥ S°vā*), 4646, †7328 (*sṛshṭā devapatnī svayaṃ S°vā*, i.e. Çrī reborn as Draupadī); II, 422 (*sabhāṃ . . . S°vaḥ*), 474 (*Viçvātmā*), 730 (*Gṛhadevīti nāmnā purā sṛshṭā S°vā*, sc. Jarā); III, 158 (told the 108 names of Sūrya), 1152 (*Prapitāmahaḥ*), 10112 (= Viçvakarman), 12191, 12204, 12890 (*Padmālayaḥ* = Vishṇu?), 13108 (*maryādāḥ S°vihitāḥ*), 14448 (*nirdishṭā tava*—i.e. Skanda's—*patnī S°vā*, sc. *Devasenā*), 15882 (*Prajāpatiḥ S°uḥ*, grandfather of Rāvaṇa), 16632 (*°uvihitāt*); IV, 1557 (*cāturvarṇyasya karmāṇi vihitāni S°vā*); V, 2172 (*B°*), 2441 (*kshatraṃ sṛshtaṃ S°vā*), 4465 (*yatha sṛshṭaḥ S°vā*), 7309 (*Bhīshmamṛtyuḥ . . . vihito vai S°vā*); VI, 2078 (*paramopetaḥ S°r iva Bhānunā*, only C., B. has *Sumerur*); VIII, 1629 (*°ūr iva Rudrasya*, sc. *sārathiḥ*), 3446 (*kṛtam andhaṃ* (so B.) *S°vā*), 4435 (*Prajāpatiṃ*), 4437 (*°o*), 4438 (*°o*), †4659 (*svayaṃ kṛtaṃ S°vā*, sc. the kirīṭa of Indra and Arjuna), †5044 (?); IX, 2479 (*Brahmā S°uḥ*); XI, 126; XII, 2149, 2151, 2181 (*proktānīha S°vā*, sc. *vyasanāni*), 2820 (*brahma kshatram idaṃ sṛshtam ekayoni S°vā*), 3380 (*dharmaḥ sṛshṭaḥ S°vā*), †6275 (*uvāca*, quotation), 7356, †7517 (?), 7569, 7570, 7615, 7661 (*anujñātāḥ S°vā*), 7990 (*rājā sṛshṭaḥ S°vā*), 8183 (*sthāpito hy asya*—i.e. the Sun's—*samayo . . . S°vā*), 8220, †8423 (*Pitāmahasyāyatane S°vaḥ*), 8534 (*vāg utsṛshṭā S°vā*), 8712 (pl., i.e. the emancipated), 8739 (*siddhiḥ S°vaḥ*), 10171 (*B°*), 10779 (?father of Dhātṛ), †12073 (*maryādā niyatā S°vā*), 12361 (*Vedāḥ sṛshṭāḥ S°vā*), 13735 (*bahavaḥ purushāḥ . . . sṛshṭāḥ S°vā*); XIII, 2558 (*dāyavidhiḥ . . . uktaḥ S°vā*), 3315 (*Pitṝṇāṃ paramaṃ bhojyaṃ tilāḥ sṛshṭāḥ S°vā*), 3225 (*B°*), 3706 (*ādishṭaḥ . . . Dakshaḥ S°vā*), 4115 (*°vaḥ . . . retaḥ*), 4346 (*°uvihito dharmaḥ*), 4347 (*°uvihitaṃ*), 4349 (*saṃkalpitā bhāgāḥ svayam eva S°vā*), 4352 (*pitaro . . . nirmitā ye S°vā*), 4353 (*saptakaḥ pitṛvaṃças tu pūrvadṛshṭaḥ S°vā*), 4377 (*°sadanaṃ*), 4380, 5371 (*gītaṃ svayam eva S°vā*), 5981 (*gāvaḥ sṛshṭāḥ S°vā*), 6453 (*sṛshṭāḥ S°vā*), 6566 (*cāturvarṇyaṃ . . . sṛshtaṃ S°vā*); XIV, 2832 (*Prajāpatiṃ*); XVIII, 216.—Do.[2] = Çiva: VII, 9507.—Do.[3] = Vishṇu (Kṛshṇa, Nārāyaṇa): II, 1324 (i.e. Kṛshṇa); III, 11864 (i.e. Nārāyaṇa), 12821; XII, 6779 (*padmaṃ sṛshṭam S°vā*?), 13489; XIII, 6954 (1000 names); XIV, 1095 (*V°*), 1223 (*V°*).

Svayambhubhavana ("the abode of Brahmán"). § 757*n* (Hastikūṭa): *Gautama* said: [*S.*] where there is no fear of cold or heat, no hunger, thirst, pain, sorrow, joy, no one that is agreeable or disagreeable, no friend and no enemy, no decrepitude and death, neither righteousness nor sin; which is free from passion, happy (*sphīte*), and where there is wisdom and *sattva* . . . . *Dhṛtarāshṭra* said: They who are freed from every attachment, possessed of purified souls (*kṛtātmānaḥ*), steady in their vow, devoted to *yoga* (*adhyātmayogasaṃsthāne yuktāḥ*), who have attained [in this life, PCR.] to the happiness of heaven, and consist of *sattva* (*sāttvikāḥ*), attain to the sacred abode of *Brahmán*: XIII, **102**, 4893.

Svayambhūta = Çiva (1000 names[2]).

Svayambhuva[1] (= Svayambhū) = Brahmán: XII, 11229(?).—Do.[2] = Çiva: XIII, 1011, 1248 (1000 names[2]).—Do.[3] = Vishṇu (Kṛshṇa): XII, 12658 (i.e. Kṛshṇa), 13494.

Svāyambhuva[1] ("son of Svayambhū [i.e. Brahmán]") = Manu[6]: I, 2963 (*M°*), 4675 (*M°*); III, 12485 (*M°*); V, 1334 (*M°*); VII, 2414 (*M°*); XII, 626 (*M°*), 1296 (*M°*), 3548 (quotation), 9595 (*M°*), 12725, 12740 (*M°*), 13040 (*M°*); XIII, 873 (*°ādyo Manavaḥ*), 4684 (*M°*), 5605 (*M°*).

Svāyambhuva[2] (do.) = Atri: XIII, 4329 (*A°*).

Svāyambhuva, adj. 1) ("relating to Svayambhū [i.e. Brahmán]"): XII, 12741 (*dharmeshu*); XIII, 677 (*kratuḥ*), 1809 (*sthānaṃ*), 3366 (*mahāsthānaṃ*), 5256 (*vimānaṃ*); 2) ("relating to Manu Svāyambhuva"): XII, 12658 (*antare*), ††13206 (*pūrve Manvantare*), 13678 (*Manoḥ S°e 'ntare*).

Svayambhuvo vana(ṃ). § 392*c* (Tīrthayātrāp.): In the *S. v. Viçvakarman* (= Svayambhū, v. 10112) on the occasion of a sacrifice had given the earth to *Kaçyapa* as dakshiṇā. Angry because she had been given to a mortal the earth sank to *Rasātala*, but appeased by *Kaçyapa* rose again from within the water in the form of an altar (*vedīrūpā*). As soon as this altar is touched by a mortal it enters (into) the sea: III, **114**, 10111.

Svayaṃçreshṭha = Çiva (1000 names[2]).

Svayamprabhā, an Apsaras. § 336 (Indralokābhigamanap.): III, **43***a*, 1784 (in the abode of Indra).

Svayaṃvara(ḥ) ("a maiden's—i.e. Kṛshṇā's—choosing a husband for herself"). § 10 (Parvasaṅgr.): I, **2**, 314 (*°o devyāḥ Pāñcālyāḥ parva*, i.e. Svayaṃvaraparva).—§ 11 (do.): I, **2**, 362 (*devyāḥ Pāñcālyāḥ*, = do.).

[Svayaṃvaraparvan(°va)] ("the section relating how Draupadī chose herself a husband", the 12th of the minor parvans of Mhbhr.). (Cf. Svayaṃvara). § 231. The *Pāṇḍavas* went to the *Pāñcāla* land in the company of *brahmans*, who told them of the *svayaṃvara*, and of *Dhṛshṭadyumna*, and *Kṛshṇā* (I, **184**). On their way they beheld *Dvaipāyana*. They took up their quarters in the house of a potter, and adopting the brahmanical profession, they began to lead a mendicant life. *Yajñasena* (= Drupada) always cherished the wish of bestowing his daughter on *Kirīṭin* (i.e. Arjuna), but never spoke of this wish to anybody. He therefore caused a very stiff bow to be made, which was incapable of being bent by anybody except *Arjuna*; and causing some machinery to be erected in the sky, he set up a mark attached to that machinery, and said: "He who with this bow and these arrows hits the mark shall obtain my daughter." Among the kings that came were *Duryodhana* and the *Kurus* and *Karṇa*. The princes entered the arena by the north-eastern gate (*çiçumāraçiraḥ prāpya*). The arena was situated to the north-east of the capital (description of it). On the 16th day *Draupadī*, having bathed, entered the arena. Then the *purohita* of the *Sōmakas* gratified *Agni*. *Dhṛshṭadyumna*, possessing a voice deep as that of a kettle-drum or of the clouds, taking hold of his sister's arm, stood in the midst of the arena, and said: "Hit the mark by means of these five arrows." Then he addressed his sister, reciting to her the names, etc. of the assembled princes (I, **185**).—§ 232. Enumeration (*a*) of the assembled princes (I, **186**).—§ 233. There came also the *devagaṇas* on their chariots; the *Rudras* and the *Ādityas*, the *Vasus* and the *Açvins*, the *Sādhyas* and all the *Maruts*, with *Yama* and *Dhaneçvara* (i.e. Kubera) walking ahead; and also the *Daityas* and *Suparṇas*, the *mahoragas*, the *Devarshis*, the *Guhyakas* and the *Cāraṇas*, *Viçvāvasu*, *Nārada* and *Parvata*, the principal *Gandharvas* with the *Apsarases*, and the *Asuras* and *Siddhas* (v. 7017), and *Halāyudha* (i.e. Balarāma), and *Janārdana* (i.e. Kṛshṇa), and the chiefs of the *Vṛshṇis*, *Andhakas*, and *Yadus*, always obedient to Kṛshṇa. *Kṛshṇa* pointed out the *Pāṇḍavas* to his brother *Rāma*. When *Duryodhana*, the *Cedi*-king *Çiçupāla* (son of *Damaghosha*), *Jarāsandha*, the *Madra*-king *Çalya*, etc. had in vain tried to string the bow, and *Karṇa*, though having succeeded in stringing it, had, as a *sūta*, been rejected by *Kṛshṇā*, *Jishṇu* (i.e. Arjuna) came forward (I, **187**). Some of the brahmans spoke reproachingly of *Arjuna's* daring undertaking, some approved of it (citing *Paraçurāma* and *Agastya's* drinking out of the Sea). *Arjuna*, bending his head to *Īçāna* and remembering *Kṛshṇa*, accomplished the task. The gods showered celestial flowers. *Drupada* was filled with joy. *Yudhishṭhira* with the twins returned home. *Kṛshṇā* approached *Arjuna*, who soon afterwards left the lists followed by her (I, **188**).—§ 234. When *Drupada* expressed his desire of bestowing his daughter on that *brahman*, the kings resolved to slay *Drupada* and burn *Kṛshṇā*, but spare *Arjuna*, whom they took for a *brahman*. They rushed at *Drupada*, who was defended by *Arjuna* with the bow and by *Bhīma* with a tree torn up by the root. *Kṛshṇa* then knew, and said to *Balarāma* that they must be the *Pāṇḍavas*, who had escaped from the fire (I, **189**). *Karṇa* was defeated by *Arjuna* ("accomplished in the *Brāhma* and the *Paurandara* weapons", v. 7105), and the *Madra*-king *Çalya* by *Bhīma*; then *Duryodhana*, etc., who had been engaged with the *brahmans*, desisted from the combat, because *brahmans*, though offending, should yet always be protected. *Kṛshṇa* said to them that those *brahmans* had justly acquired the maiden. The kings returned to their respective kingdoms. *Bhīma* and *Arjuna*, with difficulty, escaped from the throng, followed by *Kṛshṇā*.—§ 235. *Kuntī* was filled with anxiety, seeing that her sons were late in returning from their begging tour. Then, in the late afternoon, *Jishṇu* (i.e. Arjuna), accompanied by a body of *brahmans*, entered the abode of the *Bhārgava* (i.e. the potter, Nīl.) (I, **190**). *Bhīma* and *Arjuna* presented *Kṛshṇā* as their "alms", and *Kuntī*, not yet seeing them, said: "enjoy ye all." Afterwards, she was alarmed at what she had said. *Yudhishṭhira* declared that *Arjuna* should wed her; but *Arjuna* replied that it was a sin for the younger brother to marry before the elder. Meanwhile, they all fell in love with *Kṛshṇā*. Then *Yudhishṭhira* recollected the words of *Vyāsa*, and, from fear of a division amongst the brothers, said that she should be the common wife of them all. *Kṛshṇa* and *Balarāma* then paid them a visit, and again went away (I, **191**).—§ 236. When *Bhīma* and *Arjuna* were turning towards the abode of the *Bhārgava*, *Dhṛshṭadyumna* followed them and concealed himself in some part of the house. Then *Bhīma* and *Arjuna* and the twins returning from their begging tour in the evening, gave everything to *Yudhishṭhira*. *Kuntī* caused *Kṛshṇā* to distribute it, giving to *Bhīma* alone as much as to all the others, because he always ate much. Then they laid down for the night, and *Dhṛshṭadyumna* overheard their conversations. In the morning *Dhṛshṭadyumna* set out to report it to *Drupada*, who was sad, because he did not know, if perhaps a man of mean descent had taken away his daughter, though he thought it possible that it was Arjuna (I, **192**).

Svayañjāta = Vishṇu (1000 names).

Svedajāḥ = Çiva (1000 names [1]).

Svishṭakṛt, a fire. § 490 (Āṅgirasa): III, **219**, 14150.—§ 493 (do.): III, **221**, 14193 (cf. Rohiṇī[4]).

Svishṭakṛt[2] = Kṛshṇa: XII, 1510.

Syamantaka, a jewel. § 793 (Mausalap.): XVI, **3**, 79 (had been owned by Satrājit).

Syamantapañcaka, v. Sa°.

Syūmaraçmi, a ṛshi. § 684 (Mokshadh.): XII, **269**, 9604 (*ṛshiḥ*), (9613); **270**, (9640), (9674), (9676), 9676, (9694); **271**, (9740), (9743) (discourse between Kapila and *S.*).

T

Tad (or **Yat-tad**) = Vishṇu (1000 names).

Tāḍakāyana, a son of Viçvāmitra. § 721*b* (Viçvāmitrop.): XIII, **4**β, 255.

Taditprabhā, a mātṛ. § 615*u* (Skanda): IX, **46**θ, 2635.

Taijasa, name of a tīrtha. § 368 (Tīrthayātrāp.): III, **83**, 7035 (*Vāruṇam tīrtham*), 7036.—§ 615 (Baladevatīrthayātrā): IX, **46**, 2723 (*tīrtham*, there Varuṇa was installed as the lord of the waters).

Takshaçilā, name of a city. § 13 (Paushap.): I, **3**, ††682 (conquered by Janamejaya).—§ 17 (Uttaṅka): I, **3**, 834 (°*saṃstham*, sc. Janamejaya).—§ 795*b* (Janamejaya): XVIII, **5**, 181 (after the snake-sacrifice Janamejaya returned from *T.* to Hāstinapura).

Takshaka, name of a serpent-king. § 17 (Uttaṅka): I, **3**, ††774 (*nāgarājaḥ*), ††775 (do.), ††792, ††793, 802 (*yasya vāsaḥ Kurukshetre Khāṇḍave cābhavat purā / taṃ nāgarājānaṃ*), 803 (°*aç cāçvasenaç ca nityaṃ sahacarau*, dwell on the Ikshumatī, in Kurukshetra), 804 (*jaghanyajas T°ça* (read °*sya*) *Çrutaseneti yaḥ sutaḥ*), ††815, ††823 (*nāgarājena*), ††832, 840 (had bitten Parikshit, cf. § 51), 843 (*pannagādhamaḥ*), 848 (in the shape of a beggar—*kshapaṇaka*—*T.* deprived Uttaṅka of a pair of earrings but was forced to give them back).—§ 47 (Sarpanāmak.): I, **35**, 1550 (enumeration).—§ 51 (Parikshit): I, **41**, 1704 (*pannageçvaraḥ*), 1709 (*pannagottamaḥ*); **42**, 1744, 1758 (*pannagaçreshṭhaḥ*), 1760, 1762 (*pannagaçreshṭhaḥ*), (1764); **43**, (1766), 1776, (1782), 1783, 1785, 1786, 1789, 1790, 1798, 1800, 1801 (in accordance to the curse of Çṛṅgin *T.* bit Parikshit, having first prevailed upon Kāçyapa not to help Parikshit).—§ 52 (Janamejaya): I, **44,** 1804 (*pannagaçreshṭhaṃ*), †1806 (continuation).—§ 56 (Parikshit): I, **50,** 1973 (*nāgaḥ*), 1977, 1978 (*pannagottamāt*), 1979 (*pannagendraḥ*), 1980 (*bhujaṅgena*), (1982), 1984, 1985, 1987, 1988 (repetition from § 51).—§ 57 (Janamejaya): I, **50,** 1994, 1996, 2003, 2008, 2013 (Janamejaya, the son of Parikshit, wished to avenge himself on *T.*).—§ 58 (do.): I, **51,** 2017, 2019, 2022 (Janamejaya then prepared a snake-sacrifice).—§ 60 (Sarpasattra): I, **53,** 2054 (*nāgendraḥ*), 2056 (took his refuge to the palace of Indra).—§ 62 (do.): I, **56,** †2115, †2116, †2117, †2118, †2124, 2125 (*nāgaḥ*), 2126 (*pannagaṃ*), 2127, 2128, 2129, 2132, 2134 (*nāgendre*, by means of mantras *T.* was brought near to the sacrificial fire).—§ 64 (do.): I, **57,** 2149 (°*sya kule*, enumeration of the serpents of *T.'s* race who fell into the fire), 2151 (°*jā nāgāḥ*).—§ 68 (Āstīka): I, **58,** 2168, 2169 (Āstīka said thrice "stay", and *T.* remained in the air between the welkin and earth).—§ 100 (Aṃçāvat.): I, **65,** 2549 (*bhujaṅgamaḥ*, enumeration of the sons of Kadrū —*Kādraveyāḥ*).—§ 156 (Pūruvaṃç.): I, **95,** 3778 (°*duhitaraṃ Jvalāṃ*, wife of Ṛksha).—§ 254 (Khāṇḍavadahanap.): I, **223,** 8089 (*pannagaḥ*, friend of Indra, dwells in Khāṇḍava).—§ 258 (do.): I, **227,** 8236 (*nāgarājaḥ*, had gone to Kurukshetra), 8237 (*Açvasenaḥ . . . T°sya sutaḥ*); **228,** 8300 (*bhujagottamaḥ*, had gone to Kurukshetra), 8323 (°*sya niveçanāt*, i.e. Khāṇḍava).—§ 268 (Varuṇasabhāv.): II, **9,** 360 (in the palace of Varuṇa).—§ 358 (Tīrthayātrāp.): III, **82,** 5032 (*Kāçmīreshv eva nāgasya bhavanaṃ T°sya Vitastākhyaṃ*). — § 564 (Mātalīyop.): V, **103**γ, 3625 (enumeration of serpents).—§ 565 (Gālavacarita): V, **109,** 3798 (*nāgaḥ*, in Bhogavatī).—§ 586 (Bhīshmavadhap.): VI, **107,** 4900 (*yathā mahānāgas T°ḥ*).—§ 595 (Shoḍacarāj. v. Pṛthu Vainya): VII, **69,** 2415 (when the serpents milked the earth, *T.* was their calf).—§ 600 (Ghaṭotkacavadhap.): VII, **174**νν, 7873 (*Garuḍa-T°au*).—§ 603*d* (Tripura): VII, **202,** 9565 (became the avanāha (C. by error *mava°*) of Çiva's chariot).—§ 608 (Karṇap.): VIII, **79,** †4078 (°*bhogavarcasaṃ kārmukaṃ*); **87**χ, 4414 (sided with Arjuna). — § 790 (Putradarçanap.): XV, **35,** 952 (*muktaḥ*, all. to Sarpasattra). — § 793 (Mausalap.): XVI, **4**η, †119. Cf. Nāga, Nāgarāja, Nāgendra, Pannaga, Pannageçvara, Pannagendra.

Takshakaputra ("the son of Takshaka") = Açvasena: VIII, †4614.

Tala, Tāla = Çiva (1000 names[2]).

tāla ("palmyra palm"): XI, 721 (*tāladhvajarathasrajaḥ*, sc. the five Kaikayas); XVI, †62 (the device of Balarāma). Cf. Tāladhvaja, Tālaketu.

Tālacara, pl. (*āḥ*), a people. § 569 (Bhagavadyānap.): V, **140**β, 4451. Cf. Tālajaṅgha pl.

Tāladhvaja[1] ("whose banner shows the palmyra palm") = Bhīshma, q.v.—Do.[2] (do.) = Balarāma: IX, 1948 (*Rāmaḥ*), 2109, 3011.

Tālajaṅgha ("the king of the Tālajaṅghas?"). § 547 (Karṇa): III, **303,** 17014 (had been destroyed by the curse of a brahman (*brahmadaṇḍena*)).—§ 736*b* (Vītahavyop.): XIII, **30,** 1946 (Haihaya and *T.* were the sons of Vatsa). —§ 772*g* (Aurva): XIII, **154,** 7223 (°*m mahākshatram Aurveṇaikena nāçitaṃ*).

Tālajaṅgha, pl. (°*āḥ*), a people. § 387 (Sagara): III, **106,** 8832 (the Haihayas and the *T.* were vanquished by Sagara). —§ 562 (Bhagavadyānap.): V, **74**γ, 2729 (*Bahulas T°ānāṃ*). —§ 739 (Ānuçāsanik.): XIII, **34**γ, 2126 (vanquished by the Bhṛgus, cf. XIII, 7223).

Tālākaṭa, name of a city (?). § 284 (Sahadeva): II, **31,** 1169 (in the south, conquered by Sahadeva).

Tālaketu[1], a prince. § 317*b* (Kṛshṇa Vāsudeva): III, **12,** 492 (had been slain by Kṛshṇa).

Tālaketu[2] ("whose banner shows the palmyra palm") = Balarāma: IX, †2357.—Do.[3] = Bhīshma: V, 5081; VI, 1816.

Tālavana, pl. (°*āḥ*), a people. § 284 (Sahadeva): II, **31,** 1175 (in the south, vanquished by Sahadeva).

Tālin = Çiva (1000 names[2]).

Tamas[1], a brahman. § 736*b* (Vītahavyop.): XIII, **30,** 2002 (son of Çravas and father of Prakāça).

Tamas[2] = Çiva (1000 names[1]).

Tamasā, a river. § 494 (Āṅgirasa): III, **222,** 14231 (among the rivers who are mothers of fires). — § 574 (Jambūkh.): VI, **9**λ, 338.

Tamasī, a river. § 574 (Jambūkh.): VI, **9**λ, 339 (only C., B. has *Mānavī*).

***Tamoghna** ("destroying darkness") = Sūrya (the Sun): III, 193; VII, 6296.

Tamontakṛt, a warrior of Skanda. § 615*u* (Skanda): IX, **45**η, 2560.

***Tamonuda** ("dispersing darkness") = Sūrya (the Sun): III, 152, 11892, 17099; VI, 5765.

Tāmrā[1], wife of Kaçyapa (?). § 126 (Aṃçāvat.): I, **166,** 2620 (mother of five daughters: Kākī, Çyenī, Bhāsī, Dhṛtarāshṭrī, and Çukī).

Tāmrā[2], a river. § 459 (Mārkaṇḍeyas.): III, **188***a*, 12909 (seen in the body of Nārāyaṇa).—§ 574 (Jambūkh.): VI, **9**λ, 335.

Tāmracūḍa, a companion of Skanda. § 615*u* (Skanda): IX, **46,** 2669 (given to Skanda by Aruṇa; "a cock" PCR.).

Tāmracūḍā, a mātṛ. § 615*u* (Skanda): IX, **46**θ, 2636.

Tāmrāhvaya, name of a dvīpa. § 284 (Sahadeva): II, **31,** 1172 (*dvīpaṃ*, in the south, conquered by Sahadeva).

Tāmralipta ("the king of the Tāmraliptas"). § 232 (Svayaṃvarap.): I, **186,** 6993 (present at the svayaṃvara of Draupadī).—§ 280 (Bhīmasena): II, **30,** 1098 (*rājānaṃ*, in the east, conquered by Bhīmasena).

Tāmralipta, pl. (°*āḥ*), a people. § 295 (Dyūtap.): II, **52,** 1874 (brought tribute to Yudhishṭhira). Cf. next.

Tāmraliptaka, pl. (°*āḥ*), a people (= the prec.). § 574 (Jambūkh.): VI, **9**μ, 364.—§ 595 (Shoḍaçarāj., v. Rāma Jāmadagnya): VII, **70**β, 2436 (slain by Rāma Jāmadagnya). —§ 599 (Jayadrathavadhap.): VII, **119,** 4710, (ββ), 4722 (have been vanquished by Sātyaki).—§ 605 (Karṇap.): VIII, **22**ζζ, 863 (attacked the Pāñcālas), (θθ), 882 (attacked Nakula).

Tāmraparṇī[1], a tīrtha. § 377 (Dhaumyatīrthak.): III, **88,** 8340 (in the south).—Do.[2], a mountain (= Malaya). § 574 (Jambukh.): VI, **6,** 252 (C. has *T°ī çilā*, but B. reads *tāmraparṇaçilaḥ*, sc. *Malayaparvataḥ*).

Tāmrāruṇa, a tīrtha. § 370 (Tīrthayātrāp.): III, **84,** 8132. Cf. next.

Tāmrāruṇā, a river. § 775 (Ānuçāsanik.): XIII, **166***a*, 7647. Cf. the prec.

Tāmraushṭha, a Yaksha. § 269 (Vaiçravaṇasabhāv.): II, **10,** 398 (in the palace of Kubera).

Tāmravatī, a river. § 494 (Āṅgirasa): III, **222,** 14231 (among the rivers who are mothers of fires).

Tāmroshṭha = Çiva (1000 names[2]).

Taṃsu, an ancient king. § 150 (Pūruvaṃç.): I, **94,** 3704 (son of Matināra), 3705, 3706 (father of Īlina).—§ 156 (do.):

I, **95**, ††3779 (son of Matināra and Sarasvatī), 3780 (do., husband of Kālingī and father of Īlina).

Tanabāla, pl. (°*āḥ*), a people. § 574 (Jambūkh.): VI, **9**ν, 371 (in the south).

Tanaya, pl. (°*āḥ*), a people. § 574 (Jambūkh.): VI, **9**ν, 371 (in the south).

Taṇḍi, a ṛshi. § 730 (Ānuçāsanik.): XIII, **14**, 607 (*Brahmayoninā*, recited the 1000 names of Çiva); **16**, 1037 (*ṛshiḥ*, in Kṛtayuga, worshipped Çiva), (1049), 1103, 1104, 1111, 1113 (taught Upamanyu the 1000 names of Çiva); **17**, 1116 (*ṛshiṇā*), 1136 (°*kṛtaḥ*, obtained the 1000 names of Çiva from heaven), 1137, 1283 (praised Çiva with the 1000 names), 1288, 1289 (communicated them to Çukra). Cf. Brahmayoni.

Taṇḍūlikāçrama (*Taṇḍu*°, B.), a tīrtha. § 358 (Tīrthayātrāp.): III, **82**, 4084.

Tāṇḍya, one or more ṛshis. § 266 (Çakrasabhāv.): II, **7**, 294 (in the palace of Indra).—§ 677 (Mokshadh.): XII, **245**β, 8900.—§ 702 (do.): XII, **293**a, 1076 (praised Vishṇu); **297**δ, 10874.—§ 717c (Uparicara): XII, **337**ε, 12758 (*mahān ṛshiḥ*, among the sadasyas at the sacrifice of Vasu Uparicara).

Taṅgaṇa, pl. (°*āḥ*), a people. § 295 (Dyūtap.): II, **52**, 1859 (*T°āḥ para-T°āḥ*, brought tribute to Yudhishṭhira).—§ 342 (Indralokābhigamanap.): III, **51**, 1991 (had been present at the rājasūya).—§ 419 (Gandhamādanapr.): III, **140**, 10864 (*Kirāta-T°ākīrṇam*, sc. *Subāhuvishayam*).—§ 574 (Jambūkh.): VI, **9**ν, 372 (*T°āḥ para-T°āḥ*). — § 578 (Bhīshmavadhap.): VI, **50**π. 2083 (do., in the army of Yudhishṭhira).—§ 599 (Jayadrathavadhap.): VII, **121**εε, 4819 (°*āmbashṭhāḥ*, in the army of Duryodhana), (θθ), 4847 (attack Sātyaki).—§ 604 (Karṇap.): VIII, **8**, 235 (had formerly been vanquished by Karṇa).—§ 608 (do.): VIII, **73**, 3652 (only B., C. has °*Kauṅkaṇāḥ*; in the army of Duryodhana, had been vanquished by Arjuna).—§ 785 (Anugītāp.): XIV, **83**, 2469 (the sacrificial horse went to the country of the *T*.).

Tantipāla, the name which Sahadeva assumed in the palace of Virāṭa. § 549 (Pāṇḍavapraveçap.): IV, **3**, 68 (C. by error °*tri*°); **10**, 289.

Tantripāla v. Tantipāla.

Tantuvardhana = Vishṇu (1000 names).

Tanu, a ṛshi. § 641 (Mokshadh.): XII, **127**, 4665 (*ṛshim*), 4671, 4677 (*munivarottamaḥ*), 4708 (in the shape of *T*. Dharma put Vīradyumna to the test). Cf. Devarshi.

Tanuvāsas = Çiva: X, 259.

Tapaḥsakta = Çiva (1000 names[2]).

Tapaḥsuta = Yudhishṭhira: III, 17306.

Tapana[1] = Sūrya: I, 1249 (Garuḍa identified with Sūrya), 4398, 6535, 6609; III, 192, 8217 (°*sya sutā Yamunā*), 17138 (*tapatām varaḥ*); V, 4920.

Tapana[2], a Nāga (?) (according to Nīl. a Yaksha). § 46 (Garuḍa): I, **32**a, 1488.

Tapana[3], a Pāñcāla warrior. § 608 (Karṇap.): VIII, **48**ν, 2248 (slain by Karṇa).

Tapana[4] = Çiva (1000 names[1]).

Tapa(s), name of several fires. § 492 (Āṅgirasa): III, **220**, 14166, 14167, 14168 (created the fifteen *yajñamushas*).—§ 493 (do.): III, **220**, 14173 (father of Bṛhaduktha), 14174 (father of Rathantara); **221**, 14178, 14182 (father of five fires), 14183 (°*saç ca Manum putram*).—§ 500 (Skandop.): III, **228**, 14392 (°*o nāma Hutāçanaḥ*, father of seven kumārīs who became *mātṛs*).

Tapas[1] = Mahāpurusha (Mahāpurushastava).—Do.[2] = Çiva (1000 names[1]).—Do.[3] = Kṛshṇa (Vishṇu): XII, 13143.

Tāpasāraṇya, a tīrtha. § 377 (Dhaumyatīrthak.): III, **87**, 8316.

Tapasvin = Çiva (1000 names[2]).

Tapatām gati(ḥ) = Çiva: X, 257.

Tapatī, daughter of Sūrya (the Sun) and wife of Saṃvaraṇa. § 154 (Pūruvaṃç.): I, **94**, 3738 (*Saurī*, by Saṃvaraṇa, mother of Kuru).—§ 156 (do.): I, **95**, ††3791 (*Vaivasvatīm*, do.).—§ 222 (Tapatyup.): I, **171**, 6517, 6521, 6530, 6535; **172**, 6563 (6578), 6578 (*Sāvitryavarajā sutā*); **173**, 6598, 6605 (*Sāvitryavarajā sutā*), 6608, 6609, 6610, 6612, 6616, 6628, 6631, 6632 (*Vaivasvatī*, the story of Saṃvaraṇa's getting *T*. as his wife). Cf. Saurī, Sāvitryavarajā, Vaivasvatī.

Tāpatya, pl. ("descendants of Tapatī"). § 222 (Tapatyup.): I, **171**, 6517.

Tāpatya, sg. (do.) = Arjuna: I, 6514, 6516, 6632.

Tāpatya, adj. ("relating to Tapatī"). § 11 (Parvasaṅgr.): I, **2**, 387 (*ākhyānam*, i.e. Tapatyupākhyāna).

Tāpatyavardhana = Arjuna: I, 6505.

[Tapaty-upākhyāna(m)] ("the episode relating to Tapatī"). § 222 (Caitrarathap.). *Arjuna* asked why he had called him *Tāpatya*, and *Citraratha* said: "*Sūrya* had a lovely daughter *Tapatī*, the younger sister of *Sāvitrī*. *Ṛksha's* son, the king *Saṃvaraṇa*, duly worshipped *Sūrya*; to him *Sūrya* resolved to bestow his daughter. Once, when *Saṃvaraṇa* went on a hunting expedition, his steed died from fatigue on the mountain, and he began to wander on foot and saw *Tapatī* alone, and declared her his love. She did not speak a word, but disappeared. He wandered through the whole forest in search of her, and failing to find her, indulged in lamentations (I, **171**). He fell down on the earth. Then she appeared again. He asked her to marry him according to the *Gāndharva* form of marriage. She said that she loved him, but told him to ask her father *Āditya* for her hand, with worship, ascetic penances, and vows (I, **172**). *Tapatī* then ascended to the skies, and *Saṃvaraṇa* again fell down on the earth. At last his followers found him, and his minister raised him up and sprinkled his head with water, etc. Regaining his consciousness, *Saṃvaraṇa* sent away all his attendants with the exception of his minister alone, and then began to worship *Sūrya*. He also thought of his *purohita*, the *ṛshi Vasishṭha*. After the king had stayed thus on the same spot day and night, the *Viprarshi Vasishṭha* came there on the 12th day. *Vasishṭha* knew at once, by his ascetic power, what had happened and ascended to the sky in order to see *Sūrya*, and asked him to give *Tapatī* to *Saṃvaraṇa*. *Saṃvaraṇa*, with due rites, took *Tapatī's* hand on that mountain resorted to by the gods and the *Gandharvas*. And the king caused *Vasishṭha* to be proclaimed his regent in his capital and kingdom, etc., and sported with his wife in the woods on that mountain for twelve years. Now *Indra* for twelve years poured no rain in his capital and kingdom. Then *Vasishṭha* brought *Saṃvaraṇa* and his wife back into the city, and then *Indra* poured rain in abundance. *Saṃvaraṇa*, with *Tapatī*, performed sacrifices for twelve years. Their son was *Kuru*, the ancestor of *Arjuna* (I, **173**).

Tapishnu ("burning") = Sūrya (the Sun): XII, 11726.

Tapodāna, a tīrtha. § 775 (Ānuçāsanik.): XIII, **166**a, 7650.

Tapomaya, Taponidhi = Çiva (1000 names[2]).

Taponishṭha = Çiva: X, 257.

Taponitya = Çiva (1000 names[1]).
Taporata = Civa: VIII, 1449.
Taptatapas = Çiva: XIV, 204.
Tapya, Tara = Çiva (1000 names[1]).
Tāra[1], name of a monkey. § 537 (Rāma-Rāvaṇayuddha): III, **285**, 16372 (fought with Nikharvaṭa).—§ 539 (Kumbhakarṇādivadha): III, **287**, 16415 (*°prabhṛtayaḥ*).—§ 541 (Indrajidvadha): III, **289** *a*, 16468.
Tāra[2] = Vishṇu (1000 names).
Tārā[1], wife of the monkey Vālin. § 531 (Rāmopākhyānap.): III, **280**, 16108, 16110 (*tārādhipānanāṃ*), 16112 (*tārādhipaprabhā*), 16118, 16130, 16131 (*tārāpatimukhīṃ*).
Tārā[2], wife of Bṛhaspati. § 565 (Gālavacarita): V, **117**, 3972 (*reme . . . yathā . . . Bṛhaspatiç ca T°āyāṃ*).
***Tārādhipa** ("lord of the stars") = Soma (the Moon): I, 2667 (*°opamaḥ*), 2760; III, 16110 (*°ānanāṃ*), 16112 (*°prabhā*); XI, 563 (*°opamaṃ*); XII, †11096, 13017; XIII, 5861 (*sutā T°syeva*).
Tāraka[1], an Asura. § 585 (Bhīshmavadhap.): VI, **95**, 4249 (*varayasva . . . yathendras T°ṃ purā*).—§ 600 (Ghaṭotkacavadhap.): VII, **155**, 6718 (*yathāmbupatīndrau hi T°ṃ Daityasattamaṃ*, sc. *dhāvatāṃ*); **173**, 7837 (*yathendras T°ṃ pūrvaṃ Skandena saha jaghnivān*). — § 606 (Tripurākhyāna): VIII, **33**, 1395 (father of Tārāksha, Kamalāksha, and Vidyunmālin). — § 608 (Karṇap.): VIII, **53**, 2588 (*yathendraḥ . . . T°sya vadhe*).—§ 612 (Hradapraveçap.): IX, **31**ζ, 1754 (*mahā-Daityaḥ*, slain).—§ 615 (Baladevatīrthayātrāp.): IX, **43**, 2448 (*yasmin*—i.e. in Somasya tīrthaṃ — *yuddhaṃ T°ākhyaṃ sutīvraṃ yatra Skandas T°ākhyaṃ jaghāna*).—§ 615*u* (Skanda): IX, **46**λ, 2691 (*Daityendraṃ*, slain by Skanda).—§ 747*b* (Suvarṇotpatti): XIII, **84**, 4011 (*Asuraḥ*); **85**, 4015 (do.), 4017, 4028 (*°vadhopāyaḥ*), 4066 (*Asuraḥ*), 4181 (*Daityaṃ*) (*T.* scorched the gods, then Skanda was born from Agni, that he might slay *T.*).—§ 748 (Ānuçāsanik.): XIII, **86**, 4187, 4189 (*°vadhaṃ*).—§ 748*b* (Tārakavadhop.): XIII, **86**, 4212, 4213, 4214 (*Dānavaṃ*, is slain by Skanda). Cf. Asura, Daiteya, Daitya, Daityasattama, Daityendra, Dānava.
Tāraka[2] = Çiva (1000 names[1]).
Tāraka, pl., the sons of Tāraka[1]. § 606 (Tripurākhyāna): VII, **34**, 1553.
Tārakāksha, an Asura. § 603*d* (Tripura): VII, **202**, 9556 (lord of the silvern city).—§ 606 (Tripurākhyāna): VIII, **33**, 1411 (lord of the golden city, C. has by error *°akhya°*). Cf. Tārāksha.
Tārakākshasuta ("the son of Tārakāksha") = Hari[5]: VIII, 1417 (*H°*), 1419.
Tārāksha = Tārakāksha: VIII, 1395.
Tārakāmaya[1], adj. ("causing evil to Tāraka"?). § 277 (Jarāsandhavadhap.): II, **24**, 939 (*Çakra-Vishṇū hi saṅgrāmam ceratus T°e rathena tena*).—§ 279 (Arjuna): II, **27**, 1034 (*°saṅkāçaḥ*, sc. *saṅgrāmaḥ*).—§ 334*b* (Varuṇa): III, **41**, 1694 (*saṅgrāme*). — § 444 (Nivātakavacayuddhap.): III, **169**, 12102 (*astuvaṃ munayaḥ . . . yathendraṃ T°e*).—§ 584 (Bhīshmavadhap.): VI, **83**, 3664 (*yathā Vajradharaḥ pūrvaṃ saṅgrāme T°e*, sc. *nāgarājaṃ samāsthitaḥ*).—§ 597 (Pratijñāp.): VII, **84**, 2994 (*sahāmbupati-Mitrābhyāṃ yathendras T°e*, sc. *prayātaḥ*).—§ 599 (Jayadrathavadhap.): VII, **94**, 3480 (*yathā vai Brahmaṇā baddhaṃ saṅgrāme T°e Çakrasya kavacaṃ*). —§ 600 (Ghaṭotkacavadhap.): VII, **168**, 7540 (*yathendrabhayavitrastā Dānavās T°e*).—§ 605 (Karṇap.): VIII, **10**, 399 (*devair api yathā Skandaḥ saṅgrāme T°e*, sc. *vṛtaḥ*).—§ 606 (Tripurākhyāna): VIII, **33**, 1394 (*saṅgrāmaḥ*).—§ 615 (Baladevatīrthayātrā): IX, **51**, 2925 (*saṅgrāmaḥ*, took place in Somatīrtha).
Tārakāmaya[2] = Çiva (1000 names[1]).
Tārakārāja ("king of the stars") = Soma (the Moon): III, 1678.
Tārakavadhopākhyāna ("the episode relating to the destruction of Tāraka"; continuation of Suvarṇotpatti, § 747*b*). § 748*b* (Ānuçāsanik.): D. and Ṛ., reduced to great distress [by Tāraka's prowess and the conduct of Gaṅgā by throwing away Agni's seed], urged the six *Kṛttikāḥ* to rear that child [i.e. Skanda]. Amongst the celestial ladies there were none, save these, that could bear the seed of *Agni* in their wombs. *Agni* became gratified. His energy was divided into six portions, and a portion was placed in each of the *Kṛttikās*. All of them were delivered at the same time, and the six portions united into one. The Earth received the child from a heap of gold. He grew up in a celestial forest of reeds, reared by the *Kṛttikās* (whence he came to be called *Kārttikeya*; etymology of *Skanda* and *Guha*). The thirty-three gods, etc. (*α*) came to see him; Ṛ. praised him, G. sang in honour of *Kumāra*, with six faces, etc. (description). The gods gave him various kinds of toys, etc. (*β*). Rā. and As. began to walk in the train of *Skanda*. *Tāraka* in vain sought, by various means, to slay him. The gods made him the commander of their forces, and when he had grown up he slew *Tāraka* with his irresistible dart as in sport, and re-established *Indra* in the sovereignty. *Skanda* became the protector of the gods and [always] did what was agreeable to *Çaṅkara* (i.e. Çiva). Gold is the powerful energy of *Agni* and was born [from the same seed] with *Kārttikeya*; hence gold is highly auspicious. Thus did *Vasishṭha* relate to *Rāma* [*Jāmadagnya*] in days of old. By making gifts of gold *Rāma* became purified of all his sins, and [finally] attained to a high place in heaven that is not easily attainable by men (XIII, **86**).
Tarala, pl. (*°āḥ*), a people. § 604 (Karṇap.): VIII, **8**, 237 (had formerly been vanquished by Karṇa).
tārāmṛga ("star-antelope"). § 529 (Sītāharaṇa): III, **278**, 16020 (*anvadhāvan mṛgaṃ Rāmo Rudras t°ṃ yathā*). Cf. Mṛgaçiras.
Tāraṇa[1] = Çiva (1000 names[2]).—Do.[2] = Vishṇu (1000 names).
Taraṇḍaka (III, 6022), v. Arantuka.
Taraṅgāṅkitakeça = Çiva (1000 names[1]).
Taraṅgavid = Çiva (1000 names[2]).
Tarantuka, name of a dvārapala and a tīrtha belonging to him. § 362 (Tīrthayātrāp.): III, **83**, 5085 (*dvārapālaṃ*).—§ 369 (Kurukshetra): III, **83**, †7078 (v. Arantuka).—§ 615*kk* (Kurukshetrakath.): IX, **53**, †3032 (v. Arantuka).
Tārāpati ("lord of the stars") = Soma (the Moon): III, 16131 (*°mukhīṃ*), 16638 (*iva*), 17126 (*iva*); VI, 4875 (*iva*); VII, 1766 (*iva*).
Tāriṇī = Durgā (Umā): VI, 797.
***tarkaçāstra** ("philosophical treatise"): XII, 8968, 9678 (pl.), 9679 (pl.).
Tārkshya[1], one or more ṛshis, especially = Arishṭanemi. § 11 (Parvasaṅgr.): I, **2**, 467 (*saṃvādaḥ Sarasvatyās T°arsheḥ*, cf. § 456).—§ 99 (Aṃçāvat.): I, **65**, 2548.—§ 191 (Arjuna): I, **123**, 4830.—§ 266 (Çakrasabhāv.): II, **7**, 299 (in the palace of Indra).—§ 454 (Brāhmaṇamāhātmyak.): III, **184**, 12660 (*Arishṭanemnaḥ*), 12665.—§ 456 (Sarasvatī-Tārkshyasaṃv.): III, **186**, 12715 (*muninā*), (†12716), †12718, †12730, (†12731), †12733, (†12735),

(†12737), (†12740) (discourse between Sarasvatī and *T.*).—§ 700 (Mokshadh.): XII, **289,** 10615 (= Arishṭanemi).

Tārkshya[2] = Garuḍa: I, 1405, 1414, 5886 (*mārutaraṃhasaḥ*); II, 34 (*rathaṃ T° ketanaṃ*, i.e. Kṛshṇa's chariot), 1620 (*rathaṃ . . . T°pravaraketanaṃ*, do.); V, 3691, 3850, 3919, 3922; VII, 554 (°*s tan nāgam iva cākshipat*), 3675 (°-*mārutaraṃhobhiḥ*), 5769 (*hartuṃ T°a ivoragaṃ*); VIII, †816 (°*hatāv ivoragau*), 1027 (°*tulyaparākramaḥ*), 1082 (*agacchan nilayaṃ sarve T°ṃ dṛshṭveva pannagāḥ*), †4549 (°*trastā bhūmim ivoragās te*, sc. *viviçuḥ*); XII, 1586 (°*dhvajinaṃ*, sc. the chariot of Kṛshṇa); XIII, 632, 1802 (*bhavanti nirvishāḥ sarpā yathā T°sya darçanāt*).

Tārkshya[3] = Çiva (1000 names[1–2]).

Tārkshya, pl. (°*āḥ*), a people. § 295 (Dyūtap.): II, **52,** 1871 (brought tribute to Yudhishṭhira).

Tārkshyakapidhvaja, dual ("the banners of Kṛshṇa and Arjuna"): VIII, 1829.

Tārkshyaketana ("having Garuḍa in his banner") = Kṛshṇa: XII, 1712.

Tārkshyalakshaṇa (do.): XII, 1512.

Taru[1] = Çiva (1000 names[2]).—Do.[2] = Vishṇu (1000 names).

Taruṇa, name of a Gandharva (?). § 266 (Çakrasabhāv.): II, **7,** 303 (in the palace of Indra).

Taruṇaka, a serpent. § 67 (Sarpasattra): I, **57,** 2160 (of Dhṛtarāshṭra's race).

Tasthushāṃ patiḥ = Kṛshṇa: XII, 1625.

Taṭa, Taṭānāṃ pati(ḥ) = Çiva (1000 names[1]).

Tatpada = Kṛshṇa: XII, 1605.

Tattva, Tattvavid = Vishṇu (1000 names).

Taṭya = Çiva (1000 names[1]).

Tejas[1] ("light", personif.). § 270 (Brahmasabhāv.): II, **11,** 438 (in the palace of Brahmán).

Tejas[2] = Sūrya (the Sun): III, 147.—Do.[3] = Çiva (1000 names[2]).—Do.[4] = Vishṇu (1000 names).

Tejasāṃ patiḥ = Sūrya (the Sun): III, 149.

Tejaskaro nidhi(ḥ) = Çiva (1000 names[2]).

Tejasvin[1], name of one of the five Indras. § 238 (Pañcendrop.): I, **197,** 7304.

Tejasvin[2] = Çiva (1000 names[1]).

Tejeyu, son of Raudrāçva. § 150 (Pūruvaṃç.): I, **94,** 3701 (seventh son of Raudrāçva).

Tejopahārin = Çiva (1000 names[2]).

tena, pl. (XII, 10868), v. stena, pl.

Tigmamanyu = Çiva (1000 names[2]).

Tigmāṃçu[1] = Sūrya (the Sun): I, 420; III, 16981, †17125; XV, 830.—Do.[2] = Agni (q.v.).

Tigmatejas = Çiva (1000 names[2]).

Tīkshṇa, Tīkshṇadaṃshṭra = Çiva: XIV, 201.

Tīkshṇatāpa = Çiva (1000 names[2]).

Tilabhāra, pl. (°*āḥ*), a people. § 574 (Jambūkh.): VI, **9**μ, 360.

Tilottamā, name of an Apsaras. § 103 (Aṃçāvat.): I, **65,** 2557 (daughter of Prādhā).—§ 191 (Arjuna): I, **123,** 4818 (danced at the birth of Arjuna).—§ 245 (Rājyalābhap.): I, **208,** 7614, 7617 (*Apsarā devakanyā*, all. to § 246).—§ 246*b* (Sundopasundop.): *Brahmán* caused *Viçvakarman* to make a celestial maiden from small portions of every kind of gem, whence she was called *Tilottamā* (v. 7696). *Brahmán* was sitting with his face turned eastwards and the *ṛshis* facing all directions. As *T.* was walking round them, there appeared three other faces on the body of Mahādeva and 1000 eyes on Indra, while all the other celestials, only excepting Pitāmaha, and the *ṛshis* gazed at her: I, **211,** 7696 (etymology), 7698, 7707, 7710.—§ 246 (do.): I, **212,** 7719, 7723, 7732, 7736 (Sunda and Upasunda quarrelled on account of *T.*).—§ 768*b* (Umā-Maheçvarasaṃv.): XIII, **141,** 6390 (repetition from § 246*b*). — § 775 (Ānuçāsanik.): XIII, **166**β, 7641 (enumeration of Apsarases).

Timiṅgila, a king. § 284 (Sahadeva): II, **31,** 1172 (*nṛpaṃ*, in the south, vanquished by Sahadeva).

Tīragraha, pl. (°*āḥ*), a people. § 574 (Jambūkh.): VI, **9**μ, 360.

tīrtha, pl. (°*āṇi*) ("bathing-place", personif.). § 615*u* (Skanda): IX, **45**γ, 2514 (came to the investiture of Skanda).

Tīrthadeva = Çiva (1000 names[2]).

Tīrthakara = Vishṇu (1000 names).

Tīrthamahāhrada, name of a tīrtha. § 775 (Ānuçāsanik.): XIII, **166***a*, 7654.

Tīrthasenī, a mātṛ. § 615*u* (Skanda): IX, **46**θ, 2625.

Tīrthayātrā ("the pilgrimage to the tīrthas", sc. of Yudhishṭhira, etc.). § 10 (Parvasaṅgr.): I, **2,** 322 (°*ā parva . . . Kururājasya dhīmataḥ*, cf. Tīrthayātrāparvan).—§ 11 (do.): I, **2,** 440 (*Pāṇḍavānāṃ*, cf. Tīrthayātrāparvan). § 620 (Çrāddhap.): XI, **26,** 774 (°*prasaṅgena*, all. to Tīrthayātrāp.).

[Tīrthayātrāparvan(°va)] ("the episode relating to the pilgrimage to the tīrthas", the 36th of the minor parvans of Mhbhr. Cf. Tīrthayātrā). § 356: *Draupadī*, *Bhīmasena*, *Nakula*, and *Sahadeva* lamented *Arjuna*; *Sahadeva* suggested to move from the *Kāmyaka* wood (III, **80**). Then came the *devarshi Nārada* who, at the request of *Yudhishṭhira*, told them what the *brahmarshi Pulastya* had formerly said to *Bhīshma* about the merits of circumambulating (*pradakshiṇāṃ yaḥ kurute*) the earth for the purpose of visiting the *tīrthas*, when *Bhīshma* was engaged in a *pitrya vrata* at *Gaṅgādvāra* (resorted to by *devarshis*, *Gandharvas*, and gods) in the company of *munis*, and made oblations to the *pitṛs*, gods, and *ṛshis* (III, **81**). At *Bhīshma's* request *Pulastya* explained the qualities of a person who will acquire merit by visiting *tīrthas*; he said that the costly sacrifices, which only kings and very rich men are capable of affording, are not of greater merit than a sojourn in *tīrthas*, which even the poorest may accomplish.—§ 357: Then he first described *Pushkara* (q.v.).—§ 358: Then he enumerated a great many of tīrthas and the merit of visiting them.—§ 359: *Vaḍavā* (q.v.).—§ 360: *Pulastya's* enumeration of tīrthas continued (III, **82**).—§ 361: *Kurukshetra* (q.v.).—§ 362: The enumeration continued.—§ 363: *Rāmahradāḥ* (q.v.).—§ 364: The enumeration continued.—§ 365: *Maṅkaṇaka* (q.v.).—§ 366: The enumeration continued.—§ 367: *Pṛthūdaka* (q.v.).—§ 368: The enumeration continued.—§ 369: *Kurukshetra* (q.v.).—§ 370: The enumeration continued (III, **84**).—§ 371: *Tuṅgaka* (q.v.). — § 372: The enumeration continued.—§ 373: *Prayāga* (q.v.).—§ 374: The enumeration continued.—§ 375: *Gaṅgā* is equal to *Kurukshetra*, wherever one may bathe in it, especially in *Kanakhala* and in *Prayāga*, which is the most excellent; a bath in the *Gaṅgā* in that place removes 100 sins. In the *Kṛtayuga* all the tīrthas were sacred, in the *Tretāyuga Pushkara* alone, in the *Dvāpara Kurukshetra*, in the *Kaliyuga Gaṅgā*. In *Pushkara* one should practise austerities, in *Mahālaya* one should make gifts, on the *Malaya* one should ascend the funeral pyre, in *Bhṛgutuṅga* one should kill oneself by fasting; bathing in *Pushkara*, *Kurukshetra*, the *Gaṅgā*, and *Magadha* (PCR. seems to have had another reading) one purifies seven generations of one's race upwards and downwards, etc.; as long as one's bones lie in contact with the water of the *Gaṅgā*, so long does one live, honoured in heaven (*Svargaloke*). *Pitāmaha* has said that no *tīrtha* is equal to the *Gaṅgā*, no God to *Keçava*, and none is superior to brahmans. This truthful description one should recite only to the twice-born, etc. (*). In these *tīrthas* have bathed the *Vasus*, the *Sādhyas* (so B.), the *Ādityas*, the *Maruts*, the *Açvins*, and the *Ṛshis*, who are equal to the gods. Only men of piety and learning are able to visit these *tīrthas* on account of their purified senses, their belief in god (*āstikyāt*), and their acquaintance with the *Vedas* (end of *Pulastya's* discourse, in which Yudhishṭhira sometimes is addressed instead of Bhīshma).—§ 376: *Nārada* continued: Then *Pulastya* disappeared, and *Bhīshma* (who understood the *çāstras*), at the command of *Pulastya*, wandered over the earth and ended his *tīrthayātrā* at *Prayāga*. The man that so walks about the earth is rewarded after death as much as for 100 horse sacrifices. "So wilt thou *Yudhishṭhira* obtain the eight-fold (*ashṭaguṇam*) *dharma*, as *Bhīshma* did before, and because thou wilt lead the ṛshis, thy merit will be eight-fold; those *tīrthas* are infested by *Rākshasas*, and no king, save thyself, has gone there (*). The foremost of ṛshis are always there and expect thee: *Vālmīki, Kaçyapa, Ātreya, Kuṇḍajaṭhara, Viçvāmitra, Gautama, Asita Devala, Mārkaṇḍeya, Gālava, Bharadvāja, Vasishṭha, Uddālaka, Çaunaka* with his son, *Vyāsa, Durvāsas*, and *Jābāli*. With them do thou visit these *tīrthas*. The great *ṛshi Lomaça* will come to thee, do thou follow him and me to these *tīrthas*." Then *Nārada* disappeared and *Yudhishṭhira* spoke to the ascetics of the *tīrthas* (III, **85**).—§ 377: *Dhaumya-tīrthakathana* (q.v.).—§ 378: While *Dhaumya* was speaking thus, *Lomaça* arrived and told that *Arjuna* had obtained *Brahmaçiras* (*b*), learnt the *Gāndharva Veda*, etc. (III, **91**). *Lomaça* said that *Arjuna* had asked him to cause *Yudhishṭhira* to visit all *tīrthas*, like *Manu* and other *rājarshis*, and protect him from the *Rākshasas* as *Dadhīca* had protected *Indra* and *Aṅgiras* had protected the *Sun*. *Lomaça* had twice before visited the *tīrthas*. At the command of *Lomaça*, *Yudhishṭhira* caused the citizens, brahmans, and *Yatis*, who were not able to endure the privations of the journey, to return to *Hāstinapura*, where *Dhṛtarāshṭra* gave them their proper allowances from affection for *Yudhishṭhira*, and *Yudhishṭhira*, with only a small number of brahmans abode for three nights at *Kāmyaka* cheered by *Lomaça* (III, **92**). The brahmans, who dwelt in the wood, prevailed upon *Yudhishṭhira* that he allowed them to partake of the *tīrthayātrā*. Just when they were about to start, *Vyāsa, Parvata*, and *Nārada* came to *Kāmyaka*, and caused them not only to fulfil human vows by purifying the body, but even divine vows by purifying the heart, that it might be free from evil thoughts and harbour only friendly feelings towards everybody. When those celestial and human ṛshis had performed the usual propitiatory ceremonies, and when they had worshipped the feet of *Lomaça, Dvaipāyana, Nārada*, and the *devarshi Parvata*, the *Pāṇḍavas* and *Kṛshṇā* started towards the east with *Dhaumya* and the ascetics on the day following Mārgaçīrshī, when *Pushya* was in ascendance, dressed in bark and hides, with matted locks, cased in mail, and armed with swords, etc., with *Indrasena* and other attendants with some fourteen (*paricaturdaçaiḥ*) chariots and a number of cooks (III, **93**). As *Yudhishṭhira* asked why he who is virtuous is unhappy, and his enemies who are sinful, happy, *Lomaça* said that sinful men often prosper in consequence of their sins, but at last they are overtaken by destruction, even as in the *devayuga* the *Daiteyas* and *Dānavas* (*Asuras*), who practised vice (*adharma*) and did not visit the *tīrthas*, for a time prospered by their sin and vanquished the gods, who practised virtue and visited the *tīrthas*; at last, when the good qualities, prosperity, etc., left the Asuras and went to the gods, while bad qualities, adversity, etc., came to the *Asuras*, and *Kali* possessed them, they were overtaken by destruction. *Nṛga, Çibi Auçīnara, Bhagīratha, Vasumanas, Gaya, Pūru*, and *Purūravas* had by practising ascetic penances and visiting *tīrthas*, etc., obtained fame and wealth, etc., and so would *Yudhishṭhira*, and as *Ikshvāku* with his sons, etc., and *Mucukunda, Māndhātṛ*, and *Marutta*, and the gods and *devarshis* obtained fame by the power of asceticism, so would *Yudhishṭhira*, while the *Dhārtarāshṭras*, enslaved by sinfulness and ignorance, soon would be exterminated (III, **94**).—§ 379: The *Pāṇḍavas* with their followers, proceeding from place to place, at last arrived at *Naimisha*, and thence to the *Gomatī*, etc. (enumeration of *tīrthas* visited).—§ 380: *Brahmasaras* (q.v.).—§ 381: *Gaya* (q.v.).—§ 382: Thence they came to the hermitage of *Agastya*, and dwelt in *Durjayā* (i.e. *Maṇimatī*, the city of *Vātāpi*, Nīl.); there asked by *Yudhishṭhira Lomaça* told: *Agastyopākhyāna* (q.v.).—§ 383: Description of the *Gaṅgā* (*b*). Then, having at the suggestion of *Lomaça*, with his brothers and *Kṛshṇā*, bathed in *Bhṛgos tīrtham* (*c*) and gratified the gods and *Pitṛs*, *Yudhishṭhira* blazed forth in brighter effulgence and became invincible. At his request *Lomaça* told *Jāmadagnyatejohānikathana* (*b*) (v. *Rāma*[1]).—§ 384: *Yudhishṭhira* wished to hear the details of *Agastya*. *Lomaça* related: *Agastyopākhyāna* (q.v.).—§ 385: At the request of *Yudhishṭhira Lomaça* related how *Agastya* had caused *Vindhya* (q.v.) to cease to increase (§ 385), how *Agastya* drank up the Ocean (§ 386, cf. Agastyopākhyāna), *Sagara* (§ 387), *Asamañjas* (§ 388), *Gaṅgāvataraṇa* (§ 389).—§ 390: Then *Yudhishṭhira* proceeded to the rivers *Nandā* and *Aparanandā* and the *Hemakūṭa* (*b*, cf. *Ṛshabhakūṭa*) mountain. Having, at the command of *Lomaça*, bathed in *Nandā*, they proceeded to the river *Kauçikī* (*c*) with the hermitages of *Viçvāmitra* and of *Kāçyapa*, the father of *Ṛshyaçṛṅga* (*d*).—§ 391: At the request of *Yudhishṭhira Lomaça* told the history of *Ṛshyaçṛṅga* (q.v.)—§ 392: Starting from *Kauçikī*, *Yudhishṭhira* in succession repaired to all the sacred shrines (*āyatanāni*) and came to the sea where the *Gaṅgā* falls into it, and bathed in the centre of 500 rivers. Then they proceeded by the shore of the sea towards the *Kaliṅga* country. *Lomaça* said: "Here is the river *Vaitaraṇī* (*b*)." When they had all bathed in the *Vaitaraṇī*, *Yudhishṭhira* felt as if he were carried off from the region of men, and beheld all worlds, and heard the reciting of *Vaikhānasas*, whom *Lomaça* declared to be at the distance of 300,000 *yojanas*. *Lomaça* ordered him to be silent, as this was the divine forest of *Svayambhu* (*Svayambhuvo vanam*) (*c*); taught by *Lomaça* the words to be recited (*Oṃ namo viçvaguptāya*, etc. [*a*]) *Yudhishṭhira* mounted the altar of *Kaçyapa* and bathed in the sea; then he went to the *Mahendra* mountain and spent the night there (III, **114**).—§ 393: *Lomaça* told *Yudhishṭhira* the names of the ascetics (*Bhṛgus, Aṅgirases, Vāsishṭhas, Kāçyapas*), and he, with his brothers, paid a visit to them. *Akṛtavraṇa*, a follower of *Rāma Jāmadagnya*, told him when *Paraçu-Rāma* (q.v.) appeared, and that the following day was the 14th.—§ 394: At the request of *Yudhishṭhira*, *Akṛtavraṇa* (*b*) related the story of *Arjuna Kārtavīrya* (q.v.), and *Jamadagni* (q.v.), and

Paraçurāma (q.v.) (§§ 394–8) —§ 399: *Mahendrācala-gamana* (q.v.).—§ 400: On their journey to the *tīrthas* they bathed in a holy stream, and thence reached to *Godāvarī* and to the sea (in the *Draviḍa* country); then to *Agastyatīrtha* and the *Nārītīrthas*, where they heard of and praised the deed of *Arjuna*, and gave away thousands of cows, and by and by they reached *Çūrpāraka* (C. *Sūrp°*), where they saw the altar of *Ṛcīka's* son surrounded by crowds of ascetics, and the shrines of the *Vasus*, of the hosts of the *Maruts*, of the *Açvins*, *Vaivasvata*, *Āditya*, *Dhaneçvara*, *Indra*, *Vishṇu*, *Savitṛ*, *Bhava*, *Candra*, *Divākara*, and of the lord of waters, and of the host of *Sādhyas*, of *Dhātṛ*, of the *Pitṛs*, of *Rudra* with his host, of *Sarasvatī*, of the host of *Siddhas*, etc., and then returned to *Çūrpāraka*, and from this *tīrtha* at the sea they came to *Prabhāsa*, where they offered libations to the *Pitṛs* and gods, and where *Yudhishṭhira* practised austerities for twelve days, subsisting upon air and water, and performing ablutions day and night, surrounded by fires kindled on all sides. There came to them *Balarāma*, *Kṛshṇa*, *Çāmba*, etc., *Kārshṇi*, the grandson of *Çini*, and other *Vṛshṇis*, and heard what had happened to them, and wept when they saw the *Pāṇḍavas* so exceedingly lean (III, **118**).—§ 401: *Bala-Rāma* (q.v.).—§ 402: *Sātyaki*, citing *Çaibya*, etc., who did the work for *Yayāti*, recommended that *Rāma*, *Kṛshṇa*, *Pradyumna*, *Çāmba*(*b*), himself, *Aniruddha*, *Gada*, *Ulmuka*, *Bāhuka*, *Bhānu*, *Nītha*, the young hero *Niçatha*, *Sāraṇa*, and *Cārudeshṇa* should lead the united army of the *Vṛshṇis*, *Bhojas*, *Andhakas*, *Sāttvatas*, and *Çūras* (C. *Sū°*) against the *Dhārtarāshṭras* and kill them in battle, and that *Abhimanyu* should rule the earth until *Yudhishṭhira* had fulfilled his vow. *Kṛshṇa* said that the *Pāṇḍavas* would never accept the sovereignty unless it were won by their own prowess, and *Yudhishṭhira* assented to the words of *Kṛshṇa*, saying, that as *Kṛshṇa* alone knew him, so he alone knew *Kṛshṇa*, who would perceive when the time had come for bravery, and he and *Sātyaki* would then defeat *Suyodhana*. Then the *Yadus* returned home, and the *Pāṇḍavas* continued their journey accompanied by *Lomaça*, and came to the river *Payoshṇī* (*c*).—§ 403: *Lomaça* spoke of sacrifices that had formerly been performed at the *Payoshṇī* (*b*); he who bathed in the *Payoshṇī* would obtain the same *lokas* as *Gaya*.—§ 404: Having bathed in the *Payoshṇī* they went to *Vaidūryaparvata* and *Narmadā*, where they, according to the exposition of *Lomaça*, visited all the *tīrthas* and shrines, giving gifts to the brahmans by thousands. *Lomaça* said that this was the junction between the *Tretā* and *Dvāpara* age, where a person is freed of all his sins, and that here was performed the sacrifice of *Çaryāti* (*b*). *Yudhishṭhira* wished to hear more about it (III, **121**). — § 405: *Sukanyopākhyāna* (q.v.). — § 406: *Lomaça* recommended to *Yudhishṭhira* to visit the abovenamed lake, and *Sikatāksha*, and the *Saindhava* wood, and *Pushkara* (reciting the hymns of *Sthāṇu*, this being the junction of the *Dvāpara* and *Tretā*, etc.), and *Ārcīkaparvata*(*b*). Here the ṛshis eat rice boiled in milk. Here (?) is the *Yamunā*, where Kṛshṇa performed austerities; there is the holy spring of Indra, where *Dhātṛ*, *Vidhātṛ*, and *Varuṇa* rose upwards. In the *Yamunā Māndhātṛ* and *Somaka Sāhadevi* performed sacrifices (III, **125**). — § 407: *Māndhātrupākhyāna* (q.v.).—§ 408: *Jantūpākhyāna* (q.v.).—§§ 409–10: *Plakshāvataraṇa-gamana* (q.v.).—§ 411: *Çyenakapotīya* (q.v.).—§ 412: When they arrived at the hermitage of *Çvetaketu* (*b*) (who, with his sister's son *Ashṭāvakra*, was the best in that *yuga* of those conversant with the sacred lore (*brahmakṛtām*), where *Çvetaketu* beheld the goddess *Sarasvatī* in her human shape and spoke unto her, "may I be endowed with the gift of speech," *Lomaça* related: *Ashṭāvakrīya* (q.v.).—§ 413: *Lomaça* pointed out to *Yudhishṭhira Samaṅgā* [or] *Madhuvilā*, where *Indra*, after the slaughter of *Vṛtra*, became purified from all sins, *Kardamila*, *Maināka* (cf. *Aditi*), the *Kanakhala* mountains, *Gaṅgā*, the lake *Puṇya*, the mountain *Bhṛgutuṅga*, *Ushṇīgaṅga* (PCR. *Tu°*), the hermitage of *Sthūlaçiras*, and that of *Raibhya* (*b*).—§ 414: Questioned by *Yudhishṭhira*, *Lomaça* related the *Yavakrītopākhyāna* (q.v.).—§ 418: They had soon passed the mountains *Uçīrabīja*, *Maināka*, *Çveta*, and *Kālaçaila*, and saw the seven-fold *Gaṅgā* (*b*). Here was the playground of the gods marked with their footprints (*caraṇāṅkitam*). Now they should proceed to the mountains *Kālaçaila*, *Çveta*, and *Mandara* (*c*); protected by *Kubera*, etc., and by *Yātudhānas*, these mountains are difficult to ascend. There are also other followers of *Kubera*, cruel and friendly (*raudrā maitrāç ca*) *Rākshasas*. Description of *Kailāsa* (*d*). *Lomaça* asked *Varuṇa*, *Yama*, *Gaṅgā* ("the daughter of the mountain", v. 10836), *Yamunā*, the mountain, the *Maruts*, the *Açvins*, the rivers to vouchsafe *Yudhishṭhira* safety from gods, *Asuras*, and *Vasus*, and the mountains. *Yudhishṭhira* recommended them all to practise here the utmost cleanliness, and asked *Bhīma* to protect *Kṛshṇā*, who, in times of danger, even if *Arjuna* were present, ever sought protection from *Bhīma* (III, **139**).—§§ 419–23: *Gandhamādana-praveça* (q.v.).—§ 424: *Bhīma-kadalī-khaṇḍa-praveça* (q.v.).—§§ 425–6: *Hanūmad-Bhīma-saṃvāda* (q.v.).—§ 427: *Tretā-yuga* (q.v.).—§ 428: *Dvāpara-yuga* (q.v.).—§ 429: *Kali-yuga* (q.v.).—§ 430: *Hanūmad-Bhīma-saṃvāda* (q.v.). — §§ 431–4: *Saugandhikāharaṇa* (q.v.).

Tishya[1], name of a nakshatra (v. Su. Si.) = Pushya. § 460*c* (Kalkin): III, **190**, 13099 (*yadā Sūryaç ca Çandraç ca tathā T°-Bṛhaspatī ekarāçau sameshyanti pravartsyati tadā Kṛtam*).

Tishya[2], name of the fourth yuga = Kali (q.v.). § 574 (Jambūkh.): VI, **10**π, 387 (enumeration of the four yugas), 388, 391 (*°e 'smin*), 398, 399 (description of the *T.* age).—§ 668*b* (Pañcaçikhavākya): XII, **218**, 7919 (*yathā*). —§ 717*b* (Nārāyaṇīya): XII, **341**, 13092 (*tatas T°e 'tha samprāpte yuge Kalipuraskṛte / ekapādasthito dharmo yatra tatra bhavishyati*, i.e. only a quarter will remain); **350**, 13680 (*punas T°e ca samprāpte*, then the Bhāratas named Kurus will be born from Vyāsa and dissensions will break out among them).

Tiṭṭibha, an Asura. § 268 (Varuṇasabhāv.): II, **9**, 367 (in the palace of Varuṇa).

Tittira, pl. (*°āḥ*), a people. § 578 (Bhīshmavadhap.): VI, **50**π, 2084 (in the army of Yudhishṭhira).—§ 585 (do.): VI, **90**ρ, 3975 (*°jāḥ*, sc. *açvāḥ*).

Tittiri[1], a certain breed of horses: II, 1043, 1056, 1824, 2083; III, 4015; VII, 958 (C. has *Tittira-*); XII, 4560 (cf. prec. and V, 2228).

Tittiri[2], a serpent. § 47 (Sarpanāmak.): I, **35**, 1560 (enumeration).—§ 564 (Mātalīyop.): V, **103**γ, 3629 (do.).

Tittiri[3], a brahman, brother of Vaiçampāyana. § 264 (Sabhākriyāp.): II, **4***a*, 107 (waited upon Yudhishṭhira).—§ 717*c* (Uparicara): XII, **337**ε, 12760 (*Vaiçampāyanapūrvajaḥ*, among the sadasyas at the sacrifice of Vasu Uparicara).

Tomara, pl. (*°āḥ*), a people. § 574 (Jambūkh.): VI, **9**ο, 377.

Toraṇa = Çiva (1000 names[2]).

Toraṇasphāṭikā, name of a sabhā. § 298 (Dyūtap.): II,

56, †1982 (°ākhyāṃ sabhāṃ, Dhṛtarāshṭra caused it to be constructed).

Toyātman[1] = Kṛshṇa: XII, 1649.—Do.[2] = Çiva (1000 names[1]).

Traibali, a muni. § 264 (Sabhākriyāp.): II, **4a**, 108 (waited upon Yudhishṭhira).

Traiçīrsha, adj. ("relating to Triçiras [i.e. Viçvarūpa]"). § 555 (Indravijaya): V, **10**, 335 (°ayā . . . brahmahatyayā).

Traigarta[1] ("king of the Trigartas") = Suçarman: IV, 1070 (S°), 1109; VI, 3856 (*Prasthalādhipaḥ*, C. has by error *Tai°*, B. *Tri°*), 3857 (so B., C. *Tri°*), 4736 (*S°*), 5289 (*Prasthalādhipaḥ*); IX, 93 (*narādhipaḥ*, had been slain).

Traigarta[2], adj. ("belonging to the Trigartas").—§ 552 (Goharaṇap.): IV, **33**, 1117 (*balam*).

Traigarta, pl. (°āḥ), a people = Trigarta, pl. § 576 (Bhagavadgītāp.): VI, **18**δ, 688 (protected Bhīshma). — § 582 (Bhīshmavadhap.): VI, **71**γ, 3132 (supported Çakuni).— § 592 (Saṃçaptakavadhap.): VII, **18**, 727, 746 (fought with Arjuna).—§ 599 (Jayadrathavadhap.): VII, **107**, 4030 (°ānāṃ mahārathe, i.e. Vīradhanvan).

Traigartaka, adj. ("belonging to the Trigartas"). § 592 (Saṃçaptakavadhap.): VII, **18**, 726 (*bhrātṝn*). — § 785 (Anugītāp.): XIV, **74**, 2167 (°*yodhāḥ*), 2171 (°*mahārathāḥ*, vanquished by Arjuna).

Traigartī ("daughter of the Trigarta king") = Yaçodharā: I, 3788 (*Y°*).

Trailokyagoptṛ = Çiva (1000 names[1]).

Trailokyakartṛ = Brahmán: XII, 10167.—Do.[2] = Çiva: V, 7414.

Trailokyanātha = Kṛshṇa (Vishṇu): III, 1951 (*Hariḥ*).

Trailokyapati = Indra: XII, 8057.

Trailokyarāja = Indra: V, 3682.

Trailokyeça = Indra: III, 13614 (°*a ivāparaḥ*).

Traipura ("the king of Tripurā", BR.). § 284 (Sahadeva): II, **31**, 1164 (in the south, vanquished by Sahadeva).

Traipura, pl. (°āḥ), a people ("the inhabitants of Tripurā"). § 585 (Bhīshmavadhap.): VI, **87**, 3855 (followed Bṛhadbala).

***traividya** ("the three vedas"): III, 13779 (°*vṛddhāḥ*); XII, 545 (°*vṛddhānāṃ*), 8201 (°*vṛddhān*), 9721 (°*vṛddhāḥ*); XIII, 5109 (°*vṛddhebhyaḥ*); cf. trayī.—Do.[2], adj. ("familiar with the three vedas"); VI, 1190; XII, 2424 (*brāhmaṇānāṃ*), 2469 (*vipreshu*), 5972; XIII, 6455 (*brāhmaṇaḥ*).

Traiyambaka, adj. ("belonging to Tryambaka" [i.e. Çiva]) § 589 (Droṇābhishekap.): VII, **7**, 169 (*ishvastram*, known by Droṇa). § 596 (Pratijñāp.): VII, **79**, 2778 (*baliṃ*).

Trasadasyu, an ancient king. § 267 (Yamasabhāv.): II, **8**, 319 (in the palace of Yama).—§ 382 (Agastyop.): III, **98**, 8606 (*Paurukutsam*, Agastya asked him for wealth).— § 775 (Ānuçāsanik.): XIII, **166**η, 7681 (*rājā*, enumeration). Cf. Paurukutsa.

Trāsana = Çiva (1000 names[2]).

***trayī** ("the triple science"): I, 4032 (*vidyā*), 4034; II, 231; III, 11295, 11296 (°*dharmam*), 13725 (*vidyā*), 17361 (°*dharmaḥ*); VI, 1191 (°*dharmam*); XII, 231, 567, 791, 2006, 2154, †2383, 2556, 3341 (*vidyā*), 3410 (do.), 4543 (do.), 4846 (read °*īṃ vidyāṃ* with B.), 8613 (do.), 13089.

Tretā, name of the second yuga. § 8 (Parvasaṅgr.): I, **2**, 272 (°-*Dvāparayoḥ sandhau*, then Rāma Jāmadagnya slew the kshatriyas).—§ 375 (Tīrthayātrāp.): III, **85**, 8232 (*sarvaṃ Kṛtayuge puṇyaṃ T°āyāṃ Pushkaram*).—§ 403 (do.): III, **121**, 10310 (*sandhir esha, naraçreshṭha, T°āyā Dvāparasya ca*, says Lomaça to Yudhishṭhira).—§ 406 (do.): III, **125**, 10409 (do. with *dvayor* for *esha*).—§ 426 (Hanūmad-Bhīmasaṃv.): III, **149**, 11230. —§ 427 (cf. do.): In the *T.* sacrifices are introduced, religion (*dharma*) decreases by a fourth, Nārāyaṇa is red, etc.; III, **149**, 11247, 11249.— § 460 (Mārkaṇḍeyas.): III, **190**, 13018 (*tribhir aṃçaiḥ pratishṭhitaḥ T°āyāṃ*, sc. *dharmaḥ*); **191**, 13120. — § 567 (Bhagavadyānap.): V, **132**, 4475 (*rājā Kṛtayugasrashṭā T°āyāḥ*, etc.), 4476.—§ 569 (do.): V, **142**, 4819, 4821, 4823, 4825, 4827.—§ 574 (Jambūkh.): VI, **10**π, 387, 390, 395, 396 (only C.) (description).—§ 641 (Rājadh.): XII, **69**ν, 2682 (*caturtham aṃçam utsṛjya*, sc. *daṇḍanītyām*), 2693 (*rājā Kṛtayugasrashṭā T°āyāḥ*, etc.), 2694, **91**μ, 3408. —§ 649 (Āpaddh.): XII, **141a**, 5328, 5331 (°-*Dvāparayoḥ sandhau*, a twelve years' drought occurred), 5332.—§ 664 (Mokshadh.): XII, **207**, 7562 (°*prabhṛti*).—§ 677 (do.): XII, **232**, 8504 (*anye . . . dharmās T°āyāṃ*), 8505 (°*āyāṃ jñānam uttamaṃ*); **233**, 8544, 8545; **239**, 8719 (so B., error in C.), 8726 (°*ādau*).—§ 679 (do.): XII, **261**, 9262 (*anye . . . dharmās T°āyāṃ*).—§ 717b (Nārāyaṇīya): XII, **340**, 12949 (*sandhyaṃçe anuprāpte T°āyāṃ* [read °-*āyā* with B.] *Dvāparasya ca*, then Vishṇu will be incarnate as Rāma Dāçarathi).—§ 773b (Kṛshṇa Vāsudeva): XIII, **159**, 7363 (°*kāle jñānam upapannaḥ*, sc. Kṛshṇa). Cf. Tretāyuga.

Tretā[2] = Sūrya (the Sun): III, 150.

Tretāyuga, the second yuga (= Tretā). § 427 (Tretā): III, **149**, 11250.—§ 458 (Mārkaṇḍeyas.): III, **188**, 12827. —§ 459 (do.): III, **189**, 12981 (in the *T.* Nārāyaṇa is yellow). — § 574 (Jambūkh.): VI, **10**, 388. — § 661 (Mokshadh.): XII, **207**, 7556 (°*e kāle saṃsparçāj jāyate prajāḥ*).—§ 677 (do.): XII, **232**, 8496 (comprises 3,000 [celestial] years), 8502 (*pādaço hrasate vayaḥ*); **233**, 8542 (°*e tu vidhis tvesha yajñānāṃ*).—§ 683 (do.): XII, **268**, 9592 (*pādonena dharmeṇa gacchet*).—§ 717c (Uparicara): XII, **337**, 12808.—§ 717b (Nārāyaṇīya): XII, **340**, 12948 (°*e*, Vishṇu will then be incarnate as Rāma Jāmadagnya); **341**, 13089 (*yatra trayī bhavishyati*); **349**, IV, 13585.—§ 778e (Avikshit): XIV, **4**, 80 (°*mukhe*, then Kārandhama, i.e. Avikshit lived). Cf. Tretā.

Tribhuvanaçreshṭha = Vishṇu: V, 334 (*V°*).

Tribhuvanavibhu = Çiva: VIII, †1741.

Tribhuvaneçvara[1] = Brahmán: XII, 2146.

Tribhuvaneçvara[2] = Indra: III, 15411; IX, 2771 (*Çakraḥ*), 2790; XIII, 3885.

Tribhuvaneçvara[3] = Vishṇu (Kṛshṇa): II, 2293; V, 3755; XIII, 6811.

Tribhuvaneçvara, dual (°*au*) = Aruṇa and Garuḍa: I, 1461. Do. pl. (°*āḥ*): XII, 7580 (*devān*); XIII, 7091 (*Rudrāḥ*).

Tribhuvaneçvarī = Durgā (Umā): IV, 178.

Tricakshus = Kṛshṇa: XII, 1505.

Triçaṅku[1], an ancient king. § 134 (Viçvāmitra): I, **71**, 2928 (*guruçāpahatasyāpi T°oḥ çaraṇaṃ dadau*, sc. Viçvāmitra, cf. Harivaṃça, v. 717 foll.).—§ 721 (Ānuçāsanik.): XIII, **3a**, 189 (°*r bandhubhir mukta Aikshvākuḥ prītipūrvakam avākçirā divaṃ nīto dakshiṇām āçrito diçaṃ*, sc. by Viçvāmitra). Cf. Mataṅga.[1]

Triçaṅku[2] = Çiva (1000 names[2]).

Triçiras = Viçvarūpa, the son of Tvashṭṛ: V, 229, 234, 236, 243, 249, 251, 266, 270; IX, 1755 (had been slain).

Triçīrsha = Çiva (1000 names[1]).

Triçṛṅga, a mountain. § 605 (Karṇap.): VIII, **15**, 573 (*yathā*).—§ 611 (Çalyap.): IX, **10**, 475 (*iva*).

Triçukla = Çiva (1000 names[2]).

Triçūlahasta = Çiva: XIV, 207.

Triçūlakhāta, name of a tīrtha. § 370 (Tīrthayātrāp.): III, **84**, 7089.
Triçūlapāṇi = Çiva: VII, 9533.
Triçūlapāṇeḥ sthāna(m), a tīrtha. § 360 (Tīrthayātrāp.): III, **82**, 5045.
Triçūlavarapāṇi = Çiva (1000 names[1]).
Tridaça, pl. (°*āḥ*) ("the gods"): I, 2592 (°*ānāñ ca vardhikaḥ*, i.e. Viçvakarman), 2593, 3070, 3255 (°*ālayam*), 3256 (°*āvāsam*), 3281, 3551, 4784 (°*ānāṃ . . . īçvaraḥ*, i.e. Indra), 7569 (*iva*), 8162, 8261 (°*ānāṃ maheçvaraḥ*, i.e. Indra); II, 621 (°*āvaraḥ*); III, 1590, 1725 (°*ālayāḥ*), 1852 (°*ālaye*), 8089, 8162, 8346 (*Prabhāsaṃ . . . tīrthaṃ t°ānāṃ*), 8693, 8719, 8720, 8731, 8753, 8797, 8799, †8810, †8812, 8813, 8814, 8817, 8823, 8854, 8856, 9963, 10345 (dual, *Açvinau*), 10412, 11749, 13534, 13615, 14375, 14386, 14586, 14617, 14870 (°*ānāṃ . . . ātmajaiḥ*), 15853, 16495, 16528, 16533 (°*ālayāḥ*), 16807 (°*opamāḥ*), 17090; IV, 50 (°*ānāṃ yathā Çakraḥ*), 192, 2196 (°*opamān*), 2265 (°*ānām iveçvaraḥ*); V, 304, 552, †801 (*devānāṃ*), 3754, 4422, 4537 (*iva*), 5291, 5431 (°*ān iva Vajrabhṛt*), †5509 (*iva*), †5554 (do.); VI, 2455 (do.), 4427 (°*ā iva Vāsavaṃ*), 4493 (*yathā*), 4912 (°*ānām iveçvarau*), 4924, 5480, 5607; VII, 46 (°*ān iva Govindaḥ*), 1466, 1504 (*triṃçat t°sannibhāḥ*), 2230, 2513, 3437 (°*opamaḥ*), 5456 (°*ān api*), 6462 (only C.), 7341, 8207, 9554; IX, 2678, 3168; XI, 582 (°*opamān*); XII, 1832, 3591, 8417, 8419, 12819, 13802; XIII, 308, 315 (°*lokeshu*), 320 (°*loke*), 778 (°*gaṇarājyaṃ*), 927, 928, 1472, 3334, 5929, 5940, 5976 (°*vargasya*), 6045, 7480; XIV, 1570 (°*āpyāyanaṃ*), 2673 (*iva*); XIII, 13.—Do. sg. = Çiva (1000 names[2]).
Tridaça, sg. (°*ṃ*) ("heaven"): VIII, †1740 (only B., C. has *Tridivaṃ*); XIII, 3327 (only C., B. has *Tridivasya*).
Tridaçaçārdūla = Indra: XIII, 569.
Tridaçaçreshṭha = Çiva: VII, 9593.
Tridaçādhipa = Indra, q.v.
Tridaçādhipati = Indra: IX, 2767.
Tridaçādhyaksha = Vishṇu (1000 names).
Tridaçadvish, pl. (°*aḥ*) = Asura, pl.: VIII, 1528; IX, 2952; XII, 7629; XIII, 4022.
Tridaçapati = Indra: VIII, †4647.
Tridaçapuṅgava = Çiva: XII, 10688.
Tridaçāri, pl. (°*ayaḥ*) = Asura, pl.: VIII, 1518.
Tridaçarshi, pl. (°*ayaḥ*) = Devarshi, pl.: III, 8304.
Tridaçavarātmaja ("son of Indra") = Arjuna: VII, †67.
Tridaçavarāvaraja ("younger brother of Indra") = Vishṇu: VIII, †1213 (°*opamaṃ*).
Tridaçeça[1] = Brahmán: III, 10951.—Do.[2] = Indra: I, 3276 (°*ālayaṃ*); III, 1927 (°*samaḥ*, sc. Arjuna), 12213 (°*dvishaḥ*, i.e. the Asuras), 16180 (*yathā*).—Do.[3] = Kṛshṇa: XII, 1668.
Tridaçeçvara[1] = Indra: I, 1534; III, 10730, †11911, 12015, 13226, 17421 (*Vajrī*); VIII, 4440, 4443; IX, 2444; XI, 661; XII, 7338, 9530; XIII, 3913; XIV, 2882.—Do.[2] = Çiva: III, 11977; XIII, 971, 997.—Do.[3] = Kṛshṇa: VII, 6462 (wanting in B.), 8274.—Do.[4], pl. (°*āḥ*): III, 2190 (i.e. Indra, etc.); XIII, 7097.
Tridaçeçvaranātha = Kṛshṇa: VII, 6461 (wanting in B.).
Tridaçendra = Indra (q.v.).
Tridaṇḍadhṛk = Çiva (1000 names[1]).
Tridhāman = Kṛshṇa: XII, 1508.
Tridhātman = Kṛshṇa: XII, 1641.
Tridhātu = Kṛshṇa (Vishṇu): XII, 13246.
Tridiva ("heaven"): I, 161 (°*sthaṃ Dhanañjayaṃ*), †1258, 1539, †1545, 1638, 2829, 3107 (°*aukasām*), 4180 (do.), 8474; III, 1662 (°*nivāsināṃ*), 1805, 1809 (*rakshitā . . . t°ṃ Maghavān iva*), †1878 (°*gatāḥ*), 2229, †8713, 8766, 9906, 9913, 9919, 9921, 10947, 10954, 11807 (*samprāptas t°e rājyaṃ Vṛtrahā*), 11932, 12014, 12156 (°*aukasām*), 12533, 13247, 14152, 14369 (°*vāsinaḥ*), 14464 (°*ṃ Kṛttikā gatāḥ*), 14556 (°*aukasaḥ*), 16690, 16959; IV, 192; V, 271, 279, 293 (°*aukasaḥ*), †802, 2352 (*pātayet t°ād devān*), 3583 (°*aukasām*), 4180, 4603 (*iva*), †5533 (do.), †5576 (do.); VII, 1484; VIII, 1530 (°*aukasaḥ*), 1551 (°*aukasām*), †1740 (*iva*), 2201; IX, 1756, 2099 (°*aukasām*), 2101, 2111 (°*aukasaḥ*), 2293, 2300, 2444, 2792, 2821, 2983, 3011, 3014, 3022; X, †566; XI, 262 (°*aṅgatāḥ*), XII, 330 (*Çakrasya*), 1186, 1403 (*yathendras t°ṃ*, sc. *pālaya*), 1508 (°*āc cyutaḥ*, sc. Kṛshṇa), 3027 (°*aṅgama*), 7349, 13021 (°*aukasaḥ*), 13098 (°*aukaḥsu*), 13296 (°*aukasaḥ*), 13796 (°*aṅgatāḥ*), 13920 (°*aṅgataḥ*); XIII, 581, †1844, 2951, 3327 (only B.), 3673, 4747, 4748, 4750, 5198, 6262, 6277, 6442 (°*ālaye*), 7144 (°*aukasaḥ*), 7289 (do.); XIV, 246, 1053 (°*gāḥ*); XV, 339, 341; XVII, 106 (°*ālayān*); XVIII, 120 (°*ālayaiḥ*).
Tridivā, a river. § 574 (Jambūkh.): VI, **9**λ, 324, 326 (only B.).—§ 775 (Ānuçāsanik.): XIII, **166***a*, 7654.
Tridiveça, pl. (°*āḥ*) ("lords of heaven"): VIII, 1528.
Tridiveçvara = Indra, q.v.—Do. pl. (°*āḥ*): II, 2332; V, 281, 342 (*devāḥ*).
Trigaṅga, name of a tīrtha. § 370 (Tīrthayātrāp.): III, **84**, 8007.—§ 733*g* (Saptagaṅga): XIII, **25***a*, 1703.
Trigarta[1], an ancient king. § 267 (Yamasabhāv.): II, **8**, 331 (in the palace of Yama).
Trigarta[2] ("the king of the Trigartas") = Kshemaṅkara: III, 15727.
Trigarta[3] (do.) = Suçarman: IV, 1078 (*S*°), 1107; V, 7611 (?); VI, 3856 (so B., C. *Trai-*°), 3857 (B. *Trai-*°), 4664 (?); VII, 691 (*Prasthalādhipaḥ*). Cf. Traigarta[1].
Trigarta, pl. (°*āḥ*), a people, especially five brothers, Trigarta princes. § 11 (Parvasaṅgr.): I, **2**, 485 (cf. Goharaṇap.).—§ 214 (Hiḍimbavadhap.): I, **156**, 6085 (their country visited by the Pāṇḍavas).—§ 279 (Arjuna): II, **27**, 1026 (vanquished by Arjuna on his digvijaya).—§ 285 (Nakula): II, **32**, 1189 (vanquished by Nakula on his digvijaya).—§ 295 (Dyūtap.): II, **52**, 1870 (*Çibi-T°-Yaudheyāḥ*, bring tribute to Yudhishṭhira).—§ 522 (Draupadīharaṇap.): III, **271**, 15743 (ruled by Kshemaṅkara, they followed Jayadratha).—§ 552 (Goharaṇap.): IV, **25**, 868 (*mahārathaiḥ*), 880 (v. Kīcaka, § 552*b*); **30**, 971 (*rājā T°ānāṃ Suçarmā*), 981, 993 (*Suçarmā . . . T°aiḥ sahitaḥ*, rob the cattle of Virāṭa); **31**, 1007; **32**, 1036, 1037, 1055 (C. by error *Gi*°), 1056, 1059, 1060 (*rāja T°ānāṃ Suçarmā*, encounter between Suçarman and Virāṭa); **33**, 1076, 1097, 1101, 1116 (°*ānāṃ mahārathe*, i.e. Suçarman; Suçarman is made captive); **35**, 1149; **38**, 1247; **47**, 1479; **68**, 2161 (*jitvā T°ān*), 2170, 2171.—§ 556*e* (Nakula): V, **23**, 709 (Nakula had vanquished the Çibis and the T.).—§ 556 (Sañjayayānap.): V, **30**, †889 (in Duryodhana's army).—§ 561 (Yānasandhip.): V, **57**, 2249 (°*ānāñ ca vai mukhyau . . . Saṃçaptakau*).—§ 571 (Ulūkadūtāgamanap.): V, **164**ε, 5709 (the Draupadeyas are pitted against the *T.* (the five brothers?)).—§ 572 (Rathātirathasaṅkhyānap.): V, **166**, 5756 (five brothers who are *rathas* in Duryodhana's army).—§ 574 (Jambūkh.): VI, **9**ν, 368 (in the south (!)).—§ 576 (Bhagavadgītāp.): VI, **20**, †754 (in the army of Duryodhana = Saṃçaptaka, pl. ?).—§ 578 (Bhīshmavadhap.): VI, **51**σ, 2097 (protect Bhīshma).—§ 580 (do.): VI, **56***a*, 2405 (B. *Trai*°, in the head of Bhīshma's gāruḍavyūha).—§ 581 (do.): VI, **61**[3]δ, 2691

(attacked Arjuna and Abhimanyu).—§ 582 (do.): VI, **72**ε, 3168 (°*ānāṃ rathodarāḥ*, fought with Nakula).—§ 584 (do.): VI, **82**², 3589 (follow Bhīshma).—§ 586 (do.): VI, **99**δ, 4505 (follow Duryodhana); **102**, 4660 (Arjuna employed the Vāyavya weapon against the *T.*).—§ 587 (do.): VI, **114**, 5299 (°*ānāṃ mahābalaṃ*, fought with Arjuna and Bhīmasena); **117**ρ, 5485 (attacked Arjuna); **119**αα, 5649 (abandoned Bhīshma).—§ 589 (Droṇābhishekap.): VII, **4**β, 122 (had formerly been vanquished by Karṇa); **7**ζ, 183 (in the rearguard of Duryodhana's army); **11**ν, 398 (had formerly been vanquished by Kṛshṇa).—§ 591 (Saṃçaptakavadhap.): VII, **17**, 688 (five brothers Satyaratha, etc., swore to slay Arjuna or themselves die), 719 (attacked by Arjuna).—§ 592 (do.): VII, **18**, 728 (°*ānāṃ anīkinīṃ*); **19**\|β, 768 (among the Saṃçaptakas); **27**, 1205 (°*ānāṃ mahārathāḥ*, 10,000 in number).—§ 595 (Shoḍaçarāj, v. Rāma Jāmadagnya): VII, **70**β, 2436 (had formerly been slain by Rāma Jāmadagnya).—§ 599 (Jayadrathavadhap.): VII, **94**, 3482 (*rathānāñ ca sahasreṇa T°ānāṃ*, accompany Duryodhana); **107**, 4041 (Niramitra, the son of their king, is slain); **115**, 4556 (°*ānāṃ rathodarāḥ*), 4558; **123**, 4945, 4946 (°*ānāṃ trisāhasrā rathāḥ*), 4968 (°*senāpatinā*); **141**, 5843 (attacked Sātyaki), 5849.—§ 600 (Ghaṭotkacavadhap.): VII, **157**ρ, 6948 (slain by Yudhishṭhira); **164**, 7339 (in the van of Duryodhana's army).—§ 604 (Karṇap.): VIII, **8**, 235 (had formerly been vanquished by Karṇa).—§ 605 (do.): VIII, **11**σ, 417 (accompany Kṛpa); **28**, 1166 (are slain by Arjuna).—§ 608 (do.): VIII, **61**, 3110 (°*ānāṃ balaṃ*).—§ 611 (Çalyap.): IX, **8**β, 392 (follow Kṛtavarman); **14**, 705 (°*ānāṃ mahārathaiḥ*, follow Açvatthāman); **27**υυ, 1479 (°*ānāṃ mahārathāḥ*, attack Arjuna and Kṛshṇa).—§ 620 (Çrāddhap.): XI, **26**β, 791 (*mahārathāḥ*, their bodies cremated, the five brothers?).—§ 785 (Anugītāp.): XIV, **74**, 2141 (vanquished by Arjuna when he followed the sacrificial horse). Cf. Traigarta, pl. Traigartaka.

Trigartādhipati ("king of the Trigartas") = Suçarman: IV, †1073; VI, 4738; VII, 683, 1231, 1233 (°*eḥ . . bhrātaraṃ*); IX, 74 (had joined Duryodhana), 1459 (still alive).

Trigartarāj (do.) = Suçarman: VI, 4652; VII, 748.

Trigartarāja¹ (do.) = Kshemaṅkara: III, 15594 (*K*°, C. has by error °*rājñaḥ* instead of °*rājaḥ*).—Do.² = Suçarman: IV, 1113; VI, 3533, 3566, †3754, †3758, 4655, 5052; VII, 4039 (°*sya sutaḥ*, i.e. Niramitra); VIII, 1070 (?). Do.³ = Suratha: III, 15733.

Trigartarājan¹ (do.) (III, 15594), v. Trigartarāja.

Trigartarājan² (do.) = Suçarman: VI, †3760.

Trigartarājan³ (do.) = Sūryavarman: XIV, 2149 (*S*°).

Triguṇa = Mahāpurusha (Mahāpurushastava).

Trijaṭa = Çiva (1000 names¹⁻²).

Trijaṭā, a Rākshasī. § 532 (Sītāsāntvana): III, **280**, 16146 (*Rākshasī*), 16164, 16165 (consoled Sītā).—§ 533 (Sītā-Rāvaṇasaṃv.): III, **281**, 16196.—§ 543 (Rāmābhisheka): III, **291**, 16571 (honoured by Rāma). Cf. Rākshasī.

Trijaṭin = Çiva: XIII, 1161 (1000 names², only B.).

Trikakud¹ = Çiva (1000 names²).

Trikakud² = Kṛshṇa (Vishṇu): XII, 1508, 13252 (°*tvena*); XIII, 6956 (Vishṇu's 1000 names).

Trikakuda = Kṛshṇa: XII, 13252.

Trikāladhṛk = Çiva (1000 names²).

Trikarmarata = Çiva (1000 names¹).

Trikūṭa¹, a mountain. § 290 (Çiçupālavadhap.): II, **42**, 1484 (°*sthāṃ Gaṅgāṃ*, in the north?).

Trikūṭa², a mountain near Laṅkā. § 528 (Rāvaṇagamana): III, **277**, 15998 (on his way from Laṅkā to Gokarṇa Rāvaṇa crossed *T.*).—§ 534*d* (Laṅkā): III, **282**, 16252 (°*girikandare*, there Laṅkā is situated).

Trikūṭavat, a mountain. § 782*g* (Guruçishyasaṃv.): XIV, **43**η, 1173. Cf. Trikūṭa.

Trilocana = Çiva, q.v.

Trilokadhṛk = Vishṇu (1000 names).

Trilokagā = Gaṅgā: I, 3860; XVIII, 119 (*G*°).

Trilokakṛt = Brahmán: XII, ††6977 (*B*°), 10190.

Trilokapathagā = Gaṅgā: XII, 962 (*G*°).

Trilokarāja = Indra: V, 3512.

Trilokātman = Vishṇu (1000 names).

Trilokeça¹ = Brahmán: VIII, 1528 (*Pitāmahaṃ*); XII, 10182.

Trilokeça² = Çiva: XIV, 207.

Trilokeça³ = Indra: V, 3662; XII, 8348, 9527 (*Purandaraḥ*).

Trilokeça⁴ = Vishṇu: III, 8103 (*V*°); XIII, 7018 (1000 names).

Trilokeçvara¹ = Vishṇu: XIII, †510 (°*bhūtakānte*, sc. Çrī).—Do.² = Indra: XII, 1718.

Triṇayana = Çiva, q.v.

Triṇetra = Çiva (1000 names¹⁻²).

Triṇāciketa ("conversant with the three Nāciketa [fires"]): XIII, 4296.—Do.² = Mahāpurusha (Mahāpurushastava).

Tripada = Vishṇu (1000 names).

Tripāda, a Daitya. § 615*u* (Skanda): IX, **46**λ, 2693 (slain by Skanda).

Tripathagā = Gaṅgā: II, 1484 (*G*°); III, 9906, 9965 (*G*°); VI, 242; XII, 1351; XIII, 1835, †1860 (B. has *Tripathā*); XIV, 1225 (*G*°).

Tripathagāminī = Gaṅgā: I, 3903 (*G*°).

Tripishṭapa¹ ("Indra's heaven"): I, 1468 (B. *Trivishṭapa*), 7580 (°*saṅkāçaṃ Indraprastham*), 7657; II, 1257 (*Çakrasyeva T°e*), 2054 (*devair iva samavetais T°ṃ*); III, 329 (*gatā . . . Surabhī*), 5074 (*ye vasanti Kurukshetre te vasanti T°e*), 707F (do.), 8706 (°*samaprakhyaṃ*); V, 346, 347, 350, 351, 538, 3616; XII, †8332, ††13214, ††13217 (°*sthaḥ*), 13792. Cf. Trivishṭapa.

Tripishṭapa², a tīrtha. § 364 (Tīrthayatrāp.): III, **83**, 6054.

Tripura, the triple city of the Asuras. § 11 (Parvasaṅgr.): I, **2**, 543 (°*sya nipātanaṃ*, cf. § 606).—§ 320 (Saubhavadhap.): III, **22**, 880 (*Maheçvaraçaroddhūtaṃ papāta T°ṃ yathā*).—§ 334*e* (Antardhāna): III, **41**, 1703 (*Çaṅkareṇa T°ṃ nihataṃ yadā*).—§ 600 (Ghaṭotkacavadhap.): VIII, **156**, 6864 (*pureva T°ṃ dagdhvā divi devo Maheçvaraḥ*); **175**, 7979 (do.). — § 603*d* (Nārayaṇāstramokshap.). The *Asuras* had three cities in heaven: one of iron (belonging to *Vidyunmālin*), one of silver (belonging to *Tārakāksha*), and one of gold (belonging to *Kamalāksha*); *Indra* could not vanquish them; the gods repaired to *Rudra* and promised him the creatures slain in every sacrifice. *Çiva* then made *Gandhamādana* and *Vindhya* the two bamboo poles of his chariot, the earth his chariot, *Çesha* the *aksha*, the moon and sun the two wheels, *Elāpatra* and *Pushpadanta* the two pins of the yoke, the *Malaya* mountain the yoke, *Takshaka* the string for tying the yoke to the pole, and the creatures (*sattvāni*) the traces of the steeds, the four *Vedas* his four steeds, the *Upavedas* the bridle bits, *Gāyatrī* and *Sāvitrī* the reins, *om* the whip (*pratoda*), *Brahmán* the driver, *Mandara* the bow, *Vāsuki* the bowstring, *Vishṇu* the shaft, *Agni* the arrow-head, *Vāyu* the wings of the shaft (so Nīl.), *Yama Vaivasvata* the feathers in its tail, lightning the whetting stone, *Meru* the standard. Adored by gods and ṛshis he adopted a posture called after his own name, and stood immovable for 1000 years. When, however, the three cities came together in the firmament he shot that terrible shaft of three knots, inspired with the *Yuga* fire and composed of *Vishṇu* and *Soma*. While the triple city began to burn, *Pārvatī* repaired thither to behold the sight; she had on her lap a child having a bald head with five tufts of hair on it; *Indra* endeavoured to strike the child with the thunderbolt, but *Mahādeva* (i.e. the child) paralysed his arm. *Indra*, with the gods, repaired to *Brahmán*, who, understanding that it was *Çiva*, came with them and recited a hymn ($\theta\theta$). *Mahādeva* became gratified, and the arm of *Indra* reassumed its natural state: VII, **202**, 9570 (°*sya vadhārthāya*).—§ 606 (Tripurākhyāna): VIII, **33**, 1415, 1416; **34**, 1551, 1562, 1566, 1567, 1569 (the destruction of *T.* by *Çiva* is anew related, cf. § 603*d*).—§ 730*g* (Upamanyu): XIII, **14**θ, 798 (*vināçe . . . T°sya*), (ρ) 855 (*yena tat T°ṃ dagdhvā*, sc. by Çiva). Cf. XIII, 7482 foll.

Tripurā, a city. § 515 (Karṇadigvijaya): III, **254**, 15246 (conquered by Karṇa on his digvijaya).

Tripuraghna, Tripuraghātin, Tripuraharta = Çiva, q.v.

[Tripurākhyāna(ṃ)] ("the episode relating to Tripura"). § 606 (Karṇap.). The first combat between the gods and the *Asuras* was about *Tāraka* (*Tārakāmayaḥ*). The *Daityas* were defeated. Then the three sons of *Tāraka* (*Tārakāksha*, *Kamalāksha*, and *Vidyunmālin*), by practising austerities, obtained boons from *Pitāmaha* (who refused to give them immunity from death): "residing in three cities, we will rove over the earth; after 1000 years we will come together, and our three cities also will become united into one; that foremost one amongst the gods who will, with one shaft, pierce those three cities united into one will be the cause of our destruction." The great *Asura Maya* (*Viçvakarmāṇam ajaraṃ Daitya-Dānava-pūjitaṃ*) constructed the three cities: *Tārakāksha's* of gold in heaven, *Kamalāksha's* of silver in the welkin, and *Vidyunmālin's* of iron on the earth; all in such a way as to revolve in a circle; each 100 *yojanas* in breadth and 100 in length (description). Those three *Daitya* kings (*Dānavas*) soon assailed the three worlds, and millions upon millions of flesh-eating *Dānavas*, who had before been defeated by the gods, came to them and settled in the three cities; *Maya* supplied them with everything by his illusive power. *Tārakāksha's* heroic son *Hari*, by penances, obtained from *Brahmán* a boon: a lake in his city capable of reviving the dead when thrown into it. They then exterminated all cities and towns, drove the gods from all places, and roamed over celestial forests, etc., and the asylums of Ṛ. *Indra*, with the *Maruts*, having tried in vain to pierce the three cities, repaired with the gods (*Ādityas*) to *Brahmán*, complaining of the *Asuras*. *Brahmán* said that no one else, save *Sthāṇu* (*Īçāna*, *Jishṇu*, i.e. Çiva), could pierce the three cities with one shaft. They all, with *Brahmán* and Ṛ. (devoted to penances and uttering the eternal words of the *Vedas*), sought *Bhava* (*Çaṅkara*, i.e. Çiva), who had perfect knowledge of the Soul, beholding in him those diverse forms that each had individually conceived in his own heart, and praised him (***a***) (VIII, **33**). After the fears of P., D., and Ṛ. had been dispelled, *Brahmán* explained the matter to him. He said that they should fight united and with half his energy; as they said that they could not bear half his energy, he promised to slay the foes endued with half of their united energy. From that time *Çaṅkara* came to be called *Mahādeva*. Gathering portions from all forms in the three worlds they let *Viçvakarman* construct him a chariot; they made *Vishṇu* the point, *Soma* the head, and *Agni* the staff of the arrow; Earth the chariot; *Mandara* its axle; *Gaṅgā* its *jaṅghā*; the points of the compass its ornaments; the constellations its shaft; the *Kṛta*-age its yoke; *Vāsuki* its *kūbara*; *Himavat* and *Vindhya* its *apaskara* and *adhishṭhāna*; the *Udaya* and *Asta* mountains its wheels; the Ocean (the abode of the *Dānavas*) its other axle; the seven Ṛ.'s its *parishkara*; *Day* and *Night*, etc., its *anukarsha*; the planets and the stars its wooden fence; *dharma*, *artha*, and *kāma* its *triveṇu*; the herbs and the creepers, etc., its bells; the sun and moon were made its [other] wheels; *Day* and *Night* its wings; the ten foremost of Snakes *Dhṛtarāshṭra*, etc., its [other] shaft; the sky its [other] yoke; the clouds *Saṃvartaka* and *Balāhaka* the leathern strings of the yoke; the twilight, *Dhṛti*, *Medhā*, *Sthiti*, *Sannati*, and the firmament with planets and stars its covering-skins; the regents of the world (*Indra*, *Varuṇa*, *Yama*, and *Kubera*) its steeds; the cardinal and subsidiary directions its reins; *Vashaṭkāra* the goad; *Gāyatrī* the string attached to the goad; the four auspicious days (v. the note of PCR., p. 112) the traces of its steeds; the P. (*Rohakāḥ*) presiding over them the pins; Action and Truth and Penance and Profit its chords; Mind the ground; Speech the track; it was resplendent with lightning and *Indra's* bow; that space of time, which, on a former occasion, had, in the sacrifice of *Īçāna*, been fixed as a year, the bow; the goddess *Sāvitrī* the bowstring; a celestial coat of mail was made, sprung from the wheel of Time; the golden mountain *Meru* was made its flagstaff; the clouds with flashes of lightning its banners. *Çankara* placed upon it his own celestial weapons. Making the sky its flagstaff, he placed upon it his bull; *Brahmadaṇḍa*, *Kāladaṇḍa*, *Rudradaṇḍa*, and *Fever* became the protectors of the sides of the chariot; *Atharvan* and *Aṅgiras* the protectors of the wheels; the *Ṛgveda*, the *Sāmaveda*, and the *Purāṇas* stood in front of the chariot; the *itihāsa* and the *Yajurveda* were the protectors of the rear; all sacred Speeches and Sciences stood around it, and all hymns and *Vashaṭkāra*; *om* in the van. Having made the year with the six seasons his bow, he made his own shadow (i.e. the Death-night, *Raudrī kālarātrī*, *Rudra* being *Kāla*) the bowstring; *Vishṇu*, *Agni*, and *Soma* the arrow (v. supra); the universe is said to consist of *Agni* and *Soma*, and similarly to consist of *Vishṇu*, who is the soul of *Bhava*. *Çaṅkara* placed on that bow his wrath, the unbearable fire of anger, born of the wrath of *Bhṛgu* and *Aṅgiras*. The *Wind* (*Çvasana*) was caused to breathe fragrance. The great Ṛ., G., D., Aps. praised *Mahādeva* when he was about to ascend the chariot. He asked to get as his driver him who was superior to himself; the gods prevailed upon *Brahmán* to become his driver. The great Ṛ., G., D., Aps. praised *Mahādeva* after he had ascended the chariot. His bull uttered tremendous roars, so that many descendants and followers of *Tāraka* breathed their last. Frightful portents appeared. In consequence of the weight of *Soma*, etc. (β), the chariot seemed to sink. Then *Nārāyaṇa*, issuing out of the point of the arrow, assumed the form of a bull and raised the chariot. *Rudra*, standing on the head of his bull and the back of his steeds, beholding the *Dānava* city, cut off the teats of the horses and clove the hoofs of the bull; from that date the hoof of the bovine species came to be cloven and the horses to be without teats. He had united the *Pāçupata* weapon with the shaft. When the three cities became united, the D., Si., and great Ṛ. uttered the word *Jaya* adoring *Maheçvara*. When he had shot his arrow the cities began to fall down, and burning the *Asuras*, he threw them into the western ocean. The fire, born of his wrath, he quenched, lest it should reduce the three worlds to ashes. D., Ṛ., and the three worlds gratified *Sthāṇu*.

Tripuramardana, Tripuranāçana, Tripurāntaka, Tripurāntakara, Tripurārdana = Çiva, q.v.

Tripuravāsin, pl. (°*aḥ*) ("the inhabitants of Tripura"). § 603*d* (Tripura): VII, **202**, 9559.

Tripuravighna = Çiva: XIV, 205 (only C., B. has *Svadhāsvarūpāya*).

Trirāva, a Suparṇa, son of Garuḍa. § 564 (Mātalīyop.): V, **101**β, 3596 (only B., C. has *Trivāra*).

Trirvyūha = Vishṇu: XII, 13604.

Trisāman = Vishṇu (1000 names).

trisauparṇa, adj. (see Suparṇa[6]): XII, 13567 (*vratam*).

Trisauvarṇa(m) (B. Trisaup°) = Çiva (1000 names[1]) (*brahma*).

Trisrotasī, a river. § 268 (Varuṇasabhāv.): II, **9**, 375 (present in the palace of Varuṇa).

Tristhāna, a tīrtha belonging to Çiva. § 733*f* (Gaṅgādvāra): XIII, **25**, 1702 (*Maheçvarasya*).

trisuparṇa, adj. (familiar with the Trisuparṇa-verses, RV. X, 114, 3–5): XIII, 4296.

Trisuvarcaka (B. *Trishu*-°), name of a fire (?). § 491 (Āṅgirasa): III, **220**, 14156 (cf. Varca and see the footnotes, p. 40 above).

Trita, a ṛshi, brother of Ekata and Dvita. § 61 (Sarpasattra): I, **55**, †2112 (*Aurva-T°ābhyām asi tulyatejāḥ*, sc. Janamejaya). —§ 615*b* (Udapāna): IX, **36**, 2064 (*Udapānam . . . T°sya*), 2066, 2067 (*brāhmaṇasattamaḥ*), 2071, 2076, 2079, 2083, 2084, 2086, 2087, 2089, 2090, 2093, 2100, 2101, 2103, 2104 (°*yajñaḥ*), 2105 (only B.), 2108, 2112 (*T.* fell into a hole [at *Udapāna*] and was deserted by his brothers. Then he performed a mental sacrifice and was delivered, the *Sarasvatī* appearing in the hole. Then he cursed his brothers).—§ 665 (Mokshadh.): XII, **208**θ, 7597 (with Ekata and Dvita among the ṛshis of the west).—§ 717*c* (Uparicara): XII, **337**, 12757 (*Prajāpatisutāḥ . . . Ekataç ca Dvitaç caiva T°ç caiva maharshayaḥ*, among the sadasyas at the sacrifice of Vasu Uparicara), 12771 (*Ekata-Dvita-T°āḥ . . . Citraçikhaṇḍinaḥ*), 12812 (*Dvita T°matena*) —§ 717*b* (Nārāyaṇīya): XII, **340**, 12876 (*Ekataç ca Dvitaç caiva T°ç caiva maharshayaḥ*), 12950 (°*opaghātāt*, all. to § 615*b*); **342**, 13174, 13175 (*Brahmaṇaḥ putraḥ*, all. to § 615*b*).—§ 734 (Ānuçāsanik.): XIII, **26***a*, 1763 (among the ṛshis who came to see Bhīshma). —§ 770 (do.): XIII, **151**θ, 7114 (*Ekataç ca Dvitaç caiva T°ç caiva*, among the seven *Varuṇasyartvijaḥ*).—§ 775 (do.): XIII, **166**, 7668 (do., among the ṛshis of the west).

Trivāra (V, 3596) v. Trirāva.

Trivargamukhya = Dharma: III, †10257 (father of Yudhishṭhira).

Trivartman = Vishṇu: III, 12983.

Trivikrama[1] = Vishṇu (Kṛshṇa): XIII, 5378, 6815, 6892 (*Vishṇuḥ*), 7005 (Vishṇu's 1000 names), 7742 (i.e. Kṛshṇa). —Do.[2] = Çiva (1000 names[2]).

Trivikramagati = Vishṇu (Kṛshṇa): VI, 3027.

Trivishṭapa[1] (= Tripishṭapa, q.v.): III, †939 (°*m iva Çakraḥ*, sc. *viveça*), 9951 (Gaṅgā comes from *T.*), 10594 (Uçīnara ascended to *T.*), 10818; V, 1603 (*Svargam*); VI, 3549; IX, 275, 276, 2720 (°*m iva param*), 3028; XII, †2594, 3922, †10956, 12122; XIII, 4220, 4541; XIV, 916; XVIII, 1 (*Svargam*), 3 (do.), 4 (do.).

Trivishṭapa[2] = Sūrya (the Sun): III, 156.—Do.[3] = Çiva (1000 names[2]).

Triyuga[1] = Kṛshṇa: III, 8280 (dual = K. and Arjuna); V, 2541, 2542; XII, 1504.—Do.[2] = Çiva (1000 names[2]).

Truṭi, a mātṛ. § 615*u* (Skanda): IX, **46**θ, 2635.

Tryaksha = Çiva, q.v. (add X, 258; XII, 10122, 10344, 10349 (1000 names[1]); XIII, 1252 (1000 names[2]), 6542, 6565).

Tryaksha, pl. (°*āḥ*): I, 7315 (the Pāṇḍavas looked like as many *T.*, i.e. Çivas).

Tryakshan = Çiva: XIV, 193.

Tryambaka[1] = Çiva, q.v. — Do.[2], a Rudra. § 665 (Mokshadh.): XII, **208**δ, 7585.—§ 770 (Ānuçāsanik.): XIII, **151**β, 7090.—Do.[3] = Kṛshṇa: XII, 1668.

Tryambikāmbikanātha = Çiva (1000 names[1]).

Tṛṇabindu, a ṛshi. § 522 (Draupadīharaṇap.): III, **264**, 15575 (°*or ājñayā*, the Pāṇḍavas dwelt at the hermitage of *T.* when Jayadratha ravished Draupadī).—§ 550 (Samayapālanap.): IV, **13**, 327 (°*prasādāt*).—§ 615 (Gadāyuddhap.): IX, **61**, 3433 (°*or āçramam*, all. to § 522).—§ 637 (Rājadh.): XII, **47**η, 1596 (*mahāmuniḥ*, among the ṛshis who surrounded Bhīshma).

Tṛṇabindusaras ("the lake of Tṛṇabindu"). § 518 (Mṛgasvapnodbhavap.): III, **258**, 15365 (the Pāṇḍavas repaired to *T.* in the Kāmyaka forest).

Tṛṇaka, an ancient king. § 267 (Yamasabhāv.): II, **8**, 328 (in the palace of Yama).

Tṛṇāni (pl.) = Çiva (1000 names[1]).

Tṛṇapa, a Gandharva. § 191 (Arjuna): I, **123***a*, 4812 (present at the birth of Arjuna).

Tṛṇasomāṅgiras, a ṛshi. § 770 (Ānuçāsanik.): XIII, **151**η, 7112 (among the seven *Dharmarājartvijaḥ*).

Tṛptātṛptavicārin = Çiva (1000 names[1]).

Tṛtīyā, a river. § 268 (Varuṇasabhāv.): II, **9**, 373 (present in the palace of Varuṇa).

Tubha, v. Stubha.

Tuhara, a warrior of Skanda. § 615*u* (Skanda): IX, **45**η, 2573.

Tuhāra, a warrior of Skanda. § 615*u* (Skanda): IX, **45**η, 2573.

Tuhuṇḍa[1], an Asura. § 92 (Aṃçāvat.): I, **65**, 2533 (son of Danu).—§ 130 (do.): I, **67**, 2055 (*Asurottamaḥ*, incarnate as king Senābindu).

Tuhuṇḍa[2], a son of Dhṛtarāshṭra. § 232 (Svayaṃvarap.): I, **186**, 6983 (present at the svayaṃvara of Draupadī).

Tuhuṇḍa[3], pl. (°*āḥ*), a people. § 578 (Bhīshmavadhap.): VI, **50**π, 2084 (only B.).

Tukhāra, pl. (°*āḥ*) (II, 1850), v. Tushāra, pl.

Tulādhāra, a merchant. § 680*b* (Tulādhāra-Jājalisaṃv.): XII, **262**, 9277 (°*sya vākyāni*), 9284 (*vaṇigdharmā*), 9285, 9287, 9318, 9319, 9320, 9321, (9328); **263**, 9339, 9342, (9344); **264**, (9399), (9436), 9441; **265**, (9442), 9462, 9463, 9465 (discourse between *T.* and Jājali).

[Tulādhāra-Jājali-saṃvāda(ḥ)] ("the conversation of Tulādhāra with Jājali"). § 680*b* (Mokshadh.). *Bhīshma* said: There was once a brahman *Jājali*, living in a forest; he proceeded to the sea-shore and practised penances (description) for many years. Living within the waters he roamed through all the worlds with the speed of mind. Once, unseen by Ra., he thought: "there is none equal to me"; Pç. said to him that even the celebrated *Tulādhāra* (engaged in buying and selling) was not worthy of saying such words. Ṛ. wished to see *Tulādhāra*; Ra. raised him from the sea and showed him the road. Arrived at *Vārāṇasī*, he met *Tulādhāra* and spoke to him thus (!). Asked by *Yudhishṭhira*, *Bhīshma* described those difficult feats that *Jājali* had performed before; while he stood as a wooden post rapt in *yoga*, a pair of *kuliṅga* birds (*caṭakān*, v. 9317) built their nest on his head, laid their eggs there, their young ones came out, and only when the latter did not come back, even after a month, *Jājali* left that spot. Then he began to slap his armpits and proclaim loudly: "I have won great merit." Then an invisible voice in the sky said: "Thou art not equal to the wise *Tulādhāra* at *Vārāṇasī*; even he is not fit to say what thou sayest." *Jājali*, filled with wrath and desirous of meeting with *Tulādhāra*, began to roam over the whole earth, observing the vow of silence and passing the night at that spot where evening overtook him. After a considerable time he reached *Vārāṇasī* and saw *Tulādhāra* engaged in selling miscellaneous articles (*paṇyāni*). *Tulādhāra* stood up and saluted him, mentioning his dealings with the birds, etc. (XII, **262**). Asked by *Jājali*, the *vaiçya Tulādhāra* discoursed to him upon the ways of morality; "in every creature that is endued with the five senses live all the deities, *Sūrya*, etc. (*a*); the goat is *Agni*; the sheep is *Varuṇa*; the horse is *Sūrya*; Earth is *Virāj*; the cow and the calf are *Soma*; the man that sells these can never obtain success . . . In days of yore many Ṛ. (and *Yatis*) rebuked *Nahusha* for having slain a cow (which is declared in the scriptures to be like unto one's mother) and a bull (which is declared to be like to the Creator himself); in order to purify *Nahusha*, however, they divided that sin in 101 parts, and converting the fragments into diseases, threw them among all creatures, but declared that they should not be able to pour libations in his sacrifice" (XIII, **263**). *Jājali* said that *Tulādhāra's* doctrines smacked of atheism, which the latter denied, discoursing on sacrifice, saying that brahmans, having given up the sacrifice ordained for them (i.e. Yoga), had betaken themselves to the performance of sacrifices that are for *kshatriyas* (i.e. all other sacrifices). "Instead of all animals the rice-ball is a worthy offering in sacrifices; all rivers are as sacred as the *Sarasvatī*, and all mountains are sacred; the soul is itself a *tīrtha*; do not wander about on the earth to visit sacred places" (XII, **264**). *Tulādhāra* caused *Jājali* to summon the birds that had been reared by the latter; they made answer agreeably to the religion of *ahiṃsā* (Nīl.). "Faith is the daughter of *Sūrya*, etc.," quoting a verse sung by *Brahmán*, exalting Faith; "the food of a liberal usurer is acceptable, but not the food of a miser; . . . want of faith is a high sin; faith is a cleanser of sins." After a short while, *Tulādhāra* and *Jājali* both ascended to heaven. Many truths of this kind were spoken of by *Tulādhāra*; *Jājali*, having heard his words, betook himself to tranquillity (XII, **265**).

Tumbavīṇa = Çiva (1000 names[2]).

Tumbīvīṇāpriya = Çiva (1000 names[1]).

Tumbuma, pl. (°*āḥ*), a people. § 578 (Bhīshmavadhap.): VI, **50**π, 2084 (only C., B. has *Udbhasāḥ*, in the army of Yudhishṭhira).

Tumburu, a Gandharva. § 103 (Aṃçāvat.): I, **65,** 2559 (son of Prādhā, C. here *Tumbaru*).—§ 191 (Arjuna): I, **123,** 4810 (*Gandharvaiḥ sahitaḥ*, sung at the birth of Arjuna).—§ 264 (Sabhākriyāp.): II, **4,** 130 (*Dhanañjayasakhā*?), 132.—§ 266 (Çakrasabhāv.): II, **7,** 296 (in the palace of Indra).—§ 269 (Vaiçravaṇasabhāv.): II, **10,** 406 (among the Gandharva chiefs in the palace of Kubera).—§ 295 (Dyūtap.): II, **52,** 1881 (*Gandharvaḥ*, had given 100 horses to Yudhishṭhira).—§ 336 (Indralokābhigamanap.): III, **43,** 1769, 1783 (*Gandharvās T°çreshṭhāḥ*).—§ 436 (Yakshayuddhap.): III, **159,** 11656 (entertains Kubera during the parvans).—§ 552 (Goharaṇap.): IV, **56**ζ, 1771 (*Gandharvasya*, came on a vimāna to see the encounter).—§ 565 (Gālavac.): V, **117,** 3975 (*reme . . . yathā . . . T°ç caiva Rambhayā*).—§ 574 (Jambūkh.): VI, **6,** 214 (on Meru).—§ 592 (Saṃçaptakavadhap.): VII, **23**o, 969 (*dattās T°nā*, sc. horses, only B.).—§ 593*b* (Gandharvāstra): VII, **45,** 1824 (*Gandharvebhyaḥ . . . T°pramukhebhyaḥ*).—§ 608 (Karṇap.): VIII, **87**χ, 4423 (°*pramukhāḥ . . . Gandharvāḥ*).—§ 637 (Rājadh.): XII, **47**η, 1595 (? among the ṛshis who surrounded Bhīshma).—§ 695*b* (Dakshayajñavināça): XII, **285,** 10278 (°*r Nāradas tathā*).—§ 712 (Çukotpatti): XII, **325,** 12201 (°-*Nāradau*).—§ 775 (Ānuçāsanik.): XIII, **166***a*, 7640.—§ 785 (Anugītāp.): XIV, **88**ψ, 2641 (present at the açvamedha of Yudhishṭhira).—§ 789 (Putradarçanap.): XV, **29***a*, 774. Cf. Gandharva.

Tuṇḍa[1], a Rākshasa. § 537 (Rāma-Rāvaṇayuddha): III, **285**β, 16372 (fought with the monkey Nala).

Tuṇḍa[2], a prince. § 554 (Sainyodyogap.): V, **4**γ, 84 (only B., C. has *Pauṇḍraḥ*).

Tuṇḍikera[1], pl. (°*āḥ*), a people. § 604 (Karṇap.): VIII, **5**ζ, 138 (slain by Arjuna in the great battle).

Tuṇḍikera[2], sg. ("the king of the Tuṇḍikeras"). § 591 (Saṃçaptakavadhap.): VII, **17**β, 691 (among the Saṃçaptakas).

Tuṅgaka, a sacred forest. § 371 (cf. Tīrthayātrāp.). In days of old, when the *Vedas* had been lost, the ṛshi *Sārasvata* of *Aṅgiras'* race seated at ease on the upper garments of the *ṛshis* in the forest of *T.* made the *ṛshis* recollect all that they had learned before, only by distinctly pronouncing the syllable *om*. There the *ṛshis* and the gods, *Varuṇa*, *Agni*, *Prajāpati*, *Hari Nārāyaṇa*, *Mahādeva*, and *Pitāmaha*, appointed *Bhṛgu* to officiate at a sacrifice, and *Bhṛgu* once more performed the *agnyādhāna* for all these ṛshis, gratifying *Agni* with a portion of clarified butter according to the ordinance. A visit here destroys all sins, and dwelling there for a month with subdued senses, etc., leads to the *Brahmaloka* and delivers one's race: III, **85,** 8195 (*araṇyam*).

Tuṅgakāraṇya = Tuṅgaka: III, 8188.

Tuṅgaveṇā, a river. § 494 (Āṅgirasa): III, **222,** 14233 (among the rivers who are mothers of fires).—§ 574 (Jambūkh.): VI, **9**λ, 335.

***turaga,** pl. (°*āḥ*) ("horses"). § 123 (Aṃçāvat.): I, **66,** 2615 (*vyomacāriṇaḥ*, the spiritual sons of Lakshmī).

Turvasu, son of Yayāti and Devayānī. § 143 (Nahusha): I, **75,** 3159 (enumeration of the sons of Yayāti).—§ 144 (Yayāti): I, **75,** 3162 (all. to § 148).—§ 147 (Devayānī): I, **83,** 3432 (second son of Devayānī by Yayāti).—§ 148 (Yayāti): I, **84,** 3475, (3477) (would not take over the decrepitude of Yayāti and was therefore cursed), 3478 (*d:* the race of Turvasu should become extinct, he should become king of such whose practices are impure and who are non-aryan), 3481; **85,** 3520, 3525, 3533 (*d:* the Yavanas are the descendants of *T.*).—§ 156 (Pūruvaṃç.): I, **95,** ††3762 (enumeration of the sons of Yayāti).

Tushāra, pl. (°*āḥ*), a people. § 295 (Dyūtap.): II, **51,** 1850 (only B., C. has *Tukh°*, brought tribute to Yudhishṭhira).—§ 342 (Indralokābhigamanap.): III, **51,** 1991 (had been present at the rājasūya of Yudhishṭhira).—§ 449 (Ājagarap.): III, **177**, †12350 (in the north).—§ 583 (Bhīshmavadhap.): VI, **75**ε, 3297 (in the army of Duryodhana).—§ 608 (Karṇap.): VIII, **73**, 3652 (have been vanquished by Arjuna in the battle); **88**, 4506 (only B.).—§ 641 (Rājadh.): XII, **65**θ, 2429 (among the low and barbarous peoples).

Tushāragiri ("snow-mountain") = Himavat (?): XIII, 836 (°*kūṭābham*, sc. the bull of Çiva).

Tushita = Mahāpurusha (Mahāpurushastava).

Tushita, pl. (°*āḥ*), a class of gods. § 730 (Ānuçāsanik.): XIII, **18**λλ, †1371.

Tushṭa = Vishṇu (1000 names).

Tushṭājyapā = Çiva (1000 names[1]).

Tvashṭādhara, a son of Çukra. § 98 (Aṃçāvat. q.v.): I, **65**, 2548.

Tvashṭṛ, name of a god, one of the Ādityas. § 88 (Sambhavap.): I, **65**, 2524 (the eleventh of the Ādityas).—§ 191 (Arjuna): I, **123** *a*, 4824 (the tenth of the Ādityas).—§ 258 (Khāṇḍavadahanap.): I, **227**, 8266 (fought with Kṛshṇa and Arjuna).—§ 266 (Çakrasabhāv.): II, **7**, 296 (*Viçvakarmā*?, in the palace of Indra).—§ 384 (Agastyop.): III, **100**, 8711, †8713 (made the vajra of Indra).—§ 440 (Yakshayuddhap.): III, **164**, 11901 (°*uḥ*, sc. *astram*, obtained by Arjuna).—§ 535 (Setubandhana): III, **283**, 16309 (°*ur devasya tanayo balavān Viçvakarmaṇaḥ*, i.e. the monkey Nala).—§ 549 (Pāṇḍavapraveçap.): IV, **9**, 259 (Sudeshṇā asks Draupadī if she is [the wife] of *T.*).—§ 555 (Indravijaya): V, **9**, 229 (*Prajāpatiḥ*), 272 (*Prajāpatiḥ*), (274), 286, 287 (from antipathy of Indra, *T.* created Viçvarūpa Triçiras whom Indra slew, then *T.* created Vṛtra).—§ 561*h* (Arjuna): V, **56**, 2220 (*Dhātā*?, decorated the flagstaff of Arjuna).—§ 588 (Bhīshmavadhap.): VI, **121**β, 5802 (°*uḥ*, sc. *astram*, known by Arjuna).—§ 599 (Jayadrathavadhap.): VII, **94**, 3461 (°*uḥ sudurdharam tejo yena Vṛtro vinirmitaḥ*), 3462 (*T.* performed austerities and then, with the permission of Çiva, got the son Vṛtra); **99**, 3724 (°*ṭevādbhutakarmakṛt*); **108**, 4091 (*iva*).—§ 608 (Karṇap.): VIII, **68**λλλ, 3396 (had made the chariot of Arjuna).—§ 611 (Çalyap.): IX, **17**, 908, 909 (had for the use of Īçāna (i.e. Çiva) forged the weapon which Yudhishṭhira hurled against Çalya).—§ 615*u* (Skanda): IX, **45**, 2542 (gave to Skanda two companions, Cakra and Anucakra).—§ 635 (Rājadh.): XII, **30**α, 1181 (°*ṭreva nihitam yantram*).—§ 605 (Mokshadh.): XII, **208**β, 7582 (the ninth of the Ādityas), 7584 (°*uç caivātmajaḥ çrīmān Viçvarūpaḥ*).—§ 684 (Mokshadh.): XII, **269**, 9601 (Nahusha killed a cow in honour of *T.*).—§ 730 (Anuçāsanik.): XIII, **14**εε, 1003 (Çiva identified with *T.*).—§ 770 (do.): XIII, **151**γ, 7093 (the ninth of the Ādityas).—§ 782*g* (Guruçishyasaṃv.): XIV, **43**θ, 1178 (*adhirājo rūpāṇām*). Cf. Prajāpati, Viçvakarman.

Tvashṭṛ[2] = Sūrya: III, 146.—Do.[3] = Çiva (1000 names[2]).—Do.[4] = Vishṇu (1000 names).

Tvashṭṛputra ("the son of Tvashṭṛ") = Viçvarūpa: V, 235.

Tvāshṭra[1] (do.) = Viçvarūpa: V, 504 (*mahāsuraḥ*); XII, ††13207 (*V*°), ††13209 (*V*°), ††13211, ††13213 (°*otpāditam Vṛtram*).

Tvāshṭra[2] (do.) = Vṛtra: V, 512.

Tvāshṭra, adj. ("belonging to Tvashṭṛ"). § 592 (Saṃçaptakavadhap.): VII, **19**, 763 (*astram*, employed by Arjuna).—§ 599 (Jayadrathavadhap.): VII, **108**, 4091 (*astram*, employed by Bhīmasena).—§ 600 (Ghaṭotkacavadhap.): VII, **157**, 6954 (sc. *astram*, employed by Droṇa).—§ 602 (Droṇavadhap.): VII, **188**λ, 8604 (do., do.).—§ 603*b* (Nārāyaṇa): VII, **201**, †9466 (*karma*).

Tvāshṭrī ("the daughter of Tvashṭṛ"). § 119 (Aṃçāvat.): I, **66**, 2599 (wife of Savitṛ (i.e. Vivasvat) and in the shape of a mare—*vaḍavārūpadhāriṇī*—mother of the Açvins). Cf. Sañjñā.

tyāgaçāstra ("the treatise of renunciation"): XII, 7946 (sg.).

U

Uccaiḥçravas[1], a celestial horse. § 11 (Parvasaṅgr.): I, **2**, 366 (*janmo* °*aḥ*).—§ 28 (Amṛtamanthana): I, **17**, 1094 (*açvaratnam*); [**18**, 1146 (*turagaḥ pāṇḍuḥ*, arose at the churning of the ocean)].—§ 29 (Kadrū): I, **20**, 1190 (the wager of Kadrū and Vinatā about *U.*).—§ 30 (do.): I, **21**, 1206 (*turagam*, do.).—§ 60 (Sarpasattra): I, **54**, 2072 (*açvarājaḥ*, all. to § 29 foll.).—§ 201 (Droṇa): I, **130**, 5115 (*vyanadad yathaivo* °*ā hayaḥ*, sc. Açvatthāman).—§ 564 (Mātalīyop.): V, **102**, 3613 (*açvarājaḥ*, arose at the churning of the ocean, cf. § 28).—§ 576 (Bhagavadgītāp.): VI, **34**, 1231 (°*am açvānām viddhi mām*, says Kṛshṇa).—§ 589 (Droṇābhishekap.): VII, **11**, 384 (°*tulyabalam . . . hayarājānam*).—§ 603 (Nārāyaṇāstramokshap.): VII, **196**λ, 9058 (°*ā iva hreshatā*, sc. Açvatthāman).—§ 604 (Karṇap.): VIII, **8**η, 241 (*varo 'çvānām*).—§ 615*u* (Skanda): IX, **45**γ, 2518 (*hayaçreshṭhaḥ*).—§ 677 (Mokshadh.): XII, **235**, 8589 (*açvam*).—§ 785 (Anugītāp.): XIV, **87**, 2591 (*yathā*). Cf. Açvarāja.

Uccaiḥçravas[2], son of Avikshit. § 154 (Pūruvaṃç.): I, **94**, 3741 (sixth son of Avikshit).

Ucchikha, a serpent. § 64 (Sarpasattra): I, **57**, 2150 (of Takshaka's race).

Ucchṛṅga, a companion of Skanda. § 615*u* (Skanda): IX, **45**, 2551 (given to Skanda by Vindhya).

Uçanas, v. Çukra[1].

Uçaṅgava, an ancient king. § 267 (Yamasabhāv.): II, **8**, 337 (in the palace of Yama).

Uçīnara, an ancient king. § 6 (Anukram.): I, **1** *a*, 227 (in Sañjaya's enumeration).—§ 149 (Yayāti): I, **93**, †3681 (°*sya putraḥ*, i.e. Çibi).—§ 164 (Āpavop.): I, **99**, 3941 (°*sya rājarsheḥ . . . duhitā*, sc. Jitavatī).—§ 207 (Yamasabhāv.): II, **8**, 325 (in the palace of Yama). § 411 (Çyenakapotīya): III, **130**, 10557 (C. has *Ushī*°); **131**, 10584, 10589 (*rājā*), 10594 (Indra in the shape of a hawk, and Agni in that of a pigeon, put *U.* to the test; cf. the similar stories told of Çibi (§ 466) and of Vṛshadarbha (§ 738*b*)).—§ 565 (Gālavacarita): V, **118**, 3989, 3996, 3997 (resided in Bhojanagara, begat Çibi (Auçīnara) on Mādhavī, the daughter of Yayāti).—§ 656 (Khaḍgotpattik.): XII, **166**δ, 6199 (received the sword from Çunaka, from him it passed to Bhoja).—§ 746 (Ānuçāsanik.): XIII, **76**ι, 3689 (attained to heaven by way of gifts). Cf. Auçīnara[2].

Uçīnara[2] (do.) = Vṛshadarbha: XIII, 2065.

Uçīnara[3], a Vṛshṇi. § 232 (Svayaṃvarap.): I, **186**, 7000 (present at the svayaṃvara of Draupadī).

Uçīnara, pl. (°*āḥ*), a people. § 604 (Karṇap.): VIII, **5**ζ, 137 (have been slain by Arjuna in the great battle).—§ 641 (Rājadh.): XII, **101**ο, 3736 (*sarvaçastreshu kuçalāḥ sattvavanto hy Ucīnarāḥ*).—§ 739 (Ānuçāsanik.): XIII, **33** *a*, 2104 (have been degraded to çūdras).

Uçīnarasuta ("the son of Uçīnara") = Çaibya[8] (= Çibi): VII, 371.

Uçīrabīja (°*vīja*, C.), a mountain. § 418 (Tīrthayātrāp.): III, **139**, 10820 (in the north, crossed by Yudhishṭhira, etc.). —§ 565 (Gālavacarita): V, **111**, 3843 (*yatra Jāmbūnadaṃ sarah*, in the north).

***Udadhi** ("the Ocean", personif.). § 565 (Gālavacarita): V, **117**, 3969 (*reme . . . Jāhnavyāṃ yatho°ḥ*).

Udagra = Çiva (1000 names[2]).

Udakakrīḍana, name of a place. § 197 (Bhīmasenarasap.): I, **128**, 4996.

Udakapati ("lord of waters") = Varuṇa: V, 3531.

***Udāna**, one of the vital breaths. § 485 (Brāhmaṇavyādhasaṃv., v. Pativratop.): III, **213**, 13966 (description), 13970 (*Samāno°yor madhye*). — § 660*b* (Bhṛgu-Bharadvājasaṃv.): XII, **184**, 6845; **185**, 6872 (*f*: That single breath that operates in these three (i.e. Prāṇa, Samāna, and Apāna) is called Udāna).—§ 662*b* (Jāpakop.): XII, **200** ε, 7346.—§ 667 (Mokshadh.): XII, **213**, 7759 (*Vyāno°au*). — § 704 (do.): XII, **302**, 11124.—§ 714*g* (Samāna): XII, **329**, 12397 (son of Samāna and father of Vyāna).—§ 714*j* (Udvaha): XII, **329**, 12402.—§ 782*b* (Brāhmaṇagītā): XIV, **20**, 612, 614; **21**, 653; **23**, 685, 688, 692, 696, 699, 705, 706 (the contention of the vital breaths about superiority); **24**, 712, 717, 723, 724, 725, 727.—§ 782*g* (Guruçishyasaṃv.): XIV, **42**, 1109.—Do.[2] = Çiva (1000 names[1]).

Udapāna, one or more tīrthas. § 370 (Tīrthayātrāp.): III, **84**, 8088.—§ 615*b* (Baladevatīrthayātrā): Although the *Sarasvatī* seems to be lost there, yet, owing to the succulence of the herbs and the moistness of the land, holy persons know [that] the river [has an invisible current there] (IX, **35**). There the great ascetic *Trita* had lived and drunk *soma* in a pit where his two brothers had left him, and therefore were cursed by him. Requested by *Janamejaya Vaiçampāyana* related: In a former *yuga* there were three brothers who were ascetics: *Ekata*, *Dvita*, and *Trita*, like to *Prajāpati*, having by their tapas won *Brahmaloka* (*Brahmalokajitaḥ*), and being blessed with children. At last their father *Gautama* died, having passed a long life here. Those kings who had been his *yajamānas* continued to pay respect to his sons. Once, thinking of performing a sacrifice and having received animals from their *yajamānas*, those *maharshis* came towards the east. *Trita* was walking in front, *Ekata* and *Dvita* in his rear, bringing up the animals. *Ekata* and *Dvita* thought of taking the kine away and deserting *Trita*. In the night they saw a wolf. *Trita* ran in fright and fell into a deep pit on the bank of the *Sarasvatī*. Though hearing his wails of woe, his brothers deserted him. *Trita* feared to die because he had not earned the merit of drinking *soma*, and in imagination performed a sacrifice, himself being the *hotṛ* and uttering the *ṛces*, *yajushes*, and *sāmans* (description). *Bṛhaspati* prevailed upon the gods to go there lest *Trita* should become angry and create other gods. *Trita* duly gave them their shares with proper *mantras*; they granted him boons: that the gods should deliver him [from the well], and that he who bathes in that well shall have the end which is attained by persons who have drunk *soma*. At these words the *Sarasvatī*, with her waves, appeared within that well. Raised aloft by her, *Trita* emerged and worshipped the gods. Meeting his brothers he cursed them, saying that they should become wolves and have for offspring leopards and bears and apes (IX, **36**): IX, **35**, 2062 (on the Sarasvatī); **36**, 2064, 2068, 2093 (?).—§ 615 (Baladevatīrthayātrā): IX, **36**, 2118.

Udāpekshin, a son of Viçvāmitra. § 721*b* (Viçvāmitrop.): XIII, **4** β, 258.

Udaraçāṇḍilya, a ṛshi. § 266 (Çakrasabhāv.): II, **7**, 295 (in the palace of Indra).

Udāradhī = Vishṇu (1000 names).

Udarāksha (B. Udā°), a warrior of Skanda. § 615*u* (Skanda): IX, **45** η, 2565.

Udāvarta, a king. § 562 (Bhagavadyānap.): V, **74** γ, 2729 (*Haihayānāṃ*, among the wicked kings who annihilated their kinsmen and relatives; B. *Mudā°*).

Udaya, the mountain where the sun rises. § 595 (Shoḍaçarāj., v. Pṛthu Vainya): VII, **69**, 2411 (*parvataḥ*, when the mountains milked the earth, *U.* was their calf).—§ 597 (Pratijñāp.): VII, **84**, 2989 (°*ṃ Bhāskaro yathā*, sc. *āruroha*). —§ 605 (Karṇap.): VIII, **12**, 462 (°*āgrādribhavanaṃ*).—§ 608 (do.); **60**, 3016 (°*ṃ parvataṃ yadvat*). — § 611 (Çalyap.): IX, **16**, 827 (*çailāv Astodayāv iva*); **20**, †1069 (*yathodayasthaḥ Savitā*).—§ 637 (Rājadh.): XII, **45**, 1546 (*çailaṃ*). Cf. Udayācala, Udayagiri.

Udayācala = Udaya. § 601 (Droṇavadhap.): VII, **184**, †8409 (*samudiyād U°-keçarī*).

Udayagiri = Udaya. § 702 (Mokshadh.): XII, **294**, 10773 (*yatho°au dravyaṃ sannikarsheṇa dīpyate*).

Udayendu, a city of the Kurus. § 592 (Saṃçaptakavadhap.): VII, **23** ο, 971 (*pure Kurūṇām U°nāmni*, there Sutasoma was born).

Udbhasa, pl. (°*āḥ*), a people. § 578 (Bhīshmavadhap.): VI, **50** π, 2084 (only B., C. has *Tumbumāḥ*).

Udbhava[1], a prince. § 554 (Sainyodyogap.): V, **4** γ, 86.

Udbhava[2] = Vishṇu (1000 names).

Udbhid = Çiva (1000 names[2]).

Udbhijāḥ (i.e. °*ijjāḥ*) = Çiva (1000 names[1]).

Uddālaka, a ṛshi. § 14 (Paushyap.): I, **3**, 695 (= Āruṇi Pāñcālya, why he was named so).—§ 22 (Pramadvarā): I, **8** *a*, 962.—§ 59 (Sarpasattra): I, **53**, 2047 (among the sadasyas at the snake-sacrifice of Janamejaya). — § 187*b* (Çvetaketu): I, **122**, 4724 (*maharshiḥ*, father of Çvetaketu), 4735 (°*sya putreṇa . . . Çvetaketunā*).—§ 266 (Çakrasabhāv.): II, **7**, 294 (in the palace of Çakra).—§ 376 (Tīrthayātrāp.): III, **85**, 8264 (*muniḥ*, among the ṛshis who expect Yudhishṭhira).—§ 412 (Ashṭāvakrīya): III, **132**, †10603 (Kahoḍa was the disciple of *U.* and married his daughter Sujātā), †10613, †10614 (father of Çvetaketu).—§ 615*i* (Saptasārasvata): IX, **38**, 2209 (? *Auddālaki*, v. 2207; at his sacrifice the Sarasvatī appeared as the river Manoramā). — § 635 (Rājadh.): XII, **34**, 1229 (caused Çvetaketu to be begotten by a disciple of his).—§ 640 (do.): XII, **57**, 2056 (expelled his son Çvetaketu).

Uddālaki, a ṛshi. § 746 (Ānuçāsanik.): XIII, **71**, 3486 (*ṛshiḥ*), 3487 (do., father of Nāciketa), 3491 (*ṛshiḥ*, ordered Nāciketa to go to Yama).

Uddhava, a Vṛshṇi. § 232 (Svayaṃvarap.): I, **186**, 6998 (*mahāmatiḥ*, came to the svayaṃvara of Draupadī).—§ 252 (Subhadrāharaṇap.): I, **219**, 7916.—§ 253 (Haraṇāharaṇap.): I, **221**, 7990 (came to the nuptials of Arjuna and Subhadrā). —§ 294 (Dyūtap.): II, **50**, 1795 (°*o vā mahābuddhir Vṛshṇīnām arcitaḥ*). — § 320 (Saubhavadhop.): III, **15**, 644 (*Gada-Çāmbo°ādibhiḥ*), 647 (*Ugraseno°ādibhiḥ*). — § 570 (Sainyaniryāṇap.): V, **157** κ, 5330 (*Gada-Sāmbo°ādibhiḥ*).—§ 793 (Mausalap.): XVI, **3**, 67, 69 (ascends to heaven).

Uḍhra, v. Uḍra.

Udīcya, pl. (°āḥ) ("the Northerners"), a people. § 556 (Sañjayayānap.): V, **30**, †890 (*Prācyo°āḥ*, in Duryodhana's army). — § 571 (Ulūkadūtāgamanap.): V, **160**γ, †5510 (°-*Kāmboja-Çakaiḥ*); **161**, †5555 (do.).—§ 573 (Ambopākhyānap.): V, **195**ε, 7609 (*Prācyo°āḥ*, adj.?). — § 586 (Bhīshmavadhap.): VI, **106**τ, 4808 (*Pratīcyo°-Mālavāḥ*).— § 587 (do.): VI, **117**ρ, 5484 (do.); **119**αα, 5648 (do.).— § 589 (Droṇābhishekap.): VII, **7**ζ, 183 (do.). — § 599 (Jayadrathavadhap.): VII, **111**τ, 4267 (adj.?). — § 600 (Ghaṭotkacavadhap.): VII, **156**κ, 6850.—§ 604 (Karṇap.): VIII, **5**ζ, 138 (*Prācyo°āḥ*, have been slain by Arjuna in the battle).—§ 607 (do.): VIII, **45**ν, 2101.—§ 608 (do.): VIII, **70**πππ, †3511 (*hatāḥ*), (ρρρ), †3524 (do.).—§ 609 (Çalyap.): IX, **1**γ, 28 (*nihatāḥ*).

Udīrṇa = Vishṇu (1000 names).

Udra, pl. (°āḥ), a people. § 284 (Sahadeva): II, **31**, 1174 (°-*Keralaiḥ*, in the south, vanquished by Sahadeva).—§ 342 (Indralokābhigamanap.): III, **51**, 1988 (*sa-Pauṇḍro°ān*, had been present at the rājasūya of Yudhishṭhira).—§ 578 (Bhīshmavadhap.): VI, **50**π, 2084 (in the army of Yudhishṭhira, only C., with the reading *Uḍhrāḥ*, B. has *Colāḥ*). Cf. Oḍra.

Udrapāraka, a serpent. § 67 (Sarpasattra): I, **57**, 2158 (of Dhṛtarāshṭra's race).

Udrarāja ("the king of the Uḍras"). § 264 (Sabhākriyāp.): II, **4**β, 119 (*Pāṇḍyoḍrarājau*, waited upon Yudhishṭhira).

Udumbara = Vishṇu (1000 names).

Uḍupa ("lord of the stars") = Soma (the Moon): III, 11149 (*iva*).

Uḍupati (do.) = Soma (the Moon): IX, 2030 (*iva*), 2925.

Uḍurāj (do.) = Soma (the Moon): II, 1322 (*iva*); V, 1149 (*iva*); IX, 2009; XII, 1879 (*iva*); XIII, 837 (*iva*); XIV, 1897 (*iva*).

Udvaha[1], a prince. § 130 (Aṃçāvat.): I, **67**, 2700 (among the incarnations from the Krodhavaça gaṇa).

Udvaha[2], name of a wind. § 714*j* (Çukakṛtya): The wind which causes Soma (the Moon) and other luminaries to arise (in the body called *Udāna* (so C.)), and which sucks up the waters in the oceans and imparts them to the clouds and thereafter to *Parjanya*, is called *U.*: XII, **329**, 12404.

Udyat, a mountain. § 370 (Tīrthayātrāp.): III, **84**, 8071 (*Udyantaṃ . . . parvataṃ*).

Udyoga = Udyogaparvan. § 4 (Anukram.): I, **1**, 89 (*Virāṭa°-sāravān . . . Bhāratadrumaḥ*).—§ 10 (Parvasaṅgr.): I, **2**, 333 (= Sainyodyogaparvan?).—§ 585 (Bhīshmavadhap.): VI, **98**, 4484 (allusion to Ambopākhyānap.). — § 795*c* (Mahābhārata): XVIII, **6**ρ, 278. Cf. VI, 1614.

Udyogaparvan ("the book relating the preparations for war"), the fifth book of the Mhbhr. § 10 (Parvasaṅgr.): I, **2**, 329 (= Sainyodyogaparvan?).—§ 11 (do.): I, **2**, 402, 517 (said to comprise 6098 çlokas). Cf. Udyoga.

Ugra[1], a son of Dhṛtarāshṭra. § 130 (Aṃçavat.): I, **67**, 2738 (enumeration).—§ 182 (Dhṛtarāshṭraputranāmak.): I, **117**, 4551 (do.).—§ 581 (Bhīshmavadhap.): VI, **64**κ, 2838, 2843 (slain by Bhīmasena).—§ 600 (Ghaṭotkacavadhap.): VII, **157**ο, 6938 (only B.: *Ugro 'nuyāyī*, but C. has *Ugrayāyī*).

Ugra[2], a prince. § 554 (Sainyodyogap.): V, **4**γ, 75.

Ugra[3], a son of Kavi. § 747*b* (Suvarṇotpatti): XIII, **85**ι, 4150 (eighth son of Kavi).

Ugra[4] = Çiva, q.v.—Do.[5] = Vishṇu (1000 names).

ugra, name of a caste: XII, 10868 (pl.); XIII, 2568 (pl.).

Ugraçravas[1], son of Lomaharshaṇa and generally named Sauti, who recited the Mhbhr. to Çaunaka. § 1 (Anukram.): I, **1**, 1 (*Lomaharshaṇaputra U°āḥ Sautiḥ*).—§ 18 (Paulomap.): I, **4**, ††851 (*Lomaharshaṇaputra U°āḥ Sautiḥ Paurāṇikaḥ*).— § 51 (Parikshit, Āstikap.): I, **40**, 1659.—§ 775 (Ānuçāsanik.): XIII, **166**ζ, 7673 (among the ṛshis of the north).

Cf. the following synonyms:—

Laumaharshaṇi ("the son of Lomaharshaṇa"): I, 5, 8, 359, 853, 863.

Lomaharshaṇaputra (do.): I, 1, ††851.

Paurāṇika, q.v.

Sauti, Sūta, Sūtaja, Sūtanandana, Sūtaputra, q.v.

Ugraçravas[2], a son of Dhṛtarāshṭra. § 130 (Aṃçāvat.): I, **67**, 2735 (enumeration). — § 182 (Dhṛtarāshṭraputranāmak.): I, **117**, 4548 (do.).

Ugradaṇḍa = Çiva (1000 names[1]).

Ugradhanvan = Skanda: III, †14644.

Ugraka, a serpent. § 47 (Sarpanāmak.): I, **35**, 1552.

Ugrasena[1], brother of Janamejaya. § 12 (Paushyap.): I, **3**, ††662.

Ugrasena[2], a Devagandharva. § 101 (Aṃçāvat.): I, **65**, 2550 (*Bhīmaseno°au*, among the sons of Muni). — § 191 (Arjuna): I, **123**, 4811 (do., present at the birth of Arjuna). —§ 552 (Goharaṇap.): IV, **56**ζ, 1771 (came to see the encounter).

Ugrasena[3], a prince. § 130 (Aṃçāvat.): I, **67**, 2649 (incarnation of the Asura Svarbhānu).

Ugrasena[4], a son of Dhṛtarāshṭra. § 130 (Aṃçāvat.): I, **67**, 2735 (enumeration).—§ 182 (Dhṛtarāshṭraputranāmak.): I, **117**, 4548 (do.).

Ugrasena[5], son of the elder Parikshit. § 154 (Pūruvaṃç.): I, **94**, 3743.

Ugrasena[6] (probably the same as Āhuka), king of the Vṛshṇis, father of Kaṃsa. § 252 (Subhadrāharaṇap.): I, **219**, 7913 (*rājā Vṛshṇīnāṃ*).—§ 262 (Bhagavadyāna): II, **2**, 54 (*Yaduçreshṭhair U°mukhaiḥ*).—§ 264 (Sabhākriyāp.): II, **4**β, 116 (the same? waited upon Yudhishṭhira).—§ 320 (Saubhavadhop.): III, **15**, 647 (°*oddhavādibhiḥ*). — § 556 (Sañjayayānap.): V, **28**, †805 (°*ādayaḥ*).—§ 561*c* (Kṛshṇa Vāsudeva): V, **48**, †1885 (°*sya sutaṃ*, i.e. Kaṃsa; when Kṛshṇa had slain Kaṃsa, *U.* was made king). — § 641 (Rājadh.): XII, **81**, 3040 (*Babhru°yoḥ*). — § 676 (Mokshadh.): XII, **231**, 8455 (°*sya saṃvādaṃ Nārade Keçavasya ca*), (8456) (discourse between *U.* and Kṛshṇa).— § 785 (Anugītāp.): XIV, **83**, 2480 (*Vṛshṇyandhakapatiḥ*).— § 795 (Svargārohaṇap.): XVIII, **5**μ, 163 (among those who after death entered the deities). Cf. Āhuka, Bhojarāja, Kukurādhipa.

Ugrasena[7] = Janaka: III, †10651.

Ugrasenasuta ("the son of Ugrasena[6]") = Kaṃsa: I, 2703 (*K°*); V, 4296.

Ugrasenānī = Kṛshṇa: XII, 1507.

Ugratejas[1], a serpent. § 793 (Mausalap.): XVI, **4**η, †120.—Do.[2] = Çiva (1000 names[2]).

Ugrātman = Kṛshṇa: XII, 1670.

Ugrayāyin, a son of Dhṛtarāshṭra. § 182 (Dhṛtarāshṭraputranāmak.): I, **117**, 4550 (enumeration).—§ 600 (Ghaṭotkaca): VII, **157**ο, 6938 (only C., B. has *Ugro 'nuyāyī*).

Ugrāyudha[1], a son of Dhṛtarāshṭra. § 130 (Aṃçāvat.): I, **67**, 2734 (enumeration).—§ 182 (Dhṛtarāshṭraputranāmak.): I, **117**, 4546 (do.).—§ 232 (Svayaṃvarap.): I, **186**, 6982 (came to the svayaṃvara of Draupadī).—§ 604 (Karṇap.): VIII, **7**, †207 (*Bhāratarājaputraḥ?*).

Ugrāyudha[2], a Pāñcāla prince. § 608 (Karṇap.): VIII, **56**νν, 2735 (fought with Karṇa).

Ugrāyudha[3], a Kuru warrior. § 609 (Çalyap.): IX, **2**ζ, 93 (had been slain).

Ugrāyudha[4] = Çiva: VII, 9536; XII, 10676.

Ugrāyudhasuta ("the son of Ugrāyudha"), a prince. § 605 (Karṇap.): VIII, **19**, 717 (slain by Arjuna).

Ugreça = Çiva: III, 8836.

Ujjālaka, name of a lake (?). § 475 (Dhundhumārop.): III, **202**, 13530 (*samudro vālukāpūrṇaḥ*, the abode of Dhundhu).—§ 478 (do.): III, **204**, 13588 (*samudre vālukāpūrṇe*).

Ujjānaka, name of a tīrtha. § 410 (Plakshāvataraṇag.): III, **130**, 10552 (*esha U°o nāma Pāvakir yatra çāntavān / Arundhatīsahāyaç ca Vasishṭo bhagavān ṛshiḥ*). — § 733*y* (Ānuçāsanik.): By bathing in *U.* and at the hermitage of *Ārshṭishena*, and at the hermitage of *Piṅgā*, one is purified from sins, etc.: XIII, **25**α, 1741.

Ujjayana, a son of Viçvāmitra. § 721*b* (Viçvāmitrop.): XIII, **4**β, 257.

Ujjayanta, a mountain in the country of the Surāshṭras. § 377 (Dhaumyatīrthak.): III, **88**, 8347 (*çikharī*, description).

Uktha, name of a fire. § 490 (Āṅgirasa): III, **219**, 14154 (*tribhir ukthair abhishṭutaḥ*).

Ukthayajña = Kṛshṇa: XII, 1511.

Ulmucu, v. Unmucu.

Ulmuka, a Vṛshṇi. § 287 (Rājasūyikap.): II, **34**, 1275 (came to the rājasūya of Yudhishṭhira).—§ 402 (Tīrthayātrāp.): III, **120**, †10277 (*Gado°au*, will assist the Pāṇḍavas).—§ 589 (Droṇābhishekap.): VII, **11**ζ, 409.—§ 785 (Anugītāp.): XIV, **66**θ, 1939 (only B., C. has by error Unmukha).

Ulūka[1], Kaitavya, son of Çakuni. § 11 (Parvasaṅgr.): I, **2**, 515 (*°sya preshaṇam*, cf. § 571).—§ 232 (Svayaṃvarap.): I, **186**, 7002 (*Kaitavaḥ*, came to the svayaṃvara of Draupadī).—§ 561 (Yānasandhip.): V, **47**α, 1799; **57**, 2254 (Nakula wished to fight *U.*).—§ 571 (Ulūkadūtāgamanap.): V, **160**, 5412 (*Kaitavya*), 5471, 5476, 5484, 5486; **161**, 5537, (5540); **162**, 5578, 5586, 5588, 5596, 5616, 5621, 5626, 5629 (*Kaitavya*); **163**, 5666 (*Kaitavyam*), 5673, 5679, 5683, 5684, 5688 (*Kaitavyam*), 5692, 5693, 5695; **164**, 5702 (*U.* was sent by Duryodhana as an ambassador to the Pāṇḍavas).—§ 578 (Bhīshmavadhap.): VI, **45**[21], 1747, 1748 (fought with the *Cedi* king).—§ 582 (do.): VI, **72**ε, 3166 (*Çakunim U°ñ ca . . . pitāpitrau*, attacked by Sahadeva).—§ 583 (do.): VI, **79**μ, 3456 (all. to § 571).—§ 600 (Ghaṭotkacavadhap.): VII, **171**, 7715 (son of Çakuni, pierced by Arjuna), 7718.—§ 603 (Nārāyaṇāstramokshap.): VII, **193**α, 8906. — [§ 604 (Karṇap.): VIII, **7**, †208 (*Kaitavyānām adhipaḥ*).] — § 605 (do.): VIII, **11**ν, 414 (Çakuni and *U.* in the eyes of the makaravyūha of Karṇa); **25**, 993, 994, 995, 998, 1000, 1001, 1004 (encounter with Yudhishṭhira).—§ 608 (do.): VIII, **46**γ, 2134 (Çakuni and *U.* were followed by the Gāndhāras); **48**ο, 2263 (brother of Patatri, PCR.); **54**θθ, 2610; **61**, 3078 (attacked by Sahadeva), 3108, 3110, 3115.—§ 609 (Çalyap.): IX, **1**γ, 26 (*Kaitavaḥ*, among the slain).—§ 611 (do.): IX, **8**ε, 400; **11**μ, 563 (C. has by error *Ū°*); **22**, 1157 (encounter with Nakula; *Saubalasya sutam*, v. 1158); **27**υυ, 1459; **28**, 1503, 1528, 1532 (slain by Sahadeva).

Cf. the following synonyms:—

Çākuni ("the son of Çakuni"): VIII, 997.

Kaitava ("the gambler's son"): I, 7002 (*U°*); V, 5665.

Kaitavya (do.): V, 2254 (*U°*), 5412 (*U°*), 5535, 5579, 5582, 5583, 5628, 5629 (*U°*), 5643, 5644, †5651, 5666 (*U°*), 5671, 5688 (*U°*), 5698; IX, 26 (*U°*, has been slain), 96, 394.

Ulūka[2], a Nāga (?) (according to Nīl. a Yaksha). § 46 (Garuḍa): I, **32**α, 1489 (°-*Çvasanābhyām*, had an encounter with Garuḍa).

Ulūka[3], one or more ṛshis. § 573 (Ambopākhyānap.): V, **186**, 7353 (*°āçrame*).—§ 637 (Rājadh.): XII, **47**η, 1598 (*paramo vipraḥ*, among those who surrounded Bhīshma).—§ 721*b* (Viçvāmitrop.): XIII, **4**β, 250 (son of Viçvāmitra).

Ulūka[4] ("king of the Ulūkas"?) = Bṛhanta (?): II, 1019 (*°sahitaḥ*, sc. Arjuna).

Ulūka[5], pl. (*°āḥ*), a people. § 279 (Arjuna): II, **27**, 1014 (*°vāsinam . . . Bṛhantam*, in the north), 1020 (*uttarān*, vanquished by Arjuna).

***ulūka**, pl. (*°āḥ*) ("owls"). § 126 (Aṃçāvat.): I, **66**, 2621 (the offspring of Kākī). Cf. Prāvārakarṇa.

Ulūkadūtāgamana ("Ulūka's arrival as an ambassador"). § 10 (Parvasaṅgr.): I, **2**, 335 (*parva*, i.e. Ulūkadūtāgamanaparvan).

[**Ulūkadūtāgamanaparvan(°va)**] ("the section relating to Ulūka's arrival as an ambassador," the 64th of the minor parvans of Mhbhr.; cf. Ulūkadūtāgamana). § 571. When the *Pāṇḍavas* had encamped on the bank of the *Hiraṇvatī*, the *Kauravas* also fixed their encampment. Then *Duryodhana* consulted with *Karṇa*, etc. (*a*), and sent *Ulūka* to the *Pāṇḍavas* and *Somakas* in order to irritate them still more, with insulting messages to *Yudhishṭhira* (the story of the wicked cat), *Kṛshṇa*, etc. (β); before *Arjuna* he should mention the *Kāmbojas*, etc. (γ), among his troops; "I know that the *Gāṇḍīva* is full 6 cubits long" (V, **160**). *Ulūka* repeated the messages to the *Pāṇḍavas*, etc. (V, **161**), and repeated his words to *Arjuna* once more; *Bhīmasena* and the rest became furious; *Kṛshṇa* counselled *Ulūka* to retire in time; *Ulūka* once more repeated his words; they became still more enraged, especially *Bhīma*, who said that he would certainly drink *Duḥçāsana's* blood; also *Sahadeva*, etc. (δ), gave him answers for *Duryodhana*; *Sahadeva* would slay *Ulūka* before the eyes of *Çakuni*, and then *Çakuni* himself (V, **162**). *Arjuna* said that *Duryodhana's* contrivance of seeking cover behind *Bhīshma* would be of no avail, as he would himself slay *Bhīshma*; the same said *Çikhaṇḍin* ("I have been created by the Creator for the destruction of *Bhīshma*"); *Dhṛshṭadyumna* would slay *Droṇa* with all his followers and friends. *Ulūka* related it all to *Duryodhana*. Messengers instructed by *Karṇa* promulgated: "array to-morrow before sunrise" (V, **163**). *Dhṛshṭadyumna* began to select combatants in order to pit them against particular warriors of the hostile force (ε) (V, **164**).

Ulūpī, daughter of the serpent king Kauravya, wife of Arjuna. § 11 (Parvasaṅgr.): I, **2**, 397.—§ 248 (Arjunavanavāsap.): I, **214**, 7788, [7791 (*Nāgarājasutām*)], (7793), 7793 (*pannagī*), 7810 (fell in love with Arjuna and took him to the palace of Kauravya).—§ 785 (Anugītāp.): XIV, **79**, 2309 (*pannagātmajā*), 2311 (*uragātmajā*), 2312 (*pannagātmajām*); **80**, 2342 (*pannagasutām*), 2343, 2348 (*pannagātmajām*), 2352, [2371 (*nāgottamasute*)], 2382, 2397, 2399 (*Nāgendraduhitā*), 2401 (*U.* revived Arjuna).—§ 787 (Āçramavāsap.): XV, **1**α, 23 (*Nāgakanyā*); **10**ζ, 348.—§ 794 (Mahāprasthānikap.):

XVII, 1, 27 (*bhujagātmajā*, returned to the Gaṅgā). *U.* is presumably the mother of Irāvat (q.v. VI, **90**). Cf. Bhujagātmajā, Bhujagendrakanyā, Bhujagottamā, Kauravī, Kauravyaduhitṛ, Kauravyakulanandinī, Pannaganandinī, Pannagasutā, Pannagātmajā, Pannageçvarakanyā, Pannagī, Uragātmajā. Cf. also Kauravya (v. Nāga, pl.).

Ulūta, see Utūla.

Umā[1], a goddess, daughter of Himavat, wife of Çiva. § 233 (Svayaṃvarap.): I, **187**, †7008 (*cakāçire Parvatarājakanyām U°ṃ yathā devagaṇāḥ*, sc. *jigīshamāṇāḥ*).—§ 270 (Brahmasabhāv.): II, **11**, 467 (*Mahādevaḥ sahomaḥ*).—§ 330 (Indradarçana): III, **37**, 1488 (mentioned in Draupadī's blessing of Arjuna). — § 331 (Kairātap.): III, **39**, 1554 (*Devyā sahomayā*, sc. *Çivaḥ*). — § 333 (do.): III, **40**, †1663 (*sahomayā*, sc. *Içvaraḥ*).—§ 410 (Plakshāvataraṇag.): III, **130**, 10550 (*Çarvasya . . . sahomayā*).—§ 442 (Nivātakavacayuddhap.): III, **167**, 11978 (*°sahāyaḥ . . . Pinākadhṛk*). —§ 500 (Skandop.): III, **228**, 14391 (only C., cf. Agni).—§ 504 (Skandayuddha): III, **231**, 14523 (*°yonyāñ ca Rudreṇa çukraṃ siktaṃ*, from that seed Skanda was born).—§ 506 (do.): III, **231**, 14545 (*Paçupatiḥ . . . Umayā saha*).—§ 507 (do.): III, **231**, 14575.—§ 524 (Jayadrathavimokshanap.): III, **272**, 15875 (*°sahāyaḥ*, sc. *Tryambakaḥ*).—[§ 549 (Pāṇḍavapraveçap.): IV, **6**, (Yudhishṭhira hymned Durgā = Umā, who then showed herself to him).]—§ 565 (Gālavacarita): V, **111**, 3830 (*atra*—i.e. in the north—*Kāmaç ca Roshaç ca Çailaç comā ca sambabhuḥ*).—§ 574 (Jambūkh.): VI, **6**, 220 (*°sahāyaḥ . . . Bhūtabhāvanaḥ*).—§ 576 (Bhagavadgītāp.): VI, **23**, 801 (= Durgā (q.v.) hymned by Arjuna).—§ 603*d* (Tripura): VII, **202**, 9576, 9584 (*°ayā sārdhaṃ*), 9592 (had on her lap Çiva in the form of a child).—§ 615*u* (Skanda): IX, **45**γ, 2515; **46**, 2667, 2717 (*putraṃ . . . Umāyāḥ*, sc. Skanda).—§ 616 (Sauptikap.): X, **7**η, 259 (*°bhūshaṇatatparaṃ*, sc. Çiva).—§ 694*b* (Jvarotpatti): XII, **284**, (10233), (10236) (grieved at Çiva's being excluded from sacrifices). — § 695*b* (Dakshayajñavināça): XII, **285**, 10302 (partook in the destruction of Daksha's sacrifice).—§ 701*b* (Bhava-Bhārgavasamāgama): XII, **290**, 10695 (*Devīṃ*).—§ 717*b* (Nārāyaṇīya): XII, **343**, XIV, ††13222 (*Himavato girer duhitaraṃ*, Bhṛgu coveted *U.*, but she was given to Çiva).—§ 730*g* (Upamanyu): XIII, **14**, 828 (= *strīliṅgaṃ*), 836 (*Devadevaḥ sahomayā*). — § 730 (Anuçāsanik.): XIII, **14**, 1001 (*Devī*), 1022 (*Devīṃ*), **15**, 1028 (*Çarvāṇī*), (†1031); **16**, 1104 (*deva Umaya sahitaḥ*, sc. Çiva). —§ 731*b* (Ashṭāvakra-Diksaṃv.): XIII, **19**, 1400 (*Devyā*, performed austerities in order to obtain Çiva).—§ 747*b* (Suvarṇotpatti): XIII, **84**, 3993 (*Devīṃ*), 3995 (*Devī*) (the gods prevailed upon Çiva to withdraw his vital seed, *U.* then cursed the gods).—§ 768*b* (Umā-Maheçvarasaṃv.): XIII, **140**, 6338 (*Çaṅkarasyomayā sārdhaṃ saṃvādaḥ*), 6374 (6378), (6384); **141**, (6398), (6402), (6409), (6417), (6423), (6450), (6480); **142**, (6506), (6525), (6539); **143**, (6565); **144**, (6624), (6641), (6651), (6664); **145**, (6683), (6725), (6736), (6740); **146**, (6759), (6768); **148**, 6874 (*Çaṅkarasyomayā sārdhaṃ saṃvādaṃ*) (discourse between *U.* and Çiva).—§ 768 (Ānuçāsanik.): XIII, **148**, 6920 (*Çaṅkarasyomayā sārdhaṃ saṃvādaḥ*).—§ 773*d* (Çiva): XIII, **161**, 7489, 7493 (repetition from § 603*d*).—§ 778*f* (Muñjavat): XIV, **8**, 182 (*°sahāyaḥ . . . Maheçvaraḥ*).—§ 782*g* (Guruçishyasaṃv.): XIV, **43**θ, 1185 (*nārīṇām uttamām*).

Cf. also the following synonyms:—

Ambikā (?): XIII, 7106.

Āryā: III, 14495.

Bhīmā: III, 5026 (*°āyāḥ sthānaṃ*).

Çailaputrī ("daughter of the mountain"): IX, 2472, 2484; XIII, 6388, 6913.

Çailarājasutā ("daughter of the king of the mountains"): XII, 10214, 10229, 12169; XIII, 6393, 6771 (according to B. *°āṃ devīṃ*; C. has *°ā devī* = Gaṅgā).

Çākambharī, q.v.

Çarvāṇī: XIII, 1028.

Deveçī: XII, 10301.

Devī ("the goddess"): I, 2315 (praised in the Mhbhr.); II, 403 (in the palace of Kubera); III, 1554 (*U°*), 1623 (accompanied Çiva), 5027 (by bathing at *Bhīmāyāḥ sthānaṃ* one becomes the son of *D.*), 6064 (*°yās tīrthe*), 6065, 6072 (*°yās tīrthe*), 7041 (*Rudrapatnyāḥ*), 7091 (*°yāḥ sthānaṃ*, i.e. Çākambharī), 7093, 7096, [8001 (? name of a tīrtha ?)], 8113 (*Viçveçvaraṃ . . . Devyā saha*), 8161 (*Mahādevaṃ Devyā saha*, on Çrīparvata), 12285 (*Sthāṇur Devyā saha*, all. to Kairātaparvan), 14427 (*saha Devyā . . . Govṛshadhvajaḥ*), 15161, 15162 (the half of Duryodhana's body originated from *D.*); IV, 178 (*Durgāṃ*), 181, 183, 186, 189, 192, 202, 204 (hymned by Yudhishṭhira), (205), 213; V, 3829 (performed austerities in order to obtain Çiva); VI, (810) (hymned by Arjuna); VII, 9575; VIII, 1593 (*°yāḥ samīpataḥ*, sc. Çiva); IX, 2488 (*Girivarātmajā*), 2492; XII, 5789, 10238, 10239, 10273, 10286, 10287, (†10296), †10297, (10300), 10304, 10307, 10325, 10327, 10481, 10692, (10693), 10694, 10695 (*U°*), 10760, 12169 (*Çailarājasutā*), 12204; XIII, 662 (*°yā saha*, sc. Çiva), 826, 827, 871 (*°yāḥ samīpataḥ*), 977, 978 (*°yā saha Maheçvaraḥ*), 1001 (*U°*), 1022 (*U°*), 1033, 1400 (*U°*), 3992 (*Rudrāṇyāḥ*), 3993 (*U°*), 3994, 3995 (*U°*), 4001, 4008, 6364, 6413 foll. passim, 6771; XIV, 1185 (*U°*).

Durgā, q.v.

Gaurī: III, 8129; IV, †2305.

Girisutā ("daughter of the mountain"): XIII, 6368.

Girivarātmajā (do.): IX, 2488.

Kālī: X, 387.

Mahābhīmā: XII, 10304.

Mahādevī, q.v.

Mahākālī: XII, 10304.

Maheçvarī: XII, 10304.

Māheçvarī: XIV, 1184.

Parvatarājakanyā: I, †7008.

Pārvatī: III, 14542 (*sahitaṃ P°yā*, sc. Çiva), 14562 (accompanied by Gaurī, etc.); VII, 2859 (*sahitaṃ P°yā*, sc. Çiva), 9461 (*°yā sahitaṃ*, sc. Çiva), 9579, 9584; X, 206 (*°yā ca Maheçvaraḥ*); XIII, 842 (*sahitaṃ . . . P°yā Parameçvaraṃ*); XIV, 1184 (*Māheçvarī*).

Rudrāṇī: II, 458 (in the palace of Brahmán); V, 3969 (*reme . . . yathā Rudraç ca R°yāṃ*); XIII, 1411, 3992 (*Devyāḥ*), 4004, 4021, 6296.

Rudrapatnī ("wife of Rudra"): III, 7041 (*Devyāḥ*).

Tribhuvaneçvarī: IV, 178.

The following names of Umā (Durgā) occur in two separate hymns, viz. IV, 184–203, and VI, 796–808:—

Āryā (VI, 796), *Brahmaṇyā* (VI, 802), *Brahmavidyā* (VI, 803), *Caṇḍā*, *Caṇḍī* (VI, 797), *Çākambharī*, *Çvetā*, *Dhūmrākshī* (VI, 801), *Durgā* (IV, 198, 203; VI, 803), *Hiraṇyākshī* (VI, 801), *Jātavedasī* (VI, 802), *Jayā* (IV, 194; VI, 798), *Kaiṭabhanāçinī* (VI, 801), *Kālī* (IV, 195; VI, 796), *Kāpālī*, *Kapilā* (VI, 796), *Karālī*, *Kātyāyanī* (VI, 798), *Kauçikī*, *Kokamukhā* (VI, 800), *Kṛshṇā* (IV, 184, 187; VI, 801),

Kṛshṇacchavisamā (IV, 187), *Kṛshṇapiṅgalā* (VI, 796), *Kumārī* (IV, 184; VI, 796), *Mahādevī* (IV, 200; VI, 805), *Mahākālī* (IV, 195; VI, 797), *Mahishāsuranāçinī* (IV, 193), *Mandaravāsinī* (VI, 796), *Pītavāsinī* (VI, 800), *Sāvitrī* (VI, 804), *Skandamātṛ* (VI, 803), *Siddhasenānī* (VI, 796), *Tāriṇī*, *Varavarṇinī* (VI, 797), *Vijayā* (IV, 194; VI, 798), *Virūpākshī* (VI, 801).

Umā[2] = Sarasvatī: IX, 2389.

Umādhava, Umākānta = Çiva (1000 names[2]).

[Umā-Maheçvara-saṃvāda] ("the discourse between Umā and Çiva"). § 768*b* (Ānuçāsanik.): *Nārada* said: Once, *Çiva* on *Himavat*, the resort of Si. and Cā., practised severe penances, surrounded by Aps., etc. (*a*) (copious descriptions). Then came *Umā* (description) and with her hands covered the eyes of *Çiva* from behind, and darkness arose all around; but suddenly the darkness disappeared: a third eye appeared on his forehead and consumed the mountain; *Umā* stood before him with her hands joined; he directed benignant looks towards the mountain, which, in a moment, was restored to its former condition. *Umā* asked why his eastern, northern, and western faces are so handsome, and the southern so terrible (1); why his matted locks are tawny and erect (2); why his throat is blue (3); why he has always the *Pināka* in his hand (4); why he is always a *brahmacārin* with matted locks (5). *Çiva* promised to explain it to her (XIII, **140**). *Çiva* answered the above questions (1): "In days of yore *Tilottamā*, created by *Brahmán* (cf. I, ch. **211**), circumambulated me; in whatever direction she turned, a new face of mine appeared through my *yoga*-power; with my eastern face I exercise the sovereignty of the universe; with my northern I sport with thee (i.e. *Umā*); with my western I ordain the happiness of creatures; with my southern I destroy all creatures. (2 and 5): In order to do good to all creatures. (3): In days of yore, *Indra*, desirous of acquiring my prosperity hurled his thunderbolt at me, which scorched my throat. (4): In order to accomplish the purposes of the gods." *Umā:* Why hast thou selected a bull for thy vehicle? *Çiva:* In days of yore, *Brahmán* created *Surabhi* (the celestial cow); once, froth fell from one of her calves on my body; my wrath scorched all the kine which became diversified in hue; *Brahmán* pacified me and gave me this bull both as a vehicle and as a device. *Umā:* Why dost thou reside in the cemetery (description), abandoning thy many abodes in heaven? *Çiva:* I do not see any spot that is more sacred than the cemetery, and my *Bhūtas* love to reside in such spots. *Umā:* What are the indications of *dharma?* *Çiva:* Abstention from injury, etc. *Umā:* What are the duties of the four castes? *Çiva* enumerated them. *Umā:* What are the common duties of all the castes? *Çiva:* Whenever the world is created, three eternal religions are created by *Brahmán:* the *Veda*, the *smṛti*, and the practice of the righteous, etc., there are four classes of *bhikshus: kuṭīcaka, bahūdaka, haṃsa*, and *paramahaṃsa* (each in turn being superior to the preceding one; v. Nīl.). *Umā:* What is the religion of the *ṛshis* (*munis*)? *Çiva:* (1) the *Phenapas* always gather the froth from the *amṛta* that *Brahmán* drank at a great sacrifice. (2) The *Vālakhilyas* in the solar disc, adopting the practice of the birds, live by picking up grains (*uñche*), clad in deer-skins or bark of trees; they are only as big as the joint of the thumb; they have burnt all their sins by severe penances. (3) The *Cakracaras* in the *Somaloka*, near to *Pitṛloka*, live by gleaning [differently Nīl.], devoted to compassion. (4) The *Samprakshālas*, *Açmakuṭṭas*, and *Dantolūkhalikas* [v. Nīl. and the note of PCR., p. 642], near the gods [called] *Somapas* and *Ūshmapas* (C. *U*°), live by gleaning ["drinking the rays of *Soma*," PCR.], together with their wives, etc. (*Çiva* copiously described the religion of the Ṛ. in general) (XIII, **141**). *Umā:* What is the religion of the *Vānaprasthas?* *Çiva* described it (*vīrāsana, maṇḍūka-yoga, paurṇamāsya, cāturmāsya*, etc.); they attain to *Brahmaloka* or *Somaloka*. *Umā:* What is the religion of the *munis* (*munisaṅghasya*) in their doctrines of perfection (*siddhivādeshu*; i.e. *jñānagoshṭhīshu*, Nīl.; "followers of the scriptures treating of ascetic success," PCR.)? they live unrestrained in the forest, together with their wives. *Çiva:* Their characteristics are the shaving of the head, yellow robes, passing the night at home, ablutions three times a day, *hotra*, *samādhi*, adherence to the path of the good, etc. All those duties of which I have spoken before as belonging to forest-recluses, are the duties of these also, etc. (copious description). Asked by *Umā*, *Çiva* said: By fasts, etc., one attains to heaven and sports with G.; by *maṇḍūkayoga* and *dīkshā* with the *Nāgas*; by living with deer, etc., one attains to *Amarāvatī*; by subsisting upon air or water, fruits and roots, one attains to the riches of Y. and sports with Aps.; by abandoning one's body in the ocean, having lived in dependence only of himself, etc., one attains to the world of *Varuṇa*; by the same practices and piercing one's feet with a stone, one rejoices with the Gh., others obtain *Brahmaloka* (having abandoned their bodies in fire as an oblation to the gods), *Çakraloka*, etc. (XIII, **142**). Asked by *Umā*, *Çiva* expounded the circumstances under which one may be promoted or degraded to a higher or lower order when reborn (XIII, **143**). Asked by *Umā*, *Çiva* (worshipped by D. and As.) discoursed as to how men succeed in ascending to heaven, and what words, thoughts, and acts are of importance in this respect and for acquiring a long life. "This is the way that was indicated by *Brahmán* himself" (XIII, **144**). Asked by *Umā*, *Çiva* discoursed about that conduct by which a man may attain to heaven (Aps., the woods of *Nandana*), quoting *Brahmán*; the unmerciful, etc., sink into hell; they who humiliate their preceptors and seniors are reborn as *Çvapākas* and *Pukkasas*. Then (asked by *Umā*) he explained why some men become possessed of wisdom or the contrary, blind, diseased, etc.; what acts are faulty, and what faultless; why some are observant of vows, some like Rā. (*Brahmarākshasas*) in conduct, unmindful of *homa* and *vashaṭkāra* (XIII, **145**). *Nārada* said: Now *Çiva* himself became desirous of hearing. Saying that *Umā* (acquainted with all duties, etc.) used to converse every day with *Sāvitrī*, etc. (γ), who all regard their husbands as their gods, he questioned *Umā* about the duties of women; "half of my body is made up of half thy body; thou . . . art the cause of the peopling of the earth." *Umā* said she would first consult the rivers, who, with the waters of all *tīrthas*, are approaching *Çiva* in order to enable him to perform his ablutions: *Sarasvatī* (the first of all streams), going to the ocean, etc. (δ). *Gaṅgā* was selected for answering the question, and praised *Umā's* modesty; then *Umā* discoursed upon the duties of women in full. She should not cast her eyes on the moon or the sun or a tree that has a masculine name. The husband is the god of the woman. If a husband being poor, or diseased, or distressed, etc., were to command his wife to accomplish anything improper or unrighteous, the wife should, without hesitation, do so according to the practice allowable in time of distress, and she becomes entitled to a share in the merit acquired by her husband. *Nārada* said: *Çiva* applauded *Umā* and dismissed the others; Bh., etc. (ε), returned home (XIII, **146**). Asked by R̥., *Çiva* discoursed on the glory of *Vāsudeva*, i.e. Kr̥shṇa, q.v. (XIII, **147**). *Nārada* said: At the conclusion of *Çiva's* speech loud roars were heard in the firmament, etc. Some of R̥. set out on a *tīrthayātrā*, others returned whence they came.

Umāpati = Çiva, q.v.

Umlocā, an Apsaras. § 191 (Arjuna): I, **123**, 4821 (among the Apsarases who sung at the birth of Arjuna).

***uñchavr̥tti** ("one who lives by gleaning"): III, 15407 (*çilo*°); XII, 13918 (°*vrate*); XIV, 2695 foll.

[Uñchavr̥tty-upākhyāna(m)] ("the episode relating to the gleaner"). § 718*b* (Mokshadh.): *Bhīshma* said: M-r̥ *Nārada* wanders through all the worlds like *Vāyu*, not obstructed by anything; once he repaired to the abode of *Indra*, who asked him if he had perceived any wonderful incident. *Nārada* recited the following story (XII, **353**): In the town of *Mahāpadma*, on the southern bank of the *Gaṅgā*, there lived a brahman of the *Soma*-lineage (*Somānvaye*, i.e. *Atrigotre*, Nīl.), endued with amiability, etc.; he was in great trouble with regard to the value of following the ordinances of the *Vedas*, or the [*Dharma*]*çāstras*, or the duties that eminent men of former times have performed (*çishṭācīrṇa*). Then there came to him a wise brahman as a guest (XII, **354**); him he asked what he, having entrusted his duties as a householder to his son, should do in order to perform the highest duty of men, as he had no respect for the religion of the *Yatis*, who depend upon alms. The guest said that he was himself perplexed, as heaven had many doors (examples) (XII, **355**); he told him (according to what he learnt from his preceptor) to repair to *Padma*, the righteous *Nāga*, who lived in the city called after the *Nāgas* in the *Naimisha* forest, on the banks of the *Gomatī*, whence, in a former creation (*pūrvābhisarge*) the wheel of righteousness was set in motion (*dharmacakraṃ pravartitaṃ*), and where all the gods had, in days of old, performed a great sacrifice, and where king *Māndhātr̥* neglected (*atikramañ cakre*) *Indra* (XII, **356**). The host became delighted, and passed the night happily conversing with his guest about the fourth mode of life (*caturthadharma*) [i.e. *sannyāsa*, renunciation, PCR.; =*mokshadharma*, Nīl.]; the next morning, having dismissed his guest, he set out for the abode of the *Nāga* (XII, **357**), was shown the way by an ascetic, and received by the beautiful wife of the *Nāga*; as the *Nāga* had gone to draw the chariot of *Sūrya* for a month, and would be back in seven or eight days, he passed this time on the banks of the *Gomatī* (XII, **358**). On the 6th day the *Nāgas* of the city, seeing him abstaining from food and [only] reciting *mantras*, came and asked him to eat; but he wanted to keep his fast for eight days; if then the *Nāga*-chief had not come back, he would break his fast. Then the *Nāgas* returned (XII, **359**). When the *Nāga*-chief came home, he was informed by his wife about the brahman's arrival (XII, **360**). The *Nāga* doubted whether that brahman was a human being, as the *Nāgas*, even by D., As., and D-r̥, are considered to be endued with great energy; his wife told him to go and speak to the guest without the wrath which is natural to *Nāgas*; the *Nāga* himself also blamed wrath, citing *Rāvaṇa* (who became the rival of *Çakra* and was slain by *Rāma*) and the sons of *Kārtavīrya* (who were slain by *Rāma Jāmadagnya*) and *Kārtavīrya* himself (XII, **361**). The *Nāga* met with the brahman (who characterized himself as a righteous being (*dharmāraṇya* = *muni*, Nīl.)) on the banks of the *Gomatī*, engaged in Yoga and reciting the *Vedas* in order to dispel all evil from the *Nāga* (XII, **362**); he asked the *Nāga* whether he had seen anything wonderful in those regions where he had drawn the one-wheeled chariot of *Vivasvat*. The *Nāga* described the wonders of which the Sun is the source (*a*). The most wonderful was that one day, in former times, at the hour of noon, a being came through the sky like a second sun and entered *Sūrya* (XII, **363**). *Sūrya* declared it to be a brahman, who had attained to heaven on account of his having been crowned with success (*siddhaḥ*) in the gleaning-vow (*uñchavr̥ttivrate*) (description), and because he had gratified *Bhava* (Çiva) by praising him with *saṃhitāḥ*, and now he "goes round the earth staying in the disc of *Sūrya*; neither D., nor G., As., nor Pn. are superior to those creatures that attain to this excellent end" (XII, **364**). The brahman then betook himself formally to the practice of the *uñcha*-vow (XII, **365**), and having saluted the *Nāga*, he went to *Cyavana Bhārgava*, who initiated him and recited the story of the brahman in king *Janaka's* palace to D-r̥ *Nārada* > *Indra* > the foremost brahmans. "During my (i.e. Bhīshma's) battle with *Rāma*, the *Vasus* told it to me." The brahman proceeded to another forest (XII, **366**).

Unmāda[1], a companion of Skanda. § 615*u* (Skanda): IX, **45**, 2553 (given to Skanda by Pārvatī).

Unmāda[2] = Çiva (1000 names[2]).

Unmādaḥ sarvabhūtānām = Kr̥shṇa: XII, 1640.

Unmādana = Çiva (1000 names[1]).

Unmātha, a companion of Skanda. § 615*u* (Skanda): IX, **45**, 2532 (given to Skanda by Yama).

Unmattaveçaprachanna = Çiva (1000 names[2]) (B. °*vesha*°).

Unmesha = Çiva (1000 names[1]).

Unmuca, a r̥shi. § 665 (Mokshadh.): XII, **208**η, 7594 (one of the r̥shis of the south). Cf. next.

Unmucu, a r̥shi. § 770 (Ânuçâsanik.): XIII, **151**η, 7112 (the first of the seven *Dharmarājartvijaḥ*).—§ 775 (do.): XIII, **166**δ, 7665 (B. *Ulmucuḥ*, the first of the r̥shis of the south). Cf. the prec.

Unmukha (XIV, 1939) v. Ulmuka.

Upacitra, a son of Dhr̥tarāshṭra. § 130 (Aṃçāvat.): I, **67**, 2700 (enumeration).—§ 182 (Dhr̥tarāshṭraputranāmak.): I, **117**, 4543 (do.).—§ 599 (Jayadrathavadhap.): VII, **136**χχ, 5594 (slain by Bhīmasena).

Upaçānta = Çiva (1000 names[2]).

Upaçruti, a goddess. § 555 (Indravijaya): V, **13**, 426, 427 (*devīṃ*); **14**, 428 (*devīṃ*), (430), 430, 439 (*devī*, found out Indra).—§ 717*b* (Nārāyaṇīya): XII, **343**, VII), ††13215 (repetition from § 555).

Upadeçakara = Çiva (1000 names[7]).

Upagahana, son of Viçvāmitra. § 721*b* (Viçvāmitrop.): XIII, **4**β, 255.

Upajalā, a river. § 410 (Plakshāvataraṇag.): III, **130**, 10556 (*Jalāñ co°āñ caiva Yamunām abhito nadīṃ*).

Upakāra = Çiva (1000 names[2]).

Upakīcaka, pl. (°*āḥ*), followers of Kīcaka (= Kīcaka, pl.): IV, 818.

Upakr̥shṇaka, a warrior of Skanda. § 615*u* (Skanda): IX, **45**η, 2559.

Upakshaya = Çiva (1000 names[1]).

Upamanyu[1], a brahman, disciple of Āyoda Dhaumya. § 14 (Paushyap.): I, **3**, ††684.—§ 15 (cf. Paushyap.): *Upamanyu* was sent to look after the kine. His master forbade him to enjoy the alms he received before he had offered it to him; then, being deprived by the master of the whole alms, and forbidden to go begging a second time, or to drink of the milk of the cows, or the froth that the calves threw out when sucking, he ate of the leaves of the *arka* plant (*asclepias gigantea*), whence he became blind and fell into a pit. *Āyoda Dhaumya* told *U.* to glorify the Açvins, which he did; they gave him a cake which he would not apply without offering it to his preceptor, though the latter had himself formerly obtained a similar cake without offering it to his preceptor. The *Açvins* gave him teeth of gold, while those of his preceptor were of iron, and restored him to sight: I, **3,** ††697, ††698, ††700, ††704, ††708, ††711, ††717, ††718, ††721, ††739.

Upamanyu[2], **Vaiyāghrapadya** (°*pāda* C.), a ṛshi. § 730 (Ānuçāsanik.): XIII, **14,** 634 (*Vaiyāghrapādasya* (°*padya*°, B.)), 655 (Kṛshṇa came to the hermitage of *U.*, who advised him to gratify Çiva, whose granting of boons he described).—§ 730*g* (do.): *Upamanyu* said: In the *Kṛtayuga* there was a ṛshi named *Vyāghrapāda.* I was born as his son and *Dhaumya* as my younger brother. Accompanied by *Dhaumya,* I once came to the hermitage of certain ṛshis. There I saw milk, which appeared to me to be like to *amṛta.* Coming home, I asked my mother to give me some food prepared with milk. Having no milk my mother was sorry. She then took a cake (of rice) and boiled it into water and placed it before me, saying that it was milk. Knowing the nature of milk, I understood that this was not milk; this I said to my mother, who then answered me that ascetics in the wood could not have milk. "Whence shall we, who live at the river, the resort of the *Vālakhilyas,* obtain milk? In the wilderness are no offspring of *Surabhī.*" Then she told me to devote myself to *Çaṅkara* (i.e. Çiva). Questioned by me about Çiva my mother then, in accordance with the discourses of the *munis,* described the diverse forms of *Mahādeva* (i.e. Çiva) (η). I then applied myself to the practice of penances in order to gratify *Çiva.* After a thousand celestial years *Mahādeva* appeared to me in the form of *Çakra* (i.e. Indra) riding on his elephant, but I did not desire a boon from any other deity than *Mahādeva.* Questioned by Indra about the reason, I stated *Çiva* to be the existent and the non-existent, the manifest and the unmanifest, the eternal and immutable, etc., and that there was nothing superior to *Çiva* (θ). *Mahādeva* resides in the worlds named *Bhū,* etc. (ι). In all the encounters of the gods, etc. (κ), *Bhava* restores power to those who meet with destruction. It is *Maheçvara* who made futile the boons given to *Andhaka,* etc. (λ). He is adored by *yogins,* etc. (μ). *Brahmán,* etc. (ν), always say that there is none higher than *Mahādeva.* His sign (*liṅga*) is worshipped by *Brahmán,* etc. The creatures bear only the signs of *Mahādeva* and his spouse, and those of *Brahmán,* etc. (o). "I shall never acknowledge any other deity. Nor would I take the fulfilment of all my wishes from any other deity." When I had finished this speech, the celestial elephant became transformed into a white bull (description), on the back of which *Mahādeva,* with *Umā,* was seated (description of Çiva and his weapons: *Pināka* (π)). The *Pāçupata* weapon is superior to all other weapons such as the *Brāhma,* etc. (ρ), but the *çūla* (σ) is even superior. *Çiva* was also armed with the battle-axe, which he had given to *Rāma Jāmadagnya* (τ). He was surrounded by *Brahmán,* etc. (υ). The deities praised Çiva by uttering diverse hymns (ϕ). "I then praised him with a hymn (χ) and offered him *arghya* (water). *Çiva* became gratified and granted me the fulfilment of all my wishes. I once more praised him (ψ) and asked that I and my kinsmen and friends might always eat food with milk. *Çiva* granted this, and that after the expiration of a *kalpa* I should obtain the companionship of *Çiva.* Then the god disappeared": XIII, **14,** (784), (880), 928, 932.—§ 730 (do.): XIII, **14,** (964); **15,** 1034, (1036); **16,** (1037), (1104), (1109); **17,** (1115); **18,** 1358 (*U.* taught *Kṛshṇa* certain mantras by which he succeeded in seeing *Çiva, U.* afterwards recited to *Kṛshṇa* the 1000 names of *Çiva,* which had been communicated to him by *Taṇḍi*).

Upananda[1], name of a tabour. § 522 (Draupadīharaṇap.): III, **270,** †15700 (*yasya*—i.e. Yudhishṭhira's—*dhvajāgre nadato mṛdaṅgau Nando°au*). Cf. Upanandaka[3].

Upananda[2], a son of Dhṛtarāshṭra. § 608 (Karṇap.): VIII, **51**$\epsilon\epsilon$, 2458 (*Nando°au*, slain by Bhīmasena). Cf. next.

Upanandaka[1], a son of Dhṛtarāshṭra. § 130 (Aṃçāvat.): I, **67,** 2731 (*Nando°au*).—§ 182 (Dhṛtarāshṭraputranāmak.): I, **117,** 4544 (do.).—§ 578 (Bhīshmavadhap.): VI, **51**σ, 2098 (*Nando°aiḥ*). — § 583 (Bhīshmavadhap.): VI, **79,** 3470/71 (only B.).—§ 608 (Karṇap.): VIII, **51**$\delta\delta$, 2446. Cf. Upananda.

Upanandaka[2], a serpent. § 564 (Mātalīyop.): V, **103**γ, 3628 (*Nando°au*).

Upanandaka[3], name of a tabour. § 592 (Saṃçaptakavadhap.): VII, **23**π, 1032 (*mṛdaṅgau . . . Nando°au*, on the standard of Yudhishṭhira). Cf. Upananda[1].

Upanandaka[4], a warrior of Skanda. § 615*u* (Skanda): IX, **45**η, 2566.

Upāṅga, pl. (°*āni*) ("supplement to the Vedāṅgas"): I, 4004 (*sāṅgopāṅgam*); III, 2417 (*Vedāḥ sāṅgopāṅgāḥ*); XII, 11772 (*sāṅgopāṅgān . . . Vedān*), 12674 (*Vedeshu . . . sāṅgopāṅgeshu*), 13183 (*Vedān . . . sāṅgopāṅgān*).

***Upanishad** ("secret doctrine, mystery", common name of certain literary works), mostly pl.: I, 62 (*sāṅgopanishadāñ caiva Vedānām*), 112 (*dharmopanishadam*), 246 (sg., i.e. the Mhbhr.), 645 (*caturo Vedān sāṅgopanishadaḥ*), 2473 (*sāṅgopanishadān Vedān*), †3629 (*gṛhasthopanishat purāṇī*); II, 136 (*Vedopanishadāṃ vettā*, sc. Nārada); III, 1465 (sg., i.e. the Pratismṛti), 1808 (*sāṅgopanishadān Vedān*), 8641 (do.), 8676 (*Vedāç ca sāṅgopanishadaḥ*), 13653 (*sāṅgopanishado Vedān*), 13767 (*Vedasyopanishat satyaṃ satyasyopanishad damaḥ* / *damasyopanishat tyāgaḥ*), 15147 (sg., *yāç copanishadi kriyāḥ*); VII, 9601 (*Vedāṅgāḥ sopanishadaḥ*); VIII, 4414 (*Vedāḥ . . . sopavedopanishadaḥ*); XII, 1613 (*nishatsūpanishatsu*), 3520 (*rājopanishadam*), 3833 (*daṇḍopanishad*), 8484 (*Vedān . . . sāṅgopanishadaḥ*), 8898 (only C., read with B. *caturthaç caupanishado dharmaḥ*), 9074–9075 (*Vedasyopanishat satyaṃ*, etc.), 9736 (*caturthopanishadadharmaḥ*, B. and C.), 10400 (*Vedopanishadāṃ gaṇaiḥ*), 11004 (*Vedasyopanishat satyaṃ*, etc.), 11757 (sg.), †11836 (read with B. *upanishadam upākarot*), 12015 (*mokshaḥ . . . sopanishadaḥ*), 12750 (*sāṅgopanishadaṃ çāstram*), 13136 (*Purāṇe sopanishade*), 13551 (*sahopanishadān Vedān*); XIII, 3735 (*gavām up°*), 3935 (*Vedopanishadā*), 4109 (*Vedāç ca sopanishadaḥ*). Cf. Mahopanishad.

Upaplava[1] ("affliction, calamity"): VII, 4199 (PCR. = Upaplavya, but there does not seem to be any reason to take it as a proper name).

Upaplava[2] = Çiva (1000 names[1]).

Upaplavya, name of a city near to the capital of the Matsya king Virāṭa. § 11 (Parvasaṅgr.): I, **2,** 493, 512.—§ 553 (Vaivāhikap.): IV, **72,** 2349 (*Virāṭasya*).—§ 555 (Sainyodyogap.): V, **8,** 196.—§ 556 (Sañjayayānap.): V, **22,** †645; **23,** 685.—§ 562 (Bhagavadyānap.): V, **84,** 3010; **86,** 3040.—§ 569 (do.): V, **137,** 4675; **144,** 4888; **147,** 4956.—§ 570 (Sainyaniryāṇap.): V, **151,** 5157.—§ 586 (Bhīshmavadhap.): VI, **107,** 4920.—§ 598 (Jayadrathavadhap.): VII, **85,** 3030 (all. to § 562).—§ 615 (Gadāyuddhap.): IX, **35,** 1973 (only B., C. has by error °*ve*), 1976 (all. to § 562); **62,** 3482, 3491.—§ 617 (Aishīkap.): X, **11,** 578 (γ), 585; **16,** 723 (°*gatāṃ*, sc. *Uttarāṃ*).—§ 619 (Strīvilāp.): XI, **25,** 739 (all. to § 569). Cf. Upaplava.

Uparicara = Vasu, the Cedi king. § 3 (Anukram.): I, **1,** 52 (some read the Mhbhr. beginning from *U.*, i.e. v. 2334).—§ 73 (Vasu): I, **63,** 2334 (*rājo°aḥ*).—§ 75 (do.): I, **63,** 2367 (do.).—§ 76 (Matsya): I, **63,** 2392 (do.).—§ 267 (Yamasabhāv.): II, **8,** 331 (do., in the palace of Yama).—§ 717*c* (Nārāyaṇīya): *Bhīshma* said: There was, in times past, a king named *U.*, the friend of *Indra*, and devoted to *Hari Nārāyaṇa*; he won the sovereignty of the world in consequence of a boon he had obtained from *Nārāyaṇa*, and used to worship him with the *Sātvata* ritual (*Sāttvatānāṃ Pāñcarātrāṇāṃ hitaṃ*, Nīl.), revealed in days of yore by *Sūrya* himself, etc. *Indra* gave him a share in his own seat and bed. The foremost of those conversant with the *Pāñcarātra* (*Pāñcarātravidaḥ*) dwelled in his palaces. The seven ṛshis (β), named the *Citraçikhaṇḍins*, uniting together, had on *Meru* promulgated an excellent treatise on duties; they were the seven *prakṛtis* (i.e. *mahat, ahaṅkāra*, etc., Nīl.), and [*Manu*] *Svāyambhuva* was the eighth (i.e. original Prakṛti, Nīl.); they composed that treatise after having worshipped with penances *Hari Nārāyaṇa* for 1,000 celestial years, together with many other ṛshis; *Nārāyaṇa* ordered *Sarasvatī* to enter into the persons of these ṛshis and became highly pleased with the treatise, which was in accordance with the *Vedas*, etc. (γ). *Nārāyaṇa* said: "According to the authority of the scriptures I have created *Brahmán* from grace, *Rudra* from my wrath, and yourselves as representing the *prakṛti*-elements. *Sūrya*, etc. (δ) live and act in their respective spheres; guided by your treatise *Manu Svāyambhuva* will declare the duties to the world, and so will *Uçanas* and *Bṛhaspati*, when they will arise; then this science will be acquired by king *Vasu* [*Uparicara*] from *Bṛhaspati*; upon the death of that king this eternal treatise will disappear from the world." Then *Nārāyaṇa* disappeared. Subsequently, when *Bṛhaspati* was born in the *Aṅgiras* race in the *Kṛta* age, those seven ṛshis charged him with the task of promulgating their treatise, which was consistent with the *Upanishads* and the branches of the *Vedas*. Then they proceeded to the place they chose for practising penances (XII, **336**). Etymology of the name *Bṛhaspati*. King *Vasu Uparicara* became the foremost of *Bṛhaspati's* disciples, and studied at his feet that science of the *Citraçikhaṇḍins*. In his horse-sacrifice *Bṛhaspati* became the *hotṛ*, the sons of *Prajāpati*, viz. *Ekata, Dvita*, and *Trita*, the *sadasyas*, together with *Dhanusha*, etc. (ε); no animals were slain in it; *Hari* became gratified and came and took his share, visible to *Vasu*, but invisible to the others. At this *Bṛhaspati* became angry and hurled the sacrificial ladle with violence into the skies, saying: "Here I place this as *Nārāyaṇa's* share, he shall take it before my eyes." *Yudhishṭhira* asked why *Hari* only took his share invisibly. Bhīshma answered: King *Vasu* and his *sadasyas* sought to pacify *Bṛhaspati*, saying that none should feel anger in this *Kṛta* age, as *Hari* himself did not feel anger, and none could see him save he to whom he became gracious. Then the ṛshis, *Ekata, Dvita*, and *Trita* (the mindborn sons of Brahmán) narrated that they had once undergone penances for thousands of years, to the north of Meru and on the shores of the milky ocean in order to behold *Nārāyaṇa* in his own form, then an incorporeal voice directed them to *Çvetadvīpa* on the northern shore of the milky ocean; the inhabitants there are devoted to *Nārāyaṇa*, etc. (description) and adore only one god. Arrived there they could see nothing, blinded by the splendour of the deity; they then, once more, set themselves to practise austerities for 100 years, then they beheld the inhabitants (description, they are conversant with the ordinances of the *Pāñcarātra*). An incorporeal being addressed them from the sky, saying that the god could only be seen by these white men, etc.: "do ye return, after the expiration of this *Kṛta* age when the *Tretā* age comes (in the *Vaivasvata manvantara*) a great calamity will overtake the worlds, you shall then have to become the allies of the gods." Then *Ekata*, etc., returned. Hearing this *Bṛhaspati* brought the sacrifice to completion. King *U.* ruled his subjects righteously, and at last, giving up his body, ascended to heaven. After some time he, through the curse of the brahmans, fell down and sank deep into the earth; but even then he, by reciting sacred mantras having *Nārāyaṇa* for their deity, once more ascended to heaven through the grace of *Nārāyaṇa* (XII, **337**). *Yudhishṭhira* asked why king *Vasu*, who was so devoted to *Nārāyaṇa*, did fall from heaven and sink beneath the surface of the earth. *Bhīshma* cited the old narrative of a discourse between the ṛshis and the gods. The gods once said to some brahmans that sacrifices should be performed by offering goats (*aja*). The ṛshis declared that, according to a *Vedic çruti*, by *aja* was to be understood seeds; "how can animals be slain in the *Kṛta* age?" *Vasu* was coming through the skies with his troops, etc., and was asked to be their judge. Having first ascertained what opinion was entertained by each of them, *Vasu*, moved by partiality for the gods, said that sacrifices should be performed with animals. The *ṛshis* became very angry, and cursed him to fall down from heaven and sink below the surface of the earth. He immediately fell, but at the command of *Nārāyaṇa*, *Vasu's* memory did not leave him. The gods came to his hole and said that he should have the *vasor dhārā* (v. the note of PCR., p. 758) for his sustenance as long as he remained there. Then the gods and the *ṛshis* went away. *Vasu* began to adore *Hari* and to recite in silence those sacred mantras which had come out of *Nārāyaṇa's* mouth in days of yore, and worshipped him in the five sacrifices which are performed five times every day. *Hari Nārāyaṇa* (*Vishṇu*) then let *Garuḍa* take *Vasu* to *Brahmaloka* (XII, **338**): XII, **336,** 12712 (*rājo°ḥ*); **337,** 12754 (*rājo°o Vasuḥ*), 12766; **338,** 12834 (*rājo°ḥ*), 12838 (*rājo°ṃ* (!)), 12855 (*rājo°ḥ*).

Upasunda, an Asura, brother of Sunda. § 11 (Parvasaṅgr.): I, **2,** 395 (*Sundo°yoḥ . . . ākhyānam*).—§ 245 (Rājyalābhap.): I, **208,** 7613 (*Sundo°au . . . bhrātarau*), 7616 (*Sundo°āv Asurau*).—§ 246 (Sundopasundop.): I, **209,** 7621 (*Sundo°au Daityendrau*), 7636 (*Sundo°au . . . bhrātarau*), (7642) (*Sundo°au*); **210,** 7677-(*Sundo°yoḥ*); **211,** 7684 (do.), 7698 (*Sundo°ābhyāṃ*); **212,** 7723, 7726 (Sunda and *U.* subjugated the worlds, but afterwards they killed each other on account of Tilottamā).—§ 612 (Hradapraveçap.): IX, **31ζ,** 1755 (*Sund°āv Asurau kriyayā vinishūditau*).—§ 615 (Gadāyuddhap.): IX, **55,** 3107 (*Sundo°yoḥ*). Cf. Asura.

Upaveda, pl. (°*āḥ*) ("supplement to the Veda"). § 270 (Brahmasabhāv.): II, **11**, 450 (*Itihāsopavedāç ca*, in the palace of Brahmán).—§ 603*d* (Tripura): VII, **202**, 9566 (°*ān sakhilāṃç ca*, became the bridle bits of Çiva).—§ 608 (Karṇap.): VIII, **87**χ, 4414 (*so°opanishadaḥ*). — § 657 (Āpaddh.): XII, **167**, 6240 (*Vedopavedeshu*).

Upaveṇā, a river. § 494 (Āṅgirasa): III, **222**, 14232 (among the rivers who are mothers of fires).

Upavṛtta, pl. (°*āḥ*), a people. § 574 (Jambūkh.): VI, **9**μ, 356 (in the Bhāratavarsha).

Upayāja, a brahmarshi. § 218 (Draupadīsambhava): I, **167**, 6362 (*Yājopayājau Brahmarshī*), 6365, 6366, 6369, 6376, 6386, 6387, 6392 (Yāja and *U.* performed a sacrifice for Drupada, that he might obtain a son).—§ 360 (Anudyūtap.): II, **80**, 2662 (*Yājo°tapasā putraṃ lebhe sa pāvakāt*, all. to § 218). Cf. Kāçyapa, dual.

Upendra = Vishṇu: III, 171 (*devāḥ so°āḥ*); V, 2378 (*Mahendro°vikramaṃ*); VI, 2000 (only C.), 3695 (*Indro°āv ivāmarau*), 5235 (°*sadṛçaḥ*); VII, 2500 (°*sadṛçaṃ*), 6810 (*Rudro°vikramaḥ*), 7939 (do.); VIII, †1740 (= Kṛshṇa), 3667 (*Rudro°samaṃ*); IX, 1964 (*iva . . . Indro°au*); XIII, †5385, 6966 (1000 names).

Upendrā, a river. § 574 (Jambūkh.): VI, **9**λ, 334.

***Uraga**[1], mostly pl. (°*āḥ*) ("serpents"): I, 855 (*manushyo°-Gandharva-*), 986 (sg. = Sahasrapad), 2034, 2040, 2135, 2637 (*Gandharvo°-Rakshasāṃ*), 2781 (do.), 3151 (*Gandharvo°-Rākshasān*), 4410 (*Gandharvo-Rakshasāṃ*), 5901 (sg. *yathā*), 6496 (*Piçāco°-Dānavāḥ*), 7668 (*iva*), 7960 (sg. *iva*), 8035 (do.), 8295 (*Piçāco°-Rākshasān*); III, 2100 (*deva-Gandharva-manushyo°*), 2196 (*iva*), 2388 (sg.), 2407 (*Piçāco°-Rakshasān*), 4008 (dual. *iva*), 8801 (*manushyo°*), 8873 (*Asuro°-Rakshāṃsi*), 9954 (*Gandharvo°-Yakshāç ca*), 11465 (*Gandharvo°-Rakshāṃsi*), 11646 (°*ādayaḥ*), 11682 (*Gandharvo°-Rakshāṃsi*), 12021 (*Gandharvo°-Rakshasāṃ*), 12458 (sg.), 12877 (*sa-Yaksho°-Rākshasaṃ*), 12979 (*Gandharvo°-Rākshasān*), 13484 (*manushyo°-Rakshasāṃ*), 14086 (sg. *iva*), 14264 (*Kinnaro°-Rakshasāṃ*), †15590 (°-*rājakanyā*), †15646 (dual.), 15671 (*saraḥ Suparṇena hatoragaṃ*), 15823 (*Piçāco°-mānushān*); IV, 215 (sg. *yathā*), 753 (*pañcaçīrshāv ivoragau*), 2040 (*iva*); V, 337 (sg. *iva*), 464 (*Kinnaro°-Rākshasāḥ*), 2723 (sg. *iva*), 4302 (*Gandharvo°-Rākshasāḥ*), 4369 (*iva*), 4401, 5122 (*iva*), 5866 (pl.), 5994 (sg. *iva*); VI, †1261 (*divyān*), 1975 (*Piçāco°-Rākshasāḥ*), 2307 (sg. *iva*), 2467 (*Piçāco°-Rākshasāḥ*), 2705 (sg. *iva*), 3571, 3873 (*iva*), 4687 (*iva*); VII, 288 (sg. *yathā*), 573 (°*ottamaṃ*), 1463 (*sa-Yaksho°-Rākshasāḥ*), 1846 (sg. *iva*), 1848 (°*sannibhaṃ*), 2287 (*Gandharvo°-pakshiṇaḥ*), 2403 (*devāsuranaro°āḥ*), †2607, 2623 (*nāsuro°-Rākshasāḥ*), 2661 (do.), 2706 (dual. *iva*), 2806 (*Piçāco°-Rākshasāḥ*), 3444 (*Yaksho°-Rākshasāḥ*), 3745 (*iva*), 3996 (°*sannibhā*), 4591 (dual. *iva*), 4842 (°*saṅkāçaiḥ*), 5421 (dual. *iva*), 5497 (sg. *yathā*), 5769 (sg. *iva*), 6048 (*Yaksho°-Rākshasāḥ*), 6339 (do.), 6348 (*nāsuro°-Rākshasam*), 6495 (sg. *iva*), 6901 (*iva*), 6972 (*iva*), 7004 (*manushyo°*), 7021 (*Piçāco°-Rākshasaiḥ*), 7121 (°*sannibhaiḥ*), 7173 (sg. *iva*), 7183 (sg. *yathā*), 7244 (sg. *iva*), 7266 (sg. *yathā*), †7293 (*sa-Yaksho°-Kinnarāḥ*), 7807 (sg. *iva*), 8008 (sg. *iva*), 8231 (*sa-Rākshaso°āḥ*), 8402 (*yadvat*), 8444 (*nāsuro °-Rakshāṃsi*), 8584 (sg. *iva*), 8789 (sg. *iva*), 8961 (sg. *iva*), 8963 (sg. *yadvat*), 9001 (*nāsuro °-Rākshasāḥ*, only C.), 9101 (*sāsuro °-mānavān*), 9324 (sg. *iva*); VIII, 446 (*iva*), 616 (*pañcāsyo°*), †816 (dual. *iva*), 1255 (*iva*), †4327 (*yathā*), 4409 (*Piçāco°-Rākshasāḥ*), †4549 (*iva*), 4777 (*ivoragottamaḥ*), 4840 (*iva*); IX, 132 (*iva*), 3110 (dual. *iva*), 3586 (sg. *yathā*); X, 230 (sg. *iva*), 622 (*deva-Dānava-Gandharva-manushya-patago°āḥ*); XII, 2768 (*Gandharvo°-Rākshasāḥ*), 3111 (sg. *iva*), 3360 (*mānusho°-Rakshāṃsi*), 4466 (*samanushyo°vatāṃ*), 8116 (*Gandharvo°-Rākshasāḥ*), 8524 (*vayaḥ-paçu-mṛgo°ān*), 9048 (sg. *iva*), 10278 (*Piçāco°-Rākshasāḥ*), 10336 (*Piçāco°-Rākshasaiḥ*), †11096, 12570 (*Piçāco°-Rākshasaiḥ*), 13935 (°*çreshṭham*, i.e. Padmanābha); XIII, 804 (*sa-Yaksho°-Rakshasāṃ*), 1996 (sg. *iva*), 2097 (*manushyo-Rakshasāṃ*), 2977 (*pitaro°-Rākshasāḥ*), 2998 (*Kinnaro°-Rakshāṃsi*), 3171 (sg. *iva*), 3865 (*Piçāco°-Rākshasāḥ*), 3886 (*Kinnaro°-Rākshasāḥ*), 3981 (*Gandharvo°-Rākshasāḥ*), 4224 (*Gandharvo°-Rakshasāṃ*), 4701, 4731 (*deva-Yaksho°-nṛṇāṃ*), 7071 (*sa-Yaksho°-Rakshasāṃ*), 7371 (only B.), †7378; XIV, 1183 (*Gandharvo°-Rakshasāṃ*), 1226 (*Piçāco°-Rakshasāṃ . . . Īçvaraḥ prabhuḥ*).

Uraga[2], pl. (°*āḥ*), a people (? PCR.): VI, 362 (see Vātaja, pl.).

Uragā, name of a city (?). § 279 (Arjuna): II, **27**, 1027 (°*vāsinaṃ Rocamānaṃ*).

Uragapati ("lord of serpents") = Kauravya: XIV, 2406 (°*er duhitā*, i.e. Ulūpī).

Uragātmajā ("daughter of the serpent [king]") = Ulūpī: XIV, 2311 (*U°*).

Ūrdhvabāhu, a ṛshi. § 770 (Ānuçāsanik.): XIII, **151**η, 7112 (the fifth of the seven *Dharmarājartvijaḥ*).—§ 775 (do.): XIII, **166**δ, 7666 (among the ṛshis of the south).

Ūrdhvabhāj, name of a fire. § 490 (Āṅgirasa): III, **219**, 14149 (= Vaḍavāgni ?).

Ūrdhvaçāyin = Çiva (1000 names[2]).

Ūrdhvadaṃshṭrakeça = Çiva (1000 names[1]).

Ūrdhvaga = Vishṇu (1000 names).

Ūrdhvagātman = Çiva (1000 names[2]).

Ūrdhvakeça = Çiva (1000 names[1]).

Ūrdhvaliṅga = Çiva (1000 names[2]).

Ūrdhvaṃ kham iva menire = Çiva (1000 names[1]).

Ūrdhvaretas[1], a brahman. § 324 (Dvaitavanapr.): III, **26**a, 987 (waited upon Yudhishṭhira).—Do.[2] = Çiva (1000 names[2]).

Ūrdhvasaṃhanana = Çiva (1000 names[2]).

Ūrdhvavartman = Kṛshṇa: XII, 1508.

Ūrdhvaveṇīdharā, a mātṛ. § 615*u* (Skanda): IX, **46**θ, 2636.

***ūrjaskara** ("giving vigour") said of fires: III, 14181 (*pāvakān*).

Ūrjaspati = Mahāpurusha (Mahāpurushastava).

Ūrjayoni, a son of Viçvāmitra. § 721*b* (Viçvāmitrop.): XIII, **4**β, 258 (*Urjja°* C.).

Ūrjita, Ūrjitaçāsana = Vishṇu (1000 names).

Ūrmilā, wife of Yama (probably wrong reading instead of Dhūmorṇā, q.v.). § 565 (Gālavacar.): V, **117**, 3968 (*reme . . . Ū°āyāṃ yathā Yamaḥ*, B. *yathā Dhūmorṇayā Yamaḥ*).

Ūrṇanābha, a son of Dhṛtarāshṭra. § 130 (Aṃçāvat.): I, **67**, 2731 (enumeration).—§ 182 (Dhṛtarāshṭraputranāmak.): I, **117**, 4544 (do.).

Ūrṇāyu(s), a Gandharva. § 191 (Arjuna): I, **123**, 4811 (among the Devagandharvas present at the birth of Arjuna).—§ 565 (Gālavacarita): V, **117**, 3975 (*reme . . . Menakāyāṃ yatho°ḥ*).

Urukrama ("making wide strides") = Vishṇu (Kṛshṇa): III, 12984 (*Hṛshīkeçaḥ*, i.e. Nārāyaṇa): XII, 1506 (= Kṛshṇa).

Ūrva, a ṛshi. § 745*c* (Cyavana-Kuçikasaṃv.): XIII, **56**, 2907 (father of Ṛcīka, cast the fire of his anger into the mouth of the mare's head (*vaḍavāvaktre*)). Cf. Aurva.

Urvaçī[1], an Apsaras, wife of Purūravas. § 52 (Janamejaya): I, **44**, †1811 (*yatho°īṃ prāpya purā Purūravāḥ*).—§ 135

(Çak··ntalop.): I, **74**a, 3055 (among the principal Apsarases).—§ 140 (Purūravas): I, **75**, 3148 (wife of Purūravas).—§ 141 (do.): I, **75**, 3149 (°sutāḥ; by Purūravas, mother of six sons, Ayus, etc.).—§ 19 (Arjuna): I, **123**, 4823 (sung at the birth of Arjuna).—§ 269 (Vaiçravaṇasabhāv.): II, **10**, 395 (among the Apsarases in the palace of Kubera).—§ 336 (Indralokābhigamanap.): III, **43**a, 1784 (in the palace of Indra); **45**, 1800, 1801, 1803, 1814; **46**, 1817, 1833, 1835, 1837, (1838), (1858), 1864, (1865), 1867, 1868, 1872 (*U.* fell in love with Arjuna; as he refused her she cursed him saying that he should become a woman).—§ 391 (Ṛshyaçṛṅga): III, **110**, 10002 (*Apsarasam*, when Vibhāṇḍaka saw *U.* his seed come out).—§ 565 (Gālavacar.): V, **117**, 3973 (*reme . . . yathā . . . U°yāñ ca Purūravāḥ*).—§ 595 (Shoḍaçarāj. v. Bhagīratha): VII, **60**, 2254 (seems to be identified with the heavenly Gaṅgā, *tathā Bhāgīrathī Gaṅgā Urvaçī cābhavat purā*).—§ 632b (Shoḍaçarāj., v. § 595): XII, **29**, 961 (do., *Gaṅgā Bhāgīrathī tasmād Urvaçī hy abhavat purā*).—§ 716 (Çukābhipatana): XII, **333**, 12577, 12601.—§ 731b (Ashṭāvakra-Diksaṃv.): XIII, **19**β, 1424 (in the abode of Kubera).—§ 775 (Ānuçāsanik.): XIII, **166**β, 7641.

Urvaçī[2], name of a tīrtha. § 733u (Punarāvartanandā): XIII, **25**, 1732 (on the river Lauhitya). Cf. next.

Urvaçītīrtha, name of a tīrtha. § 370 (Tīrthayātrāp.): III, **84**, 8135. Cf. the prec.

Urvarā, an Apsaras. § 731b (Ashṭāvakra-Diksaṃv.): XIII, **19**β, 1424 (in the abode of Kubera).

Urvī = Bhūmi (the Earth, personif.): XII, 1788 (etymology).

Ushaṅgu[1], a ṛshi. § 665 (Mokshadh.): XII, **208**θ, 7596 (among the ṛshis of the west).—§ 775 (Ānuçāsanik.): XIII, **166**ε, 7667 (*saha sodaryaiḥ*, do.).

Ushaṅgu[2] = Çiva (1000 names[2]).—Do.[3], v. Ṛshadgu.

Ushīnara, v. Uçīnara.

Ushman (B. Ūsh°), name of a fire. § 493 (Āṅgirasa): III, **221**, 14179.—Cf. also III, 13969 (*°ā cāgnir iti jñeyo yo 'nnaṃ pacati dehināṃ*); XII, 6877 (do.).

Ushmapāḥ (pl.) (B. Ūsh°) ("steam-drinkers"), a class of pitṛs or ṛshis. § 267 (Yamasabhāv.): II, **8**, 341 (one of the classes of pitṛs).—§ 565 (Gālavacarita): V, **109**, 3780 (*°āṇāṃ devānāṃ nivāsaḥ*, in the south).—§ 576 (Bhagavadgītāp.): VI, **35**, †1268.—§ 695b (Dakshayajñavināça): XII, **285**a, 10280.—§ 730 (Ānuçāsanik.): XIII, **18**λλ, †1371.—§ 749 (do.): XIII, **91**β, 4352 (B. and C., by error *Ushṇa°*).—§ 768b (Umā-Maheçvarasaṃv.): XIII, **141**, 6495.

Ushṇa, a region in Krauñcadvīpa. § 575 (Bhūmip.): VI, **12**θ, 462, 463.

Ushṇapa, v. Ushmapa.

Ushṇaraçmi = Sūrya (the Sun): III, 16998.

Ushṇīgaṅga, a tīrtha. § 413 (Tīrthayātrāp.): III, **135**, 10698.

Ushṇīnābha, a Viçvadeva. § 749 (Ānuçāsanik.): XIII, **91**γ, 4359.

Ushṇīshin = Çiva: XIII, 1158 (1000 names[2]); XIV, 195.

Ushṭrajihva, a warrior of Skanda. § 615u (Skanda): IX, **45**η, 2564.

Ushṭrakarṇika, pl. (°āḥ), a people. § 284 (Sahadeva): II, **31**, 1175 (in the south, vanquished by Sahadeva).

Utaṅka, v. Uttaṅka.

Utathya, a ṛshi, son of Aṅgiras. § 110 (Aṃçāvat.): I, **66**, 2569 (second son of Aṅgiras).—§ 170 (Dīrghatamas): I, **104**, 4179 (husband of Mamatā), 4180 (elder brother of Bṛhaspati), 4194 (father of Dīrghatamas; Bṛhaspati violated Mamatā when she was pregnant with Dīrghatamas).—§ 641 (Rājadh.): XII, **90**, 3362 (*Aṅgirāḥ*), 3363, (3364); **91**, (3403), 3461 (instructed Māndhātṛ).—§ 717b (Nārāyaṇīya): XII, **342**, 13177, 13178 (repetition from § 170).—§ 747b (Suvarṇotpatti): XIII, **85**θ, 4147 (the second of Aṅgiras' eight sons).—§ 772j (Pavanārjunasaṃv.): *Vāyu* said: The beautiful *Bhadrā*, the daughter of *Soma*, was destined by her father to become the wife of the brahman *U.* of *Aṅgiras*' race; and she underwent severe austerities for this purpose. Then *Atri* [the father of *Soma*] invited *U.* and gave her to him. *Varuṇa* had coveted the girl from former times; he came to the forest and stole her away, when she bathed in the *Yamunā*, and carried her to his wonderful city, adorned with 600,000 lakes (read *°çata°* with B.) with palaces and *Apsarases*, etc. Having heard all this from *Nārada*, *U.* caused him to request *Varuṇa* to restore her ("thou art a *Lokapāla*, not a destroyer of the world"). As *Varuṇa* refused, and *Nārada* related to *U.* that *Varuṇa* had seized him by the throat and driven him from his house, *U.* (*Aṅgiras*) stopped the waters and drank them off, and caused the earth to dry up the 600,000 lakes, and the *Sarasvatī* to become invisible, and the region to cease to be sacred. Then *Varuṇa* restored *Bhadrā* to *U.*, who then freed the world and *Varuṇa* from distress. "Name thou a kshatriya who is superior to *U.*" (XIII, **155**): XIII, **155**, 7240 (*jātasyāṅgirase kule*), 7241, 7242, 7243, 7248, 7251, 7253, 7256, 7260, 7262, 7263, 7264. Cf. Aṅgiras[5], Āṅgirasa[2].

Utathyaputra ("the son of Utathya") = Dīrghatamas: I, 4190.

Utkala, pl. (°āḥ), a people. § 574 (Jambūkh.): VI, **9**μ, 348 (*Mekalāç co°aiḥ saha*).—§ 589 (Droṇābhishekap.): VII, **4**β, 122 (have formerly been vanquished by Karṇa for the sake of Duryodhana). — § 605 (Karṇap.): VIII, **22**θθ, 882 (*Mekalo°-Kāliṅgāḥ*).

Utkocaka, a tīrtha. § 230 (Dhaumyapurohitak.): I, **183**, 6914 (*tīrthe*, the residence of Dhaumya), 6918 (*tīrthaṃ*).

Utkrāthinī, a mātṛ. § 615u (Skanda): IX, **46**θ, 2634.

Utkroça, a companion of Skanda. § 615u (Skanda): IX, **45**, 2537 (given to Skanda by Indra).

Utpalāvana, a tīrtha. § 377 (Dhaumyatīrthak.): III, **87**, 8311 (in the east in the country of the Pāñcālas, there Viçvāmitra performed sacrifices).—§ 733o (Gaṅgāhrada): XIII, **25**, 1720.

Utpalāvatī, a river. § 571 (Jambūkh.): VI, **9**λ, 342 (only C.).

Utpalinī, a river. § 249 (Arjunavanavāsap.): I, **215**, 7817 (*nadīm*, visited by Arjuna on his tīrthayātrā).

Utpātaka, a tīrtha. § 733r (Ānuçāsanik.): By bathing in *U.* [and] in *Ashṭāvakra* and offering oblations to the *pitṛs*, and for twelve days abstaining from food one obtains to the merit of a horse-sacrifice: XIII, **25**, 1727.

Utsaṅga = Çiva (1000 names[2]).

Utsavasaṅketa, pl. (°āḥ), a people. § 279 (Arjuna): II, **27**, 1025 (*gaṇān U°ān . . . sapta*, vanquished by Arjuna). — § 285 (Nakula): II, **31**, 1191 (*gaṇān U°ān*, vanquished by Nakula). Cf. Dhvajinyutsavasaṅketa.

Uttama, a prince. § 290 (Çiçupālavadhap.): II, **44**a, 1539.

Uttama, pl. (°āḥ), a people. § 574 (Jambūkh.): VI, **9**μ, 348.

Uttamapūrusha ("the Supreme Spirit"): XII, 7828, †12696 (*Nārāyaṇena*).

Uttamaujas, a Pāñcāla prince, brother of Yudhāmanyu. § 561 (Yānasandhip.): V, **57**o, 2263 (*Pāñcālyaḥ*).—§ 569 (Bhagavadyānap.): V, **141**γ, 4749.—§ 571 (Ulūkadūtāgamanap.): V, **164**, 5707 (pitted against Kṛpa).—§ 572 (Rathātirathasaṅkhyānap.): V, **170**, 5883 (a ratha in the army of Yudhishṭhira). — § 573 (Ambopākhyānap.): V, **194** γ, 7598 (*Yudhāmanyū°au*); **196** η, 7624 (*Pāñcālyau . . . Yudhāmanyū°au*), (κ) 7638 (*Pāñcālyau Yudhāmanyū °au*).—§ 576 (Bhagavadgītāp.): VI, **15**, 606 (protects the right wheel of Arjuna); **19** ε, 714 (*Pāñcālyau Yudhāmanyū °au*, protectors of Arjuna's wheels); **25** θ, 835.—§ 585 (Bhīshmavadhap.): VI, **98**, 4494 (protects the right wheel of Arjuna). — § 589 (Droṇābhishekap.): VII, **10**, 345 (*Pāñcāleshūttamaṃ*).—§ 592 (Saṃçaptakavadhap.): VII, **21** κ, 904, 909; **23** ο, 957 (proceeded against Droṇa, description of his horses); **25**, 1101 (fought with Aṅgada). — § 593 (Abhimanyuvadhap.): VII, **35** δ, 1510.—§ 597 (Pratijñāp.): VII, **83** α, 2951 (*Pāñcālyaṃ*).—§ 598 (Jayadrathavadhap.): VII, **85** δ, 3048 (*Pāñcālyaḥ*).—§ 599 (do.): VII, **91**, 3252 (*cakrarakshau Pāñcālyau Yudhāmanyū°au*); **92**, 3289, 3290; **130**, 5336 (*cakrarakshau tu Pāñcālyau Yudhāmanyū°au*), 5345, 5346 (*Pāñcālyaḥ*), 5347 (brother of Yudhāmanyu), 5351 (*Yudhāmanyū°au*, defeated by Duryodhana); **137** ωω, 5629; **146**, 6289 (only B.); **147**, 6346 (*cakrarakshau . . . . Yudhāmanyū°au*).—§ 600 (Ghaṭotkacavadhap.): VII, **156** θ, 6765; **177** χχ, 8059 (*Yudhāmanyū°au*); **179** βββ, 8119 (do.).—§ 604 (Karṇap.); VIII, **6**, 174 (among the slain).—§ 605 (do.): VIII, **11**, 428 (*cakrarakshau tu Pāñcālyau Yudhāmanyū °au*); **30** ξξ, 1231.—§ 608 (do.): VIII, **61**, 3080 (attacked by Kṛtavarman), 3123, 3125 (vanquished by Kṛtavarman), **63** ηηη, 3199 (*pṛshṭharakshau . . . Yudhāmanyū°au*); **67** κκκ, †3374 (*Yudhāmanyuç co°āç ca çūrau pṛshṭhato māṃ rakshatām*, says Arjuna); **75**, †3812 (*Sṛñjayaḥ*, fought with Susheṇa), †3816 (slew Susheṇa); **79** η′, 4029; **82** λ′, †4195, †4200.—§ 609 (Çalyap.): IX, **1** γ, 31 (among the slain).—§ 612 (Hradapraveçap.): IX, **30** ε, 1726.—§ 616 (Sauptikap.): X, **8**, 353 (slain by Açvatthāman).—§ 620 (Çrāddhap.): XI, **26** β, 789 (his body is cremated).—§ 795 (Svargārohaṇap.): XVIII, **1** δ, 27 (*bhrātarau . . . Yudhāmanyū°au*). Cf. Pāñcālya (sg. and dual.), Sṛñjaya.

Uttaṅka (so B., C. mostly Uta°), a ṛshi. § 11 (Parvasaṅgr.): I, **2**, 364.—§ 17 (cf. Paushyap.): *U.* was the disciple of *Veda*; having resisted the temptations of the wife of *Veda*, he obtained leave to depart, but first wished to bring *Veda* some gratuity for his instruction, and having uttered this wish two times, he was ordered to procure the ear-rings of *Paushya's* queen for the wife of *Veda*. Having met with a bull (*Airāvata*) and a man (*Indra*) mounted upon it, he ate of the dung and drank of the urine (*amṛta*) of that bull, "as his master had formerly done." Coming to the abode of *Paushya*, he could not discover the queen before he had purified himself properly from the leavings of his last meal. He and *Paushya* cursed one another. Having obtained the ear-rings, *U.* returned to his master. On the road *Takshaka*, the king of the serpents, in the shape of a mendicant, stole the ear-rings and proceeded to *Nāgaloka*. *Indra*, with the thunderbolt, made a hole through which *U.* entered the *Nāgaloka*, where he hymned the serpents. He there saw two damsels (= *Dhātṛ* and *Vidhātṛ*) sitting over a loom, weaving a fabric with black and white threads (night and day), further, he saw a wheel (= the year) with twelve spokes (= the months) turned by six boys (= the seasons), and then a man (*Parjanya*) mounted on a horse (*Agni*). At the injunction of the man *U.* blew into the anus of the horse, whence there issued flames of fire with smoke, which were about to consume the *Nāgaloka*. *Takshaka* then gave back the ear-rings and *U.* was borne by the horse to his master's abode. His master explained to him all he had seen during his journey. *U.* then proceeded to *Hāstinapura* and told *Janamejaya*, who had some time before returned victorious from *Takshaçilā*, to burn *Takshaka*, who had bitten *Parikshit* to death, and caused *Kāçyapa* to turn back without relieving *Parikshit*, at a snake-sacrifice: I, **3**, ††747 (*°nāmānaṃ*), ††748, ††749, ††753, ††756, ††757 (*Utta°* also C.), ††758, ††759, ††761, ††762, ††763, ††764, ††765, ††770, ††771, ††772, ††773, ††776, ††778, ††779, ††780, ††787, ††789, ††790, ††791, ††793, ††796, ††805, ††815, ††816, ††818, ††819, ††820, ††821, ††822, ††823, ††832, 833, (836), (840), 848, 849, 850.—§ 56 (Parikshit): I, **50**, 1991 (*ṛsher U°sya*, sc. *parābhavaṃ*, all. to § 17).—§ 57 (Janamejaya): I, **50**, 2014 (*°sya priyaṃ kartum*, do.).—§ 474*b* (Dhundhumārop.): III, **201**, 13491 (*maharshiḥ*), 13492, (13494), 13504, (13505), 13507 (gratified Vishṇu who granted him boons).—§ 476 (do.): III, **202**, 13523, 13524, (13525); **203**, 13546, 13550 (*U.* urged Bṛhadaçva to slay Dhundhu, but Bṛhadaçva directed him to Kuvalāçva).—§ 478 (do.): III, **204**, 13589 (*°āçramaṃ*), 13591 (*°āçramābhyāse*, there Dhundhu had his abode), 13592, 13594, 13619 (*U.* accompanied Kuvalāçva when he set out to slay Dhundhu).—§ 784*b* (Anugītāp.): When *Kṛshṇa*, on his way from *Hāstinapura* to *Dvārakā*, had entered the desert, he beheld *U.*, who enquired whether he came after having reconciled the *Kurus* and the *Pāṇḍavas*. *Kṛshṇa* told him the matter; filled with wrath *U.* threatened to curse him; *Kṛshṇa* warned *U.* (who had practised *brahmacarya* from the day of his infancy) against destroying his penances [by a curse] (XIV, **53**). *U.* agreed that *Kṛshṇa* should first tell him "that faultless adhyātma", and *Kṛshṇa* explained his own identity with the creator and destroyer of all things. "R., V., Dai., Y., G., Rā., N., and Aps. have sprung from me; etc. *Dharma*, whose essence is compassion for all creatures, is my eldest-born offspring, and has sprung from my mind; I am *Vishṇu*, *Brahmán*, and *Çakra* (i.e. Indra)." He always acts as those beings in whose order he lives (XIV, **54**). *U.* prevailed upon *Kṛshṇa* to show him his eternal *Vaishṇava* or universal form, and praised *Kṛshṇa*, who granted him the boon to have water wherever he wished for it (water being scarce in such deserts) by thinking of *Kṛshṇa*. Once, when *U.* was wandering thirsty in the desert, and thought of *Kṛshṇa*, he saw a naked *Cāṇḍāla* (*mātaṅga*) all besmeared with dirt, surrounded by a pack of dogs, and carrying a sword, and bow, and arrows; from his urinary organs there issued copious streams of water; he invited *U.* to accept this water; *U.* refused and even censured *Kṛshṇa*, the *Cāṇḍāla* disappeared. *Kṛshṇa* came and said that the *Cāṇḍāla* was *Indra*, whom he had ordered to give *amṛta* to *U.* in the form of water, and that *Indra* at first had refused to do it, but at last had agreed on the condition that *U.* should accept it in that way. *Kṛshṇa* ordained that on those days in which *U.* would feel a desire for water, there should rise clouds raining savoury water over this desert and that they should be named *U.*-clouds; even to this day such clouds shower rain on the arid desert (XIV, **55**). Asked by *Janamejaya* about the penances of *U.*, *Vaiçampāyana* related that *U.'s* preceptor *Gautama*, having permitted thousands of disciples to return home, was so pleased with the devotion of *U.* that he would not dismiss him, even after 100 years, and decrepitude overtook *U.*; one day when he threw the load of fuel he had fetched on the earth, one of his matted locks, white as silver, had become entangled with the load and fell on the earth; beholding that sign of old age, *U.* gave himself up to loud lamentations; the beautiful daughter of his preceptor, at the command of her father, sought to hold the tears of *U.* in her hands, but her hands seemed to burn with the dropping tears, and she was obliged to let them fall on the earth; the earth was unable to hold them. Asked by *Gautama*, *U.* explained the matter. *Gautama* permitted him to leave him; as *U.* spoke of the fee, *Gautama* said that he was already highly gratified and that if *U.* became a young man of sixteen years, he would give him his daughter in marriage. *U.* again became a youth and accepted the maiden. As he spoke of the fee to his preceptor's wife, *Ahalyā* said that she was already gratified. *U.*, however, insisted, and *Ahalyā* then commanded him to bring her the celestial ear-rings which were borne by the wife of *Saudāsa*, who had [through the curse of *Çaktri*] become a cannibal. *Gautama* blamed *Ahalyā* that she had sent *U.* to the cannibal. *Ahalyā* said that she had done it unknowingly, and that *Gautama* would protect *U.* *U.* met *Saudāsa* in a deserted forest (XIV, **56**). *Saudāsa* was of frightful mien, wearing a long beard smeared with human blood, and looking like a second *Yama*; he congratulated himself that he had met *U.* at the sixth hour of the day when he was in search of food; *U.* maintained that while one is employed for the sake of his preceptor, one should not be injured; at last they agreed that when he had brought his preceptor the ear-rings he should come back; *Saudāsa* told *U.* to go and see the queen *Madayantī* (near a forest fountain), as he could not himself see her at the sixth hour. *Madayantī* told *U.* to bring her some sign from her husband, as these ear-rings, when placed on the earth, would be stolen by the *Nāgas*, if worn by one who is impure from eating, they would be taken away by the *Yakshas*, and if the wearer fell asleep, the gods would take them away; "also the *maharshis* and the *Rākshasas* watch for opportunities for carrying them away; they always produce gold and shine brightly at night; they protect against hunger, and thirst, and fear, and he who wears them grows in size" (XIV, **57**). *U.* came back to *Saudāsa*, who gave him a sign. When he had got the ear-rings, *U.* once more came back to *Saudāsa*, and asked him about the meaning of the mystic words he had caused him to say to *Madayantī*, as a sign. *Saudāsa*, referring to his own terrible condition in consequence of his being cursed [by *Çaktri*], said that he hoped that this gift to a brahman might save him. *U.* asked *Saudāsa* to give him such advice as is approved by the wise: "is it proper for me to come back to thee or not?" *Saudāsa* said that he would then tell him never to come back. When *U.*, on his way to *Ahalyā*, having bound the ear-rings in the folds of his black deerskin, had proceeded for some distance he became afflicted with hunger and climbed a *bilva*-tree (ægle marmelos), hanging his deerskin on a branch, while he plucked some fruits. Struck by some fruits the deerskin fell down, the knot was untied, and a serpent of *Airāvata's* race carried the ear-rings, holding them in his mouth, into an anthill. Filled with wrath, *U.* with his staff, pierced that anthill for thirty-five days, desirous of making a path to the nether regions; the goddess Earth became anxious; *Indra* came there in the disguise of a brahman afflicted with the sorrow of *U.*, and told him that the regions of the *Nāgas* are thousands of *yojanas* distant; as *U.* did not desist, *Indra* united the latter's staff with his thunderbolt, and struck with the thunderbolt, the earth opened a way to the *Nāgaloka* (*c*). *U.* entered the *Nāgaloka*, very cheerless; then there appeared to him a black steed with a white tail, whose face and eyes were of coppery hue. He told *U.* to blow into his anus, "which thou often didst at the retreat of *Gautama* in former days"; the horse turned out to be Agni; *U.* did as he was directed, a thick smoke enveloped the *Nāgaloka*, the *Nāgas*, headed by *Vāsuki*, gave *U.* the ear-rings, which he brought to *Ahalyā* (XIV, **58**): XIV, **53**, 1542 (*muniçreshṭham*), 1544 (*brāhmaṇaçreshṭhaḥ*), 1555, (1556); **54**, (1563); **55**, (1586), (1593), 1596, 1599, 1600, 1601, 1604, 1608, 1610, 1612, 1614, 1623 (°*meghāḥ*), 1624 (do.); **56**, 1625, 1626, 1628, 1630, 1632, 1638 (*vipraṃ*), (1640), (1645), 1653, 1656, 1657, 1660; **57**, (1664), (1666), (1673), (1675), 1676, (1678), 1680, 1681; **58**, 1692, (1699), (1701), 1721, (1723), 1730, 1734, 1737, 1746, 1750.—§ 784 (do.): XIV, **59**, 1751, 1752. Cf. Bhārgava, Bhṛgūdvaha, Bhṛgukulodvaha, Bhṛgunandana.

Uttara[1] (also called Bhūmiñjaya), son of Virāṭa. § 232 (Svayaṃvarap.): I, **186**, 6988 (*Virāṭaḥ saha putrābhyāṃ Çaṅkhenaivottareṇa ca*, present at the svayaṃvara of Draupadī).—§ 552 (Goharaṇap.): IV, **36** (1171), 1182, (1190); **37**, (1217), 1220, 1226, †1228, †1229; **38**, (1240), (1256), 1268, 1270, 1271, (1274), 1283 (*Vairāṭim*); **39**, 1285; **40**, 1304; **41**, (1312); **42**, (1325); **44**, (1367), (1373), (1377), 1390 (*ahaṃ Bhūmiñjayo nāma nāmnāhaṃ api cottaraḥ*); **45**, (1394), 1398, (1403), (1409), (1427); **46**, 1436, 1437 (°*sārathiḥ*, sc. Arjuna), 1444, 1445, (1449), 1457; **47**, 1478; **55**, 1701, (1737, only C.), 1738; **58**, 1824, 1832; **60**, 1949; **61**, 1952, 1966, 1989 (*Vairāṭim*); **67**, (†2146), †2150, †2157; **68**, 2165, 2171, 2177, 2178, 2179, 2212, 2214, 2216, 2222, (2224), 2230; **69**, (2241), (2254), 2258 (when the Kurus were ravishing the kine of Virāṭa, *U.* set out, having the disguised Arjuna for his charioteer. Arjuna disclosed to *U.* who he was and vanquished the Kurus having *U.* for his charioteer).—§ 553 (Vaivāhikap.): IV, **71**, 2300, (†2301), (2307), 2310, (2312).—§ 561 (Yānasandhip.): V, **48**, †1845 (*Virāṭaḥ . . . sahottaraḥ*); **57** ξ, 2237 (*Virāṭaḥ saha putrābhyāṃ Çaṅkhenaivottareṇa ca*), 2263 (*Vairāṭiḥ*).—§ 572 (Rathātirathasaṅkh.): V, **170**, 5879 (*Vairāṭiḥ*).—§ 578 (Bhīshmavadhap.): VI, **45**[23], 1746 (*Vairāṭim*, pierced by Vīrabāhu); **47**[28], 1842 (*Vairāṭiḥ*), 1850 (slain by Çalya).—§ 604 (Karṇap.): VIII, **6**, 187 (had been slain).—§ 619 (Strīvilāpap.): XI, **20** ε, 601 (among the slain).—§ 795 (Svargārohaṇap.): XVIII, **5** λ, 140, (μ), 164 (*saha bhrātrā Çaṅkhena*, among those who after death entered the deities). Cf. Bhūmiñjaya, Kaikeyīnandivardhana, Matsya, Mātsya, Matsyaputra, Matsyavīra, Pṛthiviñjaya, Vairaṭi, Virāṭaputra.

Uttara[2], a prince. § 277 (Jarāsandhavadhap.): II, **22**, 877 (among the kings who met with destruction on account of their having disregarded their superiors).

Uttara[3] = Vishṇu (1000 names).

Uttara[4] (= upanishad, Nīl.): XII, 11733 (*vedaḥ . . . sottaraḥ*).

Uttarā, daughter of Virāṭa, wife of Abhimanyu, mother of Parikshit. § 4 (Anukram.): I, **1**, †169.—§ 11 (Parvasaṅgr.): I, **2**, 489.—§ 56 (Parikshit): I, **49**, 1946 (°*āyāṃ ajījanat*, sc. Parikshit).—§ 160 (Pūruvaṃç.): I, **95**, †† 3835 (daughter of Virāṭa, wife of Abhimanyu).—§ 549 (Pāṇḍavapraveçap.): IV, **11**, †305.—§ 552 (Goharaṇap.): IV, **37**, 1218, 1223 (prevails upon Bṛhannalā (i.e. Arjuna) to become the charioteer of Uttara); **66**, †2116; **68**, 2186; **69**, 2257 (obtains the garments of the Kurus).—§ 553 (Vaivāhikap.): IV, **71**, 2311, 2323; **73**, 2342, 2367 (is married to Abhimanyu).—

§ 585 (Bhīshmavadhap.): VI, **98**μμ, 4459 (all. to § 552).—§ 596 (Pratijñāp.): VII, **78**, 2773 (comforted by Kṛshṇa after the death of Abhimanyu).—§ 619 (Strīvilāpap.): XI, **20**, 597.—§ 785 (Anugītāp.): XIV, **61**, 1835, 1843; **62**, 1860; **66**ι, 1940, (μ), 1953, 1957; **67**ν, 1967 (all. to § 617); **69**, 2009, 2013, 2026; **70**, 2038, 2041 (birth of Parikshit).—§ 787 (Āçramavāsap.): XV, **15**ν, †437 (*Kauravī*). Cf. Vairāṭī, Virāṭaduhitṛ, Virāṭatanayā, Abhimanyor bhāryā (XV, 670).

***uttarā**, sc. diç ("the northern region"): V, 3821 (etymology), 3847.

Uttarāgni, name of a fire. § 493 (Āṅgirasa): III, **221**, 14205.

Uttarā(ḥ) Ashāḍhāḥ, v. Ashāḍhā.

Uttarāḥ Kuravaḥ ("the northern Kurus"), a people. § 173 (Pāṇḍurājyābhisheka): I, **109**, 4346 (*uttaraiḥ Kurubhiḥ sārdhaṃ dakshiṇāḥ Kuravaḥ*).—§ 187 (Pāṇḍu): I, **122**, 4722 (among them women enjoy sexual liberty).—§ 279 (Arjuna): II, **28**, 1048 (in the north, Arjuna came to their frontier).—§ 295 (Dyūtap.): II, **52**, 1862 (*uttarebhyaḥ Kurubhyaç cāpyapoḍhaṃ mālyaṃ*).—§ 423 (Gandhamādanapr.): III, **145**, 11030.—§ 507 (Skandayuddha): III, **231**, 14612 (the head of Mahisha barred the entrance to the country of the *U.K.*).—§ 556 (Sañjayayānap.): V. **22**a, 656 (have been vanquished by Arjuna).—§ 574 (Jambūkh.): VI, **6**δ, 208.—§ 574*g* (do.): To the south of *Nīla* and to the north of *Meru* are *U.K.*, where the *Siddhas* reside, there the trees are always covered with sweet fruits and flowers, some of them yield fruits according to the will [of the plucker]; some of them are called *kshīrins* and yield milk and six different rasas (*shaḍrasaṃ*) like *amṛta*, and clothes and ornaments; the entire land has fine golden sands; a portion of it is ruby, etc., all the seasons are agreeable and nowhere does the land become miry. The men born there have fallen from the *Devaloka*, and are all of pure birth and handsome; they are born twins, and the women are like *Aps.* in beauty; they are free from illness and cheerful, they live 11,000 years. The birds named *Bhāruṇḍāḥ* take them up when dead and throw them into mountain caves: VI, **7**, 254, 266.—§ 574*i* (Jambū): VI, **7**, 278 (the river that has its origin from the juice of the jambu goes to the *U.K.*).—§ 620 (Çrāddhap.): XI, **26**, 772 (the dead warriors have attained to [the region of] the *U.K.*).—§ 745*c* (Cyavana-Kuçikasaṃv.): XIII, **54**, 2841.—§ 746 (Ānuçāsanik.): XIII, **57**, 2958 (*lokāḥ Kurushūttareshu*).—§ 757*g* (Hastikūṭa): *Gautama* said: There where the *U.K.* blaze in beauty rejoicing with the gods, where dwell the people (*lokāḥ*) sprung from Agni, water, and mountains, where *Çakra* (Indra) rains all wishes, where women live in perfect freedom, where there is no jealousy among women and men, etc. *Dhṛtarāshṭra* said: This region (*lokaḥ*) is for those who are freed from all desire, who abstain from meat, who never take up the rod of chastisement, and never inflict harm on mobile or immobile creatures, who regard themselves as identical with all creatures (*sarvabhūtātmabhūtāḥ*), who have no wishes (otherwise PCR.) and are indifferent (*nirmamāḥ*), and freed from affections regarding gain and loss, and to whom blame and praise are equal: XIII, **102**, †4867.—§ 785 (Anugītāp.): XIV, **70**, 2053 (*Kurūn . . . dakshiṇottarān*).—§ 786*e* (Agastya): XIV, **92**, 2871 (*uttarebhyaḥ Kurubhyaç ca yat kiṃcid vasu vidyate*).—§ 789 (Putradarçanap.): XV, **33**κ, 904 (some of the dead warriors proceeded to [the region of] the *U.K.*).

Uttarāḥ Phalgunyaḥ, v. Phalgunī.

Uttarāḥ Proshṭhapadāḥ, v. Proshṭhapadā.

Uttarajyotisha, a city (?). § 285 (Nakula): II, **32**, 1193 (in the west, conquered by Nakula).

Uttaramānasa, a sacred lake. § 652*b* (Indrota-Pārīkshitīya): XII, **152**β, 5646 (*Prabhāso °se*), (γ), 5662 (do.).—§ 733*z* (Kālodaka): XIII, **25**, 1746.

Uttaraṇa = Çiva (1000 names [2])

Uttāraṇa [1] = Vishṇu (1000 names).—Do.[2] = Çiva: XIV, 194 (B. *Uttaraṇāya*).

Uttarāpatha [1] ("the north"). § 664 (Mokshadh.): XII, **207**η, 7560 (*°janmanaḥ*).—Do.[2], pl. (*°āḥ*) ("the inhabitants of the north"). § 576 (Bhagavadgītāp.): VI, **15**, 604 (*Dākshiṇātyo°āḥ*).

Uttara-Yayātyupākhyāna(m), v. Yayāti (§ 149).

Uttejanī, a mātṛ. § 615*u* (Skanda): IX, **46** θ, 2624.

Utthānaḥ sarvakarmaṇāṃ = Çiva (1000 names [2]).

Utthita = Çiva (1000 names [1]).

Utūla, pl. (*°āḥ*), a people. § 574 (Jambūkh.): VI, **9**μ, 361 (so C., B. reads *Ulūtāḥ*).

V

(What is not found under **V** should be sought for under **B.**)

Vāc [1] ("Speech") = Sarasvatī: XII, 8534 (*vedamayī*), 8741 (*S°*).—Do.[2] (do.) = Çiva (1000 names [1]).

Vācaspati [1] ("the Lord of Speech"). § 639 (Rājadh.): XII, **52**, 1871 (*api*).—§ 787 (Ānuçāsanik.): XIII, **31**a, 2014.—§ 782*b* (Brāhmaṇagītā): XIV, **21**, 636 (*tato V°r jajñe taṃ manas paryavekshate*).—Do.[2] (do.) = Mahāpurusha (Mahāpurushastava).—Do.[3] (do.) = Vishṇu (1000 names).

Vācaspatya = Çiva (1000 names [2]).

Vācāviruddhāḥ (pl.), a class of gods. § 730 (Ānuçāsanik.): XIII, **18**λλ, †1372.

Vācikā, adj. ("belonging to speech," viz. one of Brahmán's births). § 717*b* (Nārāyaṇīya): XII, **348** θθ, 13490 (*janma*, the third birth of Brahmán); **349**, III), 13565 (do., do.).

Vaça, pl. (*°āḥ*), a people. § 223 (Vāsishṭha): I, **175**, 6684 (only C., B. has *Khasān*, q.v.).

Vaçakara = Çiva (1000 names [2]).

Vaçātala, pl. (*°āḥ*), a people. § 295 (Dyūtap.): II, **52**, 1871 (only B., C. has *Vaçātayaḥ*).

Vaçāti, Vaçātika, Vaçātīya, v. Vas°.

Vaçavartin = Mahāpurusha (Mahāpurushastava).

Vaçīkara = Çiva (1000 names [2]).

Vaçishṭha, Vāçishṭha, Vaçishṭhāpavāha, v. Vas°, Vās°

Vaçya = Çiva (1000 names [2]).

Vādānya, a ṛshi. § 731*b* (Ashṭāvakra-Diksaṃv.): XIII, **19**, 1391 (*ṛsheḥ*), (1396).

Vaḍavā [1], the mother of the horses. § 221 (Caitrarathap.): I, **170**, 6488.

Vaḍavā [2], name of a tirtha. § 359 (Tīrthayātrāp.): In *V.* one should in the evening offer *caru* (rice boiled in milk and butter) to the Fire; this is equal to hundred thousands of kine, hundred rājasūyas, and a thousand horse-sacrifices; here a gift to the *Pitṛs* becomes inexhaustible. Here the *ṛshis*, the *Pitṛs*, the gods, the *Gandharvas*, the *Apsarases*, the *Guhyakas*, the *Kinnaras*, the *Yakshas*, the *Siddhas*, the *Vidyādharas*, men, the *Rākshasas*, the *Daityas*, the *Rudras*, and *Brahmán* himself practised austerities for 1,000 years in order to gratify *Vishṇu*, then they cooked *caru* and praised

Keçava each with seven *ṛces*. *Keçava* conferred eightfold *aiçvarya* (superhuman power), etc., on them, and then disappeared, therefore that tīrtha became known by the name of *Saptacaru*: III, **82**, 5034.

Vaḍavā[3], a river. § 494 (Āṅgirasa): III, **222**, 14232 (among the rivers who are mothers of fires).

Vaḍavāgni = Vaḍavāmukha[1]. § 490 (Āṅgirasa): III, **219**, 14149 (*pibaty ambho yaḥ*).

Vaḍavāmukha[1], name of the submarine fire at Vaḍavāmukha(ṃ). § 30*b* (Samudra): I, **21**, 1220 (°*dīptāgnes toyahavyapradaḥ*, sc. the ocean).—§ 552 (Goharaṇap.): IV, **50**, 1580 (*agniḥ*).—§ 616 (Sauptikap.): X, **6**, 226 (*pāvakaḥ*).—§ 717*b* (Nārāyaṇīya): XII, **339**, ††12864 (*agniḥ* = Mahāpurusha). Cf. Vaḍavāvaktra.—Do.[2] = Çiva (1000 names[2]).

Vaḍavāmukha[3], a ṛshi. § 717*b* (Nārāyaṇīya): XII, **343**, XIII), ††13222 (*maharshiḥ*, incarnation of Nārāyaṇa, cursed the ocean, saying that its water should only be drinkable for the *vaḍavāmukha*).

Vaḍavāmukha(ṃ) (the mare's head, in the ocean). § 571 (Ulūkadūtāgamanap.): V, **160**, 5529 (*Kāmboja-v* °*ṃ*, sc. *purushodadhiṃ*); **161**, 5574 (do.).—§ 599 (Jayadrathavadhap.): VII, **135**, 5556 (°*madhyasthaḥ . . . mānavaḥ*).—§ 603 (Nārāyaṇāstramokshap.): VII, **202**, 9608 (°*eti* (!) *vyākhyātaṃ pivaṃs* (°*at*, B) *toyamayaṃ haviḥ*, one of the faces of Çiva).—§ 704 (Mokshadh.): XII, **302**, 11168 (°*sāgaraṃ*).—§ 717*b* (Nārāyaṇīya): XII, **343**, XIII), ††13222 (°*sañjñitena*, drinks the water of the ocean).—§ 742 (Ānuçāsanik.): XIII, **38**, 2230.—§ 773*d* (Çiva): XIII, **162**, 7531 (the face of Çiva). Cf. Vaḍavāvaktra(ṃ).

Vaḍavāvaktra, a fire = Vāḍavāmukha[1]. § 459 (Mārkaṇḍeyas.): III, **189**, 12961 (*agniḥ*).

Vaḍavāvaktra(ṃ) = Vaḍavāmukha(ṃ). § 745*c* (Cyavana-Kuçikasaṃv.): XIII, **56**, 2909 (there Ūrva will throw the fire of his wrath; cf. Aurvopākhyāna(ṃ)).

Vāddhika (VI, 1708) error in C. for Bālhīka (see additions).

Vadha = Çiva (1000 names[2]).

Vadhna, pl. v. Vadhra, pl.

Vadhra, pl. (°*āḥ*), a people. § 574 (Jambūkh.): VI, **9**μ, 363 (only B., C. has *Vadhnāḥ*).

Vadhryaçva, an ancient king. § 267 (Yamasabhāv.): II, **8**, 323 (in the palace of Yama).

Vadhūsarā, a river. § 20 (Pulomā): I, **6**, 904 (arose from the tears of Pulomā, Brahmán gave it the name V.).—[§ 383 (Paraçurāma): III, **99**, 8684 (*nadīṃ . . . Vadhūsarākṛtāhvayāṃ*).]

Vadhyā = Brahmavadhyā (personif.): XII, 10159.

Vāduli, see Vāhuli.

Vāgātman = Kṛshṇa: XII, 1635.

Vāgindra, a brahman. § 736*b* (Vītahavyop.): XIII, **30**, 2003 (of Vītahavya's race, son of Prakāça and father of Pramati).

Vāgmin[1], a prince. § 150 (Pūruvaṃç.): I, **94**, 3697 (son of Manasyu and Sauvīrī).—Do.[2] = Vishṇu (1000 names).

Vāheyika, Vahi, Vāhīka, v. Bāheyika, etc.

Vāhīkapuṅgava, so B. for Bālhīka° (q.v.).

Vāhinī[1], wife of Kuru. § 154 (Pūruvaṃç.): I, **94**, 3740.

Vāhinī[2], a river. § 574 (Jambūkh.): VI, **9**λ, 341.

Vahitṛ sarvabhūtānāṃ = Çiva (1000 names[2]).

Vahni[1] = Agni, q.v.

Vahni[2], an ancient king (an Asura?). § 673*b* (Bali-Vāsavasaṃv.): XII, **227** *a*, 8264 (among the ancient rulers of the earth).

Vahni[3], = Vishṇu (1000 names).

Vahnidaivata, adj. ("whose deity is Vahni"). § 253 (Haraṇāharaṇap.): I, **221**, 8045 (*nakshatre*, i.e. the Kṛttikās).—§ 502 (Manushyagrahak.): III, **230**, 14464 (*nakshatraṃ*, do.).

Vahniloka ("the world of Vahni"): XIII, 6557 (only B., C. has *Brahma*-°).

Vahninandana ("son of Vahni") = Skanda: III, 14626.

Vāhuli, a son of Viçvāmitra. § 721*b* (Viçvāmitrop.): XIII, **4**β, 252 (B. has *Vāduliḥ*).

Vāhyālaya, abode of out-castes, i.e. the country of the Vāhīkas (cf. Bāhīka, pl.): VIII, 2085 (B. *Vāhyanaya*).

Vaicitravīrya = Dhṛtarāshṭra[1], q.v.

Vaicitravīryaka, adj. ("belonging to Vicitravīrya"). § 788 (Āçramavāsap.): XV, **28**, 755 (°*e kshetre*, sc. *jātaḥ*, sc. Vidura).

Vaicitravīryin = Dhṛtarāshṭra[5]: IX, 2319 (*Dh*°).

Vaiçākha, name of a month. § 759 (Ānuçāsanik.): XIII, **106**β, 5155; **109**, 5377 (°*māse*).

Vaiçākhī, the day of full moon in the month of Vaiçākha. § 746 (Ānuçāsanik.): XIII, **68**, 3413 (*paurṇamāsyāṃ*).

Vaiçālāksha, adj. ("belonging to Viçālāksha [= Çiva]"). § 641 (Rājadh.): XII, **59**, 2203 (sc. *çāstraṃ*, composed by Çiva by abridging the daṇḍanīti of Brahmán; C. has by error *Vi*°).

Vaiçāleya, pl. (°*āḥ*), a family of serpents. § 608 (Karṇap.): VIII, **87**χ', 4416 (*bhoginaḥ*, sided with Arjuna).

Vaiçālī ("daughter of the king of Viçālā (?)") = Bhadrā[3]: II, 1570 (*Bh*°).

Vaiçampāyana, a ṛshi, disciple of Vyāsa; recited the Mhbhr. at the snake-sacrifice of Janamejaya: I, 11, 20, 97, 107 (*mānushe loke V°a uktavān*), 866 (°*viprāgryaiḥ*), 2227 (Vyāsa directed *V.* to tell the Mhbhr.), (2231) (*V.* gave a resumé of the Mhbhr.), (2294) (*V.* described the Mhbhr.), (2334) (*V.* began the recitation of the Mhbhr.), (2350) (only C.), (2407), 2419 (disciple of Vyāsa), (2458), (2501), (2509), (2517), (2565), (2639), (2728), (2801), (2816), (2845), (2895), (2904), (2971), (2975), (2987), (2988), (3110), (3126), (3181), (3185), (3204), (†3233), (†3236), (†3244), (†3248), (3256), (3276), (3279), (3290), (3300), (3304), (3318), (3332), (3344), (3349), (3352), (3356), (3358), (3359), (3386), (3394), (3397), (3420), (3424), (3431), (3437), (3439), (3446), (3460), (3466), (3481), (3495), (3500), (3517), (3531), (3535), (3543), (3551), (†3569), (†3589), (3679), (†3683), (†3690), (3694), (3750), (3843), (3848/49, addition in B.), (3865), (3880), (3887), (3896), (3923), (3964), (3968), (4006), (4022), (4036), (4049), (4057), (4061), (4064), (4067), (4081), (4086, only B.), (4146), (4157), (4225), (4241), (4244), (4267), (4274), (4306), (4322), (4335), (4337), (4371), (4382), (4395), (4412), (4425), (4469), (4483), (4489), (4501), (4528), (4541), (4562), (4591), (4592), (4613), (4628), (4640), (4647), (4665), (4680), (4716), (4746), (4758), (4759), (4791), (4836), (4844), (4866), (4896), (4897), (4901), (4930), (4936), (4964), (4977), (5034), (5051), (5072), (5094), (5102), (5134), (5145), (5162), (5164), (5167), (5169), (5208), (5211), (5217), (5238), (5256), (5260), (5266), (5280), (5289), (5312), (5347), (5351), (5364), (5379), (5395), (5399), (5412), (5415), (5419), (5444), (5454), (5474), (5501), (5511), (5517), (5543), (5546), (5634), (5635), (5642), (5653), (5673), (5696), (5706), (5734), (5767), (5768), (5798), (5819), (5823), (5835), (5841), (5856), (5882), (5927), (5962), (5973), (5983), (5999), (6007), (6019), (6030), (6045), (6060),

(1964), (1984), (1987), (2116), (2122), (2268), (†2714), (5962), (6120), (6126), (6210), (6219), (6231), (6238), (†6261), (6456), (10275), 12337 (disciple of Vyāsa), 12760 (*Taittiriḥ . . . V°pūrvajaḥ*), (12998), 13003, 13012, (13023), (13060), (13119), (13131), (13333), (13396), (13399), (13427), (13460), (13554), (13615), (13628), (13639), (13645), (13701), (13714); XIII, (83), 331 (*viprarshir ajñānād brāhmaṇaṃ hatvā spṛshṭo bālavadhena ca* (!)), (371), (605), (613), (1296), (1356), (1758), (1775), (1863), (1934) (ought to have been Bhīshma), (2931), (2967), (†3693), (3696), (3698), (3730), (4222), (5139), (5387), (5402), (5574), (5575), (5921), (6294), (6931), (6936), (7532), (7627), (7629), (7692), (7706), (7729), (7741), (7754), (7759), (7795); XIV, (1), (20), (119) (ought to have been Vyāsa), (†275) (do., only C.), (†292), (293), (354), (373), (408), (414), (1476), (1478), (1536), (1589), (1596), (1626), (1653), (1661), (1676), (1680) (C., by error *Saudāsa*), (1690), (1706), (1721), (1724), (1752), (1777), (1808), (1809), (1850), (1873), (1895), (1936), (1965), (1984), (2009), (2033), (2055), (2072), (2083), (2089), (2097), (2108), (2110), (2141), (2175), (2195), (2221), (2253), (2302), (2341), (2359), (2381), (2435), (2466), (2486), (2510), (2536), (2553), (2603), (2644), (2690), (2807), (2816), (2849), (2886); XV, (4), (29), (43), (60), (118), (127), (134), (153), (156), (165), (170), (261, only B.), (268), (302), (307), (352), (356), (387), (395), (410), (428), (441), (458), (495), (520), (538), (†558), (560), (574), (576), (592), (618), (636), (656), (†673), (685), (691), (715), (741), (771), (800), (862), (868), (889), (923), (939), (956), (958), (979), (983), (1011), (1050), (1087); XVI, (1), (13), (15), (33), (57), (†105), (133), (148), (177), (254), (291); XVII, (2), (47), (53), (57), (69), (73), (89), (95); XVIII, (3), (40), (81), (125), 155, 182 (°*kīrtitaṃ*), 199, (214). Cf. Brahmarshi, Vyāsaçishya.

Vaiçeshika, adj. ("relating to the Vaiçeshika-doctrine"?): XII, 1658 (*guṇaiḥ*, probably a wrong reading; cf. PCR. and his note on XII, 11874).

Vaiçravaṇa[1] = Kubera, q.v.—Do.[2] = Çiva (1000 names[2]).

Vaiçravaṇa, adj. ("belonging to Vaiçravaṇa [i.e. Kubera]"). § 269 (Vaiçravaṇasabhāv.): II, **10**, 383 (*sabhā . . . V°ī*).— § 641 (Rājadh.): XII, **124**, 4561 (*ṛddhiṃ . . . V°īṃ*).

Vaiçravaṇa-sabhā-varṇana(ṃ) ("description of the palace of Kubera"). § 269 (Lokapālas.): The *sabhā* of *Vaiçravaṇa* (i.e. *Kubera*) is 100 *yojanas* in length and 70 in breadth, acquired by *Vaiçravaṇa* by his ascetic power; it is supported by *Guhyakas* attached to the firmament, and capable of moving along it. There sits *Vaiçravaṇa* with thousands of wives, amidst the fragrance of the lotuses of the *nalinī Alakā* and the *Nandana* gardens, and the gods, *Gandharvas* (those called *Kinnaras* and those called *Naras*), *Apsarases* (enumeration), *Yakshas* (enumeration), *Lakshmī*, *Nalakūbara*, myself (i.e. *Nārada*), many *devarshis* and *brahmarshis*, *kravyādas* (i.e. *Rākshasas*), *Umāpati* (i.e. *Çiva*), with hosts of spirits (*bhūtasaṅghaiḥ*, dwarfs, etc.), and *Devī* (i.e. *Umā*), and *Gandharva* chiefs (enumeration), and *Cakradharman*, the chief of the *Vidyādharas*, *Bhagadatta*, and innumerable other kings, aud *Druma*, the chief of the *Kimpurushas*, and the *Rākshasa* king *Mahendra Gandhamādana* (according to BR., who takes it to be = *Rāvaṇa*), and *Vibhīshaṇa* (the brother of *Kubera*), and the mountains *Himavat*, etc. (enumeration), in their personified forms, and *Nandīçvara* and *Mahākāla*, and many *pārishadas* with arrowy ears and mouths, *Kāshṭha*, *Kuṭīmukha*, *Dantin*, and *Vijayā* (B. *Vijaya*), and the roaring white bull [of *Çiva*, PCR.], and *Piçācas*. *Paulastya* (i.e. *Kubera*) always adores *Çiva*, and sometimes is honoured by his visit. There also the best of jewels, *Çaṅkha* and *Padma*, those princes of all gems [in their personified forms, PCR.], accompanied by all the jewels of the earth, worship *Kubera* (II, **10**).

Vaiçvadeva, adj ("belonging to the Viçvadevas"). § 677 (Mokshadh.): XII, **244**, 8871 (sc. *loke*).—§ 704 (do.): XII, **302**ββ, 11105 (*vishayān*).—§ 746 (Ānuçāsanik.): XIII, **60**, 3060 (*tṛtīyaṃ savanaṃ*); **79**κ, 3775 (*sthānaṃ*, C. has by error *Vaiçya°*).—§ 778*b* (Saṃvartta-Maruttīya): XIV, **10**, †285 (*ukshāṇaṃ*).—§ 782*g* (Guruçishyasaṃv.): XIV, **42**, 1129 (*vāc*).—Do.[2], subst. neutr. (do.), name of a certain offering. § 309 (Āraṇyakap.): III, **2**, 105.—§ 327 (Draupadīparitāpav.): III, **30**, 1130.—§ 732 (Ānuçāsanik.): XIII, **22**, 1553.—§ 753 (do.): XIII, **97**, 4659, 4660, 4667, 4673.

Vaiçvāmitra ("son of Viçvāmitra") = Ashṭaka: III, †13301 (*A*°).

Vaiçvānara[1] = Agni, q.v. (Add VII, 2019; VIII, 2160; for II, 299, see next.)

Vaiçvānara[2], a muni. § 266 (Çakrasabhāv.): II, **7**, 299 (*muniḥ*, in the palace of Indra).

Vaiçvānara, pl. (°*āḥ*), a class of ṛshis. § 656 (Khaḍgotpattik.): XII, **166**β, 6143 (°-*Marīcipāḥ*).

Vaiçvānaramukha = Çiva: XIV, 201.

Vaiçvānarī, adj. f. ("belonging to [Agni] Vaiçvānara") said of the Earth. § 746 (Ānuçāsanik.): XIII, **62**, 3140 (C. by error *Vaiçyānarī*).

Vaiçyāḥ (pl.) = Çiva (1000 names[1]).

Vaiçyāputra ("the son of a vaiçya woman") = Yuyutsu, q.v.

Vaidambha = Çiva (1000 names[2]).

Vaidarbha ("the king of the Vidarbhas"), the father of Lopāmudrā. § 382 (Agastyop.): III, **96**, 8562; **97**, 8570.

Vaidarbhi (do.), the father of Lopāmudrā. § 767 (Ānuçāsanik.): XIII, **137***a*, 6255 (gave his daughter to Agastya).

Vaidarbhī[1] ("the daughter of the king of the Vidarbhas") = Suçravā: I, ††3770 (*S*°).

Vaidarbhī[2] (do.) = Maryādā: I, ††3771 (*M*°).

Vaidarbhī[3] (do.) = Damayantī: III, 2146, 2156, 2164, 2181, 2201, 2203, 2261, 2337, 2351, 2410, 2458, 2568, 2642, 2660, 2678, 2681, 2762, 2775, 2886, 2896, 2910, 2911, 2955, 3002 (°*jananī*), 3005, 3009, 3050, 3065.

Vaidarbhī[4] (do.) = Lopāmudrā: III, 8569 (*yuvatīṃ*); V, 3971 (*reme . . . yathā Agastyaç cāpi V°yāṃ*).

Vaidarbhī[5] (do.), wife of Sagara. § 387 (Sagara): III, **106**, 8833, 8843 (bore a gourd, from which arose sixty thousands of sons).

Vaideha[1] ("the king of the Videhas"), a prince contemporary with Yudhishṭhira. § 264 (Sabhākriyāp.): II, **4**β, 122 (waited upon Yudhishṭhira).

Vaideha[2] (do.) = Janaka: XII, 835 (*J*°), 3909, 3937, 3955, 10876, 10916, 11434 (i.e. Karālajanaka), 11840 (*J*°), 11842.

Vaideha[3] (do.) = Nimi: XII, 8600 (*N*°).

Vaideha[4], pl. (°*āḥ*), a people = Videha, pl. § 280 (Bhīmasena): II, **30**, 1089 (°*sthaḥ*, sc. Bhīmasena; on his digviyaya Bhīmasena conquered *V*. and therefrom sent expeditions).— § 574 (Jambūkh.): VI, **9**μ, 364.—§ 608 (Karṇap.): VIII, **79**, 4040 (°*āmbashṭha-Kāmbojāḥ*, had been vanquished by Arjuna in the battle).

Vaideha[5], name of a mixed caste: XIII, 2582 (sg.), 2589 (°*yāṃ*, fem.).

Vaidehaka, name of a mixed caste = Vaideha: XII, 10868 (pl.); XIII, 2571 (sg.), 2585 (do.), 2587 (do.).

Vaidehaka, adj. ("belonging to the Videhas"). § 280 (Bhīmasena): II, **30**, 1087 (°*ṃ rājānaṃ Janakaṃ*).

Vaidehī[1] ("the daughter of the king of the Videhas") = Maryādā: I, ††3776 (*M*°).

Vaidehī[2] (do.), the wife of Çatānīka[2] (the son of Janamejaya). § 160 (Pūruvamç.): I, **95**, ††3838.

Vaidehī[3] (do.) = Sītā: III, 11208, 15973 (*Janakātmajā*), 16017, 16023, 16034, 16052, 16057, 16058, 16060, 16061, 16070, 16077, 16097, 16106, 16146, 16163, 16182, 16184, 16195, 16220, 16232, 16253, 16265, 16490, 16540, 16551, 16588, 16595, 16612; IV, 652 (*duhitā Janakasya*); V, 3976 (*veme . . . V°yāñ ca yathā Rāmaḥ*); VII, 2228.

***Vaidika**, adj. ("belonging to the Vedas"): I, 4924 (°*ādhyayanāni*); VIII, †4712 (*sa-v°ḥ*, but read with B. *saved*°); XII, 317 (*karmāṇi*), 2677 (B. do., C. *sarvāṇi*), 2689 (*karmāṇi*), 2878 (*iti v°ṃ*), 2884 (do.), 2970 (*çrutiḥ*), 2974 (*sthitiḥ*), 9610 (*iti v°ṃ*), 9731 (do.), 11109 (*guṇāḥ*), 12821 (*çrutiḥ*), †13759 (*karma*); XIII, 5564 (do.); XIV, 340 (*karmāṇi*), 1014 (*çrutiḥ*), 1568 (sc. *karmāṇi*?).

Vaidūryaçikhara, a mountain. § 377 (Dhaumyatīrthak.): III, **89**, 8359 (*girivaraḥ*, in the west, description); cf. next.

Vaidūryaparvata, a mountain. § 377 (Dhaumyatīrthak.): III, **88**, 8343 (in the south).—§ 404 (Tīrthayātrāp.): III, **121**, 10306, 10310 (near Narmadā, visited by Yudhishṭhira, etc.).

***vaidya**[1], adj. ("conversant with the Vedas"): I, 6143; II, 667; III, 11634; V, †800, 1491, 3456 (*brāhmaṇāḥ*), 4485; XII, 532, 2863, 2905, 3200 (*brāhmaṇān*), 8868, 9360; XIII, 1539, 1565, 5820.—Do.[2], mostly pl. ("physicians"): III, 70, 13856; V, 110, 5156 (*cikitsakāḥ*), 5181; VI, 5745, 5747, 5749; X, 113 (sg., *yathā*); XII, 854, 878, 2654 (*caturvidhān*), 12542.—Do.[3], name of a caste: XIII, 2621 (*Vrātya-V°au*, son of a çūdra and a vaiçyā).

Vaidya[4] (XIII, 7108), v. Raibhya.

Vaidya[5] = Çiva (1000 names[2]). — Do.[6] = Vishṇu (1000 names).

Vaihāra, a mountain near Girivraja (the present Baibhār, i.e. Vaibhāra). § 277 (Jarāsandhavadhap.): II, **21**, 799 (among the four mountains which surround Girivraja).

Vaihāyasa[1], pl. (°*āḥ*) a class of ṛshis. § 421*b* (Ākāça-Gaṅgā): III, **142**, 10903.

Vaihāyasa[2], name of a lake. § 641 (Rājadh.): XII, **127**, 4662 (*hradaḥ* (C., *hṛ*°), near Badarī).

Vaijayanta[1], the standard of Indra. § 277 (Jarāsandhavadhap.): II, **22**, 872 (*Aindraḥ*, Nīl. takes it = *prāsāda*).—§ 335 (Indralokābhigamanap.): III, **42**, 1721 (*dhvajam*).

Vaijayanta[2], a mountain. § 717*d* (Brahma-Rudrasamv.): XII, **351**, 13721 (*kshīrodasya samudrasya madhye . . . V°a iti khyātaḥ parvataḥ*), 13722, 13734.

***vaijayantī**[1] ("triumphal") adj., said of garlands: I, 2318 (*mālām*); VII, 1274 (*mālā*); IX, 2667 (*mālā*).

Vaijayantī[2], dual (°*yau*), name of the bells of Airāvata. § 505 (Skandayuddha): III, **231**, 14531 (given to Skanda by Indra).

Vaikartaṇa = Karṇa, q.v.

Vaikhāna = Vishṇu (1000 names).

Vaikhānasa[1], pl. (°*āḥ*), a class of ṛshis. § 246 (Sundopasundop.): I, **211**, 7683.—§ 377 (Dhaumyatīrthak.): III, **89**, 8369 (*Pushkaraṃ . . . V°ānāṃ . . . āçramaḥ priyaḥ*).—§ 392 (Tīrthayātrāp.): III, **114**, 10109.—§ 406 (do.): III, **125**, 10413 (*Candramasas tīrtham*).—§ 565 (Gālavacarita): V, **111**, 3831 (°*āçramaḥ*, in the north).—§ 615*u* (Skanda): IX, **45**γ, 2510.—§ 626 (Rājadh.): XII, **20**, 606 (°*ānāṃ . . . vacanaṃ*, a sentence of theirs quoted?).—§ 630 (do.): XII, **26**, 773 (do., do.).—§ 641 (do.): XII, **60**, 2316 (*gāthāḥ . . . V°ānāṃ . . . munīnāṃ*, some verses sung by them quoted).—§ 677 (Mokshadh.): XII, **245**, 8897 (°*gatiṃ*), 8903.—§ 717*b* (Nārāyaṇīya): XII, **349**, I), 13561 (learnt the religion of Nārāyaṇa from the *phenapāḥ* and communicated it to Soma).—§ 747*b* (Suvarṇotpatti): XIII, **85**ζ, 4126 (arose from the ashes of the sacrificial fire).—§ 749 (Ānuçāsanik.): XIII, **90**, 4323 (°*ānāṃ vacanam ṛshīṇāṃ*, a sentence of theirs quoted?).

Vaikhānasa[2] = Mahāpurusha (Mahāpurushastava).

Vaikhānasa[3], adj. ("belonging to the Vaikhānasas"). § 772*l* (Vasishṭha): XIII, **156**, 7280 (*saraḥ*, there the gods (*Ādityāḥ*) performed a sacrifice; B., however, has *saro vai Mānasaṃ*).

Vaikuṇṭha = Vishṇu (Kṛshṇa): I, 2505; III, 8755; VI, 308 (*Vishṇuṃ*); VII, 2963 (*Vishṇo*); XII, 1503, 1652, 4079, 10019 (*Vishṇuḥ*), [12864 (Mahāpurushastava)], 13239 (°*tvaṃ*, etymology), 13403 (*avyayaṃ*); XIII, 6993 (1000 names), 7745.

Vaimānika[1], name of a tīrtha. § 733*k* (Ānuçāsanik.): By bathing in *V.* and *Kiṅkiṇīkāçrama* one acquires the merit of repairing everywhere at will. The merit of bathing in *Kālikāçrama*, etc.: XIII, **25**, 1709.

***vaimānika**[2], adj. ("celestial"): III, 171 (*gaṇāḥ*).

Vainateya[1] ("son of Vinatā") = Garuḍa: I, 1284, 1484, 1503, 1504, 1573, 1588, 2603 (*G*°), 7668 (°*ād ivoragaḥ*); II, 748 (*patato V°sya gatim anye yathā khagāḥ*); III, 550 (°*o yathā pakshī Garutmān patatāṃ varaḥ*), 11413 (°*sya sadṛçaḥ*), 16243 (°*m ivāparaṃ*); V, 3587 (°*sutaih*. six sons of *G.* enumerated), 3640, 3658, 3669 (°*parākramaṃ*), 3705, 3891, 3925, 4002, 4003; VI, 152 (*G*°), 1234 (°*aç ca pakshiṇāṃ*, sc. *asmi*, says Kṛshṇa), 4143 (°*vat*); VII, 403 (vehicle of Kṛshṇa), 573 (*yathā*), 1435 (°*vat*), 2811 (device of Kṛshṇa), 8789 (°*a ivoragaṃ*); VIII, 1803 (*Suparṇaṃ pataçreshṭhaṃ*); X, 651 (*bhujagāriḥ*, on the standard of Kṛshṇa); XII, 12587 (°*samadyutiṃ*); XIII, 870 (vehicle of Vishṇu), 915 (*pakshiṇām V°as tvam*, sc. *asi*, sc. Çiva).

Vainateya[2], a Suparṇa, son of Garuḍa. § 564 (Mātalīyop.): V, **101**β, 3595.

Vainateya[3], pl. (°*āḥ*) ("descendants of Vinatā", i.e. birds). § 99 (Aṃçāvat.): I, **65**, 2548 (enumeration). — § 191 (Arjuna): I, **123**, 4806 (present at the birth of Arjuna), 4830 (enumeration).—§ 574 (Jambūkh.): VI, **3**, 72 (omens).—§ 608 (Karṇap.): VIII, **87**χ', 4413 (sided with Arjuna).—§ 775 (Ānuçāsanik.): XIII, **166***a*, 7644.

Vaiṇavin (B. *Ve*°-) = Çiva (1000 names[2]).

Vainya ("the son of Vena") = Pṛthu: I, 466 (*Pṛthor V°sya . . . ākhyānaṃ*); II, 331 (°*ṇ*°, C.), 1929 (*P*°); III, 141, 8271 (*yathā*), 12677, 12681, 12684, 12687, 12688 (°*yajñaṃ*), 12696 (°*saṃsadi*), 12699; VI, 314 (*P*°); VII, 2394 (*P*°, C. has °*ṇ*°), 2396 (do., do.), 2397 (C. has °*ṇ*°), 2406 (*P*°, do.), 2421 (do., do.); XII, 1030 (*P*°), 1032 (*P*°), 1033, 2221, 2230, 2231, 2234 (*P*°), 2236, 2242, 6206 (*yathā*); XIII, 7125 (*P*°), 7680 (*ādirājaḥ Pṛthur V°aḥ*, C. by error has *Ve*°).

Vaiṇya, v. Vainya.

Vainyopākhyāna ("the episode relating to Vainya"). § 10 (Parvasaṅgr.): I, **1**, 332 (entered among the parvans of the fifth book of the Mhbhr., but not found there).

Vairāja[1], pl. (°*āḥ*), a class of pitṛs. § 270 (Brahmasabhāv.): II, **11**, 462 (in the palace of Brahmán).

Vairāja[2], adj. ("belonging to Virāj [i.e. Brahmán]"). § 717*d* (Brahma-Rudrasamv.): XII, **351**, 13722 (°*sadanāt*), 13730 (°*sadane*).

Vairāma, pl. (°*āḥ*), a people. § 295 (Dyūtap.): II, **51**, 1832 (brought tribute to Yudhishṭhira).

Vairāṭa, a son of Dhṛtarāshṭra. § 585 (Bhīshmavadhap.): VI, **96**θθ, 4349 (slain by Bhīmasena).

Vairāṭa, adj. ("relating to Virāṭa"). § 10 (Parvasaṅgr.): I, **2**, 327 (sc. *parva*, i.e. the fourth book of Mhbhr. [Virāṭaparvan]).—§ 11 (do.): I, **2**, 481 (*parva*, do.), 490 (do., do., said to contain 2,050 çlokas; C., however, has 2,376 çlokas).

Vairāṭi[1] ("the son of Virāṭa") = Çaṅkha: IV, 1098; VI, 1850 (v. Çveta[8]), 2010 (*Ç*°, not in B.).

Vairāṭi[2] (do.) = Çveta[8]: VI, 1850 (?), 1912, 1915/16 (only B.), 1950, 1951.

Vairāṭi[3] (do.) = Uttara: IV, 1230, 1239, 1283 (*U*°), 1303, 1317, 1352, 1355, 1374, 1390, 1402, 1454 (only B.), 1645, 1647, †1662, 1736, 1757, 1779, 1781, 1784, 1833, 1966 (*U*°), 1983, 1984, 1989 (*U*°), †2159, 2299, 2306; V, 2263 (*U*°), 5879 (*U*°); VI, 1745 (*U*°), 1842 (*U*°).

Vairāṭi[4] (XIV, 1836), v. Vairāṭī.

Vairāṭī ("the daughter of Virāṭa") = Uttarā: I, †213 (*garbhe V°yāḥ*, i.e. Parikshit), 328 (*Abhimanyoç ca V°yāḥ, parva Vaivāhikaṃ smṛtaṃ*, i.e. Vaivāhikaparvan[2], C. has by error °*ṭyā p*°); VII, 2766; XIV, 1836 (so B., C. by error *V°iḥ*), 1846, 1847, 1958, 1992, 2012; XV, 591 (°*ṭyās tanayaṃ*, i.e. Parikshit).

Vairocana ("the son of Virocana") = Bali: I, 5484 (*Indra-V°āv iva*); II, 364 (*B*°); III, 1029 (*B*°), VII, 859 (*Indra V°āv iva*), 7873 (do.); VIII, 4376 (do.), †4528 (*Sureça-V°yor yathā*, sc. *sannipātaḥ*); XII, 3385 (*B*°), 8059 (*B*°), 8117 (*B*°), 8154 (*B*°), 8232 (*B*°); XIII, 4687 (*B*°).

Vairocani (do.) = Bali: III, 976 (°*er çrīḥ*), 1044, 12068 (*B*°), 12150; V, 4368 (*Indro V°iṃ yathā*, sc. *nigṛhṇīma*); VII, 3484 (*yathā*), 5608 (*Çakra-V°ī yathā*, sc. *yuyudhāte*); XII, 8223 (*B*°), 8227, 8319; XIII, 329 (*B*°).

Vaishṇava, adj. ("belonging (or devoted) to Vishṇu"). § 440 (Yakshayuddhap.): III, **164**, 11900 (sc. *astraṃ*, acquired by Arjuna).—§ 443 (Nivātakavacayuddhap.): III, **168**, 12021 (sc. *astrāṇi*, do.).—§ 473 (Mārkaṇḍeyas.): III, **200**, †13479 (*bhūr V°ī*).—§ 476 (Dhundhumārop.): III, **202**, 13543 (*tejaḥ*).—§ 516 (Duryodhanayajña): III, **255**, 15291 (*yajñaḥ*).—§ 524*d* (Vishṇu): III, **272**, 15847 (°*añ cocyate jagat*).—§ 543 (Rāmābhisheka): III, **291**, 16596 (*nakshatre*, i.e. Çravaṇa).—§ 564 (Mātalīyop.): V, **98**, 3539 (*cakraṃ*).—§ 570*f* (Çārṅga): V, **158**, 5355 (*Çārṅgaṃ*).—§ 588 (Bhīshmavadhap.): VI, **121**β, 5801 (sc. *astraṃ*).—§ 592 (Saṃçaptakavadhap.): VII, **23**ρ, 1040 (sc. *dhanuḥ*, held by Nakula).—§ 592*c* (Vaishṇavāstra): VII, **29**, 1285 (*astraṃ*).—§ 606 (Tripurākhyāna): VIII, **34**, 1503 (°*aṃ cocyate jagat*).—§ 615*u* (Skanda): IX, **46**ι, 2656 (°*yaḥ*, sc. *mātaraḥ*).—§ 641*f* (Pṛthu Vainya): XII, **59**, 2255 (*mahattvena*).—§ 674*b* (Çrī-Vāsavasaṃv.): XII, **229**, 8345 (*padaṃ*).—§ 707 (Mokshadh.): XII, **318**, 11703 (*sthānaṃ*).—§ 717*h* (Nārāyaṇīya): XII, **341**, 13061 (*kratuṃ*); **343**, VII), ††13217 (*açvamedhaṃ yajñaṃ*).—§ 746 (Ānuçāsanik.): XIII, **76**θ, 3679 (°*ī*, said of wealth given instead of kine), †3682 (*candralokāḥ*).—§ 749 (do.): XIII, **91**β, 4350 (°*ī*, sc. the earth).—§ 768 (do.): XIII, **139**, 6317 (*tejaḥ*).—§ 784*b* (Uttaṅka): XIV, **55**, 1589 (*vapuḥ*), 1591 (*rūpaṃ*).—§ 795*c* (Mahābhārata): XVIII, **6**, 304 (a worshipper of Vishṇu), 305 (*padaṃ, yaçaḥ*), 310 (*padaṃ*).

Vaishṇavāstra ("the weapon belonging to Vishṇu"). § 592 (Saṃçaptakavadhap.): VII, **29**, 1272 (employed by Bhagadatta).—§ 592*c* (do.): Kṛshṇa has four forms: 1) one, staying on earth, engaged in ascetic austerities; 2) one, beholding good and evil deeds in the world; 3) one, coming into the world of men and engaged in action; 4) one, reposing in sleep for 1,000 years, and at the end of the 1,000 years granting, upon awakening, excellent boons. The Earth (*Pṛthivī*), knowing that that time had come, asked of him as a boon for [her son] *Naraka*, that he, possessed of the *Vaishṇavāstra*, should become incapable of being slain by gods and Asuras. The boon was granted. From *Naraka*, the king of *Prāgjyotisha* (i.e. Bhagadatta) got this weapon, that may slay even *Indra* and *Rudra*: VII, **29**, 1284, [1285 (*astraṃ* . . . *Vaishṇavaṃ*)].

Vaitahavya, pl. (°*āḥ*) ("the sons of Vītahavya"). § 736*b* (Vītahavyop.): XIII, **30**, 1965, 1974, 1976, 1978 (fought with the Kāçi kings Sudeva and Divodāsa).

***vaitālika**, pl. ("bards"): I, 6940; II, 102; IV, 2364; VII, 2912; XII, 1386.

Vaitālin, a warrior of Skanda. § 615*u* (Skanda): IX, **45**η, 2569.

Vaitaraṇī, one or more rivers, also the river in the region of Yama. § 221*b* (Gaṅgā): I, **170**, 6457 (in the regions of the Pitṛs the Gaṅgā becomes *V.*).—§ 268 (Varuṇasabhāv.): II, **9**, 373 (present in the palace of Varuṇa).—§ 364 (Tīrthayātrāp.): III, **83**, 6054 (with the tīrtha Tripishṭapa).—§ 370 (do.): III, **85**, 8148 (*sarvapāpapramocanīṃ*, C. has by error *Vat*°).—§ 392*b* (do.): On the *V. Dharma* performed sacrifices, placing himself under the protection of the gods; on the northern bank *ṛshis* formerly and now performed sacrifices; it is equal to the path of the gods (*devayānena pathā*) to a man who has attained to Svarga. There *Rudra* seized the sacrificial beast as his share, but having been satisfied by sacrifice he gave up the beast and went by the path of the gods (*devayānena*). From fear of *Rudra* the gods reserved the best of all shares for him. He, who reciting this *gāthā* performs his ablutions there, sees with his eyes the path of the gods: III, **114**, 10098 (in the country of the Kaliṅgas).—§ 392 (do.): III, **114**, 10107 (do., visited by Yudhishṭhira, etc.).—§ 565 (Gālavacarita): V, **109**, 3792 (*vaitaraṇair vṛtā*).—§ 574 (Jambūkh.): VI, **9**λ, 342 (among the rivers of Bhāratavarsha).—§ 580 (Bhīshmavadhap.): VI, **59**, †2638 (*mahā-V°īprakāçāṃ*).—§ 586 (do.): VI, **103**, 4719 (*yathā V°ī pretān Pretarājapuraṃ prati*). — § 593 (Abhimanyuvadhap.): VII, **50**, †1978 (*bhayāvahā V°īva dustarā*).—§ 599 (Jayadrathavadhap.): VII, **146**, 6189 (*ghorāṃ V°īm iva*).—§ 600 (Ghaṭotkacavadhap.): VII, **171**, 7780 (*yathā V°ī . . . Yamarāshṭraṃ prati*).—§ 608 (Karṇap.): VIII, **77**, 3905 (*yathā V°īṃ ugrāṃ dustarām akṛtātmabhiḥ*); **80**, 4098 (*mahā-V°ī yathā*); **94**, †4900 (*iva*). — § 704 (Mokshadh.): XII, **320**, 11128 (*Yamakshaye*). — § 710 (do.): XII, **322**, 12075 (*ushṇāṃ V°īṃ nadīm avagāḍhaḥ*).—§ 793 (Mausalap.): XVI, **5**, 142 (*bhīmāṃ V°īm iva*).—§ 795 (Svargārohaṇap.): XVIII, **3**, 84 (in hell).

Vaitrakīyavana, see Vetrakīyavana.

Vaittapālya, adj. ("belonging to Vittapāla [i.e. Kubera]"). § 603*b* (Nārāyaṇa): VII, **201**ζζ, 9466 (sc. *karma*).

Vaivāhika, adj. ("relating to marriage"). § 10 (Parvasaṅgr.): I, **2**, 314 (sc. *parva*, i.e. Vaivāhikaparvan[1]).—§ 11 (do.): I, **2**, 362 (do., do.).

[Vaivāhikaparvan[1]**]** ("the section relating to the marriage of Draupadī with the Pāṇḍavas", the 13th of the minor parvans of Mhbhr.). (Cf. Vaivāhika.) § 237. *Dhṛshṭadyumna* related what had happened: (*Arjuna* had large red eyes, v. 7175, and *Kṛshṇā* had followed him, catching hold of his deerskin, v. 7177); from their conversation on military subjects, he concluded that they were the *Pāṇḍavas*, of whom it had been heard that they had all escaped from the lac-house. *Drupada* (= *Saumaki*, v. 7198) sent his *purohita* to *Yudhishṭhira*, who said that there was no occasion for *Drupada* to grieve for his daughter. While *Yudhishṭhira* was saying this, another messenger from *Drupada* announced that the feast was ready (I, **193**). The *Pāṇḍavas*, with *Kuntī* and *Kṛshṇā* were conveyed to *Drupada's* palace. *Drupada* wished to ascertain to which caste they belonged, and had for that purpose made ready a large collection of various articles appertaining to different human occupations; after dinner they began to observe, with interest, the implements of war, wherefore *Drupada* and his son thought that they were of royal blood (I, **194**). *Yudhishṭhira* told *Drupada* who they were. *Drupada* vowed to restore *Yudhishṭhira* to his kingdom. *Yudhishṭhira* told him that they would all marry *Kṛshṇā*, which *Drupada* considered to be contrary to morality. While they discoursed on this matter *Vyāsa* arrived (I, **195**). *Drupada* consulted *Vyāsa* about the wedding of his daughter. *Vyāsa* desired to hear the opinion of each of them. *Drupada* regarded the practice of marrying one wife to five men as sinful, and so did *Dhṛshṭadyumna*. *Yudhishṭhira* thought it not to be sinful, because his heart, that never inclined to what was sinful, approved of it; "it is recorded in the *Purāṇa* that *Jaṭilā Gautamī* had married seven *ṛshis*, and a *muni's* daughter, born of a tree (*Vārkshī* [= *Mārishā*, BR.], see Hariv., v. 96 foll.) married the ten *Pracetases*"; moreover, their mother *Kuntī* had told them to enjoy her all. *Kuntī* was afraid that she would be guilty of a lie. *Vyāsa* said that *Yudhishṭhira* was right, and took *Drupada* apart (I, **196**) and related to him *Pañcendropākhyāna* (§§ 238–239).—§ 240. *Drupada* then consented, as it had been ordained by the gods. *Vyāsa* declared that very day to be auspicious as the moon entered in conjunction with *Pushya* (*Paushyaṃ yogam upaiti*). *Drupada* and his son made preparations for the wedding, and *Dhaumya*, performing the usual rites, married *Kṛshṇā* to *Yudhishṭhira*, and then to his brothers on successive days. *Draupadī* regained her virginity every day after her previous marriage. Then *Drupada* gave to them various kinds of excellent wealth (I, **198**). *Drupada*, after his alliance with the *Pāṇḍavas*, had all his fears dispelled. His ladies worshipped the feet of *Kuntī*. *Kuntī* pronounced a blessing upon *Kṛshṇā*. *Kṛshṇa* sent them costly presents (I, **199**).

[Vaivāhikaparvan[2]] ("the section containing the marriage of Abhimanyu and Uttarā"; the 56th of the minor parvans of Mhbhr.). § 553. On the third day the five *Pāṇḍavas*, attired in white robes after a bath, etc., entered the palace of *Virāṭa* and took their seats on the thrones reserved for kings. *Virāṭa* rebuked *Kaṅka* (*Yudhishṭhira*) for this insolence; *Arjuna* praised *Yudhishṭhira*, saying that there was none like him, even amongst D., As., men, Rā., G., Y., Ku., or M.-U., and disclosed that he was *Yudhishṭhira* (*b*) (IV, **70**). Asked by *Virāṭa* which of them then was *Arjuna*, etc., *Arjuna* pointed out *Bhīma* (β), *Nakula*, and *Sahadeva* (both beautiful and great warriors), *Draupadī*, and himself. *Uttara* spoke of *Arjuna's* prowess, and described each of them, especially *Arjuna* ("it was by him that *Bhīshma*, *Droṇa*, and *Duryodhana* were vanquished"). *Virāṭa*, thinking he had offended *Yudhishṭhira*, offered to bestow his daughter *Uttarā* on *Arjuna*, which was applauded by *Uttara*, and offered his whole kingdom, etc., to *Yudhishṭhira*. *Arjuna* accepted *Uttarā* as his daughter-in-law, saying that such an alliance between the *Matsyas* and the *Bharatas* was desirable (IV, **71**). Asked by *Virāṭa* why he himself did not wish to accept his daughter as wife, *Arjuna* alleged that she had confided in him as her father, and people might entertain suspicions against her or him; by accepting her for *Abhimanyu* he attested her purity. *Virāṭa* approved of it, and *Yudhishṭhira* gave his assent; the latter sent invitations to *Kṛshṇa*, etc., and so did *Virāṭa*. The *Pāṇḍavas* took up their abode at *Upaplavya*. *Arjuna* brought over *Abhimanyu* and *Kṛshṇa*, and many *Daçārhas* from the *Ānartta* country. The *Kāçi*-king and *Çaibya* (friendly to *Yudhishṭhira*) came, each accompanied by an *akshauhiṇī* of troops; *Yajñasena* came there with the sons of *Draupadī* and *Çikhaṇḍin*, and *Dhṛshṭadyumna* came with an *akshauhiṇī*. All the kings that came there were lords of *akshauhiṇīs* and performers of sacrifices, etc. Then came *Kṛshṇa* (decked with garlands), *Balarāma*, etc., with *Abhimanyu* and his mother. And *Indrasena*, etc., having lived at *Dvārakā* for a whole year, came with the chariots of the *Pāṇḍavas*. In the train of *Kṛshṇa* came also 10,000 elephants, 100 thousands of horses, 100 millions of chariots, 100 milliards of foot soldiers, and innumerable *Vṛshṇi*, *Andhaka*, and *Bhoja* warriors. *Kṛshṇa* gave to each of the *Pāṇḍavas* numerous female slaves, etc. Then the nuptial festival set in (description). The matrons of the *Matsyas* were headed by *Sudeshṇā*; but *Kṛshṇā* was the foremost in beauty, etc. *Virāṭa* gave [as dowry] 7,000 horses and 200 elephants, and much wealth, and offered his kingdom, etc., to the *Pāṇḍavas*. *Yudhishṭhira* gave all the wealth that had been brought by *Kṛshṇa*, etc., to the brahmans (IV, **72**).

Vaivasvata[1] ("the son of Vivasvat"): XI, 396 (= Karṇa, PCR.; it might also be taken = Yama?).

Vaivasvata[2] (do.) = Manu[7]: I, 3126 (*M*°); III, 12746 (*M*°), 12755 (*M*°), 12756 (*M*°), 12800 (*M*°); VI, 313 (*M*°); XIII, 1290 (*M*°).

Vaivasvata[3] (do.) = Yama: I, 1710 (°*sya sadanaṃ*), 3018 (*Y*°), 3136 (*Y*°), †7275, †7281, †7282; II, 280 (*Y*°), 311 (°*sya*, sc. *sabhāṃ*), 318 (*Y*°), 339, 479 (°*sabhāyāṃ*), 2557 (°*kshayaṃ*); III, 1674 (*Dharmarājaḥ*), 8521 (*gato V°ṃ prati*), 8548 (°*kshayaṃ*), 9936 (do.), †10224 (°*āditya-Dhaneçvarāṇām*, sc. *āyatanāni*), 11996 (*Lokapālaiḥ . . . V°ādibhiḥ*), †16788, 16802 (*Y*°); V, †511 (*Y*°), 519 (°*aṃ Pitṝṇām . . . ādhipatyaṃ dadau Çakraḥ*), 1253 (*Y*°), 2179 (°*kshayaṃ*), 2308, 2313 (°*kshayaṃ*), 5797 (°*opamaḥ*); VI, 3406 (°*kshayaṃ*); VII, 1179 (do.), 1820 (°*sya gṛhaṃ*), 1988 (°*kshayaṃ*), 2419 (*Y*°), 2521, 4727 (*rājā*), 6511 (°*kshayaṃ*), 7082 (°*puraṃ*), 8304 (°*kshayaṃ*), 8499 (do., only C.), 8541 (°*kshayaṃ*), 9163 (do.), 9569 (*Y*°); VIII, 99 (°*kshayaṃ*), 122 (do.), 123 (do.), 129 (do.), 132 (do.), 155 (do.), 162 (do.), 172 (do.), 181 (do.), 185 (do.), 187 (do.), 360 (°*a ivāsahyaḥ*), †665 (*pṛshatkaiḥ . . . V°daṇḍakalpaiḥ*), 1998 (°*āt daṇḍahastād api*), †4831 (*Kubera-V°-Vāsavānāṃ tulyaprabhāvāḥ*); IX, 1866 (°*m iva kruddhaṃ*); XI, 396 (see Vaivasvata[1]); XII, 168 (°*kshayaṃ*), 174 (do.), 4495 (*Y*°), 5615 (*api*), 5844 (*yathā*), 7227, †11018, 12413 (*Mṛtyu-V°au*); XIII, 1291 (*Y*°), 1739 (°*sya sadanaṃ*), †3500, †3511, 3521, †3541, 4825 (°*ṃ prāpya*), 4856 (°*sya sadane*), 7486 (*Y*°).

Vaivasvata[4], adj. *a*) ("belonging to Vivasvat"): § 588 (Bhīshmavadhap.): VI, **121**β, 5802 (*Savitur V°m*, sc. *astram*).—§ 789 (Putradarçanap.): XV, **33**κ, 903 (*lokam*).—*b*) ("belonging to Vaivasvata[2] [i.e. Manu]"): § 695 (Mokshadh.): XII, **285**, 10272 (*antare*). — § 717*c* (Uparicara): XII, **337**, 12808 (do.).—*c*) ("belonging to

Vaivasvata [i.e. Yama]"): § 611 (Çalyap.): IX, **11**, 580 (*jihvām V°īm iva*). — § 746 (Ānuçāsanik.): XIII, **71**, †3499 (*sabhām*).—§ 757*c* (Yamaloka): XIII, **102**, †4858 (*Saṃyamanī*).

Vaivasvatasya tīrtha(m), name of a tīrtha. § 733*q* (Marudgaṇa): XIII, **25**, 1725.

Vaivasvatī[1] ("daughter of Vivasvat [Sūrya]") = Tapatī: I, ††3791 (*T°*), 6632 (*T°*).

Vaivasvatī[2] (do.) = Çraddhā: XII, 9449 (*Çraddhā . . . Sūryasya duhitā*).

[Vaiyasvatopākhyāna(m)] ("story of Manu Vaivasvata"). § 457 (Mārk.). Requested by *Yudhishṭhira*, *Mārkaṇḍeya* said: The *maharshi Manu*, *Vivasvat's* son, equal to *Prajāpati* (i.e. *Brahmán*), excelled his father and grandfather in strength, etc. He practised austerities in *Badarī*, standing on one foot, etc., for 10,000 years. Once a small fish came to him on the banks of the *Cīriṇī* and asked his protection from the greater fishes. He first reared it in a water vessel, and as it grew larger, he carried it to a large tank, and thence into the *Gaṅgā*, and at last into the ocean. The fish, saying that the world was about to be destroyed, caused him to build a strong ship with a long rope and ascend it with the seven *ṛshis* and the seeds that were enumerated by the *brahmans* of old. The fish then appeared and was recognized by a horn, to which *Manu* tied the noose. And, while there was water everywhere, the fish dragged the boat through the flood for many years, until, advised by the fish, *Manu* tied the ship to the highest peak of *Himavat*, thence called *Naubandhana*. The fish told him that he was *Brahmán*, and caused *Manu* to create (again) by austerities all creatures with gods, *Asuras*, and men. This is the *Mātsyakaṃ Purāṇaṃ* (III, **187**).

Vaiyāghrapāda (°*padya*, B.) ("son of Vyāghrapāda") = Upamanyu: XIII, 634 (*U°*).

Vaiyāghrapadya = Kaṅka (the assumed name of Yudhishṭhira): IV, †224 (*K°*), 1141.

Vaiyamaka, pl. (°*āḥ*), a people. § 295 (Dyūtap.): II, **52**, 1869 (brought tribute to Yudhishṭhira).

Vaiyāsaki ("the son of Vyāsa") = Çuka: XII, 8485 (*Ç°*), 12044 (*Ç°*), 12268, 12580.

***vājapeya**, name of a certain kind of soma-sacrifice: II, 233; III, 5031, 5033, 6048, †10660; V, 4058, 4091; XIII, 4927.

Vājasana[1] = Çiva (1000 names[2]).—Do.[2] = Vishṇu (1000 names).

Vājasani = Kṛshṇa: XII, 1507.

Vājigrīva = Hayagrīva[3]: XII, †722, †725, †726, †727, †729.

***vājin**, pl. (°*aḥ*) ("horses"). § 127 (Aṃçāvat.): I, **66**, 2632 (the offspring of Gandharvī).

Vajra[1], son of Viçvāmitra. § 721*b* (Viçvāmitrop.). XIII, **4**β, 251.

Vajra[2], a Yādava prince (son of Aniruddha, acc. to Harivaṃça, v. 9204). § 793 (Mausalap.): XVI, **7**, 187, 203 (°*pradhānāḥ*), 214 (*pautram Kṛshṇasya*), 248, 252 (installed as king in Indraprastha). — § 794 (Mahāprasthānikap): XVII, **1**, 8, 9 (*Yādavaḥ*, do.).

***Vajra**[3], the thunderbolt of Indra (selected passages). § 208 (Astradarçana): I, **137**, 5430 (made from the bones of Dadhīca).—§ 221*d* (Caitrarathap.): When the thunderbolt of *Indra* was hurled at *Vṛtra's* head it broke into 1,000 pieces; that which is known in the world as glory, is a portion of the thunderbolt (the hand of the *brahman*, the chariot of the *kshatriya*, the charity of the *vaiçya*, the service of the *çūdra*), therefore the horses of the *kshatriya's* chariot ought not to be slain: I, **170**, 6485, 6486, 6487, 6488.—§ 384 (Agastyop.): III, **100**, 8712 (made by Tvashṭṛ from Dadhīca's bones). — § 634*b* (Suvarṇashṭhīvisambhavop.): XII, **31**, 1114, 1115, 1116 (Indra asked his thunderbolt (in its embodied form) to become a tiger and slay Suvarṇashṭhīvin).—§ 717*b* (Nārāyaṇīya): XII, **343**, VII), ††13213 (made by Dhātṛ from the bones of Dadhīca).—Do.[4] = Çiva (1000 names[1]).

vajra, name of a vyūha. § 576 (Bhagavadgītāp.): VI, **19**, 729 (*vyūhaḥ*).—§ 584 (Bhīshmavadhap.): VI, **81**, 3553 (*vyūham*). Cf. vajrākhya.

Vajrabāhu, a monkey. § 539 (Kumbhakarṇādivadha): III, **287**, 16414 (devoured by Kumbhakarṇa).

Vajrabhṛt = Indra, q.v.

Vajraçīrsha, a son of Bhṛgu. § 747*b* (Suvarṇotpatti): XIII, **85**, 4145 (the second son of Bhṛgu).

Vajradatta, king of Prāgjyotisha, the son of Bhagadatta. § 785 (Anugītāp.): XIV, **75**, 2176, 2187, 2191; **76**, 2196, 2199, 2200, 2203, 2204, 2214 (vanquished by Arjuna, when the latter followed the sacrificial horse). Cf. Bhagadattaja, Bhagadattasuta, Bhagadattātmaja, Prāgjyotishādhipa.

Vajradhara = Indra, q.v.

Vajradharātmaja ("the son of Indra") = Arjuna: I, 7812; XIV, 2332.

Vajradhārin, Vajradhṛk = Indra, q.v.

Vajrahasta[1] = Indra, q.v.—Do.[2] = Çiva (1000 names[2]).

Vajrahastātmajātmaja ("the grandson of Indra") = Abhimanyu: VII, 1704.

vajrākhya, name of a vyūha: VI, 704 (*vyūham*, cf. *vajram*, v. 729).

Vajranābha, a warrior of Skanda. § 615*u* (Skanda): IX, **45**η, 2565.

vajranābha, adj., said of the discus (cakra) of Kṛshṇa: I, 8196; VIII, †3853; X, 625; XVI, 60.

Vajranishkambha (V, 3595), v. Vajravishkambha.

Vajrapāṇi = Indra, q.v. Add: VI, 1900 (only B., C. has *Cakrapāṇiḥ*).

Vajrasaṅghāta = Çiva (1000 names[1]).

Vajravega, a Rākshasa, brother of Dūshaṇa and Pramāthin. § 538 (Kumbhakarṇaraṇagamana): III, **286**, 16405 (*Dūshaṇāvarajau . . . V°-Pramāthinau*), 16407 (°*-Pramāthinau*).—§ 539 (Kumbhakarṇādivadha): III, **287**, 16430 (do.), 16433 (°*-Pramathinoḥ*), 16434 (*Rakshasaḥ*, slain by Hanūmat).—Cf. Dūshaṇānuja (dual), Dūshaṇāvaraja (dual), Rakshas.

Vajravishkambha, a Suparṇa, son of Garuḍa. § 564 (Mātalīyop.): V, **101**β, 3595 (so B., C. has by error °*nish*°).

Vajrāyudha = Indra, q.v.

Vajrin[1] = Indra, q.v.—Do.[2] = Çiva: XIII, †981, 1245 (1000 names[2]), 1262 (do.).

Vajrin[3], a Viçvadeva. § 749 (Ānuçāsanik.): XIII, **91**γ, 4358.

vāka, pl. (°*āḥ*) ("recitations"): XII, 1613 (*yaṃ vākeshv anuvākeshu . . . gṛṇanti*, sc. Kṛshṇa).

Vakanaka (XIII, 257) v. Bakanakha.

Vākpati ("lord of speech)" = Kṛshṇa: XII, 1864.

Vakra, one or more princes. § 233 (Svayaṃvarap.): I, **187**, †7019 (present at the svayaṃvara of Draupadī); **188**, †7051 (do., C. has by error °*ktr*°). — § 273 (Rājasūyārambhap.): II, **14**, 575 (*Karūshādhipatiḥ*?, had joined Jarāsandha).—§ 567 (Bhagavadyānap.): V, **130**ξ, 4411 (had been slain by Kṛshṇa).—§ 621 (Rājadh.): XII, **4**ε,

113 (came to the svayaṃvara of the daughter of the Kaliṅga king Citrāṅgada). Cf. Dantavakra (?), Karūshādhipati (?).

Vakradanta: II, 577 (so B., instead of Dantavakra, q.v.).

Vakrātapa, pl. (°*āḥ*), a people. § 574 (Jambūkh.): VI, **9**μ, 352 (only C., B. has *Cakrātayaḥ*).

Vakshogrīva, son of Viçvāmitra. § 721*b* (Viçvāmitrop.): XIII, **4**β, 252.

Vālakhilya, pl. (°*āḥ*) (C. mostly Vāli°, or Bāla°, or Bāli°), certain pigmy ṛshis. § 43 (Garuḍa): I, **29**, 1386, 1392, 1398, 1399.—§ 44 (do.): I, **31**, 1423.—§ 45 (cf. Āstīkap.): *Çaunaka* asked some questions on the omens foreboding fear (cf. § 44). *Sauti* related ("as described in the *Purāṇa*"): Once when *Kaçyapa* was sacrificing from desire of offspring, assisted by the ṛshis, gods, and Gandharvas, *Indra*, who had been appointed to bring the sacrificial fuel together with the *V.* and the other deities insulted the *V.*, whose bodies were of the size of a thumb, all together carrying one single stalk of a palāça leaf (*butea frondosa*), and much afflicted when sunk in the water collected in the footstep of a cow. The *V.* then sacrificed to effect that there should be another *Indra*. *Indra* repaired to *Kaçyapa*; he reminded them that *Brahmán* himself had made *Indra* the lord of the three worlds; the *V.* then declared that their effort had also been meant for the son wished for by him. Meanwhile *Aruṇa* and *Garuḍa* were begotten and destined by *Kaçyapa* to become the brothers and helpmates of *Indra* (I, **31**): I, **31**, 1436, 1441, 1451, 1456, (1457), 1462.—§ 133 (Dushyanta): I, **70**, 2863.—§ 134 (Viçvāmitra): I, **71**, †2933.—§ 246 (Sundopasundop.): I, **211**, 7683.—§ 270 (Brahmasabhāv.): II, **11**, 437, 468 (*ṛshayaḥ*, in the palace of Brahmán).—§ 310*b* (Sūrya): III, **3**, 174.—§ 377 (Dhaumyatīrthak.): III, **90**, 8381 (*ṛshibhiḥ*, performed a sacrifice on the Sarasvatī).—§ 383 (Paraçurāma): III, **99**, 8675 (*ṛshayaḥ*).—§ 406 (Tīrthayātrāp.): III, **106**, 10413.—§ 421*b* (Ākāça-Gaṅgā): III, **142**, 10903.—§ 602 (Droṇavadhap.): VII, **190**ν, 8728.—§ 615*h* (Naimisha): IX, **37**, 2166.—§ 615*u* (Skanda): IX, **45**γ, 2510.—§ 641*f* (Pṛthu Vainya): XII, **59**, 2232 (counsellors of Pṛthu).—§ 656 (Khaḍgotpattik.): XII, **166**β, 6143.—§ 677 (Mokshadh.): XII, **245**γ, 8903.—§ 717*b* (Nārāyaṇīya): XII, **349**, II), 13564 (*ṛshīn*).—§ 726 (Ānuçāsanik.): XIII, **10**, 442.—§ 730 (do.): XIII, **14**δ, 681 (disregarded by Indra, the *V.* gratified Çiva, who granted them that they should create a bird that would rob the *amṛta* from Indra, cf. § 45).—§ 730*g* (Upamanyu): XIII, **14**, 713 (*nadīm* . . . *V°air nishevitām*).—§ 747*b* (Suvarṇotpatti): XIII, **85**ζ, 4124 (their origin).—§ 751*b* (Çapathavidhi): XIII, **94***a*, †4551, (4585).—§ 761 (Ānuçāsanik.): XIII, **115***a*, 5604.—§ 768*b* (Umā-Maheçvarasaṃv.): XIII, **141**, 6488 (°*gaṇe*, B. °*gaṇaiḥ*), 6489 (*sūryamaṇḍale*), 6490 (description).—§ 775 (Ānuçāsanik.): XIII, **166***a*, 7639.

Vālakhilya = Mahāpurusha (Mahāpurushastava).

Valgujaṅgha, a son of Viçvāmitra. § 721*b* (Viçvāmitrop.): XIII, **4**β, 251.

Vāliçikha, a serpent. § 47 (Sarpanāmak.): I, **35**, 1553.

Vālikhilya, v. Vālakhilya.

Vālin[1], an Asura. § 268 (Varuṇasabhāv.): II, **9**, 367 (among the Daityas and Dānavas present in the palace of Varuṇa).

Vālin[2], a monkey king, brother of Sugrīva. § 316 (Kirmīravadhap.): III, **11**, 432 (°-*Sugrīvayor bhrātror yathā strīkāṅkshiṇoḥ purā*).—§ 425 (Hanūmad-Bhīmasaṃv.): III, **147**, 11194 (*Çakraputram*).—§ 435 (Yakshayuddhap.): III, **157**, 11510 (°-*Sugrīvayor bhrātroḥ purā strīkāṅkshiṇor yathā*).—§ 530 (Viçvāvasumokshaṇap.): III, **279**, 16089 (*vānararājasya hemamālinaḥ*).—§ 531 (Rāmopākhyānap.): III, **280**, 16106, 16108, 16110 (*hemamālī*), 16122 (°-*Sugrīvau*), 16127 (°*iṃ* acc.), 16128, 16129, 16131 (*hate*) (*V.* had deprived Sugrīva of his kingdom and his wife Tārā. Accompanied by Rāma, Sugrīva engaged in an encounter with *V.*, who was slain by Rāma).—§ 534 (Hanūmatpratyāgamana): III, **282**, 16203 (*nihataḥ*), 16206 (°*mārgeṇa*).—§ 534*b* (Madhuvana): III, **282**, 16223 (*rakshitaṃ V°nā yat*, sc. Madhuvana).—§ 535 (Setubandhana): III, **283**, 16270 (*çvasuro V°aḥ* . . . *Susheṇaḥ*).—§ 540 (Indrajidvadha): III, **288**, 16454 (°*aḥ sutaḥ*, i.e. Aṅgada).—§ 551 (Kīcakavadhap.): IV, **22**, 752 (°-*Sugrīvayor bhrātroḥ pureva kapisiṃhayoḥ*, sc. *bāhuyuddham*).—§ 600 (Ghaṭotkacavadhap.): VII, **178**, 8102 (*yathā* . . . *V°-Sugrīvayoḥ purā*, sc. *yuddham*). — § 603 (Nārāyaṇāstramokshap.): VII, **196**, 9063 (*Rāme V°vadhād yadvad*, all. to § 531).—§ 615 (Gadāyuddhap.): IX, **55**, 3107 (°-*Sugrīvayoḥ*, sc. *sadṛçakarmāṇau*). Cf. Çakraputra.

Vāliputra ("the son of Vālin") = Aṅgada: III, 16224 (*A*°).

Vālisuta (do.) = Aṅgada: III, 16451 (*A*°).

Valkala, pl. (°*āḥ*), a people. § 574 (Jambūkh.): VI, **9**ν, 369 (C. has *Kalkalāḥ*).

Valkalājinadhārin, Valkalājinavāsas = Çiva (1000 names[1]).

Vallabha, an ancient king. § 721*b* (Viçvāmitrop.): XIII, **4**, 204 (son of Balākāçva and father of Kuçika).

Vallabha, pl. (°*āḥ*), a people. § 574 (Jambūkh.): VI, **9**ν, 370 (C.: *Mallavāç caiva tathaivāpara-V°āḥ*; B.: *Ballavāç* . . . *apara-Ballavāḥ*).

Vallyaḥ (pl.) = Çiva (1000 names[1]).

Vālmīka, a ṛshi. § 562 (Bhagavadyānap.): V, **83**η, 2946 (worshipped Kṛshṇa). Cf. next.

Vālmīki, a ṛshi. § 61 (Sarpasattra): I, **55**, †2110 (°*vat*).—§ 266 (Çakrasabhāv.): II, **7**, 297 (in the palace of Indra).—§ 376 (Tīrthayātrāp.): III, **85**, 8262.—§ 599 (Jayadrathavadhap.): VII, **143**, 6019 (*purā gītaḥ çloko V°inā*, a verse of his quoted).—§ 637 (Rājadh.): XII, **47**η, 1595.—§ 664 (Mokshadh.): XII, **207**β, 7521.—§ 730 (Ānuçāsanik.): XIII, **18**α, 1303 (was denounced as one guilty of brahmanicide, but was cleansed, having sought the protection of Çiva). Cf. Bhārgava (additions).

Vālmīki[2], a Suparṇa, son of Garuḍa. § 564 (Mātalīyop.): V, **101**β, 3596.

Vāma[1]. § 717*b* (Nārāyaṇīya): XII, **343**ψ, 13261 (°*ādeçitamārgeṇa*, Nīl. explains *V.* = Vāmadeva (= Çiva?)).

Vāma[2], a ṛshi. § 775 (Ānuçāsanik.): XIII, **166**ζ, 7671 (one of the ṛshis of the north, only C., B. *Rāmaḥ*).

Vāma[3] = Çiva (1000 names[2]).

Vāmā, a mātṛ. § 615*u* (Skanda): IX, **46**θ, 2630.

Vāmadeva[1], a ṛshi. § 266 (Çakrasabhāv.): II, **7**, 298 (in the palace of Indra).—§ 461 (Vāmadevacarita): III, **192**, ††13180, ††13181 (°*āçramam*), ††13186, (†13187), †13188, (†13189), (†13191), †13192, (†13193), (†13195), †13196, †13197, †13199, †13200, †13201, (†13202), †13203, (†13205), (†13207), †13208, (†13209) (how *V.* got back his Vāmya horses). — § 527 (Rāmopākhyānap.): III, **277**, 15981 (*Vaçishtha-V°ābhyām*).—§ 543 (Rāmābhisheka): III, **291**, 16597 (*Vaçishṭho V°aç ca*).—§ 562 (Bhagavadyānap.): V, **83**η, 2946 (do., worshipped Kṛshṇa).—§ 641 (Rājadh.): XII, **92**, 3464 (*itihāsam* . . . *gītam* . . . *V°ena*), 3465 (*maharshim*), 3467, (3468); **93**, (3482); **94**, (3522), 3534 (instructed Vasumanas).

Vāmadeva[2], a prince. § 279 (Arjuna): II, **27**, 1020 (in the north, vanquished by Arjuna on his digvijaya).

Vāmadeva[3] = Çiva (1000 names[2]).

[Vāmadeva-carita(ṃ)] ("the history of Vāmadeva"). § 461 (Mārkaṇḍeyas.). As *Yudhishṭhira* wished to hear about the greatness of *brahmans*, *Mārkaṇḍeya* related: King *Parikshit* (B. *Parīkshit*), in *Ayodhyā*, of the race of *Ikshvāku*, was, in the forest, led far away by a deer, and by a tank met with a beautiful maiden, who came along singing. He married her after having given her the pledge not to let her see water, and having arrived at his capital he lived with her in privacy, and nobody could obtain any interview with him. His chief minister, having found out the matter, made an artificial forest, with a tank covered with a net of pearls, and showed it to the king. The king told his wife to plunge into this tank. She did so, and did not reappear. When the water had been baled out a frog was found. The king ordered all frogs to be slaughtered. *Āyu*, the king of the frogs, in the shape of an ascetic (quoting two *çlokas*: "Do not wish to kill the frogs, etc."), told him that the queen was his daughter *Suçobhanā*, who had deceived many kings. She was restored to the king, but *Āyu* cursed her, saying: "Thy offspring shall prove disrespectful to brahmans." *Parikshit* begot three sons on her: *Çala*, *Dala*, and *Bala*. Having installed *Çala* on the throne, *Parikshit* retired to the wood. One day, *Çala*, as he could not overtake a deer, forced his charioteer to indicate to him, to whom the *Vāmya* horses belonged. He borrowed them from the *ṛshi Vāmadeva* and caught the deer, but did not return them. After a month, *Vāmadeva* in vain sent his disciple *Ātreya*, and then came himself, and asked for the steeds. The king, saying that such horses were not fit for brahmans, in vain offered to give him two bulls, then four asses or four mules, and as he threatened to let him be killed, *Vāmadeva*, saying that *brahmans* could not be punished, let four *Rākshasas* slay him with their lances. *Dala*, whom the *Ikshvākus* installed on the throne, attempted to shoot *Vāmadeva* with a poisoned arrow, but shot his own son *Çyenajit*, and was unable to discharge another poisoned arrow. Then he gave way, and, advised by *Vāmadeva*, he touched his queen with the arrow and was thus purified of his sin. The queen obtained the boon from *Vāmadeva*, that she might prevail upon her husband that they both should serve the *brahmans*, and he be freed from his sin, and that *Vāmadeva* should think of their weal. The king became glad and restored the *Vāmya* horses (III, **192**).

Vāmadeva(m) upākhyāna(m) ("the episode relating to Vāmadeva"). § 10 (Parvasaṅgr.): I, **2**, 332 (entered among the parvans of the fifth book, but not found there, presumably Vāmadevacarita (III, ch. **192**) is meant).

Vāmaka, name of a caste: XIII, 2622.

Vāmana[1], a serpent. § 47 (Sarpanāmak.): I, **35**, 155 (enumeration).—§ 564 (Mātalīyop.): V, **103**γ, 3626, 3639 (*dauhitro V°sya*, i.e. Sumukha).

Vāmana[2], name of a tīrtha. § 370 (Tīrthayātrāp.): III, **84**, 8108.

Vāmana[3], a Suparṇa, son of Garuḍa. § 564 (Mātalīyop.): V, **101**β, 3595.

Vāmana[4], name of one of the elephants of the quarters. § 564 (Mātalīyop.): V, **99**, 3561 (of the race of Supratīka). —§ 575c (Samā): VI, **12**, 475 (*catvāro . . . diggajāḥ . . . Vāmanairāvatādayaḥ*).—§ 581 (Bhīshmavadhap.): VI, **64**[16]μ, 2866 (among the world elephants (*diṅnāgān*) produced by way of illusion by Ghaṭotkaca).—§ 599 (Jayadrathavadhap.): VII, **121**ζζ, 4829 (*°sya*, sc. *kule jātāḥ*, sc. *kuñjarottamāḥ*).

Vāmana[5], a mountain in Krauñcadvīpa. § 575 (Bhūmip.): VI, **12**η, 459, (θ), 462. Cf. Vāmanaka[2].

Vāmana[6] ("the dwarf") = Vishṇu (Kṛshṇa) (with reference to his avatāra as a dwarf in order to deceive Bali): III, 6073, [15840 (*°ākṛtiḥ*), 15842 (*°tanuṃ*), 15843 (the story of the avatāra related in full), 17462 (*°rūpeṇa*)]; XII, 1510, 7543, 12968 (sixth avatāra of Vishṇu); XIII, 5379, 6008, 6013, 6966 (1000 names).

Vāmana[7] = Çiva: XIII, 1184 (1000 names[2]); XIV, 193.

Vāmana[8], adj. ("relating to the dwarf, [viz. Vishṇu incarnate as such]"): III, 8759 (*vapuḥ*), 15847 (*prādurbhāvaḥ*); XII, 13673 (sc. *rūpaṃ*); XIII, 6016 (*rūpaṃ*).

Vāmana, pl., a people. § 578 (Bhīshmavadhap.): VI, **51**ν, 2105 (°-*Koçalaiḥ*, B. has *Ambashṭha°*-).

Vāmanaka[1], a tīrtha. § 364 (Tīrthayātrāp.): III, **83**, 6073.

Vāmanaka[2] = Vāmana[5]: VI, 459.

Vāmanikā, a mātṛ. § 615u (Skanda): IX, **46**θ, 2641.

Vaṃça = Çiva (1000 names[2]).

Vaṃçā, one of the daughters of Prādhā. § 102 (Aṃçāvat.): I, **65**, 2553.

Vaṃçagulma, a tīrtha. § 370 (Tīrthayātrāp.): III, **85**, 8151.

Vaṃçakara = Çiva (1000 names[2]).

Vaṃçamūlaka, a tīrtha. § 364 (Tīrthayātrāp.): III, **83**, 6011.

Vaṃçanāda = Çiva (1000 names[2]).

Vaṃçavardhana = Vishṇu (1000 names).

Vāmya, dual (*au*), the horses of Vāmadeva. § 461 (Vāmadevacarita): III, **192**, ††13180, ††13182, ††13184, †13187, †13190, †13193, †11397, †13200, †13211.

Vanamālin[1] ("wearing a garland of forest flowers") = Balarāma: I, 7950; III, 10240 (*Halī*); IV, 2356 (*Halāyudhaḥ*); VII, 412 (*Halī Rāmaḥ*); IX, 2845.—Do.[2] (do.) = Çiva: VIII, 1445.—Do.[3] = Vishṇu (1000 names).

***vānara**, pl. (*°āḥ*) ("apes"). § 112 (Aṃçāvat.): I, **66**, 2571 (among the offspring of Pulastya).—§ 127 (do.): I, **66**, 2628 (among the offspring of Harī).

Vānaradhvaja, Vānaraketana, Vānaraketu = Arjuna, q.v. (cf. VI, 3585).

Vānarapravaradhvaja = Arjuna: VII, 742.

Vānararshabhalakshaṇa = Arjuna: VII, 5101.

Vānaravaryaketana = Arjuna: XIV, 1533.

Vanaspati = Mahāpurusha (Mahāpurushastava).

Vanaspatīnāṃ patiḥ = Çiva: VII, 9509.

Vānava (?), pl. (*°āḥ*), a people. § 574 (Jambūkh.): VI, **9**μ, 362 (*Vānavādarvā(ḥ)*, which by PCR. is taken as one name; cf. Darva, pl.).

Vanavāsaka (*°sika*, B.), pl. (*°āḥ*), a people. § 574 (Jambūkh.): VI, **9**ν, 366 (in the south).

Vanāyu[1], an Asura. § 93 (Aṃçāvat.): I, **65**, 2538 (among the sons of Danu).

Vanāyu[2], a prince. § 141 (Purūravas): I, **75**, 3149 (fifth son of Purūravas and Urvaçī).

Vanāyu[3], pl. (*°avaḥ*), a people. § 574 (Jambūkh.): VI, **9**μ, 363 (only B., C. has *Vātāyanāḥ*).

Vanāyuja (C. also *Vānāyuja*). adj. ("born in the country of the Vanāyus") said of horses. VI, 3974 (*vājināṃ*, C. *Vā°*-); VII, 1574 (*sādhuvāhinaḥ*, C. *Vā°*-), 4831 (*hayavarān*, C. *Vā°*-); VIII, †200 (sc. *açvaiḥ*), †4285 (*açvān*).

Vandanā, name of a river. § 574 (Jambūkh.): VI, **9**λ, 325 (only B., C. has *Gaṇḍakīṃ*).

Vandi or **Vandin** (*B*°, B.), a sūta, son of Varuṇa. § 11 (Parvasaṅgr.): I, **2**, 449.—§ 412 (Ashṭāvakrīya): III, **132**, †10600 (°*iṃ*), †10601 (do.), †10602 (do.), †10612; **133**, †10625 (°*eḥ*), 10633, 10634, †10638, †10639, †10640, †10641, †10642, †10650; **134**, †10651 (°*iṃ*), †10652, †10656 (°*iṃ*), †10657, (†10658), (†10660), (†10662), (†10664), (†10666), (†10668), (†10670), †10670, †10673, (†10674), †10679, 10680, (†10681), †10687 (having defeated many brahmans in controversies and let them be thrown into water, he was himself defeated by Ashṭāvakra, and merged then into water, having declared that he was the son of Varuṇa, and that the brahmans had been drowned in order that they might see the great sacrifice of Varuṇa). Cf. Sauti.

***vandin** (*b*°, B.), pl. ("bards"): I, 3112, 3287, 8141 (only B.); III, 14896; V, 3144, 7620; VI, †747, 3843; VII, 176, 2517, 2739, 2938, 2939 (only C.), 2996; VIII, 12, 392, 1373, 1513; IX, 3402; XI, 458, 467, 667; XII, 1323, 1376, 2233; XIII, 2573, 2821, 5768; XIV, 402, 1896, 2051; XV, 624.

Vāneya, pl. (°*āḥ*), a class of munis: IX, 2183 (*munibhiḥ*).

Vaneyu, a prince. § 150 (Pūruvaṃç.): I, **94**, 3700 (fifth son of Raudrāçva and Ghṛtācī).

Vaṅga[1], a prince. § 170 (Dīrghatamas): I, **104**, 4219 (born by Sudeshṇā, the wife of Bali from Dīrghatamas), 4220 (after him the country of the Vaṅgas is named).

Vaṅga[2], a Vaṅga king of the past. § 277 (Jarāsandhavadhap.): II, **21**, 804 (*Aṅga-V°ādayaḥ* . . . *purā*). Cf. the prec.

Vaṅga[3], the Vaṅga king at the time of Yudhishṭhira. § 264 (Sabhākriyāp.): II, **4**β, 119 (*Aṅga-V°au*, waited upon Yudhishṭhira), 120.—§ 287 (Rājasūyikap.): II, **34**, 1270 (came to the rājasūya of Yudhishṭhira).—§ 585 (Bhīshmavadhap.): VI, **92**, 4104 (*rājñā*).

Vaṅga[4], the country of the Vaṅgas. § 170 (Dīrghatamas): I, **104**, 4220 (named after Vaṅga[1]).

Vaṅga (mostly *B*° in C.), pl. (°*āḥ*), a people. § 249 (Arjunavanavāsap.): I, **215**, 7820 (*Aṅga-V°-Kaliṅgeshu yāni tīrthāni*). — § 273 (Rājasūyārambhap.): II, **14**, 584 (°-*Puṇḍra-Kirāteshu rājā* . . . *Pauṇḍrako Vāsudevaḥ*).—§ 290 (Çiçupālavadhap.): II, **44**, 1527 (*V°āṅgavishayādhyaksham* . . . *Karṇam*).—§ 295 (Dyūtap.): II, **52**, 1872 (brought tribute to Yudhishṭhira), 1874.—§ 342 (Indralokābhigamanap.): III, **51**, 1988 (*sa-V°āṅgān*, had been present at the rājasūya).—§ 515 (Karṇadigvijaya): III, **254**, 15243 (vanquished by Karṇa on his digvijaya).—§ 561*g* (Sahadeva): V, **50**, 1896 (only C. (*B*°), B. has *Aṅgān*, had been vanquished by Sahadeva).—§ 574 (Jambūkh.): VI, **9**μ, 353.—§ 585 (Bhīshmavadhap.): VI, **91**, 4074 (°*ānām adhipaḥ*); **92**, 4102 (do., fought with Ghaṭotkaca), 4107 (°*ānām īçvaraḥ*, do.).—§ 589 (Droṇābhishekap.): VII, **11**ν, 396 (had formerly been vanquished by Kṛshṇa).—§ 592 (Saṃçaptakavadhap.): VII, **24**, 1052 (had sided with Duryodhana).—§ 595 (Shoḍaçarāj. v. Rāma Jāmadagnya): VII, **70**β, 2436 (*Aṅga-V°-Kaliṅgān*, had been slain by Rāma).—§ 600 (Ghaṭotkacavadhap.): VII, **161**$\delta\delta$, 7206.—§ 604 (Karṇap.): VIII, **8**, 236 (had been vanquished by Karṇa and caused to pay tribute to Duryodhana).—§ 605 (do.): VIII, **17**, †671 (*Kaliṅga-V°āṅga°*); **22**$\zeta\zeta$, 863.—§ 608 (do.): VIII, **70**, †3500 (*Kaliṅga-V°āṅga°*). — § 785 (Anugītāp.): XIV, **82**, 2464 (*samudratīreṇa*, vanquished by Arjuna when he guarded the sacrificial horse).

Vaṅgādhipa ("the king of the Vaṅgas"). § 233 (Svayaṃvarap.): I, **187**, †7020 (sought to win Draupadī at her svayaṃvara).

Vaṅgarāja (do.). § 280 (Bhīmasena): II, **30**, 1097 (vanquished by Bhīmasena on his digvijaya).

Vāṇī[1], a river. § 574 (Jambūkh.): VI, **9**λ, 328 (only B., C. has *Vīṇām*).

Vāṇī[2] ("speech") = Sarasvatī[2]: II, 451 (*saptavidhā*); IX, 2389 (do., the river Sarasvatī identified with *V.*), 2471 (*kevalā*).

Vaṇija = Çiva (1000 names[2]).

Vaṅkshu, a river, probably the Oxus. § 295 (Dyūtap.): II, **51**, 1840 (*rāsabhān* . . . *V°tīrasamudbhavān*), 1846 (*rāsabhān* . . . *V°tīranivāsinaḥ* [*Vaṅkū-°* and *Vaṅkshu-°*], only C.).—§ 775 (Ānuçāsanik.): XIII, **166**a, 7648 (B. *Cakshuḥ*).

Vapu, an Apsaras. § 191 (Arjuna): I, **123**, 4819 (danced at the birth of Arjuna).

Vapus = Çiva (1000 names[2]).

Vapushmatī, a mātṛ. § 615*u* (Skanda): IX, **46**, 2629.

Vapushṭamā, the wife of Janamejaya Pārikshita. § 52 (Janamejaya): I, **44**, †1809 (daughter of the Kāçi king Suvarṇavarman), †1810 (married to Janamejaya), †1812.—§ 160 (Pūruvaṃç.): I, **95**, ††3838 (by Janamejaya, mother of Çatānīka and Çaṅkukarṇa).

Vara = Çiva: XII, 10373 (1000 names[1]); XIII, 1144 (1000 names[2]), 1151 (do.), 1210 (do.), 1251 (do.), 1252 (do.); XIV, 197, 210.

Varā, a river. § 574 (Jambūkh.): VI, **9**λ, 333.

***Varada**[1], adj. ("boon giving") said of various gods: = Çiva (1000 names[1–2]), = Indra: XII, ††13211 (*I*°), = Sūrya: III, 154, = Vishṇu (1000 names).—Do. fem. (°*ā*), said of a goddess: = Durgā (*Umā*): IV, 194; VI, 811.

Varada[2], a warrior of Skanda. § 615*u* (Skanda): IX, **45**η, 2566.

Varadā, a river. § 370 (Tīrthayātrāp.): III, **85**, 8177 (°*saṅgame*, a tīrtha).

Varadāna, a tīrtha. § 358 (Tīrthayātrāp.): III, **82**, 5005, 5006.

Varadhāna (VI, 2405), error in C. for Vaṭadhāna.

Varāha[1], a muni. § 264 (Sabhākriyāp.): II, **4**a, 112 (waited upon Yudhishṭhira).

Varāha[2], a mountain. § 277 (Jarāsandhavadhap.): II, **21**, 799 (near Girivraja).

Varāha[3], an Asura (?). § 673 (Bali-Vāsavasaṃv.): XII, **227**a, 8264 (among the ancient rulers of the earth; *Varāho 'çvaḥ*, C., B. has *Varāhāçvaḥ*).

Varāha[4] ("the boar") = Vishṇu (Kṛshṇa) (in his avatāra as a boar): I, 1216 (-°*rūpiṇā*); III, 10927 (*Vā*° both C. and B., *ekaçṛṅgiṇā*), 10944 (*ekaçṛṅgaḥ*, the story of the avatāra related in full), 15830 (°*vapushaṃ*, the story of the avatāra related in full), 17205 (*Vā*°, C. = Kṛshṇa); VI, 3027 (= Kṛshṇa); XII, 1506 (do.), 1635 (*yajñāṅgaḥ*), 7617, 7621, 13114 (*ekaçṛṅgāya*, = Kṛshṇa), 13450 (*mahā*°); XIII, 6013 (cf. 6008), 6858 (*mahā*°).—Do. (do.) = Çiva (1000 names[2]).

Vārāha[1] (III, 10927, 17205) v. Varāha[4].

Vārāha[2] ("named after the boar"), name of one or more tīrthas. § 362 (Tīrthayātrāp.): III, **83**, 5088 (*tīrtham*, there Vishṇu formerly stood in the form of a boar).—§ 377 (Dhaumyatīrthak.); III, **88**, 8332 (*tīrthe*, on Payoshṇī, there Nṛga performed sacrifices).

vārāha, adj. ("relating to the boar", scil. *rūpaṃ*, etc., viz. Vishṇu's): III, 5088, 8757, 12960, 15829: XII, 7619, 7633, 13252, 13410, 13673; XIII, 6016.—Do., said of mātṛs: IX, 2656.

Varāhāçva, v. Varāha[3].
Varāhadhvaja ("having a boar in his banner") = Jayadratha: VII, 6208 (cf. VI, 4134).
Varāhaka, a serpent. § 67 (Sarpasattra): I, **57**, 2159 (of Dhṛtarāshṭra's race).
Varāhakarṇa, a Yaksha. § 269 (Vaiçravaṇasabhāv.): II, **9**, 398 (in the palace of Kubera).
Vārāhaparvata (*Va*°, B.), a mountain. § 717*b* (Nārāyaṇīya): XII, **346**, 13422.
Varāhāvatāra(ḥ) ("Vishṇu's incarnation as a boar"). § 422 bis (Gandhamādanapr.). Asked by *Yudhishṭhira Lomaça* related: In the *Kṛta yuga*, when the primeval deity (*Ādidevaḥ purātanaḥ*) assumed the function of *Yama*, the creatures did not die, and multiplied to such a degree that the *Earth* sank 100 *yojanas*. She applied to *Nārāyaṇa* (= Vishṇu), who, in the shape of a boar with a single tusk (*ekaçṛnga*), lifted her up by means of that. The gods, with the *ṛshis*, became afraid of the agitation produced, but learnt the matter from *Brahmán*, and with him they went to *Nandana*, there *Vishṇu* was sitting in the shape of a boar with *Çrīvatsa* on his breast, together with *Suparṇa*, and having seen him they returned home (III, **142**).
Varajāṇuka, a muni. § 264 (Sabhākriyāp.): II, **4***a*, 108 (waited upon Yudhishṭhira, only C., B. has *Ghaṭaj*°).
Varamālyagandhavastra = Çiva (1000 names[1]).
Vāraṇa, name of a country (?). § 555 (Sainyodyogap.): V, **19**, 600 (among the regions which were overrun by the army of the Kurus).
Vāraṇāhvaya ("named after the elephant"), adj. (sc. nagara) or subst. = Hāstinapura: III, 15083; V, 6002; XV, 1098 (*nagaram*).
Vāraṇasāhvaya (do.), adj. (sc. pura) or subst. = Hāstinapura: I, 4966 (*puram*); III, 11326, 17168; IX, 3148; XIII, 7705 (*puram*); XIV, 1501, 1936 (*puram*), 2057 (do.), 2435.
Varāṇasī, a river. § 574 (Jambūkh.): VI, **9**λ, 338 (only B., C. has *Varuṇām Asīṃ*).
Vārāṇasī, a city in the country of the Kāçis, the present Benares. § 167 (Vicitravīryoparama): I, **102**, 4084 (the residence of the father of Ambā, etc.).—§ 370 (Tīrthayātrāp.): III, **84**, 8056 (a tīrtha).—§ 561*c* (Kṛshṇa Vāsudeva): V, **48**, †1883 (*nagarī*, burnt by Kṛshṇa).—§ 561 (Yānasandhip.): V, **50**, 2007 (*Kāçipatī rājā V°yām*).—§ 589*q* (Dhṛshṭadyumna): VII, **10**, 364 (at *V.* Dhṛshṭadyumna had vanquished the son of the Kāçi king).—§ 630 (Rājadh.): XII, **27**, 807 (at *V.* Bhīshma had challenged all the kings, all. to § 167).—§ 680*b* (Tulādhāra-Jājalisaṃv.): XII, **262**, 9284, 9287, 9319, 9321 (the abode of Tulādhāra).—§ 730 (Ānuçāsanik.): XIII, **14**ζ, 694 (Indra worshipped Çiva in *V.*); **18**κκ, 1333 (in *V.* Çiva made grants to Jaigīshavya).—§ 736*b* (Vītahavyop.): XIII, **30**, 1955 (built by Divodasa).—§ 763*b* (Maitreyabhikshā): XIII, **120**, 5795.—§ 778*b* (Saṃvartta-Maruttīya): XIV, **6**, 141 (the abode of Çiva), 146 (*purīṃ*). Cf. Kāçinagara, Kāçipura, Kāçipurī.
Vāraṇāvata, a city. § 11 (Parvasangr.): I, **2**, 377 (°*yātrāyāṃ*).—§ 71 (Ādivaṃçāvatāraṇap.): I, **61**, 2250 (all. to § 213).—§ 158 (Pūruvaṃç.): I, **95**, ††3822 (all. to § 213).—§ 213 (Jatugṛhap.): I, **141**, 5647; **142**, 5675, 5685, 5694; **143**, 5697, 5698, 5700, 5702, 5703, 5710, 5714; **144**, 5720, 5721, 5729; **145**, 5737, 5767; **146**, 5768, 5772; **150**, 5867, 5874; **151**, 5904 (the burning of the lac house in *V.*).—§ 215 (Bakavadhap.): I, **162**, 6257 (all. to § 213).—§ 305 (Anudyūtap.): II, **78**, 2573 (there Yudhishṭhira had been instructed by Vyāsa).—§ 317 (Arjunābhigamanap.): III, **12**, 546 (all. to § 213).—§ 556 (Sañjayayānap.): V, **31**, 934 (among the five villages which the Pāṇḍavas asked for, cf. 2595).—§ 561 (Yānasandhip.): V, **50**, 1989 (all. to § 213).—§ 562 (Bhagavadyānap.): V, **72**β, 2595 (cf. 934); **82**ζ, 2877 (do.).—§ 567 (do.): V, **128**η, 4271 (all. to § 213).—§ 589*f* (Yuyutsu): VII, **10**, 362 (in *V.* Yuyutsu had fought with many kings).—§ 608 (Karṇap.): VIII, **91**ακ', 4753 (all. to § 213).—§ 613 (Gadāyuddhap.): IX, **33**ι, 1931 (do.).—§ 615 (do.): IX, **56**ρ, 3158 (do.).—§ 617 (Aishīkap.): X, **11**δ, 597 (do.).
Vāraṇāvataka, adj. ("belonging to Vāraṇāvata"). § 213 (Jatugṛhap.): I, **146**, 5770 (*janāḥ*); **148**, 5835 (do.).
Varānga = Vishṇu (1000 names).
Varāngī, a princess, daughter of Dṛshadvat and wife of Saṃyāti. § 156 (Pūruvaṃç.): I, **95**, ††3767 (*Dṛshadvato duhitaram*).
Vārapāçyāpavāha(?), pl. (°*āḥ*), names of peoples. § 574 (Jambūkh.): VI, **9**μ, 352 (so C., B. has *Vāravāsyāyavāha*°).
Varaprada = Mahāpurusha (Mahāpurushastava).
Varāroha = Vishṇu (1000 names).
Varātivaradā = Çiva (1000 names[1]).
Vāravāsyāyavāha, pl., v. Vārapāçyāpavāha.
Varavarṇinī = Durgā (Umā): VI, 797.
Vāravatyā, a river. § 268 (Varuṇasabhāv.): II, **9**, 374 (present in the palace of Varuṇa).
Varayu, a king. § 562 (Bhagavadyānap.): V, **74**γ, 2731 (*Mahaujasāṃ*, among the wicked kings who annihilated their kinsmen and relatives).
Varcas[1], son of Soma. § 116 (Vasu, pl.): I, **66**, 2586 (*Somasya sutaḥ*, with Manoharā, father of Çiçira, Prāṇa, and Ramaṇa [or of Varcasvin (?) q.v.].—§ 130*g* (Abhimanyu): I, **67**, 2747 (*Somaputraḥ*, incarnate as Abhimanyu), 2750.—§ 795 (Svargārohaṇap.): XVIII, **5**μ, 165 (*Somaputraḥ . . . so 'bhimanyuḥ*). Cf. Somaputra.
Varcas[2] = Suvarcas: III, 14164.
Varcas[3], son of Sucetas. § 736*b* (Vītahavyop.): XIII, **30**, 2000 (son of Sucetas and father of Vihavya).
Varcasvin[1], son of Varcas[1] (?). § 116 (Vasu, pl.): I, **66**, 2586. (PCR. takes *varcasvin* as adj. ("resplendent") and attributive of Varcas; according to BR. *V*° is the name of the son of Varcas (cf. Hariv. v. 155 and 12483), and as such father of Çiçira, etc.; see Varcas[1]) —Do.[2] = Çiva (1000 names[2]).
Vārddhakshatri = Jayadratha, q.v.
Vārddhakshemi, a Vṛshṇi prince. § 232 (Svayaṃvarap.): I, **186**, 6989 (came to the svayaṃvara of Draupadī).—§ 572 (Rathātirathasankhyānap.): V, **171**, 5909 (a mahāratha in the army of Yudhishṭhira).—§ 589 (Droṇābhishekap.): VII, **10**, 360 (only B.; = Anādhṛshṭi?).—§ 592 (Saṃçaptakavadhap.): VII, **21**μ, 916; **23**ο, 985 (proceeded against Droṇa, description of his horses); **25**, 1114 (*Vārshṇeyam*, fought with Kṛpa).—§ 604 (Karṇap.): VIII, **6**, 178 (had been slain). Cf. Vārshṇeya.
Vardhakin = Çiva (1000 names[2]).
Vardhamānadvāra, name of a gate in Hāstinapura. § 787 (Āçramavāsap.): XV, **16**, 443.
Vardhamānapuradvāra = do. § 194 (Pāṇḍu): I, **126**, 4905.—§ 308 (Āraṇyakap.): III, **1**, 10.
Vardhana[1], a companion of Skanda. § 615*u* (Skanda): IX, **45**, 2540 (given to Skanda by the Açvins).—Do.[2] = Çiva (1000 names[2]).—Do.[3] = Vishṇu (1000 names).
Vareṇya[1] = Çiva (1000 names[2]).—Do.[2], according to BR.

name of the sixth son of Bhṛgu. § 747b (Suvarṇotpatti): XIII, **85**η, 4146 (PCR. takes it as adj. to Çukra). Cf. Vibhu.

Vargā, an Apsaras. § 250 (Arjunavanavāsap.): I, **216**, (7853), 7853; **217**, (7861), (7872) (*V.*, etc., had been cursed by a brahman and become crocodiles, but were delivered by Arjuna).—§ 269 (Vaiçravaṇasabhāv.): II, **10**, 394 (in the palace of Kubera).

Varin (B., *C*°), a Viçvadeva. § 749 (Ānuçāsanik.): XIII, **91**, 4358.

Vāripa ("lord of waters"): Varuṇa: XIII, 7259.

Vārisheṇa (B. *Vārisena*), an ancient king. § 267 (Yamasabhāv.): II, **8**, 331 (in the palace of Yama).

Varishṭha[1] = Kṛshṇa: XII, 1507.

Varishṭha[2], son of Manu Cākshusha. § 730 (Ānuçāsanik.): XIII, **18**κκ, 1315 (*Cākshushasya Manoḥ sutaḥ*).

Varītāksha, an Asura (?). § 673b (Bali-Vāsavasamv.): XII, **227**a, 8264 (among the ancient rulers of the earth).

Vārkshī ("born of a tree"), a daughter of a muni. § 237 (Vaivāhikap.): I, **196**, 7266 (*munijā*, wife of the ten Pracetases, acc. to Harivamça, v. 96 foll., her name is Mārishā).

Varmaka, pl. (°*āḥ*), a people. § 280 (Bhīmasena): II, **30**, 1087 (in the east, vanquished by Bhīmasena on his digvijaya).

Varṇāçramāṇām vidhivat pṛthak karmanivartī = Çiva (1000 names[1]).

Varṇadhara = Mahāpurusha (Mahāpurushastava).

Varṇakara = Çiva (1000 names[1]).

Varṇātman = Kṛshṇa: XII, 1656.

Varṇavarāḥ (pl.) = Çiva (1000 names[1]).

Varṇavibhāvin = Çiva (1000 names[2]).

Vārshagaṇya, a ṛshi. § 707 (Mokshadh.): XII, **319**β, 11782 (had instructed Viçvāvasu).

Vārshaparvaṇī = Çarmishṭhā, q.v.

Vārshṇeya[1], the charioteer of Nala, afterwards of Ṛtuparṇa. § 346 (Nalopākhyānap.): III, **60**, 2281, 2282, 2283, 2292 (*Nalasārathiḥ*).—§ 347 (do.): III, **61**, 2297.—§ 349 (do.): III, **67**, 2640 (°*Jīvalau*).—§ 351 (do.): III, **71**, 2793 (*sūtam*), 2796, 2805, 2806 (*saha-V°sārathiḥ*).—§ 352 (do.): III, **72**, 2811, 2822, 2824 (°*sārathiḥ*).—§ 353 (do.): III, **73**, 2869, 2883, 2885 (*sūtaputram*), 2887; **74**, 2902.

Vārshṇeya[2] ("the son of Vārshṇeyī") = Abhimanyu: XIV, 1828.

Vārshṇeya[3] ("of the Vṛshṇi race") = Balarāma: V, 5388 (*Rauhiṇeyaḥ*); X, 506 (preceptor of Duryodhana).

Vārshṇeya[4] (do.): Cekitāna: VI, 3715 (*C*°).

Vārshṇeya[5] (do.) = Kṛshṇa: I, 7430, 7891, 7899, 8068 (°-*Pārthayoḥ*), 8084 (°-*Pārthau*), 8293; II, 27, 644, 788, 809, 1222, 1332 (*K*°), 1335, 1338, 1378, 1591, 1888 (*Vāsudevaḥ*); III, 497, 869, 12597, 13003 (*K*°); V, 100, 138, 2816, 2821, 2851, 3003, 3060, 3070, 3115, 3130, 3155, 3166, 3243, 3246, 3272, 4128, 4369, 4650, 4755, 4769, 4783, 4809, 4811, 4839, 4842, 5216, 5361, 5363, 5464; VI, 872, 986, 1982, 1993 (*Vāsudevaḥ*), 2035, 2044, 2132, 2133, 2571, 3564, 3742, 4906, 4933, 4937, 4944, 5228 (*Vāsudevaḥ*); VII, 415, 2944, 2958, 3284, 3354 (*Vāsudevam*), 3486 (*Pārtha-V°yoḥ*), 6323, 6420, 6460 (only C.), 8077, 8268 (*K*°), 8327, 8328, 8866 (*Vāsudevaḥ*); VIII, 1331, 1351, 1631, 1956, 2194, 2863, 3756, 4041 (*Vāsudevam*), 4487; IX, 344, 1319, 1468, 1802, 3370 (*sa-V°āḥ*?), 3376, 3520; X, 509 (*K*°); XI, 492, 508, 530; XII, 1712, 1807, 1884, 1941, 3036 (*K*°), 13277; XIII, 1292, 2033; XIV, 458, 1515 (-*Kurupuṅgavau*), 1536, 1537, 1768, 1773, 1817, 1962, 1970, 1991, 1996.

Vārshṇeya[6] (do.) = Sātyaki: I, †194 (*Yuyudhānam*); V, 5708 (do.); VI, 2469, 3189, 3263, 3618, 4631, 4639, 4759, 4760, 4761; VII, 3555 (*S*°), 3557, 4179, 4197, 4217, 4224, 4719, 4725, 5109 (*S*°), 5943 (*S*°), 5963, 6010, 6334, 8802, 9181.

Vārshṇeya[7] (do.) = Vārddhakshemi: VII, 1114 (*V*°), 1115.

Vārshṇeya[8], dual (°*au*) = Kṛtavarman and Sātyaki: IX, 934.

Vārshṇeya[9], adj. ("relating to Vārshṇeya [i.e. Kṛshṇa]"). § 667 (Mokshadh.): XII, **210**, 7652 (*itihāsam*), 7654 (scil. do.).

Vārshṇeya[10], pl. (°*āḥ*), a people = Vṛshṇi, pl. § 295 (Dyūtap.): II, **51**, 1844 (brought tribute to Yudhishṭhira).—§ 556 (Sañjayayānap.): V, **28**ι, †804 (°-*Bhojāḥ*).—§ 587 (Bhīshmavadhap.): VI, **111**, 5154 (°*ānām mahāratham*, i.e. Sātyaki).—§ 793 (Mausalap.): XVI, **5**ι, 134.

Vārshṇeyī[1] ("the Vṛshṇi-princess") = Kuntī: I, 4401; V, 4914; XIV, 1846.

Vārshṇeyī[2] (do.) = Subhadrā: I, 7924; VII, 2503 (°*dayitam*, sc. Abhimanyu), 2717; XII, 16 (*vadhur me*, i.e. Yudhishṭhira's); XIV, 1839.

Vārtta, an ancient king. § 267 (Yamasabhāv.): II, **8**, 321 (in the palace of Yama).

Varuṇa, a god, one of the Ādityas; as Lord of the waters one of the Lokapālas, armed with nooses (*pāçāḥ*). § 11 (Parvasaṅgr.): I, **2**, 450 (°*syātmajena*, i.e. Vandin, cf. § 412).—§ 19 (Bhṛgu): I, **5**, 870 (°*sya kratau jātaḥ*, sc. Bhṛgu, cf. § 747b).—§ 30b (Samudra): I, **21**, 1210 (*ālayam V°sya*, i.e. the ocean).—§ 31b (Samudradarçana): I, **22**, 1230 (do., do.).—§ 49 (Vāsuki): I, **39**, 1643 (°*ālayam*, i.e. the ocean, which was churned).—§ 61 (Sarpasattra): I, **55**, †2097 (°*sya yajñaḥ*), †2107 (Janamejaya compared with *V.*).—§ 88 (Amçāvat.): I, **65**, 2523 (the fifth of the Ādityas).—§ 124 (do.): I, **66**, 2616 (husband of Devī, the daughter of Çukra, and father of Bala and Surā).—§ 135 (Çakuntalop.): I, **74**, 3072 (°*sya*, sc. *bhavanam*).—§ 147 (Devayānī): I, **82**, 3408 (°*sya*, sc. *gṛhe*).—§ 164 (Āpavop.): I, **99**, 3924 (father of Vasishṭha).—§ 171 (Vicitravīryasutotpatti): I, **105**, 4260 (*Mitra-V°yoḥ samān*).—§ 191 (Arjuna): I, **123**, 4823 (the fifth of the Ādityas, present at the birth of Arjuna).—§ 227 (Aurvop.): I, **180**, 6862 (°*ālaye*, i.e. the ocean, there Aurva threw the fire of his wrath which became the horse-head).—§ 238 (Pañcendrop.): I, **197**, †7277.—§ 257 (Khāṇḍavadahanap.): I, **225**, 8174 (*b*: one of the Lokapālas, son of Aditi, lord of the waters (*Jaleçvaram*), living in the water), 8179, 8200 (*V.* presented Arjuna with the Gāṇḍīva bow, two inexhaustible quivers, and a chariot yoked with horses).—§ 258 (do.): I, **227**, 8264 (armed with nooses (*pāçāḥ*) and *açani*, among the gods who fought with Arjuna and Kṛshṇa).—§ 259 (do.): I, **232**, 8421 (*idam vai sadma . . . V°sya parāyaṇam*).—§ 265 (Lokapālasabhākhyānap.): II, **6**, 275 (°*sya*, sc. *sabhā*), 281.—§ 267 (Yamasabhāv.): II, **8**, 352 (°*sya sabhām*).—§ 268 (Varuṇasabhāv.): II, **9**, 353 (*sabhā . . . V°sya*), 357, 358 (*Vāruṇyā ca samanvitaḥ*), 359 (*Jaleçvaram*), 364, 369 (*dharmapāçadharam*), 379 (description of his palace (*sabhā*)).—§ 270 (Brahmasabhāv.): II, **11**, 466 (waits upon Brahmán).—§ 271 (Lokapālasabhākhyānap.): II, **12**, 480 (°*sya sabhāyām*).—§ 273 (Rājasūyārambhap.): II, **14**, 578 (*rājā pratīcyām V°o yathā*, sc. *çāsti*).—§ 285 (Nakula): II, **32**, 1202 (*diçam V°pālitām*, i.e. the west).—§ 288 (Rājasūyikap.): II, **35**, 1302 (*ṛddhyā ca V°m devam spardhamānaḥ*).—§ 294 (Dyūtap.): II, **49**, 1760 (*çrīḥ . . . V°sya*).—§ 329 (Kāmyakavanapr.): III, **36**, 1442.—§ 333c (Brahmaçiras): III, **40**, 1651 (*api*, does not know the

Brahmaçiras).—§ 334 (Kairātap.): III, **41**, 1670 (*yādasāṃ bhartā*), 1691 (*yādasāṃ patiḥ*), 1692 (*Jaleçvaraḥ*, *b*: In the combat against Tāraka (*saṃgrāme Tārakāmaye*) *V.*, with his nooses, had tied thousands of Daiteyas), 1697 (gave his nooses to Arjuna).—§ 338 (Indralokābhigamanap.): III, **45**, 1812 (°*opamaḥ*).—§ 345 (Nalopākhyānap.): III, **55**, [2138 (*Apāṃ patiḥ*)], 2140, 2157; **56**, 2171 (instead of *Varuṇaṃ* read *varaṇaṃ*); [**57**, 2228 (*Apāṃ patiḥ*)] (among the Lokapālas at the svayaṃvara of Damayantī, granted Nala boons).—§ 370 (Tīrthayātrāp.): III, **84**, 8113 (*Mitra-V°yor lokān*).—§ 371 (Tuṅgaka): III, **85**, 8191 (among those who in Tuṅgaka appointed Bhṛgu to officiate at a sacrifice).—§ 377 (Dhaumyatīrthak.): III, **90**, 8386 (*devāḥ . . . sa-V°āḥ*, performed austerities at Viçākhayūpa).—§ 378 (Tīrthayātrāp.): III, **91**, 8419 (Arjuna had obtained weapons from *V.*, etc., cf. § 334).—§ 384 (Agastyop.): III, **101**, †8736 (°*syālayaṃ*, i.e. the ocean, there the Dānavas took their refuge); **103**, 8770 (°*ālayaṃ*, do.).—§ 386 (do.): III, **105**, 8806 (do., do., drunk up by Agastya).—§ 387 (Sagara): III, **107**, 8872 (°*ālayaḥ*, i.e. the ocean dug by the sons of Sagara), 8875 (*samudraṃ V°ālayaṃ*).—§ 389 (Gaṅgāvataraṇa): III, **107**, 9912 (do.); **109**, 9964 (do.).—§ 395 (Jamadagni): III, **115**, 10152 (gave 1,000 horses to Ṛcīka, cf. §§ 565 and 721*b*).—§ 406 (Tīrthayātrap.): III, **125**, 10419 (went to heaven at *Prasravaṇam Indrasya*).—§ 412 (Ashṭāvakrīya): III, **134**, †10674 (*putro V°sya*, i.e. Vandin), †10675 (°*sya . . . yajñaṃ*), 10680, †10681 (*putro V°sya*, i.e. Vandin), 10682 (Vandin, the son of *V.*, defeated brahmans in controversies and caused them to be thrown into water that they might come to the sacrifice of *V.* and officiate there).—§ 418 (Tīrthayātrāp.): III, **139**, 10833 (*rājā*, in a benediction).—§ 439 (Yakshayuddhap.): III, **163**, 11851 (*rājā*, on the mountain Asta).—§ 443 (Nivātakavacayuddhap.), III, **168**, 12005 (among the Lokapālas, repetition from § 334), 12020 (Arjuna obtained weapons from *V.*, etc., do.).—§ 461 (Vāmadevacarita): III, **192**, †13187 (*mā tvā vadhīd V°o ghorapāçaiḥ*).—§ 475*b* (Dhundhumārop.): III, **201**, 13498 (*Indra-Somāgni-V°āḥ*, praise Vishṇu).—§ 496 (Skandotpatti): III, **224**, 14269 (°*ālayaṃ*, i.e. the ocean).—§ 506 (Skandayuddha): III, **231**, 14552 (*ugrapāço V°ḥ . . . Salileçvaraḥ*).—§ 510 (Draupadī-Satyabhāmasaṃv.): III, **233**, 14704 (°*syeva nidhipūrṇam ivodadhiṃ*).—§ 522 (Draupadīharaṇap.): III, **265**, †15590 (*rājño V°sya patnī*, Draupadī was questioned if she was the wife of *V.*).—§ 534 (Hanūmatpratyāgamana). III, **282**, 16240 (°*ālayaṃ*, i.e. the ocean).—§ 535 (Setubandhana): III, **283**, 16306 (°*ālayaḥ*, do.).—§ 549 (Rāmābhisheka): III, **291** *a*, 16548, (16559).—§ 547 (Karṇa): III, **308**, 17137 (*Salileçvaraḥ*, in a blessing).—§ 552*c* (Gāṇḍīva): IV, **43**, 1348 (held the Gāṇḍīva for 100 years), 1350 (gave the Gāṇḍīva to Arjuna).—§ 552 (Goharaṇap.): IV, **45** δ, 1434; **56** ζ, 1770 (°*sya*, sc. *vimānaṃ*), —§ 552*d* (Arjuna): IV, **61**, 1982 (Arjuna obtained weapons from *V.*).—§ 555 (Indravijaya): V, **16**, 511 (among the Lokapālas who came to Indra), 519 (*i*: On *V.* Indra bestowed the sovereignty over the waters); **18**, 545.—§ 564 (Mātalīyop.): V, **98**, 3522 (Nārada will visit *V.*), 3524 (read *Nāradaṃ* with B.), 3529, 3531 (accompanied by Nārada Mātali visited *V.* in the Nāgaloka), 3532 (*putro . . . V°sya Gopateḥ*, i.e. Pushkara); **100**, 3570.—§ 565 (Gālavacarita): V, **108**, 3772 (*atra*—i.e. in the east—*Pātālam āçritya V°ḥ çriyam āpa ca*); **110**, 3801 (*dig dayitā rājño V°sya tu Gopateḥ*, i.e. the west), 3803 (installed [as king] by Kaçyapa), 3804 *atra*—i.e. in the west—*pītvā samastān vai V°sya rasān shaṭ* / *jāyate taruṇaḥ Somaḥ çuklasyādau*), 3817 (°*ālaye*); **117**, 3968 (husband of Gaurī, *reme . . . V°ç ca yathā Gauryāṃ*); **119**, 4007 (°*syālayaṃ*; *V.* gave 1,000 horses to Ṛcīka, cf. §§ 395 and 721*b*).—§ 567 (Bhagavadyānap.): V, **128**, 4303, 4304, 4305 (Dharma bound the Daityas and Dānavas [with his nooses] and handed them over to *V.*, who keeps them in the depths of the ocean); **130**, 4412 (*rājā*, had been vanquished by Kṛshṇa).—§ 570 (Sainyaniryāṇap.): V, **158** ν, 5382.—§ 571 (Ulūkadūtāgamanap.): V, **162**, 5603 (*sāgaro V°ālayaḥ*).—§ 576 (Bhagavadgītāp.): VI, **34**, 1233 (°*o yādasām aham*, sc. *asmi*, says Kṛshṇa); **35**, †1285 (Kṛshṇa identified with *V.*).—§ 578 (Bhīshmavadhap.): VI, **50**, 2039 (°*aḥ pāçabhṛd vāpi*, sc. *çakyo jetuṃ*).—§ 584 (do.): VI, **83** ι, 3679 (*ajeyaṃ . . . V°ena*, sc. Ghaṭotkaca).—§ 586 (do.): VI, **107** φ, 4902 (°*aḥ pāçadhṛg vāpi*, sc. *çakyo jetuṃ*), 4960 (*çakyo . . . jetuṃ*).—§ 587 (do.): VI, **112**, 5238 (*sadṛçaḥ . . . V°sya*).—§ 589 (Droṇābhishekap.): VII, **10**, 346 (*Yama-Vaiçravaṇāditya-Mahendra-V°opamaṃ*, sc. *Uttamaujasaṃ*); **11**, 400 (*yādobhir abhisaṃvṛtaṃ*, had been vanquished by Kṛshṇa in the sea).—§ 596 (Pratijñāp.): VII, **72**, 2521; **76** δ, 2691 (Arjuna had obtained weapons from *V.*, etc.).—§ 598 (Jayadrathavadhap.): VII, **88**, 3136 (°*aḥ pāçavān iva*).—§ 599*b* (Çrutāyudha): VII, **92**, 3304 (°*syātmajaḥ*, i.e. Çrutāyudha), 3305, 3306, 3309 (*V.* had, with the river Parṇāçā, the son Çrutāyudha, whom he gave a mace and instructed its nature).—§ 599 (Jayadrathavadhap.): VII, **92**, 3318 (*yathoktaṃ V°eṇa*, all. to § 599*b*); **127**, 5144 (*Brahmeçānendra-V°ān avahad purā rathaḥ*, sc. the chariot of Arjuna).—§ 600 (Ghaṭotkacavadhap.): VII, **155**, †6727 (°*ātmajopamāḥ*); **180** δδδ, 8194 (*Jaleçvaraḥ . . . notsahet Karṇaṃ*).—§ 603 (Nārāyaṇāstramokshap.): VII, **202** *u*, 9595 (Çiva identified with *V.*), (κκ) 9628.—§ 607 (Karṇap.): VIII, **37** γ, †1737 (*Yama V° Kubera-Vāsavāḥ*); **42**, 1998 (°*ād vāpi pāçinaḥ*); **45** ξ, 2103 (*pratīcīṃ V°ḥ pāti pālayānaḥ surān balī*).—§ 608*b* (Arjuna): VIII, **46**, 2161 (*Brahmeçānendra-V°ān kramaço yo 'vahat purā*, sc. *rathaḥ*, i.e. the chariot of Arjuna).—§ 608 (Karṇap.): VIII, **46**, 2198 (°*ṃ ko 'mbhasā hanyāt*); **87** χ', 4421 (sided with Arjuna).—§ 615*u* (Skanda): IX, **45** γ, 2507, 2524 (*yathā . . . V°ṃ Jaleçvaraṃ . . . abhyasiñcat . . . Brahmā*), 2548 (gave two companions to Skanda); **46**, 2670 (gave a nāga to Skanda).—§ 615 (Baladevatīrthayātrā); IX, **46**, 2723 (*Apāṃ patiḥ*, anointed in the tīrtha *Taijasa*, cf. § 615*v*).—§ 615*v* (do.): In the *Kṛta* age (in a former *kalpa*), all the gods [at the tīrtha *Taijasa*] installed, according to the rites in the scriptures, *V.* as the lord of all aquatic creatures, and of all the rivers, having his abode in the ocean, "as *Çakra*, the lord of the gods protects us from every fear, be thou the lord of all rivers." *V.* then began duly to protect seas and lakes, and rivers and other receptacles of water, as *Çakra* protects the gods: IX, **47**, 2733, 2736 (*sāgarālayaṃ*), 2737 (*yādasāṃ patiṃ*), 2738.—§ 615*dd* (Yamunātīrtha): IX, **49**, 2841 (*putro 'diteḥ*), 2842 (performed a rājasūya in Yamunātīrtha).—§ 615*ff* (Asita Devala): IX, **50**, 2892 (*Mitrā-V°yor lokān*).—§ 615 (Baladevatīrthayātrā): IX, **54**, 3048 (*Mitrā-V°yoḥ . . . āçramaṃ*).—§ 615 (Gadāyuddhap.): IX, **55**, 3105 (*sadṛçakarmāṇau V°sya*, sc. Bhīmasena and Duryodhana).—§ 621 (Rājadh.): XII, **5** ζ, 141 (Arjuna had obtained weapons from *V.*, etc.).—§ 623 (do.): XII, **15** β, 439 (among the gods, etc., who are slaughterers).—§ 632*b* (Shoḍaçarāj., cf. § 595, v. Marutta): XII, **29**, 911 (*sa-V°āḥ . . . devāḥ*, came to the sacrifice of Marutta).—§ 641 (Rājadh.): XII, **78**, 2922 (the sheep (*meshaḥ*) identified with *V.*); **91** ν, 3458; **122**, 4497 (*apāṃ* *rājye 'surāṇāñ* [B. *Surāṇāñ*] *ca vidadhe V°m*, sc. Vishṇu), 4511.—§ 654*b* (Pavana-çālmalīsaṃv.): XII, **155*a***, 5831 (*Jaleçvaraḥ*).—§ 664 (Mokshadh.): XII, **207**, 7553 (*yādasām asṛjan nāthaṃ V°ñ ca Jaleçvaraṃ*, sc. Kṛshṇa).—§ 665 (do.): XII, **208**β, 7581 (the fifth of the Ādityas), (η), 7595 (*Mitrā-V°yoḥ putraḥ . . . Agastyaḥ*).—§ 671*b* (Bali-Vāsavasaṃv.): XII, **223*a***, 8062 (Bali identified with *V.*).—§ 680*b* (Tulādhāra-Jājalisaṃv.): XII, **263**, 9381 (the sheep (*meshaḥ*) identified with *V.*).—§ 692 (Mokshadh.): XII, **281**β, 10052 (identified with the supreme Lord).—§ 695*b* (Dakshayajñavināça): XII, **285**, 10311 (°*ālayaḥ*, i.e. the ocean).—§ 703 (Mokshadh.): XII, **300*a***, †11095 (*Siddhiñ ca devīṃ V°sya patnīṃ*).—§ 707 (do.): XII, **319*a***, 11751, 11762 (only B., C. has by error *Vā°*).—§ 721*b* (Viçvāmitrop.): XIII, **4**, 212 (*devam Ādityam ambhasāṃ patiṃ*), 214 (*Ādityaḥ*, gave 1,000 horses to Ṛcīka, cf. §§ 395 and 565).—§ 730 (Ānuçāsanik.): XIII, **14**εε, 1003 (Çiva identified with *V.*); **16**ηη, 1059 (°*endū*, identified with Çiva); **18**λλ, †1368 (*gopaḥ*).—§ 731*b* (Ashṭāvakra-Diksaṃv.): XIII, **19**, 1472.—§ 737 (Ānuçāsanik.): XIII, **31*a***, 2013.—§ 746 (do.): XIII, **62**β, 3150; **81**, 3833 (*aiçvarye V°o rājā*).—§ 747 (do.): XIII, **84**γ, 3978 (the sheep (*meshaḥ*) identified with *V.*). — § 747*b* (Suvarṇotpatti): XIII, **85**δ, 4112 (identified with Çiva), 4115 (Çiva assumed the form of *V.* and performed a sacrifice), 4133 (*Mahādevaḥ*, do.), 4135 (= do.?), 4140 (*Īçvaraḥ*, do., *yādasāṃ patiḥ*), 4153 (*Īçvaraḥ*, do.) (at the sacrifice arose Bhṛgu, etc., who were reckoned as the offspring of *V.*).—§ 748*b* (Tārakavadhop.): XIII, **86**, 4210 (made presents to Skanda).—§ 749 (Ānuçāsanik.): XIII, **91**β, 4348, 4351.—§ 752*b* (Chattropānahotpatti): XIII, **96*a***, 4637 (*gāmbhīryaṃ V°sya*).—§ 753 (Ānuçāsanik.): XIII, **97*a***, 4661 (to *V.* offerings should be made in the west-*pratīcyāṃ*).—§ 757*j* (Varuṇaloka): XIII, **102**, 4877 (°*sya rājñaḥ sadane*).—§ 768*b* (Umā-Maheçvarasaṃv.): XIII, **146**γ, 6751 (°*sya tathā Gaurī*, sc. *sādhvī*).—§ 770 (Ānuçāsanik.): XIII, **151**ϯ, 7092 (*Jaleçvaraḥ*, the fourth of the Ādityas), (η), 7113 (*Mitrā-V°yoḥ putraḥ . . . Agastyaḥ*), (θ), 7115 (°*syartvijaḥ sapta paçcimāṃ diçam āsthitāḥ*, i.e. Dṛḍheyu, etc).—§ 772*j* (Utathya): XIII, **155**, 7244, 7248, 7251, 7252, 7253, 7261 (*V.* robbed Bhadrā, the daughter of Soma and the wife of Utathya, but was forced to give her back).—§ 773*d* (Çiva): XIII, **161**δ, 7497 (identified with Çiva).—§ 775 (Ānuçāsanik.): XIII, **166*a***, 7637 (*saha Gauryā*), (δ) 7666 (*Mitrā-V°yoḥ putraḥ . . . Agastyaḥ*).—§ 778*f* (Muñjavat): XIV, **8**, 183 (worships Çiva on Muñjavat).—§ 782*g* (Guruçishyasaṃv.): XIV, **42**ε, 1167; **43**θ, 1176 (*ambhasāṃ . . . rājā*).—§ 785 (Anugītāp.): XIV, **60**, 1787 (*Mitreṇa V°o yathā*, sc. *guptaḥ*).—§ 793 (Mausalap.): XVI, **4**η, †120 (*rājā*, in the ocean, received the nāga who issued from Balarāma).—§ 794 (Mahāprasthānikap.): XVII, **1*a***, 41 (the Gāṇḍiva had been owned by *V.* and was given back to him).—§ 795 (Svargārohaṇap.): XVIII, **5**, 176 (°*sya lokān*).

Cf. also the following synonyms:—

Aditeḥ putra(ḥ), Āditya, q.v.

Ambupa ("the lord of the waters"): VIII, †4661.

Ambupati (do.): VII, 2994 (*sahā°-Mitrābhyāṃ yathendraḥ*), 6718 (*yathā°-Mitrau*); VIII, 1485 (*Surāmbu-pretavittānāṃ patīn*).

Amburāj (do.): VII, 160.

Ambvīça (do.): VII, 37 (in the comp. *Pitṛvittāmbudeveçān*, only C.).

Apāṃ patiḥ (do.): I, 1121 (?); III, 2138, 2228, 10123 (?), †10225 (?); V, 515, 3527; IX, 2723, 2731, 2737.

Devadeva, q.v.

Gopati, q.v.

Jalādhipa ("lord of the waters"): XIII, 7262.

Jaleçvara (do.): I, 8175, 8176; II, 359 (*V°*); III, 1669 (*yādogaṇavṛtaḥ*), 1692 (*V°*); V, 4305 (*V°*); VII, 3310, 8194 (*V°*), 8444; IX, 2524 (*V°*), 2738; XII, 5831 (*V°*), 7553 (*V°*); XIII, 7092 (*V°*), 7245, 7247, 7250.

Lokapāla, q.v.

Salilarāja, Salileça, Salileçvara, Udakapati, Vāripa, q.v.

Yādasāṃ bhartā ("lord of aquatic animals"): III, 1670 (*V°*).

Yādasāṃ patiḥ (do.): IX, 2737; XIII, 4140.

Varuṇa[2], a Gandharva. § 101 (Aṃçāvat.): I, **65**, 2550 (among the Devagandharvas, sons of Muni).

Varuṇa[3], a serpent. § 793 (Mausalap.): XVI, **4**η, †119 (only C., B. has *Aruṇaḥ*).

Varuṇa[4] = Sūrya (the Sun): III, 148, 152.—Do.[5] = Vishṇu (1000 names).

Varuṇā, a river. § 574 (Jambūkh.): VI, **9**λ, 338 (only C., B. has *Varāṇasīṃ* instead of *V°āṃ Asīm* in C.).

Vāruṇa[1], a tīrtha. § 377 (Dhaumyatīrthak.): III, **88**, 8339 (in the country of the Pāṇḍyas).

Vāruṇa[2] ("the son of Varuṇa") = Bhṛgu: XIII, 4142 (*Bh°*).

Vāruṇa[3] = Vishṇu (1000 names).

Vāruṇa[4], mostly pl. (°*āḥ*) ("descendants of Varuṇa"). § 747*b* (Suvarṇotpatti): XIII, **85**, 4146, 4147 (*ashṭau Aṅgirasaḥ putrāḥ*), 4149 (*Kaveḥ putrāḥ . . . ashṭau*), 4153 (°*au Kaviṃ Bhṛguñ ca*).

Vāruṇa[5], adj. (f. °*ī*) ("belonging to Varuṇa"). § 28 (Amṛtamanthana): I, **18**, 1132 (*bhūtāni*).—§ 167 (Vicitravīryoparama): I, **102**, 4120 (*astraṃ*).—§ 208 (Astradarçana): I, **135**, 5365 (°*ena* — sc. *astreṇa* — *asṛjat payaḥ*).—§ 262 (Bhagavadyāna): II, **2**, 65 (*mahāçaṅkho Devadattaḥ*).—§ 268 (Varuṇasabhāv.): II, **9**, 380 (*mantrī*, sc. *Sunābhaḥ*), 382 (*sabhā*).—§ 272 (Rājasūyārambhap.): II, **13**, 534 (*yenābhishikto nṛpatir V°ṃ guṇam ṛcchati / tena rājā 'pi taṃ kṛtsnaṃ samrādguṇam abhīpsati*).—§ 294 (Dyūtap.): II, **49**, 1751 (*kāṃsyaṃ* (? differently Nīl.), offered by the ocean to Yudhishṭhira).—§ 296 (do.): II, **53**, 1922 (*çaṅkhaṃ*, offered by the ocean to Yudhishṭhira).—§ 300 (Prahlāda): II, **68**, 2323 (*pāçān*), 2324 (do.).—§ 305 (Anudyūtap.): II, **78**, 2578 (*saṃyame*).—§ 334*b* (Varuṇa): III, **41**, 1693 (*pāçān*).—§ 358 (Tīrthayātrāp.): III, **82**, 5011 (*lokaṃ*).—§ 368 (do.): III, **83**, 7035 (*Taijasaṃ V°ṃ tīrthaṃ*).—§ 384 (Agastyop.): III, **102**, 8737 (*samudraṃ V°ṃ nidhim ambhasaḥ*).—§ 440 (Yakshayuddhap.): III, **164**, 11900 (sc. *astraṃ*, obtained by Arjuna).—§ 515 (Karṇadigvijaya): III, **254**, 15254 (°*īm diçaṃ*, i.e. the west).—§ 552*d* (Arjuna): IV, **61**, 1982 (sc. *astraṃ*).—§ 552 (Goharaṇap.): IV, **64**, 2058 (do.).—§ 561 (Yānasandhip.): V, **60**, 2370 (°*au* [B. *dāruṇau*] *cākshayau çarapūrṇau maheshudhī*, owned by Arjuna).—§ 564 (Mātaliyop.): V, **98**, 3539 (*hrade*, in that lake is fire, the cakra of Vishṇu and that knotty bow from which the Gāṇḍiva had its origin); **102**, 3610 (*paçcimā V°ī dik*).—§ 570*e* (Gāṇḍiva): V, **158**, 5354 (*Gāṇḍivaṃ*).—§ 572 (Rathātirathasaṅkhyānap.): V, **169**, 5870 (sc. *astragrāmaḥ*, in the possession of Arjuna).—§ 573 (Ambopākhyānap.): V, **180**, 7174 (sc. *astreṇa*, employed by Rāma Jāmadagnya).—§ 584 (Bhīshmavadhap.): VI, **85**, †3779 (*astraṃ*, employed by Çikhaṇḍin).—§ 588 (do.): VI, **121**β, 5801 (sc. *astram*).—§ 599 (Jayadrathavadhap.): VII, **98**, 3658 (*astram*, employed by Sātyaki), 3659 (*astre* . . . *V°āgneye*).—§ 600 (Ghaṭotkacavadhap.): VII, **157**, 6954 (sc. *astram*, employed by Droṇa).—§ 602 (Droṇavadhap.): VII, **188**λ, 8604 (do., do.). — § 603 (Nārayaṇāstramokshap.): VII, **194**ζ, 8965 (*°āgneyam*, sc. *astram*, known by Açvatthāman); **200**, 9258 (sc. *astreṇa*, employed by Arjuna).—§ 603*b* (Nārāyaṇa): VII, **201**, †9466 (sc. *karma*).—§ 608 (Karṇap.): VIII, **89**, †4542 (sc. *astram*); **91**, 4771 (sc. *astreṇa*).—§ 615*u* (Skanda): IX, **46**ι, 2655 (*°yaḥ*, sc. *mātaraḥ*).—§ 641 (Rājadh.): XII, **95**, 3554 (*pāçaiḥ*).—§ 660*b* (Bhṛgu-Bharadvājasaṃv.): XII, **183**, 6807 (*pṛthivī parvatā meghā mūrtimantaç ca ye 'pare sarvaṃ tad V°ṃ jñeyam āpaḥ tasthambhire yataḥ*).—§ 673*b* (Bali-Vāsavasaṃv.): XII, **227**, 8229 (*pāçaiḥ*), 8301 (*pāçān*), 8323 (*pāçāḥ*).—§ 707 (Mokshadh.): XII, **319**, 11762 (read *Va°* with B.).—§ 730*g* (Upamanyu): XIII, **14**ρ, 854 (sc. *astrāt*).—§ 746 (Ānuçāsanik.): XIII, **62**, 3177 (*pāçaiḥ*, only B.); **78**, 3751 (*°īṃ diçam*, i.e. the west); **79**κ, 3771 (*lokam*).—§ 747*b* (Suvarṇotpatti): XIII, **85**, 4105 (*tanum*, *aiçvarye*), 4129 (*jyotis*, only C., B. has *dāruṇam*), 4163 (*tanum*).—§ 748*b* (Tārakavadhop.): XIII, **86**, 4210 (*°ān divyān sagajān?*).—§ 749 (Ānuçāsanik.): XIII, **89***a*, 4266 (*nakshatre*, i.e. Çatabhishā).—§ 759 (do.): XIII, **107**ζ, 5283 (*sthānam*).—§ 768*b* (Umā-Maheçvarasaṃv.): XIII, **142**, 6554 (*lokam*).—§ 789 (Putradarçanap.): XIV, **33**κ, 903 (do.).

Varuṇaçrotasa (B. *°srotasa*), a mountain. § 377 (Dhaumyatīrthak.): III, **88**, 8336 (*girim*, in the south).

[Varuṇaloka] ("the world of Varuṇa"). [§ 757*j* (Hastikūṭa): *Gautama* said: Next [to *Sūryaloka*] in the abode of king *Varuṇa*, other luminous eternal regions (*lokāḥ*) are found, free from passion, darkness, and sorrow.—*Dhṛtarāshṭra* said: This is the end of those who always perform *cāturmāsya* sacrifices, attain to 1,000 sacrifices (*ishṭīnām*), and perform *agnihotras* with faith for three years according to the *Vedas*, who bear well the yoke of duty, walk steadily on the way of the righteous, etc.: XIII, **102**, †4877 (*Varuṇasya rājñaḥ sadane*)].

[Varuṇa-sabhā-varṇana(m)] ("description of the palace of Varuṇa"). § 268 (Lokapālas.). The *sabhā* of *Varuṇa* has been built by *Viçvakarman* in the water; it is of pure white, and in dimensions similar to those of *Yama's*. There *Varuṇa* is sitting ("holding the noose of *dharma*", v. 309) with *Vāruṇī*; worshipped by the *Ādityas*, *Nāgas*, *Daityas*, and *Dānavas* ("free from death", v. 369); likewise the four oceans (v. 370); the rivers, lakes, etc., in their corporeal forms (*dehavantaḥ*, v. 376); the aquatic animals, troops of *Gandharvas* and *Apsarases*, and *Sunābha*, the minister of *Varuṇa*; he is surrounded by his sons and grandsons, and *Go* (*Gonāman*), and *Pushkara* (cf. Rām. VII, **23**, 28) (II, **9**).

Varuṇasrotasa, v. Varuṇaçrotasa.

Varuṇāstra ("the weapon belonging to Varuṇa"). § 203*b* (Arjuna): I, **132**, 5228 (*°eṇa pūrayitvā kamaṇḍalum*, sc. Arjuna).—§ 599 (Jayadrathavadhap.): VII, **145**, †6145 (employed by Arjuna). — § 603 (Nārāyaṇāstramokshap.): VII, **200**, 9259 (do.), 9269. Cf. Vāruṇa, adj.

Vāruṇi[1], a Vainateya. § 99 (Aṃçāvat.): I, **65**, 2548.

Vāruṇi[2] ("the son of Varuṇa") = Vasishṭha: I, 3926, 3928, 3937, 3947.

Vāruṇi[3] (do.) = Agastya: III, 8775, 8794, 8805.

***Vāruṇī** (wife or daughter (?) of Varuṇa), a goddess ("wine" personif.). § 268 (Varuṇasabhāv.): II, **9**, 358 (*Varuṇo V°yā samanvitaḥ*).—§ 549 (Pāṇḍavapraveçap.): IV, **9**, 259 (Sudeshṇā asked Draupadī if she was *V.*).—§ 564 (Mātalīyop.): V, **102**, 3613 (arose at the churning of the ocean). Cf. Surā.

Vāruṇya, adj. ("belonging to Vāruṇī", PCR.). § 564 (Mātalīyop.): V, **98**, 3535 (*bhavanam* . . . *V°ṃ* . . . *yat prāptāḥ suratāṃ prāptāḥ surāḥ*).

Varūthinī, an Apsaras. § 336 (Indralokābhigamanap.): III, **43***a*, 1784 (in the world of Indra).

Vasā, a river. § 574 (Jambūkh.): VI, **9**λ, 338 (*°āñ ca*, C., *°ām anyām*, B.).

Vasanta ("spring", personif.). § 533 (Sītā-Rāvaṇasaṃv.): III, **281**, 16169 (*°a iva mūrtimān*, sc. Rāvaṇa).

Vasāti[1], son of the elder Janamejaya. § 154 (Pūruvaṃç.): I, **94**, 3746 (eighth son of Janamejaya).

Vasāti (so B.) or **Vaçāti** (so mostly C.), pl. (*°ayaḥ*), a people. § 295 (Dyūtap.): II, **52**, 1871 (only C., B. has *Vaçātalāḥ*).—§ 556 (Sañjayayānap.): V, **30**, †889 (*°ç°* also B., C. has by error *Caçā°*).—§ 573 (Ambopākhyānap.): V, **195**ε, 7609 (in the army of Duryodhana).—§ 576 (Bhagavadgītap.): VI, **18**δ, 688 (*°s°* also C., do.).—§ 578 (Bhīshmavadhap.): VI, **51**σ, 2104 (*°s°* also C.).—§ 580 (do.): VI, **59**μ, †2584.—§ 586 (do.): VI, **106**ι, 4809 (*°s°* also C.).—§ 587 (do.): VI, **117**ρ, 5485 (do.).—§ 592 (Saṃçaptakavadhap.): VII, **20**ζ, 802.—§ 599 (Jayadrathavadhap.): VII, **91**β, 3254; **93**γ, 3339; **150**, 6526.—§ 602 (Droṇavadhap.): VII, **192**π, 8841.—§ 604 (Karṇap.): VIII, **5**ζ, 126.—§ 607 (do.): VIII, **44**λ, 2070 (*°s°* also C.).—§ 608 (do.): VIII, **73**, 3650.

Vasātika (*Vaç°* C.), pl. = Vasāti, pl. § 599 (Jayadrathavadhap.): VII, **157**ρ, 6949.

Vasātīya ("the king of the Vasātis"). § 593 (Abhimanyuvadhap.): VII, **44**, 1789, 1792 (slain by Abhimanyu).

Vasātīya (*Vaç°* C.), pl. = Vasāti, pl. § 593 (Abhimanyuvadhap.): VII, **49**, 1934 (read with B. *caiva Vasātīyān* for *Brahma-Vaçā°* in C.).

Vāsātya, pl. = Vasāti, pl. § 608 (Karṇap.): VIII, **56**ρρ, 2762.

Vāsava = Indra, q.v. (add. VI, 1706 (only B.)).—Do.[2] = Çiva (1000 names[2]).

Vāsava, adj. ("belonging to Vasu [Uparicara]"). § 76 (Matsya): I, **63**, 2389 (*vīryam*).

Vāsava, adj. ("belonging to Vāsava [i.e. Indra]"). § 358 (Tīrthayātrāp.): III, **82**, 5030 (*lokam*).—§ 547 (Karṇa): III, **310**, 17211 (sc. *çaktim*, i.e. Amoghā given by Indra to Karṇa).—§ 599 (Jayadrathavadhap.): VII, **147**, 6331 (sc. *çaktiḥ*, do.).—§ 600 (Ghaṭotkacavadhap.): VII, **173**, 7812 (sc. *çaktiḥ*, do.); **183**, 8302 (sc. *çaktim*, do.), 8303 (sc. *çaktiḥ*, do.), 8354 (sc. *çaktiḥ*, do.), 8356 (sc. *çaktim*, do.).—§ 611 (Çalyap.): IX, **11**, 581 (*°īm açanīm iva*).—§ 641 (Rājadh.): XII, **64**, 2399 (*rūpam*).—§ 759 (Ānuçāsanik.): XIII, **107**, 5225 (*lokam*).

Vāsava, pl. (*°āḥ*) ("the sons of Vasu [Uparicara]"). § 74 (Vasu): I, **63**, 2365 (*pañca*, i.e. Bṛhadratha, etc.).

Vāsavaguru ("the preceptor of Vāsava [i.e. Indra]") = Bṛhaspati: II, 1793 (*B°*).

Vāsavaja ("the son of Vāsava [i.e. Indra]") = Arjuna: IV, †1674.

Vāsavanandana (do.) = Arjuna: VII, 6272.

Vāsavānantaraja, Vāsavānuja, Vāsavāvaraja = Vishṇu (Kṛshṇa), v. Vishṇu.

Vāsaveya ("the son of Vāsavī [i.e. Satyavatī]") = Vyāsa: I, 59.

Vāsavi ("the son of Vāsava [i.e. Indra]") = Arjuna, q.v. (add. VII, 745, 1209, 2786, 3301, 3731; VIII, 2597).

Vāsavī ("the daughter of Vasu [Uparicara]") = Satyavatī: I, 2401.

Vashaṭkāra[1] (the exclamation *vashaṭ* or *vaushaṭ* uttered at oblations, e.g.: I, 923; VIII, 1489, 1499; X, 792; XII, 11290, cf. *nirvashaṭkāra*: XIII, 6365, 6745) = Mahāpurusha (Mahāpurushastava).—Do.[2] = Vishṇu (1000 names).

Vasishṭha (*Vaçi°* C.), a ṛshi, son of Varuṇa (or of Mitra and Varuṇa), one of the Saptarshis, husband of Arundhatī (Akshamālā), father of Çakt(r)i and grandfather of Parāçara. [Sometimes *V.* is reckoned among the Prajāpatis (spiritual sons of Brahmán)]. § 61 (Sarpasattra): I, **55**, †2110 (*°vat*).—§ 130 (Aṃçāvat.): I, **67**, 2710 (*°sya çāpena*, all. to § 164).—§ 134 (Viçvāmitra): I, **71**, 2923 (*°ṃ yaḥ putrair ishṭair vyayojayat*, cf. § 224).—§ 153 (Pūruvaṃç.): I, **94**, 3732 (*ṛshiḥ*), 3735 (became the purohita of Saṃvaraṇa, whom he installed).—§ 161 (Mahābhishop.): I, **96**, 3853 (*çaptāḥ . . . V°ena*, sc. the Vasus, cf. § 164), 3854.—§ 163 (Bhīshmotpatti): I, **98**, 3914 (*°çāpadoshеṇa*, all. to § 164).—§ 164 (Āpavop.): I, **99**, 3924 (*°nāmā sa muniḥ . . . Āpavaḥ*) (the Vasu *Dyaus* stole the *homadhenu* of *V.*; *V.* then cursed the Vasus to be reborn (Dyaus as Bhīshma)).—§ 165 (Satyavatīlābhop.): I, **100**, 4001 (Bhīshma learnt the Vedas with their Aṅgas from *V.*).—§ 188 (Madayantī): I, **122**, 4736 (*Madayantī jagāma ṛshiṃ V°ṃ . . . tasmāl lebhe ca sā putram Açmakaṃ*, cf. § 225).—§ 191 (Arjuna): I, **123**, 4807 (among the seven maharshis present at the birth of Arjuna).—§ 222 (Tapatyup.): I, **173**, 6596 (*ṛshisattamaṃ*), 6601, 6604 (*ṛshiḥ*), (6605), 6609, 6610 (*maharshiḥ*), 6612, 6614 (*ṛshiḥ*), 6615, 6617, 6619, 6627 (the purohita of Saṃvaraṇa, prevailed upon Sūrya to give Saṃvaraṇa Tapatī in marriage).—§ 223 (Vāsishṭha): I, **174**, 6635, 6636, 6638 (*Brahmaṇo mānasaḥ putro V°o 'rundhatīpatiḥ*), 6639 (only B., etymology), 6643 (*ṛshisattamaṃ*); **175**, 6649 (*Viçvāmitra-V°yoḥ*), 6654 (*°āçramaṃ*), 6655 (*ṛshiḥ*), 6657, (6665), (6668), 6670 (*°sya nandinī*), (6672), 6673, (6676), (6678), 6679 (the hostility between *V.* and *Viçvāmitra*).—§ 224 (Kalmāshapāda): I, **176**, 6701 (*°kulavardhanaṃ*, i.e. Çakt(r)i), 6710 (*Viçvāmitra-V°yoḥ*), 6712 (*ṛsheḥ putraṃ V°sya V°m iva tejasā*, i.e. Çakt(r)i), 6736 (*°syaiva putreshu*), 6737 (*putrān V°sya*) (when Kalmāshapāda had been cursed by Çakt(r)i and Viçvāmitra had caused a Rākshasa to possess him, Kalmāshapāda devoured Çakt(r)i and the other sons of *V.*).—§ 225 (Vāsishṭha): I, **176**, 6738; **177**, (6758), 6760 (*ṛshiḥ*), 6763, (6767), 6769 (*ṛshiḥ*), 6771 (6775), 6779, 6780, 6782 (*maharshiṇā*), 6787, 6788 (*ṛshiḥ*) (from grief *V.* in vain tried to commit suicide, but, hearing of his daughter-in-law being quick with child, he refrained from his purpose. *V.* afterwards delivered Kalmāshapāda from the curse, and begat Açmaka on his queen Madayantī).—§ 226 (Parāçara): I, **178**, 6794 (*muniḥ*, grandfather of Parāçara), 6795 (*muniṃ*), 6796 (*viprarshiṃ*), 6802.—§ 227 (Aurvop.): I, **178**, (6802); **179**, (6826); **180**, (6862) (told Parāçara the story of Aurva).—§ 228 (do.): I, **181**, 6865, 6868, 6871, 6882 (*ye ca Çaktryavarāḥ putrā V°sya mahāmuneḥ*), 6883, 6885.—§ 229 (Vasishṭhop.): I, **182**, 6889, 6891, 6907 (*ṛsheḥ*), 6909, 6912 (on account of a curse denounced upon Kalmāshapāda, *V.* begat a son on his queen, cf. § 225).—§ 240 (Vaivāhikap.): I, **199**, 7352 (*yathā . . . V°e cāpy Arundhatī*, sc *bhava bhartṛshu*).—§ 249 (Arjunavanavāsap.): I, **215**, 7813 (*°sya ca parvataṃ*, near Himavat (?)).—§ 259*b* (Arundhatī): I, **233**, 8456 (*Saptarshimadhyagaṃ . . . muniṃ*, his wife, Arundhatī, became jealous of him).—§ 270 (Brahmasabhāv.): II, **11**, 436 (among the *prajānāṃ patayaḥ* in the palace of Brahmán).—§ 327 (Draupadīparitāpav.): III, **31**, 1171 (among those ṛshis who have become of pure souls by virtue).—§ 347 (Nalopākhyānap.): III, **64**, 2462 (*°-Bhṛgv-Atrisamaiḥ*).—§ 358 (Tīrthayātrāp.): III, **82**, 4098 (*āçramo V°sya*, a tīrtha on the mountain Arbuda).—§ 368 (do.): III, **83**, 7050 (*°syāçramaṃ*, at Badarīpācana).—§ 370 (do.): III, **84**, 8118 (*āçramo V°sya*, a tīrtha at the Niçcirā).—§ 376 (do.): III, **85**, 8264 (among the ṛshis who expect Yudhishṭhira on his tīrthayātrā).—§ 384 (Agastyop.): III, **102**, 8739 (*°syāçrame*).—§ 391 (Ṛshyaçṛṅga): III, **113**, 10092 (*Arundhatī vā subhāgā V°ṃ . . . yathā*, sc. *paryacarat*).—§ 410 (Vipāçā): III, **130**, 10544 (*atra*—i.e. in the Vipāçā—*vai putraçokena V°o bhagavān ṛshiḥ baddhvātmānaṃ nipātito vipāçaḥ punar utthitaḥ*, cf. § 225), 10553 (*Arundhatīsahāyaḥ*, obtained tranquillity at Ujjānaka).—§ 439 (Yakshayuddhap.): III, **163**, 11855 (*sapta devarshayaḥ . . . V°pramukhāḥ*).—§ 496 (Skandotpatti): III, **224**, 14282 (*°pramukhā mukhyā viprendrāḥ*).—§ 527 (Rāmopākhyānap.): III, **277**, 15981 (*°-Vāmadevābhyāṃ*).—§ 543 (Rāmābhisheka): III, **292**, 16597 (*°o Vāmadevaç ca*, anointed Rāma Dāçarathi).—§ 562 (Bhagavadyānap.): V, **83**η, 2946 (*°o Vāmadevaç ca*, worshipped Kṛshṇa).—§ 565 (Gālavacarita): V, **106**, 3721 (*ṛshiḥ*, Dharma assumed the form of *V.*); **108**, 3773 (*atra*—i.e. in the east—*pūrvaṃ V°sya paurāṇasya, dvijarshabha, sūtiç caiva pratishṭhā ca nidhanaṃ ca prakāçate*); **117**, 3970 (*reme . . . yathā . . . V°ç cākshamālayā*).—§ 574 (Jambūkh.): VI, **2**, 65 (*Arundhatī tayā 'py esha V°ḥ pṛshṭhataḥ kṛtaḥ*, one of the stars [in Ursa major]).—§ 589 (Droṇābhishekap.): VII, **6**, 160 (*°a iva viprāṇāṃ*, sc. *çreshṭhaḥ*).—§ 599 (Jayadrathavadhap.): VII, **94**ε, 3453 (mentioned in a blessing).—§ 602 (Droṇavadhap.): VII, **190**ν, 8727.—§ 615*i* (Saptasārasvata): IX, **38**, 2212 (performed a sacrifice for Kuru in Kurukshetra).—§ 615*n* (Viçvāmitra): IX, **40**, 2302 (*°āçramaṃ*), 2303 (*Brahmaṇaḥ sutaḥ*), 2304 (*munisattamaḥ*) (*V.'s* hostility with Viçvāmitra, cf. § 223). — § 615*p* (Vasishṭhāpavāha): IX, **42**, 2358 (*°syāpavāhaḥ*), 2360, 2361 (*āçramo vai V°sya*, in Sthāṇutīrtha), 2365, 2366 (*Viçvāmitra-V°au*), 2367, 2369 (*dvijaçreshṭhaṃ*), 2374, 2376, 2377, 2378, 2380, (2381), 2383, 2392, 2393 (*ṛshisattamaṃ*) (Viçvāmitra ordered the Sarasvatī to bring *V.* to him that he might slay him)—§ 615*y* (Badarapācana): IX, **48**, 2767 (*viprarsheḥ*), 2768 (Indra assumed the form of *V.*).—§ 635 (Rājadh.): XII, **37**, 1354 (preceptor of Bhīshma).—§ 637 (do.): XII, **46**, 1568 (*°çishyaṃ*, i.e. Bhīshma); **47**η, 1594 (among the ṛshis who surrounded Bhīshma).—§ 641*g* (Mucukundop.): XII, **74**, 2814 (the purohita of Mucukunda); **122**, 4499 (*īçaṃ viprāṇāṃ*).—§ 656 (Khaḍgotpattik.): XII, **166**α, 6135 (*°āṅgirasau*, among the mind-born sons of Brahmán), (β), 6142 (*°-Gautamāgastyāḥ*).—§ 665 (Mokshadh.): XII, **208**α, 7570 (the seventh of Brahmán's seven sons), (ι), 7598 (the second of the ṛshis of the north).—§ 677 (do.): XII, **235**, 8591 (Rantideva gave lukewarm water to *V*), 8601 (*avarshati Parjanye sarvabhūtāni bhūtakṛt V°o jīvayām āsa Prajāpatir iva prajāḥ*), 8604 (Mitrasaha, i.e. Kalmāshapāda, gave his wife Madayantī to *V.* (C. *Damayantīṃ*), cf. § 225).—§ 693*b* (Vṛtravadha): XII, **282**, 10118 (restored Indra to senses by uttering the Rathantara sāman), (10119), 10124, 10130.—§ 702 (Mokshadh.): XII, **293**α, 10762; **297**, 10877 (propagator of one of the four original gotras).—

§ 705 (do.): XII, **303,** 11220 (°*sya ca saṃvādaṃ Karālajanakasya·ca*), 11221, (11226); **304,** (11263); **305,** (11317); **306,** (11339); **307,** (11373); **308,** (11418); **309,** (11466) (discourse between *V.* and Karālajanaka), 11511 (obtained the sacred knowledge from Hiraṇyagarbha and taught it to Nārada).—§ 717*b* (Nārāyaṇīya): XII, **335*a*,** 12686 (among the twenty-one Prajāpatis).—§ 717*c* (Uparicara): XII, **336*β*,** 12725 (among the seven ṛshis named Citraçikhaṇḍins).—§ 717*b* (Nārāyaṇīya): XII, **341*ν*,** 13040 (among the eight Prakṛtis), (*ξ*), 13075 (among the seven spiritual sons of Brahmán); **343,** VII). ††13209 (*Hairaṇyagarbhāt*, cursed Hiraṇyakaçipu); **350,** 13612 (°*sya sutaḥ Çaktriḥ*), †13686 (*mānasaṃ . . . Pitāmahasya*), 13697 (°*kulanandanaḥ*, i.e. Vyāsa).—§ 721 (Ānuçāsanik.): XIII, **3*a*,** 183 (°*sya . . . hataṃ putraçataṃ*, sc. by Viçvāmitra), 192 (*salile purātmānaṃ majjayan*, all. to § 225), 193.—§ 723 (do.): XIII, **6,** 296 (°*sya saṃvādaṃ Brahmaṇaç ca*, °*s*° also C.), 297 (°*s*° also C., discourse between *V.* and Brahmán).—§ 730*g* (Upamanyu): XIII, **14*χ*,** 913 (°*s tvaṃ ṛshīṇāṃ*, sc. *asi*, sc. Çiva).—§ 730 (Ānuçāsanik.): XIII, **14*ββ*,** 991.—§ 732 (do.): XIII, **24,** 1678 (*caturthas tvaṃ V°sya*, sc. Vyāsa).—§ 734 (do.): XIII, **26*a*,** 1761 (among the ṛshis who came to see Bhīshma).—§ 746 (do.): XIII, **78,** 3732 (the purohita of Saudāsa); **79,** (3757); **80,** (3785) (instructed Saudāsa about gifts of kine).—§ 747 (do.): XIII, **84*β*,** 3968 (*devarshiṃ*), 3975.—§ 747*b* (Suvarṇotpatti): XIII, **85,** (4104) (related the Suvarṇotpatti), 4183.—§ 748*b* (Tārakavadhop.): XIII, **85,** 4219 (related the Tārakavadhopākhyāna).—§ 749 (Ānuçāsanik.): XIII, **92*δ*,** 4392.—§ 750*b* (Bisastainyop.): XIII, **93*a*,** 4416 (4439), (4461), (4484) (°*s*° also C.), 4484 (do., etymology), (4515).—§ 751*b* (Çapathavidhi): XIII, **94*a*,** †4550, (4563).—§ 759 (Ānuçāsanik.): XIII, **106*δ*,** 5200.—§ 766 (do.): XIII, **126,** 6046 (*sapta . . . ṛshayaḥ . . . V°pramukhāḥ*), 6047; **130,** 6102/3 (only B.).—§ 767 (do.): XIII, **137*a*,** 6250 (Rantideva made gifts to *V.*), 6257 (*avarshati ca Parjanye sarvabhūtāni devarāṭ / V°o jīvayām āsa*), 6259 (Kakshasena made gifts to *V.*), 6262 (Mitrasaha—i.e. Kalmāshapāda—gave his wife Madayantī to *V.*).—§ 770 (do.): XIII, **151*a*,** †7088, (*ι*), 7116 (among the seven *Dhaneçvarasya guravaḥ* in the north), 7158 (*ξ*), †7160.—§ 772*b* (Pavanārjunasaṃv.): *Vāyu* said: Once the gods performing a sacrifice at the *Vaikhānasa* lake thought of the ṛshi *V.* Seeing the gods emaciated and reduced in consequence of the *dīkshā*, the gigantic *Dānavas* named *Khalins* desired to slay them. The slain *Dānavas* plunged into the lake, and in consequence of a boon granted by Brahmán they revived. Taking up mountains, etc., they agitated the lake and caused the water to rise for hundred *yojanas*. Ten thousands of them attacked the gods who repaired to *Indra*; *Indra* repaired to *V.*, who burnt the *Khalins* and caused the *Gangā*, who had gone to *Kailāsa*, to penetrate the lake, thus arose the river *Sarayū*; the place came to be named after the *Khalins* (*khalino 'bhavat*). Name thou a kshatriya superior to *V.* (XIII, **156**): XIII, **156,** 7279, 7280, 7289, 7290.—§ 773*b* (Kṛshṇa Vāsudeva): XIII, **159,** †7372 (arose from the seed of the gods, which fell into a jar.)—§ 775 (Ānuçāsanik.): XIII, **166*ζ*,** 7670 (among the ṛshis of the north).—§ 779 (Açvamedhikap.): XIV, **11,** 311 (restored Indra to senses with the Rathantara sāman, cf. XII, 10118).—§ 782*b* (Brāhmaṇagītā): XIV, **27,** 781 (*sapta saptarshayaḥ siddhā V°pramukhaiḥ saha*, read *pramukhās tathā* ?).—§ 782*g* (Guruçishyasaṃv.): XIV, **35*δ*,** 961.

Cf. also the following synonyms:—

Āpava, q.v.

Arundhatīpati ("the husband of Arundhatī"): I, 6638 (*V°*).

Brahmarshi (q.v.), **Devarshi** (q.v.).

Hairaṇyagarbha ("the son of Hiraṇyagarbha [i.e. Brahmán]"): XII, ††13209 (*V°*).

Maitrāvāruṇi ("the son of Mitra and Varuṇa"), q.v.

Vāruṇi ("the son of Varuṇa"), q.v.

Vāsishṭha[1] (*Vāç°*, C., "the son of Vasishṭha") = Çakt(r)i: I, 6699 (*ṛshisattamaṃ*), 6707, 6892 (*Ç°*); V, 3970 (*reme . . . yathā . . . Adṛçyantyāñ ca V°ḥ*).

Vāsishṭha[2], name of a tīrtha. § 370 (Tīrthayātrāp.): III, **84,** 8026 (*Vāç°*, C.). Cf. Vāsishṭhī.

Vāsishṭha[3], name of a fire (?). § 491 (Āngirasa): III, **220,** 14156 (*Vāç°*, C.).

Vāsishṭha[4] (*Vāç°*, C.), pl. (°*āḥ*) ("the descendants of Vasishṭha"). § 324 (Dvaitavanapr.): III, **26,** 970.—§ 393 (Tīrthayātrāp.): III, **115,** 10126.

Vāsishṭha (*Vāç°*, C.), adj. ("belonging or relating to Vasishṭha"). § 11 (Parvasangr.): I, **2,** 387 (*ākhyānaṃ*).—§ 223 (Vasishṭha): I, **175,** 6650 (do.), 6689 (*sainikāḥ*).—§ 565 (Gālavacarita): V, **106,** 3728 (*veshaṃ*); **109,** 3794 (*kāshṭhāṃ*, i.e. the north, Nīl. and PCR.).

Vāsishṭha(m) ("the episode relating to Vasishṭha"). § 11 (Parvas.): I, **2,** 387 (°*am ākhyanaṃ*).—§ 223 (Caitrar.). *Arjuna* wished to hear about *Vasishṭha*. The *Gandharva* said: *Vasishṭha* is *Brahmán's* spiritual son and *Arundhatī's* husband; *Kāma* and *Krodha*, who cannot be vanquished even by the immortals, used to shampoo his feet. Though his wrath was excited by *Viçvāmitra's* offence, he did not yet exterminate the *Kuçikas*. Afflicted at the loss of his sons, he did not do any dreadful deed for the destruction of *Viçvāmitra*. He did not transgress *Kṛtānta* (Death) in order to bring back his lost children from the abode of *Yama*. It was by obtaining him that the *Ikshvākus* acquired this earth, and with him as their *purohita*, they performed many great sacrifices. "Therefore acquire a fit *purohita*" (I, **174**). *Arjuna* wished to hear of the hostility between *Viçvāmitra* and *Vasishṭha*. The *Gandharva* said: This old (*purāṇa*) story of *Vasishṭha* they tell in all worlds. In *Kānyakubja* king *Gādhi*, son of *Kuçika*, had a son *Viçvāmitra*, who, with his ministers, used to go a hunting. Once he arrived at the hermitage of *Vasishṭha*, who offered him *arghya*, etc. from his cow *Nandinī*, who yielded everything desired; *Viçvāmitra* asked *Vasishṭha* to give him *Nandinī* for an *arbuda* of kine or his kingdom, but in vain. Then he wanted to take the cow by force. She repaired to *Vasishṭha*, who at first did nothing, saying, "I am a forgiving *brahman*"; but at last he said: "I do not abandon you! Stay if you can!" Hearing this word, the cow attacked *Viçvāmitra's* troops; from her tail she began to rain showers of burning coals; from her tail she brought forth *Pahlavas*, from her udders *Drāviḍas* and *Çakas*, from her womb (*yonideçāt*) *Yavanas*, from her dung (*çakṛt*) *Çabaras*, from her urine *Kāñcis*, and from her sides *Çarabhas* (B. *Çabarān* and *kāṃçcid* instead of *Kāñcīn*), and from the froth of her mouth *Pauṇḍras*, *Kirātas*, *Yavanas*, *Siṃhalas*, *Barbaras*, *Vaças* (B. *Khaçān*), *Civukas*, *Pulindas*, *Cīnas*, *Hūnas*, *Keralas*, and other *Mlecchas*, who attacked *Viçvāmitra's* soldiers. *Viçvāmitra's* troops fled, but none was deprived of life. *Viçvāmitra* then, disgusted with *kshatriya* prowess ("*brahman* prowess is true prowess"), set his mind on asceticism, and finally became a *brahman* and drank *soma* with *Indra* (I, **175**). — § 224: *Kalmāshapāda* (q.v.)—§ 225. *Vasishṭha* patiently bore his grief, and resolved rather to sacrifice his own life than exterminate the *Kauçikas*. He threw himself down from the summit of *Meru*, entered a huge fire in the forest, and tied a strong weight to his neck and threw himself into the sea, but all in vain, and, in distress of heart, he returned to his hermitage (I, **176**). Beholding it bereft of his children, he left it again and tied himself strongly with cords and flung himself into a mighty river, but the stream cut those cords and cast the *ṛshi* ashore, whence that river was called *Vipāçā*. Once more he threw himself into a river flowing from *Himavat* (*Haimavatī*), but the river immediately fled in 100 different directions, and has since been known by the name of the *Çatadru* ("*çatadhā vidrutā*", v. 6753). He now again went towards his hermitage, and was on the way addressed by *Adṛçyantī*, the wife of *Çaktri*, who had for twelve years borne his child in her womb. Hearing that child in the womb reciting the *Vedas* with the six *Angas*, *Vasishṭha* refrained from self-destruction, and, accompanied by *Adṛçyantī*, returned to his hermitage. One day he saw *Kalmāshapāda*, who would devour him; *Adṛçyantī* was terrified, but *Vasishṭha* restrained him by uttering "*huṃ*", and, sprinkling him with water sanctified by *mantras*, and freed him from his curse that had lasted twelve years. *Kalmāshapāda* promised never more to insult *brahmans*, and prevailed upon *Vasishṭha* that he accompanied him to his capital *Ayodhyā* and begat a son for him on the queen. Then he went back to his hermitage. After twelve years the queen tore open her womb by a stone, and then was born the *rājarshi Açmaka*, who founded the city of *Paudanya* (I, **177**).—§ 226 : *Parāçara* (q.v.).

Vasishṭhāpavāha ("the carrying away of Vasishṭha"), name of a tīrtha. § 615 (Baladevatīrthayātrā): IX, **41**, †2357; **42**, †2358.—§ 615*p* (do.): A great enmity arose between *Viçvāmitra* and *Vasishṭha*, due to their rivalry in respect of ascetic austerities. The hermitage of *Vasishṭha* was in *Sthāṇutīrtha*, on the bank of the *Sarasvatī*; on the opposite bank was the hermitage of *Viçvāmitra*. There (i.e. in *Sthāṇutīrtha*) *Sthāṇu* had practised penances, and having performed a sacrifice and worshipped the *Sarasvatī* he had established that tīrtha, and there the gods in days of yore installed *Skanda*. In that tīrtha on the *Sarasvatī*, the *ṛshi Viçvāmitra*, by his penances, disturbed *Vasishṭha*. *Viçvāmitra* and *Vasishṭha* every day challenged each other in respect of the superiority of their penances. *Viçvāmitra* ordered the *Sarasvatī*, notwithstanding her trembling, to bring *Vasishṭha* into his presence, that he might slay him. *Vasishṭha* willingly let her do so, lest *Viçvāmitra* should curse her. *Sarasvatī* washed away one of her banks and bore *Vasishṭha* (who praised the *Sarasvatī* (*q*)) away and informed *Kauçika* (i.e. *Viçvāmitra*) about his arrival; but while *Viçvāmitra* was looking for a weapon she quickly bore *Vasishṭha* back to the eastern bank. *Viçvāmitra* cursed her, saying that her current should be changed into blood, which is acceptable only to the *Rākshasas*. For a whole year she then flowed bearing blood mixed with water. The gods, the *Gandharvas*, and the *Apsarases* grieved. For this reason the tīrtha came to be called *V*. *Sarasvatī*, however, once more got back her own proper condition (IX, **42**), when some *munis* on a *tīrthayātrā* to the *Sarasvatī*, having bathed in all her tīrthas came to *V*. and saw the water mixed with blood, and that innumerable *Rākshasas* were drinking it. Having learnt the cause, they worshipped *Mahādeva* with penances and purified the *Sarasvatī*. The *Rākshasas*, who were *Brahma-Rākshasas* (so those among *vaiçyas*, *çūdras*, and *kshatriyas*, who hate and injure the brahmans, become *Rākshasas*), afflicted with hunger, sought the protection of the *munis*, who, having ordained what should be the food of the *Rākshasas* (*v*) solicited the *Sarasvatī*, who assumed a new shape called *Aruṇā*; bathing in that new river the *Rākshasas* abandoned their bodies and went to heaven. Ascertaining all this, *Indra* (*s*) bathed there and became purified of a grievous sin (i.e. *brahmahatyā*): IX, **42**, 2398.

Vāsishṭhī, a tīrtha (a river?). § 370 (Tīrthayātrāp.): III, **84**, 8026.

[Vasishṭhopākhyāna(m)] ("the episode relating to Vasishṭha"). § 223 (cf. Caitrarathap.). *Arjuna* asked: "Why did *Kalmāshapāda* command his queen to go to *Vasishṭha*? And was this an act of sin on the part of *Vasishṭha*?" The *Gandharva* said: Under the influence of the curse, *Kalmāshapāda*, in anger, went out of his capital, accompanied by his wife. In a solitary part of the woods he saw a *brahman* and his wife (*Āngirasī*, v. 6908) embracing each other. The couple ran away, but *Kalmāshapāda* forcibly seized the *brahman*. The *brāhmaṇī* asked him to liberate her husband, but he cruelly devoured him. The tears that the woman shed blazed up like fire and consumed everything in that place. The *brāhmaṇī* cursed the *rājarshi*, saying that he should meet with instant death when cohabiting with his wife, and that his wife should have a son from *Vasishṭha*, whose children he had devoured, and that child should be the propagator of his race. Then she entered the fire. *Vasishṭha*, by his ascetic power, immediately knew all about it. And long after this, when the *rājarshi* became freed from his curse, he approached his wife *Madayantī*, not remembering the curse of the *brāhmaṇī*. Hearing, however, the words of his wife, he recollected the curse, and, therefore, he appointed *Vasishṭha* to beget a son on his queen (I, **182**).

Vasor-dhārā[1], name of a tīrtha. § 358 (Tīrthayātrāp.): III, **82**, 5018.—Do.[2] = the river Mandākinī (according to Nīl.): XIII, 3789.—Do.[3], name of a certain libation of ghee: I, 8146; XII, 12843–44; XIII, 118.

Vastrapa, pl. (°*āḥ*), a people. § 295 (Dyūtap.): II, **52**, 1871 (brought tribute to Yudhishṭhira).

Vāstu (*Vastrā*, B.), a river. § 574 (Jāmbukh.): VI, **9**λ, 333.

Vasu[1], surnamed Uparicara, king of the Cedis. § 73 (cf. Ādivaṃçāvataraṇa). Instructed by *Indra* king *V.* won the kingdom of the *Cedis*. Some time after he dwelled in a hermitage practising austerities, from which the gods, headed by *Indra*, prevailed upon him to refrain. *Indra* gave him a crystal *vimāna* (chariot) capable of carrying him through the air like a god, and a triumphal (*vaijayantī*) garland named *Indramālā*, and a bamboo pole to protect the peaceful. After a year the king planted this pole in the ground in order to worship *Indra* (from that time all kings plant a bamboo pole, and the next day they cover it with golden clothes, etc.). *Indra* came there in the form of a swan to accept the worship, and blessed the men and kings who would observe this festivity: I, **63**, 2335 (*Pauravanandanaḥ*), 2354, 2355, 2358.—§ 74 (do.): From the country of the *Cedis V.* ruled the whole world. He installed his five sons as governors of various provinces: *Bṛhadratha* (in the country of the *Māgadhas*), *Pratyagra*, *Kuçāmba* or *Maṇivāhana*, *Māvella*, and *Yadu*; they founded kingdoms and towns, named after themselves, and created separate dynasties which lasted for long ages: I, **63**, 2360 (*Çedīçvaraḥ*), 2361 (*Cedipatiḥ*).—§ 75 (do.): Seated in his crystal chariot and coursing through the sky *V.* was adored by *Gandharvas* and *Apsarases*, and was called *Uparicara*. Near his capital flowed the river *Çuktimatī*, and from love of this river the mountain Kolāhala once barred its course. *V.* then kicked the mountain with his foot, and the river gave him the two children which she had with *Kolāhala*. *V.* made the male child the commander of his armies, and made the daughter *Girikā* his wife: I, **63**, 2368, 2370.—§ 76 (Matsya): I, **63**, 2371 (°*oḥ patnī* . . . *Girikā*) [2389 (*vīryaṃ* . . . *Vāsavaṃ*)] (the seed of *V.* fell into the Yamunā, and was swallowed by Adrikā (an Apsaras transformed into a fish), who, in consequence, bore Matsya and Satyavatī).—§ 277 (Jarāsandhavadhap.): II, **24**, 950 (the chariot which *V.* got from Indra passed over to Bṛhadratha, and from him to Jarāsandha).—§ 717*c* (Uparicara): XII, **336**, 12742 (*prajāpālaḥ*), 12746 (*rājā*); **337**, 12754 (*rājoparicaraḥ*), 12755, 12768, 12813; **338**, 12818, 12823, 12824, 12826, 12827, 12828, 12831, 12832, 12836, 12846, 12851 (*samrāḍ rājā*), 12854 (*pārthivaḥ*) (*V.* was devoted to Nārāyaṇa and a pupil of Bṛhaspati; his horse sacrifice; *V.* was cursed by some brahmans on account of a wrong explanation, and sank below the earth, where he got the libation named *vasor-dhārā* for his sustenance; at last he, by the grace of Nārāyaṇa, attained to Brahmaloka).—§ 723 (Ānuçāsanik.): XIII, **6***a*, 328 (°*r yajñaçatair ishṭvā dvitīya iva Vāsavaḥ* / *mithyābhidhānenaikena Rasātalatalaṃ gataḥ*, cf. § 717*c*).—§ 761 (do.): XIII, **115**, 5650 (*Cedipatiḥ*, questioned by the ṛshis about the eating of meat he gave a wrong answer and therefore fell down from heaven to earth and thence below the earth, cf. § 717*c*), (*c*), 5665 (among those who did not eat meat during the month of Kārttika).—§ 786 (Anugītāp.): XIV, **91**, 2828 (*nṛpatiṃ*), 2830 (*Cedīnām īçvaraṃ*) (*V.* was questioned by the ṛshis about sacrifices, he answered wrongly, and therefore sank down to Rasātala, cf. § 717*c*). Cf. Cedipa, Cedipati, Pauravanandana, Rājoparicara, Uparicara.

Vasu[2], a prince, brother of Dushyanta. § 150 (Pūruvaṃç.): I, **94**, 3708.

Vasu[3], a brahman, father of Paila. § 286 (Rājasūyikap.): II, **33**, 1239 (*Pailaḥ* . . . *V°oḥ sutaḥ*).

Vasu[4], son of Jamadagni. § 396 (Jamadagni): III, **116**, 10180.

Vasu[5], a king. § 562 (Bhagavadyānap.): V, **74**γ, 2729 (*Kṛmīṇām uddhato V°*).

Vasu[6], a ṛshi. § 770 (Ānuçāsanik.). XIII, **151**κ, 7110 (among the seven *dharaṇīdharas*).

Vasu[7] = Çiva (1000 names[2]).—Do.[8] = Vishṇu (1000 names).

Vasu[9], mostly pl. (°*avaḥ*), a class of gods. § 3 (Anukram.): I, **1***a*, 34 (issued from the primordial egg).—§ 11 (Parvasaṅgr.): I, **2**, 372 (°*ūnāṃ punarutpattiḥ*, cf. § 161 foll.).—§ 40 (Garuḍa): I, **28**, 1333.—§ 44 (do.): I, **30**, 1416.—§ 16 (do.): I, **32**, 1486.—§ 61 (Sarpasattra): I, **55**, 2111.—§ 79 (Bhīshma): I, **63**, 2420 (°*vīryāt samabhavat*, sc. Bhīshma, cf. § 161).—§ 116 (cf. Aṃçāvat.): *Paitāmaha Manu* (B. *muni*) was father of *Prajāpati*, whose sons were the eight Vasus: 1) *Dhara*, 2) *Dhruva*, 3) *Soma* (*Candramas*), 4) *Ahas*, 5) *Anila* (*Çvasana*), 6) *Anala* (*Hutāçana*, *Agni*), 7) *Pratyūsha*, 8) *Prabhāsa*; their mothers are respectively: 1–2) *Dhūmrā*, 3) *Manasvinī* (PCR. takes *manasvinyāḥ* (v. 2583) as an adjective to *Çvāsā*, who thus is the mother of both *Candramas* and *Çvasana*), 4) *Ratā*, 5) *Çvāsā*, 6) *Çāṇḍilī*, 7–8) *Prabhātā*; their sons are respectively: 1) *Draviṇa* and *Hutahavyavaha*, 2) *Kāla*, 3) *Varcas* (who [was father of *Varcasvin* (q.v.), who] with *Manoharā*, had the sons *Çiçira*, *Prāṇa*, and *Ramaṇa*), 4) *Jyotis*, *Çama*, *Çānta*, and *Muni* (? v. 2587), 5) *Manojava* and *Avijñātagati* (the mother of these two was *Çivā*), 6) *Kumāra* (*b*, v. Skanda) or *Kārttikeya*, 7) the ṛshi *Devala* (who had himself two sons), 8), *Viçvakarman* (whose mother was the sister of *Bṛhaspati*): I, **66**, 2581, 2582 (*ashṭau*), 2591.—§ 120 *bis* (Aṃçāvat.): I, **66**, 2602 (°*ūnāṃ*, sc. *pakshaḥ*).—§ 130 (do.): I, **67**, 2710 (*jajñire V°avas tv ashṭau Gaṅgāyāṃ Çāntanoḥ sutāḥ*, cf. §§ 161 foll.).—§ 133 (Dushyanta): I, **69**, 2823 (°*parākramaḥ*).—§ 145 (Kaca): I, **76**, †3229.—§ 149 (Yayāti): I, **87**, 3551.—§ 161 (Mahābhishop.): I, **96**, 3851 (*devān*), 3855, 3856, (3858), (3860), (3862), 3864 (the *V.* who had been cursed by Āpava (Vasishṭha) (v. § 164) made the arrangement with the Gaṅgā that she, having born them to Çāntanu, should throw them into the water, except the eighth).—§ 163 (Bhīshmotpatti): I, **98**, 3896 (°*ūnāṃ samayaṃ*, cf. § 161), 3914 (*ashṭau* . . . *devāḥ*), 3916 (*ashṭau*), 3917 (*devānāṃ*), 3919 (Gaṅgā threw her children into the water except the eighth (Bhīshma)).—§ 164 (Āpavop.): I, **99**, 3920, 3922 (*īçā vai sarvalokasya*), 3930 (*Pṛthvādyā V°aḥ sarve devāḥ*), 3932 (sg. i.e. Dyaus), 3935 (do., do.), 3949, 3950, 3951, 3952 (*ashṭau*), 3954, 3960 (Dyaus, one of the *V.*, had ravished the homadhenu of Vasishṭha, who then cursed the Vasus, saying that they should be reborn, but added that only Dyaus should dwell on earth for a long time).—§ 165 (Satyavatīlābhop.): I, **100**, 3987 (sg., i.e. Dyaus reborn as Devavrata, i.e. Bhīshma).—§ 191 (Arjuna): I, **123**, 4827 (*ashṭau*, present at the birth of Arjuna).—§ 233 (Svayaṃvarap.): I, **187**, †7010 (present at the svayaṃvara of Draupadī).—§ 238 (Pañcendrop.): I, **197**, †7277, †7315.—§ 258 (Khāṇḍavadahanap.): I, **227**, 8269 (among the gods who fought with Kṛshṇa and Arjuna). § 270 (Brahmasabhāv.): II, **11**, 448, 460 (in the palace of Brahmán).—§ 309 (Āraṇyakap.): III, **2**, 127.—§ 310*b* (Sūrya): III, **3**, 174.—§ 330 (Indradarçana): III, **37**, 1490.—§ 334 (Kairātap.): III, **41**, 1682 (°*sambhūtaḥ* . . . *Pitāmahaḥ*, i.e. Bhīshma).—§ 336 (Indralokābhigamanap.): III, **43**, 1768.—§ 338 (do.): III, **46**, 1840.—§ 347 (Nalopākhyānap.): III, **62**, 2356.—§ 357 (Pushkara): III, **82**, 4064 (in Pushkara).—§ 358 (Tīrthayātrāp.): III, **82**, 5020 (*saraḥ* . . . *V°ūnāṃ*).—§ 370 (do.): III, **84**, 8102.—§ 375 (do.): III, **85**, 8248 (bathe in the tīrthas), 8254 (*lokān vai V°ūnāṃ*).—§ 377 (do.): III, **90**, 8404.—§ 383 (Paraçurāma): III, **99**, 8673 (*sa°*, seen in the body of Rāma Dāçarathi).—§ 400 (Tīrthayātrāp.): III, **118**, †10224 (°*ūnāṃ*, sc. *āyatanaṃ*).—§ 412 (Ashṭāvakrīya): III, **134**, †10665 (*ashṭau*).—§ 418 (Tīrthayātrāp.): III, **139**, 10834.—§ 438 (Yakshayuddhap.): III, **162**, 11807 (*Vṛtrahā V°bhiḥ saha*).—§ 443 (Nivātakavacayuddhap.): III, **168**, 12020 (Arjuna should learn the weapons of the *Vasus*, etc.), 12043.—§ 450 (Sarasvatī-Tārkshyasaṃv.): III, **186**, †12727 (*lokā V°ūnāṃ*).—§ 459 (Mārkaṇḍeyas.): III, **188**, 12924 (seen in the body of Nārāyaṇa).—§ 506 (Skandayuddha): III, **231**, 14549.—§ 507 (do.): III, **231**, 14587.—§ 547 (Karṇa): III, **308**, 17139.—§ 548 (Āraṇeyap.): III, **313**, 17317; **314**, 17421 (Yudhishṭhira asks the Yaksha if he is one of the *V.*).—§ 549*c* (Arjuna): IV, **2**, 48 (°*ūnāṃ navamaṃ*, sc. Arjuna), 50 (°*ūnām iva Havyavāṭ*).—§ 556 (Sañjayayānap.): V, **29**, †823.—§ 561*d* (Nara-Nārāyaṇau): V, **49**, 1918 (*Agninā saha*).—§ 561 (Yānasandhip.): V, **70**, 2562 (°*tvāt* (?), etymology of the name Vāsudeva).—§ 562 (Bhagavadyānap.): V, **86**, 3043 (*Ādityā V°avo Rudrā yathā buddhiṃ Bṛhaspateḥ*, sc. *upāsante*).—§ 565 (Gālavacarita): V,

116, 3954 (*Vasumanā . . . V°bhyo vasumattaraḥ*).—§ 567 (Bhagavadyānap.): V, **128**ι, 4301; **131,** 4420, (ο), 4423 (seen in the body of Kṛshṇa).—§ 569 (do.): V, **146,** 4940 (°*avo Vāsavaṃ yathā*, sc. *namaḥ kurvanti*).—§ 570 (Sainyaniryāṇap.): V, **156,** 5290 (°*ūnām iva Havyavāṭ*, sc. *senāpatiḥ*).—§ 573 (Ambopākhyānap.): V, **185,** 7307 (*Bhīshmo V°ūnām anyatamaḥ*; sg. = Bhīshma).—§ 576 (Bhagavadgītāp.): VI, **34,** 1227 (°*ūnāṃ Pāvakaç cāsmi*, says Kṛshṇa); **35,** 1252, †1268.—§ 581 (Bhīshmavadhap.); VI, **68,** 3039 (only B.).—§ 585 (do.): VI, **96,** 4338 (°*avo Vāsavaṃ yathā*, sc. *parivārya*).—§ 587 (do.): VI, **119,** 5603 (present at Bhīshma's last encounter).—§ 589 (Droṇābhishekap.): VII, **2,** †58 (°*prabhāve V°vīryasambhave V°ūn gate eva vasudharādhipe*, i.e. Bhīshma); **6,** 159 (°*ūnām iva Pāvakaḥ*). — § 593 (Abhimanyuvadhap.): VII, **35,** 1536 (°*vagnyādityavikramaiḥ*).—§ 596 (Pratijñāp.): VII, **76,** 2682.—§ 600 (Ghaṭotkacavadhap.): VII, **156,** 6865 (sg. = Agni).—§ 608 (Karṇap.): VIII, **87**χ′, 4418 (sided with Arjuna), 4455 (°*ūnāṃ salokatvaṃ*).—§ 615*u* (Skanda): IX, **44,** 2478 (came to see Skanda): **45**γ, 2508, 2555 (gave companions to Skanda).—§ 615*ff* (Asita Devala): IX, **50,** 2893 (°*ūnāṃ*, sc. *sthānaṃ*).—§ 619 (Strīvilāpap.): XI, **19**δ, 564 (*V°ṃ Vāsavayoshitaḥ*, wrong reading in C. instead of *bahudhā varayoshitaḥ*).—§ 623 (Rājadh.): XII, **15**β, 440.—§ 626 (do.): XII, **21**β, 634 (*Rudrāḥ sa-V°avaḥ*).—§ 639 (do.): XII, **50,** 1831 (*sa tvaṃ Bhīshma mahābāho V°ūnāṃ Vāsavopamaḥ* / *nityaṃ vipraiḥ samākhyāto navamo* ('*n*°, C.) '*navamo guṇaiḥ*); **51,** †1858.—§ 641 (do.): XII, **64**η, †2395; **122,** 4499 (°*ūnāṃ Jātavedasaṃ*, sc. *īçaṃ*).—§ 656 (Khaḍgotpattik.): XII, **166**β, 6141.—§ 661 (Mokshadh.): XII, **198***a*, 7192 (*Rudrāditya-V°ūnāṃ*).—§ 664 (do.): XII, **207**ε, 7540 (sons of Dharma).—§ 665 (do.): XII, **208,** 7586 (*ashṭau*).—§ 673*b* (Bali-Vāsavasaṃv.): XII, **227,** 8220, 8288.—§ 694*b* (Jvarotpatti): XII, **284***a*, 10215.—§ 695*b* (Dakshayajñavināça): XII, **285***a*, 10279.—§ 702 (Mokshadh.): XII, **296**β, 10837.—§ 707 (do.): XII, **318,** 11704 (if the soul (*jīva*) issues through the calves, one attains to the regions of the *V.*).—§ 712 (Çukotpatti): XII, **324,** 12174.—§ 717*b* (Nārāyaṇīya): XII, **340**θ, 12916 (*ashṭau*); **341**π, 13110 (°*ūnāṃ pataye*, i.e. Vishṇu (Kṛshṇa)). — § 718*b* (Uñchavṛttyup.): XII, **366,** 13940 (told the Uñchavṛttyupākhyāna to Bhīshma).—§ 719*b* (Gautamī-lubdhaka-vyāla-Mṛtyu-Kālasaṃv.): XIII, **1***a*, 55.—§ 730*g* (Upamanyu): XIII, **14**χ, 914 (°*ūnāñ caiva Pāvakaḥ*, sc. *asi*, sc. Çiva).—§ 730 (Ānuçāsanik.): XIII, **14,** 985; **18**λλ, †1368.—§ 746 (do.): XIII, **57,** †2955 (*loko V°ūnāṃ*), 2959 (*lokān . . . V°ūnāṃ*); **79,** 3776 (°*ūnāṃ lokaṃ*).—§ 747*b* (Suvarṇotpatti): XIII, **84,** 4011; **85**ζ, 4130 (arose from the smoke of Agni).—§ 748*b* (Tārakavadhop.): XIII, **86***a*, 4201.—§ 759 (Ānuçāsanik.): XIII, **107**ζ, 5302 (*lokān V°ūnāṃ*), 5315 (do.), 5330 (°*ūnāṃ . . . lokaṃ*).—§ 766 (do.): XIII, **134**γ, 6187.—§ 768*b* (Umā-Maheçvarasaṃv.): XIII, **140***a*, 6351.—§ 770 (Ānuçāsanik.): XIII, **151**δ, 7095 (*ashṭau*, their names are: *Dhara, Dhruva, Soma, Sāvitra, Anila, Anala, Pratyūsha, Prabhāsa*), 7110 (*Rudrānala-V°prabhāḥ*), 7158 (*Çakra-V°bhiḥ*).—§ 773*b* (Kṛshṇa Vāsudeva): XIII, **159**β, 7387 (identified with Kṛshṇa).—§ 775 (Ānuçāsanik.): XIII, **166***a*, 7642.—§ 777 (Svargārohaṇik. p.): XIII, **168,** 7752; **169,** 7790 (sg. = Bhīshma), 7794 (do., do., but read with B. pl. *Vasūn*).—§ 778*f* (Muñjavat): XIV, **8,** 183 (worship Çiva on Muñjavat); **10,** †261.—§ 784*b* (Uttaṅka): XIV, **54,** 1564.—§ 785 (Anugītāp.): XIV, **81,** 2413, 2414, 2418, 2421 (on account of the slaughter of Bhīshma, the *V.* had cursed Arjuna).—§ 789 (Putradarçanap.): XV, **31**η, 858 (sg. = Bhīshma).—§ 793 (Mausalap.): XVI, **4**θ, †129.—§ 795 (Svargārohaṇap.): XVIII, **3,** 87; **4,** 145 (°*bhiḥ sahitaṃ . . . Bhīshmaṃ*); **5**μ, 158 (*ashṭau*, Bhīshma, after death, attained to the status of the *V.*).

Vasucandra, a Pāṇḍava warrior. § 600 (Ghaṭotkacavadhap.): VII, **158**χ, 7009.

Vasuçreshṭha = Çiva (1000 names[2]).

Vasuçrī, a mātṛ. § 615*u* (Skanda): IX, **46**θ, 2632.

Vasuda = Vishṇu (1000 names).

Vasudā, a mātṛ. § 615*u* (Skanda): IX, **46**θ, 2647 (B. *Viçirā*).

Vasudāmā, a mātṛ. § 615*u* (Skanda): IX, **46**θ, 2623.

Vasudāna, king of Pāṃçurāshṭra. § 264 (Sabhākriyāp.): II, **4**β, 122 (waited upon Yudhishṭhira).—§ 295 (Dyūtap.): II, **52,** 1884 (*Pāṃçurāshṭrāt*, gave tribute to Yudhishṭhira).—§ 296 (do.): II, **53,** 1914.—§ 570 (Sainyaniryāṇap.): V, **151**δ, 5161 (in the army of Yudhishṭhira).—§ 572 (Rathātirathasaṅkhyānap.): V, **171,** 5919 (do., is an atiratha).—§ 573 (Ambopākhyānap.): V, **196**μ, 7650 (followed Yudhishṭhira).—§ 578 (Bhīshmavadhap.): VI, **51**ω, 2110.—§ 585 (do.): VI, **93**ψ, 4151 (followed Bhīmasena); **95**δδ, 4255.—§ 592 (Saṃçaptakavadhap.): VII, **21**κ, 903, 909 (slain by Droṇa); **23**ο, 990 (followed Dhṛstadyumna, description of his horses).—§ 599 (Jayadrathavadhap.): VII, **113,** 4374.—§ 602 (Droṇavadhap.): VII, **190,** 8724 (slain by Droṇa).—§ 604 (Karṇap.): VIII, **6,** 174 (the son of *V.* had slain Abhibhu the Kāçi king in the battle (!)), 188 (had been slain by Droṇa). Cf. Pāṃçurāshṭrādhipa.

Vasudeva, son of Çūra, husband of Devakī, etc., father of Kṛshṇa, etc. § 82 (Kṛshṇa Vāsudeva): I, **63,** 2428 (°*āt tu Devakyāṃ prādurbhūtaḥ*, sc. Vishṇu born as Kṛshṇa).—§ 213 (Jatugṛhap.): I, **151,** 5905 (*svasāraṃ V°sya*, i.e. Kuntī).—§ 252 (Subhadrāharaṇap.): I, **219,** 7923 (*duhitā V°sya*, i.e. Subhadrā). — § 289 (Arghāharaṇap.): II, **37,** 1343 (*vṛddhe*).—§ 547 (Karṇa): III, **303,** 17021 (°*sya bhaginī*, i.e. Kuntī).—§ 599*e* (Çini): VII, **144,** 6031 (*Çauriḥ*), 6034 (°*ārthaṃ*, at the svayaṃvara of Devakī, Çini won her in behalf of *V.*).—§ 637 (Rājadh.): XII, **47**θ, 1616 (*yaṃ devaṃ Devakī devī V°ād ajījanat*, sc. Kṛshṇa).—§ 768*b* (Kṛshṇa Vāsudeva): XIII, **147,** 6837 (*Ānakadundubhiṃ*, son of Çūra and father of Kṛshṇa).—§ 785 (Anugītāp.): XIV, **60,** (1773); **61,** 1810, 1811, 1813, 1814 (Kṛshṇa related to *V.* the events of the battle); **83,** 2481 (*mātulena Kirīṭinaḥ*, B. has by error *Vāsudevena*).—§ 793 (Mausalap.): XVI, **6,** (153); **7,** 177, 191 (*Çauriḥ*, died), 192 (°*niveçane*, bewailed by his widows, Devakī, etc.).—§ 795 (Svargārohaṇap.): XVIII, **5**μ, 163 (among those who after death entered the deities).

Cf. also the following synonyms:—

Ānakadundubhi: II, 1215; III, 783; XIII, 6837 (*V*°); XVI, 148, 150.

Çauri, Çūraputra, Çūrasūnu, Çūrasuta, Çūrātmaja, q.v.

Yadūdvaha, q.v.

Vāsudeva[1] ("the son of Vasudeva") = Kṛshṇa, q.v.—Do.[2] (do.) = Balarāma: IV, 2356.

Vāsudeva[3], king of the Puṇḍras. § 232 (Svayaṃvarap.): I, **186,** 6992 (*Pauṇḍrakaḥ*, came to the svayaṃvara of Draupadī). — § 273 (Rājasūyārambhap.): II, **14,** 584 (*Vaṅga-Puṇḍra-Kirāteshu rājā . . . Pauṇḍrakaḥ*, had joined

Jarāsandha).—§ 280 (Bhīmasena): II, **30**, 1096 (*Puṇḍrādhipam*, vanquished by Bhīmasena on his digvijaya).—§ 287 (Rājasūyikap.): II, **34**, 1270 (*Pauṇḍrakaḥ*, came to the rājasūya). Cf. Pauṇḍraka, Puṇḍrādhipa.

Vasudevapitṛ ("the father of Vasudeva") = Çūra: I, 2764 (*Ç°*), 4382 (*Ç°*).

Vāsudevapriya ("dear to Vāsudeva") = Skanda: III, 14636.

Vasudevaputra ("the son of Vasudeva") = Kṛshṇa, q.v.

Vāsudevasahodarā ("the sister of Vāsudeva [i.e. Kṛshṇa]") = Subhadrā: IX, 258.

Vasudevasuta ("the son of Vasudeva") = Kṛshṇa, q.v.

Vasudevasutā ("the daughter of Vasudeva") = Subhadrā: I, 7919 (*S°*).

Vasudevātmaja ("the son of Vasudeva") = Kṛshṇa, q.v.

***Vasudhā** ("the earth", personif.): VII, 2407, (2408).

Vasudhādhara ("supporting the earth") = Çesha: XIII: 6866 (*Anantaḥ*).

Vasudharman, a Kuru warrior, a Trigarta(?). § 605 (Karṇap.): VIII, **27**λλ, 1079 (only C., attacked Arjuna).

Vasuhoma, an Aṅga king. § 641 (Rājadh.): XII, **122**, 4469 (*Aṅgeshu*), 4475, 4476, 4477, 4478 (4482) (on Muñjapṛshṭha *V.* discoursed to Māndhātṛ on chastisement).

Vāsuki, king of the serpents. § 26 (Jaratkāru): I, **14**, 1053, (1056) (gave his sister Jaratkāru to the ascetic Jaratkāru, cf. § 53).—§ 28 (Amṛtamanthana): I, **18**, 1124, 1127 (*nāgasya, V.* served as a cord at the churning of the ocean).—§ 47 (Sarpanāmak.): I, **35**, 1550 (enumeration).—§ 49 (cf. Āstīkap.): *V.* held a consultation with his brothers how to render the curse of *Kadrū* abortive; several means were proposed and rejected (I, **37**); *Elāpatra* then told that he had heard *Brahmán* say to the gods that the harmless serpents would be saved by *Āstīka*, who should be begotten by *Jaratkāru* on *V.*'s sister *Jaratkāru* (I, **38**). *V.* carefully brought up his sister. After the churning of the ocean *V.* addressed *Brahmán*, who confirmed the words of *Elāpatra*. *V.* gave order to watch the ṛshi *Jaratkāru* (I, **39**): I, **37**, 1589 (*pannagottamaḥ*), (1591), 1617 (*pannagottamam*); **38**, 1622, 1637 (*°eḥ sarparājasya Jaratkāruḥ svasā*), 1639; **39**, 1644 (*nāgaḥ*), 1645; 1652 (*nāgendraḥ*).—§ 50 (Jaratkāru): I, **40**, 1658 (*°er bhaginī*, i.e. Jaratkāru).—§ 51 (Āstīkap.): I, **40**, 1661. — § 53 (Jaratkāru): I, **46**, 1864, 1866 (*nāgendraḥ*), 1868; **47**, 1869, 1880 (*°eḥ svasā*, i.e. Jaratkāru) (*V.* gave his sister Jaratkāru to the ascetic Jaratkāru).—§ 54 (do.): I, **47**, 1884 (*°er bhaginī*, i.e. Jaratkāru), 1896 (*bhaginī* . . . *V°eḥ*, do.), 1905.—§ 55 (Āstīka): I, **48**, (1914), 1919 (*pannageçvaram*), 1921 (*nāgendraḥ*). (Jaratkāru bore Āstīka, who was reared in the house of *V.*).—§ 60 (Sarpasattra): I, **53**, 2059, 2060 (*pannagottamam*); **54**, 2067 (*nāgarājasya*), 2075, 2077 (*rājñā*), 2078 (*nāgarājaḥ*), 2080 (*pannagottamaḥ*), 2083, 2084 (*pannagottama*), (2089), 2092 (Āstīka promised *V.* to save the serpents from the curse).—§ 63 (do.): I, **57**, 2145 (enumeration of the serpents of *V.*'s race who fell into the fire), 2148 (*°jā nāgāḥ*).—§ 100 (Aṃçāvat.): I, **65**, 2549 (among the Kādraveyas, sons of Kadrū).—§ 191 (Arjuna): I, **123**, 4828 (present at the birth of Arjuna).—§ 197 (Bhīmasenarasapāna): I, **128**, 5022 (*sarparājānam*), 5025, 5027, 5028, 5031.—§ 268 (Varuṇasabhāv.): II, **9**, 360 (among the serpents in the palace of Varuṇa).—§ 370 (Tīrthayātrāp.): III, **85**, 8176 (*°er lokam*).—§ 374 (do.): III, **85**, 8228 (*Bhogavatī nāma V°es tīrtham*).—§ 549c (Arjuna): IV, **2**, 41 (*sarparājasya*; Arjuna had ravished the sister of *V.*).—§ 564 (Mātalīyop.): V, **103**, 3617 (*Bhogavatī* . . . *V°pālitā*), (γ), 3625 (enumeration of serpents).—§ 565 (Gālavacarita): V, **109**, 3797 (*Bhogavatī* . . . *V°pālitā*); **117**, 3976 (*reme* . . . *yathā* . . . *V°iḥ Çataçīrshāyām*).—§ 576 (Bhagavadgītāp.): VI, **34**, 1232 (*sarpāṇām asmi V°iḥ*, says Kṛshṇa).—§ 603d (Tripura): VII, **202**, 9568 (Çiva made *V.* his bowstring (*guṇa*)).—§ 606 (Tripurākhyāna): VIII, **34**, 1475 (became the pole (*kūbara*) of Çiva's chariot; *bhujagottamaḥ*).—§ 608 (Karṇap.): VIII, **87**χ', 4414 (sided with Arjuna)—§ 615g (Nāgadhanvan): IX, **37**, 2148 (*pannagarājasya*, resided in Nāgadhanvan), 2150 (*pannagottamam*, installed as king of the pannagas).—§ 615u (Skanda): IX, **45**γ, 2518 (*nāgarājaḥ*), 2555 (*pannageçvaraḥ*, gave two serpents as companions to Skanda).—§ 770 (Ānuçāsanik.): XIII, **151**κ, 7119 (among the seven dharaṇīdharāḥ). — § 784b (Uttaṅka): XIV, **58**, 1740 (*°pramukhānāñ ca nāgānām*), 1748 (do.).—§ 793 (Mausalap.): XVI, **4**η, †119. Cf. Nāgarāj, Nāgarāja, Nāgendra, Pannaga, Pannagarāja, Pannagarājan, Pannageçvara, Pannagendra, Sarparāja, Sarparājan.

Vasumanas[1], an ancient king [of Ayodhyā], son of Haryaçva and Mādhavī and grandson of Yayāti. § 267 (Yamasabhāv.): II, **8**, 323 (in the palace of Yama).—§ 378 (Tīrthayātrāp.): III, **94**, 8504 (had practised austerities and visited tīrthas).—§ 467 (Rājanyamahābhāgya): III, **198**, ††13302, ††13312 (did not give Nārada his flowery chariot, though he praised it).—§ 552 (Goharaṇap.): IV, **56**ζ, 1768 (came from heaven to see the encounter).—§ 565 (Gālavacarita): V, **121**, 4057; **122**, 4080 (the daughter's sons of Yayāti caused him to ascend again to heaven by means of their good deeds).—§ 641 (Rājadh.): XII, **68**, 2536, 2537 (*Kauçalyaḥ*), (2540) (Bṛhaspati's discourse to *V.*); **92**, 3465 (instructed by Vāmadeva). Cf. Vasumat, Kausalya[3].

Vasumanas[2] = Vishṇu (1000 names).

Vasumat[1] (Aushadaçvi) = Vasumanas[1]. § 149 (Yayāti): I, **86**, 3539 (*rājñā*); **92**, †3663; **93**, (†3664), †3664 (*Aushadaçviḥ*), (†3666), (†3668) (when Yayāti fell from heaven his daughter's sons, among them *V.*, offered him their worlds; they then all ascended to heaven). Cf. Aushadaçvi.

Vasumat[2], a king at the time of Yudhishṭhira. § 264 (Sabhākriyāp.): II, **4**β, 127 (waited upon Yudhishṭhira).—§ 554 (Sainyodyogap.): V, **4**γ, 84.

Vasumat[3], a rite (according to Nīl.). § 270 (Brahmasabhāv.): II, **11**, 447 (in the palace of Brahmán).

Vasumat[4], a fire, v. Dasyumat (III, 14203).

Vasumat[5], a king, son of Janaka. § 706 (Mokshadh.): XII, **310**, 11519 (*Janakātmajaḥ*).

***Vasumatī** = the earth: III, 10938; XII, 918; XIII, 4096.

Vasumitra, a king. § 130 (Aṃçāvat.): I, **67**, 2677 (incarnation of the Asura Vikshara).

***Vasundharā** (the earth, personif.): I, 2500; XII, 1676, 1850.

Vasunandinī, the wife of the Vasu Dyaus. § 164 (Āpavop.): I, **99**, 3935.

Vasuprada[1], a warrior of Skanda. § 615u (Skanda): IX, **45**η, 2565 (B. *Vasuprabhaḥ*).

Vasuprada[2] = Mahāpurusha (Mahāpurushastava).—Do.[3] = Vishṇu (1000 names).

Vasuretas[1] = Agni: I, 1021, 2168, 8221 (only B.), 8319.—Do.[2] = Çiva: VII, 2878; XIV, 206 (only C., *°suvapushe* (?)).—Do.[3] = Vishṇu (1000 names).

Vasurūpa = Çiva: XIV, 205 (only C., B. has *Bahurūpāya*).

Vasusambhava ("originating from the Vasus") = Bhīshma; VIII, 35.

Vasushena = Karṇa, q.v.
Vasuvega = Çiva (1000 names[2]).
Vasvaukasārā or **Vasvokasārā**, a river. § 459 (Mārkaṇḍeyas.): III, **188***a*, 12908 (°*o*°).—§ 574*f* (Bindusaras): VI, **6**η, 243 (C. °*o*°).
Vasvokasārā, the abode of Kubera. § 595 (Shoḍaçarāj., v. Rantideva): VII, **67**, 2371 (*vyaktaṃ V°eyaṃ*, sc. the mansion of Rantideva, PCR. translates "made of gold" (cf. also Nīl.)).
Vaṭa, a companion of Skanda. § 615*u* (Skanda): IX, **45**δ, 2536 (given to Skanda by Aṃça).
Vāta[1] = Vāyu, q.v.—Do.[2] = Çiva (1000 names[2]).
Vāṭadhāna[1] ("the king of the Vāṭadhānas"). § 130 (Aṃçāvat.): I, **67**, 2699 (among the incarnations from the Krodhavaça gaṇa).—§ 554 (Sainyodyogap.): V, **4**γ, 86.
Vāṭadhāna[2], the country of the Vāṭadhānas. § 555 (Sainyodyogap.): V, **19**, 600 (among the countries which were overrun by the armies).
Vāṭadhāna, pl. (°*āḥ*), a people. § 285 (Nakula): II, **32**, 1190 (*dvijān*, in the west, vanquished by Nakula).—§ 294 (Dyūtap.): II, **49**, 1749 (*brāhmaṇāḥ*, Nīl. and PCR. take *vāṭadhānāḥ* as an appellative).—§ 295 (do.): II, **51**, 1826 (do., do.). — § 574 (Jambūkh.): VI, **9**μ, 354. — § 580 (Bhīshmavadhap.): VI, **56***a*, 2405 (in the army of Duryodhana, C. has by error *Vāra*°).—§ 589 (Droṇābhishekap.): VII, **11**ν, 398 (had formerly been vanquished by Kṛshṇa).—§ 608 (Karṇap.): VIII, **73**, 3650 (had been slain by Arjuna).
Vātādhipa, a king. § 281 (Sahadeva): II, **31**, 1120 (in the south, vanquished by Sahadeva on his digvijaya).
Vātaghna, a son of Viçvāmitra. § 721*b* (Viçvāmitrop.): XIII, **4**β, 253.
Vātaja (?), pl. (°*āḥ*), a people. § 574 (Jambūkh.): VI, **9**μ, 362 (*Vātajāmarathoragāḥ*; PCR. "the Vātagas (!), the Amarathas, and the Uragas"); BR. suggests *Vātajāma-Rathoragāḥ*).
Vātapati, a Vṛshṇi prince. § 232 (Svayaṃvarap.): I, **186**, 7000 (came to the svayaṃvara of Draupadī).
Vātāpi or **Vātāpin**, an Asura, younger brother of Ilvala. § 11 (Anukram.): I, **2**, 442 (°*bhakshaṇaṃ*).—§ 93 (Aṃçāvat.): I, **65**, 2537 (°*ī*, nom., among the sons of Danu).—[§ 316 (Kirmīravadhap.): III, **11**, 422 (*sambhakshya jarayishyāmi yathā 'gastyo mahāsuraṃ*, all. to § 382)].—§ 382 (Agastyop.): III, **96**, 8541, 8543, 8547 (*mesharūpī*), 8549 (*Asuraṃ*), 8551 (*mahāsuraḥ*); **99**, 8616, 8617 (*mahāsuraṃ*), 8620, 8622, 8645 (*Prahrādiḥ*) (Ilvala used to kill brahmans by offering them *V.* transformed to a ram as food and again recalling him to life, but Agastya totally digested him).—§ 389 (Tīrthayātrāp.): III, **109**, 9967 (°*iç ca yathā nītaḥ kshayaṃ*, all. to § 382).—§ 479 (Pativratop.): III, **206**, 13679 (*Agastyaṃ samāsādya jīrṇaḥ . . . mahāsuraḥ*, all. to § 382).—§ 547 (Karṇa): III, **303**, 17014 (*mahāsuraḥ / nihato Brahmadaṇḍena*, all. to § 382).—§ 612 (Hradapraveçap.): IX, **31**ζ, 1755.—§ 649 (Āpaddh.): XII, **141**, 5389 (*Agastyenāsuro jagdho V°iḥ*, all. to § 382). Cf. Asura, Daitya, Ditinandana, Prāhrādi.
Vātaraṃhas = Çiva (1000 names[2]).
Vātasārathi = Agni, q.v. Add: III, 10647.
Vātaskandha, a ṛshi. § 266 (Çakrasabhāv.): II, **7**, 295 (in the palace of Indra).
Vātātmaja ("the son of the Wind") = Bhīmasena: V, 5582; VIII, †4559 (*Bhīmaḥ*).
Vātavega[1], son of Dhṛtarāshṭra. § 130 (Aṃçāvat.): I, **67**, 2737.—§ 182 (Dhṛtarāshṭraputranāmak.): I, **117**, 4549.—§ 608 (Karṇap.): VIII, **51**δδ, 2447; **84**, ξ', 4263 (slain by Bhīmasena).
Vātavega[2], a Suparṇa, son of Garuḍa. § 564 (Mātalīyop.): V, **101**β, 3595.
Vātāyana, pl. (°*āḥ*), a people. § 574 (Jambūkh.): VI, **9**μ, 363 (only C., B. has *Vanāyavaḥ*).
Vātika, a warrior of Skanda. § 615*u* (Skanda): IX, **45**η, 2569.
Vātika, pl. (°*āḥ*) ("aerial beings"): VII, 6132 (*Siddha-Cāraṇa-v°aiḥ*, only C., B. has -°*Pannagaiḥ*), 7188 (*Siddha-Cāraṇa-v°āḥ*); IX, 3090 (°*āç Cāraṇāḥ*), 3307 (°-*Cāraṇāḥ*).
Vātikakhaṇḍa (°**shaṇḍa**, B.), name of a place. § 410 (Plakshāvataraṇag.): III, **130**, 10548 (Nīl. takes *v.* as an appellative = *vātanītaḥ padmādisamūhaḥ*).
Vatsa[1], a prince, son of the Kāçi king Pratardana. § 638*b* (Rāmopākhyāna): XII, **49**, 1795 (*Pratardanasya putraḥ*, brought up among calves (*vatsaiḥ*) in a cowpen).
Vatsa[2], a prince, the ancestor of the Vatsas (?). § 736*b* (Vītahavyop.): XIII, **30**, 1946 (father of Haihaya and Tālajaṅgha af Çaryāti's race).
Vatsa, pl. (°*āḥ*), a people. § 573 (Ambop.): V, **186**, 7369. —§ 578 (Bhīshmavadhap.): VI, **50**π, 2084 (in the army of Yudhishṭhira). — § 604 (Karṇap.): VIII, **8**, 237 (had formerly been vanquished by Karṇa). Cf. Vātsya, pl.
Vatsabhūmi ("the country of the Vatsas"). § 280 (Bhīmasena): II, **30**, 1084 (in the east, conquered by Bhīmasena on his digvijaya).—§ 515 (Karṇadigvijaya): III, **254**, 15243 (conquered by Karṇa).—§ 561 (Yānasandhip.): V, **53**θ, 2107 (°*pān*, in the army of Yudhishṭhira).—§ 573 (Ambopākhyānap.): V, **186**, 7351 (*Siddha-Cāraṇasevitām*), 7366, 7367 (Ambā, with half her body, became transformed to the river of that name in *V.*).
Vatsala[1], a warrior of Skanda. § 615*u* (Skanda): IX, **45**η, 2574.—Do.[2] = Vishṇu (1000 names).
Vatsara = Vishṇu (1000 names).
Vatsarāja ("the king of the Vatsas"). § 232 (Svayaṃvarap.): I, **186**, 7002 (came to the svayaṃvara of Draupadī).
Vatsin = Vishṇu (1000 names).
Vātsya, name of one or more brahmans. § 59 (Sarpasattra): I, **53**, 2049 (among the sadasyas at the snake sacrifice of Janamejaya).—§ 637 (Rājadh.): XII, **47**η, 1592 (among those who surrounded Bhīshma).
Vātsya, pl. (°*āḥ*), a people = Vatsa, pl. § 589 (Droṇābhishekap.): VII, **11**ν, 396 (°-*Gārgya-Karūshān*, had formerly been vanquished by Kṛshṇa).—§ 736*b* (Vītahavyop.): XIII, **30**, 1951 (°*ānāṃ*, sc. *purīṃ*; = the Haihayas (?); reading of C. *Vatsyānāṃ*, B. *Vatsānāṃ*).
Vāyava, adj. (f. °*ī*) ("belonging to Vāyu [i.e. the Wind]"). § 615*u* (Skanda): IX, **46**ι, 2655 (°*yaḥ*, sc. *mātaraḥ*).
Vāyavya, adj. (do.). § 208 (Astradarçana): I, **135**, 5365 (°*ena* — sc. *astreṇa* — *asṛjat vāyuṃ*, sc. Arjuna). — § 258 (Khāṇḍavadahanap.): I, **227**, 8248 (sc. *astraṃ*, employed by Arjuna against the clouds of Indra).—§ 260 (do.): I, **234**, 8472 (sc. *astrāṇi*, will be obtained by Arjuna).—§ 440 (Yakshayuddhap.): III, **164**, 11900 (sc. *astraṃ*, obtained by Arjuna); **167**, 11964 (*mahāstraṃ*, employed by Arjuna). —§ 552 (Goharaṇap.): IV, **58**, 1876 (*astraṃ*, employed by Droṇa).—§ 552*d* (Arjuna): IV, **61**, 1982 (*astraṃ*, obtained by Arjuna from Mātariçvan, i.e. Vāyu).—§ 552 (Goharaṇap.): IV, **64**, 2058 (sc. *astraṃ*).—§ 573 (Ambopākhyānap.): V, **180**, 7173 (*astraṃ*, employed by Bhīshma).—§ 586 (Bhīshmavadhap.): VI, **102**, 4661 (*astraṃ*, employed by Arjuna).—§ 588 (do.): VI, **121**β, 5801 (sc. *astraṃ*, known by Arjuna). —§ 592 (Saṃçaptakavadhap.): VII, **23**ρ, 1038 (sc. *dhanuḥ*, owned by Bhīmasena).—§ 600 (Ghaṭotkacavadhap.): VII,

156, 6837 (*astraṃ*, employed by Açvatthāman); **175,** 7966 (*astraṃ*).—§ 602 (Droṇavadhap.): VII, **188**λ, 8604 (sc. *astraṃ*, employed by Droṇa).

Vāyavyāstra ("the weapon belonging to Vāyu [i.e. the Wind]"). § 586 (Bhīshmavadhap.): VI, **102,** 4662 (employed by Arjuna).—§ 592 (Saṃçaptakavadhap.): VII, **19,** 774 (do.).—§ 600 (Ghaṭotkacavadhap.): VII, **157,** 6953 (employed by Droṇa), 6963 (do., only B.); **161,** 7213 (do.); **162,** 7266 (do.).—§ 605 (Karṇap.): VIII, **20,** 802 (employed by the Pāṇḍya king).—§ 608 (do.): VIII, **89,** †4545 (employed by Arjuna). Cf. Vāyavya, adj.

Vāyu**[1], the god of the wind. § 4 (Anukram.): I, **1,** 112 (all. to § 190), 185 (do.).—§ 37 (Indra): I, **25,** 1288 (Indra identified with *V.*).—§ 46 (Garuḍa): I, **32,** 1478, 1479.—§ 134 (Viçvāmitra): I, **71,** †2936 (assisted Menakā).—§ 190 (Pāṇḍavotpatti): I, **123,** 4769, 4770 (Kuntī invoked *V.* who begat Bhīmasena on her).—§ 221 (Caitrarathap.): I, **170,** 6500 (among the fathers of the Pāṇḍavas).—§ 238 (Pañcendrop.): I, **197,** †7302 (among those who should beget the five Indras when they were re-born as the Pāṇḍavas).—§ 246 (Sundopasundop.): I, **211,** 7682 (*Agnir V°unā saha*).—§ 270 (Brahmasabhāv.): II, **11,** 438 (in the palace of Brahmán).—§ 283*b* (Agni): II, **31,** 1149 (*V°uḥ prāṇaṃ dadātu me*).—§ 317*b* (Kṛshṇa Vāsudeva): III, **12,** 481 (Kṛshṇa becomes *V.*, etc.).—§ 333*o* (Brahmaçiras): III, **40,** 1651 (does not know the Brahmaçiras).—§ 353 (Nalopākhyānap.): III, **76,** 2991, 2995 (bore witness to the truth of Damayantī's words).—§ 425 (Hanūmad-Bhīmasaṃv.): III, **147,** 11193 (father of Hanūmat).—§ 430 (do.): III, **150,** 11286 (*°unā parirakshitaḥ*).—§ 433 (Saugandhikāharaṇa): III, **155,** 11413 (*°samaḥ*, sc. Bhīmasena).—§ 438 (Yakshayuddhap.): III, **162,** 11818 (*°oḥ*, sc. *sutaḥ*, i.e. Bhīmasena).—§ 443 (Nivātakavacayuddhap.): III, **168,** 12020 (Arjuna learnt the use of weapons from *V.*, etc.).—§ 460 (Mārkaṇḍeyas.): III, **191,** 13122 (*°proktaṃ . . . Purāṇaṃ*).—§ 492 (Āṅgirasa): III, **220,** 14162 (*°vagnī prāṇato 'sṛjat*, sc. Pāñcajanya).—§ 506 (Skandayuddha): III, **231,** 14560.—§ 543 (Rāmābhisheka): III, **291a*, 16548, (γ), (16557), 16557 (attested the innocence of Sītā).—§ 561 (Yānasandhip.): V, **61,** 2387, 2399.—§ 564 (Mātalīyop.): V, **105**ε, 3708 (= Bhīmasena (?)).—§ 565 (Gālavacarita): V, **114,** 3896 (*°unā vardhitaṃ*, sc. the gold).—§ 576 (Bhagavadgītāp.): VI, **35,** 1285 (Kṛshṇa identified with *V.*).—§ 592 (Saṃçaptakavadhap.): VII, **19,** 775, 776 (when Arjuna employed the Vāyavyāstra, *V.* bore away the Saṃçaptakas).—§ 603*d* (Tripura): VII, **202,** 9569 (became the wings of the shafts of Çiva).—§ 603 (Nārāyaṇāstramokshap.): VII, **202**υ, 9594 (Çiva identified with *V.*), 9630 (do.).—§ 605 (Karṇap.): VIII, **16,** 635 (*jaitrena vidhināhutaṃ V°r Indram ivādhvare*, sc. *avahat*).—§ 615*u* (Skanda): IX, **44,** 2480 (*Çākho V°mūrtiḥ*); **45,** 2517 (gave two companions to Skanda).—§ 623 (Rājadh.): XII, **15**β, 440.—§ 687 (do.): XII, **47**η, 1506 (among the ṛshis who surrounded Bhīshma), (θ), 1618 (*ati-V°vindra-karmāṇaṃ Govindaṃ*), 1653 (*çarīragaḥ*, Kṛshṇa identified with *V.*), 1678 (*sapta mārgāḥ . . . V°oḥ*).—§ 639 (do.): XII, **51**δ, 1849 (do.).—§ 641 (do.): XII, **72,** 2757, (2758) (discourse with Purūravas).—§ 654*b* (Pavana-çālmalisaṃv.): XII, **156,** (5846); **157,** (5865) (discourse between *V.* and the çālmali).—§ 678 (Mṛtyu-Prajāpatisaṃv.): XII, **259,** †9226 (*devadevaḥ*).—§ 717*b* (Nārāyaṇīya): XII, **341**λ, 13017; **349,** III), 13569 (learnt the religion of Nārāyaṇa from the ṛshi Suparṇa and communicated it to the ṛshis).—§ 737 (Ānuçāsanik.): XIII, **31***a*, 2013.—§ 747*b* (Suvarṇotpatti): XIII, **85,** 4173 (*Brahma-V°vagni-Somānāṃ sālokyaṃ*).—§ 759 (Ānuçāsanik.): XIII, **107**ζ, 5304 (*°oḥ*, sc. *lokaṃ*).—§ 766 (do.): XIII, **128,** (6076).—§ 772*b* (Pavanārjunasaṃv.): XIII, **153,** 7207, 7210 (*devadūtaḥ*), 7212; **154,** (7213), 7231; **155,** (7232); **156,** 7265, 7279; **157,** 7291, 7305, (7313); **158,** (7353) (discourse between *V.* and Arjuna Kārtavīrya).—§ 773*b* (Kṛshṇa Vāsudeva): XIII, **159,** †7388 (Kṛshṇa identified with Çiva).—§ 774*d* (Çiva): XIII, **161**δ, 7496 (Çiva identified with *V.*).—§ 775 (Ānuçāsanik.): XIII, **166***a*, 7636.—§ 795 (Svargārohaṇap.): XVIII, **4**κ, 132 (*mūrtimataḥ*).

Cf. also the following synonyms:—

Āçāvaha, q.v.

Analasakha ("the friend of Anala [i.e. Agni]"): V, 3819; XII, 8418.

***Anila**: I, 2589 (one of the Vasus, husband of Çivā), 8360 (Agni identified with *A.*); III, 11195 (*prītir A°syāgninā yathā*); V, 5506 (*°o vā vahed Meruṃ*), 5551 (do.); VIII, †5042 (*Agny-anilendu-Bhānavaḥ*); XII, 5822, 5826.

***Çvasana**, q.v.

Devadeva, q.v.

***Marut**: XII, 5831.

***Māruta**: I, 897 (*mano-M°raṃhasā*), 1333, 1478, 2444 (father of Bhīmasena), 2935, 2939, 2940, ††3814 (father of Bhīmasena), 3846, 5844 (*nāvaṃ . . . mano M°gāminīm*), 5886 (*Tārkshya-M°raṃhasaḥ Bhīmasya*); II, 94; V, 7181 (*°pratimair gatau*); VII, 1035 (v. Draupadeya, pl.), 1694 (do.), 7227 (*mano-M°raṃhasaḥ*, sc. *turaṅgamān*); IX, 1188 (*mano-M°raṃhasaḥ*, sc. *rathāḥ*), 2715 (*vavau*), 2823 (do.); XII, 5812, 5823, 5827, 5856, 6778 (*Agni-M°au*), 6779 (*Agni-M°saṃyogāt*), 6794 (*Agni-M°-toyebhyaḥ*), 6795 (*Agni-M°toyānāṃ*), 6808 (*Agni-M°au*), 6813, 6818, 6838 (*Agni-M°au*), 6864, 6907, 6909 (*Agni-M°au*), 8790 (*°ākṛtiḥ*), 9089, 9091 (*°ātmā*), 10837 (*Agny-Açvi-M°āḥ*), 12080 (*Yamasya yaḥ puraḥsaraḥ*), 12081 (*antakaḥ*), 12203, 12587 (*mano-M°raṃhasaṃ*), 12626 (*°ād ūrdhvaṃ*), 12853 (*°vegavān*); XIII, 308 (*Candrārka-M°āḥ*), 1369, 3833, 5284 (*°oçanaṃ* (?), adj. sc. *lokaṃ* (?)), 7210 (*prāha*), 7352, †7393 (*avanī-M°au*); XIV, †271, 1120 (*dvitīyaṃ . . . bhūtaṃ*), 1143 (do.), 2235.

***Mātariçvan**: I, 4920 (*°vā dadau putraṃ Bhīmaṃ*, sc. to Pāṇḍu); II, 928; III, 11081 (*Pārtham ātmajaṃ M°aḥ*, i.e. Bhīmasena), 11695 (do.); IV, 1982 (Arjuna had obtained the Vāyavya weapon from *M.*); V, 2712 (*°eva Pāvakaṃ*, sc. *santejayan*), 3152, 7127; IX, 2245 (husband of Sukanyā and father of Maṅkaṇaka); XII, 271, 2750 (*Purūravasa Ailasya saṃvādaṃ M°aḥ*), (2752), 5840 (*saṅkāçaṃ M°aḥ*), 5855 (*asamaṃ M°ā*), 8798 (*sadharmā M°aḥ*), 12313 (do.); XIII, †7373 (identified with Kṛshṇa); XIV, 482.

***Pavana**: I, 1250 (Garuḍa identified with *P.*); IV, 1580; V, 3819 (*°sya niveçanaṃ*, in the west); VI, 1235 (*°ḥ pavatām asmi*, says Kṛshṇa); VIII, 4418; XII, 1756, 5804, 5813, 5814, 5816, 5841, 5850, 5851, 5853, 5859, 11616; XIII, 7186 (*°sya saṃvādam Arjunasya ca*), 7240, 7326.

***Prabhañjana**: XII, 5829.

***Samīraṇa**: III, †10257 (among the fathers of the Pāṇḍavas), †14755 (*°enātha samo balena S°syaiva sutaḥ*, i.e. Bhīmasena); VIII, †2854; XII, 5829, 5845, 5858, 5859.

***Vāta**: I, 2746 (father of Bhīmasena), 5908 (do.); III, †11386 (*°ena Kuntyāṃ . . . sujātaḥ*, sc. Bhīmasena), †11914 (Arjuna obtained weapons from *V.*), 14162 (*°-Rasāharau*, created by Pāñcajanya from his mouth); IX, 301 (*jave bale ca sadṛçam Aruṇānuja-V°yoḥ*).

Vāyu[2] = Sūrya: III, 147.—Do.[3] = Skanda: III, 14643.—Do.[4] = Çiva (1000 names[1–2]).—Do.[5] = Vishṇu (1000 names).

Vāyubala, son of Maṅkaṇaka. § 615*j* (Maṅkaṇaka): IX, **38***β*, 2221.

Vāyucakra, son of Maṅkaṇaka. § 615*j* (Maṅkaṇaka): IX, **38***β*, 2222.

Vāyuhan, son of Maṅkaṇaka. § 615*j* (Maṅkaṇaka): IX, **38***β*, 2221.

Vāyujvāla, son of Maṅkaṇaka. § 615*j* (Maṅkaṇaka): IX, **38***β*, 2222.

Vāyuloka ("the world of Vāyu [i.e. the Wind]"). § 364 (Tīrthayātrāp.): III, **83**, 6075.—§ 746 (Ānuçāsanik.): XIII, **79***κ*, 3772.

Vāyumaṇḍala, son of Maṅkaṇaka. § 615*j* (Maṅkaṇaka): IX, **38***β*, 2221.

Vāyuputra[1] ("the son of Vāyu [i.e. the Wind]") = Bhīmasena: III, 11170; V, 3707 (*Bhīmaḥ*); VII, 5518; VIII, 3885.—Do.[2] (do.) = Hanūmat, q.v.

Vāyuretas, son of Maṅkaṇaka. § 615*j* (Maṅkaṇaka): IX, **38***β*, 2222.

Vāyusuta ("the son of Vāyu [i.e. the Wind]") = Bhīmasena): III, 11095, 11116, †12321.

Vāyutanaya (do.) = Bhīmasena: III, 11169. — Do.[2] = Hanūmat, q.v.

Vāyuvāhana[1] = Çiva (1000 names[2]). — Do.[2] = Vishṇu (1000 names).

Vāyuvega[1], a prince. § 130 (Aṃçāvat.): I, **67**, 2699 (among the incarnations from the Krodhavaçagaṇa).—§ 554 (Sainyodyogap.): V, **4***γ*, 80.

Vāyuvega[2], a son of Dhṛtarāshṭra (?). § 232 (Svayaṃvarap.): I, **186**, 6982 (came to the svayaṃvara of Draupadī). Cf. Vātavega.

Vāyuvega[3], son of Maṅkaṇaka. § 615*j* (Maṅkaṇaka): IX, **38***β*, 2221.

Vāyvātman = Kṛshṇa: XII, 1654.

Veda, a brahman. § 14 (Paushyap.): I, **3**, ††684 (disciple of Āyoda Dhaumya).—§ 16 (do.): *V.* served his master with hard work a very long time uncomplainingly. He got himself three pupils, and never told them to perform any work, that they might not experience such woe as he had himself experienced from his preceptor. He was appointed *upādhyāya* by the kings *Janamejaya* and *Paushya*: I, **3**, ††740, ††742, ††746.—§ 17 (Uttaṅka): I, **3**, ††748 (preceptor of Uttaṅka).—§ 702 (Mokshadh.): XII, **297***δ*, 10874.

Veda, mostly pl. (*°āḥ*), the sacred knowledge, esp., the Vedic literature: I, 18 (*°ārthaiḥ*), 21 (*caturbhiḥ*), 48, 54 (*vyasya Vedaṃ*, sc. Vyāsa), 62 (*sāṅgopanishadāṃ*), 66 (*°ādhyātmaṃ*), 107 (*sarva-V°vidāṃ varaḥ*), 122 (*nikhilān*), 258, 260 (sg.), 261 (*Kārshṇaṃ V°ṃ*, i.e. the Mhbhr.), 264 (*caturaḥ*), 265 (*caturbhyaḥ sarahasyebhyaḥ*), 267 (*°vidhiḥ*), 309 (*loka-V°āçrayeva vāk*), 310 (*°ārthaiḥ*), 492 (*°vidushā*), 528 (do.), 645 (*caturaḥ*), †658 (*°vidushe*), ††696 (*sarve*), ††739 (do.), 872 (*°pāragaḥ*), 895 (*°dṛshṭena karmaṇā*), 917 (*°oktena vidhānena*), 1009 (*°-Vedāṅgavid*), 1010, 1013 (*°-Vedāṅgapāragāt*), 1061 (*°-Vedāṅgapāragaḥ*), 1374 (*sarve*), 1831 (*°-Vedāṅgapāragaḥ*), 1910 (do.), 1928 (*sāṅgān*), 2025 (*°vidvāṃsaḥ*), 2045 (*°vidāṃ varaḥ*), 2050 (*°pāragaḥ*), 2066 (*°vittamaṃ*), 2141 (*°vidaḥ*), 2202 (*°āçrayāḥ kathāḥ*), 2210 (*sāṅgān setitihāsān*), 2211 (*°adhyayanena*), 2212 (*vivyāsaikaṃ caturdhā yo V°ṃ V°vidāṃ varaḥ*, sc. Vyāsa), 2214 (*°-Vedāṅgapāragaiḥ*), 2236 (*°e dhanushi ca*), 2256 (*°ādhyayana-*), 2298 (*°aiḥ sammitaṃ*), 2300 (*Kārshṇaṃ V°ṃ*, i.e. the Mhbhr.), 2314 (*°ānāṃ pāragaḥ*), 2329 (*°aiḥ sammitaṃ*), 2417 (*vivyāsa V°ān*, sc. Vyāsa), 2418, 2421 (*°ārthavid*), 2473 (*sāṅgopanishadān*), 2474, 2570 (*°vidaḥ*), 2707 (*Dhanurvede V°e ca; °vidaḥ*), 2711 (*°vid*), 2743 (*°vidaḥ*), 2885 (*°pāragaiḥ*), 3049 (quotation of two çlokas), 3096 (*sarva-V°ādhigamanaṃ*), 3140 (sg., *sāṅgaṃ*), 3372 (sg.), 3426 (*°pāragaḥ*), †3583, ††3840 (*°parāḥ*), ††3841 (*°sampannāḥ*), 3842 (*°aiḥ sammitaṃ*), 4001 (*sāṅgān*), 4136 (*°pāragaiḥ*), 4176 (do.), 4177, 4182 (sg., *shaḍaṅgaṃ*), 4193 (*°vid*), 4195 (*°-Vedāṅgapāragaḥ*), 4236 (*yo vyasya V°āṃç caturaḥ*, sc. Vyāsa), 4245, 4355 (*Dhanurvede V°e ca*), 4356 (*°-Vedāṅgatattvajñāḥ*), 4555 (*°vidaḥ*), 4742 (do.), 4977 (*°oktān saṃskārān*), 5070 (*°-çāstrārthapāragaṃ*), 5073 (*°ādhyayane*), 5074, 5096 (*vidushe*), 5106, 5113 (*°-Vedāṅgavidvān*), 6087 (*Brāhmaṃ V°ṃ*), 6158 (*°çrutiṃ*), 6246 (*loka-V°viruddhaṃ*), 6332, 6494 (*°vidaḥ*), 6499 (*°e dhanushi ca*), 6510 (sg., *shaḍaṅge*), 6645 (*°dharmavid*), 6756 (*°ādhyayananiḥsvanaṃ*), 6758 (sg., *sāṅgasya*), 6759, 6765 (*sarva-V°vidāṃ vara*), 6777, 6802 (*°vidāṃ*), 6823 (sg., *shaḍaṅgaç cākhilaḥ*), 6863 (*°vidaḥ*), 6866 (*sarva-V°vidāṃ varaḥ*), 6913 (*°vid*), 6919 (*sarva-V°vidāṃ varaḥ*), 6922 (*°ārthatattvajñaḥ*), 7245 (*loka-V°viruddhaṃ*), 7257 (*dharme . . . loka-V°virodhake*), 7258 (*loka-V°yoḥ*), †7339 (*°pāragaḥ*), †7340 (do.), 7582 (*sarva-V°vidāṃ varaḥ*), 7776 (*°pāragāḥ*), 7777 (*°-Vedāṅgavidvāṃsaḥ*), 8032 (*°jñaḥ*), 8048 (*°ādhyayanaṃ*), 8054, 8056, 8141 (only B.); II, 114 (*°-Vedāṅgapāragāḥ*), 136 (*°opanishadāṃ vettā*, sc. Nārada), 150 (*°pāragaḥ*), 244, 246, 247, 277 (*°yajñaiḥ*), 818 (*°pāragāḥ*), 1146, 1237 (*iva*), 1240 (*°-Vedāṅgapāragāḥ*), 1313 (*°sampannaiḥ*), 1387 (*°-Vedāṅgavijñānaṃ*), 1395 (*agnihotramukhāḥ*), 1574 (*°çrutiṃ*), 1788/9 (only B.), 1908 (*°āntāvabhṛthaplutāḥ*), 1918 (*°pāragāḥ*), 2055 (*°vidaḥ*); III, 31 (*°oktāḥ*, sc. *guṇāḥ*), 120 (*°vacanaṃ*, quoted), 132 (*°pāragāḥ*), 169 (do.), 982 (*°vidaṃ*), 1100, 1167 (sg.), 1168 (*°ādhyāyī*), 1178 (*°-çāstrārthanindakaḥ*), 1309 (*°dhāraṇaṃ*), 1447 (*°-Vedāṅgapāragān*), 1454 (sg., *uttamaṃ*), 1760 (*°çrutivarjitāḥ*), 1808 (*sāṅgopanishadān . . . caturākhyān*), 2036 (*°vacanaṃ*), 2037, 2045 (*°dharmān*), 2074 (*°vid*), 2247 (*caturaḥ*), 2417 (*sāṅgopāṅgāḥ*), 2450 (*°vid*), 2481 (*°-Vedāṅgapāragaḥ*), 2575 (*°pāragaiḥ*), 3071 (*°-Vedāṅgapāragaiḥ*), 4025 (*yathā ca V°ān Sāvitrī*, sc. *na jahau*), 8189 (*nashṭeshu*, when the *V.* had been lost Sārasvata taught them again to the ascetics), 8220, 8225 (*°vacanāt*), 8284 (*°vidaḥ*), 8350 (*°vidaḥ*), 8385 (*°jñau; °vidvāṃsau*), 8421 (sg., *Gāndharvaṃ*), 8526 (*°pāragāḥ*), 8641 (*sāṅgopanishadān*), 8676 (*sopanishadaḥ*), 10168 (sg.), 10171 (*°ādhyayane*), 10455, †10606 (*sāṅgan*, only C.), †10626 (*°prabhāvena*), †10628 (*sarasvatīṃ . . . V°jushṭāṃ*), †10640 (*°çīlaiḥ*), †10662 (sg.), †10663 (*sarva-V°eshu*), 10707 (*°jñānāya*), 10710, 10712, 10717, 10729 (*°ārthaṃ*), 10732, 10734, 10745 (*°vidaḥ*), 10781, 10812 (sg., *Saurasya*), 10816, 11053 (*°-Vedāṅgapāragaiḥ*), 11214 (*nashṭā V°çrutir iva*), 11244 (*eka-Vedāḥ*), 11251–2 (*caturdhā V°a eva ca . . . catur-Vedās tri-Vedāḥ . . . dvi-Vedāç caika-Vedāḥ*), 11253 (*eka-Vedasya cājñānād V°ās te bahavaḥ kṛtāḥ*), 11258 (*°ācārāḥ*), 11292, 11293, 12300, 12485 (sg.), 12489 (*°-Vedāṅgapāragaḥ*), †12741 (*°vidaḥ*), 12825 (PCR. reads *devāḥ*), 12958 (*°vidushaḥ*), 12973 (sg.), 13034 (*°nindakāḥ*), ††13264 (*°ādhyayanasampannaḥ*), †13281, 13356 (*°vikrayiṇe*), 13362 (*nāvaṃ V°mayīṃ*), 13368 (*°pāragaiḥ*), 13437 (*dur-V°ā vā su-V°ā vā*), 13462, 13463, 13465 (sg.), 13466 (*°oktam āyur devānāṃ*), 13495, 13652 (*°ādhyāyī*), 13653 (*sāṅgopanishadaḥ*), 13689, 13752, 13767 (*°syopanishat satyaṃ*), 13783 (*°oktaḥ paramo dharmaḥ*), 14022 (*catvāraḥ*), 14037 (*°occāraṇakāryārthaṃ*), 14053 (*°ādhyāyī*),

14180 (°pāragāḥ), 14228 (dhishṇyān V°oktān), 14237, 14693 (°vādinaḥ), †14743 (°vidaḥ), 15148 (°-Vedāṅgapāragāḥ), 15281 (°pāragāḥ), 15825 (°pāragaiḥ), 15830 (°sammitam), 15901 (°vidaḥ), 15948 (sarahasyeshu), 16868 (sāṅgāḥ), 16927 (°vid), 17061 (°vittama), 17205 (°vidvāṃsaḥ), 17390, 17475 (°vidaḥ); IV, 1558, 1590 (catvāraḥ), 1592, 1829 (catvāraḥ), 2354 (°ādhyayana-[B. °āvabhṛtha]-sampannāḥ); V, 124 (°vid), 231, 268, 550 (sg.), 559 (°sammitam), †773 (sg.), †832 (sarva-V°ān), †878, 1032 (°vidaḥ), 1127, 1131 (brāhmaṇā V°bandhavāḥ), 1284 (sg.), 1312 (°puṇyam), 1342 (sarva-V°eshu), 1421, 1511, 1524, †1558, †1592, †1593, 1604 (°vidaḥ), †1622, 1626, †1627, 1633 (°vidvāṃsaḥ), 1661–2 (ākhyāna-pañcamair V°aiḥ . . . catur-Vedās tri-Vedāḥ . . . dvi-Vedāç caika-Vedāç ca), 1663 (ekasya V°syājñānād V°ās te bahavaḥ kṛtāḥ, C. has vedya°), 1664 (sg.), †1670 (°vedyasya), †1671 (sg.), †1672 (pl. and sg.), †1673 (do.), †1674 (do., °vidaḥ), †1675, 1678 (sg.), 1683, 1736, 1785, 3276 (°vidbhyaḥ), 3458 (°vratasamanvitaḥ), 3770, 3796 (°pāragā (°āḥ, B.)), 3797, 4731 (°pāragāḥ), 4732 (°vādān), 4912 (°ādhyayananisvanam), 5102 (°vidaḥ), 5449, 5504 (Brāhme dhanushi cācāryam V°yor antagaṃ dvayoḥ), 5549 (do.), 6054 (°vidvāṃsaḥ), 6063 (°vidāṃ vara), 7126, 7127 (°mātaraḥ), 7132 (°vid), 7147, 7511 (°pāragam), 7597 (°āntāvabhṛthasnātāḥ); VI, 5 (°ādhyayana-sampannāḥ), 36 (sarva-V°vidāṃ çreshṭhaḥ), 122 (sg.), 169 (°oktāḥ, sc. paçavaḥ), 551 (°-Vedāṅgatattvajñam), 802 (°çruti-mahāpuṇyo, sc. Durgā), 920 (°vādaratāḥ), †1152 (°vidaḥ), 1226 (°ānāṃ Sāmavedo 'smi, says Kṛshṇa), †1294 (°yajnādhyayanaiḥ), 1299, 1383 (°vid), †1397 (°vid), 1400 (sg.), 1532/3 (only B.), 2001 (°vid), 2958, 3002 (only B.); VII, 169 (sg., shaḍaṅgam), 289 (caturaḥ . . . sāṅgān), 296 (°kāmānāṃ), 988 (Dhanurvede Brāhme V°e ca pāragam), 2027 (°ādhyayanam), 2153 (°-Vedāṅgapāragāḥ), 2176 (°pāragān), 2198 (°vidyāvratasnātāḥ), 2238 (caturbhiḥ), 2288 (°-Vedāṅga-pāragāḥ), 2298 (sarva-V°vid), 2323 (°pāragāḥ), 2336, 2358, 2595 (°ādhyāyinam), 2603/4 (only B.), 2641, 2898 (°vidvāṃsau), 2925 (°vidaḥ), 2926 (°vratasnātān), 3766, 6470 (caturaḥ), 6474 (only B.), 8396, 8731 (°-Vedāṅgavidushaḥ), 8975 (°snātaḥ), 9126 (sāṅgāḥ), 9438 (°āvāsam, so B., C. has by error °āvyāsam), 9493 (°pāragaḥ), 9566 (caturaḥ), 9599 (°jñāḥ), 9601 (°āḥ sāṅgopanishadaḥ, B., C. has by error °āṅgāḥ sopanishadaḥ), 9612 (°e cāsya samākhyātam Çatarudriyam), 9639 (°aiç ca sammitam), 9647 (sg.); VIII, †1524 (caturaḥ), 2069, 2074 (°pāragaiḥ), 4113 (ākhyānapañcamāḥ), 4426 (°vidaḥ), †4573 (do.), 4743 (°āntāvabhṛthaplutaḥ), †5045 (°avaptiḥ); IX, 266, 305 (saṅgaṃç ca caturaḥ), 2086, 2191, 2201 (sg.) [2202 (nānāsvādhyāyavedinaḥ)], 2288, 2289, 2290 (°yuktaḥ), 2470 (sg., caturmūrtiḥ), 2513 (sanātanāḥ), 2832/3 (only B.), 2927 (Sārasvata taught the ṛshis the Vedas [which they had forgotten]), 2947 (do.), 2965 (do.), 2966 (do.), 2975 (do.), 2976 (°svādhyāyakāraṇāt), 3653; X, 123 (sg., agryam), 734 (°vratam), 786 (°pramāṇena); XI, 24 (°niçcayāḥ), 264 (°vidaḥ), 314, 666 (catvāraḥ); XII, 5 (°vidvāṃsaḥ), 102 (°vidyāpradaḥ), 231, 233 (°vādāḥ), 296 (°vādasya), 337 (°vāda-; °oktam), 338 (°yānena C., but read with B. deva-yānena; °niçcayāḥ), 343, 384 (°niçcayān), 456 (°nindakāḥ), 591 (°vādān), 657 (°jñānam), 661 (do.), †729, 735 (°pāragaḥ), †766, 775 (karmāṇi V°oktāni), 904 (°-Vedāṅgapāragaḥ), 1137 (°niçcitaḥ, sc. dharmaḥ), 1187 (°pāragāḥ), 1216 (loka-V°viruddhāni), 1224 (°āntagam), 1225 (°pramāṇa-), 1245 (°vide), 1303 (loka-V°yoḥ), 1312 (°-çāstrajñāḥ), 1348 (°vidāṃ varaḥ), 1354 (aṅgopavṛṃhitān), 1412 (°vidushām), 1424 (°vidvāṃsaḥ), 1461 (°ādhyayanasampannān), 1569 (sāṅgāṃç ca caturaḥ), 1592 (°vidushā), 1828 (Dhanurvede ca V°e ca), 1840 (°oktaḥ, sc. dharmaḥ ?), 1903 (catur-V°vidām), 1943 (°oktāç caiva ye dharmāḥ), 1953 (°pravādaḥ), 2015 (°āntagam), 2220 (°-Vedāṅgavid), 2262, 2326 (°m adhītya), 2333, 2338 (°ānāṃ dhāraṇam), 2342 (sg.), †2360, †2365 (°vādāḥ), 2371, 2375, †2379 (sg.), 2386 (loka-V°ottarāḥ), 2425 (°dharmāḥ), 2434 (°dharma-kriyāḥ), 2465 (°ādhyayananityatvam), 2491 (°ādhyayana-çīlānām), 2560, 2626 (°-Vedāṅgavid), †2783 (°m adhīte), 2881 (°vidaḥ), 2931 (°balinaḥ), 2968 (°vacanam), 2971, 2972, 2980 (only B.), 3373, 3409, 3619, 3651, 3994 (trayaḥ), 4066 (vidyā-V°vratasnātāḥ), 4445, 4459 (°ātmā; °pratyayaḥ), 4461 (°vishayātmakaḥ sc. vyavahāraḥ), 4462 (°prasūtātmā), 4464 (sg.), 4465 (sg.), 4515, 4662, 4697 (°vākyam), 5194 (°vidaḥ), †5407 (sg.), 5450 (°vidyāsamanvitān), 5618 (°niçcitān), 5625 (sg.), 5641, 5965, 6001, 6039 (sarva-V°āntagaḥ), 6042, 6056 (°vid), 6061 (°pāragaḥ), 6140 (°paṭhitam dharmam), 6240 (°opavedeshu), 6271 (°nindakaḥ), 6304 (°pāragaḥ), 6311 (°pāragān), 6314 (°vid), †6527, 6731 (°oktasyaiva dharmasya), 6736 (°nindakaḥ), 6780 (°mayo nidhiḥ), 6951 (°ādhyayana-sampannaḥ), 6954 (°ādhyayanasaṅgataḥ), 6955 (°ādhyayana-sampannaḥ), 6956 (tyakta-V°ḥ), ††6991 (°ābhyāsa-), 6992 (sg.), 7158 (°vādāḥ), 7202, 7265, 7266, 7268 (read with B. Vedāḥ stobhā(ḥ)), 7340, 7365, †7385, 7551 (°vidyāvidhātāram Brahmāṇam), 7647, 7651 (°vidaḥ), 7657 (°-çāstrāṇi), 7660 (setihāsān), 7661 (°vid), 7708 (°vidvāṃso V°okteshu vyavasthitāḥ), 7766 (°-çāstrajñāḥ), 7872 (°vidaḥ), 7922 (çabdāḥ), 8005 (a-V°oktavratopetāḥ; °okteshu), 8166 (vidhinā V°dṛshṭena), 8172, 8272 (°vrataparāḥ), 8398 (°vidaḥ), 8406 (do.), 8465 (°çrutibhiḥ), 8484 (akhilān sāṅgopanishadaḥ), 8503 (°vādaḥ; °syaiva yad phalam), 8533, 8534 (°mayī, sc. vāk ?), 8535, 8536 (°çabdebhyaḥ; pl.), 8538 (°vādeshu; °darçibhiḥ), 8545, 8546, 8549 (°vādāḥ), 8553, 8576 (°pārage), 8577 (akhilān), 8613 (trayīvidyām . . . V°eshūktām), 8614 (°vādeshu), 8627 (°yajñaplavena), 8650 (sarva-V°jñaḥ), 8676, 8678, 8704 (°jñāni; sg.), 8705 (°jñāni), 8706, 8715 (°vidhiḥ), 8723 (°vādeshu; °darçibhiḥ), 8726, 8727, 8729 (a-V°dharmāḥ), 8730, 8733, 8755 (°ātmā), 8804 (°vacanam, quoted), 8809, 8826 (sg.), 8833 (°vacanam), 8851 (°opavāsena), 8861 (°vidyā-vratasnātāḥ; °pāragāḥ), 8880 (°dṛshṭaḥ, sc. svargaḥ), †8944, 8963 (rahasyam sarva-V°ānām), 8967 (a-V°vidushe), 9065, 9066 (sarva-V°vid), 9074 (°syopanishat satyam), 9081 (°vid), 9231, 9263 (°vādāḥ), 9265, 9401 (°vādān), 9415 (sg., Brāhmam), 9473 (°kṛtāḥ çrutīḥ), 9475, 9477, 9604, 9606, 9607, 9628, 9631 (iti V°ā vadantīha), 9635 (°vādavidaḥ), 9651, 9652 (°vādaparijñānam), 9653 (°-çāstraiḥ), 9654, 9674 (°pramāṇyam), 9679 (°vādāḥ), 9702 (°vādam), 9705, 9707, 9708 (sg.), 9722, 9749 (pl.; °vidaḥ), 9750 (sg.; °vidaḥ), 9752, 9755, †9933, 10400 (°opanishadam gaṇaiḥ), 10467 (sg., shaḍaṅgāt), 10573 (°ādhyayanam), 10710 (çabdo Vedāçrayaḥ), 10766, 10808, 10876 (°vidaḥ), †10930, 10940, 11004 (°syo-panishat satyam), 11015, 11109, 11143 (°vādān), †11205, 11216 (°pāragaiḥ), 11333 (sg.), 11334 (pramāṇam . . . sva-V°oktam; V°-çāstradvayam), 11339 (°-çāstranidarçanam), 11340 (°-çāstrayoḥ), 11341 (sg.), 11391 (°pāragaiḥ), 11463 (sg.), †11498 (a-V°nishṭhasya), 11531 (°vid), 11573, 11574 (°-Vedāṅgapāragaiḥ), 11681, 11733 (sakhilaḥ, i.e. the Yajurveda), 11742 (sva-V°dakshiṇāyārthe), 11750 (sg. = the Yajurveda), 11771, 11772 (sāṅgopāṅgān), 11773 (°vedyam; °bhāravahaḥ), 11774 (°vid), 11840 (°vittamam), 11856 (sg.), 11857 (°vidaḥ), 11950 (°cakshuḥ), 12208 (sarahasyāḥ sasaṅgrahāḥ), 12209 (°-Vedāṅgabhāshyavid), 12210 (sarahasyān sasaṅgrahān), 12274 (°parāyaṇaḥ), 12276, 12281 (°ārtha-tattvena), 12337, 12345 (°ādhyayanasampannāḥ), 12346 (sāṅgeshu), 12352, 12353 (°ārthatattvavid), 12355 (sg.), 12360

(°*syādhyayanaṃ*), 12361 (pl.; °*pāragaṃ*), 12368, 12378 (°*dhvani*°), 12380 (°*vādavicakshaṇa*), 12384, 12385, 12386 (°*ābhyāsa-*), 12387 (°*ābhyāsaṃ*), 12393, 12420, 12422 (°*ārthaṃ*), 12598 (°*ābhyāsarate*), 12674 (°*eshu sa-Purāṇeshu sāṅgopāṅgeshu gīyase*, sc. Nārāyaṇa), 12693, †12698, ††12707, 12723 (*caturbhiḥ*), 12872 (*catur-V°ān*), 12918, 12920 (°*ānāṃ mātaram . . . Sarasvatīṃ*), 12969 (°*çrutiḥ; sa-V°āḥ*), 12976 (*mahopanishadaṃ catur-V°samanvitaṃ*), 12983 (*Purāṇaṃ V°sammitaṃ*), 13004 (°*vidaḥ*), 13007 (°*-Vedāṅgavid*), 13023 (*a-V°vidushā*), 13027 (*Mahābhāratapañcamān*), 13028, 13041 (°*-Vedāṅgasaṃyuktān yajñān*), 13052 (°*kalpitaṃ*), 13054 (*-Vedāṅgabhūshitāṃ*), 13061 (°*dṛshṭena vidhinā*), 13068 (°*kalpitān*), 13069 (°*sūtre*), 13072, 13076 (°*vidaḥ*; °*ācāryāḥ*), 13095, 13099, 13118 (°*çabdaiḥ*), 13120 (*catur-V°odgatābhiḥ*), [13124 (*sarvavedī*)], 13134 (*sa-Purāṇeshu*), 13173, 13183 (*caturaḥ sāṅgopāṅgān*), ††13205 (°*-Purāṇetihāsaprāmāṇyāt*), 13241 (°*vidushaḥ*; °*çabdārthacintakāḥ*), 13244 (°*jñaiḥ*), 13256 (°*vidaḥ*), 13279, 13312 (°*nidhim* (°*ir*, C. by error) = *Vyāsa*), 13316, 13364 (*sāṅgān*), 13382 (*Sadbhūtotpādakaṃ . . . sthānaṃ V°sañjñikaṃ*), 13407 (°*çrutiḥ*), 13457 (*Purāṇaṃ V°sammitaṃ*), 13477 (*caturaḥ*), 13478, 13479, 13480, 13481, 13482, 13483, 13485, 13494 (°*cakshuḥ*, i.e. Brahmán), 13495, 13496 (°*kāryārthaṃ*), 13498 (°*ānāṃ ālayaḥ*), 13506, 13507 (*akhilān*), 13509 (°*ānāṃ ālayaṃ*, the Vedas were recovered by Vishṇu in his form with the horsehead), 13510, 13516, 13520 (°*āpaharaṇena*), 13521 (°*satkṛtaḥ*, sc. Brahmán), 13528 (*Purāṇaṃ V°sammitaṃ*), 13529 (°*nidhiḥ*), 13530, 13551 (*sahopanishadān*), 13629 (°*āraṇyakaṃ*), 13637 (do.), †13640 (°*mahānidhānaṃ*, i.e. Vyāsa), 13645 (°*ārthān*), 13649 (*sāṅgān*), 13650 (°*ārthān*), 13651 (do.), 13677 (°*ākhyāne*), 13678, 13682, †13687 (°*nidhiḥ*), 13704 (°*ācāryaḥ*), †13711 (*sarve*), 13717 (*sarva-V°shu*), †13761 (*sarve V°āḥ sarahasyāḥ*), 13776 (sg.), 13780 (*svadharmaṃ V°oktaṃ*), 13797 (°*vrataparāḥ*), 13852 (°*dhāraṇaṃ*); XIII, 91 (*Dhanurvede ca V°e ca nirataḥ*), 101 (°*-Vedāṅgapāragaḥ*), 118 (*vidhinā V°dṛshṭena*), 135 (*vidhinā . . . V°oktena*), 363 (*sarva-V°ān*), 469 (*Atharvavede V°e ca*), 652 (°*-Vedāṅgapāragaiḥ*), 701 (°*-Vedāṅgapāragaḥ*), 915 (*Sāmavedaç ca V°ānāṃ*, sc. *asi*, sc. Çiva), 990 (so PCR. instead of *devāḥ*, C. and B.), 1006, 1012 (*vedāt*, only B., C. has *vidvān*), 1080 (°*vidaḥ*), 1102 (°*-çāstra-Purāṇoktāḥ*, sc. *gatayaḥ*), 1115 (°*-Vedāṅgasambhavaiḥ*, sc. *nāmabhiḥ*), 1116 (°*kṛtātmanā*), 1128 (*catur-V°samanvitaṃ*), 1293 (°*ena sammitaṃ*), 1339 (°*ānāṃ . . . vaktā*, sc. Vyāsa), 1350 (°*vibhūshitaṃ*), †1369 (°*vāhāḥ*), †1378 (*kṛtsnān*), 1387 (quoted), †1542 (*sarve*), †1547 (°*pāragāḥ*), 1561, 1566 (*sāṅgāṃç ca caturaḥ*), 1618 (*a-V°vratacāritrāḥ*), 1644 (pl.; °*vikrayiṇaḥ*), 1749 (°*āntagaḥ*), 1753 (*rahasyaṃ V°ānāṃ*, "gods," PCR.), 1781 (°*sambaddhāḥ*, sc. *kathāḥ*), 1948 (*Dhanurvede ca V°e ca*), 1970 (sg. *kṛtsnaṃ*), 2003 (°*-Vedāṅgapāragaḥ*), 2015 (°*vidaḥ*; °*parāyaṇān*), 2020 (sg.), 2025 (sg.), 2037 (sg., *ekaṃ*), 2179 (*sarvān*), 2194, 2195 (°*nindakaḥ*), 2299 (°*-vedāṃç ca*), 2409 (°*vidaḥ*), 2661 (°*pāragaṃ*), 2912 (sg.), 3033 (*a-V°ānāṃ*), 3054 (*vidyā-V°vratasnātān*), 3070 (°*vidaḥ*), 3138 (°*sammitāṃ*), 3140 (°*vādaṃ*), 3148 (°*vidushi*), 3276 (°*pārage*), 3355 (°*vidaḥ*), 3358 (do.), 3428 (°*prāmāṇyadarçanāt*), 3432 (sg.), †3527 (°*vidhipravṛttaḥ*), †3534 (°*āvāptiḥ*), †3581 (°*ādhyāyī*), 3624, 3640, 3648 (°*ādhyayana*), 3650 (*sarva-V°ānāṃ*), †3684 (°*āvāptiḥ*), 3845 (*vidyā-V°vratasnātāḥ*), 3935 (°*opanishadā*), 3947, 3954, 3966 (°*-çāstrajñāḥ*), 3967 (°*prāmāṇyadarçanāt*), 4018, 4109 (*sopanishadaḥ*), 4128 (°*prāmāṇyadarçanāt*), 4157 (°*vidushaḥ*), 4165 (°*çrutinidarçanāt*), 4294 (*vidyā-V°vratasnātāḥ*), 4298 (°*vidyāvratasnātaḥ*), 4305, 4309 (°*vid*), 4323 (°*pāragān*), 4397 (*a-V°oktavratāḥ*; °*okteshu*), 4401, 4523, †4557, 4573, 4591 (*sarvān*), 4622 (quoted), †4876 (°*vidāṃ*), †4881 (°*ādhyāyī*), †4902, 4926, 4990 (°*nindāṃ*), 5028 (sg.), 5065 (°*dṛshṭena karmaṇā*), 5092 (sg.), 5100 (*Dhanurvede ca Vede ca*), 5196 (*nāsti V°āt paraṃ çāstraṃ*), 5443 (*caturaḥ*), 5547 (°*puraskṛtaḥ*), 5549 (°*vṛddhebhyaḥ*), 5554 (do.), 5559 (°*vidāṃ*), 5576 (°*prāmāṇyadarçanāt*), 5611 (*sarve*), 5643, 5645 (°*oktena pramāṇena*), 5693 (*vidhinā V°dṛshṭena*), 5802 (°*vacanaṃ*; sg.), 5804 (°*oktaṃ*, quoted), 5810 (°*oktāni*), 5812, 5841 (sg.), 5842 (do.), 6119 (°*pārage*), 6129 (do.), 6440 (°*kratukriyā*), 6454 (°*oktaḥ . . . dharmaḥ*), 6477 (*dharmo V°oktaḥ*), 6519 (*pañcayajñasya V°oktasya*), 6534 (*sarva-V°eshu*), 6609 (°*pāragaḥ*), 6729 (°*vidushaḥ*), 6740 (do.), 6963 (sg. = Vishṇu, 1000 names), 7059 (°*āntagaḥ*), 7075, †7088 (*Parāçaraṃ V°nidhiṃ*), 7159 (°*vidushe*), 7334 (°*vidaḥ*), †7375 (do.), 7376 (do.), †7383 (sg.), †7389 (sg.), 7486 (*sarvān*), 7504 (°*jñāḥ*), 7524 (°*e cāsya vidur viprāḥ Çatarudriyaṃ*), 7550 (sg.), 7673 (*samavāyaç ca ṛshi-V°samanvitaḥ*, so C., but B. reads °*deva*°), 7736 (*caturaḥ sarvān*); XIV, †340 (°*ādhyayanaṃ*), 345 (only B.; *devaiḥ*, C.), 720 (so PCR.; *devasya*, C. and B.), 902 (°*vacaḥ*, quoted), 949 (°*vidyāṃ*), 1217 (*sarva-V°ānāṃ*), 1250 (°*karmasu*), 1308, 1318 (°*vidyāvyapāçrayaṃ*), 1570 (*oṃkārapramukhān*), 1903 (°*-Vedāṅgapāragaṃ*), 2118 (°*pāragaḥ*, not in B.), 2129 (°*pāragaḥ*), 2130 (°*pāragāḥ*), 2553 (°*vidaḥ*), 2621 (do.); XV, 156 (°*vidāṃ varaḥ*), 340 (°*dharmaṃ*), 429 (°*pāragaḥ*), 511 (do.), 585 (°*ādhyayaneshu*), 781 (*sarva-V°vidāṃ varaḥ*), 838 (°*vidāṃ varaḥ*), 963 (°*-Vedāṅga-vedināṃ*); XVIII, 188 (*Kārshṇaṃ V°ṃ*, i.e. the Mhbhr.), 192/3 (only B.), 200 (°*sammitaṃ*), 209/10 (only B.: *Kārshṇaṃ V°ṃ*, i.e. the Mhbhr.), 211/12 (only B.), 300 (sg.).

Vedabhū = Vishṇu: XIII, 7635.

Vedaçiras, a ṛshi. § 717*c* (Uparicara): XII, **337**ε, 12759 (among the sadasyas of Vasu Uparicara).

Vedāçvā, a river. § 574 (Jambūkh.): VI, **9**λ, 336.

Vedādhvarapati = Çiva: XII, 9162 (Ç°).

Vedadeva = Bṛhaspati: XIII, 3693 (only B., C. has *Devadeva-*°).

Vedakāra = Çiva (1000 names[2]).

Vedakartṛ = Sūrya: III, 149.

Vedamātṛ ("the mother of the Vedas") = Gāyatrī: III, 13432 (*G*°).—Do.[2] (do.) = Sāvitrī: VI, 804 (Durgā identified with *S.*); XII, 7205.

Vedāṅga, pl. (°*āni*) ("the limbs of Veda", said of the literature auxiliary to the Vedas): I, 1013 (*Veda-V°pāragāt*), 1061 (*Veda-V°pāragaḥ*), †1295 (°*eshu . . . gīyase*, sc. Indra), 1831 (*Veda-V°pāragaḥ*), 1910 (do.), 2214 (*Veda-V°pāragaiḥ*), 2777, 4150, 4195 (*Veda-V°pāragaḥ*), 4356 (*Veda-V°tattvajñāḥ*), 5106, 5113 (*Veda-V°vidvān*), 6087, 6332, 7777 (*Veda-V°vidvāṃsaḥ*); II, 114 (*Veda-V°pāragāḥ*), 450, 1240 (*Veda-V°pāragāḥ*), 1387 (*Veda-V°vijñānaṃ*); III, 1447 (*Veda-V°pāragān*), 2481 (*Veda-V°pāragaḥ*), 3071 (*Veda-V°pāragaiḥ*), 11053 (do.), 12489 (*Veda-V°pāragaḥ*), 14053 (°*ānāñ ca pāragaḥ*), 15148 (*Veda-V°pāragāḥ*); VI, 551 (*Veda-V°tattvajñaṃ*); VII, 2153 (*Veda-V°pāragāḥ*), 2288 (do.), 8731 (*Veda-V°vidushaḥ*); XII, 904 (*Veda-V°pāragāḥ*), 2220 (*Veda-V°vid*), 2626 (do.), 7661, 11574 (*Veda-V°pāragaiḥ*), 12209 (*Veda-V°bhāsyavid*), 13007 (*Veda-V°vid*), 13041 (*Veda-V°saṃyuktān yajñān*), 13054 (*Veda-V°bhūshitāṃ*); XIII, 101 (*Veda-V°pāragaḥ*), 652 (*Veda-V°pāragaiḥ*), 701 (*Veda-V°pāragaḥ*), 1093 (*çāstra-V°vidushāṃ*), 1115 (*Veda-V°sambhavaiḥ*, sc. *nāmabhiḥ*), 2003 (*Veda-V°pāragaḥ*); XIV, 1903 (*Veda-V°pāragaṃ*); XV, 963 (*Veda-V°vedināṃ*). Cf. Aṅga[10].

Vedāṅga[2], sg. = Sūrya: III, 149.—Do.[3] = Vishṇu (1000 names).

Vedāṅgapati = Vishṇu: XII, 13111.

Vedānta, mostly pl. (°*āh*), a kind of literary works, probably identical with the Upanishads: IV, 1593 (known by Droṇa); VI, 1397 (°*kṛt*, sc. Kṛshṇa); XII, 1943 (°*ādhigatah*, sc. *dharmāḥ*), 7157 (sg.), 8723, 8971 (°*eshu ca gīyate*), 10573, 11167 (°*gamanadvīpam*), 11750 (°*jñānakovidaḥ*); XIII, 1080 (sg.), 3449 (°*nishṭhasya*); XIV, 345 (*devair* (B. *Vedair*) *V°sādhanaiḥ*).—Do., sg. = Durgā: VI, 804.

Vedasmṛtā, a river. § 574 (Jambūkh.): VI, **9**λ, 324. Cf. next.

Vedasmṛti, a river. § 775 (Ānuçāsanik.): XIII, **166***a*, 7651. Cf. the prec.

Vedātman = Kṛshṇa: II, 1213; XII, 1630.

Vedavāhana = Sūrya: III, 149.

Vedavatī, a river. § 574 (Jambūkh.): VI, **9**λ, 324.—§ 775 (Ānuçāsanik.): XIII, **166***a*, 7651.

Vedavid = Vishṇu (1000 names).

Vedavyāsa = Vyāsa, q.v.

Vedayajñādhipati = Vishṇu: XII, 13111.

Vedhas[1] ("creator") = Çiva: III, 1628, 12253 (*Tripuraghnāya*); VII, 2876; XIV, 191.—Do.[2] = Dharma: V, 3196.—Do.[3] = Kṛshṇa: XII, 1996 (*K*°), 2273 (*K*°).—Do.[4], pl. = the Prajāpatis: III, 12812.—Do.[5] = Vishṇu (1000 names).

Vedī, a tīrtha. § 370 (Tīrthayātrāp.): III, **84,** 8025.—Do.[2], the wife of Brahmán (Pitāmaha): V, 3969 (only B., C. has *Devyām*).

Vedī Prajāpateḥ, a tīrtha. § 379 (Tīrthayātrāp.): III, **95,** 8516.

Vedītīrtha, a tīrtha. § 364 (Tīrthayātrāp.): III, **83,** 6069.

Vedya = Vishṇu (1000 names).

Vegavat[1], a serpent. § 67 (Sarpasattra): I, **57,** 2158 (of Dhṛtarāshṭra's race).

Vegavat[2], one or more Asuras. § 92 (Aṃçāvat.): I, **65,** 2532 (among the sons of Danu).—§ 130 (do.): I, **67,** 2646 (incarnate as one of the Kaikeya princes).—§ 320 (Saubhavadhop.): III, **16,** 675 (*Daiteyaḥ*), 676, 678 (follower of Çālva; slain by Çāmba).

Vegavat[3], a Rākshasa. § 585 (Bhīshmavadhap.): VI, **91***v*, 4083 (slain by Duryodhana).

Vegavat[4] = Vishṇu (1000 names).

Vena, one or more ancient princes. § 6 (Anukram.): I, **1***a*, 227 (in Sañjaya's enumeration).—§ 139 (Manu Vaivasvata): I, **75,** 3140 (son of Manu Vaivasvata).—§ 267 (Yamasabhāv.): II, **8,** 326 (in the palace of Yama).—§ 641 (Rājadh.): XII, **59,** 2214 (son of Atibala and Sunīthā, the daughter of Mṛtyu; *d*: *V.* was a slave of wrath and malice; the *ṛshis* slew him with *kuça* blades purified with mantras, then they bored his right thigh, thereupon came out a short-limbed person, resembling a charred brand with black red eyes and black hair, to whom they said *nishīda* ("sit down"); from him have sprung the *Nishādas* (*e*) and other *Mlecchas*, living in the *Vindhya* mountains. The *maharshis* then bored the right hand of *V.*, thence sprang a person who was a second Indra in form, etc., and acquainted with the *Vedas*, etc. (i.e. *Pṛthu* (*f*)).

Veṇā, a river. § 268 (Varuṇasabhāv.): II, **9,** 371 (°*eṇvā*, C., among the rivers present in the palace of Varuṇa).—§ 370 (Tīrthayātrāp.): III, **85,** 8175, 8177 (°*āyāḥ saṅgame snātvā vājimedhaphalam labhet*).—§ 377 (Dhaumyatīrthak.): III, **88,** 8328 (in the south).—§ 459 (Mārkaṇḍeyas.): III, **188***a*, 12909 (seen in the stomach of Nārāyaṇa).—§ 494 (Āṅgirasa): III, **222,** 14232 (among the rivers who are mothers of fires).—§ 574 (Jambūkh.): VI, **9**λ, 327 (only B.), 335.—§ 775 (Ānuçāsanik.): XIII, **166***a*, 7646, 7648 (B. *Veṇyā*).

Veṇātaṭa (C. *Veṇvā*°), pl. (°*āḥ*), a people. § 281 (Sahadeva): II, **31,** 1117 (°*ādhipam*, in the south, vanquished by Sahadeva).

Veṇavin, see Vaiṇavin.

Veṇika, pl. (°*āḥ*), a people. § 578 (Bhīshmavadhap.): VI, **51**σ, 2097 (only C., B. has *Vetrikāḥ*).

Veṇikā (?), see Sītā[3].

Veṇin, a serpent. § 66 (Sarpasattra): I, **57,** 2154 (of Kauravya's race).

Veṇīskandha, a serpent. § 66 (Sarpasattra): I, **57,** 2154 (of Kauravya's race).

Veṇudārisuta ("the son of Veṇudāri"), a prince. § 515 (Karṇadigvijaya): III, **254,** 15251 (vanquished by Karṇa on his digvijaya).

Veṇujaṅgha, a muni. § 264 (Sabhākriyāp.): II, **4***a*, 113 (waited upon Yudhishṭhira).

Veṇumaṇḍala, a varsha on Kuçadvīpa. § 575 (Bhūmip.): VI, **12**ζ, 453.

Veṇupa, pl. (°*āḥ*), a people. § 569 (Bhagavadyānap.): V, **140**β, 4751 (only B., C. has *Reṇupāḥ*).

Veṇuvīṇādhārā, a mātṛ. § 615*u* (Skanda): IX, **46**θ, 2639.

Veṇvā, Veṇyā, v. Veṇā.

Vetālajananī, a mātṛ. § 615*u* (Skanda): IX, **46**θ, 2631.

Vetasaka (*Ce*°, C.), pl., name of a place. § 594 (Mṛtyu): VII, **54,** 2095 (there Mṛtyu performed austerities).

Vetasikā, a tīrtha. § 370 (Tīrthayātrāp.): III, **84,** 8034 (°*m gatvā Pitāmahanishevitām / açvamedham avāpnoti gacched Auçanasīm gatim*).

Vetrakīyagṛha, name of the residence of a certain king. § 215 (Bakavadhap.): I, **160,** 6213 (the Rākshasa Baka lived in the territory of *V.*).

Vetrakīyavana (B. *Vaitra*°), name of a forest. § 316 (Kirmīravadhap.): III, **11,** 415 (there the Rākshasa Baka had been slain). Cf. prec.

Vetravatī, a river. § 459 (Mārkaṇḍeyas.): III, **188***a*, 12907 (seen in the stomach of Nārāyaṇa).—§ 494 (Āṅgirasa): III, **222,** 14231 (among the rivers who are mothers of fires).—§ 574 (Jambūkh.): VI, **9**λ, 323, 327 (only B., C. has *Candrabhāgam*).—§ 775 (Ānuçāsanik.): XIII, **166***a*, 7647.

Vetrika, pl. (°*āḥ*), a people. § 578 (Bhīshmavadhap.): VI, **51**σ, 2097 (only B., C. has *Veṇikāḥ*).

Vibhāga, Vibhāgajña = Çiva (1000 names[2]).

Vibhakta = Skanda: III, 14633.

Vibhāṇḍa, a ṛshi. § 637 (Rājadh.): XII, **47**η, 1598 (among the ṛshis who surrounded Bhīshma).

Vibhāṇḍaka, a ṛshi, father of Ṛshyaçṛṅga. § 391 (Ṛshyaçṛṅga): III, **110,** 9999 (*viprarshiḥ*); **111,** †10047 (*Kāçyapaḥ*, *b*: the body of Vibhāṇḍaka was covered with hair down to the tip of the nails), †10048; **113,** (†10070), †10074, †10079 (°*syātmajam*, i.e. Ṛshyaçṛṅga), †10081, †10089. Cf. Kāçyapa.

Vibhāvasu[1], a ṛshi, brother of Supratīka. § 41 (Supratīka): I, **29,** 1354 (*maharshiḥ*), 1356, 1361, 1362 (*Supratīka-V°ū*) (cursed by Supratīka, *V.* became a tortoise, who was afterwards devoured by Garuḍa).

Vibhāvasu[2], a ṛshi. § 324 (Dvaitavanap.): III, **26***a*, 987 (worshipped Yudhishṭhira).

***Vibhāvasu**[3] = Agni (the Fire): I, 1243, †2106, 7351 (*Svāhā ceva V°au*), 8149, 8160; II, 1138, 1147; III, †961 (*tejasā V°or iva*), 2662 (*prabhām iva V°oḥ*), 15932; VI, 1120; IX, 2489, 2717 (*putraṃ V°oḥ*, sc. Skanda); XII, 1644 (?), 4511 (*A°*); XIII, 114, 4033, 4040, 4079 (read with B. °*so*), 4111, 4139, 6751 (*Svāhā . . . V°oḥ*, sc. *sādhvī*).

***Vibhāvasu**[4] = Sūrya (the Sun): I, 42 (cf. Āçāvaha), †1178, 6605; III, 151, 7055, 16924, 16943, 16951, 17000, 17093, 17100, 17141 (*devo Bhānuḥ*); V, 3776; VI, 487; XII, 11736; XIII, (6055), 6117, 6134.

Vibhinna = Çiva (1000 names[1]).

Vibhīshaṇa[1], a Yaksha. § 269 (Vaiçravaṇasabhāv.): II, **10**, 398 (in the palace of Kubera).

Vibhīshaṇa[2], a Rākshasa prince, brother of Kubera and Rāvaṇa. § 269 (Vaiçravaṇasabhāv.): II, **10**, 411 (in the palace of Kubera—*bhrātaram*).—§ 284 (Sahadeva): II, **31**, 1177 (*Paulastyāya*, ruled Laṅkā, paid tribute to Sahadeva).—§ 425 (Hanūmad-Bhīmasaṃv.): III, **148**, 11213 (*Rākshasendraṃ*, installed as king of Laṅkā after Rāvaṇa had been killed, cf. § 543).—§ 526 (Rāmopākhyānap.): III, **275**, 15896 (son of Viçravas and Mālinī), 15897 (surpassed all in beauty and was very pious), (*β*), 15905 (performed austerities subsisting only on dry leaves for 1000 years), (*γ*), 15917, (15918) (asked Brahmán for swerveless righteousness and the knowledge of the Brahmāstra; this was granted, and Brahmán himself added immortality), 15924.—§ 532 (Sītāsāntvana): III, **280**, 16158 (seen in a vision by Trijaṭā).—§ 535 (Setubandhana): III, **283**, 16314 (*bhrātā Rākshasendrasya*, came to Rāma Dāçarathi), 16317 (Rāma installed *V.* in the sovereignty of the Rākshasas and made him his counsellor and the friend of Lakshmaṇa), 16318, 16320.—§ 536 (Laṅkāpraveça): III, **284**, 16346.—§ 537 (Rāma-Rāvaṇayuddha): III, **285**, 16366, (*β*), 16377 (fought with Prahasta).—§ 538 (Kumbhakarṇaraṇag.): III, **286**, 16379, 16381 (slew Prahasta).—§ 541 (Indrajidvadha): III, **289**, 16469, 16472, 16478, 16480 (°*mate*).—§ 542 (Rāvaṇavadhap.): III, **290**, 16513, 16514.—§ 543 (Rāmābhisheka): III, **291**, 16535 (Rāma gave Laṅkā to *V.*), 16536, 16582, 16587, 16598 (*Paulastyaṃ*). Cf. Paulastya.

Vibhīshaṇa[3] = Çiva (1000 names[1]).

Vibhīshaṇā, a mātṛ. § 615*u* (Skanda): IX, **46***θ*, 2640.

***vibhītaka**, the tree Terminalia Bellerica (whose fruits were used as dice): III, 2405, 2813 foll., 11570.

Vibhu[1], a prince, son of the Kāçi king. § 570 (Sainyaniryāṇap.): V, **151***δ*, 5160 (*putraḥ Kāçyasya vā V°ḥ—cābhibhūḥ*, B.).—§ 573 (Ambopākhyānap.): V, **196***μ*, 7650 (*putraḥ Kāçyasya vā V°ḥ*, both C. and B.).—§ 578 (Bhīshmavadhap.): VI, **51***ω*, 2110 (*putraḥ Kāçyasya vā V°ḥ—cābhibhūḥ*, B.).—§ 585 (do.): VI, **93***ψ*, 4151 (do., do.).—§ 592 (Saṃçaptakavadhap.): VII, **23***o*, 990 (*putraḥ Kāçyasya me* (!) *V°ḥ—cābhibhūḥ*, B.).—§ 599 (Jayadrathavadhap.): VII, **85***δ*, 3049 (*putraḥ Kāçyasya vā V°ḥ—cābhibhūḥ*, B.). Cf. Abhibhū.

Vibhu[2], the sixth son of Bhṛgu. § 747*b* (Suvarṇotpatti): XIII, **85***η*, 4146. Cf. Vareṇya[2].

***Vibhu**[3] = Çiva: I, †7297; VII, 2877, 9504 (only B.); X, 254; XIII, 1160 (1000 names[2]), 1167 (do.), 1219 (do.), 1227 (do.), 1268, 1323 (only B.).—Do.[4] = Skanda: III, 14641.—Do.[5] = Vishṇu (Kṛshṇa): II, 1521 (only C.); III, 15591, 15817; VI, 302, 1050 (?); XII, 1505, 1509, 1512, †13249; XIII, 6850 (only B.), 6975 (1000 names), 7043 (do.).

Vibhūrasi, name of a fire. § 494 (Āṅgirasa): III, **222**, 14234 (son of Adbhuta).

Vibhūti, son of Viçvāmitra. § 721*b* (Viçvāmitrop.): XIII, **4***β*, 256.

Vibudha = Çiva (1000 names[2]).

Vibudhādhipa, Vibudhādhipati ("lord of the gods") = Indra, q.v.

Vibudhaçreshṭha[1] ("the best of the gods") = Brahmán: XII, 6152 (*B°*).—Do.[2] (do.) = Çiva: III, 9942 (*Maheçvarāt*).—Do.[3] (do.) = Indra: XIII, 3159.—Do.[4] (do.) = Sūrya: III, 16945.—Do.[5] (do.) = Vishṇu: XII, 13433 (*Nārāyaṇaṃ Hariṃ*), 13454.—Do.[6] (dual) = Brahmán and Çiva: XII, 13147.

Vibudhadvish, pl. (°*aḥ*) ("enemy of the gods") = Asura, pl.: III, 849; IX, 2712, 2951, 3519.

Vibudhaloka ("the world of the gods") = Devaloka: XI, 556.

Vibudhārighna ("slayer of the enemies of the gods") = Kṛshṇa: II, 1319.

Vibudhasattama ("the best of the gods") = Skanda: IX, 2679.

Vibudhavidvish, pl. (°*aḥ*) = Vibudhadvish, pl.: I, 4801 (*Daityāḥ*).

Vibudheçvara[1] ("lord of the gods") = Brahmán: XII, 9170.—Do.[2] (do.) = Çiva: III, 9942.—Do.[3] (do.) = Indra: III, 11899; XII, 1200.

Vicakhnu (B.) or **Vicakhyu** (C.), a king. § 681 (Mokshadh.): XII, **266**, 9467 (*itihāsaṃ purātanam . . . gītaṃ rājñā V°unā*).

Vicāravid = Çiva (1000 names[2]).

Vicitra, a king. § 130 (Aṃçāvat.): I, **67**, 2697 (among the incarnations from the Krodhavaça gaṇa).

Vicitrarūpa = Hiraṇyagarbha: XII, 11232.

Vicitravīrya, a king, son of Çāntanu and Satyavatī. § 4 (Anukram.): I, **1**, 94 (*kshetre V°sya . . . Kṛshṇa-Dvaipāyanaḥ . . . trīn . . . Kauravyān janayām āsa*, all. to § 171).—§ 11 (Parvasaṅgr.): I, **2**, 375 (°*sya . . . rājye sampratipādanaṃ*).—§ 83 (Ādivaṃçāvatāraṇa): I, **63**, 2441 (*Kṛshṇa-Dvaipayanād . . . kshetre V°sya*, all. to § 171).—§ 156 (Pūruvaṃç.): I, **95**, ††3803 (*V.* and Citrāṅgada were the sons of Çāntanu and Satyavatī, cf. § 166), ††3804 (married Ambikā and Ambālikā, cf. § 167).—§ 157 (do.): I, **95**, ††3805 (died without offspring, cf. § 167), ††3807 (Vyāsa begot children on the widows of *V.*, cf. § 171).—§ 166 (Citrāṅgadop.): I, **101**, 4069 (the birth of *V.*), 4078 (after the death of Citrāṅgada, *V.*, who was still a child, was installed as king), 4079.—§ 167 (Vicitravīryoparama): I, **102**, 4126, 4131, 4137, 4138, 4140, 4142, 4145 (*V.* married Ambikā and Ambālikā, but soon died of consumption).—§ 171 (Vicitravīryasutotpatti): I, **105**, 4224 (°*kshetreshu*), 4240 (do.), 4253, 5254 (*bhrātā V°sya*, i.e. Vyāsa); **106**, 4304 (Vyāsa begot Dhṛtarāshṭra and Pāṇḍu on the widows of *V.* and Vidura on the maid of Ambikā).—§ 213 (Jatugṛhap.): I, **145**, 5744 (*Çāntanavaḥ . . . rājarshiḥ*); **151**, 5906 (*snushāṃ V°sya*, i.e. Kuntī).—§ 236 (Svayaṃvarap.): I, **192**, †7173 (°*sya sutasya*, i.e. Pāṇḍu).—§ 290 (Çiçupālavadhap.): II, **41**, 1455 (*bhrātā V°s te*, sc. Bhīshma's, all. to § 167).—§ 401 (Balarāma): III, **119**, †10248 (°*sya sutaḥ*, i.e. Dhṛtarāshṭra).—§ 569 (Bhagavadyānap.): V, **147**, 4978, 4979 (repetition from §§ 166–171).—§ 572 (Rathātirathasaṅkhyānap.): V, **172**, 5938 (all. to § 166).—§ 573 (Ambopākhyānap.): V, **173**, 5947, 5948; **174**, 5967 (repetition from § 167); **176**, 6072 (do.).—§ 744 (Ānuçāsanik.): XIII,

44β, 2441 (repetition from § 167, but with some alterations). —§ 787 (Āçramavāsap.): XV, **9**λ, 283. Cf. Kaurava, Kauravya, Kurukulodvaha.

[Vicitravīryasutotpatti(ḥ)] ("begetting of sons for Vicitravīrya"). § 171 (cf. Bhīshma-Satyavatī-saṃvāda). *Satyavatī* related to *Bhīshma* the birth of *Dvaipāyana* (cf. § 77; from the darkness of his skin he is also called *Kṛshṇa* (v. 4236)), who instantly came when *Kālī* (i.e. Satyavatī) thought of him, and promised to raise offspring in the widows of *Vicitravīrya*. As there was no time for them to observe a rigid vow for one full year, he ordered that they should tolerate his ugliness. *Satyavatī* first addressed herself to *Kausalyā* (i.e. Ambikā) and fed *brahmans, devarshis*, and guests (I, **105**). *Ambikā*, seeing *Vyāsa*, closed her eyes in fear; therefore her son, though he was destined to be mighty, etc., and to have 100 sons, had to be blind. After his (i.e. *Dhṛtarāshṭra's*) birth, *Vyāsa* approached *Ambālikā*, who became pale with fear; therefore, her son was pale and was named *Pāṇḍu*. *Ambālikā* refused to receive *Vyāsa* again and sent him a *çūdra* maid of hers, adorned with her own ornaments; on her he begat *Vidura*, who was *Dharma*, born under the curse of *Māṇḍavya*. *Vyāsa* then disappeared (I, **106**).

[Vicitravīryoparama(ḥ)] ("death of Vicitravīrya"). § 167 (cf. Citrāṅgadopākhyāna). When *Vicitravīrya* had come of age, *Bhīshma* went to *Vārāṇasī* to the *svayaṃvara* of the three daughters of the king of *Kāçi*, and, in order to marry them to *Vicitravīrya*, he carried them off with force to *Hāstinapura* (having defeated the other princes assembled, among these king *Çālva*, whom he conquered by means of the *Vāruṇa* and the *Aindra* weapons, but at last he left him with his life to return to his capital). The eldest, *Ambā*, he let free before the wedding, as she declared that she, in her heart, had chosen the *Saubha* king (i.e. Çālva), and had been chosen by him. *Ambikā* and *Ambālikā* he bestowed on *Vicitravīrya*. After seven years *Vicitravīrya* died of consumption (*yakshman*) (I, **102**).

Viçākha[1], a god, a son or form of Skanda. § 116*b* (Kumāra, v. Skanda): I, **66**, 2588 (son (?) of Skanda; acc. to PCR. brother of Skanda).—§ 266 (Çakrasabhāv.): II, **7**, 295 (the same (?), in the palace of Indra).—§ 499 (Skanda-Çakrasamāgama): III, **227**, 14384 (when Skanda's side was struck with the thunderbolt, there issued from it the youth *V*., armed with a dart and wearing celestial earrings; etymology of the name).—§ 500 (Skandop.): III, **228**, 14390 (= Skanda).—§ 505 (Skandayuddha): III, **231**, 14532 (received one of Airāvata's bells), 14533 (Kārttikeya, i.e. Skanda and *V*. had a red banner).—§ 508 (Kārttikeyastava): III, **232**, 14634 (the 38th of Skanda's 51 names).—§ 615*u* (Skanda): IX, **44**, 2487 (a form of Skanda), 2488 (joined Umā).—§ 775 (Ānuçāsanik.): XIII, **166***a*, 7636.

Viçākha[2] = Çiva (1000 names[1]).

Viçākhā, name of a nakshatra, v. Su. Si. § 546 (Kuṇḍalāharaṇap.): III, **301**, 16970 (dual, °*ayor madhyagataḥ çaçīva*). —§ 574 (Jambūkh.): VI, **3**, 95 (sg., °*āyāḥ samīpasthau Bṛhaspati-Çanaiçcarau*, omens).—§ 605 (Karṇap.): VIII, **20**, †817 (dual, °*ayor madhyagataḥ çaçī yathā*).—§ 746 (Ānuçāsanik.): XIII, **64***a*, 3270 (sg., result of making gifts under the constellation of *V*.).—§ 749 (do.): XIII, **89***a*, 4262 (pl., result of performing çrāddhas under the constellation of *V*.). —§ 759 (do.): XIII, **110**, 5392 (description of the cāndravrata).

Viçākhayūpa, name of a sacred place. § 377 (Dhaumyatīrthak.): III, **90**, 8386 (in the north, there the gods, including Varuṇa and Indra, performed austerities).—§ 449 (Ājagarap.): III, **177**, †12354 (having left the capital of Subāhu, the Pāṇḍavas, etc., dwelt for one year at *V*.).—§ 623 (Rājadh.): XII, **12**, 335 (*devānām*).

Viçām patiḥ = Çiva (1000 names[2]).

Viçāla[1] = Sūrya: III, 154.—Do.[2] = Çiva (1000 names[2]).

Viçālā[1], wife of Ajamīḍha. § 156 (Pūruvaṃç.): I, **95**, ††3790.

Viçālā[2] = Badarī (according to Nīl.): III, 10830; XII, 13390.

Viçālā[3], name of one or more rivers. § 615*i* (Saptasārasvata): IX, **38***a*, 2189 (one of the seven Sarasvatīs), 2206 (at the sacrifice of Gaya the Sarasvatī appeared in the country of the Gayas as the river *V*.).—§ 733*t* (Ānuçāsanik.): By bathing in *V*. in *Karavīrapura* and offering oblations of water to the pitṛs, and by bathing in *Devahrada* one becomes identified with *Brahman*: XIII, **25**, 1730.

Viçālaçākha = Çiva (1000 names[2]).

Viçālaka, a Yaksha. § 269 (Vaiçravaṇasabhāv.): II, **10**, 397 (in the palace of Kubera).

Viçālāksha[1], a son of Dhṛtarāshṭra. § 130 (Aṃçāvat.): I, **67**, 2736 (enumeration).—§ 182 (Dhṛtarāshṭraputranāmak.): I, **117**, 4549 (do.).—§ 585 (Bhīshmavadhap.): VI, **88**ι, 3901 (among seven sons of Dhṛtarāshṭra who attacked Bhīmasena), 3904, 3912 (slain by Bhīmasena).

Viçālāksha[2], a Matsya warrior. § 552 (Goharaṇap.): IV, **32**, 1054.

Viçālāksha[3], a Suparṇa, son of Garuḍa. § 564 (Mātalīyop.): V, **101**β, 3594.

Viçālāksha[4] = Çiva, q.v.

Viçālāksha[5] (XII, 2203), v. Vaiçālāksha.

Viçālākshī, a mātṛ. § 615*u* (Skanda): IX, **46**θ, 2621.

Viçalyā, a river. § 268 (Varuṇasabhāv.): II, **9**, 373 (present in the palace of Varuṇa).—§ 370 (Tīrthayātrāp.): III, **84**, 8092 (a tīrtha).—§ 459 (Mārkaṇḍeyas.): III, **188***a*, 12910 (seen in the stomach of Nārāyaṇa).—§ 775 (Ānuçāsanik.): XIII, **166***a*, 7646.

viçalyā, name of a certain medicinal plant: III, 16470 (cf. VI, 3540: *viçalyakaraṇīm oshadhīm*).

Viçārada = Çiva (1000 names[2]).

Viçirā, v. Vasudā.

Viçishṭa, Viçodhana = Vishṇu (1000 names).

Viçoka[1], the charioteer of Bhīmasena. § 286 (Rājasūyikap.): II, **33**, 1234.—§ 449 (Ajagarap.): III, **177**, †12352 (*sutair V°pramukhaiḥ*).—[§ 579 (Bhīshmavadhap.): VI, **54**[14], 2303 (*Açokaḥ*).]—§ 581 (do.): VI, **64**[12], 2821, 2825, 2827.—§ 583 (do.): VI, **77**[4], 3355 (*Bhīmasenasya sārathim*), 3357, 3362.—§ 585 (do.): VI, **95**, 4312.—§ 587 (do.): VI, **113**, 5264 (*sārathim*).—§ 600 (Ghaṭotkacavadhap.): VII, **155**, 6704; **156**, 6777.—§ 608 (Karṇap.): VIII, **76**, †3832, (†3836), †3844, ‖3847, (‖3848), †3860.

Viçoka[2], a Kaikeya prince. § 608 (Karṇap.): VIII, **82**, †4182 (slain by Karṇa).

Viçoka[3] = Vishṇu (1000 names).

Viçokā, a mātṛ. § 615*u* (Skanda): IX, **46**θ, 2623.

Viçoshaṇa, a celestial weapon. § 444 (Nivātakavacayuddhap.): III, **171**, 12139 (*astram*).

Viçrāma = Vishṇu (1000 names).

Viçravas, a muni or ṛshi = Pulastya. § 377 (Dhaumyatīrthak.): III, **89**, 8358 (*niketaḥ . . . V°so muneḥ*, there Kubera was born).—§ 525 (Rāmopākhyānap.): III, **274**, 15885 (Pulastya, the father of Vaiçravaṇa, i.e. Kubera, with half his own self, became the muni *V.*).—§ 526 (do.): III, **275**, 15889 (*muniḥ*, father of Kumbhakarṇa, Rāvaṇa, Vibhīshaṇa, Khara, and Çūrpaṇakhā); **276**, 15930 (°*saḥ putraḥ*, i.e. Rāvaṇa).—§ 533 (Sītā-Rāvaṇasaṃv.): III, **281**, 16179 (*putraḥ . . . viprarsheḥ sākshād V°so muneḥ*, i.e. Rāvaṇa).—§ 775 (Ānuçāsanik.): XIII, **166a**, 7638 (*mahān ṛshiḥ*).

Viçrutātman, Viçuddhātman = Vishṇu (1000 names).

Viçuṇḍi, a serpent. § 564 (Mātalīyop.): V, **103**γ, 3632.

Viçva[1], a prince. § 130 (Aṃçāvat.): I, **67**, 2672 (among the incarnations from the Krodhavaça gaṇa).

Viçva[2] = Viçvakarman: V, 7259 (*Prājāpatyaṃ V°kṛtaṃ Prasvāpaṃ*).

Viçva[3] ("omnipresent") = Çiva: XIII, 909, 1011, 1260 (1000 names[2]).—Do.[4] (do.) = *mahān ātmā*: XII, 11229, 11602, 11604.—Do.[5] (do.) = Vishṇu (Kṛshṇa): I, 2432; VI, 2945; XII, 12863, 13140, 13741; XIII, 6950 (Vishṇu's 1000 names).

Viçvā, daughter of Daksha and wife of Kaçyapa. § 87 (Aṃçāvat.): I, **65**, 2520.

Viçvabāhu[1] = Çiva (1000 names[1-2]).—Do.[2] = Vishṇu (1000 names).

Viçvabhāvana = Vishṇu (Kṛshṇa): II, 2293 (i.e. Kṛshṇa); XII, 12795.

Viçvabhū = Vishṇu (Kṛshṇa): XII, 13376.

Viçvabhuj[1], name of one of the five Indras. § 238 (Pañcendrop.): I, **197**, 7304.

Viçvabhuj[2], name of a fire. § 490 (Āṅgirasa): III, **219**, 14146.

Viçvabhuj[3] = Indra: VI, 776.

Viçvabhuj[4] = Vishṇu (Kṛshṇa): XII, 13488; XIII, 6975 (Vishṇu's 1000 names), †7367.

Viçvācī, an Apsaras. § 135 (Çakuntalop.): I, **74**, 3055 (among the six principal Apsarases).—§ 144 (Yayāti): I, **75**, 3172 (Yayāti sported with *V.*).—§ 148 (do.): I, **85**, 3508 (do.).—§ 191 (Arjuna): I, **123**, 4821 (sang at the birth of Arjuna).—§ 269 (Vaiçravaṇasabhāv.): II, **10**, 393 (in the palace of Kubera).—§ 775 (Ānuçāsanik.): XIII, **166**β, 7641.

Viçvadakshiṇa = Vishṇu (1000 names).

Viçvadaṃshṭra, an Asura (?). § 673*b* (Bali-Vāsavasaṃv.): XII, **227a**, 8264 (among the ancient rulers of the earth).

Viçvadeva = Çiva: XIII, 985 (only B.), 1216 (1000 names[2]), 1264 (do.).

Viçvadeva, pl. (°*āḥ*) = Viçve devāḥ (pl.): VII, **76**, 2682 (only B.); XII, **198**, 7191.

Viçvadṛç = Vishṇu (1000 names).

Viçvagaçva[1-2], v. Vishvagaçva.

Viçvagupta = Vishṇu: III, 10120.

Viçvajit[1], a fire. § 490 (Āṅgirasa): III, **219**, 14145.

Viçvajit[2], an Asura (?). § 673*b* (Bali-Vāsavasaṃv.): XII, **227a**, 8265 (among the ancient rulers of the earth).

Viçvajit[3] = Kṛshṇa (Vishṇu): VII, 1544; XIII, †7367.

Viçvakarmakṛt = Çiva: VII, 9597.

Viçvakarmamati = Çiva (1000 names[2]).

Viçvakarman ("who performs all works"), the celestial artificer, sometimes identified with Brahmán or Tvashṭṛ. § 39 (Rāmaṇīyaka): I, **27**, 1305 (*dvīpaṃ . . . vihitaṃ V°ṇā*).—§ 116 (Vasu, pl.): I, **66**, 2592 (*çilpaprajāpatiḥ . . . tridaçānāñ ca vardhakiḥ*, son of Prabhāsa and the sister of Bṛhaspati), 2594.—§ 246 (Sundopasundop.): I, **211**, 7688, 7689, 7693 (created Tilottamā).—§ 266 (Çakrasabhāv.): II, **7**, 296 (in the palace of Indra).—§ 267 (Yamasabhāv.): II, **8**, 311 (had built the palace of Yama), 345 (do.).—§ 268 (Varuṇasabhāv.): II, **9**, 354 (had built the palace of Varuṇa).—§ 270 (Brahmasabhāv.): II, **10**, 448 (in the palace of Brahmán). — § 296 (Dyūtap.): II, **53**, 1922 (*çaṅkhaṃ . . . sukṛtaṃ V°ṇā*). — § 392*c* (Svayambhuvo vanaṃ): III, **114**, 10111 (= Svayambhū (i.e. Brahmán), performed a sacrifice at which he gave the earth to Kaçyapa).—§ 403*b* (Payoshṇī): III, **121**, 10302 (*hiraṇmayābhir gobhiḥ kṛtābhir V°ṇā*).—§ 438 (Yakshayuddhap.): III, **161**, 11775 (had made Pushpaka, the seat (*āsanavaraṃ*) of Kubera).—§ 501 (Skandop.): III, **229**, 14426 (°*kṛtā . . . mālā*).—§ 530 (Viçvāvasumokshaṇa): III, **279**, 16056 (*purīṃ . . . nirmitāṃ V°ṇā*, sc. Laṅkā).—§ 535 (Setubandhana): III, **283**, 16309 (*Tvashṭuḥ*, father of the monkey Nala).—§ 548 (Āraṇeyap.): III, **312**, 17285 (°*kṛtaṃ yathā*, sc. *saraḥ*).—§ 552 (Goharaṇap.): IV, **46**, 1438 (*daivīṃ māyāṃ . . . vihitāṃ V°ṇā*, sc. the ape on the standard of Arjuna).—§ 578 (Bhīshmavadhap.): VI, **50**π, 2076 (*nirmito V°ṇā*, sc. the standard of Arjuna).—§ 581 (do.): VI, **66**, 2989 (had praised Kṛshṇa).—§ 596 (Pratijñāp.): VII, **79**, 2812 (*jālaiḥ . . . V°kṛtaiḥ*).—§ 597 (do.): VII, **82**, 2934 (°*kṛtaṃ . . . varāsanaṃ*).—§ 605*b* (Vijaya): VIII, **31**, 1292 (had made the bow Vijaya).—§ 606 (Tripurākhyāna): VIII, **34**, 1470 (made the chariot of Çiva).—§ 608 (Karṇap.): VIII, **53**, 2570 (°*kṛtaḥ*, sc. the ape on the standard of Arjuna). — § 617 (Aishīkap.): X, **13**, 650 (°*kṛtā . . . dhvajayashṭiḥ*, sc. Kṛshṇa's). Cf. Bhaumana, Prajāpati, Viçva, Viçvakṛt.

Viçvakarman[2] (do.) = Maya: II, 5 (*Dānavānāṃ*), 17, 84; V, 3568 (*M°*); VIII, 1406 (*M°*).

Viçvakarman[3] = Vishṇu (Kṛshṇa): I, 2430; VI, 2944, 3013 (B. *Vāsudevaḥ*); XII, 1503, 1610, 1672, 1846, 1898 (*Vāsudevena*); XIII, 6955 (1000 names), †7367; XIV, 1485, 1573, 1593.

Viçvakarman[4] = Çiva: VII, 2863; XII, 10332 (*Maheçvaraḥ*); XIII, 7498.

Viçvakartṛ = Çiva (1000 names[1]).

Viçvakṛt[1] = Brahmán: I, 928; III, 12813 (?); XIII, 2260, 2283.

Viçvakṛt[2] = Çiva (1000 names[1]).

Viçvakṛt[3] = Viçvakarman[1]: I, 7691.

Viçvakṛt[4] = Mahāpurusha (Mahāpurushastava).

Viçvakṛt[5] = Vishṇu (Kṛshṇa): III, 12813 (?); VII, 9447 (i.e. Nārāyaṇa); XII, 13363; XIII, †7382.

Viçvakṛt[6], a Viçvadeva. § 749 (Ānuçāsanik.): XIII, **91**γ, 4361.

Viçvakṛtāṃ vareṇyaḥ = Çiva (1000 names[1]).

Viçvaksena, v. Vishvaksena.

Viçvakshetra(ṃ) = Çiva (1000 names[2]).

Viçvāmitra, a ṛshi, son of Gādhi. § 5 (Anukram.): I, **1a**, 220 bis (in Nārada's enumeration of departed kings).—§ 134 (cf. Çakuntalop.): *V.* had deprived Vasishṭha of his children; though born as a kshatriya he became a brahman through his penances, and created the river *Kauçikī* for his ablutions; there, his wife, during a famine, was maintained by the *rājarshi Mataṅga*, who was living as a hunter; therefore, when the famine was over, *V.* changed the name of the river into *Pārā* and performed a sacrifice for *Mataṅga*, and *Indra* himself, from fear, came there to drink *soma*. *V.*, in anger, created another world and a series of nakshatras, beginning with *Pratiçravaṇa* (differently BR. *sub voce*), and gave protection to *Triçaṅku*, who was cursed by his *guru*; he could burn the three worlds by his splendour, and by a kick cause the earth to quake; he could sever *Meru*, and hurl it away at any distance; he could go round the earth in a moment, and *Yama*, *Soma*, the *maharshis*, the *Sādhyas*, the *Viçvas*, and the *Vālakhilyas* are afraid of his prowess. To him *Indra* sent the *Apsaras Menakā*, who, assisted by *Vāyu* and *Manmatha*, disturbed his penances (I, **71**). *V.* begat on *Menakā* a daughter, whom she abandoned on the banks of the *Mālinī* in the valleys of *Himavat*. Vultures protected the child from *Rākshasas* and carnivorous animals, until she was found and reared by *Kaṇva*, who called her *Çakuntalā*, because she had been protected by the birds (*çakuntaiḥ*): I, **71**, 2914, 2917, 2918; **72**, 2938, 2941.—§ 135 (Çakuntalop.): I, **74**, 3056 (Menakā bore Çakuntalā from *V.*), 3062 (*pitā tava*, i.e. Çakuntalā's).—§ 191 (Arjuna): I, **123**a, 4807 (among the seven maharshis present at the birth of Arjuna).—§ 208 (Astradarçana): I, **137**, 5432 (*kshatriyebhyaç ca ye jātā brāhmaṇās te ca te çrutāḥ / V°prabhṛtayaḥ prāptā brahmatvam avyayam*).—§ 223 (Vāsishṭha): I, **174**, 6639 (°*āparādhena*), 6640 (°*vināçāya*); **175**, 6649 (*vairam V°-Vasishṭhayoḥ*), 6652 (son of Gādhi), 6655, (6666), 6669, 6672, 6673 (°*bhaya-*), 6674 (°*balaiḥ*), 6680 (°*sya* . . . *sainyam*), 6688, 6689 (*sainikāḥ* . . . *V°sya*), 6690 (°*sya tat sainyam*), 6692 (the hostility between *V.* and Vasishṭha).—§ 224 (Kalmāshapāda): I, **176**, 6699, 6710 (°-*Vasishṭhayoḥ / vairam*), 6711, 6713, 6715, 6717, 6736 (*V.* caused a Rākshasa to possess Kalmāshapāda, who then devoured the sons of Vasishṭha).—§ 225 (Vāsishṭha): I, **176**, 6738 (*ghātitān* . . . *V°ena*, sc. the sons of Vasishṭha, cf. § 224).—§ 228 (Aurvop.): I, **181**, 6881 (all. to § 224).—§ 366 (Tīrthayātrāp.): III, **83**, 7009 (°*sya* . . . *tīrtham*, bathing there, one becomes a brahman).—§ 370 (do.): III, **84**, 8121 (*Kauçikaḥ*, obtained high success at *Kauçikasya muner hradam* on the Kauçikī).—§ 376 (do.): III, **85**, 8263 (among the ṛshis who expect Yudhishṭhira on his tīrthayātrā).—§ 377 (Dhaumyatīrthak.): III, **87**, 8309 (on the Kauçikī *V.* became a brahman), 8311 (*Kauçikaḥ*, performed sacrifices at Utpalāvana), 8312.—§ 390c (Kauçikī): III, **110**, 9988 (performed austerities on the Kauçikī).—§ 390 (Tīrthayātrāp.): III, **110**, 9990 (°*āçramaḥ*, on the Kauçikī, visited by Yudhishṭhira, etc.).—§ 497 (Skandotpatti): III, **226**, 14348 (had seen how Skanda was begotten by Agni on Svāhā), 14350 (performed the thirteen rites of childhood for Skanda), 14353.—§ 565 (Gālavacarita): V, **106**, 3721, 3723, 3724, 3729, 3731, 3732, 3734, 3737, 3738, 3739 (in the shape of Vasishṭha, Dharma put *V.* to the test; *V.* then became a brahman; from his disciple Gālava *V.* asked 800 horses for his fee); **107**, 3741; **113**, 3891, 3894; **114**, 3907 (°*sya çishyaḥ*, i.e. Gālava), 3911; [**117**, 3972 (*reme* . . . *yathā* . . . *Haimavatyāñ ca Kauçikaḥ*)]; **119**, 4011, 4012, 4016, 4019 (begot Ashṭaka on Mādhavī).—§ 599 (Jayadrathavadhap.): VII, **94**ε, 3453 (mentioned in a blessing to Duryodhana).—§ 602 (Droṇavadhap.): VII, **190**ν, 8727.—§ 615 (Baladevatīrthayātrā): IX, **39**, 2271 (*mahāmuniḥ*, had become a brahman), 2283; **40**, 2286.—§ 615n (do.): The great kshatriya *Gādhi Kauçika* became a great ascetic; having resolved to give up his body, he installed his son *Viçvāmitra* on the throne, notwithstanding the solicitations of his subjects, and went to heaven. *V.*, however, could not protect the earth even with his best exertions. He then heard of a great fear of *Rākshasas*, and went out with his army. In the hermitage of *Vasishṭha* his troops caused much mischief; when the brahman *Vasishṭha* came to his hermitage, he became angry and commanded his cow to create many terrible *Çabaras*, who, encountering the army of *V.*, caused a great carnage, and the troops fled away. *V.* then set his heart on ascetic austerities, and in this *tīrtha* of the *Sarasvatī* he began to emaciate his own body (description), although the gods repeatedly attempted to interrupt him. *Brahmán* (*Pitāmaha*) granted him the boon that he should become a brahman. Then he wandered over the whole earth like a celestial: IX, **40**, 2296 (son of Gādhi), 2297, 2300, 2306 (*Gādhijaḥ*), 2311.—§ 615p (Vasishṭhāpavāha): IX, **42**, 2360, 2361, 2365, 2366 (°-*Vasishṭhau*), 2367, 2370, 2372, 2378, 2381, 2391 (°*āçramaḥ*), 2395, 2396; **43**, 2400 (*V.* ordered the Sarasvatī to bring Vasishṭha into his presence that he might slay him; Sarasvatī, however, carried him back and was therefore cursed by *V.*).—[§ 637 (Rājadh.): XII, **47**η, 1594 (*Kauçikena*, among the ṛshis who surrounded Bhīshma)].—§ 638b (Rāmopākhyāna): XII, **49**, 1745 (son of Gādhi, the story of *V.*'s being born with the attributes of a brahman, cf. § 721b), 1771 (°*sya pautras tu Raibhyaputraḥ*, i.e. Parāvasu).—§ 649 (Āpaddh.): XII, **141**, 5330 (°*sya saṃvādam Cāṇḍālasya ca*), 5344, 5351, 5360, 5364, 5365, 5368, 5379, (†5387), (5389), (5391), (5393), (†5395), (†5397), (5400), (5402), (†5404), (†5406), (†5408), 5410, 5416 (discourse between *V.* and a Cāṇḍāla).—§ 665 (Mokshadh.): XII, **208**ι, 7599 (*Kauçikaḥ*, one of the ṛshis of the north).—§ 702 (do.): XII, **293**, 10759 (°*sya putratvam Ṛcīkatanayo* —i.e. Çunaḥçepha—*'gamat*, cf. XIII, 187), (*a*), 10762.—[§ 717b (Nārāyaṇīya): XII, **343**, II), ††13205 (*Kauçika*-°, cursed by Kauçika, i.e. *V.*, Indra lost his testicles, which afterwards were substituted with those of a ram)].—§ 721 (Ānuçāsanik.): XIII, **3**a, 182 (became a brahman, etc.), 187 (v. Çunaḥçepha), 190 (enumeration of the feats of *V.*); **4**, 200.—§ 721 (Viçvāmitrop.): XIII, **4**, 246 (read *brahmarshiṃ brahmavādinam*), 247 (*brāhmaṇatāṃ yātaḥ*, the wife of Gādhi bore a son *V.*, who afterwards became a brahman and founder of a race of brahmans), 259 (°*ātmajāḥ*, enumeration of the sons of *V.*), 261.—§ 730 (Ānuçāsanik.): XIII, **18**κκ, 1311 (had, by the grace of Çiva, become a brahman), 1349 (preceptor of Gālava).—§ 734 (do.): XIII, **26**a, 1762 (among the ṛshis who came to see Bhīshma).—§ 736 (do.): XIII, **30**, 1941 (°*eṇa ca purā brāhmaṇyaṃ prāptam*).—§ 745 (do.): XIII, **52**, 2720.—§ 745c (Cyavana-Kuçikasaṃv.): XIII, [**55**, 2897 (*Kauçiko dvijaḥ*, the third in descent from Kuçika will become a brahman)]; **56**, 2915 (*kshatriyaṃ viprakarmāṇam* . . . *Gādheḥ putram*), 2925 (*janma* . . . *muner V°sya*, all. to § 721b).—§ 750b (Bisastainyop.): XIII, **93**a, 4416 (4443), (4463), (4493), 4493 (etymology), (4525).—§ 751b (Çapathavidhi): XIII, **94**a, †4550, (4579).—§ 759 (Ānuçāsanik.): XIII, **106**, 5199 (became a brahman by confining himself to one meal a day during 1,000 celestial years).—§ 766 (do.): XIII, **126**, (6039).—§ 770 (do.): XIII, **151**ι, 7116 (*Kauçikaḥ*, one of the seven *Dhaneçvarasya guravaḥ*).—§ 775 (do.): XIII, **166**ζ, 7670 (one of the ṛshis of the north).—§ 782 (Anugītāp.): XIV, **35**δ, 961.—§ 786 (do.): XIV, **91**a, 2842 (°*ādayo nṛpāḥ*), 2843 (attained to high success).—§ 793 (Mausalap.): XVI, **1**, 15 (cursed Çāmba, etc.). Cf. Brahmarshi, Gādhija, Gādhinandana, Kauçika, Viprarshi.

Viçvāmitrā, a river. § 574 (Jambūkh.): VI, **9**λ, 334.

Viçvāmitraduhitṛ ("the daughter of Viçvāmitra") = Çakuntalā: I, 3782 (Ç°).

Viçvāmitranadī ("the river of Viçvāmitra"). § 377 (Dhaumyatīrthak.): III, **89**, 8362 (in the west).

Viçvāmitrapriya ("dear to Viçvāmitra") = Skanda: III, 14635.

[Viçvāmitropākhyāna(m)] ("the episode relating to Viçvāmitra"): § 721*b* (Ānuçāsanik.). *Bhīshma* said: King *Ajamīḍha* (of *Bharata's* race) > king *Jahnu* (who got *Gaṅgā* for his daughter) > *Sindhudvīpa* (virtuous) > R-ṛ *Balākāçva* > *Vallabha* > *Kuçika* > *Gādhi*, who, being childless and desiring to have a son, repaired to the forest, where the beautiful *Satyavatī* was born to him. *Cyavana's* son, *Ṛcīka Bhārgava*, asked for her hand; but as he was poor, *Gādhi* required of him as a dower 1,000 white horses having one black ear, which he obtained from *Varuṇa* (by thinking of them at *Açvatīrtha*, on the bank of the *Gaṅgā*, not far from *Kānyakubja*). *Ṛcīka* granted her a boon, that she should have a son; she related this to her mother, who prevailed upon her to obtain a son also for her; having promised them both a son, he told the mother to embrace an *açvattha* tree and *Satyavatī* an *udumbara* tree, and each of them to eat a certain *caru* (sacrificial offering), consecrated with hymns. The mother exchanged both the trees and the *carus*. *Ṛcīka* had placed the entire *brahman*-energy in *Satyavatī's caru* and the *kshatriya*-energy in that of her mother; "therefore, thy mother will give birth to an excellent brahman and thou to a terrible *kshatriya*." *Satyavatī* prevailed upon him, that not her son, but her son's son should be such. Then, by the favour of *Ṛcīka*, she gave birth to *Jamadagni*, and the wife of *Gādhi* to the Brahmarshi (read *brahmarshiṃ*) *Viçvāmitra*, versed in the *Vedas* (*brahmavādinaṃ*). *Viçvāmitra* attained to the state of a brahman, and became the founder of a race of brahmans. *Madhucchanda*, etc., (*β*), were all sons of *Viçvāmitra* (XIII, **4**).

Viçvamūrti[1] = Çiva: VII, 9506; XIII, 7499.—Do.[2] = Mahāpurusha (Mahāpurushastava).—Do.[3] = Vishṇu (Kṛshṇa): VI, †2944, 2948; XII, †12879; XIII, 7026.

Viçvanara = Çiva: VII, 9507.

Viçvāṅga = Kṛshṇa: XII, 1610.

Viçvapara = Vishṇu: III, 10120.

Viçvapati, name of a fire. § 493 (Āṅgirasa): III, **221**, 14193 (second son of the fire Manu).

Viçvaretas = Vishṇu (1000 names).

Viçvaruci, a Gandharva (?). § 595 (Shoḍaçarāj., v. Pṛthu Vainya): VII, **69**, 2418 (when the Gandharvas milked the earth *V.* was their milker).

Viçvarūpa[1], an Asura. § 268 (Varuṇasabhāv.): II, **9**, 366 (among the Daityas and Dānavas in the palace of Varuṇa).

Viçvarūpa[2], son of Tvashṭṛ. § 555 (Indravijaya): V, **8**, 230 (Tvashṭṛ created a three-headed (*triçiras*) son *V.*, whom Indra slew with his thunderbolt; Tvashṭṛ then created Vṛtra); **17**, 522 (°*vināçena*).—§ 665 (Mokshadh.): XII, **208**, 7584 (*Tvashṭuç caivātmajaḥ*).—§ 717*b* (Nārāyaṇīya): XII, **343**, VII), ††13207 (*Tvāshṭraḥ purohitaḥ devānāṃ*), ††13208 (°*mātaraṃ*), ††13209 (*Tvāshṭro V°as Triçirā devānāṃ purohitaḥ*), ††13211, ††13212, ††13213 (*V.*, the son of Tvashṭṛ and an Asura woman, was the purohita of the gods, but afterwards he joined the Asuras and was then slain by Indra with the thunderbolt, cf. § 555).—§ 778*b* (Saṃvartta-Maruttīya): XIV, **5**, 114 (°*sya nihantā*, i.e. Indra). Cf. Triçiras, Tvashṭṛputra, Tvāshṭra.

Viçvarūpa[3] = Çiva: VII, †9548, 9621 (etymology); X, 253; XII, 241 (*Mahādevaḥ*), †10438 (1000 names[1]), 11785 (*Rudrasya*); XIII, 589, 606 (*Çivāya*, B. *Vishṇurūpāya*), 727 (*Maheçvaraḥ*), 908, 1125, 1149 (1000 names[2]), 1155 (do.), 7503, 7513 (etymology); XIV, 209, 211.—Do.[4] = Hiraṇyagarbha: XII, 11233.—Do.[5] = Mahāpurusha (Mahāpurushastava).—Do.[6] = Kṛshṇa (Vishṇu); XII, †2403, 13109; XIII, †7367, †7388, †7390.

Viçvarūpadhṛk[1] = Vishṇu: XII, 12865.—Do.[2] = Vṛtra: V, 301.

Viçvasambhava[1] = Çiva: XIII, 920.—Do.[2] = Kṛshṇa: XII, 1503, 1672, 1846; XIV, 1593.

Viçvasattama = Kṛshṇa: XIV, 1485.

Viçvasena, a Gandharva (?). § 695*b* (Dakshayajñavināça): XII, **285***a*, 10279.

Viçvasṛj[1] ("creator of the universe") = Çiva: VII, 2880, 9506; XIII, 609.—Do.[2] = Kṛshṇa: VII, 1464 (*Govindaḥ*); XIII, †7367.—Do.[3], pl.: VII, 2173 (*devāḥ*); XII, 911 (do.), 1633 (*yaḥ sahasrasame sattre jajñe v°āṃ ṛshiḥ*, sc. Kṛshṇa); XIV, 1435 (*viprāḥ*), 1437 (*bhūtebhyaḥ*, i.e. Marīci, etc., Nīl.).

Viçvātman[1] ("the universal spirit") = Brahmán: II, 474.—Do.[2] = Çiva: VII, 2880, 9506, 9597; X, 307.—Do.[3] = Hiraṇyagarbha: XII, 11232.—Do.[4] = Sūrya: III, 157.—Do.[5] = Vishṇu (Kṛshṇa): II, 2293; III, 12983, 12990, 15529, 15534, 15545, 15808; XII, 1503, 1658, 1672, 1846, 12657 (*Nārāyaṇaḥ*), 13274 (do.); XIII, 6973 (1000 names); XIV, 1485, 1593.—Do.[6] = Vṛtra: XII, 10132 (*V°*).

Viçvatomukha = Sūrya: III, 157.—Do.[2] = Çiva (1000 names[1]).

Viçvāvāsa = Kṛshṇa: VI, 2949 (B. °*av*°); XIII, 7392.

Viçvāvasu, a Gandharva king. § 21 (Pramadvarā): I, **8**, 943 (*Gandharvarājaḥ*, begot Pramadvarā on Menakā).—§ 102 (Aṃçāvat.): I, **65**, 2555 (among the Devagandharvas, sons of Prādhā).—§ 191 (Arjuna): I, **123**, 4814 (among the Devagandharvas present at the birth of Arjuna).—§ 221*b* (Cākshushī): I, **170**, 6478 (learnt the Cākshushī from Soma and communicated it to Citraratha).—§ 233 (Svayaṃvarap.): I, **187**, †7011 (came to see the svayaṃvara of Draupadī).—§ 266 (Çakrasabhāv.): II, **7**, 303 (in the palace of Indra).—§ 269 (Vaiçravaṇasabhāv.): II, **10**, 406 (*Gandharvāṇāñ ca patayo V°uḥ*, etc., in the palace of Kubera).—§ 336 (Indralokābhigamanap.): III, **43**, 1773 (°*prabhṛtibhir Gandharvaiḥ*).—§ 377 (Dhaumyatīrthak.): III, **90**, 8389 (a çloka sung by *V.* quoted, PCR. has Vibhāvasu).—§ 378 (Tīrthayātrāp.): III, **91**, 8420 (°*os tu tanayād*, i.e. Citrasena).—§ 443 (Nivātakavacayuddhap.): III, **168**, 12048 (°*oç ca vai putraç Citrasenaḥ*).—§ 530 (Viçvāvasumokshaṇa): III, **279**, 16086 (*Gandharvaḥ*, had been cursed and become a Rākshasa (Kabandha), but was delivered by Rāma Dāçarathi).—§ 555 (Indravijaya): V, **11**, 356 (°*ur Nāradaç ca*).—§ 574 (Jambūkh.): VI, **6**, 214 (on Meru).—§ 595 (Shoḍaçarāj., v. Dilīpa): VII, **61**, v. 7 (only B. in a çloka wanting in C. after v. 2266; played on his vīṇā at the sacrifice of Dilīpa). § 615*d* (Gandharvāṇāṃ tīrthaṃ): IX, **37**, 2128 (°*mukhāḥ* . . . *Gandharvāḥ*).—§ 632*b* (Shoḍaçarāj., cf. § 595, v. Dilīpa): XII, **29**, 969 (played on his vīṇā at the sacrifice of Dilīpa).—§ 602*b* (Jāpakop.): XII, **200***b*, 7340.—§ 694*b* (Jvarotpatti): XII, **284***a*, 10218 (*Gandharvaḥ*).—§ 695*b* (Dakshayajñavināça): XII, **285***a*, 10279.—§ 707 (Mokshadh.): XII, **319**, 11750 (*Gandharvaḥ*), 11759, 11771, (11781), (†11807) (was instructed by Yājñavalkya).—§ 712 (Çukotpatti): XII, **324**, 12176 (*Gandharvaḥ*); **325**, 12201 (do.).—§ 730 (Ānuçāsanik.): XIII, **16** *ηη*, 1050 (?°-*Hiraṇyāksha-Puruhūtanamaskṛta*, sc. Çiva).—§ 746 (do.): XIII, **83** *ξ*, 3887.—§ 775 (do.): XIII, **166***a*, 7639.—§ 785 (Anugītāp.): XIV, **88** *ψ*, 2642.—§ 786*e* (Agastya): XIV, **92**, 2871.—

§ 789 (Putradarçanap.): XV, **29a**, 774. Cf. Gandharva, Gandharvarāja, Gandharvendra, Kāçyapa.

Viçvāvasu[2], son of Jamadagni. § 396 (Jamadagni): III, **116**, 10180.

Viçvāvasu[3] = Kṛshṇa: VI, †2944.

[**Viçvāvasumokshaṇa** ("the liberation of Viçvāvasu")]. § 530 (cf. Rāmopākhyānap.). *Jaṭāyu* (brother of *Sampāti* and son of Aruṇa and friend of Daçaratha) attacked *Rāvaṇa*, who cut off his wings. *Rāvaṇa* entered *Lankā* (built by Viçvakṛt) with *Sītā*. *Jaṭāyu* indicated to *Rāma* (*Kākutstha*) and *Lakshmaṇa* that *Rāvaṇa* had gone towards the south, and then he died. *Rāma* caused his funeral obsequies to be duly performed. *Rāma* and *Lakshmaṇa* killed a *Rākshasa* named *Kabandha*, from whose body there came out a celestial person, viz. the *Gandharva* prince *Viçvāvasu*, who had been cursed by a brahman; he directed them to *Sugrīva* (brother of the monkey king *Vālin*), who dwelled at the lake *Pampā*, near the mountain *Ṛshyamūka*, with his four counsellors; then he disappeared (III, **279**).

Viçvāvatī = Gangā: XIII, 1849.

Viçvayoni[1] ("source of the universe") = Brahmán (?): VI, 1960.—Do.[2] = Vishṇu (Kṛshṇa): XII, 1514; XIII, 6962 (1000 names), 6965 (do.).

Viçvāyu, a Viçvadeva. § 749 (Ānuçāsanik.): XIII, **91**γ, 4359 (enumeration).

Viçve [devāḥ], pl. (sometimes only *Viçve*, scil. *devāḥ*, lit. "all gods", but mostly name of a certain class of gods). § 3 (Anukramaṇik.): I, **1a**, 34 (*devāḥ ?*).—§ 15 (Upamanyu): I, **3**, †727 (*yasmin devā adhi viçve*, sc. *cakraṃ*).—§ 130 (Aṃçāvat.): I, **67**, 2762 (*devagaṇān*, incarnate as the Draupadeyas).—§ 133 (Dushyanta): I, **71**, 2933.—§ 191 (Arjuna): I, **123a**, 4827 (*devāḥ*, present at the birth of Arjuna).—§ 258 (Khāṇḍavadahanap.): I, **227**, 8270 (*devāḥ*, fought with Kṛshṇa and Arjuna).—§ 266 (Çakrasabhāv.): II, **7**, 303 (in the palace of Indra).—§ 270 (Brahmasabhāv.): II, **11**, 460 (*devāḥ*, in the palace of Brahmán).—§ 336 (Indralokābhigamanap.): III, **43**, 1768 (in the world of Indra).—§ 520 (Mudgala): III, **261**, 15446. — § 547 (Karṇa): III, **308**, 17139 (*devatāḥ*). — § 552 (Goharaṇap.): IV, **56**, 1762 (*Viçvāçvi-Marutāṃ gaṇaiḥ*).—§ 556 (Sañjayayānap.): V, **29**, †823.—§ 565 (Gālavacarita): V, **109**, 3781 (°*e . . . devāḥ Pitṛbhiḥ sārdhaṃ*, in the south).—§ 567 (Bhagavadyānap.): V, **131**o, 4424 (*devāḥ*).—§ 576 (Bhagavadgītāp.): VI, **35**, †1268.—§ 595 (Shoḍaçarāj., v. Marutta): VII, **55**, 2177 (*devāḥ*, the courtiers (*sabhāsadaḥ*) of Marutta).—§ 596 (Pratijñāp.): VII, **76**, 2682 (*devāḥ*).—§ 603*b* (Nārāyaṇa): VII, **201**ςς, †9165 (*bhūtasanghān sa-V°ān*), 9475 (?). — § 603 (Nārāyaṇāstramokshap.): VII, **202**κκ, 9621 (*devāḥ*, etymology of the name Viçvarūpa). — § 608 (Karṇap.): VIII, **87**χ', 4418 (sided with Arjuna).—§ 615*u* (Skanda): IX, **44**, 2478.—§ 615*ee* (Ādityatīrtha): IX, **49**, 2848 (*devāḥ*, in Ādityatīrtha).—§ 615*gg* (Sarasvata): IX, **51**, 2941 (°*e devāḥ sa-Pitaraḥ*).—§ 623 (Rājadh.): XII, **15**β, 440 (*devāḥ*).—§ 632*b* (Shoḍaçarāj., cf. § 595): XII, **29**, 914 (*devāḥ*, the courtiers (*sabhāsadaḥ*) of Marutta). — § 641 (Rājadh.): XII, **64**η, †2395; **122**, 4516 (°*e devāḥ . . . V°ebhyaḥ*). — § 655 (Apaddh.): XII, **165**, 6054 (*devaiḥ*).—§ 658*b* (Kṛtaghnop.): XII, **171**, 6382 (°*e devāḥ sa-Pitaraḥ*).—§ 662*b* (Jāpakop.): XII, **200**δ, 7339.—§ 664 (Mokshadh.): XII, **207**ε, 7540 (*devāḥ*, sons of Dharma).—§ 665 (do.): XII, **208**, 7589 (*devāḥ*).—§ 702 (do.): XII, **296**β, 10837 (*devāḥ*).—§ 704 (do.): XII, **301**, 11096 (*devān*). — § 730*g* (Upamanyu): XIII, **14**η, 731 (*devānāṃ*, Çiva assumes their form).—§ 730 (Ānuçāsanik.): XIII, **14**, 985 (*devāḥ*, praised Çiva); **16**ηη, 1052 (*devāḥ*), (θθ), 1105 (do.); **18**λλ, ††1368.—§ 749 (do.): XIII, **91**β, 4349 (°*e devāḥ ye nityaṃ Pitṛbhiḥ sahagocarāḥ*) (γ), 4354 (°*e cāgnimukhāḥ*, their names (sixty-four in number) enumerated), 4358 (*devāḥ*).—§ 750*b* (Bisastainyop.): XIII, **93**δ, 4493 (*devāḥ*, etymology of the name Viçvāmitra).—§ 766 (Ānuçāsanik.): XIII, **133**γ, 6186 (*devāḥ*).—§ 768*b* (Umā-Maheçvarasaṃv.): XIII, **140a**, 6351 (°*e devāḥ sa-Vāsavāḥ*).—§ 770 (Ānuçāsanik.): XIII, **151**, 7098 (*devāḥ*).—§ 773*b* (Kṛshṇa Vāsudeva): XIII, **159**β, †7387.—§ 773*d* (Çiva): XIII, **162**ε, 7513 (*devāḥ*, etymology of the name Viçvarūpa). — § 775 (Ānuçāsanik.): XIII, **166a**, 7660 (*devāḥ*).—§ 778*f* (Muñjavat): XIV, **8**, 183 (worship Çiva on Muñjavat).—§ 778*b* (Saṃvartta-Maruttīya): XIV, **10**, †261 (*devāḥ*).—§ 793 (Mausalap.): XVI, **4**θ, †129.—§ 795 (Svargārohaṇap.): XVIII, **5**μ, 164 (*devatānāṃ*). Cf. Viçvadeva, pl., Viçvedeva, pl.

Viçveça[1] ("lord of the universe") = Brahmán: V, 1920.—Do.[2] = Çiva: III, 1654; VIII, 1548; XII, 13284, 13302 (*Haraṃ*); XIII, 903.—Do.[3] = Kṛshṇa (Vishṇu): VI, †2944 XII, 13503.

Viçveçvara[1] (do.) = Brahmán: XIII, 7102 (°*kṛtān*, sc. *lokān*).—Do.[2] = Çiva: III, 7042 (*Umāpatiṃ*), 8113 (*Devyā saha*); VII, 9451, 9507, 9643; XII, ††6977 (*Umāpatiḥ*); XIII, 773; XIV, 208.—Do.[3] = Kṛshṇa (Vishṇu): VI, †1262, †2944; XII, 13322 (*Hareḥ*); XIII, 7078.—Do.[4] = Mahāpurusha (Mahāpurushastava). — Do.[5], dual (°*au*) = Brahmán and Çiva: VII, 2067; XII, 9181.

Viçveçvarasthāna, a tīrtha, sacred to Viçveçvara (Çiva). § 775 (Ānuçāsanik.): XIII, **166a**, 7649 (= Benares, PCR.).

Viçvedeva, pl. (°*āḥ*) = Viçve (pl.). § 120 bis (Aṃçāvat.): I, **66**, 2602.—§ 330 (Indradarçana): III, **37**, 1490.—§ 615*u* (Skanda): IX, **45**γ, 2508.—§ 707 (Mokshadh.): XII, **318**, 11707.—§ 753 (Ānuçāsanik.): XIII, **97a**, 4664.

Viçvedeva = Çiva: XIII, 985 (only C., B. has *Viçvadevaṃ*).

Viçvopākhyāna, v. Çvetopākhyāna.

Vidaṇḍa, a prince. § 232 (Svayaṃvarap.): I, **186**, 6992 (came to the svayaṃvara of Draupadī).

Vidabha, pl. (°*āḥ*), a people. § 574 (Jambūkh.): VI, **9**ν, 372 (only B., C. has *Daçi-Vidarbhāḥ*).

Vidāraṇa = Vishṇu (1000 names).

Vidarbha ("king of the Vidarbhas") = Bhīma: III, 2103 (*kanyāṃ V°syā*, i.e. Damayantī).

Vidarbha, pl. (°*āḥ*), a people. § 344 (Nalopākhyānap.): III, **53**, 2076 (ruled by Bhīma), 2093, 2094 (°*nagariṃ*); **54**, 2129.—§ 346 (do.): III, **60**, 2293.—§ 347 (do.): III, **61**, 2319 (*esha panthā V°āṇāṃ*); 2328, 2331; **64**, 2447, 2476.—§ 350 (do.): III, **68**, 2666 (°*sarasaḥ*); **69**, 2714 (only B., C. has °*āṃ*), 2717.—§ 351 (do.): III, **71**, 2772 (only B., C. has °*āṃ*), 2780 (°*nagarīṃ*), 2788.—§ 352 (do.): III, **72**, 2826–8 (only B., C. has °*āṃ*), 2850.—§ 353 (do.): III, **73**, 2852 (only B., C. has °*āṃ*).—§ 574 (Jambūkh.): VI, **9**μ, 351.—§ 578 (Bhīshmavadhap.): VI, **51**ρ, 2103 (in the army of Duryodhana).—§ 686 (Mokshadh.): XII, **273**, 9813. Cf. Daçi-Vidarbha, pl.

Vidarbhā, the metropolis of the Vidarbhas. § 350 (Nalopākhyānap.): III, **69**, 2714 (only C., B. has °*ān*).—§ 351 (do.): III, **71**, 2772 (do., do.).—§ 352 (do.): III, **72**, 2826–8 (do., do.).—§ 353 (do.): III, **73**, 2852 (do., do.). Cf. Kuṇḍina.

Vidarbhādhipanandinī ("daughter of the Vidarbha king") = Damayantī: III, 2409.

Vidarbhādhipati ("the king of the Vidarbhas") = Bhīma[10]: III, 2444, 2728.
Vidarbhapati (do.) = do.: III, 2108, 2873.
Vidarbharāj (do.) = do.: III, 2524.
Vidarbharāja[1] (do.) = do.: III, 2332, 2694.
Vidarbharāja[2] (do.), the father of Lopāmudrā. § 382 (Agastyop.): III, **96,** 8650.
Vidarbharāja[3] (do.), a prince. § 420 (Tīrthayātrāp.): III, **120,** †10269 (*°opacitām . . . Payoshṇīm*).
Vidarbharājan (do.) = Bhīma[10]: III, 2124 (*°jño duhitā Damayantī*).
Vidarbharājatanayā ("daughter of the Vidarbha king") = Damayantī: III, 2433 (*D°*).
Vidarbhatanayā (do.) = do.: III, 2412.
Videha, pl. (*°āḥ*), a people. § 177 (Pāṇḍudigvijaya): I, **113,** 4452 (in Mithilā, vanquished by Pāṇḍu on his digvijaya).—§ 280 (Bhīmasena): II, **29,** 1062 (vanquished by Bhīmasena on his digvijaya in the east).—§ 562 (Bhagavadyānap.): V, **74**γ, 2731 (*Hayagrīvo V°ānām*).—§ 587 (Bhīshmavadhap.): VI, **117**ρ, 5483 (attacked Arjuna).—§ 589 (Droṇābhishekap.): VII, **4**β, 120 (had formerly been vanquished by Karṇa). — § 595 (Shoḍaçarāj., v. Rāma Jāmadagnya): VII, **70**β, 2436 (have formerly been slain by Rāma Jāmadagnya).—§ 604 (Karṇap.): VIII, **3**δ, 70 (in the army of Yudhishṭhira; slain by Karṇa); **8**η, 236 (Karṇa had formerly vanquished the *V.* and caused them to pay tribute to Duryodhana); **9**θ, 283 (do.).—§ 707 (Mokshadh.): XII, **319,** 11821 (*°rājyam*, ruled by Janaka Daivarāti). — § 709*b* (Sulabha-Janakasaṃv.): XII, **321,** 11862 (*°ānāṃ purīm*, i.e. Mithilā).—§ 719 (Çukakṛti): XII, **326,** 12233, 12236 (ruled by Janaka).
Videha, sg. ("the country of the Videhas"). § 410 (Plakshāvatāraṇag.): III, **130,** 10548 (*dvāraṃ V°ād uttaram*).
Videharāja[1] ("the king of the Videhas"), a prince at the time of Yudhishṭhira. § 233 (Svayaṃvarap.): I, **188,** †7020 (present at the svayaṃvara of Draupadī).
Videharāja[2] (do.) = Janaka: III, †10600, 15880 (*J°*, father of Sītā); XII, 537 (*°mahishī*), †891, 6640 (*J°*), 9916 (an itihāsa sung by *V.* to Māṇḍavya quoted), 10941, 12270 (*J°*); XIII, 2466 (*Sukratuḥ . . . naptā V°rājasya Janakasya*).
Videharājaduhitṛ ("the daughter of the Videha king"). § 744 (Ānuçāsanik.): XIII, **46,** 2495 (a çloka sung by her quoted).
Videharājan ("the king of the Videhas") = Janaka: XII, 536.
***vidhāna** ("destiny"): I, 3370; II, 716 (*°balacoditā*), 1703 (?); XII, 850, 852, 6752, 6755, 12145, 12148 (?).
Vidharma = Kṛshṇa: XII, 1508.
Vidhātṛ ("the Ordainer, the Creator", often mentioned together with Dhātṛ, elsewhere he may be = Brahmán). § 6 (Anukramaṇik.): I, **1,** 240 (*°vihitaṃ mārgam*).—§ 17 (Uttaṅka): I, **3,** ††828 (*Dhātā V°ā ca*, seen by Uttaṅka in the world of the Nāgas in the shape of two women).—§ 27 (Kaçyapa): I, **16,** 1093 (*annaṃ vihitaṃ . . . V°trā*).—§ 33 (Garuḍa): I, **23,** 1251 (*Dhātā V°ā ca*, identified with Garuḍa).—§ 123 (Aṃçāvat.): I, **66,** 2614 (*Dhātā V°ā ca*, sons of Brahmán).—§ 235 (Svayaṃvarap.): I, **191,** 7144 (*rūpaṃ . . . V°trā vihitam*).—§ 266 (Çakrasabhāv.): II, **7,** 295 (in the palace of Indra).—§ 323 (Dvaitavanapr.): III, **25,** †960 (*yathāvad vihitaṃ V°trā*).—§ 327 (Draupadīparitāpav.): III, **30,** 1117 (*namo Dhātre V°tre ca yau mohañ cakratus tava*); **32,** 1208 (*Dhātā V°ā ca*).—§ 330 (Indradarçana): III, **37,** 1488 (*namo Dhātre V°tre ca*).—§ 340 (Indralokābhigamanap.): III, **48,** †193 (*sṛshṭo 'ntakaḥ sarvaharo V°trā*).—§ 406 (Tīrthayātrāp.): III, **125,** 10419 (*yatra*—i.e. at Prasravaṇam Indrasya—*Dhātā V°ā ca Varuṇaç cordhvam āgatāḥ*).—§ 412 (Ashṭāvakrīya): III, **134,** †10659 (*bhāryāpatī dvau vihitau V°trā*).—§ 459 (Mārkaṇḍeyas.): III, **189,** 12953 (*sarvabhūtānām*, i.e. Nārāyaṇa), 12955 (*ahaṃ Dhātā V°ā ca*, says Nārāyaṇa), 13004 (*esha Dhātā V°ā ca*, sc. Kṛshṇa).—§ 467 (Rājanyamahābhāgya): III, **198,** ††13328 (in the shape of a brahman he put Çibi to the test).—§ 480 (Pativratop.): III, **207,** 13721 (*°trā vihitaṃ . . . karma*).—§ 522 (Draupadīharaṇap.): III, **265,** †15591 (*Dhātur V°uḥ*, sc. *sadanāt*).—§ 552 (Goharaṇap.): IV, **56**ζ, 1770 (*Dhātur V°uç ca*, sc. *vimānāni*, present at the encounter).—§ 556 (Sañjayayānap.): V, **23,** †701 (*vihitaṃ V°trā*); **28,** †798 (*prāyaçcittaṃ vihitaṃ yad V°trā*).—§ 561 (Yānasandhip.): V, **53,** †2104 (*sṛshṭo 'ntakaḥ sarvaharo V°trā*).—§ 570 (Sainyaniryāṇap.): V, **151,** 5133 (*esha Dhātā V°ā ca*, sc. Kṛshṇa).—§ 571 (Ulūkadūtāgamanap.): V, **160,** 5516 (*manasaivānukulāni V°ā kurute vaçe*); **161,** 5561 (do.).—§ 599 (Jayadrathavadhap.): VII, **94**ε, 3454 (*Dhātā V°ā ca*, mentioned in a blessing to Duryodhana).—§ 603 (Nārāyaṇāstramokshap.): VII, **202***a*, 9597 (*Dhātā ca . . . V°ā ca*, identified with Çiva).—§ 615*u* (Skanda): IX, **45**γ, 2506 (*Dhātā V°ā ca*, came to the investiture of Skanda), 2545 (gave two companions to Skanda).—§ 623 (Rājadh.): XII, **15,** 458 (*daṇḍo V°trā vihitaḥ*).—§ 629 (do.): XII, **25,** †736 (*vihitaṃ V°trā*).—§ 671*b* (Bali-Vāsavasaṃv.): XII, **225,** 8157 (*na Dhātā na V°ā mām*—i.e. Çrī—*vidadhāti kathañcana / Kālas tu*, etc.).—§ 679 (Mokshadh.): XII, **261,** 9254 (*°trā vihitaṃ purā*).—§ 692 (do.): XII, **281,** 10090 (identified with Vishṇu (Kṛshṇa)).—§ 730 (Ānuçāsanik.): XIII, **14**εε, 1003 (identified with Çiva); **16,** 1059 (do.); **18,** 1324 (*Dhātā V°ā ca*, i.e. Çiva).—§ 742 (do.): XIII, **38,** †2231 (*lokā vihitā V°trā*). — § 758 (do.): XIII, **103,** †4949 (= Brahmán, discourse between him and Bhagīratha).—§ 768*b* (Umā-Maheçvarasaṃv.): XIII, **145,** 6713 (*dharmaḥ . . . V°trā svayam īritaḥ*).—§ 773*d* (Çiva): XIII, **161**δ, 7498 (*Dhātā . . . V°ā ca*, identified with Çiva).—§ 782*g* (Guruçishyasaṃv.): XIV, **42**ε, 1167 (*Dhātā V°ā ca* = mahān ātmā).
Vidhātṛ[2] = Çiva (1000 names[1–2]).—Do.[3] = Vishṇu (1000 names).
Vidheyātman = Vishṇu (1000 names).
***vidhi** ("destiny", also personified ("the Ordainer"): I, 2608 (*niyukte V°nā*), 4281 (*°nā sampracoditaḥ*); III, 323 (*°nākṛshya kāritaḥ*), 377 (*°nā sampraṇuditaḥ*), 2562 (*°eḥ saṃrambhaḥ*), 2802 (*daivena v°nā yuktāḥ*), 13803 (*balavān*), 13804 (*°nā hate*), 15169 (*daivāc ca V°nirmitāt*), 15864 (*daivaṃ ca V°nirmitam*), 16018 (*°coditā*), 17152 (*daivañ ca V°nirmitam*); V, 224 (*balavattaraḥ*), †837 (*°prakopāt*), 2916 (*daivāc ca V°nirmitāt*), 3990 (*balavān*); XI, 235 (*anatikramaṇīyaḥ*), 239 (*°eç cāpy anivartanāt*); XII, 856 (*°ceshṭitam*), 1180, 1235 (*saṃskāro vidhinoditaḥ*), †6259 (*°ir niyuṅkte; °ir balīyān*), †6679 (*°pariṇāma*), †6682 (*°niyatam*), 7639 (= Vishṇu), 8108 (*divyasya* = Kāla), 8625 (*°dṛshṭena balena*), 10011 (*kṛtāntavidhisaṃyuktaḥ*), †10079 (*svaṃ svaṃ vidhiṃ yānti*); XIII, 343 (*°nā karmaṇā caiva svargamārgam avāpnuyāt*), 5643 (*pramāṇaṃ V°nirmitam*).
Vidiçā, a river. § 268 (Varuṇasabhāv.): II, **9,** 371 (among the rivers present in the palace of Varuṇa). — § 574 (Jambūkh.): VI, **9**λ, 335.
Vidiçaḥ (pl.) = Vishṇu (1000 names).
Vidigbhānu = Mahāpurusha (Mahāpurushastava).

Vidulā, a princess, mother of Sañjaya, the Sauvīra king. § 11 (Parvasaṅgr.): I, **2**, 509 (°*āyāç ca putrasya proktaṃ cāpy anuçāsanaṃ*, i.e. Vidulāputraçāsana).—§ 568 (Vidulāputraçāsana): V, **133**, 4494 (°*āyāç ca saṃvādaṃ putrasya ca*), 4496, 4497, (4498); **134**, (4539) (the story of *V.'s* instruction of her son, which Kuntī asked Kṛshṇa to tell Yudhishṭhira).—§ 787 (Āçramavāsap.): XV, **16**, 461 (°*āyā vacobhiḥ*, all. to § 568); **17**, 487 (°*vākyaiḥ*, do.), 491 (do.).

Vidulāputraçāsana(ṃ) ("Vidulā's instruction of her son"). § 10 (Parvas.): I, **2**, 333.—§ 568 (Bhagavady.): The princess *Vidulā* one day rebuked her son *Sañjaya*, who, being defeated by the king of the *Sindhus*, was lying dejected. "Without wrath, as thou art, thou canst not be counted as a man . . . It is better to blaze up for a moment than to smoke for a long time . . . He who has not achieved a great feat, forming the subject of men's conversation, only increases the number of men; he is neither man nor woman . . . It behoves thee not to adopt the idle, wretched, infamous, and miserable profession of mendicancy that is worthy only of a coward . . . He is a man who cherishes wrath and does not forgive . . . (V, **133**) . . . The followers of the *Sindhu*-king are all discontented and waiting for the distress of their master; others will come to thee with their auxiliaries if they behold thee put forth thy prowess . . . While thou wert a child, a brahman said: 'this one, falling into great distress, will again win greatness.' *Çambara* has said 'there is not a more miserable state than that in which one does not see how to procure his food from day to day'. By slaying *Vṛtra*, *Indra* became *Mahendra* ("the great Indra"), and obtained the *soma*-cup of Mahendra (v. 4562, B.: *Māhendraṃ ca grahaṃ lebhe*), and the lordship of all the worlds . . . Sovereignty is either the door of heaven or *amṛta* . . . In the possession of wealth, rejoice, as before, with the *Sauvīra*-maidens, and be not ruled over by the *Saindhava*-maidens . . . Handed down by tradition from time immemorial, the eternal essence of *kshatriya*-virtues (*kshatrahṛdayaṃ*) has been ordained by *Prajāpati* himself . . . A *kshatriya* should rather break than yield. He should bow down to *brahmans* only and to virtue (*dharmāya*); he should rule over all other orders, destroying all evil-doers" (V. **134**). The son complained that the heart of his mother was made of steel, and blamed the *kshatriya*-practices. *Vidulā* said that if *Sañjaya* was about to be stained by infamy and she did not say it to him, her affection for him would be like that of a she-ass for her young. He ought to have recourse to virtue and profit (V, **135**) . . . "We have many treasure-houses unknown to thee . . . thou hast also more than one friend." Despair left *Sañjaya's* heart, though he was not gifted with great intelligence. He roused himself and achieved all that his mother had pointed out. Indeed, this history, named *Jaya*, should be listened to by everyone desirous of victory, etc. (V, **136**).

Vidura (also named Kshattṛ, son of Vyāsa and a çūdra woman, the maid of Ambikā, and incarnation of a portion of Dharma). § 4 (Anukramaṇik.): I, **1**, 95, 138, †151.—§ 11 (Parvasaṅgr.): I, **2**, 378, 379, 393, 503, 584, 611, 615.—§ 70 (Ādivaṃçāvatāraṇap.): I, **60**, 2213 (begotten by Vyāsa).—§ 71 (do.): I, **61**, 2244, 2245, 2252 (all. to § 213).—§ 80 (Aṇīmāṇḍavya): I, **63**, 2426 (Dharma born as *V.*).—§ 83 (Ādivaṃçāvatāraṇa): I, **63**, 2442 (*Çūdrayonau tu jajñe Dvaipāyanāt*, all. to § 171).—§ 130 (Aṃçāvat.): I, **67**, 2721*d* (incarnation of the son of Atri, i.e. Dharma).—§ 157 (Pūruvaṃç.): I, **95**, ††3808 (Dhṛtarāshṭra, Pāṇḍu, and *V.* begotten by Vyāsa, cf. § 171), ††3819.—§ 158 (do.): I, **95**, ††3823 (all. to § 213).—§ 171 (Vicitravīryasutotpatti): I, **106**, 4301 (*Dhṛtarāshṭrasya bhrātā Pāṇḍoç caiva*, begotten by Vyāsa on the maid of Ambikā), 4302 (incarnation of Dharma).—§ 172 (Anīmāṇḍavyop.): I, **108**, 4335 (Dharma born as *V*°.).—§ 173 (Pāṇḍurājyābhisheka): I, **109**, 4353, 4358, 4361 (of the *pārasava* caste), 4362.—§ 174 (Dhṛtarāshṭravivāha): I, **110**, 4369, (4370).—§ 178 (Pāṇḍu): I, **114**, 4470.—§ 179 (Viduraparinaya): I, **114**, 4481, 4482 (married a *pārasavī*, the daughter of king Devaka).—§ 180 (Gāndhārīputrotpatti): I, **115**, 4510, 4513, 4518 (when Duryodhana was born, *V.*, in vain, told Dhṛtarāshṭra to abandon him).—§ 184 (Pāṇḍu): I, **119**, 4614 (*Kshattā*).—§ 194 (do.): I, **126**, 4911 (do.).—§ 195 (do.): I, **127**, 4932, 4936, 4947, 4959, 4960 (performed the funeral ceremonies of Pāṇḍu and Mādrī).—§ 197 (Bhīmasenarasapāna): I, **129**, (5049), 5051, 5067/8 (only B.), 5070 (°*sya mate*).—§ 208 (Astradarçana): I, **134**, 5313, 5319, 5346; **135**, 5360 (5362); **136**, 5406.—§ 213 (Jatugṛhap.): I, **141**, 5637, (5640), 5643, 5646, 5656 (°*sya mate*); **143**, 5707; **145**, 5735, 5738, 5752, 5760, 5761, 5762, 5765, 5766; **147**, 5798 (°*sya suhṛt kaçcit*), 5799, 5800, 5803, 5804 (*suhṛdaṃ V°sya*), 5811, 5818 (°*āmatyāt*); **149**, 5841 (*kaviḥ*), 5843, 5844, 5848 (*Kshattā*), 5852, 5853; **150**, 5860, 5873 (*V.* warned Yudhishṭhira against the plot of Duryodhana, and sent a friend of his, a miner (*khanaka*), who saved the Pāṇḍavas from the lac-house). — § 241 (Vidurāgamanap.): I, **200**, 7380, 7382, 7385, 7390, 7392; **201**, 7396, 7397; **202**, 7439.—§ 243 (do.): I, **205**, (7488); **206**, 7524, 7527, (7533) (was sent to take the Pāṇḍavas back from Kāmpilya).—§ 244 (Rājyalābhap.): I, **207**, 7545, 7554.—§ 286 (Rājasūyikap.): II, **33**, 1259.—§ 287 (do.): II, **34**, 1264 (came to the rājasūya of Yudhishṭhira).—§ 288 (do.): II, **35**, 1294 (*Kshattā*, acted as disburser (*vyayakara*)).—§ 294 (Dyūtap.): II, **49**, 1771, 1775, 1776, 1777, (1779), 1784, 1785 (ordered by Dhṛtarāshṭra to invite Yudhishṭhira to the gambling, though he did not approve of it); **50**, 1790, 1791, 1792, 1793–4 (*b: V.* knew the whole çāstra which Bṛhaspati had revealed to Indra. *V.* was esteemed as the foremost of the Kurus as Uddhava among the Vṛshṇis).—§ 298 (do.): II, **56**, 1970, 1971, †1980, †1985 (ordered by Dhṛtarāshṭra to invite Yudhishṭhira, etc., to the gambling); **57**, 1988, (†1989), 1991 (did not approve of the gambling); **58**, †1992, †1995, (†1997), (†2002), †2003, (†2004), †2006, †2008; **60**, 2052; **62**, 2094, (2095) (quoting sentences of Kāvya, *V.* advised Dhṛtarāshṭra to abandon Duryodhana); **63**, (2111); **64**, †2121, †2126, †2127, †2131, (†2132); **65**, 2182.—§ 299 (do.): II, **66**, (†2187) (warned Duryodhana); **68**, 2263, 2307, (2308) (told the story of the quarrel between Virocana and Sudhanvan).—§ 301 (do.): II, **68**, (2337), 2338; **70**, 2378; **71**, (†2395), †2402, †2403; **73**, 2447 (*mantrī*).—§ 302 (Anudyūtap.): II, **74**, 2476.—§ 305 (do.): II, **78**, 2501, (2564), (2568) (*V.* kept Kuntī in his house and consoled Yudhishṭhira); **79**, 2614, 2619.—§ 306 (do.): II, **80**, 2620, (2623), 2628, (2629), 2651 (conversation with Dhṛtarāshṭra).—§ 307 (do.): II, **81**, 2677, 2697, 2699.—§ 308 (Āraṇyakap.): III, **1**, 12, 35.—§ 311 (do.): III, **4**, †219, (†222), †235, †238, †239 (dismissed by Dhṛtarāshṭra *V.* went to the Pāṇḍavas).—§ 312 (do.): III, **5**, 244, †245, †246, †249, †250, (†251).—§ 313 (do.): III, **6**, 262, 263, 264, 268, 269, 274, 279, 282, (283), 286 (called back by Dhṛtarāshṭra); **7**, 287, 289 (*mantrī Dhṛtarāshṭrasya*), 290; **8**, 316, 322.—§ 314 (do.): III, **9**, 324, 342.—§ 315

(Maitreyaçāpa): III, **10**, 347, 383. — § 316 (Kirmīravadhap.): III, **11**, (386), (412), (454) (related the slaughter of Kirmīra).—§ 327 (Draupadīparitāpav.): III, **29**, 1111 (*Kshattā*).—§ 342 (Indralokābhigamanap.): III, **51**, †2011. —§ 512 (Ghoshayātrāp.): III, **249**, 15084.—§ 516 (Duryodhanayajña): III, **256**, 15298, 15302, 15318, 15320; **257**, 15332.—§ 548 (Āraṇeyap.): III, **314**, 17440 (*mamāṃçajaḥ*, sc. Dharma's).—§ 549 (Pāṇḍavapr.): IV, **4**, 134.—§ 552 (Goharaṇap.): IV, **50**, 1567 (*kiṃ V°o 'bravīt*). — § 554 (Sainyodyogap.): V, **2**β, †31; **3**, 52 (only B.); **6**, 114, 117. —§ 556 (Sañjayayānap.): V, **20**, 603; **26**, †749 (*vācaḥ . . . V°sya*), †750, †753, †756; **30**, †872, †897; **31**, 926 (*Kurūṇāṃ mantradhāriṇam*).—§ 557 (Prajāgarap.): V, **33**, 971, 973, 974, 975, 977, 978, 979, (983), (986); **34**, 1095, (1097) (instructed Dhṛtarāshṭra). — § 558 (do.): V, **35**, (1182), (1192), (1203), (1221) (do., told the story of the quarrel between Virocana and Sudhanvan).—§ 559 (do.): V, **36**, (1260), †1281, (†1282), (1310); **37**, (1334), (1343); **38**, (1398); **39**, (1447), (1455); **40**, (1552) (gave further instructions to Dhṛtarāshṭra).—§ 560 (Sanatsujātap.): V, **41**, 1565, (1566), 1568, (1569), 1571, 1572, 1573, (caused Sanatsujāta to instruct Dhṛtarāshṭra); **42**, †1577.—§ 561 (Yānasandhip.): V, **47**, 1791, (*a*), 1797; **48**, †1916; **50**, 1977; **51**, 2070 (*vikrushṭaṃ V°eṇādau . . . bhayam*); **54**, 2141 (*dyūtakāle . . . proktaṃ V°eṇa*); **55**, 2151; **63**, (2438); **64**, (2455), (2462) (gave advice to Dhṛtarāshṭra); **67**, 2520.—§ 562 (Bhagavadyānap.): V, **73**, 2685; **80**ζ, 2859, 2861; **83**ι, 2967 (*Kurūṇāṃ mantradhāriṇam*), 2989; **85**κ, 3023; **87**, (3061); **88**, 3078; **89**, 3122, 3125 (Kṛshṇa stopped in the house of *V.*); **90**, 3128; **91**, 3270, 3271, 3277; **92**, 3278; **93**, 3310, 3319 (conversation between *V.* and Kṛshṇa); **94**, 3331, 3345, 3362, 3380.—§ 567 (do.): V, **124a**, 4125, (β), 4137; **125**, 4192, 4204 (*Kshattā*); **128**, 4277, (θ), 4284; **129**, 4309, 4314; **130**, 4376, 4380, 4386, 4393, 4403 (*Kshattā*), (4405) (praised Kṛshṇa); **131**, 4418, 4431.—§ 569 (do.): V, **139**, 4713; **147**, 5000 (*mataṃ . . . V°sya*); **148**, 5007, 5009, 5010, 5012, 5018, (5020), 5029, †5034, †5038; **150**, 5077, 5082, 5091, 5092. —§ 570 (Sainyaniryāṇap.): V, **154**, 5219 (*°sya . . . vākyam*), 5223, 5226, 5239.—§ 571 (Ulūkadūtāgamanap.): V, **160**, 5454 (*santyāgo V°sya*).—§ 578 (Bhīshmavadhap.): VI, **49**, 1994 (*vāryamāṇaḥ . . . V°eṇa*, sc. Duryodhana). — § 581 (do.): VI, **65**, 2900 (*°vākyāni*), 2922 (*°eṇa . . . vāryamāṇaḥ*, sc. Duryodhana). — § 583 (do.): VI, **76**, 3334 (*ukto hi V°eṇaisha*, sc. Duryodhana).—§ 585 (do.): VI, **88**κ, 3926 (*uktaṃ . . . V°eṇa*); **89**μ, 3936 (*vāryamāṇaḥ . . . V°eṇa*, sc. Duryodhana), 3942; **96**, 4324 (*dṛshṭavān purā . . . bhayaṃ*).—§ 588 (do.): VI, **121**, †5797 (*vākyaṃ . . . ucyamānaṃ V°eṇa*).—§ 598 (Jayadrathavadhap.): VII, **85**, 3035 (disapproved of the gambling), 3055 (*°vākyānāṃ*)—§ 599 (do.): VII, **114**, 4487 (*ucyase . . . V°ādibhiḥ*, sc. Dhṛtarāshṭra); **151**γ′, 6539 (*ākhyāyamānaḥ . . . V°eṇa*, sc. Duryodhana), 6540 (*°sya vacaḥ*).—§ 604 (Karṇap.): VIII, **2**γ, 30; **4**, 80 (comforted Dhṛtarāshṭra). — § 608 (do.): VIII, **69**, 3433 (*Kshattā*); **96**, 5037 (comforted Dhṛtarāshṭra).—§ 609 (Çalyap.): IX, **1**, 23, (ε), 41, 51; **2**, 115 (*uktaḥ . . . V°eṇa*, sc. Dhṛtarāshṭra, all. to § 180), 117.—§ 611 (do.): IX, **24**νν, 1306, 1310 (*uktaḥ . . . V°eṇa*, sc. Arjuna), 1312, 1313 (*uktaṃ vacanaṃ . . . V°eṇa*), 1319 (*°sya ca vākyena*).—§ 612 (Hradapraveçap.): IX, **29**, 1595 (*dṛshṭavān purā . . . vaiçasaṃ*), 1655, 1663, 1668, 1670 (met with Yuyutsu).—§ 615 (Gadāyuddhap.): IX, **61**, 3407; **63**ββ, 3548.—§ 616 (Sauptikap.): X, **1a**, 14 (*vacaḥ . . . V°sya*); **2**, 102.—§ 618 (Jalapradānikap.): XI, **1**γ, 29, 45; **2**, 46 (comforted Dhṛtarāshṭra), (47); **3**, (86); **4**, (105); **5**, (126); **6**, (152); **7**, (164); **8**, 193, (ε), 194 (*Kshattā*), (ζ), 210; **9**, 254 (*V.* again comforted Dhṛtarāshṭra); **10**, 269, 271; **13**μ, 346; **15**, 423 (*°sya vacaḥ*).—§ 619 (Strīvilāpap.): XI, **17**β, 506; **25**κ, 740.—§ 620 (Çrāddhap.): XI, **26a**, 780.—§ 621 (Rājadh.): XII, **1a**, 1; **7**η, 183.—§ 635 (do.): XII, **37**δ, 1384.—§ 637 (do.): XII, **40a**, 1447; **41**β, 1476, 1483; **42**γ, 1494; **44**δ, 1529; **45**ε, 1539, 1542.—§ 657 (Āpaddh.): XII, **167**, 6210, 6213, (6214).—§ 777 (Svargārohaṇik. p.): XIII, **168**, 7715; **169**, 7769, 7770.—§ 778 (Açvamedhikap.): XIV, **1**, 10, 11 (*uktavān V°o yad māṃ*—i.e. Dhṛtarāshṭra—all. to § 180), 17; **2**, 24.—§ 783 (Anugītāp.): XIV, **52**γ, 1503, †1531 (*°ādibhiḥ*), †1533, †1534. — § 784*b* (Uttaṅka): XIV, **53**, 1552. — § 785 (Anugītāp.): XIV, **60**, 1806; **66**, 1941, (κ), 1942; **70**, 2049; **71**π, 2061.—§ 787 (Āçramavāsap.): XV, **1**, 5, 12, 15, 16; **2**, 57; **3**γ, 79 (*uktaḥ . . . V°eṇa*, sc. Dhṛtarāshṭra), 136 (*°ādayaḥ*); **4**η, 167; **5**η, 172, 175 (*°ādayaḥ*); **7**, 255 (*uktaḥ . . . V°eṇa*, sc. Yudhishṭhira); **8**ι, 259; **11**, 356, 361, 363, 380 (all. to Dyūtaparvan); **12**, 384, 388; **13**, 395, 407, 409; **14**, 410; **15**τ, †435; **16**, 444 (went to the forest together with Dhṛtarāshṭra, etc.); **18**, 498, (ψ), 513, 515; **19**, 520, (ω), 524 (*°ādayaḥ*); **20**, 557 (being a portion of Dharma, *V.* will, after death, enter Yudhishṭhira).—§ 788 (do.): XV, **21a**, 581, 584; **26**, 689, 691, 696, 697, 699, 700, 701, 702, 703, 707 (*°sañjñakaṃ kalevaram*, entered Yudhisṭhira); **28**, 751 (*Dharmasya?*), 752 (*Māṇḍavyaçāpāt . . . Dharmo V°tāṃ gataḥ*, cf. §§ 80 and 172), 761 (*Dharmaḥ*). —§ 789 (Putradarçanap.): XV, **29**, 767 (*saṃsiddhe*); [**31**ζ, 851 (*Dharmasyāṃço 'bhavat Kshattā*)].—§ 790 (do.): XV, **35**, 941 (*yayau siddhiṃ*).—[§ 795 (Svargārohaṇap.): XVIII, **5**μ, 169 (*Kshattā*, entered Dharma)].

Cf. also the following synonyms:—
Ājamīḍha, q.v.
Bhārata, Bharatarshabha, q.v.
Kaurava, q.v.
Kshattṛ; I, 99, 393, 420, 2249, 4614, (*V°*), 4911 (*V°*), 5045, 5046, 5318, 5361, 5650, 5688, 5693, 5763, 5812, 5848 (*V°*), 7381, 7389, 7393, 7521; II, 1294 (*V°*), 1768, 1770, 1780, †1990, †1996, †2001, 2010, †2121 (*V°*), †2123, †2124, †2127 (*V°*), †2131 (*V°*), †2186, †2199, †2237, †2379 (wanting in B.), 2480 (all. to § 180), 2618, 2622, 2671, 2709; III, †246, 277, 385, 1111 (*V°*), †2012, 14801 (all. to Dyūtaparvan), 15319; V, †754 (all. to Dyūtap.), †847 (do.), †848 (do.), 972, 976, 3040, 3127, 3181, 3182, 3268, 3274, 3275, 3311, 3315, 4204 (*V°*), 4236, 4325, 4329, 4395, 4403 (*V°*), 4453, 4457, 4885, 4964, 5005 (younger brother of Pāṇḍu), †5035; VI, 3919 (*yad uktavān K°ā*), 3939 (*°ur vacanaṃ*); VII, 1057 (*yad māṃ*—i.e. Dhṛtarāshṭra—*K°ābravīt*), 5597 (*°uḥ . . . vacaḥ*), 5654 (do.), 5661 (*vilapan*), 6309 (*°a rājānam abravīt*, all. to § 180), 6548 (*°ur vākyaṃ*); VIII, 3433 (*V°*), 3728/29 (only B.); IX, 45, 46, 53, 56, 1013 (*°ur vacaḥ*), 1534 (*°ur vākyaṃ*), 1595 (*vacanaṃ K°uḥ, V°*); XI, 194 (*V°*), 274, 782; XII, 4239; XIV, 1508 (printed *Kshattvāraṃ* in C.); XV, 851 (*Dharmasyāṃçaḥ*); XVIII, 169.
Kurunandana, q.v.

Vidūra, v. Vidūratha[1].

Vidurāgamana(m) ("the arrival of Vidura"). § 10 (Parvasaṅgr.): I, **2**, 315 (*°aṃ parva*, i.e. Vidurāgamanaparvan).—§ 11 (do.): I, **2**, 362 (*°aṃ*, do.).

[Vidurāgamanaparvan(°va)] ("on the arrival of Vidura", the 14th of the minor parvans of Mhbhr.). (Cf. Vidurāgamana). § 241. The news had been reported to all the monarchs that *Draupadī* had been married to the sons of *Pāṇḍu*, whom they had thought burnt to death. They then set out for their own dominions. *Duryodhana* became greatly depressed, and, with his brothers, etc., he set out for *Hāstinapura*. *Vidura* was filled with joy, and related the news to *Dhṛtarāshṭra*, who first thought that it was *Duryodhana* who had been selected by *Draupadī*, but was very glad on hearing that it was the *Pāṇḍavas*. But *Duryodhana* and *Karṇa* tried to stir him up against them (I, **200**). *Dhṛtarāshṭra* said that he was of their opinion, but did not wish to inform *Vidura* of it; therefore he had applauded the *Pāṇḍavas* in *Vidura's* presence. *Duryodhana* suggested several plans for getting the better of the *Pāṇḍavas* (I, **201**). *Karṇa* said that the plans would not succeed; he recommended to vanquish them by prowess, while their party was yet weak. *Dhṛtarāshṭra* summoned *Bhīshma*, *Droṇa*, and *Vidura*, and consulted with them (I, **202**). *Bhīshma* recommended to give to the *Pāṇḍavas* one half of the kingdom (I, **203**). *Droṇa* approved of this, and, moreover, recommended that a messenger should be sent to *Drupada* with gifts, and say that *Dhṛtarāshṭra* was very glad of the new alliance with him, and would take the *Pāṇḍavas* to *Hāstinapura* to be installed on the throne.—§ 242. *Karṇa* spoke contemptuously of *Bhīshma* and *Droṇa*, saying that happiness depended on destiny, and not on friends, etc., mentioning the *Magadha* king *Ambuvīca* (*b*) (I, **204**).—§ 243. *Vidura* recommended the suggestion of *Bhīshma* and *Droṇa*, and said that the *Pāṇḍavas* were invincible, as they were assisted by *Rāma*, *Janārdana*, *Sātyaki*, etc. (I, **205**). *Vidura* was sent by *Dhṛtarāshṭra* with numerous jewels, etc., to *Drupada* and the *Pāṇḍavas* (also *Kṛshṇa* was present). *Vidura* said that *Dhṛtarāshṭra* was highly pleased with the alliance with *Drupada*, and asked *Drupada* to permit the *Pāṇḍavas*, with their mother and wife, to return to their paternal city (I, **206**).

[Viduraparinaya(h)] ("the marriage of Vidura"). § 179 (Sambhavap.): *Bhīshma* married king Devaka's daughter, who was by caste a *pārasavī*, to *Vidura*, who begat upon her many children as excellent as himself (I, **114**).

Vidūratha[1] (B., Vidūra), son of Kuru and Çubhāngī. § 156 (Pūruvaṃç.): I, **95**, ††3792, ††3793 (husband of Supriyā and father of Anaçvan).

Vidūratha[2], a Vṛshṇi prince. § 232 (Svayaṃvarap.): I, **186**, 6999 (among the Vṛshṇis present at the svayaṃvara of Draupadī).—§ 252 (Subhadrāharaṇap.): I, **219**, 7915.—§ 589 (Droṇābhishekap.): VII, **11** ξ, 408.—§ 795 (Svargārohaṇap.): XVIII, **5** μ, 162 (among those who, after death, became deities).

Vidūrathasuta ("the son of Vidūratha"). § 638*b* (Rāmopākhyāna): XII, **49**, 1791 (*Pauravadāyado V°ḥ . . . ṛkshaiḥ saṃvardhitaḥ . . . Ṛkshavaty atha parvate*).

Vidvat = Çiva (1000 names[2]).

Vidvattama = Vishṇu (1000 names).

Vidyā ("knowledge", personif.), a goddess. § 506 (Skandayuddha): III, **231**, 14562 (followed Umā). — Do.[2], pl. ("sciences", personif.).—§ 270 (Brahmasabhāv.): II, **11**, 438 (in the palace of Brahmán).

Vidyādhara, pl. (°*āḥ*), a class of supernatural beings: I, †2122, 8316 (°*gaṇāḥ*); III, 172 (°*ottamāḥ*), 5036, 9930 (°*ānucaritaṃ*, sc. *Himavantaṃ*), 11027 (°*samākīrṇān*, sc. *deçān*), 11562 (°*ānucaritaṃ*, sc. *Gandhamādanaṃ*), 11646 (°*gaṇāḥ*); VII, 3642 (°-*mahoragāḥ*), 5746 (°*gaṇāḥ*), †7292; IX, 2139, 2511, 2706; XII, 10220, 12622 (°*gaṇaiḥ*); XIII, 958, 996; XVIII, 216 (*nānā*°).

Vidyādharādhipa ("king of the Vidyādharas") = Cakradharman: II, 408 (*C*°).

Vidyādharendra (do.) = Jāmbavat: XIII, †630 (°*sya sutā*, i.e. Jāmbavatī).

Vidyādharī ("female Vidyādhara"): IV, 258 (Draupadī is asked if she is a *V*.).

Vidyātīrtha, name of a tīrtha. § 370 (Tīrthayātrāp.): III, **84**, 8030.

Vidyāvāsa = Mahāpurusha (Mahāpurushastava).

Vidyotā, an Apsaras. § 731*b* (Ashṭāvakra-Diksaṃv.): XIII, **19** β, 1425 (danced in the palace of Kubera).

Vidyudvarcas, a Viçvadeva. § 749 (Ānuçāsanik.): XIII, **91** γ, 4358.

Vidyujjihva, a Rākshasa. § 585 (Bhīshmavadhap.): VI, **91** v, 4083 (slain by Duryodhana).

Vidyujjihvā, a mātṛ. § 615*u* (Skanda): IX, **46** θ, 2626.

Vidyunmālin, an Asura. § 603*d* (Tripura): VII, **202**, 9557 (lord of the iron city).—§ 606 (Tripurākhyāna): VIII, **33**, 1395 (son of Tāraka), 1412 (lord of the iron city).

Vidyutā, an Apsaras. § 731*b* (Ashṭāvakra-Diksaṃv.): XIII, **19** β, 1425 (danced in the palace of Kubera).

Vidyutāksha, a warrior of Skanda. § 615*u* (Skanda): IX, **45** η, 2564.

Vidyutparṇā, an Apsaras. § 103 (Aṃçāvat.): I, **65**, 2557 (daughter of Prādhā).—§ 191 (Arjuna): I, **123**, 4818 (danced at the birth of Arjuna).

Vidyutprabha[1], a Dānava (?). § 730*e* (Ānuçāsanik.): Pleased with *V*., Mahādeva (i.e. Çiva) granted him the sovereignty of the three worlds which he enjoyed for a hundred thousand years. *Çiva* further granted him that he should become one of his attendants and obtain a hundred millions of children, and gave him the region named *Kuçadvīpa*: XIII, **14**, 671.

Vidyutprabha[2], a ṛshi. § 766 (Ānuçāsanik.): XIII, **125**, 5963 (*ṛshiḥ*), 5969 (instructed Indra).

Vidyutprabhā, pl. (°*āḥ*), name of ten Apsaras. § 565 (Gālavacarita): V, **111**, 3841 (*atra*—i.e. in the north—*V°ā nāma jagmire* (B. *jajñire*) *'psaraso daça*).

Vidyutstanitagarjita = Çiva (1000 names[1]).

Vigāhana, a king. § 562 (Bhagavadyānap.): V, **74** γ, 2732 (*Mukuṭānām*, among the wicked kings who annihilated their kinsmen and relatives).

Vighneça = Gaṇeça: I, 76, 78.

Vigraha, a companion of Skanda. § 615*u* (Skanda): IX, **45**, 2552 (given to Skanda by the Ocean).

Vihanga, a serpent. § 65 (Sarpasattra): I, **57**, 2152 (of Airāvata's race).

Vihangama ("moving in the sky") = Sūrya (the Sun): I, 6606; III, 17120.

Vihavya, a brahman. § 736*b* (Vītahavyop.): XIII, **30**, 2000 (son of Varcas), 2001 (father of Vitatya).

Vihāyasagati = Vishṇu (1000 names).

Vihṛshṭa = Çiva (1000 names[1]) (only B.).

Vijaya[1], an ancient king. § 6 (Anukram.): I, **1** *a*, 226 (in Sañjaya's enumeration).

Vijaya[2] = Arjuna, q.v.

Vijaya[3], the dart of Çiva. § 269 (Vaiçravaṇasabhāv.): II, **10**, 415 (in the palace of Kubera (only B., C. has *Vijayā*)).—

§ 506 (Skandayuddha): III, **231**, 14551 (°*o nāma Rudrasya yāti çūlaḥ svalaṃkṛtaḥ*), 14553.

Vijaya[4], name of bows. § 570*d* (Rukmin): V, **158**, 5354 (*Māhendraṃ . . . dhanuḥ*), 5356, 5359 (*dhanuḥ*, belonged to Indra and was obtained by Rukmin from Druma).—§ 605*c* (Karṇap.): *V.* was made by *Viçvakarman* for *Indra*, who, with that bow, vanquished the *Daityas*. From *Indra* it passed over to *Paraçurāma*, and from him to *Karṇa*; it is superior to the *Gāṇḍīva*: VIII, **31**, 1292 (*dhanuḥ*).—§ 605 (do.): VIII, **31**, 1303 (owned by Karṇa).—§ 607 (do.): VIII, **42**, 2001.—§ 608 (Karṇap.): VIII, **49**, 2326 (*cāpaṃ*, do.); **59**, 2916 (*dhanuḥ çreshṭhaṃ*), 2969 (*dhanuḥ*); **64**, 3259 (do.).

Vijaya[5], son of Dhṛtarāshṭra. § 592 (Saṃçaptakavadhap.): VII, **25**, 1108 (*putrās te Durjayaç caiva Jayaç ca V°aç ca*).—§ 599 (Jayadrathavadhap.): VII, **116**, 4609 (pierced by Sātyaki).—§ 600 (Ghaṭotkacavadhap.): VII, **156**κ, 6851.

Vijaya[6] a Pāṇḍava warrior. § 600 (Ghaṭotkacavadhap.): VII, **158**χ, 7012 (brother of Virāṭa?) (only C.).

Vijaya[7] = Çiva (1000 names[2]). — Do.[8] = Vishṇu (1000 names).

Vijaya, pl. (°*āḥ*), a people. § 574 (Jambūkh.): VI, **9**μ, 353.

Vijayā[1], a Daçārha princess. § 156 (Pūruvaṃç.): I, **95**, ††3786 (*Dāçārhīm*, wife of Bhumanyu and mother of Suhotra[1]).

Vijayā[2], a Madra princess. § 159 (Pūruvaṃç.): I, **95**, ††3832 (*Mādrīṃ*, daughter of Dyutimat, wife of Sahadeva Pāṇḍava, and mother of Suhotra[2]).

Vijayā[3] = Durgā (Umā): II, 415 (in the palace of Kubera, only C., B. has *Vijayaḥ*); IV, 194; VI, 798.

Vijayā[4], the garland of Kṛshṇa. § 608 (Karṇap.): VIII, **76**, †3855 (*srajaṃ*).

Vijayakālavid, Vijayāksha = Çiva (1000 names[2]).

Vijitātman = Vishṇu (1000 names).

Vikāçinī, a mātṛ. § 615*u* (Skanda): IX, **46**θ, 2636.

Vikalya (B., *Vikalpa*), pl. (°*āḥ*), a people. § 574 (Jambūkh.): VI, **9**ν, 366.

Vikarṇa[1], a son of Dhṛtarāshṭra. § 83 (Ādivaṃçāvatāraṇa): I, **63**a, 2447.—§ 130 (Aṃçāvat.): I, **67**, 2729 (enumeration).—§ 157 (Pūruvaṃç.): I, **95**, ††3810.—§ 182 (Dhṛtarāshṭraputranāmak.): I, **117**, 4543 (enumeration).—§ 209 (Drupadaçāsana): I, **138**, 5449, 5461, 5463 (among the pupils of Droṇa who assisted Droṇa when he defeated Drupada).—§ 232 (Svayaṃvarap.): I, **186**, 6981 (came to the svayaṃvara of Draupadī).—§ 241 (Vidurāgamanap.): I, **204**, 7469.—§ 244 (Rājyalābhap.): I, **207**, 7557.—§ 299 (Dyūtap.): II, **68**, 2261, 2268, 2275, 2277, 2288, 2311 (declared that the gambling away of Draupadī was invalid).—§ 302 (do.): II, **74**, 2477.—§ 402 (Tīrthayātrāp.): III, **120**, †10269.—§ 512 (Ghoshayātrāp.): III, **241**, 14897.—§ 552 (Goharaṇap.): IV, **35**a, 1151; **38**, 1243; **47**, 1488; **54**, †1668, †1669 (defeated by Arjuna); **61**, 1988 (attacked Arjuna), 1992 (defeated by Arjuna); **65**, †2092, †2096, †2098; **69**, 2245.—§ 556 (Sañjayayānap.): V, **27**, †791.—§ 561 (Yānasandhip.): V, **47**a, 1796; **55**ν, 2208 (*tavātmajaḥ*, i.e. Dhṛtarāshṭra's); **57**ξ, 2246 (assigned to Arjuna as his match in the battle), (σ), 2290; **65**δδ, 2493; **66**εε, 2503.—§ 562 (Bhagavadyānap.): V, **95**υ, 3402.—§ 567 (do.): V, **131**ρ, 4457.—§ 576 (Bhagavadgītāp.): VI, **17**, 657 (followed Açvatthāman); **18**δ, 686; **25**ι, 837.—§ 578 (Bhīshmavadhap.): VI, **44**a, 1653; **45**[16], 1726, 1727, 1728 (fought with Çrutasoma); **48**θ, 1926; **51**ρ, 2092, (σ), 2098.—§ 579 (do.): VI, **52**[1]β, 2134, (δ), 2145 (only C.), 2146 (only B.), (ε), 2148, (ζ), 2160 (*tavātmajaḥ*, i.e. Dhṛtarāshṭra's).—§ 580 (do.): VI, **57**ι, 2452 (only C.); **59**μ, †2583.—§ 581 (do.): VI, **62**ζ, 2731, 2732 (only C.); **65**, 2910, (ν), 2929.—§ 582 (do.): VI, **71**δ, 3139 (engaged in battle with Sahadeva); **72**ζ, 3163.—§ 583 (do.): VI, **76**ι, 3330; **77**κ, 3343; **78**, 3433, 3434, 3436 (defeated by Abhimanyu); **79**[13], 3475, 3477, 3478, 3479 (°*rudhira-*), 3480 (encounter with Abhimanyu).—§ 584 (do.): VI, **81**a, 3532, (β), 3558, **84**γ, 3735; **86**, 3791 (*tanayas tava*, i.e. Dhṛtarāshṭra's).—§ 585 (do.): VI, **92**χ, 4119, 4130 (struck by Ghaṭotkaca); **94**ω, 4195; **95**γγ, 4244.—§ 587 (do.): VI, **108**δ, 5050, 5104 (resisted Nakula); **111**, 5173, 5175 (fought with Nakula); **113**ι, 5240, 5243, 5250 (C. by error °*aṇa*), 5261 (encounter with Bhīmasena); **114**κ, 5293; **117**σ, 5496, 5497; **118**τ, 5520.—§ 589 (Droṇābhishekap.): VII, **7**γ, 179 (*tavātmajaḥ*, i.e. Dhṛtarāshṭra's). — § 592 (Saṃçaptakavadhap.): VII, **25**, 1099 (resisted Çikhaṇḍin). — § 596 (Pratijñāp.): VII, **74**β, 2628.—§ 598 (Jayadrathavadhap.): VII, **85**a, 3020 (*Citrasena-V°yoḥ . . . sutānāṃ me*, i.e. Dhṛtarāshṭra's), (γ), 3043; **87**θ, 3107 (*Duḥçāsanaç caiva V°ç ca tavātmajau*, i.e. Dhṛtarāshṭra's).—§ 599 (do.): VII, **95**ζ, 3525; **96**θ, 3572 (*tavātmajaḥ*, i.e. Dhṛtarāshṭra's); **106**, 3976 (*te sutaḥ*, i.e. Dhṛtarāshṭra's, proceeded against Nakula); **107**, 4042 (defeated by Nakula); **116**aa, 4604, 4608; **127**νν, 5177; **137**aaa, 5644 (slain by Bhīmasena), 5646 (*hataḥ*), 5664 (do.); **144**, 6025.—§ 600 (Ghaṭotkacavadhap.): VII, **158**ω, 7035 (had been slain); **164**, 7337 (still living (!), B., however, reads *Karṇañ ca*).—§ 604 (Karṇap.): VIII, **5**ζ, 97 (*putro V°as te*, i.e. Dhṛtarāshṭra's, had been slain by Bhīmasena); **6**, 167 (had slain Citrāyudha and Citrayodhin).—§ 609 (Çalyap.): IX, **2**, 105 (had been slain). — § 611 (do.): IX, **24**, 1295 (sc. *hate*). — § 619 (Strīvilāpap.): XI, **19**δ, 547 (*vinihataḥ*), 548, 551; **25**κ, 736. Cf. Bharatarshabha, Bharatasattama, Dhārtarāshṭra, Dhṛtarāshṭraja, Duryodhanāvara, Kurupravīra, Kuruvardhana, dual.

Vikarṇa[2], a ṛshi. § 730 (Ānuçāsanik.): XIII, **14**ζ, 688 (gratified Çiva).

Vikarṇa, pl. (°*āḥ*), a people. § 578 (Bhīshmavadhap.): VI, **51**υ, 2105 (in the army of Duryodhana).

Vikartana, V, 2206 (only B., read Vaikartana, q.v.).

Vikartṛ = Vishṇu (1000 names).

Vikaṭa[1], son of Dhṛtarāshṭra. § 130 (Aṃçāvat.): I, **67**, 2731.—§ 232 (Svayaṃvarap.): I, **186**, 6983 (came to the svayaṃvara of Draupadī).—§ 581 (Bhīshmavadhap.): VI, **64**κ, 2838 (among fourteen sons of Dhṛtarāshṭra who pierced Bhīmasena).—§ 608 (Karṇap.): VIII, **51**δδ, 2446, (εε), 2455 (slain by Bhīmasena). Cf. Vikaṭānana.

Vikaṭa[2], a warrior of Skanda. § 615*u* (Skanda): IX, **45**η, 2561.

Vikaṭānana, son of Dhṛtarāshṭra. § 182 (Dhṛtarāshṭraputranāmak.): I, **117**, 4544. Cf. Vikaṭa.

Vikhyāta = Çiva (1000 names[2]).

Vikrama[1], a companion of Skanda. § 615*u* (Skanda): IX, **45**ε, 2539 (given to Skanda by Vishṇu).—Do.[2] = Vishṇu (1000 names).

Vikramin[1], an ancient king. § 6 (Anukram.): I, **1**a, 226 (in Sañjaya's enumeration). Do.[2] = Vishṇu (1000 names).

Vikrīta, a Prajāpati. § 717*b* (Nārāyaṇīya): XII, **335**a, 12686 (PCR. has from other sources, instead of *V.*, the two names Avāk (Arvāk?) and Krīta).

Vikṛta[1]. § 662*b* (Jāpakop.): XII, **199**, 7289, (7290), 7292, 7294, (7301), (7303), (7305) (Kāma and Krodha appeared in the shape of Virūpa and *V.*). — Do.[3] = Çiva (1000 names[2]).

Vikṛtavaktra = Çiva (1000 names[1]).

Vikṛti = Kṛshṇa: XII, 1507.

Vikshara[1], an Asura. § 96 (Aṃçāvat.): I, **65**, 2541 (son of Danāyus).—§ 130 (do.): I, **67**, 2677 (*Danāyushas* (so B.) *tu putrāṇām caturṇāṃ pravaro 'suraḥ*, incarnate as king Vasumitra), 2678 (*dvitīyo V°āt . . . mahāsuraḥ*, incarnate as Pāṇḍyarāshṭrādhipa). Cf. Asura.

Vikshara[2] = Vishṇu (1000 names).

Vikshit. § 767 (Ānuçāsanik.): XIII, **137** *a*, 6260 (*Karandhamasya pautras tu Marutto V°aḥ sutaḥ*, so C., but read with B. *'vi°*). Cf. Avikshit.

Vikuñja, pl. (*°āḥ*), a people. § 580 (Bhīshmavadhap.): VI, **56** ε, 2410 (in the army of Duryodhana).

Vikuṇṭha = Vishṇu (Kṛshṇa): VI, 774. Cf. Vaikuṇṭha.

Vikuṇṭhana, a prince. § 156 (Pūruvaṃç.): I, **95**, ††3788 (son of Hastin), ††3789 (husband of Sudevā and father of Ajamīḍha).

Vikurvaṇa = Çiva (1000 names[2]).

Vilohita = Çiva: VII, 2877; X, 256; XII, 10359 (1000 names[1]); XIV, 202.

Vimala, name of a tīrtha. § 358 (Tīrthayātrāp.): III, **82**, 5029 (*tīrtham*).

Vimalā, daughter of Surabhi. § 127 (Aṃçāvat.): I, **66**, 2632.

Vimalāçoka, name of a tīrtha. § 370 (Tīrthayātrāp.): **84**, 8047.

Vimala(ṃ) saras, a tīrtha. § 775 (Ānuçāsanik.): XIII, **166** *a*, 7649.

Vimalapiṇḍaka, a serpent. § 47 (Sarpanāmak.): I, **35**, 1553.

Vimalodā or **Vimalodakā**, one of the seven Sarasvatīs. § 615*i* (Saptasārasvata): IX, **38** *a*, 2189 (*°akā*), 2214 (*°odā*, when Brahmán performed a sacrifice in the forest of Himavat, the Sarasvatī appeared there as *V.*).

Vimarsha = Çiva (1000 names[2]).

Vimça, son of Ikshvāku. § 778*b* (Saṃvartta-Maruttīya): XIV, **4**, 68 (father of Viviṃça).

Vimocana[1], a tīrtha. § 368 (Tīrthayātrāp.): III, **83**, 7032.

Vimocana[2] = Çiva (1000 names[2]).

Vimuca, a ṛshi. § 665 (Mokshadh.): XII, **208** η, 7594 (one of the ṛshis of the north).

Vimukta = Çiva (1000 names[2]).

Vimuktātman = Vishṇu (1000 names).

Viṇā, a river. § 574 (Jambūkh.): VI, **9** λ, 328 (only C., B. has *Vāṇīṃ*).

Vinaçana ("disappearance"), a tīrtha. § 360 (Tīrthayātrāp.): III, **82**, 5052 (where the Sarasvatī disappears).—§ 370 (do.): III, **84**, 8090 (another tīrtha of the same name in the east).—§ 410*b* (Plakshāvataraṇag.): The gate of the kingdom of the *Nishādas* where the *Sarasvatī* disappears from hatred of them: III, **130**, 10538 (*Sarasvatyāḥ*).—§ 615 (Baladevatīrthayātrāp.): IX, **36**, 2118; **37**, 2119 (*Çūdrābhīrapratidveshād yatra nashṭā Sarasvatī*), 2120 (etymology).

Vināçana, an Asura. § 97 (Aṃçāvat.): I, **65**, 2543 (son of Kālā). Cf. *Candrasya vināçanaḥ* (I, 2674).

Vinadī, a river. § 574 (Jambūkh.): VI, **9** λ, 335.

Vinata = Çiva (1000 names[2]).

Vinatā, daughter of Daksha and wife of Kaçyapa, mother of the Vainateyas, i.e. Garuḍa, etc. § 27 (Kaçyapa): I, **16**, 1074, 1077, 1078, 1079, 1082, 1084, 1085, 1091, 1093 (mother of Aruṇa and Garuḍa).—§ 29 (Kadrū): I, **20**, 1190 (1191) (*V.* and Kadrū bet about the colour of Uccaiḥçravas).—§ 30 (do.): I, **21**, 1205.—§ 31 (do.): I, **22**, 1227 (*Kadrūç ca Vinatā Dākshāyaṇyau*).—§ 32 (do.): I, **23**, 1235, 1237, 1238 (having lost the wager, *V.* became the slave of Kadrū).—§ 36 (Kadrū): I, **25**, 1280, 1281.—§ 40 (Garuḍa): I, **27**, 1315, (1316), (1321), (1329), 1330, (1333) (Vinatā would be delivered from the bondage if Garuḍa brought the amṛta to the Nāgas. *V.* gave directions to Garuḍa).—§ 44 (do.): I, **30**, 1424 (*putro V°āyāḥ*, i.e. Garuḍa).—§ 45 (Vālakhilya, pl.): I, **31**, 1459 (*Dākshāyaṇī*), 1468 (mother of Aruṇa and Garuḍa, cf. § 27).—§ 46 (Garuḍa): I, **34**, †1544.—§ 47 (Āstīkap.): I, **35**, 1546, 1547 (*varapradānaṃ bhartrā ca Kadrū-V°ayoḥ*, all. to § 27).—§ 48 (Çesha): I, **36**, 1573.—§ 60 (Sarpasattra): I, **54**, 2072 (*°ārthāya*, all. to § 29).—§ 87 (Aṃçāvat.): I, **65**, 2520 (daughter of Daksha and wife of Kaçyapa).—[§ 99 (do.): I, **65**, 2548 (the Vainateyas (sons of Vinatā) are six in number)].—§ 129 (do.): I, **66**, 2635 (*dvau putrau V°āyās tu vikhyātau Garuḍāruṇau*).—§ 270 (Brahmasabhāv.): II, **11**, 456 (in the palace of Brahmán).—§ 502 (Manushyagrahak.): III, **230**, 14465 (became one of the mothers of Skanda), 14480 (= Çakunigraha).—§ 564 (Mātalīyop.): V, **101**, 3588 (*°kulakartṛbhiḥ*). Cf. Dākshāyaṇī, sg. and dual.

Vinatānandavardhana ("the son of Vinatā") = Garuḍa: I, 1246.

Vinatāsūnu (do.) = Garuḍa: V, 3854.

Vinatāsuta (do.) = Garuḍa: I, 1402, 1490, 1509; V, 3699, 3906; XII, 12854.

Vinatātmaja (do.) = Garuḍa: V, 3757 (*G°*), 3850 (*Suparṇa*), 3864, 3869, 4001.

Vināyaka, pl. (*°āḥ*), a class of demons. § 696*b* (Dakshaprokta-Çivasahasranāmastotra): XII, **285**, 10477 (cf. XIII, 7103).

Vinayitṛ = Vishṇu (1000 names).

Vinda[1], an Avanti prince, brother of Anuvinda[1]. § 281 (Sahadeva): II, **31**, 1114 (*°ānuvindāv Āvantyau*, vanquished by Sahadeva on his digvijaya).—§ 290 (Çiçupālavadhap.): II, **44**, 1539 (do.).—§ 561 (Yānasandhip.): V, **66** εε, 2503 (do.).—§ 572 (Rāthātirathasaṅkhyānap.): V, **166**, 5753 (do.).—§ 573 (Ambopākhyānap.): V, **195** δ, 7607 (do.).—§ 576 (Bhagavadgītāp.): VI, **16**, 622 (*°ānuvindau*); **17**, 673 (*°ānuvindāv Āvantyau*).—§ 578 (Bhīshmavadhap.): VI, **45**[21], 1740 (do.), 1743; **47** ζ, 1851 (only B.); **49**, 2014/5 (only B.); **51** φ, 2107 (*°ānuvindāv Āvantyau*).—§ 580 (do.): VI, **56** γ, 2408 (do.); **59** μ, †2584 (*°ānuvindau*, ordered to attack Arjuna).—§ 584 (do.); VI, **81** *a*, 3533 (*°ānuvindāv Āvantyau*), (*[1]*) 3557 (do., fought with Irāvat); **83**[1], 0666; **86**[9], 3823 (*°ānuvindāv Āvantyau*, attacked Dhṛshṭadyumna), (*[10]*) 3827 (*°ānuvindau*, attacked by Yudhishṭhira).—§ 586 (do.): VI, **102** ι, 4666 (*°ānuvindāv Āvantyau*, surrounded Arjuna).—§ 587 (do.): VI, **108** δ, 5051 (do.); **113** ι, 5240 (do., fought with Bhīmasena), 5245 (do.), 5249 (*°ānuvindau*), 5261 (*°ānuvindāv Avantyau*); **114** κ, 5309 (do., fought with Arjuna).—§ 592 (Saṃçaptakavadhap.): VII, **20** ε, 801 (do.); **25**, 1083 (do., fought with Virāṭa); **32** ω, 1410 (do.).—§ 596 (Pratijñāp.): VII, **74** β, 2629 (do.).—§ 598 (Jayadrathavadhap.): VII, **85** *a*, 3025 (*°ānuvindayoḥ*).—§ 599 (do.): VII, **95** ζ, 3526 (*°ānuvindāv Āvantyau*, fought with Bhīmasena), 3533 (do.); **99**, 3691 (slain by Arjuna).—§ 604 (Karṇap.): VIII, **5** ζ, 99 (*°ānuvindāv Āvantyau*, had been slain).—§ 608 (do.): VIII, **72** υυυ, 3612 (had been vanquished by Arjuna).—§ 619 (Strīvilāpap.): XI, **25** κ, 733 (do., bewailed as slain). Cf. Āvantyau, Vinda[2].

Vinda[2], a Kaikeya prince, brother of Anuvinda[2]. § 605 (Karṇap.): VIII, **13**, 492 (°*ānuvindau Kaikeyau*, slain by Sātyaki). Cf. Kaikaya, sg. and dual, Kaikeya, sg. and dual.

Vinda[3], son of Dhṛtarāshṭra (brother of Anuvinda[3]; the quotations under Vinda[1], where *Avantyau* is not added, might also refer to these two brothers). § 130 (Aṃçāvat.): I, **67**, 2729 (°*ānuvindau*).—§ 182 (Dhṛtarāshṭraputranāmak.): I, **117**, 4542 (do.).—§ 512 (Ghoshayātrāp.): III, **242**, 14920 (do., made captive by the Gandharvas). — § 599 (Jayadrathavadhap.): VII, **127**νν, 5177 (do.), (ξξ), 5209 (do., slain by Bhīma).

Vindhaculaka, pl., v. Vindhyaculika, pl.

Vindhya, name of a mountain. § 246 (Sundopasundop.): I, **209**, 7625, 7628; **212**, 7716 (°*sya prasthe*).—§ 253 (Haraṇāharaṇap.): I, **221**, 8041 (? *prati V°ṃ*, origin of the name of Prativindhya).—§ 269 (Vaiçravaṇasabhāv.): II, **10**, 412 (present in the palace of Kubera).—§ 347 (Nalopākhyānap.): III, **61**, 2318.—§ 384 (Agastyop.): III, **103**, 8778 (°*aḥ çailo na vardhate*, all. to § 385).—§ 385 (cf. Agastyop.): *V.* once asked the Sun to honour him with circumambulations as he did *Meru*, and as the sun declared it impossible, *V.*, from wrath, began to increase and obstructed the path of the Sun, the Moon, and the *nakshatras*. As the gods could not dissuade him, they applied to *Agastya*, who, with his wife came, and, saying that he should have to go to the southern region, prevailed upon *V.* to cease to increase until he should have returned. But to this day he has not returned from the southern region: III, **104**, 8781, 8783 (*çailaḥ*), †8787, 8789, 8791, 8794, 8795.—§ 430 (Hanūmad-Bhīmasaṃv.): III, **150**, 11274 (°*parvatasannibhaṃ*, sc. *varshma*).—§ 459 (Mārkaṇḍeyas.): III, **188**, 12919 (*giriṃ uttamaṃ*, seen in the body of Nārāyaṇa).—§ 548 (Āraṇeyap.): III, **313**, 17318 (four mountains enumerated).—§ 549*f* (Durgā): IV, **6**, 195 (°*e caiva nagapṛshṭhe tava*—i.e. Durgā's (Umā's)—*sthānaṃ*).—§ 574 (Jambūkh.): VI, **9**κ, 319 (among the kulaparvatas of Bhāratavarsha). — § 599 (Jayadrathavadhap.): VII, **92**, 3313 (*iva*).—§ 600 (Ghaṭotkacavadhap.): VII, **179**, †8169 (°*tulya* (°*pāda* C.)-*pramāṇaṃ*).—§ 603*d* (Tripura): VII, **202**, 9562 (Çiva made Gandhamādana and *V.* the *vaṃçadhvajau* of his chariot).—§ 606 (Tripurākhyāna): VIII, **34**, 1475 (°*parvataḥ*, Çiva made Himavat and *V.* the *apaskara* and the *adhishṭhāna* of his chariot).—§ 615*u* (Skanda): IX, **45**γ, 2516 (personif.), 2552 (gave two companions to Skanda).—§ 641*d* (Vena): XII, **59**, 2218 (°*nilayā Mlecchāḥ*).—§ 733*v* (Rāmahrada): XIII, **25**, 1735 (a tīrtha). —§ 775 (Ānuçāsanik.): XIII, **166***a*, 7657.—§ 782*g* (Guruçishyasaṃv.): XIV, **43**η, 1173.—§ 795 (Svargārohaṇap.): XVIII, **2**, 46 (°*çailopamaiḥ pretaiḥ*).

Vindhyaculika, pl. (°*āḥ*), a people. § 574 (Jambūkh.): VI, **9**ν, 369 (only B., C. has *Vindhaculakāḥ*).

Vinītātman, an ancient king. § 6 (Anukram.): I, **1***a*, 229 (in Sañjaya's enumeration).

Vipāçā, a river. § 225 (Vāsishṭha): I, **177**, 6750 (origin of the name from Vasishṭha's becoming free from his bonds).—§ 268 (Vāruṇasabhāv.): II, **9**, 371 (present in the palace of Varuṇa).—§ 410 (Plakshāvataraṇag.): III, **130**, 10543 (*f:* there Vasishṭha became free from his bonds, cf. § 225). —§ 459 (Mārkaṇḍeyas.): III, **188***a*, 12908 (seen in the stomach of Nārāyaṇa).—§ 574 (Jambūkh.): VI, **9**λ, 323.—§ 607 (Karṇap.): VIII, **44**θ, 2055, 2064 (the Piçācas Bahi and Hīka lived in the *V.*).—§ 721 (Ānuçāsanik.): XIII, **3***a*, 193 (origin of the name).—§ 733*k* (Vaimānika): XIII, **25**, 1710.—§ 733*v* (Rāmahrada): XIII, **25**, 1733.—§ 757*m* (Goloka): XIII, **102***a*, 4888.—§ 768*b* (Umā-Maheçvarasaṃv.): XIII, **146**δ, 6764.—§ 775 (Ānuçāsanik.): XIII, **166***a*, 7645.

Vipaṇa = Çiva (1000 names[2]).

Vipāpa, name of a fire. § 490 (Āṅgirasa): III, **219**, 14142 (*agniḥ*).

Vipāpā, a river. § 574 (Jambūkh.): VI, **9**λ, 323.

Vipāpman, a Viçvadeva. § 749 (Ānuçāsanik.): XIII, **91**γ, 4355.

Vipāṭha, younger brother of Karṇa. § 592 (Saṃçaptakavadhap.): VII, **32**, 1433 (slain by Arjuna).

Vipracitta (VI, 5031; XII, 3661), v. Vipracitti.

Vipracitti, an Asura. § 92 (Aṃçāvat.): I, **65**, 2530 (eldest son of Danu).—§ 130 (do.): I, **67**, 2640 (incarnate as Jarāsandha).—§ 268 (Varuṇasabhāv.): II, **9**, 365 (in the palace of Varuṇa).—§ 585 (Bhīshmavadhap.): VI, **94**, 4212 (*yathā Çakro . . . purā vivyādha Dānavaṃ V°ṃ*). — § 587 (do.): VI, **108**, 5031 (*praikshanta . . . yudhyamānaṃ . . . V°im* (C., °*am*) *ivāmarāḥ*).—§ 612 (Hradapraveçap.): IX, **31**ζ, 1754 (had been slain).—§ 641 (Rājadh.): XII, **98**ξ, 3661 (*Daiteyaṃ*, had been slain by Indra; C. has *V°am*).—§ 656 (Khaḍgotpattik.): XII, **166**γ, 6146. — § 664 (Mokshadh.): XII, **207**, 7545 (°*pradhānān Dānavān* ["sons of Danu"]).—§ 673*b* (Bali-Vāsavasaṃv.): XII, **227***a*, 8262. Cf. Daiteya, Dānava, Dānavarshabha.

Viprarshi[1], pl. (°*ayaḥ*) = Brahmarshi, pl. § 133 (Dushyanta): I, **68**, 2800 (°*gaṇa-*).—§ 149 (Yayāti): I, **86**, 3541 (do.).—§ 459 (Mārkaṇḍeyas.): III, **189**, 12992 (do.).—§ 565 (Gālavacarita): V, **109**, 3787 (°*sadaneshu*).—§ 655 (Āpaddh.): XII, **162**, 5977 (°-*pitṛ-devatāḥ*).—§ 747 (Ānuçāsanik.): XIII, **84**, 3967 (°*gaṇāḥ*). — § 782*g* (Guruçishyasaṃv.): XIV, **51**, 1464 (°*sattamāḥ*).

Viprarshi[2], sg. = do. sg. Unnamed Viprarshis mentioned: XII, 13892, 13904, 13929; XIII, 140; XIV, 943, 2747. Names of single Viprarshis:—

Agastya: III, 8588.
Akṛtavraṇa: V, 6069.
Aṇīmāṇḍavya: I, 4318, 4332/3 (only B.).
Arishṭanemi (Tārkshya): III, 12662.
Ashṭāvakra: I, 449 (*A°*); XIII, 1462, 1521 (*A°*).
Atri: III, 12682, 12710, 12712.
Aurva: I, 6827.
Bharadvāja: IX, 2826 (*Bh°*); XII, 8481 (*Bh°*).
Bhṛgu: XII, 6950.
Cyavana: III, 10326, 10399; XIII, 2692, 2780, 2788.
Çaktri: I, 6716.
Çarmin: XIII, 3410.
Çaunaka: I, 943.
Çunaka: XIII, 2005.
Droṇa: I, 5163, 5210.
Durvāsas: III, 15551; VII, 390 (*D.*).
Gālava: V, 3767, 3810, 3870, 3923.
Gṛtsamada: XIII, 1999 (*G.*).
Jājali: XII, 9280, 9347.
Jamadagni: XIII, 4628, 4632, 4635.
Kāçyapa: XII, 6730.
Kauçika[6]: III, 13728, 13733, 13952, 14040.
Likhita: XII, 681.
Mandapāla: I, 8351.
Mārkaṇḍeya: III, 12810, 12815, 12951, 12995, 12996, 13630 (°*sattama*).
Mudgala: III, 15436.
Nārada: XII, 12695, 13771; XV, 563.

Paippalādi: XII, 7208.
Parāçara: I, 6865; XII, 11782.
Pulastya: III, 4049.
Rāma Jāmadagnya: XIII, 3973, 3980, 3989, 4003.
Ṛcīka: XIII, 243.
Ṛshabha: XII, 4660.
Saṃvarta: III, 8174 (*S*°).
Sārasvata: IX, 2976 (*S*°), 2977.
Upamanyu: XIII, 932, 1114.
Uttaṅka: I, 805; III, 13514; XIV, 1639, 1674, 1709, 1719.
Vaiçampāyana: I, 4527; VII, 3; XI, 246; XIII, 331 (*V*°); XVIII, 154.
Vasishṭha: I, 6597, 6796 (*V*°); IX, 2767 (*V*°).
Vibhāṇḍaka: III, 9999 (*V*°).
Viçravas: III, 16179 (*V*°).
Viçvāmitra: V, 3730; IX, 2360; XII, 5374.
Vipula: XIII, 2275.
Vyāsa: VI, 162 (*V*°): XII, 12382, 12643; XV, 835.
Yājñavalkya: XII, 11547, 11727.
Yavakrīta: III, 10713.

Viprthu[1], a Vṛshṇi prince. § 232 (Svayaṃvarap.): I, **186**, 6998 (came to the svayaṃvara of Draupadī).—§ 252 (Subhadrāharaṇap.): I, **219**, 7915.—§ 253 (Haraṇāharaṇap.): I, **221**, 7992.—§ 264 (Sabhākriyāp.): II, **4**β, 125.—§ 589 (Droṇābhishekap.): VII, **11**ξ, 409.

Viprthu[2], an ancient king. § 702 (Mokshadh.): XII, **295**, 10810 (after the seven ṛshis *V.* ruled the earth). Cf. Pṛthu.

Vipula[1], a Sauvīra king. § 211 (Sambhavap.): I, **139**, 5536 (*Sauvīraḥ*, vanquished by Arjuna; only B., C. has *Vitulaḥ*).

Vipula[2], a ṛshi of Bhṛgu's race. § 743 (Ânuçāsanik.): XIII, **40**, 2248, 2262.—§ 743*b* (Vipulop.): XIII, **40**, 2268, 2271, (2273), 2274, 2283, 2285, 2288, 2300, 2301, 2303, 2304; **41**, 2309, 2312, 2315 (*muniḥ*), 2316, 2320, 2325, (2327), 2334, 2336, 2337, 2338, 2339, 2340; **42**, 2344, 2355, 2356, 2363, 2364, 2365, 2367, 2369, 2370, 2371, 2375; **43**, 2378, (2379), 2393, 2403 (*V.* protected Ruci, the wife of his preceptor Devaçarman, against Indra).—§ 775 (Ânuçāsanik.): XIII, **166**ζ, 7671 (one of the ṛshis of the north). Cf. Bhārgava, Bhṛgusattama, Bhṛgūdvaha, Bhṛgūttama, Viprarshi.

[Vipulopākhyāna(m)] ("the episode about Vipula"): § 743*b* (Ânuçāsanik.). *Bhīshma* said: There was, in days of yore, a Ṛ. *Devaçarman*; his beautiful wife *Ruci* fascinated every one who saw her, both D., G., and Dā., and particularly *Indra*. *Devaçarman* knew very well the disposition of women, as well as *Indra's* coveting other men's wives. Once, desirous of performing a sacrifice, he summoned his favourite disciple *Vipula Bhārgava*, and asked him, during his absence, to protect *Ruci* against *Indra*, describing to him the disguises that *Indra* assumes (*a*). *Vipula*, by his *Yoga*-power, entered the body of *Ruci* (description) (XIII, **40**). *Indra* came, but *Ruci* was unable to move or to utter a word in reply; then, influenced by *Vipula*, she answered in *Sanskrit* (? *vāṇī saṃskārabhūshaṇā*) words that she did not intend to utter. *Indra* became perplexed, and when he with his spiritual eye discovered *Vipula* within *Ruci*, he became afraid that he might curse him. *Vipula* left the body of *Ruci* and returned to his own body which was lying near, and rebuked *Indra*, mentioning *Gautama's* curse, owing to which *Indra's* body became disfigured with 1,000 sex-marks, which, owing to *Gautama's* compassion, were afterwards changed into eyes, "see that thou dost not, with thy sons and counsellors, meet with destruction." *Çakra*, overwhelmed with shame, made himself invisible. A moment after, *Devaçarman* came back, and granted *Vipula* the boon that he should never swerve away from righteousness; dismissed by his preceptor, *Vipula* left his abode and practised the most severe austerities. *Devaçarman* also, with his spouse, began to live in the woods, perfectly fearless of *Indra* (XIII, **41**). *Vipula* became full of pride. After some time the occasion came for a ceremony of gifts, with respect to the sister of *Ruci* ~ the *Aṅga*-king *Citraratha*. Meanwhile, a celestial damsel dropped some flowers down to the earth; they were picked up by *Ruci*, who, adorned with them, went to the palace of the *Aṅga*-king. Her sister, *Prabhāvatī*, the *Aṅga*-queen, urged her to obtain some for her, and *Ruci* informed her husband, who, summoning *Vipula*, commanded him to bring him some flowers of the same kind. *Vipula* found some such flowers still lying scattered, quite fresh, and set out for *Campā*; on his way he saw a human couple moving in a circle, hand in hand; a dispute arose between them, and at last, each of them took the oath "that one of us who speaks falsely shall, in the next world, meet with the end which will be *Vipula's*". *Vipula* became very sad; proceeding a little way he beheld six other men playing with dice made of gold and silver; they were heard by *Vipula* to take the same oath as the first couple. At last he recollected the manner in which he had acted in protecting his preceptor's wife (placing limb within limb, face within face), without telling his preceptor the truth. Coming to *Campā*, he gave the flowers to his preceptor (XIII, **42**). *Devaçarman*, too, knew what he had seen on his way, and how he had acted in protecting *Ruci*; he explained that the first couple were Day and Night, the others the six Seasons. He absolved *Vipula* and ascended to heaven with his wife and his disciple. *Mārkaṇḍeya* had narrated this tale to *Bhīshma* on the banks of the *Gaṅgā* (XIII, **43**).

Vīra[1], an Asura. § 96 (Aṃçāvat.): I, **65**, 2541 (son of Danāyus). Cf. v. 2679 (*Balīvīra*, B., *Balina*, C.).

Vīra[2], a son of Dhṛtarāshṭra. § 130 (Aṃcāvat.): I, **67**, 2738 (?).

Vīra[3], a prince. § 232 (Svayaṃvarap.): I, **186**, 7000 (?).

Vīra[4], name of a fire? § 490 (Âṅgirasa): III, **219**, 14138 (*Vīra V°sya piṇḍadā* (i.e. mother Nīl.), son of Bharadvāja).

Vīra[5], a god. § 492 (Âṅgirasa): III, **220**, 14168 (among the fifteen *yajñamushaḥ*).

Vīra[6], a Bhoja prince. § 621 (Rājadh.): XII, **4**ε, 114 (*Bhojo V°ç ca nāmataḥ*).

Vīra[7] = Vishṇu (1000 names).

Vīrā[1], wife of the fire Bharadvāja. § 490 (Âṅgirasa): III, **219**, 14138 (*Bharadvājasya bhāryā*).

Vīrā[2], a river. § 574 (Jambūkh.): VI, **9**λ, 329.

Vīrabāhu[1], son of Dhṛtarāshṭra. § 130 (Aṃçāvat.): I, **67**, 2738.—§ 182 (Dhṛtarāshṭraputranāmak.): I, **117**, 4551.—§ 578 (Bhīshmavadhap.): VI, **45**[23], 1745 (attacked Uttara).—§ 581 (do.): VI, **64**[14]κ, 2838, 2844 (slain by Bhīmasena).—§ 600 (Ghaṭotkacavadhap.): VII, **157**ο, 6938 (only C., error instead of *Mahābāhu*, q.v.).

Vīrabāhu[2], a Cedi king. § 350 (Nalopākhyānap.): III, **69**, 2708 (married a daughter of the Daçārṇa king Sudāman).

Vīrabāhu[3] = Vishṇu (1000 names).

Vīrabhadra[1], a Pāṇḍava warrior. § 600 (Ghaṭotkacavadhap.): VII, **158**χ, 7011 (brother of Virāṭa?) (only C.).

Vīrabhadra[2], a divine being evolved from Çiva. § 695b (Dakshayajñavināça): XII, **285**, 10307 (created from the wrath of Çiva), (10325), 10327, 10329 (created the *Raumyas* who destroyed the sacrifice of Daksha).
Vīrāçrama, a tīrtha. § 370 (Tīrthayātrāp.): III, **84**, 8123 (°*nivāsinaṃ*, sc. *Kumāraṃ*).
Vīradhanvan, a Trigarta warrior. § 599 (Jayadrathavadhap.): VII, **107**, 4021, 4026, 4028 [4030 (*Traigartānāṃ mahārathe*)] (slain by Dhṛshṭaketu).
Vīradharman, a king. § 554 (Sainyodyogap.): V, **4**γ, 79.
Vīradyumna, a king, father of Bhūridyumna. § 641 (Rājadh.): XII, **127**, 4673 (*Bhūridyumnapitā*); **128**, 4687, 4693 (put to the test by Dharma).
Vīrahan = Vishṇu (1000 names).
Virāj[1], name of the primeval being (= Purusha), identified with Çiva and Vishṇu: XII, 1509 (= Kṛshṇa), 10429 (= Çiva, 1000 names[1]), 13143 (*purāṇaḥ Purushaḥ* = Aniruddha), 13461 (*Nārāyaṇaḥ*), 13734 (*Purushaḥ*), 13735 (do.); XIII, 7743 (= Kṛshṇa).—Do.[2] fem. = Pṛthivī: VII, 2417, 2420; XII, 2922 (*Pṛthivī*), 9381 (do.). — Do.[3], fem. = Sarasvatī ("Speech"): III, †10628 (*Sarasvatīṃ*).
Viraja[1], a tīrtha. § 370 (Tīrthayātrāp.): III, **85**, 8148.
Viraja[2]=Çiva (1000 names[2]).—Do.[3]=Vishṇu (1000 names).
Virāja, son of Avikshit. § 154 (Pūruvaṃç.): I, **94**, 3741.
Virajas[1], a serpent. § 47 (Sarpanāmak.): I, **35**, 1559.—§ 564 (Mātalīyop.): V, **103**γ, 3632.
Virajas[2], son of Dhṛtarāshṭra. § 182 (Dhṛtarāshṭraputranāmak.): I, **117**, 4553.—§ 600 (Ghaṭotkacavadhap.): VII, **157**o, 6938 (among seven sons of Dhṛtarāshṭra slain by Bhīmasena).
Virajas[3], a spiritual son of Nārāyaṇa. § 641 (Rājadh.): XII, **59**, 2209 (*mānasaṃ sutaṃ*), 2210 (father of Kīrtimat).
Virajas[4], son of Kavi. § 747b (Suvarṇotpatti): XIII, **85**, 4150.
Vīraka, pl. (°*āḥ*), a people. § 607 (Karṇap.): VIII, **44**κ, 2066.
Vīrakarā, v. Vīraṅkarā.
Vīraketu, a Pāñcāla warrior. § 599 (Jayadrathavadhap.): VII, **122**u, 4893 (*Pāñcālaputraḥ*), 4899 (slain by Droṇa). Cf. Pāñcālakulanandana, Pāñcālaputra, Pāñcālya.
Virāma[1] = Çiva (1000 names[2]). — Do.[2] = Vishṇu (1000 names).
Vīraṇa, a Prajāpati. § 717b (Nārāyaṇīya): XII, **349**, V), 13587 (*Prajāpatiḥ*), 13588 (learnt the religion of Nārāyaṇa from Sanatkumāra, and taught it to Raibhya).
Vīraṇaka, a serpent. § 67 (Sarpasattra): I, **57**, 2159 (of Dhṛtarāshṭra's race).
Vīraṅkarā (B. Vīrak°), a river. § 574 (Jambūkh.): VI, **9**λ, 333.
Vīrapramoksha, a tīrtha. § 370 (Tīrthayātrāp.): III, **84**, 8029.
Virasa, a serpent. § 564 (Mātalīyop.): V, **103**γ, 3632.
Vīrasena, king of the Nishadhas, father of Nala. § 343 (Nalopākhyānap.). III, **52**, 2067 (*Nishadheshu*, father of Nala).—§ 347 (do.): III, **64**, 2448 (*Nishadheshu mahārājaḥ*), 2497 (°*nṛpasnushā*, i.e. Damayantī).—§ 761 (Ānuçāsanik.): XIII, **115**δ, 5667 (among the kings who abstained from meat during the month of Kārttika).
Vīraseṅasuta ("the son of Vīrasena") = Nala, q.v.
vīrāshṭaka: III, 14398 (said of Çicu, v. Skandopākhyāna, ch. 228).
Virāṭa, king of the Matsyas, husband of Sudeshṇā, father of Çaṅkha, Uttara, and Uttarā. § 4 (Anukram.): I, **1**, †167 (°*rāshṭre*), †168 (do.). — § 11 (Parvasaṅgr.): I, **2**, 485 (*gograhaç ca V°sya*), 487 (*godhanaṃ V°sya*), 489, 536.—§ 130 (Aṃçāvat.): I, **67**, 2717 (incarnation of the gaṇa of the Maruts). — § 160 (Pūruvaṃç.): I, **95**, ††3835 (°*sya duhitaraṃ* . . . *Uttarāṃ*).—§ 232 (Svayaṃvarap.): I, **186**, 6988 (*saha putrābhyāṃ Çaṅkhenaivottareṇa ca*, came to the svayaṃvara of Draupadī).—§ 287 (Rājasūyikap.): II, **34**, 1272 (*saha putrābhyāṃ*, came to the rājasūya of Yudhishṭhira).—§ 290 (Çiçupālavadhap.): II, **44**a, 1538 (°-*Drupadau*).—§ 291 (Rājasūyikap.): II, **45**a, 1606.—§ 295 (Dyūtap.): II, **52**, 1883 (*Matsyena*, brought tribute to Yudhishṭhira).—§ 342 (Indralokābhigamanap.): III, **51**, 1983. — § 549 (Pāṇḍavapraveçap.): IV, **1**, 16 (*Matsyaḥ*), 22, 25 (°*rājaṃ*), 27; **2**, 28, 56, 59 (°*bhavane*); **3**, 62 (°*nṛpateḥ*), 67; **5**, 147; **7**, †214, †217 (°*rāṭ*), †221, (†225), (†227), †230 (°*rājena*); **8**, †236, †237, (†238), (†241), †243 (°*rājñaḥ*); **9**, 268, 273, 279 (°*sya bhāryayā*, i.e. Sudeshṇā); **10**, 280, (†286), (†294); **11**, †297, (†307), †309 (*sutāṃ V°sya*, i.e. Uttarā); **12**, †312 (°*rājaṃ*), (†316), (†320), †323 (°*rājñā*) (the Pāṇḍavas and Draupadī entered into the service of *V.*).—§ 550 (Samayapālanap.): IV, **13**, 328 (*saputrasya*), 330, 345, 362, 366, 367, 370, 372 (°*nṛpateḥ*).—§ 551 (Kīcakavadhap.): IV, **14**, 376 (*Kīcakaḥ* . . . *senāpatir V°sya*), †379; **15**, 433 (°*mahishī*, i.e. Sudeshṇā); **16**, 481 (486); **18**, 529 (*rājño V°sya Kīcakaḥ* . . . *senānīḥ* . . . *çyālaḥ*), 551; **19**, 559 (*sūpakaraṃ V°sya Ballavaṃ*, i.e. Bhīmasena), 560, 570 (*rājño V°sya* . . . *nartakaḥ*, i.e. Arjuna), 579 (do.), 586 (*Matsyaṃ*), 592, 598 (*açvabandho V°sya*, i.e. Nakula), 600; **20**, 634; **21**, 642 (*sabhāyāṃ V°sya*), 676 (*rājño V°sya Kīcako nāma sārathiḥ*); **23**, 799, 825 (°*sya mahānasaṃ*); **24**, 834, 845 (*rājñaḥ kanyā V°sya*, i.e. Uttarā), 856.—§ 552 (Goharaṇap.): IV, **30**, 976 (the Kurus and the Trigartas invaded the country of *V.* in order to rob his cattle); **31**, 1001, 1002, 1006, 1011 (°*sya priyo bhrātā Çatānīkaḥ*), 1015 (°*sya suto jyeshṭho vīraḥ Çaṅkhaḥ*), 1026, 1029, 1034, 1035 (*bālāgryaṃ V°sya*); **32**, 1057 (engaged in a single combat with the Trigarta king Suçarman); **33**, †1073, 1076, 1090, 1093, 1107, 1119, 1127 (made prisoner, but liberated by the Pāṇḍavas; the Trigartas were defeated); **34**, 1131, (1133), 1138, 1148; **35**, 1149, 1152; **37**, †1198 (*sutā V°sya*, i.e. Uttarā); **38**, 1266 (*putro V°sya*, i.e. Uttara), 1273 (°*sya sutaḥ*, do.); **54**, †1665 (*putro V°sya*, do.); **57**, 1820 (°*sya sutaḥ*, do.); **66**, †2120 (*putro V°sya*, do.); **67**, 2136 (°*sya dhanaṃ*), †2142 (°*rāshṭrābhimukhaṃ*, sc. Arjuna); **68**, 2160 (*vāhinīpatiḥ*), 2164 (*rājā Matsyānāṃ V°o vāhinīpatiḥ*), †2169, 2173, 2175 (°*rājaṃ*), 2182, 2189 (*purād V°sya*), (2194), (2207), 2214, 2219, (2223), 2225, 2229; **69**, (2252), 2255 (*vāhinīpatiḥ*).—§ 553 (Vaivāhikap.): IV, **70**, 2262 (°*sya sabhāṃ*), 2263, 2267; **71**, (2289), (2313), 2317, 2320; **72**, (2326), (2345), 2348, 2349 (*Upaplavyaṃ V°sya*) (Uttarā, the daughter of *V.*, was given in marriage to Abhimanyu).—§ 554 (Sainyodyogap.): V, **1**, †1, †3 (°-*Drupadau*), †5 (°*putraiḥ*); **3**, 57 (°-*Drupadau*, only B.); **5**, 100, 101, 102, 157.—§ 555 (do.): V, **19**γ, 581 (*rājā Matsyānāṃ* . . . *Pārvatīyair mahīpālaiḥ sahitaḥ*, came with his troops to Yudhishṭhira).—§ 556 (Sañjayayānap.): V, **22**β, †663 (*Mātsyeyānāṃ adhipaḥ*, among the allies of Yudhishṭhira), †683; **25**ε, †723, (ζ), †724; **27**, †784 (*Matsyo rājā rukmarathaḥ*).—§ 561 (Yānasandhip.): V, **48**, †1845 (*sahottaraḥ* . . . *Matsyaiḥ sārdhaṃ*); **50**η, 2007; **57**ξ, 2237 (*saha putrābhyāṃ Çaṅkhenaivottareṇa ca*), 2243 (*sārdhaṃ Matsyaiḥ*).—§ 562 (Bhagavadyānap.): V, **80**ε, 2856 (*sahātmajaṃ*); **83**θ, 2951.—§ 567 (do.): V,

126, 4221.—§ 569 (do.): V, **141**, 4782 (*Çaṅkhaḥ putro V°sya*); **147**, 4958 (*nṛpatīn V°pramukhān*).—§ 570 (Sainyaniryāṇap.): V, **151***a*, 5100, (*β*), 5107 (*Matsyaḥ*), 5144 (°-*Drupadau*), (*ε*), 5162; **153**, 5189 (°-*Drupadābhyām*), 5192 (°*Drupadau*), 5199; **157**, 5324 (among the seven leaders of divisions of Yudhishṭhira's army), 5336 (°-*Drupadau vṛddhau*).—§ 571 (Ulūkadūtāgamanap.): V, **160**, 5479 (°-*Drupadau*), 5496 (°*sya dāsyam*, all. to § 549), 5522 (°*sya mahānase*, do.); **161**, 5539, 5542 (= v. 5496), 5567 (= v. 5522); **162**, 5585; **163**, 5683 (°-*Drupadau vṛddhau*), 5696.—§ 572 (Rathātirathasaṅkhyānap.): V, **170**, 5886 (°-*Drupadau*).—§ 573 (Ambopākhyānap.): V, **194***γ*, 7599 (do.); **196***η*, 7624, 7632 (°-*Drupada-*), (*ν*), 7637.—§ 576 (Bhagavadgītāp.): VI, **19***ε*, 710 (*akshauhiṇīvṛtaḥ*), 720; **25***θ*, 833, (*κ*), 846.—§ 578 (Bhīshmavadhap.): VI, **45**[13], 1717, 1718, 1719 (encounter with Bhagadatta); **47**[27]*ε*, 1837 (*saha putreṇa*), ([31]*η*), 1866; **49**, 2009 (only B.); **50***ν*, 2060 (°-*Drupadau*), (*π*), 2088 (*saha Kekayaiḥ*, in the rear of Yudhishṭhira's army); **51***aa*, 2117.—§ 579 (do.): VI, **52**[1]*a*, 2128, (*ζ*), 2149; **53**[7], 2232 (°-*Drupadau vṛddhau*).—§ 580 (do.): VI, **56***ζ*, 2414; **59**, †2629 (°*rājapramukhāḥ*).—§ 582 (do.): VI, **72***ε*, 3162 (*Matsyena*); **73**, 3197.—§ 583 (do.): VI, **75***a*, 3284.—§ 584 (do.): VI, **82**, 3591, 3600 (defeated by Droṇa).—§ 585 (do.): VI, **87***θ*, 3867; **89***ν*, 3947.—§ 586 (do.): VI, **99***ζ*, 4509; **103***μ*, 4685, 4686, 4690.—§ 587 (do.): VI, **108**, 5001; **110***ζ*, 5098 (°-*Drupadau vṛddhau*), 5108 (do.); **111**, 5161 (do.), 5163, 5166 (°-*Drupadau*); **115**, 5362 (attacked Jayadratha); **116**, 5417, 5418 (encounter with Jayadratha); **118**, 5541 (°*sya priyo bhrātā Çatānīkaḥ*), (*ν*), 5555, (*φ*), 5559; **119***χ*, 5578, (*ω*), 5587 (°-*Drupadau*).—§ 589 (Droṇābhishekap.): VII, **10**, 375 (°*sya rathānīkam Matsyasya*).—§ 590 (do.): VII, **14***a*, 577 (°-*Drupadau*); **16***δ*, 650 (do.).—§ 592 (Saṃçaptakavadhap.): VII, **23***o*, 966 (*putram V°rājasya*, i.e. Uttara (?)); **25**, 1083 (*Matsyam*, attacked by Vinda and Anuvinda).—§ 593 (Abhimanyuvadhap.): VII, **35***δ*, 1510; **40***o*, 1691; **42***π*, 1743; **43***ρ*, 1769.—§ 596 (Pratijñāp.): VII, **72**, 2491.—§ 597 (do.): VII, **83***a*, 2949.—§ 598 (Jayadrathavadhap.): VII, **85***δ*, 3050.—§ 599 (do.): VII, **95**, 3533 (*Matsyam*, attacked by Vinda and Anuvinda); **96**, 3545, 3546 (encounter with Vinda and Anuvinda); **98***κ*, 3661 (*sa-Kaikayaḥ*); **111***ν*, 4283; **114***ψ*, 4503; **124***λλ*, 5002 (°-*Drupadau*).—§ 600 (Ghaṭotkacavadhap.): VII, **153**, 6627 (do.); **154***β*, 6650 (*sa-Kaikayaḥ*); **155***ε*, †6720 (*Drupada-V°-Kaikayāḥ*); **156***θ*, 6764 (*Matsyam*); **158***χ*, 7012 (°*bhrātaraḥ*); **165**, 7369 (resisted by Çalya); **167**, 7484, 7486, 7492, 7494, 7495 (defeated by Çalya).—§ 601 (Droṇavadhap.): VII, **184***a*, 8368.—§ 602 (do.): VII, **186**, 8487 (°-*Drupadau*), 8492, 8493 (°-*Drupadau*), 8495, 8499 (*V.* and Drupada slain by Droṇa).—§ 604 (Karṇap.): VIII, **6**, 156 (*V.* and Drupada with their sons had been slain by Droṇa).—§ 608 (do.): VIII, **79**, †4057 (°*sya pure*, all. to § 552); **83**, 4254 (°*bhavane*, cf. § 549 foll.).—§ 616 (Sauptikap.): X, **8**, 384 (*yac ca çishṭam V°sya balam*).—§ 617 (Aishīkap.): X, **16**, 723 (°*sya sutām . . . snushām Gāṇḍīvadhanvanaḥ*, i.e. Uttarā).—§ 619 (Strīvilāpap.): XI, **20***ε*, 598 (*nihatam*), 599.—§ 620 (Çrāddhap.): XI, **26***β*, 788 (°-*Drupadau*, their bodies are cremated).—§ 630 (Rājadh.): XII, **27***β*, 799.—§ 637 (do.): XII, **42***γ*, 1489 (his çrāddha performed).—§ 788 (Āçramavāsap.): XV, **25**, 670 (°*sya sutā*, i.e. Uttarā).—§ 789 (Putradarçanap.): XV, **32***θ*, 875 (°*Drupadau*).—§ 795 (Svargārohaṇap.): XVIII, **1***δ*, 25 (do.); **5***λ*, 148 (do.), (*μ*), 162 (do., among those who, after death, entered the deities). Cf. Matsya, Matsyapati, Matsyarāj, Matsyarāja, Matsyarājan.

Virāṭa = Virāṭaparvan: I, 89.

Virāṭaduhitṛ ("the daughter of Virāṭa") = Uttarā: IV, 2256; X, 728; XI, 571 (*snushā Gāṇḍīvadhanvanaḥ*), 572.

Virāṭajā (do.) = Uttarā: XIV, 1857.

Virāṭanagara ("the city of Virāṭa"): I, 481; III, 17436; IV, 1, 3, 17, 19, 64, 65, 178, 212, 327, 336, 384, 989, 995, 2154, 2177; V, 613, 2354, 2355, 2479, 2495, 4176, 4682, 5471, 5521, 5566, 5756; VI, 4456, 4836; VII, 5423, 6986; VIII, 1947, 2412; IX, 3160; X, 598.

Virāṭanṛpati, v. Virāṭa.

Virāṭaparvan, the fourth book of the Mhbhr. (containing the adventures of the Pāṇḍavas when living in the service of Virāṭa). § 795*c* (Mahābhārata): XVIII, **6**, 270. Cf. Vairāṭa.

Virāṭaputra[1] ("the son of Virāṭa") = Babhru (?): V, 2264 (*B°*).

Virāṭaputra[2] (do.) = Çaṅkha: V, †1846 (*jyeshṭham*); VIII, 187 (*Ç°*).

Virāṭaputra[3] (do.) = Uttara: IV, †1680, †2119.

Virāṭarāj, Viraṭarāja, Virāṭarājan, v. Virāṭa.

Virāṭatanayā ("the daughter of Virāṭa") = Uttarā: IV, 2369.

Virāva, name of a horse. § 382 (Agastyop.): III, **99**, 8631 (given to Agastya by Ilvala).

Vīravatī, a river. § 574 (Jambūkh.): VI, **9***λ*, 332.

Virāvin, a son of Dhṛtarāshṭra. § 130 (Aṃçāvat.): I, **67**, 2739.—§ 182 (Dhṛtarāshṭraputranāmak.): I, **117**, 4552.

Vīrin, pl. (°*ṇaḥ*), a family. § 267 (Yamasabhāv.): II, **8**, 334 (°*ṇām Īriṇām çatam*, B., *Īriṇāñ ca çatam tathā*, C.).

Viriñca = Brahmán. § 717*b* (Nārāyaṇīya): XII, **343***φ*, 13253 (°*a iti yat proktam Kāpilam jñānacintakaiḥ*—i.e. in the Sāṅkhya system—*sa Prajāpatiḥ*, identified with Nārāyaṇa (Vishṇu, Kṛshṇa)). Cf. next.

Viriñci = Brahmán. § 49 (Vāsuki): I, **38**, 1638.—§ 705 (Mokshadh.): XII, **303**, 11231 (= Hiraṇyagarbha).

Vīriṇī, wife of Daksha. § 138 (Daksha Prācetasa): I, **75**, 3131 (mother of 1000 sons).

Virocana[1], an Asura. § 90 (Aṃçāvat.): I, **65**, 2527 (son of Prahlāda).—§ 91 (do.): I, **65**, 2528 (father of Bali).—§ 300 (Prahlāda): II, **68**, 2315 (son of Prahlāda), 2335 (*V.'s* quarrel with Sudhanvan, cf. § 558)—§ 558 (cf. Prajāgarap.): At the svayaṃvara of *Keçinī*, *V.* and Sudhanvan staked their lives as to who of them was superior, and referred the question to Prahlāda (q.v., cf. § 300, where the same is told more in detail): V, **35**, 1186 (°*sya saṃvadaṃ Keçinyarthe Sudhanvanā*), 1187 (*Daiteyaḥ*), 1188, (1189), 1190, (1191), 1193, (1196), (1199), 1200, (1201), 1203, 1205, (1206), 1209, 1217, 1218, 1220.—§ 592 (Saṃçaptakavadhap.): VII, **26**, †1193 (°*o devavarūthinīm iva*, sc. *jagāha*).—§ 595 (Shoḍaçarāj., v. Pṛthu Vainya): VII, **69**, 2413 (when the Asuras milked the earth, *V.* was their calf).—§ 615 (Gadayuddhap.): IX, **58**, 3250 (*Çakreṇa māyayā nirjitaḥ*).—§ 641 (Rājadh.): XII, **98***ξ*, 3660 (had been slain by Indra).—§ 656 (Khaḍgotpattik.): XII, **166***γ*, 6146.—§ 671*b* (Bali-Vāsavasaṃv.): XII, **225**, 8154.—§ 673*b* (do.): XII, **227***a*, 8262 (among the ancient rulers of the earth).—§ 717*b* (Nārāyaṇīya): XII, **340**, 12943 (°*sya . . . Baliḥ putraḥ*). Cf. Daiteya, Daityendra, Prāhrādi.

Virocana[2], a son of Dhṛtarāshṭra. § 232 (Svayaṃvarap.): I, **186**, 6982 (came to the svayaṃvara of Draupadī).

Virocana[3] = Sūrya (the Sun): III, 193; V, 4920.—Do.[4] = Soma (the Moon): IX, 2025.—Do.[5] = Vishṇu (1000 names).

Virocanā, a mātṛ. § 615*u* (Skanda): IX, **46** *θ*, 2648.

Virohaṇa, a serpent. § 64 (Sarpasattra): I, **57**, 2150 (of Takshaka's race).

Virūpa[1], an Asura. § 268 (Varuṇasabhāv.): II, **9**, 366 (in the palace of Varuṇa).

Virūpa[2]. § 662*b* (Jāpakop.): XII, **199**, (7289), 7290, 7291, (7292), (7304), (7316) (Kāma and Krodha appeared in the shape of *V.* and Vikṛta).

Virūpa[3], son of Aṅgiras. § 747*b* (Suvarṇotpatti): XIII, **85** *θ*, 4148.

Virūpa[4] = Çiva (1000 names[1–2]).

Virūpāçva, an ancient king. § 761 (Ānuçāsanik.): XIII, **115** *δ*, 5667 (among the kings who abstained from meat during the month of Kārttika).

Virūpaka, an Asura (?). § 673*b* (Bali-Vāsavasaṃv.): XII, **227** *a*, 8263 (among the ancient rulers of the earth).

Virūpāksha[1] = Çiva, q.v. (add XIII, 716, 1363, 6727, 7636; XIV, 200, 209, 211).

Virūpāksha[2], an Asura. § 92 (Aṃçāvat.): I, **63**, 2533 (son of Danu).—§ 130 (do.): I, **65**, 2658 (*Daiteyaḥ . . . mahāsuraḥ*, incarnate as king Citradharman).

Virūpāksha[3], name of several Rākshasas. § 537 (Rāma-Rāvaṇayuddha): III, **285**, 16372 (follower of Rāvaṇa, fought with Sugrīva).—§ 600 (Ghaṭotkacavadhap.): VII, **175**, 7905 (*Rākshasaḥ*, charioteer of Ghaṭotkaca).—§ 658*b* (Kṛtaghnop.): XII, **170**, 6356 (*Rākshasādhipatiḥ*, lord of Meruvraja, cf. v. 6360), 6365 (do.); **171**, 6379, 6388; **172**, 6407; **173**, 6434, 6435 (°*puram*), 6436. Cf. Rākshasa, Rākshasādhipa, Rākshasādhipati, Rākshasendra.

Virūpāksha[4], a Rudra. § 665 (Mokshadh.): XII, **208** *δ*, 7585.

Virūpākshī = Durgā (Umā): VI, 801.

Vīryātman = Kṛshṇa: XII, 1664.

Vīryavat, a Viçvadeva. § 749 (Ānuçāsanik.): XIII, **91** *γ*, 4356 (enumeration).

Vīryavatī, a mātṛ. § 615*u* (Skanda): IX, **46** *θ*, 2626.

Visarga = Çiva (1000 names[2]).

Vishāgnipā, Vishāgrapād (only C.) = Çiva (1000 names[1]).

Vishama = Vishṇu (1000 names).

Vishaṇṇāṅga = Çiva (1000 names[2]).

Vishaprastha, a mountain. § 379 (Tīrthayātrāp.): III, **95**, 8513 (*girau*).

Vishayagoptṛ = Kṛshṇa: XII, 1659.

Vishkambhin = Çiva (1000 names[2]).

Vishkara, v. Viskara.

Vishṇu[1], one of the Ādityas, also named Hari, identified with the Supreme Lord Nārāyaṇa, husband of Lakshmī (Çrī, Padmā); in the Mhbhr. his principal incarnation is that as Kṛshṇa Vāsudeva. § 2 (Anukram.): I, **1**, 24 (*Hṛshīkeçaṃ . . . Hariṃ*).—§ 10 (Parvasaṅgr.): I, **2**, 357 (*çiçoç caryā V°oḥ*, sc. as Kṛshṇa).—§ 28 (Amṛtamanthana): I, [**17**, 1109 (*Nārāyaṇo devaḥ*, caused the ocean to be churned)]; **18**, 1115, 1117, 1142, (1143), [1147 (*Nārāyaṇo*, obtained the Kaustubha)]; **19**, 1159 (disguised as a woman, *V.* (Nārāyaṇa) recovered the *amṛta* from the Asuras), 1160, 1177 (defeated the Asuras with his cakra Sudarçana). — § 30*b* (Samudra): I, **22**, [1216 (*gāṃ vindatā bhagavatā Govindenāmitaujasā / varāharūpiṇā cāntarvikshobhitajalāvilaṃ*, sc. the ocean)], 1218 (*adhyātmayoganidrāñ ca Padmanābhasya sevataḥ / yugādikālaçayanaṃ V°oḥ*, sc. the ocean).—§ 33 (Garuḍa): I, **23**, 1251 (Garuḍa identified with *V.*).—§ 37 (Indra): I, **25**, 1291 (Indra identified with *V.*)—§ 46 (Garuḍa): I, **33**, 1506 (*Nārāyaṇaḥ*), 1510 (Garuḍa became his vehicle and the device of his banner), [1533 (*devadevaṃ . . . Hariṃ*)].—§ 71 (Ādivaṃçāvataraṇap.): I, **61**, 2276 (°*oḥ çatruvadheshv iva*).—§ 82 (Kṛshṇa Vāsudeva): I, **63**, 2428 (incarnate as Kṛshṇa, the son of Vasudeva and Devakī).—[§ 84 (Ādivaṃçāvataraṇap.): I, **64**, 2505 (*Nārāyaṇam amitraghnaṃ Vaikuṇṭhaṃ*)].—[§ 85 (Aṃçāvat.): I, **65**, 2509 (*Nārāyaṇena*, incarnates a portion of himself)]. — § 88 (do.): I, **65**, 2524 (the youngest of the twelve Ādityas and superior to them all).—§ 120 (do.): I, **66**, 2600 (do.):—[§ 132 (do.): I, **67**, 2785 (*Nārāyaṇaḥ . . . devadevaḥ*, a portion of him incarnate as Kṛshṇa)].—§ 133 (Dushyanta): I, **68**, 2811 (*bale V°samaḥ*, sc. Dushyanta).—§ 147 (Devayānī): I, **82**, 3408 (°*oḥ . . . gṛhe*); **83**, 3432 (*Çakra-V°ū ivāparau*, sc. Yadu and Turvasu). — § 149 (Yayāti): I, **88**, †3572 (*Çakrārka-V°pratimaprabhāvaṃ*, sc. Yayāti). — § 190*d* (Arjuna): I, **123**, 4795 (*Adityā V°nā prītir yathābhūt; °sanaḥ . . . Arjunaḥ*), 4799 (°*tulyaparākramaḥ*, sc. Arjuna).—§ 191 (do.): I, **123**, 4824 (the twelfth of the Ādityas).—§ 234 (Svayaṃvarap.): I, **190**, 7101 (*sākshād vā V°r Acyutaḥ*).—[§ 238 (Pañcendrop.): I, **197**, 7306 (*Nārāyaṇaṃ*), 7307 (*Hariḥ*) (a black and a white hair of Hari Nārāyaṇa were born as Kṛshṇa and Balarāma)].—[§ 270 (Brahmasabhāv.): II, **11**, 468 (*devo Nārāyaṇaḥ*, in the palace of Brahmán)]. — § 277 (Jarāsandhavadhap.): II, **24**, 939 (*Çakra-V°ū hi saṅgrāmaṃ caretus Tārakāmaye tena rathena*), 956 (= Kṛshṇa).—[§ 286 (Rājasūyikap.): II, **33**, 1213 (*Hariḥ* = Kṛshṇa)].—[§ 289 (Arghāharaṇap.): II, **36**, 1318 (*Hariṃ*), 1319 (*Nārāyaṇaḥ*, all. to § 85), 1321 (*Nārāyaṇaḥ Çambhuḥ . . . ajāyata Yadukshaye*)].—§ 299 (Dyūtap.): II, **68**, 2295 (= Kṛshṇa, invoked by Draupadī). — [§ 310*b* (Sūrya): III, **3**, 171 (*devāḥ . . . sopendrāḥ*, worshipped Sūrya)]. — § 317 (Arjunābhigamanap.): III, **12**, 470 (*lokanāthasya* = Kṛshṇa).—§ 317*b* (Kṛshṇa Vāsudeva): III, **12**, 484 (= Kṛshṇa), [505 (*Harir Nārāyaṇaḥ* = do.)], 511 (= do.).—§ 332 (Mahādevastava): III, **39**, 1627 (*Çivāya V°rūpāya V°ave Çivarūpāya*).—§ 333*b* (Arjuna): III, **40**, 1637 (*Purushottame* = Kṛshṇa).—§ 334 (Kairātap.): III, **41**, 1688 (= Kṛshṇa) [1698 (*Ajitena* = do.)].—§ 339 (Indralokābhigamanap.): III, **47**, 1891 (= Kṛshṇa, in Badarī), 1896 (*bhūmigataḥ çrīmān V°r Madhunisūdanaḥ Kapilo nāma devo 'sau bhagavān ajito Hariḥ* = Kapila; born as Kṛshṇa).—§ 356 (Tīrthayātrāp.): III, **80**, 3091 (*Ādityānāṃ yathā V°ḥ*).—§ 358 (do.): III, **82**, 5006 (had in the tīrtha Varadāna obtained a boon from Durvāsas), 5017 (°*unā . . . purā çaucaṃ kṛtaṃ . . . hatvā Daiteya-Dānavān*).—§ 359 (Vaḍavā): III, **82**, 5038 (worshipped by the gods, etc., in the tīrtha Vaḍavā).—[§ 360 (Tīrthayātrāp.): III, **82**, 5067 (*Keçavaṃ*, worshipped at *saṅgamaṃ . . . Sarasvatyāḥ*)].—§ 362 (do.): III, **83**, 5080 (°*oḥ sthānaṃ*, a tīrtha), 5088 (*vārāharūpeṇa*, in the tīrtha Vārāha).—§ 364 (do.): III, **83**, 6014 (had, in the tīrtha Lokoddhāra, taken up (*uddhṛtāḥ*) the worlds), [6073 (*Vāmanaṃ*, to be worshipped in the tīrtha Vishṇupada)].—[§ 368 (do.): III, **83**, 7040 (*devaiḥ . . . Nārāyaṇapurogamaiḥ*), 7043 (*Nārāyaṇaṃ . . . Padmanābhaṃ*)].—§ 370 (do.): III, **84**, 7097 (adored Çiva in the tīrtha Suvarṇa), 8099 (recovered a koṭi of tīrthas which had been carried away by an Asura in the shape of a tortoise), 8101 (in *Nārāyaṇasya sthānaṃ*), 8102 (*Çālagrāma iti khyātaḥ*), 8103 (*Trilokeçaṃ*), [8109 (*Hariṃ*, to be worshipped in the tīrtha Vāmana)], 8125 (*Mahādevaṃ*, to be worshipped in the tīrtha Agnidhārā). — [§ 371 (Tuṅgaka): III, **85**, 8192 (*Harir Nārāyaṇaḥ*, in Tuṅgaka)].—[§ 373 (Prayāga): III,

85, 8215 (*Hariḥ*, in Prayāga)].—§ 377 (Dhaumyatīrthak.): III, [**88**, 8352 (*Puṇḍarīkāksho Devadevaḥ*), 8353 (*Hariḥ . . . Madhusūdanaḥ*) (= Kṛshṇa, in Dvārakā)]; **90**, 8395 (*Nārāyaṇaḥ . . . Purushottamaḥ*, in Badarī).—§ 383 (Paraçurāma): III, **99**, 8657 (incarnate as Rāma Dāçarathi), 8677 (i.e. Rāma Dāçarathi), 8681 (do.), 8683 (do.), 8688 (do).—§ 384 (Agastyop.): III, **101**, [8722 (*Nārāyaṇaṃ prabhuṃ*)], 8723, 8724, 8725 (bestowed his energy on Indra), 8728 (*yathā mahāçailavaraḥ purastāt sa Mandaro V°karād vimuktaḥ*); [**102**, 8755 (*Vaikuṇṭhaṃ . . . Madhusūdanaṃ*)] (*c* (v. 8756 foll.): *V.* is the creator, protector (*kartā*, read *bhartā*), and destroyer (*hartā*) of the gods and the universe. His former incarnations are mentioned, viz. as a boar (*varāha*) in order to raise the sunken earth from the sea; as *narasiṃha* (half man and half lion) in order to slay the *Ādidaitya Hiraṇyakaçipu*; as a dwarf (*vāmana*) in order to deliver the three worlds from the great *Asura Bali*. He had also slain the *Asura Jambha*, the great bowman, who obstructed sacrifices); **103**, (8768), 8774 (when the Kāleyas had taken their abode in the sea, *V.* told the gods to apply to Agastya, that he might dry up the sea).—§ 386 (do.): III, **105**, 8823 (*tridaçā V°nā sārdhaṃ*, applied to Brahmán about the refilling of the sea).—§ 392 (Tīrthayātrāp.): III, **114**, †10121 (*°o retas*), †10122 (*retodhā V°oḥ*).—§ 394 (Arjuna Kārtavīrya): III, **115**, 10139 (*Devadevaṃ surārighnaṃ*, incarnate as Rāma Jāmadagnya).—§ 400 (Tīrthayātrāp.): III, **118**, †10224 (*°oḥ*, sc. *āyatanaṃ*, visited by Yudhishṭhira).—§ 407 (Mandhātrup.): III, **126**, 10424 (*iva*), 10457 (*vyajayad lokāṃs trīn V°r iva vikramaiḥ*).—§ 422*b* (Naraka): III, **142**, 10915 (*purātanena devena V°nā . . . Daityo nihataḥ*, sc. Naraka), 10919, 10921 (*devagaṇeçvaraṃ*), (10923), 10925 (slew Naraka).—§ 422 *bis* (Varāhāvatāra): III, **142**, 10926, (10942) (*V.'s* avatāra as a boar (*varāha*)).—§ 425 (Hanūmad-Bhīmasaṃv.): III, **147**, 11197 (*mānusharūpeṇa*, i.e. incarnate as Rāma Dāçarathi).—[§ 426*b* (Kṛtayuga): III, **149**, 11242 (*Nārāyaṇaḥ*, becomes white in the Kṛtayuga)].—[§ 427 (Tretāyuga): III, **149**, 11247 (*Acyutaḥ*, becomes red in the Tretāyuga)].—§ 428 (Dvāpara): III, **149**, 11251 (becomes yellow in the Dvāparayuga).—[§ 429 (Kaliyuga): III, **149**, 11257 (*Keçavaḥ*, becomes black in the Kaliyuga)].—§ 431 (Saugandhikāharaṇa): III, **151**, 11324 (*Rāmābhidhānaṃ V°ṃ*, sc. as the son of Daçaratha).—§ 439 (Yakshayuddhap.): III, **163**, [11857 (*anādinidhanaṃ devaṃ prabhuṃ Nārāyaṇaṃ paraṃ*)], 11859 (*sthānaṃ V°oḥ*), [11860 foll. (description of Nārāyaṇasthāna (near Meru))]—§ 458 (Mārkaṇḍeyas.): III, **188**, 12813 (*Nārāyaṇāṅkaprakhyaḥ*, sc. Mārkaṇḍeya, *V°oḥ*, sc. *karṇikoddharaṇaṃ* (?), at the beginning of the yuga), [12821 foll. (*Svayambhuve*, etc., i.e. Nārāyaṇa, identified with Kṛshṇa, description of the end of one [great] yuga and the beginning of the new)].—§ 459 (do.): III, **189**, 12954 (*ahaṃ Vishṇuḥ*, etc., says Nārāyaṇa explaining his nature to Mārkaṇḍeya (v. 12950–98)), 13005 (*Ādidevaṃ Ajaṃ* = Kṛshṇa).—§ 474*b* (Dhundhumārop.): III, **201**, 13492, 13504, (13506), 13514 (Uttaṅka praised *V.* with the hymn, vv. 13494–13503, and obtained the boon that Dhundhu might be slain by Kuvalāçva).—§ 476 (do.): III, **202**, 13542 (all. to § 474*b*).—§ 477 (do.): III, **203**, 13556, 13557 (*V.* (*Hari, Govinda, Keçava, Madhusūdana*), slew Madhu and Kaiṭabha at the beginning of the yuga).—§ 478 (do.): III, **204**, 13586, 13587 (Dhundhu, the son of Madhu and Kaiṭabha, assailed *V.* and the gods), 13594 (filled Kuvalāçva with his energy), 13617 (*sakhyañ ca V°nā me*, sc. Kuvalāçva's), 13625 (*°oḥ samanukīrtanaṃ*).—§ 512 (Ghoshayātrāp.): III, **249**, 15095 (*°ur devagaṇān iva*, sc. *jñātīn . . . anupaçyethāḥ*).—§ 516 (Duryodhanayajña): III, **255**, 15292 (before Duryodhana only *V.* had performed the Vaishṇava sacrifice).—§ 520 (Mudgala): III, **261**, 15482 (*Brahmaṇaḥ sadanād ūrdhvaṃ tad V°oḥ paramaṃ padaṃ*).—[§ 521 (Draupadīharaṇap.): III, **263**, 15545 (*Harir Īçvaraḥ* / *Viçvātmā*), 15553 (*Hari°* — i.e. Kṛshṇa)].—§ 524*c* (Jayadrathavimokshaṇap.): *V.* is the infinite Spirit (*pradhānapurushaḥ*), etc., who, at the termination of a *yuga* in the form of the all-consuming fire (*Kālāgniḥ*, v. 15809), burns the world and the *Nāgalokas* who dwell in the *Pātāla*, whereafter clouds appear in the sky and pour down rain that extinguishes the fire (*saṃvarttāgni-*). When, at the end of 4,000 yugas, the earth becomes flooded with water, the Supreme being (*Purusha*), under the name of *Nārāyaṇa*, with 1,000 eyes, and 1,000 feet, and 1,000 heads, sleeps upon Çesha, who has 1,000 hoods, etc., enveloping all space with nocturnal gloom. And when his creative faculty is stirred (*sattvodrekāt*) he awakes and finds the world deserted. Etymology of the name *Nārāyaṇa* (v. 15819). When he was engaged in meditation for the re-creation of the universe, a lotus came into existence from his navel, and from this the four-faced *Brahmán* came out, who, sitting on the lotus, from his mind (*mānasān*) created the nine great ṛshis *Marīci*, etc., who were equal to himself. They created the *Yakshas*, *Rākshasas*, *Bhūtas*, *Piçācas*, serpents, and men. In the form of *Brahmán* he creates, in the form of *Purusha* (*Paurushī tanuḥ*) he preserves, and in the form of *Rudra* he destroys the universe (the three conditions of *Prajāpati*): III, **272**, 15808 (*Devadevaḥ . . . Suraguruḥ*).—§ 524*d* (do.): *V.'s* incarnations are the following: (1) a boar (*yajñavarāhaḥ*, v. 15832) 10 yojanas in length; (2) half lion, half man, when he killed the *Daitya* king *Hiraṇyakaçipu*, who attacked him with his *çūla* (trident); (3) the son of *Kaçyapa* and *Aditi*, in the form of a dwarf (*vāmana*), born 1,000 years after the conception, of the hue of rain-charged clouds and with bright eyes; when he, accompanied by *Bṛhaspati*, entered the sacrificial assembly of *Bali*, the king of the *Dānavas*, he, in three paces, took in the earth (*! medinīṃ*) and gave it to *Indra*; (4) *Kṛshṇa*, with conchshell, discus, and mace, adorned with the *Çrīvatsa*, clad in yellow silken robes, who protects Arjuna, riding in the same chariot with him: III, **272**, 15825, 15846 (*devaḥ sanātanaḥ*), 15849 (*Kṛshṇeti parikīrtyate*).—§ 526 (Rāmopākhyānap.): III, **276**, 15933 (*Caturbhujaḥ*, incarnate as Rāma Dāçarathi he will slay Rāvaṇa), 15935 (*°oḥ sahāyān*, = Rāma Dāçarathi).—[§ 547 (Karṇa): III, **310**, 17205 (*Varāhaṃ aparājitaṃ* / *Nārāyaṇaṃ acintyaṃ* = Kṛshṇa)].—§ 548 (Āraṇeyap.): III, **315**, 17461 (*e*: having assumed the form of the horse-headed (*açvaçiras*), *V.* lived for a long time unrecognized, intending to enter the womb of *Aditi*, then he [born from *Aditi*] as a dwarf, took the shape of a brahman and deprived *Bali* of his kingdom by his [three] steps), [17464 (*Hariṇā*, do.: *V.* entered in the thunderbolt of Indra and lay concealed in it)], 17467 (do.: living disguised in the abode of *Daçaratha* (i.e. as Rāma Dāçarathi) *V.* slew *Daçagrīva* (i.e. Rāvaṇa) in battle).—[§ 549*f* (Durgā): IV, **6**, 186 (*Padmā Nārāyaṇaparigrahaḥ*)].—§ 553 (Vaivāhikap.): IV, **71**, 2304 (*°-Mahendrakalpau*, sc. Nakula and Sahadeva).—§ 555 (Indravijaya): V, **9**, 288; **10**, 293 (*°oḥ kshayaṃ*), 295 296 (*Sarvadeveçaṃ*), 297 (*b*: The gods and the ṛshis said: "In former times you pervaded the three worlds in three steps, you procured the *amṛta* and destroyed the *Asuras*, you suppressed the great *Asura Bali* and raised *Indra* to the throne of heaven, you are the Lord of the gods, and this entire universe is pervaded by you . . ."), (300), 328, 330, 334 (*tribhuvanaçreshṭha*) (from fear of Vṛtra the gods, etc., applied to *V.*, who promised to enter the thunderbolt of Indra); **13**, 410 (*Devadevena*), 413, 416 (distributed the sin of brahmanicide); **15**, 457; **16**, 499 (°-*tejaḥ*).—§ 556 (Sañjayayānap.): V, **22**, †674 (=Kṛshṇa), †676 (read with B. *Indrā-V°ū Daityasenāṃ yathaiva*), †677 (*Vṛshṇivīraḥ* = Kṛshṇa).—§ 561*c* (Kṛshṇa Vāsudeva): V, **48**, †1891 (= Kṛshṇa, slew Naraka).—§ 561 (Yānasandhip.): V, **48**, †1895 (i.e. Kṛshṇa); **59**, 2333 (*Indra-V°samau*, sc. Kṛshṇa and Arjuna); [**68**, 2536 (*Hariḥ* = Kṛshṇa)]; **70**, 2562 (etymology = Kṛshṇa), 2564 (= Kṛshṇa), 2571 (etymology = Kṛshṇa), [†2578 (*Hariṃ* = Kṛshṇa). — § 564 (Mātalīyop.): V, **97**, 3503 (*Ādityānāṃ hi sarveshāṃ V°r eko sanātanaḥ*); [**99**, 3551 (*Ādityo Hayagrīvaḥ*, in Pātāla)]; **100**, 3571 (*Asurāḥ Kālakañjāç ca tathā V°padodbhavāḥ*); **101**, 3592 (*kulaṃ V°parigrahaṃ*, sc. the Suparṇas), 3593 (worshipped by the Suparṇas); **104**, 3666 (*caturbhujaḥ*), 3667, 3669, (3670); **105**, 3682, 3699, 3705, 3708, 3710 (in order to save Sumukha, *V.* humiliated Garuḍa).—§ 565 (Gālavacarita): V, **107**, 3755 (*Kṛshṇaṃ*), [3759 (*Vāsavāvarajaḥ*)]; **110**, 3818 (*anādinidhanasyātra*—i.e. in the west—*V°oḥ sthāṇaṃ*); **111**, 3827 (*atra*—i.e. in the north—*V°ḥ sahasrākshaḥ sahasracaraṇo 'vyayaḥ / sahasraçirasaḥ çrīmān anekaḥ paçyati māyayā*), 3841 (*Vishṇupadaṃ . . . kramatā V°nā kṛtaṃ*); **113***a*, 3881 (*sanātanaḥ*); [**117**, 3969 (*reme . . . yathā Nārāyaṇo Lakshmyāṃ*)]. — § 574 (Jambūkh.): VI, **8**, [302 (*Hariḥ . . . Vaikuṇṭhaḥ, i:* On the north of the milky ocean (*kshīrodasya samudrasya*) *Hari Vaikuṇṭha* dwells in his chariot of gold with eight wheels, etc., and adorned with *jāmbūnada* gold; he is the lord of all creatures; in him the universe merges and from him it again emanates; he is Sacrifice's self, and fire is his mouth)], 308 (*Naro Nārāyaṇaç caiva sarvajñaḥ sarvabhūtakṛt / devā Vaikuṇṭham ity āhur narā V°m iti prabhuṃ*).—[§ 575 (Bhūmip.): VI, **12**, 450 (*Nārāyaṇo Hariḥ*, on the mountain Gomanta in Krauñcadvīpa)].—§ 576 (Bhagavadgītāp.): VI, [**21**, 774 (*Harir Vikuṇṭhaḥ* = Kṛshṇa)]; **34**, 1225 (*Ādityānām ahaṃ V°ḥ*, sc. *asmi*, says Kṛshṇa); **35**, [1255 (= Kṛshṇa, who declares himself to be the Supreme Lord)], †1270 (=Kṛshṇa), †1276 (do.); [**42**, 1531 (*Hariṃ*, do.)].—§ 578 (Bhīshmavadhap.): VI, **50**, 2074 (°*r Vajrabhṛteva*, sc. *uktaḥ*, only B., C. has *Jishṇur*).—§ 580 (Bhīshmavadhap.): VI, **59**, †2588 (°*r yathā Vṛtranisūdanasya*, sc. *cakāra sāhāyyam*), [†2610 (*Hariṃ* = Kṛshṇa)], †2611 (= Kṛshṇa).—§ 581 (do.): VI, **65**, 2960, 2968 (= Aniruddha) (Brahmán praised the Supreme Lord (Purusha, v. 2941) with the hymn 2944–72, asking him to be born on earth [as Kṛshṇa]); [**67**π, 3016 (*Purushottamaḥ* = Kṛshṇa, description of the creation, etc.), 3027 (*Madhusūdanaṃ, Varāhaç caiva Siṃhaç ca Trivikramagatiḥ prabhuḥ* = do.), 3028 (*Hariḥ* = do.)]; **68**ρ, 3039 (only B.), [3046 (*Hariḥ* = do.)].—§ 589 (Droṇābhishekap.): VII, **4**, 118 (*yathā V°r divaukasāṃ*).—§ 590 (do.): VII, **13**, 476 (*sahito devaiḥ*); **14**, 543 (*yathā V°ḥ purā . . . Hiraṇyākshena saṃyuge*).—§ 592 (Saṃçaptakavadhap.): VII, **21**, 891 (*yathā Daityagaṇe V°ḥ*, sc. *cakāra kadanaṃ mahat*).—§ 593 (Abhimanyuvadhap.): VII, **36**, 1544 (= Kṛshṇa, *mātulaṃ*, sc. Abhimanyu's), 1578 (°*r ivācintyaḥ*); **49**, 1927 (= Kṛshṇa, °*oḥ svasur nandakaraḥ*, i.e. Abhimanyu).—§ 594 (Akampana): VII, **52**, 2037 (*Indra-V°-samadyutiḥ*, sc. Hari, the son of Akampana).—§ 596 (Pratijñāp.): VII, **79**, 2783 (= Kṛshṇa, read with B., *V°r Jishṇupriyaṅkaraḥ*); **81**, 2910 (*Indra-V°ū yathā prītau Jambhasya vadhakāṅkshiṇau*).—§ 597 (do.): VII, **83**, 2963 (*Devadeveça sanātana viçātana / V°o Jishṇo Hari Kṛshṇa Purushottama* = Kṛshṇa).—§ 599*c* (Vṛtra): VII, **94**, 3460.—§ 599 (Jayadrathavadhap.): VII, **94**, 3479 (*Hiraṇyagarbheṇa yathā baddhaṃ V°oḥ purā raṇe*, sc. *kavacaṃ*); **149**, 6474 (only B.).—§ 600 (Ghaṭotkacavadhap.): VII, **170**, 7669 (*yathendraḥ samare . . . prāha V°m*); **174**, 7879 (°*r ivāhave*).—§ 602 (Droṇavadhap.): VII, **191**, 8790 (*yathā rūpaṃ purā V°or Hiraṇyakaçipor vadhe*); **192**, 8858 (*purāṇaṃ Purushaṃ*).—[§ 603 (Nārāyaṇāstramokshap.): VII, **197**, 9104 (*saṃkruddham iva garjantaṃ Hiraṇyakaçipur Hariṃ*, sc. *abravīt*)].—[§ 603*b* (Nārāyaṇa): VII, **201**, 9447 (*Nārāyaṇaḥ . . . Viçvakṛt*)].—§ 603*d* (Tripura): VII, **202**, 9568 (became the shaft of Çiva), 9574 (*çaraṃ . . . V°-Somasamāyutaṃ*, sc. Çiva's).—§ 603 (Nārāyaṇāstramokshap.): VII, **202**μ, 9600 (identified with Çiva).—§ 604 (Karṇap.): VIII, **3**, 65 (°-*Vāsavayor iva*, sc. *vikrāntaṃ*).—§ 605 (do.): VIII, **10**, 378 (°*ṃ dṛshṭveva Dānavāḥ*, sc. *dravishyanti*); **20**, †820 (*jite Balau V°m ivāmareçvaraḥ*, sc. *apūjayat*); **31**, 1268 (*Karṇasya bhujayor vīryaṃ Çakra-V°samaṃ*).—§ 606 (Tripurākhyāna): VIII, **34**, 1471 (*V.*, Soma and Agni became the arrow of Çiva), 1502 (do.), 1510 (*bāṇaṃ . . . Soma-Vishṇv-Agnisambhavaṃ*, sc. Çiva's, C. has by error °*Vishv*°), 1535 (*ishuṃ . . . V°-Somāgnisambhavaṃ*, sc. Çiva's), 1555 (*Somāgni-V°ūnāṃ*), [1556 (*Nārāyaṇaḥ*, became a bull and raised the chariot of Çiva)].—§ 607 (Karṇap.): VIII, **37**, †1720 (*Mahendra-V°pratimau*, sc. Bhīshma and Droṇa), †1726 (°-*Purandaropamaṃ*, sc. Droṇa); **45**ζ, 2105 (*Janārdanaḥ*).—§ 608 (do.): VIII, **51**, 2493 (°*r ivāsurān*, sc. *pothayām āsa*); **65**, 3304 (*hate mahāsure Jambhe Çakra-V°ū yathā Guruḥ*, sc. *abhyanandat*); **68**, †3392 (*balena V°oḥ*); **73**, 3690 (°*r iva hatvā Daiteya-Dānavān*), [3691 (*prayaccha medinīṃ rājñe Çakrāyaiva Harir yathā*)], 3692 (°*unā nihateshv eva Dānaveyeshu*); **77**, †3865 (*trailokyahetor Asurair āsīd devasya V°oḥ*, sc. *samāgamaḥ*): **79**, †4060 (*Jishṇor Vāsudevātmajasya*, i.e. Kṛshṇa); **87**, 4398 (°*vīryasamau*, sc. Karṇa and Arjuna), 4446 (*svayaṃ* = Kṛshṇa, charioteer of Arjuna); **94**, †4951 (*samānayanāv iva V°-Vāsavau*), †4961 (*sadasyahutāv iva V°-Vāsavau*); **96**, †5042, †5044, †5045.—§ 613 (Gadāyuddhap.): IX, **33**, 1914 (*yathā V°ḥ Çacīpateḥ*, sc. *prayacchorvīṃ*) —[§ 614 (do.): IX, **34**, 1964 (*Brahmāṇam iva Deveçam Indropendrau*, sc. *pūjayām āsatuḥ*)].—§ 615*u* (Skanda): IX, **44**, 2479; **45**γ, 2506 (*Indra-V°ū*), 2530 (*senāṃ V°rūpiṇīṃ*), 2539 (gave three companions to Skanda); **46**, 2667 (gave Skanda the garland Vaijayantī).—§ 615*ee* (Ādityatīrtha): IX, **49**, 2850 (having slain Madhu and Kaiṭabha *V.* performed his ablutions in Ādityatīrtha).—§ 615*kk* (Kurukshetrak.): IX, **53**, 3034 (*Brahma-V°-Maheçvaraiḥ*). — § 615 (Baladevatīrthayātrā): IX, **54**, 3039 (*devaḥ*, performed austerities).—§ 618 (Jalapradānikap.): XI, **7**, 188 (*paraṃ sthānaṃ V°oḥ*); **8**, 217 (*V.* had promised to the Earth that Duryodhana should cause her burden to be lightened by a battle in Kurukshetra).—§ 637 (Rājadh.): XII, **43**, 1503 (*Viçvakarman namas te 'stu Viçvātman Viçvasambhava / V°o Jishṇo Hare Kṛshṇa Vaikuṇṭha Purushottama*), [1506 (*Varāhaḥ . . . Urukramaḥ*), 1510 (*Vāmanaḥ*)] (Bhīshma praised Kṛshṇa as Vishṇu (Nārāyaṇa) with the hymn, vv. 1500–14); **45**, 1547 (*purushavigrahaṃ*, sc. as Kṛshṇa); **47**, 1602 (*yogeçvaraṃ Padmanābhaṃ V°ṃ Jishṇuṃ Jagatpatiṃ*), 1674, 1682, 1685 (°*mayaṃ*), 1687 (Bhīshma praised Kṛshṇa as Vishṇu (Nārāyaṇa) with the hymn vv. 1602–88).—§ 641 (do.): XII, **59**, 2208 (*Prajāpatiṃ*), [2209 (*Nārāyaṇaḥ*, created Virajas)].—§ 641*f* (Pṛthu Vainya): XII, **59**δ, 2237, 2248, 2249 (entered the body of

Pṛthu), 2252 (a golden lotus appeared on the forehead of *V.*, from that Çrī was born). — § 641 (Rājadh.): XII, **63**, †2364; **64**, 2392 (*sarvabhūteçvaraṃ Nārāyaṇaṃ*, the kings repaired to *V.* to be informed about chastisement), 2399, 2401, 2409; **65**, 2448 (*bhavanaṃ V°oḥ*) (in the form of Indra, *V.* instructed Māndhātṛ); **98**, 3654 (°*vikramakrāmī*); [**110**, 4076 (*Nārāyaṇaṃ devaṃ* = Kṛshṇa), 4080 (*Nārāyaṇaṃ Hariṃ*, do.)]; **120**ρ, †4397; **121**, 4431 (*daṇḍo hi bhagavān V°r daṇḍo hi Nārāyaṇaḥ prabhuḥ*); **122**, 4490 (*mahādevaṃ*), [4492 (*Çūlavarāyudhaḥ*), 4495 (do.)] (*V.* created chastisement and appointed leaders of the different classes of beings), 4504, 4505 (*V.* accepted chastisement from Çiva and made it over to Aṅgiras) [4515 (*Hayaçirāḥ*)].—§ 653*b* (Gṛdhragomāyusaṃv.): XII, **153***a*, 5752.—§ 656 (Khaḍgotpattik.): XII, **166**, 6185, 6186 (obtained the sword from Rudra and made it over to Marīci).—§ 660*b* (Bhṛgu-Bharadvājasaṃv.): XII, **182**, [6779 (*padmaṃ sṛshṭaṃ Svayambhuvā*)], 6784 (*anantaḥ*, created Ahaṃkāra (= Brahmán)). — § 662*b* (Jāpakop.): XII, **200**δ, 7342 (°*ḥ sahasraçīrshaç ca devó 'cintyaḥ*).—§ 663 (Mokshadh.): XII, **206**, 7497 (is superior to Kāla (Time)).—§ 664 (do.): XII, **207**, 7518, [7519 (*Nārāyaṇaṃ*, Kṛshṇa is the supreme Lord (Vishṇu Nārāyaṇa), description of the creation, etc.)], 7543 (one of the Ādityas, born as Vāmana (the dwarf)).—§ 665 (do.): XII, **208**β, 7582 (the twelfth of the Ādityas).—§ 666 (do.): XII, **209**, 7616 (*vārāharūpiṇaṃ*), 7619 (*vārāhaṃ rūpam āsthāya*), 7628, 7633 (*vārāhaṃ rūpam āsthitaḥ*) (*V.'s* incarnation as the boar = Kṛshṇa (vv. 7604 and 7636)).—§ 667 (do.): XII, **210**, 7651 (= Kṛshṇa), 7653 (*Devadevasya*, do.); **213**, 7743 (*avyaktasaṃsthānaṃ*); [**216**, 7825 (*yogeçvaro Hariḥ*)]; **217**, 7874 (*avyaktasañjñitaṃ*), [7875 (*ātmasthaṃ Hariṃ*)].—§ 673*b* (Bali-Vāsavasaṃv.): XII, **227**, 8219 (°*krānteshu lokeshu*, all. to Vishṇu's depriving Bali of the worlds by his three steps).—§ 677 (Mokshadh.): XII, **240**, 8741 (*krānte*—i.e. in the feet—*V°ḥ*).—§ 681 (do.): XII, **266**, 9476 (°*m evābhijānanti sarvayajñeshu brāhmaṇāḥ*).—§ 692 (do.): XII, **280***a*, 10019 (enumeration of names of Hari Nārāyaṇa); **281**, 10026, 10029, 10030, 10031, (β), 10052, †10075 (*sthānaṃ . . . V°oḥ*), †10076 (*devasya V°oḥ paramasya*, sc. *sthānaṃ*), †10083 (*V°or anantasya sthānaṃ*) (Sanātkumāra discoursed to Vṛtra on the greatness of *V.*).—§ 693 (do.): XII, **282**, 10098 (Vṛtra was devoted to *V.*), 10099 (*padaṃ V°oḥ*), 10101 (°*bhaktaḥ*, sc. Vṛtra).—§ 693*b* (Vṛtravadha): XII, **282***a*, 10120, 10128 (entered the thunderbolt (*vajra*)); **283**, 10152 (*vajreṇa V°yuktena*).—§ 694*b* (Jvarotpatti): XII, **284**, 10268 (*paramaṃ sthānaṃ V°oḥ*, thither went Vṛtra after death), 10269 (°*bhaktyā*, °*oḥ sthānaṃ*).—§ 695*b* (Dakshayajñavināça): XII, **285**, †10295 (°*oḥ . . . bhāgaṃ*).—§ 702 (Mokshadh.): XII, **293**, 10763 (adored by the ṛshis he granted them success); **297**, 10888 (*viçvasya . . . jagataḥ pradhānaṃ*).—§ 704 (do.): XII, **301***a*, 11094, [†11098 (*yogī . . . Nārāyaṇātmā*); **302**, 11117 (read with B. °*ṃ krānte*, cf. v. 8741), [11120 (*deve Nārāyaṇe*)], 11155 (°*or māyāçataiḥ*), [11174 (*Nārāyaṇaḥ*), 11193 (*ātmānam avyayaṃ paraṃ Nārāyaṇātmānaṃ*)]. — § 705 (do.): XII, **303**, 11251 (*pañcaviṃçatimaḥ*, i.e. the supreme Soul).—§ 707 (do.): XII, **314**, 11607 (the adhidaivata of the feet).—§ 714*b* (Himavat): XII, **328**, 12319 (*c*: *V.* performed austerities on the Himavat in order to get a son), 12323 (*e*: in order to honour Skanda *V.* did only shake the dart of Skanda, though he was able to raise it), 12326.—§ 714 (Çukakṛtya): XII, **329**, 12394 (*devayānacaro V°oḥ*), 12419 (°*or niçvāsato vātaḥ*).—[§ 717*b* (Nārāyaṇīya): XII, **335-336** (v. Nārāyaṇa)].—§ 717*c* (Uparicara): XII, **336-338** (v. Nārāyaṇa (= *Vishṇuḥ*, v. 12849)).—§ 717*b* (Nārāyaṇīya): XII, [**339-341** (v. Nārāyaṇa, description of the different avatāras (v. 12938–12968))], **342**, 13157, 13160, 13171 (etymology) (Kṛshṇa (*Hariḥ*, v. 13131), who is Vishṇu (Nārāyaṇa, q.v.), explained his names to Arjuna); **343**, 1), ††13200 (= Nārāyaṇa (q.v.), description of the creation, *V.* identified with Agni); VII) ††13213 (entered the thunderbolt (*vajra*), ††13217; VIII, ††13218 (origin of the çrīvatsa); [XIII) ††13222 (*Nārāyaṇaḥ*, born as the ṛshi Vaḍavāmukha)], [(φ) (Kṛshṇa (= Vishṇu, Nārāyaṇa (q.v.)) continued the explanation of his names)]; **344** (v. Nārāyaṇa (= *Vishṇuḥ*, v. 13324)); [**345** (v. Nārāyaṇa)]; **346**, 13425 (*V.*, Vṛshākapi in the form of the boar offered piṇḍas); **347**, 13432 (*avyayaṃ*), 13434 (= Nārāyaṇa, q.v.); **348**, 13452 (*hayaçiro mahat / havyakavyabhujo V°uḥ*, assuming a horsehead *V.* (= Nārāyaṇa, q.v.) recovered the Vedas and slew Madhu and Kaiṭabha), 13543 (*Vāsudeveti*); [**349** (v. Nārāyaṇa)]; [**350** (v. Nārāyaṇa)].—[§ 717*d* (Brahma-Rudra-saṃv.): XII, **352** (v. Nārāyaṇa)].—§ 719*b* (Gautamīlubdakavyāla-Mṛtyu-Kālasaṃv.): XIII, **1***a*, 55.—§ 723 (Ānuçāsanik.): XIII, **6***a*, 312 (*yena lokās trayaḥ sṛshṭā Daityāḥ sarvāç ca devatāḥ / sa esha bhagavān V°ḥ samudre tapyate tapaḥ*), 329 (*Baliḥ . . . V°purushakāreṇa Pātālasadanaḥ kṛtaḥ*).—[§ 727 (do.): XIII, **11** (v. Nārāyaṇa)].—§ 730 (do.): XIII, **14**, 591 (*Brahma-V°-Sureçānāṃ srashṭā*, sc. Çiva), 596 (*Nārāyaṇāt . . . çaṅkhacakragadādharāt*), 606 (= Kṛshṇa), [(β), 626 (*Hariḥ*)].—§ 730*c* (Mandara): XIII, **14**, 664 (°*oç cakraṃ*).—§ 730*g* (Upamanyu): XIII, **14**η, 731 (*Brahma-V°-Surendrāṇāṃ . . . vapur dhārayate Bhavaḥ*), (θ), 795 (*uttamaiçvaryaṃ Brahma-V°purogamaṃ*), (ξ), 824 (worships the liṅga of Çiva), (ρ), 857 (*Brahma-V°-sureshu*), [(υ), 870 (*Nārāyaṇaḥ . . . Vainateyaṃ samāruhya çaṅkhacakragadādharaḥ*), 876 (*Nārāyaṇaḥ*, praised Çiva), 877 (do., do.)], (χ), 912 (*kratūnāṃ V°r ucyate*, sc. Çiva), 914 (*Ādityānāṃ bhavān V°r*, sc. Çiva), 940 (created from the left side of Çiva).—§ 730 (Ānuçāsanik.): XIII, **14**, (971) (*Çrīc* = Kṛshṇa, so B.), (ω), 986 (*Çatakratuç ca bhagavān V°ç cāditinandanau*), (1002) (= Kṛshṇa); **16**ηη, 1052 (does not comprehend Çiva), 1058 (identified with Çiva) (θθ), 1105 (does not know Çiva truly); [**17** (v. Nārāyaṇa)]; **18**, (†1368) (= Kṛshṇa).—§ 734 (do.): XIII, **26**, 1851 (°*padīṃ . . . Jāhnavīṃ*).—§ 737 (do.): XIII, **31***a*, 2013.—§ 746 (do.): XIII, **62**β, 3150; **82**ν, 3857; **80**, 3901 (having performed austerities Aditi became quick with *V.*—*V°au garbhatāṃ āgate*).—§ 759 (do.): XIII, **109**[10], 5376 (merit of worshipping Kṛshṇa as *V.* in the month of Caitra), 5386 (the twelve names under which Vishṇu (Kṛshṇa) is to be worshipped). § 766 (do.): XIII, [**125**, 5932 (*Nārāyaṇaḥ*)]; **126**, (6006), 6015, †6043 (°*pade*); [**132**, 6165 (*yadā Nārāyaṇaḥ çrīmān ujjahāra vasundharāṃ*)]; **134**, (6189).—§ 768 (do.): XIII, **139**, 6295 (i.e. Kṛshṇa), 6306 (do.), 6307 (do., read *V°ur giriṃ* with B.). — § 768*b* (Kṛshṇa Vāsudeva): XIII, **147**, [6807 (*Hariḥ*, i.e. Kṛshṇa)], 6854 (i.e. Kṛshṇa).—§ 768*c* (Balarāma): XIII, **147**, 6866 (Balarāma is *V.*).—§ 768 (Ānuçāsanik.): XIII, **148**, 6892 (*Trivikramaḥ* = Kṛshṇa).—§ 769 (do.): XIII, **149**, 6941 (*Anādinidhanaṃ*), 6947 (°*or nāmasahasraṃ*), 6949 (°*or nāmasahasrasya*), 6950, 6977 (1000 names), 7019 (do.), 7076, 7077 (*stavaṃ . . . V°oḥ*) (Bhīshma praised *V.* = Kṛshṇa, reciting his 1000 names (v. infra)).—§ 770 (do.): XIII, **151**γ, 7093 (the twelfth of the twelve Ādityas), (ε), 7106 (*devaḥ*).—§ 773*b* (Kṛshṇa Vāsudeva): XIII, **159**, 7391 (= Kṛshṇa, only B. [= *Nārā-*

yaṇaḥ, v. †7400]).—§ 773*d* (Çiva): XIII, **161**, 7485 (Çiva made *V.* his arrow—*çarottamam*).—§ 775 (Ânuçāsanik.): XIII, **166***a*, 7635 (*Nārāyaṇaḥ*). — § 778*b* (Saṃvartta-Maruttīya): XIV, **4**, 87 (°*r ivāparaḥ*).—§ 782*b* (Brāhmaṇagītā): XIV, **21**, 631; [**25** (v. Nārāyaṇa)]. — § 782*g* (Guruçishyasaṃv.): XIV, **40**, 1085 (°*r Jishṇuḥ Çambhuç ca = mahān ātmā*), 1095 (*Svayambhūḥ*); **42**, 1126 (the adhidaivata of the feet), (ε), 1167; **43**θ, 1178 (*balavatāṃ varaḥ*), 1181 (*bhūtaṃ parataraṃ . . . na vidyate*), 1182 (*brahmamayo . . . Hariṃ*); **44**, 1223 (*Svayambhūḥ*), 1227 (*bhūtaṃ parataraṃ . . . neha vidyate*).—§ 784*b* (Uttaṅka): XIV, **54**, 1576 (i.e. Kṛshṇa); **55**, 1591 (do.); **56**, 1625 (do.).—§ 785 (Anugītāp.): XIV, **87**, 2581 (*Bhojarājanyavardhanaḥ*, i.e. Kṛshṇa). — § 788 (Âçramavāsap.): XV, **25**, †663 (°-*Mahendrakalpau*, sc. Nakula and Sahadeva). — [§ 789 (Putradarçanap.): XV, **31**η, 854 (*Nārāyaṇam*, incarnate as Hṛshīkeça, i.e. Kṛshṇa)].—§ 793 (Mausalap.): XVI, [**3**, 68 (*Hariḥ*, i.e. Kṛshṇa); **4**, †130 (*Nārāyaṇaḥ*, i.e. Kṛshṇa); **7**, 251 (*Haridhyānaikatatparāḥ*)]; **8**ν, 277 (*Janārdanaṃ* = Kṛshṇa).—[§794(Mahāprasthānikap.): XVII, **1**, 12 (*Hariṃ*), 38 (*Nārāyaṇasya*, i.e. Kṛshṇa)].—[§ 795 (Svargārohaṇap.): XVIII, **5**μ, 170 (*Nārāyaṇaḥ . . . devadevaḥ*, Kṛshṇa entered Nārāyaṇa, of whom he was a portion).]—§ 795*c* (Mahābhārata): XVIII, **6**π, 258 (°*oḥ . . . salokatāṃ*), [300 (*Hariḥ*)], 301 (°*kathā*).

Cf. Kṛshṇa (with synonyms), Nārāyaṇa, and the following synonyms:—

Abhibhū: III, 12984: XII, 1509 (= Kṛshṇa).

Acintya, q.v., add III, 17205 (*Nārāyaṇaṃ*); VII, 1578 (*V*°); XII, 7342 (*V*°), 7566 (i.e. Kṛshṇa).

Acyuta, q.v. (cf. Additions and Corrections).

Açvaciras, Âdideva, Âdikara, q.v.

Aditinandana ("the son of Aditi"): XIII, 986 (°*au = Çatakratuç ca V°ç ca*).

Âdityapati ("the lord of the Âdityas"), q.v.

Aja, q.v.

Ajita: III, 1698, 1896 (i.e. Kṛshṇa?).

Amadhya: XII, †13249

Anādi: I, 2431; VI, 1207; XII, 1658 (i.e. Kṛshṇa); XIII, 7050 (1000 names).

Anādimadhyanidhana: XII, 2398, 12716.

Anādhimadhyānta: VI, 1265, 2972.

Anādimadhyaparyanta: XII, 1623 (i.e. Kṛshṇa).

Anādinidhana: I, 2429; II, 2607; III, 11857, 12824, 13936; V, 3818; VII, 6468 (i.e. Kṛshṇa); XII, 1624 (do.), 13473, 13909; XIII, 6941, 6954 (1000 names).

Anādya: XII, †13249.

Ananta: I, 2431, 7306; III, 12984; VI, 1283 (i.e. Kṛshṇa); XII, 1663 (do.), 6784, 6798, †13249; XIII, 6939, 7019 (1000 names), 7044 (do.); XVIII, 169.

Aravindāksha, Asurasūdana, Avyakta, Avyaya, q.v.

Bhagavat, q.v.

Bhūtācārya, Bhūtarāj: XII, 7630.

Cakradhara, Cakragadāpāṇī, Cakrapāṇi, Cakrāyudha, v. Kṛshṇa.

Caturbhuja ("four-armed"): III, 15933; V, †2512 (= Kṛshṇa), 3666; XIII, 6891, 6964 (1000 names).

Caturmūrtidhṛt, q.v.

Çakrānuja ("younger brother of Indra"): VII, 6458/59 (only B.).

Çālagrāma, Çambhu, q.v.

Çaṅkhacakragadādhara, v. Kṛshṇa.

Çipivishṭa, Çrīdhara, Çūlavarāyudha, Çveta, q.v.

Devaçreshṭha (see additions), **Devadeva, Devadeveçvara, Devādhideva, Deveça**, q.v.

Ekaçṛṅga, q.v.

Govinda, v. Kṛshṇa.

Guhya, q.v.

Hari: I, 24 (*Hṛshīkeçaṃ*), 426 (i.e. Kṛshṇa), 512 (do.), 1167, 1533 (*Devadevaṃ*), 2508, †7307, 7359 (i.e. Kṛshṇa), 8318 (do.); II, 550 (do.), 1213 (= Kṛshṇa), 1318 (*Puṇḍarīkākshaṃ*, do.), 1323 (= Kṛshṇa); 1325 (*Nārāyaṇaṃ*, do.), 1385 (= Kṛshṇa), 1521 (*tejāṃçaç ca H°eḥ*, sc. Çiçupāla), 1616 (i.e. Kṛshṇa), 1623 (do.), †2229 (*Kṛshṇaṃ*), 2291 (= Kṛshṇa), 2293 (do.), †2295 (*Kṛshṇaṃ*); III, 480 (= Kṛshṇa), 498 (do.), 505 (*Nārāyaṇaḥ*, do.), 740 (*Madhunihā*, i.e. Kṛshṇa), 1896 (*Vishṇuḥ* = Kṛshṇa), 1951 (*Janārdanaḥ* = Kṛshṇa), 1985 (i.e. Kṛshṇa, will become the charioteer of Arjuna), 5080 (in the tīrtha Vishṇoḥ sthānaṃ), 5081, 8109 (in the tīrtha Vāmana), 8192 (*Nārāyaṇaḥ*, in the tīrtha Devahrada), 8215 (in Prayāga), 8353 (*Madhusūdanaḥ* = Kṛshṇa, in Dvārakā), 11863 (*Nārāyaṇaṃ*), 12560 (i.e. Kṛshṇa), 13003 (*Kṛshṇo Vārshṇeyaḥ*), 13505, 13558, 13562, 15545 (*īçvaraḥ*), 15553 (= Kṛshṇa), 15845 (incarnate as a dwarf), 17464; V, 2536 (= Kṛshṇa), †2578 (do.); VI, 301 (*Vaikuṇṭhaḥ*, in Airāvatavarsha), 450 (*Nārāyaṇaḥ*, on Gomanda), 774 (= Kṛshṇa), 1255 (= Kṛshṇa), 1531 (do.), 1532/33 (only B.), 1587 (i.e. Kṛshṇa, counsellor of Yudhishṭhira), †2610 (i.e. Kṛshṇa), †2612 (do., only B.), 3028 (do., only C.), 3046 (do.); VII, 2963 (do.), 3923 (i.e. Kṛshṇa), 6220 (*Kṛshṇaḥ*), 6474 (only B.), 9104 (*iva*); VIII, 2863 (i.e. Kṛshṇa), 3691 (*prayaccha medinīṃ rājñe Çakrāyaiva H°r yathā*), 4018 (i.e. Kṛshṇa); XI, 327 (i.e. Kṛshṇa), 328 (*Janārdanaḥ*, do.); XII, 16 (*Kṛshṇaṃ*), 1503 (= Kṛshṇa), 1606 (*Nārāyaṇaḥ*), 1611 (= Kṛshṇa), 1625 (*Nārāyaṇaṃ*, do.), 1684 (°*r ity aksharadvayaṃ*), 1690 (i.e. Kṛshṇa), 4080 (*Nārāyaṇaṃ* = Kṛshṇa), 7825 (*yogeçvaraḥ*), 7875 (*ātmasthaṃ*, i.e. the Supreme Soul), 8937 (? °*yarthaṃ*), 10018 (*Nārāyaṇaḥ*), 10043 (do.), 12658 (the third form of Nārāyaṇa born as the son of Dharma), 12667 (do.), 12712 (*Nārāyaṇaṃ*), 12729, 12767, 12788, 12797, 12839 (*Surāsuraguruḥ*), 12848 (*Surapatim, Nārāyaṇaḥ*), 12857 (*Purushaḥ . . . īçvaraḥ*), 12872 (*Nārāyaṇaḥ*), 13112, 13117 (*Īçvaraḥ*), 13130 (*Prajāpatipateḥ*), 13131 (i.e. Kṛshṇa), 13159 (*Nārāyaṇaṃ*), ††13192 (*Purushaḥ . . . avyayaḥ*), 13226 (only C., read *hare* with B.), 13227 (etymology), 13292, 13308 (*Nārāyaṇaṃ*), 13322 (*Viçveçvarasya*), 13327, 13334 (*avyayaṃ*), 13370, 13428 (*avyayaṃ*), 13433 (*Nārāyaṇaṃ*), 13437 (°*gītāsu*, i.e. the Bhagavadgītā), †13445, 13453 (*lokadhāriṇā*), 13467 (*Viçvaksenaḥ*), 13486, 13507 (*devo Hayaçirodharaḥ*), 13517, 13521, 13523, 13524 (*Açvaçirāḥ*), 13530, 13539, 13540 (*Nārāyaṇaḥ*), 13547, 13550, 13572 (*Nārāyaṇaḥ*), 13581 (*Deveçaṃ . . . Nārāyaṇaṃ*), 13586 (*Nārāyaṇaḥ*), 13590 (°*yonaye Brahmaṇe*), 13593 (?), 13594, 13600 (°*gītāsu*, i.e. the Bhagavadgītā), 13603 (*Īçvaraḥ*), 13604 (*kshetrajñaḥ*), 13619, 13624, 13656 (*Īçvaraṃ*), 13659, 13662, 18663, 13678, 13696, 13709, 13710; XIII, 602 (*Acyutaḥ* = Kṛshṇa), 626 (PCR. Agni), 6005 (*Īçvaraḥ*), 6316, 6807 (*çāçvataḥ purushaḥ*, i.e. Kṛshṇa), 6851 (*Nārāyaṇaḥ*, i.e. Kṛshṇa), 6863 (= Balarāma), 6898 (i.e. Kṛshṇa), 6909 (only C.), 6988 (1000 names), 7018 (do.); XIV, 1182 (*kartāram akṛtam*); XVI, 68 (i.e. Kṛshṇa), 251 (°*dhyānaikatatparāḥ*, do., only C.); XVII, 12 (= Kṛshṇa); XVIII, 300 (do.).

Harimedhas, Havyakavyabhuj, Hayaçiras, Hayaçirodhara, Hayamukha, q.v.

Hṛshīkeça, v. Kṛshṇa.

Içāna, Īçvara, q.v.

Indrānuja ("the younger brother of Indra"): I, 5353 (°*samaḥ*, sc. Arjuna); V, †2580 (= Kṛshṇa); VI, 2000 (°*samam*), †2614 (= Kṛshṇa).

Indrāvaraja (do.): I, †7052 (°*prabhāvaḥ*, sc. Arjuna); VIII, †701 (v. Dhanañjaya), †4698 (i.e. Kṛshṇa); IX, †901 (do.).

Jagannātha, Jagatpati, Jagatprabhu, q.v.

Janārdana, v. Kṛshṇa.

Jishṇu, Kapardin, Kapila, q.v.

Keçava, v. Kṛshṇa.

Kshetrajña, q.v.

Lokakartṛ, q.v.

Madhuhan, Madhukaiṭabhahan, Madhunihan, Madhusūdana, Madhunisūdana, q.v.

Mahābhūtādhipati, Mahādeva, Mahāpurusha, Mahāvarāha, Maheçvara, q.v.

Mahendrāvaraja ("the younger brother of Indra"): VI, 2598 (i.e. Kṛshṇa), †2601 (do.).

Muñjakeça, Muñjakeçavat, Muñjakeçin, q.v.

Nishkriya, q.v.

Padmalocana, Padmanābha, q.v.

Paramātman, Parameçvara, Parameshṭhin, q.v.

Pītavāsas, v. Kṛshṇa.

Prabhu, Prajāpati, Prajāpatipati, Puṇḍarīkāksha, Purusha, Purushavara, Purushottama, Pushkarāksha, Pushkarekshaṇa, q.v.

Rathacakrabhṛt, q.v.

Sādhya, Sahasraçirasa, Sahasraçīrsha, Sahasrāksha, Sarvabhūtapitāmaha, Sarvabhūteçvara, Sarvadeveça, Sarvalokeçvara, Siṃha, Suraçreshṭha, Suragaṇaçreshṭha, Suraguru, Surapati, Surārighna, Surāsuraguru, Suravarottama, Sureça, Svayambhū, q.v.

Tribhuvanaçreshṭha, Tribhuvaneçvara, q.v.

Tridaçavarāvaraja ("the younger brother of Indra"): VIII, †1213 (°*opamam*).

Trilokeça, Trilokeçvara, Trivartman, Trivikrama, Trivikramagati, q.v.

Upendra, Urukrama, q.v.

Vaikuṇṭha, Vāmana, Varada, Varāha, Vārāha, Vareṇya, q.v.

Vāsavānantaraja ("born immediately after Indra"): VI, †2590 (i.e. Kṛshṇa).

Vāsavānuja ("the younger brother of Indra"): V, 2947 (i.e. Kṛshṇa), 4383 (do.); XII, 1562 (do.), 1712 (do.); XIII, 6984 (1000 names).

Vāsavāvaraja (do.): V, 3759.

Vibhu, Vibudhaçreshṭha, Viçva, Viçvabhū, Viçvabhuj, Viçvagupta, Viçvakarman, Viçvakṛt, Viçvamūrti, Viçvapara, Viçvarūpa, Viçvarūpadhṛk, Viçvātman, Viçveça, Viçveçvara, Virāj, Viriñca, Vikuṇṭha, Vishvaksena, q.v.

Yajñapati, Yogeçvara, Yogīça, Yogīçvara, Yogin, q.v.

Vishṇu's 1000 names (XIII, **149,** 6950–7056). The names are the following, alphabetically arranged:—*Abhiprāya*, 7042; *Acala*, 7028; *Acintya*, 7038; *Acyuta*, 6960, 6984, 7008 (PCR. takes *Saṅkarshaṇo 'cyutaḥ* as one name); *Açoka*, 6986; *Āçrama*, 7040; *Açvattha*, 7037; *Adbhuta*, 7044; *Ādhāranilaya*, 7051; *Adhishṭhāna(ṃ)*, 6984; *Adhokshaja*, 6993; *Adhṛta*, 7039; *Ādideva*, 6985, 7001; *Āditya*, 6954, 7009; *Adṛçya*, 6982; *Agrāhya*, 6956; *Agraja*, 7044; *Agraṇī*, 6973; *Ahar*, 6959, 6974; *Aja*, 6960, 6971, 7005; *Akrūra*, 7047; *Akshara(ḥ)*, 6951; *Akshara(ṃ)*, 7000; *Akshobhya*, 7035, 7056; *Amānin*, 7029; *Amaraprabhu*, 6955; *Ambhonidhi*, 7004; *Ameyātman*, 6960, 6968; *Amitāçana*, 6989; *Amitavikrama*, 7004, 7017; *Amogha*, 6961, 6966; *Amṛta*, 6962; *Amṛtāça*, 7036; *Amṛtāṃçūdbhava*, 6980; *Amṛtapa*, 7003; *Amṛtavapus*, 7036; *Amṛtyu*, 6971; *Amūrti*, 7038; *Amūrtimat*, 7026; *Anādi*, 7050; *Anādinidhana*, 6954; *Anagha*, 6965, 7038; *Anala*, 6981, 7025; *Anāmaya*, 7022; *Ānanda*, 7005; *Ananta*, 7019 (PCR. takes *vīro 'nantaḥ* as one name), 7044; *Anantaçrī*, 7049, *Anantajit*, 6982; *Anantarūpa*, 7049; *Anantātman*, 7004; *Anartha*, 6995; *Anekamūrti*, 7026; *Anīça*, 7016; *Anila*, 6974, 7036; *Animisha*, 6972; *Anirdeçyavapus*, 6968, 7019; *Aniruddha*, 6969, 7017; *Anirviṇṇa*, 6996, 7044; *Anivartin* (C. *Anirv*°), 7013; *Anna(ṃ)*, 7054; *Annāda*, 7054; *Antaka*, 7004; *Aṇu*, 7039; *Anukūla*, 6986; *Anuttama*, 6958; *Apāṃ nidhi(ḥ)*, 6984; *Aparājita*, 7025, 7041; *Apramatta*, 6984; *Aprameya*, 6955; *Aprameyātman*, 6976; *Apratiratha*, 7017; *Araudra*, 7046; *Aravindāksha*, 6987; *Arcishmat*, 7017; *Arcita*, 7017; *Arha*, 7042; *Arka*, 7034; *Artha*, 6995; *Asaṅkhyeya*, 6976; *Asat* (neutr.), 7000; *Atīndra*, 6966; *Atīndriya*, 6967; *Ātmayoni*, 7055; *Ātmavat*, 6958; *Atula*, 6988; *Aushadha(ṃ)*, 6980; *Āvartana*, 6974; *Avijñātṛ*, 7000; *Avyakta(ḥ)*, 7026; *Avyaktarūpa*, 6982; *Avyaṅga*, 6963; *Avyaya(ḥ)*, 6951, 6953, 7045; *Ayonija*, 7010; *Babhru*, 6962; *Bahuçiras*, 6962; *Bhagahan*, 7009; *Bhagavat*, 7009; *Bhaktavatsala*, 7027; *Bhānu*, 6963, 6980; *Bhārabhṛt*, 7040; *Bhartṛ*, 6953; *Bhāskaradyuti*, 6979; *Bhāva*, 6950; *Bhāvana*, 6953; *Bhayāpaha*, 7049; *Bhayakṛt*, 7038; *Bhayanāçana*, 7038; *Bheshaja(ṃ)*, 7011; *Bhīma*, 6988, 7050; *Bhīmaparākrama*, 7050; *Bhishaj*, 7011; *Bhojana(ṃ)*, 6965, (PCR. takes *bhojanaṃ bhoktā* as one name); *Bhoktṛ*, 6965 (v. Bhojana(ṃ)), 7002, 7044; *Bhrājishṇu*, 6965; *Bhū*, 6996, 7050 (PCR. takes *bhūr bhuvaḥ* as one name), 7053 (PCR. takes *bhūr bhuvaḥ svaḥ* as one name); *Bhūçaya*, 7016; *Bhūgarbha*, 6957; *Bhujagottama*, 6970; *Bhūridakshiṇa*, 7002; *Bhūshaṇa*, 7016; *Bhūtabhāvana*, 6950; *Bhūtabhavyabhavannātha*, 6981; *Bhūtabhavyabhavatprabhu*, 6950; *Bhūtabhṛt*, 6950; *Bhūtādi*, 6953; *Bhūtakṛt*, 6950; *Bhūtamaheçvara*, 7001; *Bhūtātman*, 6950; *Bhūtāvāsa*, 7025; *Bhūti*, 7016; *Bhuvas*, 7050, 7053 (cf. Bhū); *Bīja(m) avyaya(ṃ)*, 6995; *Brahmajña*, 7020; *Brahmakṛt*, 7020; *Brahmán*, 7020; *Bráhman*, 7020; *Brāhmaṇa*, 7020; *Brāhmaṇapriya*, 7020; *Brahmaṇya*, 7020; *Brahmavid*, 7020; *Brahmavivardhana*, 7020; *Brahmin*, 7020; *Bṛhadbhānu*, 6085; *Bṛhadrūpa*, 6978; *Bṛhat* (neutr.), 7039; *Cakragadādhara*, 7007; *Cakrin*, 7046, 7056; *Cala*, 7028; *Candanāṅgadin*, 7028; *Candrāṃçu*, 6979; *Cāṇūrāndhranishūdana*, 7037; *Caturasra*, 7049; *Caturātman*, 6964, 7031; *Caturbāhu*, 7031; *Caturbhāva*, 7031; *Caturbhuja*, 6964; *Caturdaṃshṭra*, 6964; *Caturgati*, 7031; *Caturmūrti*, 7031; *Caturvedavid*, 7031; *Caturvyūha*, 6964, 7031; *Chinnasaṃçaya*, 7015; *Çabdasaha*, 7046; *Çabdātiga*, 7046; *Çaçabindu*, 6980; *Çāçvata*, 6956, 6962, 7016 (PCR. takes *çāçvataḥ sthiraḥ* as one name); *Çaktimatāṃ çreshṭha(ḥ)*, 6992; *Çama*, 7011; *Çambhu*, 6954; *Çaṅkhabhṛt*, 7056; *Çānta*, 7011, 7048;

Çānti, 7011 (PCR. takes *nishṭhāçāntiḥ parāyaṇaṃ* as one name); *Çāntida*, 7012; *Çarabha*, 6988; *Çaraṇa(ṃ)*, 6959; *Çarīrabhṛt*, 6987; *Çarīrabhūtabhṛt*, 7002; *Çarman* (neutr.), 6959; *Çārṅgadhanvan*, 7056; *Çarva*, 6953; *Çarvarīkara*, 7046; *Çāstṛ*, 6971; *Çatamūrti*, 7026; *Çatānana*, 7026; *Çatānanda*, 7015; *Çatāvarta*, 6986; *Çatrughna*, 6993; *Çatrujit*, 7037; *Çatrutāpana*, 7037; *Çauri*, 6986, 7018; *Çiçira*, 7046; *Çikhaṇḍin*, 6983; *Çipivishṭa*, 6978; *Çishṭakṛt*, 6976; *Çishṭeshṭa*, 6983; *Çiva*, 6953, 7013; *Çokanāçana*, 7016; *Çramaṇa*, 7046; *Çreshṭha*, 6957 (PCR. takes *çreshṭhaḥ prajāpatiḥ* as one name); *Çreyas* (neutr.), 7014; *Çrīça*, 7014; *Çrīda*, 7014; *Çrīdhara*, 7014; *Çrīgarbha*, 6990; *Çrīkara*, 7014; *Çrīmat*, 6952, 6968, 6973 (PCR. seems to take *çrīmān nyāyaḥ* as one name), 7014; *Çrīmatāṃ vara(ḥ)*, 7013; *Çrīnidhi*, 7014; *Çrīnivāsa*, 6969, 7014; *Çrīpati*, 7013; *Çrīvāsa*, 7013; *Çrīvatsavakshas*, 7013; *Çrīvibhāvana*, 7014; *Çrutisāgara*, 6977; *Çṛṅgin*, 7034; *Çubhāṅga*, 7012, 7033; *Çubhekshaṇa*, 6991; *Çuci*, 6966, 6976; *Çucisravas*, 6962; *Çūnya*, 7028; *Çūra*, 6986; *Çūrajaneçvara*, 7018; *Çūrasena*, 7024; *Daçārha*, 7003; *Daivakīnandana*, v. Devakīnandana; *Daksha*, 6994, 7047; *Dakshiṇa*, 7047; *Dama*, 7041; *Damana*, 6970; *Damayitṛ*, 7041; *Dāmodara*, 6989; *Daṇḍa*, 7041; *Darpada*, 7025; *Darpahan*, 7025; *Dāruṇa*, 7010; *Deva*, 6990; *Devabhṛt*, 7001 (PCR. takes *devabhṛd guruḥ* as one name); *Devakīnandana* (C. by error *Dai°*), 7055; *Deveça*, 7001; *Dhāman* (neutr.), 6956 (PCR. takes *trikakud dhāma* as one name), 6972; *Dhanañjaya*, 7019; *Dhaneçvara*, 6999; *Dhanurdhara*, 7041; *Dhanurveda*, 7041; *Dhanvin*, 6958; *Dhanya*, 7029; *Dharādhara*, 7029; *Dharaṇīdhara*, 6974; *Dharma*, 6992; *Dharmādhyaksha*, 6964; *Dharmagup*, 7000; *Dharmakṛt*, 7000; *Dharmaviduttama*, 6992; *Dharmayūpa*, 6996; *Dharmin*, 7000; *Dhātṛ*, 6954, 7051; *Dhātur uttamaḥ*, 6954 (PCR. translates "superior to Brahmán"); *Dhruva*, 6955, 6991; *Dhṛtāçis*, 7028; *Dhṛtātman*, 6966; *Dhūrya*, 6985; *Diçaḥ* (pl.), 7049; *Dīptamūrti*, 7025; *Divaspṛç*, 7010; *Draviṇaprada*, 7010; *Dṛḍha*, 7008; *Dṛpta*, 7025; *Duḥsvapnanāçana*, 7048; *Durādharsha*, 6958; *Durārihan*, 7032; *Duratikrama*, 7032; *Durāvāsa*, 7032; *Durdhara*, 6978, 7025; *Durga*, 7032; *Durgama*, 7032; *Durjaya*, 7032; *Durlabha*, 7032; *Durmarshaṇa*, 6971; *Dushkṛtihan*, 7048; *Dyutidhara*, 6979 (PCR. takes *ojas tejo dyutidharaḥ* as one word), 7030; *Eka*, 7027; *Ekapad*, 7031; *Ekātman*, 7052; *Gabhastinemi*, 7001; *Gabhīra*, 7007; *Gabhīrātman*, 7049; *Gadādhara*, 7056; *Gadāgraja*, 7030; *Gahana*, 6990, 7007; *Gaṇeçvara*, 7015 (PCR. takes *jyotir gaṇeçvaraḥ* as one word); *Garuḍadhvaja*, 6987; *Gatisattama*, 7009; *Gohita*, 7012; *Gopati*, 7002, 7012; *Goptṛ*, 7002, 7012; *Govidāṃ pati(ḥ)*, 6969; *Govinda*, 6969, 7007; *Grāmaṇī*, 6973; *Guha*, 6990; *Guhya*, 7007; *Guṇabhṛt*, 7039; *Gupta*, 7007; *Guru*, 6972, 7001 (v. *Devabhṛt*); *Gurutama*, 6972; *Halāyudha*, 7009; *Haṃsa*, 6970; *Hari*, 6988 (PCR. takes *havir hariḥ* as one word), 7018; *Havis* (neutr.), 6988 (v. *Hari*), 7023; *Hemāṅga*, 7028; *Hetu*, 6989; *Hiraṇyagarbha*, 6957, 6993; *Hiraṇyanābha*, 6970; *Hṛshīkeça*, 6955; *Hutabhuj*, 7043, 7044; *Īçāna*, 6957; *Īçvara*, 6953, 6958; *Īçvareçvara*, 7035 (PCR. takes *sarvavāg īçvareçvaraḥ* as one word); *Ijya*, 6997; *Indrakarman*, 7033; *Ishṭa*, 6983; *Jagadādija*, 6965; *Jagannātha*, 6947; *Jagataḥ setu(ḥ)*, 6980; *Jahnu*, 6975; *Janajanmādi*, 7050; *Janana*, 7050; *Janārdana*, 6963; *Janeçvara*, 6986; *Janmamṛtyujarātiga*, 7052; *Jaya*, 7003; *Jayanta*, 7034; *Jayin*, 7034; *Jetṛ*, 6965; *Jita*, 7008; *Jitakrodha*, 6998; *Jitamanyu*, 7049; *Jitāmitra*, 7005; *Jīva*, 7004; *Jīvana*, 7048; *Jñānagamya*, 7002; *Jñāna(m) uttama(ṃ)*, 6997; *Jyeshṭha*, 6957; *Jyotis* (neutr.), 7009 (PCR. takes *jyotir ādityaḥ* as one name), 7015 (v. *Gaṇeçvara*), 7043; *Ka*, 7027; *Kāla*, 6994; *Kālanemihan*, 7018; *Kāma*, 6981; *Kāmadeva*, 7019; *Kāmahan*, 6981; *Kāmakṛt*, 6981; *Kāmapāla*, 7019; *Kāmaprada*, 6981; *Kāmin*, 7019; *Kanakāṅgadin*, 7007; *Kānta*, 6981, 7019; *Kapi*, 7045; *Kapīndra*, 7002; *Kapila*, 7045; *Kapilācārya*, 7006; *Karaṇa(ṃ)*, 6990; *Kāraṇa(ṃ)*, 6990; *Kartṛ*, 6983, 6990; *Kathita*, 7040; *Kavi*, 6963; *Keçava*, 6952, 7018; *Keçihan*, 7018; *Khaṇḍaparaçu*, 7010; *Ki(ṃ)*, 7027; *Krama*, 6958; *Kratu*, 6997; *Krodhahan*, 6983; *Krodhakṛt*, 6983; *Kṛça*, 7039; *Kṛshṇa*, 6956, 7008; *Kṛtāgama*, 7019, 7033; *Kṛtajña*, 6958, 7006; *Kṛtakarman*, 7033; *Kṛtākṛta*, 6964; *Kṛtalakshaṇa* 7000; *Kṛtāntakṛt*, 7006; *Kṛti*, 6958; *Kshama*, 6996; *Kshāma*, 6996, 7040; *Kshamiṇāṃ vara(ḥ)*, 7047; *Kshara(ṃ)*, 7000; *Kshemakṛt*, 7013; *Kshetrajña*, 6951; *Kshitīça*, 7055; *Kshobhaṇa*, 6990; *Kumbha*, 7017; *Kumuda*, 7012, 7036; *Kuṇḍa*, 7036; *Kuṇḍalin*, 7046; *Kuṇḍara*, 7036; *Kuvaleçaya*, 7012; *Lakshmī*, 7050; *Lakshmīvat*, 6988; *Lohitāksha*, 6956; *Lokabandhu*, 7027; *Lokādhyaksha*, 6941, 6964; *Lokādhishṭhāna(ṃ)*, 7044; *Lokanātha*, 7027; *Lokasāraṅga*, 7033; *Lokasvāmin*, 7029; *Lokatrayāçraya*, 7014; *Mādhava*, 6957, 6967, 7027; *Madhu*, 6967; *Madhusūdana*, 6957; *Mahābala*, 6967; *Mahābhāga*, 6989; *Mahābhoga*, 6995; *Mahābhūta*, 7035; *Mahābuddhi*, 6968; *Mahāçakti*, 6968; *Mahāçana*, 6982; *Mahāçṛṅga*, 7006; *Mahādeva*, 7001; *Mahādhana*, 6995; *Mahādridhṛk*, 6968; *Mahādyuti*, 6968; *Mahāgarta*, 7035; *Mahāhavis*, 7021; *Mahāhrada*, 7035; *Mahākarman* (masc.), 7021, 7038; *Mahākoça*, 6995; *Mahākrama*, 7021; *Mahākratu*, 7021; *Mahāksha*, 6987; *Mahāmakha*, 6996; *Mahāmanas*, 7008; *Mahāmāya*, 6967; *Mahāmūrti*, 7026; *Mahānidhi*, 7035; *Maharddhi*, 6987; *Mahārha*, 7005; *Maharshi*, 7006; *Mahāsvana*, 6954; *Mahat* (masc.), 7039; *Mahātapas*, 6962; *Mahātejas*, 7021; *Mahāvarāha*, 7007; *Mahāvīrya*, 6968; *Mahāyajña*, 7021; *Mahāyajvan*, 7021; *Mahejya*, 6997; *Mahendra*, 6978; *Maheshvāsa*, 6969; *Mahībhartṛ*, 6969; *Mahīdhara*, 6983, 6989; *Mahodadhiçaya*, 7004; *Mahoraga*, 7021; *Mahotsāha*, 6967; *Mānada*, 7029; *Maṅgala(ṃ)*, 6956 (PCR. takes *pavitraṃ maṅgalaṃ paraṃ* as one name); *Manohara*, 6998; *Manojava*, 7023; *Mantra(ḥ)*, 6979; *Manu*, 6955; *Mānya*, 7029; *Mārga*, 6989, 6992 (PCR. takes *virajo mārgaḥ* as one name); *Marīci*, 6970; *Medhaja*, 7029; *Medhas* (masc.), 7008 (B. reads *Vedhāḥ*); *Medhāvin*, 6958; *Medinīpati*, 7006; *Muktānāṃ paramā gati(ḥ)*, 6951; *Mukunda*, 7004; *Nahusha*, 6983; *Naika*, 7027; *Naikaçṛṅga*, 7030; *Naikaja*, 7044; *Naikakarmakṛt*, 6999; *Naikamāya*, 6982; *Naikarūpa*, 6978; *Naikātman*, 6999; *Nakshatranemi*, 6996; *Nakshatrin*, 6996; *Nanda*, 7005; *Nandakin*, 7056; *Nandana*, 7005; *Nandi*, 7015; *Nandin*, 7009; *Nara*, 6975; *Narasiṃhavapus*, 6952; *Nārāyaṇa*, 6975; *Naya*, 6992; *Netṛ*, 6973; *Neya*, 6992; *Nidhi*, 6953; *Nigraha*, 7030; *Nimisha*, 6972; *Nirguṇa*, 7039; *Nirvāṇa(ṃ)*, 7011; *Nishṭhā*, 7011 (v. *Çānti*); *Nivṛttātman*, 6974, 7013, 7032; *Niyama*, 6966, 7041; *Niyantṛ*, 7041; *Nyagrodha*, 7037; *Nyāya*, 6973 (v. *Çrīmat*); *Ojas* (neutr.), 6979 (v. *Dyutidhara*); *Pada(m) anuttama(ṃ)*, 7027; *Padmagarbha*, 6987; *Padmanābha*, 6955, 6970, 6987; *Padmanibhekshaṇa*, 6986; *Padmin*, 6986; *Paṇa*, 7051; *Pāpanāçana*, 7055; *Para(ṃ)*, 6956 (v. *Maṅgala(ṃ)*); *Paramaspashṭa*, 6991; *Paramātman*, 6951; *Parameçvara*, 6990; *Parameshṭhin*, 6994; *Pararddhi*, 6991; *Parāyaṇa(ṃ)*, 7011 (v. *Çānti*); *Parigraha*, 6994; *Parjanya*, 7036; *Paryavasthita*, 7048; *Pavana*, 6981, 7036; *Pāvana*, 6981; *Pavitra(ṃ)*, 6956 (v. *Maṅgala(ṃ)*); *Peçala*, 7047; *Pitṛ*, 7053; *Prabhava*, 6953; *Prabhu*, 6953,

6981; *Prabhūta*, 6956; *Pradhānapurusheçvara*, 6952; *Pradyumna*, 7017; *Pragraha*, 7030; *Prāgvamça*, 7039; *Prajābhava*, 6959; *Prajāgara*, 7051; *Prajāpati*, 6957 (v. *Çreshṭha*), 6970; *Prakāçana*, 6978; *Prakāçātman*, 6979; *Pramāṇa(ṃ)*, 6995, 7052; *Prāṃçu*, 6966; *Pramodana*, 7005; *Prāṇa*, 6957, 6984, 6993; *Prāṇabhṛt*, 7052; *Prāṇada*, 6957, 6984, 6993, 7051; *Prāṇajīvana*, 7052; *Prāṇanilaya*, 7052; *Praṇava*, 6993, 7051; *Prapitāmaha*, 7053; *Prasannātman*, 6975; *Pratāpana*, 6979; *Pratardana*, 6956; *Prathita*, 6984; *Prathu* (B. *Pṛ*°), 6993; *Pratishṭhita*, 6984; *Pratyaya*, 6959; *Prītivardhana*, 7042; *Priyakṛt*, 7042; *Priyārha*, 7042; *Pṛthu*, v. *Prathu*; *Punarvasu*, 6965; *Puṇḍarīkāksha*, 6961; *Puṇya*, 7022, 7048; *Puṇyaçravaṇakīrtana*, 7047; *Puṇyakīrti*, 7022; *Purandara*, 6985; *Purātana*, 7002; *Pūrayitṛ*, 7022; *Pūrṇa*, 7022; *Purujit*, 7003; *Purusattama*, 7003; *Purusha*, 6951, 6993; *Purushottama*, 6952; *Pushkarāksha*, 6954, 7008; *Pushpahāsa*, 7051; *Pushṭa*, 6991; *Pūtātman*, 6951; *Rakshaṇa*, 7048; *Rāma*, 6992; *Raṇapriya*, 7022; *Rathāṅgapriya*, 7056; *Ratnagarbha*, 6999; *Ratnanābha*, 7034; *Ravi*, 7043; *Ravilocana*, 7043; *Rohita*, 6989; *Rucirāṅgada*, 7050; *Rudra*, 6962; *Ṛddha*, 6979, 6987; *Ṛtu*, 6994; *Sadāmarshin*, 7044; *Sadāyogin*, 6967; *Sadbhūti*, 7024; *Sadgati*, 7024; *Sādhu*, 6975; *Saha*, 6989; *Sahasrajit*, 6982; *Sahasrāksha*, 6973 (PCR. takes *sahasrākshaḥ sahasrapāt* as one name); *Sahasrāṃçu*, 7000; *Sahasramūrdhan*, 6973; *Sahasrapad*, 6973 (v. *Sahasrāksha*); *Sahasrārcis*, 7038; *Sahishṇu*, 6965, 7009; *Sākshin*, 6951, 7004; *Sama*, 6961; *Sāmaga*, 7011; *Sāmagāyana*, 7055; *Sāman* (neutr.), 7011; *Samātman*, 6961; *Samāvarta*, 7032; *Samayajña*, 6988; *Sambhava*, 6953; *Samīhana*, 6996; *Samīraṇa*, 6973; *Samitiñjaya*, 6988; *Sammita*, 6961; *Saṃnyāsakṛt*, 7011; *Sampratardana*, 6974; *Saṃsthāna(ḥ)*, 6991; *Saṃvartaka*, 6974; *Saṃvatsara*, 6959, 6994; *Saṃvṛta*, 6974; *Sanāt sanātanatama(ḥ)*, 7045; *Sandhātṛ*, 6971; *Sandhimat*, 6971; *Saṅgraha*, 6966; *Saṅkarshaṇa*, 7008 (v. *Acyuta*); *Saṅksheptṛ*, 7013; *Sannivāsa*, 7024; *Saptaidhas*, 7038; *Saptajihva*, 7038; *Saptavāhana*, 7038; *Sarga*, 6966; *Sarva*, 6953; *Sarvaçastrabhṛtāṃ vara(ḥ)*, 7030; *Sarvadarçana*, 6959; *Sarvadarçin*, 6997; *Sarvādi*, 6960; *Sarvadṛç*, 6971, 7010; *Sarvaga*, 6963; *Sarvajña*, 6997, 7036; *Sarvakāmada*, 7040; *Sarvalakshaṇalakshaṇya*, 6988; *Sarvapraharaṇāyudha*, 7056; *Sarvasaha*, 7041; *Sarvāsunilaya*, 7025; *Sarvataçcakshus*, 7016; *Sarvatomukha*, 7030; *Sarvavāsa*, 7035 (v. *Īçvareçvara*); *Sarvavid*, 6968, 7031; *Sarvayogaviniḥsṛta*, 6960; *Sarveçvara*, 6960; *Sat* (neutr.), 7000; *Satāṃ gati(ḥ)*, 6969, 6997; *Satkartṛ*, 6975; *Satkīrti*, 7015; *Satkṛta*, 6975; *Satkṛti*, 7024; *Satparāyaṇa(ḥ)*, 7024; *Satpathācāra*, 7051; *Sattā*, 7024; *Sattra(ṃ)*, 6997; *Sattvastha*, 7001; *Sattvavat*, 7042; *Sāttvika*, 7042; *Sātvatāṃ pati(ḥ)*, 7003; *Satya(ḥ)*, 6961, 6972, 7042; *Satyadharman*, 7005; *Satyadharmaparākrama*, 6980; *Satyadharmaparāyaṇa(ḥ)*, 7042; *Satyamedhas*, 7029; *Satyaparākrama*, 6972; *Satyasandha*, 7003; *Sava*, 7027; *Savitṛ*, 7043; *Siddha*, 6960, 7037; *Siddhārtha*, 6976; *Siddhasaṅkalpa*, 6976; *Siddhi*, 6960; *Siddhida*, 6976; *Siddhisādhana*, 6976; *Siṃha*, 6971, 7001; *Skanda*, 6985; *Skandadhara*, 6985; *Soma*, 7003; *Somapa*, 7003; *Spashṭākshara*, 6979; *Sragvin*, 6972; *Srashṭṛ*, 7012, 7055; *Stavapriya*, 7022; *Stavya*, 7022; *Sthānada*, 6991; *Sthāṇu*, 6953, 6962, 6995 (PCR. takes *sthāvaraḥ sthāṇuḥ* as one name); *Sthāvara*, 6995 (v. *Sthāṇu*); *Sthavira*, 6955; *Sthavishṭha*, 6955, 6996; *Sthira* 6971, 7016 (v. *Çāçvata*); *Sthūla*, 7039; *Stotra(ṃ)*, 7022; *Stotṛ*, 7022; *Stuti*, 7022; *Subhuja*, 6978; *Sudarçana*, 6994; *Sudhanvan*, 7010; *Sughosha*, 6998; *Suhṛd*, 6998; *Sukhada*, 6998, 7044; *Sūkshma*, 6998; *Sulabha*, 7037; *Sulocana*, 7034; *Sumedhas*, 7029; *Sumukha*, 6998; *Sunda*, 7034; *Sundara*, 7034; *Suparṇa*, 6970, 7040; *Suprasāda*, 6975; *Surādhyaksha*, 6964; *Surānanda*, 6969; *Surārihan*, 6971; *Sureça*, 6959; *Sureçvara*, 6980; *Suruci*, 7043; *Sūrya*, 7043; *Susheṇa*, 7007; *Sutantu*, 7033; *Sutapas*, 6970; *Suvarṇabindu*, 7035; *Suvarṇavarṇa*, 7028; *Suvīra*, 7050; *Suvrata*, 6998, 7037; *Suyāmuna*, 7024; *Svābhāvya*, 7005; *Svadhṛta*, 7037; *Svaksha*, 7015; *Svaṅga*, 7015; *Svāṅga*, 7008; *Svāpana*, 6999; *Svar*, 7053 (v. *Bhū*); *Svasti*, 7045; *Svastibhuj*, 7045; *Svastida*, 7045; *Svastidakshiṇa*, 7045; *Svastikṛt*, 7045; *Svāsya*, 7039; *Svavaça*, 6999; *Svayambhū*, 6954; *Svayañjāta*, 7055; *Tad*, 7027 (PCR. takes *yat tat* as one name); *Tantuvardhana*, 7033; *Tāra*, 6986, 7053; *Tāraṇa*, 6986; *Taru*, 7053; *Tattva(ṃ)*, 7052 (PCR. seems to take *tattvaṃ tattvavid* as one name); *Tattvavid*, 7052 (v. *Tattva(ṃ)*); *Tejas* (neutr.), 6979 (v. *Dyutidhara*), 7030; *Tīrthakara*, 7023; *Tridaçādhyaksha*, 7006; *Trikakud*, 6956 (v. *Dhāman*); *Trilokadhṛk*, 7029; *Trilokātman*, 7018; *Trilokeça*, 7018; *Tripada*, 7006; *Trisāman*, 7011; *Trivikrama*, 7005; *Tushṭa*, 6991; *Tvashṭṛ*, 6955; *Udāradhī*, 6972; *Udbhava*, 6990, 7034; *Udīrṇa*, 7016; *Udumbara*, 7037; *Ugra*, 6994; *Upendra*, 6966; *Ūrdhvaga*, 7051; *Ūrjita*, 6966; *Ūrjitaçāsana*, 7046; *Uttara*, 7002; *Uttāraṇa*, 7048; *Vācaspati*, 6972, 7010; *Vāgmin*, 6978; *Vahni*, 6974; *Vaidya*, 6967; *Vaikhāna*, 7055; *Vaikuṇṭha*, 6993; *Vājasana*, 7034; *Vāmana*, 6966; *Vaṃçavardhana*, 7039; *Vanamālin*, 7009; *Varāṅga*, 7028; *Varada*, 6985; *Varāroha*, 6962; *Vardhamāna*, 6977; *Vardhana*, 6977; *Varuṇa*, 7008; *Vāruṇa*, 7008; *Vāsavānuja*, 6984; *Vashaṭkāra*, 6950; *Vasu*, 6961, 6978, 7023; *Vasuda*, 6978; *Vāsudeva*, 6985, 7023, 7025, 7061, 7066, 7067; *Vasumanas*, 6961, 7023; *Vasuprada*, 7023; *Vasuretas*, 7023; *Vatsala*, 6999; *Vatsara*, 6999; *Vatsin*, 6999; *Vāyu*, 6993; *Vāyuvāhana*, 6985, 7040; *Veda*, 6963; *Vedāṅga*, 6963; *Vedavid*, 6963; *Vedhas* (so B., *Me*° C.), 7008; *Vedya*, 6967; *Vegavat*, 6989; *Vibhu*, 6975, 7043; *Viçishṭa*, 6976, 6983; *Viçodhana*, 7017; *Viçoka*, 7016; *Viçrāma*, 6994; *Viçrutātman*, 6971; *Viçuddhātman*, 7017; *Viçva(ṃ)*, 6950; *Viçvabāhu*, 6983; *Viçvabhuj*, 6975; *Viçvadakshiṇa*, 6994; *Viçvadṛç*, 6975; *Viçvakarman*, 6955; *Viçvamūrti*, 7026; *Viçvaretas*, 6959; *Viçvātman*, 6973; *Viçvayoni*, 6962, 6965; *Vidāraṇa*, 6998; *Vidhātṛ*, 6954, 7000; *Vidheyātman*, 7015; *Vidiçaḥ* (pl.), 7049; *Vidvattama*, 7047; *Vihāyasagati*, 7043; *Vijaya*, 6965, 7003; *Vijitātman*, 7015; *Vikartṛ*, 6990; *Vikrama*, 6958; *Vikramin*, 6958, 7046; *Vikshara*, 6980; *Vimuktātman*, 6997; *Vinayitṛ*, 7001; *Vīra*, 6992, 7018, 7019 (v. *Ananta*); *Vīrabāhu*, 6998; *Vīrahan*, 6967, 7028, 7048; *Viraja*, 6992 (v. *Mārga*); *Virāma*, 6992; *Virocana*, 7043; *Vishama*, 7028; *Vishṇu*, 6950, 6977, 7019; *Vishvaksena*, 6963; *Vistāra*, 6995; *Vītabhaya*, 7047; *Vivikta*, 6977; *Vṛddhātman*, 6987; *Vṛksha*, 7008; *Vṛsha*, 6988, 7030; *Vṛshabha*, 6977; *Vṛshabhāksha*, 7012; *Vṛshāhin*, 6977; *Vṛshākapi*, 6960; *Vṛshakarman*, 6961; *Vṛshākṛti*, 6961; *Vṛshaparvan*, 6977; *Vṛshapriya*, 7012; *Vṛshodara*, 6977; *Vyādiçaḥ* (pl.), 7049; *Vyagra*, 7030; *Vyāla*, 6959; *Vyāpin*, 6999; *Vyāpta*, 6993; *Vyāsa*, 7010; *Vyavasāya*, 6991; *Vyavasthāna*, 6991; *Yad*, 7027 (v. *Tad*); *Yaduçreshṭha*, 7024; *Yajña*, 6997, 7053; *Yajñabhṛt*, 7054; *Yajñabhuj*, 7054; *Yajñaguhya(ṃ)*, 7054; *Yajñakṛt*, 7054; *Yajñāṅga*, 7053; *Yajñāntakṛt*, 7054; *Yajñapati*, 7053; *Yajñasādhana*, 7054; *Yajñavāhana*, 7053; *Yajñin*, 7054; *Yajvan*, 7053; *Yama*, 6966, 7041; *Yoga*, 6952; *Yogavidāṃ netṛ*, 6952; *Yogin*, 7040; *Yogīça*, 7040; *Yugādikṛt*, 6982; *Yugāvarta*, 6982.

Vishṇu[2], name of a fire. § 493 (Āṅgirasa): III, **221**, 14188 (*agniḥ*). Cf. Aṅgiras[6].

Vishṇu[3] = Sūrya (the Sun): III, 148, 190.—Do.[4] = Çiva (1000 names[1–2]).

Vishṇudharman, a Suparṇa, son of Garuḍa. § 564 (Mātalīyop.): V, **101**β, 3598.

Vishṇuloka ("the world of Vishṇu"). § 358 (Tīrthayātrāp.): III, **82**, 5019.—§ 362 (do.): III, **83**, 5081.—§ 364 (do.): III, **83**, 6074.—§ 368 (do.): III, **83**, 7043.—§ 370 (do.): III, **84**, 8089, 8100, 8103, 8117.—§ 795*c* (Mahābhārata): XVIII, **6**, 261.

Vishṇupada ("Vishṇu's footmark"), name of several places. § 364 (Tīrthayātrāp.): III, **83**, 6073 (a tīrtha).—§ 410 (Plakshāvataraṇag.): III, **130**, 10543 (°*ṃ nāma . . . tīrtham uttamaṃ*).—§ 565 (Gālavacarita): V, **111**, 3841 (°*ṃ nāma kramatā Vishṇunā kṛtaṃ*, in the north).—§ 596 (Pratijñāp.): VII, **80**, 2855 (in the north, visited by Kṛshṇa and Arjuna on their way to Çiva's abode).—§ 632*b* (Shoḍaçarāj., cf. § 595, v. Paurava): XII, **29**, 928 (a mountain, Aṅga performed sacrifices *V°e girau*).—§ 766 (Ānuçāsanik.): XIII, **126**, †6043 (?, "firmament," PCR.).

Vishṇupadī = Gaṅgā: XIII, †1851 (*Jāhnavīṃ*).

Vishṇuparvan, a section of Harivaṃça. § 10 (Parvasaṅgr.): I, **2**, 357.

Vishṇuprasādita = Çiva (1000 names[2]).

Vishṇuyaças = Kalkin: III, 13101 (*Kalkī V°ā nāma*).

Vishṭaraçravas = Kṛshṇa: XII, 1370; XIV, 355.

Vishvagaçva[1] (C. *Viçv°*), one or more ancient kings. § 6 (Anukram.): I, **1***a*, 225 (in Sañjaya's enumeration).—§ 475 (Dhundhumārop.): III, **202**, 13517 (king of Ayodhyā, son of Pṛthu and father of Adri).—§ 746 (Ānuçāsanik.): XIII, **76**ι, †3689.—§ 761 (do.): XIII, **115**, 5662 (only B., C. has *Viçvaksenena*).

Vishvagaçva[2] (C. *Viçv.*), a king in the time of Yudhishṭhira. § 279 (Arjuna): II, **27**, 1023 (*Pauravaṃ*, in the north, vanquished by Arjuna on his digvijaya).

Vishvaksena[1] (C. *Viçv°*), a ṛshi. § 266 (Çakrasabhāv.): II, **7**, 300 (in the palace of Indra).

Vishvaksena[2] (C. often *Viçv°*) = Kṛshṇa (Vishṇu): V, 3010; VI, †2944 (i.e. Nārāyaṇa (Vishṇu), C. has *Viçv°*), 5599 (C. *Viçv°*); VII, 194 (°-*Dhanañjayau*), 333 (C. has *Viçv°*), 3053 (do.), 8802 (°-*Dhanañjayau*), 8803 (do.); VIII, 1096; XII, 12846 (i.e. Nārāyaṇa, C. has *Viçv°*), 13467 (*Hariḥ*, C. *Viçv°*); XIII, 6963 (Vishṇu's 1000 names), †7383, †7385, †7386, †7396, †7398.

Vishvaksena[3] (C. *Viçv°*), an ancient king. § 761 (Ānuçāsanik.): XIII, **115**γ, 5662 (among the kings who abstained from meat during the month of Kārttika, B. has *Vishvagaçvena*).

Vishvaksena[4] (C. *Viçv°*) = Mahāpurusha (Mahāpurushastava).—Do.[5] = Çiva (1000 names[2]).

Viskara, an ancient king (an Asura?). § 673*b* (Bali-Vāsavasaṃv.): XII, **227***a*, 8265 (among the ancient rulers of the earth, B. has *Vishk°*).

Vistara = Çiva (1000 names[2]).

Vistāra[1] = Çiva (1000 names[2]).—Do.[2] = Vishṇu (1000 names).

Vītabhaya = Vishṇu (1000 names).

Viṭabhūta, an Asura. § 268 (Varuṇasabhāv.): II, **9**, 367 (among the Daityas and Dānavas in the palace of Varuṇa).

Vītahavya, a king (= Haihaya[1]). § 736 (Ānuçāsanik.): XIII, **30**, 1942 (*nṛpatiḥ . . . vipratāṃ gataḥ*).—§ 736*b* (Vītahavyop.): XIII, **30**, 1944 (*rājarshir durlabhaṃ prāpto brāhmanyaṃ*), 1950 (°*dāyādaiḥ* = Vītahavya, pl.), 1983, 1984, 1989 (vanquished by the Kāçi king Pratardana), 1997 (became a brahman, father of Gṛtsamada), 2005 (*vipratām agamat*).

Vītahavya, pl. (°*āḥ*), a tribe (people) or family ("the sons or descendants of Vītahavya"). § 736*b* (Vītahavyop.): XIII, **30**, 1953 (= *Haihayāḥ*, v. 1951), 1968 (°*sahasrāṇi*), 1977 (°*ānāṃ purīṃ*).—§ 739 (Ānuçāsanik.): XIII, **34**γ, 2126 (had been vanquished by Bharadvaja). Cf. Haihaya, pl.

[Vītahavyopākhyāna(m)] ("the episode relating to Vītahavya"). § 736*b* (Ānuçāsanik.). *Bhīshma* said: While *Manu*, in days of yore, was righteously ruling his subjects, he obtained a righteous son *Çaryāti*, in whose race were born *Vatsa's* sons, the kings *Haihaya* and *Tālajaṅgha*. *Haihaya* (or *Vītahavya*) had 10 wives and 100 heroic sons, who all studied the *Vedas* and *Dhanurveda*. In *Kāçi* was king *Haryaçva*, the grandfather of *Divodāsa*. The sons of king *Haihaya* (*Vītahavya-dāyādaiḥ*) invaded *Kāçi* and slew king *Haryaçva* in a battle between the *Gaṅgā* and the *Yamunā*, and then went back to their own delightful city in the *Vatsa*-country. Meanwhile *Haryaçva's* son *Sudeva* was installed as *Kāçi*-king. The 100 sons of *Vītahavya* once more came and defeated him in battle, and then returned to their own city. After this, *Sudeva's* son *Divodāsa* became installed as *Kāçi*-king; at the command of *Indra* he built the city of *Vārāṇasī* between the *Gaṅgā* and the southern bank of the *Gomatī*. The *Haihayas* again attacked *Divodāsa*; he fought for 1,000 days, lost his army, left his capital, and fled away to the retreat of *Bharadvāja*, who was his priest, and performed a sacrifice, in consequence of which *Pratardana* was born to him. On the same day when *Pratardana* was born, he grew as great as a boy of 13 years, and mastered the *Vedas* and *Dhanurveda*, *Bharadvāja* (aided by *Yoga*) having entered into the prince and caused all the energy of the universe to enter his body (he was praised by bards and D-ṛ., etc.; description). *Divodāsa* installed *Pratardana* as *yuvarāja* and ordered him to march against the sons of *Vītahavya*. *Pratardana* speedily crossed the *Gaṅgā* and proceeded against the city of the *Vītahavyas* and slew them all. King *Vītahavya* fled away to the retreat of *Bhṛgu*. *Pratardana* followed in his footsteps and ordered *Bhṛgu* to surrender king *Vītahavya*. *Bhṛgu* said: "there is no *kshatriya* in this retreat; they who are here are all brahmans." *Pratardana* returned home, and *Vītahavya* became a Br-ṛ. in consequence of *Bhṛgu's* statement. *Vītahavya*>*Gṛtsamada* (V-ṛ., resembling *Indra* and, therefore, once afflicted by Dai.; alleged quotation from the *Ṛgveda*)>*Sutejas*>*Varcas*>*Vihavya*>*Vitatya*>*Satya*>*Santa*>R. *Çravas*>*Tamas*>*Prakāça*>*Vāgindra*>*Pramati* (B. °*mi*°) (mastering the *Vedas* and *Vedāṅgas*)>*Ruru* (begotten upon Aps. *Ghṛtācī*)>*Çunaka* (begotten upon *Pramadvarā*)>*Çaunaka* (XIII, **30**).

Vītahotra, pl., v. Vītihotra, pl.

Vitarka, son of the elder Dhṛtarāshṭra. § 154 (Pūruvaṃç.): I, **94**, 3747.

Vitastā, a river. § 268 (Varuṇasabhāv.): II, **9**, 372 (present in the palace of Varuṇa).—§ 358 (Tīrthayātrāp.): III, **82**, 5031, 5032 (*bhavanaṃ Takshakasya . . . V°ākhyaṃ*).—§ 410 (Plakshāvataraṇag.): III, **130**, 10555.—§ 459 (Mārkaṇḍeyas.): III, **188***a*, 12910 (seen in the stomach of Nārāyaṇa).—§ 565 (Gālavacarita): V, **119**, 4009 (only B.).—§ 574 (Jambūkh.): VI, **9**λ, 324.—§ 607 (Karṇap.): VIII, **44**θ, 2055. — § 733*b* (Candrabhāgā): XIII, **25**, 1694 (*ūrmimālinīm*). — § 768*b* (Umā-Maheçvarasamv.): XIII, **146**δ, 6764.—§ 775 (Ānuçāsanik.): XIII, **166***a*, 7651.

Vitatya, a brahman, son of Vihavya. § 736*b* (Vītahavyop.): XIII, **30**, 2001 (father of Satya).

Vīti, name of a fire. § 493 (Āṅgirasa): III, **221**, 14201.

Vītihotra, an ancient king ("the king of the Vītihotra's"). § 6 (Anukram.): I, **1***a*, 226 (in Sañjaya's enumeration).

Vītihotra, pl. (°*āḥ*), a people. § 595 (Shoḍaçarāj., v. Rāma Jāmadagnya): VII, **70**β, 2436 (slain by Rāma Jāmadagnya, C. has by error *Vīta*°).

Vittadā, a mātṛ. § 615*u* (Skanda): IX, **40**θ, 2646.

Vittagoptṛ, Vittānām patiḥ, Vittapati, Vitteça = Kubera, q.v.

Vitula, a Sauvīra prince. § 211 (Sambhavap.): I, **139**, 5536 (*Sauvīraḥ*, vanquished by Arjuna, only C., B. has *Vipulaḥ*).

Vivaha, name of a wind. § 714*l* (Çukakṛtya): The fifth wind is fraught with great force and speed, and is dry, and uproots and breaks down the trees. It causes calamitous phenomena of many kinds, and produces roaring sounds in the firmament. It is known by the name of *V.*: XII, **329**, 12409.

Vivardhana, a king. § 264 (Sabhākrīyāp.): II, **4**β, 116 (waited upon Yudhishṭhira).

Vivasvat**[1] ("the brilliant one"), one of the Ādityas, identical with Sūrya (sometimes a mere designation of the sun, e.g. V, 2928; VI, 5743; VIII, †4072). § 3 (Anukramanik.): I, **1**, 43 (*putrā* (so B., *purā*·C.) *V°taḥ*, v. Āçāvaha),—§ 15 (Upamanyu), I, **3**, †723 (*asitam V°taḥ*). —§ 88 (Āmçāvat.): I, **65**, 2523 (the eighth of the Ādityas). —§ 139 (Manu Vaivasvata): I, **75**, 3136 (Kaçyapa begot *Ādityān . . . Indrādīn . . . V°ntam athāpi*, father of Yama), [3137 (*Mārtaṇḍasya*, father of Manu [Vaivasvata] and Yama)].—§ 156 (Pūruvamç.): I, **95**, ††3760 (son of Aditi and father of Manu).—§ 175 (Karṇasambhava): I, **111**, 4390 (i.e. Sūrya, father of Karṇa).—§ 191 (Arjuna): I, **123**, 4824 (the eighth of the Ādityas).—§ 222 (Tapatyup.): I, **171**, 6522 (*sutā V°to vai devasya Sāvitryavarajā*, i.e. Tapatī); **173**, 6602, 6604 (i.e. Sūrya, father of Tapatī).—§ 310 (Āraṇyakap.): III, **3**, 148 (Sūrya's 108 names).—§ 310*b* (Sūrya): III, **3**, 191 (= Sūrya).—§ 310 (Āraṇyakap.): III, **3**, (201), (do.).—§ 377 (Dhaumyatīrthak.): III, **87**, 8303 (*çāmitrañ ca V°taḥ*, in the east).—§ 457 (Vaivasvatop.): III, **187**, 12747 (father of Manu [Vaivasvata]).—§ 545 (Pativratāmahātmyap.): III, **294**, 16672 (*iva*); **297**, †16788 (°*tas tvam tanayaḥ*, sc. Yama).—§ 548 (Āraṇeyap.): III, **315**, 17466 (*h:* living in concealment everywhere in the earth, *V.* at last burnt up his foes).—§ 565 (Gālavacarita): V, **109**, 3779 (gave the southern region as dakshiṇā to his guru).—§ 576 (Bhagavadgītāp.): VI, **28**, 994 (Kṛshṇa declared the system of Yoga to *V.*, and *V.* again to Manu), 997 (*janma V°taḥ*).—§ 608 (Karṇap.): VIII, **65**, 3304 (°*ān Açvināv iva*, sc. *abhyanandat*); **94**, †4923 (*bhagavān*).—§ 615*u* (Skanda): IX, **45**γ, 2507.—§ 665 (Mokshadh.): XII, **208**β, 7581 (the eighth of the Ādityas), [7583 (*Mārtaṇḍasya*, do.; father of the Açvins)].—§ 717*b* (Nārāyaṇīya): XII, **335a*, 12686 (among the twenty-one Prajāpatis); **341**π, 13114 (identified with Vishṇu); **343**, X), ††13219 (°*to dvitīyajanmany aṇḍasaṃjñitasya; Mārtaṇḍo V°ān Çrāddhadevaḥ*, son of Aditi and born from an egg); **349**, VII), 13597 (obtained the religion of Nārāyaṇa from Āditya and communicated it to Manu).—§ 718*b* (Uñchavṛttyup.): XII, **360**, 13848 (i.e. Sūrya); **363**, 13900, 13914 (do.).—§ 746 (Ānuçāsanik.): XIII, **82**ν, 3857.—[§ 770 (do.): XIII, **151**, 7096 (*Mārtaṇḍasya*, father of the Açvins who came out of the nostrils of his wife Sañjñā)].

Cf. the following synonym:—

***Mārtaṇḍa**: I, 3137 (father of Manu); III, 192, 1675 (*dvitīya iva M°o yugānte*); XII, 7583 (*Açvinau . . . M°syātmajau*), ††13219 (*V°*, etymology (?)); XIII, 7096 (°*syātmajau . . . Açvinau*).

Vivasvat[2] a Daitya. § 564 (Mātalīyop.): V, **105**, 3685 (had been slain by Garuḍa).

Vivasvat[3], a Viçvadeva. § 749 (Ānuçāsanik.): XIII, **91**γ, 4356.

Vivasvat[4] = Çiva (1000 names[2]).

Vivikta = Vishṇu (1000 names).

Vivimça[1], son of Dhṛtarāshṭra. § 609 (Çalyap.): IX, **2**ζ, 105 (only B., = Vivimçati?, had been slain).

Vivimça[2], a prince, son of Vimça. § 778*b* (Samvartta-Maruttīya): XIV, **4**, 68, 69 (father of fifteen sons, Khanīnetra, etc.).

Vivimçati, a son of Dhṛtarāshṭra. § 83 (Ādivamçāvatāraṇa): I, **63***a*, 2447 (a mahāratha).—§ 130 (Amçāvat.): I, **67**, 2729.—§ 182 (Dhṛtarāshṭraputranāmak.): I, **117**, 4543.—§ 232 (Svayamvarap.): I, **186**, 698 (came to the svayamvara of Draupadī).—§ 298 (Dyūtap.): II, **58**, †2004.—§ 512 (Ghoshayātrāp.): III, **242**, 14920 (made prisoner by the Gandharvas).—§ 552 (Goharaṇap.): IV, **35***a*, 1151; **38**, 1243; **61**, 1988 (attacked Arjuna), 1994; **63**, 2021 (attacked Arjuna); **65**, †2096; **66**, †2109.—§ 556 (Sañjayayānap.): V, **27**, †791.—§ 561 (Yānasandhip.): V, **47***a*, 1799; **55**ν, 2207; **66**εε, 2502.—§ 562 (Bhagavadyānap.): V, **94**, 3377; **95**ν, 3402.—§ 567 (do.): V, **124**β, 4138.—§ 571 (Ulūkadūtāgamanap.): V, **160**, 5528 (°*mahoragam*, sc. *purushodadhim*); **161**, 5573 (°*jhashākulam*, sc. *purushodadhim*).—§ 576 (Bhagavadgītāp.): VI, **17**, 657; **18**δ, 686. —§ 578 (Bhīshmavadhap.): VI, **44***a*, 1653; **47**[25]γ, 1809; **48**θ, 1926.—§ 581 (do.): VI, **60**β, †2672; **62**ζ, 2731, 2742.—§ 584 (do.): VI, **81***a*, 3534.—§ 585 (do.): VI, **87**, 3849; **92**χ, 4119, 4133; **94**ω, 4194; **98**νν, 4489.—§ 587 (do.): VI, **117**σ, 5495, 5497.—§ 589 (Droṇābhishekap.): VII, **7**δ, 181.—§ 590 (do.): VII, **14**, 521, 522 (fought with Bhīmasena).—§ 592 (Samçaptakavadhap.): VII, **25**, 1088, 1089 (fought with Sutasoma).—§ 593 (Abhimanyuvadhap.): VII, **37**ι, 1601, (κ), 1609. § 596 (Pratijñāp.): VII, **74**β, 2627.—§ 598 (Jayadrathavadhap.): VII, **85***a*, 3020.—§ 599 (do.): VII, **95**ζ, 3525; **96**θ, 3572; **120**δδ, 4767; **127**νν, 5176.—§ 600 (Ghaṭotkacavadhap.): VII, **158**ψ, 7031.—§ 604 (Karṇap.): VIII, **5**ζ, 96 (had been slain).—§ 619 (Strīvilāpap.): XI, **19**δ, 560, 561, 563 (lamented for as slain).

Vivimçu, a Kuru warrior. § 605 (Karṇap.) VIII, **25**, 1009.

Vivindhya, a Dānava, follower of Çalva. § 320 (Saubhavadhop.): III, **16**, 680 (*Dānavaḥ*), 681, 685 (defeated and slain by Cārudeshṇa). Cf. Dānava.

Vivitsu, a son of Dhṛtarāshṭra. § 130 (Amçāvat.): I, **67**, 2731.—§ 182 (Dhṛtarāshṭraputranāmak.): I, **117**, 4544.—§ 581 (Bhīshmavadhap.): VI, **64**κ[14], 2838 (encountered Bhīmasena).—§ 608 (Karṇap.): VIII, **51**δδ, 2446 (εε), 2451 (slain by Bhīmasena).

Vomavaktra (XIV, 197), v. Somavaktra.

Vrajana, son of Ajamīḍha. § 152 (Pūruvamç.): I, **94**, 3722 (°-*Rūpiṇau*, sons of Ajamīḍha and Keçinī), 3724.

Vrajanātha = Kṛshṇa: II, 2292.
Vratādhipa = Çiva (1000 names[2]).
Vratāvāsa = Mahāpurusha (Mahāpurushastava).
Vratavat = Çiva: X, 257.
Vrateça = Çiva: XIII, 612.
Vratin = Çiva: VIII, 1449.
vrātya ("out-caste"), pl. and sg. V, 1229 (sg.); VII, 5965 (said of the Vṛshṇis and Andhakas); VIII, 2038 (fem. pl.), 2045 (*Bāhīkeshu*), 2057 (*dāsamīyānāṃ Bāhīkānāṃ*), 2069 (*dāsamīyānāṃ*), 2090 (do.); XII, 10869 (pl. name of a certain mixed caste); XIII, 2621 (sg. do.).
Vrīhidrauṇika(ṃ) ākhyāna(ṃ). § 10 (Parvasaṅgr.): I, **2**, 325 (i.e. Vrīhidrauṇikaparvan).—§ 11 (do.): I, **2**, 472 (do.).
[Vrīhidrauṇikaparvan(°va)] ("on the droṇa of rice", the 45th of the minor parvans of Mhbhr.). § 519. Dwelling in the woods, the *Pāṇḍavas* spent eleven years in a miserable plight, *Yudhishṭhira* repenting of his act of gambling, and the others thinking of revenge. Once *Vyāsa* came to them and spoke to *Yudhishṭhira* about the meritoriousness of asceticism, saying that a wise man, knowing that life has its ups and downs, is neither filled with joy nor with grief, while foolish persons are reborn as beasts in after life; nothing in this world is more difficult to practise than charity, and therefore charity is superior to everything; even a small gift may be of great result in future life, provided that what is given away is properly acquired and, with a pure mind and in due time, bestowed on pious persons; but the bestowal of ill-gotten gains can never rescue the giver from evil (III, **259**).—§ 520: Mudgala (q.v.).
Vṛddha = Çiva (1000 names[1]).
Vṛddhaçarman, a prince. § 141 (Purūravas): I, **75**, 3150 (son of Āyus and Svarbhānavī).
Vṛddhagārgya ("old Gārgya"), a ṛshi. § 766 (Ānuçāsanik.): XIII, **125**, 5996 (questioned the Pitṛs). Cf. Gārgya.
Vṛddhakanyā ("old virgin"). § 615 (Baladevatīrthayātrā): IX, **51**, †2978.—§ 615*u* (do.): The ṛshi *Kuṇi-Garga* by penances created a fair daughter from his mind and then went to heaven. She worshipped the *Pitṛs* and the gods with fasts and practised penances in that solitary forest not wishing to marry, as she did not see a husband worthy of her. When she could no longer move, she set her heart upon departing for the other world. *Nārada* told her that she had no regions of blessedness to obtain, not having cleansed herself by the rite of marriage. She then went to a concourse of *ṛshis*, and said that she would give half her penances to him who would accept her hand in marriage. *Gālava's* son, the ṛshi *Prākçṛṅgavat*, accepted her hand on condition that he should live with her only one night. On that night she became a young lady of the finest complexion, etc., and *Gālava's* son became very happy. At morn she said: "he that will, with rapt attention, pass one night in this tīrtha after having gratified the gods with oblations of water, shall obtain the merit of the vow of *brahmacarya* for 58 years," and then she departed for heaven. He soon followed her, moved by sorrow: IX, **52**, 3003.
Vṛddhakshatra[1], king of the Sindhus (Saindhavas), father of Jayadratha. § 587 (Bhīshmavadhap.): VI, **115**, 5362 (*Jayadrathaṃ* . . . *V°sya dāyādaṃ*). — § 590 (Droṇābhishekap.): VII, **14**, 561 (*°sya dāyādaṃ*, i.e. Jayadratha). —§ 599*g* (Jayadrathavadhap.): *V.* was the father of the *Sindhu* king *Jayadratha*, at whose birth an incorporeal voice said that he would become one of the foremost of kshatriyas, but in a battle some conspicuous kshatriya would cut off his head. The *Sindhu* king *V.* then summoned all his kinsmen and pronounced the curse, that he who would cause the head of *Jayadratha* to fall to the earth, the head of that man would crack into 100 pieces. Then he installed *Jayadratha* on the throne, and, repairing to the woods, devoted himself to ascetic austerities: VII, **146**, 6258 (*Saindhavasya pitā*), 6266.—§ 599 (do.): VII, **146**, 6269, 6277, 6280 (when Arjuna cut off the head of Jayadratha, Kṛshṇa caused it to fall on the lap of *V.*; thence it fell on the earth, and according to the curse the head of *V.* broke to pieces); **148**$\phi\phi\phi$, 6412 (*nihataḥ* . . . *sahātmajaḥ*). Cf. Bṛhatkshatra[3] (see additions), Saindhava, Sindhupati.—Do.[2], a Paurava prince: VII, 9330, 9400 (only B.), v. Bṛhatkshatra[4] (see additions).
Vṛddhātman = Vishṇu (1000 names).
Vṛddhikā, pl. (°*āḥ*), a class of female ogres. § 504 (Skandayuddha): III, **231**, 14529 (*striyo mānushamāṃsādā V°ā nāma nāmataḥ*, born in trees). Cf. the reading *Vṛkshakā*, Hopkins: Epic. Mythol., p. 229.
Vṛhaka, Vṛhattvan, names of Gandharvas. § 191*b* (Arjuna): I, **123**, 4813 (B. *Bṛh°*).
Vṛjinīvat, a prince. § 768*b* (Kṛshṇa Vāsudeva): XIII, **147**, 6833 (son of Kroshṭṛ), 6834 (father of Ṛshadgu).
Vṛka[1], a prince. § 232 (Svayaṃvarap.): I, **186**, 6990 (came to the svayaṃvara of Draupadī).
Vṛka[2], a Pāṇḍava warrior. § 592 (Saṃçaptakavadhap.): VII, **21**, 867 (*Pāñcalyaḥ*, only B., the verse missing in C.), 868, 870 (slain by Droṇa).
Vṛka[3], a Kuru warrior. § 608 (Karṇap.): VIII, **85**ρ', †4307, †4321 (slain).
Vṛka[4], an ancient king. § 761 (Ānuçāsanik.): XIII, **115**δ, 5665 (among the kings who abstained from meat during the month of Kārttika).
Vṛka, pl. (°*āḥ*), a people. § 578 (Bhīshmavadhap.): VI, **51**ν, 2106 (B. *Çakaiḥ*, in Duryodhana's army).
Vṛkaratha, brother of Karṇa. § 600 (Ghaṭotkacavadhap.): VII, **157**, 6942 (*bhrātā Karṇasya*, pierced Bhīmasena).
Vṛkasthala, a village. § 556 (Sañjayayānap.): V, **31**, 934 (among the five villages for which Yudhishṭhira asked Duryodhana).—§ 562 (Bhagavadyānap.): V, **72**β, 2595 (do.); **82**ζ, 2877 (do.); **84**, 3012 (a station on Kṛshṇa's way from Upaplavya to Hāstinapura.); **85**, 3037; **86**, 3040; **89**, 3102 (°*nivāsinaḥ*).
Vṛkodara = Bhīma Pāṇḍava, q.v.
Vṛkodara, pl. a class of demons. § 615*u* (Skanda): IX, **45**, 2607 (°*nibhāḥ*, sc. some of the warriors of Skanda).
Vṛksha[1] = Çiva (1000 names[1-2]).—Do.[2] = Vishṇu (1000 names).
vṛksha, pl. (°*āḥ*) ("trees", personif.): IX, 2518.
Vṛkshākāra, Vṛkshakarṇasthiti, Vṛkshaketu = Çiva (1000 names[2]).
Vṛkshāṇāṃ kandadaḥ = Çiva (1000 names[1]).
Vṛkshāṇāṃ pati(ḥ) = Çiva: VII, 9526.
Vṛkshāraka (VII, 1872), v. Vṛndāraka.
Vṛkshavāsin, a Yaksha. § 269 (Vaiçravaṇasabhāv.): II, **10**, 399 (in the palace of Kubera; C. has by error *Vṛkshavāspaniketaç ca* instead of °*vāsy Aniketaç ca*, B.).
Vṛmhilā, v. Bṛmhitā.
Vṛndāraka, a son of Dhṛtarāshṭra. § 182 (Dhṛtarāshṭraputranāmak.): I, **117**, 4547.—§ 593 (Abhimanyuvadhap.): VII, **37**κ, 1610 (attacked Abhimanyu); **47**, 1872 (*Kurūṇāṃ kīrtivardhanaṃ*, slain by Abhimanyu, C. has by error *Vṛkshārakaṃ*).—§ 599 (Jayadrathavadhap.): VII, **127**$\nu\nu$,

5178 (among several sons of Dhṛtarāshṭra who attacked Bhīmasena), (ξξ), 5204 (*Kurūṇāṃ kīrtivardhanaṃ*, slain by Bhīmasena).

Vṛsha[1] = Karṇa, q.v.

Vṛsha[2], a Kuru warrior. § 592 (Saṃçaptakavadhap.): VII, **20**η, 804 (in Droṇa's gāruḍavyūha; B. has *Vṛshakrātho*, cf. Krātha[2]).

Vṛsha[3], a warrior of Skanda. § 615*u* (Skanda): IX, **45**η, 2566.

Vṛsha[4], an Asura(?). § 673*b* (Bali-Vāsavasaṃv.): XII, **227***a*, 8263 (among the ancient rulers of the earth).

Vṛsha[5] = Çiva: II, 1642; XII, 10372 (1000 names[1]); XIV, 199.

Vṛsha[6] = Dharma: VII, 9627; XII, 3378.

Vṛsha[7] = Kṛshṇa (Vishṇu): XII, 1507, 13247 (etymology); XIII, 6983 (1000 names), 7030 (do.).

Vṛshabha[1], a mountain near Girivraja. § 277 (Jarāsandhavadhap.): II, **21**, 799.

Vṛshabha[2], a Gāndhāra prince, brother of Çakuni. § 585 (Bhīshmavadhap.): VI, **90***v*, 3997 (six brothers of Çakuni fought with Irāvat), 4017 (the only one of the brothers who was saved).

Vṛshabha[3] = Çiva: VII, 9531.—Do.[4] = Kṛshṇa (Vishṇu): XII, 1506; XIII, 6977 (1000 names).

Vṛshabhā, a river. § 574 (Jambūkh.): VI, **9**λ, 339.

Vṛshabhadhvaja = Çiva, q.v.

Vṛshabhāksha = Vishṇu (1000 names).

Vṛshabhāṅka, Vṛshabhavāhana = Çiva, q.v.

Vṛshabhekshaṇa, Vṛshabhodāra=Çiva: VII, 9531.

Vṛshabhūta, Vṛshacara = Çiva: VII, 9532.

Vṛshaçṛṅga = Çiva: VII, 9531.

Vṛshadaṃça, a mountain. § 596 (Pratijñāp.): VII, **80**, 2852 (*çailendraṃ*, in the north, near Mahā-Mandara).

Vṛshadarbha[1], name of a king. § 267 (Yamasabhāv.): II, **8**, 337 (in the palace of Yama).—§ 465 (Mārkaṇḍeyas.): III, **196**, ††13262, ††13263, ††13267, ††13268.—§ 738*b* (Çyenakapotākhyāna): XIII, **32**, 2047 (*narendraṃ*), 2074, 2082 (king of the Kāçis, named Uçīnara (i.e. king of the Uçīnaras?, descendant of Uçīnara?) (v. 2065), the story of the hawk and the pigeon, otherwise referred to Çibi and Uçīnara, is here referred to *V.*).

Vṛshadarbha[2] = Kṛshṇa: XII, 1508.

Vṛshādarbhi, name of a king. § 655 (Āpaddh.): XII, **159***a*, 5924.—§ 677 (Mokshadh.): XII, **235**, 8598 (gave gems).—§ 750*b* (Bisastainyop.): XIII, **93**, 4415 (°*eç ca saṃvādaṃ Saptarshīṇāṃ ca*), 4424 (*Çaibyaḥ*), (4425), 4451, 4454 (*narapatiṃ*), (4455), 4474, 4538 (the story of *V.* (the son of Çibi, v. 4420) and the seven ṛshis).—§ 767 (Ānuçāsanik.): XIII, **137***a*, 6254 (*rājarshiḥ*, ascended to heaven, having given gems, etc., to the brahmans). Cf. Çaibya, Çibisūnu.

Vṛshadarpa = Çiva: VII, 9531.

Vṛshadgu, an ancient king. § 267 (Yamasabhāv.): II, **8**, 324 (in the palace of Yama; B. *Rushadgu*).

Vṛshadhvaja[1], a king. § 562 (Bhagavadyānap.): V, **74**γ, 2732 (*Pravīrāṇāṃ*, among the wicked kings who annihilated their kinsmen and relatives).

Vṛshadhvaja[2] = Çiva, q.v.

Vṛshāhin = Vishṇu (1000 names).

Vṛshaka[1], a Gandhāra prince, son of Subala, brother of Acala and Çakuni, and brother-in-law of Dhṛtarāshṭra. § 232 (Svayaṃvarap.): I, **186**, 6985 (present at the svayaṃvara of Draupadī).—§ 287 (Rājasūyikap.): II, **34**, 1266 (*Acalo V°ç caiva*, came to the rājasūya of Yudhishṭhira).—§ 572 (Rathātirathasaṅkhyānap.): V, **168**, 5808 (*Acalo Vṛshakaç caiva . . . bhrātarau*, among the rathas in the army of Duryodhana).—§ 584 (Bhīshmavadhap.): VI, **82**, 3637 (°*sya rathaṃ*).—§ 592 (Saṃçaptakavadhap.): VII, **30**, 1303 (*Gāndhārarājasya sutau . . . bhrātarau V°ācalau*), 1305, 1309 (*bhrātarau V°ācalau*), 1310 (*çyālau tava* (i.e. Dhṛtarāshṭra's) *. . . rājānau V°ācalau*), 1312 (*rājānau V°ācalau*, slain by Arjuna).—§ 604 (Karṇap.): VIII, **5**ζ, 130 (*çyālau tava . . . rājānau V°ācalau*, had been slain by Arjuna).—§ 620 (Çrāddhap.): XI, **26**β, 790 (*Acalaṃ V°ñ caiva*, their bodies are burnt).—§ 789 (Putradarçanap.): XV, **32**θ, 879 (*Acalo V°ç caiva*, among those who, summoned by Vyāsa, arose from the Gaṅgā). Cf. Gāndhāra, dual, Gāndhāramukhya, dual.

Vṛshaka[2], a prince, brother of Kaliṅga[2]. § 604 (Karṇap.): VIII, **5**ζ, 123 (*Kaliṅga-V°au bhrātarau*, had been slain).

Vṛshakāhvayā, a river. § 574 (Jambūkh.): VI, **9**λ, 343.

Vṛshākapi[1], a ṛshi. § 746 (Ānuçāsanik.): XIII, **65**ζ, 3332.

Vṛshākapi[2], one of the eleven Rudras. § 770 (Ānuçāsanik.): XIII, **151**β, 7091.

Vṛshākapi[3]=Çiva: VII, 9627 (etymology).—Do.[4]=Indra: XII, †8331.—Do.[5] = Kṛshṇa (Vishṇu): XII, 1508, 13248 (etymology), (13416), 13421 (*Devadevaḥ*), 13423; XIII, 6960 (1000 names).—Do.[6] = Sūrya: III, 191.

Vṛshakarman = Vishṇu (1000 names).

Vṛshaketana = Çiva, q.v.

Vṛshakrātha, v. Vṛsha[2].

Vṛshākṛti = Vishṇu (1000 names).

Vṛshāmitra, a brahman. § 324 (Dvaitavanapr.): III, **26***a*, 987 (waited upon Yudhishṭhira).

Vṛshaṇa = Çiva (1000 names[2]).

Vṛshanābha = Çiva: VII, 9530.

Vṛshāṇḍa, an Asura(?). § 673*b* (Bali-Vāsavasaṃv.): XII, **227***a*, 8265 (among the ancient rulers of the earth).

Vṛshāṅka = Çiva, q.v.

Vṛshaparvan[1], a rājarshi. § 11 (Parvasaṅgr.): I, **2**, 455. — § 434 (Saugandhikāharaṇa): III, **156**, 11444 (*āçramaṃ V°ṇaḥ*; *c*: the hermitage of *V.* is inhabited by Siddhas and Cāraṇas).—§ 436 (Yakshayuddhap.): III, **158**, 11543 (*āçramaṃ V°ṇaḥ*), 11544 (*rājarshiṃ*), 11546, 11547, 11549 (*āçrame V°ṇaḥ*), 11551, 11552 (the Pāṇḍavas, etc., came to the hermitage of *V.* on the Himavat; *V.* showed them the way [to the mountain Çveta]), 11556 (*yathoktaṃ V°ṇā*), 11620 (do.).—§ 449 (Ājagarap.): III, **177**, †12344 (*āçramāgryaṃ V°ṇaḥ*, the Pāṇḍavas, etc., returned to the hermitage of *V.*), †12345 (the hermitage of *V.* is frequented by gods and maharshis).—§ 450 (do.): III, **178**, 12366 (*āçramāt . . . rājarsher V°ṇaḥ*).

Vṛshaparvan[2], an Asura chief. § 92 (Aṃçāvat.): I, **65**, 2532 (among the sons of Danu).—§ 130 (do.): I, **67**, 2651 (*mahāsuraḥ*, incarnate as king Dīrghaprajña), 2652 (elder brother of Ajaka).—§ 145 (Kaca): I, **76**, 3185 (*Çukra-V°au*), 3195 (had Çukra as his purohita). — § 146 (Devayānī): I, **78**, 3284 (*Çarmishṭhā . . . duhitā V°ṇaḥ*), 3303 (*nagaraṃ V°ṇaḥ*), 3305 (*Çarmishṭhayā . . . duhitrā V°ṇaḥ*), 3309 (do.), 3312 (*Çarmishṭhā . . . duhitā V°ṇaḥ*), 3315; **79**, 3330 (*duhitur V°ṇaḥ*, i.e. Çarmishṭhā), **80**, 3332, 3336, (3338), (3342), 3344 (*mahākaviḥ*), (3346), (3348), 3356 (*duhitrā V°ṇaḥ*, i.e. Çarmishṭhā); **81**, 3368 (*duhitā Dānavendrasya Çarmishṭhā V°ṇaḥ*) (when Çarmishṭhā, the daughter of *V.*, had ill-used Devayānī, the daughter of Çukra, *V.* appeased her and Çukra by giving her Çarmishṭhā as a maid-servant).—§ 147 (do.): I, **82**, 3398 (*sutāṃ . . . V°ṇaḥ*, i.e

Çarmishṭhā); **83,** 3451 (*Çarmishṭhayā . . . duhitrā V°ṇaḥ*). —§ 156 (Pūruvaṃç.): I, **95,** ††3761 (*°ṇaç ca duhitā Çarmishṭhā*).—§ 263 (Sabhākriyāp.): II, **3,** 60 (*sabhāyāṃ V°ṇaḥ*), 75 (*sabhādravyaṃ V°ṇaḥ*, Maya brought various precious articles from the palace of *V.* in the north for the construction of the palace of Yudhishṭhira). — § 569*b* (Yayāti): V, **149,** 5044 (*Çarmishṭhayā . . . duhitrā V°ṇaḥ*). Cf. Asura, Daitya, Dānavendra.

Vṛshaparvan[3] = Vishṇu (1000 names).

Vṛshapati = Çiva: VII, 9531.

Vṛshapriya = Vishṇu (1000 names).

Vṛsharshabha = Çiva: VII, 9531.

Vṛsharūpa = Çiva (1000 names[2]).

Vṛshasāhvayā, a river. § 574 (Jambūkh.): VI, **9**λ, 342 (only B.).

Vṛshasena[1], an ancient king. § 267 (Yamasabhāv.): II, **8,** 324 (in the palace of Yama).

Vṛshasena[2], a prince. § 290 (Çiçupālavadhap.): II, **44,** 1539.

Vṛshasena[3], son of Karṇa. § 571 (Ulūkadūtāgamanap.): V, **164**ε, 5710 (Abhimanyu was pitted against *V.*).—§ 572 (Rathātirathasaṅkhyānap.): V, **167,** 5792 (*Karṇaputraḥ*, a ratha in Duryodhana's army).—§ 590 (Droṇābhishekap.): VII, **16,** 619, 620, 625 (fought with the Draupadeyas).—§ 592 (Saṃçaptakavadhap.): VII, **25,** 1121 (fought with the Pāṇḍya king).—§ 593 (Abhimanyuvadhap.): VII, **37**θ, 1590 (checked Abhimanyu); **44,** 1786 (defeated by Abhimanyu).—§ 596 (Pratijñāp.): VII, **74**β, 2627; **75**γ, 2673. —§ 598 (Jayadrathavadhap.): VII, **87**θ, 3098.—§ 599 (do.): VII, **95**η, 3540; **104**μ, 3894, 3915, 3917, 3920 (fought with Arjuna); **105**ν, 3941 (the standard of *V.* had a peacock made of gold and adorned with jewels and gems standing as if crowing, and always adorning the van of the army); **129,** 5304 (Karṇa mounted the chariot of *V.*); **143**κκκ, 6005; **145**μμμ, 6062, (οοο), 6096, 6108, 6141, 6143 (fought with Arjuna); **146,** 6228, 6247, 6250 (do.); **147**σσσ, 6363 (*Karṇasutaḥ*); **148,** 6406 (Arjuna promised to slay *V.*).—§ 600 (Ghaṭotkacavadhap.): VII, **156,** 6743 (*karçitaḥ*, sc. by Sātyaki; but the text is probably wrong in this half-çloka, as the mentioning of *V°* in this connexion is quite absurd; read with B. *Çalaç caiva mahārāja bhrātṛvyasana-karshitaḥ*), (κ), 6849; **157,** 6941 (*Karṇasya dayitaṃ putraṃ*); **158**ψ, 7030; **165,** 7368 (fought with Drupada); **168,** 7524 (do.), 7526, 7530, 7532, 7535, 7543; **170,** 7647 (pierced by Sātyaki), 7649, 7651; **172**ππ, 7746. —§ 603 (Nārāyaṇāstramokshap.): VII, **193***a*, 8908; **200***aa*, 9309, 9315 (*°sya trisāhasrān mahārathān*, they are slain by Sātyaki).—§ 604 (Karṇap.): VIII, **5**ζ, 113 (had been slain by Arjuna, all. to § 608); **9,** 321 (*hataṃ*, do.).—§ 608 (do.): VIII, **46,** 2156 (Nakula shall proceed against *V.*); **48,** 2252 (*jyeshṭhaḥ putraḥ*), 2274, 2277, 2279 (defeated by Sātyaki); **60,** 3078 (Nakula proceeded against *V.*), 3102, 3103 (fought with Nakula); **66**ιι, 3311 (protected Karṇa); **75,** †3813 (fought with Çatānīka); **84,** 4276, †4279, †4291, †4299 (defeated Nakula), †4301, †4304; **85,** †4332, †4334, †4335, †4338, †4340, †4342 (slain by Arjuna); **87,** 4372 (*hataṃ*).—§ 615 (Gadāyuddhap.): IX, **64**εε, 3613.—§ 618 (Jalapradānikap.): XI, **15,** 393 (all. to VIII, **84**), 397 (do.).—§ 619 (Strīvilāpap.): XI, **21,** 612 (*°sya mātaraṃ*, i.e. the wife of Karṇa).—§ 789 (Putradarçanap.): XV, **32**θ, 877 (*sānujaḥ*, among those who, summoned by Vyāsa, arose from the Gaṅgā). Cf. Karṇaputra, Kārṇasuta, Karṇātmaja, Kārṇi.

Vṛshaskandha = Çiva (1000 names[1]).

Vṛshavāhana = Çiva, q.v.

Vṛshavarman, a Kuru warrior. § 604 (Karṇap.): VIII, **5**ζ, 124 (had been slain by Bhīmasena).

Vṛshāvarta = Çiva: VII, 9530.

Vṛshāyudha = Çiva: VII, 9532.

Vṛshṇi, pl. (*°ayaḥ*), a people (a tribe of the Yādavas, often connected with the Andhakas and the Bhojas). § 11 (Parvasaṅgr.): I, **2,** 425 (*°īnām āgamaḥ*), 444, 616 (*°īnāṃ kadanaṃ*), 622, 624, 626 (*nāçaṃ V° kalatrāṇāṃ*). — § 82 (Kṛshṇa Vāsudeva): I, **63,** 2432 (*prajajñe 'ndhaka-V°shu*, sc. Kṛshṇa).—§ 210 (Sambhavap.): I, **139,** 5221 (*°ayaç cāndhakāç caiva*, became the pupils of Droṇa). — § 232 (Svayaṃvarap.): I, **186,** 7000 (enumeration of the *V.* who came to the svayaṃvara of Draupadī).—§ 233 (do.): I, **187,** †7012 (*°y-Andhakāḥ*).—§ 251 (Arjunavanavāsap.): I, **218,** 7902 (*Bhoja-V°y-Andhakānāṃ*), 7903 (*Bhoja-V°y-Andhakātmajaiḥ*). — § 252 (Subhadrāharaṇap.): I, **219,** 7906 (*°y-Andhakānāṃ*), 7907 (*Bhoja-V°y-Andhakāḥ*), 7910, 7913 (*rājā V°īnāṃ Ugrasenaḥ*); **220,** 7942 (*Bhoja-V°y-Andhakāḥ*), 7946 (*°vīrāḥ*), 7962 (*Bhoja-V°y-Andhakāḥ*).—§ 253 (Haraṇāharaṇap.): I, **221,** 7963 (*sarva°-*), 7975 (*°nandanaiḥ*), 7988 (*°y-Andhakamahāmātraiḥ*), 7990 (*°vīrāṇāṃ*), 7993 (*°-Bhojāndhakāḥ*), 7995 (*°cakraṃ*), 7998 (*°y-Andhakaiḥ*), 8002 (*°y-Andhakaçreshṭhān*), 8018 (*°y-Andhakamahārathān*), 8019 (*Kuru-V°y-Andhakottamaiḥ*), 8020 (*Kuru-V°ayaḥ*), 8022 (*°y-Andhakamahārathaiḥ*).—§ 264 (Sabhākriyāp.): II, **4,** 124 (*°īnāṃ . . . kumārāḥ*), 129 (*°nandanāḥ*).—§ 273 (Rājasūyārambhap.): II, **14,** 616 (*°mahārathāḥ*), 625 (*°madhye*).—§ 275 (do.): II, **19,** 767.—§ 286 (Rājasūyikap.): II, **33,** 1215 (*sarva°-*).—§ 287 (do.): II, **34,** 1276.—§ 289 (Arghāharaṇap.): II, **36,** 1322 (*kshitāv Andhaka-V°īṇāṃ*); **37,** 1360 (*°kule jātaḥ*, sc. Kṛshṇa); **39,** 1411 (*°-Pāṇḍavān*).—§ 294*b* (Vidura): II, **50,** 1795 (*Uddhavaḥ . . . V°īnām arcitaḥ*).—§ 295 (Dyūtap.): II, **52,** 1907 (*Andhaka-V°ayaḥ*). —§ 317 (Arjunābhigamanap.): III, **12,** 461 (*°ayaç cāndhakaiḥ saha*), 524.—§ 319 (Saubhavadhop.): III, **14,** 620 (*°pravīrān*), 621 (*°kulādhamaḥ*, sc. Kṛshṇa).—§ 320 (do.): III, **15,** 648 (*°y-Andhakāḥ*), 654 (*°y-Andhakapure*, i.e. Dvārakā); **16,** 666 (*°nandanāḥ*); **18,** 717, 721 (*°pravīrāṇām*), 729 (*°kule jātaḥ*), 731, 732, 737 (*°vīrāṇām*), 744 (*Andhaka-V°ayaḥ*); **19,** 751, 776; **20,** 780 (*°kulaṃ*), 784 (*°pravīrān*); **22,** 861 (*°pravīrāḥ*), 873 (*°kulaçreshṭha*, sc. Kṛshṇa).—§ 327 (Draupadīparitāpav.): III, **33,** 1352 (*°īnāṃ vṛshabheṇa*, i.e. Kṛshṇa). — § 342 (Indralokābhigamanap.): III, **51,** 1975, 1977 (*Rāma-Kṛshṇapraṇītānāṃ*).—§ 400 (Tīrthayātrāp.): III, **118,** †10231 (*sarva-V°pravarau*, i.e. Kṛshṇa and Balarāma), †10232, †10233.—§ 401 (Balarāma): III, **119,** 10237, 10238, 10239.—§ 402 (Tīrthayātrāp.): III, **120,** †10263 (*°bala-*), †10278 (*sa-V°-Bhojāndhakayodhamukhyā*).—§ 452 (Mārkaṇḍeyas.): III, **183,** †12582 (*°puraṃ*, i.e. Dvārakā). —§ 511 (Draupadī-Satyabhāmāsaṃv.): III, **235,** 14736 (*Rāmaprabhṛtayaḥ . . . Andhaka-V°ayaḥ*).—§ 515 (Karṇadigvijaya): III, **254,** 15253.—§ 522 (Draupadīharaṇap.): III, **268,** 15654 (*Janārdanaḥ sāndhaka-V°vīraḥ*).—§ 547 (Karṇa): III, **303,** 17020 (*°īnāṃ kule jātā*, sc. Kuntī).—§ 552 (Goharaṇap.): IV, **69,** 2234 (*ācāryo V°vīrāṇāṃ*, sc. Droṇa).—§ 553 (Vaivāhikap.): IV, **72,** 2360 (*°y-Andhakāḥ*). —§ 554 (Sainyodyogap.): V, **7, 131** (*°y-Andhakaiḥ*).—§ 556 (Sañjayayānap.): V, **27,** †768 (*Andhaka-V°rājye*).—§ 561*c* (Kṛshṇa Vāsudeva): V, **48,** 1885 (*°y-Andhakānāṃ madhyagataṃ*, sc. Kaṃsa).—§ 561*d* (Nara-Nārāyaṇau): V, **49,** 1939 (*°cakrasya*).—§ 561 (Yānasandhip.): V, **51,** 2056

(*Andhaka-V°ayaḥ*); **57**, 2233 (*mukhyam Andhaka-V°īnāṃ . . . Kṛshṇaṃ*); **65**, 2488 (*Andhaka-V°ishu sammataḥ*, sc. Sātyaki).—§ 562 (Bhagavadyānap.): V, **72**, 2584 (protected by Kṛshṇa); **82**, 2895; **86**, 3042 (*°rāshṭrasya bhartā goptā ca*, i.e. Kṛshṇa), 3043 (*°y-Andhakāḥ*); **88**, 3091; **93**, 3329 (*°īnām ṛshabhaḥ*, i.e. Kṛshṇa); **94**, 3344 (*Kṛshṇo V°bhiç cābhirakshitaḥ*), 3347 (*°īnāñ cāpare rathāḥ*), 3363.—§ 567 (do.): V, **128**, 4298 (*Bhāratāndhaka-V°ayaḥ*); **131**, 4420 (*Andhaka-V°ayaḥ*), 4426, 4447 (*°īnāṃ sammataḥ . . . Hārdikyaḥ*).—§ 569 (do.): V, **140**, 4735 (*mātṛpakshe*—sc. Karṇa's—*V°ayaḥ*), 4738 (*Andhaka-V°ayaḥ*), 4749 (do.).—§ 570 (Sainyaniryāṇap.): V, **153**, 5189 (in Yudhishṭhira's army); **157**, 5331 (*°mukhyaiḥ*). — § 572 (Rathātirathasaṅkhyānap.): V, **170**, 5882 (*°pravīrāṇām amarshī*, sc. Sātyaki).—§ 573 (Ambopākhyānap.): V, **196**, 7645 (*°īnāṃ pravaro rathaḥ*, sc. Sātyaki).—§ 576 (Bhagavadgītāp.): VI, **20**, 753/54 (only B.); **34**, 1241 (*°īnāṃ Vāsudevo 'smi*, says Kṛshṇa). — § 580 (Bhīshmavadhap.): VI, **59**, †2606 (*Andhaka-Vṛshṇinātha*, sc. Kṛshṇa). — § 586 (do.): VI, **107**φ, 4895. — § 589*b* (Sātyaki): VII, **10**, 342 (*°īnāṃ pravaraṃ*, i.e. Sātyaki).—§ 589 (Droṇābhishekap.): VII, **10**, 352 (do., i.e. Abhimanyu, only C.), 359; **11**, 410 (*°vīrāḥ*).—§ 596 (Pratijñāp.): VII, **74**, 2643; **78**, 2740 (*°vīreshu*), 2743 (*°vīrāṇāṃ*).—§ 597 (do.): VII, **83**, 2961 (protected by Kṛshṇa).—§ 598 (Jayadrathavadhap.): VII, **86**, 3070.—§ 599 (do.): VII, **104**, 3891 (*°y-Andhaka-Kurūttamau*, i.e. Kṛshṇa and Arjuna); **110**σ, 4194 (*saha V°bhiḥ*), 4226 (*°pravīrāṇāṃ dvāv evātirathau smṛtau*, sc. Pradyumna and Sātyaki); **115**, 4597 (*°īnām ṛshabheṇa*, i.e. Sātyaki); **126**, 5102 (*Sātyakiṃ . . . V°īnāṃ pravaraṃ rathaṃ*); **142**, 5904 (*Kuru-V°yaçaskarau*, i.e. Bhūriçravas and Sātyaki), 5906 (do.), 5931 (*°y-Andhakavyāghraṃ*, i.e. Sātyaki), 5942 (do., do.), 5946 (*pravaraṃ V°vīrāṇāṃ . . . Sātyakiṃ*); **143**, 5965 (*°y-Andhakāḥ*); **144**, 6047, 6049 (*°vīrāṇām*, C. has by error *°shṭi°*), 6052 (*°vīrāṇāṃ*), 6053 (*°pravīrāṇaṃ*).—§ 600 (Ghaṭotkacavadhap.): VII, **156**, 6732 (*dvāv eva kila V°īnāṃ tatra mukhyau mahārathau*, sc. Pradyumna and Sātyaki), 6736 (*°pāṃsana*, sc. Sātyaki, C. has by error *°shṭi°*); **158**ν, 6980; **162**, 7233 (*Kuru-V°yaçaskarau*, i.e. Somadatta and Sātyaki); **165**, 7389 (*°īnāṃ pravaro rathī*, i.e. Kṛtavarman); **171**, 7645 (*Yuyudhānaḥ . . . V°īnāṃ pravaraḥ*).—§ 602 (Droṇavadhap.): VII, **192**, 8806 (*°īnāṃ kīrtivardhanaḥ* (*°m*, C.), i.e. Sātyaki).—§ 603 (Nārāyaṇāstramokshap.): VII, **198**, 9138 (*Andhaka-V°bhiḥ*, C. has by error *°shṭi°*), 9161 (*°kulādhama*, sc. Sātyaki), 9179 (*Andhaka-V°bhyaḥ*), 9180 (*Andhaka-V°īnāṃ*), 9181 (*yathā Pāṇḍava-V°ayaḥ*); **199**, 9220 (*°y-Andhakavṛtaḥ*, sc. Sātyaki); **200**, 9322 (*°īnāṃ . . . balaṃ*).—§ 604 (Karṇap.): VIII, **8**η, 232.—§ 607 (do.): VIII, **40**, 1826 (*°vīrāṇām*).—§ 608 (do.): VIII, **73**, 3707 (*Kuru-V°yaçaskaraṃ*, i.e. Abhimanyu); **96**, 5030 (*Sātyakiḥ . . . V°īnāṃ pravaro rathaḥ*).—§ 611 (Çalyap.): IX, **21**, 1104 (*°y-Andhakamahārathau*, i.e. Sātyaki and Kṛtavarman, C. has by error *°shṭi*).—§ 615 (Gadāyuddhap.): IX, **35**, 1969 (*°bhiḥ sahitaḥ*, sc. Balarāma).—§ 617 (Aishīkap.): X, **12**, 616, 639 (*°y-Andhakamahārathaiḥ*).—§ 619 (Strīvilāpap.): XI, **25**, 752/53 (*Vṛshṇayaḥ*, only B.), 753 (*°cakrasya*, cursed by Gāndhārī). — § 621 (Rājadh.): XII, **7**, 159 (*°y-Andhakapure*, i.e. Dvārakā).—§ 635 (do.): XII, **33***a*, 1167.—§ 640 (do.): XII, **55**, 1967.—§ 641 (do.): XII, **81**, 3031 (*Andhaka-V°ayaḥ*), 3052 (do.).—§ 665 (Mokshadh.): XII, **208**, 7579 (*°vaṃçaprabhavaḥ*). — § 781 (Açvamedhikap.): XIV, **15***a*, 391 (*°puṅgavān*).—§ 783 (Anugītāp.): XIV, **52**, 1501 (do.), 1525.—§ 785 (do.): XIV, **59**, 1764 (*vihāro V°vīrāṇāṃ*), 1768 (*Bhoja-V°y-Andhakāḥ*), 1771; **60**, 1808; **66**, 1936, 1943 (*°vīreshu*), 1959 (*°y-Andhakakulaṃ*); **70**, 2042 (*°çārdūlāḥ*), 2046 (*°puṅgavāḥ*); **71**, 2056, 2066 (*°y-Andhakavyāghraiḥ*); **83**, 2478 (*Dvāravatīṃ ramyāṃ V°vīrābhipālitāṃ*); **86**, 2556; **89**, 2680 (*°vīrān*). — § 791 (Putradarçanap.): XV, **36**, 990 (*°cakraṃ*).—§ 793 (Mausalap.): XVI, **1**, 7 (*°cakrasya*), 9, (*a*), 12, 13, 14 (*°y-Andhakāḥ*), 19 (*°y-Andhakavināçāya*), 23, 26 (*°y-Andhakakule*, *°y-Andhakavināçāya*), 29 (*°y-Andhakakuleshu*); **2**, 33, 34, 36 (*°y-Andhakavināçāya*), 38 (*°veçmasu*), 40 (*°y-Andhakānāṃ*), 42, 49 (*°y-Andhakaniveçane*); **3**, 58 (*°y-Andhakān*), 60, 63 (*°y-Andhakamahārathāḥ*), 64 (*Andhaka-V°ayaḥ*), 68, 69 (*°y-Andhakamahārathāḥ*), (ε), 93 (the *V.* slew one another); **4**, †123 (*Andhaka-V°nāçaṃ*); **5**, 133 (*upasaṃhatān*), 136 (*°nilayaṃ*), 140 (*°jalāṃ*, sc. *nadīṃ*), 143 (*°puṅgavaiḥ*); **6**κ, 154 (*nidhanaṃ gatāḥ*), 155 (*°pravīrāṇāṃ*), 156 (*°nāçasya*), 167 (*°īnāṃ vaiçasaṃ mahat*); **7**λ, 181 (*°dārān*), 182 (*°vīrāṇāṃ*), 186 (*°y-Andhakajanaṃ*), 203 (*°y-Andhakakumārakāḥ*), 204, 209 (*striyaḥ . . . V°vīrāṇāṃ*), 210 (*bhṛtyās tv Andhaka-V°īnāṃ*), 213 (*putrāç cāndhaka-V°īnāṃ*), 215 (*Bhoja-V°y-Andhakastrīṇāṃ*), 216 (*°cakraṃ*), 220 (*°dārān*), 225, 233 (*°yodhāḥ*), 236 (*°bhṛtyaiḥ*), 239 (*°y-Andhaka-varastriyaḥ*), 244 (Arjuna took away from Dvārakā the remnant of the *V.*, their wives, children, and servants); **8**ν, 262 (*°vīrāṇāṃ*), 263 (*Bhoja-V°y-Andhakāḥ*, all. to ch. **3**), 270 (*°dārān*), 279 (*°y-Andhakamahārathāḥ*), 292 (*°y-Andhakakulaṃ*). — § 794 (Mahāprasthānikap.): XVII, **1**, 1 (*°y-Andhakakule*), 2 (*°īnāṃ kadanaṃ mahat*), 24 (*°kshayaṃ*).—§ 795 (Svargārohaṇap.): XVIII, **4**, 142 (*°y-Andhakamahārathān*, in heaven). Cf. Vārshṇeya, pl.

Vṛshṇi[1], sg. ("a man of the Vṛshṇi-tribe") = Kṛtavarman: VIII, 2641 (*°-Pārshatayoḥ*).—Do.[2] (do.) = Sātyaki: VII, 4681 (*°çara-*), 7665 (*°-Pārshatau*).

Vṛshṇi[3] = Çiva: XIV, 198.

Vṛshṇiçārdūla[1] = Kṛshṇa: III, 13014; IV, 2361 (*Vāsudevaṃ*); VII, 7807; XI, 468; XIII, 2015, 2042; XIV, 1977, 2584.

Vṛshṇiçārdūla[2] = Sātyaki: VII, 4791.

Vṛshṇiçreshṭha = Kṛshṇa: V, †2577.

Vṛshṇikulaçreshṭha = do.: III, 873.

Vṛshṇikulodvaha[1] = Çāmba: III, 676 (*Ç°*).

Vṛshṇikulodvaha[2] = Kṛshṇa: II, 638; XIV, 295, 1483.

Vṛshṇikulodvaha[3] = Sātyaki: I, 2714 (*S°*).

Vṛshṇinandana = Kṛshṇa: III, 614, 830; V, 2767; XI, 643 (only B.).

Vṛshṇipati = Kṛshṇa: V, †2422.

Vṛshṇipravara[1] = Balarāma: IX, 2270, †2830.

Vṛshṇipravara[2] = Kṛshṇa: III, 13005; VIII, †3297.

Vṛshṇipravīra[1] = Kṛshṇa: I, †7148; VII, 5164; XIV, 2014; XVI, 178.

Vṛshṇipravīra[2] = Pradyumna: III, 702 (*Çālva-V°yoḥ*).

Vṛshṇipravīra[3] = Sātyaki: VII, 3609 (*Yuyudhānena*), 5934; VIII, 1639.

Vṛshṇipuṅgava[1] = Kṛshṇa: XIV, 1546.

Vṛshṇipuṅgava[2] = Sātyaki: VII, 4702 (*S°*).

Vṛshṇipura = Dvārakā: III, †12582.

Vṛshṇisattama = Kṛshṇa: V, 3126.

Vṛshṇisiṃha = Kṛshṇa: II, 1425; V, †662, †675, †1851, †1857, †1907; VII, 5802, †9648 (?).—Do. = Sātyaki (?): VII, 6288 (only B.).

Vṛshṇisiṃha, dual (*°au*) = Sātyaki and Kṛtavarman: IX, 936, 1106.

Vṛshṇivara = Sātyaki: VI, 2809 (only B.); VII, 4147 (*S*°).
Vṛshṇivīra[1] = Kṛshṇa: V, †677 (*Vishṇuḥ*); VII, 411 (*Keçavena*), 2502 (*Keçavasya*), 3879; VIII, †683, †3476, 4723; XIV, 1865.
Vṛshṇivīra[2] = Sātyaki: V, 2006 (*Yuyudhānena*); VI, 2809 (only C.); VII, 3047 (*S*°), 4577, 4959, 4974 (only B.), 5111, 5113, 5824, †5836, 5993.
Vṛshṇivīra, dual (°*au*) = Kṛshṇa and Balarāma: I, †149.
Vṛshṇy-Andhakapati[1] = Kṛshṇa: XIV, 2565.—Do.[2] (do.) = Ugrasena: XIV, 2480.
Vṛshṇy - Andhakapravīra = Sātyaki: VII, 4974 (only B.).
Vṛshṇy-Andhakapura = Dvārakā: III, 654; XII, 159.
Vṛshṇy-Andhakavyāghra = Sātyaki: VII, 5931, 5942.
Vṛshṇy-Andhakottama = Kṛshṇa: VII, 3891 (*Vṛshṇy-Andhaka-Kurūttamau*).
Vṛshodara = Vishṇu (1000 names).
Vṛshya = Çiva (1000 names[1]).
Vṛtra, an Asura, slain by Indra. § 17 (Uttaṅka): I, **3,** †810 (°*sya hantā*, i.e. Indra).—§ 96 (Aṃçāvat.): I, **65,** 2541 (*mahāsuraḥ*, son of Danāyus).—§ 130 (do.): I, **67,** 2680 (*mahāsuraḥ*, incarnate as king Maṇimat).—§ 221 (Caitrarathap.): I, **170,** 6485 (the thunderbolt of Indra (*vajraṃ V°nibarhaṇam*) broke into thousand pieces on the head of *V.*).—§ 277 (Jarāsandhavadhap.): II, **23,** 914 (°-*Vāsavayor iva*, sc. *saṃyuge*).—§ 317 (Arjunābhigamanap.): III, **12,** 568 (°-*Vāsavayor iva*, sc. *yuddhaṃ*).—§ 320 (Saubhavadhop.): III, **16,** 681 (°-*Vāsavayoḥ* . . . *yathā*, sc. *yuddhaṃ*).—§ 330 (Indradarçana): III, **37,** 1469 (from fear of *V.* the gods imparted all their might to Indra).—§ 331 (Kairātap.): III, **39,** 1608 (°-*Vāsavayor iva*, sc. *yuddhaṃ*).—§ 384 (Agastyop.): III, **100,** 8692, 8693 (°*vadhe*), 8695, 8699 (headed by *V.* the Kālakeyas defeated the gods; Tvashṭṛ then constructed the thunderbolt (*vajra*) for Indra); **101,** 8714, 8721, †8726, †8730 (°*vadha*°, Indra slew *V.* with the *vajra*); **103,** 8769, 8770 (*nihataṃ*).—§ 402 (Tīrthayātrāp.): III, **120,** †10264 (*jahi* . . . *V°ṃ yathā Devapatiḥ*).—§ 413 (do.): III, **135,** 10693 (°*ṃ hatvā Çacīpatiḥ*).—§ 443 (Nivātakavacayuddhap.): III, **168,** 12073 (*Bala-V°au*, vanquished by Indra).—§ 444 (do.): **171,** 12150 (°*sya vadhe*).—§ 539 (Kumbhakarṇādivadha): III, **287,** 16428 (°*saṅkāçaṃ Kumbhakarṇam*).—§ 544 (Yudhishṭhirāçvāsa): III, **292,** 16605 (*nihataḥ*).—§ 550 (Samayapālanap.): IV, **10,** 356 (°-*Vāsavayor iva*, sc. *saṃyuge*).—§ 551 (Kīcakavadhap.): IV, **22,** 727 (*hanishyāmi V°ṃ Devapatir yathā*).—§ 552 (Goharaṇap.): IV, **58,** 1868 (°-*Vāsavayor iva*, sc. *yuddhaṃ*); **59,** 1903 (°-*Vāsavayor iva*, *kiratoḥ çarajālāni*).—§ 555 (Indravijaya): V, **9,** 275, 277, 279 (°-*Vāsavayoḥ*, sc. *yuddhaṃ*), 280, 281, 282 (*Jṛmbhikāṃ V°nāçinīṃ*), 284 (°-*Vāsavayoḥ*, sc. *yuddhaṃ*), 285, 289 (°*vadhepsavaḥ*) (Tvashṭṛ created *V.* who assailed Indra); **10,** 290, 296, 299, 303, 306, 307, 309, 310, 322, 323, 326, 327, 329, 330, 331, 334 (*hate*) (notwithstanding the compact with *V.*, Indra wilily slew him); **13,** 412 (*tvadvīryanihate*); **16,** 500 (*hataḥ*), 504, †512 (*nihataḥ*); **17,** 522 (°*āsuravadhena*).—§ 555 (Sainyodyogap.): V, **18,** 555 (°*ṃ hatvā yathā* . . . *Çakraḥ*).—§ 565 (Gālavacarita): V, **109,** 3791 (*atra*—i.e. in the south—*vṛttena V°o 'pi Çakraçatrutvam īyivān*).—§ 568 (Vidulāputraçāsana): V, **134,** 4562 (*Indro V°vadhenaiva Mahendraḥ samapadyata*).—§ 573 (Ambopākhyānap.): V, **177,** 7024 (*jahi* . . . *yathā V°ṃ Purandaraḥ*).—§ 578 (Bhīshmavadhap.): VI, **45,** 1706 (*Vṛtra-Vāsavayor iva*, only B.); **48,** 1913 (*yathā vā V°-Vāsavau*, sc. *ayudhyetāṃ*).—§ 584 (do.): VI, **84,** 3721 (°*syeva Purandaraḥ*, sc. *vadhākaṅkshī*).—§ 585 (do.): VI, **90,** 4029 (*yathā vai V°-Vāsavau*, sc. *saṅgrāme vyavatishṭhetāṃ*).—§ 586 (do.): VI, **100,** 4553 (°*o devacamūṃ iva*, sc. *dravayate*), 4580 (°-*Vāsavayoḥ*, sc. *yuddhaṃ*). — § 587 (do.): VI, **110,** 5138 (*yathā V°ṃ Purandaraḥ*, sc. *avārayat*); **111,** 5183 (*yathā V°-Mahendrayoḥ*, sc. *yuddhaṃ*). — § 589 (Droṇābhishekap.): VII, **3,** 93 (*Çatakratum ivācintyaṃ purā V°eṇa nirjitaṃ*). — § 592 (Saṃçaptakavadhap.): VII, **30,** 1310 (*Indraṃ V°balād iva*).—§ 597 (Pratijñāp.): VII, **84,** 2992 (*Vāsavam iva* (read with B. °*asyeva*) *V°ṃ hantuṃ prayāsyataḥ*).—§ 599*c* (Jayadrathavadhap.): Formerly the *Asura V.* had defeated the gods; headed by *Indra* they then applied to *Brahmán*, who applied to *Vishṇu*, who said that *Tvashṭṛ*, in days of yore, had performed ascetic penances for a million of years, and that he had created *V.* with the permission of *Maheçvara* (i.e. Çiva); "you go to *Çiva* on the *Mandara* mountain." So they did, and *Çiva* gave to *Indra* his armour cased in which *Indra* slew *V.*: VII, **94,** 3457 (*Daityena*), 3458, 3459, 3461, 3462, 3464, 3472 (only B.), 3473 (°*camūṃ*), 3475.—§ 599 (do.): VII, **102,** 3814 (*jahi* . . . *yathā V°ṃ Purandaraḥ*); **118,** †4690 (°*endrayor yuddham iva*); **124,** 5008 (*yathā V°vadhe purā*).—§ 600 (Ghaṭotkacavadhap.): VII, **153,** 6633 (°*hatyai yathā devāḥ parivavruḥ Purandaraṃ*); **159,** 7089 (*yathā V°ṃ Purandaraḥ*, sc. *pratyudyayau*); **179,** †8177 (*yathā Çakro V°vadhe*).—§ 603 (Nārāyaṇāstramokshap.): VII, **196,** 9038 (*nihate* . . . *yathā V°e mahāsure*); **200,** 9323 (*vajraṃ V°e yathā Hariḥ*, sc. *vyasṛjat*).—§ 604 (Karṇap.): VIII, **5,** 143 (*Mahendreṇa yathā V°ḥ*, sc. *nihataḥ*).—§ 605 (do.): VIII, **14,** 565 (*yathā devāsure yuddhe V°-Vāsavayor iva*, sc. *samāgamaḥ*).—§ 608 (do.): VIII, **66,** †3356 (°*e hate bhagavān ivendraḥ*); **67,** †3375 (°*eṇa Vajrīva*, sc. *sametya*); **69,** †3398 (*Marutpatir V°m ivāttavajraḥ*, sc. *ahanishyat*); **71,** †3592 (*jahi* . . . *Purandaro-V°m iva*); **73,** 3675 (°*ḥ prāpyeva Vāsavaṃ*); **83,** †4260 (°*ṃ nihatyeva Sahasranetraḥ*); **87,** 4391 (*Indra-V°āv iva*), 4406 (do.); **89,** †4530 (*Mahendra-V°āv iva samprajaghnatuḥ*); **91,** 4798 (*çiro jahāra V°sya yathā Mahendraḥ*); **94,** 4948 (*yathā purā V°vadhe Çatakratuḥ*); **96,** 4983 (*hato Vajrabhṛtā*).—§ 611 (Çalyap.): IX, **17,** 954 (°*vadhe yathendraṃ*).—§ 613 (Gadāyuddhap.): IX, **33,** 1925 (*Çakro V°m ivāhvayan*).—§ 615*u* (Skanda): IX, **46,** 2709 (*jaghānāçu V°ṃ Devapatir yathā*).—§ 615 (Gadāyuddhap.): IX, **55,** 3128 (°-*Çakrāv ivāhave*); **56,** 3156 (*Cakro V°m ivāhvayan*); **57,** 3198 (°-*Vāsavayor iva*, sc. *yuddhaṃ*), 3212 (do., do.); **58,** 3251 (*māyayā cākshipat tejo V°sya Balasūdanaḥ*); **61,** 3395 (*Indreṇeva hi V°sya vadhaḥ*), 3402 (*hate*).—§ 623 (Rājadh.): XII, **15,** 438 (*Indro V°vadhena Mahendraḥ samapadyata*).—§ 641 (do.): XII, **98**ζ, 3660 (had been slain by Indra, C. has by error *Vṛttaṃ*).—§ 692 (Mokshadh.): XII, **280,** 10002 (*Daityena*), 10004 (10005), 10014; **281,** (†10082), 10085, 10086, 10092 (*V.* was instructed by Sanatkumāra about Vishṇu).—§ 693 (do.): XII, **282,** 10098, 10101 (*vinihataḥ*), 10102 (*nirjitaḥ*).—§ 693*b* (Vṛtravadha): XII, **282,** 10104, 10106, 10107, 10109, 10110 (*Asurendrasya*), 10115 (*dharmabhṛtāṃ varaḥ*), 10116, 10117, 10118, 10126, 10127, 10128 (*Daityapatiṃ*), 10131, 10132 (*viçvātmā*); **283,** 10143, 10147, 10151 (*Daityaṃ*), 10152, 10153, 10193, 10202 (from his blood arose *çikhaṇḍas*), 10204 (*nihataḥ*), 10207 (copious description of Indra's slaying *V.*).—§ 694 (Mokshadh.): XII, **284,** 10208 (°*vadhāt*), 10209.—§ 694*b* (Jvarotpatti): XII, **284,** 10266 (*dharmabhṛtāṃ varaḥ*), 10267, 10270 (*V.* was overtaken with fever (cf. also § 693*b*), then Indra slew him with his vajra; *V.* ascended to the world of Vishṇu).—§ 717*b* (Nārāyaṇīya):

XII, **343**, VII), ††13213 (*Tvāshṭrotpāditam*, the slaughter of *V.* narrated in accordance with § 555).—§ 719*b* (Gautamī-lubdhaka-vyāla-Mṛtyu-Kālasaṃv.): XIII, **1**, †32 (°*m hatvā Devarāṭ*).—§ 778*b* (Saṃvartta-Maruttīya): XIV, **9**, †246 (*tridivaṃ prāg jahāra*).—§ 779*b* (Açvamedhikap.): In ancient times the earth was encompassed by *V.*; the seat of smell thus having been taken away, bad odours arose, and *Indra* hurled his thunderbolt at *V.*; *V.* then entered the waters, and taste thereby being taken away, *Indra* again hurled his thunderbolt at him. So it happened successively with light (colour and form), wind (touch) and ether (sound). Then *V.* suddenly entered *Indra*, who was then overcome with stupefaction (*moha*); *Vasishṭha* having restored him to consciousness by the *Rathantara sāman*, Indra in his own body slew *V.* with his invisible thunderbolt. This religious mystery was recited by *Indra* to the *maharshis* and by them to *Kṛshṇa*: XIV, **11**, 298 (*Indrasya saha V°eṇa yuddhaṃ*), 299, 301, 302, 304, 306, 308, 310, 311.—§ 785 (Anugītāp.): XIV, **76**, 2195 (°*eṇeva Çatakratoḥ*, sc. *yuddhaṃ*). Cf. Asura, Asuraçreshṭha, Asurendra, Daitya, Daityapati, Daityendra, Dānava, Dānavendra, Ditija, Surāri, Tvāshṭra, Viçvātman.

Vṛtraçatru, Vṛtrahan, Vṛtrahantṛ, Vṛtranisūdana = Indra, q.v.

[Vṛtra-vadha(ḥ)] ("the killing of Vṛtra"): § 693*b* (Mokshadh.). *Bhīshma* said: In days of yore, *Indra*, accompanied by the celestial forces, proceeded in his chariot, and beheld As. *Vṛtra*, stationed before him like a mountain, 500 *yojanas* in height and 300 in circumference. *Indra* was struck with palsy in the lower extremities. On the eve of that great battle between D. and As. there arose loud shouts from both sides, etc. *Vṛtra* felt neither awe nor fear. Then the encounter commenced; the entire welkin was enveloped by the combatants of both sides; all the gods with *Brahmán*, and Ṛ., Si., G., and Aps. on their chariots had assembled in order to see the battle. *Vṛtra* shot rocks, the gods arrows; *Vṛtra* employed illusion; *Indra* was stupefied; *Vasishṭha* restored him to his senses by the *Rathantara*, pointing out to him *Brahmán*, etc. (*a*). *Indra*, by *yoga*, dispelled the illusions of *Vṛtra*. *Bṛhaspati* (the son of *Aṅgiras*) and Ṛ. repaired to *Çiva*, whose energy became a fever and penetrated *Vṛtra*; *Vishṇu* entered the thunderbolt of *Indra*; *Bṛhaspati*, *Vasishṭha*, and Ṛ. urged *Indra* to slay *Vṛtra*, and so did *Çiva*, saying that *Vṛtra* was the soul of the universe, capable of going everywhere; for 60,000 years *Vṛtra* had practised penances in order to obtain strength; *Brahmán* had given him the boons he had solicited: the greatness of *yogins*, large powers of illusions, excess of might, etc.; *Çiva* told *Indra* to slay him with *yoga*, and imparted to him his own energy. D. and Ṛ. uttered loud cheers, etc. Suddenly all As. were afflicted with the loss of memory; in a trice their powers of illusion also disappeared. Ṛ. and D. praised *Çakra* and *Çiva* (XII, **282**). Description of the symptoms that appeared on the body of *Vṛtra* when he was overtaken by that fever: His memory issued out of his mouth in form of a dreadful jackal. Inauspicious omens. *Indra* looked hard at him; *Vṛtra* yawned and uttered superhuman cries; while *Vṛtra* was yawning *Indra* hurled his thunderbolt at him and slew him; [XII, **287**, 58 ff. = 10,267 ff.: the thunderbolt cut *Vṛtra* into two halves; *Vṛtra* then came to the highest region of *Vishṇu*, for it was by his devotion to *Vishṇu* that he had overwhelmed the universe]; then *Indra* entered heaven with that thunderbolt pervaded by *Vishṇu*. Then *Brahmavadhyā* (description) issued out of the body of the slain *Vṛtra*. A little while after, when *Indra* was proceeding towards heaven, she seized him and stuck to him. *Indra* entered the fibres of a lotus stalk and dwelt there for many years. But *Brahmavadhyā* pursued him closely, and deprived him of all his energy. At last he repaired to *Brahmán*, who made her leave *Indra* by apportioning one quarter to *Agni* (whence it should enter him who did not offer oblations of seed, etc. to *Agni*); one quarter to the trees, herbs, and all kinds of grass (whence it should possess the men who would cut or tear any of them at *parvan*-days); one quarter to the *Apsarases* (whence it should possess that man who would cohabit with women during their courses); and one quarter to the waters (whence it should possess that man who would cast into the waters phlegm and urine and excrements). With *Brahmán's* permission *Indra* then performed a horse-sacrifice and thereby became cleansed, regained his prosperity, and slew thousands of foes. From the blood of *Vṛtra* were born the *çikhaṇḍāḥ* (the crests of cocks (?) or name of a plant, BR.), which, for this reason, must not be eaten by the twice-born classes, etc. Blessing upon the reciter (XII, **283**).

Vṛtta[1], a serpent. § 47 (Sarpanāmak.): I, **35**, 1555 (read with B. *Vṛttasaṃvartakau*; C. has *Vṛttasaṃvartako*). Cf. Avṛtta.

Vṛtta[2] (XII, 3660), v. Vṛtra.

Vṛttasaṃvartaka, v. Vṛtta[1].

Vṛtti ("moral conduct", personif.) = Nīti: XII, 4432.

Vṛttāvṛttakara = Çiva (1000 names[2]).

Vudvudā, v. Budbudā.

Vyaçva, name of two ancient kings. § 267 (Yamasabhāv.): II, **8**, 323, 328 (in the palace of Yama).

Vyādha[1] ("the hunter" or "the fowler") = Dharmavyādha: III, 13696, 13703, (13713), 13761, (13762), (13843), (†13867), (13871), (13899), (13911), (13922), (13949), 13960, (13961), (14002), (14018), 14030, 14032, (14034), (14041), (14063), (14079), 14094.—Do.[2] = Çiva: VII, 2877 (C. *Vyādhyāya*), 2878 (*Vyādhāya*).

Vyādhi, pl. (°*ayaḥ*) ("diseases", personif.). § 594 (Mṛtyu): VII, **54**, 2107.—Do.[2] = Çiva (1000 names).

Vyādhi, sg., **Vyādhihan, Vyādhīnām āgamaḥ** = Çiva (1000 names[1]).

Vyādiçaḥ (pl.) = Vishṇu (1000 names).

Vyāghra = Çiva (1000 names[1-2]).

***vyāghra**, pl. (°*āḥ*) ("tigers"). § 113 (Aṃçāvat.): I, **66**, 2572 (among the offspring of Pulaha).—§ 127 (do.): I, **66**, 2629 (among the offspring of Çārdūlī).

Vyāghradatta[1], one or more Pāṇḍava warriors. § 572 (Rathātirathasaṅkhyānap.): V, **171**, 5911 (among the rathas in the army of Yudhishṭhira).—§ 590 (Droṇabhishekap.): VII, **16**δ, 650 (*Pāñcālyaḥ*), 652 (do.), 655 (slain by Droṇa).—§ 592 (Saṃçaptakavadhap.): VII, **23**ο, 1001 (proceeded against Droṇa, description of his horses). § 604 (Karṇap.): VIII, **6**, 166 (had been slain by Açvatthāman). Cf. Pāñcālya.

Vyāghradatta[2], a Kuru warrior (a Magadha prince). § 599 (Jayadrathavadhap.): VII, **106**, 3978 (resisted Sātyaki); **107**, 4044 (slain by Sātyaki) [4045 (*Māgadhasya sute*)].

Vyāghraketu, a Pāñçāla prince. § 607 (Karṇap.): VIII, **56**νν, 2735 (slain by Karṇa).

Vyāghrāksha, a warrior of Skanda. § 615*u* (Skanda): IX, **45**η, 2561.

Vyāghrapāda, a ṛshi. § 730*g* (Upamanyu): XIII, **14**, 701 (*ṛshiḥ*, father of Upamanyu, lived in the Kṛtayuga).

Vyagra = Vishṇu (1000 names).

***vyākaraṇa** ("grammar"): XII, 7372; XIII, 4303.

Vyākaraṇottara, Vyakta(ṃ) = Çiva (1000 names[2]).

Vyaktastha = Kṛshṇa: XII, 1640.

Vyaktāvyakta(ḥ) = Sūrya: III, 151. — Do.[2] = Çiva (1000 names[1-2]).

Vyaktāvyaktakara = Vishṇu: XII, 13488.

Vyāla = Vishṇu (1000 names).

Vyālarūpa = Çiva (1000 names[2]).

Vyālayajñopavītin = Kṛshṇa: XII, 1669.—Do.[2] = Çiva (1000 names[1]).

Vyāna[1], one of the vital breaths. § 485 (Brāhmaṇavyādhas., Pativratopākhyāna): III, **213**, 13967.—§ 660*b* (Bhṛgu-Bharadvājasaṃv.): XII, **184**, 6844; **185**, 6873 (*g:* That breath which operates, residing in all the joints of men's bodies, is called *V.*).—§ 662*b* (Jāpakop.): XII, **200**ϵ, 7346. —§ 667 (Mokshadh.): XII, **213**, 7759 (°*odānau*).—§ 704 (Mokshadh.): XII, **302**, 11124.—§ 714*g* (Samāna): XII, **329**, 12397 (son of Udāna; from him arose Apāna).—§ 782*b* (Brāhmaṇagītā): XIV, **20**, 612, 614; **21**, †653; **23**, 685, 687 (*vāyuḥ*), 688, 696, 697, 699, 700, 705, 706 (the contention among the vital breaths about superiority); **24**, 712, 718, 719, 722, 726, 727.—§ 782*g* (Guruçishyasaṃv.): XIV, **42**, 1109.

Vyāna[2] = Çiva (1000 names[1]).

Vyāpin, Vyāpta = Vishṇu (1000 names).

Vyāsa, a ṛshi, the supposed compiler of Mhbhr., son of Parāçara and Satyavatī, father of Çuka, and, with the wives of Vicitravīrya, of Dhṛtarāshṭra, Pāṇḍu, and Vidura; his proper name is Kṛshṇa (K.), and on account of his being born on an island (*dvīpa*) he is called Dvaipāyana (D.) and Kṛshṇa-Dvaipāyana (K.-D.); he arranged the Vedas (therefore called Vyāsa and Vedavyāsa): § 1 (Anukram.): I, **1**, [10 (*Kṛshṇa-Dvaipāyanaproktāḥ . . . kathāḥ*), 17 (*Dvaipāyanena yat proktaṃ Purāṇaṃ paramarshiṇā*, i.e. the Mhbhr.), 20 (D.)], 21 (°*sya . . . saṃhitāṃ*, i.e. the Mhbhr.).—§ 2 (do.): I, **1**, 25 (*mataṃ . . . V°sya*).—§ 4 (do.): I, **1**, [54 (*vyasya Vedaṃ sanātanam / itihāsam imaṃ cakre puṇyaṃ Satyavatīsutaḥ*, sc. the Mhbhr.), 55 (*Parāçarātmajaḥ*, D.), 56 (*ṛsheḥ*, D.), 59 (*Vāsaveyaḥ*), 60 (K.)], 75 (*Satyavatīsutaḥ*), 76 (*Vedavyāsaḥ*), 79, [80 (*muniḥ*, D.)], 83 (Gaṇeça wrote the Mhbhr. after *V.'s* dictation), [94 (K.-D., all to § 171), 99 (D., all to § 70), 103 (D., taught his disciples and his son Çuka the Mhbhr.)], 107 (*Vaiçampāyanaḥ . . . çishyo V°sya*), [†213 (D.)].—[§ 5 (do.): I, **1**, 221 (D.)].—§ 7 (do.): I, **1**, 246 (*atropanishadaṃ puṇyāṃ Kṛshṇa-Dvaipayano 'bravīt*)].—§ 10 (Parvasaṅgr.): I, **2**, 358 (*etat parvaçataṃ pūrṇaṃ V°enoktaṃ*).—§ 11 (do.): I, **2**, [368 (D.), 376 (K.-D.)], 382, 384, 405, 423, 431, 432, 519, 528, 538, [541 (*Pārāçāryeṇa*), 577 (D.)], 590 (*paramarshiṇā*), 592, [614 (*ṛsheḥ*, K.)], 627, 640 (*etad ashṭādaçam parva proktaṃ V°ena*), 646, [655 (D.)].—§ 26 (Āstīkap., Jaratkāru): I, **13**, [1025 (*Kṛshṇa-Dvaipāyanaproktaṃ*, sc. the Āstīkaparvan)]; 1026 (*çishyo V°sya*, sc. Lomaharshaṇa). —§ 59 (Sarpasattra): I, **53**, 2047 (*putraçishyasahāyavān*, among the sadasyas at the snake-sacrifice of Janamejaya).— [§ 61 (do.): I, **55**, †2103 (*Kṛshṇasya . . . Satyavatyāḥ sutasya*, performed a sacrifice), †2105 (*ṛtvik samo nāsti . . . Dvaipāyanena*)].—§ 70 (Ādivaṃçāvatāraṇap.): I, **59**, 2199 (*kathā V°sampannāḥ*), 2202 (*akathayac citram ākhyānaṃ Bhāratam*), [2203 (K.-D.), 2206 (*Kṛshṇa-Dvaipāyanamataṃ Mahābhāratam*)]; **60**, [2208 (K.-D.), 2220 (K.)], 2221, [2227 (K.-D.)], (2228) (at the snake-sacrifice of Janamejaya *V.* caused his disciple Vaiçampāyana to recite the Mhbhr.).— § 71 (do.): I, **61**, 2232 (*mataṃ . . . V°sya*).—§ 72 (do.): I, **62**, [2294 (*anukramaḥ . . . Kṛshṇa-Dvaipāyaneritaḥ*)], 2295 (*mataṃ . . . V°sya*), [2296 (*Satyavatyātmajena*)], 2305, [2309 (K.-D.), 2322 (K.-D.), 2324 (*Kṛshṇaproktāṃ . . . kathāṃ*, i.e. the Mhbhr.), 2332 (*muniḥ*, K.-D.)].—§ 77 (cf. Ādivaṃçāvatāraṇa): When *Satyavatī* plied her boat on the Yamunā, the *ṛshi Parāçara*, engaged in a tīrthayātrā, enveloped the whole region and obtained her love by promising that she should nevertheless retain her virginity, and causing her to emit a sweet scent to the distance of a yojana, whence she was named *Gandhavatī* or *Yojanagandhā*. On that very day she brought forth *Kṛshṇa*, surnamed *Dvaipāyana*, because he was born on an island (*dvīpa*) in the *Yamunā*, and *Vyāsa* because he arranged (*vivyāsa*) the *Vedas*. He set his mind on ascetism and went away, saying to his mother: "as soon as remembered by thee I shall appear": I, **63**, [2414 (*Pārāçaryaḥ*), 2415 (D.), 2416 (etymology, D.)], 2417 (etymology).—§ 78 (do.): *V.* taught *Sumantu, Jaimini, Paila*, his own son *Çuka*, and *Vaiçampāyana* the *Vedas*, of which the Mhbhr. was the fifth one, and the texts of the *Bhārata* were published by each of them separately.— [§ 83 (Ādivaṃçāvataraṇa): I, **63**, 2441 (K.-D.), 2442 (D.) (begot Dhṛtarāshṭra, Pāṇḍu, and Vidura, cf. § 171)].— [§ 130*c* (Dhṛtarāshṭra): I, **67**, 2719 (*Dhṛtarāshṭraḥ Kṛshṇa-Dvaipāyanātmajaḥ*)]. — § 133 (Dushyanta): I, **70**, 2888 (°*granthasamāçritaiḥ*, sc. *dvijaiḥ*).—[§ 156 (Pūruvaṃç.): I, **95**, 3759 (D.), ††3802 (D., son of Satyavatī and Parāçara)]. —[§ 157 (do.): I, **95**, ††3806 (D., *ṛshiṃ*, cf. § 171), ††3809 D., cf. § 180)].—§ 160 (do.): I, **95**, ††3841 (*Bhārataṃ . . . V°ena proktaṃ*).—§ 171 (Vicitravīryasutotpatti): I, **105**, [4235 (*Pārāçaryaḥ*, D.)], 4236 (°*tvaṃ*, origin of the name; K., origin of the name), [4244 (K.-D.)], 4247, (4258), (4265); **106**, 4281 (*Satyavatīsutaḥ*), 4290 (*Satyavatīputraḥ*), [4301 (*Viduraḥ Kṛshṇa-Dvaipāyanātmajaḥ*), 4302 (K.-D.), 4304 (D.)] (Satyavatī thought of *V.*, who immediately appeared, and at her injunction begot Dhṛtarāshṭra and Pāṇḍu on the wives of Vicitravīrya and Vidura on a çūdra woman).—[§ 174 (Dhṛtarāshṭravivāha): I, **110**, 4365 (K.)].—§ 180 (Gāndhārīputrotpatti): I, **115**, 4489 (*Dvaipāyanam*), [4495 (D.)], (4499), 4505 (*V.* granted Gāndhārī that she should get 100 sons and a daughter).—§ 181 (Duḥçalotpatti): I, **116**, 4525, [4536 (K.-D.)], (4537) (do.).— [§ 184 (Pāṇḍu): I, **119**, 4595 (K.-D.), all. to § 171)].— [§ 188 (do.): I, **122**, 4738 (do., do.)].—§ 196 (cf. Sambhavap.): After the çrāddha of *Pāṇḍu* was over, *V.*, foreboding the destruction of the Kauravas, prevailed upon *Satyavatī*, that she, with *Ambikā* and *Kausalyā* (i.e. Ambālikā) retired to the forest to practise *yoga*. There they practised severe austerities, and at last died: I, **128**, 4968.—§ 208 (Astradarçana): I, **134**, 5313.—§ 214 (Hiḍimbavadhap.): I, **156**, [6088 (K.-D.)], (6089), 6094 (*Satyavatīsutaḥ*), (6095), [6100 (D.)], 6102 (*ṛshiḥ*, *V.* told the Pāṇḍavas and Kuntī to go to Ekacakra).—§ 215 (Bakavadhap.): I, **162**, 6266 (*pravāca*, a statement of his quoted).—§ 220 (Caitrarathap.): I, **169**, 6421 (*Satyavatīsutaḥ*), (6426) (having narrated the story of a former birth of Draupadī, *V.* told the Pāṇḍavas to go to her svayaṃvara).—§ 221 (do.): I, **170**, 6437 (*gate*).—§ 221*b* (Gaṅgā): I, **170**, 6457 (*abravīt*, a statement of his about the Gaṅgā is quoted). — [§ 231 (Svayaṃvarap.): I, **185**, 6946 (*muniṃ*, D.)]. — § 235 (Svayaṃvarap.): I, **190**, 7128 (*mataṃ . . . V°syāpi*, all. to § 220); [**191**, 7145 (*Dvaipāyanavacaḥ*, do.)].—§ 237 (Vaivāhikap.): I, [**195**, 7251 (D.)]; **196**, [7252 (K.), 7254 (K.)], (7257), (7270), 7272 (*Dvaipāyanaḥ*), [7274

(D.)] (was questioned by Drupada about the wedding of Draupadī to the five Pāṇḍavas). — § 238 (Pañcendrop.): I, **197**, (7275), (7283), (†7289), (†7303), †7313 (told the Pañcendropākhyāna).—§ 239 (do.): I, **197**, (7319), (told of a former birth of Draupadī).—[§ 244 (Rājyalābhap.): I, **207**, 7573 (*Dvaipayanapurogamāḥ*, sc. *mahārathāḥ*, i.e. the Pāṇḍavas)].—§ 261 (Sabhākriyāp.): II, **1**, (introductory çloka). — § 264 (Sabhākriyap.): II, **4a**, 106 (K.-D.; *Vyāsaçishyāḥ* (enumerated)).—[§ 272 (Rājasūyārambhap.): II, **13**, 542 (*mantribhiḥ* . . . *Dhaumya-Dvaipāyanādyaiḥ*)].—[§ 286 (Rājasūyikap.): II, **33**, 1220 (*Dhaumya-Dvaipāyana-mukhair ṛtvigbhiḥ*), 1237 (D.), 1238 (*Satyavatīsutaḥ*, acted as brahman priest at the rājasūya of Yudhishṭhira)].—[§ 289 (Arghāharaṇap.): II, **37**, 1346 (D.)].—§ 293 (Dyūtap.): II, **46**, 1628, 1631, [1633 (K.)], 1637 (K.-D.), 1646 (do.), [1649 (D.), 1653 (D.)] (*V.* foretold the destruction that would happen after thirteen years).—§ 296 (do.): II, **53**, 1917 (present at the anointing of Yudhishṭhira).—[§ 305 (Anudyūtap.): II, **78**, 2573 (D., K. had instructed Yudhishṭhira in Vāraṇāvata)].—§ 308 (Āraṇyakap.): III, **1** (introductory çloka).—§ 313 (do.): III, [**7**, 309 (K.-D.) (warned Duryodhana, etc.)]; **8**, (311) (warned Dhṛtarāshṭra). —§ 314 (do.): III, **9**, (326), (339) (narrated the discourse between Indra and Surabhi).—§ 315 (Maitreyaçāpa): III, **10**, (349), 352 (took his leave).—§ 317*b* (Kṛshṇa Vāsudeva): III, **12**, 476 (*abravīt*, a statement of his about Kṛshṇa is quoted).—§ 317 (Arjunābhigamanap.): III, **12**, 572 (all. to § 214).—[§ 322 (Dvaitavanapr.): III, **24**, 924 (*brāhmaṇāḥ* . . . *Dvaipāyanaprabhṛtayaḥ*, wait upon Yudhishṭhira)].—[§ 324 (do.): III, **26a**, 985 (D. worshipped Yudhishṭhira)]. —§ 327 (Draupadīparitāpav.): III, **29**, 1112 (*pitāmahaḥ*); **31**, 1171. — § 329 (Kāmyakavanapr.): III, **36**, 1432 (*Satyavatīsutaḥ*), (1434), [1438 (*Pārāçaryaḥ*)], 1449 (*Satya-vatīsutaḥ*), 1451 (°*vākyam*) (*V.* imparted the Pratismṛti knowledge to Yudhishṭhira).—[§ 330 (Indradarçana): III, **37**, 1465 (K.-D., all. to § 329)].—[§ 340 (Indralokābhiga-manap.): III, **48**, 1915 (D. had told Dhṛtarāshṭra of Arjuna's arrival to the abode of Indra)].—§ 364 (Tīrtha-yātrāp.): III, **83**, 6062 (had mingled all the tīrthas into Miçraka), 6066 (in Vyāsasthalī, *V.*, from grief for his son, had resolved to give up life, but the gods revived him).—§ 367 (Pṛthūdaka): III, **83**, 7017 (had praised the tīrtha Pṛthudaka).—§ 376 (Tīrthayātrāp.): III, **85**, 8264 (*tapatām varaḥ*, among the ṛshis who expected Yudhishṭhira).—§ 377 (Dhaumyatīrthak.): III, **86**, 8279 (knew the real nature of Kṛshṇa and Arjuna).—§ 378 (Tīrthayātrāp.): III, **93**, 8475, [8482 (D.)] (came to the Pāṇḍavas in the Kāmyaka forest).—§ 519 (Vrīhidrauṇikap.): III, **259**, 15377 (*Satyavatīsutaḥ*, came to the Pāṇḍavas in the forest), 15380 (15397).—§ 520 (Mudgala): III, **260**, (15407); **261**, (15477), 15491 (told the story of Mudgala to Yudhishṭhira). — § 561 (Yāna-sandhip.): V, **51**, 2038 (*çrutaḥ* . . . *V°mukhāt*, sc. Bhīma-sena); **61**, 2385 (*Dvaipāyanaḥ*, a statement of his is quoted); **67**, 2520, [2521 (*abravīt*, K.-D.)], (†2522) (caused Sañjaya to tell Dhṛtarāshṭra of the might of Kṛshṇa and Arjuna); **69**, (2549) (warned Dhṛtarāshṭra). — § 569 (Bhagava-dyānap.): V, **147**, 4994 (*mahāmunim*, all. to § 171).—§ 573 (Ambopākhyānap.): V, **186**, 7344 (consulted by Bhīshma). —§ 574 (Jambūkh.): VI, **2**, 36 (*Satyavatīsutaḥ*), (39), 43 (only B.) (gave celestial vision to Sañjaya); **3**, (68) (described the omens), (131), (†133); **4**, 155, 162 (*viprarsheḥ*).—§ 576 (Bhagavadgītāp.): VI, [**15**, 594 (*Pārāçaryāya*, all. to § 574)]; **17**, 636 (*yatha* . . . *V°ḥ Kṛshṇa-Dvaipāyano 'bravīt*); **23**, 817 (all. to § 574), [819 (D., had prevented Duryodhana)]; **34**, 1217 (knew Kṛshṇa as the supreme Lord), 1241 (*munīnām apy aham V°aḥ*, sc. *asmi*, says Kṛshṇa); **42**, 1529 (°*prasādāt*, all. to § 574).—§ 578 (Bhīshmavadhap.): VI, **49**, 1995.—§ 581 (do.): VI, **66**ο, 2999 (Bhīshma had heard of the glory of Kṛshṇa from *V.*); [**67**ρ, 3040 (D. praised Kṛshṇa)].—[§ 588 (do.): VI, **122**, 5827 (K.-D., had told Bhīshma that Karṇa was the son of Kuntī)].—§ 594 (Abhimanyuvadhap.): VII, **52**, [2003 (K.-D., came to console Yudhishṭhira)], 2010, (2011), (2023); **54**, (2125) (told the story of Akampana to Yudhishṭhira).—§ 595 (do.): VI, **55**, (2138) (told the story of Sṛñjaya to Yudhishṭhira); **71**, (2451), (2459), 2474 (comforted Yudhishṭhira).—§ 599 (Jayadratha-vadhap.): VII, **149**, 6474 (only B.).—§ 600 (Ghaṭotkaca-vadhap.): VII, **183**, 8351, (8352), 8361 (comforted Yudhi-shṭhira).—§ 601 (Droṇavadhap.): VII, **184**, 8362.—[§ 602 (do.): VII, **192**, 8881 (*ṛsheḥ prasādāt Kṛshṇasya Satyavatyāḥ sutasya*, all. to § 574)].—§ 603 (Nārāyaṇāstramokshap.): VII, **201**, 9438 (*Vedavyāsam*), (9446), (9471) (discoursed on Nārāyaṇa to Açvatthāman); **202**, 9496, (9502), (9591), [9645 (*Parāçarasutaḥ*)] (discoursed on Çiva to Arjuna).—[§ 608 (Karṇap.): VIII, **96**αω[1], 5010 (K.-D., had several times told that Arjuna and Kṛshṇa are Nara and Nārāyaṇa)]. —[§ 612 (Hradapraveçap.): IX, **29**, 1605 (K.-D.), 1606 (D.), 1612 (D.), 1615 (K.-D.) (caused Sātyaki to set Sañjaya free)].—[§ 615*ee* (Ādityatīrtha): IX, **49**, 2848 (D.), 2851 (D., bathed in the Ādityatīrtha)].—§ 615 (Gadāyuddhap.): IX, **62**, [3491 (K.-D., a statement of his about Kṛshṇa quoted)], 3499 (only B.); **63**, [3531 (K.), 3538 (K.), 3574 (D.)], 3579.—§ 617 (Aishīkap.): X, **13**, 661 (K.-D.); **15**, [698 (D.)], (705), (720), [721 (D.)]; **16**, (739), [743 (K.)] (permitted Açvatthāman to let his aishīka weapon fall on the embryos of the Pāṇḍavas).—§ 618 (Jalapradānikap.): XI, **1**β, [14 (K.-D.)], 31; **8**ε, [194 (K.-D.), 204 (K.-D.)], (205), 242, 245 (*Satyavatīsutaḥ*) (comforted Dhṛtarāshṭra); **9**, 246 (*gate*); [**14**, 362 (*Satyavatīputraḥ*, appeased Gāndhārī)].—§ 619 (Strīvilāpap.): XI, **16**, [429 (K. gave spiritual sight to Gāndhārī)], 435.—[§ 621 (Rājadh.): XII, **1**β, 4 (D. came to the Pāṇḍavas), 9 (*munibhiḥ* . . . *Kṛshṇa-Dvaipāyanādibhiḥ*)].—§ 628 (do.): XII, **23**, [651 (D.)], (652), (668), (685), (695) (instructed Yudhishṭhira); [**24**, 698 (K.-D.)] (do.).—§ 629 (do.): XII, **25**, 732 (*Dvaipā-yanavacaḥ*), 735 (*yogavidām varaḥ*), (†736) (instructed Yudhi-shṭhira).—§ 630 (do.): XII, **27**, 826 (*munisattamaḥ*), (827) (instructed Yudhishṭhira).—§ 631 (do.): XII, **28**, 833, (834) (related the discourse delivered by Açman to Janaka). —§ 634 (Rājadh.): XII, **31**, 1133 (*yathā* . . . *prāha V°ḥ*). —§ 635 (Rājadh.): XII, **32**, [1135 (K.-D.)], (1136), (1146); **33**, [1172 (D.)], (1173); **34**, (1209); **35**, (1241); **36**, (1293) (instructed Yudhishṭhira); **37**, 1348 (*vedavidām varaḥ*, told Yudhishṭhira to consult Bhīshma), 1360 (*Satya-vatīsutam*), 1364, 1367, (γ), [1370 (D.)].—§ 637 (do.): XII, **47**η, 1592 (*vedavidushā*, among the ṛshis who surrounded Bhīshma).—§ 639 (do.): XII, **50**, 1815 (°*ādīn ṛshimukhyān*); **52**, 1883 (°*sahitāḥ* . . . *maharshayaḥ*).—§ 640 (do.): XII, **58**γ, 2116.—§ 641 (do.): XII, **59**, 2124 (°*ādīn ṛshīn*).—[§ 664 (Mokshadh.): XII, **207**β, 7520 (K.-D. had praised Kṛshṇa)].—§ 677 (do.): XII, **232**, 8483, 8485 (*Kṛshṇa-Dvaipāyanam*), (8488); **233**, (8510); **234**, (8555); **235**, (8575); **236**, (8613); **237**, (8645); **238**, (8688), (8690); **239**, (8713); **240**, (8738); **241**, (8768); [**242**, 8806 (*Parāçarasutaḥ*)]; **243**, (8828), (8836); **244**, (8854); **245**, (8887); **246**, (8916); **247**, (8951); **248**, (8975);

(8981); **249,** (8999); **250,** (9024); **251,** (9039); **252,** (†9064); **253,** (9088); **254,** (9101); **255,** (9116); [**256,** 9131 (D.)] (instructed his son Çuka).—§ 696*b* (Dakshaprokta-Çivasahasranāmastotra): XII, **285,** 10484 (*Parāçarasutaḥ*, explained the effect of reciting the 1000 names of Çiva).—§ 710 (Mokshadh.): XII, **322,** (12047), [12137 (D.)] (instructed Çuka).—§ 712 (Çukotpatti): XII, **324,** 12158 (father of Çuka), 12159 [12169 (K.-D.), 12182 (K.), 12184 (D.)]; **325,** [12187 (*Satyavatīsutaḥ*)], 12189, 12190, 12192 (*V.* gratified Çiva, who granted him that he should get a son; when *V.* one day saw Ghṛtācī his seed came out and fell on his fire-stick (*araṇi*), from that arose Çuka Āraṇeya).—§ 713 (Çukakṛti): XII, **326,** 12219 (told Çuka to go to Janaka).—§ 714 (Çukakṛtya): XII, **328,** 12337 (enumeration of his four disciples: Sumantu, etc.), 12338, 12340, 12344 (*Pārāçaryo mahāmuniḥ*), 12346, 12353 (*Parāçarātmajaḥ*); **329,** 12365 (°*çishyāḥ*), [12369 (*Parāçarasutaḥ*)], 12371, 12374, [12380 (K.-D.)], 12386, 12389, 12391, [12421 (*Parāçarasutaḥ*)] (*V.* instructed his disciples and Çuka).—§ 716 (Çukābhipatana): XII, [**332,** 12573 (K.-D., K.)]; **333,** 12577 (*suto V°sya*, i.e. Çuka); **334,** 12627, [12640 (K.-D.)], 12648 (*mahāyogī*) (*V.* grieved for his son Çuka and was comforted by Çiva).—§ 717*b* (Nārāyaṇīya): XII, [**340,** 13000 (K.-D., preceptor of Vaiçampāyana, etc.)]; **341,** 13011 (*çishyo V°sya*, i.e. Vaiçampāyana), 13025 (*Kṛshṇa-Dvaipāyano V°o Vedavyāsaḥ*), 13030 (*Parāçarasutaḥ*), (13097), (13100), [13119 (*Vedavyāsena*), 13121 (D.)] (instructed his disciples and Çuka about Nārāyaṇa (Vishṇu)); **342,** 13129; **344,** 13312 (*Kṛshṇa-Dvaipāyanam*), 13333; **347,** [13434 (*Gandhavatīsutaḥ*)], 13438 (*Kṛshṇa-Dvaipāyanam*, incarnation of Nārāyaṇa); **348,** 13457; **349,** 13610 (*gurur mama*, sc. Vaiçampāyana's), 13634 (learnt from Nārada the *ekāntagati*, i.e. the religion of Nārāyaṇa and taught it to Yudhishṭhira); **350,** [†13640 (*Nārāyaṇasyāṃçajaṃ . . . Dvaipāyanam*)], †13641 (*ajaṃ purāṇam*), [13643 (*Parāçarasya dāyadaḥ Kṛshṇa-Dvaipāyanaḥ*)], 13644, (13652), 13701 (*V.* was an incarnation of a portion of Nārāyaṇa, which was formerly born as Apāntaratamas); **351,** 13716, 13719 (discoursed on the unity of the purushas).—[§ 725 (Ānuçāsanik.): XIII, **9,** 421 (K.)].—[§ 730 (Ānuçāsanik.): XIII, **14,** 608 (*Dvaipāyanaprabhṛtayaḥ . . . ṛshayaḥ*), (δ), 680 (*Vedavyāsaç ca . . . Parāçarasutaḥ*); **18,** 1296 (K.-D. had recited the 1000 names of Çiva, when he performed austerities in order to get a son), (κκ), 1337 (*Vedavyāsaḥ*, son of Parāçara), 1338 (*K.* will become a saptarshi in the creation of Manu Sāvarṇa)]. — § 732 (do.): XIII, **24,** 1677 (instructed Bhīshma), [1679 (*Parāçara-çarīrajaḥ*)].—§ 734 (do.): XIII, **26*a*,** 1762 (among those who came to see Bhīshma).—§ 746 (do.): XIII, **81,** [3808 (K.-D.)], 3812, (3814) (instructed Çuka).—§ 762*b* (Kīṭop.): XIII, **117,** [5728 (*Dvaipāyanasya saṃvādaṃ kīṭasya ca*), 5729 (K.-D.)], (5731); **118,** (5752), (5771); **119,** [5778 (K.-D.)], (5779), [5784 (K.-D.)], (5785), 5791 (the story of *V.* and the worm).—§ 763*b* (Maitreyabhikshā): XIII, **120,** [5794 (*Maitreyasya ca saṃvādaṃ Kṛshṇa-Dvaipāyanasya ca*), 5795 (K.-D.), 5797 (K.), 5798 (K.)], (5802), 5823 (the story of Maitreya's feeding *V.*; *V.'s* discourse on gifts).—§ 766 (Ānuçāsanik.): XIII, **125,** 5922 (*yathā . . . V°ḥ purā kathitavān*); **134,** 6196 (had communicated to Bhīshma the mysteries of dharma (chapters **125-134**)).—§ 768 (do.): XIII, [**139*a*,** 6298 (K.-D.)]; **148,** 6912, 6925 (Bhīshma had heard from *V.* of the glory of Kṛshṇa and Arjuna).—§ 769 (do.): XIII, **149,** [6949 (*Vedavyāsaḥ*)], 7077 (*stavaṃ bhagavato Vishṇor V°ena kīrtitaṃ*, i.e. the 1000 names of Vishṇu).—§ 770 (do.): XIII, **151,** 7082 (°*proktaṃ mantraṃ*, i.e. vv. 7088–89), (κ), 7121.—[§ 775 (do.): XIII, **166*a*,** 7639 (K.-D.)].—§ 776 (do.): XIII, **167,** 7693 (*Satyavatīsutaḥ*), 7696.—§ 777 (Svargārohaṇik. p.): XIII, **168,** 7718 (*Pārāçaryena*), [7721 (*Dvaipāyanādīn viprān*), 7737 (*çrutaṃ devarahasyan te Kṛshṇa-Dvaipāyanād api*)], 7750 (had told that Kṛshṇa and Arjuna are Nara and Nārāyaṇa); **169,** 7762, 7764, (β), 7778, 7795.—§ 778 (Açvamedhikap.): XIV, **2,** [24 (K.-D.)], 33; **3,** (41), [59 (K.-D.)], (60), (63) (told Yudhishṭhira to perform an açvamedha with the gold left by Marutta); [**4,** 64 (D.)].—§ 778*b* (Saṃvartta-Maruttīya): XIV, **4,** (65); **5,** (94); **6,** (120), (129), (136), (146); **7,** (158); **9,** (†228), (†238); **10,** (†258), (†264), (†281) (*V.* told the Saṃvartta-Maruttīya to Yudhishṭhira).—§ 779 (Açvamedhikap.): XIV, **11,** 293.—§ 780 (do.): XIV, **14*β*,** [355 (D.-K.)], 360.—[§ 783 (Anugītāp.): XIV, **52*a*,** 1492 (K.-D., Arjuna had heard of the glory of Kṛshṇa from *V.*)].—§ 785 (do.): XIV, **62,** 1859, 1862, 1869, 1870; **63,** 1871 [1873 (D.), 1875 (K.)], 1876 (*guruṇā*), 1879, 1882; **65,** 1923 (C. has by error *Vā°*), [1934 (D.)] (at the injunction of *V.* Yudhishṭhira fetched the gold of Marutta); **70,** 2064 (*Satyavatīsutaḥ*); **71,** 2067, (2070), [2073 (K.-D.)]; **72,** 2083, (2085), 2091 (*Kṛshṇa-Dvaipāyanāya*); **73,** 2112 (initiated Yudhishṭhira for the horse-sacrifice and let the sacrificial horse loose); **88,** [2613 (*Satyavatyātmajaḥ*)], 2619, 2640 (°*çishyāḥ*); **89,** 2650 (*saçishyaḥ*), 2651 (*Satyavatīsutaḥ*), [2659 (D.-K.)], 2662 [2664 (K.-D.)], 2671 (completion of the sacrifice).—§ 787 (Āçramavāsap.): XV, **1,** 14 (*purāṇarshiḥ*); **3,** 80, 147 (*Satyavatīputraḥ*); **4,** (148), 153, 166, 167 (asked Yudhishṭhira to permit Dhṛtarāshṭra to go to the forest); **8,** 264 (κ), 275; [**10,** 305 (K.-D.), 318 (*Satyavatīsutaḥ*)]; **19,** 530 (°*āçramam*), 532; [**20*ββ*,** 539 (D.), (γγ), 552 (*Dvaipāyana-prasādāt*)].—§ 788 (do.): XV, **26,** 705 (*yogadharmaṃ* (°*ā*, C.) . . . *V°ena kathitam*); **27,** 736, 738, 739, [740 (D.)]; **28,** 741 (*Satyavatīputraḥ*) (*V.* told Dhṛtarāshṭra of Vidura's being born from Dharma).—§ 789 (Putradarçanap.): XV, **29,** 768, 772, 773, 780, 787, 815, 816; **30,** 838 (*vedavidāṃ varaḥ*); **31,** (843), 862 (explained the different incarnations of gods, etc., as actors in the battle); **32,** 868, 871, [884 (*Satyavatīputraḥ*)] (summoned by *V.* the fallen warriors arose from the Gaṅgā); **33,** 913.—§ 790 (do.): XV, **35,** 941, 942, 944, [950 (D.)] (showed to Janamejaya his father Parikshit, etc.).—§ 791 (do.): XV, **36,** [961 (*Satyavatī-putraḥ*)], 969, 975.—§ 793 (Mausalap.): XVI, **7,** 253 (*Kṛshṇa-Dvaipāyanam*); **8,** [254 (*Satyavatīsutam*), 256 (*Satyavatīsutaḥ*)], 257, (279), 291 (*V.* comforted Arjuna).—[§ 794 (Mahāprasthānikap.): XVII, **1,** 12 (D.)].—§ 795 (Svargārohaṇap.): XVIII, **1,** 2 (*maharshiṇā*); **5,** 154, [157 (*Pārāçaryaḥ*)], 182, [183 (*Kṛshṇena muninā . . . nirmitam*, sc. the Mhbhr.)]. — § 795*c* (Mahābhārata): XVIII, **5,** [192/93 (K.-D., only B.), 196 (K.-D.)], 200, [211 (D.)].

Vyāsa[2]=Çiva (1000 names[2]).—Do.[3]= Vishṇu (1000 names).

Vyāsaçishya ("the disciple of Vyāsa") = Vaiçampāyana: I, 303; II, 1788/89 (only B.); XV, 922.

Vyāsasthalī, name of a sacred place (tīrtha). § 364 (Tīrthayātrāp.): III, **83,** 6066.

Vyāsātmaja ("the son of Vyāsa") = Çuka: XII, 13647.

Vyāsavana, name of a sacred forest. § 364 (Tīrthayātrāp.): III, **83,** 6063.

Vyavasāya[1] ("eternal law", personif.). § 615*ū* (Skanda): IX, **46*κ*,** 2682. — § 641 (Rājadh.): XII, **122,** 4512

(*Brahmaṇaḥ putraḥ*), 4513.—Do.[2] = Çiva (1000 names[1-2]).—Do.[3] = Vishṇu (1000 names).

Vyavasthāna(ṃ) = Vishṇu (1000 names).

Vyaya, name of a serpent. § 67 (Sarpasattra): I, **57,** 2157 (of Dhṛtarāshṭra's race; read with B. Avyaya, q.v.).

Vyomagaṅgā ("the heavenly Gaṅgā"). § 714 (Çukakṛtya): XII, **329,** 12421.

Vyomakeça = Çiva: VII, 9626.

Vyoman = Mahāpurusha (Mahāpurushastava).

Vyomāri, a Viçvadeva. § 749 (Ānuçāsanik.): XIII, **91**γ, 4360.

Vyūka, pl. (°*āḥ*), a people. § 574 (Jambūkh.): VI, **9**λ, 369 (only B., C. has *Bakāḥ*).

Vyūḍhoraska, son of Dhṛtarāshṭra. § 585 (Bhīshmavadhap.): VI, **96,** 4345 (slain by Bhīmasena). Cf. next.

Vyūḍhoru, son of Dhṛtarāshṭra. § 130 (Aṃçāvat.): I, **67,** 2740.—§ 182 (Dhṛtarāshṭraputranāmak.): I, **117,** 4553 (B. *Vyūḍhoraḥ*).

***vyūhaçāstra** ("the science of arrays"): VI, 3866.

Vyushitāçva, an ancient king, descendant of Pūru. § 186*b* (Pāṇḍu): There was a king named *Vyushitāçva*, of the race of *Pūru*; once, when he sacrificed, the gods, with *Indra* and *Devarshis*, came there, and the gods and the *Brahmarshis* began themselves to perform a sacrifice (*cakruḥ karma svayam*); having subdued the eastern, northern, western, and southern princes, he performed a horse-sacrifice (a *gāthā* from the *Purāṇas* is cited), etc. The wife of *V.* was *Bhadrā Kākshīvatī*, whom he loved so much that he was attacked by phthisis and died sonless; *Bhadrā* conld not bear separation from him and cried out that he should show himself to her; then his voice was heard saying that she, having bathed, should lie down with him on her bed on the night of the eighth or fourteenth day of the moon, then he would beget offspring upon her. By the corpse of her husband she gave birth to seven children: three *Çālvas* and four *Madras*: I, **121,** 4686 (*Pūror vaṃçavivardhanaḥ*), 4688 (*rājarsheḥ*), 4689, 4691, 4692, 4693.—§ 187 (do.): I, **122,** 4717.

Y

Yaças = Çiva (1000 names[1]).

Yaçasvinī, a mātṛ. § 615*u* (Skanda): IX, **46**δ, 2628.

Yaçodā, wife of the cowherd Nanda. § 549*f* (Durgā): IV, **6,** 179 (°*garbhasambhūtāṃ*, sc. Durgā; cf. Harivaṃça v. 3313 foll.).

Yaçodhara, son of Kṛshṇa and Rukmiṇī. § 730 (Ānuçāsanik.): XIII, **14***a*, 621 (so B., C. has *Yaçovaraḥ*).

Yaçodharā, a Trigarta princess. § 156 (Pūruvaṃç.): I, **95,** ††3788 (*Traigartīṃ*, wife of Hastin and mother of Vikuṇṭhana).

Yaçovara (XIII, 621), v. Yaçodhara.

Yaçovāsas = Mahāpurusha (Mahāpurushastava).

Yad (or **Yat-tad**) = Vishṇu (1000 names).

Yādasāṃ bhartā, Yādasāṃ pati(ḥ) = Varuṇa (q.v.).

Yādava, pl. (°*āḥ*) ("the descendants of Yadu"), a people = Yadu, pl., commonly synonymous with Vṛshṇi, pl. § 136 (Yayātyup.): I, **75,** 3126 (°*ānāṃ imaṃ vaṃçaṃ*).—§ 148*b* (Yadu): I, **85,** 3533 (descended from Yadu). — § 156 (Pūruvaṃç.): I, **95,** ††3763 (do.).—§ 198 (Çaradvat): I, **130,** 5093 (instructed by Kṛpa).—§ 202 (Vidurāgamanap.): I, **241,** 7430 (°*vāhinīṃ*).—§ 272 (Rājasūyārambhap.): II, **13,** 553 (Yudhishṭhira sent for Kṛshṇa).—§ 273 (do.): II, **14,** 594 (oppressed by their king Kaṃsa).—§ 285 (Nakula): II, **32,** 1196 (Kṛshṇa, with the *Y.* [*Yādavaiḥ sārdhaṃ*, only C.], accepted the sway of Yudhishṭhira on Nakula's digvijaya).—§ 298 (Dyūtap.): II, **62,** 2101 (*Andhakā Y°ā Bhojāḥ*, abandoned Kaṃsa).—§ 320 (Saubhavadhop.): III, **16,** 689; **17,** 692; **20,** 784 (°*ārshabhāḥ*, Çālva attacked Dvārakā).—§ 356 (Tīrthayātrāp.): III, **80,** 4018 (had been vanquished by Arjuna when he ravished Subhadrā).—§ 448 (Ājagarap.): III, **176,** †12331 (*Kṛshṇaḥ saha Y°aiḥ*).—§ 549 (Pāṇḍavapraveçap.): IV, **4,** 140 (Indrasena, etc., went to the *Y.*).—§ 556 (Sañjayayānap.): V, **28**ι, †806.—§ 561 (Yānasandhip.): V, **71,** †2576 (*ṛshabhaṃ Y°ānāṃ*, i.e. Kṛshṇa).—§ 567 (Bhagavadyānap.): V, **128,** 4298 (*sarva-Y°āḥ*, abandoned Kaṃsa).—§ 569 (do.): V, **144**ν, 4896.—§ 569*b* (Yayāti): V, **149,** 5046 (°*ānāṃ kulakaraḥ*, i.e. Yadu).—§ 604 (Karṇap.): VIII, **8**η, 244 (°-*Kauravān*)—§ 615 (Gadāyuddhap.): IX, **35,** 1982 (*sarva-Y°aiḥ*, accompanied Balarāma).—§ 617*b* (Brahmaçiras): X, **12,** 640 (*mānitaḥ sarva-Y°aiḥ*, sc. Açvatthāman).—§ 619 (Strīvilāpap.): XI, **25,** 754 (Gāndhārī pronounced the curse that the *Y.* should fall by each other's hand, cf. § 793).—§ 641 (Rājadh.): XII, **59,** 2122 (°-*Pāṇḍavāḥ*); **81**λ, 3052, 3054.—§ 656 (Khaḍgotpattik.): XII, **166**δ, 6199 (*Bhojaḥ sa-Y°aḥ*). — § 785 (Anugītāp.): XIV, **83,** 2479 (°*ānāṃ kumārakāḥ*).—§ 793 (Mausalap.): XVI, **3,** 66, 74; **4,** †107, †113 (°*ānāṃ purīṃ*, i.e. Dvārakā) (the *Y.* slew each other, cf. § 619).

Yādava[1] ("descendant of Yadu") = Çūra: VII, 6031 (*Ç°*).

Yādava[2] (do.) = Kṛshṇa: II, 837 (*Pāṇḍava-Y°au*), 1560 (*devasya*); VI, 1287; VII, 765 (*Pāṇḍava-Y°au*); IX, 3499; XIII, 628, 2017, 2018, 2019, 2022, 2023, 2024, 2026 (B. *Keçava*), 2027, 6839, 6887 (*deveçaṃ*), 6903 (*Yādavasya*, read *yāvad asya*, B. *yāvat tasya*).

Yādava[3] (do.) = Sātyaki: V, †1857; VII, 5948 (?).

Yādava[4] (do.): Vajra: XVII, 9 (*V°*).

Yādava[5], dual (°*au*) (do.) = Kṛshṇa and Balarāma: II, 1508.

Yādava[6], adj. ("belonging to the Yadus (Yādavas) or to Yādava [= Kṛshṇa]"). § 793 (Mausalap.): XVI, **7,** 183 (*Sudharmāṃ Y°īṃ sabhāṃ*).

Yādavaçreshṭha[1] = Balarāma: IX, 3037.—Do.[2] = Kṛshṇa: II, 44 (*K°*); V, 4434; VII, 8339; IX, 3534, 3539.

Yādavaçārdūla = Kṛshṇa: V, 2989; XIII, 1024.

Yādavāgrya = Kṛshṇa: XII, †1515.

Yādavanandana = Kṛshṇa: III, 484; V, 4774; VI, 2548, 4833; VII, 8272; IX, 3518; XII, 1579; XIV, 30. Cf. Sarvayādavanandana.

Yādavarshabha = Kṛshṇa: VI, 4862 (only B., C. has *Mādhavarshabhaḥ*).

Yādaveçvara = Kṛshṇa: XIII, 1110.

Yādavī ("female descendant of Yadu") = Açmakī: I, ††3766 (*A°*).—Do.[2] = [Çrutaçravas] the mother of Çiçupāla: II, 1508.—Do.[3] = Kuntī: I, 4367.—Do.[4] = Subhadrā: XV, 844.

Yādavīmātṛ ("son of a Yādavī") = Yudhishṭhira: XV, 89.

Yādavīputra (do.) = Yudhishṭhira: XII, 2666.

Yadu[1], son of Yayāti and ancestor of the Yadus (Yādavas). § 6 (Anukram.): I, **1***a*, 225 (in Sañjaya's enumeration).—§ 143 (Nahusha): I, **75,** 3159 (his genealogy).—§ 144 (Yayāti): I, **75,** 3162, 3167 (°*prabhṛtayaḥ, Y.*, etc., would not take the decrepitude of Yayāti, cf. § 148).—§ 147 (Devayānī): I, **83,** 3432 (son of Yayāti and Devayānī).—§ 148 (Yayāti): I, **84,** 3466 (*putraṃ jyeshṭhaṃ*), 3468

(3470) (*b:* As *Y.* would not take the decrepitude of Yayāti, the latter cursed him, saying that his children should never be kings); **85**, 3519 (*jyeshṭham*), 3520 (*jyeshṭhaḥ*), 3523 (*jyeshṭhena*), 3525 (excluded from the throne), 3533 (*b:* The Yādavas are the descendants of *Y.*).—§ 149 (do.): I, **86**, 3545 (°*purogamān*).—§ 156 (Pūruvaṃç.): I, **95**, 3762 (his genealogy), ††3763 (his descendants were the Yādavas).—§ 565 (Gālavacarita): V, **120**, 4027, 4038.—§ 569*b* (Yayāti): V, **149**, 5043 (*jyeshṭhaḥ*), 5045 [5046 (*Yādavānāṃ kulakaraḥ*)], 5048 (*Y.* resided in Hāstinapura; because he disregarded his father and brothers, he was cursed by Yayāti and expelled from the kingdom, cf. § 148).—§ 599*e* (Çini): VII, **144**, 6030 (in his race Devamīḍha was born).—§ 632 (Shoḍaçarāj., v. Yayāti): XII, **29**, 991 (*antyeshu putrān nikshipya Y°-Druhyupurogamān*, sc. Yayāti, cf. § 148).—§ 768*b* (Kṛshṇa Vāsudeva): XIII, **147**, 6833 (father of Kroshṭṛ).—§ 775 (Ānuçāsanik.): XIII, **166**η, 7674. Cf. Daivayāneya.

Yadu[2], a prince. § 74 (Vasu): I, **63**, 2364 (son of Vasu Uparicara).

Yadu, pl. (°*avaḥ*) ("the descendants of Yadu[1]"), a people = Yādava, pl., commonly synonymous with Vṛshṇi, pl. § 3 (Anukram.): I, **1**, 46 (°*ūnāṃ*, sc. *vaṃçaḥ*).—§ 11 (Parvasaṅgr.): I, **2**, 623 (°*vīrāṇām āpāne vaiçasaṃ*, cf. § 793).—§ 132 (Aṃçāvat.): I, **67**, 2796 (°*ūnāṃ kule*, Kṛshṇa was born in the race of the *Y.*).—§ 233 (Svayaṃvarap.): I, **187**, †7012 (°*puṅgavāḥ*).—§ 238 (Pañcendrop.): I, **197**, †7308 (°*ūnāṃ kule*, the black hair of Nārāyaṇa was born as Kṛshṇa in the race of the *Y.*). — § 262 (Bhagavadyāna): II, **2**, 54 (°*çreshṭhair Ugrasenamukhaiḥ*).—§ 286 (Arghāharaṇap.): II, **26**, 1321 (*Nārāyaṇaḥ . . . ajāyata Y°kshaye*, sc. as Kṛshṇa).—§ 402 (Tīrthayātrāp.): III, **120**, †10288 (°*pravīrāḥ*).—§ 510 (Draupadī-Satyabhāmāsaṃv.): III, **233**, 14651 (*kathāḥ Kuru-Y°ūtthitāḥ*).—§ 524*d* (Vishṇu): III, **272**, 15848 (*ajāyata Y°kshaye*, sc. Vishṇu as Kṛshṇa).—§ 562 (Bhagavadyānap.): V, **83**, 2937 (°*ūnāṃ nandivardhanaṃ*, sc. the chariot of Kṛshṇa).—§ 580 (Bhīshmavadhap.): VI, **59**, † 2609 (had abandoned Kaṃsa).—§ 581 (do.): VI, **60**, †2659 (°*ūnām ṛshabhena*, i.e. Kṛshṇa).—§ 599 (Jayadrathavadhap.): VII, **118**, †4699 (°*ūnām ṛshabhaḥ*, i.e. Sātyaki); **140**, †5835 (do., do.).—§ 607 (Karṇap.): VIII, **37**, †1740 (°*sadanam Upendrapālitam*).—§ 608 (do.): VIII, **76**, †3853 (*cakraṃ . . . sadārcitaṃ Y°bhiḥ*).—§ 615 (Baladevatīrthayātrā): IX, **49**, 2831 (°*ūnāṃ pravaraḥ*, i.e. Balarāma).—§ 617 (Aishīkap.): X, **12**, 606 (°*ūnām ṛshabhaḥ*, i.e. Kṛshṇa); **13**, 655 (°*ūnām ṛshabhena*, i.e. Kṛshṇa).—§ 639 (Rājadh.): XII, **50**β, 1816 (°-*Kauravāḥ*).—§ 656 (Khaḍgotpattik.): XII, **166**δ, 6199.—§ 785 (Anugītāp.): XIV, **88**, 2606 (°*striyaḥ*).—§ 793 (Mausalap.): XVI, **4**, †106, †113; **6**, 168; **8**, 266.—§ 794 (Mahāprasthānikap.): XVII, **1**, 8 (°*ūnāṃ pariçeshaç ca Vajraḥ*).

Yaduçreshṭha[1] = Balarāma: IX, 3023.

Yaduçreshṭha[2] = Çūra: I, 2764 (*Ç*°), 4382 (*Ç*°).

Yaduçreshṭha[3] = Kṛshṇa (Vishṇu): II, 32, 787, 1584; III, 14739; VI, 3567; XII, 1363, 1937, 3054; XIII, 966, 6869, 7024 (Vishṇu's 1000 names).

Yaduçārdūla[1] = Balarāma: IX, 2143.

Yaduçārdūla[2] = Kṛshṇa: II, 926 (*K*°); XII, 1500, 1711.

Yadūdvaha[1] = Kṛshṇa: III, 15544.

Yadūdvaha[2] = Sātyaki: VII, 6760.

Yadūdvaha[3] = Vasudeva: XIV, 1846.

Yadukulaçreshṭha = Kṛshṇa: XIII, 1119.

Yadukula-Pāṇḍava-nandana = Kṛshṇa: VII, †8273.

Yadukulodvaha[1] = Kṛshṇa: IX, 3378, 3532; XIII, 619.

Yadukulodvaha[2] = Vasudeva: XIV, 1844.

Yadunandana[1] = Balarāma: IX, 598 (*Rāmād*), 1981, 2158, 2177, 2318; X, 505 (*Rāmaḥ*).

Yadunandana[2] = Kṛshṇa: II, 890, 925 (*K*°), 956, 1513 (*K*°), 1515 (*K*°); VIII, 3414, 3552 (*Govindaḥ*); IX, 1905, 3476; XIV, 1952, 2041, 2075, 2564, 2597 (*K*°); XVI, 91.

Yadunandanī = Subhadrā: XIV, 1841.

Yadupravīra[1] = Balarāma: I, †7151 (°*au*, i.e. B. and Kṛshṇa); IX, †2002 (*Halabhṛt*), †2009.—Do.[2] = Kṛshṇa: I, †7151 (*au*, i.e. K. and Balarāma); VI, †2608, †2610; XII, 1805; XIV, 1951.

Yadupuṅgava = Kṛshṇa: II, 31; VIII, 2583, 4989, 4997; IX, 3076; XII, 1708, 1709.

Yadusiṃha = Balarāma: IX, 3007.

Yadusukhāvaha = Kṛshṇa: V, 2947, 3329.

Yadūttama[1] = Kṛshṇa: V, 2630; IX, 3560; X, 620.

Yadūttama[2] = Sātyaki: VIII, †4204.

Yaduvaṃçavivardhana = Kṛshṇa: VI, 2964.

Yaduvara, dual (°*au*) = Balarāma and Kṛshṇa: IX, 3351.

Yaduvīra[1] = Kṛshṇa: XII, 1127.—Do.[2] = Sātyaki: VII, 6759.

Yaduvīramukhya = Kṛshṇa: I, †7013.

Yaduvṛsha = Kṛshṇa: XII, †1895.

Yaduvyāghra = Sātyaki: VI, 2353.

Yāja, a Brahmarshi, brother of Upayāja. § 218*b* (Draupadīsambhava): *Drupada* saw the two brothers of Kaçyapa's race, *Y.* and *Upayāja.* He courted *Upayāja* and asked him to perform a sacrifice, by which he might obtain a son who might slay *Droṇa*, and promised him an *arbuda* of kine. But *Upayāja* refused. *Drupada* once more began to pay homage to him, and after a year *Upayāja* said that his elder brother, *Y.*, once had taken up a fruit without inquiring of the purity of the spot, and had, in the house of his preceptor, used to eat the remains of other people's feasts; he would entertain no scruples. Describing the might of *Droṇa* ("*Droṇa* is also skilled in the *Brahmāstra*, his bow is six *aratnis* long") *Drupada* promised *Y.* to give him eight *ayutas* (cf. v. 6385: "an *arbuda*") of kine. *Y.* consented and prevailed upon *Upayāja* to assist him. *Upayāja* then spoke to Drupada of everything required for the sacrifice: I, **167**, 6362 (°*opayājau Brahmarshī*), 6376 (°*syāçramaṃ*), 6377, 6386.—§ 218 (do.): I, **167**, 6390, 6391 (6392), 6393, 6405, 6406 (in the sacrifice which *Y.* and Upayāja performed for Drupada, Dhṛshṭadyumna and Draupadī were born from the sacrificial fire).—§ 306 (Anudyūtap.): II, **80**, 2662 (°*opayājatapasā lebhe putraṃ sa pāvakāt*, sc. Drupada, all. to § 218). Cf. Kāçyapa, dual.

Yājabha (VII, 804), v. Ṛshabha.

Yajana, a tīrtha. § 360 (Tīrthayātrāp.): III, **82**, 5048.

Yājana, a tīrtha. § 360 (Tīrthayātrāp.): III, **82**, 5048.

Yajin = Çiva (1000 names[1]).

Yajña ("sacrifice", personif.): V, 3881 (BR. quote XII, 791, 2316 (*gāthā y°-gītāḥ ?*)).—Do.[2] = Çiva (1000 names[1–2]).—Do.[3] = Kṛshṇa (Vishṇu): XII, 1510, 13143; XIII, 6997 (1000 names), 7053 (do.).—Do.[4] = Mahāpurusha (Mahāpurushastava).

Yajñabhāgahara = Mahāpurusha (Mahāpurushastava).

Yajñabhāgavid = Çiva (1000 names[2]).

Yajñabhṛt = Vishṇu (1000 names).

Yajñabhuj[1] = Agni: III, 15545.—Do.[2] = Vishṇu (1000 names).

Yajñādhipa = Çiva (1000 names[1]).

Yajñagarbha = Mahāpurusha (Mahāpurushastava).
Yajñaguhya(ṃ) = Vishṇu (1000 names).
Yajñahan = Çiva (1000 names[2]).
Yajñahṛdaya = Mahāpurusha (Mahāpurushastava).
Yajñakṛt = Vishṇu (1000 names).
Yajñamṛgavyādha = Çiva (1000 names[1]).
Yajñamush, pl. (°*aḥ*) ("stealing the sacrifice"), a class of gods. § 492 (Āṅgirasa): III. **220**, 14165 (*devāḥ*), 14166 (enumeration).
Yajñānāṃ pati(ḥ) = Çiva: VII, 9540.
Yajñāṅga, pl. (°*āni*) ("parts of sacrifice"): X, 792 (*catvāri*), 802.
Yajñāṅga(ḥ) = Vishṇu (1000 names). Cf. XII, 1635 (°*o Varāhaḥ*).
Yajñāntakṛt = Vishṇu (1000 names).
Yajñapati[1] = Çiva (1000 names[2]).—Do.[2] = Vishṇu: XII, 12874; XIII, 7053 (1000 names).
Yajñāri = Çiva (1000 names[2]).
Yajñasādhana = Vishṇu (1000 names).
Yajñasamāhita = Çiva (1000 names[2]).
Yajñasambhava = Mahāpurusha (Mahāpurushastava).
Yajñasena[1] = Drupada, q.v. — Do.[2] = Kṛshṇa: XII, 1510.
Yajñasenasuta ("the son of Yajñasena [i.e. Drupada]") = Dhṛshṭadyumna: VII, 8977 (has slain Droṇa).
Yājñaseni[1] (do.) = Çikhaṇḍin: VI, 5216; VII, 350 (Ç°), 538, 1099 (Ç°), 3534 (Ç°), 3548 (?), 3549 (?), 4528, 4533, 7591; IX, 3161 (has slain Bhīshma).
Yājñaseni[2] (do.) = Dhṛshṭadyumna: V, 5162 (?); VII, 216, 4503, 8788; VIII, †3814 (*senāpatiḥ*).
Yājñasenī ("the daughter of Yajñasena [i.e. Drupada]") = Draupadī: I, 6322 (°*yāḥ svayaṃvaram*), †7131, †7133, †7137; II, 1906, 2024, †2201, †2214, †2221, †2229, †2230, 2262, 2294 (C. by error *J*°), †2295, †2363, †2383, †2399, †2523, †2524; III, †918, 1160, 1264, †1371, 10874, †12579 (*Kṛshṇām*), †12580 (*Kṛshṇe*), †12587, 14652, 14709, †15682, †15693, †15696; IV, 138, 374, 594, 695; V, †725, †851, †854, 1988; VIII, †3353, 4234/35 (only B.); IX, †3318, 3431; X, 589; XI, 420; XII, 424; XIV, 325; XVI, 179; XVII, 49, 50.
Yajñastuta = Mahāpurusha (Mahāpurushastava).
Yajñātman = Kṛshṇa: XII, 1631.
Yajñavāha[1], a warrior of Skanda. § 615*u* (Skanda): IX, **45**η, 2572.—Do.[2] = Çiva (1000 names[1]).
Yajñavāhana = Vishṇu (1000 names).
Yājñavalkya, a ṛshi. § 264 (Sabhākriyāp.): II, **4a**, 107 (*Tittirir Y°ç ca*, waited upon Yudhishṭhira). — § 266 (Çakrasabhāv.): II, **7**, 293 (in the palace of Indra).—§ 286 (Rājasūyikap.): II, **36**, 1239 (acted as adhvaryu at the rajasūya of Yudhishṭhira).—§ 707 (Mokshadh.): XII, **311**, 11545 (°*sya saṃvādaṃ Janakasya ca*), 11546 (*ṛshiçreshṭhaṃ*) (11550); **312**, (11569); **313**, (11590); **314**, (11607); **315**, (11635); **316**, (11655); **317**, (11675); **318**, (11703); **319**, (11724) (*Y.* got from Sūrya the yajushes, the Çatapatha-brāhmaṇa, etc.), 11790, (11792), (†11808) (*Y.'s* discourse with Viçvāvasu), 11818, †11836 (*Y.'s* discourse with Janaka, (ch. **311**-**319**)).—§ 721*b* (Viçvāmitrop.): XIII, **4**β, 250 (among the sons of Viçvāmitra).—§ 730 (Ānuçāsanik.): XIII, **14**δ, 679 (*ṛshiḥ*, praised Çiva).—§ 785 (Anugītāp.): XIV, **72**, 2085 (will perform rites at the açvamedha); **73**, 2129 (°*sya çishyaḥ*).—§ 794 (Mahāprasthānikap.): XVII, **1**, 12 (*Bhāradvājaṃ* ?).
Yajñayoni = Mahāpurusha (Mahāpurushastava).

Yajñendra: XIII, 806 (misprint in C. for Yakshendra, v. Yaksha, pl.).
Yajñin = Vishṇu (1000 names).
Yajuhpādabhuja = Çiva (1000 names[2]).
Yajurmaya = Çiva (1000 names[1]).
Yajurveda. § 270 (Brahmasabhāv.): II, **11**, 449 (among the Vedas present in the palace of Brahmán). — § 459 (Mārkaṇḍeyas.): III, **189**, 12963 (*Ṛgvedaḥ Sāmavedaç ca Y°o 'py Atharvaṇaḥ*, sprung from Nārāyaṇa). — § 606 (Tripurākhyāna): VIII, **34**, 1498 (*Itihāsa-Y°au*, became the pṛshṭharakshau of Çiva).—§ 717*b* (Nārāyaṇīya): XII, **342**, 13136 (*Ṛgvede sa-Y°e*); **343**, 13258 (*shaṭpañcāçatam ashṭau saptatriṃçatam ity uta / yasmiñ chākhā Y°e so 'ham ādhvaryave smṛtaḥ*, sc. Nārāyaṇa (Kṛshṇa)). Cf. next.
yajus, mostly pl. (°*ūṃshi*) ("sacrificial formula"): I, 66 (*ṛco yajūṃshi sāmāni*), 1374 (do.), 2881 (°*vidbhiḥ*); III, 966 (°*shām ṛcāṃ sāmnāñ ca*), 1103 (? °*shāṃ lokāḥ* [probably gen. pl. from *yajvan*]), 1773 (*dvijāgryaiç ca ṛg-yajuḥ-sāma-sambhavaiḥ*), 11237 (*sāma-ṛg-yajurvarṇāḥ*, did not exist in the Kṛta age), 17338 (sg.), 17339 (sg.); V, 1623 (*ṛco yajūṃshi . . . Sāmavedañ ca*), 1624 (*sāmāny ṛcaḥ . . . yajūṃshi*), †1711 (pl.), 3771 (pl., given by Sūrya); VI, 1187 (*ṛk-sāma-yajur eva ca*); IX, 2098 (*ṛco yajūṃshi sāmāni*); XII, 1632 (*yaḥ Suparṇo yajur nāma*, i.e. Kṛshṇa), 1883 (*ṛg-yajuḥ-sāmasahitair vacobhiḥ*), 2311 (*ṛg-yajuḥ-sāmavid*), 2312 (*anṛgyajur asāma ca*), †2315 (*ekam*), 2871 (*ṛg-yajuḥ-sāma-sampannāḥ*), 7045 (°*shā saṃskṛtaṃ māṃsam*), †7372 (*ṛk-sāmasaṅghāç ca yajūṃshi cāpi*), 7501 (*ṛco yajūṃshi sāmāni*), 7503 (°*shām ādiḥ*), 8543 (*ṛk-sāmāni yajūṃshi ca*), 8613 (*ṛk-sāmavarṇākSharato yajusho 'tharvaṇas tathā*), 8720 (*ṛg-sāmasu yajuḥsu ca*), 8859 (*saṃskāraṃ yajushārhati*), 8909 (sg.), 9065 (*ṛco yajūṃshi sāmāni*), 9621 (do.), 9632 (do.), 10413 (°*shāṃ Çatarudriyaṃ*, i.e. Çiva (1000 names[1])), 11532 (*ṛg-yajuḥ-sāmagaḥ*), 11725 (pl., Yājñavalkya obtained the *y.* from Sūrya), 11728 (pl.), 11744 (pl., *daçapañca*), 12736 (°*-ṛk-sāmabhiḥ*); XIII, 915 (°*shāṃ Çatarudriyaṃ*, i.e. Çiva), 1085 (*yajurmayaṃ tridhā vedyaṃ*, i.e. Çiva, so C., B. reads *yajurbhir yat*), 4107 (*mūrtimanti ca sāmāni yajūṃshi | ca sahasraçaḥ*), 4520 (pl.), 7575 (°*shā saṃskṛtaṃ māṃsaṃ*). Cf. Yajurveda.
Yajvan = Vishṇu (1000 names).
Yakṛlloma, pl. (°*āḥ*), a people. § 549 (Pāṇḍavapraveçap.): IV, **5**, 144 (*antareṇa Y°āñ Chūrasenāṃç ca*). Cf. next.
Yakṛlloman, pl. (°*ānaḥ*), a people. § 571 (Jambūkh.): VI, **9**μ, 353. Cf. the prec.
Yaksha[1], pl (°*āḥ*), a class of beings: I, 35 (issued from the primordial egg), 106 (*Gandharva-Y°-Rakshāṃsi*, Çuka recited to them the Mhbhr.), 248, 369, 454 (*Maṇimatpramukhaiḥ*), 457 (do.), 2515, 2571 (among the offspring of Pulastya), 2572 (among the offspring of Pulaha; PCR. had read *ṛkshāḥ*), 6401, 6444 (*Y°-Gandharva-Rakshasāṃ*), 6496 (°*-Rākshasa-Gandharvāḥ*, know the history of the Kurus), 7658 (°*-Raksho-gaṇan*, vanquished by Sunda and Upasunda), 7712 (*deva-Gandharva-Y°āṇāṃ*, sc. *sarvaratnāni*, robbed by Sunda and Upasunda), 8256 (°*-Rākshasa-Pannagāḥ*, attacked Arjuna), 8304 (°*Rākshasa-Gandharva-nara-Kinnara-Pannagaiḥ*); II, 399 (enumeration of the *Y.* in the palace of Kubera), 411 (*saha Y°aiḥ*, sc. Vibhīshaṇa, worship Kubera), 472 (in the palace of Brahmán), 481 (in the palace of Kubera); III, 159 (*suragaṇa-pitṛ-Y°sevitaṃ*, sc. Sūrya), 170 (°*-Guhyaka-Pannagāḥ*, follow the chariot of Sūrya), 878 (°*āṇāṃ Rāksha-sānāṃ ca Dānavānāṃ ca saṃyuge*, sc. with Kṛshṇa), 1671 (*Kuberaḥ . . . Y°air anugataḥ*), 1841 (*Siddha-Cāraṇa-Y°eshu*),

2084 (*na Y°eshu tādṛgrūpavatī*, sc. Damayantī), 5036 (in the tīrtha Vaḍavā), 5076 (in Kurukshetra), 8168 (*Bhūta-Y°-Piçācāḥ*), 8391 (*Gandharva-Y°-Rakshobhiḥ . . . sevitaṃ . . . çailaṃ*), 8674 (seen in the body of Rāma Dāçarathi), 8801 (*manushyoraga-Gandharva-Y°-Kimpurushāḥ*), 9954 (*Gandharvoraga-Y°āḥ*), 10138, 10825 (*caturgaṇāḥ*), 10831 (°-*Rākshasa-Kinnarāḥ*), 10893 (*adhyushitaṃ Y°aiḥ . . . giriṃ*), 11089 (°-*Gandharva-sura-Brahmarshigaṇasevitam*, sc. Gandhamādana), 11098 (°-*Gandharvayoshābhiḥ*), 11236 (*deva-Dānava-Gandharva-Y°-Rākshasa-pannagāḥ*, did not exist in the Kṛtayuga), 11287 (*Dhanadodyānaṃ rakshitaṃ Y°-Rākshasaiḥ*), 11359 (*pushkariṇīṃ* (sc. Kubera's) . . . *sevitām ṛshibhir divyair Y°aiḥ*), 11371, 11419 (had been slain by Bhīmasena at the lotus-tank of Kubera, cf. Rākshasa, pl.), 11654 (*adhipaṃ Y°-Rakshasāṃ*, i.e. Kubera), 11665, 11708 (°-*Rākshasa-Gandharvāḥ*), 11709 (°-*Rākshasa°*), 11713 (°-*Rakshasāṃ*), 11717 (slain by Bhīmasena, cf. Rākshasa, pl.), 11758 (*pravarā Rākshasendrāṇāṃ Y°āṇāñ ca*), 11760 (*sarva-Y°gaṇādhipaḥ*, i.e. Kubera), 11767 (*daçaçatāvarāḥ*), 11769 (*Kuberaṃ . . . Y°-Rakshogaṇāvṛtaṃ*), 11773 (°-*Gandharvāḥ*), 11777, 11784 (°-*Rakshasāṃ*), 11787 (do.), 11793, 11813 (*saha Kinnaraiḥ*), 11832, 11835 (Kubera came to the Pāṇḍavas), 12206 (*maharshi-Y°-Gandharva-Pannagāsura-Rākshasaiḥ*), 12246 (*sa°*), 12272 (*sa-Y°āsura-G°aiḥ*), 12304 (°-*Rākshasa-Gandharvāḥ*), †12362 (°-*Gandharva-maharshi-kāntāṃ*, sc. the Sarasvatī), 12364 (*nihantā Y°-Rakshasāṃ*, i.e. Bhīmasena), 12425 (*Himavāṃç ca . . . Y°-Rākshasa-saṅkulaḥ*), 12522 (*Brahmarshi-deva-Gandharva-Y°-Rākshasa-Pannagāḥ*), 12875 (*deva-Dānava-Y°āṇāṃ*), 12877 (*sa-Y°oraga-Rākshasaṃ . . . jagat*), 12891 (°-*Rākshasavarjite*, sc. *ekārṇave*), 12925 (seen in the stomach of Nārāyaṇa), 12942, 13485 (*deva-Gandharva-Y°āṇāṃ*, sc. *kathāḥ*), 13535 (*avadhyaḥ . . . Y°āṇāṃ*, sc. Dhundhu), 13584 (*deva-Dānava-Y°āṇāṃ . . . avadhyaḥ*, do.), 14264 (*deva-Dānava-Y°āṇāṃ . . . jetā*), 14507 (*āviçanti ca yaṃ Y°āḥ purushaṃ kālaparyaye / unmādayati sa tu kshipraṃ jñeyo Y°grahas tu saḥ*), 14548 (°-*Rakshobhiḥ*), †15640 (*samūheshv api Y°-Rakshasāṃ*), 15823 (°-*Rākshasa-Bhūtāni*), 15888 (°*āṇām ādhipatyaṃ*, bestowed on Kubera), 15913 (°-*Rākshasataḥ*), 15921 (*Gandharva-Y°ānugataḥ*, sc. Kubera), 15925 (*senāpatyaṃ . . . Y°-Rākshasasenayoḥ*, bestowed on Vibhīshaṇa), 16168 (*deva-Dānava-Gandharva-Y°-Kimpurushaiḥ . . . ajitaḥ*, sc. Rāvaṇa), 16177 (some *Y.* serve Rāvaṇa), 16561, 16578 (*deva-Gandharva-Y°āṇāṃ*), 16579 (°-*Rākshasa-Pannagāḥ*), 17277 (*karma tad Y°-Rakshasāṃ*); IV, 1762 (*deva-Gandharva-mahoragasamākulaṃ . . . maṇḍalaṃ*), †2176 (*devāsura-Siddha-Y°ān*), 2271 (*Gandharva-Y°pravarāḥ*); V, 332 (°-*Raksho-mahoragāḥ*), 348 (*deva-Dānava-Y°āṇāṃ*, sc. *rājā*, i.e. Nahusha), 518 (*sarva-Y°āṇāṃ*, sc. *ādhipatyaṃ*, given to Kubera), 540, †824 (*Gandharva Y°āpsarasaḥ*), 2033 (had been slain by Bhīmasena), 2353 (°-*Gandharva-bhogishu*), 3826 (*Gandharva-Y°-Siddhaiḥ*, cannot see Purusha), 3830 (*Rākshasa-Y°āṇāṃ . . . ādhipatyena*, bestowed on Kubera), 4028 (*nāga-Y°-manushyāṇāṃ*), 4175 (*devān . . . sa-Y°āsura-Pannagān*, all. to Khāṇḍavadahanaparvan), 4424 (°-*Gandharva Rakshasāṃ*), 5289 (*Kubera iva Y°āṇāṃ*, sc. *senāpatiḥ*), 5867, 7524, (7527), 7533, 7535, 7536 (°*gaṇān*), 7537; VI, 291 (°*ānugāḥ*, sc. the inhabitants of the varsha Hiraṇmaya), 814 (°-*Rakshaḥ-Piçācebhyaḥ*), 1227 (*Vitteço Y°-Rakshasāṃ*, sc. *asmi*, says Kṛshṇa), †1268 (*Gandharva-Y°āsurasaṅghāḥ*), 1430 (*yajante . . . Y°-Rakshāṃsi rājasāḥ*), 2961 (°-*Rākshasa-Pannagāḥ*); VII, 159 (*Kubera iva Y°āṇāṃ*, sc. *senāpatiḥ*), 1463 (*sa-Y°oraga-Rākshasāḥ . . . lokāḥ*), 2287 (came to the sacrifices of Māndhātṛ), 2864 (*deva-Dānava-Y°āṇāṃ . . . sādhanaṃ*, i.e. Çiva), 3444 (*sa-Y°oraga-Rākshasāḥ . . . trayo lokāḥ*), 5456 (*tridaçān . . . sa-Y°āsura-mānavān*), 6048 (°*oraga-Rākshasāḥ*), 6339 (do.), 7004 (*deva-Gandharva-Y°āṇāṃ*), 7015 (*jagat . . . sa-Y°-Rākshasagaṇaṃ*), 7021 (*devaiḥ . . . sa-Daitya-Y°-Gandharvaiḥ*), †7293 (*nāgāḥ sa-Y°oraga-Kinnarāḥ*), †7312 (*Gandharva-Y°āḥ*), †7313, 8432, 8434 (all. to Khāṇḍavadahanap.), 8611 (°-*Rākshasasaṅkulaṃ . . . ākāçaṃ*), 9197 (only B.), 9442 (do.), †9465 (*Gandharva-Y°ān*), 9474 (only B.); VIII, †1742 (*Garuḍa-Piçāca-sa-Y°-Rākshasān*, all. to Khāṇḍavadahanaparvan), 4426 (*nāga-Y°āḥ*), †4490 (*deva-nāgāsura-Siddha-Y°aiḥ*), †4962 (°-*mahoragaiḥ*); IX, 2139 (in Çaṅkhatīrtha), 2496 (*Bhūta-Y°-vihaṅgānāṃ*, sc. *aiçvaryāṇi*), 2509 (°-*Rākshasa-Pannagaiḥ*), 2531 (°-*Rakshāṃsi*), 2849 (in Ādityatīrtha), 3297; X, 438 (°-*Rakshaḥsamākīrṇe*), 441; XII, 62 (on the mountain Mahendra), 1608 (°-*Rākshasa-Pannagāḥ*, do not know Nārāyaṇa), 1830 (°-*Rākshasān*), 2240 (°-*Rākshasabhartā . . . Naravāhanaḥ*, i.e. Kubera), 2245 (°-*Rākshasa-nāgaiḥ*), 4409 (°-*Rakshaḥ-Piçācānāṃ*), 5587 (°-*Gandharva-Siddhānāṃ madhye bhrājantam Indravat*), 5773 (°-*Rākshasasevitaḥ . . . deçaḥ*), 6323 (*vanaṃ . . . Y°-Kinnara-sevitaṃ*), 6932 (°-*Rākshasa-nāgāḥ*, their creation), 7656 (°-*Rākshasān*), †8425 (*Kinnara-Y°-Rākshasāḥ*), 9771, 9809, 10216 (*Vaiçravaṇaḥ . . . Y°āṇām īçvaraḥ*), 10336 (°-*Gandharva-saṅghaiḥ*), 10666 (*Dhanadaḥ . . . Y°-Rakshodhipaḥ*, i.e. Kubera), 10838 (°-*Rākshasa-Gandharvāḥ*), †11097 (°*gaṇān*), 11003 (°*āṇāṃ vishayān*), 11244 (*trailokye . . . sa-Y°-Bhūta-Gandharve*), 12333 (°-*Rākshasa-Dānavaiḥ*), 12622 (°-*Rākshasa-saṅghaiḥ*); XIII, 308, 734 (°-*Rākshasa-sarpāṇāṃ*, Çiva assumes their forms), 804 (*devānāṃ sa-Y°oraga-R°āṃ*), 806 (°*endra-bala-Rakshaḥsu*, only B., C. has *yajñendra°*), 912 (*Kuberaḥ sarva-Y°āṇāṃ*, sc. *asi*, i.e. Çiva), 958, 1294 (°-*Rākshasāḥ*), 1373, 1421 (*Maṇibhadrapurogamāḥ . . . Kauberā Y°-Gandharva-Kinnarāḥ*), 4701, 4705 (*Gandharva-nāga-Y°ebhyaḥ*), 4711 (°-*Rākshasāḥ*), 4717 (°-*Rākshasa-bhoginām*), 4731 (*deva-Y°oraga-nṛṇāṃ*), 4734 (°*Rākshasa-pannagāḥ*), 4737 (°-*Rakshasāṃ*), †4860 (*Gandharva-Y°aiḥ*), 6344 (°-*Gandharvaiḥ*), 6351, 6547, 7071 (*sa-Y°oraga-Rākshasaṃ . . . jagat*); XIV, 184 (worship Çiva on Muñjavat), †1169, 1183 (*nara-Kinnara-Y°āṇāṃ . . . īçvaraḥ*, i.e. Vishṇu), 1226 (*nara-Kinnara-Y°āṇāṃ Īçvaraḥ prabhuḥ*), 1566 (°-*Gandharva-Rākshasān*), 1581 (°-*Rākshasayonyoḥ*), †1683, †1684, 1919 (offerings made to the *Y.*); XVIII, 146 (°-*puṇyajanaiḥ*, some of the fallen warriors joined the *Y.* after death), 174 (Ghaṭotkaca, etc., joined the gods and the *Y.* after death), 198 (in the world of the *Y.*, 1,400,000 verses of the Mhbhr. are known), 199 (Çuka recited the Mhbhr. to the *Y.* and Rakshases).

Yaksha[2], sg. (do.): III, 1590 (Arjuna asked the Kirāta if he was a *Y.*), 1592 (do.), 2151 (Nala was asked if he was a *Y.*, etc); V, 4063 (Yayāti was asked if he was a *Y.*); XII, 1076.

Names of single Yakshas:—

Amogha: III, 14548 (*mahā°*, *A°*).

Macakruka: III, 5079 (*M°*, C. has by error *Maṅkanakaḥ*), 7070 (*M°*).

Māṇivara: III, 10824 (*M°*).

Sthūṇa (Sthūṇākarṇa): I, 2453 (*Sthūṇaḥ*); V, 2003, 7476 (*Sthūṇākarṇena*), 7479 (*Sthūṇaḥ*), 7480, 7482 (°*pradhānāya*), 7483, 7484, 7485, 7486 (*mahā°*), 7487, 7495 (*Sthūṇaḥ*), †7521 (*Sthūṇasya*), 7537 (*Sthūṇaḥ*), (7542), 7544 (*Sthūṇayakshena*).

Yaksha[2], sg., said of Dharma assuming the form of a *Y.*: I, 166 (°*rūpeṇa*), (17253), (17272), (17280), 17281, (†17315), (17322), 17323, 17324, (17326), 17328, (17330), (17332), (17334), (17336), (17338), (17340), (17342), (17344), (17346), (17348), (17350), (17352), (17354), (17356), (17358), (17360), (17362), (17364), (17366), (17368), (17370), 17371, (17372), (17374), (17376), (17378), (17380), (17382), (17384), (17386), (17388), 17392), 17393, (17397), (17399), (17404), (17407), 17408, (17409), 17414, 17415, 17417, (17418), 17419, 17420, (17424), (17431).

Yakshādhipa ("lord of the Yakshas") = Kubera: III, 2554 (*Vaiçravaṇaḥ*), 16548; V, 7530.

Yakshādhipati (do.) = Kubera: III, 11755, 11761.

Yakshapati (do.) = Kubera: V, 7524, 7533.

Yakshapravara ("the principal Yaksha") = Kubera: III, 11371.

Yaksharāj ("king of the Yakshas") = Kubera: III, 1651; VIII, †4514 (?).—Do.[2] = Maṇibhadra: III, 2529 (*M°*).

Yaksharāja (do.) = Kubera: III, 11374; V, 7538.

Yaksharājan (do.) = Kubera: IX, 2756 (*K°*).

Yaksharakshodhipa ("lord of Yakshas and Rākshasas") = Kubera: XII, 10666 (*Dhanadaḥ*).

Yaksharākshasabhartṛ (do.) = Kubera: XII, 2240.

Yakshayuddha(m) ("the combat with the Yakshas"). § 10 (Parvasaṅgr.): I, **2**, 322 (i.e. Yakshayuddhaparvan).

[Yakshayuddhaparvan(°va)] ("the combat with the Yakshas", the 38th of the minor parvans of Mbhbr.; cf. Yakshayuddha). § 436. The Pāṇḍavas, etc., returned to the hermitage of *Nārāyaṇa*. Once *Yudhishṭhira* said to them: "We have passed these four years in the woods; it has been appointed by *Arjuna*, that after the fifth year he will come to the mountain *Çveta*." They then set out with the brahmans and the *Rākshasas*, and protected by *Lomaça*, sometimes going on foot, sometimes carried by the *Rākshasas*, towards the north, beholding on the way the mountains *Maināka*, *Gandhamādana*, and *Çveta*, and on the seventeenth day they reached the slopes of *Himavat*, not far from *Gandhamādana*, and were received by R.-ṛ. *Vṛshaparvan* in his hermitage, where they passed seven nights. On the eighth day they entrusted their remaining robes, their sacrificial vessels, ornaments, and jewels to *Vṛshaparvan*, and, following his instructions, set out for the north, on foot, with *Dhaumya*, *Kṛshṇā*, and *Lomaça*. On the fourth day they reached *Çveta*, and entered *Gandhamādana* (*b*) with *Draupadī* and the brahmans, and saw the great *Gaṅgā* (*c*). Thereafter, they went to the hermitage of *Ārshṭisheṇa* (III, **158**). *Ārshṭisheṇa* received the four *Pāṇḍavas* and *Kṛshṇa* and *Dhaumya*, and said that during the *parvan* days *ṛshis* living upon water and air and moving through the sky come to this mountain, sounds of kettledrums, etc., being heard on the summits, and that they should not attempt to proceed further, but wait for *Arjuna* there, as they could not go beyond *Kailāsa* (*d*) (III, **159**).—§ 437. They passed the fifth year in the hermitage of *Ārshṭisheṇa*, eating flesh of deer killed with unpoisoned shafts, listening to the stories told by *Lomaça*. *Ghaṭotkaca* had departed, promising to be present when occasion arose. *Munis* and *Cāraṇas* visited them. One day *Suparṇa* carried off a mighty *Nāga* from the lake, while the mountain trembled, etc., and the wind, raised by *Suparṇa's* wings, brought celestial flowers of five colours before the Pāṇḍavas towards the river *Açvarathā*. *Kṛshṇā* expressed to *Bhīma* the wish of seeing the top of the mountain when he had driven away the *Rākshasas*. *Bhīma* set out with bow, sword, and mace, and having ascended the summit, thereby gladdening *Kinnaras*, *Nāgas*, *Munis*, *Gandharvas*, and *Rākshasas*, he blew his shell. *Yakshas* and *Rākshasas* (*Krodhavaçāḥ*, v. 11757) assailed him with maces, clubs, etc., but were killed or defeated, and the surviving fled towards the south, forsaking their weapons. The *Rākshasa* *Maṇimat*, the friend of *Kubera*, in vain attempted to recall them, and with clubs, javelins, etc., he rushed at *Bhīma* and pierced his right arm with an iron spear with a golden haft, but at last was killed by *Bhīma* with his mace. The surviving *Rākshasas* went towards the east (III, **160**).—§ 438. Hearing various sounds and not seeing *Bhīma*, the *Pāṇḍavas* and *Kṛshṇā*, and *Dhaumya* and the brahmans were filled with anxiety, and, entrusting *Draupadī* to the charge of *Ārshṭisheṇa*, they ascended the summit of the mountain and embraced *Bhīma*, who was censured and again warned by *Yudhishṭhira*. *Kubera*, on hearing about the matter from the *Rākshasas*, in anger let yoke his carriage, and, eulogized by the gods and *Gandharvas*, and surrounded by 1,000 *Yakshas*, he set out through the firmament to *Gandhamādana*, where he seated himself on his seat *Pushpaka* (*b*), surrounded by *Yakshas*, *Rākshasas*, *Gandharvas*, and *Apsarases*, with his noose and sword and bow, and asked *Yudhishṭhira* not to be angry with *Bhīma* as *Bhīma* had only been the instrument of destiny, and said to *Bhīma* that he did not mind his act of rashness as he had thereby been delivered from the curse of *Agastya* (*c*) (III, **161**). *Kubera* then gave *Yudhishṭhira* some wise counsel, referring to the *Kṛta-yuga* (*d*); he said, that *Yudhishṭhira* ought to check the rashness of *Bhīmasena*; they should return to the hermitage of the R.-ṛ *Ārshṭisheṇa* and reside there during the first dark fortnight; the inhabitants of *Alakā* with *Gandharvas*, and *Yakshas* with *Kinnaras*, etc., should, at the command of *Kubera*, protect them, and his servants procure for them meat and drink; he praised *Arjuna* (*e*). *Arjuna* would soon join them. Then *Kubera* went to the mountain *Asta*, followed by thousands of *Yakshas* and *Rākshasas* in vehicles drawn by horses flying in the air. The dead bodies of the *Rākshasas* were, at the command of *Kubera*, removed. The *Pāṇḍavas* dwelt several nights there, being honoured by the *Rākshasas* (III, **162**).—§ 439. At sunrise, *Dhaumya* and *Ārshṭisheṇa* came to them, and *Dhaumya*, seizing *Yudhishṭhira's* hands, pointed out, towards the east, the *Mandara* mountain, the east being the region of *Indra* and *Vaiçravaṇa*, as the *South* is that of *Yama* with his abode *Saṃyamana*, and the *Asta* mountain, where the sun sets in the west, that of *Varuṇa*, together with the ocean; in the north *Meru*, with the dwelling of *Brahmán*, where *Prajāpati* creates all creatures, and the seven mind-born sons of *Brahmán* (of whom *Daksha* was the seventh), and where the seven *Devarshis* (i.e. *Saptarshayaḥ*), with *Vasishṭha* at their head, rise and set; next, to the east of *Meru*, the abode of *Nārāyaṇa* or *Vishṇu*, that cannot be seen by gods or *Dānavas*, and where even *Brahmarshis* have no access, not to speak of *Maharshis*, but only *Yatis*; thence, they do not return to this world; *Vishṇu* alone shines there. Description of the revolving around *Meru* of the sun, moon, and stars ("having coursed round *Meru*, the moon again repairs to *Mandara*", v. ii, 873) (III, **163**).—§ 440. The *Pāṇḍavas* dwelled there for a month, visited by *Gandharvas* and *Maharshis*. A night and a day became to them like a year, for since the departure of *Arjuna*, they had not felt joy. After having dwelt for five years in the abode of *Indra* and obtained all celestial weapons from him, *Āgneya, Vāruṇa, Saumya, Vāyavya, Vaishṇava, Aindra, Pāçupata, Brāhmya, Pārameshṭhya,* and those of *Prajāpati, Yama, Dhātṛ, Savitṛ, Tvashṭṛ,* and *Vaiçravaṇa. Arjuna* took leave of *Indra* and came to *Gandhamādana* (III, **164**).

Yakshendra[1] ("lord of the Yakshas") = Kubera: V, 7531, 7536; XIV, 1918 (*K*°).—Do.[2] = Māṇibhadra: III, 10826 (*M*°).—Do.[3] (do.) = Piṅgala: III, 14565 (*P*°).—Do.[4] (do.) = Taraṇḍaka (Arantuka, B.): III, 6022.

Yakshī ("female Yaksha"). § 162 (Çāntanūp.): I, **97,** 3895 (Gaṅgā was questioned if she was a *Y.*, etc.).—§ 347 (Nalopākhyānap.): III, **64,** 2519 (Damayantī was questioned if she was a *Y.*, etc.); **65,** 2558 (Damayantī supposed to be a *Y.*).—§ 522 (Draupadīharaṇap.): III, **265,** †15589 Draupadī was questioned if she was a *Y.*).—§ 549 (Pāṇḍavapraveçap.): IV, **9,** 257 (do.).

Yakshiṇī (do.). § 362 (Tīrthayātrāp.): III, **83,** 5093 (probably also name of a tīrtha).—§ 370 (do.): III, **84,** 8083 (°*ṇyā naityakaṃ prāçnīta*), 8084 (°*ṇyās tu prasādena mucyate brahmahatyayā*).

Yama[1], lord of the spirits of the dead, son of Vivasvat, often identified with Dharma. § 11 (Parvasaṅgr.): I, **2,** 535 (*Y°sādanaṃ*, only B.).—§ 51 (Parikshit): I, **41,** 1705 (*netā Y°sya sadanaṃ prati*); **42,** 1758 (*Y°sādanaṃ*). — § 61 (Sarpasattra): I, **55,** †2099 (°*sya yajño yathā*), †2107 (*Dharmarājaḥ*, comparison), †2111 (°*o yathā dharmaviniçcayajñaḥ*). — § 134 (Viçvāmitra): I, **71,** †2933.—§ 135 (Çakuntalop.): I, **74,** 3017 (among those who witness the acts of men), 3018 (*Vaivasvataḥ*), 3019 (*viyātayati duḥkṛtam*), 3072 (°*sya*, sc. *bhavanaṃ*).—§ 139 (Manu Vaivasvata): I, **75,** 3136 (*Vivasvataḥ sutaḥ . . . Vaivasvataḥ*).—§ 147 (Devayānī): I, **82,** 3408 (°*sya*, sc. *gṛhe*).—§ 151 (Pūruvaṃç.): I, **94,** 3711 (*Y°kshayaṃ*).—§ 156 (do.): I, **95,** 3784 (*retodhāḥ putra unnayati . . . Y°kshayāt*).—§ 167 (Vicitravīryop.): I, **102,** 4143 (*Y°sādanaṃ*).—§ 193 (Pāṇḍu): I, **125,** 4891 (°*sadane*).—§ 213 (Jatugṛhap.): I, **151,** 5920 (*Y°kshayaṃ*).—§ 214 (Hiḍimbavadhap.): I, **153,** 5990 (*Y°sādanaṃ*).—§ 215 (Bakavadhap.): I, **163,** 6276 (do.). — § 223 (Vāsishṭha): I **174,** 6641 (°*kshayāt*). — § 233 (Svayaṃvarap.): I, **187,** †7010 (came to see the svayaṃvara of Draupadī).—§ 238 (Pañcendrop.): I, **197,** †7276 (partook of the sacrifice of the gods in Naimishāraṇya). — § 243 (Vidurāgamanap.): I, **205,** 7505 (°*sutāv iva*). — § 246 (Sundopasundop.): I, **210,** 7671 (*Y°sādanaṃ*). — § 258 (Khāṇḍavadahanap.): I, **227,** 8264 (armed with the *Kāla-daṇḍa* he fought with Kṛshṇa and Arjuna).—§ 263 (Sabhākriyāp.): II, **3,** 72 (performs sacrifices at Bindusaras).—§ 265 (Lokapālasabhākhyānap.): II, **5,** 222 (°*vat*); **6,** 280 (*Vaivasvataṃ*). — § 267 (Yamasabhāv.): II, **8,** 318 (*Vaivasvataṃ*), 343 (°*sya purushāḥ*) (description of his palace).—§ 270 (Brahmasabhāv.): II, **11,** 466 (waits upon Brahmán).—§ 274 (Rājasūyārambhap.): II, **16,** 662 (°*o hi na vijetājau*, sc. *Jarāsandhabalaṃ*).—§ 275 (do.): II, **17,** 690 (°*āntakasamaḥ*, sc. Bṛhadratha).—§ 277 (Jarāsandhavadhap.): II, **22,** 876 (*Y°kshayaṃ*), 879 (do.).—§ 290 (Çiçupālavadhap.): II, **40,** 1427 (*netukāmo Y°kshayaṃ*).—§ 294 (Dyūtap.): II, **49,** 1760 (°*sya*, sc. *çrīḥ*). — § 298 (do.): II, **62,** 2110 (*Y°kshayaṃ*).—§ 299 (do.): II, **66,** 2188 (do.).—§ 304 (Anudyūtap.): II, **77,** 2531 ((*Y°sādanaṃ*), 2547 (do.).—§ 316 (Kirmīravadhap.): III, **11,** 428 (°*daṇḍapratīkāçam*, sc. *vṛkshaṃ*), 451 (*Y°sya sadanaṃ*). — § 317*b* (Kṛshṇa Vāsudeva): III, **12,** 480 (Kṛshṇa becomes *Y.*, etc.)—§ 319 (Saubhavadhop.): III, **14,** 625 (*Y°kshayaṃ*).—§ 320 (do.): III, **22,** 879 (*cakraṃ Kalāntaka-Y°opamaṃ*). — § 323 (Dvaitavanapr.): III, **25,** †954 (°*sya netā*, sc. Rāma Dāçarathi).—§ 325 (Draupadīparitāpav.): III, **27,** 1013 (*Kālāntaka-Y°opamaḥ*, sc. Arjuna).—§ 327 (do.): III, **29,** 1070 (*Y°sādanaṃ*).—§ 331 (Kairātap.): III, **39,** 1560 (do.), 1578 (do.), 1592 (do.), 1598 (*Y°sya sadanaṃ*).—§ 333*c* (Brahmaçiras): III, **40,** 1651 (does not know Brahmaçiras). § 334 (Kairātap.): III, **41,** 1672 (*sārdhaṃ Pitṛbhiḥ*), 1680 (*paramadharmajñaḥ*, gave a weapon to Arjuna), 1697.—§ 345 (Nalopākhyānap.): III, **55,** 2138 (*çarīrāntakaro nṛṇāṃ*), 2140, 2157; **57,** 2228 (among the Lokapālas present at the svayaṃvara of Draupadī, granted Nala boons).—§ 378 (Tīrthayātrāp.): III, **91,** 8419 (Arjuna had obtained weapons from *Y.*, etc.)—§ 402 (do.): III, **120,** †10263 (°*kshayaṃ*). — § 407 (Māndhātrup.): III, **126,** 10444 (*Y°sādanaṃ*).—§ 412 (Ashṭāvakrīya): III, **134,** †10658 (*Pitṝṇāṃ īçvaraḥ*).—§ 416 (Yavakrītop.): III, **137,** 10783 (*Kālāntaka-Y°opamaṃ*, sc. the residence of Raibhya).—§ 418 (Gandhamādanapr.): III, **139,** 10833.—§ 422*bis* (Varāhāvatāra): III, **142,** 10934 (°*tvaṃ*).—§ 424 (Bhīmakadalīkhaṇḍapr.): III, **147,** 11180 (*Y°kshayaṃ*).—§ 432 (Saugandhikāharaṇa): III, **154,** †11384 (°*daṇḍakalpāṃ mahāgadāṃ*).—§ 439 (Yakshayuddhap.): III, **163,** 11848 (*rājā*, in the south).—§ 440 (do.): III, **164,** 11901 (°*sya*, sc. *astraṃ*, obtained by Arjuna).—§ 443 (Nivātakavacayuddhap.): III, **168,** 12005 (in the south).—§ 444 (do.): III, **171,** 12160 (*Y°sādanaṃ*); **172,** 12178 (do.).—§ 450 (Ājagarap.): III, **178,** 12389 (*Kālāntaka-Y°opamaṃ*, sc. *bhujaṅgaṃ*). — § 459 (Mārkaṇḍeyas.): III, **189,** 12954 (*Pretādhipaḥ*, Nārāyaṇa identified with *Y.*).—§ 469 (do.): III, **200,** 13372 (*nopasarpanti te Y°ṃ*), 13389 (°*sya te nirvacanā bhavanti*).—§ 470 (Yamaloka): III, **200,** 13397 (°*dūtais tu Y°syājñākaraiḥ*).—§ 506 (Skandayuddha): III, **231,** 14550 (*Mṛtyunā saha*), 14551.—§ 511 (Draupadī-Satyabhāmāsaṃv.): III, **235,** 14730 (*samprasthitān . . . Y°sādanaṃ*).—§ 512 (Ghoshayātrāp.): III, **237,** 14782 (*Rudrair (!) iva Y°ḥ*, sc. *vṛtaḥ*); **245,** 14985 (*Y°sādanaṃ*).—§ 522 (Draupadīharaṇap.): III, **265,** †15590 (Draupadī was questioned if she was the wife of *Y.*).—§ 543 (Rāmābhisheka): III, **291*a*,** 16548.—§ 545 (Pativratāmāhātmyap.): III, **297,** (16758), 16763, 16765, (16766), (†16773), (†16775), (†16778), (†16780), †16781 (°*tvaṃ*), (†16784), (†16786), (†16791), (†16793), (†16798), 16802 (*Vaivasvataḥ*), 16809, 16813 (*prajāsaṃyamanaḥ*); **298,** 16895 (*Y.* came to fetch Satyavat, but gratified by Sāvitrī, he granted her several boons, among these the life of Satyavat).—§ 548 (Āraṇeyap.): III, **313,** 17314 (*Kālāntaka-Y°āt*), 17401 (*Y°ālaye*). — § 551 (Kīcakavadhap.): IV, **23,** 821 (*Y°sādanaṃ*). — § 552 (Goharaṇap.): IV, **30,** 988 (*Y°kshayaṃ*); **32,** 1039 (°*rāshṭravivardhanaḥ*, sc. *samāgamaḥ*); **45**δ, 1433; **47,** 1490 (*api*); **56**ζ, 1770 (°*sya*, sc. *vimānaṃ*); **60,** 1945 (*Y°sādanaṃ*).—§ 554 (Sainyodyogap.): V, **3,** 54 (*Y°sya sadanaṃ*), 57 (*Yamau . . . Y°-Kālopamadyutī*).—§ 555 (Indravijaya): V, **16,** †511 (*Vaivasvataḥ*, among the Lokapālas who came to Indra), 515, [519 (*Vaivasvataṃ*; *h*: Indra bestowed the sovereignty over the Pitṛs on *Y.*)]; **17,** 545.—§ 556 (Sañjayayānap.): V, **20,** 609 (*Y°sādanaṃ*); **29,** †824.—§ 558 (Prajāgarap.): V, **35,** 1253 (*pracchannapāpānāṃ çāstā Vaivasvataḥ*).—§ 560 (Sanatsujātap.): V, **42,** †1581 (°*ṃ tv eke Mṛtyum ato 'nyam āhuḥ*).—§ 561 (Yānasandhip.): V, **55,** 2187 (*Y°sādanaṃ*); **69,** 2552 (°*sya vaçam āyanti*).—§ 564 (Mātalīyop.): V, **100,** 3570.—§ 565 (Gālavacarita): V, **117,** 3968 (*reme . . . Ūrmilāyāṃ yathā*

Y°ḥ, B. *yathā Dhūmorṇayā Yamaḥ*, cf xiii, 7637).—§ 567 (Bhagavadyānap.): V, **130**, 4385 (*Y°sādanaṃ*).—§ 568 (do.): V, **137**, 4664 (*kruddhāv iva Y°āntakau*).—§ 569 (do.): V, **143**, 4837 (*Y°sādanaṃ*), (κ), 4876 (do.).—§ 570 (Sainyaniryāṇap.): V, **151**, 5123 (*°dūtasamān vege*), 5143 (*Yamau . . . Y°opamau*); **158**ν, 5381.—§ 571 (Ulūkadūtāgamanap.): V, **162**, 5601 (*Y°kshayaṃ*), 5604, 5606 (do.).—§ 573 (Ambopākhyānap.): V, **184**, 7271 (*°daṇḍasamaprabhāṃ*, sc. *çaktiṃ*). — § 574 (Jambūkh.): VI, **4**, 158 (*Y°kshayaṃ*). — § 576 (Bhagavadgītāp.): VI, **34**, 1233 (*°ḥ saṃyamatām ahaṃ*, sc. *asmi*, says Kṛshṇa); **35**, †1285 (identified with Kṛshṇa).—§ 578 (Bhīshmavadhap.): VI, **50**, 2039 (*kruddhaḥ*).—§ 579 (do.): VI, **54**, 2280 (*Kālāntaka-Y°opamaḥ*, sc. Bhīma), 2309 (*Y°sādanaṃ*), 2310 (do.), 2314 (do.); **55**, 2396 (*rūpaṃ Kālāntaka-Y°opamaṃ*).—§ 581 (do.): VI, **62**, 2774 (*°daṇḍopamāṃ . . . gadāṃ*); **63**, 2798 (do.); **64**, 2842 (*Y°sādanaṃ*), 2847 (do.).—§ 582 (do.): VI, **74**, 3260 (*°daṇḍāçanisvanān*, sc. *çaraughān*).—§ 583 (do.): VI, **75**, 3307 (*Y°sya sādanaṃ*); **79**, 3460 (*Y°sādanaṃ*), 3507 (*°rāshṭravivardhanaṃ*, sc. *yuddhaṃ*), 3509 (*Y°kshayaṃ*).—§ 584 (do.): VI, **83**, 3646 (*°rāshṭravivardhanaḥ*, sc. *prakshayaḥ*), 3654 (*Y°sādanaṃ*), 3679 (*ajeyaṃ . . . Y°ena*), 3685 (*Y°sya sadanaṃ*); **85**, †3783 (*°daṇḍakalpaiḥ . . . çaraiḥ*), †3786 (*°daṇḍakalpāṃ . . . gadāṃ*).—§ 585 (do.): VI, **87**, 3883 (*Y°kshayaṃ*); **88**, 3915 (*Y°sya sadanaṃ*); **89**, 3938 (*Y°sādanaṃ*), 3952 (*Y°kshayaṃ*), 3958 (*°rāshṭravivardhanaḥ*, sc. *saṅgrāmaḥ*); **91**, 4071 (*Kālāntaka-Y°opamaḥ*, sc. Ghaṭotkaca); **94**, 4202 (*Kālāntaka-Y°opamau*), 4203 (*Y°daṇḍopamāṃ*, sc. *gadāṃ*, only B.); **95**, 4256 (*°rāshṭravivardhanaṃ*, sc. *yuddhaṃ*); **96**, 4368 (*Y°sādanaṃ*); **98**, 4467 (do.).—§ 586 (do.): VI, **100**, 4534 (*°daṇḍopamān . . . sāyakān*); **101**, 4602 (*°daṇḍopamāḥ*, sc. *viçikhāḥ*); **103**, 4697 (*°rāshṭravivardhanaṃ*, sc. *yuddhaṃ*), 4698 *Y°sādanaṃ*), 4717 (*°rāshṭra°*); **104**, 4731 (*Y°sādanaṃ*); **106**, 4807 (*°daṇḍopamaiḥ*, sc. *bāṇaiḥ*); **107**φ, 4901, 4960, 4984 (*Y°kshayaṃ*).—§ 587 (do.): VI, **108**, 5010 (*°rāshṭravivardhanaṃ*, sc. *yuddhaṃ*); **110**, 5132 (*°daṇḍopamān*, sc. *viçikhān*), 5151 (*°daṇḍopamāṃ*, sc. *çaktiṃ*); **112**, 5238 (*sadṛçaḥ . . . Y°sya*); **116**, 5422 (*gadāṃ Y°daṇḍopamāṃ*); **118**, 5543 (*Y°sādanaṃ*); **119**, 5630 (*°dūtā iva*).—§ 589 (Droṇābhishekap.): VII, **2**, †66 (*Y°sadane*), †68 (*Yamau . . . Yamopamau*), †83 (*Y°āya*); **8**, 244 (*Y°sādanaṃ*); **10**, 346 (*°-Vaiçravaṇāditya-Mahendra-Varuṇopamaṃ*).—§ 590 (do.): VII, **14**, 509 (*Y°sādanaṃ*).—§ 592 (Saṃçaptakavadhap.): VII, **19**, 767 (do.); **21**, 909 (do.); **23**ο, 991 (*°-Vaiçravaṇopamaḥ*); **25**, 1090 (*Y°sādanaṃ*); **27**, 1223 (*°ena . . . dushkaraṃ*); **28**, 1233 (*Y°kshayaṃ*); **32**, 1447 (*°rāshṭravivardhanam*, sc. *yuddhaṃ*).—§ 593 (Abhimanyuvadhap.): VII, **46**, 1847 (*Y°sādanaṃ*).—§ 594 (Mṛtyu): VII, **54**, 2077 (*°sya bhavanaṃ*), 2107 (*lokapālaḥ*).—§ 595 (Shoḍaçarāj., v. Pṛthu Vainya): VII, **69**, 2419 (*Vaivasvataḥ*, when the puṇyajanāḥ milked the earth, *Y.* was their calf).—§ 596 (Pratijñāp.): VII, **72**, 2503 (*paçyāmi Y°sādanaṃ*, read *yāsyāmi* with B.), 2509 (*yāsyāmi Y°sādanaṃ*), 2511 (do.); **74**, 2617 (*Y°kshayaṃ*); **76**δ, 2691; **77**, 2711 (*°rāshṭravivṛddhaye*); **78**, 2741 (*Y°kshayaṃ*).—§ 597 (do.): VII, **83**, 2972 (*rājadhānīṃ Y°syādya hataḥ prāpsyati*).—§ 599 (Jayadrathavadhap.): VII, **93**, 3366 (*Y°sya sadanaṃ*); **94**, 3425 (*°daṃshṭrāntaraṃ prāptaḥ*); **100**, 3753 (*Y°sādanaṃ*); **108**, 4059 (*Y°sya sadanaṃ*); **110**, 4152 (*°daṃshṭrāntaraṃ gataṃ*); **113**, 4380 (*Y°kshayaṃ*); **116**, 4640 (*°daṇḍopamaḥ çaraḥ*); **119**, 4726 (*Kālāntaka-Y°opamaṃ*, sc. Sātyaki); **125**, 5057 (*Y°kshayaṃ*), 5071 (*Y°sya sadanaṃ*), 5072 (*°āya preshayām āsa*); **127**, 5210 (*Y°kshayaṃ*); **129**, 5303 (*Y°sādanaṃ*, only C.); **130**, 5345 (do.); **132**, 5444 (*°rāshṭropamaṃ . . . āyodhanaṃ*); **133**, 5480 (*°daṇḍopamān*, sc. *çarān*), 5489 (*Y°kshayaṃ*), 5496 (*Y°sādanaṃ*); **134**, 5520 (*Y°kshayaṃ*); **135**, 5543 (*°-Kālāntako[pa]maṃ*), 5570 (*Y°kshayaṃ*); **139**, 5750 (*°daṇḍam ivāparaṃ*); **145**, †6151 (*°rāshṭravardhanaḥ*), †6152 (*°rāshṭravardhanāḥ*); **150**, 6508 (*Y°sādanaṃ*). — § 600 (Ghaṭotkacavadhap.): VII, **153**, 6606 (*°rāshṭrāya . . . dīkshitāḥ*), 6607 (*Y°kshayaṃ*); **154**, 6680 (do.); **155**, 6716 (do.); **156**, 6908 (*°kshaya°*, C., *°rāshṭra°*, B.), 6913 (*Y°kshayaṃ*), 6915 (*°daṇḍopamaṃ*, sc. *çaraṃ*); **159**, 7090 (*Kālāntaka-Y°opamaṃ*, sc. Arjuna), 7104 (*Y°sādanaṃ*); **160**, 7174 (*Y°kshayaṃ*); **166**, 7432 (*°daṇḍopamaṃ*, sc. *çaraṃ*); **167**, 7466 (*Y°kshayaṃ*), 7491 (do.); **168**, 7558 (*rāshṭravivardhanaṃ*, sc. *yuddhaṃ*); **171**, 7698 (*Y°kshayaṃ*), 7717 (*Y°sya sadanaṃ*), 7730 (*°rāshṭraṃ*); **173**, 7777 (*Y°kshayaṃ*, only C.); **174**, 7855 (*Y°sādanaṃ*); **180**δδ, 8194 (*notsahet Karṇaṃ*).—§ 601 (Droṇavadhap.): VII, **184**, 8381 (*Y°kshayaṃ*); **185**ε, 8444.—§ 603 (Nārāyaṇāstramokshap.): VII, **200**, 9353 (*°daṇḍanibhān*, sc. *nārācān*).—§ 603*d* (Tripura): VII, **202**, 9569 (*Vaivasvataṃ*, became the *puṅkha* of Çiva's shaft).—§ 603 (Nārāyaṇāstramokshap.): VII, **202**α, 9596 (Çiva identified with *Y.*), (κκ), 9628.—§ 604 (Karṇap.): VIII, **2**γ, 42 (*Y°sādanaṃ*); **3**δ, 85 (*Y°kshayaṃ*); **5**ζ, 103 (*Y°sādanaṃ*), 105 (do.), 110 (do.), 114 (do.), 124 (do.), 135 (do.); **6**, 163 (do.), 165 (do.), 166 (do.), 167 (do.), 176 (do.), 182 (do.), 188 (do.).—§ 605 (do.): VIII, **15**, 596 (*Kālāntaka-Y°opamau*), 597 (dual, *iva*); **16**, 618 (*Y°kshayaṃ*); **21**, 830 (*°rāshṭravivardhanaḥ*, sc. *saṅgrāmaḥ*), 838 (*Y°kshayaṃ*); **22**, 878 (*°daṇḍābhaiḥ*, sc. *nārācaiḥ*); **23**, 901 (*viçikham Y°daṇḍopamatvishaṃ*); **24**, 952 (*°sya bhavanaṃ*); **27**, 1089 (*Y°kshayaṃ*), 1095 (*Y°sādanaṃ*); **30**, 1221 (*Y°kshayaṃ*).—§ 607 (do.): VIII, **37**γ, †1729 (*yāsyāmi . . . Y°āya*), †1736 (do.), †1737 (*°Varuṇa-Kubera-Vāsavāḥ*); **45**ξ, 2102 (protects the southern region inhabited by the Pitṛs.)—§ 608 (do.): VIII, **49**, 2320 (*°daṇḍanibhaṃ çaraṃ*); **51**, 2455 (*Y°kshayaṃ*), 2458 (*Y°sādanaṃ*), 2459 (*Kālāntaka-Y°opamaṃ*, sc. Bhīma); **52**, 2552 (*Y°sādanaṃ*); **54**, 2649 (do.); **56**, 2708 (*Kalāntaka-Y°opamaṃ*, sc. *rūpaṃ*), 2761 (*°daṇḍanibhaiḥ çaraiḥ*); **59**, 2910 (*°rāshṭravivardhanaḥ*, sc. *saṅgrāmaḥ*); **61**, 3109 (*Y°sya sadanam*), 3114 (*Y°kshayaṃ*); **63**, 3177 (do.); **66**, 3332 (*°tulyaḥ parākrame*); **73**, 3694 (*Y°kshayaṃ*), 3700 (do.), 3724 (do.); **74**, 3778 (*Y°rāshṭra-*); **76**, †3822 (*nayāmi . . . Y°āya*); **77**, 3876 (*Y°sya sadanaṃ*), 3878 (*Y°sādanaṃ*), 3887 (*Y°kshayaṃ*); **80**, 4118 (*niyuktān . . . Y°āya*); **81**, 4153 (*Kāladaṇḍodyataṃ*), 4155 (*Y°sādanaṃ*); **84**, 4266 (*Y°kshayaṃ*); **87**, 4390 (*°-Kālāntakopamau*), (χ'), 4421 (sided with Arjuna); **90**, †4696 (*°āgnidaṇḍapratimaiḥ*, said of arrows); **91**, †4780 (*°daṇḍakalpaṃ*, sc. *bāṇaṃ*), †4796 (*nayatāṃ Y°āya*); **92**, †4828 (*°rāshṭrakalpaṃ*, sc. *balaṃ*); **93**, 4890 (*Antako Yamaḥ*, B., *Antakopamaḥ*, C.).—§ 610 (Çalyap.): IX, **5**, 253 (*Yamāv api Y°opamau*).—§ 611 (do.): IX, **9**, 419 (*Y°kshayaṃ*, B. *°sādanaṃ*); **10**, 520 (*°rāshṭravivardhanaṃ*, sc. *yuddhaṃ*), 533 (*°rāshṭravivardhane*, sc. *saṅgrāme*); **11**, 578 (*°daṇḍapratīkāçāṃ*, sc. *gadāṃ*); **14**, 745 (*°daṇḍopamadyutiṃ*, sc. *nārācaṃ*), 750 (*°rāshṭravivardhanaṃ*, sc. *yuddhaṃ*); **15**, 762 (*Yamau . . . Y°tulyaparākramau*); **17**, †906 (*°sya dhātrīm iva*); **20**, †1070 (*°ālaye* (*°aṃ*, B)); **21**, 1100 (*Y°sādanaṃ*); **23**, 1192 (*°rāshṭravivardhanaḥ*, sc. *saṅgrāmaḥ*); **25**, 1373 (*Y°sādanaṃ*); **26**, 1426 (*°daṇḍanibhaiḥ çaraiḥ*), 1429 (*Y°kshayaṃ*); **27**, 1486 (*°daṇḍopamaṃ*, sc. *çaraṃ*); **28**, 1515 (*Y°sādanaṃ*).—§ 613

(Gadāyuddhap.): IX, **32**, 1863 (*Y°kshayam*). — § 615*u* (Skanda): IX, **45**γ, 2519 (*Kālo Y°ç ca Mṛtyuç ca Y°syānucarāç ca ye*), 2532 (gave two companions named Unmātha and Pramātha to Skanda).—§ 615*ff* (Asita Devala): IX, **50**, 2856 (*Y°vat samadarçanaḥ*).—§ 615*kk* (Kurukshetrak.): IX, **53**, 3027 (*°sya vishayam*). — § 615 (Gadāyuddhap.): IX, **55**, 3105 (*°-Vāsavayor*, sc. *sadṛçakarmāṇau*, sc. Bhīmasena and Duryodhana); **57**, 3186 (*°daṇḍopamām*, sc. *gadām*), 3202 (*°daṇḍam iva*, sc. *gadām*).—§ 616 (Sauptikap.): X, **8**, 344 (*Y°kshayam*), 401 (do.), 449 (*Y°sādanam*), 450 (*Y°sya niveçanam*).—§ 617 (Aishīkap.): X, **11**, 583 (*ātmajān . . . sampradāya Y°āya*); **13**, 669 (*Kālāntaka-Y°opamaḥ*).— § 618 (Jalapradānikap.): XI, **2**δ, 49 (*karshati*); **4**, 114 (*°dūtaiḥ*); **5**, 128 (*traset*).—§ 621 (Rājadh.): XII, **5**ζ, 141 (Arjuna had obtained a weapon from *Y.*).—§ 622 (do.): **15**, 428 (*°daṇḍabhayāt*), (β), 439.—§ 635 (do.): XII, **33***a*, 1168 (*Y°kshayam*).—§ 640 (do.): XII, **57**, 2064 (*°-Vaiçravaṇopamaḥ*).—§ 641 (do.): XII, **68**ι, 2576, 2579 (the ideal king comparable with *Y.*); **72**, 2773 (do.); **82**, 3086 (C. has by error *Mayaḥ*, some sentences of his quoted), 3092 (*gamito Y°sādanam*); **91**, 3444 (the ideal king comparable with *Y.*), 3446 (*°o yacchati bhūtāni*), (ν), 3458; **98**, 3634 (*°sādane*); **122**, 4495 (*°m Vaivasvatañ cāpi Pitṝṇām akarot prabhum*, sc. Vishṇu); **129**, 4718 (*Gautamasya ca saṃvādam Y°sya ca*), 4721 (*lokapālaḥ*), 4722, (4725) (discourse between Gautama and *Y.*).—§ 646*b* (Marjāramūshikasaṃv.): XII, **138**, 5028 (*°dūtābham*, said of a Cāṇḍāla).—§ 647*b* (Brahmadatta-Pūjanīsaṃv.): XII, **139**, 5236 (the ideal king comparable with *Y.*), 5238 (do.).—§ 652*b* (Indrota-Parīkshitīya): XII, **150**, 5612 (*°dūtāḥ*, *°kshaye*).—§ 654*b* (Pavana-çālmalisaṃv.): XII, **155***a*, 5831.—§ 661 (Mokshadh.): XII, **196**, 7156 (*°sya yat purā vṛttam Kālasya brāhmaṇasya ca*).— § 662 (do.): XII, **199**, 7198 (*Kāla-Mṛtyu-Y°ānām Ikshvākor brāhmaṇasya ca vivādaḥ* = do.).—§ 662*b* (Jāpakop.): XII, **199***a*, 7213, 7226, (7228), 7228, 7251, 7265 (different from Dharma, came to the brahman who was a *jāpaka*); **200**γ, 7332 (do.).—§ 664 (Mokshadh.): XII, **207**, 7554 (*°kṛtam bhayam*).—§ 677 (do.): XII, **236**, 8629 (*°sādanam*).— § 678*c* (Mṛtyu-Prajāpatisaṃv.): XII, **259**, 9193 (*°sya bhavane*).—§ 680*b* (Tulādhāra-Jājalisaṃv.): XII, **263***a*, 9380.—§ 692 (Mokshadh.): XII, **281**β, 10052 (identified with the supreme Lord).—§ 704 (do.): XII, **301**, 11061 (different from Mṛtyu and Antaka); **302**, 11128 (*°kshaye*). —§ 710 (do.): XII, **322**, 12078, 12079, 12080.—§ 717*b* (Nārāyaṇīya): XII, **335***a*, 12685.—§ 730 (Ānuçāsanik.): XIII, **16**ηη, 1058 (identified with Çiva); **17**, 1291 (*Vaivasvataḥ*, learnt the 1,000 names of Çiva from Nārāyaṇa and communicated them to Nāciketa).—§ 744 (do.): XIII, **45**, 2477 (*gāthā Y°odgītāḥ*, quoted).—§ 746 (do.): XIII, **62**, 3178; **68**, 3396 (*brāhmaṇasya ca saṃvādam Y°sya ca*), 3399, 3403 (*°çāsanam*), 3404, (3407), (3410), 3418 (*°çāsanam*), 3419 (*°dūtaḥ*), 3421, 3422 (discourse between *Y.* and Çarmin); **70**, 3472, 3476 (Nṛga was punished by *Y.*); **71**, 3491, †3502, †3513, 3522 (Uddālaki cursed Nāciketa to go to *Y.*, who, however, dismissed him after having instructed him); **80**, †3793 (*°sya loke*).—§ 749 (do.): XIII, **89**, 4255 (*°o tu yāni çrāddhāni provāca Çaçabindave*).—§ 753 (do.): XIII, **97***a*, 4661 (to *Y.* offerings should be made in the southern region). —§ 757*c* (Yamaloka): XIII, **102**, †4857 (*°sya . . . yātanām*).—§ 759 (Ānuçāsanik.): XIII, **104**, 5026 (*gāthā Y°odgītāḥ*, quoted).—§ 760 (do.): XIII, **111**, 5434 (*°sya purushaiḥ*), 5438 (*°sya vishayam gataḥ*), 5440 (only B.), 5441 (*°sadane divye Brahmalokasame guṇaiḥ*), 5463 (*°sya vishayam gataḥ*), 5489 (do.), 5490 (*°sya purushaiḥ*), 5491 (*°sya vishayam gataḥ*), 5514 (do.).—§ 766 (do.): XIII, **125**, 5923 (*devaguhyam . . . Y°ena* [sc. *prāptam*, Nīl.]); **130**, (6114).— § 773*d* (Çiva): XIII, **161**, 7486 (*Vaivasvatam*, became the *puṅkha* of Çiva's shaft).—§ 775 (Ānuçāsanik.): XIII, **166**, 7637 (*Dhūmorṇayā saha*, cf. V, 3968).—§ 778*f* (Muñjavat): XIV, **8**, 183 (worships Çiva on Muñjavat). — § 782 (Anugītāp.): XIV, **16**, 443 (*°kshaye*). — § 782*g* (Guruçishyasaṃv.): XIV, **43**θ, 1176 (*Pitṝṇām adhipaḥ*).—§ 784*b* (Uttaṅka): XIV, **53**, 1553 (*°kshayam*); **57**, 1662 (*°opamaḥ*, sc. Kalmāshapāda).—§ 785 (Anugītāp.): XIV, **61**, 1845 (*Yamau Y°opamau*); **68**ξ, 2006 (*Y°sādanam*); **74**, 2167 (*Kālāntaka-Y°opamam*, sc. Arjuna); **78**, 2295 (*Y°kshayam*). —§ 795 (Svargārohaṇap.): XVIII, **2**, 36 (*Yamau . . . Y°opamau*).

Cf. also Dharma and the following synonyms:—

Daṇḍin, Deveça, Kṛtānta, Lokapāla, q.v.

Pitṛīça ("lord of the Pitṛs"): VII, 37 (only C. in the comp. *Pitṛvittāmbudeveçān*).

Pitṛpati (do): VII, †1980 (*°rāshṭravardhanam*, sc. *āyodhanam*); VIII, †1210 (*°rāshṭram iva*).

Pitṛrāja (do.): I, †7077 (*iva*); 275 (*sabhām tu P°sya*), 344 (*°sabhāsadaḥ*), 1643 (*°āçritām diçam*, i.e. the south); III, 16761; VIII, †4674 (*°veçmani*).

Pitṛrājan (do.): II, 352 (*sabhā . . . P°jñaḥ*).

Pretādhipa, Pretarāj, Pretarāja, Sureça, Sūryaputra, Vaivasvata, q.v.

Yama[2], a companion of Skanda. § 615*u* (Skanda): IX, **45**, 2547 (given to Skanda by Varuṇa).

Yama[3] = Sūrya: III, 148.—Do.[4] = Çiva (1000 names[1]).— Do.[5] = Mahāpurusha (Mahāpurushastava). — Do.[6] = Vishṇu (1000 names).

Yama, dual (*°au*) ("the twins") = Nakula and Sahadeva: I, 124, 2445 (born from the Açvins), 3818, 4850 (born from the Açvins), 4851, 5820, 5839, 5872, †7014, †7016, †7058, †7139, †7158, 7227, 7235, 7505, 7547, 7994; II, 38, 41, 557, 990, 1221, 1670, 1921, †2118, 2370, 2388, †2399, 2411, 2448; III, 275, 551, 894, †903, †918, †943, 1246, †1965, 1993, 8477, 10417, †10839, 10871, 10881 (*°yoḥ pūrvajaḥ*, i.e. Arjuna), 11008, 11403, 11410, 11629, 11819, †12321, 12432, †12578, 13007, †14745, †14753, †14754, 14941, 15008, †15694, 15766, 17289, 17300; IV, 649, 1087, 1311, †2304; V, 57, 199, 619, 1959, 2215, 2916, 3177, 3200, 3403, 4887, 4949, 5232, 5642, 7598; VI, 1994, 3067, 3681, †3767, 4243, 4792, 4945, 5553; VII, †68, †81, 227, 578, 1743, 2950, 3050, †6726, 6899, 7013, 7732, 7754, 8544, 8552, 8644, 8645, 8690, 9007, 9133; VIII, 845, 1231, 1690 (*Mādrīputrau*), 1694, 1701, †1728, 2254, 2334, 2702, 2708, 3180, 3319, †3485, 3573, 3796, 4512, †4805; IX, 253, 566, 762, 1831; XII, 26, 51, 1175, 1695, 1914, 1921, 1929; XIV, 384, 1845, 1874 (*Mādrīputrau*), 2355, 2612; XV, 35, 333, 658, †663, 747, 1004; XVI, 284; XVII, 5, 20, 31 (only C.); XVIII, 36, 96, 118. Cf. Yamaja, dual.

Yāma = Sūrya: III, 150.

Yāma, pl. (*°āḥ*), a class of celestial beings, mentioned together with the Dhāmas. § 520 (Mudgala): III, **261**, 15446 (*°ā Dhāmāç ca*).—§ 615*u* (Skanda): IX, **44**, 2482 (do.).

Yāmadagnya (III, 511; VII, 2442) v. Jāmadagnya.

Yamadūta, a son of Viçvāmitra. § 721*b* (Viçvāmitrop.): XIII, **4**β, 250 (only B., C. has *Mudgalaḥ*).

Yamaja = Çiva: VII, †9457.

Yamaja, dual. (°*au*) ("the twins") = Nakula and Sahadeva: I, 5271, 6419; II, 977, 1817; III, 10858, 11019, 15063, 15375, †15608; V, 5592; XII, 1517; XV, 854. Cf. Yama, dual.

Yamaloka ("the world of Yama"). § 470 (cf. Mārkaṇḍeyas.): Asked by *Yudhishthira*, *Mārkaṇḍeya* said that the distance of *Y.* from the world of men is 86,000 yojanas, the way is terrible, and people are led along it by the messengers of *Yama* under conditions answering to their charity and fasts when alive (enumerated). There is the river *Pushpodakā*; from that river those who have given water drink clear water, while those of evil deeds have pus ordained for them: III, **200**, 13393, 13396.—§ 551 (Kīcakavadhap.): IV, **16**, 502 (°*ṃ gamishyati*); **21**, 656 (v. Sāvitrī).—§ 552 (Goharaṇap.): IV, **33**, 1099 (°*m adarçayat*).—§ 597 (Pratijñāp.): VII, **84**, 3002 (*yiyāsur Y°āya*).—§ 600 (Ghaṭotkacavadhap.): VII, **157**, 6950 (*prāhiṇod Y°āya*, B, *mṛtyu°*).—§ 618 (Strīvilāpap.): XI, **4**, 113 (°*m athāgataṃ*).—[§ 757*c* (Hastikūṭa): Gautama said: In the abode of Yama the righteous live in joy and the sinful in grief. Dhṛtarāshṭra said: Only those who are destitute of acts, and have no faith, and are atheists, and are of sinful souls, and are always engaged in gratifying their senses, are punished by Yama. Gautama said: [The city] Saṃyamanī, which belongs to Yama, where no untruth is spoken, but only truth, there the weak have their revenge (*yātayanti*) of the strong. *Dhṛtarāshṭra* said: This world is for such as conduct themselves against their elder sisters and their parents as against foes: XIII, **102**, †4856 (*Vaivasvatasya sadane*), †4858 (*Vaivasvatīṃ Saṃyamanīṃ*)]. Cf. Yāmyaloka.

Yama-sabhā-varṇana(m) ("description of the palace of Yama"). § 267 (Lokapālas.): The *sabhā* of *Yama Vaivasvata* covers an area of more than 100 *yojanas*, and was built by *Viçvakarman*; it is possessed of the splendour of the sun, and yields every thing, etc. There are many *rājarshis* (enumeration) and *Brahmarshis*, *Agastya*, *Mataṅga*, *Kāla*, *Mṛtyu*, the performers of sacrifice, *Siddhas*, *yogins* (*yogaçarīriṇaḥ*), the *Pitṛs* belonging to the classes *Agnisvāttāḥ*, *Phenapāḥ*, *Ushmapāḥ*, *Svadhāvantaḥ*, and *Barhishadaḥ*, the wheel of time, *Havyavāhana*, the sinners (*dushkṛtakarmāṇaḥ*), and those who have died during the sun's southern course, those who are employed in regulating time, and the servants (*purushāḥ*) of *Yama*; the *çiṃçapā*, *pālāça*, *kāça*, *kuça*, and other trees and plants, many *Gandharvas* and *Apsarases* (II, **8**).

Yamunā, a river, the present Jamna. § 11 (Parvasaṅgr.): I, **2**, 102 (cf. § 254).—§ 70 (Ādivaṃçāvatāraṇap.): I, **60**, 2209 (°*dvīpe*, Vyāsa was born on an island in the *Y.*). § 76 (Matsya): I, **63**, 2387 (°*āmbhasi*), 2388 (°*carī*, sc. Adrikā).—§ 77 (Vyāsa): I, **63**, 2414 (°*dvīpe*, Vyāsa was born on an island in the *Y.*)—§ 149 (Yayāti): I, **87**, 3555 (*Gaṅgā-Y°yor madhye*, there the kingdom of Pūru was situated).—§ 165 (Satyavatīlābhop.): I, **100**, 4011 (°*m abhito nadīṃ*).—§ 171 (Vicitravīryasutotpatti): I, **105**, 4229 (*nadīṃ*), 4230 (all. to § 77).—§ 221*b* (Gaṅgā): I, **170**, 6455.—§ 253 (Haraṇāharaṇap.): I, **221**, 8024 (°*tīre*).—§ 254 (Khāṇḍavadahanap.): I, **222**, 8063.—§ 273 (Rājasūyārambhap.): II, **14**, 605 (°*āmbhasi*), 607 (Ḍimbhaka and Haṃsa drowned themselves in the *Y.*).—§ 275 (do.): II, **17**, 695 (*Gaṅgā-Y°yor madhye mūrtimān iva sāgaraḥ*).—§ 312 (Āraṇyakap.): III, **5**, 241.—§ 370 (Tīrthayātrāp.): III, **84**, 8013 (*Gaṅgā-Y°yor madhye . . . saṅgame*), 8022 (°*prabhavam*).—§ 373 (Prayāga): III, **85**, 8217 (*Gaṅgayā sārdhaṃ saṅgatā*), 8218 (*Gaṅgā-Y°yor madhye* (read °*aṃ* with B.) *pṛthivyā jaghanaṃ smṛtaṃ*), 8228 (*Gaṅgā-Y°yoḥ saṅgame*, there Prayāga is situated).—§ 377 (Dhaumyatīrthak.): III, **87**, 8314 (*Gaṅgā-Y°yoḥ . . . saṅgamaṃ*); **90**, 8374 (in the north), 8378 (on the *Y.* Sahadeva[3] and Bharata had performed sacrifices).—§ 379 (Tīrthayātrāp.): III, **95**, 8515 (*Gaṅgā-Y°yoç caiva saṅgame*, i.e. at Prayāga).—§ 406 (do.): III, **125**, 10417, 10420 (*c*: on the *Y.* Somaka and Māndhātṛ had performed sacrifices).—§ 409 (Plakshāvataraṇag.): III, **129**, 10514 (on the *Y.* Ambarīsha had performed sacrifices).—§ 410 (do.): III, **130**, 10556 (*Jālāñ copajālāñ caiva Y°m abhito nadīm*),—§ 418 (Gandhamādanapr.) III, **139**, 10833.—§ 434 (Saugandhikāharaṇa): III, **156**, 11437.—§ 438 (Yakshayuddhap.): III, **161**, 11794 (°*tīraṃ*, there Agastya had performed austerities); **162**, 11827 (Çāntanu had performed sacrifices on the *Y.*).—§ 459 (Mārkaṇḍeyas.): III, **188*a***, 12907 (seen by Mārkaṇḍeya in the stomach of Nārāyaṇa).—§ 547 (Karṇa): III, **308**, 17150 (the basket in which Karṇa lay floated from the Carmaṇvatī into the *Y.*, from the *Y.* into the Gaṅgā).—§ 565 (Gālavacar.): V, **120**, 4026 (*Gaṅgā-Y°saṅgame*).—§ 573 (Ambopākhyānap.): V, **186**, 7346 (°*tīram*), 7348 (°*jalaṃ*); **187**, 7388 (°*m abhito nadīṃ*).—§ 574 (Jambūkh.): VI, **9** λ, 322.—§ 576 (Bhagavadgītāp.): VI, **18**, 694 (*Gaṅgeva Y°āntare*—°*rā*, B.).—§ 589 (Droṇābhishekap.): VII, **11**, 384 (*hayarājānaṃ Y°vanavāsinam*).—§ 595 (Shoḍaçarāj., v. Bharata): VII, **68**, 2384 (Bharata had performed 100 horse sacrifices on the *Y.*).—§ 599 (Jayadrathavadhap.): VII, **95**, 3493 (*Jāhnavī-Y°e nadyau prāvṛshīvolvaṇodake*); **150**, 6517.—§ 607 (Karṇap.): VIII, **44** η, 2029 (*bahishkṛtāḥ . . . Y°ayā*, sc. the Bāhīkas).—§ 608 (do.): VIII, **46**, 2209 (*Gaṅgā-Y°vat*, sc. *samasajjetāṃ*).—§ 615 (Baladevatīrthayātrā): IX, **54**, 3049 (*Kārapavanād Y°āyāṃ jagāma*).—§ 632*b* (Shoḍaçarāj., cf. § 595): XII, **29**, 939 (Bharata had performed 300 horse sacrifices on the *Y.*).—§ 736*b* (Vītahavyop.): XIII, **30**, 1950 (*Gaṅgā-Y°yor madhye*, there the sons of Vītahavya fought with Haryaçva).—§ 745*b* (Cyavanop.): XIII, **50**, 2646 (*Gaṅgā-Y°yor madhye*, there Cyavana entered the water), 2647 (*Gaṅgā-Y°yor vegaṃ*), 2648, 2655 (*Gaṅgā-Y°yor vāri*). — § 746 (Ānuçāsanik.): XIII, **68**, 3397 (*Gaṅgā-Y°yor madhye Yāmunasya girer adhaḥ*, there Parṇaçālā was situated).—§ 757*m* (Goloka): XIII, **102*a***, 4889.—§ 772*j* (Utathya): XIII, **155**, 7244 (Bhadrā, the daughter of Soma, bathed in the *Y.*).—§ 775 (Ānuçāsanik.): XIII, **166*a***, 7653.—§ 788 (Āçramavāsap.): XV, **23**, 633 (*nadīm*); **24**, 641. Cf. Kālindī, Kalmāshī.

Yāmuna[1], name of a mountain. § 370 (Tīrthayātrāp.): III, **84**, 8022 (?).—§ 449 (Ājagarap.): III, **177**, †12353 (*adrirājam*).—§ 555 (Sainyodyogap.): V, **19**, 600 (*parvataḥ*).—§ 746 (Ānuçāsanik.): XIII, **68**, 3397 (*Gaṅgā-Yamunayor madhye Y°sya girer adhaḥ*).

Yāmuna[2], adj. ("belonging to the Yamunā"). § 589 (Droṇābhishekap.): VII, **3**, 92 (*çrotasā Y°nenaiva* (°*neva*, B.)).

Yāmuna[3], pl. (°*āḥ*), a people. § 574 (Jambūkh.): VI, **9** μ, 358.

Yamunātīrtha[1] = Plakshāvataraṇa: III, 10525.

Yamunātīrtha[2], name of a tīrtha on the Sarasvatī. § 615*dd*: In the *Y.*, *Varuṇa*, the son of *Aditi*, had in days of yore, performed the *rājasūya* sacrifice; having subjugated both men and celestials and G. and Rā. in battle, he performed a great sacrifice in that tīrtha; during that sacrifice a terrible battle ensued between the gods and the Dānavas; after the completion of the *rājasūya* a terrible battle ensued (PCR.; *jāyate*: "usually ensues"?) among the kshatriyas (?*kshatriyān prati*): IX, **49**, 2840.

Yāmya, adj. ("belonging to Yama"). § 266 (Çakrasabhāv.): II, **7,** 310 (*sabhām*).—§ 267 (Yamasabhāv.): II, **8,** 311 (do.).—§ 268 (Varuṇasabhāv.): II, **9,** 353 (sc. *sabhā*).—§ 305 (Anudyūtap.): II, **78,** 2577 (*kopavidhāraṇe*).—§ 306 (do.): II, **80,** 2627 (*sāmāni*), 2641 (do.). — § 552 (Goharaṇap.): IV, **64,** 2058 (sc. *astram*).—§ 572 (Rathātirathasaṅkhyānap.): V, **169,** 5870 (sc. *astragrāmaḥ*).—§ 592 (Samçaptakavadhap.): VII, **23**ρ, 1041 (sc. *dhanuḥ*).—§ 600 (Ghaṭotkacavadhap.): VII, **157,** 6954 (sc. *astram*).—§ 603*b* (Nārāyaṇa): VII, **201**ξξ, †9466 (sc. *karma*).—§ 615*u* (Skanda): IX, **46**ι, 2654 (°*āḥ*, sc. *mātaraḥ*).—§ 615*ff* (Asita Devala): IX, **50**μ, 2881 (*lokam*).—§ 618 (Jalapradānikap.): XI, **7,** 181 (*ratham*, sc. the body).—§ 746 (Ānuçāsanik.): XIII, **80,** †3795 (*sabhām*).

Yāmya[2] = Çiva: VII, 9521; XIV, 193.—Do.[3] = Mahāpurusha (Mahāpurushastava).

Yāmyaloka = Yamaloka. § 746 (Ānuçāsanik.): XIII, **79**κ, 3770.

Yānasandhi ("negotiation for peace by embassy"?). § 10 (Parvasaṅgr.): I, **2,** 331 (*parva*, i.e. Yānasandhiparvan).

[Yānasandhiparvan(°va)] ("section relating to the Yānasandhi", q.v.), the 60th of the minor parvans of Mhbhr. § 561. After the night had passed away, all the princes and chiefs, *Bhīshma*, etc. (*a*) entered the court-hall (description) to hear the message of *Sañjaya* (adorned with ear-rings), who had come back from the *Pāṇḍavas* by the aid of *Saindhava* steeds. *Sañjaya* related the salutations of the *Pāṇḍavas* (V, **47**). *Sañjaya* related that *Arjuna* (! cf. § 556: Sañjayayānap., V, **23-28**) had said, with *Yudhishṭhira's* sanction, that *Sañjaya* should say to *Duryodhana* and *Karṇa*, threatening them with *Bhīmasena*, etc. (β), that if the *Dhārtarāshṭras* desired war, then all the aims of the *Pāṇḍavas* were accomplished, as *Duryodhana* should lie down on the bare earth, deprived of life, etc. *Arjuna* (*b*) trusted himself and *Kṛshṇa* (*c*); he said that *Duryodhana* often thought of imprisoning *Kṛshṇa*, and sought to create a sudden disunion between *Kṛshṇa* and *Arjuna*. "There are with us many aged *brahmans*, versed in various sciences . . . who are prophesying the great destruction of the *Kurus* and the *Sṛñjayas*, and the ultimate victory of the *Pāṇḍavas* . . . thy bow *Gāṇḍīva* yawns without being handled, etc.; on the top of my flagstaff are heard terrific voices ('when shall thy car be yoked, O *Kirīṭin?*'); innumerable jackals howl at night, and *Rākshasas* frequently alight from the sky . . . I will use the *Sthūṇākarṇa*, *Pāçupata*, and *Brāhma* weapons, and all those that *Çakra* gave me." [This speech of Arjuna is not found in § 556: Sañjayayānap.] (V, **48**). *Bhīshma* said to *Duryodhana* that *Nara* and *Nārāyaṇa* (*Nara-Nārāyaṇau*) (*d*) were *Arjuna* and *Kṛshṇa*: it was with their aid that *Çakra* vanquished the *Daityas* and *Dānavas*; *Nara* slew hundreds and thousands of *Paulomas* and *Kālakañjas* in battle; *Arjuna*, with an arrow, severed the head of the *Asura Jambha* while the latter was about to swallow him; he afflicted *Hiraṇyapura* on the other side of the ocean, having vanquished in battle 60,000 of *Nivātakavacas*; and in the same way also *Nārāyaṇa* has, in this world, destroyed numberless other *Daityas* and *Dānavas*. *Karṇa* boasted that he would slay all the *Pāṇḍavas* in battle, but was rebuked by *Bhīshma*, saying that *Karṇa* had seen his own brother slain by *Arjuna* in the city of *Virāṭa*, and alluding to the contents of the Goharaṇa-, and the Ghoshayātrāparvan. *Droṇa* also counselled peace, but got no answer from *Dhṛtarāshṭra* (V, **49**). At the request of *Dhṛtarāshṭra*, *Sañjaya* related that the *Pañcālas*, etc. (γ) looked up to *Yudhishṭhira*. As he was questioned about *Dhṛshṭadyumna* and the *Somakas*, he first fell down in a swoon. Then, regarding *Bhīmasena* (*e*) he mentioned the lac-house, etc. (δ); regarding *Arjuna*, the burning of the *Khāṇḍava* forest, etc. (ε); then *Nakula* (*f*) and *Sahadeva* (*g*); *Çikhaṇḍin* (ζ); the five *Kekaya* princes, etc. (η) (V, **50**). *Dhṛtarāshṭra* was most afraid of *Bhīma* (who was taller than *Arjuna* by the span of the thumb), with his mace (full four cubits in length, with six sides), mentioning his killing *Jarāsandha* (V, **51**). *Dhṛtarāshṭra* was also afraid of *Arjuna*, who he feared would conquer *Karṇa* (being compassionate and heedless), and *Droṇa* (being aged and having affection for his pupil Arjuna); "thirty-three years have passed since the burning of the *Khāṇḍava* forest; we have never heard of his being defeated anywhere" [but cf. the reading of B. *trayastṛṃçat samāhūya*, i.e. challenging the thirty-three gods] (V, **52**). *Dhṛtarāshṭra* was afraid of the allies of *Yudhishṭhira*: the *Pañcālas*, *Kekayas*, etc. (θ) (V, **53**). *Sañjaya* rebuked *Dhṛtarāshṭra* for his behaviour towards the *Pāṇḍavas*; "the *Matsyas*, etc. (ι) all decline to pay thee homage now" (V, **54**). *Duryodhana* said, that when the *Pāṇḍavas* had been exiled, there came to them *Kṛshṇa*, etc. (κ), all assembled in a place not far from *Indraprastha*, and suggested to *Yudhishṭhira* that he should take back the kingdom; "the people of the realm were all annoyed with us, and all our friends also were angry with us"; but *Bhīshma*, *Kṛpa*, and *Açvatthāman* had despised the foes ("inflamed with anger at the death of his father this *Bhīshma*, in days of old, had conquered all the kings of the earth, in a single chariot"). "Now the *Pāṇḍavas* are without allies; and all these kings can, for my sake, enter the fire or the sea . . . Having given up all hopes of a town, *Yudhishṭhira* craves only five villages . . . There is none on earth equal to me in an encounter with the mace. In battle, I am *Saṅkarshaṇa's* equal; I will certainly slay *Bhīma*, *Bhīshma*, etc. (λ), every one of these is singly capable of slaying the *Pāṇḍavas*." He alluded to the superhuman circumstances concerning *Bhīshma*, etc. (μ), to the resolution of the *Samçaptakas* to slay *Arjuna* or be slain by him; "our chief warriors are *Bhīshma*, etc. (ν); they have seven *akshauhiṇīs*, we have eleven; *Bṛhaspati* has said, that an army which is less by one-third ought to be encountered" (V, **55**). At the request of *Duryodhana*, *Sañjaya* described the chariots of *Arjuna* (*h*), *Yudhishṭhira* (*i*), *Bhīmasena* (*j*), *Sahadeva* (*k*), *Nakula* (*l*); "and excellent steeds, presented by the celestials, carry the sons of *Subhadrā* and *Draupadī*" (V, **56**). At the request of *Dhṛtarāshṭra*, *Sañjaya* mentioned the allies of the *Pāṇḍavas*, *Kṛshṇa*, etc. (ξ), and who had been assigned to each of them as his share: *Çikhaṇḍin* & *Bhīshma*; *Yudhishṭhira* & the *Madra* king; *Bhīmasena* & *Duryodhana's* sons and 100 brothers, the rulers of the east and the south; *Arjuna* & *Karṇa*, *Jayadratha*, etc.; the five *Kekayas* & the *Kekayas*, *Mālavas*, *Çālvakas*, *Trigartau Samçaptakau*; *Abhimanyu* & *Duryodhana's* sons (?), *Duḥçāsana's* sons, king *Bṛhadbala*; *Draupadeyāḥ* + *Dhṛshṭadyumna* & *Droṇa*; *Cekitāna* & *Somadatta*; *Sātyaki* & *Kṛtavarman*; *Sahadeva* & *Çakuni*; *Nakula* & *Ulūka*, *Sārasvatāḥ*. All the other kings had been distributed in their respective shares. Thus the *Pāṇḍava* host had been distributed into divisions. *Virāṭa* with all his *Matsya* warriors would support *Çikhaṇḍin*. *Dhṛtarāshṭra* was exceedingly afraid of *Yudhishṭhira*, etc. (ο). *Duryodhana* said that *Bhīshma*, etc. (π) were invincible. *Dhṛtarāshṭra* maintained that *Bhīshma* did not wish a battle.

Sañjaya said that *Dhṛshṭadyumna* was always urging the *Pāṇḍavas* to fight, and professed that he would alone encounter all the assembled kings: *Bhīshma*, etc. (ρ), and his words were approved by *Yudhishṭhira*; *Dhṛshṭadyumna* had told *Sañjaya* to say to the *Kurus*, etc. (σ), that they ought not to suffer themselves to be slain by *Arjuna*, who was protected by the celestials; they should send a good man to *Yudhishṭhira* and entreat him to accept the kingdom. [This is not found in Sañjayayānap., § 556] (V, **57**). *Dhṛtarāshṭra* mentioned that *Yudhishṭhira* led the *brahmacarya* mode of life from his very youth, and saying that he himself, etc. (τ) did not applaud war, he urged *Duryodhana* to desist from hostilities and give back to the *Pāṇḍavas* their kingdom, saying, that it was *Karṇa*, *Duḥçāsana*, and *Çakuni* who led *Duryodhana* astray. *Duryodhana* answered that, without depending upon *Dhṛtarāshṭra*, etc. (υ), he and *Karṇa* and *Duḥçāsana* would perform, in honour of *Yama*, a sacrifice in battle and slay the *Pāṇḍavas*; he said that he would sacrifice his life rather than surrender to the *Pāṇḍavas* even that much of land which may be covered by the sharp point of a needle. *Dhṛtarāshṭra* said that he abandoned *Duryodhana* for ever, and grieved for the kings who would be crushed by *Yuyudhāna*, etc. (φ) (V, **58**). At the request of *Dhṛtarāshṭra*, *Sañjaya* related how he had entered the inner apartments (description) in order to inform *Arjuna* and *Kṛshṇa*; he had seen two straight lines on *Arjuna's* foot-soles. *Kṛshṇa* had threatened the *Kurus*, mentioning that *Kṛshṇā* had invoked him with tears, and that D., As., men, Y., G., and N. were incapable of encountering *Arjuna* in battle, and alluding to his exploits in the city of *Virāṭa* (v. Goharaṇap.) (V, **59**). *Dhṛtarāshṭra* represented to *Duryodhana* that *Agni* would help *Arjuna*, remembering what was done to him at *Khāṇḍava*, that *Dharma*, etc., would help the *Pāṇḍavas* from parental affection, that *Arjuna* took up 500 arrows at a time, that *Bhīshma*, etc. (χ) regarded him as invincible, and said he desired peace (V, **60**). *Duryodhana*, inflamed with wrath, said that according to *Vyāsa*, *Nārada*, and *Paraçu-Rāma*, the gods never engaged in work; if *Agni*, *Vāyu*, *Dharma*, *Indra*, or the *Açvins* had ever engaged in work, the *Pārthas* could never have fallen into distress, and they and the *Maruts* would not venture to protect his foes; "charmed by me, *Agni* will be instantly extinguished . . . , my energy is greater than that of the gods; . . . it is I who set agoing all the affairs of both gods and *Asuras* . . . ; neither D. nor G., nor As. nor Rā. are capable of saving him who has incurred my displeasure . . . ; thou wilt hear of the defeat of the *Pāṇḍavas*, etc. (ψ); . . . whatever knowledge of weapons there is in *Bhīshma*, etc. (ω), exists in me as well" (V, **61**). *Karṇa* said to *Duryodhana*, mentioning the curse of *Paraçu-Rāma*, when he, by a lie, obtained the *Brāhma* weapon from him, that he would slay the *Pāñcālas*, etc. (**aa**). *Bhīshma* mentioned the *Khāṇḍava* forest, and said that the dart which *Karṇa* had got from *Indra*, would be reduced to ashes by *Kṛshṇa* with his discus, and that his other shaft (having a head like a serpent), which he respectfully worshipped with flowery garlands, would be destroyed by *Arjuna* because he was protected by *Kṛshṇa*. *Karṇa* made the pledge not to fight before *Bhīshma's* fall, and went to his own abode. *Bhīshma* ridiculed *Karṇa's* boasting before the kings of *Avanti*, etc. (ββ) (V, **62**). *Duryodhana* boasted; *Vidura* praised self-restraint (V, **63**). *Vidura* related that once two birds had flown away with the net in which they were caught, but were again caught when they began to quarrel. "So it is also with kinsmen. Once we, with some hunters and *brahmans* conversant with magic and charms, repaired to the northern mountain *Gandhamādana*, with excellent medicinal herbs, and inhabited by Si. and G. There was, on a precipice, some honey, *Kubera's* favourite drink, guarded by poisonous snakes; the *brahmans* said that a mortal drinking of it would win immortality, a sightless man obtain sight, and an old man would become a youth. The hunters desired to obtain it, and all perished. So it is with *Duryodhana*. In a single chariot *Arjuna* conquered the whole earth; *Bhīshma* and *Droṇa*, etc. were routed by him at the city of *Virāṭa*. Remember also *Drupada* and the king of the *Matsyas*" (V, **64**). *Dhṛtarāshṭra* warned *Duryodhana* against the *Pāṇḍavas*, etc. (γγ), and recommended him to follow *Bhīshma*, etc. (δδ) as his guides, mentioning the combat at the city of *Virāṭa* (V, **65**). At the request of *Dhṛtarāshṭra*, *Sañjaya* related that *Arjuna* had said that *Bhīshma*, etc. (εε) were all on the eve of death, if they did not give up to *Yudhishṭhira* his own share of the kingdom (V, **66**). As *Duryodhana* showed little regard for the words of *Sañjaya*, and the rest remained silent, the assembled kings rose and retired. *Dhṛtarāshṭra*, who always followed the counsels of his son, began to inquire in secret of *Sañjaya* about the resolves of his own party and of the foes. *Sañjaya* caused him to let *Vidura* introduce *Vyāsa* and *Gāndhārī* (V, **67**). *Sañjaya* extolled *Kṛshṇa* (*m*), and mentioned some of those whom he had vanquished (ζζ) (V, **68**). Discourse between *Dhṛtarāshṭra* and *Sañjaya* on the attributes of *Kṛshṇa*. *Dhṛtarāshṭra* told *Duryodhana* to seek refuge with *Kṛshṇa*. *Duryodhana* refused. *Dhṛtarāshṭra* complained of him to *Gāndhārī*. *Gāndhārī* threatened *Duryodhana* with *Bhīmasena*. *Vyāsa* recommended to *Dhṛtarāshṭra* to seek salvation through *Kṛshṇa*. Requested by *Dhṛtarāshṭra*, *Sañjaya* explained the path of salvation through *Kṛshṇa* (V, **69**). At the request of *Dhṛtarāshṭra*, *Sañjaya* enumerated some names of *Kṛshṇa* (V, **70**). *Dhṛtarāshṭra* complained that he could not see *Kṛshṇa*, whom he extolled under several names (ηη) (V, **71**).

Yashṭṛ = Kṛshṇa (Vishṇu): XII, 13143.

Yāska, a ṛshi. § 717*b* (Nārāyaṇīya): XII, **343**φ, 13230 (*ṛshiḥ*), 13231 (do., invoked Nārāyaṇa (Kṛshṇa) by the name of Çipivishṭa, and thus recovered the lost *Nirukta*).

Yati[1], son of Nahusha. § 143 (Nahusha): I, **75**, 3155 (eldest son of Nahusha), 3156 (*yogam āsthāya brahmabhūtaḥ*, became a muni).

Yati[2], a son of Viçvāmitra. § 721*b* (Viçvāmitrop.): XIII, **4**β, 257.

Yati[3] ("the ascetic") = Çiva: XIV, 196.

Yātudhāna, pl. (°*āḥ*), a class of demons. § 378 (Tīrthayātrāp.): III, **92**, 8438.—§ 418 (Gandhamādanapr.): III, **139**, 10828.—§ 445 (Nivātakavacayuddhap.): III, **173**, 12248 (*gadāmudgaradhāriṇām*).—§ 461 (Vāmadevacarita): III, **192**, †13191 (*suraudrāḥ*), †13198 (slew Çala).—§ 561 (Mātalīyop.): V, **100**, 3571 (*Nairṛtā Y°āç ca Brahmapādodbhavāç ca ye*, in Pātāla).—§ 567 (Bhagavadyānap.): V, **143**, 4851 (omens).—§ 600 (Ghaṭotkacavadhap.): VII, **156**, 6842 (*Paulastyair Y°aiç ca*, follow Ghaṭotkaca); **175**, 7997 (*Rākshasāç ca Piçācāç ca Y°ās tathaiva ca*, do.); **179**, †8153 (created by Ghaṭotkaca by way of illusion).—§ 608 (Karṇap.): VIII, **87**χ', 4412 (sided with Karṇa).—§ 721 (Ānuçāsanik.): XIII, **3**a, 184 (Viçvāmitra in anger created *Y.* and Rākshasas).—§ 730 (do.): XIII, **17**, 1294 (*Piçācā Y°ā vā*).—§ 749 (do.): XIII, **90**, 4292 (*Y°āç ca Piçācāç ca*, rob the havis at the sacrifice).—§ 778*f* (Muñjavat): XIV, **8**, 185 (worship Çiva on Muñjavat).—§ 795 (Svargārohaṇap.): XVIII, **5** μ, 168 (the sons of Dhṛtarāshṭra were incarnations of *Y.*).—Do., sg.: VII, **202**, 9600 (only B.).

Yātudhānī, a hag (kṛtyā), created by Vṛshadarbha. § 750*b* (Bisastainyop.): XIII, **93**, 4453, 4457, 4474, 4476, (4478), (4480), 4481, (4483), (4485), (4487), (4489), 4491, (4492), 4493, (4494), (4496), (4498), (4500), (4502), 4503, (4504), 4507, 4537.

Yaudheya, son of Yudhishṭhira and Devikā. § 159 (Pūruvaṃç.): I, **95**, ††3828.

Yaudheya, pl. (°*āḥ*), a people. § 295 (Dyūtap.): II, **52**, 1870 (*Çibi-Trigarta-Y°āḥ*, bring tribute to Yudhishṭhira).—§ 592 (Saṃçaptakavadhap.): VII, **19**, 768 (vanquished by Arjuna in the battle).—§ 600 (Ghaṭotkacavadhap.): VII, **157** ρ, 6950 (slain by Yudhishṭhira); **161** ζζ, 7208 (slain by Arjuna).—§ 604 (Karṇap.): VIII, **5** ζ, 137 (had been slain by Arjuna).

Yaudhishṭhira ("son of Yudhishṭhira") = Prativindhya: VI, 1732.

Yaudhishṭhira, pl. (°*āḥ*) ("the party of Yudhishṭhira"). § 599 (Jayadrathavadhap.): VII, **98**, 3640 (°*ādayaḥ*, C., °*āḥ sthitāḥ*, B.).

Yaudhishṭhira, adj. ("belonging to Yudhishṭhira"). § 9 (Parvasaṅgr.): I, **2**, 302 (*balaṃ*).—§ 11 (do.): I, **2**, 520 (*sainyaṃ*).—§ 524 (Jayadrathavimokshaṇap.): III, **272**, 15854 (*balaṃ*).—§ 551 (Kīcakavadhap.): IV, **19**, 569 (*çoke*)—§ 555 (Sainyodyogap.): V, **19** γ, 575 (*balaṃ*).—§ 569 (Bhagavadyānap.): V, **139**, 4715 (*çriyaṃ*); **145**, 4924 (do.); **146**, 4949 (*bale*).—§ 572 (Rathātirathasaṅkhyānap.): V, **172**, 5930 (*senāṃ*).—§ 578 (Bhīshmavadhap.): VI, **49**, 2027/28 (only B.).—§ 580 (do.): VI, **59**, 2553 (*bale*), 2574 (do.), 2575 (*balaṃ*).—§ 585 (do.): VI, **90**, 4056 (*sainye*).—§ 586 (do.): VI, **106**, 4855 (*bale*).—§ 587 (do.): VI, **117**, 5456 (do.).—§ 590 (Droṇābhishekap.): VII, **16**, 657 (do.).—§ 592 (Saṃçaptakavadhap.): VII, **20**, 822 (*sainyaṃ*); **21**, 857 (*bale*); **30**, 1335 (*anīkāṃ*, B. °*abhyanīkāni* (!)).—§ 593 (Abhimanyuvadhap.): VII, **42**, 1742 (*sainyāt*), 1762 (*balaṃ*). — § 600 (Ghaṭotkacavadhap.): VII, **156**, 6768 (*sainyaṃ*), 6918 (do.); **179**, †8126 (*balaṃ*). — § 608 (Karṇap.): VIII, **62**, 3157 (*sainyaṃ*); **73**, 3747 (*bale*).—§ 612 (Hradapraveçap.): IX, **30**, 1734 (*sainyasya*).—§ 785 (Anugītāp.): XIV, **79**, 2305 (*turagaṃ*).—§ 787 (Āçramavāsap.): XV, **16**, 469 (*çriyaṃ*).

Yaudhishṭhiri ("son of Yudhishṭhira") = Prativindhya: VII, 4061.

Yauga (VI, 1040) v. yoga, pl.

Yauna, pl. (°*āḥ*) = Yavana, pl.: XII, 7560 (°-*Kāmboja-Gāndhārāḥ*).

Yauvanāçva, Yauvanāçvi = Māndhātṛ, q.v.

Yauyudhāni ("the son of Yuyudhāna"), son of Sātyaki. § 793 (Mausalap.): XVI, **7**, 247 (*putraṃ Sātyakinaḥ*, settled on the banks of Sarasvatī).

Yavakri = Yavakrīta: III, 10759.

Yavakrī = Yavakrīta: III, 10704, 10706, 10714, 10751, 10752, 10754, 10758, 10763, 10766, 10767.

Yavakrin = Yavakrīta: III, 10733.

Yavakrīta, a ṛshi, son of Bharadvāja.—§ 11 (Parvasaṅgr.): I, **2**, 451 (°*sya . . . ākhyānaṃ*, i.e. Yavakrītopākhyana).—§ 413 (Tīrthayātrāp.): III, **135**, 10700.—§ 414 (Yavakrītop.): III, **135**, 10701, 10709, (10710), (10718), 10722, 10724, 10725, (10728), (10730), (10734) (*Y.'s* austerities and conversation with Indra).—§ 416 (do.): III, **135**, (10750); **136**, 10758, 10763, 10765, 10770, 10771 (*Y.* attempted to seduce the daughter-in-law of Raibhya and was killed by a Rākshasa created by Raibhya).—§ 417 (do.): III, **138**, 10812, 10814, 10816, 10818 (was revived).—§ 665 (Mokshadh.): XII, **207** ε, 7592 (among the ṛshis of the east).—§ 702 (do.): XII, **297** δ, 10875.—§ 734 (Ānuçāsanik.): XIII, **26** *a*, 1763 (came to see Bhīshma).—§ 770 (do.): XIII, **151** ζ, 7108 (among the seven *Mahendrasya guravaḥ* in the east).—§ 775 (do.): XIII, **166** γ, 7663 (among the ṛshis of the east). Cf. Bhāradvāja[2], Yavakri, Yavakrī, Yavakrin.

Yavakrītātmaja ("the son of Yavakrīta"). § 565 (Gālavacarita): V, **109**, 3789 (*atra*—i.e. in the south—*Sāvarṇinā caiva Y°ena ca maryādā sthāpitā, brahman, yāṃ Sūryo nātivartate*).

[Yavakrītopākhyana(m)] ("the episode relating to Yavakrīta"). § 414 (Tīrthay.). The learned *Raibhya* and the Ṛshi *Bharadvāja* were friends. *Raibhya* had two learned sons, *Arvāvasu* and *Parāvasu*; *Bharadvāja* only one son, *Yavakrīta*. As *Yavakrīta* saw that *Raibhya* and his sons were esteemed by the *brahmans*, while *Bharadvāja* was slighted, he practised austerities (exposing himself to a blazing fire) in order to acquire Vedic knowledge for himself and his father (cf. v. 10817) instead of acquiring it from a teacher during a long time. *Indra* was alarmed, and twice he in vain attempted to make *Yavakrīta* desist from his penances, saying that they never could be successful. As *Yavakrīta* declared that he would cut off his limbs and sacrifice them in the fire, *Indra* assumed the guise of an old decrepit brahman, and began to throw up a dam of sand at that spot of the *Bhāgīrathī* where *Yavakrīta* used to bathe, and declared that *Yavakrīta's* intentions were equally impossible. Then *Yavakrīta* desisted from his plan, and *Indra* granted him that the *Vedas* should be revealed to him and his father, and that he should excel other men. *Bharadvāja* said that *Yavakrīta* would become proud and uncharitable and thence destruction would soon overtake him (§ 415), and told him some gāthās, narrated by the gods, about *Medhāvin* (q.v.).—§ 416. *Bharadvāja* made *Yavakrīta* promise to shun the irritable *Raibhya* and his sons, and *Yavakrīta* began to offend other *ṛshis* (III, **135**). Once, in the month of *Mādhava*, he came to the hermitage of *Raibhya* and seduced (?) (cf. *sajjayām āsa*, var. lect. Nīl., instead of *majjayām āsa*) the wife of *Parāvasu*. When *Raibhya* came home and saw what had happened, he offered in the fire two matted locks of his hair, whence sprang out a woman resembling his daughter-in-law, who robbed *Yavakrīta* of his water-pot, and a *Rakshas*, who flew at him with his uplifted spear, as he had been deprived of his water-pot and rendered unclean (*ucchishta*). *Yavakrīta* fled to a tank and then to all the rivers, and, finding them all devoid of water, he attempted to enter into the *agnihotra* room of his father, but was stopped at the door by a blind *çūdra* warder, and killed by the *rakshas*. The *Rakshas*, with the permission of *Raibhya*, began to live with the female (III, **136**). When *Bharadvāja* returned home, the sacrificial fires, which used to welcome him every day, did not come forward to welcome him. Having heard from the *çūdra* what had happened, he cursed *Raibhya*, saying that he should be killed by his eldest son. He cremated *Yavakrīta*, and then himself entered the fire (III, **137**). At that time king *Bṛhaddyumna*, the *yājya* of *Raibhya*, employed *Arvāvasu* and *Parāvasu* at a sacrifice, while *Raibhya* stayed at home with the wife of *Parāvasu*. One day *Parāvasu*, returning home to see his wife, met in the darkness his father in the wood wrapped in the skin of a black antelope, and, mistaking him for a deer, killed him. Then, after having performed the funeral rites of his father, he prevailed upon *Arvāvasu* to observe the vow prescribed in the case of killing a brahman, while he himself conducted the sacrifice alone. When *Arvāvasu* came back, having observed the vow, *Parāvasu* caused him to be driven away from the sacrifice as a slayer of a brahman. The *brahmarshi Arvāvasu* went to the wood, and, applying to the Sun, he practised austerities and mastered the *Rahasyaveda* of the Sun. The Sun appeared to him in his embodied form, and said the gods were pleased by him. They elected *Arvāvasu* and rejected *Parāvasu*. The gods *Agni*, etc., granted him the boon that *Raibhya*, *Bharadvāja*, and *Yavakrīta* revived, that *Parāvasu* was absolved from his sin, that *Raibhya* did not recollect his having been slain, and that the *Saura Veda* should attain celebrity (*pratishṭhām*). The gods explained to *Yavakrīta* that *Raibhya* had been able to kill him because he had acquired his knowledge with great exertion and in the course of a long time, while *Yavakrīta* had learnt the *Vedas* without exertion and without a *guru*. Then *Indra* and the gods returned to heaven (III, **138**).

Yavakshā, a river. § 574 (Jambūkh.): VI, **9**λ, 338.

Yavana[1], pl. (°*āḥ*), a people. § 148*c* (Turvasu): I, **85**, 3533 (the offspring of Turvasu).—§ 223 (Vāsishṭha): I, **175**, 6683 (sprung from the womb (*yonideçāt*) of Vasishṭha's cow), 6684.—§ 264 (Sabhākriyāp.): II, **4**, 117 (*kampayām āsa Y°ān eko yaḥ*, sc. Kampana).—§ 284 (Sahadeva): II, **31**, 1175 (°*ānāṃ puraṃ*, in the south, conquered by Sahadeva on his digvijaya).—§ 285 (Nakula): II, **32**, 1199 (in the west, vanquished by Nakula on his digvijaya).—§ 295 (Dyūtap.): II, **51**, 1834 (°*aiḥ sahitaḥ . . . Bhagadattaḥ*).—§ 342 (Indralokābhigamanap.): III, **51**, 1990 (had been present at the rājasūya of Yudhishṭhira).—§ 458*b* (Kaliyuga): III, **188**, 12839 (among the barbarous people who will rule in the Kali age).—§ 515 (Karṇadigvijaya): III, **254**, 15257 (vanquished by Karṇa on his digvijaya).—§ 555 (Sainyodyogap.): V, **19**δ, 590 (°*aiç ca Çakaiḥ*, followed the Kāmboja king Sudakshiṇa).—§ 573 (Ambopākhyānap.): V, **195**ε, 7609 (in the army of Duryodhana).—§ 574 (Jambūkh.): VI, **9**ξ, 373 (in the north).—§ 576 (Bhagavadgītāp.): VI, **20**, 753 (followed Kṛpa).—§ 578 (Bhīshmavadhap.): VI, **51**σ, 2097 (protected Bhīshma).—§ 583 (do.): VI, **75**ε, 3297 (in Bhīshma's krauñcavyūha).—§ 585 (do.): VI, **87**ζ, 3856 (followed the Trigarta king).—§ 589 (Droṇābhishekap.): VII, **7**ε, 182 (in Droṇa's array).—§ 592 (Saṃçaptakavadhap.). VII, **20**γ, 798 (°-*Kāmbojāḥ*, in the neck of Droṇa's gāruḍa-vyūha). — § 599 (Jayadrathavadhap.): VII, **93**δ, 3379 (attacked Arjuna); **119**ββ, 4715, 4722, 4740, 4743, 4746, 4754 (slain by Sātyaki); **120**, 4758 (°-*Kāmbojān*); **121**εε, 4818 (attacked Sātyaki).—§ 607 (Karṇap.): VIII, **45**ν, 2107 (*sarvajñaḥ*).—§ 608 (do.): VIII, **46**ε, 2137; **56**ττ, 2807 (*ekeshu nihatair açvaiḥ Kāmbojair Y°aiḥ Çakaiḥ*); **73**, 3652; **88**, 4506 (only B.).—§ 609 (Çalyap.): IX, **1**γ, 27 (*nipātitāḥ*); **2**ζ, 74 (had joined Duryodhana).—§ 611 (do.): IX, **8**γ, 393 (follow Kṛpa).—§ 619 (Strīvilāpap.): XI, **22**η, 627 (*Kāmboja-Y°striyaḥ*, wives of Jayadratha). — § 641 (Rājadh.): XII, **65**θ, 2429; **101**π, 3737 (°-*Kāmbojāḥ*).—§ 739 (Ānuçāsanik.): XIII, **33**α, 2103 (°-*Kāmbojāḥ*, degraded to çūdras); **35**ε, 2159 (degraded to çūdras).—§ 785 (Anugītāp.): XIV, **73**, 2136 (fought with Arjuna). Cf. Yauna, pl.

Yavana[2], sg. ("the king of the Yavanas"). § 317*b* (Kṛshṇa Vāsudeva): III, **12**, 491 (*Kaserumān*, had been slain by Kṛshṇa).—§ 589 (Droṇābhishekap.): VII, **11**ν, 399 (had been vanquished by Kṛshṇa).

Yavana[3], v. Cyavana[2] (cf. Pavana[3]).

Yāvana, adj. ("belonging to the Yavanas"). § 515 (Karṇadigvijaya): III, **254**, 15254 (sc. *nṛpān*).

Yavanādhipa ("the king of the Yavanas"), one or more princes. § 211 (Sambhavap.): I, **139**, 5535 (vanquished by Arjuna).—§ 233 (Svayaṃvarap.): I, **187**, †7020 (present at the svayaṃvara of Draupadī).—§ 264 (Sabhākriyāp.): II, **4**β, 120 (waited upon Yudhishṭhira).—§ 273 (Rājasūyārambhap.): II, **14**, 578 (i.e. Bhagadatta).

Yavya, pl. (°*āḥ*), a kind of ṛshis: XII, 6143 (only C., B. reads *somavāyavyāḥ* instead of *somapā yavyāḥ*).

Yāyāta, adj. ("belonging to Yayāti"). § 144 (Yayāti): I, **75**, 3170 (*vayasā*).—§ 615 (Baladevatīrthayātrāp.): IX, **41**, 2349 (*tīrtham*, on the Sarasvatī).

Yayāti, an ancient king, son of Nahusha. § 3 (Anukramaṇik.): I, **1**, 47 (°*īkshvākuvaṃçaḥ*).—§ 5 (do.): I, **1**α, 222 *bis* (in Nārada's enumeration).—§ 61 (Janamejaya): I, **55**, †2109 (°-*Māndhātṛ - samaprabhāva*, sc. Janamejaya).—§ 143 (Nahusha): I, **75**, 3155 (second son of Nahusha), 3156 (became king), 3158 (his sons).—§ 144 (cf. Yayātyup.): Having, after 1,000 years, been attacked with decrepitude, *Y.* asked his sons, one by one, to give him their youth and take upon them his decrepitude, but only the youngest, *Pūru*, yielded to his wish, and taking upon himself the old age of *Y.* he ruled the kingdom, while *Y.*, as strong as a tiger, enjoyed the company of his two wives and, in the *Caitraratha* wood, of *Viçvācī*, but without becoming satiated. He then recited some verses (vv. 3174–3177) and took back from his son his own decrepitude, giving him back his youth. He then installed *Pūru* on the throne, saying that he was his true heir, and should continue the lineage which should be named after him. *Y.* then retired to *Bhṛgutuṅga*, and having spent a long time in ascetism, observing the vow of fasting, he died and ascended to heaven with his wives (I, **75**): I, **75**, 3164, 3171, 3172.—§ 145 (Kaca): I, **76**, 3183 (*daçamo yaḥ Prajāpateḥ*), 3185, 3186 (*Devayānyāç ca saṃyogaṃ Y°er Nāhushasya ca*).—§ 146 (Devayānī): I, **78**, 3292 (*Nahushātmajaḥ*), 3301; **81**, (3366), (3369), (3372), 3372, (3374), (3376), (3378), (3381), (3383), 3387, (3390), 3394 (*Y.* married Devayānī and promised not to cohabit with Çarmishṭhā).—§ 147 (do.): I, **82**, 3397, (3410), (3414), (3416) (Çarmishṭhā prevailed upon *Y.* to beget sons on her); **83**, 3432 (the sons of *Y.* were the foll.: with Devayānī Yadu and Turvasu, with Çarmishṭhā Druhyu, Anu and Pūru), 3434, 3450, 3452, (3455), 3460 (*Nāhushaḥ*), (3461), (3463) (Uçanas cursed *Y.* to be overcome with decrepitude, etc.).—§ 148 (cf. Yayātyup.): *Y.* transferred his decrepitude to *Pūru*, etc. (cf. § 144) and cursed his other sons, *Yadu* (*b*), *Turvasu* (*c*), *Druhyu* (*d*), *Anu* (*e*) (I, **84**). *Y.* sported with *Viçvācī* in the *Nandana* wood and in *Alakā*, and in the northern summit of *Meru*. *Y.* then recited some verses (v. 3510 foll.) and installed *Pūru* as king (cf. § 144). The offspring of *Yadu* (*b*), *Turvasu* (*c*), *Druhyu* (*d*), *Anu* (*e*), and *Pūru* (*f*) (I, **85**): I, **84**, 3466, (3467), (3474), (3478), 3481, (3482), (3485), (3488), (3490), (3492), (3498), 3499; **85**, 3500 (*Nahushātmajaḥ*), 3504, 3517 (*Nāhushaḥ*), (3522).—§ 149 (i.e. Uttara-Yayātyupākhyāna, cf. Sambhavap.): Having installed *Pūru* on the throne, *Y.* entered the wood to lead the life of a hermit for 1,000 years and then ascended to *Svarga* (I, **86**), where he was reverenced by the gods, the *Sādhyas*, the *Maruts*, and the *Vasus*, wandering about in *Devaloka* and *Brahmaloka*. One day *Indra* asked him what he had said to *Pūru* when he bestowed the kingdom upon him. *Y.* answered that he had said: "The whole country between the *Gaṅgā* and the *Yamunā* is thine, this is the central region of the earth, the outlying regions will be the dominions of thy brothers. Those without anger are ever superior to those under its sway, etc." (I, **87**). As *Y.* said that he did not know his equal in ascetic austerities among men, gods, *Gandharvas*, and *maharshis*, *Indra* declared that, owing to this haughtiness, he should fall from heaven, yet he should fall among the virtuous. When falling, he was beheld by the *rājarshi Ashṭaka* (I, **88**), of whom he was the maternal grandfather; *Y.* spoke disapprovingly of haughtiness, etc., and told that, leaving earth, he had obtained many high regions for 1,000 years, then he had dwelt in the town of *Indra* (having 1,000 gates and extending 1,000 yojanas all around) for 1,000 years, then for 1,000 years in the world of *Prajāpati*, then in the abode of *Devadeva* (i.e. Vishṇu); he had also dwelt in *Nandana* for 100 ayutas of years, assuming any form at will, sporting with the Apsarases; then there had come a messenger of the gods with a grim visage, who thrice had shouted to him "fall"; then he had fallen from *Nandana*, hearing, while falling, the compassionate exclamations of the gods, who had directed him to fall to the sacrificial place of *Ashṭaka* and his companions (I, **89**). *Y.* continued: Those who speak of their own merits after having dwelt for 60,000 or 80,000 years in heaven, are doomed to suffer the pains of the hell called *bhauma* (i.e. existence on the earth), and are attacked by certain *Rākshasas* with sharp teeth. *Y.* then taught the lore of transmigration and emancipation (I, **90**). *Y.* explained the duties of *gṛhasthas, bhikshus, brahmacārins*, and *vānaprasthas*, and the different kinds of *munis* and *mauna* (vows of silence) (I, **91**). *Y.* then said: "I now shall fall into the *bhauma* hell, the *Lokapas* of Brahmán hasten me thither." The kings *Ashṭaka*, *Pratardana* (I, **92**), *Vasumanas Aushadaçvi*, and *Çibi Auçīnara*, offered him their "*lokas*" and volunteered to go to hell (*naraka*) in his place; *Y.* did not accept the offer. Then appeared five golden chariots, in which they all five ascended to heaven, *Çibi* leaving the others behind him. *Y.* told them that he was their maternal grandfather, that he had given the whole earth with her horses, etc., to brahmans, and that the earth and the firmament and fire existed owing to his truth. *(I, **93**): I, **86**, 3535 (*Nāhusho rājā*), 3541, 3543, 3544 (*Nāhushaḥ*); **87**, 3553, (3555); **88**, †3564, (3565), (†3567), †3568, †3569; **89**, (†3577), †3577 (*Nahushasya putraḥ Pūroḥ pitā*), (†3580), †3589, (†3591), †3598; **90**, (†3601), (†3603), (†3606), (†3609), (†3613), (†3617), (†3621); **91**, (†3628), (3635), (3637); **92**, (3646), (†3651), (†3654), (†3656), (†3659), (†3661), †3663; **93**, (†3665), (†3667), (†3670), (†3672), (3674), (3676), (3678), (3681), (†3684), †3684 (*Nahushasya putraḥ Pūroḥ pitā*).—§ 156 (Pūruvaṃç.): I, **95**, ††3760 (son of Nahusha, husband of Devayānī and Çarmishṭhā, enumeration of his sons).—§ 267 (Yamasabhāv.): II, **8**, 319 (in the palace of Yama).—§ 273 (Rājasūyārambhap.): II, **14**, 570 (°*es tv eva Bhojānāṃ vistaro guṇato mahān*).—§ 296 (Dyūtap.): II, **56**, 1930 (*yathā*).—§ 320 (Saubhavadhap.): III, **21**, 841 (*prapatataḥ Y°eḥ kshīnapuṇyasya svargād iva*). —§ 345 (Nalopākhyānap.): III, **57**, 2235 (*ije cāpy açvamedhena Y°ir iva Nāhushaḥ*).—§ 376 (Tīrthayātrāp.): III, **85**, 8268 (*yathā*).—§ 377 (Dhaumyatīrthak.): III, **89**, 8363 (*Viçvāmitranadī . . . yāsyās tīre satāṃ madhye Y°ir Nahushātmajaḥ papāta sa punar lokāṃl lebhe dharmān sanātanān*, cf. § 149).—§ 378 (Tīrthayātrāp.): III, **92**, 8444 (*yathā*).—§ 402 (do.): III, **120**, †10260 (*nāthāḥ Çaibyādayaḥ . . . yathā Y°eḥ*, all. to § 149).—§ 409*c* (Plakshāvataraṇag.): *Y.* competed with *Indra*. On the place where he performed his sacrifice the ground is studded with places for the sacrificial fires of various forms, and the earth seems subsiding under the pressure of *Y.'s* pious works: III, **129**, 10516 (*Nāhushasya*), 10517.—§ 409 (do.): III, **129**, 10524 (*Nāhushaḥ*, performed sacrifices, at which Indra was pleased). —§ 412 (Ashṭāvakrīya): III, **133**, †10637 (in times of old *Y.* alone performed sacrifices). — § 464 (Mārkaṇḍeyas.): *Mārkaṇḍeya* continued: Once when King *Y. Nāhusha* was sitting on his throne, there came a brahman who asked him for wealth for his preceptor, with whom he had made the appointment always to question the giver with what feelings he would give him what he asked for. *Y.* answered that he always felt happy when giving, etc., and gave him 1,000 kine: III, **195**, ††13256 (*Nāhushaḥ*).--§ 486 (Pativratop.): III, **215**, 14047 (*rājā Y°ir dauhitraiḥ patitas tārito yathā*, all. to § 149).—§ 512 (Ghoshayātrāp.): III, **237**, 14787 (°*m iva Nāhushaṃ*).—§ 516 (Duryodhanayajña): III, **257**, 15329 (had performed the Vaishṇava sacrifice). — § 545 (Pativratāmāhātmyap.): III, **294**, 16675 (*iva*).—§ 552 (Goharaṇap.): IV, **56**ζ, 1768 (came to see the encounter). —§ 562 (Bhagavadyānap.): V. **90**ν, 3146.—§ 565 (Gālavacarita): V, **114**, 3903 (*Nāhushaḥ*), 3905 (residing in Pratisthāna); **115**, 3918 (*sarva-Kāçīçaḥ*) (gave his daughter Mādhavī to Gālava); **120**, 4037, 4039, 4041, 4045 (*Y.*, ascending to heaven after death and falling down therefrom, cf. § 149).—§ 566 (do.): As *Y.* was falling headlong towards the earth, while the kings and Si. and Aps. laughed, there came, at the command of *Indra*, a person whose business it was to hurl down those whose merits were exhausted, and told him that his pride had caused his fall. *Y.* uttered the wish that he might fall among the righteous. He fell down among his daughter's sons *Pratardana, Vasumanas, Çibi*, and *Ashṭaka*, in the *Naimisha* wood, where they performed a *vājapeya* sacrifice. They gave him their merits (*puṇya, dharma*, etc.), and the result of all their sacrifices. *Mādhavī* also came and gave him the moiety of hers, likewise *Gālava*, who gave him the eighth part of his (V, **121**). As soon as *Y.* was recognized by those virtuous persons, he rose again to heaven without touching the surface of the earth, and his four daughter's sons, in a loud voice, repeated the gift of their merits (*Ashṭaka* had performed hundreds of *puṇḍarīka, gosava*, and *vājapeya* sacrifices, *Çibi* had never spoken a falsehood) (V, **122**). *Y.* was honoured in heaven by G., Aps., D.-r,-R.-r, and the gods. *Brahmán* explained to him that it was his vanity alone that had been able to destroy all his merit (cf. also § 149). Nārada continued: "Such was the distress into which *Y.* fell in consequence of vanity and *Gālava* owing to his obstinacy. Make peace with the sons of Pāṇḍu" (V, **123**): V, **121**, 4052, 4053, 4059, 4062 (*rājarshiḥ*), (4065), 4065 (*rājarshiḥ*), (4067), 4070; **122**, 4079, 4094; **123**, 4097, (4107), 4116.—§ 567*b* (Bhagavadyānap.): *Y.*, the son of *Nahusha*, was the sixth in descent from Soma. *Y.* had five sons: *Yadu*, the son of *Devayānī*, and thus the grandson of *Çukra Kāvya* was the eldest, while *Pūru*, the son of *Çarmishṭhā* (the daughter of *Vṛshaparvan*) was the youngest. *Yadu* (the progenitor of the *Yādavas*) humiliated all the kshatriyas. He did not obey the injunctions of his father, but insulted his father and brothers. He established himself in the city named after the elephant (*nāgāhvaye*, i.e. Hāstinapura). *Y.* cursed him and expelled him from the kingdom. He also cursed his other sons who were obedient to *Yadu*, and placed his youngest son, *Pūru*, on the throne (cf. also §§ 144 and 148): V, **149**, 5042 (*Somāt . . . shaṣhṭaḥ. . . . Nahushātmajaḥ*), 5049 (*Nahushātmajaḥ*), 5050.—§ 574 (Jambūkh.): VI, **9** *aa*, 314.—§ 576 (Bhagavadgītāp.): VI, **17** *β*, 645.—§ 595 (Shoḍaçarāj.): *Y.*, the son of Nahusha; performed 100 *rājasūya* sacrifices, he gave to the brahmans the whole of the wealth in the possession of *Mlecchas*, etc.; he sided with the gods against the *Asuras*; having divided the earth into four parts, he gave it away to four persons (i.e. four *ṛtvijes*, Nīl.). His wives were *Devayānī*, daughter of *Uçanas* (*Auçanasyām*), and *Çarmishṭhā*; he roved through the celestial woods, at last he installed [his son] Pūru on the throne and retired into the forest (VII, **63**): VII, **63**, 2292 (*Nāhushaṃ*), 2300.—§ 599 (Jayadrathavadhap.): VII, **94** *ε*, 3450.—§ 599*e* (Çini): VII, **144**, 6029 (*rājarshiḥ*, son of Nahusha), 6030 (father of Yadu). — § 600 (Ghaṭotkacavadhap.): VII, **157**, 6927 (°*m iva Nāhusham*).—§ 604 (Karṇap.): VIII, **9**, 250 (do.). —§ 615 (Baladevatīrthayātrā): IX, **41**, 2350 (*Nāhushasya*), 2351, 2352 (*rājñaḥ*, performed sacrifices in Yāyātaṃ tīrthaṃ). —§ 628 (Rājadh.): XII, **24**, 700 (°*r iva Nāhushaḥ*).—§ 630 (do.): XII, **26**, 780 (*gāthā gītā Y°inā*, some verses (vv. 781–3) sung by *Y.* quoted).—§ 632*b* (Shoḍaçarāj., cf. § 595): XII, **29**, 987 (*Nāhushaṃ*), 990 (*Nahushātmajaḥ*) (repetition from § 595).—§ 638*b* (Rāmopākhyāna): XII, **49**, 1772 (°*patane*, all. to § 149).—§ 641 (Rājadh.): XII, **92**, 3467 (°*m iva Nāhushaṃ*); **93**, 3520 (*evaṃ rājopanishadaṃ Y°iḥ smāha Nāhushaḥ*).—§ 652*b* (Indrota-Parīkshitīya): XII, **152**, 5643 (*gāthāṃ gītāṃ Y°inā*, a verse (v. 5644) sung by *Y.* quoted). — § 656 (Khaḍgotpattik.): XII, **166** *δ*, 6194 (received the sword from Nahusha, from *Y.* it passed over to Pūru).—[§ 659 (Mokshadh.): XII, **178**, 6643 (*Nāhushaḥ*, questioned Bodhya)].—§ 706 (do.): XII, **310**, 11540 (°*iḥ kshīṇapuṇyo 'pi dhṛtyā lokān avāptavān*, cf. § 149).—§ 713 (Çukakṛti): XII, **327**, 12291 (*gāthāḥ purā gītāḥ . . . Y°inā*, some verses (vv. 12292–99) sung by *Y.* quoted).—§ 723 (Ānuçāsanik.): XIII, **6** *a*, 324 (*purā Y°ir vibhrashṭaç cyāvitaḥ patitaḥ kshitau / punar āropitaḥ Svargaṃ dauhitraiḥ puṇyakarmabhiḥ*, cf. § 149).—§ 746 (do.): XIII, **81** *λ*, 3806. —§ 751*b* (Çapathavidhi): XIII, **94** *a*, 4551, (4573).—§ 761 (Ānuçāsanik.): XIII, **115** *γ*, 5662 (abstained from meat during the month of Kārttika).—§ 768*b* (Kṛshṇa Vāsudeva): XIII, **147**, 6832 (son of Nahusha and father of Yadu).— § 775 (Ānuçāsanik.): XIII, **166** *η*, 7674.—§ 776 (do.): XIII, **167**, 7698 (*iva*).—§ 778*b* (Saṃvartta-Maruttīya): XIV, **5**, 103 (*iva*).

Cf. also the following synonyms:—

Nāhusha ("the son of Nahusha"): I, 3156 (*Y°*), 3161, 3186 (*Y°*), 3293, 3302, 3315, 3362, 3377, 3379, 3388, 3408, 3459, 3460 (*Y°*), 3517 (*Y°*), 3531, 3535 (*Y°*), 3544 (*Y°*); III, 2235 (*Y°*), 8777 (error in B., C. has *Nahusheṇa*), 10515, 10524 (*Y°*), 10546 (*uttarāṇāṃ sarveshām ṛshīṇāṃ N°sya ca*, sc. *saṃvādaḥ*), ††13256 (*Y°*), 14787 (*Y°*); V, 3903 (*Y°*), 3907, 4038, 4090; VII, 2292 (*Y°*), 2295 (only B.), 6927 (*Y°*); VIII, 250 (*Y°*); IX, 2350 (*Y°*); XII, 700 (*Y°*), 987 (*Y°*), 3467 (*Y°*), 3520 (*Y°*), 6643.

Nahushātmaja (do.): I, 3292 (*Y°*), 3300, 3389, 3400, 3500 (*Y°*); III, 8363 (*Y°*); V, 4043, 4055, 5042 (*Y°*), 5049 (*Y°*); XII, 990 (*Y°*).

Sarvakāçīça ("lord of all the Kāçis"): V, 3918 (*Y°*)

Yayātijā ("the daughter of Yayāti") = Mādhavī: V, 4031.

Yayātipatana ("the fall of Yāyati"), name of a tīrtha. § 358 (Tīrthayātrāp.): III, **82**, 4089.

[Yayātyupākhyāna(ṃ)] ("the episode relating to Yayāti"). § 136. *Vaiçampāyana* promised to recite the genealogy of *Prajāpati Daksha*, *Manu Vaivasvata*, *Bharata*, *Kuru*, *Pūru*, *Ājamīḍha*, the *Yādavas*, the *Kauravas*, and the *Bharatas*.—§§ 137–8: Daksha.—§ 139: Manu Vaivasvata.— §§ 140–1: Purūravas. — §§ 142–3: Nahusha. — § 144: Yayāti.—§ 145: Kaca.—§§ 146–7: Devayānī.—§ 148: Yayāti.

Yāyāvara, pl. (°*āḥ*), a family of brahmans. § 26 (Jaratkāru): I, **13**, 1030 (°*āṇāṃ pravarah*, i.e. Jaratkāru), 1036 (*ṛshayaḥ*, the ancestors (*pitaraḥ*) of Jaratkāru). — § 49 (Vāsuki): I, **38**, 1633 (°*kule . . . bhavishyati mahān ṛshir Jaratkāruḥ*).—§ 53 (Jaratkāru): I, **45**, 1828 (*ṛshayaḥ*, the ancestors (*pitaraḥ*) of Jaratkāru).—§ 677 (Mokshadh.): XII, **245**, 8902 (°*ā gaṇāḥ / ṛshīṇāṃ*).—§ 790 (Putradarçanap.): XV, **35**, 948 (°*kulotpannaṃ Jaratkārusutaṃ*, i.e. Āstīka).

Yodhya, pl. (°*āḥ*), a people. § 515 (Karṇadigvijaya): III, **254**, 15244 (vanquished by Karṇa on his digvijaya).

***Yoga** [1], name of a certain system of philosophy and religious practice. § 3 (Anukram.): I, **1**, 48 (*?*, *Vedā Y°aḥ savijñānaḥ*). —§ 265 (Lokapālasabhākhyānap.): II, **5**, 141 (*Sāṅkhya-Y°vibhāgajñaḥ*, sc. Nārada).—§ 309 (Āraṇyakap.): III, **2**, 61 (°*e Sāṅkhye ca kuçalaḥ*, sc. Çaunaka).—§ 493 (Āṅgirasa): III, **221**, 14197 (*Kapilo nāma Sāṅkhya-Y°pravartakaḥ*).— § 576 (Bhagavadgītāp.): VI, **26**, 917 (*eshā te 'bhihitā Sāṅkhye buddhir Y°e tu*); **28**, 994, 995, 996 (promulgated by Kṛshṇa to Vivasvat, by him to Manu, etc.); **29**, 1039 (*Sāṅkhya-Y°au*), 1040 (*ekaṃ Sāṅkhyañ ca Y°ñ ca*); **42**, 1529 (as propounded by Kṛshṇa in the Bhagavadgītā).— § 639 (Rājadh.): XII, **50**, 1838 (*Y°e Sāṅkhye ca niyatā ye ca dharmāḥ*).—§ 661 (Mokshadh.): XII, **196**, 7154 (*Sāṅkhya-Y°kriyāvidhiḥ*), 7157 (*Sāṅkhya-Y°au*), 7158 (do.).—§ 677 (do.): XII, **237**, 8674 (°*e Sāṅkhye 'pi*), 8685; **240**, 8736 (*Sāṅkhye vā yadi Y°e vā*); **241**, 8769 (°*kṛtyaṃ*); **254**, 9113 (°*çāstraparāḥ*).—§ 696 (Dakshaprokta-Çivasahasranāmastotra): XII, **285**, 10467 (*Sāṅkhya-Y°āt*)—.§ 704 (Mokshadh.): XII, **301**, 11037 (*Sāṅkhye Y°e ca*), 11038 (*praçaṃsanti yogā Y°ṃ*); **302**, 11110, †11205, †11206.—§ 705 (do.): XII, **306**, 11347 (*ekaṃ Sāṅkhyañ ca Y°ñ ca*), 11361 (*Sāṅkhya-Y°e ca kuçalāḥ*); **307**, 11372 (*Sāṅkhyaṃ Y°ñ ca*), 11373 (°*kṛtyaṃ*), 11374 (do.), 11393 (°*darçanaṃ*); **308**, 11461 (*Sāṅkhya-Y°au; Y°darçanaṃ*), 11465 (°*nidarçanaṃ*). § 707 (do.): XII, **314**, 11609 (°*pradarçinaḥ*); **315**, 11653; **317**, 11675 (°*jñānaṃ*), 11676 (*nāsti Y°samaṃ balaṃ*), 11678 (*ekaṃ Sāṅkhyañ ca Y°ñ ca*), 11682 (°*kṛtyaṃ*), **319**, 11735 (*Sāṅkhya-Y°epsitaṃ padam*), 11790 (°*çāstraṃ*), †11810 (°*dharme*), 11822 (°*çāstraṃ*). — § 709*b* (Sulabhā-Janakasaṃv.): XII, **321**, 11858 (°*dharmam*), 11876 (*Sāṅkhyajñāne ca Y°e ca*).—§ 713 (Çukakṛti): XII, **326**, 12218 (°*çāstraṃ*).—§ 717*b* (Nārāyaṇīya): XII, **340**, 12933 (°*çāstreshu*), 12976 (*Sāṅkhya-Y°kṛtaṃ . . . Pañcarātrānuçabditaṃ*); **342**, 13137 (°*çāstre*); **348**, 13530 (°*ç ca Sāṅkhyañ ca* = Nārāyana), 13537 (*Nārāyaṇātmakaḥ*); **349**, 13621 (*Sāṅkhya-Y°ena*), 13629 (*Sāṅkhya-Y°ṃ*); **350**, 13637 (*Sāṅkhya-Y°ṃ*), 13702 (°*ṃ*, C.; °*ḥ*, B.), †13711 (*Sāṅkhyañ ca Y°ñ ca*); **351**, 13714 (*Sāṅkhya-Y°vicāraṇe*).—§ 717*d* (Brahma-Rudrasaṃv.): XII, **352**, 13746, 13763.—§ 730*g* (Upamanyu): XIII, **14**, 789 (*Sāṅkhya-Y°ārthadaṃ*, sc. Çiva).—§ 730 (Ānuçāsanik.):

XIII, **18**λλ, †1374.—§ 746 (do.): XIII, **75**, 3642 (°*çūrāḥ*). —§ 768*b* (Umā-Maheçvarasaṃv.): XIII, **141**, 6472 (*yukto Y°ṃ prati*).—§ 769 (Ānuçāsanik.): XIII, **149**, 7075.—§ 770 (do.): XIII, **151**, 7132.—§ 782 (Anugītāp.): XIV, **19**, 546 (°*çāstraṃ*), 549 (do.).—§ 795 (Svargārohaṇap.): XVIII, **5**, 185 (*Sāṅkhya-Y°vatā*, sc. Vyāsa).

***Yoga**[2] ("application, devotion, abstract meditation and self-concentration, and the superhuman (magic) power resulting therefrom"): I, 916 (°*ena bahudhātmānaṃ kṛtvā*, sc. Agni), 1218 (*adhyātmay°nidrāñ ca Padmanābhasya* (i.e. Vishṇu) *sevataḥ*), 2591 (°*saktā*, sc. the sister of Bṛhaspati), 3156 (°*m āsthāya*, sc. Yati), 4715 (*tapoy°balānvitaḥ*, sc. Pāṇḍu), 4763 (*Dharmeṇa y°-mūrtidhareṇa*); II, 340 (°*çarīriṇaḥ*); III, 69 (*kriyāy°dvayena*), 127 (°*aiçvaryeṇa saṃyuktāḥ*, sc. the Rudras, etc.), 128 (°*siddhiṃ*), 141 (*tapoy°samādhisthaiḥ*, sc. Bhīma, etc.), 164 (°*m āsthāya*, sc. Yudhishṭhira), 1172 (*divyayogasamanvitān*, sc. Mārkaṇḍeya, etc.), 1496 (°*yuktaḥ*, sc. Arjuna), 1515 (°*samanvitaḥ*, do.), 4065 (*divyay°āḥ*, sc. the gods, etc.), 5062 (*y°m āsthāya*, sc. Çiva), 8835 (°*samanvitaḥ*, sc. Sagara), 10519 (*Ṛcīkaputrasya y°air vicarato mahīṃ*), 11818 (°*otpannaḥ*, sc. Yudhishṭhira), 11864 (°*siddhāḥ*), †12646 (°*yuktāḥ*), 13510, 13612, 13879 (*tapoy°samārambhaṃ*), 13939 (°*vidhiḥ*); 13992 (*taṃ vidyād Brahmaṇo y°ṃ viyogaṃ y°saṃjñitaṃ*), 15484 (*dhyānay°parāḥ*), 15486 (*jñānay°ena*), 16726 (*dhyānay°parāyaṇā*, sc. Sāvitrī), 16927 (°*arddhirūpavān*, sc. Sūrya), 17079 (°*āt kṛtvā dvidhātmānaṃ*, sc. Sūrya), 17125; V, 774 (°*ābhyāse*), 1031 (°*yuktaḥ*), 1311, †1689 (*paramaṃ*), †1733, 2559; VI, 592 (°*balena*), 926, 927 (*buddhiy°āt*), 928, 931, 953 (*jñānay°ena, karmay°ena*), 957 (*karmay°ṃ*), 1021 (°*yajñāḥ*), 1031 (°*saṃsiddhaḥ*), 1034 (°*saṃnyastakarmāṇaṃ*), 1035, 1036, 1037 (*karmay°ḥ*), 1041 (°*yuktaḥ*), 1042 (do.), 1056 (*Brahmay°yuktātmā*), 1067 (°*ārūḍhasya*), 1068 (°*ārūḍhaḥ*), 1076, 1080, 1081, 1083, 1084, 1087 (*taṃ vidyād duḥkhasaṃyogaviyogaṃ y°saṃjñitaṃ*), 1093 (°*yuktātmā*), 1097, 1100, 1101 (°*saṃsiddhiṃ*), 1105 (°*bhrashṭaḥ*), 1108, 1112, 1136 (°*māyāsaṃvṛtaḥ*, sc. Kṛshṇa), 1149 (*abhyāsay° yuktena cetasā*), †1151 (°*balena*), 1153 (°*dhāraṇāṃ*), 1168 (°*yuktaḥ*), 1174 (°*m aiçvaraṃ*, sc. Kṛshṇa's), 1198 (*sannyāsay°yuktātmā*), 1211, 1214 (*buddhiy°ṃ*), 1222, 1254 (°*m aiçvaraṃ*, sc. Kṛshṇa's), 1302 (°*vittamāḥ*), 1307, 1312 (*madyogam āçritaḥ*, sc. to Kṛshṇa), 1332, 1345 (*anye Sāṅkhyena y°ena karmay°ena cāpare*), 1487, 1506 (*dhyānay°paraḥ*). 1511 (*buddhiy°ṃ*), 1529, 2945 (°*parāvara*, sc. Nārāyaṇa), 2970, †2972 (*apāray°ṃ*, sc. Nārāyaṇa), 2974, 3008, 3018, 3024 (*dhyānay°ena*), 3031 (°*bhūtaṃ . . . Keçavaṃ*), 3045 (°*vidbhiḥ*), 5688 (°*m āsthāya*, sc. Bhīshma); VII, 2783 (°*m āsthāya yuktātmā*, sc. Kṛshṇa), 5986 (°*yukto 'bhavad muniḥ*, sc. Bhūriçravas), 6220 (°*ena yuktaḥ*, sc. Kṛshṇa), 8854 (°*yuktavān*, sc. Droṇa), 8858 (°*m āsthāya*, do.), 8865 (°*yuktaṃ*, do.), 8867 (°*yuktasya*, do.), 8869 (°*m āsthāya*, do.); VIII, 288 (*uktay°ḥ*, sc. Droṇa), 1439 (*y°ṃ yo veda cātmanaḥ*, sc. Çiva), †4646 (°*balena*); IX, 2465 (*mahā-y°balānvitāḥ*, sc. Skanda), 2482 (do., do.), 2486 (°*m āsthāya*, do.), 2511 (°*siddhaiḥ*), 2579 (°*yuktāḥ*), 2849 (°*siddhāḥ*), 2852 (*samprāpya paramaṃ yogaṃ*, sc. Asita Devala), 2853 (*paramaṃ y°m āsthāya*, do.), 2858 (°*m āsthāya*, sc. Jaigīshavya), 2860 (°*nityaḥ*, do.), 2876 (*prabhāvaṃ . . . y°jaṃ*), 2898 (*siddhiṃ y°sya*), 2907 (*prabhāvaṃ . . . y°jaṃ*), 2910 (*vidhiñ ca y°sya*), 2918, 2922, 3040 (°*yuktā*); XII, 589, 735 (*Vyāso y°vidāṃ varaḥ*), 777 (°*vatāṃ lokāḥ*), 1588, 1636 (°*m āsthāya*, sc. Kṛshṇa (Vishṇu)), 1690, 2490, 3882 (°*dharmavidaḥ*), 3926 (°*dharmavidaṃ*), 4190, 5981, 5986, 6616 (°*e buddhiṃ . . . dhārayan*), 7129 (*dhyānay°ñ caturvidhaṃ*), 7135 (°*vid*), 7142 (*dhyānay°vid*), 7148 (*nityay°ena*), 7353, 7360, 7624 (°*ātmā y°sārathiḥ*, sc. Vishṇu as the boar), 7641, 7683, 7684, 7814 (°*tantraiḥ*), 7948 (*tapoy°ṃ*), 8647, 8660, 8661, 8686 (°*aiçvaryaṃ*), 8723 (*karmay°ena*), 8771 (°*doshān*), 8775 (do.), 8783 (°*vid*), 8791, 8792, 8793, 8821 (°*jitātmakaṃ*), 9106 (°*yogināṃ*), 9114 (*samādhau y°m evaitac Chāṇḍilyaḥ çamam abravīt*), 9122 (°*prasādāt*), 9596, 9597 (°*dharmasya*), 9808, 9864, 9867, 9868 (°*sādhanāt* (°*ān*, B.)), 9962, 10133 (°*m āsthāya*, sc. Indra), 10240 (°*balaṃ*), 10287 (°*vid*), 10576 (*atiy°ṃ ay°ñ ca*), 10667 (°*siddhaḥ*), 10670, 10674 (*Uçanā y°siddhātmā*), 10685 (*dhyānay°ṃ*), 10916 (*karmay°ena*), 10954, 10977, 11047, 11051 (°*balāt*), 11055, 11059 (°*balaṃ*), 11060, 11065 (*balāni y°prāptāni*), 11071, 11077, 11089 (°*mārgaṃ*), 11090, 11093, 11099 (°*mārgaḥ*), 11110 (*jñānay°e*), 11131 (pl.), 11158 (*jñānay°ena Sāṅkhyena*), 11168 (*yatayaḥ siddhā jñānay°ena*), 11661 (°*dharmā*), 11679 (pl.), 11680, 11681 (*Vedeshu cāshṭaguṇinaṃ y°m āhur manīshiṇaḥ*), 11701, 11722, 11861, 11867 (°*jñā*), 11868 (°*bandhaiḥ*), 11919 (pl.), 12162 (*ātmay°ṃ*), 12166, 12167, 12170 (°*dharmaparāyaṇaḥ*, sc. Vyāsa), 12172, 12178 (*āsthitaḥ paramaṃ y°ṃ*, sc. Vyāsa), 12563, 12564 (°*ṃ samāsthāya*, sc. Çuka), 12571 (°*vīryaṃ*), 12578 (*kramay°vid*), 12582 (°*m āsthāya*, sc. Çuka), 12583, 12585 (°*m āsthāya*, sc. Çuka), 12627 (*mahāy°gatiṃ*), 12784 (*vijñānaṃ devay°jaṃ*), 12933 (°*ratiḥ*, sc. Nārāyaṇa), 13034 (°*vidaḥ*), 13080 (do.), 13142 (*prakṛtiḥ . . . y°dhāriṇī*), 13263 (*prāpya y°ṃ*, sc. Gālava), 13468 (*nidrāy°m upāgataḥ*, sc. Vishṇu (Nārāyaṇa)), 13504 (°*ṃ paramam āsthitaḥ*, do.), 13513 (*nidrāy°m upāgataṃ*, do.), 13563 (°*sthito Rudraḥ*), 13660 (*aiçvaryayogasthāṃ Buddhiṃ*), 13890 (°*yuktaḥ*); XIII, 168, 592 (°*vidbhiḥ*), 597 (°*cakshushā*), 675, 677, 813 (?), 814 (?), 987 (°*daṃ*, sc. Çiva), 1016 (*nityay°āḥ*), 1026, 1098 (*saṃyagy°japaiḥ*), 1132 (*idaṃ yogaṃ*), 1285 (°*daṃ*, sc. the 1000 names of Çiva), 1295 (*abhagnay°ḥ*), 1918, 1971, 2296, 2317, 2318 (°*bandhaiḥ*), 2319 (°*bala°*-), 2846 (°*balāt*), 2885 (°*m āsthāya*, sc. Cyavana), 2940 (°*yukte*), 3052 (*jñānavijñānatapoy°samanvitāḥ*), 3907 (°*m āsthitā*, sc. Surabhi), 5547 (°*eshv abhirataḥ*), 6393, 6501, 6513 (°*caryākṛtaiḥ*), 6514 (°*vidhaiḥ, maṇḍūkay°niyataiḥ*), 6544 (*maṇḍūkay°çāyanaḥ*), 6546 (*çītay°vahaḥ*), 6548 (*agniy°vahaḥ*), 6562 (*vīray°vahaḥ*), 6823 (°*māyaḥ*, sc. Kṛshṇa), 7761 (°*yuktasya*, sc. Bhīshma); XIV, †340, 419 (°*yuktena*, sc. Kṛshṇa), 548 (*mokshay°ṃ*), 554 (°*vidbhiḥ*), 564, 598, 742 (°*yajñaḥ*), 867 (°*m āsthitaḥ*), 868, 870, 970 (*nityay°parāyaṇāḥ*), 1089 (*nityay°āḥ*), 1195 (*pravṛttilakshaṇaḥ*), 1372 (*anāçiry°saṃyuktāḥ*), 1391 (°*vidhānavid*), 1446 (*dhyānay°ena*), 1447 (*dhyānay°ṃ*), 1448 (*dhyānay°āt*), 2841 (*mahāyogaḥ*); XV, 702 (°*balaṃ*), 705 (°*dharmā*, sc. Yudhishṭhira, so C.; B. reads °*dharmaṃ*), 758 (°*balāj jātaḥ . . . Yudhishṭhiraḥ*), 856 (°*ād evābhavad dvidhā*, sc. Soma); XVI, 67 (°*vid*, sc. Uddhava), †117 (°*yuktasya*, sc. Balarāma), †125 (*mahāy°m upetya Kṛshṇaḥ*), †126 (°*yuktaṃ*, sc. Kṛshṇa), †127 (do., do.); XVII, 30 (°*yuktāḥ*, sc. the Pāṇḍavas), 46 (°*dharmiṇaḥ*, do.), 49 (°*dharmiṇāṃ*, do.; *bhrashṭay°ā*, sc. Draupadī); XVIII, 170.

***yoga**[3], mostly pl. (°*āḥ*) ("practising yoga, followers of the Yoga system"): III, †12741, 12975; VI, 1040 (so B., C. has *Yau°*), 3036 (*yogānaṃ prabhuṃ*, i.e. Kṛshṇa, only B.); VII, 2865 (°*ānāṃ paramaṃ brahma* (*dhāma*, B.), sc. Çiva), 8260 (°*ānāṃ īçvaraṃ*, sc. Kṛshṇa); XII, 7352, 7358 (°*jāpakayoḥ*), 11038, 11039, 11043, 11048, 11050, 11052, 11054, 11055 (sg.), 11058 (sg.), 11061 (sg.), 11062 (sg.), 11064 (sg.), 11069 (sg.), 11106, 11202, 11231, 11346, 11347, 11359 (*Sāṅkhya-Y°āḥ*), 11374, 11392, 11463 (*çāstre y°ānāṃ*), 11550, 11674, 11678, 11682, 11701, 11794

(*Sāṅkhya-Y°āḥ*), 11802, 11810 (so B., C. by error *yāgo*), 11825, 13255, 13265, 13487 (*Sāṅkhya-Y°nidhe*, sc. Vishṇu); XIII, 1062 (*gataḥ Sāṅkhya-Y°ānām*, sc. Çiva), 1286 (do., do,), 4302 (pl., B., C. by error sg.), 7104 (°*bhūtagaṇāḥ*).—Do. sg. = Çiva: VII, 9508; XIII, 1238 (1000 names[2]).—Do. sg. = Vishṇu (1000 names).

Yoga[4], a ṛshi. § 770 (Ānuçāsanik.): XIII, **151**λ, 7123 (read *Sāṅkhya-yogau* with B., C. has *Sāṅkhyayogaḥ*).

Yogācārya[1] ("Yoga-teacher") = Çukra: I, 2607; XII, 2206 (*Kāvyaḥ*).—Do.[2] (do.) = Kṛshṇa: XVI, †130.—Do.[3] (do.) = Sanatkumāra: II, 441 (*S*°).

Yogādhyaksha, Yogakara = Çiva (1000 names[2]).

Yoganidrātman = Kṛshṇa: XII, 1648.

yogātman ("Yoga-soul"), said of Çiva (XII, 10444, 10685), Kṛshṇa (VI, 2944, 2952 (*sarva*°); XII, 1643, 7624), Purusha (XII, 13746), Sūrya (III, 17120), Vyāsa (XIII, 680), the yogin in general (XIII, 352, 755).

Yogavidāṃ netṛ = Vishṇu (1000 names).

Yogayogīça = Kṛshṇa: VI, 2959.

Yogeçvara[1] ("Yoga-lord") = Çiva: III, 7034 (*Sthāṇuḥ*); VII, 9508; XIII, 678, 920.—Do.[2] (do.) = Çuka: XII, 12582 (*mahā*°).—Do.[3] (do.) = Kṛshṇa (Vishṇu): I, 510 (°*tvam*, cf. V, **131**); VI, 1250, 1255 (*mahā*°, *Hariḥ*), 1529 (*K*°), 1532 (*K*°), 2055; XII, 1602, 7825 (*Hariḥ*).—Do.[4] pl. (do.): XIII, 4393 (i.e. Aṅgiras, etc.).

Yogīça[1] ("lord of the yogins") = Kṛshṇa (Vishṇu): VI, 3036 (only C.); XIII, 7040 (1000 names).

Yogīçvara[1] (do.) = Çiva: III, 5062.—Do.[2] (do.) = Kṛshṇa (Vishṇu): VI, 2945; XII, 1847.—Do.[3] (do.), pl.: XIII, 987.

yogin, sg. or pl. (°*aḥ*) ("practising yoga, followers of the Yoga system," = yoga, pl.): I, 1533 (°*inām īçvaraṃ Hariṃ*); III, 167 (°*ināṃ . . . parāyaṇaṃ*, i.e. Sūrya), 11240 (*gatir y°inām parā*), 13499, 13612 (sg.), 13975 (°*ināṃ . . . mārgaḥ*), 13978 (°*jitātmakaṃ*); V, 1738, 1740, 1742, 1744, 1746, 1748, 1750, 1752, 1754, 1756, 1759, 1761, 1763, 1765, 1767, 1769, 1771, 1773, 1775, 1777, 1779, 1781, 1783, 5363 (°*inām īçvaraṃ*, i.e. Kṛshṇa); VI, 953, 1018, 1046, 1059 (sg.), 1065 (sg.), 1066 (sg.), 1072 (sg.), 1074 (sg.), 1079 (sg.), 1083 (sg.), 1091 (sg.), 1092 (sg.), 1095 (sg.), 1096 (sg.), 1106, 1109 (sg.), 1110 (sg.), 1111, 1155 (sg.), 1164, 1166 (sg.), 1168 (sg.), †1169 (sg.), 1221 (sg.), 1315 (sg.), 1393; VII, †2466, 6220 (°*inām īçvaro Hariḥ*, i.e. Kṛshṇa); IX, 2714 (°*inām īçvaraṃ*, i.e. Skanda), 2718 (do., do.); XII, 942 (sg.), 7130, 7494, 8573, 9016 (sg.), 9106 (*yogay°ināṃ*), 10135, 11057 (sg.), 11073 (sg.), 11074 (sg.), 11076 (sg.), 11078 (sg.), 11079 (sg.), 11080 (sg.), 11082 (sg.), †11097 (sg.), †11098 (sg.), †13448 (*Sāṅkhya-Y°bhiḥ*), 13541; XIII, 813, 911, 916 (*Sanatkumāro Y°ināṃ*, sc. *asi*, sc. Çiva), 1040, 1044, 1096, 1142, 5334 (sg.); XIV, †340 (sg.), 517 (sg.), 546, 553 (sg.).—Do. said of certain persons: *Arjuna*[2] (XIII, 6901), *Çiva* XII, 10671 (*mahā*°), 10673 (do.), 10684 (do.), 13149, 13274 (*mahā*°); XIII, 901, 1142, 1153 (1000 names[2]), 1322, 1342 (*mahā*°)), *Çuka* (XII, 12196), *Çukra* (XII, 10684 (*mahā*°)), *Dadhīca* (°*ci*) (XII, 10286 (*mahā*°), ††13213 (*mahā*°)), *Gādhi* (IX, 2297 (*mahā*°)), *Kṛshṇa* (*Vishṇu*, *Nārāyaṇa*) (II, 2293 (*mahā*°); III, 8402 (*mahā*°); V, 2536 (*mahā*°), 3756; VI, 2992, 4856 (*mahā*°); VII, 6220; XII, 7630 (*mahā*°), 7635 (do.), 7636, 7638 (*mahā*°), 13540 (do.), 13653 (do.); XIII, 6967 (1000 names), 7040 (do.)), *Māṇḍavya* (I, 4307), *Mārkaṇḍeya* (III, 8330 (*mahā*°)), *Sūrya* (III, 151), *Vidura* (XV, 752 (*mahā*°)), *Vṛtra* (XII, 10268 (*mahā*°)), *Vyāsa* (I, 4235 (*mahā*°); III, 1432 (do.), 1448, 15378 (*mahā*°); XII, 12648 (do.); XIII, 1296 (do.), 1336 (do.)).

Yojanagandhā ("emitting scent to the distance of a yojana") = Satyavatī: I, 2412.

Yojya = Çiva (1000 names[2]).

Yoni, a tīrtha. § 358 (Tīrthayātrāp.): III, **82**, 5026.

Yonidvāra, a tīrtha. § 370 (Tīrthayātrāp.): III, **84**, 8073.

Yotimatsaka, v. Potimatsaka.

Yudhāmanyu, a Pāñcāla, brother of Uttamaujas. § 561 (Yānasandhip.): V, **57**ο, 2263.—§ 569 (Bhagavadyānap.): V, **141**γ, 4779.—§ 570 (Sainyaniryāṇap.): V, **153**, 5193 (*devair api durāsadaḥ*).—§ 572 (Rathātirathasaṅkhyānap.): V, **170**, 5883 (a ratha among the Pāṇḍavas' allies).—§ 573 (Ambopākhyānap.): V, **194**γ, 7598 (°*ūttamaujasau*); **195**η, 7624 (*Pāñcālyau . . . Y°ūttamaujasau*); **196**κ, 7638 (*Pāñcālyau Y°ūttamaujasau*).—§ 576 (Bhagavadgītāp.): VI, **15**, 606 (protects the left wheel of Arjuna); **19**ε, 714 (*Pāñcālyau Y°ūttamaujasau*, protectors of Arjuna's wheels); **25**θ, 835.—§ 585 (Bhīshmavadhap.): VI, **98**, 4494 (protected the left wheel of Arjuna).—§ 586 (do.): VI, **99**ζ, 4512 (only B.).—§ 587 (do.): VI, **115**ο, 5361 (fought with Duryodhana, only C., read with B. *Abhimanyuḥ*).—§ 592 (Saṃçaptakavadhap.): VII, **21**κ, 904, 911, **23**ο, 952 (proceeded against Droṇa, description of his horses).—§ 593 (Abhimanyuvadhap.): VII, **35**δ, 1510.—§ 597 (Pratijñāp.): VII, **83**a, 2951.—§ 598 (Jayadrathavadhap.): VII, **85**δ, 3048.—§ 599 (do.): VII, **91**, 3252 (*cakrarakshau Pāñcālyau Y°ūttamaujasau*); **92**, 3289, 3290; **130**, 5336 (*cakrarakshau tu Pāñcālyau Y°ūttamaujasau*), 5341, 5342, 5344, 5347 (brother of Uttamaujas), 5349, 5351 (°*ūttamaujasau*, defeated by Duryodhana); **137**ωω, 5629; **139**, 5755 (°*o rathaṃ*); **146**, 6288 (only B.); **147**, 6346 (*cakrarakshau . . . Y°ūttamaujasau*).—§ 600 (Ghaṭotkacavadhap.): VII, **156**θ, 6765; **177**χχ, 8059 (°*ūttamaujasau*); **179**βββ, 8119 (do.).—§ 604 (Karṇap.): VIII, **6**, 174 (among the slain).—§ 605 (do.): VIII, **11**, 428 (*cakrarakshau tu Pāñcālyau Y°ūttamajasau*); **13**, 523 (°*rathaṃ*); **30**ξξ, 1230.—§ 608 (do.): VIII, **59**ψψ, 2946; **61**, 3080 (attacked by Kṛpa), 3121, 3122 (defeated by Kṛpa); **63**ηηη, 3199 (*pṛshṭharakshau . . . Y°ūttamaujasau*); **67**κκκ, †3374 (°*ç cottamaujāç ca çūrau pṛshṭhato māṃ rakshatāṃ rājaputrau*, says Arjuna); **75**, †3811 (fought with Citrasena[8]); **79**η′, 4029; **82**λ, †4195, †4200, †4244, †4246 (slew Citrasena[8]); **96**aχ′, 4991 — § 609 (Çalyap.): IX, **1**γ, 31 (among the slain).—§ 612 (Hradapraveçap.): IX, **30**ε, 1726.—§ 616 (Sauptikap.): X, **8**, 354 (slain by Açvatthāman).—§ 620 (Çrāddha): XI, **26**β, 789 (his body burnt).—§ 795 (Svargārohaṇap.): XVIII, **1**δ, 27 (*bhrātarau . . . Y°ūttamaujasau*). Cf Pāñcalaja, Pāñcālya, dual, Saumaki.

Yudhishṭhira Pāṇḍava, also named Ajātaçatru and Dharmarāja (Dhr.), eldest son of Pāṇḍu and Kuntī (begotten by Dharma). § 4 (Anukram.): I, **1**, †109, 123, 128, †157, †170, †204 (Dhr.).—§ 11 (Parvasaṅgr.): I, **2**, 395, 435, 464, 522, 534 (°*nṛpājñayā*), 545 (Dhr.), 546, 593 (Dhr.), 599 (*Kururājuh*), 616 (Dhr.), 632.—§ 61 (Sarpasattra): I, **55**, †2102 (*yajñaḥ çruto divi devasyu sūnor Y°syājumīḍhasya*).—§ 71 (Ādivaṃçāvatāraṇap.): I, **61**, 2270 (Dhr., all. to § 247), 2279 (all. to Dyūtaparvan).—§ 72 (do.): I, **62**, 2291 (*suto Dharmasya*). — § 83 (Ādivaṃçāvatāraṇa): I, **63**, 2443 (*jyeshṭhaḥ*), 2444 (begotten by Dharma, cf. § 190*b*), 2451 (begat Prativindhya on Draupadī, cf. § 253). — § 130 (Aṃçāvat.): I, **67**, 2745 (*Dharmasyāṃçam*). — § 157 (Pūruvaṃç.): I, **95**, ††3814 (begotten by Dharma on Kuntī, cf. § 190*b*).—§ 159 (do.): I, **95**, ††3827 (father of Prativindhya, cf. § 253), ††3828 (married Devikā, the daughter of

Govāsana Çaibya, and on her begat Yaudheya).—§ 180 (Gāndhārīputrotp.): I, **115**, 4506 (born before Duryodhana), 4511 (*rājaputro jyeshṭhaḥ*).—§ 190*b* (Pāṇḍavotpatti): *Kuntī* bore *Y.* [from Dharma] under the conjunction of *Jyeshṭhā* (*Aindre candrasamāyukte*) at the eighth *muhūrta*, named Abhijita (*muhūrte 'bhijite 'shṭame*) *divāmadhyagate sūrye tithau pūrṇe 'tipūjite* (i.e. on the fifth tithi of the bright fortnight of *Āçvina*, Nil.; PCR. translates: of the hour of noon of that very auspicious day of the eighth moon (Kārttika), viz. the fifth of the bright fortnight). An incorporeal voice foretold his greatness: I, **123**, 4767 (*Pāṇḍoḥ prathamajaḥ putraḥ*). —§ 192 (do.): I, **124**, 4854 (*jyeshṭhaṃ*, was named *Y.* by the brahmans).—§ 194 (Pāṇḍu): I, **126**, 4919 (*sākshād Dharmād ayaṃ putras tatra jāto Y°ḥ*).—§ 197 (Bhīmasenarasap.): I, **128**, 4992, 5000; **129**, 5037, 5043 (Dhr.), 5066, 5067 (Dhr.).—§ 202 (Droṇa): I, **131**, 5158 (*Kuntīputraḥ*), (5159). —§ 205*d* (do.): *Y.* excelled everyone in driving: I, **132**, 5272 (disciple of Droṇa).—§ 206 (do.): I, **132**, 5280, 5281, 5283 (do.).—§ 208 (Astradarçana): I, **134**, 5335 (°*purogamāḥ*, sc. the Pāṇḍavas, show their proficiency in arms); **137**, †5443.—§ 209 (Drupadaçāsana): I, **138**, 5467. —§ 210 (Sambhavap.): I, **139**, 5517 (*Pāṇḍuputraḥ*, installed as *yuvarāja*), 5519 (*Kuntīputraḥ*).—§ 213 (Jatugṛhap.): I, **141**, 5663; **142**, 5682; **143**, 5706, 5709; **145**, 5746, 5747 (Dhr.), 5760 (Dhr.), (5765); **146**, 5771 (Dhr.), 5780, (5781), (5787); **147**, 5804 (*Kuntīputraḥ*), (5804); **148**, 5820 (*Kaunteyaḥ*), (5821); **149**, 5846; **150**, 5871 (*Kauravya*); **151**, 5919, 5921 (*Pāṇḍavaçreshṭhaḥ*) (Kuntī and the Pāṇḍavas escaped from the lac house).—§ 214 (Hiḍimbavadhap.): I, **154**, 6019; **155**, (6043), 6045 (*Kaunteyaṃ*), (6057); **156**, 6095 (*Dharmarāṭ*) (Vyāsa ordered the Pāṇḍavas to remain in Ekacakrā).—§ 215 (Bakavadhap.): I, **162**, 6242 (*Pāṇḍuputraḥ*), (6243), (6245), 6252, 6261; **163**, (6267).—§ 219 (Caitrarathap.): I, **168**, 6411, (6418) (Vyāsa ordered the Pāṇḍavas to go to the country of the Pāñcālas).—§ 221 (do.): I, **170**, 6469, (6471), 6472 (*Kururājaḥ*) (ordered Arjuna to spare the life of the Gandharva Citraratha).— § 231 (Svayaṃvarap.): I, **184**, (6928), (6944).—§ 233 (do.): I, **187**, †7014; **188**, †7058 (at the svayaṃvara of Draupadī Arjuna won her); [**189**, †7082 (*Dharmaputraḥ*)]. —§ 235 (do.): I, **191**, †7133, 7145 (*Kuntīputraḥ*), †7150 (*Ājamīḍhasya rājñaḥ*).—§ 236 (do.): I, **192**, †7158.—§ 237 (Vaivāhikap.): I, **193**, †7195, †7202; [**194**, †7206 (Dhr.)]; **195**, 7218, (7225) (disclosed to Drupada that they were the Pāṇḍavas), 7230, 7231, 7234 (*Kuntīputraṃ*), 7238, (7240) (asked Drupada to give Draupadī to the Pāṇḍavas as their common wife), (7246); **196**, (7264), 7269.—§ 240 (do.): I, **198**, †7339; **199**, 7365 (Dhr.) (*Y.* and his brothers married Draupadī).—§ 241 (Vidurāgamanap.): I, **201**, 7401 (*Kuntīputraṃ*). — § 244 (Rājyalābhap.): I, **207**, 7547 (*Kuntīputraḥ*), (7549), 7553 (*Pāṇḍuputraḥ*) (*Y.* became king in Indraprastha).—§ 245 (do.): I, **208**, 7601, 7604, 7605, 7607, 7611, 7615, (7616). — § 246 (Sundopasundop.): I, **209**, 7619 (*Pārtha*) (Nārada told *Y.* and his brothers the story of Sunda and Upasunda, then the Pāṇḍavas established a rule among themselves with regard to their common wife Draupadī).—§ 247 (Arjunavanavāsap.): I, **213**, 7754 (Dhr.), 7770. — § 250 (do.): I, **217**, 7884 (only B.) —[§ 252 (Subhadrāharaṇap.): I, **219**, 7930 (Dhr., *Pāṇḍavaḥ*).]— § 253 (Haraṇāharaṇap.): I, **221**, 7994, 8000, 8002 (*Kuntīputraḥ*), 8018 (Dhr.), 8029 (*Kuntīputraḥ*), 8039 (begat Prativindhya on Draupadī), 8041.—[§ 254 (Khāṇḍavadahanap.): I, **222**, 8051 (*Dharmarājānaṃ*), 8058 (Dhr.), 8066 (Dhr.).]—§ 261 (Sabhākriyāp.): II, **1**, 14 (Dhr.), 15 (Maya promised to build a palace to *Y.*).—§ 262 (Bhagavadyāna): II, **2**, 36, 41, 42, 44 (Dhr.).—[§ 263 (Sabhākriyāp.): II, **3**, 95 (Dhr.) (Maya built a palace to *Y.*).]—§ 264 (do.): II, **4**, 96, 102 (*Dharmaputraṃ*), 128 (*Kuntīputraṃ*), 134 (many ṛshis and kings waited upon *Y.*).—§ 265 (Lokapālasabhākhyānap.): II, **5**, 149, 150, (246), 248, (†262) (Nārada's discourse to *Y.*); **6**, 264 (Dhr.), 269, (271), 278 (Dhr.), (279) (Nārada described to *Y.* the sabhās of the gods (ch. **7-11**)).—§ 267 (Yamasabhāv.): II, **8**, 311.—§ 268 (Varuṇasabhāv.): II, **9**, 353, 363, 376.—§ 270 (Brahmasabhāv.): II, **11**, 456.—§ 271 (Lokapālasabhākhyānap.): II, **12**, (479), 503 (Nārada told *Y.* that Pāṇḍu wished that *Y.* should perform a rājasūya).— § 272 (Rājasūyārambhap.): II, **13**, 514, 517, 520, 527, 529, 533, 542, (Dhr.), (543), 544 (Dhr.), 552 (*Pārthaḥ*), (559) (*Y.* resolved to perform the rājasūya).—§ 274 (do.): II, **15**, (635), 650; **16**, (660), 665.—§ 275 (do.): II, **17**, (686) (Kṛshṇa told *Y.* the story of Jarāsandha).—§ 276 (Jarāsandhavadhap.): II, **20**, 775, (776) (*Y.* sent Kṛshṇa, Arjuna, and Bhīma to slay Jarāsandha).—§ 277 (do.): II, **24**, 958, 971, 974, 979 (°*mukhāḥ Pāṇḍavāḥ*) (the slaughter of Jarāsandha). —§ 278 (Digvijayap.): II, **25**, 983, 987 (Dhr.), 993 (Dhr.) (*Y.* sent his four brothers to subdue the four quarters).— § 279 (Arjuna): II, **26**, 1007 (*Dharmaputraḥ*), 1009; [**27**, 1021 (Dhr.)]; **28**, 1052 (Arjuna conquered the north for *Y.*).—[§ 280 (Bhīmasena): II, **29**, 1059 (Dhr.), 1069 (Dhr.), 1073 (Dhr.); **30**, 1104 (Dhr.) (Bhīmasena conquered the east for *Y.*).]—[§§ 281–4 (Sahadeva): II, **31**, 1105 (Dhr.), 1123 (Dhr.), 1159 (*Dharmasutasya*), 1182 (Dhr.), (Sahadeva conquered the south for *Y.*).]—§ 285 (Nakula): II, **32**, 1201 (Nakula conquered the west for *Y.*).—§ 286 (Rājasūyikap.): II, **33**, 1208, 1220, (1221), (1229), 1236 (Dhr.), 1247 (*Kuntīputraṃ*), 1248 (Dhr., *Y.* was initiated—*dīkshitaḥ*), 1258, 1259.—§ 287 (do.): II, **34**, 1284 (Dhr.).— § 288 (do.): II, **35**, 1286, 1296 (Dhr.), 1302 (performance of the rājasūya).—§ 289 (Arghāharaṇap.): II, **36**, 1314 (°*niveçane*), 1327 (Dhr.), 1328, (1331); **37**, 1361, 1367; **38**, 1369; **39**, 1414 (°*ābhishekaṃ*).—§ 290 (Çiçupālavadhap.): II, **40**, 1418, 1422 (Dhr.), 1431.—§ 292 (Rājasūyikap.): II, **45**, 1600, 1603 (Dhr.), 1611, 1616, 1618, 1622 (Dhr.), 1623 (*Kuntīputraṃ*).—§ 293 (Dyūtap.): II, **46**, 1630 (Dhr.), 1633 (Dhr.), (1634), 1649, 1653, 1661.—§ 294 (do.): II, **47**, 1683; **48**, 1702, 1716, 1718; **49**, 1725 (*rājasūyaṃ . . . Y°sya nṛpateḥ*), 1739, 1742, 1743 (°*niveçane*), 1760, 1783; **50**, 1803, 1804 (°*niveçane*), 1805 (do.), 1806.—§ 295 (do.): II, **51**, 1841 (°*niveçane*) (enumeration of the tributes given to *Y.*); **52**, 1896, 1898 (°*niveçane*), 1900, 1903 (°*niveçane*), 1904, 1905 (°*niveçane*).—§ 296 (do.): II, **53**, 1930.—§ 297 (do.): II, **54**, 1935.—§ 298 (do.): II, **56**, 1966 (*Pāṇḍuputre*), 1967 (*Kuntīputraḥ*), †1985; **57**, 1991 (*Kuntīputraṃ*); **58**, 1994 (*Dharmaputraṃ*), (†1996), (†2001), (†2003), (†2005), 2010 (commanded by Dhṛtarāshṭra, Vidura invited *Y.* to the gambling; *Y.*, together with his brothers and Draupadī, came to Hāstinapura); **59**, 2030 (*Pārthā Y°purogamāḥ*), 2032, 2033, (2034), (2038), 2043, 2044, 2045, (2047), (2050); **60**, (2056), 2059 (the gambling began); **61**, (2060), (2063), 2066, (2067), 2070, (2071), 2074, (2075), 2078, (2079), 2082, (2083), 2085, (2086), 2090, (2091), 2093; **63**, †2116; **65**, 2141, (2142), 2145, (2146), 2147, (2148), 2149, (2150), 2151, (2152), 2153, 2154, (2155), 2156, (2158), 2160, (2161), 2162, (†2164), 2166, (2168), 2169 (2173) (at the gambling *Y.* had lost his wealth, his kingdom, his four brothers, and Draupadī).—§ 299 (do.):

II, **67**, 2201, 2206, 2208, 2215, †2244, †2245 (*Kuntīsutaḥ*), †2250; **68**, 2251.—§ 301 (do.): II, **69**, 2360; **70**, †2364, 2369; **71**, †2383, 2387, †2399, 2407; **72**, 2431; **73**, (2433), 2436, 2440, 2450 (Dhr.) (the Pāṇḍavas and Draupadī were again set free).—§ 303 (Anudyūtap.): II, **76**, 2491, 2492 (2493), 2504 (2509), 2513 (at the second gambling *Y.* lost, and the Pāṇḍavas and Draupadī had to repair to the woods for twelve years, etc.).—§ 305 (do.): II, **78**, (2560), 2563, 2568, 2581, 2583.—§ 306 (do.): II, **80**, 2621 (*Dharmaputraḥ*), 2623 (*Kuntīputraḥ*), [2630 (*a*), (*Y.* had gone away, covering his face with his cloth, that he might not consume the people by the fire of his angry eyes)] (the Pāṇḍavas and Draupadī repaired to the woods).—§ 308 (Āraṇyakap.): III, **1**, (33); **2**, 48 (*Kuntīputraḥ*), (53), (58).—§ 309 (do.): III, **2**, 96, (97).—§ 310 (do.): III, **3**, 131 (*Kuntīputraḥ*), 134, 143, (166), 209 (having hymned Sūrya, *Y.* obtained an inexhaustible vessel, from which he fed the brahmans), 214, 215.—§ 311 (do.): II, **4**, †234.—§ 312 (do.): III, **5**, (†261).—§ 313 (do.): III, **6**, 273, 275, 279.—[§ 315 (Maitreyaçāpa): III, **10**, 356 (Dhr.) (visited by Maitreya).]—§ 316 (Kirmīravadhap.): III, **11**, 405, 406 (Dhr.), (410), 421, 422.—§ 317 (Arjunābhigamanap.): III, **12**, 464 (Dhr.), 467 (Dhr.), 533 (father of Prativindhya).—§ 319 (Saubhavadhop.): III, **14**, (614).—§ 320 (do.): III, **15**, (636); **20**, 794, **21**, 829 (Kṛshṇa told the Saubhavadhopākhyāna to *Y.*)—§ 321 (do.): III, **22**, 893 (Dhr.), 896, 902.—§ 322 (Dvaitavanapr.): III, **23**, †903, †918; **24**, †919 (*Kaunteyaḥ*), (930), 933.—§ 323 (do.): III, **25**, †949 (*Kuruvṛshabhaḥ*), †950.—§ 324 (do.): III, **26**, 968 (Dhr., *Kaunteyam*), 983, 984.—§ 325 (Draupadīparitāpav.): III, **27**, 1020.—§ 327 (do.): III, **29**, (1065); **30**, 1152; **31**, (1160); **32**, 1205, 1241, 1257, 1263; **33**, 1343; **34**, (†1355) (*Y.* refused to break his pledge and begin war).—§ 328 (Kāmyakavanapr.): III, **36**, 1411 (*Kuntīputraḥ*), (1415).—§ 329 (do.): III, **36**, 1433, 1434, 1438, 1450 (Vyāsa imparted the Pratismṛti knowledge to *Y.*).—§ 330 (Indradarçana): III, **37**, 1456 (Dhr.), (1459) (*Y.* imparted the Pratismṛti knowledge to Arjuna and sent him to Indra to acquire weapons).—§ 331 (Kairātap.): III, **38**, 1526 (°*niyogāt*).—§ 339 (Indralokābhigamanap.): III, **47**, 1902 (Indra sent Lomaça to *Y.*).—§ 341 (do.): III, **50**, 1960, 1963 (Dhr.).—§ 342 (do.): III, **51**, 1986, (1998).—§ 343 (Nalopākhyānap.): III, **52**, 2013, 2017, 2048 (Dhr.), 2052 (Dhr.), 2054, (2071).—§§ 344–355 (do.): III, **59**, 2271, **61**, 2305; **68**, 2684; **70**, 2765; **79**, 3089 (Bṛhadaçva told *Y.* the Nalopākhyāna and taught him the science of dice).—§§ 356–76 (Tīrthayātrāp.): III, **81**, 4027 (Dhr.), 4041 (Nārada repeated to *Y.* Pulastya's description of the tīrthas, chs. **82-85**); **82**, 4097, 5006, 5012; **83**, 5075, 5077; **84**, 8077; **85**, 8220, 8275.—§ 377 (Dhaumyatīrthak.): III, **87**, 8301; **88**, 8339, 8346, 8348; **89**, 8365; **90**, 8377, 8382, 8392 (Dhaumya described to *Y.* the tīrthas of the four quarters).—§ 378 (Tīrthayātrāp.): III, **91**, 8409 (*Dharmaputraḥ*), 8418, 8422, 8423; **92**, 8432, (8445), (8450); **93**, 8476, 8477; **94**, (8487) (Lomaça came to *Y.*, who then began the tīrthayātrā, accompanied by the brahmans).—§§ 379–91 (do.): III, [**96**, 8540 (*Kaunteyaḥ*)]; **99**, 8677; **100**, (8689); **104**, (8781); **106**, (8828); **107**, (8887); **110**, [9968 (*Kaunteyaḥ*)], (9994) (on the tīrthayātrā Lomaça pointed out the different tīrthas and told the legends relating to them).—§§ 392–99 (do.): III, **114**, 10104, (10108), 10110, †10124; **115**, (10131); **116**, 10197; [**117**, 10211 (Dhr.)] (Akṛtavraṇa told *Y.* the story of Rāma Jāmadagnya, who then appeared on the mountain Mahendra).—§ 400 (do.): III, **118**, †10231 (*Ājamīḍham*), †10234.—§ 401 (do., Balarāma): III, **119**, †10241, †10243, †10249.—§ 402 (Tīrthayātrap.): III, **120**, †10259, †10279, †10282, (†10285) (having met with the Vṛshṇis in Prabhāsa, the Pāṇḍavas continued the tīrthayātrā).—§§ 403–17 (do.): III, **121**, 10297, (10314); **125**, 10412, 10416; **126**, (10423); **127**, (10470), 10471; **132**, (†10602); **135**, 10696, (10701), 10709; **136**, 10757; **138**, 10801, 10813 (Lomaça further pointed out the different tīrthas and told the legends relating to them).—§ 418 (do.): III, **139**, (†10837).—§ 419 (Gandhamādanapr.): III, **140**, (10840), (10857).—§ 420 (do.): III, **141**, (10871).—§ 422*bis* (do., Varāhāvatāra): III, **142**, (10928), 10932.—§ 423 (Gandhamādanapr.): III, **144**, (10995), 11000 (Dhr.), 11006 (Dhr.); **145**, (11014), 11048 (*Dharmaputram*), 11051 (Dhr.).—§ 424 (Bhīmakadalīkhaṇḍapr.): III, **146**, 11101, 11102.—§ 433 (Saugandhikāharaṇa): III, **155**, 11400 (*Dharmaputraḥ*), 11403 (do.).—§ 434 (do.): III, **156**, 11430 (Dhr.), 11449 (the Pāṇḍavas at Kubera's lotus tank).—§ 435 (Jaṭāsuravadhap.): III, **157**, 11462 (Dhr.), 11477, 11478, 11481 (*Kuntīputram*), 11522.—§ 436 (Yakshayuddhap.): III, **158**, 11539, 11553, 11600; **159**, 11628, (11642), 11651, 11657.—§ 438 (do.): III, **161**, [11739 (*Ajātaçatruḥ Kaunteyaḥ*)], (11748), 11752 (*Kuntīputraḥ*), (11790); **162**, 11803, 11819, 11834 (the Pāṇḍavas' meeting with Kubera on the Gandhamādana).—§ 439 (do.): III, **163**, 11843, 11866.—§ 440 (do.): III, **164**, †11897.—§ 441 (Nivātakavacayuddhap.): III, [**165** (Arjuna's return)]; **166**, 11917 (Dhr.), 11923 (Dhr.), 11926 (*Kuntīputraḥ*), 11932 (*Kuntīputram*).—[§ 442 (do.): III, **167**, 11935 (*Dharmaputram*).]—§ 445 (do.): III, **173**, 12273 (*Kuntīputraḥ*).—§ 446 (do.): III, **174**, (12284).—§ 447 (do.): III, **175**, 12291 (Dhr.).—[§ 448 (Ājagarap.): III, **176**, 12326 (Dhr.), 12329 (Dhr.), 12333 (Dhr.).]—§ 449 (do.): III, **177**, †12357.—§ 450 (do.): III, **179**, [12398 (Dhr.)], 12435 (*Kaunteyaḥ*); **180**, 12450, (12454), (12458), 12458, (12467), 12469, (12470), 12473, (12475), (12481), 12488; **181**, (12489), (12491), (12496), (12504), (12512), (12516), 12519, 12528 (Dhr.), 12534, (*Y.'s* meeting with Nahusha, who had been transformed into an ajagara).—§ 422 (Mārkaṇḍeyas.): III, **183**, 12557 (°*purogamāḥ*), †12571, †12578.—§ 453 (do.): III, **184**, 12636, †12644.—§§ 454–509 (do.): Mārkaṇḍeya told *Y.* various legends (chs. **185-232**): III, **188**, 12805 (Dhr.); **190**, 13009 (*Kaunteyaḥ*), (13010), 13021, 13054; **191**, (13128), (13137); **193**, 13212, 13213 (*Kaunteyaḥ*, Dhr.); **200**, 13350, (13360), 13368, 13392, (13413), 13420, (13430), 13472; **201**, 13482, 13488, 13489; **203**, (13551); **204**, 13598, 13620; **205**, 13628, 13650; **206**, 13663; **208**, 13802; **209**, 13842; **210**, 13898; **213**, 13960; **214**, 14000; **216**, 14096, (14098); **217**, (14101); **232**, (14628).—§ 510 (Draupadī-Satyabhāmāsamv.): III, **233**, 14690 (°*niveçane*), 14691, 14698.—§ 512 (Ghoshayātrāp.): III, **236**, †14753; **237**, 14776, 14777; **239**, 14805, 14838 (*Kaunteyaḥ*); **240**, 14863 (*Dharmaputraḥ*); **242**, 14925, 14926; **243**, (14935); **244**, 14957; **246**, 15020 (*Kuntīputraḥ*, Dhr.), 15021, 15030, 15034 (*Kuntīputraḥ*) (*Y.* prevailed upon Citrasena to set Duryodhana free); [**247**, 15041 (Dhr.)]; **249**, 15074, 15076.—§ 516 (Duryodhanayajña): III, **255**, 15285; **256**, 15309, 15312 (Dhr.); **257**, 15327 (°*sya yajñena na samo hy esha te kratuḥ*, sc. Duryodhana's).—[§ 517 (Ghoshayātrāp.): III, **257**, 15347 (*Dharmasutaḥ*).]—§ 518 (Mṛgasvapnodbhavap.): III, **258**, 15354, 15356

(*Kaunteyaḥ*), 15359, 15360 (Dhr.) (*Y.'s* dream).—§ 519 (Vrīhidrauṇikap.): III, **259,** 15372, 15376, 15378 (*Kuntīputraḥ*), 15381, (15396), 15403.—§ 520 (do., Mudgala): III, **260,** (15405) (Vyāsa told *Y.* the story of Mudgala).—§ 521 (Draupadīharaṇap.): III, **262,** 15511; **263,** 15522, 15559. —§ 522 (do.): III, **266,** †15607; **267,** 15622 (*Kauravyaḥ . . . Kuntīputraḥ*), 15630 (*Kuntīputraḥ*); [**268,** 15643 (Dhr.), 15663 (Dhr.)]; **269,** †15668, (†15689); **270,** [†15700 (on the top of *Y.'s* flagstaff were two tabours (*mṛdaṅgau*) named Nanda and Upananda)], †15701 (*Dharmasutaṃ*), †15706 (*bhrātā ca çishyaç ca Y°sya Dhanañjayaḥ*); **271,** 15717 (*sa-Y°ān*), 15754, (15758) (Jayadratha was vanquished).—§ 523 (Jayadrathavimokshaṇap.): III, **272,** 15790, 15794, 15795, 15796 (*Dharmaputraḥ*) (*Y.* set Jayadratha free).—§§ 525-43 (Rāmopākhyānap.): Mārkaṇḍeya told *Y.* the story of Rāma Dāçarathi: III, **273,** 15860 (*Dharmarājaḥ*), (15862), (15875); **277,** (15945); **289,** 16478. — [§ 544 (Yudhishṭhirāçvāsa): III, **292** (*Y.* was comforted by Mārkaṇḍeya).] — § 545 (Pativratāmāhātmyap.): III, **293,** (16616), 16619 (Mārkaṇḍeya told *Y.* the story of Sāvitrī).—§ 546 (Kuṇḍalāharaṇap.): III, **300,** 16919 (*Pāṇḍuputraṃ*).—§ 547 (Karṇa): III, **309,** 17174.—§ 548 (Āraṇeyap.): III, **311,** 17223, 17225 (*Kuntīputraḥ*), 17235; **312,** (17242), 17246, 17250 (*Kuntīputraḥ*), 17255 (do.), 17261 (do.), 17274 (do.); **313,** 17306 (*Tapaḥsutaḥ . . . Dharmaputraḥ*), (17317), (17328), (17331), (17333), (17335), (17337), (17339), (17341), (17343), (17345), (17347), (17349), (17351), (17353), (17355), (17357), (17359), (17361), (17363), (17365), (17367), (17369), (17371), (17373), (17375), (17377), (17379), (17381), (17383), (17385), (17387), (17389), (17393), (†17398), (17400), (17405), (17408), (17413); **314,** (17420), (17430), (17433), (17441) (in the shape of a Yaksha Dharma slew the brothers of *Y.*; *Y.* answered the questions of the Yaksha, chose that Nakula should be revived, and got all his brothers revived; Dharma also granted him that they should remain unknown in the thirteenth year); **315,** 17456 (*Dharmasutaḥ*), 17469 (the Pāṇḍavas took leave of the brahmans).—§ 549 (Pāṇḍavapraveçap.): IV, **1,** 5, 6 (*Dharmaputraḥ*), (14), (22), 26; **2,** 36, (38), 58; **3,** (61), (66), (73), 78, (81); **4,** (83), (134); **5,** (148), 158 (*Dharmarājam*), 161, 169 (*Kuntīputraḥ*), 176; **6,** 178, 213 (*Y.* praised Durgā (Umā), who then appeared to him and promised him victory); **7,** †214, †221, (†224), †224, (†226) (*Y.* presented himself to Virāṭa, naming himself Kaṅka Vaiyāghrapadya, and was accepted as a courtier); **8,** †239; **10,** 288 (*jyeshṭhaḥ*), 291 (*Kururājaḥ*); **12,** 317, 319 (*Pāṇḍavaḥ*), †322.—§ 550 (Samayapālanap.): IV, **13,** 328 (*sabhāstāro Matsyānām abhavat*), 331. — § 551 (Kīcakavadhap.): IV, **16,** 460, 464 (*Bhīmasena-Y°au*), 468, 469, 490; **18,** 523 (*yasyā bhartā Y°ḥ*, sc. Draupadī), 538 (*mahārājam Indraprasthe*), 543, 547, 548 (*devitā rājñaḥ Kaṅkaḥ*), 551 (*Pāṇḍavaṃ*), 553, 554; **19,** 601; **21,** 648; **22,** 729 (*Kuntīputraḥ*).—§ 552 (Goharaṇap.): IV, [**27,** 903 (*Dharmarājaṃ*), 905 (*Ajātaçatruṃ*)]; **28,** 914, 926, 927, 928, 933, 935, 936, 940, 941; [**31,** 1024 (*rājñe*, when the Trigartas, headed by Suçarman, invaded the country of Virāṭa, *Y.*, etc. took up arms in order to assist Virāṭa)]; **33,** 1077 (*Kuntīputraḥ*), 1083 (*Dharmarājaḥ*), 1099 (*Kuntīputraḥ*), 1101, 1102, 1103, 1122, (1127) (Bhīmasena vanquished Suçarman and made him captive, but *Y.* set him free); **34,** 1136 (*Kauraveyāḥ . . . Y°purogamāḥ*), 1138, 1142 (Virāṭa thanked *Y.*); **40,** 1307, 1311; **43,** 1352; **44,** 1368 (*Kauravyaḥ*), 1371 (*sabhāstāraḥ*); **50,** 1565; **52,** 1611; **65,** †2102 (*°syāsmi nideçakārī*, said Arjuna); **68,** (2180), 2196 (*Pāṇḍaveyaḥ*), 2199, (2203), 2208 (praised Bṛhannalā (i.e. Arjuna) and was therefore struck by Virāṭa with a die); **69,** 2258 (*Pārthe*).—§ 553 (Vaivāhikap.): IV, **70,** 2261, 2275 (Dhr., *b*: Arjuna said: This one deserves to occupy the same seat as *Indra*. None, even amongst D., As., men, Rā., G., Y., Kn., or M.-U. is like to him. 10,000 elephants followed him when he dwelt among the Kurus, and 30,000 chariots, adorned with gold and drawn by the best steeds; 800 bards and minstrels praised him; like R., adoring *Indra*, etc., he made all kings pay tribute to him; 88,000 brahmans (*snātakāḥ*) were supported by him; he protected the aged and helpless, the maimed and blind as his sons, and ruled virtuously; his prosperity and prowess afflict Duryodhana, Karṇa, Çakuni, etc.); **71,** 2289 (*Kauravyaḥ Kuntīputraḥ*), 2310, 2314 (*Kuntīputraṃ*), 2319, 2320; **72,** 2347 (*Kuntīputraḥ*), 2351, 2370 (*Kuntīputraḥ*), 2373 (*Dharmaputraḥ*) (when the Pāṇḍavas had disclosed their identity, Virāṭa made an alliance with *Y.* and married Uttarā to Abhimanyu).—§ 554 (Sainyodyogap.): V, **1***a*, †4, †10 (all. to Dyūtaparvan), †19, †25 (the assembled kings joined the party of *Y.* and held a council); **2,** †30, †34, †36; **3,** 50, 63 (*Pāṇḍusutaḥ*); **5,** 101, 108; **6,** 113 (*Kuntīputraḥ*), 115 (Dhr.); **7,** 171.—§ 555 (do.): V, **8,** 185, 191, 192, 198, 205, 206, (211), 225 (Çalya promised *Y.* to dispirit Karṇa); **9,** 227; (Indravijaya): **9,** 248; **13,** 419 (Çalya told *Y.* the Indravijaya); (Sainyodyogap.): **18,** 560, 561, 566 (*Kuntīputraḥ*) (Çalya repeated his promise); **19**γ, 570, 578 (enumeration of the kings who, with their akshauhiṇīs, joined *Y.*). — § 556 (Sañjayayānap.): V, [**20,** 618 (*Dharmaputrasya*, seven akshauhiṇīs had joined *Y.*)]; **21,** 633 (*Pāṇḍuputraḥ*); **22,** †663; **23,** 686 (*Kuntīputraṃ*), (†690); **25,** (†723); **26,** (†738); **28,** (†794); **29,** (†812), (μ), †861; **30,** (†869), †902; **31,** (916), 926; **32,** †946 (*Pāṇḍuputraḥ*), †953 (Sañjaya's mission to the Pāṇḍavas).—§ 557 (Prajāgarap.): V, **33,** 986; **34,** 1178.—§ 559 (do.): V, **37,** †1376.—§ 561 (Yānasandhip.): V, **48,** †1810, †1815 (*Ājamīḍhasya*), (β), †1817, [†1834 (Dhr.)]; **50,** 1968, 1970, 1971 (*Kuntīputram*), 1973, 2009 (*°samaḥ*, sc. Abhimanyu); **53**θ, 2111, 2120; **55,** 2147, 2152, 2154, 2172 (did only ask for five villages); **56,** 2214 (*Kaunteyaḥ*), 2215, [2227 (*i*: to his chariot are yoked large steeds, white in hue as ivory)]; **57**o, 2261, 2274 (Dhr.), 2282, 2288 (*Kaunteye*), †2292 (Dhr.); **58,** 2306; **64,** 2481; **65**$\gamma\gamma$, 2484 (*Kaunteyaṃ*); **66,** †2511 (Sañjaya finished the report of his mission to the Pāṇḍavas). —§ 562 (Bhagavadyānap.): V, **72,** 2581 (Dhr.), (2586), (2663), (2670) (*Y.* agreed to send Kṛshṇa to Hāstinapura to negotiate about peace); **73,** 2679; **78,** 2802; **79,** 2831 (*°çāsanam*), 2835; **80**ϵ, 2855; [**81,** 2865 (Dhr.)]; **82,** 2876, 2879, 2916 (*°niyogena*); **83**θ, 2949 (*Kuntīputraḥ*), 2952 (Dhr.), (2956), 2968 (Kṛshṇa set out for Hāstinapura); **84,** 3015; **90,** 3149, 3177, 3200, 3202 (Kuntī sent messages to her sons through Kṛshṇa); **95**υ, 3403, 3443.—[§ 564 (Mātalīyop.): V, **97,** 3508 (*Dharmaputreṇa*).] — § 567 (Bhagavadyānap.): V, **125,** 4211; **126,** 4216; [**128,** 4281 (*Kuntīputrāya*)]; **129,** 4362; **130,** 4390; **131**o, 4425, 4455; **132,** 4463 (Kuntī sent a message to *Y.* through Kṛshṇa). —§ 569 (do.): V, **138,** 4681, 4689 (*Kuntīputraḥ*); [**139,** 4717 (Dhr.)]; **140,** 4736 (*Kaunteyaṃ pūrvajātaṃ Y°āt*, i.e. Karṇa), (*a*), 4744 (*Dharmaputraḥ*), 4745 (*Kuntīputraḥ*); **141,** 4777, 4789; **142,** 4820; **143,** 4839, (ι), 4862, 4865, 4866; **144**λ, 4888; **146,** 4949; **147,** (4960), (4962); **148,** †5039 (*Dharmaputraḥ*); **149,** †5072, †5074 (having returned to Upaplavya, Kṛshṇa told what had happened in Hāstinapura, chs. **147-150**).—§ 570 (Sainyaniryāṇap.): V, **151,** 5097 (Dhr., enumeration of the leaders of the seven akshauhiṇīs), (5130), 5155 (*Kuntīputraḥ*), 5162; **152,** 5170, 5172 (*Kuntīputraḥ*), 5183; **153,** 5188; **154,** 5216, 5232; **157,** 5317, 5319, 5326 (installed seven commanders of his divisions, cf. ch. **151**), 5337; **158,** 5368.—§ 571 (Ulūkadūtāgamanap.): V, **160,** 5456, 5477; **161,** 5535, (5537), 5540, 5557 (*Dharmaputram*); **162,** 5584, 5639, 5642; **163,** 5666, 5693 (*Dharmaputram*); **164,** 5702 (*Kuntīputraḥ*).—§ 573 (Ambopākhyānap.): V, **194,** (7582); **196,** 7622 (*Kaunteyo Dharmaputraḥ*), 7627, 7630, (λ), 7642, 7649, 7653 (*Y.* arrayed his troops).—§ 574 (Jambūkh.): VI, **1,** 7 (*Kuntīputraḥ*), 11, 12.—§ 576 (Bhagavadgītāp.): VI, **19,** 695, 719 (*Kuntīputraḥ*), 722; **21,** 760 (*Kuntīputraḥ*), 765 (*Pārtham*); **22,** 777; **25**κ, 845 (*Kuntīputraḥ*, blew his conch shell Anantavijaya).—§ 577 (Bhīshmavadhap.): VI, **43,** 1547, 1552, 1554, 1558, 1561, (1564), (1570), (1572), (1575), 1577, 1582, (1586), (1589), (1591), (1601), (1612), (1614), 1615 (*Kuntīputra*, only C.), 1621, 1623 (*Kuntīputram*), (1625), 1629 (*Y.*, etc. visited Bhīshma, etc., and asked their permission to fight).—§ 578 (do.): VI, **44,** 1666; **45**[7], 1697 (fought with Çalya), 1698 (*Kuntīputraḥ*); **49,** 1991; **50,** [2034 (Dhr.)], (π), 2081; **51***aa*, 2116 (*Kuntīputraḥ*, blew his conch shell Anantavijaya).—[§ 579 (do.): VI, **53,** 2233 (Dhr.); **54,** 2326 (Dhr.).]—§ 580 (do.): VI, [**56,** 2417 (Dhr.); **58,** 2472 (Dhr.), 2473 (*Dharmasutaḥ*), 2481 (*Dharmaputraḥ . . . Pāṇḍavaḥ*)]; **59,** 2557 (°*balam*), †2589 (°*ānīkam*).—§ 581 (do.): VI, **64,** 2880 (°*purogamāḥ*); **67,** 3035.—§ 582 (do.): VI, **69***a*, 3067; [**71,** 3138 (*Ajātaçatruḥ*, fought with Çalya)]; **72**ε, 3167.—§ 583 (do.): VI, **75,** 3280 [(*a*), 3284 (Dhr.)]; **77**[8], 3390; [**78,** 3426 (Dhr.); **79,** 3511 (Dhr.)].—§ 584 (do.): VI, **81,** 3553 (arrayed his troops in a vajra-vyūha), ([1]), 3562 (*Dharmaputraḥ*, attacked Çrutāyus); **84,** 3696, 3703 (*Dharmaputraḥ*), 3714 (do., vanquished Çrutāyus); **85**[7], †3763, †3767; **86,** 3792, 3793, 3794 (*Kauravyaḥ*, fought with Bhīshma), 3799, 3802 (*Dharmaputram*), 3805, ([10]), 3826 (attacked the two Āvantya princes), ([13]), 3835 (*Kauravyaḥ*).—§ 585 (do.): VI, **87,** 3861, (η), 3865; [**89,** 3945 (*Dharmaputrasya*)]; **93,** 4145; **95,** 4320 (attacked by Bhagadatta).—§ 586 (do.): VI, **99**ε, 4508; **102,** 4670 (attacked by Bhīshma); **103**ν, 4695 (°*purogamāḥ*, attacked Bhīshma); **105**π, 4782, 4793, 4798, 4800 (fought with Çalya); **106,** 4804, 4806 (fought with Bhīshma), 4812 (°*balam*); **107,** 4887, 4890, 4897, 4910, (4926), (4959) (asked Bhīshma about the means of slaying him).—§ 587 (do.): VI, **108,** 5000; [**110**ζ, 5099 (Dhr.), 5110 (*Dharmaputram*)]; **111,** 5189 (*Kaunteyam*, checked by Droṇa); **112,** 5218, 5232; **114,** 5328 (°*mukhāḥ Pārthāḥ*), 5347, 5351 (*Paṇḍavaḥ*), 5363 (attacked Çalya); **116,** 5415 (do.); **119,** 5638; **120,** 5755 (*Dharmaputram*).—§ 588 (do.): VI, **121**γ, 5808.—§ 589 (Droṇābhishekap.): VII, **2***a*, †67, [†81 (*Dharmaputraḥ*)], †82; **6,** 165; [**7,** 193 (Dhr.)]; **8,** 225, (η), 227, †247 (°*ānīkam*); [**9,** 284 (Dhr.); **10,** 312 (*Ajātaçatrum*), 317 (*Kaunteyam*)]; **11,** 427, 429.—§ 590 (do.): VII, **12,** 439, 448 (*Kuntīsutasya . . . Pārthe*), 453 461 (Droṇa promised to seize *Y.*); **13,** 465; **14,** 514 (°*purogamāḥ*, attacked Droṇa), (*a*), 577; **16,** 635 (°*ānīkam*), 637, 638 (fought with Droṇa), (γ), 646, 647 (*Kuntīputram*), 649, 651, 656.—§ 591 (Saṃçaptakavadhap.): VII, **17,** 675, 677, 681 (*Dharmaputram*), (714).—§ 592 (do.): VII, **19,** 790, 791; **20,** 795 (arrayed his troops), 812, 855 (Droṇa sought to seize *Y.*); **21,** 856, 858 (protected by Satyajit), 876, 877, 878, (κ), 905, 911, 912; **23**ο, 959 (description of his horses), 960, 1023, 1025 (description of his horses), (π), 1038 (Dhr., held the bow Māhendra); **24**σ, 1048, 1051; **25,** 1078 (*Pāṇḍavaçreshṭham*, fought with Çalya); **26,** 1158, 1166 (fought with Bhagadatta); **27,** 1207; **31,** 1347; [**32,** 1379 (*Ajātaçatruḥ*)].—§ 593 (Abhimanyuvadhap.): VII, **33,** 1453, 1459; **34***a*, 1484, 1490 (°*sya dhairyena . . . sadṛçaḥ*, sc. Abhimanyu); **35,** 1517, 1518, (1526), (1535); **39**ν, 1656; **40,** 1679 (Dhr., all. to Dyūtap.), (ο), 1696; **42**π, 1743; **43**ρ, 1771; **47,** 1865; [**49,** 1959 (Dhr.), 1960 (*Ajātaçatruḥ*), 1962 (Dhr.)] (Abhimanyu was slain); **51,** 1983, 1984.—§ 594 (do.): VII, **52,** 2003 (*Kuntīputram*), 2004, 2010, 2011, 2013, (2014), 2022 (*Kuntīputram*), 2032 (in order to comfort *Y.*, Vyāsa told him what Nārada had said to Akampana (q.v.), including the story of the origin of Mṛtyu); **54,** 2129.—§ 595 (do.): VII, **55,** (2135), 2169 (Vyāsa told *Y.* what Nārada had said to Sṛñjaya (q.v.), including Shoḍaçarājika); **71,** 2474, 2476.—§ 596 (Pratijñāp.): VII, **72,** 2523; **73,** (2566); [**79,** 2791 (*Dharmaputraḥ*)].—§ 597 (do.): VII, **82,** 2916, 2945 (Dhr.); **83,** 2946, 2948, 2954, 2965 (Dhr.), 2972 (only C.); **84,** 2982 (°*niveçanāt*), 3009.—§ 598 (Jayadrathavadhap.): VII, **86,** 3067 (*Kuntīputram*, all. to Dyūtaparvan).—§ 599 (do.): VII, **94,** 3431; [**95**ζ, 3529 (*Ajātaçatrum Kaunteyam*, attacked by Çalya)]; **96,** 3570 (fought with Çalya); **97,** 3574 (fought with Kṛtavarman); **98**κ, 3660; [**102,** 3815 (Dhr., all. to Dyūtaparvan)]; **106,** 3975, 3982 (*Bharataçreshṭhaḥ*), 3988, 3990 (Dhr.), 3999, 4002 (*Dharmaputrāya*), 4006, 4012 (*Kuntīputraḥ*, fled before Droṇa); **109**π, 4110, 4112 (pierced Alambusha); **110,** 4146, (4176); **111,** 4240 (Dhr.), 4252, 4257, (4278); **112,** 4356, 4359, 4368 (sent Sātyaki to assist Arjuna); [**113,** 4372 (Dhr.), 4404 (Dhr.); **115**ψ, 4501 (Dhr.), 4508 (Dhr.)]; **122,** [4880 (Dhr.)], (θθ), 4882 (*Dharmaputraḥ*); **124,** [(κκ), 4983 (Dhr.)], 5006, 5008 (fought with Duryodhana); **126,** 5099 (Dhr.), 5102 (Dhr.), 5108 (*Dharmaputraḥ*), 5121 (do.), 5125 (*Kuntīputraḥ*); **127,** 5146, 5151, [5164 (*Dharmaputraḥ*)] (sent Bhīma to assist Sātyaki); **128,** 5251 (*Dharmaputraḥ*), 5253 (do.); **129,** 5306, 5307/8 (only B.); **131**ρρ, 5360 (*Dharmaputraḥ*); **133**ττ, 5467 (*Pārthaḥ*); [**137,** 5649 (Dhr.), 5651 (Dhr.); **141,** 5858 (Dhr.), 5861 (*Dharmaputreṇa*), 5868 (Dhr.), 5876 (Dhr.), 5877 (Dhr.); **142**ζζζ, 5884 (*Dharmasutaḥ*), 5889 (Dhr.)]; **143**ηηη, 5955 (*Dharmaputram*); **144,** [(ιι), 5997 (Dhr.)], 6025; **146,** 6289 (*Dharmaputraḥ*); [**147,** 6372 (Dhr.)]; **148,** 6420, [†6445 (*Ajātaçatrum . . . Pāṇḍavam*)]; **149,** 6451 (*Dharmaputram*), 6453.—§ 600 (Ghaṭotkacavadhap.): VII, **153,** [(*a*), 6627 (*Dharmaputram*)], 6630 (only B.), 6632, 6633 (fought with Duryodhana), 6634 (only B.); **154**β, 6649; **155,** †6725, (ε), †6726; **156**η, 6745, [6746 (*Mṛdaṅgaketoḥ*)], 6759 (°*purogamāḥ*), 6762, 6765 (encounter with Droṇa), [(λ), 6853 (Dhr.), (μ), 6899 (*Dharmaputrasya*)]; **157**ξ, 6923, 6947, 6948, 6951 (°*ratham*), 6952, 6954, 6959, 6961 (*Kuntīputraḥ*) (encounter with Droṇa); **158,** 7006 (*Dharmaputraḥ*); [**159,** 7129 (Dhr.)]; **160,** 7158 (*Dharmaputraḥ*); **161,** 7204, 7207 (only C.); **162,** 7257/8 (only B.), 7259, 7260, 7261, 7262 (fought with Droṇa), 7269 (*Kuntīputram*), 7270, 7275 (Dhr.), 7277 (only C.); **165,** 7355 (*Dharmaputraḥ*), 7357 (only C.), 7360, 7378 (*Dharmaputram*), 7379, 7389, 7391 (only B.), 7392 (only C.), 7395 (*Dharmaputraḥ*), 7396 (*Dharmaputram*, vanquished by Kṛtavarman); **168,** 7544; [**170**νν, 7672 (Dhr.)]; **172,** [(ρρ), 7754 (*Dharmaputrasya*)], 7766 (°*balam*); **173,** 7779 (only B.), [7782 (*Dharmasūnunā*)], 7797, [7803

(*Dharmasutaḥ*)]; **183,** 8319 (*Dharmaputraḥ*), 8344, 8347 (°*purogamāḥ*), 8348, 8351 (*Dharmaputram*), 8354, 8357 (Vyāsa came to *Y.* and explained why Ghaṭotkaca had been slain).—§ 601 (Droṇavadhap.): VII, **184,** 8362 (Dhr.), 8363 (Dhr.).—§ 602 (do.): VII, **187** ι, 8543; [**189,** 8683 (*Dharmasutaḥ*)]; **190,** 8707, 8736 (*Kuntīputram*), 8749, 8751 (*Y.* falsely told Droṇa that Açvatthāman had been slain); **191,** 8805; **192** o, 8811, 8820 (Dhr.), 8823, [8850 (Dhr.), 8866 (Dhr.)].—§ 603 (Nārāyaṇāstramokshap.): VII, **193,** 8945 (all. to § 602), 8948 (do.); **195,** [8983 (*Dharmaputrasya*, do.), 8992 (Dhr.)], (θ), 9007; **196,** 9037, (9038); **198** o, 9133, 9165 (*Pāṇḍavaḥ*, all. to Dyūtaparvan), [9192 (Dhr.)]; **199** υ, 9199 (*Kuntīputraḥ*, all. to § 602), 9218 (Dhr.); **200,** 9266 (°*purogān*); **201** εε, 9401.—§ 604 (Karṇap.): VIII, [**7,** †199 (*Ajātaçatroḥ*, all. to § 555)]; **9** θ, 253 (°*ānīkam*), 272, 305 (Dhr.).—§ 605 (do.): VIII, **11,** [421 (Dhr.), (*aa*), 427 (Dhr.)], 432; **13,** 494 (*Dharmaputram*, attacked by Duryodhana); **24,** 965 (°*ratham*); **28,** 1119 1122 (fought with Duryodhana), 1127; **29,** 1174 (Dhr.), 1177, 1181, 1183, 1188, 1194 (fought with Duryodhana); [**30** ξξ, 1232 (Dhr.)]. — § 607 (do.): VIII, **36,** [1689 (Dhr.)], (β), 1694, [1701 (*Dharmaputram*)].—§ 608 (do.): VIII, **46,** 2125, (*a*), 2129, 2130, 2151, (2156), (η), 2204 (Dhr.); **47,** 2231 (attacked by Karṇa); **48,** 2235 (do.), [2281 (Dhr.), 2287 (Dhr.)], 2296, 2300 (°*mukhāḥ Pārthāḥ*); **49,** 2301, 2308 (attacked by Karṇa), 2310, 2329, 2332, 2346, 2350 (*Pāṇḍuputram*, encounter with Karṇa), 2360 (°*ānīkam*), 2362 2363 (Dhr.), 2398; [**51,** 2498 (*Dharmaputram*, fled before Karṇa)]; **54,** 2623 (checked by Açvatthāman); **55,** 2652, 2654, 2664, 2682 (*Droṇaçishyaḥ*), 2689 (*Dharmaputre*), 2690 (encounter with Açvatthāman); **56** ππ, 2754 (Dhr.), 2838 (retreated from the battle); **58,** 2860 (Dhr.), 2862 (*Dharmaputram*), 2864, 2898; **59,** 2909 (°*mukhāḥ Pārthāḥ*); **60,** 2976 (*Kaunteyam Dharmarājam*), 2978, 2982, 2986 (*Kuntīputram*), 2994 (*Pāṇḍavaḥ*), 2995, 2997 (*Pāṇḍaveyam*), 3026, 3033 (*Dharmaputraḥ*); **61** δδδ, 3067 (*Pāṇḍave*), 3078 (proceeded against Citrasena); **62,** 3145, 3146 (*Kuntīputraḥ*), 3147, 3148 (*Kuntīputram*), 3149, 3163 (Dhr., *Dharmaputraḥ*), 3168 (Dhr.), 3169, 3170, 3171 (Dhr.) (encounter with Karṇa); **63,** 3179, 3186, 3194, 3196, 3197, 3204, 3207 (*Kaunteyaḥ Pāṇḍuputraḥ*, retreated to the camp); **64,** 3280; **65,** †3287 (*Ājamīḍham*), †3288 (*Dharmaputraḥ*), 3300, 3305 (Dhr.), †3306; **66,** (3309); **67,** †3357; **68,** †3380 (*Y.* censured Arjuna for not having slain Karṇa); **69,** 3403, 3406, 3410, 3415, 3432 (*Pāṇḍavaḥ*), 3469, 3473 (*Pāṇḍavam*, Dhr.), 3486, 3487 (Dhr.) (Arjuna was enraged and would slay *Y.*, but was pacified by Kṛshṇa, who told him to address *Y.* as "thou"); **70,** [†3492 (Dhr.)], †3521, †3527, †3529, †3530, 3547 (Dhr.); **71,** 3553, 3559, 3564 (Dhr.), 3578 (*Dharmanandanam*), (3582), †3591 (*Y.* and Arjuna were reconciled); **72,** 3601 (Dhr.), [†3628 (Dhr.)]; **74** φφφ, [3764 (*Kuntīsutaḥ*), 3765 (do.)], 3785, 3787 (Dhr.); [**76,** 3833 (Dhr.); **79** η, 4028 (Dhr.)]; **80,** 4114; [**87** *aa'*, 4489 (Dhr.)]; **88** *a*γ', †4512; **89,** †4595 (Dhr.); **94,** †4957; **96,** 4993, 5020 (came to see the corpse of Karṇa), 5027 (Dhr.), 5029 (*Kuntīputram*), 5032.—[§ 609 (Çalyap.): IX, **1,** 10 (Dhr.)].—§ 610 (do.): IX, **3,** 186 (°*purogāṃç ca . . . Pāṇḍavān*); **4** μ, 233; **5** ν, 262; **7,** 344, 363 (Dhr.).—§ 611 (do.): IX, **8,** 377 (rushed against Çalya), [381 (Dhr.)]; [**9** ι, 451 (Dhr.)]; **10,** 461 (*Pāṇḍuputraḥ*), 463 (Dhr.), (κ), 516; **11,** 549 (*Kuntīputram*), 557 (*Ajātaçatrum Kaunteyam*), 558 (pierced by Çalya), 576 (do.); **12,** 639 (Dhr.), 642, 648 (*Kuntīputraḥ*), 652, 655 (encounter with Çalya); **13,** 673 (*Dharmaputre*, pierced by Çalya), 692 (Dhr.); [**14,** 702 (Dhr.), 703 (Dhr.)]; **15,** [764 (Dhr.)], (ρ), 768, 770 (pierced by Çalya), 774, 779; **16,** 802 (*Kuntīputraḥ*), 805, 808, 809 (Dhr.), 842, 843 (*Kuntīputre*), 852, 856 (Dhr.), 862 (encounter with Çalya); **17,** 864, 866 (χ), †875, †876, †880, †881, †886, †888 (*Dharmasutasya*), †893 (*Kuntīsutam*), †898, †912 (slew Çalya), 921, [926 (Dhr., slew the younger brother of Çalya)], 948, 950 (vanquished Kṛtavarman), 951, †954; **18,** 958 (attacked by the Madrakas), 963, 966; **19,** [999 (*Ajātaçatruṇā*)], (δδ), 1010, 1021, 1024 (*Pārthāt*), 1049 (°*purogāḥ*); **22** λλ, 1138 (pierced by Duryodhana), 1152 (attacked by Çakuni), 1155 (*Dharmaputraḥ*); **23,** 1184 (pierced Kṛpa), 1186 (pierced by Kṛpa), 1187 (*Dharmaputraḥ*), 1189, 1191 (*Kuntīputram*), 1212, 1243; **24** μμ, 1281, [(νν), 1321 (Dhr.)]; **25** oo, 1373; [**27,** 1443 (*Kuntīsutaḥ*)].—§ 612 (Hradapraveçap.): IX, **29** γ, 1651, 1667; **30** δ, 1677, 1683, 1705, 1724, 1732; **31** ζ, 1748, 1756, (1784), (θ), 1788, 1796, (1797) (*Y.* challenged Duryodhana to fight).—§ 613 (Gadāyuddhap.): IX, **32** *a*, 1823 (β), 1828, (1840), 1849, (1850), (γ), 1868, (δ), (1871) (*Y.* promised to cede the kingdom to Duryodhana, if he vanquished one of the Pāṇḍavas); **33,** 1889, (ε), 1890, (η), 1911 (Dhr.), 1918.—§ 614 (do.): IX, **34** *a*, 1954, [1964 (*Dharmasutaḥ*)].—§ 615 (do.): IX, **55,** 3081, 3087 (*Kuntīputraḥ*), 3120; **56** ρ, 3143 (Dhr.) (the encounter between Duryodhana and Bhīma began); **58,** 3254 (Duryodhana was vanquished by Bhīma); **59,** 3318, (σ), 3330, 3341 (*Dharmaputraḥ*); **60,** 3371, (3374), 3381 (Dhr.), (3386); **61,** 3400; **62** ω, 3479, 3486 (Dhr.), (3488), 3499 (only B.); **63** *aa*, 3503 (Dhr.), 3511, [3516 (Dhr.), 3532 (Dhr.)] (sent Kṛshṇa to Hāstinapura), [3556 (Dhr.)].—§ 616 (Sauptikap.): X, **9** ι, 503.—§ 617 (Aishīkap.): X, **10,** 549 (was informed about the nightly extermination of his warriors), †572; **11,** 589 (*Pāṇḍavam*, Dhr.); **12,** 606 (*Kuntīputram*); **13,** 652 (*Kururājaḥ*); **17,** 760; **18,** 799.—§ 618 (Jalapradānikap.): XI, [**1,** 2 (*Kauravaḥ . . . Dharmaputraḥ*)]; **8** ζ, 229 (all. to Rājasūyikaparvan (?)), 237; [**9,** 247 (*Kauravaḥ . . . Dharmaputraḥ*)]; **12,** 313 (Dhr.), 322 (Dhr.); **14,** 361 (Dhr.), (ξ), 376; **15** o, 385, 391, 405, 406, 407, 410 (Gāndhārī's glance blasted a nail of *Y.*'s toe) —§ 619 (Strīvilāpap.): XI, **16,** 435 (*Pāṇḍuputrāḥ . . . Y°purogamāḥ*); [**18** γ, 530 (Dhr.)]; **21** ζ, 609 (Dhr.); **23** θ, [635 (Dhr., had slain Çalya)], 640; **24** ι, 701 (all. to Dyūtaparvan).—§ 620 (Çrāddhap.): XI, **26,** 762 (Dhr.), (764), 766, (767), (774), 778, 779 (*Kuntīputraḥ*) 799 (*Kururājaḥ*) (*Y.* caused the corpses to be cremated); **27,** 813 (*Kuntīputraḥ*), 824 (Dhr.), 827 (*Kurupatiḥ*) (Kuntī disclosed to *Y.* that Karṇa was her son).—§ 621 (Rājadh.): XII, **1,** 3 (Dhr.), 7, 9 (*Dharmaputram*), 10 (13), (γ), 29 (Nārada told *Y.* the history of Karṇa, chs. **2-5**); **6,** 144, 147; **7,** 157, 200 (Dhr.) (*Y.* wished to renounce the sovereignty); [**8,** (Arjuna's speech to *Y.*)]; **9,** (243); **10,** 284 (Bhīma's speech to *Y.*).—§§ 623–629 (do.): XII, **14,** 384 (*Kaunteye*, Dhr.), 387 (*a*), 413; **17,** (511); **19,** (575); **20,** 601; **23,** 652, (667); **24,** 699, 707, 714, 718, 721; **25,** 732 (*Kaunteyaḥ*), (733), 735, 744, 760 (different speeches addressed to *Y.* in order to comfort him).—§ 630 (do.): XII, **26,** 768; **27,** (799).—§ 631 (do.): XII, **28,** 834 (Vyāsa told *Y.* the story of Açman's discourse).—§ 632 (do.): XII, **29,** 893 (*Dharmaputre*) (Kṛshṇa told *Y.* the story of Sṛñjaya, including Shoḍaçarājopākhyāna).—§ 633 (do.): XII, **30,** (1043) (Kṛshṇa told *Y.* the Nārada-Parvatopākhyāna).—[§ 634 (do.): XII, **31,**

1089 (Dhr.) (Nārada told *Y.* the Suvarṇashṭhīvisambhavopākhyāna).]—§ 635 (do.): XII, **32**, 1135, (1144); **33**, (1160), 1172; **34**, (1208); **35**, 1291 (Dhr.); **36**, (1292), 1342; **37**, (1344), (1361), 1371, 1374 (*Kuntīputraḥ*) (Vyāsa told *Y.* to apply to Bhīshma for learning the *rājadharma*; the Pāṇḍavas went to Hāstinapura); **38**ε, 1396, 1400, 1421, (1422).—§ 637 (do.): XII, **40**a, 1457 (*Kuntīputram*), 1462, 1463 (*Pāṇḍava*), 1466 (Dhr.) (*Y.* was anointed king); **41**, 1467, 1479; **42**γ, 1486, 1488, 1498 (performed the çrāddhas of his kinsmen); **43**, 1499 (praised Kṛshṇa); **44**, 1517, 1526 (*Dharmaputraḥ*), 1531; **45**, 1532, (*Dharmaputraḥ*), 1535 (*Kuntīputraḥ*), 1542; **46**, (1553), (ζ), 1573; **47**, 1694 (°-*Dhanañjayau*, the Pāṇḍavas, etc., and Kṛshṇa set out to see Bhīshma).—§ 638 (do.): XII, **48**a, 1698, 1704, (1707), 1714; **49**, 1805 (Kṛshṇa told *Y.* the history of Rāma Jāmadagnya).—§ 639 (do.): XII, **50**, 1806, 1810 (*Acyuta-Y°au*); **51**, †1861; **52**, [1873 (Dhr.) (Kṛshṇa prevailed upon Bhīshma to instruct *Y.*)], (ε), 1888; **53**, 1901, 1905, 1906, 1909 (*Dharmaputraḥ*), (1910), (ζ), 1914 (θ), 1921.—§ 640 (do.): XII, **54**a, 1929 (°*purogamāḥ*), 1936 (*Pāṇḍuputraḥ*); **55**, 1965, 1975 (Dhr.), 1984 (*Dharmaputraḥ*); **56**, 1987, (1988) (*Y.* questioned Bhīshma about the *rājadharma* and was instructed, chs. **56-58**), 1997, 2000, 2046; **57**, 2047; **58**, 2092, 2096, 2113, †2120 (°*ādayaḥ*).—§ 641 (do.): XII, **59**, 2125 (Dhr.), (2126), 2140, 2185, 2239, 2261; **60**, 2268; **61**, 2324, 2341; **62**, (†2345); **64**, 2391; **66**, (2452), 2453, 2454, 2456, 2459, 2471 (*Kaunteya*), 2476 (*Bhārata*), 2478 (*Kaunteya*), 2479, 2485; **67**, (2495); **68**, (2535); **69**, (2596), 2650, 2662, (2669), 2681; **70**, (2701), 2714; **71**, (2715), 2732, 2739; **73**, 2780; **75**, (2831), (2846), (2864); **76**, (2869); **77**, (2883); **78**, (2917), (2919), 2920, 2925, (2928), 2934, (2935), 2940, (2952); **79**, (2962), (2968); **80**, (2983); **81**, (3024); **82**, 3056; **83**, (3125); **84**, 3183; **85**, (3194), (3196); **86**, (3228); **87**, (3261), 3275, 3281, 3301; **88**, (3302); **89**, 3345, 3353, (3355), 3357; **90**, 3363; **92**, (3463); **95**, (3535), (3540); **96**, 3579; **97**, (3581); **98**, (3613), 3614; **99**, 3665, 3673; **100**, (3682), 3701; **102**, (3753), 3768, 3785; **103**, (3794), 3795; **104**. (3847), 3848; **107**, (3957); **108**, (3989), 3992, 4004; **109**, (4023); **110**, (4053); **111**, (4083), 4084; **112**, (4173), 4175, 4193; **113**, (4196); **114**, (4210); **115**, (4231); **120**, (4351); **121**, (4408), 4430, 4442, 4451, 4463; **123**, (4525); **124**, (4549), 4559 (°*niveçane*), 4562, 4613, 4620; **125**, (4622), 4629; **129**, (4710); **130**, (4727), 4732 (questioned by *Y.*, Bhīshma instructed him about the *rājadharma*).—§§ 642–655 (Āpaddh.): XII, **131**, (4779), (4787); **132**, (4793), 4799, 4814; [**133**, 4815 (*Kaunteya*); **137**, 4891 (do.)]; **138**, (4913), 4924, 5124; **139**, (5133); **140**, (5247); **141**, (5319), 5342; **142**, (5421), (5455); **143**, (5459), (5463); **149**, 5591; **150**, (5594); **153**, (5675); **154**, (5801), **158**, (5877), 5906; **159**, (5912), (5915); **160**, (5926), 5962; **162**, (5977); **163**, (6003); **164**, (6026) (questioned by *Y.*, Bhīshma instructed him).—§ 657 (do.): XII, **167**, 6210, (†6254).—§ 658 (do.): XII, **168**, (6264), 6268, (6292); [**169**, 6332 (*Kaunteya*)]; **170**, 6362; **173**, 6456 (Bhīshma told *Y.* the Kṛtaghnopākhyāna).—§§ 659–711 (Mokshadh.): XII, **174**, (6457), 6461, (6462); **175**, (6522), 6523; **176**, (6562); **177**, (6586), 6589; **178**, 6642; **179**, (6653); **180**, (6690), 6693; **181**, 6745; **182**, 6765; **193**, (7032); **194**, (7066); **196**, (7151); **197**, (7174), (7185); **198**, (7187); **199**, (7198); **200**, (7330); **201**, (7365); **207**, (7518), 7523, 7548; **208**, (7567); **209**, (7604); **210**, (7641); **212**, (7732); **218**, (7881); **220**, (7984); **221**, (8004), 8005, (8006), (8012), 8016; **222**, (8021), 8023; **223**, (8058); **226**, (8187); **227**, (8212), 8218; **229**, (8333), 8335; **230**, (8429); **231**, (8454); **232**, (8478); **245**, 8884; **256**, (9141); **257**, (9144); **260**, (9229), 9254; **261**, 9257; **262**, (9289); [**265**, 9465 (*Kaunteya*)]; **266**, (9479); **267**, (9481); **268**, (9559); **269**, (9596), 9600; **272**, (9755), 9769, 9777, 9784; **273**, (9811); **274**, (9831), 9848, 9854 (*Kaunteya*); **275**, (9855); **277**, (9914); **278**, (9928), 9929; **279**, (9967); **280**, (9990); **281**, (10086), (10092); **282**, (10098); **283**, 10198; **284**, (10208); **285**, (10346); **286**, (10485); **287**, (10532); **288**, (10553); **289**, (10612); **290**, (10659), (10679); **291**, (10697); **300**, (10992), 10993; **301**, (11037), 11043, (11046), (11078); **302**, (11098), 11141, (11150), (11177), 11191; **303**, (11214); **311**, (11543); **320**, (11837); **321**, (11852); **322**, (12044); **323**, (12138) (questioned by *Y.*, Bhīshma instructed him about the *mokshadharma*).—§ 712 (Çukotpatti): XII, **324**, (12158); **325**, 12189 (Bhīshma told *Y.* the history of Çuka (§§ 712–716, chs. **324-334**)).—§ 717 (Mokshadh.): XII, **335**, (12650); **336**, (12708); **337**, (12767); **338**, (12818), [12856 (*Kaunteya*)]; **340**, [12962 (*yajñe Dharmasutasya vai*, cf. Çiçupālavadhaparvan)], 12963, (12978), 12997 (questioned by *Y.*, Bhīshma told the Nārāyaṇīya (including the story of Uparicara)).—[§ 717*b* (Nārāyaṇīya): **349**, 13611 (Dhr., Vyāsa discoursed to *Y.* on Nārāyaṇa), 13634 (*Dharmaputrāya*, do.)]. — § 718 (Mokshadh.): XII, **353**, (13764) (questioned by *Y.*, Bhīshma told the Uñchavṛttyupākhyāna). — §§ 719–729 (Ānuçāsanik.): XIII, **1**, (1), 83; **2**, (84), 103; **3**, (181), 234, 260; **5**, (263); **6**, (295), 296; **7**, (344), 345; **8**, (374), 380, 382, 384, 393, 398; **8**, (403), 429; **10**, (433), 437, 480; **11**, (507); **12**, (528); **13**, (582) (questioned by *Y.*, Bhīshma instructed him).—§ 730 (do.): XIII, **14**, (588), 606, 614, 617, 992; [**15**, 1033 (*Bhīmapūrvaja*)]; **17**, 1114; **18**, 1303, 1326, 1333, 1342, 1353, 1357, 1367 (*Dharmaputram*) (Kṛshṇa's discourse to *Y.* on Çiva).—§§ 731–33 (do.): XIII, **19**, (1381), 1478; **21**, (1512); **22**, (1531), (1533), (1535), (1538), (1546), (1548), (1554), (1556), (1562); **23**, (1572), 1605, 1610, 1611, 1618, (1620), 1621, 1624, 1632, 1647, 1648, 1657, 1670, 1673; **24**, (1676); **25**, (1688) (questioned by *Y.*, Bhīshma instructed him).—§§ 734–744 (do.): XIII, **26**, 1759, 1766, 1775 (*Dharmasutaḥ*), (1776), 1777, 1863; **27**, (1865), 1870, 1872; **30**, (1940), 1980; **31**, (2008); **32**, (2014), 2077; **33**, (2083); **35**, 2157; **36**, 2165; **37**, (2184), (2188); **38**, (2202); **39**, (2232); [**40**, 2254 (*Kaunteya*)]; **44**, (2404), 2407, 2409, 2412, (2422), 2431; **45**, (2461), (2470); **47**, (2499), 2505, 2508, 2510, 2512, 2523, (2526), 2532, 2535, 2538, 2539, 2545, (2546), 2548; **48**, (2562), 2601; **49**, (2613), (2618), 2619, (2624), (2626), (2631), (2634), 2636 (*Y.* continued his questions to Bhīshma, who instructed him).—§ 745 (do.): XIII, **50**, (2641); **51**, 2714; **52**, (2716), **53**, (2755) (instructing *Y.*, Bhīshma told him the Cyavanopākhyāna and the Cyavana-Kuçikasaṃvāda (chs. **50-56**)).—§ 746 (do.): XIII, **57**, (2926), 2931, 2968, 2969; **58**, (2970); **59**, (3003), 3011, 3018, 3023, 3027; **60**, (†3044), 3048, 3056 (*Kaunteya*), 3060; **61**, (3064), 3075, 3100; **62**, (3103), 3106, 3153; **63**, (3200), 3227; **64-65**, (3252); **66**, (3309), 3311, (3313); **67**, (3375); **68**, (3395), 3396; **69**, (3430), 3435, (3443); **70**, 3484; **71**, (3485); **72-74**, (3542), 3619; **75**, (3622); **76**, (3665), [†3693 (Dhr.)]; **77**, 3696, (3697), [3698 (Dhr.)], (†3704), [3730 (*Ājamīḍhaḥ*

. . . *Pārthaḥ*)]; **81,** (3802), 3830, 3832; **82,** (3851); **83,** 3879, 3884, 3924 (continuation of Bhīshma's instructions to *Y.*).—§ 747 (do.): XIII, **84,** (3931); **85,** 4184 (questioned by *Y.*, Bhīshma told him the Suvarṇotpatti).—§ 748 (do.): XIII, **86,** 4186 (Bhīshma told *Y.* the Tārakavadhopākhyāna). —§ 749 (do.): XIII, **87,** (4221), 4222; **88,** (4240), 4241, 4250; **90,** (4270), 4280, 4319; **91,** 4326 (continuation of Bhīshma's instructions). —§§ 750–751 (do.): XIII, **93,** (4396), 4397, (4398), (4404), 4408, (4413) (Bhīshma told *Y.* the Bisastainyopākhyāna and the Çapathavidhi).—§ 752 (do.): XIII, **95,** (4601); **96,** (4629) (Bhīshma told (*Y.* the Chattropānahotpatti).—§§ 753–754 (do.): XIII, **97,** (4651); **98,** (4677) (continuation of Bhīshma's instructions). —§ 755 (do.): XIII, **99,** (4743); **100,** (4772) (Bhīshma told *Y.* the Nahushopākhyāna).—§ 755*b* (Nahushop.): XIII, **100,** 4801 (it is prophesied that *Y.* will rescue Nahusha from his curse, cf. § 448).—§ 756 (Ānuçāsanik.): XIII, **101,** (4813) (continuation of Bhīshma's instructions). —§ 757 (do.): XIII, **102,** (4843) (Bhīshma told *Y.* the Hastikūṭa).—§§ 758–759 (do.): XIII, **103,** (4906), 4908 (*Kaunteya*); **104,** (4954), 5035, 5072, 5090, 5109; **105,** (5113); **106,** (5133), [**106,** 5139 (*Kaunteyaṃ . . . Dharmaputraṃ*)]; **107,** (5205), 5209; **108,** (5349); **109,** (5370); **110,** 5387, (5388) (continuation of Bhīshma's instructions).— § 760 (do.): XIII, **111,** (5397), [5404 (*Dharmasutaḥ*)], (5405), (5416), (5424), (5428), (5432), 5481; **112,** (5532), 5540; **113,** (5564), 5574 (Dhr.) (Bṛhaspati instructed *Y.*).— § 761 (do.): XIII, **114,** 5575, (5576); **115,** (5594), 5602, 5603; **116,** (5680) (continuation of Bhīshma's instructions).— § 762 (do.): XIII, **117,** (5723), 5727, 5728; **119,** 5782 (Bhīshma told *Y.* the Kīṭopākhyāna).—§ 763 (do.): XIII, **120,** (5793) (Bhīshma told *Y.* the Maitreyabhikshā).— §§ 764–767 (do.): XIII, **123,** (5858); **124,** (5880); **125,** (5919); **135,** (6199); **136,** (6220), 6223; **137,** (6244), 6272, 6274; **138,** (6277) (continuation of Bhīshma's instructions).—§ 768 (do.): XIII, **139,** (6288); **148,** 6927, 6935 (Bhīshma told *Y.* the Umā-Maheçvarasaṃvāda).— §§ 769–771 (do.): XIII, **149,** 6936, 6937; **151,** (7079); **152,** (7162), 7163 (continuation of Bhīshma's instructions, including the recital of Vishṇu's 1000 names).—§ 772 (do.): XIII, **153,** (7185) (Bhīshma told *Y.* the Pavanārjunasaṃvāda).—§ 773 (do.): XIII, **159,** (7354); **160,** (7401) (Bhīshma described the glory of Kṛshṇa to *Y.*); **161,** (7458); **162,** 7502 (Kṛshṇa described the glory of Çiva to *Y.*).— §§ 774–776 (do.): XIII, **163,** 7532, (7542), 7544, (7549), (7559), (7565); **164,** (7597), 7611; **166,** 7627, (7628); **167,** 7690 (*mama pūrvapitāmahaḥ*, sc. Janamejaya's), 7694 (*Kururājaḥ*), 7696, [7703 (*Kaunteyaḥ*)] (Bhīshma concluded his instructions; *Y.*, etc., returned to Hāstinapura).—§ 777 (Svargārohaṇik. p.): XIII, **168,** [7706 (*Kuntīsutaḥ*)], 7708, 7712, 7723 (Dhr.), 7724, 7731 (*Kaunteya*), 7733, 7734 (*Dharmaputraṃ*), 7757; **169,** 7770, 7772 (present when Bhīshma ascended to heaven).—§ 778 (Açvamedhikap.): XIV, **1,** 1, 4 (*Dharmaputraṃ*), 6, 14 (*Dharmaputraṃ*), 15; **2,** 28 (Dhr.), (29); **3,** 41, 44, 45, 48, (51), (62); **4,** (64), 77; **5,** (92); [**10,** 292 (*Pāṇḍavaḥ*)] (Vyāsa narrated the Saṃvartta-Maruttīya and told *Y.* to perform a horse-sacrifice with the gold left by Marutta).—§ 779 (do.): XIV, [**11,** 295 (*Pārthaṃ . . . Dharmasutaṃ*)]; **13,** 342 (Kṛshṇa comforted *Y.*).—§ 780 (do.): XIV, **14,** 354, 358, [367 (*Dharmasutaḥ*)] (*Y.* resolved to set out for Himavat to fetch the gold).— § 781 (do.): XIV, **15,** [383 (*Dharmasutena*)], 384 (Dhr.), 393, 394, †404, †405.—§§ 782–3 (Anugītāp.): XIV, **51,** 1477; **52,** 1499, 1503, (1517), (1521), 1528 (*Kauravye Dharmarāje*), †1532 (Kṛshṇa took leave of *Y.*).—§ 785 (do.): XIV, **60,** 1795, 1796 (*Kururājaḥ*) (the events of the battle shortly related); [**62,** 1862 (Dhr.), 1869 (*Dharmātmajaṃ*), 1870 (Dhr.)]; **63,** 1873 (Dhr.), [1877 (*Dharmātmajaḥ*, set out to fetch the gold)]; **64,** 1897, [1909 (Dhr.), †1912 (*Dharmasutaṃ*)]; **65,** 1914, 1928 (Dhr.), 1932 (returned with the gold); [**66,** 1937 (*Dharmaputreṇa*), (μ), 1954 (*Dharmaputraṃ*)]; **67,** 1969 (Dhr.); **71,** 2067 (*Dharmasutaḥ*), 2072 (*Kururājaḥ*); **72,** 2083 (*Dharmaputraḥ*), (2095), (2105), 2109 (ordered Arjuna to follow the sacrificial horse); [**73,** 2111 (Dhr., was initiated for the horse-sacrifice), 2113 (*Dharmarāṭ*), 2114 (*Dharmajaḥ*), 2119 (Dhr.), 2131 (Dhr.)]; [**74,** 2147 (Dhr.), 2148 (Dhr.)]; **76,** 2215, 2217 (°*syāçvamedhaḥ*), [2219 (Dhr.)]; [**78,** 2259 (Dhr.), 2261 (Dhr.); **80,** 2349 (*Kurumukhyasya*), 2350 (Dhr.)]; **81,** 2425 (°*syāçvamedhaḥ*); **82,** 2459; **84,** 2489; **85,** 2511, 2513 (Dhr.), 2533; **86,** 2553, 2559, 2563 (Dhr.), 2565, 2566, 2578 (Dhr.); **87,** (2574), 2592; **88**χ, 2608, 2614 (the sacrifice commenced); **89,** 2650, 2652 (*Bharataçreshṭhaṃ*, Dhr.), 2653, 2659, 2661 (Dhr.), 2665, 2668, 2679 (*Kururājaḥ*).—§ 786 (do.): XIV, **90,** [2689 (Dhr.), (*b*: Nakulākhyāna): 2692 (Dhr.)]; **91,** 2814; (*f*: Jamadagni): **92,** 2899 (*Dharmaputraṃ; Dharmo hy āsīd Y°ḥ*, the mongoose despised the sacrifice of *Y.*).—§ 787 (Āçramavāsap.): XV, **1,** 11, 18 (*Kururājaḥ*), 26; **2,** 31, 41 (Dhr.), 56; **3,** 60, (β), 72 (*Kuntīputraḥ*), (γ), 86, (δ), 101, (ε), (123), 139, 146, 147; **4,** 148, 156, (ζ), 159, 164; **5,** 179, (θ), 189, 195, 198, 211; **6,** 218; **7,** 235; **8,** (258), 264, 265, (κ), 278; **9**λ, 292 (*Kuntīputraḥ*), 296; **10,** 349, 351; **11,** 356 (°*niveçanaṃ*), 357, 361, 380 (*Kuntīputraḥ*); **12,** 384 (do.), 388; **13,** 396; **14,** 416, 417; **15,** †433, †434; **16,** 445, 459 (Dhr.); **17**χ, 493; **18,** 499 (°*sya jananī*, i.e. Kuntī), 515 (°*sya jananī Kuntī*); **20,** 556 (°*sya jananī*, i.e. Kuntī), 557 (with the permission of *Y.*, Dhṛtarāshṭra, etc., retired to the forest).— § 788 (do.): XV, **23,** 624 (*Kururājaḥ*), 632, 633; **24,** 652 (*Y.*, etc., set out to visit Dhṛtarāshṭra, etc.); **25,** 658; **26,** 675 (686), 695, 696, 698, 699, [702 (Dhr.), 704 (do.), 709 (do.), 711 (*Dharmajaṃ*)] (being born from a portion of Dharma, Vidura, after death, entered the body of *Y.*, the son of Dharma); [**27,** 737 (*Kauravyaḥ Kuntīputraḥ*)]; **28,** [(ε), 747 (*Dharmasutaḥ*)], 758 (*Kururājaḥ*).—§ 789 (Putradarçanap.): XV, **29,** 769 (*Kauravyaḥ*), 775 (*Kururājaḥ*), 776; **31**η, 851 (*Dharmasyāṃçaḥ*).—§ 791 (do.): XV, **36,** 957, 966, 969, 993, (1001), 1002 (*Kauravyaṃ*), 1010 (*Y.*, etc., return to Hāstinapura).—§ 792 (Nāradāgamanap.): XV, **37,** 1011, 1012 (*Kururājaḥ*), (1016), 1052; **38,** (1057), (*a*), 1066 (°*sya jananī*, i.e. Kuntī); **39,** 1083, 1101, 1104 (Nārada communicated the death of Dhṛtarāshṭra, etc. to *Y.*, who then caused the funeral rites to be performed).—§ 793 (Mausalap.): XVI, **1,** 1 (*Kauravanandanaḥ*), 7 (*Kururājaḥ*); **2,** 54 (all. to the battle); **8,** 202.—§ 794 (Mahāprasthānikap.): XVII, **1,** 6, 15, 19 (*Kauravyo Dharmaputraḥ*), 21, 31, (*a*), 37; **2,** (52), (56), 57 (*Kaunteyaḥ*), 61, (67), 69 (Dhr.), (71); **3,** 74 (Dhr.), (79), (†81), (†83), (†87), 103, 107 (having installed Parikshit on the throne, *Y.*, etc., set out on the mahāprasthāna, his brothers and Kṛshṇā died on the way, and *Y.* alone arrived to heaven, accompanied by Dharma in the shape of a dog).—§ 795 (Svargārohaṇap.): XVIII, **1,** 3, 4 (Dhr.), 6, 12, 19 (*Kururājaḥ*); **2,** (27), 40, 56, 63, 65 (*Dharmaputraḥ*), 75, 76; **3,** 81 (Dhr.), 82 (*Kururājaḥ*), 90, 106, 110, 119 (only C.), 122 (Dhr.), 123 (*Kururājaḥ*) (having been put to test by means of illusions, *Y.*

acquired heaven); **4**, 125, 129, 135, 136, 169 (entered Dharma).

Cf. also the following synonyms:—

Ājamīḍha, Ajātaçatru, q.v.

Bhārata, Bharataçārdūla, Bharatapravarha, Bharatarshabha, Bharatasattama, Bharatasiṃha, q.v.

Bhīmapūrvaja ("the elder brother of Bhīma"): XIII, 1033.

Dharma: IV, 4 (according to the reading *Dharmo* in B., C. has *Dharmād*, cf. Dharma[1]); VI, 2063 (only B., C. *mahārājo*).

Dharmaja ("the son of Dharma"): VII, 6955 (only B.); VIII, 3554; XII, 1813, 4732 (only B.); XIII, 7722 (only B.); XIV, 2114, 2556, 2560; XV, 58, 346, 711; XVIII, 58.

Dharmanandana (do.): VIII, 3578, 4987.

Dharmaprabhava (do.): III, †14745 (*Dharmānilendra-prabhavān*).

Dharmaputra (do.): I, 418, †7082; II, 102, 1007, 1994, 2621; III, 8409, 11048, 11400, 11403, 11774, 11935, †14758, 14863, 14965, 15033, †15679, 15796, 17291, 17306; IV, 6, 2373; V, 618, 1967 (*Pāṇḍavaḥ*), 3508, 4744, †5039, 5557, 5693, 7622; VI, 2481, 3562, 3703, 3713, 3714, 3802, 3888, 3945, 4911, 4945 (only B.), 5110, 5416, 5755; VII, †81 (only C.), 681, 1772, 2791, 4002, 4882, 4896, 5108, 5121, 5164, 5251, 5253, 5360 (only C.), 5861 (do.), 5955, 6289 (only C.), 6451, 6627, 6899, 7006, 7158, 7355, 7378, 7381, 7382, 7393, 7395, 7396 (only C.), 7754, 8319 (only C.), 8351, 8983, 9218 (only B.), 9219; VIII, 494, 1171, 1182, 1701, 2498, 2668, 2689, 2862, 3033, 3163, 3165, 3288, †3482, †3483, 3560, 3787, 5005; IX, 463 (only B.), 639 (do.), 660, 670, 671, 672, 673, 692 (only B.), 959 (do.), 1187, 1779, 3341; XI, 2 (*Kauravaḥ*), 234, 247 (*Kauravaḥ*); XII, 9, 31, 893, 894, 1526, 1532, 1909, 1984, †6250, 13634; XIII, 1367, 2046, 5139, 7734; XIV, 4, 14 (only C.), 395, 400, 1937, 1954, 2083, 2899; XV, 59 (*Kauravyaḥ*), 143; XVII, 19 (*Kauravyaḥ*); XVIII, 65, 80, 89.

Dharmarāj, Dharmarāja, Dharmarājan, q.v.

Dharmasūnu ("the son of Dharma"): VI, 3698 (only B.); VII, 2981, 7782; IX, 919.

Dharmasuta (do.): I, 412; II, 57/58 (only B.), 1150, †2234, 2365; III, 4026, 4028, 11781, †14752, 15347, †15600, †15701, †15710, 17456; V, †13, 2813; VI, 2473; VII, 81 (only B.), 5884, 6474 (only B.), 7157, 7803 (only C.), 8683; VIII, 2672; IX, 690, †873, †883, †888, 1964; XII, †6263, 12962 (°*sya yajñe*, all. to Çiçupālavadhap.); XIII, 1775, 5404; XIV, 295, 367, 383, 387, 389, †1530, 1912, 2067, 2090; XV, 17, 747; XVIII, 76.

Dharmatanaya (do.): VII, 6957.

Dharmātmaja (do.): II, 1278; VII, 2942; XIV, 1869, 1887, 2091; XV, 712.

Kaunteya, q.v.

Kaurava, Kauravaçreshṭha, Kauravāgrya, Kauravanandana, Kauravanātha, Kauravarshabha, Kauravasattama, Kauravavaṃçavardhana, Kauravendra, Kauravya, q.v.

Kuntinandana, Kuntīputra, Kuntīsuta, q.v.

Kuruçārdūla, Kuruçreshṭha, Kuruçreshṭhatama, Kurūdvaha, Kurukulaçreshṭha, Kurukulodvaha, Kurumukhya, Kurunandana, Kuru-Pāṇḍavāgrya, Kurupati, Kurupravīra, Kurupuṅgava, Kururāja, Kurusattama, Kurūttama, Kuruvardhana, Kuruvīra, Kuruvṛshabha, q.v.

Mṛdaṅgaketu: VII, 6746.

Pāṇḍava, Pāṇḍavaçreshṭha, Pāṇḍavāgrya, Pāṇḍavamukhya, Pāṇḍavanandana, Pāṇḍavarshabha, Pāṇḍaveya, Pāṇḍunandana, Pāṇḍunṛpātmaja, Pāṇḍuputra, Pāṇḍusūnu, Pāṇḍusuta, Pāṇḍuvīra, q.v.

Pārtha, q.v.

Tapaḥsuta ("son of 'austerity'"): III, 17306.

Yādavīmātṛ, Yādavīputra, q.v.

Yudhishṭhirāçvāsa ("the consoling of Yudhishṭhira"). § 544 (cf. Rāmopākhyānap.): *Mārkaṇḍeya* consoled *Yudhishṭhira*, reminding him of *Rāma's* victory over *Rāvaṇa* by means of monkeys and bears: "thou acts as a *kshatriya* and has no sin, even the gods, with *Indra* and the *Asuras*, must endure the same; it was after such affliction that *Indra*, with the *Maruts*, slew *Vṛtra*, *Namuci*, and the *Rākshasī Dīrghajihvā*; *Arjuna*, *Bhīmasena*, *Nakula*, and *Sahadeva* are capable of vanquishing *Indra* with the *Maruts*; *Jayadratha*, who abducted Kṛshṇā, was vanquished" (III, **292**).

yuga (an age of the world, sg. and pl. (°*āni*)): I, 30 (°*syādau*), 38 (°*kshaye*), 39 (°*ādishu*), 66 (pl.), 1218 (°*ādikālaçayanaṃ Vishṇoḥ*), 1241 (°*āntāgnisamaprabhaḥ*), 1490 (°*āntakāle*), 2416 (*yuge yuge, yugānugaṃ*), 4341 (*Kṛtaṃ*), 5351 (°*āntānila-*), 5475 (°*āntāgnir iva*), 8208 (°*āntaṃ*), 8271 (°*ānta°-*); II, 72 (*sahasray°paryaye*), 1485 (*ānte*), 2430 (°*āntakāle*); III, 185 (*aho Brahmaṇaḥ . . . sahasray°sammitaṃ*), 496 (°*ānte*), 497 (°*ādau*), 881 (°*ānte*), 1644 (do.), 1675 (do.), 6098 (°*kshaye*), 8286 (°*ānte*), 10599 (sg.), 11231 (*yuge yuge*), 11233 (°*saṃkhyāṃ . . . yuge yuge*), 11234 (*Kṛtaṃ*), 11235 (*kāle y°ottame*), 11238 (°*saṃsarge*), 11242 (*Kṛte*), 11246 (do.), 11250 (*Dvāpare*), 11257 (*tāmasaṃ*, i.e. Kaliyuga), 11259 (pl.), 11261 (°*kshaya-*), 11262 (°*ānuvartanaṃ*), 11264 (°*saṃkhyāṃ*), 12806 (°*sahasrāntāḥ*), 12826 (*Kṛtaṃ*), 12831 (do., *dvādaçasāhasrī y°ākhyā*), 12833 (°*ānte*), 12836 (*gate yuge*), 12837 (*Kalau*), 12843 (°*ānte*), 12844 (do.), 12846 (°*kshaye*), 12847 (do.), 12854 (do.), 12860 (do), 12869 (°*sahasrānte*), 13000 (°*kshaye*), 13010 (°*ādau*), 13012 (°*kshaye*), 13019 (*tāmasaṃ*, i.e. Kaliyuga), 13021 (*anuy°ṃ*), 13027 (°*ānte*), 13028 (°*kshaye*), 13029 (do.), 13030 (do.), 13031 (do.), 13033 (do.), 13042 (°*syānte*), 13043 (°*kshaye*), 13045 (°*ānte*), 13046 (do.), 13049 (do., sg.), 13051 (°*kshaye*), 13053 (°*ānte*), 13054 (do.), 13057 (do.), 13059 (do.), 13060 (°*kshaye*), 13061 (do.), 13063 (°*ānte*), 13064 (do.), 13065 (°*kshaye*), 13069 (sg.), 13071 (°*saṃkshaye*), 13074 (do.), 13076 (°*e kshīṇe . . . y āntasya lakshaṇaṃ*), 13077 (sg.), 13078 (sg.), 13079 (*yuge yuge*), 13084 (°*ānte*), 13088 (do.), 13090 (°*kshaye*), 13091 (°*ānte*), 13093 (do.), 13094 (do.), 13095 (do.), 13097 (°*kshaye*), 13105 (*sarvasya*), 13115 (*Kṛte*), 13119 (do.), 13121 (°*saṅkhyā*), 15800 (°*āntakale*), 15814 (*catury°sahasrānte*), 17288 (°*ānte*); IV, 1709 (°*āntasamaye*), 2015 (°*ānte*); V, †1873 (*pravartayan y°m anyad y°ānte*), 2050 (°*āntaṃ*), 2534 (°*cakraṃ*), 2733 (°*ānte*), 2734 (do.), 3825 (°*āntāgnisamaprabhaḥ*), 4475 (*caturthasya*), 5506 (sg.), 5551 (do.), 5780 (°*āntāgnisamaḥ*), 5897 (°*saṅkshaye*), 7282 (°*āntam iva*), 7593 (°*ānte*); VI, 25 (do.), 244 (*sahasray°paryaye*), 387 (*catvāri*), 634 (°*ānte*), 1001 (*yuge yuge*), 1158 (*sahasray°paryayam ahar yad Brahmaṇaḥ*), 2426 (°*kshaye*), 2574 (°*āntam iva*), †2643 (°*āntakalpaṃ*, sc. *astraṃ*), 2791 (°*ānte*, only C.), 2792 (do.), 2799 (°*kshaye*, only B.), 3012 (*Dvāparasya* *yugasyānte*), 3013 (*yuge yuge*), 3086 (°*āntāgnim iva*), †3378 (°*kshaye*), †3530 (°*āntameghaughanibhaṃ*), 3703 (°*ānte*), 3707 (°*āntādityasannibhaṃ*), †3778 (°*āntāgnisamaprabhāvaṃ*), 4112 (°*ānte*), 4567 (°*kshaye*), 4656 (do.), 4732 (do.), 4855 (°*āntam iva*), 5575 (°*āntāgnisamaprakhyaḥ*), 5585 (°*kshaye*, only B.); VII, 196 (°*ānte*), 424 (sg.), 502 (°*āntakāle*), 1417 (°*āntārkaḥ*), 1418 (°*ānte*), 1485 (do.), †2611 (°*ātyaye*), 3136 (°*āntāgnir iva*), 3195 (°*kshaye*). 3237 (°*āntādityaraçmyābhaiḥ*), 3275 (°*āntāgnim iva*), 3388 (°*ānte*), 3911 (do.), 3954 (°*āntādityasannibhāḥ*), 4512 (°*āntāgnisamaprabhāṃ*), 4532 (°*āntapratimau*), 4976 (°*āntasadṛçaḥ*), 5097 (°*ānte*), †6151 (°*āntābhrasamasvanaṃ*), 6154 (°*āntavāta-*), 6791 (°*āntakālasamaye*), 6863 (°*kshaye*), 6865 (°*ānte*), 6880 (do.), 6902 (°*kshaye*), 7112 (do.), 7202 (°*ānte*), 7212 (°*kshaye*), 7978 (do.), 9001 (°*āntam iva*), 9195 (°*ānte*), 9422 (do.), 9480 (*yuge yuge*), 9485 (do.); VIII, 550 (°*ānte*), 656 (°*āntārkaḥ*), 664 (°*āntārkāv iva*), 989 (°*āntāgnim iva*), 2317 (°*ānte*), 2407 (°*āntāgnisamaprabhaṃ*), †2851 (°*āntakalpaḥ*, sc. *janakshayaḥ*), 3888 (°*kshaye*), †4070 (°*āntasūryapratimānatejasaṃ*), †4500 (°*āntasūryāv iva*), †4567 (*yuge yuge*), †4579 (°*āntavahnyarkakarаprakāçāḥ*); IX, 439 (°*saṅkshaye*), †905 (°*ānte*), 2071 (*pūrvay°e*), 2237 (°*kshaye*); X, 229 (°*ānte*), 463 (do.), 676 (°*āntānalasannibhaṃ*); XI, 280 (°*ānte*), 287 (°*āntakāle*), 610 (°*āntāgnir iva*), 649 (°*ānte*), 680 (°*āntaṃ*); XII, 1619 (°*ādishu*), 1644 (°*sahasrānte*), 1654 (pl.), †2412 (*yuge yuge*), 2441 (*Kṛte*), 2693 (*caturthasya*), 3408 (sg.), 5247 (°*kshayāt*), 5332 (°*ānte*), 5583 (°*āntāgnisamaprabhaḥ*), 7575 (pl.), 7658 (°*ādau*), 7659 (°*ādishu*), 7660 (°*ānte*), 8253 (*yuge yuge*), 8381 (°*viparyayaṃ*), 8478 (*yuge yuge*), 8497 (*Kṛtaṃ*), 8500 (*Kṛte*), 8503 (*anuy°ṃ*), 8504 (°*hrāsānurūpataḥ*), 8505 (*Kalau*), 8506 (°*ākhyāṃ*), 8508 (*sahasray°paryantam ahar yad Brahmaṇo viduḥ / rātriṃ y°sahasrāntāṃ*), 8542 (*Kṛte*), 8546 (*Dvāpare*), 8547 (*Kṛte*), 8548 (*yuge yuge*), 8550 (do.), 8574 (°*sāhasrayor ādau*), 8629, 8719 (*Kṛte*), 8726 (*Dvāpare*), 8730 (*yuge yuge*), 8899 (sg.), 9263 (*anuy°ṃ*), 9564 (*Kalau*), 9592 (*adhare*, i.e. Kaliyuga), †10063 (°*kshaye*), 10447 (°*ānte*), 11146 (pl.), 11227 (*yugaṃ dvādaçasāhasraṃ kalpaṃ viddhi caturyugaṃ*), 12658 (*Kṛte*), 12749 (*Āṅgirase*), 12788 (°*kshaye*), 12934 (°*sahasrānte*), 12969 (*Kṛte*), 13067 (*yuge yuge*), 13088 (sg.), 13091 (sg.), 13092 (*Tishye*), †13108 (°*ānte*, °*ādau*), 13150 (*yuge yuge*), 13190 (*catury°sahasrānte*), 13578 (°*dharmāṇāṃ*), 13595 (°*ādau*), 13683 (*kṛshṇe*, i.e. Kaliyuga), 13689 (*sahasray°paryayāḥ*), 13690 (*anekasahasray°paryayāḥ*); XIII, 600 (*yuge yuge*), 627 (°*paryayāḥ*), 692 (*Kṛte*), 775 (sg.), 839 (°*ānte*), 941 (do.), 942 (do.), 989 (°*paryayāḥ*), 1082 (*saṃvatsaray°ādi* = Çiva), 1798 (°*sahasraṃ*), 1799 (°*ānām ayutaṃ*), 3273 (°*çataṃ*), 4161 (°*ādinidhane*), 5257 (°*āntāgnisamaprabhaḥ*), 5267 (°*āntaṃ kalpaṃ*), 5278 (°*sahasraṃ*), 5317 (*dve y°ānāṃ sahasre*), 5321 (°*kalpasahasrāṇi trīṇi*), 6178 (*Kṛte*), 6317 (*kṛshṇavartmā yugāntābhaḥ*), 6368 (°*āntasadṛçaṃ*), 6372 (°*āgnir ivāparaḥ*), 6897 (°*āntāgnisamena*), 6901 (°*āntāgniḥ*), 6946 (*ādiyugāgame, yugakshaye*), 7128 (*Kṛte*), 7363 (do.); XIV, 1220 (*Kṛtam ādir y°ānāṃ*), 1490 (°*ānteshu*), 1578 (*calite calite yuge*), 2776 (pl.); XV, 1076 (°*kshaye*). Cf. Dvāpara(yuga), Kali(yuga), Kṛta(yuga), Tishya, Tretāyuga.

Yuga(ṃ) = Çiva (1000 names[1]).

Yugādhipa = Çiva (1000 names[2]).

Yugādi = Mahāpurusha (Mahāpurushastava).

Yugādikṛt = Vishṇu (1000 names).

Yugāgni = Kṛshṇa (Vishṇu): VI, 2954 (only C.).

Yugamadhya = Mahāpurusha (Mahāpurushastava).

Yugandhara[1], name of a place. § 409 (Plakshāvataraṇagamana): III, **129**, 10521 (°*e dadhi prāçya*).—§ 607 (Karṇap.): VIII, **44**ι, 2062 (°*e payaḥ pītvā*, in the country of the Bāhīkas?).

Yugandhara[2], a Pāṇḍava warrior. § 590 (Droṇābhishekap.): VII, **16**, 648 (attacked Droṇa), 649 (slain by Droṇa).

Yugandhara[3], pl. (°*āḥ*), a people. § 549 (Pāṇḍavapraveçap.): IV, **1**a, 12.

Yuganidhana = Mahāpurusha (Mahāpurushastava).

Yugapa, a Gandharva. § 191 (Arjuna): I, **123**a, 4812 (among the Devagandharvas present at the birth of Arjuna).

Yugarūpa, Yugāvaha = Çiva (1000 names[2]).

Yugāvarta[1] = Çiva (1000 names[1]).—Do.[2] = Vishṇu (1000 names).

Yukta, Yuktabāhu = Çiva (1000 names[2]).

Yūpadhvaja (XI, 681, 691, 692), **Yūpaketana, Yūpaketu** (also XI, 686) = Bhūriçravas, q.v.

Yuvan = Çiva (1000 names[1]).

Yuvanāçva, an ancient king. § 6 (Anukramanikāp.): I, **1**a, 226 (in Sañjaya's enumeration).—§ 407 (Māndhātrup.): III, **126**, 10427 (*Ikshvākuvaṃçaprabhavaḥ*), 10441, 10451 (*Y.* bore Māndhātṛ, who came out piercing his left side).—§ 475 (Dhundhumārop.): III, **202**, 13517 (king of Ayodhyā, son of Adri and father of Çrāva).—§ 595 (Shoḍaçarāj., v. Māndhātṛ): VII, **62**, 2274 (°*sya jaṭhare*, birth of Māndhātṛ, cf. § 407).—§ 632*b* (Shoḍaçarāj., cf. § 595): XII, **29**, 975 (do., do.).—§ 655 (Āpaddh.): XII, **159**a, 5924 (acquired heaven).—§ 656 (Khaḍgotpattik.): XII, **166**a, 6197 (received the sword from Raivata, from him it passed over to Raghu).—§ 677 (Mokshadh.): XII, **235**, 8599 (attained to heaven by way of gifts, PCR. connects *Y.* with Vṛshādarbhi, but probably wrongly; cf. XIII, 6254).—§ 761 (Ānuçāsanik.): XIII, **115**γ, 5663 (abstained from meat during the month of Kārttika). Cf. Saudyumni.

Yuvarājā Cedīnāṃ ("the crown prince of the Cedis"): VII, 9330 (cf. 9336, †9337, †9342, 9343 (slain by Açvatthāman), 9400).

Yuyudhāna = Sātyaki, q.v.

Yuyutsu, son of Dhṛtarāshṭra and a vaiçyā. § 83 (Ādivaṃçāvatāraṇa): I, **63**, 2446 (*karaṇaḥ*), (*a*), 2448 (*Vaiçyāputraḥ*, among eleven sons of Dhṛtarāshṭra who are mahārathas).—§ 130 (Aṃçāvat.): I, **67**, 2726 (*d*: *Vaiçyāputraḥ . . . Dhārtarāshṭraḥ çatādhikaḥ*), 2728, 2741 (*Vaiçyāputraḥ . . . Dhārtarāshṭraḥ·çatādhikaḥ*).—§ 180 (Gāndhārīputrotpatti): I, **115**, 4521 (*karaṇaḥ*, born from a vaiçyā), 4522 (*Vaiçyāputraḥ*).—§ 181 (Duḥçalotpatti): I, **116**, 4524 (do.).—§ 182 (Dhṛtarāshṭraputranāmak.): I, **117**, 4541 (enumeration of the sons of Dhṛtarāshṭra).—[§ 197 (Bhīmasenarasapāna): I, **129**, 5067/8 (only B., *Vaiçyāputraḥ*).]—§ 209 (Drupadaçāsana): I, **138**, 5449.—§ 232 (Svayaṃvarap.): I, **186**, 6982 (came to the svayaṃvara of Draupadī). [§ 302 (Anudyūtap.): II, **74**, 2476 (*Vaiçyāputraḥ*).]—§ 305 (do.): II, **78**, 2562.—§ 327 (Draupadīparitāpav.): III, **29**, 1112.—§ 556 (Sañjayayānap.): V, **23**δ, †697 (*Vaiçyāputraḥ*).—§ 561 (Yānasandhip.): V, **47**a, 1797; **61**, 2410 (according to Nīl.).—§ 562 (Bhagavadyānap.): V, **95**υ, 3404.—§ 567 (do.): V, **131**ρ, 4457.—§ 571 (Ulūkadūtāgamanap.): V, **160**, 5531 (°*toyaṃ*, sc. *purushodadhiṃ*, i.e. the army of Duryodhana, only C.).—§ 577 (Bhīshmavadhap.): VI, **43**, 1623, 1625, 1628 (joined the Pāṇḍavas).—§ 589 (Droṇābhishekap.): VII, **8**, 228; **10**, 364 (*f*: at Vāraṇāvata many wrathful kings battling together for six months, desiring to slay *Y.*, could not vanquish him).—§ 592 (Saṃcaptakavadhap.): VII, **23**o, 984 (cf. 1024 [v. Additions s.v. Bṛhanta], proceeded against Droṇa, description of his horses); **25**, 1076 (fought with his brother Subāhu), 1078; **26**τ, 1180, 1182, 1183, (v), 1186 (fought with the elephant of Bhagadatta).—§ 596 (Pratijñāp.): VII, **72**, 2536.—§ 597 (do.): VII, **83***a*, 2951 (*Kauravyam*). — § 605 (Karṇap.): VIII, **25**, 993, 994, 996, 999 (*°oḥ kāñcana-dhvajaḥ*), 1000, 1002 (vanquished by Ulūka); **30**ξξ, 1231 (attacked Karṇa).—§ 608 (do.): VIII, **49**χ, 2333 (attacked Vasusheṇa). — § 612 (Hradapraveçap.): IX, **29**, 1645, (1658), 1663, 1668, 1671 (returned to Hāstinapura).—§ 615 (Gadāyuddhap.): IX, **62**ψ, 3461.—§ 618 (Jalapradānikap.): XI, **12**κ, 315.—§ 620 (Çrāddhap.): XI, **26***a*, 780 (among those whom Yudhishṭhira ordered to perform the funeral rites for the dead warriors).—§ 635 (Rājadh.): XII, **37**δ, 1381 (accompanied Yudhishṭhira).—§ 637 (do.): XII, **40***a*, 1448; **41**, 1483; **43**, 1529; **44**, 1541 (*Dhārtarāshṭrasya*); **47**, 1695 (proceeded to see Bhīshma).—§ 777 (Svargārohaṇik. p.): XIII, **168**, 7715; **169**, 7769, 7771 (present when Bhīshma ascended to heaven).—§ 783 (Anugītāp.): XIV, **52**γ, 1504; **60**, 1805 (*Kauravyaḥ*, all. to the battle); **63**, 1894 (*Kauravyam . . . Dhṛtarāshṭrajam*, remained in Hāstinapura while the Pāṇḍavas fetched the gold); **66**κ, 1942; [**71**π, 2061 (*Vaiçyāputram*)].—§ 787 (Āçramavāsap.): XV, **1**, 5 (*Vaiçyāputraḥ*), 12; **3**δ, 107; **4**η, 168; **16**, 445. —§ 788 (do.): XV, **23**, 632 (remained in Hāstinapura while the Pāṇḍavas visited Dhṛtarāshṭra, etc.). — § 792 (Nāradāgamanap.): XV, **39**, 1089 (performed the funeral rites for Dhṛtarāshṭra, etc.).—§ 794 (Mahāprasthānikap.): XVII, **1**, 6 (*Vaiçyāputre*, Yudhishṭhira made over the kingdom to *Y.*, Parikshit being installed on the throne), 27.

Cf. also the following synonyms:—

Dhārtarāshṭra, Dhṛtarāshṭraja, Dhṛtarāshṭrasuta, q.v.

Karaṇa, q.v.

Kaurava, Kauravya, q.v.

Vaiçyāputra ("the son of a vaiçyā"): I, 2448 (*Y°*), 2726 (*Y°*), 2741 (*Y°*), 4522 (*Y°*), 4524 (*Y°*), 5067/8 (only B.); II, 2476; VII, 2539; IX, 1652, 1662; XIV, 2061; XV, 5 (*Y°*), †435; XVII, 6 (*Y°*).

CORRECTIONS AND ADDITIONS.

LIST OF ABBREVIATIONS.

BR. = Böhtlingh & Roth's Sanskrit Wörterbuch.
R.-ṛ. = Rājarshi.

* add under (2): or of which a complete list of quotations has not been recorded.

CONCORDANCE.

(The corrected words or numbers and the additions are given in Italics.)

§ 24, I, **9** . . . *Sahasrapad.*
§ 69, I, **58** . . . Sarpasattra (*v. Āstīkaparvan*).
(I), **59, 1–60,** 24 (*2198*–2230).
§ 70 (*a*), I, **59,** 1–10 (*2198*–2207).
§ 186, I, **121** . . . Vyushitāçvopākhyāna (*v. Vyushitāçva*).
§ 188, I, **122** . . . (*a*) *Pāṇḍu,* (*b*) Madayantī.
§ 201, I, **130** . . . (*a*) Droṇa, (*b*) *Açvatthāman.*
§ 207, I, **133** . . . Droṇa-grāha-mokshaṇa (*v. Droṇa*).
(I), **201,** 1–20 (7396–*7415*).
(I), **202,** 1–25 (*7416*–7440).
§ 242, I, **204** . . . (*a*) *Vidurāgamanaparvan,* (*b*) Ambuvīca.
§ 253 . . . *dele:* (*c*) Kṛshṇā.
§ 257, I, **225** . . . (*d*) *Sudarçana,* (*e*) *Kaumodakī.*
§ 361, III, **83,** 1–8 (*5071*–5078).
§ 383 . . . (*b*) *Gaṅgā,* (*c*) *Bhṛgos tīrtham.*
§ 392, III, **114** . . . Mahendrācalagamana (*v. Tīrthayātrāparvan*).
§ 393, III, **115** . . . Paraçurāma (*v. Tīrthayātrāparvan*).
§ 403, III, **121,** 1–15 . . . *dele :* (*c*) Gaya.
§ *407,* III, **126,** 1–47 . . . Māndhātrupākhyāna.
§ 418, III, **139** . . . *dele:* (*e*) Kṛshṇā.
III, **146** . . . *Bhīma-kadalī-khaṇḍa-praveça.*
§ 424 . . . *Bhīma-kadalī-khaṇḍa-praveça.*
§ 427 . . . Tretā-yuga (*v. Tretā*).
§ 428 . . . Dvāpara-yuga (*v. Dvāpara*).
§ 457, III, **187,** 1–58 (*12746*–12804).
(ϵ) *Skandayuddha:* III, **231.**
§ 519, III, **259,** 1–35 (15370–*15403*).
§ 520, III, **260,** 1–36 (*15404*–15440).
(III), **282,** 1–71 . . . *Hanūmat-pratyāgamana.*
§ 534, III, **282** . . . (*a*) *Hanūmatpratyāgamana.*

IV. Virāṭaparvan

§ 549 . . . (*e*) *Airāvaṇa* (elephant).
(IV), **41,** 1–12 (*1312*–1324).
(V), **59,** 1–31 (*2324*–2358).
(V), **127,** 1–25 (*4233*–4258).
(V), **136** . . . (*Vidulāputrānuçāsanasamāpti*).
(V), **148,** 1–36 (5002–*5039*).
(V), **176** . . . (*Hotravāhanā°*).
(VI), **100,** 1–54 (*4530*–4583).
(VII), **31,** 1–29 (*1344*–1372).
(VII), **188,** 1–54 (8574–*8627*).
(VII), **189,** 1–66 (*8628*–8693).
(VII), **197,** 1–44 (*9082*–9125).
(VIII), **89,** 1–97 (4524–*4621*).
(IX), **44** . . . [*Kumārābhishekopakrama*].
(IX), **64,** 1–43 (3582–*3625*).
(IX), **65,** 1–46 (*3626*–3671).
(X), **12,** 1–41 (606–*646*).
(X), **13,** 1–22 (*647*–669).
(XII), **24,** 1–34 (698–*731*).
(XII), **25,** 1–36 (*732*–767).
(XII), **35,** 1–51 (1241–*1291*).
(XII), **36,** 1–50 (*1292*–1343).
(XII), **74,** 1–22 (2808–*2830*).
(XII), **75,** 1–37 (*2831*–2868).
(XII), **82** . . . *Amātyaparīkshāyām.*
(XII), **90** . . . *Utathya-gītāḥ.*
(XII), **123** . . . *Kāmandāṅgarishṭa-saṃvāda.*
(XII), **150,** 1–19 (*5594*–5612).
(XII), **238,** 1–25 (*8688*–8712).
(XII), **290** . . . *Bhava-Bhārgava-samāgama.*
(XII), **336,** 1–55 (*12696*–12751).
(XII), **350** . . . *Dvaipāyanotpatti.*
§ 733, XIII, **25** . . . *Aṅgirasas tīrthayātrā.*
(XIII), **46** . . . *Strīpraçaṃsā.*
XCIII, Açvamedhika-Parvan (*v. Açvamedhika(m) parva(n)*).
(XIV), **21** . . . id. [*id.*].
(XIV), **70,** 1–21 (2033–*2054*).
(XIV), **71,** 1–26 (*2055*–2082).

Note.—The numbers of chapters in the Concordance refer to the Bombay edition of Çāka, 1799. Those of the Bombay edition of Çāka, 1785, are the same with the following exceptions:—

Ed. 1799.	Ed. 1785.
XII, 249–366.	**XII, 248** bis-**365.**

INDEX TO THE NAMES.

A

Adrihan = Indra: VIII, 778.
Adrija, pl. (°*āḥ*) ("mountaineers"): VII, **161**ζζ, 7208.
Ādya [3], delete this article.
Aghamarshaṇa, add: Do. (neutr.), name of a sacred hymn: XII, 5664, 7776; XIII, 1742, 6236, 6242; cf. III, 15548.
Aghaṇṭin, read **Aghaṇṭaghaṇṭin.**
***Āgneya** [1], add: § 603 (Nārāyaṇāstramokshap.): VII, **202,** 9632 (*urūbhyām ardham °aṃ*, scil. Çiva's).—Do.[2], add: I, 5107-8, 6464-66, 6915, 8472; III, 877, 14985, 14995; IV, 1876; VII, 402 (i.e. Kṛshṇa's cakra), 1424, 3657, 3659.
***Agni**, I, **4,** 854 (°-*caraṇam*), read (°-*çaraṇam*).—§ 20 (Puloma), read (Pulomā).—Add: I, **130,** 5108; **223,** 8151; **224,** 8165; **229,** 8331, 8334.—II, **7,** 302 (*Indrāgnī, Agnīshomau*); **48,** 1709.—III, **132,** †10605; **147,** 11195; **222,** 14215-17; **232,** 14519, 14522.—§ 526*a*, read: § 526 (Rāmopākhyānap.).—§ 552 (Gograhaṇap.), read: (Goharaṇap.).—Add: IV, **37,** 1211.—V, **16,** 483.—VI, **98,** 4453.—§ 594 . . . dele VII (to be inserted before **25,** 1084).—Add: VII, **35,** 1536; **66,** 2335; **101,** 3786; **194,** 8972; **201,** 9421; †9457 (*Vāgagnī*, add: B. *Vāyvagnī*); **202,** 9568, 9594, 9632-3.—VIII, **31,** 1250, 1305 (*Agnidattaḥ*, scil. the chariot of Arjuna); **34,** 1510, 1535, 1555; **37,** 1742; **46,** 2160; **60,** 2983; **96,** †5042.—§ 615: dele brought (to be inserted after 1985 (°*īn*).—Add: XII, **141,** 5343˝(°*devatāḥ*); **263,** 9381 (= 2922).—The translation of XIII, 4165, ought to be altered thus: When fire is not obtainable, gold is used as a substitute by one who knows the authorities, according to the injunction of the Veda (*pramāṇajño veda-çruti-nidarçanāt*)—and *Jāmadagnyaḥ* of the text is to be corrected into *Jāmadagnya* (vocative = Rāma).—XIII, **103,** 5142, read **106,** 5142.

Synonyms:—
Adbhuta, dele this article and see p. 12 Adbhuta [1].
Anala, add: VIII, †4787 (°*daṇḍa-sannibhaṃ*). Cf. Kālānala.
Anilasakha ("friend of the wind"): XII, 13918 (*devaḥ*).
***Anilasārathi,** add: I, 2073; XII, 2583.
***Citrabhānu,** add: I, 8226; VIII, †4680; XII, 1756 (*sa-Haihayaḥ*); XIII, 4060; XIV, 1737.
***Hiraṇyaretas,** add: I, 8408, and read XIV, 118 instead of [XIV, 118 = the sun).
Kavi: XIII, 7220.
Kṛçānu: VIII, †3402 (°*dattañ ca rathaṃ*, sc. Arjuna's).
***Kṛshṇagati**: IX, †1334.
***Kṛshṇavartman,** add: I, 8221, 8380; V, 3739.
***Saptarcis,** add: III, 5035, 5041.
***Tamonuda**: III, 14114.
Vaiçvānara, Vasuretas, Vātasārathi. Vibhāvasu, Yajñabhuj, q.v.

Agnidāyāda, Agnija = Skanda, q.v.
Agnisambhava = Aṅgiras [1]: XIII, **106,** 5142.
Agnī-Shomau, Agnīshoma, cf. also the articles Agni and Soma.
Agnisvattāḥ, read **Agnisvāttāḥ** (B. °*shvāttāḥ*).
Agnitīrtha, add: § 366 (Tīrthayātrāp.): III, **83,** 7008.
Agniveça [2], pl. (°*āḥ*), a people. § 578 (Bhīshmavadhap.): VI, **50**π, 2084 (only B.).
Agniveçya, add: § 324 (Dvaitavanapr.): III, **26***a*, 986.
Agraha, name of a fire. § 493 (Āṅgirasa): III, **221,** 14189.
Agraṇī [2], name of a fire. § 493 (Āṅgirasa): III, **221,** 14198.
Aha(ḥ), dele this article, and see Ahas.[2]
Ahalyā, add: § 772*e* (Gautama): XIII, **154,** 7218 (°*āṃ kāmayānaḥ*, sc. Indra).
Ahaṃkāra, add: III, 13916; XII, 6780 (= Brahmán), 6785 (°*asya srashṭā*, scil. Vishṇu).
Ahar [2], name of a tīrtha. § 364 (Tīrthayātrāp.): III, **83,** 6070.
Ahas [1-2], read **Ahar** [3-4].
Ahara, an asura: I, 2660 (only B., C. *Suharaḥ*, q.v.).
Ahicchatra, add: a country: I, **138,** 5515 (°*añ ca vishayaṃ Droṇaḥ samabhipadyata*).
Ahirbradhna, add: (B. always *Ahirbudhnya*).
Ahitā, a river: VI, 328 (only B., C. has *Mahitām*).
Āhuka [1], a Yādava prince, add: (= Ugrasena [6]).—V, 4297 (dele: father of Ugrasena). Cf. Dvārakādhipati (so read III, 829).
Āhuka [2]: V, 3041 (°*ānām adhipatiḥ*, add: i.e. Kṛshṇa), 5351 (add: B. has *Ākūtīnāṃ*, probably for *Ākṛtīnāṃ*).
Āhvṛti, add: (B. has *Āhutiḥ*).
Aikshvāka ("descendent of Ikshvāku") = Bhagīratha: VII, 2256 (Bh°). Cf. next.
Aikshvāku [1], add: (only C., B. has *Ikshvākuṃ*).—Do.[2], add: (B. has *Aikshvākaṃ*).—Do.[3], add: (B. has *Aikshvākaḥ*).—Do.[4] = Sāgara (the ocean): III, 16303 (only C., B. has *Aikshvākaḥ*).
Aindava, adj. ("belonging to Indu, i.e. Soma"): VII, †2467 (°*vīm ātmatanuṃ*).
***Aindra,** add: II, 278 (*vaijayantaḥ*), 2577 (*jaye*); III, 1494 (*yogena*), 12023 (*rathaṃ*); V, 5462 (*puraṃ*); VI, 83 (*nakshatraṃ Jyeshṭhāṃ*); VIII, †3238 (*jālaṃ*).
Aindrāgna, dele § 555 foll. and add: v. Aindrāgnya.
Aindrāgnya, add: V, 517 (*bhāgaḥ*, only C., B. has *Indrāgnyoḥ*); XII, 2307 (add: so C., B. reads *Aindrāgnena*).
Aindri, add: VII, †1301.
Airāvata [1], instead of § 576 (Bhagavadgītāp.): VI, **21,** read: §575*c* (Samā): VI, **12,** and insert before **31,** 1231: § 576 (Bhagavadgītāp.): VI.—VI, 2761 (read: *Airāvatopamaṃ*).—Add: VII, **26,** 1174 (only B.).—VIII, 4830, read: VII, 4830.—VIII, 6436 (read: *Airāvatopamān*).—§ 730 (Meghavāhanop., read: Ānuçāsanik.).—Cf. also III, 188 (*mahāghanāḥ sairāvatāḥ*); VII, 3639 (°*çatahradāḥ*).
Airāvati, see Irāvatī (below).
Aja [1], add: I, 2431-32.—Do.[3], add: VII, 2863, 2867, 9462, 9602; VIII, 1442.—Do.[4]: XII, 8756, read 8766; XII, 8802, add: (neutr.); Do.[5], add: I, 7306; III, 8754, 13005; V, 151; XII, 7874.—Do.[7], add: III, 15877 (father of Daçaratha).—Do.[8], add: V, 1574 (the supreme soul); XII, 11485 (do.).
Ajabindu (°*vindu*, C.), a king. § 562 (Bhagavadyānap.): V, **74**γ, 2730 (*Suvīrāṇām*).
Ajagaraparvan, read Ā°.—§ 449 . . . Mahendrasena, read Indrasena.
Ajaka, add: § 92 (Aṃçāvat.): I, **65,** 2532 (among the sons of Danu).
Ājamīḍha [2], add: III, †10231; V, †1815.—Do.[3], add: (so C., but B. has Ājamīḍha˘ (voc.) = Dhṛtarāshṭra).—Do.[4], add: II, 1962; VII, †5838 (only B., C. has °*am* = Duḥçāsana).—Do.[8], add: III, †10835 (*sarvājamīḍhāpacitam narendram*, scil. Yudhishṭhira).

Ajātaçatru, add: II, †1995; III, †254, †14757; V, †653, †681.
Ajita [3] = Kṛshṇa (Vishṇu): III, 1698, 1896, 15850.
Ajitaçatru, add: (*Ṛshabho 'jitaçatruç ca*, so C., but the reading of B. *Ṛshabho jita-*° seems to be preferable, *jitaçatru* being either adj. or nom. pr.).
Ajodara, v. Gajodara (below).
Ākhaṇḍala: VIII, 4353 (. . . *Karṇam*, read: scil. the banner of Karṇa); add: XII, 12712 (°*sakhaḥ*, i.e. Vasu Uparicara).
Akrodhana, add: (husband of Karambhā and father of Devātithi).
Akrūra [1], add: § 353 (Vaivāhikap.): IV, **72,** 2357.—§ 570 (Sainyaniryāṇap.); V, **157**κ, 5330.—XII, 3037 (add: (?) PCR.).
Ākṛshṭa, add: (B. A°).
Akṛti, read Ā° and add: § 264 (Sabhākriyāp.): II, **4**β, 126 (so B., C. has *Aṅkṛti*).
***Akshara,** add: III, 10941 (= Vishṇu), 10946 (do.); VI, 1162 (*purushaḥ paraḥ*), 1398 (*purushaḥ*).
Akshayavaṭa, a holy banyan-tree. § 370 (Tīrthayātrāp.): III, **84,** 8061 (in Gayā).—[§ 377 (Dhaumyatīrthak.): III, **87,** 8307 (*akshayyakaraṇo vaṭaḥ*).]—§ 380 (Brahmasaras): III, **95,** 8523.—[§ 595 (Shoḍaçarāj., v. Gaya): VII, **66,** 2353 (*vaṭaç cākshayyakaraṇaḥ*).—§ 749*b* (Gayā): XIII, **88,** 4253 (*akshayyakaraṇo vaṭaḥ*).]
Akshisantarjana, a celestial weapon. § 563 (Bhagavadyānap.): V, **96**φ, 3490 (to be employed by Arjuna).
Alaka, pl. (°*āḥ*), the inhabitants of Alakā. § 438 (Yakshayuddhap.): III, **162,** 11813.
Alambusha, add: VII, **167,** 7505 (only C.); **174,** 7858 (do.). Cf. Ārshyaçṛṅga (°-gi), Jāṭāsuri, Jaṭāsurasuta, Rakshas (etc.).
Alarka [1], add: III, **25,** †957.—Do.[2] . . . originally a Rākshasa, read: Asura, named Daṃça.
Alinda, read: (B. has *Aṭhidāḥ*).
Alolupa, add: § 586 (Bhīshmavadhap.): VI, **64**κ, 2838.
***Amara** [1], pl., add: I, 7715 (read *amarāv iva*); VI, 215 (read *amaraçreshṭhāṃs*); VII, 386 (°*saṃkāçaṃ*, read with B. *Antaka-*°); 2516 (°*striyaḥ*, only C., B. has *samupāsanti yaṃ purā paramastriyaḥ*); X, 771 (read with B. *aparaṃ*); XIII, † 1031 (read *Amaraprabhāva*, i.e. Kṛshṇa), 7483 (C. *mahārudraṃ*, read with B. *'marā Rudram*).—**Amaraçreshṭa**: I, 3942 (= Dyaus). — **Amaraloka** (= Devaloka): III, 8238.—**Amarāṇāṃ hradaḥ,** a tīrtha: III, **83,** 6076.
***Amaraṇa,** dele this article.
Amaraparvata, a mountain: § 285 (Nakula): II, **32,** 1193 (in the west, conquered by Nakula).
Amararāj = Indra (q.v. below).
Amaratha, pl., a people (?), see Vātaja.
Amareça [1] — Indra (q.v.).—Do.[2] = Çiva (1000 names [2]).
Amarottama [1] = Indra (q.v.).—Do.[2] = Brahmán: I, 1588.—Do.[3] = Vishṇu: V, 299.
Amatsyācin, add: B. reads *Cārumatsya*.
Ambarāvṛta, dele this article and see Ārdracarmāmbaravṛta.
Ambashṭha [1], add: V, **30,** †889 (only B., C. has *Āvantyāḥ*); VI, **51**ν, 2105 (only B., C. has *Vāmana*); VIII, **79**η', 4040.
Ambhoruda, so B. for Ambhoruha (q.v.).
[**Ambopākhyānaparvan**] in § 573 read *vīryaçulkāḥ*.
Ambuçāyin, instead of (1000 names [1]) read: XII, 10447.
Ambujekshaṇa ("lotus-eyed") = Nārāyaṇa: VII, 9447.
Ambupati, Amburāj, Ambvīça = Varuṇa, q.v.
Ambuvāhini, add: VI, 334 (only B., C. has *Madhuvāhinīṃ*).
[**Aṃçāvataraṇa(ṃ)**] § 127, instead of Krodha . . . (*Krodhavaçāḥ*) read: Krodhavaçā begat nine daughters sprung from wrath (*krodhasambhavāḥ*).
Aṃçumālin = Sūrya: III, 190.
Amoghā [2], name of the dart of Indra. § 546 (Kuṇḍalāharaṇap.): III, **302,** 16990–91 (*çaktiṃ*).—§ 547 (Karṇa): III, **310,** 17197–98, 17201, 17706–7, 17210.—§ 561 (Yānasandhip.): V, **55**μ, 2198 (*çaktyā*).—§ 600 (Ghaṭotkacavadhap.): VII, **158,** 6977 (*çaktiṃ Çakra-vinirmitāṃ*), 7022 (*çaktiḥ*); **180**δδδ, 8192 (read *çaktir Amoghā 'sya*); **182,** 8247 (*çaktiḥ*), 8253 (do.), 8258, 8262, 8264, 8276 (*çaktiṃ*).—§ 604 (Karṇap.): VIII, **3**δ, 63 (*çaktyā*).—Do.[3], name of the dart of Skanda. § 748*b* (Tārakavadhop.): XIII, **86,** 4214 (*çaktyā*).
Amūrtarayasa [1], add: probably wrong reading for *Āmūrtarayasaḥ* (= Gaya).
Amūrtarayasa [2], read **Ā**°.
Anādhṛshṭi [2], add: VII, 360 (only B., = Vārddhakshemi, q.v.).
Anādi-madhyānta = Vishṇu (q.v.).
Anagha [1], add: an ancient king. § 267 (Yamasabhāv.): II, **8,** 332 (only B., C. has *Nalaḥ*).
Analā, instead of (one of the Krodhavaçāḥ) read (daughter of Surabhi).
Analasakha = Vāyu, q.v.
Anaṅgā, a river: VI, 342 (only B., C. has *Maniṅgāṃ*).
Ananta [1], add: § 665 (Gālavac.): V, **110,** 3818 (°*asya niveçanaṃ*).—§ 768*b* (Kṛshṇa Vāsudeva): XIII, **147,** 6863, 6866 (*vasudhādharaḥ*). Cf. Phaṇīndra.
Anantavijaya, VI, 2166, read 2116.
Anantayaças, name of a ṛshi (?). § 377 (Dhaumyatīrthak.): III, **90,** 8383.
Anaraka, a tīrtha: III, 7039 (so B. prob. more correctly for Naraka [2]).
Aṇḍa, dele "the Sun" and add: Do.[2] = Vivasvat, q.v.
Andha, v. Badhirāndha (Additions).
Andha, pl., add: Do.[2] = Āndhra, pl.: V, 5510 (only C.), VI, 357 (do.).
Andhaka [2], add: § 730*g* (Upamanyu): XIII, **14**λ, 805.—§ 770 (Ānuçāsanik.): XIII, **151**μ, 7130 (slain by Çveta [1], only PCR.).
Andhaka-ghātin, dele (1000 names [1]) and add q.v.
Andhaka-nipātin = Çiva, q.v.
Andhra, pl.: VI, 357 add (C. has *Andhāḥ*); XII, 2439, read 2429.
Anenas [2], a king in Ayodhyā. § 475 (Dhundhumārop.): III, **202,** 13516 (son of Kakutstha and father of Pṛthu).
Aṅga [1], pl., add: V, **50,** 1986 (*Kāçīn Aṅga-Magadhān*, B., *Kāçī-Vaṅga-Magadhān*, C.), 1997; VI, **9,** 357.
Aṅga [8], add: VIII, **45,** 2112.
Aṅgāra [2], a people. § 574 (Jambūkh.): VI, **9**ν, 368 (*Kukkurā*°-*Mārishāḥ*).
Aṅgāraka [1], add: cf. *Kṛttikāṅgāraka* (?): XIII, 1708; Dharāputra, Lohitāṅga.
Āṅgarishṭha: XII, 4534 (. . . Kamanda, read: Kāmanda).
Aṅgiras [1], XII, **69,** 2666 (two verses sung by his son Bṛhaspati), add: so PCR., our texts read *gītāv Aṅgirasā svayaṃ*.

Aṅgirasa(ṃ), read Ā°.
Aniketa, a Yaksha. § 269 (Vaiçravaṇasabhāv.): II, **10**, 399 (in the palace of Kubera, *Vṛkshavāsy-Aniketaç, ca*, C. by error *Vṛkshavāsp-°*).
***Aṇiman**, add: XIII, 1015 (among the attributes of Çiva).
Aṇimat, read *Pāṇimān* instead of *Māṇimān*.
Aniruddha [1], add: § 232 (Svayaṃvarap.): I, **186**, 6999 (*'niruddhaḥ*). — § 287 (Rājasūyikap.): II, **34**, 1274.— § 402 (Tīrthayātrāp.): III, **120**, †10276.—XII, 13470 (read: "Bráhman develops into Purusha" instead of Brahmán, etc.).
Añjalikāçrama(?), v. Cāṇḍālikāçrama.
Aṅkṛti (or **Āṅkṛti**), probably error in C. for *Ākṛti* (B.).
Annapati [2] = Sūrya: III, 197.
Antakṛt, add: the reading of the text is *Tamontakṛt*, which probably ought to be taken as one name (q.v.).
Antardhāna, add: §208*b* (Arjuna): I, **135**, 5366 (*astreṇa*). Cf. VII, 2417, where it seems to denote the power of disappearing at will.
Antargirya, pl. (*°āḥ*), a people. § 574 (Jambūkh.): VI, **9**μ, 357 (C. by error *°aḥ*).
Antavāsa, pl. (*°āḥ*), a people. § 295 (Dyūtap.): II, **51**, 1837 (Nishādas, PCR.).
Antraçilā, v. Citraçilā.
Anudyūta, add: cf. VII, 6370 (only B.).
Anudyūtaparvan: the number § 304 after (II, 75).—ought to be inserted after (II, **76**).—
Anugītāparvan: in (XIV, **66**) correct (δ) to (θ), and in (XIV, **83**) after *Draviḍas, Andhras*, insert: *Audras* (or *Raudras* ?).
Anumati, add: § 606 (Tripurākhyāna): VIII, **34**, 1486 (among the auspicious days who became the *yoktrāṇi* of Çiva's chariot).
Ānūpa, pl. (*°āḥ*), a people. § 295 (Dyūtap.): II, **51**, 1844 (*Nīpānūpān*).
Anūpā, add: (*Arūpā*, B.).
Anūpādhipati ("the king of the sea-coast") = Nīla: VI, 4153 (*N°*), 4210 (do.).
Anūpaka, pl. (*°āḥ*), a people. § 578 (Bhīshmavadhap.): VI, **50**π, 2080.
Anūpavāsin = Nīla: VIII, 166.
Anurādhā, add: cf. Maitra (IX, 1982).
Anushṭubh, dele (1000 names) and add: XIII, 6949.
anuvākāḥ, pl., instead of "= Kṛshṇa" read: XII, 1613 (cf. vāka, pl.).
Anuvinda [1], instead of "§ 593 (Ambop.): V, **195**" read: § 573 (etc.), and instead of "VI, 1742 (do.)" read: 1740 (do.), 1742.—Add: VI, **47**ζ, 1851 (do., only B.); **49**, 2014/15 (do., do.); VII, **20**ϵ, 801.
Anvagbhānu, add: cf. Ṛceyu.
Apagā [1-2], **Apagāsuta, Apageya**, read: Āp°.
Āpagā [1], instead of "a river" read: name of various tīrthas, and add: § 368 (do.): III, **83**, 7048 (*Āpagānāṃ*, both C. and B.; read *Āpagāyāṃ*).
Apāṃ pati, add: III, 2138, 2228, 10123, †10225; V, 515, 3527.—Do. = Çiva: VII, 9540.
Aparājita [2], add: § 554 (Sainyodyogap.): V, **4**γ, 84.
Apava, read Āpava.
Apavāha, pl. (*°āḥ*), a people. § 574 (Jambūkh.): VI, **9**μ, 352 (*Vārapāçyāpavāhāḥ*, B. has *Vāravāsyāyavāhāḥ*).

Apsaras [2], add: § 412 (Ashṭāvakrīya): III, **134**, †10662 (*dṛshṭā vede pañcacūḍāpsarāḥ*).
Apta, read Āpta.
Arāli, a son of Viçvāmitra, so B. instead of Arāṇi (q.v.).
***Āraṇyaçāstra**, add: § 621 (Rājadh.): XII, **9**, 253.
Araṇyaka [1-2] and **Araṇyakaparvan**, read Āraṇya°.
Aravindavaktra = Skanda: III, 14640.
Arbuka, so B. for Arvuka (q.v.).
Ārcika = Jamadagni (q.v.).
Ardracarman, read Ārdracarmāmbaravṛta.
Arihan = Sūrya: III, 152.
Arimejaya, add: § 232 (Svayaṃvarap.): I, **186**, 6999.
Arishṭa, according to Hariv. an Asura, son of Bali, incarnate as a bull. § 567 (Bhagavadyānap.): V, **130**, 4410 (slain by Kṛshṇa), 4411 (?).
Arishṭanemi, add: cf. V, 2578 (*°-iṃ Garuḍam Suparṇaṃ Hariṃ*, in some verses praising Kṛshṇa).
Arivindavaktra, misprint for Aravindavaktra (v. above).
Ārjava(ṃ) = Çiva (1000 names [1]).
Arjuna [1], add: § 325 (Draupadīparitāpav.): III, **27**, 1012 (*bahubāhunā*).
Arjuna [2]: I, 5252, read 5257, and add: 5269, 5396, 5534–5, 5820 (6490), 7974, 8082–3, 8207; II, 666; III, (923), 1515, 1815, 11936, (11992), (12079), (12103), (12132), (12162), (12196–7), (12212), (12274), 14995, (15018), 15178, 15340, †15607, (15752), 17225, (17244), 17289; IV, 1455, 1553, (1926); V, †653; **48**, 1831 read: **49**, 1931; (2920); VI, (851), (859), (882), 1189, (†1261), (†1282), 1488, 3564, 5291, 5806/7 (only B.); VII, 1964, (2586), (3150), 3398, 4958, 6121, 6474 (only B.), 8183, 8603 (instead of 8605), 9114, 9391, 9433, (9497); VIII, 325 (only B.), †702, †710, 734, 2354 (only B.), (†3289), (3298), (†3358), (†3493), (†3587), (4010), †4621, 4706, 4798.

Add to the synonyms:—

Bībhatsu: III, 10877; V, 5429 (only B.); VI, 2466, 4658; VII, 3247, 9224 (only B.), 9392.
Bṛhannalā: IV, (1226), (1249).
Çakrātmaja: I, †7316.
***Çvetāçva**, etc., ought to have been marked by asterisks, as only selected places are quoted.
Dhanañjaya: III, 10877; IV, 1602 (only B.); VI, 2395, 4998; VII, 2662, 2840, 3246, 3383, 3396, 4279, 5960, 8190; VIII, †1983, †1984, 2415, 3630, †4076, 4766.
Gāṇḍivadhārin: V, 5932; VI, 1533.
Gāṇḍivin: V, 4869.
Guḍākeça: I, 7770; V, 4691; VI, 1224.
Jaya: III, 3088, 11525; VIII, †1742.
Jishṇu: I, 7945; III, 1523, 4019; IV, 1737 (only B.), 2075; VII, 2479, 2783 (read *Jishṇu-priyaṅkaraḥ*).—Dele: VI, 2024; VIII, 1435.
Kapidhvaja: V, 4707, 4785; VI, †786, 849, 5226, 5633 (instead of 5663); VII, 109, 2478; VIII, 1829, †3296, †4952.
Kapiketana: V, 2202; VIII, 4479.
Kapipravara, read: **Kapipravaraketana** ("with the excellent ape in the banner") and add: IV, 1442; VII, 1209; VIII, 2179.
Kapirājadhvaja (= do.): VII, 3013. — **Kapirājaketu** (= do.): VI, †2657, †2670, †2677, †2678.

Kapivaradhvaja : VII, 2821 ; VIII, 4123.
Kirīṭamālin : III, †11908 ; IV, †1689, 2029 ; VI, †2627, †2676 ; VII, 3276, †6146, †6148 ; VIII, †3287, †3866, †4514, †4582, †4615, †4797.
Kirīṭavat : VIII, 4733.
Kirīṭin : I, 535 (only B.) ; IV, 1590 (do.) ; V, 2358 ; VI, †2586, 3586, 5617 ; VII, 739 (only B.), 6535, 8081 ; VIII, 4023/4 (only B.).
Phālguna : I, 5522 (only B.) ; III, 1903 ; VII, 1453, 4241, 6458/9 (only B.), 6991, 9227 ; VIII, †3396/7 (only B.), 4105.
***Savyasācin**, add : (only selected passages).
Sitāçva ("with white horses") : III, †11898.
Tāpatya : I, 6509, 6632.—**Tāpatyavardhana** (= do.) : I, 6505.
Vānaradhvaja: VI, 3865, 5360, 5550; VII, 1416, 2495.—**Vānaraketana** : VII, 6762.—**Vānaraketu** : V, 1859.—**Vānarapravaradhvaja** : VII, 742. — **Vānararshabhalakshaṇa** : VII, 5101.
Vijaya : III, 425, 11334 ; IV, 1725 ; V, 3219 ; VI, 3619 ; VII, 3891, 4545/6 (only B.) ; VIII, 4441.
[Cf. also Ājamīḍha[6], Bhārataçreshṭha, Bhāratāgrya, Bharata-rathaçreshṭha, °-rshabha, °-sattama, Çākhāmṛgadhvaja (v. Add.), Dviyodha, Indraprabhava, Kauravanandana, °-rājaputra, °-rshabha, °-sattama, Kuntibhojātmajāputra, Kuntīmātṛ, Kuntinandana, Kuntīsuta, Kuruçārdūla, °-çreshṭha, °-udvaha, °-kulaçreshṭha, °-kulodvaha, °-mukhya, °-nandana, °-Pāṇḍavasattama, °-pravīra, °-puṅgava, °-rājaputra, °-sattama, °-ūttama, °-vīra, °-vīramukhya, Mahendratanaya, Nivātakavacāntaka, Pākaçāsana-dāyāda, °-nandana, Pāṇḍavaçreshṭha, °-āgrya, °-mukhya, °-nandana, °-rshabha, °-vīra, °-yodha, Pāṇḍuputra, °-sūnu, °-suta, °-tanaya, Purandarasuta, Saṃçaptakanihantṛ, °-nishūdana, Sarvakurūttama, Surarājaputra, Surasūnu.

Ārjuni[1], add: VII, 1708, 1857, 1869.—Do.[3] (so read instead of Arjuni[3]) : VII, 1738, read : VI, 1738.
***Arka**[1] : I, 42 (add : a son or form of Vivasvat ; cf. Āçāvaha) ; add : V, 4909 ; VII, 8681.
Ārksha ("son of Rksha") = Saṃvaraṇa : I, 3725 (*S*°).
Ārocaka (pl. °-*āḥ*), a people. § 578 (Bhīshmavadhap.) : VI, 51π, 2097 (only B., C. has *Rocakāḥ*).
Ārshabha, add : VII, **147**, 6342.
Arshṭishena[1], read : **Ā**°, and add : § 786 (Anugītāp.) : XIV, **91***a*, 2843.
Aruja, read **Ā**°.
Aruṇa[1], add : § 574*j* (Mālyavat) : VI, **7**, 285.—Dele **Aruṇa**[3] (cf. Varuṇa[4]), and insert : **Aruṇa**[3], a serpent : XVI, 119 (only B., C. has *Varuṇa*[3], q.v.).
Aruṇā[2], add : III, 7022 (see Ruṇā).
Aruṇānuja, add : IX, 301.
Arundhatī, add : cf. Akshamālā.
Aruṇī[2], read **Ā**°.
Arūpā, so B. for Anūpā, q.v.
Aryaman[2], add : VII, 21 (*vyāvṛtte 'ryamni*, B., C. has *'hani*).
Āsā (?) : III, 14451 (among the names of Devasenā).
Āshāḍha[4], read : **Ashāḍhā** (so B. always ; C. sometimes *Ā*°).
Ashṭaka, add : § 267 (Yamasabhāv.) : II, **8**, 333.—V, **122**, 4089. Cf. Kauçika, Mādhavīsuta, Vaiçvāmitra.

Ashṭamūrti = Çiva : III, 1939.
Ashṭaṅgavidyā ("medical science") : VIII, †4594 (only C.). Cf. II, 224 (*cikitsāyām ashṭaṅgāyāṁ*) and Āyurveda (II, 442).
Asi, a river. § 574 (Jambūkh.) : VI, **9**λ, 338 (*Varuṇām Asīṃ*, C., B. reads *Varāṇasīṃ*).
Asitasārathi = Arjuna : VII, 6197.
***Asta,** add : V, 3806 (*parvataḥ* (C. *sarvataḥ*)/°*o nāma*) ; IX, 827 (*çailāv Astodayāv iva*), and read IX, 1631 instead of 1651, and XI, 650 instead of X, 650.
Asti, daughter of Jarāsandha and wife of Kaṃsa. § 273 (Rājasūyārambhap.) : II, **14**, 595 (°*ḥ Prāptiç ca nāmnā te Sahadevānuje*).
Asura[1], add : I, 2750, 2795 ; III, 15341 (*surarahitaṃ*, read *surā*°) ; IV, 2176, 2206, 2271 ; V, 457, 2353, †2580 ; VI, 2990 ; VII, 454 ; XIII, 6624. Cf. Amaradvishaḥ, Amarāri, pl., devaçatru, pl., devāri, pl., devaripu, pl., suraçatru, pl., suradvish, pl., tridaçadvish, pl., tridaçāri, pl., vibudhadvish, pl.
Asura[2], add to the names of single Asuras :—

Açvagrīva : I, 2653.
Bala : II, 897.
Bāshkala : I, 2645.
Vṛshaparvan : I, 2651.
Vṛtra : I, 2541 ; VII, 3458 ; 3472 (only B.).

Āsura, adj., add : II, 12 (*abhiprāyān*), 2321 (*dharmasya*) ; VI, 1126 (*bhāvaṃ*), 1409 (*janāḥ*), 1422 (*yonim*), 5009 (*yuddhān*, read *vyūhān*) ; VII, 4646 (*camūṃ*), 6348.
Asurasūdana : XII, 3923, read XIII, 3923.
Asurāyaṇi, read **Ā**°, and add (B. has °*ṇah*).
Asurendra, add : V, 1073 (=Prahlāda).
Asuri, add : I, 6523.
Asūrya, add : (B. has *Asuryā*).
Āsyamodaka, name of a weapon. § 563 (Bhagavadyānāp.) : V, **96**φ, 3491.
Atapana, read Ā°.
Aṭavika, add (or Āṭavika) : II, 1119 ; III, 15255 (*sa-Mlecchā°ān*) ; VII, 2188 (*vasumatīṃ Mlecchā°-varjitāṃ*) ; XII, 2169.
Athida, read Aṭh°.
Ātithi(n), read A°.
Ātman[0], a son or form of Vivasvat : I, 42.
Atrisuta, add : (? *Nāsatya-Dasr'-Ātrisutodbhavādyaiḥ*, surgeons of Indra, only C.).
Aṭṭaçūlapraharaṇā, Aṭṭahāsā = Umā (Durgā), q.v.
Atula = Vishṇu (1000 names) [dele these words under **Atulya**].
Auçanasa, add : III, **285**, 16369 (*vyūhaṃ*) ; XIII, 5284 (read *Mārutauçanasaṃ* (?), B. has °*se*).
Auḍra (B. *Auṃḍrāḥ*, read *Oṃḍrāḥ*).
Audra (pl. °*aḥ*), add : (or Raudra, pl. °*āḥ*).
Aurva[2], adj. ("belonging to Aurva") ; I, 1242 (*vahniḥ*).
Aushija, add : I, 224 (only B.) (*K*°) ; II, 112.
Aushṇika (pl. °*āḥ*), a people. § 295 (Dyūtap.) : II, **51**, 1837.
Autaṅka, add : (B. Auttaṅka).
Autathya ("son of Utatha") = Dīrghatamas : I, 4182.
Āvantya : (*a*) II, 1915 (*Ā*°-*āḥ* . . . , read : *Ā*°*us* . . .) : II, 2206, add : (*Ā*°*au*, B.) ; IX, 72 (*A*°*o*, read : *Ā*°*o*) ;

—(β) add: VI, **47**ζ, 1851 (only B.), **49,** 2014/15 (do.);—(γ) IX, 93, add: (only C., B. *Ā°aḥ*); —(δ) add: § 556 (Sañjayayānap.): V, **30,** 889 (only C, B. has *Ambashṭhāḥ*).

Avikshit [2], add: § 767 (Ānuçāsanik.): XIII, **137**a, 6260 (*Marutto 'vikshitaḥ sutaḥ*). Cf. Kārandhama [2].

Avikshita, read: Āvikshita [1].

Āvikshita [2], adj.: XIV, 1882 (*dhanam*).

Avisthala, add: § 556 (Sañjayayānap.): V, **31,** 934 (only B., C. has *Kuçasthalam*).

Avṛhaka, dele this article, and see Bṛhaka (Vṛhaka).

Avṛtta: V, 3630, add: (*Saṃvṛtto Vṛtta eva ca*), cf. I, 1555 (see Vṛtta).

***Avyaya,** add: I, 1593 (*devaḥ* = Brahmán), 2430–32 (i.e. Nārāyaṇa), 2494 (*devam* = Brahmán); III, 8125 (*Vishṇum*), 10919 (*Vishṇuḥ*), 13556 (*Vishṇum*); V, 288 (do.), 3502 (= Brahmán), 4503 (*Vishṇuḥ*); VI, 1182 (*bhūtādim* = Kṛshṇa), 3000 (*Vāsudevam*); VII, 9578 (*Brahmāṇam*).

Ayati and **Āyāti.** § 136 (Yayātyup.), read: § 143 (Nahusha).

Ayavāha, pl., see Apavāha, pl. above.

Ayobhuja, son of Dhṛtarāshṭra. § 600 (Ghaṭotkacavadhap.): VII, **157**o, 6938 (slain by Bhīma). Cf. Ayobāhu.

Āyu(s), add: § 142 (Nahusha): I, **75,** 3151 (*Āyusho Nahushaḥ putraḥ*); III, **180,** 12461 (*Āyoḥ putraḥ*, i.e. Nahusha).

B

Babhru [1], add: § 589 (Droṇābhishekap.): VII, **11**ξ, 409.

Babhru [6]. a Kāçi prince. § 556 (Sañjayayānap.); V, **28,** †806 (*Kāçyaḥ*, attained to prosperity through the favour of Kṛshṇa).

Babhru [7]. § 561 (Yānasandhip.): V, **57**o, 2264 (in the army of Yudhishṭhira).

Badarī. § 333b (Arjunap.), read (Arjuna [2]).

Badhirāndha, add: (only C., B. reads *Badhirāndhau*, i.e. Badhira and Andha).

Bahirgiri (C.) or **Bahirgirya** (B.), name of a country or its people. § 574 (Jambūkh.): VI, **9**μ, 357.

Bāhuli, son of Viçvāmitra. § 721b (Viçvāmitrop.): XIII, **4**β, 252 (only C., B. has *Vāduliḥ*).

Bahurūpa, add: Do.[2], a Rudra. § 665 (Mokshadh.): XII, **208**δ, 7585.

Bahuvadyāḥ, read **Bahuvādyāḥ,** v. Bāhubādhāḥ.

Bahuvedya, read **Bahuvidya.**

Baka [5], add: (B. reads *Vyukāḥ*).

Bakanakha, add. (C. has by error *Vakanakaḥ*).

Bala [1], add: VI, 1714 (only B.); VII, 5507 (do., C. reads *badhāya*); VIII, †3869 (*yathā Marutvān °bhedane purā*), †4963 (only B., C. has *Balim*).

Bala [9], read = Çiva (1000 names [2]).

Bālabhadrāḥ, add: (B. reads *Bala°*).

Balabhedana, dele this article (cf. Bala [1] above).

Balabhid, add: I, †1586; III, 10716, 14447, 14583; V, †820; VII, †8210 (only B., C. has *Balajit*).

[**Baladevatīrthayātrā**], in (IX, **43**) the words "D. and Dā., Dai., and a Rā., named *Tāraka*" ought to be corrected into: D. and Dā., Dai., and Rā., named after the Asura *Tāraka*.

Balāhaka [2], add: § 562 (Bhagavadyānap.): V, **83,** 2938.

Balajit = Indra: VII, †8210 (only C., B. has *Balabhid*).

Balāka, add: § 641 (Rājadh.): XII, **109,** 4029 (*°o 'ndhavadhād iva*).

Balanisūdana, add: (B. always *Balanishūdana*).

Bala-Rāma, add: I, **207,** 7595 (R.)—[§ 611 (Çalyap.): IX, **12,** 598 (R., *Yadunandanāt*)].—IX, **35,** 1988 (B.D.); **52,** 3004 (Hal.); **55,** 3106 (R.); **60,** 3348 (B.D., only B.).—Dele: V, 2197; VIII, 1952.—(Cf. also the following synonyms: Bala, Balabhadra, Baladeva, Çauri, Halabhṛt, Haladhara, Halāyudha, Halin, Keçavāgraja, Keçavapūrvaja, Lāṅgaladhārin, Lāṅgaladhvaja, Lāṅgalin, Mādhava, Mādhavottama, Madhupravīra, Mushalāyudha, Nīlavāsas, Pralambahan, Rāma,[2] Rauhiṇeya, Rohiṇinandana, Rohiṇīsuta, Saṅkarshaṇa, Sarvalokeçvara, Sātvata, Sīrabhṛt, Sita, Tāladhvaja, Tālaketu, Vanamālin, Vārshṇeya, Vāsudeva, Vṛshṇipravara, Vṛshṇivīra (dual), Yādava (dual), Yaduçreshṭha, Yadunandana, Yadupravīra (sg. and dual), Yadusiṃha, Yaduvara (dual).

***Bala-Vṛtra-han,** add: III, 2120, 2233, 9992, 9996; V, 3671, 3681; XIV, 167 (only C., B. has *Balasūdanaḥ*).

Bālhī, a country. § 295 (Dyūtap.): II, **51,** 1846 (*°-Cīnasamudbhavam*, only B.).

Bālhika [3], add: § 232 (Svayaṃvarap.): I, **186,** 7001.

Bālhika [7], add: VI, 354; VIII, 2762 (B. *Vāhīkān*).

Bālhika [8], add: I, 2667 (*Prahlādo nāma*).

Bālhika-puṅgava, add: (B. reads *Vāhika-°*).

Bali [1], XI, 646 (add: B. reads *tv Ahinā yathā*).

Balina, I, 2679 (read: *Asurottamaḥ*, B. has *Balīvīra iti . . . Asurottamaḥ*).

Ballavāḥ, see also Vallabha, pl.

Bandin, (*V°*, C.), name of a sūta: III, 10612 (cf. I, 450).

Bārhaspatya, add: § 640 (Rājadharm.): XII, **56,** 2023/24 (*çāstre*, only B.).

Bhadrā [2], add: § 270 (Brahmasabhāv.): II, **11,** 458.

Bhadrā [3], add: (probably identical with Bhadrā [6]).

Bhadramanas, . . . Krodha, read Krodhavaçā.

Bhadravaṭa, add: § 358 (Tīrthayātrāp.): III, **82,** 4092 (only B., C. has *Rudravaṭam*).

Bhagadatta, add: V, †5531 (only C.); VI, 3532 (only B., C. has *Somadattaḥ*); 3855 (only C., B. has *Prāgjyotishād*); 4294; 5280/81 (only B.). Cf. the synonyms Mleccha, Parvatapati, Parvateçvara, Prāgjyotisha, Prāgjyotishādhipa, Prāgjyotishapati, Yavanādhipa.

Bhaganetrahan: II, 420, read 402.

[**Bhagavadgītāparvan**]: VI, **19,** (*çucimukha*), read (*sūcimukha*).

Bhaima (pl. patron.), add: (or adj. = relating to Bhīma).

Bhaimaseni [2], add: I, 6081/82 (only B.).

Bhaimi, add: VII, 8016 (only B., C. has *Bhīmam*).

Bhānu [2]: I, 42 (add: a son or form of Vivasvat, cf. Āçāvaha); dele XVIII, 162.—Do.[5] (a man), read: (a Vṛshṇi prince); add: § 511 (Draupadī-Satyabhāmās.): III, **235,** 14735.—§ 795 (Svargārohaṇap.): XVIII, **5**μ, 162.

Bhānudatta, one of five brothers of Çakuni. § 600 (Ghaṭotkacavadhap.): VII, **157**π, 6944/45 (in a half-çloka wanting in C.).

Bhānumat [2], add: VI, **53** [6], 2230 (*Bhānumantam*, B., C. has *Kāliṅgam*).

Bharadvāja [1], add: III, (10740), (10781); XII, 2094 (only B., C. has *Bhā°*).

Bhāradvāja [4], add: VI, 3597; VII, 3988, 7678; XII, 2094 (*Bha°*, B.).

Bharata [1], add: § 409 (Plakshāvataraṇag.): III, **129,** 10527 (performed a horse-sacrifice).

Bharata [4], add: V, 2596, 2736, 2781, 5652/53 (B.); VI, 5381/82 (B.); VII, 7696 (B.).
Bhārata [1], add: V, 5780 (°*yuddhasya*); VII, 1725 (°*sainyānām*).
Bhārata [3], add: VII, 7657 (°*ī camūḥ*, only B.), 8793 (sc. *mārgam*).
Bhārata [4-17], add: [the list of quotations is not quite complete, the name is also occasionally (wrongly) applied to other persons: VI, 2508 (C. = Sañjaya), 2509 (only B. do.), 4584 (only C., B. has *Sañjaya*)].
Bhārata [18], add: I, 100/01 (only B.); VI, 1532/33 (do.); XVIII, 192/93 (do., *mahat*); 211/12 (°*kathām*) only B.).
Bhārata [20] (= *Bha°varsha*, read: *Bhā°varsha*).
Bharataçreshṭha [1-10] (not quite complete), add: [wrongly applied to Kṛshṇa, XI, 481/82 (B.)].
Bharatarshabha [1-10] (not quite complete), add: (5) Dhṛshṭadyumna: VI, 2066 (only C., B. has *purusharshabha*).—Dele (7) Droṇa and add to (8) Duryodhana: VII, 684.—Wrongly applied to Karṇa: VIII, 1690 (only C.).
Bharatarshabhau, add: = Bhīshma and Arjuna: IV, 2057; = Bhīma and Arjuna: VI, 5298, 5301.
Bhāratasattama, add: = Yudhishṭhira: VII, 7270 (B. has *Bha°*).
Bhārgava [2], add: III, 10441 (= Bhṛgunandana [1]).
Bhārgava [4], add: III, 10374; IV, 550 read: IV, 650.
Bhārgava [8], add: (but read with B. *Bhārgavam* = Vipula).
Bhārgava [11], dele: I, 3175; III, 220 (add: (?) PCR. Uçanas); V, 1475 (add: PCR. Uçanas); add 7059, 7320; XII, 2086 (add: probably = Vālmīki, cf. Hopkins: Great Epic, p. 61).
Bhārgava [13], add: III, 10648.
Bhārgavanandana [3] = Çunaka: I, 940/41 (only B.).
***Bhāskara** [1], add: III, 200 (B.); VI, 3831; VII, 7546 (B.); VIII, †4809 (only C.); XII, 2577/78 (by error wanting in C.).
Bhauma [1], add: V, †2421 (°*sya hantā . . . Vāsudevaḥ*).
Bhaumana, add: V, †4816.
Bhīma [5] = Çiva, q.v.; dele (1000 names [2]).
Bhīma [6], add: II, (2251) (Bh.); III, 11820 (Bhs.), 12459 (Bhs.); IV, (641) (Bhs.), 712 (Bhs., only C.); VI, 1650 (Bhs., only B.), 3345 (Bhs.), 3563 (Bh., read with B. *Bhīshmam*), 5184 to be inserted after **111,** 5183; VIII, 2202–3 (Bh.).

Add to the synonyms:—
Anilātmaja: I, 6240; VIII, 3820.—**Anilaprabhava** (do.): III, †14745.
Bhārata, etc. (q.v.).
Dhanañjayāgraja (q.v.).
Māruti: VIII, 2435.—**Marutsuta** (q.v.).
Somavamçiya (q.v.).
Vātātmaja, Vāyutanaya (q.v.).
Vṛkodara: I, 2451, 4774, 5067/8 (only B.), 5520, 5902, 6279–80, 7113; II, 927, 929; III, 456, 542, 10841, †12357, 12434, 14936, 15750; V, 2061 2179, 2183, 2261; VI, 2827 (only B.), 3361 (do.), 4205 (do.); VII, 1154, 7207 (only B.), 7161/2 (do.): VIII, 3301, †4215.

Bhīma [10], add: III, 2655, 2758–59.—Cf. Vidarbha, Vidarbhādhipati, Vidarbhapati, Vidarbharāja.
Bhīmā [2], add: § 494 (Āṅgirasa): III, **222,** 14232.
Bhīmapūrvaja, add: V, 4689.
Bhīmasenānuja = Arjuna (q.v.)
Bhīṇī, add: (B. reads *Bhītī*).
Bhīshma, add to the synonyms:—

Āpagāsuta: IV, 1985.
Āpageya: I, †181; II, 1340, 1785; V, 5314, 6085, 6092, 7311; VII, 436; VIII, 18; XII, 1907, XIII, 588, 614.
Bharatasiṃha (q.v.).
Gāṅgeya: V, 7389; VI, 1958 (only B.), 2027/8 (do.), 2348 (do.), 4849 (do.), 4994; VII, 5648 (only B.); VIII, 30, 34.
Kauravāgrya, Kurusiṃha (q.v.).
Mahānadīsuta, Nadīsuta, Nimnagāsuta (q.v.).
Pitāmaha, read ***Pitāmaha** (only selected passages).
Sāgaragāsuta, Saridvarāsuta, Sarvakurūttama (q.v.).
Tālaketu (q.v.).
Vasusambhava (q.v.).

Bhīshmaka [2], add: Cf. Bhoja [2], Dākshiṇātyapati, Hiraṇyaroman.
Bhīshmavadhaparvan, after the word "Universe" **(VI, 65)** add: (v. 2967–8, according to the reading of B.).—In (VI, **106**) instead of "*Bhīshma* and the *Sauvīras*" read: *Bhīshma* + the *Sauvīras* (otherwise PCR.).—In (VI, **119**) instead of "the *Sauvīras*, etc. (*aa*), abandoned" read: did not abandon.
Bhītī, v. Bhīṇī.
Bhoja, pl. add: § 317 (Arjunābhigamanap.): III, **12,** 461.—§ 576 (Bhagavadgītāp.): VI, **20,** 753.—§ 608 (Karṇap.): VIII, **73,** 3650.
Bhoja [1], add: § 580 (do.): VI, **57**ι, 2452 (only B.).
Bhoja [2], *Dākshiṇapateḥ*, read: *Dākshiṇātyapateḥ*.
Bhoja [3] **Mārtikāvata**, read: **Mārtikavatika** (B. °*taka*). After "descendant of Mahābhoja" add: BR.).
Bhoja [4], add: VII, 5857 (*K°*); dele in XII: 3037 (?) (*Akrūra° prabhavāḥ*).
Bhoja [5] = Kaṃsa: II, 1544 (°*sya purushe*, i.e. Kṛshṇa).
Bhoja [6] = Ugrasena: XII, 3037 (*Akrūra°prabhavā*, scil. *āpad*).
Bhojyā = Rukmiṇī: III, 490.
Bhṛgu [1], I, 901, read **6,** 901: add: § 581 (Bhīshmavadhap.): VI, **68**ρ, 3039 (only B.); Cf. Prajāpatisuta, Vāruṇa,
Bhṛgūdvaha [7], read XIII, 2317.
Bhṛgunandana [3] = Cyavana, dele q.v., add: I, 900 (according to the reading of B.); XIII, 2659, 2673, 2758, 2776, 2787, 2802, 2843, 2864, 2866, 2903.
Bhṛgunandana [7] = Kuru, read Ruru.
Bhṛgusuta, add: Do.[2] = Cyavana: III, 10369.
Bhṛgūttama [2], add: VII, 5412/13 (°*dhanurdharaḥ*, so B. in a verse wanting in C.).
Bhujagendrāri = Garuḍa: V, 3858.
Bhujiṅga, pl. (°*āḥ*), a people. § 574 (Jambūkh.): VI, **9**μ, 349 (B. *Kaliṅgāḥ*).
Bhūliṅga, add: a species of bird. § 290 (Çiçupālavadhap.) II, **41,** 1450 (*prakṛtim yānti bhūtāni °-çakunir yathā*).
Bhumanyu [3], v. Sumanyu [1].
***Bhūmi**, add: I, 2496 foll. Cf. Jagatī, Kāçyapī, Medinī, Pṛthivī, Urvī.
Bhūmipati, add: Cf. I, 2499 (= Brahmán, q.v.).
Bhūrbhuva(s), a devarshi (?): XIII, **107,** 5285 (°*aç cāpi devarshim viçvarūpam*, B. has °*am*; perhaps Çiva is meant, cf. *bhūrbhuvam devam*. VII, **202,** 9502).

Bhūriçravas, add: § 555 (Sainyodyogap.): V, **19δ,** 585 (came to Duryodhana with one akshauhiṇī of troops).—VI, **84,** 3432, read 3732.

Add to the synonyms:—

Saumadatti, Somadattasuta, Yūpadhvaja, q.v. (cf. VII, 5933, 5950, where he is called *yajñaçīla*).

Bhūshika, v. Mūshika.
Bhūta, read Çiva (1000 names [1]).
***Bhūta,** pl., IX, 2442, read 2472: XII, 652, read 655.
Bhūtabhāvana [3] = Agni: I, 928.—Do.[4] = Kṛshṇa: III, 513, 11175; VI, 1219.
Bhūtabhavishyakṛt = Kṛshṇa: VIII, 3753.
Bhūta-bhavya-bhavan-nātha, add: = Kṛshṇa, II, 1214.
Bhūta-bhavyeça, add: = Çiva, VII, 9589; VIII, 1456.
Bhūtāçraya, Bhūtādi = Sūrya, q.v.
Bhūtādi, add: = Kṛshṇa, VI, 1182.
Bhūtagrāma (etc.), read: (1000 names [1]).
Bhūtakṛt [1], add: I, 2501; II, 1320; XII, 4466.—Do.[3], add: III, 12823.—Do.[5] = Indra: III, 17192.
Bhūtamaheçvara, add: (1000 names).—Do.[2] = Kṛshṇa: VI, 1180.
Bhūtamātarah (pl.). § 310*b* (Sūrya): III, **3,** 199 (= Gaurī, etc. [Nīl.]).
Bhūtapati [1], add: I, 1583 (= Brahmán); III, 153 (= Sūrya); XIV, 1177 (= Agni).
***Bhūtātman** [3] (only selected passages).
Bhūteça [1], add: V, 7379.—Do.[2], add: III, 513.—Do.[4] = Brahmán: I, 7679.
Bhūti [2], a son of Viçvāmitra: XIII, 256 (only B., C. has *Sūtiḥ*).—Do.[3-4], personif. = Çrī (Lakshmī): XII, 8354; = Umā (Durgā): VI, 808 (°*r bhūtimatām*).
Bhuvaḥ [1-2], read **Bhuvas.**
Bhuvaneçvara [1], add: VII, 9503, 9505, 9529, 9561, 9586, 9624. —Do.[4] = Indra: V, 3667.—Do.[5] = Vishṇu: III, 13499.
Bindu, read (1000 names [1-2]).
Brāhma, adj. (read: "belonging to Brahmán, or Bráhman, or to bráhman [i.e. the Brahman caste]").—Add: I, 3238 (*māyām*), 7218 (*parigrahena*); II, 476 (*çriyā*); III, 10179 (*lakshmyā*); V, 1570 (*yonim*); 1619 (*çrīḥ*), †1768 (fem. *brāhmī*, scil. *vṛtti* ?), †1782 (do.), 2979 (*çriyā*); VI, 950 (*sthitiḥ*); VII, 271 (*daive*); VIII, 1098 (neutr. °*am*, i.e. sacred knowledge); IX, 2799 (*rūpam*); XII, 5413 (*vidhinā*); XIII, 438 (°*āçramapade*), 634 (*lakshmyā*), 2147 (*çrīḥ*), 2150 (*çriyā*), 2168 (neutr. °*am*), 2178 (*durvasatīḥ*), †4886 (*vācam*), †4913 (*vratam*); XV, 517 (*rajanī*), 722 (*vapushā*), 734 (*çriyam*).
Brahmabhavana, add: III, 12832.
Brahmacāriṇī = Umā (Durgā): IV, 184.
Brahmacarya = Çiva (1000 names [1]).
***Brahmaçāpa,** add: § 717*c* (Uparicara): XII, **337,** 12814.
***Brahmadaṇḍa:** VII, 8767, read 8766; add: XII, 1440, 3820; XIII, 4506. Cf. Brahmaçapa, read °çāpa.
Brahmadeva, a Pāṇḍava warrior: V, **196,** 7646 (only B., v. Kshatrahan).
Brahmaguhā: XIII, 7370 (read: *pravishṭo . . . Bhāratāgre*).
Brahmaloka, add: IX, **12,** 635 (°*parāḥ*).
Brahmán [1], add: § 494 (Āṅgirasa): III, **222,** 14235 (°-*ṇo mānasāḥ prajāḥ*).—§ 552*m*, read: § 552*d*.—§ 561, read: § 561*d* (Nara-Nārāyaṇau).—§ 641, add: XII, **121,** 4457, 4463.—XII, **337,** 12742, read: 12772.—§ 774 (Ānuçāsanik.): XIII, **163,** 7564 (*B°aḥ putram Dharmam āhur*, B.; *brāhmaṇāḥ putra*, C.).

Add to the synonyms:—

Haṃsa, q.v.
Jalajakusumayoni, q.v.
Kamalāsana: III, 4067.
Lokapitāmaha, add: III, 15821.
Paramātman, q.v.
Pitāmaha, add: I, 8159 (only B.); III, 4067, 5028, 8672, 10961, 16632, 16634; VI, 419, 3023 (only B.); VII, 2085 (only C.), 9587; VIII, 1397, 1401, 1418, 1429, 1430, 1623; XII, †13640; XIII, (6113) (only B.).
Prapitāmaha, VII, 1626, read: VIII, 1626.
Sarvalokapitāmaha, add: III, 12989; VIII, 1398.

Bráhman, add: I, 6317 (*param*), 8424 (*vyāhṛtam*); III, 1344 (= the Vedas), ††10639 (*advaitam*), 11240 (*paramakam*), 12530; V, 1713; VI, 2951 (*anantavidita*°, scil. Nārāyaṇa), 2978 (*param padam*); VII, 8860 (*om ity ekāksharam*); XII, 1897 (*sanātanam*), 6738 (°*vākyeshu*), 7264 (*ekāksharam*), 7770 (°*ṇo rūpam*), 8509 (°*ākshayam*), 8652 (*çabda*-°), 8799 (do.), 9257 (°*lakshaṇam*), 9630 (*om iti °ṇo yoniḥ*), 9689 (°*stenāḥ*), 11924 (*brahmavidām balam*), 12354 (°*çuçrūshave*), ††13214 (*utsādanam jagāma*), †13641 (°*mahānidhānam*, scil. Vyāsa); XIII, 121 (*sanātanam*), 376 (*yeshām °a param dhanam*), 876 (*param*), 1138, 5361 (°*jñāna*°), 6247 (*nirguṇam*).
Brāhmaṇagītā: instead of (XIV, **32-33**) read: (XIV, **32**). The brahman then described himself as emancipated, and said that his wife would enter his soul (XIV, **33**).
Brahmaṇaḥ sthāna(m), add: § 573 (Ambopākhyānap.): V, **186,** 7353 (a tīrtha).
Brahmaṇya [1], add: III, 14568.
***Brahmarshi** [1], pl., add: I, 1386; V, 466, †5032; VI, 2971, 3037.—Do.[2], add: **Paraçurāma:** V, 7069.—**Viçvāmitra:** XIII 246, add: (°*iḥ*, C., °*eḥ*, B., but read with PCR. *brahmarshim*).—Do.[3], dual = Yāja and Upayāja: I, 6362.
Brahmasama, adj.: VIII, 1577 (*naye*, scil. Çalya); 4510 (scil. Droṇa); XII, 2870 (*brāhmaṇāḥ*), 2877 (do.).
Brahmayajña, add: VII, 8236 (°*vināçanāḥ*, said of Rākshasas).
Brāhmya, adj.: VII, 344, read 343; XIII, 6619 (°*m mārgam*).
Bṛhadbala [4], add from B. VI, 1851, 2014/15. Cf. Kausalendra, read: Kosalendra [2].
Bṛhadbhānu [4], the first son of Heaven: I, 42 (cf. Āçāvaha).
Bṛhaddhvanī, a river: VI, 339 (only B., C. has Bṛhadvatī).
Bṛhaka (Vṛh°, C.), a Devagandharva: I, 4813.
Bṛhanta [3], add: VII, **23,** 1024 (C. *Bṛhantam tam aridhvajāḥ*, B. *Bṛhantam tam Araṭṭajāḥ*; but that here is alluded to Yuyutsu (cf. VII, **43**) seems to be confirmed by the reading of the southern texts: *Yuyutsum makaradhvajam*).
Bṛhanta [5], add: § 573 (Ambop.): V, **196,** 7629.
Bṛhaspati, add: III, **32,** 1262 (*nītim B°-proktām*); XII, 12765. Cf. also Devācārya, Devadeva, Devaguru, Devapurohita, Devarshi, Suraguru.
Bṛhat [1] (*bṛhadbhānuḥ* of the text ought probably to have been taken as one name, cf. above).
Bṛhatkshattra [1-4] (B. more correctly °*kshatra*).
Bṛhatkshattra [2], instead of *Naishadam* read *Naishadham*.
Bṛhatkshattra [3], father of Jayadratha, otherwise named

Vṛddhakshatra (q.v.): VI, **47**ζ, 1851 (°*sya dāyādaḥ*, only B.), 2014/15 (do. do.).
Bṛhatkshattra[4] (B. *Vṛddhakshatra*), a Paurava prince. § 603 (Nārāyaṇāstramokshap.): VII, **200**γγ, 9330; **201**, 9400 (slain).
Bṛhatvan (?), see *satvāvṛhattvā*.
Bṛṃhitā (C. Bṛṃhilā, read Vṛṃhilā).
Buddhi, add: § 717*b* (Nārāyaṇīya): XII, **350**, 13658 foll.
Budha, add: Cf. Çaçija, Graha.

C

Caitra, add: § 641 (Rājadh.): XII, **69**, 2642 (*māsi*).
Caitrī: XII, 3691 (. . . *senayogaḥ*, read *senāyogaḥ*).
Cakradhara, add: Do.[2] = Kṛshṇa, q.v.
Cakramaṇḍa, dele the words: issued from the mouth of Balarāma.
Cakravyūha, add: § 596 (Pratijñāp.): VII, **72**, 2497.
Cakshurvardhanikā, add: cf. XIII, 7648 (*Vaṅkshur Mandākinī*, C., *Cakshur Mandākinī*, B.).
Cākshushā, read **Cākshushī** . . . § 221*b*, read §221*c*.
Caṇḍakauçika, add: cf. Kauçika.
***Cāṇḍāla**[1], add: XIII, **48**, 2586 (the son of a *C.* with a Māgadhī becomes a Pukkasa). Instead of XIII, 2613 read 2621.
Cāṇḍālikāçrama (B. *Āñjalikā*°), read (*Añjalikā*°).
Candanāṅgadin = Vishṇu (1000 names).
Candramaso hrada(ḥ), a lake. § 574 (Jambūkh.): VI, **6**, 224 (*hrade candramasaḥ*).
Candramauli = Çiva: VII, †9455 (only B.).
Caṇūra[1-2], correct into **Cāṇūra.**
Cārucitra, add: VI, **79**, 3470/71 (only B.).
Cārumatsya, var. lect. in B. for Amatsyāçin (q.v.).
Cāsavaktra, add: B. has (more correctly) *Cāsha*°.
Caturbāhu, add: Do.[2] = Çiva: XII, 6166.
Caturbhuja[2], add: III, 15933; V, 3666; XIV, 1531; XVI, 282.
Cedi, pl., add: VI, 2240 (only B.); VIII, 3967 (do.).
Chandas[2], instead of (1000 names) read XIII, 6949.
Cibuka, pl. (°*āḥ*), a people (so B. for Civuka, q.v.).
Cīraka, var. lect. in B. for Cīnaka (q.v.).
Citrā[2], an Apsaras: XIII, 1424 (only B., C. has *Mitrā*).
Citrabarha: **101**β, 3597, read V, **101**β, 3597.
Citrabarhin, add: § 748*b* (Tārakavadhop.): XIII, **80**β, 4206 (read: *Suparṇo 'sya dadau putraṃ mayūraṃ C°inaṃ*).
Citradarçana, son of Dhṛtarāshṭra (?): VI, **79**, 3470/71 (only B.).
Citrāṅga, add: VI, **79**, 3470/71 (only B.).
Citrāṅgada[1], add: Cf. Çāntanava, Kurumukhya, Kurusattama.
Citraratha[4], add: (v. Aṅga[1], pl.).
Citrasena[1], add: VI, 3436 (only B., C. by error has *Durjayo'tha*); 3470/71 (only B.); 5193 (do. instead of *citrahasto*, C.).
Citravāhana, add: I, **217**, 7884 (in some verses wanting in C.).
Cola[1], add: II, **27**, 1029 (only B., *Sumālān*, C.); VI, **50**π, 2084 (*Colāḥ Pāṇḍyāç ca*, B., *Pāṇḍyāç coḍhrāç ca*, C.).

Ç

Çacī: III, 10141 (°*sahayaṃ* read: °*sahāyaṃ*; III, 12003 (°*sahayaḥ*), read: (°*sahāyaḥ*).
Paulomī, add: X, 599 (°*īm iva Maghavān*).

Çāçabindava[1], add: XII, 999 (only B., C. has *Çaçabindavaḥ*).
Çaçāṅka[1], add: VIII, 3392.
Çaibya[1], add: I, 224 bis (B. has *Çvaityāya*).
Çailarājasutā[1]: add: XIII, 6771 (so C., but B. has °-*āṃ devīṃ* = Umā).
Çaka, pl., add: § 578 (Bhīshmavadhap.): VI, **51***v*, 2106 (only B., C. has *Vṛkaiḥ*).
Çākhāmṛgadhvaja ("having a monkey in his banner") = Arjuna: VII, 5802.
Çakrānuja ("younger brother of Indra") = Vishṇu (Kṛshṇa): VII, 6458/59 (only B.).
Çaktidhṛk = Skanda: III, 14383.
Çaktipāṇi = Skanda: V, 5720.
Çaktreḥ putraḥ and **Çāktreya**, read (B. Çakteḥ and Çakteya).
Çakuni, add from B. VI, 2145 (C. has *Vikarṇaḥ*); VII, 7707; IX, 1503.
Çala[2], add: VI, 1652 (only B.).—Do.[3], add: V, 5574–75 (only B.); VI, 2145 (only C., B. has *Çalyaḥ*).
Çālāvṛka, pl. (°*āḥ*), a class of brahmans. § 635 (Rājadh.): XII, **33**, 1188.
Çalu, add: (only C., B. has *Khalu*).
Çalya, add: § 241 (Vidurāgamanap.): I, **200**, 7367 (*Madrarājaṃ*).—V, **161**, 5547 (= 5529), read: 5547, 5574 (= 5529).—VI, **52**, 2145 (only B., C. has *Çaluḥ*), 2148 (only B.); **57**ι, 2452 (only B.).
Çambara, add: IX, **16**, 828 (only B.).
Çambhu[4], add: II, 2574 (instructed Yudhishṭhira).
Çaṅkhacakragadāpāṇi, Çaṅkhacakrāsipāṇi = Kṛshṇa, q.v.
Çāntanu, add. Cf. Kaurava, Paurava, Pauravanandana, Prātipeya, Satyavāc.
Çāradaṇḍāyani, add: (B. °*āyinī*).
Çarmishṭhā, add to the synonyms:—
Daityakanyā: I, 3410.
[**Çārṅgacakragadāpāṇi**, etc., delendum.]
Çaryāti: XIV, **9**, 249, add: (C. has by error *Saryāti*°).
Çatalocana[2] = Indra. VIII, 4445.
Çatānīka[1], add to the synonyms:—
Kaurava, Pāñcāleya, q.v.
Çatānīka[4], add: VII, **158**χ, 7011 (only B.).
Çataparvā: V, 3972 (. . . *Ç°āyāṃ*, read *Ç°ayā* (B. *Ç°aṇā*)).
Çatruñjaya[4], add: Cf. Suvīrarāshṭrapa.
Çauṇḍika, add. (C. has by error *Çauṇḍīkāḥ*).
Çesha: § 524, read § 524*c* (Vishṇu); add: XII, **340**, 12900 (=Saṅkarshaṇa, identified with *jīva* (Vishṇu)).—Cf. Ananta, add: Dharādhara, Nāga, pl., Pannaga, sg., Vasudhādhara.
Çibi[1]: IV, 1768 (. . . between Bhīshma and Arjuna, read: between Kṛpa and Arjuna).
Çibisūnu = Vṛshādarbha, read Vṛshādarbhi.
Çiçira[3], a mountain (in Himavat, PCR.): § 603*b* (Nārāyaṇa): VII, **201**, 9448 (*giriṃ*).
Çiçupāla, add to the synonyms:—
Sātvatīsuta, Sunītha, q.v.
Çiçupālavadhaparvan, section (*e*) read: that disguising himself he had, for the sake of the Kārūsha king, ravished the wife of his uncle (Vasudeva) *Bhadrā Vaiçālī*.
Çikhaṇḍin[1], add: VI, **59**, 2542 (only B.); VII, 368 (B. *Çaikhaṇḍinaṃ*).
Synonym: **Çikhandinī**, read: **Çikhaṇḍinī.**

Çini [2], pl., add: VII, 4470 (°*inām ṛshabham*); 5819 (°*inam*, read: *inām*).

Çinivṛshabha = Sātyaki, q.v.

Çitāçi (?), see Sītā [3].

Çiva, add to the synonyms:—

Ananta: XIII, 898 (only B.).

Bahurūpa: XIV, 205 (only B., C. *Vasurūpāya*).

Bhava: III, 788; VII, 9509 (only B.); XIII, 1312 (only B., C. *Haraḥ*), 7469 (only B.).

Bhuvaneçvara, q.v.

Candramauli: VII, †9455 (only B.).

Caturbāhu: XII, 6166.

Çarva: VII, 9584 (only B.); XIII, 7478 (only B.).

Gaura: VII, 2858.

Giriça: XII, 10422 (1000 names [1]).

Hara: IX, 1858/59 (only B.).

Kṛttivāsas: XII, †612.

Paçupati: I, 7884/85 (only B., *-eḥ sthānam*, sc. *Gokarṇam*).

Pūshṇo dantavināçana(ḥ): XIII, 6565 (B. °*nipātanaḥ*).

Rudra: III, 17478 (in some verses added in B.); VII, 1543 (only B.); VII, 2046 (do., C. *Haraḥ*); XIII, 5283 (°*devarshi-kanyābhiḥ*), insert here after 5283: (only C., read with B. *Raudram*), 5335; 7483 (*mahā-*, add: so C., read with B. *sarve 'marā Rudram jagmuḥ*),

Sarva: II, 1642 (B. *C*°, read *Ç*°); VII, 9565 (do.).—Add: III, 1628 (B. *Ç*°); XIII, 1120 (only B.), 1298 (B. *Ç*°), 1336 (do.), †1374 (do.), 1398 (do.), 6818 (do.); XIV, 208 (only B.).

Ugrāyudha: XII, 10676.

Vibudhaçreshṭha, Vibudheçvara, q.v.

Çivasahasranāmastotra(m): *Adhayaḥ*, read *Ādhayaḥ*; *Aditya*, read *Āditya*; *Bhuvaḥ*, read *Bhuvas*; *Ghaṇṭamālapriya*, read *Ghaṇṭā*°; *Huṃhuṃhuṃkārapāra*, read *Hūṃhūṃhūṃk*°; *Huṃhuṃkārapriya*, read *Hūṃhūṃk*°; *Kālapushpaphalaprada*, read *Kālapushpaphalapradā*; *Mūrtau hi te . . . sarvā vai devatā*, read *devatāḥ*; *Udbhidjāḥ*, read *Udbhijjāḥ* (B. and C. *Udbhijāḥ*); *Varātivarada*, read *Varātivaradā*; *Vishāgrapā*, read *Vishāgrapād* (B. also here *Vishāgnipā*).

Mahādevasahasranāmastotra: *Ahas*, read *Ahar*; *Paridhipatikhecara*, add: (Nīl. takes this as two separate names: *Paridhin* and *Patikhecara*); *Ushaṅga*, read *Ushaṅgu*; *Uttamaḥ sarvakarmānāṃ*, read *Utthānaḥ sarvakarmaṇāṃ*.

Çiva [4], add: = Vishṇu: XIII, 6953, 7013 (1000 names).

Çivakarṇī, add: (B. has *Mukhakarṇā*).

Çiveṇikā, see Sītā [3].

Çoṇa, add: cf. Mahāçoṇa.

Çraddhā [1], add: § 266 (Çakrasabhāv.); II, **7**, 300.

Çrīvatsa, add: III, 12933 (°*kṛtalakshaṇam*, do.), 12934 (°*dhārī*, do.), 13001 (°*vakshā Govindaḥ*); XII, 13326 (°*āṅkavibhūshaṇam*, i.e. Nārāyaṇa).

Çrutaçravas [3], a warrior in Yudhishṭhira's army. § 608 (Karṇap.): VIII, **75**, †3811 (attacked Açvatthāman; only C., B. has *çrutas tathā*).

Çrutakarman [1], add: cf. Sahadevasūnu, Sāhadevi.

Çṛgāla, add: (B. reads *Sṛgālaḥ*).

çṛṅgāṭaka, name of a vyūha: VI, 3863.

Çuci [1], °*ăshāḍa-*, read: °*-āshāḍha-* (passim).

Çūcī, see **Sūcī.**

Çuka [1], add: § 659 (Mokshadh.): XII, **177**, 6600 (*aho samyak °enoktaṃ*, a sentence of his is quoted). Cf. Dvaipāyanasuta, Kārshṇi.

Çukī, add: cf. Dāksheyī.

Çukra [1]: V, 3543 (*etac chāstraṃ* [read: *chastraṃ*] . . . *mahac Chukreṇa* [B. has *mahac cakreṇa*]).

Kāvya: IX, 2551, read: 2251.

Çunaḥçepha, add: cf. Ṛcīkatanaya, XII, 10759.

Çūra [8], pl. (°*āḥ*), add: VII, 798 (°*ābhīrāḥ*, only B., C. has *Çūdrā*°).

***Çvasana,** dele I, 1489, and add:

Çvasana [2], a nāga (Nīl. a yaksha). § 32 (Garuḍa): I, **46***a*, 1489.

Çveta [6], VI, 83 (. . . *pājvakaḥ* | read: *pāvakaḥ* |).

Çveta [8], add from B. VI, **47**, 1851; **48**, 1942, 1956 (*Bhīshmaṃ*, C. by error *Çvetam*); **49**, 2009.

Çveta [12], pl. (°*āḥ*), add: (cf. XII, †12705, 12804 (C. *drashṭāraḥ purushāḥ svetāḥ*, read with B. *dṛshṭā vaḥ purushāḥ çvetāḥ*), 12861, 13356).

Çvetagraha, VI, 3588 (°*am evoditaṃ*, read: *ivoditaṃ*, but B. reads *Çvetaṃ grahaṃ*).

D

Dāçaratha, adj., add: (Nīl. explains: "affording place for ten waggons").

Dāçārha, pl., add: V, 2889 (only B., C. has *Dāçārha*, i.e. Kṛshṇa).

Dāçārhaputraja: XI, 229, read 729; add: (is not to be read: *Dāçārhīputrajaṃ* ?).

Dāçārṇeça, VI, 2080 (only C., B. has *Dāçārṇakāḥ*).

Dāçasutā = Satyavatī: I, 7230/31 (only B.).

Dāçeyī, add: I, 4247.

Daçīvidarbha, *Ṛshīkā*, read *Ṛshikā*.

Daksha [1], add: cf. Deveça, Ka, Lokaguru, Lokapitāmaha.

Dāksheyī: XIII, 227, read 275.

Dākshiṇātya, adj.: XII, **199**, read III, **199**; add: XVI, 160 (*nṛpān*).

Dālbhya [2], add: (prob. name of the āçrama of Dālbhya, or perhaps we have to read *Dālbhyasya* instead of *Dālbhyaç ca*).

Dāmā, see Sudāmā.

Dāmin, read: name of a tīrtha and its saint: III, 5014–16.

Dānabhāri, pl. (°*ayaḥ*), a people. § 578 (Bhīshmavadhap.): VI, **50**π, 2084 (only B.).

Danadeçvara: II, 410, see: Dhanadeçvara.

Daṇḍapāṇi [1], add: III, 431 (*iva*).

Darada, pl., add: VII, 5242 (only B., C. has *Kāmbojānāṃ*).

Dasyu, pl., add: II, 527, 1054; III, 13070; IV, 704, 839, read V, 704, 838–39; V, †1877, 2564, 2719; VI, 456; VII, 2160, 2162, 2165, 2458, 4325, 4833; VIII, 2081; XIII, 7297 (°*hantā*).

Dauryodhana, add: VII, 12/13 (only B.), †8115; VIII, †4583; IX, 156 (only B.).

Devadeveça [4]: XII, 7742, read XIII, 7742.

***Devadūta** [1], add: XIII, 5936, (5947), 7210 (*Vāyuḥ*).

***Devakanyā,** add: I, 5076, 6612; III, 16175 (pl.); V, 354, 541 (pl.); XII, 6337 (°*sutaḥ*, i.e. Rājadharman); XIII, 5266 foll.—Sometimes only an appellation of an Apsaras: I, 7617; III, 15580.

Devamātṛ [1], add: XIII, †7387 (*A°*).
Devarāja [3], read **Devarāj** [3] = Vasishṭha: XIII, 6257 (*V°*).
Devasenāpati, add: IX, 2722; XIII, 4214.
Devavara [2], add: VI, †1277 (i.e. Kṛshṇa); XIII, 6812.
Devayānī: § 146 . . . *Sañjīvanī*, read *Sañjīvinī*; I, (3285), read (3286); add: 3305.
Devī [4], add: V, 3969 (B. has *Vedyām*, cf. Vedi [2]).
Devī [5] = Pṛthivī ("the Earth" personif.): I, 1941 (*P°*), 5128 (*Dharā*); II, 458 (?); VII, 1288, 8223 (*Dharām*); XI, 220; XII, 421 (*P°*), 1789 (*P°*), 11117 (Nīl.); XIII, 4096 (*P°*), 4653 (*P°*).
Dhanya = Vishṇu (1000 names). Dele: **Dhara** [4].
Dharma [1], add: I, 1940 (*vigrahavān iva*), 4919, 6500, 7302; II, 369 (*°pāçadharam*, scil. *Varuṇam*); IV, 2269 (*vigrahavān*); XII, 12878 (*°gṛhe*), 13247 (*Vṛshaḥ*), 13390 (*°asya gṛhe*); XVIII, 216 (*°āḥ*, pl., B. *°aḥ*). Cf. also Devadeva, Trivargamukhya, Yaksha.
Dharma [7] = Yudhishṭhira, q.v.
Dharmagupta, read **Dharmagup**.
***Dharmāraṇya**, add: XII, 13888 (*°am*, read *°āt* ?).
Dharmavid, read **Dharmaviduttama.**
Dharmavyādha, add: § 481 (do.): III, **210**, 13898.
Dhātrī ("mother, nurse") = Pṛthivī (personif.): XI, 215.
Dhātṛ, add: § 603 (Nārāyaṇāstramokshap.): VII, **202***cc*, 9597 (*Dhātā ca sa Vidhātā ca*, identified with Çiva).
Dhātu, read **Dhātu(r) uttama(ḥ).**
Dhaumya [1]: II, 2641 (*Nairṛtām*), read (*Nairṛtān*).
Dhenuka, pl., v. Laḍaka, pl.
Dhruva [11], a nakshatra: XIV, 1888 (cf. Anugītāparvan).
Dhṛshṭadyumna, add to the synonyms: **Drupadaputra, Drupadātmaja, Hutabhugjanman** (v. Additions), **Saumaki.**
Dhṛtarāshṭra [5], Vaicitravīryi, read Vaicitravīryin.
Dhūmapa, pl. (*°āḥ*) ("drinking smoke"), a class of beings: V, 3774; XII, 10280; XIII, †1372 (only B., C. has *Dṛshṭipāḥ*).
Dhūmaprāça, pl. (*°āḥ*) ("eating smoke"), do.: XIII, †646.
Dhūmorṇā, add: V, 3968 (only B., C. has *Ūrmilā*, q.v.).
Dīkshā = Skanda: III, 14643 (only B., C. has *Daksha*).
Dīnakṛt, read Dinakṛt.
Ditija, pl. add: V, **105***δ*, 3685.
Draupadī, in fine dele: cf. Madhusūdanī, and add: cf. Kauravarājapatnī, Mālinī [5], Pāvakātmajā.
Draupadija, read **°dija.**
Drāviḍa, pl., add: VII, 3379 (*kākavarṇā durācārāḥ strīlolāḥ kalahapriyāḥ*, only B.).
Droṇa [1], add to the synonyms:—

Çoṇāçva: VII, 954, 3266, 3426, 7213.
Kalaçottamasambhava (v. Additions). **Kumbhasambhava, Kumbhayoni** (q.v.).
Rukmavāhana (q.v.).

Droṇaputra, add: VII, 6892; VIII, 3029/30 (only B.).
Dṛçadvatī, see Dṛshadvatī.
Dṛshṭipa, pl.: XIII, †1372, add: (only C., B. has *Dhūmapāḥ*, v. additions).
Duḥsaha [1], IV, 1151, add: (B. has *Duḥçalaḥ*).
Durjaya [3], VI, 3436, add: (read with B. *Citrasenaḥ*).
Dushyanta [1], XIII, 7676, add: (C. has *Dushmantaḥ*). Cf. Paurava [4].
Dvārakā, add: cf. Ānartta-nagara and °purī (v. Ānartta [1]), Andhakapura (v. Andhaka [1]), Vṛshṇipura.
Dvijaketana ("who has a bird in his banner") = Kṛshṇa: VII, 2836.

E

Ekacandrā, so B. for Ekavaktrā (q.v.).
Ekakuṇḍalin ("having one ear-ring") = Balarāma: IX, 2132.
Ekalavyasuta, add: cf. Naishādi [2], Nishādarājan.

G

Gada, add: III, 8444 (C. *°ādayaḥ*, but read with B. *Gayādayaḥ*, v. Gaya [1]).
Gādhi(n), add: Cf. Kuçikanandana.
Gālava, pl., v. Mālava, pl.
Gajodara, add: (B. has *Ajodaraḥ*).
Gaṇḍakaṇḍa, read *Gaṇḍakaṇḍu* (B. *°ū*).
Gaṇḍakī: VI, 325, add: (B. has *Vandanā*).
Gāndhāra, pl. add: § 516*b* (Kṛshṇa Vāsudeva): V, **48**, †1882 (vanquished by Kṛshṇa).
Gandharva, pl., add: III, 4014 (*°mukhyān*), 10903; V, 5723 (read: *Gāndharva°*, adj. q.v.); VIII, 423 (only B.).
Gāndharva, ("music"), add: II, 143 (*yuddha g°-sevī*).
Gāṇḍivin, read **Gāṇḍivin.**
Gaṇeçvara, pl. ("lords of divine hosts"): IX, 2592; XII, 10308; XIII, 7102 (*sarvabhūta-°āḥ*), 7103 (*°-vināyakāḥ*).
Gaṅgā, add: Cf. also Trilokagā, Trilokapathagā.
Gardabhi, read **Gārdabhi** (so B., C. has by error *Garddhabhiḥ*).
Garuḍa [1], add: Cf. also Patagarāja, Patagendra, Patagottama Pataṅgarāja.
Gaya [1], add: II, 332 (only C., perhaps error for *Layaḥ*, B.); III, 8444 (*°ādayaḥ*, only B., C. by error *Gadā°*).—IV, 1768 (read: Kṛpa and Arjuna, instead of Bhīshma and Arjuna).
Gaya [4], son of Āyus. § 141 (Purūravas): I, **75**, 3150 (*rājiṅgayam*, C., but read with B. *Rajim Gayam*).
Gayā, add: XIII, 4888 (only B., C. has *Gaṅgām*).
Ghūrṇiā, read **Ghūrṇikā.**
Gokarṇā, add: (B. has *Gokarṇī*).
Gomatī, XIII, 6764, add: (B. has *Gautamī*, cf. v. 7647).
graha [1], add: I, 8283 (*sārkacandra-°*, adj.); II, 304 (*grahās tārāç ca*, B. probably more correctly: *grahā-stobhāç ca*, i.e. *grahāḥ stobhāç ca* [sacrificial rites ?]), 447; III, 13100; IV, 1322, 1763; V, †7; VI, 80 (sg. *mahā-°*), 94 (dual), 404 (read with B. *graham*, i.e. Rāhu), 2457 (only B., C. has *gṛhāḥ*), 3181 (do. do.), 3347 (*mahā-°*), 5209; VII, 6435, 7212 (read *grahaiḥ*), †7310 (sg., i.e. the sun), 7320; VIII, 589 (*°yuddham*), 2210, 3130, †3859, 4391 (dual), 4407 (do.).

do. (sg.) of special planets:—
Aṅgāraka: VIII, 711 (*A°*).
Çveta: VI, 3588 (*Çvetagraham*, C. *Çvetam graham*, B.).
Rāhu: VI, 86 (read 85), 95 (only B.), 404 (do.), 480 (read 481).

Guṇāvatī, a river. § 595 (Shoḍaçarāj. v. Rāma Jāmadagnya): VII, **70**, 2432 (in a passage inserted in B.).
Guru [1], add: I, 3224 (*°dehajaḥ*, i.e. Kaca).—Do.[2]: VII, 6302, 9073; VIII, †811 (*°oḥ sutāya*, i.e. Açvatthāman), †4510; XII, 50.

H

Haiḍimbasūnu, add: (C. has *Haiḍamba°*, B. *Haiḍimbi°*).
Hanūmat, add: Cf. Kesarin and the synonym Laṅkeçavanāri.
Harāhara, read: *Virūpāksho Harāharau?* (instead of *Virūpākshā*, etc.).
Hari [8], add: VII, 9323 (*vyasṛjat . . . vajraṃ Vṛtre yathā H°ḥ*).
Harivarsha, add: Cf. XII, 12228 (*Meror Hareç ca dve varshe*).
Hayaçiras, add: Cf. I, 6863 (*mahad dhayaçiro bhūtvā*, scil. the fire of Aurva's wrath).
Hayagrīva [3], add: Cf. Açvagrīva, Vājigrīva.
Hayarāja, add: = Hayarājan (C.); probably Keçin is meant, cf. Hariv. 3110, 3130, 4279 foll.
Hiḍimba, add: VII, **156,** 6841 (B. *°ānucaraiḥ saha*, C. by error *Haiḍimbo 'nucaraiḥ saha*).
Himādri = Himavat: VIII, †701 (*°kūṭa°*), †705 (do.).
Hiraṇyagarbha [4] = Skanda: III, 14407.
Hṛdika, add: VII, 4528 (*°syātmasambhavaḥ*, i.e. Kṛtavarman).
Hutabhugjanman ("arosen from fire") = Dhṛshṭadyumna: VII, 5279.

I

Īça [6] = Skanda: IX, 2721.
Īçvara [2], dele I, 6615 (*Gopatiṃ*).—Add: XIII, 792, 795, 797 (*parameçvarāt*, with incorrect sandhi, i.e. *parama īçvarāt*).
Īçvara [11] = Sūrya (the sun): I, 6615 (*Gopatiṃ*).
Ikshvāku [6], sg. = Bhagīratha: XII, 962 (= *Bh°*, only B., C. has *Aikshvākuṃ*).
Ilā [2], a river. § 434 (Saugandhikāharaṇa): III, **156,** 11437.
Indra, add: VI, 2000 (*Indraṃ*, C., *Aindraṃ*, B.); VII, 3786 (*°-Āgnyoḥ*); XII, 13802 (*°-ātikramaṃ cakre Māndhātā*).—

Synonyms:—
- **Akhaṇḍala,** read: Ākhaṇḍala.
- **Amararāj,** IV, 1573 (*Amararāṭ-samaṃ*, i.e. Arjuna).
- **Bhuvaneçvara,** q.v. (Additions).
- **Çakra,** I, 2822; VI, 3039 (only B., C. has *cakraṃ*), 4453 (only B., C. has *çatrūn*).
- **Çatalocana,** VIII, 4445.
- **Devādhipa,** XII, 3662.
- **Devarāj,** V, 5961.
- **Devarāja,** VII, 1174 (*Airāvatasthena*, only B.).
- **Hari,** VII, 9323 (*vyasṛjat . . . vajraṃ Vṛtre yathā H°ḥ*).
- **Lokādhipati,** q.v.
- **Maghavat,** VI, 4265 (only B., C. has *Bhagavān*).
- **Mahendra,** VI, †782 (so B. instead of *mahīndraṃ*, C.), 2000 (only B., C. by error *Upendra-°*).
- **Surarāj,** VII, †88.
- **Surottama,** XIII, 283 (B. *Surādhipa*).
- **Trailokyeça,** III, 13614.
- **Tridaçaçārdūla,** XIII, 569.
- **Tridaçādhipati,** dele VIII, †4647.
- **Tridaçapati,** VIII, †4647.
- **Vajrapāṇi,** VI, 1900 (only B., C. has *Cakrapāṇiḥ*).
- **Vibudhādhipa,** III, 11948.
- **Vibudhādhipati,** dele III, 11948.

Indrajāla, VI, 2633 (add: B. has *nihatendrakīlāḥ*).
Indrajit, add: I, 6081/82 (only B.).
Indraloka, add: cf. Surendraloka.
Indrasena [2], add: § 600 (Ghaṭotkacavadhap.): VII, **153,** 6630 (only B.).
Indrāstra ("the weapon of Indra"): VI, 2001 (only B., C. has *Aindrāstra*).
Irāmā, read **Īrāmā** (B. *Irāmā*).
Irāvat, add: VI, **95,** 9322. Cf. Nā rājasutāsuta, Phālguni.
Irāvatī, add: VIII, **44θ,** 2055 (*Ai[illegible]atī* both C. and B.).
itihāsa [1], add: I, 26, 54, 87, 309, 311, 648, [illegible]38, 1025, 2299, 2326–7, 3967, 4178; II, 2314; III, 1137, 3073, 3075, 3078, 15404; V, 1073, 1185, 1260, 3511, 3720, 4494; VII, 2126; VIII, 1581; XII, 305, 536, 615, 668, 744, 834, 905, 1293, 2536, 2750, 2780, 2810, 2888, 3025, 3059, 3183, 3464, 3795, 3848, 4084, 4197, 4254, 4469, 4534, 4567, 4629, 4718, 4851, 4930, 5124, 5249, 5330, 5593, 5600, 5676, 5800, 5804, 6293, 6464, 6523, 6563, 6589, 6640, 6654, 6693, 6769, 7151, 7156, 7199, 7366, 7642, 7652, 7882, 8023, 8059, 8187, 8217, 8335, 8431, 8483, 9277, 9467, 9482, 9560, 9600, 9756, 9874, 9916, 9929, 10533, 10555, 10613, 10993, 11220, 11545, 11839, 11854, 12484, 12648, 12656, 12819, 13720; XIII, 16, 87, 410, 529, 990, 1340, 1390, 1777, 1863, 1864, 1872, 2009, 2046, 2129, 2165, 2203, 2248, 2722, 3153, 3253, 3396, 3486, 3546, 3852, 3884, 3959, 4303, 4415, 4547, 4678, 4686, 4745, 4814, 4845, †4863, 4909, 5104, 5440, 5794, 5883, 7153, 7186; XIV, 599, 628, 655, 667, 684, 711, 728, 751, 793, 817, 839, 887, 935, 2849; XVIII, 183, 194, 200, 220.

J

Jagannātha [2], add: II, 779; III, 15529.
Jaguḍa, read **Jāguḍa.**
Jājñaseni (II, 2294; III, 10874), v. Yājñasenī.
Jalasandha [1 or 2], add: VI, 1926 (so B. instead of *Jārāsandhiḥ*).
Jaleçvari, a mātṛ. IX, 2631 (only B.).
Jāmbavatī, add: according to Hariv. 2072, 6701, a daughter of Jāmbavat.—Cf. Vidyādharendra(sya sutā).
Jambha [1], add: § 600 (Ghaṭotkacavadhap.): VII, **167,** 7485 (only B., C. has *Bali-°*).
Janaka, after (XIV, **32**) dele the foll. words: "who described himself as emancipated, and said that J. would enter his soul (XIV, **33**)."
Janamejaya [8], add: Cf. Somaka.
Jaṭālikā, add: (C. by error *Jāṭālikā*).
Jaya [1], add: § 580 (Bhīshmavadhap.): VI, **57ι,** 2452 (only B.) —Do.[8], add: (B. has *Jayāçvaṃ*).
Jayadratha [1], add from B.: VI, 1851, 2014/15; VII, 6456–57, 6474. Cf. also the synonym Varāhadhvaja.
Jayatsena [1], add from B.: VI, 1851, 2014–15.
Jeshṭhila, a tīrtha: III, **84,** 8112 (probably wrong reading in B. and C. for *Jyeshṭhila*, q.v.).
Jitaçatru, a ṛshi: II, 442 (so B. for Ajitaçatru, q.v.).
Jyotishka [2]: VII, **30,** 1315 (*uttamāstre*, . . . read: 1325 (*uttamāstreṇa*, only C., B. has *Jyautisheṇa*, . . .).

K

Ka [1], add: (cf. XII, 11752, 11764).
Kaca, add: cf. Guru (Additions above).
Kāçirāja [5], add: § 592 (Saṃçaptakavadhap.): VII, **23ο,** 987–88 (only B.).

Kāçisuta, read Kāçisutā.
Kāçya [2], in fine read Kāçipati [2], Kāçirāja [5].
Kaçyapa, add: III, 12955 (read so with B. instead of *Kā°*); XIII, 7237 (only B.).
Kāçyapa [1], III, 189, read III, **189**.
Kāçyapa, dual (°*au*), read = Yāja and Upayāja.
Kāçyapī, XIII, 7237 (only C., B. has *Kaçyapaḥ*).
Kadhmora, an ancient king: § 775 (Ānuçāsanik.): XIII, **166**η, 7678/79 (only B.).
Kaiçikī, III, 10095 (so C. by error instead of *Kauç°*).
Kaikaya, dele VI, 2695, etc.
Kaikeya, add: § 581 (Bhīshmavadhap.): VI, **61**ε, 2695 (attached by Dhṛshṭadyumna).
Kaikeya [1], add: VI, 1721 (read with B. *Gautamaṃ Kaikeyaḥ kruddhaḥ*).
Kaikeya [4], add: (B. has *Kekaya*).
Kākudika, read Kākudīka.
Kalā, pl., add: Do.[3] = Durgā (Umā): VI, 804.
Kalaçottamasambhava ("born from the excellent jar") = Droṇa: VII, 5019 (C. has *Kalaso°*).
Kālāgni, add: XII, 8305.
Kālakañja, IV, 1539 (*Dānavaḥ*), read: (*Dānavāḥ*).
Kālakūṭa [1], add: § 197 (Bhīmasena-rasapāna): I, **129,** 5067/68 (only B.).—§ 608 (Karṇap.): VIII, **83,** 4251 (all. to § 197).
Kali [1], § 773*b* (Kṛshṇa), read: XIII, **159,** 7363 (in the *K. yuga* Kṛshṇa is *adharma*, C. has *Kalavadharmaḥ* by error instead of *Kalāv adharmaḥ*; B. *Kalau tvadharmaḥ*).
Kālika, v. Pāṇika (additions).
Kālikeya, VII, 1933 (read: *Subaladāyādaṃ*).
Kaliṅga, pl., add: VI, 2300 (B. *Kā°*), 2314 (C. *Kā°*), 2335 (only B.); VII, 360 (only B.).
Kāliṅga [1], add: VI, 2230 (B. has *Bhānumantaṃ*); 2272/73 (only B.).
Kāliṅga, pl., add: VI, 2330 (B. *Ka°*), 2338 (do.), 3117 (C. *Ka°*); VII, 1854 (B. *Ka°*).
Kaliṅgaputra, ("son of the king of the Kaliṅgas"): VIII, †4328 (so B. probably better instead of *Kulindaputraḥ*).
Kāliṅgatanaya, (do. = Çakradeva): VI, 2258 (only B.).
Kalkin, § 460, read: § 460*c*.
Kalmāsha, a certain breed of horses: II, 1043, 1056, 1824, 2083; III, 4015; VI, 3107; VII, 958; XII, 4560. Cf. V, 2228.
kalpavṛksha, add: I, 7908.
Kāma [1], add: cf. Madana.
Kamalāsana ("having a lotus as seat") = Brahmán: III, 4067.
Kāmaṇḍa, Kāmaṇḍaka, read: Kāmanda, Kamandaka.
Kāmaratha: VII, 7012 (add: only C., B. has *Samarathaḥ*).
Kāmboja, pl.: VI, 2408 (only C., B. has *Kāmbojaḥ*, i.e. Sudakshiṇa); VII, 5242 (only C., B. has *Daradānāṃ*).
Kāmboja [1], add: VI, 1851 (only B.).
Kāmboja, adj., add: VIII, †200 (sc. horses).
Kaṃsa, add: Cf. Bhoja [5], Bhojarāja [1].
Kāñci, pl., I, 6684 (only C., B. has *kāṃçcit*).
Kānvaçira, v. Konvaçira.
Kapaṭa, add: I, 2665 (only B., C. has *Kratha*).
Kapāṭa, a city of the Pāṇḍyas (?). § 561*c* (Kṛshṇa): V, **48,** †1883 (according to a var. lect. mentioned by Nīl.: *ayaṃ Kapāṭe nijaghāna Pāṇḍyaṃ*; B.C. read *kapaṭena jaghāna*).—Cf. § 592 (Saṃçaptakavadhap.): VII, **23**ο, 1016 (*bhinne Kapāṭe Pāṇḍyānāṃ*, which Nīl. explains by *nagaraviçeshe*).
Kapiskandha, v. Pratiskandha.
Karandhama, add: § 775 (Ānuçāsanik.): XIII, **166**η, 7678/79 (only B.).
Karṇa [1], add: I, 7037 (read with B. *yat Karṇa-Çalya-pramukhaiḥ*); V, †35 (only B.); VII, 5304 (B. *Karṇaḥ samāplutya*), 7467 (B. *çaraiḥ Karṇaḥ* for *çitair bāṇaiḥ*); VIII, 333 (B. *Droṇe*), 1703 (only B.).
Ravitanaya, q.v.
Karṇa [2], add: § 600 (Ghaṭotkacavadhap.): VII, **164**θθ, 7337, (*Karṇañ ca*, B., C. has *Vikarṇaṃ*).
Kārṇaputra [1], add: VII, 7646 (only B.).
Karṇasuta [1], add: VIII, 3728/29 (only B.).
Kārshṇa, add: XVIII, 209/10 (only B.).
kāshṭhāḥ [2], add: Do. [4] = Durgā (Umā): VI, 804.
Kātyāyana, a ṛshi. § 795*c* (Mahābhārata): XVIII, **6**ξ, 216 (only B.: *muniḥ Kātyāyano varaḥ*, C. has *munibhiḥ kāyagocaraḥ*).
Kauçija, pl., add: (only C., B. has *Kosalāḥ*).
Kaulūtaka, adj. ("originating from the Kulūtas"): VII, 3897 (*hayāḥ*, only B., C. has *kulīnāç ca*).
Kaumāra, adj., add: § 11 (Parvasaṅgr.): I, **2,** 551 (°*am ākhyānam*, only B., referring to IX, **44** foll.).
Kaunteya [1], add: VI, 4654, 5620 (only B.); VII, 3873/74 (only B.); XII, 13179.—Do.[2]: VII, 5384 (only B.).—Do.[4]: I, 7884 (only B.); dele VI, 4654; VI, 4973 (only B.); VIII, 2357 (only B.); dele XII, 13179; XIII, 7721 (only B.).
Kaurava, pl., add: VII, 7061, †8155 (only C.).
Kauravya [1], add: III, 1528.
Kausalya [1], add: VI, 1851 (*B°*, only B.), 2014/15 (do. do.).—Do., pl.: VIII, 2226 (B. *Kosalaiḥ*).
Kāverakā, add: (only C., B. has *Çīveṇikā*).
Kavīndra [1] = Uçanas: XIII, 4690.—Do.[2] = Vyāsa: VI, 118.
***Kāvya** [3], adj. ("originating from Kavi [i.e. Çukra]"): V, 857 (*vācaṃ*, according to Nīl. = *Çaukraṃ*), 3327. Cf. II, 2097, 2117, 2197; V, 1262; XII, 4583 foll.
Kekaya, pl., add: VIII, 3395/96 (only B.).
Ketuvarman, so B. instead of Ketudharman (q.v.).
Ketumat [2]: VI, 2230 (*Naishādaṃ*, read *Naishādiṃ*).
Kevalī, add: (B. *Kevalā*).
Khaçira, read Khaçīra.
Khagapati = Garuḍa: V, 3888.
Khalu, see Çalu.
Khāṇḍava, add: § 595 (Shoḍaçarāj.): VII, **70,** 2432 (only B.).
Khara, add: § 539 (Kumbhakarṇādiv.): III, **287,** 16443 (only B.).
Kiṅkara [2] . . . § 345, read § 545; add: § 793 (Mausalap.): XVI, **1,** 26 (*musalaṃ °pratimaṃ*).
Kīrti, add: XII, 12919, 13536.
Koṇvaçira, read Konvaçira (B. Kānvaçira).
Kosala, pl., add: VI, 349 (only B.); VIII, 2226 (do.).
Koṭikāsya, add: Cf. Çaibya [6], Çibi, pl.
Koṭirā, a mātṛ: IX, 2632 (only C., B. has *Koṭarā*, q.v.).
krama, add: I, 2880 (*pada-°*), 2885 (°-*cikshā-viçāradaiḥ*); XII, 13527 (*Pañcālena kramaḥ prāptaḥ*).
Krauñca [1], add: VII, **134,** 5529 (*Krauñca-°*, read with B. *Krauñcaṃ*).

Krodhavaca, pl., add: § 438 (Yakshayuddhap.): III, **161,** 11757 (*gaṇāḥ*, slain by Bhīmasena).

Krodhavaçā, add: cf. Hariv. 170 (where K. is mentioned among the wives of Kaçyapa).

Kṛçānu, add: I, 5831; XIII, †1850.

Kṛpa, add: IV, 1624 (only B.); VI, 663 (B. *Māgadhasya Kṛpo yayau*, C. *Māgadhaç ca ripuṃ yayau*), 1910/11 (only B.); VII, 6314 (only B.).

Synonyms: **Acārya,** read: **Ācārya.**

Kṛshṇa[1], add: VI, **43**[4], 1532/3 (only B.), †3767 (do.); VIII, 3395/96 (do.), 4023–24 (do.); XIII, 7391 (*Kṛshṇāt*, B., C. has *kṛtsnaṃ*).

Synonyms: **Atman,** read **Ātman.**

Cakradhara: XII, 8879.

Cakrapāṇi, add: (only C.), 2604 (only B.).

Cakrāyudha: VII, 8278.

Çauri: VII, 1274 (only B.).

Dāçārha, V, 2889 (only C., B. has *Dāçārhaiḥ*).

Devakīsuta: XIII, 6949, dele (Vishṇu's 1000 names).

Dvijaketana, q.v. (Additions).

Govinda, add from B.: VI, 1532/33, 2604, 3022; VII, 6456/57.

Jagadbhartṛ, Jagadgoptṛ (q.v.).

Janārdana, add from B.: V, 4453; VI, 3028; VII. 6458/59, 6474; VIII, 3760/61; XI, 486.

Keçava, add from B.: II, 1534/35; VI, 1532/33; VII, 1296/97, 3718/19; VIII, 2357; XI, 471/72; XIII, 2026.

Madhunisūdana, Pakshivaradhvaja, Pītāmbaradhara, q.v.

Pītavāsas: III, 12882 read 12822; add: XII, 1678, 1681.

Sarveça, Sarveçvara, Tārkshyaketana, Tārkshyalakshaṇa, q.v.

Vāsudeva, add from B.: VI, 3039, 4856; VII, (2966), 7715, 8182.; VIII, 3063.

Vibudhārighna, Vṛshṇikulaçreshṭha, Yogācārya, q.v.

Kṛshṇa[4], add: VII, 7023 (*hate tu Pāṇḍave Kṛshṇe*, only B., C. has *Kṛshṇo*).

Kṛshṇa[1], dual., add: IX, 798 (only B., C. *Kṛshṇa-Pārthayoḥ*).

Kṛshṇavarṇā, add: (only C., B. has *Kṛshṇakarṇī*).

***kṛtānta,** dele XII, 7907; add: I, †1259 (*kupita*°), 1397; VI, 2773; VII, 2750 (*gatiḥ °asya*), 3066 (*°asya vidhiḥ*); XII, 10011 (*°vidhi-*); XVI, 25.

Kṛtayuga, add: cf. Ādiyuga.

Kṛttikā, pl. III, 14103 (*Radrāc ca sambhūto*), read (*Rudrāc* . . .).

Kshaṇadācara, pl. ("night-walkers") = Rākshasa, pl.: III, 11427, †15590 (°*-strī*), 16357, 16383 (sg., *Prahastaṃ*); VII, †6920.

Kshatradeva, VII, 974 (B. has *Ṛkshadevaṃ*).

Kshemakīrti, IX, 1100 (B. has *Kshemadhūrtiṃ*).

Kucirā, add: (B. *Kuvīrā*).

Kuçādya, pl. (°*āḥ*), the plural form °*āḥ* is not in our editions (B. *Kuçādyaḥ*, C. *Kulādyaḥ*), but PCR. translates "Kulādyas"; for the rest, see Adhivājya[6].

Kuçalin, name of a certain low caste (Caṇḍāla, Nīl.): XII, 10730.

Kuhū[1], add: VIII, 1486 (C. *Kuhuṃ*, was made one of the traces of Çiva's chariot).

Kukuna, add: (B. *Kukuṇaḥ*).

Kulinda, pl., add. from B.: VI, 3853; VII, 4847 (C. in both places *Pu*°).

Kulindaputra[3], add: (B. *Kaliṅga*° (v. supra)).

Kumbhāṇḍaka, add: (B. *Kumbhāṇḍakodaraḥ*).

Kumudanātha ("lord of the lotuses") = Soma (the moon): VII, 8408.

Kuṇḍabheda, add: (B. *Kuṇḍabhediṃ*).

Kundāparanta, see Kuṭṭāparanta.

Kuntinandana[1-2], read **Kuntī-°.**

Kushika: II, 321 (so B. instead of *Kuçika*, q.v.).

Kuvīrā, a river: VI, 334 (only B., C. has *Kucirā*, q.v.).

L

Labdhalaksha, add: (only C.).

***lavanodaka** (do.): III, 13677 (*sāgaraḥ*); XIII, 2136 (*samudraḥ*), 7219 (do.).

Laya, an ancient king. § 267 (Yamasabhāv.): II, **8,** 332 (only B., C. has by error *Gayaḥ*).

Lokādi[1] ("beginning of the world") = Brahmán: XII, 12914.—Do.[2] = Çiva: VII, 2863.

Lokamaheçvara = Kṛshṇa: VI, 1207.

Lokapāla, pl., add: III, 1937, 2139, 2572, 12006, 16179, 17288.

Lokapāla, sg.

Varuṇa, add: I, 8174 (*V*°).

Lokasākshin[2], add: XII, 13050.

Lokeça[2], add: VII, 2086 (only C., B. has *Deveça*); 3754, read 3454.

Lokeçvareçvara[3] = Vishṇu: VI, 2946.

Lomaça[1], add: § 746 (Ānuçāsanik.): XIII, **67,** 3383.

M

Mādhava[2], add: VI, 2604 (only B.); VII, 112 (only C.); VIII, 4654 (do.); IX, 3499 (only B.); XVI, 101 (only C.).

Mādhava[4], add: VII, 8657 (only B., C. *Sāttvataḥ*), 9179 (only C.).

Mādhava, dual, = Kṛshṇa and Sātyaki: IX, 124 (only B., C. *Sāttvatau*).

Mādhavarshabha, VI, 4862, add: (B. *Yādavarshabhaḥ*).

Madhu-mādhava, neutr., name of the two spring-months: I, 4867.

Madhumatta, pl. (°*āḥ*), add: (B. has *Madhumantaḥ*).

Madhusūdana, add: V, 4856 (only B.); VII, 8257 (only B., C. *Madhuhā*).

Madhuvāhinī, add: (B. has *Ambuvāhinīṃ*).

Madhyadeçaja, adj. ("born in the midland country"): II, 1276 (*rājānaḥ*).

Madraka, pl., add: § 600 (Ghaṭotkacavadhap.): VII, **157**ρ, 6950.

Mādrikā, add: (B. has *Ma*°).

Mādrinandana[1], add: (only C.).

Mādrīputra[3], add: V, †861 (only B., C. °*sutau*).

Mādrīsuta[2], add: VII, 7471 (only C.).

Magadha, pl.: V, 2107, add: (B. has *Mā*°); VI, 353 (only B., C. *Mā*°), 357 (do.).

Māgadha[6], add: VI, 1851 (*J*°, only B.), 2014/15 (do. do.).

Magadha [10], add: § 277 (do.): II, **21**, 803 (*vaṃçam*, only B., C. has *Mānavam*); XI, 712 (only C.).
***Māgadha**, pl., add: I, 7056; IV, 2280, 2365; V, 3144, 7620; VI, †747; VII, 2517, 2912, 2995–96, 3016; VIII, 1770 (fem. °*īnām*).
Mahābāhu [1]: VII, 6938, add: (only B., C. has *Vīrabāhu*).
Mahābhārata, add: § 164 (Āpavop.): I, **99**, 3967. Cf. also Bhārata [1] and [3].
***mahābhūta**, pl., add. VI, 172; VII, 9413; XII, 8527, 10487, 10493, 11060, 11556, 11561 (m. pl.), 11580, 12465, 13038–39; XIII, 7074; XIV, 1093–94, 1102–03–04, 1147, 1312, 1329, 1400, 1403, 1436–37; XV, 924.
Mahādeva [3], VI, 3036, add: (only C., B. *mahātmānam*).
Mahādyuti [2], XIV, 206, add: (only C.).
Mahāmegha, add: (B. *Meghavegam*).
Mahāpurusha, add: § 768 (Ānuçasanik.): XIII, **148**, 6914 (°*sambhavam*).—Do.[2] = Çiva: VII, 9483 (°*vigraham*, an image of him?).
Maheça, add: VII, 5413 (only B., *çishyo* °*sya*, sc. Rāma Jāmadagnya).
Maheçvara [4] = Purusha or Brahmán: VI, 1343 (opp. to *prakṛti*); XII, 7837, 9115.
Maheçvarapada, Maheçvarapura, read: Māheçvara°.
***Mahī** [1], add: I, 1582 foll.; XII, 1788.
Mahīja ("earth-born"), pl. (°*āḥ*) said of a particular breed of horses: VI, 3973.
***Mahoraga**, add: III, 1841 (°*gaṇeshu*); —VII, 5618, read: (*çvasan iva* °*aḥ*).
Mālava, pl., II, 1270, add: (only C., B. has *Gālavāḥ*); —add: VI, 357 (only B.), 2084 (do.).
Malla, pl., add: XII, 2655.
Mānava, adj., add: III, 186 (*jagato*, B. has '*mānavasya*); VII, 169 (*arthavidyāṃ mānavīṃ*).
Mānavarjaka, pl., add: (only C., B. has *Mālavā narāḥ*).
Mānavāstra, name of a particular weapon. § 599 (Jayadrathavadhap.): VII, **103**, 3864 (only B.).
Mandhātṛ [1], add: § 574 (Jambūkh.): VI, **9***aa*, 314 (only B.).
Manu [1], add: § 577 (Bhīshmavadhap.): VI, **43**, 1532/33 (only B.).
***Marīcipa**, pl., add: XIII, 647.
Mārkaṇḍeya, add: § 599 (Jayadrathavadhap.): VII, **149**, 6474 (only B.).
Mārttikāvataka, add: (B. has *Mārttikāvataka*).
Māruta, adj., add: § 759 (Ānuçāsanik.): XIII, **107**ζ, 5284.
Matsya [1], pl., add: § 578 (Bhīshmavadhap.); VI, **47**η, 1866 (*Cedi-Matsyeshu*, only B., C. has *Cedisainyeshu*).—VII, **198**σ, 9182 (only C.).—VIII, **78**, 3967 (do., only B.).—IX, †1087 (only C.).
Matsyanagara, dele: = Upaplavya.
Mātsyeya, pl. (°*āḥ*) = Matsya [1], pl. § 556 (Sañjayayānap.): V, **22**, †663 (°*ānām adhipo vai Virāṭaḥ*).
Maushala, v. Mausala [2].
Maya, add: I, 8324/25 (only B.); II, 57/58 (only B.).
Megharavā, add: (B. has *Meghakarṇā*).
Meghavega (only B.), v. Mahāmegha.
Meru, add: § 582 (do.): VI, **74**, 3259 (only B.).
Mitra, add: § 597 (Pratijñāp.): VII, **84**, 2994 (*sahāmbupati-Mitrābhyāṃ yathendras Tārakāmaye*).
Mitra [2] (only B.), v. Citrā.
Mitrasaha, add: I, 6891 (*nṛpaṃ*).

Mleccha, pl., add: VI, **9**μ, 365 (only B., C. has *Pauṇḍrāḥ*).
***mokshadharma**, add: III, 14000.
Mṛdaṅgaketu ("having drums in his standard") = Yudhishṭhira: VII, 6746.
Mṛgacārin, pl. (°*aḥ*), a kind of ascetics: XIII, 647.
***Mṛtyu** [1], add: XIII, 163; dele: XIII, 164 (= Dharma).
Mṛtyuloka, add: VII, 1307, 6136 (only C.), 6950 (only B.).
Mucukunda, add: § 574 (Jambūkh.): VI, **9***aa*, 314 (only B.).
Mudgala, add: III, (15481) (only C.); XIII, 250 (only C., B. has *Yamadūta*). Cf. Viprarshi.
Mukhakarṇā, a mātṛ. § 615*u* (Skanda): (IX, **46**θ, 2647 (only B., C. has *Çivakarṇī*).
Mukhasecaka, a serpent. § 67 (Sarpasattra): I, **57**, 2156 (only B., C. has *Sukhasecaka*).
Musala, Musalāyudha, so B. for Mush° (q.v.).

N

Nābhāga [2] = **Nābhāgi**: XII, 993 (B. 2nd ed. agrees with C.).
Nabhakānana, pl. v. Nalakānana.
nadija, pl., a particular breed of horses: VI, 3973; VIII, †200.
Nāga, pl., add: asterisk (*) before this heading, and the foll. passages: I, 8154 (*bahuçīrshāḥ*), 8293; III, 1899; V, 3859 (*naravaktrān*); VI, 4043, 4045; VII, 602 (°*kanyā*), 2897 (dual), †6921, †9456 (°*yajñopavītam*, sc. Çiva); VIII, 1481 (°*patīn*).

Names of single Nāgas:—
Açvasena, add: VIII, †4634 (°*vīraḥ*, only C.), †4646, †4661–62, †4673, †4675, †4682.
Çesha, add: XII, 13514 (*çayane* °*bhogāḍhye*).
Takshaka, add VI, 4900 (*T*°).
Ulūpī: XV, 23 (*U*°). Cf. Kauravya.

Nāgarājasutāsuta ("son of the daughter of the Nāga king"), i.e. Irāvat: VI, 3661 (cf. 3977).
Nāgavatmān, read: Nāgavatman (probably misprint in C. for Nāgavartman).
Nagnajita, pl. (°*āḥ*), add: or better according to B.: Nagnajit, pl. (°*aḥ*)
Nahusha [2], add: III, 8777 (B. by error *Nā*°).—§ 574 (Jambūkh.): VI, **9***aa*, 314 (only B.).—Cf. Pannaga [2].
Nakshatra [1], add: V, 1148 (*tāpyate loko* °*āṇi grahair iva*); XII, 8905 (*anakshatrāḥ* . . . *jyotishāṃ gaṇāḥ*).
Nakula, add: VIII, **48**ρ, 2286/7 (only B.).
Nala [1], add: II, 332 (B. '*naghaḥ*).
Nalakānana, add: B. reads *Nabhakānanāḥ*.
nalinī, add: II, 390 (*Alakākhyāyāḥ*); III, 11377–80, 11416–18, 12304.
Nanda [1], add: § 583 (do.): VI, **79**ν, 3470/71 (°*opanandakau*, only B.).
Nandaka [4], add: B. reads *Nandanaḥ*.
Nara [1], add: I, **224**, 8159 (°-*Nārāyaṇau*, twice in verses inserted in B.).—§ 573 (Ambop.): V, **185**, 7308/9 (= Arjuna, only B.).
Nārada [1], add: VII, **149**$\chi\chi\chi$, 6474 (only B.).—§ 615 *ff.* (Asita Devala): IX, **50**, 2919 (only B., C. has *Gālavaḥ*).—Cf. Pārameshṭha, Viprarshi.
Naraka [1], V, 4407, read 4408; add: 4409 (only B.).

Nārāyaṇa, add: I, **224,** 8159 (*Nara-*°, only B.).—VI, **67**π, 3023 (*devadevaḥ*, only B.).—VII, **149**χχχ, 6474.

Nārāyaṇa, pl., add: § 11 (Parvasaṅgr.): I, **2,** 535 (*gopālāḥ*, only B.).

***nāstika,** add: I, 2300 (*a*°), 3088 (do.); XIII, 5004 (*nāstike*, B. °*-aiḥ*).

Niçā [2] = Upaçruti (?), read = Rātrī (q.v.).

Nepāla, a country (Nepal): § 515 (Karṇadigvijaya): III, **254,** 15242/3 (°*vishaye*, only B.).

***Niçācara,** sg., add: III, 16370 (= Rāvaṇa); V, 7492 (= Sthūṇa); VI, 4075 (= Ghaṭotkaca).

Nīlavāsas, add: III, 734 (*Keçavasyāgrajo . . . Baladevaḥ*); IX, 1966.

***Niraya,** add: XII, †12074 (*parama-*°), †12075 (*mahā*°).

Nishṭhurika, add: (B. Nishṭhūrika).

P

Pāçcimānūpaka, read Pa°

Padmagarbha [2] add: VI, 2946 (only B., C. Padmanābha).

Padmanābha [1], add: VI, 1532/33 (only B.); XII, 7630.

Padmanābha [3], add: Cf. Bhogipati, Bhujagapati, Nāga, Nāgendra, Pannaga, Pannagapati, Uragaçreshṭha.

Pahlava, add: (B. sometimes Palhava) . . . VI, **20,** †753 (only B.).

Paiṅga, add: (B. has Paiṅgya).

Paippalādi, add: [XII, 7208 (*viprarshe*)].

Pakshivaradhvaja ("having the best of birds [i.e. Garuḍa] for his banner") = Kṛshṇa: VIII, †4952.

Pāñcāla, pl., add: VII, **182**ζζζ, 8269; **189,** 8689; VIII, **10**λ, 393, 395; **47**θ, 2224 [instead of 2214]; **73,** 3639 . . . and the foll. passages only from B.: VI, **9**μ, 355; VII, **167,** 7480; **170,** 7679; **183**ιιι, 8345; VIII, **73,** 3735/6, 3738/9 . . . del. (VIII) 2662 (to be inserted under Pañcāla, pl.).

Pāñcāla, sg.[1], add: VII, 7342 (only B.).

Pāñcālarāja [2], add: IX, 1379/80 (only B.).

Pāñcālarājan, add: VII, 7351 (°*rājānam*, B. °*rājaṃ ca*).

Pāñcālī, add: VIII, 3718/19 (only B.).

Pañcanada, add: Cf. III, †1364 (*pañca nadyaḥ*).

Pañcarātra, add: XII, **350,** 13637 (B. *Pā*°).

Pāṇḍava, pl., only C.: II, 1565; III, 13142; IV, 1493; VI, 2458, 2885 (B. *Pāṇḍaveyaiḥ*), 3135, 4277 (B. *Pāṇḍaveyāḥ*); VII, 463 (B. *Pāṇḍaveyeshu*), 4871, 6021, 6622, 7072, 7821; IX, 456, 1041; . . . only B.: I, 6081/82, 7884; IV, 2361; VI, 1910/11, 2197, 2433 (C. *Pāṇḍaveyānām*), 3333/34, 4292 (C. *Pāṇḍūnām*); VII, 1751, †4133, 6693 (C. *Pāṇḍaveyān*), 8268 (C. *Pāṇḍushu*); VIII, 3718/19; IX, 1218.

Pāṇḍava, sg.[1], add: VII, 6480; . . . only C.: VI, 2197; VII, 6199, †8167, 8180; VIII, 3055; . . . only B.: VI, 2458, 5131/2, 5514; VII, 1269, 6141, 6276/7; VIII, 4023/4.

Pāṇḍava, sg.[2], only C.: VI, 2850, 3357 (B. *Pāṇḍaveyaḥ*); VII, 7672; . . . only B.: VI, 1554 (C. *Pāṇḍuputre*), 2791; VII, 5362, 5660, 9264; VIII, 3055.

Pāṇḍava, sg.[5]: IX, 1218 (only C.).

Pāṇḍava sg.[6], only C.: VI, 2091, 2412; VII, 6288, 6953; XV, 736 . . . only B.: VII, 1081, 4871, 6480, 6630; IX, 1044; XIV 394.

Pāṇḍava, adj., only C.: VII, 3521 (B. *Pārshataṃ*); VIII, †4809; . . . only B.: VII, 6630 (*senā*).

Pāṇḍavarshabha [1], add: IV, 1436 (only B., C. *Pāṇḍunandanaḥ*).

Pāṇḍaveya, pl., add: VI, 4321 (only B., C. *Sṛñjayaiḥ*); VII, 7309/10 (only B.); XIV, 322 (only B., C. *Pāṇḍuputrānām*).

Pāṇḍaveya, sg.[7], add: VI, 2106 (B. *Saubaleyasya*).

Pāṇḍaveya, adj., add: VII, 7343 (B. °*vīyeshu*).

Pāṇḍu, add: § 581 (Bhīshmavadhap.): VI, **65,** 2919 (°*pūrvaja*, i.e. Dhṛtarāshṭra).

Pāṇḍu, pl., only C.: VIII, †4325. . . . only B.: VI, 2100 (C. *Pārthānām*); VII, 4545/46, 7278, 9031 (°*senām*).

Pāṇḍunandana [1], pl., only B. in a verse after III, 17478.—Do.[3], add: I, 7884 (only B.).—Do.[4], add: VII, 5302 (only C., B. *Bhīmaḥ*).—Do.[8] = Ghaṭotkaca: VII, 7924 (only B.).

Pāṇḍuputra, pl., only C.: VII, 7069, 9031; XIV, 322. . . . only B.: VIII, 3776.

Pāṇḍuputra [2], add: VII, 112 (only C.), †6145 (only B., C. °*sūnuṃ*).—Do.[6], add: VII, 6630 (only B.).

Pāṇḍusūnu [2], add: (only C., B. *Dharmasūnunā*).

Pāṇḍya [4], Çrī, read: Çrīçaila.

Pāṇika, add: (B. has *Kālikaṃ*).

Pannaga, pl., only C.: VII, 6803. . . . only B.: IV, 1801 (C. *pāvakaiḥ*); VII, 6132 (C. °*Vātikaiḥ*), 7711.

Pannaga, sg., add: IX, 49 (B. *jihmaga iva*).

Parāçara [1], add: cf. Viprarshi.

Paramātman, add: VII, 6474 (only B.).

Parameçvara, dele XIII, 792, 795, 797, and see Īçvara (Add.).

Parāvasu, III, 10757 and 10793 (read *bhāryāṃ* and *bhāryā*).

Paridhipatikhecara = Çiva (1000 names [2]), v. Additions above.

Pārshata [2], only C.: VI, 3400; VII, 7184 . . . only B.: VI, 2324.

Pārshata [4], adj. ("belonging to Dhṛshṭadyumna"): VII, 3521 (only B.).

Pārtha [1], pl., only C.: VI, 2100, 4060; VII, 1751 . . . only B.: I, 5067/8, VII, 448, 7111.

Pārtha [2], only C.: IV, 571, †1690, 1736, 1737, 1800; VI, 3207; VII, 196, 448, 1256, 6141, 7111, 7657, 8283; IX, 798 . . . only B.: IV, 1454, VI, 4849, 5099, 5486; VII, 1296/7, 3718/9, 5139/40, 5263, 5316, 6238, 6455, 6474, 6539, 6576, 7096, 7123, 7655; VIII, 300, 668/9, 3024, 3395/6, 3728/9, 4023/4.

Pārtha [3], only B.: IV, 571; VII, 1177; VIII, 3062/3; IX, 584.

Pārtha [5], only B.: VI, 2091.

***Pārvatīya** [1], pl., add: § 562 (Bhagavadyānap.): V, **86,** 3048 (*āvikaṃ . . . P°air upāhṛtaṃ*).—Do.[2], adj., add: § 793 (Mausalap.): XVI, **6**κ, 160 (*nṛpān*).

Patagendra, add: III, 665.

Patikhecara = Çiva (1000 names [2]), v. Additions above.

Patitri, read: **Patatri.**

Paurava, pl., add: VII, 7655 (only B., C. *Kauravāḥ*).

Pauravanandana [5] = Babhruvāhana: I, 7884 (only B.).

Pavana [3], an ancient king. § 775 (Ānuçāsanik.): XIII, **166**η, 7676 (only B., C. *Cyavana*. q.v.).

Picchalā, add: (B. *Picchilā*).

Piṅga, add: VII, 9541 (only B.).

Pitrīça = Yama (q.v.).

***Pitṛ,** pl., add: XIII, 6606 (read with B. *pitṛdevātithi-kṛte*).

Pitṛ-vittāmbu-deveçāḥ ("the lords of Pitṛs, riches water, and gods") = Yama, Kubera, Varuṇa, and Indra: VII, 37.
Plakshāvataraṇa . . . their king *Bharata* . . ., read: there king *Bh.*
Prabhadra, pl., (°*āḥ*), a people: VI, 2080 (only B., C. has *Prayāgāḥ*).
Prādheya, pl.: I, **65**, 2556 (only C., B. has *Prādhāyāḥ*).
Pradyumna, add: II, 622 (only B.).
Prajñāstra, add: § 319 (Saubhavadhap.): III, **20**, 816 (employed by Kṛshṇa).
***prakṛti**, add: VI, 1341/42 (only B.).
Pramāthin, pl. = Pramatha, pl.: VIII, 1507.
***Prāṇa**[3], add: XII, **237**, 8653; **240**, 8746.—XIII, **162**, 7521 (°*ápānaḥ*, sic!).
Prāṇadhāraṇa[1], add: (B. *Prāṇadhāraka*).
Prastuta, add: (B. *Prasruta*).
Prātipeya[1-2], add: (both B. and C. read *Prātip°*).—**Prātipeya**[3] (do.) = Dhṛtarāshṭra: V, †1353 (read *Prātipeya*, voc., with B.).—**Prātipeya** (pl.) (do.), add: § 301 (Dyūtap.): II, **71**, †2395.—**Prātipiya** (C. *Prātip°*, B. *Prātipeya*).
Pratiskandha, add: (B. *Kapiskandha*).
Pravīra[2] ("hero"), according to Nīl. nom. pr. of Pāṇḍya[2] (Malayadhvaja): VIII, 770/71.
***Pṛthivī**, add: I, 1941 (*devīm*).
Pṛthu Vainya, § 795, read § 775.
Pṛthuvaktrā, add: (B. *Pṛthuvastrā*).
Pulinda, pl.: VI, 3853 (add: B. *Kulindaiḥ*); VII, 4847 (add: B. *Kulindāḥ*).
Pundra, read: (I, 228).
Purushavara, add: = Kṛshṇa: VIII, †1740 (°-*ávarajā*, i.e. Subhadrā).
Pūrvadeva, add: = Kṛshṇa, VI, 3021 (only B.); = Arjuna (Nara), V, 7308 (only B.).—Do. pl.: VII, 9480 (°*ānāṃ paramau* . . . *ṛshī*, = Nara-Nārāyaṇau).
Pushpāyudha ("flower-armed") = Kāma: I, 6576.

R

Rākā[2], add: § 606 (Tripurākhyāna): VIII, **34**, 1486 (was made one of the traces of Çiva's chariot).
Rathoraga, pl., a people (BR. ?): VI, 362 (see Vātaja).
***Raudra**[5], adj., add: XIII, 5283 (scil. *sthānam*, only B., C. has by error *Rudram*).
Rāvaṇa, add: I, 6081/82 (only B.).
Rohaka, pl., a class of beings § 606 (Tripurākhyāna): VIII, **34**, 1486 (were made the pins of Çiva's chariot).
Rudra, pl., add: XVIII, 215 (only B.).
Rukmaratha[1], add: VI, 1851 (only B.), 2014/15 (only B.).—Do.[2] = Droṇa, add: VI, † 751; VII, 8629.
Rukmavāhana, add: VII, 8705.
Rushardika, read **Rusharddhika.**

Ṛ

Ṛkshadeva, son of Çikhaṇḍin. § 592 (Saṃçaptakavadhap.): VII, **23**o, 974, (only B., C. by error *Kshatradevam*).

S

Sāgara[2-4], read **Sāgara**[1-3].

V

Viçvajit[4], name of a particular sacrifice: XII, 3925.

POSTSCRIPTUM.

The author of this work, the late Professor S. Sörensen (*23rd November, 1849—†8th December, 1902), was an eminent Sanskrit scholar. While an undergraduate he strenuously applied himself to the study of Classical Philology and Sanskrit at the University of Copenhagen, where he became a pupil of J. N. Madvig and N. L. Westergaard. In 1883 he took the degree of doctor of philosophy with a most valuable and comprehensive dissertation on the "Mahābhārata and its Place in Indian Literature", in which he made an attempt at determining the oldest elements of that great epic. Unfortunately he only obtained the professorship of Indian Philology in the Copenhagen University at an advanced age. In 1902, a short time before his premature death, he succeeded V. Fausböll in the only chair of Indian Philology in the Copenhagen University.

He began to collect the materials for the present work as long ago as about the year 1880, and continued it under great difficulties and self-sacrifice. In the year 1902 the work was so far advanced that he could commence printing, but only the first four sheets (pages 1–32) had been put into type before his death. The manuscript of the preface, the concordance, and pages 33–153 had been put into final shape by him, whilst the materials for the rest of the work were left unrevised. In these circumstances it was resolved that the work should be continued, and the revision and final preparation of the manuscript was, under the superintendence of the undersigned D. Andersen, committed to the undersigned E. Olesen, who had already assisted the author for two years.

During the fu er revision, however, it was found that the collection of the material had partly been provisional, and some time had to be spent in completing it. Furthermore, it was considered advisable to add a selection of the various readings from the Bombay Edition. This accounts for the rather numerous Additions and Corrections. Several other difficulties arose during the preparation and printing of the work, especially in the time of the Great War, but they were all overcome and now we are amply rewarded for all our efforts in being able to place the great work of our compatriot before the learned world.

Our sincere thanks are due to Professor Sten Konow and to Sir George A. Grierson, who both of them have read all the proofs and given us many valuable hints. Also the printers deserve our best thanks for their accurate and skilful work. No less thanks are due to the publishers, who have been ready to carry out this far from lucrative undertaking.

Finally, we acknowledge with the deepest gratitude the subventions which have been granted by The Danish Government, The Carlsberg Fund, The Rask-Oersted Fund, and the India Office, which gracefully granted its support to the undertaking in subscribing to a number of copies.

COPENHAGEN.
January, 1925.

DINES ANDERSEN. ELOF OLESEN.